The CROSSWAY COMPREHENSIVE CONCORDANCE

The CROSSWAY COMPREHENSIVE CONCORDANCE *of the* HOLY BIBLE

ENGLISH
STANDARD
VERSION

COMPILED BY
WILLIAM D. MOUNCE

CROSSWAY BOOKS

A PUBLISHING MINISTRY OF
GOOD NEWS PUBLISHERS
WHEATON, ILLINOIS

The Crossway Comprehensive Concordance of The Holy Bible, English Standard Version

Published by Crossway Books
a publishing ministry of Good News Publishers
1300 Crescent Street
Wheaton, Illinois 60187

Cover design: Josh Dennis

First printing 2002

Printed in the United States of America

Library of Congress Cataloging-in-Publication Data

Mounce, William D.
The Crossway comprehensive concordance of the Holy Bible, English Standard Version / compiled by William D. Mounce.
p. cm.
ISBN 13: 978-1-58134-386-1
ISBN 10: 1-58134-386-8 (alk. paper)
1. Bible—Concordances, English—English Standard. I. Title.
BS425 .M68 2002
220.5'208—dc21 2002007010

RRDC 16 15 14 13 12 11 10 09 08 07 06
15 14 13 12 11 10 9 8 7 6 5 4 3 2

CONTENTS

INTRODUCTION

A concordance is one of the most useful tools available for serious Bible study. It can help locate a vaguely remembered verse and in the process uncover similar verses. But it is important to understand several basic things about concordances.

A concordance is a list of either all the words that occur in the Bible or the most important words. Under each word is a listing of the verses using that word. Each word (usually just the first letter of the word, in bold type) is shown along with enough words surrounding it to give a clue as to what the verse as a whole says. Under the heading for "world," for instance, one might find:

"For God so loved the **w**, that he gave his Jn 3:16

The phrase surrounding the "**w**" for world gives an adequate clue to lead the reader to the correct Bible passage.

In the past, the process of choosing which words to include before and after the listed word took years because it had to be done by hand. However, this concordance was produced by a custom software package that evaluated each verse and made the decision as to what words to include with the referenced word. This enabled us to produce this complete concordance to the English Standard Version within a year of the ESV's publication.

How to Use a Concordance

Next we should consider some guidelines for using a concordance. Suppose you have been reading your Bible and vaguely remember a verse that speaks about Jesus being a "propitiation." Looking up "propitiation" in this concordance will reveal that the ESV uses the word four times:

PROPITIATION (4)

God put forward as a **p** by his blood,	Rom 3:25
to make **p** for the sins of the people.	Heb 2:17
He is the **p** for our sins, and not for ours	1 Jn 2:2
sent his Son to be the **p** for our sins.	1 Jn 4:10

From this listing you should be able to identify the verse you are looking for, and in the process you will also find the other three times the word is used. These verses then help to provide the context for your verse and for the concept of "propitiation."

When you are looking for an elusive verse, pick the more specific or unusual word. Let's say you want to find the verse where Jesus talks about having "faith like a grain of mustard seed." If you look up the word "faith," you will find 278 references; looking up "seed" will locate 62 references; but "mustard" will give you a mere 5 references. It will be most efficient to find "mustard" in the concordance and look through those 5 verses. Of course, if you do not have the actual text in front of you and are not sure what specific words occur in the verse, it may take some guesswork to find the right word for your search. But by using this method you should be able to find virtually any verse in the Bible.

Do not forget about related words. You may be confident that the verse for which you are looking has the word "believe," but try as you might you cannot find the verse. As it turns out, the verse might actually have the form "believes."

Limitations of Concordances

It is good to keep in mind the limitations of using a concordance in Bible study. Suppose you want to find all the verses in the Bible that talk about prayer. You can look up the entries for "pray," "prayed," "prayer," "prayers," "praying," and "prays." These listings will show many of the verses that discuss prayer, but they will not show all of them. Why? Because sometimes the Bible talks about prayer without using any of those actual words. For example, none of these listings contain Matthew 7:7, "Ask, and it will be given to you; seek, and you will find; knock, and it will be opened to you." Not including this verse would be a serious omission in a Bible study on prayer, and it is one of the limitations inherent in the use of any concordance. Topical Bibles such as *Nave's* will make up for this limitation of concordances.

There is another limitation to concordances, but one that is easily remedied. You need to use a concordance that is based on the version of the Bible that you are reading. Let's say you want to find the verse that says, "If I speak in the tongues of men and of angels, but have not love, I am a noisy gong or a clanging cymbal." If you use a concordance based on the King James Version of the Bible, you will not find this verse listed under "love" because the KJV uses the word "charity" in place of "love" in 1 Corinthians 13:1. There are concordances based on most of the major Bible versions, and it is best to use the right concordance for the version you are reading.

Finally, a more serious limitation is that the concordance shows only a limited context for each word. "Context" is the most important tool in determining the meaning of a verse. The more context you have—that is, the more surrounding words you have—the better job you can do interpreting the verse. So let's say that you are doing a study on the "will of God" and you find this entry: "For this is the **w** of God" (1 Thes 4:3). There are insufficient words in this concordance entry to make the meaning of the verse clear. If the entry had a few more words, the verse would be clearer: "For this is the **w** of God, your sanctification." And if it had even more, the verse would be still clearer: "For this is the **w** of God, your sanctification: that you abstain from sexual immorality." Because of space limitations, of course, no concordance offers entries of that length. Therefore, once you find a verse in the concordance you should always look it up in the Bible and read the verse in its fuller context.

Types of Concordances

There are three basic types of concordances for the English reader:

1. Abbreviated concordances are found in the back of many Bibles. These concordances do not list every word in the Bible, nor do they list every verse that uses the words included. For example, the word "love" occurs 550 times in the ESV, but we only listed 120 of those verses in the concordance within the ESV's Classic Reference Edition.

2. "Complete" concordances include all the words in the Bible except for the most common (such as "a," "an," "be," etc.), and list all the verses that use each of the words included. This Crossway concordance of the ESV is a "complete" concordance, listing more than 13,700 words and every verse that includes each of those words. We omit 115 words; these are listed on page xv. Since it may seem confusing to call a concordance "complete" when it does not list every reference for every word in the Bible, it seemed more appropriate to call this present volume a "comprehensive" concordance—comprehensive in that it includes a range of words sufficient for easy access to every verse in the Bible.

3. An "exhaustive" concordance adds two more features. First, it lists every word in the Bible (including "a," "an," "be," etc., usually listed by reference only); and second, it will tell you what Hebrew, Aramaic, or Greek word lies behind each listed word. This way you can do word studies based on the original language, even if you don't know that language.

Lastly, I would mention that the English Standard Version, as an essentially literal Bible translation, is ideally suited for study with the use of a concordance. This is true because the ESV uses the same English word, as far as possible, to translate important recurring words in the original languages, and because the ESV retains key theological terms that have been of central importance for Christian doctrine through the centuries—thereby enabling the reader to locate specific words and texts, and facilitating the reading and study of the Bible.

I would encourage you also to read the "Preface to the English Standard Version," on pages xi–xiii of this volume, as this will provide further insight about the kind of translation the ESV Bible is and why it is especially useful for serious Bible study.

I trust that this concordance will help you study the Bible more effectively, give you increased access to the English Standard Version, and at the end help you understand the mind and the will of God that much better.

—William D. Mounce
April 2002

PREFACE TO THE ENGLISH STANDARD VERSION

The Bible

"This Book [is] the most valuable thing that this world affords. Here is Wisdom; this is the royal Law; these are the lively Oracles of God." With these words the Moderator of the Church of Scotland hands a Bible to the new monarch in Britain's coronation service. These words echo the King James Bible translators, who wrote in 1611: "God's sacred Word . . . is that inestimable treasure that excelleth all the riches of the earth." This assessment of the Bible is the motivating force behind the publication of the English Standard Version.

Translation Legacy

The English Standard Version (ESV) stands in the classic mainstream of English Bible translations over the past half-millennium. The fountainhead of that stream was William Tyndale's New Testament of 1526; marking its course were the King James Version of 1611 (KJV), the English Revised Version of 1885 (RV), the American Standard Version of 1901 (ASV), and the Revised Standard Version of 1952 and 1971 (RSV). In that stream, faithfulness to the text and vigorous pursuit of accuracy were combined with simplicity, beauty, and dignity of expression. Our goal has been to carry forward this legacy for a new century.

To this end each word and phrase in the ESV has been carefully weighed against the original Hebrew, Aramaic, and Greek, to ensure the fullest accuracy and clarity and to avoid under-translating or overlooking any nuance of the original text. The words and phrases themselves grow out of the Tyndale-King James legacy, and most recently out of the RSV, with the 1971 RSV text providing the starting point for our work. Archaic language has been brought to current usage and significant corrections have been made in the translation of key texts. But throughout, our goal has been to retain the depth of meaning and enduring language that have made their indelible mark on the English-speaking world and have defined the life and doctrine of the church over the last four centuries.

Translation Philosophy

The ESV is an "essentially literal" translation that seeks as far as possible to capture the precise wording of the original text and the personal style of each Bible writer. As such, its emphasis is on "word-for-word" correspondence, at the same time taking into account differences of grammar, syntax, and idiom between current literary English and the original languages. Thus it seeks to be transparent to the original text, letting the reader see as directly as possible the structure and meaning of the original.

In contrast to the ESV, some Bible versions have followed a "thought-for-thought" rather than "word-for-word" translation philosophy, emphasizing "dynamic equivalence" rather than the "essentially literal" meaning of the original. A "thought-for-thought" translation is of necessity more inclined to reflect the interpretive opinions of the translator and the influences of contemporary culture.

Every translation is at many points a trade-off between literal precision and readability, between "formal equivalence" in expression and "functional equivalence" in communication, and the ESV is no exception. Within this framework we have sought to be "as literal as possible" while maintaining clarity of expression and literary excellence. Therefore, to the extent that plain English permits and the meaning in each case allows, we have sought to use the same English word for important recurring words in the original; and, as far as grammar and syntax allow, we have rendered Old Testament passages cited in the New in ways that show their correspondence. Thus in each of these areas, as well as throughout the Bible as a whole, we have sought to capture the echoes and overtones of meaning that are so abundantly present in the original texts.

As an essentially literal translation, then, the ESV seeks to carry over every possible nuance of meaning in the original words of Scripture into our own language. As such, it is ideally suited for in-depth study of the Bible. Indeed, with its emphasis on literary excellence, the ESV is equally suited for public reading and preaching, for private reading and reflection, for both academic and devotional study, and for Scripture memorization.

Translation Style

The ESV also carries forward classic translation principles in its literary style. Accordingly it retains theological terminology—words such as grace, faith, justification, sanctification, redemption, regeneration, reconciliation, propitiation—because of their central importance for Christian doctrine and also because the underlying Greek words were already becoming key words and technical terms in New Testament times.

The ESV lets the stylistic variety of the biblical writers fully express itself—from the exalted prose that opens Genesis, to the flowing narratives of the historical books, to the rich metaphors and dramatic imagery of the poetic books, to the ringing rhetorical indictments in the prophetic books, to the smooth elegance of Luke, to the profound simplicities of John, and the closely-reasoned logic of Paul.

In punctuating, paragraphing, dividing long sentences, and rendering connectives, the ESV follows the path that seems to make the ongoing flow of thought clearest in English. The biblical languages regularly connect sentences by frequent repetition of words such as "and," "but," and "for," in a way that goes beyond the conventions of literary English. Effective translation, however, requires that these links in the original be reproduced so that the flow of the argument will be transparent to the reader. We have therefore normally translated these connectives, though occasionally we have varied the rendering by using alternatives (such as "also," "however," "now," "so," "then," or "thus") when they better capture the sense in specific instances.

In the area of gender language, the goal of the ESV is to render literally what is in the original. For example, "anyone" replaces "any man" where there is no word corresponding to "man" in the original languages, and "people" rather than "men" is regularly used where the original languages refer to both men and women. But the words "man" and "men" are retained where a male meaning component is part of the original Greek or Hebrew. Similarly, the English word "brothers" (translating the Greek word *adelphoi*) is retained as an important familial form of address between fellow-Jews and fellow-Christians in the first century. A recurring note is included to indicate that the term "brothers" (*adelphoi*) was often used in Greek to refer to both men and women, and to indicate the specific instances in the text where this is the case. In addition, the English word "sons" (translating the Greek word *huioi*) is retained in specific instances because of its meaning as a legal term in the adoption and inheritance laws of first-century Rome. As used by the apostle Paul, this term refers to the status of all Christians, both men and women, who, having been adopted into God's family, now enjoy all the privileges, obligations, and inheritance rights of God's children.

The inclusive use of the generic "he" has also regularly been retained, because this is consistent with similar usage in the original languages and because an essentially literal translation would be impossible without it. Similarly, where God and man are compared or contrasted in the original, the

ESV retains the generic use of "man" as the clearest way to express the contrast within the framework of essentially literal translation.

In each case the objective has been transparency to the original text, allowing the reader to understand the original on its own terms rather than on the terms of our present-day culture.

Textual Basis

The ESV is based on the Masoretic text of the Hebrew Bible as found in *Biblia Hebraica Stuttgartensia* (2nd ed., 1983), and on the Greek text in the 1993 editions of the *Greek New Testament* (4th corrected ed.), published by the United Bible Societies (UBS), and *Novum Testamentum Graece* (27th ed.), edited by Nestle and Aland. The currently renewed respect among Old Testament scholars for the Masoretic text is reflected in the ESV's attempt, wherever possible, to translate difficult Hebrew passages as they stand in the Masoretic text rather than resorting to emendations or to finding an alternative reading in the ancient versions. In exceptional, difficult cases, the Dead Sea Scrolls, the Septuagint, the Samaritan Pentateuch, the Syriac Peshitta, the Latin Vulgate, and other sources were consulted to shed possible light on the text, or, if necessary, to support a divergence from the Masoretic text. Similarly, in a few difficult cases in the New Testament, the ESV has followed a Greek text different from the text given preference in the UBS/Nestle-Aland 27th edition. In this regard the footnotes that accompany the ESV text are an integral part of the ESV translation, informing the reader of textual variations and difficulties and showing how these have been resolved by the ESV translation team. In addition to this, the footnotes indicate significant alternative readings and occasionally provide an explanation for technical terms or for a difficult reading in the text. Throughout, the translation team has benefited greatly from the massive textual resources that have become readily available recently, from new insights into biblical laws and culture, and from current advances in Hebrew and Greek lexicography and grammatical understanding.

Publishing Team

The ESV publishing team includes more than a hundred people. The fourteen-member Translation Oversight Committee has benefited from the work of fifty biblical experts serving as Translation Review Scholars and from the comments of the more than fifty members of the Advisory Council, all of which has been carried out under the auspices of the Good News Publishers Board of Directors. This hundred-member team, which shares a common commitment to the truth of God's Word and to historic Christian orthodoxy, is international in scope and includes leaders in many denominations.

To God's Honor and Praise

We know that no Bible translation is perfect or final; but we also know that God uses imperfect and inadequate things to his honor and praise. So to our triune God and to his people we offer what we have done, with our prayers that it may prove useful, with gratitude for much help given, and with ongoing wonder that our God should ever have entrusted to us so momentous a task.

Soli Deo Gloria!—To God alone be the glory!

*The Translation Oversight Committee**

*A complete list of the Translation Oversight Committee, the Translation Review Scholars, and the Advisory Council is available upon request from Crossway Bibles, a publishing ministry of Good News Publishers.

WORDS NOT INCLUDED IN THIS CONCORDANCE

a
about
after
against
all
also
am (except as part of God's name)
among
an
and
are
as
at
be
because
been
before
but
by
can
cannot
could
did
do
does
down
for
from
had
has
have
having
he
her
hers
herself
him
himself
his
I (except as part of God's name)
if
in
into
is
it
its
itself
like
may
me
mine (except as noun)
my
myself
no
nor
not
now
O
of
oh
on (except as proper noun)
or
our
ours
ourselves
out
over
people
said
say
saying
says
shall
she
should
so (except as proper noun)
than
that
the
their
theirs
them
themselves
then
there
these
they
this
those
through
to
under
up
upon
us
very
was
we
were
what
when
which
who
whoever
whom
whose
will (except as noun, or verb of volition)
with
would
yet
you
your
yours
yourself
yourselves

ABBREVIATIONS

Book	Abbreviation
Genesis	Gn
Exodus	Ex
Leviticus	Lv
Numbers	Nm
Deuteronomy	Dt
Joshua	Jos
Judges	Jgs
Ruth	Ru
1 Samuel	1 Sm
2 Samuel	2 Sm
1 Kings	1 Kgs
2 Kings	2 Kgs
1 Chronicles	1 Chr
2 Chronicles	2 Chr
Ezra	Ezr
Nehemiah	Neh
Esther	Est
Job	Jb
Psalms	Ps
Proverbs	Prv
Ecclesiastes	Eccl
Song of Solomon	Sg
Isaiah	Is
Jeremiah	Jer
Lamentations	Lam
Ezekiel	Ezk
Daniel	Dn
Hosea	Hos
Joel	Jl
Amos	Am
Obadiah	Ob
Jonah	Jon
Micah	Mi
Nahum	Na
Habakkuk	Hab
Zephaniah	Zep
Haggai	Hg
Zechariah	Zec
Malachi	Mal
Matthew	Mt
Mark	Mk
Luke	Lk
John	Jn
Acts	Acts
Romans	Rom
1 Corinthians	1 Cor
2 Corinthians	2 Cor
Galatians	Gal
Ephesians	Eph
Philippians	Phil
Colossians	Col
1 Thessalonians	1 Thes
2 Thessalonians	2 Thes
1 Timothy	1 Tm
2 Timothy	2 Tm
Titus	Ti
Philemon	Phlm
Hebrews	Heb
James	Jas
1 Peter	1 Pt
2 Peter	2 Pt
1 John	1 Jn
2 John	2 Jn
3 John	3 Jn
Jude	Jude
Revelation	Rv

The letter "T" in references to the Psalms (e.g., Ps 51:T) denotes the "title" of that Psalm.

CONCORDANCE

A

AARON (329)
Moses and he said, "Is there not **A**, Ex 4:14
The LORD said to **A**, "Go into the Ex 4:27
And Moses told **A** all the words of the Ex 4:28
Then Moses and **A** went and gathered Ex 4:29
A spoke all the words that the LORD had Ex 4:30
Afterward Moses and **A** went and said to Ex 5:1
king of Egypt said to them, "Moses and **A**, Ex 5:4
They met Moses and **A**, who were Ex 5:20
spoke to Moses and **A** and gave them a Ex 6:13
sister, and she bore him **A** and Moses, Ex 6:20
A took as his wife Elisheba, the daughter Ex 6:23
These are the **A** and Moses to whom the Ex 6:26
Israel from Egypt, this Moses and this **A**. Ex 6:27
and your brother **A** shall be your prophet. Ex 7:1
and your brother **A** shall tell Pharaoh to Ex 7:2
Moses and **A** did so; they did just as the Ex 7:6
years old, and **A** eighty-three years old, Ex 7:7
Then the LORD said to Moses and **A**, Ex 7:8
a miracle,' then you shall say to **A**, Ex 7:9
So Moses and **A** went to Pharaoh and did Ex 7:10
A cast down his staff before Pharaoh Ex 7:10
And the LORD said to Moses, "Say to **A**, Ex 7:19
Moses and **A** did as the LORD Ex 7:20
And the LORD said to Moses, "Say to **A**, Ex 8:5
So **A** stretched out his hand over the Ex 8:6
Pharaoh called Moses and **A** and said, Ex 8:8
So Moses and **A** went out from Pharaoh, Ex 8:12
Then the LORD said to Moses, "Say to **A**, Ex 8:16
A stretched out his hand with his staff Ex 8:17
Pharaoh called Moses and **A** and said, Ex 8:25
And the LORD said to Moses and **A**, "Take Ex 9:8
and called Moses and **A** and said to Ex 9:27
So Moses and **A** went in to Pharaoh and Ex 10:3
So Moses and **A** were brought back to Ex 10:8
hastily called Moses and **A** and said, Ex 10:16
Moses and **A** did all these wonders Ex 11:10
LORD said to Moses and **A** in the land of Ex 12:1
LORD had commanded Moses and **A**, Ex 12:28
summoned Moses and **A** by night and Ex 12:31
And the LORD said to Moses and **A**, Ex 12:43
as the LORD commanded Moses and **A**. Ex 12:50
Miriam the prophetess, the sister of **A**, Ex 15:20
against Moses and **A** in the wilderness, Ex 16:2
So Moses and **A** said to all the people of Ex 16:6
Then Moses said to **A**, "Say to the whole Ex 16:9
And as soon as **A** spoke to the whole Ex 16:10
And Moses said to **A**, "Take a jar, and Ex 16:33
so **A** placed it before the testimony to be Ex 16:34
A, and Hur went up to the top of the Ex 17:10
it, while **A** and Hur held up his hands, Ex 17:12
and **A** came with all the elders of Israel Ex 18:12
and come up bringing **A** with you. Ex 19:24
Moses, "Come up to the LORD, you and **A**, Ex 24:1
Then Moses and **A**, Nadab, and Abihu, Ex 24:9
And behold, **A** and Hur are with you. Ex 24:14
A and his sons shall tend it from Ex 27:21
"Then bring near to you **A** your brother, Ex 28:1
serve me as priests—**A** and Aaron's sons, Ex 28:1
make holy garments for **A** your brother, Ex 28:2
holy garments for **A** your brother and Ex 28:4
And **A** shall bear their names before Ex 28:12
So **A** shall bear the names of the sons of Ex 28:29
Thus **A** shall bear the judgment of the Ex 28:30
And it shall be on **A** when he ministers, Ex 28:35
and **A** shall bear any guilt from the Ex 28:38
you shall put them on **A** your brother, Ex 28:41
and they shall be on **A** and on his sons Ex 28:43
You shall bring **A** and his sons to the Ex 29:4
and put on **A** the coat and the robe of the Ex 29:5
and you shall gird **A** and his sons with Ex 29:9
Thus you shall ordain **A** and his sons. Ex 29:9
A and his sons shall lay their hands on Ex 29:10
and **A** and his sons shall lay their Ex 29:15
and **A** and his sons shall lay their Ex 29:19
of the right ear of **A** and on the tips of Ex 29:20
and sprinkle it on **A** and his garments, Ex 29:21
on the palms of **A** and on the palms Ex 29:24
It shall be for **A** and his sons as a Ex 29:28
"The holy garments of **A** shall be for Ex 29:29
And **A** and his sons shall eat the flesh Ex 29:32
you shall do to **A** and to his sons, Ex 29:35
A also and his sons I will consecrate to Ex 29:44
And **A** shall burn fragrant incense on it. Ex 30:7
and when **A** sets up the lamps at Ex 30:8
A shall make atonement on its horns Ex 30:10
with which **A** and his sons shall wash Ex 30:19
You shall anoint **A** and his sons, and Ex 30:30
the holy garments for **A** the priest and Ex 31:10
themselves together to **A** and said to Ex 32:1
So **A** said to them, "Take off the rings of Ex 32:2
in their ears and brought them to **A**. Ex 32:3
When **A** saw this, he built an altar Ex 32:5
And **A** made proclamation and said, Ex 32:5
And Moses said to **A**, "What did this Ex 32:21
And **A** said, "Let not the anger of my Ex 32:22
had broken loose (for **A** had let them Ex 32:25
made the calf, the one that **A** made. Ex 32:35
A and all the people of Israel saw Moses, Ex 34:30
and **A** and all the leaders of the Ex 34:31
the holy garments for **A** the priest, Ex 35:19
of Ithamar the son of **A** the priest. Ex 38:21
They made the holy garments for **A**, as Ex 39:1
woven of fine linen, for **A** and his sons, Ex 39:27
the holy garments for **A** the priest, Ex 39:41
Then you shall bring **A** and his sons to Ex 40:12
and put on **A** the holy garments. And Ex 40:13
with which Moses and **A** and his sons Ex 40:31
and the sons of **A** the priest shall put fire Lv 1:7
grain offering shall be for **A** and his sons; Lv 2:3
offering shall be for **A** and his sons; Lv 2:10
and the sons of **A** shall throw its blood Lv 3:13
"Command **A** and his sons, saying, This Lv 6:9
The sons of **A** shall offer it before the Lv 6:14
And the rest of it **A** and his sons shall Lv 6:16
among the children of **A** may eat of it, Lv 6:18
is the offering that **A** and his sons shall Lv 6:20
"Speak to **A** and his sons, saying, This is Lv 6:25
shared equally among all the sons of **A**. Lv 7:10
the breast shall be for **A** and his sons. Lv 7:31
among the sons of **A** offers the blood of Lv 7:33
have given them to **A** the priest and to Lv 7:34
This is the portion of **A** and of his sons Lv 7:35
"Take **A** and his sons with him, and the Lv 8:2
And Moses brought **A** and his sons and Lv 8:6
and **A** and his sons laid their hands on Lv 8:14
and **A** and his sons laid their hands on Lv 8:18
and **A** and his sons laid their hands on Lv 8:22
these in the hands of **A** and in the hands Lv 8:27
and sprinkled it on **A** and his garments, Lv 8:30
So he consecrated **A** and his garments, Lv 8:30
And Moses said to **A** and his sons, "Boil Lv 8:31
saying, '**A** and his sons shall eat it.' Lv 8:31
And **A** and his sons did all the things Lv 8:36
eighth day Moses called **A** and his sons Lv 9:1
and he said to **A**, "Take for yourself a bull Lv 9:2
Then Moses said to **A**, "Draw near to the Lv 9:7
So **A** drew near to the altar and killed the Lv 9:8
And the sons of **A** presented the blood to Lv 9:9
and the right thigh **A** waved for a wave Lv 9:21
Then **A** lifted up his hands toward the Lv 9:22
And Moses and **A** went into the tent of Lv 9:23
Now Nadab and Abihu, the sons of **A**, Lv 10:1
Then Moses said to **A**, "This is what the Lv 10:3
I will be glorified.'" And **A** held his peace. Lv 10:3
the sons of Uzziel the uncle of **A**, Lv 10:4
And Moses said to **A** and to Eleazar and Lv 10:6
And the LORD spoke to **A**, saying, Lv 10:8
Moses spoke to **A** and to Eleazar and Lv 10:12
and Ithamar, the surviving sons of **A**, Lv 10:16
And **A** said to Moses, "Behold, today Lv 10:19
And the LORD spoke to Moses and **A**, Lv 11:1
The LORD spoke to Moses and **A**, saying, Lv 13:1
he shall be brought to **A** the priest or to Lv 13:2
The LORD spoke to Moses and **A**, saying, Lv 14:33
The LORD spoke to Moses and **A**, saying, Lv 15:1
after the death of the two sons of **A**, Lv 16:1
"Tell **A** your brother not to come at any Lv 16:2
But in this way **A** shall come into the Lv 16:3
"**A** shall offer the bull as a sin offering Lv 16:6
And **A** shall cast lots over the two goats, Lv 16:8
And **A** shall present the goat on which Lv 16:9
"**A** shall present the bull as a sin Lv 16:11
And **A** shall lay both his hands on the Lv 16:21
"Then **A** shall come into the tent of Lv 16:23
"Speak to **A** and his sons and to all the Lv 17:2
"Speak to the priests, the sons of **A**, Lv 21:1
"Speak to **A**, saying, None of your Lv 21:17
of the offspring of **A** the priest who has Lv 21:21
So Moses spoke to **A** and to his sons Lv 21:24
"Speak to **A** and his sons so that they Lv 22:2
of the offspring of **A** who has a leprous Lv 22:4
"Speak to **A** and his sons and all the Lv 22:18
A shall arrange it from evening to Lv 24:3
Every Sabbath day **A** shall arrange it Lv 24:8
And it shall be for **A** and his sons, and Lv 24:9
to go to war, you and **A** shall list them, Nm 1:3
Moses and **A** took these men who had Nm 1:17
whom Moses and **A** listed with the help Nm 1:44
The LORD spoke to Moses and **A**, saying, Nm 2:1
are the generations of **A** and Moses at Nm 3:1
These are the names of the sons of **A**: Nm 3:2
These are the names of the sons of **A**, the Nm 3:3
as priests in the lifetime of **A** their father. Nm 3:4
near, and set them before **A** the priest, Nm 3:6
shall give the Levites to **A** and his sons; Nm 3:9
And you shall appoint **A** and his sons, Nm 3:10
Eleazar the son of **A** the priest was to Nm 3:32
were Moses and **A** and his sons, Nm 3:38
whom Moses and **A** listed at the Nm 3:39
give the money to **A** and his sons as Nm 3:48
redemption money to **A** and his sons, Nm 3:51
The LORD spoke to Moses and **A**, saying, Nm 4:1
A and his sons shall go in and take Nm 4:5
And when **A** and his sons have Nm 4:15
Eleazar the son of **A** the priest shall Nm 4:16
The LORD spoke to Moses and **A**, Nm 4:17
A and his sons shall go in and appoint Nm 4:19
be at the command of **A** and his sons, Nm 4:27
of Ithamar the son of **A** the priest. Nm 4:28
of Ithamar the son of **A** the priest." Nm 4:33
And Moses and **A** and the chiefs of the Nm 4:34
whom Moses and **A** listed according to Nm 4:37
whom Moses and **A** listed according to Nm 4:41
whom Moses and **A** listed according to Nm 4:45
whom Moses and **A** and the chiefs of Nm 4:46
"Speak to **A** and his sons, saying, Thus Nm 6:23
of Ithamar the son of **A** the priest. Nm 7:8
"Speak to **A** and say to him, When you Nm 8:2
And **A** did so: he set up its lamps in front Nm 8:3
and **A** shall offer the Levites before the Nm 8:11
set the Levites before **A** and his sons, Nm 8:13
Levites as a gift to **A** and his sons from Nm 8:19
Thus did Moses and **A** and all the Nm 8:20
and **A** offered them as a wave offering Nm 8:21
and **A** made atonement for them to Nm 8:21
tent of meeting before **A** and his sons; Nm 8:22
came before Moses and **A** on that day. Nm 9:6
And the sons of **A**, the priests, shall Nm 10:8
Miriam and **A** spoke against Moses Nm 12:1
said to Moses and to **A** and Miriam, Nm 12:4
of the tent and called **A** and Miriam, Nm 12:5
And **A** turned toward Miriam, and Nm 12:10
And **A** said to Moses, "Oh, my lord, do Nm 12:11
came to Moses and **A** and to all the Nm 13:26
Israel grumbled against Moses and **A**. Nm 14:2
Then Moses and **A** fell on their faces Nm 14:5
And the LORD spoke to Moses and to **A**, Nm 14:26
him to Moses and **A** and to all the Nm 15:33
Moses and against **A** and said to Nm 16:3
What is **A** that you grumble against Nm 16:11
before the LORD, you and they, and **A**, Nm 16:16
you also, and **A**, each his censer." Nm 16:17
the tent of meeting with Moses and **A**. Nm 16:18
And the LORD spoke to Moses and to **A**, Nm 16:20
Eleazar the son of **A** the priest to take Nm 16:37
who is not of the descendants of **A**, Nm 16:40
against Moses and against **A**, Nm 16:41
against Moses and against **A**, Nm 16:42
And Moses and **A** came to the front of Nm 16:43
And Moses said to **A**, "Take your Nm 16:46
So **A** took it as Moses said and ran Nm 16:47
And **A** returned to Moses at the Nm 16:50
And the staff of **A** was among their Nm 17:6
the staff of **A** for the house of Levi had Nm 17:8

the staff of **A** before the testimony, Nm 17:10
So the LORD said to **A**, "You and your Nm 18:1
Then the LORD spoke to **A**, "Behold, I Nm 18:8
And the LORD said to **A**, "You shall Nm 18:20
LORD'S contribution to **A** the priest. Nm 18:28
Now the LORD spoke to Moses and to **A**, Nm 19:1
together against Moses and against **A**. Nm 20:2
Then Moses and **A** went from the Nm 20:6
congregation, you and **A** your brother, Nm 20:8
Then Moses and **A** gathered the Nm 20:10
And the LORD said to Moses and **A**, Nm 20:12
said to Moses and **A** at Mount Hor, Nm 20:23
"Let **A** be gathered to his people, for he Nm 20:24
Take **A** and Eleazar his son and bring Nm 20:25
And strip **A** of his garments and put Nm 20:26
And **A** shall be gathered to his people Nm 20:26
And Moses stripped **A** of his garments Nm 20:28
And **A** died there on the top of the Nm 20:28
saw that **A** had perished, Nm 20:29
house of Israel wept for **A** thirty days. Nm 20:29
the son of Eleazar, son of **A** the priest, Nm 25:7
the son of Eleazar, son of **A** the priest, Nm 25:11
to Moses and to Eleazar the son of **A**, Nm 26:1
against Moses and **A** in the company Nm 26:9
she bore to Amram **A** and Moses and Nm 26:59
And to **A** were born Nadab, Abihu, Nm 26:60
those listed by Moses and **A** the priest, Nm 26:64
to your people, as your brother **A** was, Nm 27:13
under the leadership of Moses and **A**. Nm 33:1
And **A** the priest went up Mount Hor Nm 33:38
And **A** was 123 years old when he died Nm 33:39
was so angry with **A** that he was ready Dt 9:20
And I prayed for **A** also at the same time. Dt 9:20
Bene-jaakan to Moserah. There **A** died, Dt 10:6
as **A** your brother died in Mount Hor Dt 32:50
were descendants of **A** the priest received Jos 21:4
which went to the descendants of **A**, Jos 21:10
to the descendants of **A** the priest they Jos 21:13
The cities of the descendants of **A**, the Jos 21:19
And I sent Moses and **A**, and I plagued Jos 24:5
And Eleazar the son of **A** died, and they Jos 24:33
Phinehas the son of Eleazar, son of **A**, Jgs 20:28
appointed Moses and **A** and brought 1 Sm 12:6
LORD and the LORD sent Moses and **A**, 1 Sm 12:8
of Amram: **A**, Moses, and Miriam. 1 Chr 6:3
The sons of **A**: Nadab, Abihu, Eleazar, 1 Chr 6:3
But **A** and his sons made offerings on 1 Chr 6:49
These are the sons of **A**: Eleazar his 1 Chr 6:50
to the sons of **A** of the clans of 1 Chr 6:54
To the sons of **A** they gave the cities 1 Chr 6:57
prince Jehoiada, of the house of **A**, 1 Chr 12:27
together the sons of **A** and the Levites: 1 Chr 15:4
The sons of Amram: **A** and Moses. 1 Chr 23:13
A was set apart to dedicate the most 1 Chr 23:13
assist the sons of **A** for the service of 1 Chr 23:28
and to attend the sons of **A**, 1 Chr 23:32
divisions of the sons of **A** were these. 1 Chr 24:1
The sons of **A**: Nadab, Abihu, 1 Chr 24:1
for them by **A** their father, 1 Chr 24:19
just as their brothers the sons of **A**, 1 Chr 24:31
the son of Kemuel; for **A**, 1 Chr 27:17
the priests of the LORD, the sons of **A**, 2 Chr 13:9
to the LORD who are sons of **A**, 2 Chr 13:10
but for the priests the sons of **A**, 2 Chr 26:18
priests the sons of **A** to offer them on 2 Chr 29:21
And for the sons of **A**, the priests, 2 Chr 31:19
the sons of **A** were offering the 2 Chr 35:14
and for the priests the sons of **A**. 2 Chr 35:14
son of Eleazar, son of **A** the chief priest— Ezr 7:5
And the priest, the son of **A**, shall be Neh 10:38
that which was for the sons of **A**. Neh 12:47
a flock by the hand of Moses and **A**. Ps 77:20
Moses and **A** were among his priests, Ps 99:6
He sent Moses, his servant, and **A**, Ps 105:26
the camp were jealous of Moses and **A**, Ps 106:16
O house of **A**, trust in the LORD! He is Ps 115:10
of Israel; he will bless the house of **A**; Ps 115:12
Let the house of **A** say, "His steadfast Ps 118:3
down on the beard, on the beard of **A**, Ps 133:2
the LORD! O house of **A**, bless the LORD! Ps 135:19
I sent before you Moses, **A**, and Miriam. Mi 6:4
he had a wife from the daughters of **A**, Lk 1:5
saying to **A**, 'Make for us gods who Acts 7:40
only when called by God, just as **A** was. Heb 5:4
than one named after the order of **A**? Heb 7:11

AARON'S (25)
Eleazar, **A** son, took as his wife one of the Ex 6:25
But **A** staff swallowed up their staffs. Ex 7:12
serve me as priests—Aaron and **A** sons, Ex 28:1
that they make **A** garments to Ex 28:3
and they shall be on **A** heart, Ex 28:30
It shall be on **A** forehead, and Aaron Ex 28:38
"For **A** sons you shall make coats and Ex 28:40
of the ram of **A** ordination and wave it Ex 29:26
from what was **A** and his sons. Ex 29:27
and **A** sons the priests shall bring the Lv 1:5
And **A** sons the priests shall arrange the Lv 1:8
and **A** sons the priests shall throw its Lv 1:11
and bring it to **A** sons the priests. And he Lv 2:2
and **A** sons the priests shall throw the Lv 3:2
Then **A** sons shall burn it on the altar on Lv 3:5
and **A** sons shall throw its blood against Lv 3:8
The priest from among **A** sons, who is Lv 6:22
anointing oil on **A** head and anointed Lv 8:12
And Moses brought **A** sons and clothed Lv 8:13
it on the lobe of **A** right ear and on the Lv 8:23
Then he presented **A** sons, and Moses Lv 8:24
and **A** sons handed him the blood, Lv 9:12
And **A** sons handed him the blood, and Lv 9:18
and write **A** name on the staff of Levi. Nm 17:3
the manna, and **A** staff that budded, Heb 9:4

ABADDON (7)
before God, and **A** has no covering. Jb 26:6
A and Death say, 'We have heard a Jb 28:22
be a fire that consumes as far as **A**, Jb 31:12
in the grave, or your faithfulness in **A**? Ps 88:11
Sheol and **A** lie open before the LORD; Prv 15:11
Sheol and **A** are never satisfied, and Prv 27:20
His name in Hebrew is **A**, and in Greek Rv 9:11

ABAGTHA (1)
Biztha, Harbona, Bigtha and **A**, Est 1:10

ABANA (1)
Are not **A** and Pharpar, the rivers of 2 Kgs 5:12

ABANDON (6)
he will again **a** them in the Nm 32:15
grain. Let us **a** this exacting of interest. Neh 5:10
For you will not **a** my soul to Sheol, or Ps 16:10
The LORD will not **a** him to his power or Ps 37:33
his people; he will not **a** his heritage; Ps 94:14
For you will not **a** my soul to Hades, or Acts 2:27

ABANDONED (27)
the land shall be **a** by them and enjoy Lv 26:43
'It is because they **a** the covenant of the Dt 29:25
And they **a** the LORD, the God of their Jgs 2:12
They **a** the LORD and served the Baals Jgs 2:13
in the days of Jael, the highways were **a**, Jgs 5:6
were dead, they **a** their cities and fled. 1 Sm 31:7
'Because they **a** the LORD their God who 1 Kgs 9:9
But he **a** the counsel that the old men 1 Kgs 12:8
you have **a** the commandments 1 Kgs 18:18
away in the twilight and **a** their tents, 2 Kgs 7:7
And they **a** all the commandments 2 Kgs 17:16
He **a** the LORD, the God of his fathers, 2 Kgs 21:22
were dead, they **a** their cities and fled, 1 Chr 10:7
will say, 'Because they **a** the LORD, 2 Chr 7:22
But he **a** the counsel that the old men 2 Chr 10:8
was strong, he **a** the law of the LORD, 2 Chr 12:1
"Thus says the LORD, 'You **a** me, 2 Chr 12:5
so I have **a** you to the hand of 2 Chr 12:5
And they **a** the house of the LORD, 2 Chr 24:18
and you **a** them to the hand of their Neh 9:28
For he has crushed and **a** the poor; he Jb 20:19
my house; I have **a** my heritage; Jer 12:7
the Christ, that he was not **a** to Hades, Acts 2:31
hope of our being saved was at last **a**. Acts 27:20
for having **a** their former 1 Tm 5:12
way of Cain and **a** themselves for the Jude 1:11
that you have **a** the love you had at first. Rv 2:4

ABARIM (5)
into this mountain of **A** and see the Nm 27:12
and camped in the mountains of **A**, Nm 33:47
the mountains of **A** and camped in Nm 33:48
"Go up this mountain of the **A**, Mount Dt 32:49
cry out from **A**, for all your lovers are Jer 22:20

ABASE (1)
on everyone who is proud and **a** him. Jb 40:11

ABASED (2)
than this, and I will be **a** in your eyes. 2 Sm 6:22
make you despised and **a** before all the Mal 2:9

ABATE (1)
the waters continued to **a** until the tenth Gn 8:5

ABATED (3)
At the end of 150 days the waters had **a**, Gn 8:3
when the anger of King Ahasuerus had **a**, Est 2:1
Mordecai. Then the wrath of the king **a**. Est 7:10

ABBA (3)
And he said, "**A**, Father, all things are Mk 14:36
as sons, by whom we cry, "**A**! Father!" Rom 8:15
Son into our hearts, crying, "**A**! Father!" Gal 4:6

ABDA (2)
Adoniram the son of **A** was in charge 1 Kgs 4:6
and **A** the son of Shammua, son of Neh 11:17

ABDEEL (1)
Shelemiah the son of **A** to seize Baruch Jer 36:26

ABDI (3)
Ethan the son of Kishi, son of **A**, son 1 Chr 6:44
sons of Merari, Kish the son of **A**, 2 Chr 29:12
Zechariah, Jehiel, **A**, Jeremoth, Ezr 10:26

ABDIEL (1)
Ahi the son of **A**, son of Guni, was 1 Chr 5:15

ABDON (8)
pasturelands, **A** with its pasturelands, Jos 21:30
After him **A** the son of Hillel the Jgs 12:13
Then **A** the son of Hillel the Jgs 12:15
A with its pasturelands, 1 Chr 6:74
A, Zichri, Hanan, 1 Chr 8:23
son: **A**, then Zur, Kish, Baal, Nadab, 1 Chr 8:30
and his firstborn son **A**, then Zur, 1 Chr 9:36
son of Shaphan, **A** the son of Micah, 2 Chr 34:20

ABEDNEGO (15)
called Meshach, and Azariah he called **A**. Dn 1:7
and **A** over the affairs of the province of Dn 2:49
of Babylon: Shadrach, Meshach, and **A**. Dn 3:12
Shadrach, Meshach, and **A** be brought. Dn 3:13
"Is it true, O Shadrach, Meshach, and **A**, Dn 3:14
and **A** answered and said to the king, Dn 3:16
against Shadrach, Meshach, and **A**. Dn 3:19
to bind Shadrach, Meshach, and **A**, Dn 3:20
took up Shadrach, Meshach, and **A**. Dn 3:22
three men, Shadrach, Meshach, and **A**, Dn 3:23
declared, "Shadrach, Meshach, and **A**, Dn 3:26
Meshach, and **A** came out from the fire. Dn 3:26
the God of Shadrach, Meshach, and **A**, Dn 3:28
and **A** shall be torn limb from limb, Dn 3:29
and **A** in the province of Babylon. Dn 3:30

ABEL (15)
And again, she bore his brother **A**. Now Gn 4:2
Now **A** was a keeper of sheep, and Cain a Gn 4:2
and **A** also brought of the firstborn of his Gn 4:4
LORD had regard for **A** and his offering, Gn 4:4
Cain spoke to **A** his brother. And when Gn 4:8
up against his brother **A** and killed him. Gn 4:8
"Where is **A** your brother?" He said, Gn 4:9
for me another offspring instead of **A**, Gn 4:25
tribes of Israel to **A** of Beth-maacah, 2 Sm 20:14
besieged him in **A** of Beth-maacah. 2 Sm 20:15
'Let them but ask counsel at **A**,' 2 Sm 20:18
the blood of innocent **A** to the blood of Mt 23:35
from the blood of **A** to the blood of Lk 11:51
By faith **A** offered to God a more Heb 11:4
a better word than the blood of **A**. Heb 12:24

ABEL-BETH-MAACAH (2)
Ijon, Dan, **A**, and all Chinneroth, 1 Kgs 15:20
came and captured Ijon, **A**, Janoah, 2 Kgs 15:29

ABEL-KERAMIM (1)
Minnith, twenty cities, and as far as **A**, Jgs 11:33

ABEL-MAIM (1)
A, and all the store cities of Naphtali. 2 Chr 16:4

ABEL-MEHOLAH (3)
toward Zererah, as far as the border of **A**, Jgs 7:22
Jezreel, and from Beth-shean to **A**, 1 Kgs 4:12
of Shaphat of **A** you shall anoint 1 Kgs 19:16

ABEL-MIZRAIM (1)
Therefore the place was named **A**; Gn 50:11

ABEL-SHITTIM (1)
as far as **A** in the plains Nm 33:49

ABHOR (14)
you, and my soul shall not **a** you. Lv 26:11
of your idols, and my soul will **a** you. Lv 26:30
neither will I **a** them so as to destroy Lv 26:44
You shall utterly detest and **a** it, for it is Dt 7:26
"You shall not **a** an Edomite, for he is Dt 23:7
You shall not **a** an Egyptian, because Dt 23:7
into a pit, and my own clothes will **a** me. Jb 9:31
All my intimate friends **a** me, and those Jb 19:19
They **a** me; they keep aloof from me; Jb 30:10
I hate and **a** falsehood, but I love your Ps 119:163
and they **a** him who speaks the truth. Am 5:10
"I **a** the pride of Jacob and hate his Am 6:8
You who **a** idols, do you rob temples? Rom 2:22
A what is evil; hold fast to what is Rom 12:9

ABHORRED (6)
my rules and their soul **a** my statutes. Lv 26:43
has not despised or **a** the affliction of Ps 22:24
his people, and he **a** his heritage; Ps 106:40
be cursed by peoples, **a** by nations, Prv 24:24
to one deeply despised, **a** by the nation, Is 49:7
out on the open field, for you were **a**, Ezk 16:5

ABHORRENCE (1)
and they shall be an **a** to all flesh." Is 66:24

ABHORRENT (1)
the king's command was **a** to Joab. 1 Chr 21:6

ABHORS (2)
statutes, and if your soul **a** my rules, Lv 26:15
the LORD **a** the bloodthirsty and deceitful Ps 5:6

ABI (1)
mother's name was **A** the daughter of 2 Kgs 18:2

ABI-ALBON (1)
A the Arbathite, Azmaveth of 2 Sm 23:31

ABIASAPH (1)
sons of Korah: Assir, Elkanah, and **A**; Ex 6:24

ABIATHAR (30)
the son of Ahitub, named **A**, 1 Sm 22:20
And **A** told David that Saul had 1 Sm 22:21
And David said to **A**, "I knew on that 1 Sm 22:22
When **A** the son of Ahimelech had 1 Sm 23:6
And he said to **A** the priest, "Bring the 1 Sm 23:9
And David said to **A** the priest, the son 1 Sm 30:7
the ephod." So **A** brought the ephod 1 Sm 30:7
Ahimelech the son of **A** were priests, 2 Sm 8:17
And **A** came up, and behold, Zadok 2 Sm 15:24
your son, and Jonathan the son of **A**. 2 Sm 15:27
So Zadok and **A** carried the ark of 2 Sm 15:29
Are not Zadok and **A** the priests with 2 Sm 15:35
tell it to Zadok and **A** the priests. 2 Sm 15:35
said to Zadok and **A** the priests, 2 Sm 17:15
message to Zadok and **A** the priests, 2 Sm 19:11
and Zadok and **A** were priests; 2 Sm 20:25
son of Zeruiah and with **A** the priest. 1 Kgs 1:7
all the sons of the king, **A** the priest, 1 Kgs 1:19
of the army, and **A** the priest. 1 Kgs 1:25
the son of **A** the priest came. 1 Kgs 1:42
on his side are **A** the priest and Joab 1 Kgs 2:22
And to **A** the priest the king said, "Go 1 Kgs 2:26
So Solomon expelled **A** from being 1 Kgs 2:27
put Zadok the priest in the place of **A**. 1 Kgs 2:35
of the army; Zadok and **A** were priests; 1 Kgs 4:4
summoned the priests Zadok and **A**, 1 Chr 15:11
Ahimelech the son of **A** were priests; 1 Chr 18:16
the son of **A** and the heads 1 Chr 24:6
Jehoiada the son of Benaiah, and **A**. 1 Chr 27:34
of God, in the time of **A** the high priest, Mk 2:26

ABIATHAR'S (1)
Zadok's son, and Jonathan, **A** son, 2 Sm 15:36

ABIB (6)
Today, in the month of **A**, you are going Ex 13:4
the appointed time in the month of **A**, Ex 23:15
at the time appointed in the month **A**, Ex 34:18
for in the month **A** you came out from Ex 34:18
"Observe the month of **A** and keep the Dt 16:1
for in the month of **A** the LORD your God Dt 16:1

ABIDA (2)
Ephah, Epher, Hanoch, **A**, and Eldaah. Gn 25:4
Epher, Hanoch, **A**, and Eldaah. 1 Chr 1:33

ABIDAN (5)
from Benjamin, **A** the son of Gideoni; Nm 1:11
people of Benjamin being **A** the son of Nm 2:22
On the ninth day **A** the son of Gideoni, Nm 7:60
was the offering of **A** the son of Nm 7:65
people of Benjamin was **A** the son of Nm 10:24

ABIDE (24)
"My Spirit shall not **a** in man forever, Gn 6:3
His soul shall **a** in well-being, and his Ps 25:13
of the Most High will **a** in the shadow of Ps 91:1
and righteousness **a** in the fruitful field. Is 32:16
My people will **a** in a peaceful Is 32:18
believed in him, "If you **a** in my word, Jn 8:31
A in me, and I in you. As the branch Jn 15:4
neither can you, unless you **a** in me. Jn 15:4
If anyone does not **a** in me he is thrown Jn 15:6
If you **a** in me, and my words abide in Jn 15:7
you abide in me, and my words **a** in you, Jn 15:7
me, so have I loved you. **A** in my love. Jn 15:9
commandments, you will **a** in my love, Jn 15:10
Father's commandments and **a** in his Jn 15:10
bear fruit and that your fruit should **a**, Jn 15:16
So now faith, hope, and love **a**, these 1 Cor 13:13
everyone who does not **a** by all things Gal 3:10
heard from the beginning **a** in you. 1 Jn 2:24
then you too will **a** in the Son and in 1 Jn 2:24
lie, just as it has taught you—**a** in him. 1 Jn 2:27
And now, little children, **a** in him, so 1 Jn 2:28
him, how does God's love **a** in him? 1 Jn 3:17
this we know that we **a** in him and he 1 Jn 4:13
ahead and does not **a** in the teaching of 2 Jn 1:9

ABIDES (23)
In his neck **a** strength, and terror Jb 41:22
which cannot be moved, but **a** forever. Ps 125:1
my flesh and drinks my blood **a** in me, Jn 6:56
bear fruit by itself, unless it **a** in the vine, Jn 15:4
Whoever **a** in me and I in him, he it is Jn 15:5
whoever says he **a** in him ought to walk 1 Jn 2:6
loves his brother **a** in the light, 1 Jn 2:10
strong, and the word of God **a** in you, 1 Jn 2:14
whoever does the will of God **a** forever. 1 Jn 2:17
heard from the beginning **a** in you, 1 Jn 2:24
that you received from him **a** in you, 1 Jn 2:27
No one who **a** in him keeps on sinning; 1 Jn 3:6
of sinning, for God's seed **a** in him, 1 Jn 3:9
Whoever does not love **a** in death. 1 Jn 3:14
keeps his commandments **a** in him, 1 Jn 3:24
And by this we know that he **a** in us, 1 Jn 3:24
God **a** in us and his love is perfected in 1 Jn 4:12
Jesus is the Son of God, God **a** in him, 1 Jn 4:15
and whoever **a** in love abides in God, 1 Jn 4:16
and whoever abides in love **a** in God, 1 Jn 4:16
love abides in God, and God **a** in him. 1 Jn 4:16
because of the truth that **a** in us and will 2 Jn 1:2
Whoever **a** in the teaching has both the 2 Jn 1:9

ABIDING (6)
continued over the tabernacle, **a** there, Nm 9:22
are like a shadow, and there is no **a**. 1 Chr 29:15
and you do not have his word **a** in you, Jn 5:38
had a better possession and an **a** one. Heb 10:34
through the living and **a** word of God; 1 Pt 1:23
no murderer has eternal life **a** in him. 1 Jn 3:15

ABIEL (3)
whose name was Kish, the son of **A**, 1 Sm 9:1
the father of Abner was the son of **A**. 1 Sm 14:51
brooks of Gaash, **A** the Arbathite, 1 Chr 11:32

ABIEZER (6)
of Manasseh by their clans, **A**, Helek, Jos 17:2
better than the grape harvest of **A**? Jgs 8:2
A of Anathoth, Mebunnai the 2 Sm 23:27
bore Ishhod, **A** and Mahlah. 1 Chr 7:18
of Ikkesh of Tekoa, **A** of Anathoth, 1 Chr 11:28
ninth month, was **A** of Anathoth, 1 Chr 27:12

ABIEZRITE (1)
Ophrah, which belonged to Joash the **A**, Jgs 6:11

ABIEZRITES (3)
at Ophrah, which belongs to the **A**. Jgs 6:24
and the **A** were called out to follow him. Jgs 6:34
of Joash his father, at Ophrah of the **A**. Jgs 8:32

ABIGAIL (16)
Nabal, and the name of his wife **A**. 1 Sm 25:3
But one of the young men told **A**, 1 Sm 25:14
Then **A** made haste and took two 1 Sm 25:18
When **A** saw David, she hurried and 1 Sm 25:23
And David said to **A**, "Blessed be the 1 Sm 25:32
And **A** came to Nabal, and behold, 1 Sm 25:36
Then David sent and spoke to **A**, 1 Sm 25:39
of David came to **A** at Carmel, 1 Sm 25:40
And **A** hurried and rose and 1 Sm 25:42
Ahinoam of Jezreel, and **A** of Carmel, 1 Sm 27:3
of Jezreel and **A** the widow of 1 Sm 30:5
Ahinoam of Jezreel and **A** the widow of 2 Sm 2:2
of **A** the widow of Nabal of Carmel; 2 Sm 3:3
And their sisters were Zeruiah and **A**. 1 Chr 2:16
A bore Amasa, and the father of 1 Chr 2:17
second, Daniel, by **A** the Carmelite, 1 Chr 3:1

ABIGAL (1)
who had married **A** the daughter of 2 Sm 17:25

ABIHAIL (6)
clans of Merari was Zuriel the son of **A**. Nm 3:35
The name of Abishur's wife was **A**, 1 Chr 2:29
were the sons of **A** the son of Huri, 1 Chr 5:14
and of **A** the daughter of Eliab the 2 Chr 11:18
Esther the daughter of **A** the uncle of Est 2:15
Then Queen Esther, the daughter of **A**, Est 9:29

ABIHU (12)
and she bore him Nadab, **A**, Eleazar, Ex 6:23
the LORD, you and Aaron, Nadab, and **A**, Ex 24:1
Then Moses and Aaron, Nadab, and **A**, Ex 24:9
Aaron and Aaron's sons, Nadab and **A**, Ex 28:1
Now Nadab and **A**, the sons of Aaron, Lv 10:1
Nadab the firstborn, and **A**, Eleazar, and Nm 3:2
But Nadab and **A** died before the LORD Nm 3:4
Aaron were born Nadab, **A**, Eleazar, Nm 26:60
But Nadab and **A** died when they Nm 26:61
Nadab, **A**, Eleazar, and Ithamar. 1 Chr 6:3
Nadab, **A**, Eleazar, and Ithamar. 1 Chr 24:1
But Nadab and **A** died before their 1 Chr 24:2

ABIHUD (1)
And Bela had sons: Addar, Gera, **A**, 1 Chr 8:3

ABIJAH (27)
A; they were judges in Beersheba. 1 Sm 8:2
At that time **A** the son of Jeroboam 1 Kgs 14:1
Solomon was Rehoboam, **A** his son, 1 Chr 3:10
Joel his firstborn, the second **A**. 1 Chr 6:28
Omri, Jeremoth, **A**, Anathoth, 1 Chr 7:8
seventh to Hakkoz, the eighth to **A**, 1 Chr 24:10
of Absalom, who bore him **A**, 2 Chr 11:20
And Rehoboam appointed **A** the son 2 Chr 11:22
and **A** his son reigned in his place. 2 Chr 12:16
A began to reign over Judah. 2 Chr 13:1
was war between **A** and Jeroboam. 2 Chr 13:2
A went out to battle, having an army 2 Chr 13:3
Then **A** stood up on Mount 2 Chr 13:4
and all Israel before **A** and Judah. 2 Chr 13:15
A and his people struck them with 2 Chr 13:17
And **A** pursued Jeroboam and took 2 Chr 13:19
recover his power in the days of **A**. 2 Chr 13:20
But **A** grew mighty. And he took 2 Chr 13:21
The rest of the acts of **A**, his ways 2 Chr 13:22
A slept with his fathers, and they 2 Chr 14:1
mother's name was **A** the daughter of 2 Chr 29:1
Meshullam, **A**, Mijamin, Neh 10:7
Iddo, Ginnethoi, **A**, Neh 12:4
of **A**, Zichri; of Miniamin, of Neh 12:17
and Rehoboam the father of **A**, Mt 1:7
of Abijah, and **A** the father of Asaph, Mt 1:7
named Zechariah, of the division of **A**. Lk 1:5

ABIJAM (5)
And **A** his son reigned in his place. 1 Kgs 14:31
Nebat, **A** began to reign over Judah. 1 Kgs 15:1
rest of the acts of **A** and all that he 1 Kgs 15:7
was war between **A** and Jeroboam. 1 Kgs 15:7
And **A** slept with his fathers, and they 1 Kgs 15:8

ABILENE (1)
Trachonitis, and Lysanias tetrarch of **A**, Lk 3:1

ABILITY (12)
the Spirit of God, with **a** and intelligence, Ex 31:3
And I have given to all able men **a**, that Ex 31:6
houses, for they were men of great **a**. 1 Chr 26:6
and his brothers, 1,700 men of **a**, 1 Chr 26:30
men of great **a** among them were 1 Chr 26:31
and his brothers, 2,700 men of **a**, 1 Chr 26:32
According to their **a** they gave to the Ezr 2:69
another one, to each according to his **a**. Mt 25:15
everyone according to his **a**, Acts 11:29
is right, but not the **a** to carry it out. Rom 7:18
let you be tempted beyond your **a**, 1 Cor 10:13
to another the **a** to distinguish 1 Cor 12:10

ABIMAEL (2)
Obal, **A**, Sheba, Gn 10:28
Obal, **A**, Sheba, 1 Chr 1:22

ABIMELECH (64)
is my sister." And **A** king of Gerar sent Gn 20:2
But God came to **A** in a dream by night Gn 20:3
Now **A** had not approached her. So he Gn 20:4
So **A** rose early in the morning and Gn 20:8
Then **A** called Abraham and said to Gn 20:9
And **A** said to Abraham, "What did Gn 20:10
Then **A** took sheep and oxen, and male Gn 20:14
And **A** said, "Behold, my land is before Gn 20:15
prayed to God, and God healed **A**, Gn 20:17
of the house of **A** because of Sarah, Gn 20:18
At that time **A** and Phicol the Gn 21:22
When Abraham reproved **A** about a Gn 21:25
A said, "I do not know who has done Gn 21:26
sheep and oxen and gave them to **A**, Gn 21:27
And **A** said to Abraham, "What is the Gn 21:29
Then **A** and Phicol the commander of Gn 21:32
went to Gerar to **A** king of the Gn 26:1
A king of the Philistines looked out of a Gn 26:8
So **A** called Isaac and said, "Behold, she Gn 26:9
A said, "What is this you have done to Gn 26:10
So **A** warned all the people, saying, Gn 26:11
And **A** said to Isaac, "Go away from us, Gn 26:16
When **A** went to him from Gerar with Gn 26:26
him a son, and he called his name **A**. Jgs 8:31
Now **A** the son of Jerubbaal went to Jgs 9:1
and their hearts inclined to follow **A**, Jgs 9:3
Baal-berith with which **A** hired worthless Jgs 9:4
and they went and made **A** king, Jgs 9:6
and integrity when you made **A** king, Jgs 9:16
men on one stone, and have made **A**, Jgs 9:18
his house this day, then rejoice in **A**, Jgs 9:19
fire come out from **A** and devour the Jgs 9:20
and from Beth-millo and devour **A**." Jgs 9:20
lived there, because of **A** his brother. Jgs 9:21
A ruled over Israel three years. Jgs 9:22
an evil spirit between **A** and the leaders Jgs 9:23
of Shechem dealt treacherously with **A**, Jgs 9:23
their blood be laid on **A** their brother, Jgs 9:24
along that way. And it was told to **A**. Jgs 9:25
god and ate and drank and reviled **A**. Jgs 9:27
Gaal the son of Ebed said, "Who is **A**, Jgs 9:28
my hand! Then I would remove **A**. Jgs 9:29
I would say to **A**, 'Increase your army, Jgs 9:29
And he sent messengers to **A** secretly, Jgs 9:31
So **A** and all the men who were with him Jgs 9:34
and **A** and the people who were with him Jgs 9:35
mouth now, you who said, 'Who is **A**, Jgs 9:38
leaders of Shechem and fought with **A**. Jgs 9:39
And **A** chased him, and he fled before Jgs 9:40

And **A** lived at Arumah, and Zebul Jgs 9:41
went out into the field, and **A** was told. Jgs 9:42
A and the company that was with him Jgs 9:44
And **A** fought against the city all that Jgs 9:45
A was told that all the leaders of the Jgs 9:47
And **A** went up to Mount Zalmon, he Jgs 9:48
And **A** took an axe in his hand and cut Jgs 9:48
bundle and following **A** put it against Jgs 9:49
Then **A** went to Thebez and encamped Jgs 9:50
And **A** came to the tower and fought Jgs 9:52
the men of Israel saw that **A** was dead, Jgs 9:55
Thus God returned the evil of **A**, which Jgs 9:56
After **A** there arose to save Israel Tola Jgs 10:1
Who killed **A** the son of 2 Sm 11:21
when he changed his behavior before **A**, Ps 34:T

ABIMELECH'S (2)
of water that **A** servants had seized, Gn 21:25
upper millstone on **A** head and crushed Jgs 9:53

ABINADAB (11)
brought it to the house of **A** on the hill. 1 Sm 7:1
Then Jesse called **A** and made him 1 Sm 16:8
the firstborn, and next to him **A**, 1 Sm 17:13
Jonathan and **A** and Malchi-shua, 1 Sm 31:2
and brought it out of the house of **A**, 2 Sm 6:3
And Uzzah and Ahio, the sons of **A**, 2 Sm 6:3
Eliab his firstborn, **A** the second, 1 Chr 2:13
Malchi-shua, **A** and Eshbaal; 1 Chr 8:33
Malchi-shua, **A**, and Eshbaal. 1 Chr 9:39
Jonathan and **A** and Malchi-shua, 1 Chr 10:2
on a new cart, from the house of **A**, 1 Chr 13:7

ABINOAM (4)
the son of **A** from Kedesh-naphtali and Jgs 4:6
that Barak the son of **A** had gone up to Jgs 4:12
and Barak the son of **A** on that day: Jgs 5:1
lead away your captives, O son of **A**. Jgs 5:12

ABIRAM (11)
and Dathan and **A** the sons of Eliab, Nm 16:1
to call Dathan and **A** the sons of Nm 16:12
dwelling of Korah, Dathan, and **A**." Nm 16:24
Moses rose and went to Dathan and **A**, Nm 16:25
the dwelling of Korah, Dathan, and **A**. Nm 16:27
And Dathan and **A** came out and Nm 16:27
sons of Eliab: Nemuel, Dathan, and **A**. Nm 26:9
These are the Dathan and **A**, chosen Nm 26:9
he did to Dathan and **A** the sons of Eliab, Dt 11:6
at the cost of **A** his firstborn, 1 Kgs 16:34
and covered the company of **A**. Ps 106:17

ABISHAG (5)
Israel, and found **A** the Shunammite, 1 Kgs 1:3
and **A** the Shunammite was 1 Kgs 1:15
—to give me **A** the Shunammite as 1 Kgs 2:17
"Let **A** the Shunammite be given to 1 Kgs 2:21
do you ask **A** the Shunammite for 1 Kgs 2:22

ABISHAI (25)
and to Joab's brother **A** the son of 1 Sm 26:6
into the camp to Saul?" And **A** said, 1 Sm 26:6
So David and **A** went to the army by 1 Sm 26:7
Then said **A** to David, "God has given 1 Sm 26:8
But David said to **A**, "Do not destroy 1 Sm 26:9
were there, Joab, **A**, and Asahel. 2 Sm 2:18
But Joab and **A** pursued Abner. And 2 Sm 2:24
So Joab and **A** his brother killed 2 Sm 3:30
he put in the charge of **A** his brother, 2 Sm 10:10
likewise fled before **A** and entered the 2 Sm 10:14
Then **A** the son of Zeruiah said to the 2 Sm 16:9
And David said to **A** and to all his 2 Sm 16:11
under the command of **A** the son of 2 Sm 18:2
the king ordered Joab and **A** and Ittai, 2 Sm 18:5
commanded you and **A** and Ittai, 2 Sm 18:12
A the son of Zeruiah answered, 2 Sm 19:21
And David said to **A**, "Now Sheba the 2 Sm 20:6
Then Joab and **A** his brother 2 Sm 20:10
But **A** the son of Zeruiah came to his 2 Sm 21:17
Now **A**, the brother of Joab, the son 2 Sm 23:18
Zeruiah: **A**, Joab, and Asahel, three. 1 Chr 2:16
Now **A**, the brother of Joab, was 1 Chr 11:20
And **A**, the son of Zeruiah, killed 1 Chr 18:12
put in the charge of **A** his brother, 1 Chr 19:11
fled, they likewise fled before **A**, 1 Chr 19:15

ABISHALOM (2)
name was Maacah the daughter of **A**. 1 Kgs 15:2
was Maacah the daughter of **A**. 1 Kgs 15:10

ABISHUA (5)
Phinehas, Phinehas fathered **A**, 1 Chr 6:4
A fathered Bukki, Bukki fathered 1 Chr 6:5
his son, Phinehas his son, **A** his son, 1 Chr 6:50
A, Naaman, Ahoah, 1 Chr 8:4
son of **A**, son of Phinehas, son of Eleazar, Ezr 7:5

ABISHUR (1)
The sons of Shammai: Nadab and **A**. 1 Chr 2:28

ABISHUR'S (1)
The name of **A** wife was Abihail, and 1 Chr 2:29

ABITAL (2)
and the fifth, Shephatiah the son of **A**; 2 Sm 3:4
the fifth, Shephatiah, by **A**; the sixth, 1 Chr 3:3

ABITUB (1)
sons by Hushim: **A** and Elpaal. 1 Chr 8:11

ABIUD (2)
and Zerubbabel the father of **A**, and Mt 1:13
of Abiud, and **A** the father of Eliakim, Mt 1:13

ABLAZE (4)
the heat of thorns, whether green or **a**, Ps 58:9
as the flame sets the mountains **a**, Ps 83:14
The day that is coming shall set them **a**, Mal 4:1
great a forest is set **a** by such a small fire! Jas 3:5

ABLE (153)
if you are **a** to number them." Then he Gn 15:5
if you know any **a** men among them, Gn 47:6
for you. You are not **a** to do it alone. Ex 18:18
look for **a** men from all the people, Ex 18:21
will direct you, you will be **a** to endure, Ex 18:23
Moses chose **a** men out of all Israel and Ex 18:25
And I have given to all **a** men ability, Ex 31:6
And Moses was not **a** to enter the tent of Ex 40:35
all in Israel who are **a** to go to war, Nm 1:3
upward, all who were **a** to go to war: Nm 1:20
upward, all who were **a** to go to war: Nm 1:22
upward, all who were **a** to go to war: Nm 1:24
and upward, every man **a** to go to war: Nm 1:26
and upward, every man **a** to go to war: Nm 1:28
and upward, every man **a** to go to war: Nm 1:30
and upward, every man **a** to go to war: Nm 1:32
and upward, every man **a** to go to war: Nm 1:34
and upward, every man **a** to go to war: Nm 1:36
and upward, every man **a** to go to war: Nm 1:38
and upward, every man **a** to go to war: Nm 1:40
and upward, every man **a** to go to war: Nm 1:42
every man **a** to go to war in Israel— Nm 1:45
I am not **a** to carry all this people Nm 11:14
it, for we are well **a** to overcome it." Nm 13:30
"We are not **a** to go up against the Nm 13:31
the LORD was not **a** to bring this people Nm 14:16
Perhaps I shall be **a** to defeat them and Nm 22:6
Perhaps I shall be **a** to fight against Nm 22:11
to me? Am I not **a** to honor you?" Nm 22:37
I would not be **a** to go beyond the Nm 24:13
all in Israel who are **a** to go to war." Nm 26:2
to you, 'I am not **a** to bear you by myself. Dt 1:9
No one shall be **a** to stand against you Dt 7:24
the LORD was not **a** to bring them into Dt 9:28
No one shall be **a** to stand against you. Dt 11:25
so that you are not **a** to carry the tithe, Dt 14:24
Every man shall give as he is **a**, Dt 16:17
I am no longer **a** to go out and come in. Dt 31:2
No man shall be **a** to stand before you all Jos 1:5
no man has been **a** to stand before you Jos 23:9
people, "You are not **a** to serve the LORD, Jos 24:19
What have I been **a** to do in comparison Jgs 8:3
of Dan sent five **a** men from the whole Jgs 18:2
"Who is **a** to stand before the LORD, 1 Sm 6:20
If he is **a** to fight with me and kill me, 1 Sm 17:9
"You are not **a** to go against this 1 Sm 17:33
for who is **a** to govern this your great 1 Kgs 3:9
The man Jeroboam was very **a**, and 1 Kgs 11:28
them, all who were **a** to put on armor, 2 Kgs 3:21
if you are **a** on your part to set riders 2 Kgs 18:23
for he will not be **a** to deliver you out 2 Kgs 18:29
expert in war, 44,760, **a** to go to war. 1 Chr 5:18
warriors, 17,200, **a** to go to war. 1 Chr 7:11
Elzabad, whose brothers were **a** men, 1 Chr 26:7
a men qualified for the service; 1 Chr 26:8
had sons and brothers, **a** men, 1 Chr 26:9
the house of my God, so far as I was **a**, 1 Chr 29:2
that we should be **a** thus to offer 1 Chr 29:14
But who is **a** to build him a house, 2 Chr 2:6
so that none is **a** to withstand you. 2 Chr 20:6
wrecked and were not **a** to go to 2 Chr 20:37
Ahaziah had no one **a** to rule the 2 Chr 22:9
for war, **a** to handle spear and shield. 2 Chr 25:5
"The LORD is **a** to give you much 2 Chr 25:9
those lands at all **a** to deliver their 2 Chr 32:13
to destruction was **a** to deliver his 2 Chr 32:14
your God should be **a** to deliver you 2 Chr 32:14
kingdom has been **a** to deliver his 2 Chr 32:15
we will not be **a** to rebuild the wall." Neh 4:10
and said to them, "We, as far as we are **a**, Neh 5:8
through, so that they were not **a** to rise; Ps 18:38
and that he is not **a** to dispute with one Eccl 6:10
if you are **a** on your part to set riders on Is 36:8
you, for he will not be **a** to deliver you. Is 36:14
for which you will not be **a** to atone; Is 47:11
youth; perhaps you may be **a** to succeed; Is 47:12
and he is not **a** to conceal himself. Jer 49:10
that no one was **a** to touch their Lam 4:14
and gold are not **a** to deliver them in Ezk 7:19
righteous shall not be **a** to live by his Ezk 33:12
the lambs shall be as much as he is **a**, Ezk 46:5
and with the lambs as much as he is **a**, Ezk 46:7
the lambs as much as one is **a** to give, Ezk 46:11
"Are you **a** to make known to me the Dn 2:26
for you have been **a** to reveal this Dn 2:47
whom we serve is **a** to deliver us from Dn 3:17
no other god who is **a** to rescue in this Dn 3:29
my kingdom are not **a** to make known Dn 4:18
to me the interpretation, but you are **a**, Dn 4:18
who walk in pride he is **a** to humble. Dn 4:37
been **a** to deliver you from the lions?" Dn 6:20
But he is not **a** to cure you or heal your Hos 5:13
The land is not **a** to bear all his words. Am 7:10
their gold shall be **a** to deliver them on Zep 1:18
God is **a** from these stones to raise up Mt 3:9
you believe that I am **a** to do this?" They Mt 9:28
the one who is **a** to receive this receive Mt 19:12
Are you **a** to drink the cup that I am to Mt 20:22
drink?" They said to him, "We are **a**." Mt 20:22
And no one was **a** to answer him a Mt 22:46
'I am **a** to destroy the temple of God, Mt 26:61
itself, that house will not be **a** to stand. Mk 3:25
word to them, as they were **a** to hear it. Mk 4:33
to cast it out, and they were not **a**." Mk 9:18
my name will be **a** soon afterward to Mk 9:39
Are you **a** to drink the cup that I Mk 10:38
"We are **a**." And Jesus said to them, Mk 10:39
God is **a** from these stones to raise up Lk 3:8
If then you are not **a** to do as small a Lk 12:26
you, will seek to enter and will not be **a**. Lk 13:24
laid a foundation and is not **a** to finish, Lk 14:29
began to build and was not **a** to finish.' Lk 14:30
whether he is **a** with ten thousand Lk 14:31
pass from here to you may not be **a**, Lk 16:26
And they were not **a** in the presence of Lk 20:26
adversaries will be **a** to withstand or Lk 21:15
and no one is **a** to snatch them out of Jn 10:29
it, and now they were not **a** to haul it in, Jn 21:6
you will not be **a** to overthrow them. Acts 5:39
fathers nor we have been **a** to bear? Acts 15:10
which is **a** to build you up and to give Acts 20:32
yourself you will be **a** to find out from Acts 24:8
convinced that God was **a** to do what Rom 4:21
will be **a** to separate us from the love of Rom 8:39
for the Lord is **a** to make him stand. Rom 14:4
all knowledge and **a** to instruct one Rom 15:14
to him who is **a** to strengthen you Rom 16:25
and he is not **a** to understand them 1 Cor 2:14
that you may be **a** to endure it. 1 Cor 10:13
that we may be **a** to comfort those who 2 Cor 1:4
that you may be **a** to answer those 2 Cor 5:12
And God is **a** to make all grace 2 Cor 9:8
Now to him who is **a** to do far more Eph 3:20
that you may be **a** to stand against the Eph 6:11
that you may be **a** to withstand in the Eph 6:13
respectable, hospitable, **a** to teach, 1 Tm 3:2
convinced that he is **a** to guard until 2 Tm 1:12
men who will be **a** to teach others also. 2 Tm 2:2
but kind to everyone, **a** to teach, 2 Tm 2:24
learning and never **a** to arrive at 2 Tm 3:7
which are **a** to make you wise for 2 Tm 3:15
so that he may be **a** to give instruction in Ti 1:9
he is **a** to help those who are being Heb 2:18
to him who was **a** to save him from Heb 5:7
he is **a** to save to the uttermost those Heb 7:25
that God was **a** even to raise Heb 11:19
word, which is **a** to save your souls. Jas 1:21
man, **a** also to bridle his whole body. Jas 3:2
judge, he who is **a** to save and to destroy. Jas 4:12
departure you may be **a** at any time to 2 Pt 1:15
Now to him who is **a** to keep you from Jude 1:24
an open door, which no one is **a** to shut. Rv 3:8
or under the earth was **a** to open the scroll Rv 5:3

ABLE-BODIED (1)
of the Moabites, all strong, **a** men; Jgs 3:29

ABNER (62)
of his army was **A** the son of Ner, 1 Sm 14:50
Ner the father of **A** was the son of 1 Sm 14:51
against the Philistine, he said to **A**, 1 Sm 17:55
"**A**, whose son is this youth?" And 1 Sm 17:55
son is this youth?" And **A** said, 1 Sm 17:55
down of the Philistine, **A** took him, 1 Sm 17:57
sat opposite, and **A** sat by Saul's side, 1 Sm 20:25
where Saul lay, with **A** the son of Ner, 1 Sm 26:5
and **A** and the army lay around him. 1 Sm 26:7
to the army, and to **A** the son of Ner, 1 Sm 26:14
answer, **A**?" Then Abner answered, 1 Sm 26:14
answer, Abner?" Then **A** answered, 1 Sm 26:14
And David said to **A**, "Are you not a 1 Sm 26:15
But **A** the son of Ner, commander of 2 Sm 2:8
A the son of Ner, and the servants of 2 Sm 2:12

And **A** said to Joab, "Let the young 2 Sm 2:14
And **A** and the men of Israel were 2 Sm 2:17
And Asahel pursued **A**, and as he 2 Sm 2:19
hand nor to the left from following **A**. 2 Sm 2:19
Then **A** looked behind him and said, 2 Sm 2:20
A said to him, "Turn aside to your 2 Sm 2:21
And **A** said again to Asahel, "Turn 2 Sm 2:22
Therefore **A** struck him in the 2 Sm 2:23
But Joab and Abishai pursued **A**. And 2 Sm 2:24
together behind **A** and became 2 Sm 2:25
Then **A** called to Joab, "Shall the 2 Sm 2:26
And **A** and his men went all that 2 Sm 2:29
Joab returned from the pursuit of **A**. 2 Sm 2:30
A was making himself strong in the 2 Sm 3:6
And Ish-bosheth said to **A**, "Why have 2 Sm 3:7
Then **A** was very angry over the words 2 Sm 3:8
God do so to **A** and more also, if I do not 2 Sm 3:9
could not answer **A** another word, 2 Sm 3:11
And **A** sent messengers to David on 2 Sm 3:12
Then **A** said to him, "Go, return." And 2 Sm 3:16
And **A** conferred with the elders of 2 Sm 3:17
A also spoke to Benjamin. And then 2 Sm 3:19
And then **A** went to tell David at 2 Sm 3:19
When **A** came with twenty men to 2 Sm 3:20
made a feast for **A** and the men who 2 Sm 3:20
And **A** said to David, "I will arise and 2 Sm 3:21
heart desires." So David sent **A** away, 2 Sm 3:21
But **A** was not with David at Hebron, 2 Sm 3:22
"**A** the son of Ner came to the king, 2 Sm 3:23
you done? Behold, **A** came to you. 2 Sm 3:24
You know that **A** the son of Ner came 2 Sm 3:25
presence, he sent messengers after **A**, 2 Sm 3:26
And when **A** returned to Hebron, Joab 2 Sm 3:27
LORD for the blood of **A** the son of Ner. 2 Sm 3:28
and Abishai his brother killed **A**, 2 Sm 3:30
and mourn before **A**." And King 2 Sm 3:31
They buried **A** at Hebron. And the 2 Sm 3:32
his voice and wept at the grave of **A**, 2 Sm 3:32
And the king lamented for **A**, saying, 2 Sm 3:33
saying, "Should **A** die as a fool dies? 2 Sm 3:33
will to put to death **A** the son of Ner. 2 Sm 3:37
son, heard that **A** had died at Hebron, 2 Sm 4:1
buried it in the tomb of **A** at Hebron. 2 Sm 4:12
the armies of Israel, **A** the son of Ner, 1 Kgs 2:5
better than himself, **A** the son of Ner, 1 Kgs 2:32
the son of Kish and **A** the son of Ner 1 Chr 26:28
for Benjamin, Jaasiel the son of **A**; 1 Chr 27:21

ABNER'S (1)
down of Benjamin 360 of **A** men. 2 Sm 2:31

ABOARD (3)
So Simon Peter went **a** and hauled the Jn 21:11
Assos, intending to take Paul **a** there, Acts 20:13
to Phoenicia, we went **a** and set sail. Acts 21:2

ABODE (6)
them by your strength to your holy **a**. Ex 15:13
LORD, which you have made for your **a**, Ex 15:17
at the mount that God desired for his **a**, Ps 68:16
His **a** has been established in Salem, his Ps 76:2
From your lofty **a** you water the Ps 104:13
the haunt of jackals, an **a** for ostriches. Is 34:13

ABOLISH (3)
And I will **a** the bow, the sword, and Hos 2:18
that I have come to **a** the Law or the Mt 5:17
I have not come to **a** them but to fulfill Mt 5:17

ABOLISHED (1)
who **a** death and brought life and 2 Tm 1:10

ABOLISHES (1)
to do your will." He **a** the first in order Heb 10:9

ABOLISHING (1)
by **a** the law of commandments and Eph 2:15

ABOMINABLE (12)
we sacrifice offerings **a** to the Egyptians Ex 8:26
any of these **a** customs that were Lv 18:30
shall not bring an **a** thing into your Dt 7:26
for every **a** thing that the LORD hates Dt 12:31
learn to follow the **a** practices of those Dt 18:9
to all their **a** practices that they Dt 20:18
had made an **a** image for Asherah. 1 Kgs 15:13
much less one who is **a** and corrupt, Jb 15:16
God." They are corrupt, they do **a** deeds, Ps 14:1
God." They are corrupt, doing **a** iniquity; Ps 53:1
and they made their **a** images and their Ezk 7:20
your lovers, and with all your **a** idols, Ezk 16:36

ABOMINABLY (2)
He acted very **a** in going after idols, 1 Kgs 21:26
in which you acted more **a** than they, Ezk 16:52

ABOMINATION (62)
for that is an **a** to the Egyptians. Gn 43:32
shepherd is an **a** to the Egyptians." Gn 46:34
LORD our God are an **a** to the Egyptians. Ex 8:26
with a male as with a woman; it is an **a**. Lv 18:22
both of them have committed an **a**; Lv 20:13
by it, for it is an **a** to the LORD your God. Dt 7:25
certain that such an **a** has been done Dt 13:14
"You shall not eat any **a**. Dt 14:3
for that is an **a** to the LORD your God. Dt 17:1
certain that such an **a** has been done in Dt 17:4
does these things is an **a** to the LORD. Dt 18:12
does these things is an **a** to the LORD your Dt 22:5
both of these are an **a** to the LORD your Dt 23:18
defiled, for that is an **a** before the LORD. Dt 24:4
are an **a** to the LORD your God. Dt 25:16
or cast metal image, an **a** to the LORD, Dt 27:15
they have committed **a** and outrage in Jgs 20:6
after Milcom the **a** of the Ammonites. 1 Kgs 11:5
place for Chemosh the **a** of Moab, 1 Kgs 11:7
for Molech the **a** of the Ammonites, 1 Kgs 11:7
for Ashtoreth the **a** of the Sidonians, 2 Kgs 23:13
and for Chemosh the **a** of Moab, 2 Kgs 23:13
for Milcom the **a** of the Ammonites. 2 Kgs 23:13
the devious person is an **a** to the LORD, Prv 3:32
LORD hates, seven that are an **a** to him: Prv 6:16
utter truth; wickedness is an **a** to my lips. Prv 8:7
A false balance is an **a** to the LORD, but Prv 11:1
of crooked heart are an **a** to the LORD, Prv 11:20
Lying lips are an **a** to the LORD, but Prv 12:22
to turn away from evil is an **a** to fools. Prv 13:19
of the wicked is an **a** to the LORD, Prv 15:8
way of the wicked is an **a** to the LORD, Prv 15:9
of the wicked are an **a** to the LORD, Prv 15:26
is arrogant in heart is an **a** to the LORD; Prv 16:5
It is an **a** to kings to do evil, for the Prv 16:12
are both alike an **a** to the LORD. Prv 17:15
are both alike an **a** to the LORD. Prv 20:10
Unequal weights are an **a** to the LORD, Prv 20:23
The sacrifice of the wicked is an **a**; Prv 21:27
sin, and the scoffer is an **a** to mankind. Prv 24:9
hearing the law, even his prayer is an **a**. Prv 28:9
unjust man is an **a** to the righteous, Prv 29:27
way is straight is an **a** to the wicked. Prv 29:27
vain offerings; incense is an **a** to me. Is 1:13
nothing; an **a** is he who chooses you. Is 41:24
And shall I make the rest of it an **a**? Is 44:19
eating pig's flesh and the **a** and mice, Is 66:17
my land and made my heritage an **a**. Jer 2:7
they ashamed when they committed **a**? Jer 6:15
they ashamed when they committed **a**? Jer 8:12
my mind, that they should do this **a**, Jer 32:35
saying, 'Oh, do not do this **a** that I hate!' Jer 44:4
place and made your beauty an **a**, Ezk 16:25
were haughty and did an **a** before me. Ezk 16:50
up his eyes to the idols, commits **a**, Ezk 18:12
One commits **a** with his neighbor's Ezk 22:11
shall set up the **a** that makes desolate. Dn 11:31
away and the **a** that makes desolate Dn 12:11
and **a** has been committed in Israel Mal 2:11
you see the **a** of desolation spoken Mt 24:15
you see the **a** of desolation standing Mk 13:14
among men is an **a** in the sight of Lk 16:15

ABOMINATIONS (65)
and my rules and do none of these **a**, Lv 18:26
who were before you, did all of these **a**, Lv 18:27
For everyone who does any of these **a**, Lv 18:29
And because of these **a** the LORD your Dt 18:12
with **a** they provoked him to anger. Dt 32:16
according to all the **a** of the nations 1 Kgs 14:24
has committed these **a** and has done 2 Kgs 21:11
idols and all the **a** that were seen in 2 Kgs 23:24
according to the **a** of the nations 2 Chr 28:3
according to the **a** of the nations 2 Chr 33:2
took away all the **a** from all the 2 Chr 34:33
of Jehoiakim, and the **a** that he did, 2 Chr 36:8
following all the **a** of the nations. 2 Chr 36:14
from the peoples of the lands with their **a**, Ezr 9:1
with their **a** that have filled it from end Ezr 9:11
with the peoples who practice these **a**? Ezr 9:14
not, for there are seven **a** in his heart; Prv 26:25
ways, and their soul delights in their **a**; Is 66:3
—only to go on doing all these **a**? Jer 7:10
I have seen your **a**, your adulteries and Jer 13:27
filled my inheritance with their **a**." Jer 16:18
They set up their **a** in the house that is Jer 32:34
deeds and the **a** that you committed. Jer 44:22
And because of all your **a** I will do with Ezk 5:9
detestable things and with all your **a**, Ezk 5:11
that they have committed, for all their **a**. Ezk 6:9
because of all the evil **a** of the house of Ezk 6:11
and I will punish you for all your **a**. Ezk 7:3
ways, while your **a** are in your midst. Ezk 7:4
and I will punish you for all your **a**. Ezk 7:8
ways, while your **a** are in your midst. Ezk 7:9
the great **a** that the house of Israel are Ezk 8:6
But you will see still greater **a**." Ezk 8:6
and see the vile **a** that they are Ezk 8:9
see still greater **a** that they commit." Ezk 8:13
You will see still greater **a** than these." Ezk 8:15
to commit the **a** that they commit Ezk 8:17
groan over all the **a** that are committed Ezk 9:4
it all its detestable things and all its **a**. Ezk 11:18
their detestable things and their **a**, Ezk 11:21
declare all their **a** among the nations Ezk 12:16
turn away your faces from all your **a**. Ezk 14:6
man, make known to Jerusalem her **a**, Ezk 16:2
And in all your **a** and your whorings Ezk 16:22
lewdness in addition to all your **a**? Ezk 16:43
their ways and do according to their **a**; Ezk 16:47
have committed more **a** than they, Ezk 16:51
righteous by all the **a** that you have Ezk 16:51
penalty of your lewdness and your **a**, Ezk 16:58
He has done all these **a**; he shall surely Ezk 18:13
and does the same **a** that the wicked Ezk 18:24
Let them know the **a** of their fathers, Ezk 20:4
city? Then declare to her all her **a**. Ezk 22:2
Oholibah? Declare to them their **a**. Ezk 23:36
You rely on the sword, you commit **a**, Ezk 33:26
because of all their **a** that they have Ezk 33:29
for your iniquities and your **a**. Ezk 36:31
holy name by their **a** that they have Ezk 43:8
O house of Israel, enough of all your **a**, Ezk 44:6
my covenant, in addition to all your **a**. Ezk 44:7
their shame and the **a** that they have Ezk 44:13
on the wing of **a** shall come one who Dn 9:27
mouth, and its **a** from between its teeth; Zec 9:7
golden cup full of **a** and the impurities of Rv 17:4
mother of prostitutes and of earth's **a**." Rv 17:5

ABOUND (11)
the LORD will make you **a** in prosperity, Dt 28:11
they have when their grain and wine **a**. Ps 4:7
may the righteous flourish, and peace **a**, Ps 72:7
A faithful man will **a** with blessings, Prv 28:20
we to continue in sin that grace may **a**? Rom 6:1
of the Holy Spirit you may **a** in hope. Rom 15:13
God is able to make all grace **a** to you, 2 Cor 9:8
times, you may **a** in every good work. 2 Cor 9:8
that your love may **a** more and more, Phil 1:9
be brought low, and I know how to **a**. Phil 4:12
make you increase and **a** in love for 1 Thes 3:12

ABOUNDED (2)
that one man Jesus Christ **a** for many. Rom 5:15
sin increased, grace **a** all the more, Rom 5:20

ABOUNDING (12)
and **a** in steadfast love and faithfulness, Ex 34:6
slow to anger and **a** in steadfast love, Nm 14:18
slow to anger and **a** in steadfast love, Neh 9:17
a in steadfast love to all who call upon Ps 86:5
slow to anger and **a** in steadfast love Ps 86:15
slow to anger and **a** in steadfast love. Ps 103:8
slow to anger and **a** in steadfast love. Ps 145:8
there were no springs **a** with water. Prv 8:24
slow to anger, and **a** in steadfast love; Jl 2:13
slow to anger and **a** in steadfast love, Jon 4:2
always **a** in the work of the Lord, 1 Cor 15:58
as you were taught, **a** in thanksgiving. Col 2:7

ABOUNDS (1)
my lie God's truth **a** to his glory, Rom 3:7

ABOVE (164)
from the waters that were **a** the expanse. Gn 1:7
and let birds fly **a** the earth across the Gn 1:20
cursed are you **a** all livestock and above Gn 3:14
above all livestock and **a** all beasts of Gn 3:14
for the ark, and finish it to a cubit **a**, Gn 6:16
up the ark, and it rose high **a** the earth. Gn 7:17
The waters prevailed **a** the mountains, Gn 7:20
behold, the LORD stood **a** it and said, Gn 28:13
bless you with blessings of heaven **a**, Gn 49:25
likeness of anything that is in heaven **a**, Ex 20:4
shall spread out their wings **a**, Ex 25:20
with you, and from **a** the mercy seat, Ex 25:22
at its seam **a** the skillfully woven band Ex 28:27
of the veil that is **a** the ark of the Ex 30:6
of the mercy seat that is **a** the testimony, Ex 30:6
say, '**A** all you shall keep my Sabbaths, Ex 31:13
The cherubim spread out their wings **a**, Ex 37:9
at its seam **a** the skillfully woven band Ex 39:20
cord of blue to fasten it on the turban **a**, Ex 39:31
ark and set the mercy seat **a** on the ark. Ex 40:20
those that have jointed legs **a** their feet, Lv 11:21
over and **a** the number of the male Nm 3:46
who were over and **a** those redeemed by Nm 3:49
offering to the LORD **a** his Nazirite vow, Nm 6:21
speaking to him from **a** the mercy seat Nm 7:89
and about two cubits **a** the ground. Nm 11:31
you exalt yourselves **a** the assembly of Nm 16:3
LORD is God in heaven **a** and on the earth Dt 4:39
likeness of anything that is in heaven **a**, Dt 5:8
You shall be blessed **a** all peoples. There Dt 7:14
offspring after them, you **a** all peoples, Dt 10:15
as long as the heavens are **a** the earth. Dt 11:21
may not be lifted up **a** his brothers, Dt 17:20

and in honor high **a** all nations that he Dt 26:19
God will set you high **a** all the nations of Dt 28:1
you shall rise higher and higher **a** you, Dt 28:43
land, with the choicest gifts of heaven **a**, Dt 33:13
is God in the heavens **a** and on the earth Jos 2:11
coming down from **a** shall stand in Jos 3:13
coming down from **a** stood and rose Jos 3:16
honor your sons **a** me by fattening 1 Sm 2:29
who chose me **a** your father and 2 Sm 6:21
above your father and **a** all his house, 2 Sm 6:21
you exalted me **a** those who rose 2 Sm 22:49
covered with cedar **a** the chambers 1 Kgs 7:3
And **a** were costly stones, cut 1 Kgs 7:11
pillars and also **a** the rounded 1 Kgs 7:20
both **a** and below the lions and oxen, 1 Kgs 7:29
you, in heaven **a** or on earth beneath, 1 Kgs 8:23
you have done evil **a** all who were 1 Kgs 14:9
who is enthroned **a** the cherubim, 2 Kgs 19:15
and gave him a seat **a** the seats of the 2 Kgs 25:28
who sits enthroned **a** the cherubim. 1 Chr 13:6
he is to be held in awe **a** all gods. 1 Chr 16:25
and you are exalted as head **a** all. 1 Chr 29:11
made a covering **a** the ark and 2 Chr 5:8
daughter of Absalom **a** all his wives 2 Chr 11:21
the priest, and he stood **a** the people, 2 Chr 24:20
the incense altars that stood **a** them. 2 Chr 34:4
A the Horse Gate the priests repaired, Neh 3:28
all the people, for he was **a** all the people, Neh 8:5
which is exalted **a** all blessing and Neh 9:5
of the wall, **a** the house of David, Neh 12:37
on the wall, **a** the Tower of the Ovens, Neh 12:38
and **a** the Gate of Ephraim, and by the Neh 12:39
and set his throne **a** all the officials who Est 3:1
he had advanced him **a** the officials and Est 5:11
May God **a** not seek it, nor light shine Jb 3:4
in his tent, and his lamp **a** him is put out. Jb 18:6
up beneath, and his branches wither **a**. Jb 18:16
crystal; the price of wisdom is **a** pearls. Jb 28:18
my portion from God **a** and my heritage Jb 31:2
for I would have been false to God **a**. Jb 31:28
You have set your glory **a** the heavens. Ps 8:1
you exalted me **a** those who rose against Ps 18:48
and the sky **a** proclaims his handiwork. Ps 19:1
shall be lifted up **a** my enemies all Ps 27:6
He calls to the heavens **a** and to the earth, Ps 50:4
Be exalted, O God, **a** the heavens! Let Ps 57:5
Be exalted, O God, **a** the heavens! Let Ps 57:11
commanded the skies **a** and opened the Ps 78:23
and awesome **a** all who are around him? Ps 89:7
a great God, and a great King **a** all gods. Ps 95:3
to be praised; he is to be feared **a** all gods. Ps 96:4
the earth; you are exalted far **a** all gods. Ps 97:9
as high as the heavens are **a** the earth, Ps 103:11
the waters stood **a** the mountains. Ps 104:6
steadfast love is great **a** the heavens; Ps 108:4
Be exalted, O God, **a** the heavens! Let Ps 108:5
The LORD is high **a** all nations, and his Ps 113:4
all nations, and his glory **a** the heavens! Ps 113:4
I love your commandments **a** gold, Ps 119:127
above gold, **a** fine gold. Ps 119:127
is great, and that our Lord is **a** all gods. Ps 135:5
who spread out the earth **a** the waters, Ps 136:6
I do not set Jerusalem **a** my highest joy! Ps 137:6
for you have exalted **a** all things your Ps 138:2
heavens, and you waters **a** the heavens! Ps 148:4
his majesty is **a** earth and heaven. Ps 148:13
when he made firm the skies **a**, when he Prv 8:28
and shall be lifted up **a** the hills; Is 2:2
A him stood the seraphim. Each had six Is 6:2
a the stars of God I will set my throne on Is 14:13
I will ascend **a** the heights of the clouds; Is 14:14
Israel, who is enthroned **a** the cherubim, Is 37:16
It is he who sits **a** the circle of the earth, Is 40:22
"Shower, O heavens, from **a**, and let the Is 45:8
shall mourn, and the heavens **a** be dark; Jer 4:28
The heart is deceitful **a** all things, and Jer 17:9
"If the heavens **a** can be measured, Jer 31:37
a the chamber of Maaseiah the son of Jer 35:4
I will set his throne **a** these stones that I Jer 43:10
and gave him a seat **a** the seats of the Jer 52:32
And their wings were spread out **a**. Ezk 1:11
crystal, spread out **a** their heads. Ezk 1:22
came a voice from **a** the expanse over Ezk 1:25
And **a** the expanse over their heads Ezk 1:26
and seated **a** the likeness of a throne Ezk 1:26
and **a** his waist was something like the Ezk 8:2
there appeared **a** them something Ezk 10:1
never again exalt itself **a** the nations. Ezk 29:15
So it towered high **a** all the trees of the Ezk 31:5
to the space **a** the door, even to the Ezk 41:17
From the floor to **a** the door, Ezk 41:20
Daniel became distinguished **a** all the Dn 6:3
and magnify himself **a** every god, Dn 11:36
god, for he shall magnify himself **a** all. Dn 11:37
shine like the brightness of the sky **a**; Dn 12:3
who was **a** the waters of the stream, Dn 12:6
who was **a** the waters of the stream; Dn 12:7
I destroyed his fruit **a** and his roots Am 2:9
and it shall be lifted up **a** the hills; Mi 4:1
Therefore the heavens **a** you have Hg 1:10
"A disciple is not **a** his teacher, nor a Mt 10:24
his teacher, nor a servant **a** his master. Mt 10:24
the crowd, they removed the roof **a** him, Mk 2:4
A disciple is not **a** his teacher, but Lk 6:40
He who comes from **a** is above all. He Jn 3:31
He who comes from above is **a** all. He Jn 3:31
way. He who comes from heaven is **a** all. Jn 3:31
them, "You are from below; I am from **a**. Jn 8:23
all unless it had been given you from **a**. Jn 19:11
wonders in the heavens **a** and signs on Acts 2:19
But the Jerusalem **a** is free, and she is Gal 4:26
far **a** all rule and authority and power Eph 1:21
and **a** every name that is named, Eph 1:21
also ascended far **a** all the heavens, Eph 4:10
on him the name that is **a** every name, Phil 2:9
and blameless and **a** reproach before Col 1:22
with Christ, seek the things that are **a**, Col 3:1
Set your minds on things that are **a**, not Col 3:2
And **a** all these put on love, which Col 3:14
an overseer must be **a** reproach, 1 Tm 3:2
the books, and **a** all the parchments. 2 Tm 4:13
if anyone is **a** reproach, the husband of Ti 1:6
as God's steward, must be **a** reproach. Ti 1:7
sinners, and exalted **a** the heavens. Heb 7:26
A it were the cherubim of glory Heb 9:5
When he said **a**, "You have neither Heb 10:8
good gift and every perfect gift is from **a**, Jas 1:17
the wisdom that comes down from **a**, Jas 3:15
But the wisdom from **a** is first pure, then Jas 3:17
But **a** all, my brothers, do not swear, Jas 5:12
A all, keep loving one another earnestly, 1 Pt 4:8

ABRAHAM (234)

Abram, but your name shall be **A**, Gn 17:5
And God said to **A**, "As for you, you Gn 17:9
And God said to **A**, "As for Sarai your Gn 17:15
Then **A** fell on his face and laughed Gn 17:17
And **A** said to God, "Oh that Ishmael Gn 17:18
talking with him, God went up from **A**. Gn 17:22
Then **A** took Ishmael his son and all Gn 17:23
A was ninety-nine years old when he Gn 17:24
That very day **A** and his son Ishmael Gn 17:26
And **A** went quickly into the tent to Gn 18:6
And **A** ran to the herd and took a calf, Gn 18:7
Now **A** and Sarah were old, advanced Gn 18:11
The LORD said to **A**, "Why did Sarah Gn 18:13
And **A** went with them to set them on Gn 18:16
"Shall I hide from **A** what I am about Gn 18:17
seeing that **A** shall surely become a Gn 18:18
LORD may bring to **A** what he has Gn 18:19
but **A** still stood before the LORD. Gn 18:22
Then **A** drew near and said, "Will you Gn 18:23
A answered and said, "Behold, I have Gn 18:27
when he had finished speaking to **A**, Gn 18:33
Abraham, and **A** returned to his place. Gn 18:33
And **A** went early in the morning to Gn 19:27
God remembered **A** and sent Lot out of Gn 19:29
From there **A** journeyed toward the Gn 20:1
And **A** said of Sarah his wife, "She is my Gn 20:2
Then Abimelech called **A** and said to Gn 20:9
And Abimelech said to **A**, "What did Gn 20:10
A said, "I did it because I thought, Gn 20:11
female servants, and gave them to **A**, Gn 20:14
Then **A** prayed to God, and God healed Gn 20:17
Sarah conceived and bore **A** a son in his Gn 21:2
A called the name of his son who was Gn 21:3
And **A** circumcised his son Isaac when Gn 21:4
A was a hundred years old when his son Gn 21:5
would have said to **A** that Sarah would Gn 21:7
And **A** made a great feast on the day that Gn 21:8
the Egyptian, whom she had borne to **A**, Gn 21:9
So she said to **A**, "Cast out this slave Gn 21:10
very displeasing to **A** on account of Gn 21:11
But God said to **A**, "Be not displeased Gn 21:12
So **A** rose early in the morning and Gn 21:14
the commander of his army said to **A**, Gn 21:22
And **A** said, "I will swear." Gn 21:24
When **A** reproved Abimelech about a Gn 21:25
So **A** took sheep and oxen and gave Gn 21:27
A set seven ewe lambs of the flock Gn 21:28
And Abimelech said to **A**, "What is the Gn 21:29
A planted a tamarisk tree in Beersheba Gn 21:33
And **A** sojourned many days in the Gn 21:34
these things God tested **A** and said to Gn 22:1
and said to him, "**A**!" And he said, Gn 22:1
So **A** rose early in the morning, saddled Gn 22:3
On the third day **A** lifted up his eyes and Gn 22:4
Then **A** said to his young men, "Stay Gn 22:5
And **A** took the wood of the burnt Gn 22:6
And Isaac said to his father **A**, "My Gn 22:7
A said, "God will provide for himself the Gn 22:8
A built the altar there and laid the wood Gn 22:9
Then **A** reached out his hand and took Gn 22:10
and said, "**A**, Abraham!" And he said, Gn 22:11
and said, "Abraham, **A**!" And he said, Gn 22:11
And **A** lifted up his eyes and looked, Gn 22:13
And **A** went and took the ram and Gn 22:13
So **A** called the name of that place, Gn 22:14
the LORD called to **A** a second time Gn 22:15
So **A** returned to his young men, and Gn 22:19
Beersheba. And **A** lived at Beersheba. Gn 22:19
Now after these things it was told to **A**, Gn 22:20
and **A** went in to mourn for Sarah and Gn 23:2
And **A** rose up from before his dead and Gn 23:3
The Hittites answered **A**, Gn 23:5
A rose and bowed to the Hittites, the Gn 23:7
the Hittite answered **A** in the hearing Gn 23:10
Then **A** bowed down before the people Gn 23:12
Ephron answered **A**, Gn 23:14
A listened to Ephron, and Abraham Gn 23:16
and **A** weighed out for Ephron the Gn 23:16
to **A** as a possession in the presence of Gn 23:18
A buried Sarah his wife in the cave of Gn 23:19
it were made over to **A** as property for a Gn 23:20
Now **A** was old, well advanced in years. Gn 24:1
the LORD had blessed **A** in all things. Gn 24:1
And **A** said to his servant, the oldest of Gn 24:2
A said to him, "See to it that you do not Gn 24:6
under the thigh of **A** his master and Gn 24:9
he said, "O LORD, God of my master **A**, Gn 24:12
show steadfast love to my master **A**. Gn 24:12
be the LORD, the God of my master **A**, Gn 24:27
said, 'O LORD, the God of my master **A**, Gn 24:42
the LORD, the God of my master **A**, Gn 24:48
A took another wife, whose name was Gn 25:1
A gave all he had to Isaac. Gn 25:5
the sons of his concubines **A** gave gifts, Gn 25:6
A breathed his last and died in a good Gn 25:8
the field that **A** purchased from the Gn 25:10
There **A** was buried, with Sarah his Gn 25:10
After the death of **A**, God blessed Isaac Gn 25:11
Egyptian, Sarah's servant, bore to **A**. Gn 25:12
Abraham's son: **A** fathered Isaac, Gn 25:19
former famine that was in the days of **A**. Gn 26:1
the oath that I swore to **A** your father. Gn 26:3
because **A** obeyed my voice and kept Gn 26:5
had dug in the days of **A** his father.) Gn 26:15
been dug in the days of **A** his father, Gn 26:18
had stopped after the death of **A**. Gn 26:18
said, "I am the God of **A** your father. Gn 26:24
he give the blessing of **A** to you and to Gn 28:4
your sojournings that God gave to **A**!" Gn 28:4
the God of **A** your father and the God of Gn 28:13
the God of **A** and the Fear of Isaac, Gn 31:42
The God of **A** and the God of Nahor, Gn 31:53
"O God of my father **A** and God of my Gn 32:9
land that I gave to **A** and Isaac I will Gn 35:12
where **A** and Isaac had sojourned. Gn 35:27
whom my fathers **A** and Isaac walked, Gn 48:15
the name of my fathers **A** and Isaac; Gn 48:16
which **A** bought with the field from Gn 49:30
There they buried **A** and Sarah his Gn 49:31
which **A** bought with the field from Gn 50:13
this land to the land that he swore to **A**, Gn 50:24
God remembered his covenant with **A**, Ex 2:24
"I am the God of your father, the God of **A**, Ex 3:6
the God of your fathers, the God of **A**, Ex 3:15
the God of your fathers, the God of **A**, Ex 3:16
the God of their fathers, the God of **A**, Ex 4:5
I appeared to **A**, to Isaac, and to Jacob, as Ex 6:3
you into the land that I swore to give to **A**, Ex 6:8
Remember **A**, Isaac, and Israel, your Ex 32:13
Egypt, to the land of which I swore to **A**, Ex 33:1
with Isaac and my covenant with **A**, Lv 26:42
see the land that I swore to give to **A**, Nm 32:11
that the LORD swore to your fathers, to **A**, Dt 1:8
land that he swore to your fathers, to **A**, Dt 6:10
that the LORD swore to your fathers, to **A**, Dt 9:5
Remember your servants, **A**, Isaac, and Dt 9:27
and as he swore to your fathers, to **A**, Dt 29:13
the LORD swore to your fathers, to **A**, Dt 30:20
"This is the land of which I swore to **A**, Dt 34:4
Terah, the father of **A** and of Nahor; Jos 24:2
I took your father **A** from beyond the Jos 24:3
near and said, "O LORD, God of **A**, 1 Kgs 18:36
because of his covenant with **A**, 2 Kgs 13:23
Abram, that is, **A**. 1 Chr 1:27
The sons of **A**: Isaac and Ishmael. 1 Chr 1:28
A fathered Isaac. The sons of Isaac: 1 Chr 1:34
the covenant that he made with **A**, 1 Chr 16:16
O LORD, the God of **A**, Isaac, and 1 Chr 29:18
to the descendants of **A** your friend? 2 Chr 20:7
return to the LORD, the God of **A**, 2 Chr 30:6
Chaldeans and gave him the name **A**. Neh 9:7
gather as the people of the God of **A**. Ps 47:9
O offspring of **A**, his servant, children Ps 105:6

the covenant that he made with **A**, his Ps 105:9
remembered his holy promise, and **A**, Ps 105:42
thus says the LORD, who redeemed **A**, Is 29:22
whom I have chosen, the offspring of **A**, Is 41:8
Look to **A** your father and to Sarah who Is 51:2
our Father, though **A** does not know us, Is 63:16
offspring to rule over the offspring of **A**, Jer 33:26
keep saying, '**A** was only one man, Ezk 33:24
to Jacob and steadfast love to **A**, Mi 7:20
Christ, the son of David, the son of **A**. Mt 1:1
A was the father of Isaac, and Isaac the Mt 1:2
all the generations from **A** to David were Mt 1:17
to yourselves, 'We have **A** as our father,' Mt 3:9
these stones to raise up children for **A**. Mt 3:9
east and west and recline at table with **A**, Mt 8:11
'I am the God of **A**, and the God of Mt 22:32
to him, saying, 'I am the God of **A**, Mk 12:26
to **A** and to his offspring forever." Lk 1:55
the oath that he swore to our father **A**, to Lk 1:73
to yourselves, 'We have **A** as our father.' Lk 3:8
these stones to raise up children for **A**. Lk 3:8
of Jacob, the son of Isaac, the son of **A**, Lk 3:34
a daughter of **A** whom Satan bound for Lk 13:16
when you see **A** and Isaac and Jacob Lk 13:28
his eyes and saw **A** far off and Lazarus Lk 16:23
And he called out, 'Father **A**, have Lk 16:24
But **A** said, 'Child, remember that you Lk 16:25
But **A** said, 'They have Moses and the Lk 16:29
And he said, 'No, father **A**, but if Lk 16:30
to this house, since he also is a son of **A**. Lk 19:9
the Lord the God of **A** and the God of Lk 20:37
"We are offspring of **A** and have never Jn 8:33
I know that you are offspring of **A**; yet Jn 8:37
him, "**A** is our father." Jesus said to them, Jn 8:39
children, you would be doing what **A** did, Jn 8:39
I heard from God. This is not what **A** did. Jn 8:40
A died, as did the prophets, yet you say, 'If Jn 8:52
Are you greater than our father **A**, who Jn 8:53
Your father **A** rejoiced that he would see Jn 8:56
yet fifty years old, and have you seen **A**?" Jn 8:57
"Truly, truly, I say to you, before **A** was, Jn 8:58
The God of **A**, the God of Isaac, and the Acts 3:13
made with your fathers, saying to **A**, Acts 3:25
appeared to our father **A** when he was in Acts 7:2
And so **A** became the father of Isaac, Acts 7:8
in the tomb that **A** had bought for a Acts 7:16
near, which God had granted to **A**, Acts 7:17
the God of **A** and of Isaac and of Jacob.' Acts 7:32
"Brothers, sons of the family of **A**, Acts 13:26
then shall we say was gained by **A**, Rom 4:1
For if **A** was justified by works, he has Rom 4:2
"**A** believed God, and it was counted to Rom 4:3
was counted to **A** as righteousness. Rom 4:9
faith that our father **A** had before he Rom 4:12
For the promise to **A** and his offspring Rom 4:13
to the one who shares the faith of **A**, Rom 4:16
all are children of **A** because they are Rom 9:7
am an Israelite, a descendant of **A**, Rom 11:1
So am I. Are they offspring of **A**? 2 Cor 11:22
just as **A** "believed God, and it was Gal 3:6
it is those of faith who are the sons of **A**. Gal 3:7
preached the gospel beforehand to **A**, Gal 3:8
who are of faith are blessed along with **A**, Gal 3:9
Jesus the blessing of **A** might come to Gal 3:14
promises were made to **A** and to his Gal 3:16
but God gave it to **A** by a promise. Gal 3:18
For it is written that **A** had two sons, Gal 4:22
helps, but he helps the offspring of **A**. Heb 2:16
For when God made a promise to **A**, Heb 6:13
And thus **A**, having patiently waited, Heb 6:15
met **A** returning from the slaughter of Heb 7:1
and to him **A** apportioned a tenth part of Heb 7:2
man was to whom **A** the patriarch gave Heb 7:4
though these also are descended from **A**. Heb 7:5
received tithes from **A** and blessed him Heb 7:6
receives tithes, paid tithes through **A**, Heb 7:9
By faith **A** obeyed when he was called Heb 11:8
By faith **A**, when he was tested, offered Heb 11:17
Was not **A** our father justified by works Jas 2:21
was fulfilled that says, "**A** believed God, Jas 2:23
as Sarah obeyed **A**, calling him lord. 1 Pt 3:6

ABRAHAM'S (16)
every male among the men of **A** house, Gn 17:23
of Abimelech because of Sarah, **A** wife. Gn 20:18
eight Milcah bore to Nahor, **A** brother. Gn 22:23
Milcah, the wife of Nahor, **A** brother, Gn 24:15
So he said, "I am **A** servant. Gn 24:34
When **A** servant heard their words, he Gn 24:52
her nurse, and **A** servant and his men. Gn 24:59
These are the days of the years of **A** life, Gn 25:7
are the generations of Ishmael, **A** son, Gn 25:12
are the generations of Isaac, **A** son: Gn 25:19
your offspring for my servant **A** sake." Gn 26:24
the daughter of Ishmael, **A** son, Gn 28:9
The sons of Keturah, **A** concubine: 1 Chr 1:32
and was carried by the angels to **A** side. Lk 16:22
said to them, "If you were **A** children, Jn 8:39
are Christ's, then you are **A** offspring, Gal 3:29

ABRAM (55)
had lived 70 years, he fathered **A**, Gn 11:26
Terah fathered **A**, Nahor, and Haran; Gn 11:27
And **A** and Nahor took wives. The Gn 11:29
Terah took **A** his son and Lot the son Gn 11:31
Now the LORD said to **A**, "Go from your Gn 12:1
So **A** went, as the LORD had told him, and Gn 12:4
A was seventy-five years old when he Gn 12:4
And **A** took Sarai his wife, and Lot his Gn 12:5
A passed through the land to the place Gn 12:6
Then the LORD appeared to **A** and said, Gn 12:7
And **A** journeyed on, still going toward Gn 12:9
So **A** went down to Egypt to sojourn Gn 12:10
When **A** entered Egypt, the Egyptians Gn 12:14
And for her sake he dealt well with **A**; Gn 12:16
So Pharaoh called **A** and said, "What Gn 12:18
So **A** went up from Egypt, he and his Gn 13:1
Now **A** was very rich in livestock, in Gn 13:2
And there **A** called upon the name of the Gn 13:4
And Lot, who went with **A**, also had Gn 13:5
Then **A** said to Lot, "Let there be no Gn 13:8
A settled in the land of Canaan, while Gn 13:12
The LORD said to **A**, after Lot had Gn 13:14
So **A** moved his tent and came and Gn 13:18
escaped came and told **A** the Hebrew, Gn 14:13
and of Aner. These were allies of **A**. Gn 14:13
When **A** heard that his kinsman had Gn 14:14
said, "Blessed be **A** by God Most High, Gn 14:19
into your hand!" And **A** gave him a Gn 14:20
And the king of Sodom said to **A**, "Give Gn 14:21
But **A** said to the king of Sodom, "I Gn 14:22
you should say, 'I have made **A** rich.' Gn 14:23
word of the LORD came to **A** in a vision: Gn 15:1
a vision: "Fear not, **A**, I am your shield; Gn 15:1
But **A** said, "O Lord GOD, what will you Gn 15:2
And **A** said, "Behold, you have given me Gn 15:3
on the carcasses, **A** drove them away. Gn 15:11
was going down, a deep sleep fell on **A**. Gn 15:12
Then the LORD said to **A**, "Know for Gn 15:13
day the LORD made a covenant with **A**, Gn 15:18
And Sarai said to **A**, "Behold now, the Gn 16:2
children by her." And **A** listened to the Gn 16:2
after **A** had lived ten years in the land of Gn 16:3
and gave her to **A** her husband as a wife. Gn 16:3
And Sarai said to **A**, "May the wrong Gn 16:5
But **A** said to Sarai, "Behold, your Gn 16:6
And Hagar bore **A** a son, and Abram Gn 16:15
son, and **A** called the name of his son, Gn 16:15
A was eighty-six years old when Hagar Gn 16:16
old when Hagar bore Ishmael to **A**. Gn 16:16
When **A** was ninety-nine years old the Gn 17:1
the LORD appeared to **A** and said to him, Gn 17:1
Then **A** fell on his face. And God said to Gn 17:3
No longer shall your name be called **A**, Gn 17:5
A, that is, Abraham. 1 Chr 1:27
the God who chose **A** and brought him Neh 9:7

ABRAM'S (7)
wives. The name of **A** wife was Sarai, Gn 11:29
his daughter-in-law, his son **A** wife, Gn 11:31
great plagues because of Sarai, **A** wife. Gn 12:17
the herdsmen of **A** livestock and the Gn 13:7
also took Lot, the son of **A** brother, Gn 14:12
Now Sarai, **A** wife, had borne him no Gn 16:1
in the land of Canaan, Sarai, **A** wife, Gn 16:3

ABROAD (20)
these the nations spread **a** on the earth Gn 10:32
and you shall spread **a** to the west and Gn 28:14
multiplied and the more they spread **a**. Ex 1:12
the people of the LORD spreading **a**. 1 Sm 2:24
they were spread **a** over all the land, 1 Sm 30:16
let us send **a** to our brothers who 1 Chr 13:2
soon as the command was spread **a**, 2 Chr 31:5
certain people scattered **a** and dispersed Est 3:8
He wanders **a** for bread, saying, 'Where Jb 15:23
iniquity; when he goes out, he tells it **a**. Ps 41:6
Rain in abundance, O God, you shed **a**; Ps 68:9
Should your springs be scattered **a**, Prv 5:16
its shoots spread **a** and passed over the Is 16:8
For you will spread **a** to the right and to Is 54:3
horns, till you have scattered them **a**, Ezk 34:21
For I have spread you **a** as the four winds Zec 2:6
even more the report about him went **a**, Lk 5:15
the children of God who are scattered **a**. Jn 11:52
the saying spread **a** among the brothers Jn 21:23
who go **a** to the kings of the whole Rv 16:14

ABRONAH (2)
out from Jotbathah and camped at **A**. Nm 33:34
they set out from **A** and camped at Nm 33:35

ABSALOM (104)
A the son of Maacah the daughter of 2 Sm 3:3
Now **A**, David's son, had a beautiful 2 Sm 13:1
And her brother **A** said to her, "Has 2 Sm 13:20
But **A** spoke to Amnon neither good 2 Sm 13:22
good nor bad, for **A** hated Amnon, 2 Sm 13:22
two full years **A** had sheepshearers at 2 Sm 13:23
and **A** invited all the king's sons. 2 Sm 13:23
And **A** came to the king and said, 2 Sm 13:24
But the king said to **A**, "No, my son, 2 Sm 13:25
Then **A** said, "If not, please let my 2 Sm 13:26
But **A** pressed him until he let 2 Sm 13:27
Then **A** commanded his servants, 2 Sm 13:28
So the servants of **A** did to Amnon as 2 Sm 13:29
did to Amnon as **A** had commanded. 2 Sm 13:29
"**A** has struck down all the king's 2 Sm 13:30
by the command of **A** this has been 2 Sm 13:32
But **A** fled. And the young man who 2 Sm 13:34
But **A** fled and went to Talmai the 2 Sm 13:37
So **A** fled and went to Geshur, and 2 Sm 13:38
of the king longed to go out to **A**, 2 Sm 13:39
that the king's heart went out to **A**. 2 Sm 14:1
go, bring back the young man **A**." 2 Sm 14:21
Geshur and brought **A** to Jerusalem. 2 Sm 14:23
my presence." So **A** lived apart in 2 Sm 14:24
for his handsome appearance as **A**. 2 Sm 14:25
There were born to **A** three sons, and 2 Sm 14:27
So **A** lived two full years in 2 Sm 14:28
Then **A** sent for Joab, to send him to 2 Sm 14:29
arose and went to **A** at his house and 2 Sm 14:31
A answered Joab, "Behold, I sent 2 Sm 14:32
and told him, and he summoned **A**. 2 Sm 14:33
the king, and the king kissed **A**. 2 Sm 14:33
After this **A** got himself a chariot and 2 Sm 15:1
And **A** used to rise early and stand 2 Sm 15:2
A would call to him and say, 2 Sm 15:2
A would say to him, "See, your claims 2 Sm 15:3
Then **A** would say, "Oh that I were 2 Sm 15:4
Thus **A** did to all of Israel who came 2 Sm 15:6
So **A** stole the hearts of the men of 2 Sm 15:6
end of four years **A** said to the king, 2 Sm 15:7
But **A** sent secret messengers 2 Sm 15:10
then say, '**A** is king at Hebron!'" 2 Sm 15:10
With **A** went two hundred men from 2 Sm 15:11
And while **A** was offering the 2 Sm 15:12
the people with **A** kept increasing. 2 Sm 15:12
the men of Israel have gone after **A**." 2 Sm 15:13
there will be no escape for us from **A**. 2 Sm 15:14
the conspirators with **A**." And David 2 Sm 15:31
if you return to the city and say to **A**, 2 Sm 15:34
just as **A** was entering Jerusalem. 2 Sm 15:37
kingdom into the hand of your son **A**. 2 Sm 16:8
Now **A** and all the people, the men of 2 Sm 16:15
Archite, David's friend, came to **A**, 2 Sm 16:16
came to Absalom, Hushai said to **A**, 2 Sm 16:16
And **A** said to Hushai, "Is this your 2 Sm 16:17
And Hushai said to **A**, "No, for 2 Sm 16:18
Then **A** said to Ahithophel, "Give 2 Sm 16:20
Ahithophel said to **A**, "Go in to your 2 Sm 16:21
they pitched a tent for **A** on the roof. 2 Sm 16:22
And **A** went in to his father's 2 Sm 16:22
esteemed, both by David and by **A**. 2 Sm 16:23
Moreover, Ahithophel said to **A**, "Let 2 Sm 17:1
right in the eyes of **A** and all the elders 2 Sm 17:4
Then **A** said, "Call Hushai the 2 Sm 17:5
And when Hushai came to **A**, 2 Sm 17:6
came to Absalom, **A** said to him, 2 Sm 17:6
Then Hushai said to **A**, "This time the 2 Sm 17:7
among the people who follow **A**.' 2 Sm 17:9
And **A** and all the men of Israel said, 2 Sm 17:14
the LORD might bring harm upon **A**. 2 Sm 17:14
did Ahithophel counsel **A** and the 2 Sm 17:15
a young man saw them and told **A**. 2 Sm 17:18
And **A** crossed the Jordan with all 2 Sm 17:24
Now **A** had set Amasa over the army 2 Sm 17:25
And Israel and **A** encamped in the 2 Sm 17:26
with the young man **A**." And all the 2 Sm 18:5
to all the commanders about **A**. 2 Sm 18:5
And **A** happened to meet the servants 2 Sm 18:9
A was riding on his mule, and the 2 Sm 18:9
"Behold, I saw **A** hanging in an oak." 2 Sm 18:10
my sake protect the young man **A**.' 2 Sm 18:12
into the heart of **A** while he was still 2 Sm 18:14
surrounded **A** and struck him and 2 Sm 18:15
And they took **A** and threw him into 2 Sm 18:17
Now **A** in his lifetime had taken and 2 Sm 18:18
young man **A**?" Ahimaaz answered, 2 Sm 18:29
the young man **A**?" And the Cushite 2 Sm 18:32
as he went, he said, "O my son **A**, 2 Sm 18:33
son Absalom, my son, my son **A**! 2 Sm 18:33
I had died instead of you, O **A**, 2 Sm 18:33
king is weeping and mourning for **A**." 2 Sm 19:1
cried with a loud voice, "O my son **A**, 2 Sm 19:4
loud voice, "O my son Absalom, O **A**, 2 Sm 19:4
I know that if **A** were alive and all 2 Sm 19:6
he has fled out of the land from **A**. 2 Sm 19:9
But **A**, whom we anointed over us, is 2 Sm 19:10

Bichri will do us more harm than **A**. 2 Sm 20:6
man, and he was born next after **A**. 1 Kgs 1:6
me when I fled from **A** your brother. 1 Kgs 2:7
he had not supported **A**—Joab fled to 1 Kgs 2:28
third, **A**, whose mother was Maacah, 1 Chr 3:2
he took Maacah the daughter of **A**, 2 Chr 11:20
the daughter of **A** above all his 2 Chr 11:21
of David, when he fled from **A** his son. Ps 3:T

ABSALOM'S (5)
"I love Tamar, my brother **A** sister." 2 Sm 13:4
woman, in her brother **A** house. 2 Sm 13:20
it on fire." So **A** servants set the field 2 Sm 14:30
When **A** servants came to the 2 Sm 17:20
and it is called **A** monument to this 2 Sm 18:18

ABSENCE (3)
betray him to them in the **a** of a crowd. Lk 22:6
they have made up for your **a**, 1 Cor 16:17
my presence but much more in my **a**, Phil 2:12

ABSENT (5)
For though **a** in body, I am present in 1 Cor 5:3
that what we say by letter when **a**, 2 Cor 10:11
others, and I warn them now while **a**, 2 Cor 13:2
whether I come and see you or am **a**, Phil 1:27
For though I am **a** in body, yet I am with Col 2:5

ABSTAIN (8)
sons so that they **a** from the holy things Lv 22:2
"Should I weep and **a** in the fifth month, Zec 7:3
write to them to **a** from the things Acts 15:20
that you **a** from what has been Acts 15:29
that they should **a** from what has Acts 21:25
that you **a** from sexual immorality; 1 Thes 4:3
A from every form of evil. 1 Thes 5:22
and exiles to **a** from the passions 1 Pt 2:11

ABSTAINS (4)
the one who eats despise the one who **a**, Rom 14:3
not the one who **a** pass judgment on Rom 14:3
thanks to God, while the one who **a**, Rom 14:6
a in honor of the Lord and gives Rom 14:6

ABSTINENCE (1)
marriage and require **a** from foods 1 Tm 4:3

ABUNDANCE (71)
And Joseph stored up grain in great **a**, Gn 41:49
of heart, because of the **a** of all things, Dt 28:47
mountains and the **a** of the everlasting Dt 33:15
for they draw from the **a** of the seas and Dt 33:19
lay along the valley like locusts in **a**, Jgs 7:12
as the sand that is on the seashore in **a**. Jgs 7:12
olive tree said to them, 'Shall I leave my **a**, Jgs 9:9
oxen, fattened cattle, and sheep in **a**, 1 Kgs 1:19
oxen, fattened cattle, and sheep in **a**, 1 Kgs 1:25
again came such an **a** of spices as 1 Kgs 10:10
You have an **a** of workmen: 1 Chr 22:15
all this **a** that we have provided for 1 Chr 29:16
and sacrifices in **a** for all Israel. 1 Chr 29:21
to prepare timber for me in **a**, for the 2 Chr 2:9
carried away sheep in **a** and camels. 2 Chr 14:15
And Ahab killed an **a** of sheep and 2 Chr 18:2
after day, and collected money in **a**. 2 Chr 24:11
of Israel gave in **a** the firstfruits of 2 Chr 31:5
also made weapons and shields in **a**. 2 Chr 32:5
himself, and flocks and herds in **a**, 2 Chr 32:29
every ten days all kinds of wine in **a**. Neh 5:18
olive orchards and fruit trees in **a**. Neh 9:25
he judges peoples; he gives food in **a**. Jb 36:31
But I, through the **a** of your steadfast love, Ps 5:7
because of the **a** of their transgressions Ps 5:10
and they leave their **a** to their infants. Ps 17:14
They feast on the **a** of your house, and Ps 36:8
has than the **a** of many wicked. Ps 37:16
times; in the days of famine they have **a**. Ps 37:19
wealth and boast of the **a** of their riches? Ps 49:6
but trusted in the **a** of his riches and Ps 52:7
your wagon tracks overflow with **a**. Ps 65:11
you have brought us out to a place of **a**. Ps 66:12
Rain in **a**, O God, you shed abroad; you Ps 68:9
in the **a** of your steadfast love answer Ps 69:13
May there be **a** of grain in the land; on Ps 72:16
of the angels; he sent them food in **a**. Ps 78:25
gave them bread from heaven in **a**. Ps 105:40
not remember the **a** of your steadfast Ps 106:7
according to the **a** of his steadfast Ps 106:45
but in an **a** of counselors there is Prv 11:14
There is gold and **a** of costly stones, Prv 20:15
plans of the diligent lead surely to **a**, Prv 21:5
and in **a** of counselors there is victory. Prv 24:6
and because of the **a** of milk that they Is 7:22
Therefore the **a** they have gained and Is 15:7
deep and wide, with fire and wood in **a**; Is 30:33
the stability of your times, **a** of salvation, Is 33:6
Then prey and spoil in **a** will be divided; Is 33:23
because the **a** of the sea shall be turned to Is 60:5
according to the **a** of his steadfast love. Is 63:7
deeply with delight from her glorious **a**." Is 66:11
I will feast the soul of the priests with **a**, Jer 31:14
and reveal to them **a** of prosperity and Jer 33:6
wine and summer fruits in great **a**. Jer 40:12
according to the **a** of his steadfast Lam 3:32
None of them shall remain, nor their **a**, Ezk 7:11
In the **a** of your trade you were filled Ezk 28:16
gold, silver, and garments in great **a**. Zec 14:14
For out of the **a** of the heart the mouth Mt 12:34
will be given, and he will have an **a**, Mt 13:12
more be given, and he will have an **a**. Mt 25:29
For they all contributed out of their **a**, Mk 12:44
for out of the **a** of the heart his mouth Lk 6:45
not consist in the **a** of his possessions." Lk 12:15
For they all contributed out of their **a**, Lk 21:4
those who receive the **a** of grace and Rom 5:17
their **a** of joy and their extreme poverty 2 Cor 8:2
your **a** at the present time should 2 Cor 8:14
so that their **a** may supply your need, 2 Cor 8:14
facing plenty and hunger, **a** and need. Phil 4:12

ABUNDANT (29)
and on oxen, **a** provisions of flour, 1 Chr 12:40
he gave them **a** provisions and 2 Chr 11:23
Is not your evil **a**? There is no end to your Jb 22:5
my wealth was **a** or because my Jb 31:25
justice and **a** righteousness he will not Jb 37:23
Oh, how **a** is your goodness, which you Ps 31:19
land and delight themselves in **a** peace. Ps 37:11
according to your **a** mercy blot out my Ps 51:1
according to your **a** mercy, turn to me. Ps 69:16
the fame of your **a** goodness and shall Ps 145:7
Great is our Lord, and **a** in power; his Ps 147:5
but **a** crops come by the strength of the Prv 14:4
merchandise will supply **a** food and fine Is 23:18
fertile soil. He placed it beside **a** waters. Ezk 17:5
been planted on good soil by **a** waters, Ezk 17:8
full of branches by reason of **a** water. Ezk 19:10
its **a** corrosion does not go out of it. Ezk 24:12
with you because of your **a** goods; Ezk 27:16
business with you for your **a** goods, Ezk 27:18
with your **a** wealth and merchandise Ezk 27:33
its branches long from **a** water in its Ezk 31:5
for its roots went down to **a** waters. Ezk 31:7
grain and make it **a** and lay no Ezk 36:29
the tree and the increase of the field **a**, Ezk 36:30
Its leaves were beautiful and its fruit **a**, Dn 4:12
leaves were beautiful and its fruit **a**, Dn 4:21
on with a great army and **a** supplies. Dn 11:13
he has poured down for you **a** rain, the Jl 2:23
to let you know the **a** love that I have 2 Cor 2:4

ABUNDANTLY (18)
before I came, and it has increased **a**, Gn 30:30
plentiful years the earth produced **a**, Gn 41:47
his staff twice, and water came out **a**, Nm 20:11
God will make you **a** prosperous in all Dt 30:9
And they brought in **a** the tithe of 2 Chr 31:5
pour down and drop on mankind **a**. Jb 36:28
the faithful but **a** repays the one Ps 31:23
You water its furrows **a**, settling its Ps 65:10
and gave them drink **a** as from the deep. Ps 78:15
The trees of the LORD are watered **a**, the Ps 104:16
I will **a** bless her provisions; I will Ps 132:15
it shall blossom **a** and rejoice with joy Is 35:2
him, and to our God, for he will **a** pardon. Is 55:7
that they may have life and have it **a**. Jn 10:10
as we share **a** in Christ's sufferings, 2 Cor 1:5
Christ we share **a** in comfort too. 2 Cor 1:5
able to do far more **a** than all that we Eph 3:20
because your faith is growing **a**, 2 Thes 1:3

ABUSE (3)
corrects a scoffer gets himself **a**, Prv 9:7
out, and quarreling and **a** will cease. Prv 22:10
curse you, pray for those who **a** you. Lk 6:28

ABUSED (1)
they knew her and **a** her all night until Jgs 19:25

ABUSIVE (1)
arrogant, **a**, disobedient to their parents, 2 Tm 3:2

ABYSS (2)
to command them to depart into the **a**. Lk 8:31
will descend into the **a**?" (that is, Rom 10:7

ACACIA (28)
tanned rams' skins, goatskins, **a** wood, Ex 25:5
"They shall make an ark of **a** wood. Ex 25:10
shall make poles of **a** wood and overlay Ex 25:13
"You shall make a table of **a** wood. Ex 25:23
You shall make the poles of **a** wood, Ex 25:28
frames for the tabernacle of **a** wood. Ex 26:15
"You shall make bars of **a** wood, five Ex 26:26
it on four pillars of **a** overlaid with gold, Ex 26:32
make for the screen five pillars of **a**, Ex 26:37
"You shall make the altar of **a** wood, five Ex 27:1
make poles for the altar, poles of **a** wood, Ex 27:6
incense; you shall make it of **a** wood. Ex 30:1
make the poles of **a** wood and overlay Ex 30:5
rams' skins, and goatskins; **a** wood, Ex 35:7
every one who possessed **a** wood of any Ex 35:24
frames for the tabernacle of **a** wood. Ex 36:20
He made bars of **a** wood, five for the Ex 36:31
four pillars of **a** and overlaid them Ex 36:36
Bezalel made the ark of **a** wood. Two Ex 37:1
he made poles of **a** wood and overlaid Ex 37:4
He also made the table of **a** wood. Two Ex 37:10
made the poles of **a** wood to carry the Ex 37:15
He made the altar of incense of **a** wood. Ex 37:25
made the poles of **a** wood and overlaid Ex 37:28
the altar of burnt offering of **a** wood. Ex 38:1
made the poles of **a** wood and overlaid Ex 38:6
So I made an ark of **a** wood, and cut two Dt 10:3
put in the wilderness the cedar, the **a**, Is 41:19

ACCAD (1)
was Babel, Erech, **A**, and Calneh, Gn 10:10

ACCENT (1)
one of them, for your **a** betrays you." Mt 26:73

ACCEPT (54)
A it from me, that I may bury my dead Gn 23:13
see his face. Perhaps he will **a** me." Gn 32:20
then **a** my present from my hand. Gn 33:10
Please **a** my blessing that is brought to Gn 33:11
The owner shall **a** the oath, and he Ex 22:11
"**A** these from them, that they may be Nm 7:5
you shall **a** no ransom for the life of a Nm 35:31
And you shall **a** no ransom for him Nm 35:32
partiality, and you shall not **a** a bribe, Dt 16:19
A atonement, O LORD, for your people Dt 21:8
substance, and **a** the work of his hands; Dt 33:11
for he will not **a** boiled meat from you 1 Sm 2:15
which you shall **a** from their hand. 1 Sm 10:4
up against me, may he **a** an offering, 1 Sm 26:19
king, "The LORD your God **a** you." 2 Sm 24:23
so **a** now a present from your 2 Kgs 5:15
"Be pleased to **a** two talents." And he 2 Kgs 5:23
it a time to **a** money and garments, 2 Kgs 5:26
his sackcloth, but he would not **a** them. Est 4:4
roads, and do you not **a** their testimony Jb 21:29
for I will **a** his prayer not to deal with you Jb 42:8
I will not **a** a bull from your house or Ps 50:9
A my freewill offerings of praise, O Ps 119:108
Hear, my son, and **a** my words, that the Prv 4:10
He will **a** no compensation; he will Prv 6:35
Listen to advice and **a** instruction, Prv 19:20
and to **a** his lot and rejoice in his toil— Eccl 5:19
those who murmur will **a** instruction." Is 29:24
LORD their God, and did not **a** discipline; Jer 7:28
feet; therefore the LORD does not **a** them; Jer 14:10
and grain offering, I will not **a** them. Jer 14:12
if they refuse to **a** the cup from your Jer 25:28
There I will **a** them, and there I will Ezk 20:40
As a pleasing aroma I will **a** you, Ezk 20:41
your peace offerings, and I will **a** you, Ezk 43:27
and eat it, but the LORD does not **a** them. Hos 8:13
a what is good, and we will pay with Hos 14:2
and grain offerings, I will not **a** them; Am 5:22
you will fear me; you will **a** correction. Zep 3:7
will he **a** you or show you favor? Mal 1:8
and I will not **a** an offering from your Mal 1:10
Shall I **a** that from your hand? Mal 1:13
and if you are willing to **a** it, he is Mt 11:14
hear the word and **a** it and bear fruit, Mk 4:20
for us as Romans to **a** or practice." Acts 16:21
have reason to **a** your complaint. Acts 18:14
they will not **a** your testimony about Acts 22:18
way and everywhere we **a** this with all Acts 24:3
God, which these men themselves **a**, Acts 24:15
person does not **a** the things of 1 Cor 2:14
or if you **a** a different gospel from the 2 Cor 11:4
But even if you do, **a** me as a fool, so 2 Cor 11:16
say to you that if you **a** circumcision, Gal 5:2
were tortured, refusing to **a** release, Heb 11:35

ACCEPTABLE (22)
a blemish, for it will not be **a** for you. Lv 22:20
day on it shall be **a** as a food offering to Lv 22:27
of my heart be **a** in your sight, Ps 19:14
At an **a** time, O God, in the abundance Ps 69:13
lips of the righteous know what is **a**, Prv 10:32
the prayer of the upright is **a** to him. Prv 15:8
and justice is more **a** to the LORD than Prv 21:3
call this a fast, and a day **a** to the LORD? Is 58:5
Your burnt offerings are not **a**, nor your Jer 6:20
O king, let my counsel be **a** to you: Dn 4:27
to you, no prophet is **a** in his hometown. Lk 4:24
and does what is right is **a** to him. Acts 10:35
as a living sacrifice, holy and **a** to God, Rom 12:1
of God, what is good and **a** and perfect. Rom 12:2
thus serves Christ is **a** to God and Rom 14:18
the offering of the Gentiles may be **a**, Rom 15:16

for Jerusalem may be **a** to the saints, Rom 15:31
it is **a** according to what a person has, 2 Cor 8:12
a sacrifice **a** and pleasing to God. Phil 4:18
to God a more **a** sacrifice than Cain, Heb 11:4
and thus let us offer to God **a** worship, Heb 12:28
offer spiritual sacrifices **a** to God 1 Pt 2:5

ACCEPTANCE (5)
guilt offering, but the upright enjoy **a**. Prv 14:9
they shall come up with **a** on my altar, Is 60:7
what will their **a** mean but life from Rom 11:15
is trustworthy and deserving of full **a**, 1 Tm 1:15
is trustworthy and deserving of full **a**. 1 Tm 4:9

ACCEPTED (22)
If you do well, will you not be **a**? And if Gn 4:7
the face of God, and you have **a** me. Gn 33:10
that they may be **a** before the LORD. Ex 28:38
meeting, that he may be **a** before the LORD. Lv 1:3
and it shall be **a** for him to make Lv 1:4
third day, he who offers it shall not be **a**, Lv 7:18
you shall offer it so that you may be **a**. Lv 19:5
the third day, it is tainted; it will not be **a**, Lv 19:7
if it is to be **a** for you it shall be a male Lv 22:19
the flock, to be **a** it must be perfect; Lv 22:21
but for a vow offering it cannot be **a**. Lv 22:23
mutilation, they will not be **a** for you." Lv 22:25
shall sacrifice it so that you may be **a**. Lv 22:29
before the LORD, so that you may be **a**. Lv 23:11
he would not have **a** a burnt offering Jgs 13:23
So the Jews **a** what they had started to do, Est 9:23
told them, and the LORD **a** Job's prayer. Jb 42:9
and their sacrifices will be **a** on my altar; Is 56:7
For he not only **a** our appeal, but 2 Cor 8:17
a different gospel from the one you **a**, 2 Cor 11:4
you **a** it not as the word of men but 1 Thes 2:13
and you joyfully **a** the plundering of Heb 10:34

ACCEPTING (4)
in not **a** from his hand what he 2 Kgs 5:20
other churches by **a** support from 2 Cor 11:8
God commending him by **a** his gifts. Heb 11:4
the name, **a** nothing from the Gentiles. 3 Jn 1:7

ACCEPTS (6)
then man prays to God, and he **a** him; Jb 33:26
has heard my plea; the LORD **a** my prayer. Ps 6:9
The wicked **a** a bribe in secret to Prv 17:23
listens to no voice; she **a** no correction. Zep 3:2
regards the offering or **a** it with favor Mal 2:13
every man who **a** circumcision that he Gal 5:3

ACCESS (4)
you the right of **a** among those who are Zec 3:7
we have also obtained **a** by faith into Rom 5:2
him we both have **a** in one Spirit to Eph 2:18
have boldness and **a** with confidence Eph 3:12

ACCESSORIES (2)
the pillars, the bases, and all their **a**; Nm 3:36
with all their equipment and all their **a**. Nm 4:32

ACCO (1)
did not drive out the inhabitants of **A**, Jgs 1:31

ACCOMPANIED (9)
a by the instruments of David king 2 Chr 29:27
Now great crowds **a** him, and he Lk 14:25
the men who have **a** us during all the Acts 1:21
of the brothers from Joppa **a** him. Acts 10:23
These six brothers also **a** me, and we Acts 11:12
the son of Pyrrhus from Berea, **a** him; Acts 20:4
again. And they **a** him to the ship. Acts 20:38
a us until we were outside the city. Acts 21:5
Asia, we put to sea, **a** by Aristarchus, Acts 27:2

ACCOMPANY (4)
these signs will **a** those who believe: Mk 16:17
go down and **a** them without Acts 10:20
Paul wanted Timothy to **a** him, and he Acts 16:3
that I should go also, they will **a** me. 1 Cor 16:4

ACCOMPANYING (1)
confirmed the message by **a** signs.]] Mk 16:20

ACCOMPLISH (8)
if I do not **a** for David what the LORD 2 Sm 3:9
have sinned, what do you **a** against him? Jb 35:6
to **a** all that he commands them on the Jb 37:12
shall stand, and I will **a** all my purpose,' Is 46:10
but it shall **a** that which I purpose, Is 55:11
which he was about to **a** at Jerusalem. Lk 9:31
of him who sent me and to **a** his work. Jn 4:34
works that the Father has given me to **a**, Jn 5:36

ACCOMPLISHED (17)
in his own house he successfully **a**. 2 Chr 7:11
Thus was **a** all the work of Solomon 2 Chr 8:16
this work had been **a** with the help of Neh 6:16
"We have **a** a diligent search." For the Ps 64:6
We have **a** no deliverance in the earth, Is 26:18
he has executed and **a** the intents of his Jer 23:20
he has executed and **a** the intentions of Jer 30:24
and they shall be **a** before you on that Jer 39:16
your iniquity, O daughter of Zion, is **a**; Lam 4:22
shall prosper till the indignation is **a**; Dn 11:36
dot, will pass from the Law until all is **a**. Mt 5:18
all these things are about to be **a**?" Mk 13:4
of the things that have been **a** among us, Lk 1:1
how great is my distress until it is **a**! Lk 12:50
Son of Man by the prophets will be **a**. Lk 18:31
having **a** the work that you gave me to Jn 17:4
what Christ has **a** through me to Rom 15:18

ACCORD (22)
and that it has not been of my own **a**. Nm 16:28
prophets with one **a** are favorable to 1 Kgs 22:13
prophets with one **a** are favorable to 2 Chr 18:12
For they conspire with one **a**; against Ps 83:5
obeyed my voice or walked in **a** with it, Jer 9:13
of the LORD and serve him with one **a**. Zep 3:9
you, the Son can do nothing of his own **a**, Jn 5:19
from? But I have not come of my own **a**. Jn 7:28
I came not of my own **a**, but he sent me. Jn 8:42
from me, but I lay it down of my own **a**. Jn 10:18
He did not say this of his own **a**, but Jn 11:51
"Do you say this of your own **a**, Jn 18:34
these with one **a** were devoting Acts 1:14
the crowds with one **a** paid attention to Acts 8:6
It opened for them of its own **a**, and Acts 12:10
and they came to him with one **a**, Acts 12:20
good to us, having come to one **a**, Acts 15:25
one another, in **a** with Christ Jesus, Rom 15:5
What **a** has Christ with Belial? Or 2 Cor 6:15
he is going to you of his own **a**. 2 Cor 8:17
love, being in full **a** and of one mind. Phil 2:2
and not in **a** with the tradition 2 Thes 3:6

ACCORDANCE (21)
made with you in **a** with all these Ex 24:8
for in **a** with these words I have made a Ex 34:27
sanctuary shall work in **a** with all that Ex 36:1
in exact **a** with the vow that he takes, Nm 6:21
avenger of blood, in **a** with these rules. Nm 35:24
in **a** with all the curses of the covenant Dt 29:21
In **a** with all these words, and in 2 Sm 7:17
words, and in **a** with all this vision, 2 Sm 7:17
with blindness in **a** with the prayer 2 Kgs 6:18
in **a** with the word of the LORD." 2 Kgs 9:26
in **a** with all that King Ahaz had 2 Kgs 16:11
in **a** with all the Law that I 2 Kgs 17:13
In **a** with all these words, and in 1 Chr 17:15
words, and in **a** with all this vision, 1 Chr 17:15
of God and in **a** with the law and 2 Chr 31:21
the guard, in **a** with the word of the LORD, Jer 32:8
In **a** with their ways and their deeds I Ezk 36:19
for our sins in **a** with the Scriptures, 1 Cor 15:3
the third day in **a** with the Scriptures, 1 Cor 15:4
in **a** with the glorious gospel of the 1 Tm 1:11
in **a** with the prophecies previously 1 Tm 1:18

ACCORDING (627)
in which is their seed, each **a** to its kind, Gn 1:11
plants yielding seed **a** to their own Gn 1:12
in which is their seed, each **a** to its kind. Gn 1:12
the waters swarm, **a** to their kinds, Gn 1:21
and every winged bird **a** to its kind. Gn 1:21
forth living creatures **a** to their kinds Gn 1:24
beasts of the earth **a** to their kinds." And Gn 1:24
beasts of the earth **a** to their kinds and Gn 1:25
kinds and the livestock **a** to their kinds, Gn 1:25
that creeps on the ground **a** to its kind. Gn 1:25
Of the birds **a** to their kinds, and of the Gn 6:20
and of the animals **a** to their kinds, Gn 6:20
thing of the ground, **a** to its kind, Gn 6:20
they and every beast, **a** to its kind, and Gn 7:14
and all the livestock **a** to their kinds, Gn 7:14
that creeps on the earth, **a** to its kind, Gn 7:14
to its kind, and every bird, **a** to its kind, Gn 7:14
sons of Noah, **a** to their genealogies, Gn 10:32
have done altogether **a** to the outcry Gn 18:21
a to the weights current among the Gn 23:16
twelve princes **a** to their tribes. Gn 25:16
a to their clans and their dwelling Gn 36:40
a to their dwelling places in the land of Gn 36:43
to each man **a** to his dream. Gn 41:12
the firstborn **a** to his birthright and Gn 43:33
and the youngest **a** to his youth. Gn 43:33
a to the command of Pharaoh, Gn 45:21
a to the number of their dependents. Gn 47:12
of the sons of Levi **a** to their generations: Ex 6:16
of the Levites **a** to their generations. Ex 6:19
And the LORD did **a** to the word of Moses. Ex 8:13
shall take a lamb **a** to their fathers' Ex 12:3
neighbor shall take **a** to the number Ex 12:4
a to what each can eat you shall make Ex 12:4
lambs for yourselves **a** to your clans, Ex 12:21
a to the number of the persons that Ex 16:16
a to the commandment of the LORD, Ex 17:1
shall be dealt with **a** to this same rule. Ex 21:31
pillars, **a** to the twelve tribes of Israel. Ex 24:4
shall erect the tabernacle **a** to the plan Ex 26:30
stones with their names **a** to the names Ex 28:21
a to all that I have commanded you. Ex 29:35
half a shekel **a** to the shekel of the Ex 30:13
cassia, **a** to the shekel of the sanctuary, Ex 30:24
you shall make **a** to its composition, Ex 30:37
A to all that I have commanded you, Ex 31:11
the sons of Levi did **a** to the word of Ex 32:28
a to the names of the sons of Israel. Ex 39:6
stones with their names **a** to the names Ex 39:14
the people of Israel did **a** to all that the Ex 39:32
A to all that the LORD had commanded Ex 39:42
a to all that the LORD commanded him, Ex 40:16
second for a burnt offering **a** to the rule. Lv 5:10
shekels, **a** to the shekel of the sanctuary, Lv 5:15
burnt offering and offered it **a** to the rule. Lv 9:16
upon you." And they did **a** to the word of Lv 10:7
pay your neighbor **a** to the number Lv 25:15
he shall sell to you **a** to the number of Lv 25:15
of silver, **a** to the shekel of the sanctuary. Lv 27:3
priest shall value him **a** to what the Lv 27:8
shall calculate the price **a** to the years Lv 27:18
Every valuation shall be **a** to the shekel Lv 27:25
houses, **a** to the number of names, Nm 1:2
a to the number of names from twenty Nm 1:18
houses, **a** to the number of names, Nm 1:20
were listed, **a** to the number of names, Nm 1:22
houses, **a** to the number of the names, Nm 1:24
houses, **a** to the number of names, Nm 1:26
houses, **a** to the number of names, Nm 1:28
houses, **a** to the number of names, Nm 1:30
houses, **a** to the number of names, Nm 1:32
houses, **a** to the number of names, Nm 1:34
houses, **a** to the number of names, Nm 1:36
houses, **a** to the number of names, Nm 1:38
houses, **a** to the number of names, Nm 1:40
houses, **a** to the number of names, Nm 1:42
they did **a** to all that the LORD Nm 1:54
A to all that the LORD commanded Nm 2:34
one in his clan, **a** to his fathers' house. Nm 2:34
So Moses listed them **a** to the word of Nm 3:16
Their listing **a** to the number of all the Nm 3:22
A to the number of all the males, from Nm 3:28
Their listing **a** to the number of all the Nm 3:34
males, **a** to the number of names, Nm 3:43
you shall take them **a** to the shekel of Nm 3:47
and his sons, **a** to the word of the LORD, Nm 3:51
and Aaron listed **a** to the Nm 4:37
and Aaron listed **a** to the Nm 4:41
and Aaron listed **a** to the Nm 4:45
A to the commandment of the LORD Nm 4:49
Levites, to each man **a** to his service." Nm 7:5
to the sons of Gershon, **a** to their service. Nm 7:7
to the sons of Merari, **a** to their service, Nm 7:8
a to the shekel of the sanctuary, Nm 7:13
a to the shekel of the sanctuary, Nm 7:19
a to the shekel of the sanctuary, Nm 7:25
a to the shekel of the sanctuary, Nm 7:31
a to the shekel of the sanctuary, Nm 7:37
a to the shekel of the sanctuary, Nm 7:43
a to the shekel of the sanctuary, Nm 7:49
a to the shekel of the sanctuary, Nm 7:55
a to the shekel of the sanctuary, Nm 7:61
a to the shekel of the sanctuary, Nm 7:67
a to the shekel of the sanctuary, Nm 7:73
a to the shekel of the sanctuary, Nm 7:79
the vessels 2,400 shekels **a** to the shekel Nm 7:85
10 shekels apiece **a** to the shekel Nm 7:86
a to the pattern that the LORD had shown Nm 8:4
A to all that the LORD commanded Nm 8:20
a to all its statutes and all its rules you Nm 9:3
a to all that the LORD commanded Nm 9:5
a to all the statute for the Passover they Nm 9:12
a to the statute of the Passover and Nm 9:14
statute of the Passover and **a** to its rule, Nm 9:14
and **a** to the command of the LORD they Nm 9:20
then **a** to the command of the LORD Nm 9:20
Paran, **a** to the command of the LORD, Nm 13:3
a to the greatness of your steadfast Nm 14:19
said, "I have pardoned, **a** to your word. Nm 14:20
A to the number of the days in which Nm 14:34
and its drink offering, **a** to the rule, Nm 15:24
from all their chiefs **a** to their fathers' Nm 17:2
each chief, **a** to their fathers' houses, Nm 17:6
silver, **a** to the shekel of the sanctuary, Nm 18:16
The sons of Simeon **a** to their clans: of Nm 26:12
The sons of Gad **a** to their clans: of Nm 26:15
the sons of Judah **a** to their clans were: Nm 26:20
The sons of Issachar **a** to their clans: Nm 26:23
The sons of Zebulun, **a** to their clans: Nm 26:26
The sons of Joseph **a** to their clans: Nm 26:28
the sons of Ephraim **a** to their clans: Nm 26:35
are the sons of Joseph **a** to their clans. Nm 26:37

The sons of Benjamin **a** to their clans: Nm 26:38
the sons of Benjamin **a** to their clans, Nm 26:41
are the sons of Dan **a** to their clans: Nm 26:42
are the clans of Dan **a** to their clans. Nm 26:42
The sons of Asher **a** to their clans: of Nm 26:44
The sons of Naphtali **a** to their clans: Nm 26:48
the clans of Naphtali **a** to their clans, Nm 26:50
divided for inheritance **a** to the Nm 26:53
A to the names of the tribes of their Nm 26:55
shall be divided **a** to lot between Nm 26:56
the list of the Levites **a** to their clans: Nm 26:57
drink offering, **a** to the rule for them, Nm 29:6
He shall do **a** to all that proceeds out of Nm 30:2
these are their stages **a** to their starting Nm 33:2
inherit the land by lot **a** to your clans. Nm 33:54
A to the tribes of your fathers you Nm 33:54
the people of Israel **a** to the word of Nm 36:5
to the people of Israel **a** to all that the LORD Dt 1:3
its breadth, **a** to the common cubit.) Dt 3:11
"You shall not do **a** to all that we are Dt 12:8
a to the blessing of the LORD your God Dt 12:15
a to the blessing of the LORD your God Dt 16:17
your God is giving you, **a** to your tribes, Dt 16:18
Then you shall do **a** to what they Dt 17:10
shall be careful to do **a** to all that they Dt 17:10
A to the instructions that they give you, Dt 17:11
and **a** to the decision which they Dt 17:11
teach you to do **a** to all their Dt 20:18
be very careful to do **a** to all that the Dt 24:8
a to all your commandment that you Dt 26:13
I have done **a** to all that you have Dt 26:14
shall do to them **a** to the whole Dt 31:5
borders of the peoples **a** to the number of Dt 32:8
land of Moab, **a** to the word of the LORD, Dt 34:5
being careful to do **a** to all the law that Jos 1:7
may be careful to do **a** to all that is Jos 1:8
And she said, "**A** to your words, so be it." Jos 2:21
a to the number of the tribes of the people Jos 4:5
a to the number of the tribes of the people Jos 4:8
a to all that Moses had commanded Jos 4:10
You shall do **a** to the word of the Lord. Jos 8:8
a to the word of the LORD that he Jos 8:27
a to all that is written in the Book of the Jos 8:34
a to all that the LORD had spoken to Jos 11:23
an inheritance to Israel **a** to their tribal Jos 11:23
as a possession **a** to their allotments, Jos 12:7
of the people of Reuben **a** to their clans. Jos 13:15
a to their clans with their cities and Jos 13:23
to the people of Gad, **a** to their clans. Jos 13:24
of the people of Gad **a** to their clans, Jos 13:28
the people of Manasseh **a** to their clans. Jos 13:29
of the people of Machir **a** to their clans. Jos 13:31
the people of Judah **a** to their clans Jos 15:1
the people of Judah **a** to their clans. Jos 15:12
A to the commandment of the LORD to Jos 15:13
of the people of Judah **a** to their clans. Jos 15:20
with our brothers." So **a** to the mouth of Jos 17:4
the people of Benjamin **a** to its clans Jos 18:11
the people of Benjamin, **a** to their clans, Jos 18:20
the people of Benjamin **a** to their clans Jos 18:21
of the people of Benjamin **a** to its clans. Jos 18:28
of the people of Simeon, **a** to their clans, Jos 19:1
of the people of Simeon **a** to their clans. Jos 19:8
the people of Zebulun, **a** to their clans. Jos 19:10
a to their clans—these cities with their Jos 19:16
the people of Issachar, **a** to their clans. Jos 19:17
a to their clans—the cities with their Jos 19:23
of the people of Asher **a** to their clans. Jos 19:24
of the people of Asher **a** to their clans— Jos 19:31
the people of Naphtali, **a** to their clans. Jos 19:32
the people of Naphtali **a** to their clans— Jos 19:39
of the people of Dan, **a** to their clans. Jos 19:40
a to their clans—these cities with their Jos 19:48
The Merarites **a** to their clans received Jos 21:7
do to me **a** to what has gone out of your Jgs 11:36
who did with her **a** to his vow that he Jgs 11:39
took their wives, **a** to their number, Jgs 21:23
who shall do **a** to what is in my heart 1 Sm 2:35
a to the number of the lords of the 1 Sm 6:4
a to the number of all the cities of the 1 Sm 6:18
A to all the deeds that they have done, 1 Sm 8:8
a to all your heart's desire to come 1 Sm 23:20
has done to my lord **a** to all the good 1 Sm 25:30
repay the evildoer **a** to his 2 Sm 3:39
promise, and **a** to your own heart, 2 Sm 7:21
a to all that we have heard with our 2 Sm 7:22
"**A** to all that my lord the king 2 Sm 9:11
dealt with me **a** to my righteousness; 2 Sm 22:21
a to the cleanness of my hands he 2 Sm 22:21
has rewarded me **a** to my 2 Sm 22:25
a to my cleanness in his sight. 2 Sm 22:25
Act therefore **a** to your wisdom, but do 1 Kgs 2:6
behold, I now do **a** to your word. 1 Kgs 3:12
it was required, each **a** to his duty. 1 Kgs 4:28
parts, and **a** to all its specifications. 1 Kgs 6:38
of costly stones, cut **a** to measure, 1 Kgs 7:9
costly stones, cut **a** to measurement, 1 Kgs 7:11
and palm trees, **a** to the space of each, 1 Kgs 7:36
by rewarding him **a** to his 1 Kgs 8:32
you know, **a** to all his ways (for you, 1 Kgs 8:39
dwelling place and do **a** to all for 1 Kgs 8:43
Israel, **a** to all that he promised. 1 Kgs 8:56
doing **a** to all that I have commanded 1 Kgs 9:4
he spoke to them **a** to the counsel of 1 Kgs 12:14
again, **a** to the word of the LORD. 1 Kgs 12:24
a to the sign that the man of God had 1 Kgs 13:5
a to the word that the LORD spoke to 1 Kgs 13:26
for him, **a** to the word of the LORD, 1 Kgs 14:18
They did **a** to all the abominations 1 Kgs 14:24
a to the word of the LORD that he 1 Kgs 15:29
of Baasha, **a** to the word of the LORD, 1 Kgs 16:12
son Segub, **a** to the word of the LORD, 1 Kgs 16:34
So he went and did **a** to the word of 1 Kgs 17:5
a to the word of the LORD that he 1 Kgs 17:16
a to the number of the tribes of the 1 Kgs 18:31
a to the word of the LORD that he had 1 Kgs 22:38
So he died **a** to the word of the LORD 2 Kgs 1:17
day, **a** to the word that Elisha spoke. 2 Kgs 2:22
some left, **a** to the word of the LORD. 2 Kgs 4:44
a to the word of the man of God, 2 Kgs 5:14
for a shekel, **a** to the word of the LORD. 2 Kgs 7:16
woman arose and did **a** to the word of 2 Kgs 8:2
a to the word of the LORD that he 2 Kgs 10:17
the house of Ahab **a** to all that was 2 Kgs 10:30
The captains did **a** to all that 2 Kgs 11:9
by the pillar, **a** to the custom, 2 Kgs 11:14
a to what is written in the Book of the 2 Kgs 14:6
Arabah, **a** to the word of the LORD, 2 Kgs 14:25
a to all that his father Amaziah had 2 Kgs 15:3
a to all that his father Uzziah had 2 Kgs 15:34
a to the despicable practices of the 2 Kgs 16:3
this day they do **a** to the former 2 Kgs 17:34
but they did **a** to their former 2 Kgs 17:40
a to all that David his father had 2 Kgs 18:3
a to the despicable practices of the 2 Kgs 21:2
will be careful to do **a** to all that I 2 Kgs 21:8
and **a** to all the Law that my servant 2 Kgs 21:8
to do **a** to all that is written 2 Kgs 22:13
a to the word of the LORD that the 2 Kgs 23:16
He did to them **a** to all that he had 2 Kgs 23:19
his might, **a** to all the Law of Moses, 2 Kgs 23:25
a to all that his fathers had done. 2 Kgs 23:32
to give the money **a** to the command 2 Kgs 23:35
from everyone **a** to his assessment, 2 Kgs 23:35
a to all that his fathers had done. 2 Kgs 23:37
a to the word of the LORD that he 2 Kgs 24:2
Manasseh, **a** to all that he had done, 2 Kgs 24:3
LORD, **a** to all that his father had done. 2 Kgs 24:9
a to all that Jehoiakim had done. 2 Kgs 24:19
by the king, **a** to his daily needs, 2 Kgs 25:30
And their kinsmen **a** to their fathers' 1 Chr 5:13
clans of the Levites **a** to their fathers. 1 Chr 6:19
performed their service **a** to their 1 Chr 6:32
a to all that Moses the servant of God 1 Chr 6:49
their dwelling places **a** to their 1 Chr 6:54
To the Gershomites **a** to their clans 1 Chr 6:62
To the Merarites **a** to their clans were 1 Chr 6:63
generations, **a** to their fathers' houses, 1 Chr 7:4
by genealogies, **a** to their generations, 1 Chr 7:9
the sons of Jediael **a** to the heads of 1 Chr 7:11
houses, **a** to their generations, 1 Chr 8:28
and their kinsmen **a** to their 1 Chr 9:9
of fathers' houses **a** to their fathers' 1 Chr 9:9
of the Levites, **a** to their generations, 1 Chr 9:34
a to the word of the LORD by Samuel. 1 Chr 11:3
a to the word of the LORD 1 Chr 11:10
to him, **a** to the word of the LORD. 1 Chr 12:23
we did not seek him **a** to the rule." 1 Chr 15:13
Moses had commanded **a** to the 1 Chr 15:15
were to play harps **a** to Alamoth; 1 Chr 15:20
lead with lyres **a** to the Sheminith. 1 Chr 15:21
O LORD, and **a** to your own heart, 1 Chr 17:19
a to all that we have heard with our 1 Chr 17:20
as they were listed **a** to the number 1 Chr 23:24
a to the number required of them, 1 Chr 23:31
David organized them **a** to the 1 Chr 24:3
house of the LORD **a** to the procedure 1 Chr 24:19
sons of the Levites **a** to their fathers' 1 Chr 24:30
a to the promise of God to exalt him, 1 Chr 25:5
a to the use of each lampstand in 1 Chr 28:15
all the work to be done **a** to the plan. 1 Chr 28:19
by rewarding him **a** to his 2 Chr 6:23
heart you know, **a** to all his ways, 2 Chr 6:30
dwelling place and do **a** to all for 2 Chr 6:33
doing **a** to all that I have commanded 2 Chr 7:17
offering **a** to the commandment of 2 Chr 8:13
A to the ruling of David his father, he 2 Chr 8:14
spoke to them **a** to the counsel 2 Chr 10:14
and not **a** to the practices of Israel. 2 Chr 17:4
and all Judah did **a** to all that 2 Chr 23:8
with singing, **a** to the order of David. 2 Chr 23:18
death, **a** to what is written in the Law, 2 Chr 25:4
a to all that his father Amaziah had 2 Chr 26:4
in divisions **a** to the numbers in the 2 Chr 26:11
the eyes of the LORD **a** to all that his 2 Chr 27:2
a to the abominations of the nations 2 Chr 28:3
a to all that David his father had 2 Chr 29:2
a to the commandment of David 2 Chr 29:25
their accustomed posts **a** to the Law 2 Chr 30:16
even though not **a** to the 2 Chr 30:19
by division, each **a** to his service, 2 Chr 31:2
—for their service **a** to their offices, 2 Chr 31:16
of the priests was **a** to their fathers' 2 Chr 31:17
and upward was **a** to their offices, 2 Chr 31:17
did not make return **a** to the benefit 2 Chr 32:25
a to the abominations of the nations 2 Chr 33:2
to do **a** to all that is written in this 2 Chr 34:21
of Jerusalem did **a** to the covenant 2 Chr 34:32
Prepare yourselves **a** to your fathers' 2 Chr 35:4
in the Holy Place **a** to the groupings 2 Chr 35:5
and **a** to the division of the Levites by 2 Chr 35:5
to do **a** to the word of the LORD by 2 Chr 35:6
in their divisions **a** to the king's 2 Chr 35:10
might distribute them **a** to the 2 Chr 35:12
lamb with fire **a** to the rule; 2 Chr 35:13
in their place **a** to the command 2 Chr 35:15
a to the command of King Josiah. 2 Chr 35:16
and his good deeds **a** to what is 2 Chr 35:26
A to their ability they gave to the Ezr 2:69
burnt offerings by number **a** to the rule, Ezr 3:4
a to the grant that they had from Cyrus Ezr 3:7
a to the directions of David king of Ezr 3:10
a to the word sent by Darius the king, Ezr 6:13
a to the number of the tribes of Israel. Ezr 6:17
about Judah and Jerusalem **a** to the Law Ezr 7:14
you may do, **a** to the will of your God. Ezr 7:18
a to the wisdom of your God that is in Ezr 7:25
a to the counsel of my lord and of those Ezr 10:3
our God, and let it be done **a** to the Law. Ezr 10:3
houses, **a** to their fathers' houses, Ezr 10:16
And **a** to these reports you wish to Neh 6:6
my God, **a** to these things that they did, Neh 6:14
was a solemn assembly, **a** to the rule. Neh 8:18
and **a** to your great mercies you gave Neh 9:27
you delivered them **a** to your mercies. Neh 9:28
of our God, **a** to our fathers' houses, Neh 10:34
a to the commandment of David the Neh 12:24
and for the Levites **a** to the fields of Neh 12:44
a to the command of David and his Neh 12:45
and spare me **a** to the greatness of Neh 13:22
royal wine was lavished **a** to the bounty Est 1:7
And drinking was **a** to this edict: "There Est 1:8
"**A** to the law, what is to be done to Est 1:15
household and speak **a** to the language Est 1:22
edict, **a** to all that Haman commanded, Est 3:12
a to all that Mordecai commanded Est 8:9
tomorrow also to do **a** to this day's edict. Est 9:13
keep these two days **a** to what was Est 9:27
and offer burnt offerings **a** to the number Jb 1:5
For **a** to the work of a man he will repay Jb 34:11
and **a** to his ways he will make it befall Jb 34:11
not to deal with you **a** to your folly. Jb 42:8
instruments; **a** to The Sheminith. Ps 6:T
a to my righteousness and according to Ps 7:8
to my righteousness and **a** to the integrity Ps 7:8
To the choirmaster: **a** to The Gittith. A Ps 8:T
To the choirmaster: **a** to Muth-labben. A Ps 9:T
To the choirmaster: **a** to The Sheminith. Ps 12:T
dealt with me **a** to my righteousness; Ps 18:20
a to the cleanness of my hands he Ps 18:20
has rewarded me **a** to my righteousness, Ps 18:24
a to the cleanness of my hands in his Ps 18:24
choirmaster: **a** to The Doe of the Dawn. Ps 22:T
a to your steadfast love remember me, Ps 25:7
Give to them **a** to their work and Ps 28:4
to their work and **a** to the evil of Ps 28:4
give to them **a** to the work of their hands; Ps 28:4
LORD, my God, **a** to your righteousness, Ps 35:24
To the choirmaster: **a** to Lilies. A Maskil Ps 45:T
Of the Sons of Korah. **A** to Alamoth. Ps 46:T
on me, O God, **a** to your steadfast love; Ps 51:1
a to your abundant mercy blot out my Ps 51:1
To the choirmaster: **a** to Mahalath. A Ps 53:T
a to The Dove on Far-off Terebinths. Ps 56:T
To the choirmaster: **a** to Do Not Destroy. Ps 57:T
To the choirmaster: **a** to Do Not Destroy. Ps 58:T
To the choirmaster: **a** to Do Not Destroy. Ps 59:T
the choirmaster: **a** to Shushan Eduth. Ps 60:T
To the choirmaster: **a** to Jeduthun. A Ps 62:T
you will render to a man **a** to his work. Ps 62:12
To the choirmaster: **a** to Lilies. Of David. Ps 69:T
a to your abundant mercy, turn to me. Ps 69:16
To the choirmaster: **a** to Do Not Destroy. Ps 75:T
To the choirmaster: **a** to Jeduthun. A Ps 77:T
but refused to walk **a** to his law. Ps 78:10

a to your great power, preserve those Ps 79:11
To the choirmaster: **a** to Lilies. A Ps 80:T
To the choirmaster: **a** to The Gittith. Of Ps 81:T
To the choirmaster: **a** to The Gittith. A Ps 84:T
choirmaster: **a** to Mahalath Leannoth. Ps 88:T
my law and do not walk **a** to my rules, Ps 89:30
and your wrath **a** to the fear of you? Ps 90:11
He does not deal with us **a** to our sins, Ps 103:10
sins, nor repay us **a** to our iniquities. Ps 103:10
and relented **a** to the abundance of his Ps 106:45
God! Save me **a** to your steadfast love! Ps 109:26
pure? By guarding it **a** to your word. Ps 119:9
to the dust; give me life **a** to your word! Ps 119:25
sorrow; strengthen me **a** to your word! Ps 119:28
your salvation **a** to your promise; Ps 119:41
be gracious to me **a** to your promise. Ps 119:58
your servant, O LORD, **a** to your word. Ps 119:65
love comfort me **a** to your promise Ps 119:76
for me; they do not live **a** to your law. Ps 119:85
give me life, O LORD, **a** to your word! Ps 119:107
Uphold me **a** to your promise, that I Ps 119:116
with your servant **a** to your steadfast Ps 119:124
steady my steps **a** to your promise, Ps 119:133
Hear my voice **a** to your steadfast Ps 119:149
O LORD, **a** to your justice give me life. Ps 119:149
me; give me life **a** to your promise! Ps 119:154
O LORD; give me life **a** to your rules. Ps 119:156
Give me life **a** to your steadfast love. Ps 119:159
give me understanding **a** to your Ps 119:169
before you; deliver me **a** to your word. Ps 119:170
praise him **a** to his excellent greatness! Ps 150:2
A man is commended **a** to his good Prv 12:8
will he not repay man **a** to his work? Prv 24:12
Answer not a fool **a** to his folly, lest you Prv 26:4
Answer a fool **a** to his folly, lest he be Prv 26:5
to whom it happens **a** to the deeds of Eccl 8:14
to whom it happens **a** to the deeds of Eccl 8:14
If they will not speak **a** to this word, it is Is 8:20
a year, **a** to the years of a hired worker, Is 21:16
A to their deeds, so will he repay, wrath Is 59:18
LORD, **a** to all that the LORD has granted us, Is 63:7
he has granted them **a** to his compassion, Is 63:7
a to the abundance of his steadfast love. Is 63:7
So I bought a loincloth **a** to the word of Jer 13:2
mind, to give every man **a** to his ways, Jer 17:10
to his ways, **a** to the fruit of his deeds." Jer 17:10
will every one act **a** to the stubbornness Jer 18:12
will deal with us **a** to all his wonderful Jer 21:2
I will punish you **a** to the fruit of your Jer 21:14
I will recompense them **a** to their deeds Jer 25:14
rewarding each one **a** to his ways and Jer 32:19
to his ways and **a** to the fruit of Jer 32:19
whom you had set free **a** to their desire, Jer 34:16
to the LORD your God **a** to your request, Jer 42:4
us if we do not act **a** to all the word with Jer 42:5
Repay her **a** to her deeds; do to her Jer 50:29
do to her **a** to all that she has done. Jer 50:29
LORD, **a** to all that Jehoiakim had done. Jer 52:2
him by the king **a** to his daily need, Jer 52:34
will have compassion **a** to the Lam 3:32
O LORD, **a** to the work of their hands. Lam 3:64
and have not even acted **a** to the rules of Ezk 5:7
I will judge you **a** to your ways, and I will Ezk 7:3
you, and judge you **a** to your ways, Ezk 7:8
I will punish you **a** to your ways, while Ezk 7:9
A to their way I will do to them, and Ezk 7:27
and **a** to their judgments I will judge Ezk 7:27
but have acted **a** to the rules of the Ezk 11:12
ways and do **a** to their abominations; Ezk 16:47
of Israel, every one **a** to his ways, Ezk 18:30
name's sake, not **a** to your evil ways, Ezk 20:44
evil ways, nor **a** to your corrupt deeds, Ezk 20:44
Israel in you, every one **a** to his power, Ezk 22:6
shall judge you **a** to their judgments. Ezk 23:24
a to your ways and your deeds you Ezk 24:14
a to all that he has done you shall do. Ezk 24:24
shall do in Edom **a** to my anger and Ezk 25:14
to my anger and **a** to my wrath, Ezk 25:14
I will judge each of you **a** to his ways." Ezk 33:20
I will deal with you **a** to the anger and Ezk 35:11
dealt with them **a** to their uncleanness Ezk 39:24
they shall judge it **a** to my judgments. Ezk 44:24
of Israel have the land **a** to their tribes. Ezk 45:8
this land among you **a** to the tribes of Ezk 47:21
deal with your servants **a** to what you Dn 1:13
and he does **a** to his will among the host Dn 4:35
a to the law of the Medes and the Dn 6:8
a to the law of the Medes and Persians, Dn 6:12
a to the word of the LORD to Jeremiah the Dn 9:2
"O Lord, **a** to all your righteous acts, let Dn 9:16
he had spoken to me **a** to these words, Dn 10:15
nor **a** to the authority with which he Dn 11:4
I will discipline them **a** to the report Hos 7:12
and will punish Jacob **a** to his ways; Hos 12:2
ways; he will repay him **a** to his deeds. Hos 12:2
to Nineveh, **a** to the word of the LORD. Jon 3:3
Habakkuk the prophet, **a** to Shigionoth. Hab 3:1
would not be cut off **a** to all that I have Zep 3:7
a to the covenant that I made with you Hg 2:5
steals shall be cleaned out **a** to what is on Zec 5:3
shall be cleaned out **a** to what is on Zec 5:3
a to the time that he had ascertained Mt 2:16
"**A** to your faith be it done to you." Mt 9:29
will repay each person **a** to what he has Mt 16:27
to another one, to each **a** to his ability. Mt 25:15
your disciples not walk **a** to the tradition Mk 7:5
a to the custom of the priesthood, he was Lk 1:9
let it be to me **a** to your word." And the Lk 1:38
came for their purification **a** to the Law Lk 2:22
and to offer a sacrifice **a** to what is said Lk 2:24
to do for him **a** to the custom of the Law, Lk 2:27
servant depart in peace, **a** to your word; Lk 2:29
had performed everything **a** to the Law Lk 2:39
years old, they went up **a** to custom. Lk 2:42
but did not get ready or act **a** to his will, Lk 12:47
Sabbath they rested **a** to the Lk 23:56
You judge **a** to the flesh; I judge no one. Jn 8:15
and **a** to that law he ought to die because Jn 19:7
delivered up **a** to the definite plan and Acts 2:23
it, **a** to the pattern that he had seen. Acts 7:44
determined, everyone **a** to his ability, Acts 11:29
you are circumcised **a** to the custom Acts 15:1
children or walk **a** to our customs. Acts 21:21
the feet of Gamaliel **a** to the strict Acts 22:3
Ananias, a devout man **a** to the law, Acts 22:12
you sitting to judge me **a** to the law, Acts 23:3
So the soldiers, **a** to their instructions, Acts 23:31
I confess to you, that **a** to the Way, Acts 24:14
that **a** to the strictest party of our Acts 26:5
was descended from David **a** to the flesh Rom 1:3
Son of God in power **a** to the Spirit of Rom 1:4
will render to each one **a** to his works: Rom 2:6
on that day when, **a** to my gospel, God Rom 2:16
Abraham, our forefather **a** to the flesh? Rom 4:1
who walk not **a** to the flesh but Rom 8:4
to the flesh but **a** to the Spirit. Rom 8:4
For those who live **a** to the flesh set their Rom 8:5
but those who live **a** to the Spirit set Rom 8:5
not to the flesh, to live **a** to the flesh. Rom 8:12
For if you live **a** to the flesh you will Rom 8:13
intercedes for the saints **a** to the will of Rom 8:27
those who are called **a** to his purpose. Rom 8:28
brothers, my kinsmen **a** to the flesh. Rom 9:3
and from their race, **a** to the flesh, Rom 9:5
a zeal for God, but not **a** to knowledge. Rom 10:2
each **a** to the measure of faith that God Rom 12:3
Having gifts that differ **a** to the grace Rom 12:6
able to strengthen you **a** to my gospel Rom 16:25
a to the revelation of the mystery that Rom 16:25
a to the command of the eternal God, Rom 16:26
you were wise **a** to worldly standards, 1 Cor 1:26
will receive his wages **a** to his labor. 1 Cor 3:8
A to the grace of God given to me, like 1 Cor 3:10
utterance of knowledge **a** to the same 1 Cor 12:8
Do I make my plans **a** to the flesh, 2 Cor 1:17
same spirit of faith **a** to what has 2 Cor 4:13
we regard no one **a** to the flesh. 2 Cor 5:16
we once regarded Christ **a** to the flesh, 2 Cor 5:16
For they gave **a** to their means, as I can 2 Cor 8:3
it is acceptable **a** to what a person 2 Cor 8:12
has, not **a** to what he does not have. 2 Cor 8:12
suspect us of walking **a** to the flesh. 2 Cor 10:2
we are not waging war **a** to the flesh. 2 Cor 10:3
Since many boast **a** to the flesh, I too 2 Cor 11:18
age, **a** to the will of our God and Father, Gal 1:4
offspring, heirs **a** to promise. Gal 3:29
son of the slave was born **a** to the flesh, Gal 4:23
he who was born **a** to the flesh Gal 4:29
him who was born **a** to the Spirit, Gal 4:29
Jesus Christ, **a** to the purpose of his will, Eph 1:5
trespasses, **a** to the riches of his grace, Eph 1:7
the mystery of his will, **a** to his purpose, Eph 1:9
having been predestined **a** to the Eph 1:11
who works all things **a** to the counsel Eph 1:11
a to the working of his great might Eph 1:19
I was made a minister **a** to the gift of Eph 3:7
This was **a** to the eternal purpose that Eph 3:11
that **a** to the riches of his glory he may Eph 3:16
think, **a** to the power at work within us, Eph 3:20
to each one of us **a** to the measure of Eph 4:7
on those who walk **a** to the example Phil 3:17
every need of yours **a** to his riches in Phil 4:19
with all power, **a** to his glorious might, Col 1:11
became a minister **a** to the stewardship Col 1:25
and empty deceit, **a** to human tradition, Col 2:8
a to the elemental spirits of the world, Col 2:8
spirits of the world, and not **a** to Christ. Col 2:8
they are used)—**a** to human precepts Col 2:22
a to the grace of our God and the 2 Thes 1:12
by the will of God **a** to the promise of 2 Tm 1:1
unless he competes **a** to the rules. 2 Tm 2:5
the Lord will repay him **a** to his deeds. 2 Tm 4:14
in righteousness, but **a** to his own mercy, Ti 3:5
we might become heirs **a** to the hope of Ti 3:7
the Holy Spirit distributed **a** to his will. Heb 2:4
are priests who offer gifts **a** to the law. Heb 8:4
you make everything **a** to the pattern Heb 8:5
A to this arrangement, gifts and Heb 9:9
(these are offered **a** to the law), Heb 10:8
fulfill the royal law **a** to the Scripture, Jas 2:8
a to the foreknowledge of God the 1 Pt 1:2
A to his great mercy, he has caused us to 1 Pt 1:3
who judges impartially **a** to each one's 1 Pt 1:17
let those who suffer **a** to God's will 1 Pt 4:19
But **a** to his promise we are waiting for 2 Pt 3:13
also wrote to you **a** to the wisdom given 2 Pt 3:15
that if we ask anything **a** to his will he 1 Jn 5:14
that we walk **a** to his commandments; 2 Jn 1:6
in the books, **a** to what they had done. Rv 20:12
one of them, **a** to what they had done. Rv 20:13

ACCORDINGLY (3)

A, she will be called an adulteress if she Rom 7:3
A, we urged Titus that as he had 2 Cor 8:6
A, though I am bold enough in Christ Phlm 1:8

ACCORDS (3)

and the teaching that **a** with godliness, 1 Tm 6:3
of the truth, which **a** with godliness, Ti 1:1
for you, teach what **a** with sound doctrine. Ti 2:1

ACCOUNT (56)

to Abraham on **a** of his son. Gn 21:11
other use, but on no **a** shall you eat it. Lv 7:24
on the day of the plague on **a** of Peor." Nm 25:18
the LORD was angry on your **a** and said, Dt 1:37
and perish quickly on **a** of the evil of Dt 28:20
out to the LORD on **a** of the Midianites, Jgs 6:7
On this **a** that place is called Jgs 18:12
to Keilah, to destroy the city on my **a**. 1 Sm 23:10
And this is the **a** of the forced labor 1 Kgs 9:15
This is an **a** of David's mighty men: 1 Chr 11:11
were few in number, and of little **a**, 1 Chr 16:19
them; he rebuked kings on their **a**, 1 Chr 16:21
of Israel sin on **a** of such women? Neh 13:26
and the full **a** of the high honor of Est 10:2
my hand is heavy on **a** of my groaning. Jb 23:2
I would give him an **a** of all my steps; Jb 31:37
"Behold, I am of small **a**; what shall I Jb 40:4
in his heart, "You will not call to **a**"? Ps 10:13
call his wickedness to **a** till you find Ps 10:15
they were few in number, of little **a**, Ps 105:12
them; he rebuked kings on their **a**, Ps 105:14
and it went ill with Moses on their **a**, Ps 106:32
nostrils is breath, for of what **a** is he? Is 2:22
on **a** of the violence of all those who Ezk 12:19
but not on **a** of the covenant with you. Ezk 16:61
On **a** of your unclean lewdness, Ezk 24:13
one, to whom these satraps should give **a**, Dn 6:2
Shall not the land tremble on this **a**, and Am 8:8
may know on whose **a** this evil has come Jon 1:7
"Tell us on whose **a** this evil has come Jon 1:8
of evil against you falsely on my **a**. Mt 5:11
people will give **a** for every careless Mt 12:36
or persecution arises on **a** of the word, Mt 13:21
or persecution arises on **a** of the word, Mk 4:17
time past, to write an orderly **a** for you, Lk 1:3
name as evil, on **a** of the Son of Man! Lk 6:22
Turn in the **a** of your management, Lk 16:2
was, but on **a** of the crowd he could not, Lk 19:3
I said this on **a** of the people standing Jn 11:42
not only on **a** of him but also to see Jn 12:9
because on **a** of him many of the Jews Jn 12:11
or else believe on **a** of the works Jn 14:11
they will do to you on **a** of my name, Jn 15:21
But I do not **a** my life of any value nor Acts 20:24
of us will give an **a** of himself to God. Rom 14:12
by all, he is called to **a** by all, 1 Cor 14:24
is weak, and his speech of no **a**." 2 Cor 10:10
the flesh is more necessary on your **a**. Phil 1:24
On **a** of these the wrath of God is coming. Col 3:6
of Christ, on **a** of which I am in prison— Col 4:3
you anything, charge that to my **a**. Phlm 1:18
eyes of him to whom we must give **a**. Heb 4:13
as those who will have to give an **a**. Heb 13:17
but they will give **a** to him who is ready 1 Pt 4:5
tribes of the earth will wail on **a** of him. Rv 1:7
island called Patmos on **a** of the word of Rv 1:9

ACCOUNTABLE (2)

the whole world may be held **a** to God. Rom 3:19
in one point has become **a** for all of it. Jas 2:10

ACCOUNTED (4)

and are **a** as the dust on the scales; Is 40:15
they are **a** by him as less than nothing Is 40:17
servant, make many to be **a** righteous, Is 53:11
of the earth are **a** as nothing, Dn 4:35

ACCOUNTING (2)
did not ask an **a** from the men into 2 Kgs 12:15
But no **a** shall be asked from them 2 Kgs 22:7

ACCOUNTS (4)
with **a** of all his rule and his might 1 Chr 29:30
A of his sons and of the many 2 Chr 24:27
wished to settle **a** with his servants. Mt 18:23
servants came and settled **a** with them. Mt 25:19

ACCREDIT (1)
send those whom you **a** by letter to 1 Cor 16:3

ACCUMULATE (1)
ears they will **a** for themselves teachers 2 Tm 4:3

ACCURATE (1)
having a rather **a** knowledge of the Acts 24:22

ACCURATELY (2)
spoke and taught **a** the things Acts 18:25
to him the way of God more **a**. Acts 18:26

ACCURSED (11)
You rebuke the insolent, **a** ones, who Ps 119:21
sinner a hundred years old shall be **a**. Is 65:20
wicked, and the scant measure that is **a**? Mi 6:10
crowd that does not know the law is **a**." Jn 7:49
that I myself were **a** and cut off from Rom 9:3
ever says "Jesus is **a**!" and no one can 1 Cor 12:3
no love for the Lord, let him be **a**. 1 Cor 16:22
the one we preached to you, let him be **a**. Gal 1:8
to the one you received, let him be **a**. Gal 1:9
hearts trained in greed. **A** children! 2 Pt 2:14
No longer will there be anything **a**, but Rv 22:3

ACCUSATION (4)
they wrote an **a** against the inhabitants Ezr 4:6
from anyone by threats or by false **a**, Lk 3:14
"What **a** do you bring against this Jn 18:29
be here before you and to make an **a**, Acts 24:19

ACCUSATIONS (1)
today against all the **a** of the Jews, Acts 26:2

ACCUSE (13)
witness arises to **a** a person of Dt 19:16
me evil for good **a** me because I follow Ps 38:20
In return for my love they **a** me, but I Ps 109:4
Yet let no one contend, and let none **a**, Hos 4:4
standing at his right hand to **a** him. Zec 3:1
Sabbath?"—so that they might **a** him. Mt 12:10
the Sabbath, so that they might **a** him. Mk 3:2
so that they might find a reason to **a** him. Lk 6:7
And they began to **a** him, saying, "We Lk 23:2
not think that I will **a** you to the Father. Jn 5:45
summoned, Tertullus began to **a** him, Acts 24:2
about everything of which we **a** him." Acts 24:8
their conflicting thoughts **a** or even Rom 2:15

ACCUSED (11)
witness and has **a** his brother falsely, Dt 19:18
behold, he has **a** her of misconduct, Dt 22:17
with Midian?" And they **a** him fiercely. Jgs 8:1
forward and maliciously **a** the Jews. Dn 3:8
who had maliciously **a** Daniel were Dn 6:24
But when he was **a** by the chief priests Mt 27:12
And the chief priests **a** him of many Mk 15:3
why he was being **a** by the Jews, Acts 22:30
he was being **a** about questions of Acts 23:29
anyone before the **a** met the accusers Acts 25:16
And for this hope I am **a** by Jews, O Acts 26:7

ACCUSER (6)
him; I must appeal for mercy to my **a**. Jb 9:15
him; let an **a** stand at his right hand. Ps 109:6
terms quickly with your **a** while you are Mt 5:25
lest your **a** hand you over to the judge, Mt 5:25
go with your **a** before the magistrate, Lk 12:58
for the **a** of our brothers has been Rv 12:10

ACCUSERS (8)
May my **a** be put to shame and Ps 71:13
be the reward of my **a** from the LORD, Ps 109:20
I am an object of scorn to my **a**; when Ps 109:25
May my **a** be clothed with dishonor; Ps 109:29
ordering his **a** also to state before you Acts 23:30
hearing when your **a** arrive." And he Acts 23:35
the accused met the **a** face to face and Acts 25:16
When the **a** stood up, they brought Acts 25:18

ACCUSES (3)
and **a** her of misconduct and brings a Dt 22:14
There is one who **a** you: Moses, on whom Jn 5:45
who **a** them day and night before our Rv 12:10

ACCUSING (2)
scribes stood by, vehemently **a** him. Lk 23:10
charge for which they were **a** him, Acts 23:28

ACCUSTOMED (5)
if the ox has been **a** to gore in the past, Ex 21:29
that the ox has been **a** to gore in the Ex 21:36
They took their **a** posts according to 2 Chr 30:16
you can do good who are **a** to do evil. Jer 13:23
feast the governor was **a** to release for Mt 27:15

ACHAIA (10)
But when Gallio was proconsul of **A**, Acts 18:12
And when he wished to cross to **A**, the Acts 18:27
through Macedonia and **A** and go to Acts 19:21
For Macedonia and **A** have been Rom 15:26
were the first converts in **A**, 1 Cor 16:15
the saints who are in the whole of **A**: 2 Cor 1:1
saying that **A** has been ready since last 2 Cor 9:2
not be silenced in the regions of **A**. 2 Cor 11:10
the believers in Macedonia and in **A**. 1 Thes 1:7
forth from you in Macedonia and **A**, 1 Thes 1:8

ACHAICUS (1)
of Stephanas and Fortunatus and **A**, 1 Cor 16:17

ACHAN (7)
devoted things, for **A** the son of Carmi, Jos 7:1
man by man, and **A** the son of Carmi, Jos 7:18
Then Joshua said to **A**, "My son, give Jos 7:19
And **A** answered Joshua, "Truly I have Jos 7:20
Israel with him took **A** the son of Zerah, Jos 7:24
Did not **A** the son of Zerah break faith Jos 22:20
A, the troubler of Israel, who broke 1 Chr 2:7

ACHBOR (7)
Baal-hanan the son of **A** reigned in his Gn 36:38
Baal-hanan the son of **A** died, and Gn 36:39
Shaphan, and **A** the son of Micaiah, 2 Kgs 22:12
the priest, and Ahikam, and **A**, 2 Kgs 22:14
died, and Baal-hanan, the son of **A**, 1 Chr 1:49
Elnathan the son of **A** and others with Jer 26:22
of Shemaiah, Elnathan the son of **A**, Jer 36:12

ACHE (2)
the eyes and make the heart **a**. Lv 26:16
Even in laughter the heart may **a**, and Prv 14:13

ACHIEVE (1)
crafty, so that their hands **a** no success. Jb 5:12

ACHIM (2)
of Zadok, and Zadok the father of **A**, Mt 1:14
of Achim, and **A** the father of Eliud, Mt 1:14

ACHISH (21)
Saul and went to **A** the king of Gath. 1 Sm 21:10
And the servants of **A** said to him, "Is 1 Sm 21:11
was much afraid of **A** the king of 1 Sm 21:12
Then **A** said to his servants, "Behold, 1 Sm 21:14
were with him, to **A** the son of Maoch, 1 Sm 27:2
And David lived with **A** at Gath, he 1 Sm 27:3
Then David said to **A**, "If I have found 1 Sm 27:5
So that day **A** gave him Ziklag. 1 Sm 27:6
the garments, and come back to **A**. 1 Sm 27:9
When **A** asked, "Where have you 1 Sm 27:10
And **A** trusted David, thinking, "He 1 Sm 27:12
And **A** said to David, "Understand 1 Sm 28:1
David said to **A**, "Very well, you shall 1 Sm 28:2
servant can do." And **A** said to David, 1 Sm 28:2
were passing on in the rear with **A**, 1 Sm 29:2
doing here?" And **A** said to the 1 Sm 29:3
Then **A** called David and said to him, 1 Sm 29:6
And David said to **A**, "But what have I 1 Sm 29:8
And **A** answered David and said, "I 1 Sm 29:9
of Shimei's servants ran away to **A**, 1 Kgs 2:39
went to Gath to **A** to seek his servants. 1 Kgs 2:40

ACHOR (5)
they brought them up to the Valley of **A**. Jos 7:24
of that place is called the Valley of **A**. Jos 7:26
goes up to Debir from the Valley of **A**, Jos 15:7
and the Valley of **A** a place for herds to Is 65:10
make the Valley of **A** a door of hope. Hos 2:15

ACHSAH (5)
him will I give **A** my daughter as wife." Jos 15:16
And he gave him **A** his daughter as Jos 15:17
I will give him **A** my daughter for a Jgs 1:12
And he gave him **A** his daughter for a Jgs 1:13
and the daughter of Caleb was **A**. 1 Chr 2:49

ACHSHAPH (3)
king of Shimron, and to the king of **A**, Jos 11:1
one; the king of **A**, one; Jos 12:20
included Helkath, Hali, Beten, **A**, Jos 19:25

ACHZIB (4)
Keilah, **A**, and Mareshah: nine cities Jos 15:44
and it ends at the sea; Mahalab, **A**, Jos 19:29
or of Ahlab or of **A** or of Helbah or of Jgs 1:31
the houses of **A** shall be a deceitful thing Mi 1:14

ACKNOWLEDGE (24)
but he shall **a** the firstborn, the son of Dt 21:17
again to you and **a** your name and 1 Kgs 8:33
this place and **a** your name and 1 Kgs 8:35
turn again and **a** your name and 2 Chr 6:24
this place and **a** your name and 2 Chr 6:26
Then will I also **a** to you that your own Jb 40:14
In all your ways **a** him, and he will make Prv 3:6
and you who are near, **a** my might. Is 33:13
all who see them shall **a** them, that they Is 61:9
not know us, and Israel does not **a** us; Is 63:16
Only **a** your guilt, that you rebelled Jer 3:13
We **a** our wickedness, O LORD, and the Jer 14:20
Those who **a** him he shall load with Dn 11:39
until they **a** their guilt and seek my Hos 5:15
I also will **a** before my Father who is in Mt 10:32
of Man also will **a** before the angels of Lk 12:8
nor spirit, but the Pharisees **a** them all. Acts 23:8
And since they did not see fit to **a** God, Rom 1:28
he should **a** that the things I am 1 Cor 14:37
what you read and **a** and I hope you 2 Cor 1:13
and I hope you will fully **a**— 2 Cor 1:13
just as you did partially **a** us, that on 2 Cor 1:14
is, the fruit of lips that **a** his name. Heb 13:15
himself first, does not **a** our authority. 3 Jn 1:9

ACKNOWLEDGED (2)
I **a** my sin to you, and I did not cover my Ps 32:5
and having **a** that they were strangers Heb 11:13

ACKNOWLEDGES (2)
So everyone who **a** me before men, I Mt 10:32
tell you, everyone who **a** me before men, Lk 12:8

ACQUAINTANCES (3)
and an object of dread to my **a**; Ps 31:11
for him among their relatives and **a**, Lk 2:44
And all his **a** and the women who had Lk 23:49

ACQUAINTED (4)
the light, who are not **a** with its ways, Jb 24:13
lying down and are **a** with all my ways. Ps 139:3
men; a man of sorrows, and **a** with grief; Is 53:3
you have been **a** with the sacred 2 Tm 3:15

ACQUIRE (8)
Only he must not **a** many horses for Dt 17:16
to Egypt in order to **a** many horses, Dt 17:16
And he shall not **a** many wives for Dt 17:17
nor shall he **a** for himself excessive Dt 17:17
of Naomi, you also **a** Ruth the Moabite, Ru 4:5
Do not toil to **a** wealth; be discerning Prv 23:4
A no gold nor silver nor copper for your Mt 10:9
inheritance until we **a** possession of it, Eph 1:14

ACQUIRED (6)
and the people that they had **a** in Haran, Gn 12:5
that he had **a** in Paddan-aram, Gn 31:18
his property that he had **a** in the land of Gn 36:6
work on this wall, and we **a** no land, Neh 5:16
in my heart, "I have **a** great wisdom, Eccl 1:16
who have **a** livestock and goods, Ezk 38:12

ACQUIRES (1)
An intelligent heart **a** knowledge, and Prv 18:15

ACQUIT (4)
and righteous, for I will not **a** the wicked. Ex 23:7
me and do not **a** me of my iniquity. Jb 10:14
who **a** the guilty for a bribe, and deprive Is 5:23
Shall I **a** the man with wicked scales Mi 6:11

ACQUITTAL (1)
may they have no **a** from you. Ps 69:27

ACQUITTED (2)
and I would be **a** forever by my judge. Jb 23:7
against myself, but I am not thereby **a**. 1 Cor 4:4

ACQUITTING (1)
a the innocent and condemning the Dt 25:1

ACRE (1)
a furrow's length in an **a** of land. 1 Sm 14:14

ACRES (1)
For ten **a** of vineyard shall yield but one Is 5:10

ACROSS (23)
fly above the earth **a** the expanse of the Gn 1:20
took them and sent them **a** the stream, Gn 32:23
Do not take us **a** the Jordan." Nm 32:5
"If you come **a** a bird's nest in any tree or Dt 22:6
of Oreb and Zeeb to Gideon **a** the Jordan. Jgs 7:25
gold, and he drew chains of gold **a**, 1 Kgs 6:21
a great wind came **a** the wilderness and Jb 1:19
and he will lead people **a** in sandals. Is 11:15
and the kings of the coastland **a** the sea; Jer 25:22
its breadth, twenty cubits, **a** the nave. Ezk 41:4
goat came from the west **a** the face of the Dn 8:5
For you travel **a** sea and land to make a Mt 23:15
to them, "Let us go **a** to the other side." Mk 4:35
"Let us go **a** to the other side of the lake." Lk 8:22
took place in Bethany **a** the Jordan, Jn 1:28
he who was with you **a** the Jordan, Jn 3:26
boat, and started **a** the sea to Capernaum. Jn 6:17
He went away again **a** the Jordan to the Jn 10:40
with his disciples **a** the Kidron Valley, Jn 18:1
when we had sailed **a** the open sea Acts 27:5
were being driven **a** the Adriatic Sea, Acts 27:27

the cloud swung his sickle **a** the earth, Rv 14:16
angel swung his sickle **a** the earth and Rv 14:19

ACT (52)
you, my brothers, do not **a** so wickedly. Gn 19:7
her, since she was not taken in the **a**, Nm 5:13
of Israel to **a** treacherously against the Nm 31:16
beware lest you **a** corruptly by making a Dt 4:16
if you **a** corruptly by making a carved Dt 4:25
fear and not **a** presumptuously again. Dt 17:13
do such things, all who **a** dishonestly, Dt 25:16
you will surely **a** corruptly and turn Dt 31:29
"No, my brothers, do not **a** so wickedly; Jgs 19:23
May you **a** worthily in Ephrathah and Ru 4:11
A therefore according to your wisdom, 1 Kgs 2:6
hear in heaven and **a** and judge your 1 Kgs 8:32
place and forgive and **a** and render to 1 Kgs 8:39
from heaven and **a** and judge your 2 Chr 6:23
and see that you **a** quickly." But the 2 Chr 24:5
But the Levites did not **a** quickly. 2 Chr 24:5
But go, **a**, be strong for the battle. 2 Chr 25:8
had made Judah **a** sinfully and had 2 Chr 28:19
should be afraid and **a** in this way and Neh 6:13
Did not your fathers **a** in this way, Neh 13:18
great evil and **a** treacherously against Neh 13:27
he has ceased to **a** wisely and do good. Ps 36:3
to the LORD; trust in him, and he will **a**. Ps 37:5
It is time for the LORD to **a**, for your Ps 119:126
but those who **a** faithfully are his Prv 12:22
Behold, my servant shall **a** wisely; he Is 52:13
bronze and iron; all of them **a** corruptly. Jer 6:28
iniquities testify against us, **a**, O LORD, Jer 14:7
and will every one **a** according to the Jer 18:12
us if we do not **a** according to all the Jer 42:5
Therefore I will **a** in wrath. My eye will Ezk 8:18
lustful talk in their mouths they **a**; Ezk 33:31
O house of Israel, that I am about to **a**, Ezk 36:22
It is not for your sake that I will **a**, Ezk 36:32
In a dispute, they shall **a** as judges, Ezk 44:24
to the ground, and it will **a** and prosper. Dn 8:12
forgive. O Lord, pay attention and **a**. Dn 9:19
made with him he shall **a** deceitfully, Dn 11:23
but the wicked shall **a** wickedly. Dn 12:10
soles of your feet, on the day when I **a**, Mal 4:3
not get ready or **a** according to his will, Lk 12:47
has been caught in the **a** of adultery. Jn 8:4
so one **a** of righteousness leads to Rom 5:18
stand firm in the faith, **a** like men, 1 Cor 16:13
complete among you this **a** of grace. 2 Cor 8:6
that you excel in this **a** of grace also. 2 Cor 8:7
as we carry out this **a** of grace that is 2 Cor 8:19
you? Did we not **a** in the same spirit? 2 Cor 12:18
men is appointed to **a** on behalf of men Heb 5:1
promises was in the **a** of offering up Heb 11:17
desiring to **a** honorably in all things. Heb 13:18
So speak and so **a** as those who are to be Jas 2:12

ACTED (31)
brought from Egypt have **a** corruptly. Dt 9:12
they on their part **a** with cunning and Jos 9:4
if you **a** in good faith and integrity when Jgs 9:16
if you then have **a** in good faith and Jgs 9:19
Behold, I have **a** foolishly, and have 1 Sm 26:21
sinned and have **a** perversely and 1 Kgs 8:47
He **a** very abominably in going after 1 Kgs 21:26
servant, for I have **a** very foolishly." 1 Chr 21:8
sinned and have **a** perversely and 2 Chr 6:37
king of Israel, who **a** wickedly. 2 Chr 20:35
We have **a** very corruptly against you Neh 1:7
knew that they **a** arrogantly against Neh 9:10
and our fathers **a** presumptuously and Neh 9:16
Yet they **a** presumptuously and did not Neh 9:29
faithfully and we have **a** wickedly. Neh 9:33
turned away and **a** treacherously like Ps 78:57
and have not even **a** according to the Ezk 5:7
but have **a** according to the rules of Ezk 11:12
because they have **a** faithlessly, Ezk 15:8
in which you **a** more abominably Ezk 16:52
But I **a** for the sake of my name, that it Ezk 20:9
But I **a** for the sake of my name, that it Ezk 20:14
withheld my hand and **a** for the sake Ezk 20:22
Because Edom **a** revengefully against Ezk 25:12
the Philistines **a** revengefully and Ezk 25:15
done wrong and **a** wickedly and rebelled, Dn 9:5
who conceived them has **a** shamefully. Hos 2:5
going. He **a** as if he were going farther, Lk 24:28
I know that you **a** in ignorance, Acts 3:17
of the Jews **a** hypocritically along with Gal 2:13
because I had **a** ignorantly in 1 Tm 1:13

ACTING (6)
a as the rear guard of all the camps, Nm 10:25
land sins against me by **a** faithlessly, Ezk 14:13
keeps my rules by **a** faithfully—he is Ezk 18:9
mean for us, that you are **a** thus?" Ezk 24:19
and they are all **a** against the decrees of Acts 17:7
I am **a** with great boldness toward you; 2 Cor 7:4

ACTION (7)
Dress for **a** like a man; I will question Jb 38:3
"Dress for **a** like a man; I will question Jb 40:7
be enraged and take **a** against the holy Dn 11:30
their God shall stand firm and take **a**. Dn 11:32
"Stay dressed for **a** and keep your Lk 12:35
not consented to their decision and **a**; Lk 23:51
Therefore, preparing your minds for **a**, 1 Pt 1:13

ACTIONS (2)
knowledge, and by him **a** are weighed. 1 Sm 2:3
I do not understand my own **a**. For I do Rom 7:15

ACTIVE (2)
For the word of God is living and **a**, Heb 4:12
see that faith was **a** along with his Jas 2:22

ACTIVITIES (2)
and there are varieties of **a**, but it is 1 Cor 12:6
Tychicus will tell you all about my **a**. He Col 4:7

ACTIVITY (1)
one is by the **a** of Satan with all 2 Thes 2:9

ACTS (69)
arm and with great **a** of judgment. Ex 6:6
the land of Egypt by great **a** of judgment. Ex 7:4
do such works and mighty **a** as yours? Dt 3:24
The man who **a** presumptuously by Dt 17:12
Now the rest of the **a** of Solomon, 1 Kgs 11:41
in the Book of the **A** of Solomon? 1 Kgs 11:41
Now the rest of the **a** of Jeroboam, 1 Kgs 14:19
the rest of the **a** of Rehoboam and all 1 Kgs 14:29
The rest of the **a** of Abijam and all 1 Kgs 15:7
Now the rest of all the **a** of Asa, all 1 Kgs 15:23
the rest of the **a** of Nadab and all 1 Kgs 15:31
the rest of the **a** of Baasha and what 1 Kgs 16:5
Now the rest of the **a** of Elah and all 1 Kgs 16:14
Now the rest of the **a** of Zimri, and 1 Kgs 16:20
Now the rest of the **a** of Omri that he 1 Kgs 16:27
Now the rest of the **a** of Ahab and all 1 Kgs 22:39
Now the rest of the **a** of Jehoshaphat, 1 Kgs 22:45
the rest of the **a** of Ahaziah that he 2 Kgs 1:18
Now the rest of the **a** of Joram, and all 2 Kgs 8:23
Now the rest of the **a** of Jehu and all 2 Kgs 10:34
Now the rest of the **a** of Joash and all 2 Kgs 12:19
the rest of the **a** of Jehoahaz and all 2 Kgs 13:8
Now the rest of the **a** of Joash and all 2 Kgs 13:12
the rest of the **a** of Jehoash that he 2 Kgs 14:15
the rest of the **a** of Jeroboam and all 2 Kgs 14:28
Now the rest of the **a** of Azariah, and 2 Kgs 15:6
the rest of the **a** of Pekah and all 2 Kgs 15:31
the rest of the **a** of Jotham and all 2 Kgs 15:36
Now the rest of the **a** of Ahaz that he 2 Kgs 16:19
the rest of the **a** of Manasseh and all 2 Kgs 21:17
the rest of the **a** of Amon that he 2 Kgs 21:25
the rest of the **a** of Josiah and all 2 Kgs 23:28
Now the **a** of King David, from first 1 Chr 29:29
Now the rest of the **a** of Solomon, 2 Chr 9:29
Now the **a** of Rehoboam, from first 2 Chr 12:15
The rest of the **a** of Abijah, his ways 2 Chr 13:22
The **a** of Asa, from first to last, are 2 Chr 16:11
Now the rest of the **a** of Jehoshaphat, 2 Chr 20:34
Now the rest of the **a** of Uzziah, 2 Chr 26:22
Now the rest of the **a** of Jotham, and 2 Chr 27:7
the rest of his **a** and all his ways, 2 Chr 28:26
things and these **a** of faithfulness, 2 Chr 32:1
the rest of the **a** of Hezekiah and his 2 Chr 32:32
Now the rest of the **a** of Manasseh, 2 Chr 33:18
Now the rest of the **a** of Josiah, and 2 Chr 35:26
and his **a**, first and last, behold, they 2 Chr 35:27
Now the rest of the **a** of Jehoiakim, 2 Chr 36:8
And all the **a** of his power and might, Est 10:2
repays the one who **a** in pride. Ps 31:23
My mouth will tell of your righteous **a**, Ps 71:15
to Moses, his **a** to the people of Israel. Ps 103:7
Thus they became unclean by their **a**, Ps 106:39
and shall declare your mighty **a**. Ps 145:4
of his work, the first of his **a** of old. Prv 8:22
the prudent **a** with knowledge, Prv 13:16
A man of quick temper **a** foolishly, Prv 14:17
wrath falls on one who **a** shamefully. Prv 14:35
over a son who **a** shamefully and will Prv 17:2
child makes himself known by his **a**, Prv 20:11
haughty man who **a** with arrogant Prv 21:24
you, who **a** for those who wait for him. Is 64:4
my four disastrous **a** of judgment, Ezk 14:21
Lord, according to all your righteous **a**, Dn 9:16
you may know the saving **a** of the LORD." Mi 6:5
full of good works and **a** of charity. Acts 9:36
committing shameless **a** with men Rom 1:27
the one who does **a** of mercy, with Rom 12:8
no hearer who forgets but a doer who **a**, Jas 1:25
for your righteous **a** have been revealed." Rv 15:4

ACTUALLY (5)
He said to the woman, "Did God **a** say, Gn 3:1
Has he **a** said to you, 'Wash, and be 2 Kgs 5:13
Yet he is **a** not far from each one of Acts 17:27
he was **a** carried by the soldiers Acts 21:35
It is **a** reported that there is sexual 1 Cor 5:1

ADADAH (1)
Kinah, Dimonah, **A**, Jos 15:22

ADAH (8)
The name of the one was **A**, and the Gn 4:19
A bore Jabal; he was the father of those Gn 4:20
his wives: "**A** and Zillah, hear my voice; Gn 4:23
A the daughter of Elon the Hittite, Gn 36:2
And **A** bore to Esau, Eliphaz; Basemath Gn 36:4
Eliphaz the son of **A** the wife of Esau, Gn 36:10
These are the sons of **A**, Esau's wife. Gn 36:12
land of Edom; these are the sons of **A**. Gn 36:16

ADAIAH (9)
Jedidah the daughter of **A** of Bozkath. 2 Kgs 22:1
son of Ethni, son of Zerah, son of **A**, 1 Chr 6:41
A, Beraiah, and Shimrath were the 1 Chr 8:21
and **A** the son of Jeroham, son of 1 Chr 9:12
son of Obed, Maaseiah the son of **A**, 2 Chr 23:1
were Meshullam, Malluch, **A**, Jashub, Ezr 10:29
Shelemiah, Nathan, **A**, Ezr 10:39
of Col-hozeh, son of Hazaiah, son of **A**, Neh 11:5
and **A** the son of Jeroham, son of Neh 11:12

ADALIA (1)
and Poratha and **A** and Aridatha Est 9:8

ADAM (21)
But for **A** there was not found a helper Gn 2:20
And to **A** he said, "Because you have Gn 3:17
LORD God made for **A** and for his wife Gn 3:21
Now **A** knew Eve his wife, and she Gn 4:1
And **A** knew his wife again, and she Gn 4:25
This is the book of the generations of **A**. Gn 5:1
When **A** had lived 130 years, he fathered Gn 5:3
The days of **A** after he fathered Seth were Gn 5:4
all the days that **A** lived were 930 years, Gn 5:5
rose up in a heap very far away, at **A**, Jos 3:16
A, Seth, Enosh; 1 Chr 1:1
But like **A** they transgressed the Hos 6:7
son of Enos, the son of Seth, the son of **A**, Lk 3:38
Yet death reigned from **A** to Moses, Rom 5:14
was not like the transgression of **A**, Rom 5:14
For as in **A** all die, so also in Christ 1 Cor 15:22
"The first man **A** became a living 1 Cor 15:45
the last **A** became a life-giving 1 Cor 15:45
For **A** was formed first, then Eve; 1 Tm 2:13
and **A** was not deceived, but the 1 Tm 2:14
these that Enoch, the seventh from **A**, Jude 1:14

ADAMAH (1)
A, Ramah, Hazor, Jos 19:36

ADAMI-NEKEB (1)
from the oak in Zaanannim, and **A**, Jos 19:33

ADAR (9)
on the third day of the month of **A**, Ezr 6:15
twelfth month, which is the month of **A**. Est 3:7
twelfth month, which is the month of **A**, Est 3:13
twelfth month, which is the month of **A**. Est 8:12
twelfth month, which is the month of **A**, Est 9:1
of the month of **A** and they killed 300 Est 9:15
on the thirteenth day of the month of **A**, Est 9:17
day of the month of **A** as a day for Est 9:19
day of the month **A** and also the Est 9:21

ADBEEL (2)
of Ishmael; and Kedar, **A**, Mibsam, Gn 25:13
Nebaioth, and Kedar, **A**, Mibsam, 1 Chr 1:29

ADD (33)
"May the LORD **a** to me another son!" Gn 30:24
the holy thing and shall **a** a fifth to it Lv 5:16
restore it in full and shall **a** a fifth to it, Lv 6:5
he shall **a** the fifth of its value to it and Lv 22:14
it, he shall **a** a fifth to the valuation. Lv 27:13
he shall **a** a fifth to the valuation price, Lv 27:15
then he shall **a** a fifth to its valuation Lv 27:19
back at the valuation, and **a** a fifth to it; Lv 27:27
some of his tithe, he shall **a** a fifth to it. Lv 27:31
You shall not **a** to the word that I Dt 4:2
do. You shall not **a** to it or take from it. Dt 12:32
—then you shall **a** three other cities to Dt 19:9
little, I would **a** to you as much more. 2 Sm 12:8
the LORD your God **a** to the people a 2 Sm 24:3
a heavy yoke, I will **a** to your yoke. 1 Kgs 12:11
heavy, but I will **a** to your yoke. 1 Kgs 12:14
and I will **a** fifteen years to your life. I 2 Kgs 20:6
"May the LORD **a** to his people a 1 Chr 21:3
have provided. To these you must **a**. 1 Chr 22:14
a heavy yoke, I will **a** to your yoke. 2 Chr 10:11
your yoke heavy, but I will **a** to it. 2 Chr 10:14
A to them punishment upon Ps 69:27
years of life and peace they will **a** to you. Prv 3:2
Do not **a** to his words, lest he rebuke Prv 30:6
join house to house, who **a** field to field, Is 5:8

A year to year; let the feasts run their Is 29:1
of my Spirit, that they may **a** sin to sin; Is 30:1
Behold, I will **a** fifteen years to your life. Is 38:5
"**A** your burnt offerings to your Jer 7:21
by being anxious can **a** a single hour to Mt 6:27
by being anxious can **a** a single hour Lk 12:25
truth itself. We also **a** our testimony, 3 Jn 1:12
God will **a** to him the plagues described Rv 22:18

ADDAN (1)
Tel-harsha, Cherub, **A**, and Immer, Ezr 2:59

ADDAR (2)
along by Hezron, up to **A**, Jos 15:3
And Bela had sons: **A**, Gera, Abihud, 1 Chr 8:3

ADDED (23)
She **a**, "We have plenty of both straw Gn 24:25
and fresh water shall be **a** in a vessel. Nm 19:17
of our fathers and **a** to the inheritance Nm 36:3
inheritance will be **a** to the inheritance Nm 36:4
with a loud voice; and he **a** no more. Dt 5:22
for we have **a** to all our sins this evil, 1 Sm 12:19
your servant be an **a** burden to my 2 Sm 19:35
and years will be **a** to your life. Prv 9:11
nothing can be **a** to it, nor anything Eccl 3:14
many similar words were **a** to them. Jer 36:32
For the LORD has **a** sorrow to my pain. Jer 45:3
and still more greatness was **a** to me. Dn 4:36
and all these things will be **a** to you. Mt 6:33
to you, and still more will be **a** to you. Mk 4:24
a this to them all, that he locked up John Lk 3:20
and these things will be **a** to you. Lk 12:31
and there were **a** that day about three Acts 2:41
And the Lord **a** to their number day by Acts 2:47
than ever believers were **a** to the Lord, Acts 5:14
great many people were **a** to the Lord. Acts 11:24
who seemed influential **a** nothing to me. Gal 2:6
It was **a** because of transgressions, until Gal 3:19
then he **a**, "Behold, I have come to do Heb 10:9

ADDER (5)
a serpent, like the deaf **a** that stops its ear, Ps 58:4
You will tread on the lion and the **a**; the Ps 91:13
like a serpent and stings like an **a**. Prv 23:32
the serpent's root will come forth an **a**, Is 14:29
the lion, the **a** and the flying fiery serpent, Is 30:6

ADDER'S (1)
child shall put his hand on the **a** den. Is 11:8

ADDERS (1)
you serpents, **a** that cannot be charmed, Jer 8:17

ADDERS' (1)
They hatch **a** eggs; they weave the Is 59:5

ADDI (1)
the son of Melchi, the son of **A**, the son Lk 3:28

ADDICTED (1)
double-tongued, not **a** to much wine, 1 Tm 3:8

ADDING (2)
a a fifth to it and giving it to him to Nm 5:7
while **a** one thing to another to find the Eccl 7:27

ADDITION (8)
in **a** to the ram of atonement with which Nm 5:8
then he shall do in **a** to the law of the Nm 6:21
in **a** to your vow offerings and your Nm 29:39
and in **a** to them you shall give Nm 35:6
in **a** to all that I have provided for the 1 Chr 29:3
against the LORD in **a** to our present 2 Chr 28:13
committed lewdness in **a** to all your Ezk 16:43
in **a** to all your abominations. Ezk 44:7

ADDON (1)
Tel-harsha, Cherub, **A**, and Immer, Neh 7:61

ADDRESS (2)
pleasing theme; I **a** my verses to the king; Ps 45:1
could not **a** you as spiritual people, 1 Cor 3:1

ADDRESSED (7)
son of Jehiel, of the sons of Elam, **a** Ezra: Ezr 10:2
who **a** the words of this song to the LORD Ps 18:T
Pilate **a** them once more, desiring to Lk 23:20
eleven, lifted up his voice and **a** them, Acts 2:14
And when Peter saw it he **a** the people: Acts 3:12
he **a** them in the Hebrew language, Acts 21:40
Then one of the elders **a** me, saying, Rv 7:13

ADDRESSES (1)
the exhortation that **a** you as sons? Heb 12:5

ADDRESSING (2)
heard that he was **a** them in the Acts 22:2
a one another in psalms and hymns Eph 5:19

ADDS (6)
For he **a** rebellion to his sin; he claps Jb 34:37
rich, and he **a** no sorrow with it. Prv 10:22
judicious and **a** persuasiveness to Prv 16:23
no one annuls it or **a** to it once it has Gal 3:15
then he **a**, "I will remember their sins Heb 10:17
of this book: if anyone **a** to them, Rv 22:18

ADHERENT (1)
—not only to the **a** of the law but also Rom 4:16

ADHERENTS (1)
For if it is the **a** of the law who are to Rom 4:14

ADIEL (3)
Jeshohaiah, Asaiah, **A**, Jesimiel, 1 Chr 4:36
Malchijah, and Maasai the son of **A**, 1 Chr 9:12
was Azmaveth the son of **A**; 1 Chr 27:25

ADIN (4)
The sons of **A**, 454. Ezr 2:15
Of the sons of **A**, Ebed the son of Ezr 8:6
The sons of **A**, 655. Neh 7:20
Adonijah, Bigvai, **A**, Neh 10:16

ADINA (1)
A the son of Shiza the Reubenite, a 1 Chr 11:42

ADITHAIM (1)
Shaaraim, **A**, Gederah, Gederothaim: Jos 15:36

ADJOINING (13)
A the territory of Dan, from the east Ezk 48:2
A the territory of Asher, from the east Ezk 48:3
A the territory of Naphtali, from the Ezk 48:4
A the territory of Manasseh, from the Ezk 48:5
A the territory of Ephraim, from the Ezk 48:6
A the territory of Reuben, from the east Ezk 48:7
"**A** the territory of Judah, from the east Ezk 48:8
place, **a** the territory of the Levites. Ezk 48:12
A the territory of Benjamin, from the Ezk 48:24
A the territory of Simeon, from the Ezk 48:25
A the territory of Issachar, from the Ezk 48:26
A the territory of Zebulun, from the Ezk 48:27
And **a** the territory of Gad to the south, Ezk 48:28

ADJURATION (1)
sins in that he hears a public **a** to testify, Lv 5:1

ADJURE (8)
I **a** you, O daughters of Jerusalem, by the Sg 2:7
I **a** you, O daughters of Jerusalem, by the Sg 3:5
I **a** you, O daughters of Jerusalem, if you Sg 5:8
than another beloved, that you thus **a** us? Sg 5:9
I **a** you, O daughters of Jerusalem, that Sg 8:4
said to him, "I **a** you by the living God, Mt 26:63
God? I **a** you by God, do not torment me." Mk 5:7
spirits, saying, "I **a** you by the Jesus, Acts 19:13

ADLAI (1)
valleys was Shaphat the son of **A**. 1 Chr 27:29

ADMAH (5)
of Sodom, Gomorrah, **A**, and Zeboiim, Gn 10:19
king of Gomorrah, Shinab king of **A**, Gn 14:2
the king of Gomorrah, the king of **A**, Gn 14:8
Sodom and Gomorrah, **A**, and Zeboiim, Dt 29:23
O Israel? How can I make you like **A**? Hos 11:8

ADMATHA (1)
being Carshena, Shethar, **A**, Tarshish, Est 1:14

ADMIN (1)
the son of Amminadab, the son of **A**, the Lk 3:33

ADMINISTERED (3)
And David **a** justice and equity to all 2 Sm 8:15
and he **a** justice and equity to all his 1 Chr 18:14
generous gift that is being **a** by us, 2 Cor 8:20

ADMINISTRATING (1)
a, and various kinds of tongues. 1 Cor 12:28

ADMIT (2)
And their anointing shall **a** them to a Ex 40:15
Do not **a** a charge against an elder 1 Tm 5:19

ADMITTING (1)
in **a** foreigners, uncircumcised in heart Ezk 44:7

ADMONISH (5)
Hear, O my people, while I **a** you! O Ps 81:8
night or day to **a** everyone with tears. Acts 20:31
but to **a** you as my beloved children. 1 Cor 4:14
are over you in the Lord and **a** you, 1 Thes 5:12
we urge you, brothers, **a** the idle, 1 Thes 5:14

ADMONISHING (1)
teaching and **a** one another in all Col 3:16

ADNA (2)
A, Chelal, Benaiah, Maaseiah, Ezr 10:30
of Harim, **A**; of Meraioth, Helkai; Neh 12:15

ADNAH (2)
A, Jozabad, Jediael, Michael, 1 Chr 12:20
A the commander, with 300,000 2 Chr 17:14

ADONI-BEZEK (3)
They found **A** at Bezek and fought Jgs 1:5
A fled, but they pursued him and caught Jgs 1:6
And **A** said, "Seventy kings with their Jgs 1:7

ADONI-ZEDEK (2)
As soon as **A**, king of Jerusalem, heard Jos 10:1
So **A** king of Jerusalem sent to Hoham Jos 10:3

ADONIJAH (26)
and the fourth, **A** the son of Haggith; 2 Sm 3:4
Now **A** the son of Haggith exalted 1 Kgs 1:5
And they followed **A** and helped him. 1 Kgs 1:7
David's mighty men were not with **A**. 1 Kgs 1:8
A sacrificed sheep, oxen, and fattened 1 Kgs 1:9
you not heard that **A** the son of 1 Kgs 1:11
on my throne"? Why then is **A** king?' 1 Kgs 1:13
And now, behold, **A** is king, although 1 Kgs 1:18
have you said, '**A** shall reign after me, 1 Kgs 1:24
him, and saying, 'Long live King **A**!' 1 Kgs 1:25
A and all the guests who were with 1 Kgs 1:41
Abiathar the priest came. And **A** said, 1 Kgs 1:42
Jonathan answered **A**, "No, for our 1 Kgs 1:43
all the guests of **A** trembled and rose, 1 Kgs 1:49
And **A** feared Solomon. So he arose 1 Kgs 1:50
"Behold, **A** fears King Solomon, 1 Kgs 1:51
Then **A** the son of Haggith came to 1 Kgs 2:13
to speak to him on behalf of **A**. 1 Kgs 2:19
be given to **A** your brother as 1 Kgs 2:21
ask Abishag the Shunammite for **A**? 1 Kgs 2:22
if this word does not cost **A** his life! 1 Kgs 2:23
A shall be put to death this day." 1 Kgs 2:24
Joab had supported **A** although he 1 Kgs 2:28
fourth, **A**, whose mother was Haggith; 1 Chr 3:2
Jehonathan, **A**, Tobijah, 2 Chr 17:8
A, Bigvai, Adin, Neh 10:16

ADONIKAM (3)
The sons of **A**, 666. Ezr 2:13
Of the sons of **A**, those who came later, Ezr 8:13
The sons of **A**, 667. Neh 7:18

ADONIRAM (2)
and **A** the son of Abda was in charge 1 Kgs 4:6
at home. **A** was in charge of the draft. 1 Kgs 5:14

ADOPTED (1)
Pharaoh's daughter **a** him and Acts 7:21

ADOPTION (5)
have received the Spirit of **a** as sons, Rom 8:15
as we wait eagerly for **a** as sons, Rom 8:23
are Israelites, and to them belong the **a**, Rom 9:4
law, so that we might receive **a** as sons. Gal 4:5
predestined us for **a** through Jesus Eph 1:5

ADORAIM (1)
A, Lachish, Azekah, 2 Chr 11:9

ADORAM (2)
and **A** was in charge of the forced 2 Sm 20:24
Then King Rehoboam sent **A**, who 1 Kgs 12:18

ADORN (6)
"**A** yourself with majesty and dignity; Jb 40:10
that you **a** yourself with ornaments of Jer 4:30
Again you shall **a** yourself with Jer 31:4
that women should **a** themselves in 1 Tm 2:9
in everything they may **a** the doctrine of Ti 2:10
who hoped in God used to **a** themselves, 1 Pt 3:5

ADORNED (11)
painted her eyes and **a** her head and 2 Kgs 9:30
He **a** the house with settings of 2 Chr 3:6
And I **a** you with ornaments and put Ezk 16:11
Thus you were **a** with gold and silver, Ezk 16:13
eyes, and **a** yourself with ornaments. Ezk 23:40
offerings to them and **a** herself with her Hos 2:13
how it was **a** with noble stones and Lk 21:5
and **a** with gold and jewels and pearls, Rv 17:4
linen, in purple and scarlet, **a** with gold, Rv 18:16
prepared as a bride **a** for her husband. Rv 21:2
of the city were **a** with every kind of Rv 21:19

ADORNING (2)
Do not let your **a** be external—the 1 Pt 3:3
but let your **a** be the hidden person of 1 Pt 3:4

ADORNMENT (2)
life for your soul and **a** for your neck. Prv 3:22
and became tall and arrived at full **a**. Ezk 16:7

ADORNS (2)
people; he **a** the humble with salvation. Ps 149:4
and as a bride **a** herself with her jewels. Is 61:10

ADRAMMELECH (3)
in the fire to **A** and Anammelech, 2 Kgs 17:31
of Nisroch his god, **A** and Sharezer, 2 Kgs 19:37
of Nisroch his god, **A** and Sharezer, Is 37:38

ADRAMYTTIUM (1)
And embarking in a ship of **A**, which Acts 27:2

ADRIATIC (1)
were being driven across the **A** Sea, Acts 27:27

ADRIEL (2)
was given to **A** the Meholathite for 1 Sm 18:19

whom she bore to **A** the son of — 2 Sm 21:8

ADRIFT (1)
a night and a day I was **a** at sea; — 2 Cor 11:25

ADULLAM (8)
king of Libnah, one; the king of **A**, one; — Jos 12:15
Jarmuth, **A**, Socoh, Azekah, — Jos 15:35
there and escaped to the cave of **A**. — 1 Sm 22:1
time to David at the cave of **A**, — 2 Sm 23:13
to the rock to David at the cave of **A**, — 1 Chr 11:15
Beth-zur, Soco, **A**, — 2 Chr 11:7
Zanoah, **A**, and their villages, — Neh 11:30
the glory of Israel shall come to **A**. — Mi 1:15

ADULLAMITE (3)
brothers and turned aside to a certain **A**, — Gn 38:1
he and his friend Hirah the **A**. — Gn 38:12
by his friend the **A** to take back the — Gn 38:20

ADULTERER (3)
both the **a** and the adulteress shall — Lv 20:10
The eye of the **a** also waits for the — Jb 24:15
offspring of the **a** and the loose woman. — Is 57:3

ADULTERERS (7)
him, and you keep company with **a**. — Ps 50:18
For they are all **a**, a company of — Jer 9:2
For the land is full of **a**; because of the — Jer 23:10
They are all **a**; they are like a heated — Hos 7:4
against the sorcerers, against the **a**, — Mal 3:5
unjust, **a**, or even like this tax collector. — Lk 18:11
sexually immoral, nor idolaters, nor **a**, — 1 Cor 6:9

ADULTERESS (11)
the adulterer and the **a** shall surely be — Lv 20:10
from the **a** with her smooth words, — Prv 2:16
and embrace the bosom of an **a**? — Prv 5:20
from the smooth tongue of the **a**. — Prv 6:24
from the **a** with her smooth words. — Prv 7:5
is a deep pit; an **a** is a narrow well. — Prv 23:27
when he puts up security for an **a**. — Prv 27:13
This is the way of an **a**: she eats and — Prv 30:20
is loved by another man and is an **a**, — Hos 3:1
she will be called an **a** if she lives with — Rom 7:3
marries another man she is not an **a**. — Rom 7:3

ADULTERESSES (2)
on them with the sentence of **a**, — Ezk 23:45
who shed blood, because they are **a**, — Ezk 23:45

ADULTERIES (2)
saw that for all the **a** of that faithless one, — Jer 3:8
abominations, your **a** and neighings, — Jer 13:27

ADULTEROUS (6)
A wife, who receives strangers instead — Ezk 16:32
"An evil and **a** generation seeks for a — Mt 12:39
An evil and **a** generation seeks for a — Mt 16:4
words in this **a** and sinful generation, — Mk 8:38
will judge the sexually immoral and **a**. — Heb 13:4
You **a** people! Do you not know that — Jas 4:4

ADULTERY (40)
"You shall not commit **a**. — Ex 20:14
"If a man commits **a** with the wife of — Lv 20:10
"'And you shall not commit **a**. — Dt 5:18
He who commits **a** lacks sense; he who — Prv 6:32
land, committing **a** with stone and tree. — Jer 3:9
they committed **a** and trooped to the — Jer 5:7
Will you steal, murder, commit **a**, swear — Jer 7:9
thing: they commit **a** and walk in lies; — Jer 23:14
they have committed **a** with their — Jer 29:23
women who commit **a** and shed blood — Ezk 16:38
For they have committed **a**, and blood — Ezk 23:37
their idols they have committed **a**, — Ezk 23:37
I said of her who was worn out by **a**, — Ezk 23:43
face, and her **a** from between her breasts; — Hos 2:2
murder, stealing, and committing **a**; — Hos 4:2
the whore, and your brides commit **a**. — Hos 4:13
nor your brides when they commit **a**; — Hos 4:14
it was said, 'You shall not commit **a**.' — Mt 5:27
has already committed **a** with her in — Mt 5:28
immorality, makes her commit **a**. — Mt 5:32
marries a divorced woman commits **a**. — Mt 5:32
murder, **a**, sexual immorality, — Mt 15:19
and marries another, commits **a**." — Mt 19:9
not murder, You shall not commit **a**, — Mt 19:18
sexual immorality, theft, murder, **a**, — Mk 7:21
another commits **a** against her, — Mk 10:11
and marries another, she commits **a**." — Mk 10:12
'Do not murder, Do not commit **a**, Do — Mk 10:19
wife and marries another commits **a**, — Lk 16:18
from her husband commits **a**. — Lk 16:18
'Do not commit **a**, Do not murder, Do — Lk 18:20
a woman who had been caught in **a**, — Jn 8:3
woman has been caught in the act of **a**. — Jn 8:4
who say that one must not commit **a**, — Rom 2:22
commit adultery, do you commit **a**? — Rom 2:22
"You shall not commit **a**, — Rom 13:9
who said, "Do not commit **a**," also said, — Jas 2:11

If you do not commit **a** but do murder, — Jas 2:11
They have eyes full of **a**, insatiable for — 2 Pt 2:14
and those who commit **a** with her I will — Rv 2:22

ADUMMIM (2)
Gilgal, which is opposite the ascent of **A**, — Jos 15:7
which is opposite the ascent of **A**. — Jos 18:17

ADVANCE (7)
buckler and shield, and **a** for battle! — Jer 46:3
A, O horses, and rage, O chariots! Let the — Jer 46:9
the LORD: "Rise up, **a** against Kedar! — Jer 49:28
"Rise up, **a** against a nation at ease, that — Jer 49:31
You will **a**, coming on like a storm. — Ezk 38:9
to you and arrange in **a** for the gift you — 2 Cor 9:5
to me has really served to **a** the gospel, — Phil 1:12

ADVANCED (16)
and Sarah were old, **a** in years. — Gn 18:11
Now Abraham was old, well **a** in years. — Gn 24:1
Now Joshua was old and **a** in years, and — Jos 13:1
said to him, "You are old and **a** in years, — Jos 13:1
and Joshua was old and well **a** in years, — Jos 23:1
them, "I am now old and well **a** in years. — Jos 23:2
man was already old and **a** in years. — 1 Sm 17:12
King David was old and **a** in years. — 1 Kgs 1:1
and **a** her and her young women to the — Est 2:9
and **a** him and set his throne above all — Est 3:1
and how he had **a** him above the — Est 5:11
of Mordecai, to which the king **a** him, — Est 10:2
exceedingly beautiful and **a** to royalty. — Ezk 16:13
was barren, and both were **a** in years. — Lk 1:7
an old man, and my wife is **a** in years." — Lk 1:18
of the tribe of Asher. She was **a** in years, — Lk 2:36

ADVANCING (1)
And I was **a** in Judaism beyond many — Gal 1:14

ADVANTAGE (20)
"The men gained an **a** over us and — 2 Sm 11:23
that you ask, 'What **a** have I? How am I — Jb 35:3
and man has no **a** over the beasts, — Eccl 3:19
and what **a** has their owner but to see — Eccl 5:11
For what **a** has the wise man over the — Eccl 6:8
more vanity, and what is the **a** to man? — Eccl 6:11
an **a** to those who see the sun. — Eccl 7:11
and the **a** of knowledge is that wisdom — Eccl 7:12
there is no **a** to the charmer. — Eccl 10:11
but it shall not stand or be to his **a**. — Dn 11:17
the truth: it is to your **a** that I go away, — Jn 16:7
Then what **a** has the Jew? Or what is the — Rom 3:1
I do, not seeking my own **a**, — 1 Cor 10:33
no one, we have taken **a** of no one. — 2 Cor 7:2
or devours you, or takes **a** of you, — 2 Cor 11:20
Did I take **a** of you through any of — 2 Cor 12:17
with him. Did Titus take **a** of you? — 2 Cor 12:18
Christ will be of no **a** to you. — Gal 5:2
for that would be of no **a** to you. — Heb 13:17
boasters, showing favoritism to gain **a**. — Jude 1:16

ADVERSARIES (38)
of your majesty you overthrow your **a**; — Ex 15:7
enemies and an adversary to your **a**. — Ex 23:22
he shall eat up the nations, his **a**, and — Nm 24:8
lest their **a** should misunderstand, — Dt 32:27
take vengeance on my **a** and will repay — Dt 32:41
children and takes vengeance on his **a**. — Dt 32:43
for him, and be a help against his **a**." — Dt 33:7
crush the loins of his **a**, of those who — Dt 33:11
to him, "Are you for us, or for our **a**?" — Jos 5:13
The **a** of the LORD shall be broken to — 1 Sm 2:10
but if to betray me to my **a**, — 1 Chr 12:17
Now when the **a** of Judah and Benjamin — Ezr 4:1
saying, 'Surely our **a** are cut off, and — Jb 22:20
seek refuge from their **a** at your right — Ps 17:7
me to eat up my flesh, my **a** and foes, — Ps 27:2
Give me not up to the will of my **a**; for — Ps 27:12
Because of all my **a** I have become a — Ps 31:11
wound in my bones, my **a** taunt me, — Ps 42:10
And he put his **a** to rout; he put them to — Ps 78:66
him and burns up his **a** all around. — Ps 97:3
And the waters covered their **a**; not one — Ps 106:11
until he looks in triumph on his **a**. — Ps 112:8
Many are my persecutors and my **a**, — Ps 119:157
you will destroy all the **a** of my soul, — Ps 143:12
the LORD raises the **a** of Rezin against him, — Is 9:11
Let the fire for your **a** consume them. — Is 26:11
deeds, so will he repay, wrath to his **a**, — Is 59:18
our **a** have trampled down your — Is 63:18
—to make your name known to your **a**, — Is 64:2
O LORD, and listen to the voice of my **a**. — Jer 18:19
gave them into the hand of their **a**, — Ezk 39:23
Your hand shall be lifted up over your **a**, — Mi 5:9
vengeance on his **a** and keeps wrath — Na 1:2
he will make a complete end of the **a**, — Na 1:8
things, all his **a** were put to shame, — Lk 13:17
which none of your **a** will be able to — Lk 21:15
opened to me, and there are many **a**. — 1 Cor 16:9

a fury of fire that will consume the **a**. — Heb 10:27

ADVERSARY (18)
enemies and an **a** to your adversaries. — Ex 23:22
land against the **a** who oppresses you, — Nm 10:9
took his stand in the way as his **a**. — Nm 22:22
lest in the battle he become an **a** to us. — 1 Sm 29:4
should this day be as an **a** to me? — 2 Sm 19:22
side. There is neither **a** nor misfortune. — 1 Kgs 5:4
raised up an **a** against Solomon, — 1 Kgs 11:14
God also raised up as an **a** to him, — 1 Kgs 11:23
He was an **a** of Israel all the days of — 1 Kgs 11:25
me; my **a** sharpens his eyes against me. — Jb 16:9
against me and counts me as his **a**. — Jb 19:11
I had the indictment written by my **a**! — Jb 31:35
it is not an **a** who deals insolently with — Ps 55:12
Let us stand up together. Who is my **a**? — Is 50:8
"An **a** shall surround the land and — Am 3:11
saying, 'Give me justice against my **a**.' — Lk 18:3
and give the **a** no occasion for — 1 Tm 5:14
Your **a** the devil prowls around like a — 1 Pt 5:8

ADVERSARY'S (1)
Or, 'Deliver me from the **a** hand'? Or, — Jb 6:23

ADVERSITY (8)
has redeemed my life out of every **a**, — 2 Sm 4:9
has redeemed my soul out of every **a**, — 1 Kgs 1:29
their affliction and opens their ear by **a**. — Jb 36:15
all generations I shall not meet **a**." — Ps 10:6
all times, and a brother is born for **a**. — Prv 17:17
If you faint in the day of **a**, your — Prv 24:10
be joyful, and in the day of **a** consider: — Eccl 7:14
give you the bread of **a** and the water of — Is 30:20

ADVICE (11)
I will give you **a**, and God be with you! — Ex 18:19
Behold, these, on Balaam's **a**, caused — Nm 31:16
all of you, give your **a** and counsel here." — Jgs 20:7
And the **a** seemed right in the eyes of — 2 Sm 17:4
therefore come, let me give you **a**, — 1 Kgs 1:12
This **a** pleased the king and the princes, — Est 1:21
own eyes, but a wise man listens to **a**. — Prv 12:15
but with those who take **a** is wisdom. — Prv 13:10
Listen to **a** and accept instruction, — Prv 19:20
who no longer knew how to take **a**. — Eccl 4:13
opposing God!" So they took his **a**, — Acts 5:39

ADVISABLE (1)
If it seems **a** that I should go also, they — 1 Cor 16:4

ADVISE (4)
"How do you **a** me to answer this — 1 Kgs 12:6
"What do you **a** that we answer this — 1 Kgs 12:9
"How do you **a** me to answer this — 2 Chr 10:6
"What do you **a** that we answer this — 2 Chr 10:9

ADVISED (3)
had charge of the women, **a**. Now Esther — Est 2:15
was Caiaphas who had **a** the Jews that it — Jn 18:14
the Fast was already over, Paul **a** them, — Acts 27:9

ADVISER (1)
with Ahuzzath his **a** and Phicol the — Gn 26:26

ADVISERS (1)
fail, but with many **a** they succeed. — Prv 15:22

ADVOCATE (2)
They **a** customs that are not lawful — Acts 16:21
does sin, we have an **a** with the Father, — 1 Jn 2:1

AENEAS (2)
There he found a man named **A**, — Acts 9:33
said to him, "**A**, Jesus Christ heals you; — Acts 9:34

AENON (1)
John also was baptizing at **A** near Salim, — Jn 3:23

AFAR (30)
up his eyes and saw the place from **a**. — Gn 22:4
They saw him from **a**, and before he — Gn 37:18
the elders of Israel, and worship from **a**. — Ex 24:1
Like palm groves that stretch **a**, like — Nm 24:6
my knowledge from **a** and ascribe — Jb 36:3
has looked on it; man beholds it from **a**. — Jb 36:25
He smells the battle from **a**, the thunder — Jb 39:25
out the prey; his eyes behold it **a** off. — Jb 39:29
Why, O LORD, do you stand **a** off? Why — Ps 10:1
but the haughty he knows from **a**. — Ps 138:6
up; you discern my thoughts from **a**. — Ps 139:2
merchant; she brings her food from **a**. — Prv 31:14
He will raise a signal for nations **a** off, — Is 5:26
in the ruin that will come from **a**? — Is 10:3
the name of the LORD comes from **a**, — Is 30:27
they will see a land that stretches **a**. — Is 33:17
bring my sons from **a** and my daughters — Is 43:6
and give attention, you peoples from **a**. — Is 49:1
Behold, these shall come from **a**, and — Is 49:12
back, and righteousness stands **a** off; — Is 59:14
your sons shall come from **a**, and your — Is 60:4
first, to bring your children from **a**, — Is 60:9

Tubal and Javan, to the coastlands **a** off, Is 66:19
bringing against you a nation from **a**, Jer 5:15
declares the LORD, and not a God **a** off? Jer 23:23
even sent for men to come from **a**, Ezk 23:40
and shall decide for strong nations **a** off; Mi 4:3
Their horsemen come from **a**; they fly Hab 1:8
And when he saw Jesus from **a**, he ran Mk 5:6
seen them and greeted them from **a**, Heb 11:13

AFFAIR (3)
because in this **a** they dealt arrogantly Ex 18:11
those who died in the **a** of Korah. Nm 16:49
When the **a** was investigated and found Est 2:23

AFFAIRS (8)
"Why speak any more of your **a**? 2 Sm 19:29
was a turn of **a** brought about by 1 Kgs 12:15
to God and for the **a** of the king. 1 Chr 26:32
was a turn of **a** brought about by 2 Chr 10:15
lends; who conducts his **a** with justice. Ps 112:5
and Abednego over the **a** of the province Dn 2:49
appointed over the **a** of the province Dn 3:12
quietly, and to mind your own **a**, 1 Thes 4:11

AFFECTION (6)
Love one another with brotherly **a**. Rom 12:10
And his **a** for you is even greater, as 2 Cor 7:15
for you all with the **a** of Christ Jesus. Phil 1:8
in the Spirit, any **a** and sympathy, Phil 2:1
and godliness with brotherly **a**, and 2 Pt 1:7
affection, and brotherly **a** with love. 2 Pt 1:7

AFFECTIONATELY (1)
So, being **a** desirous of you, we were 1 Thes 2:8

AFFECTIONS (1)
but you are restricted in your own **a**. 2 Cor 6:12

AFFIRMING (1)
charge, **a** that all these things were so. Acts 24:9

AFFLICT (21)
over them to **a** them with heavy Ex 1:11
you shall **a** yourselves and shall do no Lv 16:29
rest to you, and you shall **a** yourselves; Lv 16:31
and you shall **a** yourselves and present Lv 23:27
solemn rest, and you shall **a** yourselves. Lv 23:32
Kittim and shall **a** Asshur and Eber; Nm 24:24
a holy convocation and **a** yourselves. Nm 29:7
and any binding oath to **a** herself, Nm 30:13
violent men shall **a** them no more, 2 Sm 7:10
from their sin, when you **a** them, 1 Kgs 8:35
And I will **a** the offspring of David 1 Kgs 11:39
from their sin, when you **a** them, 2 Chr 6:26
your people, O LORD, and **a** your heritage. Ps 94:5
you keep silent, and **a** us so terribly? Is 64:12
and those who seek their life **a** them.' Jer 19:9
he does not willingly **a** or grieve the Lam 3:33
your sins—you who **a** the righteous, Am 5:12
have afflicted you, I will **a** you no more. Na 1:12
enslave them and **a** them four hundred Acts 7:6
sincerely but thinking to **a** me in my Phil 1:17
repay with affliction those who **a** you, 2 Thes 1:6

AFFLICTED (61)
But the LORD **a** Pharaoh and his house Gn 12:17
and they will be **a** for four hundred Gn 15:13
"When a man is **a** with a leprous Lv 13:9
For whoever is not **a** on that very day Lv 23:29
of those who **a** and oppressed them. Jgs 2:18
he terrified and **a** them with tumors, 1 Sm 5:6
panic, and he **a** the men of the city, 1 Sm 5:9
And the LORD **a** the child that 2 Sm 12:15
of Israel and **a** them and gave 2 Kgs 17:20
for great disturbances **a** all the 2 Chr 15:5
against him and **a** him instead of 2 Chr 28:20
to him, and he heard the cry of the **a**— Jb 34:28
wicked alive, but gives the **a** their right. Jb 36:6
He delivers the **a** by their affliction and Jb 36:15
them; he does not forget the cry of the **a**. Ps 9:12
God, lift up your hand; forget not the **a**. Ps 10:12
O LORD, you hear the desire of the **a**; you Ps 10:17
or abhorred the affliction of the **a**, Ps 22:24
The **a** shall eat and be satisfied; those Ps 22:26
gracious to me, for I am lonely and **a**. Ps 25:16
wore sackcloth; I **a** myself with fasting; Ps 35:13
you **a** the peoples, but them you set free; Ps 44:2
But I am **a** and in pain; let your Ps 69:29
the right of the **a** and the destitute. Ps 82:3
A and close to death from my youth up, Ps 88:15
glad for as many days as you have **a** us, Ps 90:15
A Prayer of one **a**, when he is faint and Ps 102:T
even when I spoke, "I am greatly **a**"; Ps 116:10
Before I was **a** I went astray, but now I Ps 119:67
It is good for me that I was **a**, that I Ps 119:71
that in faithfulness you have **a** me. Ps 119:75
I am severely **a**; give me life, O LORD, Ps 119:107
"Greatly have they **a** me from my Ps 129:1
"Greatly have they **a** me from my Ps 129:2
LORD will maintain the cause of the **a**, Ps 140:12
All the days of the **a** are evil, but the Prv 15:15
he is poor, or crush the **a** at the gate, Prv 22:22
and pervert the rights of all the **a**. Prv 31:5
and in her the **a** of his people find Is 14:32
and will have compassion on his **a**. Is 49:13
Therefore hear this, you who are **a**, who Is 51:21
him stricken, smitten by God, and **a**. Is 53:4
He was oppressed, and he was **a**, yet he Is 53:7
"O **a** one, storm-tossed and not Is 54:11
hungry and satisfy the desire of the **a**, Is 58:10
sons of those who **a** you shall come Is 60:14
In all their affliction he was **a**, and the Is 63:9
her virgins have been **a**, and she herself Lam 1:4
because the LORD has **a** her for the Lam 1:5
the earth and turn aside the way of the **a**; Am 2:7
driven away and those whom I have **a**; Mi 4:6
Though I have **a** you, I will afflict you Na 1:12
sheep; they are **a** for lack of a shepherd. Zec 10:2
those **a** with various diseases and pains, Mt 4:24
sick and those **a** with unclean spirits, Acts 5:16
If we are **a**, it is for your comfort and 2 Cor 1:6
We are **a** in every way, but not 2 Cor 4:8
but we were **a** at every turn—fighting 2 Cor 7:5
relief to you who are **a** as well as to us, 2 Thes 1:7
feet of the saints, has cared for the **a**, 1 Tm 5:10
and goats, destitute, **a**, mistreated— Heb 11:37

AFFLICTION (66)
the LORD has listened to your **a**. Gn 16:11
the LORD has looked upon my **a**; Gn 29:32
God saw my **a** and the labor of my Gn 31:42
made me fruitful in the land of my **a**." Gn 41:52
"I have surely seen the **a** of my people who Ex 3:7
you up out of the **a** of Egypt to the land Ex 3:17
of Israel and that he had seen their **a**, Ex 4:31
the bread of **a**—for you came out of the Dt 16:3
the LORD heard our voice and saw our **a**, Dt 26:7
sickness also and every **a** that is not Dt 28:61
indeed look on the **a** of your servant 1 Sm 1:11
you shared in all my father's **a**." 1 Kgs 2:26
each knowing the **a** of his own heart 1 Kgs 8:38
LORD saw that the **a** of Israel was 2 Kgs 14:26
each knowing his own **a** and his own 2 Chr 6:29
house—and cry out to you in our **a**, 2 Chr 20:9
"And you saw the **a** of our fathers in Neh 9:9
for our **a** is not to be compared with the Est 7:4
For **a** does not come from the dust, nor Jb 5:6
filled with disgrace and look on my **a**. Jb 10:15
me; days of **a** have taken hold of me. Jb 30:16
never still; days of **a** come to meet me. Jb 30:27
in chains and caught in the cords of **a**, Jb 36:8
the afflicted by their **a** and opens their Jb 36:15
for this you have chosen rather than **a**. Jb 36:21
See my **a** from those who hate me, O you Ps 9:13
or abhorred the **a** of the afflicted, Ps 22:24
Consider my **a** and my trouble, and Ps 25:18
love, because you have seen my **a**; Ps 31:7
A will slay the wicked, and those who Ps 34:21
do you forget our **a** and oppression? Ps 44:24
of death, prisoners in **a** and in irons, Ps 107:10
because of their iniquities suffered **a**; Ps 107:17
the needy out of **a** and makes their Ps 107:41
This is my comfort in my **a**, that your Ps 119:50
delight, I would have perished in my **a**. Ps 119:92
Look on my **a** and deliver me, for I do Ps 119:153
the bread of adversity and the water of **a**, Is 30:20
I have tried you in the furnace of **a**. Is 48:10
In all their **a** he was afflicted, and the Is 63:9
But I said, "Truly this is an **a**, and I Jer 10:19
near at hand, and his **a** hastens swiftly. Jer 48:16
exile because of **a** and hard servitude; Lam 1:3
the days of her **a** and wandering all the Lam 1:7
"O LORD, behold my **a**, for the enemy Lam 1:9
man who has seen **a** under the rod of Lam 3:1
Remember my **a** and my wanderings, Lam 3:19
I saw the tents of Cushan in **a**; the Hab 3:7
disease and every **a** among the people. Mt 4:23
and healing every disease and every **a**. Mt 9:35
and to heal every disease and every **a**. Mt 10:1
all Egypt and Canaan, and great **a**, Acts 7:11
have surely seen the **a** of my people Acts 7:34
who comforts us in all our **a**, so that 2 Cor 1:4
able to comfort those who are in any **a**, 2 Cor 1:4
of the **a** we experienced in Asia. 2 Cor 1:8
you out of much **a** and anguish of 2 Cor 2:4
this slight momentary **a** is preparing 2 Cor 4:17
In all our **a**, I am overflowing with joy. 2 Cor 7:4
for in a severe test of **a**, their 2 Cor 8:2
for you received the word in much **a**, 1 Thes 1:6
beforehand that we were to suffer **a**, 1 Thes 3:4
all our distress and **a** we have been 1 Thes 3:7
just to repay with **a** those who afflict 2 Thes 1:6
publicly exposed to reproach and **a**, Heb 10:33
to visit orphans and widows in their **a**, Jas 1:27

AFFLICTIONS (10)
you and your offspring extraordinary **a**, Dt 28:59
afflictions, **a** severe and lasting, Dt 28:59
when they see the **a** of that land and the Dt 29:22
Many are the **a** of the righteous, but the Ps 34:19
out of all his **a** and gave him favor Acts 7:10
that imprisonment and **a** await me. Acts 20:23
by great endurance, in **a**, hardships, 2 Cor 6:4
is lacking in Christ's **a** for the sake of Col 1:24
that no one be moved by these **a**. For 1 Thes 3:3
persecutions and in the **a** that you are 2 Thes 1:4

AFFLICTS (1)
with which the LORD **a** the nations that Zec 14:18

AFFORD (9)
"But if he cannot **a** a lamb, then he shall Lv 5:7
"But if he cannot **a** two turtledoves or Lv 5:11
And if she cannot **a** a lamb, then she Lv 12:8
if he is poor and cannot **a** so much, Lv 14:21
or two pigeons, whichever he can **a**. Lv 14:22
or pigeons, whichever he can **a**, Lv 14:30
who cannot **a** the offerings for his Lv 14:32
him according to what the vower can **a**. Lv 27:8
above his Nazirite vow, as he can **a**, Nm 6:21

AFLAME (3)
Scoffers set a city **a**, but the wise turn Prv 29:8
at one another; their faces will be **a**. Is 13:8
to marry than to be **a** with passion. 1 Cor 7:9

AFRAID (167)
sound of you in the garden, and I was **a**, Gn 3:10
saying, "I did not laugh," for she was **a**. Gn 18:15
daughters, for he was **a** to live in Zoar. Gn 19:30
things. And the men were very much **a**. Gn 20:8
And he was **a** and said, "How awesome Gn 28:17
and said to Laban, "Because I was **a**, Gn 31:31
Then Jacob was greatly **a** and distressed. Gn 32:7
their bundles of money, they were **a**. Gn 42:35
And the men were **a** because they were Gn 43:18
He replied, "Peace to you, do not be **a**. Gn 43:23
Do not be **a** to go down to Egypt, for Gn 46:3
killed the Egyptian?" Then Moses was **a**, Ex 2:14
hid his face, for he was **a** to look at God. Ex 3:6
the people were **a** and trembled, Ex 20:18
and they were **a** to come near him. Ex 34:30
lie down, and none shall make you **a**. Lv 26:6
then were you not **a** to speak against Nm 12:8
to you, 'Do not be in dread or **a** of them. Dt 1:29
who live in Seir; and they will be **a** of you. Dt 2:4
For you were **a** because of the fire, and Dt 5:5
you shall not be **a** of them but you shall Dt 7:18
do to all the peoples of whom you are **a**. Dt 7:19
For I was **a** of the anger and hot Dt 9:19
You need not be **a** of him. Dt 18:22
your own, you shall not be **a** of them, Dt 20:1
of the LORD, and they shall be **a** of you. Dt 28:10
diseases of Egypt, of which you were **a**, Dt 28:60
said to them, "Do not be **a** or dismayed; Jos 10:25
said to Joshua, "Do not be **a** of them, Jos 11:6
do not be **a**." So he turned aside to her Jgs 4:18
because he was too **a** of his family and Jgs 6:27
But if you are **a** to go down, go down to Jgs 7:10
did not draw his sword, for he was **a**, Jgs 8:20
And Samuel was **a** to tell the vision to 1 Sm 3:15
the Philistines were **a**, for they said, "A 1 Sm 4:7
attending her said to her, "Do not be **a**, 1 Sm 4:20
of it, they were **a** of the Philistines. 1 Sm 7:7
said to the people, "Do not be **a**; 1 Sm 12:20
they were dismayed and greatly **a**. 1 Sm 17:11
fled from him and were much **a**. 1 Sm 17:24
Saul was **a** of David because the 1 Sm 18:12
Saul was even more **a** of David. So 1 Sm 18:29
heart and was much **a** of Achish the 1 Sm 21:12
do not be **a**, for he who seeks my life 1 Sm 22:23
him, "Behold, we are **a** here in Judah; 1 Sm 23:3
the army of the Philistines, he was **a**, 1 Sm 28:5
The king said to her, "Do not be **a**. 1 Sm 28:13
is it you were not **a** to put out your 2 Sm 1:14
And David was **a** of the LORD that day, 2 Sm 6:9
So the Syrians were **a** to save the 2 Sm 10:19
servants of David were **a** to tell him 2 Sm 12:18
because the people have made me **a**, 2 Sm 14:15
Then he was **a**, and he arose and ran 1 Kgs 19:3
do not be **a** of him." So he arose and 2 Kgs 1:15
He said, "Do not be **a**, for those who 2 Kgs 6:16
But they were exceedingly **a** and said, 2 Kgs 10:4
Do not be **a** because of the words that 2 Kgs 19:6
"Do not be **a** because of the 2 Kgs 25:24
for they were **a** of the Chaldeans. 2 Kgs 25:26
And David was **a** of God that day, 1 Chr 13:12
for he was **a** of the sword of the 1 Chr 21:30
Do not be **a** and do not be dismayed, 1 Chr 28:20
Then Jehoshaphat was **a** and set his 2 Chr 20:3
'Do not be **a** and do not be dismayed 2 Chr 20:15
Do not be **a** and do not be dismayed. 2 Chr 20:17

Do not be **a** or dismayed before the 2 Chr 32:7
of Judah and made them **a** to build Ezr 4:4
of the heart." Then I was very much **a**. Neh 2:2
rest of the people, "Do not be **a** of them. Neh 4:14
that I should be **a** and act in this way Neh 6:13
prophets who wanted to make me **a**. Neh 6:14
around us were **a** and fell greatly Neh 6:16
And Tobiah sent letters to make me **a**. Neh 6:19
nothing; you see my calamity and are **a**. Jb 6:21
I become **a** of all my suffering, for I know Jb 9:28
lie down, and none will make you **a**; Jb 11:19
be **a** of the sword, for wrath brings the Jb 19:29
I was timid and **a** to declare my opinion Jb 32:6
he raises himself up the mighty are **a**; Jb 41:25
I will not be **a** of many thousands of Ps 3:6
of my life; of whom shall I be **a**? Ps 27:1
Be not **a** when a man becomes rich, Ps 49:16
When I am **a**, I put my trust in you. Ps 56:3
I praise, in God I trust; I shall not be **a**. Ps 56:4
in God I trust; I shall not be **a**. What Ps 56:11
when the waters saw you, they were **a**; Ps 77:16
them in safety, so that they were not **a**, Ps 78:53
He is not **a** of bad news; his heart is Ps 112:7
he will not be **a**, until he looks in Ps 112:8
of you, and I am **a** of your judgments. Ps 119:120
If you lie down, you will not be **a**; when Prv 3:24
Do not be **a** of sudden terror or of the Prv 3:25
She is not **a** of snow for her household, Prv 31:21
they are **a** also of what is high, and Eccl 12:5
be not **a** of the Assyrians when they Is 10:24
salvation; I will trust, and will not be **a**; Is 12:2
will lie down, and none will make them **a**. Is 17:2
The sinners in Zion are **a**; trembling Is 33:14
Do not be **a** because of the words that you Is 37:6
The coastlands have seen and are **a**; the Is 41:5
Fear not, nor be **a**; have I not told you Is 44:8
are you that you are **a** of man who dies, Is 51:12
Do not be **a** of them, for I am with you to Jer 1:8
Do not be **a** of them, for they cannot do Jer 10:5
the hand of those of whom you are **a**, Jer 22:25
he was **a** and fled and escaped to Egypt. Jer 26:21
and ease, and none shall make him **a**. Jer 30:10
who heard all these words was **a**, Jer 36:24
"I am **a** of the Judeans who have Jer 38:19
the hand of the men of whom you are **a**. Jer 39:17
"Do not be **a** to serve the Chaldeans. Jer 40:9
For they were **a** of them, because Jer 41:18
king of Babylon, of whom you are **a**. Jer 42:11
of which you are **a** shall follow close Jer 42:16
and ease, and none shall make him **a**. Jer 46:27
And you, son of man, be not **a** of them, Ezk 2:6
afraid of them, nor be **a** of their words, Ezk 2:6
Be not **a** of their words, nor be dismayed Ezk 2:6
and none shall make them **a**. Ezk 34:28
their land with none to make them **a**, Ezk 39:26
I saw a dream that made me **a**. As I lay in Dn 4:5
him, and he shall be **a** and withdraw, Dn 11:30
blown in a city, and the people are not **a**? Am 3:6
Then the mariners were **a**, and each Jon 1:5
the men were exceedingly **a** and said to Jon 1:10
fig tree, and no one shall make them **a**, Mi 4:4
lie down, and none shall make them **a**." Zep 3:13
Ashkelon shall see it, and be **a**; Gaza too, Zec 9:5
of his father Herod, he was **a** to go there, Mt 2:22
And he said to them, "Why are you **a**, O Mt 8:26
When the crowds saw it, they were **a**, and Mt 9:8
saying, "Take heart; it is I. Do not be **a**." Mt 14:27
But when he saw the wind, he was **a**, Mt 14:30
say, 'From man,' we are **a** of the crowd, Mt 21:26
so I was **a**, and I went and hid your Mt 25:25
angel said to the women, "Do not be **a**, Mt 28:5
Then Jesus said to them, "Do not be **a**; Mt 28:10
He said to them, "Why are you so **a**? Mk 4:40
and in his right mind, and they were **a**. Mk 5:15
said, "Take heart; it is I. Do not be **a**." Mk 6:50
the saying, and were **a** to ask him. Mk 9:32
and those who followed were **a**. Mk 10:32
man'?"—they were **a** of the people, Mk 11:32
said nothing to anyone, for they were **a**. Mk 16:8
But the angel said to him, "Do not be **a**, Lk 1:13
And the angel said to her, "Do not be **a**, Lk 1:30
And Jesus said to Simon, "Do not be **a**; Lk 5:10
"Where is your faith?" And they were **a**, Lk 8:25
and in his right mind, and they were **a**. Lk 8:35
and they were **a** as they entered the Lk 9:34
And they were **a** to ask him about this Lk 9:45
for I was **a** of you, because you are a Lk 19:21
But he said to them, "It is I; do not be **a**." Jn 6:20
be troubled, neither let them be **a**. Jn 14:27
heard this statement, he was even more **a**. Jn 19:8
for they were **a** of being stoned by the Acts 5:26
And they were all **a** of him, for they did Acts 9:26
and they were **a** when they heard that Acts 16:38
one night in a vision, "Do not be **a**, Acts 18:9
and the tribune also was **a**, Acts 22:29
a that Paul would be torn to pieces by Acts 23:10
and he said, 'Do not be **a**, Paul; you Acts 27:24
But if you do wrong, be **a**, for he does Rom 13:4
But I am **a** that as the serpent 2 Cor 11:3
I am **a** I may have labored over you in Gal 4:11
and they were not **a** of the king's edict. Heb 11:23
not being **a** of the anger of the king, Heb 11:27

AFRESH (1)
dirt; my skin hardens, then breaks out **a**. Jb 7:5

AFTERBIRTH (1)
her **a** that comes out from between her Dt 28:57

AFTERNOON (1)
It happened, late one **a**, when David 2 Sm 11:2

AFTERWARD (68)
on the earth in those days, and also **a**, Gn 6:4
A the clans of the Canaanites Gn 10:18
and **a** they shall come out with great Gn 15:14
A his brother came out with his hand Gn 25:26
A she bore a daughter and called her Gn 30:21
ahead of me, and **a** I shall see his face. Gn 32:20
A his brother came out with the Gn 38:30
A Moses and Aaron went and said to Ex 5:1
Egypt. **A** he will let you go from here. Ex 11:1
A all the people of Israel came near, and Ex 34:32
And **a** he shall kill the burnt offering. Lv 14:19
And **a** the priest shall go in to see the Lv 14:36
and **a** he may come into the camp. Lv 16:26
and **a** he may come into the camp. Lv 16:28
and **a** he may eat of the holy things, Lv 22:7
and **a** shall make the woman drink the Nm 5:26
and **a** he may come into the camp. Nm 19:7
A you shall be gathered to your Nm 31:2
And **a** you may come into the camp." Nm 31:24
to death, and **a** the hand of all the people. Dt 13:9
to death, and **a** the hand of all the people. Dt 17:7
your vineyard, you shall not strip it **a**. Dt 24:21
returned. Then **a** you may go your way." Jos 2:16
And **a** he read all the words of the law, Jos 8:34
And **a** Joshua struck them and put Jos 10:26
A long time **a**, when the LORD had given Jos 23:1
the midst of it, and **a** I brought you out. Jos 24:5
And **a** the men of Judah went down to Jgs 1:9
and **a** your hands shall be strengthened Jgs 7:11
a those who are invited will eat. 1 Sm 9:13
And **a** David's heart struck him, 1 Sm 24:5
A David also arose and went out of the 1 Sm 24:8
A, when David heard of it, he said, "I 2 Sm 3:28
and **a** make something for yourself 1 Kgs 17:13
A Ben-hadad king of Syria mustered 2 Kgs 6:24
A Hezron went in to the daughter of 1 Chr 2:21
A he built an outer wall for the city 2 Chr 33:14
And **a** they prepared for themselves 2 Chr 35:14
and **a** you will receive me to glory. Ps 73:24
but **a** his mouth will be full of gravel. Prv 20:17
rebukes a man will **a** find more favor Prv 28:23
A you shall be called the city of Is 1:26
And **a** I will send for many hunters, Jer 16:16
A, declares the LORD, I will give Zedekiah Jer 21:7
But **a** they turned around and took Jer 34:11
A Egypt shall be inhabited as in the Jer 46:26
"But **a** I will restore the fortunes of the Jer 49:6
in one year and **a** a report in another Jer 51:46
A he shall turn his face to the Dn 11:18
A the children of Israel shall return and Hos 3:5
"And it shall come to pass **a**, that I will Jl 2:28
but **a** he changed his mind and went. Mt 21:29
you did not **a** change your minds and Mt 21:32
A the other virgins came also, saying, Mt 25:11
will be able soon **a** to speak evil of Mk 9:39
A he appeared to the eleven themselves Mk 16:14
Soon **a** he went to a town called Nain, Lk 7:11
Soon **a** he went on through cities and Lk 8:1
drink, and **a** you will eat and drink'? Lk 17:8
he refused, but **a** he said to himself, Lk 18:4
A the woman also died. Lk 20:32
A Jesus found him in the temple and said Jn 5:14
now, but **a** you will understand." Jn 13:7
follow me now, but you will follow **a**." Jn 13:36
the law, which came 430 years **a**, does Gal 3:17
saying through David so long **a**, Heb 4:7
For you know that **a**, when he desired Heb 12:17
a destroyed those who did not believe. Jude 1:5

AGABUS (2)
one of them named **A** stood up and Acts 11:28
a prophet named **A** came down from Acts 21:10

AGAG (8)
his king shall be higher than **A**, and Nm 24:7
And he took **A** the king of the 1 Sm 15:8
and the people spared **A** and the best 1 Sm 15:9
I have brought **A** the king of 1 Sm 15:20
"Bring here to me **A** the king of the 1 Sm 15:32
the Amalekites." And **A** came to him 1 Sm 15:32
A said, "Surely the bitterness of 1 Sm 15:32
And Samuel hacked **A** to pieces 1 Sm 15:33

AGAGITE (5)
King Ahasuerus promoted Haman the **A**, Est 3:1
his hand and gave it to Haman the **A**, Est 3:10
plan of Haman the **A** and the plot that Est 8:3
the letters devised by Haman the **A**, Est 8:5
For Haman the **A**, the son of Est 9:24

AGAIN (452)
And **a**, she bore his brother Abel. Now Gn 4:2
And Adam knew his wife **a**, and she Gn 4:25
and **a** he sent forth the dove out of the Gn 8:10
"I will never **a** curse the ground because Gn 8:21
Neither will I ever **a** strike down every Gn 8:21
that never **a** shall all flesh be cut off by Gn 9:11
and never **a** shall there be a flood to Gn 9:11
the waters shall never **a** become a flood Gn 9:15
A he spoke to him and said, "Suppose Gn 18:29
angry, and I will speak **a** but this once. Gn 18:32
there and worship and come **a** to you." Gn 22:5
into the trough and ran **a** to the well to Gn 24:20
And Isaac dug **a** the wells of water that Gn 26:18
so that I come **a** to my father's house in Gn 28:21
She conceived **a** and bore a son, and Gn 29:33
A she conceived and bore a son, and Gn 29:34
And she conceived **a** and bore a son, Gn 29:35
servant Bilhah conceived **a** and bore Gn 30:7
And Leah conceived **a**, and she bore Gn 30:19
I will **a** pasture your flock and keep it: Gn 30:31
God appeared to Jacob **a**, when he came Gn 35:9
She conceived **a** and bore a son, and she Gn 38:4
Yet **a** she bore a son, and she called his Gn 38:5
Shelah." And he did not know her **a**. Gn 38:26
Egypt, their father said to them, "Go **a**, Gn 43:2
brother, and arise, go **a** to the man. Gn 43:13
So we have brought it **a** with us, Gn 43:21
with you, you shall not see my face **a**.' Gn 44:23
And when our father said, 'Go **a**, buy Gn 44:25
to Egypt, and I will also bring you up **a**, Gn 46:4
you and will bring you **a** to the land of Gn 48:21
A, the LORD said to him, "Put your hand Ex 4:6
let not Pharaoh cheat **a** by not letting Ex 8:29
he sinned yet **a** and hardened his heart, Ex 9:34
never been before, nor ever will be **a**. Ex 10:14
take care never to see my face **a**, for on Ex 10:28
"As you say! I will not see your face **a**." Ex 10:29
there has never been, nor ever will be **a**. Ex 11:6
you see today, you shall never see **a**. Ex 14:13
if the man rises **a** and walks outdoors Ex 21:19
When Moses turned **a** into the camp, Ex 33:11
would put the veil over his face **a**, Ex 34:35
shall examine him **a** on the seventh Lv 13:6
he shall appear **a** before the priest. Lv 13:7
raw flesh recovers and turns white **a**, Lv 13:16
Then if it appears **a** in the garment, in Lv 13:57
the priest shall come **a** on the seventh Lv 14:39
the disease breaks out **a** in the house, Lv 14:43
will discipline you **a** sevenfold for your Lv 26:18
shall dole out your bread **a** by weight, Lv 26:26
the people of Israel also wept **a** and said, Nm 11:4
after that she may be brought in **a**." Nm 12:14
march till Miriam was brought in **a**. Nm 12:15
that there may never **a** be wrath on the Nm 18:5
Once **a** Balak sent princes, more in Nm 22:15
against the wall. So he struck her **a**. Nm 22:25
he will **a** abandon them in the Nm 32:15
us and bring us word **a** of the way by Dt 1:22
to us, and brought us word **a** and said, Dt 1:25
you; do not speak to me of this matter **a**. Dt 3:26
and fear and never **a** do any such Dt 13:11
be a heap forever. It shall not be built **a**. Dt 13:16
and fear and not act presumptuously **a**. Dt 17:13
'You shall never return that way **a**.' Dt 17:16
'Let me not hear **a** the voice of the LORD Dt 18:16
and shall never **a** commit any such evil Dt 19:20
You shall help him to lift them up **a**. Dt 22:4
away, may not take her **a** to be his wife, Dt 24:4
olive trees, you shall not go over them **a**. Dt 24:20
will bring upon you **a** all the diseases of Dt 28:60
that you should never make **a**; Dt 28:68
he will gather you **a** from all the peoples Dt 30:3
And you shall **a** obey the voice of the Dt 30:8
For the LORD will **a** take delight in Dt 30:9
who hate him, that they rise not **a**." Dt 33:11
and I brought him word **a** as it was in Jos 14:7
the people of Israel **a** did what was evil Jgs 3:12
the people of Israel **a** did what was evil Jgs 4:1
men of Penuel, "When I come **a** in peace, Jgs 8:9
of Israel turned **a** and whored after Jgs 8:33
Gaal spoke **a** and said, "Look, people are Jgs 9:37
The people of Israel **a** did what was evil Jgs 10:6
you bring me home **a** to fight with the Jgs 11:9
Jephthah **a** sent messengers to the king Jgs 11:14
the people of Israel **a** did what was evil Jgs 13:1

whom you sent come **a** to us and teach Jgs 13:8
angel of God came **a** to the woman as Jgs 13:9
of the Philistines, saying, "Come up **a**, Jgs 16:18
head began to grow **a** after it had been Jgs 16:22
him, till he spent the night there **a**. Jgs 19:7
and **a** formed the battle line in the Jgs 20:22
"Shall we **a** draw near to fight against Jgs 20:23
they lifted up their voices and wept **a**. Ru 1:14
lie down **a**." So he went and lay down. 1 Sm 3:5
And the LORD called **a**, "Samuel!" and 1 Sm 3:6
"I did not call, my son; lie down **a**." 1 Sm 3:6
LORD called Samuel **a** the third time. 1 Sm 3:8
And the LORD appeared **a** at Shiloh, for 1 Sm 3:21
and did not **a** enter the territory 1 Sm 7:13
The servant answered Saul **a**, "Here, I 1 Sm 9:8
So they inquired **a** of the LORD, "Is 1 Sm 10:22
did not see Saul **a** until the day of 1 Sm 15:35
the people answered him **a** as before. 1 Sm 17:30
And there was war **a**. And David went 1 Sm 19:8
Saul sent messengers **a** the third 1 Sm 19:21
But David vowed **a**, saying, "Your 1 Sm 20:3
made David swear **a** by his love 1 Sm 20:17
Then David inquired of the LORD **a**. 1 Sm 23:4
And Abner said **a** to Asahel, "Turn 2 Sm 2:22
And all the people wept **a** over him. 2 Sm 3:34
came up yet **a** and spread out 2 Sm 5:22
David **a** gathered all the chosen men of 2 Sm 6:1
I fast? Can I bring him back **a**? 2 Sm 12:23
me, and he shall never touch you **a**." 2 Sm 14:10
not bring his banished one home **a**. 2 Sm 14:13
which cannot be gathered up **a**. 2 Sm 14:14
And **a**, whom should I serve? Should 2 Sm 16:19
the son of Zadok said **a** to Joab, 2 Sm 18:22
There was war **a** between the 2 Sm 21:15
After this there was **a** war with the 2 Sm 21:18
And there was **a** war with the 2 Sm 21:19
And there was **a** war at Gath, where 2 Sm 21:20
A the anger of the LORD was kindled 2 Sm 24:1
Benaiah brought the king word **a**, 1 Kgs 2:30
and if they turn **a** to you and 1 Kgs 8:33
Israel and bring them **a** to the land 1 Kgs 8:34
Never **a** came such an abundance 1 Kgs 10:10
then come **a** to me." So the people 1 Kgs 12:5
said, "Come to me **a** the third day." 1 Kgs 12:12
word of the LORD and went home **a**, 1 Kgs 12:24
this people will turn **a** to their lord, 1 Kgs 12:27
the high places **a** from among all 1 Kgs 13:33
let this child's life come into him **a**." 1 Kgs 17:21
the life of the child came into him **a**, 1 Kgs 17:22
And he said, "Go **a**," seven times. 1 Kgs 18:43
he ate and drank and lay down **a**. 1 Kgs 19:6
of the LORD came **a** a second time and 1 Kgs 19:7
And he said to him, "Go back **a**, 1 Kgs 19:20
The messengers came **a** and said, 1 Kgs 20:5
departed and brought him word **a**. 1 Kgs 20:9
A the king sent to him another 2 Kgs 1:11
A the king sent the captain of a third 2 Kgs 1:13
to the man of God and come back **a**." 2 Kgs 4:22
Then he got up **a** and walked once 2 Kgs 4:35
And Elisha came **a** to Gilgal when 2 Kgs 4:38
Syrians did not come **a** on raids into 2 Kgs 6:23
A the watchman reported, "He 2 Kgs 9:20
of Jehoahaz took **a** from Ben-hadad 2 Kgs 13:25
So he sent messengers **a** to Hezekiah, 2 Kgs 19:9
of Judah shall **a** take root downward 2 Kgs 19:30
Egypt did not come **a** out of his land, 2 Kgs 24:7
the first to dwell **a** in their possessions 1 Chr 9:2
Then let us bring **a** the ark of our 1 Chr 13:3
the Philistines yet **a** made a raid 1 Chr 14:13
And when David **a** inquired of God, 1 Chr 14:14
And there was **a** war with the 1 Chr 20:5
And there was **a** war at Gath, where 1 Chr 20:6
and they turn **a** and acknowledge 2 Chr 6:24
Israel and bring them **a** to the land 2 Chr 6:25
"Come to me **a** in three days." So the 2 Chr 10:5
said, "Come to me **a** the third day." 2 Chr 10:12
And he went out **a** among the people, 2 Chr 19:4
to him from Ephraim to go home **a**. 2 Chr 25:10
the Edomites had **a** invaded and 2 Chr 28:17
that he may turn **a** to the remnant of 2 Chr 30:6
and brought him **a** to Jerusalem 2 Chr 33:13
your commandments **a** and intermarry Ezr 9:14
they had rest they did evil **a** before you, Neh 9:28
If you do so **a**, I will lay hands on Neh 13:21
that Vashti is never **a** to come before Est 1:19
She would not go in to the king **a**, unless Est 2:14
after the feast, the king **a** said to Esther, Est 7:2
Then Esther spoke **a** to the king. She fell Est 8:3
A there was a day when the sons of God Jb 2:1
is a breath; my eye will never **a** see good. Jb 7:7
like a lion and **a** work wonders against Jb 10:16
tree, if it be cut down, that it will sprout **a**, Jb 14:7
so a man lies down and rises not **a**; till Jb 14:12
If a man dies, shall he live **a**? All the Jb 14:14
But you, come on **a**, all of you, and I Jb 17:10

down riches and vomits them up **a**; Jb 20:15
And Job **a** took up his discourse, and Jb 27:1
And Job **a** took up his discourse, and Jb 29:1
After I spoke they did not speak **a**, and Jb 29:22
the battle—you will not do it **a**! Jb 41:8
slept; I woke **a**, for the LORD sustained me. Ps 3:5
Look away from me, that I may smile **a**, Ps 39:13
he will not rise **a** from where he lies." Ps 41:8
for I shall **a** praise him, my salvation Ps 42:5
for I shall **a** praise him, my salvation Ps 42:11
for I shall **a** praise him, my salvation Ps 43:5
of his fathers, who will never **a** see light. Ps 49:19
and calamities will revive me **a**; Ps 71:20
of the earth you will bring me up **a**. Ps 71:20
my greatness and comfort me **a**. Ps 71:21
spurn forever, and never **a** be favorable? Ps 77:7
a wind that passes and comes not **a**. Ps 78:39
They tested God **a** and again and Ps 78:41
God again and **a** and provoked the Ps 78:41
Turn **a**, O God of hosts! Look down Ps 80:14
Restore us **a**, O God of our salvation, and Ps 85:4
Will you not revive us **a**, that your Ps 85:6
so that they might not **a** cover the earth. Ps 104:9
say to your neighbor, "Go, and come **a**, Prv 3:28
him, you will only have to do it **a**. Prv 19:19
righteous falls seven times and rises **a**, Prv 24:16
the streams flow, there they flow **a**. Eccl 1:7
A I saw all the oppressions that are done Eccl 4:1
A, I saw vanity under the sun: Eccl 4:7
A, if two lie together, they keep warm, Eccl 4:11
from his mother's womb he shall go **a**, Eccl 5:15
A I saw that under the sun the race is Eccl 9:11
a tenth remain in it, it will be burned **a**, Is 6:13
A the LORD spoke to Ahaz, Is 7:10
The LORD spoke to me **a**: Is 8:5
on Jacob and will **a** choose Israel, Is 14:1
you will inquire, inquire; come back **a**." Is 21:12
upon it, and it falls, and will not rise **a**. Is 24:20
I will **a** do wonderful things with this Is 29:14
of Judah shall **a** take root downward Is 37:31
"I will not **a** give your grain to be food for Is 62:8
or missed; it shall not be made **a**. Jer 3:16
pass your hand **a** over its branches." Jer 6:9
LORD: When men fall, do they not rise **a**? Jer 8:4
one to spread my tent **a** and to set up Jer 10:20
A the LORD said to me, "A conspiracy Jer 11:9
up, I will **a** have compassion on them, Jer 12:15
I will bring them **a** each to his heritage Jer 12:15
die, and he shall never see this land **a**." Jer 22:12
throne of David and ruling **a** in Judah." Jer 22:30
A I will build you, and you shall be Jer 31:4
A you shall adorn yourself with Jer 31:4
A you shall plant vineyards on the Jer 31:5
and vineyards shall **a** be bought in Jer 32:15
or beast, there shall be heard **a** Jer 33:10
there shall **a** be habitations of Jer 33:12
flocks shall **a** pass under the hands of Jer 33:13
so that they would not be enslaved **a**. Jer 34:10
She shall never **a** have people, nor be Jer 50:39
he turns his hand **a** and again the Lam 3:3
his hand again and **a** the whole day Lam 3:3
A, if a righteous person turns from his Ezk 3:20
And of these **a** you shall take some and Ezk 5:4
and the like of which I will never do **a**. Ezk 5:9
A the word of the LORD came to me: Ezk 16:1
"When I passed by you **a** and saw you, Ezk 16:8
open your mouth **a** because of your Ezk 16:63
A, when a wicked person turns away Ezk 18:27
its sheath; it shall not be sheathed **a**. Ezk 21:5
The word of the LORD came to me **a**: Ezk 21:18
sought for, you will never be found **a**, Ezk 26:21
and never **a** exalt itself above the Ezk 29:15
that they will never **a** rule over the Ezk 29:15
And it shall never **a** be the reliance of Ezk 29:16
A, though I say to the wicked, 'You Ezk 33:14
you may never **a** suffer the disgrace Ezk 36:30
A he measured a thousand, and led me Ezk 47:4
A he measured a thousand, and led me Ezk 47:4
A he measured a thousand, and it was a Ezk 47:5
it shall be built **a** with squares and Dn 9:25
A one having the appearance of a man Dn 10:18
and **a** shall carry the war as far as his Dn 11:10
of the north shall **a** raise a multitude, Dn 11:13
She conceived **a** and bore a daughter. Hos 1:6
And the LORD said to me, "Go **a**, love a Hos 3:1
I will return **a** to my place, until they Hos 5:15
anger; I will not **a** destroy Ephraim; Hos 11:9
I will **a** make you dwell in tents, as in Hos 12:9
nor will be **a** after them through the years Jl 2:2
my people shall never **a** be put to shame. Jl 2:26
my people shall never **a** be put to shame. Jl 2:27
strangers shall never **a** pass through it. Jl 3:17
people Israel; I will never **a** pass by them; Am 7:8
but never **a** prophesy at Bethel, for it is Am 7:13
people Israel; I will never **a** pass by them. Am 8:2

the Nile, and be tossed about and sink **a**, Am 8:8
lives,' they shall fall, and never rise **a**." Am 8:14
all of it rises like the Nile, and sinks **a**, Am 9:5
and they shall never **a** be uprooted out Am 9:15
Yet I shall **a** look upon your holy temple.' Jon 2:4
I will **a** bring a conqueror to you, Mi 1:15
He will **a** have compassion on us; he will Mi 7:19
for never **a** shall the worthless pass Na 1:15
your midst; you shall never **a** fear evil. Zep 3:15
Cry out **a**, Thus says the LORD of hosts: Zec 1:17
My cities shall **a** overflow with Zec 1:17
and the LORD will **a** comfort Zion and Zec 1:17
comfort Zion and **a** choose Jerusalem.'" Zec 1:17
land, and will **a** choose Jerusalem." Zec 2:12
talked with me came **a** and woke me, Zec 4:1
A I lifted my eyes and saw, and behold, a Zec 5:1
A I lifted my eyes and saw, and behold, Zec 6:1
and old women shall **a** sit in the streets Zec 8:4
so **a** have I purposed in these days to Zec 8:15
no oppressor shall **a** march over them, Zec 9:8
while Jerusalem shall **a** be inhabited in Zec 12:6
And if anyone **a** prophesies, his father Zec 13:3
for there shall never **a** be a decree of Zec 14:11
Jesus said to him, "**A** it is written, 'You Mt 4:7
A, the devil took him to a very high Mt 4:8
"**A** you have heard that it was said to Mt 5:33
"**A**, the kingdom of heaven is like a Mt 13:45
"**A**, the kingdom of heaven is like a net Mt 13:47
A I say to you, if two of you agree on Mt 18:19
A I tell you, it is easier for a camel to go Mt 19:24
Going out **a** about the sixth hour and Mt 20:5
ever come from you **a**!" And the fig tree Mt 21:19
A he sent other servants, more than the Mt 21:36
And **a** Jesus spoke to them in parables, Mt 22:1
A he sent other servants, saying, 'Tell Mt 22:4
For I tell you, you will not see me **a**, Mt 23:39
you I will not drink **a** of this fruit of the Mt 26:29
A, for the second time, he went away Mt 26:42
And **a** he came and found them Mt 26:43
So, leaving them **a**, he went away and Mt 26:44
third time, saying the same words **a**. Mt 26:44
And **a** he denied it with an oath: "I do Mt 26:72
The governor **a** said to them, "Which Mt 27:21
And Jesus cried out **a** with a loud voice Mt 27:50
He went out **a** beside the sea, and all the Mk 2:13
A he entered the synagogue, and a man Mk 3:1
went home, and the crowd gathered **a**, Mk 3:20
A he began to teach beside the sea. And a Mk 4:1
when Jesus had crossed **a** in the boat to Mk 5:21
the people to him **a** and said to them, Mk 7:14
days, when **a** a great crowd had gathered, Mk 8:1
And he left them, got into the boat **a**, Mk 8:13
Then Jesus laid his hands on his eyes **a**; Mk 8:25
and be killed, and after three days rise **a**. Mk 8:31
out of him and never enter him **a**." Mk 9:25
saltiness, how will you make it salty **a**? Mk 9:50
Jordan, and crowds gathered to him **a**. Mk 10:1
crowds gathered to him again. And **a**, Mk 10:1
disciples asked him **a** about this Mk 10:10
But Jesus said to them **a**, "Children, Mk 10:24
And taking the twelve **a**, he began to Mk 10:32
eat fruit from you **a**." And his disciples Mk 11:14
And they came **a** to Jerusalem. And as Mk 11:27
A he sent to them another servant, and Mk 12:4
In the resurrection, when they rise **a**, Mk 12:23
I will not drink **a** of the fruit of the Mk 14:25
And **a** he went away and prayed, Mk 14:39
And **a** he came and found them Mk 14:40
A the high priest asked him, "Are you Mk 14:61
girl saw him and began **a** to say to the Mk 14:69
But **a** he denied it. And after a little Mk 14:70
while the bystanders **a** said to Peter, Mk 14:70
And Pilate **a** asked him, "Have you no Mk 15:4
And Pilate **a** said to them, "Then what Mk 15:12
And they cried out **a**, "Crucify him." Mk 15:13
nor **a** does a bad tree bear good fruit, Lk 6:43
And **a** he said, "To what shall I Lk 13:20
this my son was dead, and is alive **a**; Lk 15:24
And when you have turned **a**, Lk 22:32
The next day **a** John was standing with Jn 1:35
unless one is born **a** he cannot see the Jn 3:3
that I said to you, 'You must be born **a**.' Jn 3:7
he left Judea and departed **a** for Galilee. Jn 4:3
who drinks of this water will be thirsty **a**, Jn 4:13
So he came **a** to Cana in Galilee, where Jn 4:46
Jesus withdrew **a** to the mountain by Jn 6:15
in the morning he came **a** to the temple. Jn 8:2
A Jesus spoke to them, saying, "I am the Jn 8:12
So he said to them **a**, "I am going away, Jn 8:21
So the Pharisees **a** asked him how he had Jn 9:15
So they said **a** to the blind man, "What Jn 9:17
not listen. Why do you want to hear it **a**? Jn 9:27
So Jesus **a** said to them, "Truly, truly, I Jn 10:7
lay down my life that I may take it up **a**. Jn 10:17
and I have authority to take it up **a**. Jn 10:18

There was **a** a division among the Jews Jn 10:19
Jews picked up stones **a** to stone him. Jn 10:31
A they sought to arrest him, but he Jn 10:39
He went away **a** across the Jordan to the Jn 10:40
to the disciples, "Let us go to Judea **a**." Jn 11:7
to stone you, and are you going there **a**?" Jn 11:8
said to her, "Your brother will rise **a**." Jn 11:23
that he will rise **a** in the resurrection on Jn 11:24
Then Jesus, deeply moved **a**, came to the Jn 11:38
have glorified it, and I will glorify it **a**." Jn 12:28
they could not believe. For **a** Isaiah said, Jn 12:39
I will come **a** and will take you to myself, Jn 14:3
and **a** a little while, and you will see Jn 16:16
you will not see me, and **a** a little while, Jn 16:17
and **a** a little while and you will see me'? Jn 16:19
but I will see you **a** and your hearts will Jn 16:22
So he asked them **a**, "Whom do you Jn 18:7
Peter **a** denied it, and at once a rooster Jn 18:27
entered his headquarters **a** and called Jn 18:33
They cried out **a**, "Not this man, but Jn 18:40
Pilate went out **a** and said to them, "See, I Jn 19:4
He entered his headquarters **a** and said to Jn 19:9
And **a** another Scripture says, "They Jn 19:37
Jesus said to them **a**, "Peace be with you. Jn 20:21
days later, his disciples were inside **a**, Jn 20:26
Jesus revealed himself **a** to the disciples Jn 21:1
Repent therefore, and turn **a**, that your Acts 3:19
voice came to him **a** a second time, Acts 10:15
and all was drawn up **a** into heaven. Acts 11:10
said, "We will hear you **a** about this." Acts 17:32
the kingdom will see my face **a**. Acts 20:25
that they would not see his face **a**. Acts 20:38
took a sounding **a** and found fifteen Acts 27:28
raised from the dead will never die **a**; Rom 6:9
God has the power to graft them in **a**. Rom 11:23
For to this end Christ died and lived **a**, Rom 14:9
And **a** it is said, "Rejoice, O Gentiles, Rom 15:10
And **a**, "Praise the Lord, all you Rom 15:11
And **a** Isaiah says, "The root of Jesse Rom 15:12
and **a**, "The Lord knows the thoughts 1 Cor 3:20
but then come together **a**, so that 1 Cor 7:5
need of you," nor **a** the head to the 1 Cor 12:21
set our hope that he will deliver us **a**. 2 Cor 1:10
I refrained from coming **a** to Corinth. 2 Cor 1:23
beginning to commend ourselves **a**? 2 Cor 3:1
ourselves to you **a** but giving you 2 Cor 5:12
that when I come **a** my God may 2 Cor 12:21
that if I come **a** I will not spare them 2 Cor 13:2
As we have said before, so now I say **a**: If Gal 1:9
Arabia, and returned **a** to Damascus. Gal 1:17
years I went up **a** to Jerusalem with Gal 2:1
can you turn back **a** to the weak and Gal 4:9
for whom I am **a** in the anguish of Gal 4:19
and do not submit **a** to a yoke of slavery. Gal 5:1
I testify **a** to every man who accepts Gal 5:3
Jesus, because of my coming to you **a**. Phil 1:26
that you may rejoice at seeing him **a**, Phil 2:28
in the Lord always; **a** I will say, Rejoice. Phil 4:4
sent me help for my needs once and **a**. Phil 4:16
a and again—but Satan hindered 1 Thes 2:18
again and **a**—but Satan hindered 1 Thes 2:18
we believe that Jesus died and rose **a**, 1 Thes 4:14
Son, today I have begotten you"? Or **a**, Heb 1:5
And **a**, when he brings the firstborn into Heb 1:6
And **a**, "I will put my trust in him." Heb 2:13
"I will put my trust in him." And **a**, Heb 2:13
And **a** in this passage he said, "They Heb 4:5
a he appoints a certain day, "Today," Heb 4:7
to teach you **a** the basic principles Heb 5:12
not laying **a** a foundation of repentance Heb 6:1
impossible to restore **a** to repentance Heb 6:4
they are crucifying once **a** the Son of Heb 6:6
I will repay." And **a**, "The Lord will Heb 10:30
that they might rise **a** to a better life. Heb 11:35
of peace who brought **a** from the dead Heb 13:20
Then he prayed **a**, and heaven gave rain, Jas 5:18
caused us to be born **a** to a living hope 1 Pt 1:3
since you have been born **a**, not of 1 Pt 1:23
they are **a** entangled in them and 2 Pt 2:20
I had heard from heaven spoke to me **a**, Rv 10:8
"You must **a** prophesy about many Rv 10:11
are lost to you, never to be found **a**!" Rv 18:14

AGATE (4)
and the third row a jacinth, an **a**, and Ex 28:19
and the third row, a jacinth, an **a**, and Ex 39:12
I will make your pinnacles of **a**, your Is 54:12
jasper, the second sapphire, the third **a**, Rv 21:19

AGE (57)
you shall be buried in a good old **a**. Gn 15:15
a son in his old **a** at the time of which Gn 21:2
Yet I have borne him a son in his old **a**." Gn 21:7
his last and died in a good old **a**, Gn 25:8
because he was the son of his old **a**. Gn 37:3
a young brother, the child of his old **a**. Gn 44:20
Now the eyes of Israel were dim with **a**, Gn 48:10
And from the **a** of fifty years they shall Nm 8:25
of the LORD, died at the **a** of 110 years. Jgs 2:8
died in a good old **a** and was buried in Jgs 8:32
of life and a nourisher of your old **a**, Ru 4:15
for his eyes were dim because of his **a**. 1 Kgs 14:4
But in his old **a** he was diseased in 1 Kgs 15:23
count those below twenty years of **a**, 1 Chr 27:23
Then he died at a good **a**, full of 1 Chr 29:28
shall come to your grave in ripe old **a**, Jb 5:26
Why do the wicked live, reach old **a**, and Jb 21:7
Do not cast me off in the time of old **a**; Ps 71:9
So even to old **a** and gray hairs, O God, Ps 71:18
They still bear fruit in old **a**; they are Ps 92:14
even to your old **a** I am he, and to gray Is 46:4
you majestic forever, a joy from **a** to age. Is 60:15
you majestic forever, a joy from age to **a**. Is 60:15
you, behold, you were at the **a** for love, Ezk 16:8
than the youths who are of your own **a**? Dn 1:10
with staff in hand because of great **a**. Zec 8:4
either in this **a** or in the age to come. Mt 12:32
either in this age or in the **a** to come. Mt 12:32
The harvest is the close of the **a**, and Mt 13:39
fire, so will it be at the close of the **a**. Mt 13:40
So it will be at the close of the **a**. The Mt 13:49
your coming and of the close of the **a**?" Mt 24:3
with you always, to the end of the **a**." Mt 28:20
walking (for she was twelve years of **a**), Mk 5:42
and in the **a** to come eternal life. Mk 10:30
in her old **a** has also conceived Lk 1:36
his ministry, was about thirty years of **a**, Lk 3:23
only daughter, about twelve years of **a**, Lk 8:42
time, and in the **a** to come eternal life." Lk 18:30
"The sons of this **a** marry and are Lk 20:34
to attain to that **a** and to the Lk 20:35
who opened his eyes. Ask him; he is of **a**. Jn 9:21
Therefore his parents said, "He is of **a**; Jn 9:23
Where is the debater of this **a**? 1 Cor 1:20
not a wisdom of this **a** or of the rulers 1 Cor 2:6
of this age or of the rulers of this **a**, 1 Cor 2:6
of the rulers of this **a** understood this, 1 Cor 2:8
you thinks that he is wise in this **a**, 1 Cor 3:18
sins to deliver us from the present evil **a**, Gal 1:4
many of my own **a** among my people, Gal 1:14
not only in this **a** but also in the one to Eph 1:21
if she is not less than sixty years of **a**, 1 Tm 5:9
As for the rich in this present **a**, 1 Tm 6:17
upright, and godly lives in the present **a**, Ti 2:12
of God and the powers of the **a** to come, Heb 6:5
(which is symbolic for the present **a**). Heb 9:9
even when she was past the **a**, Heb 11:11

AGED (12)
Barzillai was a very **a** man, eighty 2 Sm 19:32
young man or virgin, old man or **a**. 2 Chr 36:17
Wisdom is with the **a**, and Jb 12:12
the gray-haired and the **a** are among us, Jb 15:10
and withdrew, and the **a** rose and stood; Jb 29:8
said: "I am young in years, and you are **a**; Jb 32:6
nor the **a** who understand what is right. Jb 32:9
I understand more than the **a**, for I Ps 119:100
Grandchildren are the crown of the **a**, Prv 17:6
full of marrow, of **a** wine well refined. Is 25:6
on the **a** you made your yoke exceedingly Is 47:6
shall be taken, the elderly and the very **a**. Jer 6:11

AGEE (1)
Shammah, the son of **A** the Hararite. 2 Sm 23:11

AGENTS (1)
governors and the royal **a** also helped the Est 9:3

AGES (14)
"For inquire, please, of bygone **a**, and Jb 8:8
renown, O LORD, throughout all **a**. Ps 135:13
A ago I was set up, at the first, before the Prv 8:23
It has been already in the **a** before us. Eccl 1:10
that was kept secret for long **a** Rom 16:25
God decreed before the **a** for our glory. 1 Cor 2:7
on whom the end of the **a** has come. 1 Cor 10:11
that in the coming **a** he might show the Eph 2:7
the mystery hidden for **a** in God who Eph 3:9
mystery hidden for **a** and generations Col 1:26
To the King of **a**, immortal, invisible, 1 Tm 1:17
us in Christ Jesus before the **a** began, 2 Tm 1:9
never lies, promised before the **a** began Ti 1:2
all at the end of the **a** to put away sin by Heb 9:26

AGHAST (1)
in labor. They will look **a** at one another; Is 13:8

AGILE (1)
his arms were made **a** by the hands of Gn 49:24

AGITATING (1)
too, **a** and stirring up the crowds. Acts 17:13

AGO (26)
says the LORD, the God of Israel, 'Long **a**, Jos 24:2
donkeys that were lost three days **a**, 1 Sm 9:20
because I fell sick three days **a**. 1 Sm 30:13
heard that I determined it long **a**? 2 Kgs 19:25
the house that was built many years **a**, Ezr 5:11
For long **a** in the days of David and Neh 12:46
consider the days of old, the years long **a**. Ps 77:5
Ages **a** I was set up, at the first, before Prv 8:23
did it, or see him who planned it long **a**. Is 22:11
not heard that I determined it long **a**? Is 37:26
counsel together! Who told this long **a**? Is 45:21
They are created now, not long **a**; before Is 48:7
in days of old, the generations of long **a**. Is 51:9
"For long **a** I broke your yoke and burst Jer 2:20
word, which he commanded long **a**; Lam 2:17
in darkness like the dead of long **a**. Lam 3:6
have repented long **a** in sackcloth and Mt 11:21
Sidon, they would have repented long **a**, Lk 10:13
the mouth of his holy prophets long **a**. Acts 3:21
And Cornelius said, "Four days **a**, Acts 10:30
who a year **a** started not only to do 2 Cor 8:10
who fourteen years **a** was caught up 2 Cor 12:2
Long **a**, at many times and in many Heb 1:1
condemnation from long **a** is not idle, 2 Pt 2:3
this fact, that the heavens existed long **a**, 2 Pt 3:5
unnoticed who long **a** were designated Jude 1:4

AGONY (5)
of the disease, and he died in great **a**. 2 Chr 21:19
be dismayed: pangs and **a** will seize them; Is 13:8
to Egypt; Pelusium shall be in great **a**; Ezk 30:16
And being in an **a** he prayed more Lk 22:44
in birth pains and the **a** of giving birth. Rv 12:2

AGREE (15)
this condition will we **a** with you— Gn 34:15
condition will the men **a** to dwell with Gn 34:22
Only let us **a** with them, and they will Gn 34:23
"**A** with God, and be at peace; thereby Jb 22:21
if two of you **a** on earth about anything Mt 18:19
Did you not **a** with me for a denarius? Mt 20:13
him, but their testimony did not **a**. Mk 14:56
about this their testimony did not **a**. Mk 14:59
with this the words of the prophets **a**, Acts 15:15
do what I do not want, I **a** with the law, Rom 7:16
that all of you **a** and that there be no 1 Cor 1:10
one another, **a** with one another, 2 Cor 13:11
and I entreat Syntyche to **a** in the Lord. Phil 4:2
doctrine and does not **a** with the sound 1 Tm 6:3
water and the blood; and these three **a**. 1 Jn 5:8

AGREED (11)
the frogs, as he had **a** with Pharaoh. Ex 8:12
So the priests **a** that they should take 2 Kgs 12:8
All the assembly **a** to do so, for the 1 Chr 13:4
the whole assembly **a** together to 2 Chr 30:23
You have **a** to speak lying and corrupt Dn 2:9
and the governors are **a** that the king Dn 6:7
together, unless they have **a** to meet? Am 3:3
they were glad, and **a** to give him money. Lk 22:5
the Jews had already **a** that if anyone Jn 9:22
is it that you have **a** together to test the Acts 5:9
"The Jews have **a** to ask you to bring Acts 23:20

AGREEING (1)
After **a** with the laborers for a denarius a Mt 20:2

AGREEMENT (9)
with death, and with Sheol we have an **a**, Is 28:15
and your **a** with Sheol will not stand; Is 28:18
and satraps came by **a** to the king and Dn 6:6
these men came by **a** and found Daniel Dn 6:11
these men came by **a** to the king and Dn 6:15
to the king of the north to make an **a**. Dn 11:6
bring terms of an **a** and perform them. Dn 11:17
except perhaps by **a** for a limited time, 1 Cor 7:5
What **a** has the temple of God with 2 Cor 6:16

AGRIPPA (11)
A the king and Bernice arrived at Acts 25:13
Then **A** said to Festus, "I would like Acts 25:22
on the next day **A** and Bernice came Acts 25:23
"King **A** and all who are present with Acts 25:24
all, and especially before you, King **A**, Acts 25:26
So **A** said to Paul, "You have Acts 26:1
fortunate that it is before you, King **A**, Acts 26:2
"Therefore, O King **A**, I was not Acts 26:19
King **A**, do you believe the prophets? I Acts 26:27
And **A** said to Paul, "In a short time Acts 26:28
And **A** said to Festus, "This man Acts 26:32

AGROUND (3)
that they would run **a** on the Syrtis, Acts 27:17
But we must run **a** on some island." Acts 27:26
striking a reef, they ran the vessel **a**. Acts 27:41

AGUR (1)
The words of **A** son of Jakeh. The Prv 30:1

AH (29)
A, sinful nation, a people laden with Is 1:4
"**A**, I will get relief from my enemies and Is 1:24

A, Assyria, the rod of my anger; the staff Is 10:5
A, the thunder of many peoples; they Is 17:12
A, the roar of nations; they roar like the Is 17:12
A, land of whirring wings that is beyond Is 18:1
A, the proud crown of the drunkards of Is 28:1
A, Ariel, Ariel, the city where David Is 29:1
A, you who hide deep from the LORD Is 29:15
"**A**, stubborn children," declares the Is 30:1
A, you destroyer, who yourself have not Is 33:1
Then I said, "**A**, Lord GOD! Behold, I do not Jer 1:6
Then I said, "**A**, Lord GOD, surely you Jer 4:10
"**A**, Lord GOD, behold, the prophets say Jer 14:13
for him, saying, '**A**, my brother!' Jer 22:18
for him, saying, 'Ah, my brother!' or '**A**, Jer 22:18
not lament for him, saying, '**A**, lord!' Jer 22:18
for him, saying, 'Ah, lord!' or '**A**, Jer 22:18
'**A**, Lord GOD! It is you who has made Jer 32:17
A, sword of the LORD! How long till you Jer 47:6
A, this is the day we longed for; now we Lam 2:16
Then I said, "**A**, Lord GOD! Behold, I Ezk 4:14
upon my face, and cried, "**A**, Lord GOD! Ezk 9:8
a loud voice and said, "**A**, Lord GOD! Ezk 11:13
Then I said, "**A**, Lord GOD! They are Ezk 20:49
A, it is made like lightning; it is taken Ezk 21:15
A, shepherds of Israel who have been Ezk 34:2
Ephraim has said, "**A**, but I am rich; I Hos 12:8
"**A**, now you are speaking plainly and Jn 16:29

AHA (13)
When the trumpet sounds, he says '**A**!' Jb 39:25
mouths against me; they say, "**A**, Aha! Ps 35:21
say, "Aha, **A**! our eyes have seen it!" Ps 35:21
"**A**, our heart's desire!" Let them not Ps 35:25
of their shame who say to me, "**A**, Aha!" Ps 40:15
of their shame who say to me, "Aha, **A**!" Ps 40:15
of their shame who say, "**A**, Aha!" Ps 70:3
of their shame who say, "Aha, **A**!" Ps 70:3
warms himself and says, "**A**, I am warm, Is 44:16
'**A**!' over my sanctuary when it was Ezk 25:3
'**A**, the gate of the peoples is broken; Ezk 26:2
Because the enemy said of you, '**A**!' and, Ezk 36:2
"**A**! You who would destroy the temple Mk 15:29

AHAB (93)
and **A** his son reigned in his place. 1 Kgs 16:28
A the son of Omri began to reign 1 Kgs 16:29
and **A** the son of Omri reigned over 1 Kgs 16:29
And **A** the son of Omri did evil in 1 Kgs 16:30
And **A** made an Asherah. Ahab did 1 Kgs 16:33
A did more to provoke the LORD, the 1 Kgs 16:33
of Tishbe in Gilead, said to **A**, 1 Kgs 17:1
year, saying, "Go, show yourself to **A**, 1 Kgs 18:1
So Elijah went to show himself to **A**. 1 Kgs 18:2
And **A** called Obadiah, who was over 1 Kgs 18:3
And **A** said to Obadiah, "Go through 1 Kgs 18:5
A went in one direction by himself, 1 Kgs 18:6
give your servant into the hand of **A**, 1 Kgs 18:9
I come and tell **A** and he cannot find 1 Kgs 18:12
So Obadiah went to meet **A**, and told 1 Kgs 18:16
told him. And **A** went to meet Elijah. 1 Kgs 18:16
When **A** saw Elijah, Ahab said to 1 Kgs 18:17
Ahab saw Elijah, **A** said to him, 1 Kgs 18:17
So **A** sent to all the people of Israel 1 Kgs 18:20
And Elijah said to **A**, "Go up, eat and 1 Kgs 18:41
So **A** went up to eat and to drink. 1 Kgs 18:42
sea." And he said, "Go up, say to **A**, 1 Kgs 18:44
rain. And **A** rode and went to Jezreel. 1 Kgs 18:45
and ran before **A** to the entrance 1 Kgs 18:46
A told Jezebel all that Elijah had 1 Kgs 19:1
into the city to **A** king of Israel and 1 Kgs 20:2
came near to **A** king of Israel 1 Kgs 20:13
And **A** said, "By whom?" He said, 1 Kgs 20:14
father did in Samaria." And **A** said, 1 Kgs 20:34
the palace of **A** king of Samaria. 1 Kgs 21:1
And after this **A** said to Naboth, 1 Kgs 21:2
But Naboth said to **A**, "The LORD 1 Kgs 21:3
And **A** went into his house vexed and 1 Kgs 21:4
and was dead, Jezebel said to **A**, 1 Kgs 21:15
And as soon as **A** heard that Naboth 1 Kgs 21:16
A arose to go down to the vineyard 1 Kgs 21:16
go down to meet **A** king of Israel, 1 Kgs 21:18
A said to Elijah, "Have you found 1 Kgs 21:20
and will cut off from **A** every male, 1 Kgs 21:21
Anyone belonging to **A** who dies in 1 Kgs 21:24
evil in the sight of the LORD like **A**, 1 Kgs 21:25
And when **A** heard those words, he 1 Kgs 21:27
you seen how **A** has humbled 1 Kgs 21:29
the LORD said, 'Who will entice **A**, 1 Kgs 22:20
rest of the acts of **A** and all that he 1 Kgs 22:39
So **A** slept with his fathers, and 1 Kgs 22:40
in the fourth year of **A** king of Israel. 1 Kgs 22:41
the son of **A** said to Jehoshaphat, 1 Kgs 22:49
Ahaziah the son of **A** began to reign 1 Kgs 22:51
After the death of **A**, Moab rebelled 2 Kgs 1:1
the son of **A** became king over 2 Kgs 3:1
But when **A** died, the king of Moab 2 Kgs 3:5
In the fifth year of Joram the son of **A**, 2 Kgs 8:16
of Israel, as the house of **A** had done, 2 Kgs 8:18
for the daughter of **A** was his wife. 2 Kgs 8:18
the twelfth year of Joram the son of **A**, 2 Kgs 8:25
of the house of **A** and did what was 2 Kgs 8:27
the LORD, as the house of **A** had done, 2 Kgs 8:27
he was son-in-law to the house of **A**. 2 Kgs 8:27
Joram the son of **A** to make war 2 Kgs 8:28
to see Joram the son of **A** in Jezreel, 2 Kgs 8:29
down the house of **A** your master, 2 Kgs 9:7
For the whole house of **A** shall perish, 2 Kgs 9:8
and I will cut off from **A** every male, 2 Kgs 9:8
make the house of **A** like the house of 2 Kgs 9:9
rode side by side behind **A** his father, 2 Kgs 9:25
eleventh year of Joram the son of **A**, 2 Kgs 9:29
Now **A** had seventy sons in Samaria. 2 Kgs 10:1
and to the guardians of the sons of **A**, 2 Kgs 10:1
spoke concerning the house of **A**, 2 Kgs 10:10
of the house of **A** in Jezreel, 2 Kgs 10:11
all who remained to **A** in Samaria, 2 Kgs 10:17
said to them, "**A** served Baal a little, 2 Kgs 10:18
to the house of **A** according to all 2 Kgs 10:30
as **A** king of Israel had done, 2 Kgs 21:3
the plumb line of the house of **A**, 2 Kgs 21:13
he made a marriage alliance with **A**. 2 Chr 18:1
years he went down to **A** in Samaria. 2 Chr 18:2
And **A** killed an abundance of sheep 2 Chr 18:2
A king of Israel said to Jehoshaphat 2 Chr 18:3
'Who will entice **A** the king of 2 Chr 18:19
of Israel, as the house of **A** had done, 2 Chr 21:6
for the daughter of **A** was his wife. 2 Chr 21:6
as the house of **A** led Israel into 2 Chr 21:13
walked in the ways of the house of **A**, 2 Chr 22:3
the LORD, as the house of **A** had done. 2 Chr 22:4
Jehoram the son of **A** king of Israel to 2 Chr 22:5
to see Joram the son of **A** in Jezreel, 2 Chr 22:6
anointed to destroy the house of **A**. 2 Chr 22:7
judgment on the house of **A**, 2 Chr 22:8
concerning **A** the son of Kolaiah and Jer 29:21
LORD make you like Zedekiah and **A**, Jer 29:22
and all the works of the house of **A**; Mi 6:16

AHAB'S (1)
wrote letters in **A** name and sealed 1 Kgs 21:8

AHARAH (1)
Ashbel the second, **A** the third, 1 Chr 8:1

AHARHEL (1)
Anub, Zobebah, and the clans of **A**, 1 Chr 4:8

AHASBAI (1)
Eliphelet the son of **A** of Maacah, 2 Sm 23:34

AHASUERUS (31)
And in the reign of **A**, in the beginning of Ezr 4:6
Now in the days of **A**, the Ahasuerus who Est 1:1
the **A** who reigned from India to Ethiopia Est 1:1
those days when King **A** sat on his royal Est 1:2
in the palace that belonged to King **A**. Est 1:9
who served in the presence of King **A**, Est 1:10
command of King **A** delivered by the Est 1:15
who are in all the provinces of King **A**. Est 1:16
'King **A** commanded Queen Vashti to Est 1:17
is never again to come before King **A**. Est 1:19
when the anger of King **A** had abated, Est 2:1
each young woman to go in to King **A**, Est 2:12
was taken to King **A** into his royal Est 2:16
and sought to lay hands on King **A**. Est 2:21
these things King **A** promoted Haman Est 3:1
throughout the whole kingdom of **A**. Est 3:6
of Nisan, in the twelfth year of King **A**, Est 3:7
Then Haman said to King **A**, "There is a Est 3:8
the name of King **A** and sealed with the Est 3:12
who had sought to lay hands on King **A**. Est 6:2
Then King **A** said to Queen Esther, "Who Est 7:5
On that day King **A** gave to Queen Esther Est 8:1
Then King **A** said to Queen Esther and to Est 8:7
in the name of King **A** and sealed it with Est 8:10
throughout all the provinces of King **A**, Est 8:12
the provinces of King **A** to lay hands on Est 9:2
who were in all the provinces of King **A**, Est 9:20
the 127 provinces of the kingdom of **A**, Est 9:30
King **A** imposed tax on the land and on Est 10:1
the Jew was second in rank to King **A**, Est 10:3
In the first year of Darius the son of **A**, by Dn 9:1

AHAVA (3)
them to the river that runs to **A**, Ezr 8:15
I proclaimed a fast there, at the river **A**, Ezr 8:21
departed from the river **A** on the twelfth Ezr 8:31

AHAZ (45)
and **A** his son reigned in his place. 2 Kgs 15:38
son of Remaliah, **A** the son of Jotham, 2 Kgs 16:1
A was twenty years old when he 2 Kgs 16:2
and they besieged **A** but could not 2 Kgs 16:5
So **A** sent messengers to 2 Kgs 16:7
A also took the silver and gold that 2 Kgs 16:8
When King **A** went to Damascus to 2 Kgs 16:10
And King **A** sent to Uriah the priest 2 Kgs 16:10
with all that King **A** had sent from 2 Kgs 16:11
before King **A** arrived from 2 Kgs 16:11
And King **A** commanded Uriah the 2 Kgs 16:15
did all this, as King **A** commanded. 2 Kgs 16:16
And King **A** cut off the frames of the 2 Kgs 16:17
the rest of the acts of **A** that he did, 2 Kgs 16:19
And **A** slept with his fathers and was 2 Kgs 16:20
In the twelfth year of **A** king of Judah, 2 Kgs 17:1
king of Israel, Hezekiah the son of **A**, 2 Kgs 18:1
it had gone down on the steps of **A**. 2 Kgs 20:11
the roof of the upper chamber of **A**, 2 Kgs 23:12
A his son, Hezekiah his son, 1 Chr 3:13
Pithon, Melech, Tarea, and **A**. 1 Chr 8:35
A fathered Jehoaddah, and Jehoaddah 1 Chr 8:36
Pithon, Melech, Tahrea, and **A**. 1 Chr 9:41
And **A** fathered Jarah, and Jarah 1 Chr 9:42
and **A** his son reigned in his place. 2 Chr 27:9
A was twenty years old when he 2 Chr 28:1
At that time King **A** sent to the king 2 Chr 28:16
Judah because of **A** king of Israel, 2 Chr 28:19
For **A** took a portion from the house 2 Chr 28:21
to the LORD—this same King **A**. 2 Chr 28:22
And **A** gathered together the vessels 2 Chr 28:24
And **A** slept with his fathers, and 2 Chr 28:27
utensils that King **A** discarded in 2 Chr 29:19
days of Uzziah, Jotham, **A**, and Hezekiah, Is 1:1
In the days of **A** the son of Jotham, son of Is 7:1
Ephraim," the heart of **A** and the heart of Is 7:2
the LORD said to Isaiah, "Go out to meet **A**, Is 7:3
Again the LORD spoke to **A**, Is 7:10
But **A** said, "I will not ask, and I will not Is 7:12
the year that King **A** died came this Is 14:28
sun on the dial of **A** turn back ten steps." Is 38:8
of Uzziah, Jotham, **A**, and Hezekiah, Hos 1:1
in the days of Jotham, **A**, and Hezekiah, Mi 1:1
of Jotham, and Jotham the father of **A**, Mt 1:9
of Ahaz, and **A** the father of Hezekiah, Mt 1:9

AHAZIAH (39)
and **A** his son reigned in his place. 1 Kgs 22:40
Then **A** the son of Ahab said to 1 Kgs 22:49
A the son of Ahab began to reign 1 Kgs 22:51
Now **A** fell through the lattice in his 2 Kgs 1:2
king of Judah, because **A** had no son. 2 Kgs 1:17
the rest of the acts of **A** that he did, 2 Kgs 1:18
and **A** his son reigned in his place. 2 Kgs 8:24
king of Israel, **A** the son of Jehoram, 2 Kgs 8:25
A was twenty-two years old when he 2 Kgs 8:26
And **A** the son of Jehoram king of 2 Kgs 8:29
And **A** king of Judah had come down 2 Kgs 9:16
king of Israel and **A** king of Judah set 2 Kgs 9:21
reined about and fled, saying to **A**, 2 Kgs 9:23
saying to Ahaziah, "Treachery, O **A**!" 2 Kgs 9:23
When **A** the king of Judah saw this, 2 Kgs 9:27
of Ahab, **A** began to reign over Judah. 2 Kgs 9:29
met the relatives of **A** king of Judah, 2 Kgs 10:13
answered, "We are the relatives of **A**, 2 Kgs 10:13
the mother of **A** saw that her 2 Kgs 11:1
daughter of King Joram, sister of **A**, 2 Kgs 11:2
Joash the son of **A** and stole him 2 Kgs 11:2
and Jehoram and **A** his fathers, 2 Kgs 12:18
year of Joash the son of **A**, 2 Kgs 13:1
Judah, the son of Jehoash, son of **A**, 2 Kgs 14:13
Joram his son, **A** his son, Joash his 1 Chr 3:11
Judah joined with **A** king of Israel, 2 Chr 20:35
"Because you have joined with **A**, 2 Chr 20:37
of Jerusalem made **A** his youngest 2 Chr 22:1
So **A** the son of Jehoram king of 2 Chr 22:1
A was twenty-two years old when he 2 Chr 22:2
And **A** the son of Jehoram king of 2 Chr 22:6
the downfall of **A** should come about 2 Chr 22:7
Ahaziah's brothers, who attended **A**, 2 Chr 22:8
He searched for **A**, and he was 2 Chr 22:9
And the house of **A** had no one able 2 Chr 22:9
the mother of **A** saw that her 2 Chr 22:10
Joash the son of **A** and stole him 2 Chr 22:11
priest, because she was a sister of **A**, 2 Chr 22:11
of Judah, the son of Joash, son of **A**, 2 Chr 25:23

AHAZIAH'S (1)
of Judah and the sons of **A** brothers, 2 Chr 22:8

AHBAN (1)
and she bore him **A** and Molid. 1 Chr 2:29

AHEAD (30)
"Pass on **a** of me and put a space Gn 32:16
going? And whose are these **a** of you?' Gn 32:17
him with the present that goes **a** of me, Gn 32:20
So the present passed on **a** of him, and Gn 32:21
on our way, and I will go **a** of you." Gn 33:12
Let my lord pass on **a** of his servant, Gn 33:14
of the livestock that are **a** of me and at Gn 33:14
He had sent Judah **a** of him to Joseph to Gn 46:28
of the LORD went **a** and stood in a Nm 22:26

"He is; behold, he is just **a** of you. 1 Sm 9:12
arose and went to Ziph **a** of Saul. 1 Sm 23:24
Gehazi went on **a** and laid the staff on 2 Kgs 4:31
he had sent a man **a** of them, Joseph, Ps 105:17
of understanding walks straight **a**. Prv 15:21
but each shall go out straight **a**. Ezk 46:9
the breaches, each one straight **a**; Am 4:3
all the towns and got there **a** of them. Mk 6:33
and Jesus was walking **a** of them. Mk 10:32
And he sent messengers **a** of him, who Lk 9:52
others and sent them on **a** of him, Lk 10:1
So he ran on **a** and climbed up into a Lk 19:4
he had said these things, he went on **a**, Lk 19:28
These went on **a** and were waiting for Acts 20:5
But going **a** to the ship, we set sail for Acts 20:13
I decided to go **a** and send him. Acts 25:25
each one goes **a** with his own meal. 1 Cor 11:21
brothers to go on **a** to you and arrange 2 Cor 9:5
and straining forward to what lies **a**, Phil 3:13
the Lord may speed **a** and be honored, 2 Thes 3:1
Everyone who goes on **a** and does not 2 Jn 1:9

AHER (1)
the sons of Ir, Hushim the son of **A**. 1 Chr 7:12

AHI (1)
A the son of Abdiel, son of Guni, was 1 Chr 5:15

AHIAH (1)
A, Hanan, Anan, Neh 10:26

AHIAM (2)
A the son of Sharar the Hararite, 2 Sm 23:33
A the son of Sachar the Hararite, 1 Chr 11:35

AHIAN (1)
The sons of Shemida were **A**, 1 Chr 7:19

AHIEZER (6)
from Dan, **A** the son of Ammishaddai; Nm 1:12
people of Dan being **A** the son of Nm 2:25
On the tenth day **A** the son of Nm 7:66
was the offering of **A** the son of Nm 7:71
over their company was **A** the son of Nm 10:25
The chief was **A**, then Joash, both 1 Chr 12:3

AHIHUD (2)
of Asher a chief, **A** the son of Shelomi. Nm 34:27
is, Heglam, who fathered Uzza and **A**. 1 Chr 8:7

AHIJAH (24)
including **A** the son of Ahitub, 1 Sm 14:3
So Saul said to **A**, "Bring the ark of 1 Sm 14:18
Elihoreph and **A** the sons of Shisha 1 Kgs 4:3
the prophet **A** the Shilonite found 1 Kgs 11:29
Now **A** had dressed himself in a new 1 Kgs 11:29
Then **A** laid hold of the new 1 Kgs 11:30
the LORD spoke by **A** the Shilonite to 1 Kgs 12:15
Behold, **A** the prophet is there, who 1 Kgs 14:2
to Shiloh and came to the house of **A**. 1 Kgs 14:4
Now **A** could not see, for his eyes were 1 Kgs 14:4
And the LORD said to **A**, "Behold, the 1 Kgs 14:5
But when **A** heard the sound of her 1 Kgs 14:6
spoke by his servant **A** the prophet. 1 Kgs 14:18
Baasha the son of **A**, of the house of 1 Kgs 15:27
spoke by his servant **A** the Shilonite. 1 Kgs 15:29
Baasha the son of **A** began to reign 1 Kgs 15:33
the house of Baasha the son of **A**, 1 Kgs 21:22
like the house of Baasha the son of **A**. 2 Kgs 9:9
firstborn, Bunah, Oren, Ozem, and **A**. 1 Chr 2:25
Naaman, **A**, and Gera, that is, Heglam, 1 Chr 8:7
the Mecherathite, **A** the Pelonite, 1 Chr 11:36
A had charge of the treasuries of the 1 Chr 26:20
in the prophecy of **A** the Shilonite, 2 Chr 9:29
he spoke by **A** the Shilonite to 2 Chr 10:15

AHIKAM (20)
the priest, and **A** the son of Shaphan, 2 Kgs 22:12
So Hilkiah the priest, and **A**, and 2 Kgs 22:14
he appointed Gedaliah the son of **A**, 2 Kgs 25:22
Hilkiah, **A** the son of Shaphan, 2 Chr 34:20
But the hand of **A** the son of Shaphan Jer 26:24
entrusted him to Gedaliah the son of **A**, Jer 39:14
then return to Gedaliah the son of **A**, Jer 40:5
Jeremiah went to Gedaliah the son of **A**, Jer 40:6
Gedaliah the son of **A** governor in the Jer 40:7
Gedaliah the son of **A**, son of Shaphan, Jer 40:9
had appointed Gedaliah the son of **A**, Jer 40:11
Gedaliah the son of **A** would not believe Jer 40:14
Gedaliah the son of **A** said to Johanan Jer 40:16
with ten men to Gedaliah the son of **A**, Jer 41:1
and struck down Gedaliah the son of **A**, Jer 41:2
"Come in to Gedaliah the son of **A**." Jer 41:6
committed to Gedaliah the son of **A**. Jer 41:10
down Gedaliah the son of **A**—soldiers, Jer 41:16
had struck down Gedaliah the son of **A**, Jer 41:18
had left with Gedaliah the son of **A**, Jer 43:6

AHILUD (5)
the son of **A** was recorder, 2 Sm 8:16
the son of **A** was the recorder; 2 Sm 20:24
Jehoshaphat the son of **A** was recorder; 1 Kgs 4:3
Baana the son of **A**, in Taanach, 1 Kgs 4:12
the son of **A** was recorder; 1 Chr 18:15

AHIMAAZ (15)
was Ahinoam the daughter of **A**. 1 Sm 14:50
with your two sons, **A** your son, 2 Sm 15:27
are with them there, **A**, Zadok's son, 2 Sm 15:36
Now Jonathan and **A** were waiting at 2 Sm 17:17
"Where are **A** and Jonathan?" And 2 Sm 17:20
Then **A** the son of Zadok said, "Let 2 Sm 18:19
Then **A** the son of Zadok said again 2 Sm 18:22
"Run." Then **A** ran by the way of the 2 Sm 18:23
like the running of **A** the son of 2 Sm 18:27
Then **A** cried out to the king, "All is 2 Sm 18:28
young man Absalom?" **A** answered, 2 Sm 18:29
A, in Naphtali (he had taken 1 Kgs 4:15
fathered Zadok, Zadok fathered **A**, 1 Chr 6:8
A fathered Azariah, Azariah fathered 1 Chr 6:9
Zadok his son, **A** his son. 1 Chr 6:53

AHIMAN (4)
A, Sheshai, and Talmai, the Nm 13:22
of Anak, Sheshai and **A** and Talmai, Jos 15:14
defeated Sheshai and **A** and Talmai. Jgs 1:10
A, and their kinsmen (Shallum was 1 Chr 9:17

AHIMELECH (18)
David came to Nob to **A** the priest. 1 Sm 21:1
And **A** came to meet David trembling 1 Sm 21:1
And David said to **A** the priest, "The 1 Sm 21:2
Then David said to **A**, "Then have 1 Sm 21:8
to Nob, to **A** the son of Ahitub, 1 Sm 22:9
king sent to summon **A** the priest, 1 Sm 22:11
Then **A** answered the king, "And 1 Sm 22:14
A, you and all your father's house." 1 Sm 22:16
of the sons of **A** the son of Ahitub, 1 Sm 22:20
Abiathar the son of **A** had fled to 1 Sm 23:6
Then David said to **A** the Hittite, and 1 Sm 26:6
to Abiathar the priest, the son of **A**, 1 Sm 30:7
son of Ahitub and **A** the son of 2 Sm 8:17
son of Ahitub and **A** the son of 1 Chr 18:16
Eleazar, and **A** of the sons of Ithamar, 1 Chr 24:3
Zadok the priest and **A** the son of 1 Chr 24:6
A, and the heads of fathers' houses 1 Chr 24:31
"David has come to the house of **A**." Ps 52:T

AHIMOTH (1)
The sons of Elkanah: Amasai and **A**, 1 Chr 6:25

AHINADAB (1)
A the son of Iddo, in Mahanaim; 1 Kgs 4:14

AHINOAM (7)
of Saul's wife was **A** the daughter of 1 Sm 14:50
David also took **A** of Jezreel, and 1 Sm 25:43
David with his two wives, **A** of Jezreel, 1 Sm 27:3
A of Jezreel and Abigail the widow of 1 Sm 30:5
A of Jezreel and Abigail the widow of 2 Sm 2:2
firstborn was Amnon, of **A** of Jezreel; 2 Sm 3:2
firstborn, Amnon, by **A** the Jezreelite; 1 Chr 3:1

AHIO (6)
And Uzzah and **A**, the sons of 2 Sm 6:3
ark of God, and **A** went before the ark. 2 Sm 6:4
and **A**, Shashak, and Jeremoth. 1 Chr 8:14
Gedor, **A**, Zecher, 1 Chr 8:31
Gedor, **A**, Zechariah, and Mikloth; 1 Chr 9:37
and Uzzah and **A** were driving the 1 Chr 13:7

AHIRA (5)
from Naphtali, **A** the son of Enan." Nm 1:15
people of Naphtali being **A** the son of Nm 2:29
On the twelfth day **A** the son of Enan, Nm 7:78
was the offering of **A** the son of Enan. Nm 7:83
people of Naphtali was **A** the son of Nm 10:27

AHIRAM (1)
the clan of the Ashbelites; of **A**, Nm 26:38

AHIRAMITES (1)
of Ahiram, the clan of the **A**; Nm 26:38

AHISAMACH (3)
with him Oholiab, the son of **A**, Ex 31:6
and Oholiab the son of **A** of the tribe of Ex 35:34
with him was Oholiab the son of **A**, Ex 38:23

AHISHAHAR (1)
Zethan, Tarshish, and **A**. 1 Chr 7:10

AHISHAR (1)
A was in charge of the palace; and 1 Kgs 4:6

AHITHOPHEL (20)
sacrifices, he sent for **A** the Gilonite, 2 Sm 15:12
"**A** is among the conspirators with 2 Sm 15:31
the counsel of **A** into foolishness." 2 Sm 15:31
will defeat for me the counsel of **A**. 2 Sm 15:34
came to Jerusalem, and **A** with him. 2 Sm 16:15
Then Absalom said to **A**, "Give your 2 Sm 16:20
A said to Absalom, "Go in to your 2 Sm 16:21
days the counsel that **A** gave was as 2 Sm 16:23
so was all the counsel of **A** esteemed, 2 Sm 16:23
Moreover, **A** said to Absalom, "Let me 2 Sm 17:1
said to him, "Thus has **A** spoken; 2 Sm 17:6
time the counsel that **A** has given is 2 Sm 17:7
than the counsel of **A**." For the LORD 2 Sm 17:14
to defeat the good counsel of **A**, 2 Sm 17:14
and so did **A** counsel Absalom and 2 Sm 17:15
and so has **A** counseled against 2 Sm 17:21
When **A** saw that his counsel was 2 Sm 17:23
Maacah, Eliam the son of **A** of Gilo, 2 Sm 23:34
A was the king's counselor, and 1 Chr 27:33
A was succeeded by Jehoiada the 1 Chr 27:34

AHITUB (15)
including Ahijah the son of **A**, 1 Sm 14:3
to Nob, to Ahimelech the son of **A**, 1 Sm 22:9
Ahimelech the priest, the son of **A**, 1 Sm 22:11
now, son of **A**." And he answered, 1 Sm 22:12
the sons of Ahimelech the son of **A**, 1 Sm 22:20
the son of **A** and Ahimelech the 2 Sm 8:17
Amariah, Amariah fathered **A**, 1 Chr 6:7
A fathered Zadok, Zadok fathered 1 Chr 6:8
Amariah, Amariah fathered **A**, 1 Chr 6:11
A fathered Zadok, Zadok fathered 1 Chr 6:12
his son, Amariah his son, **A** his son, 1 Chr 6:52
of Zadok, son of Meraioth, son of **A**, 1 Chr 9:11
the son of **A** and Ahimelech the 1 Chr 18:16
son of Shallum, son of Zadok, son of **A**, Ezr 7:2
of Zadok, son of Meraioth, son of **A**, Neh 11:11

AHLAB (1)
of Sidon or of **A** or of Achzib or Jgs 1:31

AHLAI (2)
Ishi: Sheshan. The son of Sheshan: **A**. 1 Chr 2:31
the Hittite, Zabad the son of **A**, 1 Chr 11:41

AHOAH (1)
Abishua, Naaman, **A**, 1 Chr 8:4

AHOHI (1)
was Eleazar the son of Dodo, son of **A**. 2 Sm 23:9

AHOHITE (4)
Zalmon the **A**, Maharai of 2 Sm 23:28
was Eleazar the son of Dodo, the **A**. 1 Chr 11:12
Sibbecai the Hushathite, Ilai the **A**, 1 Chr 11:29
Dodai the **A** was in charge of the 1 Chr 27:4

AHUMAI (1)
and Jahath fathered **A** and Lahad. 1 Chr 4:2

AHUZZAM (1)
Naarah bore him **A**, Hepher, Temeni, 1 Chr 4:6

AHUZZATH (1)
him from Gerar with **A** his adviser and Gn 26:26

AHZAI (1)
Amashsai, the son of Azarel, son of **A**, Neh 11:13

AI (37)
Bethel on the west and **A** on the east. Gn 12:8
at the beginning, between Bethel and **A**, Gn 13:3
Joshua sent men from Jericho to **A**, Jos 7:2
And the men went up and spied out **A**. Jos 7:2
three thousand men go up and attack **A**. Jos 7:3
people. And they fled before the men of **A**, Jos 7:4
and the men of **A** killed about thirty-six Jos 7:5
men with you, and arise, go up to **A**. Jos 8:1
I have given into your hand the king of **A**, Jos 8:1
And you shall do to **A** and its king as you Jos 8:2
all the fighting men arose to go up to **A**. Jos 8:3
of ambush and lay between Bethel and **A**, Jos 8:9
between Bethel and Ai, to the west of **A**, Jos 8:9
the elders of Israel, before the people to **A**. Jos 8:10
and encamped on the north side of **A**, Jos 8:11
of Ai, with a ravine between them and **A**. Jos 8:11
them in ambush between Bethel and **A**, Jos 8:12
And as soon as the king of **A** saw this, he Jos 8:14
a man was left in **A** or Bethel who did Jos 8:17
javelin that is in your hand toward **A**, Jos 8:18
So when the men of **A** looked back, Jos 8:20
back and struck down the men of **A**. Jos 8:21
But the king of **A** they took alive, and Jos 8:23
all the inhabitants of **A** in the open Jos 8:24
all Israel returned to **A** and struck it Jos 8:24
women, were 12,000, all the people of **A**. Jos 8:25
all the inhabitants of **A** to destruction. Jos 8:26
So Joshua burned **A** and made it forever Jos 8:28
he hanged the king of **A** on a tree until Jos 8:29
what Joshua had done to Jericho and to **A**, Jos 9:3
Joshua had captured **A** and had devoted Jos 10:1
doing to **A** and its king as he had done to Jos 10:1
cities, and because it was greater than **A**, Jos 10:2
the king of **A**, which is beside Bethel, Jos 12:9
The men of Bethel and **A**, 223. Ezr 2:28
The men of Bethel and **A**, 123. Neh 7:32
"Wail, O Heshbon, for **A** is laid waste! Jer 49:3

AIAH (6)
are the sons of Zibeon: **A** and Anah; Gn 36:24

to them went down **a** into Sheol, Nm 16:33
lying with him keep **a** for yourselves. Nm 31:18
fast to the LORD your God are all **a** today. Dt 4:4
but with us, who are all of us here **a** today. Dt 5:3
good always, that he might preserve us **a**, Dt 6:24
you shall save **a** nothing that breathes, Dt 20:16
even today while I am yet **a** with you, Dt 31:27
is no god besides me; I kill and I make **a**; Dt 32:39
that you will save **a** my father and Jos 2:13
all who belonged to her, Joshua saved **a**. Jos 6:25
But the king of Ai they took **a**, and Jos 8:23
now, behold, the LORD has kept me **a**, Jos 14:10
the LORD lives, if you had saved them **a**, Jgs 8:19
whom they had saved **a** of the women Jgs 21:14
of the Amalekites **a** and devoted to 1 Sm 15:8
If I am still **a**, show me the steadfast 1 Sm 20:14
leave neither man nor woman **a**, 1 Sm 27:9
man nor woman **a** to bring news 1 Sm 27:11
"Behold, while the child was yet **a**, 2 Sm 12:18
wept for the child while he was **a**; 2 Sm 12:21
He said, "While the child was still **a**, 2 Sm 12:22
while he was still **a** in the oak. 2 Sm 18:14
that if Absalom were **a** and all of us 2 Sm 19:6
one says, 'This is my son that is **a**, 1 Kgs 3:23
woman whose son was **a** said to the 1 Kgs 3:26
his father while he was yet **a**, 1 Kgs 12:6
and save the horses and mules **a**, 1 Kgs 18:5
come out for peace, take them **a**. 1 Kgs 20:18
come out for war, take them **a**." 1 Kgs 20:18
you for money, for Naboth is not **a**, 1 Kgs 21:15
said, "Am I God, to kill and to make **a**, 2 Kgs 5:7
we shall take them **a** and get into the 2 Kgs 7:12
"Take them **a**." And they took them 2 Kgs 10:14
they took them **a** and slaughtered 2 Kgs 10:14
2,000 donkeys, and 100,000 men **a**. 1 Chr 5:21
his father while he was yet **a**, 2 Chr 10:6
fell until none remained **a**, 2 Chr 14:13
captured another 10,000 **a** and took 2 Chr 25:12
get grain, that we may eat and keep **a**." Neh 5:2
He does not keep the wicked **a**, but gives Jb 36:6
the one who could not keep himself **a**. Ps 22:29
from death and keep them **a** in famine. Ps 33:19
the LORD protects him and keeps him **a**; Ps 41:2
over them; let them go down to Sheol **a**; Ps 55:15
they would have swallowed us up **a**, Ps 124:3
like Sheol let us swallow them **a**, and Prv 1:12
fortunate than the living who are still **a**. Eccl 4:2
day a man will keep **a** a young cow and Is 7:21
fatherless children; I will keep them **a**; Jer 49:11
they flung me **a** into the pit and cast Lam 3:53
"Yet I will leave some of you **a**. When Ezk 6:8
my people and keep your own souls **a**? Ezk 13:18
die and keeping **a** souls who should Ezk 13:19
killed, and whom he would, he kept **a**; Dn 5:19
and perish, and one third shall be left **a**. Zec 13:8
which today is **a** and tomorrow is Mt 6:30
that impostor said, while he was still **a**, Mt 27:63
heard that he was **a** and had been seen Mk 16:11
the grass, which is **a** in the field today, Lk 12:28
this my son was dead, and is **a** again; Lk 15:24
for this your brother was dead, and is **a**; Lk 15:32
of angels, who said that he was **a**. Lk 24:23
he presented himself **a** after his Acts 1:3
so that they would not be kept **a**. Acts 7:19
saints and widows, he presented her **a**. Acts 9:41
And they took the youth away **a**, and Acts 20:12
dead, but whom Paul asserted to be **a**. Acts 25:19
dead to sin and **a** to God in Christ Rom 6:11
another man while her husband is **a**. Rom 7:3
I was once **a** apart from the law, but Rom 7:9
came, sin came **a** and I died. Rom 7:9
at one time, most of whom are still **a**, 1 Cor 15:6
so also in Christ shall all be made **a**. 1 Cor 15:22
made us **a** together with Christ—by Eph 2:5
flesh, God made **a** together with him, Col 2:13
why, as if you were still **a** in the world, Col 2:20
from the Lord, that we who are **a**, 1 Thes 4:15
Then we who are **a**, who are left, will 1 Thes 4:17
as long as the one who made it is **a**. Heb 9:17
in the flesh but made **a** in the spirit, 1 Pt 3:18
I died, and behold I am **a** forevermore, Rv 1:18
You have the reputation of being **a**, but Rv 3:1
These two were thrown **a** into the lake Rv 19:20

ALLAMMELECH (1)
A, Amad, and Mishal. On the west it Jos 19:26

ALLEGIANCE (4)
that point kept their **a** to the house 1 Chr 12:29
pledged their **a** to King Solomon. 1 Chr 29:24
of Canaan and swear **a** to the LORD of Is 19:18
shall bow, every tongue shall swear **a**.' Is 45:23

ALLEGORICALLY (1)
Now this may be interpreted **a**: these Gal 4:24

ALLIANCE (5)
made a marriage **a** with Pharaoh king 1 Kgs 3:1
he made a marriage **a** with Ahab. 2 Chr 18:1
a plan, but not mine, and who make an **a**, Is 30:1
After some years they shall make an **a**, Dn 11:6
the time that an **a** is made with him Dn 11:23

ALLIED (1)
Can wicked rulers be **a** with you, those Ps 94:20

ALLIES (3)
and of Aner. These were **a** of Abram. Gn 14:13
Though they hire **a** among the nations, Hos 8:10
All your **a** have driven you to your Ob 1:7

ALLON (1)
Ziza the son of Shiphi, son of **A**, son 1 Chr 4:37

ALLON-BACUTH (1)
below Bethel. So he called its name **A**. Gn 35:8

ALLOT (4)
Only **a** the land to Israel for an Jos 13:6
"When you **a** the land as an Ezk 45:1
You shall **a** it as an inheritance for Ezk 47:22
that you shall **a** as an inheritance Ezk 48:29

ALLOTMENT (6)
The **a** for the tribe of the people of Judah Jos 15:1
The **a** of the people of Joseph went from Jos 16:1
Then **a** was made to the people of Jos 17:1
power. You shall not have one **a** only, Jos 17:17
shall have an **a** measuring 25,000 Ezk 48:10
shall have an **a** 25,000 cubits in Ezk 48:13

ALLOTMENTS (4)
to Israel according to their tribal **a**. Jos 11:23
as a possession according to their **a**, Jos 12:7
And **a** were made to the rest of the people Jos 17:2
These shall be the **a** of the holy Ezk 48:10

ALLOTS (1)
from me! To an apostate he **a** our fields." Mi 2:4

ALLOTTED (26)
the LORD your God has **a** to all the peoples Dt 4:19
and whom he had not **a** to them. Dt 29:26
is his people, Jacob his **a** heritage. Dt 32:9
It was **a** to the half-tribe of the people of Jos 13:29
These were **a** to the people of Machir Jos 13:31
commanded Moses; they **a** the land. Jos 14:5
of Gilead, were **a** Gilead and Bashan, Jos 17:1
The land of Gilead was **a** to the rest of Jos 17:6
and the territory **a** to it fell between the Jos 18:11
the cities **a** to them were out of the tribe Jos 21:20
those **a** to them were in all twelve cities. Jos 21:40
I have **a** to you as an inheritance for Jos 23:4
up with me into the territory **a** to me, Jgs 1:3
you into the territory **a** to you." So Jgs 1:3
their clans were **a** thirteen cities out 1 Chr 6:62
to their clans were **a** twelve cities out 1 Chr 6:63
of the Merarites were **a** out of the 1 Chr 6:77
and to his sons was **a** the gatehouse. 1 Chr 26:15
and peoples and **a** to them every Neh 9:22
so I am **a** months of emptiness, and nights Jb 7:3
not rest on the land **a** to the righteous, Ps 125:3
and diminished your **a** portion and Ezk 16:27
they shall be **a** an inheritance among Ezk 47:22
shall stand in your **a** place at the end Dn 12:13
among us and was **a** his share in this Acts 1:17
having determined **a** periods and the Acts 17:26

ALLOW (13)
door and will not **a** the destroyer to Ex 12:23
you shall **a** a redemption of the land. Lv 25:24
But Sihon would not **a** Israel to pass Nm 21:23
for they did not **a** them to come down to Jgs 1:34
Moabites and did not **a** anyone to pass Jgs 3:28
But her father would not **a** him to go in. Jgs 15:1
And she did not **a** the birds of the air 2 Sm 21:10
chief of the eunuchs to **a** him not to defile Dn 1:8
enter yourselves nor **a** those who would Mt 23:13
And he would not **a** anyone to carry Mk 11:16
them and would not **a** them to speak, Lk 4:41
but the Spirit of Jesus did not **a** them. Acts 16:7
as the wind did not **a** us to go farther, Acts 27:7

ALLOWANCE (10)
priests had a fixed **a** from Pharaoh and Gn 47:22
and lived on the **a** that Pharaoh gave Gn 47:22
and assigned him an **a** of food and 1 Kgs 11:18
and for his **a**, a regular allowance 2 Kgs 25:30
a regular **a** was given him by the 2 Kgs 25:30
brothers ate the food **a** of the governor. Neh 5:14
not demand the food **a** of the governor, Neh 5:18
the guard gave him an **a** of food and a Jer 40:5
and for his **a**, a regular allowance was Jer 52:34
a regular **a** was given him by the king Jer 52:34

ALLOWED (22)
LORD your God has not **a** you to do this. Dt 18:14
he **a** no one to oppress them; he 1 Chr 16:21
for no one was **a** to enter the king's gate Est 4:2
saying that the king **a** the Jews who were Est 8:11
are in Susa be **a** tomorrow also to do Est 9:13
no evil shall be **a** to befall you, no Ps 91:10
he **a** no one to oppress them; he Ps 105:14
hardness of heart Moses **a** you to divorce Mt 19:8
Am I not **a** to do what I choose with Mt 20:15
And he **a** no one to follow him except Mk 5:37
"Moses **a** a man to write a certificate of Mk 10:4
the house, he **a** no one to enter with him, Lk 8:51
past generations he **a** all the nations Acts 14:16
earth! For he should not be **a** to live." Acts 22:22
the sea, Justice has not **a** him to live." Acts 28:4
Rome, Paul was **a** to stay by himself, Acts 28:16
They were **a** to torment them for five Rv 9:5
and it was **a** to exercise authority for Rv 13:5
Also it was **a** to make war on the saints Rv 13:7
the signs that it is **a** to work in the Rv 13:14
And it was **a** to give breath to the image Rv 13:15
and it was **a** to scorch people with fire. Rv 16:8

ALLOWS (1)
"The man who **a** any of those whom 2 Kgs 10:24

ALLOY (1)
dross as with lye and remove all your **a**. Is 1:25

ALLURE (1)
"Therefore, behold, I will **a** her, and Hos 2:14

ALLURED (1)
He also **a** you out of distress into a Jb 36:16

ALMIGHTY (58)
to Abram and said to him, "I am God **A**; Gn 17:1
God **A** bless you and make you fruitful Gn 28:3
And God said to him, "I am God **A**: be Gn 35:11
May God **A** grant you mercy before the Gn 43:14
"God **A** appeared to me at Luz in the Gn 48:3
by the **A** who will bless you with Gn 49:25
to Isaac, and to Jacob, as God **A**, Ex 6:3
of God, who sees the vision of the **A**, Nm 24:4
High, who sees the vision of the **A**, Nm 24:16
for the **A** has dealt very bitterly with me. Ru 1:20
me and the **A** has brought calamity Ru 1:21
despise not the discipline of the **A**. Jb 5:17
For the arrows of the **A** are in me; my Jb 6:4
from a friend forsakes the fear of the **A**. Jb 6:14
justice? Or does the **A** pervert the right? Jb 8:3
seek God and plead with the **A** for mercy, Jb 8:5
God? Can you find out the limit of the **A**? Jb 11:7
But I would speak to the **A**, and I desire to Jb 13:3
his hand against God and defies the **A**, Jb 15:25
What is the **A**, that we should serve Jb 21:15
and let them drink of the wrath of the **A**. Jb 21:20
Is it any pleasure to the **A** if you are in the Jb 22:3
from us,' and 'What can the **A** do to us?' Jb 22:17
If you return to the **A** you will be built Jb 22:23
then the **A** will be your gold and your Jb 22:25
delight yourself in the **A** and lift up Jb 22:26
my heart faint; the **A** has terrified me; Jb 23:16
are not times of judgment kept by the **A**, Jb 24:1
who has taken away my right, and the **A**, Jb 27:2
Will he take delight in the **A**? Will he Jb 27:10
what is with the **A** I will not conceal. Jb 27:11
that oppressors receive from the **A**: Jb 27:13
when the **A** was yet with me, when my Jb 29:5
and my heritage from the **A** on high? Jb 31:2
is my signature! Let the **A** answer me!) Jb 31:35
it is the spirit in man, the breath of the **A**, Jb 32:8
me, and the breath of the **A** gives me life. Jb 33:4
and from the **A** that he should do Jb 34:10
and the **A** will not pervert justice. Jb 34:12
an empty cry, nor does the **A** regard it. Jb 35:13
The **A**—we cannot find him; he is great Jb 37:23
"Shall a faultfinder contend with the **A**? Jb 40:2
When the **A** scatters kings there, let Ps 68:14
High will abide in the shadow of the **A**. Ps 91:1
as destruction from the **A** it will come! Is 13:6
of many waters, like the sound of the **A**, Ezk 1:24
like the voice of God **A** when he speaks. Ezk 10:5
and as destruction from the **A** it comes. Jl 1:15
daughters to me, says the Lord **A**." 2 Cor 6:18
and who was and who is to come, the **A**." Rv 1:8
say, "Holy, holy, holy, is the Lord God **A**, Rv 4:8
"We give thanks to you, Lord God **A**, Rv 11:17
are your deeds, O Lord God the **A**! Rv 15:3
the altar saying, "Yes, Lord God the **A**, Rv 16:7
for battle on the great day of God the **A**. Rv 16:14
For the Lord our God the **A** reigns. Rv 19:6
of the fury of the wrath of God the **A**. Rv 19:15
is the Lord God the **A** and the Lamb. Rv 21:22

ALMODAD (2)
Joktan fathered **A**, Sheleph, Gn 10:26
Joktan fathered **A**, Sheleph, 1 Chr 1:20

ALMON (1)
and **A** with its pasturelands—four Jos 21:18

ALMON-DIBLATHAIM (2)
out from Dibon-gad and camped at **A**. Nm 33:46
they set out from **A** and camped in the Nm 33:47

ALMOND (9)
sticks of poplar and **a** and plane trees, Gn 30:37
three cups made like **a** blossoms, each Ex 25:33
and three cups made like **a** blossoms, Ex 25:33
be four cups made like **a** blossoms, Ex 25:34
three cups made like **a** blossoms, each Ex 37:19
and three cups made like **a** blossoms, Ex 37:19
were four cups made like **a** blossoms, Ex 37:20
the **a** tree blossoms, the grasshopper Eccl 12:5
you see?" And I said, "I see an **a** branch." Jer 1:11

ALMONDS (2)
gum, myrrh, pistachio nuts, and **a**. Gn 43:11
produced blossoms, and it bore ripe **a**. Nm 17:8

ALMOST (7)
people? They are **a** ready to stone me." Ex 17:4
But as for me, my feet had **a** stumbled, Ps 73:2
They have **a** made an end of me on Ps 119:87
The next Sabbath **a** the whole city Acts 13:44
in Ephesus but in **a** all of Asia this Acts 19:26
the seven days were **a** completed, Acts 21:27
under the law **a** everything is purified Heb 9:22

ALMS (8)
But give as **a** those things that are Lk 11:41
Beautiful Gate to ask **a** of those entering Acts 3:2
go into the temple, he asked to receive **a**. Acts 3:3
Gate of the temple, asking for **a**. Acts 3:10
gave **a** generously to the people, Acts 10:2
prayers and your **a** have ascended as Acts 10:4
heard and your **a** have been Acts 10:31
I came to bring **a** to my nation and Acts 24:17

ALMUG (3)
great amount of **a** wood and 1 Kgs 10:11
made of the **a** wood supports for 1 Kgs 10:12
No such **a** wood has come or been 1 Kgs 10:12

ALOES (5)
a river, like **a** that the LORD has planted, Nm 24:6
fragrant with myrrh and **a** and cassia. Ps 45:8
my bed with myrrh, **a**, and cinnamon. Prv 7:17
all trees of frankincense, myrrh and **a**, Sg 4:14
bringing a mixture of myrrh and **a**, Jn 19:39

ALOFT (3)
it towered **a** among the thick boughs; Ezk 19:11
Though you soar **a** like the eagle, though Ob 1:4
Jerusalem shall remain **a** on its site Zec 14:10

ALONE (131)
"It is not good that the man should be **a**; Gn 2:18
And Jacob was left **a**. And a man Gn 32:24
and he **a** is left of his mother's Gn 44:20
land of the priests **a** did not become Gn 47:26
So he let him **a**. It was then that she said, Ex 4:26
to eat, that **a** may be prepared by you. Ex 12:16
'Leave us **a** that we may serve the Ex 14:12
Why do you sit **a**, and all the people Ex 18:14
for you. You are not able to do it **a**. Ex 18:18
be her master's, and he shall go out **a**. Ex 21:4
to any god, other than the LORD **a**, Ex 22:20
Moses **a** shall come near to the LORD, but Ex 24:2
Now therefore let me **a**, that my wrath Ex 32:10
disease. He is unclean. He shall live **a**. Lv 13:46
I am not able to carry all this people **a**; Nm 11:14
so that you may not bear it yourself **a**. Nm 11:17
behold, a people dwelling **a**, and not Nm 23:9
know that man does not live by bread **a**, Dt 8:3
Let me **a**, that I may destroy them and Dt 9:14
It is not with you **a** that I am making Dt 29:14
the LORD **a** guided him, no foreign god Dt 32:12
So Israel lived in safety, Jacob lived **a**, in Dt 33:28
did Israel burn, except Hazor **a**; Jos 11:13
and in Edrei (he **a** was left of the Jos 13:12
the tribe of Levi **a** Moses gave no Jos 13:14
he did not perish **a** for his iniquity.'" Jos 22:20
him as he was sitting **a** in his cool roof Jgs 3:20
If there is dew on the fleece **a**, and it is Jgs 6:37
be done for me: leave me **a** two months, Jgs 11:37
and said to him, "Why are you **a**, 1 Sm 21:1
She fell at his feet and said, "On me **a**, 1 Sm 25:24
the king's sons, for Amnon **a** is dead. 2 Sm 13:32
sons are dead, for Amnon **a** is dead." 2 Sm 13:33
Leave him **a**, and let him curse, for 2 Sm 16:11
looked, he saw a man running **a**. 2 Sm 18:24
And the king said, "If he is **a**, there is 2 Sm 18:25
another man running **a**!" The king 2 Sm 18:26
Give up him **a**, and I will withdraw 2 Sm 20:21
also gave birth. And we were **a**. 1 Kgs 3:18
two of them were **a** in the open 1 Kgs 11:29
the man of God said, "Leave her **a**, 2 Kgs 4:27
cherubim, you are the God, you **a**, 2 Kgs 19:15
know that you, O LORD, are God **a**." 2 Kgs 19:19
his bones." So they let his bones **a**, 2 Kgs 23:18
my son, whom **a** God has chosen, 1 Chr 29:1
but we **a** will build to the LORD, the God of Ezr 4:3
Let the work on this house of God **a**. Let Ezr 6:7
"You are the LORD, you **a**. You have Neh 9:6
he disdained to lay hands on Mordecai **a**. Est 3:6
sword, and I **a** have escaped to tell you." Jb 1:15
them, and I **a** have escaped to tell you." Jb 1:16
sword, and I **a** have escaped to tell you." Jb 1:17
are dead, and I **a** have escaped to tell you." Jb 1:19
Leave me **a**, for my days are a breath. Jb 7:16
me, nor leave me **a** till I swallow my spit? Jb 7:19
who **a** stretched out the heavens and Jb 9:8
Then cease, and leave me **a**, that I may Jb 10:20
look away from him and leave him **a**, Jb 14:6
to whom **a** the land was given, and no Jb 15:19
or have eaten my morsel **a**, and the Jb 31:17
for you **a**, O LORD, make me dwell in Ps 4:8
For God **a** my soul waits in silence; from Ps 62:1
For God **a**, O my soul, wait in silence, for Ps 62:5
them of your righteousness, yours **a**. Ps 71:16
of Israel, who **a** does wondrous things. Ps 72:18
that they may know that you **a**, whose Ps 83:18
and do wondrous things; you **a** are God. Ps 86:10
to him who **a** does great wonders, for Ps 136:4
of the LORD, for his name **a** is exalted; Ps 148:13
Let them be for yourself **a**, and not for Prv 5:17
yourself; if you scoff, you **a** will bear it. Prv 9:12
woe to him who is **a** when he falls and Eccl 4:10
warm, but how can one keep warm **a**? Eccl 4:11
might prevail against one who is **a**, Eccl 4:12
See, this **a** I found, that God made man Eccl 7:29
and the LORD **a** will be exalted in that day. Is 2:11
and the LORD **a** will be exalted in that day. Is 2:17
you are made to dwell **a** in the midst of the Is 5:8
but your name **a** we bring to Is 26:13
the cherubim, you are the God, you **a**, Is 37:16
may know that you **a** are the LORD." Is 37:20
things, who **a** stretched out the heavens, Is 44:24
Behold, I was left **a**; from where have Is 49:21
"I have trodden the winepress **a**, and from Is 63:3
I sat **a**, because your hand was upon Jer 15:17
that has no gates or bars, that dwells **a**. Jer 49:31
Let him sit **a** in silence when it is laid Lam 3:28
while they were striking, and I was left **a**, Ezk 9:8
They **a** would be delivered, but the Ezk 14:16
but they **a** would be delivered. Ezk 14:18
who **a** among the sons of Levi may Ezk 40:46
And I, Daniel, **a** saw the vision, for the Dn 10:7
So I was left **a** and saw this great vision, Dn 10:8
Ephraim is joined to idols; leave him **a**. Hos 4:17
to Assyria, a wild donkey wandering **a**; Hos 8:9
who dwell **a** in a forest in the midst of a Mi 7:14
is written, "'Man shall not live by bread **a**, Mt 4:4
When evening came, he was there **a**, Mt 14:23
Let them **a**; they are blind guides. And Mt 15:14
him his fault, between you and him **a**. Mt 18:15
Who can forgive sins but God **a**?" Mk 2:7
And when he was **a**, those around him Mk 4:10
out on the sea, and he was **a** on the land. Mk 6:47
me good? No one is good except God **a**. Mk 10:18
But Jesus said, "Leave her **a**. Why do Mk 14:6
written, 'Man shall not live by bread **a**.'" Lk 4:4
Who can forgive sins but God **a**?" Lk 5:21
it happened that as he was praying **a**, Lk 9:18
the voice had spoken, Jesus was found **a**. Lk 9:36
that my sister has left me to serve **a**? Lk 10:40
answered him, 'Sir, let it **a** this year also, Lk 13:8
me good? No one is good except God **a**. Lk 18:19
If I **a** bear witness about myself, my Jn 5:31
but that his disciples had gone away **a**. Jn 6:22
and Jesus was left **a** with the woman Jn 8:9
is true, for it is not I **a** who judge, Jn 8:16
He has not left me **a**, for I always do the Jn 8:29
Jesus said, "Leave her **a**, so that she may Jn 12:7
into the earth and dies, it remains **a**; Jn 12:24
to his own home, and will leave me **a**. Jn 16:32
Yet I am not **a**, for the Father is with me. Jn 16:32
away from these men and let them **a**, Acts 5:38
to him" were not written for his sake **a**, Rom 4:23
your altars, and I **a** am left, Rom 11:3
boast will be in himself **a** and not in his Gal 6:4
willing to be left behind at Athens **a**, 1 Thes 3:1
She who is truly a widow, left all **a**, has 1 Tm 5:5
who **a** has immortality, who dwells 1 Tm 6:16
Luke **a** is with me. Get Mark and 2 Tm 4:11
is justified by works and not by faith **a**. Jas 2:24
glorify your name? For you **a** are holy. Rv 15:4

ALONG (105)
it on her shoulder, **a** with the child, Gn 21:14
all the Egyptians dug **a** the Nile for water Ex 7:24
a pillar of cloud to lead them **a** the way, Ex 13:21
a with her two sons. The name of the one Ex 18:3
for a guilt offering, **a** with the log of oil, Lv 14:12
burnt offering, **a** with a grain offering. Lv 14:31
the scarlet yarn, **a** with the live bird, Lv 14:51
Levites were not listed **a** with them by Nm 1:47
dwell by the sea, and **a** the Jordan." Nm 13:29
We will go **a** the King's Highway. Nm 20:17
to Hazar-addar, and pass **a** to Azmon. Nm 34:4
the pursuers searched all **a** the way and Jos 2:22
and in the lowland all **a** the coast of the Jos 9:1
the ascent of Akrabbim, passes **a** to Zin, Jos 15:3
south of Kadesh-barnea, **a** by Hezron, Jos 15:3
passes **a** to Azmon, goes out by the Jos 15:4
Beth-hoglah and passes **a** north of Jos 15:6
And the boundary passes **a** to the waters Jos 15:7
passes **a** to the northern shoulder of Jos 15:10
and passes **a** by Timnah. Jos 15:10
Shikkeron and passes **a** to Mount Jos 15:11
Bethel to Luz, it passes **a** to Ataroth, Jos 16:2
Taanath-shiloh and passes **a** beyond it Jos 16:6
us an inheritance **a** with our brothers." Jos 17:4
received an inheritance **a** with his sons. Jos 17:6
the boundary goes **a** southward to the Jos 17:7
since all **a** the LORD has blessed me?" Jos 17:14
the boundary passes **a** southward in Jos 18:13
From there it passes **a** on the east Jos 19:13
a with their pasturelands for our Jos 21:2
a with the pasturelands around it. Jos 21:11
a with all the nations that I have already Jos 23:4
of the East lay **a** the valley like locusts Jgs 7:12
all who passed by them **a** that way. Jgs 9:25
image and went **a** with the people. Jgs 18:20
for all **a** I have been speaking out of 1 Sm 1:16
with her, **a** with a three-year-old bull, 1 Sm 1:24
of Beth-shemesh **a** one highway, 1 Sm 6:12
arose and went, **a** with his men, 1 Sm 18:27
while Shimei went **a** on the hillside 2 Sm 16:13
a with the daughter of Pharaoh: 1 Kgs 11:1
put him to death **a** with the Jews and 2 Kgs 25:25
a with all their villages that were 1 Chr 4:33
And **a** with them, by their generations, 1 Chr 7:4
number of them **a** with their 1 Chr 25:7
a with the sons of Henadad and the Ezr 3:9
whatever passes **a** the paths of the seas. Ps 8:8
gladness they are led **a** as they enter the Ps 45:15
so that all who pass **a** the way pluck its Ps 80:12
passing **a** the street near her corner, Prv 7:8
with a pestle **a** with crushed grain, Prv 27:22
a with that youth who was to stand in Eccl 4:15
the grasshopper drags itself **a**, Eccl 12:5
with their eyes, mincing **a** as they go, Is 3:16
They shall feed **a** the ways; on all bare Is 49:9
him bound in chains **a** with all the Jer 40:1
he had struck down **a** with Gedaliah was Jer 41:9
All who pass **a** the way clap their Lam 2:15
went, and the wheels rose **a** with them, Ezk 1:20
the earth, the wheels rose **a** with them, Ezk 1:21
I will give it **a** with the Ammonites to Ezk 25:10
And the pavement ran **a** the side of the Ezk 40:18
a the Jordan between Gilead and the Ezk 47:18
from there **a** the Brook of Egypt to the Ezk 47:19
from there **a** the Brook of Egypt to the Ezk 48:28
the winter house **a** with the summer Am 3:15
the idolatrous priests **a** with the priests, Zep 1:4
as he sowed, some seeds fell **a** the path, Mt 13:4
This is what was sown **a** the path. Mt 13:19
you root up the wheat **a** with them. Mt 13:29
take one or two others **a** with you, Mt 18:16
disciples to him, **a** with the Herodians, Mt 22:16
as he sowed, some seed fell **a** the path, Mk 4:4
And these are the ones **a** the path, where Mk 4:15
some fell **a** the path and was trampled Lk 8:5
The ones **a** the path are those who have Lk 8:12
As they were going **a** the road, someone Lk 9:57
he was passing **a** between Samaria and Lk 17:11
And as he rode **a**, they spread their Lk 19:36
a with the Gentiles and the peoples of Acts 4:27
as they were going **a** the road they Acts 8:36
they went out and went **a** one street, Acts 12:10
And he rejoiced **a** with his entire Acts 16:34
For as I passed **a** and observed the Acts 17:23
and purify yourself **a** with them and Acts 21:24
he purified himself **a** with them and Acts 21:26
therefore you, **a** with the council, Acts 23:15
to sail to the ports **a** the coast of Asia, Acts 27:2
across the open sea **a** the coast of Acts 27:5
Coasting **a** it with difficulty, we came Acts 27:8
weighed anchor and sailed **a** Crete, Acts 27:13
we gave way to it and were driven **a**. Acts 27:15
the gear, and thus they were driven **a**. Acts 27:17
the right to take **a** a believing wife, 1 Cor 9:5
not be condemned **a** with the world. 1 Cor 11:32
been thinking all **a** that we have 2 Cor 12:19
with Barnabas, taking Titus **a** with me. Gal 2:1
Jews acted hypocritically **a** with him, Gal 2:13
are of faith are blessed **a** with Abraham, Gal 3:9
put away from you, **a** with all malice. Eph 4:31
a with those who call on the Lord 2 Tm 2:22
that faith was active **a** with his works, Jas 2:22

as they were carried **a** by the Holy — 2 Pt 1:21
world is passing away **a** with its desires, — 1 Jn 2:17
waterless clouds, swept **a** by winds; — Jude 1:12

ALONGSIDE (7)
be from the wilderness of Zin **a** Edom, — Nm 34:3
"**A** the portion set apart as the holy — Ezk 45:6
a the holy district and the property of — Ezk 45:7
And **a** the territory of the priests, the — Ezk 48:13
of the length **a** the holy portion — Ezk 48:18
west, and it shall be **a** the holy portion. — Ezk 48:18
Passing **a** the Sea of Galilee, he saw — Mk 1:16

ALOOF (5)
you yourself would have stood **a**." — 2 Sm 18:13
They abhor me; they keep **a** from me; — Jb 30:10
and companions stand **a** from my — Ps 38:11
honor for a man to keep **a** from strife, — Prv 20:3
On the day that you stood **a**, on the day — Ob 1:11

ALOUD (43)
Then Jacob kissed Rachel and wept **a**. — Gn 29:11
And he wept **a**, so that the Egyptians — Gn 45:2
Mount Gerizim and cried **a** and said to — Jgs 9:7
of the people, and all the people wept **a**. — 1 Sm 11:4
and went away, crying **a** as she went. — 2 Sm 13:19
all the land wept **a** as all the people — 2 Sm 15:23
Elijah mocked them, saying, "Cry **a**, — 1 Kgs 18:27
And they cried **a** and cut themselves — 1 Kgs 18:28
laid, though many shouted **a** for joy, — Ezr 3:12
I cried **a** to the LORD, and he answered me — Ps 3:4
proclaiming thanksgiving **a**, and telling — Ps 26:7
Hear, O LORD, when I cry **a**; be gracious — Ps 27:7
tongue will sing **a** of your — Ps 51:14
I will sing **a** of your steadfast love in the — Ps 59:16
I cry **a** to God, aloud to God, and he will — Ps 77:1
I cry aloud to God, **a** to God, and he will — Ps 77:1
Sing **a** to God our strength; shout for joy — Ps 81:1
and shall sing **a** of your righteousness. — Ps 145:7
Wisdom cries **a** in the street, in the — Prv 1:20
at the entrance of the portals she cries **a**: — Prv 8:3
Cry **a**, O daughter of Gallim! Give — Is 10:30
a bare hill raise a signal; cry **a** to them; — Is 13:2
therefore the armed men of Moab cry **a**; — Is 15:4
He will not cry **a** or lift up his voice, or — Is 42:2
he cries out, he shouts **a**, he shows — Is 42:13
break forth into singing and cry **a**, you — Is 54:1
"Cry **a**; do not hold back; lift up your — Is 58:1
cry **a** and say, 'Assemble, and let us go — Jer 4:5
"Sing **a** with gladness for Jacob, and — Jer 31:7
shall come and sing **a** on the height of — Jer 31:12
Sigh, but not **a**; make no mourning — Ezk 24:17
and shout **a** over you and cry out — Ezk 27:30
And the herald proclaimed **a**, "You are — Dn 3:4
He proclaimed **a** and said thus: 'Chop — Dn 4:14
Now why do you cry **a**? Is there no king — Mi 4:9
is bitter; the mighty man cries **a** there. — Zep 1:14
Sing **a**, O daughter of Zion; shout, O — Zep 3:14
greatly, O daughter of Zion! Shout **a**, — Zec 9:9
two blind men followed him, crying **a**, — Mt 9:27
He will not quarrel or cry **a**, nor will — Mt 12:19
break forth and cry **a**, you who are not — Gal 4:27
is the one who reads **a** the words of this — Rv 1:3
her torment, weeping and mourning **a**, — Rv 18:15

ALPHA (3)
"I am the **A** and the Omega," says the — Rv 1:8
"It is done! I am the **A** and the Omega, — Rv 21:6
I am the **A** and the Omega, the first and — Rv 22:13

ALPHAEUS (5)
James the son of **A**, and Thaddaeus; — Mt 10:3
saw Levi the son of **A** sitting at the tax — Mk 2:14
and Thomas, and James the son of **A**, — Mk 3:18
and Thomas, and James the son of **A**, — Lk 6:15
James the son of **A** and Simon the — Acts 1:13

ALREADY (60)
seventy persons; Joseph was **a** in Egypt. — Ex 1:5
the plague had **a** begun among the — Nm 16:47
with all the nations that I have **a** cut off, — Jos 23:4
of Zebah and Zalmunna **a** in your hand, — Jgs 8:6
Zebah and Zalmunna **a** in your hand, — Jgs 8:15
the man was **a** old and advanced — 1 Sm 17:12
and five sheep **a** prepared and five — 1 Sm 25:18
of Israel who have **a** perished. — 2 Kgs 7:13
For our guilt is **a** great, and there is — 2 Chr 28:13
of our daughters have **a** been enslaved, — Neh 5:5
full of all good things, cisterns **a** hewn, — Neh 9:25
It has been **a** in the ages before us. — Eccl 1:10
the king? Only what has **a** been done. — Eccl 2:12
That which is, **a** has been; that which — Eccl 3:15
been; that which is to be, **a** has been; — Eccl 3:15
the dead who are **a** dead more fortunate — Eccl 4:2
has come to be has **a** been named, — Eccl 6:10
hate and their envy have **a** perished, — Eccl 9:6
for God has **a** approved what you do. — Eccl 9:7
others to him besides those **a** gathered." — Is 56:8
a they are among the nations as a — Hos 8:8
Indeed, I have **a** cursed them, because — Mal 2:2
lustful intent has **a** committed adultery — Mt 5:28
But I tell you that Elijah has **a** come, — Mt 17:12
the boat, so that the boat was **a** filling. — Mk 4:37
around at everything, as it was **a** late, — Mk 11:11
to hear that he should have **a** died. — Mk 15:44
he asked him whether he was **a** dead. — Mk 15:44
earth, and would that it were **a** kindled! — Lk 12:49
was drawing near—**a** on the way down — Lk 19:37
and know that the summer is **a** near. — Lk 21:30
whoever does not believe is condemned **a**, — Jn 3:18
A the one who reaps is receiving wages — Jn 4:36
and knew that he had **a** been there a long — Jn 5:6
for the Jews had **a** agreed that if anyone — Jn 9:22
He answered them, "I have told you **a**, — Jn 9:27
found that Lazarus had **a** been in the — Jn 11:17
when the devil had **a** put it into the heart — Jn 13:2
A you are clean because of the word that — Jn 15:3
to Jesus and saw that he was **a** dead, — Jn 19:33
until the next day, for it was **a** evening. — Acts 4:3
because even the Fast was **a** over, — Acts 27:9
at all. For we have **a** charged that all, — Rom 3:9
not where Christ has **a** been named, — Rom 15:20
A you have all you want! Already you — 1 Cor 4:8
you want! **A** you have become rich! — 1 Cor 4:8
I have **a** pronounced judgment on the — 1 Cor 5:3
with one another is **a** a defeat for you. — 1 Cor 6:7
at the time of his call **a** circumcised? — 1 Cor 7:18
boasting of work **a** done in — 2 Cor 10:16
Not that I have **a** obtained this or am — Phil 3:12
already obtained this or am **a** perfect, — Phil 3:12
though we had **a** suffered and been — 1 Thes 2:2
mystery of lawlessness is **a** at work. — 2 Thes 2:7
For some have **a** strayed after Satan. — 1 Tm 5:15
that the resurrection has **a** happened. — 2 Tm 2:18
For I am **a** being poured out as a drink — 2 Tm 4:6
so long afterward, in the words **a** quoted, — Heb 4:7
away and the true light is **a** shining. — 1 Jn 2:8
was coming and now is in the world **a**. — 1 Jn 4:3

ALTAR (380)
Then Noah built an **a** to the LORD and — Gn 8:20
and offered burnt offerings on the **a**. — Gn 8:20
land." So he built there an **a** to the LORD, — Gn 12:7
And there he built an **a** to the LORD and — Gn 12:8
where he had made an **a** at the first. — Gn 13:4
and there he built an **a** to the LORD. — Gn 13:18
Abraham built the **a** there and laid the — Gn 22:9
Isaac his son and laid him on the **a**, — Gn 22:9
So he built an **a** there and called upon — Gn 26:25
There he erected an **a** and called it — Gn 33:20
Make an **a** there to the God who — Gn 35:1
I may make there an **a** to the God who — Gn 35:3
there he built an **a** and called the place — Gn 35:7
And Moses built an **a** and called the — Ex 17:15
An **a** of earth you shall make for me — Ex 20:24
If you make me an **a** of stone, you shall — Ex 20:25
you shall not go up by steps to my **a**, — Ex 20:26
you shall take him from my **a**, — Ex 21:14
the morning and built an **a** at the foot of — Ex 24:4
half of the blood he threw against the **a**. — Ex 24:6
"You shall make the **a** of acacia wood, — Ex 27:1
The **a** shall be square, and its height — Ex 27:1
under the ledge of the **a** so that the net — Ex 27:5
that the net extends halfway down the **a**. — Ex 27:5
And you shall make poles for the **a**, poles — Ex 27:6
the two sides of the **a** when it is carried. — Ex 27:7
they come near the **a** to minister in the — Ex 28:43
on the horns of the **a** with your finger, — Ex 29:12
you shall pour out at the base of the **a**. — Ex 29:12
is on them, and burn them on the **a**. — Ex 29:13
and throw it against the sides of the **a**. — Ex 29:16
and burn the whole ram on the **a**. It is a — Ex 29:18
of the blood against the sides of the **a**. — Ex 29:20
take part of the blood that is on the **a**, — Ex 29:21
and burn them on the **a** on top of the — Ex 29:25
Also you shall purify the **a**, when you — Ex 29:36
atonement for the **a** and consecrate it, — Ex 29:37
it, and the **a** shall be most holy. — Ex 29:37
Whatever touches the **a** shall become — Ex 29:37
this is what you shall offer on the **a**: — Ex 29:38
the tent of meeting and the **a**. — Ex 29:44
"You shall make an **a** on which to burn — Ex 30:1
it between the tent of meeting and the **a**, — Ex 30:18
when they come near the **a** to minister, — Ex 30:20
and its utensils, and the **a** of incense, — Ex 30:27
and the **a** of burnt offering with all its — Ex 30:28
with all its utensils, and the **a** of incense, — Ex 31:8
and the **a** of burnt offering with all its — Ex 31:9
Aaron saw this, he built an **a** before it. — Ex 32:5
and the **a** of incense, with its poles, and — Ex 35:15
the **a** of burnt offering, with its grating — Ex 35:16
He made the **a** of incense of acacia — Ex 37:25
He made the **a** of burnt offering of — Ex 38:1
And he made all the utensils of the **a**, the — Ex 38:3
And he made for the **a** a grating, a — Ex 38:4
on the sides of the **a** to carry it with — Ex 38:7
the bronze **a** and the bronze grating for — Ex 38:30
for it and all the utensils of the **a**, — Ex 38:30
the golden **a**, the anointing oil and the — Ex 39:38
the bronze **a**, and its grating of bronze, — Ex 39:39
shall put the golden **a** for incense before — Ex 40:5
You shall set the **a** of burnt offering — Ex 40:6
between the tent of meeting and the **a**, — Ex 40:7
shall also anoint the **a** of burnt offering — Ex 40:10
all its utensils, and consecrate the **a**, — Ex 40:10
so that the **a** may become most holy. — Ex 40:10
He put the golden **a** in the tent of — Ex 40:26
And he set the **a** of burnt offering at the — Ex 40:29
between the tent of meeting and the **a**, — Ex 40:30
and when they approached the **a**, — Ex 40:32
court around the tabernacle and the **a**, — Ex 40:33
against the sides of the **a** that is at the — Lv 1:5
put fire on the **a** and arrange wood on — Lv 1:7
fat, on the wood that is on the fire on the **a**; — Lv 1:8
And the priest shall burn all of it on the **a**, — Lv 1:9
on the north side of the **a** before the LORD, — Lv 1:11
throw its blood against the sides of the **a**. — Lv 1:11
on the wood that is on the fire on the **a**, — Lv 1:12
shall offer all of it and burn it on the **a**; — Lv 1:13
shall bring it to the **a** and wring off its — Lv 1:15
wring off its head and burn it on the **a**. — Lv 1:15
shall be drained out on the side of the **a**. — Lv 1:15
and cast it beside the **a** on the east side, — Lv 1:16
And the priest shall burn it on the **a**, on — Lv 1:17
this as its memorial portion on the **a**, — Lv 2:2
to the priest, he shall bring it to the **a**. — Lv 2:8
memorial portion and burn this on the **a**, — Lv 2:9
be offered on the **a** for a pleasing aroma. — Lv 2:12
throw the blood against the sides of the **a**. — Lv 3:2
shall burn it on the **a** on top of the burnt — Lv 3:5
throw its blood against the sides of the **a**. — Lv 3:8
shall burn it on the **a** as a food offering — Lv 3:11
throw its blood against the sides of the **a**. — Lv 3:13
burn them on the **a** as a food offering — Lv 3:16
the horns of the **a** of fragrant incense — Lv 4:7
at the base of the **a** of burnt offering that — Lv 4:7
burn them on the **a** of burnt offering. — Lv 4:10
on the horns of the **a** that is in the tent — Lv 4:18
at the base of the **a** of burnt offering that — Lv 4:18
he shall take from it and burn on the **a**. — Lv 4:19
the horns of the **a** of burnt offering and — Lv 4:25
at the base of the **a** of burnt offering. — Lv 4:25
And all its fat he shall burn on the **a**, — Lv 4:26
the horns of the **a** of burnt offering and — Lv 4:30
the rest of its blood at the base of the **a**. — Lv 4:30
burn it on the **a** for a pleasing aroma — Lv 4:31
the horns of the **a** of burnt offering and — Lv 4:34
the rest of its blood at the base of the **a**. — Lv 4:34
and the priest shall burn it on the **a**, — Lv 4:35
of the sin offering on the side of the **a**, — Lv 5:9
shall be drained out at the base of the **a**; — Lv 5:9
portion and burn this on the **a**, — Lv 5:12
on the hearth on the **a** all night until the — Lv 6:9
and the fire of the **a** shall be kept burning — Lv 6:9
burnt offering on the **a** and put them — Lv 6:10
on the altar and put them beside the **a**. — Lv 6:10
The fire on the **a** shall be kept burning — Lv 6:12
be kept burning on the **a** continually; — Lv 6:13
offer it before the LORD in front of the **a**. — Lv 6:14
this as its memorial portion on the **a**, — Lv 6:15
shall be thrown against the sides of the **a**. — Lv 7:2
burn them on the **a** as a food offering — Lv 7:5
The priest shall burn the fat on the **a**, — Lv 7:31
sprinkled some of it on the **a** seven times, — Lv 8:11
and anointed the **a** and all its utensils — Lv 8:11
the horns of the **a** around it and purified — Lv 8:15
it and purified the **a** and poured out the — Lv 8:15
at the base of the **a** and consecrated it to — Lv 8:15
fat, and Moses burned them on the **a**. — Lv 8:16
threw the blood against the sides of the **a**. — Lv 8:19
Moses burned the whole ram on the **a**. — Lv 8:21
threw the blood against the sides of the **a**. — Lv 8:24
burned them on the **a** with the burnt — Lv 8:28
that was on the **a** and sprinkled it on — Lv 8:30
"Draw near to the **a** and offer your sin — Lv 9:7
drew near to the **a** and killed the calf — Lv 9:8
on the horns of the **a** and poured out the — Lv 9:9
poured out the blood at the base of the **a**. — Lv 9:9
from the sin offering he burned on the **a**, — Lv 9:10
and he threw it against the sides of the **a**. — Lv 9:12
the head, and he burned them on the **a**. — Lv 9:13
them with the burnt offering on the **a**. — Lv 9:14
a handful of it, and burned it on the **a**, — Lv 9:17
and he threw it against the sides of the **a**. — Lv 9:18
and he burned the fat pieces on the **a**, — Lv 9:20
offering and the pieces of fat on the **a**, — Lv 9:24
and eat it unleavened beside the **a**, — Lv 10:12
offering and the grain offering on the **a**. — Lv 14:20
coals of fire from the **a** before the LORD, — Lv 16:12

shall go out to the **a** that is before the Lv 16:18
put it on the horns of the **a** all around. Lv 16:18
Place and the tent of meeting and the **a**, Lv 16:20
the sin offering he shall burn on the **a**. Lv 16:25
for the tent of meeting and for the **a**, Lv 16:33
throw the blood on the **a** of the LORD at Lv 17:6
for you on the **a** to make atonement for Lv 17:11
go through the veil or approach the **a**, Lv 21:23
to the LORD as a food offering on the **a**. Lv 22:22
that is around the tabernacle and the **a**, Nm 3:26
And over the golden **a** they shall spread Nm 4:11
the ashes from the **a** and spread a Nm 4:13
shall put on it all the utensils of the **a**, Nm 4:14
and the basins, all the utensils of the **a**; Nm 4:14
that is around the tabernacle and the **a**, Nm 4:26
before the LORD and bring it to the **a**. Nm 5:25
portion, and burn it on the **a**, Nm 5:26
and consecrated the **a** with all its Nm 7:1
for the dedication of the **a** on the day it Nm 7:10
offered their offering before the **a**. Nm 7:10
each day, for the dedication of the **a**." Nm 7:11
dedication offering for the **a** on the day Nm 7:84
dedication offering for the **a** after it was Nm 7:88
plates as a covering for the **a**, Nm 16:38
hammered out as a covering for the **a**, Nm 16:39
on it from off the **a** and lay incense on Nm 16:46
of the sanctuary or to the **a** lest they, Nm 18:3
over the sanctuary and over the **a**, Nm 18:5
all that concerns the **a** and that is Nm 18:7
their blood on the **a** and shall burn Nm 18:17
Balaam offered on each **a** a bull and a Nm 23:2
I have offered on each **a** a bull and a Nm 23:4
offered a bull and a ram on each **a**. Nm 23:14
offered a bull and a ram on each **a**. Nm 23:30
blood, on the **a** of the LORD your God. Dt 12:27
be poured out on the **a** of the LORD your Dt 12:27
an Asherah beside the **a** of the LORD Dt 16:21
set it down before the **a** of the LORD your Dt 26:4
you shall build an **a** to the LORD your Dt 27:5
altar to the LORD your God, an **a** of stones. Dt 27:5
you shall build an **a** to the LORD your Dt 27:6
and whole burnt offerings on your **a**. Dt 33:10
that time Joshua built an **a** to the LORD, Jos 8:30
the Law of Moses, "an **a** of uncut stones, Jos 8:31
congregation and for the **a** of the LORD, Jos 9:27
built there an **a** by the Jordan, Jos 22:10
by the Jordan, an **a** of imposing size. Jos 22:10
have built the **a** at the frontier Jos 22:11
by building yourselves an **a** this day in Jos 22:16
for yourselves an **a** other than the Jos 22:19
altar other than the **a** of the LORD our Jos 22:19
for building an **a** to turn away from Jos 22:23
we said, 'Let us now build an **a**, Jos 22:26
'Behold, the copy of the **a** of the LORD, Jos 22:28
by building an **a** for burnt offering, Jos 22:29
other than the **a** of the LORD our God Jos 22:29
the people of Gad called the **a** Witness, Jos 22:34
Then Gideon built an **a** there to the LORD Jgs 6:24
and pull down the **a** of Baal that your Jgs 6:25
and build an **a** to the LORD your God on Jgs 6:26
behold, the **a** of Baal was broken down, Jgs 6:28
was offered on the **a** that had been built. Jgs 6:28
has broken down the **a** of Baal and cut Jgs 6:30
because his **a** has been broken down." Jgs 6:31
him," because he broke down his **a**. Jgs 6:32
went up toward heaven from the **a**, Jgs 13:20
the LORD went up in the flame of the **a**. Jgs 13:20
and built there an **a** and offered burnt Jgs 21:4
Israel to be my priest, to go up to my **a**, 1 Sm 2:28
cut off from my **a** shall be spared to 1 Sm 2:33
And he built there an **a** to the LORD. 1 Sm 7:17
And Saul built an **a** to the LORD; it 1 Sm 14:35
it was the first **a** that he built to the 1 Sm 14:35
raise an **a** to the LORD on the 2 Sm 24:18
in order to build an **a** to the LORD, 2 Sm 24:21
David built there an **a** to the LORD 2 Sm 24:25
and took hold of the horns of the **a**. 1 Kgs 1:50
he has laid hold of the horns of the **a**, 1 Kgs 1:51
they brought him down from the **a**. 1 Kgs 1:53
and caught hold of the horns of the **a**. 1 Kgs 2:28
is beside the **a**," Solomon sent 1 Kgs 2:29
a thousand burnt offerings on that **a**. 1 Kgs 3:4
gold. He also overlaid an **a** of cedar. 1 Kgs 6:20
Also the whole **a** that belonged to the 1 Kgs 6:22
the golden **a**, the golden table for the 1 Kgs 7:48
stood before the **a** of the LORD 1 Kgs 8:22
his oath before your **a** in this house, 1 Kgs 8:31
he arose from before the **a** of the LORD, 1 Kgs 8:54
because the bronze **a** that was before 1 Kgs 8:64
peace offerings on the **a** that he built 1 Kgs 9:25
and he offered sacrifices on the **a**. 1 Kgs 12:32
went up to the **a** that he had made 1 Kgs 12:33
went up to the **a** to make offerings. 1 Kgs 12:33
standing by the **a** to make offerings. 1 Kgs 13:1
man cried against the **a** by the word 1 Kgs 13:2
the word of the LORD and said, "O **a**, 1 Kgs 13:2
said, "O altar, **a**, thus says the LORD: 1 Kgs 13:2
'Behold, the **a** shall be torn down, and 1 Kgs 13:3
he cried against the **a** at Bethel, 1 Kgs 13:4
stretched out his hand from the **a**, 1 Kgs 13:4
The **a** also was torn down, and the 1 Kgs 13:5
and the ashes poured out from the **a**, 1 Kgs 13:5
the LORD against the **a** in Bethel and 1 Kgs 13:32
He erected an **a** for Baal in the house 1 Kgs 16:32
limped around the **a** that they had 1 Kgs 18:26
And he repaired the **a** of the LORD 1 Kgs 18:30
stones he built an **a** in the name of 1 Kgs 18:32
And he made a trench about the **a**, 1 Kgs 18:32
water ran around the **a** and filled the 1 Kgs 18:35
around the **a** and the house on 2 Kgs 11:11
and set it beside the **a** on the right side 2 Kgs 12:9
he saw the **a** that was at Damascus. 2 Kgs 16:10
to Uriah the priest a model of the **a**, 2 Kgs 16:10
And Uriah the priest built the **a**; in 2 Kgs 16:11
Damascus, the king viewed the **a**. 2 Kgs 16:12
drew near to the **a** and went up on 2 Kgs 16:12
blood of his peace offerings on the **a**. 2 Kgs 16:13
And the bronze **a** that was before the 2 Kgs 16:14
place between his **a** and the house 2 Kgs 16:14
and put it on the north side of his **a**. 2 Kgs 16:14
"On the great **a** burn the morning 2 Kgs 16:15
but the bronze **a** shall be for me to 2 Kgs 16:15
worship before this **a** in Jerusalem"? 2 Kgs 18:22
not come up to the **a** of the LORD in 2 Kgs 23:9
Moreover, the **a** at Bethel, the high 2 Kgs 23:15
that **a** with the high place he pulled 2 Kgs 23:15
burned them on the **a** and defiled it, 2 Kgs 23:16
have done against the **a** at Bethel." 2 Kgs 23:17
offerings on the **a** of burnt offering 1 Chr 6:49
offering and on the **a** of incense for 1 Chr 6:49
the LORD on the **a** of burnt offering 1 Chr 16:40
go up and raise an **a** to the LORD on 1 Chr 21:18
may build on it an **a** to the LORD— 1 Chr 21:22
David built there an **a** to the LORD 1 Chr 21:26
heaven upon the **a** of burnt offering. 1 Chr 21:26
and the **a** of burnt offering were at 1 Chr 21:29
God and here the **a** of burnt offering 1 Chr 22:1
for the **a** of incense made of refined 1 Chr 28:18
the bronze **a** that Bezalel the son of 2 Chr 1:5
there to the bronze **a** before the LORD, 2 Chr 1:6
He made an **a** of bronze, twenty cubits 2 Chr 4:1
the golden **a**, the tables for the bread 2 Chr 4:19
stood east of the **a** with 120 priests 2 Chr 5:12
stood before the **a** of the LORD 2 Chr 6:12
his oath before your **a** in this house, 2 Chr 6:22
because the bronze **a** Solomon had 2 Chr 7:7
the dedication of the **a** seven days and 2 Chr 7:9
to the LORD on the **a** of the LORD that 2 Chr 8:12
and he repaired the **a** of the LORD that 2 Chr 15:8
house, around the **a** and the house. 2 Chr 23:10
to burn incense on the **a** of incense. 2 Chr 26:16
of the LORD, by the **a** of incense. 2 Chr 26:19
the **a** of burnt offering and all its 2 Chr 29:18
they are before the **a** of the LORD." 2 Chr 29:19
to offer them on the **a** of the LORD. 2 Chr 29:21
the blood and threw it against the **a**. 2 Chr 29:22
blood was thrown against the **a**. 2 Chr 29:22
blood was thrown against the **a**. 2 Chr 29:22
offering with their blood on the **a**, 2 Chr 29:24
burnt offering be offered on the **a**. 2 Chr 29:27
"Before one **a** you shall worship, 2 Chr 32:12
He also restored the **a** of the LORD 2 Chr 33:16
burnt offerings on the **a** of the LORD, 2 Chr 35:16
and they built the **a** of the God of Israel, Ezr 3:2
They set the **a** in its place, for fear was on Ezr 3:3
shall offer them on the **a** of the house of Ezr 7:17
to burn on the **a** of the LORD our God, Neh 10:34
in innocence and go around your **a**, Ps 26:6
Then I will go to the **a** of God, to God my Ps 43:4
then bulls will be offered on your **a**. Ps 51:19
with cords, up to the horns of the **a**! Ps 118:27
that he had taken with tongs from the **a**. Is 6:6
day there will be an **a** to the LORD in the Is 19:19
"You shall worship before this **a**"? Is 36:7
their sacrifices will be accepted on my **a**; Is 56:7
shall come up with acceptance on my **a**, Is 60:7
The Lord has scorned his **a**, disowned Lam 2:7
north, and behold, north of the **a** gate, Ezk 8:5
the LORD, between the porch and the **a**, Ezk 8:16
went in and stood beside the bronze **a**. Ezk 9:2
the priests who have charge of the **a**. Ezk 40:46
And the **a** was in front of the temple. Ezk 40:47
an **a** of wood, three cubits high, two Ezk 41:22
measurements of the **a** by cubits (the Ezk 43:13
And this shall be the height of the **a**: Ezk 43:13
and the **a** hearth, four cubits; and Ezk 43:15
and from the **a** hearth projecting Ezk 43:15
The **a** hearth shall be square, twelve Ezk 43:16
The steps of the **a** shall face east." Ezk 43:17
These are the ordinances for the **a**: Ezk 43:18
the four horns of the **a** and on the four Ezk 43:20
shall purify the **a** and make Ezk 43:20
and the **a** shall be purified, as it was Ezk 43:22
atonement for the **a** and cleanse it, Ezk 43:26
offer on the **a** your burnt offerings Ezk 43:27
the four corners of the ledge of the **a**, Ezk 45:19
threshold of the temple, south of the **a**. Ezk 47:1
O priests; wail, O ministers of the **a**. Jl 1:13
the vestibule and the **a** let the priests, Jl 2:17
down beside every **a** on garments taken Am 2:8
and the horns of the **a** shall be cut off Am 3:14
I saw the LORD standing beside the **a**, and Am 9:1
bowl, drenched like the corners of the **a**. Zec 9:15
LORD shall be as the bowls before the **a**. Zec 14:20
By offering polluted food upon my **a**. But Mal 1:7
might not kindle fire on my **a** in vain! Mal 1:10
You cover the LORD'S **a** with tears, with Mal 2:13
your gift at the **a** and there remember Mt 5:23
leave your gift there before the **a** and go. Mt 5:24
you say, 'If anyone swears by the **a**, Mt 23:18
swears by the gift that is on the **a**, Mt 23:18
the gift or the **a** that makes the gift Mt 23:19
whoever swears by the **a** swears by it Mt 23:20
between the sanctuary and the **a**. Mt 23:35
on the right side of the **a** of incense. Lk 1:11
perished between the **a** and the Lk 11:51
found also an **a** with this inscription, Acts 17:23
who serve at the **a** share in the 1 Cor 9:13
the sacrifices participants in the **a**? 1 Cor 10:18
which no one has ever served at the **a**. Heb 7:13
having the golden **a** of incense and the Heb 9:4
We have an **a** from which those who Heb 13:10
he offered up his son Isaac on the **a**? Jas 2:21
I saw under the **a** the souls of those who Rv 6:9
and stood at the **a** with a golden censer, Rv 8:3
saints on the golden **a** before the throne, Rv 8:3
it with fire from the **a** and threw it on the Rv 8:5
four horns of the golden **a** before God, Rv 9:13
of God and the **a** and those who worship Rv 11:1
another angel came out from the **a**, Rv 14:18
And I heard the **a** saying, "Yes, Lord God Rv 16:7

ALTARS (63)

shall tear down their **a** and break their Ex 34:13
cut down your incense **a** and cast your Lv 26:30
the ark, the table, the lampstand, the **a**, Nm 3:31
to Balak, "Build for me here seven **a**, Nm 23:1
have arranged the seven **a** and I have Nm 23:4
and built seven **a** and offered a bull Nm 23:14
for me here seven **a** and prepare for Nm 23:29
shall break down their **a** and dash in Dt 7:5
shall tear down their **a** and dash in Dt 12:3
this land; you shall break down their **a**.' Jgs 2:2
covenant, thrown down your **a**, 1 Kgs 19:10
covenant, thrown down your **a**, 1 Kgs 19:14
his **a** and his images they broke in 2 Kgs 11:18
the priest of Baal before the **a**. 2 Kgs 11:18
high places and **a** Hezekiah has 2 Kgs 18:22
and he erected **a** for Baal and made 2 Kgs 21:3
And he built **a** in the house of the 2 Kgs 21:4
And he built **a** for all the host of 2 Kgs 21:5
And the **a** on the roof of the upper 2 Kgs 23:12
and the **a** that Manasseh had made 2 Kgs 23:12
high places who were there, on the **a**, 2 Kgs 23:20
took away the foreign **a** and the high 2 Chr 14:3
the high places and the incense **a**. 2 Chr 14:5
his **a** and his images they broke in 2 Chr 23:17
the priest of Baal before the **a**. 2 Chr 23:17
he made himself **a** in every corner 2 Chr 28:24
and removed the **a** that were in 2 Chr 30:14
and all the **a** for burning incense 2 Chr 30:14
places and the **a** throughout all 2 Chr 31:1
places and his **a** and commanded 2 Chr 32:12
down, and he erected **a** to the Baals, 2 Chr 33:3
And he built **a** in the house of the 2 Chr 33:4
And he built **a** for all the host of 2 Chr 33:5
and all the **a** that he had built on 2 Chr 33:15
they chopped down the **a** of the Baals 2 Chr 34:4
down the incense **a** that stood above 2 Chr 34:4
priests on their **a** and cleansed Judah 2 Chr 34:5
he broke down the **a** and beat the 2 Chr 34:7
all the incense **a** throughout all the 2 Chr 34:7
where she may lay her young, at your **a**, Ps 84:3
He will not look to the **a**, the work of his Is 17:8
either the Asherim or the **a** of incense. Is 17:8
stones of the **a** like chalkstones crushed Is 27:9
Asherim or incense **a** will remain Is 27:9
high places and **a** Hezekiah has removed, Is 36:7
of Jerusalem are the **a** you have set up Jer 11:13
to shame, **a** to make offerings to Baal. Jer 11:13
their heart, and on the horns of their **a**, Jer 17:1
children remember their **a** and their Jer 17:2
Your **a** shall become desolate, and your Ezk 6:4
and your incense **a** shall be broken, Ezk 6:4
I will scatter your bones around your **a**. Ezk 6:5
so that your **a** will be waste and ruined, Ezk 6:6

and destroyed, your incense **a** cut down, Ezk 6:6
lie among their idols around their **a**, Ezk 6:13
Ephraim has multiplied **a** for sinning, Hos 8:11
they have become to him **a** for sinning. Hos 8:11
his fruit increased, the more **a** he built; Hos 10:1
break down their **a** and destroy their Hos 10:2
and thistle shall grow up on their **a**, Hos 10:8
their **a** also are like stone heaps on the Hos 12:11
I will punish the **a** of Bethel, Am 3:14
they have demolished your **a**, Rom 11:3

ALTER (2)
who shall put out a hand to **a** this, Ezr 6:12
violate my covenant or **a** the word that Ps 89:34

ALTERED (1)
the appearance of his face was **a**, Lk 9:29

ALTERS (1)
a decree that if anyone **a** this edict, Ezr 6:11

ALTHOUGH (42)
my daughters, **a** no one is with us, Gn 31:50
land of the Philistines, **a** that was near. Ex 13:17
a neither the ark of the covenant of Nm 14:44
inheritance, **a** I am a numerous people, Jos 17:14
him, and **a** he had nothing in his hand, Jgs 14:6
A the people of Israel had sworn to 2 Sm 21:2
And **a** they covered him with clothes, 1 Kgs 1:1
now, behold, Adonijah is king, **a** you, 1 Kgs 1:18
had supported Adonijah **a** he had not 1 Kgs 2:28
my father, **a** I am but a little child. 1 Kgs 3:7
a I your servant have feared the LORD 1 Kgs 18:12
a there is no wrong in my hands, 1 Chr 12:17
no breach left in it (**a** up to that time I Neh 6:1
a you incited me against him to destroy Jb 2:3
a you know that I am not guilty, and Jb 10:7
a there is no violence in my hands, and Jb 16:17
a they had declared Job to be in the Jb 32:3
a man's trouble lies heavy on him. Eccl 8:6
in his death, **a** he had done no violence, Is 53:9
prophesy in my name **a** I did not send Jer 14:15
a the LORD persistently sent to you all his Jer 25:4
the LORD,' **a** I have not spoken?" Ezk 13:7
falsely, **a** I have not grieved him, Ezk 13:22
possession of them'—**a** the LORD was Ezk 35:10
A I trained and strengthened their Hos 7:15
And **a** they were seeking to arrest him, Mt 21:46
(**a** Jesus himself did not baptize, but only Jn 4:2
A the doors were locked, Jesus came and Jn 20:26
And **a** there were so many, the net was Jn 21:11
the ground, and **a** his eyes were opened, Acts 9:8
a we gave them no instructions, Acts 15:24
For **a** they knew God, they did not Rom 1:21
a the Law and the Prophets bear Rom 3:21
you, **a** the body is dead because of sin, Rom 8:10
off, and you, **a** a wild olive shoot, Rom 11:17
a it is not a wisdom of this age or of the 1 Cor 2:6
For **a** there may be so-called gods in 1 Cor 8:5
So **a** I wrote to you, it was not for the 2 Cor 7:12
not enter my rest,'" **a** his works were Heb 4:3
A he was a son, he learned obedience Heb 5:8
a I was very eager to write to you about Jude 1:3
to remind you, **a** you once fully knew it, Jude 1:5

ALTOGETHER (12)
they have done **a** according to the Gn 18:21
a his sons and his daughters Gn 46:15
your hands, so that you will be **a** joyful. Dt 16:15
me, and now you have destroyed me **a**. Jb 10:8
why then have you become **a** vain? Jb 27:12
of the LORD are true, and righteous **a**. Ps 19:9
shame and disappointed **a** who rejoice Ps 35:26
But transgressors shall be **a** destroyed; Ps 37:38
shame and disappointed **a** who seek to Ps 40:14
tongue, behold, O LORD, you know it **a**. Ps 139:4
You are **a** beautiful, my love; there is no Sg 4:7
is most sweet, and he is **a** desirable. Sg 5:16

ALUSH (2)
out from Dophkah and camped at **A**. Nm 33:13
they set out from **A** and camped at Nm 33:14

ALVAH (2)
names: the chiefs Timna, **A**, Jetheth, Gn 36:40
Edom were: chiefs Timna, **A**, Jetheth, 1 Chr 1:51

ALVAN (2)
A, Manahath, Ebal, Shepho, and Gn 36:23
A, Manahath, Ebal, Shepho, and 1 Chr 1:40

ALWAYS (79)
So it was **a**: the cloud covered it by day Nm 9:16
Oh that they had such a mind as this **a**, Dt 5:29
to fear the LORD our God, for our good **a**, Dt 6:24
his rules, and his commandments **a**. Dt 11:1
eyes of the LORD your God are **a** upon it, Dt 11:12
may learn to fear the LORD your God **a**. Dt 14:23
been kept from us as **a** when I go on 1 Sm 21:5
therefore he shall **a** be my servant." 1 Sm 27:12
father, and you shall eat at my table **a**." 2 Sm 9:7
master's grandson shall **a** eat at my 2 Sm 9:10
for he ate **a** at the king's table. 2 Sm 9:13
of his father, for Hiram **a** loved David. 1 Kgs 5:1
my servant may **a** have a lamp 1 Kgs 11:36
for you, you shall **a** be careful to do. 2 Kgs 17:37
but **a** evil." And Jehoshaphat said, 2 Chr 18:7
For the needy shall not **a** be forgotten, Ps 9:18
I have set the LORD **a** before me; because Ps 16:8
a at ease, they increase in riches. Ps 73:12
He will not **a** chide, nor will he keep his Ps 103:9
delight; be intoxicated **a** in her love. Prv 5:19
Bind them on your heart **a**; tie them Prv 6:21
his delight, rejoicing before him **a**, Prv 8:30
Blessed is the one who fears the LORD **a**, Prv 28:14
Let your garments be **a** white. Let not Eccl 9:8
contend forever, nor will I **a** be angry; Is 57:16
in heaven their angels **a** see the face of Mt 18:10
For you **a** have the poor with you, but Mt 26:11
with you, but you will not **a** have me. Mt 26:11
And behold, I am with you **a**, to the end Mt 28:20
the mountains he was **a** crying out and Mk 5:5
For you **a** have the poor with you, and Mk 14:7
for them. But you will not **a** have me. Mk 14:7
he said to him, 'Son, you are **a** with me, Lk 15:31
effect that they ought **a** to pray and not Lk 18:1
said to him, "Sir, give us this bread **a**." Jn 6:34
has not yet come, but your time is **a** here. Jn 7:6
for I **a** do the things that are pleasing to Jn 8:29
I knew that you **a** hear me, but I said Jn 11:42
The poor you **a** have with you, but you Jn 12:8
with you, but you do not **a** have me." Jn 12:8
I have **a** taught in synagogues and in Jn 18:20
him, "'I saw the Lord **a** before me, Acts 2:25
and ears, you **a** resist the Holy Spirit. Acts 7:51
So I **a** take pains to have a clear Acts 24:16
a in my prayers, asking that somehow Rom 1:10
thanks to my God **a** for you because of 1 Cor 1:4
a abounding in the work of the 1 Cor 15:58
Yes and No, but in him it is **a** Yes. 2 Cor 1:19
who in Christ **a** leads us in 2 Cor 2:14
a carrying in the body the death of 2 Cor 4:10
we who live are **a** being given over to 2 Cor 4:11
So we are **a** of good courage. We know 2 Cor 5:6
as sorrowful, yet **a** rejoicing; as poor, 2 Cor 6:10
It is **a** good to be made much of for a Gal 4:18
giving thanks **a** and for everything to Eph 5:20
a in every prayer of mine for you all Phil 1:4
full courage now as **a** Christ will be Phil 1:20
my beloved, as you have **a** obeyed, Phil 2:12
Rejoice in the Lord **a**; again I will say, Phil 4:4
We **a** thank God, the Father of our Lord Col 1:3
Let your speech **a** be gracious, seasoned Col 4:6
a struggling on your behalf in his Col 4:12
give thanks to God **a** for all of you, 1 Thes 1:2
be saved—so as **a** to fill up the 1 Thes 2:16
reported that you **a** remember us 1 Thes 3:6
and so we will **a** be with the Lord. 1 Thes 4:17
but **a** seek to do good to one another 1 Thes 5:15
Rejoice **a**, 1 Thes 5:16
We ought **a** to give thanks to God for 2 Thes 1:3
To this end we **a** pray for you, that 2 Thes 1:11
But we ought **a** to give thanks to 2 Thes 2:13
a learning and never able to arrive at a 2 Tm 3:7
As for you, **a** be sober-minded, endure 2 Tm 4:5
of their own, said, "Cretans are **a** liars, Ti 1:12
I thank my God **a** when I remember Phlm 1:4
said, 'They **a** go astray in their heart; Heb 3:10
since he **a** lives to make intercession Heb 7:25
a being prepared to make a defense to 1 Pt 3:15
Therefore I intend **a** to remind you of 2 Pt 1:12

AM (3) [Part of God's Name]
to Moses, "I **A** WHO I AM." And he said, Ex 3:14
to Moses, "I AM WHO I **A**." And he said, Ex 3:14
people of Israel, 'I **A** has sent me to you.'" Ex 3:14

AMAD (1)
Allammelech, **A**, and Mishal. On the Jos 19:26

AMAL (1)
Zophah, Imna, Shelesh, and **A**. 1 Chr 7:35

AMALEK (22)
Esau's son; she bore **A** to Eliphaz.) Gn 36:12
Korah, Gatam, and **A**; these are the Gn 36:16
Then **A** came and fought with Israel at Ex 17:8
for us men, and go out and fight with **A**. Ex 17:9
as Moses told him, and fought with **A**, Ex 17:10
he lowered his hand, **A** prevailed. Ex 17:11
And Joshua overwhelmed **A** and his Ex 17:13
the memory of **A** from under heaven." Ex 17:14
have war with **A** from generation to Ex 17:16
Then he looked on **A** and took up his Nm 24:20
"**A** was the first among the nations, Nm 24:20
"Remember what **A** did to you on the Dt 25:17
the memory of **A** from under heaven; Dt 25:19
'I have noted what **A** did to Israel in 1 Sm 15:2
Now go and strike **A** and devote to 1 Sm 15:3
came to the city of **A** and lay in wait 1 Sm 15:5
I have brought Agag the king of **A**, 1 Sm 15:20
carry out his fierce wrath against **A**, 1 Sm 28:18
A, and from the spoil of Hadadezer the 2 Sm 8:12
Gatam, Kenaz, and of Timna, **A**. 1 Chr 1:36
Ammonites, the Philistines and **A**. 1 Chr 18:11
Gebal and Ammon and **A**, Philistia with Ps 83:7

AMALEKITE (3)
man of Egypt, servant to an **A**, 1 Sm 30:13
are you?' I answered him, 'I am an **A**.' 2 Sm 1:8
"I am the son of a sojourner, an **A**." 2 Sm 1:13

AMALEKITES (25)
and defeated all the country of the **A**, Gn 14:7
The **A** dwell in the land of the Negeb. Nm 13:29
since the **A** and the Canaanites dwell Nm 14:25
For there the **A** and the Canaanites Nm 14:43
Then the **A** and the Canaanites who Nm 14:45
to himself the Ammonites and the **A**, Jgs 3:13
the Midianites and the **A** and the people of Jgs 6:3
the Midianites and the **A** and the people Jgs 6:33
the Midianites and the **A** and all the Jgs 7:12
and the **A** and the Maonites oppressed Jgs 10:12
Ephraim, in the hill country of the **A**. Jgs 12:15
and struck the **A** and delivered Israel 1 Sm 14:48
go down from among the **A**, lest I 1 Sm 15:6
Kenites departed from among the **A**. 1 Sm 15:6
Saul defeated the **A** from Havilah as 1 Sm 15:7
the king of the **A** alive and devoted to 1 Sm 15:8
have brought them from the **A**, 1 Sm 15:15
to destruction the sinners, the **A**, 1 Sm 15:18
I have devoted the **A** to destruction. 1 Sm 15:20
the king of the **A**." And Agag came 1 Sm 15:32
the Geshurites, the Girzites, and the **A**, 1 Sm 27:8
the **A** had made a raid against the 1 Sm 30:1
recovered all that the **A** had taken, 1 Sm 30:18
returned from striking down the **A**, 2 Sm 1:1
remnant of the **A** who had escaped, 1 Chr 4:43

AMAM (1)
A, Shema, Moladah, Jos 15:26

AMANA (1)
Depart from the peak of **A**, from the peak Sg 4:8

AMARIAH (16)
Meraioth fathered **A**, Amariah 1 Chr 6:7
fathered Amariah, **A** fathered Ahitub, 1 Chr 6:7
Azariah fathered **A**, Amariah 1 Chr 6:11
Amariah, **A** fathered Ahitub, 1 Chr 6:11
Meraioth his son, **A** his son, Ahitub 1 Chr 6:52
Jeriah the chief, **A** the second, 1 Chr 23:19
Jeriah the chief, **A** the second, 1 Chr 24:23
A the chief priest is over you in all 2 Chr 19:11
A, and Shecaniah were faithfully 2 Chr 31:15
son of **A**, son of Azariah, son of Meraioth, Ezr 7:3
Shallum, **A**, and Joseph. Ezr 10:42
Pashhur, **A**, Malchijah, Neh 10:3
of Uzziah, son of Zechariah, son of **A**, Neh 11:4
A, Malluch, Hattush, Neh 12:2
of Ezra, Meshullam; of **A**, Jehohanan; Neh 12:13
son of Cushi, son of Gedaliah, son of **A**, Zep 1:1

AMASA (17)
Absalom had set **A** over the army 2 Sm 17:25
A was the son of a man named Ithra 2 Sm 17:25
And say to **A**, 'Are you not my bone 2 Sm 19:13
Then the king said to **A**, "Call the 2 Sm 20:4
So **A** went to summon Judah, but he 2 Sm 20:5
is in Gibeon, **A** came to meet them. 2 Sm 20:8
And Joab said to **A**, "Is it well with 2 Sm 20:9
And Joab took **A** by the beard 2 Sm 20:9
But **A** did not observe the sword that 2 Sm 20:10
men took his stand by **A** and said, 2 Sm 20:11
And **A** lay wallowing in his blood in 2 Sm 20:12
he carried **A** out of the highway into 2 Sm 20:12
the son of Ner, and **A** the son of Jether, 1 Kgs 2:5
of Israel, and **A** the son of Jether, 1 Kgs 2:32
Abigail bore **A**, and the father of 1 Chr 2:17
and the father of **A** was Jether the 1 Chr 2:17
of Shallum, and **A** the son of Hadlai, 2 Chr 28:12

AMASAI (5)
sons of Elkanah: **A** and Ahimoth, 1 Chr 6:25
of Elkanah, son of Mahath, son of **A**, 1 Chr 6:35
Then the Spirit clothed **A**, chief of 1 Chr 12:18
Joshaphat, Nethanel, **A**, Zechariah, 1 Chr 15:24
Levites arose, Mahath the son of **A**, 2 Chr 29:12

AMASHSAI (1)
heads of fathers' houses, 242; and **A**, Neh 11:13

AMASIAH (1)
and next to him **A** the son of Zichri, 2 Chr 17:16

AMAW (1)
the River in the land of the people of **A**, Nm 22:5

AMAZED (22)
righteousness, do not be **a** at the matter, Eccl 5:8
And all the people were **a**, and said, Mt 12:23
so that the governor was greatly **a**. Mt 27:14
And they were all **a**, so that they Mk 1:27
so that they were all **a** and glorified God, Mk 2:12
were greatly **a** and ran up to him and Mk 9:15
And the disciples were **a** at his words. Mk 10:24
And they were **a**, and those who Mk 10:32
no further answer, so that Pilate was **a**. Mk 15:5
heard him were **a** at his understanding Lk 2:47
And they were all **a** and said to one Lk 4:36
And her parents were **a**, but he charged Lk 8:56
some women of our company **a** us. Lk 24:22
And they were **a** and astonished, saying, Acts 2:7
And all were **a** and perplexed, saying to Acts 2:12
Moses saw it, he was **a** at the sight, Acts 7:31
in the city and **a** the people of Samaria, Acts 8:9
long time he had **a** them with his Acts 8:11
great miracles performed, he was **a**. Acts 8:13
all who heard him were **a** and said, Acts 9:21
who had come with Peter were **a**, Acts 10:45
opened, they saw him and were **a**. Acts 12:16

AMAZEMENT (4)
the men looked at one another in **a**. Gn 43:33
were immediately overcome with **a**. Mk 5:42
And **a** seized them all, and they glorified Lk 5:26
filled with wonder and **a** at what had Acts 3:10

AMAZIAH (39)
and **A** his son reigned in his place. 2 Kgs 12:21
he fought against **A** king of Judah, 2 Kgs 13:12
king of Israel, **A** the son of Joash, 2 Kgs 14:1
Then **A** sent messengers to Jehoash 2 Kgs 14:8
of Israel sent word to **A** king of Judah, 2 Kgs 14:9
But **A** would not listen. So Jehoash 2 Kgs 14:11
and he and **A** king of Judah faced 2 Kgs 14:11
of Israel captured **A** king of Judah, 2 Kgs 14:13
how he fought with **A** king of Judah, 2 Kgs 14:15
A the son of Joash, king of Judah, 2 Kgs 14:17
Now the rest of the deeds of **A**, are 2 Kgs 14:18
him king instead of his father **A**. 2 Kgs 14:21
the fifteenth year of **A** the son of 2 Kgs 14:23
king of Israel, Azariah the son of **A**, 2 Kgs 15:1
to all that his father **A** had done. 2 Kgs 15:3
A his son, Azariah his son, Jotham 1 Chr 3:12
Jamlech, Joshah the son of **A**, 1 Chr 4:34
son of Hashabiah, son of **A**, son of 1 Chr 6:45
And **A** his son reigned in his place. 2 Chr 24:27
A was twenty-five years old when he 2 Chr 25:1
Then **A** assembled the men of Judah 2 Chr 25:5
And **A** said to the man of God, "But 2 Chr 25:9
Then **A** discharged the army that 2 Chr 25:10
But **A** took courage and led out his 2 Chr 25:11
of the army whom **A** sent back, 2 Chr 25:13
After **A** came from striking down 2 Chr 25:14
LORD was angry with **A** and sent to 2 Chr 25:15
Then **A** king of Judah took counsel 2 Chr 25:17
Israel sent word to **A** king of Judah, 2 Chr 25:18
But **A** would not listen, for it was of 2 Chr 25:20
and he and **A** king of Judah faced 2 Chr 25:21
of Israel captured **A** king of Judah, 2 Chr 25:23
A the son of Joash, king of Judah, 2 Chr 25:25
Now the rest of the deeds of **A**, from 2 Chr 25:26
him king instead of his father **A**. 2 Chr 26:1
to all that his father **A** had done. 2 Chr 26:4
Then **A** the priest of Bethel sent to Am 7:10
And **A** said to Amos, "O seer, go, flee Am 7:12
Then Amos answered and said to **A**, "I Am 7:14

AMAZING (3)
man answered, "Why, this is an **a** thing! Jn 9:30
saw another sign in heaven, great and **a**, Rv 15:1
saying, "Great and **a** are your deeds, Rv 15:3

AMBASSADOR (1)
for which I am an **a** in chains, that I Eph 6:20

AMBASSADORS (3)
which sends **a** by the sea, in vessels of Is 18:2
against him by sending his **a** to Egypt, Ezk 17:15
Therefore, we are **a** for Christ, God 2 Cor 5:20

AMBITION (3)
I make it my **a** to preach the gospel, Rom 15:20
jealousy and selfish **a** in your hearts, Jas 3:14
For where jealousy and selfish **a** exist, Jas 3:16

AMBUSH (36)
Lay an **a** against the city, behind it." Jos 8:2
you shall lie in **a** against the city, Jos 8:4
shall rise up from the **a** and seize the city, Jos 8:7
to the place of **a** and lay between Bethel Jos 8:9
and set them in **a** between Bethel and Ai, Jos 8:12
that there was an **a** against him behind Jos 8:14
And the men in the **a** rose quickly out of Jos 8:19
Israel saw that the **a** had captured the Jos 8:21
Shechem put men in **a** against him on Jgs 9:25
are with you, and set an **a** in the field. Jgs 9:32
night and set an **a** against Shechem in Jgs 9:34
who were with him rose from the **a**. Jgs 9:35
companies and set an **a** in the fields. Jgs 9:43
the place and set an **a** for him all night Jgs 16:2
had men lying in **a** in an inner Jgs 16:9
the men lying in **a** were in an inner Jgs 16:12
So Israel set men in **a** around Gibeah. Jgs 20:29
Israel who were in **a** rushed out of their Jgs 20:33
trusted the men in **a** whom they had set Jgs 20:36
Then the men in **a** hurried and rushed Jgs 20:37
the men in **a** moved out and struck all Jgs 20:37
men in the main **a** was that when they Jgs 20:38
"Go and lie in **a** in the vineyards Jgs 21:20
had sent an **a** around to come 2 Chr 13:13
Judah, and the **a** was behind them. 2 Chr 13:13
the LORD set an **a** against the men of 2 Chr 20:22
He sits in **a** in the villages; in hiding Ps 10:8
he lurks in **a** like a lion in his thicket; he Ps 10:9
to tear, as a young lion lurking in **a**. Ps 17:12
shooting from **a** at the blameless, Ps 64:4
let us **a** the innocent without reason; Prv 1:11
blood; they set an **a** for their own lives. Prv 1:18
but in his heart he plans an **a** for him. Jer 9:8
son of Paul's sister heard of their **a**, Acts 23:16
of their men are lying in **a** for him, Acts 23:21
they were planning an **a** to kill him on Acts 25:3

AMBUSHES (2)
of the enemy and from **a** by the way. Ezr 8:31
strong; set up watchmen; prepare the **a**; Jer 51:12

AMEN (56)
And the woman shall say, '**A**, Amen.' Nm 5:22
And the woman shall say, 'Amen, **A**.' Nm 5:22
all the people shall answer and say, '**A**.' Dt 27:15
And all the people shall say, '**A**.' Dt 27:16
And all the people shall say, '**A**.' Dt 27:17
And all the people shall say, '**A**.' Dt 27:18
And all the people shall say, '**A**.' Dt 27:19
And all the people shall say, '**A**.' Dt 27:20
And all the people shall say, '**A**.' Dt 27:21
And all the people shall say, '**A**.' Dt 27:22
And all the people shall say, '**A**.' Dt 27:23
And all the people shall say, '**A**.' Dt 27:24
And all the people shall say, '**A**.' Dt 27:25
And all the people shall say, '**A**.' Dt 27:26
answered the king, "**A**! May the LORD, 1 Kgs 1:36
said, "**A**!" and praised the LORD. 1 Chr 16:36
the assembly said "**A**" and praised the Neh 5:13
"**A**, Amen," lifting up their hands. Neh 8:6
"Amen, **A**," lifting up their hands. Neh 8:6
everlasting to everlasting! **A** and Amen. Ps 41:13
everlasting to everlasting! Amen and **A**. Ps 41:13
be filled with his glory! **A** and Amen! Ps 72:19
be filled with his glory! Amen and **A**! Ps 72:19
be the LORD forever! **A** and Amen. Ps 89:52
be the LORD forever! Amen and **A**. Ps 89:52
all the people say, "**A**!" Praise the LORD! Ps 106:48
Jeremiah said, "**A**! May the LORD do so; Jer 28:6
the Creator, who is blessed forever! **A**. Rom 1:25
who is God over all, blessed forever. **A**. Rom 9:5
things. To him be glory forever. **A**. Rom 11:36
the God of peace be with you all. **A**. Rom 15:33
forevermore through Jesus Christ! **A**. Rom 16:27
an outsider say "**A**" to your 1 Cor 14:16
be with you all in Christ Jesus. **A**. 1 Cor 16:24
him that we utter our **A** to God for his 2 Cor 1:20
to whom be the glory forever and ever. **A**. Gal 1:5
Christ be with your spirit, brothers. **A**. Gal 6:18
all generations, forever and ever. **A**. Eph 3:21
Father be glory forever and ever. **A**. Phil 4:20
honor and glory forever and ever. **A**. 1 Tm 1:17
be honor and eternal dominion. **A**. 1 Tm 6:16
him be the glory forever and ever. **A**. 2 Tm 4:18
to whom be glory forever and ever. **A**. Heb 13:21
and dominion forever and ever. **A**. 1 Pt 4:11
be the dominion forever and ever. **A**. 1 Pt 5:11
both now and to the day of eternity. **A**. 2 Pt 3:18
before all time and now and forever. **A**. Jude 1:25
glory and dominion forever and ever. **A**. Rv 1:6
will wail on account of him. Even so. **A**. Rv 1:7
'The words of the **A**, the faithful and true Rv 3:14
"**A**!" and the elders fell down and Rv 5:14
"**A**! Blessing and glory and wisdom and Rv 7:12
be to our God forever and ever! **A**." Rv 7:12
on the throne, saying, "**A**. Hallelujah!" Rv 19:4
says, "Surely I am coming soon." **A**. Rv 22:20
grace of the Lord Jesus be with all. **A**. Rv 22:21

AMEND (4)
A your ways and your deeds, and I will let Jer 7:3
"For if you truly **a** your ways and your Jer 7:5
way, and **a** your ways and your deeds.' Jer 18:11
from his evil way, and **a** your deeds, Jer 35:15

AMENDS (2)
and they make **a** for their iniquity, Lv 26:41
they shall make **a** for their iniquity, Lv 26:43

AMETHYST (3)
third row a jacinth, an agate, and an **a**; Ex 28:19
third row, a jacinth, an agate, and an **a**; Ex 39:12
the eleventh jacinth, the twelfth **a**. Rv 21:20

AMI (1)
and the sons of **A**. Ezr 2:57

AMID (8)
A thoughts from visions of the night, Jb 4:13
they come; **a** the crash they roll on. Jb 30:14
I lie down **a** fiery beasts—the children Ps 57:4
They shall fall **a** those who are slain Ezk 32:20
bronze, **a** the tender grass of the field. Dn 4:15
of Kerioth, and Moab shall die **a** uproar, Am 2:2
a shouting and the sound of the trumpet; Am 2:2
forward the top stone **a** shouts of 'Grace, Zec 4:7

AMISS (1)
for what he has done **a** in the holy thing Lv 5:16

AMITTAI (2)
by his servant Jonah the son of **A**, 2 Kgs 14:25
of the LORD came to Jonah the son of **A**, Jon 1:1

AMMAH (1)
going down they came to the hill of **A**, 2 Sm 2:24

AMMIEL (6)
the tribe of Dan, **A** the son of Gemalli; Nm 13:12
is in the house of Machir the son of **A**, 2 Sm 9:4
from the house of Machir the son of **A**, 2 Sm 9:5
Machir the son of **A** from Lo-debar, 2 Sm 17:27
four by Bath-shua, the daughter of **A**; 1 Chr 3:5
A the sixth, Issachar the seventh, 1 Chr 26:5

AMMIHUD (10)
from Ephraim, Elishama the son of **A**, Nm 1:10
Ephraim being Elishama the son of **A**, Nm 2:18
the seventh day Elishama the son of **A**, Nm 7:48
the offering of Elishama the son of **A**. Nm 7:53
company was Elishama the son of **A**. Nm 10:22
of Simeon, Shemuel the son of **A**. Nm 34:20
Naphtali a chief, Pedahel the son of **A**. Nm 34:28
fled and went to Talmai the son of **A**, 2 Sm 13:37
Ladan his son, **A** his son, Elishama 1 Chr 7:26
Uthai the son of **A**, son of Omri, son of 1 Chr 9:4

AMMINADAB (16)
the daughter of **A** and the sister of Ex 6:23
from Judah, Nahshon the son of **A**; Nm 1:7
of Judah being Nahshon the son of **A**, Nm 2:3
the first day was Nahshon the son of **A**, Nm 7:12
the offering of Nahshon the son of **A**. Nm 7:17
company was Nahshon the son of **A**. Nm 10:14
Hezron fathered Ram, Ram fathered **A**, Ru 4:19
A fathered Nahshon, Nahshon fathered Ru 4:20
Ram fathered **A**, and Amminadab 1 Chr 2:10
and **A** fathered Nahshon, 1 Chr 2:10
A his son, Korah his son, Assir his 1 Chr 6:22
of the sons of Uzziel, **A** the chief, 1 Chr 15:10
Asaiah, Joel, Shemaiah, Eliel, and **A**, 1 Chr 15:11
and Ram the father of **A**, and Mt 1:4
and **A** the father of Nahshon, Mt 1:4
the son of **A**, the son of Admin, the son Lk 3:33

AMMISHADDAI (5)
from Dan, Ahiezer the son of **A**; Nm 1:12
of Dan being Ahiezer the son of **A**, Nm 2:25
On the tenth day Ahiezer the son of **A**, Nm 7:66
was the offering of Ahiezer the son of **A**. Nm 7:71
company was Ahiezer the son of **A**. Nm 10:25

AMMIZABAD (1)
A his son was in charge of his 1 Chr 27:6

AMMON (13)
approach the territory of the people of **A**, Dt 2:19
land of the people of **A** as a possession, Dt 2:19
land of the sons of **A** you did not draw Dt 2:37
the people of Israel and the people of **A**." Jgs 11:27
the men of **A** and Moab and Mount 2 Chr 20:10
an ambush against the men of **A**, 2 Chr 20:22
For the men of **A** and Moab rose 2 Chr 20:23
women of Ashdod, **A**, and Moab. Neh 13:23
Gebal and **A** and Amalek, Philistia with Ps 83:7
Egypt, Judah, Edom, the sons of **A**, Jer 9:26
Edom, Moab, and the sons of **A**; Jer 25:21
king of Moab, the king of the sons of **A**, Jer 27:3
pasture for camels and **A** a fold for Ezk 25:5

AMMONITE (14)
"No **A** or Moabite may enter the Dt 23:3
Then Nahash the **A** went up and 1 Sm 11:1
But Nahash the **A** said to them, "On 1 Sm 11:2
Zelek the **A**, Naharai of Beeroth, the 2 Sm 23:37
Moabite, **A**, Edomite, Sidonian, and 1 Kgs 11:1
mother's name was Naamah the **A**. 1 Kgs 14:21

mother's name was Naamah the **A**. 1 Kgs 14:31
Zelek the **A**, Naharai of Beeroth, the 1 Chr 11:39
mother's name was Naamah the **A**. 2 Chr 12:13
Zabad the son of Shimeath the **A**, 2 Chr 24:26
Horonite and Tobiah, the **A** servant, Neh 2:10
and Tobiah the **A** servant and Geshem Neh 2:19
Tobiah the **A** was beside him, and he Neh 4:3
written that no **A** or Moabite should Neh 13:1

AMMONITES (100)
He is the father of the **A** to this day. Gn 19:38
to the Jabbok, as far as to the **A**, Nm 21:24
for the border of the **A** was strong. Nm 21:24
—but the **A** call them Zamzummim Dt 2:20
the LORD destroyed them before the **A**, Dt 2:21
bed of iron. Is it not in Rabbah of the **A**? Dt 3:11
as the river Jabbok, the border of the **A**; Dt 3:16
the river Jabbok, the boundary of the **A**, Jos 12:2
as far as the boundary of the **A**; Jos 13:10
of Gilead, and half the land of the **A**, Jos 13:25
to himself the **A** and the Amalekites, Jgs 3:13
the gods of Moab, the gods of the **A**, Jgs 10:6
Philistines and into the hand of the **A**, Jgs 10:7
And the **A** crossed the Jordan to fight Jgs 10:9
from the **A** and from the Philistines? Jgs 10:11
Then the **A** were called to arms, and Jgs 10:17
who will begin to fight against the **A**? Jgs 10:18
After a time the **A** made war against Jgs 11:4
And when the **A** made war against Jgs 11:5
leader, that we may fight with the **A**." Jgs 11:6
us and fight with the **A** and be our head Jgs 11:8
me home again to fight with the **A**, Jgs 11:9
to the king of the **A** and said, Jgs 11:12
king of the **A** answered the messengers Jgs 11:13
sent messengers to the king of the **A** Jgs 11:14
the land of Moab or the land of the **A**, Jgs 11:15
But the king of the **A** did not listen to Jgs 11:28
Mizpah of Gilead he passed on to the **A**. Jgs 11:29
"If you will give the **A** into my hand, Jgs 11:30
in peace from the **A** shall be the LORD'S, Jgs 11:31
crossed over to the **A** to fight against Jgs 11:32
So the **A** were subdued before the Jgs 11:33
you on your enemies, on the **A**." Jgs 11:36
to fight against the **A** and did not call Jgs 12:1
people had a great dispute with the **A**, Jgs 12:2
my hand and crossed over against the **A**, Jgs 12:3
and struck down the **A** until the heat 1 Sm 11:11
the king of the **A** came against you, 1 Sm 12:12
side, against Moab, against the **A**, 1 Sm 14:47
from Edom, Moab, the **A**, the 2 Sm 8:12
After this the king of the **A** died, and 2 Sm 10:1
servants came into the land of the **A**. 2 Sm 10:2
the princes of the **A** said to Hanun 2 Sm 10:3
When the **A** saw that they had 2 Sm 10:6
the **A** sent and hired the Syrians of 2 Sm 10:6
And the **A** came out and drew up in 2 Sm 10:8
and he arrayed them against the **A**. 2 Sm 10:10
but if the **A** are too strong for you, 2 Sm 10:11
And when the **A** saw that the Syrians 2 Sm 10:14
fighting against the **A** and came to 2 Sm 10:14
were afraid to save the **A** anymore. 2 Sm 10:19
they ravaged the **A** and besieged 2 Sm 11:1
killed him with the sword of the **A**. 2 Sm 12:9
Rabbah of the **A** and took the 2 Sm 12:26
thus he did to all the cities of the **A**. 2 Sm 12:31
of Nahash from Rabbah of the **A**, 2 Sm 17:27
Milcom the abomination of the **A**. 1 Kgs 11:5
for Molech the abomination of the **A**, 1 Kgs 11:7
Moab, and Milcom the god of the **A**, 1 Kgs 11:33
Milcom the abomination of the **A**. 2 Kgs 23:13
of the Moabites and bands of the **A**, 2 Kgs 24:2
nations, from Edom, Moab, the **A**, 1 Chr 18:11
this Nahash the king of the **A** died, 1 Chr 19:1
the land of the **A** to Hanun to console 1 Chr 19:2
the princes of the **A** said to Hanun, 1 Chr 19:3
When the **A** saw that they had 1 Chr 19:6
Hanun and the **A** sent 1,000 talents of 1 Chr 19:6
And the **A** were mustered from their 1 Chr 19:7
And the **A** came out and drew up in 1 Chr 19:9
and they were arrayed against the **A**. 1 Chr 19:11
but if the **A** are too strong for you, 1 Chr 19:12
And when the **A** saw that the 1 Chr 19:15
not willing to save the **A** any more. 1 Chr 19:19
the country of the **A** and came and 1 Chr 20:1
David did to all the cities of the **A**. 1 Chr 20:3
After this the Moabites and **A**, and 2 Chr 20:1
The **A** paid tribute to Uzziah, and his 2 Chr 26:8
king of the **A** and prevailed against 2 Chr 27:5
And the **A** gave him that year 100 2 Chr 27:5
The **A** paid him the same amount in 2 Chr 27:5
the Perizzites, the Jebusites, the **A**, Ezr 9:1
the Arabs and the **A** and the Ashdodites Neh 4:7
and Moab, and the **A** shall obey them. Is 11:14
Moab and among the **A** and in Edom Jer 40:11
the king of the **A** has sent Ishmael the Jer 40:14
and set out to cross over to the **A**. Jer 41:10
with eight men, and went to the **A**. Jer 41:15
Concerning the **A**. Thus says the LORD: Jer 49:1
cry to be heard against Rabbah of the **A**; Jer 49:2
I will restore the fortunes of the **A**, Jer 49:6
to Rabbah of the **A** and to Judah, Ezk 21:20
concerning the **A** and concerning Ezk 21:28
face toward the **A** and prophesy against Ezk 25:2
Say to the **A**, Hear the word of the Lord Ezk 25:3
give it along with the **A** to the people of Ezk 25:10
that the **A** may be remembered no Ezk 25:10
and Moab and the main part of the **A**. Dn 11:41
"For three transgressions of the **A**, and Am 1:13
of Moab and the revilings of the **A**, Zep 2:8
like Sodom, and the **A** like Gomorrah, Zep 2:9

AMNON (25)
his firstborn was **A**, of Ahinoam of 2 Sm 3:2
And after a time **A**, David's son, loved 2 Sm 13:1
And **A** was so tormented that he made 2 Sm 13:2
seemed impossible to **A** to do 2 Sm 13:2
But **A** had a friend, whose name was 2 Sm 13:3
Will you not tell me?" **A** said to him, 2 Sm 13:4
So **A** lay down and pretended to be ill. 2 Sm 13:6
came to see him, **A** said to the king, 2 Sm 13:6
him, but he refused to eat. And **A** said, 2 Sm 13:9
Then **A** said to Tamar, "Bring the 2 Sm 13:10
into the chamber to **A** her brother. 2 Sm 13:10
Then **A** hated her with very great 2 Sm 13:15
loved her. And **A** said to her, "Get up! 2 Sm 13:15
"Has **A** your brother been with you? 2 Sm 13:20
Absalom spoke to **A** neither good 2 Sm 13:22
good nor bad, for Absalom hated **A**, 2 Sm 13:22
please let my brother **A** go with us." 2 Sm 13:26
him until he let **A** and all the king's 2 Sm 13:27
and when I say to you, 'Strike **A**,' 2 Sm 13:28
of Absalom did to **A** as Absalom had 2 Sm 13:29
the king's sons, for **A** alone is dead. 2 Sm 13:32
sons are dead, for **A** alone is dead." 2 Sm 13:33
because he was comforted about **A**, 2 Sm 13:39
A, by Ahinoam the Jezreelite; 1 Chr 3:1
A, Rinnah, Ben-hanan, and Tilon. 1 Chr 4:20

AMNON'S (3)
to your brother **A** house and prepare 2 Sm 13:7
Tamar went to her brother **A** house, 2 Sm 13:8
"Mark when **A** heart is merry with 2 Sm 13:28

AMOK (2)
Sallu, **A**, Hilkiah, Jedaiah. These were Neh 12:7
of Sallai, Kallai; of **A**, Eber; Neh 12:20

AMON (18)
take him back to **A** the governor of 1 Kgs 22:26
and **A** his son reigned in his place. 2 Kgs 21:18
A was twenty-two years old when he 2 Kgs 21:19
the servants of **A** conspired against 2 Kgs 21:23
who had conspired against King **A**, 2 Kgs 21:24
the rest of the acts of **A** that he did, 2 Kgs 21:25
A his son, Josiah his son. 1 Chr 3:14
take him back to **A** the governor of 2 Chr 18:25
and **A** his son reigned in his place. 2 Chr 33:20
A was twenty-two years old when he 2 Chr 33:21
A sacrificed to all the images that 2 Chr 33:22
but this **A** incurred guilt more and 2 Chr 33:23
who had conspired against King **A**. 2 Chr 33:25
of Pochereth-hazzebaim, the sons of **A**. Neh 7:59
came in the days of Josiah the son of **A**, Jer 1:2
the thirteenth year of Josiah the son of **A**, Jer 25:3
punishment upon **A** of Thebes, Jer 46:25
in the days of Josiah the son of **A**, Zep 1:1

AMORITE (8)
was living by the oaks of Mamre the **A**, Gn 14:13
his daughters captives, to an **A** king, Nm 21:29
I have given into your hand Sihon the **A**, Dt 2:24
land of the Canaanite, the Hittite, the **A**, Neh 9:8
your father was an **A** and your mother Ezk 16:3
was a Hittite and your father an **A**. Ezk 16:45
it was I who destroyed the **A** before them, Am 2:9
wilderness, to possess the land of the **A**. Am 2:10

AMORITES (79)
and the Jebusites, the **A**, the Gn 10:16
and also the **A** who were dwelling in Gn 14:7
the iniquity of the **A** is not yet Gn 15:16
the **A**, the Canaanites, the Girgashites Gn 15:21
the hand of the **A** with my sword and Gn 48:22
place of the Canaanites, the Hittites, the **A**, Ex 3:8
of the Canaanites, the Hittites, the **A**, Ex 3:17
of the Canaanites, the Hittites, the **A**, Ex 13:5
brings you to the **A** and the Hittites and Ex 23:23
I will drive out the Canaanites, the **A**, Ex 33:2
I will drive out before you the **A**, Ex 34:11
and the **A** dwell in the hill country. Nm 13:29
that extends from the border of the **A**, Nm 21:13
of Moab, between Moab and the **A**. Nm 21:13
messengers to Sihon king of the **A**, Nm 21:21
Israel settled in all the cities of the **A**, Nm 21:25
the city of Sihon the king of the **A**, Nm 21:26
Thus Israel lived in the land of the **A**. Nm 21:31
and dispossessed the **A** who were Nm 21:32
him as you did to Sihon king of the **A**, Nm 21:34
saw all that Israel had done to the **A**. Nm 22:2
Sihon king of the **A** and the kingdom Nm 32:33
and dispossessed the **A** who were in it. Nm 32:39
he had defeated Sihon the king of the **A**, Dt 1:4
the hill country of the **A** and to all their Dt 1:7
on the way to the hill country of the **A**, Dt 1:19
have come to the hill country of the **A**, Dt 1:20
Egypt, to give us into the hand of the **A**, Dt 1:27
Then the **A** who lived in that hill Dt 1:44
him as you did to Sihon the king of the **A**, Dt 3:2
two kings of the **A** who were beyond the Dt 3:8
Hermon Sirion, while the **A** call it Senir), Dt 3:9
in the land of Sihon the king of the **A**, Dt 4:46
king of Bashan, the two kings of the **A**, Dt 4:47
you, the Hittites, the Girgashites, the **A**, Dt 7:1
destruction, the Hittites and the **A**, Dt 20:17
did to Sihon and Og, the kings of the **A**, Dt 31:4
two kings of the **A** who were beyond the Jos 2:10
the Perizzites, the Girgashites, the **A**, Jos 3:10
the kings of the **A** who were beyond the Jos 5:1
at all, to give us into the hands of the **A**, Jos 7:7
Sea toward Lebanon, the Hittites, the **A**, Jos 9:1
two kings of the **A** who were beyond the Jos 9:10
Then the five kings of the **A**, the king of Jos 10:5
all the kings of the **A** who dwell in the Jos 10:6
the LORD gave the **A** over to the sons Jos 10:12
in the east and the west, the **A**, Jos 11:3
Sihon king of the **A** who lived at Jos 12:2
the Negeb, the land of the Hittites, the **A**, Jos 12:8
to Aphek, to the boundary of the **A**, Jos 13:4
and all the cities of Sihon king of the **A**, Jos 13:10
all the kingdom of Sihon king of the **A**, Jos 13:21
Then I brought you to the land of the **A**, Jos 24:8
fought against you, and also the **A**, Jos 24:11
out before you, the two kings of the **A**; Jos 24:12
or the gods of the **A** in whose land you Jos 24:15
the peoples, the **A** who lived in the land. Jos 24:18
The **A** pressed the people of Dan back Jgs 1:34
The **A** persisted in dwelling in Mount Jgs 1:35
the border of the **A** ran from the ascent Jgs 1:36
among the Canaanites, the Hittites, the **A**, Jgs 3:5
fear the gods of the **A** in whose land you Jgs 6:10
beyond the Jordan in the land of the **A**, Jgs 10:8
from the Egyptians and from the **A**, Jgs 10:11
sent messengers to Sihon king of the **A**, Jgs 11:19
took possession of all the land of the **A**, Jgs 11:21
the territory of the **A** from the Arnon to Jgs 11:22
dispossessed the **A** from before his Jgs 11:23
peace also between Israel and the **A**. 1 Sm 7:14
of Israel but of the remnant of the **A**. 2 Sm 21:2
of Sihon king of the **A** and of Og king 1 Kgs 4:19
All the people who were left of the **A**, 1 Kgs 9:20
going after idols, as the **A** had done, 1 Kgs 21:26
more evil than all that the **A** did, 2 Kgs 21:11
and the Jebusites, the **A**, the 1 Chr 1:14
who were left of the Hittites, the **A**, 2 Chr 8:7
the Moabites, the Egyptians, and the **A**. Ezr 9:1
Sihon, king of the **A**, and Og, king of Ps 135:11
Sihon, king of the **A**, for his steadfast Ps 136:19

AMOS (10)
The words of **A**, who was among the Am 1:1
to me, "**A**, what do you see?" And I said, Am 7:8
"**A** has conspired against you in the Am 7:10
For thus **A** has said, "'Jeroboam shall Am 7:11
And Amaziah said to **A**, "O seer, go, flee Am 7:12
Then **A** answered and said to Amaziah, Am 7:14
he said, "**A**, what do you see?" And I said, Am 8:2
and Manasseh the father of **A**, Mt 1:10
of Amos, and **A** the father of Josiah, Mt 1:10
the son of Mattathias, the son of **A**, the Lk 3:25

AMOUNT (8)
shall calculate the **a** of the valuation Lv 27:23
the spoil of the city, a very great **a**. 2 Sm 12:30
Ophir a very great **a** of almug wood 1 Kgs 10:11
David took a large **a** of bronze. 1 Chr 18:8
out the spoil of the city, a very great **a**. 1 Chr 20:2
paid him the same **a** in the second 2 Chr 27:5
so that we have this large **a** left." 2 Chr 31:10
lend to sinners, to get back the same **a**. Lk 6:34

AMOZ (13)
to the prophet Isaiah the son of **A**. 2 Kgs 19:2
Isaiah the son of **A** sent to Hezekiah, 2 Kgs 19:20
prophet the son of **A** came to him and 2 Kgs 20:1
the prophet the son of **A** wrote. 2 Chr 26:22
and Isaiah the prophet, the son of **A**, 2 Chr 32:20
of Isaiah the prophet the son of **A**, 2 Chr 32:32
The vision of Isaiah the son of **A**, which he Is 1:1
Isaiah the son of **A** saw concerning Judah Is 2:1
Babylon which Isaiah the son of **A** saw. Is 13:1
the LORD spoke by Isaiah the son of **A**, Is 20:2

to the prophet Isaiah the son of **A**. Is 37:2
Isaiah the son of **A** sent to Hezekiah, Is 37:21
the prophet the son of **A** came to him, Is 38:1

AMPHIPOLIS (1)
had passed through **A** and Apollonia, Acts 17:1

AMPLE (2)
you have **a** goods laid up for many Lk 12:19
me you may have **a** cause to glory in Phil 1:26

AMPLIATUS (1)
Greet **A**, my beloved in the Lord. Rom 16:8

AMRAM (13)
A, Izhar, Hebron, and Uzziel, the years of Ex 6:18
A took as his wife Jochebed his father's Ex 6:20
the years of the life of **A** being 137 years. Ex 6:20
clans: **A**, Izhar, Hebron, and Uzziel. Nm 3:19
And Kohath was the father of **A**. Nm 26:58
And she bore to **A** Aaron and Moses Nm 26:59
Kohath: **A**, Izhar, Hebron, and Uzziel. 1 Chr 6:2
The children of **A**: Aaron, Moses, and 1 Chr 6:3
Kohath: **A**, Izhar, Hebron and Uzziel. 1 Chr 6:18
A, Izhar, Hebron, and Uzziel, four. 1 Chr 23:12
The sons of **A**: Aaron and Moses. 1 Chr 23:13
of Levi: of the sons of **A**, Shubael; 1 Chr 24:20
Of the sons of Bani: Maadai, **A**, Uel, Ezr 10:34

AMRAM'S (1)
The name of **A** wife was Jochebed the Nm 26:59

AMRAMITES (2)
the clan of the **A** and the clan of Nm 3:27
Of the **A**, the Izharites, the 1 Chr 26:23

AMRAPHEL (2)
In the days of **A** king of Shinar, Arioch Gn 14:1
Tidal king of Goiim, **A** king of Shinar, Gn 14:9

AMULETS (1)
the sashes, the perfume boxes, and the **a**; Is 3:20

AMZI (2)
son of **A**, son of Bani, son of Shemer, 1 Chr 6:46
of Jeroham, son of Pelaliah, son of **A**, Neh 11:12

ANAB (2)
from Hebron, from Debir, from **A**, Jos 11:21
A, Eshtemoh, Anim, Jos 15:50

ANAH (12)
the daughter of **A** the daughter of Gn 36:2
the daughter of **A** the daughter of Gn 36:14
of Oholibamah the daughter of **A**, Gn 36:18
of the land: Lotan, Shobal, Zibeon, **A**, Gn 36:20
are the sons of Zibeon: Aiah and **A**; Gn 36:24
he is the **A** who found the hot springs Gn 36:24
These are the children of **A**: Dishon Gn 36:25
and Oholibamah the daughter of **A**. Gn 36:25
the chiefs Lotan, Shobal, Zibeon, **A**, Gn 36:29
Lotan, Shobal, Zibeon, **A**, Dishon, 1 Chr 1:38
The sons of Zibeon: Aiah and **A**. 1 Chr 1:40
The son of **A**: Dishon. The sons of 1 Chr 1:41

ANAHARATH (1)
Hapharaim, Shion, **A**, Jos 19:19

ANAIAH (2)
him stood Mattithiah, Shema, **A**, Uriah, Neh 8:4
Pelatiah, Hanan, **A**, Neh 10:22

ANAK (9)
and Talmai, the descendants of **A**, Nm 13:22
we saw the descendants of **A** there. Nm 13:28
we saw the Nephilim (the sons of **A**, Nm 13:33
'Who can stand before the sons of **A**?' Dt 9:2
is, Hebron (Arba was the father of **A**). Jos 15:13
out from there the three sons of **A**, Jos 15:14
and Talmai, the descendants of **A**. Jos 15:14
(Arba being the father of **A**), Jos 21:11
he drove out from it the three sons of **A**. Jgs 1:20

ANAKIM (9)
we have seen the sons of the **A** there.'" Dt 1:28
people great and many, and tall as the **A**. Dt 2:10
Like the **A** they are also counted as Dt 2:11
people great and many, and tall as the **A**; Dt 2:21
a people great and tall, the sons of the **A**, Dt 9:2
and cut off the **A** from the hill country, Jos 11:21
There was none of the **A** left in the land Jos 11:22
heard on that day how the **A** were there, Jos 14:12
was the greatest man among the **A**.) Jos 14:15

ANAMIM (2)
Egypt fathered Ludim, **A**, Lehabim, Gn 10:13
Egypt fathered Ludim, **A**, Lehabim, 1 Chr 1:11

ANAMMELECH (1)
in the fire to Adrammelech and **A**, 2 Kgs 17:31

ANAN (1)
Ahiah, Hanan, **A**, Neh 10:26

ANANI (1)
Akkub, Johanan, Delaiah, and **A**, 1 Chr 3:24

ANANIAH (2)
son of **A** repaired beside his own house. Neh 3:23
Anathoth, Nob, **A**, Neh 11:32

ANANIAS (11)
But a man named **A**, with his wife Acts 5:1
"**A**, why has Satan filled your heart to Acts 5:3
When **A** heard these words, he fell down Acts 5:5
was a disciple at Damascus named **A**. Acts 9:10
to him in a vision, "**A**." And he said, Acts 9:10
vision a man named **A** come in and Acts 9:12
But **A** answered, "Lord, I have heard Acts 9:13
So **A** departed and entered the house. Acts 9:17
"And one **A**, a devout man according Acts 22:12
the high priest **A** commanded those Acts 23:2
days the high priest **A** came down with Acts 24:1

ANATH (2)
After him was Shamgar the son of **A**, Jgs 3:31
"In the days of Shamgar, son of **A**, in the Jgs 5:6

ANATHOTH (20)
A with its pasturelands, and Almon Jos 21:18
Abiezer of **A**, Mebunnai the 2 Sm 23:27
the priest the king said, "Go to **A**, 1 Kgs 2:26
and **A** with its pasturelands. 1 Chr 6:60
Jeremoth, Abijah, **A**, and Alemeth. 1 Chr 7:8
of Ikkesh of Tekoa, Abiezer of **A**, 1 Chr 11:28
of Azmaveth; Beracah, Jehu of **A**, 1 Chr 12:3
the ninth month, was Abiezer of **A**, 1 Chr 27:12
The men of **A**, 128. Ezr 2:23
The men of **A**, 128. Neh 7:27
Hariph, **A**, Nebai, Neh 10:19
A, Nob, Ananiah, Neh 11:32
Give attention, O Laishah! O Poor **A**! Is 10:30
the priests who were in **A** in the land of Jer 1:1
says the LORD concerning the men of **A**, Jer 11:21
I will bring disaster upon the men of **A**, Jer 11:23
rebuked Jeremiah of **A** who is Jer 29:27
to you and say, 'Buy my field that is at **A**, Jer 32:7
my field that is at **A** in the land of Jer 32:8
bought the field at **A** from Hanamel my Jer 32:9

ANCESTOR (3)
Dan, after the name of Dan their **a**. Jos 19:47
city Dan, after the name of Dan their **a**, Jgs 18:29
loins of his **a** when Melchizedek met Heb 7:10

ANCESTORS (1)
I thank God whom I serve, as did my **a**, 2 Tm 1:3

ANCESTRAL (2)
the chiefs of their **a** tribes, Nm 1:16
listed along with them by their **a** tribe. Nm 1:47

ANCHOR (2)
they weighed **a** and sailed along Acts 27:13
as a sure and steadfast **a** of the soul, Heb 6:19

ANCHORS (3)
they let down four **a** from the stern Acts 27:29
pretense of laying out **a** from the bow, Acts 27:30
So they cast off the **a** and left them in Acts 27:40

ANCIENT (26)
produce of the **a** mountains and the Dt 33:15
Kishon swept them away, the **a** torrent, Jgs 5:21
to Lehem (now the records are **a**). 1 Chr 4:22
And be lifted up, O **a** doors, that the King Ps 24:7
And lift them up, O **a** doors, that the Ps 24:9
who rides in the heavens, the **a** heavens; Ps 68:33
not move the **a** landmark that your Prv 22:28
Do not move an **a** landmark or enter Prv 23:10
am a son of the wise, a son of **a** kings"? Is 19:11
it before me, since I appointed an **a** people. Is 44:7
beginning and from **a** times things not Is 46:10
And your **a** ruins shall be rebuilt; you Is 58:12
They shall build up the **a** ruins; they Is 61:4
it is an **a** nation, a nation whose Jer 5:15
roads, and look, and ask for the **a** paths, Jer 6:16
stumble in their ways, in the **a** roads, Jer 18:15
and me from **a** times prophesied war, Jer 28:8
'The **a** heights have become our Ezk 36:2
placed, and the **A** of days took his seat; Dn 7:9
and he came to the **A** of Days and was Dn 7:13
until the **A** of Days came, and judgment Dn 7:22
whose origin is from of old, from **a** days. Mi 5:2
For from **a** generations Moses has Acts 15:21
if he did not spare the **a** world, but 2 Pt 2:5
dragon was thrown down, that **a** serpent, Rv 12:9
And he seized the dragon, that **a** serpent, Rv 20:2

ANCIENTS (1)
As the proverb of the **a** says, 'Out of 1 Sm 24:13

ANDREW (13)
(who is called Peter) and **A** his brother, Mt 4:18
who is called Peter, and **A** his brother; Mt 10:2
he saw Simon and **A** the brother of Mk 1:16
and entered the house of Simon and **A**, Mk 1:29
A, and Philip, and Bartholomew, and Mk 3:18
and John and **A** asked him privately, Mk 13:3
he named Peter, and **A** his brother, Lk 6:14
John speak and followed Jesus was **A**, Jn 1:40
from Bethsaida, the city of **A** and Peter. Jn 1:44
of his disciples, **A**, Simon Peter's brother, Jn 6:8
Philip went and told **A**; Andrew and Jn 12:22
A and Philip went and told Jesus. Jn 12:22
Peter and John and James and **A**, Acts 1:13

ANDRONICUS (1)
Greet **A** and Junia, my kinsmen and Rom 16:7

ANEM (1)
and **A** with its pasturelands; 1 Chr 6:73

ANER (3)
Amorite, brother of Eshcol and of **A**. Gn 14:13
of the men who went with me. Let **A**, Gn 14:24
of Manasseh, **A** with its pasturelands, 1 Chr 6:70

ANGEL (203)
The **a** of the LORD found her by a spring Gn 16:7
The **a** of the LORD said to her, "Return to Gn 16:9
The **a** of the LORD also said to her, "I Gn 16:10
And the **a** of the LORD said to her, Gn 16:11
and the **a** of God called to Hagar from Gn 21:17
But the **a** of the LORD called to him Gn 22:11
And the **a** of the LORD called to Gn 22:15
this land,' he will send his **a** before you, Gn 24:7
will send his **a** with you and prosper Gn 24:40
Then the **a** of God said to me in the Gn 31:11
the **a** who has redeemed me from all Gn 48:16
And the **a** of the LORD appeared to him in a Ex 3:2
Then the **a** of God who was going Ex 14:19
I send an **a** before you to guard you on Ex 23:20
"When my **a** goes before you and Ex 23:23
you; behold, my **a** shall go before you. Ex 32:34
I will send an **a** before you, and I will Ex 33:2
voice and sent an **a** and brought us Nm 20:16
and the **a** of the LORD took his stand in Nm 22:22
the donkey saw the **a** of the LORD Nm 22:23
Then the **a** of the LORD stood in a Nm 22:24
the donkey saw the **a** of the LORD, Nm 22:25
Then the **a** of the LORD went ahead Nm 22:26
the donkey saw the **a** of the LORD, Nm 22:27
and he saw the **a** of the LORD standing Nm 22:31
And the **a** of the LORD said to him, Nm 22:32
Then Balaam said to the **a** of the LORD, Nm 22:34
And the **a** of the LORD said to Balaam, Nm 22:35
Now the **a** of the LORD went up from Jgs 2:1
As soon as the **a** of the LORD spoke these Jgs 2:4
"Curse Meroz, says the **a** of the LORD, Jgs 5:23
Now the **a** of the LORD came and sat Jgs 6:11
And the **a** of the LORD appeared to him Jgs 6:12
And the **a** of God said to him, "Take the Jgs 6:20
Then the **a** of the LORD reached out the Jgs 6:21
And the **a** of the LORD vanished from his Jgs 6:21
perceived that he was the **a** of the LORD. Jgs 6:22
now I have seen the **a** of the LORD face to Jgs 6:22
And the **a** of the LORD appeared to the Jgs 13:3
was like the appearance of the **a** of God, Jgs 13:6
and the **a** of God came again to the Jgs 13:9
And the **a** of the LORD said to Manoah, Jgs 13:13
Manoah said to the **a** of the LORD, Jgs 13:15
And the **a** of the LORD said to Manoah, Jgs 13:16
know that he was the **a** of the LORD.) Jgs 13:16
And Manoah said to the **a** of the LORD, Jgs 13:17
And the **a** of the LORD said to him, Jgs 13:18
the **a** of the LORD went up in the flame Jgs 13:20
The **a** of the LORD appeared no more to Jgs 13:21
knew that he was the **a** of the LORD. Jgs 13:21
blameless in my sight as an **a** of God. 1 Sm 29:9
king is like the **a** of God to discern 2 Sm 14:17
the wisdom of the **a** of God to know 2 Sm 14:20
my lord the king is like the **a** of God; 2 Sm 19:27
And when the **a** stretched out his 2 Sm 24:16
and said to the **a** who was working 2 Sm 24:16
your hand." And the **a** of the LORD 2 Sm 24:16
when he saw the **a** who was striking 2 Sm 24:17
and an **a** spoke to me by the word of 1 Kgs 13:18
an **a** touched him and said to him, 1 Kgs 19:5
And the **a** of the LORD came again a 1 Kgs 19:7
But the **a** of the LORD said to Elijah the 2 Kgs 1:3
Then the **a** of the LORD said to Elijah, 2 Kgs 1:15
And that night the **a** of the LORD 2 Kgs 19:35
with the **a** of the LORD destroying 1 Chr 21:12
And God sent the **a** to Jerusalem to 1 Chr 21:15
he said to the **a** who was working 1 Chr 21:15
your hand." And the **a** of the LORD 1 Chr 21:15
eyes and saw the **a** of the LORD 1 Chr 21:16
Now the **a** of the LORD had 1 Chr 21:18
He turned and saw the **a**, and his 1 Chr 21:20
Then the LORD commanded the **a**, 1 Chr 21:27
of the sword of the **a** of the LORD. 1 Chr 21:30
And the LORD sent an **a**, who cut off 2 Chr 32:21
If there be for him an **a**, a mediator, one Jb 33:23
The **a** of the LORD encamps around those Ps 34:7

with the **a** of the LORD driving them Ps 35:5
with the **a** of the LORD pursuing them! Ps 35:6
And the **a** of the LORD went out and Is 37:36
and the **a** of his presence saved them; Is 63:9
who has sent his **a** and delivered his Dn 3:28
My God sent his **a** and shut the lions' Dn 6:22
He strove with the **a** and prevailed; he Hos 12:4
The **a** who talked with me said to me, 'I Zec 1:9
And they answered the **a** of the LORD Zec 1:11
Then the **a** of the LORD said, 'O LORD of Zec 1:12
words to the **a** who talked with Zec 1:13
So the **a** who talked with me said to me, Zec 1:14
And I said to the **a** who talked with me, Zec 1:19
the **a** who talked with me came forward, Zec 2:3
and another **a** came forward to meet him Zec 2:3
priest standing before the **a** of the LORD, Zec 3:1
Now Joshua was standing before the **a**, Zec 3:3
And the **a** said to those who were Zec 3:4
And the **a** of the LORD was standing by. Zec 3:5
And the **a** of the LORD solemnly assured Zec 3:6
And the **a** who talked with me came Zec 4:1
And I said to the **a** who talked with me, Zec 4:4
Then the **a** who talked with me answered Zec 4:5
Then the **a** who talked with me came Zec 5:5
Then I said to the **a** who talked with me, Zec 5:10
and said to the **a** who talked with me, Zec 6:4
And the **a** answered and said to me, Zec 6:5
shall be like God, like the **a** of the LORD, Zec 12:8
an **a** of the Lord appeared to him in a Mt 1:20
he did as the **a** of the Lord commanded Mt 1:24
an **a** of the Lord appeared to Joseph in a Mt 2:13
an **a** of the Lord appeared in a dream to Mt 2:19
for an **a** of the Lord descended from Mt 28:2
But the **a** said to the women, "Do not be Mt 28:5
appeared to him an **a** of the Lord Lk 1:11
But the **a** said to him, "Do not be afraid, Lk 1:13
And Zechariah said to the **a**, "How shall Lk 1:18
And the **a** answered him, "I am Gabriel, Lk 1:19
the sixth month the **a** Gabriel was sent Lk 1:26
And the **a** said to her, "Do not be afraid, Lk 1:30
And Mary said to the **a**, "How will this Lk 1:34
And the **a** answered her, "The Holy Lk 1:35
word." And the **a** departed from her. Lk 1:38
And an **a** of the Lord appeared to them, Lk 2:9
And the **a** said to them, "Fear not, for Lk 2:10
there was with the **a** a multitude of the Lk 2:13
name given by the **a** before he was Lk 2:21
appeared to him an **a** from heaven, Lk 22:43
Others said, "An **a** has spoken to him." Jn 12:29
during the night an **a** of the Lord Acts 5:19
that his face was like the face of an **a**. Acts 6:15
an **a** appeared to him in the wilderness Acts 7:30
the hand of the **a** who appeared to him Acts 7:35
the wilderness with the **a** who spoke to Acts 7:38
Now an **a** of the Lord said to Philip, Acts 8:26
clearly in a vision an **a** of God come in Acts 10:3
When the **a** who spoke to him had Acts 10:7
directed by a holy **a** to send for you Acts 10:22
he had seen the **a** stand in his house Acts 11:13
an **a** of the Lord stood next to him, Acts 12:7
And the **a** said to him, "Dress yourself Acts 12:8
what was being done by the **a** was real, Acts 12:9
street, and immediately the **a** left him. Acts 12:10
Lord has sent his **a** and rescued me Acts 12:11
so, and they kept saying, "It is his **a**!" Acts 12:15
Immediately an **a** of the Lord struck Acts 12:23
say that there is no resurrection, nor **a**, Acts 23:8
What if a spirit or an **a** spoke to him?" Acts 23:9
stood before me an **a** of the God to Acts 27:23
disguises himself as an **a** of light. 2 Cor 11:14
if we or an **a** from heaven should preach Gal 1:8
me, but received me as an **a** of God, Gal 4:14
known by sending his **a** to his servant Rv 1:1
"To the **a** of the church in Ephesus write: Rv 2:1
"And to the **a** of the church in Smyrna Rv 2:8
"And to the **a** of the church in Rv 2:12
"And to the **a** of the church in Thyatira Rv 2:18
"And to the **a** of the church in Sardis Rv 3:1
"And to the **a** of the church in Rv 3:7
"And to the **a** of the church in Laodicea Rv 3:14
I saw a strong **a** proclaiming with a loud Rv 5:2
Then I saw another **a** ascending from the Rv 7:2
And another **a** came and stood at the altar Rv 8:3
rose before God from the hand of the **a**. Rv 8:4
Then the **a** took the censer and filled it Rv 8:5
The first **a** blew his trumpet, and there Rv 8:7
The second **a** blew his trumpet, and Rv 8:8
The third **a** blew his trumpet, and a Rv 8:10
The fourth **a** blew his trumpet, and a Rv 8:12
And the fifth **a** blew his trumpet, and I Rv 9:1
king over them the **a** of the bottomless Rv 9:11
Then the sixth **a** blew his trumpet, and I Rv 9:13
saying to the sixth **a** who had the Rv 9:14
saw another mighty **a** coming down Rv 10:1
And the **a** whom I saw standing on the Rv 10:5
call to be sounded by the seventh **a**, Rv 10:7
in the hand of the **a** who is standing on Rv 10:8
So I went to the **a** and told him to give me Rv 10:9
scroll from the hand of the **a** and ate it. Rv 10:10
Then the seventh **a** blew his trumpet, Rv 11:15
I saw another **a** flying directly overhead, Rv 14:6
Another **a**, a second, followed, saying, Rv 14:8
And another **a**, a third, followed them, Rv 14:9
And another **a** came out of the temple, Rv 14:15
Then another **a** came out of the temple Rv 14:17
And another **a** came out from the altar, Rv 14:18
the **a** who has authority over the fire, Rv 14:18
So the **a** swung his sickle across the Rv 14:19
So the first **a** went and poured out his Rv 16:2
The second **a** poured out his bowl into Rv 16:3
The third **a** poured out his bowl into the Rv 16:4
And I heard the **a** in charge of the waters Rv 16:5
The fourth **a** poured out his bowl on the Rv 16:8
The fifth **a** poured out his bowl on the Rv 16:10
The sixth **a** poured out his bowl on the Rv 16:12
The seventh **a** poured out his bowl into Rv 16:17
But the **a** said to me, "Why do you Rv 17:7
And the **a** said to me, "The waters that Rv 17:15
this I saw another **a** coming down from Rv 18:1
Then a mighty **a** took up a stone like a Rv 18:21
And the **a** said to me, "Write this: Blessed Rv 19:9
Then I saw an **a** standing in the sun, Rv 19:17
Then I saw an **a** coming down from Rv 20:1
Then the **a** showed me the river of the Rv 22:1
has sent his **a** to show his servants what Rv 22:6
at the feet of the **a** who showed them to Rv 22:8
have sent my **a** to testify to you about Rv 22:16

ANGEL'S (1)
which is also an **a** measurement. Rv 21:17

ANGELS (91)
The two **a** came to Sodom in the Gn 19:1
As morning dawned, the **a** urged Lot, Gn 19:15
the **a** of God were ascending and Gn 28:12
on his way, and the **a** of God met him. Gn 32:1
no trust, and his **a** he charges with error; Jb 4:18
Man ate of the bread of the **a**; he sent Ps 78:25
and distress, a company of destroying **a**. Ps 78:49
will command his **a** concerning you to Ps 91:11
Bless the LORD, O you his **a**, you Ps 103:20
Praise him, all his **a**; praise him, all his Ps 148:2
will command his **a** concerning you,' Mt 4:6
a came and were ministering to him. Mt 4:11
close of the age, and the reapers are **a**. Mt 13:39
The Son of Man will send his **a**, and Mt 13:41
The **a** will come out and separate the Mt 13:49
going to come with his **a** in the glory of Mt 16:27
that in heaven their **a** always see the Mt 18:10
in marriage, but are like **a** in heaven. Mt 22:30
will send out his **a** with a loud trumpet Mt 24:31
no one knows, not even the **a** of heaven, Mt 24:36
in his glory, and all the **a** with him, Mt 25:31
fire prepared for the devil and his **a**. Mt 25:41
send me more than twelve legions of **a**? Mt 26:53
and the **a** were ministering to him. Mk 1:13
the glory of his Father with the holy **a**." Mk 8:38
in marriage, but are like **a** in heaven. Mk 12:25
will send out the **a** and gather his elect Mk 13:27
one knows, not even the **a** in heaven, Mk 13:32
When the **a** went away from them into Lk 2:15
will command his **a** concerning you, Lk 4:10
the glory of the Father and of the holy **a**. Lk 9:26
will acknowledge before the **a** of God, Lk 12:8
men will be denied before the **a** of God. Lk 12:9
there is joy before the **a** of God over one Lk 15:10
was carried by the **a** to Abraham's side. Lk 16:22
they are equal to **a** and are sons of Lk 20:36
that they had even seen a vision of **a**, Lk 24:23
and the **a** of God ascending and Jn 1:51
And she saw two **a** in white, sitting Jn 20:12
law as delivered by **a** and did not keep Acts 7:53
neither death nor life, nor **a** nor rulers, Rom 8:38
become a spectacle to the world, to **a**, 1 Cor 4:9
you not know that we are to judge **a**? 1 Cor 6:3
on her head, because of the **a**. 1 Cor 11:10
speak in the tongues of men and of **a**, 1 Cor 13:1
in place through **a** by an intermediary. Gal 3:19
on asceticism and worship of **a**, Col 2:18
from heaven with his mighty **a** 2 Thes 1:7
vindicated by the Spirit, seen by **a**, 1 Tm 3:16
Jesus and of the elect **a** I charge you to 1 Tm 5:21
as much superior to **a** as the name he Heb 1:4
For to which of the **a** did God ever say, Heb 1:5
he says, "Let all God's **a** worship him." Heb 1:6
Of the **a** he says, "He makes his angels Heb 1:7
angels he says, "He makes his **a** winds, Heb 1:7
And to which of the **a** has he ever said, Heb 1:13
the message declared by **a** proved to be Heb 2:2
it was not to **a** that God subjected the Heb 2:5
him for a little while lower than the **a**; Heb 2:7
a little while was made lower than the **a**, Heb 2:9
For surely it is not **a** that he helps, but Heb 2:16
and to innumerable **a** in festal Heb 12:22
some have entertained **a** unawares. Heb 13:2
things into which **a** long to look. 1 Pt 1:12
and is at the right hand of God, with **a**, 1 Pt 3:22
if God did not spare **a** when they sinned, 2 Pt 2:4
whereas **a**, though greater in might 2 Pt 2:11
And the **a** who did not stay within their Jude 1:6
seven stars are the **a** of the seven Rv 1:20
name before my Father and before his **a**. Rv 3:5
and the elders the voice of many **a**, Rv 5:11
After this I saw four **a** standing at the four Rv 7:1
voice to the four **a** who had been given Rv 7:2
And all the **a** were standing around the Rv 7:11
I saw the seven **a** who stand before God, Rv 8:2
Now the seven **a** who had the seven Rv 8:6
trumpets that the three **a** are about to Rv 8:13
"Release the four **a** who are bound at the Rv 9:14
So the four **a**, who had been prepared for Rv 9:15
Michael and his **a** fighting against the Rv 12:7
And the dragon and his **a** fought back, Rv 12:7
and his **a** were thrown down with him. Rv 12:9
presence of the holy **a** and in the Rv 14:10
amazing, seven **a** with seven plagues, Rv 15:1
came the seven **a** with the seven Rv 15:6
gave to the seven **a** seven golden bowls Rv 15:7
plagues of the seven **a** were finished. Rv 15:8
voice from the temple telling the seven **a**, Rv 16:1
one of the seven **a** who had the seven Rv 17:1
one of the seven **a** who had the seven Rv 21:9
twelve gates, and at the gates twelve **a**, Rv 21:12

ANGER (269)
until your brother's **a** turns away from Gn 27:45
Jacob's **a** was kindled against Rachel, Gn 30:2
servant treated me," his **a** was kindled. Gn 39:19
and let not your **a** burn against your Gn 44:18
For in their **a** they killed men, Gn 49:6
Cursed be their **a**, for it is fierce, and Gn 49:7
Then the **a** of the LORD was kindled Ex 4:14
And he went out from Pharaoh in hot **a**. Ex 11:8
from your burning **a** and relent from Ex 32:12
and the dancing, Moses' **a** burned hot, Ex 32:19
said, "Let not the **a** of my lord burn hot. Ex 32:22
a God merciful and gracious, slow to **a**, Ex 34:6
the LORD heard it, his **a** was kindled, Nm 11:1
And the **a** of the LORD blazed hotly, Nm 11:10
the **a** of the LORD was kindled against Nm 11:33
And the **a** of the LORD was kindled Nm 12:9
LORD is slow to **a** and abounding in Nm 14:18
But God's **a** was kindled because he Nm 22:22
Balaam. And Balaam's **a** was kindled, Nm 22:27
And Balak's **a** was kindled against Nm 24:10
And the **a** of the LORD was kindled Nm 25:3
that the fierce **a** of the LORD may turn Nm 25:4
And the LORD'S **a** was kindled on that Nm 32:10
And the LORD'S **a** was kindled against Nm 32:13
still more the fierce **a** of the LORD Nm 32:14
LORD your God, so as to provoke him to **a**, Dt 4:25
lest the **a** of the LORD your God be kindled Dt 6:15
Then the **a** of the LORD would be kindled Dt 7:4
the sight of the LORD to provoke him to **a**. Dt 9:18
was afraid of the **a** and hot displeasure Dt 9:19
then the **a** of the LORD will be kindled Dt 11:17
the fierceness of his **a** and show you Dt 13:17
of blood in hot **a** pursue the manslayer Dt 19:6
but rather the **a** of the LORD and his Dt 29:20
the LORD overthrew in his **a** and wrath— Dt 29:23
What caused the heat of this great **a**?' Dt 29:24
Therefore the **a** of the LORD was kindled Dt 29:27
from their land in **a** and fury and great Dt 29:28
Then my **a** will be kindled against Dt 31:17
provoking him to **a** through the work Dt 31:29
abominations they provoked him to **a**. Dt 32:16
have provoked me to **a** with their idols. Dt 32:21
will provoke them to **a** with a foolish Dt 32:21
For a fire is kindled by my **a**, and it Dt 32:22
And the **a** of the LORD burned against the Jos 7:1
the LORD turned from his burning **a**. Jos 7:26
Then the **a** of the LORD will be kindled Jos 23:16
them. And they provoked the LORD to **a**. Jgs 2:12
So the **a** of the LORD was kindled against Jgs 2:14
So the **a** of the LORD was kindled against Jgs 2:20
Therefore the **a** of the LORD was kindled Jgs 3:8
to God, "Let not your **a** burn against me; Jgs 6:39
you?" Then their **a** against him subsided Jgs 8:3
Gaal the son of Ebed, his **a** was kindled. Jgs 9:30
So the **a** of the LORD was kindled against Jgs 10:7
In hot **a** he went back to his father's Jgs 14:19
words, and his **a** was greatly kindled. 1 Sm 11:6
And Eliab's **a** was kindled against 1 Sm 17:28
Then Saul's **a** was kindled against 1 Sm 20:30
the table in fierce **a** and ate no food 1 Sm 20:34
And the **a** of the LORD was kindled 2 Sm 6:7
then, if the king's **a** rises, and if he 2 Sm 11:20

Then David's **a** was greatly kindled 2 Sm 12:5
Again the **a** of the LORD was kindled 2 Sm 24:1
and metal images, provoking me to **a**, 1 Kgs 14:9
Asherim, provoking the LORD to **a**. 1 Kgs 14:15
and because of the **a** to which he 1 Kgs 15:30
provoking me to **a** with their sins, 1 Kgs 16:2
provoking him to **a** with the work of 1 Kgs 16:7
God of Israel to **a** with their idols. 1 Kgs 16:13
the God of Israel, to **a** by their idols. 1 Kgs 16:26
to **a** than all the kings of Israel who 1 Kgs 16:33
for the **a** to which you have 1 Kgs 21:22
to **a** in every way that his father had 1 Kgs 22:53
And the **a** of the LORD was kindled 2 Kgs 13:3
things, provoking the LORD to **a**, 2 Kgs 17:11
of the LORD, provoking him to **a**. 2 Kgs 17:17
sight of the LORD, provoking him to **a**. 2 Kgs 21:6
sight and have provoked me to **a**, 2 Kgs 21:15
might provoke me to **a** with all the 2 Kgs 22:17
had made, provoking the LORD to **a**. 2 Kgs 23:19
by which his **a** was kindled against 2 Kgs 23:26
For because of the **a** of the LORD it 2 Kgs 24:20
And the **a** of the LORD was kindled 1 Chr 13:10
against Jehoram the **a** of the 2 Chr 21:16
and returned home in fierce **a**. 2 Chr 25:10
other gods, provoking to **a** the LORD, 2 Chr 28:25
that his fierce **a** may turn away 2 Chr 29:10
that his fierce **a** may turn away from 2 Chr 30:8
sight of the LORD, provoking him to **a**. 2 Chr 33:6
might provoke me to **a** with all the 2 Chr 34:25
have provoked you to **a** in the presence Neh 4:5
slow to **a** and abounding in steadfast Neh 9:17
enraged, and his **a** burned within him. Est 1:12
when the **a** of King Ahasuerus had Est 2:1
by the blast of his **a** they are consumed. Jb 4:9
it not, when he overturns them in his **a**, Jb 9:5
"God will not turn back his **a**; beneath Jb 9:13
You who tear yourself in your **a**, shall Jb 18:4
send his burning **a** against him and Jb 20:23
That God distributes pains in his **a**? Jb 21:17
of the family of Ram, burned with **a**. Jb 32:2
He burned with **a** at Job because he Jb 32:2
He burned with **a** also at Job's three Jb 32:3
of these three men, he burned with **a**. Jb 32:5
now, because his **a** does not punish, Jb 35:15
"The godless in heart cherish **a**; they do Jb 36:13
Pour out the overflowings of your **a**, Jb 40:11
"My **a** burns against you and against Jb 42:7
O LORD, rebuke me not in your **a**, nor Ps 6:1
Arise, O LORD, in your **a**; lift yourself up Ps 7:6
Turn not your servant away in **a**, O you Ps 27:9
For his **a** is but for a moment, and his Ps 30:5
Refrain from **a**, and forsake wrath! Fret Ps 37:8
O LORD, rebuke me not in your **a**, nor Ps 38:1
and in **a** they bear a grudge against me. Ps 55:3
and let your burning **a** overtake them. Ps 69:24
Why does your **a** smoke against the Ps 74:1
before you when once your **a** is roused? Ps 76:7
Has he in **a** shut up his compassion?" Ps 77:9
against Jacob; his **a** rose against Israel, Ps 78:21
the **a** of God rose against them, and he Ps 78:31
he restrained his **a** often and did not stir Ps 78:38
He let loose on them his burning **a**, Ps 78:49
He made a path for his **a**; he did not Ps 78:50
they provoked him to **a** with their high Ps 78:58
Pour out your **a** on the nations that do Ps 79:6
your wrath; you turned from your hot **a**. Ps 85:3
you prolong your **a** to all generations? Ps 85:5
slow to **a** and abounding in steadfast Ps 86:15
For we are brought to an end by your **a**; Ps 90:7
Who considers the power of your **a**, and Ps 90:11
because of your indignation and **a**; for Ps 102:10
slow to **a** and abounding in steadfast Ps 103:8
chide, nor will he keep his **a** forever. Ps 103:9
the LORD to **a** with their deeds, Ps 106:29
Then the **a** of the LORD was kindled Ps 106:40
when their **a** was kindled against us; Ps 124:3
slow to **a** and abounding in steadfast Ps 145:8
is slow to **a** has great understanding, Prv 14:29
wrath, but a harsh word stirs up **a**. Prv 15:1
he who is slow to **a** quiets contention. Prv 15:18
Whoever is slow to **a** is better than the Prv 16:32
Good sense makes one slow to **a**, and it Prv 19:11
provokes him to **a** forfeits his life. Prv 20:2
A gift in secret averts **a**, and a Prv 21:14
no friendship with a man given to **a**, Prv 22:24
and turn away his **a** from him. Prv 24:18
Wrath is cruel, **a** is overwhelming, but Prv 27:4
one given to **a** causes much Prv 29:22
blood, and pressing **a** produces strife. Prv 30:33
in much vexation and sickness and **a**. Eccl 5:17
for **a** lodges in the bosom of fools. Eccl 7:9
If the **a** of the ruler rises against you, Eccl 10:4
Therefore the **a** of the LORD was kindled Is 5:25
For all this his **a** has not turned away, Is 5:25
at the fierce **a** of Rezin and Syria and the Is 7:4
For all this his **a** has not turned away, Is 9:12
For all this his **a** has not turned away, Is 9:17
For all this his **a** has not turned away, Is 9:21
For all this his **a** has not turned away, Is 10:4
Ah, Assyria, the rod of my **a**; the staff in Is 10:5
and my **a** will be directed to their Is 10:25
were angry with me, your **a** turned away, Is 12:1
my mighty men to execute my **a**, Is 13:3
comes, cruel, with wrath and fierce **a**, Is 13:9
LORD of hosts in the day of his fierce **a**. Is 13:13
the nations in **a** with unrelenting Is 14:6
comes from afar, burning with his **a**, Is 30:27
in furious **a** and a flame of devouring Is 30:30
him the heat of his **a** and the might of Is 42:25
"For my name's sake I defer my **a**, for the Is 48:9
In overflowing **a** for a moment I hid my Is 54:8
I trod them in my **a** and trampled them in Is 63:3
I trampled down the peoples in my **a**; I Is 63:6
the whirlwind, to render his **a** in fury, Is 66:15
surely his **a** has turned from me.' Jer 2:35
I will not look on you in **a**, for I am Jer 3:12
for the fierce **a** of the LORD has not turned Jer 4:8
ruins before the LORD, before his fierce **a**. Jer 4:26
to other gods, to provoke me to **a**. Jer 7:18
my **a** and my wrath will be poured out Jer 7:20
they provoked me to **a** with their carved Jer 8:19
not in your **a**, lest you bring me to Jer 10:24
provoking me to **a** by making offerings Jer 11:17
because of the fierce **a** of the LORD." Jer 12:13
for in my **a** a fire is kindled that shall Jer 15:14
for in my **a** a fire is kindled that shall Jer 17:4
deal with them in the time of your **a**. Jer 18:23
arm, in **a** and in fury and in great wrath. Jer 21:5
The **a** of the LORD will not turn back Jer 23:20
or provoke me to **a** with the work of your Jer 25:6
might provoke me to **a** with the work of Jer 25:7
because of the fierce **a** of the LORD. Jer 25:37
oppressor, and because of his fierce **a**." Jer 25:38
The fierce **a** of the LORD will not turn Jer 30:24
out to other gods, to provoke me to **a**. Jer 32:29
but provoke me to **a** by the work of Jer 32:30
This city has aroused my **a** and wrath, Jer 32:31
to provoke me to **a**—their kings and Jer 32:32
drove them in my **a** and my wrath and Jer 32:37
shall strike down in my **a** and my wrath, Jer 33:5
for great is the **a** and wrath that the LORD Jer 36:7
As my **a** and my wrath were poured out Jer 42:18
that they committed, provoking me to **a**, Jer 44:3
my wrath and my **a** were poured out and Jer 44:6
you provoke me to **a** with the works of Jer 44:8
bring disaster upon them, my fierce **a**, Jer 49:37
his life from the fierce **a** of the LORD! Jer 51:45
For because of the **a** of the LORD things Jer 52:3
inflicted on the day of his fierce **a**. Lam 1:12
the Lord in his **a** has set the daughter Lam 2:1
his footstool in the day of his **a**. Lam 2:1
has cut down in fierce **a** all the might of Lam 2:3
have killed them in the day of your **a**, Lam 2:21
on the day of the **a** of the LORD no one Lam 2:22
wrapped yourself with **a** and pursued Lam 3:43
pursue them in **a** and destroy them Lam 3:66
he poured out his hot **a**, and he Lam 4:11
"Thus shall my **a** spend itself, and I will Ezk 5:13
judgments on you in **a** and fury, Ezk 5:15
you, and I will send my **a** upon you; Ezk 7:3
upon you, and spend my **a** against you, Ezk 7:8
and provoke me still further to **a**? Ezk 8:17
there shall be a deluge of rain in my **a**, Ezk 13:13
your whoring, to provoke me to **a**. Ezk 16:26
them and spend my **a** against them in Ezk 20:8
them and spend my **a** against them in Ezk 20:21
gather you in my **a** and in my wrath, Ezk 22:20
according to my **a** and according to Ezk 25:14
you according to the **a** and envy that Ezk 35:11
GOD, my wrath will be roused in my **a**. Ezk 38:18
so I have consumed them in my **a**. Ezk 43:8
let your **a** and your wrath turn away Dn 9:16
be broken, neither in **a** nor in battle. Dn 11:20
their intrigue; all night their **a** smolders; Hos 7:6
O Samaria. My **a** burns against them. Hos 8:5
I will not execute my burning **a**; I will Hos 11:9
I gave you a king in my **a**, and I took Hos 13:11
freely, for my **a** has turned from them. Hos 14:4
for he is gracious and merciful, slow to **a**, Jl 2:13
off all pity, and his **a** tore perpetually, Am 1:11
and relent and turn from his fierce **a**, Jon 3:9
slow to **a** and abounding in steadfast Jon 4:2
And in **a** and wrath I will execute Mi 5:15
He does not retain his **a** forever, because Mi 7:18
The LORD is slow to **a** and great in power, Na 1:3
Who can endure the heat of his **a**? Na 1:6
Was your **a** against the rivers, or your Hab 3:8
in fury; you threshed the nations in **a**. Hab 3:12
upon you the burning **a** of the LORD, Zep 2:2
upon you the day of the **a** of the LORD. Zep 2:2
be hidden on the day of the **a** of the LORD. Zep 2:3
them my indignation, all my burning **a**; Zep 3:8
Therefore great **a** came from the LORD Zec 7:12
"My **a** is hot against the shepherds, and Zec 10:3
And in **a** his master delivered him to Mt 18:34
And he looked around at them with **a**, Mk 3:5
be quarreling, jealousy, **a**, hostility, 2 Cor 12:20
sorcery, enmity, strife, jealousy, fits of **a**, Gal 5:20
do not let the sun go down on your **a**, Eph 4:26
and wrath and **a** and clamor and Eph 4:31
do not provoke your children to **a**, Eph 6:4
a, wrath, malice, slander, and obscene Col 3:8
holy hands without **a** or quarreling; 1 Tm 2:8
not being afraid of the **a** of the king, Heb 11:27
quick to hear, slow to speak, slow to **a**; Jas 1:19
for the **a** of man does not produce the Jas 1:20
full strength into the cup of his **a**, Rv 14:10

ANGERED (3)
the LORD heard your words and was **a**, Dt 1:34
because our fathers had **a** the God of Ezr 5:12
They **a** him at the waters of Meribah, Ps 106:32

ANGLE (1)
and at the Valley Gate and at the **A**, 2 Chr 26:9

ANGRY (94)
So Cain was very **a**, and his face fell. Gn 4:5
The LORD said to Cain, "Why are you **a**, Gn 4:6
Then he said, "Oh let not the Lord be **a**, Gn 18:30
Then he said, "Oh let not the Lord be **a**, Gn 18:32
"Let not my lord be **a** that I cannot rise Gn 31:35
Then Jacob became **a** and berated Gn 31:36
and the men were indignant and very **a**, Gn 34:7
And Pharaoh was **a** with his two Gn 40:2
When Pharaoh was **a** with his Gn 41:10
be distressed or **a** with yourselves Gn 45:5
and stank. And Moses was **a** with them. Ex 16:20
And he was **a** with Eleazar and Lv 10:16
And Moses was very **a** and said to the Nm 16:15
and will you be **a** with all the Nm 16:22
And Moses was **a** with the officers of Nm 31:14
me the LORD was **a** on your account and Dt 1:37
But the LORD was **a** with me because of Dt 3:26
the LORD was **a** with me because of you, Dt 4:21
and the LORD was so **a** with you that he Dt 9:8
the LORD was so **a** with Aaron that he Dt 9:20
tomorrow he will be **a** with the whole Jos 22:18
among us, lest **a** fellows fall upon you, Jgs 18:25
And Samuel was **a**, 1 Sm 15:11
And Saul was very **a**, and this saying 1 Sm 18:8
well with your servant, but if he is **a**, 1 Sm 20:7
of the Philistines were **a** with him. 1 Sm 29:4
Then Abner was very **a** over the words 2 Sm 3:8
And David was **a** because the LORD had 2 Sm 6:8
of all these things, he was very **a**. 2 Sm 13:21
then are you **a** over this matter? 2 Sm 19:42
and quaked, because he was **a**. 2 Sm 22:8
—and you are **a** with them and give 1 Kgs 8:46
And the LORD was **a** with Solomon, 1 Kgs 11:9
But Naaman was **a** and went away, 2 Kgs 5:11
man of God was **a** with him and 2 Kgs 13:19
the LORD was very **a** with Israel and 2 Kgs 17:18
And David was **a** because the LORD 1 Chr 13:11
—and you are **a** with them and give 2 Chr 6:36
Then Asa was **a** with the seer and 2 Chr 16:10
they became very **a** with Judah and 2 Chr 25:10
the LORD was **a** with Amaziah and 2 Chr 25:15
Then Uzziah was **a**. Now he had a 2 Chr 26:19
when he became **a** with the priests, 2 Chr 26:19
of your fathers, was **a** with Judah, 2 Chr 28:9
Would you not be **a** with us until you Ezr 9:14
the wall, he was **a** and greatly enraged, Neh 4:1
beginning to be closed, they were very **a**. Neh 4:7
I was very **a** when I heard their outcry Neh 5:6
And I was very **a**, and I threw all the Neh 13:8
became **a** and sought to lay hands on Est 2:21
Kiss the Son, lest he be **a**, and you perish Ps 2:12
Be **a**, and do not sin; ponder in your own Ps 4:4
trembled and quaked, because he was **a**. Ps 18:7
broken our defenses; you have been **a**; Ps 60:1
long, O LORD? Will you be **a** forever? Ps 79:5
long will you be **a** with your people's Ps 80:4
Will you be **a** with us forever? Will you Ps 85:5
The wicked man sees it and is **a**; he Ps 112:10
whom the LORD is **a** will fall into it. Prv 22:14
and a backbiting tongue, **a** looks. Prv 25:23
Why should God be **a** at your voice and Eccl 5:6
Be not quick in your spirit to become **a**, Eccl 7:9
My mother's sons were **a** with me; they Sg 1:6
O LORD, for though you were **a** with me, Is 12:1
I was **a** with my people; I profaned my Is 47:6
I have sworn that I will not be **a** with you, Is 54:9
contend forever, nor will I always be **a**; Is 57:16
of the iniquity of his unjust gain I was **a**, Is 57:17
I hid my face and was **a**, but he went on Is 57:17
Behold, you were **a**, and we sinned; in our Is 64:5

Be not so terribly **a**, O LORD, and Is 64:9
will he be **a** forever, will he be indignant Jer 3:5
declares the LORD; I will not be **a** forever. Jer 3:12
and you remain exceedingly **a** with us. Lam 5:22
I will be calm and will no more be **a**. Ezk 16:42
of this the king was **a** and very furious, Dn 2:12
Jonah exceedingly, and he was **a**. Jon 4:1
the LORD said, "Do you do well to be **a**?" Jon 4:4
you do well to be **a** for the plant?" And he Jon 4:9
And he said, "Yes, I do well to be **a**, Jon 4:9
I do well to be angry, **a** enough to die." Jon 4:9
"The LORD was very **a** with your fathers. Zec 1:2
you have been **a** these seventy years?' Zec 1:12
I am exceedingly **a** with the nations Zec 1:15
for while I was **a** but a little, they Zec 1:15
people with whom the LORD is **a** forever.'" Mal 1:4
that everyone who is **a** with his brother Mt 5:22
The king was **a**, and he sent his troops Mt 22:7
of the house became **a** and said to his Lk 14:21
But he was **a** and refused to go in. His Lk 15:28
are you **a** with me because on the Jn 7:23
Now Herod was **a** with the people of Acts 12:20
a foolish nation I will make you **a**." Rom 10:19
Be **a** and do not sin; do not let the sun Eph 4:26

ANGUISH (39)
tremble and be in **a** because of you.' Dt 2:25
me and kill me, for **a** has seized me, 2 Sm 1:9
mouth; I will speak in the **a** of my spirit; Jb 7:11
distress and **a** terrify him; they prevail Jb 15:24
of them there, **a** as of a woman in labor. Ps 48:6
My heart is in **a** within me; the terrors of Ps 55:4
hold on me; I suffered distress and **a**. Ps 116:3
Trouble and **a** have found me out, Ps 119:143
when distress and **a** come upon you. Prv 1:27
distress and darkness, the gloom of **a**. Is 8:22
will be no gloom for her who was in **a**. Is 9:1
they will be in **a** like a woman in labor. Is 13:8
Therefore my loins are filled with **a**; Is 21:3
they will be in **a** over the report about Is 23:5
Through a land of trouble and **a**, from Is 30:6
Out of the **a** of his soul he shall see and Is 53:11
My **a**, my anguish! I writhe in pain! Oh Jer 4:19
My anguish, my **a**! I writhe in pain! Oh Jer 4:19
a as of one giving birth to her first child, Jer 4:31
struck them down, but they felt no **a**; Jer 5:3
a has taken hold of us, pain as of a Jer 6:24
I have made **a** and terror fall upon them Jer 15:8
a and sorrows have taken hold of her, Jer 49:24
a seized him, pain as of a woman in Jer 50:43
When **a** comes, they will seek peace, Ezk 7:25
upon Egypt, and **a** shall be in Cush, Ezk 30:4
and **a** shall come upon them on the day Ezk 30:9
Daniel was, he cried out in a tone of **a**. Dn 6:20
Before them peoples are in **a**; all faces grow Jl 2:6
melt and knees tremble; **a** is in all loins; Na 2:10
is that day, a day of distress and **a**, Zep 1:15
be afraid; Gaza too, and shall writhe in **a**; Zec 9:5
my tongue, for I am in **a** in this flame.' Lk 16:24
he is comforted here, and you are in **a**. Lk 16:25
baby, she no longer remembers the **a**, Jn 16:21
sorrow and unceasing **a** in my heart. Rom 9:2
of much affliction and **a** of heart and 2 Cor 2:4
am again in the **a** of childbirth until Gal 4:19
People gnawed their tongues in **a** Rv 16:10

ANIAM (1)
were Ahian, Shechem, Likhi, and **A**. 1 Chr 7:19

ANIM (1)
Anab, Eshtemoh, **A**, Jos 15:50

ANIMAL (35)
some of every clean **a** and some of every Gn 8:20
say that a fierce **a** has devoured him, Gn 37:20
robe. A fierce **a** has devoured him. Gn 37:33
and slaughter an **a** and make ready, Gn 43:16
"Whoever lies with an **a** shall be put to Ex 22:19
offering, if he offers an **a** from the herd, Lv 3:1
offering to the LORD is an **a** from the flock, Lv 3:6
of an unclean wild **a** or a carcass of Lv 5:2
The fat of an **a** that dies of itself and the Lv 7:24
of the fat of an **a** of which a food offering Lv 7:25
blood whatever, whether of fowl or of **a**, Lv 7:26
Every **a** that parts the hoof but is not Lv 11:26
"And if any **a** which you may eat dies, Lv 11:39
not lie with any **a** and so make yourself Lv 18:23
woman give herself to an **a** to lie with it: Lv 18:23
If a man lies with an **a**, he shall surely Lv 20:15
be put to death, and you shall kill the **a**. Lv 20:15
woman approaches any **a** and lies with Lv 20:16
it, you shall kill the woman and the **a**; Lv 20:16
Any **a** that has its testicles bruised or Lv 22:24
Whoever kills an **a** shall make it good, Lv 24:21
"If the vow is an **a** that may be offered as Lv 27:9
in fact substitute one **a** for another, Lv 27:10
if it is any unclean **a** that may not be Lv 27:11
he shall stand the **a** before the priest, Lv 27:11
And if it is an unclean **a**, then he shall Lv 27:27
every tenth **a** of all that pass under the Lv 27:32
the likeness of any **a** that is on the earth, Dt 4:17
Every **a** that parts the hoof and has the Dt 14:6
be anyone who lies with any kind of **a**.' Dt 27:21
he sacrificed an ox and a fattened **a**. 2 Sm 6:13
said to her servant, "Urge the **a** on; 2 Kgs 4:24
There was no **a** with me but the one on Neh 2:12
no room for the **a** that was under me Neh 2:14
him on his own **a** and brought him to Lk 10:34

ANIMAL'S (1)
Whoever takes an **a** life shall make it Lv 24:18

ANIMALS (38)
man and **a** and creeping things and birds Gn 6:7
and of the **a** according to their kinds, Gn 6:20
Take with you seven pairs of all clean **a**, Gn 7:2
and a pair of the **a** that are not clean, Gn 7:2
Of clean **a**, and of animals that are not Gn 7:8
animals, and of **a** that are not clean, Gn 7:8
man and **a** and creeping things and Gn 7:23
flesh—birds and **a** and every creeping Gn 8:17
the firstborn of your **a** that are males Ex 13:12
firstborn of man and the firstborn of **a**. Ex 13:15
may eat among all the **a** that are on the Lv 11:2
and chews the cud, among the **a**, Lv 11:3
paws, among the **a** that go on all fours, Lv 11:27
A blind or disabled or mutilated or Lv 22:22
your God any such **a** gotten from a Lv 22:25
cattle and for the wild **a** that are in your Lv 25:7
"But a firstborn of **a**, which as a Lv 27:26
firstborn of unclean **a** you shall Nm 18:15
These are the **a** you may eat: the ox, the Dt 14:4
in two and chews the cud, among the **a**, Dt 14:6
alive, and not lose some of the **a**." 1 Kgs 18:5
army or for the **a** that followed them. 2 Kgs 3:9
you, your livestock, and your **a**.' 2 Kgs 3:17
to you burnt offerings of fattened **a**, Ps 66:15
But wild **a** will lie down there, and their Is 13:21
And wild **a** shall meet with hyenas; the Is 34:14
with the men and **a** that are on the earth, Jer 27:5
has died of itself or is torn by wild **a**. Ezk 44:31
the peace offerings of your fattened **a**, Am 5:22
When you offer blind **a** in sacrifice, is Mal 1:8
And he was with the wild **a**, and the Mk 1:13
were all kinds of **a** and reptiles and Acts 10:12
I observed **a** and beasts of prey and Acts 11:6
man and birds and **a** and reptiles. Rom 1:23
one kind for humans, another for **a**, 1 Cor 15:39
the bodies of those **a** whose blood is Heb 13:11
But these, like irrational **a**, creatures of 2 Pt 2:12
by all that they, like unreasoning **a**, Jude 1:10

ANKLE-DEEP (1)
led me through the water, and it was **a**. Ezk 47:3

ANKLES (1)
his feet and **a** were made strong. Acts 3:7

ANKLETS (1)
the Lord will take away the finery of the **a**, Is 3:18

ANNA (1)
prophetess, **A**, the daughter of Phanuel, Lk 2:36

ANNAS (4)
the high priesthood of **A** and Caiaphas, Lk 3:2
First they led him to **A**, for he was the Jn 18:13
A then sent him bound to Caiaphas the Jn 18:24
with **A** the high priest and Caiaphas Acts 4:6

ANNIHILATE (2)
to destroy, to kill, and to **a** all Jews, Est 3:13
and to **a** any armed force of any people Est 8:11

ANNIHILATED (1)
to be destroyed, to be killed, and to be **a**. Est 7:4

ANNOUNCE (5)
the women who **a** the news are a great Ps 68:11
set a watchman; let him **a** what he sees. Is 21:6
of hosts, the God of Israel, I **a** to you. Is 21:10
this time forth I **a** to you new things, Is 48:6
a to Jerusalem, "Besiegers come from a Jer 4:16

ANNOUNCED (8)
or now **a** to us such things as these." Jgs 13:23
went out from my mouth and I **a** them; Is 48:3
before they came to pass I **a** them to you, Is 48:5
You have brought the day you **a**; now Lam 1:21
Magdalene went and **a** to the disciples, Jn 20:18
killed those who **a** beforehand the Acts 7:52
that have now been **a** to you through 1 Pt 1:12
just as he **a** to his servants the prophets. Rv 10:7

ANNOYED (2)
greatly **a** because they were teaching Acts 4:2
Paul, having become greatly **a**, Acts 16:18

ANNUAL (1)
and the three **a** feasts—the Feast of 2 Chr 8:13

ANNUL (2)
of hosts has purposed, and who will **a** it? Is 14:27
does not **a** a covenant previously Gal 3:17

ANNULLED (2)
your covenant with death will be **a**, Is 28:18
So it was **a** on that day, and the sheep Zec 11:11

ANNULLING (2)
a the covenant that I had made with Zec 11:10
a the brotherhood between Judah and Zec 11:14

ANNULS (1)
no one **a** it or adds to it once it has been Gal 3:15

ANOINT (34)
and shall **a** them and ordain them and Ex 28:41
oil and pour it on his head and **a** him. Ex 29:7
for it, and shall **a** it to consecrate it. Ex 29:36
With it you shall **a** the tent of meeting Ex 30:26
You shall **a** Aaron and his sons, and Ex 30:30
anointing oil and **a** the tabernacle and Ex 40:9
You shall also **a** the altar of burnt Ex 40:10
You shall also **a** the basin and its Ex 40:11
And you shall **a** him and consecrate Ex 40:13
and **a** them, as you anointed their Ex 40:15
but you shall not **a** yourself with the Dt 28:40
trees once went out to **a** a king over them, Jgs 9:8
Wash therefore and **a** yourself, and put Ru 3:3
and you shall **a** him to be prince over 1 Sm 9:16
LORD sent me to **a** you king over his 1 Sm 15:1
And you shall **a** for me him whom I 1 Sm 16:3
And the LORD said, "Arise, **a** him, for 1 Sm 16:12
Do not **a** yourself with oil, but behave 2 Sm 14:2
the prophet there **a** him king over 1 Kgs 1:34
you shall **a** Hazael to be king over 1 Kgs 19:15
of Nimshi you shall **a** to be king 1 Kgs 19:16
Abel-meholah you shall **a** to be 1 Kgs 19:16
says the LORD, I **a** you king over Israel.' 2 Kgs 9:3
I **a** you king over the people of the 2 Kgs 9:6
the LORD, I **a** you king over Israel.'" 2 Kgs 9:12
of my enemies; you **a** my head with oil; Ps 23:5
and prophet, and to **a** a most holy place. Dn 9:24
my mouth, nor did I **a** myself at all, Dn 10:3
wine in bowls and **a** themselves with the Am 6:6
olives, but not **a** yourselves with oil; Mi 6:15
fast, **a** your head and wash your face, Mt 6:17
spices, so that they might go and **a** him. Mk 16:1
You did not **a** my head with oil, but she Lk 7:46
not be seen, and salve to **a** your eyes, Rv 3:18

ANOINTED (99)
where you **a** a pillar and made a vow to Gn 31:13
they shall be **a** in them and ordained in Ex 29:29
and anoint them, as you **a** their father, Ex 40:15
if it is the **a** priest who sins, thus bringing Lv 4:3
And the **a** priest shall take some of the Lv 4:5
Then the **a** priest shall bring some of the Lv 4:16
offer to the LORD on the day when he is **a**: Lv 6:20
Aaron's sons, who is **a** to succeed him, Lv 6:22
of Israel, from the day that he **a** them. Lv 7:36
anointing oil and **a** the tabernacle and Lv 8:10
and **a** the altar and all its utensils and Lv 8:11
Aaron's head and **a** him to consecrate Lv 8:12
the priest who is **a** and consecrated as Lv 16:32
names of the sons of Aaron, the **a** priests, Nm 3:3
tabernacle and had **a** and consecrated it Nm 7:1
furnishings and had **a** and consecrated Nm 7:1
of the altar on the day it was **a**; Nm 7:10
for the altar on the day when it was **a**, Nm 7:84
offering for the altar after it was **a**. Nm 7:88
high priest who was **a** with the holy Nm 35:25
his king and exalt the power of his **a**." 1 Sm 2:10
go in and out before my **a** forever. 1 Sm 2:35
"Has not the LORD **a** you to be prince 1 Sm 10:1
that the LORD has **a** you to be prince 1 Sm 10:1
me before the LORD and before his **a**. 1 Sm 12:3
you, and his **a** is witness this day, 1 Sm 12:5
The LORD **a** you king over Israel. 1 Sm 15:17
"Surely the LORD'S **a** is before him." 1 Sm 16:6
horn of oil and **a** him in the midst 1 Sm 16:13
do this thing to my lord, the LORD'S **a**, 1 Sm 24:6
against him, seeing he is the LORD'S **a**." 1 Sm 24:6
my lord, for he is the LORD'S **a**.' 1 Sm 24:10
against the LORD'S **a** and be guiltless?" 1 Sm 26:9
out my hand against the LORD'S **a**. 1 Sm 26:11
watch over your lord, the LORD'S **a**. 1 Sm 26:16
out my hand against the LORD'S **a**. 1 Sm 26:23
your hand to destroy the LORD'S **a**?" 2 Sm 1:14
saying, 'I have killed the LORD'S **a**.'" 2 Sm 1:16
the shield of Saul, not **a** with oil. 2 Sm 1:21
and there they **a** David king over the 2 Sm 2:4
house of Judah has **a** me king over 2 Sm 2:7
I was gentle today, though **a** king. 2 Sm 3:39
LORD, and they **a** David king over Israel. 2 Sm 5:3

David had been **a** king over Israel, 2 Sm 5:17
God of Israel, 'I **a** you king over Israel, 2 Sm 12:7
and washed and **a** himself and 2 Sm 12:20
But Absalom, whom we **a** over us, is 2 Sm 19:10
because he cursed the LORD'S **a**?" 2 Sm 19:21
and shows steadfast love to his **a**, 2 Sm 22:51
on high, the **a** of the God of Jacob, 2 Sm 23:1
of oil from the tent and **a** Solomon. 1 Kgs 1:39
the prophet have **a** him king at 1 Kgs 1:45
heard that they had **a** him king in 1 Kgs 5:1
proclaimed him king and **a** him, 2 Kgs 11:12
the son of Josiah, and **a** him, 2 Kgs 23:30
And they **a** David king over Israel, 1 Chr 11:3
that David had been **a** king over all 1 Chr 14:8
saying, "Touch not my **a** ones, do 1 Chr 16:22
and they **a** him as prince for the 1 Chr 29:22
not turn away the face of your **a** one! 2 Chr 6:42
whom the LORD had **a** to destroy the 2 Chr 22:7
and Jehoiada and his sons **a** him, 2 Chr 23:11
with food and drink, and **a** them, 2 Chr 28:15
against the LORD and against his **a**, Ps 2:2
king, and shows steadfast love to his **a**, Ps 18:50
Now I know that the LORD saves his **a**; he Ps 20:6
people; he is the saving refuge of his **a**. Ps 28:8
has **a** you with the oil of gladness beyond Ps 45:7
shield, O God; look on the face of your **a**! Ps 84:9
servant; with my holy oil I have **a** him, Ps 89:20
you are full of wrath against your **a**. Ps 89:38
they mock the footsteps of your **a**. Ps 89:51
saying, "Touch not my **a** ones, do my Ps 105:15
not turn away the face of your **a** one. Ps 132:10
I have prepared a lamp for my **a**. Ps 132:17
Thus says the LORD to his **a**, to Cyrus, Is 45:1
because the LORD has **a** me to bring good Is 61:1
breath of our nostrils, the LORD'S **a**, Lam 4:20
blood from you and **a** you with oil. Ezk 16:9
You were an **a** guardian cherub. I Ezk 28:14
Jerusalem to the coming of an **a** one, Dn 9:25
an **a** one shall be cut off and shall have Dn 9:26
your people, for the salvation of your **a**. Hab 3:13
"These are the two **a** ones who stand by Zec 4:14
out many demons and **a** with oil many Mk 6:13
she has **a** my body beforehand for Mk 14:8
because he has **a** me to proclaim good Lk 4:18
kissed his feet and **a** them with the Lk 7:38
oil, but she has **a** my feet with ointment. Lk 7:46
Then he **a** the man's eyes with the mud Jn 9:6
Jesus made mud and **a** my eyes and said Jn 9:11
It was Mary who **a** the Lord with Jn 11:2
and **a** the feet of Jesus and wiped his feet Jn 12:3
against the Lord and against his **A**'— Acts 4:26
your holy servant Jesus, whom you **a**, Acts 4:27
how God **a** Jesus of Nazareth with the Acts 10:38
us with you in Christ, and has **a** us, 2 Cor 1:21
has **a** you with the oil of gladness Heb 1:9
But you have been **a** by the Holy One, 1 Jn 2:20

ANOINTING (27)

spices for the **a** oil and for the fragrant Ex 25:6
You shall take the **a** oil and pour it on Ex 29:7
that is on the altar, and of the **a** oil, Ex 29:21
of these a sacred **a** oil blended as by Ex 30:25
by the perfumer; it shall be a holy **a** oil. Ex 30:25
shall be my holy **a** oil throughout your Ex 30:31
and the **a** oil and the fragrant incense Ex 31:11
spices for the **a** oil and for the fragrant Ex 35:8
and the **a** oil and the fragrant incense, Ex 35:15
and oil for the light, and for the **a** oil, Ex 35:28
He made the holy **a** oil also, and the Ex 37:29
altar, the **a** oil and the fragrant incense, Ex 39:38
you shall take the **a** oil and anoint the Ex 40:9
And their **a** shall admit them to a Ex 40:15
the garments and the **a** oil and the bull Lv 8:2
Then Moses took the **a** oil and anointed Lv 8:10
poured some of the **a** oil on Aaron's head Lv 8:12
Moses took some of the **a** oil and of the Lv 8:30
for the **a** oil of the LORD is upon you." Lv 10:7
on whose head the **a** oil is poured and Lv 21:10
the consecration of the **a** oil of his God Lv 21:12
the regular grain offering, and the **a** oil, Nm 4:16
good faith you are **a** me king over you, Jgs 9:15
your **a** oils are fragrant; your name is oil Sg 1:3
a him with oil in the name of the Lord. Jas 5:14
But the **a** that you received from him 1 Jn 2:27
But as his **a** teaches you about 1 Jn 2:27

ANOINTS (1)

relative, the one who **a** him for burial, Am 6:10

ANOTHER (463)

appointed for me **a** offspring instead of Gn 4:25
He waited **a** seven days, and again he Gn 8:10
Then he waited **a** seven days and sent Gn 8:12
And they said to one **a**, "Come, let us Gn 11:3
Abraham took **a** wife, whose name was Gn 25:1
Then they dug **a** well, and they Gn 26:21
he moved from there and dug **a** well, Gn 26:22
in return for serving me **a** seven years." Gn 29:27
and served Laban for **a** seven years. Gn 29:30
"May the LORD add to me **a** son!" Gn 30:24
her, "Do not fear, for you have **a** son." Gn 35:17
Then he dreamed **a** dream and told it to Gn 37:9
said, "Behold, I have dreamed **a** dream. Gn 37:9
They said to one **a**, "Here comes this Gn 37:19
to his sons, "Why do you look at one **a**?" Gn 42:1
Then they said to one **a**, "In truth we Gn 42:21
and they turned trembling to one **a**, Gn 42:28
to tell the man that you had **a** brother?" Gn 43:6
still alive? Do you have **a** brother?' Gn 43:7
the men looked at one **a** in amazement. Gn 43:33
They did not see one **a**, nor did anyone Ex 10:23
people of Israel saw it, they said to one **a**, Ex 16:15
and I decide between one person and **a**, Ex 18:16
If he takes **a** wife to himself, he shall Ex 21:10
a man willfully attacks **a** to kill him Ex 21:14
beast loose and it feeds in **a** man's field, Ex 22:5
with their wings, their faces one to **a**; Ex 25:20
Five curtains shall be coupled to one **a**, Ex 26:3
five curtains shall be coupled to one **a**. Ex 26:3
set; the loops shall be opposite one **a**. Ex 26:5
frame, and two bases under **a** frame. Ex 26:25
He coupled five curtains to one **a**, and Ex 36:10
other five curtains he coupled to one **a**. Ex 36:10
set. The loops were opposite one **a**. Ex 36:12
their wings, with their faces one to **a**; Ex 37:9
priest shall shut him up for **a** seven days. Lv 13:5
the itching disease for **a** seven days. Lv 13:33
and he shall shut it up for **a** seven days. Lv 13:54
brought up in the family or in **a** home. Lv 18:9
deal falsely; you shall not lie to one **a**. Lv 19:11
assigned to **a** man and not yet Lv 19:20
neighbor, you shall not wrong one **a**. Lv 25:14
You shall not wrong one **a**, but you Lv 25:17
shall not rule, one over **a** ruthlessly. Lv 25:46
They shall stumble over one **a**, as if to Lv 26:37
does in fact substitute one animal for **a**, Lv 27:10
field, or if he has sold the field to **a** man, Lv 27:20
and you shall take **a** bull from the herd Nm 8:8
And they said to one **a**, "Let us choose a Nm 14:4
him, "Please come with me to **a** place, Nm 23:13
"Come now, I will take you to **a** place. Nm 23:27
not be transferred from one tribe to **a**, Nm 36:7
shall be transferred from one tribe to **a**, Nm 36:9
for himself from the midst of **a** nation, Dt 4:34
between one kind of homicide and **a**, Dt 17:8
another, one kind of legal right and **a**, Dt 17:8
another, or one kind of assault and **a**, Dt 17:8
he die in the battle and **a** man dedicate it. Dt 20:5
in the battle and **a** man enjoy its fruit. Dt 20:6
he die in the battle and **a** man take her.' Dt 20:7
is found lying with the wife of **a** man, Dt 22:22
if she goes and becomes **a** man's wife, Dt 24:2
men fight with one **a** and the wife of Dt 25:11
a wife, but **a** man shall ravish her. Dt 28:30
daughters shall be given to **a** people, Dt 28:32
great wrath, and cast them into **a** land, Dt 29:28
Then the boundary goes in **a** direction, Jos 18:14
And there arose **a** generation after them Jgs 2:10
And they said to one **a**, "Who has done Jgs 6:29
the leaders of Gilead, said one to **a**, Jgs 10:18
house, for you are the son of **a** woman." Jgs 11:2
not go to glean in **a** field or leave this one, Ru 2:8
women, lest in **a** field you be assaulted." Ru 2:22
but arose before one could recognize **a**. Ru 3:14
a carrying three loaves of bread, 1 Sm 10:3
bread, and **a** carrying a skin of wine. 1 Sm 10:3
with them and be turned into **a** man. 1 Sm 10:6
leave Samuel, God gave him **a** heart. 1 Sm 10:9
the prophets, the people said to one **a**, 1 Sm 10:11
a company turned toward 1 Sm 13:18
and **a** company turned toward the 1 Sm 13:18
he turned away from him toward **a**, 1 Sm 17:30
sang to one **a** as they celebrated, 1 Sm 18:7
And they kissed one **a** and wept with 1 Sm 20:41
one another and wept with one **a**, 1 Sm 20:41
not sing to one **a** of him in dances, 1 Sm 21:11
of whom they sing to one **a** in dances, 1 Sm 29:5
could not answer Abner **a** word, 2 Sm 3:11
sword devours now one and now **a**. 2 Sm 11:25
they quarreled with one **a** in the field. 2 Sm 14:6
You may carry news **a** day, but 2 Sm 18:20
The watchman saw **a** man running. 2 Sm 18:26
a man running alone!" The king 2 Sm 18:26
So he went **a** way and did not return 1 Kgs 13:10
came, she pretended to be **a** woman. 1 Kgs 14:5
Why do you pretend to be **a**? 1 Kgs 14:6
Obadiah went in **a** direction by 1 Kgs 18:6
encamped opposite one **a** seven days. 1 Kgs 20:29
Then he found **a** man and said, 1 Kgs 20:37
you, I will give you **a** vineyard for it.' 1 Kgs 21:6
"Is there not here **a** prophet of the 1 Kgs 22:7
said one thing, and **a** said another. 1 Kgs 22:20
said one thing, and another said **a**. 1 Kgs 22:20
king sent to him **a** captain of fifty 2 Kgs 1:11
together and struck one **a** down. 2 Kgs 3:23
"Bring me **a** vessel." And he said to her, 2 Kgs 4:6
"There is not **a**." Then the oil stopped 2 Kgs 4:6
And they said to one **a**, "Why are we 2 Kgs 7:3
a great army, so that they said to one **a**, 2 Kgs 7:6
back and entered **a** tent and carried 2 Kgs 7:8
Then they said to one **a**, "We are not 2 Kgs 7:9
(**a** third being at the gate Sur and a 2 Kgs 11:6
"Come, let us look one **a** in the face." 2 Kgs 14:8
of Judah faced one **a** in battle at 2 Kgs 14:11
filled Jerusalem from one end to **a**, 2 Kgs 21:16
Jerahmeel also had **a** wife, whose 1 Chr 2:26
from one kingdom to **a** people, 1 Chr 16:20
"Is there not here **a** prophet of the 2 Chr 18:6
said one thing, and **a** said another. 2 Chr 18:19
said one thing, and another said **a**. 2 Chr 18:19
Seir, they all helped to destroy one **a**. 2 Chr 20:23
of Judah captured **a** 10,000 alive and 2 Chr 25:12
let us look one **a** in the face." 2 Chr 25:17
of Judah faced one **a** in battle at 2 Chr 25:21
to keep the feast for **a** seven days. 2 Chr 30:23
they kept it for **a** seven days with 2 Chr 30:23
upon it, and outside it he built **a** wall, 2 Chr 32:5
of Pahath-moab repaired **a** section and Neh 3:11
repaired **a** section opposite the ascent Neh 3:19
of Zabbai repaired **a** section from the Neh 3:20
of Hakkoz repaired **a** section from the Neh 3:21
the son of Henadad repaired **a** section, Neh 3:24
the Tekoites repaired **a** section opposite Neh 3:27
sixth son of Zalaph repaired **a** section. Neh 3:30
separated on the wall, far from one **a**. Neh 4:19
for **a** quarter of it they made confession Neh 9:3
her royal position to **a** who is better Est 1:19
will rise for the Jews from **a** place, Est 4:14
on which they send gifts of food to one **a**. Est 9:19
gifts of food to one **a** and gifts to the Est 9:22
was yet speaking, there came **a** and said, Jb 1:16
was yet speaking, there came **a** and said, Jb 1:17
was yet speaking, there came **a** and said, Jb 1:18
and my eyes shall behold, and not **a**. Jb 19:27
A dies in bitterness of soul, never Jb 21:25
then let me sow, and **a** eat, and let what Jb 31:8
then let my wife grind for **a**, and let Jb 31:10
One is so near to **a** that no air can come Jb 41:16
They are joined one to **a**; they clasp Jb 41:17
those who run after **a** god shall multiply; Ps 16:4
Truly no man can ransom **a**, or give to Ps 49:7
I proclaim your might to **a** generation, Ps 71:18
putting down one and lifting up **a**. Ps 75:7
nation, from one kingdom to **a** people, Ps 105:13
his days be few; may **a** take his office! Ps 109:8
shall commend your works to **a**, Ps 145:4
a withholds what he should give, and Prv 11:24
a pretends to be poor, yet has great Prv 13:7
shall I awake? I must have **a** drink." Prv 23:35
Let **a** praise you, and not your own Prv 27:2
iron, and one man sharpens **a**. Prv 27:17
If one is burdened with the blood of **a**, Prv 28:17
he falls and has not **a** to lift him up! Eccl 4:10
adding one thing to **a** to find the Eccl 7:27
is your beloved more than **a** beloved, Sg 5:9
is your beloved more than **a** beloved, Sg 5:9
And the people will oppress one **a**, every Is 3:5
And one called to **a** and said: "Holy, holy, Is 6:3
are like fuel for the fire; no one spares **a**. Is 9:19
They will look aghast at one **a**; their faces Is 13:8
each against **a** and each against his Is 19:2
LORD'S,' **a** will call on the name of Jacob, Is 44:5
of Jacob, and **a** will write on his hand, Is 44:5
profaned? My glory I will not give to **a**. Is 48:11
but his servants he will call by **a** name. Is 65:15
They shall not build and **a** inhabit; they Is 65:22
inhabit; they shall not plant and **a** eat; Is 65:22
goes from him and becomes **a** man's wife, Jer 3:1
if you truly execute justice one with **a**, Jer 7:5
And I will dash them one against **a**, Jer 13:14
hand, and he reworked it into **a** vessel, Jer 18:4
mother who bore you into **a** country, Jer 22:26
by their dreams that they tell one **a**, Jer 23:27
LORD, who steal my words from one **a**. Jer 23:30
of the north, far and near, one after **a**, Jer 25:26
There was **a** man who prophesied in Jer 26:20
the words, they turned one to **a** in fear. Jer 36:16
"Take **a** scroll and write on it all the Jer 36:28
Then Jeremiah took **a** scroll and gave it Jer 36:32
and they fell, and they said one to **a**, Jer 46:16
One runner runs to meet **a**, and one Jer 51:31
another, and one messenger to meet **a**, Jer 51:31
year and afterward a report in **a** year, Jer 51:46
their wings touched one **a**. Each one of Ezk 1:9
each of which touched the wing of **a**, Ezk 1:11
stretched out straight, one toward **a**. Ezk 1:23
living creatures as they touched one **a**, Ezk 3:13

and water, and look at one **a** in dismay, Ezk 4:17
from your place to **a** place in their Ezk 12:3
"And there was **a** great eagle with great Ezk 17:7
she took **a** of her cubs and made him a Ezk 19:5
a lewdly defiles his daughter-in-law; Ezk 22:11
a in you violates his sister, his father's Ezk 22:11
in your iniquities and groan to one **a**. Ezk 24:23
at the doors of the houses, say to one **a**, Ezk 33:30
then take **a** stick and write on it, 'For Ezk 37:16
And join them one to **a** into one stick, Ezk 37:17
were in three stories, one over **a**, Ezk 41:6
north, and **a** door toward the south. Ezk 41:11
A section, 25,000 cubits long and Ezk 45:5
corner of the court there was **a** court— Ezk 46:21
A kingdom inferior to you shall arise Dn 2:39
so they will mix with one **a** in marriage, Dn 2:43
shall the kingdom be left to **a** people. Dn 2:44
for yourself, and give your rewards to **a**. Dn 5:17
up out of the sea, different from one **a**. Dn 7:3
And behold, **a** beast, a second one, like a Dn 7:5
I looked, and behold, **a**, like a leopard, Dn 7:6
there came up among them **a** horn, Dn 7:8
shall arise, and **a** shall arise after them; Dn 7:24
and **a** holy one said to the one who Dn 8:13
woman who is loved by **a** man and is an Hos 3:1
not play the whore, or belong to **a** man; Hos 3:3
and their children to **a** generation. Jl 1:3
They do not jostle one **a**; each marches in Jl 2:8
on one city, and send no rain on **a** city; Am 4:7
cities would wander to **a** city to drink Am 4:8
And they said to one **a**, "Come, let us cast Jon 1:7
and **a** angel came forward to meet him Zec 2:3
show kindness and mercy to one **a**, Zec 7:9
you devise evil against **a** in your heart." Zec 7:10
you shall do: Speak the truth to one **a**; Zec 8:16
devise evil in your hearts against one **a**, Zec 8:17
inhabitants of one city shall go to **a**, Zec 8:21
who are left devour the flesh of one **a**." Zec 11:9
so that each will seize the hand of **a**, Zec 14:13
Why then are we faithless to one **a**, Mal 2:10
who feared the LORD spoke with one **a**. Mal 3:16
departed to their own country by **a** way. Mt 2:12
I say to one, 'Go,' and he goes, and to **a**, Mt 8:9
A of the disciples said to him, "Lord, let Mt 8:21
who is to come, or shall we look for **a**?" Mt 11:3
in one case a hundredfold, in **a** sixty, Mt 13:23
in another sixty, and in **a** thirty." Mt 13:23
He put **a** parable before them, saying, Mt 13:24
He put **a** parable before them, saying, Mt 13:31
He told them **a** parable. "The kingdom Mt 13:33
for sexual immorality, and marries **a**, Mt 19:9
"Hear **a** parable. There was a master of Mt 21:33
it to tenants, and went into **a** country. Mt 21:33
took his servants and beat one, killed **a**, Mt 21:35
beat one, killed another, and stoned **a**. Mt 21:35
off, one to his farm, **a** to his business, Mt 22:5
here one stone upon **a** that will not be Mt 24:2
away and betray one **a** and hate one Mt 24:10
and betray one another and hate one **a**. Mt 24:10
To one he gave five talents, to **a** two, to Mt 25:15
five talents, to another two, to **a** one, Mt 25:15
people one from **a** as a shepherd Mt 25:32
and began to say to him one after **a**, Mt 26:22
to the entrance, **a** servant girl saw him, Mt 26:71
filled with great fear and said to one **a**, Mk 4:41
discussing with one **a** the fact that Mk 8:16
had argued with one **a** about who was Mk 9:34
yourselves, and be at peace with one **a**." Mk 9:50
wife and marries **a** commits adultery Mk 10:11
divorces her husband and marries **a**, Mk 10:12
And they discussed it with one **a**, Mk 11:31
it to tenants and went into **a** country. Mk 12:1
Again he sent to them **a** servant, and Mk 12:4
And he sent **a**, and him they killed. And Mk 12:5
But those tenants said to one **a**, 'This is Mk 12:7
and heard them disputing with one **a**, Mk 12:28
here one stone upon **a** that will not be Mk 13:2
and to say to him one after **a**, Mk 14:19
hands, and in three days I will build **a**, Mk 14:58
with the scribes mocked him to one **a**, Mk 15:31
And they were saying to one **a**, "Who Mk 16:3
things he appeared in **a** form to two of Mk 16:12
into heaven, the shepherds said to one **a**, Lk 2:15
they were all amazed and said to one **a**, Lk 4:36
On **a** Sabbath, he entered the synagogue Lk 6:6
discussed with one **a** what they might Lk 6:11
he goes; and to **a**, 'Come,' and he comes; Lk 7:8
who is to come, or shall we look for **a**?" Lk 7:19
who is to come, or shall we look for **a**?'" Lk 7:20
in the marketplace and calling to one **a**, Lk 7:32
and they marveled, saying to one **a**, Lk 8:25
And they went on to **a** village. Lk 9:56
To **a** he said, "Follow me." But he said, Lk 9:59
Yet **a** said, "I will follow you, Lord, but Lk 9:61
together that they were trampling one **a**, Lk 12:1
And **a** said, 'I have bought five yoke of Lk 14:19
And **a** said, 'I have married a wife, and Lk 14:20
going out to encounter **a** king in war, Lk 14:31
Then he said to **a**, 'And how much do Lk 16:7
wife and marries **a** commits adultery, Lk 16:18
Then **a** came, saying, 'Lord, here is Lk 19:20
will not leave one stone upon **a** in you, Lk 19:44
And they discussed it with one **a**, saying, Lk 20:5
tenants and went into **a** country for a Lk 20:9
And he sent **a** servant. But they also Lk 20:11
here one stone upon **a** that will not be Lk 21:6
And they began to question one **a**, Lk 22:23
of about an hour still **a** insisted, Lk 22:59
So the disciples said to one **a**, "Has Jn 4:33
saying holds true, 'One sows and **a** reaps.' Jn 4:37
while I am going **a** steps down before me." Jn 5:7
There is **a** who bears witness about me, Jn 5:32
If **a** comes in his own name, you will Jn 5:43
receive glory from one **a** and do not seek Jn 5:44
The Jews said to one **a**, "Where does this Jn 7:35
by the door but climbs in by **a** way, Jn 10:1
and saying to one **a** as they stood in Jn 11:56
So the Pharisees said to one **a**, "You see Jn 12:19
The disciples looked at one **a**, uncertain Jn 13:22
I give to you, that you love one **a**: Jn 13:34
loved you, you also are to love one **a**. Jn 13:34
my disciples, if you have love for one **a**." Jn 13:35
Father, and he will give you **a** Helper, Jn 14:16
that you love one **a** as I have loved you. Jn 15:12
you, so that you will love one **a**. Jn 15:17
So some of his disciples said to one **a**, Jn 16:17
followed Jesus, and so did **a** disciple. Jn 18:15
so they said to one **a**, "Let us not tear it, Jn 19:24
And again **a** Scripture says, "They will Jn 19:37
and **a** will dress you and carry you Jn 21:18
dwell in it'; and "'Let **a** take his office.' Acts 1:20
amazed and perplexed, saying to one **a**, Acts 2:12
the council, they conferred with one **a**, Acts 4:15
there arose over Egypt **a** king who did Acts 7:18
with or to visit anyone of **a** nation, Acts 10:28
Then he departed and went to **a** place. Acts 12:17
Therefore he says also in **a** psalm, Acts 13:35
of Caesar, saying that there is **a** king, Acts 17:7
some cried out one thing, some **a**, Acts 19:32
them bring charges against one **a**. Acts 19:38
and said farewell to one **a**. Then we Acts 21:6
were shouting one thing, some **a**. Acts 21:34
one synagogue after **a** I imprisoned Acts 22:19
had withdrawn, they said to one **a**, Acts 26:31
from his hand, they said to one **a**, Acts 28:4
were consumed with passion for one **a**, Rom 1:27
passing judgment on **a** you condemn Rom 2:1
if she lives with **a** man while her Rom 7:3
and if she marries **a** man she is not an Rom 7:3
of Christ, so that you may belong to **a**, Rom 7:4
see in my members **a** law waging war Rom 7:23
honored use and **a** for dishonorable Rom 9:21
and individually members one of **a**. Rom 12:5
Love one **a** with brotherly affection. Rom 12:10
Outdo one **a** in showing honor. Rom 12:10
Live in harmony with one **a**. Do not Rom 12:16
the one who loves **a** has fulfilled the Rom 13:8
to pass judgment on the servant of **a**? Rom 14:4
esteems one day as better than **a**, Rom 14:5
another, while **a** esteems all days alike. Rom 14:5
pass judgment on one **a** any longer, Rom 14:13
anyone to make **a** stumble by what Rom 14:20
to live in such harmony with one **a**, Rom 15:5
Therefore welcome one **a** as Christ Rom 15:7
knowledge and able to instruct one **a**. Rom 15:14
Greet one **a** with a holy kiss. All the Rom 16:16
when one says, "I follow Paul," and **a**, 1 Cor 3:4
be puffed up in favor of one against **a**. 1 Cor 4:6
one of you has a grievance against **a**, 1 Cor 6:1
at all with one **a** is already a defeat 1 Cor 6:7
Do not deprive one **a**, except perhaps 1 Cor 7:5
God, one of one kind and one of **a**. 1 Cor 7:7
One goes hungry, **a** gets drunk. 1 Cor 11:21
come together to eat, wait for one **a**— 1 Cor 11:33
and to **a** the utterance of knowledge 1 Cor 12:8
to **a** faith by the same Spirit, to 1 Cor 12:9
to **a** gifts of healing by the one Spirit, 1 Cor 12:9
to **a** the working of miracles, to 1 Cor 12:10
working of miracles, to **a** prophecy, 1 Cor 12:10
to **a** the ability to distinguish 1 Cor 12:10
to **a** various kinds of tongues, 1 Cor 12:10
to **a** the interpretation of tongues. 1 Cor 12:10
may have the same care for one **a**. 1 Cor 12:25
revelation is made to **a** sitting there, 1 Cor 14:30
one kind for humans, **a** for animals, 1 Cor 15:39
another for animals, **a** for birds, 1 Cor 15:39
another for birds, and **a** for fish. 1 Cor 15:39
and the glory of the earthly is of **a**. 1 Cor 15:40
of the sun, and **a** glory of the moon, 1 Cor 15:41
of the moon, and **a** glory of the stars; 1 Cor 15:41
Greet one **a** with a holy kiss. 1 Cor 16:20
mind not to make **a** painful visit to 2 Cor 2:1
image from one degree of glory to **a**. 2 Cor 3:18
themselves by one **a** and compare 2 Cor 10:12
and compare themselves with one **a**, 2 Cor 10:12
comes and proclaims **a** Jesus than 2 Cor 11:4
Aim for restoration, comfort one **a**, 2 Cor 13:11
one another, agree with one **a**, 2 Cor 13:11
Greet one **a** with a holy kiss. 2 Cor 13:12
not that there is **a** one, but there are some Gal 1:7
the flesh, but through love serve one **a**. Gal 5:13
But if you bite and devour one **a**, watch Gal 5:15
that you are not consumed by one **a**. Gal 5:15
not become conceited, provoking one **a**, Gal 5:26
provoking one another, envying one **a**. Gal 5:26
patience, bearing with one **a** in love, Eph 4:2
neighbor, for we are members one of **a**. Eph 4:25
Be kind to one **a**, tenderhearted, Eph 4:32
another, tenderhearted, forgiving one **a**, Eph 4:32
addressing one **a** in psalms and hymns Eph 5:19
submitting to one **a** out of reverence Eph 5:21
Do not lie to one **a**, seeing that you have Col 3:9
bearing with one **a** and, if one has a Col 3:13
and, if one has a complaint against **a**, Col 3:13
and admonishing one **a** in all wisdom, Col 3:16
abound in love for one **a** and for all, 1 Thes 3:12
been taught by God to love one **a**, 1 Thes 4:9
encourage one **a** with these 1 Thes 4:18
encourage one **a** and build 1 Thes 5:11
one another and build one **a** up, 1 Thes 5:11
to do good to one **a** and to everyone. 1 Thes 5:15
one of you for one **a** is increasing. 2 Thes 1:3
envy, hated by others and hating one **a**. Ti 3:3
But exhort one **a** every day, as long as it Heb 3:13
would not have spoken of **a** day later on. Heb 4:8
as he says also in **a** place, "You are a Heb 5:6
there have been for **a** priest to arise Heb 7:11
things are spoken belonged to **a** tribe, Heb 7:13
more evident when **a** priest arises in Heb 7:15
how to stir up one **a** to love and good Heb 10:24
habit of some, but encouraging one **a**, Heb 10:25
messengers and sent them out by **a** way? Jas 2:25
Do not speak evil against one **a**, Jas 4:11
Do not grumble against one **a**, brothers, Jas 5:9
your sins to one **a** and pray for one Jas 5:16
sins to one another and pray for one **a**, Jas 5:16
love one **a** earnestly from a pure heart, 1 Pt 1:22
Above all, keep loving one **a** earnestly, 1 Pt 4:8
hospitality to one **a** without grumbling. 1 Pt 4:9
has received a gift, use it to serve one **a**, 1 Pt 4:10
all of you, with humility toward one **a**, 1 Pt 5:5
Greet one **a** with the kiss of love. Peace 1 Pt 5:14
the light, we have fellowship with one **a**, 1 Jn 1:7
beginning, that we should love one **a**. 1 Jn 3:11
of his Son Jesus Christ and love one **a**, 1 Jn 3:23
Beloved, let us love one **a**, for love is from 1 Jn 4:7
so loved us, we also ought to love one **a**. 1 Jn 4:11
if we love one **a**, God abides in us and 1 Jn 4:12
from the beginning—that we love one **a**. 2 Jn 1:5
And out came **a** horse, bright red. Its rider Rv 6:4
the earth, so that men should slay one **a**, Rv 6:4
Then I saw **a** angel ascending from the Rv 7:2
And **a** angel came and stood at the altar Rv 8:3
Then I saw **a** mighty angel coming Rv 10:1
And **a** sign appeared in heaven: behold, a Rv 12:3
Then I saw **a** beast rising out of the Rv 13:11
Then I saw **a** angel flying directly Rv 14:6
A angel, a second, followed, saying, Rv 14:8
And **a** angel, a third, followed them, Rv 14:9
And **a** angel came out of the temple, Rv 14:15
Then **a** angel came out of the temple in Rv 14:17
And **a** angel came out from the altar, Rv 14:18
Then I saw **a** sign in heaven, great and Rv 15:1
After this I saw **a** angel coming down Rv 18:1
Then I heard **a** voice from heaven Rv 18:4
Then **a** book was opened, which is the Rv 20:12

ANOTHER'S (8)

they may not understand one **a** speech." Gn 11:7
and me, when we are out of one **a** sight. Gn 31:49
"When one man's ox butts **a**, so that it Ex 21:35
himself, and do not reveal **a** secret, Prv 25:9
not been faithful in that which is **a**, Lk 16:12
feet, you also ought to wash one **a** feet. Jn 13:14
already done in **a** area of influence. 2 Cor 10:16
Bear one **a** burdens, and so fulfill the law Gal 6:2

ANSWER (162)

So my honesty will **a** for me later, Gn 30:33
God will give Pharaoh a favorable **a**." Gn 41:16
we told him was in **a** to these questions. Gn 43:7
But his brothers could not **a** him, Gn 45:3
And she shall **a** and say, 'So shall it be Dt 25:9
And all the people shall **a** and say, Dt 27:15
of Manasseh said in **a** to the heads of Jos 22:21
Her wisest princesses **a**, indeed, she Jgs 5:29

up, let us be going." But there was no **a**. Jgs 19:28
But she did not **a** or pay attention. 1 Sm 4:20
the LORD will not **a** you in that day." 1 Sm 8:18
But he did not **a** him that day. 1 Sm 14:37
son of Ner, saying, "Will you not **a**, 1 Sm 26:14
of the LORD, the LORD did not **a** him, 1 Sm 28:6
could not **a** Abner another 2 Sm 3:11
to the LORD, but he did not **a** them. 2 Sm 22:42
and decide what **a** I shall return to 2 Sm 24:13
do you advise me to **a** this people?" 1 Kgs 12:6
words to them when you **a** them, 1 Kgs 12:7
you advise that we **a** this people who 1 Kgs 12:9
And the people did not **a** him a word. 1 Kgs 18:21
Baal, **a** us!" But there was no voice, 1 Kgs 18:26
A me, O LORD, answer me, that this 1 Kgs 18:37
Answer me, O LORD, **a** me, that this 1 Kgs 18:37
command was, "Do not **a** him." 2 Kgs 18:36
Now decide what **a** I shall return to 1 Chr 21:12
do you advise me to **a** this people?" 2 Chr 10:6
you advise that we **a** this people who 2 Chr 10:9
The king sent an **a**: "To Rehum the Ezr 4:17
Darius and then an **a** be returned by Ezr 5:5
"Call now; is there anyone who will **a** you? Jb 5:1
one could not **a** him once in a thousand Jb 9:3
How then can I **a** him, choosing my Jb 9:14
I am in the right, I cannot **a** him; Jb 9:15
is not a man, as I am, that I might **a** him, Jb 9:32
Then call, and I will **a**; or let me speak, Jb 13:22
You would call, and I would **a** you; you Jb 14:15
a wise man **a** with windy knowledge, Jb 15:2
end? Or what provokes you that you **a**? Jb 16:3
call to my servant, but he gives me no **a**; Jb 19:16
"Therefore my thoughts **a** me, because of Jb 20:2
what he would **a** me and understand Jb 23:5
cry to you for help and you do not **a** me; Jb 30:20
he makes inquiry, what shall I **a** him? Jb 31:14
my signature! Let the Almighty **a** me!) Jb 31:35
So these three men ceased to **a** Job, Jb 32:1
friends because they had found no **a**, Jb 32:3
saw that there was no **a** in the mouth of Jb 32:5
and I will not **a** him with your speeches. Jb 32:14
"They are dismayed; they **a** no more; Jb 32:15
they stand there, and **a** no more? Jb 32:16
I also will **a** with my share; I also will Jb 32:17
find relief; I must open my lips and **a**. Jb 32:20
A me, if you can; set your words in order Jb 33:5
I will **a** you, for God is greater than Jb 33:12
saying, 'He will **a** none of man's words'? Jb 33:13
If you have any words, **a** me; speak, for I Jb 33:32
I will **a** you and your friends with you. Jb 35:4
There they cry out, but he does not **a**, Jb 35:12
He who argues with God, let him **a** it." Jb 40:2
am of small account; what shall I **a** you? Jb 40:4
I have spoken once, and I will not **a**; Jb 40:5
A me when I call, O God of my Ps 4:1
Consider and **a** me, O LORD my God; light Ps 13:3
I call upon you, for you will **a** me, O God; Ps 17:6
cried to the LORD, but he did not **a** them. Ps 18:41
May the LORD **a** you in the day of trouble! Ps 20:1
he will **a** him from his holy heaven with Ps 20:6
save the king! May he **a** us when we call. Ps 20:9
O my God, I cry by day, but you do not **a**, Ps 22:2
I cry aloud; be gracious to me and **a** me! Ps 27:7
it is you, O Lord my God, who will **a**. Ps 38:15
Attend to me, and **a** me; I am restless in Ps 55:2
salvation by your right hand and **a** us! Ps 60:5
awesome deeds you **a** us with Ps 65:5
of your steadfast love **a** me in your Ps 69:13
A me, O LORD, for your steadfast love is Ps 69:16
for I am in distress; make haste to **a** me. Ps 69:17
Incline your ear, O LORD, and **a** me, for I Ps 86:1
my trouble I call upon you, for you **a** me. Ps 86:7
When he calls to me, I will **a** him; I will Ps 91:15
a me speedily in the day when I call! Ps 102:2
salvation by your right hand and **a** me! Ps 108:6
shall I have an **a** for him who taunts Ps 119:42
my whole heart I cry; **a** me, O LORD! Ps 119:145
In your faithfulness **a** me, in your Ps 143:1
A me quickly, O LORD! My spirit fails! Ps 143:7
they will call upon me, but I will not **a**; Prv 1:28
A soft **a** turns away wrath, but a harsh Prv 15:1
To make an apt **a** is a joy to a man, Prv 15:23
of the righteous ponders how to **a**, Prv 15:28
but the **a** of the tongue is from the LORD. Prv 16:1
If one gives an **a** before he hears, it is Prv 18:13
use entreaties, but the rich **a** roughly. Prv 18:23
may give a true **a** to those who sent Prv 22:21
gives an honest **a** kisses the lips. Prv 24:26
A not a fool according to his folly, lest Prv 26:4
A a fool according to his folly, lest he be Prv 26:5
than seven men who can **a** sensibly. Prv 26:16
that I may **a** him who reproaches me. Prv 27:11
him not; I called him, but he gave no **a**. Sg 5:6
All of them will **a** and say to you: 'You Is 14:10
What will one **a** the messengers of the Is 14:32
king's command was, "Do not **a** him." Is 36:21
with thirst, I the LORD will **a** them; Is 41:17
counselor who, when I ask, gives an **a**. Is 41:28
it does not **a** or save him from his trouble. Is 46:7
why, when I called, was there no one to **a**? Is 50:2
Then you shall call, and the LORD will **a**; Is 58:9
because, when I called, you did not **a**; Is 65:12
Before they call I will **a**; while they are Is 65:24
and when I called you, you did not **a**, Jer 7:13
call to them, but they will not **a** you. Jer 7:27
And they will **a**, "Because they have Jer 22:9
Call to me and I will **a** you, and will tell Jer 33:3
all the people who had given him this **a**: Jer 44:20
I the LORD will **a** him as he comes with Ezk 14:4
him, I the LORD will **a** him myself. Ezk 14:7
we have no need to **a** you in this matter. Dn 3:16
And there she shall **a** as in the days of Hos 2:15
"And in that day I will **a**, declares the Hos 2:21
declares the LORD, I will **a** the heavens, Hos 2:21
the heavens, and they shall **a** the earth, Hos 2:21
and the earth shall **a** the grain, the Hos 2:22
and the oil, and they shall **a** Jezreel, Hos 2:22
idols? It is I who **a** and look after you. Hos 14:8
cry to the LORD, but he will not **a** them; Mi 3:4
their lips, for there is no **a** from God. Mi 3:7
to you? How have I wearied you? **A** me! Mi 6:3
what I will **a** concerning my complaint. Hab 2:1
the LORD their God and I will **a** them. Zec 10:6
call upon my name, and I will **a** them. Zec 13:9
But he did not **a** her a word. And his Mt 15:23
one question, and if you tell me the **a**, Mt 21:24
And no one was able to **a** him a word, Mt 22:46
Then the righteous will **a** him, saying, Mt 25:37
And the King will **a** them, 'Truly, I say Mt 25:40
Then they also will **a**, saying, 'Lord, Mt 25:44
Then he will **a** them, saying, 'Truly, I Mt 25:45
up and said, "Have you no **a** to make? Mt 26:62
chief priests and elders, he gave no **a**. Mt 27:12
But he gave him no **a**, not even to a Mt 27:14
a me, and I will tell you by what Mk 11:29
from heaven or from man? **A** me." Mk 11:30
and they did not know what to **a** him. Mk 14:40
asked Jesus, "Have you no **a** to make? Mk 14:60
But he remained silent and made no **a**. Mk 14:61
asked him, "Have you no **a** to make? Mk 15:4
But Jesus made no further **a**, so that Mk 15:5
and he will **a** from within, 'Do not Lk 11:7
'Lord, open to us,' then he will **a** you, Lk 13:25
marveling at his **a** they became silent. Lk 20:26
not to meditate beforehand how to **a**, Lk 21:14
and if I ask you, you will not **a**. Lk 22:68
him at some length, but he made no **a**. Lk 23:9
We need to give an **a** to those who sent Jn 1:22
"Is that how you **a** the high priest?" Jn 18:22
are you from?" But Jesus gave him no **a**. Jn 19:9
servant girl named Rhoda came to **a**. Acts 12:13
who are you, O man, to **a** back to God? Rom 9:20
may be able to **a** those who boast 2 Cor 5:12
know how you ought to **a** each person. Col 4:6

ANSWERED (433)

Abraham **a** and said, "Behold, I have Gn 18:27
"Suppose forty are found there." He **a**, Gn 18:29
Suppose thirty are found there." He **a**, "I Gn 18:30
Suppose twenty are found there." He **a**, Gn 18:31
Suppose ten are found there." He **a**, Gn 18:32
The Hittites **a** Abraham, Gn 23:5
Ephron the Hittite **a** Abraham in the Gn 23:10
Ephron **a** Abraham, Gn 23:14
Then Laban and Bethuel **a** and said, Gn 24:50
to him, "My son"; and he **a**, "Here I am." Gn 27:1
found it so quickly, my son?" He **a**, Gn 27:20
"Are you really my son Esau?" He **a**, Gn 27:24
said to him, "Who are you?" He **a**, Gn 27:32
Isaac **a** and said to Esau, "Behold, I Gn 27:37
Then Isaac his father **a** and said to Gn 27:39
Then Rachel and Leah **a** and said to Gn 31:14
Jacob **a** and said to Laban, "Because I Gn 31:31
Then Laban **a** and said to Jacob, "The Gn 31:43
all this company that I met?" Jacob **a**, Gn 33:8
The sons of Jacob **a** Shechem and his Gn 34:13
He **a**, "I will send you a young goat Gn 38:17
And Joseph **a** and said, "This is its Gn 40:18
Joseph **a** Pharaoh, "It is not in me; God Gn 41:16
And Reuben **a** them, "Did I not tell you Gn 42:22
And Joseph **a**, "Give your livestock, Gn 47:16
bury me in their burying place." He **a**, Gn 47:30
And Pharaoh **a**, "Go up, and bury your Gn 50:6
He **a**, "Who made you a prince and a Ex 2:14
Then Moses **a**, "But behold, they will not Ex 4:1
All the people **a** together and said, "All Ex 19:8
spoke, and God **a** him in thunder. Ex 19:19
And all the people **a** with one voice and Ex 24:3
But Balaam **a** and said to the servants Nm 22:18
And he **a** and said, "Must I not take Nm 23:12
But Balaam **a** Balak, "Did I not tell Nm 23:26
of Gad and the people of Reuben **a**, Nm 32:31
And you **a** me, 'The thing that you have Dt 1:14
"Then you **a** me, 'We have sinned Dt 1:41
And they **a** Joshua, "All that you have Jos 1:16
And Achan **a** Joshua, "Truly I have Jos 7:20
They **a** Joshua, "Because it was told to Jos 9:24
Then the people **a**, "Far be it from us Jos 24:16
And his comrade **a**, "This is no other Jgs 7:14
and the men of Penuel **a** him as the men Jgs 8:8
him as the men of Succoth had **a**. Jgs 8:8
whom you killed at Tabor?" They **a**, Jgs 8:18
And they **a**, "We will willingly give Jgs 8:25
of the Ammonites **a** the messengers of Jgs 11:13
woman who was murdered, **a** and said, Jgs 20:4
"The LORD be with you!" And they **a**, Ru 2:4
who was in charge of the reapers **a**, Ru 2:6
But Boaz **a** her, "All that you have done Ru 2:11
He said, "Who are you?" And she **a**, "I am Ru 3:9
But Hannah **a**, "No, my lord, I am a 1 Sm 1:15
Then Eli **a**, "Go in peace, and the God 1 Sm 1:17
He who brought the news **a** and said, 1 Sm 4:17
the ark of the God of Israel?" They **a**, 1 Sm 5:8
that we shall return to him?" They **a**, 1 Sm 6:4
the LORD for Israel, and the LORD **a** him. 1 Sm 7:9
The servant **a** Saul again, "Here, I have 1 Sm 9:8
They **a**, "He is; behold, he is just ahead 1 Sm 9:12
Samuel **a** Saul, "I am the seer. Go up 1 Sm 9:19
Saul **a**, "Am I not a Benjaminite, from 1 Sm 9:21
And a man of the place **a**, "And who 1 Sm 10:12
among all the people who **a** him. 1 Sm 14:39
have you not **a** your servant this 1 Sm 14:41
One of the young men **a**, "Behold, I 1 Sm 16:18
And the people **a** him in the same 1 Sm 17:27
and the people **a** him again as before. 1 Sm 17:30
are you, young man?" And David **a**, 1 Sm 17:58
he has escaped?" And Michal **a** Saul, 1 Sm 19:17
Jonathan **a** Saul, "David earnestly 1 Sm 20:28
Then Jonathan **a** Saul his father, 1 Sm 20:32
And the priest **a** David, "I have no 1 Sm 21:4
And David **a** the priest, "Truly women 1 Sm 21:5
Then **a** Doeg the Edomite, who stood 1 Sm 22:9
"Hear now, son of Ahitub." And he **a**, 1 Sm 22:12
Then Ahimelech **a** the king, "And 1 Sm 22:14
And the LORD **a** him, "Arise, go down 1 Sm 23:4
And Nabal **a** David's servants, 1 Sm 25:10
not answer, Abner?" Then Abner **a**, 1 Sm 26:14
And David **a** and said, "Here is the 1 Sm 26:22
me by bringing me up?" Saul **a**, 1 Sm 28:15
And Achish **a** David and said, "I 1 Sm 29:9
Shall I overtake them?" He **a** him, 1 Sm 30:8
Tell me." And he **a**, "The people fled 2 Sm 1:4
and called to me. And I **a**, 'Here I am.' 2 Sm 1:7
he said to me, 'Who are you?' I **a** him, 2 Sm 1:8
do you come from?" And he **a**, 2 Sm 1:13
and said, "Is it you, Asahel?" And he **a**, 2 Sm 2:20
But David **a** Rechab and Baanah his 2 Sm 4:9
David said, "Mephibosheth!" And he **a**, 2 Sm 9:6
She **a** him, "No, my brother, do not 2 Sm 13:12
to her, "What is your trouble?" She **a**, 2 Sm 14:5
Then the king **a** the woman, "Do not 2 Sm 14:18
in all this?" The woman **a** and said, 2 Sm 14:19
Absalom **a** Joab, "Behold, I sent word 2 Sm 14:32
But Ittai **a** the king, "As the LORD 2 Sm 15:21
have you brought these?" Ziba **a**, 2 Sm 16:2
young man Absalom?" Ahimaaz **a**, 2 Sm 18:29
man Absalom?" And the Cushite **a**, 2 Sm 18:32
Abishai the son of Zeruiah **a**, "Shall 2 Sm 19:21
He **a**, "My lord, O king, my servant 2 Sm 19:26
And the king **a**, "Chimham shall go 2 Sm 19:38
the men of Judah **a** the men of Israel, 2 Sm 19:42
the men of Israel **a** the men of Judah, 2 Sm 19:43
woman said, "Are you Joab?" He **a**, 2 Sm 20:17
the words of your servant." And he **a**, 2 Sm 20:17
Joab **a**, "Far be it from me, far be it, 2 Sm 20:20
Then King David **a**, "Call Bathsheba 1 Kgs 1:28
the son of Jehoiada **a** the king, 1 Kgs 1:36
Jonathan **a** Adonijah, "No, for our 1 Kgs 1:43
King Solomon **a** his mother, "And 1 Kgs 2:22
"Thus said Joab, and thus he **a** me." 1 Kgs 2:30
Then the king **a** and said, "Give the 1 Kgs 3:27
And Solomon **a** all her questions; 1 Kgs 10:3
And the king **a** the people harshly, 1 Kgs 12:13
listen to them, the people **a** the king, 1 Kgs 12:16
And he **a** him, "It is I. Go, tell your 1 Kgs 18:8
And he **a**, "I have not troubled Israel, 1 Kgs 18:18
fire, he is God." And all the people **a**, 1 Kgs 18:24
there was no voice, and no one **a**. 1 Kgs 18:26
No one **a**; no one paid attention. 1 Kgs 18:29
And the king of Israel **a**, "As you say, 1 Kgs 20:4
And the king of Israel **a**, "Tell him, 1 Kgs 20:11
"Who shall begin the battle?" He **a**, 1 Kgs 20:14
And he **a**, 'I will not give you my 1 Kgs 21:6
you found me, O my enemy?" He **a**, 1 Kgs 21:20
or shall we refrain?" And he **a** him, 1 Kgs 22:15
They **a** him, "He wore a garment of 2 Kgs 1:8

But Elijah **a** the captain of fifty, "If I 2 Kgs 1:10
And he **a** and said to him, "O man of 2 Kgs 1:11
But Elijah **a** them, "If I am a man of 2 Kgs 1:12
your master from over you?" And he **a**, 2 Kgs 2:5
way shall we march?" Jehoram **a**, 2 Kgs 3:8
one of the king of Israel's servants **a**, 2 Kgs 3:11
the commander of the army?'" She **a**, 2 Kgs 4:13
then is to be done for her?" Gehazi **a**, 2 Kgs 4:14
Is all well with the child?'" And she **a**, 2 Kgs 4:26
a place for us to dwell there." And he **a**, 2 Kgs 6:2
to go with your servants." And he **a**, 2 Kgs 6:3
He **a**, "You shall not strike them 2 Kgs 6:22
her, "What is your trouble?" She **a**, 2 Kgs 6:28
the captain had **a** the man of God, "If 2 Kgs 7:19
said, "Why does my lord weep?" He **a**, 2 Kgs 8:12
should do this great thing?" Elisha **a**, 2 Kgs 8:13
did Elisha say to you?" And he **a**, 2 Kgs 8:14
has said, 'Is it peace?'" And Jehu **a**, 2 Kgs 9:19
Jehu, he said, "Is it peace, Jehu?" He **a**, 2 Kgs 9:22
he said, "Who are you?" And they **a**, 2 Kgs 10:13
mine is to yours?" And Jehonadab **a**, 2 Kgs 10:15
people were silent and **a** him not a 2 Kgs 18:36
And Hezekiah **a**, "It is an easy thing 2 Kgs 20:10
in your house?" And Hezekiah **a**, 2 Kgs 20:15
and the LORD **a** him with fire from 1 Chr 21:26
that the LORD had **a** him at the 1 Chr 21:28
God **a** Solomon, "Because this was in 2 Chr 1:11
the king of Tyre **a** in a letter that 2 Chr 2:11
And Solomon **a** all her questions. 2 Chr 9:2
And the king **a** them harshly; and 2 Chr 10:13
listen to them, the people **a** the king, 2 Chr 10:16
me to Ramoth-gilead?" He **a** him, 2 Chr 18:3
battle, or shall I refrain?" And he **a**, 2 Chr 18:14
army of Israel?" The man of God **a**, 2 Chr 25:9
was of the house of Zadok, **a** him, 2 Chr 31:10
and he **a** him and gave him a sign. 2 Chr 32:24
Then Hilkiah **a** and said to 2 Chr 34:15
Then all the assembly **a** with a loud Ezr 10:12
way, and I **a** them in the same manner. Neh 6:4
LORD, the great God, and all the people **a**, Neh 8:6
Then Esther **a**, "My wish and my request Est 5:7
Then Queen Esther **a**, "If I have found Est 7:3
have you come?" Satan **a** the LORD and Jb 1:7
Then Satan **a** the LORD and said, "Does Job Jb 1:9
have you come?" Satan **a** the LORD and Jb 2:2
Then Satan **a** the LORD and said, "Skin for Jb 2:4
Then Eliphaz the Temanite **a** and said: Jb 4:1
Then Job **a** and said: Jb 6:1
Then Bildad the Shuhite **a** and said: Jb 8:1
Then Job **a** and said: Jb 9:1
If I summoned him and he **a** me, I would Jb 9:16
Then Zophar the Naamathite **a** and said: Jb 11:1
Then Job **a** and said: Jb 12:1
I, who called to God and he **a** me, a just Jb 12:4
Then Eliphaz the Temanite **a** and said: Jb 15:1
Then Job **a** and said: Jb 16:1
Then Bildad the Shuhite **a** and said: Jb 18:1
Then Job **a** and said: Jb 19:1
but I am not **a**; I call for help, but there is Jb 19:7
Then Zophar the Naamathite **a** and said: Jb 20:1
Then Job **a** and said: Jb 21:1
Then Eliphaz the Temanite **a** and said: Jb 22:1
Then Job **a** and said: Jb 23:1
Then Bildad the Shuhite **a** and said: Jb 25:1
Then Job **a** and said: Jb 26:1
the son of Barachel the Buzite **a** and said: Jb 32:6
you who refuted Job or who **a** his words. Jb 32:12
Then Elihu **a** and said: Jb 34:1
And Elihu **a** and said: Jb 35:1
Then the LORD **a** Job out of the whirlwind Jb 38:1
Then Job **a** the LORD and said: Jb 40:3
Then the LORD **a** Job out of the whirlwind Jb 40:6
Then Job **a** the LORD and said: Jb 42:1
the LORD, and he **a** me from his holy hill. Ps 3:4
and he **a** me and delivered me from all Ps 34:4
I **a** you in the secret place of thunder; Ps 81:7
They called to the LORD, and he **a** them. Ps 99:6
O LORD our God, you **a** them; you were a Ps 99:8
the LORD; the LORD **a** me and set me free. Ps 118:5
you that you have **a** me and have Ps 118:21
When I told of my ways, you **a** me; Ps 119:26
I called to the LORD, and he **a** me. Ps 120:1
On the day I called, you **a** me; my Ps 138:3
poor will himself call out and not be **a**. Prv 21:13
riders, horsemen in pairs!" And he **a**, Is 21:9
they were silent and **a** him not a word, Is 36:21
they seen in your house?" Hezekiah **a**, Is 39:4
the LORD: "In a time of favor I have **a** you; Is 49:8
them, because when I called, no one **a**, Is 66:4
and honey, as at this day." Then I **a**, Jer 11:5
to his brother, 'What has the LORD **a**?' Jer 23:35
the prophet, 'What has the LORD **a** you?' Jer 23:37
But they **a**, "We will drink no wine, for Jer 35:6
called to them and they have not **a**." Jer 35:17
Baruch **a** them, "He dictated all these Jer 36:18
and he **a** them as the king had Jer 38:27
in the land of Egypt, **a** Jeremiah: Jer 44:15
of man, can these bones live?" And I **a**, Ezk 37:3
The king **a** and said to the Chaldeans, Dn 2:5
They **a** a second time and said, "Let the Dn 2:7
The king **a** and said, "I know with Dn 2:8
The Chaldeans **a** the king and said, Dn 2:10
Daniel **a** and said: "Blessed be the name Dn 2:20
Daniel **a** the king and said, "No wise Dn 2:27
The king **a** and said to Daniel, "Truly, Dn 2:47
Nebuchadnezzar **a** and said to them, "Is Dn 3:14
and Abednego **a** and said to the king, Dn 3:16
into the fire?" They **a** and said to the Dn 3:24
He **a** and said, "But I see four men Dn 3:25
Nebuchadnezzar **a** and said, "Blessed be Dn 3:28
alarmed him. The king **a** and said, Dn 4:19
alarm you." Belteshazzar **a** and said, Dn 4:19
and the king **a** and said, "Is not this Dn 4:30
The king **a** and said to Daniel, "You are Dn 5:13
Then Daniel **a** and said before the king, Dn 5:17
the den of lions?" The king **a** and said, Dn 6:12
Then they **a** and said before the king, Dn 6:13
The LORD **a** and said to his people, Jl 2:19
Then Amos **a** and said to Amaziah, "I Am 7:14
the LORD, out of my distress, and he **a** me; Jon 2:2
and what Balaam the son of Beor **a** him, Mi 6:5
And the LORD **a** me: "Write the vision; Hab 2:2
it become holy?'" The priests **a** and said, Hg 2:12
unclean?" The priests **a** and said, Hg 2:13
Then Haggai **a** and said, "So is it with Hg 2:14
was standing among the myrtle trees **a**, Zec 1:10
And they **a** the angel of the LORD who Zec 1:11
And the LORD **a** gracious and Zec 1:13
who talked with me **a** and said to me, Zec 4:5
And a second time I **a** and said to him, Zec 4:12
he said to me, "What do you see?" I **a**, Zec 5:2
Then I **a** and said to the angel who talked Zec 6:4
And the angel **a** and said to me, "These Zec 6:5
But Jesus **a** him, "Let it be so now, for Mt 3:15
But he **a**, "It is written, "'Man shall not Mt 4:4
And Jesus **a** them, "Go and tell John Mt 11:4
of the scribes and Pharisees **a** him, Mt 12:38
But he **a** them, "An evil and adulterous Mt 12:39
And he **a** them, "To you it has been Mt 13:11
He **a**, "The one who sows the good seed Mt 13:37
And Peter **a** him, "Lord, if it is you, Mt 14:28
He **a** them, "And why do you break the Mt 15:3
He **a**, "Every plant that my heavenly Mt 15:13
He **a**, "I was sent only to the lost sheep Mt 15:24
And he **a**, "It is not right to take the Mt 15:26
Then Jesus **a** her, "O woman, great is Mt 15:28
He **a** them, "When it is evening, you say, Mt 16:2
And Jesus **a** him, "Blessed are you, Mt 16:17
He **a**, "Elijah does come, and he will Mt 17:11
And Jesus **a**, "O faithless and twisted Mt 17:17
He **a**, "Have you not read that he who Mt 19:4
Jesus **a**, "You do not know what you Mt 20:22
And Jesus **a** them, "Truly, I say to you, Mt 21:21
Jesus **a** them, "I also will ask you one Mt 21:24
So they **a** Jesus, "We do not know." And Mt 21:27
And he **a**, 'I will not,' but afterward he Mt 21:29
And he **a**, 'I go, sir,' but did not go. Mt 21:30
But Jesus **a** them, "You are wrong, Mt 22:29
But he **a** them, "You see all these, do you Mt 24:2
And Jesus **a** them, "See that no one leads Mt 24:4
But the wise **a**, saying, 'Since there will Mt 25:9
But he **a**, 'Truly, I say to you, I do not Mt 25:12
But his master **a** him, 'You wicked and Mt 25:26
He **a**, "He who has dipped his hand in Mt 26:23
Judas, who would betray him, **a**, "Is it I, Mt 26:25
Peter **a** him, "Though they all fall Mt 26:33
What is your judgment?" They **a**, "He Mt 26:66
And all the people **a**, "His blood be on Mt 27:25
And he **a** them, "Who are my mother Mk 3:33
But he **a** them, "You give them Mk 6:37
But she **a** him, "Yes, Lord; yet even the Mk 7:28
And his disciples **a** him, "How can one Mk 8:4
who do you say that I am?" Peter **a** him, Mk 8:29
And someone from the crowd **a** him, Mk 9:17
And he **a** them, "O faithless generation, Mk 9:19
He **a** them, "What did Moses command Mk 10:3
And Jesus **a** them, "Have faith in God. Mk 11:22
So they **a** Jesus, "We do not know." Mk 11:33
and seeing that he **a** them well, Mk 12:28
Jesus **a**, "The most important is, 'Hear, Mk 12:29
And when Jesus saw that he **a** wisely, Mk 12:34
the King of the Jews?" And he **a** him, Mk 15:2
And he **a** them, saying, "Do you want Mk 15:9
And the angel **a** him, "I am Gabriel, who Lk 1:19
And the angel **a** her, "The Holy Spirit Lk 1:35
but his mother **a**, "No; he shall be called Lk 1:60
And he **a** them, "Whoever has two Lk 3:11
John **a** them all, saying, "I baptize you Lk 3:16
And Jesus **a** him, "It is written, 'Man shall Lk 4:4
And Jesus **a** him, "It is written, "'You Lk 4:8
And Jesus **a** him, "It is said, 'You shall Lk 4:12
And Simon **a**, "Master, we toiled all night Lk 5:5
perceived their thoughts, he **a** them, Lk 5:22
And Jesus **a** them, "Those who are well Lk 5:31
And Jesus **a** them, "Have you not read Lk 6:3
And he **a** them, "Go and tell John what Lk 7:22
have something to say to you." And he **a**, Lk 7:40
Simon **a**, "The one, I suppose, for whom Lk 7:43
But he **a** them, "My mother and my Lk 8:21
But Jesus on hearing this **a** him, "Do not Lk 8:50
And they **a**, "John the Baptist. But others Lk 9:19
who do you say that I am?" And Peter **a**, Lk 9:20
Jesus **a**, "O faithless and twisted Lk 9:41
John **a**, "Master, we saw someone Lk 9:49
And he **a**, "You shall love the Lord Lk 10:27
he said to him, "You have **a** correctly; Lk 10:28
But the Lord **a** her, "Martha, Martha, Lk 10:41
One of the lawyers **a** him, "Teacher, in Lk 11:45
And he **a** them, "Do you think that these Lk 13:2
And he **a** him, 'Sir, let it alone this year Lk 13:8
Then the Lord **a** him, "You hypocrites! Lk 13:15
but he **a** his father, 'Look, these many Lk 15:29
Then Jesus **a**, "Were not ten cleansed? Lk 17:17
of God would come, he **a** them, Lk 17:20
He **a**, "I tell you, if these were silent, the Lk 19:40
He **a** them, "I also will ask you a Lk 20:3
So they **a** that they did not know where it Lk 20:7
Then some of the scribes **a**, "Teacher, Lk 20:39
you the King of the Jews?" And he **a** him, Lk 23:3
one of them, named Cleopas, **a** him, Lk 24:18
not." "Are you the Prophet?" And he **a**, Jn 1:21
John **a** them, "I baptize with water, but Jn 1:26
"How do you know me?" Jesus **a** him, Jn 1:48
Nathanael **a** him, "Rabbi, you are the Jn 1:49
Jesus **a** him, "Because I said to you, 'I saw Jn 1:50
Jesus **a** them, "Destroy this temple, and in Jn 2:19
Jesus **a** him, "Truly, truly, I say to you, Jn 3:3
Jesus **a**, "Truly, truly, I say to you, unless Jn 3:5
Jesus **a** him, "Are you the teacher of Jn 3:10
John **a**, "A person cannot receive even Jn 3:27
Jesus **a** her, "If you knew the gift of God, Jn 4:10
The woman **a** him, "I have no husband." Jn 4:17
The sick man **a** him, "Sir, I have no one to Jn 5:7
But he **a** them, "The man who healed me, Jn 5:11
But Jesus **a** them, "My Father is working Jn 5:17
Philip **a** him, "Two hundred denarii Jn 6:7
Jesus **a** them, "Truly, truly, I say to you, Jn 6:26
Jesus **a** them, "This is the work of God, Jn 6:29
Jesus **a** them, "Do not grumble among Jn 6:43
Simon Peter **a** him, "Lord, to whom shall Jn 6:68
Jesus **a** them, "Did I not choose you, the Jn 6:70
So Jesus **a** them, "My teaching is not Jn 7:16
The crowd **a**, "You have a demon! Who Jn 7:20
Jesus **a** them, "I did one deed, and you all Jn 7:21
The officers **a**, "No one ever spoke like Jn 7:46
The Pharisees **a** them, "Have you also Jn 7:47
Jesus **a**, "Even if I do bear witness about Jn 8:14
"Where is your Father?" Jesus **a**, Jn 8:19
They **a** him, "We are offspring of Jn 8:33
Jesus **a** them, "Truly, truly, I say to you, Jn 8:34
They **a** him, "Abraham is our father." Jn 8:39
The Jews **a** him, "Are we not right in Jn 8:48
Jesus **a**, "I do not have a demon, but I Jn 8:49
Jesus **a**, "If I glorify myself, my glory is Jn 8:54
Jesus **a**, "It was not that this man sinned, Jn 9:3
He **a**, "The man called Jesus made mud Jn 9:11
His parents **a**, "We know that this is our Jn 9:20
He **a**, "Whether he is a sinner I do not Jn 9:25
He **a** them, "I have told you already, and Jn 9:27
The man **a**, "Why, this is an amazing Jn 9:30
They **a** him, "You were born in utter sin, Jn 9:34
He **a**, "And who is he, sir, that I may Jn 9:36
Jesus **a** them, "I told you, and you do not Jn 10:25
Jesus **a** them, "I have shown you many Jn 10:32
The Jews **a** him, "It is not for a good Jn 10:33
Jesus **a** them, "Is it not written in your Jn 10:34
Jesus **a**, "Are there not twelve hours in the Jn 11:9
And Jesus **a** them, "The hour has come Jn 12:23
Jesus **a**, "This voice has come for your Jn 12:30
So the crowd **a** him, "We have heard Jn 12:34
Jesus **a** him, "What I am doing you do Jn 13:7
shall never wash my feet." Jesus **a** him, Jn 13:8
Jesus **a**, "It is he to whom I will give this Jn 13:26
where are you going?" Jesus **a** him, Jn 13:36
Jesus **a**, "Will you lay down your life for Jn 13:38
Jesus **a** him, "If anyone loves me, he will Jn 14:23
Jesus **a** them, "Do you now believe? Jn 16:31
They **a** him, "Jesus of Nazareth." Jesus Jn 18:5
Jesus **a**, "I told you that I am he. So, if you Jn 18:8
Jesus **a** him, "I have spoken openly to Jn 18:20
Jesus **a** him, "If what I said is wrong, Jn 18:23
They **a** him, "If this man were not doing Jn 18:30
Jesus **a**, "Do you say this of your own Jn 18:34
Pilate **a**, "Am I a Jew? Your own nation Jn 18:35
Jesus **a**, "My kingdom is not of this Jn 18:36

to him, "So you are a king?" Jesus **a**, Jn 18:37
The Jews **a** him, "We have a law, and Jn 19:7
Jesus **a** him, "You would have no Jn 19:11
crucify your King?" The chief priests **a**, Jn 19:15
Pilate **a**, "What I have written I have Jn 19:22
Thomas **a** him, "My Lord and my Jn 20:28
do you have any fish?" They **a** him, Jn 21:5
But Peter and John **a** them, "Whether Acts 4:19
But Peter and the apostles **a**, "We must Acts 5:29
And Simon **a**, "Pray for me to the Lord, Acts 8:24
But Ananias **a**, "Lord, I have heard Acts 9:13
But the voice **a** a second time from Acts 11:9
But the evil spirit **a** them, "Jesus I Acts 19:15
Then Paul **a**, "What are you doing, Acts 21:13
And I **a**, 'Who are you, Lord?' And he Acts 22:8
The tribune **a**, "I bought this Acts 22:28
a, "To Caesar you have appealed; Acts 25:12
I **a** them that it was not the custom of Acts 25:16

ANSWERING (1)
And Jesus **a** said to him, "Simon, I have Lk 7:40

ANSWERS (12)
altar to the God who **a** me in the day of Gn 35:3
princesses answer, indeed, she **a** herself, Jgs 5:29
me if your father **a** you roughly?" 1 Sm 20:10
away from me and **a** me no more, 1 Sm 28:15
the LORD, and the God who **a** by fire, 1 Kgs 18:24
out of my understanding a spirit **a** me. Jb 20:3
is nothing left of your **a** but falsehood." Jb 21:34
the end, because he **a** like wicked men. Jb 34:36
life, and money **a** everything. Eccl 10:19
cry. As soon as he hears it, he **a** you. Is 30:19
and whatever the LORD **a** you I will tell Jer 42:4
amazed at his understanding and his **a**. Lk 2:47

ANT (1)
Go to the **a**, O sluggard; consider her Prv 6:6

ANTELOPE (2)
roebuck, the wild goat, the ibex, the **a**, Dt 14:5
the head of every street like an **a** in a net; Is 51:20

ANTHOTHIJAH (1)
Hananiah, Elam, **A**, 1 Chr 8:24

ANTICHRIST (4)
as you have heard that **a** is coming, 1 Jn 2:18
This is the **a**, he who denies the Father 1 Jn 2:22
This is the spirit of the **a**, which you 1 Jn 4:3
Such a one is the deceiver and the **a**. 2 Jn 1:7

ANTICHRISTS (1)
is coming, so now many **a** have come. 1 Jn 2:18

ANTIMONY (2)
stones for setting, **a**, colored stones, 1 Chr 29:2
behold, I will set your stones in **a**, Is 54:11

ANTIOCH (19)
and Nicolaus, a proselyte of **A**. Acts 6:5
far as Phoenicia and Cyprus and **A**, Acts 11:19
who on coming to **A** spoke to the Acts 11:20
and they sent Barnabas to **A**. Acts 11:22
had found him, he brought him to **A**. Acts 11:26
And in **A** the disciples were first Acts 11:26
came down from Jerusalem to **A**. Acts 11:27
the church at **A** prophets and teachers, Acts 13:1
from Perga and came to **A** in Pisidia. Acts 13:14
But Jews came from **A** and Iconium, Acts 14:19
to Lystra and to Iconium and to **A**, Acts 14:21
and from there they sailed to **A**, where Acts 14:26
and send them to **A** with Paul and Acts 15:22
of the Gentiles in **A** and Syria and Acts 15:23
were sent off, they went down to **A**, Acts 15:30
Paul and Barnabas remained in **A**, Acts 15:35
the church, and then went down to **A**. Acts 18:22
But when Cephas came to **A**, I opposed Gal 2:11
sufferings that happened to me at **A**, 2 Tm 3:11

ANTIPAS (1)
in the days of **A** my faithful witness, Rv 2:13

ANTIPATRIS (1)
Paul and brought him by night to **A**. Acts 23:31

ANTS (1)
the **a** are a people not strong, yet they Prv 30:25

ANUB (1)
Koz fathered **A**, Zobebah, and the 1 Chr 4:8

ANVIL (1)
with the hammer him who strikes the **a**, Is 41:7

ANXIETIES (2)
I want you to be free from **a**. The 1 Cor 7:32
casting all your **a** on him, because he 1 Pt 5:7

ANXIETY (6)
out of my great **a** and vexation." 1 Sm 1:16
A in a man's heart weighs him down, Prv 12:25
shall eat bread by weight and with **a**, Ezk 4:16
water with trembling and with **a**. Ezk 12:18
They shall eat their bread with **a**, and Ezk 12:19
on me of my **a** for all the churches. 2 Cor 11:28

ANXIOUS (25)
the donkeys and become **a** about us." 1 Sm 9:5
about the donkeys and is **a** about you, 1 Sm 10:2
go late to rest, eating the bread of **a** toil; Ps 127:2
Say to those who have an **a** heart, "Be Is 35:4
green, and is not **a** in the year of drought, Jer 17:8
me, Daniel, my spirit within me was **a**, Dn 7:15
I tell you, do not be **a** about your life, Mt 6:25
of you by being **a** can add a single Mt 6:27
And why are you **a** about clothing? Mt 6:28
Therefore do not be **a**, saying, 'What Mt 6:31
"Therefore do not be **a** about tomorrow, Mt 6:34
for tomorrow will be **a** for itself. Mt 6:34
do not be **a** how you are to speak or Mt 10:19
do not be **a** beforehand what you are Mk 13:11
you are **a** and troubled about many Lk 10:41
do not be **a** about how you should Lk 12:11
I tell you, do not be **a** about your life, Lk 12:22
of you by being **a** can add a single Lk 12:25
as that, why are you **a** about the rest? Lk 12:26
unmarried man is **a** about the things 1 Cor 7:32
married man is **a** about worldly 1 Cor 7:33
betrothed woman is **a** about the 1 Cor 7:34
married woman is **a** about worldly 1 Cor 7:34
him again, and that I may be less **a**. Phil 2:28
do not be **a** about anything, but in Phil 4:6

ANXIOUSLY (1)
inhabitants of Maroth wait **a** for good, Mi 1:12

ANY (518)
was more crafty than **a** other beast of the Gn 3:1
shall not eat of **a** tree in the garden'?" Gn 3:1
lest **a** who found him should attack Gn 4:15
And they took as their wives **a** they chose. Gn 6:2
your money from a foreigner who is Gn 17:12
A uncircumcised male who is not Gn 17:14
daughters who have not known **a** man. Gn 19:8
that I should give her to **a** other man; Gn 29:19
"Is there **a** portion or inheritance left to Gn 31:14
before **a** king reigned over the Gn 36:31
loved Joseph more than **a** other of his Gn 37:3
Could we in **a** way know that he would Gn 43:7
was five times as much as **a** of theirs. Gn 43:34
and if you know **a** able men among Gn 47:6
and **a** woman who lives in her house, Ex 3:22
dog shall growl against **a** of the people of Ex 11:7
Do not eat **a** of it raw or boiled in water, Ex 12:9
had they prepared **a** provisions for Ex 12:39
you shall not take **a** of the flesh outside Ex 12:46
and you shall not break **a** of its bones. Ex 12:46
"Let no one leave **a** of it over till the Ex 16:19
but **a** small matter they shall decide Ex 18:22
A hard case they brought to Moses, but Ex 18:26
but **a** small matter they decided Ex 18:26
or **a** likeness of anything that is in Ex 20:4
On it you shall not do **a** work, you, or Ex 20:10
for a cloak, or for **a** kind of lost thing, Ex 22:9
an ox or a sheep or **a** beast to keep safe, Ex 22:10
"Whoever sacrifices to **a** god, other Ex 22:20
shall not mistreat **a** widow or fatherless Ex 22:22
you lend money to **a** of my people with Ex 22:25
you shall not eat **a** flesh that is torn Ex 22:31
and Aaron shall bear **a** guilt from the Ex 28:38
And if **a** of the flesh for the ordination Ex 29:34
Whoever compounds **a** like it or Ex 30:33
like it or whoever puts **a** of it on an Ex 30:33
Whoever makes **a** like it to use as Ex 30:38
Whoever does **a** work on it, that soul Ex 31:14
Whoever does **a** work on the Sabbath Ex 31:15
them, 'Let **a** who have gold take it off.' Ex 32:24
created in all the earth or in **a** nation. Ex 34:10
not make for yourself **a** gods of cast Ex 34:17
Whoever does **a** work on it shall be put Ex 35:2
possessed acacia wood of **a** use in the Ex 35:24
by a weaver—by **a** sort of workman or Ex 35:35
know how to do **a** work in the Ex 36:1
When **a** one of you brings an offering to Lv 1:2
burn no leaven nor **a** honey as a food Lv 2:11
sins unintentionally in **a** of the LORD'S Lv 4:2
not to be done, and does **a** one of them, Lv 4:2
and they do **a** one of the things that by Lv 4:13
doing unintentionally **a** one of all the Lv 4:22
unintentionally in doing **a** one of the Lv 4:27
good, **a** sort of rash oath that people swear, Lv 5:4
it, and he realizes his guilt in **a** of these; Lv 5:4
realizes his guilt in **a** of these and Lv 5:5
he has committed in **a** one of these Lv 5:13
and sins unintentionally in **a** of the holy Lv 5:15
doing **a** of the things that by the LORD'S Lv 5:17
swearing falsely—in **a** of all the things Lv 6:3
shall be forgiven for **a** of the things that Lv 6:7
and when **a** of its blood is splashed on a Lv 6:27
be eaten from which **a** blood is brought Lv 6:30
priest who offers **a** man's burnt offering Lv 7:8
He shall not leave **a** of it until the Lv 7:15
If **a** of the flesh of the sacrifice of his Lv 7:18
"Flesh that touches **a** unclean thing Lv 7:19
unclean beast or **a** unclean detestable Lv 7:21
torn by beasts may be put to **a** other use, Lv 7:24
of animal, in **a** of your dwelling places. Lv 7:26
Whoever eats **a** blood, that person shall Lv 7:27
You shall not eat **a** of their flesh, and Lv 11:8
you shall not eat **a** of their flesh, and Lv 11:11
the kite, the falcon of **a** kind, Lv 11:14
every raven of **a** kind, Lv 11:15
the sea gull, the hawk of **a** kind, Lv 11:16
the stork, the heron of **a** kind, the Lv 11:19
the locust of **a** kind, the bald locust of Lv 11:22
of any kind, the bald locust of **a** kind, Lv 11:22
of any kind, the cricket of **a** kind, Lv 11:22
kind, and the grasshopper of **a** kind. Lv 11:22
and whoever carries **a** part of their Lv 11:25
the mouse, the great lizard of **a** kind, Lv 11:29
And anything on which **a** of them falls Lv 11:32
a article that is used for any purpose. Lv 11:32
any article that is used for **a** purpose. Lv 11:32
And if **a** of them falls into any Lv 11:33
of them falls into **a** earthenware vessel, Lv 11:33
A food in it that could be eaten, on Lv 11:34
everything on which **a** part of their Lv 11:35
And if **a** part of their carcass falls upon Lv 11:37
carcass falls upon **a** seed grain that Lv 11:37
on the seed and **a** part of their carcass Lv 11:38
"And if **a** animal which you may eat Lv 11:39
a swarming thing that swarms on the Lv 11:42
detestable with **a** swarming thing Lv 11:43
yourselves with **a** swarming thing Lv 11:44
or the woof or in **a** article made of skin, Lv 13:49
or **a** article made of skin that is Lv 13:52
or the woof or in **a** article made of skin, Lv 13:53
or the woof, or in **a** article made of skin, Lv 13:57
or **a** article made of skin from which Lv 13:58
or the woof, or in **a** article made of skin, Lv 13:59
is the law for **a** case of leprous disease: Lv 14:54
When **a** man has a discharge from his Lv 15:2
And **a** saddle on which the one with the Lv 15:9
And if **a** man lies with her and her Lv 15:24
not to come at **a** time into the Holy Lv 16:2
If **a** one of the house of Israel kills an ox Lv 17:3
say to them, **A** one of the house of Israel, Lv 17:8
"If **a** one of the house of Israel or of the Lv 17:10
who sojourn among them eats **a** blood, Lv 17:10
neither shall **a** stranger who sojourns Lv 17:12
"**A** one also of the people of Israel, or of Lv 17:13
who takes in hunting **a** beast or bird Lv 17:13
shall not eat the blood of **a** creature, Lv 17:14
of you shall approach **a** one of his close Lv 18:6
You shall not give **a** of your children to Lv 18:21
shall not lie with **a** animal and so Lv 18:23
neither shall **a** woman give herself to Lv 18:23
yourselves unclean by **a** of these Lv 18:24
everyone who does **a** of these Lv 18:29
never to practice **a** of these abominable Lv 18:30
or make for yourselves **a** gods of cast Lv 19:4
the land and plant **a** kind of tree for Lv 19:23
"You shall not eat **a** flesh with the Lv 19:26
You shall not make **a** cuts on your Lv 19:28
A one of the people of Israel or of the Lv 20:2
in Israel who gives **a** of his children to Lv 20:2
a woman approaches **a** animal and lies Lv 20:16
beards, nor make **a** cuts on their body. Lv 21:5
And the daughter of **a** priest, if she Lv 21:9
not go in to **a** dead bodies nor make Lv 21:11
'If **a** one of all your offspring throughout Lv 22:3
When **a** one of the house of Israel or of Lv 22:18
for **a** of their vows or freewill offerings Lv 22:18
A animal that has its testicles bruised Lv 22:24
of your God **a** such animals gotten Lv 22:25
you shall not do **a** ordinary work. Lv 23:7
you shall not do **a** ordinary work." Lv 23:8
You shall not do **a** ordinary work. Lv 23:21
You shall not do **a** ordinary work, and Lv 23:25
you shall not do **a** work on that very Lv 23:28
And whoever does **a** work on that very Lv 23:30
You shall not do **a** work. It is a statute Lv 23:31
you shall not do **a** ordinary work. Lv 23:35
you shall not do **a** ordinary work. Lv 23:36
may redeem at **a** time the houses Lv 25:32
And if it is **a** unclean animal that may Lv 27:11
And if **a** outsider comes near, he shall Nm 1:51
But if **a** outsider comes near, he shall Nm 3:10
And **a** outsider who came near was to Nm 3:38
man or woman commits **a** of the sins Nm 5:6
If **a** man's wife goes astray and breaks Nm 5:12
and shall not drink **a** juice of grapes or Nm 6:3
"And if **a** man dies very suddenly beside Nm 6:9
If **a** one of you or of your descendants is Nm 9:10
the morning, nor break **a** of its bones; Nm 9:12

and **a** outsider who comes near shall Nm 18:7
shall you have **a** portion among Nm 18:20
And you may eat it in **a** place, you Nm 18:31
the dead body of **a** person shall be Nm 19:11
Have I now **a** power of my own to Nm 22:38
You shall not do **a** ordinary work, Nm 28:18
You shall not do **a** ordinary work. Nm 28:25
You shall not do **a** ordinary work, Nm 28:26
You shall not do **a** ordinary work. Nm 29:1
You shall not do **a** ordinary work, Nm 29:12
You shall not do **a** ordinary work, Nm 29:35
her vows or **a** thoughtless utterance of Nm 30:6
(But **a** vow of a widow or of a divorced Nm 30:9
A vow and any binding oath to afflict Nm 30:13
Any vow and **a** binding oath to afflict Nm 30:13
you has killed **a** person and whoever Nm 31:19
and whoever has touched **a** slain, Nm 31:19
manslayer who kills **a** person without Nm 35:11
anyone who kills **a** person without Nm 35:15
manslayer shall at **a** time go beyond Nm 35:26
if they are married to **a** of the sons of Nm 36:3
an inheritance in **a** tribe of the Nm 36:8
for I will not give you **a** of their land, Dt 2:5
for I will not give you **a** of their land for a Dt 2:9
for I will not give you **a** of the land of the Dt 2:19
for yourselves, in the form of **a** figure, Dt 4:16
the likeness of **a** animal that is on the Dt 4:17
the likeness of **a** winged bird that flies in Dt 4:17
the likeness of **a** fish that is in the water Dt 4:18
Did **a** people ever hear the voice of a god Dt 4:33
Or has **a** god ever attempted to go and Dt 4:34
or **a** likeness of anything that is in heaven Dt 5:8
On it you shall not do **a** work, you or Dt 5:14
ox or your donkey or **a** of your livestock, Dt 5:14
the voice of the LORD our God **a** more, Dt 5:25
more in number than **a** other people that Dt 7:7
your burnt offerings at **a** place that you Dt 12:13
and eat meat within **a** of your towns, Dt 12:15
or **a** of your vow offerings that you vow, Dt 12:17
then you may kill **a** of your herd or Dt 12:21
never again do **a** such wickedness as Dt 13:11
yourselves or make **a** baldness on your Dt 14:1
"You shall not eat **a** abomination. Dt 14:3
the kite, the falcon of **a** kind; Dt 14:13
every raven of **a** kind; Dt 14:14
the sea gull, the hawk of **a** kind; Dt 14:15
the stork, the heron of **a** kind; the Dt 14:18
in **a** of your towns within your land that Dt 15:7
But if it has **a** blemish, if it is lame or Dt 15:21
blind or has **a** serious blemish Dt 15:21
nor shall **a** of the flesh that you sacrifice Dt 16:4
Passover sacrifice within **a** of your Dt 16:5
"You shall not plant **a** tree as an Dt 16:21
in which is a blemish, **a** defect whatever, Dt 17:1
within **a** of your towns that the LORD Dt 17:2
sun or the moon or **a** of the host of Dt 17:3
"If **a** case arises requiring decision Dt 17:8
a case within your towns that is too Dt 17:8
a Levite comes from **a** of your towns out Dt 18:6
my God or see this great fire **a** more, Dt 18:16
so that **a** manslayer can flee to them. Dt 19:3
against a person for **a** crime or for any Dt 19:15
any crime or for **a** wrong in connection Dt 19:15
in connection with **a** offense that he Dt 19:15
never again commit **a** such evil among Dt 19:20
'Is there **a** man who has built a new Dt 20:5
And is there **a** man who has planted a Dt 20:6
And is there **a** man who has betrothed a Dt 20:7
'Is there **a** man who is fearful and Dt 20:8
or with **a** lost thing of your brother's, Dt 22:3
across a bird's nest in **a** tree or on the Dt 22:6
"If **a** man takes a wife and goes in to her Dt 22:13
"If **a** man among you becomes unclean Dt 23:10
LORD your God in payment for **a** vow, Dt 23:18
but you shall not put **a** in your bag. Dt 23:24
army or be liable for **a** other public duty. Dt 24:5
make your neighbor a loan of **a** sort, Dt 24:10
have not transgressed **a** of your Dt 26:13
or removed **a** of it while I was unclean, Dt 26:14
unclean, or offered **a** of it to the dead. Dt 26:14
anyone who lies with **a** kind of animal.' Dt 27:21
not turn aside from **a** of the words that Dt 28:14
your eyes, but you shall not eat **a** of it. Dt 28:31
he will not give to **a** of them any of the Dt 28:55
give to any of them **a** of the flesh of his Dt 28:55
no spirit left in **a** man because of you, Jos 2:11
there was no longer **a** spirit in them Jos 5:1
neither shall **a** word go out of your Jos 6:10
devoted them you take **a** of the devoted Jos 6:18
his tongue against **a** of the people Jos 10:21
and they did not leave **a** who breathed. Jos 11:14
manslayer who strikes **a** person without Jos 20:3
They did not drop **a** of their practices or Jgs 2:19
drive out before them **a** of the nations Jgs 2:21
tent, and if **a** man comes and asks you, Jgs 4:20
Now are you **a** better than Balak the Jgs 11:25
And when **a** of the fugitives of Ephraim Jgs 12:5
or strong drink, or eat **a** unclean thing. Jgs 13:14
become weak and be like **a** other man." Jgs 16:7
weak and be like **a** other man." Jgs 16:11
weak and be like **a** other man." Jgs 16:13
weak and be like **a** other man." Jgs 16:17
will not give them **a** of our daughters for Jgs 21:7
was that when **a** man offered 1 Sm 2:13
he was taller than **a** of the people. 1 Sm 9:2
he was taller than **a** of the people 1 Sm 10:23
taken anything from **a** man's hand." 1 Sm 12:4
in the hand of **a** of the people with 1 Sm 13:22
And when Saul saw **a** strong man, or 1 Sm 14:52
any strong man, or **a** valiant man, 1 Sm 14:52
saw it or knew it, nor did **a** awake, 1 Sm 26:12
of seeking me **a** longer within the 1 Sm 27:1
will not give them **a** of the spoil that 1 Sm 30:22
"Shall I go up into **a** of the cities of 2 Sm 2:1
I speak a word with **a** of the judges of 2 Sm 7:7
And when **a** man had a dispute to 2 Sm 15:2
"Why speak **a** more of your affairs? 2 Sm 19:29
expense? Or has he given us **a** gift?" 2 Sm 19:42
it for us to put **a** man to death in 2 Sm 21:4
had never at **a** time displeased him 1 Kgs 1:6
go out from there to **a** place whatever. 1 Kgs 2:36
go out and go to **a** place whatever, 1 Kgs 2:42
hammer nor axe nor **a** tool of iron was 1 Kgs 6:7
skill for making **a** work in bronze. 1 Kgs 7:14
plea is made by **a** man or by all 1 Kgs 8:38
of it was never made in **a** kingdom. 1 Kgs 10:20
A who would, he ordained to be 1 Kgs 13:33
if by **a** means he is missing, your 1 Kgs 20:39
offering or sacrifice to **a** god but the 2 Kgs 5:17
should I wait for the LORD **a** longer?" 2 Kgs 6:33
man who allows **a** of those whom 2 Kgs 10:24
the house wherever **a** need of repairs 2 Kgs 12:5
and for **a** outlay for the repairs of the 2 Kgs 12:12
bowls, trumpets, or **a** vessels of gold, 2 Kgs 12:13
pierce the hand of **a** man who leans 2 Kgs 18:21
Has **a** of the gods of the nations ever 2 Kgs 18:33
nor did **a** like him arise after him. 2 Kgs 23:25
of Edom before **a** king reigned over 1 Chr 1:43
I speak a word with **a** of the judges of 1 Chr 17:6
to save the Ammonites **a** more. 1 Chr 19:19
the tabernacle or **a** of the things 1 Chr 23:26
and **a** work for the service of the 1 Chr 23:28
who has skill for **a** kind of service; 1 Chr 28:21
had not been on **a** king before him 1 Chr 29:25
engraving and execute **a** design that 2 Chr 2:14
plea is made by **a** man or by all 2 Chr 6:29
and Levites concerning **a** matter and 2 Chr 8:15
like it was ever made for **a** kingdom. 2 Chr 9:19
enter who was in **a** way unclean. 2 Chr 23:19
for no god of **a** nation or kingdom 2 Chr 32:15
dwell there overthrow **a** king or people Ezr 6:12
should be no remnant, nor **a** to escape? Ezr 9:14
bring in goods or **a** grain on the Neh 10:31
know that if **a** man or woman Est 4:11
palace you will escape **a** more than all Est 4:13
and to annihilate **a** armed force of any Est 8:11
any armed force of **a** people or province Est 8:11
or is there **a** taste in the juice of the Jb 6:6
Have I **a** help in me, when resource is Jb 6:13
Is there **a** injustice on my tongue? Jb 6:30
down, they wither before **a** other plant. Jb 8:12
that I had died before **a** eye had seen me Jb 10:18
like deep shadow without **a** order, Jb 10:22
nor will his place **a** more behold him. Jb 20:9
Will **a** teach God knowledge, seeing Jb 21:22
Is it **a** pleasure to the Almighty if you are Jb 22:3
Is there **a** number to his armies? Upon Jb 25:3
does not reproach me for **a** of my days. Jb 27:6
eyes, and if **a** spot has stuck to my hands, Jb 31:7
not show partiality to **a** man or use Jb 32:21
man or use flattery toward **a** person. Jb 32:21
If you have **a** words, answer me; speak, Jb 33:32
and had no regard for **a** of his ways, Jb 34:27
punishment; I will not offend **a** more; Jb 34:31
God is mighty, and does not despise **a**; Jb 36:5
he does not regard **a** who are wise in Jb 37:24
to see if there are **a** who understand, Ps 14:2
man to see if there are **a** who understand, Ps 53:2
there is no longer **a** prophet, and there is Ps 74:9
men you shall die, and fall like **a** prince." Ps 82:7
O Lord, nor are there **a** works like yours. Ps 86:8
they loathed **a** kind of food, and they Ps 107:18
nor **a** to pity his fatherless children! Ps 109:12
nor do **a** who go down into silence. Ps 115:17
nor is there **a** breath in their mouths. Ps 135:17
see if there be **a** grievous way in me, Ps 139:24
Do not let my heart incline to **a** evil, to Ps 141:4
has not dealt thus with **a** other nation; Ps 147:20
is a net spread in the sight of **a** bird, Prv 1:17
and do not choose **a** of his ways, Prv 3:31
Without having **a** chief, officer, or ruler, Prv 6:7
but sin is a reproach to **a** people. Prv 14:34
and does not turn back before **a**; Prv 30:30
will there be **a** remembrance of later Eccl 1:11
more than **a** who had been before me in Eccl 2:7
the fragrance of your oils than **a** spice! Sg 4:10
up, nor will **a** of its cords be broken. Is 33:20
nor shall **a** ravenous beast come up on it; Is 35:9
pierce the hand of **a** man who leans on Is 36:6
LORD will deliver us." Has **a** of the gods of Is 36:18
formed, nor shall there be **a** after me. Is 43:10
me? There is no Rock; I know not **a**." Is 44:8
it, and keeps his hand from doing **a** evil." Is 56:2
neighbor, and put no trust in **a** brother, Jer 9:4
But if **a** nation will not listen, then I Jer 12:17
Are there **a** among the false gods of the Jer 14:22
the desert, and shall not see **a** good come. Jer 17:6
houses on the Sabbath or do **a** work, Jer 17:22
If at **a** time I declare concerning a nation Jer 18:7
And if at **a** time I declare concerning a Jer 18:9
us not pay attention to **a** of his words." Jer 18:18
or speak **a** more in his name," there is in Jer 20:9
be dismayed, neither shall **a** be missing, Jer 23:4
"'"But if **a** nation or kingdom will not Jer 27:8
But **a** nation that will bring its neck Jer 27:11
has spoken concerning **a** nation that Jer 27:13
neither the king nor **a** of his servants Jer 36:24
"Is there **a** word from the LORD?" Jer 37:17
by the mouth of **a** man of Judah in Jer 44:26
see if there is **a** sorrow like my sorrow, Lam 1:12
me into darkness without **a** light; Lam 3:2
nor **a** of the inhabitants of the world, Lam 4:12
they went in **a** of their four directions Ezk 1:17
and **a** of you who survive I will scatter Ezk 5:10
And if **a** survivors escape, they will be Ezk 7:16
they went in **a** of their four directions Ezk 10:11
shall be no more **a** false vision or Ezk 12:24
of my words will be delayed **a** longer, Ezk 12:28
A one of the house of Israel who takes Ezk 14:4
For **a** one of the house of Israel, or of the Ezk 14:7
the wood of the vine surpass **a** wood, Ezk 15:2
take a peg from it to hang **a** vessel on it? Ezk 15:3
to do **a** of these things to you out of Ezk 16:5
your whorings on **a** passerby; Ezk 16:15
offering yourself to **a** passerby and Ezk 16:25
does not lend at interest or take **a** profit, Ezk 18:8
of blood, who does **a** of these things Ezk 18:10
Have I **a** pleasure in the death of the Ezk 18:23
then wherever they saw **a** high hill or Ezk 20:28
they saw any high hill or **a** leafy tree, Ezk 20:28
after piece, without making **a** choice. Ezk 24:6
sword comes and takes **a** one of them, Ezk 33:6
or with **a** of their transgressions. Ezk 37:23
field or cut down **a** out of the forests, Ezk 39:10
nor come near **a** of my holy things Ezk 44:13
prince makes a gift to **a** of his sons as Ezk 46:16
shall not take **a** of the inheritance Ezk 46:18
They shall not sell or exchange **a** of it. Ezk 48:14
a thing of **a** magician or enchanter Dn 2:10
not because of **a** wisdom that I have Dn 2:30
fire had not had **a** power over the bodies Dn 3:27
serve and worship **a** god except their Dn 3:28
A people, nation, or language that Dn 3:29
find no ground for complaint or **a** fault, Dn 6:4
shall not find **a** ground for complaint Dn 6:5
whoever makes petition to **a** god or man Dn 6:7
who makes petition to **a** god or man Dn 6:12
shall not pay attention to **a** other god, Dn 11:37
I will never forget **a** of their deeds. Am 8:7
Can I forget **a** longer the treasures of Mi 6:10
or stew or wine or oil or **a** kind of food, Hg 2:12
with a dead body touches **a** of these, Hg 2:13
no wage for man or **a** wage for beast, Zec 8:10
neither was there **a** safety from the foe Zec 8:10
And if **a** of the families of the earth do Zec 14:17
hand, will he show favor to **a** of you? Mal 1:9
a descendant of the man who does this, Mal 2:12
side, they had forgotten to bring **a** bread. Mt 16:5
lawful to divorce one's wife for **a** cause?" Mt 19:3
dare to ask him **a** more questions. Mt 22:46
for the crowd **a** one prisoner whom Mt 27:15
it is not lawful for **a** but the priests to Mk 2:26
Why trouble the Teacher **a** further?" Mk 5:35
And if **a** place will not receive you and Mk 6:11
dared to ask him **a** more questions. Mk 12:34
and if they drink **a** deadly poison, it Mk 16:18
all those who had **a** who were sick with Lk 4:40
which is not lawful for **a** but the priests to Lk 6:4
do not trouble the Teacher **a** more." Lk 8:49
a one of you who does not renounce all Lk 14:33
"Will **a** one of you who has a servant Lk 17:7
no longer dared to ask him **a** question. Lk 20:40
this man guilty of **a** of your charges Lk 23:14
without him was not **a** thing made that Jn 1:3
Have **a** of the authorities or the Pharisees Jn 7:48

do you have **a** fish?" They answered him, Jn 21:5
the proceeds to all, as **a** had need. Acts 2:45
no one said that **a** of the things that Acts 4:32
was distributed to each as **a** had need. Acts 4:35
for he had not yet fallen on **a** of them, Acts 8:16
that if he found **a** belonging to the Way, Acts 9:2
should not call **a** person common or Acts 10:28
if you have **a** word of exhortation for Acts 13:15
Gallio paid no attention to **a** of this. Acts 18:17
account my life of **a** value nor as Acts 20:24
temple, without **a** crowd or tumult. Acts 24:18
Caesar have I committed **a** offense." Acts 25:8
that he ought not to live **a** longer. Acts 25:24
it thought incredible by **a** of you that Acts 26:8
is to perish from the head of **a** of you." Acts 27:34
lest **a** should swim away and escape. Acts 27:42
reported or spoken **a** evil about you. Acts 28:21
What then? Are we Jews **a** better off? Rom 3:9
Who shall bring **a** charge against Rom 8:33
covet," and **a** other commandment, Rom 13:9
judgment on one another **a** longer, Rom 14:13
I no longer have **a** room for work in Rom 15:23
you are not lacking in **a** spiritual gift, 1 Cor 1:7
judged by you or by **a** human court. 1 Cor 4:3
the Lord) that if **a** brother has a wife 1 Cor 7:12
If **a** woman has a husband who is an 1 Cor 7:13
not to lay **a** restraint upon you, 1 Cor 7:35
a vineyard without eating **a** of its fruit? 1 Cor 9:7
have made no use of **a** of these rights, 1 Cor 9:15
things to secure **a** such provision. 1 Cor 9:15
without raising **a** question on 1 Cor 10:25
you without raising **a** question on 1 Cor 10:27
would not make it **a** less a part of 1 Cor 12:15
would not make it **a** less a part of 1 Cor 12:16
If **a** speak in a tongue, let there be 1 Cor 14:27
I worked harder than **a** of them, 1 Cor 15:10
comfort those who are in **a** affliction, 2 Cor 1:4
refrain from burdening you in **a** way. 2 Cor 11:9
of you through **a** of those whom 2 Cor 12:17
For I did not receive it from **a** man, nor Gal 1:12
if anyone is caught in **a** transgression, Gal 6:1
spot or wrinkle or **a** such thing, Eph 5:27
So if there is **a** encouragement in Christ, Phil 2:1
in Christ, **a** comfort from love, Phil 2:1
from love, **a** participation in the Spirit, Phil 2:1
in the Spirit, **a** affection and sympathy, Phil 2:1
that by **a** means possible I may attain Phil 3:11
is commendable, if there is **a** excellence, Phil 4:8
In **a** and every circumstance, I have Phil 4:12
or impurity or **a** attempt to deceive, 1 Thes 2:3
we might not be a burden to **a** of you, 1 Thes 2:9
Let no one deceive you in **a** way. For 2 Thes 2:3
you keep away from **a** brother who is 2 Thes 3:6
we might not be a burden to **a** of you. 2 Thes 3:8
not to teach **a** different doctrine, 1 Tm 1:3
If **a** believing woman has relatives 1 Tm 5:16
disobedient, unfit for **a** good work. Ti 1:16
lest there be in **a** of you an evil, Heb 3:12
let us fear lest **a** of you should seem to Heb 4:1
active, sharper than **a** two-edged sword, Heb 4:12
no longer have **a** consciousness of sin? Heb 10:2
there is no longer **a** offering for sin. Heb 10:18
If **a** of you lacks wisdom, let him ask God, Jas 1:5
heaven or by earth or by **a** other oath, Jas 5:12
may be able at **a** time to recall these 2 Pt 1:15
you, not wishing that **a** should perish, 2 Pt 3:9
into your house or give him **a** greeting, 2 Jn 1:10
I say, I do not lay on you **a** other burden. Rv 2:24
blow on earth or sea or against **a** tree. Rv 7:1
not strike them, nor **a** scorching heat. Rv 7:16
grass of the earth or **a** green plant or any Rv 9:4
of the earth or any green plant or **a** tree, Rv 9:4
there was no longer **a** place for them in Rv 12:8
and a craftsman of **a** craft will be Rv 18:22
might not deceive the nations **a** longer, Rv 20:3

ANYMORE (25)

dove, and she did not return to him **a**. Gn 8:12
man, it shall not be redeemed **a**. Lv 27:20
Israel no more, nor did they fight **a**. 2 Sm 2:28
were afraid to save the Ammonites **a**. 2 Sm 10:19
of Israel to wander **a** out of the land 2 Kgs 21:8
house, nor does his place know him **a**. Jb 7:10
nation, neither shall they learn war **a**. Is 2:4
of Tarshish; there is no restraint **a**. Is 23:10
yet your Teacher will not hide himself **a**, Is 30:20
be uprooted or overthrown **a** forever." Jer 31:40
nor defile themselves **a** with all their Ezk 14:11
eyes to them or remember Egypt **a**. Ezk 23:27
shall not be cleansed **a** till I have Ezk 24:13
no foot of man shall trouble them **a**, Ezk 32:13
not let you hear **a** the reproach of the Ezk 36:15
not defile themselves **a** with their idols Ezk 37:23
not let my holy name be profaned **a**. Ezk 39:7
them remaining among the nations **a**. Ezk 39:28
I will not hide my face **a** from them, Ezk 39:29
nation, neither shall they learn war **a**; Mi 4:3
And no one could bind him **a**, not even Mk 5:3
for they cannot die **a**, because they are Lk 20:36
shall hunger no more, neither thirst **a**; Rv 7:16
for her, since no one buys their cargo **a**, Rv 18:11
be mourning nor crying nor pain **a**, Rv 21:4

ANYONE (252)

If **a** kills Cain, vengeance shall be taken Gn 4:15
men said to Lot, "Have you **a** else here? Gn 19:12
daughters, or **a** you have in the city, Gn 19:12
A with whom you find your gods shall Gn 31:32
nor did **a** rise from his place for three Ex 10:23
houses, for if **a** eats what is leavened, Ex 12:15
If **a** eats what is leavened, that person Ex 12:19
him, and **a** found in possession of him, Ex 21:16
or is driven away, without **a** seeing it, Ex 22:10
"When **a** brings a grain offering as an Lv 2:1
If **a** sins unintentionally in any of the Lv 4:2
"If **a** of the common people sins Lv 4:27
"If **a** sins in that he hears a public Lv 5:1
or if **a** touches an unclean thing, whether Lv 5:2
or if **a** utters with his lips a rash oath to do Lv 5:4
"If **a** commits a breach of faith and sins Lv 5:15
"If **a** sins, doing any of the things that by Lv 5:17
"If **a** sins and commits a breach of faith Lv 6:2
And if **a** touches an unclean thing, Lv 7:21
And **a** who touches his bed shall wash Lv 15:5
A whom the one with the discharge Lv 15:11
her menstrual impurity, that is, for **a**, Lv 15:33
For **a** who curses his father or his Lv 20:9
and **a** born in his house may eat of his Lv 22:11
And if **a** eats of a holy thing Lv 22:14
And when **a** offers a sacrifice of peace Lv 22:21
If **a** injures his neighbor, as he has Lv 24:19
If **a** makes a special vow to the LORD Lv 27:2
whatever **a** gives to the priest shall be Nm 5:10
But if **a** who is clean and is not on a Nm 9:13
or **a** is living permanently among Nm 15:14
person, the body of **a** who has died, Nm 19:13
and **a** who touches it shall be unclean Nm 19:22
And if a serpent bit **a**, he would look at Nm 21:9
Wherever the lot falls for **a**, that shall Nm 33:54
that **a** who kills any person without Nm 35:15
"If **a** kills a person, the murderer shall Nm 35:30
You shall not be intimidated by **a**, for Dt 1:17
a who kills his neighbor Dt 4:42
be found among you **a** who burns his Dt 18:10
a who practices divination or tells Dt 18:10
If **a** kills his neighbor unintentionally Dt 19:4
"But if **a** hates his neighbor and lies in Dt 19:11
upon your house, if **a** should fall from it. Dt 22:8
"'Cursed be **a** who dishonors his father Dt 27:16
"'Cursed be **a** who moves his Dt 27:17
"'Cursed be **a** who misleads a blind Dt 27:18
"'Cursed be **a** who perverts the justice Dt 27:19
"'Cursed be **a** who lies with his father's Dt 27:20
"'Cursed be **a** who lies with any kind of Dt 27:21
"'Cursed be **a** who lies with his sister, Dt 27:22
"'Cursed be **a** who lies with his Dt 27:23
"'Cursed be **a** who strikes down his Dt 27:24
"'Cursed be **a** who takes a bribe to shed Dt 27:25
"'Cursed be **a** who does not confirm the Dt 27:26
Then if **a** goes out of the doors of your Jos 2:19
if a hand is laid on **a** who is with you in Jos 2:19
that **a** who killed a person without Jos 20:9
and did not allow **a** to pass over. Jgs 3:28
man comes and asks you, 'Is **a** here?' Jgs 4:20
for you there, and **a** of whom I say to you, Jgs 7:4
go with you, and **a** of whom I say to you, Jgs 7:4
Sidonians and had no dealings with **a**. Jgs 18:7
Sidon, and they had no dealings with **a**. Jgs 18:28
"Is there still **a** left of the house of Saul, 2 Sm 9:1
king said, "If **a** says anything to you, 2 Sm 14:10
Shall **a** be put to death in Israel this 2 Sm 19:22
And **a** who came by, seeing him, 2 Sm 20:12
A belonging to Jeroboam who dies 1 Kgs 14:11
and **a** who dies in the open country 1 Kgs 14:11
A belonging to Baasha who dies in 1 Kgs 16:4
and **a** of his who dies in the field the 1 Kgs 16:4
A belonging to Ahab who dies in 1 Kgs 21:24
and **a** of his who dies in the open 1 Kgs 21:24
If you meet **a**, do not greet him, and if 2 Kgs 4:29
do not greet him, and if **a** greets you, 2 Kgs 4:29
you tell us. We will not make **a** king. 2 Kgs 10:5
with the sword **a** who follows her." 2 Kgs 11:15
and **a** who follows her is to be put to 2 Chr 23:14
I make a decree that if **a** alters this edict, Ezr 6:11
I make a decree that **a** of the people of Ezr 7:13
custom, or toll on **a** of the priests, Ezr 7:24
and that if **a** did not come within three Ezr 10:8
send portions to **a** who has nothing Neh 8:10
perish forever without **a** regarding it. Jb 4:20
"Call now; is there **a** who will answer you? Jb 5:1
in a valley away from where **a** lives; Jb 28:4
if I have seen **a** perish for lack of Jb 31:19
"For has **a** said to God, 'I have borne Jb 34:31
Can **a** understand the spreading of the Jb 36:29
If **a** returns evil for good, evil will not Prv 17:13
it. Lest **a** punish it, I keep it night and day; Is 27:3
If **a** stirs up strife, it is not from me; Is 54:15
nor shall **a** give him the cup of Jer 16:7
He shall not have **a** living among this Jer 29:32
murder of Gedaliah, before **a** knew of it, Jer 41:4
does not oppress **a**, but restores to the Ezk 18:7
does not oppress **a**, exacts no pledge, Ezk 18:16
I have no pleasure in the death of **a**, Ezk 18:32
then if **a** who hears the sound of the Ezk 33:4
through the land and **a** sees a human Ezk 39:15
of the month for **a** who has sinned Ezk 45:20
that **a** who makes petition to any god or Dn 6:12
"Is there still **a** with you?" he shall say, Am 6:10
And if **a** again prophesies, his father Zec 13:3
But if **a** slaps you on the right cheek, Mt 5:39
And if **a** would sue you and take your Mt 5:40
And if **a** forces you to go one mile, go Mt 5:41
to him, "See that you say nothing to **a**, Mt 8:4
And if **a** will not receive you or listen to Mt 10:14
except the Son and **a** to whom the Son Mt 11:27
nor will **a** hear his voice in the streets; Mt 12:19
When **a** hears the word of the kingdom Mt 13:19
say, 'If **a** tells his father or his mother, Mt 15:5
unwashed hands does not defile **a**." Mt 15:20
his disciples, "If **a** would come after me, Mt 16:24
If **a** says anything to you, you shall say, Mt 21:3
and when it falls on **a**, it will crush Mt 21:44
nor from that day did **a** dare to ask him Mt 22:46
who say, 'If **a** swears by the temple, Mt 23:16
but if **a** swears by the gold of the Mt 23:16
And you say, 'If **a** swears by the altar, it Mt 23:18
but if **a** swears by the gift that is on the Mt 23:18
Then if **a** says to you, 'Look, here is the Mt 24:23
to him, "See that you say nothing to **a**, Mk 1:44
If **a** has ears to hear, let him hear." Mk 4:23
a house and did not want **a** to know, Mk 7:24
said to them, "If **a** would come after me, Mk 8:34
they no longer saw **a** with them but Jesus Mk 9:8
Galilee. And he did not want **a** to know, Mk 9:30
And he said to them, "If **a** would be first, Mk 9:35
If **a** says to you, 'Why are you doing Mk 11:3
would not allow **a** to carry anything Mk 11:16
if you have anything against **a**, Mk 11:25
And then if **a** says to you, 'Look, here Mk 13:21
seized them, and they said nothing to **a**, Mk 16:8
not extort money from **a** by threats or Lk 3:14
she could not be healed by **a**. Lk 8:43
he said to all, "If **a** would come after me, Lk 9:23
except the Son and **a** to whom the Son Lk 10:22
"If **a** comes to me and does not hate his Lk 14:26
And if I have defrauded **a** of anything, I Lk 19:8
If **a** asks you, 'Why are you untying it?' Lk 19:31
broken to pieces, and when it falls on **a**, Lk 20:18
"Has **a** brought him something to eat?" Jn 4:33
not that **a** has seen the Father except he Jn 6:46
If **a** eats of this bread, he will live forever. Jn 6:51
Jesus stood up and cried out, "If **a** thirsts, Jn 7:37
and have never been enslaved to **a**. Jn 8:33
truly, I say to you, if **a** keeps my word, Jn 8:51
prophets, yet you say, 'If **a** keeps my word, Jn 8:52
agreed that if **a** should confess Jesus Jn 9:22
but if **a** is a worshiper of God and does Jn 9:31
it been heard that **a** opened the eyes of Jn 9:32
If **a** enters by me, he will be saved and Jn 10:9
If **a** walks in the day, he does not Jn 11:9
But if **a** walks in the night, he stumbles, Jn 11:10
given orders that if **a** knew where he Jn 11:57
If **a** serves me, he must follow me; and Jn 12:26
If **a** serves me, the Father will honor Jn 12:26
If **a** hears my words and does not keep Jn 12:47
Jesus answered him, "If **a** loves me, he Jn 14:23
If **a** does not abide in me he is thrown Jn 15:6
and do not need **a** to question you; Jn 16:30
"It is not lawful for us to put **a** to death." Jn 18:31
If you forgive the sins of **a**, they are Jn 20:23
if you withhold forgiveness from **a**, it is Jn 20:23
to speak no more to **a** in this name." Acts 4:17
so that **a** on whom I lay my hands Acts 8:19
with or to visit **a** of another nation, Acts 10:28
but in every nation **a** who fears him Acts 10:35
"Can **a** withhold water for baptizing Acts 10:47
with him have a complaint against **a**, Acts 19:38
me disputing with **a** or stirring up Acts 24:12
to give up **a** before the accused Acts 25:16
present yourselves to **a** as obedient Rom 6:16
A who does not have the Spirit of Christ Rom 8:9
it is unclean for **a** who thinks it Rom 14:14
it is wrong for **a** to make another Rom 14:20
not know whether I baptized **a** else.) 1 Cor 1:16
Now if **a** builds on the foundation 1 Cor 3:12
If the work that **a** has built on the 1 Cor 3:14
If **a** destroys God's temple, God will 1 Cor 3:17

If **a** among you thinks that he is wise 1 Cor 3:18
not to associate with **a** who bears the 1 Cor 5:11
Was **a** at the time of his call already 1 Cor 7:18
Was **a** at the time of his call 1 Cor 7:18
If **a** thinks that he is not behaving 1 Cor 7:36
If **a** imagines that he knows 1 Cor 8:2
But if **a** loves God, he is known by God. 1 Cor 8:3
For if **a** sees you who have knowledge 1 Cor 8:10
rather die than have **a** deprive me of 1 Cor 9:15
Therefore let **a** who thinks that he 1 Cor 10:12
If **a** is inclined to be contentious, we 1 Cor 11:16
For **a** who eats and drinks without 1 Cor 11:29
if **a** is hungry, let him eat at home— 1 Cor 11:34
how will **a** know what is played? 1 Cor 14:7
how will **a** know what is said? 1 Cor 14:9
how can **a** in the position of an 1 Cor 14:16
If **a** thinks that he is a prophet, or 1 Cor 14:37
If **a** does not recognize this, he is not 1 Cor 14:38
If **a** has no love for the Lord, let him 1 Cor 16:22
Now if **a** has caused pain, he has 2 Cor 2:5
A whom you forgive, I also forgive. 2 Cor 2:10
Therefore, if **a** is in Christ, he is a new 2 Cor 5:17
If **a** is confident that he is Christ's, let 2 Cor 10:7
and was in need, I did not burden **a**, 2 Cor 11:9
But whatever **a** else dares to boast of 2 Cor 11:21
If **a** is preaching to you a gospel contrary Gal 1:9
I did not immediately consult with **a**; Gal 1:16
if **a** is caught in any transgression, Gal 6:1
For if **a** thinks he is something, when he Gal 6:3
something to share with **a** in need. Eph 4:28
knowing that whatever good **a** does, this Eph 6:8
If **a** else thinks he has reason for Phil 3:4
you have no need for **a** to write to you, 1 Thes 4:9
See that no one repays **a** evil for evil, 1 Thes 5:15
If **a** is not willing to work, let him 2 Thes 3:10
If **a** does not obey what we say in 2 Thes 3:14
If **a** aspires to the office of overseer, he 1 Tm 3:1
But if **a** does not provide for his 1 Tm 5:8
If **a** teaches a different doctrine and 1 Tm 6:3
if **a** cleanses himself from what is 2 Tm 2:21
if **a** is above reproach, the husband of one Ti 1:6
A who has set aside the law of Moses Heb 10:28
For if **a** is a hearer of the word and not a Jas 1:23
If **a** thinks he is religious and does not Jas 1:26
and if **a** does not stumble in what he says, Jas 3:2
Is **a** among you suffering? Let him pray. Jas 5:13
suffering? Let him pray. Is **a** cheerful? Jas 5:13
Is **a** among you sick? Let him call for Jas 5:14
if **a** among you wanders from the truth Jas 5:19
to make a defense to **a** who asks you for 1 Pt 3:15
Yet if **a** suffers as a Christian, let him 1 Pt 4:16
that you may not sin. But if **a** does sin, 1 Jn 2:1
If **a** loves the world, the love of the 1 Jn 2:15
have no need that **a** should teach you. 1 Jn 2:27
But if **a** has the world's goods and sees 1 Jn 3:17
A who does not love does not know God, 1 Jn 4:8
If **a** says, "I love God," and hates his 1 Jn 4:20
If **a** sees his brother committing a sin 1 Jn 5:16
If **a** comes to you and does not bring 2 Jn 1:10
If **a** hears my voice and opens the door, I Rv 3:20
And if **a** would harm them, fire pours Rv 11:5
If **a** would harm them, this is how he is Rv 11:5
If **a** has an ear, let him hear: Rv 13:9
If **a** is to be taken captive, to captivity Rv 13:10
if **a** is to be slain with the sword, with Rv 13:10
"If **a** worships the beast and its image Rv 14:9
nor **a** who does what is detestable or Rv 21:27
if **a** adds to them, God will add to him Rv 22:18
and if **a** takes away from the words of Rv 22:19

ANYONE'S (7)
and you do not care about **a** opinion, Mt 22:16
true and do not care about **a** opinion. Mk 12:14
If **a** will is to do God's will, he will know Jn 7:17
If **a** work is burned up, he will suffer 1 Cor 3:15
We put no obstacle in **a** way, so that 2 Cor 6:3
nor did we eat **a** bread without paying 2 Thes 3:8
And if **a** name was not found written in Rv 20:15

ANYTHING (153)
or a sandal strap or **a** that is yours, Gn 14:23
Is **a** too hard for the LORD? At the Gn 18:14
your hand on the boy or do **a** to him, Gn 22:12
Jacob said, "You shall not give me **a**. Gn 30:31
him, "Be careful not to say **a** to Jacob, Gn 31:24
'Be careful not to say **a** to Jacob, Gn 31:29
had no concern about **a** but the food he Gn 39:6
has no concern about **a** in the house, Gn 39:8
has he kept back **a** from me except Gn 39:9
paid no attention to **a** that was in Gn 39:23
a that remains until the morning you Ex 12:10
or any likeness of **a** that is in heaven Ex 20:4
donkey, or **a** that is your neighbor's." Ex 20:17
"If a man borrows **a** of his neighbor, Ex 22:14
blood of my sacrifice with **a** leavened, Ex 23:18
blood of my sacrifice with **a** leavened, Ex 34:25
moved them to bring **a** for the work Ex 35:29
man or woman do **a** more for the Ex 36:6
or **a** about which he has sworn falsely, he Lv 6:5
But **a** in the seas or the rivers that has Lv 11:10
And **a** on which any of them falls when Lv 11:32
She shall not touch **a** holy, nor come Lv 12:4
wool, or in a skin or in **a** made of skin, Lv 13:48
And whoever sits on **a** on which the one Lv 15:6
And whoever touches **a** that was under Lv 15:10
And whoever touches **a** on which she Lv 15:22
it is the bed or **a** on which she sits, Lv 15:23
and **a** left over until the third day shall Lv 19:6
by bird or by **a** with which the ground Lv 20:25
Whoever touches **a** that is unclean Lv 22:4
You shall not offer **a** that has a Lv 22:20
devotes to the LORD, of **a** that he has, Lv 27:28
for him who does **a** unintentionally, Nm 15:29
the person who does **a** with a high Nm 15:30
now any power of my own to speak **a**? Nm 22:38
a by which she has bound herself, Nm 30:9
or hurled **a** on him without lying in Nm 35:22
the likeness of **a** that creeps on the Dt 4:18
the form of **a** that the LORD your God has Dt 4:23
making a carved image in the form of **a**, Dt 4:25
or any likeness of **a** that is in heaven Dt 5:8
his donkey, or **a** that is your neighbor's.' Dt 5:21
"You shall not eat **a** that has died Dt 14:21
he may not see **a** indecent among you Dt 23:14
interest on **a** that is lent for interest. Dt 23:19
of you shall never be **a** but servants, Jos 9:23
may not eat of **a** that comes from the Jgs 13:14
there is no lack of **a** that is in the Jgs 18:10
your servants. There is no lack of **a**." Jgs 19:19
and more also if **a** but death parts me Ru 1:17
more also if you hide **a** from me of all 1 Sm 3:17
had spoken, he did not tell him **a**. 1 Sm 10:16
us or taken **a** from any man's 1 Sm 12:4
you have not found **a** in my hand." 1 Sm 12:5
you. And if I learn **a** I will tell you." 1 Sm 19:3
Yet Saul did not say **a** that day, for he 1 Sm 20:26
'Let no one know **a** of the matter 1 Sm 21:2
not the king impute **a** to his servant 1 Sm 22:15
we did not miss **a** when we were in 1 Sm 25:15
spoil or **a** that had been taken. 1 Sm 30:19
if I taste bread or **a** else till the sun 2 Sm 3:35
impossible to Amnon to do **a** to her. 2 Sm 13:2
king said, "If anyone says **a** to you, 2 Sm 14:10
not hide from me **a** I ask you." And 2 Sm 14:18
or to the left from **a** that my lord the 2 Sm 14:19
was not considered as **a** in the days 1 Kgs 10:21
turn aside from **a** that he 1 Kgs 15:5
was not considered as **a** in the days of 2 Chr 9:20
he will not let **a** in which he delights Jb 20:20
"If I have withheld **a** that the poor Jb 31:16
set before my eyes **a** that is worthless. Ps 101:3
can be added to it, nor **a** taken from it. Eccl 3:14
it has not seen the sun or known **a**, Eccl 6:5
may not find out **a** that will be after Eccl 7:14
My son, beware of **a** beyond these. Of Eccl 12:12
God of all flesh. Is **a** too hard for me? Jer 32:27
the LORD your God in **a** that he sent me Jer 42:21
Is wood taken from it to make **a**? Do Ezk 15:3
middle of it is charred, is it useful for **a**? Ezk 15:4
it is charred, can it ever be used for **a**! Ezk 15:5
nor his army got **a** from Tyre to pay Ezk 29:18
bind themselves with **a** that causes Ezk 44:18
The priests shall not eat of **a**, whether Ezk 44:31
language that speaks **a** against the God Dn 3:29
has not been done **a** like what has been Dn 9:12
man nor beast, herd nor flock, taste **a**. Jon 3:7
no longer good for **a** except to be thrown Mt 5:13
'No'; **a** more than this comes from evil. Mt 5:37
"Never was **a** like this seen in Israel." Mt 9:33
of you agree on earth about **a** they ask, Mt 18:19
If anyone says **a** to you, you shall say, Mt 21:3
God, saying, "We never saw **a** like this!" Mk 2:12
nor is **a** secret except to come to light. Mk 4:22
permit him to do **a** for his father or Mk 7:12
on him, he asked him, "Do you see **a**?" Mk 8:23
But if you can do **a**, have compassion Mk 9:22
cannot be driven out by **a** but prayer." Mk 9:29
he went to see if he could find **a** on it. Mk 11:13
anyone to carry **a** through the temple. Mk 11:16
forgive, if you have **a** against anyone, Mk 11:25
nor enter his house, to take **a** out, Mk 13:15
nor is **a** secret that will not be known Lk 8:17
no one in those days **a** of what they had Lk 9:36
in bed. I cannot get up and give you **a**'? Lk 11:7
get up and give him **a** because he is his Lk 11:8
the pigs ate, and no one gave him **a**. Lk 15:16
And if I have defrauded anyone of **a**, I Lk 19:8
but they did not find **a** they could do, Lk 19:48
or sandals, did you lack **a**?" They said, Lk 22:35
said to them, "Have you **a** here to eat?" Lk 24:41
"Can **a** good come out of Nazareth?" Jn 1:46
If you ask me **a** in my name, I will do it. Jn 14:14
I have never eaten **a** that is common Acts 10:14
hands, as though he needed **a**, Acts 17:25
But if you seek **a** further, it shall be Acts 19:39
declaring to you **a** that was Acts 20:20
should they have **a** against me. Acts 24:19
and if there is **a** wrong about the man, Acts 25:5
and have committed **a** for which I Acts 25:11
nor depth, nor **a** else in all creation, Rom 8:39
Owe no one **a**, except to love each Rom 13:8
One person believes he may eat **a**, Rom 14:2
drink wine or do **a** that causes your Rom 14:21
to speak of **a** except what Christ Rom 15:18
he who plants nor he who waters is **a**, 1 Cor 3:7
I am not aware of **a** against myself, but 1 Cor 4:4
For who sees **a** different in you? What 1 Cor 4:7
me," but I will not be enslaved by **a**. 1 Cor 6:12
counts for **a** nor uncircumcision, 1 Cor 7:19
but we endure **a** rather than put an 1 Cor 9:12
That food offered to idols is **a**, or that 1 Cor 10:19
is anything, or that an idol is **a**? 1 Cor 10:19
If there is **a** they desire to learn, let 1 Cor 14:35
not writing to you **a** other than what 2 Cor 1:13
I have forgiven, if I have forgiven **a**, 2 Cor 2:10
ourselves to claim **a** as coming from 2 Cor 3:5
For we cannot do **a** against the truth, 2 Cor 13:8
nor uncircumcision counts for **a**, Gal 5:6
For neither circumcision counts for **a**, Gal 6:15
But when **a** is exposed by the light, it Eph 5:13
for **a** that becomes visible is light. Eph 5:14
not frightened in **a** by your opponents. Phil 1:28
way, and if in **a** you think otherwise, Phil 3:15
do not be anxious about **a**, but in Phil 4:6
excellence, if there is **a** worthy of praise, Phil 4:8
everywhere, so that we need not say **a**. 1 Thes 1:8
have no need to have **a** written to you. 1 Thes 5:1
and we cannot take **a** out of the world. 1 Tm 6:7
has wronged you at all, or owes you **a**, Phlm 1:18
that he will receive **a** from the Lord; Jas 1:7
and do not fear **a** that is frightening. 1 Pt 3:6
that if we ask **a** according to his will he 1 Jn 5:14
No longer will there be **a** accursed, but Rv 22:3

ANYWHERE (1)
not look back or stop **a** in the valley. Gn 19:17

APART (59)
set seven ewe lambs of the flock **a**. Gn 21:28
seven ewe lambs that you have set **a**?" Gn 21:29
put his own droves **a** and did not put Gn 30:40
him who was set **a** from his brothers. Gn 49:26
that day I will set **a** the land of Goshen, Ex 8:22
you shall set **a** to the LORD all that first Ex 13:12
which I have set **a** for you to hold Lv 20:25
words, the ground under them split **a**. Nm 16:31
Then Moses set **a** three cities in the east Dt 4:41
that time the LORD set **a** the tribe of Levi Dt 10:8
you shall set **a** three cities for yourselves Dt 19:2
you, You shall set **a** three cities. Dt 19:7
the towns that were set **a** for the people of Jos 16:9
So they set **a** Kedesh in Galilee in the hill Jos 20:7
the men of Israel, **a** from Benjamin, Jgs 20:17
"Let him dwell **a** in his own house; 2 Sm 14:24
So Absalom lived **a** in his own 2 Sm 14:24
Aaron was set **a** to dedicate the most 1 Chr 23:13
the service also set **a** for the service 1 Chr 25:1
his officials had set **a** to attend the Ezr 8:20
Then I set **a** twelve of the leading priests: Ezr 8:24
and they set **a** that which was for the Neh 12:47
and the Levites set **a** that which was Neh 12:47
I was at ease, and he broke me **a**; he Jb 16:12
us burst their bonds **a** and cast away their Ps 2:3
the LORD has set **a** the godly for himself; Ps 4:3
lest like a lion they tear my soul **a**, Ps 7:2
are my Lord; I have no good **a** from you." Ps 16:2
you who forget God, lest I tear you **a**, Ps 50:22
of death, and burst their bonds **a**. Ps 107:14
for **a** from him who can eat or who Eccl 2:25
is utterly broken, the earth is split **a**, Is 24:19
and set them **a** for the day of slaughter. Jer 12:3
They will set **a** men to travel through Ezk 39:14
you shall set **a** for the LORD a portion of Ezk 45:1
"Alongside the portion set **a** as the holy Ezk 45:6
be the portion which you shall set **a**, Ezk 48:8
that you shall set **a** for the LORD shall Ezk 48:9
that you shall set **a** shall be 25,000 Ezk 48:20
off you and will burst your bonds **a**." Na 1:13
fall to the ground **a** from your Father. Mt 10:29
chains, but he wrenched the chains **a**, Mk 5:4
took them and withdrew **a** to a town Lk 9:10
fruit, for **a** from me you can do nothing. Jn 15:5
"Set **a** for me Barnabas and Saul for Acts 13:2
be an apostle, set **a** for the gospel of God, Rom 1:1
has been manifested **a** from the law, Rom 3:21
is justified by faith **a** from works of Rom 3:28
counts righteousness **a** from works: Rom 4:6

A from the law, sin lies dead. Rom 7:8
I was once alive **a** from the law, but Rom 7:9
And, **a** from other things, there is 2 Cor 11:28
he who had set me **a** before I was born, Gal 1:15
vessel for honorable use, set **a** as holy, 2 Tm 2:21
that **a** from us they should not be Heb 11:40
Show me your faith **a** from your works, Jas 2:18
that faith **a** from works is useless? Jas 2:20
For as the body **a** from the spirit is dead, Jas 2:26
dead, so also faith **a** from works is dead. Jas 2:26

APELLES (1)
Greet **A**, who is approved in Christ. Rom 16:10

APES (2)
gold, silver, ivory, **a**, and peacocks. 1 Kgs 10:22
gold, silver, ivory, **a**, and peacocks. 2 Chr 9:21

APHEK (8)
the king of **A**, one; the king of Jos 12:18
that belongs to the Sidonians, to **A**, Jos 13:4
A and Rehob—twenty-two cities with Jos 19:30
and the Philistines encamped at **A**. 1 Sm 4:1
had gathered all their forces at **A**. 1 Sm 29:1
and went up to **A** to fight against 1 Kgs 20:26
And the rest fled into the city of **A**, 1 Kgs 20:30
the Syrians in **A** until you have 2 Kgs 13:17

APHEKAH (1)
Janim, Beth-tappuah, **A**, Jos 15:53

APHIAH (1)
son of Zeror, son of Becorath, son of **A**, 1 Sm 9:1

APHIK (1)
Achzib or of Helbah or of **A** or of Rehob, Jgs 1:31

APIECE (2)
weighing 10 shekels **a** according to the Nm 7:86
The double doors had two leaves **a**, Ezk 41:24

APOLLONIA (1)
passed through Amphipolis and **A**, Acts 17:1

APOLLOS (10)
Now a Jew named **A**, a native of Acts 18:24
happened that while **A** was at Corinth, Acts 19:1
Paul," or "I follow **A**," or "I follow 1 Cor 1:12
"I follow **A**," are you not being merely 1 Cor 3:4
What then is **A**? What is Paul? 1 Cor 3:5
I planted, **A** watered, but God gave the 1 Cor 3:6
whether Paul or **A** or Cephas or the 1 Cor 3:22
to myself and **A** for your benefit, 1 Cor 4:6
Now concerning our brother **A**, I 1 Cor 16:12
Zenas the lawyer and **A** on their way; Ti 3:13

APOLLYON (1)
is Abaddon, and in Greek he is called **A**. Rv 9:11

APOLOGIZED (1)
So they came and **a** to them. And they Acts 16:39

APOSTASIES (1)
transgressions are many, their **a** are great. Jer 5:6

APOSTASY (2)
you, and your **a** will reprove you. Jer 2:19
I will heal their **a**; I will love them Hos 14:4

APOSTATE (1)
it from me! To an **a** he allots our fields." Mi 2:4

APOSTLE (19)
of Christ Jesus, called to be an **a**, Rom 1:1
then as I am an **a** to the Gentiles, Rom 11:13
will of God to be an **a** of Christ Jesus, 1 Cor 1:1
Am I not free? Am I not an **a**? Have I 1 Cor 9:1
If to others I am not an **a**, at least I am 1 Cor 9:2
apostles, unworthy to be called an **a**, 1 Cor 15:9
an **a** of Christ Jesus by the will of God, 2 Cor 1:1
of a true **a** were performed among 2 Cor 12:12
an **a**—not from men nor through man, Gal 1:1
an **a** of Christ Jesus by the will of God, Eph 1:1
an **a** of Christ Jesus by the will of God, Col 1:1
an **a** of Christ Jesus by command of 1 Tm 1:1
a preacher and an **a** (I am telling the 1 Tm 2:7
an **a** of Christ Jesus by the will of God 2 Tm 1:1
a preacher and **a** and teacher, 2 Tm 1:11
a servant of God and an **a** of Jesus Christ, Ti 1:1
the **a** and high priest of our confession, Heb 3:1
Peter, an **a** of Jesus Christ, To those who 1 Pt 1:1
Peter, a servant and **a** of Jesus Christ, 2 Pt 1:1

APOSTLES (52)
The names of the twelve **a** are these: first, Mt 10:2
(whom he also named **a**) so that they Mk 3:14
The **a** returned to Jesus and told him all Mk 6:30
from them twelve, whom he named **a**: Lk 6:13
On their return the **a** told him all that Lk 9:10
said, 'I will send them prophets and **a**, Lk 11:49
The **a** said to the Lord, "Increase our Lk 17:5
reclined at table, and the **a** with him. Lk 22:14
them who told these things to the **a**, Lk 24:10
Holy Spirit to the **a** whom he had Acts 1:2
he was numbered with the eleven **a**. Acts 1:26
and said to Peter and the rest of the **a**, Acts 2:37
signs were being done through the **a**. Acts 2:43
great power the **a** were giving their Acts 4:33
called by the **a** Barnabas (which Acts 4:36
the people by the hands of the **a**. Acts 5:12
they arrested the **a** and put them in the Acts 5:18
But Peter and the **a** answered, "We Acts 5:29
and when they had called in the **a**, they Acts 5:40
These they set before the **a**, and they Acts 6:6
of Judea and Samaria, except the **a**. Acts 8:1
Now when the **a** at Jerusalem heard Acts 8:14
brought him to the **a** and declared to Acts 9:27
Now the **a** and the brothers who were Acts 11:1
with the Jews and some with the **a**. Acts 14:4
But when the **a** Barnabas and Paul Acts 14:14
to Jerusalem to the **a** and the elders Acts 15:2
by the church and the **a** and the elders, Acts 15:4
The **a** and the elders were gathered Acts 15:6
it seemed good to the **a** and the elders, Acts 15:22
brothers, both the **a** and the elders, Acts 15:23
been reached by the **a** and elders who Acts 16:4
They are well known to the **a**, and they Rom 16:7
God has exhibited us **a** as last of all, 1 Cor 4:9
as do the other **a** and the brothers of 1 Cor 9:5
has appointed in the church first **a**, 1 Cor 12:28
Are all **a**? Are all prophets? Are all 1 Cor 12:29
he appeared to James, then to all the **a**. 1 Cor 15:7
For I am the least of the **a**, unworthy 1 Cor 15:9
For such men are false **a**, deceitful 2 Cor 11:13
disguising themselves as **a** of Christ. 2 Cor 11:13
to those who were **a** before me, Gal 1:17
none of the other **a** except James the Gal 1:19
the foundation of the **a** and prophets, Eph 2:20
revealed to his holy **a** and prophets by Eph 3:5
And he gave the **a**, the prophets, the Eph 4:11
have made demands as **a** of Christ. 1 Thes 2:6
of the Lord and Savior through your **a**, 2 Pt 3:2
the predictions of the **a** of our Lord Jude 1:17
those who call themselves **a** and are not, Rv 2:2
and you saints and **a** and prophets, Rv 18:20
names of the twelve **a** of the Lamb. Rv 21:14

APOSTLES' (5)
themselves to the **a** teaching and Acts 2:42
and laid it at the **a** feet, and it was Acts 4:35
the money and laid it at the **a** feet. Acts 4:37
only a part of it and laid it at the **a** feet. Acts 5:2
through the laying on of the **a** hands, Acts 8:18

APOSTLESHIP (3)
this ministry and **a** from which Judas Acts 1:25
received grace and **a** to bring about Rom 1:5
for you are the seal of my **a** in the Lord. 1 Cor 9:2

APOSTOLIC (1)
through Peter for his **a** ministry to the Gal 2:8

APPAIM (2)
The sons of Nadab: Seled and **A**; and 1 Chr 2:30
The son of **A**: Ishi. The son of Ishi: 1 Chr 2:31

APPALLED (21)
enemies who settle in it shall be **a** at it. Lv 26:32
hair from my head and beard and sat **a**. Ezr 9:3
me while I sat **a** until the evening Ezr 9:4
The upright are **a** at this, and the Jb 17:8
They of the west are **a** at his day, and Jb 18:20
Look at me and be **a**, and lay your hand Jb 21:5
Let those be **a** because of their shame Ps 40:15
within me; my heart within me is **a**. Ps 143:4
My heart staggers; horror has **a** me; the Is 21:4
I was **a**, but there was no one to uphold; Is 63:5
Be **a**, O heavens, at this; be shocked, be Jer 2:12
The priests shall be **a** and the prophets Jer 4:9
Surely their fold shall be **a** at their fate. Jer 49:20
who passes by Babylon shall be **a**, Jer 50:13
surely their fold shall be **a** at their fate. Jer 50:45
and the land was **a** and all who were in Ezk 19:7
every moment and be **a** at you. Ezk 26:16
of the coastlands are **a** at you, Ezk 27:35
you among the peoples are **a** at you; Ezk 28:19
I will make many peoples **a** at you, Ezk 32:10
but I was **a** by the vision and did not Dn 8:27

APPALLING (1)
An **a** and horrible thing has happened Jer 5:30

APPAREL (7)
who put ornaments of gold on your **a**. 2 Sm 1:24
from Bozrah, he who is splendid in his **a**, Is 63:1
Why is your **a** red, and your garments Is 63:2
on my garments, and stained all my **a**. Is 63:3
two men stood by them in dazzling **a**. Lk 24:4
I coveted no one's silver or gold or **a**. Acts 20:33
adorn themselves in respectable **a**, 1 Tm 2:9

APPEAL (18)
she went to **a** to the king for her house 2 Kgs 8:3
him; I must **a** for mercy to my accuser. Jb 9:15
Then I said, "I will **a** to this, to the years Ps 77:10
you think that I cannot **a** to my Father, Mt 26:53
give me up to them. I **a** to Caesar." Acts 25:11
I was compelled to **a** to Caesar— Acts 28:19
I **a** to you therefore, brothers, by the Rom 12:1
I **a** to you, brothers, by our Lord Jesus Rom 15:30
I **a** to you, brothers, to watch out for Rom 16:17
I **a** to you, brothers, by the name of 1 Cor 1:10
God making his **a** through us. 2 Cor 5:20
we **a** to you not to receive the grace of 2 Cor 6:1
For he not only accepted our **a**, but 2 Cor 8:17
For our **a** does not spring from error 1 Thes 2:3
for love's sake I prefer to **a** to you—I, Phlm 1:9
I **a** to you for my child, Onesimus, Phlm 1:10
I **a** to you, brothers, bear with my Heb 13:22
the body but as an **a** to God for a good 1 Pt 3:21

APPEALED (6)
he had restored to life **a** to the king for 2 Kgs 8:5
fever, and they **a** to him on her behalf. Lk 4:38
answered, "To Caesar you have **a**; Acts 25:12
But when Paul had **a** to be kept in Acts 25:21
And as he himself **a** to the emperor, I Acts 25:25
set free if he had not **a** to Caesar." Acts 26:32

APPEALING (2)
centurion came forward to him, **a** to him, Mt 8:5
it necessary to write **a** to you to contend Jude 1:3

APPEALS (1)
Elijah, how he **a** to God against Israel? Rom 11:2

APPEAR (39)
and let the dry land **a**." And it was so. Gn 1:9
they will say, 'The LORD did not **a** to you.'" Ex 4:1
None shall **a** before me empty-handed. Ex 23:15
shall all your males **a** before the Lord Ex 23:17
And none shall **a** before me Ex 34:20
shall all your males **a** before the LORD Ex 34:23
you go up to **a** before the LORD your Ex 34:24
with oil, for today the LORD will **a** to you.'" Lv 9:4
that the glory of the LORD may **a** to you." Lv 9:6
he shall **a** again before the priest. Lv 13:7
For I will **a** in the cloud over the mercy Lv 16:2
all your males shall **a** before the LORD Dt 16:16
They shall not **a** before the LORD Dt 16:16
to the dispute shall **a** before the LORD, Dt 19:17
all Israel comes to **a** before the LORD Dt 31:11
so that he may **a** in the presence of the 1 Sm 1:22
them as a blazing oven when you **a**. Ps 21:9
When shall I come and **a** before God? Ps 42:2
The flowers **a** on the earth, the time of Sg 2:12
"When you come to **a** before me, who has Is 1:12
'**A**.' They shall feed along the ways; Is 49:9
made your sisters **a** righteous by all Ezk 16:51
have made your sisters **a** righteous. Ezk 16:52
your deeds your sins **a**—because you Ezk 21:24
from him shall **a** and profane the Dn 11:31
Then the LORD will **a** over them, and his Zec 9:14
tombs, which outwardly **a** beautiful, Mt 23:27
you also outwardly **a** righteous to Mt 23:28
Then will **a** in heaven the sign of the Mt 24:30
kingdom of God was to **a** immediately. Lk 19:11
on the third day and made him to **a**, Acts 10:40
and to those in which I will **a** to you, Acts 26:16
we must all **a** before the judgment 2 Cor 5:10
do not want to **a** to be frightening you 2 Cor 10:9
—not that we may **a** to have met the 2 Cor 13:7
then you also will **a** with him in glory. Col 3:4
but the sins of others **a** later. 1 Tm 5:24
now to **a** in the presence of God on our Heb 9:24
the sins of many, will **a** a second time, Heb 9:28

APPEARANCE (69)
that you are a woman beautiful in **a**, Gn 12:11
young woman was very attractive in **a**, Gn 24:16
because she was attractive in **a**. Gn 26:7
Rachel was beautiful in form and **a**. Gn 29:17
Joseph was handsome in form and **a**. Gn 39:6
Now the **a** of the glory of the LORD was Ex 24:17
like the **a** of leprous disease in the skin Lv 13:43
And if the **a** of the diseased area has not Lv 13:55
the tabernacle like the **a** of fire until Nm 9:15
it by day and the **a** of fire by night. Nm 9:16
seed, and its **a** like that of bdellium. Nm 11:7
and his **a** was like the appearance of the Jgs 13:6
appearance was like the **a** of the angel of Jgs 13:6
"Do not look on his **a** or on the height 1 Sm 16:7
man looks on the outward **a**, but the 1 Sm 16:7
a youth, ruddy and handsome in **a**. 1 Sm 17:42
to her, "What is his **a**?" And she said, 1 Sm 28:14
for his handsome **a** as Absalom. 2 Sm 14:25
It stood still, but I could not discern its **a**. Jb 4:16
His **a** is like Lebanon, choice as the Sg 5:15
astonished at you—his **a** was so marred, Is 52:14
And this was their **a**: they had a human Ezk 1:5
their **a** was like burning coals of fire, Ezk 1:13

like the **a** of torches moving to and fro Ezk 1:13
fro, like the **a** of a flash of lightning. Ezk 1:14
As for the **a** of the wheels and their Ezk 1:16
their **a** was like the gleaming of beryl. Ezk 1:16
their **a** and construction being as it Ezk 1:16
likeness of a throne, in **a** like sapphire; Ezk 1:26
throne was a likeness with a human **a**. Ezk 1:26
from what had the **a** of his waist I Ezk 1:27
like the **a** of fire enclosed all around. Ezk 1:27
from what had the **a** of his waist I Ezk 1:27
of his waist I saw as it were the **a** of fire, Ezk 1:27
Like the **a** of the bow that is in the Ezk 1:28
so was the **a** of the brightness all Ezk 1:28
Such was the **a** of the likeness of the Ezk 1:28
behold, a form that had the **a** of a man. Ezk 8:2
was something like the **a** of brightness, Ezk 8:2
like a sapphire, in **a** like a throne. Ezk 10:1
and the **a** of the wheels was like Ezk 10:9
And as for their **a**, the four had the Ezk 10:10
the same faces whose **a** I had seen by Ezk 10:22
all of them having the **a** of officers, Ezk 23:15
was a man whose **a** was like bronze, Ezk 40:3
of good **a** and skillful in all wisdom, Dn 1:4
Then let our **a** and the appearance of the Dn 1:13
our appearance and the **a** of the youths Dn 1:13
they were better in **a** and fatter in flesh Dn 1:15
before you, and its **a** was frightening. Dn 2:31
and the **a** of the fourth is like a son of Dn 3:25
before me one having the **a** of a man. Dn 8:15
beryl, his face like the **a** of lightning, Dn 10:6
My radiant **a** was fearfully changed, Dn 10:8
Again one having the **a** of a man Dn 10:18
Their **a** is like the appearance of horses, Jl 2:4
Their appearance is like the **a** of horses, Jl 2:4
know how to interpret the **a** of the sky, Mt 16:3
His **a** was like lightning, and his Mt 28:3
until the day of his public **a** to Israel. Lk 1:80
praying, the **a** of his face was altered, Lk 9:29
how to interpret the **a** of earth and sky, Lk 12:56
boast about outward **a** and not about 2 Cor 5:12
These have indeed an **a** of wisdom in Col 2:23
to nothing by the **a** of his coming. 2 Thes 2:8
having the **a** of godliness, but denying 2 Tm 3:5
sat there had the **a** of jasper and Rv 4:3
a rainbow that had the **a** of an emerald. Rv 4:3
In **a** the locusts were like horses prepared Rv 9:7

APPEARANCES (3)
opinion, for you are not swayed by **a**. Mt 22:16
For you are not swayed by **a**, but truly Mk 12:14
Do not judge by **a**, but judge with right Jn 7:24

APPEARED (83)
Then the LORD **a** to Abram and said, "To Gn 12:7
an altar to the LORD, who had **a** to him. Gn 12:7
years old the LORD **a** to Abram and said Gn 17:1
And the LORD **a** to him by the oaks of Gn 18:1
And the LORD **a** to him and said, "Do not Gn 26:2
And the LORD **a** to him the same night Gn 26:24
there to the God who **a** to you when you Gn 35:1
God **a** to Jacob again, when he came Gn 35:9
"God Almighty **a** to me at Luz in the Gn 48:3
the angel of the LORD **a** to him in a flame Ex 3:2
of Isaac, and of Jacob, has **a** to me, Ex 3:16
Isaac, and the God of Jacob, has **a** to you." Ex 4:5
I **a** to Abraham, to Isaac, and to Jacob, as Ex 6:3
its normal course when the morning **a**. Ex 14:27
the glory of the LORD **a** in the cloud. Ex 16:10
the glory of the LORD **a** to all the people. Lv 9:23
the glory of the LORD **a** at the tent of Nm 14:10
glory of the LORD **a** to all the Nm 16:19
covered it, and the glory of the LORD **a**. Nm 16:42
And the glory of the LORD **a** to them, Nm 20:6
And the LORD **a** in the tent in a pillar of Dt 31:15
the angel of the LORD **a** to him and said Jgs 6:12
angel of the LORD **a** to the woman and Jgs 13:3
came to me the other day has **a** to me." Jgs 13:10
angel of the LORD **a** no more to Manoah Jgs 13:21
And as morning **a**, the woman came Jgs 19:26
And the LORD **a** again at Shiloh, for 1 Sm 3:21
At Gibeon the LORD **a** to Solomon in a 1 Kgs 3:5
the LORD **a** to Solomon a second time, 1 Kgs 9:2
time, as he had **a** to him at Gibeon. 1 Kgs 9:2
God of Israel, who had **a** to him twice 1 Kgs 11:9
In that night God **a** to Solomon, and 2 Chr 1:7
where the LORD had **a** to David his 2 Chr 3:1
Then the LORD **a** to Solomon in the 2 Chr 7:12
the LORD **a** to him from far away. I have Jer 31:3
Below what **a** to be his waist was fire, Ezk 8:2
the cherubim there **a** above them Ezk 10:1
The cherubim **a** to have the form of a Ezk 10:8
of a human hand **a** and wrote on the Dn 5:5
reign of King Belshazzar a vision **a** to me, Dn 8:1
after that which **a** to me at the first. Dn 8:1
an angel of the Lord **a** to him in a Mt 1:20
from them what time the star had **a**. Mt 2:7
an angel of the Lord **a** to Joseph in a Mt 2:13
an angel of the Lord **a** in a dream to Mt 2:19
and bore grain, then the weeds **a** also. Mt 13:26
there **a** to them Moses and Elijah, Mt 17:3
went into the holy city and **a** to many. Mt 27:53
John **a**, baptizing in the wilderness and Mk 1:4
And there **a** to them Elijah with Moses, Mk 9:4
the week, he **a** first to Mary Magdalene, Mk 16:9
these things he **a** in another form Mk 16:12
Afterward he **a** to the eleven Mk 16:14
And there **a** to him an angel of the Lord Lk 1:11
And an angel of the Lord **a** to them, and Lk 2:9
by some that Elijah had **a**, and by others Lk 9:8
who **a** in glory and spoke of his Lk 9:31
And there **a** to him an angel from Lk 22:43
has risen indeed, and has **a** to Simon!" Lk 24:34
tongues as of fire **a** to them and rested Acts 2:3
The God of glory **a** to our father Acts 7:2
the following day he **a** to them as they Acts 7:26
an angel **a** to him in the wilderness of Acts 7:30
hand of the angel who **a** to him in the Acts 7:35
the Lord Jesus who **a** to you on the Acts 9:17
for many days he **a** to those who had Acts 13:31
And a vision **a** to Paul in the night: a Acts 16:9
for I have **a** to you for this purpose, Acts 26:16
sun nor stars **a** for many days, Acts 27:20
and that he **a** to Cephas, then to the 1 Cor 15:5
Then he **a** to more than five hundred 1 Cor 15:6
Then he **a** to James, then to all the 1 Cor 15:7
to one untimely born, he **a** also to me. 1 Cor 15:8
For the grace of God has **a**, bringing Ti 2:11
and loving kindness of God our Savior **a**, Ti 3:4
But when Christ **a** as a high priest of Heb 9:11
he has **a** once for all at the end of the Heb 9:26
now, and what we will be has not yet **a**; 1 Jn 3:2
You know that he **a** to take away sins, 1 Jn 3:5
the Son of God **a** was to destroy the 1 Jn 3:8
And a great sign **a** in heaven: a woman Rv 12:1
And another sign **a** in heaven: behold, a Rv 12:3
And I saw what **a** to be a sea of glass Rv 15:2

APPEARING (6)
a to them during forty days and Acts 1:3
from reproach until the **a** of our Lord 1 Tm 6:14
manifested through the **a** of our 2 Tm 1:10
dead, and by his **a** and his kingdom: 2 Tm 4:1
but also to all who have loved his **a**. 2 Tm 4:8
the **a** of the glory of our great God and Ti 2:13

APPEARS (22)
white and the disease **a** to be deeper than Lv 13:3
of his body and **a** no deeper than the Lv 13:4
But when raw flesh **a** on him, he shall Lv 13:14
and if it **a** deeper than the skin and its Lv 13:20
turned white and it **a** deeper than the Lv 13:25
And if it **a** deeper than the skin, and the Lv 13:30
itching disease and it **a** no deeper than Lv 13:31
and the itch **a** to be no deeper than the Lv 13:32
in the skin and it **a** to be no deeper than Lv 13:34
Then if it **a** again in the garment, in the Lv 13:57
and if it **a** to be deeper than the surface, Lv 14:37
strength; each one **a** before God in Zion. Ps 84:7
LORD builds up Zion; he **a** in his glory; Ps 102:16
the new growth **a** and the vegetation Prv 27:25
coming, and who can stand when he **a**? Mal 3:2
man comes from, and when the Christ **a**, Jn 7:27
They said, "When the Christ **a**, will he do Jn 7:31
When Christ who is your life **a**, then you Col 3:4
you are a mist that **a** for a little time and Jas 4:14
And when the chief Shepherd **a**, you will 1 Pt 5:4
so that when he **a** we may have 1 Jn 2:28
we know that when he **a** we shall be like 1 Jn 3:2

APPEASE (2)
"I may **a** him with the present that goes Gn 32:20
of death, and a wise man will **a** it. Prv 16:14

APPETITE (12)
strong drink, whatever your **a** craves. Dt 14:26
My **a** refuses to touch them; they are as Jb 6:7
bread, and his **a** the choicest food. Jb 33:20
lion, or satisfy the **a** of the young lions, Jb 38:39
steals to satisfy his **a** when he is Prv 6:30
righteous has enough to satisfy his **a**, Prv 13:25
A worker's **a** works for him; his Prv 16:26
to your throat if you are given to **a**. Prv 23:2
for his mouth, yet his **a** is not satisfied. Eccl 6:7
of the eyes than the wandering of the **a**: Eccl 6:9
Sheol has enlarged its **a** and opened its Is 5:14
The dogs have a mighty **a**; they never Is 56:11

APPETITES (1)
our Lord Christ, but their own **a**, Rom 16:18

APPHIA (1)
and **A** our sister and Archippus our Phlm 1:2

APPIUS (1)
the Forum of **A** and Three Taverns Acts 28:15

APPLE (7)
for him, he kept him as the **a** of his eye. Dt 32:10
Keep me as the **a** of your eye; hide me in Ps 17:8
keep my teaching as the **a** of your eye; Prv 7:2
As an **a** tree among the trees of the forest, Sg 2:3
beloved? Under the **a** tree I awakened you. Sg 8:5
Pomegranate, palm, and **a**, all the trees of Jl 1:12
who touches you touches the **a** of his eye: Zec 2:8

APPLES (3)
word fitly spoken is like **a** of gold in a Prv 25:11
refresh me with **a**, for I am sick with love. Sg 2:5
vine, and the scent of your breath like **a**, Sg 7:8

APPLIED (5)
with gold evenly **a** on the carved 1 Kgs 6:35
And I **a** my heart to seek and to search Eccl 1:13
And I **a** my heart to know wisdom and Eccl 1:17
When I **a** my heart to know wisdom, Eccl 8:16
I have **a** all these things to myself and 1 Cor 4:6

APPLIES (1)
"This **a** to the Levites: from twenty-five Nm 8:24

APPLY (3)
and **a** your heart to my knowledge, Prv 22:17
A your heart to instruction and your Prv 23:12
take a cake of figs and **a** it to the boil, Is 38:21

APPLYING (1)
this I observed while **a** my heart to all Eccl 8:9

APPOINT (33)
Pharaoh proceed to **a** overseers over Gn 41:34
then I will **a** for you a place to which he Ex 21:13
But **a** the Levites over the tabernacle of Nm 1:50
And you shall **a** Aaron and his sons, Nm 3:10
sons shall go in and **a** them each to his Nm 4:19
flesh, **a** a man over the congregation Nm 27:16
men, and I will **a** them as your heads.' Dt 1:13
"You shall **a** judges and officers in all Dt 16:18
the people of Israel, '**A** the cities of refuge, Jos 20:2
Now **a** for us a king to judge us like all 1 Sm 8:5
take your sons and **a** them to his 1 Sm 8:11
And he will **a** for himself 1 Sm 8:12
house, to **a** me as prince over Israel, 2 Sm 6:21
And I will **a** a place for my people 2 Sm 7:10
of the Levites to **a** their brothers as 1 Chr 15:16
And I will **a** a place for my people 1 Chr 17:9
a magistrates and judges who may Ezr 7:25
A guards from among the inhabitants Neh 7:3
And let the king **a** officers in all the Est 2:3
be past, that you would **a** me a set time, Jb 14:13
a steadfast love and faithfulness to watch Ps 61:7
the set time that I **a** I will judge with Ps 75:2
A a wicked man against him; let an Ps 109:6
I will **a** over them four kinds of Jer 15:3
And I will **a** over her whomever I Jer 49:19
and I will **a** over her whomever I Jer 50:44
Ashkenaz; **a** a marshal against her; Jer 51:27
Yet I will **a** them to keep charge of the Ezk 44:14
and requested the king to **a** him a time, Dn 2:16
and they shall **a** for themselves one Hos 1:11
of wisdom, whom we will **a** to this duty. Acts 6:3
to **a** you as a servant and witness to Acts 26:16
and **a** elders in every town as I directed Ti 1:5

APPOINTED (156)
"God has **a** for me another offspring Gn 4:25
At the **a** time I will return to you about Gn 18:14
one whom you have **a** for your servant Gn 24:14
whom the LORD has **a** for my master's Gn 24:44
captain of the guard **a** Joseph to be with Gn 40:4
this statute at its **a** time from year to Ex 13:10
seven days at the **a** time in the month Ex 23:15
And behold, I have **a** with him Oholiab, Ex 31:6
you, at the time **a** in the month Abib, Ex 34:18
These are the **a** feasts of the LORD that Lv 23:2
holy convocations; they are my **a** feasts. Lv 23:2
"These are the **a** feasts of the LORD, the Lv 23:4
shall proclaim at the time **a** for them. Lv 23:4
"These are the **a** feasts of the LORD, Lv 23:37
people of Israel the **a** feasts of the LORD. Lv 23:44
And the **a** guard duty of the sons of Nm 3:36
of Israel keep the Passover at its **a** time. Nm 9:2
at twilight, you shall keep it at its **a** time; Nm 9:3
LORD'S offering at its **a** time among the Nm 9:7
bring the LORD'S offering at its **a** time; Nm 9:13
and at your **a** feasts and at the Nm 10:10
as a freewill offering or at your **a** feasts, Nm 15:3
be careful to offer to me at its **a** time.' Nm 28:2
shall offer to the LORD at your **a** feasts, Nm 29:39
then commanders shall be **a** at the head Dt 20:9
from the people of Israel, whom he had **a**, Jos 4:4
out early to the **a** place toward the Jos 8:14
they **a** Bezer in the wilderness on the Jos 20:8
Now the **a** signal between the men of Jgs 20:38
it was kept for you until the hour **a**, 1 Sm 9:24
who **a** Moses and Aaron and brought 1 Sm 12:6

seven days, the time **a** by Samuel. 1 Sm 13:8
you did not come within the days **a**, 1 Sm 13:11
you and has **a** you prince over 1 Sm 25:30
the time that I **a** judges over my people 2 Sm 7:11
the set time that had been **a** him. 2 Sm 20:5
from the morning until the **a** time. 2 Sm 24:15
And I have **a** him to be ruler over 1 Kgs 1:35
high places and **a** priests from 1 Kgs 12:31
And Jeroboam **a** a feast on the 1 Kgs 12:32
Now the king had **a** the captain on 2 Kgs 7:17
So the king **a** an official for her, 2 Kgs 8:6
the LORD and **a** from among 2 Kgs 17:32
he **a** Gedaliah the son of Ahikam, 2 Kgs 25:22
Babylon had **a** Gedaliah governor, 2 Kgs 25:23
brothers the Levites were **a** for all the 1 Chr 6:48
of them were **a** over the furniture 1 Chr 9:29
So the Levites **a** Heman the son of 1 Chr 15:17
Then he **a** some of the Levites as 1 Chr 16:4
day David first **a** that thanksgiving 1 Chr 16:7
sons of Jeduthun were **a** to the gate. 1 Chr 16:42
the time that I **a** judges over my 1 Chr 17:10
according to the **a** duties in their 1 Chr 24:3
These had as their **a** duty in their 1 Chr 24:19
his sons were **a** to external duties 1 Chr 26:29
King David **a** him and his brothers, 1 Chr 26:32
new moons and the **a** feasts of the LORD 2 Chr 2:4
father, at the place that David had **a**, 2 Chr 3:1
he **a** the divisions of the priests for 2 Chr 8:14
and he **a** his own priests for the high 2 Chr 11:15
And Rehoboam **a** Abijah the son of 2 Chr 11:22
He **a** judges in the land in all the 2 Chr 19:5
Jerusalem Jehoshaphat **a** certain 2 Chr 19:8
he **a** those who were to sing to the 2 Chr 20:21
And Hezekiah **a** the divisions of the 2 Chr 31:2
the new moons, and the **a** feasts, 2 Chr 31:3
the land that I **a** for your fathers, 2 Chr 33:8
He **a** the priests to their offices and 2 Chr 35:2
moon and at all the **a** feasts of the LORD, Ezr 3:5
They **a** the Levites, from twenty years old Ezr 3:8
taken foreign wives come at **a** times, Ezr 10:14
time that I was **a** to be their governor Neh 5:14
the singers, and the Levites had been **a**, Neh 7:1
stiffened their neck and **a** a leader to Neh 9:17
the new moons, the **a** feasts, Neh 10:33
to our fathers' houses, at times **a**, Neh 10:34
onto the wall and **a** two great choirs Neh 12:31
day men were **a** over the storerooms, Neh 12:44
who was **a** over the chambers of the Neh 13:4
And I **a** as treasurers over the Neh 13:13
for the wood offering at **a** times, Neh 13:31
eunuchs, who had been **a** to attend her, Est 4:5
was written and at the time **a** every year, Est 9:27
should be observed at their **a** seasons, Est 9:31
and you have **a** his limits that he cannot Jb 14:5
to death and to the house **a** for all living. Jb 30:23
awake for me; you have **a** a judgment. Ps 7:6
Like sheep they are **a** for Sheol; Death Ps 49:14
testimony in Jacob and **a** a law in Israel, Ps 78:5
time to favor her; the **a** time has come. Ps 102:13
down to the place that you **a** for them. Ps 104:8
You have **a** your testimonies in Ps 119:138
new moons and your **a** feasts my soul Is 1:14
every stroke of the **a** staff that the LORD Is 30:32
Behold Zion, the city of our **a** feasts! Is 33:20
it before me, since I **a** an ancient people. Is 44:7
you; I **a** you a prophet to the nations." Jer 1:5
keeps for us the weeks **a** for the harvest.' Jer 5:24
and night will not come at their **a** time, Jer 33:20
the king of Babylon **a** governor of the Jer 40:5
king of Babylon had **a** Gedaliah the son Jer 40:7
in Judah and had **a** Gedaliah the son of Jer 40:11
king of Babylon had **a** governor in the Jer 41:2
and against the seashore he has **a** it." Jer 47:7
near, the **a** time of your years has come. Ezk 22:4
flock at Jerusalem during her **a** feasts, Ezk 36:38
be burned in the **a** place belonging to Ezk 43:21
and my statutes in all my **a** feasts, Ezk 44:24
all the **a** feasts of the house of Israel: Ezk 45:17
come before the LORD at the **a** feasts, Ezk 46:9
"At the feasts and the **a** festivals, the Ezk 46:11
whom the king had **a** to destroy the wise Dn 2:24
request of the king, and he **a** Shadrach, Dn 2:49
Jews whom you have **a** over the affairs Dn 3:12
for it refers to the **a** time of the end. Dn 8:19
for the end is yet to be at the time **a**. Dn 11:27
"At the time **a** he shall return and Dn 11:29
of the end, for it still awaits the **a** time. Dn 11:35
her Sabbaths, and all her **a** feasts. Hos 2:11
For you also, O Judah, a harvest is **a**, Hos 6:11
will you do on the day of the **a** festival, Hos 9:5
in tents, as in the days of the **a** feast. Hos 12:9
And the LORD **a** a great fish to swallow Jon 1:17
Now the LORD God **a** a plant and made it Jon 4:6
God **a** a worm that attacked the plant, Jon 4:7
sun rose, God **a** a scorching east wind, Jon 4:8
"Hear of the rod and of him who **a** it! Mi 6:9
For still the vision awaits its **a** time; it Hab 2:3
to all that I have **a** against you.' Zep 3:7
And he **a** twelve (whom he also named Mk 3:14
He **a** the twelve: Simon (to whom he Mk 3:16
this child is **a** for the fall and rising of Lk 2:34
this the Lord **a** seventy-two others and Lk 10:1
I chose you and **a** you that you should Jn 15:16
that he may send the Christ **a** for you, Acts 3:20
that he is the one **a** by God to be judge Acts 10:42
On an **a** day Herod put on his royal Acts 12:21
as many as were **a** to eternal life Acts 13:48
And when they had **a** elders for them Acts 14:23
some of the others were **a** to go up to Acts 15:2
by a man whom he has **a**; Acts 17:31
will be told all that is **a** for you to do.' Acts 22:10
God of our fathers **a** you to know his Acts 22:14
When they had **a** a day for him, they Acts 28:23
the authorities resists what God has **a**, Rom 13:2
the **a** time has grown very short. 1 Cor 7:29
And God has **a** in the church first 1 Cor 12:28
but he has been **a** by the churches to 2 Cor 8:19
For this I was **a** a preacher and an 1 Tm 2:7
for which I was **a** a preacher and 2 Tm 1:11
Son, whom he **a** the heir of all things, Heb 1:2
who was faithful to him who **a** him, just Heb 3:2
from among men is **a** to act on behalf Heb 5:1
but was **a** by him who said to him, Heb 5:5
every high priest is **a** to offer gifts and Heb 8:3
And just as it is **a** for man to die once, Heb 9:27

APPOINTING (1)
me faithful, **a** me to his service, 1 Tm 1:12

APPOINTMENT (5)
out into the field to the **a** with David, 1 Sm 20:35
I have made an **a** with the young men 1 Sm 21:2
by the **a** of Hezekiah the king and 2 Chr 31:13
They made an **a** together to come to Jb 2:11
By your **a** they stand this day, for all Ps 119:91

APPOINTS (4)
For he will complete what he **a** for me, Jb 23:14
again he **a** a certain day, "Today," Heb 4:7
For the law **a** men in their weakness as Heb 7:28
a a Son who has been made perfect Heb 7:28

APPORTION (2)
to **a** the contribution reserved for 2 Chr 31:14
the land, to **a** the desolate heritages, Is 49:8

APPORTIONED (6)
whose inheritance had not yet been **a**. Jos 18:2
And there Joshua **a** the land to the Jos 18:10
and nights of misery are **a** to me. Jb 7:3
wind its weight and **a** the waters by Jb 28:25
he **a** them for a possession and settled Ps 78:55
and to him Abraham **a** a tenth part of Heb 7:2

APPORTIONS (1)
who **a** to each one individually as he 1 Cor 12:11

APPROACH (18)
"None of you shall **a** any one of his close Lv 18:6
brother, that is, you shall not **a** his wife; Lv 18:14
"You shall not **a** a woman to uncover Lv 18:19
has a blemish may **a** to offer the bread Lv 21:17
not go through the veil or **a** the altar, Lv 21:23
And when you **a** the territory of the Dt 2:19
"Behold, the days **a** when you must die. Dt 31:14
the people who are with me will **a** the city. Jos 8:5
my steps; like a prince I would **a** him. Jb 31:37
strength; let them **a**, then let them speak; Is 41:1
him draw near, and he shall **a** me, Jer 30:21
for who would dare of himself to **a** me? Jer 30:21
Jerusalem at the **a** of Pharaoh's army, Jer 37:11
his neighbor's wife or **a** a woman in Ezk 18:6
where the priests who **a** the LORD shall Ezk 42:13
sanctuary, and they shall **a** my table, Ezk 44:16
in the sanctuary and **a** the LORD to Ezk 45:4
hearts like an oven they **a** their intrigue; Hos 7:6

APPROACHED (11)
Now Abimelech had not **a** her. So he Gn 20:4
of meeting, and when they **a** the altar, Ex 40:32
who were over those who were listed, **a** Nm 7:2
They **a** Eleazar the priest and Joshua the Jos 17:4
Then Saul **a** Samuel in the gate and 1 Sm 9:18
in his hand, and he **a** the Philistine. 1 Sm 17:40
they **a** Zerubbabel and the heads of Ezr 4:2
been done, the officials **a** me and said, Ezr 9:1
Then Esther **a** and touched the tip of the Est 5:2
I **a** one of those who stood there and Dn 7:16
as he went on his way, he **a** Damascus, Acts 9:3

APPROACHES (4)
If a woman **a** any animal and lies with Lv 20:16
throughout your generations **a** the holy Lv 22:3
And whoever **a** the ranks is to be put 2 Kgs 11:8
where no thief **a** and no moth destroys. Lk 12:33

APPROACHING (2)
days of mourning for my father are **a**; Gn 27:41
were on their journey and **a** the city, Acts 10:9

APPROVAL (5)
without our husbands' **a** that we made Jer 44:19
do them but give **a** to those who Rom 1:32
is good, and you will receive his **a**, Rom 13:3
By their **a** of this service, they will 2 Cor 9:13
For am I now seeking the **a** of man, or Gal 1:10

APPROVE (5)
Nevertheless, the lords do not **a** of you. 1 Sm 29:6
yet after them people **a** of their boasts. Ps 49:13
in his lawsuit, the Lord does not **a**. Lam 3:36
know his will and **a** what is excellent, Rom 2:18
so that you may **a** what is excellent, Phil 1:10

APPROVED (12)
offering today, would the LORD have **a**?" Lv 10:19
And when Moses heard that, he **a**. Lv 10:20
of this law, **a** by the Levitical priests. Dt 17:18
fathers' houses, **a**, mighty warriors, 1 Chr 7:40
me blessed, and when the eye saw, it **a**, Jb 29:11
for God has already **a** what you do. Eccl 9:7
And Saul **a** of his execution. And there Acts 8:1
is acceptable to God and **a** by men. Rom 14:18
Greet Apelles, who is **a** in Christ. Rom 16:10
who commends himself who is **a**, 2 Cor 10:18
just as we have been **a** by God to be 1 Thes 2:4
to present yourself to God as one **a**, 2 Tm 2:15

APPROVES (1)
judgment on himself for what he **a**. Rom 14:22

APPROVING (1)
standing by and **a** and watching over Acts 22:20

APRONS (1)
even handkerchiefs or **a** that had Acts 19:12

APT (1)
To make an **a** answer is a joy to a Prv 15:23

AQUILA (6)
And he found a Jew named **A**, a native Acts 18:2
Syria, and with him Priscilla and **A**. Acts 18:18
but when Priscilla and **A** heard him, Acts 18:26
Greet Prisca and **A**, my fellow workers Rom 16:3
A and Prisca, together with the 1 Cor 16:19
Greet Prisca and **A**, and the 2 Tm 4:19

AR (6)
valleys that extends to the seat of **A**, Nm 21:15
city of Sihon. It devoured **A** of Moab, Nm 21:28
because I have given **A** to the people of Lot Dt 2:9
you are to cross the border of Moab at **A**. Dt 2:18
the Moabites who live in **A** did for me, Dt 2:29
Because **A** of Moab is laid waste in a Is 15:1

ARA (1)
of Jether: Jephunneh, Pispa, and **A**. 1 Chr 7:38

ARAB (5)
A, Dumah, Eshan, Jos 15:52
servant and Geshem the **A** heard of it, Neh 2:19
Tobiah and Geshem the **A** and the rest Neh 6:1
no **A** will pitch his tent there; Is 13:20
lovers like an **A** in the wilderness. Jer 3:2

ARABAH (26)
in the wilderness, in the **A** opposite Suph, Dt 1:1
and to all their neighbors in the **A**, Dt 1:7
away from the **A** road from Elath and Dt 2:8
the **A** also, with the Jordan as the border, Dt 3:17
Chinnereth as far as the Sea of the **A**, Dt 3:17
together with all the **A** on the east side of Dt 4:49
of the Jordan as far as the Sea of the **A**, Dt 4:49
of the Canaanites who live in the **A**, Dt 11:30
flowing down toward the Sea of the **A**, Jos 3:16
place toward the **A** to meet Israel Jos 8:14
and in the **A** south of Chinneroth, Jos 11:2
the lowland and the **A** and the hill Jos 11:16
Mount Hermon, with all the **A** eastward: Jos 12:1
and the **A** to the Sea of Chinneroth Jos 12:3
of Beth-jeshimoth, to the Sea of the **A**, Jos 12:3
hill country, in the lowland, in the **A**, Jos 12:8
of Beth-arabah it goes down to the **A**. Jos 18:18
in the **A** to the south of Jeshimon. 1 Sm 23:24
went all that night through the **A**. 2 Sm 2:29
and went by the way of the **A** all night, 2 Sm 4:7
as far as the Sea of the **A**, 2 Kgs 14:25
they went in the direction of the **A**. 2 Kgs 25:4
two walls; and they went toward the **A**. Jer 39:4
And they went in the direction of the **A**. Jer 52:7
region and goes down into the **A**, Ezk 47:8
Lebo-hamath to the Brook of the **A**." Am 6:14

ARABIA (8)
all the kings of **A** and the governors 2 Chr 9:14
The oracle concerning **A**. In the Is 21:13
In the thickets in **A** you will lodge, O Is 21:13

all the kings of **A** and all the kings of Jer 25:24
A and all the princes of Kedar were Ezk 27:21
Cush, and Put, and Lud, and all **A**, and Ezk 30:5
before me, but I went away into **A**, Gal 1:17
Now Hagar is Mount Sinai in **A**; she Gal 4:25

ARABIANS (5)
and the **A** also brought him 7,700 2 Chr 17:11
and of the **A** who are near 2 Chr 21:16
that came with the **A** to the camp 2 Chr 22:1
and against the **A** who lived in 2 Chr 26:7
Cretans and **A**—we hear them telling Acts 2:11

ARABS (1)
Tobiah and the **A** and the Ammonites Neh 4:7

ARAD (5)
When the Canaanite, the king of **A**, Nm 21:1
And the Canaanite, the king of **A**, Nm 33:40
of Hormah, one; the king of **A**, one; Jos 12:14
Judah, which lies in the Negeb near **A**, Jgs 1:16
Zebadiah, **A**, Eder, 1 Chr 8:15

ARAH (4)
sons of Ulla: **A**, Hanniel, and Rizia. 1 Chr 7:39
The sons of **A**, 775. Ezr 2:5
son-in-law of Shecaniah the son of **A**: Neh 6:18
The sons of **A**, 652. Neh 7:10

ARAM (11)
Asshur, Arpachshad, Lud, and **A**. Gn 10:22
The sons of **A**: Uz, Hul, Gether, and Gn 10:23
his brother, Kemuel the father of **A**, Gn 22:21
said, "From **A** Balak has brought me, Nm 23:7
David put garrisons in **A** of Damascus, 2 Sm 8:6
a vow while I lived at Geshur in **A**, 2 Sm 15:8
Asshur, Arpachshad, Lud, and **A**. 1 Chr 1:17
And the sons of **A**: Uz, Hul, Gether, 1 Chr 1:17
But Geshur and **A** took from them 1 Chr 2:23
brother: Rohgah, Jehubbah, and **A**. 1 Chr 7:34
Jacob fled to the land of **A**; there Israel Hos 12:12

ARAM-MAACAH (1)
from **A** and from Zobah. 1 Chr 19:6

ARAM-NAHARAIM (1)
he strove with **A** and with Aram-zobah, Ps 60:T

ARAM-ZOBAH (1)
with Aram-naharaim and with **A**, Ps 60:T

ARAMAIC (9)
"Please speak to your servants in **A**, 2 Kgs 18:26
letter was written in **A** and translated. Ezr 4:7
"Please speak to your servants in **A**, Is 36:11
the Chaldeans said to the king in **A**, Dn 2:4
Sheep Gate a pool, in **A** called Bethesda, Jn 5:2
Stone Pavement, and in **A** Gabbatha. Jn 19:13
a skull, which in **A** is called Golgotha. Jn 19:17
near the city, and it was written in **A**, Jn 19:20
She turned and said to him in **A**, Jn 20:16

ARAMEAN (7)
of Bethuel the **A** of Paddan-aram, Gn 25:20
the sister of Laban the **A**. Gn 25:20
to Laban, the son of Bethuel the **A**, Gn 28:5
And Jacob tricked Laban the **A**, by not Gn 31:20
came to Laban the **A** in a dream by Gn 31:24
God, 'A wandering **A** was my father. Dt 26:5
Asriel, whom his **A** concubine bore; 1 Chr 7:14

ARAN (2)
are the sons of Dishan: Uz and **A**. Gn 36:28
Akan. The sons of Dishan: Uz and **A**. 1 Chr 1:42

ARARAT (4)
ark came to rest on the mountains of **A**. Gn 8:4
and escaped into the land of **A**. 2 Kgs 19:37
after they escaped into the land of **A**, Is 37:38
against her the kingdoms, **A**, Minni, Jer 51:27

ARAUNAH (9)
the threshing floor of **A** the Jebusite. 2 Sm 24:16
the threshing floor of **A** the Jebusite." 2 Sm 24:18
And when **A** looked down, he saw 2 Sm 24:20
And **A** went out and paid homage to 2 Sm 24:20
And **A** said, "Why has my lord the 2 Sm 24:21
Then **A** said to David, "Let my lord 2 Sm 24:22
A gives to the king." And Araunah 2 Sm 24:23
to the king." And **A** said to the king, 2 Sm 24:23
But the king said to **A**, "No, but I will 2 Sm 24:24

ARBA (3)
(**A** was the greatest man among the Jos 14:15
is, Hebron (**A** was the father of Anak). Jos 15:13
gave them Kiriath-arba (**A** being the Jos 21:11

ARBATHITE (2)
Abi-albon the **A**, Azmaveth of 2 Sm 23:31
of the brooks of Gaash, Abiel the **A**, 1 Chr 11:32

ARBITE (1)
Hezro of Carmel, Paarai the **A**, 2 Sm 23:35

ARBITER (1)
There is no **a** between us, who might lay Jb 9:33

ARBITRATOR (1)
who made me a judge or **a** over you?" Lk 12:14

ARCHANGEL (2)
of command, with the voice of an **a**, 1 Thes 4:16
But when the **a** Michael, contending Jude 1:9

ARCHELAUS (1)
when he heard that **A** was reigning over Mt 2:22

ARCHER (3)
Like an **a** who wounds everyone is one Prv 26:10
noise of horseman and **a** every city takes Jer 4:29
Let not the **a** bend his bow, and let him Jer 51:3

ARCHERS (10)
The **a** bitterly attacked him, shot at Gn 49:23
against Saul, and the **a** found him, 1 Sm 31:3
and he was badly wounded by the **a**. 1 Sm 31:3
Then the **a** shot at your servants 2 Sm 11:24
against Saul, and the **a** found him, 1 Chr 10:3
him, and he was wounded by the **a**. 1 Chr 10:3
And the **a** shot King Josiah. And the 2 Chr 35:23
his **a** surround me. He slashes open my Jb 16:13
the remainder of the **a** of the mighty Is 21:17
"Summon **a** against Babylon, all those Jer 50:29

ARCHIPPUS (2)
And say to **A**, "See that you fulfill the Col 4:17
our sister and **A** our fellow soldier, Phlm 1:2

ARCHITE (5)
Hushai the **A** came to meet him with 2 Sm 15:32
And when Hushai the **A**, David's 2 Sm 16:16
said, "Call Hushai the **A** also, 2 Sm 17:5
of Hushai the **A** is better than 2 Sm 17:14
and Hushai the **A** was the king's 1 Chr 27:33

ARCHITES (1)
along to Ataroth, the territory of the **A**. Jos 16:2

ARCHIVES (2)
be made in the royal **a** there in Babylon, Ezr 5:17
the house of the **a** where the documents Ezr 6:1

ARD (3)
Ehi, Rosh, Muppim, Huppim, and **A**. Gn 46:21
the sons of Bela were **A** and Naaman: Nm 26:40
of Bela were Ard and Naaman: of **A**, Nm 26:40

ARDITES (1)
Naaman: of Ard, the clan of the **A**; Nm 26:40

ARDON (1)
were her sons: Jesher, Shobab, and **A**. 1 Chr 2:18

AREA (19)
in the field, throughout its whole **a**, Gn 23:17
shall examine the diseased **a** on the skin Lv 13:3
hair in the diseased **a** has turned white Lv 13:3
and if the diseased **a** has faded and the Lv 13:6
forehead a reddish-white diseased **a**, Lv 13:42
of the diseased **a** has not changed, Lv 13:55
and if the diseased **a** has faded after it Lv 13:56
their iniquities on itself to a remote **a**, Lv 16:22
into three parts the **a** of the land that Dt 19:3
priests, the men of the surrounding **a**, Neh 3:22
all around the outside of the temple **a**, Ezk 40:5
Thus the temple had a broad **a** upward, Ezk 41:7
measuring the interior of the temple **a**, Ezk 42:15
and measured the temple **a** all around. Ezk 42:15
to the temple, outside the sacred **a**. Ezk 43:21
of the city an **a** 5,000 cubits broad and Ezk 45:6
with regard to the **a** of influence God 2 Cor 10:13
our **a** of influence among you may 2 Cor 10:15
done in another's **a** of influence. 2 Cor 10:16

ARELI (2)
Haggi, Shuni, Ezbon, Eri, Arodi, and **A**. Gn 46:16
of Arod, the clan of the Arodites; of **A**, Nm 26:17

ARELITES (1)
Arodites; of Areli, the clan of the **A**. Nm 26:17

AREOPAGITE (1)
were Dionysius the **A** and a woman Acts 17:34

AREOPAGUS (2)
of him and brought him to the **A**, Acts 17:19
Paul, standing in the midst of the **A**, Acts 17:22

ARETAS (1)
under King **A** was guarding 2 Cor 11:32

ARGOB (5)
them—sixty cities, the whole region of **A**, Dt 3:4
of Og, that is, all the region of **A**, Dt 3:13
the Manassite took all the region of **A**, Dt 3:14
in Gilead, and he had the region of **A**, 1 Kgs 4:13
the king's house with **A** and Arieh; 2 Kgs 15:25

ARGUE (8)
and I desire to **a** my case with God. Jb 13:3
in him; yet I will **a** my ways to his face. Jb 13:15
Should he **a** in unprofitable talk, or in Jb 15:3
that he would **a** the case of a man with Jb 16:21
There an upright man could **a** with him, Jb 23:7
A your case with your neighbor Prv 25:9
me in remembrance; let us **a** together; Is 43:26
came and began to **a** with him, Mk 8:11

ARGUED (2)
the way they had **a** with one another Mk 9:34
Paul **a** in his defense, "Neither against Acts 25:8

ARGUES (1)
with the Almighty? He who **a** with God, Jb 40:2

ARGUING (3)
the people were **a** throughout all the 2 Sm 19:9
around them, and scribes **a** with them. Mk 9:14
"What are you **a** about with them?" Mk 9:16

ARGUMENT (4)
Hear now my **a** and listen to the Jb 13:6
and make my disgrace an **a** against me, Jb 19:5
If a wise man has an **a** with a fool, the Prv 29:9
An **a** arose among them as to which of Lk 9:46

ARGUMENTATIVE (1)
they are to be well-pleasing, not **a**, Ti 2:9

ARGUMENTS (3)
before him and fill my mouth with **a**. Jb 23:4
We destroy **a** and every lofty opinion 2 Cor 10:5
no one may delude you with plausible **a**. Col 2:4

ARID (1)
I have given the **a** plain for his home Jb 39:6

ARIDAI (1)
and Arisai and **A** and Vaizatha, Est 9:9

ARIDATHA (1)
and Poratha and Adalia and **A** Est 9:8

ARIEH (1)
the king's house with Argob and **A**; 2 Kgs 15:25

ARIEL (6)
Then I sent for Eliezer, **A**, Shemaiah, Ezr 8:16
Ah, **A**, Ariel, the city where David Is 29:1
Ariel, **A**, the city where David encamped! Is 29:1
Yet I will distress **A**, and there shall be Is 29:2
and she shall be to me like an **A**. Is 29:2
of all the nations that fight against **A**, Is 29:7

ARIELS (1)
He struck down two **a** of Moab. 2 Sm 23:20

ARIMATHEA (4)
there came a rich man from **A**, Mt 27:57
Joseph of **A**, a respected member of the Mk 15:43
Joseph, from the Jewish town of **A**. Lk 23:50
After these things Joseph of **A**, who was Jn 19:38

ARIOCH (7)
king of Shinar, **A** king of Ellasar, Gn 14:1
king of Shinar, and **A** king of Ellasar, Gn 14:9
with prudence and discretion to **A**, Dn 2:14
He declared to **A**, the king's captain, Dn 2:15
so urgent?" Then **A** made the matter Dn 2:15
Therefore Daniel went in to **A**, whom Dn 2:24
Then **A** brought in Daniel before the Dn 2:25

ARISAI (1)
and Parmashta and **A** and Aridai and Est 9:9

ARISE (124)
A, walk through the length and the Gn 13:17
"Let my father **a** and eat of his son's Gn 27:31
A, flee to Laban my brother in Haran Gn 27:43
A, go to Paddan-aram to the house of Gn 28:2
a pillar and made a vow to me. Now **a**, Gn 31:13
"**A**, go up to Bethel and dwell there. Gn 35:1
Then let us **a** and go up to Bethel, so that Gn 35:3
after them there will **a** seven years of Gn 41:30
the boy with me, and we will **a** and go, Gn 43:8
Take also your brother, and **a**, go Gn 43:13
the ark set out, Moses said, "**A**, O LORD, Nm 10:35
to me, '**A**, go down quickly from here, Dt 9:12
'**A**, go on your journey at the head of the Dt 10:11
then you shall **a** and go up to the place Dt 17:8
Now therefore **a**, go over this Jordan, you Jos 1:2
all the fighting men with you, and **a**, Jos 8:1
A, Barak, lead away your captives, O son Jgs 5:12
to him, "**A**, go down against the camp, Jgs 7:9
"**A**, for the LORD has given the host of Jgs 7:15
said, "**A**, and let us go up against them, Jgs 18:9
and tomorrow you shall **a** early in the Jgs 19:9
one of the young men with you, and **a**, 1 Sm 9:3
And the LORD said, "**A**, anoint him, 1 Sm 16:12
answered him, "**A**, go down to Keilah, 1 Sm 23:4
the young men **a** and compete before 2 Sm 2:14
us." And Joab said, "Let them **a**." 2 Sm 2:14
"I will **a** and go and gather all 2 Sm 3:21
him at Jerusalem, "**A**, and let us flee, 2 Sm 15:14
and I will **a** and pursue David tonight. 2 Sm 17:1

"**A**, and go quickly over the water, 2 Sm 17:21
Now therefore **a**, go out and speak 2 Sm 19:7
and none like you shall **a** after you. 1 Kgs 3:12
to his wife, "**A**, and disguise yourself, 1 Kgs 14:2
A therefore, go to your house. When 1 Kgs 14:12
"**A**, go to Zarephath, which belongs 1 Kgs 17:9
him and said to him, "**A** and eat." 1 Kgs 19:5
touched him and said, "**A** and eat, 1 Kgs 19:7
A and eat bread and let your heart be 1 Kgs 21:7
"**A**, take possession of the vineyard 1 Kgs 21:15
"**A**, go down to meet Ahab king of 1 Kgs 21:18
"**A**, go up to meet the messengers of the 2 Kgs 1:3
"**A**, and depart with your household, 2 Kgs 8:1
nor did any like him **a** after him. 2 Kgs 23:25
bronze, and iron. **A** and work! 1 Chr 22:16
A and build the sanctuary of the 1 Chr 22:19
"And now **a**, O LORD God, and go to 2 Chr 6:41
A, for it is your task, and we are with Ezr 10:4
and we his servants will **a** and build, Neh 2:20
with Urim and Thummim should **a**. Neh 7:65
When I lie down I say, 'When shall I **a**?' Jb 7:4
Upon whom does his light not **a**? Jb 25:3
A, O LORD! Save me, O my God! For you Ps 3:7
A, O LORD, in your anger; lift yourself up Ps 7:6
A, O LORD! Let not man prevail; let the Ps 9:19
A, O LORD; O God, lift up your hand; Ps 10:12
needy groan, I will now **a**," says the LORD; Ps 12:5
A, O LORD! Confront him, subdue him! Ps 17:13
shall not fear; though war **a** against me, Ps 27:3
God shall **a**, his enemies shall be Ps 68:1
A, O God, defend your cause; remember Ps 74:22
and **a** and tell them to their children, Ps 78:6
A, O God, judge the earth; for you shall Ps 82:8
You will **a** and have pity on Zion; it is Ps 102:13
They **a** and are put to shame, but your Ps 109:28
A, O LORD, and go to your resting place, Ps 132:8
When will you **a** from your sleep? Prv 6:9
"**A**, my love, my beautiful one, and come Sg 2:10
A, my love, my beautiful one, and come Sg 2:13
they drink. **A**, O princes; oil the shield! Is 21:5
a, cross over to Cyprus, even there you Is 23:12
not live; they are shades, they will not **a**; Is 26:14
but will **a** against the house of the Is 31:2
"Now I will **a**," says the LORD, "now I will Is 33:10
servant of rulers: "Kings shall see and **a**; Is 49:7
Shake yourself from the dust and **a**; be Is 52:2
A, shine, for your light has come, and the Is 60:1
but the LORD will **a** upon you, and his Is 60:2
a, and say to them everything that I Jer 1:17
of their trouble they say, '**A** and save us!' Jer 2:27
Let them **a**, if they can save you, in your Jer 2:28
against her; **a**, and let us attack at noon! Jer 6:4
A, and let us attack by night and destroy Jer 6:5
which is around your waist, and **a**, Jer 13:4
LORD said to me, "**A**, go to the Euphrates, Jer 13:6
"**A**, and go down to the potter's house, Jer 18:2
'**A**, and let us go up to Zion, to the LORD Jer 31:6
'**A**, and let us go back to our own people Jer 46:16
"**A**, cry out in the night, at the Lam 2:19
he said to me, "**A**, go out into the valley, Ezk 3:22
inferior to you shall **a** after you, Dn 2:39
and it was told, '**A**, devour much flesh.' Dn 7:5
four kings who shall **a** out of the earth. Dn 7:17
out of this kingdom ten kings shall **a**, Dn 7:24
arise, and another shall **a** after them; Dn 7:24
four kingdoms shall **a** from his nation, Dn 8:22
one who understands riddles, shall **a**. Dn 8:23
three more kings shall **a** in Persia, Dn 11:2
Then a mighty king shall **a**, who shall Dn 11:3
from her roots one shall **a** in his place. Dn 11:7
"Then shall **a** in his place one who Dn 11:20
his place shall **a** a contemptible person Dn 11:21
"At that time shall **a** Michael, the great Dn 12:1
of war shall **a** among your people, Hos 10:14
"**A**, go to Nineveh, that great city, and Jon 1:2
you sleeper? **A**, call out to your god! Jon 1:6
"**A**, go to Nineveh, that great city, and Jon 3:2
A and go, for this is no place to rest, Mi 2:10
A and thresh, O daughter of Zion, for I Mi 4:13
A, plead your case before the mountains, Mi 6:1
are before me; strife and contention **a**. Hab 1:3
Will not your debtors suddenly **a**, and Hab 2:7
to a silent stone, **A**! Can this teach? Hab 2:19
false prophets will **a** and lead many Mt 24:11
false prophets will **a** and perform great Mt 24:24
means, "Little girl, I say to you, **a**." Mk 5:41
false prophets will **a** and perform signs Mk 13:22
he said, "Young man, I say to you, **a**." Lk 7:14
by the hand he called, saying, "Child, **a**." Lk 8:54
I will **a** and go to my father, and I will Lk 15:18
and why do doubts **a** in your hearts? Lk 24:38
"Tabitha, **a**." And she opened her eyes, Acts 9:40
own selves will **a** men speaking Acts 20:30
"Awake, O sleeper, and **a** from the dead, Eph 5:14
for another priest to **a** after the order of Heb 7:11

ARISEN (5)
And there has not **a** a prophet since in Dt 34:10
and see how this sin has **a** today. 1 Sm 14:38
And as soon as he has **a**, his kingdom Dn 11:4
of women there has **a** no one greater Mt 11:11
"A great prophet has **a** among us!" and Lk 7:16

ARISES (8)
a dreamer of dreams **a** among you and Dt 13:1
"If any case **a** requiring decision between Dt 17:8
If a malicious witness **a** to accuse a Dt 19:16
or persecution **a** on account Mt 13:21
or persecution **a** on account Mk 4:17
and see that no prophet **a** from Galilee." Jn 7:52
even he who **a** to rule the Gentiles; Rom 15:12
when another priest **a** in the likeness Heb 7:15

ARISTARCHUS (5)
dragging with them Gaius and **A**, Acts 19:29
of the Thessalonians, **A** and Secundus; Acts 20:4
Asia, we put to sea, accompanied by **A**, Acts 27:2
A my fellow prisoner greets you, and Col 4:10
and so do Mark, **A**, Demas, and Luke, Phlm 1:24

ARISTOBULUS (1)
those who belong to the family of **A**. Rom 16:10

ARK (226)
Make yourself an **a** of gopher wood. Gn 6:14
Make rooms in the **a**, and cover it inside Gn 6:14
the length of the **a** 300 cubits, its Gn 6:15
Make a roof for the **a**, and finish it to a Gn 6:16
and set the door of the **a** in its side. Gn 6:16
with you, and you shall come into the **a**, Gn 6:18
every sort into the **a** to keep them alive Gn 6:19
the LORD said to Noah, "Go into the **a**, Gn 7:1
him went into the **a** to escape the waters Gn 7:7
and female, went into the **a** with Noah, Gn 7:9
of his sons with them entered the **a**, Gn 7:13
They went into the **a** with Noah, two Gn 7:15
The waters increased and bore up the **a**, Gn 7:17
and the **a** floated on the face of the Gn 7:18
and those who were with him in the **a**. Gn 7:23
the livestock that were with him in the **a**. Gn 8:1
the **a** came to rest on the mountains of Gn 8:4
the window of the **a** that he had made Gn 8:6
her foot, and she returned to him to the **a**, Gn 8:9
her and brought her into the **a** with him. Gn 8:9
again he sent forth the dove out of the **a**. Gn 8:10
the covering of the **a** and looked, Gn 8:13
"Go out from the **a**, you and your wife, Gn 8:16
earth, went out by families from the **a**. Gn 8:19
with you, as many as came out of the **a**; Gn 9:10
who went forth from the **a** were Shem, Gn 9:18
"They shall make an **a** of acacia wood. Ex 25:10
on the sides of the **a** to carry the ark by Ex 25:14
sides of the ark to carry the **a** by them. Ex 25:14
poles shall remain in the rings of the **a**; Ex 25:15
shall put into the **a** the testimony that I Ex 25:16
put the mercy seat on the top of the **a**, Ex 25:21
and in the **a** you shall put the Ex 25:21
that are on the **a** of the testimony, Ex 25:22
and bring the **a** of the testimony in Ex 26:33
mercy seat on the **a** of the testimony in Ex 26:34
veil that is above the **a** of the testimony, Ex 30:6
of meeting and the **a** of the testimony, Ex 30:26
of meeting, and the **a** of the testimony, Ex 31:7
the **a** with its poles, the mercy seat, and Ex 35:12
Bezalel made the **a** of acacia wood. Two Ex 37:1
on the sides of the **a** to carry the ark. Ex 37:5
on the sides of the ark to carry the **a**. Ex 37:5
the **a** of the testimony with its poles and Ex 39:35
you shall put in it the **a** of the testimony, Ex 40:3
and you shall screen the **a** with the veil. Ex 40:3
for incense before the **a** of the testimony, Ex 40:5
took the testimony and put it into the **a**, Ex 40:20
put the poles on the **a** and set the mercy Ex 40:20
and set the mercy seat above on the **a**. Ex 40:20
he brought the **a** into the tabernacle Ex 40:21
and screened the **a** of the testimony, Ex 40:21
before the mercy seat that is on the **a**, Lv 16:2
And their guard duty involved the **a**, Nm 3:31
screen and cover the **a** of the testimony Nm 4:5
seat that was on the **a** of the testimony, Nm 7:89
And the **a** of the covenant of the LORD Nm 10:33
And whenever the **a** set out, Moses Nm 10:35
although neither the **a** of the Nm 14:44
the mountain and make an **a** of wood. Dt 10:1
broke, and you shall put them in the **a**.' Dt 10:2
So I made an **a** of acacia wood, and cut Dt 10:3
put the tablets in the **a** that I had made. Dt 10:5
of Levi to carry the **a** of the covenant of Dt 10:8
who carried the **a** of the covenant of the Dt 31:9
who carried the **a** of the covenant Dt 31:25
by the side of the **a** of the covenant of Dt 31:26
soon as you see the **a** of the covenant of Jos 3:3
"Take up the **a** of the covenant and pass Jos 3:6
So they took up the **a** of the covenant and Jos 3:6
the priests who bear the **a** of the covenant, Jos 3:8
the **a** of the covenant of the Lord of all Jos 3:11
of the priests bearing the **a** of the LORD, Jos 3:13
the priests bearing the **a** of the covenant Jos 3:14
as those bearing the **a** had come as far Jos 3:15
the priests bearing the **a** were dipped in Jos 3:15
the priests bearing the **a** of the covenant Jos 3:17
"Pass on before the **a** of the LORD your Jos 4:5
cut off before the **a** of the covenant of Jos 4:7
the priests bearing the **a** of the covenant Jos 4:9
the priests bearing the **a** stood in the Jos 4:10
the **a** of the LORD and the priests passed Jos 4:11
the priests bearing the **a** of the testimony Jos 4:16
the priests bearing the **a** of the covenant Jos 4:18
trumpets of rams' horns before the **a**. Jos 6:4
"Take up the **a** of the covenant and let Jos 6:6
of rams' horns before the **a** of the LORD." Jos 6:6
men pass on before the **a** of the LORD." Jos 6:7
with the **a** of the covenant of the LORD Jos 6:8
the rear guard was walking after the **a**, Jos 6:9
So he caused the **a** of the LORD to circle Jos 6:11
and the priests took up the **a** of the LORD. Jos 6:12
rams' horns before the **a** of the LORD Jos 6:13
was walking after the **a** of the LORD, Jos 6:13
on his face before the **a** of the LORD until Jos 7:6
sides of the **a** before the Levitical Jos 8:33
priests who carried the **a** of the covenant Jos 8:33
of the LORD (for the **a** of the covenant of Jgs 20:27
of the LORD, where the **a** of God was. 1 Sm 3:3
Let us bring the **a** of the covenant of 1 Sm 4:3
from there the **a** of the covenant 1 Sm 4:4
were there with the **a** of the covenant of 1 Sm 4:4
As soon as the **a** of the covenant of the 1 Sm 4:5
they learned that the **a** of the LORD had 1 Sm 4:6
And the **a** of God was captured, and 1 Sm 4:11
for his heart trembled for the **a** of God. 1 Sm 4:13
and the **a** of God has been captured." 1 Sm 4:17
As soon as he mentioned the **a** of God, 1 Sm 4:18
the news that the **a** of God was 1 Sm 4:19
from Israel!" because the **a** of God had 1 Sm 4:21
for the **a** of God has been captured." 1 Sm 4:22
the Philistines captured the **a** of God, 1 Sm 5:1
the Philistines took the **a** of God and 1 Sm 5:2
on the ground before the **a** of the LORD. 1 Sm 5:3
on the ground before the **a** of the LORD, 1 Sm 5:4
"The **a** of the God of Israel must not 1 Sm 5:7
shall we do with the **a** of the God of 1 Sm 5:8
"Let the **a** of the God of Israel be 1 Sm 5:8
So they brought the **a** of the God of 1 Sm 5:8
So they sent the **a** of God to Ekron. But 1 Sm 5:10
But as soon as the **a** of God came to 1 Sm 5:10
around to us the **a** of the God of 1 Sm 5:10
"Send away the **a** of the God of Israel, 1 Sm 5:11
The **a** of the LORD was in the country of 1 Sm 6:1
shall we do with the **a** of the LORD? 1 Sm 6:2
"If you send away the **a** of the God of 1 Sm 6:3
And take the **a** of the LORD and place it 1 Sm 6:8
And they put the **a** of the LORD on the 1 Sm 6:11
they lifted up their eyes and saw the **a**, 1 Sm 6:13
Levites took down the **a** of the LORD 1 Sm 6:15
they set down the **a** of the LORD is 1 Sm 6:18
they looked upon the **a** of the LORD. 1 Sm 6:19
have returned the **a** of the LORD. 1 Sm 6:21
came and took up the **a** of the LORD and 1 Sm 7:1
to have charge of the **a** of the LORD. 1 Sm 7:1
the day that the **a** was lodged at 1 Sm 7:2
"Bring the **a** of God here." For the 1 Sm 14:18
of God here." For the **a** of God went at 1 Sm 14:18
to bring up from there the **a** of God, 2 Sm 6:2
And they carried the **a** of God on a new 2 Sm 6:3
with the **a** of God, and Ahio went before 2 Sm 6:4
ark of God, and Ahio went before the **a**. 2 Sm 6:4
out his hand to the **a** of God and took 2 Sm 6:6
and he died there beside the **a** of God. 2 Sm 6:7
"How can the **a** of the LORD come to 2 Sm 6:9
willing to take the **a** of the LORD into 2 Sm 6:10
And the **a** of the LORD remained in the 2 Sm 6:11
because of the **a** of God." So David 2 Sm 6:12
and brought up the **a** of God from the 2 Sm 6:12
those who bore the **a** of the LORD had 2 Sm 6:13
Israel brought up the **a** of the LORD 2 Sm 6:15
As the **a** of the LORD came into the city 2 Sm 6:16
they brought in the **a** of the LORD and 2 Sm 6:17
cedar, but the **a** of God dwells in a tent." 2 Sm 7:2
"The **a** and Israel and Judah dwell in 2 Sm 11:11
bearing the **a** of the covenant of God. 2 Sm 15:24
they set down the **a** of God until the 2 Sm 15:24
"Carry the **a** of God back into the 2 Sm 15:25
Abiathar carried the **a** of God back 2 Sm 15:29
because you carried the **a** of the Lord 1 Kgs 2:26
and stood before the **a** of the covenant 1 Kgs 3:15
to set there the **a** of the covenant of 1 Kgs 6:19
to bring up the **a** of the covenant of the 1 Kgs 8:1
came, and the priests took up the **a**. 1 Kgs 8:3

And they brought up the **a** of the LORD, 1 Kgs 8:4
him, were with him before the **a**, 1 Kgs 8:5
priests brought the **a** of the covenant 1 Kgs 8:6
out their wings over the place of the **a**, 1 Kgs 8:7
cherubim overshadowed the **a** and its 1 Kgs 8:7
was nothing in the **a** except the two 1 Kgs 8:9
there I have provided a place for the **a**, 1 Kgs 8:21
of the LORD after the **a** rested there. 1 Chr 6:31
let us bring again the **a** of our God to 1 Chr 13:3
to bring the **a** of God from 1 Chr 13:5
to bring up from there the **a** of God, 1 Chr 13:6
And they carried the **a** of God on a 1 Chr 13:7
put out his hand to take hold of the **a**, 1 Chr 13:9
he put out his hand to the **a**, 1 Chr 13:10
can I bring the **a** of God home to 1 Chr 13:12
did not take the **a** home into the city 1 Chr 13:13
And the **a** of God remained with the 1 Chr 13:14
a place for the **a** of God and pitched 1 Chr 15:1
the Levites may carry the **a** of God, 1 Chr 15:2
them to carry the **a** of the LORD and 1 Chr 15:2
to bring up the **a** of the LORD to 1 Chr 15:3
you may bring up the **a** of the LORD, 1 Chr 15:12
to bring up the **a** of the LORD, 1 Chr 15:14
the Levites carried the **a** of God on 1 Chr 15:15
were to be gatekeepers for the **a**. 1 Chr 15:23
the trumpets before the **a** of God. 1 Chr 15:24
were to be gatekeepers for the **a**. 1 Chr 15:24
to bring up the **a** of the covenant of 1 Chr 15:25
were carrying the **a** of the covenant 1 Chr 15:26
the Levites who were carrying the **a**, 1 Chr 15:27
brought up the **a** of the covenant 1 Chr 15:28
And as the **a** of the covenant of the 1 Chr 15:29
they brought in the **a** of God and set 1 Chr 16:1
as ministers before the **a** of the LORD, 1 Chr 16:4
regularly before the **a** of the covenant 1 Chr 16:6
there before the **a** of the covenant 1 Chr 16:37
regularly before the **a** as each day 1 Chr 16:37
but the **a** of the covenant of the LORD 1 Chr 17:1
so that the **a** of the covenant of the 1 Chr 22:19
of rest for the **a** of the covenant of 1 Chr 28:2
and covered the **a** of the covenant 1 Chr 28:18
had brought up the **a** of God from 2 Chr 1:4
to bring up the **a** of the covenant of the 2 Chr 5:2
came, and the Levites took up the **a**. 2 Chr 5:4
And they brought up the **a**, the tent of 2 Chr 5:5
before him, were before the **a**, 2 Chr 5:6
priests brought the **a** of the covenant 2 Chr 5:7
out their wings over the place of the **a**, 2 Chr 5:8
a covering above the **a** and its poles. 2 Chr 5:8
was nothing in the **a** except the two 2 Chr 5:10
And there I have set the **a**, in which is 2 Chr 6:11
place, you and the **a** of your might. 2 Chr 6:41
places to which the **a** of the LORD has 2 Chr 8:11
"Put the holy **a** in the house that 2 Chr 35:3
place, you and the **a** of your might. Ps 132:8
"The **a** of the covenant of the LORD." It Jer 3:16
until the day when Noah entered the **a**, Mt 24:38
until the day when Noah entered the **a**, Lk 17:27
of incense and the **a** of the covenant Heb 9:4
fear constructed an **a** for the saving Heb 11:7
Noah, while the **a** was being prepared, 1 Pt 3:20
and the **a** of his covenant was seen Rv 11:19

ARKITES (2)
the Hivites, the **A**, the Sinites, Gn 10:17
the Hivites, the **A**, the Sinites, 1 Chr 1:15

ARM (70)
you with an outstretched **a** and with great Ex 6:6
because of the greatness of your **a**, they Ex 15:16
"**A** men from among you for the war, Nm 31:3
by a mighty hand and an outstretched **a**, Dt 4:34
a mighty hand and an outstretched **a**. Dt 5:15
the mighty hand, and the outstretched **a**, Dt 7:19
great power and by your outstretched **a**.' Dt 9:29
his mighty hand and his outstretched **a**, Dt 11:2
a mighty hand and an outstretched **a**, Dt 26:8
like a lion; he tears off **a** and scalp. Dt 33:20
head and the armlet that was on his **a**, 2 Sm 1:10
hand, and of your outstretched **a**), 1 Kgs 8:42
to worship there, leaning on my **a**, 2 Kgs 5:18
power and with an outstretched **a**. 2 Kgs 17:36
hand and your outstretched **a**, 2 Chr 6:32
of the seat were **a** rests and two lions 2 Chr 9:18
two lions standing beside the **a** rests, 2 Chr 9:18
With him is an **a** of flesh, but with 2 Chr 32:8
you have saved the **a** that has no Jb 26:2
and let my **a** be broken from its socket. Jb 31:22
for help because of the **a** of the mighty. Jb 35:9
withheld, and their uplifted **a** is broken. Jb 38:15
Have you an **a** like God, and can you Jb 40:9
Break the **a** of the wicked and evildoer; Ps 10:15
the land, nor did their own **a** save them, Ps 44:3
them, but your right hand and your **a**, Ps 44:3
You with your **a** redeemed your people, Ps 77:15
they are the strong **a** of the children of Ps 83:8
your enemies with your mighty **a**. Ps 89:10
You have a mighty **a**; strong is your Ps 89:13
him; my **a** also shall strengthen him. Ps 89:21
and his holy **a** have worked salvation Ps 98:1
a strong hand and an outstretched **a**, Ps 136:12
upon your heart, as a seal upon your **a**, Sg 8:6
each devours the flesh of his own **a**, Is 9:20
grain and his **a** harvests the ears, Is 17:5
the descending blow of his **a** to be seen, Is 30:30
Battling with brandished **a**, he will fight Is 30:32
we wait for you. Be our **a** every morning, Is 33:2
with might, and his **a** rules for him; Is 40:10
and works it with his strong **a**. Is 44:12
and his **a** shall be against the Is 48:14
hope for me, and for my **a** they wait. Is 51:5
awake, put on strength, O **a** of the LORD; Is 51:9
has bared his holy **a** before the eyes of Is 52:10
And to whom has the **a** of the LORD been Is 53:1
then his own **a** brought him salvation, Is 59:16
by his right hand and by his mighty **a**: Is 62:8
so my own **a** brought me salvation, Is 63:5
who caused his glorious **a** to go at the Is 63:12
with outstretched hand and strong **a**, Jer 21:5
and my outstretched **a** have made the Jer 27:5
power and by your outstretched **a**! Jer 32:17
with a strong hand and outstretched **a**, Jer 32:21
of Moab is cut off, and his **a** is broken, Jer 48:25
the siege of Jerusalem, with your **a** bared, Ezk 4:7
not take a strong **a** or many people to Ezk 17:9
and an outstretched **a** and with wrath Ezk 20:33
a mighty hand and an outstretched **a**, Ezk 20:34
I have broken the **a** of Pharaoh king Ezk 30:21
both the strong **a** and the one that was Ezk 30:22
yes, those who were its **a**, who lived Ezk 31:17
she shall not retain the strength of her **a**, Dn 11:6
arm, and he and his **a** shall not endure, Dn 11:6
the sword strike his **a** and his right Zec 11:17
Let his **a** be wholly withered, his right Zec 11:17
He has shown strength with his **a**; he Lk 1:51
and to whom has the **a** of the Lord been Jn 12:38
and with uplifted **a** he led them out of Acts 13:17
a yourselves with the same way of 1 Pt 4:1

ARMAGEDDON (1)
at the place that in Hebrew is called **A**. Rv 16:16

ARMED (32)
each tribe, twelve thousand **a** for war. Nm 31:5
and every **a** man of you will pass over Nm 32:21
pass over, every man who is **a** for war, Nm 32:27
every man who is **a** to battle before Nm 32:29
if they will not pass over with you **a**, Nm 32:30
We will pass over **a** before the LORD Nm 32:32
shall cross over **a** before your brothers, Dt 3:18
shall pass over **a** before your brothers Jos 1:14
Manasseh passed over **a** before the Jos 4:12
the city and let the **a** men pass on before Jos 6:7
The **a** men were walking before the Jos 6:9
And the **a** men were walking before Jos 6:13
to the outposts of the **a** men who were in Jgs 7:11
the tribe of Dan, **a** with weapons of war, Jgs 18:11
Danites, **a** with their weapons of war, Jgs 18:16
with the 600 men **a** with weapons of Jgs 18:17
and he was **a** with a coat of mail, 1 Sm 17:5
and who was **a** with a new sword, 2 Sm 21:16
divisions of the **a** troops who came 1 Chr 12:23
shield and spear were 6,800 **a** troops. 1 Chr 12:24
were 37,000 men **a** with shield and 1 Chr 12:34
120,000 men **a** with all the weapons 1 Chr 12:37
a with large shields and spears, 2 Chr 14:8
with 200,000 men **a** with bow and 2 Chr 17:17
Jehozabad with 180,000 **a** for war. 2 Chr 17:18
So the **a** men left the captives and 2 Chr 28:14
and to annihilate any **a** force of any Est 8:11
The Ephraimites, **a** with the bow, turned Ps 78:9
like a robber, and want like an **a** man. Prv 6:11
like a robber, and want like an **a** man. Prv 24:34
therefore the **a** men of Moab cry aloud; Is 15:4
When a strong man, fully **a**, guards Lk 11:21

ARMIES (20)
with all their **a** and encamped against Jos 10:5
Philistines gathered their **a** for battle. 1 Sm 17:1
he should defy the **a** of the living 1 Sm 17:26
he has defied the **a** of the living God." 1 Sm 17:36
of hosts, the God of the **a** of Israel, 1 Sm 17:45
Keilah against the **a** of the 1 Sm 23:3
the two commanders of the **a** of Israel, 1 Kgs 2:5
commanders of his **a** against the 1 Kgs 15:20
commanders of his **a** against the 2 Chr 16:4
Is there any number to his **a**? Upon Jb 25:3
us and have not gone out with our **a**. Ps 44:9
You do not go forth, O God, with our **a**. Ps 60:10
"The kings of the **a**—they flee, they Ps 68:12
You do not go out, O God, with our **a**. Ps 108:11
as upon a dance before two **a**? Sg 6:13
A shall be utterly swept away before Dn 11:22
you see Jerusalem surrounded by **a**, Lk 21:20
mighty in war, put foreign **a** to flight. Heb 11:34
And the **a** of heaven, arrayed in fine Rv 19:14
the earth with their **a** gathered to make Rv 19:19

ARMLET (1)
on his head and the **a** that was on his 2 Sm 1:10

ARMLETS (3)
and earrings and signet rings and **a**, Ex 35:22
articles of gold, **a** and bracelets, Nm 31:50
the headdresses, the **a**, the sashes, the Is 3:20

ARMONI (1)
bore to Saul, **A** and Mephibosheth; 2 Sm 21:8

ARMOR (25)
to the young man who carried his **a**, 1 Sm 14:1
to the young man who carried his **a**, 1 Sm 14:6
And he had bronze **a** on his legs, and 1 Sm 17:6
Then Saul clothed David with his **a**. 1 Sm 17:38
David strapped his sword over his **a**. 1 Sm 17:39
but he put his **a** in his tent. 1 Sm 17:54
him and gave it to David, and his **a**, 1 Sm 18:4
stripped off his **a** and sent messengers 1 Sm 31:9
They put his **a** in the temple of 1 Sm 31:10
straps on his **a** boast himself like 1 Kgs 20:11
between the scale **a** and the 1 Kgs 22:34
them, all who were able to put on **a**, 2 Kgs 3:21
him and took his head and his **a**, 1 Chr 10:9
And they put his **a** in the temple of 1 Chr 10:10
between the scale **a** and the 2 Chr 18:33
strap on your **a** and be shattered; Is 8:9
shattered; strap on your **a** and be shattered. Is 8:9
polish your spears, put on your **a**! Jer 46:4
bow, and let him not stand up in his **a**. Jer 51:3
warriors clothed in full **a**, Ezk 23:12
horsemen, all of them clothed in full **a**, Ezk 38:4
he takes away his **a** in which he trusted Lk 11:22
of darkness and put on the **a** of light. Rom 13:12
Put on the whole **a** of God, that you Eph 6:11
Therefore take up the whole **a** of God, Eph 6:13

ARMOR-BEARER (18)
to the young man his **a** and said to him, Jgs 9:54
And his **a** said to him, "Do all that is 1 Sm 14:7
hailed Jonathan and his **a** and said, 1 Sm 14:12
a thing." And Jonathan said to his **a**, 1 Sm 14:12
hands and feet, and his **a** after him. 1 Sm 14:13
and his **a** killed them after him. 1 Sm 14:13
which Jonathan and his **a** made, 1 Sm 14:14
Jonathan and his **a** were not there. 1 Sm 14:17
him greatly, and he became his **a**. 1 Sm 16:21
Then Saul said to his **a**, "Draw your 1 Sm 31:4
mistreat me." But his **a** would not, 1 Sm 31:4
And when his **a** saw that Saul was 1 Sm 31:5
died, and his three sons, and his **a**, 1 Sm 31:6
the **a** of Joab the son of Zeruiah, 2 Sm 23:37
Then Saul said to his **a**, "Draw your 1 Chr 10:4
mistreat me." But his **a** would not, 1 Chr 10:4
And when his **a** saw that Saul was 1 Chr 10:5
the **a** of Joab the son of Zeruiah, 1 Chr 11:39

ARMOR-BEARERS (1)
And ten young men, Joab's **a**, 2 Sm 18:15

ARMORY (4)
the spices, the precious oil, his **a**, 2 Kgs 20:13
the ascent to the **a** at the buttress. Neh 3:19
the spices, the precious oil, his whole **a**, Is 39:2
LORD has opened his **a** and brought out Jer 50:25

ARMPITS (1)
clothes between your **a** and the ropes." Jer 38:12

ARMRESTS (2)
of the seat were **a** and two lions 1 Kgs 10:19
and two lions standing beside the **a**, 1 Kgs 10:19

ARMS (40)
bracelets for her **a** weighing ten gold Gn 24:22
ring and the bracelets on his sister's **a**, Gn 24:30
on her nose and the bracelets on her **a**. Gn 24:47
his **a** were made agile by the hands of Gn 49:24
but we will take up **a**, ready to go Nm 32:17
if you will take up **a** to go before the Nm 32:20
and underneath are the everlasting **a**. Dt 33:27
Then the Ammonites were called to **a**, Jgs 10:17
The men of Ephraim were called to **a**, Jgs 12:1
that were on his **a** became as flax that Jgs 15:14
the ropes off his **a** like a thread. Jgs 16:12
drink from his cup and lie in his **a**, 2 Sm 12:3
wives into your **a** and gave you 2 Sm 12:8
so that my **a** can bend a bow of 2 Sm 22:35
who touches them **a** himself with 2 Sm 23:7
Let her lie in your **a**, that my lord the 1 Kgs 1:2
him from her **a** and carried him 1 Kgs 17:19
and the **a** of the fatherless were crushed. Jb 22:9
so that my **a** can bend a bow of bronze. Ps 18:34
For the **a** of the wicked shall be broken, Ps 37:17
hand nor the binder of sheaves his **a**, Ps 129:7

with strength and makes her **a** strong. Prv 31:17
His **a** are rods of gold, set with jewels. His Sg 5:14
he will gather the lambs in his **a**; Is 40:11
gone out, and my **a** will judge the peoples; Is 51:5
and I will tear them from your **a**, Ezk 13:20
king of Egypt and will break his **a**, Ezk 30:22
I will strengthen the **a** of the king of Ezk 30:24
but I will break the **a** of Pharaoh, Ezk 30:24
I will strengthen the **a** of the king of Ezk 30:25
but the **a** of Pharaoh shall fall. Ezk 30:25
was of fine gold, its chest and **a** of silver, Dn 2:32
his **a** and legs like the gleam of Dn 10:6
I trained and strengthened their **a**, Hos 7:15
I took them up by their **a**, but they did Hos 11:3
your mouth from her who lies in your **a**; Mi 7:5
midst of them, and taking him in his **a**, Mk 9:36
took them in his **a** and blessed them, Mk 10:16
him up in his **a** and blessed God and Lk 2:28
over him, and taking him in his **a**, Acts 20:10

ARMY (189)
commander of his **a** said to Abraham, Gn 21:22
the commander of his **a** rose up and Gn 21:32
and Phicol the commander of his **a**, Gn 26:26
his chariot and took his **a** with him, Ex 14:6
chariots and his horsemen and his **a**, Ex 14:9
them with a large **a** and with a strong Nm 20:20
was angry with the officers of the **a**, Nm 31:14
to the men in the **a** who had gone to Nm 31:21
the spoil that the **a** took was 675,000 Nm 31:32
of those who had gone out in the **a**, Nm 31:36
of the men who had served in the **a**— Nm 31:42
who were over the thousands of the **a**, Nm 31:48
(The men in the **a** had each taken Nm 31:53
and what he did to the **a** of Egypt, to their Dt 11:4
and chariots and an **a** larger than your Dt 20:1
not go out with the **a** or be liable for any Dt 24:5
am the commander of the **a** of the LORD. Jos 5:14
of the LORD'S **a** said to Joshua, Jos 5:15
The commander of his **a** was Sisera, who Jgs 4:2
draw out Sisera, the general of Jabin's **a**, Jgs 4:7
chariots and all his **a** before Barak by Jgs 4:15
and the **a** to Harosheth-hagoyim, Jgs 4:16
and all the **a** of Sisera fell by the edge of Jgs 4:16
around the camp, and all the **a** ran. Jgs 7:21
his comrade and against all the **a**. Jgs 7:22
And the **a** fled as far as Beth-shittah Jgs 7:22
that we should give bread to your **a**?" Jgs 8:6
Zalmunna were in Karkor with their **a**, Jgs 8:10
were left of all the **a** of the people of the Jgs 8:10
and Jogbehah and attacked the **a**, Jgs 8:11
attacked the army, for the **a** felt secure. Jgs 8:11
and he threw all the **a** into a panic. Jgs 8:12
say to Abimelech, 'Increase your **a**, Jgs 9:29
all the people of Israel, the whole **a**, Jgs 20:26
Sisera, commander of the **a** of Hazor, 1 Sm 12:9
went up after Saul to meet the **a**; 1 Sm 13:15
commander of his **a** was Abner the 1 Sm 14:50
drew up for battle, **a** against army. 1 Sm 17:21
drew up for battle, army against **a**. 1 Sm 17:21
to Abner, the commander of the **a**, 1 Sm 17:55
son of Ner, the commander of his **a**. 1 Sm 26:5
while the **a** was encamped around 1 Sm 26:5
and Abishai went to the **a** by night. 1 Sm 26:7
and Abner and the **a** lay around him. 1 Sm 26:7
And David called to the **a**, and to 1 Sm 26:14
men are to go out with me in the **a**." 1 Sm 28:1
Saul saw the **a** of the Philistines, 1 Sm 28:5
LORD will give the **a** of Israel also into 1 Sm 28:19
the son of Ner, commander of Saul's **a**, 2 Sm 2:8
Joab and all the **a** that was with him 2 Sm 3:23
strike down the **a** of the Philistines." 2 Sm 5:24
had defeated the whole **a** of Hadadezer, 2 Sm 8:9
the son of Zeruiah was over the **a**, 2 Sm 8:16
commander of the **a** of Hadadezer at 2 Sm 10:16
Shobach the commander of their **a**, 2 Sm 10:18
set Amasa over the **a** instead of Joab. 2 Sm 17:25
And David sent out the **a**, one third 2 Sm 18:2
while all the **a** marched out by 2 Sm 18:4
So the **a** went out into the field against 2 Sm 18:6
commander of my **a** from now on 2 Sm 19:13
in command of all the **a** of Israel; 2 Sm 20:23
said to Joab, the commander of the **a**, 2 Sm 24:2
Joab and the commanders of the **a**. 2 Sm 24:4
commanders of the **a** went out from 2 Sm 24:4
and Joab the commander of the **a**, 1 Kgs 1:19
king's sons, the commanders of the **a**, 1 Kgs 1:25
of Ner, commander of the **a** of Israel, 1 Kgs 2:32
Jether, commander of the **a** of Judah. 1 Kgs 2:32
of Jehoiada over the **a** in place of Joab, 1 Kgs 2:35
of Jehoiada was in command of the **a**; 1 Kgs 4:4
the commander of the **a** went up to 1 Kgs 11:15
the commander of the **a** was dead, 1 Kgs 11:21
Omri, the commander of the **a**, 1 Kgs 16:16
of Syria gathered all his **a** together. 1 Kgs 20:1
districts and the **a** that followed 1 Kgs 20:19
and muster an **a** like the army that 1 Kgs 20:25
an army like the **a** that you have 1 Kgs 20:25
sunset a cry went through the **a**, 1 Kgs 22:36
no water for the **a** or for the animals 2 Kgs 3:9
commander of the **a**?'" She answered, 2 Kgs 4:13
commander of the **a** of the king of 2 Kgs 5:1
horses and chariots and a great **a**, 2 Kgs 6:14
an **a** with horses and chariots was all 2 Kgs 6:15
mustered his entire **a** and went up 2 Kgs 6:24
Lord had made the **a** of the Syrians 2 Kgs 7:6
and of horses, the sound of a great **a**, 2 Kgs 7:6
sent them after the **a** of the Syrians, 2 Kgs 7:14
surrounded him, but his **a** fled home. 2 Kgs 8:21
commanders of the **a** were in council. 2 Kgs 9:5
the captains who were set over the **a**, 2 Kgs 11:15
left to Jehoahaz an **a** of more than 2 Kgs 13:7
with a great **a** from Lachish to 2 Kgs 18:17
with all his **a** against Jerusalem and 2 Kgs 25:1
But the **a** of the Chaldeans pursued 2 Kgs 25:5
and all his **a** was scattered from him. 2 Kgs 25:5
And all the **a** of the Chaldeans, who 2 Kgs 25:10
commander of the **a** who mustered 2 Kgs 25:19
houses, were units of the **a** for war, 1 Chr 7:4
valley saw that the **a** had fled and 1 Chr 10:7
when the **a** of Philistines was 1 Chr 11:15
These Gadites were officers of the **a**; 1 Chr 12:14
and were commanders in the **a**. 1 Chr 12:21
help him, until there was a great **a**, 1 Chr 12:22
was a great army, like an **a** of God. 1 Chr 12:22
strike down the **a** of the Philistines." 1 Chr 14:15
down the Philistine **a** from Gibeon 1 Chr 14:16
defeated the whole **a** of Hadadezer, 1 Chr 18:9
the son of Zeruiah was over the **a**; 1 Chr 18:15
and the king of Maacah with his **a**, 1 Chr 19:7
Joab and all the **a** of the mighty men. 1 Chr 19:8
commander of the **a** of Hadadezer at 1 Chr 19:16
the commander of their **a**. 1 Chr 19:18
Joab led out the **a** and ravaged the 1 Chr 20:1
to Joab and the commanders of the **a**, 1 Chr 21:2
commanders of the **a** had dedicated. 1 Chr 26:26
was commander of the king's **a**. 1 Chr 27:34
having an **a** of valiant men of war, 2 Chr 13:3
And Asa had an **a** of 300,000 from 2 Chr 14:8
against them with an **a** of a million 2 Chr 14:9
broken before the LORD and his **a**. 2 Chr 14:13
the **a** of the king of Syria has escaped 2 Chr 16:7
the Libyans a huge **a** with very many 2 Chr 16:8
holy attire, as they went before the **a**, 2 Chr 20:21
the captains who were set over the **a**, 2 Chr 23:14
of the year the **a** of the Syrians came 2 Chr 24:23
Though the **a** of the Syrians had 2 Chr 24:24
into their hand a very great **a**, 2 Chr 24:24
do not let the **a** of Israel go with you, 2 Chr 25:7
have given to the **a** of Israel?" The 2 Chr 25:9
Amaziah discharged the **a** that had 2 Chr 25:10
men of the **a** whom Amaziah sent 2 Chr 25:13
Uzziah had an **a** of soldiers, 2 Chr 26:11
their command was an **a** of 307,500, 2 Chr 26:13
Uzziah prepared for all the **a** shields, 2 Chr 26:14
out to meet the **a** that came to 2 Chr 28:9
the commanders of the **a** of the king 2 Chr 33:11
put commanders of the **a** in all the 2 Chr 33:14
with me officers of the **a** and horsemen. Neh 2:9
of his brothers and of the **a** of Samaria, Neh 4:2
The **a** of Persia and Media and the nobles Est 1:3
Though an **a** encamp against me, my Ps 27:3
The king is not saved by his great **a**; a Ps 33:16
and a king whose **a** is with him. Prv 30:31
Jerusalem, awesome as an **a** with banners. Sg 6:4
the sun, awesome as an **a** with banners?" Sg 6:10
Hezekiah at Jerusalem, with a great **a**. Is 36:2
forth chariot and horse, **a** and warrior; Is 43:17
At that time the **a** of the king of Babylon Jer 32:2
Babylon and all his **a** and all the Jer 34:1
when the **a** of the king of Babylon was Jer 34:7
into the hand of the **a** of the king of Jer 34:21
for fear of the **a** of the Chaldeans and Jer 35:11
the Chaldeans and the **a** of the Syrians.' Jer 35:11
The **a** of Pharaoh had come out of Jer 37:5
Pharaoh's **a** that came to help you is Jer 37:7
defeat the whole **a** of Chaldeans who Jer 37:10
when the Chaldean **a** had withdrawn Jer 37:11
at the approach of Pharaoh's **a**, Jer 37:11
into the hand of the **a** of the king of Jer 38:3
and all his **a** came against Jerusalem Jer 39:1
But the **a** of the Chaldeans pursued them Jer 39:5
Concerning the **a** of Pharaoh Neco, Jer 46:2
men; devote to destruction all her **a**. Jer 51:3
came with all his **a** against Jerusalem, Jer 52:4
But the **a** of the Chaldeans pursued the Jer 52:8
And all his **a** was scattered from him. Jer 52:8
And all the **a** of the Chaldeans, who Jer 52:14
commander of the **a** who mustered the Jer 52:25
sound of tumult like the sound of an **a**. Ezk 1:24
might give him horses and a large **a**. Ezk 17:15
with his mighty **a** and great company Ezk 17:17
and Put were in your **a** as your men of Ezk 27:10
Babylon made his **a** labor hard Ezk 29:18
he nor his **a** got anything from Ezk 29:18
it; and it shall be the wages for his **a**. Ezk 29:19
his multitude, Pharaoh and all his **a**, Ezk 32:31
on their feet, an exceedingly great **a**. Ezk 37:10
and I will bring you out, and all your **a**, Ezk 38:4
on horses, a great host, a mighty **a**. Ezk 38:15
mighty men of his **a** to bind Shadrach, Dn 3:20
shall come against the **a** and enter the Dn 11:7
with a great **a** and abundant supplies. Dn 11:13
the king of the south with a great **a**. Dn 11:25
an exceedingly great and mighty **a**, Dn 11:25
His **a** shall be swept away, and many Dn 11:26
like a powerful **a** drawn up for battle. Jl 2:5
The LORD utters his voice before his **a**, for Jl 2:11
the destroyer, and the cutter, my great **a**, Jl 2:25
sitting on the horse and against his **a**. Rv 19:19

ARNAN (1)
his son Rephaiah, his son **A**, 1 Chr 3:21

ARNI (1)
the son of Admin, the son of **A**, Lk 3:33

ARNON (25)
and camped on the other side of the **A**, Nm 21:13
for the **A** is the border of Moab, Nm 21:13
in Suphah, and the valleys of the **A**, Nm 21:14
of his land from the **A** to the Jabbok, Nm 21:24
land out of his hand, as far as the **A**. Nm 21:26
and swallowed the heights of the **A**. Nm 21:28
Moab, on the border formed by the **A**, Nm 22:36
journey and go over the Valley of the **A**. Dt 2:24
is on the edge of the Valley of the **A**, Dt 2:36
the Valley of the **A** to Mount Hermon Dt 3:8
is on the edge of the Valley of the **A**, Dt 3:12
from Gilead as far as the Valley of the **A**, Dt 3:16
is on the edge of the Valley of the **A**, Dt 4:48
the Valley of the **A** to Mount Hermon, Jos 12:1
is on the edge of the Valley of the **A**, Jos 12:2
is on the edge of the Valley of the **A**, Jos 13:9
is on the edge of the Valley of the **A**, Jos 13:16
from the **A** to the Jabbok and to the Jgs 11:13
and camped on the other side of the **A**. Jgs 11:18
for the **A** was the boundary of Moab. Jgs 11:18
the Amorites from the **A** to the Jabbok Jgs 11:22
cities that are on the banks of the **A**, Jgs 11:26
which is by the Valley of the **A**, 2 Kgs 10:33
daughters of Moab at the fords of the **A**. Is 16:2
Tell it beside the **A**, that Moab is laid Jer 48:20

AROD (1)
of **A**, the clan of the Arodites; of Areli, Nm 26:17

ARODI (1)
Haggi, Shuni, Ezbon, Eri, **A**, and Areli. Gn 46:16

ARODITES (1)
of Arod, the clan of the **A**; of Areli, the Nm 26:17

AROER (16)
people of Gad built Dibon, Ataroth, **A**, Nm 32:34
From **A**, which is on the edge of the Dt 2:36
the Gadites the territory beginning at **A**, Dt 3:12
from **A**, which is on the edge of the Dt 4:48
who lived at Heshbon and ruled from **A**, Jos 12:2
from **A**, which is on the edge of the Jos 13:9
So their territory was from **A**, which is Jos 13:16
half the land of the Ammonites, to **A**, Jos 13:25
its villages, and in **A** and its villages, Jgs 11:26
struck them from **A** to the Jgs 11:33
in **A**, in Siphmoth, in Eshtemoa, 1 Sm 30:28
crossed the Jordan and began from **A**, 2 Sm 24:5
and the Manassites, from **A**, 2 Kgs 10:33
of Shema, son of Joel, who lived in **A**, 1 Chr 5:8
The cities of **A** are deserted; they will be Is 17:2
the way and watch, O inhabitant of **A**! Jer 48:19

AROERITE (1)
and Jeiel the sons of Hotham the **A**, 1 Chr 11:44

AROMA (42)
when the LORD smelled the pleasing **a**, Gn 8:21
It is a pleasing **a**, a food offering to the Ex 29:18
offering, as a pleasing **a** before the LORD. Ex 29:25
as in the morning, for a pleasing **a**, Ex 29:41
food offering with a pleasing **a** to the LORD. Lv 1:9
offering with a pleasing **a** to the LORD. Lv 1:13
offering with a pleasing **a** to the LORD. Lv 1:17
food offering with a pleasing **a** to the LORD. Lv 2:2
food offering with a pleasing **a** to the LORD. Lv 2:9
be offered on the altar for a pleasing **a**. Lv 2:12
food offering with a pleasing **a** to the LORD. Lv 3:5
altar as a food offering with a pleasing **a**. Lv 3:16
on the altar for a pleasing **a** to the LORD. Lv 4:31
on the altar, a pleasing **a** to the LORD. Lv 6:15
and offer it for a pleasing **a** to the LORD. Lv 6:21
It was a burnt offering with a pleasing **a**, Lv 8:21

an ordination offering with a pleasing **a**, Lv 8:28
burn the fat for a pleasing **a** to the LORD. Lv 17:6
offering to the LORD with a pleasing **a**, Lv 23:13
offering with a pleasing **a** to the LORD. Lv 23:18
feasts, to make a pleasing **a** to the LORD, Nm 15:3
a hin of wine, a pleasing **a** to the LORD. Nm 15:7
food offering, a pleasing **a** to the LORD. Nm 15:10
offering, with a pleasing **a** to the LORD. Nm 15:13
offering, with a pleasing **a** to the LORD, Nm 15:14
offering, a pleasing **a** to the LORD, Nm 15:24
offering, with a pleasing **a** to the LORD. Nm 18:17
for my food offerings, my pleasing **a**, Nm 28:2
at Mount Sinai for a pleasing **a**, Nm 28:6
offering, with a pleasing **a** to the LORD. Nm 28:8
for a burnt offering with a pleasing **a**, Nm 28:13
offering, with a pleasing **a** to the LORD. Nm 28:24
offering, with a pleasing **a** to the LORD: Nm 28:27
offering, for a pleasing **a** to the LORD: Nm 29:2
to the rule for them, for a pleasing **a**, Nm 29:6
burnt offering to the LORD, a pleasing **a**: Nm 29:8
offering, with a pleasing **a** to the LORD, Nm 29:13
offering, with a pleasing **a** to the LORD: Nm 29:36
they offered pleasing **a** to all their Ezk 6:13
—you set before them for a pleasing **a**; Ezk 16:19
As a pleasing **a** I will accept you, when Ezk 20:41
For we are the **a** of Christ to God 2 Cor 2:15

AROMAS (2)
and I will not smell your pleasing **a**. Lv 26:31
there they sent up their pleasing **a**, and Ezk 20:28

AROMATIC (1)
as much, that is, 250, and 250 of **a** cane, Ex 30:23

AROSE (132)
when she lay down or when she **a**. Gn 19:33
And the younger **a** and lay with him, Gn 19:35
when she lay down or when she **a**. Gn 19:35
the burnt offering and **a** and went to the Gn 22:3
and they **a** and went together to Gn 22:19
and he **a** and went to Mesopotamia to Gn 24:10
When they **a** in the morning, he said, Gn 24:54
and her young women **a** and rode on Gn 24:61
So Jacob **a** and set his sons and his Gn 31:17
that he had and **a** and crossed the Gn 31:21
in the morning Laban **a** and kissed his Gn 31:55
The same night he **a** and took his two Gn 32:22
behold, my sheaf **a** and stood upright. Gn 37:7
Then she **a** and went away, and taking Gn 38:19
They **a** and went down to Egypt and Gn 43:15
Now there **a** a new king over Egypt, who Ex 1:8
and all the fighting men **a** to go up to Ai. Jos 8:3
Joshua **a** early in the morning and Jos 8:10
So the men **a** and went, and Joshua Jos 18:8
of Moab, **a** and fought against Israel. Jos 24:9
And there **a** another generation after Jgs 2:10
God for you." And he **a** from his seat. Jgs 3:20
woman." Then Deborah **a** and went with Jgs 4:9
ceased in Israel; they ceased to be until I **a**; Jgs 5:7
I arose; I, Deborah, **a** as a mother in Israel. Jgs 5:7
strength." And Gideon **a** and killed Jgs 8:21
After Abimelech there **a** to save Israel Jgs 10:1
After him **a** Jair the Gileadite, who Jgs 10:3
And Manoah **a** and went after his wife Jgs 13:11
and at midnight he **a** and took hold of Jgs 16:3
Then her husband **a** and went after her, Jgs 19:3
the fourth day they **a** early in the Jgs 19:5
the fifth day he **a** early in the morning Jgs 19:8
And all the people **a** as one man, saying, Jgs 20:8
The people of Israel **a** and went up to Jgs 20:18
Then she **a** with her daughters-in-law to Ru 1:6
but **a** before one could recognize Ru 3:14
"Samuel!" and Samuel **a** and went to 1 Sm 3:6
And he **a** and went to Eli and said, 1 Sm 3:8
send you on your way." So Saul **a**, 1 Sm 9:26
And Samuel **a** and went up from 1 Sm 13:15
And if he **a** against me, I caught him 1 Sm 17:35
When the Philistine **a** and came and 1 Sm 17:48
David **a** and went, along with his 1 Sm 18:27
a and departed from Keilah, 1 Sm 23:13
And they **a** and went to Ziph ahead 1 Sm 23:24
you.'" Then David **a** and stealthily cut 1 Sm 24:4
Afterward David also **a** and went out 1 Sm 24:8
So Saul **a** and went down to the 1 Sm 26:2
So David **a** and went over, he and the 1 Sm 27:2
So he **a** from the earth and sat on the 1 Sm 28:23
all the valiant men **a** and went all 1 Sm 31:12
Then they **a** and passed over by 2 Sm 2:15
And David **a** and went with all the 2 Sm 6:2
when David **a** from his couch and 2 Sm 11:2
Then David **a** from the earth and 2 Sm 12:20
the child died, you **a** and ate food." 2 Sm 12:21
Then all the king's sons **a**, and each 2 Sm 13:29
Then the king **a** and tore his 2 Sm 13:31
So Joab **a** and went to Geshur and 2 Sm 14:23
Then Joab **a** and went to Absalom at 2 Sm 14:31
in peace." So he **a** and went to Hebron. 2 Sm 15:9
Then David **a**, and all the people who 2 Sm 17:22
Then the king **a** and took his seat in 2 Sm 19:8
And when David **a** in the morning, 2 Sm 24:11
So he **a** and went and took hold of the 1 Kgs 1:50
Shimei **a** and saddled a donkey and 1 Kgs 2:40
And she **a** at midnight and took my 1 Kgs 3:20
he **a** from before the altar of the LORD, 1 Kgs 8:54
But Jeroboam **a** and fled into Egypt, 1 Kgs 11:40
She **a** and went to Shiloh and came to 1 Kgs 14:4
Jeroboam's wife **a** and departed 1 Kgs 14:17
So he **a** and went to Zarephath. And 1 Kgs 17:10
and he **a** and ran for his life and 1 Kgs 19:3
And he **a** and ate and drank, and 1 Kgs 19:8
Then he **a** and went after Elijah and 1 Kgs 19:21
Ahab **a** to go down to the vineyard 1 Kgs 21:16
of him." So he **a** and went down with 2 Kgs 1:15
leave you." So he **a** and followed her. 2 Kgs 4:30
So they **a** at twilight to go to the camp 2 Kgs 7:5
So the woman **a** and did according to 2 Kgs 8:2
So he **a** and went into the house. And 2 Kgs 9:6
she **a** and destroyed all the royal 2 Kgs 11:1
His servants **a** and made a 2 Kgs 12:20
And when people **a** early in the 2 Kgs 19:35
captains of the forces **a** and went to 2 Kgs 25:26
all the valiant men **a** and took away 1 Chr 10:12
And after this there **a** war with the 1 Chr 20:4
she **a** and destroyed all the royal 2 Chr 22:10
Then the Levites **a**, Mahath the son 2 Chr 29:12
and the Levites **a** and blessed the 2 Chr 30:27
Then **a** Jeshua the son of Jozadak, with Ezr 3:2
the son of Jozadak **a** and began to rebuild Ezr 5:2
Then Ezra **a** and made the leading Ezr 10:5
Then I **a** in the night, I and a few men Neh 2:12
And I looked and **a** and said to the Neh 4:14
Now there **a** a great outcry of the people Neh 5:1
And the king **a** in his wrath from the Est 7:7
Then Job **a** and tore his robe and shaved Jb 1:20
when God **a** to establish judgment, to Ps 76:9
I **a** to open to my beloved, and my hands Sg 5:5
And when people **a** early in the Is 37:36
the elders of the land **a** and spoke to all Jer 26:17
So I **a** and went out into the valley, and Ezk 3:23
the king **a** and went in haste to the den Dn 6:19
broken, in place of which four others **a**, Dn 8:22
So Jonah **a** and went to Nineveh, Jon 3:3
of Nineveh, and he **a** from his throne, Jon 3:6
behold, there **a** a great storm on the sea, Mt 8:24
and took her by the hand, and the girl **a**. Mt 9:25
And a great windstorm **a**, and the waves Mk 4:37
And from there he **a** and went away to Mk 7:24
by the hand and lifted him up, and he **a**. Mk 9:27
In those days Mary **a** and went with Lk 1:39
And he **a** and left the synagogue and Lk 4:38
And when a flood **a**, the stream broke Lk 6:48
An argument **a** among them as to Lk 9:46
a severe famine **a** in that country, Lk 15:14
And he **a** and came to his father. But Lk 15:20
A dispute also **a** among them, as to Lk 22:24
company of them **a** and brought him Lk 23:1
Now a discussion **a** between some of Jn 3:25
by the Hellenists **a** against the Hebrews Acts 6:1
until there **a** over Egypt another king Acts 7:18
And there **a** on that day a great Acts 8:1
the persecution that **a** over Stephen Acts 11:19
And there **a** a sharp disagreement, so Acts 15:39
that time there **a** no little disturbance Acts 19:23
a dissension **a** between the Pharisees Acts 23:7
Then a great clamor **a**, and some of Acts 23:9
false prophets also **a** among the people, 2 Pt 2:1
Now war **a** in heaven, Michael and his Rv 12:7

AROUND (354)
is the one that flowed **a** the whole land of Gn 2:11
is the one that flowed **a** the whole land of Gn 2:13
fell upon the cities that were **a** them, Gn 35:5
your sheaves gathered **a** it and bowed Gn 37:7
every city the food from the fields **a** it. Gn 41:48
But God led the people **a** by the way of Ex 13:18
in the morning dew lay **a** the camp. Ex 16:13
the people stood **a** Moses from morning Ex 18:13
the people stand **a** you from morning Ex 18:14
you shall set limits for the people all **a**, Ex 19:12
'Set limits **a** the mountain and Ex 19:23
shall make on it a molding of gold **a** it. Ex 25:11
gold and make a molding of gold **a** it. Ex 25:24
shall make a rim **a** it a handbreadth Ex 25:25
wide, and a molding of gold **a** the rim. Ex 25:25
All the pillars **a** the court shall be Ex 27:17
it, with a woven binding **a** the opening, Ex 28:32
and purple and scarlet yarns, **a** its hem, Ex 28:33
a pomegranate, **a** the hem of the robe. Ex 28:34
gold, its top and **a** its sides and its horns. Ex 30:3
you shall make a molding of gold **a** it. Ex 30:3
And all the sons of Levi gathered **a** him. Ex 32:26
outside, and made a molding of gold **a** it. Ex 37:2
gold, and made a molding of gold **a** it. Ex 37:11
he made a rim **a** it a handbreadth wide, Ex 37:12
and made a molding of gold **a** the rim. Ex 37:12
its top and **a** its sides and its horns. Ex 37:26
And he made a molding of gold **a** it, Ex 37:26
All the hangings **a** the court were of Ex 38:16
and for the court all **a** were of bronze. Ex 38:20
the bases **a** the court, and the bases of Ex 38:31
tabernacle, and all the pegs **a** the court. Ex 38:31
garment, with a binding **a** the opening, Ex 39:23
the pomegranates all **a** the hem of Ex 39:25
bell and a pomegranate **a** the hem of Ex 39:26
And you shall set up the court all **a**, and Ex 40:8
erected the court **a** the tabernacle and Ex 40:33
and tied the sash **a** his waist and clothed Lv 8:7
skillfully woven band of the ephod **a** him, Lv 8:7
coats and tied sashes **a** their waists and Lv 8:13
horns of the altar **a** it and purified the Lv 8:15
the inside of the house scraped all **a**, Lv 14:41
he shall tie the linen sash **a** his waist, Lv 16:4
and put it on the horns of the altar all **a**. Lv 16:18
You shall not go **a** as a slanderer Lv 19:16
that have no wall **a** them shall be Lv 25:31
from among the nations that are **a** you. Lv 25:44
of it and shall camp **a** the tabernacle. Nm 1:50
Levites shall camp **a** the tabernacle of Nm 1:53
the court that is **a** the tabernacle and Nm 3:26
also the pillars **a** the court, with their Nm 3:37
the court that is **a** the tabernacle and Nm 4:26
and the pillars **a** the court with their Nm 4:32
the people and placed them **a** the tent. Nm 11:24
journey on the other side, **a** the camp, Nm 11:31
out for themselves all **a** the camp. Nm 11:32
all Israel who were **a** them fled at their Nm 16:34
to the Red Sea, to go **a** the land of Edom. Nm 21:4
horde will now lick up all that is **a** us, Nm 22:4
land as defined by its borders all **a**." Nm 34:12
to the Levites pasturelands **a** the cities. Nm 35:2
city outward a thousand cubits all **a**. Nm 35:4
for many days we traveled **a** Mount Seir. Dt 2:1
have been traveling **a** this mountain Dt 2:3
the gods of the peoples who are **a** you, Dt 6:14
gives you rest from all your enemies **a**, Dt 12:10
of the gods of the peoples who are **a** you, Dt 13:7
me, like all the nations that are **a** me,' Dt 17:14
you rest from all your enemies **a** you, Dt 25:19
You shall march **a** the city, all the men of Jos 6:3
all the men of war going **a** the city once. Jos 6:3
day you shall march **a** the city seven Jos 6:4
March **a** the city and let the armed men Jos 6:7
day they marched **a** the city once, Jos 6:14
and marched **a** the city in the same Jos 6:15
day that they marched **a** the city seven Jos 6:15
the boundary bends **a** to Baalah (that Jos 15:9
the boundary bends **a** to Shikkeron Jos 15:11
This is the boundary **a** the people of Jos 15:12
boundary turns **a** toward Jos 16:6
clans, boundary by boundary all **a**. Jos 18:20
with all the villages **a** these cities as far Jos 19:8
Judah, along with the pasturelands **a** it. Jos 21:11
cities each had its pasturelands **a** it. Jos 21:42
the gods of the peoples who were **a** them, Jgs 2:12
man stood in his place **a** the camp, Jgs 7:21
the collars that were **a** the necks of their Jgs 8:26
fellows collected **a** Jephthah and Jgs 11:3
the wilderness and went **a** the land of Jgs 11:18
Dan, who turned **a** and said to Micah, Jgs 18:23
So Israel set men in ambush **a** Gibeah. Jgs 20:29
of Israel be brought **a** to Gath." So they 1 Sm 5:8
But after they had brought it **a**, the 1 Sm 5:9
"They have brought **a** to us the ark of 1 Sm 5:10
while the army was encamped **a** him. 1 Sm 26:5
and Abner and the army lay **a** him. 1 Sm 26:7
built the city all **a** from the Millo 2 Sm 5:9
go **a** to their rear, and come against 2 Sm 5:23
He made darkness **a** him his canopy, 2 Sm 22:12
and from Dan they went **a** to Sidon, 2 Sm 24:6
of war on the belt **a** his waist and on 1 Kgs 2:5
of the LORD and the wall **a** Jerusalem. 1 Kgs 3:1
And he had peace on all sides **a** him. 1 Kgs 4:24
running **a** the walls of the house, 1 Kgs 6:5
And he made side chambers all **a**. 1 Kgs 6:5
For **a** the outside of the house he made 1 Kgs 6:6
A all the walls of the house he carved 1 Kgs 6:29
had three courses of cut stone all **a**, 1 Kgs 7:12
in two rows **a** the one latticework 1 Kgs 7:18
pomegranates in two rows all **a**, 1 Kgs 7:20
ten cubits, compassing the sea all **a**. 1 Kgs 7:24
the space of each, with wreaths all **a**. 1 Kgs 7:36
the king turned **a** and blessed all 1 Kgs 8:14
And they limped **a** the altar that 1 Kgs 18:26
And the water ran **a** the altar and 1 Kgs 18:35
us put sackcloth **a** our waists and 1 Kgs 20:31
they tied sackcloth **a** their waists 1 Kgs 20:32
"Turn **a** and carry me out of the 1 Kgs 22:34
And he turned **a**, and when he saw 2 Kgs 2:24

horses and chariots was all **a** the city. 2 Kgs 6:15
and chariots of fire all **a** Elisha. 2 Kgs 6:17
Turn **a** and ride behind me." And the 2 Kgs 9:18
peace? Turn **a** and ride behind me." 2 Kgs 9:19
a the altar and the house on behalf 2 Kgs 11:11
he caused to go **a** the house of the 2 Kgs 16:18
the nations that were **a** them, 2 Kgs 17:15
at the cities of Judah and **a** Jerusalem; 2 Kgs 23:5
it. And they built siegeworks all **a** it. 2 Kgs 25:1
though the Chaldeans were **a** the city. 2 Kgs 25:4
broke down the walls **a** Jerusalem. 2 Kgs 25:10
all of bronze, were all **a** the capital. 2 Kgs 25:17
villages that were **a** these cities as 1 Chr 4:33
And they lodged **a** the house of God, 1 Chr 9:27
built the city all **a** from the Millo in 1 Chr 11:8
go **a** and come against them 1 Chr 14:14
ten cubits, compassing the sea all **a**. 2 Chr 4:3
Then the king turned **a** and blessed all 2 Chr 6:3
sent an ambush **a** to come upon 2 Chr 13:13
they attacked all the cities **a** Gerar, 2 Chr 14:14
and the LORD gave them rest all **a**. 2 Chr 15:15
of the lands that were **a** Judah, 2 Chr 17:10
"Turn **a** and carry me out of the 2 Chr 18:33
for his God gave him rest all **a**. 2 Chr 20:30
the house, **a** the altar and the house. 2 Chr 23:10
Fish Gate, and carried it **a** Ophel, 2 Chr 33:14
far as Naphtali, in their ruins all **a**, 2 Chr 34:6
gathered **a** me while I sat appalled until Ezr 9:4
to us from the nations that were **a** us. Neh 5:17
all the nations **a** us were afraid and fell Neh 6:16
for themselves villages **a** Jerusalem. Neh 12:29
you not put a hedge **a** him and his house Jb 1:10
you will look **a** and take your rest in Jb 11:18
against me and encamp **a** my tent. Jb 19:12
Therefore snares are all **a** you, and Jb 22:10
me, when my children were all **a** me, Jb 29:5
They turn **a** and around by his Jb 37:12
turn around and **a** by his guidance, Jb 37:12
doors of his face? **A** his teeth is terror. Jb 41:14
who have set themselves against me all **a**. Ps 3:6
his covering, his canopy **a** him, Ps 18:11
hands in innocence and go **a** your altar, Ps 26:6
be lifted up above my enemies all **a** me, Ps 27:6
of the LORD encamps **a** those who fear Ps 34:7
the derision and scorn of those **a** us. Ps 44:13
Walk about Zion, go **a** her, number Ps 48:12
devouring fire, **a** him a mighty tempest. Ps 50:3
Day and night they go **a** it on its walls, Ps 55:10
let all **a** him bring gifts to him who is to Ps 76:11
of their camp, all **a** their dwellings. Ps 78:28
their blood like water all **a** Jerusalem, Ps 79:3
mocked and derided by those **a** us. Ps 79:4
and awesome above all who are **a** him? Ps 89:7
O LORD, with your faithfulness all **a** you? Ps 89:8
Clouds and thick darkness are all **a** him; Ps 97:2
him and burns up his adversaries all **a**. Ps 97:3
be like a garment that he wraps **a** him, Ps 109:19
will be like olive shoots **a** your table. Ps 128:3
forsake you; bind them **a** your neck; Prv 3:3
heart always; tie them **a** your neck. Prv 6:21
to the south and goes **a** to the north; Eccl 1:6
a and around goes the wind, and on its Eccl 1:6
around and **a** goes the wind, and on its Eccl 1:6
A it are sixty mighty men, some of the Sg 3:7
For a cry has gone **a** the land of Moab; Is 15:8
and whirl you **a** and around, and throw Is 22:18
and whirl you around and **a**, and throw Is 22:18
And I will encamp against you all **a**, and Is 29:3
bare, and tie sackcloth **a** your waist. Is 32:11
it set him on fire all **a**, but he did not Is 42:25
Lift up your eyes **a** and see; they all Is 49:18
Lift up your eyes all **a**, and see; they all Is 60:4
all its walls all **a** and against all the Jer 1:15
of a field are they against her all **a**, Jer 4:17
her; they shall pitch their tents **a** her; Jer 6:3
Are the birds of prey against her all **a**? Jer 12:9
a linen loincloth and put it **a** your waist, Jer 13:1
word of the LORD, and put it **a** my waist. Jer 13:2
you have bought, which is **a** your waist, Jer 13:4
of Judah and the places **a** Jerusalem, Jer 17:26
and it shall devour all that is **a** her." Jer 21:14
all the people gathered **a** Jeremiah in the Jer 26:9
afterward they turned **a** and took back Jer 34:11
but then you turned **a** and profaned my Jer 34:16
from Mizpah turned **a** and came back, Jer 41:14
for the sword shall devour **a** you.' Jer 46:14
Grieve for him, all you who are **a** him, Jer 48:17
are gashes, and **a** the waist is sackcloth. Jer 48:37
and a horror to all that are **a** him." Jer 48:39
GOD of hosts, from all who are **a** you, Jer 49:5
in array against Babylon all **a**, Jer 50:14
Raise a shout against her all **a**; she has Jer 50:15
who bend the bow. Encamp **a** her; Jer 50:29
and it will devour all that is **a** him. Jer 50:32
to it. And they built siegeworks all **a** it. Jer 52:4
while the Chaldeans were **a** the city. Jer 52:7
broke down all the walls **a** Jerusalem. Jer 52:14
all of bronze, were **a** the capital. Jer 52:22
were a hundred upon the network all **a**. Jer 52:23
flaming fire in Jacob, consuming all **a**. Lam 2:3
and a great cloud, with brightness **a** it, Ezk 1:4
rims of all four were full of eyes all **a**. Ezk 1:18
the appearance of fire enclosed all **a**. Ezk 1:27
of fire, and there was brightness **a** him. Ezk 1:27
the appearance of the brightness all **a**. Ezk 1:28
and plant battering rams against it all **a**. Ezk 4:2
and strike with the sword all **a** the city. Ezk 5:2
of the nations, with countries all **a** her. Ezk 5:5
more than the countries all **a** her; Ezk 5:6
than the nations that are all **a** you, Ezk 5:7
the rules of the nations that are all **a** you, Ezk 5:7
part shall fall by the sword all **a** you; Ezk 5:12
among the nations all **a** you and in the Ezk 5:14
and a horror, to the nations all **a** you, Ezk 5:15
I will scatter your bones **a** your altars. Ezk 6:5
lie among their idols **a** their altars, Ezk 6:13
And there, engraved on the wall all **a**, Ezk 8:10
were full of eyes all **a**—the wheels that Ezk 10:12
rules of the nations that are **a** you." Ezk 11:12
toward every wind all who are **a** him, Ezk 12:14
daughters of Syria and all those **a** her, Ezk 16:57
those all **a** who despise you. Ezk 16:57
and Helech were on your walls all **a**, Ezk 27:11
hung their shields on your walls all **a**; Ezk 27:11
making its rivers flow **a** the place of its Ezk 31:4
all her company, its graves all **a** it, Ezk 32:22
and her company is all **a** her grave, all Ezk 32:23
and all her multitude **a** her grave; Ezk 32:24
all her multitude, her graves all **a** it, Ezk 32:25
all her multitude, her graves all **a** it, Ezk 32:26
and the places all **a** my hill a blessing, Ezk 34:26
derision to the rest of the nations all **a**, Ezk 36:4
that are all **a** you shall themselves Ezk 36:7
that are left all **a** you shall know that Ezk 36:36
And he led me **a** among them, and Ezk 37:2
gone, and will gather them from all **a**, Ezk 37:21
gather from all **a** to the sacrificial Ezk 39:17
there was a wall all **a** the outside of the Ezk 40:5
And **a** the vestibule of the gateway was Ezk 40:14
And the gateway had windows all **a**, Ezk 40:16
the vestibule had windows all **a** inside, Ezk 40:16
and a pavement, all **a** the court. Ezk 40:17
it and its vestibule had windows all **a**, Ezk 40:25
it and its vestibule had windows all **a**. Ezk 40:29
And there were vestibules all **a**, Ezk 40:30
it and its vestibule had windows all **a**. Ezk 40:33
as the others, and it had windows all **a**. Ezk 40:36
long, were fastened all **a** within. Ezk 40:43
chambers, four cubits, all **a** the temple. Ezk 41:5
There were offsets all **a** the wall of the Ezk 41:6
was enclosed upward all **a** the temple. Ezk 41:7
the temple had a raised platform all **a**; Ezk 41:8
of twenty cubits all **a** the temple on Ezk 41:10
of the free space was five cubits all **a**. Ezk 41:11
building was five cubits thick all **a**, Ezk 41:12
and the galleries all **a** the three of Ezk 41:16
were paneled with wood all **a**, Ezk 41:16
And on all the walls all **a**, inside and Ezk 41:17
were carved on the whole temple all **a**. Ezk 41:19
and measured the temple area all **a**. Ezk 42:15
cubits by the measuring reed all **a**. Ezk 42:16
cubits by the measuring reed all **a**. Ezk 42:17
It had a wall **a** it, 500 cubits long and Ezk 42:20
of the mountain all **a** shall be most Ezk 43:12
with a rim of one span **a** its edge. Ezk 43:13
with a rim **a** it half a cubit broad, Ezk 43:17
broad, and its base one cubit all **a**. Ezk 43:17
of the ledge and upon the rim all **a**. Ezk 43:20
linen undergarments **a** their waists. Ezk 44:18
with fifty cubits for an open space **a** it. Ezk 45:2
court and led me **a** to the four corners Ezk 46:21
a each of the four courts was a row of Ezk 46:23
made at the bottom of the rows all **a**. Ezk 46:23
gate and led me **a** on the outside to Ezk 47:2
have a chain of gold **a** his neck and shall Dn 5:7
a chain of gold **a** your neck and shall Dn 5:16
a chain of gold was put **a** his neck, Dn 5:29
a byword among all who are **a** us. Dn 9:16
belt of fine gold from Uphaz **a** his waist. Dn 10:5
that sat by the Nile, with water **a** her, Na 3:8
LORD'S right hand will come **a** to you, Hab 2:16
And I will be to her a wall of fire all **a**, Zec 2:5
and prosperous, with her cities **a** her, Zec 7:7
hair and a leather belt **a** his waist, Mt 3:4
when Jesus saw a great crowd **a** him, Mt 8:18
they sent **a** to all that region and Mt 14:35
great millstone fastened **a** his neck and Mt 18:6
vineyard and put a fence **a** it and dug a Mt 21:33
wore a leather belt **a** his waist and ate Mk 1:6
And he looked **a** at them with anger, Mk 3:5
the Jordan and from **a** Tyre and Sidon. Mk 3:8
had diseases pressed **a** him to touch Mk 3:10
And a crowd was sitting **a** him, and Mk 3:32
looking about at those who sat **a** him, Mk 3:34
those **a** him with the twelve asked him Mk 4:10
him, "You see the crowd pressing **a** you, Mk 5:31
And he looked **a** to see who had done it. Mk 5:32
And suddenly, looking **a**, they no longer Mk 9:8
they saw a great crowd **a** them, Mk 9:14
millstone were hung **a** his neck and Mk 9:42
And Jesus looked **a** and said to his Mk 10:23
when he had looked **a** at everything, Mk 11:11
vineyard and put a fence **a** it and dug a Mk 12:1
who like to walk **a** in long robes and Mk 12:38
and the glory of the Lord shone **a** them, Lk 2:9
he went into all the region **a** the Jordan, Lk 3:3
And after looking **a** at them all he said Lk 6:10
As Jesus went, the people pressed **a** him. Lk 8:42
also, until I dig **a** it and put on manure. Lk 13:8
a millstone were hung **a** his neck and he Lk 17:2
set up a barricade **a** you and surround Lk 19:43
who like to walk **a** in long robes, Lk 20:46
when those who were **a** him saw what Lk 22:49
So the Jews gathered **a** him and said to Jn 10:24
on account of the people standing **a**, Jn 11:42
and taking a towel, tied it **a** his waist. Jn 13:4
with the towel that was wrapped **a** him. Jn 13:5
she turned **a** and saw Jesus standing, Jn 20:14
gathered from the towns **a** Jerusalem, Acts 5:16
a light from heaven flashed **a** him. Acts 9:3
"Wrap your cloak **a** you and follow Acts 12:8
from heaven suddenly shone **a** me. Acts 22:6
down from Jerusalem stood **a** him, Acts 25:7
that shone **a** me and those who Acts 26:13
and all the way **a** to Illyricum I have Rom 15:19
the devil prowls **a** like a roaring 1 Pt 5:8
robe and with a golden sash **a** his chest. Rv 1:13
and **a** the throne was a rainbow that had Rv 4:3
A the throne were twenty-four thrones, Rv 4:4
And **a** the throne, on each side of the Rv 4:6
six wings, are full of eyes all **a** and within, Rv 4:8
and I heard **a** the throne and the living Rv 5:11
angels were standing **a** the throne and Rv 7:11
around the throne and **a** the elders and Rv 7:11
linen, with golden sashes **a** their chests. Rv 15:6

AROUSED (2)
This city has **a** my anger and wrath, Jer 32:31
flesh, our sinful passions, **a** by the law, Rom 7:5

ARPACHSHAD (9)
Elam, Asshur, **A**, Lud, and Aram. Gn 10:22
A fathered Shelah; and Shelah fathered Gn 10:24
he fathered **A** two years after the flood. Gn 11:10
lived after he fathered **A** 500 years and Gn 11:11
When **A** had lived 35 years, he fathered Gn 11:12
And **A** lived after he fathered Shelah Gn 11:13
Elam, Asshur, **A**, Lud, and Aram. 1 Chr 1:17
A fathered Shelah, and Shelah 1 Chr 1:18
Shem, **A**, Shelah; 1 Chr 1:24

ARPAD (6)
are the gods of Hamath and **A**? 2 Kgs 18:34
is the king of Hamath, the king of **A**, 2 Kgs 19:13
like Carchemish? Is not Hamath like **A**? Is 10:9
Where are the gods of Hamath and **A**? Is 36:19
is the king of Hamath, the king of **A**, Is 37:13
"Hamath and **A** are confounded, Jer 49:23

ARPHAXAD (1)
the son of Cainan, the son of **A**, the son Lk 3:36

ARRANGE (9)
And you shall bring in the table and **a** it, Ex 40:4
fire on the altar and **a** wood on the fire. Lv 1:7
Aaron's sons the priests shall **a** the pieces, Lv 1:8
and the priest shall **a** them on the wood Lv 1:12
and he shall **a** the burnt offering on it Lv 6:12
Aaron shall **a** it from evening to Lv 24:3
He shall **a** the lamps on the lampstand of Lv 24:4
Sabbath day Aaron shall **a** it before the Lv 24:8
ahead to you and **a** in advance for the 2 Cor 9:5

ARRANGED (4)
and **a** the bread on it before the LORD, as Ex 40:23
"I have **a** the seven altars and I have Nm 23:4
Paul aboard there, for so he had **a**, Acts 20:13
it is, God **a** the members in the body, 1 Cor 12:18

ARRANGEMENT (3)
and for the regular **a** of the showbread, 2 Chr 2:4
to them the design of the temple, its **a**, Ezk 43:11
According to this **a**, gifts and sacrifices Heb 9:9

ARRANGEMENTS (1)
with the same exits and **a** and doors, Ezk 42:11

ARRANGING (1)
and studying and **a** many proverbs Eccl 12:9

ARRAY (9)
and set themselves in **a** against Gibeah, Jgs 20:30
and set themselves in **a** at Baal-tamar, Jgs 20:33
drew up in battle **a** at the entrance of 2 Sm 10:8
drew up in battle **a** at the entrance of 1 Chr 19:9
the battle in **a** against the Syrians, 1 Chr 19:17
on horses, set in **a** as a man for battle, Jer 6:23
And they shall **a** themselves against her. Jer 50:9
Set yourselves in **a** against Babylon all Jer 50:14
sons and all who **a** themselves in foreign Zep 1:8

ARRAYED (17)
men of Israel and **a** them against the 2 Sm 10:9
and he **a** them against the 2 Sm 10:10
The Syrians **a** themselves against 2 Sm 10:17
on their thrones, **a** in their robes, 1 Kgs 22:10
these, men of war, **a** in battle order, 1 Chr 12:38
of Israel and **a** them against the 1 Chr 19:10
and they were **a** against the 1 Chr 19:11
sons and kinsmen, **a** in fine linen, 2 Chr 5:12
on their thrones, **a** in their robes. 2 Chr 18:9
poison; the terrors of God are **a** against me. Jb 6:4
that I wage, for many are **a** against me. Ps 55:18
a as a man for battle against you, Jer 50:42
all his glory was not **a** like one of these. Mt 6:29
all his glory was not **a** like one of these. Lk 12:27
it on his head and **a** him in a purple robe. Jn 19:2
The woman was **a** in purple and scarlet, Rv 17:4
the armies of heaven, **a** in fine linen, Rv 19:14

ARRAYING (1)
Then, **a** him in splendid clothing, he Lk 23:11

ARREST (10)
although they were seeking to **a** him, Mt 21:46
together in order to **a** Jesus by stealth Mt 26:4
they were seeking to **a** him but feared Mk 12:12
were seeking how to **a** him by stealth Mk 14:1
So they were seeking to **a** him, but no one Jn 7:30
and Pharisees sent officers to **a** him. Jn 7:32
Some of them wanted to **a** him, but no Jn 7:44
Again they sought to **a** him, but he Jn 10:39
them know, so that they might **a** him. Jn 11:57
the Jews, he proceeded to **a** Peter also. Acts 12:3

ARRESTED (8)
when he heard that John had been **a**, Mt 4:12
Now after John was **a**, Jesus came into Mk 1:14
but no one **a** him, because his hour had Jn 8:20
officers of the Jews **a** Jesus and bound Jn 18:12
became a guide to those who **a** Jesus. Acts 1:16
And they **a** them and put them in Acts 4:3
they **a** the apostles and put them in the Acts 5:18
came up and **a** him and ordered Acts 21:33

ARRIVAL (1)
tabernacle was set up before their **a**. Nm 10:21

ARRIVE (7)
nothing till you **a** there." Therefore the Gn 19:22
must serve the LORD until we **a** there." Ex 10:26
And when you **a**, you shall anoint 1 Kgs 19:15
And when you **a**, look there for Jehu 2 Kgs 9:2
when your accusers **a**." And he Acts 23:35
And when I **a**, I will send those whom 1 Cor 16:3
and never able to **a** at a knowledge of 2 Tm 3:7

ARRIVED (31)
When he **a**, he sounded the trumpet in Jgs 3:27
the land of Moab and **a** on the east side Jgs 11:18
and departed and **a** opposite Jebus (that Jgs 19:10
When he **a**, Eli was sitting on his seat 1 Sm 4:13
servants of David **a** with Joab from 2 Sm 3:22
were with him, **a** weary at the Jordan. 2 Sm 16:14
before the messenger **a** Elisha said to 2 Kgs 6:32
King Ahaz **a** from Damascus. 2 Kgs 16:11
When they **a**, they came and stood 2 Kgs 18:17
the king's eunuchs **a** and hurried to Est 6:14
eighty men **a** from Shechem and Shiloh Jer 41:5
of the LORD. And they **a** at Tahpanhes. Jer 43:7
The time has come; the day has **a**. Let Ezk 7:12
became tall and **a** at full adornment. Ezk 16:7
and Jedaiah, who have **a** from Babylon, Zec 6:10
for a friend of mine has **a** on a journey, Lk 11:6
When the day of Pentecost **a**, they were Acts 2:1
And when he **a**, they took him to the Acts 9:39
moment three men **a** at the house Acts 11:11
When they **a** at Salamis, they Acts 13:5
And when they **a** and gathered the Acts 14:27
and when they **a** they went into the Acts 17:10
Silas and Timothy **a** from Macedonia, Acts 18:5
When he **a**, he greatly helped those Acts 18:27
voyage from Tyre, we **a** at Ptolemais, Acts 21:7
days after Festus had **a** in the province, Acts 25:1
When he had **a**, the Jews who had Acts 25:7
king and Bernice **a** at Caesarea and Acts 25:13
of days and **a** with difficulty off Acts 27:7
we made a circuit and **a** at Rhegium. Acts 28:13
but when he **a** in Rome he searched 2 Tm 1:17

ARRIVES (2)
until the ninth year, when its crop **a**. Lv 25:22
is he who waits and **a** at the 1,335 days. Dn 12:12

ARROGANCE (8)
let not **a** come from your mouth; 1 Sm 2:3
In **a** the wicked hotly pursue the poor; let Ps 10:2
Let not the foot of **a** come upon me, nor Ps 36:11
Pride and **a** and the way of evil and Prv 8:13
who say in pride and in **a** of heart: Is 9:9
how proud he is!—of his **a**, his pride, Is 16:6
of his loftiness, his pride, and his **a**, Jer 48:29
As it is, you boast in your **a**. All such Jas 4:16

ARROGANT (19)
I was envious of the **a** when I saw the Ps 73:3
They pour out their **a** words; all the Ps 94:4
a haughty look and an **a** heart I will not Ps 101:5
The **a** have hidden a trap for me, and Ps 140:5
Everyone who is **a** in heart is an Prv 16:5
"Scoffer" is the name of the **a**, haughty Prv 21:24
haughty man who acts with **a** pride. Prv 21:24
the speech of the **a** heart of the king Is 10:12
I will put an end to the pomp of the **a**, Is 13:11
a traitor, an **a** man who is never at rest. Hab 2:5
And now we call the **a** blessed. Mal 3:15
when all the **a** and all evildoers will be Mal 4:1
do not be **a** toward the branches. If Rom 11:18
Some are **a**, as though I were not 1 Cor 4:18
the talk of these **a** people but their 1 Cor 4:19
And you are **a**! Ought you not rather 1 Cor 5:2
love does not envy or boast; it is not **a** 1 Cor 13:4
self, lovers of money, proud, **a**, abusive, 2 Tm 3:2
He must not be **a** or quick-tempered or a Ti 1:7

ARROGANTLY (4)
this affair they dealt **a** with the people." Ex 18:11
that they acted **a** against our fathers. Neh 9:10
transgressions, that they are behaving **a**. Jb 36:9
to pity; with their mouths they speak **a**. Ps 17:10

ARROW (20)
boy ran, he shot an **a** beyond him. 1 Sm 20:36
the place of the **a** that Jonathan had 1 Sm 20:37
and said, "Is not the **a** beyond you?" 1 Sm 20:37
so that the **a** pierced his heart, 2 Kgs 9:24
he said, "The LORD'S **a** of victory, 2 Kgs 13:17
victory, the **a** of victory over Syria! 2 Kgs 13:17
into this city or shoot an **a** there, 2 Kgs 19:32
a bronze **a** will strike him through. Jb 20:24
The **a** cannot make him flee; for him Jb 41:28
they have fitted their **a** to the string to Ps 11:2
But God shoots his **a** at them; they are Ps 64:7
of the night, nor the **a** that flies by day, Ps 91:5
till an **a** pierces its liver; as a bird Prv 7:23
a war club, or a sword, or a sharp **a**. Prv 25:18
city or shoot an **a** there or come before Is 37:33
hand he hid me; he made me a polished **a**; Is 49:2
Their tongue is a deadly **a**; it speaks Jer 9:8
bow and set me as a target for his **a**. Lam 3:12
as my bow; I have made Ephraim its **a**. Zec 9:13
and his **a** will go forth like lightning; Zec 9:14

ARROWS (43)
and pierce them through with his **a**. Nm 24:8
upon them; I will spend my **a** on them; Dt 32:23
I will make my **a** drunk with blood, Dt 32:42
And I will shoot three **a** to the side of 1 Sm 20:20
young man, saying, 'Go, find the **a**.' 1 Sm 20:21
'Look, the **a** are on this side of you, 1 Sm 20:21
youth, 'Look, the **a** are beyond you,' 1 Sm 20:22
"Run and find the **a** that I shoot." As 1 Sm 20:36
boy gathered up the **a** and came to 1 Sm 20:38
he sent out **a** and scattered them; 2 Sm 22:15
"Take a bow and **a**." So he took a 2 Kgs 13:15
arrows." So he took a bow and **a**. 2 Kgs 13:15
"Take the **a**," and he took them. 2 Kgs 13:18
and could shoot **a** and sling stones 1 Chr 12:2
corners, to shoot **a** and great stones. 2 Chr 26:15
For the **a** of the Almighty are in me; my Jb 6:4
weapons, making his **a** fiery shafts. Ps 7:13
he sent out his **a** and scattered them; Ps 18:14
For your **a** have sunk into me, and your Ps 38:2
Your **a** are sharp in the heart of the Ps 45:5
of man, whose teeth are spears and **a**, Ps 57:4
when he aims his **a**, let them be blunted. Ps 58:7
like swords, who aim bitter words like **a**, Ps 64:3
There he broke the flashing **a**, the shield, Ps 76:3
thunder; your **a** flashed on every side. Ps 77:17
A warrior's sharp **a**, with glowing coals Ps 120:4
Like **a** in the hand of a warrior are the Ps 127:4
them; send out your **a** and rout them! Ps 144:6
who throws firebrands, **a**, and death Prv 26:18
their **a** are sharp, all their bows bent, Is 5:28
With bow and **a** a man will come there, Is 7:24
Their **a** are like a skilled warrior who Jer 50:9
shoot at her, spare no **a**, for she has Jer 50:14
"Sharpen the **a**! Take up the shields! Jer 51:11
into my kidneys the **a** of his quiver; Lam 3:13
against you the deadly **a** of famine, Ezk 5:16
arrows of famine, **a** for destruction, Ezk 5:16
He shakes the **a**; he consults the Ezk 21:21
and will make your **a** drop out of your Ezk 39:3
them, shields and bucklers, bow and **a**, Ezk 39:9
from your bow, calling for many **a**. Hab 3:9
place at the light of your **a** as they sped, Hab 3:11
pierced with his own **a** the heads of his Hab 3:14

ART (2)
spices prepared by the perfumer's **a**, 2 Chr 16:14
formed by the **a** and imagination of Acts 17:29

ARTAXERXES (14)
In the days of **A**, Bishlam and Ezr 4:7
their associates wrote to **A** king of Persia. Ezr 4:7
letter against Jerusalem to **A** the king as Ezr 4:8
"To **A** the king: Your servants, the men Ezr 4:11
Cyrus and Darius and **A** king of Persia; Ezr 6:14
after this, in the reign of **A** king of Persia, Ezr 7:1
in the seventh year of **A** the king, Ezr 7:7
of the letter that King **A** gave to Ezra the Ezr 7:11
"**A**, king of kings, to Ezra the priest, the Ezr 7:12
"And I, **A** the king, make a decree to all Ezr 7:21
Babylonia, in the reign of **A** the king: Ezr 8:1
Nisan, in the twentieth year of King **A**, Neh 2:1
to the thirty-second year of **A** the king, Neh 5:14
thirty-second year of **A** king of Neh 13:6

ARTAXERXES' (1)
the copy of King **A** letter was read Ezr 4:23

ARTEMAS (1)
When I send **A** or Tychicus to you, do Ti 3:12

ARTEMIS (5)
who made silver shrines of **A**, Acts 19:24
the great goddess **A** may be counted Acts 19:27
out, "Great is **A** of the Ephesians!" Acts 19:28
voice, "Great is **A** of the Ephesians!" Acts 19:34
is temple keeper of the great **A**, Acts 19:35

ARTICLE (10)
whether it is an **a** of wood or a garment Lv 11:32
any **a** that is used for any purpose. Lv 11:32
or the woof or in any **a** made of skin, Lv 13:49
or any **a** made of skin that is diseased, Lv 13:52
or the woof or in any **a** made of skin, Lv 13:53
or the woof, or in any **a** made of skin, Lv 13:57
or any **a** made of skin from which the Lv 13:58
or the woof, or in any **a** made of skin, Lv 13:59
purify every garment, every **a** of skin, Nm 31:20
of goats' hair, and every **a** of wood." Nm 31:20

ARTICLES (8)
what each man found, **a** of gold, Nm 31:50
from them the gold, all crafted **a**. Nm 31:51
Joram brought with him **a** of silver, 2 Sm 8:10
his present, **a** of silver and gold, 1 Kgs 10:25
And he sent all sorts of **a** of gold, of 1 Chr 18:10
his present, **a** of silver and of gold, 2 Chr 9:24
of scented wood, all kinds of **a** of ivory, Rv 18:12
of ivory, all kinds of **a** of costly wood, Rv 18:12

ARTIFICIAL (1)
the tombs of David, as far as the **a** pool, Neh 3:16

ARTISANS (1)
Babylon, together with the rest of the **a** Jer 52:15

ARTISTIC (2)
to devise **a** designs, to work in gold, Ex 31:4
to devise **a** designs, to work in gold and Ex 35:32

ARTS (5)
Egypt, also did the same by their secret **a**. Ex 7:11
of Egypt did the same by their secret **a**. Ex 7:22
same by their secret **a** and made frogs Ex 8:7
tried by their secret **a** to produce gnats, Ex 8:18
had practiced magic **a** brought their Acts 19:19

ARUBBOTH (1)
in **A** (to him belonged Socoh and all 1 Kgs 4:10

ARUMAH (1)
And Abimelech lived at **A**, and Zebul Jgs 9:41

ARVAD (2)
of Sidon and **A** were your rowers; Ezk 27:8
Men of **A** and Helech were on your Ezk 27:11

ARVADITES (2)
the **A**, the Zemarites, and the Gn 10:18
the **A**, the Zemarites, and the 1 Chr 1:16

ARZA (1)
himself drunk in the house of **A**, 1 Kgs 16:9

ASA (58)
And **A** his son reigned in his place. 1 Kgs 15:8
of Israel, **A** began to reign over Judah, 1 Kgs 15:9
And **A** did what was right in the eyes 1 Kgs 15:11
And **A** cut down her image and 1 Kgs 15:13
the heart of **A** was wholly true to the 1 Kgs 15:14

was war between **A** and Baasha 1 Kgs 15:16
out or come in to **A** king of Judah. 1 Kgs 15:17
Then **A** took all the silver and the 1 Kgs 15:18
And King **A** sent them to Ben-hadad 1 Kgs 15:18
listened to King **A** and sent the 1 Kgs 15:20
Then King **A** made a proclamation 1 Kgs 15:22
and with them King **A** built Geba of 1 Kgs 15:22
Now the rest of all the acts of **A**, all 1 Kgs 15:23
And **A** slept with his fathers and was 1 Kgs 15:24
the second year of **A** king of Judah, 1 Kgs 15:25
the third year of **A** king of Judah 1 Kgs 15:28
was war between **A** and Baasha 1 Kgs 15:32
In the third year of **A** king of Judah, 1 Kgs 15:33
twenty-sixth year of **A** king of Judah, 1 Kgs 16:8
twenty-seventh year of **A** king of 1 Kgs 16:10
twenty-seventh year of **A** king of 1 Kgs 16:15
thirty-first year of **A** king of Judah, 1 Kgs 16:23
thirty-eighth year of **A** king of 1 Kgs 16:29
the son of **A** began to reign 1 Kgs 22:41
walked in all the way of **A** his father. 1 Kgs 22:43
remained in the days of his father **A**. 1 Kgs 22:46
Abijah his son, **A** his son, 1 Chr 3:10
and Berechiah the son of **A**, 1 Chr 9:16
And **A** his son reigned in his place. 2 Chr 14:1
And **A** did what was good and right 2 Chr 14:2
And **A** had an army of 300,000 from 2 Chr 14:8
And **A** went out to meet him, and 2 Chr 14:10
And **A** cried to the LORD his God, "O 2 Chr 14:11
the Ethiopians before **A** and before 2 Chr 14:12
A and the people who were with him 2 Chr 14:13
went out to meet **A** and said to him, 2 Chr 15:2
me, **A**, and all Judah and Benjamin: 2 Chr 15:2
As soon as **A** heard these words, the 2 Chr 15:8
of the fifteenth year of the reign of **A**. 2 Chr 15:10
King **A** removed from being queen 2 Chr 15:16
A cut down her image, crushed it, 2 Chr 15:16
the heart of **A** was wholly true all 2 Chr 15:17
the thirty-fifth year of the reign of **A**. 2 Chr 15:19
the thirty-sixth year of the reign of **A**, 2 Chr 16:1
go out or come in to **A** king of Judah. 2 Chr 16:1
Then **A** took silver and gold from the 2 Chr 16:2
listened to King **A** and sent the 2 Chr 16:4
Then King **A** took all Judah, and 2 Chr 16:6
the seer came to **A** king of Judah and 2 Chr 16:7
Then **A** was angry with the seer and 2 Chr 16:10
And **A** inflicted cruelties upon some 2 Chr 16:10
The acts of **A**, from first to last, are 2 Chr 16:11
year of his reign **A** was diseased in 2 Chr 16:12
And **A** slept with his fathers, dying 2 Chr 16:13
of Ephraim that **A** his father had 2 Chr 17:2
in the way of **A** his father and did 2 Chr 20:32
or in the ways of **A** king of Judah, 2 Chr 21:12
large cistern that King **A** had made for Jer 41:9

ASAHEL (18)
were there, Joab, Abishai, and **A**. 2 Sm 2:18
Now **A** was as swift of foot as a wild 2 Sm 2:18
And **A** pursued Abner, and as he 2 Sm 2:19
said, "Is it you, **A**?" And he answered, 2 Sm 2:20
take his spoil." But **A** would not turn 2 Sm 2:21
And Abner said again to **A**, "Turn 2 Sm 2:22
to the place where **A** had fallen and 2 Sm 2:23
servants nineteen men besides **A**. 2 Sm 2:30
And they took up **A** and buried him 2 Sm 2:32
he died, for the blood of **A** his brother. 2 Sm 3:27
had put their brother **A** to death in the 2 Sm 3:30
A the brother of Joab was one of the 2 Sm 23:24
Zeruiah: Abishai, Joab, and **A**, three. 1 Chr 2:16
mighty men were **A** the brother of 1 Chr 11:26
A the brother of Joab was fourth, for 1 Chr 27:7
Zebadiah, **A**, Shemiramoth, 2 Chr 17:8
Azaziah, Nahath, **A**, Jerimoth, 2 Chr 31:13
Jonathan the son of **A** and Jahzeiah the Ezr 10:15

ASAIAH (8)
secretary, and **A** the king's servant, 2 Kgs 22:12
and **A** went to Huldah the 2 Kgs 22:14
Jaakobah, Jeshohaiah, **A**, Adiel, 1 Chr 4:36
son, Haggiah his son, and **A** his son. 1 Chr 6:30
A the firstborn, and his sons. 1 Chr 9:5
of the sons of Merari, **A** the chief, 1 Chr 15:6
and the Levites Uriel, **A**, Joel, 1 Chr 15:11
secretary, and **A** the king's servant, 2 Chr 34:20

ASAPH (48)
the secretary, and Joah the son of **A**, 2 Kgs 18:18
the secretary, and Joah the son of **A**, 2 Kgs 18:37
and his brother **A**, who stood on his 1 Chr 6:39
namely, **A** the son of Berechiah, 1 Chr 6:39
son of Mica, son of Zichri, son of **A**; 1 Chr 9:15
and of his brothers **A** the son of 1 Chr 15:17
The singers, Heman, **A**, and Ethan, 1 Chr 15:19
A was the chief, and second to him 1 Chr 16:5
lyres; **A** was to sound the cymbals, 1 Chr 16:5
to the LORD by **A** and his brothers. 1 Chr 16:7
So David left **A** and his brothers 1 Chr 16:37
set apart for the service the sons of **A**, 1 Chr 25:1
Of the sons of **A**: Zaccur, Joseph, 1 Chr 25:2
and Asharelah, sons of **A**, 1 Chr 25:2
of Asaph, under the direction of **A**, 1 Chr 25:2
A, Jeduthun, and Heman were under 1 Chr 25:6
The first lot fell for **A** to Joseph; the 1 Chr 25:9
the son of Kore, of the sons of **A**. 1 Chr 26:1
all the Levitical singers, **A**, Heman, 2 Chr 5:12
Mattaniah, a Levite of the sons of **A**, 2 Chr 20:14
and of the sons of **A**, Zechariah and 2 Chr 29:13
the words of David and of **A** the seer. 2 Chr 29:30
The singers, the sons of **A**, were in 2 Chr 35:15
to the command of David, and **A**, 2 Chr 35:15
The singers: the sons of **A**, 128. Ezr 2:41
trumpets, and the Levites, the sons of **A**, Ezr 3:10
and a letter to **A**, the keeper of the king's Neh 2:8
The singers: the sons of **A**, 148. Neh 7:44
son of Mica, son of Zabdi, son of **A**, Neh 11:17
son of Mica, of the sons of **A**, Neh 11:22
of Micaiah, son of Zaccur, son of **A**; Neh 12:35
of David and **A** there were directors Neh 12:46
A Psalm of **A**. Ps 50:T
A Psalm of **A**. Ps 73:T
A Maskil of **A**. Ps 74:T
to Do Not Destroy. A Psalm of **A**. Ps 75:T
stringed instruments. A Psalm of **A**. Ps 76:T
according to Jeduthun. A Psalm of **A**. Ps 77:T
A Maskil of **A**. Ps 78:T
A Psalm of **A**. Ps 79:T
to Lilies. A Testimony. Of **A**, a Psalm. Ps 80:T
according to The Gittith. Of **A**. Ps 81:T
A Psalm of **A**. Ps 82:T
A Song. A Psalm of **A**. Ps 83:T
the secretary, and Joah the son of **A**, Is 36:3
the secretary, and Joah the son of **A**, Is 36:22
of Abijah, and Abijah the father of **A**, Mt 1:7
and **A** the father of Jehoshaphat, and Mt 1:8

ASAREL (1)
Jehallelel: Ziph, Ziphah, Tiria, and **A**. 1 Chr 4:16

ASCEND (7)
'Who will **a** to heaven for us and bring Dt 30:12
Who shall **a** the hill of the LORD? And Ps 24:3
If I **a** to heaven, you are there! If I make Ps 139:8
said in your heart, 'I will **a** to heaven; Is 14:13
I will **a** above the heights of the clouds; I Is 14:14
For David did not **a** into the heavens, Acts 2:34
'Who will **a** into heaven?'" (that is, Rom 10:6

ASCENDED (9)
When Jehoram had **a** the throne of 2 Chr 21:4
You **a** on high, leading a host of Ps 68:18
Who has **a** to heaven and come down? Prv 30:4
No one has **a** into heaven except he who Jn 3:13
to me, for I have not yet **a** to the Father; Jn 20:17
and your alms have **a** as a memorial Acts 10:4
"When he **a** on high he led a host of Eph 4:8
"He **a**," what does it mean but that he Eph 4:9
is the one who also **a** far above all the Eph 4:10

ASCENDING (5)
of God were **a** and descending on Gn 28:12
the angels of God **a** and descending on Jn 1:51
see the Son of Man **a** to where he was Jn 6:62
'I am **a** to my Father and your Father, Jn 20:17
I saw another angel **a** from the rising of Rv 7:2

ASCENT (15)
shall turn south of the **a** of Akrabbim, Nm 34:4
the way of the **a** of Beth-horon and Jos 10:10
were going down the **a** of Beth-horon, Jos 10:11
out southward of the **a** of Akrabbim, Jos 15:3
which is opposite the **a** of Adummim, Jos 15:7
which is opposite the **a** of Adummim. Jos 18:17
Amorites ran from the **a** of Akrabbim, Jgs 1:36
from the battle by the **a** of Heres. Jgs 8:13
David went up the **a** of the Mount of 2 Sm 15:30
him in the chariot at the **a** of Gur, 2 Kgs 9:27
they will come up by the **a** of Ziz. 2 Chr 20:16
section opposite the **a** to the armory Neh 3:19
the city of David, at the **a** of the wall, Neh 12:37
For at the **a** of Luhith they go up weeping; Is 15:5
For at the **a** of Luhith they go up Jer 48:5

ASCENTS (15)
A Song of **A**. Ps 120:T
A Song of **A**. Ps 121:T
A Song of **A**. Of David. Ps 122:T
A Song of **A**. Ps 123:T
A Song of **A**. Of David. Ps 124:T
A Song of **A**. Ps 125:T
A Song of **A**. Ps 126:T
A Song of **A**. Of Solomon. Ps 127:T
A Song of **A**. Ps 128:T
A Song of **A**. Ps 129:T
A Song of **A**. Ps 130:T
A Song of **A**. Of David. Ps 131:T
A Song of **A**. Ps 132:T
A Song of **A**. Of David. Ps 133:T
A Song of **A**. Ps 134:T

ASCERTAINED (3)
the weight of the bronze was not **a**. 1 Kgs 7:47
wise men secretly and **a** from them what Mt 2:7
time that he had **a** from the wise men. Mt 2:16

ASCETICISM (2)
insisting on **a** and worship of angels, Col 2:18
self-made religion and **a** and severity to Col 2:23

ASCRIBE (12)
name of the LORD; **a** greatness to our God! Dt 32:3
A to the LORD, O clans of the peoples, 1 Chr 16:28
a to the LORD glory and strength! 1 Chr 16:28
A to the LORD the glory due his 1 Chr 16:29
from afar and **a** righteousness to my Jb 36:3
A to the LORD, O heavenly beings, ascribe Ps 29:1
beings, **a** to the LORD glory and strength. Ps 29:1
A to the LORD the glory due his name; Ps 29:2
A power to God, whose majesty is over Ps 68:34
A to the LORD, O families of the peoples, Ps 96:7
peoples, **a** to the LORD glory and strength! Ps 96:7
A to the LORD the glory due his name; Ps 96:8

ASCRIBED (2)
"They have **a** to David ten thousands, 1 Sm 18:8
and to me they have **a** thousands, 1 Sm 18:8

ASENATH (3)
And he gave him in marriage **A**, the Gn 41:45
A, the daughter of Potiphera priest of Gn 41:50
Manasseh and Ephraim, whom **A**, Gn 46:20

ASH (5)
the camp to a clean place, to the **a** heap, Lv 4:12
On the **a** heap it shall be burned up. Lv 4:12
the needy from the **a** heap to make 1 Sm 2:8
dust and lifts the needy from the **a** heap, Ps 113:7
brought up in purple embrace **a** heaps. Lam 4:5

ASHAMED (63)
his wife were both naked and were not **a**. Gn 2:25
meet them, for the men were greatly **a**. 2 Sm 10:5
steal in who are **a** when they flee in 2 Sm 19:3
when they urged him till he was **a**, 2 Kgs 2:17
them, for the men were greatly **a**. 1 Chr 19:5
the priests and the Levites were **a**, 2 Chr 30:15
For I was **a** to ask the king for a band of Ezr 8:22
I am **a** and blush to lift my face to you, Ezr 9:6
They are **a** because they were confident; Jb 6:20
upon me; are you not **a** to wrong me? Jb 19:3
enemies shall be **a** and greatly troubled; Ps 6:10
they shall be **a** who are wantonly Ps 25:3
radiant, and their faces shall never be **a**. Ps 34:5
For they shall be **a** of the oaks that you Is 1:29
shall be dismayed and **a** because of Cush Is 20:5
Be **a**, O Sidon, for the sea has spoken, the Is 23:4
moon will be confounded and the sun **a**, Is 24:23
see your zeal for your people, and be **a**. Is 26:11
"Jacob shall no more be **a**, no more Is 29:22
shall come and be **a** all who were Is 45:24
"Fear not, for you will not be **a**; be not Is 54:4
the forehead of a whore; you refuse to be **a**. Jer 3:3
Were they **a** when they committed Jer 6:15
No, they were not at all **a**; they did not Jer 6:15
Were they **a** when they committed Jer 8:12
No, they were not at all **a**; they did not Jer 8:12
They shall be **a** of their harvests Jer 12:13
they are **a** and confounded and cover Jer 14:3
is no rain on the land, the farmers are **a**; Jer 14:4
you will be **a** and confounded because Jer 22:22
I was **a**, and I was confounded, because Jer 31:19
Then Moab shall be **a** of Chemosh, as Jer 48:13
as the house of Israel was **a** of Bethel, Jer 48:13
who were **a** of your lewd behavior. Ezk 16:27
So be **a**, you also, and bear your Ezk 16:52
your disgrace and be **a** of all that you Ezk 16:54
your ways and be **a** when you take Ezk 16:61
Be **a** and confounded for your ways, O Ezk 36:32
that they may be **a** of their iniquities; Ezk 43:10
And if they are **a** of all that they have Ezk 43:11
and they shall be **a** because of their Hos 4:19
shame, and Israel shall be **a** of his idol. Hos 10:6
Be **a**, O tillers of the soil; wail, O Jl 1:11
shall see and be **a** of all their might; Mi 7:16
every prophet will be **a** of his vision Zec 13:4
For whoever is **a** of me and of my words Mk 8:38
Son of Man also be **a** when he comes in Mk 8:38
For whoever is **a** of me and of my words, Lk 9:26
the Son of Man be **a** when he comes in Lk 9:26
strong enough to dig, and I am **a** to beg. Lk 16:3
For I am not **a** of the gospel, for it is the Rom 1:16
the things of which you are now **a**? Rom 6:21
not write these things to make you **a**, 1 Cor 4:14
not for destroying you, I will not be **a**. 2 Cor 10:8
and hope that I will not be at all **a**, Phil 1:20
to do with him, that he may be **a**. 2 Thes 3:14

Therefore do not be **a** of the testimony 2 Tm 1:8
But I am not **a**, for I know whom I 2 Tm 1:12
me and was not **a** of my chains, 2 Tm 1:16
a worker who has no need to be **a**, 2 Tm 2:15
is why he is not **a** to call them brothers, Heb 2:11
Therefore God is not **a** to be called Heb 11:16
suffers as a Christian, let him not be **a**, 1 Pt 4:16

ASHAN (4)
Libnah, Ether, **A**, Jos 15:42
and **A**—four cities with their villages, Jos 19:7
Etam, Ain, Rimmon, Tochen, and **A**, 1 Chr 4:32
A with its pasturelands, and 1 Chr 6:59

ASHARELAH (1)
Zaccur, Joseph, Nethaniah, and **A**, 1 Chr 25:2

ASHBEL (3)
Bela, Becher, **A**, Gera, Naaman, Ehi, Gn 46:21
of Bela, the clan of the Belaites; of **A**, Nm 26:38
Bela his firstborn, **A** the second, 1 Chr 8:1

ASHBELITES (1)
Belaites; of Ashbel, the clan of the **A**; Nm 26:38

ASHDOD (20)
in Gath, and in **A** did some remain. Jos 11:22
Philistines, those of Gaza, **A**, Ashkelon, Jos 13:3
to the sea, all that were by the side of **A**, Jos 15:46
A, its towns and its villages; Gaza, its Jos 15:47
they brought it from Ebenezer to **A**. 1 Sm 5:1
when the people of **A** rose early the next 1 Sm 5:3
the threshold of Dagon in **A** to this day. 1 Sm 5:5
LORD was heavy against the people of **A**, 1 Sm 5:6
with tumors, both **A** and its territory. 1 Sm 5:6
when the men of **A** saw how things 1 Sm 5:7
one for **A**, one for Gaza, one for 1 Sm 6:17
the wall of Jabneh and the wall of **A**, 2 Chr 26:6
the territory of **A** and elsewhere 2 Chr 26:6
Jews who had married women of **A**, Neh 13:23
children spoke the language of **A**, Neh 13:24
came to **A** and fought against it and Is 20:1
Gaza, Ekron, and the remnant of **A**); Jer 25:20
I will cut off the inhabitants from **A**, and Am 1:8
to the strongholds in **A** and to the Am 3:9
a mixed people shall dwell in **A**, and I Zec 9:6

ASHDOD'S (1)
A people shall be driven out at noon, and Zep 2:4

ASHDODITES (1)
the Ammonites and the **A** heard that the Neh 4:7

ASHER (44)
me happy." So she called his name **A**. Gn 30:13
of Zilpah, Leah's servant: Gad and **A**. Gn 35:26
The sons of **A**: Imnah, Ishvah, Ishvi, Gn 46:17
Dan and Naphtali, Gad and **A**. Ex 1:4
from **A**, Pagiel the son of Ochran; Nm 1:13
Of the people of **A**, their generations, by Nm 1:40
listed of the tribe of **A** were 41,500. Nm 1:41
next to him shall be the tribe of **A**, Nm 2:27
of the people of **A** being Pagiel the son Nm 2:27
of Ochran, the chief of the people of **A**: Nm 7:72
of the people of **A** was Pagiel the son Nm 10:26
from the tribe of **A**, Sethur the son of Nm 13:13
The sons of **A** according to their Nm 26:44
name of the daughter of **A** was Serah. Nm 26:46
of the sons of **A** as they were listed, Nm 26:47
of the tribe of the people of **A** a chief, Nm 34:27
Reuben, Gad, **A**, Zebulun, Dan, and Dt 27:13
And of **A** he said, "Most blessed of sons Dt 33:24
he said, "Most blessed of sons be **A**; Dt 33:24
reached from **A** to Michmethath, Jos 17:7
On the north **A** is reached, and on the Jos 17:10
Issachar and in **A** Manasseh had Jos 17:11
of the people of **A** according to their Jos 19:24
of the people of **A** according to their Jos 19:31
at the south and **A** on the west and Jos 19:34
the tribe of Issachar, from the tribe of **A**, Jos 21:6
and out of the tribe of **A**, Mishal with Jos 21:30
A did not drive out the inhabitants of Jgs 1:31
A sat still at the coast of the sea, staying Jgs 5:17
And he sent messengers to **A**, Zebulun, Jgs 6:35
from Naphtali and from **A** and from all Jgs 7:23
the son of Hushai, in **A** and Bealoth; 1 Kgs 4:16
Benjamin, Naphtali, Gad, and **A**. 1 Chr 2:2
A, Naphtali and Manasseh in 1 Chr 6:62
out of the tribe of **A**: Mashal with its 1 Chr 6:74
The sons of **A**: Imnah, Ishvah, Ishvi, 1 Chr 7:30
All of these were men of **A**, heads of 1 Chr 7:40
Of **A** 40,000 seasoned troops ready 1 Chr 12:36
However, some men of **A**, of 2 Chr 30:11
the east side to the west, **A**, one portion. Ezk 48:2
Adjoining the territory of **A**, from the Ezk 48:3
gates, the gate of Gad, the gate of **A**, Ezk 48:34
daughter of Phanuel, of the tribe of **A**. Lk 2:36
12,000 from the tribe of **A**, 12,000 from Rv 7:6

ASHER'S (1)
"**A** food shall be rich, and he shall Gn 49:20

ASHERAH (19)
plant any tree as an **A** beside the altar of Dt 16:21
has, and cut down the **A** that is beside it Jgs 6:25
with the wood of the **A** that you shall cut Jgs 6:26
down, and the **A** beside it was cut down, Jgs 6:28
of Baal and cut down the **A** beside it." Jgs 6:30
made an abominable image for **A**. 1 Kgs 15:13
And Ahab made an **A**. Ahab did 1 Kgs 16:33
of Baal and the 400 prophets of **A**, 1 Kgs 18:19
and the **A** also remained in Samaria.) 2 Kgs 13:6
they made an **A** and worshiped all 2 Kgs 17:16
broke the pillars and cut down the **A**. 2 Kgs 18:4
altars for Baal and made an **A**, 2 Kgs 21:3
the carved image of **A** that he had 2 Kgs 21:7
all the vessels made for Baal, for **A**, 2 Kgs 23:4
he brought out the **A** from the house 2 Kgs 23:6
the women wove hangings for the **A**. 2 Kgs 23:7
it to dust. He also burned the **A**. 2 Kgs 23:15
had made a detestable image for **A**. 2 Chr 15:16
root out your **A** images from among Mi 5:14

ASHERAHS (2)
for you destroyed the **A** out of the 2 Chr 19:3
altars to the Baals, and made **A**, 2 Chr 33:3

ASHERIM (18)
their pillars and cut down their **A** Ex 34:13
and chop down their **A** and burn their Dt 7:5
their pillars and burn their **A** with fire. Dt 12:3
because they have made their **A**, 1 Kgs 14:15
and pillars and **A** on every high 1 Kgs 14:23
themselves pillars and **A** on every 2 Kgs 17:10
and cut down the **A** and filled their 2 Kgs 23:14
down the pillars and cut down the **A** 2 Chr 14:3
high places and the **A** out of Judah. 2 Chr 17:6
and served the **A** and the idols. 2 Chr 24:18
and cut down the **A** and broke down 2 Chr 31:1
and set up the **A** and the images, 2 Chr 33:19
Jerusalem of the high places, the **A**, 2 Chr 34:3
broke in pieces the **A** and the carved 2 Chr 34:4
altars and beat the **A** and the images 2 Chr 34:7
made, either the **A** or the altars of incense. Is 17:8
no **A** or incense altars will remain Is 27:9
remember their altars and their **A**, Jer 17:2

ASHERITES (1)
so the **A** lived among the Canaanites, Jgs 1:32

ASHEROTH (1)
their God and served the Baals and the **A**. Jgs 3:7

ASHES (37)
to the Lord, I who am but dust and **a**. Gn 18:27
shall make pots for it to receive its **a**, Ex 27:3
altar on the east side, in the place for **a**. Lv 1:16
he shall take up the **a** to which the fire Lv 6:10
and carry the **a** outside the camp Lv 6:11
shall take away the **a** from the altar Nm 4:13
shall gather up the **a** of the heifer and Nm 19:9
one who gathers the **a** of the heifer Nm 19:10
they shall take some **a** of the burnt Nm 19:17
And Tamar put **a** on her head and 2 Sm 13:19
and the **a** that are on it shall be 1 Kgs 13:3
and the **a** poured out from the altar, 1 Kgs 13:5
Kidron and carried their **a** to Bethel. 2 Kgs 23:4
his clothes and put on sackcloth and **a**, Est 4:1
many of them lay in sackcloth and **a**. Est 4:3
to scrape himself while he sat in the **a**. Jb 2:8
Your maxims are proverbs of **a**; your Jb 13:12
and I have become like dust and **a**. Jb 30:19
despise myself, and repent in dust and **a**." Jb 42:6
For I eat **a** like bread and mingle tears Ps 102:9
like wool; he scatters hoarfrost like **a**. Ps 147:16
He feeds on **a**; a deluded heart has led Is 44:20
to spread sackcloth and **a** under him? Is 58:5
them a beautiful headdress instead of **a**, Is 61:3
people, put on sackcloth, and roll in **a**; Jer 6:26
shepherds, and cry out, and roll in **a**, Jer 25:34
valley of the dead bodies and the **a**, Jer 31:40
on gravel, and made me cower in **a**; Lam 3:16
dust on their heads and wallow in **a**; Ezk 27:30
and I turned you to **a** on the earth in Ezk 28:18
mercy with fasting and sackcloth and **a**. Dn 9:3
himself with sackcloth, and sat in **a**. Jon 3:6
for they will be **a** under the soles of your Mal 4:3
repented long ago in sackcloth and **a**. Mt 11:21
long ago, sitting in sackcloth and **a**. Lk 10:13
bulls and with the **a** of a heifer Heb 9:13
and Gomorrah to **a** he condemned them 2 Pt 2:6

ASHHUR (2)
his father, and she bore him **A**, 1 Chr 2:24
A, the father of Tekoa, had two wives, 1 Chr 4:5

ASHIMA (1)
Nergal, the men of Hamath made **A**, 2 Kgs 17:30

ASHKELON (13)
those of Gaza, Ashdod, **A**, Gath, Jos 13:3
its territory, and **A** with its territory, Jgs 1:18
he went down to **A** and struck down Jgs 14:19
for Ashdod, one for Gaza, one for **A**, 1 Sm 6:17
Gath, publish it not in the streets of **A**, 2 Sm 1:20
kings of the land of the Philistines (**A**, Jer 25:20
has come upon Gaza; **A** has perished. Jer 47:5
Against **A** and against the seashore he Jer 47:7
and him who holds the scepter from **A**; Am 1:8
and **A** shall become a desolation; Zep 2:4
in the houses of **A** they shall lie down Zep 2:7
A shall see it, and be afraid; Gaza too, Zec 9:5
from Gaza; **A** shall be uninhabited; Zec 9:5

ASHKENAZ (3)
of Gomer: **A**, Riphath, and Togarmah. Gn 10:3
of Gomer: **A**, Riphath, and Togarmah. 1 Chr 1:6
the kingdoms, Ararat, Minni, and **A**; Jer 51:27

ASHNAH (2)
And in the lowland, Eshtaol, Zorah, **A**, Jos 15:33
Iphtah, **A**, Nezib, Jos 15:43

ASHORE (5)
men drew it **a** and sat down and sorted Mt 13:48
When he went **a** he saw a great crowd, Mt 14:14
When he went **a** he saw a great crowd, Mk 6:34
Peter went aboard and hauled the net **a**, Jn 21:11
planned if possible to run the ship **a**. Acts 27:39

ASHPENAZ (1)
Then the king commanded **A**, his chief Dn 1:3

ASHTAROTH (12)
of Bashan, who lived in **A** and in Edrei. Dt 1:4
to Og king of Bashan, who lived in **A**. Jos 9:10
the Rephaim, who lived at **A** and at Edrei Jos 12:4
who reigned in **A** and in Edrei (he Jos 13:12
and half Gilead, and **A**, and Edrei, the Jos 13:31
the LORD and served the Baals and the **A**. Jgs 2:13
the LORD and served the Baals and the **A**, Jgs 10:6
gods and the **A** from among you 1 Sm 7:3
of Israel put away the Baals and the **A**, 1 Sm 7:4
and have served the Baals and the **A**. 1 Sm 12:10
put his armor in the temple of **A**, 1 Sm 31:10
its pasturelands and **A** with its 1 Chr 6:71

ASHTERATHITE (1)
Uzzia the **A**, Shama and Jeiel the 1 Chr 11:44

ASHTEROTH-KARNAIM (1)
came and defeated the Rephaim in **A**, Gn 14:5

ASHTORETH (3)
Solomon went after **A** the goddess of 1 Kgs 11:5
me and worshiped **A** the goddess of 1 Kgs 11:33
had built for **A** the abomination of 2 Kgs 23:13

ASHURITES (1)
over Gilead and the **A** and Jezreel and 2 Sm 2:9

ASHVATH (1)
of Japhlet: Pasach, Bimhal, and **A**. 1 Chr 7:33

ASIA (18)
Judea and Cappadocia, Pontus and **A**, Acts 2:9
and of those from Cilicia and **A**, Acts 6:9
the Holy Spirit to speak the word in **A**. Acts 16:6
all the residents of **A** heard the word Acts 19:10
he himself stayed in **A** for a while. Acts 19:22
in almost all of **A** this Paul has Acts 19:26
she whom all **A** and the world Acts 19:27
he might not have to spend time in **A**, Acts 20:16
from the first day that I set foot in **A**, Acts 20:18
almost completed, the Jews from **A**, Acts 21:27
or tumult. But some Jews from **A**— Acts 24:18
to sail to the ports along the coast of **A**, Acts 27:2
was the first convert to Christ in **A**. Rom 16:5
The churches of **A** send you 1 Cor 16:19
of the affliction we experienced in **A**. 2 Cor 1:8
all who are in **A** turned away from 2 Tm 1:15
Galatia, Cappadocia, **A**, and Bithynia, 1 Pt 1:1
John to the seven churches that are in **A**: Rv 1:4

ASIANS (1)
and the **A**, Tychicus and Trophimus. Acts 20:4

ASIARCHS (1)
And even some of the **A**, who were Acts 19:31

ASIDE (105)
please turn **a** to your servant's house Gn 19:2
so they turned **a** to him and entered his Gn 19:3
his brothers and turned **a** to a certain Gn 38:1
said, "I will turn **a** to see this great sight, Ex 3:3
the LORD saw that he turned **a** to see, Ex 3:4
that is left over lay **a** to be kept till the Ex 16:23
So they laid it **a** till the morning, as Ex 16:24
They have turned **a** quickly out of the Ex 32:8
have not turned **a** to uncleanness while Nm 5:19
We will not turn **a** to the right hand Nm 20:17
We will not turn **a** into field or Nm 21:22

And the donkey turned **a** out of the Nm 22:23
saw me and turned **a** before me these Nm 22:33
If she had not turned **a** from me, Nm 22:33
I will turn **a** neither to the right nor to Dt 2:27
You shall not turn **a** to the right hand or Dt 5:32
They have turned **a** quickly out of the Dt 9:12
You had turned **a** quickly from the way Dt 9:16
and you turn **a** and serve other gods Dt 11:16
but turn **a** from the way that I am Dt 11:28
You shall not turn **a** from the verdict Dt 17:11
may not turn **a** from the Dt 17:20
if you do not turn **a** from any of the Dt 28:14
act corruptly and turn **a** from the way Dt 31:29
turning **a** from it neither to the right Jos 23:6
They soon turned **a** from the way in Jgs 2:17
to meet Sisera and said to him, "Turn **a**, Jgs 4:18
him, "Turn aside, my lord; turn **a** to me; Jgs 4:18
be afraid." So he turned **a** to her into the Jgs 4:18
And he turned **a** to see the carcass of the Jgs 14:8
And they turned **a** and said to him, Jgs 18:3
And they turned **a** there and came to Jgs 18:15
let us turn **a** to this city of the Jebusites Jgs 19:11
"We will not turn **a** into the city of Jgs 19:12
and they turned **a** there, to go in and Jgs 19:15
So Boaz said, "Turn **a**, friend; sit down Ru 4:1
here." And he turned **a** and sat down. Ru 4:1
in his ways but turned **a** after gain. 1 Sm 8:3
you, of which I said to you, 'Put it **a**.'" 1 Sm 9:23
Yet do not turn **a** from following the 1 Sm 12:20
And do not turn **a** after empty things 1 Sm 12:21
"Turn **a** to your right hand or to your 2 Sm 2:21
would not turn **a** from following him. 2 Sm 2:21
Asahel, "Turn **a** from following me. 2 Sm 2:22
But he refused to turn **a**. Therefore 2 Sm 2:23
Joab took him **a** into the midst of the 2 Sm 3:27
But David took it **a** to the house of 2 Sm 6:10
"Turn **a** and stand here." So he 2 Sm 18:30
here." So he turned **a** and stood still. 2 Sm 18:30
from his statutes I did not turn **a**. 2 Sm 22:23
But if you turn **a** from following me, 1 Kgs 9:6
did not turn **a** from anything that 1 Kgs 15:5
He did not turn **a** from it, doing 1 Kgs 22:43
vessels. And when one is full, set it **a**." 2 Kgs 4:4
Jehu did not turn **a** from the sins of 2 Kgs 10:29
and he did not turn **a** to the right or to 2 Kgs 22:2
but took it **a** to the house of 1 Chr 13:13
"But if you turn **a** and forsake my 2 Chr 7:19
they did not turn **a** from what the 2 Chr 8:15
his father and did not turn **a** from it, 2 Chr 20:32
he did not turn **a** to the right hand 2 Chr 34:2
And they set **a** the burnt offerings 2 Chr 35:12
The caravans turn **a** from their course; Jb 6:18
kept his way and have not turned **a**. Jb 23:11
if my step has turned **a** from the way and Jb 31:7
he may turn man **a** from his deed and Jb 33:17
because they turned **a** from following Jb 34:27
the greatness of the ransom turn you **a**. Jb 36:18
They have all turned **a**; together they Ps 14:3
I do not turn **a** from your rules, for Ps 119:102
But those who turn **a** to their crooked Ps 125:5
Let not your heart turn **a** to her ways; Prv 7:25
of the upright turns **a** from evil; Prv 16:17
to turn **a** the needy from justice and to Is 10:2
with an empty plea turn **a** him who is in Is 29:21
leave the way, turn **a** from the path, let Is 30:11
heart; they have turned **a** and gone away. Jer 5:23
like a traveler who turns **a** to tarry for a Jer 14:8
Who will turn **a** to ask about your Jer 15:5
he turned **a** my steps and tore me to Lam 3:11
in him, and set **a** the king's command, Dn 3:28
turning **a** from your commandments Dn 9:5
has transgressed your law and turned **a**, Dn 9:11
men themselves go **a** with prostitutes Hos 4:14
of the earth and turn **a** the way of the Am 2:7
bribe, and turn **a** the needy in the gate. Am 5:12
But you have turned **a** from the way. Mal 2:8
those who thrust **a** the sojourner, Mal 3:5
you have turned **a** from my statutes Mal 3:7
And Peter took him **a** and began to Mt 16:22
he took the twelve disciples **a**, Mt 20:17
And taking him **a** from the crowd Mk 7:33
And Peter took him **a** and began to Mk 8:32
He laid **a** his outer garments, and taking Jn 13:4
from which Judas turned **a** to go to his Acts 1:25
wronging his neighbor thrust him **a**, Acts 7:27
refused to obey him, but thrust him **a**, Acts 7:39
you thrust it **a** and judge yourselves Acts 13:46
and going **a** asked him privately, Acts 23:19
All have turned **a**; together they have Rom 3:12
is to put something **a** and store it up, 1 Cor 16:2
This he set **a**, nailing it to the cross. Col 2:14
commandment is set **a** because of its Heb 7:18
Anyone who has set **a** the law of Heb 10:28
witnesses, let us also lay **a** every weight, Heb 12:1

ASIEL (1)
of Joshibiah, son of Seraiah, son of **A**, 1 Chr 4:35

ASK (140)
us call the young woman and **a** her." Gn 24:57
is it that you **a** my name?" And there Gn 32:29
A me for as great a bride price and gift Gn 34:12
has sent me to you,' and they **a** me, Ex 3:13
each woman shall **a** of her neighbor, Ex 3:22
in the hearing of the people, that they **a**, Ex 11:2
"For **a** now of the days that are past, Dt 4:32
and **a** from one end of heaven to the Dt 4:32
and make search and **a** diligently. Dt 13:14
a your father, and he will show you, your Dt 32:7
When your children **a** in time to come, Jos 4:6
"When your children **a** their fathers in Jos 4:21
but did not **a** counsel from the LORD. Jos 9:14
she urged him to **a** her father for a field. Jos 15:18
she urged him to **a** her father for a field. Jgs 1:14
I did not **a** him where he was from, and Jgs 13:6
said to him, "Why do you **a** my name, Jgs 13:18
How then do you **a** me, 'What is the Jgs 18:24
I will do for you all that you **a**, for all my Ru 3:11
this evil, to **a** for ourselves a king." 1 Sm 12:19
A your young men, and they will tell 1 Sm 25:8
said, "Why then do you **a** me, 1 Sm 28:16
to **a** about his health and to bless him 2 Sm 8:10
from me anything I **a** you." And the 2 Sm 14:18
that I may send you to the king, to **a**, 2 Sm 14:32
'Let them but **a** counsel at Abel,' 2 Sm 20:18
"Please **a** King Solomon—he will not 1 Kgs 2:17
why do you **a** Abishag the 1 Kgs 2:22
A for him the kingdom also, for he is 1 Kgs 2:22
God said, "**A** what I shall give you." 1 Kgs 3:5
to Elisha, "**A** what I shall do for you, 2 Kgs 2:9
she said, "Did I **a** my lord for a son? 2 Kgs 4:28
they did not **a** an accounting from 2 Kgs 12:15
to **a** about his health and to bless 1 Chr 18:10
said to him, "**A** what I shall give you." 2 Chr 1:7
For I was ashamed to **a** the king for a Ezr 8:22
"But **a** the beasts, and they will teach Jb 12:7
that you **a**, 'What advantage have I? How Jb 35:3
A of me, and I will make the nations your Ps 2:8
they **a** me of things that I do not know. Ps 35:11
My eyes long for your promise; I **a**, Ps 119:82
Two things I **a** of you; deny them not to Prv 30:7
it is not from wisdom that you **a** this. Eccl 7:10
"**A** a sign of the LORD your God; let it be Is 7:11
But Ahaz said, "I will not **a**, and I will not Is 7:12
there is no counselor who, when I **a**, Is 41:28
formed him: "**A** me of things to come; Is 45:11
God; they **a** of me righteous judgments; Is 58:2
be sought by those who did not **a** for me; Is 65:1
and look, and **a** for the ancient paths, Jer 6:16
And when they **a** you, 'Where shall we Jer 15:2
will turn aside to **a** about your welfare? Jer 15:5
A among the nations, Who has heard Jer 18:13
A now, and see, can a man bear a child? Jer 30:6
to Jeremiah, "I will **a** you a question; Jer 38:14
A him who flees and her who escapes; Jer 48:19
They shall **a** the way to Zion, with faces Jer 50:5
let the house of Israel **a** me to do for Ezk 36:37
the prince and the judge **a** for a bribe, and Mi 7:3
of hosts: **A** the priests about the law: Hg 2:11
A rain from the LORD in the season of Zec 10:1
knows what you need before you **a** him. Mt 6:8
"**A**, and it will be given to you; seek, and Mt 7:7
give good things to those who **a** him! Mt 7:11
oath to give her whatever she might **a**. Mt 14:7
agree on earth about anything they **a**, Mt 18:19
"Why do you **a** me about what is good? Mt 19:17
And whatever you **a** in prayer, you will Mt 21:22
them, "I also will **a** you one question, Mt 21:24
did anyone dare to **a** him any more Mt 22:46
the crowd to **a** for Barabbas and Mt 27:20
the girl, "**A** me for whatever you wish, Mk 6:22
he vowed to her, "Whatever you **a** me, Mk 6:23
"For what should I **a**?" And she said, Mk 6:24
the saying, and were afraid to **a** him. Mk 9:32
you to do for us whatever we **a** of you." Mk 10:35
I tell you, whatever you **a** in prayer, Mk 11:24
to them, "I will **a** you one question; Mk 11:29
no one dared to **a** him any more Mk 12:34
came up and began to **a** Pilate to do as Mk 15:8
And Jesus said to them, "I **a** you, is it Lk 6:9
they were afraid to **a** him about this Lk 9:45
I tell you, **a**, and it will be given to you; Lk 11:9
the Holy Spirit to those who **a** him!" Lk 11:13
them, "I also will **a** you a question. Lk 20:3
no longer dared to **a** him any question. Lk 20:40
and if I **a** you, you will not answer. Lk 22:68
and Levites from Jerusalem to **a** him, Jn 1:19
is it that you, a Jew, **a** for a drink from me, Jn 4:9
And as they continued to **a** him, he stood Jn 8:7
who opened his eyes. **A** him; he is of age. Jn 9:21
his parents said, "He is of age; **a** him." Jn 9:23
I know that whatever you **a** from God, Jn 11:22
motioned to him to **a** Jesus of whom he Jn 13:24
Whatever you **a** in my name, this I will Jn 14:13
If you **a** me anything in my name, I will Jn 14:14
And I will **a** the Father, and he will give Jn 14:16
words abide in you, **a** whatever you wish, Jn 15:7
so that whatever you **a** the Father in my Jn 15:16
Jesus knew that they wanted to **a** him, Jn 16:19
In that day you will **a** nothing of me. Jn 16:23
whatever you **a** of the Father in my Jn 16:23
A, and you will receive, that your joy Jn 16:24
In that day you will **a** in my name, and I Jn 16:26
to you that I will **a** the Father on your Jn 16:26
I do not **a** that you take them out of the Jn 17:15
"I do not **a** for these only, but also for Jn 17:20
Why do you **a** me? Ask those who have Jn 18:21
A those who have heard me what I said Jn 18:21
Now none of the disciples dared **a** him, Jn 21:12
the Beautiful Gate to **a** alms of those Acts 3:2
said to Philip, "About whom, I **a** you, Acts 8:34
called out to **a** whether Simon who Acts 10:18
I **a** then why you sent for me." Acts 10:29
to Joppa and **a** for Simon who Acts 10:32
Jews have agreed to **a** you to bring Acts 23:20
But I **a**, have they not heard? Indeed Rom 10:18
But I **a**, did Israel not understand? Rom 10:19
myself to those who did not **a** for me." Rom 10:20
I **a**, then, has God rejected his people? Rom 11:1
So I **a**, did they stumble in order that Rom 11:11
let them **a** their husbands at home. 1 Cor 14:35
But someone will **a**, "How are the 1 Cor 15:35
Let me **a** you only this: Did you receive Gal 3:2
So I **a** you not to lose heart over what I Eph 3:13
abundantly than all that we **a** or think, Eph 3:20
Yes, I **a** you also, true companion, help Phil 4:3
we **a** and urge you in the Lord Jesus, 1 Thes 4:1
We **a** you, brothers, to respect those 1 Thes 5:12
gathered together to him, we **a** you, 2 Thes 2:1
any of you lacks wisdom, let him **a** God, Jas 1:5
But let him **a** in faith, with no doubting, Jas 1:6
You do not have, because you do not **a**. Jas 4:2
You **a** and do not receive, because you Jas 4:3
do not receive, because you **a** wrongly, Jas 4:3
and whatever we **a** we receive from 1 Jn 3:22
that if we **a** anything according to his 1 Jn 5:14
that he hears us in whatever we **a**, 1 Jn 5:15
a sin not leading to death, he shall **a**, 1 Jn 5:16
And now I **a** you, dear lady—not as 2 Jn 1:5

ASKED (156)
Then I **a** her, 'Whose daughter are Gn 24:47
men of the place **a** him about his wife, Gn 26:7
Then Jacob **a** him, "Please tell me your Gn 32:29
And the man **a** him, "What are you Gn 37:15
And he **a** the men of the place, "Where Gn 38:21
So he **a** Pharaoh's officers who were Gn 40:7
My lord **a** his servants, saying, 'Have Gn 44:19
set over them, were beaten and were **a**, Ex 5:14
And the LORD did as Moses **a**, and Ex 8:31
for they had **a** the Egyptians for silver Ex 12:35
so that they let them have what they **a**. Ex 12:36
And they **a** each other of their welfare Ex 18:7
LORD they gave him the city that he **a**, Jos 19:50
He **a** water and she gave him milk; she Jgs 5:25
of Micah, and **a** him about his welfare. Jgs 18:15
said, "I have **a** for him from the LORD." 1 Sm 1:20
for the petition she **a** of the LORD." So 1 Sm 2:20
have chosen, for whom you have **a**; 1 Sm 12:13
And he **a**, "Where are Samuel and 1 Sm 19:22
'David earnestly **a** leave of me to run 1 Sm 20:6
"David earnestly **a** leave of me to go 1 Sm 20:28
When Achish **a**, "Where have you 1 Sm 27:10
David **a** how Joab was doing and how 2 Sm 11:7
And when he **a**, they set food before 2 Sm 12:20
the Lord that Solomon had **a** this. 1 Kgs 3:10
said to him, "Because you have **a** this, 1 Kgs 3:11
and have not **a** for yourself long life 1 Kgs 3:11
but have **a** for yourself 1 Kgs 3:11
I give you also what you have not **a**, 1 Kgs 3:13
whatever she **a** besides what was 1 Kgs 10:13
And he **a** that he might die, saying, "It 1 Kgs 19:4
he said, "You have **a** a hard thing; 2 Kgs 2:10
And the king **a** her, "What is your 2 Kgs 6:28
And when the king **a** the woman, she 2 Kgs 8:6
accounting shall be **a** from them for 2 Kgs 22:7
pain!" And God granted what he **a**. 1 Chr 4:10
and you have not **a** possessions, 2 Chr 1:11
you, and have not even **a** long life, 2 Chr 1:11
but have **a** wisdom and knowledge 2 Chr 1:11
whatever she **a** besides what she had 2 Chr 9:12
They also **a** them this: "What are the Ezr 5:4
Then we **a** those elders and spoke to them Ezr 5:9
We also **a** them their names, for your Ezr 5:10
and the king granted him all that he **a**, Ezr 7:6
And I **a** them concerning the Jews who Neh 1:2
And the king granted me what I **a**, Neh 2:8

after some time I **a** leave of the king Neh 13:6
she **a** for nothing except what Hegai the Est 2:15
may do as Esther has **a**." So the king and Est 5:5
Have you not **a** those who travel the Jb 21:29
He **a** life of you; you gave it to him, Ps 21:4
One thing have I **a** of the LORD, that will I Ps 27:4
They **a**, and he brought quail, and Ps 105:40
he gave them what they **a**, but sent a Ps 106:15
Then they **a** Baruch, "Tell us, please, Jer 36:17
officials came to Jeremiah and **a** him, Jer 38:27
Therefore he **a** the chief of the eunuchs to Dn 1:8
and powerful king has **a** such a thing of Dn 2:10
made known to me what we **a** of you, Dn 2:23
king the mystery that the king has **a**, Dn 2:27
who stood there and **a** him the truth Dn 7:16
And he **a** that he might die and said, "It is Jon 4:8
And they **a** him, "Is it lawful to heal on Mt 12:10
and to test him they **a** him to show them Mt 16:1
of Caesarea Philippi, he **a** his disciples, Mt 16:13
And the disciples **a** him, "Then why do Mt 17:10
before him she **a** him for something. Mt 20:20
and they **a** him a question, Mt 22:23
a lawyer, **a** him a question to test him. Mt 22:35
together, Jesus **a** them a question, Mt 22:41
the governor, and the governor **a** him, Mt 27:11
He went to Pilate and **a** for the body of Mt 27:58
him with the twelve **a** him about the Mk 4:10
And Jesus **a** him, "What is your name?" Mk 5:9
with haste to the king and **a**, Mk 6:25
And the Pharisees and the scribes **a** him, Mk 7:5
his disciples **a** him about the parable. Mk 7:17
And he **a** them, "How many loaves do Mk 8:5
and laid his hands on him, he **a** him, Mk 8:23
And on the way he **a** his disciples, Mk 8:27
And he **a** them, "But who do you say Mk 8:29
And they **a** him, "Why do the scribes Mk 9:11
And he **a** them, "What are you arguing Mk 9:16
So I **a** your disciples to cast it out, and Mk 9:18
And Jesus **a** his father, "How long has Mk 9:21
the house, his disciples **a** him privately, Mk 9:28
when he was in the house he **a** them, Mk 9:33
came up and in order to test him **a**, Mk 10:2
house the disciples **a** him again about Mk 10:10
up and knelt before him and **a** him, Mk 10:17
And they **a** him a question, saying, Mk 12:18
that he answered them well, **a** him, Mk 12:28
and John and Andrew **a** him privately, Mk 13:3
stood up in the midst and **a** Jesus, Mk 14:60
Again the high priest **a** him, "Are you Mk 14:61
And Pilate **a** him, "Are you the King of Mk 15:2
And Pilate again **a** him, "Have you no Mk 15:4
for them one prisoner for whom they **a**. Mk 15:6
went to Pilate and **a** for the body of Mk 15:43
he **a** him whether he was already dead. Mk 15:44
And he **a** for a writing tablet and wrote, Lk 1:63
And the crowds **a** him, "What then Lk 3:10
Soldiers also **a** him, "And we, what shall Lk 3:14
he **a** him to put out a little from the land. Lk 5:3
One of the Pharisees **a** him to eat with Lk 7:36
And when his disciples **a** him what this Lk 8:9
Jesus then **a** him, "What is your name?" Lk 8:30
country of the Gerasenes **a** him to depart Lk 8:37
And he **a** them, "Who do the crowds say Lk 9:18
a Pharisee **a** him to dine with him, Lk 11:37
of the servants and **a** what these things Lk 15:26
Being **a** by the Pharisees when the Lk 17:20
And a ruler **a** him, "Good Teacher, Lk 18:18
And when he came near, he **a** him, Lk 18:40
So they **a** him, "Teacher, we know that Lk 20:21
and they **a** him a question, saying, Lk 20:28
And they **a** him, "Teacher, when will Lk 21:7
And Pilate **a** him, "Are you the King of Lk 23:3
he **a** whether the man was a Galilean. Lk 23:6
and murder, for whom they **a**, Lk 23:25
went to Pilate and **a** for the body of Lk 23:52
And they **a** him, "What then? Are you Jn 1:21
They **a** him, "Then why are you Jn 1:25
'Give me a drink,' you would have **a** him, Jn 4:10
to him, they **a** him to stay with them, Jn 4:40
he went to him and **a** him to come down Jn 4:47
So he **a** them the hour when he began to Jn 4:52
They **a** him, "Who is the man who said Jn 5:12
And his disciples **a** him, "Rabbi, who Jn 9:2
So the Pharisees again **a** him how he had Jn 9:15
and **a** them, "Is this your son, who you Jn 9:19
from Bethsaida in Galilee, and **a** him, Jn 12:21
Until now you have **a** nothing in my Jn 16:24
So he **a** them again, "Whom do you Jn 18:7
a, "Did I not see you in the garden with Jn 18:26
the Jews **a** Pilate that their legs might be Jn 19:31
a Pilate that he might take away the Jn 19:38
they had come together, they **a** him, Acts 1:6
go into the temple, he **a** to receive alms. Acts 3:3
and **a** for a murderer to be granted to Acts 3:14
sight of God and **a** to find a dwelling Acts 7:46
him reading Isaiah the prophet and **a**, Acts 8:30
and **a** him for letters to the synagogues Acts 9:2
Then they **a** him to remain for some Acts 10:48
king's chamberlain, they **a** for peace, Acts 12:20
Then they **a** for a king, and God gave Acts 13:21
they **a** Pilate to have him executed. Acts 13:28
took them out and **a** them to leave the Acts 16:39
When they **a** him to stay for a longer Acts 18:20
prisoner called me and **a** me to bring Acts 23:18
and going aside **a** him privately, Acts 23:19
he **a** what province he was from. Acts 23:34
I **a** whether he wanted to go to Acts 25:20
I have **a** to see you and speak with Acts 28:20
Only, they **a** us to remember the poor, Gal 2:10
the requests that we have **a** of him. 1 Jn 5:15

ASKING (20)
is what you are **a**." And they were Ex 10:11
the people who were **a** for a king from 1 Sm 8:10
the LORD, in **a** for yourselves a king." 1 Sm 12:17
never at any time displeased him by **a**, 1 Kgs 1:6
let my mouth sin by **a** for his life with a Jb 31:30
to Egypt, without **a** for my direction, Is 30:2
LORD, and he delights in them." Or by **a**, Mal 2:17
stood outside, **a** to speak to him. Mt 12:46
came up to him and tested him by **a**, Mt 19:3
"You do not know what you are **a**. Mt 20:22
"You do not know what you are **a**. Mk 10:38
listening to them and **a** them questions. Lk 2:46
Jews, **a** him to come and heal his servant. Lk 7:3
also blindfolded him and kept **a** him, Lk 22:64
them, "Is this what you are **a** yourselves, Jn 16:19
Gate of the temple, **a** for alms. Acts 3:10
a as a favor against Paul that he Acts 25:3
a for a sentence of condemnation Acts 25:15
a that somehow by God's will I may Rom 1:10
a that you may be filled with the Col 1:9

ASKS (18)
Esau my brother meets you and **a** you, Gn 32:17
when in time to come your son **a** you, Ex 13:14
"When your son **a** you in time to come, Dt 6:20
tent, and if any man comes and **a** you, Jgs 4:20
satisfied with riches, so that he never **a**, Eccl 4:8
people, or a prophet or a priest **a** you, Jer 23:33
The thing that the king **a** is difficult, Dn 2:11
And if one **a** him, 'What are these Zec 13:6
For everyone who **a** receives, and the one Mt 7:8
one of you, if his son **a** him for bread, Mt 7:9
Or if he **a** for a fish, will give him a Mt 7:10
For everyone who **a** receives, and the Lk 11:10
among you, if his son **a** for a fish, Lk 11:11
or if he **a** for an egg, will give him a Lk 11:12
sends a delegation and **a** for terms of Lk 14:32
If anyone **a** you, 'Why are you untying Lk 19:31
him who sent me, and none of you **a** me, Jn 16:5
defense to anyone who **a** you for a 1 Pt 3:15

ASLEEP (26)
And he fell **a** and dreamed a second Gn 41:5
he was lying fast **a** from weariness. Jgs 4:21
did any awake, for they were all **a**, 1 Sm 26:12
or perhaps he is **a** and must be 1 Kgs 18:27
ship and had lain down and was fast **a**. Jon 1:5
Your shepherds are **a**, O king of Assyria; Na 3:18
swamped by the waves; but he was **a**. Mt 8:24
the saints who had fallen **a** were raised, Mt 27:52
and stole him away while we were **a**.' Mt 28:13
he was in the stern, **a** on the cushion. Mk 4:38
lest he come suddenly and find you **a**. Mk 13:36
he said to Peter, "Simon, are you **a**? Mk 14:37
and as they sailed he fell **a**. And a Lk 8:23
them, "Our friend Lazarus has fallen **a**, Jn 11:11
said to him, "Lord, if he has fallen **a**, Jn 11:12
And when he had said this, he fell **a**. Acts 7:60
fell **a** and was laid with his fathers Acts 13:36
still alive, though some have fallen **a**. 1 Cor 15:6
who have fallen **a** in Christ have 1 Cor 15:18
firstfruits of those who have fallen **a**. 1 Cor 15:20
brothers, about those who are **a**, 1 Thes 4:13
with him those who have fallen **a**. 1 Thes 4:14
not precede those who have fallen **a**. 1 Thes 4:15
we are awake or **a** we might live 1 Thes 5:10
is not idle, and their destruction is not **a**. 2 Pt 2:3
For ever since the fathers fell **a**, all 2 Pt 3:4

ASNAH (1)
the sons of **A**, the sons of Meunim, the Ezr 2:50

ASPATHA (1)
killed Parshandatha and Dalphon and **A** Est 9:7

ASPIRE (1)
and to **a** to live quietly, and to mind 1 Thes 4:11

ASPIRES (1)
If anyone **a** to the office of overseer, he 1 Tm 3:1

ASPS (3)
of serpents and the cruel venom of **a**. Dt 32:33
and under their lips is the venom of **a**. Ps 140:3
"The venom of **a** is under their Rom 3:13

ASRIEL (3)
and of **A**, the clan of the Asrielites; Nm 26:31
their clans, Abiezer, Helek, **A**, Shechem, Jos 17:2
A, whom his Aramean concubine 1 Chr 7:14

ASRIELITES (1)
and of Asriel, the clan of the **A**; and of Nm 26:31

ASSAIL (1)
When evildoers **a** me to eat up my flesh, Ps 27:2

ASSAILANTS (2)
ears have heard the doom of my evil **a**. Ps 92:11
and thoughts of my **a** are against me Lam 3:62

ASSAILED (2)
me, the torrents of destruction **a** me; 2 Sm 22:5
me; the torrents of destruction **a** me; Ps 18:4

ASSASSINS (1)
thousand men of the **A** out into the Acts 21:38

ASSAULT (4)
so that he may **a** us and fall upon us to Gn 43:18
another, or one kind of **a** and another, Dt 17:8
every dispute and every **a** shall be settled. Dt 21:5
"Will he even **a** the queen in my Est 7:8

ASSAULTED (1)
women, lest in another field you be **a**." Ru 2:22

ASSAULTS (1)
over me; your dreadful **a** destroy me. Ps 88:16

ASSEMBLE (24)
"**A** and listen, O sons of Jacob, listen to Gn 49:2
And **a** all the congregation at the Lv 8:3
of meeting and **a** the whole Nm 8:9
"Take the staff, and **a** the congregation, Nm 20:8
A the people, men, women, and little Dt 31:12
A to me all the elders of your tribes and Dt 31:28
exiles that they should **a** at Jerusalem, Ezr 10:7
it into my heart to **a** the nobles and the Neh 7:5
the nations and will **a** the banished of Is 11:12
nations gather together, and the peoples **a**. Is 43:9
Let them all **a**, let them stand forth. Is 44:11
"**A** yourselves and come; draw near Is 45:20
"**A**, all of you, and listen! who among Is 48:14
'**A**, and let us go into the fortified cities!' Jer 4:5
Go, **a** all the wild beasts; bring them to Jer 12:9
from the peoples and **a** you out of the Ezk 11:17
to all beasts of the field, '**A** and come, Ezk 39:17
shall wage war and **a** a multitude of Dn 11:10
Consecrate the congregation; **a** the elders; Jl 2:16
"**A** yourselves on the mountains of Am 3:9
I will surely **a** all of you, O Jacob; I will Mi 2:12
I will **a** the lame and gather those who Mi 4:6
is to gather nations, to **a** kingdoms, Zep 3:8
to **a** them for battle on the great day of Rv 16:14

ASSEMBLED (43)
Moses **a** all the congregation of the Ex 35:1
the congregation was **a** at the entrance Lv 8:4
they **a** the whole congregation together, Nm 1:18
They **a** themselves together against Nm 16:3
Then Korah **a** all the congregation Nm 16:19
the congregation had **a** against Moses Nm 16:42
And they **a** themselves together against Nm 20:2
of the people of Israel **a** at Shiloh and set Jos 18:1
and the congregation **a** as one man to Jgs 20:1
And all Israel **a** and mourned for him, 1 Sm 25:1
The Philistines **a** and came and 1 Sm 28:4
all the Bichrites **a** and followed him 2 Sm 20:14
Then Solomon **a** the elders of Israel 1 Kgs 8:1
the men of Israel **a** to King Solomon at 1 Kgs 8:2
of Israel, who had **a** before him, 1 Kgs 8:5
he **a** all the house of Judah and the 1 Kgs 12:21
Then Jehu **a** all the people and said 2 Kgs 10:18
So David **a** all Israel from the Nile of 1 Chr 13:5
And David **a** all Israel at Jerusalem to 1 Chr 15:3
David **a** all the leaders of Israel and 1 Chr 23:2
David **a** at Jerusalem all the officials 1 Chr 28:1
Then Solomon **a** the elders of Israel 2 Chr 5:2
the men of Israel **a** before the king at 2 Chr 5:3
of Israel, who had **a** before him, 2 Chr 5:6
he **a** the house of Judah and 2 Chr 11:1
And Judah **a** to seek help from the 2 Chr 20:4
the fourth day they **a** in the Valley 2 Chr 20:26
Then Amaziah **a** the men of Judah 2 Chr 25:5
and the Levites and **a** them in the 2 Chr 29:4
nor had the people **a** in Jerusalem— 2 Chr 30:3
Judah and Benjamin **a** at Jerusalem Ezr 10:9
people of Israel were **a** with fasting and Neh 9:1
For behold, the kings **a**; they came on Ps 48:4
of utter ruin in the **a** congregation." Prv 5:14
land arose and spoke to all the **a** people, Jer 26:17
and all your hosts that are **a** about you, Ezk 38:7
Have you **a** your hosts to carry off Ezk 38:13

the nations and then **a** them into their — Ezk 39:28
Now many nations are **a** against you, — Mi 4:11
And when they had **a** with the elders — Mt 28:12
the crowds that had **a** for this spectacle, — Lk 23:48
When you are **a** in the name of the — 1 Cor 5:4
And they **a** them at the place that in — Rv 16:16

ASSEMBLIES (2)
Mount Zion and over her **a** a cloud by day, — Is 4:5
and I take no delight in your solemn **a**. — Am 5:21

ASSEMBLING (1)
and **a** all the chief priests and scribes of — Mt 2:4

ASSEMBLY (118)
when the whole **a** of the congregation of — Ex 12:6
On the first day you shall hold a holy **a**, — Ex 12:16
and on the seventh day a holy **a**. — Ex 12:16
to kill this whole **a** with hunger." — Ex 16:3
the thing is hidden from the eyes of the **a**, — Lv 4:13
the **a** shall offer a bull from the herd for — Lv 4:14
first bull; it is the sin offering for the **a**. — Lv 4:21
for his house and for all the **a** of Israel. — Lv 16:17
the priests and for all the people of the **a**. — Lv 16:33
It is a solemn **a**; you shall not do any — Lv 23:36
But when the **a** is to be gathered — Nm 10:7
before all the **a** of the congregation — Nm 14:5
For the **a**, there shall be one statute for — Nm 15:15
of the congregation, chosen from the **a**, — Nm 16:2
yourselves above the **a** of the LORD?" — Nm 16:3
they perished from the midst of the **a**. — Nm 16:33
said and ran into the midst of the **a**. — Nm 16:47
be cut off from the midst of the **a**, — Nm 19:20
have you brought the **a** of the LORD into — Nm 20:4
the presence of the **a** to the entrance of — Nm 20:6
Aaron gathered the **a** together before — Nm 20:10
shall not bring this **a** into the land — Nm 20:12
eighth day you shall have a solemn **a**. — Nm 29:35
spoke to all your **a** at the mountain out — Dt 5:22
of the midst of the fire on the day of the **a**. — Dt 9:10
of the midst of the fire on the day of the **a**. — Dt 10:4
shall be a solemn **a** to the LORD your — Dt 16:8
your God at Horeb on the day of the **a**, — Dt 18:16
is cut off shall enter the **a** of the LORD. — Dt 23:1
union may enter the **a** of the LORD. — Dt 23:2
descendants may enter the **a** of the LORD. — Dt 23:2
or Moabite may enter the **a** of the LORD. — Dt 23:3
them may enter the **a** of the LORD forever, — Dt 23:3
generation may enter the **a** of the LORD. — Dt 23:8
finished, in the ears of all the **a** of Israel: — Dt 31:30
a law, as a possession for the **a** of Jacob. — Dt 33:4
did not read before all the **a** of Israel, — Jos 8:35
the whole **a** of the people of Israel — Jos 22:12
themselves in the **a** of the people — Jgs 20:2
not come up in the **a** to the LORD?" For — Jgs 21:5
to the camp from Jabesh-gilead, to the **a**. — Jgs 21:8
and that all this **a** may know that — 1 Sm 17:47
around and blessed all the **a** of Israel, — 1 Kgs 8:14
of Israel, while all the **a** of Israel stood. — 1 Kgs 8:14
presence of all the **a** of Israel and — 1 Kgs 8:22
and blessed all the **a** of Israel with a — 1 Kgs 8:55
and all Israel with him, a great **a**, — 1 Kgs 8:65
Jeroboam and all the **a** of Israel came — 1 Kgs 12:3
called him to the **a** and made him — 1 Kgs 12:20
"Sanctify a solemn **a** for Baal." So — 2 Kgs 10:20
And David said to all the **a** of Israel, — 1 Chr 13:2
All the **a** agreed to do so, for the thing — 1 Chr 13:4
sight of all Israel, the **a** of the LORD, — 1 Chr 28:8
And David the king said to all the **a**, — 1 Chr 29:1
the LORD in the presence of all the **a**. — 1 Chr 29:10
Then David said to all the **a**, "Bless — 1 Chr 29:20
God." And all the **a** blessed the LORD, — 1 Chr 29:20
And Solomon, and all the **a** with him, — 2 Chr 1:3
And Solomon and the **a** resorted to it. — 2 Chr 1:5
around and blessed all the **a** of Israel, — 2 Chr 6:3
of Israel, while all the **a** of Israel stood. — 2 Chr 6:3
presence of all the **a** of Israel and — 2 Chr 6:12
in the presence of all the **a** of Israel, — 2 Chr 6:13
and all Israel with him, a very great **a**, — 2 Chr 7:8
the eighth day they held a solemn **a**, — 2 Chr 7:9
stood in the **a** of Judah and — 2 Chr 20:5
sons of Asaph, in the midst of the **a**. — 2 Chr 20:14
And all the **a** made a covenant with — 2 Chr 23:3
before the princes and all the **a**. — 2 Chr 28:14
were brought to the king and the **a**, — 2 Chr 29:23
The whole **a** worshiped, and the — 2 Chr 29:28
LORD." And the **a** brought sacrifices — 2 Chr 29:31
offerings that the **a** brought was 70 — 2 Chr 29:32
and all the **a** in Jerusalem had — 2 Chr 30:2
seemed right to the king and all the **a**. — 2 Chr 30:4
in the second month, a very great **a**. — 2 Chr 30:13
were many in the **a** who had not — 2 Chr 30:17
Then the whole **a** agreed together to — 2 Chr 30:23
of Judah gave the **a** 1,000 bulls and — 2 Chr 30:24
princes gave the **a** 1,000 bulls and — 2 Chr 30:24
The whole **a** of Judah, and the — 2 Chr 30:25
and the whole **a** that came out of — 2 Chr 30:25
and their daughters, the whole **a**, — 2 Chr 31:18
The whole **a** together was 42,360, — Ezr 2:64
the house of God, a very great **a** of men, — Ezr 10:1
Then all the **a** answered with a loud — Ezr 10:12
Let our officials stand for the whole **a**. — Ezr 10:14
And I held a great **a** against them — Neh 5:7
And all the **a** said "Amen" and — Neh 5:13
The whole **a** together was 42,360, — Neh 7:66
the priest brought the Law before the **a**, — Neh 8:2
And all the **a** of those who had — Neh 8:17
on the eighth day there was a solemn **a**, — Neh 8:18
Moabite should ever enter the **a** of God, — Neh 13:1
sun; I stand up in the **a** and cry for help. — Jb 30:28
Let the **a** of the peoples be gathered about — Ps 7:7
I hate the **a** of evildoers, and I will not sit — Ps 26:5
in the great **a** I will bless the LORD. — Ps 26:12
your faithfulness in the **a** of the holy — Ps 89:5
and praise him in the **a** of the elders. — Ps 107:32
song, his praise in the **a** of the godly! — Ps 149:1
good sense will rest in the **a** of the dead. — Prv 21:16
wickedness will be exposed in the **a**. — Prv 26:26
I cannot endure iniquity and solemn **a**. — Is 1:13
sit on the mount of **a** in the far reaches — Is 14:13
all the women who stood by, a great **a**, — Jer 44:15
he summoned an **a** against me to — Lam 1:15
Consecrate a fast; call a solemn **a**. Gather — Jl 1:14
in Zion; consecrate a fast; call a solemn **a**; — Jl 2:15
to cast the line by lot in the **a** of the LORD. — Mi 2:5
the **a** of the elders of the people gathered — Lk 22:66
And all the **a** fell silent, and they — Acts 15:12
another, for the **a** was in confusion, — Acts 19:32
it shall be settled in the regular **a**. — Acts 19:39
said these things, he dismissed the **a**. — Acts 19:41
the Sadducees, and the **a** was divided. — Acts 23:7
and to the **a** of the firstborn who are — Heb 12:23
ring and fine clothing comes into your **a**, — Jas 2:2

ASSERTED (1)
dead, but whom Paul **a** to be alive. — Acts 25:19

ASSERTIONS (1)
about which they make confident **a**. — 1 Tm 1:7

ASSESSED (1)
which each man is **a**—the money — 2 Kgs 12:4

ASSESSMENT (2)
the money from the **a** of persons— — 2 Kgs 12:4
from everyone according to his **a**, — 2 Kgs 23:35

ASSHUR (6)
Elam, **A**, Arpachshad, Lud, and Aram. — Gn 10:22
be burned when **A** takes you away — Nm 24:22
Kittim and shall afflict **A** and Eber; — Nm 24:24
Elam, **A**, Arpachshad, Lud, and — 1 Chr 1:17
A also has joined them; they are the — Ps 83:8
A, and Chilmad traded with you. — Ezk 27:23

ASSHURIM (1)
The sons of Dedan were **A**, Letushim, — Gn 25:3

ASSIGN (7)
And you shall **a** to their charge all that — Nm 4:27
For I **a** to you a number of days, 390 — Ezk 4:5
Forty days I **a** you, a day for each year. — Ezk 4:6
I **a** to you cow's dung instead of human — Ezk 4:15
district you shall **a** for the property — Ezk 45:6
there you shall **a** him his inheritance, — Ezk 47:23
and I **a** to you, as my Father assigned to — Lk 22:29

ASSIGNED (17)
a to another man and not yet ransomed — Lv 19:20
to the place to which you have **a** him. — 1 Sm 29:4
he **a** Uriah to the place where he — 2 Sm 11:16
a house and **a** him an allowance — 1 Kgs 11:18
And Solomon **a** 70,000 men to bear — 2 Chr 2:2
any design that may be **a** him, — 2 Chr 2:14
of them he **a** to bear burdens, — 2 Chr 2:18
Levites in Judah were **a** to Benjamin. — Neh 11:36
when he **a** to the sea its limit, so that the — Prv 8:29
The king **a** them a daily portion of the — Dn 1:5
king, who **a** your food and your drink; — Dn 1:10
chief of the eunuchs had **a** over Daniel, — Dn 1:11
I assign to you, as my Father **a** to me, — Lk 22:29
to the measure of faith that God has **a**. — Rom 12:3
you believed, as the Lord **a** to each. — 1 Cor 3:5
the life that the Lord has **a** to him, — 1 Cor 7:17
to the area of influence God **a** to us, — 2 Cor 10:13

ASSIGNING (1)
you do to the Levites in **a** their duties." — Nm 8:26

ASSIGNS (1)
the day when he **a** his possessions as an — Dt 21:16

ASSIR (4)
of Korah: **A**, Elkanah, and Abiasaph; — Ex 6:24
his son, Korah his son, **A** his son, — 1 Chr 6:22
his son, Ebiasaph his son, **A** his son, — 1 Chr 6:23
son of Tahath, son of **A**, son of — 1 Chr 6:37

ASSIST (4)
the names of the men who shall **a** you. — Nm 1:5
their duty was to **a** the sons of — 1 Chr 23:28
was also to **a** with the showbread, — 1 Chr 23:29
the Jews. And they had John to **a** them. — Acts 13:5

ASSISTANT (5)
So Moses rose with his **a** Joshua, and — Ex 24:13
the camp, his **a** Joshua the son of Nun, — Ex 33:11
Nun, the **a** of Moses from his youth, — Nm 11:28
said to Joshua the son of Nun, Moses' **a**, — Jos 1:1
and as their **a** Hanan the son of — Neh 13:13

ASSISTED (2)
and went after Elijah and **a** him. — 1 Kgs 19:21
be **a** by the men of his place with silver — Ezr 1:4

ASSISTING (2)
were overseers **a** Conaniah and — 2 Chr 31:13
Shecaniah were faithfully **a** him in — 2 Chr 31:15

ASSOCIATE (7)
so that you **a** with them and they with — Jos 23:12
therefore do not **a** with a simple — Prv 20:19
is for a Jew to **a** with or to visit anyone — Acts 10:28
not be haughty, but **a** with the lowly. — Rom 12:16
letter not to **a** with sexually immoral — 1 Cor 5:9
to you not to **a** with anyone who — 1 Cor 5:11
Therefore do not **a** with them; — Eph 5:7

ASSOCIATED (3)
and the people of Israel **a** with him'; — Ezk 37:16
and all the house of Israel **a** with him.' — Ezk 37:16
and the tribes of Israel **a** with him. — Ezk 37:19

ASSOCIATES (8)
the rest of their **a** wrote to Artaxerxes — Ezr 4:7
the scribe, and the rest of their **a**, — Ezr 4:9
the rest of their **a** who live in Samaria — Ezr 4:17
and Shimshai the scribe and their **a**, — Ezr 4:23
Shethar-bozenai and their **a** came to — Ezr 5:3
Shethar-bozenai and his **a** the governors — Ezr 5:6
and your **a** the governors who are in the — Ezr 6:6
and their **a** did with all diligence what — Ezr 6:13

ASSOCIATION (1)
But some, through former **a** with idols, — 1 Cor 8:7

ASSOS (2)
ahead to the ship, we set sail for **A**, — Acts 20:13
And when he met us at **A**, we took — Acts 20:14

ASSUAGE (1)
the solace of my lips would **a** your pain. — Jb 16:5

ASSUAGED (1)
"If I speak, my pain is not **a**, and if I — Jb 16:6

ASSUMING (2)
a that you have heard of the stewardship — Eph 3:2
a that you have heard about him and — Eph 4:21

ASSURANCE (6)
be in dread and have no **a** of your life. — Dt 28:66
of this he has given **a** to all by raising — Acts 17:31
the riches of full **a** of understanding and — Col 2:2
to have the full **a** of hope until the — Heb 6:11
with a true heart in full **a** of faith, — Heb 10:22
Now faith is the **a** of things hoped for, — Heb 11:1

ASSURED (5)
Be **a**, an evil person will not go — Prv 11:21
is an abomination to the LORD; be **a**, — Prv 16:5
I will give you **a** peace in this place.'" — Jer 14:13
the angel of the LORD solemnly **a** Joshua, — Zec 3:6
stand mature and fully **a** in all the will — Col 4:12

ASSYRIA (130)
river is the Tigris, which flows east of **A**. — Gn 2:14
land he went into **A** and built Nineveh, — Gn 10:11
is opposite Egypt in the direction of **A**. — Gn 25:18
Pul the king of **A** came against the — 2 Kgs 15:19
every man, to give to the king of **A**. — 2 Kgs 15:20
So the king of **A** turned back and — 2 Kgs 15:20
Tiglath-pileser king of **A** came and — 2 Kgs 15:29
he carried the people captive to **A**. — 2 Kgs 15:29
to Tiglath-pileser king of **A**, — 2 Kgs 16:7
and sent a present to the king of **A**. — 2 Kgs 16:8
And the king of **A** listened to him. — 2 Kgs 16:9
The king of **A** marched up against — 2 Kgs 16:9
to meet Tiglath-pileser king of **A**, — 2 Kgs 16:10
of the LORD, because of the king of **A**. — 2 Kgs 16:18
him came up Shalmaneser king of **A**. — 2 Kgs 17:3
But the king of **A** found treachery in — 2 Kgs 17:4
offered no tribute to the king of **A**, — 2 Kgs 17:4
Therefore the king of **A** shut him up — 2 Kgs 17:4
Then the king of **A** invaded all the — 2 Kgs 17:5
the king of **A** captured Samaria, — 2 Kgs 17:6
Israelites away to **A** and placed them — 2 Kgs 17:6
their own land to **A** until this day. — 2 Kgs 17:23
the king of **A** brought people from — 2 Kgs 17:24
So the king of **A** was told, "The — 2 Kgs 17:26
Then the king of **A** commanded, — 2 Kgs 17:27

against the king of **A** and would not 2 Kgs 18:7
Shalmaneser king of **A** came up 2 Kgs 18:9
The king of **A** carried the Israelites 2 Kgs 18:11
Israelites away to **A** and put them 2 Kgs 18:11
Sennacherib king of **A** came up 2 Kgs 18:13
sent to the king of **A** at Lachish, 2 Kgs 18:14
the king of **A** required of Hezekiah 2 Kgs 18:14
overlaid and gave it to the king of **A**. 2 Kgs 18:16
And the king of **A** sent the Tartan, 2 Kgs 18:17
says the great king, the king of **A**: 2 Kgs 18:19
wager with my master the king of **A**: 2 Kgs 18:23
of the great king, the king of **A**! 2 Kgs 18:28
given into the hand of the king of **A**.' 2 Kgs 18:30
for thus says the king of **A**: 2 Kgs 18:31
out of the hand of the king of **A**? 2 Kgs 18:33
master the king of **A** has sent to 2 Kgs 19:4
of the king of **A** have reviled me. 2 Kgs 19:6
the king of **A** fighting against 2 Kgs 19:8
given into the hand of the king of **A**. 2 Kgs 19:10
what the kings of **A** have done to all 2 Kgs 19:11
the kings of **A** have laid waste the 2 Kgs 19:17
Sennacherib king of **A** I have heard. 2 Kgs 19:20
the LORD concerning the king of **A**: 2 Kgs 19:32
Sennacherib king of **A** departed and 2 Kgs 19:36
city out of the hand of the king of **A**, 2 Kgs 20:6
to the king of **A** to the river 2 Kgs 23:29
Tiglath-pileser king of **A** carried away 1 Chr 5:6
stirred up the spirit of Pul king of **A**, 1 Chr 5:26
the spirit of Tiglath-pileser king of **A**, 1 Chr 5:26
Ahaz sent to the king of **A** for help. 2 Chr 28:16
king of **A** came against 2 Chr 28:20
and gave tribute to the king of **A**, 2 Chr 28:21
from the hand of the kings of **A**. 2 Chr 30:6
Sennacherib king of **A** came and 2 Chr 32:1
should the kings of **A** come and find 2 Chr 32:4
before the king of **A** and all the horde 2 Chr 32:7
After this, Sennacherib, king of **A**, 2 Chr 32:9
"Thus says Sennacherib king of **A**, 2 Chr 32:10
us from the hand of the king of **A**"? 2 Chr 32:11
in the camp of the king of **A**. 2 Chr 32:21
Sennacherib king of **A** and from 2 Chr 32:22
of the army of the king of **A**, 2 Chr 33:11
of Esarhaddon king of **A** who brought us Ezr 4:2
the heart of the king of **A** to them, Ezr 6:22
time of the kings of **A** until this day. Neh 9:32
departed from Judah—the king of **A**." Is 7:17
and for the bee that is in the land of **A**. Is 7:18
—with the king of **A**—the head and the Is 7:20
will be carried away before the king of **A**." Is 8:4
and many, the king of **A** and all his glory. Is 8:7
Ah, **A**, the rod of my anger; the staff in Is 10:5
of the king of **A** and the boastful look Is 10:12
that remains of his people, from **A**, Is 11:11
be a highway from **A** for the remnant Is 11:16
there will be a highway from Egypt to **A**, Is 19:23
to Assyria, and **A** will come into Egypt, Is 19:23
will come into Egypt, and Egypt into **A**, Is 19:23
Israel will be the third with Egypt and **A**, Is 19:24
my people, and **A** the work of my hands, Is 19:25
who was sent by Sargon the king of **A**, Is 20:1
shall the king of **A** lead away the Is 20:4
help to be delivered from the king of **A**! Is 20:6
was not; **A** destined it for wild beasts. Is 23:13
lost in the land of **A** and those who were Is 27:13
Sennacherib king of **A** came up against Is 36:1
And the king of **A** sent the Rabshakeh Is 36:2
'Thus says the great king, the king of **A**: Is 36:4
a wager with my master the king of **A**: Is 36:8
words of the great king, the king of **A**! Is 36:13
be given into the hand of the king of **A**." Is 36:15
For thus says the king of **A**: Make your Is 36:16
land out of the hand of the king of **A**? Is 36:18
his master the king of **A** has sent to mock Is 37:4
men of the king of **A** have reviled me. Is 37:6
the king of **A** fighting against Libnah, Is 37:8
be given into the hand of the king of **A**. Is 37:10
what the kings of **A** have done to all Is 37:11
the kings of **A** have laid waste all the Is 37:18
me concerning Sennacherib king of **A**, Is 37:21
says the LORD concerning the king of **A**: Is 37:33
Sennacherib king of **A** departed and Is 37:37
this city out of the hand of the king of **A**, Is 38:6
gain by going to **A** to drink the waters Jer 2:18
by Egypt as you were put to shame by **A**. Jer 2:36
First the king of **A** devoured him, and Jer 50:17
his land, as I punished the king of **A**. Jer 50:18
have given the hand to Egypt, and to **A**, Lam 5:6
the choicest men of **A** all of them, Ezk 23:7
Behold, **A** was a cedar in Lebanon, with Ezk 31:3
"**A** is there, and all her company, its Ezk 32:22
his wound, then Ephraim went to **A**, Hos 5:13
sense, calling to Egypt, going to **A**. Hos 7:11
For they have gone up to **A**, a wild Hos 8:9
and they shall eat unclean food in **A**. Hos 9:3
shall be carried to **A** as tribute to the Hos 10:6
land of Egypt, but **A** shall be their king, Hos 11:5
and like doves from the land of **A**, Hos 11:11
they make a covenant with **A**, and oil is Hos 12:1
A shall not save us; we will not ride on Hos 14:3
shepherd the land of **A** with the sword, Mi 5:6
to you, from **A** and the cities of Egypt, Mi 7:12
Your shepherds are asleep, O king of **A**; Na 3:18
hand against the north and destroy **A**, Zep 2:13
of Egypt, and gather them from **A**, Zec 10:10
The pride of **A** shall be laid low, and Zec 10:11

ASSYRIAN (5)
that I will break the **A** in my land, and Is 14:25
"And the **A** shall fall by a sword, not of Is 31:8
and the **A** oppressed them for nothing. Is 52:4
When the **A** comes into our land and Mi 5:5
deliver us from the **A** when he comes into Mi 5:6

ASSYRIANS (10)
down 185,000 in the camp of the **A**. 2 Kgs 19:35
not afraid of the **A** when they strike with Is 10:24
the Egyptians will worship with the **A**. Is 19:23
The **A** will be terror-stricken at the Is 30:31
thousand in the camp of the **A**. Is 37:36
You played the whore also with the **A**, Ezk 16:28
and she lusted after her lovers the **A**, Ezk 23:5
of her lovers, into the hands of the **A**, Ezk 23:9
She lusted after the **A**, governors and Ezk 23:12
and Koa, and all the **A** with them, Ezk 23:23

ASTONISH (1)
A yourselves and be astonished; blind Is 29:9

ASTONISHED (23)
passing by it will be **a** and will hiss, 1 Kgs 9:8
passing by will be **a** and say, 2 Chr 7:21
Astonish yourselves and be **a**; blind Is 29:9
As many were **a** at you—his appearance Is 52:14
King Nebuchadnezzar was **a** and rose Dn 3:24
the crowds were **a** at his teaching, Mt 7:28
in their synagogue, so that they were **a**, Mt 13:54
disciples heard this, they were greatly **a**, Mt 19:25
heard it, they were **a** at his teaching. Mt 22:33
And they were **a** at his teaching, for he Mk 1:22
and many who heard him were **a**, Mk 6:2
And they were **a** beyond measure, Mk 7:37
And they were exceedingly **a**, and said Mk 10:26
all the crowd was **a** at his teaching. Mk 11:18
when his parents saw him, they were **a**. Lk 2:48
and they were **a** at his teaching, for his Lk 4:32
who were with him were **a** at the catch of Lk 5:9
And all were **a** at the majesty of God. But Lk 9:43
The Pharisee was **a** to see that he did Lk 11:38
And they were amazed and **a**, saying, Acts 2:7
common men, they were **a**. Acts 4:13
for he was **a** at the teaching of the Acts 13:12
I am **a** that you are so quickly deserting Gal 1:6

ASTONISHING (1)
and shall speak **a** things against the Dn 11:36

ASTONISHMENT (2)
made them an object of horror, of **a**, 2 Chr 29:8
for trembling and **a** had seized them, Mk 16:8

ASTOUNDED (7)
heaven tremble and are **a** at his rebuke. Jb 26:11
As soon as they saw it, they were **a**; they Ps 48:5
shall be appalled and the prophets **a**." Jer 4:9
the nations, and see; wonder and be **a**. Hab 1:5
wind ceased. And they were utterly **a**, Mk 6:51
in the portico called Solomon's, **a**. Acts 3:11
"'Look, you scoffers, be **a** and perish; Acts 13:41

ASTRAY (59)
your enemy's ox or his donkey going **a**, Ex 23:4
any man's wife goes **a** and breaks faith Nm 5:12
But if you have gone **a**, though you are Nm 5:20
authority, goes **a** and defiles herself, Nm 5:29
ox or his sheep going **a** and ignore them. Dt 22:1
and Manasseh led them **a** to do more 2 Kgs 21:9
whoredom and made Judah go **a**. 2 Chr 21:11
and the inhabitants of Jerusalem **a**, 2 Chr 33:9
make me understand how I have gone **a**. Jb 6:24
to the proud, to those who go **a** after a lie! Ps 40:4
from the womb; they go **a** from birth, Ps 58:3
are a people who go **a** in their heart, Ps 95:10
Before I was afflicted I went **a**, but now Ps 119:67
all who go **a** from your statutes, Ps 119:118
I have gone **a** like a lost sheep; seek Ps 119:176
and because of his great folly he is led **a**. Prv 5:23
he who rejects reproof leads others **a**. Prv 10:17
the way of the wicked leads them **a**. Prv 12:26
Do they not go **a** who devise evil? Prv 14:22
and whoever is led **a** by it is not wise. Prv 20:1
this people have been leading them **a**, Is 9:16
And those who go **a** in spirit will come Is 29:24
jaws of the peoples a bridle that leads **a**. Is 30:28
even if they are fools, they shall not go **a**. Is 35:8
a deluded heart has led him **a**, and he Is 44:20
wisdom and your knowledge led you **a**, Is 47:10
All we like sheep have gone **a**; we have Is 53:6
by Baal and led my people Israel **a**. Jer 23:13
and lead my people **a** by their lies and Jer 23:32
that you have gone **a** at the cost of your Jer 42:20
Their shepherds have led them **a**, Jer 50:6
of Israel may no more go **a** from me, Ezk 14:11
going **a** from me after their idols when Ezk 44:10
me after their idols when Israel went **a**, Ezk 44:10
the people of Israel went **a** from me, Ezk 44:15
who did not go **a** when the people of Ezk 48:11
when the people of Israel went **a**, Ezk 48:11
a spirit of whoredom has led them **a**, Hos 4:12
statutes, but their lies have led them **a**, Am 2:4
the prophets who lead my people **a**, Mi 3:5
sheep and one of them has gone **a**, Mt 18:12
and go in search of the one that went **a**? Mt 18:12
over the ninety-nine that never went **a**. Mt 18:13
them, "See that no one leads you **a**. Mt 24:4
the Christ,' and they will lead many **a**. Mt 24:5
prophets will arise and lead many **a**. Mt 24:11
great signs and wonders, so as to lead **a**, Mt 24:24
to them, "See that no one leads you **a**. Mk 13:5
'I am he!' and they will lead many **a**. Mk 13:6
perform signs and wonders, to lead **a**, Mk 13:22
And he said, "See that you are not led **a**. Lk 21:8
said, "No, he is leading the people **a**." Jn 7:12
pagans you were led **a** to mute idols, 1 Cor 12:2
thoughts will be led **a** from a sincere 2 Cor 11:3
Barnabas was led **a** by their hypocrisy. Gal 2:13
sins and led **a** by various passions, 2 Tm 3:6
were once foolish, disobedient, led **a**, Ti 3:3
said, 'They always go **a** in their heart; Heb 3:10
the right way, they have gone **a**. 2 Pt 2:15

ASTROLOGERS (4)
or **a** can show to the king the mystery Dn 2:27
the Chaldeans, and the **a** came in, Dn 4:7
the enchanters, the Chaldeans, and the **a**. Dn 5:7
enchanters, Chaldeans, and **a**, Dn 5:11

ASYNCRITUS (1)
Greet **A**, Phlegon, Hermes, Patrobas, Rom 16:14

ATAD (2)
they came to the threshing floor of **A**, Gn 50:10
mourning on the threshing floor of **A**, Gn 50:11

ATARAH (1)
had another wife, whose name was **A**; 1 Chr 2:26

ATAROTH (4)
"**A**, Dibon, Jazer, Nimrah, Heshbon, Nm 32:3
people of Gad built Dibon, **A**, Aroer, Nm 32:34
from Bethel to Luz, it passes along to **A**, Jos 16:2
down from Janoah to **A** and to Naarah, Jos 16:7

ATAROTH-ADDAR (2)
on the east was **A** as far as Upper Jos 16:5
then the boundary goes down to **A**, Jos 18:13

ATE (112)
make one wise, she took of its fruit and **a**, Gn 3:6
her husband who was with her, and he **a**. Gn 3:6
she gave me fruit of the tree, and I **a**." Gn 3:12
said, "The serpent deceived me, and I **a**." Gn 3:13
by them under the tree while they **a**. Gn 18:8
baked unleavened bread, and they **a**. Gn 19:3
men who were with him **a** and drank, Gn 24:54
loved Esau because he **a** of his game, Gn 25:28
and he **a** and drank and rose and went Gn 25:34
them a feast, and they **a** and drank. Gn 26:30
So he brought it near to him, and he **a**; Gn 27:25
it to me, and I **a** it all before you came, Gn 27:33
a heap, and they **a** there by the heap. Gn 31:46
They **a** bread and spent the night in Gn 31:54
about anything but the food he **a**. Gn 39:6
thin cows **a** up the seven attractive, Gn 41:4
ugly cows **a** up the first seven plump Gn 41:20
and the Egyptians who **a** with him by Gn 43:32
and they **a** all the plants in the land and Ex 10:15
by the meat pots and **a** bread to the full, Ex 16:3
The people of Israel **a** the manna forty Ex 16:35
They **a** the manna till they came to the Ex 16:35
they beheld God, and **a** and drank. Ex 24:11
He neither **a** bread nor drank water. Ex 34:28
remember the fish we **a** in Egypt that Nm 11:5
and the people **a** and bowed down to Nm 25:2
nights. I neither **a** bread nor drank water. Dt 9:9
I neither **a** bread nor drank water, Dt 9:18
land, and he **a** the produce of the field, Dt 32:13
who **a** the fat of their sacrifices and Dt 32:38
day, they **a** of the produce of the land, Jos 5:11
the day after they **a** of the produce of Jos 5:12
but they **a** of the fruit of the land of Jos 5:12
of their god and **a** and drank and reviled Jgs 9:27
and gave some to them, and they **a**. Jgs 14:9
So they **a** and drank and spent the night Jgs 19:4
of them sat and **a** and drank together. Jgs 19:6

wait until the day declines." So they **a**, Jgs 19:8
washed their feet, and **a** and drank. Jgs 19:21
And she **a** until she was satisfied, and Ru 2:14
Then the woman went her way and **a**, 1 Sm 1:18
guests." So Saul **a** with Samuel that 1 Sm 9:24
And the people **a** them with the 1 Sm 14:32
in fierce anger and **a** no food the 1 Sm 20:34
Saul and his servants, and they **a**. 1 Sm 28:25
And they gave him bread and he **a**. 1 Sm 30:11
do." So Mephibosheth **a** at David's 2 Sm 9:11
for he **a** always at the king's table. 2 Sm 9:13
and he **a** in his presence and drank, 2 Sm 11:13
they set food before him, and he **a**. 2 Sm 12:20
the child died, you arose and **a** food." 2 Sm 12:21
They **a** and drank and were happy. 1 Kgs 4:20
back with him and **a** bread in his 1 Kgs 13:19
and her household **a** for many days. 1 Kgs 17:15
And he **a** and drank and lay down 1 Kgs 19:6
And he arose and **a** and drank, and 1 Kgs 19:8
and gave it to the people, and they **a**. 1 Kgs 19:21
And they **a** and had some left, 2 Kgs 4:44
So we boiled my son and **a** him. And 2 Kgs 6:29
they went into a tent and **a** and drank, 2 Kgs 7:8
Then he went in and **a** and drank. 2 Kgs 9:34
but they **a** unleavened bread among 2 Kgs 23:9
And they **a** and drank before the 1 Chr 29:22
yet they **a** the Passover otherwise 2 Chr 30:18
So they **a** the food of the festival for 2 Chr 30:22
I nor my brothers **a** the food allowance Neh 5:14
So they **a** and were filled and became Neh 9:25
and **a** bread with him in his house. Jb 42:11
in whom I trusted, who **a** my bread, Ps 41:9
Man **a** of the bread of the angels; he sent Ps 78:25
And they **a** and were well filled, for he Ps 78:29
in their land and **a** up the fruit of Ps 105:35
and **a** sacrifices offered to the dead; Ps 106:28
spice, I **a** my honeycomb with my honey, Sg 5:1
All who **a** of it incurred guilt; disaster Jer 2:3
Your words were found, and I **a** them, Jer 15:16
As they **a** bread together there at Mizpah, Jer 41:1
fill your stomach with it." Then I **a** it, Ezk 3:3
You **a** fine flour and honey and oil. Ezk 16:13
a daily portion of the food that the king **a**, Dn 1:5
all the youths who **a** the king's food. Dn 1:15
from among men and **a** grass like an Dn 4:33
I **a** no delicacies, no meat or wine Dn 10:3
the house of God and **a** the bread of the Mt 12:4
And they all **a** and were satisfied. And Mt 14:20
And those who **a** were about five Mt 14:21
And they all **a** and were satisfied. And Mt 15:37
Those who **a** were four thousand men, Mt 15:38
around his waist and **a** locusts and wild Mk 1:6
priest, and **a** the bread of the Presence, Mk 2:26
And they all **a** and were satisfied. Mk 6:42
And those who **a** the loaves were five Mk 6:44
some of his disciples **a** with hands that Mk 7:2
And they **a** and were satisfied. And they Mk 8:8
And he **a** nothing during those days. Lk 4:2
his disciples plucked and **a** some heads of Lk 6:1
of God and took and **a** the bread of the Lk 6:4
And they all **a** and were satisfied. And Lk 9:17
say, 'We **a** and drank in your presence, Lk 13:26
to be fed with the pods that the pigs **a**, Lk 15:16
and he took it and **a** before them. Lk 24:43
but because you **a** your fill of the loaves. Jn 6:26
Our fathers **a** the manna in the Jn 6:31
Your fathers **a** the manna in the Jn 6:49
heaven, not as the fathers **a** and died. Jn 6:58
'He who **a** my bread has lifted his heel Jn 13:18
without sight, and neither **a** nor drank. Acts 9:9
who **a** and drank with him after he Acts 10:41
men and **a** with them." Acts 11:3
were encouraged and **a** some food Acts 27:36
and all **a** the same spiritual food, 1 Cor 10:3
from the hand of the angel and **a** it. Rv 10:10

ATER (5)
The sons of **A**, namely of Hezekiah, 98. Ezr 2:16
the sons of Shallum, the sons of **A**, the Ezr 2:42
The sons of **A**, namely of Hezekiah, 98. Neh 7:21
the sons of Shallum, the sons of **A**, the Neh 7:45
A, Hezekiah, Azzur, Neh 10:17

ATHACH (1)
in Hormah, in Bor-ashan, in **A**, 1 Sm 30:30

ATHAIAH (1)
A the son of Uzziah, son of Zechariah, Neh 11:4

ATHALIAH (17)
His mother's name was **A**; she was a 2 Kgs 8:26
Now when **A** the mother of Ahaziah 2 Kgs 11:1
Thus they hid him from **A**, so that he 2 Kgs 11:2
LORD, while **A** reigned over the land. 2 Kgs 11:3
When **A** heard the noise of the 2 Kgs 11:13
And **A** tore her clothes and cried, 2 Kgs 11:14
city was quiet after **A** had been put 2 Kgs 11:20
Shamsherai, Shehariah, **A**, 1 Chr 8:26
His mother's name was **A**, the 2 Chr 22:2
Now when **A** the mother of Ahaziah 2 Chr 22:10
a sister of Ahaziah, hid him from **A**, 2 Chr 22:11
God, while **A** reigned over the land. 2 Chr 22:12
When **A** heard the noise of the 2 Chr 23:12
And **A** tore her clothes and cried, 2 Chr 23:13
city was quiet after **A** had been put 2 Chr 23:21
For the sons of **A**, that wicked 2 Chr 24:7
the sons of Elam, Jeshaiah the son of **A**, Ezr 8:7

ATHARIM (1)
that Israel was coming by the way of **A**, Nm 21:1

ATHENIANS (1)
Now all the **A** and the foreigners who Acts 17:21

ATHENS (5)
Paul brought him as far as **A**, Acts 17:15
while Paul was waiting for them at **A**, Acts 17:16
"Men of **A**, I perceive that in every Acts 17:22
After this Paul left **A** and went to Acts 18:1
willing to be left behind at **A** alone, 1 Thes 3:1

ATHLAI (1)
Jehohanan, Hananiah, Zabbai, and **A**. Ezr 10:28

ATHLETE (2)
Every **a** exercises self-control in all 1 Cor 9:25
An **a** is not crowned unless he 2 Tm 2:5

ATONE (5)
against me, you **a** for our transgressions. Ps 65:3
deliver us, and **a** for our sins, for your Ps 79:9
you, for which you will not be able to **a**; Is 47:11
when I **a** for you for all that you have Ezk 16:63
put an end to sin, and to **a** for iniquity, Dn 9:24

ATONED (7)
Israel, so that their blood guilt be **a** for.' Dt 21:8
house shall not be **a** for by sacrifice 1 Sm 3:14
a for their iniquity and did not destroy Ps 78:38
love and faithfulness iniquity is **a** for, Prv 16:6
guilt is taken away, and your sin **a** for. Is 6:7
iniquity will not be **a** for you until you Is 22:14
by this the guilt of Jacob will be **a** for, Is 27:9

ATONEMENT (90)
those things with which **a** was made at Ex 29:33
shall offer a bull as a sin offering for **a**. Ex 29:36
the altar, when you make **a** for it, Ex 29:36
days you shall make **a** for the altar and Ex 29:37
Aaron shall make **a** on its horns once a Ex 30:10
the sin offering of **a** he shall make Ex 30:10
atonement he shall make **a** for it once Ex 30:10
LORD'S offering to make **a** for your lives. Ex 30:15
You shall take the **a** money from the Ex 30:16
LORD, so as to make **a** for your lives." Ex 30:16
perhaps I can make **a** for your sin." Ex 32:30
be accepted for him to make **a** for him. Lv 1:4
And the priest shall make **a** for them, Lv 4:20
So the priest shall make **a** for him for his Lv 4:26
And the priest shall make **a** for him, and Lv 4:31
the priest shall make **a** for him for the Lv 4:35
the priest shall make **a** for him for his Lv 5:6
the priest shall make **a** for him for the Lv 5:10
the priest shall make **a** for him for the Lv 5:13
the priest shall make **a** for him with the Lv 5:16
the priest shall make **a** for him for the Lv 5:18
the priest shall make **a** for him before the Lv 6:7
of meeting to make **a** in the Holy Place; Lv 6:30
The priest who makes **a** with it shall have Lv 7:7
altar and consecrated it to make **a** for it. Lv 8:15
to be done to make **a** for you. Lv 8:34
offering and make **a** for yourself and Lv 9:7
of the people and make **a** for them, Lv 9:7
to make **a** for them before the LORD? Lv 10:17
it before the LORD and make **a** for her. Lv 12:7
And the priest shall make **a** for her, and Lv 12:8
the priest shall make **a** for him before Lv 14:18
to make **a** for him who is to be cleansed Lv 14:19
Thus the priest shall make **a** for him, Lv 14:20
offering to be waved, to make **a** for him, Lv 14:21
to make **a** for him before the LORD. Lv 14:29
the priest shall make **a** before the LORD Lv 14:31
So he shall make **a** for the house, and it Lv 14:53
the priest shall make **a** for him before Lv 15:15
the priest shall make **a** for her before Lv 15:30
and shall make **a** for himself and Lv 16:6
alive before the LORD to make **a** over it, Lv 16:10
and shall make **a** for himself and for Lv 16:11
Thus he shall make **a** for the Holy Lv 16:16
he enters to make **a** in the Holy Place Lv 16:17
out and has made **a** for himself and for Lv 16:17
is before the LORD and make **a** for it, Lv 16:18
the people and make **a** for himself and Lv 16:24
brought in to make **a** in the Holy Place, Lv 16:27
For on this day shall **a** be made for you Lv 16:30
priest in his father's place shall make **a**, Lv 16:32
He shall make **a** for the holy sanctuary, Lv 16:33
and he shall make **a** for the tent of Lv 16:33
and he shall make **a** for the priests and Lv 16:33
that **a** may be made for the people of Lv 16:34
on the altar to make **a** for your souls, Lv 17:11
it is the blood that makes **a** by the life. Lv 17:11
the priest shall make **a** for him with the Lv 19:22
of this seventh month is the Day of **A**. Lv 23:27
on that very day, for it is a Day of **A**, Lv 23:28
to make **a** for you before the LORD your Lv 23:28
On the Day of **A** you shall sound the Lv 25:9
to the ram of **a** with which atonement is Nm 5:8
of atonement with which **a** is made for Nm 5:8
a burnt offering, and make **a** for him, Nm 6:11
to the LORD to make **a** for the Levites. Nm 8:12
meeting and to make **a** for the people of Nm 8:19
and Aaron made **a** for them to cleanse Nm 8:21
the priest shall make **a** for all the Nm 15:25
priest shall make **a** before the LORD Nm 15:28
unintentionally, to make **a** for him, Nm 15:28
congregation and make **a** for them, Nm 16:46
the incense and made **a** for the people. Nm 16:47
his God and made **a** for the people of Nm 25:13
for a sin offering, to make **a** for you. Nm 28:22
with one male goat, to make **a** for you. Nm 28:30
for a sin offering, to make **a** for you; Nm 29:5
offering, besides the sin offering of **a**, Nm 29:11
to make **a** for ourselves before the Nm 31:50
and no **a** can be made for the land for Nm 35:33
Accept **a**, O LORD, for your people Israel, Dt 21:8
And how shall I make **a**, that you 2 Sm 21:3
Holy Place, and to make **a** for Israel, 1 Chr 6:49
on the altar, to make **a** for all Israel. 2 Chr 29:24
the sin offerings to make **a** for Israel, Neh 10:33
purify the altar and make **a** for it. Ezk 43:20
days shall they make **a** for the altar Ezk 43:26
peace offerings, to make **a** for them, Ezk 45:15
to make **a** on behalf of the house of Ezk 45:17
so you shall make **a** for the temple. Ezk 45:20

ATONING (1)
has made an end of **a** for the Holy Place Lv 16:20

ATROTH-BETH-JOAB (1)
A and half of the Manahathites, 1 Chr 2:54

ATROTH-SHOPHAN (1)
A, Jazer, Jogbehah, Nm 32:35

ATTACH (5)
and you shall **a** the corded chains to Ex 28:14
two cords you shall **a** to the two settings Ex 28:25
and so **a** it in front to the shoulder Ex 28:25
and **a** them in front to the lower part of Ex 28:27
join them and will **a** themselves to the Is 14:1

ATTACHED (7)
this time my husband will be **a** to me, Gn 29:34
have two shoulder pieces **a** to its two Ex 28:7
They **a** the two ends of the two cords to Ex 39:18
Thus they **a** it in front to the shoulder Ex 39:18
and **a** them in front to the lower part of Ex 39:20
valiant man, he **a** him to himself. 1 Sm 14:52
of gold, which were **a** to the throne, 2 Chr 9:18

ATTACHING (1)
made for the ephod **a** shoulder pieces, Ex 39:4

ATTACK (27)
lest any who found him should **a** him. Gn 4:15
I fear him, that he may come and **a** me, Gn 32:11
themselves against me and **a** me, Gn 34:30
or three thousand men go up and **a** Ai. Jos 7:3
But the people of Israel did not **a** them, Jos 9:18
your enemies; **a** their rear guard. Jos 10:19
me that you will not **a** me yourselves." Jgs 15:12
the Philistines drew near to **a** Israel. 1 Sm 7:10
I go and **a** these Philistines?" And 1 Sm 23:2
"Go and **a** the Philistines and save 1 Sm 23:2
and did not permit them to **a** Saul. 1 Sm 24:7
the water shaft to **a** 'the lame and the 2 Sm 5:8
Strengthen your **a** against the city 2 Sm 11:25
as some of the people fall at the first **a**, 2 Sm 17:9
and you shall **a** every fortified city 2 Kgs 3:19
people or province that might **a** them, Est 8:11
me all day long, for many **a** me proudly. Ps 56:2
long will all of you **a** a man to batter Ps 62:3
destroy me, those who **a** me with lies. Ps 69:4
words of hate, and **a** me without cause. Ps 109:3
it, but could not yet mount an **a** against it. Is 7:1
against her; arise, and let us **a** at noon! Jer 6:4
and let us **a** by night and destroy her Jer 6:5
end, the king of the south shall **a** him, Dn 11:40
them underfoot and turn to **a** you. Mt 7:6
and no one will **a** you to harm you, Acts 18:10
Jews made a united **a** on Paul and Acts 18:12

ATTACKED (9)
The archers bitterly **a** him, shot at Gn 49:23
how he **a** you on the way when you Dt 25:18
of Nobah and Jogbehah and **a** the army, Jgs 8:11

to his aid and **a** the Philistine and 2 Sm 21:17
he **a** and killed with the sword two 1 Kgs 2:32
and the slingers surrounded and **a** it. 2 Kgs 3:25
And they **a** all the cities around 2 Chr 14:14
God appointed a worm that **a** the plant, Jon 4:7
in an uproar, and **a** the house of Jason, Acts 17:5

ATTACKER (1)
on me; all day long an **a** oppresses me; Ps 56:1

ATTACKING (4)
that of a man **a** and murdering his Dt 22:26
of the king of Israel, who are **a** me." 2 Kgs 16:7
he shall refrain from **a** the king of the Dn 11:8
The crowd joined in **a** them, and the Acts 16:22

ATTACKS (5)
"If Esau comes to the one camp and **a** it, Gn 32:8
if a man willfully **a** another to kill him Ex 21:14
wait for him and **a** him and strikes him Dt 19:11
"He who **a** Kiriath-sepher and captures Jgs 1:12
stronger than he **a** him and overcomes Lk 11:22

ATTAI (4)
Jarha his slave, and she bore him **A**. 1 Chr 2:35
A fathered Nathan, and Nathan 1 Chr 2:36
A sixth, Eliel seventh, 1 Chr 12:11
who bore him Abijah, **A**, Ziza, 2 Chr 11:20

ATTAIN (9)
but he did not **a** to the three. 2 Sm 23:19
thirty, but he did not **a** to the three. 2 Sm 23:23
but he did not **a** to the three. 1 Chr 11:21
thirty, but he did not **a** to the three. 1 Chr 11:25
for me; it is high; I cannot **a** it. Ps 139:6
are considered worthy to **a** to that age Lk 20:35
to which our twelve tribes hope to **a**, as Acts 26:7
until we all **a** to the unity of the faith Eph 4:13
possible I may **a** the resurrection from Phil 3:11

ATTAINABLE (1)
perfection had been **a** through the Heb 7:11

ATTAINED (3)
and they have not **a** to the days of the Gn 47:9
did not pursue righteousness have **a** it, Rom 9:30
Only let us hold true to what we have **a**. Phil 3:16

ATTALIA (1)
word in Perga, they went down to **A**, Acts 14:25

ATTEMPT (2)
When an **a** was made by both Gentiles Acts 14:5
error or impurity or any **a** to deceive, 1 Thes 2:3

ATTEMPTED (4)
Or has any god ever **a** to go and take a Dt 4:34
to Jerusalem, he **a** to join the disciples. Acts 9:26
up to Mysia, they **a** to go into Bithynia, Acts 16:7
when they **a** to do the same, Heb 11:29

ATTEND (9)
and to **a** the sons of Aaron, 1 Chr 23:32
officials had set apart to **a** the Levites. Ezr 8:20
who had been appointed to **a** her, Est 4:5
Hear a just cause, O LORD; **a** to my cry! Ps 17:1
A to me, and answer me; I am restless in Ps 55:2
is wise, let him **a** to these things; Ps 107:43
A to my cry, for I am brought very low! Ps 142:6
will **a** and listen for the time to come? Is 42:23
Behold, I will **a** to you for your evil deeds, Jer 23:2

ATTENDANCE (3)
his officials, and the **a** of his servants, 1 Kgs 10:5
his officials, and the **a** of his servants, 2 Chr 9:4
one of the eunuchs in **a** on the king, Est 7:9

ATTENDANT (1)
and gave it back to the **a** and sat down. Lk 4:20

ATTENDANTS (3)
"Silence." And all his **a** went out from Jgs 3:19
but she shall be given up, and her **a**, Dn 11:6
Then the king said to the **a**, 'Bind him Mt 22:13

ATTENDED (11)
found favor in his sight and **a** him, Gn 39:4
Joseph to be with them, and he **a** them. Gn 40:4
and her five young women **a** her. 1 Sm 25:42
was of service to the king and **a** to him, 1 Kgs 1:4
son of Hachmoni **a** the king's sons. 1 Chr 27:32
Ahaziah's brothers, who **a** Ahaziah, 2 Chr 22:8
the king's young men who **a** him said, Est 2:2
The king's young men who **a** him said, Est 6:3
he has **a** to the voice of my prayer. Ps 66:19
them away, and you have not **a** to them. Jer 23:2
soldier from among those who **a** him, Acts 10:7

ATTENDING (5)
her death the women **a** her said to her, 1 Sm 4:20
the Shunammite was **a** to the king). 1 Kgs 1:15
a the temple together and breaking Acts 2:46
be prevented from **a** to his needs. Acts 24:23
ministers of God, **a** to this very thing. Rom 13:6

ATTENTION (56)
the prison paid no **a** to anything that Gn 39:23
but whoever did not pay **a** to the word of Ex 9:21
"Pay **a** to all that I have said to you, and Ex 23:13
Pay careful **a** to him and obey his Ex 23:21
son." But she did not answer or pay **a**. 1 Sm 4:20
'If your sons pay close **a** to their way, 1 Kgs 2:4
your sons pay close **a** to their way, 1 Kgs 8:25
No one answered; no one paid **a**. 1 Kgs 18:29
your sons pay close **a** to their way, 2 Chr 6:16
them, but they would not pay **a**. 2 Chr 24:19
and to his people, but they paid no **a**. 2 Chr 33:10
law or paid **a** to your commandments Neh 9:34
of his power? No; he would pay **a** to me. Jb 23:6
I gave you my **a**, and, behold, there was Jb 32:12
Pay **a**, O Job, listen to me; be silent, and I Jb 33:31
Give **a** to the sound of my cry, my King Ps 5:2
your flocks, and give **a** to your herds, Prv 27:23
Cry aloud, O daughter of Gallim! Give **a**, Is 10:30
Give ear, and hear my voice; give **a**, and Is 28:23
and the ears of those who hear will give **a**. Is 32:3
Draw near, O nations, to hear, and give **a**, Is 34:1
you had paid **a** to my commandments! Is 48:18
Listen to me, O coastlands, and give **a**, Is 49:1
"Give **a** to me, my people, and give ear to Is 51:4
'Pay **a** to the sound of the trumpet!' Jer 6:17
But they said, 'We will not pay **a**.' Jer 6:17
they have not paid **a** to my words; Jer 6:19
I have paid **a** and listened, but they have Jer 8:6
and let us not pay **a** to any of his Jer 18:18
or who has paid **a** to his word and Jer 23:18
because they did not pay **a** to my words, Jer 29:19
These men, O king, pay no **a** to you; Dn 3:12
the exiles from Judah, pays no **a** to you, Dn 6:13
O Lord, forgive. O Lord, pay **a** and act. Dn 9:19
turn back and pay **a** to those who Dn 11:30
He shall pay no **a** to the gods of his Dn 11:37
He shall not pay **a** to any other god, Dn 11:37
Hear this, O priests! Pay **a**, O house of Hos 5:1
Hear, you peoples, all of you; pay **a**, O Mi 1:2
But they did not hear or pay **a** to me, Zec 1:4
they refused to pay **a** and turned a Zec 7:11
The LORD paid **a** and heard them, Mal 3:16
But they paid no **a** and went off, one to Mt 22:5
said to them, "Pay **a** to what you hear: Mk 4:24
Pay **a** to yourselves! If your brother sins, Lk 17:3
And he fixed his **a** on them, expecting to Acts 3:5
with one accord paid **a** to what was Acts 8:6
They all paid **a** to him, from the least Acts 8:10
And they paid **a** to him because for a Acts 8:11
her heart to pay **a** to what was said Acts 16:14
But Gallio paid no **a** to any of this. Acts 18:17
Pay careful **a** to yourselves and to all Acts 20:28
the centurion paid more **a** to the pilot Acts 27:11
must pay much closer **a** to what we Heb 2:1
and if you pay **a** to the one who wears the Jas 2:3
will do well to pay **a** as to a lamp 2 Pt 1:19

ATTENTIVE (11)
open and your ears **a** to the prayer of 2 Chr 6:40
open and my ears **a** to the prayer that 2 Chr 7:15
let your ear be **a** and your eyes open, to Neh 1:6
let your ear be **a** to the prayer of your Neh 1:11
of all the people were **a** to the Book of the Neh 8:3
Let your ears be **a** to the voice of my Ps 130:2
making your ear **a** to wisdom and Prv 2:2
O sons, a father's instruction, and be **a**, Prv 4:1
My son, be **a** to my words; incline your Prv 4:20
My son, be **a** to my wisdom; incline your Prv 5:1
me, and be **a** to the words of my mouth. Prv 7:24

ATTEST (1)
the son of Jeberechiah, to **a** for me." Is 8:2

ATTESTED (2)
a man **a** to you by God with mighty Acts 2:22
and it was **a** to us by those who heard, Heb 2:3

ATTESTING (1)
and this was the manner of **a** in Israel. Ru 4:7

ATTIRE (4)
the LORD and praise him in holy **a**, 2 Chr 20:21
forget her ornaments, or a bride her **a**? Jer 2:32
all who array themselves in foreign **a**. Zep 1:8
hair and gold or pearls or costly **a**, 1 Tm 2:9

ATTRACTIVE (6)
saw that the daughters of man were **a**. Gn 6:2
woman was very **a** in appearance, Gn 24:16
because she was **a** in appearance. Gn 26:7
out of the Nile seven cows **a** and plump, Gn 41:2
the ugly, thin cows ate up the seven **a**, Gn 41:4
Seven cows, plump and **a**, came up out Gn 41:18

ATTRIBUTES (1)
For his invisible **a**, namely, his eternal Rom 1:20

AUDIENCE (1)
and they entered the **a** hall with the Acts 25:23

AUGUSTAN (1)
centurion of the **A** Cohort named Acts 27:1

AUGUSTUS (1)
went out from Caesar **A** that all the world Lk 2:1

AUNT (1)
not approach his wife; she is your **a**. Lv 18:14

AUTHOR (1)
and you killed the **A** of life, whom God Acts 3:15

AUTHORITIES (15)
synagogues and the rulers and the **a**, Lk 12:11
Can it be that the **a** really know that this Jn 7:26
Have any of the **a** or the Pharisees Jn 7:48
many even of the **a** believed in him, Jn 12:42
some of the brothers before the city **a**, Acts 17:6
and the city **a** were disturbed when Acts 17:8
person be subject to the governing **a**. Rom 13:1
whoever resists the **a** resists what God Rom 13:2
taxes, for the **a** are ministers of God, Rom 13:6
to the rulers and **a** in the heavenly Eph 3:10
but against the rulers, against the **a**, Eph 6:12
dominions or rulers or **a**—all things Col 1:16
disarmed the rulers and **a** and put them Col 2:15
them to be submissive to rulers and **a**, Ti 3:1
a, and powers having been subjected to 1 Pt 3:22

AUTHORITY (99)
up grain under the **a** of Pharaoh for Gn 41:35
you were under your husband's **a**, Nm 5:19
you are under your husband's **a**, Nm 5:20
a wife, though under her husband's **a**, Nm 5:29
shall invest him with some of your **a**, Nm 27:20
250, who exercised **a** over the people. 2 Chr 8:10
Elkanah the next in **a** to the king. 2 Chr 28:7
Mordecai the Jew gave full written **a**, Est 9:29
and will commit your **a** to his hand. Is 22:21
nor according to the **a** with which he Dn 11:4
and his **a** shall be a great authority. Dn 11:5
and his authority shall be a great **a**. Dn 11:5
he was teaching them as one who had **a**, Mt 7:29
For I too am a man under **a**, with soldiers Mt 8:9
the Son of Man has **a** on earth to forgive Mt 9:6
God, who had given such **a** to men. Mt 9:8
and gave them **a** over unclean spirits, Mt 10:1
their great ones exercise **a** over them. Mt 20:25
"By what **a** are you doing these things, Mt 21:23
these things, and who gave you this **a**?" Mt 21:23
will tell you by what **a** I do these things. Mt 21:24
I tell you by what **a** I do these things. Mt 21:27
"All **a** in heaven and on earth has been Mt 28:18
for he taught them as one who had **a**, Mk 1:22
"What is this? A new teaching with **a**! Mk 1:27
the Son of Man has **a** on earth to forgive Mk 2:10
and have **a** to cast out demons. Mk 3:15
and gave them **a** over the unclean spirits. Mk 6:7
their great ones exercise **a** over them. Mk 10:42
"By what **a** are you doing these things, Mk 11:28
or who gave you this **a** to do them?" Mk 11:28
tell you by what **a** I do these things. Mk 11:29
I tell you by what **a** I do these things." Mk 11:33
you I will give all this **a** and their glory, Lk 4:6
at his teaching, for his word possessed **a**. Lk 4:32
For with **a** and power he commands the Lk 4:36
the Son of Man has **a** on earth to forgive Lk 5:24
For I too am a man set under **a**, with Lk 7:8
gave them power and **a** over all demons Lk 9:1
I have given you **a** to tread on serpents Lk 10:19
after he has killed, has **a** to cast into hell. Lk 12:5
little, you shall have **a** over ten cities.' Lk 19:17
"Tell us by what **a** you do these things, Lk 20:2
things, or who it is that gave you this **a**." Lk 20:2
I tell you by what **a** I do these things." Lk 20:8
him up to the **a** and jurisdiction of the Lk 20:20
and those in **a** over them are called Lk 22:25
he has given him **a** to execute judgment, Jn 5:27
or whether I am speaking on my own **a**. Jn 7:17
speaks on his own **a** seeks his own glory, Jn 7:18
he, and that I do nothing on my own **a**, Jn 8:28
I have **a** to lay it down, and I have Jn 10:18
it down, and I have **a** to take it up again. Jn 10:18
For I have not spoken on my own **a**, but Jn 12:49
I say to you I do not speak on my own **a**, Jn 14:10
for he will not speak on his own **a**, Jn 16:13
since you have given him **a** over all flesh, Jn 17:2
know that I have **a** to release you and Jn 19:10
to release you and **a** to crucify you?" Jn 19:10
"You would have no **a** over me at all Jn 19:11
that the Father has fixed by his own **a**. Acts 1:7
And here he has **a** from the chief Acts 9:14
"let the men of **a** among you go down Acts 25:5
prison after receiving **a** from the Acts 26:10
with the **a** and commission Acts 26:12
For there is no **a** except from God, and Rom 13:1
have no fear of the one who is in **a**? Rom 13:3
wife does not have **a** over her own 1 Cor 7:4

husband does not have **a** over his own 1 Cor 7:4
Do I say these things on human **a**? 1 Cor 9:8
to have a symbol of **a** on her head, 1 Cor 11:10
every rule and every **a** and power. 1 Cor 15:24
if I boast a little too much of our **a**, 2 Cor 10:8
not with the Lord's **a** but as a fool. 2 Cor 11:17
in my use of the **a** that the Lord has 2 Cor 13:10
above all rule and **a** and power and Eph 1:21
him, who is the head of all rule and **a**. Col 2:10
to teach or to exercise **a** over a man; 1 Tm 2:12
things; exhort and rebuke with all **a**. Ti 2:15
lust of defiling passion and despise **a**. 2 Pt 2:10
first, does not acknowledge our **a**. 3 Jn 1:9
not stay within their own position of **a**, Jude 1:6
on their dreams, defile the flesh, reject **a**, Jude 1:8
be glory, majesty, dominion, and **a**, Jude 1:25
end, to him I will give **a** over the nations, Rv 2:26
I myself have received **a** from my Father. Rv 2:27
And they were given **a** over a fourth of the Rv 6:8
And I will grant **a** to my two witnesses, Rv 11:3
of our God and the **a** of his Christ have Rv 12:10
his power and his throne and great **a**. Rv 13:2
for he had given his **a** to the beast, Rv 13:4
allowed to exercise **a** for forty-two Rv 13:5
And **a** was given it over every tribe and Rv 13:7
It exercises all the **a** of the first beast in Rv 13:12
altar, the angel who has **a** over the fire, Rv 14:18
they are to receive **a** as kings for one Rv 17:12
over their power and **a** to the beast. Rv 17:13
down from heaven, having great **a**, Rv 18:1
those to whom the **a** to judge was Rv 20:4

AUTHORIZED (1)
"Collect no more than you are **a** to do." Lk 3:13

AUTUMN (3)
The sluggard does not plow in the **a**; he Prv 20:4
its season, the **a** rain and the spring rain, Jer 5:24
fruitless trees in late **a**, twice dead, Jude 1:12

AVAIL (8)
your cry for help **a** to keep you from Jb 36:19
the sword reaches him, it does not **a**, Jb 41:26
I held my peace to no **a**, and my distress Ps 39:2
no counsel can **a** against the LORD. Prv 21:30
you trust in deceptive words to no **a**. Jer 7:8
lies at the same table, but to no **a**, Dn 11:27
Spirit who gives life; the flesh is of no **a**. Jn 6:63
a yourself of the opportunity. 1 Cor 7:21

AVEN (2)
The high places of **A**, the sin of Israel, Hos 10:8
off the inhabitants from the Valley of **A**, Am 1:5

AVENGE (12)
"**A** the people of Israel on the Nm 31:2
you, may the LORD **a** me against you, 1 Sm 24:12
so that I may **a** on Jezebel the blood of 2 Kgs 9:7
he said, "May the LORD see and **a**!" 2 Chr 24:22
from my enemies and **a** myself on my Is 1:24
and shall I not **a** myself on a nation such Jer 5:9
and shall I not **a** myself on a nation Jer 5:29
and shall I not **a** myself on a nation such Jer 9:9
of vengeance, to **a** himself on his foes. Jer 46:10
I will **a** their blood, blood I have not Jl 3:21
Beloved, never **a** yourselves, but leave Rom 12:19
you will judge and **a** our blood on those Rv 6:10

AVENGED (13)
slave dies under his hand, he shall be **a**. Ex 21:20
survives a day or two, he is not to be **a**, Ex 21:21
that the LORD has **a** you on your Jgs 11:36
is what you do, I swear I will be **a** on you, Jgs 15:7
that I may be **a** on the Philistines for Jgs 16:28
evening and I am **a** on my enemies." 1 Sm 14:24
that he may be **a** of the king's 1 Sm 18:25
the LORD who has **a** the insult I 1 Sm 25:39
The LORD has **a** my lord the king this 2 Sm 4:8
The LORD has **a** on you all the blood of 2 Sm 16:8
avenge their blood, blood I have not **a**, Jl 3:21
oppressed man and **a** him by striking Acts 7:24
and has **a** on her the blood of his Rv 19:2

AVENGER (18)
shall be for you a refuge from the **a**, Nm 35:12
The **a** of blood shall himself put the Nm 35:19
The **a** of blood shall put the murderer Nm 35:21
the manslayer and the **a** of blood, Nm 35:24
from the hand of the **a** of blood, Nm 35:25
and the **a** of blood finds him outside Nm 35:27
and the **a** of blood kills the Nm 35:27
lest the **a** of blood in hot anger pursue Dt 19:6
and hand him over to the **a** of blood, Dt 19:12
be for you a refuge from the **a** of blood. Jos 20:3
And if the **a** of blood pursues him, they Jos 20:5
not die by the hand of the **a** of blood, Jos 20:9
God, that the **a** of blood kill no more, 2 Sm 14:11
of your foes, to still the enemy and the **a**. Ps 8:2
at the sight of the enemy and the **a** Ps 44:16

to them, but an **a** of their wrongdoings. Ps 99:8
an **a** who carries out God's wrath on Rom 13:4
the Lord is an **a** in all these things, 1 Thes 4:6

AVENGES (2)
for he **a** the blood of his children and Dt 32:43
For he who **a** blood is mindful of them; Ps 9:12

AVENGING (5)
bloodguilt and from **a** myself with 1 Sm 25:33
a in time of peace for blood that had 1 Kgs 2:5
their God?" Let the **a** of the outpoured Ps 79:10
The LORD is a jealous and **a** God; the LORD Na 1:2
avenging God; the LORD is **a** and wrathful; Na 1:2

AVERT (2)
and pleaded with him to **a** the evil plan of Est 8:3
even sacrificial flesh **a** your doom? Jer 11:15

AVERTED (3)
plague may be **a** from the people." 2 Sm 24:21
and the plague was **a** from Israel. 2 Sm 24:25
plague may be **a** from the people." 1 Chr 21:22

AVERTS (1)
A gift in secret **a** anger, and a Prv 21:14

AVITH (2)
his place, the name of his city being **A**. Gn 36:35
place, the name of his city being **A**. 1 Chr 1:46

AVOID (8)
A it; do not go on it; turn away from it Prv 4:15
not only to **a** God's wrath but also for Rom 13:5
that you have been taught; **a** them. Rom 16:17
A the irreverent babble and 1 Tm 6:20
But **a** irreverent babble, for it will 2 Tm 2:16
but denying its power. **A** such people. 2 Tm 3:5
to speak evil of no one, to **a** quarreling, to Ti 3:2
But **a** foolish controversies, genealogies, Ti 3:9

AVOIDED (2)
and whom they **a** and did not 2 Chr 20:10
of your lips I have **a** the ways of the Ps 17:4

AVVA (1)
from Babylon, Cuthah, **A**, Hamath, 2 Kgs 17:24

AVVIM (3)
As for the **A**, who lived in villages as far Dt 2:23
Gath, and Ekron), and those of the **A**, Jos 13:3
A, Parah, Ophrah, Jos 18:23

AVVITES (1)
and the **A** made Nibhaz and Tartak; 2 Kgs 17:31

AWAIT (2)
imprisonment and afflictions **a** me. Acts 20:23
is in heaven, and from it we **a** a Savior, Phil 3:20

AWAITING (1)
waysides you have sat **a** lovers like an Jer 3:2

AWAITS (2)
the end, for it still **a** the appointed time. Dn 11:35
For still the vision **a** its appointed time; Hab 2:3

AWAKE (49)
"**A**, awake, Deborah! Awake, awake, Jgs 5:12
"Awake, **a**, Deborah! Awake, awake, Jgs 5:12
Deborah! **A**, awake, break out in a song! Jgs 5:12
Deborah! Awake, **a**, break out in a song! Jgs 5:12
man saw it or knew it, nor did any **a**, 1 Sm 26:12
no more he will not **a** or be roused out Jb 14:12
against the fury of my enemies; **a** for me; Ps 7:6
when I **a**, I shall be satisfied with your Ps 17:15
A and rouse yourself for my Ps 35:23
A! Why are you sleeping, O Lord? Ps 44:23
A, my glory! Awake, O harp and lyre! I Ps 57:8
Awake, my glory! **A**, O harp and lyre! I Ps 57:8
O harp and lyre! I will **a** the dawn! Ps 57:8
ready. **A**, come to meet me, and see! Ps 59:4
I lie **a**; I am like a lonely sparrow on the Ps 102:7
A, O harp and lyre! I will awake the Ps 108:2
O harp and lyre! I will **a** the dawn! Ps 108:2
My eyes are **a** before the watches of Ps 119:148
the city, the watchman stays **a** in vain. Ps 127:1
them, they are more than the sand. I **a**, Ps 139:18
and when you **a**, they will talk with Prv 6:22
but I did not feel it. When shall I **a**? Prv 23:35
A, O north wind, and come, O south Sg 4:16
I slept, but my heart was **a**. A sound! My Sg 5:2
who dwell in the dust, **a** and sing for joy! Is 26:19
A, awake, put on strength, O arm of the Is 51:9
Awake, **a**, put on strength, O arm of the Is 51:9
a, as in days of old, the generations of Is 51:9
A, awake, put on your strength, O Zion; Is 52:1
Awake, **a**, put on your strength, O Zion; Is 52:1
who sleep in the dust of the earth shall **a**, Dn 12:2
A, you drunkards, and weep, and wail, all Jl 1:5
and those **a** who will make you Hab 2:7
to a wooden thing, **A**; to a silent stone, Hab 2:19
"**A**, O sword, against my shepherd, Zec 13:7
Therefore, stay **a**, for you do not know Mt 24:42

he would have stayed **a** and would not Mt 24:43
Be on guard, keep **a**. For you do not Mk 13:33
commands the doorkeeper to stay **a**. Mk 13:34
Therefore stay **a**—for you do not Mk 13:35
what I say to you I say to all: Stay **a**." Mk 13:37
when they became fully **a** they saw his Lk 9:32
the master finds **a** when he comes. Lk 12:37
or in the third, and finds them **a**, Lk 12:38
But stay **a** at all times, praying that you Lk 21:36
Therefore it says, "**A**, O sleeper, and Eph 5:14
do, but let us keep **a** and be sober. 1 Thes 5:6
that whether we are **a** or asleep we 1 Thes 5:10
Blessed is the one who stays **a**, keeping Rv 16:15

AWAKEN (4)
you not stir up or **a** love until it pleases. Sg 2:7
you not stir up or **a** love until it pleases. Sg 3:5
you not stir up or **a** love until it pleases. Sg 8:4
has fallen asleep, but I go to **a** him." Jn 11:11

AWAKENED (5)
perhaps he is asleep and must be **a**." 1 Kgs 18:27
and told him, "The child has not **a**." 2 Kgs 4:31
her beloved? Under the apple tree I **a** you. Sg 8:5
the end has come; it has **a** against you. Ezk 7:6
me, like a man who is **a** out of his sleep. Zec 4:1

AWAKENS (2)
Morning by morning he **a**; he awakens Is 50:4
he **a** my ear to hear as those who are Is 50:4

AWAKES (3)
Like a dream when one **a**, O Lord, when Ps 73:20
he is eating and **a** with his hunger not Is 29:8
man dreams he is drinking and **a** faint, Is 29:8

AWARD (1)
judge, will **a** to me on that Day, 2 Tm 4:8

AWARE (9)
Before I was **a**, my desire set me among Sg 6:12
Jesus, **a** of this, withdrew from there. Mt 12:15
But Jesus, **a** of this, said, "O you of little Mt 16:8
But Jesus, **a** of their malice, said, "Why Mt 22:18
But Jesus, **a** of this, said to them, "Why Mt 26:10
And Jesus, **a** of this, said to them, "Why Mk 8:17
I am not **a** of anything against myself, 1 Cor 4:4
yourselves are fully **a** that the day 1 Thes 5:2
You are **a** that all who are in Asia 2 Tm 1:15

AWAY (874)
driven me today **a** from the ground, Gn 4:14
Then Cain went **a** from the presence of Gn 4:16
and they sent him **a** with his wife and Gn 12:20
on the carcasses, Abram drove them **a**. Gn 15:11
you indeed sweep **a** the righteous with Gn 18:23
Will you then sweep **a** the place and Gn 18:24
lest you be swept **a** in the punishment Gn 19:15
Escape to the hills, lest you be swept **a**." Gn 19:17
along with the child, and sent her **a**. Gn 21:14
he said, "Send me **a** to my master." Gn 24:54
Send me **a** that I may go to my master." Gn 24:56
So they sent **a** Rebekah their sister and Gn 24:59
living he sent them **a** from his son Gn 25:6
said to Isaac, "Go **a** from us, Gn 26:16
me and have sent me **a** from you?" Gn 26:27
but good and have sent you **a** in peace. Gn 26:29
and he has taken **a** your blessing." Gn 27:35
two times. He took **a** my birthright, Gn 27:36
he has taken **a** my blessing." Then Gn 27:36
a from the fatness of the earth shall Gn 27:39
and **a** from the dew of heaven on high. Gn 27:39
until your brother's fury turns **a**— Gn 27:44
your brother's anger turns **a** from you, Gn 27:45
Thus Isaac sent Jacob **a**. And he went to Gn 28:5
and sent him **a** to Paddan-aram to Gn 28:6
that you have taken **a** my husband? Gn 30:15
Would you take **a** my son's Gn 30:15
said, "God has taken **a** my reproach." Gn 30:23
Jacob said to Laban, "Send me **a**, Gn 30:25
Thus God has taken **a** the livestock of Gn 31:9
that God has taken **a** from our father Gn 31:16
He drove **a** all his livestock, all his Gn 31:18
me and driven **a** my daughters like Gn 31:26
might have sent you **a** with mirth and Gn 31:27
you have gone **a** because you longed Gn 31:30
would have sent me **a** empty-handed. Gn 31:42
out of Shechem's house and went **a**. Gn 34:26
"Put **a** the foreign gods that are among Gn 35:2
went into a land **a** from his brother Gn 36:6
And the man said, "They have gone **a**, Gn 37:17
Then she arose and went **a**, and taking Gn 38:19
Then he turned **a** from them and wept. Gn 42:24
the men were sent **a** with their donkeys. Gn 44:3
Then he sent his brothers **a**, and as Gn 45:24
"Take this child **a** and nurse him for me, Ex 2:9
The shepherds came and drove them **a**, Ex 2:17
do you take the people **a** from their work? Ex 5:4
with the LORD to take **a** the frogs from me Ex 8:8

The frogs shall go **a** from you and your Ex 8:11
only you must not go very far **a**. Ex 8:28
Pharaoh said to him, "Get **a** from me; Ex 10:28
you go, he will drive you **a** completely. Ex 11:1
that you have taken us **a** to die in the Ex 14:11
inhabitants of Canaan have melted **a**. Ex 15:15
and he went **a** to his own country. Ex 18:27
and it dies or is injured or is driven **a**, Ex 22:10
I will take sickness **a** from among you. Ex 23:25
Then I will take **a** my hand, and you Ex 33:23
carry your brothers **a** from the front of Lv 10:4
it may be sent **a** into the wilderness to Lv 16:10
goat and send it **a** into the wilderness Lv 16:21
are left shall rot **a** in your enemies' Lv 26:39
their fathers they shall rot **a** like them. Lv 26:39
And they shall take **a** the ashes from Nm 4:13
makes your thigh fall **a** and your body Nm 5:21
womb swell and your thigh fall **a**.' Nm 5:22
shall swell, and her thigh shall fall **a**, Nm 5:27
flesh is half eaten **a** when he comes Nm 12:12
Get **a** from the dwelling of Korah, Nm 16:24
lest you be swept **a** with all their sins." Nm 16:26
So they got **a** from the dwelling of Nm 16:27
"Get **a** from the midst of this Nm 16:45
territory, so Israel turned **a** from him. Nm 20:21
that he take **a** the serpents from us." So Nm 21:7
when Asshur takes you **a** captive." Nm 24:22
of the LORD may turn **a** from Israel." Nm 25:4
our father be taken **a** from his clan Nm 27:4
For if you turn **a** from following him, Nm 32:15
So it will be taken **a** from the lot of our Nm 36:3
So we went on, **a** from our brothers, the Dt 2:8
a from the Arabah road from Elath and Dt 2:8
you be drawn **a** and bow down to them Dt 4:19
it, and clears **a** many nations before you, Dt 7:1
for they would turn **a** your sons from Dt 7:4
the LORD will take **a** from you all Dt 7:15
God will clear **a** these nations before Dt 7:22
sought to draw you **a** from the LORD Dt 13:10
and have drawn **a** the inhabitants of Dt 13:13
wives for himself, lest his heart turn **a**, Dt 17:17
among you and turn **a** from you. Dt 23:14
her former husband, who sent her **a**, Dt 24:4
there shall be no one to frighten them **a**. Dt 28:26
peoples where the LORD will lead you **a**. Dt 28:37
bring a nation against you from far **a**, Dt 28:49
whose heart is turning **a** today from the Dt 29:18
lead to the sweeping **a** of moist and dry Dt 29:19
But if your heart turns **a**, and you will Dt 30:17
but are drawn **a** to worship other gods Dt 30:17
inhabitants of the land melt **a** before you. Jos 2:9
words, so be it." Then she sent them **a**, Jos 2:21
of the land melt **a** because of us." Jos 2:24
stood and rose up in a heap very far **a**, Jos 3:16
"Today I have rolled **a** the reproach of Jos 5:9
until you take **a** the devoted things Jos 7:13
we have drawn them **a** from the city. Jos 8:6
Joshua they were drawn **a** from the city. Jos 8:16
So Joshua blessed them and sent them **a**, Jos 22:6
when Joshua sent them **a** to their homes Jos 22:7
of Israel in turning **a** this day from Jos 22:16
you too must turn **a** this day from Jos 22:18
an altar to turn **a** from following the Jos 22:23
the LORD and turn **a** this day from Jos 22:29
Put **a** the gods that your fathers served Jos 24:14
"Then put **a** the foreign gods that are Jos 24:23
So Joshua sent the people **a**, every man Jos 24:28
he sent **a** the people who carried the Jgs 3:18
pitched his tent as far **a** as the oak in Jgs 4:11
from his chariot and fled **a** on foot. Jgs 4:15
But Sisera fled **a** on foot to the tent of Jgs 4:17
Arise, Barak, lead **a** your captives, O son Jgs 5:12
The torrent Kishon swept them **a**, the Jgs 5:21
home and hurry **a** from Mount Gilead.'" Jgs 7:3
And Jotham ran **a** and fled and went to Jgs 9:21
So they put **a** the foreign gods from Jgs 10:16
coming up from Egypt took **a** my land, Jgs 11:13
Israel did not take **a** the land of Moab Jgs 11:15
Then he sent her **a** for two months, Jgs 11:38
he threw **a** the jawbone out of his hand. Jgs 15:17
from his sleep and pulled **a** the pin, Jgs 16:14
that I made and the priest, and go **a**, Jgs 18:24
and she went **a** from him to her father's Jgs 19:2
man rose up and went **a** to his home. Jgs 19:28
people and were drawn **a** from the city. Jgs 20:31
flee and draw them **a** from the city to Jgs 20:32
I went **a** full, and the LORD has brought Ru 1:21
drunk? Put **a** your wine from you." 1 Sm 1:14
"Send **a** the ark of the God of Israel, 1 Sm 5:11
"If you send **a** the ark of the God of 1 Sm 6:3
his hand does not turn **a** from you." 1 Sm 6:3
them, did they not send the people **a**, 1 Sm 6:6
take their calves home, **a** from them. 1 Sm 6:7
to whom shall he go up **a** from us?" 1 Sm 6:20
then put **a** the foreign gods and the 1 Sm 7:3
people of Israel put **a** the Baals and the 1 Sm 7:4
Then Samuel sent all the people **a**, 1 Sm 10:25
do wickedly, you shall be swept **a**, 1 Sm 12:25
As Samuel turned to go **a**, Saul seized 1 Sm 15:27
Philistine and takes **a** the reproach 1 Sm 17:26
And he turned **a** from him toward 1 Sm 17:30
window, and he fled **a** and escaped. 1 Sm 19:12
not disclose it to you and send you **a**, 1 Sm 20:13
then go, for the LORD has sent you **a**. 1 Sm 20:22
let me get **a** and see my brothers.' 1 Sm 20:29
by hot bread on the day it is taken **a**. 1 Sm 21:6
and brought **a** their livestock 1 Sm 23:5
was hurrying to get **a** from Saul. 1 Sm 23:26
his enemy, will he let him go **a** safe? 1 Sm 24:19
who are breaking **a** from their 1 Sm 25:10
young men turned **a** and came back 1 Sm 25:12
from Saul's head, and they went **a**. 1 Sm 26:12
fall to the earth **a** from the presence 1 Sm 26:20
alive, but would take **a** the sheep, 1 Sm 27:9
and God has turned **a** from me and 1 Sm 28:15
they rose and went **a** that night. 1 Sm 28:25
each man may lead **a** his wife and 1 Sm 30:22
heart desires." So David sent Abner **a**, 2 Sm 3:21
at Hebron, for he had sent him **a**, 2 Sm 3:22
Why is it that you have sent him **a**, so 2 Sm 3:24
David and his men carried them **a**. 2 Sm 5:21
Saul, whom I put **a** from before you. 2 Sm 7:15
middle, at their hips, and sent them **a**. 2 Sm 10:4
"The LORD also has put **a** your sin; 2 Sm 12:13
in sending me **a** is greater than 2 Sm 13:16
her hand on her head and went **a**, 2 Sm 13:19
But God will not take **a** life, and he 2 Sm 14:14
of them went **a** quickly and came 2 Sm 17:18
Judah stolen you **a** and brought the 2 Sm 19:41
are all like thorns that are thrown **a**, 2 Sm 23:6
please take **a** the iniquity of your 2 Sm 24:10
and thus take **a** from me and from 1 Kgs 2:31
of Shimei's servants ran **a** to Achish, 1 Kgs 2:39
that they are carried **a** captive to the 1 Kgs 8:46
the eighth day he sent the people **a**, 1 Kgs 8:66
they will turn **a** your heart after 1 Kgs 11:2
And his wives turned **a** his heart. 1 Kgs 11:3
old his wives turned **a** his heart after 1 Kgs 11:4
his heart had turned **a** from the LORD, 1 Kgs 11:9
I will not tear **a** all the kingdom, 1 Kgs 11:13
He said to them, "Go **a** for three days, 1 Kgs 12:5
again to me." So the people went **a**. 1 Kgs 12:5
And as he went **a** a lion met him on 1 Kgs 13:24
tore the kingdom **a** from the house 1 Kgs 14:8
He took **a** the treasures of the house 1 Kgs 14:26
king's house. He took **a** everything. 1 Kgs 14:26
He also took **a** all the shields of gold 1 Kgs 14:26
He put **a** the male cult prostitutes 1 Kgs 15:12
the high places were not taken **a**. 1 Kgs 15:14
and they carried **a** the stones of 1 Kgs 15:22
I will utterly sweep **a** Baasha and his 1 Kgs 16:3
now, O LORD, take **a** my life, for I am 1 Kgs 19:4
and they seek my life, to take it **a**." 1 Kgs 19:10
and they seek my life, to take it **a**." 1 Kgs 19:14
whatever pleases you and take it **a**.'" 1 Kgs 20:6
to take the bandage **a** from his eyes, 1 Kgs 20:41
his bed and turned **a** his face and 1 Kgs 21:4
Yet the high places were not taken **a**, 1 Kgs 22:43
the LORD will take **a** your master from 2 Kgs 2:3
the LORD will take **a** your master from 2 Kgs 2:5
for he put **a** the pillar of Baal that his 2 Kgs 3:2
feet. And Gehazi came to push her **a**. 2 Kgs 4:27
But Naaman was angry and went **a**, 2 Kgs 5:11
So he turned and went **a** in a rage. 2 Kgs 5:12
in the house, and he sent the men **a**, 2 Kgs 5:24
had eaten and drunk, he sent them **a**, 2 Kgs 6:23
So they fled **a** in the twilight and 2 Kgs 7:7
Syrians had thrown **a** in their haste. 2 Kgs 7:15
and stole him **a** from among the 2 Kgs 11:2
the high places were not taken **a**; 2 Kgs 12:3
Then Hazael went **a** from Jerusalem. 2 Kgs 12:18
the high places were not taken **a**. 2 Kgs 15:4
He did not turn **a** from the sins of 2 Kgs 15:24
carried the Israelites **a** to Assyria and 2 Kgs 17:6
the LORD carried **a** before them. 2 Kgs 17:11
you have carried **a** and placed in 2 Kgs 17:26
whom you carried **a** from there, 2 Kgs 17:27
they had carried **a** from Samaria 2 Kgs 17:28
whom they had been carried **a**. 2 Kgs 17:33
carried the Israelites **a** to Assyria 2 Kgs 18:11
I come and take you **a** to a land like 2 Kgs 18:32
be born to you, shall be taken **a**, 2 Kgs 20:18
Josiah put **a** the mediums and the 2 Kgs 23:24
But he took Jehoahaz **a**, and he 2 Kgs 23:34
He carried **a** all Jerusalem and all 2 Kgs 24:14
And he carried **a** Jehoiachin to 2 Kgs 24:15
And they took **a** the pots and the 2 Kgs 25:14
captain of the guard took **a** as gold, 2 Kgs 25:15
king of Assyria carried **a** into exile; 1 Chr 5:6
after he had sent **a** Hushim and Baara 1 Chr 8:8
men arose and took **a** the body of 1 Chr 10:12
took counsel and sent him **a**, 1 Chr 12:19
middle, at their hips, and sent them **a**; 1 Chr 19:4
please take **a** the iniquity of your 1 Chr 21:8
that they are carried **a** captive to a 2 Chr 6:36
do not turn **a** the face of your 2 Chr 6:42
he sent the people **a** to their homes, 2 Chr 7:10
in three days." So the people went **a**. 2 Chr 10:5
He took **a** the treasures of the house 2 Chr 12:9
king's house. He took **a** everything. 2 Chr 12:9
He also took **a** the shields of gold that 2 Chr 12:9
He took **a** the foreign altars and the 2 Chr 14:3
of Judah carried **a** very much spoil. 2 Chr 14:13
livestock and carried **a** sheep in 2 Chr 14:15
courage and put **a** the detestable idols 2 Chr 15:8
and they carried **a** the stones of 2 Chr 16:6
him; God drew them **a** from him. 2 Chr 18:31
places, however, were not taken **a**; 2 Chr 20:33
it and carried **a** all the possessions 2 Chr 21:17
and stole him **a** from among the 2 Chr 22:11
when he turned **a** from the LORD 2 Chr 25:27
Judah and carried **a** captives. 2 Chr 28:17
and have turned **a** their faces from 2 Chr 29:6
his fierce anger may turn **a** from us. 2 Chr 29:10
fierce anger may turn **a** from you. 2 Chr 30:8
and will not turn **a** his face from you, 2 Chr 30:9
incense they took **a** and threw into 2 Chr 30:14
same Hezekiah taken **a** his high 2 Chr 32:12
And he took **a** the foreign gods and 2 Chr 33:15
And Josiah took **a** all the 2 Chr 34:33
did not turn **a** from following the 2 Chr 34:33
Josiah did not turn **a** from him, 2 Chr 35:22
said to his servants, "Take me **a**, 2 Chr 35:23
had carried **a** from Jerusalem Ezr 1:7
shout, and the sound was heard far **a**. Ezr 3:13
this house and carried **a** the people to Ezr 5:12
in the province Beyond the River, keep **a**. Ezr 6:6
our God to put **a** all these wives and Ezr 10:3
over this matter is turned **a** from us." Ezr 10:14
pledged themselves to put **a** their wives, Ezr 10:19
I said, "Should such a man as I run **a**? Neh 6:11
the joy of Jerusalem was heard far **a**. Neh 12:43
had been carried **a** from Jerusalem Est 2:6
the captives carried **a** with Jeconiah king Est 2:6
king of Babylon had carried **a**. Est 2:6
Mordecai then went **a** and did Est 4:17
who feared God and turned **a** from evil. Jb 1:1
who fears God and turns **a** from evil?" Jb 1:8
The LORD gave, and the LORD has taken **a**; Jb 1:21
who fears God and turns **a** from evil? Jb 2:3
as torrential streams that pass **a**, Jb 6:15
How long will you not look **a** from me, Jb 7:19
transgression and take **a** my iniquity? Jb 7:21
Behold, he snatches **a**; who can turn him Jb 9:12
are swifter than a runner; they flee **a**; Jb 9:25
Let him take his rod **a** from me, and let Jb 9:34
If iniquity is in your hand, put it far **a**, Jb 11:14
it as waters that have passed **a**. Jb 11:16
He leads counselors **a** stripped, and Jb 12:17
He leads priests **a** stripped and Jb 12:19
trusted and takes **a** the discernment of Jb 12:20
he enlarges nations, and leads them **a**. Jb 12:23
He takes **a** understanding from the Jb 12:24
Man wastes **a** like a rotten thing, like a Jb 13:28
look **a** from him and leave him alone, Jb 14:6
a lake and a river wastes **a** and dries up, Jb 14:11
the mountain falls and crumbles **a**, Jb 14:18
the waters wear **a** the stones; the torrents Jb 14:19
the torrents wash **a** the soil of the earth; Jb 14:19
his countenance, and send him **a**. Jb 14:20
But you are doing **a** with the fear of God Jb 15:4
Why does your heart carry you **a**, and Jb 15:12
He will fly **a** like a dream and not be Jb 20:8
he will be chased **a** like a vision of the Jb 20:8
of his house will be carried **a**, Jb 20:28
and like chaff that the storm carries **a**? Jb 21:18
You have sent widows **a** empty, and the Jb 22:9
They were snatched **a** before their time; Jb 22:16
time; their foundation was washed **a**. Jb 22:16
They drive **a** the donkey of the fatherless; Jb 24:3
and heat snatch **a** the snow waters; Jb 24:19
"As God lives, who has taken **a** my right, Jb 27:2
die I will not put **a** my integrity from me. Jb 27:5
cuts him off, when God takes **a** his life? Jb 27:8
shafts in a valley **a** from where anyone Jb 28:4
hang in the air, far **a** from mankind; Jb 28:4
and to turn **a** from evil is Jb 28:28
the rabble rise; they push **a** my feet; Jb 30:12
my prosperity has passed **a** like a cloud. Jb 30:15
else my Maker would soon take me **a**. Jb 32:22
His flesh is so wasted **a** that it cannot be Jb 33:21
the right, and God has taken **a** my right; Jb 34:5
the people are shaken and pass **a**, Jb 34:20
the mighty are taken **a** by no human Jb 34:20
but are like chaff that the wind drives **a**. Ps 1:4

bonds apart and cast **a** their cords from Ps 2:3
My eye wastes **a** because of grief; it grows Ps 6:7
and his statutes I did not put **a** from me. Ps 18:22
Do not sweep my soul **a** with sinners, nor Ps 26:9
Turn not your servant **a** in anger, O you Ps 27:9
of my iniquity, and my bones waste **a**. Ps 31:10
my bones wasted **a** through my Ps 32:3
so that he drove him out, and he went **a**. Ps 34:T
Turn **a** from evil and do good; seek Ps 34:14
the angel of the LORD driving them **a**! Ps 35:5
nor the hand of the wicked drive me **a**. Ps 36:11
they vanish—like smoke they vanish **a**. Ps 37:20
Turn **a** from evil and do good; so shall Ps 37:27
But he passed **a**, and behold, he was no Ps 37:36
Look **a** from me, that I may smile Ps 39:13
altogether who seek to snatch **a** my life; Ps 40:14
when he dies he will carry nothing **a**; Ps 49:17
Cast me not **a** from your presence, and Ps 51:11
They have all fallen **a**; together they have Ps 53:3
like a dove! I would fly **a** and be at rest; Ps 55:6
yes, I would wander far **a**; I would lodge Ps 55:7
Let them vanish like water that runs **a**; Ps 58:7
green or ablaze, may he sweep them **a**! Ps 58:9
As smoke is driven **a**, so you shall drive Ps 68:2
is driven away, so you shall drive them **a**; Ps 68:2
in a moment, swept **a** utterly by terrors! Ps 73:19
but turned **a** and acted treacherously Ps 78:57
and put **a** your indignation toward us! Ps 85:4
O LORD, why do you cast my soul **a**? Ps 88:14
You sweep them **a** as with a flood; they Ps 90:5
all our days pass **a** under your wrath; Ps 90:9
they are soon gone, and we fly **a**. Ps 90:10
I hate the work of those who fall **a**; it Ps 101:3
For my days pass **a** like smoke, and my Ps 102:3
evening shadow; I wither **a** like grass. Ps 102:11
"take me not **a** in the midst of my days Ps 102:24
them like a robe, and they will pass **a**, Ps 102:26
they steal **a** and lie down in their dens. Ps 104:22
when you take **a** their breath, they die Ps 104:29
to turn **a** his wrath from destroying Ps 106:23
their courage melted **a** in their evil Ps 107:26
he gnashes his teeth and melts **a**; Ps 112:10
Take **a** from me scorn and contempt, Ps 119:22
My soul melts **a** for sorrow; strengthen Ps 119:28
Turn **a** the reproach that I dread, for Ps 119:39
me, but I do not turn **a** from your law. Ps 119:51
then the flood would have swept us **a**, Ps 124:4
ways the LORD will lead **a** with evildoers! Ps 125:5
do not turn **a** the face of your anointed Ps 132:10
he gave a decree, and it shall not pass **a**. Ps 148:6
gain; it takes **a** the life of its possessors. Prv 1:19
the simple are killed by their turning **a**, Prv 1:32
eyes; fear the LORD, and turn **a** from evil. Prv 3:7
and do not turn **a** from the words of my Prv 4:5
not go on it; turn **a** from it and pass on. Prv 4:15
Put **a** from you crooked speech, and put Prv 4:24
or to the left; turn your foot **a** from evil. Prv 4:27
get, and his disgrace will not be wiped **a**. Prv 6:33
that one may turn **a** from the snares of Prv 13:14
but to turn **a** from evil is an Prv 13:19
but it is swept **a** through injustice. Prv 13:23
wise is cautious and turns **a** from evil, Prv 14:16
that one may turn **a** from the snares of Prv 14:27
A soft answer turns **a** wrath, but a Prv 15:1
he may turn **a** from Sheol beneath. Prv 15:24
fear of the LORD one turns **a** from evil. Prv 16:6
his father and chases **a** his mother is a Prv 19:26
says the buyer, but when he goes **a**, Prv 20:14
Blows that wound cleanse **a** evil; Prv 20:30
of the wicked will sweep them **a**, Prv 21:7
those who are being taken **a** to death; Prv 24:11
and turn **a** his anger from him. Prv 24:18
Take **a** the dross from the silver, and Prv 25:4
take **a** the wicked from the presence of Prv 25:5
is near than a brother who is far **a**. Prv 27:10
If one turns **a** his ear from hearing the Prv 28:9
a city aflame, but the wise turn **a** wrath. Prv 29:8
a time to cast **a** stones, and a time to Eccl 3:5
lose; a time to keep, and a time to cast **a**; Eccl 3:6
and God seeks what has been driven **a**. Eccl 3:15
toil that he may carry **a** in his hand. Eccl 5:15
heart, and put **a** pain from your body, Eccl 11:10
my love, my beautiful one, and come **a**, Sg 2:10
my love, my beautiful one, and come **a**. Sg 2:13
I will go **a** to the mountain of myrrh and Sg 4:6
me, they bruised me, they took **a** my veil, Sg 5:7
Turn **a** your eyes from me, for they Sg 6:5
you and will smelt **a** your dross as with Is 1:25
And the idols shall utterly pass **a**. Is 2:18
day mankind will cast **a** their idols of Is 2:20
of hosts is taking **a** from Jerusalem and Is 3:1
day the Lord will take **a** the finery of the Is 3:18
called by your name; take **a** our reproach." Is 4:1
Lord shall have washed **a** the filth of the Is 4:4
For all this his anger has not turned **a**, Is 5:25
your guilt is taken **a**, and your sin atoned Is 6:7
and the LORD removes people far **a**, and Is 6:12
the feet, and it will sweep **a** the beard also. Is 7:20
Samaria will be carried **a** before the king Is 8:4
For all this his anger has not turned **a**, Is 9:12
For all this his anger has not turned **a**, Is 9:17
For all this his anger has not turned **a**, Is 9:21
For all this his anger has not turned **a**, Is 10:4
it will be as when a sick man wastes **a**. Is 10:18
were angry with me, your anger turned **a**, Is 12:1
but you are cast out, **a** from your grave, Is 14:19
laid up they carry **a** over the Brook of Is 15:7
gladness are taken **a** from the fruitful Is 16:10
yet the harvest will flee **a** in a day of grief Is 17:11
rebuke them, and they will flee far **a**, Is 17:13
branches he lops off and clears **a**. Is 18:5
and dry up, reeds and rushes will rot **a**. Is 19:6
the Nile will be parched, will be driven **a**, Is 19:7
of Assyria lead **a** the Egyptian captives Is 20:4
were captured, though they had fled far **a**. Is 22:3
Therefore I said: "Look **a** from me; let me Is 22:4
He has taken **a** the covering of Judah. In Is 22:8
the LORD will hurl you **a** violently, Is 22:17
old, whose feet carried her to settle far **a**? Is 23:7
One. But I say, "I waste **a**, I waste away. Is 24:16
One. But I say, "I waste away, I waste **a**. Is 24:16
Lord GOD will wipe **a** tears from all faces, Is 25:8
people he will take **a** from all the earth, Is 25:8
and hail will sweep **a** the refuge of lies, Is 28:17
upon horses"; therefore you shall flee **a**; Is 30:16
day everyone shall cast **a** his idols of Is 31:7
His rock shall pass **a** in terror, and his Is 31:9
Lebanon is confounded and withers **a**; Is 33:9
All the host of heaven shall rot **a**, and the Is 34:4
joy, and sorrow and sighing shall flee **a**. Is 35:10
I come and take you **a** to a land like Is 36:17
whom you will father, shall be taken **a**, Is 39:7
them, and the wind shall carry them **a**, Is 41:16
you will not know how to charm **a**; Is 47:11
polished arrow; in his quiver he hid me **a**. Is 49:2
who swallowed you up will be far **a**. Is 49:19
bereaved and barren, exiled and put **a**, Is 49:21
of divorce, with which I sent her **a**? Is 50:1
transgressions your mother was sent **a**. Is 50:1
joy, and sorrow and sighing shall flee **a**. Is 51:11
that my people are taken **a** for nothing? Is 52:5
oppression and judgment he was taken **a**; Is 53:8
devout men are taken **a**, while no one Is 57:1
righteous man is taken **a** from calamity; Is 57:1
them off, a breath will take them **a**. Is 57:13
If you take **a** the yoke from your midst, Is 58:9
our iniquities, like the wind, take us **a**. Is 64:6
a boiling pot, facing **a** from the north." Jer 1:13
too you will come **a** with your hands on Jer 2:37
I had sent her **a** with a decree of divorce. Jer 3:8
strip **a** her branches, for they are not the Jer 5:10
heart; they have turned aside and gone **a**. Jer 5:23
Your iniquities have turned these **a**, and Jer 5:25
"'Cut off your hair and cast it **a**; raise a Jer 7:29
the earth, and none will frighten them **a**. Jer 7:33
again? If one turns **a**, does he not return? Jer 8:4
this people turned **a** in perpetual Jer 8:5
I gave them has passed **a** from them." Jer 8:13
leave my people and go **a** from them! Jer 9:2
in it the beasts and the birds are swept **a**, Jer 12:4
has grown feeble; she has fainted **a**; Jer 15:9
In your forbearance take me not **a**; Jer 15:15
for I have taken **a** my peace from this Jer 16:5
whose heart turns **a** from the LORD. Jer 17:5
those who turn **a** from you shall be Jer 17:13
I have not run **a** from being your Jer 17:16
them, to turn **a** your wrath from them. Jer 18:20
but weep bitterly for him who goes **a**, Jer 22:10
father, and who went **a** from this place: Jer 22:11
my flock and have driven them **a**, Jer 23:2
up and cast you **a** from my presence, Jer 23:39
whom I have sent **a** from this place to Jer 24:5
king of Babylon did not take **a**, Jer 27:20
king of Babylon took **a** from this place Jer 28:3
exiles whom I sent **a** from Jerusalem to Jer 29:20
for behold, I will save you from far **a**, Jer 30:10
the LORD appeared to him from far **a**. I Jer 31:3
and declare it in the coastlands far **a**; Jer 31:10
For after I had turned **a**, I relented, and Jer 31:19
I will not turn **a** from doing good to Jer 32:40
Chaldeans will surely go **a** from us," for Jer 37:9
go away from us," for they will not go **a**. Jer 37:9
in the mud, they turn **a** from you.' Jer 38:22
Ishmael had carried **a** captive from Jer 41:14
burn them and carry them **a** captive. Jer 43:12
and he shall go **a** from there in peace. Jer 43:12
The swift cannot flee **a**, nor the warrior Jer 46:6
makes a sound like a serpent gliding **a**; Jer 46:22
for behold, I will save you from far **a**, Jer 46:27
"Give wings to Moab, for she would fly **a**, Jer 48:9
joy have been taken **a** from the fruitful Jer 48:33
suddenly make him run **a** from her. Jer 49:19
ones of the flock shall be dragged **a**. Jer 49:20
their camels shall be led **a** from them, Jer 49:29
Flee, wander far **a**, dwell in the depths, Jer 49:30
in it; both man and beast shall flee **a**. Jer 50:3
turning them **a** on the mountains. Jer 50:6
is a hunted sheep driven **a** by lions. Jer 50:17
suddenly make them run **a** from her, Jer 50:44
ones of their flock shall be dragged **a**; Jer 50:45
Remember the LORD from far **a**, and let Jer 51:50
of the guard carried **a** captive some of Jer 52:15
And they took **a** the pots and the Jer 52:18
the captain of the guard took **a** as gold, Jer 52:19
Nebuchadnezzar carried **a** captive: Jer 52:28
he carried **a** captive from Jer 52:29
of the guard carried **a** captive of the Jer 52:30
her children have gone **a**, captives Lam 1:5
she herself groans and turns her face **a**. Lam 1:8
made my flesh and my skin waste **a**; Lam 3:4
the victims of hunger, who wasted **a**, Lam 4:9
"**A**! Unclean!" people cried at them. Lam 4:15
people cried at them. "**A**! Away! Lam 4:15
A! Do not touch!" So they became Lam 4:15
The Spirit lifted me up and took me **a**, Ezk 3:14
and rot **a** because of their punishment. Ezk 4:17
GOD: Repent and turn **a** from your idols, Ezk 14:6
and turn **a** your faces from all your Ezk 14:6
strikes it—wither **a** on the bed where Ezk 17:10
chief men of the land he had taken **a**), Ezk 17:13
a wicked person turns **a** from all his Ezk 18:21
righteous person turns **a** from his Ezk 18:24
righteous person turns **a** from his Ezk 18:26
wicked person turns **a** from the Ezk 18:27
considered and turned **a** from all the Ezk 18:28
Cast **a** from you all the transgressions Ezk 18:31
Cast **a** the detestable things your eyes Ezk 20:7
of them cast **a** the detestable things Ezk 20:8
clothes and take **a** your beautiful Ezk 23:26
in hatred and take **a** all the fruit of Ezk 23:29
delight of your eyes **a** from you at a Ezk 24:16
but you shall rot **a** in your iniquities Ezk 24:23
in Egypt, and her wealth is carried **a**, Ezk 30:4
the earth have gone **a** from its shadow Ezk 31:12
drag her **a**, and all her multitudes. Ezk 32:20
and the sword comes and takes him **a**, Ezk 33:4
that person is taken **a** in his iniquity, Ezk 33:6
us, and we rot **a** because of them. Ezk 33:10
off plunder, to carry **a** silver and gold, Ezk 38:13
gold, to take **a** livestock and goods, Ezk 38:13
galleries took more **a** from them than Ezk 42:5
Now let them put **a** their whoring and Ezk 43:9
Put **a** violence and oppression, and Ezk 45:9
So the steward took **a** their food and the Dn 1:16
and the wind carried them **a**, so that not Dn 2:35
the beasts, their dominion was taken **a**, Dn 7:12
dominion, which shall not pass **a**, Dn 7:14
and his dominion shall be taken **a**, Dn 7:26
burnt offering was taken **a** from him, Dn 8:11
who are near and those who are far **a**, Dn 9:7
and your wrath turn **a** from your city Dn 9:16
And when the multitude is taken **a**, his Dn 11:12
shall be utterly swept **a** before him and Dn 11:22
His army shall be swept **a**, and many Dn 11:26
and shall take **a** the regular burnt Dn 11:31
offering is taken **a** and the Dn 12:11
that she put **a** her whoring from her Hos 2:2
and I will take **a** my wool and my flax, Hos 2:9
and even the fish of the sea are taken **a**. Hos 4:3
wine, which take **a** the understanding. Hos 4:11
I, even I, will tear and go **a**; I will carry Hos 5:14
cloud, like the dew that goes early **a**. Hos 6:4
they are going **a** from destruction; Hos 9:6
Ephraim's glory shall fly **a** like a bird— Hos 9:11
they were called, the more they went **a**; Hos 11:2
people are bent on turning **a** from me, Hos 11:7
mist or like the dew that goes early **a**, Hos 13:3
anger, and I took him **a** in my wrath. Hos 13:11
LORD; say to him, "Take **a** all iniquity; Hos 14:2
sell them to the Sabeans, to a nation far **a**, Jl 3:8
the mighty shall flee **a** naked in that Am 2:16
when they shall take you **a** with hooks, Am 4:2
the sword, and carried **a** your horses, Am 4:10
Take **a** from me the noise of your Am 5:23
O you who put far **a** the day of disaster Am 6:3
who stretch themselves out shall pass **a**." Am 6:7
must go into exile **a** from his land.'" Am 7:11
"O seer, go, flee **a** to the land of Judah, Am 7:12
surely go into exile **a** from its land.'" Am 7:17
the sword; not one of them shall flee **a**; Am 9:1
a from the presence of the LORD. Jon 1:3
I said, 'I am driven **a** from your sight; Jon 2:4
When my life was fainting **a**, I Jon 2:7
of Beth-ezel shall take **a** from you its Mi 1:11
seize them, and houses, and take them **a**; Mi 2:2

children you take **a** my splendor forever. Mi 2:9
who have been driven **a** and those whom Mi 4:6
you shall put **a**, but not preserve, and Mi 6:14
many, they will be cut down and pass **a**. Na 1:12
river gates are opened; the palace melts **a**; Na 2:6
is like a pool whose waters run **a**. Na 2:8
The locust spreads its wings and flies **a**. Na 3:16
of cold—when the sun rises, they fly **a**; Na 3:17
will utterly sweep **a** everything from the Zep 1:2
"I will sweep **a** man and beast; I will Zep 1:3
I will sweep **a** the birds of the heavens Zep 1:3
before the day passes **a** like chaff— Zep 2:2
LORD has taken **a** the judgments against Zep 3:15
you; he has cleared **a** your enemies. Zep 3:15
when you brought it home, I blew it **a**. Hg 1:9
I have taken your iniquity **a** from you, Zec 3:4
I will take **a** its blood from its mouth, Zec 9:7
and you shall be taken **a** with it. Mal 2:3
to you, until heaven and earth pass **a**, Mt 5:18
you to sin, tear it out and throw it **a**. Mt 5:29
you to sin, cut it off and throw it **a**. Mt 5:30
us out, send us **a** into the herd of pigs." Mt 8:31
the bridegroom is taken **a** from them, Mt 9:15
for the patch tears **a** from the garment, Mt 9:16
he said, "Go **a**, for the girl is not dead but Mt 9:24
But they went **a** and spread his fame Mt 9:31
As they were going **a**, behold, a Mt 9:32
As they went **a**, Jesus began to speak to Mt 11:7
since they had no root, they withered **a**. Mt 13:6
not, even what he has will be taken **a**. Mt 13:12
comes and snatches **a** what has been Mt 13:19
of the word, immediately he falls **a**. Mt 13:21
weeds among the wheat and went **a**. Mt 13:25
into containers but threw **a** the bad. Mt 13:48
these parables, he went **a** from there, Mt 13:53
send the crowds **a** to go into the villages Mt 14:15
But Jesus said, "They need not go **a**; you Mt 14:16
And Jesus went **a** from there and Mt 15:21
and begged him, saying, "Send her **a**, Mt 15:23
I am unwilling to send them **a** hungry, Mt 15:32
And after sending **a** the crowds, he got Mt 15:39
you to sin, cut it off and throw it **a**. Mt 18:8
you to sin, tear it out and throw it **a**. Mt 18:9
he went **a** from Galilee and entered the Mt 19:1
certificate of divorce and to send her **a**?" Mt 19:7
he laid his hands on them and went **a**. Mt 19:15
man heard this he went **a** sorrowful, Mt 19:22
God will be taken **a** from you and Mt 21:43
And they left him and went **a**. Mt 22:22
Jesus left the temple and was going **a**, Mt 24:1
then many will fall **a** and betray one Mt 24:10
will not pass **a** until all these Mt 24:34
Heaven and earth will pass **a**, but my Mt 24:35
away, but my words will not pass **a**. Mt 24:35
the flood came and swept them all **a**, Mt 24:39
to his ability. Then he went **a**. Mt 25:15
not, even what he has will be taken **a**. Mt 25:29
these will go **a** into eternal Mt 25:46
"You will all fall **a** because of me this Mt 26:31
"Though they all fall **a** because of you, Mt 26:33
because of you, I will never fall **a**." Mt 26:33
the second time, he went **a** and prayed, Mt 26:42
he went **a** and prayed for the third time, Mt 26:44
him and led him **a** and delivered him Mt 27:2
on him and led him **a** to crucify him. Mt 27:31
to the entrance of the tomb and went **a**. Mt 27:60
go and steal him **a** and tell the people, Mt 27:64
night and stole him **a** while we were Mt 28:13
charged him and sent him **a** at once, Mk 1:43
the bridegroom is taken **a** from them, Mk 2:20
If he does, the patch tears **a** from it, the Mk 2:21
and since it had no root, it withered **a**. Mk 4:6
comes and takes **a** the word that Mk 4:15
of the word, immediately they fall **a**. Mk 4:17
not, even what he has will be taken **a**." Mk 4:25
And he went **a** and began to proclaim Mk 5:20
He went **a** from there and came to his Mk 6:1
"Come **a** by yourselves to a desolate Mk 6:31
And they went **a** in the boat to a Mk 6:32
Send them **a** to go into the surrounding Mk 6:36
he arose and went **a** to the region of Mk 7:24
if I send them **a** hungry to their homes, Mk 8:3
some of them have come from far **a**." Mk 8:3
thousand people. And he sent them **a**. Mk 8:9
certificate of divorce and to send her **a**." Mk 10:4
by the saying, he went **a** sorrowful, Mk 10:22
And they went **a** and found a colt tied at Mk 11:4
saw the fig tree withered **a** to its roots. Mk 11:20
him and sent him **a** empty-handed. Mk 12:3
them. So they left him and went **a**. Mk 12:12
will not pass **a** until all these Mk 13:30
Heaven and earth will pass **a**, but my Mk 13:31
away, but my words will not pass **a**. Mk 13:31
Jesus said to them, "You will all fall **a**, Mk 14:27
to him, "Even though they all fall **a**, Mk 14:29
And again he went **a** and prayed, Mk 14:39
him and lead him **a** under guard." Mk 14:44
he left the linen cloth and ran **a** naked. Mk 14:52
Jesus and led him **a** and delivered him Mk 15:1
the soldiers led him **a** inside the palace Mk 15:16
"Who will roll **a** the stone for us from Mk 16:3
to take **a** my reproach among people." Lk 1:25
things, and the rich he has sent empty **a**. Lk 1:53
When the angels went **a** from them into Lk 2:15
passing through their midst, he went **a**. Lk 4:30
the bridegroom is taken **a** from them, Lk 5:35
from one who takes **a** your cloak do not Lk 6:29
from one who takes **a** your goods do not Lk 6:30
the rock, and as it grew up, it withered **a**, Lk 8:6
devil comes and takes **a** the word from Lk 8:12
for a while, and in time of testing fall **a**. Lk 8:13
he thinks that he has will be taken **a**." Lk 8:18
be with him, but Jesus sent him **a**, Lk 8:38
God has done for you." And he went **a**, Lk 8:39
Now the day began to wear **a**, and the Lk 9:12
"Send the crowd **a** to go into the Lk 9:12
which will not be taken **a** from her." Lk 10:42
he takes **a** his armor in which he Lk 11:22
For you have taken **a** the key of Lk 11:52
As he went **a** from there, the scribes Lk 11:53
the manger and lead it **a** to water it? Lk 13:15
and said to him, "Get **a** from here, Lk 13:31
should perish **a** from Jerusalem.' Lk 13:33
him and healed him and sent him **a**. Lk 14:4
or for the manure pile. It is thrown **a**. Lk 14:35
is taking the management **a** from me? Lk 16:3
and earth to pass **a** than for one dot Lk 16:17
house, not come down to take them **a**, Lk 17:31
which I kept laid **a** in a handkerchief; Lk 19:20
not, even what he has will be taken **a**. Lk 19:26
who were sent went **a** and found it just Lk 19:32
him and sent him **a** empty-handed. Lk 20:10
and sent him **a** empty-handed. Lk 20:11
generation will not pass **a** until all has Lk 21:32
Heaven and earth will pass **a**, but my Lk 21:33
away, but my words will not pass **a**. Lk 21:33
He went **a** and conferred with the chief Lk 22:4
Then they seized him and led him **a**, Lk 22:54
And they led him **a** to their council, Lk 22:66
cried out together, "**A** with this man, Lk 23:18
And as they led him **a**, they seized one Lk 23:26
were led **a** to be put to death with him. Lk 23:32
found the stone rolled **a** from the tomb, Lk 24:2
of God, who takes **a** the sin of the world! Jn 1:29
sold the pigeons, "Take these things **a**; Jn 2:16
his disciples had gone **a** into the city to Jn 4:8
water jar and went **a** into town and said Jn 4:28
The man went **a** and told the Jews that it Jn 5:15
After this Jesus went **a** to the other side of Jn 6:1
but that his disciples had gone **a** alone. Jn 6:22
Twelve, "Do you want to go **a** as well?" Jn 6:67
they heard it, they went **a** one by one, Jn 8:9
So he said to them again, "I am going **a**, Jn 8:21
He went **a** again across the Jordan to the Jn 10:40
Jesus said, "Take **a** the stone." Martha, Jn 11:39
So they took **a** the stone. And Jesus lifted Jn 11:41
will come and take **a** both our place Jn 11:48
the Jews were going **a** and believing in Jn 12:11
You heard me say to you, 'I am going **a**, Jn 14:28
mine that does not bear fruit he takes **a**, Jn 15:2
in me he is thrown **a** like a branch and Jn 15:6
things to you to keep you from falling **a**. Jn 16:1
it is to your advantage that I go **a**, for if I Jn 16:7
that I go away, for if I do not go **a**, Jn 16:7
They cried out, "**A** with him, away with Jn 19:15
cried out, "Away with him, **a** with him, Jn 19:15
broken and that they might be taken **a**. Jn 19:31
that he might take **a** the body of Jesus, Jn 19:38
So he came and took **a** his body. Jn 19:38
stone had been taken **a** from the tomb. Jn 20:1
to them, "They have taken **a** my Lord, Jn 20:13
to him, "Sir, if you have carried him **a**, Jn 20:15
have laid him, and I will take him **a**." Jn 20:15
Jerusalem, a Sabbath day's journey **a**. Acts 1:12
the census and drew **a** some of the Acts 5:37
keep **a** from these men and let them Acts 5:38
But God turned **a** and gave them over Acts 7:42
For his life is taken **a** from the earth." Acts 8:33
the Spirit of the Lord carried Philip **a**, Acts 8:39
day he rose and went **a** with them, Acts 10:23
to turn the proconsul **a** from the faith. Acts 13:8
with him and sailed **a** to Cyprus, Acts 15:39
sent Paul and Silas **a** by night to Acts 17:10
his skin were carried **a** to the sick, Acts 19:12
persuaded and turned **a** a great many Acts 19:26
but we sailed **a** from Philippi after the Acts 20:6
And they took the youth **a** alive, and Acts 20:12
to draw **a** the disciples after them. Acts 20:30
followed, crying out, "**A** with him!" Acts 21:36
be baptized and wash **a** your sins, Acts 22:16
I will send you far **a** to the Gentiles.'" Acts 22:21
"**A** with such a fellow from the earth! Acts 22:22
and take him **a** from among them Acts 23:10
and said, "Go **a** for the present. Acts 24:25
Then the soldiers cut **a** the ropes of Acts 27:32
lest any should swim **a** and escape. Acts 27:42
with them when I take **a** their sins." Rom 11:27
of this age, who are doomed to pass **a**. 1 Cor 2:6
form of this world is passing **a**. 1 Cor 7:31
If I give **a** all I have, and if I deliver up 1 Cor 13:3
As for prophecies, they will pass **a**; as 1 Cor 13:8
cease; as for knowledge, it will pass **a**. 1 Cor 13:8
perfect comes, the partial will pass **a**. 1 Cor 13:10
only through Christ is it taken **a**. 2 Cor 3:14
our outer nature is wasting **a**, 2 Cor 4:16
in the body we are **a** from the Lord, 2 Cor 5:6
we would rather be **a** from the body 2 Cor 5:8
So whether we are at home or **a**, we 2 Cor 5:9
The old has passed **a**; behold, the new 2 Cor 5:17
but bold toward you when I am **a**! 2 Cor 10:1
these things while I am **a** from you, 2 Cor 13:10
before me, but I went **a** into Arabia, Gal 1:17
by the law; you have fallen **a** from grace. Gal 5:4
Therefore, having put **a** falsehood, let Eph 4:25
clamor and slander be put **a** from you, Eph 4:31
But now you must put them all **a**: anger, Col 3:8
But since we were torn **a** from you, 1 Thes 2:17
a from the presence of the Lord and 2 Thes 1:9
that you keep **a** from any brother 2 Thes 3:6
have wandered **a** into vain discussion, 1 Tm 1:6
passions draw them **a** from Christ, 1 Tm 5:11
some have wandered **a** from the faith 1 Tm 6:10
all who are in Asia turned **a** from me, 2 Tm 1:15
and will turn **a** from listening to the 2 Tm 4:4
of people who turn **a** from the truth. Ti 1:14
we have heard, lest we drift **a** from it. Heb 2:1
leading you to fall **a** from the living Heb 3:12
if they then fall **a**, since they are Heb 6:6
and growing old is ready to vanish **a**. Heb 8:13
of the ages to put **a** sin by the sacrifice Heb 9:26
blood of bulls and goats to take **a** sins. Heb 10:4
which can never take **a** sins. Heb 10:11
do not throw **a** your confidence, Heb 10:35
Do not be led **a** by diverse and strange Heb 13:9
like a flower of the grass he will pass **a**. Jas 1:10
will the rich man fade **a** in the midst of Jas 1:11
Therefore put **a** all filthiness and Jas 1:21
at himself and goes **a** and at once forgets Jas 1:24
So put **a** all malice and all deceit and 1 Pt 2:1
let him turn **a** from evil and do good; 1 Pt 3:11
the heavens will pass **a** with a roar, 2 Pt 3:10
you are not carried **a** with the error of 2 Pt 3:17
the darkness is passing **a** and the true 1 Jn 2:8
the world is passing **a** along with its 1 Jn 2:17
know that he appeared to take **a** sins, 1 Jn 3:5
and God will wipe **a** every tear from their Rv 7:17
the woman, to sweep her **a** with a flood. Rv 12:15
And every island fled **a**, and no Rv 16:20
And he carried me **a** in the Spirit into a Rv 17:3
From his presence earth and sky fled **a**, Rv 20:11
heaven and the first earth had passed **a**, Rv 21:1
He will wipe **a** every tear from their eyes, Rv 21:4
for the former things have passed **a**." Rv 21:4
And he carried me **a** in the Spirit to a Rv 21:10
and if anyone takes **a** from the words of Rv 22:19
God will take **a** his share in the tree of Rv 22:19

AWE (16)
and they stood in **a** of him just as they Jos 4:14
him just as they had stood in **a** of Moses, Jos 4:14
success, he stood in fearful **a** of him. 1 Sm 18:15
and they stood in **a** of the king, 1 Kgs 3:28
he is to be held in **a** above all gods. 1 Chr 16:25
glorify him, and stand in **a** of him, Ps 22:23
of the world stand in **a** of him! Ps 33:8
ends of the earth are in **a** at your signs. Ps 65:8
my heart stands in **a** of your words. Ps 119:161
Jacob and will stand in **a** of the God of Is 29:23
he feared me. He stood in **a** of my name. Mal 2:5
place, they were filled with **a** and said, Mt 27:54
they glorified God and were filled with **a**, Lk 5:26
And **a** came upon every soul, and Acts 2:43
do not become proud, but stand in **a**. Rom 11:20
worship, with reverence and **a**, Heb 12:28

AWE-INSPIRING (1)
of an expanse, shining like **a** crystal, Ezk 1:22

AWESOME (32)
afraid and said, "How **a** is this place! Gn 28:17
in holiness, **a** in glorious deeds, Ex 15:11
for it is an **a** thing that I will do with Ex 34:10
God is in your midst, a great and **a** God. Dt 7:21
the great, the mighty, and the **a** God, Dt 10:17
you may fear this glorious and **a** name, Dt 28:58
appearance of the angel of God, very **a**. Jgs 13:6
them great and **a** things by driving 2 Sm 7:23

a name for great and **a** things, 1 Chr 17:21
the great and **a** God who keeps covenant Neh 1:5
the Lord, who is great and **a**, Neh 4:14
the great, the mighty, and the **a** God, Neh 9:32
splendor; God is clothed with **a** majesty. Jb 37:22
let your right hand teach you **a** deeds! Ps 45:4
By **a** deeds you answer us with Ps 65:5
Say to God, "How **a** are your deeds! So Ps 66:3
he is **a** in his deeds toward the children of Ps 66:5
A is God from his sanctuary; the God of Ps 68:35
and **a** above all who are around him? Ps 89:7
Let them praise your great and **a** name! Ps 99:3
of Ham, and **a** deeds by the Red Sea. Ps 106:22
forever. Holy and **a** is his name! Ps 111:9
shall speak of the might of your **a** deeds, Ps 145:6
as Jerusalem, **a** as an army with banners. Sg 6:4
as the sun, **a** as an army with banners?" Sg 6:10
When you did **a** things that we did not Is 64:3
And their rims were tall and **a**, and the Ezk 1:18
saying, "O Lord, the great and **a** God, Dn 9:4
For the day of the LORD is great and very **a**; Jl 2:11
before the great and **a** day of the LORD Jl 2:31
The LORD will be **a** against them; for he Zep 2:11
before the great and **a** day of the LORD Mal 4:5

AWL (2)
shall bore his ear through with an **a**, Ex 21:6
then you shall take an **a**, and put it Dt 15:17

AWNING (1)
from the coasts of Elishah was your **a**. Ezk 27:7

AWOKE (12)
When Noah **a** from his wine and knew Gn 9:24
Then Jacob **a** from his sleep and said, Gn 28:16
attractive, plump cows. And Pharaoh **a**. Gn 41:4
And Pharaoh **a**, and behold, it was a Gn 41:7
as ugly as at the beginning. Then I **a**. Gn 41:21
Samson!" But he **a** from his sleep and Jgs 16:14
Samson!" And he **a** from his sleep and Jgs 16:20
And Solomon **a**, and behold, it was a 1 Kgs 3:15
Then the Lord **a** as from sleep, like a Ps 78:65
At this I **a** and looked, and my sleep was Jer 31:26
And he **a** and rebuked the wind and Mk 4:39
perishing!" And he **a** and rebuked the Lk 8:24

AXE (11)
and his hand swings the **a** to cut down a Dt 19:5
its trees by wielding an **a** against them. Dt 20:19
And Abimelech took an **a** in his hand Jgs 9:48
his plowshare, his mattock, his **a**, 1 Sm 13:20
neither hammer nor **a** nor any tool 1 Kgs 6:7
a log, his **a** head fell into the water, 2 Kgs 6:5
Shall the **a** boast over him who hews Is 10:15
down the thickets of the forest with an **a**, Is 10:34
and worked with an **a** by the hands of Jer 10:3
Even now the **a** is laid to the root of the Mt 3:10
Even now the **a** is laid to the root of the Lk 3:9

AXES (6)
for sharpening the **a** and for setting 1 Sm 13:21
picks and iron **a** and made them 2 Sm 12:31
with saws and iron picks and **a**. 1 Chr 20:3
were like those who swing **a** in a forest of Ps 74:5
come against her with **a** like those who Jer 46:22
and with his **a** he will break down your Ezk 26:9

AXLES (3)
four bronze wheels and **a** of bronze, 1 Kgs 7:30
The **a** of the wheels were of one piece 1 Kgs 7:32
made like a chariot wheel; their **a**, 1 Kgs 7:33

AYYAH (1)
and its towns, and **A** and its towns; 1 Chr 7:28

AZAL (1)
of the mountains shall reach to **A**. Zec 14:5

AZALIAH (2)
the king sent Shaphan the son of **A**, 2 Kgs 22:3
house, he sent Shaphan the son of **A**, 2 Chr 34:8

AZANIAH (1)
Jeshua the son of **A**, Binnui of the sons Neh 10:9

AZAREL (6)
Elkanah, Isshiah, **A**, Joezer, and 1 Chr 12:6
the eleventh to **A**, his sons and his 1 Chr 25:18
for Dan, **A** the son of Jeroham. 1 Chr 27:22
A, Shelemiah, Shemariah, Ezr 10:41
and Amashsai, the son of **A**, son of Neh 11:13
his relatives, Shemaiah, **A**, Milalai, Neh 12:36

AZARIAH (49)
A the son of Zadok was the priest; 1 Kgs 4:2
A the son of Nathan was over the 1 Kgs 4:5
And all the people of Judah took **A**, 2 Kgs 14:21
king of Israel, **A** the son of Amaziah, 2 Kgs 15:1
Now the rest of the acts of **A**, and all 2 Kgs 15:6
And **A** slept with his fathers, and they 2 Kgs 15:7
thirty-eighth year of **A** king of Judah, 2 Kgs 15:8
thirty-ninth year of **A** king of Judah, 2 Kgs 15:17
the fiftieth year of **A** king of Judah, 2 Kgs 15:23
fifty-second year of **A** king of Judah, 2 Kgs 15:27
and Ethan's son was **A**. 1 Chr 2:8
fathered Jehu, and Jehu fathered **A**. 1 Chr 2:38
A fathered Helez, and Helez fathered 1 Chr 2:39
Amaziah his son, **A** his son, Jotham 1 Chr 3:12
Ahimaaz fathered **A**, Azariah fathered 1 Chr 6:9
fathered Azariah, **A** fathered Johanan, 1 Chr 6:9
and Johanan fathered **A** (it was he 1 Chr 6:10
A fathered Amariah, Amariah 1 Chr 6:11
fathered Hilkiah, Hilkiah fathered **A**, 1 Chr 6:13
A fathered Seraiah, Seraiah fathered 1 Chr 6:14
son of Elkanah, son of Joel, son of **A**, 1 Chr 6:36
and **A** the son of Hilkiah, son of 1 Chr 9:11
of God came upon **A** the son of Oded, 2 Chr 15:1
the prophecy of **A** the son of Oded, 2 Chr 15:8
A, Jehiel, Zechariah, Azariah, 2 Chr 21:2
Jehiel, Zechariah, **A**, Michael, 2 Chr 21:2
of hundreds, **A** the son of Jeroham, 2 Chr 23:1
son of Jehohanan, **A** the son of Obed, 2 Chr 23:1
But **A** the priest went in after him, 2 Chr 26:17
And **A** the chief priest and all the 2 Chr 26:20
of Ephraim, **A** the son of Johanan, 2 Chr 28:12
son of Amasai, and Joel the son of **A**, 2 Chr 29:12
of Abdi, and **A** the son of Jehallelel; 2 Chr 29:12
A the chief priest, who was of the 2 Chr 31:10
the king and **A** the chief officer 2 Chr 31:13
Persia, Ezra the son of Seraiah, son of **A**, Ezr 7:1
son of Amariah, son of **A**, son of Ezr 7:3
After them **A** the son of Maaseiah, son Neh 3:23
from the house of **A** to the buttress Neh 3:24
Jeshua, Nehemiah, **A**, Raamiah, Neh 7:7
Hodiah, Maaseiah, Kelita, **A**, Jozabad, Neh 8:7
Seraiah, **A**, Jeremiah, Neh 10:2
and **A**, Ezra, Meshullam, Neh 12:33
A the son of Hoshaiah and Johanan the Jer 43:2
Mishael, and **A** of the tribe of Judah. Dn 1:6
Meshach, and **A** he called Abednego. Dn 1:7
over Daniel, Hananiah, Mishael, and **A**, Dn 1:11
like Daniel, Hananiah, Mishael, and **A**. Dn 1:19
known to Hananiah, Mishael, and **A**, Dn 2:17

AZAZ (1)
and Bela the son of **A**, son of Shema, 1 Chr 5:8

AZAZEL (4)
lot for the LORD and the other lot for **A**. Lv 16:8
the lot fell for **A** shall be presented alive Lv 16:10
be sent away into the wilderness to **A**. Lv 16:10
the goat go to **A** shall wash his clothes Lv 16:26

AZAZIAH (3)
and **A** were to lead with lyres 1 Chr 15:21
Ephraimites, Hoshea the son of **A**; 1 Chr 27:20
while Jehiel, **A**, Nahath, Asahel, 2 Chr 31:13

AZBUK (1)
After him Nehemiah the son of **A**, Neh 3:16

AZEKAH (7)
them as far as **A** and Makkedah. Jos 10:10
from heaven on them as far as **A**, Jos 10:11
Jarmuth, Adullam, Socoh, **A**, Jos 15:35
and encamped between Socoh and **A**, 1 Sm 17:1
Adoraim, Lachish, **A**, 2 Chr 11:9
and its fields, and **A** and its villages. Neh 11:30
of Judah that were left, Lachish and **A**, Jer 34:7

AZEL (6)
his son, Eleasah his son, **A** his son. 1 Chr 8:37
A had six sons, and these are their 1 Chr 8:38
Hanan. All these were the sons of **A**. 1 Chr 8:38
his son, Eleasah his son, **A** his son. 1 Chr 9:43
A had six sons and these are their 1 Chr 9:44
and Hanan; these were the sons of **A**. 1 Chr 9:44

AZGAD (4)
The sons of **A**, 1,222. Ezr 2:12
Of the sons of **A**, Johanan the son of Ezr 8:12
The sons of **A**, 2,322. Neh 7:17
Bunni, **A**, Bebai, Neh 10:15

AZIEL (1)
Zechariah, **A**, Shemiramoth, Jehiel, 1 Chr 15:20

AZIZA (1)
Mattaniah, Jeremoth, Zabad, and **A**. Ezr 10:27

AZMAVETH (8)
the Arbathite, **A** of Bahurim, 2 Sm 23:31
fathered Alemeth, **A**, and Zimri. 1 Chr 8:36
fathered Alemeth, **A**, and Zimri. 1 Chr 9:42
A of Baharum, Eliahba the 1 Chr 11:33
also Jeziel and Pelet, the sons of **A**; 1 Chr 12:3
king's treasuries was **A** the son of 1 Chr 27:25
The sons of **A**, 42. Ezr 2:24
and from the region of Geba and **A**, Neh 12:29

AZMON (3)
on to Hazar-addar, and pass along to **A**. Nm 34:4
border shall turn from **A** to the Brook Nm 34:5
passes along to **A**, goes out by the Brook Jos 15:4

AZNOTH-TABOR (1)
turns westward to **A** and goes from Jos 19:34

AZOR (2)
of Eliakim, and Eliakim the father of **A**, Mt 1:13
and **A** the father of Zadok, and Zadok Mt 1:14

AZOTUS (1)
But Philip found himself at **A**, and as Acts 8:40

AZRIEL (3)
Epher, Ishi, Eliel, **A**, Jeremiah, 1 Chr 5:24
for Naphtali, Jeremoth the son of **A**; 1 Chr 27:19
Seraiah the son of **A** and Shelemiah the Jer 36:26

AZRIKAM (6)
Elioenai, Hizkiah, and **A**, three. 1 Chr 3:23
A, Bocheru, Ishmael, Sheariah, 1 Chr 8:38
the son of Hasshub, son of **A**, 1 Chr 9:14
A, Bocheru, Ishmael, Sheariah, 1 Chr 9:44
king's son and **A** the commander of 2 Chr 28:7
the son of Hasshub, son of **A**, Neh 11:15

AZUBAH (4)
mother's name was **A** the daughter 1 Kgs 22:42
fathered children by his wife **A**, 1 Chr 2:18
When **A** died, Caleb married 1 Chr 2:19
mother's name was **A** the daughter 2 Chr 20:31

AZZAN (1)
Issachar a chief, Paltiel the son of **A**. Nm 34:26

AZZUR (3)
Ater, Hezekiah, **A**, Neh 10:17
the fourth year, Hananiah the son of **A**, Jer 28:1
among them Jaazaniah the son of **A**, Ezk 11:1

B

BAAL (66)
So Israel yoked himself to **B** of Peor. Nm 25:3
have yoked themselves to **B** of Peor." Nm 25:5
all the men who followed the **B** of Peor. Dt 4:3
down the altar of **B** that your father has, Jgs 6:25
behold, the altar of **B** was broken down, Jgs 6:28
down the altar of **B** and cut down the Jgs 6:30
against him, "Will you contend for **B**? Jgs 6:31
"Let **B** contend against him," because he Jgs 6:32
went and served **B** and worshiped 1 Kgs 16:31
erected an altar for **B** in the house of 1 Kgs 16:32
an altar for Baal in the house of **B**, 1 Kgs 16:32
the 450 prophets of **B** and the 400 1 Kgs 18:19
but if **B**, then follow him." And the 1 Kgs 18:21
Elijah said to the prophets of **B**, 1 Kgs 18:25
the name of **B** from morning until 1 Kgs 18:26
morning until noon, saying, "O **B**, 1 Kgs 18:26
to them, "Seize the prophets of **B**; 1 Kgs 18:40
the knees that have not bowed to **B**, 1 Kgs 19:18
He served **B** and worshiped him and 1 Kgs 22:53
away the pillar of **B** that his father had 2 Kgs 3:2
said to them, "Ahab served **B** a little, 2 Kgs 10:18
call to me all the prophets of **B**, 2 Kgs 10:19
I have a great sacrifice to offer to **B**. 2 Kgs 10:19
order to destroy the worshipers of **B**. 2 Kgs 10:19
solemn assembly for **B**." So they 2 Kgs 10:20
and all the worshipers of **B** came, 2 Kgs 10:21
And they entered the house of **B**, and 2 Kgs 10:21
and the house of **B** was filled from 2 Kgs 10:21
the worshipers of **B**." So he brought 2 Kgs 10:22
the house of **B** with Jehonadab the 2 Kgs 10:23
and he said to the worshipers of **B**, 2 Kgs 10:23
you, but only the worshipers of **B**." 2 Kgs 10:23
the inner room of the house of **B**, 2 Kgs 10:25
was in the house of **B** and burned it. 2 Kgs 10:26
And they demolished the pillar of **B**, 2 Kgs 10:27
Baal, and demolished the house of **B**, 2 Kgs 10:27
Thus Jehu wiped out **B** from Israel. 2 Kgs 10:28
to the house of **B** and tore it down; 2 Kgs 11:18
the priest of **B** before the altars. 2 Kgs 11:18
all the host of heaven and served **B**. 2 Kgs 17:16
he erected altars for **B** and made an 2 Kgs 21:3
of the LORD all the vessels made for **B**, 2 Kgs 23:4
those also who burned incense to **B**, 2 Kgs 23:5
were around these cities as far as **B**. 1 Chr 4:33
his son, Reaiah his son, **B** his son, 1 Chr 5:5
Abdon, then Zur, Kish, **B**, Nadab, 1 Chr 8:30
son Abdon, then Zur, Kish, **B**, Ner, 1 Chr 9:36
to the house of **B** and tore it down; 2 Chr 23:17
the priest of **B** before the altars. 2 Chr 23:17
they yoked themselves to the **B** of Peor, Ps 106:28
prophets prophesied by **B** and went after Jer 2:8
swear falsely, make offerings to **B**, Jer 7:9
to shame, altars to make offerings to **B**. Jer 11:13
me to anger by making offerings to **B**." Jer 11:17
as they taught my people to swear by **B**, Jer 12:16

the high places of **B** to burn their sons Jer 19:5
sons in the fire as burnt offerings to **B**, Jer 19:5
they prophesied by **B** and led my people Jer 23:13
as their fathers forgot my name for **B**? Jer 23:27
been made to **B** and drink offerings Jer 32:29
the high places of **B** in the Valley of Jer 32:35
silver and gold, which they used for **B**. Hos 2:8
and no longer will you call me 'My **B**.' Hos 2:16
he incurred guilt through **B** and died. Hos 13:1
place the remnant of **B** and the name of Zep 1:4
who have not bowed the knee to **B**." Rom 11:4

BAAL'S (1)
LORD, but **B** prophets are 450 men. 1 Kgs 18:22

BAAL-BERITH (2)
after the Baals and made **B** their god. Jgs 8:33
of the house of **B** with which Abimelech Jgs 9:4

BAAL-GAD (3)
as far as **B** in the Valley of Lebanon Jos 11:17
from **B** in the Valley of Lebanon to Jos 12:7
from **B** below Mount Hermon to Jos 13:5

BAAL-HAMON (1)
Solomon had a vineyard at **B**; he let out Sg 8:11

BAAL-HANAN (5)
and **B** the son of Achbor reigned in his Gn 36:38
B the son of Achbor died, and Hadar Gn 36:39
Shaul died, and **B**, the son of Achbor, 1 Chr 1:49
B died, and Hadad reigned in his 1 Chr 1:50
in the Shephelah was **B** the Gederite; 1 Chr 27:28

BAAL-HAZOR (1)
Absalom had sheepshearers at **B**, 2 Sm 13:23

BAAL-HERMON (2)
from Mount **B** as far as Lebo-hamath. Jgs 3:3
very numerous from Bashan to **B**, 1 Chr 5:23

BAAL-MEON (3)
and **B** (their names were changed), Nm 32:38
lived in Aroer, as far as Nebo and **B**. 1 Chr 5:8
Beth-jeshimoth, **B**, and Kiriathaim. Ezk 25:9

BAAL-PEOR (2)
eyes have seen what the LORD did at **B**, Dt 4:3
they came to **B** and consecrated Hos 9:10

BAAL-PERAZIM (4)
And David came to **B**, and David 2 Sm 5:20
the name of that place is called **B**. 2 Sm 5:20
And he went up to **B**, and David 1 Chr 14:11
the name of that place is called **B**. 1 Chr 14:11

BAAL-SHALISHAH (1)
A man came from **B**, bringing the 2 Kgs 4:42

BAAL-TAMAR (1)
place and set themselves in array at **B**, Jgs 20:33

BAAL-ZEBUB (4)
telling them, "Go, inquire of **B**, 2 Kgs 1:2
that you are going to inquire of **B**, 2 Kgs 1:3
that you are sending to inquire of **B**, 2 Kgs 1:6
have sent messengers to inquire of **B**, 2 Kgs 1:16

BAAL-ZEPHON (3)
Migdol and the sea, in front of **B**; Ex 14:2
at the sea, by Pi-hahiroth, in front of **B**. Ex 14:9
back to Pi-hahiroth, which is east of **B**, Nm 33:7

BAALAH (5)
boundary bends around to **B** (that is, Jos 15:9
circles west of **B** to Mount Seir, Jos 15:10
passes along to Mount **B** and goes out Jos 15:11
B, Iim, Ezem, Jos 15:29
David and all Israel went up to **B**, 1 Chr 13:6

BAALATH (3)
Eltekeh, Gibbethon, **B**, Jos 19:44
and **B** and Tamar in the wilderness, 1 Kgs 9:18
and **B**, and all the store cities that 2 Chr 8:6

BAALATH-BEER (1)
villages around these cities as far as **B**, Jos 19:8

BAALE-JUDAH (1)
were with him from **B** to bring up from 2 Sm 6:2

BAALIS (1)
"Do you know that **B** the king of the Jer 40:14

BAALS (19)
in the sight of the LORD and served the **B**. Jgs 2:11
and served the **B** and the Ashtaroth. Jgs 2:13
God and served the **B** and the Asheroth. Jgs 3:7
whored after the **B** and made Baal-berith Jgs 8:33
and served the **B** and the Ashtaroth, Jgs 10:6
our God and have served the **B**." Jgs 10:10
put away the **B** and the Ashtaroth, 1 Sm 7:4
have served the **B** and the Ashtaroth. 1 Sm 12:10
of the LORD and followed the **B**. 1 Kgs 18:18
father David. He did not seek the **B**, 2 Chr 17:3
of the house of the LORD for the **B**. 2 Chr 24:7
He even made metal images for the **B**, 2 Chr 28:2
down, and he erected altars to the **B**, 2 Chr 33:3
the altars of the **B** in his presence, 2 Chr 34:4
not unclean, I have not gone after the **B**'? Jer 2:23
own hearts and have gone after the **B**, Jer 9:14
feast days of the **B** when she burned Hos 2:13
the names of the **B** from her mouth, Hos 2:17
sacrificing to the **B** and burning Hos 11:2

BAANA (3)
B the son of Ahilud, in Taanach, 1 Kgs 4:12
B the son of Hushai, in Asher and 1 Kgs 4:16
to them Zadok the son of **B** repaired. Neh 3:4

BAANAH (9)
the name of the one was **B**, and the 2 Sm 4:2
Rimmon the Beerothite, Rechab and **B**, 2 Sm 4:5
Then Rechab and **B** his brother 2 Sm 4:6
answered Rechab and **B** his brother, 2 Sm 4:9
Heleb the son of **B** of Netophah, Ittai 2 Sm 23:29
Heled the son of **B** of Netophah, 1 Chr 11:30
Bilshan, Mispar, Bigvai, Rehum, and **B**. Ezr 2:2
Bilshan, Mispereth, Bigvai, Nehum, **B**. Neh 7:7
Malluch, Harim, **B**. Neh 10:27

BAARA (1)
sent away Hushim and **B** his wives. 1 Chr 8:8

BAASEIAH (1)
son of Michael, son of **B**, son of 1 Chr 6:40

BAASHA (28)
between Asa and **B** king of Israel 1 Kgs 15:16
B king of Israel went up against 1 Kgs 15:17
your covenant with **B** king of Israel, 1 Kgs 15:19
And when **B** heard of it, he stopped 1 Kgs 15:21
with which **B** had been building, 1 Kgs 15:22
B the son of Ahijah, of the house of 1 Kgs 15:27
And **B** struck him down at 1 Kgs 15:27
So **B** killed him in the third year of 1 Kgs 15:28
between Asa and **B** king of Israel 1 Kgs 15:32
B the son of Ahijah began to reign 1 Kgs 15:33
to Jehu the son of Hanani against **B**, 1 Kgs 16:1
utterly sweep away **B** and his house, 1 Kgs 16:3
Anyone belonging to **B** who dies in 1 Kgs 16:4
rest of the acts of **B** and what he did, 1 Kgs 16:5
And **B** slept with his fathers and was 1 Kgs 16:6
of Hanani against **B** and his house, 1 Kgs 16:7
Elah the son of **B** began to reign over 1 Kgs 16:8
he struck down all the house of **B**. 1 Kgs 16:11
Zimri destroyed all the house of **B**, 1 Kgs 16:12
he spoke against **B** by Jehu the 1 Kgs 16:12
for all the sins of **B** and the sins of 1 Kgs 16:13
like the house of **B** the son of 1 Kgs 21:22
like the house of **B** the son of Ahijah. 2 Kgs 9:9
B king of Israel went up against 2 Chr 16:1
your covenant with **B** king of Israel, 2 Chr 16:3
And when **B** heard of it, he stopped 2 Chr 16:5
with which **B** had been building, 2 Chr 16:6
made for defense against **B** king of Israel; Jer 41:9

BABBLE (3)
Should your **b** silence men, and when Jb 11:3
the irreverent **b** and contradictions 1 Tm 6:20
But avoid irreverent **b**, for it will lead 2 Tm 2:16

BABBLER (2)
do not associate with a simple **b**. Prv 20:19
"What does this **b** wish to say?" Acts 17:18

BABBLING (2)
but a **b** fool will come to ruin. Prv 10:8
trouble, but a **b** fool will come to ruin. Prv 10:10

BABEL (2)
The beginning of his kingdom was **B**, Gn 10:10
Therefore its name was called **B**, Gn 11:9

BABES (1)
Out of the mouth of **b** and infants, you Ps 8:2

BABIES (2)
because infants and **b** faint in the Lam 2:11
infants and nursing **b** you have Mt 21:16

BABY (6)
the child, and behold, the **b** was crying. Ex 2:6
of Mary, the **b** leaped in her womb. Lk 1:41
ears, the **b** in my womb leaped for joy. Lk 1:44
you will find a **b** wrapped in swaddling Lk 2:12
and Joseph, and the **b** lying in a manger. Lk 2:16
come, but when she has delivered the **b**, Jn 16:21

BABYLON (288)
of Assyria brought people from **B**, 2 Kgs 17:24
men of **B** made Succoth-benoth, 2 Kgs 17:30
the son of Baladan, king of **B**, 2 Kgs 20:12
come from a far country, from **B**." 2 Kgs 20:14
up till this day, shall be carried to **B**. 2 Kgs 20:17
in the palace of the king of **B**." 2 Kgs 20:18
Nebuchadnezzar king of **B** came up, 2 Kgs 24:1
for the king of **B** had taken all that 2 Kgs 24:7
Nebuchadnezzar king of **B** came up 2 Kgs 24:10
Nebuchadnezzar king of **B** came to 2 Kgs 24:11
gave himself up to the king of **B**, 2 Kgs 24:12
The king of **B** took him prisoner in 2 Kgs 24:12
he carried away Jehoiachin to **B**. 2 Kgs 24:15
into captivity from Jerusalem to **B**. 2 Kgs 24:15
the king of **B** brought captive to 2 Kgs 24:16
brought captive to **B** all the men 2 Kgs 24:16
And the king of **B** made Mattaniah, 2 Kgs 24:17
rebelled against the king of **B**. 2 Kgs 24:20
king of **B** came with 2 Kgs 25:1
him up to the king of **B** at Riblah, 2 Kgs 25:6
him in chains and took him to **B**. 2 Kgs 25:7
king of **B**—Nebuzaradan, 2 Kgs 25:8
bodyguard, a servant of the king of **B**, 2 Kgs 25:8
who had deserted to the king of **B**, 2 Kgs 25:11
pieces and carried the bronze to **B**. 2 Kgs 25:13
them to the king of **B** at Riblah. 2 Kgs 25:20
the king of **B** struck them down 2 Kgs 25:21
Nebuchadnezzar king of **B** had left, 2 Kgs 25:22
the king of **B** had appointed 2 Kgs 25:23
in the land and serve the king of **B**, 2 Kgs 25:24
month, Evil-merodach king of **B**, 2 Kgs 25:27
the kings who were with him in **B**. 2 Kgs 25:28
taken into exile in **B** because of their 1 Chr 9:1
of the envoys of the princes of **B**, 2 Chr 32:31
of bronze and brought him to **B**. 2 Chr 33:11
king of **B** and bound 2 Chr 36:6
him in chains to take him to **B**. 2 Chr 36:6
of the LORD to **B** and put them in 2 Chr 36:7
and put them in his palace in **B**. 2 Chr 36:7
sent and brought him to **B**, 2 Chr 36:10
princes, all these he brought to **B**. 2 Chr 36:18
took into exile in **B** those who had 2 Chr 36:20
the king of **B** had carried captive Ezr 2:1
the hand of Nebuchadnezzar king of **B**, Ezr 5:12
in the first year of Cyrus king of **B**, Ezr 5:13
and brought into the temple of **B**, Ezr 5:14
the king took out of the temple of **B**, Ezr 5:14
made in the royal archives there in **B**, Ezr 5:17
that is in Jerusalem and brought to **B**, Ezr 6:5
the king of **B** had carried into Neh 7:6
of Artaxerxes king of **B** I went to the Neh 13:6
Nebuchadnezzar king of **B** had carried Est 2:6
who know me I mention Rahab and **B**; Ps 87:4
By the waters of **B**, there we sat down Ps 137:1
O daughter of **B**, doomed to be Ps 137:8
The oracle concerning **B** which Isaiah Is 13:1
And **B**, the glory of kingdoms, the Is 13:19
take up this taunt against the king of **B**: Is 14:4
will cut off from **B** name and remnant, Is 14:22
And he answered, "Fallen, fallen is **B**; Is 21:9
the son of Baladan, king of **B**, Is 39:1
come to me from a far country, from **B**." Is 39:3
up till this day, shall be carried to **B**. Is 39:6
eunuchs in the palace of the king of **B**." Is 39:7
your sake I send to **B** and bring them all Is 43:14
and sit in the dust, O virgin daughter of **B**; Is 47:1
he shall perform his purpose on **B**, and Is 48:14
Go out from **B**, flee from Chaldea, Is 48:20
all Judah into the hand of the king of **B**. Jer 20:4
He shall carry them captive to **B**, and Jer 20:4
and seize them and carry them to **B**. Jer 20:5
To **B** you shall go, and there you shall Jer 20:6
Nebuchadnezzar king of **B** is making Jer 21:2
against the king of **B** and against the Jer 21:4
Nebuchadnezzar king of **B** and into the Jer 21:7
be given into the hand of the king of **B**, Jer 21:10
Nebuchadnezzar king of **B** and into the Jer 22:25
Nebuchadnezzar king of **B** had taken Jer 24:1
workers, and had brought them to **B**, Jer 24:1
first year of Nebuchadnezzar king of **B**), Jer 25:1
and for Nebuchadnezzar the king of **B**, Jer 25:9
shall serve the king of **B** seventy years. Jer 25:11
punish the king of **B** and that nation, Jer 25:12
after them the king of **B** shall drink. Jer 25:26
hand of Nebuchadnezzar, the king of **B**, Jer 27:6
serve this Nebuchadnezzar king of **B**, Jer 27:8
its neck under the yoke of the king of **B**, Jer 27:8
you, 'You shall not serve the king of **B**.' Jer 27:9
the yoke of the king of **B** and serve him, Jer 27:11
necks under the yoke of the king of **B**, Jer 27:12
nation that will not serve the king of **B**? Jer 27:13
you, 'You shall not serve the king of **B**,' Jer 27:14
now shortly be brought back from **B**,' Jer 27:16
to them; serve the king of **B** and live. Jer 27:17
and in Jerusalem may not go to **B**. Jer 27:18
Nebuchadnezzar king of **B** did not take Jer 27:20
from Jerusalem to **B** Jeconiah the son Jer 27:20
shall be carried to **B** and remain there Jer 27:22
I have broken the yoke of the king of **B**. Jer 28:2
Nebuchadnezzar king of **B** took away Jer 28:3
away from this place and carried to **B**. Jer 28:3
all the exiles from Judah who went to **B**, Jer 28:4
I will break the yoke of the king of **B**." Jer 28:4
to this place from **B** the vessels of the Jer 28:6

Nebuchadnezzar king of **B** from the Jer 28:11
to serve Nebuchadnezzar king of **B**, Jer 28:14
had taken into exile from Jerusalem to **B**. Jer 29:1
Judah sent to **B** to Nebuchadnezzar king Jer 29:3
Babylon to Nebuchadnezzar king of **B**. Jer 29:3
have sent into exile from Jerusalem to **B**: Jer 29:4
seventy years are completed for **B**, Jer 29:10
LORD has raised up prophets for us in **B**,' Jer 29:15
whom I sent away from Jerusalem to **B**: Jer 29:20
the hand of Nebuchadnezzar king of **B**, Jer 29:21
used by all the exiles from Judah in **B**: Jer 29:22
whom the king of **B** roasted in the fire," Jer 29:22
For he has sent to us in **B**, saying, Jer 29:28
of the king of **B** was besieging Jerusalem, Jer 32:2
this city into the hand of the king of **B**, Jer 32:3
be given into the hand of the king of **B**, Jer 32:4
And he shall take Zedekiah to **B**, and Jer 32:5
the hand of Nebuchadnezzar king of **B**, Jer 32:28
into the hand of the king of **B** by sword, Jer 32:36
Nebuchadnezzar king of **B** and all his Jer 34:1
this city into the hand of the king of **B**, Jer 34:2
shall see the king of **B** eye to eye and Jer 34:3
him face to face. And you shall go to **B**.' Jer 34:3
of the king of **B** was fighting against Jer 34:7
of the king of **B** which has withdrawn Jer 34:21
Nebuchadnezzar king of **B** came up Jer 35:11
that the king of **B** will certainly come Jer 36:29
Nebuchadnezzar king of **B** made king Jer 37:1
into the hand of the king of **B**." Jer 37:17
'The king of **B** will not come against Jer 37:19
the army of the king of **B** and be taken." Jer 38:3
to the officials of the king of **B**, Jer 38:17
to the officials of the king of **B**, Jer 38:18
of the king of **B** and were saying, Jer 38:22
but shall be seized by the king of **B**, Jer 38:23
Nebuchadnezzar king of **B** and all his Jer 39:1
officials of the king of **B** came and sat in Jer 39:3
all the rest of the officers of the king of **B**. Jer 39:3
him up to Nebuchadnezzar king of **B**, Jer 39:5
The king of **B** slaughtered the sons of Jer 39:6
and the king of **B** slaughtered all the Jer 39:6
bound him in chains to take him to **B**. Jer 39:7
carried into exile to **B** the rest of the Jer 39:9
king of **B** gave command Jer 39:11
all the chief officers of the king of **B** Jer 39:13
and Judah who were being exiled to **B**. Jer 40:1
seems good to you to come with me to **B**, Jer 40:4
wrong to you to come with me to **B**, Jer 40:4
the king of **B** appointed governor of Jer 40:5
the king of **B** had appointed Gedaliah Jer 40:7
who had not been taken into exile to **B**, Jer 40:7
Dwell in the land and serve the king of **B**, Jer 40:9
that the king of **B** had left a remnant Jer 40:11
the king of **B** had appointed governor Jer 41:2
the king of **B** had made governor Jer 41:18
Do not fear the king of **B**, of whom you Jer 42:11
may kill us or take us into exile in **B**." Jer 43:3
take Nebuchadnezzar the king of **B**, Jer 43:10
the hand of Nebuchadnezzar king of **B**, Jer 44:30
Nebuchadnezzar king of **B** defeated in Jer 46:2
Nebuchadnezzar king of **B** to strike the Jer 46:13
Nebuchadnezzar king of **B** and his Jer 46:26
king of **B** struck down. Jer 49:28
Nebuchadnezzar king of **B** has made a Jer 49:30
word that the LORD spoke concerning **B**, Jer 50:1
'**B** is taken, Bel is put to shame, Jer 50:2
"Flee from the midst of **B**, and go out of Jer 50:8
and bringing against **B** a gathering of Jer 50:9
who passes by **B** shall be appalled, Jer 50:13
in array against **B** all around, Jer 50:14
Cut off from **B** the sower, and the one Jer 50:16
Nebuchadnezzar king of **B** has gnawed Jer 50:17
on the king of **B** and his land, Jer 50:18
How **B** has become a horror among the Jer 50:23
snare for you and you were taken, O **B**, Jer 50:24
They flee and escape from the land of **B**, Jer 50:28
"Summon archers against **B**, all those Jer 50:29
but unrest to the inhabitants of **B**. Jer 50:34
LORD, and against the inhabitants of **B**, Jer 50:35
beasts shall dwell with hyenas in **B**, Jer 50:39
for battle against you, O daughter of **B**! Jer 50:42
"The king of **B** heard the report of Jer 50:43
plan that the LORD has made against **B**, Jer 50:45
of the capture of **B** the earth shall Jer 50:46
stir up the spirit of a destroyer against **B**, Jer 51:1
and I will send to **B** winnowers, and they Jer 51:2
"Flee from the midst of **B**; let every one Jer 51:6
B was a golden cup in the LORD'S hand, Jer 51:7
Suddenly **B** has fallen and been broken; Jer 51:8
We would have healed **B**, but she was Jer 51:9
his purpose concerning **B** is to destroy Jer 51:11
up a standard against the walls of **B**; Jer 51:12
spoke concerning the inhabitants of **B**. Jer 51:12
"I will repay **B** and all the inhabitants Jer 51:24
for the LORD'S purposes against **B** stand, Jer 51:29
to make the land of **B** a desolation, Jer 51:29
The warriors of **B** have ceased fighting; Jer 51:30
to tell the king of **B** that his city is Jer 51:31
The daughter of **B** is like a threshing Jer 51:33
the king of **B** has devoured me; Jer 51:34
kinsmen be upon **B**," let the inhabitant Jer 51:35
and **B** shall become a heap of ruins, the Jer 51:37
"How **B** is taken, the praise of the whole Jer 51:41
How **B** has become a horror among the Jer 51:41
The sea has come up on **B**; she is Jer 51:42
And I will punish Bel in **B**, and take out Jer 51:44
flow to him; the wall of **B** has fallen. Jer 51:44
when I will punish the images of **B**; Jer 51:47
is in them, shall sing for joy over **B**, Jer 51:48
B must fall for the slain of Israel, just as Jer 51:49
just as for **B** have fallen the slain of all Jer 51:49
Though **B** should mount up to heaven, Jer 51:53
"A voice! A cry from **B**! The noise of Jer 51:54
the LORD is laying **B** waste and stilling Jer 51:55
a destroyer has come upon her, upon **B**; Jer 51:56
The broad wall of **B** shall be leveled to Jer 51:58
went with Zedekiah king of Judah to **B**, Jer 51:59
the disaster that should come upon **B**, Jer 51:60
words that are written concerning **B**. Jer 51:60
"When you come to **B**, see that you Jer 51:61
and say, 'Thus shall **B** sink, to rise no Jer 51:64
Zedekiah rebelled against the king of **B**. Jer 52:3
Nebuchadnezzar king of **B** came with Jer 52:4
up to the king of **B** at Riblah in the land Jer 52:9
The king of **B** slaughtered the sons of Jer 52:10
and the king of **B** took him to Babylon, Jer 52:11
and the king of Babylon took him to **B**, Jer 52:11
king of **B**—Nebuzaradan the captain Jer 52:12
bodyguard, who served the king of **B**, Jer 52:12
who had deserted to the king of **B**, Jer 52:15
pieces, and carried all the bronze to **B**. Jer 52:17
them to the king of **B** at Riblah. Jer 52:26
And the king of **B** struck them down, Jer 52:27
of the month, Evil-merodach king of **B**, Jer 52:31
of the kings who were with him in **B**. Jer 52:32
And I will bring him to **B**, the land of Ezk 12:13
the king of **B** came to Jerusalem, Ezk 17:12
and brought them to him to **B**. Ezk 17:12
with him he broke, in **B** he shall die. Ezk 17:16
will bring him to **B** and enter into Ezk 17:20
cage and brought him to the king of **B**; Ezk 19:9
for the sword of the king of **B** to come. Ezk 21:19
For the king of **B** stands at the parting Ezk 21:21
The king of **B** has laid siege to Ezk 24:2
the north Nebuchadnezzar king of **B**, Ezk 26:7
Nebuchadnezzar king of **B** made his Ezk 29:18
Egypt to Nebuchadnezzar king of **B**; Ezk 29:19
hand of Nebuchadnezzar king of **B**. Ezk 30:10
of the king of **B** and put my sword Ezk 30:24
strengthen the arms of the king of **B**, Ezk 30:25
of the king of **B** and he stretches it Ezk 30:25
of the king of **B** shall come upon you. Ezk 32:11
Nebuchadnezzar king of **B** came to Dn 1:1
that all the wise men of **B** be destroyed. Dn 2:12
had gone out to kill the wise men of **B**. Dn 2:14
with the rest of the wise men of **B**. Dn 2:18
appointed to destroy the wise men of **B**. Dn 2:24
him, "Do not destroy the wise men of **B**; Dn 2:24
whole province of **B** and chief prefect Dn 2:48
chief prefect over all the wise men of **B**. Dn 2:48
over the affairs of the province of **B**. Dn 2:49
on the plain of Dura, in the province of **B**. Dn 3:1
over the affairs of the province of **B**: Dn 3:12
and Abednego in the province of **B**. Dn 3:30
the wise men of **B** should be brought Dn 4:6
on the roof of the royal palace of **B**, Dn 4:29
answered and said, "Is not this great **B**, Dn 4:30
The king declared to the wise men of **B**, Dn 5:7
In the first year of Belshazzar king of **B**, Dn 7:1
in the open country; you shall go to **B**. Mi 4:10
you who dwell with the daughter of **B**. Zec 2:7
and Jedaiah, who have arrived from **B**, Zec 6:10
at the time of the deportation to **B**. Mt 1:11
And after the deportation to **B**: Mt 1:12
deportation to **B** fourteen generations, Mt 1:17
from the deportation to **B** to the Christ Mt 1:17
I will send you into exile beyond **B**.' Acts 7:43
She who is at **B**, who is likewise chosen, 1 Pt 5:13
saying, "Fallen, fallen is **B** the great, Rv 14:8
fell, and God remembered **B** the great, Rv 16:19
"**B** the great, mother of prostitutes and of Rv 17:5
voice, "Fallen, fallen is **B** the great! Rv 18:2
You great city, you mighty city, **B**! Rv 18:10
"So will **B** the great city be thrown Rv 18:21

BABYLONIA (8)

were brought up from **B** to Jerusalem. Ezr 1:11
king of Babylon had carried captive to **B**. Ezr 2:1
house and carried away the people to **B**. Ezr 5:12
a decree, and search was made in **B**, Ezr 6:1
this Ezra went up from **B**. He was a scribe Ezr 7:6
the first month he began to go up from **B**, Ezr 7:9
shall find in the whole province of **B**, Ezr 7:16
of those who went up with me from **B**, Ezr 8:1

BABYLONIANS (4)

the Persians, the men of Erech, the **B**, Ezr 4:9
a likeness of **B** whose native land was Ezk 23:15
And the **B** came to her into the bed of Ezk 23:17
the **B** and all the Chaldeans, Pekod Ezk 23:23

BACA (1)

go through the Valley of **B** they make it a Ps 84:6

BACK (396)

And the dove came **b** to him in the Gn 8:11
Then they turned **b** and came to Gn 14:7
Then he brought **b** all the possessions, Gn 14:16
and also brought **b** his kinsman Lot Gn 14:16
And they shall come **b** here in the Gn 15:16
But they said, "Stand **b**!" And they said, Gn 19:9
Do not look **b** or stop anywhere in the Gn 19:17
But Lot's wife, behind him, looked **b**, Gn 19:26
I then take your son **b** to the land from Gn 24:5
to it that you do not take my son **b** there. Gn 24:6
only you must not take my son **b** there." Gn 24:8
go, and will bring you **b** to this land. Gn 28:15
and put the stone **b** in its place over the Gn 29:3
Adullamite to take **b** the pledge from Gn 38:20
But as he drew **b** his hand, behold, his Gn 38:29
nor has he kept **b** anything from me Gn 39:9
brothers, "My money has been put **b**; Gn 42:28
two sons if I do not bring him **b** to you. Gn 42:37
hands, and I will bring him **b** to you." Gn 42:37
I do not bring him **b** to you and set him Gn 43:9
Carry **b** with you the money that was Gn 43:12
and may he send **b** your other brother Gn 43:14
our sacks we brought **b** to you from the Gn 44:8
"When we went **b** to your servant my Gn 44:24
saying, 'If I do not bring him **b** to you, Gn 44:32
and let the boy go **b** with his brothers. Gn 44:33
For how can I go **b** to my father if the Gn 44:34
load your beasts and go **b** to the land of Gn 45:17
hate us and pay us **b** for all the evil Gn 50:15
"Put your hand **b** inside your cloak." So Ex 4:7
So he put his hand **b** inside his cloak, Ex 4:7
Moses went **b** to Jethro his father-in-law Ex 4:18
"Please let me go **b** to my brothers in Ex 4:18
said to Moses in Midian, "Go **b** to Egypt, Ex 4:19
donkey, and went **b** to the land of Egypt. Ex 4:20
said to Moses, "When you go **b** to Egypt, Ex 4:21
from their work? Get **b** to your burdens." Ex 5:4
and Aaron were brought **b** to Pharaoh. Ex 10:8
of Israel to turn **b** and encamp in front Ex 14:2
LORD drove the sea **b** by a strong east Ex 14:21
water may come **b** upon the Egyptians, Ex 14:26
the LORD brought **b** the waters of the sea Ex 15:19
going astray, you shall bring it **b** to him. Ex 23:4
shall hang over the **b** of the tabernacle. Ex 26:12
front and on the **b** they were written. Ex 32:15
away my hand, and you shall see my **b**, Ex 33:23
the rot is on the **b** or on the front. Lv 13:55
he sold it and pay **b** the balance to the Lv 25:27
and go **b** to his own clan and return to Lv 25:41
then he shall buy it **b** at the valuation, Lv 27:27
They brought **b** word to them and to Nm 13:26
it not be better for us to go **b** to Egypt?" Nm 14:3
us choose a leader and go **b** to Egypt." Nm 14:4
you have turned **b** from following the Nm 14:43
"Put **b** the staff of Aaron before the Nm 17:10
tonight, and I will bring **b** word to you, Nm 22:8
if it is evil in your sight, I will turn **b**." Nm 22:34
the LORD has held you **b** from honor." Nm 24:11
Balaam rose and went **b** to his place. Nm 24:25
has turned **b** my wrath from the Nm 25:11
Etham and turned **b** to Pi-hahiroth, Nm 33:7
dedicated it? Let him go **b** to his house, Dt 20:5
its fruit? Let him go **b** to his house, Dt 20:6
not taken her? Let him go **b** to his house, Dt 20:7
fainthearted? Let him go **b** to his house, Dt 20:8
You shall take them **b** to your brother. Dt 22:1
with it and turn **b** and cover up your Dt 23:13
in the field, you shall not go **b** to get it. Dt 24:19
LORD will bring you **b** in ships to Egypt, Dt 28:68
So when the men of Ai looked **b**, behold, Jos 8:20
the wilderness turned **b** against the Jos 8:20
then they turned **b** and struck down the Jos 8:21
Joshua did not draw **b** his hand with Jos 8:26
Israel with him turned **b** to Debir and Jos 10:38
And Joshua turned **b** at that time and Jos 11:10
"Go **b** to your tents with much wealth Jos 22:8
of Israel, and brought **b** word to them. Jos 22:32
God will push them **b** before you and Jos 23:5
For if you turn **b** and cling to the Jos 23:12
the people of Dan **b** into the hill country, Jgs 1:34
they turned **b** and were more corrupt Jgs 2:19
But he himself turned **b** at the idols near Jgs 3:19
the LORD, and I cannot take **b** my vow." Jgs 11:35

hot anger he went **b** to his father's Jgs 14:19
him, he turned and went **b** to his home. Jgs 18:26
to speak kindly to her and bring her **b**. Jgs 19:3
of Israel turned **b** against the people Jgs 20:48
But Naomi said, "Turn **b**, my Ru 1:11
Turn **b**, my daughters; go your way, for Ru 1:12
sister-in-law has gone **b** to her people Ru 1:15
and the LORD has brought me **b** empty. Ru 1:21
who came **b** with Naomi from the Ru 2:6
must not go **b** empty-handed to your Ru 3:17
who has come **b** from the country of Ru 4:3
then they went **b** to their house at 1 Sm 1:19
took Dagon and put him **b** in his place. 1 Sm 5:3
who was with him, "Come, let us go **b**, 1 Sm 9:5
he turned his **b** to leave Samuel, 1 Sm 10:9
he has turned **b** from following me 1 Sm 15:11
So Samuel turned **b** after Saul, and 1 Sm 15:31
but David went **b** and forth from 1 Sm 17:15
of Israel came **b** from chasing the 1 Sm 17:53
and come **b** to me with sure 1 Sm 23:23
away and came **b** and told him 1 Sm 25:12
and has kept **b** his servant from 1 Sm 25:39
the garments, and come **b** to Achish. 1 Sm 27:9
said to him, "Send the man **b**, 1 Sm 29:4
So go **b** now; and go peaceably, that 1 Sm 29:7
had been taken. David brought **b** all. 1 Sm 30:19
the bow of Jonathan turned not **b**, 2 Sm 1:22
so that the spear came out at his **b**. 2 Sm 2:23
they brought him **b** from the cistern 2 Sm 3:26
will send you **b**." So Uriah remained 2 Sm 11:12
fighting, and then draw **b** from him, 2 Sm 11:15
but we drove them **b** to the entrance 2 Sm 11:23
I fast? Can I bring him **b** again? 2 Sm 12:23
bring **b** the young man Absalom." 2 Sm 14:21
will indeed bring me **b** to Jerusalem, 2 Sm 15:8
Go **b** and stay with the king, for you 2 Sm 15:19
Go **b** and take your brothers with 2 Sm 15:20
"Carry the ark of God **b** into the city. 2 Sm 15:25
he will bring me **b** and let me see 2 Sm 15:25
Go **b** to the city in peace, with your 2 Sm 15:27
the ark of God **b** to Jerusalem, 2 Sm 15:29
Israel will give me **b** the kingdom of 2 Sm 16:3
will bring all the people **b** to you as a 2 Sm 17:3
the troops came **b** from pursuing 2 Sm 18:16
about bringing the king **b**?" 2 Sm 19:10
last to bring the king **b** to his house, 2 Sm 19:11
you be the last to bring **b** the king?' 2 Sm 19:12
So the king came **b** to the Jordan, 2 Sm 19:15
until the day he came **b** in safety. 2 Sm 19:24
speak of bringing **b** our king?" But 2 Sm 19:43
and did not turn **b** until they were 2 Sm 22:38
LORD will bring **b** his bloody deeds 1 Kgs 2:32
shall their blood come **b** on the head 1 Kgs 2:33
the LORD will bring **b** your harm on 1 Kgs 2:44
dwell, in the other court **b** of the hall, 1 Kgs 7:8
measure, sawed with saws, **b** and front, 1 Kgs 7:9
she turned and went **b** to her own 1 Kgs 10:13
and at the **b** of the throne was a 1 Kgs 10:19
kingdom will turn **b** to the house 1 Kgs 12:26
that he could not draw it **b** to himself. 1 Kgs 13:4
'Bring him **b** with you into your 1 Kgs 13:18
So he went **b** with him and ate bread 1 Kgs 13:19
prophet who had brought him **b**. 1 Kgs 13:20
but have come **b** and have eaten 1 Kgs 13:22
prophet whom he had brought **b**. 1 Kgs 13:23
had brought him **b** from the way 1 Kgs 13:26
donkey and brought it **b** to the city 1 Kgs 13:29
and have cast me behind your **b**, 1 Kgs 14:9
and brought them **b** to the 1 Kgs 14:28
that you have turned their hearts **b**." 1 Kgs 18:37
And he said to him, "Go **b** again, 1 Kgs 19:20
and take him **b** to Amon the 1 Kgs 22:26
they turned **b** from pursuing him. 1 Kgs 22:33
to us, 'Go **b** to the king who sent you, 2 Kgs 1:6
from him and went **b** and stood on 2 Kgs 2:13
And they came **b** to him while he was 2 Kgs 2:18
the man of God and come **b** again." 2 Kgs 4:22
again and walked once **b** and forth in 2 Kgs 4:35
Then they came **b** and entered another 2 Kgs 7:8
them, but he is not coming **b**." 2 Kgs 9:18
them, but he is not coming **b**. 2 Kgs 9:20
When they came **b** and told him, he 2 Kgs 9:36
king of Assyria turned **b** and did not 2 Kgs 15:20
and I will turn you **b** on the way by 2 Kgs 19:28
"Turn **b**, and say to Hezekiah the 2 Kgs 20:5
forward ten steps, or go **b** ten steps?" 2 Kgs 20:9
let the shadow go **b** ten steps." 2 Kgs 20:10
he brought the shadow **b** ten steps, 2 Kgs 20:11
And they brought **b** word to the 2 Kgs 22:20
all Israel and came **b** to Jerusalem. 1 Chr 21:4
he put his sword **b** into its sheath. 1 Chr 21:27
she turned and went **b** to her own 2 Chr 9:12
and brought them **b** to the 2 Chr 12:11
and take him **b** to Amon the 2 Chr 18:25
they turned **b** from pursuing him. 2 Chr 18:32

and brought them **b** to the LORD, 2 Chr 19:4
them to bring them **b** to the LORD. 2 Chr 24:19
of the army whom Amaziah sent **b**, 2 Chr 25:13
and send **b** the captives from your 2 Chr 28:11
And they brought **b** word to the 2 Chr 34:28
be restored and brought **b** to the temple Ezr 6:5
and I turned **b** and entered by the Neh 2:15
Turn **b** their taunt on their own heads Neh 4:4
have bought **b** our Jewish brothers who Neh 5:8
law behind their **b** and killed your Neh 9:26
them in order to turn them **b** to you, Neh 9:26
in order to turn them **b** to your law. Neh 9:29
and I brought **b** there the vessels of the Neh 13:9
he snatches away; who can turn him **b**? Jb 9:12
"God will not turn **b** his anger; beneath Jb 9:13
the court, who can turn him **b**? Jb 11:10
and his hands will give **b** his wealth. Jb 20:10
He will give **b** the fruit of his toil and Jb 20:18
and who can turn him **b**? Jb 23:13
he keeps **b** his soul from the pit, his life Jb 33:18
to bring **b** his soul from the pit, that he Jb 33:30
he does not turn **b** from the sword. Jb 39:22
His **b** is made of rows of shields, shut up Jb 41:15
they shall turn **b** and be put to shame in Ps 6:10
When my enemies turn **b**, they stumble Ps 9:3
and did not turn **b** till they were Ps 18:37
Keep **b** your servant also from Ps 19:13
them be turned **b** and disappointed who Ps 35:4
wicked borrows but does not pay **b**, Ps 37:21
let those be turned **b** and brought to Ps 40:14
You have made us turn **b** from the foe, Ps 44:10
Our heart has not turned **b**, nor have Ps 44:18
my enemies will turn **b** in the day when Ps 56:9
Each evening they come **b**, howling like Ps 59:6
Each evening they come **b**, howling Ps 59:14
said, "I will bring them **b** from Bashan, Ps 68:22
I will bring them **b** from the depths of Ps 68:22
Let them be turned **b** and brought to Ps 70:2
Let them turn **b** because of their shame Ps 70:3
Therefore his people turn **b** to them, Ps 73:10
Why do you hold **b** your hand, your Ps 74:11
not the downtrodden turn **b** in shame; Ps 74:21
the bow, turned **b** on the day of battle. Ps 78:9
Then we shall not turn **b** from you; Ps 80:18
saints; but let them not turn **b** to folly. Ps 85:8
You have also turned **b** the edge of his Ps 89:43
He will bring **b** on them their iniquity Ps 94:23
sea looked and fled; Jordan turned **b**. Ps 114:3
you flee? O Jordan, that you turn **b**? Ps 114:5
I hold **b** my feet from every evil way, Ps 119:101
The plowers plowed upon my **b**; they Ps 129:3
oath from which he will not turn **b**: Ps 132:11
them; hold **b** your foot from their paths, Prv 1:15
none who go to her come **b**, nor do they Prv 2:19
a rod is for the **b** of him who lacks Prv 10:13
people curse him who holds **b** grain, Prv 11:26
work of a man's hand comes **b** to him. Prv 12:14
mouth of a fool comes a rod for his **b**, Prv 14:3
will not even bring it **b** to his mouth. Prv 19:24
righteous gives and does not hold **b**. Prv 21:26
hold **b** those who are stumbling to the Prv 24:11
I will pay the man **b** for what he has Prv 24:29
the donkey, and a rod for the **b** of fools. Prv 26:3
him out to bring it **b** to his mouth. Prv 26:15
a stone will come **b** on him who starts Prv 26:27
but a wise man quietly holds it **b**. Prv 29:11
beasts and does not turn **b** before any; Prv 30:30
He made its posts of silver, its **b** of gold, Sg 3:10
is stretched out, and who will turn it **b**? Is 14:27
will inquire, inquire; come **b** again." Is 21:12
to those who turn **b** the battle at the Is 28:6
he does not call **b** his words, but will arise Is 31:2
and I will turn you **b** on the way by Is 37:29
the dial of Ahaz turn **b** ten steps." So the Is 38:8
steps." So the sun turned **b** on the dial the Is 38:8
have cast all my sins behind your **b**. Is 38:17
They are turned **b** and utterly put to Is 42:17
hand; I work, and who can turn it **b**?" Is 43:13
who turns wise men **b** and makes their Is 44:25
to be his servant, to bring Jacob **b** to him; Is 49:5
Jacob and to bring **b** the preserved of Is 49:6
I gave my **b** to those who strike, and my Is 50:6
you have made your **b** like the ground Is 51:23
be stretched out; do not hold **b**; Is 54:2
"Cry aloud; do not hold **b**; lift up your Is 58:1
"If you turn **b** your foot from the Is 58:13
and turning **b** from following our God, Is 59:13
Justice is turned **b**, and righteousness Is 59:14
your compassion are held **b** from me. Is 63:15
For they have turned their **b** to me, and Jer 2:27
of the LORD has not turned **b** from us." Jer 4:8
I have not relented, nor will I turn **b**." Jer 4:28
They have turned **b** to the iniquities of Jer 11:10
I will bring them **b** to their own land Jer 16:15
I will show them my **b**, not my face, in Jer 18:17

I will turn **b** the weapons of war that are Jer 21:4
and I will bring them **b** to their fold, Jer 23:3
LORD will not turn **b** until he has Jer 23:20
and I will bring them **b** to this land. Jer 24:6
to speak to them; do not hold **b** a word. Jer 26:2
shortly be brought **b** from Babylon,' Jer 27:16
I will bring them **b** and restore them to Jer 27:22
two years I will bring **b** to this place all Jer 28:3
I will also bring **b** to this place Jeconiah Jer 28:4
and bring **b** to this place from Babylon Jer 28:6
promise and bring you **b** to this place. Jer 29:10
and I will bring you **b** to the place from Jer 29:14
and I will bring them **b** to the land that I Jer 30:3
LORD will not turn **b** until he has Jer 30:24
with pleas for mercy I will lead them **b**, Jer 31:9
and they shall come **b** from the land of Jer 31:16
children shall come **b** to their own Jer 31:17
bring me **b** that I may be restored, for Jer 31:18
turned to me their **b** and not their face. Jer 32:33
I will bring them **b** to this place, and I Jer 32:37
turned around and took **b** the male and Jer 34:11
each of you took **b** his male and female Jer 34:16
LORD, and will bring them **b** to this city. Jer 34:22
Chaldeans shall come **b** and fight Jer 37:8
and do not send me **b** to the house of Jer 37:20
he would not send me **b** to the house of Jer 38:26
Mizpah turned around and came **b**, Jer 41:14
Johanan brought **b** from Gibeon. Jer 41:16
tell you. I will keep nothing **b** from you." Jer 42:4
they look not **b**—terror on every side! Jer 46:5
and let us go **b** to our own people and to Jer 46:16
the fathers look not **b** to their children, Jer 47:3
is he who keeps **b** his sword from Jer 48:10
How Moab has turned his **b** in shame! Jer 48:39
Flee, turn **b**, dwell in the depths, O Jer 49:8
a net for my feet; he turned me **b**; Lam 1:13
it had writing on the front and on the **b**, Ezk 2:10
all their multitude; it shall not turn **b**; Ezk 7:13
case at his waist, brought **b** word, Ezk 9:11
me and cast me behind your **b**, Ezk 23:35
I will not go **b**; I will not spare; I will Ezk 24:14
Egypt and bring them **b** to the land of Ezk 29:14
turn from his way and live; turn **b**, Ezk 33:11
back, turn **b** from your evil ways, Ezk 33:11
gives **b** what he has taken by robbery, Ezk 33:15
up, the strayed you have not brought **b**, Ezk 34:4
the lost, and I will bring **b** the strayed, Ezk 34:16
have brought them **b** from the peoples Ezk 39:27
that was at the **b** and its galleries on Ezk 41:15
chambers were set **b** from the ground Ezk 42:6
Then he brought me **b** to the outer gate Ezk 44:1
Then he brought me **b** to the door of Ezk 47:1
this?" Then he led me **b** to the bank of Ezk 47:6
As I went **b**, I saw on the bank of the Ezk 47:7
with four wings of a bird on its **b**. Dn 7:6
shall turn his insolence **b** upon him. Dn 11:18
turn his face **b** toward the fortresses Dn 11:19
and shall turn **b** and be enraged and Dn 11:30
He shall turn **b** and pay attention to Dn 11:30
Therefore I will take **b** my grain in its Hos 2:9
Are you paying me **b** for something? Jl 3:4
If you are paying me **b**, I will return your Jl 3:4
the men rowed hard to get **b** to dry land, Jon 1:13
"Halt! Halt!" they cry, but none turns **b**. Na 2:8
who have turned **b** from following the Zep 1:6
And he thrust her **b** into the basket, Zec 5:8
I will bring them **b** because I have Zec 10:6
'What are these wounds on your **b**?' Zec 13:6
in the field not turn **b** to take his cloak. Mt 24:18
him, "Put your sword **b** into its place. Mt 26:52
mind and brought **b** the thirty pieces Mt 27:3
and came and rolled **b** the stone and sat Mt 28:2
it and will send it **b** here immediately.'" Mk 11:3
the field not turn **b** to take his cloak. Mk 13:16
the stone had been rolled **b**—it was very Mk 16:4
And they went **b** and told the rest, but Mk 16:13
scroll and gave it **b** to the attendant and Lk 4:20
away your goods do not demand them **b**. Lk 6:30
to sinners, to get **b** the same amount. Lk 6:34
you use it will be measured **b** to you." Lk 6:38
the boy, and gave him **b** to his father. Lk 9:42
to the plow and looks **b** is fit for the Lk 9:62
spend, I will repay you when I come **b**.' Lk 10:35
he has received him **b** safe and sound.' Lk 15:27
he saw that he was healed, turned **b**, Lk 17:15
the one who is in the field not turn **b**. Lk 17:31
clothing, he sent him **b** to Pilate. Lk 23:11
did Herod, for he sent him **b** to us. Lk 23:15
they came **b** saying that they had even Lk 24:23
Just then his disciples came **b**. They Jn 4:27
of his disciples turned **b** and no longer Jn 6:66
So he went and washed and came **b** seeing. Jn 9:7
come from God and was going **b** to God, Jn 13:3
So that disciple, leaning **b** against Jesus, Jn 13:25
"I am he," they drew **b** and fell to the Jn 18:6

he went **b** outside to the Jews and told Jn 18:38
the disciples went **b** to their homes. Jn 20:10
knowledge he kept **b** for himself some Acts 5:2
Spirit and to keep **b** for yourself part of Acts 5:3
they were carried **b** to Shechem and Acts 7:16
the spirit of slavery to fall **b** into fear, Rom 8:15
are you, O man, to answer **b** to God? Rom 9:20
be grafted **b** into their own olive tree. Rom 11:24
and to come **b** to you from 2 Cor 1:16
came he drew **b** and separated himself, Gal 2:12
how can you turn **b** again to the weak Gal 4:9
this he will receive **b** from the Lord, Eph 6:8
wrongdoer will be paid **b** for the wrong Col 3:25
I am sending him **b** to you, sending Phlm 1:12
that you might have him **b** forever, Phlm 1:15
shall live by faith, and if he shrinks **b**, Heb 10:38
those who shrink **b** and are destroyed, Heb 10:39
speaking, he did receive him **b**. Heb 11:19
Women received **b** their dead by Heb 11:35
your fields, which you kept **b** by fraud, Jas 5:4
the truth and someone brings him **b**, Jas 5:19
that whoever brings **b** a sinner from Jas 5:20
knowing it to turn **b** from the holy 2 Pt 2:21
a scroll written within and on the **b**, Rv 5:1
holding **b** the four winds of the earth, Rv 7:1
And the dragon and his angels fought **b**, Rv 12:7
Pay her **b** as she herself has paid back Rv 18:6
back as she herself has paid **b** others, Rv 18:6

BACKBITING (1)
brings forth rain, and a **b** tongue, Prv 25:23

BACKBONE (1)
the whole fat tail, cut off close to the **b**, Lv 3:9

BACKS (13)
all your enemies turn their **b** to you. Ex 23:27
you, and you shall tread upon their **b**." Dt 33:29
has turned their **b** before their enemies! Jos 7:8
They turn their **b** before their enemies, Jos 7:12
they turned their **b** before the men Jgs 20:42
made my enemies turn their **b** to me, 2 Sm 22:41
of the LORD and turned their **b**. 2 Chr 29:6
made my enemies turn their **b** to me, Ps 18:40
you laid a crushing burden on our **b**; Ps 66:11
scoffers, and beating for the **b** of fools. Prv 19:29
carry their riches on the **b** of donkeys, Is 30:6
with their **b** to the temple of the LORD, Ezk 8:16
cannot see, and bend their **b** forever." Rom 11:10

BACKSLIDER (1)
The **b** in heart will be filled with the Prv 14:14

BACKSLIDING (2)
but he went on **b** in the way of his own Is 57:17
this people turned away in perpetual **b**? Jer 8:5

BACKSLIDINGS (2)
your name's sake; for our **b** are many; Jer 14:7
them from all the **b** in which they Ezk 37:23

BACKWARD (11)
and walked **b** and covered the Gn 9:23
Their faces were turned **b**, and they did Gn 9:23
horse's heels so that his rider falls **b**. Gn 49:17
Eli fell over **b** from his seat by the side 1 Sm 4:18
I go forward, but he is not there, and **b**, Jb 23:8
Zion be put to shame and turned **b**! Ps 129:5
a little, that they may go, and fall **b**, Is 28:13
and I was not rebellious; I turned not **b**. Is 50:5
evil hearts, and went **b** and not forward. Jer 7:24
you keep going **b**, so I have stretched out Jer 15:6
They are dismayed and have turned **b**. Jer 46:5

BAD (49)
we cannot speak to you **b** or good. Gn 24:50
anything to Jacob, either good or **b**." Gn 31:24
anything to Jacob, either good or **b**.' Gn 31:29
And Joseph brought a **b** report of them Gn 37:2
it or make a substitute for it, good for **b**, Lv 27:10
for it, good for bad, or **b** for good; Lv 27:10
priest shall value it as either good or **b**; Lv 27:12
priest shall value it as either good or **b**; Lv 27:14
not differentiate between good or **b**, Lv 27:33
land that they dwell in is good or **b**, Nm 13:19
people of Israel a **b** report of the land Nm 13:32
by bringing up a **b** report about the Nm 14:36
who brought up a **b** report of the land Nm 14:37
to do either good or **b** of my own will. Nm 24:13
and brings a **b** name upon her, Dt 22:14
he has brought a **b** name upon a virgin Dt 22:19
spoke to Amnon neither good nor **b**, 2 Sm 13:22
as my lord sees, but the water is **b**, 2 Kgs 2:19
could give me a **b** name in order to Neh 6:13
He is not afraid of **b** news; his heart is Ps 112:7
"**B**, Bad," says the buyer, but when he Prv 20:14
"Bad, **B**," says the buyer, but when he Prv 20:14
of trouble is like a **b** tooth or a foot Prv 25:19
those riches were lost in a **b** venture. Eccl 5:14
figs, but the other basket had very **b** figs, Jer 24:2
figs, so **b** that they could not be eaten. Jer 24:2
figs very good, and the **b** figs very bad, Jer 24:3
figs very good, and the bad figs very **b**, Jer 24:3
bad, so **b** that they cannot be eaten." Jer 24:3
Like the **b** figs that are so bad they Jer 24:8
figs that are so **b** they cannot be eaten, Jer 24:8
Whether it is good or **b**, we will obey the Jer 42:6
for they have heard **b** news; they melt Jer 49:23
the Most High that good and **b** come? Lam 3:38
but if your eye is **b**, your whole body Mt 6:23
fruit, but the diseased tree bears **b** fruit. Mt 7:17
A healthy tree cannot bear **b** fruit, nor Mt 7:18
or make the tree **b** and its fruit bad, Mt 12:33
or make the tree bad and its fruit **b**, Mt 12:33
into containers but threw away the **b**. Mt 13:48
all whom they found, both **b** and good. Mt 22:10
"For no good tree bears **b** fruit, nor Lk 6:43
nor again does a **b** tree bear good fruit, Lk 6:43
body is full of light, but when it is **b**, Lk 11:34
and Lazarus in like manner **b** things; Lk 16:25
nothing either good or **b**—in order Rom 9:11
not a terror to good conduct, but to **b**. Rom 13:3
"**B** company ruins good morals." 1 Cor 15:33
impostors will go on from **b** to worse, 2 Tm 3:13

BADGER (2)
And the rock **b**, because it chews the Lv 11:5
the camel, the hare, and the rock **b**, Dt 14:7

BADGERS (2)
the rocks are a refuge for the rock **b**. Ps 104:18
the rock **b** are a people not mighty, yet Prv 30:26

BADLY (4)
did you treat me so **b** as to tell the man Gn 43:6
the man was harsh and **b** behaved; 1 Sm 25:3
and he was **b** wounded by the archers. 1 Sm 31:3
me away, for I am **b** wounded." 2 Chr 35:23

BAG (11)
but you shall not put any in your **b**. Dt 23:24
not have in your **b** two kinds of Dt 25:13
put his hand in his **b** and took out a 1 Sm 17:49
transgression would be sealed up in a **b**, Jb 14:17
he took a **b** of money with him; at full Prv 7:20
all the weights in the **b** are his work. Prv 16:11
scales and with a **b** of deceitful weights? Mi 6:11
does so to put them into a **b** with holes. Hg 1:6
no **b** for your journey, nor two tunics Mt 10:10
journey except a staff—no bread, no **b**, Mk 6:8
nothing for your journey, no staff, nor **b**, Lk 9:3

BAGGAGE (15)
he has hidden himself among the **b**." 1 Sm 10:22
of the keeper of the **b** and ran to the 1 Sm 17:22
two hundred remained with the **b**. 1 Sm 25:13
his share be who stays by the **b**. 1 Sm 30:24
Migron; at Michmash he stores his **b**; Is 10:28
Prepare yourselves **b** for exile, O Jer 46:19
man, prepare for yourself an exile's **b**, Ezk 12:3
shall bring out your **b** by day in their Ezk 12:4
by day in their sight, as **b** for exile, Ezk 12:4
wall, and bring your **b** out through it. Ezk 12:5
you shall lift the **b** upon your shoulder Ezk 12:6
I brought out my **b** by day, as baggage Ezk 12:7
out my baggage by day, as **b** for exile, Ezk 12:7
I brought out my **b** at dusk, carrying it Ezk 12:7
shall lift his **b** upon his shoulder Ezk 12:12

BAGGED (1)
came up and they **b** and counted the 2 Kgs 12:10

BAGPIPE (4)
trigon, harp, **b**, and every kind of music, Dn 3:5
trigon, harp, **b**, and every kind of music, Dn 3:7
trigon, harp, **b**, and every kind of music, Dn 3:10
trigon, harp, **b**, and every kind of music, Dn 3:15

BAGS (3)
gave orders to fill their **b** with grain, Gn 42:25
the choice fruits of the land in your **b**, Gn 43:11
tied up two talents of silver in two **b**, 2 Kgs 5:23

BAHARUM (1)
Azmaveth of **B**, Eliahba the 1 Chr 11:33

BAHURIM (6)
her, weeping after her all the way to **B**. 2 Sm 3:16
When King David came to **B**, there 2 Sm 16:5
and came to the house of a man at **B**, 2 Sm 17:18
son of Gera, the Benjaminite, from **B**, 2 Sm 19:16
the Arbathite, Azmaveth of **B**, 2 Sm 23:31
son of Gera, the Benjaminite from **B**, 1 Kgs 2:8

BAKBAKKAR (1)
and **B**, Heresh, Galal and Mattaniah 1 Chr 9:15

BAKBUK (2)
the sons of **B**, the sons of Hakupha, the Ezr 2:51
the sons of **B**, the sons of Hakupha, the Neh 7:53

BAKBUKIAH (3)
of the praise, who gave thanks, and **B**, Neh 11:17
And **B** and Unni and their brothers Neh 12:9
Mattaniah, **B**, Obadiah, Meshullam, Neh 12:25

BAKE (5)
b what you will bake and boil what Ex 16:23
bake what you will **b** and boil what Ex 16:23
take fine flour and **b** twelve loaves from Lv 24:5
ten women shall **b** your bread in a Lv 26:26
where they shall **b** the grain offering, Ezk 46:20

BAKED (16)
them a feast and **b** unleavened bread, Gn 19:3
were all sorts of **b** food for Pharaoh, Gn 40:17
And they **b** unleavened cakes of the Ex 12:39
bring a grain offering **b** in the oven as Lv 2:4
offering is a grain offering **b** on a griddle, Lv 2:5
It shall not be **b** with leaven. I have given Lv 6:17
mixed, in **b** pieces like a grain offering, Lv 6:21
And every grain offering **b** in the oven Lv 7:9
flour, and they shall be **b** with leaven, Lv 23:17
it was like the taste of cakes **b** with oil. Nm 11:8
kneaded it and **b** unleavened bread 1 Sm 28:24
cakes in his sight and **b** the cakes. 2 Sm 13:8
your God lives, I have nothing **b**, 1 Kgs 17:12
his head a cake **b** on hot stones and 1 Kgs 19:6
of unleavened bread, the **b** offering, 1 Chr 23:29
in the fire; I also **b** bread on its coals; Is 44:19

BAKER (9)
of Egypt and his **b** committed an offense Gn 40:1
the chief cupbearer and the chief **b**, Gn 40:2
—the cupbearer and the **b** of the king of Gn 40:5
When the chief **b** saw that the Gn 40:16
head of the chief **b** among his servants. Gn 40:20
But he hanged the chief **b**, as Joseph Gn 40:22
me and the chief **b** in custody in the Gn 41:10
to my office, and the **b** was hanged." Gn 41:13
a heated oven whose **b** ceases to stir the Hos 7:4

BAKERS (1)
to be perfumers and cooks and **b**. 1 Sm 8:13

BAKERS' (1)
was given him daily from the **b** street, Jer 37:21

BAKES (1)
himself; he kindles a fire and **b** bread. Is 44:15

BAKING (1)
b it in their sight on human dung." Ezk 4:12

BALAAM (62)
sent messengers to **B** the son of Beor at Nm 22:5
And they came to **B** and gave him Nm 22:7
So the princes of Moab stayed with **B**. Nm 22:8
And God came to **B** and said, "Who are Nm 22:9
And **B** said to God, "Balak the son of Nm 22:10
God said to **B**, "You shall not go with Nm 22:12
So **B** rose in the morning and said to Nm 22:13
and said, "**B** refuses to come with us." Nm 22:14
And they came to **B** and said to him, Nm 22:16
But **B** answered and said to the Nm 22:18
And God came to **B** at night and said Nm 22:20
So **B** rose in the morning and saddled Nm 22:21
And **B** struck the donkey, to turn her Nm 22:23
of the LORD, she lay down under **B**. Nm 22:27
of the donkey, and she said to **B**, Nm 22:28
And **B** said to the donkey, "Because Nm 22:29
And the donkey said to **B**, "Am I not Nm 22:30
Then the LORD opened the eyes of **B**, Nm 22:31
Then **B** said to the angel of the LORD, "I Nm 22:34
And the angel of the LORD said to **B**, Nm 22:35
that I tell you." So **B** went on with the Nm 22:35
When Balak heard that **B** had come, Nm 22:36
And Balak said to **B**, "Did I not send to Nm 22:37
B said to Balak, "Behold, I have come Nm 22:38
Then **B** went with Balak, and they Nm 22:39
and sent for **B** and for the princes who Nm 22:40
morning Balak took **B** and brought Nm 22:41
And **B** said to Balak, "Build for me here Nm 23:1
Balak did as **B** had said. And Balak and Nm 23:2
And Balak and **B** offered on each altar Nm 23:2
And **B** said to Balak, "Stand beside Nm 23:3
and God met **B**. And Balaam said to Nm 23:4
And **B** said to him, "I have arranged the Nm 23:4
And **B** took up his discourse and said, Nm 23:7
And Balak said to **B**, "What have you Nm 23:11
B said to Balak, "Stand here beside Nm 23:15
And the LORD met **B** and put a word in Nm 23:16
And **B** took up his discourse and said, Nm 23:18
And Balak said to **B**, "Do not curse Nm 23:25
But **B** answered Balak, "Did I not tell Nm 23:26
And Balak said to **B**, "Come now, I Nm 23:27
So Balak took **B** to the top of Peor, Nm 23:28
And **B** said to Balak, "Build for me Nm 23:29
And Balak did as **B** had said, and Nm 23:30
When **B** saw that it pleased the LORD to Nm 24:1
And **B** lifted up his eyes and saw Israel Nm 24:2

said, "The oracle of **B** the son of Beor, Nm 24:3
Balak's anger was kindled against **B**, Nm 24:10
And Balak said to **B**, "I called you to Nm 24:10
And **B** said to Balak, "Did I not tell Nm 24:12
said, "The oracle of **B** the son of Beor, Nm 24:15
Then **B** rose and went back to his Nm 24:25
And they also killed **B** the son of Beor Nm 31:8
they hired against you **B** the son of Beor Dt 23:4
the LORD your God would not listen to **B**; Dt 23:5
B also, the son of Beor, the one who Jos 13:22
he sent and invited **B** the son of Beor Jos 24:9
but I would not listen to **B**. Indeed, he Jos 24:10
but hired **B** against them to curse Neh 13:2
and what **B** the son of Beor answered him, Mi 6:5
They have followed the way of **B**, the 2 Pt 2:15
some there who hold the teaching of **B**, Rv 2:14

BALAAM'S (5)
the wall and pressed **B** foot against the Nm 22:25
And **B** anger was kindled, and he Nm 22:27
LORD put a word in **B** mouth and said, Nm 23:5
Behold, these, on **B** advice, caused the Nm 31:16
sake of gain to **B** error and perished in Jude 1:11

BALADAN (2)
Merodach-baladan the son of **B**, 2 Kgs 20:12
that time Merodach-baladan the son of **B**, Is 39:1

BALAH (1)
Hazar-shual, **B**, Ezem, Jos 19:3

BALAK (42)
And **B** the son of Zippor saw all that Nm 22:2
of the field." So **B** the son of Zippor, Nm 22:4
said to God, "**B** the son of Zippor, Nm 22:10
morning and said to the princes of **B**, Nm 22:13
of Moab rose and went to **B** and said, Nm 22:14
Once again **B** sent princes, more in Nm 22:15
him, "Thus says **B** the son of Zippor: Nm 22:16
answered and said to the servants of **B**, Nm 22:18
"Though **B** were to give me his house Nm 22:18
Balaam went on with the princes of **B**. Nm 22:35
When **B** heard that Balaam had Nm 22:36
And **B** said to Balaam, "Did I not send Nm 22:37
Balaam said to **B**, "Behold, I have Nm 22:38
Then Balaam went with **B**, and they Nm 22:39
And **B** sacrificed oxen and sheep, and Nm 22:40
in the morning **B** took Balaam and Nm 22:41
And Balaam said to **B**, "Build for me Nm 23:1
B did as Balaam had said. And Balak Nm 23:2
And **B** and Balaam offered on each Nm 23:2
And Balaam said to **B**, "Stand beside Nm 23:3
mouth and said, "Return to **B**, Nm 23:5
said, "From Aram **B** has brought me, Nm 23:7
And **B** said to Balaam, "What have Nm 23:11
And **B** said to him, "Please come with Nm 23:13
Balaam said to **B**, "Stand here beside Nm 23:15
in his mouth and said, "Return to **B**, Nm 23:16
And **B** said to him, "What has the Nm 23:17
discourse and said, "Rise, **B**, and hear; Nm 23:18
And **B** said to Balaam, "Do not curse Nm 23:25
But Balaam answered **B**, "Did I not tell Nm 23:26
And **B** said to Balaam, "Come now, I Nm 23:27
So **B** took Balaam to the top of Peor, Nm 23:28
And Balaam said to **B**, "Build for me Nm 23:29
And **B** did as Balaam had said, and Nm 23:30
And **B** said to Balaam, "I called you to Nm 24:10
And Balaam said to **B**, "Did I not tell Nm 24:12
'If **B** should give me his house full of Nm 24:13
to his place. And **B** also went his way. Nm 24:25
Then **B** the son of Zippor, king of Moab, Jos 24:9
you any better than **B** the son of Jgs 11:25
remember what **B** king of Moab devised, Mi 6:5
who taught **B** to put a stumbling block Rv 2:14

BALAK'S (2)
to Balaam and gave him **B** message. Nm 22:7
And **B** anger was kindled against Nm 24:10

BALANCE (5)
it and pay back the **b** to the man to Lv 25:27
(Let me be weighed in a just **b**, and let Jb 31:6
A false **b** is an abomination to the LORD, Prv 11:1
A just **b** and scales are the LORD'S; all Prv 16:11
in scales and the hills in a **b**? Is 40:12

BALANCES (8)
You shall have just **b**, just weights, a Lv 19:36
and all my calamity laid in the **b**! Jb 6:2
estate are a delusion; in the **b** they go up; Ps 62:9
Then take **b** for weighing and divide the Ezk 5:1
"You shall have just **b**, a just ephah, Ezk 45:10
weighed in the **b** and found wanting; Dn 5:27
merchant, in whose hands are false **b**, Hos 12:7
great and deal deceitfully with false **b**, Am 8:5

BALANCINGS (1)
Do you know the **b** of the clouds, the Jb 37:16

BALD (14)
of any kind, the **b** locust of any kind, Lv 11:22
hair falls out from his head, he is **b**; Lv 13:40
if there is on the **b** head or the bald Lv 13:42
head or the **b** forehead a reddish-white Lv 13:42
breaking out on his **b** head or his bald Lv 13:42
out on his bald head or his **b** forehead. Lv 13:42
is reddish-white on his **b** head or on his Lv 13:43
on his bald head or on his **b** forehead, Lv 13:43
They shall not make **b** patches on their Lv 21:5
cut himself or make himself **b** for them. Jer 16:6
they make themselves **b** for you and Ezk 27:31
Every head was made **b**, and every Ezk 29:18
Make yourselves **b** and cut off your Mi 1:16
make yourselves as **b** as the eagle, Mi 1:16

BALDHEAD (2)
jeered at him, saying, "Go up, you **b**! 2 Kgs 2:23
"Go up, you baldhead! Go up, you **b**!" 2 Kgs 2:23

BALDNESS (8)
his forehead, he has **b** of the forehead; Lv 13:41
or make any **b** on your foreheads Dt 14:1
well-set hair, **b**; and instead of a rich robe, Is 3:24
On every head is **b**; every beard is shorn; Is 15:2
mourning, for **b** and wearing sackcloth; Is 22:12
B has come upon Gaza; Ashkelon has Jer 47:5
is on all faces, and **b** on all their heads. Ezk 7:18
on every waist and **b** on every head; Am 8:10

BALL (1)
and throw you like a **b** into a wide land. Is 22:18

BALLAD (1)
Therefore the **b** singers say, "Come to Nm 21:27

BALM (6)
camels bearing gum, **b**, and myrrh, Gn 37:25
to the man, a little **b** and a little honey, Gn 43:11
Is there no **b** in Gilead? Is there no Jer 8:22
Go up to Gilead, and take **b**, O virgin Jer 46:11
Take **b** for her pain; perhaps she may be Jer 51:8
of Minnith, meal, honey, oil, and **b**. Ezk 27:17

BALSAM (4)
against them opposite the **b** trees. 2 Sm 5:23
of marching in the tops of the **b** trees, 2 Sm 5:24
against them opposite the **b** trees. 1 Chr 14:14
marching in the tops of the **b** trees, 1 Chr 14:15

BAMAH (1)
go? So its name is called **B** to this day.) Ezk 20:29

BAMOTH (2)
to Nahaliel, and from Nahaliel to **B**, Nm 21:19
and from **B** to the valley lying in the Nm 21:20

BAMOTH-BAAL (2)
Balaam and brought him up to **B**, Nm 22:41
Dibon, and **B**, and Beth-baal-meon, Jos 13:17

BAND (31)
And the skillfully woven **b** on it shall be Ex 28:8
the skillfully woven **b** of the ephod. Ex 28:27
on the skillfully woven **b** of the ephod, Ex 28:28
with the skillfully woven **b** of the ephod. Ex 29:5
And the skillfully woven **b** on it was of Ex 39:5
the skillfully woven **b** of the ephod. Ex 39:20
on the skillfully woven **b** of the ephod, Ex 39:21
tied the skillfully woven **b** of the ephod Lv 8:7
around him, binding it to him with the **b**. Lv 8:7
the LORD, "Shall I pursue after this **b**? 1 Sm 30:8
me down to this **b**?" And he said, 1 Sm 30:15
and I will take you down to this **b**." 1 Sm 30:15
our hand the **b** that came against 1 Sm 30:23
when a **b** of Philistines was 2 Sm 23:13
there was a round **b** half a cubit 1 Kgs 7:35
became leader of a marauding **b**, 1 Kgs 11:24
a marauding **b** was seen and the 2 Kgs 13:21
out of Mount Zion a **b** of survivors. 2 Kgs 19:31
David against the **b** of raiders, 1 Chr 12:21
for the **b** of men that came with the 2 Chr 22:1
the king for a **b** of soldiers and Ezr 8:22
and thick darkness its swaddling **b**, Jb 38:9
a **b** of ruthless men seek my life, and Ps 86:14
They **b** together against the life of the Ps 94:21
and when a **b** of shepherds is called out Is 31:4
and out of Mount Zion a **b** of survivors. Is 37:32
bound with a **b** of iron and bronze, Dn 4:15
bound with a **b** of iron and bronze, Dn 4:23
wait for a man, so the priests **b** together; Hos 6:9
having procured a **b** of soldiers and some Jn 18:3
So the **b** of soldiers and their captain Jn 18:12

BANDAGE (3)
himself with a **b** over his eyes. 1 Kgs 20:38
hurried to take the **b** away from his 1 Kgs 20:41
up, to heal it by binding it with a **b**, Ezk 30:21

BANDITS (1)
thief breaks in, and the **b** raid outside. Hos 7:1

BANDS (9)
men who were captains of raiding **b**; 2 Sm 4:2
Now **b** of Moabites used to invade 2 Kgs 13:20
sent against him **b** of the Chaldeans 2 Kgs 24:2
of the Chaldeans and **b** of the Syrians 2 Kgs 24:2
of the Syrians and **b** of the Moabites 2 Kgs 24:2
the Moabites and **b** of the 2 Kgs 24:2
who sew magic **b** upon all wrists, Ezk 13:18
against your magic **b** with which you Ezk 13:20
cords of kindness, with the **b** of love, Hos 11:4

BANI (15)
of Nathan of Zobah, **B** the Gadite, 2 Sm 23:36
son of Amzi, son of **B**, son of Shemer, 1 Chr 6:46
son of Omri, son of Imri, son of **B**, 1 Chr 9:4
The sons of **B**, 642. Ezr 2:10
Of the sons of **B**, Shelomith the son of Ezr 8:10
Of the sons of **B** were Meshullam, Ezr 10:29
Of the sons of **B**: Maadai, Amram, Uel, Ezr 10:34
Levites repaired: Rehum the son of **B**. Neh 3:17
Also Jeshua, **B**, Sherebiah, Jamin, Neh 8:7
of the Levites stood Jeshua, **B**, Kadmiel, Neh 9:4
Bunni, Sherebiah, **B**, and Chenani; Neh 9:4
Jeshua, Kadmiel, **B**, Hashabneiah, Neh 9:5
Hodiah, **B**, Beninu. Neh 10:13
Pahath-moab, Elam, Zattu, **B**, Neh 10:14
in Jerusalem was Uzzi the son of **B**, Neh 11:22

BANISH (3)
I will **b** from them the voice of mirth Jer 25:10
of peace and **b** wild beasts from Ezk 34:25
he will **b** ungodliness from Jacob"; Rom 11:26

BANISHED (4)
not bring his **b** one home again. 2 Sm 14:13
means so that the **b** one will not 2 Sm 14:14
and will assemble the **b** of Israel, Is 11:12
dark; the gladness of the earth is **b**. Is 24:11

BANISHMENT (1)
for death or for **b** or for confiscation of Ezr 7:26

BANK (15)
by the other cows on the **b** of the Nile. Gn 41:3
placed it among the reeds by the river **b**. Ex 2:3
Stand on the **b** of the Nile to meet him, Ex 7:15
and stood on the **b** of the Jordan. 2 Kgs 2:13
he led me back to the **b** of the river. Ezk 47:6
I saw on the **b** of the river very many Ezk 47:7
a ram standing on the **b** of the canal. Dn 8:3
I had seen standing on the **b** of the canal, Dn 8:6
I was standing on the **b** of the great river Dn 10:4
one on this **b** of the stream and one on Dn 12:5
stream and one on that **b** of the stream. Dn 12:5
rushed down the steep **b** into the sea and Mt 8:32
rushed down the steep **b** into the sea Mk 5:13
rushed down the steep **b** into the lake Lk 8:33
did you not put my money in the **b**, Lk 19:23

BANKERS (1)
to have invested my money with the **b**, Mt 25:27

BANKS (9)
I was standing on the **b** of the Nile. Gn 41:17
to all the **b** of the river Jabbok and the Dt 2:37
overflows all its **b** throughout the time Jos 3:15
to their place and overflowed all its **b**, Jos 4:18
cities that are on the **b** of the Arnon, Jgs 11:26
when it was overflowing all its **b**, 1 Chr 12:15
over all its channels and go over all its **b**, Is 8:7
And on the **b**, on both sides of the Ezk 47:12
a man's voice between the **b** of the Ulai, Dn 8:16

BANNED (2)
and he himself **b** from the congregation Ezr 10:8
"I am **b** from going to the house of the Jer 36:5

BANNER (5)
called the name of it, The LORD is my **b**, Ex 17:15
You have set up a **b** for those who fear Ps 60:4
house, and his **b** over me was love. Sg 2:4
and proclaim, set up a **b** and proclaim, Jer 50:2
Egypt was your sail, serving as your **b**; Ezk 27:7

BANNERS (4)
with the **b** of their fathers' houses. Nm 2:2
and in the name of our God set up our **b**! Ps 20:5
as Jerusalem, awesome as an army with **b**. Sg 6:4
as the sun, awesome as an army with **b**?" Sg 6:10

BANQUET (5)
his birthday gave a **b** for his nobles and Mk 6:21
him, "When you give a dinner or a **b**, Lk 14:12
once gave a great **b** and invited many. Lk 14:16
at the time for the **b** he sent his servant Lk 14:17
who were invited shall taste my **b**.'" Lk 14:24

BANQUETING (2)
He brought me to the **b** house, and his Sg 2:4
king and his lords, came into the **b** hall, Dn 5:10

BAPTISM (20)
Pharisees and Sadducees coming for **b**, Mt 3:7
The **b** of John, from where did it come? Mt 21:25
and proclaiming a **b** of repentance for Mk 1:4
be baptized with the **b** with which I Mk 10:38
and with the **b** with which I am Mk 10:39
Was the **b** of John from heaven or Mk 11:30
proclaiming a **b** of repentance for the Lk 3:3
having been baptized with the **b** of John, Lk 7:29
I have a **b** to be baptized with, and how Lk 12:50
Was the **b** of John from heaven or from Lk 20:4
beginning from the **b** of John until the Acts 1:22
Galilee after the **b** that John Acts 10:37
had proclaimed a **b** of repentance to Acts 13:24
though he knew only the **b** of John. Acts 18:25
baptized?" They said, "Into John's **b**." Acts 19:3
baptized with the **b** of repentance, Acts 19:4
therefore with him by **b** into death, Rom 6:4
one Lord, one faith, one **b**, Eph 4:5
having been buried with him in **b**, in Col 2:12
B, which corresponds to this, now 1 Pt 3:21

BAPTIST (14)
those days John the **B** came preaching in Mt 3:1
arisen no one greater than John the **B**. Mt 11:11
days of John the **B** until now the Mt 11:12
said to his servants, "This is John the **B**. Mt 14:2
the head of John the **B** here on a platter." Mt 14:8
And they said, "Some say John the **B**, Mt 16:14
he was speaking to them of John the **B**. Mt 17:13
"John the **B** has been raised from the Mk 6:14
And she said, "The head of John the **B**." Mk 6:24
the head of John the **B** on a platter." Mk 6:25
And they told him, "John the **B**; and Mk 8:28
they said, "John the **B** has sent us to you, Lk 7:20
For John the **B** has come eating no Lk 7:33
And they answered, "John the **B**. But Lk 9:19

BAPTIZE (10)
"I **b** you with water for repentance, but Mt 3:11
He will **b** you with the Holy Spirit and Mt 3:11
but he will **b** you with the Holy Spirit." Mk 1:8
them all, saying, "I **b** you with water, Lk 3:16
He will **b** you with the Holy Spirit and Lk 3:16
John answered them, "I **b** with water, but Jn 1:26
he who sent me to **b** with water said to Jn 1:33
(although Jesus himself did not **b**, but Jn 4:2
(I did **b** also the household of 1 Cor 1:16
did not send me to **b** but to preach the 1 Cor 1:17

BAPTIZED (51)
and they were **b** by him in the river Mt 3:6
to the Jordan to John, to be **b** by him. Mt 3:13
him, saying, "I need to be **b** by you, Mt 3:14
And when Jesus was **b**, immediately he Mt 3:16
to him and were being **b** by him in the Mk 1:5
I have **b** you with water, but he will Mk 1:8
of Galilee and was **b** by John in the Mk 1:9
or to be **b** with the baptism with Mk 10:38
with the baptism with which I am **b**?" Mk 10:38
with the baptism with which I am **b**, Mk 10:39
which I am baptized, you will be **b**, Mk 10:39
believes and is **b** will be saved, Mk 16:16
the crowds that came out to be **b** by him, Lk 3:7
also came to be **b** and said to him, Lk 3:12
Now when all the people were **b**, and Lk 3:21
Jesus also had been **b** and was praying, Lk 3:21
having been **b** with the baptism of John, Lk 7:29
themselves, not having been **b** by him.) Lk 7:30
I have a baptism to be **b** with, and how Lk 12:50
and people were coming and being **b** Jn 3:23
for John **b** with water, but you will be Acts 1:5
but you will be **b** with the Holy Spirit Acts 1:5
"Repent and be **b** every one of you in Acts 2:38
So those who received his word were **b**, Acts 2:41
the name of Jesus Christ, they were **b**, Acts 8:12
and after being **b** he continued with Acts 8:13
they had only been **b** in the name of Acts 8:16
What prevents me from being **b**?" Acts 8:36
Philip and the eunuch, and he **b** him. Acts 8:38
his sight. Then he rose and was **b**; Acts 9:18
them to be **b** in the name Acts 10:48
Lord, how he said, 'John **b** with water, Acts 11:16
but you will be **b** with the Holy Acts 11:16
And after she was **b**, and her Acts 16:15
and he was **b** at once, he and all his Acts 16:33
hearing Paul believed and were **b**. Acts 18:8
what then were you **b**?" They said, Acts 19:3
"John **b** with the baptism of Acts 19:4
they were **b** in the name of the Lord Acts 19:5
Rise and be **b** and wash away your Acts 22:16
us who have been **b** into Christ Jesus Rom 6:3
into Christ Jesus were **b** into his death? Rom 6:3
Or were you **b** in the name of Paul? 1 Cor 1:13
thank God that I **b** none of you except 1 Cor 1:14
may say that you were **b** in my name. 1 Cor 1:15
not know whether I **b** anyone else.) 1 Cor 1:16
and all were **b** into Moses in the 1 Cor 10:2
Spirit we were all **b** into one body— 1 Cor 12:13
people mean by being **b** on behalf of 1 Cor 15:29
why are people **b** on their behalf? 1 Cor 15:29
of you as were **b** into Christ have put Gal 3:27

BAPTIZES (1)
this is he who **b** with the Holy Spirit.' Jn 1:33

BAPTIZING (11)
b them in the name of the Father and Mt 28:19
b in the wilderness and proclaiming a Mk 1:4
They asked him, "Then why are you **b**, if Jn 1:25
across the Jordan, where John was **b**. Jn 1:28
but for this purpose I came **b** with water, Jn 1:31
he remained there with them and was **b**. Jn 3:22
John also was **b** at Aenon near Salim, Jn 3:23
to whom you bore witness—look, he is **b**, Jn 3:26
was making and **b** more disciples than Jn 4:1
the place where John had been **b** at first, Jn 10:40
withhold water for **b** these people, Acts 10:47

BAR (6)
The middle **b**, halfway up the frames, Ex 26:28
he made the middle **b** to run from end Ex 36:33
and a **b** of gold weighing 50 shekels, Jos 7:21
silver and the cloak and the **b** of gold, Jos 7:24
two posts, and pulled them up, **b** and all, Jgs 16:3
guard, let them shut and **b** the doors. Neh 7:3

BAR-JESUS (1)
a Jewish false prophet named **B**. Acts 13:6

BAR-JONAH (1)
him, "Blessed are you, Simon **B**! Mt 16:17

BARABBAS (11)
had then a notorious prisoner called **B**. Mt 27:16
you: **B**, or Jesus who is called Christ?" Mt 27:17
crowd to ask for **B** and destroy Jesus. Mt 27:20
to release for you?" And they said, "**B**." Mt 27:21
Then he released for them **B**, and Mt 27:26
insurrection, there was a man called **B**. Mk 15:7
to have him release for them **B** instead. Mk 15:11
satisfy the crowd, released for them **B**, Mk 15:15
with this man, and release to us **B**"— Lk 23:18
but **B**!" Now Barabbas was a robber. Jn 18:40
but Barabbas!" Now **B** was a robber. Jn 18:40

BARACHEL (2)
Then Elihu the son of **B** the Buzite, of the Jb 32:2
Elihu the son of **B** the Buzite answered Jb 32:6

BARACHIAH (1)
to the blood of Zechariah the son of **B**, Mt 23:35

BARAK (15)
She sent and summoned **B** the son of Jgs 4:6
B said to her, "If you will go with me, I Jgs 4:8
arose and went with **B** to Kedesh. Jgs 4:9
And **B** called out Zebulun and Naphtali Jgs 4:10
Sisera was told that **B** the son of Jgs 4:12
And Deborah said to **B**, "Up! For this is Jgs 4:14
out before you?" So **B** went down from Jgs 4:14
and all his army before **B** by the edge of Jgs 4:15
And **B** pursued the chariots and the Jgs 4:16
And behold, as **B** was pursuing Sisera, Jgs 4:22
Then sang Deborah and **B** the son of Jgs 5:1
Arise, **B**, lead away your captives, O son Jgs 5:12
Deborah, and Issachar faithful to **B**; Jgs 5:15
sent Jerubbaal and **B** and Jephthah 1 Sm 12:11
fail me to tell of Gideon, **B**, Samson, Heb 11:32

BARBARIAN (1)
and uncircumcised, **b**, Scythian, Col 3:11

BARBARIANS (1)
obligation both to Greeks and to **b**, Rom 1:14

BARBER'S (1)
Use it as a **b** razor and pass it over your Ezk 5:1

BARBS (1)
remain shall be as **b** in your eyes and Nm 33:55

BARE (36)
you shall not strip your vineyard **b**, Lv 19:10
tell you." And he went to a **b** height, Nm 23:3
foundations of the world were laid **b**, 2 Sm 22:16
and put it under him on the **b** steps, 2 Kgs 9:13
of the world were laid **b** at your rebuke, Ps 18:15
deer give birth and strips the forests **b**, Ps 29:9
of Jerusalem, how they said, "Lay it **b**, Ps 137:7
how they said, "Lay it bare, lay it **b**, Ps 137:7
and the LORD will lay **b** their secret parts. Is 3:17
On a **b** hill raise a signal; cry aloud to Is 13:2
There will be **b** places by the Nile, on the Is 19:7
siege towers, they stripped her palaces **b**, Is 23:13
strip, and make yourselves **b**, and tie Is 32:11
I will open rivers on the **b** heights, and Is 41:18
on all **b** heights shall be their pasture; Is 49:9
Lift up your eyes to the **b** heights, and see! Jer 3:2
A voice on the **b** heights is heard, the Jer 3:21
hot wind from the **b** heights in the desert Jer 4:11
raise a lamentation on the **b** heights, for Jer 7:29
Upon all the **b** heights in the desert Jer 12:12
wild donkeys stand on the **b** heights; Jer 14:6
But I have stripped Esau **b**; I have Jer 49:10
become drunk and strip yourself **b**. Lam 4:21
so that its foundation will be laid **b**. Ezk 13:14
had grown; yet you were naked and **b**. Ezk 16:7
youth, when you were naked and **b**, Ezk 16:22
jewels and leave you naked and **b**. Ezk 16:39
labor and leave you naked and **b**, Ezk 23:29
is in her midst; she put it on the **b** rock; Ezk 24:7
I have set on the **b** rock the blood she Ezk 24:8
soil from her and make her a **b** rock. Ezk 26:4
I will make you a **b** rock. You shall be Ezk 26:14
and every shoulder was rubbed **b**, Ezk 29:18
laying him **b** from thigh to neck. Hab 3:13
for her cedar work will be laid **b**. Zep 2:14
the body that is to be, but a **b** kernel, 1 Cor 15:37

BARED (2)
The LORD has **b** his holy arm before the Is 52:10
the siege of Jerusalem, with your arm **b**, Ezk 4:7

BAREFOOT (4)
went, **b** and with his head covered. 2 Sm 15:30
feet," and he did so, walking naked and **b**. Is 20:2
has walked naked and **b** for three years as Is 20:3
both the young and the old, naked and **b**, Is 20:4

BARELY (3)
and with their ears they can **b** hear, Mt 13:15
and with their ears they can **b** hear, Acts 28:27
those who are **b** escaping from those 2 Pt 2:18

BARGAIN (2)
the fatherless, and **b** over your friend. Jb 6:27
Will traders **b** over him? Will they Jb 41:6

BARIAH (1)
Hattush, Igal, **B**, Neariah, and 1 Chr 3:22

BARK (2)
they cannot **b**, dreaming, lying down, Is 56:10
has stripped off their **b** and thrown it down; Jl 1:7

BARKOS (2)
the sons of **B**, the sons of Sisera, the sons Ezr 2:53
the sons of **B**, the sons of Sisera, the Neh 7:55

BARLEY (36)
(The flax and the **b** were struck down, Ex 9:31
for the **b** was in the ear and the flax was Ex 9:31
A homer of **b** seed shall be valued at Lv 27:16
of her, a tenth of an ephah of **b** flour. Nm 5:15
a land of wheat and **b**, of vines and fig Dt 8:8
a cake of **b** bread tumbled into the Jgs 7:13
at the beginning of **b** harvest. Ru 1:22
gleaned, and it was about an ephah of **b**. Ru 2:17
the end of the **b** and wheat harvests. Ru 2:23
he is winnowing **b** tonight at the Ru 3:2
out six measures of **b** and put it on Ru 3:15
"These six measures of **b** he gave to me, Ru 3:17
is next to mine, and he has **b** there; 2 Sm 14:30
and earthen vessels, wheat, **b**, flour, 2 Sm 17:28
harvest, at the beginning of **b** harvest. 2 Sm 21:9
B also and straw for the horses and 1 Kgs 4:28
twenty loaves of **b** and fresh ears of 2 Kgs 4:42
shekel, and two seahs of **b** for a shekel, 2 Kgs 7:1
and two seahs of **b** for a shekel, 2 Kgs 7:16
"Two seahs of **b** shall be sold for a 2 Kgs 7:18
There was a plot of ground full of **b**, 1 Chr 11:13
of crushed wheat, 20,000 cors of **b**, 2 Chr 2:10
Now therefore the wheat and **b**, oil 2 Chr 2:15
10,000 cors of wheat and 10,000 of **b**. 2 Chr 27:5
foul weeds instead of **b**." The words of Jb 31:40
wheat in rows and **b** in its proper place, Is 28:25
death, for we have stores of wheat, **b**, oil, Jer 41:8
"And you, take wheat and **b**, beans and Ezk 4:9
And you shall eat it as a **b** cake, baking Ezk 4:12
people for handfuls of **b** and for pieces Ezk 13:19
of an ephah from each homer of **b**, Ezk 45:13
of silver and a homer and a lethech of **b**. Hos 3:2
O vinedressers, for the wheat and the **b**, Jl 1:11
here who has five **b** loaves and two fish, Jn 6:9
with fragments from the five **b** loaves, Jn 6:13
and three quarts of **b** for a denarius, Rv 6:6

BARN (7)
the **b** owl, the tawny owl, the carrion Lv 11:18
owl and the short-eared owl, the **b** owl Dt 14:16
Is the seed yet in the **b**? Indeed, the vine, Hg 2:19
floor and gather his wheat into the **b**, Mt 3:12
but gather the wheat into my **b**.'" Mt 13:30
floor and to gather the wheat into his **b**, Lk 3:17
they have neither storehouse nor **b**, Lk 12:24

BARNABAS (29)
by the apostles **B** (which means son Acts 4:36
But **B** took him and brought him to Acts 9:27
and they sent **B** to Antioch. Acts 11:22

So **B** went to Tarsus to look for Saul, Acts 11:25
the elders by the hand of **B** and Saul. Acts 11:30
And **B** and Saul returned from Acts 12:25
B, Simeon who was called Niger, Acts 13:1
"Set apart for me **B** and Saul for the Acts 13:2
who summoned **B** and Saul and Acts 13:7
to Judaism followed Paul and **B**, Acts 13:43
And Paul and **B** spoke out boldly, Acts 13:46
up persecution against Paul and **B**, Acts 13:50
B they called Zeus, and Paul, Hermes, Acts 14:12
when the apostles **B** and Paul heard Acts 14:14
next day he went on with **B** to Derbe. Acts 14:20
And after Paul and **B** had no small Acts 15:2
Paul and **B** and some of the others Acts 15:2
and they listened to **B** and Paul as Acts 15:12
them to Antioch with Paul and **B**. Acts 15:22
to you with our beloved **B** and Paul, Acts 15:25
But Paul and **B** remained in Antioch, Acts 15:35
And after some days Paul said to **B**, Acts 15:36
Now **B** wanted to take with them Acts 15:37
B took Mark with him and sailed Acts 15:39
Or is it only **B** and I who have no right 1 Cor 9:6
I went up again to Jerusalem with **B**, Gal 2:1
the right hand of fellowship to **B** and me, Gal 2:9
so that even **B** was led astray by their Gal 2:13
the cousin of **B** (concerning whom you Col 4:10

BARNS (4)
blessing on you in your **b** and in all that Dt 28:8
then your **b** will be filled with plenty, Prv 3:10
neither sow nor reap nor gather into **b**, Mt 6:26
will tear down my **b** and build larger Lk 12:18

BARRACKS (6)
ordered him to be brought into the **b**. Acts 21:34
was about to be brought into the **b**, Acts 21:37
ordered him to be brought into the **b**, Acts 22:24
by force and bring him into the **b**. Acts 23:10
went and entered the **b** and told Paul. Acts 23:16
on the next day they returned to the **b**, Acts 23:32

BARREN (19)
Now Sarai was **b**; she had no child. Gn 11:30
LORD for his wife, because she was **b**. Gn 25:21
opened her womb, but Rachel was **b**. Gn 29:31
shall miscarry or be **b** in your land; Ex 23:26
be male or female **b** among you or Dt 7:14
And his wife was **b** and had no children. Jgs 13:2
you are **b** and have not borne children, Jgs 13:3
The **b** has borne seven, but she who 1 Sm 2:5
Behold, let that night be **b**; let no joyful Jb 3:7
For the company of the godless is **b**, and Jb 15:34
"They wrong the **b** childless woman, Jb 24:21
He gives the **b** woman a home, making Ps 113:9
Sheol, the **b** womb, the land never Prv 30:16
I was bereaved and **b**, exiled and put Is 49:21
"Sing, O **b** one, who did not bear; break Is 54:1
had no child, because Elizabeth was **b**, Lk 1:7
sixth month with her who was called **b**. Lk 1:36
'Blessed are the **b** and the wombs that Lk 23:29
"Rejoice, O **b** one who does not bear; Gal 4:27

BARRENNESS (1)
he considered the **b** of Sarah's womb. Rom 4:19

BARRICADE (1)
will set up a **b** around you and Lk 19:43

BARRIER (2)
the sea, a perpetual **b** that it cannot pass; Jer 5:22
There was a **b** before the side rooms, Ezk 40:12

BARS (44)
"You shall make **b** of acacia wood, five Ex 26:26
and five **b** for the frames of the other Ex 26:27
and five **b** for the frames of the side of Ex 26:27
their rings of gold for holders for the **b**, Ex 26:29
and you shall overlay the **b** with gold. Ex 26:29
covering, its hooks and its frames, its **b**, Ex 35:11
He made **b** of acacia wood, five for the Ex 36:31
and five **b** for the frames of the other Ex 36:32
and five **b** for the frames of the Ex 36:32
their rings of gold for holders for the **b**, Ex 36:34
the bars, and overlaid the **b** with gold. Ex 36:34
its utensils, its hooks, its frames, its **b**, Ex 39:33
I have broken the **b** of your yoke and Lv 26:13
the frames of the tabernacle, the **b**, Nm 3:36
the frames of the tabernacle, with its **b**, Nm 4:31
fortified with high walls, gates, and **b**, Dt 3:5
Your **b** shall be iron and bronze, and as Dt 33:25
entering a town that has gates and **b**." 1 Sm 23:7
great cities with walls and bronze **b**); 1 Kgs 4:13
fortified cities with walls, gates, and **b**, 2 Chr 8:5
with walls and towers, gates and **b**. 2 Chr 14:7
and set its doors, its bolts, and its **b**. Neh 3:3
and set its doors, its bolts, and its **b**. Neh 3:6
it and set its doors, its bolts, and its **b**, Neh 3:13
it and set its doors, its bolts, and its **b**. Neh 3:14
it and set its doors, its bolts, and its **b**. Neh 3:15
Will it go down to the **b** of Sheol? Shall Jb 17:16
limits for it and set **b** and doors, Jb 38:10
tubes of bronze, his limbs like **b** of iron. Jb 40:18
of bronze and cuts in two the **b** of iron. Ps 107:16
For he strengthens the **b** of your gates; Ps 147:13
and quarreling is like the **b** of a castle. Prv 18:19
of bronze and cut through the **b** of iron, Is 45:2
You have broken wooden **b**, but you Jer 28:13
you have made in their place **b** of iron. Jer 28:13
the LORD, that has no gates or **b**, Jer 49:31
dwellings are on fire; her **b** are broken. Jer 51:30
he has ruined and broken her **b**; Lam 2:9
I break there the yoke **b** of Egypt, Ezk 30:18
LORD, when I break the **b** of their yoke, Ezk 34:27
walls, and having no **b** or gates,' Ezk 38:11
cities, consume the **b** of their gates, Hos 11:6
to the land whose **b** closed upon me Jon 2:6
your enemies; fire has devoured your **b**. Na 3:13

BARSABBAS (2)
they put forward two, Joseph called **B**, Acts 1:23
They sent Judas called **B**, and Silas, Acts 15:22

BARTER (1)
were in you to **b** for your wares. Ezk 27:9

BARTERED (1)
and calamus were **b** for your Ezk 27:19

BARTHOLOMEW (4)
Philip and **B**; Thomas and Matthew the Mt 10:3
Andrew, and Philip, and **B**, and Mk 3:18
and James and John, and Philip, and **B**, Lk 6:14
Philip and Thomas, **B** and Matthew, Acts 1:13

BARTIMAEUS (1)
and a great crowd, **B**, a blind beggar, Mk 10:46

BARUCH (26)
After him **B** the son of Zabbai repaired Neh 3:20
Daniel, Ginnethon, **B**, Neh 10:6
and Maaseiah the son of **B**, son of Neh 11:5
deed of purchase to **B** the son of Neriah Jer 32:12
I charged **B** in their presence, saying, Jer 32:13
deed of purchase to **B** the son of Neriah, Jer 32:16
Then Jeremiah called **B** the son of Jer 36:4
and **B** wrote on a scroll at the dictation Jer 36:4
And Jeremiah ordered **B**, saying, "I am Jer 36:5
And **B** the son of Neriah did all that Jer 36:8
B read the words of Jeremiah from the Jer 36:10
when **B** read the scroll in the hearing of Jer 36:13
of Shelemiah, son of Cushi, to say to **B**, Jer 36:14
and come." So **B** the son of Neriah took Jer 36:14
down and read it." So **B** read it to them. Jer 36:15
And they said to **B**, "We must report all Jer 36:16
Then they asked **B**, "Tell us, please, Jer 36:17
B answered them, "He dictated all these Jer 36:18
Then the officials said to **B**, "Go and Jer 36:19
of Abdeel to seize **B** the secretary and Jer 36:26
the words that **B** wrote at Jeremiah's Jer 36:27
scroll and gave it to **B** the scribe, Jer 36:32
but **B** the son of Neriah has set you Jer 43:3
Jeremiah the prophet and **B** the son of Jer 43:6
the prophet spoke to **B** the son of Neriah, Jer 45:1
the LORD, the God of Israel, to you, O **B**: Jer 45:2

BARZILLAI (12)
and **B** the Gileadite from Rogelim, 2 Sm 17:27
Now **B** the Gileadite had come down 2 Sm 19:31
B was a very aged man, eighty years 2 Sm 19:32
And the king said to **B**, "Come over 2 Sm 19:33
But **B** said to the king, "How many 2 Sm 19:34
the king kissed **B** and blessed him, 2 Sm 19:39
to Adriel the son of **B** the Meholathite; 2 Sm 21:8
loyally with the sons of **B** the Gileadite, 1 Kgs 2:7
and the sons of **B** (who had taken a wife Ezr 2:61
from the daughters of **B** the Gileadite, Ezr 2:61
the sons of **B** (who had taken a wife of Neh 7:63
of the daughters of **B** the Gileadite and Neh 7:63

BASE (18)
shall be made of hammered work: its **b**, Ex 25:31
you shall pour out at the **b** of the altar. Ex 29:12
lampstand of hammered work. Its **b**, Ex 37:17
for the hundred talents, a talent a **b**. Ex 38:27
shall pour out at the **b** of the altar of Lv 4:7
shall pour out at the **b** of the altar of Lv 4:18
of its blood at the **b** of the altar of burnt Lv 4:25
the rest of its blood at the **b** of the altar. Lv 4:30
the rest of its blood at the **b** of the altar. Lv 4:34
shall be drained out at the **b** of the altar; Lv 5:9
out the blood at the **b** of the altar and Lv 8:15
poured out the blood at the **b** of the altar. Lv 9:9
From its **b** to its flowers, it was Nm 8:4
Its corners, its **b**, and its walls were of Ezk 41:22
its **b** shall be one cubit high and one Ezk 43:13
from the **b** on the ground to the lower Ezk 43:14
broad, and its **b** one cubit all around. Ezk 43:17
will set the basket down there on its **b**." Zec 5:11

BASED (3)
it by faith, but as if it were **b** on works. Rom 9:32
the righteousness that is **b** on the law, Rom 10:5
But the righteousness **b** on faith says, Rom 10:6

BASEMATH (7)
and **B** the daughter of Elon the Hittite, Gn 26:34
and **B**, Ishmael's daughter, the sister of Gn 36:3
bore to Esau, Eliphaz; **B** bore Reuel; Gn 36:4
Reuel the son of **B** the wife of Esau. Gn 36:10
These are the sons of **B**, Esau's wife. Gn 36:13
these are the sons of **B**, Esau's wife. Gn 36:17
(he had taken **B** the daughter of 1 Kgs 4:15

BASES (55)
and forty **b** of silver you shall make Ex 26:19
two **b** under one frame for its two Ex 26:19
and two **b** under the next frame for its Ex 26:19
and their forty **b** of silver, two bases Ex 26:21
bases of silver, two **b** under one frame, Ex 26:21
frame, and two **b** under the next frame. Ex 26:21
be eight frames, with their **b** of silver, Ex 26:25
with their bases of silver, sixteen **b**; Ex 26:25
two **b** under one frame, and two bases Ex 26:25
frame, and two **b** under another frame. Ex 26:25
with hooks of gold, on four **b** of silver. Ex 26:32
you shall cast five **b** of bronze for them. Ex 26:37
pillars and their twenty **b** shall be of Ex 27:10
its pillars twenty and their **b** twenty, Ex 27:11
fifty cubits, with ten pillars and ten **b**. Ex 27:12
with their three pillars and three **b**. Ex 27:14
with their three pillars and three **b**. Ex 27:15
have four pillars and with them four **b**. Ex 27:16
shall be of silver, and their **b** of bronze. Ex 27:17
of fine twined linen and **b** of bronze. Ex 27:18
its frames, its bars, its pillars, and its **b**; Ex 35:11
of the court, its pillars and its **b**, Ex 35:17
And he made forty **b** of silver under the Ex 36:24
two **b** under one frame for its two Ex 36:24
and two **b** under the next frame for its Ex 36:24
and their forty **b** of silver, two bases Ex 36:26
two **b** under one frame and two bases Ex 36:26
one frame and two **b** under the next Ex 36:26
were eight frames with their **b** of silver: Ex 36:30
with their bases of silver: sixteen **b**, Ex 36:30
sixteen bases, under every frame two **b**. Ex 36:30
and he cast for them four **b** of silver. Ex 36:36
of gold, but their five **b** were of bronze. Ex 36:38
and their twenty **b** were of bronze, Ex 38:10
pillars, their twenty **b** were of bronze, Ex 38:11
cubits, their ten pillars, and their ten **b**; Ex 38:12
with their three pillars and three **b**. Ex 38:14
their three pillars and their three **b**. Ex 38:15
And the **b** for the pillars were of bronze, Ex 38:17
Their four **b** were of bronze, their Ex 38:19
were for casting the **b** of the sanctuary Ex 38:27
of the sanctuary and the **b** of the veil; Ex 38:27
a hundred **b** for the hundred talents, a Ex 38:27
it he made the **b** for the entrance of Ex 38:30
the **b** around the court, and the bases of Ex 38:31
court, and the **b** of the gate of the court, Ex 38:31
its frames, its bars, its pillars, and its **b**; Ex 39:33
of the court, its pillars, and its **b**, Ex 39:40
He laid its **b**, and set up its frames, and Ex 40:18
tabernacle, the bars, the pillars, the **b**, Nm 3:36
court, with their **b** and pegs and cords Nm 3:37
tabernacle, with its bars, pillars, and **b**, Nm 4:31
pillars around the court with their **b**, Nm 4:32
On what were its **b** sunk, or who laid its Jb 38:6
are alabaster columns, set on **b** of gold. Sg 5:15

BASHAN (60)
turned and went up by the way to **B**. Nm 21:33
Og the king of **B** came out against Nm 21:33
and the kingdom of Og king of **B**, Nm 32:33
lived in Heshbon, and Og the king of **B**, Dt 1:4
we turned and went up the way to **B**. Dt 3:1
And Og the king of **B** came out against us, Dt 3:1
gave into our hand Og also, the king of **B**, Dt 3:3
region of Argob, the kingdom of Og in **B**. Dt 3:4
of the tableland and all Gilead and all **B**, Dt 3:10
Edrei, cities of the kingdom of Og in **B**. Dt 3:10
only Og the king of **B** was left of the Dt 3:11
The rest of Gilead, and all **B**, the Dt 3:13
(All that portion of **B** is called the land of Dt 3:13
B, as far as the border of the Geshurites Dt 3:14
and Golan in **B** for the Manassites. Dt 4:43
land and the land of Og, the king of **B**, Dt 4:47
Og the king of **B** came out against us Dt 29:7
with fat of lambs, rams of **B** and goats, Dt 32:14
"Dan is a lion's cub that leaps from **B**." Dt 33:22
king of Heshbon, and to Og king of **B**, Jos 9:10
and Og king of **B**, one of the remnant of Jos 12:4
and Salecah and all **B** to the boundary Jos 12:5
Mount Hermon, and all **B** to Salecah; Jos 13:11
all the kingdom of Og in **B**, who Jos 13:12
from Mahanaim, through all **B**, Jos 13:30

the whole kingdom of Og king of **B**, Jos 13:30
all the towns of Jair, which are in **B**, Jos 13:30
the cities of the kingdom of Og in **B**. Jos 13:31
of Gilead, were allotted Gilead and **B**, Jos 17:1
besides the land of Gilead and **B**, Jos 17:5
from the tribe of Gad, and Golan in **B**, Jos 20:8
from the half-tribe of Manasseh in **B**, Jos 21:6
Golan in **B** with its pasturelands, Jos 21:27
Moses had given a possession in **B**, Jos 22:7
the region of Argob, which is in **B**, 1 Kgs 4:13
of the Amorites and of Og king of **B**. 1 Kgs 4:19
of the Arnon, that is, Gilead and **B**. 2 Kgs 10:33
in the land of **B** as far as Salecah: 1 Chr 5:11
the second, Janai, and Shaphat in **B**. 1 Chr 5:12
lived in Gilead, in **B** and in its towns, 1 Chr 5:16
numerous from **B** to Baal-hermon, 1 Chr 5:23
Asher, Naphtali and Manasseh in **B**. 1 Chr 6:62
Golan in **B** with its pasturelands and 1 Chr 6:71
Heshbon and the land of Og king of **B**. Neh 9:22
me; strong bulls of **B** surround me; Ps 22:12
O mountain of God, mountain of **B**; O Ps 68:15
mountain, mountain of **B**! Ps 68:15
said, "I will bring them back from **B**, Ps 68:22
of the Amorites, and Og, king of **B**, Ps 135:11
and Og, king of **B**, for his steadfast love Ps 136:20
lifted up; and against all the oaks of **B**; Is 2:13
and **B** and Carmel shake off their leaves. Is 33:9
and cry out, and lift up your voice in **B**; Jer 22:20
and he shall feed on Carmel and in **B**, Jer 50:19
Of oaks of **B** they made your oars; they Ezk 27:6
of bulls, all of them fat beasts of **B**. Ezk 39:18
"Hear this word, you cows of **B**, who are Am 4:1
let them graze in **B** and Gilead as in the Mi 7:14
up all the rivers; **B** and Carmel wither; Na 1:4
Wail, oaks of **B**, for the thick forest has Zec 11:2

BASIC (1)
teach you again the **b** principles of the Heb 5:12

BASIN (31)
and dip it in the blood that is in the **b**, Ex 12:22
with the blood that is in the **b**. Ex 12:22
"You shall also make a **b** of bronze, Ex 30:18
all its utensils and the **b** and its stand. Ex 30:28
all its utensils, and the **b** and its stand, Ex 31:9
and all its utensils, the **b** and its stand; Ex 35:16
He made the **b** of bronze and its stand of Ex 38:8
and all its utensils; the **b** and its stand; Ex 39:39
and place the **b** between the tent of Ex 40:7
shall also anoint the **b** and its stand, Ex 40:11
He set the **b** between the tent of meeting Ex 40:30
all its utensils and the **b** and its stand, Lv 8:11
130 shekels, one silver **b** of 70 shekels, Nm 7:13
130 shekels, one silver **b** of 70 shekels, Nm 7:19
130 shekels, one silver **b** of 70 shekels, Nm 7:25
130 shekels, one silver **b** of 70 shekels, Nm 7:31
130 shekels, one silver **b** of 70 shekels, Nm 7:37
130 shekels, one silver **b** of 70 shekels, Nm 7:43
130 shekels, one silver **b** of 70 shekels, Nm 7:49
130 shekels, one silver **b** of 70 shekels, Nm 7:55
130 shekels, one silver **b** of 70 shekels, Nm 7:61
130 shekels, one silver **b** of 70 shekels, Nm 7:67
130 shekels, one silver **b** of 70 shekels, Nm 7:73
130 shekels, one silver **b** of 70 shekels, Nm 7:79
weighing 130 shekels and each **b** 70, Nm 7:85
four corners were supports for a **b**. 1 Kgs 7:30
Each **b** held forty baths, each basin 1 Kgs 7:38
baths, each **b** measured four cubits, 1 Kgs 7:38
and there was a **b** for each of the ten 1 Kgs 7:38
and removed the **b** from them, 2 Kgs 16:17
poured water into a **b** and began to wash Jn 13:5

BASINS (23)
took half of the blood and put it in **b**, Ex 24:6
and shovels and **b** and forks and fire Ex 27:3
of the altar, the pots, the shovels, the **b**, Ex 38:3
pans, the forks, the shovels, and the **b**, Nm 4:14
twelve silver plates, twelve silver **b**, Nm 7:84
brought beds, **b**, and earthen vessels, 2 Sm 17:28
And he made ten **b** of bronze. Each 1 Kgs 7:38
made the pots, the shovels, and the **b**. 1 Kgs 7:40
stands, and the ten **b** on the stands; 1 Kgs 7:43
Now the pots, the shovels, and the **b**, 1 Kgs 7:45
cups, snuffers, **b**, dishes for incense, 1 Kgs 7:50
for the house of the LORD **b** of silver, 2 Kgs 12:13
for the forks, the **b** and the cups; 1 Chr 28:17
He also made ten **b** in which to wash, 2 Chr 4:6
And he made a hundred **b** of gold. 2 Chr 4:8
made the pots, the shovels, and the **b**. 2 Chr 4:11
stands also, and the **b** on the stands, 2 Chr 4:14
the snuffers, **b**, dishes for incense, 2 Chr 4:22
30 **b** of gold, 1,000 basins of silver, 29 Ezr 1:9
30 basins of gold, 1,000 **b** of silver, 29 Ezr 1:9
the treasury 1,000 darics of gold, 50 **b**, Neh 7:70
the snuffers and the **b** and the dishes Jer 52:18
the fire pans and the **b** and the pots and Jer 52:19

BASIS (2)
grace, it is no longer on the **b** of works; Rom 11:6
not on the **b** of a legal requirement Heb 7:16

BASKET (35)
and in the uppermost **b** there were all Gn 40:17
were eating it out of the **b** on my head." Gn 40:17
took for him a **b** made of bulrushes and Ex 2:3
She saw the **b** among the reeds and sent Ex 2:5
put them in one **b** and bring them in Ex 29:3
in one basket and bring them in the **b**, Ex 29:3
wafer out of the **b** of unleavened bread Ex 29:23
bread that is in the **b** in the entrance of Ex 29:32
two rams and the **b** of unleavened bread. Lv 8:2
and out of the **b** of unleavened bread Lv 8:26
that is in the **b** of ordination offerings, Lv 8:31
and a **b** of unleavened bread, loaves of Nm 6:15
LORD, with the **b** of unleavened bread. Nm 6:17
loaf out of the **b** and one unleavened Nm 6:19
is giving you, and you shall put it in a **b**, Dt 26:2
priest shall take the **b** from your hand Dt 26:4
shall be your **b** and your kneading Dt 28:5
shall be your **b** and your kneading Dt 28:17
The meat he put in a **b**, and the broth he Jgs 6:19
your hands were freed from the **b**. Ps 81:6
One **b** had very good figs, like first-ripe Jer 24:2
figs, but the other **b** had very bad figs, Jer 24:2
showed me: behold, a **b** of summer fruit. Am 8:1
"A **b** of summer fruit." Then the LORD Am 8:2
"This is the **b** that is going out." And he Zec 5:6
and there was a woman sitting in the **b**! Zec 5:7
And he thrust her back into the **b**, Zec 5:8
they lifted up the **b** between earth and Zec 5:9
me, "Where are they taking the **b**?" Zec 5:10
they will set the **b** down there on its Zec 5:11
people light a lamp and put it under a **b**, Mt 5:15
a lamp brought in to be put under a **b**, Mk 4:21
a lamp puts it in a cellar or under a **b**, Lk 11:33
in the wall, lowering him in a **b**. Acts 9:25
let down in a **b** through a window in 2 Cor 11:33

BASKETS (14)
there were three cake **b** on my head, Gn 40:16
the three **b** are three days. Gn 40:18
put their heads in **b** and sent them to 2 Kgs 10:7
two **b** of figs placed before the temple of Jer 24:1
they took up twelve **b** full of the broken Mt 14:20
they took up seven **b** full of the broken Mt 15:37
and how many **b** you gathered? Mt 16:9
and how many **b** you gathered? Mt 16:10
they took up twelve **b** full of broken Mk 6:43
the broken pieces left over, seven **b** full. Mk 8:8
how many **b** full of broken pieces did Mk 8:19
how many **b** full of broken pieces did Mk 8:20
picked up, twelve **b** of broken pieces. Lk 9:17
and filled twelve **b** with fragments from Jn 6:13

BAT (2)
of any kind, the hoopoe, and the **b**. Lv 11:19
of any kind; the hoopoe and the **b**. Dt 14:18

BATH (5)
acres of vineyard shall yield but one **b**, Is 5:10
balances, a just ephah, and a just **b**. Ezk 45:10
The ephah and the **b** shall be of the Ezk 45:11
the **b** containing one tenth of a Ezk 45:11
one tenth of a **b** from each cor (the Ezk 45:14

BATH-RABBIM (1)
are pools in Heshbon, by the gate of **B**. Sg 7:4

BATH-SHUA (2)
these three **B** the Canaanite bore to 1 Chr 2:3
Nathan and Solomon, four by **B**, 1 Chr 3:5

BATHE (26)
of Pharaoh came down to **b** at the river, Ex 2:5
off all his hair and **b** himself in water, Lv 14:8
wash his clothes and **b** his body in Lv 14:9
wash his clothes and **b** himself in water Lv 15:5
wash his clothes and **b** himself in water Lv 15:6
wash his clothes and **b** himself in water Lv 15:7
wash his clothes and **b** himself in water Lv 15:8
his clothes and **b** himself in water Lv 15:10
his clothes and **b** himself in water Lv 15:11
And he shall **b** his body in fresh water Lv 15:13
he shall **b** his whole body in water and Lv 15:16
of them shall **b** themselves in water Lv 15:18
his clothes and **b** himself in water Lv 15:21
his clothes and **b** himself in water Lv 15:22
his clothes and **b** himself in water Lv 15:27
He shall **b** his body in water and then Lv 16:4
And he shall **b** his body in water in a Lv 16:24
wash his clothes and **b** his body in Lv 16:26
wash his clothes and **b** his body in Lv 16:28
his clothes and **b** himself in water Lv 17:15
if he does not wash them or **b** his flesh, Lv 17:16
wash his clothes and **b** his body in Nm 19:7
clothes in water and **b** his body in Nm 19:8
his clothes and **b** himself in water, Nm 19:19
comes, he shall **b** himself in water, Dt 23:11
he will **b** his feet in the blood of the Ps 58:10

BATHED (6)
things unless he has **b** his body in water. Lv 22:6
how could I put it on? I had **b** my feet; Sg 5:3
doves beside streams of water, **b** in milk, Sg 5:12
Then I **b** you with water and washed off Ezk 16:9
For them you **b** yourself, painted your Ezk 23:40
"The one who has **b** does not need to Jn 13:10

BATHING (1)
that he saw from the roof a woman **b**; 2 Sm 11:2

BATHS (9)
of a lily. It held two thousand **b**. 1 Kgs 7:26
Each basin held forty **b**, each basin 1 Kgs 7:38
cors of barley, 20,000 **b** of wine, 2 Chr 2:10
baths of wine, and 20,000 **b** of oil." 2 Chr 2:10
like the flower of a lily. It held 3,000 **b**. 2 Chr 4:5
silver, 100 cors of wheat, 100 **b** of wine, Ezr 7:22
of wheat, 100 baths of wine, 100 **b** of oil, Ezr 7:22
the fixed portion of oil, measured in **b**, Ezk 45:14
cor, like the homer, contains ten **b**). Ezk 45:14

BATHSHEBA (11)
And one said, "Is not this **B**, the 2 Sm 11:3
B, and went in to her and lay with 2 Sm 12:24
Then Nathan said to **B** the mother of 1 Kgs 1:11
So **B** went to the king in his chamber 1 Kgs 1:15
B bowed and paid homage to the 1 Kgs 1:16
"Call **B** to me." So she came into the 1 Kgs 1:28
Then **B** bowed with her face to the 1 Kgs 1:31
of Haggith came to **B** the mother of 1 Kgs 2:13
B said, "Very well; I will speak for you 1 Kgs 2:18
So **B** went to King Solomon to speak 1 Kgs 2:19
went to him, after he had gone in to **B**. Ps 51:T

BATS (1)
to worship, to the moles and to the **b**, Is 2:20

BATTALION (2)
they gathered the whole **b** before him. Mt 27:27
and they called together the whole **b**. Mk 15:16

BATTER (1)
will all of you attack a man to **b** him, Ps 62:3

BATTERED (1)
left in the city; the gates are **b** into ruins. Is 24:12

BATTERING (6)
and they were **b** the wall to throw it 2 Sm 20:15
a **b** down of walls and a shouting to the Is 22:5
and plant **b** rams against it all around. Ezk 4:2
for Jerusalem, to set **b** rams, Ezk 21:22
to set **b** rams against the gates, Ezk 21:22
the shock of his **b** rams against your Ezk 26:9

BATTLE (173)
and they joined **b** in the Valley of Gn 14:8
out of the land of Egypt equipped for **b**. Ex 13:18
he and all his people, to **b** at Edrei. Nm 21:33
men in the army who had gone to **b**: Nm 31:21
who went out to **b** and all the Nm 31:27
the men of war who went out to **b**, Nm 31:28
is armed for war, before the LORD to **b**, Nm 32:27
who is armed to **b** before the LORD, Nm 32:29
harass Moab or contend with them in **b**, Dt 2:9
possession, and contend with him in **b**. Dt 2:24
us, he and all his people, to **b** at Jahaz. Dt 2:32
us, he and all his people, to **b** at Edrei. Dt 3:1
And when you draw near to the **b**, the Dt 20:2
drawing near for **b** against your Dt 20:3
he die in the **b** and another man dedicate Dt 20:5
he die in the **b** and another man enjoy Dt 20:6
lest he die in the **b** and another man take Dt 20:7
king of Bashan came out against us to **b**, Dt 29:7
for war passed over before the LORD for **b**, Jos 4:13
toward the Arabah to meet Israel in **b**. Jos 8:14
of Gibeon. They took them all in **b**. Jos 11:19
they should come against Israel in **b**, Jos 11:20
Joash returned from the **b** by the ascent Jgs 8:13
to go out to **b** against the people of Jgs 20:14
Israel drew up the **b** line against them Jgs 20:20
and again formed the **b** line in the Jgs 20:22
once more to **b** against our brothers, Jgs 20:28
out of all Israel, and the **b** was hard, Jgs 20:34
the men of Israel should turn in **b**. Jgs 20:39
are defeated before us, as in the first **b**." Jgs 20:39
wilderness, but the **b** overtook them. Jgs 20:42
for each man of them his wife in **b**, Jgs 21:22
went out to **b** against the Philistines. 1 Sm 4:1
against Israel, and when the **b** spread, 1 Sm 4:2
four thousand men on the field of **b**. 1 Sm 4:2
ran from the **b** line and came 1 Sm 4:12
"I am he who has come from the **b**; 1 Sm 4:16
I fled from the **b** today." And he said, 1 Sm 4:16
the day of the **b** there was neither 1 Sm 13:22
with him rallied and went into the **b**. 1 Sm 14:20

too followed hard after them in the **b**. 1 Sm 14:22
And the **b** passed beyond Beth-aven. 1 Sm 14:23
gathered their armies for **b**. 1 Sm 17:1
up in line of **b** against the Philistines. 1 Sm 17:2
have you come out to draw up for **b**? 1 Sm 17:8
of Jesse had followed Saul to the **b**. 1 Sm 17:13
who went to the **b** were Eliab the 1 Sm 17:13
the host was going out to the **b** line, 1 Sm 17:20
and the Philistines drew up for **b**, 1 Sm 17:21
you have come down to see the **b**." 1 Sm 17:28
For the **b** is the LORD'S, and he will 1 Sm 17:47
quickly toward the **b** line to meet 1 Sm 17:48
of the Philistines came out to **b**, 1 Sm 18:30
or he will go down into **b** and perish. 1 Sm 26:10
He shall not go down with us to **b**, lest 1 Sm 29:4
lest in the **b** he become an adversary 1 Sm 29:4
'He shall not go up with us to the **b**.' 1 Sm 29:9
share is who goes down into the **b**, 1 Sm 30:24
The **b** pressed hard against Saul, and 1 Sm 31:3
answered, "The people fled from the **b**, 2 Sm 1:4
have fallen in the midst of the **b**! 2 Sm 1:25
And the **b** was very fierce that day. 2 Sm 2:17
Asahel to death in the **b** at Gibeon. 2 Sm 3:30
and drew up in **b** array at the 2 Sm 10:8
Joab saw that the **b** was set against 2 Sm 10:9
drew near to **b** against the Syrians, 2 Sm 10:13
year, the time when kings go out to **b**, 2 Sm 11:1
and that you go to **b** in person. 2 Sm 17:11
and the **b** was fought in the forest of 2 Sm 18:6
The **b** spread over the face of all the 2 Sm 18:8
who are ashamed when they flee in **b**. 2 Sm 19:3
we anointed over us, is dead in **b**. 2 Sm 19:10
shall no longer go out with us to **b**, 2 Sm 21:17
equipped me with strength for the **b**; 2 Sm 22:40
who were gathered there for **b**, 2 Sm 23:9
go out to **b** against their enemy, 1 Kgs 8:44
shall begin the **b**?" He answered, 1 Kgs 20:14
on the seventh day the **b** was joined. 1 Kgs 20:29
went out into the midst of the **b**, 1 Kgs 20:39
with me to **b** at Ramoth-gilead?" And 1 Kgs 22:4
I go to **b** against Ramoth-gilead, 1 Kgs 22:6
shall we go to Ramoth-gilead to **b**, 1 Kgs 22:15
"I will disguise myself and go into **b**, 1 Kgs 22:30
disguised himself and went into **b**. 1 Kgs 22:30
around and carry me out of the **b**, 1 Kgs 22:34
And the **b** continued that day, and 1 Kgs 22:35
go with me to **b** against Moab?" And 2 Kgs 3:7
saw that the **b** was going against 2 Kgs 3:26
one another in **b** at Beth-shemesh, 2 Kgs 14:11
for they cried out to God in the **b**, 1 Chr 5:20
The **b** pressed hard against Saul, and 1 Chr 10:3
were gathered there for **b**. 1 Chr 11:13
Philistines for the **b** against Saul. 1 Chr 12:19
equipped for **b** with all the weapons 1 Chr 12:33
Danites 28,600 men equipped for **b**. 1 Chr 12:35
40,000 seasoned troops ready for **b**. 1 Chr 12:36
men of war, arrayed in **b** order, 1 Chr 12:38
of the balsam trees, then go out to **b**, 1 Chr 14:15
from their cities and came to **b**. 1 Chr 19:7
and drew up in **b** array at the 1 Chr 19:9
Joab saw that the **b** was set against 1 Chr 19:10
drew near before the Syrians for **b**, 1 Chr 19:14
David set the **b** in array against 1 Chr 19:17
year, the time when kings go out to **b**, 1 Chr 20:1
go out to **b** against their enemies, 2 Chr 6:34
Abijah went out to **b**, having an 2 Chr 13:3
up his line of **b** against him with 2 Chr 13:3
priests with their **b** trumpets to 2 Chr 13:12
to sound the call to **b** against you. 2 Chr 13:12
the **b** was in front of and behind 2 Chr 13:14
the men of Judah raised the **b** shout. 2 Chr 13:15
up their lines of **b** in the Valley of 2 Chr 14:10
we go to **b** against Ramoth-gilead, 2 Chr 18:5
shall we go to Ramoth-gilead to **b**, 2 Chr 18:14
"I will disguise myself and go into **b**, 2 Chr 18:29
himself, and they went into **b**. 2 Chr 18:29
around and carry me out of the **b**, 2 Chr 18:33
And the **b** continued that day, and 2 Chr 18:34
came against Jehoshaphat for **b**. 2 Chr 20:1
for the **b** is not yours but God's. 2 Chr 20:15
You will not need to fight in this **b**. 2 Chr 20:17
But go, act, be strong for the **b**. Why 2 Chr 25:8
not letting them go with him to **b**, 2 Chr 25:13
one another in **b** at Beth-shemesh, 2 Chr 25:21
against him, like a king ready for **b**. Jb 15:24
of trouble, for the day of **b** and war? Jb 38:23
He smells the **b** from afar, the thunder Jb 39:25
remember the **b**—you will not do it Jb 41:8
equipped me with strength for the **b**; Ps 18:39
and mighty, the LORD, mighty in **b**! Ps 24:8
soul in safety from the **b** that I wage, Ps 55:18
the bow, turned back on the day of **b**. Ps 78:9
and you have not made him stand in **b**. Ps 89:43
have covered my head in the day of **b**. Ps 140:7
my hands for war, and my fingers for **b**; Ps 144:1
horse is made ready for the day of **b**, Prv 21:31
not to the swift, nor the **b** to the strong, Eccl 9:11
by the sword and your mighty men in **b**. Is 3:25
tramping warrior in **b** tumult and every Is 9:5
LORD of hosts is mustering a host for **b**. Is 13:4
the bent bow, and from the press of **b**. Is 21:15
are not slain with the sword or dead in **b**. Is 22:2
Would that I had thorns and briers to **b**! Is 27:4
to those who turn back the **b** at the gate. Is 28:6
the heat of his anger and the might of **b**; Is 42:25
on horses, set in array as a man for **b**, Jer 6:23
like a horse plunging headlong into **b**. Jer 8:6
be struck down by the sword in **b**. Jer 18:21
buckler and shield, and advance for **b**! Jer 46:3
when I will cause the **b** cry to be heard Jer 49:2
come against her, and rise up for **b**! Jer 49:14
The noise of **b** is in the land, and great Jer 50:22
arrayed as a man for **b** against you, Jer 50:42
everything ready, but none goes to **b**, Ezk 7:14
that it might stand in **b** in the day of Ezk 13:5
be broken, neither in anger nor in **b**. Dn 11:20
destroyed Beth-arbel on the day of **b**; Hos 10:14
like a powerful army drawn up for **b**. Jl 2:5
with shouting on the day of **b**, Am 1:14
"Rise up! Let us rise against her for **b**!" Ob 1:1
the ramparts; watch the road; dress for **b**; Na 2:1
of trumpet blast and **b** cry against the Zep 1:16
and the **b** bow shall be cut off, and he Zec 9:10
make them like his majestic steed in **b**. Zec 10:3
him the tent peg, from him the **b** bow, Zec 10:4
They shall be like mighty men in **b**, Zec 10:5
all the nations against Jerusalem to **b**, Zec 14:2
nations as when he fights on a day of **b**. Zec 14:3
sound, who will get ready for **b**? 1 Cor 14:8
locusts were like horses prepared for **b**: Rv 9:7
chariots with horses rushing into **b**. Rv 9:9
to assemble them for **b** on the great day Rv 16:14
Gog and Magog, to gather them for **b**; Rv 20:8

BATTLEMENT (1)
is a wall, we will build on her a **b** of silver, Sg 8:9

BATTLEMENTS (2)
fortified cities and against the lofty **b**. Zep 1:16
have cut off nations; their **b** are in ruins; Zep 3:6

BATTLES (5)
and go out before us and fight our **b**." 1 Sm 8:20
fight the LORD'S **b**." For Saul thought, 1 Sm 18:17
my lord is fighting the **b** of the LORD, 1 Sm 25:28
spoil won in **b** they dedicated gifts 1 Chr 26:27
and to fight our **b**." And the people 2 Chr 32:8

BATTLING (1)
B with brandished arm, he will fight Is 30:32

BAVVAI (1)
B the son of Henadad, ruler of half the Neh 3:18

BAY (4)
Sea, from the **b** that faces southward. Jos 15:2
north side runs from the **b** of the sea at Jos 15:5
ends at the northern **b** of the Salt Sea, Jos 18:19
but they noticed a **b** with a beach, Acts 27:39

BAZAARS (1)
you may establish **b** for yourself in 1 Kgs 20:34

BAZLITH (1)
the sons of **B**, the sons of Mehida, the Neh 7:54

BAZLUTH (1)
the sons of **B**, the sons of Mehida, the Ezr 2:52

BDELLIUM (2)
land is good; **b** and onyx stone are there. Gn 2:12
seed, and its appearance like that of **b**. Nm 11:7

BEACH (4)
And the whole crowd stood on the **b**. Mt 13:2
And kneeling down on the **b**, we Acts 21:5
land, but they noticed a bay with a **b**, Acts 27:39
to the wind they made for the **b**. Acts 27:40

BEADS (1)
signet rings, earrings, and **b**, Nm 31:50

BEALIAH (1)
Eluzai, Jerimoth, **B**, Shemariah, 1 Chr 12:5

BEALOTH (2)
Ziph, Telem, **B**, Jos 15:24
the son of Hushai, in Asher and **B**; 1 Kgs 4:16

BEAM (6)
of his spear was like a weaver's **b**, 1 Sm 17:7
of whose spear was like a weaver's **b**. 2 Sm 21:19
his hand a spear like a weaver's **b**, 1 Chr 11:23
of whose spear was like a weaver's **b**. 1 Chr 20:5
a **b** shall be pulled out of his house, Ezr 6:11
and the **b** from the woodwork respond. Hab 2:11

BEAMS (12)
that the supporting **b** should not be 1 Kgs 6:6
of the house of **b** and planks of cedar. 1 Kgs 6:9
cut stone and one course of cedar **b**. 1 Kgs 6:36
pillars, with cedar **b** on the pillars. 1 Kgs 7:2
all around, and a course of cedar **b**; 1 Kgs 7:12
So he lined the house with gold—its **b**, 2 Chr 3:7
for binders and **b** for the buildings 2 Chr 34:11
me timber to make **b** for the gates of Neh 2:8
They laid its **b** and set its doors, its bolts, Neh 3:3
They laid its **b** and set its doors, its bolts, Neh 3:6
He lays the **b** of his chambers on the Ps 104:3
the **b** of our house are cedar; our rafters Sg 1:17

BEANS (2)
flour, parched grain, **b** and lentils, 2 Sm 17:28
take wheat and barley, **b** and lentils, Ezk 4:9

BEAR (213)
"My punishment is greater than I can **b**. Gn 4:13
you are pregnant and shall **b** a son. Gn 16:11
who is ninety years old, **b** a child?" Gn 17:17
but Sarah your wife shall **b** you a son, Gn 17:19
whom Sarah shall **b** to you at this time Gn 17:21
laugh and say, 'Shall I indeed **b** a child, Gn 18:13
you, then let me **b** the blame forever. Gn 43:9
then I shall **b** the blame before my Gn 44:32
so he bowed his shoulder to **b**, Gn 49:15
and they will **b** the burden with you. Ex 18:22
"You shall not **b** false witness against Ex 20:16
evil, nor shall you **b** witness in a lawsuit, Ex 23:2
And Aaron shall **b** their names before Ex 28:12
So Aaron shall **b** the names of the sons Ex 28:29
Thus Aaron shall **b** the judgment of Ex 28:30
and Aaron shall **b** any guilt from the Ex 28:38
the Holy Place, lest they **b** guilt and die. Ex 28:43
yet does not speak, he shall **b** his iniquity; Lv 5:1
realizes his guilt, he shall **b** his iniquity. Lv 5:17
and he who eats of it shall **b** his iniquity. Lv 7:18
you that you may **b** the iniquity of the Lv 10:17
The goat shall **b** all their iniquities on Lv 16:22
bathe his flesh, he shall **b** his iniquity." Lv 17:16
everyone who eats it shall **b** his iniquity, Lv 19:8
take vengeance or **b** a grudge against Lv 19:18
nakedness, and he shall **b** his iniquity. Lv 20:17
relative; they shall **b** their iniquity. Lv 20:19
nakedness; they shall **b** their sin; Lv 20:20
lest they **b** sin for it and die thereby Lv 22:9
so cause them to **b** iniquity and guilt, Lv 22:16
curses his God shall **b** his sin. Lv 24:15
but the woman shall **b** her iniquity." Nm 5:31
time; that man shall **b** his sin. Nm 9:13
and they shall **b** the burden of the Nm 11:17
that you may not **b** it yourself alone. Nm 11:17
you shall **b** your iniquity forty years, Nm 14:34
with you shall **b** iniquity connected Nm 18:1
with you shall **b** iniquity connected Nm 18:1
tent of meeting, lest they **b** sin and die. Nm 18:22
and they shall **b** their iniquity. Nm 18:23
And you shall **b** no sin by reason of it, Nm 18:32
of them, then he shall **b** her iniquity." Nm 30:15
to you, 'I am not able to **b** you by myself. Dt 1:9
How can I **b** by myself the weight and Dt 1:12
you shall not **b** false witness against Dt 5:20
command the priests who **b** the ark of the Jos 3:8
Seven priests shall **b** seven trumpets of Jos 6:4
and let seven priests **b** seven trumpets of Jos 6:6
Zebulun those who **b** the lieutenant's Jgs 5:14
but you shall conceive and **b** a son. Jgs 13:3
behold, you shall conceive and **b** a son. Jgs 13:5
'Behold, you shall conceive and **b** a son. Jgs 13:7
a husband this night and should **b** sons, Ru 1:12
And when there came a lion, or a **b**, 1 Sm 17:34
the paw of the **b** will deliver me from 1 Sm 17:37
like a **b** robbed of her cubs in the 2 Sm 17:8
on me I will **b**." And the king of 2 Kgs 18:14
root downward and **b** fruit upward. 2 Kgs 19:30
70,000 men to **b** burdens and 80,000 2 Chr 2:2
of them he assigned to **b** burdens, 2 Chr 2:18
strength of those who **b** the burdens is Neh 4:10
For how can I **b** to see the calamity that Est 8:6
Or how can I **b** to see the destruction of Est 8:6
who made the **B** and Orion, the Pleiades Jb 9:9
B with me, and I will speak, and after I Jb 21:3
"**B** with me a little, and I will show you, Jb 36:2
can you guide the **B** with its children? Jb 38:32
Make them **b** their guilt, O God; let them Ps 5:10
and in anger they **b** a grudge against me. Ps 55:3
who taunts me—then I could **b** it; Ps 55:12
at Jerusalem kings shall **b** gifts to you. Ps 68:29
Let the mountains **b** prosperity for the Ps 72:3
and how I **b** in my heart the insults of Ps 89:50
On their hands they will **b** you up, lest Ps 91:12
They still **b** fruit in old age; they are Ps 92:14
yourself; if you scoff, you alone will **b** it. Prv 9:12
but a crushed spirit who can **b**? Prv 18:14
lion or a charging **b** is a wicked ruler Prv 28:15
trembles; under four it cannot **b** up: Prv 30:21

from the washing, all of which **b** twins, Sg 4:2
up from the washing; all of them **b** twins; Sg 6:6
the virgin shall conceive and **b** a son, Is 7:14
and a branch from his roots shall **b** fruit. Is 11:1
The cow and the **b** shall graze; their Is 11:7
take root downward and **b** fruit upward. Is 37:31
salvation and righteousness may **b** fruit; Is 45:8
I have made, and I will **b**; I will carry and Is 46:4
you who **b** the vessels of the LORD. Is 52:11
and he shall **b** their iniquities. Is 53:11
"Sing, O barren one, who did not **b**; break Is 54:1
labor in vain or **b** children for calamity, Is 65:23
this is an affliction, and I must **b** it." Jer 10:19
know that for your sake I **b** reproach. Jer 15:15
drought, for it does not cease to **b** fruit." Jer 17:8
and do not **b** a burden on the Sabbath Jer 17:21
and not to **b** a burden and enter by the Jer 17:27
that they may **b** sons and daughters; Jer 29:6
Ask now, and see, can a man **b** a child? Jer 30:6
LORD could no longer **b** your evil deeds Jer 44:22
He is a **b** lying in wait for me, a lion in Lam 3:10
for a man that he **b** the yoke in his Lam 3:27
are no more; and we **b** their iniquities. Lam 5:7
lie on it, you shall **b** their punishment. Ezk 4:4
So long shall you **b** the punishment of Ezk 4:5
and **b** the punishment of the house of Ezk 4:6
And they shall **b** their punishment— Ezk 14:10
B your disgrace, you also, for you Ezk 16:52
you also, and **b** your disgrace, Ezk 16:52
that you may **b** your disgrace and be Ezk 16:54
You **b** the penalty of your lewdness Ezk 16:58
produce branches and **b** fruit and Ezk 17:8
that it may **b** branches and produce Ezk 17:23
you yourself must **b** the consequences Ezk 23:35
and you shall **b** the penalty for your Ezk 23:49
and they **b** their shame with those Ezk 32:24
and they **b** their shame with those Ezk 32:25
and **b** their shame with those who go Ezk 32:30
you shall no longer **b** the disgrace of Ezk 36:15
went astray, shall **b** their punishment. Ezk 44:10
and they shall **b** their punishment. Ezk 44:12
but they shall **b** their shame and the Ezk 44:13
but they will **b** fresh fruit every Ezk 47:12
another beast, a second one, like a **b**. Dn 7:5
root is dried up; they shall **b** no fruit. Hos 9:16
is false; now they must **b** their guilt. Hos 10:2
upon them like a **b** robbed of her cubs; Hos 13:8
Samaria shall **b** her guilt, because she Hos 13:16
man fled from a lion, and a **b** met him, Am 5:19
The land is not able to **b** all his words. Am 7:10
so you shall **b** the scorn of my people." Mi 6:16
I will **b** the indignation of the LORD Mi 7:9
of the LORD and shall **b** royal honor, Zec 6:13
your vine in the field shall not fail to **b**, Mal 3:11
She will **b** a son, and you shall call his Mt 1:21
the virgin shall conceive and **b** a son, Mt 1:23
B fruit in keeping with repentance. Mt 3:8
therefore that does not **b** good fruit is cut Mt 3:10
and "'On their hands they will **b** you up, Mt 4:6
A healthy tree cannot **b** bad fruit, nor Mt 7:18
nor can a diseased tree **b** good fruit. Mt 7:18
tree that does not **b** good fruit is cut Mt 7:19
to **b** witness before them and the Mt 10:18
you? How long am I to **b** with you? Mt 17:17
not steal, You shall not **b** false witness, Mt 19:18
They tie up heavy burdens, hard to **b**, Mt 23:4
hear the word and accept it and **b** fruit, Mk 4:20
with you? How long am I to **b** with you? Mk 9:19
Do not steal, Do not **b** false witness, Mk 10:19
for my sake, to **b** witness before them. Mk 13:9
your wife Elizabeth will **b** you a son, Lk 1:13
conceive in your womb and **b** a son, Lk 1:31
B fruits in keeping with repentance. And Lk 3:8
therefore that does not **b** good fruit is cut Lk 3:9
and "'On their hands they will **b** you up, Lk 4:11
nor again does a bad tree **b** good fruit, Lk 6:43
good heart, and **b** fruit with patience. Lk 8:15
am I to be with you and **b** with you? Lk 9:41
load people with burdens hard to **b**, Lk 11:46
Then if it should **b** fruit next year, well Lk 13:9
Whoever does not **b** his own cross and Lk 14:27
Do not steal, Do not **b** false witness, Lk 18:20
will be your opportunity to **b** witness. Lk 21:13
as a witness, to **b** witness about the light, Jn 1:7
but came to **b** witness about the light. Jn 1:8
needed no one to **b** witness about man, Jn 2:25
and **b** witness to what we have seen, Jn 3:11
You yourselves **b** me witness, that I said, Jn 3:28
If I alone **b** witness about myself, my Jn 5:31
b witness about me that the Father has Jn 5:36
and it is they that **b** witness about me, Jn 5:39
"Even if I do **b** witness about myself, Jn 8:14
is because you cannot **b** to hear my Jn 8:43
my Father's name **b** witness about me, Jn 10:25
from the dead continued to **b** witness. Jn 12:17
mine that does not **b** fruit he takes away, Jn 15:2
every branch that does **b** fruit he prunes, Jn 15:2
fruit he prunes, that it may **b** more fruit. Jn 15:2
As the branch cannot **b** fruit by itself, Jn 15:4
that you **b** much fruit and so prove to be Jn 15:8
you should go and **b** fruit and that your Jn 15:16
the Father, he will **b** witness about me. Jn 15:26
And you also will **b** witness, because Jn 15:27
say to you, but you cannot **b** them now. Jn 16:12
is wrong, **b** witness about the wrong; Jn 18:23
the world—to **b** witness to the truth. Jn 18:37
all the prophets **b** witness that Acts 10:43
fathers nor we have been able to **b**? Acts 15:10
council of elders can **b** me witness. Acts 22:5
Law and the Prophets **b** witness to it— Rom 3:21
in order that we may **b** fruit for God. Rom 7:4
in our members to **b** fruit for death. Rom 7:5
I **b** them witness that they have a zeal Rom 10:2
for he does not **b** the sword in vain. Rom 13:4
an obligation to **b** with the failings Rom 15:1
we shall also **b** the image of the man 1 Cor 15:49
I wish you would **b** with me in a little 2 Cor 11:1
in a little foolishness. Do **b** with me! 2 Cor 11:1
For you gladly **b** with fools, being 2 Cor 11:19
For you **b** it if someone makes 2 Cor 11:20
"Rejoice, O barren one who does not **b**; Gal 4:27
who is troubling you will **b** the penalty, Gal 5:10
B one another's burdens, and so fulfill Gal 6:2
For each will have to **b** his own load. Gal 6:5
for I **b** on my body the marks of Jesus. Gal 6:17
For I **b** him witness that he has worked Col 4:13
when we could **b** it no longer, 1 Thes 3:1
reason, when I could **b** it no longer, 1 Thes 3:5
younger widows marry, **b** children, 1 Tm 5:14
been offered once to **b** the sins of many, Heb 9:28
the camp and **b** the reproach he Heb 13:13
b with my word of exhortation, Heb 13:22
Can a fig tree, my brothers, **b** olives, or a Jas 3:12
and how you cannot **b** with those who are Rv 2:2

BEAR'S (1)
its feet were like a **b**, and its mouth was Rv 13:2

BEARABLE (4)
it will be more **b** on the day of Mt 10:15
it will be more **b** on the day of Mt 11:22
it will be more **b** on that day for Sodom Lk 10:12
it will be more **b** in the judgment for Lk 10:14

BEARD (17)
has a disease on the head or the **b**, Lv 13:29
a leprous disease of the head or the **b**. Lv 13:30
off all his hair from his head, his **b**, Lv 14:9
temples or mar the edges of your **b**. Lv 19:27
him by his **b** and struck him 1 Sm 17:35
and let his spittle run down his **b**. 1 Sm 21:13
shaved off half the **b** of each and cut 2 Sm 10:4
nor trimmed his **b** nor washed his 2 Sm 19:24
took Amasa by the **b** with his right 2 Sm 20:9
from my head and **b** and sat appalled. Ezr 9:3
oil on the head, running down on the **b**, Ps 133:2
down on the beard, on the **b** of Aaron, Ps 133:2
the feet, and it will sweep away the **b** also. Is 7:20
every head is baldness; every **b** is shorn; Is 15:2
my cheeks to those who pull out the **b**; Is 50:6
head is shaved and every **b** cut off. Jer 48:37
and pass it over your head and your **b**. Ezk 5:1

BEARDED (2)
the eagle, the **b** vulture, the black Lv 11:13
the eagle, the **b** vulture, the black Dt 14:12

BEARDS (4)
heads, nor shave off the edges of their **b**, Lv 21:5
Jericho until your **b** have grown and 2 Sm 10:5
Jericho until your **b** have grown and 1 Chr 19:5
with their **b** shaved and their clothes Jer 41:5

BEARERS (1)
touched the bier, and the **b** stood still. Lk 7:14

BEARING (40)
and fruit trees **b** fruit in which is their Gn 1:11
and trees **b** fruit in which is their seed, Gn 1:12
LORD has prevented me from **b** children. Gn 16:2
his name Judah. Then she ceased **b**. Gn 29:35
saw that she had ceased **b** children, Gn 30:9
from Gilead, with their camels **b** gum, Gn 37:25
Gershonites, in serving and **b** burdens: Nm 4:24
and the service of **b** burdens in the tent Nm 4:47
you a root **b** poisonous and bitter Dt 29:18
catching them, **b** them on its pinions, Dt 32:11
the feet of the priests **b** the ark of the Jos 3:13
Jordan with the priests **b** the ark of the Jos 3:14
and as soon as those **b** the ark had come Jos 3:15
feet of the priests **b** the ark were dipped Jos 3:15
Now the priests **b** the ark of the Jos 3:17
the feet of the priests **b** the ark of the Jos 4:9
For the priests **b** the ark stood in the Jos 4:10
"Command the priests **b** the ark of the Jos 4:16
And when the priests **b** the ark of the Jos 4:18
the seven priests **b** the seven trumpets of Jos 6:8
the seven priests **b** the seven trumpets Jos 6:13
b the ark of the covenant of God. 2 Sm 15:24
b two hundred loaves of bread, 2 Sm 16:1
with camels **b** spices and very much 1 Kgs 10:2
men of Judah **b** shield and spear 1 Chr 12:24
retinue and camels **b** spices and very 2 Chr 9:1
goes out weeping, **b** the seed for sowing, Ps 126:6
suffering no mishap or failure in **b**; Ps 144:14
a burden to me; I am weary of **b** them. Is 1:14
made cakes for her **b** her image and Jer 44:19
him, "You are **b** witness about yourself; Jn 8:13
and he went out, **b** his own cross, to the Jn 19:17
disciple who is **b** witness about these Jn 21:24
Mount Sinai, **b** children for slavery; Gal 4:24
patience, **b** with one another in love, Eph 4:2
whole world it is **b** fruit and growing— Col 1:6
b fruit in every good work and Col 1:10
b with one another and, if one has a Col 3:13
firm foundation stands, **b** this seal: 2 Tm 2:19
are enduring patiently and **b** up for my Rv 2:3

BEARS (32)
is a doe let loose that **b** beautiful fawns. Gn 49:21
a wife and she **b** him sons or daughters, Ex 21:4
a woman conceives and **b** a male child, Lv 12:2
But if she **b** a female child, then she Lv 12:5
This is the law for her who **b** a child, Lv 12:7
first son whom she **b** shall succeed to the Dt 25:6
her feet and her children whom she **b**, Dt 28:57
has struck down both lions and **b**, 1 Sm 17:36
Blessed be the Lord, who daily **b** us up; Ps 68:19
but the root of the righteous **b** fruit. Prv 12:12
A man who **b** false witness against his Prv 25:18
look on their faces **b** witness against them; Is 3:9
We all growl like **b**; we moan and moan Is 59:11
wilderness are green; the tree **b** its fruit; Jl 2:22
So, every healthy tree **b** good fruit, but Mt 7:17
fruit, but the diseased tree **b** bad fruit. Mt 7:17
He indeed **b** fruit and yields, in one case Mt 13:23
"For no good tree **b** bad fruit, nor again Lk 6:43
He **b** witness to what he has seen and Jn 3:32
is another who **b** witness about me, Jn 5:32
the testimony that he **b** about me is true. Jn 5:32
I am the one who **b** witness about myself, Jn 8:18
Father who sent me **b** witness about me." Jn 8:18
alone; but if it dies, it **b** much fruit. Jn 12:24
and I in him, he it is that **b** much fruit, Jn 15:5
while their conscience also **b** witness, Rom 2:15
The Spirit himself **b** witness with our Rom 8:16
my conscience **b** me witness in the Rom 9:1
with anyone who **b** the name of 1 Cor 5:11
Love **b** all things, believes all things, 1 Cor 13:7
But if it **b** thorns and thistles, it is Heb 6:8
the Holy Spirit also **b** witness to us; Heb 10:15

BEAST (124)
And to every **b** of the earth and to every Gn 1:30
LORD God formed every **b** of the field and Gn 2:19
of the heavens and to every **b** of the field. Gn 2:20
crafty than any other **b** of the field that Gn 3:1
they and every **b**, according to its kind, Gn 7:14
Every **b**, every creeping thing, and every Gn 8:19
shall be upon every **b** of the earth and Gn 9:2
from every **b** I will require it and from Gn 9:5
and every **b** of the earth with you, Gn 9:10
of the ark; it is for every **b** of the earth. Gn 9:10
and there were gnats on man and **b**. Ex 8:17
not. So there were gnats on man and **b**. Ex 8:18
sores on man and **b** throughout all the Ex 9:9
breaking out in sores on man and **b**. Ex 9:10
for every man and **b** that is in the field Ex 9:19
on man and **b** and every plant of the Ex 9:22
in all the land of Egypt, both man and **b**. Ex 9:25
of the people of Israel, either man or **b**, Ex 11:7
in the land of Egypt, both man and **b**; Ex 12:12
people of Israel, both of man and of **b**, Ex 13:2
whether **b** or man, he shall not live.' Ex 19:13
to its owner, and the dead **b** shall be his. Ex 21:34
and the dead **b** also they shall share. Ex 21:35
ox for ox, and the dead **b** shall be his. Ex 21:36
If the stolen **b** is found alive in his Ex 22:4
or lets his **b** loose and it feeds in another Ex 22:5
an ox or a sheep or any **b** to keep safe, Ex 22:10
or an unclean **b** or any unclean Lv 7:21
is the law about **b** and bird and every Lv 11:46
takes in hunting any **b** or bird that Lv 17:13
separate the clean **b** from the unclean, Lv 20:25
yourselves detestable by **b** or by bird Lv 20:25
that he has, whether man or **b**, Lv 27:28
in Israel, both of man and of **b**. Nm 3:13
Israel are mine, both of man and of **b**. Nm 8:17
womb of all flesh, whether man or **b**, Nm 18:15
all the plunder, both of man and of **b**. Nm 31:11

that was taken, both of man and of **b**, Nm 31:26
and a wild **b** of Lebanon passed by 2 Kgs 14:9
and a wild **b** of Lebanon passed by 2 Chr 25:18
and that the wild **b** may trample them. Jb 39:15
like the great deep; man and **b** you save, Ps 36:6
For every **b** of the forest is mine, the Ps 50:10
and ignorant; I was like a **b** toward you. Ps 73:22
they give drink to every **b** of the field; Ps 104:11
of Egypt, both of man and of **b**; Ps 135:8
has regard for the life of his **b**, Prv 12:10
the spirit of the **b** goes down into the Eccl 3:21
nor shall any ravenous **b** come up on it; Is 35:9
out on this place, upon man and **b**, Jer 7:20
of this city, both man and **b**. Jer 21:6
with the seed of man and the seed of **b**. Jer 31:27
'It is a desolation, without man or **b**; Jer 32:43
say, 'It is a waste without man or **b**,' Jer 33:10
without man or inhabitant or **b**, Jer 33:10
place that is waste, without man or **b**, Jer 33:12
and will cut off from it man and **b**?" Jer 36:29
in it; both man and **b** shall flee away. Jer 50:3
shall dwell in it, neither man nor **b**, Jer 51:62
it, and cut off from it man and **b**, Ezk 14:13
land, and I cut off from it man and **b**, Ezk 14:17
blood, to cut off from it man and **b**, Ezk 14:19
to cut off from it man and **b**! Ezk 14:21
Edom and cut off from it man and **b**. Ezk 25:13
and will cut off from you man and **b**, Ezk 29:8
and no foot of **b** shall pass through it; Ezk 29:11
I will multiply on you man and **b**, Ezk 36:11
not eat of anything, whether bird or **b**, Ezk 44:31
and his mind was made like that of a **b**, Dn 5:21
And behold, another **b**, a second one, like Dn 7:5
And the **b** had four heads, and dominion Dn 7:6
the night visions, and behold, a fourth **b**, Dn 7:7
And as I looked, the **b** was killed, and its Dn 7:11
to know the truth about the fourth **b**, Dn 7:19
'As for the fourth **b**, there shall be a Dn 7:23
No **b** could stand before him, and there Dn 8:4
a lion, as a wild **b** would rip them open. Hos 13:8
Let neither man nor **b**, herd nor flock, Jon 3:7
but let man and **b** be covered with Jon 3:8
"I will sweep away man and **b**; I will Zep 1:3
the ground brings forth, on man and **b**, Hg 1:11
was no wage for man or any wage for **b**, Zec 8:10
and on a colt, the foal of a **b** of burden.'" Mt 21:5
"If even a **b** touches the mountain, Heb 12:20
For every kind of **b** and bird, of reptile Jas 3:7
the **b** that rises from the bottomless pit Rv 11:7
And I saw a **b** rising out of the sea, with Rv 13:1
And the **b** that I saw was like a leopard; Rv 13:2
earth marveled as they followed the **b**. Rv 13:3
for he had given his authority to the **b**, Rv 13:4
to the beast, and they worshiped the **b**, Rv 13:4
the beast, saying, "Who is like the **b**, Rv 13:4
And the **b** was given a mouth uttering Rv 13:5
Then I saw another **b** rising out of the Rv 13:11
authority of the first **b** in its presence, Rv 13:12
and its inhabitants worship the first **b**, Rv 13:12
the presence of the **b** it deceives those Rv 13:14
an image for the **b** that was wounded Rv 13:14
to give breath to the image of the **b**, Rv 13:15
the image of the **b** might even speak Rv 13:15
worship the image of the **b** to be slain. Rv 13:15
the name of the **b** or the number of its Rv 13:17
calculate the number of the **b**, Rv 13:18
"If anyone worships the **b** and its image Rv 14:9
these worshipers of the **b** and its image, Rv 14:11
who had conquered the **b** and its image Rv 15:2
the mark of the **b** and worshiped its Rv 16:2
out his bowl on the throne of the **b**, Rv 16:10
of the mouth of the **b** and out of the Rv 16:13
sitting on a scarlet **b** that was full of Rv 17:3
and of the **b** with seven heads and ten Rv 17:7
The **b** that you saw was, and is not, and Rv 17:8
of the world will marvel to see the **b**, Rv 17:8
As for the **b** that was and is not, it is an Rv 17:11
kings for one hour, together with the **b**. Rv 17:12
over their power and authority to the **b**. Rv 17:13
they and the **b** will hate the prostitute. Rv 17:16
handing over their royal power to the **b**, Rv 17:17
for every unclean and detestable **b**. Rv 18:2
And I saw the **b** and the kings of the Rv 19:19
And the **b** was captured, and with it the Rv 19:20
the mark of the **b** and those who Rv 19:20
had not worshiped the **b** or its image and Rv 20:4
and sulfur where the **b** and the false Rv 20:10

BEAST'S (1)
man's, and let a **b** mind be given to him; Dn 4:16

BEASTS (123)
and creeping things and **b** of the earth Gn 1:24
And God made the **b** of the earth Gn 1:25
all livestock and above all **b** of the field; Gn 3:14
b, all swarming creatures that swarm Gn 7:21
Noah and all the **b** and all the livestock Gn 8:1
was torn by wild **b** I did not bring Gn 31:39
their property and all their **b** be ours? Gn 34:23
of his household, his livestock, all his **b**, Gn 36:6
load your **b** and go back to the land of Gn 45:17
If it is torn by **b**, let him bring it as Ex 22:13
any flesh that is torn by **b** in the field; Ex 22:31
what they leave the **b** of the field may Ex 23:11
and the wild **b** multiply against you. Ex 23:29
one that is torn by **b** may be put to any Lv 7:24
what dies of itself or what is torn by **b**, Lv 17:15
not eat what dies of itself or is torn by **b**, Lv 22:8
I will remove harmful **b** from the land, Lv 26:6
I will let loose the wild **b** against you, Lv 26:22
of every 50, both of persons and of **b**, Nm 31:47
for their livestock and for all their **b**. Nm 35:3
lest the wild **b** grow too numerous for Dt 7:22
of the air and for the **b** of the earth, Dt 28:26
I will send the teeth of **b** against them, Dt 32:24
men and **b** and all that they found. Jgs 20:48
of the air and to the **b** of the field." 1 Sm 17:44
the air and to the wild **b** of the earth, 1 Sm 17:46
by day, or the **b** of the field by night. 2 Sm 21:10
He spoke also of **b**, and of birds, and 1 Kgs 4:33
silver and gold, with goods and with **b**, Ezr 1:4
of silver, with gold, with goods, with **b**, Ezr 1:6
and shall not fear the **b** of the earth. Jb 5:22
and the **b** of the field shall be at peace Jb 5:23
"But ask the **b**, and they will teach you; Jb 12:7
The proud **b** have not trodden it; the lion Jb 28:8
us more than the **b** of the earth and Jb 35:11
Then the **b** go into their lairs, and Jb 37:8
food for him where all the wild **b** play. Jb 40:20
sheep and oxen, and also the **b** of the field, Ps 8:7
not remain; he is like the **b** that perish. Ps 49:12
understanding is like the **b** that perish. Ps 49:20
I lie down amid fiery **b**—the children of Ps 57:4
Rebuke the **b** that dwell among the Ps 68:30
the soul of your dove to the wild **b**; Ps 74:19
flesh of your faithful to the **b** of the earth. Ps 79:2
when all the **b** of the forest creep Ps 104:20
He gives to the **b** their food, and to the Ps 147:9
B and all livestock, creeping things Ps 148:10
She has slaughtered her **b**; she has mixed Prv 9:2
is mightiest among **b** and does not Prv 30:30
see that they themselves are but **b**. Eccl 3:18
and what happens to the **b** is the same; Eccl 3:19
and man has no advantage over the **b**, Eccl 3:19
offerings of rams and the fat of well-fed **b**; Is 1:11
the mountains and to the **b** of the earth. Is 18:6
and all the **b** of the earth will winter on Is 18:6
was not; Assyria destined it for wild **b**. Is 23:13
An oracle on the **b** of the Negeb. Is 30:6
nor are its **b** enough for a burnt Is 40:16
The wild **b** will honor me, the jackals Is 43:20
stoops; their idols are on **b** and livestock; Is 46:1
carry are borne as burdens on weary **b**. Is 46:1
All you **b** of the field, come to devour— Is 56:9
come to devour—all you **b** in the forest. Is 56:9
birds of the air, and for the **b** of the earth, Jer 7:33
of the air and the **b** have fled and are Jer 9:10
who dwell in it the **b** and the birds are Jer 12:4
Go, assemble all the wild **b**; bring them Jer 12:9
of the air and the **b** of the earth to devour Jer 15:3
birds of the air and for the **b** of the earth. Jer 16:4
birds of the air and to the **b** of the earth. Jer 19:7
have given him also the **b** of the field to Jer 27:6
given to him even the **b** of the field.'" Jer 28:14
birds of the air and the **b** of the earth. Jer 34:20
"Therefore wild **b** shall dwell with Jer 50:39
what died of itself or was torn by **b**, Ezk 4:14
send famine and wild **b** against you, Ezk 5:17
of creeping things and loathsome **b**, Ezk 8:10
"If I cause wild **b** to pass through the Ezk 14:15
may pass through because of the **b**, Ezk 14:15
of judgment, sword, famine, wild **b**, Ezk 14:21
To the **b** of the earth and to the birds of Ezk 29:5
its branches all the **b** of the field gave Ezk 31:6
its branches are all the **b** of the field. Ezk 31:13
and I will gorge the **b** of the whole earth Ezk 32:4
will destroy all its **b** from beside many Ezk 32:13
nor shall the hoofs of **b** trouble them. Ezk 32:13
field I will give to the **b** to be devoured, Ezk 33:27
and they became food for all the wild **b**. Ezk 34:5
have become food for all the wild **b**, Ezk 34:8
and banish wild **b** from the land, Ezk 34:25
nor shall the **b** of the land devour Ezk 34:28
the heavens and the **b** of the field and Ezk 38:20
every sort and to the **b** of the field to be Ezk 39:4
of every sort and to all **b** of the field, Ezk 39:17
of bulls, all of them fat **b** of Bashan. Ezk 39:18
the children of man, the **b** of the field, Dn 2:38
The **b** of the field found shade under it, Dn 4:12
Let the **b** flee from under it and the birds Dn 4:14
his portion be with the **b** in the grass of Dn 4:15
under which **b** of the field found shade, Dn 4:21
let his portion be with the **b** of the field, Dn 4:23
dwelling shall be with the **b** of the field. Dn 4:25
dwelling shall be with the **b** of the field. Dn 4:32
And four great **b** came up out of the sea, Dn 7:3
different from all the **b** that were before it, Dn 7:7
As for the rest of the **b**, their dominion Dn 7:12
'These four great **b** are four kings who Dn 7:17
and the **b** of the field shall devour them. Hos 2:12
on that day with the **b** of the field, Hos 2:18
and also the **b** of the field and the birds Hos 4:3
How the **b** groan! The herds of cattle are Jl 1:18
Even the **b** of the field pant for you Jl 1:20
Fear not, you **b** of the field, for the Jl 2:22
like a lion among the **b** of the forest, Mi 5:8
destruction of the **b** that terrified them, Hab 2:17
lie down in her midst, all kinds of **b**; Zep 2:14
she has become, a lair for wild **b**! Zep 2:15
and whatever **b** may be in those Zec 14:15
you bring to me slain **b** and sacrifices, Acts 7:42
I observed animals and **b** of prey and Acts 11:6
I fought with **b** at Ephesus? 1 Cor 15:32
said, "Cretans are always liars, evil **b**, Ti 1:12
with pestilence and by wild **b** of the earth. Rv 6:8

BEAT (40)
You shall **b** some of it very small, and Ex 30:36
it in handmills or **b** it in mortars and Nm 11:8
you as bees do and **b** you down in Seir as Dt 1:44
When you **b** your olive trees, you shall Dt 24:20
should go on to **b** him with more stripes Dt 25:3
"Then loud **b** the horses' hoofs with the Jgs 5:22
Then she **b** out what she had gleaned, Ru 2:17
I **b** them fine as the dust of the earth; 2 Sm 22:43
the brook Kidron and **b** it to dust and 2 Kgs 23:6
the altars and **b** the Asherim and 2 Chr 34:7
and cursed them and **b** some of them Neh 13:25
I **b** them fine as dust before the wind; I Ps 18:42
say, "but I was not hurt; they **b** me, Prv 23:35
as they went about in the city; they **b** me, Sg 5:7
and they shall **b** their swords into Is 2:4
B your breasts for the pleasant fields, for Is 32:12
you trust they shall **b** down with the Jer 5:17
Then Pashhur **b** Jeremiah the prophet, Jer 20:2
and they **b** him and imprisoned him in Jer 37:15
B your plowshares into swords, and your Jl 3:10
and the sun **b** down on the head of Jonah Jon 4:8
and they shall **b** their swords into Mi 4:3
you shall **b** in pieces many peoples; Mi 4:13
and the winds blew and **b** on that house, Mt 7:25
winds blew and **b** against that house, Mt 7:27
tenants took his servants and **b** one, Mt 21:35
and begins to **b** his fellow servants and Mt 24:49
they took him and **b** him and sent him Mk 12:3
some they **b**, and some they killed. Mk 12:5
stripped him and **b** him and departed, Lk 10:30
and begins to **b** the male and female Lk 12:45
so that she will not **b** me down by her Lk 18:5
up his eyes to heaven, but **b** his breast, Lk 18:13
But the tenants **b** him and sent him Lk 20:10
But they also **b** and treated him Lk 20:11
were mocking him as they **b** him. Lk 22:63
they **b** them and charged them not to Acts 5:40
and gave orders to **b** them with rods. Acts 16:22
and **b** him in front of the tribunal. Acts 18:17
I imprisoned and **b** those who Acts 22:19

BEATEN (30)
set over them, were **b** and were asked, Ex 5:14
And behold, your servants are **b**; but the Ex 5:16
bring to you pure **b** olive oil for the Ex 27:20
mingled with a fourth of a hin of **b** oil, Ex 29:40
two handfuls of sweet incense **b** small, Lv 16:12
you pure oil from **b** olives for the lamp, Lv 24:2
mixed with a quarter of a hin of **b** oil. Nm 28:5
then if the guilty man deserves to be **b**, Dt 25:2
to lie down and be **b** in his presence with Dt 25:2
Israel pretended to be **b** before them and Jos 8:15
of Israel were **b** before the servants 2 Sm 2:17
household, and 20,000 cors of **b** oil. 1 Kgs 5:11
made 200 large shields of **b** gold; 1 Kgs 10:16
And he made 300 shields of **b** gold; 1 Kgs 10:17
made 200 large shields of **b** gold; 2 Chr 9:15
600 shekels of **b** gold went into each 2 Chr 9:15
And he made 300 shields of **b** gold; 2 Chr 9:16
and evening they are **b** to pieces; Jb 4:20
when an olive tree is **b**—two or three Is 17:6
the nations, as when an olive tree is **b**, Is 24:13
through, you will be **b** down by it. Is 28:18
cumin, but dill is **b** out with a stick, Is 28:27
B silver is brought from Tarshish, and Jer 10:9
Their warriors are **b** down and have fled Jer 46:5
All her carved images shall be **b** to pieces, Mi 1:7
way from the land, **b** by the waves, Mt 14:24
and you will be **b** in synagogues, Mk 13:9
to them, "They have **b** us publicly, Acts 16:37

Three times I was **b** with rods. Once 2 Cor 11:25
is it if, when you sin and are **b** for it, 1 Pt 2:20

BEATING (15)
and he saw an Egyptian **b** a Hebrew, Ex 2:11
hand of him who is **b** him and puts out Dt 25:11
his son Gideon was **b** out wheat in the Jgs 6:11
surrounded the house, **b** on the door. Jgs 19:22
into a fight, and his mouth invites a **b**. Prv 18:6
scoffers, and **b** for the backs of fools. Prv 19:29
the poor is a **b** rain that leaves no Prv 28:3
My heart is **b** wildly; I cannot keep Jer 4:19
moaning like doves and **b** their breasts. Na 2:7
to his will, will receive a severe **b**. Lk 12:47
not know, and did what deserved a **b**, Lk 12:48
a beating, will receive a light **b**. Lk 12:48
place, returned home **b** their breasts. Lk 23:48
and the soldiers, they stopped **b** Paul. Acts 21:32
I do not box as one **b** the air. 1 Cor 9:26

BEATINGS (2)
b, imprisonments, riots, labors, 2 Cor 6:5
imprisonments, with countless **b**, 2 Cor 11:23

BEAUTIFUL (76)
that you are a woman **b** in appearance, Gn 12:11
saw that the woman was very **b**. Gn 12:14
but Rachel was **b** in form and Gn 29:17
is a doe let loose that bears **b** fawns. Gn 49:21
you see among the captives a **b** woman, Dt 21:11
among the spoil a **b** cloak from Shinar, Jos 7:21
not her younger sister more **b** than she? Jgs 15:2
was ruddy and had **b** eyes and was 1 Sm 16:12
The woman was discerning and **b**, 1 Sm 25:3
bathing; and the woman was very **b**. 2 Sm 11:2
Absalom, David's son, had a **b** sister, 2 Sm 13:1
was Tamar. She was a **b** woman. 2 Sm 14:27
sought for a **b** young woman 1 Kgs 1:3
The young woman was very **b**, and 1 Kgs 1:4
"Let **b** young virgins be sought out for Est 2:2
to gather all the **b** young virgins to the Est 2:3
young woman had a **b** figure and was Est 2:7
were no women so **b** as Job's daughters. Jb 42:15
places; indeed, I have a **b** inheritance. Ps 16:6
b in elevation, is the joy of all the earth, Ps 48:2
she will bestow on you a **b** crown." Prv 4:9
snout is a **b** woman without Prv 11:22
He has made everything **b** in its time. Eccl 3:11
do not know, O most **b** among women, Sg 1:8
Behold, you are **b**, my love; behold, you Sg 1:15
are beautiful, my love; behold, you are **b**; Sg 1:15
Behold, you are **b**, my beloved, truly Sg 1:16
"Arise, my love, my **b** one, and come Sg 2:10
Arise, my love, my **b** one, and come Sg 2:13
Behold, you are **b**, my love, behold, you Sg 4:1
are beautiful, my love, behold, you are **b**! Sg 4:1
You are altogether **b**, my love; there is no Sg 4:7
How **b** is your love, my sister, my bride! Sg 4:10
beloved, O most **b** among women? Sg 5:9
beloved gone, O most **b** among women? Sg 6:1
You are **b** as Tirzah, my love, lovely as Sg 6:4
down like the dawn, **b** as the moon, Sg 6:10
How **b** are your feet in sandals, O noble Sg 7:1
How **b** and pleasant you are, O loved one, Sg 7:6
of Tarshish, and against all the **b** craft. Is 2:16
of the LORD shall be **b** and glorious, Is 4:2
shall be desolate, large and **b** houses, Is 5:9
put on your **b** garments, O Jerusalem, the Is 52:1
How **b** upon the mountains are the feet of Is 52:7
my altar, and I will beautify my **b** house. Is 60:7
One of Israel, because he has made you **b**. Is 60:9
to give them a **b** headdress instead of Is 61:3
himself like a priest with a **b** headdress, Is 61:10
see, from your holy and **b** habitation. Is 63:15
Our holy and **b** house, where our fathers Is 64:11
land, a heritage most **b** of all nations. Jer 3:19
'a green olive tree, **b** with good fruit.' Jer 11:16
for your **b** crown has come down from Jer 13:18
flock that was given you, your **b** flock? Jer 13:20
"A **b** heifer is Egypt, but a biting fly Jer 46:20
His **b** ornament they used for pride, and Ezk 7:20
your ears and a **b** crown on your Ezk 16:12
You grew exceedingly **b** and advanced Ezk 16:13
You also took your **b** jewels of my Ezk 16:17
and take your **b** jewels and leave Ezk 16:39
clothes and take away your **b** jewels. Ezk 23:26
women, and **b** crowns on their heads. Ezk 23:42
with **b** branches and forest shade, Ezk 31:3
It was **b** in its greatness, in the length of Ezk 31:7
I made it **b** in the mass of its branches, Ezk 31:9
lustful songs with a **b** voice and plays Ezk 33:32
Its leaves were **b** and its fruit abundant, Dn 4:12
whose leaves were **b** and its fruit Dn 4:21
tombs, which outwardly appear **b**, Mt 23:27
For she has done a **b** thing to me. Mt 26:10
her? She has done a **b** thing to me. Mk 14:6
that is called the **B** Gate to ask alms Acts 3:2
one who sat at the **B** Gate of the temple, Acts 3:10
was born; and he was **b** in God's sight. Acts 7:20
"How **b** are the feet of those who Rom 10:15
because they saw that the child was **b**, Heb 11:23

BEAUTIFY (4)
to **b** the house of the LORD that is in Ezr 7:27
my altar, and I will **b** my beautiful house. Is 60:7
the pine, to **b** the place of my sanctuary, Is 60:13
eyes with paint? In vain you **b** yourself. Jer 4:30

BEAUTIFYING (1)
this was the regular period of their **b**, Est 2:12

BEAUTY (37)
Aaron your brother, for glory and for **b**. Ex 28:2
You shall make them for glory and **b**. Ex 28:40
show the peoples and the princes her **b**, Est 1:11
to gaze upon the **b** of the LORD and to Ps 27:4
and the king will desire your **b**. Since Ps 45:11
Out of Zion, the perfection of **b**, God Ps 50:2
strength and **b** are in his sanctuary. Ps 96:6
Do not desire her **b** in your heart, and Prv 6:25
Charm is deceitful, and **b** is vain, but Prv 31:30
of sackcloth; and branding instead of **b**. Is 3:24
and the fading flower of its glorious **b**, Is 28:1
and the fading flower of its glorious **b**, Is 28:4
be a crown of glory, and a diadem of **b**, Is 28:5
Your eyes will behold the king in his **b**; Is 33:17
and all its **b** is like the flower of the field. Is 40:6
the figure of a man, with the **b** of a man, Is 44:13
him, and no **b** that we should desire him. Is 53:2
shall be a crown of **b** in the hand of the Is 62:3
city that was called the perfection of **b**, Lam 2:15
the **b** of their form was like sapphire. Lam 4:7
among the nations because of your **b**, Ezk 16:14
you trusted in your **b** and played the Ezk 16:15
on any passerby; your **b** became his. Ezk 16:15
and made your **b** an abomination, Ezk 16:25
but I will set **b** in the land of the Ezk 26:20
Tyre, you have said, 'I am perfect in **b**.' Ezk 27:3
your builders made perfect your **b**. Ezk 27:4
all around; they made perfect your **b**. Ezk 27:11
swords against the **b** of your wisdom Ezk 28:7
full of wisdom and perfect in **b**. Ezk 28:12
heart was proud because of your **b**; Ezk 28:17
in the garden of God was its equal in **b**. Ezk 31:8
'Whom do you surpass in **b**? Go down Ezk 32:19
his **b** shall be like the olive, and his Hos 14:6
is his goodness, and how great his **b**! Zec 9:17
grass; its flower falls, and its **b** perishes. Jas 1:11
heart with the imperishable **b** of a gentle 1 Pt 3:4

BEBAI (6)
The sons of **B**, 623. Ezr 2:11
Of the sons of **B**, Zechariah, the son of Ezr 8:11
sons of Bebai, Zechariah, the son of **B**, Ezr 8:11
Of the sons of **B** were Jehohanan, Ezr 10:28
The sons of **B**, 628. Neh 7:16
Bunni, Azgad, **B**, Neh 10:15

BECAME (229)
of life, and the man **b** a living creature. Gn 2:7
and there it divided and **b** four rivers. Gn 2:10
of the wine and **b** drunk and lay Gn 9:21
looked back, and she **b** a pillar of salt. Gn 19:26
daughters of Lot **b** pregnant by their Gn 19:36
of my mother, and she **b** my wife. Gn 20:12
in the wilderness and **b** an expert with Gn 21:20
and took Rebekah, and she **b** his wife, Gn 24:67
and the man **b** rich, and gained more Gn 26:13
and more until he **b** very wealthy. Gn 26:13
Then Jacob **b** angry and berated Gn 31:36
with Joseph, and he **b** a successful man, Gn 39:2
For your servant **b** a pledge of safety Gn 44:32
land of Egypt." And his heart **b** numb, Gn 45:26
severe on them. The land **b** Pharaoh's. Gn 47:20
to bear, and **b** a servant at forced labor. Gn 49:15
to Pharaoh's daughter, and he **b** her son. Ex 2:10
threw it on the ground, and it **b** a serpent, Ex 4:3
caught it, and it **b** a staff in his hand— Ex 4:4
and his servants, and it **b** a serpent. Ex 7:10
cast down his staff, and they **b** serpents. Ex 7:12
the dust of the earth **b** gnats in all the Ex 8:17
and it **b** boils breaking out in sores on Ex 9:10
all the land of Egypt since it **b** a nation. Ex 9:24
it into the water, and the water **b** sweet. Ex 15:25
and the land **b** unclean, so that I Lv 18:25
so that the land **b** unclean), Lv 18:27
them before the LORD, and they **b** holy. Nm 16:38
And the people **b** impatient on the way. Nm 21:4
250 men, and they **b** a warning. Nm 26:10
few in number, and there he **b** a nation, Dt 26:5
Thus the LORD **b** king in Jeshurun, when Dt 33:5
hearts of the people melted and **b** as water. Jos 7:5
them live." So they **b** cutters of wood and Jos 9:21
Therefore Hebron **b** the inheritance of Jos 14:14
It **b** an inheritance of the descendants Jos 24:32
them, but **b** subject to forced labor. Jgs 1:30
and of Beth-anath **b** subject to forced Jgs 1:33
them, and they **b** subject to forced labor. Jgs 1:35
and it **b** a snare to Gideon and to his Jgs 8:27
and he **b** impatient over the misery of Jgs 10:16
a man, and it **b** a custom in Israel Jgs 11:39
that were on his arms **b** as flax that has Jgs 15:14
one of his sons, who **b** his priest. Jgs 17:5
and the young man **b** to him like one Jgs 17:11
Levite, and the young man **b** his priest, Jgs 17:12
So Boaz took Ruth, and she **b** his wife. Ru 4:13
and laid him on her lap and **b** his nurse. Ru 4:16
When Samuel **b** old, he made his sons 1 Sm 8:1
father?" Therefore it **b** a proverb, 1 Sm 10:12
quaked, and it **b** a very great panic. 1 Sm 14:15
to his mouth, and his eyes **b** bright. 1 Sm 14:27
greatly, and he **b** his armor-bearer. 1 Sm 16:21
to him. And he **b** captain over them. 1 Sm 22:2
died within him, and he **b** as a stone. 1 Sm 25:37
messengers of David and **b** his wife. 1 Sm 25:42
Jezreel, and both of them **b** his wives. 1 Sm 25:43
behind Abner and **b** one group and 2 Sm 2:25
the house of Saul **b** weaker and weaker. 2 Sm 3:1
she fled in her haste, he fell and **b** lame. 2 Sm 4:4
And David **b** greater and greater, for 2 Sm 5:10
forever. And you, O LORD, **b** their God. 2 Sm 7:24
And the Moabites **b** servants to David 2 Sm 8:2
and the Syrians **b** servants to David 2 Sm 8:6
all the Edomites **b** David's servants. 2 Sm 8:14
Ziba's house **b** Mephibosheth's 2 Sm 9:12
with Israel and **b** subject to them. 2 Sm 10:19
and she **b** his wife and bore him a 2 Sm 11:27
wife bore to David, and he **b** sick. 2 Sm 12:15
of the thirty and **b** their commander, 2 Sm 23:19
men about him and **b** leader of a 1 Kgs 11:24
Then this thing **b** a sin, for the 1 Kgs 12:30
restored to him and **b** as it was before. 1 Kgs 13:6
And this thing **b** sin to the house of 1 Kgs 13:34
So Tibni died, and Omri **b** king. 1 Kgs 16:22
the mistress of the house, **b** ill. 1 Kgs 17:17
Jehoram **b** king in his place in the 2 Kgs 1:17
the son of Ahab **b** king over Israel in 2 Kgs 3:1
him, the flesh of the child **b** warm. 2 Kgs 4:34
died. And Hazael **b** king in his place. 2 Kgs 8:15
thirty-two years old when he **b** king, 2 Kgs 8:17
Ben-hadad his son **b** king in his 2 Kgs 13:24
And Hoshea **b** his vassal and paid 2 Kgs 17:3
went after false idols and **b** false, 2 Kgs 17:15
those days Hezekiah **b** sick and was 2 Kgs 20:1
and Jehoiakim **b** his servant three 2 Kgs 24:1
eighteen years old when he **b** king, 2 Kgs 24:8
years old when he **b** king, 2 Kgs 24:18
though Judah **b** strong among his 1 Chr 5:2
Zeruiah went up first, so he **b** chief. 1 Chr 11:6
And David **b** greater and greater, for 1 Chr 11:9
the thirty and **b** their commander, 1 Chr 11:21
and you, O LORD, **b** their God. 1 Chr 17:22
and the Moabites **b** servants to David 1 Chr 18:2
and the Syrians **b** servants to David 1 Chr 18:6
all the Edomites **b** David's servants. 1 Chr 18:13
with David and **b** subject to him. 1 Chr 19:19
therefore they **b** counted as a single 1 Chr 23:11
so Eleazar and Ithamar **b** the priests. 1 Chr 24:2
in his feet, and his disease **b** severe. 2 Chr 16:12
thirty-two years old when he **b** king, 2 Chr 21:5
And they **b** very angry with Judah 2 Chr 25:10
border of Egypt, for he **b** very strong. 2 Chr 26:8
and when he **b** angry with the 2 Chr 26:19
So Jotham **b** mighty, because he 2 Chr 27:6
his distress he **b** yet more faithless 2 Chr 28:22
those days Hezekiah **b** sick and was 2 Chr 32:24
was eight years old when he **b** king, 2 Chr 36:9
and they **b** servants to him and to 2 Chr 36:20
and were filled and **b** fat and delighted Neh 9:25
At this the king **b** enraged, and his Est 1:12
b angry and sought to lay hands on Est 2:21
My heart **b** hot within me. As I mused, Ps 39:3
my soul with fasting, it **b** my reproach. Ps 69:10
my clothing, I **b** a byword to them. Ps 69:11
at En-dor, who **b** dung for the ground. Ps 83:10
He rebuked the Red Sea, and it **b** dry, Ps 106:9
their idols, which **b** a snare to them. Ps 106:36
Thus they **b** unclean by their acts, Ps 106:39
Judah **b** his sanctuary, Israel his Ps 114:2
So I **b** great and surpassed all who were Eccl 2:9
In those days Hezekiah **b** sick and was at Is 38:1
not deal falsely." And he **b** their Savior. Is 63:8
after worthlessness, and **b** worthless? Jer 2:5
and your words **b** to me a joy and the Jer 15:16
and they **b** a waste and a desolation, Jer 44:6
twenty-one years old when he **b** king; Jer 52:1
of Babylon, in the year that he **b** king, Jer 52:31
grievously; therefore she **b** filthy; Lam 1:8
they **b** their food during the Lam 4:10
touch!" So they **b** fugitives and Lam 4:15

you grew up and **b** tall and arrived at Ezk 16:7
declares the Lord GOD, and you **b** mine. Ezk 16:8
on any passerby; your beauty **b** his. Ezk 16:15
and it sprouted and **b** a low spreading Ezk 17:6
So it **b** a vine and produced branches Ezk 17:6
he **b** a young lion, and he learned to Ezk 19:3
he **b** a young lion, and he learned to Ezk 19:6
Its strong stems **b** rulers' scepters; it Ezk 19:11
the name of her sister. They **b** mine, Ezk 23:4
and she **b** a byword among women, Ezk 23:10
and she **b** more corrupt than her Ezk 23:11
and they **b** food for all the wild beasts. Ezk 34:5
so that you **b** the possession of the rest Ezk 36:3
and you **b** the talk and evil gossip of the Ezk 36:3
And it **b** broader as it wound upward to Ezk 41:7
their idols and **b** a stumbling block Ezk 44:12
and **b** like the chaff of the summer Dn 2:35
struck the image **b** a great mountain Dn 2:35
The tree grew and **b** strong, and its top Dn 4:11
tree you saw, which grew and **b** strong, Dn 4:20
Then this Daniel **b** distinguished above Dn 6:3
power. He did as he pleased and **b** great. Dn 8:4
Then the goat **b** exceedingly great, but Dn 8:8
It **b** great, even as great as the Prince of Dn 8:11
the princes **b** sick with the heat of wine; Hos 7:5
and **b** detestable like the thing they Hos 9:10
and I **b** to them as one who eases the Hos 11:4
but when they had grazed, they **b** full, Hos 13:6
Then the LORD **b** jealous for his land and Jl 2:18
Yet she **b** an exile; she went into Na 3:10
So I **b** the shepherd of the flock doomed Zec 11:7
But I **b** impatient with them, and they Zec 11:8
been tricked by the wise men, **b** furious, Mt 2:16
the sun, and his clothes **b** white as light. Mt 17:2
was returning to the city, he **b** hungry. Mt 21:18
was delayed, they all **b** drowsy and slept. Mt 25:5
guards trembled and **b** like dead men. Mt 28:4
and his clothes **b** radiant, intensely Mk 9:3
the child grew and **b** strong in spirit, Lk 1:80
And the child grew and **b** strong, filled Lk 2:40
and Judas Iscariot, who **b** a traitor. Lk 6:16
and his clothing **b** dazzling white. Lk 9:29
but when they **b** fully awake they saw Lk 9:32
For as Jonah **b** a sign to the people of Lk 11:30
in his garden, and it grew and **b** a tree, Lk 13:19
master of the house **b** angry and said to Lk 14:21
he heard these things, he **b** very sad, Lk 18:23
marveling at his answer they **b** silent. Lk 20:26
and his sweat **b** like great drops of Lk 22:44
Herod and Pilate **b** friends with each Lk 23:12
And the Word **b** flesh and dwelt among Jn 1:14
The sea **b** rough because a strong wind Jn 6:18
who **b** a guide to those who arrested Acts 1:16
And it **b** known to all the inhabitants Acts 1:19
many of the priests **b** obedient to the Acts 6:7
And so Abraham **b** the father of Isaac, Acts 7:8
day, and Isaac **b** the father of Jacob, Acts 7:8
and Joseph's family **b** known to Acts 7:13
retort Moses fled and **b** an exile in the Acts 7:29
where he **b** the father of two sons. Acts 7:29
but their plot **b** known to Saul. They Acts 9:24
In those days she **b** ill and died, and Acts 9:37
And it **b** known throughout all Joppa, Acts 9:42
And he **b** hungry and wanted Acts 10:10
But when some **b** stubborn and Acts 19:9
And this **b** known to all the residents Acts 19:17
language, they **b** even more quiet. Acts 22:2
And when the dissension **b** violent, Acts 23:10
but they **b** futile in their thinking, Rom 1:21
Claiming to be wise, they **b** fools, Rom 1:22
I tell you that Christ **b** a servant to the Rom 15:8
For I **b** your father in Christ Jesus 1 Cor 4:15
To the Jews I **b** as a Jew, in order to 1 Cor 9:20
under the law I **b** as one under the 1 Cor 9:20
outside the law I **b** as one outside the 1 Cor 9:21
To the weak I **b** weak, that I might 1 Cor 9:22
like a child. When I **b** a man, 1 Cor 13:11
first man Adam **b** a living being"; 1 Cor 15:45
the last Adam **b** a life-giving spirit. 1 Cor 15:45
was rich, yet for your sake he **b** poor, 2 Cor 8:9
and of which I, Paul, **b** a minister. Col 1:23
of which I **b** a minister according to the Col 1:25
And you **b** imitators of us and of the 1 Thes 1:6
so that you **b** an example to all the 1 Thes 1:7
b imitators of the churches of God 1 Thes 2:14
was deceived and **b** a transgressor. 1 Tm 2:14
whose father I **b** in my Phlm 1:10
he **b** the source of eternal salvation to all Heb 5:9
those who formerly **b** priests were Heb 7:20
condemned the world and **b** an heir of Heb 11:7
out of weakness, **b** mighty in war, Heb 11:34
and the sun **b** black as sackcloth, Rv 6:12
as sackcloth, the full moon **b** like blood, Rv 6:12
into the sea, and a third of the sea **b** blood. Rv 8:8
A third of the waters **b** wormwood, and Rv 8:11
Then the dragon **b** furious with the Rv 12:17
sea, and it **b** like the blood of a corpse, Rv 16:3
the springs of water, and they **b** blood. Rv 16:4

BECHER (5)
Bela, **B**, Ashbel, Gera, Naaman, Ehi, Gn 46:21
the clan of the Shuthelahites; of **B**, Nm 26:35
of Benjamin: Bela, **B**, and Jediael, three. 1 Chr 7:6
The sons of **B**: Zemirah, Joash, Eliezer, 1 Chr 7:8
Alemeth. All these were the sons of **B**. 1 Chr 7:8

BECHERITES (1)
of Becher, the clan of the **B**; Nm 26:35

BECOME (337)
to his wife, and they shall **b** one flesh. Gn 2:24
the man has **b** like one of us in Gn 3:22
waters shall never again **b** a flood to Gn 9:15
will bless her, and she shall **b** nations; Gn 17:16
Abraham shall surely **b** a great and Gn 18:18
to sojourn, and he has **b** the judge! Gn 19:9
against its people has **b** great before the Gn 19:13
blessed my master, and he has **b** great. Gn 24:35
may you **b** thousands of ten Gn 24:60
that you may **b** a company of peoples. Gn 28:3
Jordan, and now I have **b** two camps. Gn 32:10
you—that you will **b** as we are by Gn 34:15
will dwell with you and **b** one people. Gn 34:16
to dwell with us to **b** one people—when Gn 34:22
we will see what will **b** of his dreams." Gn 37:20
the priests alone did not **b** Pharaoh's. Gn 47:26
He also shall **b** a people, and he also Gn 48:19
his offspring shall **b** a multitude of Gn 48:19
he shall **b** a haven for ships, and his Gn 49:13
take from the Nile will **b** blood on the dry Ex 4:9
before Pharaoh, that it may **b** a serpent.'" Ex 7:9
pools of water, so that they may **b** blood, Ex 7:19
so that it may **b** gnats in all the land of Ex 8:16
It shall **b** fine dust over all the land of Ex 9:9
and **b** boils breaking out in sores on man Ex 9:9
my song, and he has **b** my salvation; Ex 15:2
your wives shall **b** widows and your Ex 22:24
lest the land **b** desolate and the wild Ex 23:29
touches the altar shall **b** holy. Ex 29:37
Whatever touches them will **b** holy. Ex 30:29
we do not know what has **b** of him." Ex 32:1
we do not know what has **b** of him.' Ex 32:23
you go, lest it **b** a snare in your midst. Ex 34:12
all its furniture, so that it may **b** holy. Ex 40:9
altar, so that the altar may **b** most holy. Ex 40:10
hidden from him and he has **b** unclean, Lv 5:2
that one may do and thereby **b** guilty." Lv 6:7
Whatever touches them shall **b** holy." Lv 6:18
"And by these you shall **b** unclean. Lv 11:24
them, and **b** unclean through them. Lv 11:43
driving out before you have **b** unclean, Lv 18:24
and the land **b** full of depravity. Lv 19:29
and the woman shall **b** a curse among Nm 5:27
wives and our little ones will **b** a prey. Nm 14:3
ones, who you said would **b** a prey, Nm 14:31
fire far and wide, for they have **b** holy. Nm 16:37
lest he **b** like Korah and his company Nm 16:40
the seventh day, he will not **b** clean. Nm 19:12
little ones, who you said would **b** a prey, Dt 1:39
your house and **b** devoted to destruction Dt 7:26
you, one of your brothers should **b** poor, Dt 15:7
this day you have **b** the people of the Dt 27:9
And you shall **b** a horror, a proverb, Dt 28:37
because they have **b** devoted for Jos 7:12
you, but they shall **b** thorns in your sides, Jgs 2:3
and you have **b** the cause of great Jgs 11:35
then I shall **b** weak and be like any Jgs 16:7
then I shall **b** weak and be like any Jgs 16:11
then I shall **b** weak and be like any Jgs 16:13
and I shall **b** weak and be like any Jgs 16:17
he has hired me, and I have **b** his priest." Jgs 18:4
womb that they may **b** your husbands? Ru 1:11
lest you **b** slaves to the Hebrews as they 1 Sm 4:9
the donkeys and **b** anxious about us." 1 Sm 9:5
also that Israel had **b** a stench to the 1 Sm 13:4
how my eyes have **b** bright because I 1 Sm 14:29
Now then **b** the king's son-in-law.'" 1 Sm 18:22
little thing to **b** the king's 1 Sm 18:23
that he might **b** the king's 1 Sm 18:27
turned from you and **b** your enemy? 1 Sm 28:16
in the battle he **b** an adversary to us. 1 Sm 29:4
saw that they had **b** a stench to David, 2 Sm 10:6
son of Haggith has **b** king and David 1 Kgs 1:11
has turned about and **b** my brother's, 1 Kgs 2:15
and Israel will **b** a proverb and a 1 Kgs 9:7
And this house will **b** a heap of ruins. 1 Kgs 9:8
neither did the jug of oil **b** empty, 1 Kgs 17:16
and have **b** like plants of the field 2 Kgs 19:26
and they shall **b** a prey and a spoil to 2 Kgs 21:14
that they should **b** a desolation and 2 Kgs 22:19
saw that they had **b** a stench to 1 Chr 19:6
to these reports you wish to **b** their king. Neh 6:6
For you have now **b** nothing; you see my Jb 6:21
mark? Why have I **b** a burden to you? Jb 7:20
I **b** afraid of all my suffering, for I know Jb 9:28
which were ready to **b** heaps of ruins; Jb 15:28
I have **b** a foreigner in their eyes. Jb 19:15
why then have you **b** altogether vain? Jb 27:12
"And now I have **b** their song; I am a Jb 30:9
mire, and I have **b** like dust and ashes. Jb 30:19
let his flesh **b** fresh with youth; let him Jb 33:25
The waters **b** hard like stone, and the Jb 38:30
Their young ones **b** strong; they grow up Jb 39:4
aside; together they have **b** corrupt; Ps 14:3
me, I **b** like those who go down to the pit. Ps 28:1
all my adversaries I have **b** a reproach, Ps 31:11
is dead; I have **b** like a broken vessel. Ps 31:12
and his children **b** a blessing. Ps 37:26
I have **b** like a man who does not hear, Ps 38:14
away; together they have **b** corrupt; Ps 53:3
I have **b** a stranger to my brothers, an Ps 69:8
their own table before them **b** a snare; Ps 69:22
when they are at peace, let it **b** a trap. Ps 69:22
We have **b** a taunt to our neighbors, Ps 79:4
me; my companions have **b** darkness. Ps 88:18
he has **b** the scorn of his neighbors. Ps 89:41
But the LORD has **b** my stronghold, and Ps 94:22
my body has **b** gaunt, with no fat. Ps 109:24
Those who make them **b** like them; so Ps 115:8
and my song; he has **b** my salvation. Ps 118:14
me and have **b** my salvation. Ps 118:21
rejected has **b** the cornerstone. Ps 118:22
For I have **b** like a wineskin in the Ps 119:83
Those who make them **b** like them, so Ps 135:18
Be not quick in your spirit to **b** angry, Eccl 7:9
been like Sodom, and **b** like Gomorrah. Is 1:9
soul hates; they have **b** a burden to me; Is 1:14
red like crimson, they shall **b** like wool. Is 1:18
How the faithful city has **b** a whore, she Is 1:21
Your silver has **b** dross, your best wine Is 1:22
And the strong shall **b** tinder, and his Is 1:31
shekels of silver, will **b** briers and thorns. Is 7:23
but they will **b** a place where cattle are let Is 7:25
And he will **b** a sanctuary and a stone of Is 8:14
The light of Israel will **b** a fire, and his Is 10:17
my song, and he has **b** my salvation." Is 12:2
to you: 'You too have **b** as weak as we! Is 14:10
as weak as we! You have **b** like us!' Is 14:10
to be a city and will **b** a heap of ruins. Is 17:1
and its canals will **b** foul, and the Is 19:6
The princes of Zoan have **b** fools, and Is 19:13
the land of Judah will **b** a terror to the Is 19:17
and he will **b** a throne of honor to his Is 22:23
vision of all this has **b** to you like the Is 29:11
and the watchtower will **b** dens forever, Is 32:14
sulfur; her land shall **b** burning pitch. Is 34:9
the burning sand shall **b** a pool, and the Is 35:7
down, the grass shall **b** reeds and rushes. Is 35:7
and have **b** like plants of the field and Is 37:27
the uneven ground shall **b** level, and the Is 40:4
they have **b** plunder with none to rescue, Is 42:22
LORD, and my God has **b** my strength— Is 49:5
The least one shall **b** a clan, and the Is 60:22
We have **b** like those over whom you Is 63:19
We have all **b** like one who is unclean, Is 64:6
Your holy cities have **b** a wilderness; Is 64:10
a wilderness; Zion has **b** a wilderness, Is 64:10
and all our pleasant places have **b** ruins. Is 64:11
Sharon shall **b** a pasture for flocks, and Is 65:10
servant? Why then has he **b** a prey? Jer 2:14
you turned degenerate and **b** a wild vine? Jer 2:21
The prophets will **b** wind; the word is not Jer 5:13
therefore they have **b** great and rich; Jer 5:27
name, **b** a den of robbers in your eyes? Jer 7:11
of the bride, for the land shall **b** a waste. Jer 7:34
For your gods have **b** as many as your Jer 11:13
My heritage has **b** to me like a lion in Jer 12:8
let their wives **b** childless and widowed. Jer 18:21
I have **b** a laughingstock all the day; Jer 20:7
word of the LORD has **b** for me a reproach Jer 20:8
that this house shall **b** a desolation. Jer 22:5
all of them have **b** like Sodom to me, Jer 23:14
This whole land shall **b** a ruin and a Jer 25:11
for their land has **b** a waste because of Jer 25:38
Jerusalem shall **b** a heap of ruins, and Jer 26:18
Why should this city **b** a desolation? Jer 27:17
go to Egypt. You shall **b** an execration, Jer 42:18
may be cut off and **b** a curse and a taunt Jer 44:8
by famine, and they shall **b** an oath, Jer 44:12
your land has **b** a desolation and Jer 44:22
For Memphis shall **b** a waste, a ruin, Jer 46:19
and shall **b** an overflowing torrent; Jer 47:2
her cities shall **b** a desolation, with no Jer 48:9
waters of Nimrim also have **b** desolate. Jer 48:34
So Moab has **b** a derision and a horror Jer 48:39
it shall **b** a desolate mound, and its Jer 49:2
the LORD, that Bozrah shall **b** a horror, Jer 49:13

"Edom shall **b** a horror. Everyone who Jer 49:17
Damascus has **b** feeble, she turned to Jer 49:24
Their camels shall **b** plunder, their Jer 49:32
Hazor shall **b** a haunt of jackals, an Jer 49:33
How Babylon has **b** a horror among Jer 50:23
the diviners, that they may **b** fools! Jer 50:36
in her midst, that they may **b** women! Jer 50:37
strength has failed; they have **b** women; Jer 51:30
and Babylon shall **b** a heap of ruins, Jer 51:37
them drunk, that they may **b** merry, Jer 51:39
How Babylon has **b** a horror among Jer 51:41
Her cities have **b** a horror, a land of Jer 51:43
and they shall **b** exhausted.'" Thus far Jer 51:64
How like a widow has she **b**, she who Lam 1:1
among the provinces has **b** a slave. Lam 1:1
with her; they have **b** her enemies. Lam 1:2
Her foes have **b** the head; her enemies Lam 1:5
Her princes have **b** like deer that find Lam 1:6
Jerusalem has **b** a filthy thing among Lam 1:17
The Lord has **b** like an enemy; he has Lam 2:5
I have **b** the laughingstock of all Lam 3:14
the daughter of my people has **b** cruel, Lam 4:3
on their bones; it has **b** as dry as wood. Lam 4:8
you shall **b** drunk and strip yourself Lam 4:21
We have **b** orphans, fatherless; our Lam 5:3
For this our heart has **b** sick, for these Lam 5:17
Your altars shall **b** desolate, and your Ezk 6:4
and the land shall **b** a desolation; Ezk 12:20
Now you have **b** an object of reproach Ezk 16:57
and bear fruit and **b** a noble vine. Ezk 17:8
and produce fruit and **b** a noble cedar. Ezk 17:23
lamentation and has **b** a lamentation. Ezk 19:14
You have **b** guilty by the blood that Ezk 22:4
the house of Israel has **b** dross to me; Ezk 22:18
Because you have all **b** dross, Ezk 22:19
upon the coals, that it may **b** hot, Ezk 24:11
And she shall **b** plunder for the Ezk 26:5
and your heart has **b** proud in your Ezk 28:5
so that it may **b** strong to wield the Ezk 30:21
surely because my sheep have **b** a prey, Ezk 34:8
and my sheep have **b** food for all the Ezk 34:8
waste, and you shall **b** a desolation, Ezk 35:4
ancient heights have **b** our possession,' Ezk 36:2
which have **b** a prey and derision to the Ezk 36:4
that was desolate has **b** like the garden Ezk 36:35
that they may **b** one in your hand. Ezk 37:17
After he has **b** clean, they shall count Ezk 44:26
flows into the sea, the water will **b** fresh. Ezk 47:8
that the waters of the sea may **b** fresh; Ezk 47:9
swamps and marshes will not **b** fresh; Ezk 47:11
O king, who have grown and **b** strong. Dn 4:22
and in his own mind he shall **b** great. Dn 8:25
your people have **b** a byword among Dn 9:16
And when he has **b** strong through his Dn 11:2
and he shall **b** strong with a small Dn 11:23
He shall **b** ruler of the treasures of gold Dn 11:43
whore, O Israel, let not Judah **b** guilty. Hos 4:15
Ephraim shall **b** a desolation in the day Hos 5:9
princes of Judah have **b** like those who Hos 5:10
they have **b** to him altars for sinning. Hos 8:11
"Egypt shall **b** a desolation and Edom a Jl 3:19
of the temple shall **b** wailings in that Am 8:3
he should see what would **b** of the city. Jon 4:5
Jerusalem shall **b** a heap of ruins, and Mi 3:12
For I have **b** as when the summer fruit Mi 7:1
and Ashkelon shall **b** a desolation; Zep 2:4
The seacoast shall **b** the possession of Zep 2:7
God of Israel, "Moab shall **b** like Sodom, Zep 2:9
one else." What a desolation she has **b**, Zep 2:15
does it **b** holy?'" The priests answered Hg 2:12
does it **b** unclean?" The priests answered Hg 2:13
answered and said, "It does **b** unclean." Hg 2:13
and they shall **b** plunder for those who Zec 2:9
Before Zerubbabel you shall **b** a plain. Zec 4:7
Then Ephraim shall **b** like a mighty Zec 10:7
"**B** shepherd of the flock doomed to Zec 11:4
say, 'Blessed be the LORD, I have **b** rich,' Zec 11:5
these stones to **b** loaves of bread." Mt 4:3
unless you turn and **b** like children, Mt 18:3
to his wife, and they shall **b** one flesh'? Mt 19:5
builders rejected has **b** the cornerstone; Mt 21:42
and I will make you **b** fishers of men." Mk 1:17
of it, for Jesus' name had **b** known. Mk 6:14
and they shall **b** one flesh.' So they are Mk 10:8
rejected has **b** the cornerstone; Mk 12:10
low, and the crooked shall **b** straight, Lk 3:5
and the rough places shall **b** level ways, Lk 3:5
of God, command this stone to **b** bread." Lk 4:3
than for one dot of the Law to **b** void. Lk 16:17
rejected has **b** the cornerstone'? Lk 20:17
greatest among you **b** as the youngest, Lk 22:26
he gave the right to **b** children of God, Jn 1:12
of the feast tasted the water now **b** wine, Jn 2:9
I will give him will **b** in him a spring of Jn 4:14
How is it that you say, 'You will **b** free'?" Jn 8:33
Do you also want to **b** his disciples?" Jn 9:27
may see, and those who see may **b** blind." Jn 9:39
that you may **b** sons of light." When Jn 12:36
in me, that they may **b** perfectly one, Jn 17:23
of Psalms, "'May his camp **b** desolate, Acts 1:20
of these men must **b** with us a witness Acts 1:22
builders, which has **b** the cornerstone. Acts 4:11
we do not know what has **b** of him.' Acts 7:40
the soldiers over what had **b** of Peter. Acts 12:18
Paul, having **b** greatly annoyed, Acts 16:18
me this day might **b** such as I am Acts 26:29
aside; together they have **b** worthless; Rom 3:12
that he should **b** the father of many Rom 4:18
slaves of sin have **b** obedient from the Rom 6:17
sin, have **b** slaves of righteousness. Rom 6:18
free from sin and have **b** slaves of God, Rom 6:22
commandment might **b** sinful Rom 7:13
like Sodom and **b** like Gomorrah." Rom 9:29
"Let their table **b** a snare and a trap, Rom 11:9
So do not **b** proud, but stand in awe. Rom 11:20
each one's work will **b** manifest, for 1 Cor 3:13
let him **b** a fool that he may become 1 Cor 3:18
become a fool that he may **b** wise. 1 Cor 3:18
all you want! Already you have **b** rich! 1 Cor 4:8
rich! Without us you have **b** kings! 1 Cor 4:8
because we have **b** a spectacle to the 1 Cor 4:9
We have **b**, and are still, like the 1 Cor 4:13
is written, "The two will **b** one flesh." 1 Cor 6:16
with a price; do not **b** slaves of men. 1 Cor 7:23
does not somehow **b** a stumbling 1 Cor 8:9
I have **b** all things to all people, that 1 Cor 9:22
him we might **b** the righteousness of 2 Cor 5:21
that you by his poverty might **b** rich. 2 Cor 8:9
Brothers, I entreat you, **b** as I am, for I Gal 4:12
as I am, for I also have **b** as you are. Gal 4:12
What then has **b** of the blessing you Gal 4:15
Have I then **b** your enemy by telling Gal 4:16
Let us not **b** conceited, provoking one Gal 5:26
They have **b** callous and have given Eph 4:19
his wife, and the two shall **b** one flesh." Eph 5:31
so that it has **b** known throughout the Phil 1:13
having **b** confident in the Lord by my Phil 1:14
your children, lest they **b** discouraged. Col 3:21
because you had **b** very dear to us. 1 Thes 2:8
or he may **b** puffed up with conceit 1 Tm 3:6
his grace we might **b** heirs according to Ti 3:7
of your faith may **b** effective for the Phlm 1:6
having **b** as much superior to angels as Heb 1:4
so that he might **b** a merciful and Heb 2:17
since you have **b** dull of hearing. Heb 5:11
having **b** a high priest forever after the Heb 6:20
who has **b** a priest, not on the basis of a Heb 7:16
trouble, and by it many **b** defiled; Heb 12:15
among yourselves and **b** judges with evil Jas 2:4
in one point has **b** accountable for all of Jas 2:10
you have **b** a transgressor of the law. Jas 2:11
Not many of you should **b** teachers, my Jas 3:1
builders rejected has **b** the cornerstone," 1 Pt 2:7
what will **b** of the ungodly and the 1 Pt 4:18
them you may **b** partakers of the 2 Pt 1:4
the last state has **b** worse for them than 2 Pt 2:20
that it might **b** plain that they all are 1 Jn 2:19
of the world has **b** the kingdom of our Rv 11:15
the dwellers on earth have **b** drunk." Rv 17:2
She has **b** a dwelling place for demons, a Rv 18:2

BECOMES (35)

which they have committed **b** known, Lv 4:14
may be with which one **b** unclean, Lv 5:3
and the raw flesh of the burn **b** a spot, Lv 13:24
"If your brother **b** poor and sells part of Lv 25:25
and then himself **b** prosperous and Lv 25:26
"If your brother **b** poor and cannot Lv 25:35
"If your brother **b** poor beside you and Lv 25:39
stranger or sojourner with you **b** rich, Lv 25:47
brother beside him **b** poor and sells Lv 25:47
your nostrils and **b** loathsome to you, Nm 11:20
man among you **b** unclean because of Dt 23:10
and if she goes and **b** another man's wife, Dt 24:2
bull or seven rams **b** a priest of what 2 Chr 13:9
Be not afraid when a man **b** rich, when Ps 49:16
Whoever walks with the wise **b** wise, Prv 13:20
scoffer is punished, the simple **b** wise; Prv 21:11
a slave when he **b** king, and a fool Prv 30:22
is over, and the flower **b** a ripening grape, Is 18:5
and the wilderness **b** a fruitful field, Is 32:15
it with his strong arm. He **b** hungry, Is 44:12
Then it **b** fuel for a man. He takes a part Is 44:15
goes from him and **b** another man's wife, Jer 3:1
than all the garden plants and **b** a tree, Mt 13:32
proselyte, and when he **b** a proselyte, Mt 23:15
soon as its branch **b** tender and puts Mt 24:32
it grows up and **b** larger than all the Mk 4:32
foams and grinds his teeth and **b** rigid. Mk 9:18
soon as its branch **b** tender and puts Mk 13:28
circumcision **b** uncircumcision. Rom 2:25
Then what **b** of our boasting? It is Rom 3:27
joined to a prostitute **b** one body with 1 Cor 6:16
joined to the Lord **b** one spirit with 1 Cor 6:17
is exposed by the light, it **b** visible, Eph 5:13
for anything that **b** visible is light. Eph 5:14
This **b** even more evident when Heb 7:15

BECOMING (7)

emission of semen, **b** unclean thereby; Lv 15:32
Fine speech is not **b** to a fool; still less is Prv 17:7
have done, **b** a consolation to them. Ezk 16:54
curse of the law by **b** a curse for us— Gal 3:13
humbled himself by **b** obedient to the Phil 2:8
his sufferings, **b** like him in his death, Phil 3:10
And what is **b** obsolete and growing Heb 8:13

BECORATH (1)

the son of Abiel, son of Zeror, son of **B**, 1 Sm 9:1

BED (86)

bowed himself upon the head of his **b**. Gn 47:31
summoned his strength and sat up in **b**. Gn 48:2
because you went up to your father's **b**; Gn 49:4
his feet into the **b** and breathed his last Gn 49:33
bedroom and on your **b** and into the Ex 8:3
the man does not die but takes to his **b**, Ex 21:18
Every **b** on which the one with the Lv 15:4
who touches his **b** shall wash his Lv 15:5
whoever touches her **b** shall wash his Lv 15:21
Whether it is the **b** or anything on Lv 15:23
and every **b** on which he lies shall be Lv 15:24
Every **b** on which she lies, all the days Lv 15:26
shall be to her as the **b** of her impurity. Lv 15:26
Rephaim. Behold, his **b** was a bed of iron. Dt 3:11
Rephaim. Behold, his bed was a **b** of iron. Dt 3:11
a **b** was spread for Saul on the roof, 1 Sm 9:25
and laid it on the **b** and put a pillow 1 Sm 19:13
"Bring him up to me in the **b**, 1 Sm 19:15
in, behold, the image was in the **b**, 1 Sm 19:16
from the earth and sat on the **b**. 1 Sm 28:23
as he lay on his **b** in his bedroom, 2 Sm 4:7
man in his own house on his **b**, 2 Sm 4:11
"Lie down on your **b** and pretend to be 2 Sm 13:5
And the king bowed himself on the **b**. 1 Kgs 1:47
lodged, and laid him on his own **b**. 1 Kgs 17:19
lay down on his **b** and turned away 1 Kgs 21:4
come down from the **b** to which you 2 Kgs 1:4
come down from the **b** to which you 2 Kgs 1:6
come down from the **b** to which you 2 Kgs 1:16
with walls and put there for him a **b**, 2 Kgs 4:10
and laid him on the **b** of the man of 2 Kgs 4:21
he saw the child lying dead on his **b**. 2 Kgs 4:32
day he took the **b** cloth and dipped it 2 Kgs 8:15
the priest, and killed him on his **b**. 2 Chr 24:25
When I say, 'My **b** will comfort me, my Jb 7:13
my house, if I make my **b** in darkness, Jb 17:13
Ophir among the stones of the torrent **b**, Jb 22:24
He goes to **b** rich, but will do so no Jb 27:19
with pain on his **b** and with continual Jb 33:19
every night I flood my **b** with tears; Ps 6:6
He plots trouble while on his **b**; he sets Ps 36:4
when I remember you upon my **b**, and Ps 63:6
not enter my house or get into my **b**, Ps 132:3
If I make my **b** in Sheol, you are there! Ps 139:8
I have perfumed my **b** with myrrh, Prv 7:17
why should your **b** be taken from Prv 22:27
its hinges, so does a sluggard on his **b**. Prv 26:14
She makes **b** coverings for herself; her Prv 31:22
On my **b** by night I sought him whom Sg 3:1
maggots are laid as a **b** beneath you, Is 14:11
For the **b** is too short to stretch oneself Is 28:20
and lofty mountain you have set your **b**, Is 57:7
deserting me, you have uncovered your **b**, Is 57:8
with them, you have loved their **b**, Is 57:8
toward him from the **b** where it was Ezk 17:7
away on the **b** where it sprouted?" Ezk 17:10
came to her into the **b** of love, Ezk 23:17
have made her a **b** among the slain Ezk 32:25
of your head as you lay in **b** are these: Dn 2:28
as you lay in **b** came thoughts of what Dn 2:29
As I lay in **b** the fancies and the visions of Dn 4:5
of my head as I lay in **b** were these: Dn 4:10
in the visions of my head as I lay in **b**, Dn 4:13
and visions of his head as he lay in his **b**. Dn 7:1
the corner of a couch and part of a **b**. Am 3:12
brought to him a paralytic, lying on a **b**. Mt 9:2
—"Rise, pick up your **b** and go home." Mt 9:6
they let down the **b** on which the Mk 2:4
or to say, 'Rise, take up your **b** and walk'? Mk 2:9
"I say to you, rise, pick up your **b**, and Mk 2:11
picked up his **b** and went out Mk 2:12
to be put under a basket, or under a **b**, Mk 4:21
the child lying in **b** and the demon Mk 7:30
were bringing on a **b** a man who was Lk 5:18
him down with his **b** through the tiles Lk 5:19
you, rise, pick up your **b** and go home." Lk 5:24
covers it with a jar or puts it under a **b**, Lk 8:16

shut, and my children are with me in **b**. Lk 11:7
in that night there will be two in one **b**. Lk 17:34
Jesus said to him, "Get up, take up your **b**, Jn 5:8
healed, and he took up his **b** and walked. Jn 5:9
it is not lawful for you to take up your **b**." Jn 5:10
that man said to me, 'Take up your **b**, Jn 5:11
said to you, 'Take up your **b** and walk'?" Jn 5:12
and make your **b**." And immediately Acts 9:34
all, and let the marriage **b** be undefiled, Heb 13:4

BEDAD (2)
Husham died, and Hadad the son of **B**, Gn 36:35
died, and Hadad the son of **B**, 1 Chr 1:46

BEDAN (1)
The son of Ulam: **B**. These were the 1 Chr 7:17

BEDECKED (1)
body is polished ivory, **b** with sapphires. Sg 5:14

BEDEIAH (1)
Benaiah, **B**, Cheluhi, Ezr 10:35

BEDRIDDEN (1)
man named Aeneas, **b** for eight years, Acts 9:33

BEDROOM (6)
house and into your **b** and on your bed Ex 8:3
the house, as he lay on his bed in his **b**, 2 Sm 4:7
the words that you speak in your **b**." 2 Kgs 6:12
and she put him and his nurse in a **b**. 2 Kgs 11:2
she put him and his nurse in a **b**. 2 Chr 22:11
king, nor in your **b** curse the rich, Eccl 10:20

BEDS (11)
brought **b**, basins, and earthen 2 Sm 17:28
on men, while they slumber on their **b**, Jb 33:15
ponder in your own hearts on your **b**, and Ps 4:4
in glory; let them sing for joy on their **b**. Ps 149:5
His cheeks are like **b** of spices, mounds Sg 5:13
gone down to his garden to the **b** of spices, Sg 6:2
they rest in their **b** who walk in their Is 57:2
the heart, but they wail upon their **b**; Hos 7:14
to those who lie on **b** of ivory and stretch Am 6:4
wickedness and work evil on their **b**! Mi 2:1
sick people on their **b** to wherever they Mk 6:55

BEE (1)
and for the **b** that is in the land of Is 7:18

BEELIADA (1)
Elishama, **B** and Eliphelet. 1 Chr 14:7

BEELZEBUL (7)
have called the master of the house **B**, Mt 10:25
heard it, they said, "It is only by **B**, Mt 12:24
And if I cast out demons by **B**, by Mt 12:27
"He is possessed by **B**," and "by the Mk 3:22
them said, "He casts out demons by **B**, Lk 11:15
you say that I cast out demons by **B**. Lk 11:18
And if I cast out demons by **B**, by Lk 11:19

BEER (2)
And from there they continued to **B**; Nm 21:16
and fled and went to **B** and lived there, Jgs 9:21

BEER-ELIM (1)
to Eglaim; her wailing reaches to **B**. Is 15:8

BEER-LAHAI-ROI (3)
Therefore the well was called **B**; it lies Gn 16:14
had returned from **B** and was dwelling Gn 24:62
Isaac his son. And Isaac settled at **B**. Gn 25:11

BEERA (1)
Shamma, Shilshah, Ithran, and **B**. 1 Chr 7:37

BEERAH (1)
B his son, whom Tiglath-pileser king 1 Chr 5:6

BEERI (2)
Judith the daughter of **B** the Hittite to Gn 26:34
LORD that came to Hosea, the son of **B**, Hos 1:1

BEEROTH (9)
Israel journeyed from **B** Bene-jaakan to Dt 10:6
Chephirah, **B**, and Kiriath-jearim. Jos 9:17
Gibeon, Ramah, **B**, Jos 18:25
of Benjamin from **B** (for Beeroth also 2 Sm 4:2
from Beeroth (for **B** also is counted 2 Sm 4:2
Zelek the Ammonite, Naharai of **B**, 2 Sm 23:37
Zelek the Ammonite, Naharai of **B**, 1 Chr 11:39
sons of Kiriath-arim, Chephirah, and **B**, Ezr 2:25
of Kiriath-jearim, Chephirah, and **B**, Neh 7:29

BEEROTHITE (2)
Now the sons of Rimmon the **B**, 2 Sm 4:5
his brother, the sons of Rimmon the **B**, 2 Sm 4:9

BEEROTHITES (1)
the **B** fled to Gittaim and have been 2 Sm 4:3

BEERSHEBA (34)
and wandered in the wilderness of **B**. Gn 21:14
Therefore that place was called **B**, Gn 21:31
So they made a covenant at **B**. Then Gn 21:32
a tamarisk tree in **B** and called there Gn 21:33
and they arose and went together to **B**. Gn 22:19
to Beersheba. And Abraham lived at **B**. Gn 22:19
From there he went up to **B**. Gn 26:23
the name of the city is **B** to this day. Gn 26:33
Jacob left **B** and went toward Haran. Gn 28:10
with all that he had and came to **B**, Gn 46:1
Then Jacob set out from **B**. The sons of Gn 46:5
Hazar-shual, **B**, Biziothiah, Jos 15:28
And they had for their inheritance **B**, Jos 19:2
people of Israel came out, from Dan to **B**, Jgs 20:1
from Dan to **B** knew that Samuel 1 Sm 3:20
second, Abijah; they were judges in **B**. 1 Sm 8:2
Israel and over Judah, from Dan to **B**." 2 Sm 3:10
be gathered to you, from Dan to **B**, 2 Sm 17:11
all the tribes of Israel, from Dan to **B**, 2 Sm 24:2
went out to the Negeb of Judah at **B**. 2 Sm 24:7
people from Dan to **B** 70,000 men. 2 Sm 24:15
lived in safety, from Dan even to **B**, 1 Kgs 4:25
and ran for his life and came to **B**, 1 Kgs 19:3
His mother's name was Zibiah of **B**. 2 Kgs 12:1
had made offerings, from Geba to **B**. 2 Kgs 23:8
They lived in **B**, Moladah, 1 Chr 4:28
"Go, number Israel, from **B** to Dan, 1 Chr 21:2
from **B** to the hill country of 2 Chr 19:4
His mother's name was Zibiah of **B**. 2 Chr 24:1
throughout all Israel, from **B** to Dan, 2 Chr 30:5
in Hazar-shual, in **B** and its villages, Neh 11:27
they encamped from **B** to the valley Neh 11:30
not enter into Gilgal or cross over to **B**; Am 5:5
O Dan,' and, 'As the Way of **B** lives,' Am 8:14

BEES (3)
you and chased you as **b** do and beat you Dt 1:44
there was a swarm of **b** in the body of Jgs 14:8
They surrounded me like **b**; they went Ps 118:12

BEESHTERAH (1)
and **B** with its pasturelands—two Jos 21:27

BEFALL (4)
and no plague will **b** you to destroy Ex 12:13
And in the days to come evil will **b** you, Dt 31:29
to his ways he will make it **b** him. Jb 34:11
no evil shall be allowed to **b** you, no Ps 91:10

BEFALLEN (2)
because disaster had **b** his house. 1 Chr 7:23
Remember, O LORD, what has **b** us; Lam 5:1

BEFALLS (3)
comes upon me, and what I dread **b** me. Jb 3:25
No ill **b** the righteous, but the wicked Prv 12:21
but trouble **b** the income of the wicked. Prv 15:6

BEFITS (2)
O you righteous! Praise **b** the upright. Ps 33:1
holiness **b** your house, O LORD, Ps 93:5

BEFOREHAND (15)
beginning, that we might know, and **b**, Is 41:26
See, I have told you **b**. Mt 24:25
do not be anxious **b** what you are to Mk 13:11
on guard; I have told you all things **b**. Mk 13:23
she has anointed my body **b** for burial. Mk 14:8
minds not to meditate **b** how to answer, Lk 21:14
the Holy Spirit spoke **b** by the mouth Acts 1:16
those who announced **b** the coming of Acts 7:52
which he promised **b** through his Rom 1:2
which he has prepared **b** for glory— Rom 9:23
faith, preached the gospel **b** to Abraham, Gal 3:8
for good works, which God prepared **b**, Eph 2:10
we kept telling you **b** that we were to 1 Thes 3:4
we told you **b** and solemnly warned 1 Thes 4:6
You therefore, beloved, knowing this **b**, 2 Pt 3:17

BEFRIEND (1)
dwell in the land and **b** faithfulness. Ps 37:3

BEG (17)
and said, "I **b** you, my brothers, do not Gn 19:7
go to the king to **b** his favor and plead Est 4:8
but Haman stayed to **b** for his life from Est 7:7
May his children wander about and **b**, Ps 109:10
for thirst; the children **b** for food, Lam 4:4
And they began to **b** Jesus to depart Mk 5:17
Jesus, Son of the Most High God? I **b** you, Lk 8:28
out, "Teacher, I **b** you to look at my son, Lk 9:38
enough to dig, and I am ashamed to **b**. Lk 16:3
And he said, 'Then I **b** you, father, to Lk 16:27
this not the man who used to sit and **b**?" Jn 9:8
a citizen of no obscure city. I **b** you, Acts 21:39
I **b** you in your kindness to hear us Acts 24:4
Therefore I **b** you to listen to me Acts 26:3
So I **b** you to reaffirm your love for 2 Cor 2:8
I **b** of you that when I am present I 2 Cor 10:2
made the hearers **b** that no further Heb 12:19

BEGAN (186)
At that time people **b** to call upon the Gn 4:26
When man **b** to multiply on the face of Gn 6:1
Noah **b** to be a man of the soil, and he Gn 9:20
the seven years of famine **b** to come, Gn 41:54
the people **b** to whore with the Nm 25:1
side their boundary **b** at the Jordan. Jos 18:12
the Spirit of the LORD **b** to stir him in Jgs 13:25
Then she **b** to torment him, and his Jgs 16:19
hair of his head **b** to grow again after Jgs 16:22
And as the dawn **b** to break, they let Jgs 19:25
at other times they **b** to strike and kill Jgs 20:31
But when the signal **b** to rise out of the Jgs 20:40
was ... years old when he **b** to reign, 1 Sm 13:1
years old when he **b** to reign over 2 Sm 2:10
was thirty years old when he **b** to reign, 2 Sm 5:4
crossed the Jordan and **b** from Aroer, 2 Sm 24:5
he **b** to build the house of the LORD. 1 Kgs 6:1
years old when he **b** to reign, 1 Kgs 14:21
Nebat, Abijam **b** to reign over Judah. 1 Kgs 15:1
of Israel, Asa **b** to reign over Judah, 1 Kgs 15:9
the son of Jeroboam **b** to reign over 1 Kgs 15:25
the son of Ahijah **b** to reign over all 1 Kgs 15:33
the son of Baasha **b** to reign over 1 Kgs 16:8
When he **b** to reign, as soon as he 1 Kgs 16:11
of Judah, Omri **b** to reign over Israel, 1 Kgs 16:23
the son of Omri **b** to reign over 1 Kgs 16:29
the son of Asa **b** to reign over Judah 1 Kgs 22:41
years old when he **b** to reign, 1 Kgs 22:42
the son of Ahab **b** to reign over 1 Kgs 22:51
king of Judah, **b** to reign. 2 Kgs 8:16
of Jehoram, king of Judah, **b** to reign. 2 Kgs 8:25
years old when he **b** to reign, 2 Kgs 8:26
Ahab, Ahaziah **b** to reign over Judah. 2 Kgs 9:29
those days the LORD **b** to cut off parts 2 Kgs 10:32
seven years old when he **b** to reign. 2 Kgs 11:21
year of Jehu, Jehoash **b** to reign, 2 Kgs 12:1
the son of Jehu **b** to reign over Israel 2 Kgs 13:1
the son of Jehoahaz **b** to reign over 2 Kgs 13:10
of Joash, king of Judah, **b** to reign. 2 Kgs 14:1
years old when he **b** to reign, 2 Kgs 14:2
king of Israel, **b** to reign in Samaria, 2 Kgs 14:23
of Amaziah, king of Judah, **b** to reign. 2 Kgs 15:1
sixteen years old when he **b** to reign, 2 Kgs 15:2
the son of Jabesh **b** to reign in the 2 Kgs 15:13
the son of Gadi **b** to reign over Israel, 2 Kgs 15:17
the son of Menahem **b** to reign over 2 Kgs 15:23
the son of Remaliah **b** to reign over 2 Kgs 15:27
of Uzziah, king of Judah, **b** to reign. 2 Kgs 15:32
years old when he **b** to reign, 2 Kgs 15:33
those days the LORD **b** to send Rezin 2 Kgs 15:37
of Jotham, king of Judah, **b** to reign. 2 Kgs 16:1
twenty years old when he **b** to reign, 2 Kgs 16:2
the son of Elah **b** to reign in Samaria 2 Kgs 17:1
son of Ahaz, king of Judah, **b** to reign. 2 Kgs 18:1
years old when he **b** to reign, 2 Kgs 18:2
twelve years old when he **b** to reign, 2 Kgs 21:1
years old when he **b** to reign, 2 Kgs 21:19
eight years old when he **b** to reign, 2 Kgs 22:1
years old when he **b** to reign, 2 Kgs 23:31
years old when he **b** to reign, 2 Kgs 23:36
in the year that he **b** to reign, 2 Kgs 25:27
Joab the son of Zeruiah **b** to count, 1 Chr 27:24
Then Solomon **b** to build the house of 2 Chr 3:1
He **b** to build in the second month of 2 Chr 3:2
years old when he **b** to reign, 2 Chr 12:13
Abijah **b** to reign over Judah. 2 Chr 13:1
And when they **b** to sing and praise, 2 Chr 20:22
years old when he **b** to reign, 2 Chr 20:31
years old when he **b** to reign, 2 Chr 21:20
years old when he **b** to reign, 2 Chr 22:2
seven years old when he **b** to reign, 2 Chr 24:1
years old when he **b** to reign, 2 Chr 25:1
sixteen years old when he **b** to reign, 2 Chr 26:3
years old when he **b** to reign, 2 Chr 27:1
years old when he **b** to reign, 2 Chr 27:8
twenty years old when he **b** to reign, 2 Chr 28:1
Hezekiah **b** to reign when he was 2 Chr 29:1
They **b** to consecrate on the first 2 Chr 29:17
And when the burnt offering **b**, the 2 Chr 29:27
began, the song to the LORD **b** also, 2 Chr 29:27
the third month they **b** to pile up the 2 Chr 31:7
"Since they **b** to bring the 2 Chr 31:10
twelve years old when he **b** to reign, 2 Chr 33:1
years old when he **b** to reign, 2 Chr 33:21
eight years old when he **b** to reign, 2 Chr 34:1
he **b** to seek the God of David his 2 Chr 34:3
the twelfth year he **b** to purge Judah 2 Chr 34:3
years old when he **b** to reign, 2 Chr 36:2
years old when he **b** to reign, 2 Chr 36:5
years old when he **b** to reign, 2 Chr 36:11
the seventh month they **b** to offer burnt Ezr 3:6
of Jozadak arose and **b** to rebuild the Ezr 5:2
of the first month he **b** to go up from Ezr 7:9
As soon as it **b** to grow dark at the Neh 13:19
the morning since your days **b**, Jb 38:12
my sanctuary." So they **b** with the elders Ezk 9:6
is in Gilgal; there I **b** to hate them. Hos 9:15
Jonah **b** to go into the city, going a day's Jon 3:4

From that time Jesus **b** to preach, Mt 4:17
left her, and she rose and **b** to serve him. Mt 8:15
Jesus **b** to speak to the crowds Mt 11:7
Then he **b** to denounce the cities where Mt 11:20
and they **b** to pluck heads of grain and Mt 12:1
And they **b** discussing it among Mt 16:7
From that time Jesus **b** to show his Mt 16:21
took him aside and **b** to rebuke him, Mt 16:22
When he **b** to settle, one was brought Mt 18:24
and seizing him, he **b** to choke him, Mt 18:28
were very sorrowful and **b** to say to Mt 26:22
he **b** to be sorrowful and troubled. Mt 26:37
Then he **b** to invoke a curse on himself Mt 26:74
fever left her, and she **b** to serve them. Mk 1:31
he went out and **b** to talk freely about Mk 1:45
his disciples **b** to pluck heads of grain. Mk 2:23
Again he **b** to teach beside the sea. And a Mk 4:1
And they **b** to beg Jesus to depart from Mk 5:17
he went away and **b** to proclaim in the Mk 5:20
girl got up and **b** walking (for she was Mk 5:42
And on the Sabbath he **b** to teach in the Mk 6:2
called the twelve and **b** to send them out Mk 6:7
And he **b** to teach them many things. Mk 6:34
the whole region and **b** to bring the Mk 6:55
Pharisees came and **b** to argue with Mk 8:11
And they **b** discussing with one Mk 8:16
And he **b** to teach them that the Son of Mk 8:31
took him aside and **b** to rebuke him. Mk 8:32
Peter **b** to say to him, "See, we have left Mk 10:28
he **b** to tell them what was to happen Mk 10:32
they **b** to be indignant at James and Mk 10:41
of Nazareth, he **b** to cry out and say, Mk 10:47
entered the temple and **b** to drive out Mk 11:15
And he **b** to speak to them in parables. Mk 12:1
And Jesus **b** to say to them, "See that no Mk 13:5
They **b** to be sorrowful and to say to Mk 14:19
and **b** to be greatly distressed and Mk 14:33
And some **b** to spit on him and to Mk 14:65
girl saw him and **b** again to say to Mk 14:69
But he **b** to invoke a curse on himself Mk 14:71
crowd came up and **b** to ask Pilate to Mk 15:8
And they **b** to salute him, "Hail, King Mk 15:18
at that very hour she **b** to give thanks to Lk 2:38
but then they **b** to search for him Lk 2:44
Jesus, when he **b** his ministry, was Lk 3:23
And he **b** to say to them, "Today this Lk 4:21
she rose and **b** to serve them. Lk 4:39
both the boats, so that they **b** to sink. Lk 5:7
scribes and the Pharisees **b** to question, Lk 5:21
And the dead man sat up and **b** to speak, Lk 7:15
Jesus **b** to speak to the crowds Lk 7:24
she **b** to wet his feet with her tears and Lk 7:38
at table with him **b** to say among Lk 7:49
Now the day **b** to wear away, and the Lk 9:12
the crowds were increasing, he **b** to say, Lk 11:29
and the Pharisees **b** to press him Lk 11:53
another, he **b** to say to his disciples first, Lk 12:1
But they all alike **b** to make excuses. Lk 14:18
'This man **b** to build and was not able Lk 14:30
in that country, and he **b** to be in need. Lk 15:14
and is found.' And they **b** to celebrate. Lk 15:24
of his disciples **b** to rejoice and Lk 19:37
entered the temple and **b** to drive out Lk 19:45
And he **b** to tell the people this parable: Lk 20:9
And they **b** to question one another, Lk 22:23
And they **b** to accuse him, saying, "We Lk 23:2
them the hour when he **b** to get better, Jn 4:52
went up into the temple and **b** teaching. Jn 7:14
Never since the world **b** has it been heard Jn 9:32
into a basin and **b** to wash the disciples' Jn 13:5
with all that Jesus **b** to do and teach, Acts 1:1
the Holy Spirit and **b** to speak in other Acts 2:4
And leaping up he stood and **b** to walk, Acts 3:8
the temple at daybreak and **b** to teach. Acts 5:21
But Peter **b** and explained it to them in Acts 11:4
As I **b** to speak, the Holy Spirit fell on Acts 11:15
with jealousy and **b** to contradict Acts 13:45
they **b** rejoicing and glorifying the Acts 13:48
And he sprang up and **b** walking. Acts 14:10
He **b** to speak boldly in the Acts 18:26
and they **b** speaking in tongues and Acts 19:6
Tertullus **b** to accuse him, Acts 24:2
they **b** the next day to jettison the Acts 27:18
of all he broke it and **b** to eat. Acts 27:35
that he who **b** a good work in you will Phil 1:6
us in Christ Jesus before the ages **b**, 2 Tm 1:9
who never lies, promised before the ages **b** Ti 1:2
and I **b** to weep loudly because no one was Rv 5:4

BEGETTING (1)
who says to a father, 'What are you **b**?' Is 45:10

BEGGAR (2)
a great crowd, Bartimaeus, a blind **b**, Mk 10:46
had seen him before as a **b** were saying, Jn 9:8

BEGGED (16)
when he **b** us and we did not listen. Gn 42:21
And the demons **b** him, saying, "If you Mt 8:31
him, they **b** him to leave their region. Mt 8:34
And his disciples came and **b** him, Mt 15:23
And he **b** him earnestly not to send Mk 5:10
and they **b** him, saying, "Send us to the Mk 5:12
possessed with demons **b** him that he Mk 5:18
And she **b** him to cast the demon out of Mk 7:26
and they **b** him to lay his hand on him. Mk 7:32
a blind man and **b** him to touch him. Mk 8:22
saw Jesus, he fell on his face and **b** him, Lk 5:12
And they **b** him not to command them Lk 8:31
and they **b** him to let them enter these. Lk 8:32
the demons had gone **b** that he might be Lk 8:38
And I **b** your disciples to cast it out, but Lk 9:40
the people **b** that these things might Acts 13:42

BEGGING (3)
forsaken or his children **b** for bread. Ps 37:25
man was sitting by the roadside **b**. Lk 18:35
b us earnestly for the favor of taking 2 Cor 8:4

BEGIN (19)
B to take possession, and contend with Dt 2:24
This day I will **b** to put the dread and fear Dt 2:25
B to take possession, that you may Dt 2:31
B to count the seven weeks from the time Dt 16:9
"Today I will **b** to exalt you in the sight of Jos 3:7
the man who will **b** to fight against the Jgs 10:18
and he shall **b** to save Israel from the Jgs 13:5
"Who shall **b** the battle?" He 1 Kgs 20:14
I **b** to work disaster at the city that is Jer 25:29
And **b** at my sanctuary." So they began Ezk 9:6
And do not **b** to say to yourselves, 'We Lk 3:8
and you **b** to stand outside and to Lk 13:25
Then you will **b** to say, 'We ate and Lk 13:26
and then you will **b** with shame to take Lk 14:9
to finish, all who see it **b** to mock him, Lk 14:29
Now when these things **b** to take place, Lk 21:28
Then they will **b** to say to the Lk 23:30
Much in every way. To **b** with, the Jews Rom 3:2
for judgment to **b** at the household 1 Pt 4:17

BEGINNING (97)
In the **b**, God created the heavens and the Gn 1:1
The **b** of his kingdom was Babel, Gn 10:10
and this is only the **b** of what they will Gn 11:6
place where his tent had been at the **b**, Gn 13:3
for they were still as ugly as at the **b**. Gn 41:21
b with the eldest and ending with the Gn 44:12
month shall be for you the **b** of months. Ex 12:2
ninth day of the month **b** at evening, Lv 23:32
and the Gadites the territory **b** at Aroer, Dt 3:12
from the **b** of the year to the end of the Dt 11:12
of the camp at the **b** of the middle watch, Jgs 7:19
to Bethlehem at the **b** of barley harvest. Ru 1:22
concerning his house, from **b** to end. 1 Sm 3:12
of harvest, at the **b** of barley harvest. 2 Sm 21:9
from the **b** of harvest until rain fell 2 Sm 21:10
And at the **b** of their dwelling there, 2 Kgs 17:25
and Jeshua the son of Jozadak made a **b**, Ezr 3:8
reign of Ahasuerus, in the **b** of his reign, Ezr 4:6
that the breaches were **b** to be closed, Neh 4:7
And though your **b** was small, your latter Jb 8:7
the latter days of Job more than his **b**. Jb 42:12
fear of the LORD is the **b** of wisdom; Ps 111:10
fear of the LORD is the **b** of knowledge; Prv 1:7
The **b** of wisdom is this: Get wisdom, and Prv 4:7
LORD possessed me at the **b** of his work, Prv 8:22
up, at the first, before the **b** of the earth. Prv 8:23
The fear of the LORD is the **b** of wisdom, Prv 9:10
The **b** of strife is like letting out water, Prv 17:14
gained hastily in the **b** will not be Prv 20:21
God has done from the **b** to the end. Eccl 3:11
Better is the end of a thing than its **b**, Eccl 7:8
The **b** of the words of his mouth is Eccl 10:13
the first, and your counselors as at the **b**. Is 1:26
Has it not been told you from the **b**? Is 40:21
this, calling the generations from the **b**? Is 41:4
Who declared it from the **b**, that we Is 41:26
the end from the **b** and from ancient Is 46:10
from the **b** I have not spoken in secret, Is 48:16
set on high from the **b** is the place of Jer 17:12
In the **b** of the reign of Jehoiakim the son Jer 26:1
In the **b** of the reign of Zedekiah the son Jer 27:1
at the **b** of the reign of Zedekiah king of Jer 28:1
in the **b** of the reign of Zedekiah king of Jer 49:34
night, at the **b** of the night watches! Lam 2:19
year of our exile, at the **b** of the year, Ezk 40:1
an entrance at the **b** of the passage, Ezk 42:12
B at the northern extreme, beside the Ezk 48:1
At the **b** of your pleas for mercy a word Dn 9:23
the latter growth was just **b** to sprout, Am 7:1
it was the **b** of sin to the daughter of Mi 1:13
was afraid, and **b** to sink he cried out, Mt 14:30
them from the **b** made them male Mt 19:4
your wives, but from the **b** it was not so. Mt 19:8
pay them their wages, **b** with the last, Mt 20:8
All these are but the **b** of the birth pains. Mt 24:8
not been from the **b** of the world until Mt 24:21
nothing, but rather that a riot was **b**, Mt 27:24
The **b** of the gospel of Jesus Christ, the Mk 1:1
But from the **b** of creation, 'God made Mk 10:6
These are but the **b** of the birth pains. Mk 13:8
not been from the **b** of the creation Mk 13:19
who from the **b** were eyewitnesses and Lk 1:2
of Preparation, and the Sabbath was **b**. Lk 23:54
And **b** with Moses and all the Prophets, Lk 24:27
name to all nations, **b** from Jerusalem. Lk 24:47
In the **b** was the Word, and the Word was Jn 1:1
He was in the **b** with God. Jn 1:2
Jesus knew from the **b** who those were Jn 6:64
away one by one, **b** with the older ones, Jn 8:9
what I have been telling you from the **b**. Jn 8:25
He was a murderer from the **b**, and has Jn 8:44
you have been with me from the **b**. Jn 15:27
not say these things to you from the **b**, Jn 16:4
b from the baptism of John until the Acts 1:22
and **b** with this Scripture he told him Acts 8:35
b from Galilee after the baptism that Acts 10:37
fell on them just as on us at the **b**. Acts 11:15
spent from the **b** among my own Acts 26:4
Are we **b** to commend ourselves 2 Cor 3:1
know that in the **b** of the gospel, Phil 4:15
He is the **b**, the firstborn from the dead, Col 1:18
the foundation of the earth in the **b**, Heb 1:10
having neither **b** of days nor end of life, Heb 7:3
as they were from the **b** of creation." 2 Pt 3:4
That which was from the **b**, which we 1 Jn 1:1
that you had from the **b**. 1 Jn 2:7
you know him who is from the **b**. 1 Jn 2:13
you know him who is from the **b**. 1 Jn 2:14
you heard from the **b** abide in you. 1 Jn 2:24
you heard from the **b** abides in you, 1 Jn 2:24
the devil has been sinning from the **b**. 1 Jn 3:8
that you have heard from the **b**, 1 Jn 3:11
we have had from the **b**—that we love 2 Jn 1:5
just as you have heard from the **b**, 2 Jn 1:6
and true witness, the **b** of God's creation. Rv 3:14
Alpha and the Omega, the **b** and the end. Rv 21:6
the first and the last, the **b** and the end." Rv 22:13

BEGINNINGS (2)
feasts and at the **b** of your months, Nm 10:10
"At the **b** of your months, you shall Nm 28:11

BEGINS (4)
the southern side **b** at the outskirts Jos 18:15
and **b** to beat his fellow servants and Mt 24:49
and **b** to beat the male and female Lk 12:45
and if it **b** with us, what will be the 1 Pt 4:17

BEGOTTEN (5)
a father, or who has **b** the drops of dew? Jb 38:28
me, "You are my Son; today I have **b** you. Ps 2:7
are my Son, today I have **b** you.' Acts 13:33
"You are my Son, today I have **b** you"? Heb 1:5
"You are my Son, today I have **b** you"; Heb 5:5

BEGRUDGE (3)
refined among you will **b** food to his Dt 28:54
will **b** to the husband she embraces, Dt 28:56
to me? Or do you **b** my generosity?' Mt 20:15

BEGS (2)
Give to the one who **b** from you, and do Mt 5:42
Give to everyone who **b** from you, and Lk 6:30

BEGUILED (1)
with which they **b** you in the matter Nm 25:18

BEGUN (12)
out from the LORD; the plague has **b**." Nm 16:46
plague had already **b** among the Nm 16:47
I have **b** to give Sihon and his land over Dt 2:31
you have only **b** to show your servant Dt 3:24
Now Benjamin had **b** to strike and kill Jgs 20:39
whose eyesight had **b** to grow dim so 1 Sm 3:2
before whom you have **b** to fall, Est 6:13
her whoring that she had **b** in Egypt; Ezk 23:8
and your whoring **b** in the land Ezk 23:27
because it had **b** to rain and was cold. Acts 28:2
Having **b** by the Spirit, are you now Gal 3:3
taken your great power and **b** to reign. Rv 11:17

BEHALF (35)
her, so that she may give birth on my **b**, Gn 30:3
all these words on his **b** in the ears of all Jgs 9:3
sent messengers to David on his **b**, 2 Sm 3:12
sought God on **b** of the child. 2 Sm 12:16
to speak to him on **b** of Adonijah. 1 Kgs 2:19
word spoken on your **b** to the king or 2 Kgs 4:13
house of the LORD on **b** of the king, 2 Kgs 11:7
altar and the house on **b** of the king. 2 Kgs 11:11
the salvation of the LORD on your **b**, 2 Chr 20:17
and plead with him on **b** of her people. Est 4:8

found in Susa, and hold a fast on my **b**, Est 4:16
I have yet something to say on God's **b**. Jb 36:2
deal on my **b** for your name's sake; Ps 109:21
inquire of the dead on **b** of the living? Is 8:19
or lift up a cry or prayer on their **b**, Jer 11:14
into exile, and pray to the LORD on its **b**, Jer 29:7
have intervened on **b** of your sisters. Ezk 16:52
to make atonement on **b** of the house Ezk 45:17
on **b** of my people and my heritage Israel, Jl 3:2
fever, and they appealed to him on her **b**. Lk 4:38
you that I will ask the Father on your **b**; Jn 16:26
me in your prayers to God on my **b**, Rom 15:30
by being baptized on **b** of the dead? 1 Cor 15:29
why are people baptized on their **b**? 1 Cor 15:29
give thanks on our **b** for the blessing 2 Cor 1:11
We implore you on **b** of Christ, be 2 Cor 5:20
On **b** of this man I will boast, but on 2 Cor 12:5
but on my own **b** I will not boast, 2 Cor 12:5
for Christ Jesus on **b** of you Gentiles— Eph 3:1
is a faithful minister of Christ on your **b** Col 1:7
struggling on your **b** in his prayers, Col 4:12
me on your **b** during my Phlm 1:13
appointed to act on **b** of men in relation Heb 5:1
has gone as a forerunner on our **b**, Heb 6:20
appear in the presence of God on our **b**. Heb 9:24

BEHAVE (3)
this fellow to **b** as a madman 1 Sm 21:15
but **b** like a woman who has been 2 Sm 14:2
how one ought to **b** in the household 1 Tm 3:15

BEHAVED (2)
but the man was harsh and badly **b**; 1 Sm 25:3
our conscience that we **b** in the world 2 Cor 1:12

BEHAVING (3)
that they are **b** arrogantly. Jb 36:9
not of the flesh and **b** only in a human 1 Cor 3:3
that he is not **b** properly toward his 1 Cor 7:36

BEHAVIOR (7)
So he changed his **b** before them and 1 Sm 21:13
For the queen's **b** will be made known Est 1:17
heard of the queen's **b** will say the same Est 1:18
he changed his **b** before Abimelech, Ps 34:T
who were ashamed of your lewd **b**. Ezk 16:27
women likewise are to be reverent in **b**, Ti 2:3
who revile your good **b** in Christ may 1 Pt 3:16

BEHEADED (6)
him and put him to death and **b** him. 2 Sm 4:7
He sent and had John **b** in the prison, Mt 14:10
heard of it, he said, "John, whom I **b**, Mk 6:16
head. He went and **b** him in the prison Mk 6:27
Herod said, "John I **b**, but who is this Lk 9:9
those who had been **b** for the testimony Rv 20:4

BEHELD (2)
men of the people of Israel; they **b** God, Ex 24:11
He has not **b** misfortune in Jacob, nor Nm 23:21

BEHEMOTH (1)
"Behold, **B**, which I made as I made you; Jb 40:15

BEHIND (78)
was listening at the tent door **b** him. Gn 18:10
But Lot's wife, **b** him, looked back, and Gn 19:26
looked, and behold, **b** him was a ram, Gn 22:13
lord Esau. And moreover, he is **b** us.'" Gn 32:18
your servant Jacob is **b** us.'" For he Gn 32:20
your flocks and your herds remain **b**." Ex 10:24
not a hoof shall be left **b**, for we must Ex 10:26
of the slave girl who is **b** the handmill, Ex 11:5
host of Israel moved and went **b** them, Ex 14:19
from before them and stood **b** them, Ex 14:19
were to camp **b** the tabernacle on Nm 3:23
your tail, those who were lagging **b** you, Dt 25:18
Lay an ambush against the city, **b** it." Jos 8:2
shall lie in ambush against the city, **b** it. Jos 8:4
was an ambush against him **b** the city. Jos 8:14
of the roof chamber **b** him and locked Jgs 3:23
the Benjaminites looked **b** them, Jgs 20:40
was coming from the field **b** the oxen. 1 Sm 11:5
is here wrapped in a cloth **b** the ephod. 1 Sm 21:9
king!" And when Saul looked **b** him, 1 Sm 24:8
where those who were left **b** stayed. 1 Sm 30:9
Two hundred stayed **b**, who were too 1 Sm 30:10
my master left me **b** because I fell 1 Sm 30:13
And when he looked **b** him, he saw me, 2 Sm 1:7
Then Abner looked **b** him and said, 2 Sm 2:20
themselves together **b** Abner and 2 Sm 2:25
coming from the road **b** him by the 2 Sm 13:34
anger, and have cast me **b** your back, 1 Kgs 14:9
and shut the door **b** yourself and your 2 Kgs 4:4
and shut the door **b** herself and her 2 Kgs 4:5
and shut the door **b** him and went 2 Kgs 4:21
and shut the door **b** the two of them 2 Kgs 4:33
the sound of his master's feet **b** him?" 2 Kgs 6:32
Turn around and ride **b** me." And the 2 Kgs 9:18
peace? Turn around and ride **b** me." 2 Kgs 9:19
I rode side by side **b** Ahab his father, 2 Kgs 9:25
third at the gate **b** the guards) shall 2 Kgs 11:6
she wags her head **b** you—the 2 Kgs 19:21
around to come upon them from **b**. 2 Chr 13:13
Judah, and the ambush was **b** them. 2 Chr 13:13
battle was in front of and **b** them. 2 Chr 13:14
the lowest parts of the space **b** the wall, Neh 4:13
the leaders stood **b** the whole house Neh 4:16
and cast your law **b** their back and Neh 9:26
B him he leaves a shining wake; one Jb 41:32
her virgin companions following **b** her. Ps 45:14
and you cast my words **b** you. Ps 50:17
You hem me in, **b** and before, and lay Ps 139:5
Behold, there he stands **b** our wall, gazing Sg 2:9
beautiful! Your eyes are doves **b** your veil. Sg 4:1
like halves of a pomegranate **b** your veil. Sg 4:3
like halves of a pomegranate **b** your veil. Sg 6:7
chambers, and shut your doors **b** you; Is 26:20
And your ears shall hear a word **b** you, Is 30:21
she wags her head **b** you—the daughter Is 37:22
you have cast all my sins **b** your back. Is 38:17
B the door and the doorpost you have set Is 57:8
and I heard **b** me the voice of a great Ezk 3:12
me and cast me **b** your back, Ezk 23:35
whom you left **b** shall fall by Ezk 24:21
before them, and **b** them a flame burns. Jl 2:3
them, but **b** them a desolate wilderness, Jl 2:3
and relent, and leave a blessing **b** him, Jl 2:14
trees in the glen, and **b** him were red, Zec 1:8
years came up **b** him and touched Mt 9:20
he turned and said to Peter, "Get **b** me, Mt 16:23
Jesus and came up **b** him in the crowd Mk 5:27
he rebuked Peter and said, "Get **b** me, Mk 8:33
the boy Jesus stayed **b** in Jerusalem. Lk 2:43
and standing **b** him at his feet, weeping, Lk 7:38
She came up **b** him and touched the Lk 8:44
on him the cross, to carry it **b** Jesus. Lk 23:26
forgetting what lies **b** and straining Phil 3:13
willing to be left **b** at Athens alone, 1 Thes 3:1
into the inner place **b** the curtain, Heb 6:19
B the second curtain was a second Heb 9:3
and I heard **b** me a loud voice like a Rv 1:10
creatures, full of eyes in front and **b**: Rv 4:6

BEHOLD (1102)
"**B**, I have given you every plant yielding Gn 1:29
saw everything that he had made, and **b**, Gn 1:31
"**B**, the man has become like one of us Gn 3:22
B, you have driven me today away from Gn 4:14
And God saw the earth, and **b**, it was Gn 6:12
B, I will destroy them with the earth. Gn 6:13
For **b**, I will bring a flood of waters upon Gn 6:17
back to him in the evening, and **b**, Gn 8:11
covering of the ark and looked, and **b**, Gn 8:13
"**B**, I establish my covenant with you and Gn 9:9
the LORD said, "**B**, they are one people, Gn 11:6
"**B**, you have given me no offspring, Gn 15:3
And **b**, the word of the LORD came to Gn 15:4
a deep sleep fell on Abram. And **b**, Gn 15:12
b, a smoking fire pot and a flaming Gn 15:17
And Sarai said to Abram, "**B** now, the Gn 16:2
Sarai, "**B**, your servant is in your power; Gn 16:6
"**B**, you are pregnant and shall bear a Gn 16:11
"**B**, my covenant is with you, and you Gn 17:4
b, I have blessed him and will make Gn 17:20
He lifted up his eyes and looked, and **b**, Gn 18:2
"**B**, I have undertaken to speak to the Gn 18:27
"**B**, I have undertaken to speak to the Gn 18:31
B, I have two daughters who have not Gn 19:8
B, your servant has found favor in Gn 19:19
B, this city is near enough to flee to, Gn 19:20
to him, "**B**, I grant you this favor also, Gn 19:21
b, the smoke of the land went up like Gn 19:28
"**B**, I lay last night with my father. Gn 19:34
"**B**, you are a dead man because of the Gn 20:3
said, "**B**, my land is before you; Gn 20:15
"**B**, I have given your brother a Gn 20:16
son." He said, "**B**, the fire and the wood, Gn 22:7
lifted up his eyes and looked, and **b**, Gn 22:13
"**B**, Milcah also has borne children to Gn 22:20
B, I am standing by the spring of water, Gn 24:13
he had finished speaking, **b**, Rebekah, Gn 24:15
to me," he went to the man. And **b**, Gn 24:30
b, I am standing by the spring of water. Gn 24:43
b, Rebekah came out with her water Gn 24:45
B, Rebekah is before you; take her and Gn 24:51
he lifted up his eyes and saw, and **b**, Gn 24:63
b, there were twins in her womb. Gn 25:24
Isaac and said, "**B**, she is your wife. Gn 26:9
He said, "**B**, I am old; I do not know the Gn 27:2
"**B**, my brother Esau is a hairy man, Gn 27:11
He took away my birthright, and **b**, Gn 27:36
"**B**, I have made him lord over you, Gn 27:37
"**B**, away from the fatness of the earth Gn 27:39
"**B**, your brother Esau comforts Gn 27:42
And he dreamed, and **b**, there was a Gn 28:12
the top of it reached to heaven. And **b**, Gn 28:12
And **b**, the LORD stood above it and Gn 28:13
B, I am with you and will keep you Gn 28:15
looked, he saw a well in the field, and **b**, Gn 29:2
He said, "**B**, it is still high day; it is not Gn 29:7
And in the morning, **b**, it was Leah! Gn 29:25
lifted up his eyes and looked, and **b**, Gn 33:1
dwell in the land and trade in it, for **b**, Gn 34:21
B, we were binding sheaves in the field, Gn 37:7
were binding sheaves in the field, and **b**, Gn 37:7
sheaf arose and stood upright. And **b**, Gn 37:7
said, "**B**, I have dreamed another dream. Gn 37:9
B, the sun, the moon, and eleven stars Gn 37:9
his hand, **b**, his brother came out. Gn 38:29
"**B**, because of me my master has no Gn 39:8
and **b**, there came up out of the Nile Gn 41:2
And **b**, seven other cows, ugly and thin, Gn 41:3
and dreamed a second time. And **b**, Gn 41:5
And **b**, after them sprouted seven ears, Gn 41:6
And Pharaoh awoke, and **b**, it was a Gn 41:7
"**B**, in my dream I was standing on the Gn 41:17
"**B**, I have heard that there is grain for Gn 42:2
one man in the land of Canaan, and **b**, Gn 42:13
b, every man's bundle of money was in Gn 42:35
B, the money that we found in the Gn 44:8
b, we are my lord's servants, both we Gn 44:16
"**B**, I have this day bought you and Gn 47:23
"**B**, your father is ill." So he took with Gn 48:1
'**B**, I will make you fruitful and multiply Gn 48:4
never expected to see your face; and **b**, Gn 48:11
said to Joseph, "**B**, I am about to die, Gn 48:21
and said, "**B**, we are your servants." Gn 50:18
"**B**, the people of Israel are too many and Ex 1:9
she opened it, she saw the child, and **b**, Ex 2:6
b, two Hebrews were struggling together. Ex 2:13
He looked, and **b**, the bush was burning, Ex 3:2
b, the cry of the people of Israel has come Ex 3:9
Then Moses answered, "But **b**, they will Ex 4:1
it out, **b**, his hand was leprous like snow. Ex 4:6
b, it was restored like the rest of his flesh. Ex 4:7
B, he is coming out to meet you, and Ex 4:14
him go, **b**, I will kill your firstborn son.'" Ex 4:23
"**B**, the people of the land are now many, Ex 5:5
yet they say to us, 'Make bricks!' And **b**, Ex 5:16
"**B**, the people of Israel have not listened Ex 6:12
the LORD, "**B**, I am of uncircumcised lips. Ex 6:30
b, with the staff that is in my hand I will Ex 7:17
b, I will plague all your country with Ex 8:2
b, I will send swarms of flies on you and Ex 8:21
"**B**, I am going out from you and I will Ex 8:29
b, the hand of the LORD will fall with a Ex 9:3
And Pharaoh sent, and **b**, not one of the Ex 9:7
B, about this time tomorrow I will cause Ex 9:18
b, tomorrow I will bring locusts into Ex 10:4
of Israel lifted up their eyes, and **b**, Ex 14:10
"**B**, I am about to rain bread from Ex 16:4
looked toward the wilderness, and **b**, Ex 16:10
B, I will stand before you there on the Ex 17:6
"**B**, I am coming to you in a thick cloud, Ex 19:9
"**B**, I send an angel before you to guard Ex 23:20
"**B** the blood of the covenant that the Ex 24:8
for us until we return to you. And **b**, Ex 24:14
And **b**, I have appointed with him Ex 31:6
to Moses, "I have seen this people, and **b**, Ex 32:9
to you; **b**, my angel shall go before you. Ex 32:34
"**B**, there is a place by me where you Ex 33:21
he said, "**B**, I am making a covenant. Ex 34:10
B, I will drive out before you the Ex 34:11
the people of Israel saw Moses, and **b**, Ex 34:30
And Moses saw all the work, and **b**, Ex 39:43
the goat of the sin offering, and **b**, Lv 10:16
B, its blood was not brought into the Lv 10:18
"**B**, today they have offered their sin Lv 10:19
"**B**, I have taken the Levites from Nm 3:12
over the tent, **b**, Miriam was leprous, Nm 12:10
Aaron turned toward Miriam, and **b**, Nm 12:10
toward the tent of meeting. And **b**, Nm 16:42
into the midst of the assembly. And **b**, Nm 16:47
into the tent of the testimony, and **b**, Nm 17:8
of Israel said to Moses, "**B**, we perish, Nm 17:12
And **b**, I have taken your brothers the Nm 18:6
"**B**, I have given you charge of the Nm 18:8
"**B**, a people has come out of Egypt. Nm 22:5
'**B**, a people has come out of Egypt, Nm 22:11
B, I have come out to oppose you Nm 22:32
said to Balak, "**B**, I have come to you! Nm 22:38
And he returned to him, and **b**, he and Nm 23:6
crags I see him, from the hills I **b** him; Nm 23:9
b, a people dwelling alone, and not Nm 23:9
took you to curse my enemies, and **b**, Nm 23:11
And he came to him, and **b**, he was Nm 23:17
B, I received a command to bless: he Nm 23:20
B, a people! As a lioness it rises up and Nm 23:24
you to curse my enemies, and **b**, Nm 24:10
And now, **b**, I am going to my people. Nm 24:14

I see him, but not now; I **b** him, but	Nm 24:17
And **b**, one of the people of Israel came	Nm 25:6
'B, I give to him my covenant of peace,	Nm 25:12
B, these, on Balaam's advice, caused	Nm 31:16
of Jazer and the land of Gilead, and **b**,	Nm 32:1
And **b**, you have risen in your fathers'	Nm 32:14
b, you have sinned against the LORD,	Nm 32:23
your God has multiplied you, and **b**,	Dt 1:10
B, I have given into your hand Sihon the	Dt 2:24
'**B**, I have begun to give Sihon and his	Dt 2:31
Rephaim. **B**, his bed was a bed of iron.	Dt 3:11
'**B**, the LORD our God has shown us his	Dt 5:24
said to me, 'I have seen this people, and **b**,	Dt 9:13
And I looked, and **b**, you had sinned	Dt 9:16
B, to the LORD your God belong heaven	Dt 10:14
make search and ask diligently. And **b**,	Dt 13:14
and **b**, he has accused her of	Dt 22:17
And **b**, now I bring the first of the fruit	Dt 26:10
"**B**, the days approach when you must	Dt 31:14
"**B**, you are about to lie down with your	Dt 31:16
B, even today while I am yet alive with	Dt 31:27
"**B**, men of Israel have come here tonight	Jos 2:2
B, when we come into the land, you	Jos 2:18
B, the ark of the covenant of the Lord of	Jos 3:11
he lifted up his eyes and looked, and **b**,	Jos 5:13
and they ran to the tent; and **b**,	Jos 7:22
"**B**, you shall lie in ambush against the	Jos 8:4
b, the smoke of the city went up to	Jos 8:20
you, but now, **b**, it is dry and crumbly.	Jos 9:12
were new when we filled them, and **b**,	Jos 9:13
And now, **b**, we are in your hand.	Jos 9:25
And now, **b**, the LORD has kept me alive,	Jos 14:10
b, I am this day eighty-five years old.	Jos 14:10
"**B**, the people of Reuben and the people	Jos 22:11
say, '**B**, the copy of the altar of the LORD,	Jos 22:28
B, I have allotted to you as an	Jos 23:4
"**B**, this stone shall be a witness against	Jos 24:27
b, I have given the land into his hand."	Jgs 1:2
And **b**, as Barak was pursuing Sisera,	Jgs 4:22
B, my clan is the weakest in Manasseh,	Jgs 6:15
b, the altar of Baal was broken down,	Jgs 6:28
b, I am laying a fleece of wool on the	Jgs 6:37
b, a man was telling a dream to his	Jgs 7:13
And he said, "**B**, I dreamed a dream, and	Jgs 7:13
said, "Behold, I dreamed a dream, and **b**,	Jgs 7:13
and said, "**B** Zebah and Zalmunna,	Jgs 8:15
"**B**, Gaal the son of Ebed and his	Jgs 9:31
came to his home at Mizpah. And **b**,	Jgs 11:34
"**B**, you are barren and have not borne	Jgs 13:3
for **b**, you shall conceive and bear a son.	Jgs 13:5
'**B**, you shall conceive and bear a son.	Jgs 13:7
"**B**, the man who came to me the other	Jgs 13:10
to the vineyards of Timnah. And **b**,	Jgs 14:5
aside to see the carcass of the lion, and **b**,	Jgs 14:8
"**B**, I have not told my father nor my	Jgs 14:16
"**B**, you have mocked me and told me	Jgs 16:10
it in my ears, **b**, the silver is with me;	Jgs 17:2
them, for we have seen the land, and **b**,	Jgs 18:9
this day; **b**, it is west of Kiriath-jearim.	Jgs 18:12
"**B**, now the day has waned toward	Jgs 19:9
the night. **B**, the day draws to its close.	Jgs 19:9
And **b**, an old man was coming from	Jgs 19:16
hearts merry, **b**, the men of the city,	Jgs 19:22
B, here are my virgin daughter and his	Jgs 19:24
b, there was his concubine lying at the	Jgs 19:27
B, you people of Israel, all of you, give	Jgs 20:7
looked behind them, and **b**,	Jgs 20:40
come up to the LORD to Mizpah?" And **b**,	Jgs 21:8
b, not one of the inhabitants of	Jgs 21:9
"**B**, there is the yearly feast of the LORD	Jgs 21:19
And **b**, Boaz came from Bethlehem. And	Ru 2:4
man was startled and turned over, and **b**,	Ru 3:8
up to the gate and sat down there. And **b**,	Ru 4:1
B, the days are coming when I will cut	1 Sm 2:31
"**B**, I am about to do a thing in Israel	1 Sm 3:11
b, Dagon had fallen face downward on	1 Sm 5:3
b, Dagon had fallen face downward on	1 Sm 5:4
"**B**, you are old and your sons do not	1 Sm 8:5
"**B**, there is a man of God in this city,	1 Sm 9:6
"He is; **b**, he is just ahead of you.	1 Sm 9:12
go down before me to Gilgal. And **b**,	1 Sm 10:8
b, a group of prophets met him,	1 Sm 10:10
"**B**, he has hidden himself among the	1 Sm 10:22
b, Saul was coming from the field	1 Sm 11:5
"**B**, I have obeyed your voice in all	1 Sm 12:1
now, **b**, the king walks before you,	1 Sm 12:2
you, and I am old and gray; and **b**,	1 Sm 12:2
And now **b** the king whom you have	1 Sm 12:13
b, the LORD has set a king over you.	1 Sm 12:13
the burnt offering, **b**, Samuel came.	1 Sm 13:10
B, I am with you heart and soul."	1 Sm 14:7
said, "**B**, we will cross over to the men,	1 Sm 14:8
Gibeah of Benjamin looked, and **b**,	1 Sm 14:16
b, Jonathan and his armor-bearer	1 Sm 14:17
and went into the battle. And **b**,	1 Sm 14:20
b, there was honey on the ground.	1 Sm 14:25
the forest, **b**, the honey was dropping,	1 Sm 14:26
"**B**, the people are sinning against the	1 Sm 14:33
"Saul came to Carmel, and **b**,	1 Sm 15:12
B, to obey is better than sacrifice,	1 Sm 15:22
remains yet the youngest, but **b**,	1 Sm 16:11
Saul's servants said to him, "**B** now,	1 Sm 16:15
"**B**, I have seen a son of Jesse the	1 Sm 16:18
talked with them, **b**, the champion,	1 Sm 17:23
say, '**B**, the king has delight in you,	1 Sm 18:22
came in, **b**, the image was in the bed,	1 Sm 19:16
"**B**, David is at Naioth in Ramah."	1 Sm 19:19
"**B**, they are at Naioth in Ramah."	1 Sm 19:22
B, my father does nothing either great	1 Sm 20:2
"**B**, tomorrow is the new moon,	1 Sm 20:5
b, if he is well disposed toward David,	1 Sm 20:12
And **b**, I will send the young man,	1 Sm 20:21
b, the LORD is between you and me	1 Sm 20:23
b, it is here wrapped in a cloth behind	1 Sm 21:9
servants, "**B**, you see the man is mad.	1 Sm 21:14
"**B**, the Philistines are fighting against	1 Sm 23:1
him, "**B**, we are afraid here in Judah;	1 Sm 23:3
"**B**, David is in the wilderness of	1 Sm 24:1
'**B**, I will give your enemy into your	1 Sm 24:4
who say, '**B**, David seeks your harm'?	1 Sm 24:9
B, this day your eyes have seen how	1 Sm 24:10
b, I know that you shall surely be	1 Sm 24:20
"**B**, David sent messengers out of the	1 Sm 25:14
b, I come after you." But she did not	1 Sm 25:19
b, David and his men came down	1 Sm 25:20
And Abigail came to Nabal, and **b**,	1 Sm 25:36
"**B**, your handmaid is a servant to	1 Sm 25:41
B, I have acted foolishly, and have	1 Sm 26:21
B, as your life was precious this day	1 Sm 26:24
him, "**B**, there is a medium at En-dor."	1 Sm 28:7
"**B**, your servant has obeyed you.	1 Sm 28:21
b, they were spread abroad over all	1 Sm 30:16
day, **b**, a man came from Saul's camp,	2 Sm 1:2
was Saul leaning on his spear, and **b**,	2 Sm 1:6
b, it is written in the Book of Jashar.	2 Sm 1:18
Make your covenant with me, and **b**,	2 Sm 3:12
have you done? **B**, Abner came to you.	2 Sm 3:24
when one told me, '**B**, Saul is dead,'	2 Sm 4:10
said, "**B**, we are your bone and flesh.	2 Sm 5:1
he answered, "**B**, I am your servant."	2 Sm 9:6
'**B**, I will raise up evil against you out	2 Sm 12:11
said, "**B**, while the child was yet alive,	2 Sm 12:18
"**B**, your servant has sheepshearers.	2 Sm 13:24
lifted up his eyes and looked, and **b**,	2 Sm 13:34
king, "**B**, the king's sons have come;	2 Sm 13:35
b, the king's sons came and lifted up	2 Sm 13:36
Then the king said to Joab, "**B** now, I	2 Sm 14:21
answered Joab, "**B**, I sent word to you,	2 Sm 14:32
"**B**, your servants are ready to do	2 Sm 15:15
And Abiathar came up, and **b**,	2 Sm 15:24
no pleasure in you,' **b**, here I am,	2 Sm 15:26
b, Hushai the Archite came to meet	2 Sm 15:32
B, their two sons are with them there,	2 Sm 15:36
the king, "**B**, he remains in Jerusalem,	2 Sm 16:3
"**B**, all that belonged to Mephibosheth	2 Sm 16:4
"**B**, my own son seeks my life;	2 Sm 16:11
B, even now he has hidden himself in	2 Sm 17:9
"**B**, I saw Absalom hanging in an	2 Sm 18:10
And **b**, the Cushite came, and the	2 Sm 18:31
"**B**, the king is weeping and mourning	2 Sm 19:1
"**B**, the king is sitting in the gate." And	2 Sm 19:8
Therefore, **b**, I have come this day,	2 Sm 19:20
"**B**, his head shall be thrown to you	2 Sm 20:21
people, and said, "**B**, I have sinned,	2 Sm 24:17
And now, **b**, Adonijah is king,	1 Kgs 1:18
army, and Abiathar the priest. And **b**,	1 Kgs 1:25
b, Jonathan the son of Abiathar the	1 Kgs 1:42
"**B**, Adonijah fears King Solomon,	1 Kgs 1:51
Adonijah fears King Solomon, for **b**,	1 Kgs 1:51
has fled to the tent of the LORD, and **b**,	1 Kgs 2:29
"**B**, your servants are in Gath,"	1 Kgs 2:39
b, I now do according to your word.	1 Kgs 3:12
B, I give you a wise and discerning	1 Kgs 3:12
And Solomon awoke, and **b**, it was a	1 Kgs 3:15
to nurse my child, **b**, he was dead.	1 Kgs 3:21
b, he was not the child that I had	1 Kgs 3:21
B, heaven and the highest heaven	1 Kgs 8:27
and my own eyes had seen it. And **b**,	1 Kgs 10:7
'**B**, I am about to tear the kingdom	1 Kgs 11:31
B your gods, O Israel, who brought	1 Kgs 12:28
And **b**, a man of God came out of	1 Kgs 13:1
'**B**, a son shall be born to the house of	1 Kgs 13:2
'**B**, the altar shall be torn down, and	1 Kgs 13:3
And **b**, men passed by and saw the	1 Kgs 13:25
B, Ahijah the prophet is there, who	1 Kgs 14:2
"**B**, the wife of Jeroboam is coming to	1 Kgs 14:5
therefore **b**, I will bring harm upon	1 Kgs 14:10
b, they are written in the Book of the	1 Kgs 14:19
B, I am sending to you a present of	1 Kgs 15:19
b, I will utterly sweep away Baasha	1 Kgs 16:3
B, I have commanded a widow there	1 Kgs 17:9
b, a widow was there gathering	1 Kgs 17:10
was on the way, **b**, Elijah met him.	1 Kgs 18:7
Go, tell your lord, '**B**, Elijah is here.'"	1 Kgs 18:8
tell your lord, "**B**, Elijah is here."'	1 Kgs 18:11
tell your lord, "**B**, Elijah is here"';	1 Kgs 18:14
"**B**, a little cloud like a man's hand	1 Kgs 18:44
and slept under a broom tree. And **b**,	1 Kgs 19:5
And he looked, and **b**, there was at his	1 Kgs 19:6
to a cave and lodged in it. And **b**,	1 Kgs 19:9
the mount before the LORD." And **b**,	1 Kgs 19:11
at the entrance of the cave. And **b**,	1 Kgs 19:13
And **b**, a prophet came near to Ahab	1 Kgs 20:13
B, I will give it into your hand this	1 Kgs 20:13
his servants said to him, "**B** now,	1 Kgs 20:31
b, as soon as you have gone from	1 Kgs 20:36
into the midst of the battle, and **b**,	1 Kgs 20:39
b, he is in the vineyard of Naboth,	1 Kgs 21:18
B, I will bring disaster upon you. I	1 Kgs 21:21
"**B**, the words of the prophets with	1 Kgs 22:13
Now therefore **b**, the LORD has put a	1 Kgs 22:23
"**B**, you shall see on that day when	1 Kgs 22:25
B, fire came down from heaven and	2 Kgs 1:14
b, chariots of fire and horses of fire	2 Kgs 2:11
And they said to him, "**B** now, there	2 Kgs 2:16
"**B**, the situation of this city is	2 Kgs 2:19
b, water came from the direction of	2 Kgs 3:20
And she said to her husband, "**B** now, I	2 Kgs 4:9
"**B**, I thought that he would surely	2 Kgs 5:11
"**B**, I know that there is no God in all	2 Kgs 5:15
It was told him, "**B**, he is in Dothan."	2 Kgs 6:13
b, an army with horses and chariots	2 Kgs 6:15
of the young man, and he saw, and **b**,	2 Kgs 6:17
opened their eyes and they saw, and **b**,	2 Kgs 6:20
wall—and the people looked, and **b**,	2 Kgs 6:30
the Syrians, **b**, there was no one there.	2 Kgs 7:5
"**B**, the king of Israel has hired against	2 Kgs 7:6
to the camp of the Syrians, and **b**,	2 Kgs 7:10
after them as far as the Jordan, and **b**,	2 Kgs 7:15
b, the woman whose son he had	2 Kgs 8:5
b, the commanders of the army were	2 Kgs 9:5
"**B**, the two kings could not stand	2 Kgs 10:4
b, a marauding band was seen and	2 Kgs 13:21
b, they are written in the Book of the	2 Kgs 15:11
b, they are written in the Book of the	2 Kgs 15:15
b, they are written in the Book of the	2 Kgs 15:26
b, they are written in the Book of the	2 Kgs 15:31
has sent lions among them, and **b**,	2 Kgs 17:26
B, you are trusting now in Egypt,	2 Kgs 18:21
B, I will put a spirit in him, so that he	2 Kgs 19:7
"**B**, he has set out to fight against	2 Kgs 19:9
B, you have heard what the kings of	2 Kgs 19:11
b, these were all dead bodies.	2 Kgs 19:35
seen your tears. **B**, I will heal you.	2 Kgs 20:5
B, the days are coming, when all	2 Kgs 20:17
B, I am bringing upon Jerusalem	2 Kgs 21:12
b, I will bring disaster upon this	2 Kgs 22:16
b, I will gather you to your fathers,	2 Kgs 22:20
said, "**B**, we are your bone and flesh.	1 Chr 11:1
"**B**, I dwell in a house of cedar,	1 Chr 17:1
B, a son shall be born to you who	1 Chr 22:9
And **b** the divisions of the priests	1 Chr 28:21
B, I am about to build a house for the	2 Chr 2:4
B, heaven and the highest heaven	2 Chr 6:18
and my own eyes had seen it. And **b**,	2 Chr 9:6
b, God is with us at our head, and	2 Chr 13:12
b, the battle was in front of and	2 Chr 13:14
B, I am sending to you silver and	2 Chr 16:3
"**B**, the words of the prophets with	2 Chr 18:12
Now therefore **b**, the LORD has put a	2 Chr 18:22
"**B**, you shall see on that day when	2 Chr 18:24
And **b**, Amariah the chief priest is	2 Chr 19:11
b, they are in Hazazon-tamar" (that	2 Chr 20:2
And now **b**, the men of Ammon and	2 Chr 20:10
b, they reward us by coming to	2 Chr 20:11
B, they will come up by the ascent	2 Chr 20:16
they looked toward the horde, and **b**,	2 Chr 20:24
b, the LORD will bring a great plague	2 Chr 21:14
said to them, "**B**, the king's son!	2 Chr 23:3
all the priests looked at him, and **b**,	2 Chr 26:20
b, they are written in the Book of the	2 Chr 27:7
said to them, "**B**, because the LORD,	2 Chr 28:9
b, they are written in the Book of the	2 Chr 28:26
For **b**, our fathers have fallen by the	2 Chr 29:9
made ready and consecrated, and **b**,	2 Chr 29:19
b, they are written in the vision of	2 Chr 32:32
b, they are in the Chronicles of the	2 Chr 33:18
b, they are written in the Chronicles	2 Chr 33:19
b, I will bring disaster upon this	2 Chr 34:24
B, I will gather you to your fathers,	2 Chr 34:28
b, they are written in the Laments.	2 Chr 35:25
b, they are written in the Book of the	2 Chr 35:27
b, they are written in the Book of the	2 Chr 36:8
B, we are before you in our guilt, for	Ezr 9:15
B, we are slaves this day; in the land	Neh 9:36

fruit and its good gifts, **b**, we are slaves. Neh 9:36
"**B**, I have given Esther the house of Est 8:7
Satan, "**B**, all that he has is in your hand. Jb 1:12
and **b**, a great wind came across the Jb 1:19
LORD said to Satan, "**B**, he is in your hand; Jb 2:6
B, let that night be barren; let no joyful Jb 3:7
B, you have instructed many, and you Jb 4:3
"**B**, blessed is the one whom God Jb 5:17
B, this we have searched out; it is true. Jb 5:27
eye of him who sees me will **b** me no more; Jb 7:8
B, this is the joy of his way, and out of the Jb 8:19
"**B**, God will not reject a blameless man, Jb 8:20
B, he passes by me, and I see him not; he Jb 9:11
B, he snatches away; who can turn him Jb 9:12
it is a contest of strength, **b**, he is mighty! Jb 9:19
"**B**, my eye has seen all this, my ear has Jb 13:1
B, I have prepared my case; I know that I Jb 13:18
B, God puts no trust in his holy ones, Jb 15:15
Even now, **b**, my witness is in heaven, Jb 16:19
B, I cry out, 'Violence!' but I am not Jb 19:7
see for myself, and my eyes shall **b**, Jb 19:27
more, nor will his place any more **b** him. Jb 20:9
B, is not their prosperity in their hand? Jb 21:16
"**B**, I know your thoughts and your Jb 21:27
"**B**, I go forward, but he is not there, and Jb 23:8
hand when he is working, I do not **b** him; Jb 23:9
B, like wild donkeys in the desert the poor Jb 24:5
B, even the moon is not bright, and the Jb 25:5
B, these are but the outskirts of his Jb 26:14
B, all of you have seen it yourselves; Jb 27:12
he said to man, '**B**, the fear of the Lord, Jb 28:28
"**B**, I waited for your words, I listened for Jb 32:11
b, there was none among you who Jb 32:12
B, my belly is like wine that has no Jb 32:19
B, I open my mouth; the tongue in my Jb 33:2
B, I am toward God as you are; I too was Jb 33:6
B, no fear of me need terrify you; my Jb 33:7
B, he finds occasions against me, he Jb 33:10
"**B**, in this you are not right. I will Jb 33:12
"**B**, God does all these things, twice, Jb 33:29
he hides his face, who can **b** him, Jb 34:29
and **b** the clouds, which are higher than Jb 35:5
"**B**, God is mighty, and does not despise Jb 36:5
B, God is exalted in his power; who is a Jb 36:22
B, God is great, and we know him not; Jb 36:26
B, he scatters his lightning about him Jb 36:30
spies out the prey; his eyes **b** it afar off. Jb 39:29
"**B**, I am of small account; what shall I Jb 40:4
"**B**, Behemoth, which I made as I made Jb 40:15
B, his strength in his loins, and his Jb 40:16
B, if the river is turbulent he is not Jb 40:23
B, the hope of a man is false; he is laid Jb 41:9
B, the wicked man conceives evil and is Ps 7:14
for **b**, the wicked bend the bow; they Ps 11:2
deeds; the upright shall **b** his face. Ps 11:7
come! Let your eyes **b** the right! Ps 17:2
me, I shall **b** your face in righteousness; Ps 17:15
B, the eye of the LORD is on those who Ps 33:18
But he passed away, and **b**, he was no Ps 37:36
Mark the blameless and **b** the upright, Ps 37:37
B, you have made my days a few Ps 39:5
Then I said, "**B**, I have come; in the scroll Ps 40:7
b, I have not restrained my lips, as you Ps 40:9
Come, **b** the works of the LORD, how he Ps 46:8
For **b**, the kings assembled; they came Ps 48:4
B, I was brought forth in iniquity, and in Ps 51:5
B, you delight in truth in the inward Ps 51:6
B, God is my helper; the Lord is the Ps 54:4
For **b**, they lie in wait for my life; fierce Ps 59:3
b, he sends out his voice, his mighty Ps 68:33
B, these are the wicked; always at ease, Ps 73:12
For **b**, those who are far from you shall Ps 73:27
For **b**, your enemies make an uproar; Ps 83:2
B our shield, O God; look on the face of Ps 84:9
b, Philistia and Tyre, with Cush— Ps 87:4
For **b**, your enemies, O LORD, for behold, Ps 92:9
For behold, your enemies, O LORD, for **b**, Ps 92:9
that I may **b** wondrous things out of Ps 119:18
B, I long for your precepts; in your Ps 119:40
B, he who keeps Israel will neither Ps 121:4
B, as the eyes of servants look to the Ps 123:2
B, children are a heritage from the Ps 127:3
B, thus shall the man be blessed who Ps 128:4
B, we heard of it in Ephrathah; we Ps 132:6
B, how good and pleasant it is when Ps 133:1
a word is on my tongue, **b**, O LORD, Ps 139:4
b, I will pour out my spirit to you; Prv 1:23
And **b**, the woman meets him, dressed Prv 7:10
"**B**, we did not know this," does not he Prv 24:12
and **b**, it was all overgrown with Prv 24:31
that is done under the sun, and **b**, Eccl 1:14
enjoy yourself." But **b**, this also was Eccl 2:1
toil I had expended in doing it, and **b**, Eccl 2:11
that are done under the sun. And **b**, Eccl 4:1
B, what I have seen to be good and Eccl 5:18
B, this is what I found, says the Eccl 7:27
B, you are beautiful, my love; behold, Sg 1:15
beautiful, my love; **b**, you are beautiful; Sg 1:15
B, you are beautiful, my beloved, truly Sg 1:16
B, he comes, leaping over the mountains, Sg 2:8
B, there he stands behind our wall, gazing Sg 2:9
for **b**, the winter is past; the rain is over Sg 2:11
B, it is the litter of Solomon! Around it are Sg 3:7
B, you are beautiful, my love, behold, you Sg 4:1
beautiful, my love, **b**, you are beautiful! Sg 4:1
For **b**, the Lord GOD of hosts is taking away Is 3:1
and he looked for justice, but **b**, bloodshed; Is 5:7
for righteousness, but **b**, an outcry! Is 5:7
them from the ends of the earth; and **b**, Is 5:26
to the land, **b**, darkness and distress; Is 5:30
and said: "**B**, this has touched your lips; Is 6:7
B, the virgin shall conceive and bear a Is 7:14
b, the Lord is bringing up against them Is 8:7
B, I and the children whom the LORD has Is 8:18
And they will look to the earth, but **b**, Is 8:22
B, the Lord GOD of hosts will lop the Is 10:33
"**B**, God is my salvation; I will trust, and Is 12:2
B, the day of the LORD comes, cruel, with Is 13:9
B, I am stirring up the Medes against Is 13:17
B, Damascus will cease to be a city and Is 17:1
At evening time, **b**, terror! Before Is 17:14
B, the LORD is riding on a swift cloud and Is 19:1
'**B**, this is what has happened to those in Is 20:6
And **b**, here come riders, horsemen in Is 21:9
and **b**, joy and gladness, killing oxen Is 22:13
B, the LORD will hurl you away violently, Is 22:17
B the land of the Chaldeans! This is the Is 23:13
B, the LORD will empty the earth and Is 24:1
be said on that day, "**B**, this is our God; Is 25:9
For **b**, the LORD is coming out from his Is 26:21
B, the Lord has one who is mighty and Is 28:2
"**B**, I am the one who has laid as a Is 28:16
b, I will again do wonderful things with Is 29:14
B, the name of the LORD comes from Is 30:27
B, a king will reign in righteousness, and Is 32:1
B, their heroes cry in the streets; the Is 33:7
Your eyes will **b** the king in his beauty; Is 33:17
B Zion, the city of our appointed feasts! Is 33:20
b, it descends for judgment upon Edom, Is 34:5
B, your God will come with vengeance, Is 35:4
B, you are trusting in Egypt, that broken Is 36:6
B, I will put a spirit in him, so that he Is 37:7
B, you have heard what the kings of Is 37:11
morning, **b**, these were all dead bodies. Is 37:36
tears. **B**, I will add fifteen years to your life. Is 38:5
B, I will make the shadow cast by the Is 38:8
B, it was for my welfare that I had great Is 38:17
B, the days are coming, when all that is in Is 39:6
say to the cities of Judah, "**B** your God!" Is 40:9
B, the Lord GOD comes with might, and Is 40:10
b, his reward is with him, and his Is 40:10
B, the nations are like a drop from a Is 40:15
b, he takes up the coastlands like fine Is 40:15
B, all who are incensed against you Is 41:11
B, I make of you a threshing sledge, new, Is 41:15
B, you are nothing, and your work is Is 41:24
"**B**, here they are!" and I give to Is 41:27
B, they are all a delusion; their works are Is 41:29
B my servant, whom I uphold, my Is 42:1
B, the former things have come to pass, Is 42:9
B, I am doing a new thing; now it Is 43:19
B, all his companions shall be put to Is 44:11
B, they are like stubble; the fire Is 47:14
lest you should say, '**B**, I knew them.' Is 48:7
B, I have refined you, but not as silver; I Is 48:10
B, these shall come from afar, and Is 49:12
these shall come from afar, and **b**, Is 49:12
B, I have engraved you on the palms of Is 49:16
B, I was left alone; from where have these Is 49:21
"**B**, I will lift up my hand to the nations, Is 49:22
B, for your iniquities you were sold, and Is 50:1
B, by my rebuke I dry up the sea, I make Is 50:2
B, the Lord GOD helps me; who will Is 50:9
B, all of them will wear out like a Is 50:9
B, all you who kindle a fire, who equip Is 50:11
"**B**, I have taken from your hand the cup Is 51:22
B, my servant shall act wisely; he shall Is 52:13
b, I will set your stones in antimony, Is 54:11
B, I have created the smith who blows Is 54:16
B, I made him a witness to the peoples, a Is 55:4
B, you shall call a nation that you do not Is 55:5
not the eunuch say, "**B**, I am a dry tree." Is 56:3
B, in the day of your fast you seek your Is 58:3
B, you fast only to quarrel and to fight Is 58:4
B, the LORD'S hand is not shortened, that it Is 59:1
we hope for light, and **b**, darkness, and for Is 59:9
For **b**, darkness shall cover the earth, and Is 60:2
B, the LORD has proclaimed to the end of Is 62:11
of Zion, "**B**, your salvation comes; Is 62:11
b, his reward is with him, and his Is 62:11
B, you were angry, and we sinned; in our Is 64:5
B, please look, we are all your people. Is 64:9
B, it is written before me: "I will not keep Is 65:6
"**B**, my servants shall eat, but you shall Is 65:13
b, my servants shall drink, but you Is 65:13
b, my servants shall rejoice, but you Is 65:13
b, my servants shall sing for gladness of Is 65:14
"For **b**, I create new heavens and a new Is 65:17
forever in that which I create; for **b**, Is 65:18
"**B**, I will extend peace to her like a river, Is 66:12
"For **b**, the LORD will come in fire, and Is 66:15
B, I do not know how to speak, for I am Jer 1:6
"**B**, I have put my words in your mouth. Jer 1:9
For **b**, I am calling all the tribes of the Jer 1:15
I, **b**, I make you this day a fortified city, Jer 1:18
O generation, **b** the word of the LORD. Jer 2:31
B, I will bring you to judgment for Jer 2:35
B, you have spoken, but you have done all Jer 3:5
I will heal your faithlessness." "**B**, we Jer 3:22
B, he comes up like clouds; his chariots Jer 4:13
I looked on the earth, and **b**, it was Jer 4:23
I looked on the mountains, and **b**, they Jer 4:24
I looked, and **b**, there was no man, and Jer 4:25
I looked, and **b**, the fruitful land was a Jer 4:26
b, I am making my words in your Jer 5:14
B, I am bringing against you a nation Jer 5:15
B, their ears are uncircumcised, they Jer 6:10
b, the word of the LORD is to them an Jer 6:10
b, I am bringing disaster upon this Jer 6:19
'**B**, I will lay before this people stumbling Jer 6:21
"**B**, a people is coming from the north Jer 6:22
"**B**, you trust in deceptive words to no Jer 7:8
B, I myself have seen it, declares the Jer 7:11
b, my anger and my wrath will be Jer 7:20
Therefore, **b**, the days are coming, Jer 7:32
and the law of the LORD is with us'? But **b**, Jer 8:8
b, they have rejected the word of the LORD, Jer 8:9
came; for a time of healing, but **b**, terror. Jer 8:15
For **b**, I am sending among you serpents, Jer 8:17
B, the cry of the daughter of my people Jer 8:19
"**B**, I will refine them and test them, for Jer 9:7
B, I will feed this people with bitter food, Jer 9:15
"**B**, the days are coming, declares the Jer 9:25
"**B**, I am slinging out the inhabitants of Jer 10:18
A voice, a rumor! **B**, it comes!— Jer 10:22
b, I am bringing disaster upon them Jer 11:11
LORD of hosts: "**B**, I will punish them. Jer 11:22
"**B**, I will pluck them up from their Jer 12:14
the place where I had hidden it. And **b**, Jer 13:7
B, I will fill with drunkenness all the Jer 13:13
Lord GOD, **b**, the prophets say to them, Jer 14:13
the field, **b**, those pierced by the sword! Jer 14:18
enter the city, **b**, the diseases of famine! Jer 14:18
for a time of healing, but **b**, terror. Jer 14:19
B, I will silence in this place, before your Jer 16:9
done worse than your fathers, for **b**, Jer 16:12
"Therefore, **b**, the days are coming, Jer 16:14
"**B**, I am sending for many fishers, Jer 16:16
"Therefore, **b**, I will make them know, Jer 16:21
B, they say to me, "Where is the word of Jer 17:15
B, like the clay in the potter's hand, so Jer 18:6
b, I am shaping disaster against you Jer 18:11
B, I am bringing such disaster upon this Jer 19:3
therefore, **b**, days are coming, declares Jer 19:6
b, I am bringing upon this city and Jer 19:15
B, I will make you a terror to yourself Jer 20:4
B, I will turn back the weapons of war Jer 21:4
B, I set before you the way of life and the Jer 21:8
"**B**, I am against you, O inhabitant of Jer 21:13
B, I will attend to you for your evil deeds, Jer 23:2
"**B**, the days are coming, declares the Jer 23:5
"Therefore, **b**, the days are coming, Jer 23:7
"**B**, I will feed them with bitter food and Jer 23:15
B, the storm of the LORD! Wrath has Jer 23:19
Therefore, **b**, I am against the prophets, Jer 23:30
B, I am against the prophets, declares Jer 23:31
B, I am against those who prophesy Jer 23:32
b, I will surely lift you up and cast you Jer 23:39
b, two baskets of figs placed before the Jer 24:1
b, I will send for all the tribes of the Jer 25:9
For **b**, I begin to work disaster at the Jer 25:29
B, disaster is going forth from nation to Jer 25:32
But as for me, **b**, I am in your hands. Jer 26:14
'**B**, the vessels of the LORD'S house will Jer 27:16
'**B**, I will remove you from the face of Jer 28:16
hosts, **b**, I am sending on them sword, Jer 29:17
B, I will deliver them into the hand of Jer 29:21
B, I will punish Shemaiah of Nehelam Jer 29:32
For **b**, days are coming, declares the Jer 30:3
LORD, nor be dismayed, O Israel; for **b**, Jer 30:10
B, I will restore the fortunes of the tents Jer 30:18
B the storm of the LORD! Wrath has Jer 30:23
B, I will bring them from the north Jer 31:8
"**B**, the days are coming, declares the Jer 31:27
"**B**, the days are coming, declares the Jer 31:31

“**B**, the days are coming, declares the Jer 31:38
B, I am giving this city into the hand of Jer 32:3
B, Hanamel the son of Shallum your Jer 32:7
B, the siege mounds have come up to Jer 32:24
you spoke has come to pass, and **b**, Jer 32:24
“**B**, I am the LORD, the God of all flesh. Is Jer 32:27
B, I am giving this city into the hands Jer 32:28
B, I will gather them from all the Jer 32:37
B, I will bring to it health and healing, Jer 33:6
“**B**, the days are coming, declares the Jer 33:14
B, I am giving this city into the hand of Jer 34:2
b, I proclaim to you liberty to the Jer 34:17
B, I will command, declares the LORD, Jer 34:22
B, I am bringing upon Judah and all Jer 35:17
‘**B**, Pharaoh’s army that came to help Jer 37:7
Zedekiah said, “**B**, he is in your hands, Jer 38:5
B, all the women left in the house of the Jer 38:22
B, I will fulfill my words against this Jer 39:16
b, I release you today from the chains on Jer 40:4
B, I will pray to the LORD your God Jer 42:4
B, I will send and take Nebuchadnezzar Jer 43:10
B, this day they are a desolation, and no Jer 44:2
B, I will set my face against you for Jer 44:11
B, I have sworn by my great name, says Jer 44:26
B, I am watching over them for disaster Jer 44:27
b, I will give Pharaoh Hophra king of Jer 44:30
B, what I have built I am breaking Jer 45:4
Seek them not, for **b**, I am bringing Jer 45:5
“**B**, I am bringing punishment upon Jer 46:25
nor be dismayed, O Israel, for **b**, Jer 46:27
B, waters are rising out of the north, and Jer 47:2
“Therefore, **b**, the days are coming, Jer 48:12
“**B**, one shall fly swiftly like an eagle Jer 48:40
Therefore, **b**, the days are coming, Jer 49:2
B, I will bring terror upon you, declares Jer 49:5
For **b**, I will make you small among Jer 49:15
B, like a lion coming up from the Jer 49:19
B, one shall mount up and fly swiftly Jer 49:22
“**B**, I will break the bow of Elam, the Jer 49:35
For **b**, I am stirring up and bringing Jer 50:9
B, she shall be the last of the nations, a Jer 50:12
B, I am bringing punishment on the Jer 50:18
“**B**, I am against you, O proud one, Jer 50:31
“**B**, a people comes from the north; a Jer 50:41
“**B**, like a lion coming up from the Jer 50:44
“**B**, I will stir up the spirit of a destroyer Jer 51:1
“**B**, I am against you, O destroying Jer 51:25
“**B**, I will plead your cause and take Jer 51:36
b, the days are coming when I will Jer 51:47
“Therefore, **b**, the days are coming, Jer 51:52
“O LORD, **b** my affliction, for the enemy Lam 1:9
B their sitting and their rising; I am Lam 3:63
b, a stormy wind came out of the north, Ezk 1:4
b, a hand was stretched out to me, Ezk 2:9
a hand was stretched out to me, and **b**, Ezk 2:9
B, I have made your face as hard as their Ezk 3:8
and went out into the valley, and **b**, Ezk 3:23
man, **b**, cords will be placed upon you, Ezk 3:25
And **b**, I will place cords upon you, so Ezk 4:8
GOD! **B**, I have never defiled myself. Ezk 4:14
b, I will break the supply of bread in Ezk 4:16
Lord GOD: **B**, I, even I, am against you. Ezk 5:8
B, I, even I, will bring a sword upon you, Ezk 6:3
GOD: Disaster after disaster! **B**, it comes. Ezk 7:5
it has awakened against you. **B**, it comes. Ezk 7:6
“**B**, the day! Behold, it comes! Your Ezk 7:10
“Behold, the day! **B**, it comes! Your Ezk 7:10
Then I looked, and **b**, a form that had Ezk 8:2
And **b**, the glory of the God of Israel was Ezk 8:4
up my eyes toward the north, and **b**, Ezk 8:5
I looked, **b**, there was a hole in the wall. Ezk 8:7
in the wall.” So I dug in the wall, and **b**, Ezk 8:8
gate of the house of the LORD, and **b**, Ezk 8:14
court of the house of the LORD. And **b**, Ezk 8:16
B, they put the branch to their nose. Ezk 8:17
And **b**, six men came from the direction Ezk 9:2
And **b**, the man clothed in linen, with Ezk 9:11
Then I looked, and **b**, on the expanse Ezk 10:1
And I looked, and **b**, there were four Ezk 10:9
of the LORD, which faces east. And **b**, Ezk 11:1
man, **b**, they of the house of Israel say, Ezk 12:27
and seen lying visions, therefore **b**, Ezk 13:8
B, I am against your magic bands Ezk 13:20
But **b**, some survivors will be left in it, Ezk 14:22
b, when they come out to you, and Ezk 14:22
B, it is given to the fire for fuel. When Ezk 15:4
B, when it was whole, it was used for Ezk 15:5
saw you, **b**, you were at the age for love, Ezk 16:8
B, therefore, I stretched out my hand Ezk 16:27
b, I will gather all your lovers with Ezk 16:37
b, I have returned your deeds upon Ezk 16:43
“**B**, everyone who uses proverbs will Ezk 16:44
B, this was the guilt of your sister Ezk 16:49
great wings and much plumage, and **b**, Ezk 17:7
B, it is planted; will it thrive? Will it Ezk 17:10

b, the king of Babylon came to Ezk 17:12
oath in breaking the covenant, and **b**, Ezk 17:18
B, all souls are mine; the soul of the Ezk 18:4
people, **b**, he shall die for his iniquity. Ezk 18:18
Lord GOD, **B**, I will kindle a fire in you, Ezk 20:47
B, I am against you and will draw my Ezk 21:3
B, it is coming, and it will be fulfilled,’” Ezk 21:7
“**B**, the princes of Israel in you, every Ezk 22:6
“**B**, I strike my hand at the dishonest Ezk 22:13
b, I will gather you into the midst of Ezk 22:19
“**B**, I will stir up against you your Ezk 23:22
B, I will deliver you into the hands of Ezk 23:28
my sanctuary to profane it. And **b**, Ezk 23:39
to whom a messenger was sent; and **b**, Ezk 23:40
b, I am about to take the delight of Ezk 24:16
B, I will profane my sanctuary, the Ezk 24:21
therefore **b**, I am handing you over to Ezk 25:4
b, I have stretched out my hand against Ezk 25:7
‘**B**, the house of Judah is like all the Ezk 25:8
B, I will stretch out my hand against Ezk 25:16
B, I am against you, O Tyre, and will Ezk 26:3
B, I will bring against Tyre from the Ezk 26:7
b, I will bring foreigners upon you, Ezk 28:7
“**B**, I am against you, O Sidon, and I Ezk 28:22
“**B**, I am against you, Pharaoh king of Ezk 29:3
B, I will bring a sword upon you, and Ezk 29:8
b, I am against you and against your Ezk 29:10
B, I will give the land of Egypt to Ezk 29:19
day of Egypt’s doom; for, **b**, it comes! Ezk 30:9
arm of Pharaoh king of Egypt, and **b**, Ezk 30:21
B, I am against Pharaoh king of Egypt Ezk 30:22
B, Assyria was a cedar in Lebanon, Ezk 31:3
And **b**, you are to them like one who Ezk 33:32
GOD, **B**, I am against the shepherds, Ezk 34:10
B, I, I myself will search for my sheep Ezk 34:11
B, I judge between sheep and sheep, Ezk 34:17
B, I, I myself will judge between the fat Ezk 34:20
B, I am against you, Mount Seir, and I Ezk 35:3
B, I have spoken in my jealous wrath, Ezk 36:6
For **b**, I am for you, and I will turn to Ezk 36:9
he led me around among them, and **b**, Ezk 37:2
on the surface of the valley, and **b**, Ezk 37:2
B, I will cause breath to enter you, and Ezk 37:5
I prophesied, there was a sound, and **b**, Ezk 37:7
And I looked, and **b**, there were sinews Ezk 37:8
B, they say, ‘Our bones are dried up, Ezk 37:11
B, I will open your graves and raise Ezk 37:12
B, I am about to take the stick of Ezk 37:19
B, I will take the people of Israel from Ezk 37:21
B, I am against you, O Gog, chief prince Ezk 38:3
B, I am against you, O Gog, chief prince Ezk 39:1
B, it is coming and it will be brought Ezk 39:8
b, there was a man whose appearance Ezk 40:3
And **b**, there was a wall all around the Ezk 40:5
me into the outer court. And **b**, Ezk 40:17
he led me toward the south, and **b**, Ezk 40:24
And **b**, the glory of the God of Israel was Ezk 43:2
brought me into the inner court; and **b**, Ezk 43:5
holy. **B**, this is the law of the temple. Ezk 43:12
front of the temple, and I looked, and **b**, Ezk 44:4
holy chambers for the priests, and **b**, Ezk 46:19
to the four corners of the court. And **b**, Ezk 46:21
back to the door of the temple, and **b**, Ezk 47:1
gate that faces toward the east; and **b**, Ezk 47:2
“You saw, O king, and **b**, a great image. Dn 2:31
I saw, and **b**, a tree in the midst of the Dn 4:10
visions of my head as I lay in bed, and **b**, Dn 4:13
“I saw in my vision by night, and **b**, Dn 7:2
And **b**, another beast, a second one, like a Dn 7:5
After this I looked, and **b**, another, like a Dn 7:6
this I saw in the night visions, and **b**, Dn 7:7
I considered the horns, and **b**, there came Dn 7:8
were plucked up by the roots. And **b**, Dn 7:8
I saw in the night visions, and **b**, with Dn 7:13
I raised my eyes and saw, and **b**, a ram Dn 8:3
b, a male goat came from the west across Dn 8:5
vision, I sought to understand it. And **b**, Dn 8:15
“**B**, I will make known to you what shall Dn 8:19
I lifted up my eyes and looked, and **b**, a Dn 10:5
And **b**, a hand touched me and set me Dn 10:10
And **b**, one in the likeness of the Dn 10:16
out, **b**, the prince of Greece will come. Dn 10:20
B, three more kings shall arise in Persia, Dn 11:2
Then I, Daniel, looked, and **b**, two others Dn 12:5
“Therefore, **b**, I will allure her, and Hos 2:14
For **b**, they are going away from Hos 9:6
his people, “**B**, I am sending to you grain, Jl 2:19
“For **b**, in those days and at that time, Jl 3:1
B, I will stir them up from the place to Jl 3:7
“**B**, I will press you down in your place, Am 2:13
that, **b**, the days are coming upon you, Am 4:2
For **b**, he who forms the mountains Am 4:13
For **b**, the LORD commands, and the Am 6:11
“For **b**, I will raise up against you a Am 6:14
b, he was forming locusts when the Am 7:1

was just beginning to sprout, and **b**, Am 7:1
b, the Lord GOD was calling for a Am 7:4
b, the Lord was standing beside a wall Am 7:7
“**B**, I am setting a plumb line in the Am 7:8
showed me: **b**, a basket of summer fruit. Am 8:1
“**B**, the days are coming,” declares the Am 8:11
B, the eyes of the Lord GOD are upon the Am 9:8
“For **b**, I will command, and shake the Am 9:9
“**B**, the days are coming,” declares the Am 9:13
B, I will make you small among the Ob 1:2
For **b**, the LORD is coming out of his place, Mi 1:3
b, against this family I am devising Mi 2:3
B, upon the mountains, the feet of him Na 1:15
B, I am against you, declares the LORD of Na 2:13
B, I am against you, declares the LORD of Na 3:5
B, your troops are women in your midst. Na 3:13
For **b**, I am raising up the Chaldeans, Hab 1:6
“**B**, his soul is puffed up; it is not upright Hab 2:4
B, is it not from the LORD of hosts that Hab 2:13
B, it is overlaid with gold and silver, Hab 2:19
B, at that time I will deal with all your Zep 3:19
You looked for much, and **b**, it came to Hg 1:9
“I saw in the night, and **b**, a man riding Zec 1:8
‘We have patrolled the earth, and **b**, Zec 1:11
And I lifted my eyes and saw, and **b**, Zec 1:18
And I lifted my eyes and saw, and **b**, a Zec 2:1
And **b**, the angel who talked with me Zec 2:3
“**B**, I will shake my hand over them, and Zec 2:9
and rejoice, O daughter of Zion, for **b**, Zec 2:10
“**B**, I have taken your iniquity away from Zec 3:4
b, I will bring my servant the Branch. Zec 3:8
For **b**, on the stone that I have set before Zec 3:9
“What do you see?” I said, “I see, and **b**, Zec 4:2
Again I lifted my eyes and saw, and **b**, a Zec 5:1
And **b**, the leaden cover was lifted, and Zec 5:7
Then I lifted my eyes and saw, and **b**, two Zec 5:9
Again I lifted my eyes and saw, and **b**, Zec 6:1
“**B**, those who go toward the north Zec 6:8
“**B**, the man whose name is the Branch: Zec 6:12
b, I will save my people from the east Zec 8:7
But **b**, the Lord will strip her of her Zec 9:4
b, your king is coming to you; righteous Zec 9:9
B, I will cause each of them to fall into Zec 11:6
For **b**, I am raising up in the land a Zec 11:16
“**B**, I am about to make Jerusalem a cup Zec 12:2
B, a day is coming for the LORD, when Zec 14:1
B, I will rebuke your offspring, and Mal 2:3
“**B**, I send my messenger and he will Mal 3:1
in whom you delight, **b**, he is coming, Mal 3:1
“For **b**, the day is coming, burning like Mal 4:1
“**B**, I will send you Elijah the prophet Mal 4:5
b, an angel of the Lord appeared to him Mt 1:20
“**B**, the virgin shall conceive and bear a Mt 1:23
b, wise men from the east came to Mt 2:1
the king, they went on their way. And **b**, Mt 2:9
b, an angel of the Lord appeared to Mt 2:13
b, an angel of the Lord appeared in a Mt 2:19
he went up from the water, and **b**, Mt 3:16
and **b**, a voice from heaven said, “This is Mt 3:17
Then the devil left him, and **b**, angels Mt 4:11
And **b**, a leper came to him and knelt Mt 8:2
And **b**, there arose a great storm on the Mt 8:24
And **b**, they cried out, “What have you Mt 8:29
came out and went into the pigs, and **b**, Mt 8:32
And **b**, all the city came out to meet Mt 8:34
And **b**, some people brought to him a Mt 9:2
And **b**, some of the scribes said to Mt 9:3
b, many tax collectors and sinners Mt 9:10
b, a ruler came in and knelt before him, Mt 9:18
And **b**, a woman who had suffered from Mt 9:20
b, a demon-oppressed man who was Mt 9:32
“**B**, I am sending you out as sheep in Mt 10:16
B, those who wear soft clothing are in Mt 11:8
“‘**B**, I send my messenger before your Mt 11:10
“**B**, my servant whom I have chosen, Mt 12:18
at the preaching of Jonah, and **b**, Mt 12:41
to hear the wisdom of Solomon, and **b**, Mt 12:42
b, his mother and his brothers stood Mt 12:46
And **b**, a Canaanite woman from that Mt 15:22
And **b**, there appeared to them Moses Mt 17:3
b, a bright cloud overshadowed them, Mt 17:5
And **b**, a man came up to him, saying, Mt 19:16
And **b**, there were two blind men Mt 20:30
of Zion, ‘**B**, your king is coming to you, Mt 21:5
And **b**, one of those who were with Mt 26:51
And **b**, the curtain of the temple was Mt 27:51
And **b**, there was a great earthquake, for Mt 28:2
that he has risen from the dead, and **b**, Mt 28:7
And **b**, Jesus met them and said, Mt 28:9
b, some of the guard went into the city Mt 28:11
all that I have commanded you. And **b**, Mt 28:20
“**B**, I send my messenger before your Mk 1:2
it said, “**B**, he is calling Elijah.” Mk 15:35
And **b**, you will be silent and unable to Lk 1:20
And **b**, you will conceive in your womb Lk 1:31

And **b**, your relative Elizabeth in her old Lk 1:36
said, "**B**, I am the servant of the Lord; Lk 1:38
For **b**, when the sound of your greeting Lk 1:44
the humble estate of his servant. For **b**, Lk 1:48
the angel said to them, "Fear not, for **b**, Lk 2:10
"**B**, this child is appointed for the fall Lk 2:34
B, your father and I have been searching Lk 2:48
And **b**, some men were bringing on a Lk 5:18
in that day, and leap for joy, for **b**, Lk 6:23
b, a man who had died was being Lk 7:12
B, those who are dressed in splendid Lk 7:25
"'**B**, I send my messenger before your Lk 7:27
And **b**, a woman of the city, who was a Lk 7:37
And **b**, two men were talking with him, Lk 9:30
And **b**, a man from the crowd cried out, Lk 9:38
And **b**, a spirit seizes him, and he Lk 9:39
b, I am sending you out as lambs in the Lk 10:3
B, I have given you authority to tread Lk 10:19
And **b**, a lawyer stood up to put him to Lk 10:25
to hear the wisdom of Solomon, and **b**, Lk 11:31
at the preaching of Jonah, and **b**, Lk 11:32
those things that are within, and **b**, Lk 11:41
And **b**, some are last who will be first, Lk 13:30
'**B**, I cast out demons and perform Lk 13:32
B, your house is forsaken. And I tell Lk 13:35
And **b**, there was a man before him who Lk 14:2
or 'There!' for **b**, the kingdom of God is Lk 17:21
stood and said to the Lord, "**B**, Lord, Lk 19:8
"**B**, when you have entered the city, Lk 22:10
But **b**, the hand of him who betrays me Lk 22:21
Simon, **b**, Satan demanded to have you, Lk 22:31
b, I did not find this man guilty of any Lk 23:14
For **b**, the days are coming when they Lk 23:29
b, two men stood by them in dazzling Lk 24:4
And **b**, I am sending the promise of my Lk 24:49
him, and said, "**B**, the Lamb of God, Jn 1:29
by and said, "**B**, the Lamb of God!" Jn 1:36
and said of him, "**B**, an Israelite indeed, Jn 1:47
b, your king is coming, sitting on a Jn 12:15
B, the hour is coming, indeed it has Jn 16:32
robe. Pilate said to them, "**B** the man!" Jn 19:5
hour. He said to the Jews, "**B** your King!" Jn 19:14
to his mother, "Woman, **b**, your son!" Jn 19:26
"**B**, your mother!" And from that hour Jn 19:27
b, two men stood by them in white Acts 1:10
B, the feet of those who have buried Acts 5:9
he said, "**B**, I see the heavens opened, Acts 7:56
for a man of Tarsus named Saul, for **b**, Acts 9:11
b, the men who were sent by Acts 10:17
"**B**, three men are looking for you. Acts 10:19
in my house at the ninth hour, and **b**, Acts 10:30
And **b**, at that very moment three Acts 11:11
And **b**, an angel of the Lord stood next Acts 12:7
b, the hand of the Lord is upon you, Acts 13:11
No, but **b**, after me one is coming, the Acts 13:25
life, **b**, we are turning to the Gentiles. Acts 13:46
And now, **b**, I am going to Jerusalem, Acts 20:22
b, I know that none of you among Acts 20:25
you must stand before Caesar. And **b**, Acts 27:24
"**B**, I am laying in Zion a stone of Rom 9:33
B! I tell you a mystery. We shall not 1 Cor 15:51
passed away; **b**, the new has come. 2 Cor 5:17
day of salvation I have helped you." **B**, 2 Cor 6:2
time; **b**, now is the day of salvation. 2 Cor 6:2
well known; as dying, and **b**, we live; 2 Cor 6:9
"**B**, I and the children God has given Heb 2:13
"**B**, the days are coming, declares the Heb 8:8
I said, '**B**, I have come to do your will, Heb 10:7
"**B**, I have come to do your will." He Heb 10:9
B, the wages of the laborers who mowed Jas 5:4
b, the Judge is standing at the door. Jas 5:9
B, we consider those blessed who Jas 5:11
"**B**, I am laying in Zion a stone, a 1 Pt 2:6
"**B**, the Lord came with ten thousands Jude 1:14
B, he is coming with the clouds, and every Rv 1:7
I died, and **b** I am alive forevermore, and Rv 1:18
B, the devil is about to throw some of Rv 2:10
B, I will throw her onto a sickbed, and Rv 2:22
B, I have set before you an open door, Rv 3:8
B, I will make those of the synagogue of Rv 3:9
that they are Jews and are not, but lie—**b**, Rv 3:9
B, I stand at the door and knock. If Rv 3:20
After this I looked, and **b**, a door standing Rv 4:1
At once I was in the Spirit, and **b**, a throne Rv 4:2
b, the Lion of the tribe of Judah, the Root Rv 5:5
And I looked, and **b**, a white horse! And Rv 6:2
say, "Come!" And I looked, and **b**, Rv 6:5
And I looked, and **b**, a pale horse! And its Rv 6:8
he opened the sixth seal, I looked, and **b**, Rv 6:12
After this I looked, and **b**, a great Rv 7:9
has passed; **b**, two woes are still to come. Rv 9:12
passed; **b**, the third woe is soon to come. Rv 11:14
b, a great red dragon, with seven heads Rv 12:3
Then I looked, and **b**, on Mount Zion Rv 14:1
Then I looked, and **b**, a white cloud, Rv 14:14
("**B**, I am coming like a thief! Blessed is Rv 16:15
Then I saw heaven opened, and **b**, a Rv 19:11
"**B**, the dwelling place of God is with Rv 21:3
"**B**, I am making all things new." Also he Rv 21:5
"And **b**, I am coming soon. Blessed is the Rv 22:7
"**B**, I am coming soon, bringing my Rv 22:12

BEHOLDING (2)

the sanctuary, **b** your power and glory. Ps 63:2
unveiled face, **b** the glory of the Lord, 2 Cor 3:18

BEHOLDS (2)

riddles, and he **b** the form of the LORD. Nm 12:8
has looked on it; man **b** it from afar. Jb 36:25

BEING (265)

the hand, the LORD **b** merciful to him, Gn 19:16
every male among you **b** circumcised. Gn 34:15
the name of his city **b** Dinhabah. Gn 36:32
his place, the name of his city **b** Avith. Gn 36:35
his place, the name of his city **b** Pau; Gn 36:39
Joseph, **b** seventeen years old, was Gn 37:2
As she was **b** brought out, she sent Gn 38:25
So Joseph died, **b** 110 years old. They Gn 50:26
the years of the life of Levi **b** 137 years. Ex 6:16
years of the life of Kohath **b** 133 years. Ex 6:18
years of the life of Amram **b** 137 years. Ex 6:20
their kneading bowls **b** bound up in Ex 12:34
the waters **b** a wall to them on their Ex 14:22
the waters **b** a wall to them on their Ex 14:29
injured or dies, the owner not **b** with it, Ex 22:14
which is **b** shown you on the Ex 25:40
the LORD for him who is **b** cleansed. Lv 14:31
each man **b** the head of the house of his Nm 1:4
the people of Judah **b** Nahshon the son Nm 2:3
his company as listed **b** 74,600. Nm 2:4
people of Issachar **b** Nethanel the son Nm 2:5
his company as listed **b** 54,400. Nm 2:6
the people of Zebulun **b** Eliab the son of Nm 2:7
his company as listed **b** 57,400. Nm 2:8
the people of Reuben **b** Elizur the son of Nm 2:10
his company as listed **b** 46,500. Nm 2:11
people of Simeon **b** Shelumiel the son Nm 2:12
his company as listed **b** 59,300. Nm 2:13
the people of Gad **b** Eliasaph the son of Nm 2:14
his company as listed **b** 45,650. Nm 2:15
people of Ephraim **b** Elishama the son Nm 2:18
his company as listed **b** 40,500. Nm 2:19
people of Manasseh **b** Gamaliel the son Nm 2:20
his company as listed **b** 32,200. Nm 2:21
people of Benjamin **b** Abidan the son Nm 2:22
his company as listed **b** 35,400. Nm 2:23
the people of Dan **b** Ahiezer the son of Nm 2:25
his company as listed **b** 62,700. Nm 2:26
the people of Asher **b** Pagiel the son of Nm 2:27
his company as listed **b** 41,500. Nm 2:28
the people of Naphtali **b** Ahira the son Nm 2:29
his company as listed **b** 53,400. Nm 2:30
all the gold of the dishes **b** 120 shekels; Nm 7:86
cubits, the city **b** in the middle. Nm 35:5
without **b** at enmity with him in time Dt 4:42
b careful to do all this commandment Dt 15:5
b careful to do all his commandments Dt 28:1
you today, **b** careful to do them, Dt 28:13
b careful to do according to all the law Jos 1:7
the LORD your God **b** carried by the Jos 3:3
land to the south **b** Ephraim's and that Jos 17:10
and that to the north **b** Manasseh's, Jos 17:10
them Kiriath-arba (Arba **b** the father Jos 21:11
of the LORD, died, **b** 110 years old. Jos 24:29
food she had left over after **b** satisfied. Ru 2:18
"How long will you go on **b** drunk? 1 Sm 1:14
rejected me from **b** king over them. 1 Sm 8:7
has also rejected you from **b** king." 1 Sm 15:23
rejected you from **b** king over 1 Sm 15:26
rejected him from **b** king over Israel? 1 Sm 16:1
to her, and **b** stronger than she, 2 Sm 13:14
expelled Abiathar from **b** priest to the 1 Kgs 2:27
heard in the house while it was **b** built. 1 Kgs 6:7
servants, Hadad still **b** a little child. 1 Kgs 11:17
his mother from **b** queen mother 1 Kgs 15:13
in **b** like the house of Jeroboam, 1 Kgs 16:7
you see me as I am **b** taken from you, 2 Kgs 2:10
king's sons who were **b** put to death, 2 Kgs 11:2
(another third **b** at the gate Sur and a 2 Kgs 11:6
And as a man was **b** buried, behold, 2 Kgs 13:21
the name of his city **b** Dinhabah. 1 Chr 1:43
place, the name of his city **b** Avith. 1 Chr 1:46
his place, the name of his city **b** Pai; 1 Chr 1:50
number in the days of David **b** 22,600. 1 Chr 7:2
one father's house **b** chosen for 1 Chr 24:6
b a man of understanding and a 1 Chr 27:32
Asa removed from **b** queen mother 2 Chr 15:16
and **b** a leper lived in a separate 2 Chr 26:21
saw the foundation of this house **b** laid, Ezr 3:12
It is **b** built with huge stones, and timber Ezr 5:8
came later, their names **b** Eliphelet, Ezr 8:13
the men next to him **b** Carshena, Est 1:14
after **b** twelve months under the Est 2:12
inside the inner court without **b** called, Est 4:11
b publicly displayed to all peoples, Est 8:13
full vigor, **b** wholly at ease and secure, Jb 21:23
heart is glad, and my whole **b** rejoices; Ps 16:9
you delight in truth in the inward **b**, Ps 51:6
the mountains, **b** girded with might; Ps 65:6
Yet he, **b** compassionate, atoned for Ps 78:38
sing praise to my God while I have **b**. Ps 104:33
sing and make melody with all my **b**! Ps 108:1
you, when I was **b** made in secret, Ps 139:15
praises to my God while I have my **b**. Ps 146:2
O simple ones, will you love **b** simple? Prv 1:22
and will keep your foot from **b** caught. Prv 3:26
My inmost **b** will exult when your lips Prv 23:16
Rescue those who are **b** taken away to Prv 24:11
Besides **b** wise, the Preacher also Eccl 12:9
not run away from **b** your shepherd, Jer 17:16
of Israel cease from **b** a nation before Jer 31:36
the king of Judah were **b** led out to the Jer 38:22
and Judah who were **b** exiled to Babylon. Jer 40:1
let us cut her off from **b** a nation!' Jer 48:2
appearance and construction **b** as it Ezk 1:16
the hand of the LORD **b** strong upon me. Ezk 3:14
instead of **b** the desolation that it was Ezk 36:34
each **b** a cubit and a handbreadth in Ezk 40:5
by cubits (the cubit **b** a cubit and a Ezk 43:13
gates of the city **b** named after the Ezk 48:31
kingdom, **b** about sixty-two years old. Dn 5:31
I reject you from **b** a priest to me. Hos 4:6
which came into **b** in a night and Jon 4:10
does not care for those **b** destroyed, Zec 11:16
b a just man and unwilling to put her to Mt 1:19
And **b** warned in a dream not to return Mt 2:12
and **b** warned in a dream he withdrew to Mt 2:22
which of you by **b** anxious can add a Mt 6:27
that the boat was **b** swamped by the Mt 8:24
the marketplaces and **b** called rabbi by Mt 23:7
are you to escape **b** sentenced to hell? Mt 23:33
cut short, no human **b** would be saved. Mt 24:22
to him and were **b** baptized by him in Mk 1:5
forty days, **b** tempted by Satan. Mk 1:13
And as for the dead **b** raised, have you Mk 12:26
the days, no human **b** would be saved. Mk 13:20
b delivered from the hand of our Lk 1:74
Pontius Pilate **b** governor of Judea, Lk 3:1
of Judea, and Herod **b** tetrarch of Galilee, Lk 3:1
b the son (as was supposed) of Joseph, Lk 3:23
for forty days, **b** tempted by the devil. And Lk 4:2
in their synagogues, **b** glorified by all. Lk 4:15
a man who had died was **b** carried out, Lk 7:12
which of you by **b** anxious can add a Lk 12:25
and in Hades, **b** in torment, he lifted up Lk 16:23
B asked by the Pharisees when the Lk 17:20
and marrying and **b** given in Lk 17:27
sons of God, **b** sons of the resurrection. Lk 20:36
And **b** in an agony he prayed more Lk 22:44
and people were coming and **b** baptized Jn 3:23
for blasphemy, because you, **b** a man, Jn 10:33
but **b** high priest that year he Jn 11:51
joy that a human **b** has been born into Jn 16:21
the doors **b** locked where the disciples Jn 20:19
B therefore a prophet, and knowing Acts 2:30
B therefore exalted at the right hand of Acts 2:33
and signs were **b** done through the Acts 2:43
day by day those who were **b** saved. Acts 2:47
a man lame from birth was **b** carried, Acts 3:2
if we are **b** examined today concerning Acts 4:9
they were afraid of **b** stoned by the Acts 5:26
their widows were **b** neglected in the Acts 6:1
And seeing one of them **b** wronged, he Acts 7:24
attention to what was **b** said by Philip Acts 8:6
and after **b** baptized he continued with Acts 8:13
What prevents me from **b** baptized?" Acts 8:36
Samaria had peace and was **b** built up. Acts 9:31
b let down by its four corners upon Acts 10:11
b let down from heaven by its four Acts 11:5
know that what was **b** done by the Acts 12:9
So, **b** sent out by the Holy Spirit, they Acts 13:4
So, **b** sent on their way by the church, Acts 15:3
in it, **b** Lord of heaven and earth, Acts 17:24
we live and move and have our **b**'; Acts 17:28
B then God's offspring, we ought not Acts 17:29
think that the divine **b** is like gold or Acts 17:29
And **b** fervent in spirit, he spoke and Acts 18:25
in danger of **b** charged with rioting Acts 19:40
And **b** overcome by sleep, he fell down Acts 20:9
b sorrowful most of all because of the Acts 20:38
b zealous for God as all of you are this Acts 22:3
of Stephen your witness was **b** shed, Acts 22:20
reason why he was **b** accused by the Acts 22:30
that he was **b** accused about Acts 23:29
reforms are **b** made for this nation, Acts 24:2
that Paul was **b** kept at Caesarea Acts 25:4

B at a loss how to investigate these	Acts 25:20
by **b** the first to rise from the dead,	Acts 26:23
all hope of our **b** saved was at last	Acts 27:20
as we were **b** driven across the	Acts 27:27
and the stern was **b** broken up by the	Acts 27:41
for every human **b** who does evil,	Rom 2:9
why am I still **b** condemned as a	Rom 3:7
the law no human **b** will be justified	Rom 3:20
who believe without **b** circumcised,	Rom 4:11
We know that Christ **b** raised from the	Rom 6:9
in the law of God, in my inner **b**,	Rom 7:22
your sake we are **b** killed all the day	Rom 8:36
b ignorant of the righteousness that	Rom 10:3
but to us who are **b** saved it is the	1 Cor 1:18
so that no human **b** might boast in	1 Cor 1:29
are you not **b** merely human?	1 Cor 3:4
b under no necessity but having his	1 Cor 7:37
an idol, and their conscience, **b** weak,	1 Cor 8:7
law (though not **b** myself under the	1 Cor 9:20
outside the law (not **b** outside the law	1 Cor 9:21
the other person is not **b** built up.	1 Cor 14:17
and by which you are **b** saved, if you	1 Cor 15:2
people mean by **b** baptized on	1 Cor 15:29
first man Adam became a living **b**";	1 Cor 15:45
those who are **b** saved and among	2 Cor 2:15
glory, which was **b** brought to an end,	2 Cor 3:7
For if what was **b** brought to an end	2 Cor 3:11
outcome of what was **b** brought to an	2 Cor 3:13
are **b** transformed into the same	2 Cor 3:18
who live are always **b** given over to	2 Cor 4:11
our inner nature is **b** renewed day by	2 Cor 4:16
b burdened—not that we would be	2 Cor 5:4
but **b** himself very earnest he is going	2 Cor 8:17
of grace that is **b** ministered by us,	2 Cor 8:19
gift that is **b** administered by us,	2 Cor 8:20
nothing of you—for **b** so confident.	2 Cor 9:4
b ready to punish every disobedience,	2 Cor 10:6
bear with fools, **b** wise yourselves!	2 Cor 11:19
So to keep me from **b** too elated by the	2 Cor 12:7
me, to keep me from **b** too elated.	2 Cor 12:7
are you now **b** perfected by the flesh?	Gal 3:3
why am I still **b** persecuted?	Gal 5:11
But God, **b** rich in mercy, because of the	Eph 2:4
Christ Jesus himself **b** the cornerstone,	Eph 2:20
the whole structure, **b** joined together,	Eph 2:21
him you also are **b** built together into a	Eph 2:22
through his Spirit in your inner **b**,	Eph 3:16
you, **b** rooted and grounded in love,	Eph 3:17
complete my joy by **b** of the same mind,	Phil 2:2
love, **b** in full accord and of one mind.	Phil 2:2
a servant, **b** born in the likeness of men.	Phil 2:7
And **b** found in human form, he	Phil 2:8
Not that I am speaking of **b** in need, for	Phil 4:11
be encouraged, **b** knit together in love,	Col 2:2
which is **b** renewed in knowledge after	Col 3:10
b watchful in it with thanksgiving.	Col 4:2
So, **b** affectionately desirous of you,	1 Thes 2:8
Christ and our **b** gathered together to	2 Thes 2:1
b trained in the words of the faith and	1 Tm 4:6
after **b** captured by him to do his will.	2 Tm 2:26
to worse, deceiving and **b** deceived.	2 Tm 3:13
For I am already **b** poured out as a	2 Tm 4:6
so that **b** justified by his grace we might	Ti 3:7
is able to help those who are **b** tempted.	Heb 2:18
And **b** made perfect, he became the	Heb 5:9
b designated by God a high priest after	Heb 5:10
it is worthless and near to **b** cursed,	Heb 6:8
for all time those who are **b** sanctified.	Heb 10:14
sometimes **b** publicly exposed to	Heb 10:33
and sometimes **b** partners with those	Heb 10:33
b warned by God concerning events as	Heb 11:7
not **b** afraid of the anger of the king,	Heb 11:27
"I am **b** tempted by God," for God	Jas 1:13
b no hearer who forgets but a doer who	Jas 1:25
but no human **b** can tame the tongue. It	Jas 3:8
fruit of the earth, **b** patient about it,	Jas 5:7
God's power are **b** guarded through faith	1 Pt 1:5
minds for action, and **b** sober-minded,	1 Pt 1:13
like living stones are **b** built up as a	1 Pt 2:5
always **b** prepared to make a defense to	1 Pt 3:15
b put to death in the flesh but made	1 Pt 3:18
of Noah, while the ark was **b** prepared,	1 Pt 3:20
charge, but **b** examples to the flock.	1 Pt 5:3
of suffering are **b** experienced by your	1 Pt 5:9
keep you from **b** ineffective or	2 Pt 1:8
b kept until the day of judgment and	2 Pt 3:7
You have the reputation of **b** alive, but	Rv 3:1
vanished like a scroll that is **b** rolled up,	Rv 6:14
out his purpose by **b** of one mind and	Rv 17:17

BEINGS (4)

than the heavenly **b** and crowned him	Ps 8:5
Ascribe to the LORD, O heavenly **b**,	Ps 29:1
Who among the heavenly **b** is like the	Ps 89:6
they exchanged human **b** and vessels	Ezk 27:13

BEKA (1)

a **b** a head (that is, half a shekel, by the	Ex 38:26

BEL (3)

B bows down; Nebo stoops; their idols are	Is 46:1
'Babylon is taken, **B** is put to shame,	Jer 50:2
And I will punish **B** in Babylon, and	Jer 51:44

BELA (14)

of Zeboiim, and the king of **B** (that is,	Gn 14:2
of Zeboiim, and the king of **B** (that is,	Gn 14:8
B the son of Beor reigned in Edom, the	Gn 36:32
B died, and Jobab the son of Zerah of	Gn 36:33
B, Becher, Ashbel, Gera, Naaman, Ehi,	Gn 46:21
according to their clans: of **B**,	Nm 26:38
And the sons of **B** were Ard and	Nm 26:40
B the son of Beor, the name of his city	1 Chr 1:43
B died, and Jobab the son of Zerah of	1 Chr 1:44
and **B** the son of Azaz, son of Shema,	1 Chr 5:8
B, Becher, and Jediael, three.	1 Chr 7:6
The sons of **B**: Ezbon, Uzzi, Uzziel,	1 Chr 7:7
Benjamin fathered **B** his firstborn,	1 Chr 8:1
And **B** had sons: Addar, Gera, Abihud,	1 Chr 8:3

BELAITES (1)

their clans: of Bela, the clan of the **B**;	Nm 26:38

BELIAL (1)

What accord has Christ with **B**? Or	2 Cor 6:15

BELIEF (1)

by the Spirit and **b** in the truth.	2 Thes 2:13

BELIEVE (149)

became numb, for he did not **b** them.	Gn 45:26
they will not **b** me or listen to my voice,	Ex 4:1
"that they may **b** that the LORD, the God of	Ex 4:5
"If they will not **b** you," God said, "or	Ex 4:8
to the first sign, they may **b** the latter sign.	Ex 4:8
If they will not **b** even these two signs or	Ex 4:9
and may also **b** you forever." When	Ex 19:9
And how long will they not **b** in me,	Nm 14:11
Aaron, "Because you did not **b** in me,	Nm 20:12
word you did not **b** the LORD your God,	Dt 1:32
your God and did not **b** him or obey his	Dt 9:23
but I did not **b** the reports until I	1 Kgs 10:7
who did not **b** in the LORD their God.	2 Kgs 17:14
but I did not **b** the reports until I came	2 Chr 9:6
B in the LORD your God, and you	2 Chr 20:20
b his prophets, and you will	2 Chr 20:20
in this fashion, and do not **b** him,	2 Chr 32:15
I would not **b** that he was listening to my	Jb 9:16
He does not **b** that he will return out of	Jb 15:22
I **b** that I shall look upon the goodness	Ps 27:13
because they did not **b** in God and did	Ps 78:22
despite his wonders, they did not **b**.	Ps 78:32
for I **b** in your commandments.	Ps 119:66
when he speaks graciously, **b** him not,	Prv 26:25
may know and **b** me and understand	Is 43:10
do not **b** them, though they speak	Jer 12:6
the son of Ahikam would not **b** them.	Jer 40:14
The kings of the earth did not **b**, nor	Lam 4:12
your days that you would not **b** if told.	Hab 1:5
"Do you **b** that I am able to do this?"	Mt 9:28
of these little ones who **b** in me to sin,	Mt 18:6
to us, 'Why then did you not **b** him?'	Mt 21:25
righteousness, and you did not **b** him,	Mt 21:32
change your minds and **b** him.	Mt 21:32
the Christ!' or 'There he is!' do not **b** it.	Mt 24:23
he is in the inner rooms,' do not **b** it.	Mt 24:26
from the cross, and we will **b** in him.	Mt 27:42
is at hand; repent and **b** in the gospel."	Mk 1:15
of the synagogue, "Do not fear, only **b**."	Mk 5:36
of the child cried out and said, "I **b**;	Mk 9:24
of these little ones who **b** in me to sin,	Mk 9:42
in prayer, **b** that you have received it,	Mk 11:24
say, 'Why then did you not **b** him?'	Mk 11:31
or 'Look, there he is!' do not **b** it.	Mk 13:21
we may see and **b**." Those who were	Mk 15:32
been seen by her, they would not **b** it.	Mk 16:11
told the rest, but they did not **b** them.	Mk 16:13
whoever does not **b** will be	Mk 16:16
signs will accompany those who **b**:	Mk 16:17
place, because you did not **b** my words,	Lk 1:20
so that they may not **b** and be saved.	Lk 8:12
they **b** for a while, and in time of testing	Lk 8:13
this answered him, "Do not fear; only **b**,	Lk 8:50
he will say, 'Why did you not **b** him?'	Lk 20:5
to them, "If I tell you, you will not **b**,	Lk 22:67
an idle tale, and they did not **b** them.	Lk 24:11
slow of heart to **b** all that the prophets	Lk 24:25
the light, that all might **b** through him.	Jn 1:7
'I saw you under the fig tree,' do you **b**?	Jn 1:50
told you earthly things and you do not **b**,	Jn 3:12
how can you **b** if I tell you heavenly	Jn 3:12
whoever does not **b** is condemned	Jn 3:18
Jesus said to her, "Woman, **b** me, the	Jn 4:21
because of what you said that we **b**,	Jn 4:42
see signs and wonders you will not **b**."	Jn 4:48
for you do not **b** the one whom he has	Jn 5:38
How can you **b**, when you receive glory	Jn 5:44
If you believed Moses, you would **b** me;	Jn 5:46
But if you do not **b** his writings, how will	Jn 5:47
his writings, how will you **b** my words?"	Jn 5:47
that you **b** in him whom he has sent."	Jn 6:29
do you do, that we may see and **b** you?	Jn 6:30
that you have seen me and yet do not **b**.	Jn 6:36
you who do not **b**." (For Jesus knew from	Jn 6:64
beginning who those were who did not **b**,	Jn 6:64
for unless you **b** that I am he you will die	Jn 8:24
because I tell the truth, you do not **b** me.	Jn 8:45
If I tell the truth, why do you not **b** me?	Jn 8:46
The Jews did not **b** that he had been	Jn 9:18
he said, "Do you **b** in the Son of Man?"	Jn 9:35
who is he, sir, that I may **b** in him?"	Jn 9:36
said, "Lord, I **b**," and he worshiped him.	Jn 9:38
them, "I told you, and you do not **b**.	Jn 10:25
but you do not **b** because you are not	Jn 10:26
works of my Father, then do not **b** me;	Jn 10:37
I do them, even though you do not **b** me,	Jn 10:38
you do not believe me, **b** the works,	Jn 10:38
that I was not there, so that you may **b**.	Jn 11:15
in me shall never die. Do you **b** this?"	Jn 11:26
I **b** that you are the Christ, the Son of	Jn 11:27
that they may **b** that you sent me."	Jn 11:42
go on like this, everyone will **b** in him,	Jn 11:48
While you have the light, **b** in the light,	Jn 12:36
before them, they still did not **b** in him,	Jn 12:37
Therefore they could not **b**. For again	Jn 12:39
does take place you may **b** that I am he.	Jn 13:19
be troubled. **B** in God; believe also in me.	Jn 14:1
be troubled. Believe in God; **b** also in me.	Jn 14:1
Do you not **b** that I am in the Father	Jn 14:10
B me that I am in the Father and the	Jn 14:11
or else **b** on account of the works	Jn 14:11
that when it does take place you may **b**.	Jn 14:29
sin, because they do not **b** in me;	Jn 16:9
this is why we **b** that you came from	Jn 16:30
Jesus answered them, "Do you now **b**?	Jn 16:31
for those who will **b** in me through	Jn 17:20
that the world may **b** that you have sent	Jn 17:21
telling the truth—that you also may **b**.	Jn 19:35
my hand into his side, I will never **b**."	Jn 20:25
it in my side. Do not disbelieve, but **b**."	Jn 20:27
so that you may **b** that Jesus is the	Jn 20:31
for they did not **b** that he was a	Acts 9:26
your days, a work that you will not **b**,	Acts 13:41
hear the word of the gospel and **b**.	Acts 15:7
But we **b** that we will be saved	Acts 15:11
And they said, "**B** in the Lord Jesus,	Acts 16:31
telling the people to **b** in the one who	Acts 19:4
King Agrippa, do you **b** the prophets?	Acts 26:27
the prophets? I know that you **b**."	Acts 26:27
faith in Jesus Christ for all who **b**.	Rom 3:22
of all who **b** without being	Rom 4:11
counted to us who **b** in him who	Rom 4:24
we **b** that we will also live with him.	Rom 6:8
Jesus is Lord and **b** in your heart that	Rom 10:9
how are they to **b** in him of whom	Rom 10:14
what we preach to save those who **b**.	1 Cor 1:21
among you. And I **b** it in part,	1 Cor 11:18
"I believed, and so I spoke," we also **b**,	2 Cor 4:13
Christ might be given to those who **b**.	Gal 3:22
of his power toward us who **b**,	Eph 1:19
you should not only **b** in him but also	Phil 1:29
For since we **b** that Jesus died and	1 Thes 4:14
so that they may **b** what is false,	2 Thes 2:11
who did not **b** the truth but	2 Thes 2:12
those who were to **b** in him for	1 Tm 1:16
by those who **b** and know the	1 Tm 4:3
all people, especially of those who **b**.	1 Tm 4:10
near to God must **b** that he exists and	Heb 11:6
You **b** that God is one; you do well. Even	Jas 2:19
well. Even the demons **b**—and shudder!	Jas 2:19
you **b** in him and rejoice with joy that is	1 Pt 1:8
So the honor is for you who **b**, but for	1 Pt 2:7
who believe, but for those who do not **b**,	1 Pt 2:7
that we **b** in the name of his Son Jesus	1 Jn 3:23
Beloved, do not **b** every spirit, but test the	1 Jn 4:1
to know and to **b** the love that God	1 Jn 4:16
Whoever does not **b** God has made	1 Jn 5:10
things to you who **b** in the name of	1 Jn 5:13
afterward destroyed those who did not **b**.	Jude 1:5

BELIEVED (82)

And he **b** the LORD, and he counted it to	Gn 15:6
And the people **b**; and when they heard	Ex 4:31
and they **b** in the LORD and in his	Ex 14:31
Then they **b** his words; they sang his	Ps 106:12
I **b**, even when I spoke, "I am greatly	Ps 116:10
Who has **b** what they heard from us?	Is 53:1
And the people of Nineveh **b** God. They	Jon 3:5
you as you have **b**." And the servant was	Mt 8:13
collectors and the prostitutes **b** him.	Mt 21:32

because they had not **b** those who saw Mk 16:14
blessed is she who **b** that there would be Lk 1:45
who did receive him, who **b** in his name, Jn 1:12
his glory. And his disciples **b** in him. Jn 2:11
and they **b** the Scripture and the word Jn 2:22
many **b** in his name when they saw the Jn 2:23
because he has not **b** in the name of the Jn 3:18
from that town **b** in him because Jn 4:39
And many more **b** because of his word. Jn 4:41
will live." The man **b** the word that Jesus Jn 4:50
"Your son will live." And he himself **b**, Jn 4:53
If you **b** Moses, you would believe me; for Jn 5:46
and we have **b**, and have come to know, Jn 6:69
For not even his brothers **b** in him. Jn 7:5
Yet many of the people **b** in him. They Jn 7:31
whom those who **b** in him were to Jn 7:39
authorities or the Pharisees **b** in him? Jn 7:48
was saying these things, many **b** in him. Jn 8:30
Jesus said to the Jews who had **b** in him, Jn 8:31
And many **b** in him there. Jn 10:42
tell you that if you **b** you would see the Jn 11:40
and had seen what he did, **b** in him, Jn 11:45
who has **b** what he heard from us, Jn 12:38
many even of the authorities **b** in him, Jn 12:42
loved me and have **b** that I came from Jn 16:27
you; and they have **b** that you sent me. Jn 17:8
first, also went in, and he saw and **b**; Jn 20:8
"Have you **b** because you have seen me? Jn 20:29
who have not seen and yet have **b**." Jn 20:29
And all who **b** were together and had Acts 2:44
of those who had heard the word **b**, Acts 4:4
number of those who **b** were of one Acts 4:32
But when they **b** Philip as he preached Acts 8:12
Even Simon himself **b**, and after being Acts 8:13
all Joppa, and many **b** in the Lord. Acts 9:42
to us when we **b** in the Lord Jesus Acts 11:17
a great number who **b** turned to the Acts 11:21
Then the proconsul **b**, when he saw Acts 13:12
as were appointed to eternal life **b**. Acts 13:48
number of both Jews and Greeks **b**. Acts 14:1
to the Lord in whom they had **b**. Acts 14:23
household that he had **b** in God. Acts 16:34
Many of them therefore **b**, with not a Acts 17:12
But some men joined him and **b**, Acts 17:34
ruler of the synagogue, **b** in the Lord, Acts 18:8
Corinthians hearing Paul **b** and were Acts 18:8
those who through grace had **b**, Acts 18:27
Spirit when you **b**?" And they said, Acts 19:2
among the Jews of those who have **b**. Acts 21:20
But as for the Gentiles who have **b**, we Acts 21:25
and beat those who **b** in you. Acts 22:19
the Scripture say? "Abraham **b** God, Rom 4:3
the presence of the God in whom he **b**, Rom 4:17
In hope he **b** against hope, that he Rom 4:18
on him in whom they have not **b**? Rom 10:14
who has **b** what he has heard from Rom 10:16
to us now than when we first **b**. Rom 13:11
Servants through whom you **b**, as the 1 Cor 3:5
to you—unless you **b** in vain. 1 Cor 15:2
I or they, so we preach and so you **b**. 1 Cor 15:11
to what has been written, "I **b**, 2 Cor 4:13
so we also have **b** in Christ Jesus, Gal 2:16
just as Abraham "**b** God, and it was Gal 3:6
gospel of your salvation, and **b** in him, Eph 1:13
marveled at among all who have **b**, 2 Thes 1:10
because our testimony to you was **b**. 2 Thes 1:10
among the nations, **b** on in the world, 1 Tm 3:16
ashamed, for I know whom I have **b**, 2 Tm 1:12
you have learned and have firmly **b**, 2 Tm 3:14
so that those who have **b** in God may be Ti 3:8
For we who have **b** enter that rest, as he Heb 4:3
fulfilled that says, "Abraham **b** God, Jas 2:23
because he has not **b** in the testimony 1 Jn 5:10

BELIEVER (2)
son of a Jewish woman who was a **b**, Acts 16:1
what portion does a **b** share with an 2 Cor 6:15

BELIEVERS (13)
And more than ever **b** were added to Acts 5:14
And the **b** from among the Acts 10:45
But some **b** who belonged to the party Acts 15:5
many of those who were now **b** came, Acts 19:18
a sign not for **b** but for unbelievers, 1 Cor 14:22
a sign not for unbelievers but for **b**. 1 Cor 14:22
to all the **b** in Macedonia and 1 Thes 1:7
was our conduct toward you **b**. 1 Thes 2:10
of God, which is at work in you **b**. 1 Thes 2:13
but set the **b** an example in speech, 1 Tm 4:12
their good service are **b** and beloved. 1 Tm 6:2
and his children are **b** and not open to the Ti 1:6
who through him are **b** in God, who 1 Pt 1:21

BELIEVES (33)
The simple **b** everything, but the Prv 14:15
'Whoever **b** will not be in haste.' Is 28:16
All things are possible for one who **b**." Mk 9:23
but **b** that what he says will come to Mk 11:23
Whoever **b** and is baptized will be Mk 16:16
that whoever **b** in him may have eternal Jn 3:15
that whoever **b** in him should not perish Jn 3:16
Whoever **b** in him is not condemned, Jn 3:18
Whoever **b** in the Son has eternal life; Jn 3:36
hears my word and **b** him who sent me Jn 5:24
and whoever **b** in me shall never thirst. Jn 6:35
on the Son and **b** in him should have Jn 6:40
I say to you, whoever **b** has eternal life. Jn 6:47
Whoever **b** in me, as the Scripture has Jn 7:38
Whoever **b** in me, though he die, yet Jn 11:25
everyone who lives and **b** in me shall Jn 11:26
cried out and said, "Whoever **b** in me, Jn 12:44
b not in me but in him who sent me. Jn 12:44
so that whoever **b** in me may not Jn 12:46
whoever **b** in me will also do the works Jn 14:12
that everyone who **b** in him receives Acts 10:43
by him everyone who **b** is freed from Acts 13:38
God for salvation to everyone who **b**, Rom 1:16
and whoever **b** in him will not be put Rom 9:33
for righteousness to everyone who **b**. Rom 10:4
with the heart one **b** and is justified, Rom 10:10
"Everyone who **b** in him will not be Rom 10:11
One person **b** he may eat anything, Rom 14:2
Love bears all things, **b** all things, 1 Cor 13:7
and whoever **b** in him will not be put to 1 Pt 2:6
Everyone who **b** that Jesus is the Christ 1 Jn 5:1
except the one who **b** that Jesus is the 1 Jn 5:5
Whoever **b** in the Son of God has the 1 Jn 5:10

BELIEVING (7)
the Jews were going away and **b** in Jesus. Jn 12:11
and that by **b** you may have life in his Jn 20:31
b everything laid down by the Law Acts 24:14
fill you with all joy and peace in **b**, Rom 15:13
have the right to take along a **b** wife, 1 Cor 9:5
If any **b** woman has relatives who are 1 Tm 5:16
Those who have **b** masters must not 1 Tm 6:2

BELITTLES (1)
Whoever **b** his neighbor lacks sense, Prv 11:12

BELL (4)
a golden **b** and a pomegranate, a golden Ex 28:34
a golden **b** and a pomegranate, Ex 28:34
a **b** and a pomegranate, a bell and a Ex 39:26
a **b** and a pomegranate around the hem Ex 39:26

BELLOWING (1)
b with their mouths with swords in their Ps 59:7

BELLOWS (1)
The **b** blow fiercely; the lead is Jer 6:29

BELLS (4)
its hem, with **b** of gold between them, Ex 28:33
They also made **b** of pure gold, and put Ex 39:25
and put the **b** between the Ex 39:25
be inscribed on the **b** of the horses, Zec 14:20

BELLY (20)
on your **b** you shall go, and dust you Gn 3:14
Whatever goes on its **b**, and whatever Lv 11:42
of Israel and the woman through her **b**. Nm 25:8
his right thigh, and thrust it into his **b**. Jgs 3:21
for he did not pull the sword out of his **b**; Jgs 3:22
and fill his **b** with the east wind? Jb 15:2
up again; God casts them out of his **b**. Jb 20:15
he knew no contentment in his **b**, Jb 20:20
To fill his **b** to the full God will send his Jb 20:23
my **b** is like wine that has no vent; Jb 32:19
and his power in the muscles of his **b**. Jb 40:16
to the dust; our **b** clings to the ground. Ps 44:25
but the **b** of the wicked suffers want. Prv 13:25
Your **b** is a heap of wheat, encircled with Sg 7:2
feed your **b** with this scroll that I give Ezk 3:3
And Jonah was in the **b** of the fish three Jon 1:17
to the LORD his God from the **b** of the fish, Jon 2:1
out of the **b** of Sheol I cried, and you Jon 2:2
three nights in the **b** of the great fish, Mt 12:40
end is destruction, their god is their **b**, Phil 3:19

BELONG (51)
you and asks you, 'To whom do you **b**? Gn 32:17
say, 'They **b** to your servant Jacob. Gn 32:18
"By the man to whom these **b**, Gn 38:25
them, "Do not interpretations **b** to God? Gn 40:8
pan or a griddle shall **b** to the priest who Lv 7:9
It shall **b** to the priest who throws the Lv 7:14
the walled city shall **b** in perpetuity to Lv 25:30
This shall **b** to them as pastureland for Nm 35:5
the LORD your God **b** heaven and the Dt 10:14
"The secret things **b** to the LORD our Dt 29:29
things that are revealed **b** to us and to Dt 29:29
and sisters, and all who **b** to them, Jos 2:13
there the woman and all who **b** to her, Jos 6:22
the cities of Manasseh, **b** to Ephraim. Jos 17:9
who do not **b** to the people of Israel, Jgs 19:12
as one male of all who **b** to him." 1 Sm 25:22
said to him, "To whom do you **b**? 1 Sm 30:13
saying, "To whom does the land **b**? 2 Sm 3:12
For the shields of the earth **b** to God; he is Ps 47:9
the Lord, **b** deliverances from death. Ps 68:20
The plans of the heart **b** to man, but the Prv 16:1
It shall **b** to those who walk on the way; Is 35:8
your offerings, shall **b** to the priests. Ezk 44:30
It shall **b** to the whole house of Israel. Ezk 45:6
to the prince shall **b** the land on both Ezk 45:7
his inheritance, it shall **b** to his sons. Ezk 46:16
his inheritance—it shall **b** to his sons. Ezk 46:17
And it shall **b** to them as a special Ezk 48:12
of the city shall **b** to the prince. Ezk 48:21
tribal portions, it shall **b** to the prince. Ezk 48:21
and ever, to whom **b** wisdom and might. Dn 2:20
Lord our God **b** mercy and forgiveness, Dn 9:9
not play the whore, or **b** to another man; Hos 3:3
to drink because you **b** to Christ will Mk 9:41
God to whom I **b** and whom I Acts 27:23
you who are called to **b** to Jesus Christ, Rom 1:6
of Christ, so that you may **b** to another, Rom 7:4
the Spirit of Christ does not **b** to him. Rom 8:9
Israelites, and to them **b** the adoption, Rom 9:4
To them **b** the patriarchs, and from Rom 9:5
are descended from Israel **b** to Israel, Rom 9:6
Greet those who **b** to the family of Rom 16:10
in the Lord who **b** to the family of Rom 16:11
I do not **b** to the body," that would 1 Cor 12:15
I do not **b** to the body," that would 1 Cor 12:16
at his coming those who **b** to Christ. 1 Cor 15:23
And those who **b** to Christ Jesus have Gal 5:24
But since we **b** to the day, let us be 1 Thes 5:8
things—things that **b** to salvation. Heb 6:9
To him **b** glory and dominion forever 1 Pt 4:11
and glory and power **b** to our God, Rv 19:1

BELONGED (42)
To Gershon **b** the clan of the Libnites Nm 3:21
To Kohath **b** the clan of the Nm 3:27
To Merari **b** the clan of the Mahlites Nm 3:33
all the people who **b** to Korah and all Nm 16:32
they and all that **b** to them went down Nm 16:33
and brothers and all who **b** to her. Jos 6:23
father's household and all who **b** to her, Jos 6:25
The land of Tappuah **b** to Manasseh, Jos 17:8
boundary of Manasseh **b** to the people Jos 17:8
of the Kohathites who **b** to the people of Jos 21:10
Ophrah, which **b** to Joash the Abiezrite, Jgs 6:11
had made, and the priest who **b** to him, Jgs 18:27
parcel of land that **b** to our relative Ru 4:3
of Naomi all that **b** to Elimelech and all Ru 4:9
Elimelech and all that **b** to Chilion and Ru 4:9
was missed of all that **b** to him, 1 Sm 25:21
Therefore Ziklag has **b** to the kings of 1 Sm 27:6
"All that **b** to Saul and to all his house I 2 Sm 9:9
all that **b** to Mephibosheth is now 2 Sm 16:4
in Arubboth (to him **b** Socoh and all 1 Kgs 4:10
the whole altar that **b** to the inner 1 Kgs 6:22
which **b** to the Philistines, 1 Kgs 15:27
which **b** to the Philistines, 1 Kgs 16:15
house of the LORD; it **b** to the priests. 2 Kgs 12:16
had taken all that **b** to the king of 2 Kgs 24:7
former inhabitants there **b** to Ham. 1 Chr 4:40
him, yet the birthright **b** to Joseph), 1 Chr 5:2
they found that **b** to the king's 2 Chr 21:17
the burial field that **b** to the kings, 2 Chr 26:23
all the territory that **b** to the people 2 Chr 34:33
their descent, whether they **b** to Israel: Ezr 2:59
their descent, whether they **b** to Israel: Neh 7:61
in the palace that **b** to King Ahasuerus. Est 1:9
the twenty cubits that **b** to the inner Ezk 42:3
facing the pavement that **b** to the outer Ezk 42:3
learned that he **b** to Herod's jurisdiction, Lk 23:7
any of the things that **b** to him was his Acts 4:32
sold a field that **b** to him and brought Acts 4:37
some of those who **b** to the synagogue of Acts 6:9
hands on some who **b** to the church. Acts 12:1
But some believers who **b** to the party Acts 15:5
things are spoken **b** to another tribe, Heb 7:13

BELONGING (24)
All the persons **b** to Jacob who came Gn 46:26
the fields of pastureland **b** to their cities Lv 25:34
of a father's house **b** to the Simeonites. Nm 25:14
The cities **b** to the tribe of the people of Jos 15:21
a city **b** to the people of Judah. Jos 18:14
of the Kohathites **b** to the Kohathite Jos 21:20
to come to the part of the field **b** to Boaz, Ru 2:3
cities of the Philistines **b** to the five 1 Sm 6:18
Anyone **b** to Jeroboam who dies in 1 Kgs 14:11
Anyone **b** to Baasha who dies in the 1 Kgs 16:4
Anyone **b** to Ahab who dies in the 1 Kgs 21:24
the plot of ground **b** to Naboth the 2 Kgs 9:25
Their kinsmen **b** to all the clans of 1 Chr 7:5
sons of the Gershonites **b** to Ladan, 1 Chr 26:21
of the fathers' houses **b** to Ladan the 1 Chr 26:21

of common land **b** to their cities, 2 Chr 31:19
characters, '**B** to Maher-shalal-hashbaz.' Is 8:1
you hunt down souls **b** to my people Ezk 13:18
toward the north, **b** to the outer court, Ezk 40:20
in the appointed place **b** to the temple, Ezk 43:21
and the parts of Libya **b** to Cyrene, Acts 2:10
be sojourners in a land **b** to others, Acts 7:6
so that if he found any **b** to the Way, Acts 9:2
that place were lands **b** to the chief Acts 28:7

BELONGINGS (3)
lied and put them among their own **b**. Jos 7:11
of the city, all its gains, all its prized **b**, Jer 20:5
possessions and **b** and distributing Acts 2:45

BELONGS (47)
away from our father **b** to us and to Gn 31:16
that nothing of all that **b** to the people of Ex 9:4
to him to whom it **b** on the day he realizes Lv 6:5
like the sin offering, **b** to the priest; Lv 14:13
to whom the land **b** as a possession. Lv 27:24
which as a firstborn **b** to the LORD, Lv 27:26
its furnishings, and over all that **b** to it. Nm 1:50
them up with all that **b** to them, Nm 16:30
if the firstborn son **b** to the unloved, Dt 21:15
and Mearah that **b** to the Sidonians, Jos 13:4
on the side that **b** to the people of Jos 22:11
at Ophrah, which **b** to the Abiezrites. Jgs 6:24
was in the valley that **b** to Beth-rehob. Jgs 18:28
near Gibeah, which **b** to Benjamin, Jgs 19:14
"I came to Gibeah that **b** to Benjamin, Jgs 20:4
gathered at Socoh, which **b** to Judah, 1 Sm 17:1
against that which **b** to Judah and 1 Sm 30:14
of Obed-edom and all that **b** to him, 2 Sm 6:12
go to Zarephath, which **b** to Sidon, 1 Kgs 17:9
came to Beersheba, which **b** to Judah, 1 Kgs 19:3
know that Ramoth-gilead **b** to us, 1 Kgs 22:3
at Beth-shemesh, which **b** to Judah. 2 Kgs 14:11
is, to Kiriath-jearim that **b** to Judah, 1 Chr 13:6
at Beth-shemesh, which **b** to Judah. 2 Chr 25:21
Salvation **b** to the LORD; your blessing be Ps 3:8
For kingship **b** to the LORD, and he rules Ps 22:28
have I heard this: that power **b** to God, Ps 62:11
and that to you, O Lord, **b** steadfast love. Ps 62:12
For our shield **b** to the LORD, our king to Ps 89:18
of battle, but the victory **b** to the LORD. Prv 21:31
comes, the one to whom judgment **b**, Ezk 21:27
midst of that which **b** to the prince. Ezk 48:22
To you, O Lord, **b** righteousness, but to Dn 9:7
To us, O Lord, **b** open shame, to our Dn 9:8
I will pay. Salvation **b** to the LORD!" Jon 2:9
for to such **b** the kingdom of heaven." Mt 19:14
Take what **b** to you and go. I choose to Mt 20:14
to do what I choose with what **b** to me? Mt 20:15
for to such **b** the kingdom of God. Mk 10:14
for to such **b** the kingdom of God. Lk 18:16
who is of the earth **b** to the earth and Jn 3:31
the surpassing power **b** to God and 2 Cor 4:7
to the one hope that **b** to your call— Eph 4:4
which **b** to your former manner of life Eph 4:22
to come, but the substance **b** to Christ. Col 2:17
"Salvation **b** to our God who sits on the Rv 7:10
not, it is an eighth but it **b** to the seven, Rv 17:11

BELOVED (110)
said, "The **b** of the LORD dwells in safety. Dt 33:12
"Saul and Jonathan, **b** and lovely! In 2 Sm 1:23
like him, and he was **b** by his God, Neh 13:26
That your **b** ones may be delivered, give Ps 60:5
You have caused my **b** and my friend Ps 88:18
That your **b** ones may be delivered, give Ps 108:6
anxious toil; for he gives to his **b** sleep. Ps 127:2
My **b** is to me a sachet of myrrh that lies Sg 1:13
My **b** is to me a cluster of henna Sg 1:14
Behold, you are beautiful, my **b**, truly Sg 1:16
forest, so is my **b** among the young men. Sg 2:3
The voice of my **b**! Behold, he comes, Sg 2:8
My **b** is like a gazelle or a young stag. Sg 2:9
My **b** speaks and says to me: "Arise, my Sg 2:10
My **b** is mine, and I am his; he grazes Sg 2:16
and the shadows flee, turn, my **b**, Sg 2:17
Let my **b** come to his garden, and eat its Sg 4:16
was awake. A sound! My **b** is knocking. Sg 5:2
My **b** put his hand to the latch, and my Sg 5:4
I arose to open to my **b**, and my hands Sg 5:5
I opened to my **b**, but my beloved had Sg 5:6
beloved, but my **b** had turned and gone. Sg 5:6
daughters of Jerusalem, if you find my **b**, Sg 5:8
What is your **b** more than another Sg 5:9
is your beloved more than another **b**, Sg 5:9
What is your **b** more than another Sg 5:9
is your beloved more than another **b**, Sg 5:9
My **b** is radiant and ruddy, distinguished Sg 5:10
This is my **b** and this is my friend, O Sg 5:16
Where has your **b** gone, O most beautiful Sg 6:1
Where has your **b** turned, that we may Sg 6:1
My **b** has gone down to his garden to the Sg 6:2
I am my beloved's and my **b** is mine; he Sg 6:3
It goes down smoothly for my **b**, gliding Sg 7:9
Come, my **b**, let us go out into the fields Sg 7:11
which I have laid up for you, O my **b**. Sg 7:13
up from the wilderness, leaning on her **b**? Sg 8:5
Make haste, my **b**, and be like a gazelle Sg 8:14
me sing for my **b** my love song Is 5:1
My **b** had a vineyard on a very fertile hill. Is 5:1
What right has my **b** in my house, Jer 11:15
I have given the **b** of my soul into the Jer 12:7
his fathers, or to the one **b** by women. Dn 11:37
I will put their **b** children to death. Hos 9:16
from heaven said, "This is my **b** Son, Mt 3:17
my **b** with whom my soul is well Mt 12:18
from the cloud said, "This is my **b** Son, Mt 17:5
came from heaven, "You are my **b** Son; Mk 1:11
out of the cloud, "This is my **b** Son; Mk 9:7
He had still one other, a **b** son. Finally Mk 12:6
came from heaven, "You are my **b** Son; Lk 3:22
I will send my **b** son; perhaps they will Lk 20:13
you with our **b** Barnabas and Paul, Acts 15:25
her who was not **b** I will call Rom 9:25
who was not beloved I will call '**b**.'" Rom 9:25
they are **b** for the sake of their Rom 11:28
B, never avenge yourselves, but leave Rom 12:19
Greet my **b** Epaenetus, who was the Rom 16:5
Greet Ampliatus, my **b** in the Lord. Rom 16:8
worker in Christ, and my **b** Stachys. Rom 16:9
Greet the **b** Persis, who has worked Rom 16:12
to admonish you as my **b** children. 1 Cor 4:14
my **b** and faithful child in the Lord, 1 Cor 4:17
Therefore, my **b**, flee from idolatry. 1 Cor 10:14
Therefore, my **b** brothers, be 1 Cor 15:58
b, let us cleanse ourselves from every 2 Cor 7:1
and all for your upbuilding, **b**. 2 Cor 12:19
with which he has blessed us in the **B**. Eph 1:6
be imitators of God, as **b** children. Eph 5:1
Tychicus the **b** brother and faithful Eph 6:21
Therefore, my **b**, as you have always Phil 2:12
stand firm thus in the Lord, my **b**. Phil 4:1
it from Epaphras our **b** fellow servant. Col 1:7
us to the kingdom of his **b** Son, Col 1:13
then, as God's chosen ones, holy and **b**, Col 3:12
He is a **b** brother and faithful minister Col 4:7
Onesimus, our faithful and **b** brother, Col 4:9
Luke the **b** physician greets you, as Col 4:14
God for you, brothers **b** by the Lord, 2 Thes 2:13
their good service are believers and **b**. 1 Tm 6:2
To Timothy, my **b** child: Grace, 2 Tm 1:2
To Philemon our **b** fellow worker Phlm 1:1
as a **b** brother—especially to me, Phlm 1:16
b, we feel sure of better things—things Heb 6:9
Do not be deceived, my **b** brothers. Jas 1:16
Know this, my **b** brothers: let every Jas 1:19
Listen, my **b** brothers, has not God Jas 2:5
B, I urge you as sojourners and exiles to 1 Pt 2:11
B, do not be surprised at the fiery trial 1 Pt 4:12
the Majestic Glory, "This is my **b** Son, 2 Pt 1:17
second letter that I am writing to you, **b**. 2 Pt 3:1
b, that with the Lord one day is as a 2 Pt 3:8
b, since you are waiting for these, 2 Pt 3:14
just as our **b** brother Paul also wrote to 2 Pt 3:15
therefore, **b**, knowing this beforehand, 2 Pt 3:17
B, I am writing you no new 1 Jn 2:7
B, we are God's children now, and what 1 Jn 3:2
B, if our heart does not condemn us, we 1 Jn 3:21
B, do not believe every spirit, but test the 1 Jn 4:1
B, let us love one another, for love is 1 Jn 4:7
B, if God so loved us, we also ought to 1 Jn 4:11
The elder to the **b** Gaius, whom I love in 3 Jn 1:1
B, I pray that all may go well with you 3 Jn 1:2
B, it is a faithful thing you do in all your 3 Jn 1:5
B, do not imitate evil but imitate good. 3 Jn 1:11
b in God the Father and kept for Jesus Jude 1:1
B, although I was very eager to write to Jude 1:3
b, the predictions of the apostles of our Jude 1:17
b, build yourselves up in your most Jude 1:20
the camp of the saints and the **b** city, Rv 20:9

BELOVED'S (2)
I am my **b** and my beloved is mine; he Sg 6:3
I am my **b**, and his desire is for me. Sg 7:10

BELOW (23)
she was buried under an oak **b** Bethel. Gn 35:8
Valley of Lebanon **b** Mount Hermon. Jos 11:17
from Baal-gad **b** Mount Hermon to Jos 13:5
camp of Midian was **b** him in the valley. Jgs 7:8
and struck them, as far as **b** Beth-car. 1 Sm 7:11
that is beside Zarethan **b** Jezreel, 1 Kgs 4:12
both above and **b** the lions and oxen, 1 Kgs 7:29
not count those **b** twenty years of 1 Chr 27:23
together; bind their faces in the world **b**. Jb 40:13
of the earth **b** can be explored, Jer 31:37
B what appeared to be his waist was fire, Ezk 8:2
will make you to dwell in the world **b**, Ezk 26:20
all given over to death, to the world **b**, Ezk 31:14
water, were comforted in the world **b**. Ezk 31:16
with the trees of Eden to the world **b**. Ezk 31:18
of majestic nations, to the world **b**, Ezk 32:18
uncircumcised into the world **b**, Ezk 32:24
B these chambers was an entrance on Ezk 42:9
was issuing from **b** the threshold of Ezk 47:1
was flowing down from **b** the south end Ezk 47:1
And as Peter was **b** in the courtyard, Mk 14:66
He said to them, "You are from **b**; I am Jn 8:23
above and signs on the earth **b**, Acts 2:19

BELSHAZZAR (8)
King **B** made a great feast for a thousand Dn 5:1
B, when he tasted the wine, commanded Dn 5:2
Then King **B** was greatly alarmed, and Dn 5:9
son, **B**, have not humbled your heart, Dn 5:22
Then **B** gave the command, and Daniel Dn 5:29
That very night **B** the Chaldean king Dn 5:30
In the first year of **B** king of Babylon, Dn 7:1
of the reign of King **B** a vision appeared to Dn 8:1

BELT (19)
with your **b** fastened, your sandals on Ex 12:11
even his sword and his bow and his **b**. 1 Sm 18:4
give you ten pieces of silver and a **b**." 2 Sm 18:11
and over it was a **b** with a sword in its 2 Sm 20:8
of war on the **b** around his waist and 1 Kgs 2:5
with a **b** of leather about his waist." 2 Kgs 1:8
princes and loosens the **b** of the strong. Jb 12:21
of wrath you will put on like a **b**. Ps 76:10
is robed; he has put on strength as his **b**. Ps 93:1
like a **b** that he puts on every day! Ps 109:19
be rottenness; and instead of a **b**, a rope; Is 3:24
Righteousness shall be the **b** of his waist, Is 11:5
waist, and faithfulness the **b** of his loins. Is 11:5
with a **b** of fine gold from Uphaz Dn 10:5
hair and a leather **b** around his waist, Mt 3:4
and wore a leather **b** around his waist Mk 1:6
he took Paul's **b** and bound his own Acts 21:11
who owns this **b** and deliver him Acts 21:11
having fastened on the **b** of truth, Eph 6:14

BELTESHAZZAR (10)
Daniel he called **B**, Hananiah he called Dn 1:7
king said to Daniel, whose name was **B**, Dn 2:26
—he who was named **B** after the name of Dn 4:8
"O **B**, chief of the magicians, because I Dn 4:9
And you, O **B**, tell me the interpretation, Dn 4:18
Then Daniel, whose name was **B**, was Dn 4:19
"**B**, let not the dream or the Dn 4:19
alarm you." **B** answered and Dn 4:19
in this Daniel, whom the king named **B**. Dn 5:12
revealed to Daniel, who was named **B**. Dn 10:1

BELTS (4)
before him and to loose the **b** of kings, Is 45:1
wearing **b** on their waists, with Ezk 23:15
no gold nor silver nor copper for your **b**, Mt 10:9
no bread, no bag, no money in their **b**— Mk 6:8

BEN-ABINADAB (1)
B, in all Naphath-dor (he had 1 Kgs 4:11

BEN-AMMI (1)
also bore a son and called his name **B**. Gn 19:38

BEN-DEKER (1)
B, in Makaz, Shaalbim, Beth-shemesh, 1 Kgs 4:9

BEN-GEBER (1)
B, in Ramoth-gilead (he had the 1 Kgs 4:13

BEN-HADAD (27)
Asa sent them to **B** the son of 1 Kgs 15:18
And **B** listened to King Asa and sent 1 Kgs 15:20
B the king of Syria gathered all his 1 Kgs 20:1
Israel and said to him, "Thus says **B**: 1 Kgs 20:2
came again and said, "Thus says **B**: 1 Kgs 20:5
So he said to the messengers of **B**, 1 Kgs 20:9
B sent to him and said, "The gods do 1 Kgs 20:10
When **B** heard this message as he 1 Kgs 20:12
while **B** was drinking himself 1 Kgs 20:16
And **B** sent out scouts, and they 1 Kgs 20:17
but **B** king of Syria escaped on a 1 Kgs 20:20
B mustered the Syrians and went up 1 Kgs 20:26
B also fled and entered an inner 1 Kgs 20:30
and said, "Your servant **B** says, 1 Kgs 20:32
"Yes, your brother **B**." Then he said, 1 Kgs 20:33
bring him." Then **B** came out to 1 Kgs 20:33
And **B** said to him, "The cities that 1 Kgs 20:34
Afterward **B** king of Syria mustered 2 Kgs 6:24
B the king of Syria was sick. 2 Kgs 8:7
"Your son **B** king of Syria has sent me 2 Kgs 8:9
into the hand of **B** the son of Hazael. 2 Kgs 13:3
B his son became king in his place. 2 Kgs 13:24
took again from **B** the son of 2 Kgs 13:25
and sent them to **B** king of Syria, 2 Chr 16:2
And **B** listened to King Asa and sent 2 Chr 16:4
it shall devour the strongholds of **B**." Jer 49:27

and it shall devour the strongholds of **B**. Am 1:4

BEN-HAIL (1)
he sent his officials, **B**, Obadiah, 2 Chr 17:7

BEN-HANAN (1)
Amnon, Rinnah, **B**, and Tilon. 1 Chr 4:20

BEN-HESED (1)
B, in Arubboth (to him belonged 1 Kgs 4:10

BEN-HUR (1)
B, in the hill country of Ephraim; 1 Kgs 4:8

BEN-ONI (1)
she was dying), she called his name **B**; Gn 35:18

BEN-ZOHETH (1)
The sons of Ishi: Zoheth and **B**. 1 Chr 4:20

BENAIAH (44)
and **B** the son of Jehoiada was over the 2 Sm 8:18
and **B** the son of Jehoiada was in 2 Sm 20:23
And **B** the son of Jehoiada was a 2 Sm 23:20
but **B** went down to him with a staff 2 Sm 23:21
These things did **B** the son of 2 Sm 23:22
B of Pirathon, Hiddai of the brooks 2 Sm 23:30
Zadok the priest and **B** the son of 1 Kgs 1:8
the prophet or **B** or the mighty 1 Kgs 1:10
the priest, and **B** the son of Jehoiada, 1 Kgs 1:26
and **B** the son of Jehoiada." So they 1 Kgs 1:32
And **B** the son of Jehoiada answered 1 Kgs 1:36
prophet, and **B** the son of Jehoiada, 1 Kgs 1:38
prophet, and **B** the son of Jehoiada, 1 Kgs 1:44
So King Solomon sent **B** the son of 1 Kgs 2:25
the altar," Solomon sent **B** the son of 1 Kgs 2:29
So **B** came to the tent of the LORD and 1 Kgs 2:30
die here." Then **B** brought the king 1 Kgs 2:30
Then **B** the son of Jehoiada went up 1 Kgs 2:34
The king put **B** the son of Jehoiada 1 Kgs 2:35
the king commanded **B** the son of 1 Kgs 2:46
B the son of Jehoiada was in command 1 Kgs 4:4
Asaiah, Adiel, Jesimiel, **B**, 1 Chr 4:36
And **B** the son of Jehoiada was a 1 Chr 11:22
but **B** went down to him with a staff 1 Chr 11:23
These things did **B** the son of 1 Chr 11:24
people of Benjamin, **B** of Pirathon, 1 Chr 11:31
Jehiel, Unni, Eliab, **B**, Maaseiah, 1 Chr 15:18
and **B** were to play harps according 1 Chr 15:20
Amasai, Zechariah, **B**, and Eliezer, 1 Chr 15:24
Mattithiah, Eliab, **B**, Obed-edom, 1 Chr 16:5
and **B** and Jahaziel the priests were to 1 Chr 16:6
and **B** the son of Jehoiada was over 1 Chr 18:17
for the third month, was **B**, 1 Chr 27:5
This is the **B** who was a mighty man 1 Chr 27:6
eleventh month, was **B** of Pirathon, 1 Chr 27:14
succeeded by Jehoiada the son of **B**, 1 Chr 27:34
the son of Zechariah, son of **B**, 2 Chr 20:14
and **B** were overseers assisting 2 Chr 31:13
Mijamin, Eleazar, Hashabiah, and **B**. Ezr 10:25
Adna, Chelal, **B**, Maaseiah, Mattaniah, Ezr 10:30
B, Bedeiah, Cheluhi, Ezr 10:35
Zabad, Zebina, Jaddai, Joel, and **B**. Ezr 10:43
son of Azzur, and Pelatiah the son of **B**, Ezk 11:1
that Pelatiah the son of **B** died. Ezk 11:13

BEND (9)
that my arms can **b** a bow of bronze. 2 Sm 22:35
for behold, the wicked **b** the bow; they Ps 11:2
so that my arms can **b** a bow of bronze. Ps 18:34
draw the sword and **b** their bows to Ps 37:14
They **b** their tongue like a bow; falsehood Jer 9:3
all around, all you who **b** the bow; Jer 50:14
Babylon, all those who **b** the bow. Jer 50:29
Let not the archer **b** his bow, and let him Jer 51:3
see, and **b** their backs forever." Rom 11:10

BENDING (1)
afflicted you shall come **b** low to you, Is 60:14

BENDS (4)
Then the boundary **b** around to Baalah Jos 15:9
then the boundary **b** around to Jos 15:11
Then it **b** in a northerly direction Jos 18:17
going on to Rimmon it **b** toward Neah, Jos 19:13

BENE-BERAK (1)
Jehud, **B**, Gath-rimmon, Jos 19:45

BENE-JAAKAN (3)
out from Moseroth and camped at **B**. Nm 33:31
they set out from **B** and camped at Nm 33:32
journeyed from Beeroth **B** to Moserah. Dt 10:6

BENEATH (21)
blessings of the deep that crouches **b**, Gn 49:25
in heaven above, or that is in the earth **b**, Ex 20:4
they shall be separate **b**, but joined at Ex 26:24
And they were separate **b** but joined at Ex 36:29
God in heaven above and on the earth **b**; Dt 4:39
in heaven above, or that is on the earth **b**, Dt 5:8
above, and of the deep that crouches **b**, Dt 33:13
in the heavens above and on the earth **b**. Jos 2:11
you, in heaven above or on earth **b**, 1 Kgs 8:23
he had sackcloth **b** on his body— 2 Kgs 6:30
b him bowed the helpers of Rahab. Jb 9:13
His roots dry up **b**, and his branches Jb 18:16
that he may turn away from Sheol **b**. Prv 15:24
of heart with which he toils **b** the sun? Eccl 2:22
Sheol **b** is stirred up to meet you when Is 14:9
maggots are laid as a bed **b** you, and Is 14:11
to the heavens, and look at the earth **b**; Is 51:6
shall return and dwell **b** my shadow; Hos 14:7
destroyed his fruit above and his roots **b**. Am 2:9
bread have set a trap **b** you—you have no Ob 1:7
into my bones; my legs tremble **b** me. Hab 3:16

BENEFACTORS (1)
in authority over them are called **b**. Lk 22:25

BENEFIT (10)
according to the **b** done to him, 2 Chr 32:25
who love you, what **b** is that to you? Lk 6:32
do good to you, what **b** is that to you? Lk 6:33
to myself and Apollos for your **b**, 1 Cor 4:6
I say this for your own **b**, not to lay 1 Cor 7:35
how will I **b** you unless I bring you 1 Cor 14:6
partner and fellow worker for your **b**. 2 Cor 8:23
better since those who **b** by their good 1 Tm 6:2
I want some **b** from you in the Lord. Phlm 1:20
the message they heard did not **b** them, Heb 4:2

BENEFITED (1)
which have not **b** those devoted to Heb 13:9

BENEFITS (4)
O my soul, and forget not all his **b**, Ps 103:2
I render to the LORD for all his **b** to me? Ps 116:12
A man who is kind **b** himself, but a Prv 11:17
I give my judgment: this **b** you, 2 Cor 8:10

BENINU (1)
Hodiah, Bani, **B**. Neh 10:13

BENJAMIN (162)
Ben-oni; but his father called him **B**. Gn 35:18
The sons of Rachel: Joseph and **B**. Gn 35:24
But Jacob did not send **B**, Joseph's Gn 42:4
is no more, and now you would take **B**. Gn 42:36
send back your other brother and **B**. Gn 43:14
double the money with them, and **B**. Gn 43:15
When Joseph saw **B** with them, he said Gn 43:16
up his eyes and saw his brother **B**, Gn 43:29
see, and the eyes of my brother **B** see, Gn 45:12
and wept, and **B** wept upon his neck. Gn 45:14
but to **B** he gave three hundred shekels Gn 45:22
of Rachel, Jacob's wife: Joseph and **B**. Gn 46:19
And the sons of **B**: Bela, Becher, Gn 46:21
"**B** is a ravenous wolf, in the morning Gn 49:27
Issachar, Zebulun, and **B**, Ex 1:3
from **B**, Abidan the son of Gideoni; Nm 1:11
Of the people of **B**, their generations, by Nm 1:36
those listed of the tribe of **B** were 35,400. Nm 1:37
Then the tribe of **B**, the chief of the Nm 2:22
of the people of **B** being Abidan the son Nm 2:22
of Gideoni, the chief of the people of **B**: Nm 7:60
of the people of **B** was Abidan the son Nm 10:24
from the tribe of **B**, Palti the son of Nm 13:9
The sons of **B** according to their Nm 26:38
are the sons of **B** according to their Nm 26:41
Of the tribe of **B**, Elidad the son of Nm 34:21
Levi, Judah, Issachar, Joseph, and **B**. Dt 27:12
Of **B** he said, "The beloved of the LORD Dt 33:12
of the people of **B** according to its clans Jos 18:11
is the inheritance of the people of **B**, Jos 18:20
of the people of **B** according to their Jos 18:21
of the people of **B** according to its clans. Jos 18:28
from the tribes of Judah, Simeon, and **B**, Jos 21:4
then out of the tribe of **B**, Gibeon with Jos 21:17
But the people of **B** did not drive out the Jgs 1:21
with the people of **B** in Jerusalem to this Jgs 1:21
following you, **B**, with your kinsmen; Jgs 5:14
Judah and against **B** and against the Jgs 10:9
them near Gibeah, which belongs to **B**, Jgs 19:14
(Now the people of **B** heard that the Jgs 20:3
"I came to Gibeah that belongs to **B**, Jgs 20:4
they come they may repay Gibeah of **B**, Jgs 20:10
sent men through all the tribe of **B**, Jgs 20:12
Then the people of **B** came together out Jgs 20:14
And the people of **B** mustered out of Jgs 20:15
And the men of Israel, apart from **B**, Jgs 20:17
against the people of **B**?" And the LORD Jgs 20:18
of Israel went out to fight against **B**, Jgs 20:20
The people of **B** came out of Gibeah Jgs 20:21
the people of **B**?" And the LORD said, Jgs 20:23
against the people of **B** the second day. Jgs 20:24
And **B** went against them out of Jgs 20:25
against our brothers, the people of **B**, Jgs 20:28
against the people of **B** on the third day Jgs 20:30
And the people of **B** went out against Jgs 20:31
And the people of **B** said, "They are Jgs 20:32
And the LORD defeated **B** before Israel, Jgs 20:35
destroyed 25,100 men of **B** that day. Jgs 20:35
So the people of **B** saw that they were Jgs 20:36
The men of Israel gave ground to **B**, Jgs 20:36
Now **B** had begun to strike and kill Jgs 20:39
and the men of **B** were dismayed, Jgs 20:41
Eighteen thousand men of **B** fell, all of Jgs 20:44
fell that day of **B** were 25,000 men who Jgs 20:46
the people of **B** and struck them Jgs 20:48
give his daughter in marriage to **B**." Jgs 21:1
had compassion for **B** their brother and Jgs 21:6
word to the people of **B** who were at the Jgs 21:13
And **B** returned at that time. And they Jgs 21:14
had compassion on **B** because the LORD Jgs 21:15
the women are destroyed out of **B**?" Jgs 21:16
an inheritance for the survivors of **B**, Jgs 21:17
"Cursed be he who gives a wife to **B**." Jgs 21:18
And they commanded the people of **B**, Jgs 21:20
of Shiloh, and go to the land of **B**. Jgs 21:21
And the people of **B** did so and took Jgs 21:23
A man of **B** ran from the battle line 1 Sm 4:12
was a man of **B** whose name was Kish, 1 Sm 9:1
they passed through the land of **B**, 1 Sm 9:4
send to you a man from the land of **B**, 1 Sm 9:16
of all the clans of the tribe of **B**? 1 Sm 9:21
tomb in the territory of **B** at Zelzah, 1 Sm 10:2
and the tribe of **B** was taken by lot. 1 Sm 10:20
brought the tribe of **B** near by its 1 Sm 10:21
were with Jonathan in Gibeah of **B**. 1 Sm 13:2
went up from Gilgal to Gibeah of **B**. 1 Sm 13:15
with them stayed in Geba of **B**, 1 Sm 13:16
of Saul in Gibeah of **B** looked, 1 Sm 14:16
about him, "Hear now, people of **B**; 1 Sm 22:7
and Ephraim and **B** and all Israel. 2 Sm 2:9
twelve for **B** and Ish-bosheth the son 2 Sm 2:15
the people of **B** gathered themselves 2 Sm 2:25
had struck down of **B** 360 of Abner's 2 Sm 2:31
Abner also spoke to **B**. And then 2 Sm 3:19
the whole house of **B** thought good to 2 Sm 3:19
Rimmon a man of **B** from Beeroth (for 2 Sm 4:2
(for Beeroth also is counted part of **B**; 2 Sm 4:2
him were a thousand men from **B**. 2 Sm 19:17
Jonathan in the land of **B** in Zela, 2 Sm 21:14
of Ribai of Gibeah of the people of **B**, 2 Sm 23:29
Shimei the son of Ela, in **B**; 1 Kgs 4:18
house of Judah and the tribe of **B**, 1 Kgs 12:21
and to all the house of Judah and **B**, 1 Kgs 12:23
Asa built Geba of **B** and Mizpah. 1 Kgs 15:22
Dan, Joseph, **B**, Naphtali, Gad, and 1 Chr 2:2
and from the tribe of **B**, Gibeon, Geba 1 Chr 6:60
and **B** these cities that are mentioned 1 Chr 6:65
The sons of **B**: Bela, Becher, and 1 Chr 7:6
Jeush, **B**, Ehud, Chenaanah, Zethan, 1 Chr 7:10
B fathered Bela his firstborn, Ashbel 1 Chr 8:1
of the people of Judah, **B**, Ephraim, 1 Chr 9:3
of Ribai of Gibeah of the people of **B**, 1 Chr 11:31
of the men of **B** and Judah came to 1 Chr 12:16
include Levi and **B** in the 1 Chr 21:6
Iddo the son of Zechariah; for **B**, 1 Chr 27:21
assembled the house of Judah and **B**, 2 Chr 11:1
and to all Israel in Judah and **B**, 2 Chr 11:3
cities that are in Judah and in **B**. 2 Chr 11:10
very strong. So he held Judah and **B**. 2 Chr 11:12
all the districts of Judah and **B**, 2 Chr 11:23
280,000 men from **B** that carried 2 Chr 14:8
"Hear me, Asa, and all Judah and **B**: 2 Chr 15:2
land of Judah and **B** and from the 2 Chr 15:8
And he gathered all Judah and **B**, and 2 Chr 15:9
Of **B**: Eliada, a mighty man of valor, 2 Chr 17:17
and of hundreds for all Judah and **B**. 2 Chr 25:5
altars throughout all Judah and **B**, 2 Chr 31:1
from all Judah and **B** and from the 2 Chr 34:9
in Jerusalem and in **B** stand to it. 2 Chr 34:32
of the fathers' houses of Judah and **B**, Ezr 1:5
adversaries of Judah and **B** heard that the Ezr 4:1
of Judah and **B** assembled at Jerusalem Ezr 10:9
B, Malluch, and Shemariah. Ezr 10:32
After them **B** and Hasshub repaired Neh 3:23
the sons of Judah and of the sons of **B**. Neh 11:4
And these are the sons of **B**: Sallu the Neh 11:7
The people of **B** also lived from Geba Neh 11:31
Levites in Judah were assigned to **B**. Neh 11:36
Judah, **B**, Shemaiah, and Jeremiah, Neh 12:34
There is **B**, the least of them, in the lead, Ps 68:27
Before Ephraim and **B** and Manasseh, Ps 80:2
who were in Anathoth in the land of **B**, Jer 1:1
Flee for safety, O people of **B**, from the Jer 6:1
around Jerusalem, from the land of **B**, Jer 17:26
were in the upper **B** Gate of the house Jer 20:2
field that is at Anathoth in the land of **B**, Jer 32:8
sealed and witnessed, in the land of **B**, Jer 32:44
the cities of the Negeb, in the land of **B**, Jer 33:13
go to the land of **B** to receive his portion Jer 37:12
When he was at the **B** Gate, a sentry Jer 37:13

—the king was sitting in the **B** Gate— Jer 38:7
of Judah and the territory of **B**. Ezk 48:22
the east side to the west, **B**, one portion. Ezk 48:23
Adjoining the territory of **B**, from the Ezk 48:24
gates, the gate of Joseph, the gate of **B**, Ezk 48:32
alarm at Beth-aven; we follow you, O **B**! Hos 5:8
of Samaria, and **B** shall possess Gilead. Ob 1:19
site from the Gate of **B** to the place of Zec 14:10
son of Kish, a man of the tribe of **B**, Acts 13:21
Abraham, a member of the tribe of **B**. Rom 11:1
of the people of Israel, of the tribe of **B**, Phil 3:5
12,000 from the tribe of **B** were sealed. Rv 7:8

BENJAMIN'S (3)
but **B** portion was five times as much Gn 43:34
And the cup was found in **B** sack. Gn 44:12
fell upon his brother **B** neck and wept, Gn 45:14

BENJAMINITE (10)
a deliverer, Ehud, the son of Gera, the **B**, Jgs 3:15
son of Becorath, son of Aphiah, a **B**, 1 Sm 9:1
Saul answered, "Am I not a **B**, from 1 Sm 9:21
how much more now may this **B**! 2 Sm 16:11
And Shimei the son of Gera, the **B**, 2 Sm 19:16
was Sheba, the son of Bichri, a **B**. 2 Sm 20:1
the son of Gera, the **B** from Bahurim, 1 Kgs 2:8
was Abiezer of Anathoth, a **B**; 1 Chr 27:12
of Jair, son of Shimei, son of Kish, a **B**, Est 2:5
LORD concerning the words of Cush, a **B**. Ps 7:T

BENJAMINITES (9)
Gibeah. The men of the place were **B**. Jgs 19:16
from Israel." But the **B** would not listen Jgs 20:13
but the **B** did not know that disaster Jgs 20:34
of smoke, the **B** looked behind them, Jgs 20:40
Surrounding the **B**, they pursued them Jgs 20:43
and grandsons, 150. All these were **B**. 1 Chr 8:40
Of the **B**: Sallu the son of Meshullam, 1 Chr 9:7
hand; they were **B**, Saul's kinsmen. 1 Chr 12:2
Of the **B**, the kinsmen of Saul, 3,000, 1 Chr 12:29

BENO (2)
and Mushi. The sons of Jaaziah: **B**. 1 Chr 24:26
of Jaaziah, **B**, Shoham, Zaccur and 1 Chr 24:27

BENT (16)
his sword; he has **b** and readied his bow; Ps 7:12
tremble, and the strong men are **b**, Eccl 12:3
their arrows are sharp, all their bows **b**, Is 5:28
from the drawn sword, from the **b** bow, Is 21:15
He has **b** his bow like an enemy, with Lam 2:4
he **b** his bow and set me as a target for Lam 3:12
this vine **b** its roots toward him and Ezk 17:7
power, have been **b** on shedding blood. Ezk 22:6
their hearts shall be **b** on doing evil. Dn 11:27
and I **b** down to them and fed them. Hos 11:4
My people are **b** on turning away from Hos 11:7
For I have **b** Judah as my bow; I have Zec 9:13
She was **b** over and could not fully Lk 13:11
Jesus **b** down and wrote with his finger on Jn 8:6
And once more he **b** down and wrote on Jn 8:8
But Paul went down and **b** over him, Acts 20:10

BEON (1)
Heshbon, Elealeh, Sebam, Nebo, and **B**, Nm 32:3

BEOR (11)
Bela the son of **B** reigned in Edom, the Gn 36:32
to Balaam the son of **B** at Pethor, Nm 22:5
"The oracle of Balaam the son of **B**, Nm 24:3
"The oracle of Balaam the son of **B**, Nm 24:15
Balaam the son of **B** with the sword. Nm 31:8
Balaam the son of **B** from Pethor of Dt 23:4
Balaam also, the son of **B**, the one who Jos 13:22
Balaam the son of **B** to curse you, Jos 24:9
Bela the son of **B**, the name of his city 1 Chr 1:43
what Balaam the son of **B** answered him, Mi 6:5
the way of Balaam, the son of **B**, 2 Pt 2:15

BEQUEATH (1)
You may **b** them to your sons after you Lv 25:46

BERA (1)
kings made war with **B** king of Sodom, Gn 14:2

BERACAH (3)
of Azmaveth; **B**, Jehu of Anathoth, 1 Chr 12:3
they assembled in the Valley of **B**, 2 Chr 20:26
called the Valley of **B** to this day. 2 Chr 20:26

BERAIAH (1)
B, and Shimrath were the sons of 1 Chr 8:21

BERATED (1)
Jacob became angry and **b** Laban. Gn 31:36

BEREA (4)
Paul and Silas away by night to **B**, Acts 17:10
was proclaimed by Paul at **B** also, Acts 17:13
Sopater of **B**, the son of Pyrrhus from Acts 20:4
of Berea, the son of Pyrrhus from **B**, Acts 20:4

BEREAVE (6)
which shall **b** you of your children and Lv 26:22
Outdoors the sword shall **b**, and Dt 32:25
shall no longer **b** them of children. Ezk 36:12
and you **b** your nation of children,' Ezk 36:13
people and no longer **b** your nation of Ezk 36:14
children, I will **b** them till none is left. Hos 9:12

BEREAVED (5)
them, "You have **b** me of my children: Gn 42:36
as for me, if I am **b** of my children, Gn 43:14
I am bereaved of my children, I am **b**." Gn 43:14
has borne me these? I was **b** and barren, Is 49:21
in the gates of the land; I have **b** them; Jer 15:7

BEREAVEMENT (1)
The children of your **b** will yet say in Is 49:20

BEREAVES (1)
In the street the sword **b**; in the house Lam 1:20

BERECHIAH (11)
and Hashubah, Ohel, **B**, Hasadiah, 1 Chr 3:20
hand, namely, Asaph the son of **B**, 1 Chr 6:39
of Jeduthun, and **B** the son of Asa, 1 Chr 9:16
of his brothers Asaph the son of **B**; 1 Chr 15:17
B and Elkanah were to be 1 Chr 15:23
B the son of Meshillemoth, 2 Chr 28:12
next to them Meshullam the son of **B**, Neh 3:4
the son of **B** repaired opposite his Neh 3:30
of Meshullam the son of **B** as his wife. Neh 6:18
to the prophet Zechariah, the son of **B**, Zec 1:1
to the prophet Zechariah, the son of **B**, Zec 1:7

BERED (2)
it lies between Kadesh and **B**. Gn 16:14
Shuthelah, and **B** his son, Tahath his 1 Chr 7:20

BEREFT (3)
Why should I be **b** of you both in one Gn 27:45
repay me evil for good; my soul is **b**. Ps 35:12
my soul is **b** of peace; I have forgotten Lam 3:17

BERI (1)
Suah, Harnepher, Shual, **B**, Imrah. 1 Chr 7:36

BERIAH (11)
Ishvah, Ishvi, **B**, with Serah their sister. Gn 46:17
And the sons of **B**: Heber and Malchiel. Gn 46:17
of Ishvi, the clan of the Ishvites; of **B**, Nm 26:44
Of the sons of **B**: of Heber, the clan of Nm 26:45
And he called his name **B**, because 1 Chr 7:23
Ishvi, **B**, and their sister Serah. 1 Chr 7:30
The sons of **B**: Heber, and Malchiel, 1 Chr 7:31
and **B** and Shema (they were heads of 1 Chr 8:13
Ishpah, and Joha were sons of **B**. 1 Chr 8:16
Jahath, Zina, and Jeush and **B**. 1 Chr 23:10
but Jeush and **B** did not have many 1 Chr 23:11

BERIITES (1)
Ishvites; of Beriah, the clan of the **B**. Nm 26:44

BERNICE (3)
the king and **B** arrived at Caesarea Acts 25:13
day Agrippa and **B** came with great Acts 25:23
the governor and **B** and those who Acts 26:30

BEROTHAH (1)
B, Sibraim (which lies on the border Ezk 47:16

BEROTHAI (1)
And from Betah and from **B**, cities of 2 Sm 8:8

BERRIES (1)
is beaten—two or three **b** in the top of the Is 17:6

BERYL (7)
and the fourth row a **b**, an onyx, and a Ex 28:20
and the fourth row, a **b**, an onyx, and a Ex 39:13
appearance was like the gleaming of **b**. Ezk 1:16
of the wheels was like sparkling **b**. Ezk 10:9
sardius, topaz, and diamond, **b**, onyx, Ezk 28:13
His body was like **b**, his face like the Dn 10:6
the seventh chrysolite, the eighth **b**, Rv 21:20

BESAI (2)
Uzza, the sons of Paseah, the sons of **B**, Ezr 2:49
the sons of **B**, the sons of Meunim, the Neh 7:52

BESET (1)
since he himself is **b** with weakness. Heb 5:2

BESIDE (122)
behold, three flocks of sheep lying **b** it, Gn 29:2
to her, to lie **b** her or to be with her. Gn 39:10
he left his garment **b** me and fled and Gn 39:15
he left his garment **b** me and fled out of Gn 39:18
her young women walked **b** the river. Ex 2:5
its contents and cast it **b** the altar on the Lv 1:16
on the altar and put them **b** the altar. Lv 6:10
and eat it unleavened **b** the altar, Lv 10:12
God, that your brother may live **b** you. Lv 25:36
brother becomes poor **b** you and sells Lv 25:39
and your brother **b** him becomes poor Lv 25:47
man dies very suddenly **b** him and he Nm 6:9
the sea and let them fall **b** the camp, Nm 11:31
to Balak, "Stand **b** your burnt offering, Nm 23:3
Moab were standing **b** his burnt Nm 23:6
"Stand here **b** your burnt offering, Nm 23:15
he was standing **b** his burnt offering, Nm 23:17
that stretch afar, like gardens **b** a river, Nm 24:6
planted, like cedar trees **b** the waters. Nm 24:6
opposite Gilgal, **b** the oak of Moreh? Dt 11:30
any tree as an Asherah **b** the altar of the Dt 16:21
at Adam, the city that is **b** Zarethan, Jos 3:16
the king of Ai, which is **b** Bethel, one; Jos 12:9
given a possession **b** their brothers in Jos 22:7
and cut down the Asherah that is **b** it Jgs 6:25
and the Asherah **b** it was cut down, Jgs 6:28
of Baal and cut down the Asherah **b** it." Jgs 6:30
rose early and encamped **b** the spring of Jgs 7:1
in the wine." So she sat **b** the reapers, Ru 2:14
sitting on the seat **b** the doorpost of the 1 Sm 1:9
house of Dagon and set it up **b** Dagon. 1 Sm 5:2
of the LORD and the box that was **b** it, 1 Sm 6:15
The great stone **b** which they set 1 Sm 6:18
go out and stand **b** my father in the 1 Sm 19:3
hand, and remain **b** the stone heap. 1 Sm 20:19
David rose from **b** the stone heap 1 Sm 20:41
which is **b** the road on the east of 1 Sm 26:3
he said to me 'Stand **b** me and kill me, 2 Sm 1:9
So I stood **b** him and killed him, 2 Sm 1:10
feet and hanged them **b** the pool at 2 Sm 4:12
and he died there **b** the ark of God. 2 Sm 6:7
the elders of his house stood **b** him, 2 Sm 12:17
to rise early and stand **b** the way of the 2 Sm 15:2
them and won a name **b** the three. 2 Sm 23:18
and won a name **b** the three mighty 2 Sm 23:22
Serpent's Stone, which is **b** En-rogel, 1 Kgs 1:9
he is **b** the altar," Solomon sent 1 Kgs 2:29
and took my son from **b** me, 1 Kgs 3:20
Beth-shean that is **b** Zarethan below 1 Kgs 4:12
which was **b** the latticework. 1 Kgs 7:20
two lions standing **b** the armrests, 1 Kgs 10:19
the road, and the donkey stood **b** it; 1 Kgs 13:24
it; the lion also stood **b** the body. 1 Kgs 13:24
and the lion standing **b** the body. 1 Kgs 13:28
is buried; lay my bones **b** his bones. 1 Kgs 13:31
b the palace of Ahab king of 1 Kgs 21:1
of heaven standing **b** him on his 1 Kgs 22:19
and the trumpeters **b** the king, 2 Kgs 11:14
of it and set it **b** the altar on the right 2 Kgs 12:9
them and won a name **b** the three. 1 Chr 11:20
and won a name **b** the three mighty 1 Chr 11:24
two lions standing **b** the arm rests, 2 Chr 9:18
and the trumpeters **b** the king, 2 Chr 23:13
said to me (the queen sitting **b** him), Neh 2:6
of Ananiah repaired **b** his own house. Neh 3:23
Tobiah the Ammonite was **b** him, and Neh 4:3
who sounded the trumpet was **b** me. Neh 4:18
And **b** him stood Mattithiah, Shema, Neh 8:4
plowing and the donkeys feeding **b** them, Jb 1:14
at the crashing they are **b** themselves. Jb 41:25
green pastures. He leads me **b** still waters. Ps 23:2
B them the birds of the heavens dwell; Ps 104:12
b the way they have set snares for me. Ps 140:5
neighbor, who dwells trustingly **b** you. Prv 3:29
On the heights **b** the way, at the Prv 8:2
b the gates in front of the town, at the Prv 8:3
then I was **b** him, like a master Prv 8:30
daily at my gates, waiting **b** my doors. Prv 8:34
one who veils herself **b** the flocks of your Sg 1:7
your young goats **b** the shepherds' tents. Sg 1:8
eyes are like doves **b** streams of water, Sg 5:12
bathed in milk, sitting **b** a full pool. Sg 5:12
and **b** our doors are all choice fruits, Sg 7:13
Happy are you who sow **b** all waters, Is 32:20
b every green tree and on the high hills, Jer 17:2
all the officials who stood **b** the king. Jer 36:21
wail and cry! Tell it **b** the Arnon, that Jer 48:20
on the earth **b** the living creatures, Ezk 1:15
creatures went, the wheels went **b** them; Ezk 1:19
and the sound of the wheels **b** them, Ezk 3:13
went in and stood **b** the bronze altar. Ezk 9:2
he went in and stood **b** a wheel. Ezk 10:6
there were four wheels **b** the cherubim, Ezk 10:9
the cherubim, one **b** each cherub, Ezk 10:9
went, the wheels went **b** them. Ezk 10:16
the wheels did not turn from **b** them. Ezk 10:16
they went out, with the wheels **b** them. Ezk 10:19
their wings, with the wheels **b** them, Ezk 11:22
soil. He placed it **b** abundant waters. Ezk 17:5
all its beasts from **b** many waters; Ezk 32:13
And there were pillars **b** the jambs, Ezk 40:49
While the man was standing **b** me, I Ezk 43:6
and their doorposts **b** my doorposts, Ezk 43:8
Fishermen will stand **b** the sea. From Ezk 47:10
b the way of Hethlon to Lebo-hamath, Ezk 48:1
like a leopard I will lurk **b** the way. Hos 13:7
lay themselves down **b** every altar on Am 2:8

the Lord was standing **b** a wall built Am 7:7
I saw the LORD standing **b** the altar, and Am 9:1
which are **b** the two golden pipes from Zec 4:12
went out of the house and sat **b** the sea. Mt 13:1
from there and walked **b** the Sea of Mt 15:29
He went out again **b** the sea, and all the Mk 2:13
Again he began to teach **b** the sea. And a Mk 4:1
and the whole crowd was **b** the sea on the Mk 4:1
about him, and he was **b** the sea. Mk 5:21
from his journey, was sitting **b** the well. Jn 4:6
man who was healed standing **b** them, Acts 4:14
her out and buried her **b** her husband. Acts 5:10
the widows stood **b** him weeping and Acts 9:39
For if we are **b** ourselves, it is for God; 2 Cor 5:13
standing **b** the sea of glass with harps of Rv 15:2

BESIDES (90)

B, she is indeed my sister, the daughter Gn 20:12
b the former famine that was in the Gn 26:1
and took as his wife, **b** the wives he had, Gn 28:9
or if you take wives **b** my daughters, Gn 31:50
men on foot, **b** women and children. Ex 12:37
b the burnt offering of the morning. Lv 9:17
b the LORD'S Sabbaths and besides your Lv 23:38
LORD'S Sabbaths and **b** your gifts and Lv 23:38
besides your gifts and **b** all your vow Lv 23:38
vow offerings and **b** all your freewill Lv 23:38
are fortified and very large. And **b**, Nm 13:28
b those who died in the affair of Nm 16:49
b the regular burnt offering and its Nm 28:10
it shall be offered **b** the regular burnt Nm 28:15
shall offer these **b** the burnt offering Nm 28:23
It shall be offered **b** the regular burnt Nm 28:24
B the regular burnt offering and its Nm 28:31
b the burnt offering of the new moon, Nm 29:6
b the sin offering of atonement, Nm 29:11
offering, **b** the regular burnt offering, Nm 29:16
b the regular burnt offering and its Nm 29:19
b the regular burnt offering and its Nm 29:22
offering, **b** the regular burnt offering, Nm 29:25
b the regular burnt offering and its Nm 29:28
b the regular burnt offering, its grain Nm 29:31
b the regular burnt offering, its grain Nm 29:34
b the regular burnt offering and its Nm 29:38
great and fortified up to heaven. And **b**, Dt 1:28
and bars, **b** very many unwalled villages. Dt 3:5
the LORD is God; there is no other **b** him. Dt 4:35
b what he receives from the sale of his Dt 18:8
b the covenant that he had made with Dt 29:1
even I, am he, and there is no god **b** me; Dt 32:39
b the land of Gilead and Bashan, Jos 17:5
b the crescent ornaments and the Jgs 8:26
and **b** the collars that were around the Jgs 8:26
b her he had neither son nor daughter. Jgs 11:34
the sword, **b** the inhabitants of Gibeah, Jgs 20:15
Ruth the Moabite said, "**B**, he said to me, Ru 2:21
for there is no one **b** you to redeem it, Ru 4:4
holy like the LORD; there is none **b** you; 1 Sm 2:2
servants nineteen men **b** Asahel. 2 Sm 2:30
like you, and there is no God **b** you, 2 Sm 7:22
B, your father is expert in war; he will 2 Sm 17:8
cattle, a hundred sheep, **b** deer, 1 Kgs 4:23
b Solomon's 3,300 chief officers who 1 Kgs 5:16
whatever she asked **b** what was 1 Kgs 10:13
b that which came from the 1 Kgs 10:15
b the sin that he made Judah to sin 2 Kgs 21:16
sons, **b** the sons of the concubines, 1 Chr 3:9
b their kinsmen, heads of their 1 Chr 9:13
O LORD, and there is no God **b** you, 1 Chr 17:20
b great quantities of onyx and stones 1 Chr 29:2
whatever she asked **b** what she had 2 Chr 9:12
b that which the explorers and 2 Chr 9:14
b those whom the king had placed 2 Chr 17:19
B the great number of burnt 2 Chr 29:35
b freewill offerings for the house of God Ezr 1:4
costly wares, **b** all that was freely offered. Ezr 1:6
b their male and female servants, of Ezr 2:65
b 220 of the temple servants, whom Ezr 8:20
b those who came to us from the Neh 5:17
b their male and female servants, of Neh 7:67
is nothing on earth that I desire **b** you. Ps 73:25
B being wise, the Preacher also taught Eccl 12:9
other lords **b** you have ruled over us, Is 26:13
the LORD, and **b** me there is no savior. Is 43:11
and I am the last; **b** me there is no god. Is 44:6
are my witnesses! Is there a God **b** me? Is 44:8
there is no other, **b** me there is no God; Is 45:5
from the west, that there is none **b** me; Is 45:6
and there is no other, no god **b** him.'" Is 45:14
And there is no other god **b** me, a Is 45:21
God and a Savior; there is none **b** me. Is 45:21
heart, "I am, and there is no one **b** me; Is 47:8
heart, "I am, and there is no one **b** me." Is 47:10
others to him **b** those already gathered." Is 56:8
by the ear, no eye has seen a God **b** you, Is 64:4
be plucked up and go to others **b** these. Dn 11:4
but me, and **b** me there is no savior. Hos 13:4
thousand men, **b** women and children. Mt 14:21
thousand men, **b** women and children. Mt 15:38
B, while he was sitting on the judgment Mt 27:19
he is one, and there is no other **b** him. Mk 12:32
And **b** all this, between us and you a Lk 16:26
Yes, and **b** all this, it is now the third Lk 24:21
B this you know the time, that the Rom 13:11
And **b** our own comfort, we rejoiced 2 Cor 7:13
B that, they learn to be idlers, going 1 Tm 5:13
B this, we have had earthly fathers who Heb 12:9

BESIEGE (7)

war against you, then you shall **b** it. Dt 20:12
"When you **b** a city for a long time, Dt 20:19
"They shall **b** you in all your towns, Dt 28:52
And they shall **b** you in all your towns Dt 28:52
to Keilah, to **b** David and his men. 1 Sm 23:8
if their enemies **b** them in the land at 2 Chr 6:28
and will **b** you with towers and I will raise Is 29:3

BESIEGED (20)

human, that they should be **b** by you? Dt 20:19
went up and **b** Jabesh-gilead, 1 Sm 11:1
the Ammonites and **b** Rabbah. 2 Sm 11:1
with Joab came and **b** him in Abel 2 Sm 20:15
Israel with him, and they **b** Tirzah. 1 Kgs 16:17
army and went up and **b** Samaria. 2 Kgs 6:24
great famine in Samaria, as they **b** it, 2 Kgs 6:25
and they **b** Ahaz but could not 2 Kgs 16:5
Samaria, and for three years he **b** it. 2 Kgs 17:5
came up against Samaria and **b** it, 2 Kgs 18:9
up to Jerusalem, and the city was **b**. 2 Kgs 24:10
So the city was **b** till the eleventh year 2 Kgs 25:2
and came and **b** Rabbah. 1 Chr 20:1
love to me when I was in a **b** city. Ps 31:21
a great king came against it and **b** it, Eccl 9:14
a lodge in a cucumber field, like a **b** city. Is 1:8
army came against Jerusalem and **b** it. Jer 39:1
So the city was **b** till the eleventh year of Jer 52:5
he has **b** and enveloped me with Lam 3:5
of Babylon came to Jerusalem and **b** it. Dn 1:1

BESIEGERS (1)

Jerusalem, "**B** come from a distant land; Jer 4:16

BESIEGES (1)

if their enemy **b** them in the land at 1 Kgs 8:37

BESIEGING (7)

And as Joab was **b** the city, he 2 Sm 11:16
the city while his servants were **b** it, 2 Kgs 24:11
who was **b** Lachish with all his 2 Chr 32:9
the Chaldeans who are **b** you outside the Jer 21:4
the Chaldeans who are **b** you shall live Jer 21:9
of the king of Babylon was **b** Jerusalem, Jer 32:2
Chaldeans who were **b** Jerusalem heard Jer 37:5

BESODEIAH (1)

the son of **B** repaired the Gate Neh 3:6

BESOR (3)

him, and they came to the brook **B**, 1 Sm 30:9
too exhausted to cross the brook **B**. 1 Sm 30:10
who had been left at the brook **B**. 1 Sm 30:21

BEST (49)

Rebekah took the **b** garments of Esau Gn 27:15
I will give you the **b** of the land of Gn 45:18
for the **b** of all the land of Egypt is Gn 45:20
and your brothers in the **b** of the land. Gn 47:6
the land of Egypt, in the **b** of the land, Gn 47:11
make restitution from the **b** in his own Ex 22:5
"The **b** of the firstfruits of your ground Ex 23:19
The **b** of the firstfruits of your ground Ex 34:26
All the **b** of the oil and all the best of Nm 18:12
the oil and all the **b** of the wine and of Nm 18:12
from each its **b** part is to be dedicated.' Nm 18:29
you have offered from it the **b** of it, Nm 18:30
when you have contributed the **b** of it. Nm 18:32
'Let them marry whom they think **b**, Nm 36:6
with the **b** gifts of the earth and its Dt 33:16
He chose the **b** of the land for himself, Dt 33:21
companion, who had been his **b** man. Jgs 14:20
said to her, "Do what seems **b** to you; 1 Sm 1:23
He will take the **b** of your fields and 1 Sm 8:14
servants and the **b** of your young 1 Sm 8:16
spared Agag and the **b** of the sheep 1 Sm 15:9
the people spared the **b** of the sheep 1 Sm 15:15
the **b** of the things devoted to 1 Sm 15:21
chose some of the **b** men of Israel and 2 Sm 10:9
"Whatever seems **b** to you I will do." 2 Sm 18:4
your **b** wives and children also are 1 Kgs 20:3
select the **b** and fittest of your 2 Kgs 10:3
chose some of the **b** men of Israel 1 Chr 19:10
young women to the **b** place in the Est 2:9
and your mouth like the **b** wine. It goes Sg 7:9
dross, your **b** wine mixed with water. Is 1:22
for your wares the **b** of all kinds of Ezk 27:22
of Eden, the choice and **b** of Lebanon, Ezk 31:16
shall not stand, or even his **b** troops, Dn 11:15
The **b** of them is like a brier, the most Mi 7:4
at feasts and the **b** seats in the Mt 23:6
and have the **b** seats in the synagogues Mk 12:39
For you love the **b** seat in the Lk 11:43
his servants, 'Bring quickly the **b** robe, Lk 15:22
the marketplaces and the **b** seats in the Lk 20:46
But Paul thought **b** not to take with Acts 15:38
making the **b** use of the time, because Eph 5:16
outsiders, making the **b** use of the time. Col 4:5
Do your **b** to present yourself to God 2 Tm 2:15
Do your **b** to come to me soon. 2 Tm 4:9
Do your **b** to come before winter. 2 Tm 4:21
do your **b** to come to me at Nicopolis, Ti 3:12
Do your **b** to speed Zenas the lawyer and Ti 3:13
a short time as it seemed **b** to them, Heb 12:10

BESTOW (4)

so that he might **b** a blessing upon you Ex 32:29
splendor and majesty you **b** on him. Ps 21:5
she will **b** on you a beautiful crown." Prv 4:9
less honorable we **b** the greater 1 Cor 12:23

BESTOWED (7)

prosperity that shall be **b** on Israel, 1 Sm 2:32
of all Israel and **b** on him such 1 Chr 29:25
distinction has been **b** on Mordecai for Est 6:3
the splendor that I had **b** on you, Ezk 16:14
She **b** her whoring upon them, the Ezk 23:7
and on many who were blind he **b** sight. Lk 7:21
highly exalted him and **b** on him the Phil 2:9

BESTOWER (1)

this against Tyre, the **b** of crowns, Is 23:8

BESTOWING (1)

b his riches on all who call on him. Rom 10:12

BESTOWS (1)

and shield; the LORD **b** favor and honor. Ps 84:11

BETAH (1)

And from **B** and from Berothai, cities 2 Sm 8:8

BETEN (1)

included Helkath, Hali, **B**, Achshaph, Jos 19:25

BETH-ANATH (3)

B, and Beth-shemesh—nineteen cities Jos 19:38
Beth-shemesh, or the inhabitants of **B**, Jgs 1:33
Beth-shemesh and of **B** became subject Jgs 1:33

BETH-ANOTH (1)

Maarath, **B**, and Eltekon: six cities with Jos 15:59

BETH-ARABAH (4)

and passes along north of **B**. Jos 15:6
In the wilderness, **B**, Middin, Secacah, Jos 15:61
of the shoulder of **B** it goes down to Jos 18:18
B, Zemaraim, Bethel, Jos 18:22

BETH-ARBEL (1)

as Shalman destroyed **B** on the day of Hos 10:14

BETH-ASHBEA (1)

of the house of linen workers at **B**; 1 Chr 4:21

BETH-AVEN (7)

men from Jericho to Ai, which is near **B**, Jos 7:2
and it ends at the wilderness of **B**. Jos 18:12
in Michmash, to the east of **B**. 1 Sm 13:5
day. And the battle passed beyond **B**. 1 Sm 14:23
Enter not into Gilgal, nor go up to **B**, Hos 4:15
Sound the alarm at **B**; we follow you, O Hos 5:8
of Samaria tremble for the calf of **B**. Hos 10:5

BETH-AZMAVETH (1)

The men of **B**, 42. Neh 7:28

BETH-BAAL-MEON (1)

Dibon, and Bamoth-baal, and **B**, Jos 13:17

BETH-BARAH (2)

the waters against them, as far as **B**, Jgs 7:24
and they captured the waters as far as **B**, Jgs 7:24

BETH-BIRI (1)

Hazar-susim, **B**, and Shaaraim. 1 Chr 4:31

BETH-CAR (1)

and struck them, as far as below **B**. 1 Sm 7:11

BETH-DAGON (2)

Gederoth, **B**, Naamah, and Makkedah: Jos 15:41
then it turns eastward, it goes to **B**, and Jos 19:27

BETH-DIBLATHAIM (1)

and Dibon, and Nebo, and **B**, Jer 48:22

BETH-EDEN (1)

and him who holds the scepter from **B**; Am 1:5

BETH-EKED (2)

when he was at **B** of the Shepherds, 2 Kgs 10:12
and slaughtered them at the pit of **B**, 2 Kgs 10:14

BETH-EMEK (1)

of Iphtahel northward to **B** and Neiel. Jos 19:27

BETH-EZEL (1)
the lamentation of **B** shall take away Mi 1:11

BETH-GADER (1)
and Hareph the father of **B**. 1 Chr 2:51

BETH-GAMUL (1)
and Kiriathaim, and **B**, and Beth-meon, Jer 48:23

BETH-GILGAL (1)
also from **B** and from the region of Neh 12:29

BETH-HACCHEREM (2)
son of Rechab, ruler of the district of **B**, Neh 3:14
trumpet in Tekoa, and raise a signal on **B**, Jer 6:1

BETH-HAGGAN (1)
saw this, he fled in the direction of **B**. 2 Kgs 9:27

BETH-HARAM (1)
and in the valley **B**, Beth-nimrah, Jos 13:27

BETH-HARAN (1)
Beth-nimrah and **B**, fortified cities, Nm 32:36

BETH-HOGLAH (3)
boundary goes up to **B** and passes along Jos 15:6
on to the north of the shoulder of **B**. Jos 18:19
their clans were Jericho, **B**, Emek-keziz, Jos 18:21

BETH-HORON (14)
of the ascent of **B** and struck them as Jos 10:10
they were going down the ascent of **B**, Jos 10:11
as far as the territory of Lower **B**, Jos 16:3
was Ataroth-addar as far as Upper **B**, Jos 16:5
mountain that lies south of Lower **B**. Jos 18:13
that lies to the south, opposite **B**, Jos 18:14
B with its pasturelands—four cities; Jos 21:22
another company turned toward **B**; 1 Sm 13:18
Solomon rebuilt Gezer) and Lower **B** 1 Kgs 9:17
pasturelands, **B** with its pasturelands, 1 Chr 6:68
who built both Lower and Upper **B**, 1 Chr 7:24
also built Upper **B** and Lower 2 Chr 8:5
built Upper Beth-horon and Lower **B**, 2 Chr 8:5
cities of Judah, from Samaria to **B**, 2 Chr 25:13

BETH-JESHIMOTH (4)
by the Jordan from **B** as far as Nm 33:49
eastward, and in the direction of **B**, Jos 12:3
and the slopes of Pisgah, and **B**, Jos 13:20
the glory of the country, **B**, Baal-meon, Ezk 25:9

BETH-LE-APHRAH (1)
at all; in **B** roll yourselves in the dust. Mi 1:10

BETH-LEBAOTH (1)
B, and Sharuhen—thirteen cities with Jos 19:6

BETH-MAACAH (2)
all the tribes of Israel to Abel of **B**, 2 Sm 20:14
came and besieged him in Abel of **B**. 2 Sm 20:15

BETH-MARCABOTH (2)
Ziklag, **B**, Hazar-susah, Jos 19:5
B, Hazar-susim, Beth-biri, and 1 Chr 4:31

BETH-MEON (1)
Kiriathaim, and Beth-gamul, and **B**, Jer 48:23

BETH-MILLO (3)
of Shechem came together, and all **B**, Jgs 9:6
devour the leaders of Shechem and **B**; Jgs 9:20
Shechem and from **B** and devour Jgs 9:20

BETH-NIMRAH (2)
B and Beth-haran, fortified cities, and Nm 32:36
in the valley Beth-haram, **B**, Succoth, Jos 13:27

BETH-PAZZEZ (1)
Remeth, En-gannim, En-haddah, **B**. Jos 19:21

BETH-PELET (2)
Hazar-gaddah, Heshmon, **B**, Jos 15:27
and in Jeshua and in Moladah and **B**, Neh 11:26

BETH-PEOR (4)
So we remained in the valley opposite **B**. Dt 3:29
the Jordan in the valley opposite **B**, Dt 4:46
the valley in the land of Moab opposite **B**; Dt 34:6
and **B**, and the slopes of Pisgah, and Jos 13:20

BETH-RAPHA (1)
Eshton fathered **B**, Paseah, and 1 Chr 4:12

BETH-REHOB (2)
It was in the valley that belongs to **B**. Jgs 18:28
sent and hired the Syrians of **B**, 2 Sm 10:6

BETH-SHAN (3)
fastened his body to the wall of **B**. 1 Sm 31:10
bodies of his sons from the wall of **B**, 1 Sm 31:12
them from the public square of **B**, 2 Sm 21:12

BETH-SHEAN (6)
Asher Manasseh had **B** and its villages, Jos 17:11
both those in **B** and its villages and Jos 17:16
out the inhabitants of **B** and its villages, Jgs 1:27
and all **B** that is beside Zarethan 1 Kgs 4:12
Jezreel, and from **B** to Abel-meholah, 1 Kgs 4:12
of the Manassites, **B** and its towns, 1 Chr 7:29

BETH-SHEMESH (22)
and goes down to **B** and passes along Jos 15:10
touches Tabor, Shahazumah, and **B**, Jos 19:22
and **B**—nineteen cities with their Jos 19:38
B with its pasturelands—nine cities Jos 21:16
did not drive out the inhabitants of **B**, Jgs 1:33
the inhabitants of **B** and of Beth-anath Jgs 1:33
goes up on the way to its own land, to **B**, 1 Sm 6:9
the direction of **B** along one highway, 1 Sm 6:12
after them as far as the border of **B**. 1 Sm 6:12
Now the people of **B** were reaping their 1 Sm 6:13
field of Joshua of **B** and stopped there. 1 Sm 6:14
the men of **B** offered burnt offerings 1 Sm 6:15
to this day in the field of Joshua of **B**. 1 Sm 6:18
And he struck some of the men of **B**, 1 Sm 6:19
Then the men of **B** said, "Who is able 1 Sm 6:20
Shaalbim, **B**, and Elonbeth-hanan; 1 Kgs 4:9
faced one another in battle at **B**, 2 Kgs 14:11
son of Jehoash, son of Ahaziah, at **B**, 2 Kgs 14:13
and **B** with its pasturelands; 1 Chr 6:59
faced one another in battle at **B**, 2 Chr 25:21
son of Joash, son of Ahaziah, at **B**, 2 Chr 25:23
Negeb of Judah, and had taken **B**, 2 Chr 28:18

BETH-SHITTAH (1)
the army fled as far as **B** toward Zererah, Jgs 7:22

BETH-TAPPUAH (1)
Janim, **B**, Aphekah, Jos 15:53

BETH-TOGARMAH (2)
From **B** they exchanged horses, war Ezk 27:14
B from the uttermost parts of the north Ezk 38:6

BETH-ZUR (4)
Halhul, **B**, Gedor, Jos 15:58
Maon; and Maon fathered **B**. 1 Chr 2:45
B, Soco, Adullam, 2 Chr 11:7
of Azbuk, ruler of half the district of **B**, Neh 3:16

BETHANY (12)
out of the city to **B** and lodged there. Mt 21:17
Now when Jesus was at **B** in the house of Mt 26:6
near to Jerusalem, to Bethphage and **B**, Mk 11:1
late, he went out to **B** with the twelve. Mk 11:11
day, when they came from **B**, Mk 11:12
And while he was at **B** in the house of Mk 14:3
he drew near to Bethphage and **B**, Lk 19:29
Then he led them out as far as **B**, and Lk 24:50
things took place in **B** across the Jordan, Jn 1:28
Now a certain man was ill, Lazarus of **B**, Jn 11:1
B was near Jerusalem, about two miles Jn 11:18
the Passover, Jesus therefore came to **B**, Jn 12:1

BETHEL (72)
on the east of **B** and pitched his tent, Gn 12:8
with **B** on the west and Ai on the east. Gn 12:8
the Negeb as far as **B** to the place where Gn 13:3
at the beginning, between **B** and Ai, Gn 13:3
He called the name of that place **B**, but Gn 28:19
I am the God of **B**, where you anointed Gn 31:13
Jacob, "Arise, go up to **B** and dwell there. Gn 35:1
Then let us arise and go up to **B**, so that I Gn 35:3
is, **B**), which is in the land of Canaan, Gn 35:6
she was buried under an oak below **B**. Gn 35:8
where God had spoken with him **B**. Gn 35:15
Then they journeyed from **B**. When Gn 35:16
to Ai, which is near Beth-aven, east of **B**, Jos 7:2
of ambush and lay between **B** and Ai, Jos 8:9
set them in ambush between **B** and Ai, Jos 8:12
was left in Ai or **B** who did not go out Jos 8:17
the king of Ai, which is beside **B**, one; Jos 12:9
of Makkedah, one; the king of **B**, one; Jos 12:16
from Jericho into the hill country to **B**. Jos 16:1
Then going from **B** to Luz, it passes Jos 16:2
B), then the boundary goes down to Jos 18:13
Beth-arabah, Zemaraim, **B**, Jos 18:22
house of Joseph also went up against **B**, Jgs 1:22
And the house of Joseph scouted out **B**. Jgs 1:23
between Ramah and **B** in the hill Jgs 4:5
and went up to **B** and inquired of God, Jgs 20:18
army, went up and came to **B** and wept. Jgs 20:26
of which goes up to **B** and the other to Jgs 20:31
the people came to **B** and sat there till Jgs 21:2
the LORD at Shiloh, which is north of **B**, Jgs 21:19
that goes up from **B** to Shechem, Jgs 21:19
he went on a circuit year by year to **B**, 1 Sm 7:16
up to God at **B** will meet you there, 1 Sm 10:3
Michmash and the hill country of **B**, 1 Sm 13:2
It was for those in **B**, in Ramoth of 1 Sm 30:27
And he set one in **B**, and the other he 1 Kgs 12:29
So he did in **B**, sacrificing to the 1 Kgs 12:32
And he placed in **B** the priests of the 1 Kgs 12:32
he had made in **B** on the fifteenth 1 Kgs 12:33
of Judah by the word of the LORD to **B**. 1 Kgs 13:1
which he cried against the altar at **B**, 1 Kgs 13:4
return by the way that he came to **B**. 1 Kgs 13:10
Now an old prophet lived in **B**. And 1 Kgs 13:11
man of God had done that day in **B**. 1 Kgs 13:11
against the altar in **B** and against all 1 Kgs 13:32
In his days Hiel of **B** built Jericho. 1 Kgs 16:34
sent me as far as **B**." But Elisha said, 2 Kgs 2:2
not leave you." So they went down to **B**. 2 Kgs 2:2
prophets who were in **B** came out to 2 Kgs 2:3
He went up from there to **B**, and while 2 Kgs 2:23
calves that were in **B** and in Dan. 2 Kgs 10:29
and lived in **B** and taught them 2 Kgs 17:28
Kidron and carried their ashes to **B**. 2 Kgs 23:4
Moreover, the altar at **B**, the high 2 Kgs 23:15
have done against the altar at **B**." 2 Kgs 23:17
to all that he had done at **B**. 2 Kgs 23:19
and settlements were **B** and its towns, 1 Chr 7:28
B with its villages and Jeshanah 2 Chr 13:19
The men of **B** and Ai, 223. Ezr 2:28
The men of **B** and Ai, 123. Neh 7:32
at Michmash, Aija, **B** and its villages, Neh 11:31
as the house of Israel was ashamed of **B**, Jer 48:13
Thus it shall be done to you, O **B**, Hos 10:15
He met God at **B**, and there God spoke Hos 12:4
I will punish the altars of **B**, Am 3:14
"Come to **B**, and transgress; to Gilgal, Am 4:4
but do not seek **B**, and do not enter into Am 5:5
into exile, and **B** shall come to nothing." Am 5:5
it devour, with none to quench it for **B**, Am 5:6
the priest of **B** sent to Jeroboam Am 7:10
but never again prophesy at **B**, for it is Am 7:13
Now the people of **B** had sent Sharezer Zec 7:2

BETHESDA (1)
Sheep Gate a pool, in Aramaic called **B**, Jn 5:2

BETHLEHEM (49)
on the way to Ephrath (that is, **B**), Gn 35:19
there on the way to Ephrath (that is, **B**)." Gn 48:7
and **B**—twelve cities with their villages. Jos 19:15
After him Ibzan of **B** judged Israel. Jgs 12:8
Then Ibzan died and was buried at **B**. Jgs 12:10
there was a young man of **B** in Judah, Jgs 17:7
from the town of **B** in Judah to sojourn Jgs 17:8
said to him, "I am a Levite of **B** in Judah, Jgs 17:9
to himself a concubine from **B** in Judah. Jgs 19:1
him to her father's house at **B** in Judah, Jgs 19:2
"We are passing from **B** in Judah to the Jgs 19:18
I went to **B** in Judah, and I am going to Jgs 19:18
and a man of **B** in Judah went to sojourn Ru 1:1
They were Ephrathites from **B** in Judah. Ru 1:2
of them went on until they came to **B**. Ru 1:19
And when they came to **B**, the whole Ru 1:19
And they came to **B** at the beginning of Ru 1:22
And behold, Boaz came from **B**. And he Ru 2:4
in Ephrathah and be renowned in **B**, Ru 4:11
the LORD commanded and came to **B**. 1 Sm 16:4
son of an Ephrathite of **B** in Judah, 1 Sm 17:12
Saul to feed his father's sheep at **B**. 1 Sm 17:15
asked leave of me to run to **B** his city, 1 Sm 20:6
asked leave of me to go to **B**. 1 Sm 20:28
tomb of his father, which was at **B**. 2 Sm 2:32
of the Philistines was then at **B**. 2 Sm 23:14
from the well of **B** that is by the 2 Sm 23:15
out of the well of **B** that was by the 2 Sm 23:16
thirty; Elhanan the son of Dodo of **B**, 2 Sm 23:24
Salma, the father of **B**, and Hareph 1 Chr 2:51
B, the Netophathites, 1 Chr 2:54
firstborn of Ephrathah, the father of **B**. 1 Chr 4:4
of the Philistines was then at **B**. 1 Chr 11:16
from the well of **B** that is by the 1 Chr 11:17
out of the well of **B** that was by the 1 Chr 11:18
Joab, Elhanan the son of Dodo of **B**, 1 Chr 11:26
He built **B**, Etam, Tekoa, 2 Chr 11:6
The sons of **B**, 123. Ezr 2:21
The men of **B** and Netophah, 188. Neh 7:26
and stayed at Geruth Chimham near **B**, Jer 41:17
But you, O **B** Ephrathah, who are too little Mi 5:2
after Jesus was born in **B** of Judea in the Mt 2:1
They told him, "In **B** of Judea, for so it is Mt 2:5
"'And you, O **B**, in the land of Judah, are Mt 2:6
And he sent them to **B**, saying, "Go and Mt 2:8
all the male children in **B** and in all that Mt 2:16
to the city of David, which is called **B**, Lk 2:4
"Let us go over to **B** and see this thing Lk 2:15
offspring of David, and comes from **B**, Jn 7:42

BETHLEHEMITE (4)
I will send you to Jesse the **B**, for I have 1 Sm 16:1
I have seen a son of Jesse the **B**, 1 Sm 16:18
the son of your servant Jesse the **B**." 1 Sm 17:58
the son of Jaare-oregim, the **B**, 2 Sm 21:19

BETHPHAGE (3)
drew near to Jerusalem and came to **B**, Mt 21:1
near to Jerusalem, to **B** and Bethany, Mk 11:1
When he drew near to **B** and Bethany, Lk 19:29

BETHSAIDA (7)
B! For if the mighty works done in you Mt 11:21

and go before him to the other side, to **B**, Mk 6:45
And they came to **B**. And some people Mk 8:22
and withdrew apart to a town called **B**. Lk 9:10
B! For if the mighty works done in you Lk 10:13
Now Philip was from **B**, the city of Jn 1:44
to Philip, who was from **B** in Galilee, Jn 12:21

BETHUEL (10)
Chesed, Hazo, Pildash, Jidlaph, and **B**." Gn 22:22
(**B** fathered Rebekah.) These eight Gn 22:23
who was born to **B** the son of Milcah, Gn 24:15
am the daughter of **B** the son of Gn 24:24
She said, 'The daughter of **B**, Nahor's Gn 24:47
Then Laban and **B** answered and said, Gn 24:50
the daughter of **B** the Aramean of Gn 25:20
to the house of **B** your mother's father, Gn 28:2
to Laban, the son of **B** the Aramean, Gn 28:5
B, Hormah, Ziklag, 1 Chr 4:30

BETHUL (1)
Eltolad, **B**, Hormah, Jos 19:4

BETONIM (1)
Heshbon to Ramath-mizpeh and **B**, Jos 13:26

BETRAY (20)
but if to **b** me to my adversaries, 1 Chr 12:17
have finished betraying, they will **b** you. Is 33:1
will fall away and **b** one another and Mt 24:10
he sought an opportunity to **b** him. Mt 26:16
I say to you, one of you will **b** me." Mt 26:21
his hand in the dish with me will **b** me. Mt 26:23
Judas, who would **b** him, answered, "Is Mt 26:25
chief priests in order to **b** him to them. Mk 14:10
he sought an opportunity to **b** him. Mk 14:11
I say to you, one of you will **b** me, Mk 14:18
officers how he might **b** him to them. Lk 22:4
sought an opportunity to **b** him to them Lk 22:6
would you **b** the Son of Man with a Lk 22:48
and who it was who would **b** him.) Jn 6:64
one of the Twelve, was going to **b** him. Jn 6:71
disciples (he who was about to **b** him), Jn 12:4
of Judas Iscariot, Simon's son, to **b** him, Jn 13:2
For he knew who was to **b** him; that Jn 13:11
truly, I say to you, one of you will **b** me." Jn 13:21
"Lord, who is it that is going to **b** you?" Jn 21:20

BETRAYAL (1)
with **b** the traitors have betrayed." Is 24:16

BETRAYED (15)
thus," I would have **b** the generation of Ps 73:15
For the traitors have **b**, with betrayal the Is 24:16
with betrayal the traitors have **b**." Is 24:16
destroyed, you traitor, whom none has **b**! Is 33:1
and Judas Iscariot, who **b** him. Mt 10:4
man by whom the Son of Man is **b**! Mt 26:24
the Son of Man is **b** into the hands of Mt 26:45
and Judas Iscariot, who **b** him. Mk 3:19
man by whom the Son of Man is **b**! Mk 14:21
The Son of Man is **b** into the hands of Mk 14:41
but woe to that man by whom he is **b**!" Lk 22:22
Now Judas, who **b** him, also knew the Jn 18:2
to them, "I am he." Judas, who **b** him, Jn 18:5
whom you have now **b** and murdered, Acts 7:52
the night when he was **b** took bread, 1 Cor 11:23

BETRAYER (5)
let us be going; see, my **b** is at hand." Mt 26:46
Now the **b** had given them a sign, Mt 26:48
Then when Judas, his **b**, saw that Jesus Mt 27:3
let us be going; see, my **b** is at hand." Mk 14:42
Now the **b** had given them a sign, Mk 14:44

BETRAYING (2)
and when you have finished **b**, they will Is 33:1
have sinned by **b** innocent blood." They Mt 27:4

BETRAYS (4)
the traitor **b**, and the destroyer destroys. Is 21:2
who **b** nations with her whorings, Na 3:4
one of them, for your accent **b** you." Mt 26:73
the hand of him who **b** me is with me Lk 22:21

BETROTH (4)
You shall **b** a wife, but another man Dt 28:30
And I will **b** you to me forever. I will Hos 2:19
I will **b** you to me in righteousness and Hos 2:19
I will **b** you to me in faithfulness. And Hos 2:20

BETROTHED (15)
there any man who has **b** a wife and has Dt 20:7
"If there is a **b** virgin, and a man meets Dt 22:23
a man meets a young woman who is **b**, Dt 22:25
and though the **b** young woman cried Dt 22:27
"If a man meets a virgin who is not **b**, Dt 22:28
his mother Mary had been **b** to Joseph, Mt 1:18
to a virgin **b** to a man whose name was Lk 1:27
to be registered with Mary, his **b**, who was Lk 2:5
Now concerning the **b**, I have no 1 Cor 7:25
sinned, and if a **b** woman marries, 1 Cor 7:28
the unmarried or **b** woman is 1 Cor 7:34
not behaving properly toward his **b**, 1 Cor 7:36
this in his heart, to keep her as his **b**, 1 Cor 7:37
then he who marries his **b** does well, 1 Cor 7:38
for you, for I **b** you to one husband, 2 Cor 11:2

BETTER (121)
"It is **b** that I give her to you than that I Gn 29:19
For it would have been **b** for us to serve Ex 14:12
For it was **b** for us in Egypt." Nm 11:18
Would it not be **b** for us to go back to Nm 14:3
the grapes of Ephraim **b** than the grape Jgs 8:2
leaders of Shechem, 'Which is **b** for you, Jgs 9:2
Now are you any **b** than Balak the son Jgs 11:25
Is it **b** for you to be priest to the house Jgs 18:19
How much **b** if the people had eaten 1 Sm 14:30
Behold, to obey is **b** than sacrifice, 1 Sm 15:22
of yours, who is **b** than you. 1 Sm 15:28
There is nothing **b** for me than that I 1 Sm 27:1
It would be **b** for me to be there still." 2 Sm 14:32
the Archite is **b** than the counsel 2 Sm 17:14
Therefore it is **b** that you send us help 2 Sm 18:3
more righteous and **b** than himself, 1 Kgs 2:32
life, for I am no **b** than my fathers." 1 Kgs 19:4
and I will give you a **b** vineyard for it; 1 Kgs 21:2
b than all the waters of Israel? 2 Kgs 5:12
house, who were **b** than yourself, 2 Chr 21:13
position to another who is **b** than she. Est 1:19
I? How am I **b** off than if I had sinned?' Jb 35:3
B is the little that the righteous has Ps 37:16
Because your steadfast love is **b** than life, Ps 63:3
in your courts is **b** than a thousand Ps 84:10
It is **b** to take refuge in the LORD than to Ps 118:8
It is **b** to take refuge in the LORD than to Ps 118:9
of your mouth is **b** to me than Ps 119:72
gain from her is **b** than gain from Prv 3:14
from silver and her profit **b** than gold. Prv 3:14
for wisdom is **b** than jewels, and all that Prv 8:11
My fruit is **b** than gold, even fine gold, Prv 8:19
B to be lowly and have a servant than to Prv 12:9
B is a little with the fear of the LORD Prv 15:16
B is a dinner of herbs where love is Prv 15:17
B is a little with righteousness than Prv 16:8
How much **b** to get wisdom than gold! Prv 16:16
It is **b** to be of a lowly spirit with the Prv 16:19
is slow to anger is **b** than the mighty, Prv 16:32
B is a dry morsel with quiet than a Prv 17:1
B is a poor person who walks in his Prv 19:1
love, and a poor man is **b** than a liar. Prv 19:22
It is **b** to live in a corner of the housetop Prv 21:9
It is **b** to live in a desert land than with Prv 21:19
and favor is **b** than silver or gold. Prv 22:1
for it is **b** to be told, "Come up here," Prv 25:7
It is **b** to live in a corner of the Prv 25:24
B is open rebuke than hidden love. Prv 27:5
B is a neighbor who is near than a Prv 27:10
B is a poor man who walks in his Prv 28:6
There is nothing **b** for a person than Eccl 2:24
that there is nothing **b** for them than Eccl 3:12
that there is nothing **b** than that a Eccl 3:22
But **b** than both is he who has not yet Eccl 4:3
B is a handful of quietness than two Eccl 4:6
Two are **b** than one, because they have Eccl 4:9
B was a poor and wise youth than an Eccl 4:13
draw near to listen is **b** than to offer the Eccl 5:1
It is **b** that you should not vow than Eccl 5:5
that a stillborn child is **b** off than he. Eccl 6:3
B is the sight of the eyes than the Eccl 6:9
good name is **b** than precious ointment, Eccl 7:1
It is **b** to go to the house of mourning Eccl 7:2
Sorrow is **b** than laughter, for by Eccl 7:3
It is **b** for a man to hear the rebuke of Eccl 7:5
B is the end of a thing than its Eccl 7:8
patient in spirit is **b** than the proud in Eccl 7:8
the former days **b** than these?" For Eccl 7:10
for a living dog is **b** than a dead lion. Eccl 9:4
But I say that wisdom is **b** than might, Eccl 9:16
heard in quiet are **b** than the shouting Eccl 9:17
Wisdom is **b** than weapons of war, but Eccl 9:18
his mouth! For your love is **b** than wine; Sg 1:2
How much **b** is your love than wine, and Sg 4:10
monument and a name **b** than sons and Is 56:5
seen that they were **b** in appearance and Dn 1:15
found them ten times **b** than all the Dn 1:20
for it was **b** for me then than now.' Hos 2:7
Are you **b** than these kingdoms? Am 6:2
me, for it is **b** for me to die than to live." Jon 4:3
said, "It is **b** for me to die than to live." Jon 4:8
Are you **b** than Thebes that sat by the Na 3:8
For it is **b** that you lose one of your Mt 5:29
For it is **b** that you lose one of your Mt 5:30
it would be **b** for him to have a great Mt 18:6
It is **b** for you to enter life crippled or Mt 18:8
It is **b** for you to enter life with one eye Mt 18:9
man with his wife, it is **b** not to marry." Mt 19:10
It would have been **b** for that man if he Mt 26:24
and was no **b** but rather grew worse. Mk 5:26
it would be **b** for him if a great Mk 9:42
It is **b** for you to enter life crippled than Mk 9:43
It is **b** for you to enter life lame than Mk 9:45
It is **b** for you to enter the kingdom of Mk 9:47
It would have been **b** for that man if Mk 14:21
It would be **b** for him if a millstone were Lk 17:2
them the hour when he began to get **b**, Jn 4:52
understand that it is **b** for you that one Jn 11:50
What then? Are we Jews any **b** off? No, Rom 3:9
esteems one day as **b** than another, Rom 14:5
For it is **b** to marry than to be aflame 1 Cor 7:9
from marriage will do even **b**. 1 Cor 7:38
if we do not eat, and no **b** off if we do. 1 Cor 8:8
it is not for the **b** but for the worse. 1 Cor 11:17
I am a **b** one—I am talking like a 2 Cor 11:23
say, and got the **b** of you by deceit. 2 Cor 12:16
and be with Christ, for that is far **b**. Phil 1:23
must serve all the **b** since those who 1 Tm 6:2
we feel sure of **b** things—things that Heb 6:9
the other hand, a **b** hope is introduced, Heb 7:19
Jesus the guarantor of a **b** covenant. Heb 7:22
the old as the covenant he mediates is **b**, Heb 8:6
better, since it is enacted on **b** promises. Heb 8:6
themselves with **b** sacrifices than Heb 9:23
yourselves had a **b** possession and an Heb 10:34
But as it is, they desire a **b** country, Heb 11:16
that they might rise again to a **b** life. Heb 11:35
God had provided something **b** for us, Heb 11:40
blood that speaks a **b** word than the Heb 12:24
For it is **b** to suffer for doing good, if 1 Pt 3:17
it would have been **b** for them never to 2 Pt 2:21

BETWEEN (234)
I will put enmity **b** you and the woman, Gn 3:15
and **b** your offspring and her offspring; Gn 3:15
covenant that I make **b** me and you and Gn 9:12
sign of the covenant **b** me and the earth. Gn 9:13
my covenant that is **b** me and you and Gn 9:15
the everlasting covenant **b** God and Gn 9:16
that I have established **b** me and all Gn 9:17
Resen **b** Nineveh and Calah; that is the Gn 10:12
been at the beginning, **b** Bethel and Ai, Gn 13:3
and there was strife **b** the herdsmen of Gn 13:7
Lot, "Let there be no strife **b** you and me, Gn 13:8
and **b** your herdsmen and my Gn 13:8
a flaming torch passed **b** these pieces. Gn 15:17
May the LORD judge **b** you and me!" Gn 16:5
it lies **b** Kadesh and Bered. Gn 16:14
may make my covenant **b** me and you, Gn 17:2
establish my covenant **b** me and you Gn 17:7
b me and you and your offspring after Gn 17:10
a sign of the covenant **b** me and you. Gn 17:11
the Negeb and lived **b** Kadesh and Shur; Gn 20:1
of silver, what is that **b** you and me? Gn 23:15
we said, let there be a sworn pact **b** us, Gn 26:28
a sworn pact between us, **b** you and us, Gn 26:28
three days' journey **b** himself and Gn 30:36
that they may decide **b** us two. Gn 31:37
And let it be a witness **b** you and me." Gn 31:44
heap is a witness **b** you and me today." Gn 31:48
said, "The LORD watch **b** you and me, Gn 31:49
us, see, God is witness **b** you and me." Gn 31:50
pillar, which I have set **b** you and me. Gn 31:51
judge **b** us." So Jacob swore by the Fear Gn 31:53
me and put a space **b** drove and drove." Gn 32:16
for there was an interpreter **b** them. Gn 42:23
nor the ruler's staff from **b** his feet, Gn 49:10
donkey, crouching **b** the sheepfolds. Gn 49:14
will put a division **b** my people and your Ex 8:23
will make a distinction **b** the livestock of Ex 9:4
makes a distinction **b** Egypt and Israel. Ex 11:7
hand and as a memorial **b** your eyes, Ex 13:9
on your hand or frontlets **b** your eyes, Ex 13:16
of Pi-hahiroth, **b** Migdol and the sea, Ex 14:2
coming **b** the host of Egypt and the Ex 14:20
of Sin, which is **b** Elim and Sinai, Ex 16:1
me and I decide **b** one person and Ex 18:16
by the LORD shall be **b** them both to see Ex 22:11
from **b** the two cherubim that are on Ex 25:22
its hem, with bells of gold **b** them, Ex 28:33
You shall put it **b** the tent of meeting Ex 30:18
this is a sign **b** me and you throughout Ex 31:13
It is a sign forever **b** me and the people Ex 31:17
put the bells **b** the pomegranates all Ex 39:25
hem of the robe, **b** the pomegranates— Ex 39:25
and place the basin **b** the tent of meeting Ex 40:7
He set the basin **b** the tent of meeting Ex 40:30
You are to distinguish **b** the holy and Lv 10:10
and **b** the unclean and the clean, Lv 10:10
make a distinction **b** the unclean and Lv 11:47
and the clean and **b** the living creature Lv 11:47
that the LORD made **b** him and the Lv 26:46
shall not differentiate **b** good or bad, Lv 27:33
testimony, from **b** the two cherubim; Nm 7:89
While the meat was yet **b** their teeth, Nm 11:33

they carried it on a pole **b** two of them; Nm 13:23
And he stood **b** the dead and the Nm 16:48
of Moab, **b** Moab and the Amorites. Nm 21:13
in a narrow path **b** the vineyards, Nm 22:24
according to lot **b** the larger and Nm 26:56
into two parts **b** the warriors who Nm 31:27
shall judge **b** the manslayer Nm 35:24
opposite Suph, **b** Paran and Tophel, Dt 1:1
time, 'Hear the cases **b** your brothers, Dt 1:16
and judge righteously **b** a man and his Dt 1:16
while I stood **b** the LORD and you at that Dt 5:5
and they shall be as frontlets **b** your eyes. Dt 6:8
they shall be as frontlets **b** your eyes. Dt 11:18
arises requiring decision **b** one kind of Dt 17:8
there is a dispute **b** men and they come Dt 25:1
into court and the judges decide **b** them, Dt 25:1
that comes out from **b** her feet and her Dt 28:57
day long, and dwells **b** his shoulders." Dt 33:12
Yet there shall be a distance **b** you and it, Jos 3:4
place of ambush and lay **b** Bethel and Ai, Jos 8:9
side of Ai, with a ravine **b** them and Ai. Jos 8:11
set them in ambush **b** Bethel and Ai, Jos 8:12
allotted to it fell **b** the people of Judah Jos 18:11
the Jordan a boundary **b** us and you, Jos 22:25
but to be a witness **b** us and you, and Jos 22:27
you, and **b** our generations after us, Jos 22:27
but to be a witness **b** us and you.' Jos 22:28
"it is a witness **b** us that the LORD is Jos 22:34
he put darkness **b** you and the Jos 24:7
the palm of Deborah **b** Ramah and Bethel Jgs 4:5
for there was peace **b** Jabin the king of Jgs 4:17
B her feet he sank, he fell, he lay still; Jgs 5:27
fell, he lay still; **b** her feet he sank, he fell; Jgs 5:27
sent an evil spirit **b** Abimelech and the Jgs 9:23
"The LORD will be witness **b** us, Jgs 11:10
decide this day **b** the people of Israel Jgs 11:27
in Mahaneh-dan, **b** Zorah and Eshtaol. Jgs 13:25
tail and put a torch **b** each pair of tails. Jgs 15:4
They made him stand **b** the pillars. Jgs 16:25
and buried him **b** Zorah and Eshtaol Jgs 16:31
Now the appointed signal **b** the men of Jgs 20:38
and set it up **b** Mizpah and Shen and 1 Sm 7:12
There was peace also **b** Israel and the 1 Sm 7:14
"Cast the lot **b** me and my son 1 Sm 14:42
and encamped **b** Socoh and Azekah, 1 Sm 17:1
the other side, with a valley **b** them. 1 Sm 17:3
of bronze slung **b** his shoulders. 1 Sm 17:6
there is but a step **b** me and death." 1 Sm 20:3
the LORD is **b** you and me forever." 1 Sm 20:23
'The LORD shall be **b** me and you, 1 Sm 20:42
and **b** my offspring and your 1 Sm 20:42
May the LORD judge **b** me and you, 1 Sm 24:12
and give sentence **b** me and you, 1 Sm 24:15
of the hill, with a great space **b** them. 1 Sm 26:13
was a long war **b** the house of Saul 2 Sm 3:1
While there was war **b** the house of 2 Sm 3:6
he was suspended **b** heaven and earth, 2 Sm 18:9
David was sitting **b** the two gates, 2 Sm 18:24
of silver or gold **b** us and Saul or 2 Sm 21:4
the oath of the LORD that was **b** them, 2 Sm 21:7
b David and Jonathan the son of Saul. 2 Sm 21:7
was war again **b** the Philistines and 2 Sm 21:15
that I may discern **b** good and evil, 1 Kgs 3:9
there was peace **b** Hiram and 1 Kgs 5:12
the clay ground **b** Succoth and 1 Kgs 7:46
there was war **b** Rehoboam and 1 Kgs 14:30
there was war **b** Rehoboam and 1 Kgs 15:6
there was war **b** Abijam and 1 Kgs 15:7
there was war **b** Asa and Baasha 1 Kgs 15:16
there be a covenant **b** me and you, 1 Kgs 15:19
as there was **b** my father and your 1 Kgs 15:19
there was war **b** Asa and Baasha 1 Kgs 15:32
they divided the land **b** them to pass 1 Kgs 18:6
you go limping **b** two different 1 Kgs 18:21
earth and put his face **b** his knees. 1 Kgs 18:42
the king of Israel **b** the scale armor 1 Kgs 22:34
and shot Joram **b** the shoulders, 2 Kgs 9:24
army, "Bring her out **b** the ranks, 2 Kgs 11:15
made a covenant **b** the LORD and 2 Kgs 11:17
and also **b** the king and the people. 2 Kgs 11:17
from the place **b** his altar and the 2 Kgs 16:14
by the way of the gate **b** the two walls, 2 Kgs 25:4
the LORD standing **b** earth and 1 Chr 21:16
the clay ground **b** Succoth and 2 Chr 4:17
continual wars **b** Rehoboam and 2 Chr 12:15
there was war **b** Abijah and 2 Chr 13:2
to help, **b** the mighty and the weak. 2 Chr 14:11
"There is a covenant **b** me and you, 2 Chr 16:3
as there was **b** my father and your 2 Chr 16:3
the king of Israel **b** the scale armor 2 Chr 18:33
to them, "Bring her out **b** the ranks, 2 Chr 23:14
made a covenant **b** himself and all 2 Chr 23:16
And **b** the upper chamber of the Neh 3:32
B morning and evening they are beaten Jb 4:20
There is no arbiter **b** us, who might lay Jb 9:33
at the boundary **b** light and darkness. Jb 26:10
to another that no air can come **b** them. Jb 41:16
b them virgins playing tambourines: Ps 68:25
in the valleys; they flow **b** the hills; Ps 104:10
and decides **b** powerful contenders. Prv 18:18
a sachet of myrrh that lies **b** my breasts. Sg 1:13
He shall judge **b** the nations, and shall Is 2:4
of Judah, judge **b** me and my vineyard. Is 5:3
You made a reservoir **b** the two walls for Is 22:11
have made a separation **b** you and your Is 59:2
they cut in two and passed **b** its parts— Jer 34:18
of the land who passed **b** the parts of the Jer 34:19
rags and clothes **b** your armpits and Jer 38:12
garden through the gate **b** the two walls; Jer 39:4
by the way of a gate **b** the two walls, Jer 52:7
it as an iron wall **b** you and the city; Ezk 4:3
Spirit lifted me up **b** earth and heaven Ezk 8:3
of the LORD, **b** the porch and the altar, Ezk 8:16
burning coals from **b** the cherubim, Ezk 10:2
"Take fire from **b** the whirling wheels, Ezk 10:6
from **b** the cherubim," he went in and Ezk 10:6
out his hand from **b** the cherubim to Ezk 10:7
to the fire that was **b** the cherubim, Ezk 10:7
executes true justice **b** man and man, Ezk 18:8
Sabbaths, as a sign **b** me and them, Ezk 20:12
that they may be a sign **b** me and you, Ezk 20:20
made no distinction **b** the holy and Ezk 22:26
taught the difference **b** the unclean Ezk 22:26
Behold, I judge **b** sheep and sheep, Ezk 34:17
and sheep, **b** rams and male goats. Ezk 34:17
I myself will judge **b** the fat sheep and Ezk 34:20
And I will judge **b** sheep and sheep. Ezk 34:22
broad; and the space **b** the side rooms, Ezk 40:7
The free space **b** the side chambers of Ezk 41:9
a palm tree **b** cherub and cherub. Ezk 41:18
to make a separation **b** the holy and Ezk 42:20
with only a wall **b** me and them. Ezk 43:8
people the difference **b** the holy and Ezk 44:23
how to distinguish **b** the unclean and Ezk 44:23
on the border **b** Damascus and Ezk 47:16
boundary shall run **b** Hauran and Ezk 47:18
along the Jordan **b** Gilead and the Ezk 47:18
the prince shall lie **b** the territory of Ezk 48:22
It had three ribs in its mouth **b** its teeth; Dn 7:5
goat had a conspicuous horn **b** his eyes. Dn 8:5
I heard a man's voice **b** the banks of the Dn 8:16
And the great horn **b** his eyes is the first Dn 8:21
pitch his palatial tents **b** the sea and Dn 11:45
and her adultery from **b** her breasts; Hos 2:2
B the vestibule and the altar let the priests, Jl 2:17
He shall judge **b** many peoples, and shall Mi 4:3
lifted up the basket **b** earth and heaven. Zec 5:9
came out from **b** two mountains. Zec 6:1
counsel of peace shall be **b** them both."' Zec 6:13
and its abominations from **b** its teeth; Zec 9:7
the brotherhood **b** Judah and Zec 11:14
the LORD was witness **b** you and the Mal 2:14
see the distinction **b** the righteous and Mal 3:18
b one who serves God and one who Mal 3:18
tell him his fault, **b** you and him alone. Mt 18:15
whom you murdered **b** the sanctuary Mt 23:35
who perished **b** the altar and the Lk 11:51
And he divided his property **b** them. Lk 15:12
b us and you a great chasm has been Lk 16:26
was passing along **b** Samaria and Lk 17:11
Now a discussion arose **b** some of John's Jn 3:25
one on either side, and Jesus **b** them. Jn 19:18
Peter was sleeping **b** two soldiers, Acts 12:6
he made no distinction **b** us and them, Acts 15:9
a dissension arose **b** the Pharisees and Acts 23:7
is no distinction **b** Jew and Greek; Rom 10:12
you have, keep **b** yourself and God. Rom 14:22
to settle a dispute **b** the brothers, 1 Cor 6:5
the ability to distinguish **b** spirits, 1 Cor 12:10
I am hard pressed **b** the two. My desire Phil 1:23
there is one mediator **b** God and men, 1 Tm 2:5
And **b** the throne and the four living Rv 5:6

BEVELED (1)
oxen, there were wreaths of **b** work. 1 Kgs 7:29

BEWAIL (1)
b the burning that the LORD has kindled. Lv 10:6

BEWARE (23)
b lest you act corruptly by making a Dt 4:16
And **b** lest you raise your eyes to heaven, Dt 4:19
B lest you say in your heart, 'My power Dt 8:17
B lest there be among you a man or Dt 29:18
B lest there be among you a root Dt 29:18
"**B** that you do not pass this place, 2 Kgs 6:9
B lest you say, 'We have found wisdom; Jb 32:13
B lest wrath entice you into scoffing, Jb 36:18
My son, **b** of anything beyond these. Eccl 12:12
B lest Hezekiah mislead you by saying, Is 36:18
Let everyone **b** of his neighbor, and put Jer 9:4
"**B** of practicing your righteousness Mt 6:1
"**B** of false prophets, who come to you in Mt 7:15
B of men, for they will deliver you over Mt 10:17
"Watch and **b** of the leaven of the Mt 16:6
B of the leaven of the Pharisees and Mt 16:11
did not tell them to **b** of the leaven of Mt 16:12
b of the leaven of the Pharisees and the Mk 8:15
his teaching he said, "**B** of the scribes, Mk 12:38
first, "**B** of the leaven of the Pharisees, Lk 12:1
"**B** of the scribes, who like to walk Lk 20:46
B, therefore, lest what is said in the Acts 13:40
B of him yourself, for he strongly 2 Tm 4:15

BEWILDERED (1)
came together, and they were **b**, Acts 2:6

BEWITCHED (1)
O foolish Galatians! Who has **b** you? It Gal 3:1

BEYOND (121)
and pitched his tent **b** the tower of Gn 35:21
father are mighty **b** the blessings of Gn 49:26
floor of Atad, which is **b** the Jordan, Gn 50:10
Abel-mizraim; it is **b** the Jordan. Gn 50:11
if she has a discharge **b** the time of her Lv 15:25
the plains of Moab **b** the Jordan at Nm 22:1
I could not go **b** the command of the Nm 22:18
not be able to go **b** the word of the Nm 24:13
on the other side of the Jordan and **b**, Nm 32:19
shall remain with us **b** the Jordan." Nm 32:32
their inheritance **b** the Jordan Nm 34:15
shall give three cities **b** the Jordan, Nm 35:14
at any time go **b** the boundaries of his Nm 35:26
spoke to all Israel **b** the Jordan in the Dt 1:1
B the Jordan, in the land of Moab, Moses Dt 1:5
of the Amorites who were **b** the Jordan, Dt 3:8
LORD your God gives them **b** the Jordan. Dt 3:20
over and see the good land **b** the Jordan, Dt 3:25
apart three cities in the east **b** the Jordan, Dt 4:41
b the Jordan in the valley opposite Dt 4:46
who lived to the east **b** the Jordan; Dt 4:47
Are they not **b** the Jordan, west of the Dt 11:30
Neither is it **b** the sea, that you should Dt 30:13
land that Moses gave you **b** the Jordan, Jos 1:14
the LORD gave you **b** the Jordan toward Jos 1:15
of the Amorites who were **b** the Jordan, Jos 2:10
the Amorites who were **b** the Jordan to the Jos 5:1
had been content to dwell **b** the Jordan! Jos 7:7
all the kings who were **b** the Jordan in the Jos 9:1
of the Amorites who were **b** the Jordan, Jos 9:10
of their land **b** the Jordan toward Jos 12:1
Moses gave them, **b** the Jordan eastward, Jos 13:8
of Chinnereth, eastward **b** the Jordan. Jos 13:27
of Moab, **b** the Jordan east of Jericho. Jos 13:32
the two and one-half tribes **b** the Jordan, Jos 14:3
and passes along **b** it on the Jos 16:6
received their inheritance **b** the Jordan Jos 18:7
And **b** the Jordan east of Jericho, they Jos 20:8
ago, your fathers lived **b** the Euphrates, Jos 24:2
father Abraham from **b** the River and Jos 24:3
that your fathers served **b** the River and Jos 24:14
fathers served in the region **b** the River, Jos 24:15
and he passed **b** the idols and escaped to Jgs 3:26
Gilead stayed **b** the Jordan; and Dan, Jgs 5:17
of Israel who were **b** the Jordan in the Jgs 10:8
And the battle passed **b** Beth-aven. 1 Sm 14:23
youth, 'Look, the arrows are **b** you,' 1 Sm 20:22
the boy ran, he shot an arrow **b** him. 1 Sm 20:36
and said, "Is not the arrow **b** you?" 1 Sm 20:37
the valley and those **b** the Jordan saw 1 Sm 31:7
Syrians who were **b** the Euphrates. 2 Sm 10:16
had passed a little **b** the summit, 2 Sm 16:1
but he delayed **b** the set time that had 2 Sm 20:5
and understanding **b** measure, 1 Kgs 4:29
and scatter them **b** the Euphrates, 1 Kgs 14:15
of all these vessels was **b** weight. 2 Kgs 25:16
and **b** the Jordan at Jericho, on the 1 Chr 6:78
of Manasseh from **b** the Jordan, 1 Chr 12:37
Syrians who were **b** the Euphrates, 1 Chr 19:16
as bronze in quantities **b** weighing, 1 Chr 22:3
and bronze and iron **b** weighing, 1 Chr 22:14
you from Edom, from **b** the sea; 2 Chr 20:2
in the rest of the province **B** the River. Ezr 4:10
the men of the province **B** the River, Ezr 4:11
possession in the province **B** the River." Ezr 4:16
in the rest of the province **B** the River, Ezr 4:17
over the whole province **B** the River, Ezr 4:20
governor of the province **B** the River and Ezr 5:3
governor of the province **B** the River and Ezr 5:6
were in the province **B** the River sent to Ezr 5:6
governor of the province **B** the River, Ezr 6:6
who are in the province **B** the River, Ezr 6:6
tribute of the province from **B** the River. Ezr 6:8
the governor of the province **B** the River, Ezr 6:13
treasurers in the province **B** the River: Ezr 7:21
the people in the province **B** the River, Ezr 7:25
governors of the province **B** the River, Ezr 8:36
governors of the province **B** the River, Neh 2:7

of the province **B** the River and Neh 2:9
the governor of the province **B** the River. Neh 3:7
who does great things **b** searching out, Jb 9:10
out, and marvelous things **b** number. Jb 9:10
evils have encompassed me **b** number; Ps 40:12
the oil of gladness **b** your companions; Ps 45:7
power; his understanding is **b** measure. Ps 147:5
a moment he will be broken **b** healing. Prv 6:15
will suddenly be broken **b** healing. Prv 29:1
My son, beware of anything **b** these. Eccl 12:12
appetite and opened its mouth **b** measure, Is 5:14
a razor that is hired **b** the River—with the Is 7:20
the way of the sea, the land **b** the Jordan, Is 9:1
whirring wings that is **b** the rivers of Is 18:1
was so marred, **b** human semblance, Is 52:14
and his form **b** that of the children of Is 52:14
will be like this day, great **b** measure." Is 56:12
dragged and dumped **b** the gates of Jer 22:19
bronze of all these things was **b** weight. Jer 52:20
against my land, powerful and **b** number; Jl 1:6
you into exile **b** Damascus," says the Am 5:27
From **b** the rivers of Cush my Zep 3:10
"Great is the LORD **b** the border of Israel!" Mal 1:5
the way of the sea, **b** the Jordan, Mt 4:15
and Judea, and from **b** the Jordan. Mt 4:25
entered the region of Judea **b** the Jordan. Mt 19:1
and Idumea and from **b** the Jordan and Mk 3:8
And they were astonished **b** measure, Mk 7:37
to the region of Judea and **b** the Jordan, Mk 10:1
I will send you into exile **b** Babylon.' Acts 7:43
might become sinful **b** measure. Rom 7:13
B that, I do not know whether I 1 Cor 1:16
learn by us not to go **b** what is written, 1 Cor 4:6
let you be tempted **b** your ability, 1 Cor 10:13
so utterly burdened **b** our strength 2 Cor 1:8
weight of glory **b** all comparison, 2 Cor 4:17
as I can testify, and **b** their means, 2 Cor 8:3
But we will not boast **b** limits, but 2 Cor 10:13
We do not boast **b** limit in the 2 Cor 10:15
preach the gospel in lands **b** you, 2 Cor 10:16
advancing in Judaism **b** many of my Gal 1:14
the oil of gladness **b** your companions." Heb 1:9
It is **b** dispute that the inferior is blessed Heb 7:7

BEZAI (3)
The sons of **B**, 323. Ezr 2:17
The sons of **B**, 324. Neh 7:23
Hodiah, Hashum, **B**, Neh 10:18

BEZALEL (9)
I have called by name **B** the son of Uri, Ex 31:2
has called by name **B** the son of Uri, Ex 35:30
"**B** and Oholiab and every craftsman in Ex 36:1
And Moses called **B** and Oholiab and Ex 36:2
B made the ark of acacia wood. Two Ex 37:1
B the son of Uri, son of Hur, of the tribe Ex 38:22
Hur fathered Uri, and Uri fathered **B**. 1 Chr 2:20
the bronze altar that **B** the son of Uri, 2 Chr 1:5
Maaseiah, Mattaniah, **B**, Binnui, Ezr 10:30

BEZEK (3)
and they defeated 10,000 of them at **B**. Jgs 1:4
found Adoni-bezek at **B** and fought Jgs 1:5
When he mustered them at **B**, the 1 Sm 11:8

BEZER (5)
B in the wilderness on the tableland for Dt 4:43
they appointed **B** in the wilderness on Jos 20:8
of Reuben, **B** with its pasturelands, Jos 21:36
B in the wilderness with its 1 Chr 6:78
B, Hod, Shamma, Shilshah, Ithran, 1 Chr 7:37

BICHRI (8)
whose name was Sheba, the son of **B**, 2 Sm 20:1
and followed Sheba the son of **B**. 2 Sm 20:2
Sheba the son of **B** will do us more 2 Sm 20:6
to pursue Sheba the son of **B**. 2 Sm 20:7
brother pursued Sheba the son of **B**. 2 Sm 20:10
Joab to pursue Sheba the son of **B**. 2 Sm 20:13
Ephraim, called Sheba the son of **B**, 2 Sm 20:21
Sheba the son of **B** and threw it out 2 Sm 20:22

BICHRITES (1)
and all the **B** assembled and followed 2 Sm 20:14

BIDKAR (1)
Jehu said to **B** his aide, "Take him up 2 Kgs 9:25

BIER (3)
And King David followed the **b**. 2 Sm 3:31
laid him on a **b** that had been filled 2 Chr 16:14
Then he came up and touched the **b**, Lk 7:14

BIG (8)
right hand and on the **b** toe of his right Lv 8:23
hands and on the **b** toes of their right Lv 8:24
right hand and on the **b** toe of his right Lv 14:14
right hand and on the **b** toe of his right Lv 14:17
right hand and on the **b** toe of his right Lv 14:25
right hand and on the **b** toe of his right Lv 14:28
and cut off his thumbs and his **b** toes. Jgs 1:6
their thumbs and their **b** toes cut off used Jgs 1:7

BIGTHA (1)
Biztha, Harbona, **B** and Abagtha, Est 1:10

BIGTHAN (1)
sitting at the king's gate, **B** and Teresh, Est 2:21

BIGTHANA (1)
Mordecai had told about **B** and Teresh, Est 6:2

BIGVAI (6)
Mordecai, Bilshan, Mispar, **B**, Rehum, Ezr 2:2
The sons of **B**, 2,056. Ezr 2:14
Of the sons of **B**, Uthai and Zaccur, and Ezr 8:14
Bilshan, Mispereth, **B**, Nehum, Neh 7:7
The sons of **B**, 2,067. Neh 7:19
Adonijah, **B**, Adin, Neh 10:16

BILDAD (5)
Eliphaz the Temanite, **B** the Shuhite, Jb 2:11
Then **B** the Shuhite answered and said: Jb 8:1
Then **B** the Shuhite answered and said: Jb 18:1
Then **B** the Shuhite answered and said: Jb 25:1
the Temanite and **B** the Shuhite and Jb 42:9

BILE (1)
my **b** is poured out to the ground Lam 2:11

BILEAM (1)
and **B** with its pasturelands, 1 Chr 6:70

BILGAH (3)
the fifteenth to **B**, the sixteenth to 1 Chr 24:14
Mijamin, Maadiah, **B**, Neh 12:5
of **B**, Shammua; of Shemaiah, Neh 12:18

BILGAI (1)
Maaziah, **B**, Shemaiah; these are the Neh 10:8

BILHAH (11)
his female servant **B** to his daughter Gn 29:29
Then she said, "Here is my servant **B**; go Gn 30:3
So she gave him her servant **B** as a wife, Gn 30:4
And **B** conceived and bore Jacob a son. Gn 30:5
Rachel's servant **B** conceived again and Gn 30:7
and lay with **B** his father's concubine. Gn 35:22
The sons of **B**, Rachel's servant: Dan Gn 35:25
was a boy with the sons of **B** and Zilpah, Gn 37:2
These are the sons of **B**, whom Laban Gn 46:25
B, Ezem, Tolad, 1 Chr 4:29
and Shallum, the descendants of **B**. 1 Chr 7:13

BILHAN (4)
the sons of Ezer: **B**, Zaavan, and Akan. Gn 36:27
sons of Ezer: **B**, Zaavan, and Akan. 1 Chr 1:42
of Jediael: **B**. And the sons of Bilhan: 1 Chr 7:10
And the sons of **B**: Jeush, Benjamin, 1 Chr 7:10

BILL (2)
He said to him, 'Take your **b**, and sit Lk 16:6
He said to him, 'Take your **b**, and write Lk 16:7

BILLOWS (1)
your waves and your **b** passed over me. Jon 2:3

BILSHAN (2)
Seraiah, Reelaiah, Mordecai, **B**, Mispar, Ezr 2:2
Nahamani, Mordecai, **B**, Mispereth, Neh 7:7

BIMHAL (1)
of Japhlet: Pasach, **B**, and Ashvath. 1 Chr 7:33

BIND (40)
And they shall **b** the breastpiece by its Ex 28:28
sons with sashes and **b** caps on them. Ex 29:9
swears an oath to **b** himself by a Nm 30:2
You shall **b** them as a sign on your hand, Dt 6:8
and you shall **b** them as a sign on your Dt 11:18
it into money and **b** up the money in Dt 14:25
said, "We have come up to **b** Samson, Jgs 15:10
to him, "We have come down to **b** you, Jgs 15:12
we will only **b** you and give you into Jgs 15:13
that we may **b** him to humble him. Jgs 16:5
"If they **b** me with seven fresh Jgs 16:7
"If they **b** me with new ropes that have Jgs 16:11
broken, but the feeble **b** on strength. 1 Sm 2:4
shoulder; I would **b** it on me as a crown; Jb 31:36
"Can you **b** the chains of the Pleiades or Jb 38:31
Can you **b** him in the furrow with Jb 39:10
b their faces in the world below. Jb 40:13
to **b** his princes at his pleasure and to Ps 105:22
B the festal sacrifice with cords, up to Ps 118:27
to **b** their kings with chains and their Ps 149:8
forsake you; **b** them around your neck; Prv 3:3
B them on your heart always; tie them Prv 6:21
b them on your fingers; write them on Prv 7:3
B up the testimony; seal the teaching Is 8:16
your robe, and will **b** your sash on him, Is 22:21
you shall **b** them on as a bride does. Is 49:18
he has sent me to **b** up the brokenhearted, Is 61:1
a small number and **b** them in the Ezk 5:3
B on your turban, and put your shoes Ezk 24:17
the strayed, and I will **b** up the injured, Ezk 34:16
They shall not **b** themselves with Ezk 44:18
mighty men of his army to **b** Shadrach, Dn 3:20
has struck us down, and he will **b** us up. Hos 6:1
the weeds first and **b** them in bundles Mt 13:30
and whatever you **b** on earth shall be Mt 16:19
whatever you **b** on earth shall be Mt 18:18
'**B** him hand and foot and cast him Mt 22:13
And no one could **b** him anymore, not Mk 5:3
the chief priests to **b** all who call on Acts 9:14
Jews at Jerusalem will **b** the man who Acts 21:11

BINDER (1)
his hand nor the **b** of sheaves his arms, Ps 129:7

BINDERS (1)
and timber for **b** and beams for the 2 Chr 34:11

BINDING (9)
Behold, we were **b** sheaves in the field, Gn 37:7
B his foal to the vine and his donkey's Gn 49:11
it, with a woven **b** around the opening, Ex 28:32
garment, with a **b** around the opening, Ex 39:23
around him, **b** it to him with the band. Lv 8:7
Any vow and any **b** oath to afflict Nm 30:13
up, to heal it by **b** it with a bandage, Ezk 30:21
b and delivering to prison both men Acts 22:4
—that the law is **b** on a person only as Rom 7:1

BINDS (12)
to the LORD and **b** herself by a pledge, Nm 30:3
For he wounds, but he **b** up; he shatters, Jb 5:18
bonds of kings and **b** a waistcloth on Jb 12:18
He **b** up the waters in his thick clouds, Jb 26:8
it **b** me about like the collar of my Jb 30:18
do not cry for help when he **b** them. Jb 36:13
the brokenhearted and **b** up their Ps 147:3
Like one who **b** the stone in the sling is Prv 26:8
day when the LORD **b** up the brokenness Is 30:26
unless he first **b** the strong man? Mt 12:29
goods, unless he first **b** the strong man. Mk 3:27
which **b** everything together in perfect Col 3:14

BINEA (2)
Moza fathered **B**; Raphah was his 1 Chr 8:37
Moza fathered **B**, and Rephaiah was 1 Chr 9:43

BINNUI (7)
son of Jeshua and Noadiah the son of **B**. Ezr 8:33
Mattaniah, Bezalel, **B**, and Manasseh. Ezr 10:30
Of the sons of **B**: Shimei, Ezr 10:38
After him **B** the son of Henadad Neh 3:24
The sons of **B**, 648. Neh 7:15
of Azaniah, **B** of the sons of Henadad, Neh 10:9
Jeshua, **B**, Kadmiel, Sherebiah, Judah, Neh 12:8

BIRD (41)
and every winged **b** according to its Gn 1:21
earth and to every **b** of the heavens and Gn 1:30
the field and every **b** of the heavens and Gn 2:19
earth, according to its kind, and every **b**, Gn 7:14
beast, every creeping thing, and every **b**, Gn 8:19
some of every clean **b** and offered burnt Gn 8:20
earth and upon every **b** of the heavens, Gn 9:2
law about beast and **b** and every living Lv 11:46
shall take the live **b** with the cedarwood Lv 14:6
dip them and the live **b** in the blood of Lv 14:6
in the blood of the **b** that was killed over Lv 14:6
and shall let the living **b** go into the open Lv 14:7
the scarlet yarn, along with the live **b**, Lv 14:51
in the blood of the **b** that was killed and Lv 14:51
the blood of the **b** and with the fresh Lv 14:52
and with the live **b** and with the Lv 14:52
he shall let the live **b** go out of the city Lv 14:53
hunting any beast or **b** that may be Lv 17:13
and the unclean **b** from the clean. Lv 20:25
by beast or by **b** or by anything with Lv 20:25
likeness of any winged **b** that flies in the Dt 4:17
"That path no **b** of prey knows, and the Jb 28:7
Will you play with him as with a **b**, or Jb 41:5
soul, "Flee like a **b** to your mountain, Ps 11:1
have escaped like a **b** from the snare of Ps 124:7
is a net spread in the sight of any **b**, Prv 1:17
like a **b** from the hand of the fowler. Prv 6:5
its liver; as a **b** rushes into a snare; Prv 7:23
Like a **b** that strays from its nest is a Prv 27:8
for a **b** of the air will carry your Eccl 10:20
and one rises up at the sound of a **b**, Eccl 12:4
there the night **b** settles and finds for Is 34:14
calling a **b** of prey from the east, the Is 46:11
been hunted like a **b** by those who Lam 3:52
under it will dwell every kind of **b**; Ezk 17:23
eat of anything, whether **b** or beast, Ezk 44:31
with four wings of a **b** on its back. Dn 7:6
glory shall fly away like a **b**—no birth, Hos 9:11
Does a **b** fall in a snare on the earth, Am 3:5
For every kind of beast and **b**, of reptile Jas 3:7
spirit, a haunt for every unclean **b**, Rv 18:2

BIRD'S (1)
"If you come across a **b** nest in any tree Dt 22:6

BIRDS (93)
and let **b** fly above the earth across the Gn 1:20
seas, and let **b** multiply on the earth." Gn 1:22
sea and over the **b** of the heavens and Gn 1:26
sea and over the **b** of the heavens and Gn 1:28
livestock and to the **b** of the heavens Gn 2:20
and creeping things and **b** of the heavens, Gn 6:7
Of the **b** according to their kinds, and of Gn 6:20
seven pairs of the **b** of the heavens also, Gn 7:3
of animals that are not clean, and of **b**, Gn 7:8
that moved on the earth, **b**, livestock, Gn 7:21
creeping things and **b** of the heavens. Gn 7:23
of all flesh—**b** and animals and every Gn 8:17
living creature that is with you, the **b**, Gn 9:10
other. But he did not cut the **b** in half. Gn 15:10
And when **b** of prey came down on the Gn 15:11
but the **b** were eating it out of the Gn 40:17
And the **b** will eat the flesh from you." Gn 40:19
to the LORD is a burnt offering of **b**, Lv 1:14
these you shall detest among the **b**; Lv 11:13
two live clean **b** and cedarwood and Lv 14:4
kill one of the **b** in an earthenware vessel Lv 14:5
of the house he shall take two small **b**, Lv 14:49
kill one of the **b** in an earthenware Lv 14:50
"You may eat all clean **b**. Dt 14:11
shall be food for all **b** of the air and for Dt 28:26
give your flesh to the **b** of the air and 1 Sm 17:44
this day to the **b** of the air and 1 Sm 17:46
she did not allow the **b** of the air to 2 Sm 21:10
He spoke also of beasts, and of **b**, and 1 Kgs 4:33
open country the **b** of the heavens 1 Kgs 14:11
in the field the **b** of the heavens shall 1 Kgs 16:4
open country the **b** of the heavens 1 Kgs 21:24
was one ox and six choice sheep and **b**, Neh 5:18
the **b** of the heavens, and they will tell Jb 12:7
and concealed from the **b** of the air. Jb 28:21
us wiser than the **b** of the heavens?' Jb 35:11
the **b** of the heavens, and the fish of the Ps 8:8
I know all the **b** of the hills, and all that Ps 50:11
dust, winged **b** like the sand of the seas; Ps 78:27
your servants to the **b** of the heavens for Ps 79:2
Beside them the **b** of the heavens dwell; Ps 104:12
In them the **b** build their nests; the Ps 104:17
creeping things and flying **b**! Ps 148:10
and like **b** that are caught in a snare, Eccl 9:12
Like fleeing **b**, like a scattered nest, so are Is 16:2
them be left to the **b** of prey of the Is 18:6
And the **b** of prey will summer on them, Is 18:6
Like **b** hovering, so the LORD of hosts will Is 31:5
no man, and all the **b** of the air had fled. Jer 4:25
Like a cage full of **b**, their houses are full Jer 5:27
people will be food for the **b** of the air, Jer 7:33
both the **b** of the air and the beasts have Jer 9:10
in it the beasts and the **b** are swept away, Jer 12:4
Are the **b** of prey against her all around? Jer 12:9
and the **b** of the air and the beasts of the Jer 15:3
shall be food for the **b** of the air and for Jer 16:4
bodies for food to the **b** of the air and to Jer 19:7
shall be food for the **b** of the air and the Jer 34:20
with which you hunt the souls like **b**, Ezk 13:20
you hunt go free, the souls like **b**. Ezk 13:20
shade of its branches **b** of every sort Ezk 17:23
the earth and to the **b** of the heavens I Ezk 29:5
All the **b** of the heavens made their Ezk 31:6
trunk dwell all the **b** of the heavens, Ezk 31:13
will cause all the **b** of the heavens to Ezk 32:4
of the sea and the **b** of the heavens and Ezk 38:20
I will give you to **b** of prey of every sort Ezk 39:4
Speak to the **b** of every sort and to all Ezk 39:17
of the field, and the **b** of the heavens, Dn 2:38
and the **b** of the heavens lived in its Dn 4:12
under it and the **b** from its branches. Dn 4:14
in whose branches the **b** of the heavens Dn 4:21
beasts of the field, the **b** of the heavens, Hos 2:18
of the field and the **b** of the heavens, Hos 4:3
bring them down like **b** of the heavens; Hos 7:12
come trembling like **b** from Egypt, Hos 11:11
will sweep away the **b** of the heavens and Zep 1:3
Look at the **b** of the air: they neither sow Mt 6:26
have holes, and **b** of the air have nests, Mt 8:20
and the **b** came and devoured them. Mt 13:4
so that the **b** of the air come and make Mt 13:32
the path, and the **b** came and devoured it. Mk 4:4
so that the **b** of the air can make nests Mk 4:32
underfoot, and the **b** of the air devoured it. Lk 8:5
have holes, and **b** of the air have nests, Lk 9:58
much more value are you than the **b**! Lk 12:24
and the **b** of the air made nests in its Lk 13:19
animals and reptiles and **b** of the air. Acts 10:12
of prey and reptiles and **b** of the air. Acts 11:6
mortal man and **b** and animals and Rom 1:23
another for animals, another for **b**, 1 Cor 15:39
called to all the **b** that fly directly Rv 19:17
and all the **b** were gorged with their Rv 19:21

BIRDS' (1)
and his nails were like **b** claws. Dn 4:33

BIRSHA (1)
king of Sodom, **B** king of Gomorrah, Gn 14:2

BIRTH (72)
Ishmael, named in the order of their **b**: Gn 25:13
her days to give **b** were completed, Gn 25:24
so that she may give **b** on my behalf, Gn 30:3
vigorous and give **b** before the midwife Ex 1:19
She gave **b** to a son, and he called his Ex 2:22
the other stone, in the order of their **b**. Ex 28:10
Did I give them **b**, that you should say Nm 11:12
and you forgot the God who gave you **b**. Dt 32:18
than seven sons, has given **b** to him." Ru 4:15
was pregnant, about to give **b**. 1 Sm 4:19
were dead, she bowed and gave **b**, 1 Sm 4:19
and I gave **b** to a child while she was 1 Kgs 3:17
Then on the third day after I gave **b**, 1 Kgs 3:18
I gave birth, this woman also gave **b**. 1 Kgs 3:18
children have come to the point of **b**, 2 Kgs 19:3
his mouth and cursed the day of his **b**. Jb 3:1
"Why did I not die at **b**, come out from Jb 3:11
conceive trouble and give **b** to evil, Jb 15:35
and who has given **b** to the frost of Jb 38:29
know when the mountain goats give **b**? Jb 39:1
do you know the time when they give **b**, Jb 39:2
with mischief and gives **b** to lies. Ps 7:14
On you was I cast from my **b**, and from Ps 22:10
makes the deer give **b** and strips the Ps 29:9
they go astray from **b**, speaking lies. Ps 58:3
you I have leaned from before my **b**; Ps 71:6
and the day of death than the day of **b**. Eccl 7:1
"I have neither labored nor given **b**, I Is 23:4
her pangs when she is near to giving **b**, Is 26:17
we writhed, but we have given **b** to wind. Is 26:18
and the earth will give **b** to the dead. Is 26:19
conceive chaff; you give **b** to stubble; Is 33:11
children have come to the point of **b**, and Is 37:3
been borne by me from before your **b**, Is 46:3
and that from before **b** you were called a Is 48:8
conceive mischief and give **b** to iniquity. Is 59:4
"Before she was in labor she gave **b**; Is 66:7
bring to the point of **b** and not cause to Is 66:9
father,' and to a stone, 'You gave me **b**.' Jer 2:27
as of one giving **b** to her first child, Jer 4:31
our own people and to the land of our **b**, Jer 46:16
the heart of a woman in her **b** pains; Jer 48:41
the heart of a woman in her **b** pains." Jer 49:22
Your origin and your **b** are of the land Ezk 16:3
And as for your **b**, on the day you were Ezk 16:4
beasts of the field gave **b** to their young, Ezk 31:6
glory shall fly away like a bird—no **b**, Hos 9:11
Even though they give **b**, I will put their Hos 9:16
when she who is in labor has given **b**; Mi 5:3
Now the **b** of Jesus Christ took place in Mt 1:18
her not until she had given **b** to a son. Mt 1:25
are eunuchs who have been so from **b**, Mt 19:12
are but the beginning of the **b** pains. Mt 24:8
was a Gentile, a Syrophoenician by **b**. Mk 7:26
are but the beginning of the **b** pains. Mk 13:8
gladness, and many will rejoice at his **b**, Lk 1:14
the time came for Elizabeth to give **b**, Lk 1:57
there, the time came for her to give **b**. Lk 2:6
And she gave **b** to her firstborn son and Lk 2:7
he passed by, he saw a man blind from **b**. Jn 9:1
When a woman is giving **b**, she has Jn 16:21
a man lame from **b** was being carried, Acts 3:2
He was crippled from **b** and had never Acts 14:8
Paul said, "But I am a citizen by **b**." Acts 22:28
powerful, not many were of noble **b**. 1 Cor 1:26
ourselves are Jews by **b** and not Gentile Gal 2:15
when it has conceived gives **b** to sin, Jas 1:15
was crying out in **b** pains and the agony Rv 12:2
in birth pains and the agony of giving **b**. Rv 12:2
the woman who was about to give **b**, Rv 12:4
She gave **b** to a male child, one who is to Rv 12:5
woman who had given **b** to the male Rv 12:13

BIRTHDAY (3)
the third day, which was Pharaoh's **b**, Gn 40:20
But when Herod's **b** came, the daughter Mt 14:6
when Herod on his **b** gave a banquet for Mk 6:21

BIRTHRIGHT (9)
Jacob said, "Sell me your **b** now." Gn 25:31
about to die; of what use is a **b** to me?" Gn 25:32
swore to him and sold his **b** to Jacob. Gn 25:33
his way. Thus Esau despised his **b**. Gn 25:34
He took away my **b**, and behold, now Gn 27:36
according to his **b** and the youngest Gn 43:33
his **b** was given to the sons of Joseph 1 Chr 5:1
him, yet the **b** belonged to Joseph), 1 Chr 5:2
Esau, who sold his **b** for a single meal. Heb 12:16

BIRTHSTOOL (1)
Hebrew women and see them on the **b**, Ex 1:16

BIRZAITH (1)
Heber, and Malchiel, who fathered **B**. 1 Chr 7:31

BISHLAM (1)
B and Mithredath and Tabeel and the Ezr 4:7

BIT (6)
the people, and they **b** the people, Nm 21:6
And if a serpent **b** anyone, he would Nm 21:9
your nose and my **b** in your mouth, 2 Kgs 19:28
must be curbed with **b** and bridle, Ps 32:9
in your nose and my **b** in your mouth, Is 37:29
against the wall, and a serpent **b** him. Am 5:19

BITE (4)
and a serpent will **b** him who breaks Eccl 10:8
and they shall **b** you," declares the LORD. Jer 8:17
the serpent, and it shall **b** them. Am 9:3
But if you **b** and devour one another, Gal 5:15

BITES (3)
that **b** the horse's heels so that his rider Gn 49:17
In the end it **b** like a serpent and stings Prv 23:32
If the serpent **b** before it is charmed, Eccl 10:11

BITHIAH (1)
These are the sons of **B**, the daughter 1 Chr 4:17

BITHYNIA (2)
to Mysia, they attempted to go into **B**, Acts 16:7
Galatia, Cappadocia, Asia, and **B**, 1 Pt 1:1

BITING (1)
but a **b** fly from the north has come Jer 46:20

BITS (2)
fragments, and the little house into **b**. Am 6:11
If we put **b** into the mouths of horses so Jas 3:3

BITTEN (1)
set it on a pole, and everyone who is **b**, Nm 21:8

BITTER (47)
and they made life **b** for Isaac and Gn 26:35
exceedingly great and **b** cry and said Gn 27:34
and made their lives **b** with hard service, Ex 1:14
unleavened bread and **b** herbs they shall Ex 12:8
the water of Marah because it was **b**; Ex 15:23
shall enter into her and cause **b** pain. Nm 5:24
shall enter into her and cause **b** pain, Nm 5:27
it with unleavened bread and **b** herbs. Nm 9:11
a root bearing poisonous and **b** fruit, Dt 29:18
grapes of poison; their clusters are **b**; Dt 32:32
for it is exceedingly **b** to me for your Ru 1:13
debt, and everyone who was **b** in soul, 1 Sm 22:2
because all the people were **b** in soul, 1 Sm 30:6
you not know that the end will be **b**? 2 Sm 2:26
her alone, for she is in **b** distress, 2 Kgs 4:27
the affliction of Israel was very **b**, 2 Kgs 14:26
and he cried out with a loud and **b** cry. Est 4:1
who is in misery, and life to the **b** in soul, Jb 3:20
For you write **b** things against me and Jb 13:26
"Today also my complaint is **b**; my hand Jb 23:2
the Almighty, who has made my soul **b**, Jb 27:2
swords, who aim **b** words like arrows, Ps 64:3
for they made his spirit **b**, and he Ps 106:33
but in the end she is **b** as wormwood, Prv 5:4
who is hungry everything **b** is sweet. Prv 27:7
and wine to those in **b** distress; Prv 31:6
I find something more **b** than death: Eccl 7:26
who put **b** for sweet and sweet for bitter! Is 5:20
who put bitter for sweet and sweet for **b**! Is 5:20
"Look away from me; let me weep **b** tears; Is 22:4
strong drink is **b** to those who drink it. Is 24:9
that it is evil and **b** for you to forsake the Jer 2:19
This is your doom, and it is **b**; it has Jer 4:18
as for an only son, most **b** lamentation, Jer 6:26
Behold, I will feed this people with **b** food, Jer 9:15
will feed them with **b** food and give Jer 23:15
in Ramah, lamentation and **b** weeping. Jer 31:15
with breaking heart and **b** grief, groan Ezk 21:6
bitterness of soul, with **b** mourning. Ezk 27:31
Ephraim has given **b** provocation; so Hos 12:14
only son and the end of it like a **b** day. Am 8:10
the Chaldeans, that **b** and hasty nation, Hab 1:6
the sound of the day of the LORD is **b**; Zep 1:14
But if you have **b** jealousy and selfish Jas 3:14
the water, because it had been made **b**. Rv 8:11
it will make your stomach **b**, but in Rv 10:9
I had eaten it my stomach was made **b**. Rv 10:10

BITTERLY (18)
The archers **b** attacked him, shot at Gn 49:23
they lifted up their voices and wept **b**. Jgs 21:2
the Almighty has dealt very **b** with me. Ru 1:20
and prayed to the LORD and wept **b**. 1 Sm 1:10
also and all his servants wept very **b**. 2 Sm 13:36
in your sight." And Hezekiah wept **b**. 2 Kgs 20:3
him out of Israel, for the people wept **b**. Ezr 10:1

in the streets; the envoys of peace weep **b**. Is 33:7
in your sight." And Hezekiah wept **b**. Is 38:3
my eyes will weep **b** and run down with Jer 13:17
but weep **b** for him who goes away, Jer 22:10
She weeps **b** in the night, with tears on Lam 1:2
been afflicted, and she herself suffers **b**. Lam 1:4
shout aloud over you and cry out **b**. Ezk 27:30
up a taunt song against you and moan **b**, Mi 2:4
an only child, and weep **b** over him, Zec 12:10
times." And he went out and wept **b**. Mt 26:75
And he went out and wept **b**. Lk 22:62

BITTERNESS (21)
have the water of **b** that brings the Nm 5:18
from this water of **b** that brings the Nm 5:19
and wash them off into the water of **b**. Nm 5:23
drink the water of **b** that brings the Nm 5:24
said, "Surely the **b** of death is past." 1 Sm 15:32
I will complain in the **b** of my soul. Jb 7:11
let me get my breath, but fills me with **b**. Jb 9:18
I will speak in the **b** of my soul. Jb 10:1
Another dies in **b** of soul, never having Jb 21:25
The heart knows its own **b**, and no Prv 14:10
to his father and **b** to her who bore Prv 17:25
all my years because of the **b** of my soul. Is 38:15
it was for my welfare that I had great **b**; Is 38:17
enveloped me with **b** and tribulation; Lam 3:5
He has filled me with **b**; he has sated Lam 3:15
and I went in **b** in the heat of my spirit, Ezk 3:14
and they weep over you in **b** of soul, Ezk 27:31
are in the gall of **b** and in the bond of Acts 8:23
"Their mouth is full of curses and **b**." Rom 3:14
Let all **b** and wrath and anger and Eph 4:31
that no "root of **b**" springs up and Heb 12:15

BITUMEN (3)
had brick for stone, and **b** for mortar. Gn 11:3
the Valley of Siddim was full of **b** pits, Gn 14:10
and daubed it with **b** and pitch. Ex 2:3

BIZIOTHIAH (1)
Hazar-shual, Beersheba, **B**, Jos 15:28

BIZTHA (1)
he commanded Mehuman, **B**, Harbona, Est 1:10

BLACK (17)
and spotted sheep and every **b** lamb, Gn 30:32
the goats and **b** among the lambs, Gn 30:33
white on it, and every lamb that was **b**, Gn 30:35
the striped and all the **b** in the flock of Gn 30:40
the bearded vulture, the **b** vulture, Lv 11:13
the skin and there is no **b** hair in it, Lv 13:31
is unchanged and **b** hair has grown Lv 13:37
the bearded vulture, the **b** vulture, Dt 14:12
the heavens grew **b** with clouds and 1 Kgs 18:45
My skin turns **b** and falls from me, and Jb 30:30
gold; his locks are wavy, **b** as a raven. Sg 5:11
and the day shall be **b** over them; Mi 3:6
had red horses, the second **b** horses, Zec 6:2
chariot with the **b** horses goes toward Zec 6:6
you cannot make one hair white or **b**. Mt 5:36
And I looked, and behold, a **b** horse! Rv 6:5
and the sun became **b** as sackcloth, Rv 6:12

BLACKER (1)
Now their face is **b** than soot; they are Lam 4:8

BLACKNESS (3)
dwell upon it; let the **b** of the day terrify it. Jb 3:5
the heavens with **b** and make sackcloth Is 50:3
Like **b** there is spread upon the mountains Jl 2:2

BLACKSMITH (1)
Now there was no **b** to be found 1 Sm 13:19

BLADE (4)
And the hilt also went in after the **b**, and Jgs 3:22
the blade, and the fat closed over the **b**, Jgs 3:22
then let my shoulder **b** fall from my Jb 31:22
The earth produces by itself, first the **b**, Mk 4:28

BLAME (3)
you, then let me bear the **b** forever. Gn 43:9
I shall bear the **b** before my father all Gn 44:32
that no one should **b** us about this 2 Cor 8:20

BLAMELESS (50)
was a righteous man, **b** in his generation. Gn 6:9
Almighty; walk before me, and be **b**, Gn 17:1
You shall be **b** before the LORD your Dt 18:13
know that you are as **b** in my sight as 1 Sm 29:9
I was **b** before him, and I kept myself 2 Sm 22:24
with the **b** man you show yourself 2 Sm 22:26
blameless man you show yourself **b**; 2 Sm 22:26
refuge and has made my way **b**. 2 Sm 22:33
to those whose heart is **b** toward him. 2 Chr 16:9
was Job, and that man was **b** and upright, Jb 1:1
him on the earth, a **b** and upright man, Jb 1:8
him on the earth, a **b** and upright man, Jb 2:3
"Behold, God will not reject a **b** man, nor Jb 8:20
though I am **b**, he would prove me Jb 9:20
I am **b**; I regard not myself; I loathe my Jb 9:21
He destroys both the **b** and the wicked. Jb 9:22
and he answered me, a just and **b** man, Jb 12:4
it gain to him if you make your ways **b**? Jb 22:3
I was **b** before him, and I kept myself Ps 18:23
with the **b** man you show yourself Ps 18:25
blameless man you show yourself **b**; Ps 18:25
me with strength and made my way **b**. Ps 18:32
Then I shall be **b**, and innocent of great Ps 19:13
The LORD knows the days of the **b**, and Ps 37:18
Mark the **b** and behold the upright, for Ps 37:37
in your words and **b** in your judgment. Ps 51:4
shooting from ambush at the **b**, Ps 64:4
I will ponder the way that is **b**. Oh when Ps 101:2
the way that is **b** shall minister to me. Ps 101:6
Blessed are those whose way is **b**, who Ps 119:1
May my heart be **b** in your statutes, Ps 119:80
of the LORD is a stronghold to the **b**, Prv 10:29
righteousness of the **b** keeps his way Prv 11:5
but those of **b** ways are his delight. Prv 11:20
guards him whose way is **b**, Prv 13:6
but the **b** will have a goodly Prv 28:10
hate one who is **b** and seek the life Prv 29:10
You were **b** in your ways from the day Ezk 28:15
me, because I was found **b** before him; Dn 6:22
we should be holy and **b** before him. Eph 1:4
and so be pure and **b** for the day of Phil 1:10
that you may be **b** and innocent, Phil 2:15
as to righteousness, under the law **b**. Phil 3:6
you holy and **b** and above reproach Col 1:22
and righteous and **b** was our 1 Thes 2:10
establish your hearts **b** in holiness 1 Thes 3:13
and body be kept **b** at the coming of 1 Thes 5:23
as deacons if they prove themselves **b**. 1 Tm 3:10
to present you **b** before the presence Jude 1:24
mouth no lie was found, for they are **b**. Rv 14:5

BLAMELESSLY (2)
He who walks **b** and does what is right Ps 15:2
walking **b** in all the commandments and Lk 1:6

BLASPHEME (6)
and tried to make them **b**, Acts 26:11
to Satan that they may learn not to **b**. 1 Tm 1:20
not the ones who **b** the honorable name Jas 2:7
not tremble as they **b** the glorious ones, 2 Pt 2:10
authority, and **b** the glorious ones. Jude 1:8
But these people **b** all that they do not Jude 1:10

BLASPHEMED (4)
the Israelite woman's son **b** the Name, Lv 24:11
In this also your fathers **b** me, by Ezk 20:27
name of God is **b** among the Gentiles Rom 2:24
of them the way of truth will be **b**. 2 Pt 2:2

BLASPHEMER (1)
though formerly I was a **b**, 1 Tm 1:13

BLASPHEMERS (1)
neither sacrilegious nor **b** of our Acts 19:37

BLASPHEMES (4)
Whoever **b** the name of the LORD shall Lv 24:16
well as the native, when he **b** the Name, Lv 24:16
but whoever **b** against the Holy Spirit Mk 3:29
but the one who **b** against the Holy Lk 12.10

BLASPHEMIES (5)
of Egypt,' and had committed great **b**, Neh 9:18
to you, and they committed great **b**. Neh 9:26
of man, and whatever **b** they utter, Mk 3:28
saying, "Who is this who speaks **b**? Lk 5:21
opened its mouth to utter **b** against God, Rv 13:6

BLASPHEMING (7)
knew, because his sons were **b** God, 1 Sm 3:13
said to themselves, "This man is **b**." Mt 9:3
does this man speak like that? He is **b**! Mk 2:7
many other things against him, **b** him. Lk 22:65
and sent into the world, 'You are **b**,' Jn 10:36
b about matters of which they are 2 Pt 2:12
God, **b** his name and his dwelling, Rv 13:6

BLASPHEMOUS (6)
heard him speak **b** words against Acts 6:11
not pronounce a **b** judgment against 2 Pt 2:11
presume to pronounce a **b** judgment, Jude 1:9
on its horns and **b** names on its heads. Rv 13:1
a mouth uttering haughty and **b** words, Rv 13:5
a scarlet beast that was full of **b** names, Rv 17:3

BLASPHEMY (6)
every sin and **b** will be forgiven people, Mt 12:31
but the **b** against the Spirit will not be Mt 12:31
his robes and said, "He has uttered **b**. Mt 26:65
do we need? You have now heard his **b**. Mt 26:65
You have heard his **b**. What is your Mk 14:64
that we are going to stone you but for **b**, Jn 10:33

BLAST (10)
At the **b** of your nostrils the waters piled Ex 15:8
When the trumpet sounds a long **b**, Ex 19:13
mountain and a very loud trumpet **b**, Ex 19:16
proclaimed with **b** of trumpets, Lv 23:24
together, you shall blow a long **b**, Nm 10:7
they make a long **b** with the ram's horn, Jos 6:5
at the **b** of the breath of his nostrils. 2 Sm 22:16
and by the **b** of his anger they are Jb 4:9
at the **b** of the breath of your nostrils. Ps 18:15
a day of trumpet **b** and battle cry Zep 1:16

BLASTS (1)
at the **b** of the other trumpets that the Rv 8:13

BLASTUS (1)
one accord, and having persuaded **B**, Acts 12:20

BLAZE (1)
to take up the censers out of the **b**. Nm 16:37

BLAZED (1)
And the anger of the LORD **b** hotly, and Nm 11:10

BLAZES (1)
in the morning it **b** like a flaming fire. Hos 7:6

BLAZING (6)
make them as a **b** oven when you Ps 21:9
The **b** flame shall not be quenched, Ezk 20:47
jealousy and in my **b** wrath I declare, Ezk 38:19
clans of Judah like a **b** pot in the midst Zec 12:6
a **b** fire and darkness and gloom and Heb 12:18
star fell from heaven, **b** like a torch, Rv 8:10

BLEACH (1)
white, as no one on earth could **b** them. Mk 9:3

BLEATING (1)
"What then is this **b** of the sheep in 1 Sm 15:14

BLEMISH (69)
Your lamb shall be without **b**, a male a Ex 12:5
bull of the herd and two rams without **b**, Ex 29:1
the herd, he shall offer a male without **b**. Lv 1:3
goats, he shall bring a male without **b**, Lv 1:10
he shall offer it without **b** before the LORD. Lv 3:1
male or female, he shall offer it without **b**. Lv 3:6
from the herd without **b** to the LORD for Lv 4:3
as his offering a goat, a male without **b**, Lv 4:23
his offering a goat, a female without **b**, Lv 4:28
he shall bring a female without **b** Lv 4:32
a ram without **b** out of the flock, Lv 5:15
priest a ram without **b** out of the flock, Lv 5:18
the LORD a ram without **b** out of the flock, Lv 6:6
ram for a burnt offering, both without **b**, Lv 9:2
and a lamb, both a year old without **b**, Lv 9:3
shall take two male lambs without **b**, Lv 14:10
and one ewe lamb a year old without **b**, Lv 14:10
who has a **b** may approach to Lv 21:17
no one who has a **b** shall draw near, Lv 21:18
priest who has a **b** shall come near to Lv 21:21
since he has a **b**, he shall not come Lv 21:21
approach the altar, because he has a **b**, Lv 21:23
for you it shall be a male without **b**, Lv 22:19
shall not offer anything that has a **b**, Lv 22:20
be perfect; there shall be no **b** in it. Lv 22:21
Since there is a **b** in them, because of Lv 22:25
a year old without **b** as a burnt offering Lv 23:12
seven lambs a year old without **b**, Lv 23:18
a year old without **b** for a burnt Nm 6:14
a year old without **b** as a sin offering, Nm 6:14
and one ram without **b** as a peace Nm 6:14
without defect, in which there is no **b**, Nm 19:2
two male lambs a year old without **b**, Nm 28:3
two male lambs a year old without **b**, Nm 28:9
male lambs a year old without **b**; Nm 28:11
a year old; see that they are without **b**; Nm 28:19
offering. See that they are without **b**. Nm 28:31
seven male lambs a year old without **b**; Nm 29:2
a year old: see that they are without **b**. Nm 29:8
a year old; they shall be without **b**; Nm 29:13
male lambs a year old without **b**, Nm 29:17
male lambs a year old without **b**, Nm 29:20
male lambs a year old without **b**, Nm 29:23
male lambs a year old without **b**, Nm 29:26
male lambs a year old without **b**, Nm 29:29
male lambs a year old without **b**, Nm 29:32
male lambs a year old without **b**, Nm 29:36
But if it has any **b**, if it is lame or blind Dt 15:21
or blind or has any serious **b** whatever, Dt 15:21
God an ox or a sheep in which is a **b**, Dt 17:1
of his head there was no **b** in him. 2 Sm 14:25
you will lift up your face without **b**; Jb 11:15
a male goat without **b** for a sin Ezk 43:22
from the herd without **b** and a ram Ezk 43:23
and a ram from the flock without **b**. Ezk 43:23
and a ram from the flock, without **b**, Ezk 43:25
take a bull from the herd without **b**, Ezk 45:18
bulls and seven rams without **b**, Ezk 45:23

be six lambs without **b** and a ram Ezk 46:4
without blemish and a ram without **b**. Ezk 46:4
offer a bull from the herd without **b**, Ezk 46:6
and a ram, which shall be without **b**. Ezk 46:6
a year old without **b** for a burnt Ezk 46:13
youths without **b**, of good appearance Dn 1:4
that she might be holy and without **b**. Eph 5:27
children of God without **b** in the midst Phil 2:15
Spirit offered himself without **b** to God, Heb 9:14
like that of a lamb without **b** or spot. 1 Pt 1:19
to be found by him without spot or **b**, 2 Pt 3:14

BLEMISHED (2)
longer his children because they are **b**; Dt 32:5
and yet sacrifices to the Lord what is **b**. Mal 1:14

BLEMISHES (2)
They are blots and **b**, reveling in their 2 Pt 2:13
These are **b** on your love feasts, as they Jude 1:12

BLENDED (3)
a sacred anointing oil **b** as by the Ex 30:25
and make an incense **b** as by the Ex 30:35
fragrant incense, **b** as by the perfumer. Ex 37:29

BLESS (130)
and I will **b** you and make your name Gn 12:2
I will **b** those who bless you, and him Gn 12:3
I will bless those who **b** you, and him Gn 12:3
I will **b** her, and moreover, I will give Gn 17:16
I will **b** her, and she shall become Gn 17:16
I will surely **b** you, and I will surely Gn 22:17
and I will be with you and will **b** you, Gn 26:3
with you and will **b** you and multiply Gn 26:24
that my soul may **b** you before I die." Gn 27:4
I may eat it and **b** you before the LORD Gn 27:7
so that he may **b** you before he dies." Gn 27:10
of my game, that your soul may **b** me." Gn 27:19
my son's game and **b** you." So he Gn 27:25
of his son's game, that you may **b** me." Gn 27:31
bitter cry and said to his father, "**B** me, Gn 27:34
B me, even me also, O my father." And Gn 27:38
God Almighty **b** you and make you Gn 28:3
"I will not let you go unless you **b** me." Gn 32:26
them to me, please, that I may **b** them." Gn 48:9
redeemed me from all evil, **b** the boys; Gn 48:16
Almighty who will **b** you with Gn 49:25
have said, and be gone, and **b** me also!" Ex 12:32
I will come to you and **b** you. Ex 20:24
and he will **b** your bread and your Ex 23:25
Thus you shall **b** the people of Israel: Nm 6:23
The LORD **b** you and keep you; Nm 6:24
the people of Israel, and I will **b** them." Nm 6:27
I know that he whom you **b** is blessed, Nm 22:6
you have done nothing but **b** them." Nm 23:11
Behold, I received a command to **b**: he Nm 23:20
them at all, and do not **b** them at all." Nm 23:25
saw that it pleased the LORD to **b** Israel, Nm 24:1
Blessed are those who **b** you, and Nm 24:9
times as many as you are and **b** you, Dt 1:11
He will love you, **b** you, and multiply Dt 7:13
He will also **b** the fruit of your womb Dt 7:13
and you shall **b** the LORD your God for Dt 8:10
to minister to him and to **b** in his name, Dt 10:8
the LORD your God may **b** you in all the Dt 14:29
for the LORD will **b** you in the land that Dt 15:4
For the LORD your God will **b** you, as he Dt 15:6
LORD your God will **b** you in all your Dt 15:10
the LORD your God will **b** you in all that Dt 15:18
LORD your God will **b** you in all your Dt 16:15
minister to him and to **b** in the name of Dt 21:5
LORD your God may **b** you in all that Dt 23:20
he may sleep in his cloak and **b** you. Dt 24:13
the LORD your God may **b** you in all the Dt 24:19
and **b** your people Israel and the ground Dt 26:15
on Mount Gerizim to **b** the people: Dt 27:12
And he will **b** you in the land that the Dt 28:8
in its season and to **b** all the work of Dt 28:12
LORD your God will **b** you in the land Dt 30:16
B, O LORD, his substance, and accept the Dt 33:11
at the first, to **b** the people of Israel. Jos 8:33
offered themselves willingly, **b** the LORD! Jgs 5:2
willingly among the people. **B** the LORD. Jgs 5:9
And they answered, "The LORD **b** you." Ru 2:4
Then Eli would **b** Elkanah and his 1 Sm 2:20
comes, since he must **b** the sacrifice; 1 Sm 9:13
David returned to **b** his household. 2 Sm 6:20
it please you to **b** the house of your 2 Sm 7:29
his health and to **b** him because he 2 Sm 8:10
that you may **b** the heritage of the 2 Sm 21:3
that you would **b** me and enlarge 1 Chr 4:10
went home to **b** his household. 1 Chr 16:43
have been pleased to **b** the house of 1 Chr 17:27
his health and to **b** him because he 1 Chr 18:10
"**B** the LORD your God." And all the 1 Chr 29:20
"Stand up and **b** the LORD your God Neh 9:5
For you **b** the righteous, O LORD; you Ps 5:12
I **b** the LORD who gives me counsel; in the Ps 16:7
in the great assembly I will **b** the LORD. Ps 26:12
save your people and **b** your heritage! Ps 28:9
May the LORD **b** his people with peace! Ps 29:11
I will **b** the LORD at all times; his praise Ps 34:1
They **b** with their mouths, but inwardly Ps 62:4
So I will **b** you as long as I live; in your Ps 63:4
B our God, O peoples; let the sound of his Ps 66:8
be gracious to us and **b** us and make his Ps 67:1
its increase; God, our God, shall **b** us. Ps 67:6
God shall **b** us; let all the ends of the Ps 67:7
"**B** God in the great congregation, the Ps 68:26
Sing to the LORD, **b** his name; tell of his Ps 96:2
praise! Give thanks to him; **b** his name! Ps 100:4
B the LORD, O my soul, and all that is Ps 103:1
all that is within me, **b** his holy name! Ps 103:1
B the LORD, O my soul, and forget not all Ps 103:2
B the LORD, O you his angels, you Ps 103:20
B the LORD, all his hosts, his ministers, Ps 103:21
B the LORD, all his works, in all places Ps 103:22
his dominion. **B** the LORD, O my soul! Ps 103:22
B the LORD, O my soul! O LORD my God, Ps 104:1
be no more! **B** the LORD, O my soul! Ps 104:35
Let them curse, but you will **b**! They Ps 109:28
LORD has remembered us; he will **b** us; Ps 115:12
bless us; he will **b** the house of Israel; Ps 115:12
of Israel; he will **b** the house of Aaron; Ps 115:12
he will **b** those who fear the LORD, both Ps 115:13
But we will **b** the LORD from this time Ps 115:18
We **b** you from the house of the LORD. Ps 118:26
The LORD **b** you from Zion! May you Ps 128:5
We **b** you in the name of the LORD!" Ps 129:8
I will abundantly **b** her provisions; I Ps 132:15
Come, **b** the LORD, all you servants of Ps 134:1
hands to the holy place and **b** the LORD! Ps 134:2
May the LORD **b** you from Zion, he who Ps 134:3
O house of Israel, **b** the LORD! O house Ps 135:19
LORD! O house of Aaron, **b** the LORD! Ps 135:19
O house of Levi, **b** the LORD! You who Ps 135:20
You who fear the LORD, **b** the LORD! Ps 135:20
and **b** your name forever and ever. Ps 145:1
Every day I will **b** you and praise your Ps 145:2
LORD, and all your saints shall **b** you! Ps 145:10
and let all flesh **b** his holy name Ps 145:21
fathers and do not **b** their mothers. Prv 30:11
that I might **b** him and multiply him. Is 51:2
in the land shall **b** himself by the God Is 65:16
then nations shall **b** themselves in him, Jer 4:2
"'The LORD **b** you, O habitation of Jer 31:23
But from this day on I will **b** you." Hg 2:19
b those who curse you, pray for those Lk 6:28
to **b** you by turning every one of you Acts 3:26
B those who persecute you; bless and Rom 12:14
you; **b** and do not curse them. Rom 12:14
When reviled, we **b**; when persecuted, 1 Cor 4:12
The cup of blessing that we **b**, is it 1 Cor 10:16
"Surely I will **b** you and multiply you." Heb 6:14
With it we **b** our Lord and Father, and Jas 3:9
contrary, **b**, for to this you were called, 1 Pt 3:9

BLESSED (306)
And God **b** them, saying, "Be fruitful Gn 1:22
And God **b** them. And God said to them, Gn 1:28
So God **b** the seventh day and made it Gn 2:3
and he **b** them and named them Man Gn 5:2
And God **b** Noah and his sons and said to Gn 9:1
He also said, "**B** be the LORD, the God of Gn 9:26
all the families of the earth shall be **b**." Gn 12:3
And he **b** him and said, "Blessed be Gn 14:19
said, "**B** be Abram by God Most High, Gn 14:19
and **b** be God Most High, who has Gn 14:20
I have **b** him and will make him Gn 17:20
nations of the earth shall be **b** in him? Gn 18:18
shall all the nations of the earth be **b**, Gn 22:18
And the LORD had **b** Abraham in all Gn 24:1
and said, "**B** be the LORD, the God of my Gn 24:27
He said, "Come in, O **b** of the LORD. Gn 24:31
The LORD has greatly **b** my master, and Gn 24:35
worshiped the LORD and **b** the LORD, Gn 24:48
And they **b** Rebekah and said to her, Gn 24:60
of Abraham, God **b** Isaac his son. Gn 25:11
all the nations of the earth shall be **b**, Gn 26:4
year a hundredfold. The LORD **b** him, Gn 26:12
peace. You are now the **b** of the LORD." Gn 26:29
his brother Esau's hands. So he **b** him. Gn 27:23
of his garments and **b** him and said, Gn 27:27
the smell of a field that the LORD has **b**! Gn 27:27
and **b** be everyone who blesses you!" Gn 27:29
all before you came, and I have **b** him? Gn 27:33
blessed him? Yes, and he shall be **b**." Gn 27:33
with which his father had **b** him, Gn 27:41
called Jacob and **b** him and directed Gn 28:1
saw that Isaac had **b** Jacob and sent Gn 28:6
and that as he **b** him he directed him, Gn 28:6
shall all the families of the earth be **b**. Gn 28:14
that the LORD has **b** me because of you. Gn 30:27
and the LORD has **b** you wherever I Gn 30:30
and his daughters and **b** them. Gn 31:55
ask my name?" And there he **b** him. Gn 32:29
came from Paddan-aram, and **b** him. Gn 35:9
he had the LORD **b** the Egyptian's house Gn 39:5
before Pharaoh, and Jacob **b** Pharaoh. Gn 47:7
And Jacob **b** Pharaoh and went out Gn 47:10
at Luz in the land of Canaan and **b** me, Gn 48:3
And he **b** Joseph and said, "The God Gn 48:15
So he **b** them that day, saying, "By you Gn 48:20
their father said to them as he **b** them, Gn 49:28
Jethro said, "**B** be the LORD, who has Ex 18:10
Therefore the LORD **b** the Sabbath day Ex 20:11
had they done it. Then Moses **b** them. Ex 39:43
his hands toward the people and **b** them, Lv 9:22
when they came out they **b** the people, Lv 9:23
for I know that he whom you bless is **b**, Nm 22:6
not curse the people, for they are **b**." Nm 22:12
bless: he has **b**, and I cannot revoke it. Nm 23:20
B are those who bless you, and cursed Nm 24:9
you have **b** them these three times. Nm 24:10
the LORD your God has **b** you in all the Dt 2:7
You shall be **b** above all peoples. There Dt 7:14
in which the LORD your God has **b** you. Dt 12:7
As the LORD your God has **b** you, you Dt 15:14
B shall you be in the city, and blessed Dt 28:3
the city, and **b** shall you be in the field. Dt 28:3
B shall be the fruit of your womb and Dt 28:4
B shall be your basket and your Dt 28:5
B shall you be when you come in, and Dt 28:6
in, and **b** shall you be when you go out. Dt 28:6
the man of God **b** the people of Israel Dt 33:1
he said, "**B** by the LORD be his land, Dt 33:13
Gad he said, "**B** be he who enlarges Gad! Dt 33:20
Asher he said, "Most **b** of sons be Asher; Dt 33:24
Then Joshua **b** him, and he gave Jos 14:13
since all along the LORD has **b** me?" Jos 17:14
So Joshua **b** them and sent them away, Jos 22:6
them away to their homes and **b** them, Jos 22:7
the people of Israel **b** God and spoke no Jos 22:33
not listen to Balaam. Indeed, he **b** you. Jos 24:10
"Most **b** of women be Jael, the wife of Jgs 5:24
Kenite, of tent-dwelling women most **b**. Jgs 5:24
young man grew, and the LORD **b** him. Jgs 13:24
mother said, "**B** be my son by the LORD." Jgs 17:2
B be the man who took notice of you." Ru 2:19
"May he be **b** by the LORD, Ru 2:20
And he said, "May you be **b** by the LORD, Ru 3:10
women said to Naomi, "**B** be the LORD, Ru 4:14
said to him, "**B** be you to the LORD. 1 Sm 15:13
said, "May you be **b** by the LORD, 1 Sm 23:21
David said to Abigail, "**B** be the LORD, 1 Sm 25:32
B be your discretion, and blessed be 1 Sm 25:33
be your discretion, and **b** be you, 1 Sm 25:33
"**B** be the LORD who has avenged the 1 Sm 25:39
Then Saul said to David, "**B** be you, 1 Sm 26:25
to them, "May you be **b** by the LORD, 2 Sm 2:5
and the LORD **b** Obed-edom and all his 2 Sm 6:11
"The LORD has **b** the household of 2 Sm 6:12
he **b** the people in the name of the 2 Sm 6:18
house of your servant be **b** forever." 2 Sm 7:29
and paid homage and **b** the king. 2 Sm 14:22
and said, "**B** be the LORD your God, 2 Sm 18:28
the king kissed Barzillai and **b** him, 2 Sm 19:39
"The LORD lives, and **b** be my rock, 2 Sm 22:47
And the king also said, '**B** be the LORD, 1 Kgs 1:48
But King Solomon shall be **b**, and the 1 Kgs 2:45
and said, "**B** be the LORD this day, 1 Kgs 5:7
turned around and **b** all the 1 Kgs 8:14
And he said, "**B** be the LORD, the God 1 Kgs 8:15
And he stood and **b** all the assembly 1 Kgs 8:55
"**B** be the LORD who has given rest to 1 Kgs 8:56
and they **b** the king and went to their 1 Kgs 8:66
B be the LORD your God, who has 1 Kgs 10:9
And the LORD **b** the household of 1 Chr 13:14
he **b** the people in the name of the 1 Chr 16:2
B be the LORD, the God of Israel, 1 Chr 16:36
for it is you, O LORD, who have **b**, 1 Chr 17:27
have blessed, and it is **b** forever." 1 Chr 17:27
Peullethai the eighth, for God **b** him. 1 Chr 26:5
Therefore David **b** the LORD in the 1 Chr 29:10
"**B** are you, O LORD, the God of Israel 1 Chr 29:10
And all the assembly **b** the LORD, 1 Chr 29:20
also said, "**B** be the LORD God of Israel, 2 Chr 2:12
turned around and **b** all the assembly 2 Chr 6:3
And he said, "**B** be the LORD, the God of 2 Chr 6:4
B be the LORD your God, who has 2 Chr 9:8
Beracah, for there they **b** the LORD. 2 Chr 20:26
the Levites arose and **b** the people, 2 Chr 30:27
they **b** the LORD and his people Israel. 2 Chr 31:8
left, for the LORD has **b** his people, 2 Chr 31:10
B be the LORD, the God of our fathers, Ezr 7:27
And Ezra **b** the LORD, the great God, and Neh 8:6
B be your glorious name, which is Neh 9:5
And the people **b** all the men who Neh 11:2

You have **b** the work of his hands, and Jb 1:10
taken away; **b** be the name of the LORD." Jb 1:21
"Behold, **b** is the one whom God reproves; Jb 5:17
When the ear heard, it called me **b**, and Jb 29:11
if his body has not **b** me, and if he was Jb 31:20
And the LORD **b** the latter days of Job Jb 42:12
B is the man who walks not in the Ps 1:1
B are all who take refuge in him. Ps 2:12
The LORD lives, and **b** be my rock, and Ps 18:46
For you make him most **b** forever; you Ps 21:6
B be the LORD! for he has heard the voice Ps 28:6
B be the LORD, for he has wondrously Ps 31:21
B is the one whose transgression is Ps 32:1
B is the man against whom the LORD Ps 32:2
B is the nation whose God is the LORD, Ps 33:12
B is the man who takes refuge in him! Ps 34:8
for those **b** by the LORD shall inherit the Ps 37:22
B is the man who makes the LORD his Ps 40:4
B is the one who considers the poor! In Ps 41:1
him alive; he is called **b** in the land; Ps 41:2
B be the LORD, the God of Israel, from Ps 41:13
lips; therefore God has **b** you forever. Ps 45:2
while he lives, he counts himself **b**, Ps 49:18
B is the one you choose and bring near, Ps 65:4
B be God, because he has not rejected Ps 66:20
B be the Lord, who daily bears us up; Ps 68:19
and strength to his people. **B** be God! Ps 68:35
May people be **b** in him, all nations call Ps 72:17
blessed in him, all nations call him **b**! Ps 72:17
B be the LORD, the God of Israel, who Ps 72:18
B be his glorious name forever; may the Ps 72:19
B are those who dwell in your house, ever Ps 84:4
B are those whose strength is in you, in Ps 84:5
of hosts, **b** is the one who trusts in you! Ps 84:12
B are the people who know the festal Ps 89:15
B be the LORD forever! Amen and Amen. Ps 89:52
B is the man whom you discipline, O Ps 94:12
B are they who observe justice, who do Ps 106:3
B be the LORD, the God of Israel, from Ps 106:48
B is the man who fears the LORD, who Ps 112:1
the generation of the upright will be **b**. Ps 112:2
B be the name of the LORD from this Ps 113:2
May you be **b** by the LORD, who made Ps 115:15
B is he who comes in the name of the Ps 118:26
B are those whose way is blameless, Ps 119:1
B are those who keep his testimonies, Ps 119:2
B are you, O LORD; teach me your Ps 119:12
B be the LORD, who has not given us as Ps 124:6
B is the man who fills his quiver with Ps 127:5
B is everyone who fears the LORD, who Ps 128:1
you shall be **b**, and it shall be well with Ps 128:2
shall the man be **b** who fears the LORD. Ps 128:4
B be the LORD from Zion, he who Ps 135:21
b shall he be who repays you with what Ps 137:8
B shall he be who takes your little ones Ps 137:9
B be the LORD, my rock, who trains my Ps 144:1
B are the people to whom such Ps 144:15
B are the people whose God is the LORD! Ps 144:15
B is he whose help is the God of Jacob, Ps 146:5
B is the one who finds wisdom, and the Prv 3:13
those who hold her fast are called **b**. Prv 3:18
Let your fountain be **b**, and rejoice in Prv 5:18
to me: **b** are those who keep my ways. Prv 8:32
B is the one who listens to me, watching Prv 8:34
but **b** is he who is generous to the Prv 14:21
and **b** is he who trusts in the LORD. Prv 16:20
in his integrity—**b** are his children Prv 20:7
the beginning will not be **b** in the end. Prv 20:21
Whoever has a bountiful eye will be **b**, Prv 22:9
B is the one who fears the LORD always, Prv 28:14
but **b** is he who keeps the law. Prv 29:18
Her children rise up and call her **b**; Prv 31:28
young women saw her and called her **b**; Sg 6:9
whom the LORD of hosts has **b**, saying, Is 19:25
blessed, saying, "**B** be Egypt my people, Is 19:25
justice; **b** are all those who wait for him. Is 30:18
B is the man who does this, and the son of Is 56:2
that they are an offspring the LORD has **b**. Is 61:9
be the offspring of the **b** of the LORD, Is 65:23
"**B** is the man who trusts in the LORD, Jer 17:7
my mother bore me, let it not be **b**! Jer 20:14
"**B** be the glory of the LORD from its Ezk 3:12
night. Then Daniel **b** the God of heaven. Dn 2:19
"**B** be the name of God forever and ever, Dn 2:20
and said, "**B** be the God of Shadrach, Dn 3:28
returned to me, and I **b** the Most High, Dn 4:34
B is he who waits and arrives at the Dn 12:12
those who sell them say, '**B** be the LORD, Zec 11:5
Then all nations will call you **b**, for Mal 3:12
And now we call the arrogant **b**. Mal 3:15
"**B** are the poor in spirit, for theirs is the Mt 5:3
"**B** are those who mourn, for they shall be Mt 5:4
"**B** are the meek, for they shall inherit the Mt 5:5
"**B** are those who hunger and thirst for Mt 5:6
"**B** are the merciful, for they shall receive Mt 5:7
"**B** are the pure in heart, for they shall see Mt 5:8
"**B** are the peacemakers, for they shall be Mt 5:9
"**B** are those who are persecuted for Mt 5:10
"**B** are you when others revile you and Mt 5:11
And **b** is the one who is not offended by Mt 11:6
But **b** are your eyes, for they see, and Mt 13:16
And Jesus answered him, "**B** are you, Mt 16:17
B is he who comes in the name of the Mt 21:9
'**B** is he who comes in the name of the Mt 23:39
B is that servant whom his master will Mt 24:46
'Come, you who are **b** by my Father, Mt 25:34
And having **b** them, he said that these Mk 8:7
he took them in his arms and **b** them, Mk 10:16
B is he who comes in the name of the Mk 11:9
B is the coming kingdom of our father Mk 11:10
"Are you the Christ, the Son of the **B**?" Mk 14:61
a loud cry, "**B** are you among women, Lk 1:42
women, and **b** is the fruit of your womb! Lk 1:42
And **b** is she who believed that there Lk 1:45
now on all generations will call me **b**; Lk 1:48
"**B** be the Lord God of Israel, for he has Lk 1:68
him up in his arms and **b** God and said, Lk 2:28
And Simeon **b** them and said to Mary Lk 2:34
"**B** are you who are poor, for yours is the Lk 6:20
"**B** are you who are hungry now, for you Lk 6:21
"**B** are you who weep now, for you shall Lk 6:21
"**B** are you when people hate you and Lk 6:22
And **b** is the one who is not offended by Lk 7:23
"**B** are the eyes that see what you see! Lk 10:23
to him, "**B** is the womb that bore you, Lk 11:27
"**B** rather are those who hear the word Lk 11:28
B are those servants whom the master Lk 12:37
finds them awake, **b** are those servants! Lk 12:38
B is that servant whom his master will Lk 12:43
'**B** is he who comes in the name of the Lk 13:35
and you will be **b**, because they cannot Lk 14:14
"**B** is everyone who will eat bread in the Lk 14:15
"**B** is the King who comes in the name Lk 19:38
'**B** are the barren and the wombs that Lk 23:29
took the bread and **b** and broke it and Lk 24:30
and lifting up his hands he **b** them. Lk 24:50
While he **b** them, he parted from them Lk 24:51
B is he who comes in the name of the Jn 12:13
these things, **b** are you if you do them. Jn 13:17
B are those who have not seen and yet Jn 20:29
shall all the families of the earth be **b**.' Acts 3:25
'It is more **b** to give than to receive.'" Acts 20:35
than the Creator, who is **b** forever! Rom 1:25
"**B** are those whose lawless deeds are Rom 4:7
b is the man against whom the Lord Rom 4:8
Christ who is God over all, **b** forever. Rom 9:5
B is the one who has no reason to Rom 14:22
B be the God and Father of our Lord 2 Cor 1:3
the Lord Jesus, he who is **b** forever, 2 Cor 11:31
"In you shall all the nations be **b**." Gal 3:8
are of faith are **b** along with Abraham, Gal 3:9
B be the God and Father of our Lord Eph 1:3
who has **b** us in Christ with every Eph 1:3
with which he has **b** us in the Beloved. Eph 1:6
gospel of the **b** God with which 1 Tm 1:11
—he who is the **b** and only Sovereign, 1 Tm 6:15
waiting for our **b** hope, the appearing of Ti 2:13
the slaughter of the kings and **b** him, Heb 7:1
from Abraham and **b** him who had Heb 7:6
that the inferior is **b** by the superior. Heb 7:7
dying, **b** each of the sons of Joseph, Heb 11:21
B is the man who remains steadfast Jas 1:12
doer who acts, he will be **b** in his doing. Jas 1:25
we consider those **b** who remained Jas 5:11
B be the God and Father of our Lord 1 Pt 1:3
for righteousness' sake, you will be **b**. 1 Pt 3:14
for the name of Christ, you are **b**, 1 Pt 4:14
B is the one who reads aloud the words of Rv 1:3
this prophecy, and **b** are those who hear, Rv 1:3
B are the dead who die in the Lord from Rv 14:13
Lord from now on." "**B** indeed," says the Rv 14:13
B is the one who stays awake, keeping Rv 16:15
B are those who are invited to the Rv 19:9
B and holy is the one who shares in the Rv 20:6
B is the one who keeps the words of the Rv 22:7
B are those who wash their robes, so Rv 22:14

BLESSES (9)
and blessed be everyone who **b** you!" Gn 27:29
tithe, when the LORD your God **b** you, Dt 14:24
shall give as the LORD your God **b** you. Dt 16:10
sworn covenant, **b** himself in his heart, Dt 29:19
gates; he **b** your children within you. Ps 147:13
but he **b** the dwelling of the righteous. Prv 3:33
Whoever **b** his neighbor with a loud Prv 27:14
So that he who **b** himself in the land Is 65:16
of frankincense, like one who **b** an idol. Is 66:3

BLESSING (80)
your name great, so that you will be a **b**. Gn 12:2
a curse upon myself and not a **b**." Gn 27:12
As soon as Isaac had finished **b** Jacob, Gn 27:30
and he has taken away your **b**." Gn 27:35
has taken away my **b**." Then he said, Gn 27:36
"Have you not reserved a **b** for me?" Gn 27:36
said to his father, "Have you but one **b**, Gn 27:38
Jacob because of the **b** with which his Gn 27:41
May he give the **b** of Abraham to you Gn 28:4
Please accept my **b** that is brought to Gn 33:11
the **b** of the LORD was on all that he had, Gn 39:5
b each with the blessing suitable to Gn 49:28
each with the **b** suitable to him. Gn 49:28
he might bestow a **b** upon you this Ex 32:29
I will command my **b** on you in the Lv 25:21
before you today a **b** and a curse: Dt 11:26
the **b**, if you obey the commandments Dt 11:27
you shall set the **b** on Mount Gerizim Dt 11:29
according to the **b** of the LORD your God Dt 12:15
according to the **b** of the LORD your God Dt 16:17
God turned the curse into a **b** for you, Dt 23:5
LORD will command the **b** on you in Dt 28:8
come upon you, the **b** and the curse, Dt 30:1
before you life and death, **b** and curse. Dt 30:19
This is the **b** with which Moses the man Dt 33:1
with favor, and full of the **b** of the LORD, Dt 33:23
the words of the law, the **b** and the curse, Jos 8:34
She said to him, "Give me a **b**. Since Jos 15:19
She said to him, "Give me a **b**. Since you Jgs 1:15
and with your **b** shall the house of 2 Sm 7:29
he would not go but gave him his **b**. 2 Sm 13:25
which is exalted above all **b** and praise. Neh 9:5
—yet our God turned the curse into a **b**. Neh 13:2
The **b** of him who was about to perish Jb 29:13
to the LORD; your **b** be on your people! Ps 3:8
He will receive **b** from the LORD and Ps 24:5
and his children become a **b**. Ps 37:26
it with showers, and **b** its growth. Ps 65:10
By his **b** they multiply greatly, and he Ps 107:38
He did not delight in **b**; may it be far Ps 109:17
This **b** has fallen to me, that I have Ps 119:56
by say, "The **b** of the LORD be upon you! Ps 129:8
there the LORD has commanded the **b**, Ps 133:3
The memory of the righteous is a **b**, but Prv 10:7
The **b** of the LORD makes rich, and he Prv 10:22
By the **b** of the upright a city is exalted, Prv 11:11
Whoever brings **b** will be enriched, Prv 11:25
but a **b** is on the head of him who sells Prv 11:26
and a good **b** will come upon them. Prv 24:25
Assyria, a **b** in the midst of the earth, Is 19:24
offspring, and my **b** on your descendants. Is 44:3
'Do not destroy it, for there is a **b** in it,' Is 65:8
and the places all around my hill a **b**, Ezk 34:26
season; they shall be showers of **b**. Ezk 34:26
that a **b** may rest on your house. Ezk 44:30
and relent, and leave a **b** behind him, Jl 2:14
so will I save you, and you shall be a **b**. Zec 8:13
pour down for you a **b** until there is no Mal 3:10
he looked up to heaven and said a **b**. Mt 14:19
and after **b** it broke it and gave it to the Mt 26:26
heaven and said a **b** and broke the Mk 6:41
and after **b** it broke it and gave it to Mk 14:22
his tongue loosed, and he spoke, **b** God. Lk 1:64
up to heaven and said a **b** over them. Lk 9:16
were continually in the temple **b** God. Lk 24:53
David also speaks of the **b** of the one to Rom 4:6
Is this **b** then only for the circumcised, Rom 4:9
in the fullness of the **b** of Christ. Rom 15:29
The cup of **b** that we bless, is it not a 1 Cor 10:16
behalf for the **b** granted us through 2 Cor 1:11
Christ Jesus the **b** of Abraham might Gal 3:14
then has become of the **b** you felt? Gal 4:15
with every spiritual **b** in the heavenly Eph 1:3
it is cultivated, receives a **b** from God. Heb 6:7
when he desired to inherit the **b**, Heb 12:17
the same mouth come **b** and cursing. Jas 3:10
were called, that you may obtain a **b**. 1 Pt 3:9
and might and honor and glory and **b**!" Rv 5:12
to the Lamb be **b** and honor and glory Rv 5:13
B and glory and wisdom and Rv 7:12

BLESSINGS (19)
"By you Israel will pronounce **b**, Gn 48:20
will bless you with **b** of heaven above, Gn 49:25
b of the deep that crouches beneath, Gn 49:25
b of the breasts and of the womb. Gn 49:25
The **b** of your father are mighty Gn 49:26
mighty beyond the **b** of my parents, Gn 49:26
And all these **b** shall come upon you and Dt 28:2
him and pronounce **b** in his name 1 Chr 23:13
For you meet him with rich **b**; you set a Ps 21:3
and **b** invoked for him all the day! Ps 72:15
are the people to whom such **b** fall! Ps 144:15
B are on the head of the righteous, but Prv 10:6
A faithful man will abound with **b**, Prv 28:20
curse upon you and I will curse your **b**. Mal 2:2
you the holy and sure **b** of David.' Acts 13:34
come to share in their spiritual **b**, Rom 15:27

to be of service to them in material **b**. Rom 15:27
that I may share with them in its **b**. 1 Cor 9:23
Isaac invoked future **b** on Jacob and Heb 11:20

BLEW (26)
You **b** with your wind; the sea covered Ex 15:10
ark, while the trumpets **b** continually. Jos 6:9
on, and they **b** the trumpets continually. Jos 6:13
LORD, while the trumpets **b** continually. Jos 6:13
And they **b** the trumpets and smashed Jgs 7:19
the three companies **b** the trumpets and Jgs 7:20
When they **b** the 300 trumpets, the LORD Jgs 7:22
And Saul **b** the trumpet throughout 1 Sm 13:3
So Joab **b** the trumpet, and all the 2 Sm 2:28
Then Joab **b** the trumpet, and the 2 Sm 18:16
And he **b** the trumpet and said, "We 2 Sm 20:1
it out to Joab. So he **b** the trumpet, 2 Sm 20:22
Solomon. Then they **b** the trumpet, 1 Kgs 1:39
and they **b** the trumpet and 2 Kgs 9:13
LORD, and the priests **b** the trumpets. 2 Chr 13:14
when you brought it home, I **b** it away. Hg 1:9
and the winds **b** and beat on that house, Mt 7:25
and the winds **b** and beat against that Mt 7:27
Now when the south wind **b** gently, Acts 27:13
The first angel **b** his trumpet, and there Rv 8:7
The second angel **b** his trumpet, and Rv 8:8
The third angel **b** his trumpet, and a Rv 8:10
The fourth angel **b** his trumpet, and a Rv 8:12
And the fifth angel **b** his trumpet, and I Rv 9:1
Then the sixth angel **b** his trumpet, and Rv 9:13
Then the seventh angel **b** his trumpet, Rv 11:15

BLIGHT (5)
drought and with **b** and with mildew. Dt 28:22
there is pestilence or **b** or mildew or 1 Kgs 8:37
there is pestilence or **b** or mildew or 2 Chr 6:28
"I struck you with **b** and mildew; your Am 4:9
of your toil with **b** and with mildew and Hg 2:17

BLIGHTED (5)
seven ears, thin and **b** by the east wind. Gn 41:6
withered, thin, and **b** by the east wind, Gn 41:23
the seven empty ears **b** by the east wind Gn 41:27
the housetops, **b** before it is grown. 2 Kgs 19:26
on the housetops, **b** before it is grown. Is 37:27

BLIND (80)
him mute, or deaf, or seeing, or **b**? Ex 4:11
or put a stumbling block before the **b**, Lv 19:14
shall draw near, a man **b** or lame, Lv 21:18
Animals **b** or disabled or mutilated or Lv 22:22
if it is lame or **b** or has any serious Dt 15:21
anyone who misleads a **b** man on the Dt 27:18
at noonday, as the **b** grope in darkness, Dt 28:29
I taken a bribe to **b** my eyes with it? 1 Sm 12:3
but the **b** and the lame will ward you 2 Sm 5:6
shaft to attack 'the lame and the **b**,' 2 Sm 5:8
"The **b** and the lame shall not come 2 Sm 5:8
I was eyes to the **b** and feet to the lame. Jb 29:15
the LORD opens the eyes of the **b**. The Ps 146:8
and their ears heavy, and **b** their eyes; Is 6:10
be astonished; **b** yourselves and be blind! Is 29:9
be astonished; blind yourselves and be **b**! Is 29:9
and darkness the eyes of the **b** shall see. Is 29:18
Then the eyes of the **b** shall be opened, Is 35:5
to open the eyes that are **b**, to bring out Is 42:7
And I will lead the **b** in a way that they Is 42:16
Hear, you deaf, and look, you **b**, that you Is 42:18
Who is **b** but my servant, or deaf as my Is 42:19
Who is **b** as my dedicated one, or blind Is 42:19
one, or **b** as the servant of the LORD? Is 42:19
Bring out the people who are **b**, yet have Is 43:8
His watchmen are **b**; they are all Is 56:10
We grope for the wall like the **b**; we Is 59:10
earth, among them the **b** and the lame, Jer 31:8
They wandered, **b**, through the streets; Lam 4:14
so that they shall walk like the **b**, Zep 1:17
When you offer **b** animals in sacrifice, Mal 1:8
on from there, two **b** men followed him, Mt 9:27
the house, the **b** men came to him, Mt 9:28
the **b** receive their sight and the lame Mt 11:5
man who was **b** and mute was Mt 12:22
Let them alone; they are **b** guides. And Mt 15:14
guides. And if the **b** lead the blind, Mt 15:14
And if the blind lead the **b**, both will Mt 15:14
bringing with them the lame, the **b**, Mt 15:30
the lame walking, and the **b** seeing. Mt 15:31
there were two **b** men sitting by the Mt 20:30
And the **b** and the lame came to him in Mt 21:14
"Woe to you, **b** guides, who say, 'If Mt 23:16
You **b** fools! For which is greater, the Mt 23:17
You **b** men! For which is greater, the Mt 23:19
You **b** guides, straining out a gnat and Mt 23:24
You **b** Pharisee! First clean the inside Mt 23:26
brought to him a **b** man and begged Mk 8:22
And he took the **b** man by the hand Mk 8:23
a great crowd, Bartimaeus, a **b** beggar, Mk 10:46
him." And they called the **b** man, Mk 10:49
for you?" And the **b** man said to him, Mk 10:51
captives and recovering of sight to the **b**, Lk 4:18
"Can a **b** man lead a blind man? Lk 6:39
"Can a blind man lead a **b** man? Lk 6:39
on many who were **b** he bestowed sight. Lk 7:21
the **b** receive their sight, the lame walk, Lk 7:22
the poor, the crippled, the lame, the **b**, Lk 14:13
the poor and crippled and **b** and lame.' Lk 14:21
a **b** man was sitting by the roadside Lk 18:35
In these lay a multitude of invalids—**b**, Jn 5:3
he passed by, he saw a man **b** from birth. Jn 9:1
man or his parents, that he was born **b**?" Jn 9:2
the man who had formerly been **b**. Jn 9:13
So they said again to the **b** man, "What Jn 9:17
that he had been **b** and had received his Jn 9:18
this your son, who you say was born **b**? Jn 9:19
this is our son and that he was born **b**. Jn 9:20
man who had been **b** and said to him, Jn 9:24
thing I do know, that though I was **b**, Jn 9:25
anyone opened the eyes of a man born **b**. Jn 9:32
see, and those who see may become **b**." Jn 9:39
things, and said to him, "Are we also **b**?" Jn 9:40
Jesus said to them, "If you were **b**, you Jn 9:41
Can a demon open the eyes of the **b**?" Jn 10:21
the eyes of the **b** man also have kept Jn 11:37
and you will be **b** and unable to see Acts 13:11
that you yourself are a guide to the **b**, Rom 2:19
qualities is so nearsighted that he is **b**, 2 Pt 1:9
wretched, pitiable, poor, **b**, and naked. Rv 3:17

BLINDED (4)
withered, his right eye utterly **b**!" Zec 11:17
"He has **b** their eyes and hardened their Jn 12:40
of this world has **b** the minds of the 2 Cor 4:4
because the darkness has **b** his eyes. 1 Jn 2:11

BLINDFOLDED (1)
They also **b** him and kept asking him, Lk 22:64

BLINDNESS (5)
And they struck with **b** the men who Gn 19:11
with madness and **b** and confusion of Dt 28:28
this people with **b**." So he struck 2 Kgs 6:18
struck them with **b** in accordance 2 Kgs 6:18
strike every horse of the peoples with **b**. Zec 12:4

BLINDS (2)
for a bribe **b** the clear-sighted and Ex 23:8
for a bribe **b** the eyes of the wise and Dt 16:19

BLOCK (14)
or put a stumbling **b** before the blind, Lv 19:14
Shall I fall down before a **b** of wood?" Is 44:19
and I lay a stumbling **b** before him, Ezk 3:20
it was the stumbling **b** of their iniquity. Ezk 7:19
set the stumbling **b** of their iniquity Ezk 14:3
and sets the stumbling **b** of his iniquity Ezk 14:4
putting the stumbling **b** of his iniquity Ezk 14:7
east of the sea. It will **b** the travelers, Ezk 39:11
became a stumbling **b** of iniquity to Ezk 44:12
a stumbling **b** and a retribution for Rom 11:9
to put a stumbling **b** or hindrance in Rom 14:13
a stumbling **b** to Jews and folly to 1 Cor 1:23
become a stumbling **b** to the weak. 1 Cor 8:9
to put a stumbling **b** before the sons of Rv 2:14

BLOCKED (2)
or his body is **b** up by his discharge, Lv 15:3
he has **b** my ways with blocks of Lam 3:9

BLOCKS (2)
this people stumbling **b** against which Jer 6:21
has blocked my ways with **b** of stones; Lam 3:9

BLOOD (425)
voice of your brother's **b** is crying to me Gn 4:10
receive your brother's **b** from your Gn 4:11
not eat flesh with its life, that is, its **b**. Gn 9:4
"Whoever sheds the **b** of man, by man Gn 9:6
of man, by man shall his **b** be shed, Gn 9:6
And Reuben said to them, "Shed no **b**; Gn 37:22
we kill our brother and conceal his **b**? Gn 37:26
a goat and dipped the robe in the **b**. Gn 37:31
there comes a reckoning for his **b**." Gn 42:22
wine and his vesture in the **b** of grapes. Gn 49:11
the Nile will become **b** on the dry Ex 4:9
you are a bridegroom of **b** to me!" Ex 4:25
"A bridegroom of **b**," because of the Ex 4:26
is in the Nile, and it shall turn into **b**. Ex 7:17
of water, so that they may become **b**, Ex 7:19
and there shall be **b** throughout all the Ex 7:19
all the water in the Nile turned into **b**. Ex 7:20
There was **b** throughout all the land of Ex 7:21
shall take some of the **b** and put it on the Ex 12:7
The **b** shall be a sign for you, on the Ex 12:13
And when I see the **b**, I will pass over Ex 12:13
and dip it in the **b** that is in the basin, Ex 12:22
two doorposts with the **b** that is in the Ex 12:22
and when he sees the **b** on the lintel and Ex 12:23
shall not offer the **b** of my sacrifice Ex 23:18
Moses took half of the **b** and put it in Ex 24:6
and half of the **b** he threw against the Ex 24:6
And Moses took the **b** and threw it on Ex 24:8
"Behold the **b** of the covenant that the Ex 24:8
shall take part of the **b** of the bull and Ex 29:12
and the rest of the **b** you shall pour out Ex 29:12
and shall take its **b** and throw it Ex 29:16
and take part of its **b** and put it on the Ex 29:20
the rest of the **b** against the sides of Ex 29:20
shall take part of the **b** that is on the Ex 29:21
With the **b** of the sin offering of Ex 30:10
shall not offer the **b** of my sacrifice Ex 34:25
priests shall bring the **b** and throw the Lv 1:5
blood and throw the **b** against the sides of Lv 1:5
priests shall throw its **b** against the sides Lv 1:11
Its **b** shall be drained out on the side of Lv 1:15
priests shall throw the **b** against the sides Lv 3:2
sons shall throw its **b** against the sides of Lv 3:8
Aaron shall throw its **b** against the sides Lv 3:13
places, that you eat neither fat nor **b**." Lv 3:17
shall take some of the **b** of the bull and Lv 4:5
dip his finger in the **b** and sprinkle part of Lv 4:6
sprinkle part of the **b** seven times before Lv 4:6
shall put some of the **b** on the horns of the Lv 4:7
and all the rest of the **b** of the bull he shall Lv 4:7
shall bring some of the **b** of the bull into Lv 4:16
his finger in the **b** and sprinkle it seven Lv 4:17
shall put some of the **b** on the horns of Lv 4:18
and the rest of the **b** he shall pour out at Lv 4:18
take some of the **b** of the sin offering Lv 4:25
pour out the rest of its **b** at the base of the Lv 4:25
take some of its **b** with his finger and Lv 4:30
out all the rest of its **b** at the base of the Lv 4:30
take some of the **b** of the sin offering Lv 4:34
out all the rest of its **b** at the base of the Lv 4:34
sprinkle some of the **b** of the sin offering Lv 5:9
while the rest of the **b** shall be drained out Lv 5:9
and when any of its **b** is splashed on a Lv 6:27
eaten from which any **b** is brought into Lv 6:30
and its **b** shall be thrown against the sides Lv 7:2
priest who throws the **b** of the peace Lv 7:14
Moreover, you shall eat no **b** whatever, Lv 7:26
Whoever eats any **b**, that person shall be Lv 7:27
of Aaron offers the **b** of the peace Lv 7:33
And he killed it, and Moses took the **b**, Lv 8:15
altar and poured out the **b** at the base of Lv 8:15
and Moses threw the **b** against the sides Lv 8:19
Moses took some of its **b** and put it on Lv 8:23
Moses put some of the **b** on the lobes of Lv 8:24
And Moses threw the **b** against the sides Lv 8:24
oil and of the **b** that was on the Lv 8:30
the sons of Aaron presented the **b** to him, Lv 9:9
dipped his finger in the **b** and put it on the Lv 9:9
altar and poured out the **b** at the base of Lv 9:9
and Aaron's sons handed him the **b**, Lv 9:12
And Aaron's sons handed him the **b**, Lv 9:18
its **b** was not brought into the inner Lv 10:18
days in the **b** of her purifying. Lv 12:4
shall continue in the **b** of her purifying Lv 12:5
she shall be clean from the flow of her **b**. Lv 12:7
the live bird in the **b** of the bird that was Lv 14:6
take some of the **b** of the guilt offering, Lv 14:14
foot, on top of the **b** of the guilt offering. Lv 14:17
take some of the **b** of the guilt offering Lv 14:25
the place where the **b** of the guilt Lv 14:28
and dip them in the **b** of the bird that Lv 14:51
the house with the **b** of the bird and Lv 14:52
and the discharge in her body is **b**, Lv 15:19
has a discharge of **b** for many days, Lv 15:25
shall take some of the **b** of the bull and Lv 16:14
sprinkle some of the **b** with his finger Lv 16:14
people and bring its **b** inside the veil Lv 16:15
veil and do with its **b** as he did with the Lv 16:15
blood as he did with the **b** of the bull, Lv 16:15
shall take some of the **b** of the bull and Lv 16:18
the bull and some of the **b** of the goat, Lv 16:18
sprinkle some of the **b** on it with his Lv 16:19
whose **b** was brought in to make Lv 16:27
He has shed **b**, and that man shall be cut Lv 17:4
priest shall throw the **b** on the altar of Lv 17:6
who sojourn among them eats any **b**, Lv 17:10
that person who eats **b** and will cut Lv 17:10
For the life of the flesh is in the **b**, and I Lv 17:11
for it is the **b** that makes atonement by Lv 17:11
No person among you shall eat **b**, Lv 17:12
who sojourns among you eat **b**. Lv 17:12
shall pour out its **b** and cover it with Lv 17:13
For the life of every creature is its **b**: its Lv 17:14
creature is its blood: its **b** is its life. Lv 17:14
You shall not eat the **b** of any creature, Lv 17:14
for the life of every creature is its **b**. Lv 17:14
shall not eat any flesh with the **b** in it. Lv 19:26
father or his mother; his **b** is upon him. Lv 20:9
be put to death; their **b** is upon them. Lv 20:11

perversion; their **b** is upon them. Lv 20:12
be put to death; their **b** is upon them. Lv 20:13
be put to death; their **b** is upon them. Lv 20:16
has uncovered the fountain of her **b**. Lv 20:18
stones; their **b** shall be upon them." Lv 20:27
You shall sprinkle their **b** on the altar Nm 18:17
shall take some of its **b** with his finger, Nm 19:4
sprinkle some of its **b** toward the front Nm 19:4
Its skin, its flesh, and its **b**, with its Nm 19:5
the prey and drunk the **b** of the slain." Nm 23:24
The avenger of **b** shall himself put the Nm 35:19
The avenger of **b** shall put the Nm 35:21
the manslayer and the avenger of **b**, Nm 35:24
from the hand of the avenger of **b**, Nm 35:25
the avenger of **b** finds him outside Nm 35:27
the avenger of **b** kills the manslayer, Nm 35:27
manslayer, he shall not be guilty of **b**. Nm 35:27
you live, for **b** pollutes the land, Nm 35:33
for the land for the **b** that is shed in it, Nm 35:33
except by the **b** of the one who shed it. Nm 35:33
Only you shall not eat the **b**; you shall Dt 12:16
Only be sure that you do not eat the **b**, Dt 12:23
do not eat the blood, for the **b** is the life, Dt 12:23
burnt offerings, the flesh and the **b**, Dt 12:27
The **b** of your sacrifices shall be poured Dt 12:27
Only you shall not eat its **b**; you shall Dt 15:23
lest the avenger of **b** in hot anger pursue Dt 19:6
lest innocent **b** be shed in your land Dt 19:10
and hand him over to the avenger of **b**, Dt 19:12
the guilt of innocent **b** from Israel, Dt 19:13
testify, 'Our hands did not shed this **b**, Dt 21:7
set the guilt of innocent **b** in the midst of Dt 21:8
Israel, so that their **b** guilt be atoned for.' Dt 21:8
the guilt of innocent **b** from your midst, Dt 21:9
not bring the guilt of **b** upon your house, Dt 22:8
who takes a bribe to shed innocent **b**.' Dt 27:25
wine made from the **b** of the grape. Dt 32:14
I will make my arrows drunk with **b**, Dt 32:42
flesh—with the **b** of the slain and Dt 32:42
for he avenges the **b** of his children and Dt 32:43
street, his **b** shall be on his own head, Jos 2:19
in the house, his **b** shall be on our head. Jos 2:19
for you a refuge from the avenger of **b**. Jos 20:3
And if the avenger of **b** pursues him, Jos 20:5
not die by the hand of the avenger of **b**, Jos 20:9
and their **b** be laid on Abimelech their Jgs 9:24
And the people ate them with the **b**. 1 Sm 14:32
by eating with the **b**." And he said, 1 Sm 14:33
by eating with the **b**.'" So every one 1 Sm 14:34
sin against innocent **b** by killing 1 Sm 19:5
for having shed **b** without cause or 1 Sm 25:31
let not my **b** fall to the earth away 1 Sm 26:20
said to him, "Your **b** be on your head, 2 Sm 1:16
"From the **b** of the slain, from the fat 2 Sm 1:22
died, for the **b** of Asahel his brother. 2 Sm 3:27
the LORD for the **b** of Abner the son 2 Sm 3:28
not now require his **b** at your hand 2 Sm 4:11
that the avenger of **b** kill no more, 2 Sm 14:11
"Get out, get out, you man of **b**, 2 Sm 16:7
on you all the **b** of the house of 2 Sm 16:8
evil is on you, for you are a man of **b**." 2 Sm 16:8
wallowing in his **b** in the highway. 2 Sm 20:12
Shall I drink the **b** of the men who 2 Sm 23:17
time of peace for **b** that had been shed 1 Kgs 2:5
and putting the **b** of war on the belt 1 Kgs 2:5
his gray head down with **b** to Sheol." 1 Kgs 2:9
the guilt for the **b** that Joab shed 1 Kgs 2:31
So shall their **b** come back on the 1 Kgs 2:33
Your **b** shall be on your own head." 1 Kgs 2:37
until the **b** gushed out upon them. 1 Kgs 18:28
dogs licked up the **b** of Naboth shall 1 Kgs 21:19
shall dogs lick your own **b**."'" 1 Kgs 21:19
And the **b** of the wound flowed into 1 Kgs 22:35
and the dogs licked up his **b**, 1 Kgs 22:38
the water opposite them as red as **b**. 2 Kgs 3:22
And they said, "This is **b**; the kings 2 Kgs 3:23
avenge on Jezebel the **b** of my servants 2 Kgs 9:7
and the **b** of all the servants of the 2 Kgs 9:7
I saw yesterday the **b** of Naboth and 2 Kgs 9:26
of Naboth and the **b** of his sons— 2 Kgs 9:26
And some of her **b** spattered on the 2 Kgs 9:33
offering and threw the **b** of his peace 2 Kgs 16:13
on it all the **b** of the burnt offering 2 Kgs 16:15
and all the **b** of the sacrifice, 2 Kgs 16:15
shed very much innocent **b**, 2 Kgs 21:16
also for the innocent **b** that he had 2 Kgs 24:4
he filled Jerusalem with innocent **b**, 2 Kgs 24:4
have shed much **b** and have waged 1 Chr 22:8
have shed so much **b** before me on 1 Chr 22:8
are a man of war and have shed **b**.' 1 Chr 28:3
him because of the **b** of the son of 2 Chr 24:25
priests received the **b** and threw it 2 Chr 29:22
rams and their **b** was thrown 2 Chr 29:22
lambs and their **b** was thrown 2 Chr 29:22
offering with their **b** on the altar, 2 Chr 29:24
priests threw the **b** that they 2 Chr 30:16
priests threw the **b** that they 2 Chr 35:11
"O earth, cover not my **b**, and let my cry Jb 16:18
His young ones suck up **b**, and where Jb 39:30
For he who avenges **b** is mindful of Ps 9:12
their drink offerings of **b** I will not pour Ps 16:4
flesh of bulls or drink the **b** of goats? Ps 50:13
men of **b** and treachery shall not live Ps 55:23
bathe his feet in the **b** of the wicked. Ps 58:10
that you may strike your feet in their **b**, Ps 68:23
life, and precious is their **b** in his sight. Ps 72:14
He turned their rivers to **b**, so that they Ps 78:44
have poured out their **b** like water all Ps 79:3
of the outpoured **b** of your servants Ps 79:10
their waters into **b** and caused their Ps 105:29
they poured out innocent **b**, the blood Ps 106:38
the **b** of their sons and daughters, Ps 106:38
and the land was polluted with **b**. Ps 106:38
O God! O men of **b**, depart from me! Ps 139:19
"Come with us, let us lie in wait for **b**; Prv 1:11
to evil, and they make haste to shed **b**. Prv 1:16
these men lie in wait for their own **b**; Prv 1:18
and hands that shed innocent **b**, Prv 6:17
words of the wicked lie in wait for **b**, Prv 12:6
one is burdened with the **b** of another, Prv 28:17
curds, pressing the nose produces **b**, Prv 30:33
I do not delight in the **b** of bulls, or of Is 1:11
I will not listen; your hands are full of **b**. Is 1:15
every garment rolled in **b** will be burned Is 9:5
For the waters of Dibon are full of **b**; for I Is 15:9
the earth will disclose the **b** shed on it, Is 26:21
the mountains shall flow with their **b**. Is 34:3
The LORD has a sword; it is sated with **b**; it Is 34:6
with fat, with the **b** of lambs and goats, Is 34:6
Their land shall drink its fill of **b**, and Is 34:7
be drunk with their own **b** as with wine. Is 49:26
hands are defiled with **b** and your fingers Is 59:3
evil, and they are swift to shed innocent **b**; Is 59:7
grain offering, like one who offers pig's **b**; Is 66:3
widow, or shed innocent **b** in this place, Jer 7:6
filled this place with the **b** of innocents, Jer 19:4
nor shed innocent **b** in this place. Jer 22:3
gain, for shedding innocent **b**, Jer 22:17
will bring innocent **b** upon yourselves Jer 26:15
and be sated and drink its fill of their **b**. Jer 46:10
"My **b** be upon the inhabitants of Jer 51:35
the midst of her the **b** of the righteous. Lam 4:13
were so defiled with **b** that no one was Lam 4:14
but his **b** I will require at your hand. Ezk 3:18
but his **b** I will require at your hand. Ezk 3:20
Pestilence and **b** shall pass through Ezk 5:17
The land is full of **b**, and the city full of Ezk 9:9
pour out my wrath upon it with **b**, Ezk 14:19
you and saw you wallowing in your **b**, Ezk 16:6
in your blood, I said to you in your **b**, Ezk 16:6
'Live!' I said to you in your **b**, 'Live!' Ezk 16:6
and washed off your **b** from you and Ezk 16:9
naked and bare, wallowing in your **b**. Ezk 16:22
and because of the **b** of your children Ezk 16:36
adultery and shed **b** are judged, Ezk 16:38
bring upon you the **b** of wrath and Ezk 16:38
a son who is violent, a shedder of **b**, Ezk 18:10
die; his **b** shall be upon himself. Ezk 18:13
Your **b** shall be in the midst of the Ezk 21:32
A city that sheds **b** in her midst, so that Ezk 22:3
become guilty by the **b** that you have Ezk 22:4
power, have been bent on shedding **b**. Ezk 22:6
are men in you who slander to shed **b**, Ezk 22:9
In you they take bribes to shed **b**; you Ezk 22:12
and at the **b** that has been in your Ezk 22:13
wolves tearing the prey, shedding **b**, Ezk 22:27
adultery, and **b** is on their hands. Ezk 23:37
the sentence of women who shed **b**, Ezk 23:45
adulteresses, and **b** is on their hands." Ezk 23:45
For the **b** she has shed is in her midst; Ezk 24:7
set on the bare rock the **b** she has shed, Ezk 24:8
into her, and **b** into her streets; Ezk 28:23
to the mountains with your flowing **b**, Ezk 32:6
his **b** shall be upon his own head. Ezk 33:4
warning; his **b** shall be upon himself. Ezk 33:5
but his **b** I will require at the Ezk 33:6
but his **b** I will require at your hand. Ezk 33:8
eat flesh with the **b** and lift up your Ezk 33:25
up your eyes to your idols and shed **b**; Ezk 33:25
the Lord GOD, I will prepare you for **b**, Ezk 35:6
you for blood, and **b** shall pursue you; Ezk 35:6
therefore **b** shall pursue you. Ezk 35:6
upon them for the **b** that they had Ezk 36:18
and you shall eat flesh and drink **b**. Ezk 39:17
and drink the **b** of the princes of the Ezk 39:18
filled, and drink **b** till you are drunk, Ezk 39:19
upon it and for throwing **b** against it, Ezk 43:18
shall take some of its **b** and put it on Ezk 43:20
offer to me my food, the fat and the **b**. Ezk 44:7
before me to offer me the fat and the **b**, Ezk 44:15
take some of the **b** of the sin offering Ezk 45:19
the house of Jehu for the **b** of Jezreel, Hos 1:4
is a city of evildoers, tracked with **b**. Hos 6:8
earth, **b** and fire and columns of smoke. Jl 2:30
be turned to darkness, and the moon to **b**, Jl 2:31
they have shed innocent **b** in their land. Jl 3:19
I will avenge their **b**, blood I have not Jl 3:21
avenge their blood, **b** I have not avenged, Jl 3:21
life, and lay not on us innocent **b**, Jon 1:14
build Zion with **b** and Jerusalem with Mi 3:10
they all lie in wait for **b**, and each hunts Mi 7:2
for the **b** of man and violence to the Hab 2:8
builds a town with **b** and founds a city Hab 2:12
for the **b** of man and violence to the Hab 2:17
their **b** shall be poured out like dust, Zep 1:17
I will take away its **b** from its mouth, Zec 9:7
because of the **b** of my covenant with Zec 9:11
from a discharge of **b** for twelve years Mt 9:20
For flesh and **b** has not revealed this to Mt 16:17
them in shedding the **b** of the prophets.' Mt 23:30
come all the righteous **b** shed on earth, Mt 23:35
from the **b** of innocent Abel to the Mt 23:35
Abel to the **b** of Zechariah the Mt 23:35
for this is my **b** of the covenant, which Mt 26:28
by betraying innocent **b**." They said, Mt 27:4
into the treasury, since it is **b** money." Mt 27:6
has been called the Field of **B** to this day. Mt 27:8
saying, "I am innocent of this man's **b**; Mt 27:24
"His **b** be on us and on our children!" Mt 27:25
had a discharge of **b** for twelve years, Mk 5:25
And immediately the flow of **b** dried up, Mk 5:29
them, "This is my **b** of the covenant, Mk 14:24
had a discharge of **b** for twelve years, Lk 8:43
immediately her discharge of **b** ceased. Lk 8:44
so that the **b** of all the prophets, shed Lk 11:50
from the **b** of Abel to the blood of Lk 11:51
the blood of Abel to the **b** of Zechariah, Lk 11:51
the Galileans whose **b** Pilate had Lk 13:1
for you is the new covenant in my **b**. Lk 22:20
like great drops of **b** falling down to the Lk 22:44
not of **b** nor of the will of the flesh nor of Jn 1:13
flesh of the Son of Man and drink his **b**, Jn 6:53
flesh and drinks my **b** has eternal life, Jn 6:54
flesh is true food, and my **b** is true drink. Jn 6:55
my flesh and drinks my **b** abides in me, Jn 6:56
and at once there came out **b** and water. Jn 19:34
Akeldama, that is, Field of **B**.) Acts 1:19
signs on the earth below, **b**, and fire, Acts 2:19
turned to darkness and the moon to **b**, Acts 2:20
intend to bring this man's **b** upon us." Acts 5:28
what has been strangled, and from **b**. Acts 15:20
been sacrificed to idols, and from **b**, Acts 15:29
them, "Your **b** be on your own heads! Acts 18:6
I am innocent of the **b** of all of you, Acts 20:26
which he obtained with his own **b**. Acts 20:28
been sacrificed to idols, and from **b**, Acts 21:25
And when the **b** of Stephen your Acts 22:20
"Their feet are swift to shed **b**; Rom 3:15
put forward as a propitiation by his **b**, Rom 3:25
we have now been justified by his **b**, Rom 5:9
a participation in the **b** of Christ? 1 Cor 10:16
cup is the new covenant in my **b**. 1 Cor 11:25
the body and **b** of the Lord. 1 Cor 11:27
flesh and **b** cannot inherit the 1 Cor 15:50
him we have redemption through his **b**, Eph 1:7
been brought near by the **b** of Christ. Eph 2:13
we do not wrestle against flesh and **b**, Eph 6:12
making peace by the **b** of his cross. Col 1:20
the children share in flesh and **b**, Heb 2:14
once a year, and not without taking **b**, Heb 9:7
by means of the **b** of goats and calves Heb 9:12
and calves but by means of his own **b**, Heb 9:12
defiled persons with the **b** of goats and Heb 9:13
how much more will the **b** of Christ, Heb 9:14
covenant was inaugurated without **b**. Heb 9:18
he took the **b** of calves and goats, Heb 9:19
"This is the **b** of the covenant that God Heb 9:20
he sprinkled with the **b** both the tent Heb 9:21
almost everything is purified with **b**, Heb 9:22
without the shedding of **b** there is no Heb 9:22
places every year with **b** not his own, Heb 9:25
is impossible for the **b** of bulls and Heb 10:4
enter the holy places by the **b** of Jesus, Heb 10:19
has profaned the **b** of the covenant Heb 10:29
kept the Passover and sprinkled the **b**, Heb 11:28
resisted to the point of shedding your **b**. Heb 12:4
and to the sprinkled **b** that speaks a Heb 12:24
a better word than the **b** of Abel. Heb 12:24
those animals whose **b** is brought Heb 13:11
the people through his own **b**. Heb 13:12
by the **b** of the eternal covenant, Heb 13:20
Christ and for sprinkling with his **b**: 1 Pt 1:2
but with the precious **b** of Christ, like 1 Pt 1:19
and the **b** of Jesus his Son cleanses us 1 Jn 1:7
came by water and **b**—Jesus Christ; 1 Jn 5:6

water only but by the water and the **b**. 1 Jn 5:6
the Spirit and the water and the **b**; and 1 Jn 5:8
us and has freed us from our sins by his **b** Rv 1:5
and by your **b** you ransomed people for Rv 5:9
judge and avenge our **b** on those who Rv 6:10
sackcloth, the full moon became like **b**, Rv 6:12
made them white in the **b** of the Lamb. Rv 7:14
there followed hail and fire, mixed with **b**, Rv 8:7
the sea, and a third of the sea became **b**. Rv 8:8
to turn them into **b** and to strike the Rv 11:6
conquered him by the **b** of the Lamb Rv 12:11
city, and **b** flowed from the winepress, Rv 14:20
sea, and it became like the **b** of a corpse, Rv 16:3
the springs of water, and they became **b**. Rv 16:4
they have shed the **b** of saints and Rv 16:6
and you have given them **b** to drink. Rv 16:6
woman, drunk with the **b** of the saints, Rv 17:6
the saints, the **b** of the martyrs of Jesus. Rv 17:6
her was found the **b** of prophets and of Rv 18:24
avenged on her the **b** of his servants." Rv 19:2
He is clothed in a robe dipped in **b**, and Rv 19:13

BLOODGUILT (7)
that he dies, there shall be no **b** for him, Ex 22:2
risen on him, there shall be **b** for him. Ex 22:3
LORD, **b** shall be imputed to that man. Lv 17:4
restrained you from **b** and from 1 Sm 25:26
this day from **b** and from avenging 1 Sm 25:33
"There is **b** on Saul and on his house, 2 Sm 21:1
Lord will leave his **b** on him and will Hos 12:14

BLOODGUILTINESS (1)
Deliver me from **b**, O God, O God of my Ps 51:14

BLOODSHED (9)
and so the guilt of **b** be upon you. Dt 19:10
live in their cities, concerning **b**, 2 Chr 19:10
justice, but behold, **b**; for righteousness, Is 5:7
ears from hearing of **b** and shuts his Is 33:15
is he who keeps back his sword from **b**. Jer 48:10
because you did not hate **b**, therefore Ezk 35:6
With pestilence and **b** I will enter into Ezk 38:22
all bounds, and **b** follows bloodshed. Hos 4:2
all bounds, and bloodshed follows **b**. Hos 4:2

BLOODSTAINS (1)
Zion and cleansed the **b** of Jerusalem from Is 4:4

BLOODTHIRSTY (4)
the LORD abhors the **b** and deceitful man. Ps 5:6
with sinners, nor my life with **b** men, Ps 26:9
who work evil, and save me from **b** men. Ps 59:2
B men hate one who is blameless and Prv 29:10

BLOODY (6)
will bring back his **b** deeds on his 1 Kgs 2:32
the land is full of **b** crimes and the city Ezk 7:23
you judge, will you judge the **b** city? Ezk 22:2
Woe to the **b** city, to the pot whose Ezk 24:6
says the Lord GOD: Woe to the **b** city! Ezk 24:9
Woe to the **b** city, all full of lies and Na 3:1

BLOOM (3)
whether the pomegranates were in **b**. Sg 6:11
opened and the pomegranates are in **b**. Sg 7:12
Carmel wither; the **b** of Lebanon withers. Na 1:4

BLOSSOM (13)
and cast off his **b** like the olive tree. Jb 15:33
and may people **b** in the cities like the Ps 72:16
tree ripens its figs, and the vines are in **b**; Sg 2:13
vineyards, for our vineyards are in **b**." Sg 2:15
as rottenness, and their **b** go up like dust; Is 5:24
and make them **b** in the morning that Is 17:11
For before the harvest, when the **b** is over, Is 18:5
Israel shall **b** and put forth shoots and fill Is 27:6
desert shall rejoice and **b** like the crocus; Is 35:1
it shall **b** abundantly and rejoice with joy Is 35:2
the dew to Israel; he shall **b** like the lily; Hos 14:5
like the grain; they shall **b** like the vine; Hos 14:7
Though the fig tree should not **b**, nor Hab 3:17

BLOSSOMED (1)
Your doom has come; the rod has **b**; Ezk 7:10

BLOSSOMS (12)
As soon as it budded, its **b** shot forth, Gn 40:10
three cups made like almond **b**, each Ex 25:33
and three cups made like almond **b**, Ex 25:33
shall be four cups made like almond **b**, Ex 25:34
three cups made like almond **b**, each Ex 37:19
and three cups made like almond **b**, Ex 37:19
were four cups made like almond **b**, Ex 37:20
and put forth buds and produced **b**, Nm 17:8
the almond tree **b**, the grasshopper Eccl 12:5
a cluster of henna **b** in the vineyards of Sg 1:14
nut orchard to look at the **b** of the valley, Sg 6:11
whether the grape **b** have opened and the Sg 7:12

BLOT (15)
"I will **b** out man whom I have created Gn 6:7
I have made I will **b** out from the face of Gn 7:4
that I will utterly **b** out the memory of Ex 17:14
and the Jebusites, and I **b** them out, Ex 23:23
please **b** me out of your book that you Ex 32:32
against me, I will **b** out of my book. Ex 32:33
may destroy them and **b** out their name Dt 9:14
you shall **b** out the memory of Amalek Dt 25:19
and the LORD will **b** out his name from Dt 29:20
said that he would **b** out the name of 2 Kgs 14:27
your abundant mercy **b** out my Ps 51:1
my sins, and **b** out all my iniquities. Ps 51:9
nor **b** out their sin from your sight. Jer 18:23
When I **b** you out, I will cover the Ezk 32:7
and I will never **b** his name out of the Rv 3:5

BLOTS (2)
I am he who **b** out your transgressions Is 43:25
the daytime. They are **b** and blemishes, 2 Pt 2:13

BLOTTED (11)
He **b** out every living thing that was on Gn 7:23
They were **b** out from the earth. Gn 7:23
that his name may not be **b** out of Israel. Dt 25:6
that a tribe not be **b** out from Israel. Jgs 21:17
not their sin be **b** out from your sight, Neh 4:5
you have **b** out their name forever and Ps 9:5
Let them be **b** out of the book of the Ps 69:28
may his name be **b** out in the second Ps 109:13
let not the sin of his mother be **b** out! Ps 109:14
I have **b** out your transgressions like a Is 44:22
again, that your sins may be **b** out, Acts 3:19

BLOW (48)
And God made a wind **b** over the earth, Gn 8:1
But if they **b** only one, then the chiefs, Nm 10:4
When you **b** an alarm, the camps that Nm 10:5
And when you **b** an alarm the second Nm 10:6
together, you shall **b** a long blast, Nm 10:7
Aaron, the priests, shall **b** the trumpets. Nm 10:8
you shall **b** the trumpets over your Nm 10:10
It is a day for you to **b** the trumpets, Nm 29:1
he who struck the **b** shall be put to Nm 35:21
and the priests shall **b** the trumpets. Jos 6:4
them with a great **b** at Gibeon and Jos 10:10
them with a great **b** until they were Jos 10:20
When I **b** the trumpet, I and all who are Jgs 7:18
then **b** the trumpets also on every side of Jgs 7:18
in their right hands the trumpets to **b**. Jgs 7:20
as far as Abel-keramim, with a great **b**. Jgs 11:33
them hip and thigh with a great **b**, Jgs 15:8
had struck the people with a great **b**. 1 Sm 6:19
and struck them with a great **b**, 1 Sm 19:8
and struck them with a great **b**. 1 Sm 23:5
ground without striking a second **b**, 2 Sm 20:10
Then **b** the trumpet and say, 'Long 1 Kgs 1:34
struck the Syrians with a great **b**. 1 Kgs 20:21
should **b** the trumpets before the 1 Chr 15:24
priests were to **b** trumpets regularly 1 Chr 16:6
the east wind to **b** in the heavens, Ps 78:26
B the trumpet at the new moon, at the Ps 81:3
he makes his wind **b** and the waters Ps 147:18
B upon my garden, let its spices flow. Sg 4:16
and heals the wounds inflicted by his **b**. Is 30:26
heard and the descending **b** of his arm Is 30:30
and say, "**B** the trumpet through the land; Jer 4:5
B the trumpet in Tekoa, and raise a signal Jer 6:1
The bellows **b** fiercely; the lead is Jer 6:29
a great wound, with a very grievous **b**. Jer 14:17
for I have dealt you the **b** of an enemy, Jer 30:14
b the trumpet among the nations; Jer 51:27
I will **b** upon you with the fire of my Ezk 21:31
to **b** the fire on it in order to melt it, Ezk 22:20
will gather you and **b** on you with the Ezk 22:21
coming and does not **b** the trumpet, Ezk 33:6
B the horn in Gibeah, the trumpet in Hos 5:8
B a trumpet in Zion; sound an alarm on Jl 2:1
B the trumpet in Zion; consecrate a fast; Jl 2:15
Therefore I strike you with a grievous **b**, Mi 6:13
that no wind might **b** on earth or sea or Rv 7:1
the seven trumpets prepared to **b** them. Rv 8:6
that the three angels are about to **b**!" Rv 8:13

BLOWING (6)
the LORD went forward, **b** the trumpets, Jos 6:8
the priests who were **b** the trumpets, Jos 6:9
the land rejoicing and **b** trumpets. 2 Kgs 11:14
the land rejoicing and **b** trumpets, 2 Chr 23:13
And when you see the south wind **b**, Lk 12:55
rough because a strong wind was **b**. Jn 6:18

BLOWN (8)
And when both are **b**, all the Nm 10:3
alarm is to be **b** whenever they are to Nm 10:6
when the priests had **b** the trumpets, Jos 6:16
people shouted, and the trumpets were **b**. Jos 6:20
look! When a trumpet is **b**, hear! Is 18:3
in that day a great trumpet will be **b**, Is 27:13
"They have **b** the trumpet and made Ezk 7:14
Is a trumpet **b** in a city, and the people Am 3:6

BLOWS (11)
than a hundred **b** into a fool. Prv 17:10
B that wound cleanse away evil; Prv 20:30
The wind **b** to the south and goes Eccl 1:6
the peoples in wrath with unceasing **b**, Is 14:6
fades when the breath of the LORD **b** on it; Is 40:7
root in the earth, when he **b** on them, Is 40:24
created the smith who **b** the fire of coals Is 54:16
upon the land and **b** the trumpet and Ezk 33:3
And the guards received him with **b**. Mk 14:65
The wind **b** where it wishes, and you hear Jn 3:8
had inflicted many **b** upon them, Acts 16:23

BLUE (46)
b and purple and scarlet yarns and fine Ex 25:4
fine twined linen and **b** and purple and Ex 26:1
you shall make loops of **b** on the edge of Ex 26:4
make a veil of **b** and purple and scarlet Ex 26:31
of **b** and purple and scarlet yarns and Ex 26:36
of **b** and purple and scarlet yarns and Ex 27:16
gold, **b** and purple and scarlet yarns, Ex 28:5
gold, of **b** and purple and scarlet yarns, Ex 28:6
of gold, **b** and purple and scarlet yarns, Ex 28:8
of gold, **b** and purple and scarlet yarns, Ex 28:15
the rings of the ephod with a lace of **b**, Ex 28:28
make the robe of the ephod all of **b**. Ex 28:31
make pomegranates of **b** and purple Ex 28:33
fasten it on the turban by a cord of **b**. Ex 28:37
b and purple and scarlet yarns and fine Ex 35:6
every one who possessed **b** or purple or Ex 35:23
they had spun in **b** and purple and Ex 35:25
by an embroiderer in **b** and purple and Ex 35:35
fine twined linen and **b** and purple and Ex 36:8
He made loops of **b** on the edge of the Ex 36:11
made the veil of **b** and purple and Ex 36:35
of **b** and purple and scarlet yarns and Ex 36:37
with needlework in **b** and purple and Ex 38:18
and embroiderer in **b** and purple and Ex 38:23
From the **b** and purple and scarlet yarns Ex 39:1
of gold, **b** and purple and scarlet yarns, Ex 39:2
to work into the **b** and purple and the Ex 39:3
of gold, **b** and purple and scarlet yarns, Ex 39:5
of gold, **b** and purple and scarlet yarns, Ex 39:8
the rings of the ephod with a lace of **b**, Ex 39:21
the robe of the ephod woven all of **b**, Ex 39:22
made pomegranates of **b** and purple Ex 39:24
twined linen and of **b** and purple and Ex 39:29
tied to it a cord of **b** to fasten it on the Ex 39:31
and spread on top of that a cloth all of **b**, Nm 4:6
shall spread a cloth of **b** and put on it Nm 4:7
take a cloth of **b** and cover the Nm 4:9
spread a cloth of **b** and cover it with Nm 4:11
in a cloth of **b** and cover them with Nm 4:12
to put a cord of **b** on the tassel of each Nm 15:38
and in purple, crimson, and **b** fabrics, 2 Chr 2:7
b, and crimson fabrics and fine 2 Chr 2:14
made the veil of **b** and purple and 2 Chr 3:14
the king in royal robes of **b** and white, Est 8:15
b and purple from the coasts of Elishah Ezk 27:7
in clothes of **b** and embroidered work, Ezk 27:24

BLUNT (1)
If the iron is **b**, and one does not Eccl 10:10

BLUNTED (1)
when he aims his arrows, let them be **b**. Ps 58:7

BLUSH (4)
I am ashamed and **b** to lift my face to Ezr 9:6
and you shall **b** for the gardens that you Is 1:29
ashamed; they did not know how to **b**. Jer 6:15
ashamed; they did not know how to **b**. Jer 8:12

BOANERGES (1)
of James (to whom he gave the name **B**, Mk 3:17

BOAR (1)
The **b** from the forest ravages it, and all Ps 80:13

BOARD (5)
So he paid the fare and went on **b**, to go Jon 1:3
we took him on **b** and went to Acts 20:14
Then we went on **b** the ship, and they Acts 21:6
sailing for Italy and put us on **b**. Acts 27:6
they put on **b** whatever we needed. Acts 28:10

BOARDS (6)
You shall make it hollow, with **b**. As it Ex 27:8
it with them. He made it hollow, with **b**. Ex 38:7
house on the inside with **b** of cedar. 1 Kgs 6:15
floor of the house with **b** of cypress. 1 Kgs 6:15
of the house with **b** of cedar from the 1 Kgs 6:16
a door, we will enclose her with **b** of cedar. Sg 8:9

BOAST (57)
into their hand, lest Israel **b** over me, Jgs 7:2
on his armor **b** himself like he 1 Kgs 20:11
My soul makes its **b** in the LORD; let the Ps 34:2
who **b** against me when my foot slips!" Ps 38:16

in their wealth and **b** of the abundance Ps 49:6
Why do you **b** of evil, O mighty man? Ps 52:1
I say to the boastful, 'Do not **b**,' and to the Ps 75:4
their arrogant words; all the evildoers **b**. Ps 94:4
who make their **b** in worthless idols; Ps 97:7
Do not **b** about tomorrow, for you do Prv 27:1
Shall the axe **b** over him who hews with Is 10:15
of Cush their hope and of Egypt their **b**. Is 20:5
nations, and in their glory you shall **b**. Is 61:6
"Let not the wise man **b** in his wisdom, Jer 9:23
let not the mighty man **b** in his might, Jer 9:23
let not the rich man **b** in his riches, Jer 9:23
but let him who boasts **b** in this, that he Jer 9:24
Why do you **b** of your valleys, O Jer 49:4
their ruin; do not **b** in the day of distress. Ob 1:12
a Jew and rely on the law and **b** in God Rom 2:17
You who **b** in the law dishonor God Rom 2:23
by works, he has something to **b** about, Rom 4:2
human being might **b** in the 1 Cor 1:29
the one who boasts, **b** in the Lord." 1 Cor 1:31
So let no one **b** in men. For all things 1 Cor 3:21
why do you **b** as if you did not receive 1 Cor 4:7
and kind; love does not envy or **b**; 1 Cor 13:4
For our **b** is this: the testimony of our 2 Cor 1:12
our Lord Jesus you will **b** of us as we 2 Cor 1:14
will boast of us as we will **b** of you. 2 Cor 1:14
but giving you cause to **b** about us, 2 Cor 5:12
answer those who **b** about outward 2 Cor 5:12
of which I **b** about you to the people of 2 Cor 9:2
For even if I **b** a little too much of our 2 Cor 10:8
But we will not **b** beyond limits, but 2 Cor 10:13
but will **b** only with regard to the 2 Cor 10:13
We do not **b** beyond limit in the 2 Cor 10:15
the one who boasts, **b** in the Lord." 2 Cor 10:17
as a fool, so that I too may **b** a little. 2 Cor 11:16
Since many **b** according to the 2 Cor 11:18
according to the flesh, I too will **b**. 2 Cor 11:18
anyone else dares to **b** of—I am 2 Cor 11:21
as a fool—I also dare to **b** of that. 2 Cor 11:21
If I must **b**, I will boast of the things 2 Cor 11:30
I will **b** of the things that show my 2 Cor 11:30
On behalf of this man I will **b**, but on 2 Cor 12:5
but on my own behalf I will not **b**, 2 Cor 12:5
Though if I should wish to **b**, I would 2 Cor 12:6
Therefore I will **b** all the more 2 Cor 12:9
then his reason to **b** will be in himself Gal 6:4
that they may **b** in your flesh. Gal 6:13
be it from me to **b** except in the cross of Gal 6:14
a result of works, so that no one may **b**. Eph 2:9
Therefore we ourselves **b** about you 2 Thes 1:4
Let the lowly brother **b** in his exaltation, Jas 1:9
hearts, do not **b** and be false to the truth. Jas 3:14
As it is, you **b** in your arrogance. All Jas 4:16

BOASTED (3)
In God we have **b** continually, and we Ps 44:8
they taunted and **b** against the people Zep 2:10
that in their **b** mission they work 2 Cor 11:12

BOASTERS (1)
they are loud-mouthed **b**, showing Jude 1:16

BOASTFUL (5)
The **b** shall not stand before your eyes; Ps 5:5
I say to the **b**, 'Do not boast,' and to the Ps 75:4
of Assyria and the **b** look in his eyes. Is 10:12
insolent, haughty, **b**, inventors of evil, Rom 1:30
I am saying with this **b** confidence, 2 Cor 11:17

BOASTFULNESS (1)
your heart has lifted you up in **b**. 2 Chr 25:19

BOASTING (14)
his insolence; in his idle **b** he is not right. Is 16:6
Then what becomes of our **b**? It is Rom 3:27
Your **b** is not good. Do you not know 1 Cor 5:6
deprive me of my ground for **b**. 1 Cor 9:15
gospel, that gives me no ground for **b**. 1 Cor 9:16
so also our **b** before Titus has proved 2 Cor 7:14
love and of our **b** about you to these 2 Cor 8:24
brothers so that our **b** about you may 2 Cor 9:3
without **b** of work already done in 2 Cor 10:16
this **b** of mine will not be silenced in 2 Cor 11:10
I must go on **b**. Though there is 2 Cor 12:1
joy or crown of **b** before our Lord 1 Thes 2:19
our confidence and our **b** in our hope. Heb 3:6
in your arrogance. All such **b** is evil. Jas 4:16

BOASTS (13)
For the wicked **b** of the desires of his Ps 10:3
lips, the tongue that makes great **b**, Ps 12:3
yet after them people approve of their **b**. Ps 49:13
but when he goes away, then he **b**. Prv 20:14
rain is a man who **b** of a gift he does Prv 25:14
but let him who **b** boast in this, that he Jer 9:24
LORD; his **b** are false, his deeds are false. Jer 48:30
people and made **b** against their Zep 2:8
as it is written, "Let the one who **b**, 1 Cor 1:31
For whatever **b** I made to him about 2 Cor 7:14
"Let the one who **b**, boast in the 2 Cor 10:17
a small member, yet it **b** of great things. Jas 3:5
For, speaking loud **b** of folly, they 2 Pt 2:18

BOAT (47)
in the **b** with Zebedee their father, Mt 4:21
they left the **b** and their father Mt 4:22
And when he got into the **b**, his disciples Mt 8:23
so that the **b** was being swamped by the Mt 8:24
And getting into a **b** he crossed over and Mt 9:1
so that he got into a **b** and sat down. Mt 13:2
from there in a **b** to a desolate place Mt 14:13
disciples get into the **b** and go before Mt 14:22
but the **b** by this time was a long way Mt 14:24
Peter got out of the **b** and walked on the Mt 14:29
And when they got into the **b**, the wind Mt 14:32
And those in the **b** worshiped him, Mt 14:33
he got into the **b** and went to the region Mt 15:39
who were in their **b** mending the nets. Mk 1:19
father Zebedee in the **b** with the hired Mk 1:20
disciples to have a **b** ready for him Mk 3:9
so that he got into a **b** and sat in it on the Mk 4:1
they took him with them in the **b**, Mk 4:36
and the waves were breaking into the **b**, Mk 4:37
boat, so that the **b** was already filling. Mk 4:37
And when Jesus had stepped out of the **b**, Mk 5:2
As he was getting into the **b**, the man Mk 5:18
crossed again in the **b** to the other side, Mk 5:21
went away in the **b** to a desolate place Mk 6:32
disciples get into the **b** and go before Mk 6:45
evening came, the **b** was out on the sea, Mk 6:47
And he got into the **b** with them, and Mk 6:51
And when they got out of the **b**, the Mk 6:54
he got into the **b** with his disciples and Mk 8:10
And he left them, got into the **b** again, Mk 8:13
had only one loaf with them in the **b**. Mk 8:14
down and taught the people from the **b**. Lk 5:3
partners in the other **b** to come and help Lk 5:7
day he got into a **b** with his disciples, Lk 8:22
fear. So he got into the **b** and returned. Lk 8:37
got into a **b**, and started across the sea to Jn 6:17
on the sea and coming near the **b**, Jn 6:19
they were glad to take him into the **b**, Jn 6:21
and immediately the **b** was at the land to Jn 6:21
saw that there had been only one **b** there, Jn 6:22
had not entered the **b** with his disciples, Jn 6:22
you." They went out and got into the **b**, Jn 21:3
"Cast the net on the right side of the **b**, Jn 21:6
The other disciples came in the **b**, Jn 21:8
with difficulty to secure the ship's **b**. Acts 27:16
had lowered the ship's **b** into the sea Acts 27:30
the ropes of the ship's **b** and let it go. Acts 27:32

BOATS (7)
as he was. And other **b** were with him. Mk 4:36
and he saw two **b** by the lake, but the Lk 5:2
Getting into one of the **b**, which was Lk 5:3
And they came and filled both the **b**, so Lk 5:7
when they had brought their **b** to land, Lk 5:11
Other **b** from Tiberias came near the Jn 6:23
themselves got into the **b** and went to Jn 6:24

BOAZ (28)
the clan of Elimelech, whose name was **B**. Ru 2:1
to the part of the field belonging to **B**, Ru 2:3
And behold, **B** came from Bethlehem. Ru 2:4
Then **B** said to his young man who was Ru 2:5
Then **B** said to Ruth, "Now, listen, my Ru 2:8
But **B** answered her, "All that you have Ru 2:11
And at mealtime **B** said to her, "Come Ru 2:14
to glean, **B** instructed his young men, Ru 2:15
name with whom I worked today is **B**." Ru 2:19
she kept close to the young women of **B**, Ru 2:23
Is not **B** our relative, with whose young Ru 3:2
And when **B** had eaten and drunk, and Ru 3:7
Now **B** had gone up to the gate and sat Ru 4:1
the redeemer, of whom **B** had spoken, Ru 4:1
Boaz had spoken, came by. So **B** said, Ru 4:1
Then **B** said, "The day you buy the field Ru 4:5
So when the redeemer said to **B**, "Buy it Ru 4:8
Then **B** said to the elders and all the Ru 4:9
So **B** took Ruth, and she became his Ru 4:13
Salmon fathered **B**, Boaz fathered Obed, Ru 4:21
Salmon fathered Boaz, **B** fathered Obed, Ru 4:21
on the north and called its name **B**. 1 Kgs 7:21
fathered Salmon, Salmon fathered **B**, 1 Chr 2:11
B fathered Obed, Obed fathered Jesse. 1 Chr 2:12
Jachin, and that on the north **B**. 2 Chr 3:17
and Salmon the father of **B** by Rahab, Mt 1:5
Rahab, and **B** the father of Obed by Ruth, Mt 1:5
son of Jesse, the son of Obed, the son of **B**, Lk 3:32

BOCHERU (2)
Azrikam, **B**, Ishmael, Sheariah, 1 Chr 8:38
Azrikam, **B**, Ishmael, Sheariah, 1 Chr 9:44

BOCHIM (2)
of the LORD went up from Gilgal to **B**. Jgs 2:1
And they called the name of that place **B**. Jgs 2:5

BODIES (58)
of my lord but our **b** and our land. Gn 47:18
in to any dead **b** nor make himself Lv 21:11
and cast your dead **b** upon the dead Lv 26:30
bodies upon the dead **b** of your idols, Lv 26:30
your dead **b** shall fall in this Nm 14:29
your dead **b** shall fall in this Nm 14:32
last of your dead **b** lies in the Nm 14:33
I will give the dead **b** of the host of 1 Sm 17:46
of Saul and the **b** of his sons from 1 Sm 31:12
behold, these were all dead **b**. 2 Kgs 19:35
body of Saul and the **b** of his sons, 1 Chr 10:12
there were dead **b** lying on the 2 Chr 20:24
They rule over our **b** and over our Neh 9:37
until death; their **b** are fat and sleek. Ps 73:4
They have given the **b** of your servants Ps 79:2
Your dead shall live; their **b** shall rise. Is 26:19
morning, behold, these were all dead **b**. Is 37:36
and look on the dead **b** of the men who Is 66:24
And the dead **b** of this people will be food Jer 7:33
'The dead **b** of men shall fall like dung Jer 9:22
and their dead **b** shall be food for the Jer 16:4
I will give their dead **b** for food to the Jer 19:7
valley of the dead **b** and the ashes, Jer 31:40
fill them with the dead **b** of men whom I Jer 33:5
Their dead **b** shall be food for the birds Jer 34:20
their clothes torn, and their **b** gashed, Jer 41:5
had thrown all the **b** of the men whom Jer 41:9
their **b** were more ruddy than coral, the Lam 4:7
of another, while two covered their **b**. Ezk 1:11
I will lay the dead **b** of the people of Israel Ezk 6:5
and by the dead **b** of their kings at Ezk 43:7
whoring and the dead **b** of their kings Ezk 43:9
had any power over the **b** of those men. Dn 3:27
and yielded up their **b** rather than serve Dn 3:28
"So many dead **b**!" "They are thrown Am 8:3
dead **b** without end—they stumble over Na 3:3
without end—they stumble over the **b**! Na 3:3
And many **b** of the saints who had Mt 27:52
and so that the **b** would not remain on Jn 19:31
of their **b** among themselves, Rom 1:24
sin therefore reign in your mortal **b**, Rom 6:12
to your mortal **b** through his Spirit Rom 8:11
as sons, the redemption of our **b**. Rom 8:23
to present your **b** as a living sacrifice, Rom 12:1
not know that your **b** are members of 1 Cor 6:15
There are heavenly **b** and earthly 1 Cor 15:40
are heavenly bodies and earthly **b**, 1 Cor 15:40
may also be manifested in our **b**. 2 Cor 4:10
into Macedonia, our **b** had no rest, 2 Cor 7:5
should love their wives as their own **b**. Eph 5:28
sinned, whose **b** fell in the wilderness? Heb 3:17
conscience and our **b** washed with Heb 10:22
For the **b** of those animals whose Heb 13:11
obey us, we guide their whole **b** as well. Jas 3:3
and the heavenly **b** will be burned up 2 Pt 3:10
and the heavenly **b** will melt as they 2 Pt 3:12
and their dead **b** will lie in the street of Rv 11:8
will gaze at their dead **b** and refuse to let Rv 11:9

BODILY (6)
Holy Spirit descended on him in **b** form, Lk 3:22
strong, but his **b** presence is weak, 2 Cor 10:10
was because of a **b** ailment that I Gal 4:13
him the whole fullness of deity dwells **b**, Col 2:9
for while **b** training is of some value, 1 Tm 4:8
requirement concerning **b** descent, Heb 7:16

BODY (232)
out red, all his **b** like a hairy cloak, Gn 25:25
kings shall come from your own **b**. Gn 35:11
covering, and it is his cloak for his **b**; Ex 22:27
be poured on the **b** of an ordinary Ex 30:32
put his linen undergarment on his **b**, Lv 6:10
on the skin of his **b** a swelling or an Lv 13:2
of leprous disease on the skin of his **b**, Lv 13:2
the diseased area on the skin of his **b**. Lv 13:3
to be deeper than the skin of his **b**, Lv 13:3
the skin of his **b** and appears no deeper Lv 13:4
leprous disease in the skin of his **b**, Lv 13:11
leprous disease has covered all his **b**, Lv 13:13
in the skin of one's **b** a boil and it heals, Lv 13:18
when the **b** has a burn on its skin and Lv 13:24
a woman has spots on the skin of the **b**, Lv 13:38
on the skin of the **b** are of a dull white, Lv 13:39
of leprous disease in the skin of the **b**, Lv 13:43
his clothes and bathe his **b** in water, Lv 14:9
any man has a discharge from his **b**, Lv 15:2
whether his **b** runs with his discharge, Lv 15:3
or his **b** is blocked up by his discharge, Lv 15:3
And whoever touches the **b** of the one Lv 15:7
he shall bathe his **b** in fresh water and Lv 15:13
shall bathe his whole **b** in water and be Lv 15:16

and the discharge in her **b** is blood, Lv 15:19
have the linen undergarment on his **b**, Lv 16:4
He shall bathe his **b** in water and then Lv 16:4
And he shall bathe his **b** in water in a Lv 16:24
his clothes and bathe his **b** in water, Lv 16:26
his clothes and bathe his **b** in water, Lv 16:28
any cuts on your **b** for the dead or Lv 19:28
beards, nor make any cuts on their **b**. Lv 21:5
unless he has bathed his **b** in water. Lv 22:6
your thigh fall away and your **b** swell. Nm 5:21
to the LORD he shall not go near a dead **b**. Nm 6:6
he sinned by reason of the dead **b**. Nm 6:11
let them go with a razor over all their **b**, Nm 8:7
unclean through touching a dead **b**, Nm 9:6
are unclean through touching a dead **b**. Nm 9:7
is unclean through touching a dead **b**, Nm 9:10
his clothes and bathe his **b** in water, Nm 19:7
water and bathe his **b** in water and Nm 19:8
touches the dead **b** of any person Nm 19:11
person, the **b** of anyone who has died, Nm 19:13
his **b** shall not remain all night on the Dt 21:23
And your dead **b** shall be food for all Dt 28:26
and they took his **b** down from the tree Jos 8:29
was a swarm of bees in the **b** of the lion, Jgs 14:8
and they fastened his **b** to the wall of 1 Sm 31:10
night and took the **b** of Saul and the 1 Sm 31:12
you, who shall come from your **b**, 2 Sm 7:12
no water," your **b** shall not come 1 Kgs 13:22
And his **b** was thrown in the road, 1 Kgs 13:24
it; the lion also stood beside the **b**. 1 Kgs 13:24
by and saw the **b** thrown in the road 1 Kgs 13:25
road and the lion standing by the **b**. 1 Kgs 13:25
went and found his **b** thrown in the 1 Kgs 13:28
and the lion standing beside the **b**. 1 Kgs 13:28
had not eaten the **b** or torn the 1 Kgs 13:28
prophet took up the **b** of the man of 1 Kgs 13:29
And he laid the **b** in his own grave. 1 Kgs 13:30
he had sackcloth beneath on his **b**— 2 Kgs 6:30
and took away the **b** of Saul and the 1 Chr 10:12
He feels only the pain of his own **b**, and Jb 14:22
him and rain it upon him into his **b**. Jb 20:23
It is drawn forth and comes out of his **b**; Jb 20:25
if his **b** has not blessed me, and if he Jb 31:20
from grief; my soul and my **b** also. Ps 31:9
may it soak into his **b** like water, like Ps 109:18
my **b** has become gaunt, with no fat. Ps 109:24
of the sons of your **b** I will set on your Ps 132:11
when your flesh and **b** are consumed, Prv 5:11
to the soul and health to the **b**. Prv 16:24
go down into the inner parts of the **b**. Prv 18:8
go down into the inner parts of the **b**. Prv 26:22
how to cheer my **b** with wine—my Eccl 2:3
and put away pain from your **b**, Eccl 11:10
His **b** is polished ivory, bedecked with Sg 5:14
the LORD will destroy, both soul and **b**, Is 10:18
the pit, like a dead **b** trampled underfoot. Is 14:19
from the **b** of my mother he named my Is 49:1
and dumped his dead **b** into the burial Jer 26:23
and his dead **b** shall be cast out to the Jer 36:30
creature had two wings covering its **b**. Ezk 1:23
And their whole **b**, their rims, and Ezk 10:12
and his **b** was wet with the dew of Dn 4:33
and his **b** was wet with the dew of Dn 5:21
and its **b** destroyed and given over to be Dn 7:11
His **b** was like beryl, his face like the Dn 10:6
the fruit of my **b** for the sin of my soul?" Mi 6:7
I hear, and my **b** trembles; my lips Hab 3:16
contact with a dead **b** touches any of Hg 2:13
than that your whole **b** be thrown into Mt 5:29
than that your whole **b** go into hell. Mt 5:30
"The eye is the lamp of the **b**. So, if your Mt 6:22
your whole **b** will be full of light, Mt 6:22
your whole **b** will be full of darkness. Mt 6:23
what you will drink, nor about your **b**, Mt 6:25
food, and the **b** more than clothing? Mt 6:25
those who kill the **b** but cannot kill the Mt 10:28
can destroy both soul and **b** in hell. Mt 10:28
came and took the **b** and buried it, Mt 14:12
In pouring this ointment on my **b**, she Mt 26:12
and said, "Take, eat; this is my **b**." Mt 26:26
to Pilate and asked for the **b** of Jesus. Mt 27:58
And Joseph took the **b** and wrapped it Mt 27:59
and she felt in her **b** that she was healed Mk 5:29
they came and took his **b** and laid it in Mk 6:29
has anointed my **b** beforehand for Mk 14:8
to them, and said, "Take; this is my **b**." Mk 14:22
nothing but a linen cloth about his **b**. Mk 14:51
to Pilate and asked for the **b** of Jesus. Mk 15:43
Your eye is the lamp of your **b**. When Lk 11:34
is healthy, your whole **b** is full of light, Lk 11:34
it is bad, your **b** is full of darkness. Lk 11:34
If then your whole **b** is full of light, Lk 11:36
friends, do not fear those who kill the **b**, Lk 12:4
what you will eat, nor about your **b**, Lk 12:22
food, and the **b** more than clothing. Lk 12:23
gave it to them, saying, "This is my **b**, Lk 22:19
to Pilate and asked for the **b** of Jesus. Lk 23:52
saw the tomb and how his **b** was laid. Lk 23:55
they did not find the **b** of the Lord Jesus. Lk 24:3
and when they did not find his **b**, they Lk 24:23
was speaking about the temple of his **b**. Jn 2:21
Sabbath I made a man's whole **b** well? Jn 7:23
that he might take away the **b** of Jesus, Jn 19:38
So he came and took away his **b**. Jn 19:38
So they took the **b** of Jesus and bound it Jn 19:40
sitting where the **b** of Jesus had lain, Jn 20:12
and turning to the **b** he said, "Tabitha, Acts 9:40
in faith when he considered his own **b**, Rom 4:19
him in order that the **b** of sin might be Rom 6:6
died to the law through the **b** of Christ, Rom 7:4
will deliver me from this **b** of death? Rom 7:24
although the **b** is dead because of sin, Rom 8:10
you put to death the deeds of the **b**, Rom 8:13
For as in one **b** we have many Rom 12:4
we, though many, are one **b** in Christ, Rom 12:5
For though absent in **b**, I am present 1 Cor 5:3
The **b** is not meant for sexual 1 Cor 6:13
for the Lord, and the Lord for the **b**. 1 Cor 6:13
a prostitute becomes one **b** with her? 1 Cor 6:16
sin a person commits is outside the **b**, 1 Cor 6:18
person sins against his own **b**. 1 Cor 6:18
not know that your **b** is a temple of 1 Cor 6:19
with a price. So glorify God in your **b**. 1 Cor 6:20
not have authority over her own **b**, 1 Cor 7:4
not have authority over his own **b**, 1 Cor 7:4
Lord, how to be holy in **b** and spirit. 1 Cor 7:34
But I discipline my **b** and keep it 1 Cor 9:27
a participation in the **b** of Christ? 1 Cor 10:16
bread, we who are many are one **b**, 1 Cor 10:17
said, "This is my **b** which is for you. 1 Cor 11:24
of profaning the **b** and blood of 1 Cor 11:27
without discerning the **b** eats and 1 Cor 11:29
For just as the **b** is one and has 1 Cor 12:12
and all the members of the **b**, 1 Cor 12:12
the body, though many, are one **b**, 1 Cor 12:12
all baptized into one **b**—Jews or 1 Cor 12:13
For the **b** does not consist of one 1 Cor 12:14
not belong to the **b**," that would not 1 Cor 12:15
not make it any less a part of the **b**. 1 Cor 12:15
not belong to the **b**," that would not 1 Cor 12:16
not make it any less a part of the **b**. 1 Cor 12:16
If the whole **b** were an eye, where 1 Cor 12:17
hearing? If the whole **b** were an ear, 1 Cor 12:17
God arranged the members in the **b**, 1 Cor 12:18
member, where would the **b** be? 1 Cor 12:19
it is, there are many parts, yet one **b**. 1 Cor 12:20
the parts of the **b** that seem to be 1 Cor 12:22
those parts of the **b** that we think 1 Cor 12:23
But God has so composed the **b**, 1 Cor 12:24
there may be no division in the **b**, 1 Cor 12:25
Now you are the **b** of Christ and 1 Cor 12:27
and if I deliver up my **b** to be burned, 1 Cor 13:3
With what kind of **b** do they come?" 1 Cor 15:35
you sow is not the **b** that is to be, 1 Cor 15:37
God gives it a **b** as he has chosen, 1 Cor 15:38
and to each kind of seed its own **b**. 1 Cor 15:38
It is sown a natural **b**; it is raised a 1 Cor 15:44
body; it is raised a spiritual **b**. 1 Cor 15:44
If there is a natural **b**, there is also a 1 Cor 15:44
body, there is also a spiritual **b**. 1 Cor 15:44
For this perishable **b** must put on 1 Cor 15:53
and this mortal **b** must put on 1 Cor 15:53
always carrying in the **b** the death of 2 Cor 4:10
are at home in the **b** we are away from 2 Cor 5:6
be away from the **b** and at home with 2 Cor 5:8
is due for what he has done in the **b**, 2 Cor 5:10
from every defilement of **b** and spirit, 2 Cor 7:1
—whether in the **b** or out of the 2 Cor 12:2
body or out of the **b** I do not know, 2 Cor 12:2
—whether in the **b** or out of the 2 Cor 12:3
body or out of the **b** I do not know, 2 Cor 12:3
for I bear on my **b** the marks of Jesus. Gal 6:17
which is his **b**, the fullness of him who Eph 1:23
out the desires of the **b** and the mind, Eph 2:3
both to God in one **b** through the cross, Eph 2:16
are fellow heirs, members of the same **b**, Eph 3:6
There is one **b** and one Spirit—just as Eph 4:4
for building up the **b** of Christ, Eph 4:12
from whom the whole **b**, joined and Eph 4:16
makes the **b** grow so that it builds itself Eph 4:16
Christ is the head of the church, his **b**, Eph 5:23
because we are members of his **b**. Eph 5:30
always Christ will be honored in my **b**, Phil 1:20
will transform our lowly **b** to be like Phil 3:21
lowly body to be like his glorious **b**, Phil 3:21
And he is the head of the **b**, the church. Col 1:18
now reconciled in his **b** of flesh by his Col 1:22
Christ's afflictions for the sake of his **b**, Col 1:24
For though I am absent in **b**, yet I am Col 2:5
hands, by putting off the **b** of the flesh, Col 2:11
to the Head, from whom the whole **b**, Col 2:19
and asceticism and severity to the **b**, Col 2:23
which indeed you were called in one **b**. Col 3:15
to control his own **b** in holiness and 1 Thes 4:4
and soul and **b** be kept blameless 1 Thes 5:23
regulations for the **b** imposed until the Heb 9:10
but a **b** have you prepared for me; Heb 10:5
the offering of the **b** of Jesus Christ Heb 10:10
mistreated, since you also are in the **b**. Heb 13:3
giving them the things needed for the **b**, Jas 2:16
For as the **b** apart from the spirit is dead, Jas 2:26
man, able also to bridle his whole **b**. Jas 3:2
our members, staining the whole **b**, Jas 3:6
bore our sins in his **b** on the tree, 1 Pt 2:24
of dirt from the **b** but as an appeal 1 Pt 3:21
think it right, as long as I am in this **b**, 2 Pt 1:13
the putting off of my **b** will be soon, 2 Pt 1:14
was disputing about the **b** of Moses, Jude 1:9

BODYGUARD (6)
son-in-law, and captain over your **b**, 1 Sm 22:14
well, I will make you my **b** for life." 1 Sm 28:2
three. And David set him over his **b**. 2 Sm 23:23
—Nebuzaradan, the captain of the **b**, 2 Kgs 25:8
three. And David set him over his **b**. 1 Chr 11:25
—Nebuzaradan the captain of the **b**, Jer 52:12

BOG (1)
the pit of destruction, out of the miry **b**, Ps 40:2

BOHAN (2)
up to the stone of **B** the son of Reuben. Jos 15:6
to the stone of **B** the son of Reuben, Jos 18:17

BOIL (21)
you will bake and **b** what you will boil, Ex 16:23
you will bake and boil what you will **b**, Ex 16:23
"You shall not **b** a young goat in its Ex 23:19
ram of ordination and **b** its flesh in a Ex 29:31
You shall not **b** a young goat in its Ex 34:26
"**B** the flesh at the entrance of the tent of Lv 8:31
the skin of one's body a **b** and it heals, Lv 13:18
the place of the **b** there comes a white Lv 13:19
disease that has broken out in the **b**. Lv 13:20
does not spread, it is the scar of the **b**, Lv 13:23
"You shall not **b** a young goat in its Dt 14:21
and **b** stew for the sons of the 2 Kgs 4:38
And let them take and lay it on the **b**, 2 Kgs 20:7
He makes the deep **b** like a pot; he Jb 41:31
take a cake of figs and apply it to the **b**, Is 38:21
the fire causes water to **b**—to make your Is 64:2
the flock; pile the logs under it; **b** it well; Ezk 24:5
logs, kindle the fire, **b** the meat well, Ezk 24:10
the priests shall **b** the guilt offering Ezk 46:20
at the temple shall **b** the sacrifices of Ezk 46:24
and take of them and **b** the meat of the Zec 14:21

BOILED (10)
Do not eat any of it raw or **b** in water, Ex 12:9
vessel in which it is **b** shall be broken. Lv 6:28
broken. But if it is **b** in a bronze vessel, Lv 6:28
the shoulder of the ram, when it is **b**, Nm 6:19
beat it in mortars and **b** it in pots and Nm 11:8
he will not accept **b** meat from you 1 Sm 2:15
sacrificed them and **b** their flesh 1 Kgs 19:21
So we **b** my son and ate him. And on 2 Kgs 6:29
and they **b** the holy offerings in 2 Chr 35:13
women have **b** their own Lam 4:10

BOILING (3)
would come, while the meat was **b**, 1 Sm 2:13
as from a **b** pot and burning rushes. Jb 41:20
do you see?" And I said, "I see a **b** pot, Jer 1:13

BOILS (6)
and become **b** breaking out in sores on Ex 9:9
and it became **b** breaking out in sores Ex 9:10
not stand before Moses because of the **b**, Ex 9:11
for the **b** came upon the magicians and Ex 9:11
LORD will strike you with the **b** of Egypt, Dt 28:27
the legs with grievous **b** of which you Dt 28:35

BOLD (10)
him, and with **b** face she says to him, Prv 7:13
A wicked man puts on a **b** face, but Prv 21:29
but the righteous are **b** as a lion. Prv 28:1
reached their limit, a king of **b** face, Dn 8:23
Then Isaiah is so **b** as to say, "I have Rom 10:20
we have such a hope, we are very **b**, 2 Cor 3:12
but **b** toward you when I am away! 2 Cor 10:1
are much more **b** to speak the word Phil 1:14
though I am **b** enough in Christ to Phlm 1:8
B and willful, they do not tremble as 2 Pt 2:10

BOLDLY (10)
he had preached **b** in the name Acts 9:27
preaching **b** in the name of the Lord. Acts 9:28
And Paul and Barnabas spoke out **b**, Acts 13:46
a long time, speaking **b** for the Lord, Acts 14:3
began to speak **b** in the synagogue, Acts 18:26

and for three months spoke **b**, Acts 19:8
these things, and to him I speak **b**. Acts 26:26
written to you very **b** by way of Rom 15:15
opening my mouth **b** to proclaim the Eph 6:19
in chains, that I may declare it **b**, Eph 6:20

BOLDNESS (8)
when they saw the **b** of Peter and John, Acts 4:13
to speak your word with all **b**, Acts 4:29
to speak the word of God with **b**. Acts 4:31
Christ with all **b** and without Acts 28:31
I am acting with great **b** toward you; I 2 Cor 7:4
have to show **b** with such confidence 2 Cor 10:2
in whom we have **b** and access with Eph 3:12
we had **b** in our God to declare to you 1 Thes 2:2

BOLT (2)
of my presence and **b** the door after 2 Sm 13:17
liquid myrrh, on the handles of the **b**. Sg 5:5

BOLTED (1)
put her out and **b** the door after her. 2 Sm 13:18

BOLTS (6)
laid its beams and set its doors, its **b**, Neh 3:3
laid its beams and set its doors, its **b**, Neh 3:6
They rebuilt it and set its doors, its **b**, Neh 3:13
He rebuilt it and set its doors, its **b**, and Neh 3:14
it and covered it and set its doors, its **b**, Neh 3:15
and fiery lightning **b** through their Ps 105:32

BOND (9)
and there is none remaining, **b** or free. Dt 32:36
every male, both **b** and free in Israel, 1 Kgs 14:10
off from Ahab every male, **b** or free, 1 Kgs 21:21
off from Ahab every male, **b** or free, 2 Kgs 9:8
for there was none left, **b** or free, 2 Kgs 14:26
bring you into the **b** of the covenant. Ezk 20:37
be loosed from this **b** on the Sabbath Lk 13:16
of bitterness and in the **b** of iniquity." Acts 8:23
the unity of the Spirit in the **b** of peace. Eph 4:3

BONDAGE (3)
and brought you out of the house of **b**. Jgs 6:8
the land of Egypt, out of the house of **b**, Jer 34:13
set free from its **b** to decay and obtain Rom 8:21

BONDS (17)
fire, and his **b** melted off his hands. Jgs 15:14
Neco put him in **b** at Riblah in the 2 Kgs 23:33
He looses the **b** of kings and binds a Jb 12:18
Who has loosed the **b** of the swift Jb 39:5
"Let us burst their **b** apart and cast away Ps 2:3
of death, and burst their **b** apart. Ps 107:14
maidservant. You have loosed my **b**. Ps 116:16
do not scoff, lest your **b** be made strong; Is 28:22
loose the **b** from your neck, O captive Is 52:2
to loose the **b** of wickedness, to undo the Is 58:6
ago I broke your yoke and burst your **b**; Jer 2:20
broken the yoke; they had burst the **b**. Jer 5:5
off your neck, and I will burst your **b**, Jer 30:8
off you and will burst your **b** apart." Na 1:13
he would break the **b** and be driven by Lk 8:29
and everyone's **b** were unfastened. Acts 16:26
and bring them in **b** to Jerusalem to be Acts 22:5

BONE (14)
"This at last is **b** of my bones and flesh Gn 2:23
"Surely you are my **b** and my flesh!" Gn 29:14
or touches a human **b** or a grave, Nm 19:16
there and on whoever touched the **b**, Nm 19:18
also that I am your **b** and your flesh." Jgs 9:2
said, "Behold, we are your **b** and flesh. 2 Sm 5:1
brothers; you are my **b** and my flesh. 2 Sm 19:12
'Are you not my **b** and my flesh? 2 Sm 19:13
"Behold, we are your **b** and flesh. 1 Chr 11:1
your hand and touch his **b** and his flesh, Jb 2:5
and a soft tongue will break a **b**. Prv 25:15
the bones came together, **b** to its bone. Ezk 37:7
the bones came together, bone to its **b**. Ezk 37:7
the land and anyone sees a human **b**, Ezk 39:15

BONES (96)
last is bone of my **b** and flesh of my Gn 2:23
you shall carry up my **b** from here." Gn 50:25
and you shall not break any of its **b**. Ex 12:46
Moses took the **b** of Joseph with him, Ex 13:19
shall carry up my **b** with you from Ex 13:19
the morning, nor break any of its **b**; Nm 9:12
and shall break their **b** in pieces and Nm 24:8
As for the **b** of Joseph, which the people Jos 24:32
they took their **b** and buried them 1 Sm 31:13
went and took the **b** of Saul and the 2 Sm 21:12
of Saul and the **b** of his son Jonathan 2 Sm 21:12
up from there the **b** of Saul and the 2 Sm 21:13
of Saul and the **b** of his son 2 Sm 21:13
and they gathered the **b** of those who 2 Sm 21:13
And they buried the **b** of Saul and 2 Sm 21:14
and human **b** shall be burned on 1 Kgs 13:2
is buried; lay my **b** beside his bones. 1 Kgs 13:31
is buried; lay my bones beside his **b**. 1 Kgs 13:31
as the man touched the **b** of Elisha, 2 Kgs 13:21
filled their places with the **b** of men. 2 Kgs 23:14
sent and took the **b** out of the tombs 2 Kgs 23:16
no man move his **b**." So they let his 2 Kgs 23:18
his bones." So they let his **b** alone, 2 Kgs 23:18
with the **b** of the prophet who came 2 Kgs 23:18
and burned human **b** on them. 2 Kgs 23:20
they buried their **b** under the oak 1 Chr 10:12
He also burned the **b** of the priests on 2 Chr 34:5
trembling, which made all my **b** shake. Jb 4:14
strangling and death rather than my **b**. Jb 7:15
and knit me together with **b** and sinews. Jb 10:11
My **b** stick to my skin and to my flesh, Jb 19:20
His **b** are full of his youthful vigor, but Jb 20:11
of milk and the marrow of his **b** moist. Jb 21:24
The night racks my **b**, and the pain Jb 30:17
from me, and my **b** burn with heat. Jb 30:30
bed and with continual strife in his **b**, Jb 33:19
and his **b** that were not seen stick out. Jb 33:21
His **b** are tubes of bronze, his limbs like Jb 40:18
heal me, O LORD, for my **b** are troubled. Ps 6:2
like water, and all my **b** are out of joint; Ps 22:14
I can count all my **b**—they stare and Ps 22:17
of my iniquity, and my **b** waste away. Ps 31:10
my **b** wasted away through my groaning Ps 32:3
He keeps all his **b**; not one of them is Ps 34:20
All my **b** shall say, "O LORD, who is like Ps 35:10
is no health in my **b** because of my sin. Ps 38:3
As with a deadly wound in my **b**, my Ps 42:10
let the **b** that you have broken rejoice. Ps 51:8
For God scatters the **b** of him who Ps 53:5
smoke, and my **b** burn like a furnace. Ps 102:3
my loud groaning my **b** cling to my Ps 102:5
his body like water, like oil into his **b**! Ps 109:18
so shall our **b** be scattered at the mouth Ps 141:7
to your flesh and refreshment to your **b**. Prv 3:8
shame is like rottenness in his **b**. Prv 12:4
to the flesh, but envy makes the **b** rot. Prv 14:30
heart, and good news refreshes the **b**. Prv 15:30
but a crushed spirit dries up the **b**. Prv 17:22
spirit comes to the **b** in the womb of Eccl 11:5
morning; like a lion he breaks all my **b**; Is 38:13
places and make your **b** strong; Is 58:11
your **b** shall flourish like the grass; Is 66:14
the LORD, the **b** of the kings of Judah, Jer 8:1
of the kings of Judah, the **b** of its officials, Jer 8:1
bones of its officials, the **b** of the priests, Jer 8:1
bones of the priests, the **b** of the prophets, Jer 8:1
and the **b** of the inhabitants of Jerusalem Jer 8:1
it were a burning fire shut up in my **b**, Jer 20:9
is broken within me; all my **b** shake; Jer 23:9
king of Babylon has gnawed his **b**. Jer 50:17
sent fire; into my **b** he made it descend; Lam 1:13
skin waste away; he has broken my **b**; Lam 3:4
their skin has shriveled on their **b**; Lam 4:8
I will scatter your **b** around your altars. Ezk 6:5
and the shoulder; fill it with choice **b**. Ezk 24:4
it; boil it well; seethe also its **b** in it. Ezk 24:5
the spices, and let the **b** be burned up. Ezk 24:10
and whose iniquities are upon their **b**; Ezk 32:27
the middle of the valley; it was full of **b**. Ezk 37:1
man, can these **b** live?" And I answered, Ezk 37:3
he said to me, "Prophesy over these **b**, Ezk 37:4
these bones, and say to them, O dry **b**, Ezk 37:4
Thus says the Lord GOD to these **b**: Ezk 37:5
a rattling, and the **b** came together, Ezk 37:7
these **b** are the whole house of Israel. Ezk 37:11
Behold, they say, 'Our **b** are dried up, Ezk 37:11
them and broke all their **b** in pieces. Dn 6:24
he burned to lime the **b** of the king of Am 2:1
him up to bring the **b** out of the house, Am 6:10
my people and their flesh from off their **b**, Mi 3:2
and break their **b** in pieces and chop Mi 3:3
the sound; rottenness enters into my **b**; Hab 3:16
of dead people's **b** and all uncleanness. Mt 23:27
not have flesh and **b** as you see that Lk 24:39
"Not one of his **b** will be broken." Jn 19:36
and gave directions concerning his **b**. Heb 11:22

BOOK (157)
This is the **b** of the generations of Adam. Gn 5:1
as a memorial in a **b** and recite it in the Ex 17:14
Then he took the **B** of the Covenant and Ex 24:7
me out of your **b** that you have Ex 32:32
against me, I will blot out of my **b**. Ex 32:33
these curses in a **b** and wash them off Nm 5:23
it is said in the **B** of the Wars of the Nm 21:14
write for himself in a **b** a copy of this Dt 17:18
of this law that are written in this **b**, Dt 28:58
that is not recorded in the **b** of this law, Dt 28:61
curses written in this **b** will settle upon Dt 29:20
covenant written in this **B** of the Law. Dt 29:21
upon it all the curses written in this **b**, Dt 29:27
that are written in this **B** of the Law, Dt 30:10
words of this law in a **b** to the very end, Dt 31:24
"Take this **B** of the Law and put it by Dt 31:26
This **B** of the Law shall not depart from Jos 1:8
it is written in the **B** of the Law of Moses, Jos 8:31
to all that is written in the **B** of the Law. Jos 8:34
Is this not written in the **B** of Jashar? Jos 10:13
land and wrote in a **b** a description of it Jos 18:9
that is written in the **B** of the Law of Jos 23:6
wrote these words in the **B** of the Law of Jos 24:26
he wrote them in a **b** and laid it up 1 Sm 10:25
behold, it is written in the **B** of Jashar. 2 Sm 1:18
not written in the **B** of the Acts of 1 Kgs 11:41
written in the **B** of the Chronicles 1 Kgs 14:19
written in the **B** of the Chronicles 1 Kgs 14:29
not written in the **B** of the Chronicles 1 Kgs 15:7
written in the **B** of the Chronicles 1 Kgs 15:23
written in the **B** of the Chronicles 1 Kgs 15:31
not written in the **B** of the Chronicles 1 Kgs 16:5
written in the **B** of the Chronicles 1 Kgs 16:14
written in the **B** of the Chronicles 1 Kgs 16:20
written in the **B** of the Chronicles 1 Kgs 16:27
written in the **B** of the Chronicles 1 Kgs 22:39
written in the **B** of the Chronicles 1 Kgs 22:45
not written in the **B** of the Chronicles 2 Kgs 1:18
not written in the **B** of the Chronicles 2 Kgs 8:23
written in the **B** of the Chronicles 2 Kgs 10:34
written in the **B** of the Chronicles 2 Kgs 12:19
not written in the **B** of the Chronicles 2 Kgs 13:8
written in the **B** of the Chronicles 2 Kgs 13:12
what is written in the **B** of the Law of 2 Kgs 14:6
written in the **B** of the Chronicles 2 Kgs 14:15
written in the **B** of the Chronicles 2 Kgs 14:18
written in the **B** of the Chronicles 2 Kgs 14:28
not written in the **B** of the Chronicles 2 Kgs 15:6
written in the **B** of the Chronicles 2 Kgs 15:11
written in the **B** of the Chronicles 2 Kgs 15:15
written in the **B** of the Chronicles 2 Kgs 15:21
written in the **B** of the Chronicles 2 Kgs 15:26
written in the **B** of the Chronicles 2 Kgs 15:31
written in the **B** of the Chronicles 2 Kgs 15:36
written in the **B** of the Chronicles 2 Kgs 16:19
written in the **B** of the Chronicles 2 Kgs 20:20
written in the **B** of the Chronicles 2 Kgs 21:17
written in the **B** of the Chronicles 2 Kgs 21:25
"I have found the **B** of the Law in the 2 Kgs 22:8
And Hilkiah gave the **b** to Shaphan, 2 Kgs 22:8
given me a **b**." And Shaphan read 2 Kgs 22:10
heard the words of the **B** of the Law, 2 Kgs 22:11
the words of this **b** that has been 2 Kgs 22:13
have not obeyed the words of this **b**, 2 Kgs 22:13
the words of the **b** that the king of 2 Kgs 22:16
the words of the **B** of the Covenant 2 Kgs 23:2
covenant that were written in this **b**. 2 Kgs 23:3
is written in this **B** of the Covenant." 2 Kgs 23:21
written in the **b** that Hilkiah the 2 Kgs 23:24
written in the **B** of the Chronicles 2 Kgs 23:28
not written in the **B** of the Chronicles 2 Kgs 24:5
are written in the **B** of the Kings of 1 Chr 9:1
are written in the **B** of the Kings of 2 Chr 16:11
having the **B** of the Law of the LORD 2 Chr 17:9
are recorded in the **B** of the Kings of 2 Chr 20:34
in the Story of the **B** of the Kings. 2 Chr 24:27
written in the Law, in the **B** of Moses, 2 Chr 25:4
not written in the **B** of the Kings of 2 Chr 25:26
are written in the **B** of the Kings of 2 Chr 27:7
are written in the **B** of the Kings of 2 Chr 28:26
in the **B** of the Kings of Judah and 2 Chr 32:32
the priest found the **B** of the Law of 2 Chr 34:14
"I have found the **B** of the Law in the 2 Chr 34:15
And Hilkiah gave the **b** to Shaphan. 2 Chr 34:15
Shaphan brought the **b** to the king, 2 Chr 34:16
given me a **b**." And Shaphan read 2 Chr 34:18
the words of the **b** that has been 2 Chr 34:21
to all that is written in this **b**." 2 Chr 34:21
are written in the **b** that was read 2 Chr 34:24
the words of the **B** of the Covenant 2 Chr 34:30
covenant that were written in this **b**. 2 Chr 34:31
as it is written in the **B** of Moses. 2 Chr 35:12
are written in the **B** of the Kings of 2 Chr 35:27
are written in the **B** of the Kings of 2 Chr 36:8
may be made in the **b** of the records of Ezr 4:15
You will find in the **b** of the records and Ezr 4:15
as it is written in the **B** of Moses. Ezr 6:18
And I found the **b** of the genealogy of Neh 7:5
the scribe to bring the **B** of the Law of Neh 8:1
people were attentive to the **B** of the Law. Neh 8:3
And Ezra opened the **b** in the sight of all Neh 8:5
They read from the **b**, from the Law of Neh 8:8
he read from the **B** of the Law of God. Neh 8:18
place and read from the **B** of the Law of Neh 9:3
written in the **B** of the Chronicles Neh 12:23
they read from the **B** of Moses in the Neh 13:1
was recorded in the **b** of the chronicles Est 2:23
orders to bring the **b** of memorable deeds, Est 6:1
not written in the **B** of the Chronicles of Est 10:2
Oh that they were inscribed in a **b**! Jb 19:23

in the scroll of the **b** it is written of me: Ps 40:7
in your bottle. Are they not in your **b**? Ps 56:8
be blotted out of the **b** of the living; Ps 69:28
substance; in your **b** were written, Ps 139:16
to you like the words of a **b** that is sealed. Is 29:11
when they give the **b** to one who cannot Is 29:12
day the deaf shall hear the words of a **b**, Is 29:18
them on a tablet and inscribe it in a **b**, Is 30:8
Seek and read from the **b** of the LORD: Is 34:16
against it, everything written in this **b**, Jer 25:13
Write in a **b** all the words that I have Jer 30:2
these words in a **b** at the dictation of Jer 45:1
Jeremiah wrote in a **b** all the disaster Jer 51:60
When you finish reading this **b**, tie a Jer 51:63
me, and behold, a scroll of a **b** was in it. Ezk 2:9
you what is inscribed in the **b** of truth: Dn 10:21
name shall be found written in the **b**. Dn 12:1
Daniel, shut up the words and seal the **b**, Dn 12:4
The **b** of the vision of Nahum of Elkosh. Na 1:1
and a **b** of remembrance was written Mal 3:16
The **b** of the genealogy of Jesus Christ, the Mt 1:1
have you not read in the **b** of Moses, Mk 12:26
it is written in the **b** of the words of Isaiah Lk 3:4
David himself says in the **B** of Psalms, Lk 20:42
which are not written in this **b**; Jn 20:30
In the first **b**, O Theophilus, I have dealt Acts 1:1
"For it is written in the **B** of Psalms, Acts 1:20
as it is written in the **b** of the prophets: Acts 7:42
all things written in the **B** of the Law, Gal 3:10
whose names are in the **b** of life. Phil 4:3
and sprinkled both the **b** itself and all Heb 9:19
is written of me in the scroll of the **b**.'" Heb 10:7
what you see in a **b** and send it to the Rv 1:11
never blot his name out of the **b** of life. Rv 3:5
of the world in the **b** of life of the Lamb Rv 13:8
not been written in the **b** of life from the Rv 17:8
opened. Then another **b** was opened, Rv 20:12
book was opened, which is the **b** of life. Rv 20:12
was not found written in the **b** of life, Rv 20:15
who are written in the Lamb's **b** of life. Rv 21:27
the words of the prophecy of this **b**." Rv 22:7
with those who keep the words of this **b**. Rv 22:9
up the words of the prophecy of this **b**, Rv 22:10
the words of the prophecy of this **b**: Rv 22:18
to him the plagues described in this **b**, Rv 22:18
the words of the **b** of this prophecy, Rv 22:19
holy city, which are described in this **b**. Rv 22:19

BOOKS (8)
Of making many **b** there is no end, Eccl 12:12
sat in judgment, and the **b** were opened. Dn 7:10
perceived in the **b** the number of years Dn 9:2
could not contain the **b** that would be Jn 21:25
arts brought their **b** together and Acts 19:19
I left with Carpus at Troas, also the **b**, 2 Tm 4:13
before the throne, and **b** were opened. Rv 20:12
judged by what was written in the **b**, Rv 20:12

BOOT (1)
For every **b** of the tramping warrior in Is 9:5

BOOTH (9)
like a **b** that a watchman makes. Jb 27:18
of Zion is left like a **b** in a vineyard, Is 1:8
There will be a **b** for shade by day from the Is 4:6
He has laid waste his **b** like a garden, Lam 2:6
I will raise up the **b** of David that is Am 9:11
the city and made a **b** for himself there. Jon 4:5
a man called Matthew sitting at the tax **b**, Mt 9:9
the son of Alphaeus sitting at the tax **b**, Mk 2:14
named Levi, sitting at the tax **b**. Lk 5:27

BOOTHS (22)
a house and made **b** for his livestock. Gn 33:17
seven days is the Feast of **B** to the LORD. Lv 23:34
You shall dwell in **b** for seven days. All Lv 23:42
All native Israelites shall dwell in **b**, Lv 23:42
of Israel dwell in **b** when I brought Lv 23:43
shall keep the Feast of **B** seven days, Dt 16:13
Feast of Weeks, and at the Feast of **B**. Dt 16:16
in the year of release, at the Feast of **B**, Dt 31:10
ark and Israel and Judah dwell in **b**, 2 Sm 11:11
drinking with the kings in the **b**, 1 Kgs 20:12
drinking himself drunk in the **b**, 1 Kgs 20:16
Feast of Weeks, and the Feast of **B**. 2 Chr 8:13
And they kept the Feast of **B**, as it is Ezr 3:4
should dwell in **b** during the feast Neh 8:14
palm, and other leafy trees to make **b**, Neh 8:15
them and made **b** for themselves, Neh 8:16
from the captivity made **b** and lived in Neh 8:17
made booths and lived in the **b**, Neh 8:17
of hosts, and to keep the Feast of **B**. Zec 14:16
that do not go up to keep the Feast of **B**. Zec 14:18
that do not go up to keep the Feast of **B**. Zec 14:19
Now the Jews' Feast of **B** was at hand. Jn 7:2

BOR-ASHAN (1)
in Hormah, in **B**, in Athach, 1 Sm 30:30

BORDER (60)
as El-paran on the **b** of the wilderness. Gn 14:6
for ships, and his **b** shall be at Sidon. Gn 49:13
till they came to the **b** of the land of Ex 16:35
And I will set your **b** from the Red Sea Ex 23:31
Hor, on the **b** of the land of Edom, Nm 20:23
extends from the **b** of the Amorites, Nm 21:13
for the Arnon is the **b** of Moab, Nm 21:13
of Ar, and leans to the **b** of Moab." Nm 21:15
for the **b** of the Ammonites was Nm 21:24
Moab, on the **b** formed by the Arnon, Nm 22:36
the Arnon, at the extremity of the **b**. Nm 22:36
and your southern **b** shall run from Nm 34:3
And your **b** shall turn south of the Nm 34:4
And the **b** shall turn from Azmon to Nm 34:5
"For the western **b**, you shall have the Nm 34:6
its coast. This shall be your western **b**. Nm 34:6
"This shall be your northern **b**: from Nm 34:7
and the limit of the **b** shall be at Zedad. Nm 34:8
Then the **b** shall extend to Ziphron, Nm 34:9
This shall be your northern **b**. Nm 34:9
for your eastern **b** from Hazar-enan to Nm 34:10
And the **b** shall go down from Nm 34:11
And the **b** shall go down and reach to Nm 34:11
And the **b** shall go down to the Jordan, Nm 34:12
you are to cross the **b** of Moab at Ar. Dt 2:18
as far as the **b** of the Geshurites and the Dt 3:14
with the middle of the valley as a **b**, Dt 3:16
river Jabbok, the **b** of the Ammonites; Dt 3:16
Arabah also, with the Jordan as the **b**, Dt 3:17
at Gilgal on the east **b** of Jericho. Jos 4:19
And the **b** of the people of Reuben was Jos 13:23
goes down to the **b** of the mountain Jos 18:16
of the Jordan: this is the southern **b**. Jos 18:19
And the **b** of the Amorites ran from the Jgs 1:36
as far as the **b** of Abel-meholah, Jgs 7:22
them as far as the **b** of Beth-shemesh. 1 Sm 6:12
turned toward the **b** that looks down 1 Sm 13:18
the Philistines and to the **b** of Egypt. 1 Kgs 4:21
out and were drawn up at the **b**. 2 Kgs 3:21
He restored the **b** of Israel from 2 Kgs 14:25
would bless me and enlarge my **b**, 1 Chr 4:10
the Philistines and to the **b** of Egypt. 2 Chr 9:26
fame spread even to the **b** of Egypt, 2 Chr 26:8
of Egypt, and a pillar to the LORD at its **b**. Is 19:19
in its proper place, and emmer as the **b**? Is 28:25
I will judge you at the **b** of Israel, and Ezk 11:10
of it. I will judge you at the **b** of Israel, Ezk 11:11
to Syene, as far as the **b** of Cush. Ezk 29:10
lies on the **b** between Damascus and Ezk 47:16
which is on the **b** of Hauran. Ezk 47:16
is on the northern **b** of Damascus, Ezk 47:17
with the **b** of Hamath to the north. Ezk 47:17
is on the northern **b** of Damascus over Ezk 48:1
cubits of the holy portion to the east **b**, Ezk 48:21
from the 25,000 cubits to the west **b**, Ezk 48:21
order to remove them far from their own **b**. Jl 3:6
Gilead, that they might enlarge their **b**. Am 1:13
All your allies have driven you to your **b**; Ob 1:7
into our land and treads within our **b**. Mi 5:6
is the LORD beyond the **b** of Israel!" Mal 1:5

BORDERS (12)
nations before you and enlarge your **b**; Ex 34:24
the land of Canaan as defined by its **b**), Nm 34:2
land as defined by its **b** all around." Nm 34:12
he fixed the **b** of the peoples according to Dt 32:8
clear it and possess it to its farthest **b**. Jos 17:18
me any longer within the **b** of Israel, 1 Sm 27:1
to their settlements within their **b**: 1 Chr 6:54
He makes peace in your **b**; he fills you Ps 147:14
you have enlarged all the **b** of the land. Is 26:15
or destruction within your **b**; Is 60:18
Your **b** are in the heart of the seas; your Ezk 27:4
and on Hamath also, which **b** on it, Tyre Zec 9:2

BORE (144)
his wife, and she conceived and **b** Cain, Gn 4:1
And again, she **b** his brother Abel. Now Gn 4:2
wife, and she conceived and **b** Enoch. Gn 4:17
Adah **b** Jabal; he was the father of those Gn 4:20
Zillah also **b** Tubal-cain; he was the Gn 4:22
and she **b** a son and called his name Gn 4:25
of man and they **b** children to them. Gn 6:4
The waters increased and **b** up the ark, Gn 7:17
And Hagar **b** Abram a son, and Gn 16:15
the name of his son, whom Hagar **b**, Gn 16:15
old when Hagar **b** Ishmael to Abram. Gn 16:16
The firstborn **b** a son and called his Gn 19:37
The younger also **b** a son and called Gn 19:38
female slaves so that they **b** children. Gn 20:17
Sarah conceived and **b** Abraham a son Gn 21:2
was born to him, whom Sarah **b** him, Gn 21:3
These eight Milcah **b** to Nahor, Gn 22:23
whose name was Reumah, **b** Tebah, Gn 22:24
son of Milcah, whom she **b** to Nahor." Gn 24:24
Sarah my master's wife **b** a son to my Gn 24:36
Nahor's son, whom Milcah **b** to him.' Gn 24:47
She **b** him Zimran, Jokshan, Medan, Gn 25:2
Sarah's servant, **b** to Abraham. Gn 25:12
was sixty years old when she **b** them. Gn 25:26
And Leah conceived and **b** a son, and Gn 29:32
She conceived again and **b** a son, and Gn 29:33
Again she conceived and **b** a son, and Gn 29:34
And she conceived again and **b** a son, Gn 29:35
saw that she **b** Jacob no children, Gn 30:1
Bilhah conceived and **b** Jacob a son. Gn 30:5
conceived again and **b** Jacob a second Gn 30:7
Leah's servant Zilpah **b** Jacob a son. Gn 30:10
Leah's servant Zilpah **b** Jacob a second Gn 30:12
and she conceived and **b** Jacob a fifth Gn 30:17
again, and she **b** Jacob a sixth son. Gn 30:19
Afterward she **b** a daughter and called Gn 30:21
She conceived and **b** a son and said, Gn 30:23
your wages,' then all the flock **b** spotted; Gn 31:8
your wages,' then all the flock **b** striped. Gn 31:8
bring to you. I **b** the loss of it myself. Gn 31:39
And Adah **b** to Esau, Eliphaz; Basemath Gn 36:4
to Esau, Eliphaz; Basemath **b** Reuel; Gn 36:4
and Oholibamah **b** Jeush, Jalam, and Gn 36:5
Esau's son; she **b** Amalek to Eliphaz.) Gn 36:12
she **b** to Esau Jeush, Jalam, and Korah. Gn 36:14
and she conceived and **b** a son, and he Gn 38:3
She conceived again and **b** a son, and Gn 38:4
Yet again she **b** a son, and she called his Gn 38:5
Judah was in Chezib when she **b** him. Gn 38:5
Potiphera priest of On, **b** them to him. Gn 41:50
know that my wife **b** me two sons. Gn 44:27
whom she **b** to Jacob in Paddan-aram, Gn 46:15
and these she **b** to Jacob—sixteen Gn 46:18
of Potiphera the priest of On, **b** to him. Gn 46:20
and these she **b** to Jacob—seven Gn 46:25
The woman conceived and **b** a son, and Ex 2:2
sister, and she **b** him Aaron and Moses, Ex 6:20
of Nahshon, and she **b** him Nadab, Ex 6:23
of Putiel, and she **b** him Phinehas. Ex 6:25
and how I **b** you on eagles' wings and Ex 19:4
And his master shall **b** his ear through Ex 21:6
blossoms, and it **b** ripe almonds. Nm 17:8
And she **b** to Amram Aaron and Nm 26:59
displeasure that the LORD **b** against you, Dt 9:19
were unmindful of the Rock that **b** you, Dt 32:18
who was in Shechem also **b** him a son, Jgs 8:31
And Gilead's wife also **b** him sons. And Jgs 11:2
And the woman **b** a son and called his Jgs 13:24
of Perez, whom Tamar **b** to Judah, Ru 4:12
gave her conception, and she **b** a son. Ru 4:13
time Hannah conceived and **b** a son, 1 Sm 1:20
she conceived and **b** three sons and 1 Sm 2:21
And when those who **b** the ark of the 2 Sm 6:13
became his wife and **b** him a son. 2 Sm 11:27
child that Uriah's wife **b** to David, 2 Sm 12:15
and lay with her, and she **b** a son, 2 Sm 12:24
of Aiah, whom she **b** to Saul, 2 Sm 21:8
whom she **b** to Adriel the son of 2 Sm 21:8
sister of Tahpenes **b** him Genubath 1 Kgs 11:20
and she **b** a son about that time the 2 Kgs 4:17
concubine: she **b** Zimran, 1 Chr 1:32
Bath-shua the Canaanite **b** to him. 1 Chr 2:3
Tamar also **b** him Perez 1 Chr 2:4
Abigail **b** Amasa, and the father of 1 Chr 2:17
married Ephrath, who **b** him Hur. 1 Chr 2:19
sixty years old, and she **b** him Segub. 1 Chr 2:21
his father, and she **b** him Ashhur, 1 Chr 2:24
and she **b** him Ahban and Molid. 1 Chr 2:29
Jarha his slave, and she **b** him Attai. 1 Chr 2:35
also, Caleb's concubine, **b** Haran, 1 Chr 2:46
concubine, **b** Sheber and Tirhanah. 1 Chr 2:48
She also **b** Shaaph the father of 1 Chr 2:49
Naarah **b** him Ahuzzam, Hepher, 1 Chr 4:6
saying, "Because I **b** him in pain." 1 Chr 4:9
and she conceived and **b** Miriam, 1 Chr 4:17
his Judahite wife **b** Jered the father 1 Chr 4:18
whom his Aramean concubine **b**; 1 Chr 7:14
she **b** Machir the father of Gilead. 1 Chr 7:14
Maacah the wife of Machir **b** a son, 1 Chr 7:16
his sister Hammolecheth **b** Ishhod, 1 Chr 7:18
wife, and she conceived and **b** a son. 1 Chr 7:23
and she **b** him sons, Jeush, 2 Chr 11:19
of Absalom, who **b** him Abijah, 2 Chr 11:20
Many years you **b** with them and Neh 9:30
and bitterness to her who **b** him. Prv 17:25
be glad; let her who **b** you rejoice. Prv 23:25
one of her mother, pure to her who **b** her. Sg 6:9
you; there she who **b** you was in labor. Sg 8:5
prophetess, and she conceived and **b** a son. Is 8:3
And Elam **b** the quiver with chariots and Is 22:6
your father and to Sarah who **b** you; Is 51:2
yet he **b** the sin of many, and makes Is 53:12
She who **b** seven has grown feeble; she Jer 15:9
Woe is me, my mother, that you **b** me, Jer 15:10

the mothers who **b** them and the Jer 16:3
The day when my mother **b** me, let it Jer 20:14
and the mother who **b** you into another Jer 22:26
because I **b** the disgrace of my youth.' Jer 31:19
and she who **b** you shall be disgraced. Jer 50:12
mine, and they **b** sons and daughters. Ezk 23:4
and she conceived and **b** him a son. Hos 1:3
She conceived again and **b** a daughter. Hos 1:6
No Mercy, she conceived and **b** a son. Hos 1:8
father and mother who **b** him will say Zec 13:3
and mother who **b** him shall pierce Zec 13:3
took our illnesses and **b** our diseases." Mt 8:17
when the plants came up and **b** grain, Mt 13:26
For many **b** false witness against him, Mk 14:56
stood up and **b** false witness against Mk 14:57
Elizabeth to give birth, and she **b** a son. Lk 1:57
him, "Blessed is the womb that **b** you, Lk 11:27
the wombs that never **b** and the breasts Lk 23:29
(John **b** witness about him, and cried Jn 1:15
And John **b** witness: "I saw the Spirit Jn 1:32
Jordan, to whom you **b** witness—look, Jn 3:26
other words he **b** witness and Acts 2:40
who **b** witness to the word of his grace, Acts 14:3
knows the heart, **b** witness to them, Acts 15:8
while God also **b** witness by signs and Heb 2:4
gave rain, and the earth **b** its fruit. Jas 5:18
He himself **b** our sins in his body on 1 Pt 2:24
who **b** witness to the word of God and to Rv 1:2
so that when she **b** her child he might Rv 12:4
upon the people who **b** the mark of the Rv 16:2

BORED (1)
priest took a chest and **b** a hole in the 2 Kgs 12:9

BORN (137)
To Enoch was **b** Irad, and Irad fathered Gn 4:18
To Seth also a son was **b**, and he called Gn 4:26
of the land and daughters were **b** to them, Gn 6:1
Sons were **b** to them after the flood. Gn 10:1
brother of Japheth, children were **b**. Gn 10:21
To Eber were **b** two sons: the name of Gn 10:25
forth his trained men, **b** in his house, Gn 14:14
whether **b** in your house or bought Gn 17:12
both he who is **b** in your house and he Gn 17:13
"Shall a child be **b** to a man who is a Gn 17:17
his son and all those **b** in his house or Gn 17:23
those **b** in the house and those bought Gn 17:27
the name of his son who was **b** to him, Gn 21:3
old when his son Isaac was **b** to him. Gn 21:5
who was **b** to Bethuel the son of Gn 24:15
of Jacob who were **b** to him in Gn 35:26
sons of Esau who were **b** to him in the Gn 36:5
are the chiefs **b** of Oholibamah the Gn 36:18
came, two sons were **b** to Joseph. Gn 41:50
of Egypt were **b** Manasseh and Gn 46:20
who were **b** to Jacob—fourteen persons Gn 46:22
of Joseph, who were **b** to him in Egypt, Gn 46:27
who were **b** to you in the land of Egypt Gn 48:5
"Every son that is **b** to the Hebrews you Ex 1:22
and anyone **b** in his house may eat of Lv 22:11
"When an ox or sheep or goat is **b**, it Lv 22:27
you, who have been **b** in your land, Lv 25:45
of Levi, who was **b** to Levi in Egypt. Nm 26:59
And to Aaron were **b** Nadab, Abihu, Nm 26:60
firstborn males that are **b** of your herd Dt 15:19
"No one **b** of a forbidden union may Dt 23:2
Children **b** to them in the third Dt 23:8
all the people who were **b** on the way in Jos 5:5
all Israel, sojourner as well as native **b**, Jos 8:33
are to do with the child who will be **b**." Jgs 13:8
Dan their ancestor, who was **b** to Israel; Jgs 18:29
"A son has been **b** to Naomi." They Ru 4:17
And sons were **b** to David at Hebron: 2 Sm 3:2
wife. These were **b** to David in Hebron. 2 Sm 3:5
sons and daughters were **b** to David. 2 Sm 5:13
of those who were **b** to him in 2 Sm 5:14
the child who is **b** to you shall die." 2 Sm 12:14
There were **b** to Absalom three sons, 2 Sm 14:27
and he was **b** next after Absalom. 1 Kgs 1:6
son who shall be **b** to you shall build 1 Kgs 8:19
a son shall be **b** to the house of David, 1 Kgs 13:2
own sons, who shall be **b** to you, 2 Kgs 20:18
To Eber were **b** two sons: the name of 1 Chr 1:19
The sons of Hezron that were **b** to him: 1 Chr 2:9
of David who were **b** to him in 1 Chr 3:1
six were **b** to him in Hebron, where he 1 Chr 3:4
These were **b** to him in Jerusalem: 1 Chr 3:5
of Gath who were **b** in the land killed, 1 Chr 7:21
names of the children **b** to him in 1 Chr 14:4
a son shall be **b** to you who shall be a 1 Chr 22:9
Shemaiah were sons **b** who were 1 Chr 26:6
son who shall be **b** to you shall build 2 Chr 6:9
There were **b** to him seven sons and three Jb 1:2
"Let the day perish on which I was **b**, and Jb 3:3
but man is **b** to trouble as the sparks fly Jb 5:7
when a wild donkey's colt is **b** a man! Jb 11:12
"Man who is **b** of a woman is few of days Jb 14:1
"Are you the first man who was **b**? Or Jb 15:7
Or he who is **b** of a woman, that he can Jb 15:14
How can he who is **b** of woman be pure? Jb 25:4
You know, for you were **b** then, and the Jb 38:21
Cush—"This one was **b** there," they say. Ps 87:4
"This one and that one were **b** in her"; Ps 87:5
the peoples, "This one was **b** there." Selah Ps 87:6
times, and a brother is **b** for adversity. Prv 17:17
and had slaves who were **b** in my house. Eccl 2:7
a time to be **b**, and a time to die; a time Eccl 3:2
his own kingdom he had been **b** poor. Eccl 4:14
For to us a child is **b**, to us a son is given; Is 9:6
things? Shall a land be **b** in one day? Is 66:8
and before you were **b** I consecrated you; Jer 1:5
and daughters who are **b** in this place, Jer 16:3
Cursed be the day on which I was **b**! Jer 20:14
"A son is **b** to you," making him very Jer 20:15
another country, where you were not **b**, Jer 22:26
the day you were **b** your cord was not Ezk 16:4
abhorred, on the day that you were **b**. Ezk 16:5
and make her as in the day she was **b**, Hos 2:3
husband of Mary, of whom Jesus was **b**, Mt 1:16
Now after Jesus was **b** in Bethlehem of Mt 2:1
is he who has been **b** king of the Jews? Mt 2:2
of them where the Christ was to be **b**. Mt 2:4
among those **b** of women there has Mt 11:11
for that man if he had not been **b**." Mt 26:24
for that man if he had not been **b**." Mk 14:21
the child to be **b** will be called holy Lk 1:35
For unto you is **b** this day in the city of Lk 2:11
among those **b** of women none is greater Lk 7:28
who were **b**, not of blood nor of the will of Jn 1:13
unless one is **b** again he cannot see the Jn 3:3
"How can a man be **b** when he is old? Jn 3:4
time into his mother's womb and be **b**?" Jn 3:4
you, unless one is **b** of water and the Spirit, Jn 3:5
That which is **b** of the flesh is flesh, and Jn 3:6
and that which is **b** of the Spirit is spirit. Jn 3:6
that I said to you, 'You must be **b** again.' Jn 3:7
it is with everyone who is **b** of the Spirit." Jn 3:8
"We were not **b** of sexual immorality. Jn 8:41
man or his parents, that he was **b** blind?" Jn 9:2
this your son, who you say was **b** blind? Jn 9:19
this is our son and that he was **b** blind. Jn 9:20
anyone opened the eyes of a man **b** blind. Jn 9:32
answered him, "You were **b** in utter sin, Jn 9:34
being has been **b** into the world. Jn 16:21
this purpose I was **b** and for this Jn 18:37
At this time Moses was **b**; and he was Acts 7:20
"I am a Jew, **b** in Tarsus in Cilicia, but Acts 22:3
they were not yet **b** and had done Rom 9:11
man, so man is now **b** of woman. 1 Cor 11:12
Last of all, as to one untimely **b**, he 1 Cor 15:8
he who had set me apart before I was **b**, Gal 1:15
God sent forth his Son, **b** of woman, Gal 4:4
Son, born of woman, **b** under the law, Gal 4:4
of the slave was **b** according to the Gal 4:23
the free woman was **b** through promise. Gal 4:23
time he who was **b** according to the Gal 4:29
him who was **b** according to the Gal 4:29
servant, being **b** in the likeness of men. Phil 2:7
were **b** descendants as many as the Heb 11:12
By faith Moses, when he was **b**, was Heb 11:23
has caused us to be **b** again to a living 1 Pt 1:3
since you have been **b** again, not of 1 Pt 1:23
instinct, **b** to be caught and destroyed, 2 Pt 2:12
righteousness has been **b** of him. 1 Jn 2:29
No one **b** of God makes a practice of 1 Jn 3:9
sinning because he has been **b** of God. 1 Jn 3:9
whoever loves has been **b** of God and 1 Jn 4:7
Jesus is the Christ has been **b** of God, 1 Jn 5:1
Father loves whoever has been **b** of him. 1 Jn 5:1
who has been **b** of God overcomes 1 Jn 5:4
everyone who has been **b** of God does 1 Jn 5:18
but he who was **b** of God protects him, 1 Jn 5:18

BORNE (36)
Abram's wife, had **b** him no children. Gn 16:1
Yet I have **b** him a son in his old age." Gn 21:7
Egyptian, whom she had **b** to Abraham, Gn 21:9
Milcah also has **b** children to your Gn 22:20
because I have **b** him three sons." Gn 29:34
because I have **b** him six sons." So she Gn 30:20
As soon as Rachel had **b** Joseph, Jacob Gn 30:25
for their children whom they have **b**? Gn 31:43
of Leah, whom she had **b** to Jacob, Gn 34:1
and the unloved have **b** him children, Dt 21:15
you are barren and have not **b** children, Jgs 13:3
The barren has **b** seven, but she who 1 Sm 2:5
for you have **b** a son." But she did not 1 Sm 4:20
he was not the child that I had **b**." 1 Kgs 3:21
of the women had even **b** children. Ezr 10:44
said to God, 'I have **b** punishment; Jb 34:31
it is for your sake that I have **b** reproach, Ps 69:7
things you carry are **b** as burdens on Is 46:1
who have been **b** by me from before your Is 46:3
say in your heart: 'Who has **b** me these? Is 49:21
guide her among all the sons she has **b**; Is 51:18
Surely he has **b** our griefs and carried our Is 53:4
daughters, whom you had **b** to me, Ezk 16:20
the children whom they had **b** to me. Ezk 23:37
the LORD; for they have **b** alien children. Hos 5:7
to us who have **b** the burden of the Mt 20:12
have seen and have **b** witness that this is Jn 1:34
to John, and he has **b** witness to the truth. Jn 5:33
sent me has himself **b** witness about me. Jn 5:37
who saw it has **b** witness—his Jn 19:35
Just as we have **b** the image of the 1 Cor 15:49
and the voice was **b** to him by the 2 Pt 1:17
heard this very voice **b** from heaven, 2 Pt 1:18
God that he has **b** concerning his Son. 1 Jn 5:9
that God has **b** concerning his Son. 1 Jn 5:10
of God and for the witness they had **b**. Rv 6:9

BORROW (4)
to many nations, but you shall not **b**, Dt 15:6
to many nations, but you shall not **b**. Dt 28:12
b vessels from all your neighbors, 2 Kgs 4:3
refuse the one who would **b** from you. Mt 5:42

BORROWED (3)
cried out, "Alas, my master! It was **b**." 2 Kgs 6:5
"We have **b** money for the king's tax on Neh 5:4
I have not lent, nor have I **b**, yet all of Jer 15:10

BORROWER (2)
poor, and the **b** is the slave of the lender. Prv 22:7
the seller; as with the lender, so with the **b**; Is 24:2

BORROWS (2)
"If a man **b** anything of his neighbor, Ex 22:14
The wicked **b** but does not pay back, Ps 37:21

BOSOM (11)
say to me, 'Carry them in your **b**, Nm 11:12
do by hiding my iniquity in my **b**, Jb 31:33
and embrace the **b** of an adulteress? Prv 5:20
angry, for anger lodges in the **b** of fools. Eccl 7:9
he will carry them in his **b**, and gently Is 40:11
they shall bring your sons in their **b**, Is 49:22
will repay; I will indeed repay into their **b** Is 65:6
measure into their **b** payment for their Is 65:7
life is poured out on their mothers' **b**. Lam 2:12
handled her virgin **b** and poured out Ezk 23:8
Egyptians handled your **b** and pressed Ezk 23:21

BOSOMS (1)
pressed and their virgin **b** handled. Ezk 23:3

BOSSED (1)
against him with a thickly **b** shield; Jb 15:26

BOTH (260)
and his wife were **b** naked and were not Gn 2:25
Then the eyes of **b** were opened, and they Gn 3:7
a garment, laid it on **b** their shoulders, Gn 9:23
could not support **b** of them dwelling Gn 13:6
b he who is born in your house and he Gn 17:13
the men of Sodom, **b** young and old, Gn 19:4
of the house, **b** small and great, Gn 19:11
Thus **b** the daughters of Lot became Gn 19:36
because there **b** of them swore an oath. Gn 21:31
knife. So they went **b** of them together. Gn 22:6
son." So they went **b** of them together. Gn 22:8
"We have plenty of **b** straw and fodder, Gn 24:25
should I be bereft of you **b** in one day?" Gn 27:45
be destroyed, **b** I and my household." Gn 34:30
And one night they **b** dreamed—the Gn 40:5
b we and you and also our little ones. Gn 43:8
b we and he also in whose hand the Gn 44:16
even until now, **b** we and our fathers,' Gn 46:34
before your eyes, **b** we and our land? Gn 47:19
And Joseph took them **b**, Ephraim in Gn 48:13
up with him **b** chariots and horsemen. Gn 50:9
mouth and will teach you **b** what to do. Ex 4:15
all the land of Egypt, **b** man and beast. Ex 9:25
in the land of Egypt, **b** man and beast; Ex 12:12
people, **b** you and the people of Israel; Ex 12:31
much livestock, **b** flocks and herds. Ex 12:38
people of Israel, **b** of man and of beast, Ex 13:2
b the firstborn of man and the Ex 13:15
the case of **b** parties shall come before Ex 22:9
shall be between them **b** to see whether Ex 22:11
Thus shall it be with **b** of them; they Ex 26:24
tablets that were written on **b** sides; Ex 32:15
So they came, **b** men and women. All Ex 35:22
b him and Oholiab the son of Ex 35:34
On **b** sides of the gate of the court were Ex 38:15
for a burnt offering, **b** without blemish, Lv 9:2
and a lamb, **b** a year old without blemish, Lv 9:3
b of them shall bathe themselves in Lv 15:18
And Aaron shall lay **b** his hands on the Lv 16:21
b the adulterer and the adulteress shall Lv 20:10
b of them shall surely be put to death; Lv 20:11
b of them shall surely be put to death; Lv 20:12

b of them have committed an Lv 20:13
B of them shall be cut off from among Lv 20:18
b of the most holy and of the holy Lv 21:22
then **b** it and the substitute shall be Lv 27:10
then **b** it and the substitute shall be Lv 27:33
in Israel, **b** of man and of beast. Nm 3:13
You shall put out **b** male and female, Nm 5:3
b of them full of fine flour mixed with Nm 7:13
b of them full of fine flour mixed with Nm 7:19
b of them full of fine flour mixed with Nm 7:25
b of them full of fine flour mixed with Nm 7:31
b of them full of fine flour mixed with Nm 7:37
b of them full of fine flour mixed with Nm 7:43
b of them full of fine flour mixed with Nm 7:49
b of them full of fine flour mixed with Nm 7:55
b of them full of fine flour mixed with Nm 7:61
b of them full of fine flour mixed with Nm 7:67
b of them full of fine flour mixed with Nm 7:73
b of them full of fine flour mixed with Nm 7:79
Israel are mine, **b** of man and of beast. Nm 8:17
b for the sojourner and for the native." Nm 9:14
And when **b** are blown, all the Nm 10:3
and Miriam, and they **b** came forward. Nm 12:5
we should die here, **b** we and our cattle? Nm 20:4
the chamber and pierced **b** of them, Nm 25:8
b he and all the people of Israel with Nm 27:21
all the plunder, **b** of man and of beast. Nm 31:11
that was taken, **b** of man and of beast, Nm 31:26
of every 50, **b** of persons and of beasts, Nm 31:47
then **b** parties to the dispute shall Dt 19:17
and **b** the loved and the unloved have Dt 21:15
of another man, **b** of them shall die, Dt 22:22
you shall bring them **b** out to the gate Dt 22:24
for **b** of these are an abomination to the Dt 23:18
city to destruction, **b** men and women, Jos 6:21
all who fell that day, **b** men and women, Jos 8:25
b those in Beth-shean and its villages Jos 17:16
locusts in number—**b** they and their Jgs 6:5
the day declines." So they ate, **b** of them. Jgs 19:8
and **b** Mahlon and Chilion died, so that Ru 1:5
continued to grow **b** in stature and 1 Sm 2:26
b of them shall die on the same day. 1 Sm 2:34
head of Dagon and **b** his hands were 1 Sm 5:4
tumors, **b** Ashdod and its territory. 1 Sm 5:6
the men of the city, **b** young and old, 1 Sm 5:9
b fortified cities and unwalled 1 Sm 6:18
and **b** he and Samuel went out into 1 Sm 9:26
and if **b** you and the king who reigns 1 Sm 12:14
swept away, **b** you and your king." 1 Sm 12:25
So **b** of them showed themselves to 1 Sm 14:11
them, but kill **b** man and woman, 1 Sm 15:3
has struck down **b** lions and bears, 1 Sm 17:36
the field." So they **b** went out into the 1 Sm 20:11
because we have sworn **b** of us in the 1 Sm 20:42
b man and woman, child and 1 Sm 22:19
were a wall to us **b** by night and by 1 Sm 25:16
and **b** of them became his wives. 1 Sm 25:43
all who were in it, **b** small and great. 1 Sm 30:2
of Israel, **b** men and women, 2 Sm 6:19
table. Now he was lame in **b** his feet. 2 Sm 9:13
was set against him **b** in front and in 2 Sm 10:9
and let me see **b** it and his dwelling 2 Sm 15:25
b by David and by Absalom. 2 Sm 16:23
So **b** of them went away quickly and 2 Sm 17:18
b you and all your servants." 2 Sm 19:14
have not asked, **b** riches and honor, 1 Kgs 3:13
b the nave and the inner sanctuary. 1 Kgs 6:5
b cherubim had the same measure 1 Kgs 6:25
b above and below the lions and 1 Kgs 7:29
male, **b** bond and free in Israel, 1 Kgs 14:10
b because of all the evil that he did in 1 Kgs 16:7
as they **b** were standing by the Jordan. 2 Kgs 2:7
all the people, **b** small and great. 2 Kgs 23:2
all the people, **b** small and great, 2 Kgs 25:26
who built **b** Lower and Upper 1 Chr 7:24
Joash, **b** sons of Shemaah of Gibeah; 1 Chr 12:3
to all Israel, **b** men and women, 1 Chr 16:3
was set against him **b** in front and 1 Chr 19:10
officers of God among **b** the sons of 1 Chr 24:5
B riches and honor come from you, 1 Chr 29:12
b for the service and for the burnt 2 Chr 24:14
b in the Shephelah and in the plain, 2 Chr 26:10
b he and the inhabitants of 2 Chr 32:26
all the people **b** great and small. 2 Chr 34:30
b men and women and all who could Neh 8:2
So **b** choirs of those who gave thanks Neh 12:40
in Susa, the citadel, **b** great and small, Est 1:5
the men were **b** hanged on the gallows. Est 2:23
of King Ahasuerus, **b** near and far, Est 9:20
He destroys **b** the blameless and the Jb 9:22
us, who might lay his hand on us **b**. Jb 9:33
B the gray-haired and the aged are Jb 15:10
In peace I will **b** lie down and sleep; for Ps 4:8
b low and high, rich and poor together! Ps 49:2
of Jacob, **b** rider and horse lay stunned. Ps 76:6
living things **b** small and great. Ps 104:25
B we and our fathers have sinned; we Ps 106:6
the LORD, **b** the small and the great. Ps 115:13
of Egypt, **b** of man and of beast; Ps 135:8
the righteous are **b** alike an Prv 17:15
unequal measures are **b** alike an Prv 20:10
seeing eye, the LORD has made them **b**. Prv 20:12
the ruin that will come from them **b**? Prv 24:22
a fool's provocation is heavier than **b**. Prv 27:3
the LORD gives light to the eyes of **b**. Prv 29:13
I got singers, **b** men and women, and Eccl 2:8
But better than **b** is he who has not yet Eccl 4:3
God shall come out from **b** of them. Eccl 7:18
man does not know; **b** are before him. Eccl 9:1
that, or whether **b** alike will be good. Eccl 11:6
spark, and **b** of them shall burn together, Is 1:31
a rock of stumbling to **b** houses of Israel, Is 8:14
the LORD will destroy, **b** soul and body, Is 10:18
Cushite exiles, **b** the young and the old, Is 20:4
fruit; let the earth cause them **b** to sprout; Is 45:8
b your iniquities and your fathers' Is 65:7
courage shall fail **b** king and officials. Jer 4:9
b husband and wife shall be taken, the Jer 6:11
b the birds of the air and the beasts have Jer 9:10
They are **b** stupid and foolish; the Jer 10:8
For **b** prophet and priest ply their trade Jer 14:18
B great and small shall die in this land. Jer 16:6
of this city, **b** man and beast. Jer 21:6
"**B** prophet and priest are ungodly; even Jer 23:11
b this sealed deed of purchase and this Jer 32:14
to her, as we did, **b** we and our fathers, Jer 44:17
warrior; they have **b** fallen together." Jer 46:12
in it; **b** man and beast shall flee away. Jer 50:3
for the LORD has **b** planned and done Jer 51:12
the fire has consumed **b** ends of it, Ezk 15:4
b the fortunes of Sodom and her Ezk 16:53
sisters, **b** your elder and your younger, Ezk 16:61
off from you **b** righteous and wicked. Ezk 21:3
off from you **b** righteous and wicked, Ezk 21:4
B of them shall come from the same Ezk 21:19
was defiled; they **b** took the same way. Ezk 23:13
b the strong arm and the one that was Ezk 30:22
B it and its vestibule had windows all Ezk 40:25
and **b** it and its vestibule had windows Ezk 40:29
and **b** it and its vestibule had windows Ezk 40:33
belong the land on **b** sides of the holy Ezk 45:7
on the banks, on **b** sides of the river, Ezk 47:12
"What remains on **b** sides of the holy Ezk 48:21
b of the royal family and of the nobility, Dn 1:3
It had two horns, and **b** horns were high, Dn 8:3
to seal **b** vision and prophet, Dn 9:24
and consume it, **b** timber and stones." Zec 5:4
of peace shall be between them **b**."' Zec 6:13
fresh wineskins, and so **b** are preserved." Mt 9:17
him who can destroy **b** soul and body Mt 10:28
Let **b** grow together until the harvest, Mt 13:30
lead the blind, **b** will fall into a pit." Mt 15:14
all whom they found, **b** bad and good. Mt 22:10
And they were **b** righteous before God, Lk 1:6
barren, and **b** were advanced in years. Lk 1:7
And they came and filled **b** the boats, so Lk 5:7
man? Will they not **b** fall into a pit? Lk 6:39
could not pay, he cancelled the debt of **b**. Lk 7:42
he who invited you **b** will come and say Lk 14:9
ready to go with you **b** to prison and to Lk 22:33
together, **b** chief priests and scribes. Lk 22:66
come and take away **b** our place and Jn 11:48
have seen and hated **b** me and my Jn 15:24
B of them were running together, but the Jn 20:4
b Jews and proselytes, Cretans and Acts 2:11
patriarch David that he **b** died and was Acts 2:29
God has made him **b** Lord and Christ, Acts 2:36
anointed, **b** Herod and Pontius Pilate, Acts 4:27
multitudes of **b** men and women, Acts 5:14
man God sent as **b** ruler and redeemer Acts 7:35
they were baptized, **b** men and women. Acts 8:12
and they **b** went down into the water, Acts 8:38
of all that he did **b** in the country of Acts 10:39
a great number of **b** Jews and Greeks Acts 14:1
was made by **b** Gentiles and Jews, Acts 14:5
they passed through **b** Phoenicia and Acts 15:3
b the apostles and the elders, Acts 15:23
word of the Lord, **b** Jews and Greeks. Acts 19:10
of Ephesus, **b** Jews and Greeks. Acts 19:17
testifying **b** to Jews and to Greeks of Acts 20:21
delivering to prison **b** men and Acts 22:4
be a resurrection of **b** the just and the Acts 24:15
clear conscience toward **b** God and Acts 24:16
me, **b** in Jerusalem and here, Acts 25:24
I stand here testifying **b** to small and Acts 26:22
would proclaim light **b** to our people Acts 26:23
facing **b** southwest and northwest, Acts 27:12
them about Jesus **b** from the Law Acts 28:23
each other's faith, **b** yours and mine. Rom 1:12
I am under obligation **b** to Greeks and Rom 1:14
b to the wise and to the foolish. Rom 1:14
charged that all, **b** Jews and Greeks, Rom 3:9
he might be Lord **b** of the dead and Rom 14:9
Jesus Christ, **b** their Lord and ours: 1 Cor 1:2
who are called, **b** Jews and Greeks, 1 Cor 1:24
and God will destroy **b** one and the 1 Cor 6:13
who has made us **b** one and has Eph 2:14
and might reconcile us **b** to God in one Eph 2:16
For through him we **b** have access in Eph 2:18
that he who is **b** their Master and yours Eph 6:9
b in my imprisonment and in the Phil 1:7
b to will and to work for his good Phil 2:13
who killed **b** the Lord Jesus and the 1 Thes 2:15
you will save **b** yourself and your 1 Tm 4:16
but **b** their minds and their consciences Ti 1:15
to you, **b** in the flesh and in the Lord. Phlm 1:16
and sprinkled **b** the book itself and all Heb 9:19
sprinkled with the blood **b** the tent and Heb 9:21
from the same opening **b** fresh and salt Jas 3:11
In **b** of them I am stirring up your 2 Pt 3:1
To him be the glory **b** now and to the 2 Pt 3:18
in the teaching has **b** the Father and the 2 Jn 1:9
who fear your name, **b** small and great, Rv 11:18
Also it causes all, **b** small and great, Rv 13:16
both small and great, **b** rich and poor, Rv 13:16
both rich and poor, **b** free and slave, Rv 13:16
the flesh of all men, **b** free and slave, Rv 19:18
both free and slave, **b** small and great." Rv 19:18

BOTHER (1)
will answer from within, 'Do not **b** me; Lk 11:7

BOTHERING (1)
yet because this widow keeps **b** me, I will Lk 18:5

BOTTLE (1)
of my tossings; put my tears in your **b**. Ps 56:8

BOTTOM (7)
flowed into the **b** of the chariot. 1 Kgs 22:35
hearths made at the **b** of the rows all Ezk 46:23
before they reached the **b** of the den, Dn 6:24
hide from my sight at the **b** of the sea, Am 9:3
temple was torn in two, from top to **b**. Mt 27:51
temple was torn in two, from top to **b**. Mk 15:38
woven in one piece from top to **b**, Jn 19:23

BOTTOMLESS (6)
was given the key to the shaft of the **b** pit. Rv 9:1
He opened the shaft of the **b** pit, and from Rv 9:2
as king over them the angel of the **b** pit. Rv 9:11
that rises from the **b** pit will make war Rv 11:7
about to rise from the **b** pit and go to Rv 17:8
hand the key to the **b** pit and a great Rv 20:1

BOUGH (3)
"Joseph is a fruitful **b**, a fruitful bough Gn 49:22
fruitful bough, a fruitful **b** by a spring; Gn 49:22
or three berries in the top of the highest **b**, Is 17:6

BOUGHS (9)
of palm trees and **b** of leafy trees and Lv 23:40
will lop the **b** with terrifying power; Is 10:33
When its **b** are dry, they are broken; Is 27:11
and produced branches and put out **b**. Ezk 17:6
it towered aloft among the thick **b**; Ezk 19:11
its **b** grew large and its branches long Ezk 31:5
of the heavens made their nests in its **b**; Ezk 31:6
not rival it, nor the fir trees equal its **b**; Ezk 31:8
and its **b** have been broken in all the Ezk 31:12

BOUGHT (47)
in your house or **b** with your money Gn 17:12
and he who is **b** with your money, Gn 17:13
born in his house or **b** with his money, Gn 17:23
house and those **b** with money from Gn 17:27
he **b** for a hundred pieces of money the Gn 33:19
had **b** him from the Ishmaelites who Gn 39:1
in exchange for the grain that they **b**. Gn 47:14
So Joseph **b** all the land of Egypt for Gn 47:20
I have this day **b** you and your land for Gn 47:23
which Abraham **b** with the field from Gn 49:30
that is in it were **b** from the Hittites." Gn 49:32
which Abraham **b** with the field from Gn 50:13
every slave that is **b** for money may eat Ex 12:44
to the LORD a field that he has **b**, Lv 27:22
return to him from whom it was **b**, Lv 27:24
of land that Jacob **b** from the sons of Jos 24:32
this day that I have **b** from the hand of Ru 4:9
of Mahlon, I have **b** to be my wife, Ru 4:10
one little ewe lamb, which he had **b**. 2 Sm 12:3
nothing." So David **b** the threshing 2 Sm 24:24
He **b** the hill of Samaria from 1 Kgs 16:24
have **b** back our Jewish brothers who Neh 5:8
It cannot be **b** for gold, and silver Jb 28:15
I **b** male and female slaves, and had Eccl 2:7
You have not **b** me sweet cane with Is 43:24
So I **b** a loincloth according to the word Jer 13:2
"Take the loincloth that you have **b**, Jer 13:4
"And I **b** the field at Anathoth from Jer 32:9

vineyards shall again be **b** in this land.' Jer 32:15
Fields shall be **b** in this land of which Jer 32:43
Fields shall be **b** for money, and deeds Jer 32:44
we drink; the wood we get must be **b**. Lam 5:4
So I **b** her for fifteen shekels of silver and Hos 3:2
went and sold all that he had and **b** it. Mt 13:46
out all who sold and **b** in the temple, Mt 21:12
they took counsel and **b** with them the Mt 27:7
sold and those who **b** in the temple, Mk 11:15
And Joseph **b** a linen shroud, and Mk 15:46
mother of James and Salome **b** spices, Mk 16:1
The first said to him, 'I have **b** a field, Lk 14:18
said, 'I have **b** five yoke of oxen, Lk 14:19
(Now this man **b** a field with the Acts 1:18
tomb that Abraham had **b** for a sum Acts 7:16
"I **b** this citizenship for a large sum." Acts 22:28
for you were **b** with a price. So glorify 1 Cor 6:20
You were **b** with a price; do not 1 Cor 7:23
even denying the Master who **b** them, 2 Pt 2:1

BOUNCED (1)
upon her hip, and **b** upon her knees. Is 66:12

BOUND (83)
wood in order and **b** Isaac his son and Gn 22:9
from them and **b** him before their Gn 42:24
then, as his life is **b** up in the boy's life, Gn 44:30
kneading bowls being **b** up in their Ex 12:34
And they **b** the breastpiece by its rings Ex 39:21
around their waists and **b** caps on them, Lv 8:13
by which she has **b** herself and says Nm 30:4
by which she has **b** herself shall stand. Nm 30:4
by which she has **b** herself shall stand. Nm 30:5
of her lips by which she has **b** herself, Nm 30:6
by which she has **b** herself shall stand. Nm 30:7
of her lips by which she **b** herself. Nm 30:8
anything by which she has **b** herself, Nm 30:9
her husband's house or **b** herself by a Nm 30:10
by which she **b** herself shall stand. Nm 30:11
and he **b** it on his right thigh under his Jgs 3:16
kill you." So they **b** him with two new Jgs 15:13
strength lies, and how you might be **b**, Jgs 16:6
been dried, and she **b** him with them. Jgs 16:8
Please tell me how you might be **b**." Jgs 16:10
took new ropes and **b** him with them Jgs 16:12
how you might be **b**." And he said to Jgs 16:13
down to Gaza and **b** him with bronze Jgs 16:21
my lord shall be **b** in the bundle of 1 Sm 25:29
Your hands were not **b**; your feet were 2 Sm 3:34
shut him up and **b** him in prison. 2 Kgs 17:4
eyes of Zedekiah and **b** him in chains 2 Kgs 25:7
with hooks and **b** him with chains 2 Chr 33:11
of Babylon and **b** him in chains 2 Chr 36:6
many in Judah were **b** by oath to him, Neh 6:18
And if they are **b** in chains and caught Jb 36:8
built as a city that is **b** firmly together, Ps 122:3
Folly is **b** up in the heart of a child, Prv 22:15
are not pressed out or **b** up or softened with Is 1:6
opening of the prison to those who are **b**; Is 61:1
eyes of Zedekiah and **b** him in chains to Jer 39:7
when he took him **b** in chains along Jer 40:1
eyes of Zedekiah, and **b** him in chains, Jer 52:11
"My transgressions were **b** into a yoke; Lam 1:14
you, and you shall be **b** with them, Ezk 3:25
b with cords and made secure. Ezk 27:24
and behold, it has not been **b** up, Ezk 30:21
healed, the injured you have not **b** up, Ezk 34:4
Then these men were **b** in their cloaks, Dn 3:21
fell **b** into the burning fiery furnace. Dn 3:23
not cast three men **b** into the fire?" They Dn 3:24
earth, **b** with a band of iron and bronze, Dn 4:15
earth, **b** with a band of iron and bronze, Dn 4:23
them when they are **b** up for their Hos 10:10
The iniquity of Ephraim is **b** up; his Hos 13:12
and all her great men were **b** in chains. Na 3:10
had seized John and **b** him and put him Mt 14:3
you bind on earth shall be **b** in heaven, Mt 16:19
you bind on earth shall be **b** in heaven, Mt 18:18
gold of the temple, he is **b** by his oath.' Mt 23:16
that is on the altar, he is **b** by his oath.' Mt 23:18
And they **b** him and led him away and Mt 27:2
he had often been **b** with shackles and Mk 5:4
and seized John and **b** him in prison for Mk 6:17
And they **b** Jesus and led him away and Mk 15:1
kept under guard and **b** with chains and Lk 8:29
He went to him and **b** up his wounds, Lk 10:34
Abraham whom Satan **b** for eighteen Lk 13:16
his hands and feet **b** with linen strips, Jn 11:44
of the Jews arrested Jesus and **b** him. Jn 18:12
Annas then sent him **b** to Caiaphas the Jn 18:24
the body of Jesus and **b** it in linen cloths Jn 19:40
he might bring them **b** to Jerusalem. Acts 9:2
to bring them **b** before the chief Acts 9:21
two soldiers, **b** with two chains, Acts 12:6
took Paul's belt and **b** his own feet Acts 21:11
ordered him to be **b** with two chains. Acts 21:33
citizen and that he had **b** him. Acts 22:29
made a plot and **b** themselves by an Acts 23:12
"We have strictly **b** ourselves by an Acts 23:14
who have **b** themselves by an oath Acts 23:21
a married woman is **b** by law to her Rom 7:2
Are you **b** to a wife? Do not seek to be 1 Cor 7:27
A wife is **b** to her husband as long as 1 Cor 7:39
suffering, **b** with chains as a criminal. 2 Tm 2:9
criminal. But the word of God is not **b**! 2 Tm 2:9
four angels who are **b** at the great river Rv 9:14
Satan, and **b** him for a thousand years, Rv 20:2

BOUNDARIES (7)
any time go beyond the **b** of his city of Nm 35:26
finds him outside the **b** of his city of Nm 35:27
him within the **b** of his inheritance Jgs 2:9
You have fixed all the **b** of the earth; Ps 74:17
proud but maintains the widow's **b**. Prv 15:25
I remove the **b** of peoples, and plunder Is 10:13
periods and the **b** of their dwelling Acts 17:26

BOUNDARY (71)
river Jabbok, the **b** of the Ammonites, Jos 12:2
all Bashan to the **b** of the Geshurites and Jos 12:5
half of Gilead to the **b** of Sihon king of Jos 12:5
of Egypt, northward to the **b** of Ekron, Jos 13:3
to Aphek, to the **b** of the Amorites, Jos 13:4
as far as the **b** of the Ammonites; Jos 13:10
people of Reuben was the Jordan as a **b**. Jos 13:23
of Heshbon, having the Jordan as a **b**, Jos 13:27
reached southward to the **b** of Edom, Jos 15:1
And their south **b** ran from the end of Jos 15:2
at the sea. This shall be your south **b**. Jos 15:4
And the east **b** is the Salt Sea, to the Jos 15:5
And the **b** on the north side runs from Jos 15:5
And the **b** goes up to Beth-hoglah and Jos 15:6
And the **b** goes up to the stone of Bohan Jos 15:6
And the **b** goes up to Debir from the Jos 15:7
And the **b** passes along to the waters of Jos 15:7
Then the **b** goes up by the Valley of the Jos 15:8
And the **b** goes up to the top of the Jos 15:8
Then the **b** extends from the top of the Jos 15:9
Then the **b** bends around to Baalah Jos 15:9
And the **b** circles west of Baalah to Jos 15:10
The **b** goes out to the shoulder of the Jos 15:11
then the **b** bends around to Shikkeron Jos 15:11
Then the **b** comes to an end at the sea. Jos 15:11
And the west **b** was the Great Sea with Jos 15:12
This is the **b** around the people of Jos 15:12
extreme south, toward the **b** of Edom, Jos 15:21
the **b** of their inheritance on the east was Jos 16:5
and the **b** goes from there to the sea. Jos 16:6
on the east the **b** turns around toward Jos 16:6
From Tappuah the **b** goes westward to Jos 16:8
Then the **b** goes along southward to the Jos 17:7
Tappuah on the **b** of Manasseh Jos 17:8
Then the **b** went down to the brook Jos 17:9
Then the **b** of Manasseh goes on the Jos 17:9
Manasseh's, with the sea forming its **b**. Jos 17:10
the north side their **b** began at the Jos 18:12
Then the **b** goes up to the shoulder Jos 18:12
From there the **b** passes along Jos 18:13
then the **b** goes down to Ataroth-addar, Jos 18:13
Then the **b** goes in another direction, Jos 18:14
And the **b** goes from there to Ephron, Jos 18:15
Then the **b** goes down to the border of Jos 18:16
Then the **b** passes on to the north of the Jos 18:19
And the **b** ends at the northern bay of Jos 18:19
The Jordan forms its **b** on the eastern Jos 18:20
their clans, **b** by boundary all around. Jos 18:20
their clans, boundary by **b** all around. Jos 18:20
Then their **b** goes up westward and on Jos 19:11
the sunrise to the **b** of Chisloth-tabor. Jos 19:12
on the north the **b** turns about to Jos 19:14
The **b** also touches Tabor, Jos 19:22
and its **b** ends at the Jordan—sixteen Jos 19:22
Then the **b** turns to Ramah, reaching Jos 19:29
Then the **b** turns to Hosah, and it ends Jos 19:29
And their **b** ran from Heleph, from the Jos 19:33
Then the **b** turns westward to Jos 19:34
made the Jordan a **b** between us and Jos 22:25
for the Arnon was the **b** of Moab. Jgs 11:18
the waters at the **b** between light and Jb 26:10
You set a **b** that they may not pass, Ps 104:9
I placed the sand as the **b** for the sea, Jer 5:22
from the western to the eastern **b** Ezk 45:7
"This is the **b** by which you shall Ezk 47:13
"This shall be the **b** of the land: On Ezk 47:15
So the **b** shall run from the sea to Ezk 47:17
the **b** shall run between Hauran and Ezk 47:18
Sea shall be the **b** to a point opposite Ezk 47:20
the **b** shall run from Tamar to the Ezk 48:28
In that day the **b** shall be far extended. Mi 7:11

BOUNDING (2)
over the mountains, **b** over the hills. Sg 2:8
the wheel, galloping horse and **b** chariot! Na 3:2

BOUNDS (2)
They know no **b** in deeds of evil; they Jer 5:28
they break all **b**, and bloodshed follows Hos 4:2

BOUNTIES (1)
up to the **b** of the everlasting hills. Gn 49:26

BOUNTIFUL (1)
Whoever has a **b** eye will be blessed, for Prv 22:9

BOUNTIFULLY (6)
the LORD, because he has dealt **b** with me. Ps 13:6
rest; for the LORD has dealt **b** with you. Ps 116:7
Deal **b** with your servant, that I may Ps 119:17
me, for you will deal **b** with me. Ps 142:7
and whoever sows **b** will also reap 2 Cor 9:6
sows bountifully will also reap **b**. 2 Cor 9:6

BOUNTY (3)
given her by the **b** of King Solomon. 1 Kgs 10:13
lavished according to the **b** of the king. Est 1:7
You crown the year with your **b**; your Ps 65:11

BOW (109)
I have set my **b** in the cloud, and it shall Gn 9:13
over the earth and the **b** is seen in the Gn 9:14
When the **b** is in the clouds, I will see it Gn 9:16
and became an expert with the **b**. Gn 21:20
your weapons, your quiver and your **b**, Gn 27:3
serve you, and nations **b** down to you. Gn 27:29
your mother's sons **b** down to you. Gn 27:29
indeed come to **b** ourselves to the Gn 37:10
"**B** the knee!" Thus he set him over all Gn 41:43
with my sword and with my **b**." Gn 48:22
father's sons shall **b** down before you. Gn 49:8
yet his **b** remained unmoved; his arms Gn 49:24
come down to me and **b** down to me, Ex 11:8
You shall not **b** down to them or serve Ex 20:5
you shall not **b** down to their gods nor Ex 23:24
stone in your land to **b** down to it, Lv 26:1
be drawn away and **b** down to them and Dt 4:19
You shall not **b** down to them or serve Dt 5:9
b down to him, all gods, for he avenges Dt 32:43
them or serve them or **b** down to them, Jos 23:7
serve other gods and **b** down to them. Jos 23:16
it was not by your sword or by your **b**. Jos 24:12
that I may **b** before the LORD your 1 Sm 15:30
even his sword and his **b** and his belt. 1 Sm 18:4
the **b** of Jonathan turned not back, 2 Sm 1:22
my arms can bend a **b** of bronze. 2 Sm 22:35
man drew his **b** at random and 1 Kgs 22:34
and I **b** myself in the house of 2 Kgs 5:18
when I **b** myself in the house of 2 Kgs 5:18
with your sword and with your **b**? 2 Kgs 6:22
And Jehu drew his **b** with his full 2 Kgs 9:24
"Take a **b** and arrows." So he took a 2 Kgs 13:15
arrows." So he took a **b** and arrows. 2 Kgs 13:15
Israel, "Draw the **b**," and he drew it. 2 Kgs 13:16
other gods or **b** yourselves to them 2 Kgs 17:35
You shall **b** yourselves to him, and 2 Kgs 17:36
shield and sword, and drew the **b**, 1 Chr 5:18
men armed with **b** and shield; 2 Chr 17:17
man drew his **b** at random and 2 Chr 18:33
But Mordecai did not **b** down or pay Est 3:2
that Mordecai did not **b** down or pay Est 3:5
me, and my **b** ever new in my hand.' Jb 29:20
another, and let others **b** down on her. Jb 31:10
I will **b** down toward your holy temple in Ps 5:7
his sword; he has bent and readied his **b**; Ps 7:12
for behold, the wicked bend the **b**; they Ps 11:2
that my arms can bend a **b** of bronze. Ps 18:34
before him shall **b** all who go down to Ps 22:29
For not in my **b** do I trust, nor can my Ps 44:6
beauty. Since he is your lord, **b** to him. Ps 45:11
he breaks the **b** and shatters the spear; Ps 46:9
you, that they may flee to it from the **b**. Ps 60:4
May desert tribes **b** down before him and Ps 72:9
The Ephraimites, armed with the **b**, Ps 78:9
fathers; they twisted like a deceitful **b**. Ps 78:57
you shall not **b** down to a foreign god. Ps 81:9
Oh come, let us worship and **b** down; let Ps 95:6
I **b** down toward your holy temple and Ps 138:2
B your heavens, O LORD, and come Ps 144:5
The evil **b** down before the good, the Prv 14:19
they **b** down to the work of their hands, to Is 2:8
With **b** and arrows a man will come Is 7:24
from the drawn sword, from the bent **b**, Is 21:15
without the **b** they were captured. Is 22:3
his sword, like driven stubble with his **b**. Is 41:2
come over in chains and **b** down to you. Is 45:14
'To me every knee shall **b**, every tongue Is 45:23
They stoop; they **b** down together; they Is 46:2
to the ground they shall **b** down to you, Is 49:23
who have said to you, '**B** down, Is 51:23
Is it to **b** down his head like a reed, and to Is 58:5
who despised you shall **b** down at your Is 60:14
all of you shall **b** down to the slaughter, Is 65:12
Tarshish, Pul, and Lud, who draw the **b**, Is 66:19

They lay hold on **b** and javelin; they are Jer 6:23
They bend their tongue like a **b**; Jer 9:3
men of Lud, skilled in handling the **b**. Jer 46:9
"Behold, I will break the **b** of Elam, the Jer 49:35
all around, all you who bend the **b**; Jer 50:14
Babylon, all those who bend the **b**. Jer 50:29
They lay hold of **b** and spear; they are Jer 50:42
Let not the archer bend his **b**, and let Jer 51:3
He has bent his **b** like an enemy, with Lam 2:4
he bent his **b** and set me as a target for Lam 3:12
the appearance of the **b** that is in the Ezk 1:28
I will strike your **b** from your left hand, Ezk 39:3
shields and bucklers, **b** and arrows, Ezk 39:9
of the land shall **b** down at the entrance Ezk 46:3
day I will break the **b** of Israel in the Hos 1:5
will not save them by **b** or by sword or Hos 1:7
And I will abolish the **b**, the sword, and Hos 2:18
upward; they are like a treacherous **b**; Hos 7:16
he who handles the **b** shall not stand, Am 2:15
and you shall **b** down no more to the Mi 5:13
LORD, and **b** myself before God on high? Mi 6:6
You stripped the sheath from your **b**, Hab 3:9
those who **b** down on the roofs to the Zep 1:5
those who **b** down and swear to the LORD Zep 1:5
of the earth, and to him shall **b** down, Zep 2:11
and the battle **b** shall be cut off, and he Zec 9:10
For I have bent Judah as my **b**; I have Zec 9:13
him the tent peg, from him the battle **b**, Zec 10:4
of laying out anchors from the **b**, Acts 27:30
The **b** stuck and remained Acts 27:41
the Lord, every knee shall **b** to me, Rom 14:11
For this reason I **b** my knees before the Eph 3:14
the name of Jesus every knee should **b**, Phil 2:10
make them come and **b** down before your Rv 3:9
And its rider had a **b**, and a crown was Rv 6:2

BOWED (71)
to meet them and **b** himself to the earth Gn 18:2
to meet them and **b** himself with his Gn 19:1
Abraham rose and **b** to the Hittites, the Gn 23:7
Then Abraham **b** down before the Gn 23:12
The man **b** his head and worshiped the Gn 24:26
Then I **b** my head and worshiped the Gn 24:48
he **b** himself to the earth before the Gn 24:52
they and their children, and **b** down. Gn 33:6
and her children drew near and **b** down. Gn 33:7
and Rachel drew near, and they **b** down. Gn 33:7
gathered around it and **b** down to my Gn 37:7
brothers came and **b** themselves before Gn 42:6
had with them and **b** down to him to Gn 43:26
still alive." And they **b** their heads and Gn 43:28
Then Israel **b** himself upon the head of Gn 47:31
and he **b** himself with his face to the Gn 48:12
pleasant, so he **b** his shoulder to bear, Gn 49:15
they **b** their heads and worshiped. Ex 4:31
And the people **b** their heads and Ex 12:27
his father-in-law and **b** down and kissed Ex 18:7
And Moses quickly **b** his head toward Ex 34:8
And he **b** down and fell on his face. Nm 22:31
the people ate and **b** down to their gods. Nm 25:2
were around them, and **b** down to them. Jgs 2:12
after other gods and **b** down to them. Jgs 2:17
the Philistines." Then he **b** with all his Jgs 16:30
were dead, she **b** and gave birth, 1 Sm 4:19
Saul, and Saul **b** before the LORD. 1 Sm 15:31
face to the ground and **b** three times. 1 Sm 20:41
David **b** with his face to the earth and 1 Sm 24:8
on her face and **b** to the ground. 1 Sm 25:23
And she rose and **b** with her face to 1 Sm 25:41
and he **b** with his face to the ground 1 Sm 28:14
to the king and **b** himself on his face 2 Sm 14:33
seen." The Cushite **b** before Joab, 2 Sm 18:21
is well." And he **b** before the king 2 Sm 18:28
He **b** the heavens and came down; 2 Sm 22:10
Bathsheba **b** and paid homage to the 1 Kgs 1:16
before the king, he **b** before the king, 1 Kgs 1:23
Then Bathsheba **b** with her face to 1 Kgs 1:31
And the king **b** himself on the bed. 1 Kgs 1:47
rose to meet her and **b** down to her. 1 Kgs 2:19
And he **b** himself down on the earth 1 Kgs 18:42
all the knees that have not **b** to Baal, 1 Kgs 19:18
to meet him and **b** to the ground 2 Kgs 2:15
and **b** their heads and paid homage 1 Chr 29:20
they **b** down with their faces to the 2 Chr 7:3
Then Jehoshaphat **b** his head with 2 Chr 20:18
present with him **b** themselves and 2 Chr 29:29
and they **b** down and worshiped. 2 Chr 29:30
And they **b** their heads and worshiped Neh 8:6
at the king's gate **b** down and paid Est 3:2
beneath him **b** the helpers of Rahab. Jb 9:13
He **b** the heavens and came down; thick Ps 18:9
I prayed with head **b** on my chest. Ps 35:13
his mother, I **b** down in mourning. Ps 35:14
I am utterly **b** down and prostrate; all the Ps 38:6
For our soul is **b** down to the dust; our Ps 44:25
a net for my steps; my soul was **b** down. Ps 57:6
So he **b** their hearts down with hard Ps 107:12
and raises up all who are **b** down. Ps 145:14
The LORD lifts up those who are **b** down; Ps 146:8
labor; I am **b** down so that I cannot hear; Is 21:3
from the dust your speech will be **b** down; Is 29:4
He who is **b** down shall speedily be Is 51:14
every green tree you **b** down like a Jer 2:20
of Jerusalem have **b** their heads to Lam 2:10
it and is **b** down within me. Lam 3:20
they were frightened and **b** their faces to Lk 24:5
is finished," and he **b** his head and gave Jn 19:30
men who have not **b** the knee to Baal." Rom 11:4

BOWELS (6)
curse pass into your **b** and make your Nm 5:22
sickness with a disease of your **b**, 2 Chr 21:15
until your **b** come out because of 2 Chr 21:15
him in his **b** with an incurable 2 Chr 21:18
his **b** came out because of the 2 Chr 21:19
in the middle and all his **b** gushed out. Acts 1:18

BOWING (6)
b himself to the ground seven times, Gn 33:3
and eleven stars were **b** down to me." Gn 37:9
gods, serving them and **b** down to them. Jgs 2:19
she fell on her face, **b** to the ground, Ru 2:10
and fell at his feet, **b** to the ground. 2 Kgs 4:37
b in worship over the head of his staff. Heb 11:21

BOWL (19)
be your basket and your kneading **b**. Dt 28:5
be your basket and your kneading **b**. Dt 28:17
she brought him curds in a noble's **b**. Jgs 5:25
dew from the fleece to fill a **b** with water. Jgs 6:38
He said, "Bring me a new **b**, and put 2 Kgs 2:20
is snapped, or the golden **b** is broken, Eccl 12:6
navel is a rounded **b** that never lacks Sg 7:2
who have drunk to the dregs the **b**, Is 51:17
the **b** of my wrath you shall drink no Is 51:22
all of gold, with a **b** on the top of it, Zec 4:2
on the right of the **b** and the other on its Zec 4:3
if drunk with wine, and be full like a **b**, Zec 9:15
went and poured out his **b** on the earth, Rv 16:2
angel poured out his **b** into the sea, Rv 16:3
angel poured out his **b** into the rivers Rv 16:4
angel poured out his **b** on the sun, Rv 16:8
angel poured out his **b** on the throne of Rv 16:10
angel poured out his **b** on the great Rv 16:12
angel poured out his **b** into the air, Rv 16:17

BOWLS (27)
into your ovens and your kneading **b**. Ex 8:3
their kneading **b** being bound up in Ex 12:34
and its flagons and **b** with which to Ex 25:29
and its **b** and flagons with which to Ex 37:16
it the plates, the dishes for incense, the **b**, Nm 4:7
the two **b** of the capitals that were on 1 Kgs 7:41
to cover the two **b** of the capitals that 1 Kgs 7:41
to cover the two **b** of the capitals that 1 Kgs 7:42
of silver, snuffers, **b**, trumpets, 2 Kgs 12:13
the fire pans also and the **b**. What 2 Kgs 25:15
for the golden **b** and the weight of 1 Chr 28:17
for the silver **b** and the weight of 1 Chr 28:17
the two pillars, the **b**, and the two 2 Chr 4:12
to cover the two **b** of the capitals that 2 Chr 4:12
to cover the two **b** of the capitals that 2 Chr 4:13
30 **b** of gold, 410 bowls of silver, and Ezr 1:10
30 bowls of gold, 410 **b** of silver, and Ezr 1:10
20 **b** of gold worth 1,000 darics, and two Ezr 8:27
also the small **b** and the fire pans and Jer 52:19
incense and the **b** for drink offerings. Jer 52:19
drink wine in **b** and anoint themselves Am 6:6
LORD shall be as the **b** before the altar. Zec 14:20
a harp, and golden **b** full of incense, Rv 5:8
seven angels seven golden **b** full of the Rv 15:7
on the earth the seven **b** of the wrath of Rv 16:1
who had the seven **b** came and said to Rv 17:1
who had the seven **b** full of the seven Rv 21:9

BOWMEN (2)
b, having many sons and grandsons, 1 Chr 8:40
They were **b** and could shoot arrows 1 Chr 12:2

BOWS (12)
The **b** of the mighty are broken, but 1 Sm 2:4
that carried shields and drew **b**. 2 Chr 14:8
of mail, **b**, and stones for slinging. 2 Chr 26:14
their swords, their spears, and their **b**. Neh 4:13
the spears, shields, **b**, and coats of mail. Neh 4:16
you will aim at their faces with your **b**. Ps 21:12
sword and bend their **b** to bring down Ps 37:14
own heart, and their **b** shall be broken. Ps 37:15
their arrows are sharp, all their **b** bent, Is 5:28
Their **b** will slaughter the young men; Is 13:18
Bel **b** down; Nebo stoops; their idols are Is 46:1
their **b** are broken in pieces, for the Jer 51:56

BOWSHOT (1)
good way off, about the distance of a **b**, Gn 21:16

BOWSTRINGS (3)
me with seven fresh **b** that have not Jgs 16:7
up to her seven fresh **b** that had not been Jgs 16:8
you, Samson!" But he snapped the **b**, Jgs 16:9

BOX (7)
cart and put in a **b** at its side the figures 1 Sm 6:8
the cart and the **b** with the golden 1 Sm 6:11
the LORD and the **b** that was beside it, 1 Sm 6:15
putting money into the offering **b**. Mk 12:41
who are contributing to the offering **b**. Mk 12:43
putting their gifts into the offering **b**, Lk 21:1
I do not **b** as one beating the air. 1 Cor 9:26

BOXES (1)
the armlets, the sashes, the perfume **b**, Is 3:20

BOY (43)
because of the **b** and because of Gn 21:12
And God heard the voice of the **b**, and Gn 21:17
heard the voice of the **b** where he is. Gn 21:17
Lift up the **b**, and hold him fast with Gn 21:18
skin with water and gave the **b** a drink. Gn 21:19
And God was with the **b**, and he grew Gn 21:20
I and the **b** will go over there and Gn 22:5
your hand on the **b** or do anything to Gn 22:12
He was a **b** with the sons of Bilhah and Gn 37:2
his brothers and said, "The **b** is gone, Gn 37:30
I not tell you not to sin against the **b**? Gn 42:22
to Israel his father, "Send the **b** with me, Gn 43:8
lord, 'The **b** cannot leave his father, Gn 44:22
my father, and the **b** is not with us, Gn 44:30
as he sees that the **b** is not with us, Gn 44:31
a pledge of safety for the **b** to my father, Gn 44:32
remain instead of the **b** as a servant to Gn 44:33
and let the **b** go back with his Gn 44:33
to my father if the **b** is not with me? Gn 44:34
And the **b** ministered to the LORD in 1 Sm 2:11
LORD, a **b** clothed with a linen ephod. 1 Sm 2:18
said, "Inquire whose son the **b** is." 1 Sm 17:56
with David, and with him a little **b**. 1 Sm 20:35
And he said to his **b**, "Run and find 1 Sm 20:36
arrows that I shoot." As the **b** ran, 1 Sm 20:36
And when the **b** came to the place of 1 Sm 20:37
Jonathan called after the **b** and said, 1 Sm 20:37
And Jonathan called after the **b**, 1 Sm 20:38
stay!" So Jonathan's **b** gathered up 1 Sm 20:38
But the **b** knew nothing. Only 1 Sm 20:39
his weapons to his **b** and said to him, 1 Sm 20:40
And as soon as the **b** had gone, 1 Sm 20:41
year of his reign, while he was yet a **b**, 2 Chr 34:3
For before the **b** knows how to refuse the Is 7:16
for before the **b** knows how to cry 'My Is 8:4
people, and have traded a **b** for a prostitute, Jl 3:3
of him, and the **b** was healed instantly. Mt 17:18
And they brought the **b** to him. And Mk 9:20
him, immediately it convulsed the **b**, Mk 9:20
it came out, and the **b** was like a corpse, Mk 9:26
the **b** Jesus stayed behind in Jerusalem. Lk 2:43
the unclean spirit and healed the **b**, Lk 9:42
"There is a **b** here who has five barley Jn 6:9

BOY'S (1)
as his life is bound up in the **b** life, Gn 44:30

BOYS (8)
When the **b** grew up, Esau was a Gn 25:27
redeemed me from all evil, bless the **b**; Gn 48:16
some small **b** came out of the city 2 Kgs 2:23
the woods and tore forty-two of the **b**. 2 Kgs 2:24
They send out their little **b** like a flock, Jb 21:11
And I will make **b** their princes, and Is 3:4
and **b** stagger under loads of wood. Lam 5:13
city shall be full of **b** and girls playing in Zec 8:5

BOZEZ (1)
The name of the one was **B**, and the 1 Sm 14:4

BOZKATH (2)
Lachish, **B**, Eglon, Jos 15:39
Jedidah the daughter of Adaiah of **B**. 2 Kgs 22:1

BOZRAH (8)
son of Zerah of **B** reigned in his place. Gn 36:33
son of Zerah of **B** reigned in his place. 1 Chr 1:44
For the LORD has a sacrifice in **B**, a great Is 34:6
Edom, in crimsoned garments from **B**, Is 63:1
and Kerioth, and **B**, and all the cities of Jer 48:24
the LORD, that **B** shall become a horror, Jer 49:13
eagle and spread his wings against **B**, Jer 49:22
it shall devour the strongholds of **B**." Am 1:12

BRACELETS (7)
and two **b** for her arms weighing ten Gn 24:22
the ring and the **b** on his sister's arms, Gn 24:30
on her nose and the **b** on her arms. Gn 24:47
found, articles of gold, armlets and **b**, Nm 31:50
the pendants, the **b**, and the scarves; Is 3:19
ornaments and put **b** on your wrists Ezk 16:11
and they put **b** on the hands of the Ezk 23:42

BRAIDED (1)
not with **b** hair and gold or pearls or 1 Tm 2:9

BRAIDING (1)
adorning be external—the **b** of hair, 1 Pt 3:3

BRAMBLE (4)
Then all the trees said to the **b**, 'You Jgs 9:14
And the **b** said to the trees, 'If in good Jgs 9:15
come out of the **b** and devour the cedars Jgs 9:15
nor are grapes picked from a **b** bush. Lk 6:44

BRAMBLES (1)
As a lily among **b**, so is my love among Sg 2:2

BRANCH (29)
each with calyx and flower, on one **b**, Ex 25:33
on the other **b**—so for the six branches Ex 25:33
each with calyx and flower, on one **b**, Ex 37:19
on the other **b**—so for the six branches Ex 37:19
down from there a **b** with a single Nm 13:23
his time, and his **b** will not be green. Jb 15:32
In that day the **b** of the LORD shall be Is 4:2
and tail, palm **b** and reed in one day— Is 9:14
and a **b** from his roots shall bear fruit. Is 11:1
away from your grave, like a loathed **b**, Is 14:19
Egypt that head or tail, palm **b** or reed, Is 19:15
the land forever, the **b** of my planting, Is 60:21
you see?" And I said, "I see an almond **b**." Jer 1:11
I will raise up for David a righteous **B**, Jer 23:5
will cause a righteous **B** to spring up Jer 33:15
Behold, they put the **b** to their nose. Ezk 8:17
the vine **b** that is among the trees of the Ezk 15:2
"And from a **b** from her roots one shall Dn 11:7
behold, I will bring my servant the **B**. Zec 3:8
"Behold, the man whose name is the **B**: Zec 6:12
for he shall **b** out from his place, and he Zec 6:12
that it will leave them neither root nor **b**. Mal 4:1
as soon as its **b** becomes tender and Mt 24:32
as soon as its **b** becomes tender and Mk 13:28
Every **b** of mine that does not bear fruit Jn 15:2
and every **b** that does bear fruit he Jn 15:2
As the **b** cannot bear fruit by itself, Jn 15:4
he is thrown away like a **b** and withers; Jn 15:6
sour wine on a hyssop **b** and held it to Jn 19:29

BRANCHES (72)
and on the vine there were three **b**. As Gn 40:10
the three **b** are three days. Gn 40:12
by a spring; his **b** run over the wall. Gn 49:22
And there shall be six **b** going out of its Ex 25:32
three **b** of the lampstand out of one side Ex 25:32
of it and three **b** of the lampstand out Ex 25:32
—so for the six **b** going out of the Ex 25:33
pair of the six **b** going out from the Ex 25:35
Their calyxes and their **b** shall be of Ex 25:36
And there were six **b** going out of its Ex 37:18
three **b** of the lampstand out of one side Ex 37:18
of it and three **b** of the lampstand out Ex 37:18
—so for the six **b** going out of the Ex 37:19
each pair of the six **b** going out of it. Ex 37:21
Their calyxes and their **b** were of one Ex 37:22
b of palm trees and boughs of leafy Lv 23:40
went under the thick **b** of a great 2 Sm 18:9
out to the hills and bring **b** of olive, Neh 8:15
bud and put out **b** like a young plant. Jb 14:9
dry up beneath, and his **b** wither above. Jb 18:16
waters, with the dew all night on my **b**, Jb 29:19
its shade, the mighty cedars with its **b**. Ps 80:10
It sent out its **b** to the sea and its shoots Ps 80:11
heavens dwell; they sing among the **b**. Ps 104:12
of the nations have struck down its **b**, Is 16:8
bough, four or five on the **b** of a fruit tree, Is 17:6
and the spreading **b** he lops off and clears Is 18:5
and the **b** of Egypt's Nile will diminish Is 19:6
grazes; there it lies down and strips its **b**. Is 27:10
strip away her **b**, for they are not the Jer 5:10
pass your hand again over its **b**." Jer 6:9
set fire to it, and its **b** will be consumed. Jer 11:16
Your **b** passed over the sea, reached to Jer 48:32
vine, and its **b** turned toward him, Ezk 17:6
a vine and produced **b** and put out Ezk 17:6
and shot forth its **b** toward him from Ezk 17:7
that it might produce **b** and bear fruit Ezk 17:8
that it may bear **b** and produce fruit Ezk 17:23
in the shade of its **b** birds of every sort Ezk 17:23
fruitful and full of **b** by reason of Ezk 19:10
in its height with the mass of its **b**. Ezk 19:11
with beautiful **b** and forest shade, Ezk 31:3
large and its **b** long from abundant Ezk 31:5
under its **b** all the beasts of the field Ezk 31:6
in its greatness, in the length of its **b**; Ezk 31:7
neither were the plane trees like its **b**; Ezk 31:8
I made it beautiful in the mass of its **b**, Ezk 31:9
and in all the valleys its **b** have fallen, Ezk 31:12
and on its **b** are all the beasts of the Ezk 31:13
shall shoot forth your **b** and yield your Ezk 36:8
the birds of the heavens lived in its **b**, Dn 4:12
'Chop down the tree and lop off its **b**, Dn 4:14
from under it and the birds from its **b**. Dn 4:14
and in whose **b** the birds of the heavens Dn 4:21
thrown it down; their **b** are made white. Jl 1:7
have plundered them and ruined their **b**. Na 2:2
"What are these two **b** of the olive trees, Zec 4:12
the air come and make nests in its **b**." Mt 13:32
and others cut **b** from the trees and Mt 21:8
the garden plants and puts out large **b**, Mk 4:32
and others spread leafy **b** that they had Mk 11:8
the birds of the air made nests in its **b**." Lk 13:19
So they took **b** of palm trees and went Jn 12:13
I am the vine; you are the **b**. Whoever Jn 15:5
and withers; and the **b** are gathered, Jn 15:6
and if the root is holy, so are the **b**. Rom 11:16
But if some of the **b** were broken off, Rom 11:17
do not be arrogant toward the **b**. If Rom 11:18
"**B** were broken off so that I might be Rom 11:19
if God did not spare the natural **b**, Rom 11:21
much more will these, the natural **b**, Rom 11:24
white robes, with palm **b** in their hands, Rv 7:9

BRAND (2)
and you were as a **b** plucked out of the Am 4:11
Is not this a **b** plucked from the fire?" Zec 3:2

BRANDING (1)
of sackcloth; and **b** instead of beauty. Is 3:24

BRANDISH (1)
you, when I **b** my sword before them. Ezk 32:10

BRANDISHED (2)
Battling with **b** arm, he will fight with Is 30:32
musters them; the cypress spears are **b**. Na 2:3

BRASS (1)
is an iron sinew and your forehead **b**, Is 48:4

BRAVEST (1)
sent 12,000 of their **b** men there and Jgs 21:10

BRAWLER (1)
Wine is a mocker, strong drink a **b**, Prv 20:1

BRAY (2)
Does the wild donkey **b** when he has grass, Jb 6:5
Among the bushes they **b**; under the Jb 30:7

BRAZEN (1)
things, the deeds of a **b** prostitute, Ezk 16:30

BREACH (23)
"What a **b** you have made for Gn 38:29
For every **b** of trust, whether it is for an Ex 22:9
"If anyone commits a **b** of faith and sins Lv 5:15
sins and commits a **b** of faith against the Lv 6:2
'What is this **b** of faith that you have Jos 22:16
in rebellion or in **b** of faith against the Jos 22:22
not committed this **b** of faith against Jos 22:31
the LORD had made a **b** in the tribes of Jgs 21:15
and closed up the **b** of the city of 1 Kgs 11:27
Then a **b** was made in the city, and 2 Kgs 25:4
in Babylon because of their **b** of faith. 1 Chr 9:1
So Saul died for his **b** of faith. He 1 Chr 10:13
that there was no **b** left in it (although Neh 6:1
He breaks me with **b** upon breach; he Jb 16:14
He breaks me with breach upon **b**; he Jb 16:14
As through a wide **b** they come; amid Jb 30:14
chosen one, stood in the **b** before him, Ps 106:23
shall be to you like a **b** in a high wall, Is 30:13
you shall be called the repairer of the **b**, Is 58:12
of the month, a **b** was made in the city. Jer 39:2
Then a **b** was made in the city, and all Jer 52:7
and stand in the **b** before me for the Ezk 22:30
He who opens the **b** goes up before them; Mi 2:13

BREACHED (3)
You have **b** all his walls; you have laid Ps 89:40
as men enter a city that has been **b**. Ezk 26:10
Thebes shall be **b**, and Memphis shall Ezk 30:16

BREACHES (6)
and that the **b** were beginning to Neh 4:7
torn it open; repair its **b**, for it totters. Ps 60:2
and you saw that the **b** of the city of Is 22:9
You have not gone up into the **b**, or Ezk 13:5
And you shall go out through the **b**, Am 4:3
of David that is fallen and repair its **b**, Am 9:11

BREAD (331)
By the sweat of your face you shall eat **b**, Gn 3:19
king of Salem brought out **b** and wine. Gn 14:18
while I bring a morsel of **b**, that you Gn 18:5
them a feast and baked unleavened **b**, Gn 19:3
the morning and took **b** and a skin of Gn 21:14
Jacob gave Esau **b** and lentil stew, Gn 25:34
she put the delicious food and the **b**, Gn 27:17
and will give me **b** to eat and clothing Gn 28:20
and called his kinsmen to eat **b**. Gn 31:54
They ate **b** and spent the night in the Gn 31:54
but in all the land of Egypt there was **b**. Gn 41:54
the people cried to Pharaoh for **b**. Gn 41:55
they heard that they should eat **b** there. Gn 43:25
b, and provision for his father on the Gn 45:23
the man? Call him, that he may eat **b**." Ex 2:20
with unleavened **b** and bitter herbs they Ex 12:8
Seven days you shall eat unleavened **b**. Ex 12:15
observe the Feast of Unleavened **B**, Ex 12:17
shall eat unleavened **b** until the Ex 12:18
places you shall eat unleavened **b**." Ex 12:20
this place. No leavened **b** shall be eaten. Ex 13:3
Seven days you shall eat unleavened **b**, Ex 13:6
Unleavened **b** shall be eaten for seven Ex 13:7
no leavened **b** shall be seen with you, Ex 13:7
sat by the meat pots and ate **b** to the full, Ex 16:3
am about to rain **b** from heaven for you, Ex 16:4
to eat and in the morning **b** to the full, Ex 16:8
the morning you shall be filled with **b**. Ex 16:12
"It is the **b** that the LORD has given you Ex 16:15
day they gathered twice as much **b**, Ex 16:22
sixth day he gives you **b** for two days. Ex 16:29
that they may see the **b** with which I fed Ex 16:32
Israel to eat **b** with Moses' father-in-law Ex 18:12
shall keep the Feast of Unleavened **B**. Ex 23:15
shall eat unleavened **b** for seven days Ex 23:15
he will bless your **b** and your water, Ex 23:25
you shall set the **b** of the Presence on Ex 25:30
and unleavened **b**, unleavened cakes Ex 29:2
and one loaf of **b** and one cake of bread Ex 29:23
bread and one cake of **b** made with oil, Ex 29:23
basket of unleavened **b** that is before Ex 29:23
of the ram and the **b** that is in the Ex 29:32
ordination or of the **b** remain until the Ex 29:34
shall keep the Feast of Unleavened **B**. Ex 34:18
Seven days you shall eat unleavened **b**, Ex 34:18
He neither ate **b** nor drank water. Ex 34:28
its utensils, and the **b** of the Presence; Ex 35:13
its utensils, and the **b** of the Presence; Ex 39:36
and arranged the **b** on it before the Ex 40:23
his offering with loaves of leavened **b**. Lv 7:13
two rams and the basket of unleavened **b**. Lv 8:2
basket of unleavened **b** that was before Lv 8:26
loaf and one loaf of **b** with oil and one Lv 8:26
there eat it and the **b** that is in the basket Lv 8:31
of the flesh and the **b** you shall burn up Lv 8:32
LORD'S food offerings, the **b** of their God; Lv 21:6
him, for he offers the **b** of your God. Lv 21:8
may approach to offer the **b** of his God. Lv 21:17
not come near to offer the **b** of his God. Lv 21:21
He may eat the **b** of his God, both of the Lv 21:22
shall you offer as the **b** of your God any Lv 22:25
is the Feast of Unleavened **b** to the LORD; Lv 23:6
seven days you shall eat unleavened **b**. Lv 23:6
shall eat neither **b** nor grain parched Lv 23:14
places two loaves of **b** to be waved, Lv 23:17
shall present with the **b** seven lambs a Lv 23:18
wave them with the **b** of the firstfruits Lv 23:20
may go with the **b** as a memorial Lv 24:7
And you shall eat your **b** to the full and Lv 26:5
When I break your supply of **b**, ten Lv 26:26
women shall bake your **b** in a single Lv 26:26
shall dole out your **b** again by weight, Lv 26:26
the table of the **b** of the Presence they Nm 4:7
the regular show **b** also shall be on it. Nm 4:7
and a basket of unleavened **b**, loaves of Nm 6:15
LORD, with the basket of unleavened **b**. Nm 6:17
it with unleavened **b** and bitter herbs. Nm 9:11
people of the land, for they are **b** for us. Nm 14:9
and when you eat of the **b** of the land, Nm 15:19
days shall unleavened **b** be eaten. Nm 28:17
know that man does not live by **b** alone, Dt 8:3
in which you will eat **b** without scarcity, Dt 8:9
nights. I neither ate **b** nor drank water. Dt 9:9
nights. I neither ate **b** nor drank water, Dt 9:18
You shall eat no leavened **b** with it. Dt 16:3
days you shall eat it with unleavened **b**, Dt 16:3
the **b** of affliction—for you came out of Dt 16:3
For six days you shall eat unleavened **b**, Dt 16:8
at the Feast of Unleavened **B**, at the Dt 16:16
not meet you with **b** and with water on Dt 23:4
You have not eaten **b**, and you have not Dt 29:6
Here is our **b**. It was still warm when we Jos 9:12
a cake of barley **b** tumbled into the Jgs 7:13
"Please give loaves of **b** to the people who Jgs 8:5
that we should give **b** to your army?" Jgs 8:6
that we should give **b** to your men who Jgs 8:15
your heart with a morsel of **b**, Jgs 19:5
with **b** and wine for me and your Jgs 19:19
here and eat some **b** and dip your morsel Ru 2:14
full have hired themselves out for **b**, 1 Sm 2:5
of silver or a loaf of **b** and shall say, 1 Sm 2:36
places, that I may eat a morsel of **b**."'" 1 Sm 2:36
For the **b** in our sacks is gone, and 1 Sm 9:7
another carrying three loaves of **b**, 1 Sm 10:3
greet you and give you two loaves of **b**, 1 Sm 10:4
a donkey laden with **b** and a skin of 1 Sm 16:20

Give me five loaves of **b**, or whatever 1 Sm 21:3
"I have no common **b** on hand, 1 Sm 21:4
but there is holy **b**—if the young men 1 Sm 21:4
So the priest gave him the holy **b**, for 1 Sm 21:6
for there was no **b** there but the bread 1 Sm 21:6
bread there but the **b** of the Presence, 1 Sm 21:6
to be replaced by hot **b** on the day it is 1 Sm 21:6
you have given him **b** and a sword 1 Sm 22:13
Shall I take my **b** and my water and 1 Sm 25:11
Let me set a morsel of **b** before you; 1 Sm 28:22
it and baked unleavened **b** of it, 1 Sm 28:24
And they gave him **b** and he ate. 1 Sm 30:11
he had not eaten **b** or drunk water 1 Sm 30:12
falls by the sword or who lacks **b**!" 2 Sm 3:29
persuade David to eat **b** while it was 2 Sm 3:35
if I taste **b** or anything else till the sun 2 Sm 3:35
both men and women, a cake of **b**, 2 Sm 6:19
master's grandson may have **b** to eat. 2 Sm 9:10
Tamar come and give me **b** to eat, 2 Sm 13:5
bearing two hundred loaves of **b**, 2 Sm 16:1
the **b** and summer fruit for the young 2 Sm 16:2
golden table for the **b** of the Presence, 1 Kgs 7:48
And I will not eat **b** or drink water in 1 Kgs 13:8
shall neither eat **b** nor drink water 1 Kgs 13:9
"Come home with me and eat **b**." 1 Kgs 13:15
neither will I eat **b** nor drink water 1 Kgs 13:16
shall neither eat **b** nor drink water 1 Kgs 13:17
that he may eat **b** and drink water.'" 1 Kgs 13:18
with him and ate **b** in his house and 1 Kgs 13:19
and have eaten **b** and drunk water 1 Kgs 13:22
"Eat no **b** and drink no water," your 1 Kgs 13:22
And after he had eaten **b** and drunk, 1 Kgs 13:23
ravens brought him **b** and meat in 1 Kgs 17:6
and **b** and meat in the evening, 1 Kgs 17:6
me a morsel of **b** in your hand." 1 Kgs 17:11
cave and fed them with **b** and water.) 1 Kgs 18:4
cave and fed them with **b** and water? 1 Kgs 18:13
Arise and eat **b** and let your heart be 1 Kgs 21:7
him meager rations of **b** and water, 1 Kgs 22:27
the man of God **b** of the firstfruits, 2 Kgs 4:42
Set **b** and water before them, that they 2 Kgs 6:22
and wine, a land of **b** and vineyards, 2 Kgs 18:32
they ate unleavened **b** among their 2 Kgs 23:9
men and women, to each a loaf of **b**, 1 Chr 16:3
offering, the wafers of unleavened **b**, 1 Chr 23:29
the tables for the **b** of the Presence, 2 Chr 4:19
feasts—the Feast of Unleavened **B**, 2 Chr 8:13
meager rations of **b** and water until 2 Chr 18:26
Feast of Unleavened **B** in the second 2 Chr 30:13
Feast of Unleavened **B** seven days 2 Chr 30:21
Feast of Unleavened **B** seven days. 2 Chr 35:17
Feast of Unleavened **B** seven days with Ezr 6:22
neither eating **b** nor drinking water, Ezr 10:6
You gave them **b** from heaven for their Neh 9:15
the people of Israel with **b** and water, Neh 13:2
For my sighing comes instead of my **b**, Jb 3:24
He wanders abroad for **b**, saying, Jb 15:23
you have withheld **b** from the hungry. Jb 22:7
and his descendants have not enough **b**. Jb 27:14
As for the earth, out of it comes **b**, but Jb 28:5
so that his life loathes **b**, and his Jb 33:20
before, and ate **b** with him in his house. Jb 42:11
my people as they eat **b** and do not call Ps 14:4
forsaken or his children begging for **b**. Ps 37:25
friend in whom I trusted, who ate my **b**, Ps 41:9
who eat up my people as they eat **b**, Ps 53:4
Can he also give **b** or provide meat for Ps 78:20
Man ate of the **b** of the angels; he sent Ps 78:25
fed them with the **b** of tears and given Ps 80:5
and has withered; I forget to eat my **b**. Ps 102:4
I eat ashes like **b** and mingle tears with Ps 102:9
face shine and **b** to strengthen man's Ps 104:15
on the land and broke all supply of **b**, Ps 105:16
and gave them **b** from heaven in Ps 105:40
late to rest, eating the **b** of anxious toil; Ps 127:2
I will satisfy her poor with **b**. Ps 132:15
For they eat the **b** of wickedness and Prv 4:17
she prepares her **b** in summer and Prv 6:8
price of a prostitute is only a loaf of **b**, Prv 6:26
eat of my **b** and drink of the wine I have Prv 9:5
sweet, and **b** eaten in secret is pleasant." Prv 9:17
than to play the great man and lack **b**. Prv 12:9
works his land will have plenty of **b**, Prv 12:11
eyes, and you will have plenty of **b**. Prv 20:13
B gained by deceit is sweet to a man, Prv 20:17
for he shares his **b** with the poor. Prv 22:9
Do not eat the **b** of a man who is stingy; Prv 23:6
enemy is hungry, give him **b** to eat, Prv 25:21
works his land will have plenty of **b**, Prv 28:19
but for a piece of **b** a man will do Prv 28:21
and does not eat the **b** of idleness. Prv 31:27
Go, eat your **b** in joy, and drink your Eccl 9:7
battle to the strong, nor **b** to the wise, Eccl 9:11
B is made for laughter, and wine Eccl 10:19
Cast your **b** upon the waters, for you Eccl 11:1

Judah support and supply, all support of **b**, Is 3:1
in my house there is neither **b** nor cloak; Is 3:7
"We will eat our own **b** and wear our own Is 4:1
meet the fugitive with **b**, O inhabitants Is 21:14
Does one crush grain for **b**? No, he does Is 28:28
Lord give you the **b** of adversity and the Is 30:20
with which you sow the ground, and **b**, Is 30:23
of rocks; his **b** will be given him; Is 33:16
and wine, a land of **b** and vineyards. Is 36:17
himself; he kindles a fire and bakes **b**. Is 44:15
in the fire; I also baked **b** on its coals; Is 44:19
to the pit, neither shall his **b** be lacking. Is 51:14
your money for that which is not **b**, Is 55:2
seed to the sower and **b** to the eater, Is 55:10
not to share your **b** with the hungry and Is 58:7
No one shall break **b** for the mourner, to Jer 16:7
And a loaf of **b** was given him daily Jer 37:21
until all the **b** of the city was gone. Jer 37:21
hunger, for there is no **b** left in the city." Jer 38:9
As they ate **b** together there at Mizpah, Jer 41:1
of the trumpet or be hungry for **b**, Jer 42:14
her people groan as they search for **b**; Lam 1:11
"Where is **b** and wine?" as they faint Lam 2:12
Egypt, and to Assyria, to get **b** enough. Lam 5:6
We get our **b** at the peril of our lives, Lam 5:9
vessel and make your **b** from them. Ezk 4:9
the people of Israel eat their **b** unclean, Ezk 4:13
on which you may prepare your **b**." Ezk 4:15
will break the supply of **b** in Jerusalem. Ezk 4:16
They shall eat **b** by weight and with Ezk 4:16
do this that they may lack **b** and water, Ezk 4:17
upon you and break your supply of **b**. Ezk 5:16
"Son of man, eat your **b** with quaking, Ezk 12:18
They shall eat their **b** with anxiety, Ezk 12:19
handfuls of barley and for pieces of **b**, Ezk 13:19
break its supply of **b** and send famine Ezk 14:13
Also my **b** that I gave you—I fed you Ezk 16:19
gives his **b** to the hungry and covers Ezk 18:7
but gives his **b** to the hungry and Ezk 18:16
cover your lips, nor eat the **b** of men." Ezk 24:17
cover your lips, nor eat the **b** of men. Ezk 24:22
may sit in it to eat **b** before the LORD. Ezk 44:3
seven days unleavened **b** shall be Ezk 45:21
lovers, who give me my **b** and my water, Hos 2:5
It shall be like mourners' **b** to them; all Hos 9:4
for their **b** shall be for their hunger only; Hos 9:4
cities, and lack of **b** in all your places, Am 4:6
to the land of Judah, and eat **b** there, Am 7:12
famine on the land—not a famine of **b**, Am 8:11
those who eat your **b** have set a trap Ob 1:7
touches with his fold **b** or stew or wine Hg 2:12
these stones to become loaves of **b**." Mt 4:3
is written, "'Man shall not live by **b** alone, Mt 4:4
Give us this day our daily **b**, Mt 6:11
one of you, if his son asks him for **b**, Mt 7:9
of God and ate the **b** of the Presence, Mt 12:4
to take the children's **b** and throw it to Mt 15:26
we to get enough **b** in such a desolate Mt 15:33
side, they had forgotten to bring any **b**. Mt 16:5
themselves, saying, "We brought no **b**." Mt 16:7
yourselves the fact that you have no **b**? Mt 16:8
that I did not speak about **b**? Mt 16:11
tell them to beware of the leaven of **b**, Mt 16:12
day of Unleavened **B** the disciples came Mt 26:17
Now as they were eating, Jesus took **b**, Mt 26:26
priest, and ate the **b** of the Presence, Mk 2:26
for their journey except a staff—no **b**, Mk 6:8
hundred denarii worth of **b** and give it Mk 6:37
to take the children's **b** and throw it to Mk 7:27
feed these people with **b** here in this Mk 8:4
Now they had forgotten to bring **b**, and Mk 8:14
one another the fact that they had no **b**. Mk 8:16
discussing the fact that you have no **b**? Mk 8:17
and the Feast of Unleavened **B**. Mk 14:1
And on the first day of Unleavened **B**, Mk 14:12
one who is dipping **b** into the dish Mk 14:20
And as they were eating, he took **b**, Mk 14:22
God, command this stone to become **b**." Lk 4:3
written, 'Man shall not live by **b** alone.'" Lk 4:4
and took and ate the **b** of the Presence, Lk 6:4
has come eating no **b** and drinking no Lk 7:33
for your journey, no staff, nor bag, nor **b**, Lk 9:3
Give us each day our daily **b**, Lk 11:3
who will eat **b** in the kingdom Lk 14:15
servants have more than enough **b**, Lk 15:17
the Feast of Unleavened **B** drew near, Lk 22:1
Then came the day of Unleavened **B**, on Lk 22:7
And he took **b**, and when he had given Lk 22:19
he took the **b** and blessed and broke it Lk 24:30
to them in the breaking of the **b**. Lk 24:35
said to Philip, "Where are we to buy **b**, Jn 6:5
would not buy enough **b** for each of them Jn 6:7
they had eaten the **b** after the Lord had Jn 6:23
'He gave them **b** from heaven to eat.'" Jn 6:31
Moses who gave you the **b** from heaven, Jn 6:32

Father gives you the true **b** from heaven. Jn 6:32
For the **b** of God is he who comes down Jn 6:33
said to him, "Sir, give us this **b** always." Jn 6:34
Jesus said to them, "I am the **b** of life; Jn 6:35
"I am the **b** that came down from Jn 6:41
I am the **b** of life. Jn 6:48
This is the **b** that comes down from Jn 6:50
I am the living **b** that came down from Jn 6:51
If anyone eats of this **b**, he will live Jn 6:51
And the **b** that I will give for the life of the Jn 6:51
This is the **b** that came down from Jn 6:58
feeds on this **b** will live forever." Jn 6:58
'He who ate my **b** has lifted his heel Jn 13:18
give this morsel of **b** when I have dipped Jn 13:26
So, after receiving the morsel of **b**, he Jn 13:30
in place, with fish laid out on it, and **b**. Jn 21:9
Jesus came and took the **b** and gave it to Jn 21:13
to the breaking of **b** and the prayers. Acts 2:42
together and breaking **b** in their Acts 2:46
was during the days of Unleavened **B**. Acts 12:3
after the days of Unleavened **B**, Acts 20:6
we were gathered together to break **b**, Acts 20:7
gone up and had broken **b** and eaten, Acts 20:11
he had said these things, he took **b**, Acts 27:35
with the unleavened **b** of sincerity and 1 Cor 5:8
The **b** that we break, is it not a 1 Cor 10:16
Because there is one **b**, we who are 1 Cor 10:17
body, for we all partake of the one **b**. 1 Cor 10:17
night when he was betrayed took **b**, 1 Cor 11:23
as you eat this **b** and drink the cup, 1 Cor 11:26
eats the **b** or drinks the cup of the 1 Cor 11:27
and so eat of the **b** and drink of the 1 Cor 11:28
to the sower and **b** for food will 2 Cor 9:10
we eat anyone's **b** without paying for 2 Thes 3:8
and the table and the **b** of the Presence. Heb 9:2

BREADTH (65)
of the ark 300 cubits, its **b** 50 cubits, Gn 6:15
the length and the **b** of the land, Gn 13:17
be its length, a cubit and a half its **b**, Ex 25:10
its length, and a cubit and a half its **b**. Ex 25:17
cubits shall be its length, a cubit its **b**, Ex 25:23
and the **b** of each curtain four cubits; Ex 26:2
and the **b** of each curtain four cubits. Ex 26:8
a cubit and a half the **b** of each frame. Ex 26:16
And for the **b** of the court on the west Ex 27:12
The **b** of the court on the front to the Ex 27:13
shall be a hundred cubits, the **b** fifty, Ex 27:18
a span its length and a span its **b**. Ex 28:16
shall be its length, and a cubit its **b**. Ex 30:2
and the **b** of each curtain four cubits. Ex 36:9
and the **b** of each curtain four cubits. Ex 36:15
a cubit and a half the **b** of each frame. Ex 36:21
was its length, a cubit and a half its **b**, Ex 37:1
its length, and a cubit and a half its **b**. Ex 37:6
Two cubits was its length, a cubit its **b**, Ex 37:10
was a cubit, and its **b** was a cubit. Ex 37:25
was its length, and five cubits its **b**. Ex 38:1
long and five cubits high in its **b**, Ex 38:18
its length and a span its **b** when doubled. Ex 39:9
was its length, and four cubits its **b**, Dt 3:11
and **b** of mind like the sand on the 1 Kgs 4:29
cubits and its **b** fifty cubits and 1 Kgs 7:2
was fifty cubits, and its **b** thirty cubits. 1 Kgs 7:6
sixty cubits, and the **b** twenty cubits. 2 Chr 3:3
corresponding to the **b** of the house, 2 Chr 3:8
cubits, and its **b** was twenty cubits. 2 Chr 3:8
be sixty cubits and its **b** sixty cubits, Ezr 6:3
outspread wings will fill the **b** of your land, Is 8:8
people from the length and **b** of the land: Jer 8:19
of the other, a **b** of twenty-five cubits; Ezk 40:13
he measured its length and its **b**. Ezk 40:20
cubits, and its **b** twenty-five cubits. Ezk 40:21
cubits, and its **b** twenty-five cubits. Ezk 40:25
cubits, and its **b** twenty-five cubits. Ezk 40:29
cubits, and its **b** twenty-five cubits. Ezk 40:33
cubits, and its **b** twenty-five cubits. Ezk 40:36
And the **b** of the gate was fourteen Ezk 40:48
twenty cubits, and the **b** twelve cubits, Ezk 40:49
side six cubits was the **b** of the jambs. Ezk 41:1
And the **b** of the entrance was ten Ezk 41:2
of the nave, forty cubits, and its **b**, Ezk 41:2
of the room, twenty cubits, and its **b**, Ezk 41:4
thick, and the **b** of the side chambers, Ezk 41:5
chambers was a **b** of twenty cubits Ezk 41:10
And the **b** of the free space was five Ezk 41:11
also the **b** of the east front of the Ezk 41:14
hundred cubits, and the **b** fifty cubits. Ezk 42:2
the north, of the same length and **b**, Ezk 42:11
two cubits, with a **b** of one cubit; Ezk 43:14
four cubits, with a **b** of one cubit; Ezk 43:14
you shall set apart, 25,000 cubits in **b**, Ezk 48:8
cubits in length, and 20,000 in **b**. Ezk 48:9
10,000 cubits in **b** on the western side, Ezk 48:10
side, 10,000 in **b** on the eastern side, Ezk 48:10
cubits in length and 10,000 in **b**. Ezk 48:13

be 25,000 cubits and the **b** 20,000. Ezk 48:13
5,000 cubits in **b** and 25,000 in length, Ezk 48:15
was sixty cubits and its **b** six cubits. Dn 3:1
great city, three days' journey in **b**. Jon 3:3
who march through the **b** of the earth, Hab 1:6
saints what is the **b** and length and Eph 3:18

BREAK (135)
Lot, and drew near to **b** the door down. Gn 19:9
grow restless you shall **b** his yoke from Gn 27:40
and you shall not **b** any of its bones. Ex 12:46
will not redeem it you shall **b** its neck. Ex 13:13
lest they **b** through to the LORD to look Ex 19:21
lest the LORD **b** out against them." Ex 19:22
and the people **b** through to come Ex 19:24
to the LORD, lest he **b** out against them." Ex 19:24
overthrow them and **b** their pillars in Ex 23:24
loose (for Aaron had let them **b** loose, Ex 32:25
their altars and **b** their pillars and Ex 34:13
will not redeem it you shall **b** its neck. Ex 34:20
You shall **b** it in pieces and pour oil on it; Lv 2:6
it shall be unclean, and you shall **b** it. Lv 11:33
And he shall **b** down the house, its Lv 14:45
commandments, but **b** my covenant, Lv 26:15
and I will **b** the pride of your power, and Lv 26:19
When I **b** your supply of bread, ten Lv 26:26
them utterly and **b** my covenant with Lv 26:44
the morning, nor **b** any of its bones; Nm 9:12
and shall **b** their bones in pieces and Nm 24:8
forehead of Moab and **b** down all the Nm 24:17
by a pledge, he shall not **b** his word. Nm 30:2
you shall **b** down their altars and dash in Dt 7:5
and shall **b** the heifer's neck there in the Dt 21:4
forsake me and **b** my covenant that Dt 31:16
and despise me and **b** my covenant. Dt 31:20
the son of Zerah **b** faith in the matter Jos 22:20
'I will never **b** my covenant with you, Jgs 2:1
this land; you shall **b** down their altars.' Jgs 2:2
Awake, awake, **b** out in a song! Jgs 5:12
again in peace, I will **b** down this tower." Jgs 8:9
And as the dawn began to **b**, they let Jgs 19:25
Then at the **b** of dawn Samuel called 1 Sm 9:26
b your covenant with Baasha king 1 Kgs 15:19
him 700 swordsmen to **b** through, 2 Kgs 3:26
b your covenant with Baasha king of 2 Chr 16:3
'Why do you **b** the commandments 2 Chr 24:20
shall we **b** your commandments again Ezr 9:14
on it he will **b** down their stone wall!" Neh 4:3
the spears from the **b** of dawn until the Neh 4:21
you torment me and **b** me in pieces with Jb 19:2
They **b** up my path; they promote my Jb 30:13
You shall **b** them with a rod of iron and Ps 2:9
the cheek; you **b** the teeth of the wicked. Ps 3:7
B the arm of the wicked and evildoer; Ps 10:15
But God will **b** you down forever; he will Ps 52:5
O God, **b** the teeth in their mouths; tear Ps 58:6
b forth into joyous song and sing Ps 98:4
and a soft tongue will **b** a bone. Prv 25:15
a time to **b** down, and a time to build Eccl 3:3
I will **b** down its wall, and it shall be Is 5:5
rest and quiet; they **b** forth into singing. Is 14:7
that I will **b** the Assyrian in my land, Is 14:25
For waters **b** forth in the wilderness, and Is 35:6
a bruised reed he will not **b**, and a faintly Is 42:3
b forth into singing, O mountains, O Is 44:23
I will **b** in pieces the doors of bronze and Is 45:2
b forth, O mountains, into singing! Is 49:13
B forth together into singing, you waste Is 52:9
b forth into singing and cry aloud, you Is 54:1
before you shall **b** forth into singing, Is 55:12
the oppressed go free, and to **b** every yoke? Is 58:6
Then shall your light **b** forth like the Is 58:8
kingdoms, to pluck up and to **b** down, Jer 1:10
"**B** up your fallow ground, and sow not Jer 4:3
and do not **b** your covenant with Jer 14:21
Can one **b** iron, iron from the north, Jer 15:12
No one shall **b** bread for the mourner, to Jer 16:7
will pluck up and **b** down and destroy it, Jer 18:7
"Then you shall **b** the flask in the sight Jer 19:10
So will I **b** this people and this city, as Jer 19:11
for I will **b** the yoke of the king of Jer 28:4
Even so will I **b** the yoke of Jer 28:11
that I will **b** his yoke from off your neck, Jer 30:8
over them to pluck up and **b** down, Jer 31:28
If you can **b** my covenant with the day Jer 33:20
He shall **b** the obelisks of Heliopolis, Jer 43:13
empty his vessels and **b** his jars in Jer 48:12
"Behold, I will **b** the bow of Elam, the Jer 49:35
of war: with you I **b** nations in pieces; Jer 51:20
with you I **b** in pieces the horse and his Jer 51:21
with you I **b** in pieces the chariot and Jer 51:21
with you I **b** in pieces man and woman; Jer 51:22
with you I **b** in pieces the old man and Jer 51:22
with you I **b** in pieces the young man Jer 51:22
with you I **b** in pieces the shepherd and Jer 51:23
with you I **b** in pieces the farmer and Jer 51:23
with you I **b** in pieces governors and Jer 51:23
I will **b** the supply of bread in Ezk 4:16
famine upon you and **b** your supply of Ezk 5:16
will fall, and a stormy wind **b** out. Ezk 13:11
make a stormy wind **b** out in my Ezk 13:13
And I will **b** down the wall that you Ezk 13:14
hand against it and **b** its supply of Ezk 14:13
vaulted chamber and **b** down your Ezk 16:39
Can he **b** the covenant and yet escape? Ezk 17:15
I will **b** off from the topmost of its Ezk 17:22
walls of Tyre and **b** down her towers, Ezk 26:4
his axes he will **b** down your towers. Ezk 26:9
They will **b** down your walls and Ezk 26:12
when I **b** there the yoke bars of Egypt, Ezk 30:18
king of Egypt and will **b** his arms, Ezk 30:22
but I will **b** the arms of Pharaoh, Ezk 30:24
LORD, when I **b** the bars of their yoke, Ezk 34:27
crushes, it shall **b** and crush all these. Dn 2:40
It shall **b** in pieces all these kingdoms Dn 2:44
b off your sins by practicing Dn 4:27
Then, at **b** of day, the king arose and Dn 6:19
and trample it down, and **b** it to pieces. Dn 7:23
those who eat his food shall **b** him. Dn 11:26
on that day I will **b** the bow of Israel in Hos 1:5
they **b** all bounds, and bloodshed Hos 4:2
The LORD will **b** down their altars and Hos 10:2
b up your fallow ground, for it is the Hos 10:12
I will **b** the gate-bar of Damascus, and Am 1:5
lest he **b** out like fire in the house of Am 5:6
sea, so that the ship threatened to **b** up. Jon 1:4
they **b** through and pass the gate, going Mi 2:13
and **b** their bones in pieces and chop Mi 3:3
And now I will **b** his yoke from off you Na 1:13
destroy and where thieves **b** in and steal, Mt 6:19
and where thieves do not **b** in and steal. Mt 6:20
a bruised reed he will not **b**, and a Mt 12:20
do your disciples **b** the tradition of Mt 15:2
why do you **b** the commandment of Mt 15:3
he did not want to **b** his word to her. Mk 6:26
but he would **b** the bonds and be driven Lk 8:29
was already dead, they did not **b** his legs. Jn 19:33
we were gathered together to **b** bread, Acts 20:7
you obey the law, but if you **b** the law, Rom 2:25
code and circumcision but **b** the law. Rom 2:27
The bread that we **b**, is it not a 1 Cor 10:16
b forth and cry aloud, you who are not Gal 4:27
worthy to open the scroll and **b** its seals?" Rv 5:2

BREAKERS (1)
all your **b** and your waves have gone Ps 42:7

BREAKFAST (2)
"Come and have **b**." Now none of the Jn 21:12
When they had finished **b**, Jesus said to Jn 21:15

BREAKING (25)
with him until the **b** of the day. Gn 32:24
and become boils **b** out in sores on man Ex 9:9
and it became boils **b** out in sores on Ex 9:10
"If a thief is found **b** in and is struck so Ex 22:2
it is a leprous disease **b** out on his bald Lv 13:42
that people commit by **b** faith with the Nm 5:6
the congregation and for **b** camp. Nm 10:2
days who are **b** away from their 1 Sm 25:10
to collapse, whose **b** comes suddenly, Is 30:13
and its **b** is like that of a potter's vessel Is 30:14
of heart and shall wail for **b** of spirit. Is 65:14
poor; you did not find them **b** in. Jer 2:34
Behold, what I have built I am **b** down, Jer 45:4
despised the oath in **b** the covenant, Ezk 16:59
despised the oath in **b** the covenant, Ezk 17:18
with **b** heart and bitter grief, groan Ezk 21:6
and the waves were **b** into the boat, Mk 4:37
number of fish, and their nets were **b**. Lk 5:6
known to them in the **b** of the bread. Lk 24:35
because not only was he **b** the Sabbath, Jn 5:18
Just as day was **b**, Jesus stood on the Jn 21:4
to the **b** of bread and the prayers. Acts 2:42
temple together and **b** bread in their Acts 2:46
you doing, weeping and **b** my heart? Acts 21:13
in the law dishonor God by **b** the law. Rom 2:23

BREAKS (22)
lest they multiply, and, if war **b** out, Ex 1:10
"If fire **b** out and catches in thorns so Ex 22:6
if the leprous disease **b** out in the skin, Lv 13:12
"If the disease **b** out again in the house, Lv 14:43
wife goes astray and **b** faith with him, Nm 5:12
dirt; my skin hardens, then **b** out afresh. Jb 7:5
He **b** me with breach upon breach; he Jb 16:14
He **b** me down on every side, and I am Jb 19:10
The voice of the LORD **b** the cedars; the Ps 29:5
cedars; the LORD **b** the cedars of Lebanon. Ps 29:5
he **b** the bow and shatters the spear; Ps 46:9
As when one plows and **b** up the earth, Ps 141:7
of life, but perverseness in it **b** the spirit. Prv 15:4
water, so quit before the quarrel **b** out. Prv 17:14
he **b** out against all sound judgment. Prv 18:1
will bite him who **b** through a wall. Eccl 10:8
morning; like a lion he **b** all my bones; Is 38:13
a lamb, like one who **b** a dog's neck; Is 66:3
and this city, as one **b** a potter's vessel, Jer 19:11
like a hammer that **b** the rock in Jer 23:29
because iron **b** to pieces and shatters all Dn 2:40
the thief **b** in, and the bandits raid Hos 7:1

BREAST (21)
"You shall take the **b** of the ram of Ex 29:26
you shall consecrate the **b** of the wave Ex 29:27
He shall bring the fat with the **b**, that the Lv 7:30
that the **b** may be waved as a wave Lv 7:30
but the **b** shall be for Aaron and his Lv 7:31
For the **b** that is waved and the thigh Lv 7:34
And Moses took the **b** and waved it for a Lv 8:29
But the **b** that is waved and the thigh Lv 10:14
is contributed and the **b** that is waved Lv 10:15
together with the **b** that is waved and Nm 6:20
as the **b** that is waved and as the right Nm 18:18
servant slept, and laid him at her **b**, 1 Kgs 3:20
breast, and laid her dead son at my **b**. 1 Kgs 3:20
snatch the fatherless child from the **b**, Jb 24:9
is like wax; it is melted within my **b**; Ps 22:14
from the milk, those taken from the **b**? Is 28:9
you shall nurse at the **b** of kings; Is 60:16
and be satisfied from her consoling **b**; Is 66:11
Even jackals offer the **b**; they nurse Lam 4:3
I will tear open their **b**, and there I will Hos 13:8
up his eyes to heaven, but beat his **b**, Lk 18:13

BREASTPIECE (25)
for setting, for the ephod and for the **b**. Ex 25:7
the garments that they shall make: a **b**, Ex 28:4
"You shall make a **b** of judgment, in Ex 28:15
shall make for the **b** twisted chains like Ex 28:22
shall make for the **b** two rings of gold, Ex 28:23
the two rings on the two edges of the **b**. Ex 28:23
in the two rings at the edges of the **b**. Ex 28:24
and put them at the two ends of the **b**, Ex 28:26
they shall bind the **b** by its rings to Ex 28:28
so that the **b** shall not come loose from Ex 28:28
of Israel in the **b** of judgment on his Ex 28:29
And in the **b** of judgment you shall put Ex 28:30
of the ephod, and the ephod, and the **b**, Ex 29:5
for setting, for the ephod and for the **b**. Ex 35:9
to be set, for the ephod and for the **b**, Ex 35:27
He made the **b**, in skilled work, in the Ex 39:8
They made the **b** doubled, a span its Ex 39:9
they made on the **b** twisted chains like Ex 39:15
the two rings on the two edges of the **b**. Ex 39:16
in the two rings at the edges of the **b**. Ex 39:17
and put them at the two ends of the **b**, Ex 39:19
And they bound the **b** by its rings to Ex 39:21
and that the **b** should not come loose Ex 39:21
And he placed the **b** on him, and in the Lv 8:8
and in the **b** he put the Urim and the Lv 8:8

BREASTPLATE (5)
between the scale armor and the **b**. 1 Kgs 22:34
between the scale armor and the **b**. 2 Chr 18:33
He put on righteousness as a **b**, and a Is 59:17
having put on the **b** of righteousness, Eph 6:14
having put on the **b** of faith and love, 1 Thes 5:8

BREASTPLATES (3)
they had **b** like breastplates of iron, and Rv 9:9
they had breastplates like **b** of iron, and Rv 9:9
they wore **b** the color of fire and of Rv 9:17

BREASTS (25)
blessings of the **b** and of the womb. Gn 49:25
they put the fat pieces on the **b**, and he Lv 9:20
but the **b** and the right thigh Aaron Lv 9:21
me? Or why the **b**, that I should nurse? Jb 3:12
made me trust you at my mother's **b**. Ps 22:9
Let her **b** fill you at all times with Prv 5:19
sachet of myrrh that lies between my **b**. Sg 1:13
Your two **b** are like two fawns, twins of a Sg 4:5
Your two **b** are like two fawns, twins of a Sg 7:3
palm tree, and your **b** are like its clusters. Sg 7:7
Oh may your **b** be like clusters of the Sg 7:8
to me who nursed at my mother's **b**! Sg 8:1
We have a little sister, and she has no **b**. Sg 8:8
I was a wall, and my **b** were like towers; Sg 8:10
Beat your **b** for the pleasant fields, for Is 32:12
Your **b** were formed, and your hair had Ezk 16:7
there their **b** were pressed and their Ezk 23:3
bosom and pressed your young **b**." Ezk 23:21
and gnaw its shards, and tear your **b**; Ezk 23:34
and her adultery from between her **b**; Hos 2:2
them a miscarrying womb and dry **b**. Hos 9:14
moaning like doves and beating their **b**. Na 2:7
you, and the **b** at which you nursed!" Lk 11:27
bore and the **b** that never nursed!' Lk 23:29
place, returned home beating their **b**. Lk 23:48

BREATH (68)
earth, everything that has the **b** of life, Gn 1:30
breathed into his nostrils the **b** of life, Gn 2:7
in which is the **b** of life under heaven. Gn 6:17
all flesh in which there was the **b** of life. Gn 7:15
in whose nostrils was the **b** of life died. Gn 7:22
at the blast of the **b** of his nostrils. 2 Sm 22:16
the LORD, there was no more **b** in her. 1 Kgs 10:5
that there was no **b** left in him. 1 Kgs 17:17
the LORD, there was no more **b** in her. 2 Chr 9:4
By the **b** of God they perish, and by the Jb 4:9
"Remember that my life is a **b**; my eye will Jb 7:7
Leave me alone, for my days are a **b**. Jb 7:16
he will not let me get my **b**, but fills me Jb 9:18
living thing and the **b** of all mankind. Jb 12:10
and by the **b** of his mouth he will Jb 15:30
My **b** is strange to my wife, and I am a Jb 19:17
and whose **b** has come out from you? Jb 26:4
as long as my **b** is in me, and the spirit of Jb 27:3
the spirit in man, the **b** of the Almighty, Jb 32:8
and the **b** of the Almighty gives me life. Jb 33:4
gather to himself his spirit and his **b**, Jb 34:14
By the **b** of God ice is given, and the Jb 37:10
His **b** kindles coals, and a flame comes Jb 41:21
at the blast of the **b** of your nostrils. Ps 18:15
and by the **b** of his mouth all their host. Ps 33:6
Surely all mankind stands as a mere **b**! Ps 39:5
to him; surely all mankind is a mere **b**! Ps 39:11
Those of low estate are but a **b**; those of Ps 62:9
go up; they are together lighter than a **b**. Ps 62:9
So he made their days vanish like a **b**, Ps 78:33
thoughts of man, that they are but a **b**. Ps 94:11
when you take away their **b**, they die Ps 104:29
nor is there any **b** in their mouths. Ps 135:17
Man is like a **b**; his days are like a Ps 144:4
When his **b** departs he returns to the Ps 146:4
everything that has **b** praise the LORD! Ps 150:6
They all have the same **b**, and man Eccl 3:19
vine, and the scent of your **b** like apples, Sg 7:8
regarding man in whose nostrils is **b**, Is 2:22
and with the **b** of his lips he shall kill the Is 11:4
over the River with his scorching **b**, Is 11:15
for the **b** of the ruthless is like a storm Is 25:4
them with his fierce **b** in the day of Is 27:8
his **b** is like an overflowing stream that Is 30:28
the **b** of the LORD, like a stream of sulfur, Is 30:33
your **b** is a fire that will consume you. Is 33:11
flower fades when the **b** of the LORD blows Is 40:7
who gives **b** to the people on it and spirit Is 42:5
carry them off, a **b** will take them away. Is 57:13
before me, and the **b** of life that I made. Is 57:16
of the daughter of Zion gasping for **b**, Jer 4:31
are false, and there is no **b** in them. Jer 10:14
are false, and there is no **b** in them. Jer 51:17
The **b** of our nostrils, the LORD'S Lam 4:20
Behold, I will cause **b** to enter you, and Ezk 37:5
cover you with skin, and put **b** in you, Ezk 37:6
them. But there was no **b** in them. Ezk 37:8
Then he said to me, "Prophesy to the **b**; Ezk 37:9
prophesy, son of man, and say to the **b**, Ezk 37:9
Come from the four winds, O **b**, and Ezk 37:9
me, and the **b** came into them, Ezk 37:10
but the God in whose hand is your **b**, Dn 5:23
remains in me, and no **b** is left in me." Dn 10:17
and silver, and there is no **b** at all in it. Hab 2:19
mankind life and **b** and everything. Acts 17:25
will kill with the **b** of his mouth and 2 Thes 2:8
and a half days a **b** of life from God Rv 11:11
it was allowed to give **b** to the image of Rv 13:15

BREATHE (4)
them, and their hope is to **b** their last." Jb 11:20
and made its owners **b** their last, Jb 31:39
against me, and they **b** out violence. Ps 27:12
winds, O breath, and **b** on these slain, Ezk 37:9

BREATHED (17)
from the ground and **b** into his nostrils Gn 2:7
Abraham **b** his last and died in a good Gn 25:8
He **b** his last and died, and was Gn 25:17
And Isaac **b** his last, and he died and Gn 35:29
feet into the bed and **b** his last and was Gn 49:33
but devoted to destruction all that **b**, Jos 10:40
destruction; there was none left that **b**. Jos 11:11
and they did not leave any who **b**. Jos 11:14
house of Jeroboam not one that **b**, 1 Kgs 15:29
Jesus uttered a loud cry and **b** his last. Mk 15:37
him, saw that in this way he **b** his last, Mk 15:39
And having said this he **b** his last. Lk 23:46
this, he **b** on them and said to them, Jn 20:22
these words, he fell down and **b** his last. Acts 5:5
she fell down at his feet and **b** her last. Acts 5:10
he was eaten by worms and **b** his last. Acts 12:23
All Scripture is **b** out by God and 2 Tm 3:16

BREATHES (9)
you shall save alive nothing that **b**, Dt 20:16
low; man **b** his last, and where is he? Jb 14:10
a false witness who **b** out lies, and one Prv 6:19
not lie, but a false witness **b** out lies. Prv 14:5
but one who **b** out lies is deceitful. Prv 14:25
and he who **b** out lies will not escape. Prv 19:5
and he who **b** out lies will perish. Prv 19:9
Until the day **b** and the shadows flee, Sg 2:17
Until the day **b** and the shadows flee, I will Sg 4:6

BREATHING (1)
still **b** threats and murder against the Acts 9:1

BRED (5)
And since they **b** when they came to Gn 30:38
the flocks **b** in front of the sticks and Gn 30:39
morning, and it **b** worms and stank. Ex 16:20
the king's service, **b** from the royal stud, Est 8:10
The lovely and delicately **b** I will destroy, Jer 6:2

BREED (3)
that they might **b** among the sticks, Gn 30:41
not let your cattle **b** with a different Lv 19:19
you know that they **b** quarrels. 2 Tm 2:23

BREEDER (1)
Mesha king of Moab was a sheep **b**, 2 Kgs 3:4

BREEDING (2)
the stronger of the flock were **b**, Gn 30:41
In the **b** season of the flock I lifted up Gn 31:10

BREEDS (1)
Their bull **b** without fail; their cow Jb 21:10

BRIBE (20)
God, who are trustworthy and hate a **b**, Ex 18:21
And you shall take no **b**, for a bribe Ex 23:8
for a **b** blinds the clear-sighted and Ex 23:8
God, who is not partial and takes no **b**. Dt 10:17
partiality, and you shall not accept a **b**, Dt 16:19
for a **b** blinds the eyes of the wise and Dt 16:19
anyone who takes a **b** to shed innocent Dt 27:25
have I taken a **b** to blind my eyes 1 Sm 12:3
Or, 'From your wealth offer a **b** for me'? Jb 6:22
does not take a **b** against the innocent. Ps 15:5
A **b** is like a magic stone in the eyes of Prv 17:8
The wicked accepts a **b** in secret to Prv 17:23
secret averts anger, and a concealed **b**, Prv 21:14
madness, and a **b** corrupts the heart. Eccl 7:7
Everyone loves a **b** and runs after gifts. Is 1:23
who acquit the guilty for a **b**, and deprive Is 5:23
who shakes his hands, lest they hold a **b**, Is 33:15
who afflict the righteous, who take a **b**, Am 5:12
Its heads give judgment for a **b**; its Mi 3:11
the prince and the judge ask for a **b**, and Mi 7:3

BRIBED (1)
and **b** counselors against them to Ezr 4:5

BRIBERY (1)
and fire consumes the tents of **b**. Jb 15:34

BRIBES (5)
They took **b** and perverted justice. 1 Sm 8:3
our God, or partiality or taking **b**." 2 Chr 19:7
and whose right hands are full of **b**. Ps 26:10
but he who hates **b** will live. Prv 15:27
In you they take **b** to shed blood; you Ezk 22:12

BRIBING (1)
b them to come to you from every side Ezk 16:33

BRICK (5)
thoroughly." And they had **b** for stone, Gn 11:3
with hard service, in mortar and **b**, Ex 1:14
and made them toil at the **b** kilns. 2 Sm 12:31
of man, take a **b** and lay it before you, Ezk 4:1
the mortar; take hold of the **b** mold! Na 3:14

BRICKS (9)
to one another, "Come, let us make **b**, Gn 11:3
no longer give the people straw to make **b**, Ex 5:7
But the number of **b** that they made in Ex 5:8
task of making **b** today and yesterday, Ex 5:14
servants, yet they say to us, 'Make **b**!' Ex 5:16
still deliver the same number of **b**." Ex 5:18
by no means reduce your number of **b**, Ex 5:19
"The **b** have fallen, but we will build with Is 9:10
in gardens and making offerings on **b**; Is 65:3

BRIDAL (1)
whom I paid the **b** price of a hundred 2 Sm 3:14

BRIDE (24)
me for as great a **b** price and gift as you Gn 34:12
back to you as a **b** comes home to her 2 Sm 17:3
Come with me from Lebanon, my **b**; Sg 4:8
have captivated my heart, my sister, my **b**; Sg 4:9
beautiful is your love, my sister, my **b**! Sg 4:10
Your lips drip nectar, my **b**; honey and Sg 4:11
A garden locked is my sister, my **b**, a Sg 4:12
I came to my garden, my sister, my **b**, I Sg 5:1
you shall bind them on as a **b** does. Is 49:18
and as a **b** adorns herself with her Is 61:10
and as the bridegroom rejoices over the **b**, Is 62:5
devotion of your youth, your love as a **b**, Jer 2:2
forget her ornaments, or a **b** her attire? Jer 2:32
of the bridegroom and the voice of the **b**, Jer 7:34
of the bridegroom and the voice of the **b**. Jer 16:9
the bridegroom and the voice of the **b**, Jer 25:10
the bridegroom and the voice of the **b**, Jer 33:11
leave his room, and the **b** her chamber. Jl 2:16
one who has the **b** is the bridegroom. Jn 3:29
of bridegroom and **b** will be heard Rv 18:23
come, and his **B** has made herself ready; Rv 19:7
prepared as a **b** adorned for her Rv 21:2
saying, "Come, I will show you the **B**, Rv 21:9
The Spirit and the **B** say, "Come." And Rv 22:17

BRIDE-PRICE (3)
he shall give the **b** for her and make Ex 22:16
pay money equal to the **b** for virgins. Ex 22:17
king desires no **b** except a hundred 1 Sm 18:25

BRIDEGROOM (26)
said, "Surely you are a **b** of blood to me!" Ex 4:25
"A **b** of blood," because of the Ex 4:26
comes out like a **b** leaving his chamber, Ps 19:5
as a **b** decks himself like a priest with a Is 61:10
you, and as the **b** rejoices over the bride, Is 62:5
the voice of the **b** and the voice of the Jer 7:34
the voice of the **b** and the voice of the Jer 16:9
the voice of the **b** and the voice of the Jer 25:10
the voice of the **b** and the voice of the Jer 33:11
wearing sackcloth for the **b** of her youth. Jl 1:8
Let the **b** leave his room, and the bride her Jl 2:16
mourn as long as the **b** is with them? Mt 9:15
will come when the **b** is taken away Mt 9:15
took their lamps and went to meet the **b**. Mt 25:1
As the **b** was delayed, they all became Mt 25:5
midnight there was a cry, 'Here is the **b**! Mt 25:6
they were going to buy, the **b** came, Mt 25:10
guests fast while the **b** is with them? Mk 2:19
As long as they have the **b** with them, Mk 2:19
will come when the **b** is taken away Mk 2:20
guests fast while the **b** is with them? Lk 5:34
will come when the **b** is taken away Lk 5:35
knew), the master of the feast called the **b** Jn 2:9
The one who has the bride is the **b**. The Jn 3:29
The friend of the **b**, who stands and hears Jn 3:29
and the voice of **b** and bride will be Rv 18:23

BRIDEGROOM'S (1)
hears him, rejoices greatly at the **b** voice. Jn 3:29

BRIDES (2)
whore, and your **b** commit adultery. Hos 4:13
nor your **b** when they commit Hos 4:14

BRIDLE (7)
Who would come near him with a **b**? Jb 41:13
which must be curbed with bit and **b**, Ps 32:9
A whip for the horse, a **b** for the donkey, Prv 26:3
jaws of the peoples a **b** that leads astray. Is 30:28
religious and does not **b** his tongue but Jas 1:26
man, able also to **b** his whole body. Jas 3:2
the winepress, as high as a horse's **b**, Rv 14:20

BRIEF (2)
But now for a **b** moment favor has been Ezr 9:8
For a **b** moment I deserted you, but with Is 54:7

BRIEFLY (4)
beg you in your kindness to hear us **b**. Acts 24:4
to me by revelation, as I have written **b**. Eph 3:3
for I have written to you **b**. Heb 13:22
as I regard him, I have written **b** to you, 1 Pt 5:12

BRIER (3)
instead of the **b** shall come up the Is 55:13
shall be no more a **b** to prick or a Ezk 28:24
The best of them is like a **b**, the most Mi 7:4

BRIERS (11)
the thorns of the wilderness and with **b**." Jgs 8:7
of the wilderness and **b** and with them Jgs 8:16
or hoed, and **b** and thorns shall grow up; Is 5:6
of silver, will become **b** and thorns. Is 7:23
for all the land will be **b** and thorns. Is 7:24
not come there for fear of **b** and thorns, Is 7:25
like a fire; it consumes **b** and thorns; Is 9:18
and devour his thorns and **b** in one day. Is 10:17
Would that I had thorns and **b** to battle! Is 27:4
my people growing up in thorns and **b**, Is 32:13
though **b** and thorns are with you and Ezk 2:6

BRIGHT (18)
to his mouth, and his eyes became **b**. 1 Sm 14:27
eyes have become **b** because I tasted 1 Sm 14:29
two vessels of fine **b** bronze as precious Ezr 8:27
Behold, even the moon is not **b**, and the Jb 25:5
on the light when it is **b** in the skies, Jb 37:21
dark to you; the night is **b** as the day, Ps 139:12
beautiful as the moon, **b** as the sun, Sg 6:10
And the fire was **b**, and out of the fire Ezk 1:13

All the **b** lights of heaven will I make Ezk 32:8
behold, a **b** cloud overshadowed them, Mt 17:5
no part dark, it will be wholly **b**, Lk 11:36
a man stood before me in **b** clothing Acts 10:30
And out came another horse, **b** red. Its Rv 6:4
seven plagues, clothed in pure, **b** linen, Rv 15:6
and the earth was made **b** with his glory. Rv 18:1
b and pure"—for the fine linen is the Rv 19:8
the river of the water of life, **b** as crystal, Rv 22:1
of David, the **b** morning star." Rv 22:16

BRIGHTEN (1)
that our God may **b** our eyes and grant Ezr 9:8

BRIGHTER (4)
your life will be **b** than the noonday; Jb 11:17
which shines **b** and brighter until full Prv 4:18
shines brighter and **b** until full day. Prv 4:18
a light from heaven, **b** than the sun, Acts 26:13

BRIGHTNESS (16)
Out of the **b** before him coals of fire 2 Sm 22:13
Out of the **b** before him hailstones and Ps 18:12
for light, and behold, darkness, and for **b**, Is 59:9
light, and kings to the **b** of your rising. Is 60:3
nor for **b** shall the moon give you light; Is 60:19
until her righteousness goes forth as **b**, Is 62:1
and a great cloud, with **b** around it, Ezk 1:4
of fire, and there was **b** around him. Ezk 1:27
was the appearance of the **b** all around. Ezk 1:28
was something like the appearance of **b**, Ezk 8:2
was filled with the **b** of the glory of Ezk 10:4
This image, mighty and of exceeding **b**, Dn 2:31
shall shine like the **b** of the sky above; Dn 12:3
not light, and gloom with no **b** in it? Am 5:20
His **b** was like the light; rays flashed Hab 3:4
not see because of the **b** of that light, Acts 22:11

BRIM (10)
round, ten cubits from **b** to brim, 1 Kgs 7:23
round, ten cubits from brim to **b**, 1 Kgs 7:23
Under its **b** were gourds, for ten 1 Kgs 7:24
and its **b** was made like the brim of a 1 Kgs 7:26
its brim was made like the **b** of a cup, 1 Kgs 7:26
was round, ten cubits from **b** to brim, 2 Chr 4:2
was round, ten cubits from brim to **b**, 2 Chr 4:2
And its **b** was made like the brim of a 2 Chr 4:5
its brim was made like the **b** of a cup, 2 Chr 4:5
water." And they filled them up to the **b**. Jn 2:7

BRIMSTONE (1)
whole land burned out with **b** and salt, Dt 29:23

BRING (684)
"Let the earth **b** forth living creatures Gn 1:24
in pain you shall **b** forth children. Gn 3:16
and thistles it shall **b** forth for you; Gn 3:18
cursed this one shall **b** us relief from Gn 5:29
I will **b** a flood of waters upon the earth Gn 6:17
you shall **b** two of every sort into the ark Gn 6:19
B out with you every living thing that is Gn 8:17
When I **b** clouds over the earth and the Gn 9:14
to him, "**B** me a heifer three years old, Gn 15:9
But I will **b** judgment on the nation Gn 15:14
while I **b** a morsel of bread, that you Gn 18:5
that the LORD may **b** to Abraham what Gn 18:19
B them out to us, that we may know Gn 19:5
Let me **b** them out to you, and do to Gn 19:8
in the city, **b** them out of the place. Gn 19:12
as I love, and **b** it to me so that I may eat, Gn 27:4
to the field to hunt for game and **b** it, Gn 27:5
'**B** me game and prepare for me Gn 27:7
to the flock and **b** me two good young Gn 27:9
And you shall **b** it to your father to eat, Gn 27:10
be mocking him and **b** a curse upon Gn 27:12
obey my voice, and go, **b** them to me." Gn 27:13
Then he said, "**B** it near to me, that I Gn 27:25
Then I will send and **b** you from there. Gn 27:45
go, and will **b** you back to this land. Gn 28:15
torn by wild beasts I did not **b** to you. Gn 31:39
and **b** me word." So he sent him from Gn 37:14
And Judah said, "**B** her out, Gn 38:24
God, and God will shortly **b** it about. Gn 41:32
one of you, and let him **b** your brother, Gn 42:16
and **b** your youngest brother to me. So Gn 42:20
B your youngest brother to me. Then I Gn 42:34
two sons if I do not **b** him back to you. Gn 42:37
hands, and I will **b** him back to you." Gn 42:37
you would **b** down my gray hairs with Gn 42:38
he would say, '**B** your brother down'?" Gn 43:7
If I do not **b** him back to you and set Gn 43:9
his house, "**B** the men into the house, Gn 43:16
to your servants, '**B** him down to me, Gn 44:21
you will **b** down my gray hairs in evil Gn 44:29
and your servants will **b** down the gray Gn 44:31
saying, 'If I do not **b** him back to you, Gn 44:32
Hurry and **b** my father down here." Gn 45:13
and for your wives, and **b** your father, Gn 45:19
to Egypt, and I will also **b** you up again, Gn 46:4
me here." And he said, "**B** them to me, Gn 48:9
be with you and will **b** you again to the Gn 48:21
to **b** it about that many people should Gn 50:20
God will visit you and **b** you up out of Gn 50:24
of the Egyptians and to **b** them up out of Ex 3:8
to Pharaoh that you may **b** my people, Ex 3:10
go to Pharaoh and **b** the children of Ex 3:11
I promise that I will **b** you up out of the Ex 3:17
and I will **b** you out from under the Ex 6:6
I will **b** you into the land that I swore to Ex 6:8
to **b** the people of Israel out of the land of Ex 6:13
"**B** out the people of Israel from the land Ex 6:26
lay my hand on Egypt and **b** my hosts, Ex 7:4
hand against Egypt and **b** out the people Ex 7:5
tomorrow I will **b** locusts into your Ex 10:4
plague more I will **b** upon Pharaoh and Ex 11:1
LORD, to **b** them out of the land of Egypt; Ex 12:42
You will **b** them in and plant them on Ex 15:17
day, when they prepare what they **b** in, Ex 16:5
said, "Why did you **b** us up out of Egypt, Ex 17:3
people before God and **b** their cases to Ex 18:19
Every great matter they shall **b** to you, Ex 18:22
then his master shall **b** him to God, and Ex 21:6
and he shall **b** him to the door or the Ex 21:6
torn by beasts, let him **b** it as evidence. Ex 22:13
going astray, you shall **b** it back to him. Ex 23:4
your ground you shall **b** into the house Ex 23:19
on the way and to **b** you to the place Ex 23:20
and **b** the ark of the testimony in there Ex 26:33
of Israel that they **b** to you pure beaten Ex 27:20
"Then **b** near to you Aaron your Ex 28:1
to **b** them to regular remembrance Ex 28:29
in one basket and **b** them in the basket, Ex 29:3
basket, and **b** the bull and the two rams. Ex 29:3
You shall **b** Aaron and his sons to the Ex 29:4
Then you shall **b** his sons and put coats Ex 29:8
"Then you shall **b** the bull before the Ex 29:10
that it may **b** the people of Israel to Ex 30:16
and your daughters, and **b** them to me." Ex 32:2
say, 'With evil intent did he **b** them out, Ex 32:12
"See, you say to me, '**B** up this people,' Ex 33:12
go with me, do not **b** us up from here. Ex 33:15
your ground you shall **b** to the house of Ex 34:26
heart, let him **b** the LORD'S contribution: Ex 35:5
heart moved them to **b** anything for the Ex 35:29
"The people **b** much more than enough Ex 36:5
And you shall **b** in the table and arrange Ex 40:4
and you shall **b** in the lampstand and set Ex 40:4
Then you shall **b** Aaron and his sons Ex 40:12
You shall **b** his sons also and put coats Ex 40:14
you shall **b** your offering of livestock Lv 1:2
He shall **b** it to the entrance of the tent of Lv 1:3
sons the priests shall **b** the blood and Lv 1:5
he shall **b** a male without blemish, Lv 1:10
then he shall **b** his offering of Lv 1:14
And the priest shall **b** it to the altar and Lv 1:15
and **b** it to Aaron's sons the priests. And Lv 2:2
"When you **b** a grain offering baked in Lv 2:4
And you shall **b** the grain offering that is Lv 2:8
to the priest, he shall **b** it to the altar. Lv 2:8
grain offering that you **b** to the LORD Lv 2:11
of firstfruits you may **b** them to the Lv 2:12
He shall **b** the bull to the entrance of the Lv 4:4
blood of the bull and **b** it into the tent of Lv 4:5
for a sin offering and **b** it in front of the Lv 4:14
the anointed priest shall **b** some of the Lv 4:16
to him, he shall **b** as his offering a goat, Lv 4:23
to him, he shall **b** for his offering a goat, Lv 4:28
he shall **b** a female without blemish Lv 4:32
he shall **b** to the LORD as his Lv 5:6
then he shall **b** to the LORD as his Lv 5:7
He shall **b** them to the priest, who shall Lv 5:8
then he shall **b** as his offering for the sin Lv 5:11
And he shall **b** it to the priest, and the Lv 5:12
he shall **b** to the LORD as his Lv 5:15
He shall **b** to the priest a ram without Lv 5:18
And he shall **b** to the priest as his Lv 6:6
You shall **b** it well mixed, in baked Lv 6:21
thanksgiving he shall **b** his offering Lv 7:13
to the LORD shall **b** his offering to the Lv 7:29
His own hands shall **b** the LORD'S food Lv 7:30
He shall **b** the fat with the breast, that Lv 7:30
people of Israel to **b** their offerings to the Lv 7:38
and **b** the offering of the people and make Lv 9:7
is waved they shall **b** with the food Lv 10:15
she shall **b** to the priest at the entrance of Lv 12:6
eighth day he shall **b** them for his Lv 14:23
or two pigeons and **b** them to the priest, Lv 15:29
small, and he shall **b** it inside the veil Lv 16:12
for the people and **b** its blood inside the Lv 16:15
and does not **b** it to the entrance of the Lv 17:4
of Israel may **b** their sacrifices that Lv 17:5
field, that they may **b** them to the LORD, Lv 17:5
and does not **b** it to the entrance of the Lv 17:9
but he shall **b** his compensation to the Lv 19:21
you shall **b** the sheaf of the firstfruits of Lv 23:10
You shall **b** from your dwelling places Lv 23:17
the people of Israel to **b** you pure oil from Lv 24:2
"**B** out of the camp the one who cursed, Lv 24:14
And I will **b** a sword upon you, that Lv 26:25
"**B** the tribe of Levi near, and set them Nm 3:6
of Israel, which they **b** to the priest, Nm 5:9
then the man shall **b** his wife to the Nm 5:15
to the priest and **b** the offering required Nm 5:15
"And the priest shall **b** her near and set Nm 5:16
before the LORD and **b** it to the altar. Nm 5:25
eighth day he shall **b** two turtledoves or Nm 6:10
of his separation and **b** a male lamb a Nm 6:12
and he shall **b** his gift to the LORD, one Nm 6:14
And the priest shall **b** them before the Nm 6:16
And you shall **b** the Levites before the Nm 8:9
When you **b** the Levites before the Nm 8:10
because he did not **b** the LORD'S offering Nm 9:13
and **b** them to the tent of meeting, Nm 11:16
of good courage and **b** some of the Nm 13:20
he will **b** us into this land and give it to Nm 14:8
was not able to **b** this people into the Nm 14:16
I will **b** into the land into which he Nm 14:24
said would become a prey, I will **b** in, Nm 14:31
come into the land to which I **b** you Nm 15:18
is holy, and will **b** him near to him. Nm 16:5
he chooses he will **b** near to him. Nm 16:5
of Israel, to **b** you near to himself, Nm 16:9
every one of you **b** before the LORD his Nm 16:17
And with you **b** your brothers also, the Nm 18:2
their land, which they **b** to the LORD, Nm 18:13
the people of Israel to **b** you a red heifer Nm 19:2
up out of Egypt to **b** us to this evil Nm 20:5
So you shall **b** water out of the rock for Nm 20:8
shall we **b** water for you out of this Nm 20:10
you shall not **b** this assembly into Nm 20:12
Eleazar his son and **b** them up to Nm 20:25
tonight, and I will **b** back word to you, Nm 22:8
shall lead them out and **b** them in, Nm 27:17
is too hard for you, you shall **b** to me, Dt 1:17
the land for us and **b** us word again of Dt 1:22
mightier than yourselves, to **b** you in, Dt 4:38
that he might **b** us in and give us the Dt 6:23
you shall not **b** an abominable thing Dt 7:26
was not able to **b** them into the land Dt 9:28
there you shall **b** your burnt offerings Dt 12:6
there you shall **b** all that I command Dt 12:11
three years you shall **b** out all the tithe Dt 14:28
then you shall **b** out to your gates that Dt 17:5
of that city shall **b** the heifer down to Dt 21:4
and you **b** her home to your house, she Dt 21:12
take hold of him and **b** him out to the Dt 21:19
he is, you shall **b** it home to your house, Dt 22:2
that you may not **b** the guilt of blood Dt 22:8
shall take and **b** out the evidence Dt 22:15
then they shall **b** out the young woman Dt 22:21
then you shall **b** them both out to the Dt 22:24
You shall not **b** the fee of a prostitute or Dt 23:18
And you shall not **b** sin upon the land Dt 24:4
make the loan shall **b** the pledge out to Dt 24:11
now I **b** the first of the fruit of the Dt 26:10
"The LORD will **b** you and your king Dt 28:36
The LORD will **b** a nation against you Dt 28:49
then the LORD will **b** on you and your Dt 28:59
And he will **b** upon you again all the Dt 28:60
of this law, the LORD will **b** upon you, Dt 28:61
And the LORD will **b** you back in ships Dt 28:68
LORD your God will **b** you into the land Dt 30:5
ascend to heaven for us and **b** it to us, Dt 30:12
will go over the sea for us and **b** it to us, Dt 30:13
for you shall **b** the people of Israel into Dt 31:23
of Judah, and **b** him in to his people. Dt 33:7
"**B** out the men who have come to you, Jos 2:3
and **b** them over with you and lay them Jos 4:3
for destruction and **b** trouble upon it. Jos 6:18
prostitute's house and **b** out from there Jos 6:22
said, "Why did you **b** trouble on us? Jos 7:25
of the cave and **b** those five kings out Jos 10:22
seven divisions and **b** the description Jos 18:6
so the LORD will **b** upon you all the evil Jos 23:15
'Did not the LORD **b** us up from Egypt?' Jgs 6:13
I come to you and **b** out my present and Jgs 6:18
the town said to Joash, "**B** out your son, Jgs 6:30
of Gilead went to **b** Jephthah from the Jgs 11:5
"If you **b** me home again to fight with Jgs 11:9
to speak kindly to her and **b** her back. Jgs 19:3
"**B** out the man who came into your Jgs 19:22
his concubine. Let me **b** them out now. Jgs 19:24
to **b** provisions for the people, Jgs 20:10
"**B** the garment you are wearing and Ru 3:15
as the child is weaned, I will **b** him, 1 Sm 1:22
Let us **b** the ark of the covenant of the 1 Sm 4:3
"But if we go, what can we **b** the man? 1 Sm 9:7
there is no present to **b** to the man of 1 Sm 9:7

to the cook, “**B** the portion I gave you, 1 Sm 9:23
and thus **b** disgrace on all Israel.” 1 Sm 11:2
B the men, that we may put them to 1 Sm 11:12
said, “**B** the burnt offering here to me, 1 Sm 13:9
“**B** the ark of God here.” For the ark 1 Sm 14:18
‘Let every man **b** his ox or his sheep 1 Sm 14:34
“**B** here to me Agag the king of the 1 Sm 15:32
who can play well and **b** him to me.” 1 Sm 16:17
well, and **b** some token from them.” 1 Sm 17:18
saying, “**B** him up to me in the bed, 1 Sm 19:15
for why should you **b** me to your 1 Sm 20:8
Therefore send and **b** him to me, 1 Sm 20:31
the priest, “**B** the ephod here.” 1 Sm 23:9
nor woman alive to **b** news to Gath, 1 Sm 27:11
by a spirit and **b** up for me whomever 1 Sm 28:8
trap for my life to **b** about my death?” 1 Sm 28:9
“Whom shall I **b** up for you?” He 1 Sm 28:11
you?” He said, “**B** up Samuel for me.” 1 Sm 28:11
“**B** me the ephod.” So Abiathar 1 Sm 30:7
shall be with you to **b** over all Israel to 2 Sm 3:12
see my face unless you first **b** Michal, 2 Sm 3:13
Now then **b** it about, for the LORD has 2 Sm 3:18
from Baale-judah to **b** up from there 2 Sm 6:2
for him and shall **b** in the produce, 2 Sm 9:10
I fast? Can I **b** him back again? 2 Sm 12:23
“**B** the food into the chamber, 2 Sm 13:10
says anything to you, **b** him to me, 2 Sm 14:10
the king does not **b** his banished one 2 Sm 14:13
b back the young man Absalom.” 2 Sm 14:21
the LORD will indeed **b** me back to 2 Sm 15:8
us quickly and **b** down ruin on 2 Sm 15:14
he will **b** me back and let me see 2 Sm 15:25
and I will **b** all the people back to you 2 Sm 17:3
then all Israel will **b** ropes to that 2 Sm 17:13
the LORD might **b** harm upon 2 Sm 17:14
you be the last to **b** the king back to 2 Sm 19:11
you be the last to **b** back the king?’ 2 Sm 19:12
the king and to **b** the king over the 2 Sm 19:15
crossed the ford to **b** over the king’s 2 Sm 19:18
are on the haughty to **b** them down. 2 Sm 22:28
own mule, and **b** him down to Gihon. 1 Kgs 1:33
are a worthy man and **b** good news.” 1 Kgs 1:42
and you shall **b** his gray head down 1 Kgs 2:9
The LORD will **b** back his bloody 1 Kgs 2:32
So the LORD will **b** back your harm 1 Kgs 2:44
“**B** me a sword.” So a sword was 1 Kgs 3:24
My servants shall **b** it down to the sea 1 Kgs 5:9
to **b** up the ark of the covenant of the 1 Kgs 8:1
people Israel and **b** them again to 1 Kgs 8:34
‘**B** him back with you into your 1 Kgs 13:18
I will **b** harm upon the house of 1 Kgs 14:10
said, “**B** me a little water in a vessel, 1 Kgs 17:10
And as she was going to **b** it, he 1 Kgs 17:11
“**B** me a morsel of bread in your 1 Kgs 17:11
me a little cake of it and **b** it to me, 1 Kgs 17:13
come to me to **b** my sin to 1 Kgs 17:18
“Go and **b** him.” Then Ben-hadad 1 Kgs 20:33
and let them **b** a charge against 1 Kgs 21:10
Behold, I will **b** disaster upon you. I 1 Kgs 21:21
I will not **b** the disaster in his days; 1 Kgs 21:29
son’s days I will **b** the disaster upon 1 Kgs 21:29
“**B** quickly Micaiah the son of 1 Kgs 22:9
He said, “**B** me a new bowl, and put 2 Kgs 2:20
But now **b** me a musician.” And 2 Kgs 3:15
“**B** me another vessel.” And he said to 2 Kgs 4:6
“Then **b** flour.” And he threw it into 2 Kgs 4:41
and I will **b** you to the man whom 2 Kgs 6:19
“**B** out the vestments for all the 2 Kgs 10:22
army, “**B** her out between the ranks, 2 Kgs 11:15
prompts him to **b** into the house 2 Kgs 12:4
there is no strength to **b** them forth. 2 Kgs 19:3
days of old what now I **b** to pass, 2 Kgs 19:25
And Isaiah said, “**B** a cake of figs. 2 Kgs 20:7
I will **b** disaster upon this place and 2 Kgs 22:16
that I will **b** upon this place.’” 2 Kgs 22:20
of the threshold to **b** out of the temple 2 Kgs 23:4
that it might not **b** me pain!” And 1 Chr 4:10
Then let us **b** again the ark of our 1 Chr 13:3
to **b** the ark of God from 1 Chr 13:5
to **b** up from there the ark of God, 1 Chr 13:6
“How can I **b** the ark of God home 1 Chr 13:12
Israel at Jerusalem to **b** up the ark of 1 Chr 15:3
so that you may **b** up the ark of the 1 Chr 15:12
consecrated themselves to **b** up the 1 Chr 15:14
of thousands went to **b** up the ark of 1 Chr 15:25
b an offering and come before him! 1 Chr 16:29
Beersheba to Dan, and **b** me a report, 1 Chr 21:2
need from Lebanon and **b** it to you in 2 Chr 2:16
to **b** up the ark of the covenant of the 2 Chr 5:2
people Israel and **b** them again to 2 Chr 6:25
“**B** quickly Micaiah the son of 2 Chr 18:8
the LORD will **b** a great plague on 2 Chr 21:14
them, “**B** her out between the ranks, 2 Chr 23:14
the Levites to **b** in from Judah 2 Chr 24:6
Judah and Jerusalem to **b** in for the 2 Chr 24:9
among them to **b** them back to 2 Chr 24:19
and it will **b** you no honor from the 2 Chr 26:18
“You shall not **b** the captives in 2 Chr 28:13
for you propose to **b** upon us guilt 2 Chr 28:13
for they did not **b** him into the 2 Chr 28:27
b sacrifices and thank offerings to 2 Chr 29:31
they began to **b** the contributions 2 Chr 31:10
I will **b** disaster upon this place and 2 Chr 34:24
disaster that I will **b** upon this place 2 Chr 34:28
All these did Sheshbazzar **b** up, when Ezr 1:11
and the Tyrians to **b** cedar trees from Ezr 3:7
and the vessels, to **b** them to Jerusalem, Ezr 8:30
them from there and **b** them to the place Neh 1:9
told Ezra the scribe to **b** the Book of the Neh 8:1
out to the hills and **b** branches of olive, Neh 8:15
peoples of the land **b** in goods or any Neh 10:31
to **b** it into the house of our God, Neh 10:34
obligate ourselves to **b** the firstfruits Neh 10:35
also to **b** to the house of our God, to Neh 10:36
and to **b** the first of our dough, and Neh 10:37
and to **b** to the Levites the tithes from Neh 10:37
And the Levites shall **b** up the tithe of Neh 10:38
of Levi shall **b** the contribution of Neh 10:39
the people cast lots to **b** one out of ten Neh 11:1
to **b** them to Jerusalem to celebrate Neh 12:27
did not our God **b** all this disaster on Neh 13:18
to **b** Queen Vashti before the king with Est 1:11
Then the king said, “**B** Haman quickly, Est 5:5
he gave orders to **b** the book of Est 6:1
arrived and hurried to **b** Haman to the Est 6:14
me; you **b** fresh troops against me. Jb 10:17
“Why did you **b** me out from the Jb 10:18
are secure, who **b** their god in their hand. Jb 12:6
such a one and **b** me into judgment with Jb 14:3
Who can **b** a clean thing out of an Jb 14:4
spirit against God and **b** such words out Jb 15:13
I know that you will **b** me to death and Jb 30:23
the pit, and his life to those who **b** death. Jb 33:22
to **b** back his soul from the pit, that he Jb 33:30
to **b** rain on a land where no man is, on Jb 38:26
they crouch, **b** forth their offspring, Jb 39:3
who is proud and **b** him low and tread Jb 40:12
him who made him **b** near his sword! Jb 40:19
but the haughty eyes you **b** down. Ps 18:27
are enlarged; **b** me out of my distresses. Ps 25:17
He will **b** forth your righteousness as the Ps 37:6
bend their bows to **b** down the poor and Ps 37:14
let them **b** me to your holy hill and to Ps 43:3
totter by your power and **b** them down, Ps 59:11
Who will **b** me to the fortified city? Who Ps 60:9
Blessed is the one you choose and **b** near, Ps 65:4
said, “I will **b** them back from Bashan, Ps 68:22
I will **b** them back from the depths of Ps 68:22
of the earth you will **b** me up again. Ps 71:20
the kings of Sheba and Seba **b** gifts! Ps 72:10
let all around him **b** gifts to him who is Ps 76:11
we **b** our years to an end like a sigh. Ps 90:9
He will **b** back on them their iniquity Ps 94:23
b an offering, and come into his courts! Ps 96:8
that he may **b** forth food from the Ps 104:14
Who will **b** me to the fortified city? Ps 108:10
B me out of prison, that I may give Ps 142:7
In your righteousness **b** my soul out Ps 143:11
may our sheep **b** forth thousands and Ps 144:13
like the clouds that **b** the spring rain. Prv 16:15
dish and will not even **b** it back to his Prv 19:24
do not hastily **b** into court, for what Prv 25:8
he who hears you **b** shame upon you, Prv 25:10
it wears him out to **b** it back to his Prv 26:15
for you do not know what a day may **b**. Prv 27:1
One’s pride will **b** him low, but he who Prv 29:23
Who can **b** him to see what will be Eccl 3:22
things God will **b** you into judgment. Eccl 11:9
For God will **b** every deed into Eccl 12:14
I would lead you and **b** you into the house Sg 8:2
each one was to **b** for its fruit a thousand Sg 8:11
B no more vain offerings; incense is an Is 1:13
b justice to the fatherless, plead the Is 1:17
They do not **b** justice to the fatherless, Is 1:23
The LORD will **b** upon you and upon your Is 7:17
like a bull I **b** down those who sit on Is 10:13
will take them and **b** them to their place, Is 14:2
for I will **b** upon Dibon even more, a lion Is 15:9
the sighing she has caused I **b** to an end. Is 21:2
To the thirsty **b** water; meet the fugitive Is 21:14
of his walls he will **b** down, Is 25:12
your name alone we **b** to remembrance. Is 26:13
and there is no strength to **b** them forth. Is 37:3
from days of old what now I **b** to pass, Is 37:26
from day to night you **b** me to an end; Is 38:12
from day to night you **b** me to an end. Is 38:13
b your proofs, says the King of Jacob. Is 41:21
Let them **b** them, and tell us what is to Is 41:22
him; he will **b** forth justice to the nations. Is 42:1
quench; he will faithfully **b** forth justice. Is 42:3
to **b** out the prisoners from the dungeon, Is 42:7
I will **b** your offspring from the east, and Is 43:5
b my sons from afar and my daughters Is 43:6
B out the people who are blind, yet have Is 43:8
Let them **b** their witnesses to prove them Is 43:9
send to Babylon and **b** them all down as Is 43:14
I have spoken, and I will **b** it to pass; I Is 46:11
I **b** near my righteousness; it is not far Is 46:13
to be his servant, to **b** Jacob back to him; Is 49:5
of Jacob and to **b** back the preserved of Is 49:6
and they shall **b** your sons in their Is 49:22
the earth, making it **b** forth and sprout, Is 55:10
these I will **b** to my holy mountain, and Is 56:7
with the hungry and **b** the homeless poor Is 58:7
They shall **b** gold and frankincense, and Is 60:6
and frankincense, and shall **b** good news, Is 60:6
first, to **b** your children from afar, Is 60:9
that people may **b** to you the wealth of Is 60:11
Instead of bronze I will **b** gold, and Is 60:17
gold, and instead of iron I will **b** silver; Is 60:17
has anointed me to **b** good news to the Is 61:1
I will **b** forth offspring from Jacob, and Is 65:9
treatment for them and **b** their fears upon Is 66:4
Shall I **b** to the point of birth and not Is 66:9
and not cause to **b** forth?” says the LORD; Is 66:9
“shall I, who cause to **b** forth, shut the Is 66:9
And they shall **b** all your brothers from Is 66:20
as the Israelites **b** their grain offering Is 66:20
I will **b** you to judgment for saying, Jer 2:35
from a family, and I will **b** you to Zion. Jer 3:14
stay not, for I **b** disaster from the north, Jer 4:6
this time, and I will **b** distress on them, Jer 10:18
in your anger, lest you **b** me to nothing. Jer 10:24
For I will **b** disaster upon the men of Jer 11:23
all the wild beasts; **b** them to devour. Jer 12:9
and I will **b** them again each to his Jer 12:15
gods of the nations that can **b** rain? Jer 14:22
For I will **b** them back to their own Jer 16:15
b upon them the day of disaster; Jer 17:18
on the Sabbath day or **b** it in by the Jer 17:21
and **b** in no burden by the gates of this Jer 17:24
when you **b** the plunderer suddenly Jer 18:22
And I will **b** them together into the midst Jer 21:4
and I will **b** them back to their fold, Jer 23:3
for I will **b** disaster upon them in the Jer 23:12
And I will **b** upon you everlasting Jer 23:40
and I will **b** them back to this land. Jer 24:6
and I will **b** them against this land and Jer 25:9
I will **b** upon that land all the words Jer 25:13
you will **b** innocent blood upon Jer 26:15
we are about to **b** great disaster upon Jer 26:19
any nation that will **b** its neck under Jer 27:11
“**B** your necks under the yoke of the Jer 27:12
Then I will **b** them back and restore Jer 27:22
two years I will **b** back to this place Jer 28:3
I will also **b** back to this place Jeconiah Jer 28:4
and **b** back to this place from Babylon Jer 28:6
you my promise and **b** you back to this Jer 29:10
and I will **b** you back to the place from Jer 29:14
and I will **b** them back to the land that I Jer 30:3
I will **b** them from the north country Jer 31:8
b me back that I may be restored, for Jer 31:18
to overthrow, destroy, and **b** harm, Jer 31:28
them by the hand to **b** them out of the Jer 31:32
I will **b** them back to this place, and I Jer 32:37
so I will **b** upon them all the good that I Jer 32:42
Behold, I will **b** to it health and healing, Jer 33:6
as they **b** thank offerings to the house Jer 33:11
LORD, and will **b** them back to this city. Jer 34:22
speak with them and **b** them to the Jer 35:2
I will **b** upon them and upon the Jer 36:31
the disaster that I will **b** upon them. Jer 42:17
And I will **b** to an end in Moab, Jer 48:35
For I will **b** these things upon Moab, Jer 48:44
Behold, I will **b** terror upon you, declares Jer 49:5
For I will **b** the calamity of Esau upon Jer 49:8
eagle’s, I will **b** you down from there, Jer 49:16
and I will **b** their calamity from every Jer 49:32
And I will **b** upon Elam the four winds Jer 49:36
I will **b** disaster upon them, my fierce Jer 49:37
her; **b** up horses like bristling locusts. Jer 51:27
I will **b** them down like lambs to the Jer 51:40
and when I **b** more and more famine Ezk 5:16
you, and I will **b** the sword upon you. Ezk 5:17
I, even I, will **b** a sword upon you, Ezk 6:3
I will **b** the worst of the nations to take Ezk 7:24
“**B** near the executioners of the city, Ezk 9:1
I will **b** their deeds upon their heads.” Ezk 9:10
sword, and I will **b** the sword upon you, Ezk 11:8
And I will **b** you out of the midst of it, Ezk 11:9
I will **b** their deeds upon their own Ezk 11:21
You shall **b** out your baggage by day Ezk 12:4
and **b** your baggage out through it. Ezk 12:5
the wall to **b** him out through Ezk 12:12
snare. And I will **b** him to Babylon, Ezk 12:13

and **b** it down to the ground, Ezk 13:14
"Or if I **b** a sword upon that land and Ezk 14:17
and **b** upon you the blood of wrath Ezk 16:38
They shall **b** up a crowd against you, Ezk 16:40
and I will **b** him to Babylon and enter Ezk 17:20
I **b** low the high tree, and make high Ezk 17:24
to them that I would **b** them out of the Ezk 20:6
that I would not **b** them into the land Ezk 20:15
I will **b** you out from the peoples and Ezk 20:34
And I will **b** you into the wilderness of Ezk 20:35
and I will **b** you into the bond of the Ezk 20:37
I will **b** them out of the land where Ezk 20:38
when I **b** you out from the peoples and Ezk 20:41
when I **b** you into the land of Israel, Ezk 20:42
is low, and **b** low that which is exalted. Ezk 21:26
and I will **b** them against you from Ezk 23:22
"**B** up a vast host against them, and Ezk 23:46
and will **b** up many nations against Ezk 26:3
I will **b** against Tyre from the north Ezk 26:7
when I **b** up the deep over you, Ezk 26:19
I will **b** you to a dreadful end, and you Ezk 26:21
behold, I will **b** foreigners upon you, Ezk 28:7
Behold, I will **b** a sword upon you, and Ezk 29:8
fortunes of Egypt and **b** them back to Ezk 29:14
I will **b** desolation upon the land and Ezk 30:12
when I **b** your destruction among the Ezk 32:9
"They shall **b** to ruin the pride of Ezk 32:12
to them, If I **b** the sword upon a land, Ezk 33:2
And I will **b** them out from the peoples Ezk 34:13
and will **b** them into their own land. Ezk 34:13
the lost, and I will **b** back the strayed, Ezk 34:16
all the countries and **b** you into your Ezk 36:24
And I will **b** you into the land of Israel. Ezk 37:12
around, and **b** them to their own land. Ezk 37:21
into your jaws, and I will **b** you out, Ezk 38:4
latter days I will **b** you against my Ezk 38:16
that I would **b** you against them? Ezk 38:17
and **b** you up from the uttermost parts Ezk 39:2
and it will **b** them renown on the day Ezk 39:13
in order not to **b** them out into the Ezk 46:20
eunuch, to **b** some of the people of Israel, Dn 1:3
b me in before the king, and I will show Dn 2:24
all these kingdoms and **b** them to an Dn 2:44
king called loudly to **b** in the enchanters, Dn 5:7
to **b** in everlasting righteousness, Dn 9:24
and he shall **b** terms of an agreement Dn 11:17
her, and **b** her into the wilderness, Hos 2:14
I will **b** them down like birds of the Hos 7:12
Even if they **b** up children, I will Hos 9:12
all the nations and **b** them down to the Jl 3:2
there. **B** down your warriors, O LORD. Jl 3:11
the land and **b** down your defenses Am 3:11
your husbands, '**B**, that we may drink!' Am 4:1
b your sacrifices every morning, your Am 4:4
"Did you **b** to me sacrifices and Am 5:25
the day of disaster and **b** near the seat of Am 6:3
shall take him up to **b** the bones out of Am 6:10
on the needy and **b** the poor of the Am 8:4
I will **b** sackcloth on every waist and Am 8:10
heaven, from there I will **b** them down. Am 9:2
"Did I not **b** up Israel from the land of Am 9:7
"Who will **b** me down to the ground?" Ob 1:3
the stars, from there I will **b** you down, Ob 1:4
I will again **b** a conqueror to you, Mi 1:15
He will **b** me out to the light; I shall look Mi 7:9
I will **b** distress on mankind, so that Zep 1:17
my dispersed ones, shall **b** my offering. Zep 3:10
At that time I will **b** you in, at the time Zep 3:20
up to the hills and **b** wood and build the Hg 1:8
behold, I will **b** my servant the Branch. Zec 3:8
And he shall **b** forward the top stone Zec 4:7
and I will **b** them to dwell in the midst of Zec 8:8
"As I purposed to **b** disaster to you when Zec 8:14
in these days to **b** good to Jerusalem and Zec 8:15
I will **b** them back because I have Zec 10:6
I will **b** them home from the land of Zec 10:10
and I will **b** them to the land of Gilead Zec 10:10
You **b** what has been taken by Mal 1:13
sick, and this you **b** as your offering! Mal 1:13
and they will **b** offerings in Mal 3:3
B the full tithes into the storehouse, Mal 3:10
when you have found him, **b** me word, Mt 2:8
that I have come to **b** peace to the earth. Mt 10:34
I have not come to **b** peace, but a Mt 10:34
And he said, "**B** them here to me." Mt 14:18
side, they had forgotten to **b** any bread. Mt 16:5
I to bear with you? **B** him here to me." Mt 17:17
with her. Untie them and **b** them to me. Mt 21:2
with orders to **b** John's head. Mk 6:27
region and began to **b** the sick people Mk 6:55
Now they had forgotten to **b** bread, and Mk 8:14
am I to bear with you? **B** him to me." Mk 9:19
no one has ever sat. Untie it and **b** it. Mk 11:2
B me a denarius and let me look at it." Mk 12:15
And when they **b** you to trial and Mk 13:11
how many charges they **b** against you." Mk 15:4
to you and to **b** you this good news. Lk 1:19
I **b** you good news of a great joy that will Lk 2:10
they were seeking to **b** him in and lay Lk 5:18
but finding no way to **b** him in, because Lk 5:19
and bear with you? **B** your son here." Lk 9:41
And when they **b** you before the Lk 12:11
and **b** in the poor and crippled and Lk 14:21
his servants, '**B** quickly the best robe, Lk 15:22
And **b** the fattened calf and kill it, and Lk 15:23
b them here and slaughter them before Lk 19:27
has ever yet sat. Untie it and **b** it here. Lk 19:30
said to them, "Why did you not **b** him?" Jn 7:45
might have some charge to **b** against him. Jn 8:6
are not of this fold. I must **b** them also, Jn 10:16
all things and **b** to your remembrance Jn 14:26
accusation do you **b** against this man?" Jn 18:29
"**B** some of the fish that you have just Jn 21:10
and you intend to **b** this man's blood Acts 5:28
"'Did you **b** to me slain beasts and Acts 7:42
he might **b** them bound to Jerusalem. Acts 9:2
to **b** them bound before the chief Acts 9:21
men to Joppa and **b** one Simon who is Acts 10:5
'Send to Joppa and **b** Simon who is Acts 11:13
after the Passover to **b** him out to the Acts 12:4
when Herod was about to **b** him out, Acts 12:6
And we **b** you the good news that Acts 13:32
that you may **b** salvation to the ends Acts 13:47
with you, and we **b** you good news, Acts 14:15
seeking to **b** them out to the crowd. Acts 17:5
For you **b** some strange things to our Acts 17:20
Let them **b** charges against one Acts 19:38
who were there and **b** them in bonds to Acts 22:5
them by force and **b** him into the Acts 23:10
to the tribune to **b** him down to you, Acts 23:15
and asked me to **b** this young man to Acts 23:18
to ask you to **b** Paul down to the Acts 23:20
Paul to ride and **b** him safely to Felix Acts 23:24
you what they now **b** up against me. Acts 24:13
years I came to **b** alms to my nation Acts 24:17
man, let them **b** charges against him." Acts 25:5
no charge to **b** against my nation. Acts 28:19
and apostleship to **b** about the Rom 1:5
which is good, then, **b** death to me? Rom 7:13
Who shall **b** any charge against God's Rom 8:33
heaven?'" (that is, to **b** Christ down) Rom 10:6
(that is, to **b** Christ up from the dead). Rom 10:7
through me to **b** the Gentiles to Rom 15:18
to **b** about the obedience of faith— Rom 16:26
not, to **b** to nothing things that are, 1 Cor 1:28
who will **b** to light the things now 1 Cor 4:5
you unless I **b** you some revelation 1 Cor 14:6
also with Jesus and **b** us with you 2 Cor 4:14
so that they might **b** us into slavery— Gal 2:4
and to **b** to light for everyone what is the Eph 3:9
but **b** them up in the discipline and Eph 6:4
work in you will **b** it to completion at Phil 1:6
God will **b** with him those who have 1 Thes 4:14
of his mouth and **b** to nothing by the 2 Thes 2:8
me. Get Mark and **b** him with you, 2 Tm 4:11
b the cloak that I left with Carpus at 2 Tm 4:13
every evil deed and **b** me safely into 2 Tm 4:18
them by the hand to **b** them out of the Heb 8:9
you do not know what tomorrow will **b**. Jas 4:14
that he might **b** us to God, 1 Pt 3:18
who will secretly **b** in destructive 2 Pt 2:1
to you and does not **b** this teaching, 2 Jn 1:10
if I come, I will **b** up what he is doing, 3 Jn 1:10
of the earth will **b** their glory into it, Rv 21:24
They will **b** into it the glory and the Rv 21:26

BRINGING (72)
king of Egypt about **b** out the people of Ex 6:27
you done to us in **b** us out of Egypt? Ex 14:11
down, and come up **b** Aaron with you. Ex 19:24
that he had spoken of **b** on his people. Ex 32:14
They still kept **b** him freewill offerings Ex 36:3
So the people were restrained from **b**, Ex 36:6
priest who sins, thus **b** guilt on the people, Lv 4:3
land of Canaan, to which I am **b** you. Lv 18:3
the land where I am **b** you to live may Lv 20:22
b iniquity to remembrance. Nm 5:15
are we kept from **b** the LORD'S offering at Nm 9:7
Why is the LORD **b** us into this land, to Nm 14:3
grumble against him by **b** up a bad Nm 14:36
the LORD your God is **b** you into a good Dt 8:7
will take delight in **b** ruin upon you Dt 28:63
b upon it all the curses written in this Dt 29:27
you disturbed me by **b** me up?" Saul 1 Sm 28:15
from a raid, **b** much spoil with them. 2 Sm 3:22
and thought he was **b** good news, 2 Sm 4:10
say nothing about **b** the king 2 Sm 19:10
first to speak of **b** back our king?" 2 Sm 19:43
the guilty by **b** his conduct on 1 Kgs 8:32
of Tarshish used to come **b** gold, 1 Kgs 10:22
b the man of God bread of the 2 Kgs 4:42
men of the city, who were **b** them up. 2 Kgs 10:6
I am **b** upon Jerusalem and Judah 2 Kgs 21:12
came **b** food on donkeys and on 1 Chr 12:40
the guilty by **b** his conduct on 2 Chr 6:23
of Tarshish used to come **b** gold, 2 Chr 9:21
While they were **b** out the money 2 Chr 34:14
and **b** in heaps of grain and loading Neh 13:15
Now you are **b** more wrath on Israel Neh 13:18
He was **b** up Hadassah, that is Esther, the Est 2:7
of your name, **b** it down to the ground. Ps 74:7
shouts of joy, **b** his sheaves with him. Ps 126:6
the Lord is **b** up against them the waters of Is 8:7
I am **b** against you a nation from afar, Jer 5:15
behold, I am **b** disaster upon this people, Jer 6:19
I am **b** disaster upon them that they Jer 11:11
b burnt offerings and sacrifices, Jer 17:26
and **b** thank offerings to the house of Jer 17:26
I am **b** such disaster upon this place that Jer 19:3
I am **b** upon this city and upon all its Jer 19:15
I am **b** upon Judah and all the Jer 35:17
b grain offerings and incense to present Jer 41:5
for behold, I am **b** disaster upon all flesh, Jer 45:5
I am **b** punishment upon Amon of Jer 46:25
am stirring up and **b** against Babylon a Jer 50:9
I am **b** punishment on the king of Jer 50:18
of the disaster that I am **b** upon her, Jer 51:64
known to them in **b** them out of the Ezk 20:9
ruled us, by **b** upon us a great calamity. Dn 9:12
came to him, **b** with them the lame, Mt 15:30
came forward, **b** five talents more, Mt 25:20
b to him a paralytic carried by four Mk 2:3
And they were **b** children to him that Mk 10:13
some men were **b** on a bed a man who Lk 5:18
proclaiming and **b** the good news of the Lk 8:1
Now they were **b** even infants to him Lk 18:15
b him into the high priest's house, Lk 22:54
I am **b** him out to you that you may Jn 19:4
came **b** a mixture of myrrh and aloes, Jn 19:39
b the sick and those afflicted with Acts 5:16
their service, **b** with them John, Acts 12:25
b us to the house of Mnason of Acts 21:16
b many and serious charges against Acts 25:7
am going to Jerusalem **b** aid to the Rom 15:25
b holiness to completion in the fear of 2 Cor 7:1
has appeared, **b** salvation for all people, Ti 2:11
things exist, in **b** many sons to glory, Heb 2:10
b upon themselves swift destruction. 2 Pt 2:1
soon, **b** my recompense with me, Rv 22:12

BRINGS (82)
And when the LORD **b** you into the land Ex 13:5
"When the LORD **b** you into the land of Ex 13:11
goes before you and **b** you to the Ex 23:23
When any one of you **b** an offering to the Lv 1:2
"When anyone **b** a grain offering as an Lv 2:1
"If he **b** a lamb as his offering for a sin Lv 4:32
the water of bitterness that **b** the curse. Nm 5:18
this water of bitterness that **b** the curse. Nm 5:19
May this water that **b** the curse pass Nm 5:22
the water of bitterness that **b** the curse, Nm 5:24
and the water that **b** the curse shall Nm 5:24
the water that **b** the curse shall enter Nm 5:27
then he who **b** his offering shall offer to Nm 15:4
God **b** them out of Egypt and is for Nm 23:22
God **b** him out of Egypt and is for him Nm 24:8
the LORD your God **b** you into the land Dt 6:10
the LORD your God **b** you into the land Dt 7:1
the LORD your God **b** you into the land Dt 11:29
her of misconduct and **b** a bad name Dt 22:14
The LORD **b** trouble on you today." And Jos 7:25
The LORD **b** kills and **b** to life; he brings 1 Sm 2:6
life; he **b** down to Sheol and raises up. 1 Sm 2:6
and makes rich; he **b** low and he exalts. 1 Sm 2:7
The king said, "He also **b** news." 2 Sm 18:26
Great salvation he **b** to his king, and 2 Sm 22:51
When disaster **b** sudden death, he mocks Jb 9:23
out of darkness and **b** deep darkness to Jb 12:22
for wrath **b** the punishment of the Jb 19:29
thing that is hidden he **b** out to light. Jb 28:11
Great salvation he **b** to his king, and Ps 18:50
The LORD **b** the counsel of the nations Ps 33:10
for the rain and **b** forth the wind from Ps 135:7
but the way of the wicked he **b** to ruin. Ps 146:9
sleeps in harvest is a son who **b** shame. Prv 10:5
but the mouth of a fool **b** ruin near. Prv 10:14
The hope of the righteous **b** joy, but Prv 10:28
of the righteous **b** forth wisdom, Prv 10:31
Whoever **b** blessing will be enriched, Prv 11:25
but she who **b** shame is like rottenness Prv 12:4
but the tongue of the wise **b** healing. Prv 12:18
but the wicked **b** shame and disgrace. Prv 13:5
despises the word **b** destruction on Prv 13:13
but a faithful envoy **b** healing. Prv 13:17
wealth, but the folly of fools **b** folly. Prv 14:24
he who purses his lips **b** evil to pass. Prv 16:30
room for him and **b** him before the Prv 18:16

When a man's folly **b** his way to ruin, Prv 19:3
Wealth **b** many new friends, but a poor Prv 19:4
is a son who **b** shame and reproach. Prv 19:26
the mighty and **b** down the stronghold Prv 21:22
much more when he **b** it with evil Prv 21:27
The north wind **b** forth rain, and a Prv 25:23
child left to himself **b** shame to his Prv 29:15
merchant; she **b** her food from afar. Prv 31:14
profit them, that **b** neither help nor profit, Is 30:5
And yet he is wise and **b** disaster; he does Is 31:2
who **b** princes to nothing, and makes Is 40:23
He who **b** out their host by number, Is 40:26
who **b** forth chariot and horse, army Is 43:17
are the feet of him who **b** good news, Is 52:7
peace, who **b** good news of happiness, Is 52:7
For as the earth **b** forth its sprouts, and Is 61:11
and he **b** forth the wind from his Jer 10:13
LORD your God before he **b** darkness, Jer 13:16
and he **b** forth the wind from his Jer 51:16
but he **b** their guilt to remembrance, Ezk 21:23
against you, as the sea **b** up its waves. Ezk 26:3
the feet of him who **b** good news, Na 1:15
He **b** all of them up with a hook; he Hab 1:15
the oil, on what the ground **b** forth, Hg 1:11
who **b** an offering to the LORD of hosts! Mal 2:12
quench, until he **b** justice to victory; Mt 12:20
out of his good treasure **b** forth good, Mt 12:35
out of his evil treasure **b** forth evil. Mt 12:35
Then it goes and **b** with it seven other Mt 12:45
who **b** out of his treasure what is new Mt 13:52
Then it goes and **b** seven other spirits Lk 11:26
For the law **b** wrath, but where there is Rom 4:15
when he **b** the firstborn into the world, Heb 1:6
sin when it is fully grown **b** forth death. Jas 1:15
the truth and someone **b** him back, Jas 5:19
him know that whoever **b** back a sinner Jas 5:20

BRINK (4)
'When you come to the **b** of the waters of Jos 3:8
were dipped in the **b** of the water (now Jos 3:15
I am at the **b** of utter ruin in the Prv 5:14
places by the Nile, on the **b** of the Nile, Is 19:7

BRISTLE (1)
their kings shall **b** with horror Ezk 32:10

BRISTLES (1)
the hair of their kings **b** with horror; Ezk 27:35

BRISTLING (1)
her; bring up horses like **b** locusts. Jer 51:27

BRITTLE (1)
shall be partly strong and partly **b**. Dn 2:42

BROAD (37)
up out of that land to a good and **b** land, Ex 3:8
wood, five cubits long and five cubits **b**. Ex 27:1
He brought me out into a **b** place; he 2 Sm 22:20
The lowest story was five cubits **b**, the 1 Kgs 6:6
broad, the middle one was six cubits **b**, 1 Kgs 6:6
and the third was seven cubits **b**. 1 Kgs 6:6
pasture, and the land was very **b**, 1 Chr 4:40
restored Jerusalem as far as the **B** Wall. Neh 3:8
the Tower of the Ovens, to the **B** Wall, Neh 12:38
of distress into a **b** place where there Jb 36:16
is given, and the **b** waters are frozen fast. Jb 37:10
He brought me out into a **b** place; he Ps 18:19
enemy; you have set my feet in a **b** place. Ps 31:8
your commandment is exceedingly **b**. Ps 119:96
be for us a place of **b** rivers and streams, Is 33:21
The **b** wall of Babylon shall be leveled Jer 51:58
rooms, one reed long and one reed **b**; Ezk 40:7
cubits long and five cubits **b**. Ezk 40:30
a half long, and a cubit and a half **b**, Ezk 40:42
cubits long and a hundred cubits **b**, Ezk 40:47
Thus the temple had a **b** area upward, Ezk 41:7
on the west side was seventy cubits **b**, Ezk 41:12
two cubits long, and two cubits **b**. Ezk 41:22
it, 500 cubits long and 500 cubits **b**, Ezk 42:20
be one cubit high and one cubit **b**, Ezk 43:13
square, twelve cubits long by twelve **b**. Ezk 43:16
fourteen cubits long by fourteen **b**, Ezk 43:17
with a rim around it half a cubit **b**, Ezk 43:17
25,000 cubits long and 20,000 cubits **b**. Ezk 45:1
25,000 cubits long and 10,000 **b**, Ezk 45:3
25,000 cubits long and 10,000 cubits **b**, Ezk 45:5
area 5,000 cubits **b** and 25,000 cubits Ezk 45:6
courts, forty cubits long and thirty **b**; Ezk 46:22
feed them like a lamb in a **b** pasture? Hos 4:16
noon and darken the earth in **b** daylight. Am 8:9
make their phylacteries **b** and their Mt 23:5
marched up over the **b** plain of the earth Rv 20:9

BROADER (2)
longer than the earth and **b** than the sea. Jb 11:9
And it became **b** as it wound upward to Ezk 41:7

BROILED (1)
They gave him a piece of **b** fish, Lk 24:42

BROKE (88)
plant of the field and **b** every tree of the Ex 9:25
out of his hands and **b** them at the foot Ex 32:19
were on the first tablets, which you **b**. Ex 34:1
my two hands and **b** them before your Dt 9:17
that were on the first tablets that you **b**, Dt 10:2
because you **b** faith with me in the Dt 32:51
But the people of Israel **b** faith in regard to Jos 7:1
him," because he **b** down his altar. Jgs 6:32
blew the trumpets and **b** the jars. Jgs 7:20
And he **b** down the tower of Penuel and Jgs 8:17
and old, so that tumors **b** out on them. 1 Sm 5:9
and the day **b** upon them at Hebron. 2 Sm 2:32
three mighty men **b** through the 2 Sm 23:16
the mountains and **b** in pieces the 1 Kgs 19:11
and his images they **b** in pieces, 2 Kgs 11:18
to Jerusalem and **b** down the wall 2 Kgs 14:13
the high places and **b** the pillars and 2 Kgs 18:4
And he **b** in pieces the bronze serpent 2 Kgs 18:4
And he **b** down the houses of the 2 Kgs 23:7
And he **b** down the high places of the 2 Kgs 23:8
he pulled down and **b** in pieces and 2 Kgs 23:12
And he **b** in pieces the pillars and 2 Kgs 23:14
b down the walls around Jerusalem. 2 Kgs 25:10
the Chaldeans **b** in pieces and 2 Kgs 25:13
who **b** faith in the matter of the 1 Chr 2:7
But they **b** faith with the God of their 1 Chr 5:25
He **b** faith with the LORD in that he 1 Chr 10:13
three mighty men **b** through the 1 Chr 11:18
the LORD our God **b** out against us, 1 Chr 15:13
high places and **b** down the pillars 2 Chr 14:3
and his images they **b** in pieces, 2 Chr 23:17
to Jerusalem and **b** down the wall 2 Chr 25:23
the Philistines and **b** through the 2 Chr 26:6
leprosy **b** out on his forehead in the 2 Chr 26:19
cities of Judah and **b** in pieces the 2 Chr 31:1
the Asherim and **b** down the high 2 Chr 31:1
And he **b** in pieces the Asherim and 2 Chr 34:4
he **b** down the altars and beat the 2 Chr 34:7
house of God and **b** down the wall of 2 Chr 36:19
I was at ease, and he **b** me apart; he Jb 16:12
I **b** the fangs of the unrighteous and Jb 29:17
and coals of fire **b** through his clouds. Ps 18:12
carved wood they **b** down with hatchets Ps 74:6
you **b** the heads of the sea monsters on Ps 74:13
There he **b** the flashing arrows, the Ps 76:3
on the land and **b** all supply of bread, Ps 105:16
Fire also **b** out in their company; the Ps 106:18
and a plague **b** out among them. Ps 106:29
by his knowledge the deeps **b** open, and Prv 3:20
and you **b** down the houses to fortify the Is 22:10
"For long ago I **b** your yoke and burst Jer 2:20
of Jeremiah the prophet and **b** them. Jer 28:10
land of Egypt, my covenant that they **b**, Jer 31:32
and **b** down the walls of Jerusalem. Jer 39:8
b down all the walls around Jerusalem. Jer 52:14
of the LORD, the Chaldeans **b** in pieces, Jer 52:17
He **b** off the topmost of its young twigs Ezk 17:4
and whose covenant with him he **b**, Ezk 17:16
despised, and my covenant that he **b**. Ezk 17:19
you **b** and tore all their shoulders; Ezk 29:7
you **b** and made all their loins to shake. Ezk 29:7
of iron and clay, and **b** them in pieces. Dn 2:34
hand, and that it **b** in pieces the iron, Dn 2:45
overpowered them and **b** all their bones Dn 6:24
it devoured and **b** in pieces and stamped Dn 7:7
and which devoured and **b** in pieces and Dn 7:19
and struck the ram and **b** his two horns. Dn 8:7
And I took my staff Favor, and I **b** it, Zec 11:10
Then I **b** my second staff Union, Zec 11:14
Then he **b** the loaves and gave them to Mt 14:19
given thanks he **b** them and gave Mt 15:36
and after blessing it **b** it and gave it to Mt 26:26
apart, and he **b** the shackles in pieces. Mk 5:4
said a blessing and **b** the loaves and Mk 6:41
he **b** them and gave them to his disciples Mk 8:6
When I **b** the five loaves for the five Mk 8:19
and she **b** the flask and poured it over Mk 14:3
and after blessing it **b** it and gave it to Mk 14:22
three times." And he **b** down and wept. Mk 14:72
the stream **b** against that house and Lk 6:48
When the stream **b** against it, Lk 6:49
Then he **b** the loaves and gave them to Lk 9:16
thanks, he **b** it and gave it to them, Lk 22:19
bread and blessed and **b** it and gave it Lk 24:30
the soldiers came and **b** the legs of the Jn 19:32
the meeting of the synagogue **b** up, Acts 13:43
presence of all he **b** it and began to Acts 27:35
when he had given thanks, he **b** it, 1 Cor 11:24

BROKEN (143)
his people; he has **b** my covenant." Gn 17:14
go, for the day has **b**." But Jacob said, Gn 32:26
because of their **b** spirit and harsh Ex 6:9
people, since he has **b** faith with her. Ex 21:8
that the people had **b** loose (for Aaron Ex 32:25
vessel in which it is boiled shall be **b**. Lv 6:28
oven or stove, it shall be **b** in pieces. Lv 11:35
leprous disease that has **b** out in the Lv 13:20
It has **b** out in the burn, and the priest Lv 13:25
is leukoderma that has **b** out in the Lv 13:39
with the discharge touches shall be **b**, Lv 15:12
And I have **b** the bars of your yoke and Lv 26:13
defiled herself and has **b** faith with her Nm 5:27
LORD and has **b** his commandment, Nm 15:31
heifer whose neck was **b** in the valley, Dt 21:6
behold, the altar of Baal was **b** down, Jgs 6:28
for he has **b** down the altar of Baal and Jgs 6:30
because his altar has been **b** down." Jgs 6:31
The bows of the mighty are **b**, but the 1 Sm 2:4
of the LORD shall be **b** to pieces; 1 Sm 2:10
gate, and his neck was **b** and he died, 1 Sm 4:18
And I will have them **b** up there, and 1 Kgs 5:9
now in Egypt, that **b** reed of a staff, 2 Kgs 18:21
the LORD had **b** out against Uzzah. 1 Chr 13:11
"God has **b** through my enemies by 1 Chr 14:11
for they were **b** before the LORD and 2 Chr 14:13
They were **b** in pieces. Nation was 2 Chr 15:6
woman, had **b** into the house of God, 2 Chr 24:7
the wall that was **b** down and raised 2 Chr 32:5
that his father Hezekiah had **b** down, 2 Chr 33:3
"We have **b** faith with our God and Ezr 10:2
"You have **b** faith and married foreign Ezr 10:10
The wall of Jerusalem is **b** down, and its Neh 1:3
of Jerusalem that were **b** down and its Neh 2:13
he took a piece of **b** pottery with which to Jb 2:8
lion, the teeth of the young lions are **b**. Jb 4:10
My spirit is **b**; my days are extinct; the Jb 17:1
my plans are **b** off, the desires of my Jb 17:11
so wickedness is **b** like a tree.' Jb 24:20
and let my arm be **b** from its socket. Jb 31:22
is withheld, and their uplifted arm is **b**. Jb 38:15
is dead; I have become like a **b** vessel. Ps 31:12
all his bones; not one of them is **b**. Ps 34:20
own heart, and their bows shall be **b**. Ps 37:15
For the arms of the wicked shall be **b**, Ps 37:17
yet you have **b** us in the place of jackals Ps 44:19
let the bones that you have **b** rejoice. Ps 51:8
The sacrifices of God are a **b** spirit; a Ps 51:17
a **b** and contrite heart, O God, you will Ps 51:17
God, you have rejected us, **b** our defenses; Ps 60:1
Reproaches have **b** my heart, so that I Ps 69:20
Why then have you **b** down its walls, so Ps 80:12
He has **b** my strength in midcourse; Ps 102:23
LORD to act, for your law has been **b**. Ps 119:126
the snare is **b**, and we have escaped! Ps 124:7
a moment he will be **b** beyond healing. Prv 6:15
nettles, and its stone wall was **b** down. Prv 24:31
is like a city **b** into and left without Prv 25:28
will suddenly be **b** beyond healing. Prv 29:1
—a threefold cord is not quickly **b**. Eccl 4:12
is snapped, or the golden bowl is **b**, Eccl 12:6
fountain, or the wheel **b** at the cistern, Eccl 12:6
rebels and sinners shall be **b** together, Is 1:28
a waistband is loose, not a sandal strap **b**; Is 5:27
years Ephraim will be **b** to pieces so that Is 7:8
Be **b**, you peoples, and be shattered; give Is 8:9
They shall fall and be **b**; they shall be Is 8:15
you have **b** as on the day of Midian. Is 9:4
the yoke will be **b** because of the fat." Is 10:27
The LORD has **b** the staff of the wicked, the Is 14:5
of you, that the rod that struck you is **b**, Is 14:29
the statutes, **b** the everlasting covenant. Is 24:5
The wasted city is **b** down; every house Is 24:10
The earth is utterly **b**, the earth is split Is 24:19
When its boughs are dry, they are **b**; Is 27:11
may go, and fall backward, and be **b**, Is 28:13
Covenants are **b**; cities are despised; there Is 33:8
up, nor will any of its cords be **b**. Is 33:20
are trusting in Egypt, that **b** reed of a staff, Is 36:6
b cisterns that can hold no water. Jer 2:13
God." But they all alike had **b** the yoke; Jer 5:5
is destroyed, and all my cords are **b**; Jer 10:20
of Judah have **b** my covenant that Jer 11:10
Is this man Coniah a despised, **b** pot, a Jer 22:28
the prophets: My heart is **b** within me; Jer 23:9
I have **b** the yoke of the king of Babylon. Jer 28:2
prophet Hananiah had **b** the yoke-bars Jer 28:12
says the LORD: You have **b** wooden bars, Jer 28:13
with David my servant may be **b**, Jer 33:21
the fortress is put to shame and **b** down; Jer 48:1
say, 'How the mighty scepter is **b**, the Jer 48:17
Moab is put to shame, for it is **b**; wail Jer 48:20
of Moab is cut off, and his arm is **b**, Jer 48:25
for I have **b** Moab like a vessel for Jer 48:38
How it is **b**! How they wail! How Moab Jer 48:39
of the whole earth is cut down and **b**! Jer 50:23
Babylon has fallen and been **b**; Jer 51:8
her dwellings are on fire; her bars are **b**. Jer 51:30
their bows are **b** in pieces, for the LORD Jer 51:56
wrath he has **b** down the strongholds Lam 2:2

ground; he has ruined and **b** her bars; Lam 2:9
skin waste away; he has **b** my bones; Lam 3:4
and your incense altars shall be **b**, Ezk 6:4
and ruined, your idols **b** and destroyed, Ezk 6:6
how I have been **b** over their whoring Ezk 6:9
'Aha, the gate of the peoples is **b**; Ezk 26:2
fire to Egypt, and all her helpers are **b**. Ezk 30:8
I have **b** the arm of Pharaoh king of Ezk 30:21
the strong arm and the one that was **b**, Ezk 30:22
its boughs have been **b** in all the Ezk 31:12
you shall be **b** and lie among the Ezk 32:28
the blood. You have **b** my covenant, Ezk 44:7
the gold, all together were **b** in pieces, Dn 2:35
he was strong, the great horn was **b**, Dn 8:8
As for the horn that was **b**, in place of Dn 8:22
and he shall be **b**—but by no human Dn 8:25
kingdom shall be **b** and divided toward Dn 11:4
But within a few days he shall be **b**, Dn 11:20
utterly swept away before him and **b**, Dn 11:22
The calf of Samaria shall be **b** to pieces. Hos 8:6
and the rocks are **b** into pieces by him. Na 1:6
baskets full of the **b** pieces left over. Mt 14:20
baskets full of the **b** pieces left over. Mt 15:37
falls on this stone will be **b** to pieces; Mt 21:44
would not have let his house be **b** into. Mt 24:43
twelve baskets full of **b** pieces and of the Mk 6:43
And they took up the **b** pieces left over, Mk 8:8
many baskets full of **b** pieces did you Mk 8:19
many baskets full of **b** pieces did you Mk 8:20
picked up, twelve baskets of **b** pieces. Lk 9:17
not have left his house to be **b** into. Lk 12:39
falls on that stone will be **b** to pieces, Lk 20:18
so that the law of Moses may not be **b**, Jn 7:23
came—and Scripture cannot be **b**— Jn 10:35
their legs might be **b** and that they Jn 19:31
"Not one of his bones will be **b**." Jn 19:36
gone up and had **b** bread and eaten, Acts 20:11
the stern was being **b** up by the surf. Acts 27:41
if some of the branches were **b** off, Rom 11:17
"Branches were **b** off so that I might Rom 11:19
They were **b** off because of their Rom 11:20
both one and has **b** down in his flesh Eph 2:14
as when earthen pots are **b** in pieces, Rv 2:27

BROKENHEARTED (4)
is near to the **b** and saves the crushed Ps 34:18
pursued the poor and needy and the **b**, Ps 109:16
He heals the **b** and binds up their Ps 147:3
he has sent me to bind up the **b**, to Is 61:1

BROKENNESS (1)
the LORD binds up the **b** of his people, Is 30:26

BRONZE (153)
forger of all instruments of **b** and iron. Gn 4:22
receive from them: gold, silver, and **b**, Ex 25:3
"You shall make fifty clasps of **b**, and Ex 26:11
you shall cast five bases of **b** for them. Ex 26:37
with it, and you shall overlay it with **b**. Ex 27:2
You shall make all its utensils of **b**. Ex 27:3
make for it a grating, a network of **b**, Ex 27:4
you shall make four **b** rings at its four Ex 27:4
acacia wood, and overlay them with **b**. Ex 27:6
and their twenty bases shall be of **b**, Ex 27:10
twenty and their bases twenty, of **b**, Ex 27:11
shall be of silver, and their bases of **b**. Ex 27:17
of fine twined linen and bases of **b**. Ex 27:18
all the pegs of the court, shall be of **b**. Ex 27:19
"You shall also make a basin of **b**, with Ex 30:18
a basin of bronze, with its stand of **b**, Ex 30:18
designs, to work in gold, silver, and **b**, Ex 31:4
LORD'S contribution: gold, silver, and **b**; Ex 35:5
of burnt offering, with its grating of **b**, Ex 35:16
of silver or **b** brought it as Ex 35:24
to work in gold and silver and **b**, Ex 35:32
made fifty clasps of **b** to couple the tent Ex 36:18
of gold, but their five bases were of **b**. Ex 36:38
piece with it, and he overlaid it with **b**. Ex 38:2
fire pans. He made all its utensils of **b**. Ex 38:3
for the altar a grating, a network of **b**, Ex 38:4
four corners of the **b** grating as holders Ex 38:5
acacia wood and overlaid them with **b**. Ex 38:6
He made the basin of **b** and its stand of Ex 38:8
the basin of bronze and its stand of **b**, Ex 38:8
pillars and their twenty bases were of **b**, Ex 38:10
pillars, their twenty bases were of **b**, Ex 38:11
And the bases for the pillars were of **b**, Ex 38:17
Their four bases were of **b**, their hooks Ex 38:19
and for the court all around were of **b**. Ex 38:20
The **b** that was offered was seventy Ex 38:29
the **b** altar and the bronze grating for it Ex 38:30
bronze altar and the **b** grating for it Ex 38:30
the **b** altar, and its grating of bronze, its Ex 39:39
the bronze altar, and its grating of **b**, its Ex 39:39
But if it is boiled in a **b** vessel, that shall Lv 6:28
heavens like iron and your earth like **b**. Lv 26:19
Eleazar the priest took the **b** censers, Nm 16:39
So Moses made a **b** serpent and set it on Nm 21:9
he would look at the **b** serpent and live. Nm 21:9
only the gold, the silver, the **b**, the Nm 31:22
the heavens over your head shall be **b**, Dt 28:23
Your bars shall be iron and **b**, and as Dt 33:25
and gold, and every vessel of **b** and iron, Jos 6:19
gold, and the vessels of **b** and of iron, Jos 6:24
livestock, with silver, gold, **b**, and iron, Jos 22:8
Gaza and bound him with **b** shackles. Jgs 16:21
He had a helmet of **b** on his head, and 1 Sm 17:5
coat was five thousand shekels of **b**. 1 Sm 17:5
And he had **b** armor on his legs, and a 1 Sm 17:6
and a javelin of **b** slung between his 1 Sm 17:6
He put a helmet of **b** on his head and 1 Sm 17:38
King David took very much **b**. 2 Sm 8:8
him articles of silver, of gold, and of **b**. 2 Sm 8:10
weighed three hundred shekels of **b**, 2 Sm 21:16
that my arms can bend a bow of **b**. 2 Sm 22:35
great cities with walls and **b** bars); 1 Kgs 4:13
was a man of Tyre, a worker in **b**. 1 Kgs 7:14
and skill for making any work in **b**. 1 Kgs 7:14
He cast two pillars of **b**. Eighteen 1 Kgs 7:15
two capitals of cast **b** to set on the 1 Kgs 7:16
He also made the ten stands of **b**. 1 Kgs 7:27
stand had four **b** wheels and axles 1 Kgs 7:30
four bronze wheels and axles of **b**, 1 Kgs 7:30
And he made ten basins of **b**. Each 1 Kgs 7:38
King Solomon, were of burnished **b**. 1 Kgs 7:45
weight of the **b** was not ascertained. 1 Kgs 7:47
because the **b** altar that was before 1 Kgs 8:64
made in their place shields of **b**, 1 Kgs 14:27
And the **b** altar that was before the 2 Kgs 16:14
but the **b** altar shall be for me to 2 Kgs 16:15
sea from off the **b** oxen that were 2 Kgs 16:17
in pieces the **b** serpent that Moses 2 Kgs 18:4
And the pillars of **b** that were in the 2 Kgs 25:13
the stands and the **b** sea that were in 2 Kgs 25:13
pieces and carried the **b** to Babylon. 2 Kgs 25:13
all the vessels of **b** used in the temple 2 Kgs 25:14
the **b** of all these vessels was beyond 2 Kgs 25:16
cubits, and on it was a capital of **b**. 2 Kgs 25:17
and pomegranates, all of **b**, 2 Kgs 25:17
Ethan, were to sound **b** cymbals; 1 Chr 15:19
David took a large amount of **b**. 1 Chr 18:8
it Solomon made the **b** sea and the 1 Chr 18:8
and the pillars and the vessels of **b**. 1 Chr 18:8
of articles of gold, of silver, and of **b**. 1 Chr 18:10
as well as **b** in quantities beyond 1 Chr 22:3
and **b** and iron beyond weighing, 1 Chr 22:14
gold, silver, **b**, and iron. Arise and 1 Chr 22:16
and the **b** for the things of bronze, 1 Chr 29:2
and the bronze for the things of **b**, 1 Chr 29:2
18,000 talents of **b** and 100,000 1 Chr 29:7
the **b** altar that Bezalel the son of Uri, 2 Chr 1:5
up there to the **b** altar before the LORD, 2 Chr 1:6
to work in gold, silver, **b**, and iron, 2 Chr 2:7
to work in gold, silver, **b**, iron, 2 Chr 2:14
He made an altar of **b**, twenty cubits 2 Chr 4:1
court and overlaid their doors with **b**. 2 Chr 4:9
made of burnished **b** for King 2 Chr 4:16
the weight of the **b** was not sought. 2 Chr 4:18
had made a **b** platform five cubits 2 Chr 6:13
because the **b** altar Solomon had 2 Chr 7:7
place shields of **b** and committed 2 Chr 12:10
workers in iron and **b** to repair the 2 Chr 24:12
with chains of **b** and brought him 2 Chr 33:11
vessels of fine bright **b** as precious as Ezr 8:27
the strength of stones, or is my flesh **b**? Jb 6:12
a **b** arrow will strike him through. Jb 20:24
His bones are tubes of **b**, his limbs like Jb 40:18
iron as straw, and **b** as rotten wood. Jb 41:27
so that my arms can bend a bow of **b**. Ps 18:34
shatters the doors of **b** and cuts in two Ps 107:16
pieces the doors of **b** and cut through the Is 45:2
Instead of **b** I will bring gold, and Is 60:17
instead of wood, **b**, instead of stones, Is 60:17
fortified city, an iron pillar, and **b** walls, Jer 1:18
about with slanders; they are **b** and iron; Jer 6:28
break iron, iron from the north, and **b**? Jer 15:12
you to this people a fortified wall of **b**; Jer 15:20
And the pillars of **b** that were in the Jer 52:17
the stands and the **b** sea that were in Jer 52:17
pieces, and carried all the **b** to Babylon. Jer 52:17
all the vessels of **b** used in the temple Jer 52:18
the twelve **b** bulls that were under the Jer 52:20
the **b** of all these things was beyond Jer 52:20
On it was a capital of **b**. The height of Jer 52:22
A network and pomegranates, all of **b**, Jer 52:22
And they sparkled like burnished **b**. Ezk 1:7
they went in and stood beside the **b** altar. Ezk 9:2
all of them are **b** and tin and iron and Ezk 22:18
one gathers silver and **b** and iron and Ezk 22:20
and vessels of **b** for your merchandise. Ezk 27:13
a man whose appearance was like **b**, Ezk 40:3
of silver, its middle and thighs of **b**, Dn 2:32
Then the iron, the clay, the **b**, the silver, Dn 2:35
after you, and yet a third kingdom of **b**, Dn 2:39
that it broke in pieces the iron, the **b**, Dn 2:45
earth, bound with a band of iron and **b**, Dn 4:15
earth, bound with a band of iron and **b**, Dn 4:23
the gods of gold and silver, **b**, iron, Dn 5:4
praised the gods of silver and gold, of **b**, Dn 5:23
with its teeth of iron and claws of **b**, Dn 7:19
and legs like the gleam of burnished **b**, Dn 10:6
horn iron, and I will make your hoofs **b**; Mi 4:13
the mountains were mountains of **b**. Zec 6:1
his feet were like burnished **b**, refined in Rv 1:15
fire, and whose feet are like burnished **b**. Rv 2:18
gold and silver and **b** and stone and Rv 9:20
of costly wood, **b**, iron and marble, Rv 18:12

BROOCHES (1)
willing heart brought **b** and earrings Ex 35:22

BROOD (9)
your fathers' place, a **b** of sinful men, Nm 32:14
A senseless, a nameless **b**, they have been Jb 30:8
partridge that gathers a **b** that she did Jer 17:11
he said to them, "You **b** of vipers! Mt 3:7
You **b** of vipers! How can you speak Mt 12:34
You serpents, you **b** of vipers, how are Mt 23:33
as a hen gathers her **b** under her wings, Mt 23:37
to be baptized by him, "You **b** of vipers! Lk 3:7
as a hen gathers her **b** under her wings, Lk 13:34

BROOK (46)
of leafy trees and willows of the **b**, Lv 23:40
turn from Azmon to the **B** of Egypt, Nm 34:5
'Now rise up and go over the **b** Zered.' So Dt 2:13
Zered.' So we went over the **b** Zered. Dt 2:13
we crossed the **b** Zered was thirty-eight Dt 2:14
dust of it into the **b** that ran down from Dt 9:21
to Azmon, goes out by the **B** of Egypt, Jos 15:4
towns and its villages; to the **B** of Egypt, Jos 15:47
goes westward to the **b** Kanah and ends Jos 16:8
boundary went down to the **b** Kanah. Jos 17:9
These cities, to the south of the **b**, Jos 17:9
the north side of the **b** and ends at the Jos 17:9
then the **b** that is east of Jokneam. Jos 19:11
stones from the **b** and put them 1 Sm 17:40
him, and they came to the **b** Besor, 1 Sm 30:9
too exhausted to cross the **b** Besor. 1 Sm 30:10
and who had been left at the **b** Besor. 1 Sm 30:21
and the king crossed the **b** Kidron, 2 Sm 15:23
have gone over the **b** of water." And 2 Sm 17:20
you go out and cross the **b** Kidron, 1 Kgs 2:37
from Lebo-hamath to the **B** of Egypt, 1 Kgs 8:65
and burned it at the **b** Kidron. 1 Kgs 15:13
and hide yourself by the **b** Cherith, 1 Kgs 17:3
You shall drink from the **b**, and I 1 Kgs 17:4
and lived by the **b** Cherith that is east 1 Kgs 17:5
the evening, and he drank from the **b**. 1 Kgs 17:6
And after a while the **b** dried up, 1 Kgs 17:7
down to the **b** Kishon and 1 Kgs 18:40
outside Jerusalem, to the **b** Kidron, 2 Kgs 23:6
burned it at the **b** Kidron and beat it 2 Kgs 23:6
the dust of them into the **b** Kidron. 2 Kgs 23:12
of Egypt from the **B** of Egypt to the 2 Kgs 24:7
from Lebo-hamath to the **B** of Egypt. 2 Chr 7:8
it, and burned it at the **b** Kidron. 2 Chr 15:16
it and carried it out to the **b** Kidron. 2 Chr 29:16
springs and the **b** that flowed 2 Chr 32:4
him; the willows of the **b** surround him. Jb 40:22
He will drink from the **b** by the way; Ps 110:7
fountain of wisdom is a bubbling **b**. Prv 18:4
carry away over the **B** of the Willows. Is 15:7
river Euphrates to the **B** of Egypt the Is 27:12
Will you be to me like a deceitful **b**, Jer 15:18
and all the fields as far as the **b** Kidron, Jer 31:40
from there along the **B** of Egypt to the Ezk 47:19
from there along the **B** of Egypt to the Ezk 48:28
Lebo-hamath to the **B** of the Arabah." Am 6:14

BROOKS (8)
you into a good land, a land of **b** of water, Dt 8:7
to Jotbathah, a land with **b** of water. Dt 10:7
Pirathon, Hiddai of the **b** of Gaash, 2 Sm 23:30
Hurai of the **b** of Gaash, Abiel the 1 Chr 11:32
You split open springs and **b**; you dried Ps 74:15
hill there will be **b** running with water, Is 30:25
I will make them walk by **b** of water, Jer 31:9
for you because the water **b** are dried up, Jl 1:20

BROOM (5)
came and sat down under a **b** tree. 1 Kgs 19:4
he lay down and slept under a **b** tree. 1 Kgs 19:5
and the roots of the **b** tree for their food. Jb 30:4
arrows, with glowing coals of the **b** tree! Ps 120:4
it with the **b** of destruction," declares Is 14:23

BROTH (3)
put in a basket, and the **b** he put in a pot, Jgs 6:19
and pour the **b** over them." And he did Jgs 6:20

and **b** of tainted meat is in their vessels; Is 65:4

BROTHER (341)

And again, she bore his **b** Abel. Now Gn 4:2
Cain spoke to Abel his **b**. And when they Gn 4:8
rose up against his **b** Abel and killed Gn 4:8
to Cain, "Where is Abel your **b**?" He said, Gn 4:9
children of Eber, the elder **b** of Japheth, Gn 10:21
also took Lot, the son of Abram's **b**, Gn 14:12
the Amorite, **b** of Eshcol and of Aner. Gn 14:13
sister'? And she herself said, 'He is my **b**.' Gn 20:5
we come, say of me, He is my **b**.'" Gn 20:13
I have given your **b** a thousand pieces Gn 20:16
has borne children to your **b** Nahor: Gn 22:20
Uz his firstborn, Buz his **b**, Kemuel the Gn 22:21
Milcah bore to Nahor, Abraham's **b**. Gn 22:23
the wife of Nahor, Abraham's **b**, Gn 24:15
Rebekah had a **b** whose name was Gn 24:29
He also gave to her **b** and to her mother Gn 24:53
Her **b** and her mother said, "Let the Gn 24:55
Afterward his **b** came out with his Gn 25:26
heard your father speak to your **b** Esau, Gn 27:6
"Behold, my **b** Esau is a hairy man, Gn 27:11
were hairy like his **b** Esau's hands. Gn 27:23
Esau his **b** came in from his hunting. Gn 27:30
But he said, "Your **b** came deceitfully, Gn 27:35
shall live, and you shall serve your **b**; Gn 27:40
then I will kill my **b** Jacob." Gn 27:41
your **b** Esau comforts himself about Gn 27:42
Arise, flee to Laban my **b** in Haran Gn 27:43
daughters of Laban your mother's **b**. Gn 28:2
Bethuel the Aramean, the **b** of Rebekah, Gn 28:5
the daughter of Laban his mother's **b**, Gn 29:10
and the sheep of Laban his mother's **b**, Gn 29:10
the flock of Laban his mother's **b**. Gn 29:10
before him to Esau his **b** in the land of Gn 32:3
saying, "We came to your **b** Esau, Gn 32:6
deliver me from the hand of my **b**, Gn 32:11
him he took a present for his **b** Esau, Gn 32:13
"When Esau my **b** meets you and asks Gn 32:17
seven times, until he came near to his **b**. Gn 33:3
But Esau said, "I have enough, my **b**; Gn 33:9
you when you fled from your **b** Esau." Gn 35:1
himself to him when he fled from his **b**. Gn 35:7
went into a land away from his **b** Jacob. Gn 36:6
if we kill our **b** and conceal his blood? Gn 37:26
our hand be upon him, for he is our **b**, Gn 37:27
her, and raise up offspring for your **b**." Gn 38:8
so as not to give offspring to his **b**. Gn 38:9
back his hand, behold, his **b** came out. Gn 38:29
Afterward his **b** came out with the Gn 38:30
Jacob did not send Benjamin, Joseph's **b**, Gn 42:4
unless your youngest **b** comes here. Gn 42:15
one of you, and let him bring your **b**, Gn 42:16
and bring your youngest **b** to me. So Gn 42:20
truth we are guilty concerning our **b**, Gn 42:21
Bring your youngest **b** to me. Then I Gn 42:34
men, and I will deliver your **b** to you, Gn 42:34
not go down with you, for his **b** is dead, Gn 42:38
see my face unless your **b** is with you.' Gn 43:3
If you will send our **b** with us, we will go Gn 43:4
see my face, unless your **b** is with you.'" Gn 43:5
to tell the man that you had another **b**?" Gn 43:6
still alive? Do you have another **b**?' Gn 43:7
he would say, 'Bring your **b** down'?" Gn 43:7
Take also your **b**, and arise, go again Gn 43:13
send back your other **b** and Benjamin. Gn 43:14
up his eyes and saw his **b** Benjamin, Gn 43:29
son, and said, "Is this your youngest **b**, Gn 43:29
his compassion grew warm for his **b**, Gn 43:30
saying, 'Have you a father, or a **b**?' Gn 44:19
a father, an old man, and a young **b**, Gn 44:20
His **b** is dead, and he alone is left of his Gn 44:20
'Unless your youngest **b** comes down Gn 44:23
down. If our youngest **b** goes with us, Gn 44:26
face unless our youngest **b** is with us.' Gn 44:26
And he said, "I am your **b**, Joseph, Gn 45:4
see, and the eyes of my **b** Benjamin see, Gn 45:12
fell upon his **b** Benjamin's neck and Gn 45:14
his younger **b** shall be greater than he, Gn 48:19
and he said, "Is there not Aaron, your **b**, Ex 4:14
and your **b** Aaron shall be your prophet. Ex 7:1
and your **b** Aaron shall tell Pharaoh to let Ex 7:2
"Then bring near to you Aaron your **b**, Ex 28:1
make holy garments for Aaron your **b**, Ex 28:2
garments for Aaron your **b** and his sons Ex 28:4
you shall put them on Aaron your **b**, Ex 28:41
of you kill his **b** and his companion Ex 32:27
one at the cost of his son and of his **b**, Ex 32:29
"Tell Aaron your **b** not to come at any Lv 16:2
the nakedness of your father's **b**, Lv 18:14
shall not hate your **b** in your heart, Lv 19:17
his father, his son, his daughter, his **b**, Lv 21:2
"If your **b** becomes poor and sells part Lv 25:25
come and redeem what his **b** has sold. Lv 25:25
"If your **b** becomes poor and cannot Lv 25:35
God, that your **b** may live beside you. Lv 25:36
"If your **b** becomes poor beside you and Lv 25:39
and your **b** beside him becomes poor Lv 25:47
father or for his mother, for **b** or sister, Nm 6:7
congregation, you and Aaron your **b**, Nm 20:8
of Edom: "Thus says your **b** Israel: Nm 20:14
to your people, as your **b** Aaron was, Nm 27:13
of Zelophehad our **b** to his daughters. Nm 36:2
a man and his **b** or the alien who Dt 1:16
"If your **b**, the son of your mother, or Dt 13:6
shall not exact it of his neighbor, his **b**, Dt 15:2
yours is with your **b** your hand shall Dt 15:3
or shut your hand against your poor **b**, Dt 15:7
eye look grudgingly on your poor **b**, Dt 15:9
shall open wide your hand to your **b**, Dt 15:11
"If your **b**, a Hebrew man or a Hebrew Dt 15:12
a foreigner over you, who is not your **b**. Dt 17:15
witness and has accused his **b** falsely, Dt 19:18
to him as he had meant to do to his **b**. Dt 19:19
You shall take them back to your **b**. Dt 22:1
shall stay with you until your **b** seeks it. Dt 22:2
not abhor an Edomite, for he is your **b**. Dt 23:7
not charge interest on loans to your **b**, Dt 23:19
you may not charge your **b** interest, Dt 23:20
these, your **b** be degraded in your sight. Dt 25:3
Her husband's **b** shall go in to her and Dt 25:5
perform the duty of a husband's **b** to her. Dt 25:5
shall succeed to the name of his dead **b**, Dt 25:6
'My husband's **b** refuses to perpetuate Dt 25:7
perform the duty of a husband's **b** to me.' Dt 25:7
among you will begrudge food to his **b**, Dt 28:54
as Aaron your **b** died in Mount Hor and Dt 32:50
the son of Kenaz, the **b** of Caleb, Jos 15:17
And Judah said to Simeon his **b**, "Come Jgs 1:3
the son of Kenaz, Caleb's younger **b**, Jgs 1:13
And Judah went with Simeon his **b**, and Jgs 1:17
the son of Kenaz, Caleb's younger **b**. Jgs 3:9
Abimelech, for they said, "He is our **b**." Jgs 9:3
lived there, because of Abimelech his **b**. Jgs 9:21
blood be laid on Abimelech their **b**, Jgs 9:24
for Benjamin their **b** and said, Jgs 21:6
the son of Ahitub, Ichabod's **b**, 1 Sm 14:3
Eliab his eldest **b** heard when he 1 Sm 17:28
and my **b** has commanded me to be 1 Sm 20:29
and to Joab's **b** Abishai the son of 1 Sm 26:6
am distressed for you, my **b** Jonathan; 2 Sm 1:26
I lift up my face to your **b** Joab?" 2 Sm 2:22
he died, for the blood of Asahel his **b**. 2 Sm 3:27
Joab and Abishai his **b** killed Abner, 2 Sm 3:30
he had put their **b** Asahel to death in 2 Sm 3:30
Rechab and Baanah his **b** escaped. 2 Sm 4:6
answered Rechab and Baanah his **b**, 2 Sm 4:9
put in the charge of Abishai his **b**, 2 Sm 10:10
the son of Shimeah, David's **b**. 2 Sm 13:3
love Tamar, my **b** Absalom's sister." 2 Sm 13:4
"Go to your **b** Amnon's house and 2 Sm 13:7
Tamar went to her **b** Amnon's house, 2 Sm 13:8
into the chamber to Amnon her **b**. 2 Sm 13:10
She answered him, "No, my **b**, do not 2 Sm 13:12
But she said to him, "No, my **b**, for 2 Sm 13:16
And her **b** Absalom said to her, "Has 2 Sm 13:20
"Has Amnon your **b** been with you? 2 Sm 13:20
He is your **b**; do not take this to 2 Sm 13:20
woman, in her **b** Absalom's house. 2 Sm 13:20
please let my **b** Amnon go with us." 2 Sm 13:26
the son of Shimeah, David's **b**, 2 Sm 13:32
'Give up the man who struck his **b**, 2 Sm 14:7
for the life of his **b** whom he killed.' 2 Sm 14:7
Abishai the son of Zeruiah, Joab's **b**, 2 Sm 18:2
my **b**?" And Joab took Amasa by the 2 Sm 20:9
and Abishai his **b** pursued Sheba 2 Sm 20:10
the son of Shimei, David's **b**, 2 Sm 21:21
Now Abishai, the **b** of Joab, the son 2 Sm 23:18
Asahel the **b** of Joab was one of the 2 Sm 23:24
or the mighty men or Solomon his **b**. 1 Kgs 1:10
me when I fled from Absalom your **b**. 1 Kgs 2:7
given to Adonijah your **b** as his wife." 1 Kgs 2:21
kingdom also, for he is my older **b**, 1 Kgs 2:22
my **b**?" So they are called the land of 1 Kgs 9:13
over him, saying, "Alas, my **b**!" 1 Kgs 13:30
said, "Does he still live? He is my **b**." 1 Kgs 20:32
your **b** Ben-hadad." Then he said, 1 Kgs 20:33
The sons of Jada, Shammai's **b**: 1 Chr 2:32
The sons of Caleb the **b** of Jerahmeel: 1 Chr 2:42
Chelub, the **b** of Shuhah, fathered 1 Chr 4:11
and his **b** Asaph, who stood on his 1 Chr 6:39
and the name of his **b** was Sheresh; 1 Chr 7:16
The sons of Shemer his **b**: Rohgah, 1 Chr 7:34
The sons of Helem his **b**: Zophah, 1 Chr 7:35
The sons of Eshek his **b**: Ulam his 1 Chr 8:39
Now Abishai, the **b** of Joab, was 1 Chr 11:20
men were Asahel the **b** of Joab, 1 Chr 11:26
Joel the **b** of Nathan, Mibhar the 1 Chr 11:38
the son of Shimri, and Joha his **b**, 1 Chr 11:45
put in the charge of Abishai his **b**, 1 Chr 19:11
fled before Abishai, Joab's **b**, 1 Chr 19:15
down Lahmi the **b** of Goliath the 1 Chr 20:5
the son of Shimea, David's **b**, 1 Chr 20:7
The **b** of Micah, Isshiah; of the sons 1 Chr 24:25
house and his younger **b** alike, 1 Chr 24:31
of Jehieli, Zetham, and Joel his **b**, 1 Chr 26:22
Asahel the **b** of Joab was fourth, for 1 Chr 27:7
Levite, with Shimei his **b** as second, 2 Chr 31:12
Conaniah and Shimei his **b**, 2 Chr 31:13
made Eliakim his **b** king over Judah 2 Chr 36:4
took Jehoahaz his **b** and carried him 2 Chr 36:4
and made his **b** Zedekiah king over 2 Chr 36:10
each from his **b**." And I held a great Neh 5:7
I gave my **b** Hanani and Hananiah the Neh 7:2
I am a **b** of jackals and a companion of Jb 30:29
though I grieved for my friend or my **b**; Ps 35:14
You sit and speak against your **b**; you Ps 50:20
all times, and a **b** is born for adversity. Prv 17:17
in his work is a **b** to him who destroys. Prv 18:9
A **b** offended is more unyielding than Prv 18:19
is a friend who sticks closer than a **b**. Prv 18:24
who is near than a **b** who is far away. Prv 27:10
who has no other, either son or **b**, Eccl 4:8
that you were like a **b** to me who nursed at Sg 8:1
will take hold of his **b** in the house of his Is 3:6
helps his neighbor and says to his **b**, Is 41:6
of his neighbor, and put no trust in any **b**, Jer 9:4
in any brother, for every **b** is a deceiver, Jer 9:4
not lament for him, saying, 'Ah, my **b**!' Jer 22:18
to his neighbor and every one to his **b**, Jer 23:35
one teach his neighbor and each his **b**, Jer 31:34
that no one should enslave a Jew, his **b**. Jer 34:9
every one to his **b** and to his neighbor; Jer 34:17
he practiced extortion, robbed his **b**, Ezk 18:18
say to one another, each to his **b**, Ezk 33:30
man's sword will be against his **b**. Ezk 38:21
for **b** or unmarried sister they may Ezk 44:25
In the womb he took his **b** by the heel, Hos 12:3
he pursued his **b** with the sword Am 1:11
of the violence done to your **b** Jacob, Ob 1:10
over the day of your **b** in the day of his Ob 1:12
go down, every one by the sword of his **b**. Hg 2:22
not Esau Jacob's **b**?" declares the LORD. Mal 1:2
(who is called Peter) and Andrew his **b**, Mt 4:18
James the son of Zebedee and John his **b**, Mt 4:21
who is angry with his **b** will be liable to Mt 5:22
whoever insults his **b** will be liable to Mt 5:22
remember that your **b** has something Mt 5:23
First be reconciled to your **b**, and then Mt 5:24
Or how can you say to your **b**, 'Let me Mt 7:4
who is called Peter, and Andrew his **b**; Mt 10:2
the son of Zebedee, and John his **b**; Mt 10:2
B will deliver brother over to death, and Mt 10:21
Brother will deliver **b** over to death, and Mt 10:21
in heaven is my **b** and sister and Mt 12:50
the sake of Herodias, his **b** Philip's wife, Mt 14:3
him Peter and James, and John his **b**, Mt 17:1
"If your **b** sins against you, go and tell Mt 18:15
listens to you, you have gained your **b**. Mt 18:15
how often will my **b** sin against me, Mt 18:21
do not forgive your **b** from your heart." Mt 18:35
his **b** must marry the widow and raise Mt 22:24
widow and raise up children for his **b**.' Mt 22:24
no children left his wife to his **b**. Mt 22:25
and Andrew the **b** of Simon casting Mk 1:16
the son of Zebedee and John his **b**, Mk 1:19
Zebedee and John the **b** of James (to Mk 3:17
God, he is my **b** and sister and mother." Mk 3:35
and James and John the **b** of James. Mk 5:37
the son of Mary and **b** of James and Joses Mk 6:3
the sake of Herodias, his **b** Philip's wife, Mk 6:17
us that if a man's **b** dies and leaves a Mk 12:19
widow and raise up offspring for his **b**. Mk 12:19
And **b** will deliver brother over to Mk 13:12
brother will deliver **b** over to death, Mk 13:12
and his **b** Philip tetrarch of the region of Lk 3:1
he named Peter, and Andrew his **b**, Lk 6:14
How can you say to your **b**, 'Brother, let Lk 6:42
'**B**, let me take out the speck that is in Lk 6:42
tell my **b** to divide the inheritance with Lk 12:13
And he said to him, 'Your **b** has come, Lk 15:27
and be glad, for this your **b** was dead, Lk 15:32
If your **b** sins, rebuke him, and if he Lk 17:3
wrote for us that if a man's **b** dies, Lk 20:28
widow and raise up offspring for his **b**. Lk 20:28
Jesus was Andrew, Simon Peter's **b**. Jn 1:40
first found his own **b** Simon and said to Jn 1:41
of his disciples, Andrew, Simon Peter's **b**, Jn 6:8
with her hair, whose **b** Lazarus was ill. Jn 11:2
to console them concerning their **b**. Jn 11:19
been here, my **b** would not have died. Jn 11:21
said to her, "Your **b** will rise again." Jn 11:23
been here, my **b** would not have died." Jn 11:32
his hands on him he said, "**B** Saul, Acts 9:17
He killed James the **b** of John with the Acts 12:2

b, how many thousands there are Acts 21:20
standing by me said to me, '**B** Saul, Acts 22:13
do you pass judgment on your **b**? Rom 14:10
Or you, why do you despise your **b**? Rom 14:10
block or hindrance in the way of a **b**. Rom 14:13
For if your **b** is grieved by what you Rom 14:15
that causes your **b** to stumble. Rom 14:21
the city treasurer, and our **b** Quartus, Rom 16:23
of Christ Jesus, and our **b** Sosthenes, 1 Cor 1:1
bears the name of **b** if he is guilty 1 Cor 5:11
but **b** goes to law against brother, and 1 Cor 6:6
but brother goes to law against **b**, and 1 Cor 6:6
the Lord) that if any **b** has a wife who 1 Cor 7:12
In such cases the **b** or sister is not 1 Cor 7:15
the **b** for whom Christ died. 1 Cor 8:11
if food makes my **b** stumble, 1 Cor 8:13
eat meat, lest I make my **b** stumble. 1 Cor 8:13
Now concerning our **b** Apollos, I 1 Cor 16:12
by the will of God, and Timothy our **b**, 2 Cor 1:1
I did not find my **b** Titus there. 2 Cor 2:13
we are sending the **b** who is famous 2 Cor 8:18
we are sending our **b** whom we have 2 Cor 8:22
Titus to go, and sent the **b** with him. 2 Cor 12:18
other apostles except James the Lord's **b**. Gal 1:19
Tychicus the beloved **b** and faithful Eph 6:21
you Epaphroditus my **b** and fellow Phil 2:25
by the will of God, and Timothy our **b**, Col 1:1
He is a beloved **b** and faithful minister Col 4:7
Onesimus, our faithful and beloved **b**, Col 4:9
our **b** and God's coworker in the 1 Thes 3:2
and wrong his **b** in this matter, 1 Thes 4:6
away from any **b** who is walking 2 Thes 3:6
as an enemy, but warn him as a **b**. 2 Thes 3:15
for Christ Jesus, and Timothy our **b**, Phlm 1:1
joy and comfort from your love, my **b**, Phlm 1:7
as a beloved **b**—especially to me, Phlm 1:16
b, I want some benefit from you in Phlm 1:20
one his neighbor and each one his **b**, Heb 8:11
know that our **b** Timothy has been Heb 13:23
Let the lowly **b** boast in his exaltation, Jas 1:9
If a **b** or sister is poorly clothed and Jas 2:15
who speaks against a **b** or judges his Jas 4:11
speaks against a brother or judges his **b**, Jas 4:11
Silvanus, a faithful **b** as I regard him, 1 Pt 5:12
just as our beloved **b** Paul also wrote to 2 Pt 3:15
light and hates his **b** is still in darkness. 1 Jn 2:9
Whoever loves his **b** abides in the 1 Jn 2:10
But whoever hates his **b** is in the 1 Jn 2:11
nor is the one who does not love his **b**. 1 Jn 3:10
was of the evil one and murdered his **b**. 1 Jn 3:12
who hates his **b** is a murderer, 1 Jn 3:15
world's goods and sees his **b** in need, 1 Jn 3:17
says, "I love God," and hates his **b**, 1 Jn 4:20
does not love his **b** whom he has seen 1 Jn 4:20
loves God must also love his **b**. 1 Jn 4:21
If anyone sees his **b** committing a sin 1 Jn 5:16
a servant of Jesus Christ and **b** of James, Jude 1:1
your **b** and partner in the tribulation and Rv 1:9

BROTHER'S (34)

said, "I do not know; am I my **b** keeper?" Gn 4:9
The voice of your **b** blood is crying to Gn 4:10
to receive your **b** blood from your Gn 4:11
His **b** name was Jubal; he was the father Gn 4:21
divided, and his **b** name was Joktan. Gn 10:25
took Sarai his wife, and Lot his **b** son, Gn 12:5
a while, until your **b** fury turns away— Gn 27:44
until your **b** anger turns away from Gn 27:45
"Go in to your **b** wife and perform the Gn 38:8
he went in to his **b** wife he would waste Gn 38:9
uncover the nakedness of your **b** wife; Lv 18:16
brother's wife; it is your **b** nakedness. Lv 18:16
If a man takes his **b** wife, it is impurity. Lv 20:21
He has uncovered his **b** nakedness; Lv 20:21
"You shall not see your **b** ox or his sheep Dt 22:1
or with any lost thing of your **b**, Dt 22:3
shall not see your **b** donkey or his ox Dt 22:4
the man does not wish to take his **b** wife, Dt 25:7
then his **b** wife shall go up to the gate to Dt 25:7
to perpetuate his **b** name in Israel; Dt 25:7
then his **b** wife shall go up to him in the Dt 25:9
man who does not build up his **b** house.' Dt 25:9
has turned about and become my **b**, 1 Kgs 2:15
divided), and his **b** name was Joktan. 1 Chr 1:19
drinking wine in their oldest **b** house, Jb 1:13
drinking wine in their oldest **b** house, Jb 1:18
do not go to your **b** house in the day of Prv 27:10
do you see the speck that is in your **b** eye, Mt 7:3
clearly to take the speck out of your **b** eye. Mt 7:5
not lawful for you to have your **b** wife." Mk 6:18
reproved by him for Herodias, his **b** wife, Lk 3:19
you see the speck that is in your **b** eye, Lk 6:41
take out the speck that is in your **b** eye. Lk 6:42
deeds were evil and his **b** righteous. 1 Jn 3:12

BROTHER-IN-LAW (1)

wife and perform the duty of a **b** to her, Gn 38:8

BROTHERHOOD (4)

and did not remember the covenant of **b**. Am 1:9
annulling the **b** between Judah and Zec 11:14
Honor everyone. Love the **b**. Fear God. 1 Pt 2:17
experienced by your **b** throughout the 1 Pt 5:9

BROTHERLY (7)

Love one another with **b** affection. Rom 12:10
Now concerning **b** love you have no 1 Thes 4:9
Let **b** love continue. Heb 13:1
to the truth for a sincere **b** love, 1 Pt 1:22
have unity of mind, sympathy, **b** love, 1 Pt 3:8
and godliness with **b** affection, and 2 Pt 1:7
affection, and **b** affection with love. 2 Pt 1:7

BROTHERS (505)

of his father and told his two **b** outside. Gn 9:22
servant of servants shall he be to his **b**." Gn 9:25
and said, "I beg you, my **b**, do not act so Gn 19:7
Be lord over your **b**, and may your Gn 27:29
and all his **b** I have given to him for Gn 27:37
Jacob said to them, "My **b**, where do you Gn 29:4
also said to her father and to her **b**, Gn 34:11
of Jacob, Simeon and Levi, Dinah's **b**, Gn 34:25
old, was pasturing the flock with his **b**. Gn 37:2
But when his **b** saw that their father Gn 37:4
father loved him more than all his **b**, Gn 37:4
he told it to his **b** they hated him even Gn 37:5
His **b** said to him, "Are you indeed to Gn 37:8
dream and told it to his **b** and said, Gn 37:9
he told it to his father and to his **b**, Gn 37:10
mother and your **b** indeed come to Gn 37:10
And his **b** were jealous of him, but his Gn 37:11
Now his **b** went to pasture their Gn 37:12
"Are not your **b** pasturing the flock at Gn 37:13
is well with your **b** and with the flock, Gn 37:14
"I am seeking my **b**," he said. "Tell me, Gn 37:16
Joseph went after his **b** and found them Gn 37:17
So when Joseph came to his **b**, they Gn 37:23
Then Judah said to his **b**, "What profit Gn 37:26
own flesh." And his **b** listened to him. Gn 37:27
and returned to his **b** and said, "The Gn 37:30
went down from his **b** and turned aside Gn 38:1
he feared that he would die, like his **b**. Gn 38:11
So ten of Joseph's **b** went down to buy Gn 42:3
Benjamin, Joseph's brother, with his **b**, Gn 42:4
And Joseph's **b** came and bowed Gn 42:6
Joseph saw his **b** and recognized them, Gn 42:7
And Joseph recognized his **b**, but they Gn 42:8
said, "We, your servants, are twelve **b**, Gn 42:13
one of your **b** remain confined where Gn 42:19
He said to his **b**, "My money has been Gn 42:28
We are twelve **b**, sons of our father. Gn 42:32
leave one of your **b** with me, and take Gn 42:33
Judah and his **b** came to Joseph's Gn 44:14
and let the boy go back with his **b**. Gn 44:33
Joseph made himself known to his **b**. Gn 45:1
And Joseph said to his **b**, "I am Joseph! Is Gn 45:3
still alive?" But his **b** could not answer Gn 45:3
So Joseph said to his **b**, "Come near to Gn 45:4
he kissed all his **b** and wept upon Gn 45:15
them. After that his **b** talked with him. Gn 45:15
"Joseph's **b** have come," it pleased Gn 45:16
Pharaoh said to Joseph, "Say to your **b**, Gn 45:17
Then he sent his **b** away, and as they Gn 45:24
Joseph said to his **b** and to his father's Gn 46:31
him, 'My **b** and my father's household, Gn 46:31
and told Pharaoh, "My father and my **b**, Gn 47:1
And from among his **b** he took five men Gn 47:2
Pharaoh said to his **b**, "What is your Gn 47:3
"Your father and your **b** have come to Gn 47:5
your father and your **b** in the best of Gn 47:6
his father and his **b** and gave them a Gn 47:11
And Joseph provided his father, his **b**, Gn 47:12
the name of their **b** in their inheritance. Gn 48:6
than to your **b** one mountain slope Gn 48:22
"Simeon and Levi are **b**; weapons of Gn 49:5
"Judah, your **b** shall praise you; your Gn 49:8
of him who was set apart from his **b**. Gn 49:26
as all the household of Joseph, his **b**, Gn 50:8
to Egypt with his **b** and all who had Gn 50:14
When Joseph's **b** saw that their father Gn 50:15
transgression of your **b** and their sin, Gn 50:17
His **b** also came and fell down before Gn 50:18
And Joseph said to his **b**, "I am about Gn 50:24
died, and all his **b** and all that generation. Ex 1:6
me go back to my **b** in Egypt to see Ex 4:18
carry your **b** away from the front of the Lv 10:4
but let your **b**, the whole house of Israel, Lv 10:6
"The priest who is chief among his **b**, Lv 21:10
but over your **b** the people of Israel you Lv 25:46
One of his **b** may redeem him, Lv 25:48
They minister to their **b** in the tent of Nm 8:26
and all your **b** the sons of Levi with Nm 16:10
And with you bring your **b** also, the Nm 18:2
I have taken your **b** the Levites from Nm 18:6
perished when our **b** perished before Nm 20:3
us a possession among our father's **b**." Nm 27:4
among their father's **b** and transfer the Nm 27:7
you shall give his inheritance to his **b**. Nm 27:9
And if he has no **b**, then you shall Nm 27:10
give his inheritance to his father's **b**. Nm 27:10
And if his father has no **b**, then you Nm 27:11
"Shall your **b** go to the war while you Nm 32:6
married to sons of their father's **b**. Nm 36:11
time, 'Hear the cases between your **b**, Dt 1:16
Our **b** have made our hearts melt, Dt 1:28
to pass through the territory of your **b**, Dt 2:4
So we went on, away from our **b**, the Dt 2:8
shall cross over armed before your **b**, Dt 3:18
until the LORD gives rest to your **b**, as to Dt 3:20
has no portion or inheritance with his **b**. Dt 10:9
you, one of your **b** should become poor, Dt 15:7
One from among your **b** you shall set Dt 17:15
heart may not be lifted up above his **b**, Dt 17:20
have no inheritance among their **b**; Dt 18:2
from your **b**—it is to him you shall Dt 18:15
a prophet like you from among their **b**. Dt 18:18
"If a man is found stealing one of his **b**, Dt 24:7
he is one of your **b** or one of the Dt 24:14
"If **b** dwell together, and one of them dies Dt 25:5
he disowned his **b** and ignored his Dt 33:9
pate of him who is prince among his **b**. Dt 33:16
let him be the favorite of his **b**, and let Dt 33:24
over armed before your **b** and shall help Jos 1:14
LORD gives rest to your **b** as he has to Jos 1:15
my father and mother, my **b** and sisters, Jos 2:13
house your father and mother, your **b**, Jos 2:18
father and mother and **b** and all who Jos 6:23
But my **b** who went up with me made Jos 14:8
along with our **b**." So according to Jos 17:4
inheritance among the **b** of their father. Jos 17:4
not forsaken your **b** these many days, Jos 22:3
LORD your God has given rest to your **b**, Jos 22:4
a possession beside their **b** in the land Jos 22:7
the spoil of your enemies with your **b**." Jos 22:8
And he said, "They were my **b**, the sons Jgs 8:19
Ophrah and killed his **b** the sons of Jgs 9:5
strengthened his hands to kill his **b**. Jgs 9:24
his father in killing his seventy **b**. Jgs 9:56
Jephthah fled from his **b** and lived in the Jgs 11:3
Then his **b** and all his family came Jgs 16:31
they came to their **b** at Zorah and Jgs 18:8
Zorah and Eshtaol, their **b** said to them, Jgs 18:8
out the country of Laish said to their **b**, Jgs 18:14
to them and said to them, "No, my **b**, Jgs 19:23
would not listen to the voice of their **b**, Jgs 20:13
again draw near to fight against our **b**, Jgs 20:23
out once more to battle against our **b**, Jgs 20:28
fathers or their **b** come to complain Jgs 21:22
off from among his **b** and from the gate Ru 4:10
anointed him in the midst of his **b**. 1 Sm 16:13
"Take for your **b** an ephah of this 1 Sm 17:17
them quickly to the camp to your **b**. 1 Sm 17:17
See if your **b** are well, and bring 1 Sm 17:18
ranks and went and greeted his **b**. 1 Sm 17:22
eyes, let me get away and see my **b**.' 1 Sm 20:29
And when his **b** and all his father's 1 Sm 22:1
said, "You shall not do so, my **b**, 1 Sm 30:23
to turn from the pursuit of their **b**?" 2 Sm 2:26
pursuit of their **b** until the morning." 2 Sm 2:27
the house of Saul your father, to his **b**, 2 Sm 3:8
Go back and take your **b** with you, 2 Sm 15:20
You are my **b**; you are my bone and 2 Sm 19:12
"Why have our **b** the men of Judah 2 Sm 19:41
En-rogel, and he invited all his **b**, 1 Kgs 1:9
ate unleavened bread among their **b**. 2 Kgs 23:9
Jabez was more honorable than his **b**; 1 Chr 4:9
but his **b** did not have many 1 Chr 4:27
strong among his **b** and a chief 1 Chr 5:2
On the left hand were their **b**, the 1 Chr 6:44
And their **b** the Levites were 1 Chr 6:48
days, and his **b** came to comfort him. 1 Chr 7:22
for their **b** had made preparation for 1 Chr 12:39
send abroad to our **b** who remain in 1 Chr 13:2
Uriel the chief, with 120 of his **b**; 1 Chr 15:5
Asaiah the chief, with 220 of his **b**; 1 Chr 15:6
Joel the chief, with 130 of his **b**; 1 Chr 15:7
the chief, with 200 of his **b**; 1 Chr 15:8
Eliel the chief, with 80 of his **b**; 1 Chr 15:9
the chief, with 112 of his **b**. 1 Chr 15:10
yourselves, you and your **b**, 1 Chr 15:12
to appoint their **b** as the singers 1 Chr 15:16
and of his **b** Asaph the son of 1 Chr 15:17
and of the sons of Merari, their **b**, 1 Chr 15:17
and with them their **b** of the second 1 Chr 15:18
sung to the LORD by Asaph and his **b**. 1 Chr 16:7
left Asaph and his **b** there before the 1 Chr 16:37
Obed-edom and his sixty-eight **b**, 1 Chr 16:38

priest and his **b** the priests before 1 Chr 16:39
to attend the sons of Aaron, their **b**, 1 Chr 23:32
just as their **b** the sons of Aaron, 1 Chr 24:31
number of them along with their **b**, 1 Chr 25:7
to him and his **b** and his sons, 1 Chr 25:9
third to Zaccur, his sons and his **b**, 1 Chr 25:10
the fourth to Izri, his sons and his **b**, 1 Chr 25:11
to Nethaniah, his sons and his **b**, 1 Chr 25:12
to Bukkiah, his sons and his **b**, 1 Chr 25:13
to Jesharelah, his sons and his **b**, 1 Chr 25:14
to Jeshaiah, his sons and his **b**, 1 Chr 25:15
to Mattaniah, his sons and his **b**, 1 Chr 25:16
tenth to Shimei, his sons and his **b**, 1 Chr 25:17
to Azarel, his sons and his **b**, 1 Chr 25:18
to Hashabiah, his sons and his **b**, 1 Chr 25:19
Shubael, his sons and his **b**, 1 Chr 25:20
Mattithiah, his sons and his **b**, 1 Chr 25:21
to Jeremoth, his sons and his **b**, 1 Chr 25:22
to Hananiah, his sons and his **b**, 1 Chr 25:23
Joshbekashah, his sons and his **b**, 1 Chr 25:24
to Hanani, his sons and his **b**, 1 Chr 25:25
to Mallothi, his sons and his **b**, 1 Chr 25:26
to Eliathah, his sons and his **b**, 1 Chr 25:27
to Hothir, his sons and his **b**, 1 Chr 25:28
to Giddalti, his sons and his **b**, 1 Chr 25:29
to Mahazioth, his sons and his **b**, 1 Chr 25:30
to Romamti-ezer, his sons and his **b**, 1 Chr 25:31
and Elzabad, whose **b** were able men, 1 Chr 26:7
of Obed-edom with their sons and **b**, 1 Chr 26:8
And Meshelemiah had sons and **b**, 1 Chr 26:9
all the sons and **b** of Hosah were 1 Chr 26:11
men, had duties, just as their **b** did, 1 Chr 26:12
His **b**: from Eliezer were his son 1 Chr 26:25
Shelomoth and his **b** were in charge 1 Chr 26:26
in the care of Shelomoth and his **b**. 1 Chr 26:28
Hebronites, Hashabiah and his **b**, 1 Chr 26:30
David appointed him and his **b**, 1 Chr 26:32
for Judah, Elihu, one of David's **b**; 1 Chr 27:18
said: "Hear me, my **b** and my people. 1 Chr 28:2
as chief prince among his **b**, 2 Chr 11:22
to you from your **b** who live in their 2 Chr 19:10
not come upon you and your **b**. 2 Chr 19:10
He had **b**, the sons of Jehoshaphat: 2 Chr 21:2
he killed all his **b** with the sword, 2 Chr 21:4
and also you have killed your **b**, 2 Chr 21:13
of Judah and the sons of Ahaziah's **b**, 2 Chr 22:8
gathered their **b** and consecrated 2 Chr 29:15
their **b** the Levites helped them, 2 Chr 29:34
not be like your fathers and your **b**, 2 Chr 30:7
your **b** and your children will find 2 Chr 30:9
to distribute the portions to their **b**, 2 Chr 31:15
houses of your **b** the lay people, 2 Chr 35:5
yourselves, and prepare for your **b**, 2 Chr 35:6
and Shemaiah and Nethanel his **b**, 2 Chr 35:9
for their **b** the Levites prepared for 2 Chr 35:15
And Jeshua with his sons and his **b**, and Ezr 3:9
and the Levites, their sons and **b**. Ezr 3:9
good to you and your **b** to do with the Ezr 7:18
to Iddo and his **b** and the temple Ezr 8:17
of Jeshua the son of Jozadak and his **b**. Ezr 10:18
that Hanani, one of my **b**, came with Neh 1:2
high priest rose up with his **b** the priests, Neh 3:1
After him their **b** repaired: Bavvai the Neh 3:18
in the presence of his **b** and of the army Neh 4:2
and awesome, and fight for your **b**, Neh 4:14
neither I nor my **b** nor my servants Neh 4:23
and of their wives against their Jewish **b**. Neh 5:1
Now our flesh is as the flesh of our **b**, Neh 5:5
back our Jewish **b** who have been Neh 5:8
you even sell your **b** that they may be Neh 5:8
I and my **b** and my servants are Neh 5:10
neither I nor my **b** ate the food Neh 5:14
and their **b**, Shebaniah, Hodiah, Neh 10:10
join with their **b**, their nobles, and Neh 10:29
and his **b**, men of valor, 928. Neh 11:8
and their **b** who did the work of the Neh 11:12
and his **b**, heads of fathers' houses, Neh 11:13
and their **b**, mighty men of valor, 128; Neh 11:14
Bakbukiah, the second among his **b**; Neh 11:17
Akkub, Talmon and their **b**, Neh 11:19
the priests and of their **b** in the days of Neh 12:7
who with his **b** was in charge of the Neh 12:8
Unni and their **b** stood opposite them Neh 12:9
with their **b** who stood opposite them, Neh 12:24
their duty was to distribute to their **b**. Neh 13:13
and popular with the multitude of his **b**, Est 10:3
My **b** are treacherous as a torrent-bed, as Jb 6:15
"He has put my **b** far from me, and Jb 19:13
exacted pledges of your **b** for nothing and Jb 22:6
came to him all his **b** and sisters and all Jb 42:11
them an inheritance among their **b**. Jb 42:15
I will tell of your name to my **b**; in the Ps 22:22
I have become a stranger to my **b**, an Ps 69:8
For my **b** and companions' sake I will Ps 122:8
pleasant it is when **b** dwell in unity! Ps 133:1

and one who sows discord among **b**. Prv 6:19
share the inheritance as one of the **b**. Prv 17:2
All a poor man's **b** hate him; how Prv 19:7
"Your **b** who hate you and cast you out Is 66:5
shall bring all your **b** from all the Is 66:20
For even your **b** and the house of your Jer 12:6
of Habazziniah and his **b** and all his Jer 35:3
His children are destroyed, and his **b**, Jer 49:10
"Son of man, your **b**, even your Ezk 11:15
of man, your brothers, even your **b**, Ezk 11:15
Say to your **b**, "You are my people," and Hos 2:1
he may flourish among his **b**, Hos 13:15
then the rest of his **b** shall return to the Mi 5:3
and Jacob the father of Judah and his **b**, Mt 1:2
Josiah the father of Jechoniah and his **b**, Mt 1:11
by the Sea of Galilee, he saw two **b**, Mt 4:18
going on from there he saw two other **b**, Mt 4:21
And if you greet only your **b**, what more Mt 5:47
his mother and his **b** stood outside, Mt 12:46
is my mother, and who are my **b**?" Mt 12:48
said, "Here are my mother and my **b**! Mt 12:49
And are not his **b** James and Joseph Mt 13:55
has left houses or **b** or sisters or father Mt 19:29
it, they were indignant at the two **b**. Mt 20:24
Now there were seven **b** among us. The Mt 22:25
you have one teacher, and you are all **b**. Mt 23:8
did it to one of the least of these my **b**, Mt 25:40
afraid; go and tell my **b** to go to Galilee, Mt 28:10
And his mother and his **b** came, and Mk 3:31
"Your mother and your **b** are outside, Mk 3:32
"Who are my mother and my **b**?" Mk 3:33
he said, "Here are my mother and my **b**! Mk 3:34
has left house or **b** or sisters or mother Mk 10:29
houses and **b** and sisters and mothers Mk 10:30
There were seven **b**; the first took a Mk 12:20
his mother and his **b** came to him, Lk 8:19
mother and your **b** are standing outside, Lk 8:20
"My mother and my **b** are those who Lk 8:21
your friends or your **b** or your relatives Lk 14:12
wife and children and **b** and sisters, Lk 14:26
for I have five **b**—so that he may warn Lk 16:28
house or wife or **b** or parents or Lk 18:29
Now there were seven **b**. The first took Lk 20:29
by parents and **b** and relatives and Lk 21:16
have turned again, strengthen your **b**." Lk 22:32
his mother and his **b** and his disciples, Jn 2:12
So his **b** said to him, "Leave here and go to Jn 7:3
For not even his **b** believed in him. Jn 7:5
But after his **b** had gone up to the feast, Jn 7:10
Father; but go to my **b** and say to them, Jn 20:17
abroad among the **b** that this disciple Jn 21:23
Mary the mother of Jesus, and his **b**. Acts 1:14
stood up among the **b** (the company of Acts 1:15
"**B**, the Scripture had to be fulfilled, Acts 1:16
"**B**, I may say to you with confidence Acts 2:29
of the apostles, "**B**, what shall we do?" Acts 2:37
b, I know that you acted in ignorance, Acts 3:17
for you a prophet like me from your **b**. Acts 3:22
b, pick out from among you seven men Acts 6:3
Stephen said: "**B** and fathers, hear me. Acts 7:2
Joseph made himself known to his **b**, Acts 7:13
old, it came into his heart to visit his **b**, Acts 7:23
supposed that his **b** would understand Acts 7:25
them, saying, 'Men, you are **b**. Acts 7:26
for you a prophet like me from your **b**.' Acts 7:37
And when the **b** learned this, they Acts 9:30
some of the **b** from Joppa Acts 10:23
apostles and the **b** who were Acts 11:1
These six **b** also accompanied me, Acts 11:12
to send relief to the **b** living in Judea. Acts 11:29
James and to the **b**." Then he departed Acts 12:17
"**B**, if you have any word of Acts 13:15
"**B**, sons of the family of Abraham, Acts 13:26
b, that through this man forgiveness Acts 13:38
poisoned their minds against the **b**. Acts 14:2
from Judea and were teaching the **b**, Acts 15:1
and brought great joy to all the **b**. Acts 15:3
"**B**, you know that in the early days Acts 15:7
James replied, "**B**, listen to me. Acts 15:13
and Silas, leading men among the **b**, Acts 15:22
with the following letter: "The **b**, both Acts 15:23
to the **b** who are of the Gentiles in Acts 15:23
and strengthened the **b** with many Acts 15:32
off in peace by the **b** to those who had Acts 15:33
return and visit the **b** in every city Acts 15:36
commended by the **b** to the grace Acts 15:40
spoken of by the **b** at Lystra and Acts 16:2
And when they had seen the **b**, they Acts 16:40
and some of the **b** before the city Acts 17:6
The **b** immediately sent Paul and Acts 17:10
Then the **b** immediately sent Paul off Acts 17:14
took leave of the **b** and set sail for Acts 18:18
the **b** encouraged him and wrote to Acts 18:27
and we greeted the **b** and stayed with Acts 21:7
to Jerusalem, the **b** received us gladly. Acts 21:17

"**B** and fathers, hear the defense that I Acts 22:1
From them I received letters to the **b**, Acts 22:5
"**B**, I have lived my life before God in Acts 23:1
know, **b**, that he was the high priest, Acts 23:5
out in the council, "**B**, I am a Pharisee, Acts 23:6
There we found **b** and were invited to Acts 28:14
And the **b** there, when they heard Acts 28:15
"**B**, though I had done nothing Acts 28:17
and none of the **b** coming here has Acts 28:21
b, that I have often intended to come to Rom 1:13
b—for I am speaking to those who Rom 7:1
Likewise, my **b**, you also have died to Rom 7:4
So then, **b**, we are debtors, not to the Rom 8:12
be the firstborn among many **b**. Rom 8:29
cut off from Christ for the sake of my **b**, Rom 9:3
B, my heart's desire and prayer to God Rom 10:1
b: a partial hardening has come Rom 11:25
therefore, **b**, by the mercies of God, Rom 12:1
myself am satisfied about you, my **b**, Rom 15:14
b, by our Lord Jesus Christ and by Rom 15:30
and the **b** who are with them. Rom 16:14
b, to watch out for those who cause Rom 16:17
b, by the name of our Lord Jesus 1 Cor 1:10
there is quarreling among you, my **b**. 1 Cor 1:11
b: not many of you were wise 1 Cor 1:26
b, did not come proclaiming to you 1 Cor 2:1
b, could not address you as spiritual 1 Cor 3:1
b, that you may learn by us not to go 1 Cor 4:6
to settle a dispute between the **b**, 1 Cor 6:5
wrong and defraud—even your own **b**! 1 Cor 6:8
b, in whatever condition each was 1 Cor 7:24
b: the appointed time has grown very 1 Cor 7:29
against your **b** and wounding 1 Cor 8:12
other apostles and the **b** of the Lord 1 Cor 9:5
b, that our fathers were all under the 1 Cor 10:1
So then, my **b**, when you come 1 Cor 11:33
b, I do not want you to be 1 Cor 12:1
b, if I come to you speaking in 1 Cor 14:6
B, do not be children in your 1 Cor 14:20
then, **b**? When you come together, 1 Cor 14:26
So, my **b**, earnestly desire to 1 Cor 14:39
you, **b**, of the gospel I preached to you, 1 Cor 15:1
than five hundred **b** at one time, 1 Cor 15:6
I protest, **b**, by my pride in you, 1 Cor 15:31
b: flesh and blood cannot inherit 1 Cor 15:50
Therefore, my beloved **b**, be 1 Cor 15:58
for I am expecting him with the **b**. 1 Cor 16:11
him to visit you with the other **b**, 1 Cor 16:12
b—you know that the household of 1 Cor 16:15
All the **b** send you greetings. Greet 1 Cor 16:20
b, of the affliction we experienced in 2 Cor 1:8
b, about the grace of God that has 2 Cor 8:1
And as for our **b**, they are messengers 2 Cor 8:23
I am sending the **b** so that our 2 Cor 9:3
necessary to urge the **b** to go on ahead 2 Cor 9:5
for the **b** who came from Macedonia 2 Cor 11:9
danger at sea, danger from false **b**; 2 Cor 11:26
Finally, **b**, rejoice. Aim for 2 Cor 13:11
and all the **b** who are with me, To the Gal 1:2
b, that the gospel that was preached by Gal 1:11
because of false **b** secretly brought in Gal 2:4
b: even with a man-made covenant, Gal 3:15
B, I entreat you, become as I am, for I Gal 4:12
Now you, **b**, like Isaac, are children of Gal 4:28
b, we are not children of the slave but of Gal 4:31
But if I, **b**, still preach circumcision, Gal 5:11
For you were called to freedom, **b**. Gal 5:13
B, if anyone is caught in any Gal 6:1
Christ be with your spirit, **b**. Amen. Gal 6:18
Peace be to the **b**, and love with faith, Eph 6:23
b, that what has happened to me has Phil 1:12
And most of the **b**, having become Phil 1:14
Finally, my **b**, rejoice in the Lord. To Phil 3:1
B, I do not consider that I have made it Phil 3:13
B, join in imitating me, and keep your Phil 3:17
Therefore, my **b**, whom I love and long Phil 4:1
Finally, **b**, whatever is true, whatever is Phil 4:8
The **b** who are with me greet you. Phil 4:21
the saints and faithful **b** in Christ at Col 1:2
Give my greetings to the **b** at Laodicea, Col 4:15
For we know, **b** loved by God, that he 1 Thes 1:4
b, that our coming to you was not in 1 Thes 2:1
you remember, **b**, our labor and toil: 1 Thes 2:9
b, became imitators of the churches 1 Thes 2:14
away from you, **b**, for a short time, 1 Thes 2:17
b, in all our distress and affliction we 1 Thes 3:7
b, we ask and urge you in the Lord 1 Thes 4:1
to all the **b** throughout Macedonia. 1 Thes 4:10
you, **b**, to do this more and more, 1 Thes 4:10
b, about those who are asleep, 1 Thes 4:13
b, you have no need to have anything 1 Thes 5:1
b, for that day to surprise you like a 1 Thes 5:4
b, to respect those who labor among 1 Thes 5:12
we urge you, **b**, admonish the idle, 1 Thes 5:14
B, pray for us. 1 Thes 5:25

Greet all the **b** with a holy kiss. 1 Thes 5:26
to have this letter read to all the **b**. 1 Thes 5:27
thanks to God for you, **b**, as is right, 2 Thes 1:3
together to him, we ask you, **b**, 2 Thes 2:1
God for you, **b** beloved by the Lord, 2 Thes 2:13
b, stand firm and hold to the 2 Thes 2:15
Finally, **b**, pray for us, that the word 2 Thes 3:1
b, in the name of our Lord Jesus 2 Thes 3:6
b, do not grow weary in doing good. 2 Thes 3:13
If you put these things before the **b**, 1 Tm 4:6
a father. Treat younger men like **b**, 1 Tm 5:1
on the ground that they are **b**; 1 Tm 6:2
and Linus and Claudia and all the **b**. 2 Tm 4:21
why he is not ashamed to call them **b**, Heb 2:11
"I will tell of your name to my **b**; Heb 2:12
to be made like his **b** in every respect, Heb 2:17
Therefore, holy **b**, you who share in a Heb 3:1
b, lest there be in any of you an evil, Heb 3:12
from the people, that is, from their **b**, Heb 7:5
b, since we have confidence to enter Heb 10:19
b, bear with my word of exhortation, Heb 13:22
Count it all joy, my **b**, when you meet Jas 1:2
Do not be deceived, my beloved **b**. Jas 1:16
Know this, my beloved **b**: let every Jas 1:19
My **b**, show no partiality as you hold the Jas 2:1
Listen, my beloved **b**, has not God chosen Jas 2:5
What good is it, my **b**, if someone says Jas 2:14
of you should become teachers, my **b**, Jas 3:1
come blessing and cursing. My **b**, Jas 3:10
Can a fig tree, my **b**, bear olives, or a Jas 3:12
Do not speak evil against one another, **b**. Jas 4:11
therefore, **b**, until the coming of the Lord. Jas 5:7
b, so that you may not be judged; Jas 5:9
b, take the prophets who spoke in the Jas 5:10
But above all, my **b**, do not swear, either Jas 5:12
My **b**, if anyone among you wanders Jas 5:19
b, be all the more diligent to make 2 Pt 1:10
surprised, **b**, that the world hates you. 1 Jn 3:13
of death into life, because we love the **b**. 1 Jn 3:14
ought to lay down our lives for the **b**. 1 Jn 3:16
greatly when the **b** came and testified 3 Jn 1:3
you do in all your efforts for these **b**, 3 Jn 1:5
with that, he refuses to welcome the **b**, 3 Jn 1:10
servants and their **b** should be complete, Rv 6:11
the accuser of our **b** has been thrown Rv 12:10
with you and your **b** who hold to the Rv 19:10
with you and your **b** the prophets, Rv 22:9

BROUGHT (799)

The earth **b** forth vegetation, plants Gn 1:12
of the heavens and **b** them to the man Gn 2:19
into a woman and **b** her to the man. Gn 2:22
the course of time Cain **b** to the LORD an Gn 4:3
and Abel also **b** of the firstborn of his Gn 4:4
hand and took her and **b** her into the ark Gn 8:9
Then he **b** back all the possessions, Gn 14:16
and also **b** back his kinsman Lot with Gn 14:16
king of Salem **b** out bread and Gn 14:18
And he **b** him outside and said, "Look Gn 15:5
"I am the LORD who **b** you out from Ur Gn 15:7
And he **b** him all these, cut them in Gn 15:10
Let a little water be **b**, and wash your Gn 18:4
out their hands and **b** Lot into the Gn 19:10
and they **b** him out and set him Gn 19:16
And as they **b** them out, one said, Gn 19:17
that you have **b** on me and my Gn 20:9
And the servant **b** out jewelry of silver Gn 24:53
Then Isaac **b** her into the tent of Sarah Gn 24:67
and you would have **b** guilt upon us." Gn 26:10
and took them and **b** them to his Gn 27:14
and bless you." So he **b** it near to him, Gn 27:25
to him, and he ate; and he **b** him wine, Gn 27:25
prepared delicious food and **b** it to his Gn 27:31
then that hunted game and **b** it to me, Gn 27:33
and kissed him and **b** him to his Gn 29:13
his daughter Leah and **b** her to Jacob, Gn 29:23
in the field and **b** them to his mother Gn 30:14
sticks and so the flocks **b** forth striped, Gn 30:39
accept my blessing that is **b** to you, Gn 33:11
"You have **b** trouble on me by making Gn 34:30
And Joseph **b** a bad report of them to Gn 37:2
of many colors and **b** it to their father Gn 37:32
As she was being **b** out, she sent word Gn 38:25
Now Joseph had been **b** down to Egypt, Gn 39:1
Ishmaelites who had **b** him down there. Gn 39:1
he has **b** among us a Hebrew to laugh Gn 39:14
servant, whom you have **b** among us, Gn 39:17
and they quickly **b** him out of the pit. Gn 41:14
the grain that they had **b** from Egypt, Gn 43:2
Joseph told him and **b** the men to Gn 43:17
because they were **b** to Joseph's house, Gn 43:18
sacks the first time, that we are **b** in, Gn 43:18
weight. So we have **b** it again with us, Gn 43:21
and we have **b** other money down with Gn 43:22
your money." Then he **b** Simeon out to Gn 43:23
when the man had **b** the men into Gn 43:24

they **b** into the house to him the Gn 43:26
of our sacks we **b** back to you from Gn 44:8
All his offspring he **b** with him into Gn 46:7
and they have **b** their flocks and their Gn 46:32
Then Joseph **b** in Jacob his father and Gn 47:7
And Joseph **b** the money into Gn 47:14
So they **b** their livestock to Joseph, and Gn 47:17
So Joseph **b** them near him, and he Gn 48:10
right hand, and **b** them near him. Gn 48:13
up, she **b** him to Pharaoh's daughter, Ex 2:10
when you have **b** the people out of Egypt, Ex 3:12
who has **b** you out from under the Ex 6:7
the field and is not **b** home will die when Ex 9:19
and Aaron were **b** back to Pharaoh. Ex 10:8
and the LORD **b** an east wind upon the Ex 10:13
the east wind had **b** the locusts. Ex 10:13
on this very day I **b** your hosts out of Ex 12:17
the dough that they had **b** out of Egypt, Ex 12:39
very day the LORD **b** the people of Israel Ex 12:51
strong hand the LORD **b** you out from Ex 13:3
hand the LORD has **b** you out of Egypt. Ex 13:9
strong hand the LORD **b** us out of Egypt, Ex 13:14
strong hand the LORD **b** us out of Ex 13:16
the LORD **b** back the waters of the sea Ex 15:19
for you have **b** us out into this Ex 16:3
it was the LORD who **b** you out of the land Ex 16:6
when I **b** you out of the land of Egypt.'" Ex 16:32
how the LORD had **b** Israel out of Egypt. Ex 18:1
b a burnt offering and sacrifices to Ex 18:12
Any hard case they **b** to Moses, but any Ex 18:26
on eagles' wings and **b** you to myself. Ex 19:4
Then Moses **b** the people out of the Ex 19:17
God, who **b** you out of the land of Egypt, Ex 20:2
who **b** them out of the land of Egypt Ex 29:46
the man who **b** us up out of the land of Ex 32:1
were in their ears and **b** them to Aaron. Ex 32:3
who **b** you up out of the land of Egypt!" Ex 32:4
burnt offerings and **b** peace offerings. Ex 32:6
whom you **b** up out of the land of Egypt, Ex 32:7
who **b** you up out of the land of Egypt!'" Ex 32:8
whom you have **b** out of the land of Ex 32:11
to you that you have **b** such a great sin Ex 32:21
the man who **b** us up out of the land of Ex 32:23
people whom you have **b** up out of the Ex 33:1
and **b** the LORD'S contribution to be Ex 35:21
a willing heart **b** brooches and Ex 35:22
rams' skins or goatskins **b** them. Ex 35:23
of silver or bronze **b** it as the LORD'S Ex 35:24
acacia wood of any use in the work **b** it. Ex 35:24
and they all **b** what they had spun in Ex 35:25
And the leaders **b** onyx stones and Ex 35:27
by Moses to be done **b** it as a freewill Ex 35:29
people of Israel had **b** for doing the work Ex 36:3
Then they **b** the tabernacle to Moses, Ex 39:33
And he **b** the ark into the tabernacle Ex 40:21
which any blood is **b** into the tent of Lv 6:30
And Moses **b** Aaron and his sons and Lv 8:6
And Moses **b** Aaron's sons and clothed Lv 8:13
Then he **b** the bull of the sin offering, Lv 8:14
And they **b** what Moses commanded in Lv 9:5
its blood was not **b** into the inner part Lv 10:18
I am the LORD who **b** you up out of the Lv 11:45
then he shall be **b** to Aaron the priest or Lv 13:2
disease, he shall be **b** to the priest, Lv 13:9
his cleansing. He shall be **b** to the priest, Lv 14:2
whose blood was **b** in to make Lv 16:27
whether **b** up in the family or in another Lv 18:9
daughter, **b** up in your father's family, Lv 18:11
who **b** you out of the land of Egypt. Lv 19:36
who **b** you out of the land of Egypt to be Lv 22:33
until you have **b** the offering of your Lv 23:14
from the day that you **b** the sheaf of the Lv 23:15
in booths when I **b** them out of the Lv 23:43
and cursed. Then they **b** him to Moses. Lv 24:11
and they **b** out of the camp the one who Lv 24:23
who **b** you out of the land of Egypt to Lv 25:38
whom I **b** out of the land of Egypt; Lv 25:42
my servants whom I **b** out of the land Lv 25:55
who **b** you out of the land of Egypt, Lv 26:13
contrary to them and **b** them into the Lv 26:41
whom I **b** out of the land of Egypt in the Lv 26:45
he shall be **b** to the entrance of the tent Nm 6:13
and **b** their offerings before the LORD, six Nm 7:3
ox. They **b** them before the tabernacle. Nm 7:3
and it **b** quail from the sea and let Nm 11:31
and after that she may be **b** in again." Nm 12:14
the march till Miriam was **b** in again. Nm 12:15
they also **b** some pomegranates and Nm 13:23
They **b** back word to them and to all Nm 13:26
So they **b** to the people of Israel a bad Nm 13:32
for you **b** up this people in your might Nm 14:13
the men who **b** up a bad report of the Nm 14:37
and they have **b** their offering, Nm 15:25
him gathering sticks **b** him to Moses Nm 15:33
all the congregation **b** him outside Nm 15:36

who **b** you out of the land of Egypt to Nm 15:41
and that he has **b** you near him, and Nm 16:10
thing that you have **b** us up out of Nm 16:13
you have not **b** us into a land flowing Nm 16:14
Then Moses **b** out all the staffs from Nm 17:9
Why have you **b** the assembly of the Nm 20:4
sent an angel and **b** us out of Egypt. Nm 20:16
"Why have you **b** us up out of Egypt to Nm 21:5
Balak took Balaam and **b** him up to Nm 22:41
and said, "From Aram Balak has **b** me, Nm 23:7
Israel came and **b** a Midianite woman Nm 25:6
Moses **b** their case before the LORD. Nm 27:5
Then they **b** the captives and the Nm 31:12
And we have **b** the LORD'S offering, Nm 31:50
and **b** it into the tent of meeting, Nm 31:54
until we have **b** them to their place. Nm 32:17
the fruit of the land and **b** it down to us, Dt 1:25
to us, and **b** us word again and said, Dt 1:25
LORD hated us he has **b** us out of the land Dt 1:27
LORD has taken you and **b** you out of the Dt 4:20
offspring after them and **b** you out of Dt 4:37
God, who **b** you out of the land of Egypt, Dt 5:6
the LORD your God **b** you out from there Dt 5:15
LORD, who **b** you out of the land of Egypt, Dt 6:12
And the LORD **b** us out of Egypt with a Dt 6:21
And he **b** us out from there, that he Dt 6:23
that the LORD has **b** you out with a mighty Dt 7:8
by which the LORD your God **b** you out. Dt 7:19
God, who **b** you out of the land of Egypt, Dt 8:14
who **b** you water out of the flinty rock, Dt 8:15
that the LORD has **b** me in to possess Dt 9:4
whom you have **b** from Egypt have Dt 9:12
whom you have **b** out of Egypt with a Dt 9:26
lest the land from which you **b** us say, Dt 9:28
he has **b** them out to put them to death Dt 9:28
whom you **b** out by your great power Dt 9:29
who **b** you out of the land of Egypt and Dt 13:5
God, who **b** you out of the land of Egypt, Dt 13:10
the LORD your God **b** you out of Egypt Dt 16:1
who **b** you up out of the land of Egypt. Dt 20:1
because he has **b** a bad name upon a Dt 22:19
And the LORD **b** us out of Egypt with a Dt 26:8
And he **b** us into this place and gave us Dt 26:9
with them when he **b** them out of the Dt 29:25
For when I have **b** them into the land Dt 31:20
before I have **b** them into the land that I Dt 31:21
But she had **b** them up to the roof and hid Jos 2:6
spies went in and **b** out Rahab and her Jos 6:23
And they **b** all her relatives and put Jos 6:23
why have you **b** this people over the Jos 7:7
therefore you shall be **b** near by your Jos 7:14
in the morning and **b** Israel near tribe Jos 7:16
And he **b** near the clans of Judah, and Jos 7:17
And he **b** near the clan of the Zerahites Jos 7:17
And he **b** near his household man by Jos 7:18
out of the tent and **b** them to Joshua and Jos 7:23
And they **b** them up to the Valley of Jos 7:24
took alive, and **b** him near to Joshua. Jos 8:23
and **b** those five kings out to him from Jos 10:23
And when they **b** those kings out to Jos 10:24
and I **b** him word again as it was in my Jos 14:7
of Israel, and **b** back word to them. Jos 22:32
the midst of it, and afterward I **b** you out. Jos 24:5
"Then I **b** your fathers out of Egypt, and Jos 24:6
Then I **b** you to the land of the Amorites, Jos 24:8
LORD our God who **b** us and our fathers Jos 24:17
the people of Israel **b** up from Egypt, Jos 24:32
repaid me." And they **b** him to Jerusalem, Jgs 1:7
"I **b** you up from Egypt and brought you Jgs 2:1
up from Egypt and **b** you into the land Jgs 2:1
who had **b** them out of the land of Egypt. Jgs 2:12
milk; she **b** him curds in a noble's bowl. Jgs 5:25
And Israel was **b** very low because of Jgs 6:6
you up from Egypt and **b** you out of the Jgs 6:8
and **b** them to him under the terebinth Jgs 6:19
So he **b** the people down to the water. And Jgs 7:5
and they **b** the heads of Oreb and Zeeb to Jgs 7:25
You have **b** me very low, and you have Jgs 11:35
thirty daughters he **b** in from outside Jgs 12:9
they **b** thirty companions to be with Jgs 14:11
two new ropes and **b** him up from the Jgs 15:13
lords of the Philistines **b** up to her seven Jgs 16:8
up to her and **b** the money in their Jgs 16:18
out his eyes and **b** him down to Gaza Jgs 16:21
and took him and **b** him up and Jgs 16:31
aside and said to him, "Who **b** you here? Jgs 18:3
And she **b** him into her father's house. Jgs 19:3
So he **b** him into his house and gave Jgs 19:21
and they **b** them to the camp at Shiloh, Jgs 21:12
full, and the LORD has **b** me back empty. Ru 1:21
the Almighty has **b** calamity upon me?" Ru 1:21
She also **b** out and gave her what food Ru 2:18
and she **b** him to the house of the 1 Sm 1:24
the bull, and they **b** the child to Eli. 1 Sm 1:25
All that the fork **b** up the priest would 1 Sm 2:14

sent to Shiloh and **b** from there the ark 1 Sm 4:4
He who **b** the news answered and said, 1 Sm 4:17
they **b** it from Ebenezer to Ashdod. 1 Sm 5:1
the ark of God and **b** it into the house 1 Sm 5:2
God of Israel be **b** around to Gath." So 1 Sm 5:8
to Gath." So they **b** the ark of the 1 Sm 5:8
But after they had **b** it around, the 1 Sm 5:9
"They have **b** around to us the ark of 1 Sm 5:10
ark of the LORD and **b** it to the house of 1 Sm 7:1
from the day I **b** them up out of Egypt 1 Sm 8:8
his young man and **b** them into the 1 Sm 9:22
of Israel, 'I **b** up Israel out of Egypt, 1 Sm 10:18
Then Samuel **b** all the tribes of 1 Sm 10:20
He **b** the tribe of Benjamin near by 1 Sm 10:21
despised him and **b** him no present. 1 Sm 10:27
and Aaron and **b** your fathers up 1 Sm 12:6
who **b** your fathers out of Egypt and 1 Sm 12:8
one of the people **b** his ox with him 1 Sm 14:34
"They have **b** them from the 1 Sm 15:15
I have **b** Agag the king of Amalek, 1 Sm 15:20
And he sent and **b** him in. Now he 1 Sm 16:12
the Philistine and **b** it to Jerusalem, 1 Sm 17:54
and **b** him before Saul with the head 1 Sm 17:57
And David **b** their foreskins, 1 Sm 18:27
because his deeds have **b** good to you. 1 Sm 19:4
And Jonathan **b** David to Saul, and he 1 Sm 19:7
for you have **b** your servant into a 1 Sm 20:8
For I have **b** neither my sword nor my 1 Sm 21:8
Why then have you **b** him to me? 1 Sm 21:14
that you have **b** this fellow to behave 1 Sm 21:15
the Philistines and **b** away their 1 Sm 23:5
that your servant has **b** to my lord 1 Sm 25:27
from her hand what she had **b** him. 1 Sm 25:35
ephod." So Abiathar **b** the ephod to 1 Sm 30:7
open country and **b** him to David. 1 Sm 30:11
had been taken. David **b** back all. 1 Sm 30:19
and I have **b** them here to my lord." 2 Sm 1:10
And David **b** up his men who were 2 Sm 2:3
son of Saul and **b** him over to 2 Sm 2:8
and they **b** him back from the cistern 2 Sm 3:26
and **b** the head of Ish-bosheth to David 2 Sm 4:8
it was you who led out and **b** in Israel. 2 Sm 5:2
on a new cart and **b** it out of the house 2 Sm 6:3
So David went and **b** up the ark of 2 Sm 6:12
all the house of Israel **b** up the ark of 2 Sm 6:15
And they **b** in the ark of the LORD and 2 Sm 6:17
house since the day I **b** up the people of 2 Sm 7:6
house, that you have **b** me thus far? 2 Sm 7:18
you have **b** about all this greatness, 2 Sm 7:21
servants to David and **b** tribute. 2 Sm 8:2
servants to David and **b** tribute. 2 Sm 8:6
of Hadadezer and **b** them to Jerusalem. 2 Sm 8:7
And Joram **b** with him articles of 2 Sm 8:10
King David sent and **b** him from the 2 Sm 9:5
Hadadezer sent and **b** out the Syrians 2 Sm 10:16
David sent and **b** her to his house, 2 Sm 11:27
which he had bought. And he **b** it up, 2 Sm 12:3
And he **b** out the spoil of the city, a 2 Sm 12:30
And he **b** out the people who were in 2 Sm 12:31
she had made and **b** them into the 2 Sm 13:10
But when she **b** them near him to 2 Sm 13:11
sent to Tekoa and **b** from there a wise 2 Sm 14:2
to Geshur and **b** Absalom to 2 Sm 14:23
"Why have you **b** these?" Ziba 2 Sm 16:2
b beds, basins, and earthen vessels, 2 Sm 17:28
of Israel, **b** the king on his way. 2 Sm 19:40
stolen you away and **b** the king and 2 Sm 19:41
And he **b** up from there the bones of 2 Sm 21:13
He **b** me out into a broad place; he 2 Sm 22:20
me vengeance and **b** down peoples 2 Sm 22:48
who **b** me out from my enemies; you 2 Sm 22:49
And the LORD **b** about a great victory 2 Sm 23:10
gate and carried and **b** it to David. 2 Sm 23:16
Shunammite, and **b** her to the king. 1 Kgs 1:3
Has this thing been **b** about by my 1 Kgs 1:27
David's mule and **b** him to Gihon. 1 Kgs 1:38
and they **b** him down from the altar. 1 Kgs 1:53
and had a seat **b** for the king's 1 Kgs 2:19
here." Then Benaiah **b** the king word 1 Kgs 2:30
Shimei went and **b** his servants from 1 Kgs 2:40
Pharaoh's daughter and **b** her into the 1 Kgs 3:1
So a sword was **b** before the king. 1 Kgs 3:24
They **b** tribute and served Solomon 1 Kgs 4:21
and swift steeds they **b** to the place 1 Kgs 4:28
Solomon sent and **b** Hiram from 1 Kgs 7:13
And Solomon **b** in the things that 1 Kgs 7:51
And they **b** up the ark of the LORD, the 1 Kgs 8:4
the priests and the Levites **b** them up. 1 Kgs 8:4
Then the priests **b** the ark of the 1 Kgs 8:6
the day that I **b** my people Israel out 1 Kgs 8:16
when he **b** them out of the land of 1 Kgs 8:21
heritage, which you **b** out of Egypt, 1 Kgs 8:51
when you **b** our fathers out of Egypt, 1 Kgs 8:53
LORD their God who **b** their fathers out 1 Kgs 9:9
the LORD has **b** all this disaster 1 Kgs 9:9

went to Ophir and **b** from there gold, 1 Kgs 9:28
and they **b** it to King Solomon. 1 Kgs 9:28
of Hiram, which **b** gold from Ophir, 1 Kgs 10:11
b from Ophir a very great amount 1 Kgs 10:11
Every one of them **b** his present, 1 Kgs 10:25
a turn of affairs **b** about by the LORD 1 Kgs 12:15
who **b** you up out of the land of 1 Kgs 12:28
to the prophet who had **b** him back. 1 Kgs 13:20
the prophet whom he had **b** back. 1 Kgs 13:23
prophet who had **b** him back from 1 Kgs 13:26
it on the donkey and **b** it back to the 1 Kgs 13:29
carried them and **b** them back to 1 Kgs 14:28
And he **b** into the house of the LORD 1 Kgs 15:15
And the ravens **b** him bread and 1 Kgs 17:6
have you **b** calamity even upon the 1 Kgs 17:20
the child and **b** him down from 1 Kgs 17:23
And Elijah **b** them down to the 1 Kgs 18:40
messengers departed and **b** him word 1 Kgs 20:9
a soldier turned and **b** a man to me 1 Kgs 20:39
the worthless men **b** a charge 1 Kgs 21:13
the king died, and was **b** to Samaria. 1 Kgs 22:37
and put salt in it." So they **b** it to him. 2 Kgs 2:20
as she poured they **b** the vessels to her. 2 Kgs 4:5
had lifted him and **b** him to his 2 Kgs 4:20
And he **b** the letter to the king of Israel, 2 Kgs 5:6
accepting from his hand what he **b**. 2 Kgs 5:20
"They have **b** the heads of the king's 2 Kgs 10:8
of Baal." So he **b** out the vestments 2 Kgs 10:22
and they **b** out the pillar that was in 2 Kgs 10:26
Jehoiada sent and **b** the captains of 2 Kgs 11:4
and they each **b** his men who were to 2 Kgs 11:9
Then he **b** out the king's son and 2 Kgs 11:12
and they **b** the king down from the 2 Kgs 11:19
holy things that is **b** into the house of 2 Kgs 12:4
the money that was **b** into the house 2 Kgs 12:9
the money that was **b** into the house 2 Kgs 12:13
offerings was not **b** into the house 2 Kgs 12:16
And they **b** him on horses; and he 2 Kgs 14:20
who had **b** them up out of the land of 2 Kgs 17:7
king of Assyria **b** people from 2 Kgs 17:24
who **b** you out of the land of Egypt 2 Kgs 17:36
and he **b** the shadow back ten steps, 2 Kgs 20:11
and the conduit and **b** water into the 2 Kgs 20:20
money that has been **b** into the house 2 Kgs 22:4
place.'" And they **b** back word to 2 Kgs 22:20
And he **b** out the Asherah from the 2 Kgs 23:6
And he **b** all the priests out of the 2 Kgs 23:8
from Megiddo and **b** him to 2 Kgs 23:30
king of Babylon **b** captive to 2 Kgs 24:16
captured the king and **b** him up to 2 Kgs 25:6
guard took them and **b** them to the 2 Kgs 25:20
of Manasseh, and **b** them to Halah, 1 Chr 5:26
them when they were **b** in and taken 1 Chr 9:28
of his sons, and **b** them to Jabesh. 1 Chr 10:12
was you who led out and **b** in Israel. 1 Chr 11:2
gate and took it and **b** it to David. 1 Chr 11:18
of their lives they **b** it." Therefore he 1 Chr 11:19
and the LORD **b** the fear of him upon 1 Chr 14:17
So all Israel **b** up the ark of the 1 Chr 15:28
And they **b** in the ark of God and set 1 Chr 16:1
since the day I **b** up Israel to this 1 Chr 17:5
house, that you have **b** me thus far? 1 Chr 17:16
servants to David and **b** tribute. 1 Chr 18:2
servants to David and **b** tribute. 1 Chr 18:6
of Hadadezer and **b** them to 1 Chr 18:7
sent messengers and **b** out the 1 Chr 19:16
And he **b** out the spoil of the city, a 1 Chr 20:2
And he **b** out the people who were in 1 Chr 20:3
and Tyrians **b** great quantities 1 Chr 22:4
of God may be **b** into a house built 1 Chr 22:19
(But David had **b** up the ark of God 2 Chr 1:4
And Solomon **b** in the things that 2 Chr 5:1
And they **b** up the ark, the tent of 2 Chr 5:5
tent; the Levitical priests **b** them up. 2 Chr 5:5
Then the priests **b** the ark of the 2 Chr 5:7
'Since the day that I **b** my people out of 2 Chr 6:5
of their fathers who **b** them out of the 2 Chr 7:22
Therefore he has **b** all this disaster 2 Chr 7:22
Solomon **b** Pharaoh's daughter up 2 Chr 8:11
of Solomon and **b** from there 450 2 Chr 8:18
talents of gold and **b** it to King 2 Chr 8:18
of Solomon, who **b** gold from Ophir, 2 Chr 9:10
b algum wood and precious stones. 2 Chr 9:10
besides what she had **b** to the king. 2 Chr 9:12
the explorers and merchants **b**. 2 Chr 9:14
of the land **b** gold and silver 2 Chr 9:14
Every one of them **b** his present, 2 Chr 9:24
a turn of affairs **b** about by God 2 Chr 10:15
carried them and **b** them back to 2 Chr 12:11
spoil that they had **b** 700 oxen and 2 Chr 15:11
And he **b** into the house of God the 2 Chr 15:18
And all Judah **b** tribute to 2 Chr 17:5
the Philistines **b** Jehoshaphat 2 Chr 17:11
the Arabians also **b** him 7,700 rams 2 Chr 17:11
and **b** them back to the LORD, 2 Chr 19:4

and he was **b** to Jehu and put to 2 Chr 22:9
and they each **b** his men, 2 Chr 23:8
Then they **b** out the king's son and 2 Chr 23:11
Jehoiada the priest **b** out the 2 Chr 23:14
and they **b** the king down from the 2 Chr 23:20
people rejoiced and **b** their tax and 2 Chr 24:10
the chest was **b** to the king's 2 Chr 24:11
they **b** the rest of the money before 2 Chr 24:14
he **b** the gods of the men of Seir and 2 Chr 25:14
and **b** him to Jerusalem and broke 2 Chr 25:23
And they **b** him upon horses, and 2 Chr 25:28
his people and **b** them to Damascus. 2 Chr 28:5
spoil from them and **b** the spoil to 2 Chr 28:8
they **b** them to their kinsfolk at 2 Chr 28:15
He **b** in the priests and the Levites 2 Chr 29:4
and they **b** out all the uncleanness 2 Chr 29:16
And they **b** seven bulls, seven rams, 2 Chr 29:21
the sin offering were **b** to the king 2 Chr 29:23
And the assembly **b** sacrifices and 2 Chr 29:31
of a willing heart **b** burnt offerings. 2 Chr 29:31
that the assembly **b** was 70 bulls, 2 Chr 29:32
themselves and **b** burnt offerings 2 Chr 30:15
And they **b** in abundantly the tithe of 2 Chr 31:5
cities of Judah also **b** in the tithe of 2 Chr 31:6
And they faithfully **b** in the 2 Chr 31:12
And many **b** gifts to the LORD to 2 Chr 32:23
Therefore the LORD **b** upon them the 2 Chr 33:11
of bronze and **b** him to Babylon. 2 Chr 33:11
heard his plea and **b** him again to 2 Chr 33:13
that had been **b** into the house 2 Chr 34:9
that had been **b** into the house 2 Chr 34:14
Shaphan **b** the book to the king, 2 Chr 34:16
And they **b** back word 2 Chr 34:28
second chariot and **b** him to 2 Chr 35:24
Nebuchadnezzar sent and **b** him to 2 Chr 36:10
Therefore he **b** up against them the 2 Chr 36:17
princes, all these he **b** to Babylon. 2 Chr 36:18
Cyrus the king also **b** out the vessels of Ezr 1:7
Cyrus king of Persia **b** these out in Ezr 1:8
the exiles were **b** up from Babylonia Ezr 1:11
king of Assyria who **b** us here." Ezr 4:2
was in Jerusalem and **b** into the temple Ezr 5:14
that is in Jerusalem and **b** to Babylon, Ezr 6:5
be restored and **b** back to the temple that Ezr 6:5
on us, they **b** us a man of discretion, Ezr 8:18
and I **b** charges against the nobles and Neh 5:7
So Ezra the priest **b** the Law before the Neh 8:2
people went out and **b** them and made Neh 8:16
who chose Abram and **b** him out of Ur Neh 9:7
for their hunger and **b** water for them Neh 9:15
'This is your God who **b** you up out of Neh 9:18
and you **b** them into the land that you Neh 9:23
Then I **b** the leaders of Judah up onto Neh 12:31
and I **b** back there the vessels of the Neh 13:9
Then all Judah **b** the tithe of the Neh 13:12
which they **b** into Jerusalem on the Neh 13:15
b in fish and all kinds of goods and Neh 13:16
no load might be **b** in on the Sabbath Neh 13:19
Queen Vashti to be **b** before him, Est 1:17
just as when she was **b** up by him. Est 2:20
and he sent and **b** his friends and his Est 5:10
let royal robes be **b**, which the king has Est 6:8
"Now a word was **b** to me stealthily; my Jb 4:12
schemes of the wily are **b** to a quick end. Jb 5:13
it; they are **b** low, and he perceives it not. Jb 14:21
Or were you **b** forth before the hills? Jb 15:7
which he trusted and is **b** to the king of Jb 18:14
they are **b** low and gathered up like all Jb 24:24
when they **b** a complaint against me, Jb 31:13
the evil that the LORD had **b** upon him. Jb 42:11
He **b** me out into a broad place; he Ps 18:19
LORD, you have **b** up my soul from Sheol; Ps 30:3
be condemned when he is **b** to trial. Ps 37:33
be turned back and **b** to dishonor who Ps 40:14
how he has **b** desolations on the earth. Ps 46:8
Behold, I was **b** forth in iniquity, and in Ps 51:5
They are **b** to ruin, with their own Ps 64:8
tell what God has **b** about and ponder Ps 64:9
You **b** us into the net; you laid a Ps 66:11
yet you have **b** us out to a place of Ps 66:12
who seek you be **b** to dishonor through Ps 69:6
be turned back and **b** to dishonor who Ps 70:2
And he **b** them to his holy land, to the Ps 78:54
the nursing ewes he **b** him to shepherd Ps 78:71
speedily to meet us, for we are **b** very low. Ps 79:8
You **b** a vine out of Egypt; you drove out Ps 80:8
who **b** you up out of the land of Egypt. Ps 81:10
Before the mountains were **b** forth, or Ps 90:2
For we are **b** to an end by your anger; by Ps 90:7
Then he **b** out Israel with silver and Ps 105:37
They asked, and he **b** quail, and gave Ps 105:40
So he **b** his people out with joy, his Ps 105:43
and they were **b** into subjection under Ps 106:42
purposes and were **b** low through their Ps 106:43
He **b** them out of darkness and the Ps 107:14

and he **b** them to their desired haven. Ps 107:30
are diminished and **b** low through Ps 107:39
simple; when I was **b** low, he saved me. Ps 116:6
and **b** Israel out from among them, for Ps 136:11
Attend to my cry, for I am **b** very low! Ps 142:6
there were no depths I was **b** forth, Prv 8:24
shaped, before the hills, I was **b** forth, Prv 8:25
all the daughters of song are **b** low— Eccl 12:4
The king has **b** me into his chambers. Sg 1:4
He **b** me to the banqueting house, and his Sg 2:4
go until I had **b** him into my mother's Sg 3:4
"Children have I reared and **b** up, but they Is 1:2
and each one is **b** low—do not forgive Is 2:9
haughty looks of man shall be **b** low, Is 2:11
all that is lifted up—and it shall be **b** low; Is 2:12
and the lofty pride of men shall be **b** low, Is 2:17
them! For they have **b** evil on themselves. Is 3:9
Man is humbled, and each one is **b** low, Is 5:15
and the eyes of the haughty are **b** low. Is 5:15
the former time he **b** into contempt the Is 9:1
hewn down, and the lofty will be **b** low. Is 10:33
Your pomp is **b** down to Sheol, the Is 14:11
But you are **b** down to Sheol, to the far Is 14:15
glory of Moab will be **b** into contempt, Is 16:14
that day the glory of Jacob will be **b** low, Is 17:4
that time tribute will be **b** to the LORD of Is 18:7
young men nor **b** up young women." Is 23:4
And you will be **b** low; from the earth you Is 29:4
You have not **b** me your sheep for burnt Is 43:23
I have **b** him, and he will prosper in his Is 48:15
and put away, but who has **b** up these? Is 49:21
hand among all the sons she has **b** up. Is 51:18
was the chastisement that **b** us peace, Is 53:5
offering, you have **b** a grain offering. Is 57:6
then his own arm **b** him salvation, and Is 59:16
so my own arm **b** me salvation, and my Is 63:5
Where is he who **b** them up out of the Is 63:11
Shall a nation be **b** forth in one moment? Is 66:8
was in labor she **b** forth her children. Is 66:8
'Where is the LORD who **b** us up from the Jer 2:6
And I **b** you into a plentiful land to enjoy Jer 2:7
Have you not **b** this upon yourself by Jer 2:17
and your deeds have **b** this upon you. Jer 4:18
in the day that I **b** them out of the land Jer 7:22
of Jerusalem shall be **b** out of their tombs. Jer 8:1
Beaten silver is **b** from Tarshish, and Jer 10:9
your fathers when I **b** them out of the Jer 11:4
your fathers when I **b** them up out of Jer 11:7
Therefore I **b** upon them all the words of Jer 11:8
I have **b** against the mothers of young Jer 15:8
the LORD lives who **b** up the people of Jer 16:14
the LORD lives who **b** up the people of Jer 16:15
be the man who **b** the news to my Jer 20:15
'As the LORD lives who **b** up the people of Jer 23:7
'As the LORD lives who **b** up and led the Jer 23:8
workers, and had **b** them to Babylon, Jer 24:1
Uriah from Egypt and **b** him to King Jer 26:23
now shortly be **b** back from Babylon,' Jer 27:16
You **b** your people Israel out of the land Jer 32:21
Just as I have **b** all this great disaster Jer 32:42
and **b** them into subjection as slaves. Jer 34:11
your fathers when I **b** them out of the Jer 34:13
and you **b** them into subjection to be Jer 34:16
I **b** them to the house of the LORD into the Jer 35:4
and seized Jeremiah and **b** him to the Jer 37:14
they **b** him up to Nebuchadnezzar king Jer 39:5
The LORD has **b** it about, and has done as Jer 40:3
whom Johanan **b** back from Gibeon. Jer 41:16
the disaster that I **b** upon Jerusalem and Jer 44:2
also, O Madmen, shall be **b** to silence; Jer 48:2
his armory and **b** out the weapons Jer 50:25
The LORD has **b** about our vindication; Jer 51:10
captured the king and **b** him up to the Jer 52:9
guard took them and **b** them to the Jer 52:26
king of Judah and **b** him out of prison. Jer 52:31
my sorrow, which was **b** upon me, Lam 1:12
You have **b** the day you announced; Lam 1:21
he has **b** down to the ground in Lam 2:2
he has driven and **b** me into darkness Lam 3:2
those who were **b** up in purple embrace Lam 4:5
earth and heaven and **b** me in visions of Ezk 8:3
And he **b** me to the entrance of the court, Ezk 8:7
Then he **b** me to the entrance of the Ezk 8:14
And he **b** me into the inner court of the Ezk 8:16
writing case at his waist, **b** back word, Ezk 9:11
Spirit lifted me up and **b** me to the east Ezk 11:1
but you shall be **b** out of the midst of it. Ezk 11:7
lifted me up and **b** me in the vision Ezk 11:24
I **b** out my baggage by day, as baggage Ezk 12:7
I **b** out my baggage at dusk, carrying it Ezk 12:7
sons and daughters who will be **b** out; Ezk 14:22
disaster that I have **b** upon Jerusalem, Ezk 14:22
Jerusalem, for all that I have **b** upon it. Ezk 14:22
and her princes and **b** them to him to Ezk 17:12
And she **b** up one of her cubs; he Ezk 19:3
and they **b** him with hooks to the land Ezk 19:4
him in a cage and **b** him to the king of Ezk 19:9
they **b** him into custody, that his voice Ezk 19:9
land of Egypt and **b** them into the Ezk 20:10
in whose sight I had **b** them out. Ezk 20:14
in whose sight I had **b** them out. Ezk 20:22
For when I had **b** them into the land Ezk 20:28
made, and you have **b** your days near, Ezk 22:4
have **b** this upon you, because you Ezk 23:30
sort drunkards were **b** from the Ezk 23:42
they **b** you in payment ivory tusks Ezk 27:15
"Your rowers have **b** you out into the Ezk 27:26
so I **b** fire out from your midst; Ezk 28:18
field, and not be **b** together or gathered. Ezk 29:5
shall be **b** in to destroy the land, Ezk 30:11
You shall be **b** down with the trees of Ezk 31:18
up, the strayed you have not **b** back, Ezk 34:4
and he **b** me out in the Spirit of the Ezk 37:1
Its people were **b** out from the peoples Ezk 38:8
it is coming and it will be **b** about, Ezk 39:8
when I have **b** them back from the Ezk 39:27
was upon me, and he **b** me to the city. Ezk 40:1
In visions of God he **b** me to the land of Ezk 40:2
When he **b** me there, behold, there was Ezk 40:3
for you were **b** here in order that I Ezk 40:4
Then he **b** me into the outer court. Ezk 40:17
Then he **b** me to the inner court Ezk 40:28
Then he **b** me to the inner court on Ezk 40:32
Then he **b** me to the north gate, and Ezk 40:35
Then he **b** me to the vestibule of the Ezk 40:48
Then he **b** me to the nave and Ezk 41:1
and he **b** me to the chambers that were Ezk 42:1
lifted me up and **b** me into the inner Ezk 43:5
Then he **b** me back to the outer gate of Ezk 44:1
Then he **b** me by way of the north gate Ezk 44:4
Then he **b** me through the entrance, Ezk 46:19
Then he **b** me out to the outer court Ezk 46:21
Then he **b** me back to the door of the Ezk 47:1
Then he **b** me out by way of the north Ezk 47:2
And he **b** them to the land of Shinar, to Dn 1:2
commanded that they should be **b** in, Dn 1:18
chief of the eunuchs **b** them in before Dn 1:18
Then Arioch **b** in Daniel before the Dn 2:25
Meshach, and Abednego be **b**. Dn 3:13
So they **b** these men before the king. Dn 3:13
men of Babylon should be **b** before me, Dn 4:6
taken out of the temple in Jerusalem be **b**, Dn 5:2
Then they **b** in the golden vessels that Dn 5:3
Then Daniel was **b** in before the king. Dn 5:13
whom the king my father **b** from Judah. Dn 5:13
have been **b** in before me to read this Dn 5:15
he was **b** down from his kingly throne, Dn 5:20
of his house have been **b** in before you, Dn 5:23
of your kingdom and **b** it to an end; Dn 5:26
and Daniel was **b** and cast into the den Dn 6:16
And a stone was **b** and laid on the Dn 6:17
no diversions were **b** to him, and sleep Dn 6:18
accused Daniel were **b** and cast into Dn 6:24
ready the calamity and has **b** it upon us, Dn 9:14
who **b** your people out of the land of Dn 9:15
a prophet the LORD **b** Israel up from Hos 12:13
Also it was I who **b** you up out of the Am 2:10
the whole family that I **b** up out of the Am 3:1
yet you **b** up my life from the pit, O LORD Jon 2:6
For I **b** you up from the land of Egypt and Mi 6:4
And when you **b** it home, I blew it away. Hg 1:9
all Syria, and they **b** him all the sick, Mt 4:24
That evening they **b** to him many who Mt 8:16
behold, some people **b** to him a paralytic, Mt 9:2
man who was mute was **b** to him. Mt 9:32
heaven? You will be **b** down to Hades. Mt 11:23
who was blind and mute was **b** to him, Mt 12:22
and his head was **b** on a platter and Mt 14:11
to the girl, and she **b** it to her mother. Mt 14:11
to all that region and **b** to him all who Mt 14:35
themselves, saying, "We **b** no bread." Mt 16:7
And I **b** him to your disciples, and they Mt 17:16
one was **b** to him who owed him ten Mt 18:24
Then children were **b** to him that he Mt 19:13
They **b** the donkey and the colt and put Mt 21:7
the tax." And they **b** him a denarius. Mt 22:19
changed his mind and **b** back the thirty Mt 27:3
evening at sundown they **b** to him all Mk 1:32
"Is a lamp **b** in to be put under a basket, Mk 4:21
and **b** his head on a platter and gave it Mk 6:28
And they **b** to him a man who was deaf Mk 7:32
And some people **b** to him a blind man Mk 8:22
him, "Teacher, I **b** my son to you, Mk 9:17
And they **b** the boy to him. And when Mk 9:20
And they **b** the colt to Jesus and threw Mk 11:7
And they **b** one. And he said to them, Mk 12:16
And they **b** him to the place called Mk 15:22
he has **b** down the mighty from their Lk 1:52
they **b** him up to Jerusalem to present Lk 2:22
and when the parents **b** in the child Lk 2:27
to Nazareth, where he had been **b** up. Lk 4:16
out of the town and **b** him to the brow of Lk 4:29
with various diseases **b** them to him, Lk 4:40
And when they had **b** their boats to Lk 5:11
house, **b** an alabaster flask of ointment, Lk 7:37
heaven? You shall be **b** down to Hades. Lk 10:15
his own animal and **b** him to an inn Lk 10:34
and charges were **b** to him that this Lk 16:1
and commanded him to be **b** to him. Lk 18:40
And they **b** it to Jesus, and throwing Lk 19:35
and you will be **b** before kings and Lk 21:12
of them arose and **b** him before Pilate. Lk 23:1
"You **b** me this man as one who was Lk 23:14
He **b** him to Jesus. Jesus looked at him Jn 1:42
"Has anyone **b** him something to eat?" Jn 4:33
scribes and the Pharisees **b** a woman who Jn 8:3
They **b** to the Pharisees the man who Jn 9:13
When he has **b** out all his own, he goes Jn 10:4
kept watch at the door, and **b** Peter in. Jn 18:16
he **b** Jesus out and sat down on the Jn 19:13
houses sold them and **b** the proceeds of Acts 4:34
belonged to him and **b** the money and Acts 4:37
of the proceeds and **b** only a part of Acts 5:2
the prison doors and **b** them out, Acts 5:19
and sent to the prison to have them **b**. Acts 5:21
with the officers went and **b** them, Acts 5:26
And when they had **b** them, they set Acts 5:27
and seized him and **b** him before the Acts 6:12
And he was **b** up for three months in Acts 7:20
adopted him and **b** him up as Acts 7:21
Our fathers in turn **b** it in with Joshua Acts 7:45
by the hand and **b** him into Damascus. Acts 9:8
Barnabas took him and **b** him to the Acts 9:27
they **b** him down to Caesarea and sent Acts 9:30
had found him, he **b** him to Antioch. Acts 11:26
how the Lord had **b** him out of the Acts 12:17
man's offspring God has **b** to Israel a Acts 13:23
b oxen and garlands to the gates and Acts 14:13
and **b** great joy to all the brothers. Acts 15:3
of divination and **b** her owners much Acts 16:16
And when they had **b** them to the Acts 16:20
Then he **b** them out and said, "Sirs, Acts 16:30
Then he **b** them up into his house Acts 16:34
who conducted Paul **b** him as far Acts 17:15
hold of him and **b** him to the Acts 17:19
attack on Paul and **b** him before the Acts 18:12
practiced magic arts **b** their books Acts 19:19
b no little business to the craftsmen. Acts 19:24
For you have **b** these men here who Acts 19:37
he even **b** Greeks into the temple and Acts 21:28
that Paul had **b** him into the Acts 21:29
him to be **b** into the barracks. Acts 21:34
was about to be **b** into the barracks, Acts 21:37
Tarsus in Cilicia, but **b** up in this city, Acts 22:3
him to be **b** into the barracks, Acts 22:24
and he **b** Paul down and set him Acts 22:30
he took him and **b** him to the tribune Acts 23:18
him, I **b** him down to their council. Acts 23:28
took Paul and **b** him by night to Acts 23:31
the tribunal and ordered Paul to be **b**. Acts 25:6
tribunal and ordered the man to be **b**. Acts 25:17
they **b** no charge in his case of such Acts 25:18
command of Festus, Paul was **b** in. Acts 25:23
Therefore I have **b** him before you Acts 25:26
so it was that all were **b** safely to land. Acts 27:44
After we were **b** safely through, we Acts 28:1
one trespass **b** condemnation, Rom 5:16
many trespasses **b** justification. Rom 5:16
the body of sin might be **b** to nothing, Rom 6:6
those who have been **b** from death to Rom 6:13
its glory, which was being **b** to an end, 2 Cor 3:7
if what was being **b** to an end came 2 Cor 3:11
of what was being **b** to an end. 2 Cor 3:13
of false brothers secretly **b** in—who Gal 2:4
far off have been **b** near by the blood Eph 2:13
I know how to be **b** low, and I know Phil 4:12
and has **b** us the good news of your 1 Thes 3:6
if she has **b** up children, has shown 1 Tm 5:10
for we **b** nothing into the world, and 1 Tm 6:7
abolished death and **b** life and 2 Tm 1:10
whose blood is **b** into the holy Heb 13:11
God of peace who **b** again from the Heb 13:20
Of his own will he **b** us forth by the Jas 1:18
the grace that will be **b** to you at the 1 Pt 1:13
persons, were **b** safely through water. 1 Pt 3:20
when he **b** a flood upon the world of the 2 Pt 2:5
and who was, for you **b** these judgments. Rv 16:5

BROW (2)

and on the **b** of him who was set apart Gn 49:26
and brought him to the **b** of the hill on Lk 4:29

BRUISE (2)

and her offspring; he shall **b** your head, Gn 3:15
your head, and you shall **b** his heel." Gn 3:15

BRUISED (4)
that has its testicles **b** or crushed or Lv 22:24
they beat me, they **b** me, they took away Sg 5:7
a **b** reed he will not break, and a faintly Is 42:3
a **b** reed he will not break, and a Mt 12:20

BRUISES (1)
in it, but **b** and sores and raw wounds; Is 1:6

BRUISING (1)
crying out and **b** himself with stones. Mk 5:5

BRUSHWOOD (2)
cut down a bundle of **b** and took it up Jgs 9:48
as when fire kindles **b** and the fire causes Is 64:2

BRUTAL (1)
self-control, **b**, not loving good, 2 Tm 3:3

BRUTISH (2)
I was **b** and ignorant; I was like a beast Ps 73:22
deliver you into the hands of **b** men, Ezk 21:31

BUBBLING (1)
the fountain of wisdom is a **b** brook. Prv 18:4

BUCKET (1)
the nations are like a drop from a **b**, Is 40:15

BUCKETS (1)
Water shall flow from his **b**, and his Nm 24:7

BUCKLER (5)
hold of shield and **b** and rise for my Ps 35:2
refuge; his faithfulness is a shield and **b**. Ps 91:4
"Prepare **b** and shield, and advance for Jer 46:3
against you on every side with **b**, Ezk 23:24
host, all of them with **b** and shield, Ezk 38:4

BUCKLERS (1)
weapons and burn them, shields and **b**, Ezk 39:9

BUD (2)
was in the ear and the flax was in **b**. Ex 9:31
of water it will **b** and put out branches Jb 14:9

BUDDED (5)
As soon as it **b**, its blossoms shot forth, Gn 40:10
the valley, to see whether the vines had **b**, Sg 6:11
and see whether the vines have **b**, Sg 7:12
the rod has blossomed; pride has **b**. Ezk 7:10
the manna, and Aaron's staff that **b**, Heb 9:4

BUDS (1)
and put forth **b** and produced Nm 17:8

BUFFETED (1)
poorly dressed and **b** and homeless, 1 Cor 4:11

BUGLE (1)
And if the **b** gives an indistinct 1 Cor 14:8

BUILD (142)
let us **b** ourselves a city and a tower with Gn 11:4
stone, you shall not **b** it of hewn stones, Ex 20:25
to Balak, "**B** for me here seven altars, Nm 23:1
"**B** for me here seven altars and Nm 23:29
"We will **b** sheepfolds here for our Nm 32:16
B cities for your little ones and folds Nm 32:24
great and good cities that you did not **b**, Dt 6:10
that you may **b** siegeworks against the Dt 20:20
"When you **b** a new house, you shall Dt 22:8
man who does not **b** up his brother's Dt 25:9
And there you shall **b** an altar to the Dt 27:5
you shall **b** an altar to the LORD your God Dt 27:6
shall ravish her. You shall **b** a house, Dt 28:30
we said, 'Let us now **b** an altar, Jos 22:26
and **b** an altar to the LORD your God on Jgs 6:26
And I will **b** him a sure house, and he 1 Sm 2:35
Would you **b** me a house to dwell in? 2 Sm 7:5
He shall **b** a house for my name, and I 2 Sm 7:13
servant, saying, 'I will **b** you a house.' 2 Sm 7:27
in order to **b** an altar to the LORD, 2 Sm 24:21
"**B** yourself a house in Jerusalem and 1 Kgs 2:36
my father could not **b** a house for the 1 Kgs 5:3
And so I intend to **b** a house for the 1 Kgs 5:5
place, shall **b** the house for my name.' 1 Kgs 5:5
timber and the stone to **b** the house. 1 Kgs 5:18
he began to **b** the house of the LORD. 1 Kgs 6:1
tribes of Israel in which to **b** a house, 1 Kgs 8:16
David my father to **b** a house for the 1 Kgs 8:17
was in your heart to **b** a house for my 1 Kgs 8:18
you shall not **b** the house, 1 Kgs 8:19
born to you shall **b** the house for my 1 Kgs 8:19
and all that Solomon desired to **b**, 1 Kgs 9:1
Solomon drafted to **b** the house of 1 Kgs 9:15
Solomon desired to **b** in Jerusalem, 1 Kgs 9:19
with you and will **b** you a sure 1 Kgs 11:38
and carpenters to **b** a house for 1 Chr 14:1
is not you who will **b** me a house to 1 Chr 17:4
that the LORD will **b** you a house. 1 Chr 17:10
He shall **b** a house for me, and I will 1 Chr 17:12
servant that you will **b** a house for 1 Chr 17:25
floor that I may **b** on it an altar 1 Chr 21:22
and charged him to **b** a house for the 1 Chr 22:6
it in my heart to **b** a house to the 1 Chr 22:7
You shall not **b** a house to my name, 1 Chr 22:8
He shall **b** a house for my name. He 1 Chr 22:10
Arise and **b** the sanctuary of the 1 Chr 22:19
it in my heart to **b** a house of rest for 1 Chr 28:2
'You may not **b** a house for my 1 Chr 28:3
your son who shall **b** my house and 1 Chr 28:6
has chosen you to **b** a house for the 1 Chr 28:10
and that he may **b** the palace for 1 Chr 29:19
Solomon purposed to **b** a temple for 2 Chr 2:1
sent him cedar to **b** himself a house to 2 Chr 2:3
I am about to **b** a house for the name 2 Chr 2:4
The house that I am to **b** will be great, 2 Chr 2:5
But who is able to **b** him a house, 2 Chr 2:6
him? Who am I to **b** a house for him, 2 Chr 2:6
the house I am to **b** will be great and 2 Chr 2:9
who will **b** a temple for the LORD and 2 Chr 2:12
Solomon began to **b** the house of 2 Chr 3:1
He began to **b** in the second month of 2 Chr 3:2
tribes of Israel in which to **b** a house, 2 Chr 6:5
of David my father to **b** a house for the 2 Chr 6:7
was in your heart to **b** a house for my 2 Chr 6:8
it is not you who shall **b** the house, 2 Chr 6:9
born to you shall **b** the house for my 2 Chr 6:9
Solomon desired to **b** in Jerusalem, 2 Chr 8:6
"Let us **b** these cities and surround 2 Chr 14:7
has charged me to **b** him a house at 2 Chr 36:23
he has charged me to **b** him a house at Ezr 1:2
and said to them, "Let us **b** with you, Ezr 4:2
but we alone will **b** to the LORD, the God Ezr 4:3
of Judah and made them afraid to **b** Ezr 4:4
gave you a decree to **b** this house and to Ezr 5:3
gave you a decree to **b** this house and to Ezr 5:9
Come, let us **b** the wall of Jerusalem, Neh 2:17
us rise up and **b**." So they strengthened Neh 2:18
and we his servants will arise and **b**, Neh 2:20
he has seized a house that he did not **b**. Jb 20:19
tear them down and **b** them up no more. Ps 28:5
pleasure; **b** up the walls of Jerusalem; Ps 51:18
God will save Zion and **b** up the cities of Ps 69:35
and **b** your throne for all generations.'" Ps 89:4
In them the birds **b** their nests; the Ps 104:17
the house, those who **b** it labor in vain. Ps 127:1
the field, and after that **b** your house. Prv 24:27
time to break down, and a time to **b** up; Eccl 3:3
we will **b** on her a battlement of silver, Sg 8:9
fallen, but we will **b** with dressed stones; Is 9:10
he shall **b** my city and set my exiles free, Is 45:13
And it shall be said, "**B** up, build up, Is 57:14
And it shall be said, "Build up, **b** up, Is 57:14
Foreigners shall **b** up your walls, and Is 60:10
They shall **b** up the ancient ruins; they Is 61:4
the people; **b** up, build up the highway; Is 62:10
the people; build up, **b** up the highway; Is 62:10
They shall **b** houses and inhabit them; Is 65:21
They shall not **b** and another inhabit; Is 65:22
is the house that you would **b** for me, Is 66:1
and to overthrow, to **b** and to plant." Jer 1:10
or a kingdom that I will **b** and plant it, Jer 18:9
'I will **b** myself a great house with Jer 22:14
them back to this land. I will **b** them up, Jer 24:6
B houses and live in them; plant gardens Jer 29:5
b houses and live in them, and plant Jer 29:28
Again I will **b** you, and you shall be Jer 31:4
will watch over them to **b** and to plant, Jer 31:28
You shall not **b** a house; you shall not Jer 35:7
and not to **b** houses to dwell in. We have Jer 35:9
then I will **b** you up and not pull you Jer 42:10
against it, and **b** a siege wall against it, Ezk 4:2
say, 'The time is not near to **b** houses. Ezk 11:3
and because, when the people **b** a wall, Ezk 13:10
to cast up mounds, to **b** siege towers. Ezk 21:22
them who should **b** up the wall Ezk 22:30
and they shall **b** houses and plant Ezk 28:26
word to restore and **b** Jerusalem to the Dn 9:25
thorns, and I will **b** a wall against her, Hos 2:6
who **b** Zion with blood and Jerusalem Mi 3:10
Though they **b** houses, they shall not Zep 1:13
the hills and bring wood and **b** the house, Hg 1:8
the land of Shinar, to **b** a house for it. Zec 5:11
and he shall **b** the temple of the LORD. Zec 6:12
It is he who shall **b** the temple of the Zec 6:13
come and help to **b** the temple of the Zec 6:15
the LORD of hosts says, "They may **b**, Mal 1:4
and on this rock I will **b** my church, Mt 16:18
For you **b** the tombs of the prophets Mt 23:29
and in three days I will **b** another, Mk 14:58
For you **b** the tombs of the prophets Lk 11:47
killed them, and you **b** their tombs. Lk 11:48
tear down my barns and **b** larger ones, Lk 12:18
For which of you, desiring to **b** a tower, Lk 14:28
'This man began to **b** and was not able Lk 14:30
has taken forty-six years to **b** this temple, Jn 2:20
What kind of house will you **b** for me, Acts 7:49
which is able to **b** you up and to give Acts 20:32
his neighbor for his good, to **b** him up. Rom 15:2
lest I **b** on someone else's foundation, Rom 15:20
are lawful," but not all things **b** up. 1 Cor 10:23
one another and **b** one another up, 1 Thes 5:11
b yourselves up in your most holy Jude 1:20

BUILDER (4)
like a skilled master **b** I laid a 1 Cor 3:10
more glory as the **b** of a house has Heb 3:3
someone, but the **b** of all things is God.) Heb 3:4
whose designer and **b** is God. Heb 11:10

BUILDERS (16)
So Solomon's **b** and Hiram's builders 1 Kgs 5:18
builders and Hiram's **b** and the men 1 Kgs 5:18
carpenters and the **b** who worked on 2 Kgs 12:11
is, to the carpenters, and to the **b**, 2 Kgs 22:6
carpenters and the **b** to buy 2 Chr 34:11
And when the **b** laid the foundation of Ezr 3:10
you to anger in the presence of the **b**. Neh 4:5
And each of the **b** had his sword Neh 4:18
stone that the **b** rejected has become Ps 118:22
Your **b** make haste; your destroyers and Is 49:17
seas; your **b** made perfect your beauty. Ezk 27:4
stone that the **b** rejected has become Mt 21:42
stone that the **b** rejected has become Mk 12:10
stone that the **b** rejected has become Lk 20:17
stone that was rejected by you, the **b**, Acts 4:11
stone that the **b** rejected has become 1 Pt 2:7

BUILDING (53)
all the earth, and they left off **b** the city. Gn 11:8
the LORD by **b** yourselves an altar Jos 22:16
us as rebels by **b** for yourselves an Jos 22:19
for **b** an altar to turn away from Jos 22:23
following the LORD by **b** an altar for Jos 22:29
until he had finished **b** his own house 1 Kgs 3:1
this house that you are **b**, 1 Kgs 6:12
He was seven years in **b** it. 1 Kgs 6:38
Solomon was **b** his own house thirteen 1 Kgs 7:1
Solomon had finished **b** the house of 1 Kgs 9:1
heard of it, he stopped **b** Ramah, 1 Kgs 15:21
with which Baasha had been **b**, 1 Kgs 15:22
dressed stones for **b** the house of 1 Chr 22:2
you may succeed in **b** the house of 1 Chr 22:11
God, and I made preparations for **b**. 1 Chr 28:2
we have provided for **b** you a house 1 Chr 29:16
measurements for **b** the house 2 Chr 3:3
he stopped **b** Ramah and let his work 2 Chr 16:5
with which Baasha had been **b**, 2 Chr 16:6
He joined him in **b** ships to go to 2 Chr 20:36
LORD and did much **b** on the wall of 2 Chr 27:3
the returned exiles were **b** a temple to the Ezr 4:1
to do with us in **b** a house to our God; Ezr 4:3
of the men who are **b** this building?" Ezr 5:4
of the men who are building this **b**?" Ezr 5:4
that time until now it has been in **b**, Ezr 5:16
They finished their **b** by decree of the Ezr 6:14
Sanballat heard that we were **b** the wall, Neh 4:1
what they are **b**—if a fox goes up on it Neh 4:3
who were **b** on the wall. Those who Neh 4:17
to rebel; that is why you are **b** the wall. Neh 6:6
it, **b** great siegeworks against it. Eccl 9:14
b your vaulted chamber at the head of Ezk 16:31
The **b** that was facing the separate Ezk 41:12
the wall of the **b** was five cubits thick Ezk 41:12
and the yard and the **b** with its walls, a Ezk 41:13
the length of the **b** facing the yard that Ezk 41:15
yard and opposite the **b** on the north. Ezk 42:1
The length of the **b** whose door faced Ezk 42:2
lower and middle chambers of the **b**. Ezk 42:5
opposite the yard and opposite the **b**, Ezk 42:10
A day for the **b** of your walls! In that day Mi 7:11
he is like a man **b** a house, who dug deep Lk 6:48
buying and selling, planting and **b**, Lk 17:28
workers. You are God's field, God's **b**. 1 Cor 3:9
and someone else is **b** upon it. 1 Cor 3:10
strive to excel in **b** up the church. 1 Cor 14:12
Let all things be done for **b** up. 1 Cor 14:26
is destroyed, we have a **b** from God, 2 Cor 5:1
the Lord gave for **b** you up and not 2 Cor 10:8
has given me for **b** up and not for 2 Cor 13:10
of ministry, for **b** up the body of Christ, Eph 4:12
but only such as is good for **b** up, Eph 4:29

BUILDINGS (4)
and beams for the **b** that the kings 2 Chr 34:11
to point out to him the **b** of the temple. Mt 24:1
stones and what wonderful **b**!" Mk 13:1
said to him, "Do you see these great **b**? Mk 13:2

BUILDS (15)
He **b** his house like a moth's, like a Jb 27:18
For the LORD **b** up Zion; he appears in Ps 102:16
Unless the LORD **b** the house, those who Ps 127:1
The LORD **b** up Jerusalem; he gathers Ps 147:2
The wisest of women **b** her house, but Prv 14:1

By justice a king **b** up the land, but he Prv 29:4
"Woe to him who **b** his house by Jer 22:13
who **b** his upper chambers in the Am 9:6
"Woe to him who **b** a town with blood Hab 2:12
each one take care how he **b** upon it. 1 Cor 3:10
Now if anyone **b** on the foundation 1 Cor 3:12
"knowledge" puffs up, but love **b** up. 1 Cor 8:1
who speaks in a tongue **b** up himself, 1 Cor 14:4
one who prophesies **b** up the church. 1 Cor 14:4
body grow so that it **b** itself up in love. Eph 4:16

BUILT (203)
and bore Enoch. When he **b** a city, Gn 4:17
Then Noah **b** an altar to the LORD and Gn 8:20
he went into Assyria and **b** Nineveh, Gn 10:11
tower, which the children of man had **b**. Gn 11:5
give this land." So he **b** there an altar to Gn 12:7
And there he **b** an altar to the LORD and Gn 12:8
and there he **b** an altar to the LORD. Gn 13:18
Abraham **b** the altar there and laid the Gn 22:9
So he **b** an altar there and called upon Gn 26:25
and **b** himself a house and made Gn 33:17
and there he **b** an altar and called the Gn 35:7
They **b** for Pharaoh store cities, Pithom Ex 1:11
And Moses **b** an altar and called the Ex 17:15
in the morning and **b** an altar at the Ex 24:4
Aaron saw this, he **b** an altar before it. Ex 32:5
(Hebron was **b** seven years before Nm 13:22
say, "Come to Heshbon, let it be **b**; Nm 21:27
and **b** seven altars and offered a bull Nm 23:14
And the people of Gad **b** Dibon, Nm 32:34
And the people of Reuben **b** Heshbon, Nm 32:37
other names to the cities that they **b**. Nm 32:38
are full and have **b** good houses and live Dt 8:12
a heap forever. It shall not be **b** again. Dt 13:16
any man who has **b** a new house and Dt 20:5
for her house was **b** into the city wall, Jos 2:15
At that time Joshua **b** an altar to the Jos 8:30
half-tribe of Manasseh **b** there an altar Jos 22:10
of Manasseh have **b** the altar at Jos 22:11
labored and cities that you had not **b**, Jos 24:13
of the Hittites and **b** a city and called Jgs 1:26
Then Gideon **b** an altar there to the LORD Jgs 6:24
was offered on the altar that had been **b**. Jgs 6:28
people rose early and **b** there an altar Jgs 21:4
who together **b** up the house of Israel. Ru 4:11
And he **b** there an altar to the LORD. 1 Sm 7:17
And Saul **b** an altar to the LORD; it 1 Sm 14:35
the first altar that he **b** to the LORD. 1 Sm 14:35
And David **b** the city all around from 2 Sm 5:9
and masons who **b** David a house. 2 Sm 5:11
"Why have you not **b** me a house of 2 Sm 7:7
And David **b** there an altar to the 2 Sm 24:25
house had yet been **b** for the name of 1 Kgs 3:2
that King Solomon **b** for the LORD 1 Kgs 6:2
He also **b** a structure against the wall 1 Kgs 6:5
When the house was **b**, it was with 1 Kgs 6:7
in the house while it was being **b**. 1 Kgs 6:7
So he **b** the house and finished it, and 1 Kgs 6:9
He **b** the structure against the whole 1 Kgs 6:10
So Solomon **b** the house and finished 1 Kgs 6:14
He **b** twenty cubits of the rear of the 1 Kgs 6:16
and he **b** this within as an inner 1 Kgs 6:16
He **b** the inner court with three 1 Kgs 6:36
He **b** the House of the Forest of 1 Kgs 7:2
and it was **b** on four rows of cedar 1 Kgs 7:2
I have indeed **b** you an exalted house, 1 Kgs 8:13
and I have **b** the house for the name 1 Kgs 8:20
much less this house that I have **b**! 1 Kgs 8:27
house that I have **b** is called by your 1 Kgs 8:43
house that I have **b** for your name, 1 Kgs 8:44
house that I have **b** for your name, 1 Kgs 8:48
this house that you have **b**, 1 Kgs 9:3
which Solomon had **b** the two 1 Kgs 9:10
house that Solomon had **b** for her. 1 Kgs 9:24
built for her. Then he **b** the Millo. 1 Kgs 9:24
on the altar that he **b** to the LORD, 1 Kgs 9:25
King Solomon **b** a fleet of ships at 1 Kgs 9:26
of Solomon, the house that he had **b**, 1 Kgs 10:4
Then Solomon **b** a high place for 1 Kgs 11:7
Solomon **b** the Millo, and closed up 1 Kgs 11:27
you a sure house, as I **b** for David, 1 Kgs 11:38
Then Jeroboam **b** Shechem in the 1 Kgs 12:25
went out from there and **b** Penuel. 1 Kgs 12:25
For they also **b** for themselves high 1 Kgs 14:23
up against Judah and **b** Ramah, 1 Kgs 15:17
them King Asa **b** Geba of Benjamin 1 Kgs 15:22
that he did, and the cities that he **b**, 1 Kgs 15:23
name of the city that he **b** Samaria, 1 Kgs 16:24
of Baal, which he **b** in Samaria. 1 Kgs 16:32
In his days Hiel of Bethel **b** Jericho. 1 Kgs 16:34
with the stones he **b** an altar in the 1 Kgs 18:32
ivory house that he **b** and all the 1 Kgs 22:39
he built and all the cities that he **b**, 1 Kgs 22:39
He **b** Elath and restored it to Judah, 2 Kgs 14:22
He **b** the upper gate of the house of 2 Kgs 15:35
And Uriah the priest **b** the altar; in 2 Kgs 16:11
that had been **b** inside the house 2 Kgs 16:18
They **b** for themselves high places in 2 Kgs 17:9
And he **b** altars in the house of the 2 Kgs 21:4
And he **b** altars for all the host of 2 Kgs 21:5
of Israel had **b** for Ashtoreth the 2 Kgs 23:13
And they **b** siegeworks all around it. 2 Kgs 25:1
house that Solomon **b** in Jerusalem). 1 Chr 6:10
meeting until Solomon **b** the house 1 Chr 6:32
who **b** both Lower and Upper 1 Chr 7:24
who **b** Ono and Lod with its towns, 1 Chr 8:12
And he **b** the city all around from the 1 Chr 11:8
David **b** houses for himself in the 1 Chr 15:1
"Why have you not **b** me a house of 1 Chr 17:6
And David **b** there an altar to the 1 Chr 21:26
that is to be **b** for the LORD must 1 Chr 22:5
into a house **b** for the name 1 Chr 22:19
But I have **b** you an exalted house, a 2 Chr 6:2
and I have **b** the house for the name 2 Chr 6:10
much less this house that I have **b**! 2 Chr 6:18
house that I have **b** is called by your 2 Chr 6:33
house that I have **b** for your name, 2 Chr 6:34
house that I have **b** for your name, 2 Chr 6:38
in which Solomon had **b** the house of 2 Chr 8:1
He **b** Tadmor in the wilderness and all 2 Chr 8:4
the store cities that he **b** in Hamath. 2 Chr 8:4
He also **b** Upper Beth-horon and 2 Chr 8:5
to the house that he had **b** for her, 2 Chr 8:11
that he had **b** before the vestibule, 2 Chr 8:12
of Solomon, the house that he had **b**, 2 Chr 9:3
and he **b** cities for defense in Judah. 2 Chr 11:5
He **b** Bethlehem, Etam, Tekoa, 2 Chr 11:6
He **b** fortified cities in Judah, for the 2 Chr 14:6
every side." So they **b** and prospered. 2 Chr 14:7
went up against Judah and **b** Ramah, 2 Chr 16:1
with them he **b** Geba and Mizpah. 2 Chr 16:6
He **b** in Judah fortresses and store 2 Chr 17:12
lived in it and have **b** for you in it a 2 Chr 20:8
and they **b** the ships in Ezion-geber. 2 Chr 20:36
He **b** Eloth and restored it to Judah, 2 Chr 26:2
and he **b** cities in the territory of 2 Chr 26:6
Uzziah **b** towers in Jerusalem at the 2 Chr 26:9
And he **b** towers in the wilderness 2 Chr 26:10
He **b** the upper gate of the house of 2 Chr 27:3
he **b** cities in the hill country of 2 Chr 27:4
to work resolutely and **b** up all the 2 Chr 32:5
it, and outside it he **b** another wall, 2 Chr 32:5
And he **b** altars in the house of the 2 Chr 33:4
And he **b** altars for all the host of 2 Chr 33:5
Afterward he **b** an outer wall for the 2 Chr 33:14
that he had **b** on the mountain 2 Chr 33:15
sites on which he **b** high places and 2 Chr 33:19
the son of David, king of Israel, **b**. 2 Chr 35:3
and they **b** the altar of the God of Israel, Ezr 3:2
great God. It is being **b** with huge stones, Ezr 5:8
the house that was **b** many years ago, Ezr 5:11
a great king of Israel **b** and finished. Ezr 5:11
of the Jews **b** and prospered through Ezr 6:14
the priests, and they **b** the Sheep Gate. Neh 3:1
And next to him the men of Jericho **b**. Neh 3:2
next to them Zaccur the son of Imri **b**. Neh 3:2
The sons of Hassenaah **b** the Fish Gate. Neh 3:3
And he **b** the wall of the Pool of Shelah Neh 3:15
So we **b** the wall. And all the wall was Neh 4:6
sword strapped at his side while he **b**. Neh 4:18
heard that I had **b** the wall and that Neh 6:1
when the wall had been **b** and I had set Neh 7:1
the singers had **b** for themselves Neh 12:29
return to the Almighty you will be **b** up; Jb 22:23
He **b** his sanctuary like the high Ps 78:69
I said, "Steadfast love will be **b** up forever; Ps 89:2
Jerusalem—**b** as a city that is bound Ps 122:3
Wisdom has **b** her house; she has hewn Prv 9:1
By wisdom a house is **b**, and by Prv 24:3
I **b** houses and planted vineyards for Eccl 2:4
like the tower of David, **b** in rows of stone; Sg 4:4
he **b** a watchtower in the midst of it, and Is 5:2
of the cities of Judah, 'They shall be **b**, Is 44:26
saying of Jerusalem, 'She shall be **b**,' and Is 44:28
And they have **b** the high places of Jer 7:31
then they shall be **b** up in the midst of Jer 12:16
and have **b** the high places of Baal to Jer 19:5
I will build you, and you shall be **b**, Jer 31:4
wrath, from the day it was **b** to this day, Jer 32:31
They **b** the high places of Baal in the Jer 32:35
what I have **b** I am breaking down, Jer 45:4
it. And they **b** siegeworks all around it. Jer 52:4
or **b** up a wall for the house of Israel, Ezk 13:5
you **b** yourself a vaulted chamber and Ezk 16:24
of every street you **b** your lofty place Ezk 16:25
up and siege walls **b** to cut off many Ezk 17:17
which I have **b** by my mighty power as Dn 4:30
weeks it shall be **b** again with squares Dn 9:25
has forgotten his Maker and **b** palaces, Hos 8:14
fruit increased, the more altars he **b**; Hos 10:1
him, you have **b** houses of hewn stone, Am 5:11
standing beside a wall **b** with a plumb Am 7:7
my house shall be **b** in it, declares the Zec 1:16
was laid, that the temple might be **b**. Zec 8:9
Tyre has **b** herself a rampart and heaped Zec 9:3
like a wise man who **b** his house on the Mt 7:24
a foolish man who **b** his house on the Mt 7:26
winepress in it and **b** a tower and leased Mt 21:33
a pit for the winepress and **b** a tower, Mk 12:1
of the hill on which their town was **b**, Lk 4:29
not shake it, because it had been well **b**. Lk 6:48
is like a man who **b** a house on the Lk 6:49
he is the one who **b** us our synagogue." Lk 7:5
it was Solomon who **b** a house for Acts 7:47
had peace and was being **b** up. Acts 9:31
that anyone has **b** on the foundation 1 Cor 3:14
so that the church may be **b** up. 1 Cor 14:5
the other person is not being **b** up. 1 Cor 14:17
b on the foundation of the apostles and Eph 2:20
you also are being **b** together into a Eph 2:22
rooted and **b** up in him and established Col 2:7
(For every house is **b** by someone, but Heb 3:4
living stones are being **b** up as a 1 Pt 2:5
The wall was **b** of jasper, while the city Rv 21:18

BUKKI (5)
of Dan a chief, **B** the son of Jogli. Nm 34:22
Abishua fathered **B**, Bukki fathered 1 Chr 6:5
fathered Bukki, **B** fathered Uzzi, 1 Chr 6:5
B his son, Uzzi his son, Zerahiah his 1 Chr 6:51
son of Zerahiah, son of Uzzi, son of **B**, Ezr 7:4

BUKKIAH (2)
B, Mattaniah, Uzziel, Shebuel and 1 Chr 25:4
the sixth to **B**, his sons and his 1 Chr 25:13

BUL (1)
the eleventh year, in the month of **B**, 1 Kgs 6:38

BULGING (1)
you like a breach in a high wall, **b** out, Is 30:13

BULL (101)
Take one **b** of the herd and two rams Ex 29:1
and bring the **b** and the two rams. Ex 29:3
you shall bring the **b** before the tent of Ex 29:10
lay their hands on the head of the **b**. Ex 29:10
you shall kill the **b** before the LORD at Ex 29:11
of the blood of the **b** and put it on the Ex 29:12
But the flesh of the **b** and its skin and Ex 29:14
day you shall offer a **b** as a sin offering Ex 29:36
Then he shall kill the **b** before the LORD, Lv 1:5
he has committed a **b** from the herd Lv 4:3
He shall bring the **b** to the entrance of the Lv 4:4
on the head of the **b** and kill the bull Lv 4:4
of the bull and kill the **b** before the LORD. Lv 4:4
of the blood of the **b** and bring it into the Lv 4:5
of the blood of the **b** he shall pour out at Lv 4:7
all the fat of the **b** of the sin offering he Lv 4:8
But the skin of the **b** and all its flesh, Lv 4:11
all the rest of the **b**—he shall carry Lv 4:12
assembly shall offer a **b** from the herd Lv 4:14
on the head of the **b** before the LORD, Lv 4:15
and the **b** shall be killed before the LORD. Lv 4:15
of the blood of the **b** into the tent of Lv 4:16
Thus shall he do with the **b**. As he did Lv 4:20
As he did with the **b** of the sin offering, Lv 4:20
he shall carry the **b** outside the camp Lv 4:21
and burn it up as he burned the first **b**; Lv 4:21
anointing oil and the **b** of the sin offering Lv 8:2
Then he brought the **b** of the sin Lv 8:14
on the head of the **b** of the sin offering. Lv 8:14
But the **b** and its skin and its flesh and Lv 8:17
"Take for yourself a **b** calf for a sin Lv 9:2
with a **b** from the herd for a sin offering Lv 16:3
"Aaron shall offer the **b** as a sin offering Lv 16:6
"Aaron shall present the **b** as a sin Lv 16:11
He shall kill the **b** as a sin offering for Lv 16:11
the blood of the **b** and sprinkle it with Lv 16:14
blood as he did with the blood of the **b**, Lv 16:15
of the blood of the **b** and some of the Lv 16:18
And the **b** for the sin offering and the Lv 16:27
You may present a **b** or a lamb that Lv 22:23
and one **b** from the herd and two rams. Lv 23:18
one **b** from the herd, one ram, one male Nm 7:15
one **b** from the herd, one ram, one male Nm 7:21
one **b** from the herd, one ram, one male Nm 7:27
one **b** from the herd, one ram, one male Nm 7:33
one **b** from the herd, one ram, one male Nm 7:39
one **b** from the herd, one ram, one male Nm 7:45
one **b** from the herd, one ram, one male Nm 7:51
one **b** from the herd, one ram, one male Nm 7:57
one **b** from the herd, one ram, one male Nm 7:63
one **b** from the herd, one ram, one male Nm 7:69
one **b** from the herd, one ram, one male Nm 7:75
one **b** from the herd, one ram, one male Nm 7:81
let them take a **b** from the herd and Nm 8:8
you shall take another **b** from the herd Nm 8:8

when you offer a **b** as a burnt offering Nm 15:8
shall offer with the **b** a grain offering of Nm 15:9
it shall be done for each **b** or ram, Nm 15:11
shall offer one **b** from the herd Nm 15:24
offered on each altar a **b** and a ram. Nm 23:2
offered on each altar a **b** and a ram." Nm 23:4
altars and offered a **b** and a ram on Nm 23:14
and offered a **b** and a ram on each Nm 23:30
offering, mixed with oil, for each **b**, Nm 28:12
shall be half a hin of wine for a **b**, Nm 28:14
of an ephah shall you offer for a **b**, Nm 28:20
three tenths of an ephah for each **b**, Nm 28:28
one **b** from the herd, one ram, seven Nm 29:2
oil, three tenths of an ephah for the **b**, Nm 29:3
one **b** from the herd, one ram, seven Nm 29:8
oil, three tenths of an ephah for the **b**, Nm 29:9
a pleasing aroma to the LORD: one **b**, Nm 29:36
and the drink offerings for the **b**, Nm 29:37
A firstborn **b**—he has majesty, and his Dt 33:17
LORD said to him, "Take your father's **b**, Jgs 6:25
bull, and the second **b** seven years old, Jgs 6:25
Then take the second **b** and offer it as a Jgs 6:26
and the second **b** was offered on the altar Jgs 6:28
her, along with a three-year-old **b**, 1 Sm 1:24
Then they slaughtered the **b**, and they 1 Sm 1:25
them choose one **b** for themselves 1 Kgs 18:23
will prepare the other **b** and lay it on 1 Kgs 18:23
for yourselves one **b** and prepare it 1 Kgs 18:25
And they took the **b** that was given 1 Kgs 18:26
order and cut the **b** in pieces and 1 Kgs 18:33
with a young **b** or seven rams 2 Chr 13:9
Their **b** breeds without fail; their cow Jb 21:10
I will not accept a **b** from your house or Ps 50:9
than an ox or a **b** with horns and hoofs. Ps 69:31
like a **b** I bring down those who sit on Is 10:13
a **b** from the herd for a sin offering. Ezk 43:19
shall also take the **b** of the sin Ezk 43:21
purified, as it was purified with the **b**. Ezk 43:22
you shall offer a **b** from the herd Ezk 43:23
a **b** from the herd and a ram from the Ezk 43:25
you shall take a **b** from the herd Ezk 45:18
the land a young **b** for a sin offering. Ezk 45:22
a grain offering an ephah for each **b**, Ezk 45:24
he shall offer a **b** from the herd without Ezk 46:6
an ephah with the **b** and an ephah with Ezk 46:7
offering with a young **b** shall be an Ezk 46:11

BULLS (58)
and their calves, forty cows and ten **b**, Gn 32:15
of the **b** or the sheep or the goats. Lv 22:19
cattle for the burnt offering twelve **b**, Nm 7:87
of peace offerings twenty-four **b**, Nm 7:88
lay their hands on the heads of the **b**, Nm 8:12
for me here seven **b** and seven rams." Nm 23:1
for me here seven **b** and seven rams." Nm 23:29
two **b** from the herd, one ram, seven Nm 28:11
two **b** from the herd, one ram, and Nm 28:19
two **b** from the herd, one ram, seven Nm 28:27
to the LORD, thirteen **b** from the herd, Nm 29:13
of an ephah for each of the thirteen **b**, Nm 29:14
the second day twelve **b** from the herd, Nm 29:17
and the drink offerings for the **b**, Nm 29:18
"On the third day eleven **b**, two rams, Nm 29:20
and the drink offerings for the **b**, Nm 29:21
"On the fourth day ten **b**, two rams, Nm 29:23
and the drink offerings for the **b**, Nm 29:24
"On the fifth day nine **b**, two rams, Nm 29:26
and the drink offerings for the **b**, Nm 29:27
"On the sixth day eight **b**, two rams, Nm 29:29
and the drink offerings for the **b**, Nm 29:30
"On the seventh day seven **b**, two Nm 29:32
and the drink offerings for the **b**, Nm 29:33
Let two **b** be given to us, and let 1 Kgs 18:23
they sacrificed seven **b** and seven 1 Chr 15:26
burnt offerings to the LORD, 1,000 **b**, 1 Chr 29:21
And they brought seven **b**, seven 2 Chr 29:21
So they slaughtered the **b**, and the 2 Chr 29:22
the assembly brought was 70 **b**, 2 Chr 29:32
offerings were 600 **b** and 3,000 2 Chr 29:33
the assembly 1,000 **b** and 7,000 2 Chr 30:24
the assembly 1,000 **b** and 10,000 2 Chr 30:24
to the number of 30,000, and 3,000 **b**; 2 Chr 35:7
2,600 Passover lambs and 300 **b**. 2 Chr 35:8
lambs and young goats and 500 **b**. 2 Chr 35:9
of Moses. And so they did with the **b**. 2 Chr 35:12
And whatever is needed—**b**, rams, or Ezr 6:9
dedication of this house of God 100 **b**, Ezr 6:17
then, you shall with all diligence buy **b**, Ezr 7:17
the God of Israel, twelve **b** for all Israel, Ezr 8:35
therefore take seven **b** and seven rams Jb 42:8
Many **b** encompass me; strong bulls of Ps 22:12
me; strong **b** of Bashan surround me; Ps 22:12
I eat the flesh of **b** or drink the blood of Ps 50:13
then **b** will be offered on your altar. Ps 51:19
I will make an offering of **b** and goats. Ps 66:15
the herd of **b** with the calves of the Ps 68:30
I do not delight in the blood of **b**, or of Is 1:11
and young steers with the mighty **b**. Is 34:7
Kill all her **b**; let them go down to the Jer 50:27
the twelve bronze **b** that were under the Jer 52:20
rams, of lambs, and of he-goats, of **b**, Ezk 39:18
LORD seven young **b** and seven rams Ezk 45:23
to nothing: in Gilgal they sacrifice **b**; Hos 12:11
and we will pay with **b** the vows of our Hos 14:2
blood of goats and **b** and with the ashes Heb 9:13
for the blood of **b** and goats to take Heb 10:4

BULRUSHES (1)
a basket made of **b** and daubed it with Ex 2:3

BULWARKS (2)
city; he sets up salvation as walls and **b**. Is 26:1
she has surrendered; her **b** have fallen; Jer 50:15

BUNAH (1)
Ram, his firstborn, **B**, Oren, Ozem, 1 Chr 2:25

BUNCH (1)
Take a **b** of hyssop and dip it in the Ex 12:22

BUNCHES (1)
of bread, a hundred **b** of raisins, 2 Sm 16:1

BUNDLE (6)
every man's **b** of money was in his Gn 42:35
and cut down a **b** of brushwood and Jgs 9:48
cut down his **b** and following Jgs 9:49
be bound in the **b** of the living in 1 Sm 25:29
Gather up your **b** from the ground, O Jer 10:17
Paul had gathered a **b** of sticks and Acts 28:3

BUNDLES (3)
and their father saw their **b** of money, Gn 42:35
out some from the **b** for her and leave Ru 2:16
first and bind them in **b** to be burned, Mt 13:30

BUNNI (3)
Kadmiel, Shebaniah, **B**, Sherebiah, Neh 9:4
B, Azgad, Bebai, Neh 10:15
Azrikam, son of Hashabiah, son of **B**; Neh 11:15

BURDEN (44)
you, and they will bear the **b** with you. Ex 18:22
who hates you lying down under its **b**, Ex 23:5
them each to his task and to his **b**, Nm 4:19
that you lay the **b** of all this people on Nm 11:11
people alone; the **b** is too heavy for me. Nm 11:14
they shall bear the **b** of the people Nm 11:17
myself the weight and **b** of you and your Dt 1:12
go on with me, you will be a **b** to me. 2 Sm 15:33
servant be an added **b** to my lord the 2 Sm 19:35
mark? Why have I become a **b** to you? Jb 7:20
like a heavy **b**, they are too heavy for me. Ps 38:4
Cast your **b** on the LORD, and he will Ps 55:22
you laid a crushing **b** on our backs; Ps 66:11
"I relieved your shoulder of the **b**; your Ps 81:6
soul hates; they have become a **b** to me; Is 1:14
For the yoke of his **b**, and the staff for his Is 9:4
in that day his **b** will depart from your Is 10:27
them, and his **b** from their shoulder." Is 14:25
they cannot save the **b**, but themselves go Is 46:2
and do not bear a **b** on the Sabbath day Jer 17:21
do not carry a **b** out of your houses Jer 17:22
and bring in no **b** by the gates of this Jer 17:24
and not to bear a **b** and enter by the Jer 17:27
asks you, 'What is the **b** of the LORD?' Jer 23:33
you shall say to them, 'You are the **b**, Jer 23:33
the people who says, 'The **b** of the LORD,' Jer 23:34
But 'the **b** of the LORD' you shall Jer 23:36
for the **b** is every man's own word, Jer 23:36
But if you say, 'The **b** of the LORD,' thus Jer 23:38
"The **b** of the LORD," when I sent to you, Jer 23:38
"You shall not say, 'The **b** of the LORD,'" Jer 23:38
The **b** of the word of the LORD is against Zec 9:1
The **b** of the word of the LORD Zec 12:1
For my yoke is easy, and my **b** is light." Mt 11:30
us who have borne the **b** of the day and Mt 20:12
and on a colt, the foal of a beast of **b**.'" Mt 21:5
you no greater **b** than these Acts 15:28
and was in need, I did not **b** anyone, 2 Cor 11:9
except that I myself did not **b** you? 2 Cor 12:13
And I will not be a **b**, for I seek not 2 Cor 12:14
granting that I myself did not **b** you, 2 Cor 12:16
we might not be a **b** to any of you, 1 Thes 2:9
we might not be a **b** to any of you. 2 Thes 3:8
I say, I do not lay on you any other **b**. Rv 2:24

BURDEN-BEARERS (2)
also had 70,000 **b** and 80,000 1 Kgs 5:15
were over the **b** and directed all who 2 Chr 34:13

BURDENED (8)
If one is **b** with the blood of another, Prv 28:17
I have not **b** you with offerings, Is 43:23
But you have **b** me with your sins; you Is 43:24
were so utterly **b** beyond our strength 2 Cor 1:8
being **b**—not that we would be 2 Cor 5:4
others should be eased and you **b**, 2 Cor 8:13
Let the church not be **b**, so that it 1 Tm 5:16
b with sins and led astray by various 2 Tm 3:6

BURDENING (1)
and will refrain from **b** you in any 2 Cor 11:9

BURDENS (18)
over them to afflict them with heavy **b**. Ex 1:11
out to his people and looked on their **b**, Ex 2:11
from their work? Get back to your **b**." Ex 5:4
and you make them rest from their **b**!" Ex 5:5
out from under the **b** of the Egyptians, Ex 6:6
out from under the **b** of the Egyptians. Ex 6:7
Gershonites, in serving and bearing **b**: Nm 4:24
the service of bearing **b** in the tent of Nm 4:47
70,000 men to bear **b** and 80,000 to 2 Chr 2:2
of them he assigned to bear **b**, 2 Chr 2:18
of those who bear the **b** is failing. Neh 4:10
Those who carried **b** were loaded in Neh 4:17
before me laid heavy **b** on the people Neh 5:15
you carry are borne as **b** on weary beasts. Is 46:1
They tie up heavy **b**, hard to bear, and Mt 23:4
you load people with **b** hard to bear, Lk 11:46
do not touch the **b** with one of your Lk 11:46
Bear one another's **b**, and so fulfill the Gal 6:2

BURDENSOME (2)
lest we be **b** to you." He pressed him, 2 Sm 13:25
And his commandments are not **b**. 1 Jn 5:3

BURIAL (13)
one knows the place of his **b** to this day. Dt 34:6
fathers in the **b** field that belonged 2 Chr 26:23
life's good things, and he also has no **b**, Eccl 6:3
You will not be joined with them in **b**, Is 14:20
With the **b** of a donkey he shall be Jer 22:19
dead body into the **b** place of the Jer 26:23
will give to Gog a place for **b** in Israel, Ezk 39:11
relative, the one who anoints him for **b**, Am 6:10
she has done it to prepare me for **b**. Mt 26:12
potter's field as a **b** place for strangers. Mt 27:7
anointed my body beforehand for **b**. Mk 14:8
that she may keep it for the day of my **b**. Jn 12:7
the spices, as is the **b** custom of the Jews. Jn 19:40

BURIED (105)
peace; you shall be **b** in a good old age. Gn 15:15
Abraham **b** Sarah his wife in the cave Gn 23:19
and Ishmael his sons **b** him in the cave Gn 25:9
There Abraham was **b**, with Sarah his Gn 25:10
and she was **b** under an oak below Gn 35:8
and she was **b** on the way to Ephrath Gn 35:19
And his sons Esau and Jacob **b** him. Gn 35:29
and I **b** her there on the way to Ephrath Gn 48:7
There they **b** Abraham and Sarah his Gn 49:31
There they **b** Isaac and Rebekah his Gn 49:31
Rebekah his wife, and there I **b** Leah— Gn 49:31
land of Canaan and **b** him in the cave Gn 50:13
After he had **b** his father, Joseph Gn 50:14
because there they **b** the people who Nm 11:34
Miriam died there and was **b** there. Nm 20:1
There Aaron died, and there he was **b**. Dt 10:6
and he **b** him in the valley in the land of Dt 34:6
And they **b** him in his own inheritance Jos 24:30
from Egypt, they **b** them at Shechem, Jos 24:32
Aaron died, and they **b** him at Gibeah, Jos 24:33
And they **b** him within the boundaries of Jgs 2:9
good old age and was **b** in the tomb of Jgs 8:32
Then he died and was **b** at Shamir. Jgs 10:2
And Jair died and was **b** in Kamon. Jgs 10:5
Gileadite died and was **b** in his city in Jgs 12:7
Ibzan died and was **b** at Bethlehem. Jgs 12:10
died and was **b** at Aijalon in Jgs 12:12
died and was **b** at Pirathon in Jgs 12:15
him up and **b** him between Zorah Jgs 16:31
you die I will die, and there will I be **b**. Ru 1:17
and they **b** him in his house at 1 Sm 25:1
for him and **b** him in Ramah, 1 Sm 28:3
their bones and **b** them under the 1 Sm 31:13
the men of Jabesh-gilead who **b** Saul," 2 Sm 2:4
loyalty to Saul your lord and **b** him. 2 Sm 2:5
took up Asahel and **b** him in the 2 Sm 2:32
They **b** Abner at Hebron. And the 2 Sm 3:32
head of Ish-bosheth and **b** it in the 2 Sm 4:12
and he died and was **b** in the tomb of 2 Sm 17:23
And they **b** the bones of Saul and his 2 Sm 21:14
his fathers and was **b** in the city of 1 Kgs 2:10
And he was **b** in his own house in the 1 Kgs 2:34
his fathers and was **b** in the city of 1 Kgs 11:43
And after he had **b** him, he said to 1 Kgs 13:31
grave in which the man of God is **b**; 1 Kgs 13:31
And all Israel **b** him and mourned 1 Kgs 14:18
fathers and was **b** with his fathers 1 Kgs 14:31
and they **b** him in the city of David. 1 Kgs 15:8
fathers and was **b** with his fathers 1 Kgs 15:24
with his fathers and was **b** at Tirzah, 1 Kgs 16:6
his fathers and was **b** in Samaria, 1 Kgs 16:28

And they **b** the king in Samaria. 1 Kgs 22:37
fathers and was **b** with his fathers 1 Kgs 22:50
his fathers and was **b** with his fathers 2 Kgs 8:24
and **b** him in his tomb with his 2 Kgs 9:28
fathers, and they **b** him in Samaria. 2 Kgs 10:35
And they **b** him with his fathers in 2 Kgs 12:21
fathers, and they **b** him in Samaria, 2 Kgs 13:9
And Joash was **b** in Samaria with 2 Kgs 13:13
So Elisha died, and they **b** him. Now 2 Kgs 13:20
And as a man was being **b**, behold, 2 Kgs 13:21
fathers and was **b** in Samaria with 2 Kgs 14:16
and he was **b** in Jerusalem with his 2 Kgs 14:20
and they **b** him with his fathers in 2 Kgs 15:7
fathers and was **b** with his fathers 2 Kgs 15:38
fathers and was **b** with his fathers 2 Kgs 16:20
his fathers and was **b** in the garden 2 Kgs 21:18
And he was **b** in his tomb in the 2 Kgs 21:26
him to Jerusalem and **b** him in his 2 Kgs 23:30
And they **b** their bones under the 1 Chr 10:12
his fathers and was **b** in the city of 2 Chr 9:31
his fathers and was **b** in the city of 2 Chr 12:16
and they **b** him in the city of David. 2 Chr 14:1
They **b** him in the tomb that he had 2 Chr 16:14
his fathers and was **b** with his fathers 2 Chr 21:1
They **b** him in the city of David, but 2 Chr 21:20
to Jehu and put to death. They **b** him, 2 Chr 22:9
And they **b** him in the city of David 2 Chr 24:16
and they **b** him in the city of David, 2 Chr 24:25
and he was **b** with his fathers in the 2 Chr 25:28
and they **b** him with his fathers in 2 Chr 26:23
and they **b** him in the city of David, 2 Chr 27:9
fathers, and they **b** him in the city, 2 Chr 28:27
and they **b** him in the upper part of 2 Chr 32:33
and they **b** him in his house, 2 Chr 33:20
he died and was **b** in the tombs of 2 Chr 35:24
Then I saw the wicked **b**. They used to Eccl 8:10
And they shall not be gathered or **b**. Jer 8:2
not be lamented, nor shall they be **b**. Jer 16:4
They shall not be **b**, and no one shall Jer 16:6
you shall die, and there you shall be **b**, Jer 20:6
the burial of a donkey he shall be **b**, Jer 22:19
shall not be lamented, or gathered, or **b**; Jer 25:33
Gog and all his multitude will be **b**. Ezk 39:11
till the buriers have **b** it in the Valley Ezk 39:15
came and took the body and **b** it, Mt 14:12
side. The rich man also died and was **b**, Lk 16:22
David that he both died and was **b**, Acts 2:29
him up and carried him out and **b** him. Acts 5:6
of those who have **b** your husband are Acts 5:9
carried her out and **b** her beside her Acts 5:10
Devout men **b** Stephen and made great Acts 8:2
We were **b** therefore with him by Rom 6:4
that he was **b**, that he was raised on 1 Cor 15:4
having been **b** with him in baptism, in Col 2:12

BURIERS (1)
till the **b** have buried it in the Valley Ezk 39:15

BURIES (3)
who survive him the pestilence **b**, Jb 27:15
The sluggard **b** his hand in the dish Prv 19:24
The sluggard **b** his hand in the dish; it Prv 26:15

BURN (126)
and **b** them thoroughly." And they had Gn 11:3
not your anger **b** against your servant, Gn 44:18
remains until the morning you shall **b**. Ex 12:10
b for burn, wound for wound, stripe for Ex 21:25
burn for **b**, wound for wound, stripe for Ex 21:25
and my wrath will **b**, and I will kill you Ex 22:24
a lamp may regularly be set up to **b**. Ex 27:20
is on them, and **b** them on the altar. Ex 29:13
its dung you shall **b** with fire outside Ex 29:14
and **b** the whole ram on the altar. It is a Ex 29:18
from their hands and **b** them on the Ex 29:25
then you shall **b** the remainder with Ex 29:34
make an altar on which to **b** incense; Ex 30:1
And Aaron shall **b** fragrant incense on Ex 30:7
when he dresses the lamps he shall **b** it, Ex 30:7
up the lamps at twilight, he shall **b** it, Ex 30:8
to **b** a food offering to the LORD, Ex 30:20
that my wrath may **b** hot against them Ex 32:10
does your wrath **b** hot against your Ex 32:11
"Let not the anger of my lord **b** hot. Ex 32:22
And the priest shall **b** all of it on the altar, Lv 1:9
shall offer all of it and **b** it on the altar; Lv 1:13
wring off its head and **b** it on the altar. Lv 1:15
And the priest shall **b** it on the altar, Lv 1:17
and the priest shall **b** this as its memorial Lv 2:2
its memorial portion and **b** this on the Lv 2:9
for you shall **b** no leaven nor any honey Lv 2:11
And the priest shall **b** as its memorial Lv 2:16
Then Aaron's sons shall **b** it on the altar Lv 3:5
And the priest shall **b** it on the altar as a Lv 3:11
And the priest shall **b** them on the altar Lv 3:16
and the priest shall **b** them on the altar Lv 4:10
heap, and shall **b** it up on a fire of wood. Lv 4:12
he shall take from it and **b** on the altar. Lv 4:19
bull outside the camp and **b** it up as he Lv 4:21
And all its fat he shall **b** on the altar, like Lv 4:26
and the priest shall **b** it on the altar for a Lv 4:31
and the priest shall **b** it on the altar, Lv 4:35
its memorial portion and **b** this on the Lv 5:12
The priest shall **b** wood on it every Lv 6:12
offering on it and shall **b** on it the fat of Lv 6:12
the grain offering and **b** this as its Lv 6:15
The priest shall **b** them on the altar as a Lv 7:5
The priest shall **b** the fat on the altar, Lv 7:31
and the bread you shall **b** up with fire. Lv 8:32
when the body has a **b** on its skin and Lv 13:24
the raw flesh of the **b** becomes a spot, Lv 13:24
It has broken out in the **b**, and the Lv 13:25
has faded, it is a swelling from the **b**, Lv 13:28
him clean, for it is the scar of the **b**. Lv 13:28
And he shall **b** the garment, or the Lv 13:52
You shall **b** it in the fire, whether the Lv 13:55
You shall **b** with fire whatever has the Lv 13:57
the sin offering he shall **b** on the altar. Lv 16:25
the tent of meeting and **b** the fat for a Lv 17:6
memorial portion, and **b** it on the altar, Nm 5:26
draw near to **b** incense before the Nm 16:40
on the altar and shall **b** their fat as a Nm 18:17
their Asherim and **b** their carved images Dt 7:5
of their gods you shall **b** with fire. Dt 7:25
their pillars and **b** their Asherim with Dt 12:3
for they even **b** their sons and their Dt 12:31
of its open square and **b** the city and all Dt 13:16
their horses and **b** their chariots with Jos 11:6
that stood on mounds did Israel **b**, Jos 11:13
God, "Let not your anger **b** against me; Jgs 6:39
to the door of the tower to **b** it with fire. Jgs 9:52
We will **b** your house over you with Jgs 12:1
lest we **b** you and your father's house Jgs 14:15
said to him, "Let them **b** the fat first, 1 Sm 2:16
to go up to my altar, to **b** incense, 1 Sm 2:28
and will **b** up the house of 1 Kgs 14:10
I will utterly **b** you up, and will cut 1 Kgs 21:21
the great altar **b** the morning burnt 2 Kgs 16:15
that no one might **b** his son or his 2 Kgs 23:10
of pure gold to **b** before the inner 2 Chr 4:20
that its lamps may **b** every evening. 2 Chr 13:11
of the LORD to **b** incense on the altar 2 Chr 26:16
Uzziah, to **b** incense to the LORD, 2 Chr 26:18
who are consecrated to **b** incense. 2 Chr 26:18
a censer in his hand to **b** incense, 2 Chr 26:19
on it you shall **b** your sacrifices"? 2 Chr 32:12
to **b** on the altar of the LORD our God, Neh 10:34
from me, and my bones **b** with heat. Jb 30:30
and it would **b** to the root all my Jb 31:12
forever? Will your jealousy **b** like fire? Ps 79:5
How long will your wrath **b** like fire? Ps 89:46
smoke, and my bones **b** like a furnace. Ps 102:3
spark, and both of them shall **b** together, Is 1:31
and it will **b** and devour his thorns and Is 10:17
against them, I would **b** them up together. Is 27:4
you who **b** with lust among the oaks, Is 57:5
like fire, and **b** with none to quench it, Jer 4:4
ground; it will **b** and not be quenched." Jer 7:20
to **b** their sons and their daughters in the Jer 7:31
a fire is kindled that shall **b** forever." Jer 15:14
a fire is kindled that shall **b** forever." Jer 17:4
high places of Baal to **b** their sons in the Jer 19:5
of Babylon, and he shall **b** it with fire.' Jer 21:10
like fire, and **b** with none to quench it, Jer 21:12
come and set this city on fire and **b** it, Jer 32:29
burnt offerings, to **b** grain offerings, Jer 33:18
of Babylon, and he shall **b** it with fire. Jer 34:2
so people shall **b** spices for you and Jer 34:5
against it and take it and **b** it with fire. Jer 34:22
urged the king not to **b** the scroll, Jer 36:25
They shall capture it and **b** it with fire. Jer 37:8
would rise up and **b** this city with fire.'" Jer 37:10
Chaldeans, and they shall **b** it with fire, Jer 38:18
and he shall **b** them and carry them Jer 43:12
the gods of Egypt he shall **b** with fire.'" Jer 43:13
A third part you shall **b** in the fire in the Ezk 5:2
midst of the fire and **b** them in the fire. Ezk 5:4
And they shall **b** your houses and Ezk 16:41
daughters, and **b** up their houses. Ezk 23:47
become hot, and its copper may **b**, Ezk 24:11
make fires of the weapons and **b** them, Ezk 39:9
the mountains and **b** offerings on the Hos 4:13
they shall **b** them and consume them, Ob 1:18
and I will **b** your chariots in smoke, Na 2:13
chaff he will **b** with unquenchable fire." Mt 3:12
the temple of the Lord and **b** incense. Lk 1:9
chaff he will **b** with unquenchable fire." Lk 3:17
"Did not our hearts **b** within us while Lk 24:32
the heavenly bodies will melt as they **b**! 2 Pt 3:12
devour her flesh and **b** her up with fire, Rv 17:16

BURNED (139)
said, "Bring her out, and let her be **b**." Gn 38:24
this great sight, why the bush is not **b**." Ex 3:3
and the dancing, Moses' anger **b** hot, Ex 32:19
they had made and **b** it with fire and Ex 32:20
and **b** fragrant incense on it, as the Ex 40:27
of wood. On the ash heap it shall be **b** up. Lv 4:12
and burn it up as he **b** the first bull; Lv 4:21
forever. The whole of it shall be **b**. Lv 6:22
offering of a priest shall be wholly **b**. Lv 6:23
the Holy Place; it shall be **b** up with fire. Lv 6:30
on the third day shall be **b** up with fire. Lv 7:17
not be eaten. It shall be **b** up with fire. Lv 7:19
their fat, and Moses **b** them on the altar. Lv 8:16
and its dung he **b** up with fire outside Lv 8:17
and Moses **b** the head and the pieces and Lv 8:20
and Moses **b** the whole ram on the altar. Lv 8:21
from their hands and **b** them on the Lv 8:28
from the sin offering he **b** on the altar, Lv 9:10
and the skin he **b** up with fire outside Lv 9:11
and the head, and he **b** them on the altar. Lv 9:13
and the legs and **b** them with the burnt Lv 9:14
took a handful of it, and **b** it on the altar, Lv 9:17
and he **b** the fat pieces on the altar, Lv 9:20
sin offering, and behold, it was **b** up! Lv 10:16
leprous disease. It shall be **b** in the fire. Lv 13:52
and their dung shall be **b** up with fire. Lv 16:27
the third day shall be **b** up with fire. Lv 19:6
he and they shall be **b** with fire, that Lv 20:14
her father; she shall be **b** with fire. Lv 21:9
fire of the LORD **b** among them and Nm 11:1
the fire of the LORD **b** among them. Nm 11:3
which those who were **b** had offered, Nm 16:39
And the heifer shall be **b** in his sight. Nm 19:5
and its blood, with its dung, shall be **b**. Nm 19:5
Kain shall be **b** when Asshur takes Nm 24:22
their encampments, they **b** with fire, Nm 31:10
while the mountain **b** with fire to the Dt 4:11
made, and **b** it with fire and crushed it, Dt 9:21
the whole land **b** out with brimstone Dt 29:23
And they **b** the city with fire, and Jos 6:24
anger of the LORD **b** against the people of Jos 7:1
the devoted things shall be **b** with fire, Jos 7:15
They **b** them with fire and stoned them Jos 7:25
So Joshua **b** Ai and made it forever a Jos 8:28
their horses and **b** their chariots with Jos 11:9
breathed. And he **b** Hazor with fire. Jos 11:11
except Hazor alone; that Joshua **b**. Jos 11:13
Philistines came up and **b** her and her Jgs 15:6
of the sword and **b** the city with fire. Jgs 18:27
Moreover, before the fat was **b**, the 1 Sm 2:15
overcome Ziklag and **b** it with fire 1 Sm 30:1
to the city, they found it **b** with fire, 1 Sm 30:3
of Caleb, and we **b** Ziklag with fire." 1 Sm 30:14
came to Jabesh and **b** them there. 1 Sm 31:12
and captured Gezer and **b** it with fire, 1 Kgs 9:16
human bones shall be **b** on you.'" 1 Kgs 13:2
down her image and **b** it at the 1 Kgs 15:13
king's house and **b** the king's house 1 Kgs 16:18
was in the house of Baal and **b** it. 2 Kgs 10:26
He even **b** his son as an offering, 2 Kgs 16:3
and **b** his burnt offering and his 2 Kgs 16:13
And they **b** their sons and their 2 Kgs 17:17
and the Sepharvites **b** their children 2 Kgs 17:31
And he **b** his son as an offering and 2 Kgs 21:6
He **b** them outside Jerusalem in the 2 Kgs 23:4
those also who **b** incense to Baal, 2 Kgs 23:5
and **b** it at the brook Kidron and beat 2 Kgs 23:6
And he **b** the chariots of the sun 2 Kgs 23:11
high place he pulled down and **b**, 2 Kgs 23:15
it to dust. He also **b** the Asherah. 2 Kgs 23:15
of the tombs and **b** them on the 2 Kgs 23:16
and **b** human bones on them. 2 Kgs 23:20
And he **b** the house of the LORD and 2 Kgs 25:9
every great house he **b** down. 2 Kgs 25:9
gave command, and they were **b**. 1 Chr 14:12
it, and **b** it at the brook Kidron. 2 Chr 15:16
Son of Hinnom and **b** his sons as an 2 Chr 28:3
and have not **b** incense or offered 2 Chr 29:7
And he **b** his sons as an offering in 2 Chr 33:6
He also **b** the bones of the priests on 2 Chr 34:5
And they **b** the house of God and 2 Chr 36:19
of Jerusalem and **b** all its palaces 2 Chr 36:19
Jerusalem lies in ruins with its gates **b**. Neh 2:17
heaps of rubbish, and **b** ones at that?" Neh 4:2
enraged, and his anger **b** within him. Est 1:12
fell from heaven and **b** up the sheep and Jb 1:16
of the family of Ram, **b** with anger. Jb 32:2
He **b** with anger at Job because he Jb 32:2
He **b** with anger also at Job's three friends Jb 32:3
of these three men, he **b** with anger. Jb 32:5
As I mused, the fire **b**; then I spoke with Ps 39:3
they **b** all the meeting places of God in Ps 74:8
They have **b** it with fire; they have cut it Ps 80:16
company; the flame **b** up the wicked. Ps 106:18
to his chest and his clothes not be **b**? Prv 6:27
lies desolate; your cities are **b** with fire; Is 1:7

a tenth remain in it, it will be **b** again, Is 6:13
rolled in blood will be **b** as fuel for the fire. Is 9:5
And the peoples will be as if **b** to lime, Is 33:12
thorns cut down, that are **b** in the fire." Is 33:12
it **b** him up, but he did not take it to Is 42:25
you walk through fire you shall not be **b**, Is 43:2
to say, "Half of it I **b** in the fire; Is 44:19
fathers praised you, has been **b** by fire, Is 64:11
And as spices were **b** for your fathers, the Jer 34:5
after the king had **b** the scroll with the Jer 36:27
Jehoiakim the king of Judah has **b**. Jer 36:28
says the LORD, You have **b** this scroll, Jer 36:29
king of Judah had **b** in the fire. Jer 36:32
and this city shall not be **b** with fire, Jer 38:17
and this city shall be **b** with fire." Jer 38:23
The Chaldeans **b** the king's house and Jer 39:8
and its villages shall be **b** with fire; Jer 49:2
been seized, the marshes are **b** with fire, Jer 51:32
and her high gates shall be **b** with fire. Jer 51:58
And he **b** the house of the LORD, and the Jer 52:13
every great house he **b** down. Jer 52:13
he has **b** like a flaming fire in Jacob, Lam 2:3
the spices, and let the bones be **b** up. Ezk 24:10
and it shall be **b** in the appointed Ezk 43:21
and given over to be **b** with fire. Dn 7:11
the Baals when she **b** offerings to them Hos 2:13
and flame has **b** all the trees of the field. Jl 1:19
because he **b** to lime the bones of the Am 2:1
pieces, all her wages shall be **b** with fire, Mi 1:7
first and bind them in bundles to be **b**, Mt 13:30
the weeds are gathered and **b** with fire, Mt 13:40
those murderers and **b** their city. Mt 22:7
are gathered, thrown into the fire, and **b**. Jn 15:6
books together and **b** them in the Acts 19:19
If anyone's work is **b** up, he will 1 Cor 3:15
and if I deliver up my body to be **b**, 1 Cor 13:3
to being cursed, and its end is to be **b**. Heb 6:8
for sin are **b** outside the camp. Heb 13:11
bodies will be **b** up and dissolved, 2 Pt 3:10
And a third of the earth was **b** up, and a Rv 8:7
up, and a third of the trees were **b** up, Rv 8:7
burned up, and all green grass was **b** up. Rv 8:7
famine, and she will be **b** up with fire; Rv 18:8

BURNING (59)
He looked, and behold, the bush was **b**, Ex 3:2
Turn from your **b** anger and relent Ex 32:12
the fire of the altar shall be kept **b** on it. Lv 6:9
The fire on the altar shall be kept **b** on it; Lv 6:12
Fire shall be kept **b** on the altar Lv 6:13
bewail the **b** that the LORD has kindled. Lv 10:6
that a light may be kept **b** regularly. Lv 24:2
throw them into the fire **b** the heifer. Nm 19:6
while the mountain was **b** with fire, Dt 5:23
and the mountain was **b** with fire. Dt 9:15
Then the LORD turned from his **b** anger. Jos 7:26
not turn from the **b** of his great 2 Kgs 23:26
it to him for the **b** of incense of sweet 2 Chr 2:4
all the altars for **b** incense they took 2 Chr 30:14
God will send his **b** anger against him Jb 20:23
as from a boiling pot and **b** rushes. Jb 41:20
For my sides are filled with **b**, and there Ps 38:7
and let your **b** anger overtake them. Ps 69:24
He let loose on them his **b** anger, wrath, Ps 78:49
Let **b** coals fall upon them! Let them Ps 140:10
for you will heap **b** coals on his head, Prv 25:22
by a spirit of judgment and by a spirit of **b**. Is 4:4
having in his hand a **b** coal that he had Is 6:6
and under his glory a **b** will be kindled, Is 10:16
will be kindled, like the **b** of fire. Is 10:16
LORD comes from afar, **b** with his anger, Is 30:27
For a **b** place has long been prepared; Is 30:33
sulfur; her land shall become **b** pitch. Is 34:9
the **b** sand shall become a pool, and the Is 35:7
and a faintly **b** wick he will not quench; Is 42:3
who equip yourselves with **b** torches! Is 50:11
and her salvation as a **b** torch. Is 62:1
heart as it were a **b** fire shut up in my Jer 20:9
and there was a fire **b** in the fire pot Jer 36:22
as an oven with the **b** heat of famine. Lam 5:10
appearance was like **b** coals of fire, Ezk 1:13
your hands with **b** coals from between Ezk 10:2
be cast into a **b** fiery furnace." Dn 3:6
shall be cast into a **b** fiery furnace. Dn 3:11
be cast into a **b** fiery furnace. Dn 3:15
to deliver us from the **b** fiery furnace, Dn 3:17
to cast them into the **b** fiery furnace. Dn 3:20
were thrown into the **b** fiery furnace. Dn 3:21
fell bound into the **b** fiery furnace. Dn 3:23
near to the door of the **b** fiery furnace; Dn 3:26
was fiery flames; its wheels were **b** fire. Dn 7:9
to the Baals and **b** offerings to idols. Hos 11:2
I will not execute my **b** anger; I will not Hos 11:9
were as a brand plucked out of the **b**; Am 4:11
comes upon you the **b** anger of the LORD, Zep 2:2
them my indignation, all my **b** anger; Zep 3:8
the day is coming, **b** like an oven, Mal 4:1
for action and keep your lamps **b**, Lk 12:35
He was a **b** and shining lamp, and you Jn 5:35
doing you will heap **b** coals on his Rom 12:20
before the throne were **b** seven torches of Rv 4:5
like a great mountain, **b** with fire, Rv 8:8
her when they see the smoke of her **b**. Rv 18:9
out as they saw the smoke of her **b**, Rv 18:18

BURNINGS (1)
us can dwell with everlasting **b**?" Is 33:14

BURNISHED (6)
for King Solomon, were of **b** bronze. 1 Kgs 7:45
Huram-abi made of **b** bronze for 2 Chr 4:16
foot. And they sparkled like **b** bronze. Ezk 1:7
and legs like the gleam of **b** bronze, Dn 10:6
his feet were like **b** bronze, refined in a Rv 1:15
of fire, and whose feet are like **b** bronze. Rv 2:18

BURNS (15)
And he who **b** them shall wash his Lv 16:28
The one who **b** the heifer shall wash Nm 19:8
among you anyone who **b** his son or Dt 18:10
anger, and it **b** to the depths of Sheol, Dt 32:22
as a man **b** up dung until it is all 1 Kgs 14:10
"My anger **b** against you and against Jb 42:7
the spear; he **b** the chariots with fire. Ps 46:9
goes before him and **b** up his adversaries Ps 97:3
For wickedness **b** like a fire; it consumes Is 9:18
Half of it he **b** in the fire. Over the half he Is 44:16
in my nostrils, a fire that **b** all the day. Is 65:5
O Samaria. My anger **b** against them. Hos 8:5
before them, and behind them a flame **b**. Jl 2:3
into the lake of fire that **b** with sulfur. Rv 19:20
be in the lake that **b** with fire and sulfur, Rv 21:8

BURNT (301)
clean bird and offered **b** offerings on the Gn 8:20
offer him there as a **b** offering on one of Gn 22:2
the wood for the **b** offering and arose Gn 22:3
the wood of the **b** offering and laid it Gn 22:6
but where is the lamb for a **b** offering?" Gn 22:7
for himself the lamb for a **b** offering, Gn 22:8
it up as a **b** offering instead of his Gn 22:13
let us have sacrifices and **b** offerings, Ex 10:25
brought a **b** offering and sacrifices to Ex 18:12
on it your **b** offerings and your Ex 20:24
who offered **b** offerings and sacrificed Ex 24:5
the altar. It is a **b** offering to the LORD. Ex 29:18
on the altar on top of the **b** offering, Ex 29:25
be a regular **b** offering throughout Ex 29:42
incense on it, or a **b** offering, Ex 30:9
and the altar of **b** offering with all its Ex 30:28
and the altar of **b** offering with all its Ex 31:9
day and offered **b** offerings and brought Ex 32:6
the altar of **b** offering, with its grating Ex 35:16
made the altar of **b** offering of acacia Ex 38:1
set the altar of **b** offering before the door Ex 40:6
anoint the altar of **b** offering and all its Ex 40:10
set the altar of **b** offering at the Ex 40:29
offered on it the **b** offering and the Ex 40:29
his offering is a **b** offering from the herd, Lv 1:3
lay his hand on the head of the **b** offering, Lv 1:4
he shall flay the **b** offering and cut it Lv 1:6
burn all of it on the altar, as a **b** offering, Lv 1:9
"If his gift for a **b** offering is from the Lv 1:10
it is a **b** offering, a food offering with a Lv 1:13
to the LORD is a **b** offering of birds, Lv 1:14
It is a **b** offering, a food offering with a Lv 1:17
it on the altar on top of the **b** offering, Lv 3:5
base of the altar of **b** offering that is at the Lv 4:7
burn them on the altar of **b** offering. Lv 4:10
base of the altar of **b** offering that is at Lv 4:18
where they kill the **b** offering before the Lv 4:24
of the altar of **b** offering and pour out Lv 4:25
at the base of the altar of **b** offering. Lv 4:25
the sin offering in the place of **b** offering. Lv 4:29
of the altar of **b** offering and pour out Lv 4:30
the place where they kill the **b** offering. Lv 4:33
of the altar of **b** offering and pour out Lv 4:34
sin offering and the other for a **b** offering. Lv 5:7
the second for a **b** offering according to Lv 5:10
saying, This is the law of the **b** offering. Lv 6:9
The **b** offering shall be on the hearth on Lv 6:9
fire has reduced the **b** offering on the Lv 6:10
he shall arrange the **b** offering on it and Lv 6:12
the place where the **b** offering is killed Lv 6:25
where they kill the **b** offering they shall Lv 7:2
offers any man's **b** offering shall have Lv 7:8
the skin of the **b** offering that he has Lv 7:8
This is the law of the **b** offering, of the Lv 7:37
he presented the ram of the **b** offering, Lv 8:18
It was a **b** offering with a pleasing Lv 8:21
them on the altar with the **b** offering. Lv 8:28
a sin offering and a ram for a **b** offering, Lv 9:2
year old without blemish, for a **b** offering, Lv 9:3
offering and your **b** offering and make Lv 9:7
Then he killed the **b** offering, and Lv 9:12
And they handed the **b** offering to him, Lv 9:13
burned them with the **b** offering on the Lv 9:14
he presented the **b** offering and offered Lv 9:16
besides the **b** offering of the morning. Lv 9:17
sin offering and the **b** offering and the Lv 9:22
and consumed the **b** offering and the Lv 9:24
offering and their **b** offering before the Lv 10:19
a lamb a year old for a **b** offering, Lv 12:6
one for a **b** offering and the other for a Lv 12:8
kill the sin offering and the **b** offering, Lv 14:13
afterward he shall kill the **b** offering. Lv 14:19
priest shall offer the **b** offering and the Lv 14:20
a sin offering and the other a **b** offering. Lv 14:22
offering and the other for a **b** offering, Lv 14:31
offering and the other for a **b** offering. Lv 15:15
offering and the other for a **b** offering. Lv 15:30
a sin offering and a ram for a **b** offering. Lv 16:3
offering, and one ram for a **b** offering. Lv 16:5
out and offer his **b** offering and the Lv 16:24
burnt offering and the **b** offering of the Lv 16:24
them, who offers a **b** offering or sacrifice Lv 17:8
in Israel presents a **b** offering as his Lv 22:18
without blemish as a **b** offering to the Lv 23:12
They shall be a **b** offering to the LORD, Lv 23:18
b offerings and grain offerings, Lv 23:37
offering and the other for a **b** offering, Nm 6:11
old without blemish for a **b** offering, Nm 6:14
offer his sin offering and his **b** offering, Nm 6:16
male lamb a year old, for a **b** offering; Nm 7:15
male lamb a year old, for a **b** offering; Nm 7:21
male lamb a year old, for a **b** offering; Nm 7:27
male lamb a year old, for a **b** offering; Nm 7:33
male lamb a year old, for a **b** offering; Nm 7:39
male lamb a year old, for a **b** offering; Nm 7:45
male lamb a year old, for a **b** offering; Nm 7:51
male lamb a year old, for a **b** offering; Nm 7:57
male lamb a year old, for a **b** offering; Nm 7:63
male lamb a year old, for a **b** offering; Nm 7:69
male lamb a year old, for a **b** offering; Nm 7:75
male lamb a year old, for a **b** offering; Nm 7:81
cattle for the **b** offering twelve bulls, Nm 7:87
the other for a **b** offering to the LORD Nm 8:12
trumpets over your **b** offerings and Nm 10:10
food offering or a **b** offering or a Nm 15:3
and you shall offer with the **b** offering, Nm 15:5
offer a bull as a **b** offering or sacrifice, Nm 15:8
bull from the herd for a **b** offering, Nm 15:24
take some ashes of the **b** sin offering, Nm 19:17
to Balak, "Stand beside your **b** offering, Nm 23:3
were standing beside his **b** offering. Nm 23:6
"Stand here beside your **b** offering, Nm 23:15
he was standing beside his **b** offering, Nm 23:17
It is a regular **b** offering, which was Nm 28:6
this is the **b** offering of every Sabbath, Nm 28:10
besides the regular **b** offering and its Nm 28:10
you shall offer a **b** offering to the Nm 28:11
for a **b** offering with a pleasing Nm 28:13
This is the **b** offering of each month Nm 28:14
besides the regular **b** offering and its Nm 28:15
food offering, a **b** offering to the LORD: Nm 28:19
offer these besides the **b** offering of the Nm 28:23
which is for a regular **b** offering. Nm 28:23
besides the regular **b** offering and its Nm 28:24
but offer a **b** offering, with a pleasing Nm 28:27
Besides the regular **b** offering and its Nm 28:31
and you shall offer a **b** offering, for a Nm 29:2
besides the **b** offering of the new moon, Nm 29:6
and the regular **b** offering and its grain Nm 29:6
you shall offer a **b** offering to the LORD, Nm 29:8
and the regular **b** offering and its Nm 29:11
And you shall offer a **b** offering, a Nm 29:13
besides the regular **b** offering, Nm 29:16
besides the regular **b** offering and its Nm 29:19
besides the regular **b** offering and its Nm 29:22
besides the regular **b** offering, Nm 29:25
besides the regular **b** offering and its Nm 29:28
besides the regular **b** offering, its Nm 29:31
besides the regular **b** offering, its Nm 29:34
but you shall offer a **b** offering, a food Nm 29:36
besides the regular **b** offering and its Nm 29:38
freewill offerings, for your **b** offerings, Nm 29:39
shall bring your **b** offerings and your Dt 12:6
your **b** offerings and your sacrifices, Dt 12:11
do not offer your **b** offerings at any Dt 12:13
there you shall offer your **b** offerings, Dt 12:14
and offer your **b** offerings, the flesh and Dt 12:27
as a whole **b** offering to the LORD your Dt 13:16
And you shall offer **b** offerings on it to Dt 27:6
you and whole **b** offerings on your Dt 33:10
they offered on it **b** offerings to the LORD Jos 8:31
did so to offer **b** offerings or grain Jos 22:23
now build an altar, not for **b** offering, Jos 22:26
presence with our **b** offerings and Jos 22:27

our fathers made, not for **b** offerings, Jos 22:28
by building an altar for **b** offering, Jos 22:29
and offer it as a **b** offering with the wood Jgs 6:26
and I will offer it up for a **b** offering." Jgs 11:31
But if you prepare a **b** offering, then Jgs 13:16
not have accepted a **b** offering and a Jgs 13:23
and offered **b** offerings and peace Jgs 20:26
altar and offered **b** offerings and peace Jgs 21:4
the cows as a **b** offering to the LORD. 1 Sm 6:14
Beth-shemesh offered **b** offerings and 1 Sm 6:15
it as a whole **b** offering to the LORD. 1 Sm 7:9
Samuel was offering up the **b** offering, 1 Sm 7:10
to you to offer **b** offerings and to 1 Sm 10:8
said, "Bring the **b** offering here to me, 1 Sm 13:9
And he offered the **b** offering. 1 Sm 13:9
had finished offering the **b** offering, 1 Sm 13:10
myself, and offered the **b** offering." 1 Sm 13:12
great delight in **b** offerings and 1 Sm 15:22
And David offered **b** offerings and 2 Sm 6:17
finished offering the **b** offerings and 2 Sm 6:18
the oxen for the **b** offering and the 2 Sm 24:22
I will not offer **b** offerings to the LORD 2 Sm 24:24
LORD and offered **b** offerings and 2 Sm 24:25
to offer a thousand **b** offerings on that 1 Kgs 3:4
and offered up **b** offerings and peace 1 Kgs 3:15
there he offered the **b** offering and the 1 Kgs 8:64
small to receive the **b** offering and the 1 Kgs 8:64
used to offer up **b** offerings and peace 1 Kgs 9:25
and his **b** offerings that he offered at 1 Kgs 10:5
pour it on the **b** offering and on the 1 Kgs 18:33
and consumed the **b** offering and 1 Kgs 18:38
offered him for a **b** offering on the 2 Kgs 3:27
will not offer **b** offering or sacrifice 2 Kgs 5:17
in to offer sacrifices and **b** offerings. 2 Kgs 10:24
an end of offering the **b** offering, 2 Kgs 10:25
and burned his **b** offering and his 2 Kgs 16:13
burn the morning **b** offering and 2 Kgs 16:15
and the king's **b** offering and his 2 Kgs 16:15
with the **b** offering of all the people 2 Kgs 16:15
the blood of the **b** offering and all 2 Kgs 16:15
on the altar of **b** offering and on the 1 Chr 6:49
and they offered **b** offerings and 1 Chr 16:1
finished offering the **b** offerings and 1 Chr 16:2
to offer **b** offerings to the LORD on 1 Chr 16:40
the altar of **b** offering regularly 1 Chr 16:40
give the oxen for **b** offerings and the 1 Chr 21:23
nor offer **b** offerings that cost me 1 Chr 21:24
LORD and presented **b** offerings and 1 Chr 21:26
heaven upon the altar of **b** offering. 1 Chr 21:26
and the altar of **b** offering were at 1 Chr 21:29
here the altar of **b** offering for Israel." 1 Chr 22:1
and whenever **b** offerings were 1 Chr 23:31
next day offered **b** offerings to the 1 Chr 29:21
offered a thousand **b** offerings on it. 2 Chr 1:6
and for **b** offerings morning and 2 Chr 2:4
off what was used for the **b** offering, 2 Chr 4:6
and consumed the **b** offering and the 2 Chr 7:1
there he offered the **b** offering and the 2 Chr 7:7
could not hold the **b** offering and the 2 Chr 7:7
Solomon offered up **b** offerings to the 2 Chr 8:12
and his **b** offerings that he offered at 2 Chr 9:4
and every evening **b** offerings and 2 Chr 13:11
LORD, to offer **b** offerings to the LORD, 2 Chr 23:18
the service and for the **b** offerings, 2 Chr 24:14
And they offered **b** offerings in the 2 Chr 24:14
incense or offered **b** offerings in the 2 Chr 29:7
the altar of **b** offering and all its 2 Chr 29:18
commanded that the **b** offering and 2 Chr 29:24
commanded that the **b** offering be 2 Chr 29:27
And when the **b** offering began, the 2 Chr 29:27
continued until the **b** offering was 2 Chr 29:28
a willing heart brought **b** offerings. 2 Chr 29:31
number of the **b** offerings that the 2 Chr 29:32
these were for a **b** offering to the 2 Chr 29:32
could not flay all the **b** offerings, 2 Chr 29:34
the great number of **b** offerings, 2 Chr 29:35
drink offerings for the **b** offerings. 2 Chr 29:35
and brought **b** offerings into 2 Chr 30:15
for **b** offerings and peace offerings, 2 Chr 31:2
possessions was for the **b** offerings: 2 Chr 31:3
the **b** offerings of morning and 2 Chr 31:3
and the **b** offerings for the Sabbaths, 2 Chr 31:3
set aside the **b** offerings that they 2 Chr 35:12
were offering the **b** offerings and the 2 Chr 35:14
and to offer **b** offerings on the 2 Chr 35:16
the God of Israel, to offer **b** offerings on it, Ezr 3:2
and they offered **b** offerings on it to the Ezr 3:3
LORD, **b** offerings morning and evening. Ezr 3:3
offered the daily **b** offerings by number Ezr 3:4
and after that the regular **b** offerings, the Ezr 3:5
they began to offer **b** offerings to the Ezr 3:6
or sheep for **b** offerings to the God of Ezr 6:9
offered **b** offerings to the God of Israel, Ezr 8:35
All this was a **b** offering to the LORD. Ezr 8:35
grain offering, the regular **b** offering, Neh 10:33
morning and offer **b** offerings according Jb 1:5
and offer up a **b** offering for yourselves. Jb 42:8
and regard with favor your **b** sacrifices! Ps 20:3
B offering and sin offering you have not Ps 40:6
your **b** offerings are continually before Ps 50:8
will not be pleased with a **b** offering. Ps 51:16
in **b** offerings and whole burnt Ps 51:19
burnt offerings and whole **b** offerings; Ps 51:19
come into your house with **b** offerings; Ps 66:13
will offer to you **b** offerings of fattened Ps 66:15
have had enough of **b** offerings of rams Is 1:11
are its beasts enough for a **b** offering. Is 40:16
brought me your sheep for **b** offerings, Is 43:23
their **b** offerings and their sacrifices will Is 56:7
Your **b** offerings are not acceptable, nor Jer 6:20
"Add your **b** offerings to your sacrifices, Jer 7:21
them concerning **b** offerings and Jer 7:22
though they offer **b** offering and grain Jer 14:12
bringing **b** offerings and sacrifices, Jer 17:26
sons in the fire as **b** offerings to Baal, Jer 19:5
in my presence to offer **b** offerings, Jer 33:18
the crags, and make you a **b** mountain. Jer 51:25
where the **b** offering was to be washed. Ezk 40:38
on which the **b** offering and the sin Ezk 40:39
tables of hewn stone for the **b** offering, Ezk 40:42
with which the **b** offerings and the Ezk 40:42
erected for offering **b** offerings upon it Ezk 43:18
them up as a **b** offering to the LORD. Ezk 43:24
on the altar your **b** offerings and your Ezk 43:27
shall slaughter the **b** offering and the Ezk 44:11
of Israel for grain offering, **b** offering, Ezk 45:15
duty to furnish the **b** offerings, Ezk 45:17
offerings, grain offerings, **b** offerings, Ezk 45:17
shall provide as a **b** offering to the Ezk 45:23
provision for sin offerings, **b** offerings, Ezk 45:25
priests shall offer his **b** offering and his Ezk 46:2
The **b** offering that the prince offers to Ezk 46:4
either a **b** offering or peace offerings Ezk 46:12
he shall offer his **b** offering or his Ezk 46:12
without blemish for a **b** offering to the Ezk 46:13
by morning, for a regular **b** offering. Ezk 46:15
And the regular **b** offering was taken Dn 8:11
with the regular **b** offering because of Dn 8:12
concerning the regular **b** offering, Dn 8:13
shall take away the regular **b** offering. Dn 11:31
that the regular **b** offering is taken Dn 12:11
of God rather than **b** offerings. Hos 6:6
you offer me your **b** offerings and grain Am 5:22
Shall I come before him with **b** offerings, Mi 6:6
than all whole **b** offerings and Mk 12:33
in **b** offerings and sin offerings you Heb 10:6
and offerings and **b** offerings and sin Heb 10:8

BURST (20)
the fountains of the great deep **b** forth, Gn 7:11
we filled them, and behold, they have **b**. Jos 9:13
"The LORD has **b** through my enemies 2 Sm 5:20
the LORD had **b** forth against Uzzah. 2 Sm 6:8
no vent; like new wineskins ready to **b**. Jb 32:19
with doors when it **b** out from the womb, Jb 38:8
"Let us **b** their bonds apart and cast away Ps 2:3
of death, and **b** their bonds apart. Ps 107:14
ago I broke your yoke and **b** your bonds; Jer 2:20
broken the yoke; they had **b** the bonds. Jer 5:5
it will **b** upon the head of the wicked. Jer 23:19
off your neck, and I will **b** your bonds, Jer 30:8
it will **b** upon the head of the wicked. Jer 30:23
you **b** forth in your rivers, trouble the Ezk 32:2
they **b** through the weapons and are not Jl 2:8
off you and will **b** your bonds apart." Na 1:13
the skins **b** and the wine is spilled and Mt 9:17
the wine will **b** the skins—and the wine Mk 2:22
the new wine will **b** the skins and it will Lk 5:37
and falling headlong he **b** open in the Acts 1:18

BURSTING (3)
me like a **b** flood." Therefore the 2 Sm 5:20
like a **b** flood." Therefore the name 1 Chr 14:11
and your vats will be **b** with wine. Prv 3:10

BURY (36)
that I may **b** my dead out of my sight." Gn 23:4
B your dead in the choicest of our Gn 23:6
willing that I should **b** my dead out of Gn 23:8
my people I give it to you. **B** your dead." Gn 23:11
from me, that I may **b** my dead there." Gn 23:13
between you and me? **B** your dead." Gn 23:15
truly with me. Do not **b** me in Egypt, Gn 47:29
out of Egypt and **b** me in their burying Gn 47:30
b me with my fathers in the cave that Gn 49:29
land of Canaan, there shall you **b** me.' Gn 50:5
let me please go up and **b** my father. Gn 50:5
answered, "Go up, and **b** your father, Gn 50:6
So Joseph went up to **b** his father. With Gn 50:7
had gone up with him to **b** his father. Gn 50:14
tree, but you shall **b** him the same day, Dt 21:23
has said, strike him down and **b** him, 1 Kgs 2:31
of the army went up to **b** the slain, 1 Kgs 11:15
to the city to mourn and to **b** him. 1 Kgs 13:29
b me in the grave in which the man 1 Kgs 13:31
shall mourn for him and **b** him, 1 Kgs 14:13
and none shall **b** her." Then he 2 Kgs 9:10
now to this cursed woman and **b** her, 2 Kgs 9:34
But when they went to **b** her, they 2 Kgs 9:35
but they did not **b** him in the tombs 2 Chr 24:25
and there was no one to **b** them. Ps 79:3
for they will **b** in Topheth, because there Jer 7:32
sword, with none to **b** them—them, Jer 14:16
Men shall **b** in Topheth because there Jer 19:11
because there will be no place else to **b**. Jer 19:11
All the people of the land will **b** them, Ezk 39:13
land regularly and **b** those travelers Ezk 39:14
gather them; Memphis shall **b** them. Hos 9:6
"Lord, let me first go and **b** my father." Mt 8:21
and leave the dead to **b** their own dead." Mt 8:22
"Lord, let me first go and **b** my father." Lk 9:59
"Leave the dead to **b** their own dead. Lk 9:60

BURYING (9)
me property among you for a **b** place, Gn 23:4
tomb to hinder you from **b** your dead." Gn 23:6
your presence as property for a **b** place." Gn 23:9
as property for a **b** place by the Hittites. Gn 23:20
me in their **b** place." He answered, Gn 47:30
the Hittite to possess as a **b** place. Gn 49:30
the Hittite to possess as a **b** place. Gn 50:13
the Egyptians were **b** all their firstborn, Nm 33:4
the house of Israel will be **b** them, Ezk 39:12

BUSH (11)
When no **b** of the field was yet in the land Gn 2:5
in a flame of fire out of the midst of a **b**. Ex 3:2
looked, and behold, the **b** was burning, Ex 3:2
this great sight, why the **b** is not burned." Ex 3:3
aside to see, God called to him out of the **b**, Ex 3:4
the favor of him who dwells in the **b**. Dt 33:16
of Moses, in the passage about the **b**, Mk 12:26
nor are grapes picked from a bramble **b**. Lk 6:44
showed, in the passage about the **b**, Lk 20:37
Mount Sinai, in a flame of fire in a **b**. Acts 7:30
angel who appeared to him in the **b**. Acts 7:35

BUSHES (4)
she put the child under one of the **b**. Gn 21:15
or the **b** of the earth, and they will teach Jb 12:8
they pick saltwort and the leaves of **b**, Jb 30:4
Among the **b** they bray; under the nettles Jb 30:7

BUSIES (1)
while each of you **b** himself with his own Hg 1:9

BUSINESS (25)
If you do not tell this **b** of ours, then Jos 2:14
But if you tell this **b** of ours, then we Jos 2:20
in this place? What is your **b** here?" Jgs 18:3
because the king's **b** required haste." 1 Sm 21:8
in Maon whose **b** was in Carmel. 1 Sm 25:2
and from the **b** of the merchants, 1 Kgs 10:15
of those who have charge of the king's **b**, Est 3:9
in ships, doing **b** on the great waters; Ps 107:23
It is an unhappy **b** that God has given Eccl 1:13
he has given the **b** of gathering and Eccl 2:26
I have seen the **b** that God has given to Eccl 3:10
This also is vanity and an unhappy **b**. Eccl 4:8
For a dream comes with much **b**, and a Eccl 5:3
and to see the **b** that is done on earth, Eccl 8:16
who have done **b** with you from your Is 47:15
"Tarshish did **b** with you because of Ezk 27:12
Syria did **b** with you because of your Ezk 27:16
Damascus did **b** with you for your Ezk 27:18
goats; in these they did **b** with you. Ezk 27:21
Then I rose and went about the king's **b**, Dn 8:27
off, one to his farm, another to his **b**, Mt 22:5
to them, 'Engage in **b** until I come.' Lk 19:13
what they had gained by doing **b**. Lk 19:15
brought no little **b** to the craftsmen. Acts 19:24
know that from this **b** we have our Acts 19:25

BUSY (6)
your servant was **b** here and there, 1 Kgs 20:40
to **b** myself with wicked deeds in Ps 141:4
to the children of man to be **b** with. Eccl 1:13
to the children of man to be **b** with. Eccl 3:10
folly, and his heart is **b** with iniquity, Is 32:6
you walk in idleness, not **b** at work, 2 Thes 3:11

BUSYBODIES (2)
in idleness, not busy at work, but **b**. 2 Thes 3:11
only idlers, but also gossips and **b**, 1 Tm 5:13

BUTT (1)
in the stomach with the **b** of his spear, 2 Sm 2:23

BUTTER (2)
when my steps were washed with **b**, and Jb 29:6
His speech was smooth as **b**, yet war Ps 55:21

BUTTOCKS (1)
naked and barefoot, with **b** uncovered, Is 20:4

BUTTRESS (5)
the ascent to the armory at the **b**. Neh 3:19
another section from the **b** to the door Neh 3:20
from the house of Azariah to the **b** Neh 3:24
repaired opposite the **b** and the tower Neh 3:25
the living God, a pillar and **b** of truth. 1 Tm 3:15

BUTTS (1)
"When one man's ox **b** another's, so Ex 21:35

BUY (57)
came to Egypt to Joseph to **b** grain, Gn 41:57
Go down and **b** grain for us there, that Gn 42:2
brothers went down to **b** grain in Egypt. Gn 42:3
of Israel came to **b** among the others Gn 42:5
"From the land of Canaan, to **b** food." Gn 42:7
your servants have come to **b** food. Gn 42:10
to them, "Go again, **b** us a little food." Gn 43:2
with us, we will go down and **b** you food. Gn 43:4
we came down the first time to **b** food. Gn 43:20
other money down with us to **b** food. Gn 43:22
father said, 'Go again, **b** us a little food,' Gn 44:25
B us and our land for food, and we with Gn 47:19
the land of the priests he did not **b**, Gn 47:22
When you **b** a Hebrew slave, he shall Ex 21:2
your neighbor or **b** from your Lv 25:14
you may **b** male and female slaves Lv 25:44
You may also **b** from among the Lv 25:45
then he shall **b** it back at the valuation, Lv 27:27
and you shall also **b** water of them for Dt 2:6
'**B** it in the presence of those sitting here Ru 4:4
"The day you **b** the field from the hand of Ru 4:5
"**B** it for yourself," he drew off his sandal. Ru 4:8
"To **b** the threshing floor from you, 2 Sm 24:21
but I will **b** it from you for a price. 2 Sm 24:24
as well as to **b** timber and quarried 2 Kgs 12:12
but I will **b** them for the full price. 1 Chr 21:24
king's traders would **b** them from 2 Chr 1:16
and the builders to **b** quarried stone, 2 Chr 34:11
you shall with all diligence **b** bulls, Ezr 7:17
we will not **b** from them on the Neh 10:31
in his hand to **b** wisdom when he has Prv 17:16
B truth, and do not sell it; buy wisdom, Prv 23:23
b wisdom, instruction, and Prv 23:23
he who has no money, come, **b** and eat! Is 55:1
b wine and milk without money and Is 55:1
"Go and **b** a linen loincloth and put it Jer 13:1
LORD, "Go, **b** a potter's earthenware flask, Jer 19:1
and say, '**B** my field that is at Anathoth, Jer 32:7
'**B** my field that is at Anathoth in the Jer 32:8
redemption is yours; **b** it for yourself.' Jer 32:8
"**B** the field for money and get Jer 32:25
that we may **b** the poor for silver and the Am 8:6
Those who **b** them slaughter them and Zec 11:5
the villages and **b** food for themselves." Mt 14:15
to the dealers and **b** for yourselves.' Mt 25:9
And while they were going to **b**, the Mt 25:10
villages and **b** themselves something Mk 6:36
"Shall we go and **b** two hundred denarii Mk 6:37
we are to go and **b** food for all these Lk 9:13
has no sword sell his cloak and **b** one. Lk 22:36
had gone away into the city to **b** food.) Jn 4:8
said to Philip, "Where are we to **b** bread, Jn 6:5
denarii would not **b** enough bread for Jn 6:7
"**B** what we need for the feast," or that he Jn 13:29
and those who **b** as though they had 1 Cor 7:30
I counsel you to **b** from me gold refined Rv 3:18
so that no one can **b** or sell unless he Rv 13:17

BUYER (7)
in the hand of the **b** until the year of Lv 25:28
city shall belong in perpetuity to the **b**, Lv 25:30
shall calculate with his **b** from the year Lv 25:50
female slaves, but there will be no **b**." Dt 28:68
"Bad, Bad," says the **b**, but when he Prv 20:14
mistress; as with the **b**, so with the seller; Is 24:2
Let not the **b** rejoice, nor the seller Ezk 7:12

BUYING (2)
them use it for **b** timber and quarried 2 Kgs 22:6
eating and drinking, **b** and selling, Lk 17:28

BUYS (4)
but if a priest **b** a slave as his property Lv 22:11
She considers a field and **b** it; with the Prv 31:16
sells all that he has and **b** that field. Mt 13:44
since no one **b** their cargo anymore, Rv 18:11

BUZ (3)
Uz his firstborn, **B** his brother, Gn 22:21
of Jeshishai, son of Jahdo, son of **B**. 1 Chr 5:14
B, and all who cut the corners of their Jer 25:23

BUZI (1)
came to Ezekiel the priest, the son of **B**, Ezk 1:3

BUZITE (2)
Then Elihu the son of Barachel the **B**, of Jb 32:2
son of Barachel the **B** answered and said: Jb 32:6

BYGONE (1)
"For inquire, please, of **b** ages, and Jb 8:8

BYSTANDERS (6)
girl saw him, and she said to the **b**, Mt 26:71
a little while the **b** came up and said Mt 26:73
And some of the **b**, hearing it, said, Mt 27:47
him and began again to say to the **b**, Mk 14:69
a little while the **b** again said to Peter, Mk 14:70
And some of the **b** hearing it said, Mk 15:35

BYWAYS (1)
abandoned, and travelers kept to the **b**. Jgs 5:6

BYWORD (14)
and a **b** among all the peoples where the Dt 28:37
a proverb and a **b** among all peoples. 1 Kgs 9:7
a proverb and a **b** among all peoples. 2 Chr 7:20
"He has made me a **b** of the peoples, and I Jb 17:6
become their song; I am a **b** to them. Jb 30:9
have made us a **b** among the nations, Ps 44:14
my clothing, I became a **b** to them. Ps 69:11
of the earth, to be a reproach, a **b**, Jer 24:9
him a sign and a **b** and cut him off Ezk 14:8
your sister Sodom a **b** in your mouth Ezk 16:56
and she became a **b** among women, Ezk 23:10
people have become a **b** among all who Dn 9:16
a reproach, a **b** among the nations. Jl 2:17
you have been a **b** of cursing among Zec 8:13

C

CABBON (1)
C, Lahmam, Chitlish, Jos 15:40

CABUL (2)
Then it continues in the north to **C**, Jos 19:27
are called the land of **C** to this day. 1 Kgs 9:13

CAESAR (20)
Is it lawful to pay taxes to **C**, or not?" Mt 22:17
"Therefore render to **C** the things that Mt 22:21
Is it lawful to pay taxes to **C**, or not? Mk 12:14
"Render to **C** the things that are Mk 12:17
decree went out from **C** Augustus that all Lk 2:1
fifteenth year of the reign of Tiberius **C**, Lk 3:1
Is it lawful for us to give tribute to **C**, or Lk 20:22
"Then render to **C** the things that are Lk 20:25
and forbidding us to give tribute to **C**, Lk 23:2
who makes himself a king opposes **C**." Jn 19:12
answered, "We have no king but **C**." Jn 19:15
are all acting against the decrees of **C**, Acts 17:7
nor against **C** have I committed any Acts 25:8
give me up to them. I appeal to **C**." Acts 25:11
answered, "To **C** you have appealed; Acts 25:12
you have appealed; to **C** you shall go." Acts 25:12
be held until I could send him to **C**." Acts 25:21
set free if he had not appealed to **C**." Acts 26:32
Paul; you must stand before **C**. Acts 27:24
compelled to appeal to **C**—though I Acts 28:19

CAESAR'S (9)
They said, "**C**." Then he said to them, Mt 22:21
render to Caesar the things that are **C**, Mt 22:21
is this?" They said to him, "**C**." Mk 12:16
to Caesar the things that are **C**, Mk 12:17
does it have?" They said, "**C**." Lk 20:24
render to Caesar the things that are **C**, Lk 20:25
release this man, you are not **C** friend. Jn 19:12
"I am standing before **C** tribunal, Acts 25:10
you, especially those of **C** household. Phil 4:22

CAESAREA (17)
came into the district of **C** Philippi, Mt 16:13
disciples to the villages of **C** Philippi. Mk 8:27
to all the towns until he came to **C**. Acts 8:40
brought him down to **C** and sent him Acts 9:30
At **C** there was a man named Acts 10:1
on the following day they entered **C**. Acts 10:24
in which we were, sent to me from **C**. Acts 11:11
down from Judea to **C** and spent time Acts 12:19
When he had landed at **C**, he went up Acts 18:22
next day we departed and came to **C**, Acts 21:8
of the disciples from **C** went with us, Acts 21:16
to go as far as **C** at the third hour of Acts 23:23
they had come to **C** and delivered the Acts 23:33
he went up to Jerusalem from **C**. Acts 25:1
was being kept at **C** and that he Acts 25:4
eight or ten days, he went down to **C**. Acts 25:6
Bernice arrived at **C** and greeted Acts 25:13

CAGE (2)
Like a **c** full of birds, their houses are Jer 5:27
they put him in a **c** and brought him to Ezk 19:9

CAIAPHAS (9)
of the high priest, whose name was **C**, Mt 26:3
Jesus led him to **C** the high priest, Mt 26:57
the high priesthood of Annas and **C**, Lk 3:2
them, **C**, who was high priest that year, Jn 11:49
for he was the father-in-law of **C**, Jn 18:13
It was **C** who had advised the Jews that it Jn 18:14
sent him bound to **C** the high priest. Jn 18:24
from the house of **C** to the governor's Jn 18:28
the high priest and **C** and John and Acts 4:6

CAIN (18)
his wife, and she conceived and bore **C**, Gn 4:1
of sheep, and **C** a worker of the ground. Gn 4:2
the course of time **C** brought to the LORD Gn 4:3
but for **C** and his offering he had no Gn 4:5
So **C** was very angry, and his face fell. Gn 4:5
The LORD said to **C**, "Why are you angry, Gn 4:6
C spoke to Abel his brother. And when Gn 4:8
C rose up against his brother Abel and Gn 4:8
Then the LORD said to **C**, "Where is Abel Gn 4:9
C said to the LORD, "My punishment is Gn 4:13
If anyone kills **C**, vengeance shall be Gn 4:15
And the LORD put a mark on **C**, Gn 4:15
Then **C** went away from the presence of Gn 4:16
C knew his wife, and she conceived and Gn 4:17
instead of Abel, for **C** killed him." Gn 4:25
a more acceptable sacrifice than **C**, Heb 11:4
We should not be like **C**, who was of 1 Jn 3:12
the way of **C** and abandoned Jude 1:11

CAIN'S (1)
If **C** revenge is sevenfold, then Lamech's Gn 4:24

CAINAN (2)
the son of **C**, the son of Arphaxad, the Lk 3:36
the son of Mahalaleel, the son of **C**, Lk 3:37

CAKE (13)
there were three **c** baskets on my head, Gn 40:16
of bread and one **c** of bread made with Ex 29:23
a **c** of barley bread tumbled into the Jgs 7:13
him a piece of a **c** of figs and two 1 Sm 30:12
both men and women, a **c** of bread, 2 Sm 6:19
of meat, and a **c** of raisins to each one. 2 Sm 6:19
make me a little **c** of it and bring 1 Kgs 17:13
at his head a **c** baked on hot stones 1 Kgs 19:6
And Isaiah said, "Bring a **c** of figs. 2 Kgs 20:7
a portion of meat, and a **c** of raisins. 1 Chr 16:3
"Let them take a **c** of figs and apply it to Is 38:21
And you shall eat it as a barley **c**, Ezk 4:12
the peoples; Ephraim is a **c** not turned. Hos 7:8

CAKES (22)
of fine flour! Knead it, and make **c**." Gn 18:6
they baked unleavened **c** of the dough Ex 12:39
bread, unleavened **c** mixed with oil, Ex 29:2
and boiled it in pots and made **c** of it. Nm 11:8
it was like the taste of **c** baked with oil. Nm 11:8
land, unleavened **c** and parched grain. Jos 5:11
goat and unleavened **c** from an ephah Jgs 6:19
"Take the meat and the unleavened **c**, Jgs 6:20
touched the meat and the unleavened **c**. Jgs 6:21
the flesh and the unleavened **c**. Jgs 6:21
of raisins and two hundred **c** of figs, 1 Sm 25:18
and make a couple of **c** in my sight, 2 Sm 13:6
kneaded it and made **c** in his sight 2 Sm 13:8
cakes in his sight and baked the **c**. 2 Sm 13:8
And Tamar took the **c** she had made 2 Sm 13:10
Take with you ten loaves, some **c**, 1 Kgs 14:3
was entrusted with making the flat **c**. 1 Chr 9:31
provisions of flour, **c** of figs, 1 Chr 12:40
stricken, for the raisin **c** of Kir-hareseth. Is 16:7
to make **c** for the queen of heaven. Jer 7:18
that we made **c** for her bearing Jer 44:19
turn to other gods and love **c** of raisins." Hos 3:1

CALAH (2)
built Nineveh, Rehoboth-Ir, **C**, and Gn 10:11
Resen between Nineveh and **C**; that is Gn 10:12

CALAMITIES (4)
from all your **c** and your distresses, 1 Sm 10:19
see many troubles and **c** will revive me Ps 71:20
endurance, in afflictions, hardships, **c**, 2 Cor 6:4
hardships, persecutions, and **c**. 2 Cor 12:10

CALAMITY (44)
out from all the tribes of Israel for **c**, Dt 29:21
for the day of their **c** is at hand, and Dt 32:35
the Almighty has brought **c** upon me?" Ru 1:21
confronted me in the day of my **c**, 2 Sm 22:19
LORD relented from the **c** and said to 2 Sm 24:16
have you brought **c** even upon the 1 Kgs 17:20
saw, and he relented from the **c**. 1 Chr 21:15
I bear to see the **c** that is coming to my Est 8:6
and all my **c** laid in the balances! Jb 6:2
nothing; you see my **c** and are afraid. Jb 6:21
Cannot my palate discern the cause of **c**? Jb 6:30
death, he mocks at the **c** of the innocent. Jb 9:23

and **c** is ready for his stumbling. Jb 18:12
out? That their **c** comes upon them? Jb 21:17
the evil man is spared in the day of **c**, Jb 21:30
break up my path; they promote my **c**; Jb 30:13
Is not **c** for the unrighteous, and disaster Jb 31:3
For I was in terror of **c** from God, and I Jb 31:23
They confronted me in the day of my **c**, Ps 18:18
altogether who rejoice at my **c**! Ps 35:26
I also will laugh at your **c**; I will mock Prv 1:26
a storm and your **c** comes like a Prv 1:27
therefore **c** will come upon him Prv 6:15
who is glad at **c** will not go unpunished. Prv 17:5
with a dishonest tongue falls into **c**. Prv 17:20
Whoever sows injustice will reap **c**, and Prv 22:8
but the wicked stumble in times of **c**. Prv 24:16
brother's house in the day of your **c**. Prv 27:10
hardens his heart will fall into **c**. Prv 28:14
darkness, I make well-being and create **c**, Is 45:7
the righteous man is taken away from **c**; Is 57:1
not labor in vain or bear children for **c**, Is 65:23
not my face, in the day of their **c**." Jer 18:17
the day of their **c** has come upon them, Jer 46:21
The **c** of Moab is near at hand, and his Jer 48:16
For I will bring the **c** of Esau upon him, Jer 49:8
I will bring their **c** from every side of Jer 49:32
power of the sword at the time of their **c**, Ezk 35:5
ruled us, by bringing upon us a great **c**. Dn 9:12
of Moses, all this **c** has come upon us; Dn 9:13
has kept ready the **c** and has brought it Dn 9:14
gate of my people in the day of their **c**; Ob 1:13
gloat over his disaster in the day of his **c**; Ob 1:13
do not loot his wealth in the day of his **c**. Ob 1:13

CALAMUS (2)
nard and saffron, **c** and cinnamon, with Sg 4:14
and **c** were bartered for your Ezk 27:19

CALCOL (2)
Ezrahite, and Heman, **C**, and Darda, 1 Kgs 4:31
Zimri, Ethan, Heman, **C**, and Dara, 1 Chr 2:6

CALCULATE (6)
let him **c** the years since he sold it and Lv 25:27
He shall **c** with his buyer from the year Lv 25:50
he shall **c** and pay for his redemption Lv 25:52
the priest shall **c** the price according Lv 27:18
then the priest shall **c** the amount of Lv 27:23
who has understanding **c** the number Rv 13:18

CALCULATING (1)
for he is like one who is inwardly **c**. Prv 23:7

CALEB (32)
tribe of Judah, **C** the son of Jephunneh; Nm 13:6
But **C** quieted the people before Moses Nm 13:30
son of Nun and **C** the son of Nm 14:6
But my servant **C**, because he has a Nm 14:24
except **C** the son of Jephunneh and Nm 14:30
son of Nun and **C** the son of Nm 14:38
except **C** the son of Jephunneh and Nm 26:65
none except **C** the son of Jephunneh Nm 32:12
of Judah, **C** the son of Jephunneh. Nm 34:19
except **C** the son of Jephunneh. He shall Dt 1:36
And **C** the son of Jephunneh the Jos 14:6
he gave Hebron to **C** the son of Jos 14:13
became the inheritance of **C** the son of Jos 14:14
he gave to **C** the son of Jephunneh a Jos 15:13
And **C** drove out from there the three Jos 15:14
And **C** said, "Whoever strikes Jos 15:16
the son of Kenaz, the brother of **C**, Jos 15:17
got off her donkey, and **C** said to her, Jos 15:18
had been given to **C** the son of Jos 21:12
And **C** said, "He who attacks Jgs 1:12
from her donkey, and **C** said to her, Jgs 1:14
springs of water." And **C** gave her the Jgs 1:15
And Hebron was given to **C**, as Moses Jgs 1:20
to Judah and against the Negeb of **C**, 1 Sm 30:14
C the son of Hezron fathered children 1 Chr 2:18
Azubah died, **C** married Ephrath, 1 Chr 2:19
of Hezron, **C** went in to Ephrathah, 1 Chr 2:24
The sons of **C** the brother of 1 Chr 2:42
and the daughter of **C** was Achsah. 1 Chr 2:49
These were the descendants of **C**. The 1 Chr 2:50
The sons of **C** the son of Jephunneh: 1 Chr 4:15
villages they gave to **C** the son of 1 Chr 6:56

CALEB'S (4)
the son of Kenaz, **C** younger brother, Jgs 1:13
the son of Kenaz, **C** younger brother. Jgs 3:9
Ephah also, **C** concubine, bore 1 Chr 2:46
Maacah, **C** concubine, bore Sheber 1 Chr 2:48

CALEBITE (1)
harsh and badly behaved; he was a **C**. 1 Sm 25:3

CALF (31)
Abraham ran to the herd and took a **c**, Gn 18:7
and milk and the **c** that he had Gn 18:8
with a graving tool and made a golden **c**. Ex 32:4
themselves a golden **c** and have Ex 32:8
camp and saw the **c** and the dancing, Ex 32:19
He took the **c** that they had made and Ex 32:20
it into the fire, and out came this **c**." Ex 32:24
on the people, because they made the **c**, Ex 32:35
for yourself a bull **c** for a sin offering Lv 9:2
for a sin offering, and a **c** and a lamb, Lv 9:3
altar and killed the **c** of the sin offering, Lv 9:8
You had made yourselves a golden **c**. Dt 9:16
sinful thing, the **c** that you had made, Dt 9:21
had a fattened **c** in the house, 1 Sm 28:24
for themselves a golden **c** and said, Neh 9:18
He makes Lebanon to skip like a **c**, and Ps 29:6
They made a **c** in Horeb and Ps 106:19
and the **c** and the lion and the fattened Is 11:6
and the lion and the fattened **c** together; Is 11:6
like the wilderness; there the **c** grazes; Is 27:10
I was disciplined, like an untrained **c**; Jer 31:18
make them like the **c** that they cut in Jer 34:18
who passed between the parts of the **c**. Jer 34:19
I have spurned your **c**, O Samaria. My Hos 8:5
The **c** of Samaria shall be broken to Hos 8:6
Samaria tremble for the **c** of Beth-aven. Hos 10:5
Ephraim was a trained **c** that loved to Hos 10:11
And bring the fattened **c** and kill it, Lk 15:23
your father has killed the fattened **c**, Lk 15:27
you killed the fattened **c** for him!' Lk 15:30
And they made a **c** in those days, and Acts 7:41

CALF'S (2)
the back of the throne was a **c** head, 1 Kgs 10:19
of their feet were like the sole of a **c** foot. Ezk 1:7

CALL (196)
to the man to see what he would **c** them. Gn 2:19
time people began to **c** upon the name of Gn 4:26
You shall **c** his name Ishmael, Gn 16:11
wife, you shall not **c** her name Sarai, Gn 17:15
a son, and you shall **c** his name Isaac. Gn 17:19
"Let us **c** the young woman and ask Gn 24:57
"Shall I go and **c** you a nurse from the Ex 2:7
the man? **C** him, that he may eat bread." Ex 2:20
Moses sent to **c** Dathan and Abiram Nm 16:12
land of the people of Amaw, to **c** him, Nm 22:5
him, "If the men have come to **c** you, Nm 22:20
"Did I not send to you to **c** you? Nm 22:37
but the Moabites **c** them Emim. Dt 2:11
the Ammonites **c** them Zamzummim Dt 2:20
(the Sidonians **c** Hermon Sirion, while the Dt 3:9
Sirion, while the Amorites **c** it Senir), Dt 3:9
God is to us, whenever we **c** upon him? Dt 4:7
I **c** heaven and earth to witness against Dt 4:26
of his city shall **c** him and speak to Dt 25:8
and you **c** them to mind among all the Dt 30:1
I **c** heaven and earth to witness against Dt 30:19
C Joshua and present yourselves in the Dt 31:14
in their ears and **c** heaven and earth to Dt 31:28
They shall **c** peoples to their mountain; Dt 33:19
not to **c** us when you went to fight with Jgs 8:1
Ammonites and did not **c** us to go with Jgs 12:1
were merry, they said, "**C** Samson, Jgs 16:25
She said to them, "Do not **c** me Naomi; Ru 1:20
c me Mara, for the Almighty has dealt Ru 1:20
Why **c** me Naomi, when the LORD has Ru 1:21
you called me." But he said, "I did not **c**; 1 Sm 3:5
you called me." But he said, "I did not **c**, 1 Sm 3:6
I will **c** upon the LORD, that he may 1 Sm 12:17
Absalom would **c** to him and say, 2 Sm 15:2
said, "**C** Hushai the Archite also, 2 Sm 17:5
"**C** the men of Judah together to me 2 Sm 20:4
I **c** upon the LORD, who is worthy to be 2 Sm 22:4
"**C** Bathsheba to me." So she came 1 Kgs 1:28
David said, "**C** to me Zadok the priest, 1 Kgs 1:32
ear to them whenever they **c** to you. 1 Kgs 8:52
And you **c** upon the name of your 1 Kgs 18:24
and I will **c** upon the name of the 1 Kgs 18:24
and **c** upon the name of your god, 1 Kgs 18:25
"**C** this Shunammite." When he had 2 Kgs 4:12
"**C** her." And when he had called her, 2 Kgs 4:15
"**C** this Shunammite." So he called 2 Kgs 4:36
me and stand and **c** upon the name of 2 Kgs 5:11
Now therefore **c** to me all the 2 Kgs 10:19
thanks to the LORD; **c** upon his name; 1 Chr 16:8
to sound the **c** to battle against 2 Chr 13:12
"**C** now; is there anyone who will answer Jb 5:1
Then **c**, and I will answer; or let me Jb 13:22
You would **c**, and I would answer you; Jb 14:15
I **c** for help, but there is no justice. Jb 19:7
I **c** to my servant, but he gives me no Jb 19:16
Will he **c** upon God at all times? Jb 27:10
they **c** for help because of the arm of the Jb 35:9
Answer me when I **c**, O God of my Ps 4:1
himself; the LORD hears when I **c** to him. Ps 4:3
his heart, "You will not **c** to account"? Ps 10:13
c his wickedness to account till you Ps 10:15
eat bread and do not **c** upon the LORD? Ps 14:4
I **c** upon you, for you will answer me, O Ps 17:6
I **c** upon the LORD, who is worthy to be Ps 18:3
the king! May he answer us when we **c**. Ps 20:9
To you, O LORD, I **c**; my rock, be not deaf Ps 28:1
not be put to shame, for I **c** upon you; Ps 31:17
and **c** upon me in the day of trouble; I Ps 50:15
they eat bread, and do not **c** upon God? Ps 53:4
But I **c** to God, and the LORD will save Ps 55:16
will turn back in the day when I **c**. Ps 56:9
end of the earth I **c** to you when my heart Ps 61:2
in him, all nations **c** him blessed! Ps 72:17
that do not **c** upon your name! Ps 79:6
us life, and we will **c** upon your name! Ps 80:18
in steadfast love to all who **c** upon you. Ps 86:5
In the day of my trouble I **c** upon you, for Ps 86:7
Every day I **c** upon you, O LORD; I spread Ps 88:9
answer me speedily in the day when I **c**! Ps 102:2
thanks to the LORD; **c** upon his name; Ps 105:1
therefore I will **c** on him as long as I Ps 116:2
cup of salvation and **c** on the name of Ps 116:13
of thanksgiving and **c** on the name Ps 116:17
I **c** to you; save me, that I may Ps 119:146
O LORD, I **c** upon you; hasten to me! Ps 141:1
Give ear to my voice when I **c** to you! Ps 141:1
The LORD is near to all who **c** on him, Ps 145:18
on him, to all who **c** on him in truth. Ps 145:18
Then they will **c** upon me, but I will not Prv 1:28
if you **c** out for insight and raise your Prv 2:3
my sister," and **c** insight your intimate Prv 7:4
Does not wisdom **c**? Does not Prv 8:1
"To you, O men, I **c**, and my cry is to the Prv 8:4
her young women to **c** from the highest Prv 9:3
the poor will himself **c** out and not be Prv 21:13
Her children rise up and **c** her blessed; Prv 31:28
Woe to those who **c** evil good and good Is 5:20
a son, and shall **c** his name Immanuel. Is 7:14
me, "**C** his name Maher-shalal-hashbaz; Is 8:3
"Do not **c** conspiracy all that this people Is 8:12
thanks to the LORD, **c** upon his name, Is 12:4
that day I will **c** my servant Eliakim the Is 22:20
disaster; he does not **c** back his words, Is 31:2
—there is no one there to **c** it a kingdom, Is 34:12
the sun, and he shall **c** upon my name; Is 41:25
"Yet you did not **c** upon me, O Jacob; Is 43:22
another will **c** on the name of Jacob, Is 44:5
God of Israel, who **c** you by your name. Is 45:3
Israel my chosen, I **c** you by your name, Is 45:4
For they **c** themselves after the holy city, Is 48:2
out the heavens; when I **c** to them, Is 48:13
you shall **c** a nation that you do not Is 55:5
be found; **c** upon him while he is near; Is 55:6
Will you **c** this a fast, and a day Is 58:5
Then you shall **c**, and the LORD will Is 58:9
and **c** the Sabbath a delight and the holy Is 58:13
they shall **c** you the City of the LORD, the Is 60:14
you shall **c** your walls Salvation, and Is 60:18
his servants he will **c** by another name. Is 65:15
Before they **c** I will answer; while they Is 65:24
And I thought you would **c** me, My Jer 3:19
not listen to you. You shall **c** to them, Jer 7:27
and **c** for the mourning women to come; Jer 9:17
on the peoples that **c** not on your name, Jer 10:25
will not listen when they **c** to me in the Jer 11:14
LORD does not **c** your name Pashhur, Jer 20:3
Then you will **c** upon me and come Jer 29:12
day when watchmen will **c** in the hill Jer 31:6
C to me and I will answer you, and will Jer 33:3
C the name of Pharaoh, king of Egypt, Jer 46:17
though I **c** and cry for help, he shuts Lam 3:8
But this I **c** to mind, and therefore I Lam 3:21
LORD said to him, "**C** his name Jezreel, Hos 1:4
said to him, "**C** her name No Mercy, Hos 1:6
LORD said, "**C** his name Not My People, Hos 1:9
the LORD, you will **c** me 'My Husband,' Hos 2:16
and no longer will you **c** me 'My Baal.' Hos 2:16
and though they **c** out to the Most Hos 11:7
Consecrate a fast; **c** a solemn assembly. Jl 1:14
To you, O LORD, I **c**. For fire has devoured Jl 1:19
consecrate a fast; **c** a solemn assembly; Jl 2:15
They shall **c** the farmers to mourning Am 5:16
that great city, and **c** out against it, Jon 1:2
you sleeper? Arise, **c** out to your god! Jon 1:6
and **c** out against it the message that I tell Jon 3:2
and let them **c** out mightily to God. Jon 3:8
that all of them may **c** upon the name of Zep 3:9
They will **c** upon my name, and I will Zec 13:9
Then all nations will **c** you blessed, for Mal 3:12
And now we **c** the arrogant blessed. Mal 3:15
a son, and you shall **c** his name Jesus, Mt 1:21
and they shall **c** his name Immanuel" Mt 1:23
For I came not to **c** the righteous, but Mt 9:13
'**C** the laborers and pay them their Mt 20:8
sent his servants to **c** those who were Mt 22:3
And **c** no man your father on earth, for Mt 23:9
out his angels with a loud trumpet **c**, Mt 24:31
I came not to **c** the righteous, but Mk 2:17

said to him, “Why do you **c** me good? Mk 10:18
“**C** him.” And they called the blind Mk 10:49
do with the man you **c** the King of the Mk 15:12
a son, and you shall **c** his name John. Lk 1:13
a son, and you shall **c** his name Jesus. Lk 1:31
on all generations will **c** me blessed; Lk 1:48
have not come to **c** the righteous but Lk 5:32
“Why do you **c** me ‘Lord, Lord,’ and not Lk 6:46
said to him, “Why do you **c** me good? Lk 18:19
Jesus said to her, “Go, **c** your husband, Jn 4:16
You **c** me Teacher and Lord, and you Jn 13:13
No longer do I **c** you servants, for the Jn 15:15
to bind all who **c** on your name.” Acts 9:14
has made clean, do not **c** common.” Acts 10:15
I should not **c** any person common Acts 10:28
has made clean, do not **c** common.’ Acts 11:9
to the Way, which they **c** a sect, Acts 24:14
But if you **c** yourself a Jew and rely on Rom 2:17
of works but because of his **c**— Rom 9:11
were not my people I will **c** ‘my people,’ Rom 9:25
who was not beloved I will **c** ‘beloved.’” Rom 9:25
his riches on all who **c** on him. Rom 10:12
how are they to **c** on him in whom Rom 10:14
who in every place **c** upon the name of 1 Cor 1:2
time of his **c** already circumcised? 1 Cor 7:18
at the time of his **c** uncircumcised? 1 Cor 7:18
But I **c** God to witness against me—it 2 Cor 1:23
to the one hope that belongs to your **c**— Eph 4:4
prize of the upward **c** of God in Christ Phil 3:14
along with those who **c** on the Lord 2 Tm 2:22
he is not ashamed to **c** them brothers, Heb 2:11
Let him **c** for the elders of the church, Jas 5:14
And if you **c** on him as Father who 1 Pt 1:17
tested those who **c** themselves apostles Rv 2:2
not learned what some **c** the deep things Rv 2:24
days of the trumpet **c** to be sounded by Rv 10:7
Here is a **c** for the endurance and faith Rv 13:10
Here is a **c** for the endurance of the Rv 14:12

CALLED (586)

God **c** the light Day, and the darkness he Gn 1:5
light Day, and the darkness he **c** Night. Gn 1:5
And God **c** the expanse Heaven. And there Gn 1:8
God **c** the dry land Earth, and the waters Gn 1:10
that were gathered together he **c** Seas. Gn 1:10
whatever the man **c** every living Gn 2:19
she shall be **c** Woman, because she was Gn 2:23
But the LORD God **c** to the man and said to Gn 3:9
The man **c** his wife's name Eve, because Gn 3:20
he **c** the name of the city after the name Gn 4:17
and she bore a son and **c** his name Seth, Gn 4:25
son was born, and he **c** his name Enosh. Gn 4:26
and **c** his name Noah, saying, “Out of Gn 5:29
Therefore its name was **c** Babel, Gn 11:9
altar to the LORD and **c** upon the name of Gn 12:8
So Pharaoh **c** Abram and said, “What Gn 12:18
And there Abram **c** upon the name of Gn 13:4
So she **c** the name of the LORD who Gn 16:13
Therefore the well was **c** Beer-lahai-roi; Gn 16:14
son, and Abram **c** the name of his son, Gn 16:15
No longer shall your name be **c** Abram, Gn 17:5
And they **c** to Lot, “Where are the men Gn 19:5
the name of the city was **c** Zoar. Gn 19:22
bore a son and **c** his name Moab. Gn 19:37
bore a son and **c** his name Ben-ammi. Gn 19:38
in the morning and **c** all his servants Gn 20:8
Then Abimelech **c** Abraham and said Gn 20:9
Abraham **c** the name of his son who Gn 21:3
the angel of God **c** to Hagar from Gn 21:17
Therefore that place was **c** Beersheba, Gn 21:31
tree in Beersheba and **c** there on the Gn 21:33
angel of the LORD **c** to him from heaven Gn 22:11
So Abraham **c** the name of that place, Gn 22:14
angel of the LORD **c** to Abraham a Gn 22:15
And they **c** Rebekah and said to her, Gn 24:58
a hairy cloak, so they **c** his name Esau. Gn 25:25
Esau's heel, so his name was **c** Jacob. Gn 25:26
(Therefore his name was **c** Edom.) Gn 25:30
So Abimelech **c** Isaac and said, “Behold, Gn 26:9
water is ours.” So he **c** the name of the Gn 26:20
over that also, so he **c** its name Sitnah. Gn 26:21
So he **c** its name Rehoboth, saying, Gn 26:22
an altar there and **c** upon the name of Gn 26:25
He **c** it Shibah; therefore the name of Gn 26:33
he **c** Esau his older son and said to him, Gn 27:1
So she sent and **c** Jacob her younger Gn 27:42
Then Isaac **c** Jacob and blessed him Gn 28:1
He **c** the name of that place Bethel, but Gn 28:19
a son, and she **c** his name Reuben, Gn 29:32
son also.” And she **c** his name Simeon. Gn 29:33
sons.” Therefore his name was **c** Levi. Gn 29:34
LORD.” Therefore she **c** his name Judah. Gn 29:35
a son.” Therefore she **c** his name Dan. Gn 30:6
prevailed.” So she **c** his name Naphtali. Gn 30:8
has come!” so she **c** his name Gad. Gn 30:11
For women have **c** me happy.” So she Gn 30:13
me happy.” So she **c** his name Asher. Gn 30:13
husband.” So she **c** his name Issachar. Gn 30:18
six sons.” So she **c** his name Zebulun. Gn 30:20
a daughter and **c** her name Dinah. Gn 30:21
And she **c** his name Joseph, saying, Gn 30:24
So Jacob sent and **c** Rachel and Leah Gn 31:4
Laban **c** it Jegar-sahadutha, but Jacob Gn 31:47
Jegar-sahadutha, but Jacob **c** it Galeed. Gn 31:47
the hill country and **c** his kinsmen to Gn 31:54
is God's camp!” So he **c** the name of that Gn 32:2
name shall no longer be **c** Jacob, Gn 32:28
So Jacob **c** the name of the place Gn 32:30
the name of the place is **c** Succoth. Gn 33:17
an altar and **c** it El-Elohe-Israel. Gn 33:20
built an altar and **c** the place El-bethel, Gn 35:7
Bethel. So he **c** its name Allon-bacuth. Gn 35:8
no longer shall your name be **c** Jacob, Gn 35:10
your name.” So he **c** his name Israel. Gn 35:10
So Jacob **c** the name of the place where Gn 35:15
was dying), she **c** his name Ben-oni; Gn 35:18
but his father **c** him Benjamin. Gn 35:18
and bore a son, and he **c** his name Er. Gn 38:3
bore a son, and she **c** his name Onan. Gn 38:4
bore a son, and she **c** his name Shelah. Gn 38:5
Therefore his name was **c** Perez. Gn 38:29
his hand, and his name was **c** Zerah. Gn 38:30
she **c** to the men of her household and Gn 39:14
and he sent and **c** for all the magicians Gn 41:8
Then Pharaoh sent and **c** Joseph, and Gn 41:14
And they **c** out before him, “Bow the Gn 41:43
And Pharaoh **c** Joseph's name Gn 41:45
Joseph **c** the name of the firstborn Gn 41:51
The name of the second he **c** Ephraim, Gn 41:52
he **c** his son Joseph and said to him, Gn 47:29
They shall be **c** by the name of their Gn 48:6
Then Jacob **c** his sons and said, “Gather Gn 49:1
the king of Egypt **c** the midwives and Ex 1:18
So the girl went and **c** the child's mother. Ex 2:8
to a son, and he **c** his name Gershom, Ex 2:22
aside to see, God **c** to him out of the bush, Ex 3:4
Then Pharaoh **c** Moses and Aaron and Ex 8:8
Then Pharaoh **c** Moses and Aaron and Ex 8:25
Pharaoh sent and **c** Moses and Aaron Ex 9:27
Then Pharaoh hastily **c** Moses and Ex 10:16
Then Pharaoh **c** Moses and said, “Go, Ex 10:24
Then Moses **c** all the elders of Israel Ex 12:21
the house of Israel **c** its name manna. Ex 16:31
And he **c** the name of the place Massah Ex 17:7
built an altar and **c** the name of it, Ex 17:15
The LORD **c** to him out of the mountain, Ex 19:3
So Moses came and **c** the elders of the Ex 19:7
And the LORD **c** Moses to the top of the Ex 19:20
on the seventh day he **c** to Moses out of Ex 24:16
I have **c** by name Bezalel the son of Uri, Ex 31:2
the camp, and he **c** it the tent of meeting. Ex 33:7
But Moses **c** to them, and Aaron and all Ex 34:31
the LORD has **c** by name Bezalel the son Ex 35:30
And Moses **c** Bezalel and Oholiab and Ex 36:2
The LORD **c** Moses and spoke to him from Lv 1:1
the eighth day Moses **c** Aaron and his Lv 9:1
And Moses **c** Mishael and Elzaphan, the Lv 10:4
the name of that place was **c** Taberah, Nm 11:3
that place was **c** Kibroth-hattaavah, Nm 11:34
of the tent and **c** Aaron and Miriam, Nm 12:5
And Moses **c** Hoshea the son of Nun Nm 13:16
That place was **c** the Valley of Eshcol, Nm 13:24
the name of the place was **c** Hormah. Nm 21:3
Balaam, “I **c** you to curse my enemies, Nm 24:10
villages, and **c** them Havvoth-jair. Nm 32:41
and its villages, and **c** it Nobah, Nm 32:42
portion of Bashan is **c** the land of Dt 3:13
and **c** the villages after his own name, Dt 3:14
name of his house shall be **c** in Israel, Dt 25:10
shall see that you are **c** by the name of Dt 28:10
Then Joshua **c** the twelve men from the Jos 4:4
name of that place is **c** Gilgal to this day. Jos 5:9
the son of Nun **c** the priests and said Jos 6:6
of that place is **c** the Valley of Achor. Jos 7:26
in the city were **c** together to pursue Jos 8:16
the people of Gad **c** the altar Witness, Jos 22:34
So the name of the city was **c** Hormah. Jgs 1:17
and built a city and **c** its name Luz. Jgs 1:26
And they **c** the name of that place Jgs 2:5
And Barak **c** out Zebulun and Naphtali Jgs 4:10
Sisera **c** out all his chariots, 900 Jgs 4:13
built an altar there to the LORD and **c** it, Jgs 6:24
on that day Gideon was **c** Jerubbaal, Jgs 6:32
and the Abiezrites were **c** out to follow Jgs 6:34
and they too were **c** out to follow him. Jgs 6:35
men of Israel were **c** out from Naphtali Jgs 7:23
So all the men of Ephraim were **c** out, Jgs 7:24
a son, and he **c** his name Abimelech. Jgs 8:31
Then he **c** quickly to the young man his Jgs 9:54
thirty cities, **c** Havvoth-jair to this day, Jgs 10:4
Then the Ammonites were **c** to arms, Jgs 10:17
The men of Ephraim were **c** to arms, Jgs 12:1
with the Ammonites, and when I **c** you, Jgs 12:2
bore a son and **c** his name Samson. Jgs 13:24
And that place was **c** Ramath-lehi. Jgs 15:17
and he **c** upon the LORD and said, Jgs 15:18
the name of it was **c** En-hakkore; Jgs 15:19
she sent and **c** the lords of the Jgs 16:18
And she **c** a man and had him shave Jgs 16:19
entertain us.” So they **c** Samson out of Jgs 16:25
Then Samson **c** to the LORD and said, Jgs 16:28
that place is **c** Mahaneh-dan to this Jgs 18:12
houses near Micah's house were **c** out, Jgs 18:22
a son, and she **c** his name Samuel, 1 Sm 1:20
Then the LORD **c** Samuel, and he said, 1 Sm 3:4
“Here I am, for you **c** me.” But he said, 1 Sm 3:5
And the LORD **c** again, “Samuel!” and 1 Sm 3:6
“Here I am, for you **c** me.” But he said, 1 Sm 3:6
And the LORD **c** Samuel again the third 1 Sm 3:8
for you **c** me.” Then Eli perceived that 1 Sm 3:8
But Eli **c** Samuel and said, “Samuel, 1 Sm 3:16
And the Philistines **c** for the priests and 1 Sm 6:2
and Shen and **c** its name Ebenezer; 1 Sm 7:12
“prophet” was formerly **c** a seer.) 1 Sm 9:9
break of dawn Samuel **c** to Saul on 1 Sm 9:26
Now Samuel **c** the people together to 1 Sm 10:17
So Samuel **c** upon the LORD, and the 1 Sm 12:18
And the people were **c** out to join Saul 1 Sm 13:4
Then Jesse **c** Abinadab and made 1 Sm 16:8
And Jonathan **c** David, and Jonathan 1 Sm 19:7
Jonathan **c** after the boy and said, 1 Sm 20:37
And Jonathan **c** after the boy, 1 Sm 20:38
that place was **c** the Rock of 1 Sm 23:28
went out of the cave, and **c** after Saul, 1 Sm 24:8
And David **c** to the army, and to 1 Sm 26:14
Then Achish **c** David and said to 1 Sm 29:6
behind him, he saw me, and **c** to me. 2 Sm 1:7
Then David **c** one of the young men 2 Sm 1:15
that place was **c** Helkath-hazzurim, 2 Sm 2:16
Then Abner **c** to Joab, “Shall the 2 Sm 2:26
in the stronghold and **c** it the city of 2 Sm 5:9
name of that place is **c** Baal-perazim. 2 Sm 5:20
which is **c** by the name of the LORD of 2 Sm 6:2
And that place is **c** Perez-uzzah, to this 2 Sm 6:8
was Ziba, and they **c** him to David. 2 Sm 9:2
Then the king **c** Ziba, Saul's servant, 2 Sm 9:9
a son, and he **c** his name Solomon. 2 Sm 12:24
So he **c** his name Jedidiah, because 2 Sm 12:25
the city and it be **c** by my name.” 2 Sm 12:28
He **c** the young man who served him 2 Sm 13:17
in remembrance.” He **c** the pillar 2 Sm 18:18
and it is **c** Absalom's monument to 2 Sm 18:18
The watchman **c** out and told the 2 Sm 18:25
And the watchman **c** to the gate and 2 Sm 18:26
Then a wise woman **c** from the city, 2 Sm 20:16
Ephraim, **c** Sheba the son of Bichri, 2 Sm 20:21
So the king **c** the Gibeonites and 2 Sm 21:2
“In my distress I **c** upon the LORD; to 2 Sm 22:7
I called upon the LORD; to my God I **c**. 2 Sm 22:7
on the south and **c** its name Jachin, 1 Kgs 7:21
on the north and **c** its name Boaz. 1 Kgs 7:21
that I have built is **c** by your name. 1 Kgs 8:43
brother?” So they are **c** the land of 1 Kgs 9:13
And they sent and **c** him, and 1 Kgs 12:3
they sent and **c** him to the assembly 1 Kgs 12:20
the saying that he **c** out by the word 1 Kgs 13:32
fortified the hill and **c** the name of 1 Kgs 16:24
And he **c** to her and said, “Bring me 1 Kgs 17:10
to bring it, he **c** to her and said, 1 Kgs 17:11
And Ahab **c** Obadiah, who was over 1 Kgs 18:3
prepared it and **c** upon the name 1 Kgs 18:26
the king of Israel **c** all the elders of 1 Kgs 20:7
The LORD has **c** these three kings to 2 Kgs 3:10
the LORD who has **c** these three kings 2 Kgs 3:13
were **c** out and were drawn up at the 2 Kgs 3:21
Shunammite.” When he had **c** her, 2 Kgs 4:12
“Call her.” And when he had **c** her, 2 Kgs 4:15
Then she **c** to her husband and said, 2 Kgs 4:22
“Call this Shunammite.” So he **c** her. 2 Kgs 4:36
and he **c** his servants and said to 2 Kgs 6:11
So they came and **c** to the gatekeepers 2 Kgs 7:10
Then the gatekeepers **c** out, and it 2 Kgs 7:11
can, for the LORD has **c** for a famine, 2 Kgs 8:1
Then Elisha the prophet **c** one of the 2 Kgs 9:1
took Sela by storm, and **c** it Joktheel, 2 Kgs 14:7
offerings to it (it was **c** Nehushtan). 2 Kgs 18:4
And when they **c** for the king, there 2 Kgs 18:18
the Rabshakeh stood and **c** out in a 2 Kgs 18:28
And Isaiah the prophet **c** to the LORD, 2 Kgs 20:11
and his mother **c** his name Jabez, 1 Chr 4:9
Jabez **c** upon the God of Israel, 1 Chr 4:10
a son, and she **c** his name Peresh; 1 Chr 7:16
And he **c** his name Beriah, because 1 Chr 7:23
therefore it was **c** the city of David. 1 Chr 11:7
which is **c** by the name of the LORD 1 Chr 13:6
that place is **c** Perez-uzza to this 1 Chr 13:11

of that place is **c** Baal-perazim. 1 Chr 14:11
peace offerings and **c** on the LORD, 1 Chr 21:26
Then he **c** for Solomon his son and 1 Chr 22:6
that on the south he **c** Jachin, and 2 Chr 3:17
that I have built is **c** by your name. 2 Chr 6:33
my people who are **c** by my name 2 Chr 7:14
And they sent and **c** him. And 2 Chr 10:3
that place has been **c** the Valley of 2 Chr 20:26
the Gileadite, and was **c** by their name). Ezr 2:61
you say." And I **c** the priests and made Neh 5:12
the Gileadite and was **c** by their name). Neh 7:63
Then Esther **c** for Hathach, one of the Est 4:5
inside the inner court without being **c**, Est 4:11
I have not been **c** to come in to the king Est 4:11
Therefore they **c** these days Purim, after Est 9:26
I, who **c** to God and he answered me, a Jb 12:4
When the ear heard, it **c** me blessed, Jb 29:11
gold my trust or **c** fine gold my Jb 31:24
And he **c** the name of the first daughter Jb 42:14
In my distress I **c** upon the LORD; to my Ps 18:6
him alive; he is **c** blessed in the land; Ps 41:2
though they **c** lands by their own Ps 49:11
In distress you **c**, and I delivered you; I Ps 81:7
was among those who **c** upon his name. Ps 99:6
They **c** to the LORD, and he answered Ps 99:6
Then I **c** on the name of the LORD: "O Ps 116:4
Out of my distress I **c** on the LORD; the Ps 118:5
In my distress I **c** to the LORD, and he Ps 120:1
On the day I **c**, you answered me; my Ps 138:3
Because I have **c** and you refused to Prv 1:24
those who hold her fast are **c** blessed. Prv 3:18
The wise of heart is **c** discerning, and Prv 16:21
plans to do evil will be **c** a schemer. Prv 24:8
I sought him, but found him not; I **c** him, Sg 5:6
young women saw her and **c** her blessed; Sg 6:9
Afterward you shall be **c** the city of Is 1:26
clothes, only let us be **c** by your name; Is 4:1
and remains in Jerusalem will be **c** holy, Is 4:3
And one **c** to another and said: "Holy, holy, Is 6:3
shook at the voice of him who **c**, Is 6:4
his name shall be **c** Wonderful Counselor, Is 9:6
of these will be **c** the City of Destruction. Is 19:18
Lord GOD of hosts **c** for weeping and Is 22:12
therefore I have **c** her "Rahab who sits Is 30:7
band of shepherds is **c** out against him is Is 31:4
The fool will no more be **c** noble, nor the Is 32:5
and it shall be **c** the Way of Holiness; Is 35:8
the Rabshakeh stood and **c** out in a loud Is 36:13
the earth, and **c** from its farthest corners, Is 41:9
the LORD; I have **c** you in righteousness; Is 42:6
you; I have **c** you by name, you are mine. Is 43:1
everyone who is **c** by my name, whom I Is 43:7
shall no more be **c** tender and delicate. Is 47:1
shall no more be **c** the mistress of Is 47:5
of Jacob, who are **c** by the name of Israel, Is 48:1
that from before birth you were **c** a rebel. Is 48:8
to me, O Jacob, and Israel, whom I **c**! Is 48:12
I, even I, have spoken and **c** him; I have Is 48:15
The LORD **c** me from the womb, from the Is 49:1
why, when I **c**, was there no one to Is 50:2
for he was but one when I **c** him, that I Is 51:2
the God of the whole earth he is **c**. Is 54:5
For the LORD has **c** you like a wife deserted Is 54:6
for my house shall be **c** a house of prayer Is 56:7
you shall be **c** the repairer of the breach, Is 58:12
that they may be **c** oaks of righteousness, Is 61:3
but you shall be **c** the priests of the LORD; Is 61:6
and you shall be **c** by a new name that Is 62:2
but you shall be **c** My Delight Is in Her, Is 62:4
And they shall be **c** The Holy People, Is 62:12
and you shall be **c** Sought Out, A City Is 62:12
like those who are not **c** by your name. Is 63:19
I," to a nation that was not **c** by my name. Is 65:1
to the slaughter, because, when I **c**, Is 65:12
their fears upon them, because when I **c**, Is 66:4
Have you not just now **c** to me, 'My father, Jer 3:4
time Jerusalem shall be **c** the throne of Jer 3:17
Rejected silver they are **c**, for the LORD Jer 6:30
in this house, which is **c** by my name, Jer 7:10
Has this house, which is **c** by my name, Jer 7:11
you did not listen, and when I **c** you, Jer 7:13
do to the house that is **c** by my name, Jer 7:14
in the house that is **c** by my name, Jer 7:30
LORD, when it will no more be **c** Topheth, Jer 7:32
The LORD once **c** you 'a green olive tree, Jer 11:16
midst of us, and we are **c** by your name; Jer 14:9
of my heart, for I am **c** by your name, Jer 15:16
this place shall no more be **c** Topheth, Jer 19:6
this is the name by which he will be **c**: Jer 23:6
at the city that is **c** by my name, Jer 25:29
because they have **c** you an outcast: Jer 30:17
in the house that is **c** by my name, Jer 32:34
this is the name by which it will be **c**: Jer 33:16
me in the house that is **c** by my name, Jer 34:15
I have **c** to them and they have not Jer 35:17
Then Jeremiah **c** Baruch the son of Jer 36:4
"I **c** to my lovers, but they deceived me; Lam 1:19
the city that was **c** the perfection of Lam 2:15
"I **c** on your name, O LORD, from the Lam 3:55
You came near when I **c** on you; you Lam 3:57
And he **c** to the man clothed in linen, Ezk 9:3
they were **c** in my hearing "the Ezk 10:13
So its name is **c** Bamah to this day.) Ezk 20:29
It will be **c** the Valley of Hamon-gog. Ezk 39:11
Daniel he **c** Belteshazzar, Hananiah he Dn 1:7
Belteshazzar, Hananiah he **c** Shadrach, Dn 1:7
called Shadrach, Mishael he **c** Meshach, Dn 1:7
Meshach, and Azariah he **c** Abednego. Dn 1:7
The king **c** loudly to bring in the Dn 5:7
Now let Daniel be **c**, and he will show Dn 5:12
between the banks of the Ulai, and it **c**, Dn 8:16
and the city that is **c** by your name. Dn 9:18
and your people are **c** by your name." Dn 9:19
loved him, and out of Egypt I **c** my son. Hos 11:1
The more they were **c**, the more they Hos 11:2
the nations who are **c** by my name," Am 9:12
Therefore they **c** out to the LORD, "O Jon 1:14
saying, "I **c** out to the LORD, out of my Jon 2:2
And he **c** out, "Yet forty days, and Jon 3:4
They **c** for a fast and put on sackcloth, Jon 3:5
And I have **c** for a drought on the land Hg 1:11
"As I **c**, and they would not hear, so they Zec 7:13
and they would not hear, so they **c**, Zec 7:13
Jerusalem shall be **c** the faithful city, Zec 8:3
and they will be **c** 'the wicked country,' Mal 1:4
whom Jesus was born, who is **c** Christ. Mt 1:16
birth to a son. And he **c** his name Jesus. Mt 1:25
the prophet, "Out of Egypt I **c** my son." Mt 2:15
he went and lived in a city **c** Nazareth, Mt 2:23
be fulfilled: "He shall be **c** a Nazarene." Mt 2:23
Simon (who is **c** Peter) and Andrew his Mt 4:18
mending their nets, and he **c** them. Mt 4:21
for they shall be **c** sons of God. Mt 5:9
the same will be **c** least in the kingdom Mt 5:19
teaches them will be **c** great in the Mt 5:19
he saw a man **c** Matthew sitting at the tax Mt 9:9
And he **c** to him his twelve disciples and Mt 10:1
first, Simon, who is **c** Peter, and Andrew Mt 10:2
If they have **c** the master of the house Mt 10:25
son? Is not his mother **c** Mary? Mt 13:55
And he **c** the people to him and said to Mt 15:10
Then Jesus **c** his disciples to him and Mt 15:32
But Jesus **c** them to him and said, "You Mt 20:25
And stopping, Jesus **c** them and said, Mt 20:32
'My house shall be **c** a house of prayer,' Mt 21:13
For many are **c**, but few are chosen." Mt 22:14
marketplaces and being **c** rabbi by Mt 23:7
But you are not to be **c** rabbi, for you Mt 23:8
Neither be **c** instructors, for you have Mt 23:10
who **c** his servants and entrusted to Mt 25:14
with them to a place **c** Gethsemane, Mt 26:36
that field has been **c** the Field of Blood Mt 27:8
then a notorious prisoner **c** Barabbas. Mt 27:16
Barabbas, or Jesus who is **c** Christ?" Mt 27:17
with Jesus who is **c** Christ?" They all Mt 27:22
to a place **c** Golgotha (which means Mt 27:33
And immediately he **c** them, and they Mk 1:20
on the mountain and **c** to him those Mk 3:13
And he **c** them to him and said to them Mk 3:23
outside they sent to him and **c** him. Mk 3:31
And he **c** the twelve and began to send Mk 6:7
And he **c** the people to him again and Mk 7:14
he **c** his disciples to him and said to Mk 8:1
And he **c** to him the crowd with his Mk 8:34
And he sat down and **c** the twelve. And Mk 9:35
And Jesus **c** them to him and said to Mk 10:42
"Call him." And they **c** the blind man, Mk 10:49
'My house shall be **c** a house of prayer Mk 11:17
And he **c** his disciples to him and said Mk 12:43
they went to a place **c** Gethsemane. Mk 14:32
there was a man **c** Barabbas. Mk 15:7
and they **c** together the whole Mk 15:16
to the place **c** Golgotha (which means Mk 15:22
be great and will be **c** the Son of the Lk 1:32
to be born will be **c** holy—the Son of Lk 1:35
sixth month with her who was **c** barren. Lk 1:36
they would have **c** him Zechariah after Lk 1:59
answered, "No; he shall be **c** John." Lk 1:60
of your relatives is **c** by this name." Lk 1:61
inquiring what he wanted him to be **c**. Lk 1:62
will be **c** the prophet of the Most High; Lk 1:76
the city of David, which is **c** Bethlehem, Lk 2:4
he was circumcised, he was **c** Jesus, Lk 2:21
the womb shall be **c** holy to the Lord") Lk 2:23
he **c** his disciples and chose from them Lk 6:13
and Simon who was **c** the Zealot, Lk 6:15
afterward he went to a town **c** Nain, Lk 7:11
Mary, **c** Magdalene, from whom seven Lk 8:2
As he said these things, he **c** out, Lk 8:8
But taking her by the hand he **c**, saying, Lk 8:54
And he **c** the twelve together and gave Lk 9:1
withdrew apart to a town **c** Bethsaida. Lk 9:10
And she had a sister **c** Mary, who sat at Lk 10:39
saw her, he **c** her over and said to her, Lk 13:12
I am no longer worthy to be **c** your son. Lk 15:19
am no longer worthy to be **c** your son.' Lk 15:21
And he **c** one of the servants and asked Lk 15:26
And he **c** him and said to him, 'What is Lk 16:2
And he **c** out, 'Father Abraham, have Lk 16:24
But Jesus **c** them to him, saying, "Let Lk 18:16
he had given the money to be **c** to him, Lk 19:15
Bethany, at the mount that is **c** Olivet, Lk 19:29
out and lodged on the mount **c** Olivet. Lk 21:37
drew near, which is **c** the Passover. Lk 22:1
Then Satan entered into Judas **c** Iscariot, Lk 22:3
authority over them are **c** benefactors. Lk 22:25
came a crowd, and the man **c** Judas, Lk 22:47
Pilate then **c** together the chief priests Lk 23:13
came to the place that is **c** The Skull, Lk 23:33
You shall be **c** Cephas" (which means Jn 1:42
Jesus answered him, "Before Philip **c** you, Jn 1:48
the master of the feast **c** the bridegroom Jn 2:9
So he came to a town of Samaria **c** Sychar, Jn 4:5
Messiah is coming (he who is **c** Christ). Jn 4:25
Sheep Gate a pool, in Aramaic **c** Bethesda, Jn 5:2
"The man **c** Jesus made mud and Jn 9:11
until they **c** the parents of the man who Jn 9:18
the second time they **c** the man who had Jn 9:24
If he **c** them gods to whom the word of Jn 10:35
So Thomas, **c** the Twin, said to his Jn 11:16
this, she went and **c** her sister Mary, Jn 11:28
the wilderness, to a town **c** Ephraim, Jn 11:54
with him when he **c** Lazarus out of the Jn 12:17
but I have **c** you friends, for all that I Jn 15:15
headquarters again and **c** Jesus and said Jn 18:33
seat at a place **c** The Stone Pavement, Jn 19:13
cross, to the place **c** the place of a skull, Jn 19:17
skull, which in Aramaic is **c** Golgotha. Jn 19:17
Thomas, one of the Twelve, **c** the Twin, Jn 20:24
Simon Peter, Thomas (**c** the Twin), Jn 21:2
to Jerusalem from the mount **c** Olivet, Acts 1:12
that the field was **c** in their own Acts 1:19
put forward two, Joseph **c** Barsabbas, Acts 1:23
Barsabbas, who was also **c** Justus, Acts 1:23
the temple that is **c** the Beautiful Gate to Acts 3:2
to them in the portico **c** Solomon's, Acts 3:11
So they **c** them and charged them not Acts 4:18
who was also **c** by the apostles Acts 4:36
they **c** together the council and all the Acts 5:21
and when they had **c** in the apostles, Acts 5:40
of the Freedmen (as it was **c**), Acts 6:9
as they were stoning Stephen, he **c** out, Acts 7:59
is the power of God that is **c** Great." Acts 8:10
"Rise and go to the street **c** Straight, Acts 9:11
of those who **c** upon this name? Acts 9:21
and bring one Simon who is **c** Peter. Acts 10:5
he **c** two of his servants and a devout Acts 10:7
and **c** out to ask whether Simon who Acts 10:18
Simon who was **c** Peter was lodging Acts 10:18
them and had **c** together his relatives Acts 10:24
and ask for Simon who is **c** Peter. Acts 10:32
and bring Simon who is **c** Peter; Acts 11:13
the disciples were first **c** Christians. Acts 11:26
Barnabas, Simeon who was **c** Niger, Acts 13:1
for the work to which I have **c** them." Acts 13:2
But Saul, who was also **c** Paul, filled Acts 13:9
Barnabas they **c** Zeus, and Paul, Acts 14:12
the Gentiles who are **c** by my name, Acts 15:17
They sent Judas **c** Barsabbas, and Acts 15:22
to take with them John **c** Mark. Acts 15:37
that God had **c** us to preach Acts 16:10
And the jailer **c** for lights and rushed Acts 16:29
sent to Ephesus and **c** the elders of the Acts 20:17
Paul **c** one of the centurions and said, Acts 23:17
"Paul the prisoner **c** me and asked Acts 23:18
Then he **c** two of the centurions and Acts 23:23
we came to a place **c** Fair Havens, Acts 27:8
tempestuous wind, **c** the northeaster, Acts 27:14
the lee of a small island **c** Cauda, Acts 27:16
learned that the island was **c** Malta. Acts 28:1
three days he **c** together the local Acts 28:17
of Christ Jesus, **c** to be an apostle, Rom 1:1
including you who are **c** to belong to Rom 1:6
who are loved by God and **c** to be saints: Rom 1:7
she will be **c** an adulteress if she lives Rom 7:3
for those who are **c** according to his Rom 8:28
those whom he predestined he also **c**, Rom 8:30
and those whom he **c** he also justified, Rom 8:30
even us whom he has **c**, not from the Rom 9:24
there they will be **c** 'sons of the living Rom 9:26
c by the will of God to be an apostle of 1 Cor 1:1
c to be saints together with all those 1 Cor 1:2
whom you were **c** into the fellowship 1 Cor 1:9
but to those who are **c**, both Jews and 1 Cor 1:24
not enslaved. God has **c** you to peace. 1 Cor 7:15

to him, and to which God has c him. 1 Cor 7:17
in the condition in which he was c. 1 Cor 7:20
Were you a slave when c? Do not be 1 Cor 7:21
For he who was c in the Lord as a 1 Cor 7:22
he who was free when c is a slave of 1 Cor 7:22
in whatever condition each was c, 1 Cor 7:24
by all, he is c to account by all, 1 Cor 14:24
apostles, unworthy to be c an apostle, 1 Cor 15:9
quickly deserting him who c you in the Gal 1:6
I was born, and who c me by his grace, Gal 1:15
For you were c to freedom, brothers. Gal 5:13
what is the hope to which he has c you, Eph 1:18
c "the uncircumcision" by what is Eph 2:11
by what is c the circumcision, Eph 2:11
of the calling to which you have been c, Eph 4:1
—just as you were c to the one hope that Eph 4:4
to which indeed you were c in one body. Col 3:15
and Jesus who is c Justus. These are the Col 4:11
For God has not c us for impurity, 1 Thes 4:7
To this he c you through our gospel, 2 Thes 2:14
which you were c and about which 1 Tm 6:12
of what is falsely c "knowledge," 1 Tm 6:20
who saved us and c us to a holy 2 Tm 1:9
as long as it is c "today," that none of Heb 3:13
for himself, but only when c by God, Heb 5:4
of the Presence. It is c the Holy Place. Heb 9:2
was a second section c the Most Holy Heb 9:3
that those who are c may receive the Heb 9:15
obeyed when he was c to go out to Heb 11:8
God is not ashamed to be c their God, Heb 11:16
refused to be c the son of Pharaoh's Heb 11:24
honorable name by which you were c? Jas 2:7
—and he was c a friend of God. Jas 2:23
but as he who c you is holy, you also 1 Pt 1:15
excellencies of him who c you out of 1 Pt 2:9
For to this you have been c, because 1 Pt 2:21
contrary, bless, for to this you were c, 1 Pt 3:9
who has c you to his eternal glory in 1 Pt 5:10
knowledge of him who c us to his own 2 Pt 1:3
us, that we should be c children of God; 1 Jn 3:1
brother of James, To those who are c, Jude 1:1
was on the island c Patmos on account of Rv 1:9
and he c with a loud voice to the four Rv 7:2
Abaddon, and in Greek he is c Apollyon. Rv 9:11
and c out with a loud voice, like a lion Rv 10:3
When he c out, the seven thunders Rv 10:3
that symbolically is c Sodom and Egypt, Rv 11:8
serpent, who is c the devil and Satan, Rv 12:9
and he c with a loud voice to the one Rv 14:18
place that in Hebrew is c Armageddon. Rv 16:16
those with him are c and chosen and Rv 17:14
And he c out with a mighty voice, Rv 18:2
one sitting on it is c Faithful and True, Rv 19:11
name by which he is c is The Word of Rv 19:13
with a loud voice he c to all the birds Rv 19:17

CALLING (36)
of it and settled in it, c Leshem, Jos 19:47
that the LORD was c the young man. 1 Sm 3:8
came and stood, c as at other times, 1 Sm 3:10
c to those who pass by, who are going Prv 9:15
and Sabbath and the c of convocations— Is 1:13
One is c to me from Seir, "Watchman, Is 21:11
host by number, c them all by name, Is 40:26
c the generations from the beginning? Is 41:4
c a bird of prey from the east, the man of Is 46:11
I am c all the tribes of the kingdoms of Jer 1:15
silly and without sense, c to Egypt, Hos 7:11
the Lord GOD was c for a judgment by Am 7:4
from your bow, c for many arrows. Hab 3:9
the marketplaces and c to their Mt 11:16
And c to him a child, he put him in the Mt 18:2
hearing it, said, "This man is c Elijah." Mt 27:47
him, "Take heart. Get up; he is c you." Mk 10:49
it said, "Behold, he is c Elijah." Mk 15:35
c two of his disciples to him, sent them Lk 7:19
in the marketplace and c to one another, Lk 7:32
C ten of his servants, he gave them ten Lk 19:13
Then Jesus, c out with a loud voice, Lk 23:46
but he was even c God his own Father, Jn 5:18
"The Teacher is here and is c for you." Jn 11:28
Then c the saints and widows, he Acts 9:41
wash away your sins, c on his name.' Acts 22:16
the gifts and the c of God are Rom 11:29
For consider your c, brothers: not 1 Cor 1:26
manner worthy of the c to which you Eph 4:1
you worthy of his c and may fulfill 2 Thes 1:11
who saved us and called us to a holy c, 2 Tm 1:9
brothers, you who share in a heavenly c, Heb 3:1
as Sarah obeyed Abraham, c him lord. 1 Pt 3:6
to make your c and election sure, 2 Pt 1:10
c to the mountains and rocks, "Fall on Rv 6:16
c with a loud voice to him who sat on Rv 14:15

CALLOUS (1)
They have become c and have given Eph 4:19

CALLS (34)
When Pharaoh c you and says, 'What Gn 46:33
Samuel, "Go, lie down, and if he c you, 1 Sm 3:9
"Who are you who c to the king?" 1 Sm 26:14
to all for which the foreigner c to you, 1 Kgs 8:43
all for which the foreigner c to you, 2 Chr 6:33
Deep c to deep at the roar of your Ps 42:7
He c to the heavens above and to the Ps 50:4
For he delivers the needy when he c, the Ps 72:12
When he c to me, I will answer him; I Ps 91:15
all that this people c conspiracy, Is 8:12
There is no one who c upon your name, Is 64:7
fallen, and none of them c upon me. Hos 7:7
pass that everyone who c on the name of Jl 2:32
survivors shall be those whom the LORD c. Jl 2:32
who c for the waters of the sea and pours Am 5:8
who c for the waters of the sea and pours Am 9:6
that David, in the Spirit, c him Lord, Mt 22:43
If then David c him Lord, how is he his Mt 22:45
David himself c him Lord. So how is Mk 12:37
he c together his friends and his Lk 15:6
she c together her friends and Lk 15:9
where he c the Lord the God of Lk 20:37
David thus c him Lord, so how is he Lk 20:44
and he c his own sheep by name and Jn 10:3
that everyone who c upon the name Acts 2:21
whom the Lord our God c to himself." Acts 2:39
to the dead and c into existence the Rom 4:17
For "everyone who c on the name of Rom 10:13
persuasion is not from him who c you. Gal 5:8
who c you into his own kingdom 1 Thes 2:12
He who c you is faithful; he will 1 Thes 5:24
who c herself a prophetess and is Rv 2:20
This c for wisdom: let the one who has Rv 13:18
This c for a mind with wisdom: the Rv 17:9

CALM (4)
I will be c and will no more be angry. Ezk 16:42
and the sea, and there was a great c. Mt 8:26
the wind ceased, and there was a great c. Mk 4:39
and they ceased, and there was a c. Lk 8:24

CALMED (3)
So the Levites c all the people, saying, Neh 8:11
But I have c and quieted my soul, like a Ps 131:2
I c myself until morning; like a lion he Is 38:13

CALMNESS (1)
for c will lay great offenses to rest. Eccl 10:4

CALNEH (2)
was Babel, Erech, Accad, and C, Gn 10:10
Pass over to C, and see, and from there Am 6:2

CALNO (1)
Is not C like Carchemish? Is not Hamath Is 10:9

CALVES (21)
thirty milking camels and their c, Gn 32:15
cows to the cart, but take their c home, 1 Sm 6:7
the cart and shut up their c at home. 1 Sm 6:10
and oxen and c and slaughtered 1 Sm 14:32
and of the fattened c and the lambs, 1 Sm 15:9
counsel and made two c of gold. 1 Kgs 12:28
sacrificing to the c that he made. 1 Kgs 12:32
the golden c that were in Bethel and 2 Kgs 10:29
themselves metal images of two c; 2 Kgs 17:16
idols and for the c that he had made. 2 Chr 11:15
you the golden c that Jeroboam made 2 Chr 13:8
fail; their cow c and does not miscarry. Jb 21:10
herd of bulls with the c of the peoples. Ps 68:30
soldiers in her midst are like fattened c; Jer 46:21
who offer human sacrifice kiss c!" Hos 13:2
from the flock and c from the midst of Am 6:4
with burnt offerings, with c a year old? Mi 6:6
shall go out leaping like c from the stall. Mal 4:2
and my fat c have been slaughtered, Mt 22:4
blood of goats and c but by means of Heb 9:12
people, he took the blood of c and goats, Heb 9:19

CALVING (1)
birth? Do you observe the c of the does? Jb 39:1

CALYX (6)
blossoms, each with c and flower, Ex 25:33
blossoms, each with c and flower, Ex 25:33
and a c of one piece with it under each Ex 25:35
blossoms, each with c and flower, Ex 37:19
blossoms, each with c and flower, Ex 37:19
and a c of one piece with it under each Ex 37:21

CALYXES (6)
its base, its stem, its cups, its c, and its Ex 25:31
blossoms, with their c and flowers, Ex 25:34
Their c and their branches shall be of Ex 25:36
Its base, its stem, its cups, its c, and its Ex 37:17
blossoms, with their c and flowers, Ex 37:20
Their c and their branches were of one Ex 37:22

CAME (1574)
the sons of God c in to the daughters Gn 6:4
when the flood of waters c upon the earth. Gn 7:6
the waters of the flood c upon the earth. Gn 7:10
the ark c to rest on the mountains of Gn 8:4
And the dove c back to him in the Gn 8:11
with you, as many as c out of the ark; Gn 9:10
(from whom the Philistines c), Gn 10:14
And the LORD c down to see the city and Gn 11:5
of Canaan, but when they c to Haran, Gn 11:31
When they c to the land of Canaan, Gn 12:5
moved his tent and c and settled by the Gn 13:18
who were with him c and defeated the Gn 14:5
turned back and c to En-mishpat (that Gn 14:7
who had escaped c and told Abram Gn 14:13
the word of the LORD c to Abram in a Gn 15:1
behold, the word of the LORD c to him: Gn 15:4
when birds of prey c down on the Gn 15:11
The two angels c to Sodom in the Gn 19:1
are the men who c to you tonight? Gn 19:5
And they said, "This fellow c to sojourn, Gn 19:9
risen on the earth when Lot c to Zoar. Gn 19:23
But God c to Abimelech in a dream by Gn 20:3
When they c to the place of which God Gn 22:9
back to the land from which you c?" Gn 24:5
c out with her water jar on her Gn 24:15
the spring and filled her jar and c up. Gn 24:16
So the man c to the house and Gn 24:32
"I c today to the spring and said, 'O Gn 24:42
Rebekah c out with her water jar on Gn 24:45
The first c out red, all his body like a Gn 25:25
Afterward his brother c out with his Gn 25:26
cooking stew, Esau c in from the field, Gn 25:29
day Isaac's servants c and told him Gn 26:32
So he c near and kissed him. And Isaac Gn 27:27
Esau his brother c in from his Gn 27:30
it to me, and I ate it all before you c, Gn 27:33
he said, "Your brother c deceitfully, Gn 27:35
And he c to a certain place and stayed Gn 28:11
went on his journey and c to the land of Gn 29:1
them, Rachel c with her father's sheep, Gn 29:9
Jacob c near and rolled the stone from Gn 29:10
When Jacob c from the field in the Gn 30:16
For you had little before I c, and it has Gn 30:30
places, where the flocks c to drink. Gn 30:38
since they bred when they c to drink, Gn 30:38
But God c to Laban the Aramean in a Gn 31:24
saying, "We c to your brother Esau, Gn 32:6
times, until he c near to his brother. Gn 33:3
And Jacob c safely to the city of Gn 33:18
so Jacob held his peace until they c. Gn 34:5
and his son Shechem c to the gate of Gn 34:20
their swords and c against the city Gn 34:25
The sons of Jacob c upon the slain and Gn 34:27
And Jacob c to Luz (that is, Bethel), Gn 35:6
again, when he c from Paddan-aram, Gn 35:9
And Jacob c to his father Isaac at Gn 35:27
of Hebron, and he c to Shechem. Gn 37:14
and before he c near to them they Gn 37:18
So when Joseph c to his brothers, they Gn 37:23
When the time of her labor c, there Gn 38:27
his hand, saying, "This one c out first." Gn 38:28
his hand, behold, his brother c out. Gn 38:29
Afterward his brother c out with the Gn 38:30
He c in to me to lie with me, and I cried Gn 39:14
by her until his master c home, Gn 39:16
among us, c in to me to laugh at me. Gn 39:17
When Joseph c to them in the morning, Gn 40:6
there c up out of the Nile seven cows Gn 41:2
and thin, c up out of the Nile after them, Gn 41:3
as he interpreted to us, so it c about. Gn 41:13
his clothes, he c in before Pharaoh. Gn 41:14
c up out of the Nile and fed in the reed Gn 41:18
Seven other cows c up after them, poor Gn 41:19
and ugly cows that c up after them are Gn 41:27
Before the year of famine c, two sons Gn 41:50
in the land of Egypt c to an end, Gn 41:53
all the earth c to Egypt to Joseph to buy Gn 41:57
the sons of Israel c to buy among the Gn 42:5
came to buy among the others who c, Gn 42:5
And Joseph's brothers c and bowed Gn 42:6
When they c to Jacob their father in Gn 42:29
we c down the first time to buy food. Gn 43:20
And when we c to the lodging place we Gn 43:21
When Joseph c home, they brought Gn 43:26
Then he washed his face and c out. Gn 43:31
and his brothers c to Joseph's house, Gn 44:14
near to me, please." And they c near. Gn 45:4
up out of Egypt and c to the land of Gn 45:25
with all that he had and c to Beersheba, Gn 46:1
in the land of Canaan, and c into Egypt, Gn 46:6
descendants of Israel, who c into Egypt, Gn 46:8
belonging to Jacob who c into Egypt, Gn 46:26
house of Jacob who c into Egypt were Gn 46:27
and they c into the land of Goshen. Gn 46:28
all the Egyptians c to Joseph and said, Gn 47:15
they c to him the following year and Gn 47:18

land of Egypt before I **c** to you in Egypt, Gn 48:5
As for me, when I **c** from Paddan, to my Gn 48:7
When they **c** to the threshing floor of Gn 50:10
His brothers also **c** and fell down Gn 50:18
sons of Israel who **c** to Egypt with Jacob, Ex 1:1
the daughter of Pharaoh **c** down to bathe Ex 2:5
and they **c** and drew water and filled the Ex 2:16
The shepherds **c** and drove them away, Ex 2:17
When they **c** home to their father Reuel, Ex 2:18
cry for rescue from slavery **c** up to God. Ex 2:23
west side of the wilderness and **c** to Horeb, Ex 3:1
the people of Israel **c** and cried to Ex 5:15
for them, as they **c** out from Pharaoh; Ex 5:20
For since I **c** to Pharaoh to speak in your Ex 5:23
and the frogs **c** up and covered the land of Ex 8:6
There **c** great swarms of flies into the Ex 8:24
for the boils **c** upon the magicians and Ex 9:11
from the day they **c** on earth to this Ex 10:6
The locusts **c** up over all the land of Ex 10:14
this day in which you **c** out from Egypt, Ex 13:3
LORD did for me when I **c** out of Egypt.' Ex 13:8
When they **c** to Marah, they could not Ex 15:23
Then they **c** to Elim, where there were Ex 15:27
the people of Israel **c** to the wilderness of Ex 16:1
In the evening quail **c** up and covered Ex 16:13
of the congregation **c** and told Moses, Ex 16:22
years, till they **c** to a habitable land. Ex 16:35
the manna till they **c** to the border of Ex 16:35
Then Amalek **c** and fought with Israel Ex 17:8
c with his sons and his wife to Moses in Ex 18:5
and Aaron **c** with all the elders of Israel Ex 18:12
on that day they **c** into the wilderness of Ex 19:1
from Rephidim and **c** into the wilderness Ex 19:2
So Moses **c** and called the elders of the Ex 19:7
The LORD **c** down on Mount Sinai, to Ex 19:20
if it was hired, it **c** for its hiring fee. Ex 22:15
of Abib, for in it you **c** out of Egypt. Ex 23:15
Moses **c** and told the people all the words Ex 24:3
And as soon as he **c** near the camp and Ex 32:19
it into the fire, and out **c** this calf." Ex 32:24
the month Abib you **c** out from Egypt. Ex 34:18
When Moses **c** down from Mount Ex 34:29
his hand as he **c** down from the Ex 34:29
Afterward all the people of Israel **c** near, Ex 34:32
would remove the veil, until he **c** out. Ex 34:34
And when he **c** out and told the people Ex 34:34
And they **c**, everyone whose heart Ex 35:21
So they **c**, both men and women. All Ex 35:22
every sort of task on the sanctuary **c**, Ex 36:4
and he **c** down from offering the sin Lv 9:22
and when they **c** out they blessed the Lv 9:23
And fire **c** out from before the LORD and Lv 9:24
And fire **c** out from before the LORD and Lv 10:2
So they **c** near and carried them in their Lv 10:5
And any outsider who **c** near was to be Nm 3:38
and they **c** before Moses and Aaron on Nm 9:6
Then the LORD **c** down in the cloud Nm 11:25
meeting." And the three of them **c** out. Nm 12:4
And the LORD **c** down in a pillar of Nm 12:5
and Miriam, and they both **c** forward. Nm 12:5
up into the Negeb and **c** to Hebron. Nm 13:22
And they **c** to the Valley of Eshcol and Nm 13:23
And they **c** to Moses and Aaron and to Nm 13:26
"We **c** to the land to which you sent Nm 13:27
that hill country **c** down and defeated Nm 14:45
Dathan and Abiram **c** out and stood Nm 16:27
And fire **c** out from the LORD and Nm 16:35
And Moses and Aaron **c** to the front of Nm 16:43
c into the wilderness of Zin in the first Nm 20:1
twice, and water **c** out abundantly, Nm 20:11
through." And Edom **c** out against Nm 20:20
whole congregation, **c** to Mount Hor. Nm 20:22
Moses and Eleazar **c** down from the Nm 20:28
And the people **c** to Moses and said, Nm 21:7
to the wilderness and **c** to Jahaz and Nm 21:23
For fire **c** out from Heshbon, flame Nm 21:28
king of Bashan **c** out against them, Nm 21:33
And they **c** to Balaam and gave him Nm 22:7
And God **c** to Balaam and said, "Who Nm 22:9
And they **c** to Balaam and said to Nm 22:16
And God **c** to Balaam at night and Nm 22:20
Balak, and they **c** to Kiriath-huzoth. Nm 22:39
And he **c** to him, and behold, he was Nm 23:17
And the Spirit of God **c** upon him, Nm 24:2
the people of Israel **c** and brought a Nm 25:6
people of Israel who **c** out of the land Nm 26:4
so the plague **c** among the Nm 31:16
of hundreds, **c** near to Moses Nm 31:48
the people of Reuben **c** and said to Nm 32:2
of the men who **c** up out of Egypt, Nm 32:11
Then they **c** near to him and said, Nm 32:16
they set out from Marah and **c** to Elim; Nm 33:9
c near and spoke before Moses and Nm 36:1
us. And we **c** to Kadesh-barnea. Dt 1:19
Then all of you **c** near me and said, 'Let Dt 1:22

and **c** to the Valley of Eshcol and spied it Dt 1:24
that you went until you **c** to this place.' Dt 1:31
in that hill country **c** out against you Dt 1:44
the Caphtorim, who **c** from Caphtor, Dt 2:23
Then Sihon **c** out against us, he and all Dt 2:32
Og the king of Bashan **c** out against us, Dt 3:1
And you **c** near and stood at the foot of Dt 4:11
people of Israel when they **c** out of Egypt, Dt 4:45
Israel defeated when they **c** out of Egypt. Dt 4:46
was burning with fire, you **c** near to me, Dt 5:23
From the day you **c** out of the land of Dt 9:7
the land of Egypt until you **c** to this place, Dt 9:7
So I turned and **c** down from the Dt 9:15
Then I turned and **c** down from the Dt 10:5
the wilderness, until you **c** to this place, Dt 11:5
of affliction—for you **c** out of the land of Dt 16:3
the day when you **c** out of the land Dt 16:3
at sunset, at the time you **c** out of Egypt. Dt 16:6
this woman, and when I **c** near her, Dt 22:14
on the way, when you **c** out of Egypt, Dt 23:4
Miriam on the way as you **c** out of Egypt. Dt 24:9
to you on the way as you **c** out of Egypt, Dt 25:17
And when you **c** to this place, Sihon the Dt 29:7
the king of Bashan **c** out against us to Dt 29:7
and how we **c** through the midst of the Dt 29:16
Moses **c** and recited all the words of this Dt 32:44
"The LORD **c** from Sinai and dawned Dt 33:2
he **c** from the ten thousands of holy ones, Dt 33:2
and he **c** with the heads of the people, Dt 33:21
And they went and **c** into the house of Jos 2:1
And she said, "True, the men **c** to me, but Jos 2:4
lay down, she **c** up to them on the roof Jos 2:8
Sea before you when you **c** out of Egypt, Jos 2:10
They **c** down from the hills and passed Jos 2:23
and passed over and **c** to Joshua the son Jos 2:23
And they **c** to the Jordan, he and all the Jos 3:1
covenant of the LORD **c** up from the Jos 4:18
The people **c** up out of the Jordan on the Jos 4:19
males of the people who **c** out of Egypt, Jos 5:4
all the people who **c** out had been Jos 5:5
the men of war who **c** out of Egypt, Jos 5:6
of Israel. None went out, and none **c** in. Jos 6:1
And they **c** into the camp and spent the Jos 6:11
And the others **c** out from the city Jos 8:22
So Joshua **c** upon them suddenly, Jos 10:9
these kings." Then they **c** near and put Jos 10:24
Horam king of Gezer **c** up to help Jos 10:33
And they **c** out with all their troops, a Jos 11:4
their forces and **c** and encamped Jos 11:5
all his warriors **c** suddenly against them Jos 11:7
And Joshua **c** at that time and cut off Jos 11:21
the people of Judah **c** to Joshua at Gilgal. Jos 14:6
When she **c** to him, she urged him to Jos 15:18
Then they **c** to Joshua to the camp at Jos 18:9
Benjamin according to its clans **c** up, Jos 18:11
The second lot **c** out for Simeon, for the Jos 19:1
The third lot **c** up for the people of Jos 19:10
The fourth lot **c** out for Issachar, for Jos 19:17
The fifth lot **c** out for the tribe of the Jos 19:24
The sixth lot **c** out for the people of Jos 19:32
The seventh lot **c** out for the tribe of the Jos 19:40
houses of the Levites **c** to Eleazar the Jos 21:1
The lot **c** out for the clans of the Jos 21:4
house of Israel had failed; all **c** to pass. Jos 21:45
And when they **c** to the region of the Jos 22:10
And they **c** to the people of Reuben, the Jos 22:15
and for which there **c** a plague upon Jos 22:17
fathers out of Egypt, and you **c** to the sea. Jos 24:6
went over the Jordan and **c** to Jericho, Jos 24:11
When she **c** to him, she urged him to Jgs 1:14
And Ehud **c** to him as he was sitting Jgs 3:20
out of his belly; and the dung **c** out. Jgs 3:22
When he had gone, the servants **c**, and Jgs 3:24
and the people of Israel **c** up to her for Jgs 4:5
And Jael **c** out to meet Sisera and said to Jgs 4:18
the princes of Issachar **c** with Deborah, Jgs 5:15
"The kings **c**, they fought; then fought Jgs 5:19
that they laid waste the land as they **c** in. Jgs 6:5
the angel of the LORD **c** and sat under the Jgs 6:11
and the people of the East **c** together, Jgs 6:33
When Gideon **c**, behold, a man was Jgs 7:13
the camp of Midian and **c** to the tent and Jgs 7:13
who were with him **c** to the outskirts of Jgs 7:19
And Gideon **c** to the Jordan and crossed Jgs 8:4
And he **c** to the men of Succoth and Jgs 8:15
And all the leaders of Shechem **c** together, Jgs 9:6
And Abimelech **c** to the tower and Jgs 9:52
and upon them **c** the curse of Jotham Jgs 9:57
And the people of Israel **c** together, and Jgs 10:17
but when they **c** up from Egypt, Israel Jgs 11:16
to the Red Sea and **c** to Kadesh. Jgs 11:16
Then Jephthah **c** to his home at Jgs 11:34
his daughter **c** out to meet him with Jgs 11:34
Then the woman **c** and told her Jgs 13:6
her husband, "A man of God **c** to me, Jgs 13:6

the angel of God **c** again to the woman Jgs 13:9
the man who **c** to me the other day has Jgs 13:10
after his wife and **c** to the man and Jgs 13:11
Then he **c** up and told his father and Jgs 14:2
and they **c** to the vineyards of Timnah. Jgs 14:5
a young lion **c** toward him roaring. Jgs 14:5
And he **c** to his father and mother and Jgs 14:9
"Out of the eater **c** something to eat. Jgs 14:14
of the strong **c** something sweet." And Jgs 14:14
And the Philistines **c** up and burned Jgs 15:6
Then the Philistines **c** up and encamped Jgs 15:9
When he **c** to Lehi, the Philistines Jgs 15:14
the Philistines **c** shouting to meet him. Jgs 15:14
that is at Lehi, and water **c** out from it. Jgs 15:19
lords of the Philistines **c** up to her and Jgs 16:5
lords of the Philistines **c** up to her and Jgs 16:18
and all his family **c** down and took Jgs 16:31
he **c** to the hill country of Ephraim to Jgs 17:8
the land." And they **c** to the hill country Jgs 18:2
five men departed and **c** to Laish and Jgs 18:7
And when they **c** to their brothers at Jgs 18:8
Ephraim, and **c** to the house of Micah. Jgs 18:13
turned aside there and **c** to the house of Jgs 18:15
belonged to him, and they **c** to Laish, Jgs 18:27
saw him, he **c** with joy to meet him. Jgs 19:3
out the man who **c** into your house, Jgs 19:22
the woman **c** and fell down at the door Jgs 19:26
that the people of Israel **c** up out of the Jgs 19:30
Then all the people of Israel **c** out, from Jgs 20:1
"I **c** to Gibeah that belongs to Benjamin, Jgs 20:4
people of Benjamin **c** together out of Jgs 20:14
people of Benjamin **c** out of Gibeah Jgs 20:21
the people of Israel **c** near against the Jgs 20:24
went up and **c** to Bethel and wept. Jgs 20:26
And there **c** against Gibeah 10,000 Jgs 20:34
And those who **c** out of the cities were Jgs 20:42
And the people **c** to Bethel and sat there Jgs 21:2
them went on until they **c** to Bethlehem. Ru 1:19
And when they **c** to Bethlehem, the Ru 1:19
And they **c** to Bethlehem at the Ru 1:22
And behold, Boaz **c** from Bethlehem. And Ru 2:4
who **c** back with Naomi from the Ru 2:6
So she **c**, and she has continued from Ru 2:7
your native land and **c** to a people that Ru 2:11
Then she **c** softly and uncovered his feet Ru 3:7
that the woman **c** to the threshing Ru 3:14
And when she **c** to her mother-in-law, Ru 3:16
of whom Boaz had spoken, **c** by. Ru 4:1
Shiloh to all the Israelites who **c** there. 1 Sm 2:14
And there **c** a man of God to Eli and 1 Sm 2:27
And the LORD **c** and stood, calling as 1 Sm 3:10
And the word of Samuel **c** to all Israel. 1 Sm 4:1
And when the troops **c** to the camp, the 1 Sm 4:3
covenant of the LORD **c** into the camp, 1 Sm 4:5
the battle line and **c** to Shiloh the 1 Sm 4:12
And when the man **c** into the city and 1 Sm 4:13
the man hurried and **c** and told Eli. 1 Sm 4:14
gave birth, for her pains **c** upon her. 1 Sm 4:19
as soon as the ark of God **c** to Ekron, 1 Sm 5:10
The cart **c** into the field of Joshua of 1 Sm 6:14
men of Kiriath-jearim **c** and took up 1 Sm 7:1
gathered together and **c** to Samuel at 1 Sm 8:4
When they **c** to the land of Zuph, Saul 1 Sm 9:5
Now the day before Saul **c**, the LORD 1 Sm 9:15
And when they **c** down from the high 1 Sm 9:25
And all these signs **c** to pass that day. 1 Sm 10:9
When they **c** to Gibeah, behold, a 1 Sm 10:10
prophesying, he **c** to the high place. 1 Sm 10:13
When the messengers **c** to Gibeah of 1 Sm 11:4
the people, and they **c** out as one man. 1 Sm 11:7
When the messengers **c** and told the 1 Sm 11:9
And they **c** into the midst of the 1 Sm 11:11
of the Ammonites **c** against you, 1 Sm 12:12
They **c** up and encamped in 1 Sm 13:5
the burnt offering, behold, Samuel **c**. 1 Sm 13:10
And raiders **c** out of the camp of the 1 Sm 13:17
when all the people **c** to the forest, 1 Sm 14:25
the way when they **c** up out of Egypt. 1 Sm 15:2
And Saul **c** to the city of Amalek and 1 Sm 15:5
of Israel when they **c** up out of Egypt." 1 Sm 15:6
The word of the LORD **c** to Samuel: 1 Sm 15:10
was told Samuel, "Saul **c** to Carmel, 1 Sm 15:12
And Samuel **c** to Saul, and Saul said 1 Sm 15:13
Amalekites." And Agag **c** to him 1 Sm 15:32
commanded and **c** to Bethlehem. 1 Sm 16:4
elders of the city **c** to meet him 1 Sm 16:4
When they **c**, he looked on Eliab and 1 Sm 16:6
And David **c** to Saul and entered his 1 Sm 16:21
And there **c** out from the camp of the 1 Sm 17:4
days the Philistine **c** forward and 1 Sm 17:16
And he **c** to the encampment as the 1 Sm 17:20
c up out of the ranks of the 1 Sm 17:23
And when there **c** a lion, or a bear, 1 Sm 17:34
moved forward and **c** near to David, 1 Sm 17:41
Philistine arose and **c** and drew near 1 Sm 17:48

people of Israel **c** back from chasing 1 Sm 17:53
the women **c** out of all the cities of 1 Sm 18:6
he went out and **c** in before the 1 Sm 18:13
for he went out and **c** in before them. 1 Sm 18:16
of the Philistines **c** out to battle, 1 Sm 18:30
as often as they **c** out David had 1 Sm 18:30
spirit from the LORD **c** upon Saul, 1 Sm 19:9
And when the messengers **c** in, 1 Sm 19:16
and he **c** to Samuel at Ramah and 1 Sm 19:18
Spirit of God **c** upon the messengers 1 Sm 19:20
went to Ramah and **c** to the great 1 Sm 19:22
the Spirit of God **c** upon him also, 1 Sm 19:23
he prophesied until he **c** to Naioth in 1 Sm 19:23
in Ramah and **c** and said before 1 Sm 20:1
And when the new moon **c**, the king 1 Sm 20:24
And when the boy **c** to the place of 1 Sm 20:37
up the arrows and **c** to his master. 1 Sm 20:38
Then David **c** to Nob to Ahimelech 1 Sm 21:1
And Ahimelech **c** to meet David 1 Sm 21:1
at Nob, and all of them **c** to the king. 1 Sm 22:11
a messenger **c** to Saul, saying, 1 Sm 23:27
And he **c** to the sheepfolds by the way, 1 Sm 24:3
When David's young men **c**, they said 1 Sm 25:9
turned away and **c** back and told 1 Sm 25:12
the donkey and **c** down under cover 1 Sm 25:20
and his men **c** down toward her, 1 Sm 25:20
And Abigail **c** to Nabal, and behold, 1 Sm 25:36
the servants of David **c** to Abigail at 1 Sm 25:40
Then the Ziphites **c** to Saul at Gibeah, 1 Sm 26:1
he saw that Saul **c** after him into the 1 Sm 26:3
Then David rose and **c** to the place 1 Sm 26:5
one of the people **c** in to destroy the 1 Sm 26:15
assembled and **c** and encamped 1 Sm 28:4
And they **c** to the woman by night. 1 Sm 28:8
And the woman **c** to Saul, and when 1 Sm 28:21
of your lord who **c** with you, 1 Sm 29:10
David and his men **c** to Ziklag on the 1 Sm 30:1
when David and his men **c** to the city, 1 Sm 30:3
him, and they **c** to the brook Besor, 1 Sm 30:9
Then David **c** to the two hundred 1 Sm 30:21
And when David **c** near to the people 1 Sm 30:21
our hand the band that **c** against us. 1 Sm 30:23
When David **c** to Ziklag, he sent part 1 Sm 30:26
And the Philistines **c** and lived in 1 Sm 31:7
when the Philistines **c** to strip the 1 Sm 31:8
and they **c** to Jabesh and burned 1 Sm 31:12
behold, a man **c** from Saul's camp, 2 Sm 1:2
And when he **c** to David, he fell to the 2 Sm 1:2
And the men of Judah **c**, and there they 2 Sm 2:4
so that the spear **c** out at his back. 2 Sm 2:23
And all who **c** to the place where 2 Sm 2:23
was going down they **c** to the hill of 2 Sm 2:24
whole morning, they **c** to Mahanaim. 2 Sm 2:29
When Abner **c** with twenty men to 2 Sm 3:20
and all the army that was with him **c**, 2 Sm 3:23
"Abner the son of Ner **c** to the king, 2 Sm 3:23
you done? Behold, Abner **c** to you. 2 Sm 3:24
the son of Ner **c** to deceive you and 2 Sm 3:25
When Joab **c** out from David's 2 Sm 3:26
all the people **c** to persuade David 2 Sm 3:35
Saul and Jonathan **c** from Jezreel, 2 Sm 4:4
heat of the day they **c** to the house of 2 Sm 4:5
And they **c** into the midst of the house 2 Sm 4:6
When they **c** into the house, as he lay 2 Sm 4:7
the tribes of Israel **c** to David at Hebron 2 Sm 5:1
all the elders of Israel **c** to the king at 2 Sm 5:3
Jerusalem, after he **c** from Hebron, 2 Sm 5:13
And David **c** to Baal-perazim, and 2 Sm 5:20
And the Philistines **c** up yet again and 2 Sm 5:22
And when they **c** to the threshing floor 2 Sm 6:6
the ark of the LORD **c** into the city of 2 Sm 6:16
the daughter of Saul **c** out to meet 2 Sm 6:20
night the word of the LORD **c** to Nathan, 2 Sm 7:4
Syrians of Damascus **c** to help 2 Sm 8:5
c to David and fell on his face and paid 2 Sm 9:6
And David's servants **c** into the land 2 Sm 10:2
And the Ammonites **c** out and drew 2 Sm 10:8
the Ammonites and **c** to Jerusalem. 2 Sm 10:14
They **c** to Helam, with Shobach the 2 Sm 10:16
crossed the Jordan and **c** to Helam. 2 Sm 10:17
and took her, and she **c** to him, 2 Sm 11:4
When Uriah **c** to him, David asked 2 Sm 11:7
men of the city **c** out and fought 2 Sm 11:17
messenger went and **c** and told 2 Sm 11:22
over us and **c** out against us 2 Sm 11:23
He **c** to him and said to him, "There 2 Sm 12:1
Now there **c** a traveler to the rich 2 Sm 12:4
And when the king **c** to see him, 2 Sm 13:6
And Absalom **c** to the king and said, 2 Sm 13:24
were on the way, news **c** to David, 2 Sm 13:30
the king's sons **c** and lifted up their 2 Sm 13:36
the woman of Tekoa **c** to the king, 2 Sm 14:4
So he **c** to the king and bowed 2 Sm 14:33
And whenever a man **c** near to pay 2 Sm 15:5
to all of Israel who **c** to the king for 2 Sm 15:6

And a messenger **c** to David, saying, 2 Sm 15:13
You **c** only yesterday, and shall I 2 Sm 15:20
And Abiathar **c** up, and behold, 2 Sm 15:24
Zadok **c** also with all the Levites, 2 Sm 15:24
Hushai the Archite **c** to meet him 2 Sm 15:32
David's friend, **c** into the city, 2 Sm 15:37
When King David **c** to Bahurim, 2 Sm 16:5
there **c** out a man of the family of the 2 Sm 16:5
and as he **c** he cursed continually. 2 Sm 16:5
the men of Israel, **c** to Jerusalem, 2 Sm 16:15
David's friend, **c** to Absalom, 2 Sm 16:16
And when Hushai **c** to Absalom, 2 Sm 17:6
away quickly and **c** to the house 2 Sm 17:18
When Absalom's servants **c** to the 2 Sm 17:20
gone, the men **c** up out of the well, 2 Sm 17:21
Then David **c** to Mahanaim. And 2 Sm 17:24
When David **c** to Mahanaim, Shobi 2 Sm 17:27
and the troops **c** back from 2 Sm 18:16
And behold, the Cushite **c**, and the 2 Sm 18:31
Then Joab **c** into the house to the 2 Sm 19:5
And all the people **c** before the king. 2 Sm 19:8
So the king **c** back to the Jordan, and 2 Sm 19:15
and Judah **c** to Gilgal to meet the 2 Sm 19:15
the son of Saul **c** down to meet the 2 Sm 19:24
until the day he **c** back in safety. 2 Sm 19:24
And when he **c** to Jerusalem to meet 2 Sm 19:25
the men of Israel **c** to the king and 2 Sm 19:41
And David **c** to his house at 2 Sm 20:3
is in Gibeon, Amasa **c** to meet them. 2 Sm 20:8
And anyone who **c** by, seeing him, 2 Sm 20:12
were with Joab **c** and besieged him 2 Sm 20:15
And he **c** near her, and the woman 2 Sm 20:17
the son of Zeruiah **c** to his aid and 2 Sm 21:17
my voice, and my cry **c** to his ears. 2 Sm 22:7
He bowed the heavens and **c** down; 2 Sm 22:10
Foreigners **c** cringing to me; as soon 2 Sm 22:45
lost heart and **c** trembling out of 2 Sm 22:46
went down and **c** about harvest time 2 Sm 23:13
Then they **c** to Gilead, and to Kadesh 2 Sm 24:6
land of the Hittites; and they **c** to Dan, 2 Sm 24:6
and **c** to the fortress of Tyre and to all 2 Sm 24:7
they **c** to Jerusalem at the end of nine 2 Sm 24:8
word of the LORD **c** to the prophet 2 Sm 24:11
So Gad **c** to David and told him, and 2 Sm 24:13
And Gad **c** that day to David and 2 Sm 24:18
the king, Nathan the prophet **c** in. 1 Kgs 1:22
prophet." And when he **c** in before the 1 Kgs 1:23
to me." So she **c** into the king's 1 Kgs 1:28
Jehoiada." So they **c** before the king. 1 Kgs 1:32
the son of Abiathar the priest **c**. 1 Kgs 1:42
the king's servants **c** to congratulate 1 Kgs 1:47
And he **c** and paid homage to King 1 Kgs 1:53
But when he **c** down to meet me at the 1 Kgs 2:8
the son of Haggith **c** to Bathsheba the 1 Kgs 2:13
When the news **c** to Joab—for Joab 1 Kgs 2:28
So Benaiah **c** to the tent of the LORD 1 Kgs 2:30
Then he **c** to Jerusalem and stood 1 Kgs 3:15
Then two prostitutes **c** to the king 1 Kgs 3:16
and for all who **c** to King Solomon's 1 Kgs 4:27
people of all nations **c** to hear the 1 Kgs 4:34
the people of Israel **c** out of the land 1 Kgs 6:1
the word of the LORD **c** to Solomon, 1 Kgs 6:11
He **c** to King Solomon and did all his 1 Kgs 7:14
And all the elders of Israel **c**, and the 1 Kgs 8:3
when they **c** out of the land of Egypt. 1 Kgs 8:9
And when the priests **c** out of the 1 Kgs 8:10
But when Hiram **c** from Tyre to see 1 Kgs 9:12
she **c** to test him with hard questions. 1 Kgs 10:1
She **c** to Jerusalem with a very great 1 Kgs 10:2
And when she **c** to Solomon, she told 1 Kgs 10:2
the reports until I **c** and my own eyes 1 Kgs 10:7
Never again **c** such an abundance 1 Kgs 10:10
weight of gold that **c** to Solomon in 1 Kgs 10:14
besides that which **c** from the 1 Kgs 10:15
out from Midian and **c** to Paran and 1 Kgs 11:18
them from Paran and **c** to Egypt, 1 Kgs 11:18
the assembly of Israel **c** and said to 1 Kgs 12:3
all the people **c** to Rehoboam the 1 Kgs 12:12
When Rehoboam **c** to Jerusalem, he 1 Kgs 12:21
the word of God **c** to Shemaiah the 1 Kgs 12:22
a man of God **c** out of Judah by the 1 Kgs 13:1
nor return by the way that you **c**.'" 1 Kgs 13:9
by the way that he **c** to Bethel. 1 Kgs 13:10
And his sons **c** and told him all that 1 Kgs 13:11
man of God who **c** from Judah had 1 Kgs 13:12
of God who **c** from Judah?" And 1 Kgs 13:14
nor return by the way that you **c**.'" 1 Kgs 13:17
word of the LORD **c** to the prophet 1 Kgs 13:20
the man of God who **c** from Judah, 1 Kgs 13:21
And they **c** and told it in the city 1 Kgs 13:25
went to Shiloh and **c** to the house of 1 Kgs 14:4
shall you say to her." When she **c**, 1 Kgs 14:5
of her feet, as she **c** in at the door, 1 Kgs 14:6
arose and departed and **c** to Tirzah. 1 Kgs 14:17
And as she **c** to the threshold of the 1 Kgs 14:17

king of Egypt **c** up against 1 Kgs 14:25
the word of the LORD **c** to Jehu the son 1 Kgs 16:1
word of the LORD **c** by the prophet 1 Kgs 16:7
Zimri **c** in and struck him down 1 Kgs 16:10
And the word of the LORD **c** to him, 1 Kgs 17:2
Then the word of the LORD **c** to him, 1 Kgs 17:8
And when he **c** to the gate of the city, 1 Kgs 17:10
the life of the child **c** into him again, 1 Kgs 17:22
days the word of the LORD **c** to Elijah, 1 Kgs 18:1
And Elijah **c** near to all the people 1 Kgs 18:21
And all the people **c** near to him. 1 Kgs 18:30
to whom the word of the LORD **c**, 1 Kgs 18:31
Elijah the prophet **c** near and said, 1 Kgs 18:36
ran for his life and **c** to Beersheba, 1 Kgs 19:3
the wilderness and **c** and sat down 1 Kgs 19:4
angel of the LORD **c** again a second 1 Kgs 19:7
There he **c** to a cave and lodged in it. 1 Kgs 19:9
behold, the word of the LORD **c** to him, 1 Kgs 19:9
there **c** a voice to him and said, 1 Kgs 19:13
The messengers **c** again and said, 1 Kgs 20:5
a prophet **c** near to Ahab king of 1 Kgs 20:13
Then the prophet **c** near to the king 1 Kgs 20:22
And a man of God **c** near and said to 1 Kgs 20:28
him." Then Ben-hadad **c** out to him, 1 Kgs 20:33
vexed and sullen and **c** to Samaria. 1 Kgs 20:43
But Jezebel his wife **c** to him and said 1 Kgs 21:5
the two worthless men **c** in and sat 1 Kgs 21:13
word of the LORD **c** to Elijah the 1 Kgs 21:17
word of the LORD **c** to Elijah the 1 Kgs 21:28
the king of Judah **c** down to the king 1 Kgs 22:2
Then a spirit **c** forward and stood 1 Kgs 22:21
son of Chenaanah **c** near and 1 Kgs 22:24
to him, "There **c** a man to meet us, 2 Kgs 1:6
of man was he who **c** to meet you and 2 Kgs 1:7
fifty." Then fire **c** down from heaven 2 Kgs 1:10
the fire of God **c** down from heaven 2 Kgs 1:12
of fifty went up and **c** and fell on his 2 Kgs 1:13
fire **c** down from heaven and 2 Kgs 1:14
who were in Bethel **c** out to Elisha and 2 Kgs 2:3
not leave you." So they **c** to Jericho. 2 Kgs 2:4
on Elisha." And they **c** to meet him 2 Kgs 2:15
And they **c** back to him while he was 2 Kgs 2:18
some small boys **c** out of the city and 2 Kgs 2:23
And two she-bears **c** out of the woods 2 Kgs 2:24
the hand of the LORD **c** upon him. 2 Kgs 3:15
water **c** from the direction of Edom, 2 Kgs 3:20
But when they **c** to the camp of Israel, 2 Kgs 3:24
And there **c** great wrath against 2 Kgs 3:27
She **c** and told the man of God, and he 2 Kgs 4:7
One day he **c** there, and he turned 2 Kgs 4:11
So she set out and **c** to the man of God 2 Kgs 4:25
And when she **c** to the mountain to 2 Kgs 4:27
feet. And Gehazi **c** to push her away. 2 Kgs 4:27
When Elisha **c** into the house, he saw 2 Kgs 4:32
And when she **c** to him, he said, 2 Kgs 4:36
She **c** and fell at his feet, bowing to 2 Kgs 4:37
And Elisha **c** again to Gilgal when 2 Kgs 4:38
and **c** and cut them up into the pot of 2 Kgs 4:39
A man **c** from Baal-shalishah, 2 Kgs 4:42
So Naaman **c** with his horses and 2 Kgs 5:9
But his servants **c** near and said to 2 Kgs 5:13
and he **c** and stood before him. 2 Kgs 5:15
And when he **c** to the hill, he took 2 Kgs 5:24
them. And when they **c** to the Jordan, 2 Kgs 6:4
and they **c** by night and surrounded 2 Kgs 6:14
when the Syrians **c** down against 2 Kgs 6:18
the messenger **c** down to him and 2 Kgs 6:33
But when they **c** to the edge of the 2 Kgs 7:5
And when these lepers **c** to the edge of 2 Kgs 7:8
Then they **c** back and entered another 2 Kgs 7:8
So they **c** and called to the 2 Kgs 7:10
"We **c** to the camp of the Syrians, 2 Kgs 7:10
said when the king **c** down to him. 2 Kgs 7:17
Now Elisha **c** to Damascus. 2 Kgs 8:7
When he **c** and stood before him, he 2 Kgs 8:9
from Elisha and **c** to his master, 2 Kgs 8:14
And when he **c**, behold, the 2 Kgs 9:5
When Jehu **c** out to the servants of 2 Kgs 9:11
the company of Jehu as he **c** and said, 2 Kgs 9:17
horseman, who **c** to them and said, 2 Kgs 9:19
When Jehu **c** to Jezreel, Jezebel heard 2 Kgs 9:30
When they **c** back and told him, he 2 Kgs 9:36
And as soon as the letter **c** to them, 2 Kgs 10:7
When the messenger **c** and told him, 2 Kgs 10:8
and we **c** down to visit the royal 2 Kgs 10:13
And when he **c** to Samaria, he 2 Kgs 10:17
and all the worshipers of Baal **c**, 2 Kgs 10:21
Sabbath, and **c** to Jehoiada the priest. 2 Kgs 11:9
and the high priest **c** up and they 2 Kgs 12:10
and **c** to Jerusalem and broke down 2 Kgs 14:13
generation." And so it **c** to pass.) 2 Kgs 15:12
the son of Gadi **c** up from Tirzah 2 Kgs 15:14
up from Tirzah and **c** to Samaria, 2 Kgs 15:14
king of Assyria **c** against the land, 2 Kgs 15:19
king of Assyria **c** and captured Ijon, 2 Kgs 15:29

Israel, **c** up to wage war on Jerusalem, 2 Kgs 16:5
Elath, and the Edomites **c** to Elath, 2 Kgs 16:6
when the king **c** from Damascus, 2 Kgs 16:12
Against him **c** up Shalmaneser king 2 Kgs 17:3
all the land and **c** to Samaria, 2 Kgs 17:5
away from Samaria **c** and lived in 2 Kgs 17:28
king of Assyria **c** up against Samaria 2 Kgs 18:9
king of Assyria **c** up against all 2 Kgs 18:13
they went up and **c** to Jerusalem. 2 Kgs 18:17
they **c** and stood by the conduit of 2 Kgs 18:17
there **c** out to them Eliakim the son 2 Kgs 18:18
c to Hezekiah with their clothes torn 2 Kgs 18:37
servants of King Hezekiah **c** to Isaiah, 2 Kgs 19:5
back on the way by which you **c**. 2 Kgs 19:28
By the way that he **c**, by the same he 2 Kgs 19:33
the son of Amoz **c** to him and said 2 Kgs 20:1
court, the word of the LORD **c** to him: 2 Kgs 20:4
Isaiah the prophet **c** to King 2 Kgs 20:14
the day their fathers **c** out of Egypt, 2 Kgs 21:15
Shaphan the secretary **c** to the king, 2 Kgs 22:9
man of God who **c** from Judah and 2 Kgs 23:17
of the prophet who **c** out of Samaria. 2 Kgs 23:18
and he **c** to Egypt and died there. 2 Kgs 23:34
king of Babylon **c** up, 2 Kgs 24:1
Surely this **c** upon Judah at the 2 Kgs 24:3
king of Babylon **c** up to Jerusalem, 2 Kgs 24:10
king of Babylon **c** to the city 2 Kgs 24:11
anger of the LORD it **c** to the point in 2 Kgs 24:20
king of Babylon **c** with all his 2 Kgs 25:1
the king of Babylon, **c** to Jerusalem. 2 Kgs 25:8
they **c** with their men to Gedaliah at 2 Kgs 25:23
c with ten men and struck down 2 Kgs 25:25
(from whom the Philistines **c**), 1 Chr 1:12
from these **c** the Zorathites and the 1 Chr 2:53
the Kenites who **c** from Hammath, 1 Chr 2:55
by name, **c** in the days of Hezekiah, 1 Chr 4:41
his brothers and a chief **c** from him, 1 Chr 5:2
because they **c** down to raid their 1 Chr 7:21
and his brothers **c** to comfort him. 1 Chr 7:22
and the Philistines **c** and lived in 1 Chr 10:7
when the Philistines **c** to strip the 1 Chr 10:8
all the elders of Israel **c** to the king at 1 Chr 11:3
are the men who **c** to David at Ziklag, 1 Chr 12:1
Benjamin and Judah **c** to the 1 Chr 12:16
David when he **c** with the 1 Chr 12:19
day to day men **c** to David to help 1 Chr 12:22
the armed troops who **c** to David in 1 Chr 12:23
c to Hebron with full intent to make 1 Chr 12:38
c bringing food on donkeys and on 1 Chr 12:40
And when they **c** to the threshing 1 Chr 13:9
covenant of the LORD **c** to the city of 1 Chr 15:29
the word of the LORD **c** to Nathan, 1 Chr 17:3
Syrians of Damascus **c** to help 1 Chr 18:5
And David's servants **c** to the land of 1 Chr 19:2
who **c** and encamped before Medeba. 1 Chr 19:7
from their cities and **c** to battle. 1 Chr 19:7
And the Ammonites **c** out and drew 1 Chr 19:9
the city. Then Joab **c** to Jerusalem. 1 Chr 19:15
the Jordan and **c** to them and 1 Chr 19:17
the Ammonites and **c** and besieged 1 Chr 20:1
all Israel and **c** back to Jerusalem. 1 Chr 21:4
So Gad **c** to David and said to him, 1 Chr 21:11
As David **c** to Ornan, Ornan looked 1 Chr 21:21
But the word of the LORD **c** to me, 1 Chr 22:8
and his lot **c** out for the north. 1 Chr 26:14
Obed-edom's **c** out for the south, 1 Chr 26:15
Shuppim and Hosah it **c** out for the 1 Chr 26:16
the divisions that **c** and went, 1 Chr 27:1
Yet wrath **c** upon Israel for this, and 1 Chr 27:24
the circumstances that **c** upon him 1 Chr 29:30
So Solomon **c** from the high place at 2 Chr 1:13
And all the elders of Israel **c**, and the 2 Chr 5:4
of Israel, when they **c** out of Egypt. 2 Chr 5:10
And when the priests **c** out of the 2 Chr 5:11
fire **c** down from heaven and 2 Chr 7:1
she **c** to Jerusalem to test him with 2 Chr 9:1
And when she **c** to Solomon, she told 2 Chr 9:1
the reports until I **c** and my own eyes 2 Chr 9:6
weight of gold that **c** to Solomon in 2 Chr 9:13
Jeroboam and all Israel **c** and said to 2 Chr 10:3
all the people **c** to Rehoboam the 2 Chr 10:12
When Rehoboam **c** to Jerusalem, he 2 Chr 11:1
word of the LORD **c** to Shemaiah the 2 Chr 11:2
their holdings and **c** to Judah and 2 Chr 11:14
LORD God of Israel **c** after them from 2 Chr 11:16
king of Egypt **c** up against Jerusalem 2 Chr 12:2
without number who **c** with him 2 Chr 12:3
cities of Judah and **c** as far as 2 Chr 12:4
the prophet **c** to Rehoboam 2 Chr 12:5
the word of the LORD **c** to Shemaiah: 2 Chr 12:7
king of Egypt **c** up against Jerusalem. 2 Chr 12:9
the guard **c** and carried them and 2 Chr 12:11
Zerah the Ethiopian **c** out against 2 Chr 14:9
chariots, and **c** as far as Mareshah. 2 Chr 14:9
The Spirit of God **c** upon Azariah the 2 Chr 15:1
who went out or to him who **c** in, 2 Chr 15:5
time Hanani the seer **c** to Asa king of 2 Chr 16:7
Then a spirit **c** forward and stood 2 Chr 18:20
son of Chenaanah **c** near and 2 Chr 18:23
c against Jehoshaphat for battle. 2 Chr 20:1
Some men **c** and told Jehoshaphat, 2 Chr 20:2
cities of Judah they **c** to seek the LORD. 2 Chr 20:4
invade when they **c** from the land 2 Chr 20:10
of the LORD **c** upon Jahaziel the 2 Chr 20:14
When Judah **c** to the watchtower of 2 Chr 20:24
and his people **c** to take their 2 Chr 20:25
They **c** to Jerusalem with harps and 2 Chr 20:28
the fear of God **c** on all the 2 Chr 20:29
And a letter **c** to him from Elijah 2 Chr 21:12
And they **c** up against Judah and 2 Chr 21:17
his bowels **c** out because of the 2 Chr 21:19
of men that **c** with the Arabians 2 Chr 22:1
For when he **c** there, he went out with 2 Chr 22:7
of Israel, and they **c** to Jerusalem. 2 Chr 23:2
princes of Judah **c** and paid homage 2 Chr 24:17
And wrath **c** upon Judah and 2 Chr 24:18
of the Syrians **c** up against Joash. 2 Chr 24:23
They **c** to Judah and Jerusalem and 2 Chr 24:23
But a man of God **c** to him and said, 2 Chr 25:7
After Amaziah **c** from striking 2 Chr 25:14
meet the army that **c** to Samaria and 2 Chr 28:9
king of Assyria **c** against him and 2 Chr 28:20
wrath of the LORD **c** on Judah and 2 Chr 29:8
of the month they **c** to the vestibule 2 Chr 29:17
for the thing **c** about suddenly. 2 Chr 29:36
themselves and **c** to Jerusalem. 2 Chr 30:11
And many people **c** together in 2 Chr 30:13
whole assembly that **c** out of Israel, 2 Chr 30:25
and the sojourners who **c** out of the 2 Chr 30:25
and their prayer **c** to his holy 2 Chr 30:27
and the princes **c** and saw the 2 Chr 31:8
king of Assyria **c** and invaded Judah 2 Chr 32:1
And when he **c** into the house of his 2 Chr 32:21
Therefore wrath **c** upon him and 2 Chr 32:25
They **c** to Hilkiah the high priest and 2 Chr 34:9
but **c** to fight in the plain of 2 Chr 35:22
Against him **c** up Nebuchadnezzar 2 Chr 36:6
people of the province who **c** up out of the Ezr 2:1
They **c** with Zerubbabel, Jeshua, Ezr 2:2
were those who **c** up from Tel-melah, Ezr 2:59
when they **c** to the house of the LORD Ezr 2:68
When the seventh month **c**, and the Ezr 3:1
in their vestments **c** forward with Ezr 3:10
king that the Jews who **c** up from you to Ezr 4:12
and their associates **c** to them and Ezr 5:3
Then this Sheshbazzar **c** and laid the Ezr 5:16
And he **c** to Jerusalem in the fifth month, Ezr 7:8
day of the fifth month he **c** to Jerusalem, Ezr 7:9
sons of Adonikam, those who **c** later, Ezr 8:13
We **c** to Jerusalem, and there we Ezr 8:32
c with certain men from Judah. Neh 1:2
Then I **c** to the governors of the Neh 2:9
lived near them **c** from all directions Neh 4:12
the break of dawn until the stars **c** out. Neh 4:21
besides those who **c** to us from the Neh 5:17
Tobiah, and Tobiah's letters **c** to them. Neh 6:17
genealogy of those who **c** up at the first, Neh 7:5
of the province who **c** up out of the Neh 7:6
They **c** with Zerubbabel, Jeshua, Neh 7:7
were those who **c** up from Tel-melah, Neh 7:61
c together to Ezra the scribe in order to Neh 8:13
You **c** down on Mount Sinai and spoke Neh 9:13
the Levites who **c** up with Zerubbabel Neh 12:1
and they **c** to a halt at the Gate of the Neh 12:39
and **c** to Jerusalem, and I then Neh 13:7
Now when the turn **c** for each young Est 2:12
When the turn **c** for Esther the Est 2:15
And this **c** to the knowledge of Est 2:22
women and her eunuchs **c** and told her, Est 4:4
So the king and Haman **c** to the feast that Est 5:5
So Haman **c** in, and the king said to him, Est 6:6
And Mordecai **c** before the king, for Est 8:1
But when it **c** before the king, he gave Est 9:25
the sons of God **c** to present themselves Jb 1:6
the LORD, and Satan also **c** among them. Jb 1:6
and there **c** a messenger to Job and said, Jb 1:14
yet speaking, there **c** another and said, Jb 1:16
yet speaking, there **c** another and said, Jb 1:17
yet speaking, there **c** another and said, Jb 1:18
a great wind **c** across the wilderness and Jb 1:19
"Naked I **c** from my mother's womb, Jb 1:21
the sons of God **c** to present themselves Jb 2:1
and Satan also **c** among them to present Jb 2:1
him, they **c** each from his own place, Jb 2:11
dread **c** upon me, and trembling, which Jb 4:14
who was about to perish **c** upon me, Jb 29:13
But when I hoped for good, evil **c**, and Jb 30:26
and when I waited for light, darkness **c**. Jb 30:26
Then **c** to him all his brothers and Jb 42:11
The enemy **c** to an end in everlasting Ps 9:6
He bowed the heavens and **c** down; thick Ps 18:9
he **c** swiftly on the wings of the wind. Ps 18:10
obeyed me; foreigners **c** cringing to me. Ps 18:44
lost heart and **c** trembling out of Ps 18:45
For he spoke, and it **c** to be; he Ps 33:9
the kings assembled; they **c** on together. Ps 48:4
when Doeg, the Edomite, **c** and told Saul, Ps 52:T
until what he had said **c** to pass, the Ps 105:19
Then Israel **c** to Egypt; Jacob Ps 105:23
He spoke, and there **c** swarms of flies, Ps 105:31
He spoke, and the locusts **c**, young Ps 105:34
As he **c** from his mother's womb he Eccl 5:15
he shall go again, naked as he **c**, Eccl 5:15
just as he **c**, so shall he go, and what Eccl 5:16
and a great king **c** against it and Eccl 9:14
I **c** to my garden, my sister, my bride, I Sg 5:1
the king of Israel **c** up to Jerusalem to Is 7:1
for Israel when they **c** up from the land Is 11:16
year that King Ahaz died **c** this oracle: Is 14:28
c to Ashdod and fought against it and Is 20:1
king of Assyria **c** up against all Is 36:1
And there **c** out to him Eliakim the son of Is 36:3
c to Hezekiah with their clothes torn, Is 36:22
the servants of King Hezekiah **c** to Isaiah, Is 37:5
you back on the way by which you **c**.' Is 37:29
By the way that he **c**, by the same he Is 37:34
the prophet the son of Amoz **c** to him, Is 38:1
Then the word of the LORD **c** to Isaiah: Is 38:4
Isaiah the prophet **c** to King Hezekiah, Is 39:3
and who **c** from the waters of Judah, Is 48:1
suddenly I did them and they **c** to pass. Is 48:3
before they **c** to pass I announced them to Is 48:5
from the time it **c** to be I have been Is 48:16
Why, when I **c**, was there no man; why, Is 50:2
that we did not look for, you **c** down, Is 64:3
has made, and so all these things **c** to be, Is 66:2
before her pain **c** upon her she delivered a Is 66:7
the word of the LORD **c** in the days of Jer 1:2
It **c** also in the days of Jehoiakim the son Jer 1:3
Now the word of the LORD **c** to me, saying, Jer 1:4
And the word of the LORD **c** to me, saying, Jer 1:11
The word of the LORD **c** to me a second Jer 1:13
The word of the LORD **c** to me, saying, Jer 2:1
disaster **c** upon them, declares the LORD." Jer 2:3
But when you **c** in, you defiled my land Jer 2:7
The word that **c** to Jeremiah from the Jer 7:1
day that your fathers **c** out of the land Jer 7:25
We looked for peace, but no good **c**; for a Jer 8:15
The word that **c** to Jeremiah from the Jer 11:1
the word of the LORD **c** to me a second Jer 13:3
Then the word of the LORD **c** to me: Jer 13:8
the LORD that **c** to Jeremiah concerning Jer 14:1
We looked for peace, but no good **c**; for Jer 14:19
The word of the LORD **c** to me: Jer 16:1
You know what **c** out of my lips; it was Jer 17:16
The word that **c** to Jeremiah from the Jer 18:1
Then the word of the LORD **c** to me: Jer 18:5
Then Jeremiah **c** from Topheth, where Jer 19:14
is the word that **c** to Jeremiah from the Jer 21:1
Then the word of the LORD **c** to me: Jer 24:4
The word that **c** to Jeremiah concerning Jer 25:1
king of Judah, this word **c** from the LORD: Jer 26:1
they **c** up from the king's house to the Jer 26:10
this word **c** to Jeremiah from the LORD. Jer 27:1
the word of the LORD **c** to Jeremiah: Jer 28:12
the word of the LORD **c** to Jeremiah: Jer 29:30
The word that **c** to Jeremiah from the Jer 30:1
The word that **c** to Jeremiah from the Jer 32:1
said, "The word of the LORD **c** to me: Jer 32:6
Then Hanamel my cousin **c** to me in the Jer 32:8
The word of the LORD **c** to Jeremiah: Jer 32:26
word of the LORD **c** to Jeremiah a second Jer 33:1
The word of the LORD **c** to Jeremiah: Jer 33:19
The word of the LORD **c** to Jeremiah: Jer 33:23
The word that **c** to Jeremiah from the Jer 34:1
The word that **c** to Jeremiah from the Jer 34:8
word of the LORD **c** to Jeremiah from the Jer 34:12
The word that **c** to Jeremiah from the Jer 35:1
king of Babylon **c** up against the Jer 35:11
the word of the LORD **c** to Jeremiah: Jer 35:12
this word **c** to Jeremiah from the LORD: Jer 36:1
all the people who **c** from the cities of Jer 36:9
the scroll in his hand and **c** to them. Jer 36:14
the word of the LORD **c** to Jeremiah: Jer 36:27
word of the LORD **c** to Jeremiah the Jer 37:6
Pharaoh's army that **c** to help you is Jer 37:7
Then all the officials **c** to Jeremiah and Jer 38:27
all his army **c** against Jerusalem and Jer 39:1
of the king of Babylon **c** and sat in the Jer 39:3
word of the LORD **c** to Jeremiah while he Jer 39:15
The word that **c** to Jeremiah from the Jer 40:1
had been driven and **c** to the land of Jer 40:12
in the open country **c** to Gedaliah at Jer 40:13
c with ten men to Gedaliah the son of Jer 41:1
the son of Nethaniah **c** out from Mizpah Jer 41:6

Mizpah to meet them, weeping as he **c**. Jer 41:6
When they **c** into the city, Ishmael the Jer 41:7
They **c** upon him at the great pool that Jer 41:12
Mizpah turned around and **c** back, Jer 41:14
from the least to the greatest, **c** near Jer 42:1
days the word of the LORD **c** to Jeremiah. Jer 42:7
And they **c** into the land of Egypt, for Jer 43:7
word of the LORD **c** to Jeremiah in Jer 43:8
The word that **c** to Jeremiah concerning Jer 44:1
who **c** to the land of Egypt to live, Jer 44:28
of the LORD that **c** to Jeremiah the Jer 46:1
of the LORD that **c** to Jeremiah the Jer 47:1
strength, for fire **c** out from Heshbon, Jer 48:45
If grape-gatherers **c** to you, would they Jer 49:9
leave gleanings? If thieves **c** by night, Jer 49:9
of the LORD that **c** to Jeremiah the Jer 49:34
anger of the LORD things **c** to the point in Jer 52:3
king of Babylon **c** with all his Jer 52:4
Who has spoken and it **c** to pass, Lam 3:37
You **c** near when I called on you; you Lam 3:57
word of the LORD **c** to Ezekiel the priest, Ezk 1:3
behold, a stormy wind **c** out of the north, Ezk 1:4
from the midst of it **c** the likeness of four Ezk 1:5
And there **c** a voice from above the Ezk 1:25
And I **c** to the exiles at Tel-abib, who Ezk 3:15
days, the word of the LORD **c** to me: Ezk 3:16
The word of the LORD **c** to me: Ezk 6:1
The word of the LORD **c** to me: Ezk 7:1
six men **c** from the direction of the upper Ezk 9:2
And it **c** to pass, while I was Ezk 11:13
And the word of the LORD **c** to me: Ezk 11:14
The word of the LORD **c** to me: Ezk 12:1
morning the word of the LORD **c** to me: Ezk 12:8
And the word of the LORD **c** to me: Ezk 12:17
And the word of the LORD **c** to me: Ezk 12:21
And the word of the LORD **c** to me: Ezk 12:26
The word of the LORD **c** to me: Ezk 13:1
of the elders of Israel **c** to me and sat Ezk 14:1
And the word of the LORD **c** to me: Ezk 14:2
And the word of the LORD **c** to me: Ezk 14:12
And the word of the LORD **c** to me: Ezk 15:1
Again the word of the LORD **c** to me: Ezk 16:1
The word of the LORD **c** to me: Ezk 17:1
c to Lebanon and took the top of the Ezk 17:3
Then the word of the LORD **c** to me: Ezk 17:11
the king of Babylon **c** to Jerusalem, Ezk 17:12
The word of the LORD **c** to me: Ezk 18:1
of the elders of Israel **c** to inquire of the Ezk 20:1
And the word of the LORD **c** to me: Ezk 20:2
And the word of the LORD **c** to me: Ezk 20:45
The word of the LORD **c** to me: Ezk 21:1
And the word of the LORD **c** to me: Ezk 21:8
The word of the LORD **c** to me again: Ezk 21:18
And the word of the LORD **c** to me, Ezk 22:1
And the word of the LORD **c** to me: Ezk 22:17
And the word of the LORD **c** to me: Ezk 22:23
The word of the LORD **c** to me: Ezk 23:1
And the Babylonians **c** to her into the Ezk 23:17
same day they **c** into my sanctuary Ezk 23:39
was sent; and behold, they **c**. Ezk 23:40
month, the word of the LORD **c** to me: Ezk 24:1
The word of the LORD **c** to me: Ezk 24:15
them, "The word of the LORD **c** to me: Ezk 24:20
The word of the LORD **c** to me: Ezk 25:1
month, the word of the LORD **c** to me: Ezk 26:1
The word of the LORD **c** to me: Ezk 27:1
When your wares **c** from the seas, you Ezk 27:33
The word of the LORD **c** to me: Ezk 28:1
the word of the LORD **c** to me: Ezk 28:11
The word of the LORD **c** to me: Ezk 28:20
month, the word of the LORD **c** to me: Ezk 29:1
month, the word of the LORD **c** to me: Ezk 29:17
The word of the LORD **c** to me: Ezk 30:1
month, the word of the LORD **c** to me: Ezk 30:20
month, the word of the LORD **c** to me: Ezk 31:1
month, the word of the LORD **c** to me: Ezk 32:1
month, the word of the LORD **c** to me: Ezk 32:17
The word of the LORD **c** to me: Ezk 33:1
a fugitive from Jerusalem **c** to me and Ezk 33:21
me the evening before the fugitive **c**; Ezk 33:22
by the time the man **c** to me in the Ezk 33:22
The word of the LORD **c** to me: Ezk 33:23
The word of the LORD **c** to me: Ezk 34:1
The word of the LORD **c** to me: Ezk 35:1
The word of the LORD **c** to me: Ezk 36:16
But when they **c** to the nations, Ezk 36:20
came to the nations, wherever they **c**, Ezk 36:20
among the nations to which they **c**. Ezk 36:21
among the nations to which you **c**. Ezk 36:22
a rattling, and the bones **c** together, Ezk 37:7
me, and the breath **c** into them, Ezk 37:10
The word of the LORD **c** to me: Ezk 37:15
The word of the LORD **c** to me: Ezk 38:1
I had seen when he **c** to destroy the city, Ezk 43:3
king of Babylon **c** to Jerusalem and Dn 1:1

So they **c** in and stood before the king. Dn 2:2
you lay in bed **c** thoughts of what would Dn 2:29
time certain Chaldeans **c** forward and Dn 3:8
Then Nebuchadnezzar **c** near to the Dn 3:26
and Abednego **c** out from the fire. Dn 3:26
the Chaldeans, and the astrologers **c** in, Dn 4:7
At last Daniel **c** in before me—he who Dn 4:8
a holy one, **c** down from heaven. Dn 4:13
All this **c** upon King Nebuchadnezzar. Dn 4:28
Then all the king's wise men **c** in, but Dn 5:8
his lords, **c** into the banqueting hall, Dn 5:10
presidents and satraps **c** by agreement to Dn 6:6
Then these men **c** by agreement and Dn 6:11
Then they **c** near and said before the Dn 6:12
Then these men **c** by agreement to the Dn 6:15
As he **c** near to the den where Daniel Dn 6:20
And four great beasts **c** up out of the sea, Dn 7:3
there **c** up among them another horn, Dn 7:8
of fire issued and **c** out from before him; Dn 7:10
clouds of heaven there **c** one like a son Dn 7:13
and he **c** to the Ancient of Days and was Dn 7:13
the other horn that **c** up and before Dn 7:20
until the Ancient of Days **c**, and Dn 7:22
and the time **c** when the saints possessed Dn 7:22
the other, and the higher one **c** up last. Dn 8:3
a male goat **c** from the west across the Dn 8:5
He **c** to the ram with the two horns, Dn 8:6
instead of it there **c** up four conspicuous Dn 8:8
Out of one of them **c** a little horn, which Dn 8:9
So he **c** near where I stood. And when he Dn 8:17
And when he **c**, I was frightened and fell Dn 8:17
c to me in swift flight at the time of the Dn 9:21
one of the chief princes, **c** to help me, Dn 10:13
and **c** to make you understand what is Dn 10:14
The word of the LORD that **c** to Hosea, the Hos 1:1
at the time when she **c** out of the land of Hos 2:15
But they **c** to Baal-peor and consecrated Hos 9:10
The word of the LORD that **c** to Joel, the son Jl 1:1
If thieves **c** to you, if plunderers came by Ob 1:5
if plunderers **c** by night—how you have Ob 1:5
If grape gatherers **c** to you, would they Ob 1:5
the word of the LORD **c** to Jonah the son of Jon 1:1
So the captain **c** and said to him, "What Jon 1:6
the LORD, and my prayer **c** to you, Jon 2:7
word of the LORD **c** to Jonah the second Jon 3:1
But when dawn **c** up the next day, God Jon 4:7
which **c** into being in a night and Jon 4:10
of the LORD that **c** to Micah of Moresheth Mi 1:1
in the days when you **c** out of the land of Mi 7:15
From you **c** one who plotted evil against Na 1:11
God **c** from Teman, and the Holy One Hab 3:3
who **c** like a whirlwind to scatter me, Hab 3:14
of the LORD that **c** to Zephaniah the son Zep 1:1
the word of the LORD **c** by the hand of Hg 1:1
the word of the LORD **c** by the hand of Hg 1:3
looked for much, and behold, it **c** to little. Hg 1:9
And they **c** and worked on the house of Hg 1:14
the word of the LORD **c** by the hand of Hg 2:1
I made with you when you **c** out of Egypt. Hg 2:5
word of the LORD **c** by Haggai the Hg 2:10
When one **c** to a heap of twenty Hg 2:16
When one **c** to the wine vat to draw fifty Hg 2:16
The word of the LORD **c** a second time to Hg 2:20
word of the LORD **c** to the prophet Zec 1:1
word of the LORD **c** to the prophet Zec 1:7
the angel who talked with me **c** forward, Zec 2:3
and another angel **c** forward to meet him Zec 2:3
who talked with me **c** again and woke Zec 4:1
Then the word of the LORD **c** to me, Zec 4:8
who talked with me **c** forward and said Zec 5:5
four chariots **c** out from between two Zec 6:1
When the strong horses **c** out, they were Zec 6:7
And the word of the LORD **c** to me: Zec 6:9
word of the LORD **c** to Zechariah on the Zec 7:1
the word of the LORD of hosts **c** to me: Zec 7:4
And the word of the LORD **c** to Zechariah, Zec 7:8
Therefore great anger **c** from the LORD Zec 7:12
And the word of the LORD of hosts **c**, Zec 8:1
the foe for him who went out or **c** in, Zec 8:10
the word of the LORD of hosts **c** to me, Zec 8:18
before they **c** together she was found to Mt 1:18
wise men from the east **c** to Jerusalem, Mt 2:1
went before them until it **c** to rest over the Mt 2:9
days John the Baptist **c** preaching in the Mt 3:1
Then Jesus **c** from Galilee to the Jordan Mt 3:13
And the tempter **c** and said to him, "If you Mt 4:3
angels **c** and were ministering to him. Mt 4:11
when he sat down, his disciples **c** to him. Mt 5:1
And the rain fell, and the floods **c**, and Mt 7:25
And the rain fell, and the floods **c**, and Mt 7:27
When he **c** down from the mountain, Mt 8:1
a leper **c** to him and knelt before him, Mt 8:2
a centurion **c** forward to him, Mt 8:5
And a scribe **c** up and said to him, Mt 8:19
And when he **c** to the other side, to the Mt 8:28

"Go." So they **c** out and went into the Mt 8:32
behold, all the city **c** out to meet Jesus, Mt 8:34
he crossed over and **c** to his own city. Mt 9:1
collectors and sinners **c** and were Mt 9:10
For I **c** not to call the righteous, but Mt 9:13
Then the disciples of John **c** to him, Mt 9:14
a ruler **c** in and knelt before him, Mt 9:18
blood for twelve years **c** up behind him Mt 9:20
And when Jesus **c** to the ruler's house Mt 9:23
the house, the blind men **c** to him, Mt 9:28
For John **c** neither eating nor drinking, Mt 11:18
The Son of Man **c** eating and drinking, Mt 11:19
for she **c** from the ends of the earth to Mt 12:42
return to my house from which I **c**.' Mt 12:44
and the birds **c** and devoured them. Mt 13:4
Then the disciples **c** and said to him, Mt 13:10
his enemy **c** and sowed weeds among Mt 13:25
So when the plants **c** up and bore Mt 13:26
master of the house **c** and said to him, Mt 13:27
And his disciples **c** to him, saying, Mt 13:36
But when Herod's birthday **c**, the Mt 14:6
And his disciples **c** and took the body Mt 14:12
the disciples **c** to him and said, Mt 14:15
When evening **c**, he was there alone, Mt 14:23
fourth watch of the night he **c** to them, Mt 14:25
and walked on the water and **c** to Jesus. Mt 14:29
over, they **c** to land at Gennesaret. Mt 14:34
Pharisees and scribes **c** to Jesus from Mt 15:1
Then the disciples **c** and said to him, Mt 15:12
woman from that region **c** out and was Mt 15:22
And his disciples **c** and begged him, Mt 15:23
But she **c** and knelt before him, saying, Mt 15:25
And great crowds **c** to him, bringing Mt 15:30
And the Pharisees and Sadducees **c**, and Mt 16:1
Now when Jesus **c** into the district of Mt 16:13
But Jesus **c** and touched them, saying, Mt 17:7
And when they **c** to the crowd, a man Mt 17:14
to the crowd, a man **c** up to him and, Mt 17:14
him, and the demon **c** out of him, Mt 17:18
Then the disciples **c** to Jesus privately Mt 17:19
When they **c** to Capernaum, the Mt 17:24
"Yes." And when he **c** into the house, Mt 17:25
At that time the disciples **c** to Jesus, Mt 18:1
Then Peter **c** up and said to him, "Lord, Mt 18:21
And Pharisees **c** up to him and tested Mt 19:3
And behold, a man **c** up to him, Mt 19:16
And when evening **c**, the owner of the Mt 20:8
those hired about the eleventh hour **c**, Mt 20:9
Now when those hired first **c**, they Mt 20:10
of the sons of Zebedee **c** up to him with Mt 20:20
as the Son of Man **c** not to be served Mt 20:28
near to Jerusalem and **c** to Bethphage, Mt 21:1
the blind and the lame **c** to him in the Mt 21:14
the elders of the people **c** up to him as Mt 21:23
For John **c** to you in the way of Mt 21:32
"But when the king **c** in to look at the Mt 22:11
The same day Sadducees **c** to him, who Mt 22:23
when his disciples **c** to point out to him Mt 24:1
Olives, the disciples **c** to him privately, Mt 24:3
until the flood **c** and swept them Mt 24:39
were going to buy, the bridegroom **c**, Mt 25:10
Afterward the other virgins **c** also, Mt 25:11
of those servants **c** and settled accounts Mt 25:19
had received the five talents **c** forward, Mt 25:20
also who had the two talents **c** forward, Mt 25:22
had received the one talent **c** forward, Mt 25:24
me, I was in prison and you **c** to me.' Mt 25:36
a woman **c** up to him with an alabaster Mt 26:7
Bread the disciples **c** to Jesus, Mt 26:17
And he **c** to the disciples and found Mt 26:40
And again he **c** and found them Mt 26:43
Then he **c** to the disciples and said to Mt 26:45
While he was still speaking, Judas **c**, Mt 26:47
And he **c** up to Jesus at once and said, Mt 26:49
do what you **c** to do." Then they came Mt 26:50
to do." Then they **c** up and laid hands Mt 26:50
many false witnesses **c** forward. Mt 26:60
came forward. At last two **c** forward Mt 26:60
And a servant girl **c** up to him and Mt 26:69
while the bystanders **c** up and said Mt 26:73
When morning **c**, all the chief priests Mt 27:1
And when they **c** to a place called Mt 27:33
there **c** a rich man from Arimathea, Mt 27:57
from heaven and **c** and rolled back Mt 28:2
"Greetings!" And they **c** up and took Mt 28:9
'His disciples **c** by night and stole him Mt 28:13
And Jesus **c** and said to them, "All Mt 28:18
In those days Jesus **c** from Nazareth of Mk 1:9
And when he **c** up out of the water, Mk 1:10
And a voice **c** from heaven, "You are Mk 1:11
John was arrested, Jesus **c** into Galilee, Mk 1:14
out with a loud voice, **c** out of him. Mk 1:26
And he **c** and took her by the hand and Mk 1:31
there also, for that is why I **c** out." Mk 1:38
And a leper **c** to him, imploring him, Mk 1:40

And they **c**, bringing to him a paralytic	Mk 2:3
I **c** not to call the righteous, but	Mk 2:17
And people **c** and said to him, "Why do	Mk 2:18
all that he was doing, they **c** to him.	Mk 3:8
whom he desired, and they **c** to him.	Mk 3:13
the scribes who **c** down from Jerusalem	Mk 3:22
And his mother and his brothers **c**, and	Mk 3:31
the path, and the birds **c** and devoured it.	Mk 4:4
They **c** to the other side of the sea, to the	Mk 5:1
And the unclean spirits **c** out, and	Mk 5:13
And people **c** to see what it was that had	Mk 5:14
And they **c** to Jesus and saw the	Mk 5:15
Then **c** one of the rulers of the	Mk 5:22
about Jesus and **c** up behind him	Mk 5:27
c in fear and trembling and fell down	Mk 5:33
there **c** from the ruler's house some	Mk 5:35
They **c** to the house of the ruler of the	Mk 5:38
away from there and **c** to his hometown,	Mk 6:1
But an opportunity **c** when Herod on	Mk 6:21
when Herodias's daughter **c** in and	Mk 6:22
And she **c** in immediately with haste to	Mk 6:25
they **c** and took his body and laid it in a	Mk 6:29
late, his disciples **c** to him and said,	Mk 6:35
And when evening **c**, the boat was out	Mk 6:47
fourth watch of the night he **c** to them,	Mk 6:48
they **c** to land at Gennesaret and	Mk 6:53
And wherever he **c**, in villages, cities, or	Mk 6:56
heard of him and **c** and fell down at	Mk 7:25
The Pharisees **c** and began to argue	Mk 8:11
And they **c** to Bethsaida. And some	Mk 8:22
them, and a voice **c** out of the cloud,	Mk 9:7
And when they **c** to the disciples, they	Mk 9:14
saw that a crowd **c** running together,	Mk 9:25
and convulsing him terribly, it **c** out,	Mk 9:26
And they **c** to Capernaum. And when	Mk 9:33
And Pharisees **c** up and in order to test	Mk 10:2
Zebedee, **c** up to him and said to him,	Mk 10:35
even the Son of Man **c** not to be served	Mk 10:45
And they **c** to Jericho. And as he was	Mk 10:46
his cloak, he sprang up and **c** to Jesus.	Mk 10:50
day, when they **c** from Bethany,	Mk 11:12
find anything on it. When he **c** to it,	Mk 11:13
And they **c** to Jerusalem. And he	Mk 11:15
And when evening **c** they went out of	Mk 11:19
And they **c** again to Jerusalem. And as	Mk 11:27
the scribes and the elders **c** to him,	Mk 11:27
When the season **c**, he sent a servant to	Mk 12:2
And they **c** and said to him, "Teacher,	Mk 12:14
And Sadducees **c** to him, who say that	Mk 12:18
one of the scribes **c** up and heard them	Mk 12:28
And a poor widow **c** and put in two	Mk 12:42
And as he **c** out of the temple, one of his	Mk 13:1
a woman **c** with an alabaster flask of	Mk 14:3
it was evening, he **c** with the twelve.	Mk 14:17
And he **c** and found them sleeping,	Mk 14:37
And again he **c** and found them	Mk 14:40
And he **c** the third time and said to	Mk 14:41
while he was still speaking, Judas **c**,	Mk 14:43
And when he **c**, he went up to him at	Mk 14:45
the elders and the scribes **c** together.	Mk 14:53
of the servant girls of the high priest **c**,	Mk 14:66
And the crowd **c** up and began to ask	Mk 15:8
other women who **c** up with him	Mk 15:41
And when he **c** out, he was unable to	Lk 1:22
And he **c** to her and said, "Greetings, O	Lk 1:28
the sound of your greeting **c** to my ears,	Lk 1:44
Now the time **c** for Elizabeth to give	Lk 1:57
the eighth day they **c** to circumcise the	Lk 1:59
And fear **c** on all their neighbors. And	Lk 1:65
were there, the time **c** for her to give birth.	Lk 2:6
when the time **c** for their purification	Lk 2:22
And he **c** in the Spirit into the temple,	Lk 2:27
down with them and **c** to Nazareth and	Lk 2:51
the word of God **c** to John the son of	Lk 3:2
to the crowds that **c** out to be baptized	Lk 3:7
Tax collectors also **c** to be baptized and	Lk 3:12
and a voice **c** from heaven, "You are my	Lk 3:22
And he **c** to Nazareth, where he had	Lk 4:16
and a great famine **c** over all the land,	Lk 4:25
down in their midst, he **c** out of him,	Lk 4:35
And demons also **c** out of many, crying,	Lk 4:41
the people sought him and **c** to him,	Lk 4:42
And they **c** and filled both the boats, so	Lk 5:7
the cities, there **c** a man full of leprosy.	Lk 5:12
And when day **c**, he called his disciples	Lk 6:13
And he **c** down with them and stood on	Lk 6:17
who **c** to hear him and to be healed of	Lk 6:18
for power **c** out from him and healed	Lk 6:19
And when they **c** to Jesus, they pleaded	Lk 7:4
Then he **c** up and touched the bier, and	Lk 7:14
but from the time I **c** in she has not	Lk 7:45
and people from town after town **c** to him,	Lk 8:4
his mother and his brothers **c** to him,	Lk 8:19
And a windstorm **c** down on the lake,	Lk 8:23
Then the demons **c** out of the man and	Lk 8:33
and they **c** to Jesus and found the man	Lk 8:35
And there **c** a man named Jairus, who	Lk 8:41
She **c** up behind him and touched the	Lk 8:44
she was not hidden, she **c** trembling,	Lk 8:47
from the ruler's house **c** and said,	Lk 8:49
And when he **c** to the house, he allowed	Lk 8:51
away, and the twelve **c** and said to him,	Lk 9:12
a cloud **c** and overshadowed them,	Lk 9:34
And a voice **c** out of the cloud, saying,	Lk 9:35
when he **c** to the place and saw him,	Lk 10:32
as he journeyed, **c** to where he was,	Lk 10:33
return to my house from which I **c**.'	Lk 11:24
for she **c** from the ends of the earth to	Lk 11:31
"I **c** to cast fire on the earth, and would	Lk 12:49
and he **c** seeking fruit on it and found	Lk 13:6
very hour some Pharisees **c** and said to	Lk 13:31
So the servant **c** and reported these	Lk 14:21
"But when he **c** to himself, he said,	Lk 15:17
And he arose and **c** to his father. But	Lk 15:20
and as he **c** and drew near to the house,	Lk 15:25
in. His father **c** out and entreated him,	Lk 15:28
But when this son of yours **c**, who has	Lk 15:30
even the dogs **c** and licked his sores.	Lk 16:21
and the flood **c** and destroyed them all.	Lk 17:27
And when he **c** near, he asked him,	Lk 18:40
And when Jesus **c** to the place, he looked	Lk 19:5
So he hurried and **c** down and received	Lk 19:6
For the Son of Man **c** to seek and to	Lk 19:10
The first **c** before him, saying, 'Lord,	Lk 19:16
And the second **c**, saying, 'Lord, your	Lk 19:18
Then another **c**, saying, 'Lord, here is	Lk 19:20
and the scribes with the elders **c** up	Lk 20:1
that they did not know where it **c** from.	Lk 20:7
When the time **c**, he sent a servant to	Lk 20:10
There **c** to him some Sadducees, those	Lk 20:27
morning all the people **c** to him in the	Lk 21:38
Then **c** the day of Unleavened Bread, on	Lk 22:7
And when the hour **c**, he reclined at	Lk 22:14
And he **c** out and went, as was his	Lk 22:39
And when he **c** to the place, he said to	Lk 22:40
he **c** to the disciples and found them	Lk 22:45
he was still speaking, there **c** a crowd,	Lk 22:47
When day **c**, the assembly of the elders	Lk 22:66
And when they **c** to the place that is	Lk 23:33
they **c** back saying that they had even	Lk 24:23
He **c** as a witness, to bear witness about	Jn 1:7
light, but **c** to bear witness about the light.	Jn 1:8
He **c** to his own, and his own people did	Jn 1:11
grace and truth **c** through Jesus Christ.	Jn 1:17
for this purpose I **c** baptizing with water,	Jn 1:31
you will see." So they **c** and saw where he	Jn 1:39
not know where it **c** from (though the	Jn 2:9
This man **c** to Jesus by night and said to	Jn 3:2
And they **c** to John and said to him,	Jn 3:26
So he **c** to a town of Samaria called	Jn 4:5
There **c** a woman of Samaria to draw	Jn 4:7
Just then his disciples **c** back. They	Jn 4:27
So when the Samaritans **c** to him, they	Jn 4:40
So when he **c** to Galilee, the Galileans	Jn 4:45
So he **c** again to Cana in Galilee, where	Jn 4:46
When evening **c**, his disciples went down	Jn 6:16
boats from Tiberias **c** near the place	Jn 6:23
am the bread that **c** down from heaven."	Jn 6:41
living bread that **c** down from heaven.	Jn 6:51
is the bread that **c** down from heaven,	Jn 6:58
The officers then **c** to the chief priests	Jn 7:45
in the morning he **c** again to the temple.	Jn 8:2
All the people **c** to him, and he sat down	Jn 8:2
for I know where I **c** from and where I am	Jn 8:14
love me, for I **c** from God and I am here.	Jn 8:42
I **c** not of my own accord, but he sent me.	Jn 8:42
So he went and washed and **c** back seeing.	Jn 9:7
said, "For judgment I **c** into this world,	Jn 9:39
All who **c** before me are thieves and	Jn 10:8
I **c** that they may have life and have it	Jn 10:10
the word of God **c**—and Scripture	Jn 10:35
And many **c** to him. And they said,	Jn 10:41
Now when Jesus **c**, he found that	Jn 11:17
Now when Mary **c** to where Jesus was	Jn 11:32
deeply moved again, **c** to the tomb.	Jn 11:38
The man who had died **c** out, his hands	Jn 11:44
Passover, Jesus therefore **c** to Bethany,	Jn 12:1
Jews learned that Jesus was there, they **c**,	Jn 12:9
So these **c** to Philip, who was from	Jn 12:21
name." Then a voice **c** from heaven:	Jn 12:28
He **c** to Simon Peter, who said to him,	Jn 13:6
me and have believed that I **c** from God.	Jn 16:27
I **c** from the Father and have come into	Jn 16:28
is why we believe that you **c** from God."	Jn 16:30
come to know in truth that I **c** from you;	Jn 17:8
to him, **c** forward and said to them,	Jn 18:4
They **c** up to him, saying, "Hail, King of	Jn 19:3
So Jesus **c** out, wearing the crown of	Jn 19:5
So the soldiers **c** and broke the legs of	Jn 19:32
But when they **c** to Jesus and saw that	Jn 19:33
and at once there **c** out blood and water.	Jn 19:34
So he **c** and took away his body.	Jn 19:38
c bringing a mixture of myrrh and	Jn 19:39
the week Mary Magdalene **c** to the tomb	Jn 20:1
Then Simon Peter **c**, following him, and	Jn 20:6
Jesus **c** and stood among them and said	Jn 20:19
Twin, was not with them when Jesus **c**.	Jn 20:24
Jesus **c** and stood among them and said,	Jn 20:26
The other disciples **c** in the boat,	Jn 21:8
Jesus **c** and took the bread and gave it to	Jn 21:13
And suddenly there **c** from heaven a	Acts 2:2
at this sound the multitude **c** together,	Acts 2:6
And awe **c** upon every soul, and many	Acts 2:43
Samuel and those who **c** after him,	Acts 3:24
temple and the Sadducees **c** upon them,	Acts 4:1
number of the men **c** to about five	Acts 4:4
And great fear **c** upon all who heard of	Acts 5:5
of about three hours his wife **c** in,	Acts 5:7
When the young men **c** in they found	Acts 5:10
And great fear **c** upon the whole	Acts 5:11
that as Peter **c** by at least his shadow	Acts 5:15
Now when the high priest **c**, and those	Acts 5:21
But when the officers **c**, they did not	Acts 5:22
And someone **c** and told them, "Look!	Acts 5:25
him were dispersed and **c** to nothing.	Acts 5:36
and they **c** upon him and seized him	Acts 6:12
Now there **c** a famine throughout all	Acts 7:11
it **c** into his heart to visit his brothers,	Acts 7:23
to look, there **c** the voice of the Lord:	Acts 7:31
For unclean spirits **c** out of many who	Acts 8:7
who **c** down and prayed for them that	Acts 8:15
along the road they **c** to some water,	Acts 8:36
And when they **c** up out of the water,	Acts 8:39
to all the towns until he **c** to Caesarea.	Acts 8:40
road by which you **c** has sent me so	Acts 9:17
he **c** down also to the saints who lived	Acts 9:32
And there **c** a voice to him: "Rise,	Acts 10:13
And the voice **c** to him again a	Acts 10:15
I was sent for, I **c** without objection.	Acts 10:29
its four corners, and it **c** down to me.	Acts 11:5
The report of this **c** to the ears of the	Acts 11:22
When he **c** and saw the grace of God,	Acts 11:23
these days prophets **c** down from	Acts 11:27
they **c** to the iron gate leading into the	Acts 12:10
When Peter **c** to himself, he said,	Acts 12:11
girl named Rhoda **c** to answer.	Acts 12:13
Now when day **c**, there was no little	Acts 12:18
and they **c** to him with one accord,	Acts 12:20
they **c** upon a certain magician,	Acts 13:6
sail from Paphos and **c** to Perga in	Acts 13:13
on from Perga and **c** to Antioch in	Acts 13:14
But Jews **c** from Antioch and	Acts 14:19
through Pisidia and **c** to Pamphylia.	Acts 14:24
But some men **c** down from Judea and	Acts 15:1
When they **c** to Jerusalem, they were	Acts 15:4
Paul **c** also to Derbe and to Lystra. A	Acts 16:1
of her." And it **c** out that very hour.	Acts 16:18
So they **c** and apologized to them.	Acts 16:39
and Apollonia, they **c** to Thessalonica,	Acts 17:1
by Paul at Berea also, they **c** there too,	Acts 17:13
And they **c** to Ephesus, and he left	Acts 18:19
a native of Alexandria, **c** to Ephesus.	Acts 18:24
the inland country and **c** to Ephesus.	Acts 19:1
on them, the Holy Spirit **c** on them,	Acts 19:6
and the evil spirits **c** out of them.	Acts 19:12
of those who were now believers **c**,	Acts 19:18
them and found it **c** to fifty thousand	Acts 19:19
much encouragement, he **c** to Greece.	Acts 20:2
and in five days we **c** to them at Troas,	Acts 20:6
from there we **c** the following day	Acts 20:15
And when they **c** to him, he said to	Acts 20:18
sail, we **c** by a straight course to Cos,	Acts 21:1
day we departed and **c** to Caesarea,	Acts 21:8
prophet named Agabus **c** down from	Acts 21:10
word **c** to the tribune of the cohort	Acts 21:31
Then the tribune **c** up and arrested	Acts 21:33
And when he **c** to the steps, he was	Acts 21:35
were with me, and **c** into Damascus.	Acts 22:11
c to me, and standing by me said to	Acts 22:13
So the tribune **c** and said to him,	Acts 22:27
by them when I **c** upon them with the	Acts 23:27
high priest Ananias **c** down with some	Acts 24:1
after several years I **c** to bring alms to	Acts 24:17
After some days Felix **c** with his wife	Acts 24:24
So when they **c** together here, I made	Acts 25:17
Agrippa and Bernice **c** with great	Acts 25:23
and Pamphylia, we **c** to Myra in Lycia.	Acts 27:5
we **c** to a place called Fair Havens,	Acts 27:8
a viper **c** out because of the heat and	Acts 28:3
had diseases also **c** and were cured.	Acts 28:9
and on the second day we **c** to Puteoli.	Acts 28:13
for seven days. And so we **c** to Rome.	Acts 28:14
c as far as the Forum of Appius and	Acts 28:15
And when we **c** into Rome, Paul was	Acts 28:16
they **c** to him at his lodging in greater	Acts 28:23

and welcomed all who **c** to him, Acts 28:30
just as sin **c** into the world through Rom 5:12
Now the law **c** in to increase the Rom 5:20
law, but when the commandment **c**, Rom 7:9
came, sin **c** alive and I died. Rom 7:9
And I, when I **c** to you, brothers, did 1 Cor 2:1
it from you that the word of God **c**? 1 Cor 14:36
For as by a man **c** death, by a man 1 Cor 15:21
so that when I **c** I might not suffer pain 2 Cor 2:3
When I **c** to Troas to preach the 2 Cor 2:12
c with such glory that the Israelites 2 Cor 3:7
being brought to an end **c** with glory, 2 Cor 3:11
For even when we **c** into Macedonia, 2 Cor 7:5
the brothers who **c** from Macedonia 2 Cor 11:9
But when Cephas **c** to Antioch, I Gal 2:11
For before certain men **c** from James, Gal 2:12
but when they **c** he drew back and Gal 2:12
the law, which **c** 430 years afterward, Gal 3:17
Now before faith **c**, we were held captive Gal 3:23
law was our guardian until Christ **c**, Gal 3:24
And he **c** and preached peace to you Eph 2:17
because our gospel **c** to you not only 1 Thes 1:5
For we never **c** with words of flattery, 1 Thes 2:5
that Christ Jesus **c** into the world to 1 Tm 1:15
first defense no one **c** to stand by me, 2 Tm 4:16
For good news **c** to us just as to them, Heb 4:2
of the oath, which **c** later than the law, Heb 7:28
when Christ **c** into the world, Heb 10:5
This is he who **c** by water and blood— 1 Jn 5:6
when the brothers **c** and testified to 3 Jn 1:3
the Lord **c** with ten thousands of his Jude 1:14
from his mouth **c** a sharp two-edged Rv 1:16
first and the last, who died and **c** to life. Rv 2:8
From the throne **c** flashes of lightning, Rv 4:5
given to him, and he **c** out conquering, Rv 6:2
And out **c** another horse, bright red. Its Rv 6:4
And another angel **c** and stood at the altar Rv 8:3
Then from the smoke **c** locusts on the Rv 9:3
and smoke and sulfur **c** out of their Rv 9:17
The nations raged, but your wrath **c**, Rv 11:18
But the earth **c** to the help of the Rv 12:16
And another angel **c** out of the temple, Rv 14:15
Then another angel **c** out of the temple Rv 14:17
And another angel **c** out from the altar, Rv 14:18
out of the sanctuary **c** the seven angels Rv 15:6
and painful sores **c** upon the people Rv 16:2
air, and a loud voice **c** out of the temple, Rv 16:17
had the seven bowls **c** and said to me, Rv 17:1
And from the throne **c** a voice saying, Rv 19:5
by the sword that **c** from the mouth of Rv 19:21
They **c** to life and reigned with Christ for Rv 20:4
but fire **c** down from heaven and Rv 20:9
Then **c** one of the seven angels who had Rv 21:9

CAMEL (10)

saw Isaac, she dismounted from the **c** Gn 24:64
the hoof, you shall not eat these: The **c**, Lv 11:4
hoof cloven you shall not eat these: the **c**, Dt 14:7
infant, ox and sheep, **c** and donkey.'" 1 Sm 15:3
of goods of Damascus, forty **c** loads. 2 Kgs 8:9
a restless young **c** running here and Jer 2:23
it is easier for a **c** to go through the eye Mt 19:24
out a gnat and swallowing a **c**! Mt 23:24
It is easier for a **c** to go through the eye Mk 10:25
it is easier for a **c** to go through the eye Lk 18:25

CAMEL'S (3)

and put them in the **c** saddle and sat on Gn 31:34
wore a garment of **c** hair and a leather Mt 3:4
John was clothed with **c** hair and wore a Mk 1:6

CAMELS (48)

servants, female donkeys, and **c**. Gn 12:16
took ten of his master's **c** and departed, Gn 24:10
And he made the **c** kneel down outside Gn 24:11
and I will water your **c**'—let her be the Gn 24:14
said, "I will draw water for your **c** also, Gn 24:19
draw water, and she drew for all his **c**. Gn 24:20
When the **c** had finished drinking, the Gn 24:22
he was standing by the **c** at the spring. Gn 24:30
the house and a place for the **c**." Gn 24:31
to the house and unharnessed the **c**, Gn 24:32
and gave straw and fodder to the **c**, Gn 24:32
and female servants, **c** and donkeys. Gn 24:35
I will draw for your **c** also," let her be Gn 24:44
and I will give your **c** drink also.' Gn 24:46
I drank, and she gave the **c** drink also. Gn 24:46
and rode on the **c** and followed the Gn 24:61
saw, and behold, there were **c** coming. Gn 24:63
and male servants, and **c** and donkeys. Gn 30:43
and set his sons and his wives on **c**. Gn 31:17
him, and the flocks and herds and **c**, Gn 32:7
thirty milking **c** and their calves, forty Gn 32:15
from Gilead, with their **c** bearing gum, Gn 37:25
in the field, the horses, the donkeys, the **c**, Ex 9:3
both they and their **c** could not be Jgs 6:5
and their **c** were without number, Jgs 7:12
that were on the necks of their **c**. Jgs 8:21
that were around the necks of their **c**. Jgs 8:26
the sheep, the oxen, the donkeys, the **c**, 1 Sm 27:9
men, who mounted **c** and fled. 1 Sm 30:17
with **c** bearing spices and very much 1 Kgs 10:2
50,000 of their **c**, 250,000 sheep, 2,000 1 Chr 5:21
on donkeys and on **c** and on mules 1 Chr 12:40
Over the **c** was Obil the Ishmaelite; 1 Chr 27:30
great retinue and **c** bearing spices and 2 Chr 9:1
away sheep in abundance and **c**. 2 Chr 14:15
their **c** were 435, and their donkeys were Ezr 2:67
their **c** 435, and their donkeys 6,720. Neh 7:69
He possessed 7,000 sheep, 3,000 **c**, 500 yoke Jb 1:3
made a raid on the **c** and took them and Jb 1:17
And he had 14,000 sheep, 6,000 **c**, 1,000 Jb 42:12
in pairs, riders on donkeys, riders on **c**, Is 21:7
and their treasures on the humps of **c**, Is 30:6
A multitude of **c** shall cover you, the Is 60:6
you, the young **c** of Midian and Ephah; Is 60:6
their **c** shall be led away from them, Jer 49:29
Their **c** shall become plunder, their Jer 49:32
Rabbah a pasture for **c** and Ammon a Ezk 25:5
fall on the horses, the mules, the **c**, Zec 14:15

CAMP (178)

"This is God's **c**!" So he called the name Gn 32:2
Esau comes to the one **c** and attacks it, Gn 32:8
it, then the **c** that is left will escape." Gn 32:8
he himself stayed that night in the **c**. Gn 32:21
quail came up and covered the **c**, Ex 16:13
in the morning dew lay around the **c**. Ex 16:13
so that all the people in the **c** trembled. Ex 19:16
the people out of the **c** to meet God, Ex 19:17
you shall burn with fire outside the **c**; Ex 29:14
"There is a noise of war in the **c**." Ex 32:17
as he came near the **c** and saw the calf Ex 32:19
stood in the gate of the **c** and said, Ex 32:26
fro from gate to gate throughout the **c**, Ex 32:27
to take the tent and pitch it outside the **c**, Ex 33:7
it outside the camp, far off from the **c**, Ex 33:7
tent of meeting, which was outside the **c**. Ex 33:7
When Moses turned again into the **c**, Ex 33:11
word was proclaimed throughout the **c**, Ex 36:6
shall carry outside the **c** to a clean place, Lv 4:12
the bull outside the **c** and burn it up Lv 4:21
the ashes outside the **c** to a clean place. Lv 6:11
he burned up with fire outside the **c**, Lv 8:17
he burned up with fire outside the **c**. Lv 9:11
front of the sanctuary and out of the **c**." Lv 10:4
carried them in their coats out of the **c**, Lv 10:5
His dwelling shall be outside the **c**. Lv 13:46
and the priest shall go out of the **c**, and Lv 14:3
And after that he may come into the **c**, Lv 14:8
and afterward he may come into the **c**. Lv 16:26
Place, shall be carried outside the **c**. Lv 16:27
and afterward he may come into the **c**. Lv 16:28
kills an ox or a lamb or a goat in the **c**, Lv 17:3
goat in the camp, or kills it outside the **c**, Lv 17:3
son and a man of Israel fought in the **c**, Lv 24:10
"Bring out of the **c** the one who cursed, Lv 24:14
brought out of the **c** the one who had Lv 24:23
of it and shall **c** around the tabernacle. Nm 1:50
man in his own **c** and each man by Nm 1:52
the Levites shall **c** around the Nm 1:53
people of Israel shall **c** each by his own Nm 2:2
They shall **c** facing the tent of meeting Nm 2:2
Those to **c** on the east side toward the Nm 2:3
of the standard of the **c** of Judah by their Nm 2:3
Those to **c** next to him shall be the tribe Nm 2:5
All those listed of the **c** of Judah, by their Nm 2:9
the standard of the **c** of Reuben by their Nm 2:10
And those to **c** next to him shall be the Nm 2:12
All those listed of the **c** of Reuben, by Nm 2:16
with the **c** of the Levites in the midst of Nm 2:17
as they **c**, so shall they set out, each in Nm 2:17
the standard of the **c** of Ephraim by Nm 2:18
All those listed of the **c** of Ephraim, by Nm 2:24
be the standard of the **c** of Dan by their Nm 2:25
And those to **c** next to him shall be the Nm 2:27
those listed of the **c** of Dan were Nm 2:31
Gershonites were to **c** behind the Nm 3:23
of Kohath were to **c** on the south side Nm 3:29
They were to **c** on the north side of the Nm 3:35
who were to **c** before the tabernacle Nm 3:38
When the **c** is to set out, Aaron and his Nm 4:5
of the sanctuary, as the **c** sets out, Nm 4:15
put out of the **c** everyone who is leprous Nm 5:2
and female, putting them outside the **c**, Nm 5:3
camp, that they may not defile their **c**, Nm 5:3
Israel did so, and put them outside the **c**; Nm 5:4
the tabernacle, they remained in **c**. Nm 9:18
of the LORD they remained in **c**; Nm 9:20
of Israel remained in **c** and did not set Nm 9:22
the congregation and for breaking **c**. Nm 10:2
The standard of the **c** of the people of Nm 10:14
the standard of the **c** of Reuben set out Nm 10:18
the standard of the **c** of the people of Nm 10:22
the standard of the **c** of the people of Nm 10:25
where we should **c** in the wilderness, Nm 10:31
day, whenever they set out from the **c**. Nm 10:34
consumed some outlying parts of the **c**. Nm 11:1
the dew fell upon the **c** in the night, Nm 11:9
Now two men remained in the **c**, one Nm 11:26
tent, and so they prophesied in the **c**. Nm 11:26
and Medad are prophesying in the **c**." Nm 11:27
the elders of Israel returned to the **c**. Nm 11:30
the sea and let them fall beside the **c**, Nm 11:31
on the other side, around the **c**, Nm 11:31
out for themselves all around the **c**. Nm 11:32
her be shut outside the **c** seven days, Nm 12:14
was shut outside the **c** seven days, Nm 12:15
LORD nor Moses departed out of the **c**. Nm 14:44
stone him with stones outside the **c**." Nm 15:35
him outside the **c** and stoned him Nm 15:36
taken outside the **c** and slaughtered Nm 19:3
and afterward he may come into the **c**. Nm 19:7
deposit them outside the **c** in a clean Nm 19:9
at the **c** on the plains of Moab by the Nm 31:12
went to meet them outside the **c**. Nm 31:13
Encamp outside the **c** seven days. Nm 31:19
afterward you may come into the **c**." Nm 31:24
the men of war, had perished from the **c**, Dt 2:14
against them, to destroy them from the **c**, Dt 2:15
emission, then he shall go outside the **c**. Dt 23:10
camp. He shall not come inside the **c**, Dt 23:10
the sun sets, he may come inside the **c**. Dt 23:11
"You shall have a place outside the **c**, Dt 23:12
your God walks in the midst of your **c**, Dt 23:14
you, therefore your **c** must be holy, Dt 23:14
and the sojourner who is in your **c**, Dt 29:11
the midst of the **c** and command the Jos 1:11
three days the officers went through the **c** Jos 3:2
their places in the **c** until they were Jos 5:8
they came into the **c** and spent the night Jos 6:11
the camp and spent the night in the **c**. Jos 6:11
the city once, and returned into the **c**. Jos 6:14
things and make the **c** of Israel a thing Jos 6:18
and put them outside the **c** of Israel. Jos 6:23
went to Joshua in the **c** at Gilgal and said Jos 9:6
Gibeon sent to Joshua at the **c** in Gilgal, Jos 10:6
all Israel with him, to the **c** at Gilgal. Jos 10:15
safe to Joshua in the **c** at Makkedah. Jos 10:21
all Israel with him, to the **c** at Gilgal. Jos 10:43
they came to Joshua to the **c** at Shiloh, Jos 18:9
And the **c** of Midian was north of them, Jgs 7:1
And the **c** of Midian was below him in Jgs 7:8
said to him, "Arise, go down against the **c**, Jgs 7:9
go down to the **c** with Purah your Jgs 7:10
go down against the **c**." Then he went Jgs 7:11
of the armed men who were in the **c**. Jgs 7:11
bread tumbled into the **c** of Midian and Jgs 7:13
into his hand Midian and all the **c**." Jgs 7:14
he returned to the **c** of Israel and said, Jgs 7:15
When I come to the outskirts of the **c**, do Jgs 7:17
also on every side of all the **c** and shout, Jgs 7:18
the outskirts of the **c** at the beginning of Jgs 7:19
man stood in his place around the **c**, Jgs 7:21
had come to the **c** from Jabesh-gilead, Jgs 21:8
they brought them to the **c** at Shiloh, Jgs 21:12
And when the troops came to the **c**, the 1 Sm 4:3
covenant of the LORD came into the **c**, 1 Sm 4:5
great shouting in the **c** of the Hebrews 1 Sm 4:6
the ark of the LORD had come to the **c**, 1 Sm 4:6
has come into the **c**." And they said, 1 Sm 4:7
the midst of the **c** in the morning 1 Sm 11:11
came out of the **c** of the Philistines 1 Sm 13:17
And there was a panic in the **c**, in the 1 Sm 14:15
the tumult in the **c** of the Philistines 1 Sm 14:19
had gone up with them into the **c**, 1 Sm 14:21
came out from the **c** of the Philistines 1 Sm 17:4
quickly to the **c** to your brothers. 1 Sm 17:17
and they plundered their **c**. 1 Sm 17:53
with me into the **c** to Saul?" And 1 Sm 26:6
day, behold, a man came from Saul's **c**, 2 Sm 1:2
"I have escaped from the **c** of Israel." 2 Sm 1:3
broke through the **c** of the 2 Sm 23:16
king over Israel that day in the **c**. 1 Kgs 16:16
But when they came to the **c** of Israel, 2 Kgs 3:24
such and such a place shall be my **c**." 2 Kgs 6:8
let us go over to the **c** of the Syrians. 2 Kgs 7:4
at twilight to go to the **c** of the Syrians. 2 Kgs 7:5
came to the edge of the **c** of the Syrians, 2 Kgs 7:5
their donkeys, leaving the **c** as it was, 2 Kgs 7:7
these lepers came to the edge of the **c**, 2 Kgs 7:8
"We came to the **c** of the Syrians, 2 Kgs 7:10
gone out of the **c** to hide themselves 2 Kgs 7:12
and plundered the **c** of the Syrians. 2 Kgs 7:16
185,000 in the **c** of the Assyrians. 2 Kgs 19:35
been in charge of the **c** of the LORD, 1 Chr 9:19
broke through the **c** of the 1 Chr 11:18
the Arabians to the **c** had killed all 2 Chr 22:1

in the gates of the **c** of the LORD and to 2 Chr 31:2
and officers in the **c** of the king of 2 Chr 32:21
May their **c** be a desolation; let no one Ps 69:25
he let them fall in the midst of their **c**, Ps 78:28
When men in the **c** were jealous of Ps 106:16
thousand in the **c** of the Assyrians. Is 37:36
his army, for his **c** is exceedingly great; Jl 2:11
the stench of your **c** go up into your Am 4:10
Psalms, "'May his **c** become desolate, Acts 1:20
for sin are burned outside the **c**. Heb 13:11
to him outside the **c** and bear the Heb 13:13
earth and surrounded the **c** of the saints Rv 20:9

CAMPAIGN (1)
march out and in with me in the **c**. 1 Sm 29:6

CAMPED (56)
Paddan-aram, and he **c** before the city. Gn 33:18
of the LORD, and **c** at Rephidim, Ex 17:1
Moses, so they **c** by their standards, Nm 2:34
settled down, there the people of Israel **c**. Nm 9:17
and at the command of the LORD they **c**. Nm 9:18
At the command of the LORD they **c**, Nm 9:23
and **c** in the wilderness of Paran. Nm 12:16
people of Israel set out and **c** in Oboth. Nm 21:10
out from Oboth and **c** at Iye-abarim, Nm 21:11
they set out and **c** in the Valley of Nm 21:12
they set out and **c** on the other side Nm 21:13
of Israel set out and **c** in the plains of Nm 22:1
set out from Rameses and **c** at Succoth. Nm 33:5
set out from Succoth and **c** at Etham, Nm 33:6
Baal-zephon, and they **c** before Migdol. Nm 33:7
wilderness of Etham and **c** at Marah. Nm 33:8
seventy palm trees, and they **c** there. Nm 33:9
out from Elim and **c** by the Red Sea. Nm 33:10
the Red Sea and **c** in the wilderness of Nm 33:11
wilderness of Sin and **c** at Dophkah. Nm 33:12
set out from Dophkah and **c** at Alush. Nm 33:13
set out from Alush and **c** at Rephidim, Nm 33:14
from Rephidim and **c** in the Nm 33:15
of Sinai and **c** at Kibroth-hattaavah. Nm 33:16
Kibroth-hattaavah and **c** at Hazeroth. Nm 33:17
out from Hazeroth and **c** at Rithmah. Nm 33:18
Rithmah and **c** at Rimmon-perez. Nm 33:19
from Rimmon-perez and **c** at Libnah. Nm 33:20
set out from Libnah and **c** at Rissah. Nm 33:21
out from Rissah and **c** at Kehelathah. Nm 33:22
from Kehelathah and **c** at Mount Nm 33:23
Mount Shepher and **c** at Haradah. Nm 33:24
from Haradah and **c** at Makheloth. Nm 33:25
out from Makheloth and **c** at Tahath. Nm 33:26
set out from Tahath and **c** at Terah. Nm 33:27
set out from Terah and **c** at Mithkah. Nm 33:28
from Mithkah and **c** at Hashmonah. Nm 33:29
from Hashmonah and **c** at Moseroth. Nm 33:30
from Moseroth and **c** at Bene-jaakan. Nm 33:31
Bene-jaakan and **c** at Hor-haggidgad. Nm 33:32
Hor-haggidgad and **c** at Jotbathah. Nm 33:33
from Jotbathah and **c** at Abronah. Nm 33:34
from Abronah and **c** at Ezion-geber. Nm 33:35
from Ezion-geber and **c** in the Nm 33:36
out from Kadesh and **c** at Mount Hor, Nm 33:37
from Mount Hor and **c** at Zalmonah. Nm 33:41
out from Zalmonah and **c** at Punon. Nm 33:42
set out from Punon and **c** at Oboth. Nm 33:43
out from Oboth and **c** at Iye-abarim, Nm 33:44
set out from Iyim and **c** at Dibon-gad. Nm 33:45
Dibon-gad and **c** at Nm 33:46
from Almon-diblathaim and **c** in the Nm 33:47
of Abarim and **c** in the plains Nm 33:48
they **c** by the Jordan from Nm 33:49
land of Moab and **c** on the other side Jgs 11:18
to Ahava, and there we **c** three days. Ezr 8:15

CAMPING (2)
his eyes and saw Israel **c** tribe by tribe. Nm 24:2
of my lord are **c** in the open field. 2 Sm 11:11

CAMPS (11)
flocks and herds and camels, into two **c**, Gn 32:7
Jordan, and now I have become two **c**. Gn 32:10
of the Levites in the midst of the **c**; Nm 2:17
those listed in the **c** by their companies Nm 2:32
the **c** that are on the east side shall set Nm 10:5
the **c** that are on the south side shall set Nm 10:6
acting as the rear guard of all the **c**, Nm 10:25
they dwell in are **c** or strongholds, Nm 13:19
the gatekeepers of the **c** of the Levites. 1 Chr 9:18
Set **c** also against it, and plant battering Ezk 4:2
whatever beasts may be in those **c**. Zec 14:15

CANA (4)
day there was a wedding at **C** in Galilee, Jn 2:1
first of his signs, Jesus did at **C** in Galilee, Jn 2:11
So he came again to **C** in Galilee, where Jn 4:46
the Twin), Nathanael of **C** in Galilee, Jn 21:2

CANAAN (87)
and Japheth. (Ham was the father of **C**.) Gn 9:18
And Ham, the father of **C**, saw the Gn 9:22
he said, "Cursed be **C**; a servant of Gn 9:25
God of Shem; and let **C** be his servant. Gn 9:26
tents of Shem, and let **C** be his servant." Gn 9:27
sons of Ham: Cush, Egypt, Put, and **C**. Gn 10:6
C fathered Sidon his firstborn and Gn 10:15
the Chaldeans to go into the land of **C**, Gn 11:31
and they set out to go to the land of **C**. Gn 12:5
When they came to the land of **C**, Gn 12:5
Abram settled in the land of **C**, while Gn 13:12
had lived ten years in the land of **C**, Gn 16:3
of your sojournings, all the land of **C**, Gn 17:8
(that is, Hebron) in the land of **C**, Gn 23:2
(that is, Hebron) in the land of **C**. Gn 23:19
go to the land of **C** to his father Isaac. Gn 31:18
of Shechem, which is in the land of **C**, Gn 33:18
is, Bethel), which is in the land of **C**, Gn 35:6
who were born to him in the land of **C**. Gn 36:5
that he had acquired in the land of **C**. Gn 36:6
father's sojournings, in the land of **C**. Gn 37:1
for the famine was in the land of **C**. Gn 42:5
They said, "From the land of **C**, to buy Gn 42:7
the sons of one man in the land of **C**, Gn 42:13
to Jacob their father in the land of **C**, Gn 42:29
day with our father in the land of **C**.' Gn 42:32
brought back to you from the land of **C**. Gn 44:8
beasts and go back to the land of **C**, Gn 45:17
to the land of **C** to their father Jacob. Gn 45:25
which they had gained in the land of **C**, Gn 46:6
Er and Onan died in the land of **C**); Gn 46:12
household, who were in the land of **C**, Gn 46:31
possess, have come from the land of **C**. Gn 47:1
for the famine is severe in the land of **C**. Gn 47:4
the land of **C** languished by reason Gn 47:13
the land of Egypt and in the land of **C**, Gn 47:14
the land of Egypt and in the land of **C**, Gn 47:15
at Luz in the land of **C** and blessed me, Gn 48:3
Rachel died in the land of **C** on the way, Gn 48:7
to the east of Mamre, in the land of **C**, Gn 49:30
I hewed out for myself in the land of **C**, Gn 50:5
him to the land of **C** and buried him in Gn 50:13
with them to give them the land of **C**, Ex 6:4
the inhabitants of **C** have melted away. Ex 15:15
came to the border of the land of **C**. Ex 16:35
"When you come into the land of **C**, Lv 14:34
shall not do as they do in the land of **C**, Lv 18:3
land of Egypt to give you the land of **C**, Lv 25:38
"Send men to spy out the land of **C**, Nm 13:2
spy out the land of **C** and said to them, Nm 13:17
Er and Onan died in the land of **C**. Nm 26:19
among you in the land of **C**." Nm 32:30
before the LORD into the land of **C**, Nm 32:32
lived in the Negeb in the land of **C**, Nm 33:40
over the Jordan into the land of **C**, Nm 33:51
you enter the land of **C** (this is the land Nm 34:2
the land of **C** as defined by its borders), Nm 34:2
the people of Israel in the land of **C**." Nm 34:29
cross the Jordan into the land of **C**, Nm 35:10
and three cities in the land of **C**, Nm 35:14
opposite Jericho, and view the land of **C**, Dt 32:49
ate of the fruit of the land of **C** that year. Jos 5:12
people of Israel received in the land of **C**, Jos 14:1
said to them at Shiloh in the land of **C**, Jos 21:2
at Shiloh, which is in the land of **C**, Jos 22:9
of the Jordan that is in the land of **C**, Jos 22:10
the altar at the frontier of the land of **C**, Jos 22:11
in the land of Gilead to the land of **C**, Jos 22:32
and led him through all the land of **C**, Jos 24:3
had not experienced all the wars in **C**. Jgs 3:1
them into the hand of Jabin king of **C**, Jgs 4:2
Jabin the king of **C** before the people of Jgs 4:23
and harder against Jabin the king of **C**, Jgs 4:24
until they destroyed Jabin king of **C**. Jgs 4:24
then fought the kings of **C**, at Taanach, Jgs 5:19
at Shiloh, which is in the land of **C**. Jgs 21:12
sons of Ham: Cush, Egypt, Put, and **C**. 1 Chr 1:8
C fathered Sidon his firstborn and 1 Chr 1:13
"To you I will give the land of **C**, 1 Chr 16:18
give the land of **C** as your portion for Ps 105:11
whom they sacrificed to the idols of **C**, Ps 106:38
of Bashan, and all the kingdoms of **C**, Ps 135:11
the language of **C** and swear allegiance Is 19:18
command concerning **C** to destroy Is 23:11
The word of the LORD is against you, O **C**, Zep 2:5
a famine throughout all Egypt and **C**, Acts 7:11
seven nations in the land of **C**, Acts 13:19

CANAANITE (12)
must not take a wife from the **C** women. Gn 28:1
not take a wife from the **C** women," Gn 28:6
Esau saw that the **C** women did not Gn 28:8
of a certain **C** whose name was Gn 38:2
and Shaul, the son of a **C** woman. Gn 46:10
Zohar, and Shaul, the son of a **C** woman; Ex 6:15
When the **C**, the king of Arad, who Nm 21:1
And the **C**, the king of Arad, who lived Nm 33:40
boundary of Ekron, it is counted as **C**; Jos 13:3
three Bath-shua the **C** bore to him. 1 Chr 2:3
to give to his offspring the land of the **C**, Neh 9:8
a **C** woman from that region came out Mt 15:22

CANAANITES (63)
Afterward the clans of the **C** dispersed. Gn 10:18
territory of the **C** extended from Sidon Gn 10:19
At that time the **C** were in the land. Gn 12:6
At that time the **C** and the Perizzites Gn 13:7
the Amorites, the **C**, the Girgashites Gn 15:21
for my son from the daughters of the **C**, Gn 24:3
my son from the daughters of the **C**, Gn 24:37
of the land, the **C** and the Perizzites. Gn 34:30
Esau took his wives from the **C**: Adah Gn 36:2
the inhabitants of the land, the **C**, Gn 50:11
milk and honey, to the place of the **C**, Ex 3:8
affliction of Egypt to the land of the **C**, Ex 3:17
LORD brings you into the land of the **C**, Ex 13:5
LORD brings you into the land of the **C**, Ex 13:11
the Hittites and the Perizzites and the **C**, Ex 23:23
which shall drive out the Hivites, the **C**, Ex 23:28
before you, and I will drive out the **C**, Ex 33:2
out before you the Amorites, the **C**, Ex 34:11
And the **C** dwell by the sea, and along Nm 13:29
the Amalekites and the **C** dwell in the Nm 14:25
Amalekites and the **C** are facing you, Nm 14:43
the Amalekites and the **C** who lived in Nm 14:45
the voice of Israel and gave over the **C**, Nm 21:3
and by the seacoast, the land of the **C**, Dt 1:7
the Girgashites, the Amorites, the **C**, Dt 7:1
in the land of the **C** who live in the Dt 11:30
the Amorites, the **C** and the Perizzites, Dt 20:17
fail drive out from before you the **C**, Jos 3:10
all the kings of the **C** who were by the sea, Jos 5:1
For the **C** and all the inhabitants of the Jos 7:9
Lebanon, the Hittites, the Amorites, the **C**, Jos 9:1
to the **C** in the east and the west, the Jos 11:3
land of the Hittites, the Amorites, the **C**, Jos 12:8
in the south, all the land of the **C**, and Jos 13:4
not drive out the **C** who lived in Gezer, Jos 16:10
so the **C** have lived in the midst of Jos 16:10
but the **C** persisted in dwelling in that Jos 17:12
strong, they put the **C** to forced labor, Jos 17:13
Yet all the **C** who dwell in the plain Jos 17:16
For you shall drive out the **C**, though Jos 17:18
also the Amorites, the Perizzites, the **C**, Jos 24:11
shall go up first for us against the **C**, Jgs 1:1
to me, that we may fight against the **C**. Jgs 1:3
the LORD gave the **C** and the Perizzites into Jgs 1:4
him and defeated the **C** and the Perizzites. Jgs 1:5
to fight against the **C** who lived in the Jgs 1:9
Judah went against the **C** who lived in Jgs 1:10
they defeated the **C** who inhabited Jgs 1:17
for the **C** persisted in dwelling in that Jgs 1:27
strong, they put the **C** to forced labor, Jgs 1:28
not drive out the **C** who lived in Gezer, Jgs 1:29
so the **C** lived in Gezer among them. Jgs 1:29
of Nahalol, so the **C** lived among them, Jgs 1:30
so the Asherites lived among the **C**, the Jgs 1:32
Beth-anath, so they lived among the **C**, Jgs 1:33
and all the **C** and the Sidonians Jgs 3:3
So the people of Israel lived among the **C**, Jgs 3:5
to all the cities of the Hivites and **C**; 2 Sm 24:7
and had killed the **C** who lived in the 1 Kgs 9:16
with their abominations, from the **C**, Ezr 9:1
the inhabitants of the land, the **C**, Neh 9:24
and your birth are of the land of the **C**; Ezk 16:3
the land of the **C** as far as Zarephath, Ob 1:20

CANAL (11)
I was among the exiles by the Chebar **c**, Ezk 1:1
land of the Chaldeans by the Chebar **c**, Ezk 1:3
who were dwelling by the Chebar **c**, Ezk 3:15
glory that I had seen by the Chebar **c**, Ezk 3:23
creatures that I saw by the Chebar **c**. Ezk 10:15
the God of Israel by the Chebar **c**; Ezk 10:20
I had seen by the Chebar **c**. Ezk 10:22
vision that I had seen by the Chebar **c**. Ezk 43:3
saw in the vision, and I was at the Ulai **c**. Dn 8:2
a ram standing on the bank of the **c**. Dn 8:3
I had seen standing on the bank of the **c**, Dn 8:6

CANALS (3)
waters of Egypt, over their rivers, their **c**, Ex 7:19
the rivers, over the **c** and over the pools, Ex 8:5
and its **c** will become foul, and the Is 19:6

CANANAEAN (2)
Simon the **C**, and Judas Iscariot, who Mt 10:4
and Thaddaeus, and Simon the **C**, Mk 3:18

CANCELING (1)
by **c** the record of debt that stood Col 2:14

CANCELLED (2)
they could not pay, he **c** the debt of both. Lk 7:42
for whom he **c** the larger debt." And he Lk 7:43

CANDACE (1)
a eunuch, a court official of **C**, Acts 8:27

CANE (3)
that is, 250, and 250 of aromatic **c**, Ex 30:23
not bought me sweet **c** with money, Is 43:24
Sheba, or sweet **c** from a distant land? Jer 6:20

CANNEH (1)
Haran, **C**, Eden, traders of Sheba, Ezk 27:23

CANOPIES (1)
chambers of the temple, and the **c**. Ezk 41:26

CANOPY (6)
He made darkness around him his **c**, 2 Sm 22:12
with pillars, and a **c** in front of them. 1 Kgs 7:6
his covering, his **c** around him, Ps 18:11
for over all the glory there will be a **c**. Is 4:5
he will spread his royal **c** over them. Jer 43:10
And there was a **c** of wood in front of Ezk 41:25

CAPERNAUM (16)
he went and lived in **C** by the sea, Mt 4:13
When he entered **C**, a centurion came Mt 8:5
you, **C**, will you be exalted to heaven? Mt 11:23
When they came to **C**, the collectors of Mt 17:24
And they went into **C**, and immediately Mk 1:21
when he returned to **C** after some days, Mk 2:1
And they came to **C**. And when he was Mk 9:33
What we have heard you did at **C**, do Lk 4:23
And he went down to **C**, a city of Galilee. Lk 4:31
in the hearing of the people, he entered **C**. Lk 7:1
you, **C**, will you be exalted to heaven? Lk 10:15
After this he went down to **C**, with his Jn 2:12
And at **C** there was an official whose son Jn 4:46
a boat, and started across the sea to **C**. Jn 6:17
got into the boats and went to **C**, Jn 6:24
in the synagogue, as he taught at **C**. Jn 6:59

CAPHTOR (3)
Gaza, the Caphtorim, who came from **C**, Dt 2:23
the remnant of the coastland of **C**. Jer 47:4
the Philistines from **C** and the Syrians Am 9:7

CAPHTORIM (3)
whom the Philistines came), and **C**. Gn 10:14
lived in villages as far as Gaza, the **C**, Dt 2:23
whom the Philistines came), and **C**. 1 Chr 1:12

CAPITAL (19)
height of the one **c** was five cubits, 1 Kgs 7:16
height of the other **c** was five cubits. 1 Kgs 7:16
a lattice for the one **c** and a lattice for 1 Kgs 7:17
capital and a lattice for the other **c**. 1 Kgs 7:17
latticework to cover the **c** that was on 1 Kgs 7:18
and he did the same with the other **c**. 1 Kgs 7:18
all around, and so with the other **c**. 1 Kgs 7:20
cubits, and on it was a **c** of bronze. 2 Kgs 25:17
The height of the **c** was three cubits. 2 Kgs 25:17
all of bronze, were all around the **c**. 2 Kgs 25:17
with a **c** of five cubits on the top of 2 Chr 3:15
the **c** that is in the province of Media, Ezr 6:2
the twentieth year, as I was in Susa the **c**, Neh 1:1
sat on his royal throne in Susa, the **c**, Est 1:2
young virgins to the harem in Susa the **c**, Est 2:3
On it was a **c** of bronze. The height of Jer 52:22
The height of the one **c** was five cubits. Jer 52:22
all of bronze, were around the **c**. Jer 52:22
and when I saw, I was in Susa the **c**, Dn 8:2

CAPITALS (16)
He overlaid their **c**, and their fillets were Ex 36:38
The overlaying of their **c** was also of Ex 38:17
the overlaying of their **c** and their fillets Ex 38:19
and overlaid their **c** and made fillets Ex 38:28
He also made two **c** of cast bronze to 1 Kgs 7:16
of chain work for the **c** on the tops of 1 Kgs 7:17
Now the **c** that were on the tops of the 1 Kgs 7:19
The **c** were on the two pillars and also 1 Kgs 7:20
two bowls of the **c** that were on the 1 Kgs 7:41
two bowls of the **c** that were on the 1 Kgs 7:41
two bowls of the **c** that were on the 1 Kgs 7:42
and the two **c** on the top of the pillars; 2 Chr 4:12
two bowls of the **c** that were on the 2 Chr 4:12
two bowls of the **c** that were on the 2 Chr 4:13
"Strike the **c** until the thresholds shake, Am 9:1
and the hedgehog shall lodge in her **c**; Zep 2:14

CAPPADOCIA (2)
residents of Mesopotamia, Judea and **C**, Acts 2:9
dispersion in Pontus, Galatia, **C**, Asia, 1 Pt 1:1

CAPS (4)
you shall make coats and sashes and **c**. Ex 28:40
sons with sashes and bind **c** on them. Ex 29:9
of fine linen, and the **c** of fine linen, Ex 39:28
their waists and bound **c** on them, Lv 8:13

CAPTAIN (51)
officer of Pharaoh, the **c** of the guard. Gn 37:36
an officer of Pharaoh, the **c** of the guard, Gn 39:1
in the house of the **c** of the guard, Gn 40:3
The **c** of the guard appointed Joseph to Gn 40:4
in the house of the **c** of the guard, Gn 41:10
with us, a servant of the **c** of the guard. Gn 41:12
to him. And he became **c** over them. 1 Sm 22:2
and **c** over your bodyguard, 1 Sm 22:14
king sent to him a **c** of fifty men with 2 Kgs 1:9
But Elijah answered the **c** of fifty, "If I 2 Kgs 1:10
sent to him another **c** of fifty men 2 Kgs 1:11
the king sent the **c** of a third fifty 2 Kgs 1:13
And the third **c** of fifty went up and 2 Kgs 1:13
Then the **c** on whose hand the king 2 Kgs 7:2
had appointed the **c** on whose hand 2 Kgs 7:17
the **c** had answered the man of God, 2 Kgs 7:19
Pekah the son of Remaliah, his **c**, 2 Kgs 15:25
repulse a single **c** among the least 2 Kgs 18:24
the **c** of the bodyguard, 2 Kgs 25:8
who were with the **c** of the guard, 2 Kgs 25:10
Nebuzaradan the **c** of the guard 2 Kgs 25:11
But the **c** of the guard left some of 2 Kgs 25:12
was of gold the **c** of the guard took 2 Kgs 25:15
And the **c** of the guard took Seraiah 2 Kgs 25:18
And Nebuzaradan the **c** of the 2 Kgs 25:20
the **c** of fifty and the man of rank, the Is 3:3
you repulse a single **c** among the least of Is 36:9
Then Nebuzaradan, the **c** of the guard, Jer 39:9
Nebuzaradan, the **c** of the guard, left in Jer 39:10
Nebuzaradan, the **c** of the guard, Jer 39:11
So Nebuzaradan the **c** of the guard, Jer 39:13
after Nebuzaradan the **c** of the guard Jer 40:1
The **c** of the guard took Jeremiah and Jer 40:2
right to go." So the **c** of the guard gave Jer 40:5
Nebuzaradan, the **c** of the guard, Jer 41:10
whom Nebuzaradan the **c** of the guard Jer 43:6
—Nebuzaradan the **c** of the bodyguard, Jer 52:12
who were with the **c** of the guard, Jer 52:14
And Nebuzaradan the **c** of the guard Jer 52:15
But Nebuzaradan the **c** of the guard left Jer 52:16
was of gold the **c** of the guard took Jer 52:19
And the **c** of the guard took Seraiah the Jer 52:24
And Nebuzaradan the **c** of the guard Jer 52:26
Nebuzaradan the **c** of the guard carried Jer 52:30
to Arioch, the **c** of the king's guard, Dn 2:14
He declared to Arioch, the king's **c**, Dn 2:15
So the **c** came and said to him, "What do Jon 1:6
of soldiers and their **c** and the officers of Jn 18:12
the priests and the **c** of the temple and Acts 4:1
Now when the **c** of the temple and the Acts 5:24
Then the **c** with the officers went and Acts 5:26

CAPTAINS (24)
two men who were **c** of raiding bands; 2 Sm 4:2
his officials, his commanders, his **c**, 1 Kgs 9:22
commanded the thirty-two **c** of his 1 Kgs 22:31
And when the **c** of the chariots saw 1 Kgs 22:32
And when the **c** of the chariots saw 1 Kgs 22:33
the two former **c** of fifty men 2 Kgs 1:14
sent and brought the **c** of the Carites 2 Kgs 11:4
The **c** did according to all that 2 Kgs 11:9
priest gave to the **c** the spears and 2 Kgs 11:10
and the **c** and the trumpeters beside 2 Kgs 11:14
priest commanded the **c** who were 2 Kgs 11:15
And he took the **c**, the Carites, the 2 Kgs 11:19
Now when all the **c** and their men 2 Kgs 25:23
and the **c** of the forces arose and 2 Kgs 25:26
had commanded the **c** of his 2 Chr 18:30
As soon as the **c** of the chariots saw 2 Chr 18:31
as soon as the **c** of the chariots saw 2 Chr 18:32
priest gave to the **c** the spears and the 2 Chr 23:9
and the **c** and the trumpeters beside 2 Chr 23:13
brought out the **c** who were set 2 Chr 23:14
And he took the **c**, the nobles, the 2 Chr 23:20
battle from afar, the thunder of the **c**, Jb 39:25
When all the **c** of the forces in the open Jer 40:7
to eat the flesh of kings, the flesh of **c**, Rv 19:18

CAPTIVATED (2)
You have **c** my heart, my sister, my bride; Sg 4:9
you have **c** my heart with one glance of Sg 4:9

CAPTIVE (50)
that his kinsman had been taken **c**, Gn 14:14
to the firstborn of the **c** who was in the Ex 12:29
Israel, and took some of them **c**. Nm 21:1
when Asshur takes you away **c**." Nm 24:22
people of Israel took **c** the women of Nm 31:9
into your hand and you take them **c**, Dt 21:10
and taken **c** the women and all who 1 Sm 30:2
and sons and daughters taken **c**. 1 Sm 30:3
two wives also had been taken **c**, 1 Sm 30:5
they are carried away **c** to the land of 1 Kgs 8:46
to which they have been carried **c**, 1 Kgs 8:47
of their enemies, who carried them **c**, 1 Kgs 8:48
the sight of those who carried them **c**, 1 Kgs 8:50
you have taken **c** with your sword 2 Kgs 6:22
he carried the people **c** to Assyria. 2 Kgs 15:29
took it, carrying its people **c** to Kir, 2 Kgs 16:9
of Babylon brought **c** to Babylon all 2 Kgs 24:16
and the sons of Jeconiah, the **c**: 1 Chr 3:17
they are carried away **c** to a land far 2 Chr 6:36
to which they have been carried **c**, 2 Chr 6:37
to which they were carried **c**, 2 Chr 6:38
him and took **c** a great number 2 Chr 28:5
men of Israel took **c** 200,000 of their 2 Chr 28:8
of Babylon had carried **c** to Babylonia. Ezr 2:1
be pitied by all those who held them **c**. Ps 106:46
treacherous are taken **c** by their lust. Prv 11:6
like purple; a king is held **c** in the tresses. Sg 7:5
They will take **c** those who were their Is 14:2
from your neck, O **c** daughter of Zion. Is 52:2
the LORD'S flock has been taken **c**. Jer 13:17
He shall carry them **c** to Babylon, and Jer 20:4
place where they have carried him **c**, Jer 22:12
Then Ishmael took **c** all the rest of the Jer 41:10
of Nethaniah took them **c** and set out Jer 41:10
had carried away **c** from Mizpah Jer 41:14
burn them and carry them away **c**. Jer 43:12
for your sons have been taken **c**, Jer 48:46
All who took them **c** have held them Jer 50:33
the guard carried away **c** some of the Jer 52:15
Nebuchadnezzar carried away **c**: Jer 52:28
he carried away **c** from Jerusalem 832 Jer 52:29
the guard carried away **c** of the Judeans Jer 52:30
the nations where they are carried **c**, Ezk 6:9
sword and be led **c** among all nations, Lk 21:24
having died to that which held us **c**, Rom 7:6
mind and making me **c** to the law of Rom 7:23
take every thought **c** to obey Christ, 2 Cor 10:5
came, we were held **c** under the law, Gal 3:23
no one takes you **c** by philosophy and Col 2:8
If anyone is to be taken **c**, to captivity Rv 13:10

CAPTIVES (25)
my daughters like **c** of the sword? Gn 31:26
sons fugitives, and his daughters **c**, Nm 21:29
they brought the **c** and the plunder Nm 31:12
yourselves and your **c** on the third Nm 31:19
see among the **c** a beautiful woman, Dt 21:11
—with the blood of the slain and the **c**, Dt 32:42
Arise, Barak, lead away your **c**, O son of Jgs 5:12
the mighty men of valor, 10,000 **c**, 2 Kgs 24:14
send back the **c** from your relatives 2 Chr 28:11
"You shall not bring the **c** in here, 2 Chr 28:13
armed men left the **c** and the spoil 2 Chr 28:14
by name rose and took the **c**, 2 Chr 28:15
defeated Judah and carried away **c**. 2 Chr 28:17
be plundered in a land where they are **c**. Neh 4:4
Jerusalem among the **c** carried away Est 2:6
leading a host of **c** in your train and Ps 68:18
lead away the Egyptian **c** and the Cushite Is 20:4
mighty, or the **c** of a tyrant be rescued? Is 49:24
"Even the **c** of the mighty shall be taken, Is 49:25
to proclaim liberty to the **c**, Is 61:1
along with all the **c** of Jerusalem and Jer 40:1
have gone away, **c** before the foe. Lam 1:5
faces forward. They gather **c** like sand. Hab 1:9
liberty to the **c** and recovering of Lk 4:18
he ascended on high he led a host of **c**, Eph 4:8

CAPTIVITY (34)
not be yours, for they shall go into **c**. Dt 28:41
until the day of the **c** of the land. Jgs 18:30
he took into **c** from Jerusalem to 2 Kgs 24:15
plead with you in the land of their **c**, 2 Chr 6:37
the land of their **c** to which they were 2 Chr 6:38
and our wives are in **c** for this. 2 Chr 29:9
up out of the **c** of those exiles whom Ezr 2:1
who had come to Jerusalem from the **c**. Ezr 3:8
that time those who had come from **c**, Ezr 8:35
the kings of the lands, to the sword, to **c**, Ezr 9:7
up out of the **c** of those exiles whom Neh 7:6
returned from the **c** made booths and Neh 8:17
and delivered his power to **c**, his glory to Ps 78:61
save the burden, but themselves go into **c**. Is 46:2
until the **c** of Jerusalem in the fifth Jer 1:3
to famine, and those who are for **c**, Jer 15:2
and those who are for captivity, to **c**.' Jer 15:2
who dwell in your house, shall go into **c**. Jer 20:6
and your lovers shall go into **c**; Jer 22:22
your offspring from the land of their **c**. Jer 30:10
foes, every one of them, shall go into **c**; Jer 30:16
to **c** those who are doomed to captivity, Jer 43:11
to captivity those who are doomed to **c**, Jer 43:11
your offspring from the land of their **c**. Jer 46:27
captive, and your daughters into **c**. Jer 48:46
and my young men have gone into **c**. Lam 1:18
them. They shall go into exile, into **c**.' Ezk 12:11
sword, and the women shall go into **c**. Ezk 30:17
and her daughters shall go into **c**. Ezk 30:18
of Israel went into **c** for their iniquity, Ezk 39:23

by sword and flame, by **c** and plunder. Dn 11:33
if they go into **c** before their enemies, Am 9:4
Yet she became an exile; she went into **c**; Na 3:10
is to be taken captive, to **c** he goes; Rv 13:10

CAPTORS (4)
plead with you in the land of their **c**, 1 Kgs 8:47
compassion with their **c** and return 2 Chr 30:9
For there our **c** required of us songs, Ps 137:3
will take captive those who were their **c**, Is 14:2

CAPTURE (11)
the Midianites and **c** the waters against Jgs 7:24
in on David and his men to **c** them, 1 Sm 23:26
do not let her **c** you with her eyelashes; Prv 6:25
of the king of Babylon, and he shall **c** it; Jer 32:3
king of Babylon, and he shall **c** it. Jer 32:28
city. They shall **c** it and burn it with fire. Jer 37:8
the sound of the **c** of Babylon the earth Jer 50:46
coastlands and shall **c** many of them, Dn 11:18
robber, with swords and clubs to **c** me? Mt 26:55
with swords and clubs to **c** me? Mk 14:48
into households and **c** weak women, 2 Tm 3:6

CAPTURED (59)
in the houses, they **c** and plundered. Gn 34:29
and they **c** its villages and Nm 21:32
of Manasseh went to Gilead and **c** it, Nm 32:39
of Manasseh went and **c** their villages, Nm 32:41
Nobah went and **c** Kenath and its Nm 32:42
And we **c** all his cities at that time and Dt 2:34
with the plunder of the cities that we **c**. Dt 2:35
in which she was **c** and shall remain in Dt 21:13
straight before him, and they **c** the city. Jos 6:20
they ran and entered the city and **c** it. Jos 8:19
saw that the ambush had **c** the city, Jos 8:21
heard how Joshua had **c** Ai and had Jos 10:1
Joshua **c** it on that day and struck it, Jos 10:28
and he **c** it on the second day and Jos 10:32
And they **c** it on that day, and struck it Jos 10:35
and **c** it and struck it with the edge of Jos 10:37
and he **c** it with its king and all its Jos 10:39
And Joshua **c** all these kings and their Jos 10:42
at that time and **c** Hazor and struck its Jos 11:10
kings, and all their kings, Joshua **c**, Jos 11:12
And he **c** all their kings and struck Jos 11:17
son of Kenaz, the brother of Caleb, **c** it. Jos 15:17
against Jerusalem and **c** it and struck Jgs 1:8
of Kenaz, Caleb's younger brother, **c** it. Jgs 1:13
Judah also **c** Gaza with its territory, and Jgs 1:18
and they **c** the waters as far as Jgs 7:24
And they **c** the two princes of Midian, Jgs 7:25
he pursued them and **c** the two kings of Jgs 8:12
And he **c** a young man of Succoth and Jgs 8:14
He **c** the city and killed the people who Jgs 9:45
and encamped against Thebez and **c** it. Jgs 9:50
And the Gileadites **c** the fords of the Jgs 12:5
And the ark of God was **c**, and the two 1 Sm 4:11
dead, and the ark of God has been **c**." 1 Sm 4:17
the news that the ark of God was **c**, 1 Sm 4:19
of God had been **c** and because of her 1 Sm 4:21
Israel, for the ark of God has been **c**." 1 Sm 4:22
When the Philistines **c** the ark of God, 1 Sm 5:1
David also **c** all the flocks and herds, 1 Sm 30:20
had gone up and **c** Gezer and burned 1 Kgs 9:16
king of Israel **c** Amaziah king of 2 Kgs 14:13
king of Assyria came and **c** Ijon, 2 Kgs 15:29
the king of Assyria **c** Samaria, 2 Kgs 17:6
Then they **c** the king and brought 2 Kgs 25:6
of Ephraim that Asa his father had **c**. 2 Chr 17:2
and he was **c** while hiding in 2 Chr 22:9
men of Judah **c** another 10,000 alive 2 Chr 25:12
king of Israel **c** Amaziah king of 2 Chr 25:23
who **c** Manasseh with hooks and 2 Chr 33:11
And they **c** fortified cities and a rich Neh 9:25
to Ashdod and fought against it and **c** it— Is 20:1
fled together; without the bow they were **c**. Is 22:3
All of you who were found were **c**, though Is 22:3
but shall surely be **c** and delivered into Jer 34:3
Then they **c** the king and brought him Jer 52:9
the LORD'S anointed, was **c** in their pits, Lam 4:20
our own strength **c** Karnaim for Am 6:13
after being **c** by him to do his will. 2 Tm 2:26
And the beast was **c**, and with it the Rv 19:20

CAPTURES (3)
strikes Kiriath-sepher and **c** it, Jos 15:16
"He who attacks Kiriath-sepher and **c** it, Jgs 1:12
tree of life, and whoever **c** souls is wise. Prv 11:30

CAPTURING (1)
and after **c** it and striking it with the Jos 19:47

CARAVAN (1)
up they saw a **c** of Ishmaelites coming Gn 37:25

CARAVANS (3)
The **c** turn aside from their course; they Jb 6:18
The **c** of Tema look, the travelers of Jb 6:19
Arabia you will lodge, O **c** of Dedanites. Is 21:13

CARBUNCLE (3)
topaz, and **c** shall be the first row; Ex 28:17
sardius, topaz, and **c** was the first row; Ex 39:10
and jasper, sapphire, emerald, and **c**; Ezk 28:13

CARBUNCLES (1)
your pinnacles of agate, your gates of **c**, Is 54:12

CARCASS (18)
whether a **c** of an unclean wild animal or Lv 5:2
wild animal or a **c** of unclean livestock or Lv 5:2
livestock or a **c** of unclean swarming Lv 5:2
Whoever touches their **c** shall be Lv 11:24
any part of their **c** shall wash his Lv 11:25
Whoever touches their **c** shall be Lv 11:27
he who carries their **c** shall wash his Lv 11:28
any part of their **c** falls shall be Lv 11:35
but whoever touches a **c** in them shall Lv 11:36
if any part of their **c** falls upon any seed Lv 11:37
seed and any part of their **c** falls on it, Lv 11:38
whoever touches its **c** shall be unclean Lv 11:39
whoever eats of its **c** shall wash his Lv 11:40
whoever carries the **c** shall wash his Lv 11:40
he turned aside to see the **c** of the lion, Jgs 14:8
scraped the honey from the **c** of the lion. Jgs 14:9
You crushed Rahab like a **c**; you Ps 89:10
and fill the valleys with your **c**. Ezk 32:5

CARCASSES (5)
birds of prey came down on the **c**, Gn 15:11
flesh, and you shall not touch their **c**; Lv 11:8
their flesh, and you shall detest their **c**. Lv 11:11
not eat, and their **c** you shall not touch. Dt 14:8
my land with the **c** of their detestable Jer 16:18

CARCHEMISH (3)
up to fight at **C** on the Euphrates 2 Chr 35:20
Is not Calno like **C**? Is not Hamath like Is 10:9
river Euphrates at **C** and which Jer 46:2

CARE (64)
nursing flocks and herds are a **c** to me. Gn 33:13
take **c** never to see my face again, for on Ex 10:28
'Take **c** not to go up into the mountain Ex 19:12
Take **c**, lest you make a covenant with Ex 34:12
and they shall take **c** of it and shall Nm 1:50
"Must I not take **c** to speak what the Nm 23:12
"Only take **c**, and keep your soul Dt 4:9
Take **c**, lest you forget the covenant of Dt 4:23
then take **c** lest you forget the LORD, who Dt 6:12
"Take **c** lest you forget the LORD your Dt 8:11
Take **c** lest your heart be deceived, and Dt 11:16
Take **c** that you do not offer your burnt Dt 12:13
Take **c** that you do not neglect the Dt 12:19
take **c** that you be not ensnared to Dt 12:30
Take **c** lest there be an unworthy Dt 15:9
"Take **c**, in a case of leprous disease, to Dt 24:8
whether they will take **c** to walk in the Jgs 2:22
be to you; I will **c** for all your wants. Jgs 19:20
my father cease to **c** about the donkeys 1 Sm 9:5
has ceased to **c** about the donkeys 1 Sm 10:2
of the living in the **c** of the LORD your 1 Sm 25:29
For if we flee, they will not **c** about us. 2 Sm 18:3
half of us die, they will not **c** about us. 2 Sm 18:3
He had neither taken **c** of his feet nor 2 Sm 19:24
he had left to **c** for the house and 2 Sm 20:3
having the **c** of the courts and the 1 Chr 23:28
gifts were in the **c** of Shelomoth and 1 Chr 26:28
LORD, in the **c** of Jehiel the Gershonite. 1 Chr 29:8
and **c** for the golden lampstand that 2 Chr 13:11
of God, in the **c** of Obed-edom. 2 Chr 25:24
And take **c** not to be slack in this Ezr 4:22
love, and your **c** has preserved my spirit. Jb 10:12
For what do they **c** for their houses after Jb 21:21
Take **c**; do not turn to iniquity, for this Jb 36:21
and the son of man that you **c** for him? Ps 8:4
many proverbs with great **c**. Eccl 12:9
see, or send to Kedar and examine with **c**; Jer 2:10
Take **c** for the sake of your lives, and do Jer 17:21
the shepherds who **c** for my people: Jer 23:2
over them who will **c** for them, Jer 23:4
forgotten you; they **c** nothing for you; Jer 30:14
womb, the children of their tender **c**? Lam 2:20
who does not **c** for those being Zec 11:16
you do not **c** about anyone's opinion, Mt 22:16
do you not **c** that we are perishing?" Mk 4:38
and do not **c** about anyone's opinion. Mk 12:14
Take **c** then how you hear, for to the one Lk 8:18
him to an inn and took **c** of him. Lk 10:34
the innkeeper, saying, 'Take **c** of him, Lk 10:35
do you not **c** that my sister has left me Lk 10:40
And he said to them, "Take **c**, and be Lk 12:15
take **c** what you are about to do with Acts 5:35
overseers, to **c** for the church of God, Acts 20:28
Let each one take **c** how he builds 1 Cor 3:10
But take **c** that this right of yours does 1 Cor 8:9
have the same **c** for one another. 1 Cor 12:25
Titus the same earnest **c** I have for 2 Cor 8:16
nursing mother taking **c** of her own 1 Thes 2:7
how will he **c** for God's church? 1 Tm 3:5
who are widows, let her **c** for them. 1 Tm 5:16
so that it may **c** for those who are 1 Tm 5:16
or the son of man, that you **c** for him? Heb 2:6
Take **c**, brothers, lest there be in any of Heb 3:12
take **c** that you are not carried away 2 Pt 3:17

CARED (4)
he encircled him, he **c** for him, he kept Dt 32:10
this, not because he **c** about the poor, Jn 12:6
leave to go to his friends and be **c** for. Acts 27:3
of the saints, has **c** for the afflicted, 1 Tm 5:10

CAREFREE (1)
The sound of a **c** multitude was with Ezk 23:42

CAREFUL (53)
"Be **c** not to say anything to Jacob, Gn 31:24
'Be **c** not to say anything to Jacob, Gn 31:29
Pay **c** attention to him and obey his Ex 23:21
you shall be **c** to offer to me at its Nm 28:2
they will be afraid of you. So be very **c**. Dt 2:4
you shall learn them and be **c** to do them. Dt 5:1
You shall be **c** therefore to do as the LORD Dt 5:32
therefore, O Israel, and be **c** to do them, Dt 6:3
if we are **c** to do all this commandment Dt 6:25
You shall therefore be **c** to do the Dt 7:11
command you today you shall be **c** to do, Dt 8:1
For if you will be **c** to do all this Dt 11:22
you shall be **c** to do all the statutes and Dt 11:32
rules that you shall be **c** to do in the land Dt 12:1
Be **c** to obey all these words that I Dt 12:28
I command you, you shall be **c** to do. Dt 12:32
being **c** to do all this commandment Dt 15:5
and you shall be **c** to observe these Dt 16:12
And you shall be **c** to do according to Dt 17:10
provided you are **c** to keep all this Dt 19:9
You shall be **c** to do what has passed Dt 23:23
to be very **c** to do according to all that Dt 24:8
them, so you shall be **c** to do. Dt 24:8
You shall therefore be **c** to do them Dt 26:16
being **c** to do all his commandments Dt 28:1
you today, being **c** to do them, Dt 28:13
LORD your God or be **c** to do all his Dt 28:15
"If you are not **c** to do all the words of Dt 28:58
and be **c** to do all the words of this law, Dt 31:12
that they may be **c** to do all the words of Dt 32:46
being **c** to do according to all the law that Jos 1:7
so that you may be **c** to do according to Jos 1:8
but have been **c** to keep the charge of the Jos 22:3
Only be very **c**, therefore, to observe the Jos 22:5
Be very **c**, therefore, to love the LORD Jos 23:11
Therefore be **c** and drink no wine or Jgs 13:4
all that I said to the woman let her be **c**. Jgs 13:13
But Jehu was not **c** to walk in the 2 Kgs 10:31
for you, you shall always be **c** to do. 2 Kgs 17:37
only they will be **c** to do according to 2 Kgs 21:8
prosper if you are **c** to observe the 1 Chr 22:13
Be **c** now, for the LORD has chosen 1 Chr 28:10
Be **c** what you do, for there is no 2 Chr 19:7
if only they will be **c** to do all that I 2 Chr 33:8
And say to him, 'Be **c**, be quiet, do not fear, Is 7:4
and has been **c** to observe all my Ezk 18:19
statutes, and be **c** to obey my rules, Ezk 20:19
statutes and were not **c** to obey my Ezk 20:21
my statutes and be **c** to obey my rules. Ezk 36:27
my rules and be **c** to obey my statutes. Ezk 37:24
Therefore be **c** lest the light in you be Lk 11:35
Pay **c** attention to yourselves and to Acts 20:28
in God may be **c** to devote themselves to Ti 3:8

CAREFULLY (8)
man questioned us **c** about ourselves Gn 43:7
"But if you **c** obey his voice and do all Ex 23:22
"Therefore watch yourselves very **c**. Dt 4:15
more; though you look **c** at his place, Ps 37:10
a ruler, observe **c** what is before you, Prv 23:1
Pharisees, they were watching him **c**. Lk 14:1
Look **c** then how you walk, not as Eph 5:15
to be yours searched and inquired **c**, 1 Pt 1:10

CARELESS (2)
from evil, but a fool is reckless and **c**. Prv 14:16
account for every **c** word they speak, Mt 12:36

CARES (13)
a land that the LORD your God **c** for. The Dt 11:12
When the **c** of my heart are many, your Ps 94:19
remains to me; no one **c** for my soul. Ps 142:4
broken pot, a vessel no one **c** for? Jer 22:28
outcast: 'It is Zion, for whom no one **c**!' Jer 30:17
Moab like a vessel for which no one **c**, Jer 48:38
for the LORD of hosts **c** for his flock, the Zec 10:3
but the **c** of the world and the Mt 13:22
but the **c** of the world and the Mk 4:19

are choked by the **c** and riches and Lk 8:14
and drunkenness and **c** of this life, Lk 21:34
a hired hand and **c** nothing for the Jn 10:13
anxieties on him, because he **c** for you. 1 Pt 5:7

CARGO (6)
And they hurled the **c** that was in the Jon 1:5
for there the ship was to unload its **c**. Acts 21:3
loss, not only of the **c** and the ship, Acts 27:10
began the next day to jettison the **c**. Acts 27:18
her, since no one buys their **c** anymore, Rv 18:11
c of gold, silver, jewels, pearls, fine Rv 18:12

CARITES (2)
the captains of the **C** and of the 2 Kgs 11:4
And he took the captains, the **C**, the 2 Kgs 11:19

CARKAS (1)
Bigtha and Abagtha, Zethar and **C**, Est 1:10

CARMEL (28)
one; the king of Jokneam in **C**, one; Jos 12:22
Maon, **C**, Ziph, Juttah, Jos 15:55
west it touches **C** and Shihor-libnath, Jos 19:26
it was told Samuel, "Saul came to **C**, 1 Sm 15:12
in Maon whose business was in **C**. 1 Sm 25:2
goats. He was shearing his sheep in **C**. 1 Sm 25:2
said to the young men, "Go up to **C**, 1 Sm 25:5
nothing all the time they were in **C**. 1 Sm 25:7
of David came to Abigail at **C**, 1 Sm 25:40
Ahinoam of Jezreel, and Abigail of **C**, 1 Sm 27:3
and Abigail the widow of Nabal of **C**. 1 Sm 30:5
and Abigail the widow of Nabal of **C**. 2 Sm 2:2
of Abigail the widow of Nabal of **C**; 2 Sm 3:3
Hezro of **C**, Paarai the Arbite, 2 Sm 23:35
gather all Israel to me at Mount **C**, 1 Kgs 18:19
the prophets together at Mount **C**. 1 Kgs 18:20
went up to the top of Mount **C**. 1 Kgs 18:42
From there he went on to Mount **C**, 2 Kgs 2:25
came to the man of God at Mount **C**. 2 Kgs 4:25
Hezro of **C**, Naarai the son of Ezbai, 1 Chr 11:37
Your head crowns you like **C**, and your Sg 7:5
and Bashan and **C** shake off their leaves. Is 33:9
given to it, the majesty of **C** and Sharon. Is 35:2
the mountains and like **C** by the sea, Jer 46:18
and he shall feed on **C** and in Bashan, Jer 50:19
mourn, and the top of **C** withers." Am 1:2
If they hide themselves on the top of **C**, Am 9:3
up all the rivers; Bashan and **C** wither; Na 1:4

CARMELITE (1)
the second, Daniel, by Abigail the **C**, 1 Chr 3:1

CARMI (8)
Reuben: Hanoch, Pallu, Hezron, and **C**. Gn 46:9
of Israel: Hanoch, Pallu, Hezron, and **C**; Ex 6:14
Hezron, the clan of the Hezronites; of **C**, Nm 26:6
devoted things, for Achan the son of **C**, Jos 7:1
man by man, and Achan the son of **C**, Jos 7:18
The son of **C**: Achan, the troubler of 1 Chr 2:7
Perez, Hezron, **C**, Hur, and Shobal. 1 Chr 4:1
Israel: Hanoch, Pallu, Hezron, and **C**. 1 Chr 5:3

CARMITES (1)
Hezronites; of Carmi, the clan of the **C**. Nm 26:6

CARNELIAN (2)
there had the appearance of jasper and **c**, Rv 4:3
the fifth onyx, the sixth **c**, the seventh Rv 21:20

CARPENTER (2)
The **c** stretches a line; he marks it out Is 44:13
Is not this the **c**, the son of Mary and Mk 6:3

CARPENTER'S (1)
Is not this the **c** son? Is not his mother Mt 13:55

CARPENTERS (8)
also **c** and masons who built David a 2 Sm 5:11
it out to the **c** and the builders who 2 Kgs 12:11
(that is, to the **c**, and to the builders, 2 Kgs 22:6
also masons and **c** to build a house 1 Chr 14:1
c, and all kinds of craftsmen 1 Chr 22:15
hired masons and **c** to restore the 2 Chr 24:12
gave it to the **c** and the builders to 2 Chr 34:11
gave money to the masons and the **c**, Ezr 3:7

CARPETS (2)
you who sit on rich **c** and you who walk Jgs 5:10
work, and in **c** of colored material, Ezk 27:24

CARPUS (1)
the cloak that I left with **C** at Troas, 2 Tm 4:13

CARRIAGE (1)
Solomon made himself a **c** from the wood Sg 3:9

CARRIED (149)
The sons of Israel **c** Jacob their father, Gn 46:5
and in them let my name be **c** on, and Gn 48:16
for his sons **c** him to the land of Gn 50:13
gold, and the table shall be **c** with these. Ex 25:28
on the two sides of the altar when it is **c**. Ex 27:7
they came near and **c** them in their Lv 10:5
Holy Place, shall be **c** outside the camp. Lv 16:27
things that had to be **c** on the shoulder. Nm 7:9
sons of Merari, who **c** the tabernacle, Nm 10:17
and they **c** it on a pole between two of Nm 13:23
have seen how the LORD your God **c** you, Dt 1:31
who **c** the ark of the covenant of the Dt 31:9
the Levites who **c** the ark of Dt 31:25
LORD your God being **c** by the Levitical Jos 3:3
And they **c** them over with them to the Jos 4:8
the Levitical priests who **c** the ark of the Jos 8:33
sent away the people who **c** the tribute. Jgs 3:18
on his shoulders and **c** them to the top Jgs 16:3
from the dancers whom they **c** off. Jgs 21:23
to the young man who **c** his armor, 1 Sm 14:1
to the young man who **c** his armor, 1 Sm 14:6
but **c** them off and went their way. 1 Sm 30:2
and David and his men **c** them away. 2 Sm 5:21
And they **c** the ark of God on a new 2 Sm 6:3
of gold that were **c** by the servants of 2 Sm 8:7
So Zadok and Abiathar **c** the ark of 2 Sm 15:29
he **c** Amasa out of the highway into 2 Sm 20:12
by the gate and **c** and brought it to 2 Sm 23:16
because you **c** the ark of the Lord 1 Kgs 2:26
of the people who **c** on the work. 1 Kgs 5:16
so that they are **c** away captive to the 1 Kgs 8:46
to which they have been **c** captive, 1 Kgs 8:47
of their enemies, who **c** them captive, 1 Kgs 8:48
the sight of those who **c** them captive, 1 Kgs 8:50
of the people who **c** on the work. 1 Kgs 9:23
the guard **c** them and brought them 1 Kgs 14:28
and they **c** away the stones of 1 Kgs 15:22
from her arms and **c** him up into 1 Kgs 17:19
one of their raids had **c** off a little girl 2 Kgs 5:2
And they **c** them before Gehazi. 2 Kgs 5:23
and they **c** off silver and gold and 2 Kgs 7:8
another tent and **c** off things from 2 Kgs 7:8
His servants **c** him in a chariot to 2 Kgs 9:28
and he **c** the people captive to 2 Kgs 15:29
and he **c** the Israelites away to 2 Kgs 17:6
whom the LORD **c** away before them. 2 Kgs 17:11
that you have **c** away and placed 2 Kgs 17:26
priests whom you **c** away from 2 Kgs 17:27
whom they had **c** away from 2 Kgs 17:28
whom they had been **c** away. 2 Kgs 17:33
king of Assyria **c** the Israelites away 2 Kgs 18:11
till this day, shall be **c** to Babylon. 2 Kgs 20:17
of the Kidron and **c** their ashes to 2 Kgs 23:4
And his servants **c** him dead in a 2 Kgs 23:30
and **c** off all the treasures of the 2 Kgs 24:13
He **c** away all Jerusalem and all the 2 Kgs 24:14
And he **c** away Jehoiachin to 2 Kgs 24:15
the captain of the guard **c** into exile. 2 Kgs 25:11
broke in pieces and **c** the bronze to 2 Kgs 25:13
king of Assyria **c** away into exile; 1 Chr 5:6
valiant men who **c** shield and sword, 1 Chr 5:18
They **c** off their livestock: 50,000 of 1 Chr 5:21
and they were **c** into exile to 1 Chr 8:6
And they **c** the ark of God on a new 1 Chr 13:7
And the Levites **c** the ark of God on 1 Chr 15:15
of gold that were **c** by the servants of 1 Chr 18:7
gold that he had **c** off from all the 1 Chr 18:11
so that they are **c** away captive to a 2 Chr 6:36
to which they have been **c** captive, 2 Chr 6:37
to which they were **c** captive, 2 Chr 6:38
guard came and **c** them and 2 Chr 12:11
from Benjamin that **c** shields and 2 Chr 14:8
men of Judah **c** away very much 2 Chr 14:13
had livestock and **c** away sheep in 2 Chr 14:15
and they **c** away the stones of Ramah 2 Chr 16:6
and invaded it and **c** away all the 2 Chr 21:17
defeated Judah and **c** away captives. 2 Chr 28:17
the Levites took it and **c** it out to the 2 Chr 29:16
Fish Gate, and **c** it around Ophel, 2 Chr 33:14
and **c** them quickly to all the lay 2 Chr 35:13
of the chariot and **c** him in his 2 Chr 35:24
his brother and **c** him to Egypt. 2 Chr 36:4
Nebuchadnezzar also **c** part of the 2 Chr 36:7
that Nebuchadnezzar had **c** away from Ezr 1:7
of Babylon had **c** captive to Babylonia. Ezr 2:1
this house and **c** away the people Ezr 5:12
Those who **c** burdens were loaded in Neh 4:17
the king of Babylon had **c** into exile. Neh 7:6
who had been **c** away from Jerusalem Est 2:6
among the captives **c** away with Jeconiah Est 2:6
king of Babylon had **c** away. Est 2:6
and edict were about to be **c** out, Est 9:1
not been, **c** from the womb to the grave. Jb 10:19
possessions of his house will be **c** away, Jb 20:28
When he is **c** to the grave, watch is kept Jb 21:32
of Samaria will be **c** away before the king Is 8:4
of old, whose feet **c** her to settle far away? Is 23:7
up till this day, shall be **c** to Babylon. Is 39:6
from before your birth, **c** from the womb; Is 46:3
daughters shall be **c** on their shoulders. Is 49:22
has borne our griefs and **c** our sorrows, Is 53:4
and your daughters shall be **c** on the hip. Is 60:4
he lifted them up and **c** them all the days Is 63:9
shall nurse, you shall be **c** upon her hip, Is 66:12
they have to be **c**, for they cannot walk. Jer 10:5
place where they have **c** him captive, Jer 22:12
They shall be **c** to Babylon and remain Jer 27:22
away from this place and **c** to Babylon. Jer 28:3
c into exile to Babylon the rest of the Jer 39:9
whom Ishmael had **c** away captive Jer 41:14
of the guard **c** away captive some Jer 52:15
pieces, and **c** all the bronze to Babylon. Jer 52:17
whom Nebuchadnezzar **c** away Jer 52:28
of Nebuchadnezzar he **c** away captive Jer 52:29
captain of the guard **c** away captive of Jer 52:30
he has **c** out his word, which he Lam 2:17
the nations where they are **c** captive, Ezk 6:9
of its young twigs and **c** it to a land of Ezk 17:4
But she **c** her whoring further. She Ezk 23:14
When she **c** on her whoring so openly Ezk 23:18
fall in Egypt, and her wealth is **c** away, Ezk 30:4
and the wind **c** them away, so that not a Dn 2:35
thing itself shall be **c** to Assyria as Hos 10:6
with Assyria, and oil is **c** to Egypt. Hos 12:1
and have **c** my rich treasures into your Jl 3:5
because they **c** into exile a whole people Am 1:6
the sword, and **c** away your horses, Am 4:10
the day that strangers **c** off his wealth Ob 1:11
she is **c** off, her slave girls lamenting, Na 2:7
to him a paralytic **c** by four men. Mk 2:3
a man who had died was being **c** out, Lk 7:12
man died and was **c** by the angels to Lk 16:22
from them and was **c** up into heaven. Lk 24:51
that his deeds have been **c** out in God." Jn 3:21
to him, "Sir, if you have **c** him away, Jn 20:15
a man lame from birth was being **c**, Acts 3:2
wrapped him up and **c** him out and Acts 5:6
and they **c** her out and buried her Acts 5:10
so that they even **c** out the sick into the Acts 5:15
and they were **c** back to Shechem and Acts 7:16
the Spirit of the Lord **c** Philip away, Acts 8:39
And when they had **c** out all that was Acts 13:29
touched his skin were **c** away to the Acts 19:12
he was actually **c** by the soldiers Acts 21:35
by the waves and **c** about by every Eph 4:14
God as they were **c** along by the Holy 2 Pt 1:21
that you are not **c** away with the error 2 Pt 3:17
And he **c** me away in the Spirit into a Rv 17:3
And he **c** me away in the Spirit to a Rv 21:10

CARRIES (13)
and whoever **c** any part of their carcass Lv 11:25
and he who **c** their carcass shall wash Lv 11:28
And whoever **c** the carcass shall wash Lv 11:40
And whoever **c** such things shall wash Lv 15:10
bosom, as a nurse **c** a nursing child,' Nm 11:12
God carried you, as a man **c** his son, Dt 1:31
and like chaff that the storm **c** away? Jb 21:18
in the night a whirlwind **c** him off. Jb 27:20
over the man who **c** out evil devices! Ps 37:7
and the tempest **c** them off like stubble. Is 40:24
'If someone **c** holy meat in the fold of his Hg 2:12
an avenger who **c** out God's wrath on Rom 13:4
seven heads and ten horns that **c** her. Rv 17:7

CARRION (2)
barn owl, the tawny owl, the **c** vulture, Lv 11:18
owl, the **c** vulture and the cormorant, Dt 14:17

CARRY (108)
on their way to **c** it down to Egypt. Gn 37:25
the rest go and **c** grain for the famine Gn 42:19
bags, and **c** a present down to the man, Gn 43:11
C back with you the money that was Gn 43:12
sacks with food, as much as they can **c**, Gn 44:1
wagons that Joseph had sent to **c** him, Gn 45:27
wagons that Pharaoh had sent to **c** him. Gn 46:5
C me out of Egypt and bury me in Gn 47:30
and you shall **c** up my bones from Gn 50:25
and you shall **c** up my bones with you Ex 13:19
sides of the ark to **c** the ark by them. Ex 25:14
as holders for the poles to **c** the table. Ex 25:27
be holders for poles with which to **c** it. Ex 30:4
rings on the sides of the ark to **c** the ark. Ex 37:5
as holders for the poles to **c** the table. Ex 37:14
the poles of acacia wood to **c** the table, Ex 37:15
holders for the poles with which to **c** it. Ex 37:27
on the sides of the altar to **c** it with them. Ex 38:7
the bull—he shall **c** outside the camp to Lv 4:12
And he shall **c** the bull outside the camp Lv 4:21
other garments and **c** the ashes outside Lv 6:11
c your brothers away from the front of Lv 10:4
and he shall **c** them out of the city to an Lv 14:45
They are to **c** the tabernacle and all its Nm 1:50
sons of Kohath shall come to **c** these, Nm 4:15
that the sons of Kohath are to **c**. Nm 4:15
they shall **c** the curtains of the Nm 4:25
all that they are to **c** and in all that they Nm 4:27

to their charge all that they are to **c**. Nm 4:27
And this is what they are charged to **c**, Nm 4:31
the objects that they are required to **c**. Nm 4:32
and the priest shall **c** out for her all this Nm 5:30
say to me, '**C** them in your bosom, Nm 11:12
I am not able to **c** all this people alone; Nm 11:14
incense on it and **c** it quickly to the Nm 16:46
the tribe of Levi to **c** the ark of the Dt 10:8
so that you are not able to **c** the tithe, Dt 14:24
You shall **c** much seed into the field Dt 28:38
and **c** them quickly to the camp to 1 Sm 17:17
to him, "Go and **c** them to the city." 1 Sm 20:40
LORD and did not **c** out his fierce 1 Sm 28:18
to **c** the good news to the house of 1 Sm 31:9
for me, where could I **c** my shame? 2 Sm 13:13
"**C** the ark of God back into the city. 2 Sm 15:25
"Let me run and **c** news to the king 2 Sm 18:19
to him, "You are not to **c** news today. 2 Sm 18:20
You may **c** news another day, but 2 Sm 18:20
day, but today you shall **c** no news, 2 Sm 18:20
of the LORD will **c** you I know not 1 Kgs 18:12
"Turn around and **c** me out of the 1 Kgs 22:34
to his servant, "**C** him to his mother." 2 Kgs 4:19
of the Philistines to **c** the good news 1 Chr 10:9
but the Levites may **c** the ark of God, 1 Chr 15:2
had chosen them to **c** the ark of the 1 Chr 15:2
Because you did not **c** it the first 1 Chr 15:13
longer need to **c** the tabernacle or 1 Chr 23:26
"Turn around and **c** me out of the 2 Chr 18:33
until they could **c** no more. 2 Chr 20:25
and **c** out the filth from the Holy 2 Chr 29:5
You need not **c** it on your shoulders. 2 Chr 35:3
and also to **c** the silver and gold that the Ezr 7:15
Why does your heart **c** you away, and Jb 15:12
clothing; hungry, they **c** the sheaves; Jb 24:10
Surely I would **c** it on my shoulder; I Jb 31:36
Be their shepherd and **c** them forever. Ps 28:9
when he dies he will **c** nothing away; Ps 49:17
Can a man **c** fire next to his chest and Prv 6:27
toil that he may **c** away in his hand. Eccl 5:15
for a bird of the air will **c** your voice, Eccl 10:20
prey; they **c** it off, and none can rescue. Is 5:29
have laid up they **c** away over the Brook Is 15:7
declares the LORD, "who **c** out a plan, Is 30:1
they **c** their riches on the backs of Is 30:6
he will **c** them in his bosom, and gently Is 40:11
them, and the wind shall **c** them away, Is 41:16
no knowledge who **c** about their wooden Is 45:20
these things you **c** are borne as burdens Is 46:1
age I am he, and to gray hairs I will **c** you. Is 46:4
and I will bear; I will **c** and will save. Is 46:4
They lift it to their shoulders, they **c** it, Is 46:7
The wind will **c** them off, a breath will Is 57:13
And do not **c** a burden out of your Jer 17:22
He shall **c** them captive to Babylon, and Jer 20:4
and seize them and **c** them to Babylon. Jer 20:5
burn them and **c** them away captive. Jer 43:12
upon your shoulder and **c** it out at Ezk 12:6
and he shall **c** off its wealth and Ezk 29:19
to seize spoil and **c** off plunder, to turn Ezk 38:12
assembled your hosts to **c** off plunder, Ezk 38:13
off plunder, to **c** away silver and gold, Ezk 38:13
and all its statutes and **c** them out. Ezk 43:11
He shall also **c** off to Egypt their gods Dn 11:8
and again shall **c** the war as far as his Dn 11:10
I will **c** off, and no one shall rescue. Hos 5:14
I, whose sandals I am not worthy to **c**. Mt 3:11
compelled this man to **c** his cross. Mt 27:32
allow anyone to **c** anything through Mk 11:16
of Alexander and Rufus, to **c** his cross. Mk 15:21
C no moneybag, no knapsack, no Lk 10:4
on him the cross, to **c** it behind Jesus. Lk 23:26
will dress you and **c** you where you do Jn 21:18
are at the door, and they will **c** you out." Acts 5:9
of mine to **c** my name before Acts 9:15
is right, but not the ability to **c** it out. Rom 7:18
for the Lord will **c** out his sentence Rom 9:28
accredit by letter to **c** your gift to 1 Cor 16:3
travel with us as we **c** out this act of 2 Cor 8:19
into their hearts to **c** out his purpose by Rv 17:17

CARRYING (18)
of goatskin and put it on the **c** frame. Nm 4:10
goatskin and put them on the **c** frame. Nm 4:12
each one with his task of serving or **c**. Nm 4:49
Kohathites set out, **c** the holy things, Nm 10:21
you there, one **c** three young goats, 1 Sm 10:3
goats, another **c** three loaves of bread, 1 Sm 10:3
of bread, and another **c** a skin of wine. 1 Sm 10:3
have done well in **c** out what is right 2 Kgs 10:30
and took it, **c** its people captive to Kir, 2 Kgs 16:9
the Levites who were **c** the ark of the 1 Chr 15:26
all the Levites who were **c** the ark, 1 Chr 15:27
and **c** all the feeble among them on 2 Chr 28:15
dusk, **c** it on my shoulder in their sight. Ezk 12:7
and a man **c** a jar of water will meet Mk 14:13
a man **c** a jar of water will meet you. Lk 22:10
kept them from **c** out their plan. Acts 27:43
always **c** in the body the death of 2 Cor 4:10
c out the desires of the body and the Eph 2:3

CARSHENA (1)
the men next to him being **C**, Shethar, Est 1:14

CART (15)
and prepare a new **c** and two milk cows 1 Sm 6:7
a yoke, and yoke the cows to the **c**, 1 Sm 6:7
and place it on the **c** and put in a box 1 Sm 6:8
yoked them to the **c** and shut up their 1 Sm 6:10
of the LORD on the **c** and the box with 1 Sm 6:11
The **c** came into the field of Joshua of 1 Sm 6:14
the wood of the **c** and offered the cows 1 Sm 6:14
of God on a new **c** and brought it out of 2 Sm 6:3
of Abinadab, were driving the new **c**, 2 Sm 6:3
carried the ark of God on a new **c**, 1 Chr 13:7
Uzzah and Ahio were driving the **c**. 1 Chr 13:7
falsehood, who draw sin as with **c** ropes, Is 5:18
nor is a **c** wheel rolled over cumin, Is 28:27
when he drives his **c** wheel over it with Is 28:28
as a **c** full of sheaves presses down. Am 2:13

CARVE (1)
on the height and **c** a dwelling for Is 22:16

CARVED (45)
shall not make for yourself a **c** image, Ex 20:4
by making a **c** image for yourselves, Dt 4:16
he made with you, and make a **c** image, Dt 4:23
corruptly by making a **c** image in the Dt 4:25
shall not make for yourself a **c** image, Dt 5:8
and burn their **c** images with fire. Dt 7:5
The **c** images of their gods you shall Dt 7:25
shall chop down the **c** images of their Dt 12:3
man who makes a **c** or cast metal Dt 27:15
to make a **c** image and a metal image. Jgs 17:3
who made it into a **c** image and a metal Jgs 17:4
an ephod, household gods, a **c** image, Jgs 18:14
up and entered and took the **c** image, Jgs 18:17
Micah's house and took the **c** image, Jgs 18:18
gods and the **c** image and went Jgs 18:20
Dan set up the **c** image for themselves, Jgs 18:30
they set up Micah's **c** image that he Jgs 18:31
within the house was **c** in the form of 1 Kgs 6:18
of the house he **c** engraved figures of 1 Kgs 6:29
On them he **c** cherubim and palm 1 Kgs 6:35
gold evenly applied on the **c** work. 1 Kgs 6:35
and on its panels, he **c** cherubim, 1 Kgs 7:36
LORD and also served their **c** images. 2 Kgs 17:41
And the **c** image of Asherah that he 2 Kgs 21:7
doors—and he **c** cherubim on the 2 Chr 3:7
And the **c** image of the idol that he 2 Chr 33:7
and the **c** and the metal images. 2 Chr 34:3
the Asherim and the **c** and the metal 2 Chr 34:4
And all its **c** wood they broke down with Ps 74:6
whose **c** images were greater than those Is 10:10
and all the **c** images of her gods he has Is 21:9
you will defile your **c** idols overlaid with Is 30:22
I give to no other, nor my praise to **c** idols. Is 42:8
put to shame, who trust in **c** idols, Is 42:17
my **c** image and my metal image Is 48:5
to anger with their **c** images and with Jer 8:19
It was **c** of cherubim and palm trees, a Ezk 41:18
They were **c** on the whole temple all Ezk 41:19
door, cherubim and palm trees were **c**; Ezk 41:20
the nave were **c** cherubim and palm Ezk 41:25
trees, such as were **c** on the walls. Ezk 41:25
All her **c** images shall be beaten to pieces, Mi 1:7
will cut off your **c** images and your Mi 5:13
I will cut off the **c** image and the metal Na 1:14
ministry of death, **c** in letters on stone, 2 Cor 3:7

CARVING (2)
cutting stones for setting, and in **c** wood, Ex 31:5
stones for setting, and in **c** wood, Ex 35:33

CARVINGS (2)
of olivewood with **c** of cherubim, 1 Kgs 6:32
At its opening there were **c**, and its 1 Kgs 7:31

CASE (58)
Any hard **c** they brought to Moses, but Ex 18:26
the **c** of both parties shall come before Ex 22:9
and it turns into a **c** of leprous disease on Lv 13:2
of his body, it is a **c** of leprous disease. Lv 13:3
It is a **c** of leprous disease that has Lv 13:20
him unclean; it is a **c** of leprous disease. Lv 13:25
him unclean; it is a **c** of leprous disease. Lv 13:27
"When there is a **c** of leprous disease in Lv 13:47
made of skin, it is a **c** of leprous disease, Lv 13:49
is the law for a **c** of leprous disease in a Lv 13:59
if the **c** of leprous disease is healed in the Lv 14:3
him in whom is a **c** of leprous disease, Lv 14:32
and I put a **c** of leprous disease in a Lv 14:34
to me to be some **c** of disease in my Lv 14:35
is the law for any **c** of leprous disease: Lv 14:54
Moses brought their **c** before the LORD. Nm 27:5
And the **c** that is too hard for you, you Dt 1:17
"If any **c** arises requiring decision Dt 17:8
any **c** within your towns that is too Dt 17:8
For this **c** is like that of a man Dt 22:26
"Take care, in a **c** of leprous disease, to Dt 24:8
the city and explain his **c** to the elders of Jos 20:4
whenever a **c** comes to you from 2 Chr 19:10
and I desire to argue my **c** with God. Jb 13:3
him? Will you plead the **c** for God? Jb 13:8
Behold, I have prepared my **c**; I know Jb 13:18
that he would argue the **c** of a man with Jb 16:21
I would lay my **c** before him and fill my Jb 23:4
do not see him, that the **c** is before him, Jb 35:14
draw up our **c** because of darkness. Jb 37:19
one who states his **c** first seems right, Prv 18:17
Argue your **c** with your neighbor Prv 25:9
Set forth your **c**, says the LORD; bring Is 41:21
set forth your **c**, that you may be proved Is 43:26
Declare and present your **c**; let them Is 45:21
you; yet I would plead my **c** before you. Jer 12:1
in linen, with a writing **c** at his waist. Ezk 9:2
linen, who had the writing **c** at his waist. Ezk 9:3
in linen, with the writing **c** at his waist, Ezk 9:11
Arise, plead your **c** before the mountains, Mi 6:1
in their **c** the prophecy of Isaiah is Mt 13:14
fruit and yields, in one **c** a hundredfold, Mt 13:23
"If such is the **c** of a man with his wife, Mt 19:10
So in the present **c** I tell you, keep away Acts 5:38
to determine his **c** more exactly. Acts 23:15
the governor their **c** against Paul. Acts 24:1
comes down, I will decide your **c**." Acts 24:22
the Jews laid out their **c** against Paul, Acts 25:2
Festus laid Paul's **c** before the king, Acts 25:14
the Jews laid out their **c** against him, Acts 25:15
no charge in his **c** of such evils as Acts 25:18
reason for the death penalty in my **c**. Acts 28:18
Indeed, in this **c**, what once had glory 2 Cor 3:10
In their **c** the god of this world has 2 Cor 4:4
In that **c** the offense of the cross has Gal 5:11
we speak in this way, yet in your **c**, Heb 6:9
In the one **c** tithes are received by mortal Heb 7:8
by mortal men, but in the other **c**, Heb 7:8

CASES (8)
before God and bring their **c** to God, Ex 18:19
"This is the law in **c** of jealousy, when Nm 5:29
time, 'Hear the **c** between your brothers, Dt 1:16
for the LORD and to decide disputed **c**. 2 Chr 19:8
are you incompetent to try trivial **c**? 1 Cor 6:2
So if you have such **c**, why do you lay 1 Cor 6:4
In such **c** the brother or sister is not 1 Cor 7:15
works, so as to help **c** of urgent need, Ti 3:14

CASIPHIA (2)
to Iddo, the leading man at the place **C**, Ezr 8:17
and the temple servants at the place **C**, Ezr 8:17

CASKS (1)
and **c** of wine from Uzal they Ezk 27:19

CASLUHIM (2)
C (from whom the Philistines came), Gn 10:14
C (from whom the Philistines 1 Chr 1:12

CASSIA (3)
and 500 of **c**, according to the shekel of Ex 30:24
all fragrant with myrrh and aloes and **c**. Ps 45:8
c, and calamus were bartered for your Ezk 27:19

CAST (246)
"**C** out this slave woman with her son, Gn 21:10
c him into this pit here in the Gn 37:22
they took him and **c** him into a pit. Gn 37:24
time his master's wife **c** her eyes on Gn 39:7
to the Hebrews you shall **c** into the Nile, Ex 1:22
'Take your staff and **c** it down before Ex 7:9
Aaron **c** down his staff before Pharaoh Ex 7:10
For each man **c** down his staff, and they Ex 7:12
chariots and his host he **c** into the sea, Ex 15:4
You shall **c** four rings of gold for it and Ex 25:12
and you shall **c** five bases of bronze for Ex 26:37
make for yourself any gods of **c** metal. Ex 34:17
For I will **c** out nations before you and Ex 34:24
and he **c** for them four bases of silver. Ex 36:36
And he **c** for it four rings of gold for its Ex 37:3
He **c** for it four rings of gold and Ex 37:13
He **c** four rings on the four corners of the Ex 38:5
with its contents and **c** it beside the altar Lv 1:16
And Aaron shall **c** lots over the two Lv 16:8
make for yourselves any gods of **c** metal: Lv 19:4
incense altars and **c** your dead bodies Lv 26:30
who makes a carved or **c** metal image, Dt 27:15
wrath, and **c** them into another land, Dt 29:28
And I will **c** lots for you here before the Jos 18:6
And I will **c** lots for you here before the Jos 18:8
and Joshua **c** lots for them in Shiloh Jos 18:10
"**C** the lot between me and my son 1 Sm 14:42

not a woman **c** an upper millstone 2 Sm 11:21
They **c** up a mound against the city, 2 Sm 20:15
He **c** two pillars of bronze. Eighteen 1 Kgs 7:15
made two capitals of **c** bronze to set 1 Kgs 7:16
Then he made the sea of **c** metal. It 1 Kgs 7:23
two rows, **c** with it when it was cast. 1 Kgs 7:24
two rows, cast with it when it was **c**. 1 Kgs 7:24
The supports were **c** with wreaths at 1 Kgs 7:30
spokes, and their hubs were all **c**. 1 Kgs 7:33
All of them were **c** alike, of the same 1 Kgs 7:37
plain of the Jordan the king **c** them, 1 Kgs 7:46
for my name I will **c** out of my sight, 1 Kgs 9:7
and have **c** me behind your back, 1 Kgs 14:9
passed by him and **c** his cloak upon 1 Kgs 19:19
whom the LORD **c** out before the 1 Kgs 21:26
caught him up and **c** him upon some 2 Kgs 2:16
and the officers **c** them out and 2 Kgs 10:25
nor has he **c** them from his presence 2 Kgs 13:23
until he had **c** them out of his sight. 2 Kgs 17:20
and have **c** their gods into the fire, 2 Kgs 19:18
with a shield or **c** up a siege mound 2 Kgs 19:32
beat it to dust and **c** the dust of it 2 Kgs 23:6
broke in pieces and **c** the dust of 2 Kgs 23:12
and I will **c** off this city that I have 2 Kgs 23:27
and Judah that he **c** them out from 2 Kgs 24:20
his younger brother alike, **c** lots, 1 Chr 24:31
And they **c** lots for their duties, small 1 Chr 25:8
And they **c** lots by fathers' houses, 1 Chr 26:13
They **c** lots also for his son 1 Chr 26:14
forsake him, he will **c** you off forever. 1 Chr 28:9
Then he made the sea of **c** metal. It 2 Chr 4:2
in two rows, **c** with it when it was cast. 2 Chr 4:3
in two rows, cast with it when it was **c**. 2 Chr 4:3
plain of the Jordan the king **c** them, 2 Chr 4:17
for my name, I will **c** out of my sight, 2 Chr 7:20
and his sons **c** them out from 2 Chr 11:14
that God will **c** you down before 2 Chr 25:8
God has power to help or to **c** down." 2 Chr 25:8
he wrote letters to **c** contempt on the 2 Chr 32:17
and you **c** their pursuers into the Neh 9:11
against you and **c** your law behind Neh 9:26
have likewise **c** lots for the wood Neh 10:34
the rest of the people **c** lots to bring one Neh 11:1
of King Ahasuerus, they **c** Pur (that is, Est 3:7
they **c** lots) before Haman day after day; Est 3:7
and they **c** it month after month till the Est 3:7
to destroy them, and had **c** Pur (that is, Est 9:24
them, and had cast Pur (that is, **c** lots), Est 9:24
You would even **c** lots over the fatherless, Jb 6:27
and **c** off his blossom like the olive tree. Jb 15:33
For he is **c** into a net by his own feet, and Jb 18:8
ten times you have **c** reproach upon me; Jb 19:3
they have **c** up their siege ramp against Jb 19:12
the light of my face they did not **c** down. Jb 29:24
they have **c** off restraint in my presence. Jb 30:11
they **c** up against me their ways of Jb 30:12
God has **c** me into the mire, and I have Jb 30:19
out the skies, hard as a **c** metal mirror? Jb 37:18
firmly **c** on him and immovable. Jb 41:23
their bonds apart and **c** away their cords Ps 2:3
of their transgressions **c** them out, Ps 5:10
they set their eyes to **c** us to the ground. Ps 17:11
I **c** them out like the mire of the streets. Ps 18:42
On you was I **c** from my birth, and Ps 22:10
them, and for my clothing they **c** lots. Ps 22:18
C me not off; forsake me not, O God of Ps 27:9
he fall, he shall not be **c** headlong, Ps 37:24
Why are you **c** down, O my soul, and Ps 42:5
my God. My soul is **c** down within me; Ps 42:6
Why are you **c** down, O my soul, and Ps 42:11
Why are you **c** down, O my soul, and Ps 43:5
and you **c** my words behind you. Ps 50:17
C me not away from your presence, and Ps 51:11
C your burden on the LORD, and he will Ps 55:22
will **c** them down into the pit of Ps 55:23
In wrath **c** down the peoples, O God! Ps 56:7
my washbasin; upon Edom I **c** my shoe; Ps 60:8
Do not **c** me off in the time of old age; Ps 71:9
O God, why do you **c** us off forever? Why Ps 74:1
O LORD, why do you **c** my soul away? Ps 88:14
But now you have **c** off and rejected; Ps 89:38
splendor to cease and **c** his throne to the Ps 89:44
washbasin; upon Edom I **c** my shoe; Ps 108:9
Let them be **c** into fire, into miry pits, Ps 140:10
The lot is **c** into the lap, but its every Prv 16:33
vision the people **c** off restraint, Prv 29:18
a time to **c** away stones, and a time to Eccl 3:5
a time to keep, and a time to **c** away; Eccl 3:6
C your bread upon the waters, for you Eccl 11:1
that day mankind will **c** away their idols Is 2:20
but you are **c** out, away from your Is 14:19
and lament, all who **c** a hook in the Nile; Is 19:8
the covering that is **c** over all peoples, Is 25:7
down, lay low, and **c** to the ground, Is 25:12
that day everyone shall **c** away his idols Is 31:7
Their slain shall be **c** out, and the stench Is 34:3
He has **c** the lot for them; his hand has Is 34:17
and have **c** their gods into the fire. For Is 37:19
it with a shield or **c** up a siege mound Is 37:33
will make the shadow **c** by the declining Is 38:8
for you have **c** all my sins behind your Is 38:17
I have chosen you and not **c** you off"; Is 41:9
like a wife of youth when she is **c** off, Is 54:6
who hate you and **c** you out for my Is 66:5
c up a siege mound against Jerusalem. Jer 6:6
And I will **c** you out of my sight, as I cast Jer 7:15
of my sight, as I **c** out all your kinsmen, Jer 7:15
"'Cut off your hair and **c** it away; raise a Jer 7:29
because they have **c** down our Jer 9:19
they prophesy shall be **c** out in the Jer 14:16
your choicest cedars and **c** them into the Jer 22:7
his children hurled and **c** into a land Jer 22:28
are the burden, and I will **c** you off, Jer 23:33
lift you up and **c** you away from my Jer 23:39
then I will **c** off all the offspring of Jer 31:37
his dead body shall be **c** out to the heat Jer 36:30
they took Jeremiah and **c** him into the Jer 38:6
him slaughtered them and **c** them into a Jer 41:7
tie a stone to it and **c** it into the midst of Jer 51:63
and Judah that he **c** them out from his Jer 52:3
He has **c** down from heaven to earth the Lam 2:1
For the Lord will not **c** off forever, Lam 3:31
alive into the pit and **c** stones on me; Lam 3:53
against it, and **c** up a mound against it. Ezk 4:2
shall take some and **c** them into the Ezk 5:4
and I will **c** down your slain before your Ezk 6:4
They **c** their silver into the streets, and Ezk 7:19
but you were **c** out on the open field, Ezk 16:5
when mounds are **c** up and siege walls Ezk 17:17
C away from you all the Ezk 18:31
up in fury, **c** down to the ground; Ezk 19:12
C away the detestable things your eyes Ezk 20:7
None of them **c** away the detestable Ezk 20:8
against the gates, to **c** up mounds, Ezk 21:22
forgotten me and **c** me behind your Ezk 23:35
and soil they will **c** into the midst of Ezk 26:12
They **c** dust on their heads and Ezk 27:30
so I **c** you as a profane thing from the Ezk 28:16
I **c** you to the ground; I exposed you Ezk 28:17
And I will **c** you out into the wilderness, Ezk 29:5
its wickedness deserves. I have **c** it out. Ezk 31:11
when I **c** it down to Sheol with those Ezk 31:16
And I will **c** you on the ground; on the Ezk 32:4
shall immediately be **c** into a burning Dn 3:6
and worship shall be **c** into a burning Dn 3:11
shall immediately be **c** into a burning Dn 3:15
and to **c** them into the burning fiery Dn 3:20
"Did we not **c** three men bound into the Dn 3:24
O king, shall be **c** into the den of lions. Dn 6:7
shall be **c** into the den of lions?" The Dn 6:12
Daniel was brought and **c** into the den Dn 6:16
Daniel were brought and **c** into the den Dn 6:24
but he **c** him down to the ground and Dn 8:7
and he shall **c** down tens of thousands, Dn 11:12
and have **c** lots for my people, and have Jl 3:3
with the sword and **c** off all pity, Am 1:11
and you shall be **c** out into Harmon," Am 4:3
to wormwood and **c** down righteousness Am 5:7
his gates and **c** lots for Jerusalem, Ob 1:11
said to one another, "Come, let us **c** lots, Jon 1:7
evil has come upon us." So they **c** lots, Jon 1:7
For you **c** me into the deep, into the heart Jon 2:3
you will have none to **c** the line by lot in Mi 2:5
the remnant, and those who were **c** off, Mi 4:7
You will **c** all our sins into the depths of Mi 7:19
for her honored men lots were **c**, and all Na 3:10
to **c** down the horns of the nations who Zec 1:21
name, and **c** out demons in your name, Mt 7:22
and he **c** out the spirits with a word and Mt 8:16
begged him, saying, "If you **c** us out, Mt 8:31
And when the demon had been **c** out, Mt 9:33
over unclean spirits, to **c** them out, Mt 10:1
the dead, cleanse lepers, **c** out demons. Mt 10:8
And if I **c** out demons by Beelzebul, by Mt 12:27
by whom do your sons **c** them out? Mt 12:27
the Spirit of God that I **c** out demons, Mt 12:28
and said, "Why could we not **c** it out?" Mt 17:19
go to the sea and **c** a hook and take the Mt 17:27
hand and foot and **c** him into the outer Mt 22:13
And **c** the worthless servant into the Mt 25:30
diseases, and **c** out many demons. Mk 1:34
and have authority to **c** out demons. Mk 3:15
parables, "How can Satan **c** out Satan? Mk 3:23
And they **c** out many demons and Mk 6:13
she begged him to **c** the demon out of Mk 7:26
So I asked your disciples to **c** it out, and Mk 9:18
And it has often **c** him into fire and into Mk 9:22
privately, "Why could we not **c** it out?" Mk 9:28
from whom he had **c** out seven demons. Mk 16:9
in my name they will **c** out demons; Mk 16:17
And I begged your disciples to **c** it out, Lk 9:40
you say that I **c** out demons by Lk 11:18
And if I **c** out demons by Beelzebul, by Lk 11:19
by whom do your sons **c** them out? Lk 11:19
the finger of God that I **c** out demons, Lk 11:20
has killed, has authority to **c** into hell. Lk 12:5
"I came to **c** fire on the earth, and Lk 12:49
of God but you yourselves **c** out. Lk 13:28
I **c** out demons and perform cures Lk 13:32
his neck and he were **c** into the sea than Lk 17:2
This one also they wounded and **c** out. Lk 20:12
they do." And they **c** lots to divide his Lk 23:34
whoever comes to me I will never **c** out. Jn 6:37
you teach us?" And they **c** him out. Jn 9:34
Jesus heard that they had **c** him out, and Jn 9:35
now will the ruler of this world be **c** out. Jn 12:31
but **c** lots for it to see whose it shall be." Jn 19:24
for my clothing they **c** lots." So the Jn 19:24
"**C** the net on the right side of the boat, Jn 21:6
and you will find some." So they **c** it, Jn 21:6
And they **c** lots for them, and the lot Acts 1:26
Then they **c** him out of the city and Acts 7:58
put to death I **c** my vote against them. Acts 26:10
So they **c** off the anchors and left Acts 27:40
So then let us **c** off the works of Rom 13:12
"**C** out the slave woman and her son, Gal 4:30
but **c** them into hell and committed 2 Pt 2:4
They **c** their crowns before the throne, Rv 4:10
stars of heaven and **c** them to the earth. Rv 12:4

CASTANETS (1)
and tambourines and **c** and cymbals. 2 Sm 6:5

CASTING (13)
of silver were for **c** the bases of the Ex 38:27
weeping and **c** himself down before the Ezr 10:1
Jeremiah the prophet by **c** him into the Jer 38:9
Andrew his brother, **c** a net into the sea, Mt 4:18
his garments among them by **c** lots. Mt 27:35
the brother of Simon **c** a net into the Mk 1:16
in their synagogues and **c** out demons. Mk 1:39
we saw someone **c** out demons in your Mk 9:38
among them, **c** lots for them, Mk 15:24
we saw someone **c** out demons in your Lk 9:49
Now he was **c** out a demon that was Lk 11:14
c all your anxieties on him, because he 1 Pt 5:7
sea, **c** up the foam of their own shame; Jude 1:13

CASTLE (2)
governor of the **c** charge over Jerusalem, Neh 7:2
and quarreling is like the bars of a **c**. Prv 18:19

CASTS (15)
to the ungodly and **c** me into the hands Jb 16:11
up again; God **c** them out of his belly. Jb 20:15
humble; he **c** the wicked to the ground. Ps 147:6
Slothfulness **c** into a deep sleep, and an Prv 19:15
lays it low to the ground, **c** it to the dust. Is 26:5
he **c** down to the earth with his hand. Is 28:2
A craftsman **c** it, and a goldsmith Is 40:19
it with gold and **c** for it silver chains. Is 40:19
Who fashions a god or **c** an idol that is Is 44:10
"He **c** out demons by the prince of Mt 9:34
demons, that this man **c** out demons." Mt 12:24
And if Satan **c** out Satan, he is divided Mt 12:26
prince of demons he **c** out the demons." Mk 3:22
said, "He **c** out demons by Beelzebul, Lk 11:15
fear in love, but perfect love **c** out fear. 1 Jn 4:18

CATCH (11)
"Put out your hand and **c** it by the tail"— Ex 4:4
C the foxes for us, the little foxes that Sg 2:15
in wait. They set a trap; they **c** men. Jer 5:26
the LORD, and they shall **c** them. Jer 16:16
a young lion, and he learned to **c** prey; Ezk 19:3
a young lion, and he learned to **c** prey; Ezk 19:6
the deep and let down your nets for a **c**." Lk 5:4
were astonished at the **c** of fish that they Lk 5:9
to **c** him in something he might say. Lk 11:54
that they might **c** him in something he Lk 20:20
of the people to **c** him in what he Lk 20:26

CATCHES (3)
"If fire breaks out and **c** in thorns so that Ex 22:6
He **c** the wise in their own craftiness, and Jb 5:13
"He **c** the wise in their craftiness," 1 Cor 3:19

CATCHING (2)
young, spreading out its wings, **c** them, Dt 32:11
afraid; from now on you will be **c** men." Lk 5:10

CATERPILLAR (3)
or blight or mildew or locust or **c**, 1 Kgs 8:37
or blight or mildew or locust or **c**, 2 Chr 6:28
your spoil is gathered as the **c** gathers; Is 33:4

CATTLE (39)
handmill, and all the firstborn of the **c**. Ex 11:5
shall not let your **c** breed with a Lv 19:19
and for your **c** and for the wild animals Lv 25:7

and the **c** of the Levites instead of all Nm 3:41
the firstborn among the **c** of the people Nm 3:41
and the **c** of the Levites instead of their Nm 3:45
cattle of the Levites instead of their **c**. Nm 3:45
all the **c** for the burnt offering twelve Nm 7:87
and all the **c** for the sacrifice of peace Nm 7:88
we should die here, both we and our **c**? Nm 20:4
drink to the congregation and their **c**." Nm 20:8
and they took as plunder all their **c**, Nm 31:9
donkeys, and of the flocks, of all the **c**, Nm 31:30
72,000 **c**, Nm 31:33
The **c** were 36,000, of which the LORD'S Nm 31:38
36,000 **c**, Nm 31:44
our wives, our livestock, and all our **c**, Nm 32:26
shall be for their **c** and for their Nm 35:3
destruction, all who are in it and its **c**, Dt 13:15
of your ground and the fruit of your **c**, Dt 28:4
the offspring of your **c** and the fruit of Dt 28:51
in the fruit of your **c** and in the fruit of Dt 30:9
and fattened **c** by the Serpent's Stone, 1 Kgs 1:9
He has sacrificed oxen, fattened **c**, 1 Kgs 1:19
and has sacrificed oxen, fattened **c**, 1 Kgs 1:25
ten fat oxen, and twenty pasture-fed **c**, 1 Kgs 4:23
brought in the tithe of **c** and sheep, 2 Chr 31:6
and stalls for all kinds of **c**, and 2 Chr 32:28
the firstborn of our sons and of our **c**, Neh 10:36
Why are we counted as **c**? Why are we Jb 18:3
presence; the **c** also declare that he rises. Jb 36:33
forest is mine, the **c** on a thousand hills. Ps 50:10
He gave over their **c** to the hail and their Ps 78:48
may our **c** be heavy with young, Ps 144:14
become a place where **c** are let loose and Is 7:25
and the lowing of **c** is not heard; Jer 9:10
The herds of **c** are perplexed because there Jl 1:18
hand from their left, and also much **c**?" Jon 4:11
wine, oil, fine flour, wheat, **c** and sheep, Rv 18:13

CAUDA (1)
the lee of a small island called **C**, Acts 27:16

CAUGHT (37)
was a ram, **c** in a thicket by his horns. Gn 22:13
she **c** him by his garment, saying, "Lie Gn 39:12
the tail"—so he put out his hand and **c** it, Ex 4:4
they pursued him and **c** him and cut off Jgs 1:6
So Samson went and **c** 300 foxes and Jgs 15:4
his arms became as flax that has **c** fire, Jgs 15:14
I **c** him by his beard and struck him 1 Sm 17:35
And each **c** his opponent by the head 2 Sm 2:16
and his head **c** fast in the oak, 2 Sm 18:9
of the LORD and **c** hold of the horns 1 Kgs 2:28
of the LORD has **c** him up and cast 2 Kgs 2:16
the man of God, she **c** hold of his feet. 2 Kgs 4:27
are bound in chains and **c** in the cords of Jb 36:8
that they hid their own foot has been **c**. Ps 9:15
let them be **c** in the schemes that they Ps 10:2
and will keep your foot from being **c**. Prv 3:26
mouth, **c** in the words of your mouth, Prv 6:2
but if he is **c**, he will pay sevenfold; he Prv 6:31
to the slaughter, or as a stag is **c** fast Prv 7:22
net, and like birds that are **c** in a snare, Eccl 9:12
and whoever is **c** will fall by the sword. Is 13:15
out of the pit shall be **c** in the snare. Is 24:18
"As a thief is shamed when **c**, so the Jer 2:26
out of the pit shall be **c** in the snare. Jer 48:44
you were found and **c**, because you Jer 50:24
he was **c** in their pit, and they brought Ezk 19:4
a woman who had been **c** in adultery, Jn 8:3
this woman has been **c** in the act of Jn 8:4
the boat, but that night they **c** nothing. Jn 21:3
some of the fish that you have just **c**." Jn 21:10
when the ship was **c** and could not Acts 27:15
fourteen years ago was **c** up to the 2 Cor 12:2
that this man was **c** up into paradise 2 Cor 12:3
if anyone is **c** in any transgression, Gal 6:1
will be **c** up together with them in 1 Thes 4:17
of instinct, born to be **c** and destroyed, 2 Pt 2:12
but her child was **c** up to God and to his Rv 12:5

CAULDRON (5)
it into the pan or kettle or **c** or pot. 1 Sm 2:14
This city is the **c**, and we are the meat.' Ezk 11:3
they are the meat, and this city is the **c**, Ezk 11:7
This city shall not be your **c**, nor Ezk 11:11
up like meat in a pot, like flesh in a **c**. Mi 3:3

CAULDRONS (1)
the holy offerings in pots, in **c**, 2 Chr 35:13

CAULKERS (1)
your mariners and your pilots, your **c**, Ezk 27:27

CAULKING (1)
skilled men were in you, **c** your seams; Ezk 27:9

CAUSE (117)
time tomorrow I will **c** very heavy hail to Ex 9:18
In every place where I **c** my name to be Ex 20:24
and subverts the **c** of those who Ex 23:8
and so **c** them to bear iniquity and Lv 22:16
shall enter into her and **c** bitter pain. Nm 5:24
shall enter into her and **c** bitter pain, Nm 5:27
with a stone tool that could **c** death, Nm 35:17
with a wooden tool that could **c** death, Nm 35:18
or used a stone that could **c** death, and Nm 35:23
him, for he shall **c** Israel to inherit it. Dt 1:38
wise and subverts the **c** of the righteous. Dt 16:19
horses for himself or **c** the people to Dt 17:16
the judge shall **c** him to lie down and be Dt 25:2
"The LORD will **c** your enemies who rise Dt 28:7
"The LORD will **c** you to be defeated Dt 28:25
for you shall **c** this people to inherit the Jos 1:6
you have become the **c** of great trouble Jgs 11:35
blood by killing David without **c**?" 1 Sm 19:5
it and plead my **c** and deliver me 1 Sm 24:15
lord shall have no **c** of grief or pangs 1 Sm 25:31
shed blood without **c** or for my 1 Sm 25:31
with a dispute or **c** might come to me, 2 Sm 15:4
For will he not **c** to prosper all my 2 Sm 23:5
the blood that Joab shed without **c**. 1 Kgs 2:31
and their plea, and maintain their **c**. 1 Kgs 8:45
and their plea, and maintain their **c** 1 Kgs 8:49
may he maintain the **c** of his servant 1 Kgs 8:59
his servant and the **c** of his people 1 Kgs 8:59
remembrance and to **c** the death of 1 Kgs 17:18
And I will not **c** the feet of Israel to 2 Kgs 21:8
should it be a **c** of guilt for Israel?" 1 Chr 21:3
and their plea, and maintain their **c**. 2 Chr 6:35
and maintain their **c** and forgive 2 Chr 6:39
Jerusalem and to **c** confusion in it. Neh 4:8
God, and to God would I commit my **c**, Jb 5:8
my palate discern the **c** of calamity? Jb 6:30
and multiplies my wounds without **c**; Jb 9:17
and I searched out the **c** of him whom I Jb 29:16
I have rejected the **c** of my manservant Jb 31:13
evil or plundered my enemy without **c**, Ps 7:4
For you have maintained my just **c**; you Ps 9:4
Hear a just **c**, O LORD; attend to my cry! Ps 17:1
For without **c** they hid their net for me; Ps 35:7
me; without **c** they dug a pit for my life. Ps 35:7
wink the eye who hate me without **c**. Ps 35:19
yourself for my vindication, for my **c**, Ps 35:23
and defend my **c** against an ungodly Ps 43:1
out victoriously for the **c** of truth and Ps 45:4
I will **c** your name to be remembered in Ps 45:17
All day long they injure my **c**; all their Ps 56:5
head are those who hate me without **c**; Ps 69:4
May he defend the **c** of the poor of the Ps 72:4
Arise, O God, defend your **c**; remember Ps 74:22
You **c** the grass to grow for the Ps 104:14
words of hate, and attack me without **c**. Ps 109:3
Plead my **c** and redeem me; give me Ps 119:154
Princes persecute me without **c**, but Ps 119:161
will maintain the **c** of the afflicted, Ps 140:12
LORD will plead their **c** and rob of life Prv 22:23
he will plead their **c** against you. Prv 23:11
Who has wounds without **c**? Prv 23:29
against your neighbor without **c**, Prv 24:28
Do not take your stand in an evil **c**, for Eccl 8:3
to the fatherless, plead the widow's **c**. Is 1:17
and the widow's **c** does not come to them. Is 1:23
And the LORD will **c** his majestic voice to Is 30:30
a year of recompense for the **c** of Zion. Is 34:8
fruit; let the earth **c** them both to sprout; Is 45:8
your God who pleads the **c** of his people: Is 51:22
Lord GOD will **c** righteousness and Is 61:11
of birth and not **c** to bring forth?" says Is 66:9
"shall I, who **c** to bring forth, shut the Is 66:9
not with justice the **c** of the fatherless, Jer 5:28
for to you have I committed my **c**. Jer 11:20
and will **c** their people to fall by the Jer 19:7
for to you have I committed my **c**. Jer 20:12
He judged the **c** of the poor and needy; Jer 22:16
There is none to uphold your **c**, no Jer 30:13
do this abomination, to **c** Judah to sin. Jer 32:35
that time I will **c** a righteous Branch to Jer 33:15
when I will **c** the battle cry to be heard Jer 49:2
He will surely plead their **c**, that he may Jer 50:34
I will plead your **c** and take vengeance Jer 51:36
but, though he **c** grief, he will have Lam 3:32
my eyes **c** me grief at the fate of all the Lam 3:51
those who were my enemies without **c**; Lam 3:52
"You have taken up my **c**, O Lord; you Lam 3:58
wrong done to me, O LORD; judge my **c**. Lam 3:59
"If I **c** wild beasts to pass through the Ezk 14:15
have not done without **c** all that I have Ezk 14:23
"On that day I will **c** a horn to spring Ezk 29:21
and will **c** all the birds of the heavens to Ezk 32:4
I will **c** your multitude to fall by the Ezk 32:12
clear, and **c** their rivers to run like oil, Ezk 32:14
And I will **c** you to be inhabited as in Ezk 36:11
peoples and no longer **c** your nation to Ezk 36:15
and **c** you to walk in my statutes and Ezk 36:27
I will **c** the cities to be inhabited, Ezk 36:33
Behold, I will **c** breath to enter you, and Ezk 37:5
you, and will **c** flesh to come upon you, Ezk 37:6
and he shall **c** fearful destruction and Dn 8:24
he pleads my **c** and executes judgment Mi 7:9
And I will **c** the remnant of this people Zec 8:12
I will **c** each of them to fall into the Zec 11:6
it lawful to divorce one's wife for any **c**?" Mt 19:3
than that he should **c** one of these little Lk 17:2
be fulfilled: 'They hated me without a **c**.' Jn 15:25
since there is no **c** that we can give to Acts 19:40
for those who **c** divisions and create Rom 16:17
For if I **c** you pain, who is there to 2 Cor 2:2
not to **c** you pain but to let you know 2 Cor 2:4
but giving you **c** to boast about 2 Cor 5:12
From now on let no one **c** me trouble, Gal 6:17
you may have ample **c** to glory in Phil 1:26
and in him there is no **c** for stumbling. 1 Jn 2:10
It is these who **c** divisions, worldly Jude 1:19
speak and might **c** those who would Rv 13:15

CAUSED (33)
the LORD God had not **c** it to rain on the Gn 2:5
So the LORD God **c** a deep sleep to fall Gn 2:21
And when God **c** me to wander from Gn 20:13
him and that the LORD **c** all that he did Gn 39:3
c the people of Israel to act Nm 31:16
flock, until they have **c** you to perish. Dt 28:51
What **c** the heat of this great anger?' Dt 29:24
So he **c** the ark of the LORD to circle the Jos 6:11
and he **c** him to come up into the 1 Kgs 20:33
for the king he **c** to go around the 2 Kgs 16:18
who **c** the inhabitants of Gath to 1 Chr 8:13
the God who has **c** his name to dwell Ezr 6:12
and I **c** the widow's heart to sing for joy. Jb 29:13
or have **c** the eyes of the widow to fail, Jb 31:16
so that they **c** the cry of the poor to Jb 34:28
and **c** the dawn to know its place, Jb 38:12
of the rock and **c** waters to flow down Ps 78:16
He **c** the east wind to blow in the Ps 78:26
You have **c** my companions to shun me; Ps 88:8
You have **c** my beloved and my friend Ps 88:18
waters into blood and **c** their fish to Ps 105:29
He **c** them to be pitied by all those who Ps 106:46
He has **c** his wondrous works to be Ps 111:4
all the sighing she has **c** I bring to an end. Is 21:2
who **c** his glorious arm to go at the right Is 63:12
my neck; he **c** my strength to fail; Lam 1:14
he **c** rampart and wall to lament; Lam 2:8
went down to Sheol I **c** mourning; Ezk 31:15
the terror that they **c** by their might; Ezk 32:30
You have **c** many to stumble by your Mal 2:8
Now if anyone has **c** pain, he has 2 Cor 2:5
has caused pain, he has **c** it not to me, 2 Cor 2:5
he has **c** us to be born again to a living 1 Pt 1:3

CAUSELESS (1)
flying, a curse that is **c** does not alight. Prv 26:2

CAUSES (24)
"If a man **c** a field or vineyard to be Ex 22:5
for his land or for love, he **c** it to happen. Jb 37:13
upon them and **c** the lightning of Jb 37:15
A slack hand **c** poverty, but the hand of Prv 10:4
Whoever winks the eye **c** trouble, but Prv 10:10
given to anger **c** much transgression. Prv 29:22
and as a garden **c** what is sown in it to Is 61:11
brushwood and the fire **c** water to boil— Is 64:2
with anything that **c** sweat. Ezk 44:18
If your right eye **c** you to sin, tear it out Mt 5:29
And if your right hand **c** you to sin, cut Mt 5:30
out of his kingdom all **c** of sin and all Mt 13:41
but whoever **c** one of these little ones Mt 18:6
if your hand or your foot **c** you to sin, Mt 18:8
And if your eye **c** you to sin, tear it out Mt 18:9
"Whoever **c** one of these little ones who Mk 9:42
And if your hand **c** you to sin, cut it off. Mk 9:43
And if your foot **c** you to sin, cut it off. It Mk 9:45
And if your eye **c** you to sin, tear it out. Mk 9:47
or do anything that **c** your brother to Rom 14:21
bitterness" springs up and **c** trouble, Heb 12:15
What **c** quarrels and what causes fights Jas 4:1
quarrels and what **c** fights among you? Jas 4:1
Also it **c** all, both small and great, both Rv 13:16

CAUSING (2)
against the city, **c** a very great panic, 1 Sm 5:9
c them to look at their husbands with Est 1:17

CAUTIONED (1)
And he **c** them, saying, "Watch out; Mk 8:15

CAUTIOUS (1)
who is wise is **c** and turns away from Prv 14:16

CAVE (35)
he lived in a **c** with his two daughters. Gn 19:30
he may give me the **c** of Machpelah, Gn 23:9
field, and I give you the **c** that is in it. Gn 23:11
the field with the **c** that was in it and Gn 23:17

Sarah his wife in the **c** of the field of Gn 23:19
The field and the **c** that is in it were Gn 23:20
sons buried him in the **c** of Machpelah, Gn 25:9
with my fathers in the **c** that is in the Gn 49:29
in the **c** that is in the field at Gn 49:30
the field and the **c** that is in it were Gn 49:32
and buried him in the **c** of the field at Gn 50:13
hid themselves in the **c** at Makkedah. Jos 10:16
found, hidden in the **c** at Makkedah." Jos 10:17
the mouth of the **c** and set men by Jos 10:18
the mouth of the **c** and bring those five Jos 10:22
those five kings out to me from the **c**." Jos 10:22
those five kings out to him from the **c**, Jos 10:23
threw them into the **c** where they had Jos 10:27
large stones against the mouth of the **c**, Jos 10:27
in the pomegranate **c** at Migron. 1 Sm 14:2
there and escaped to the **c** of Adullam. 1 Sm 22:1
by the way, where there was a **c**, 1 Sm 24:3
sitting in the innermost parts of the **c**. 1 Sm 24:3
rose up and left the **c** and went on his 1 Sm 24:7
David also arose and went out of the **c**, 1 Sm 24:8
you today into my hand in the **c**. 1 Sm 24:10
time to David at the **c** of Adullam, 2 Sm 23:13
by fifties in a **c** and fed them with 1 Kgs 18:4
by fifties in a **c** and fed them with 1 Kgs 18:13
There he came to a **c** and lodged in it. 1 Kgs 19:9
and stood at the entrance of the **c**. 1 Kgs 19:13
rock to David at the **c** of Adullam, 1 Chr 11:15
David, when he fled from Saul, in the **c**. Ps 57:T
Maskil of David, when he was in the **c**. Ps 142:T
It was a **c**, and a stone lay against it. Jn 11:38

CAVERNS (1)
to enter the **c** of the rocks and the clefts of Is 2:21

CAVES (7)
mountains and the **c** and the Jgs 6:2
hid themselves in **c** and in holes 1 Sm 13:6
people shall enter the **c** of the rocks and Is 2:19
in strongholds and in **c** shall die by Ezk 33:27
he filled his **c** with prey and his dens Na 2:12
and in dens and **c** of the earth. Heb 11:38
hid themselves in the **c** and among the Rv 6:15

CEASE (35)
and winter, day and night, shall not **c**." Gn 8:22
The thunder will **c**, and there will be no Ex 9:29
I will make to **c** from me the Nm 17:5
For there will never **c** to be poor in the Dt 15:11
make our children **c** to worship the Jos 22:25
or shall we **c**?" And the LORD said, Jgs 20:28
"Do not **c** to cry out to the LORD our 1 Sm 7:8
lest my father **c** to care about the 1 Sm 9:5
building Ramah and let his work **c**. 2 Chr 16:5
C opposing God, who is with me, 2 Chr 35:21
a decree that these men be made to **c**, Ezr 4:21
and by force and power made them **c**. Ezr 4:23
of these days **c** among their Est 9:28
There the wicked **c** from troubling, and Jb 3:17
Are not my days few? Then **c**, and leave Jb 10:20
again, and that its shoots will not **c**. Jb 14:7
He makes wars **c** to the end of the earth; Ps 46:9
made his splendor to **c** and cast his Ps 89:44
C to hear instruction, my son, and Prv 19:27
out, and quarreling and abuse will **c**. Prv 22:10
and the grinders **c** because they are Eccl 12:3
deeds from before my eyes; **c** to do evil, Is 1:16
Damascus will **c** to be a city and will Is 17:1
shall come to nothing and the scoffer **c**, Is 29:20
tears night and day, and let them not **c**, Jer 14:17
of drought, for it does not **c** to bear fruit." Jer 17:8
the offspring of Israel **c** from being a Jer 31:36
made the wine **c** from the winepresses; Jer 48:33
C your evictions of my people, declares Ezk 45:9
Then I said, "O Lord GOD, please **c**! How Am 7:5
they did not **c** teaching and preaching Acts 5:42
three years I did not **c** night or day to Acts 20:31
pass away; as for tongues, they will **c**; 1 Cor 13:8
I do not **c** to give thanks for you, Eph 1:16
and day and night they never **c** to say, Rv 4:8

CEASED (35)
way of women had **c** to be with Sarah. Gn 18:11
his name Judah. Then she **c** bearing. Gn 29:35
saw that she had **c** bearing children, Gn 30:9
sand of the sea, until he **c** to measure it, Gn 41:49
the LORD, and the thunder and the hail **c**, Ex 9:33
rain and the hail and the thunder had **c**, Ex 9:34
And the manna **c** the day after they ate Jos 5:12
The villagers **c** in Israel; they ceased to be Jgs 5:7
ceased in Israel; they **c** to be until I arose; Jgs 5:7
who were hungry have **c** to hunger. 1 Sm 2:5
now your father has **c** to care about 1 Sm 10:2
and it **c** until the second year of the Ezr 4:24
So these three men **c** to answer Job, Jb 32:1
deceit; he has **c** to act wisely and do good. Ps 36:3
Has his steadfast love forever **c**? Are his Ps 77:8
"How the oppressor has **c**, the insolent Is 14:4
oppressor has ceased, the insolent fury **c**! Is 14:4
is no more and destruction has **c**, Is 16:4
fruit and your harvest the shout has **c**. Is 16:9
is stilled, the noise of the jubilant has **c**, Is 24:8
When you have **c** to destroy, you will be Is 33:1
warriors of Babylon have **c** fighting; Jer 51:30
The joy of our hearts has **c**; our Lam 5:15
the sea, and the sea **c** from its raging. Jon 1:15
when they got into the boat, the wind **c**. Mt 14:32
Be still!" And the wind **c**, and there was Mk 4:39
into the boat with them, and the wind **c**. Mk 6:51
I came in she has not **c** to kiss my feet. Lk 7:45
wind and the raging waves, and they **c**, Lk 8:24
immediately her discharge of blood **c**. Lk 8:44
After the uproar **c**, Paul sent for the Acts 20:1
not be persuaded, we **c** and said, Acts 21:14
we heard, we have not **c** to pray for you, Col 1:9
would they not have **c** to be offered, Heb 10:2
has suffered in the flesh has **c** from sin, 1 Pt 4:1

CEASES (5)
there is no whisperer, quarreling **c**. Prv 26:20
The highways lie waste; the traveler **c**. Is 33:8
The steadfast love of the LORD never **c**; Lam 3:22
heated oven whose baker **c** to stir the Hos 7:4
"This man never **c** to speak words Acts 6:13

CEASING (5)
against the LORD by **c** to pray for you, 1 Sm 12:23
I did not know tore at me without **c**; Ps 35:15
"My eyes will flow without **c**, without Lam 3:49
of his Son, that without **c** I mention you Rom 1:9
pray without **c**, 1 Thes 5:17

CEDAR (51)
planted, like **c** trees beside the waters. Nm 24:6
sent messengers to David, and **c** trees, 2 Sm 5:11
"See now, I dwell in a house of **c**, 2 Sm 7:2
have you not built me a house of **c**?'" 2 Sm 7:7
from the **c** that is in Lebanon to the 1 Kgs 4:33
in the matter of **c** and cypress timber. 1 Kgs 5:8
all the timber of **c** and cypress that he 1 Kgs 5:10
of the house of beams and planks of **c**. 1 Kgs 6:9
joined to the house with timbers of **c**. 1 Kgs 6:10
house on the inside with boards of **c**. 1 Kgs 6:15
house with boards of **c** from the floor 1 Kgs 6:16
The **c** within the house was carved in 1 Kgs 6:18
flowers. All was **c**; no stone was seen. 1 Kgs 6:18
gold. He also overlaid an altar of **c**. 1 Kgs 6:20
cut stone and one course of **c** beams. 1 Kgs 6:36
it was built on four rows of **c** pillars, 1 Kgs 7:2
pillars, with **c** beams on the pillars. 1 Kgs 7:2
was covered with **c** above the 1 Kgs 7:3
It was finished with **c** from floor to 1 Kgs 7:7
according to measurement, and **c**. 1 Kgs 7:11
all around, and a course of **c** beams; 1 Kgs 7:12
supplied Solomon with **c** and cypress 1 Kgs 9:11
and he made **c** as plentiful as the 1 Kgs 10:27
on Lebanon sent to a **c** on Lebanon, 2 Kgs 14:9
sent messengers to David, and **c** trees, 1 Chr 14:1
"Behold, I dwell in a house of **c**, 1 Chr 17:1
have you not built me a house of **c**?'" 1 Chr 17:6
and **c** timbers without number, for 1 Chr 22:4
great quantities of **c** to David. 1 Chr 22:4
and he made **c** as plentiful as the 2 Chr 1:15
father and sent him **c** to build himself 2 Chr 2:3
Send me also **c**, cypress, and algum 2 Chr 2:8
and he made **c** as plentiful as the 2 Chr 9:27
on Lebanon sent to a **c** on Lebanon, 2 Chr 25:18
Tyrians to bring **c** trees from Lebanon Ezr 3:7
He makes his tail stiff like a **c**; the Jb 40:17
palm tree and grow like a **c** in Lebanon. Ps 92:12
the beams of our house are **c**; our rafters Sg 1:17
door, we will enclose her with boards of **c**. Sg 8:9
I will put in the wilderness the **c**, the Is 41:19
He plants a **c** and the rain nourishes it. Is 44:14
paneling it with **c** and painting it with Jer 22:14
are a king because you compete in **c**? Jer 22:15
to Lebanon and took the top of the **c**. Ezk 17:3
the lofty top of the **c** and will set it out. Ezk 17:22
produce fruit and become a noble **c**. Ezk 17:23
they took a **c** from Lebanon to make a Ezk 27:5
Behold, Assyria was a **c** in Lebanon, Ezk 31:3
On the day the **c** went down to Sheol I Ezk 31:15
for her **c** work will be laid bare. Zep 2:14
Wail, O cypress, for the **c** has fallen, for Zec 11:2

CEDARS (19)
bramble and devour the **c** of Lebanon.' Jgs 9:15
therefore command that **c** of Lebanon 1 Kgs 5:6
I felled its tallest **c**, its choicest 2 Kgs 19:23
The voice of the LORD breaks the **c**; the Ps 29:5
the LORD breaks the **c** of Lebanon. Ps 29:5
shade, the mighty **c** with its branches. Ps 80:10
the **c** of Lebanon that he planted. Ps 104:16
and all hills, fruit trees and all **c**! Ps 148:9
is like Lebanon, choice as the **c**. Sg 5:15
against all the **c** of Lebanon, lofty and Is 2:13
down, but we will put **c** in their place." Is 9:10
cypresses rejoice at you, the **c** of Lebanon, Is 14:8
of Lebanon, to cut down its tallest **c**, Is 37:24
He cuts down **c**, or he chooses a cypress Is 44:14
cut down your choicest **c** and cast them Jer 22:7
of Lebanon, nested among the **c**, Jer 22:23
The **c** in the garden of God could not Ezk 31:8
like the height of the **c** and who was as Am 2:9
that the fire may devour your **c**! Zec 11:1

CEDARWOOD (6)
live clean birds and **c** and scarlet yarn Lv 14:4
live bird with the **c** and the scarlet yarn Lv 14:6
with **c** and scarlet yarn and hyssop, Lv 14:49
and shall take the **c** and the hyssop and Lv 14:51
bird and with the **c** and hyssop and Lv 14:52
the priest shall take **c** and hyssop and Nm 19:6

CEILING (4)
and he made the **c** of the house of 1 Kgs 6:9
floor of the house to the walls of the **c**, 1 Kgs 6:15
the gate from the **c** of the one side Ezk 40:13
the one side room to the **c** of the other, Ezk 40:13

CELEBRATE (11)
you shall **c** the feast of the LORD seven Lv 23:39
You shall **c** it as a feast to the LORD for Lv 23:41
you shall **c** it in the seventh month. Lv 23:41
to Jerusalem to **c** the dedication with Neh 12:27
and the voices of those who **c**. Jer 30:19
you shall **c** the Feast of the Passover, Ezk 45:21
calf and kill it, and let us eat and **c**. Lk 15:23
lost, and is found.' And they began to **c**. Lk 15:24
goat, that I might **c** with my friends. Lk 15:29
It was fitting to **c** and be glad, for this Lk 15:32
Let us therefore **c** the festival, not with 1 Cor 5:8

CELEBRATED (2)
women sang to one another as they **c**, 1 Sm 18:7
c the dedication of this house of God Ezr 6:16

CELEBRATION (1)
instruments leading in the **c**. 2 Chr 23:13

CELL (1)
next to him, and a light shone in the **c**. Acts 12:7

CELLAR (1)
a lamp puts it in a **c** or under a basket, Lk 11:33

CELLARS (1)
for the wine **c** was Zabdi the 1 Chr 27:27

CELLS (1)
to the dungeon **c** and remained there Jer 37:16

CENCHREAE (2)
At **C** he had cut his hair, for he was Acts 18:18
Phoebe, a servant of the church at **C**, Rom 16:1

CENSER (11)
each took his **c** and put fire in it and laid Lv 10:1
And he shall take a **c** full of coals of fire Lv 16:12
of you take his **c** and put incense on Nm 16:17
one of you bring before the LORD his **c**, Nm 16:17
you also, and Aaron, each his **c**." Nm 16:17
every man took his **c** and put fire in Nm 16:18
Moses said to Aaron, "Take your **c**, Nm 16:46
Now he had a **c** in his hand to burn 2 Chr 26:19
them. Each had his **c** in his hand, Ezk 8:11
and stood at the altar with a golden **c**, Rv 8:3
the angel took the **c** and filled it with Rv 8:5

CENSERS (6)
Do this: take **c**, Korah and all his Nm 16:6
before the LORD his censer, 250 **c**; Nm 16:17
priest to take up the **c** out of the blaze. Nm 16:37
As for the **c** of these men who have Nm 16:38
Eleazar the priest took the bronze **c**, Nm 16:39
of gold, 1,000 basins of silver, 29 **c**, Ezr 1:9

CENSURE (1)
I hear **c** that insults me, and out of my Jb 20:3

CENSUS (12)
"When you take the **c** of the people of Ex 30:12
is numbered in the **c** shall give this: Ex 30:13
Everyone who is numbered in the **c**, Ex 30:14
"Take a **c** of all the congregation of the Nm 1:2
shall not take a **c** of them among the Nm 1:49
"Take a **c** of the sons of Kohath from Nm 4:2
"Take a **c** of the sons of Gershon also, Nm 4:22
listed in the **c** from twenty years old Nm 14:29
"Take a **c** of all the congregation of the Nm 26:2
"Take a **c** of the people, from twenty Nm 26:4
after the **c** of them that David his 2 Chr 2:17
the days of the **c** and drew away some Acts 5:37

CENTER (3)
are coming down from the **c** of the land, Jgs 9:37
I have set her in the **c** of the nations, with Ezk 5:5
goods, who dwell at the **c** of the earth. Ezk 38:12

CENTURION (21)
Capernaum, a **c** came forward to him, Mt 8:5
But the **c** replied, "Lord, I am not worthy Mt 8:8
And to the **c** Jesus said, "Go; let it be done Mt 8:13
When the **c** and those who were with Mt 27:54
And when the **c**, who stood facing Mk 15:39
And summoning the **c**, he asked him Mk 15:44
he learned from the **c** that he was dead, Mk 15:45
Now a **c** had a servant who was sick and Lk 7:2
When the **c** heard about Jesus, he sent to Lk 7:3
not far from the house, the **c** sent friends, Lk 7:6
Now when the **c** saw what had taken Lk 23:47
a **c** of what was known as the Italian Acts 10:1
And they said, "Cornelius, a **c**, an Acts 10:22
Paul said to the **c** who was standing Acts 22:25
When the **c** heard this, he went to the Acts 22:26
gave orders to the **c** that he should be Acts 24:23
other prisoners to a **c** of the Augustan Acts 27:1
There the **c** found a ship of Alexandria Acts 27:6
But the **c** paid more attention to the Acts 27:11
Paul said to the **c** and the soldiers, Acts 27:31
But the **c**, wishing to save Paul, kept Acts 27:43

CENTURIONS (3)
took soldiers and **c** and ran down Acts 21:32
Paul called one of the **c** and said, Acts 23:17
Then he called two of the **c** and said, Acts 23:23

CEPHAS (9)
shall be called **C**" (which means Peter). Jn 1:42
Apollos," or "I follow **C**," or "I follow 1 Cor 1:12
Paul or Apollos or **C** or the world or 1 Cor 3:22
and the brothers of the Lord and **C**? 1 Cor 9:5
and that he appeared to **C**, then to the 1 Cor 15:5
Jerusalem to visit **C** and remained with Gal 1:18
and when James and **C** and John, who Gal 2:9
But when **C** came to Antioch, I opposed Gal 2:11
of the gospel, I said to **C** before them all, Gal 2:14

CERTAIN (52)
"Know for **c** that your offspring will be Gn 15:13
he came to a **c** place and stayed there Gn 28:11
and turned aside to a **c** Adullamite, Gn 38:1
daughter of a **c** Canaanite whose name Gn 38:2
And there were **c** men who were unclean Nm 9:6
that **c** worthless fellows have gone out Dt 13:13
it be true and **c** that such an Dt 13:14
it is true and **c** that such an Dt 17:4
know for **c** that the LORD your God will Jos 23:13
And a **c** woman threw an upper Jgs 9:53
There was a **c** man of Zorah, of the tribe Jgs 13:2
a **c** Levite was sojourning in the remote Jgs 19:1
There was a **c** man of 1 Sm 1:1
Now a **c** man of the servants of Saul 1 Sm 21:7
him, "There were two men in a **c** city, 2 Sm 12:1
And a **c** man saw it and told Joab, 2 Sm 18:10
Kidron, know for **c** that you shall die. 1 Kgs 2:37
'Know for **c** that on the day you go 1 Kgs 2:42
together with **c** Edomites of his 1 Kgs 11:17
And a **c** man of the sons of the 1 Kgs 20:35
But a **c** man drew his bow at 1 Kgs 22:34
and **c** worthless scoundrels gathered 2 Chr 13:7
But a **c** man drew his bow at 2 Chr 18:33
Jehoshaphat appointed **c** Levites and 2 Chr 19:8
C chiefs also of the men of 2 Chr 28:12
brothers, came with **c** men from Judah. Neh 1:2
And in Jerusalem lived **c** of the sons of Neh 11:4
And **c** divisions of the Levites in Neh 11:36
and **c** of the priests' sons with Neh 12:35
"There is a **c** people scattered abroad and Est 3:8
Only know for **c** that if you put me to Jer 26:15
And **c** of the elders of the land arose and Jer 26:17
King Jehoiakim sent to Egypt **c** men, Jer 26:22
Then **c** of the elders of Israel came to Ezk 14:1
c of the elders of Israel came to inquire Ezk 20:1
The dream is **c**, and its interpretation Dn 2:45
at that time **c** Chaldeans came forward Dn 3:8
There are **c** Jews whom you have Dn 3:12
into the city to a **c** man and say to him, Mt 26:18
"A **c** moneylender had two debtors. One Lk 7:41
Now Jesus was praying in a **c** place, and Lk 11:1
"In a **c** city there was a judge who Lk 18:2
Now a **c** man was ill, Lazarus of Jn 11:1
therefore know for **c** that God has Acts 2:36
Paphos, they came upon a **c** magician, Acts 13:6
Rather they had **c** points of dispute Acts 25:19
own religion and about a **c** Jesus, Acts 25:19
For before **c** men came from James, he Gal 2:12
that you may charge **c** persons not to 1 Tm 1:3
C persons, by swerving from these, 1 Tm 1:6
again he appoints a **c** day, "Today," Heb 4:7
For **c** people have crept in unnoticed Jude 1:4

CERTAINLY (18)
with you will **c** wear yourselves out, Ex 18:18
You **c** ought to have eaten it in the Lv 10:18
I said, 'I will **c** honor you,' but the Nm 24:11
For the LORD will **c** make my lord a 1 Sm 25:28
for I will **c** give the Philistines into 2 Sm 5:19
"Go, say to him, 'You shall **c** recover,' 2 Kgs 8:10
has shown me that he shall **c** die." 2 Kgs 8:10
told me that you would **c** recover." 2 Kgs 8:14
of Babylon will **c** come and destroy Jer 36:29
Son of Man will **c** suffer at their Mt 17:12
to Peter, "**C** you too are one of them, Mt 26:73
said to Peter, "**C** you are one of them, Mk 14:70
saying, "**C** this man also was with him, Lk 22:59
saying, "**C** this man was innocent!" Lk 23:47
They will **c** hear that you have come. Acts 21:22
we shall **c** be united with him in a Rom 6:5
is Christ then a servant of sin? **C** not! Gal 2:17
contrary to the promises of God? **C** not! Gal 3:21

CERTAINTY (5)
your servants for a **c** that the LORD your Jos 9:24
Know for a **c** that I have warned you Jer 42:19
therefore know for a **c** that you shall Jer 42:22
"I know with **c** that you are trying to gain Dn 2:8
you may have **c** concerning the things Lk 1:4

CERTIFICATE (6)
and he writes her a **c** of divorce and puts Dt 24:1
her and writes her a **c** of divorce and puts Dt 24:3
"Where is your mother's **c** of divorce, Is 50:1
his wife, let him give her a **c** of divorce.' Mt 5:31
one to give a **c** of divorce and to Mt 19:7
a man to write a **c** of divorce and to Mk 10:4

CHAFF (16)
frighten a driven leaf and pursue dry **c**? Jb 13:25
and like **c** that the storm carries away? Jb 21:18
but are like **c** that the wind drives away. Ps 1:4
Let them be like **c** before the wind, with Ps 35:5
whirling dust, like **c** before the wind. Ps 83:13
chased like **c** on the mountains before Is 17:13
multitude of the ruthless like passing **c**. Is 29:5
You conceive **c**; you give birth to Is 33:11
and you shall make the hills like **c**; Is 41:15
will scatter you like **c** driven by the Jer 13:24
and became like the **c** of the summer Dn 2:35
like the **c** that swirls from the Hos 13:3
of sandals and sell the **c** of the wheat?" Am 8:6
day passes away like **c**—before there Zep 2:2
but the **c** he will burn with Mt 3:12
but the **c** he will burn with Lk 3:17

CHAIN (10)
linen and put a gold **c** about his neck. Gn 41:42
work with wreaths of **c** work for the 1 Kgs 7:17
"Forge a **c**! For the land is full of Ezk 7:23
on your wrists and a **c** on your neck. Ezk 16:11
purple and have a **c** of gold around his Dn 5:7
purple and have a **c** of gold around your Dn 5:16
a **c** of gold was put around his neck, Dn 5:29
bind him anymore, not even with a **c**, Mk 5:3
of Israel that I am wearing this **c**." Acts 28:20
key to the bottomless pit and a great **c**. Rv 20:1

CHAINS (36)
and two **c** of pure gold, twisted like Ex 28:14
shall attach the corded **c** to the settings. Ex 28:14
for the breastpiece twisted **c** like cords, Ex 28:22
on the breastpiece twisted **c** like cords, Ex 39:15
gold, and he drew **c** of gold across, 1 Kgs 6:21
and bound him in **c** and took him to 2 Kgs 25:7
fine gold and made palms and **c** on it. 2 Chr 3:5
He made **c** like a necklace and put 2 Chr 3:16
pomegranates and put them on the **c**. 2 Chr 3:16
bound him with **c** of bronze and 2 Chr 33:11
and bound him in **c** to take him to 2 Chr 36:6
if they are bound in **c** and caught in the Jb 36:8
"Can you bind the **c** of the Pleiades or Jb 38:31
their kings with **c** and their nobles Ps 149:8
it with gold and casts for it silver **c**. Is 40:19
shall come over in **c** and bow down to Is 45:14
and bound him in **c** to take him to Jer 39:7
took him bound in **c** along with all the Jer 40:1
you today from the **c** on your hands. Jer 40:4
eyes of Zedekiah, and bound him in **c**, Jer 52:11
escape; he has made my **c** heavy; Lam 3:7
and all her great men were bound in **c**. Na 3:10
often been bound with shackles and **c**, Mk 5:4
and chains, but he wrenched the **c** apart, Mk 5:4
guard and bound with **c** and shackles, Lk 8:29
two soldiers, bound with two **c**, Acts 12:6
up quickly." And the **c** fell off his Acts 12:7
ordered him to be bound with two **c**. Acts 21:33
such as I am—except for these **c**." Acts 26:29
for which I am an ambassador in **c**, Eph 6:20
with my own hand. Remember my **c**. Col 4:18
me and was not ashamed of my **c**, 2 Tm 1:16
suffering, bound with **c** as a criminal. 2 Tm 2:9
and even **c** and imprisonment. Heb 11:36
committed them to **c** of gloomy 2 Pt 2:4
kept in eternal **c** under gloomy Jude 1:6

CHAIR (1)
put there for him a bed, a table, a **c**, 2 Kgs 4:10

CHALDEA (8)
Go out from Babylon, flee from **C**, Is 48:20
C shall be plundered; all who plunder Jer 50:10
the inhabitants of **C** before your very Jer 51:24
the inhabitants of **C**," let Jerusalem say. Jer 51:35
the vision by the Spirit of God into **C**, Ezk 11:24
also with the trading land of **C**, Ezk 16:29
whose native land was **C**. Ezk 23:15
and sent messengers to them in **C**. Ezk 23:16

CHALDEAN (6)
be afraid because of the **C** officials. 2 Kgs 25:24
king of Babylon, the **C**, Ezr 5:12
Now when the **C** army had withdrawn Jer 37:11
and the **C** soldiers who happened to be Jer 41:3
of any magician or enchanter or **C**. Dn 2:10
night Belshazzar the **C** king was killed. Dn 5:30

CHALDEANS (77)
the land of his kindred, in Ur of the **C**. Gn 11:28
together from Ur of the **C** to go into the Gn 11:31
out from Ur of the **C** to give you this Gn 15:7
him bands of the **C** and bands of the 2 Kgs 24:2
though the **C** were around the city. 2 Kgs 25:4
the army of the **C** pursued the king 2 Kgs 25:5
And all the army of the **C**, who were 2 Kgs 25:10
the **C** broke in pieces and carried 2 Kgs 25:13
the Jews and the **C** who were with 2 Kgs 25:25
Egypt, for they were afraid of the **C**. 2 Kgs 25:26
up against them the king of the **C**, 2 Chr 36:17
out of Ur of the **C** and gave him the Neh 9:7
"The **C** formed three groups and made a Jb 1:17
the splendor and pomp of the **C**, Is 13:19
Behold the land of the **C**! This is the Is 23:13
them all down as fugitives, even the **C**, Is 43:14
without a throne, O daughter of the **C**! Is 47:1
go into darkness, O daughter of the **C**; Is 47:5
and his arm shall be against the **C**. Is 48:14
and against the **C** who are besieging Jer 21:4
surrenders to the **C** who are besieging Jer 21:9
of Babylon and into the hand of the **C**. Jer 22:25
away from this place to the land of the **C**. Jer 24:5
and that nation, the land of the **C**, Jer 25:12
shall not escape out of the hand of the **C**, Jer 32:4
Though you fight against the **C**, you Jer 32:5
the hands of the **C** who are fighting Jer 32:24
city is given into the hands of the **C**.'" Jer 32:25
the hands of the **C** and into the hand Jer 32:28
The **C** who are fighting against this Jer 32:29
beast; it is given into the hand of the **C**.' Jer 32:43
in to fight against the **C** and to fill them Jer 33:5
of the army of the **C** and the army of Jer 35:11
And when the **C** who were besieging Jer 37:5
And the **C** shall come back and fight Jer 37:8
"The **C** will surely go away from us," for Jer 37:9
the whole army of **C** who are fighting Jer 37:10
saying, "You are deserting to the **C**." Jer 37:13
deserting to the **C**." But Irijah would Jer 37:14
but he who goes out to the **C** shall live. Jer 38:2
shall be given into the hand of the **C**, Jer 38:18
the Judeans who have deserted to the **C**, Jer 38:19
and your sons shall be led out to the **C**, Jer 38:23
the army of the **C** pursued them and Jer 39:5
The **C** burned the king's house and the Jer 39:8
saying, "Do not be afraid to serve the **C**. Jer 40:9
you before the **C** who will come Jer 40:10
because of the **C**. For they were afraid Jer 41:18
us, to deliver us into the hand of the **C**, Jer 43:3
Babylon, concerning the land of the **C**, Jer 50:1
Babylon, and go out of the land of the **C**, Jer 50:8
has a work to do in the land of the **C**. Jer 50:25
"A sword against the **C**, declares the Jer 50:35
he has formed against the land of the **C**: Jer 50:45
shall fall down slain in the land of the **C**, Jer 51:4
but the land of the **C** is full of guilt Jer 51:5
destruction from the land of the **C**! Jer 51:54
garden, while the **C** were around the city. Jer 52:7
the army of the **C** pursued the king and Jer 52:8
And all the army of the **C**, who were Jer 52:14
of the LORD, the **C** broke in pieces, Jer 52:17
in the land of the **C** by the Chebar canal, Ezk 1:3
him to Babylon, the land of the **C**, Ezk 12:13
images of the **C** portrayed in Ezk 23:14
the Babylonians and all the **C**, Pekod Ezk 23:23
the literature and language of the **C**. Dn 1:4
and the **C** be summoned to tell the king Dn 2:2
Then the **C** said to the king in Aramaic, Dn 2:4
The king answered and said to the **C**, Dn 2:5
The **C** answered the king and said, Dn 2:10
at that time certain **C** came forward and Dn 3:8
the magicians, the enchanters, the **C**, Dn 4:7
loudly to bring in the enchanters, the **C**, Dn 5:7
enchanters, **C**, and astrologers, Dn 5:11
was made king over the realm of the **C**— Dn 9:1

For behold, I am raising up the **C**, that Hab 1:6
the land of the **C** and lived in Haran. Acts 7:4

CHALKSTONES (1)
of the altars like **c** crushed to pieces, Is 27:9

CHAMBER (50)
And he entered his **c** and wept there. Gn 43:30
of Israel into the **c** and pierced both of Nm 25:8
as he was sitting alone in his cool roof **c**. Jgs 3:20
doors of the roof **c** behind him and Jgs 3:23
that the doors of the roof **c** were locked, Jgs 3:24
himself in the closet of the cool **c**." Jgs 3:24
still did not open the doors of the roof **c**, Jgs 3:25
my wife in the **c**." But her father would Jgs 15:1
had men lying in ambush in an inner **c**. Jgs 16:9
lying in ambush were in an inner **c**. Jgs 16:12
to Tamar, "Bring the food into the **c**, 2 Sm 13:10
them into the **c** to Amnon her 2 Sm 13:10
went up to the **c** over the gate and 2 Sm 18:33
the king in his **c** (now the king was 1 Kgs 1:15
up into the upper **c** where he lodged, 1 Kgs 17:19
from the upper **c** into the house 1 Kgs 17:23
and entered an inner **c** in the city. 1 Kgs 20:30
go into an inner **c** to hide yourself." 1 Kgs 22:25
the lattice in his upper **c** in Samaria, 2 Kgs 1:2
he turned into the **c** and rested there. 2 Kgs 4:11
his fellows, and lead him to an inner **c**. 2 Kgs 9:2
by the **c** of Nathan-melech the 2 Kgs 23:11
on the roof of the upper **c** of Ahaz, 2 Kgs 23:12
go into an inner **c** to hide yourself." 2 Chr 18:24
and went to the **c** of Jehohanan the son Ezr 10:6
of Berechiah repaired opposite his **c**. Neh 3:30
Gate, and to the upper **c** of the corner. Neh 3:31
And between the upper **c** of the corner Neh 3:32
for Tobiah a large **c** where they had Neh 13:5
preparing for him a **c** in the courts of Neh 13:7
furniture of Tobiah out of the **c**. Neh 13:8
From its **c** comes the whirlwind, and Jb 37:9
out like a bridegroom leaving his **c**, Ps 19:5
All glorious is the princess in her **c**, Ps 45:13
and into the **c** of her who conceived me. Sg 3:4
of the LORD into the **c** of the sons of Jer 35:4
which was near the **c** of the officials, Jer 35:4
above the **c** of Maaseiah the son of Jer 35:4
in the **c** of Gemariah the son of Jer 36:10
the king's house, into the secretary's **c**, Jer 36:12
the scroll in the **c** of Elishama the Jer 36:20
took it from the **c** of Elishama the Jer 36:21
yourself a vaulted **c** and made Ezk 16:24
building your vaulted **c** at the head of Ezk 16:31
down your vaulted **c** and break down Ezk 16:39
There was a **c** with its door in the Ezk 40:38
This **c** that faces south is for the Ezk 40:45
and the **c** that faces north is for the Ezk 40:46
in his upper **c** open toward Jerusalem. Dn 6:10
leave his room, and the bride her **c**. Jl 2:16

CHAMBERLAIN (2)
chamber of Nathan-melech the **c**, 2 Kgs 23:11
persuaded Blastus, the king's **c**, Acts 12:20

CHAMBERS (53)
And he made side **c** all around. 1 Kgs 6:5
with cedar above the **c** that were on the 1 Kgs 7:3
to be over the **c** and the treasures of 1 Chr 9:26
were in the **c** of the temple free from 1 Chr 9:33
the care of the courts and the **c**, 1 Chr 23:28
its upper rooms, and its inner **c**, 1 Chr 28:11
of the LORD, all the surrounding **c**, 1 Chr 28:12
And he overlaid the upper **c** with gold. 2 Chr 3:9
them to prepare **c** in the house 2 Chr 31:11
within the **c** of the house of the LORD." Ezr 8:29
to the **c** of the house of our God; Neh 10:37
of our God, to the **c** of the storehouse. Neh 10:38
of grain, wine, and oil to the **c**, Neh 10:39
was appointed over the **c** of the house Neh 13:4
I gave orders, and they cleansed the **c**, Neh 13:9
Orion, the Pleiades and the **c** of the south; Jb 9:9
lays the beams of his **c** on the waters; Ps 104:3
with frogs, even in the **c** of their kings. Ps 105:30
to Sheol, going down to the **c** of death. Prv 7:27
run. The king has brought me into his **c**. Sg 1:4
Come, my people, enter your **c**, and shut Is 26:20
to the house of the LORD, into one of the **c**; Jer 35:2
behold, there were **c** and a pavement, Ezk 40:17
court. Thirty **c** faced the pavement. Ezk 40:17
gateway there were two **c** in the inner Ezk 40:44
thick, and the breadth of the side **c**, Ezk 41:5
And the side **c** were in three stories, one Ezk 41:6
to serve as supports for the side **c**, Ezk 41:6
as it wound upward to the side **c**, Ezk 41:7
of the side **c** measured a full Ezk 41:8
outer wall of the side **c** was five cubits. Ezk 41:9
space between the side **c** of the temple Ezk 41:9
other **c** was a breadth of twenty cubits Ezk 41:10
doors of the side **c** opened on the free Ezk 41:11
the vestibule, the side **c** of the temple, Ezk 41:26
brought me to the **c** that were opposite Ezk 42:1
And before the **c** was a passage inward, Ezk 42:4
Now the upper **c** were narrower, for the Ezk 42:5
the lower and middle **c** of the building. Ezk 42:5
Thus the upper **c** were set back from Ezk 42:6
was a wall outside parallel to the **c**, Ezk 42:7
toward the outer court, opposite the **c**, Ezk 42:7
For the **c** on the outer court were fifty Ezk 42:8
Below these **c** was an entrance on the Ezk 42:9
and opposite the building, there were **c** Ezk 42:10
were similar to the **c** on the north, Ezk 42:11
the entrances of the **c** on the south. Ezk 42:12
"The north **c** and the south chambers Ezk 42:13
and the south **c** opposite the yard Ezk 42:13
opposite the yard are the holy **c**, Ezk 42:13
and lay them in the holy **c**. Ezk 44:19
north row of the holy **c** for the priests, Ezk 46:19
who builds his upper **c** in the heavens Am 9:6

CHAMELEON (1)
the lizard, the sand lizard, and the **c**. Lv 11:30

CHAMPION (3)
the Philistines a **c** named Goliath of 1 Sm 17:4
he talked with them, behold, the **c**, 1 Sm 17:23
Philistines saw that their **c** was dead, 1 Sm 17:51

CHANCE (5)
"By **c** I happened to be on Mount 2 Sm 1:6
but time and **c** happen to them all. Eccl 9:11
Now by **c** a priest was going down that Lk 10:31
on the **c** that somehow they could Acts 27:12
rejected, for he found no **c** to repent, Heb 12:17

CHANGE (25)
purify yourselves and **c** your garments. Gn 35:2
and all of them he gave a **c** of clothes, Gn 45:22
"Lest the people **c** their minds when Ex 13:17
of man, that he should **c** his mind. Nm 23:19
In order to **c** the course of things 2 Sm 14:20
you **c** his countenance, and send him Jb 14:20
swears to his own hurt and does not **c**; Ps 15:4
because they do not **c** and do not fear Ps 55:19
You will **c** them like a robe, and they Ps 102:26
has sworn and will not **c** his mind, Ps 110:4
Can the Ethiopian **c** his skin or the Jer 13:23
corrupt words before me till the times **c**. Dn 2:9
thoughts alarm you or your color **c**. Dn 5:10
and shall think to **c** the times and the Dn 7:25
me; I will **c** their glory into shame. Hos 4:7
at that time I will **c** the speech of the Zep 3:9
and I will **c** their shame into praise and Zep 3:19
"For I the LORD do not **c**; therefore you, O Mal 3:6
did not afterward **c** your minds and Mt 21:32
this place and will **c** the customs that Acts 6:14
be present with you now and **c** my tone, Gal 4:20
For when there is a **c** in the priesthood, Heb 7:12
there is necessarily a **c** in the law as Heb 7:12
has sworn and will not **c** his mind, Heb 7:21
there is no variation or shadow due to **c**. Jas 1:17

CHANGED (33)
has cheated me and **c** my wages ten Gn 31:7
and you have **c** my wages ten times. Gn 31:41
had shaved himself and **c** his clothes, Gn 41:14
and his servants was **c** toward the people, Ex 14:5
of the diseased area has not **c**, Lv 13:55
and Baal-meon (their names were **c**), Nm 32:38
So he **c** his behavior before them 1 Sm 21:13
anointed himself and **c** his clothes. 2 Sm 12:20
father, and **c** his name to Jehoiakim. 2 Kgs 23:34
place, and **c** his name to Zedekiah. 2 Kgs 24:17
and **c** his name to Jehoiakim. 2 Chr 36:4
It is **c** like clay under the seal, and its Jb 38:14
when he **c** his behavior before Ps 34:T
shine, and the hardness of his face is **c**. Eccl 8:1
Has a nation **c** its gods, even though they Jer 2:11
But my people have **c** their glory for that Jer 2:11
remains in him, and his scent is not **c**. Jer 48:11
has grown dim, how the pure gold is **c**! Lam 4:1
of his face was **c** against Shadrach, Dn 3:19
Let his mind be **c** from a man's, and let Dn 4:16
Then the king's color **c**, and his thoughts Dn 5:6
was greatly alarmed, and his color **c**, Dn 5:9
sign the document, so that it cannot be **c**, Dn 6:8
that the king establishes can be **c**." Dn 6:15
nothing might be **c** concerning Daniel. Dn 6:17
greatly alarmed me, and my color **c**, Dn 7:28
My radiant appearance was fearfully **c**, Dn 10:8
but afterward he **c** his mind and went. Mt 21:29
he **c** his mind and brought back the Mt 27:3
they **c** their minds and said that he Acts 28:6
not all sleep, but we shall all be **c**, 1 Cor 15:51
imperishable, and we shall be **c**. 1 Cor 15:52
them up, like a garment they will be **c**. Heb 1:12

CHANGES (6)
shekels of silver and five **c** of clothes. Gn 45:22
linen garments and thirty **c** of clothes, Jgs 14:12
garments and thirty **c** of clothes." And Jgs 14:13
shekels of gold, and ten **c** of clothes. 2 Kgs 5:5
He **c** times and seasons; he removes Dn 2:21
ruined; he **c** the portion of my people; Mi 2:4

CHANGING (1)
How much you go about, **c** your way! Jer 2:36

CHANNEL (1)
"Who has cleft a **c** for the torrents of Jb 38:25

CHANNELS (5)
Then the **c** of the sea were seen; the 2 Sm 22:16
He cuts out **c** in the rocks, and his eye Jb 28:10
Then the **c** of the sea were seen, and the Ps 18:15
it will rise over all its **c** and go over all its Is 8:7
breath, and strike it into seven **c**, Is 11:15

CHANT (2)
the daughters of the nations shall **c** it; Ezk 32:16
over all her multitude, shall they **c** it, Ezk 32:16

CHANTED (1)
This is a lamentation that shall be **c**; Ezk 32:16

CHARACTER (4)
When he lies, he speaks out of his own **c**, Jn 8:44
and endurance produces **c**, and Rom 5:4
character, and **c** produces hope, Rom 5:4
promise the unchangeable **c** of his Heb 6:17

CHARACTERS (1)
a large tablet and write on it in common **c**, Is 8:1

CHARCOAL (3)
As **c** to hot embers and wood to fire, so Prv 26:21
servants and officers had made a **c** fire, Jn 18:18
got out on land, they saw a **c** fire in place, Jn 21:9

CHARGE (130)
household, who had **c** of all that he had, Gn 24:2
obeyed my voice and kept my **c**, Gn 26:5
black, and put them in **c** of his sons. Gn 30:35
house and put him in **c** of all that he Gn 39:4
So he left all that he had in Joseph's **c**, Gn 39:6
has put everything that he has in my **c**. Gn 39:8
prison put Joseph in **c** of all the Gn 39:22
to anything that was in Joseph's **c**, Gn 39:23
them, put them in **c** of my livestock." Gn 47:6
and gave them a **c** about the people of Ex 6:13
Keep far from a false **c**, and do not kill Ex 23:7
So keep my **c** never to practice any of Lv 18:30
They shall therefore keep my **c**, lest they Lv 22:9
the priest shall have **c** of the oil for Nm 4:16
shall assign to their **c** all that they are Nm 4:27
of Israel kept the **c** of the LORD and Nm 9:19
set out. They kept the **c** of the LORD, Nm 9:23
I have given you **c** of the contributions Nm 18:8
But **c** Joshua, and encourage and Dt 3:28
love the LORD your God and keep his **c**, Dt 11:1
three witnesses shall a **c** be established. Dt 19:15
"You shall not **c** interest on loans to Dt 23:19
You may **c** a foreigner interest, but you Dt 23:20
you may not **c** your brother interest, Dt 23:20
careful to keep the **c** of the LORD your Jos 22:3
young man who was in **c** of the reapers, Ru 2:5
servant who was in **c** of the reapers Ru 2:6
his son Eleazar to have **c** of the ark of 1 Sm 7:1
and the **c** was two-thirds of a shekel 1 Sm 13:21
not heard his father **c** the people with 1 Sm 14:27
left the things in **c** of the keeper of 1 Sm 17:22
And yet you **c** me today with a fault 2 Sm 3:8
he put in the **c** of Abishai his 2 Sm 10:10
and Adoram was in **c** of the forced 2 Sm 20:24
and keep the **c** of the LORD your God, 1 Kgs 2:3
Ahishar was in **c** of the palace; and 1 Kgs 4:6
of Abda was in **c** of the forced labor. 1 Kgs 4:6
Adoniram was in **c** of the draft. 1 Kgs 5:14
who had **c** of the people who carried 1 Kgs 5:16
550 who had **c** of the people who 1 Kgs 9:23
he gave him **c** over all the 1 Kgs 11:28
and let them bring a **c** against him, 1 Kgs 21:10
men brought a **c** against Naboth in 1 Kgs 21:13
we dwell under your **c** is too small for 2 Kgs 6:1
hand he leaned to have **c** of the gate. 2 Kgs 7:17
him who was in **c** of the wardrobe, 2 Kgs 10:22
whom David put in **c** of the service of 1 Chr 6:31
were in **c** of the work of the service, 1 Chr 9:19
fathers had been in **c** of the camp of 1 Chr 9:19
their sons were in **c** of the gates of 1 Chr 9:23
and they had **c** of opening it every 1 Chr 9:27
Some of them had **c** of the utensils of 1 Chr 9:28
the Kohathites had **c** of the 1 Chr 9:32
he put in the **c** of Abishai his 1 Chr 19:11
when he gives you **c** over Israel you 1 Chr 22:12
"shall have **c** of the work in the 1 Chr 23:4
they were to keep **c** of the tent of 1 Chr 23:32

Ahijah had **c** of the treasuries of the 1 Chr 26:20
were in **c** of the treasuries of the 1 Chr 26:22
chief officer in **c** of the treasuries. 1 Chr 26:24
his brothers were in **c** of all the 1 Chr 26:26
of Zabdiel was in **c** of the first 1 Chr 27:2
the Ahohite was in **c** of the division 1 Chr 27:4
his son was in **c** of his division. 1 Chr 27:6
For we keep the **c** of the LORD our 2 Chr 13:11
people shall keep the **c** of the LORD. 2 Chr 23:6
organized to be in **c** of the house of 2 Chr 23:18
it to those who had **c** of the work of 2 Chr 24:12
The chief officer in **c** of them was 2 Chr 31:12
brought these out in **c** of Mithredath the Ezr 1:8
governor of the castle **c** over Jerusalem, Neh 7:2
his brothers was in **c** of the songs of Neh 12:8
king's eunuch, who is in **c** of the women. Est 2:3
of Hegai, who had **c** of the women. Est 2:8
who was in **c** of the concubines. Est 2:14
eunuch, who had **c** of the women, Est 2:15
of those who have **c** of the king's Est 3:9
this Job did not sin or **c** God with wrong. Jb 1:22
Who gave him **c** over the earth, and Jb 34:13
I rebuke you and lay the **c** before you. Ps 50:21
when I did not send them or **c** them. Jer 23:32
Give them this **c** for their masters: 'Thus Jer 27:4
to have **c** in the house of the LORD over Jer 29:26
be quiet when the LORD has given it a **c**? Jer 47:7
the priests who have **c** of the temple, Ezk 40:45
for the priests who have **c** of the altar. Ezk 40:46
you have not kept **c** of my holy things, Ezk 44:8
set others to keep my **c** for you in my Ezk 44:8
appoint them to keep **c** of the temple, Ezk 44:14
who kept the **c** of my sanctuary when Ezk 44:15
to me, and they shall keep my **c**. Ezk 44:16
the sons of Zadok, who kept my **c**, Ezk 48:11
great prince who has **c** of your people. Dn 12:1
Like warriors they **c**; like soldiers they Jl 2:7
will walk in my ways and keep my **c**, Zec 3:7
rule my house and have **c** of my courts, Zec 3:7
of our keeping his **c** or of walking as Mal 3:14
that every **c** may be established by the Mt 18:16
him no answer, not even to a single **c**, Mt 27:14
his head they put the **c** against him, Mt 27:37
home and puts his servants in **c**, Mk 13:34
inscription of the **c** against him read, Mk 15:26
they might have some **c** to bring against Jn 8:6
This **c** I have received from my Father." Jn 10:18
and having **c** of the moneybag he used to Jn 12:6
who was in **c** of all her treasure. Acts 8:27
desiring to know the **c** for which they Acts 23:28
The Jews also joined in the **c**, Acts 24:9
defense concerning the **c** laid against Acts 25:16
they brought no **c** in his case of such Acts 25:18
though I had no **c** to bring against Acts 28:19
some people slanderously **c** us with Rom 3:8
shall bring any **c** against God's elect? Rom 8:33
To the married I give this **c** (not I, but 1 Cor 7:10
I may present the gospel free of **c**, 1 Cor 9:18
God's gospel to you free of **c**? 2 Cor 11:7
Every **c** must be established by the 2 Cor 13:1
that you may **c** certain persons not 1 Tm 1:3
The aim of our **c** is love that issues 1 Tm 1:5
This **c** I entrust to you, Timothy, my 1 Tm 1:18
Do not admit a **c** against an elder 1 Tm 5:19
the elect angels I **c** you to keep these 1 Tm 5:21
I **c** you in the presence of God, who 1 Tm 6:13
age, **c** them not to be haughty, 1 Tm 6:17
and **c** them before God not to quarrel 2 Tm 2:14
I **c** you in the presence of God and of 2 Tm 4:1
not open to the **c** of debauchery or Ti 1:6
you anything, **c** that to my account. Phlm 1:18
not domineering over those in your **c**, 1 Pt 5:3
I heard the angel in **c** of the waters say, Rv 16:5

CHARGED (36)

days, performing what the LORD has **c**, Lv 8:35
And this is what they are **c** to carry, as Nm 4:31
because they were **c** with the service of Nm 7:9
And I **c** your judges at that time, 'Hear Dt 1:16
That day Moses **c** the people, saying, Dt 27:11
and Joshua **c** those who went to write the Jos 18:8
Have I not **c** the young men not to touch Ru 2:9
"Your father strictly **c** the people 1 Sm 14:28
"The king has **c** me with a matter and 1 Sm 21:2
you, and with which I have **c** you.' 1 Sm 21:2
For I am **c** with unbearable news for 1 Kgs 14:6
Solomon his son and **c** him to build 1 Chr 22:6
And he **c** them: "Thus you shall do 2 Chr 19:9
and he has **c** me to build him a 2 Chr 36:23
and he has **c** me to build him a house at Ezr 1:2
I **c** Baruch in their presence, saying, Jer 32:13
Then he strictly **c** the disciples to tell Mt 16:20
And Jesus sternly **c** him and sent him Mk 1:43
And he strictly **c** them that no one Mk 5:43
He **c** them to take nothing for their Mk 6:8
And Jesus **c** them to tell no one. But the Mk 7:36
But the more he **c** them, the more Mk 7:36
And he strictly **c** them to tell no one Mk 8:30
he **c** them to tell no one what they had Mk 9:9
And he **c** him to tell no one, but "go and Lk 5:14
but he **c** them to tell no one what had Lk 8:56
And he strictly **c** and commanded them Lk 9:21
may be **c** against this generation, Lk 11:50
they called them and **c** them not to Acts 4:18
"We strictly **c** you not to teach in this Acts 5:28
they beat them and **c** them not to Acts 5:40
danger of being **c** with rioting today, Acts 19:40
but **c** with nothing deserving death Acts 23:29
For we have already **c** that all, both Rom 3:9
encouraged you and **c** you to walk 1 Thes 2:12
me. May it not be **c** against them! 2 Tm 4:16

CHARGES (12)

and I brought **c** against the nobles and Neh 5:7
no trust, and his angels he **c** with error; Jb 4:18
for help; yet God **c** no one with wrong. Jb 24:12
See how many **c** they bring against Mk 15:4
and **c** were brought to him that this Lk 16:1
guilty of any of your **c** against him. Lk 23:14
Let them bring **c** against one Acts 19:38
man, let them bring **c** against him." Acts 25:5
many and serious **c** against him that Acts 25:7
there be tried on these **c** before me?" Acts 25:9
there is nothing to their **c** against me, Acts 25:11
not to indicate the **c** against him." Acts 25:27

CHARGING (4)

a roaring lion or a **c** bear is a wicked Prv 28:15
I saw the ram **c** westward and northward Dn 8:4
Horsemen **c**, flashing sword and Na 3:3
dismissed the young man, **c** him, Acts 23:22

CHARIOT (56)

And he made him ride in his second **c**. Gn 41:43
Joseph prepared his **c** and went up Gn 46:29
he made ready his **c** and took his army Ex 14:6
clogging their **c** wheels so that they Ex 14:25
got down from his **c** and fled away on Jgs 4:15
lattice: 'Why is his **c** so long in coming? Jgs 5:28
hamstrung all the **c** horses but left 2 Sm 8:4
Absalom got himself a **c** and horses, 2 Sm 15:1
The wheels were made like a **c** wheel; 1 Kgs 7:33
his **c** commanders and his 1 Kgs 9:22
he stationed in the **c** cities and with 1 Kgs 10:26
A **c** could be imported from Egypt 1 Kgs 10:29
hurried to mount his **c** to flee to 1 Kgs 12:18
Ahab, 'Prepare your **c** and go down, 1 Kgs 18:44
horse for horse, and **c** for chariot. 1 Kgs 20:25
horse for horse, and chariot for **c**. 1 Kgs 20:25
caused him to come up into the **c**. 1 Kgs 20:33
he said to the driver of his **c**, 1 Kgs 22:34
up in his **c** facing the Syrians, 1 Kgs 22:35
flowed into the bottom of the **c**. 1 Kgs 22:35
And they washed the **c** by the pool of 1 Kgs 22:38
got down from the **c** to meet him and 2 Kgs 5:21
man turned from his **c** to meet you? 2 Kgs 5:26
he and his **c** commanders struck the 2 Kgs 8:21
Then Jehu mounted his **c** and went to 2 Kgs 9:16
ready." And they made ready his **c**. 2 Kgs 9:21
king of Judah set out, each in his **c**, 2 Kgs 9:21
his heart, and he sank in his **c**. 2 Kgs 9:24
they shot him in the **c** at the ascent of 2 Kgs 9:27
carried him in a **c** to Jerusalem, 2 Kgs 9:28
took him up with him into the **c**. 2 Kgs 10:15
LORD." So he had him ride in his **c**. 2 Kgs 10:16
him dead in a **c** from Megiddo and 2 Kgs 23:30
David hamstrung all the **c** horses, 1 Chr 18:4
for the golden **c** of the cherubim 1 Chr 28:18
he stationed in the **c** cities and with 2 Chr 1:14
They imported a **c** from Egypt for 2 Chr 1:17
he stationed in the **c** cities and with 2 Chr 9:25
quickly mounted his **c** to flee to 2 Chr 10:18
he said to the driver of his **c**, 2 Chr 18:33
up in his **c** facing the Syrians 2 Chr 18:34
him and his **c** commanders. 2 Chr 21:9
him out of the **c** and carried him in 2 Chr 35:24
in his second **c** and brought him 2 Chr 35:24
the waters; he makes the clouds his **c**; Ps 104:3
who brings forth **c** and horse, army and Is 43:17
in pieces the **c** and the charioteer; Jer 51:21
wheel, galloping horse and bounding **c**! Na 3:2
on your horses, on your **c** of salvation? Hab 3:8
The first **c** had red horses, the second Zec 6:2
and the fourth **c** dappled horses—all of Zec 6:3
The **c** with the black horses goes toward Zec 6:6
will cut off the **c** from Ephraim and the Zec 9:10
and was returning, seated in his **c**, and Acts 8:28
to Philip, "Go over and join this **c**." Acts 8:29
And he commanded the **c** to stop, and Acts 8:38

CHARIOTEER (1)

I break in pieces the chariot and the **c**; Jer 51:21

CHARIOTEERS (1)

be filled at my table with horses and **c**, Ezk 39:20

CHARIOTS (110)

went up with him both **c** and horsemen. Gn 50:9
took six hundred chosen **c** and all the Ex 14:7
and all the other **c** of Egypt with officers Ex 14:7
Pharaoh's horses and **c** and his Ex 14:9
over Pharaoh and all his host, his **c**, Ex 14:17
I have gotten glory over Pharaoh, his **c**, Ex 14:18
of the sea, all Pharaoh's horses, his **c**, Ex 14:23
back upon the Egyptians, upon their **c**, Ex 14:26
and covered the **c** and the horsemen; Ex 14:28
"Pharaoh's **c** and his host he cast into Ex 15:4
Pharaoh with his **c** and his horsemen Ex 15:19
of Egypt, to their horses and to their **c**, Dt 11:4
and see horses and **c** and an army larger Dt 20:1
seashore, with very many horses and **c**. Jos 11:4
their horses and burn their **c** with fire." Jos 11:6
their horses and burned their **c** with fire. Jos 11:9
who dwell in the plain have **c** of iron, Jos 17:16
though they have **c** of iron, Jos 17:18
your fathers with **c** and horsemen to Jos 24:6
of the plain because they had **c** of iron. Jgs 1:19
for he had 900 **c** of iron and he oppressed Jgs 4:3
river Kishon with his **c** and his troops, Jgs 4:7
Sisera called out all his **c**, 900 chariots Jgs 4:13
called out all his chariots, 900 **c** of iron, Jgs 4:13
Sisera and all his **c** and all his army Jgs 4:15
And Barak pursued the **c** and the army Jgs 4:16
Why tarry the hoofbeats of his **c**?' Jgs 5:28
appoint them to his **c** and to be his 1 Sm 8:11
his horsemen and to run before his **c**. 1 Sm 8:11
of war and the equipment of his **c**. 1 Sm 8:12
thirty thousand **c** and six thousand 1 Sm 13:5
the **c** and the horsemen were close 2 Sm 1:6
horses but left enough for a hundred **c**. 2 Sm 8:4
of the Syrians the men of 700 **c**, 2 Sm 10:18
prepared for himself **c** and horsemen, 1 Kgs 1:5
had 40,000 stalls of horses for his **c**, 1 Kgs 4:26
Solomon had, and the cities for his **c**, 1 Kgs 9:19
gathered together **c** and horsemen. 1 Kgs 10:26
He had 1,400 **c** and 12,000 1 Kgs 10:26
Zimri, commander of half his **c**, 1 Kgs 16:9
were with him, and horses and **c**. 1 Kgs 20:1
out and struck the horses and **c**, 1 Kgs 20:21
the thirty-two captains of his **c**, 1 Kgs 22:31
captains of the **c** saw Jehoshaphat, 1 Kgs 22:32
the captains of the **c** saw that it was 1 Kgs 22:33
c of fire and horses of fire separated 2 Kgs 2:11
The **c** of Israel and its horsemen!" 2 Kgs 2:12
with his horses and **c** and stood at the 2 Kgs 5:9
sent there horses and **c** and a great 2 Kgs 6:14
with horses and **c** was all around 2 Kgs 6:15
full of horses and **c** of fire all around 2 Kgs 6:17
hear the sound of **c** and of horses, 2 Kgs 7:6
Zair with all his **c** and rose by night, 2 Kgs 8:21
and there are with you **c** and horses, 2 Kgs 10:2
horsemen and ten **c** and ten 2 Kgs 13:7
The **c** of Israel and its horsemen!" 2 Kgs 13:14
in Egypt for **c** and for horsemen? 2 Kgs 18:24
'With my many **c** I have gone up 2 Kgs 19:23
And he burned the **c** of the sun with 2 Kgs 23:11
And David took from him 1,000 **c**, 1 Chr 18:4
horses, but left enough for 100 **c**. 1 Chr 18:4
of silver to hire **c** and horsemen from 1 Chr 19:6
They hired 32,000 **c** and the king of 1 Chr 19:7
the men of 7,000 **c** and 40,000 foot 1 Chr 19:18
gathered together **c** and horsemen. 2 Chr 1:14
He had 1,400 **c** and 12,000 horsemen, 2 Chr 1:14
all the cities for his **c** and the cities for 2 Chr 8:6
his officers, the commanders of his **c**, 2 Chr 8:9
had 4,000 stalls for horses and **c**, 2 Chr 9:25
with 1,200 **c** and 60,000 horsemen. 2 Chr 12:3
an army of a million men and 300 **c**, 2 Chr 14:9
with very many **c** and horsemen? 2 Chr 16:8
commanded the captains of his **c**, 2 Chr 18:30
captains of the **c** saw Jehoshaphat, 2 Chr 18:31
the captains of the **c** saw that it was 2 Chr 18:32
with his commanders and all his **c**, 2 Chr 21:9
Some trust in **c** and some in horses, but Ps 20:7
the spear; he burns the **c** with fire. Ps 46:9
The **c** of God are twice ten thousand, Ps 68:17
my love, to a mare among Pharaoh's **c**. Sg 1:9
set me among the **c** of my kinsman, Sg 6:12
with horses, and there is no end to their **c**. Is 2:7
bore the quiver with **c** and horsemen, Is 22:6
Your choicest valleys were full of **c**, and Is 22:7
die, and there shall be your glorious **c**, Is 22:18
who trust in **c** because they are many Is 31:1
trust in Egypt for **c** and for horsemen? Is 36:9
With my many **c** I have gone up the Is 37:24
in fire, and his **c** like the whirlwind, Is 66:15
on horses and in **c** and in litters and on Is 66:20
up like clouds; his **c** like the whirlwind; Jer 4:13
of David, riding in **c** and on horses, Jer 17:25

of David, riding in c and on horses, Jer 22:4
Advance, O horses, and rage, O c! Let the Jer 46:9
of his stallions, at the rushing of his c, Jer 47:3
against her horses and against her c, Jer 50:37
the north with c and wagons and Ezk 23:24
king of kings, with horses and c, Ezk 26:7
of the horsemen and wagons and c, Ezk 26:10
a whirlwind, with c and horsemen, Dn 11:40
As with the rumbling of c, they leap on the Jl 2:5
Harness the steeds to the c, inhabitants Mi 1:13
among you and will destroy your c; Mi 5:10
The c come with flashing metal on the Na 2:3
The c race madly through the streets; Na 2:4
hosts, and I will burn your c in smoke, Na 2:13
and overthrow the c and their riders. Hg 2:22
four c came out from between two Zec 6:1
the noise of many c with horses rushing Rv 9:9
wheat, cattle and sheep, horses and c, Rv 18:13

CHARITY (1)
was full of good works and acts of c. Acts 9:36

CHARM (2)
C is deceitful, and beauty is vain, but Prv 31:30
which you will not know how to c away; Is 47:11

CHARMED (2)
If the serpent bites before it is c, there Eccl 10:11
you serpents, adders that cannot be c, Jer 8:17

CHARMER (2)
or a c or a medium or a wizard or a Dt 18:11
there is no advantage to the c. Eccl 10:11

CHARMERS (1)
not hear the voice of c or of the cunning Ps 58:5

CHARMS (3)
the skillful magician and the expert in c. Is 3:3
of the prostitute, graceful and of deadly c, Na 3:4
her whorings, and peoples with her c. Na 3:4

CHARRED (2)
both ends of it, and the middle of it is c, Ezk 15:4
the fire has consumed it and it is c, Ezk 15:5

CHASE (4)
You shall c your enemies, and they shall Lv 26:7
Five of you shall c a hundred, and a Lv 26:8
a hundred of you shall c ten thousand, Lv 26:8
on every side, and c him at his heels. Jb 18:11

CHASED (10)
out against you and c you as bees do Dt 1:44
How could one have c a thousand, and Dt 32:30
of their men and c them before the gate Jos 7:5
blow at Gibeon and c them by the way Jos 10:10
who struck them and c them as far as Jos 11:8
And Abimelech c him, and he fled Jgs 9:40
Horonite. Therefore I c him from me. Neh 13:28
he will be c away like a vision of the Jb 20:8
c like chaff on the mountains before the Is 17:13
heavens; they c us on the mountains; Lam 4:19

CHASES (1)
to his father and c away his mother is Prv 19:26

CHASING (1)
came back from c the Philistines, 1 Sm 17:53

CHASM (1)
us and you a great c has been fixed, Lk 16:26

CHASTISE (1)
Your evil will c you, and your apostasy Jer 2:19

CHASTISEMENT (2)
upon him was the c that brought us Is 53:5
For the c of the daughter of my people Lam 4:6

CHASTISES (1)
and c every son whom he receives." Heb 12:6

CHEAT (3)
Only let not Pharaoh c again by not Ex 8:29
of those who c me surrounds me, Ps 49:5
Cursed be the c who has a male in his Mal 1:14

CHEATED (2)
For he has c me these two times. Gn 27:36
yet your father has c me and changed Gn 31:7

CHEBAR (8)
as I was among the exiles by the C canal, Ezk 1:1
land of the Chaldeans by the C canal, Ezk 1:3
who were dwelling by the C canal, Ezk 3:15
the glory that I had seen by the C canal, Ezk 3:23
creatures that I saw by the C canal. Ezk 10:15
the God of Israel by the C canal; Ezk 10:20
appearance I had seen by the C canal. Ezk 10:22
vision that I had seen by the C canal. Ezk 43:3

CHECKED (1)
eyes the disease is c and the disease has Lv 13:5

CHECKER (3)
an ephod, a robe, a coat of c work, Ex 28:4
weave the coat in c work of fine linen, Ex 28:39
were lattices of c work with wreaths 1 Kgs 7:17

CHEDORLAOMER (5)
Arioch king of Ellasar, C king of Elam, Gn 14:1
Twelve years they had served C, but in Gn 14:4
In the fourteenth year C and the kings Gn 14:5
with C king of Elam, Tidal king of Gn 14:9
from the defeat of C and the kings who Gn 14:17

CHEEK (8)
struck Micaiah on the c and said, 1 Kgs 22:24
struck Micaiah on the c and said, 2 Chr 18:23
they have struck me insolently on the c; Jb 16:10
For you strike all my enemies on the c; Ps 3:7
let him give his c to the one who Lam 3:30
rod they strike the judge of Israel on the c. Mi 5:1
But if anyone slaps you on the right c, Mt 5:39
To one who strikes you on the c, offer Lk 6:29

CHEEKS (7)
shoulder and the two c and the stomach. Dt 18:3
Your c are lovely with ornaments, your Sg 1:10
Your c are like halves of a pomegranate Sg 4:3
His c are like beds of spices, mounds of Sg 5:13
Your c are like halves of a pomegranate Sg 6:7
and my c to those who pull out the beard; Is 50:6
bitterly in the night, with tears on her c; Lam 1:2

CHEER (5)
will put off my sad face, and be of good c,' Jb 9:27
leave me alone, that I may find a little c Jb 10:20
are many, your consolations c my soul. Ps 94:19
my heart how to c my body with wine Eccl 2:3
and let your heart c you in the days of Eccl 11:9

CHEERED (1)
so that I too may be c by news of you. Phil 2:19

CHEERFUL (6)
and eat bread and let your heart be c; 1 Kgs 21:7
A glad heart makes a c face, but by Prv 15:13
but the c of heart has a continual Prv 15:15
seasons of joy and gladness and c feasts. Zec 8:19
compulsion, for God loves a c giver. 2 Cor 9:7
suffering? Let him pray. Is anyone c? Jas 5:13

CHEERFULLY (2)
And Agag came to him c. 1 Sm 15:32
over this nation, I c make my defense. Acts 24:10

CHEERFULNESS (1)
the one who does acts of mercy, with c. Rom 12:8

CHEERS (2)
I leave my wine that c God and men and Jgs 9:13
no songs are sung, no c are raised; Is 16:10

CHEESE (2)
curds and sheep and c from the herd, 2 Sm 17:29
me out like milk and curdle me like c? Jb 10:10

CHEESES (1)
take these ten c to the commander 1 Sm 17:18

CHELAL (1)
Adna, C, Benaiah, Maaseiah, Ezr 10:30

CHELUB (2)
C, the brother of Shuhah, fathered 1 Chr 4:11
tilling the soil was Ezri the son of C; 1 Chr 27:26

CHELUBAI (1)
born to him: Jerahmeel, Ram, and C. 1 Chr 2:9

CHELUHI (1)
Benaiah, Bedeiah, C, Ezr 10:35

CHEMOSH (8)
Moab! You are undone, O people of C! Nm 21:29
you not possess what C your god gives Jgs 11:24
high place for C the abomination of 1 Kgs 11:7
of the Sidonians, C the god of Moab, 1 Kgs 11:33
and for C the abomination of Moab, 2 Kgs 23:13
and C shall go into exile with his priests Jer 48:7
Then Moab shall be ashamed of C, as Jer 48:13
The people of C are undone, for your Jer 48:46

CHENAANAH (5)
the son of C made for himself 1 Kgs 22:11
the son of C came near and 1 Kgs 22:24
Jeush, Benjamin, Ehud, C, Zethan, 1 Chr 7:10
the son of C made for himself 2 Chr 18:10
the son of C came near and 2 Chr 18:23

CHENANI (1)
Bunni, Sherebiah, Bani, and C; Neh 9:4

CHENANIAH (3)
C, leader of the Levites in music, 1 Chr 15:22
and the singers and C the leader of 1 Chr 15:27
C and his sons were appointed to 1 Chr 26:29

CHEPHAR-AMMONI (1)
C, Ophni, Geba—twelve cities with Jos 18:24

CHEPHIRAH (4)
their cities were Gibeon, C, Beeroth, Jos 9:17
Mizpeh, C, Mozah, Jos 18:26
sons of Kiriath-arim, C, and Beeroth, Ezr 2:25
men of Kiriath-jearim, C, and Beeroth, Neh 7:29

CHERAN (2)
Hemdan, Eshban, Ithran, and C. Gn 36:26
Hemdan, Eshban, Ithran, and C. 1 Chr 1:41

CHERETHITES (10)
the Negeb of the C and against that 1 Sm 30:14
was over the C and the Pelethites, 2 Sm 8:18
passed by him, and all the C, 2 Sm 15:18
men and the C and the Pelethites, 2 Sm 20:7
command of the C and the 2 Sm 20:23
and the C and the Pelethites went 1 Kgs 1:38
and the C and the Pelethites. 1 Kgs 1:44
was over the C and the Pelethites; 1 Chr 18:17
I will cut off the C and destroy the rest Ezk 25:16
of the seacoast, you nation of the C! Zep 2:5

CHERISH (2)
"The godless in heart c anger; they do Jb 36:13
they have forsaken the LORD to c Hos 4:10

CHERISHED (2)
If I had c iniquity in my heart, the Lord Ps 66:18
Because you c perpetual enmity and Ezk 35:5

CHERISHES (1)
his own flesh, but nourishes and c it, Eph 5:29

CHERITH (2)
and hide yourself by the brook C, 1 Kgs 17:3
lived by the brook C that is east of 1 Kgs 17:5

CHERUB (27)
Make one c on the one end, and one Ex 25:19
the one end, and one c on the other end. Ex 25:19
one c on the one end, and one cherub on Ex 37:8
the one end, and one c on the other end. Ex 37:8
He rode on a c and flew; he was seen 2 Sm 22:11
was the length of one wing of the c, 1 Kgs 6:24
the length of the other wing of the c; 1 Kgs 6:24
The other c also measured ten cubits; 1 Kgs 6:25
The height of one c was ten cubits, 1 Kgs 6:26
cubits, and so was that of the other c. 1 Kgs 6:26
wing of the other c touched the other 1 Kgs 6:27
touched the wing of the other c; 2 Chr 3:11
and of this c, one wing, of five cubits, 2 Chr 3:12
was joined to the wing of the first c. 2 Chr 3:12
from Tel-melah, Tel-harsha, C, Addan, Ezr 2:59
Tel-melah, Tel-harsha, C, Addon, Neh 7:61
He rode on a c and flew; he came swiftly Ps 18:10
gone up from the c on which it rested Ezk 9:3
went up from the c to the threshold of Ezk 10:4
And a c stretched out his hand from Ezk 10:7
beside the cherubim, one beside each c, Ezk 10:9
the first face was the face of the c, and Ezk 10:14
You were an anointed guardian c. I Ezk 28:14
and I destroyed you, O guardian c, Ezk 28:16
a palm tree between c and cherub. Ezk 41:18
a palm tree between cherub and c. Ezk 41:18
and cherub. Every c had two faces: Ezk 41:18

CHERUBIM (67)
Eden he placed the c and a flaming Gn 3:24
And you shall make two c of gold; of Ex 25:18
shall you make the c on its two ends. Ex 25:19
The c shall spread out their wings Ex 25:20
mercy seat shall the faces of the c be. Ex 25:20
from between the two c that are on the Ex 25:22
make them with c skillfully worked into Ex 26:1
be made with c skillfully worked into Ex 26:31
scarlet yarns, with c skillfully worked. Ex 36:8
with c skillfully worked into it he made Ex 36:35
And he made two c of gold. He made Ex 37:7
mercy seat he made the c on its two ends. Ex 37:8
The c spread out their wings above, Ex 37:9
the mercy seat were the faces of the c. Ex 37:9
the testimony, from between the two c; Nm 7:89
of hosts, who is enthroned on the c. 1 Sm 4:4
of hosts who sits enthroned on the c. 2 Sm 6:2
he made two c of olivewood, 1 Kgs 6:23
both c had the same measure and the 1 Kgs 6:25
He put the c in the innermost part of 1 Kgs 6:27
the wings of the c were spread out so 1 Kgs 6:27
And he overlaid the c with gold. 1 Kgs 6:28
engraved figures of c and palm trees 1 Kgs 6:29
doors of olivewood with carvings of c, 1 Kgs 6:32
spread gold on the c and on the palm 1 Kgs 6:32
On them he carved c and palm trees 1 Kgs 6:35
in the frames were lions, oxen, and c. 1 Kgs 7:29
stays and on its panels, he carved c, 1 Kgs 7:36
Place, underneath the wings of the c. 1 Kgs 8:6
For the c spread out their wings over 1 Kgs 8:7
so that the c overshadowed the ark and 1 Kgs 8:7
Israel, who is enthroned above the c, 2 Kgs 19:15
LORD who sits enthroned above the c. 1 Chr 13:6

chariot of the **c** that spread their 1 Chr 28:18
doors—and he carved **c** on the walls. 2 Chr 3:7
Place he made two **c** of wood and 2 Chr 3:10
wings of the **c** together extended 2 Chr 3:11
wings of these **c** extended twenty 2 Chr 3:13
The **c** stood on their feet, facing the 2 Chr 3:13
and fine linen, and he worked **c** on it. 2 Chr 3:14
Place, underneath the wings of the **c**. 2 Chr 5:7
The **c** spread out their wings over the 2 Chr 5:8
so that the **c** made a covering above 2 Chr 5:8
You who are enthroned upon the **c**, Ps 80:1
He sits enthroned upon the **c**; let the Ps 99:1
of Israel, who is enthroned above the **c**, Is 37:16
the heads of the **c** there appeared above Ezk 10:1
the whirling wheels underneath the **c**. Ezk 10:2
with burning coals from between the **c**, Ezk 10:2
Now the **c** were standing on the south Ezk 10:3
of the wings of the **c** was heard as far as Ezk 10:5
from between the **c**," he went in and Ezk 10:6
hand from between the **c** to the fire that Ezk 10:7
to the fire that was between the **c**, Ezk 10:7
The **c** appeared to have the form of a Ezk 10:8
there were four wheels beside the **c**, Ezk 10:9
And the **c** mounted up. These were the Ezk 10:15
And when the **c** went, the wheels went Ezk 10:16
And when the **c** lifted up their wings Ezk 10:16
of the house, and stood over the **c**. Ezk 10:18
And the **c** lifted up their wings and Ezk 10:19
canal; and I knew that they were **c**. Ezk 10:20
Then the **c** lifted up their wings, with Ezk 11:22
It was carved of **c** and palm trees, a Ezk 41:18
the door, **c** and palm trees were carved; Ezk 41:20
the nave were carved **c** and palm trees, Ezk 41:25
it were the **c** of glory overshadowing Heb 9:5

CHESALON (1)
shoulder of Mount Jearim (that is, **C**), Jos 15:10

CHESED (1)
C, Hazo, Pildash, Jidlaph, and Bethuel." Gn 22:22

CHESIL (1)
Eltolad, **C**, Hormah, Jos 15:30

CHEST (10)
the priest took a **c** and bored a hole 2 Kgs 12:9
there was much money in the **c**, 2 Kgs 12:10
and they made a **c** and set it outside 2 Chr 24:8
dropped it into the **c** until they had 2 Chr 24:10
And whenever the **c** was brought to 2 Chr 24:11
come and empty the **c** and take it 2 Chr 24:11
I prayed with head bowed on my **c**. Ps 35:13
fire next to his **c** and his clothes not Prv 6:27
was of fine gold, its **c** and arms of silver, Dn 2:32
and with a golden sash around his **c**. Rv 1:13

CHESTS (1)
linen, with golden sashes around their **c**. Rv 15:6

CHESULLOTH (1)
territory included Jezreel, **C**, Shunem, Jos 19:18

CHEW (6)
among those that **c** the cud or part the Lv 11:4
is cloven-footed but does not **c** the cud, Lv 11:7
cloven-footed or does not **c** the cud is Lv 11:26
Yet of those that **c** the cud or have the Dt 14:7
because they **c** the cud but do not part Dt 14:7
it parts the hoof but does not **c** the cud, Dt 14:8

CHEWS (5)
hoof and is cloven-footed and **c** the cud, Lv 11:3
because it **c** the cud but does not part the Lv 11:4
because it **c** the cud but does not part the Lv 11:5
because it **c** the cud but does not part the Lv 11:6
has the hoof cloven in two and **c** the cud, Dt 14:6

CHEZIB (1)
Judah was in **C** when she bore him. Gn 38:5

CHIDE (1)
He will not always **c**, nor will he keep Ps 103:9

CHIDON (1)
they came to the threshing floor of **C**, 1 Chr 13:9

CHIEF (213)
Horites, **c** by chief in the land of Seir. Gn 36:30
Horites, chief by **c** in the land of Seir. Gn 36:30
the **c** cupbearer and the chief baker, Gn 40:2
the chief cupbearer and the **c** baker, Gn 40:2
So the **c** cupbearer told his dream to Gn 40:9
When the **c** baker saw that the Gn 40:16
the head of the **c** cupbearer and the Gn 40:20
the head of the **c** baker among his Gn 40:20
He restored the **c** cupbearer to his Gn 40:21
But he hanged the **c** baker, as Joseph Gn 40:22
Yet the **c** cupbearer did not remember Gn 40:23
Then the **c** cupbearer said to Pharaoh, Gn 41:9
put me and the **c** baker in custody in Gn 41:10
lay his hand on the **c** men of the people Ex 24:11
priest who is **c** among his brothers, Lv 21:10
the **c** of the people of Judah being Nm 2:3
the **c** of the people of Issachar being Nm 2:5
the **c** of the people of Zebulun being Nm 2:7
the **c** of the people of Reuben being Nm 2:10
the **c** of the people of Simeon being Nm 2:12
the **c** of the people of Gad being Nm 2:14
the **c** of the people of Ephraim being Nm 2:18
the **c** of the people of Manasseh being Nm 2:20
the **c** of the people of Benjamin being Nm 2:22
the **c** of the people of Dan being Ahiezer Nm 2:25
the **c** of the people of Asher being Nm 2:27
the **c** of the people of Naphtali being Nm 2:29
the son of Lael as **c** of the fathers' house Nm 3:24
son of Uzziel as **c** of the fathers' house Nm 3:30
the priest was to be **c** over the chiefs of Nm 3:32
And the **c** of the fathers' house of the Nm 3:35
offer their offerings, one **c** each day, Nm 7:11
the son of Zuar, the **c** of Issachar, Nm 7:18
of Helon, the **c** of the people of Zebulun: Nm 7:24
Shedeur, the **c** of the people of Reuben: Nm 7:30
the **c** of the people of Simeon: Nm 7:36
son of Deuel, the **c** of the people of Gad: Nm 7:42
the **c** of the people of Ephraim: Nm 7:48
the **c** of the people of Manasseh: Nm 7:54
the **c** of the people of Benjamin: Nm 7:60
the **c** of the people of Dan: Nm 7:66
of Ochran, the **c** of the people of Asher: Nm 7:72
of Enan, the **c** of the people of Naphtali: Nm 7:78
a man, every one a **c** among them." Nm 13:2
chiefs gave him staffs, one for each **c**, Nm 17:6
c of a father's house belonging to the Nm 25:14
the daughter of the **c** of Midian, Nm 25:18
You shall take one **c** from every tribe Nm 34:18
Of the tribe of the people of Dan a **c**, Nm 34:22
tribe of the people of Manasseh a **c**, Nm 34:23
the tribe of the people of Ephraim a **c**, Nm 34:24
the tribe of the people of Zebulun a **c**, Nm 34:25
the tribe of the people of Issachar a **c**, Nm 34:26
of the tribe of the people of Asher a **c**, Nm 34:27
the tribe of the people of Naphtali a **c**, Nm 34:28
the Edomite, the **c** of Saul's herdsmen. 1 Sm 21:7
Tahchemonite; he was **c** of the three. 2 Sm 23:8
three of the thirty **c** men went down 2 Sm 23:13
son of Zeruiah, was **c** of the thirty. 2 Sm 23:18
Solomon's 3,300 **c** officers who 1 Kgs 5:16
These were the **c** officers who were 1 Kgs 9:23
and the **c** men of the land he took 2 Kgs 24:15
took Seraiah the **c** priest and 2 Kgs 25:18
his brothers and a **c** came from him, 1 Chr 5:2
into exile; he was a **c** of the Reubenites. 1 Chr 5:6
their generations was recorded: the **c**, 1 Chr 5:7
Joel the **c**, Shapham the second, 1 Chr 5:12
Guni, was **c** in their fathers' houses, 1 Chr 5:15
Isshiah, all five of them were **c** men. 1 Chr 7:3
to their generations, **c** men. 1 Chr 8:28
the **c** officer of the house of God; 1 Chr 9:11
their kinsmen (Shallum was the **c**); 1 Chr 9:17
of Eleazar was the **c** officer over them 1 Chr 9:20
for the four **c** gatekeepers, who were 1 Chr 9:26
first shall be **c** and commander." 1 Chr 11:6
went up first, so he became **c**. 1 Chr 11:6
a Hachmonite, was **c** of the three. 1 Chr 11:11
of the thirty **c** men went down 1 Chr 11:15
brother of Joab, was **c** of the thirty. 1 Chr 11:20
The **c** was Ahiezer, then Joash, both 1 Chr 12:3
Ezer the **c**, Obadiah second, Eliab 1 Chr 12:9
clothed Amasai, **c** of the thirty, 1 Chr 12:18
of the sons of Kohath, Uriel the **c**, 1 Chr 15:5
of the sons of Merari, Asaiah the **c**, 1 Chr 15:6
of the sons of Gershom, Joel the **c**, 1 Chr 15:7
sons of Elizaphan, Shemaiah the **c**, 1 Chr 15:8
of the sons of Hebron, Eliel the **c**, 1 Chr 15:9
sons of Uzziel, Amminadab the **c**, 1 Chr 15:10
Asaph was the **c**, and second to him 1 Chr 16:5
sons were the **c** officials in the 1 Chr 18:17
Jehiel the **c**, and Zetham, and Joel, 1 Chr 23:8
Jahath was the **c**, and Zizah the 1 Chr 23:11
sons of Gershom: Shebuel the **c**. 1 Chr 23:16
The sons of Eliezer: Rehabiah the **c**. 1 Chr 23:17
The sons of Izhar: Shelomith the **c**. 1 Chr 23:18
Jeriah the **c**, Amariah the second, 1 Chr 23:19
Micah the **c** and Isshiah the second. 1 Chr 23:20
Since more **c** men were found among 1 Chr 24:4
the sons of Rehabiah, Isshiah the **c**. 1 Chr 24:21
Jeriah the **c**, Amariah the second, 1 Chr 24:23
Shimri the **c** (for though he was not 1 Chr 26:10
firstborn, his father made him **c**), 1 Chr 26:10
corresponding to their **c** men, 1 Chr 26:12
was **c** officer in charge of the 1 Chr 26:24
Jerijah was **c** of the Hebronites of 1 Chr 26:31
of Perez and was **c** of all the 1 Chr 27:3
the son of Jehoiada the **c** priest; 1 Chr 27:5
the son of Zichri was **c** officer; 1 Chr 27:16
And these were the **c** officers of King 2 Chr 8:10
of Maacah as **c** prince among his 2 Chr 11:22
Amariah the **c** priest is over you in 2 Chr 19:11
summoned Jehoiada the **c** and said to 2 Chr 24:6
officer of the **c** priest would come 2 Chr 24:11
And Azariah the **c** priest and all the 2 Chr 26:20
Azariah the **c** priest, who was of the 2 Chr 31:10
The **c** officer in charge of them was 2 Chr 31:12
king and Azariah the **c** officer of the 2 Chr 31:13
the **c** officers of the house of God, 2 Chr 35:8
son of Eleazar, son of Aaron the **c** priest— Ezr 7:5
weigh them before the **c** priests and the Ezr 8:29
of the officials and **c** men has been Ezr 9:2
I chose their way and sat as **c**, and I Jb 29:25
Without having any **c**, officer, or ruler, Prv 6:7
myrrh and aloes, with all **c** spices— Sg 4:14
In the year that the commander in **c**, who Is 20:1
who was **c** officer in the house of the Jer 20:1
and raise shouts for the **c** of the nations; Jer 31:7
and all the **c** officers of the king of Jer 39:13
family, one of the **c** officers of the king, Jer 41:1
of the guard took Seraiah the **c** priest, Jer 52:24
him under oath (the **c** men of the land Ezk 17:13
the **c** prince of Meshech and Tubal, Ezk 38:2
O Gog, **c** prince of Meshech and Tubal. Ezk 38:3
O Gog, **c** prince of Meshech and Tubal. Ezk 39:1
commanded Ashpenaz, his **c** eunuch, Dn 1:3
And the **c** of the eunuchs gave them Dn 1:7
Therefore he asked the **c** of the eunuchs Dn 1:8
in the sight of the **c** of the eunuchs, Dn 1:9
and the **c** of the eunuchs said to Daniel, Dn 1:10
the steward whom the **c** of the eunuchs Dn 1:11
the **c** of the eunuchs brought them in Dn 1:18
of Babylon and **c** prefect over all Dn 2:48
"O Belteshazzar, **c** of the magicians, Dn 4:9
king—made him **c** of the magicians, Dn 5:11
days, but Michael, one of the **c** princes, Dn 10:13
assembling all the **c** priests and scribes Mt 2:4
the elders and **c** priests and scribes, Mt 16:21
over to the **c** priests and scribes, Mt 20:18
But when the **c** priests and the scribes Mt 21:15
the **c** priests and the elders of the people Mt 21:23
When the **c** priests and the Pharisees Mt 21:45
Then the **c** priests and the elders of the Mt 26:3
was Judas Iscariot, went to the **c** priests Mt 26:14
from the **c** priests and the elders of the Mt 26:47
Now the **c** priests and the whole Mt 26:59
all the **c** priests and the elders of the Mt 27:1
of silver to the **c** priests and the elders, Mt 27:3
But the **c** priests, taking the pieces of Mt 27:6
was accused by the **c** priests and elders, Mt 27:12
Now the **c** priests and the elders Mt 27:20
So also the **c** priests, with the scribes Mt 27:41
the **c** priests and the Pharisees gathered Mt 27:62
city and told the **c** priests all that had Mt 28:11
the elders and the **c** priests and the Mk 8:31
delivered over to the **c** priests and the Mk 10:33
And the **c** priests and the scribes heard Mk 11:18
the **c** priests and the scribes and the Mk 11:27
And the **c** priests and the scribes were Mk 14:1
went to the **c** priests in order to betray Mk 14:10
from the **c** priests and the scribes and Mk 14:43
And all the **c** priests and the elders and Mk 14:53
Now the **c** priests and the whole Mk 14:55
the **c** priests held a consultation with Mk 15:1
And the **c** priests accused him of many Mk 15:3
of envy that the **c** priests had delivered Mk 15:10
But the **c** priests stirred up the crowd Mk 15:11
So also the **c** priests with the scribes Mk 15:31
by the elders and **c** priests and scribes, Lk 9:22
He was a **c** tax collector and was rich. Lk 19:2
The **c** priests and the scribes and the Lk 19:47
the **c** priests and the scribes with the Lk 20:1
The scribes and the **c** priests sought to Lk 20:19
And the **c** priests and the scribes were Lk 22:2
conferred with the **c** priests and officers Lk 22:4
Jesus said to the **c** priests and officers of Lk 22:52
together, both **c** priests and scribes. Lk 22:66
Pilate said to the **c** priests and the Lk 23:4
The **c** priests and the scribes stood by, Lk 23:10
called together the **c** priests and the Lk 23:13
and how our **c** priests and rulers Lk 24:20
and the **c** priests and Pharisees sent Jn 7:32
then came to the **c** priests and Pharisees, Jn 7:45
So the **c** priests and the Pharisees Jn 11:47
Now the **c** priests and the Pharisees had Jn 11:57
So the **c** priests made plans to put Jn 12:10
some officers from the **c** priests and the Jn 18:3
nation and the **c** priests have delivered Jn 18:35
When the **c** priests and the officers saw Jn 19:6
your King?" The **c** priests answered, Jn 19:15
So the **c** priests of the Jews said to Pilate, Jn 19:21
and reported what the **c** priests and the Acts 4:23
the temple and the **c** priests heard these Acts 5:24
authority from the **c** priests to bind Acts 9:14
them bound before the **c** priests?" Acts 9:21
because he was the **c** speaker. Acts 14:12

and commanded the **c** priests and all — Acts 22:30
They went to the **c** priests and elders — Acts 23:14
And the **c** priests and the principal — Acts 25:2
the **c** priests and the elders of the Jews — Acts 25:15
authority from the **c** priests, — Acts 26:10
and commission of the **c** priests. — Acts 26:12
lands belonging to the **c** man of the — Acts 28:7
And when the **c** Shepherd appears, you — 1 Pt 5:4

CHIEFS (62)
These are the **c** of the sons of Esau. The — Gn 36:15
the firstborn of Esau: the **c** Teman, — Gn 36:15
these are the **c** of Eliphaz in the land of — Gn 36:16
of Reuel, Esau's son: the **c** Nahath, — Gn 36:17
these are the **c** of Reuel in the land of — Gn 36:17
Oholibamah, Esau's wife: the **c** Jeush, — Gn 36:18
these are the **c** born of Oholibamah — Gn 36:18
(that is, Edom), and these are their **c**. — Gn 36:19
Dishan; these are the **c** of the Horites, — Gn 36:21
These are the **c** of the Horites: the — Gn 36:29
the chiefs of the Horites: the **c** Lotan, — Gn 36:29
Dishan; these are the **c** of the Horites, — Gn 36:30
These are the names of the **c** of Esau, — Gn 36:40
places, by their names: the **c** Timna, — Gn 36:40
these are the **c** of Edom (that is, Esau, — Gn 36:43
Now are the **c** of Edom dismayed; — Ex 15:15
men over the people as **c** of thousands, — Ex 18:21
heads over the people, **c** of thousands, — Ex 18:25
the **c** of their ancestral tribes, — Nm 1:16
listed with the help of the **c** of Israel, — Nm 1:44
was to be chief over the **c** of the Levites, — Nm 3:32
Aaron and the **c** of the congregation — Nm 4:34
and Aaron and the **c** of Israel listed, — Nm 4:46
the **c** of Israel, heads of their fathers' — Nm 7:2
houses, who were the **c** of the tribes, — Nm 7:2
oxen, a wagon for every two of the **c**, — Nm 7:3
And the **c** offered offerings for the — Nm 7:10
and the **c** offered their offering before — Nm 7:10
it was anointed, from the **c** of Israel: — Nm 7:84
But if they blow only one, then the **c**, — Nm 10:4
of Israel, 250 **c** of the congregation, — Nm 16:2
from all their **c** according to their — Nm 17:2
Israel. And all their **c** gave him staffs, — Nm 17:6
"Take all the **c** of the people and hang — Nm 25:4
priest and before the **c** and all the — Nm 27:2
and all the **c** of the congregation — Nm 31:13
priest and to the **c** of the congregation, — Nm 32:2
spoke before Moses and before the **c**, — Nm 36:1
Israel and said to the **c** of the men of — Jos 10:24
and with him ten **c**, one from each of — Jos 22:14
the priest and the **c** of the congregation, — Jos 22:30
the son of Eleazar the priest, and the **c**, — Jos 22:32
And the **c** of all the people, of all the — Jgs 20:2
The **c** of Edom were: chiefs Timna, — 1 Chr 1:51
Edom were: **c** Timna, Alvah, Jetheth, — 1 Chr 1:51
and Iram; these are the **c** of Edom. — 1 Chr 1:54
mighty warriors, **c** of the princes. — 1 Chr 7:40
these are the **c** of David's mighty — 1 Chr 11:10
c of thousands in Manasseh. — 1 Chr 12:20
know what Israel ought to do, 200 **c**, — 1 Chr 12:32
also commanded the **c** of the Levites — 1 Chr 15:16
David and the **c** of the service also set — 1 Chr 25:1
Certain **c** also of the men of — 2 Chr 28:12
Jeiel and Jozabad, the **c** of the Levites, — 2 Chr 35:9
The **c** of the people: Parosh, — Neh 10:14
These are the **c** of the province who — Neh 11:3
and Jozabad, of the **c** of the Levites, — Neh 11:16
These were the **c** of the priests and of — Neh 12:7
And the **c** of the Levites: Hashabiah, — Neh 12:24
understanding from the **c** of the people — Jb 12:24
he will shatter **c** over the wide earth. — Ps 110:6
The mighty **c** shall speak of them, — Ezk 32:21

CHILD (166)
Now Sarai was barren; she had no **c**. — Gn 11:30
"Shall a **c** be born to a man who is a — Gn 17:17
who is ninety years old, bear a **c**?" — Gn 17:17
laugh and say, 'Shall I indeed bear a **c**, — Gn 18:13
And the **c** grew and was weaned. And — Gn 21:8
it on her shoulder, along with the **c**, — Gn 21:14
she put the **c** under one of the bushes. — Gn 21:15
on the death of the **c**." And as she sat — Gn 21:16
a young brother, the **c** of his old age. — Gn 44:20
and when she saw that he was a fine **c**, — Ex 2:2
She put the **c** in it and placed it among the — Ex 2:3
When she opened it, she saw the **c**, and — Ex 2:6
Hebrew women to nurse the **c** for you?" — Ex 2:7
"Take this **c** away and nurse him for me, — Ex 2:9
So the woman took the **c** and nursed him. — Ex 2:9
When the **c** grew up, she brought him to — Ex 2:10
not mistreat any widow or fatherless **c**. — Ex 22:22
a woman conceives and bears a male **c**, — Lv 12:2
But if she bears a female **c**, then she — Lv 12:5
This is the law for her who bears a **c**, — Lv 12:7
divorced and has no **c** and returns to — Lv 22:13
as a nurse carries a nursing **c**,' — Nm 11:12
the nursing **c** with the man of gray — Dt 32:25
She was his only **c**; besides her he had — Jgs 11:34
for the **c** shall be a Nazirite to God from — Jgs 13:5
for the **c** shall be a Nazirite to God from — Jgs 13:7
are to do with the **c** who will be born." — Jgs 13:8
Then Naomi took the **c** and laid him on — Ru 4:16
husband, "As soon as the **c** is weaned, — 1 Sm 1:22
LORD at Shiloh. And the **c** was young. — 1 Sm 1:24
the bull, and they brought the **c** to Eli. — 1 Sm 1:25
For this **c** I prayed, and the LORD has — 1 Sm 1:27
And she named the **c** Ichabod, saying, — 1 Sm 4:21
both man and woman, **c** and infant, — 1 Sm 15:3
both man and woman, **c** and infant, — 1 Sm 22:19
of Saul had no **c** to the day of — 2 Sm 6:23
the **c** who is born to you shall die." — 2 Sm 12:14
LORD afflicted the **c** that Uriah's wife — 2 Sm 12:15
sought God on behalf of the **c**. — 2 Sm 12:16
On the seventh day the **c** died. And — 2 Sm 12:18
afraid to tell him that the **c** was dead, — 2 Sm 12:18
"Behold, while the **c** was yet alive, — 2 Sm 12:18
then can we say to him the **c** is dead? — 2 Sm 12:18
understood that the **c** was dead. — 2 Sm 12:19
servants, "Is the **c** dead?" They said, — 2 Sm 12:19
and wept for the **c** while he was alive; — 2 Sm 12:21
but when the **c** died, you arose and — 2 Sm 12:21
He said, "While the **c** was still alive, I — 2 Sm 12:22
gracious to me, that the **c** may live?' — 2 Sm 12:22
my father, although I am but a little **c**. — 1 Kgs 3:7
I gave birth to a **c** while she was in — 1 Kgs 3:17
I rose in the morning to nurse my **c**, — 1 Kgs 3:21
he was not the **c** that I had borne." — 1 Kgs 3:21
said, "No, the living **c** is mine, — 1 Kgs 3:22
and the dead **c** is yours." The first — 1 Kgs 3:22
first said, "No, the dead **c** is yours, — 1 Kgs 3:22
and the living **c** is mine." Thus they — 1 Kgs 3:22
king said, "Divide the living **c** in two, — 1 Kgs 3:25
"Oh, my lord, give her the living **c**, — 1 Kgs 3:26
"Give the living **c** to the first woman, — 1 Kgs 3:27
servants, Hadad still being a little **c**. — 1 Kgs 11:17
tell you what shall happen to the **c**." — 1 Kgs 14:3
feet enter the city, the **c** shall die. — 1 Kgs 14:12
threshold of the house, the **c** died. — 1 Kgs 14:17
himself upon the **c** three times and — 1 Kgs 17:21
the life of the **c** came into him — 1 Kgs 17:22
Elijah took the **c** and brought him — 1 Kgs 17:23
When the **c** had grown, he went out — 2 Kgs 4:18
mother, the **c** sat on her lap till noon, — 2 Kgs 4:20
well with the **c**?'" And she answered, — 2 Kgs 4:26
And lay my staff on the face of the **c**." — 2 Kgs 4:29
Then the mother of the **c** said, "As the — 2 Kgs 4:30
and laid the staff on the face of the **c**, — 2 Kgs 4:31
told him, "The **c** has not awakened." — 2 Kgs 4:31
he saw the **c** lying dead on his bed. — 2 Kgs 4:32
Then he went up and lay on the **c**, — 2 Kgs 4:34
him, the flesh of the **c** became warm. — 2 Kgs 4:34
The **c** sneezed seven times, and the — 2 Kgs 4:35
times, and the **c** opened his eyes. — 2 Kgs 4:35
was restored like the flesh of a little **c**, — 2 Kgs 5:14
Or why was I not as a hidden stillborn **c**, — Jb 3:16
snatch the fatherless **c** from the breast, — Jb 24:9
like the stillborn **c** who never sees the — Ps 58:8
soul, like a weaned **c** with its mother; — Ps 131:2
like a weaned **c** is my soul within me. — Ps 131:2
Even a **c** makes himself known by his — Prv 20:11
Train up a **c** in the way he should go; — Prv 22:6
Folly is bound up in the heart of a **c**, — Prv 22:15
Do not withhold discipline from a **c**; if — Prv 23:13
but a **c** left to himself brings shame to — Prv 29:15
I say that a stillborn **c** is better off than — Eccl 6:3
to you, O land, when your king is a **c**, — Eccl 10:16
bones in the womb of a woman with **c**, — Eccl 11:5
For to us a **c** is born, to us a son is given; — Is 9:6
be so few that a **c** can write them down. — Is 10:19
together; and a little **c** shall lead them. — Is 11:6
The nursing **c** shall play over the hole of — Is 11:8
and the weaned **c** shall put his hand on — Is 11:8
"Can a woman forget her nursing **c**, — Is 49:15
as of one giving birth to her first **c**, — Jer 4:31
Ask now, and see, can a man bear a **c**? — Jer 30:6
my dear son? Is he my darling **c**? — Jer 31:20
you man and woman, infant and **c**, — Jer 44:7
When Israel was a **c**, I loved him, and — Hos 11:1
for him, as one mourns for an only **c**, — Zec 12:10
found to be with **c** from the Holy Spirit. — Mt 1:18
"Go and search diligently for the **c**, — Mt 2:8
to rest over the place where the **c** was. — Mt 2:9
house they saw the **c** with Mary his — Mt 2:11
said, "Rise, take the **c** and his mother, — Mt 2:13
for Herod is about to search for the **c**, — Mt 2:13
rose and took the **c** and his mother by — Mt 2:14
take the **c** and his mother and go to the — Mt 2:20
rose and took the **c** and his mother and — Mt 2:21
over to death, and the father his **c**, — Mt 10:21
And calling to him a **c**, he put him in — Mt 18:2
himself like this **c** is the greatest — Mt 18:4
receives one such **c** in my name — Mt 18:5
twice as much a **c** of hell as yourselves. — Mt 23:15
The **c** is not dead but sleeping." — Mk 5:39
with him and went in where the **c** was. — Mk 5:40
home and found the **c** lying in bed and — Mk 7:30
the father of the **c** cried out and said, — Mk 9:24
And he took a **c** and put him in the — Mk 9:36
receives one such **c** in my name — Mk 9:37
of God like a **c** shall not enter it." — Mk 10:15
dies and leaves a wife, but leaves no **c**, — Mk 12:19
over to death, and the father his **c**, — Mk 13:12
But they had no **c**, because Elizabeth was — Lk 1:7
therefore the **c** to be born will be called — Lk 1:35
day they came to circumcise the **c**. — Lk 1:59
"What then will this **c** be?" For the — Lk 1:66
c, will be called the prophet of the Most — Lk 1:76
And the **c** grew and became strong in — Lk 1:80
with Mary, his betrothed, who was with **c**. — Lk 2:5
had been told them concerning this **c**. — Lk 2:17
when the parents brought in the **c** Jesus, — Lk 2:27
this **c** is appointed for the fall and rising — Lk 2:34
And the **c** grew and became strong, — Lk 2:40
and the father and mother of the **c**. — Lk 8:51
by the hand he called, saying, "**C**, arise." — Lk 8:54
to look at my son, for he is my only **c**. — Lk 9:38
hearts, took a **c** and put him by his side — Lk 9:47
"Whoever receives this **c** in my name — Lk 9:48
'**C**, remember that you in your lifetime — Lk 16:25
of God like a **c** shall not enter it." — Lk 18:17
him, "Sir, come down before my **c** dies." — Jn 4:49
offspring after him, though he had no **c**. — Acts 7:5
beloved and faithful **c** in the Lord, — 1 Cor 4:17
When I was a **c**, I spoke like a child, — 1 Cor 13:11
When I was a child, I spoke like a **c**, — 1 Cor 13:11
spoke like a child, I thought like a **c**, — 1 Cor 13:11
like a child, I reasoned like a **c**. — 1 Cor 13:11
I mean that the heir, as long as he is a **c**, — Gal 4:1
To Timothy, my true **c** in the faith: — 1 Tm 1:2
I entrust to you, Timothy, my **c**, — 1 Tm 1:18
To Timothy, my beloved **c**: Grace, — 2 Tm 1:2
You then, my **c**, be strengthened by — 2 Tm 2:1
To Titus, my true **c** in a common faith: — Ti 1:4
I appeal to you for my **c**, Onesimus, — Phlm 1:10
word of righteousness, since he is a **c**. — Heb 5:13
they saw that the **c** was beautiful, — Heb 11:23
when she bore her **c** he might devour it. — Rv 12:4
She gave birth to a male **c**, one who is to — Rv 12:5
but her **c** was caught up to God and to — Rv 12:5
who had given birth to the male **c**. — Rv 12:13

CHILD'S (5)
So the girl went and called the **c** mother. — Ex 2:8
true, what is to be the **c** manner of life, — Jgs 13:12
let this **c** life come into him again." — 1 Kgs 17:21
for those who sought the **c** life are dead." — Mt 2:20
and took the **c** father and mother — Mk 5:40

CHILDBEARING (2)
"I will surely multiply your pain in **c**; — Gn 3:16
will be saved through **c**—if they — 1 Tm 2:15

CHILDBIRTH (3)
The pangs of **c** come for him, but he — Hos 13:13
together in the pains of **c** until now. — Rom 8:22
in the anguish of **c** until Christ is — Gal 4:19

CHILDHOOD (3)
pampers his servant from **c** will in the — Prv 29:21
to him?" And he said, "From **c**. — Mk 9:21
and how from **c** you have been — 2 Tm 3:15

CHILDISH (1)
I became a man, I gave up **c** ways. — 1 Cor 13:11

CHILDLESS (10)
what will you give me, for I continue **c**, — Gn 15:2
shall bear their sin; they shall die **c**. — Lv 20:20
brother's nakedness; they shall be **c**. — Lv 20:21
"As your sword has made women **c**, — 1 Sm 15:33
your mother be **c** among women." — 1 Sm 15:33
Seled and Appaim; and Seled died **c**. — 1 Chr 2:30
and Jonathan; and Jether died **c**. — 1 Chr 2:32
"They wrong the barren **c** woman, and — Jb 24:21
let their wives become **c** and widowed. — Jer 18:21
"Write this man down as **c**, a man who — Jer 22:30

CHILDREN (498)
in pain you shall bring forth **c**. — Gn 3:16
of man and they bore **c** to them. — Gn 6:4
also, the father of all the **c** of Eber, — Gn 10:21
elder brother of Japheth, **c** were born. — Gn 10:21
the tower, which the **c** of man had built. — Gn 11:5
Abram's wife, had borne him no **c**. — Gn 16:1
LORD has prevented me from bearing **c**. — Gn 16:2
that I shall obtain **c** by her." And — Gn 16:2
may command his **c** and his — Gn 18:19
and female slaves so that they bore **c**. — Gn 20:17
to Abraham that Sarah would nurse **c**? — Gn 21:7
also has borne **c** to your brother — Gn 22:20

Eldaah. All these were the **c** of Keturah. Gn 25:4
The **c** struggled together within her, Gn 25:22
Rachel saw that she bore Jacob no **c**, Gn 30:1
She said to Jacob, "Give me **c**, or I shall Gn 30:1
that even I may have **c** through her." Gn 30:3
Leah saw that she had ceased bearing **c**, Gn 30:9
my wives and my **c** for whom I have Gn 30:26
our father belongs to us and to our **c**. Gn 31:16
my daughters, the **c** are my children, Gn 31:43
my daughters, the children are my **c**, Gn 31:43
or for their **c** whom they have Gn 31:43
and attack me, the mothers with the **c**. Gn 32:11
two female servants, and his eleven **c**, Gn 32:22
So he divided the **c** among Leah and Gn 33:1
he put the servants with their **c** in front, Gn 33:2
children in front, then Leah with her **c**, Gn 33:2
up his eyes and saw the women and **c**, Gn 33:5
"The **c** whom God has graciously given Gn 33:5
the servants drew near, they and their **c**, Gn 33:6
Leah likewise and her **c** drew near and Gn 33:7
"My lord knows that the **c** are frail, Gn 33:13
ahead of me and at the pace of the **c**, Gn 33:14
These are the **c** of Anah: Dishon and Gn 36:25
them, "You have bereaved me of my **c**: Gn 42:36
as for me, if I am bereaved of my **c**, Gn 43:14
and he alone is left of his mother's **c**, Gn 44:20
you and your **c** and your children's Gn 45:10
your children and your children's **c**, Gn 45:10
And the **c** that you fathered after them Gn 48:6
Only their **c**, their flocks, and their Gn 50:8
Joseph saw Ephraim's **c** of the third Gn 50:23
The **c** also of Machir the son of Gn 50:23
them, but let the male **c** live. Ex 1:17
you done this, and let the male **c** live?" Ex 1:18
and said, "This is one of the Hebrews' **c**." Ex 2:6
you may bring my people, the **c** of Israel, Ex 3:10
Pharaoh and bring the **c** of Israel out of Ex 3:11
bring my hosts, my people the **c** of Israel, Ex 7:4
And when your **c** say to you, 'What do Ex 12:26
men on foot, besides women and **c**. Ex 12:37
kill us and our **c** and our livestock with Ex 17:3
of the fathers on the **c** to the third and Ex 20:5
the wife and her **c** shall be her master's, Ex 21:4
'I love my master, my wife, and my **c**; Ex 21:5
woman, so that her **c** come out, Ex 21:22
become widows and your **c** fatherless. Ex 22:24
the fathers on the **c** and the children's Ex 34:7
on the children and the children's **c**, Ex 34:7
Every male among the **c** of Aaron may Lv 6:18
not give any of your **c** to offer them to Lv 18:21
gives any of his **c** to Molech shall surely Lv 20:2
he has given one of his **c** to Molech, Lv 20:3
when he gives one of his **c** to Molech, Lv 20:4
off in the sight of the **c** of their people. Lv 20:17
go out from you, he and his **c** with him, Lv 25:41
then he and his **c** with him shall be Lv 25:54
bereave you of your **c** and destroy your Lv 26:22
wilderness of Sinai, and they had no **c**. Nm 3:4
she shall be free and shall conceive **c**. Nm 5:28
the iniquity of the fathers on the **c**, Nm 14:18
And your **c** shall be shepherds in the Nm 14:33
to him and to his **c** I will give the land Dt 1:36
said would become a prey, and your **c**, Dt 1:39
every city, men, women, and **c**. Dt 2:34
every city, men, women, and **c**. Dt 3:6
known to your **c** and your children's Dt 4:9
to your children and your children's **c**— Dt 4:9
and that they may teach their **c** so.' Dt 4:10
"When you father **c** and children's Dt 4:25
you father children and children's **c**, Dt 4:25
well with you and with your **c** after you, Dt 4:40
of the fathers on the **c** to the third and Dt 5:9
You shall teach them diligently to your **c**, Dt 6:7
not speaking to your **c** who have not Dt 11:2
You shall teach them to your **c**, talking Dt 11:19
the days of your **c** may be multiplied in Dt 11:21
well with you and with your **c** after you, Dt 12:25
you and with your **c** after you forever, Dt 12:28
long in his kingdom, he and his **c**, Dt 17:20
and the unloved have borne him **c**, Dt 21:15
C born to them in the third generation Dt 23:8
not be put to death because of their **c**, Dt 24:16
nor shall **c** be put to death because of Dt 24:16
and to the last of the **c** whom he has left, Dt 28:54
of the flesh of his **c** whom he is eating, Dt 28:55
her feet and her **c** whom she bears, Dt 28:57
your **c** who rise up after you, Dt 29:22
belong to us and to our **c** forever, Dt 29:29
to the LORD your God, you and your **c**, Dt 30:2
and that their **c**, who have not known Dt 31:13
are no longer his **c** because they are Dt 32:5
c in whom is no faithfulness. Dt 32:20
the blood of his **c** and takes vengeance Dt 32:43
you may command them to your **c**, Dt 32:46
disowned his brothers and ignored his **c**. Dt 33:9

When your **c** ask in time to come, 'What Jos 4:6
"When your **c** ask their fathers in times Jos 4:21
then you shall let your **c** know, 'Israel Jos 4:22
So it was their **c**, whom he raised up in Jos 5:7
inheritance for you and your **c** forever, Jos 14:9
time to come your **c** might say to our Jos 22:24
come your children might say to our **c**, Jos 22:24
So your **c** might make our children Jos 22:25
might make our **c** cease to worship Jos 22:25
so your **c** will not say to our children Jos 22:27
will not say to our **c** in time to come, Jos 22:27
but Jacob and his **c** went down to Egypt. Jos 24:4
And his wife was barren and had no **c**. Jgs 13:2
you are barren and have not borne **c**, Jgs 13:3
And Peninnah had **c**, but Hannah had 1 Sm 1:2
had children, but Hannah had no **c**. 1 Sm 1:2
but she who has many **c** is forlorn. 1 Sm 2:5
the LORD give you **c** by this woman for 1 Sm 2:20
man may lead away his wife and **c**, 1 Sm 30:22
it grew up with him and with his **c**. 2 Sm 12:3
will dwell among the **c** of Israel and 1 Kgs 6:13
the hearts of all the **c** of mankind), 1 Kgs 8:39
from following me, you or your **c**, 1 Kgs 9:6
your best wives and **c** also are mine.'" 1 Kgs 20:3
your gold, your wives and your **c**." 1 Kgs 20:5
he sent to me for my wives and my **c**, 1 Kgs 20:7
to take my two **c** to be his slaves." 2 Kgs 4:1
put to death the **c** of the murderers, 2 Kgs 14:6
not be put to death because of their **c**, 2 Kgs 14:6
nor shall **c** be put to death because of 2 Kgs 14:6
Sepharvites burned their **c** in the 2 Kgs 17:31
the LORD commanded the **c** of Jacob, 2 Kgs 17:34
Their **c** did likewise, and their 2 Kgs 17:41
and their children's **c**—as their 2 Kgs 17:41
c have come to the point of birth, and 2 Kgs 19:3
son of Hezron fathered **c** by his wife 1 Chr 2:18
his brothers did not have many **c**, 1 Chr 4:27
The **c** of Amram: Aaron, Moses, and 1 Chr 6:3
are the names of the **c** born to him in 1 Chr 14:4
died before their father and had no **c**, 1 Chr 24:2
inheritance to your **c** after you 1 Chr 28:8
know the hearts of the **c** of mankind, 2 Chr 6:30
little ones, their wives, and their **c**. 2 Chr 20:13
great plague on your people, your **c**, 2 Chr 21:14
But he did not put their **c** to death, 2 Chr 25:4
shall not die because of their **c**, 2 Chr 25:4
nor **c** die because of their fathers, 2 Chr 25:4
brothers and your **c** will find 2 Chr 30:9
were enrolled with all their little **c**, 2 Chr 31:18
and the **c** of Israel were in the towns, Ezr 3:1
him a safe journey for ourselves, our **c**, Ezr 8:21
it for an inheritance to your **c** forever.' Ezr 9:12
great assembly of men, women, and **c**, Ezr 10:1
to put away all these wives and their **c**, Ezr 10:3
some of the women had even borne **c**. Ezr 10:44
our brothers, our **c** are as their children. Neh 5:5
our brothers, our children are as their **c**. Neh 5:5
You multiplied their **c** as the stars of Neh 9:23
joy; the women and **c** also rejoiced. Neh 12:43
half of their **c** spoke the language Neh 13:24
all Jews, young and old, women and **c**, Est 3:13
attack them, **c** and women included, Est 8:11
Job said, "It may be that my **c** have sinned, Jb 1:5
His **c** are far from safety; they are crushed Jb 5:4
If your **c** have sinned against him, he has Jb 8:4
their property—the eyes of his **c** will fail. Jb 17:5
am a stench to the **c** of my own mother. Jb 19:17
Even young **c** despise me; when I rise Jb 19:18
His **c** will seek the favor of the poor, and Jb 20:10
boys like a flock, and their **c** dance. Jb 21:11
'God stores up their iniquity for their **c**.' Jb 21:19
the wasteland yields food for their **c**. Jb 24:5
If his **c** are multiplied, it is for the sword, Jb 27:14
with me, when my **c** were all around me, Jb 29:5
or can you guide the Bear with its **c**? Jb 38:32
his eyes see, his eyelids test, the **c** of man. Ps 11:4
vanished from among the **c** of man. Ps 12:1
vileness is exalted among the **c** of man. Ps 12:8
down from heaven on the **c** of man, Ps 14:2
they are satisfied with **c**, and they leave Ps 17:14
offspring from among the **c** of man. Ps 21:10
in you, in the sight of the **c** of mankind! Ps 31:19
from heaven; he sees all the **c** of man; Ps 33:13
Come, O **c**, listen to me; I will teach you Ps 34:11
The **c** of mankind take refuge in the Ps 36:7
forsaken or his **c** begging for bread. Ps 37:25
and his **c** become a blessing. Ps 37:26
but the **c** of the wicked shall be cut off. Ps 37:28
down from heaven on the **c** of man to see Ps 53:2
down amid fiery beasts—the **c** of man, Ps 57:4
Do you judge the **c** of man uprightly? Ps 58:1
in his deeds toward the **c** of man. Ps 66:5
give deliverance to the **c** of the needy, Ps 72:4
have betrayed the generation of your **c**. Ps 73:15
your people, the **c** of Jacob and Joseph. Ps 77:15

We will not hide them from their **c**, but Ps 78:4
our fathers to teach to their **c**, Ps 78:5
might know them, the **c** yet unborn, Ps 78:6
and arise and tell them to their **c**, Ps 78:6
they are the strong arm of the **c** of Lot. Ps 83:8
If his **c** forsake my law and do not walk Ps 89:30
you have created all the **c** of man! Ps 89:47
to dust and say, "Return, O **c** of man!" Ps 90:3
and your glorious power to their **c**. Ps 90:16
The **c** of your servants shall dwell Ps 102:28
As a father shows compassion to his **c**, Ps 103:13
and his righteousness to children's **c**, Ps 103:17
of Abraham, his servant, **c** of Jacob, Ps 105:6
for his wondrous works to the **c** of men! Ps 107:8
his wondrous works to the **c** of men! Ps 107:15
his wondrous works to the **c** of men! Ps 107:21
his wondrous works to the **c** of men! Ps 107:31
May his **c** be fatherless and his wife a Ps 109:9
May his **c** wander about and beg, Ps 109:10
to him, nor any to pity his fatherless **c**! Ps 109:12
making her the joyous mother of **c**. Ps 113:9
give you increase, you and your **c**! Ps 115:14
the earth he has given to the **c** of man. Ps 115:16
Behold, **c** are a heritage from the LORD, Ps 127:3
of a warrior are the **c** of one's youth. Ps 127:4
your **c** will be like olive shoots around Ps 128:3
May you see your children's **c**! Peace be Ps 128:6
make known to the **c** of man your Ps 145:12
gates; he blesses your **c** within you. Ps 147:13
and maidens together, old men and **c**! Ps 148:12
let the **c** of Zion rejoice in their King! Ps 149:2
I call, and my cry is to the **c** of man. Prv 8:4
world and delighting in the **c** of man. Prv 8:31
an inheritance to his children's **c**, Prv 13:22
and his **c** will have a refuge. Prv 14:26
much more the hearts of the **c** of man! Prv 15:11
aged, and the glory of **c** is their fathers. Prv 17:6
integrity—blessed are his **c** after him! Prv 20:7
Her **c** rise up and call her blessed; her Prv 31:28
God has given to the **c** of man to be Eccl 1:13
what was good for the **c** of man to do Eccl 2:3
concubines, the delight of the **c** of man. Eccl 2:8
God has given to the **c** of man to be Eccl 3:10
with regard to the **c** of man that God Eccl 3:18
what happens to the **c** of man and Eccl 3:19
fathers a hundred **c** and lives many Eccl 6:3
the heart of the **c** of man is fully set to Eccl 8:11
the hearts of the **c** of man are full of evil, Eccl 9:3
so the **c** of man are snared at an evil Eccl 9:12
"**C** have I reared and brought up, but they Is 1:2
of evildoers, **c** who deal corruptly! Is 1:4
they strike hands with the **c** of foreigners. Is 2:6
I and the **c** whom the LORD has given me Is 8:18
of the womb; their eyes will not pity **c**. Is 13:18
will be like the glory of the **c** of Israel, Is 17:3
they deserted because of the **c** of Israel, Is 17:9
For when he sees his **c**, the work of my Is 29:23
"Ah, stubborn **c**," declares the LORD, "who Is 30:1
For they are a rebellious people, lying **c**, Is 30:9
c unwilling to hear the instruction of the Is 30:9
people have deeply revolted, O **c** of Israel. Is 31:6
c have come to the point of birth, and Is 37:3
makes known to the **c** your faithfulness. Is 38:19
me concerning my **c** and the work Is 45:11
not sit as a widow or know the loss of **c**": Is 47:8
the loss of **c** and widowhood shall come Is 47:9
The **c** of your bereavement will yet say Is 49:20
contend with you, and I will save your **c**. Is 49:25
form beyond that of the **c** of mankind— Is 52:14
For the **c** of the desolate one will be more Is 54:1
will be more than the **c** of her who is Is 54:1
All your **c** shall be taught by the LORD, Is 54:13
and great shall be the peace of your **c**. Is 54:13
Are you not **c** of transgression, the Is 57:4
tree, who slaughter your **c** in the valleys, Is 57:5
Tarshish first, to bring your **c** from afar, Is 60:9
c who will not deal falsely." And he Is 63:8
not labor in vain or bear **c** for calamity, Is 65:23
was in labor she brought forth her **c**. Is 66:8
and with your children's **c** I will contend. Jer 2:9
In vain have I struck your **c**; they took Jer 2:30
Return, O faithless **c**, declares the LORD; Jer 3:14
they know me not; they are stupid **c**; Jer 4:22
Your **c** have forsaken me and have sworn Jer 5:7
"Pour it out upon the **c** in the street, and Jer 6:11
The **c** gather wood, the fathers kindle Jer 7:18
cutting off the **c** from the streets and the Jer 9:21
my **c** have gone from me, and they are Jer 10:20
while their **c** remember their altars and Jer 17:2
Therefore deliver up their **c** to famine; Jer 18:21
are he and his **c** hurled and cast into Jer 22:28
Their **c** shall be as they were of old, and Jer 30:20
Rachel is weeping for her **c**; she refuses Jer 31:15
she refuses to be comforted for her **c**, Jer 31:15
and your **c** shall come back to their Jer 31:17

the guilt of fathers to their **c** after them, Jer 32:18
are open to all the ways of the **c** of man, Jer 32:19
For the **c** of Israel and the children of Jer 32:30
of Israel and the **c** of Judah have done Jer 32:30
The **c** of Israel have done nothing but Jer 32:30
all the evil of the **c** of Israel and the Jer 32:32
of Israel and the **c** of Judah that they Jer 32:32
good and the good of their **c** after them. Jer 32:39
committed to him men, women, and **c**, Jer 40:7
—soldiers, women, **c**, and eunuchs, Jer 41:16
the men, the women, the **c**, the Jer 43:6
the fathers look not back to their **c**, Jer 47:3
His **c** are destroyed, and his brothers, Jer 49:10
Leave your fatherless **c**; I will keep Jer 49:11
her **c** have gone away, captives before Lam 1:5
my **c** are desolate, for the enemy has Lam 1:16
hands to him for the lives of your **c**, Lam 2:19
their womb, the **c** of their tender care? Lam 2:20
willingly afflict or grieve the **c** of men. Lam 3:33
the **c** beg for food, but no one gives to Lam 4:4
women have boiled their own **c**; Lam 4:10
you, and they will rob you of your **c**. Ezk 5:17
men and maidens, little **c** and women, Ezk 9:6
you slaughtered my **c** and delivered Ezk 16:21
of the blood of your **c** that you gave to Ezk 16:36
who loathed her husband and her **c**; Ezk 16:45
loathed their husbands and their **c**. Ezk 16:45
"And I said to their **c** in the wilderness, Ezk 20:18
But the **c** rebelled against me. They Ezk 20:21
your gifts and offer up your **c** in fire, Ezk 20:31
them for food the **c** whom they had Ezk 23:37
had slaughtered their **c** in sacrifice to Ezk 23:39
the world below, among the **c** of man, Ezk 31:14
you shall no longer bereave them of **c**. Ezk 36:12
and you bereave your nation of **c**,' Ezk 36:13
no longer bereave your nation of **c**, Ezk 36:14
They and their **c** and their children's Ezk 37:25
and their children's **c** shall dwell there Ezk 37:25
you and have had **c** among you. Ezk 47:22
be to you as native-born **c** of Israel. Ezk 47:22
given, wherever they dwell, the **c** of man, Dn 2:38
driven from among the **c** of mankind, Dn 5:21
cast into the den of lions—they, their **c**, Dn 6:24
the likeness of the **c** of man touched Dn 10:16
of whoredom and have **c** of whoredom, Hos 1:2
the number of the **c** of Israel shall be Hos 1:10
be said to them, "**C** of the living God." Hos 1:10
And the **c** of Judah and the children of Hos 1:11
of Judah and the **c** of Israel shall be Hos 1:11
Upon her **c** also I will have no mercy, Hos 2:4
mercy, because they are **c** of whoredom. Hos 2:4
even as the LORD loves the **c** of Israel, Hos 3:1
For the **c** of Israel shall dwell many days Hos 3:4
Afterward the **c** of Israel shall return and Hos 3:5
Hear the word of the LORD, O **c** of Israel, Hos 4:1
law of your God, I also will forget your **c**. Hos 4:6
the LORD; for they have borne alien **c**. Hos 5:7
Even if they bring up **c**, I will bereave Hos 9:12
must lead his **c** out to slaughter. Hos 9:13
birth, I will put their beloved **c** to death. Hos 9:16
were dashed in pieces with their **c**. Hos 10:14
his **c** shall come trembling from the Hos 11:10
Tell your **c** of it, and let your children tell Jl 1:3
of it, and let your **c** tell their children, Jl 1:3
of it, and let your children tell their **c**, Jl 1:3
children, and their **c** to another generation. Jl 1:3
and gladness dries up from the **c** of man. Jl 1:12
elders; gather the **c**, even nursing infants. Jl 2:16
"Be glad, O **c** of Zion, and rejoice in the Jl 2:23
off your hair, for the **c** of your delight; Mi 1:16
from their young **c** you take away my Mi 2:9
not for a man nor wait for the **c** of man. Mi 5:7
Their **c** shall see it and be glad; their Zec 10:7
and with their **c** they shall live and Zec 10:9
therefore you, O **c** of Jacob, are not Mal 3:6
of fathers to their **c** and the hearts of Mal 4:6
and the hearts of **c** to their fathers, Mal 4:6
killed all the male **c** in Bethlehem and Mt 2:16
lamentation, Rachel weeping for her **c**; Mt 2:18
these stones to raise up **c** for Abraham. Mt 3:9
know how to give good gifts to your **c**, Mt 7:11
and **c** will rise against parents and Mt 10:21
It is like **c** sitting in the marketplaces Mt 11:16
and revealed them to little **c**; Mt 11:25
the good seed is the **c** of the kingdom. Mt 13:38
thousand men, besides women and **c**. Mt 14:21
thousand men, besides women and **c**. Mt 15:38
you, unless you turn and become like **c**, Mt 18:3
with his wife and **c** and all that he had, Mt 18:25
Then **c** were brought to him that he Mt 19:13
"Let the little **c** come to me and do not Mt 19:14
or father or mother or **c** or lands, Mt 19:29
did, and the **c** crying out in the temple, Mt 21:15
Moses said, 'If a man dies having no **c**, Mt 22:24
widow and raise up **c** for his brother.' Mt 22:24

and having no **c** left his wife to his Mt 22:25
I have gathered your **c** together as a Mt 23:37
"His blood be on us and on our **c**!" Mt 27:25
all sins will be forgiven the **c** of man, Mk 3:28
And he said to her, "Let the **c** be fed first, Mk 7:27
And they were bringing **c** to him that Mk 10:13
said to them, "Let the **c** come to me; Mk 10:14
"**C**, how difficult it is to enter the Mk 10:24
or mother or father or **c** or lands, Mk 10:29
sisters and mothers and **c** and lands, Mk 10:30
and **c** will rise against parents and Mk 13:12
will turn many of the **c** of Israel to the Lk 1:16
to turn the hearts of the fathers to the **c**, Lk 1:17
these stones to raise up **c** for Abraham. Lk 3:8
They are like **c** sitting in the Lk 7:32
Yet wisdom is justified by all her **c**." Lk 7:35
and revealed them to little **c**; Lk 10:21
now shut, and my **c** are with me in bed. Lk 11:7
know how to give good gifts to your **c**, Lk 11:13
I have gathered your **c** together as a Lk 13:34
and wife and **c** and brothers and Lk 14:26
to him, saying, "Let the **c** come to me, Lk 18:16
or wife or brothers or parents or **c**, Lk 18:29
the ground, you and your **c** within you. Lk 19:44
brother dies, having a wife but no **c**, Lk 20:28
first took a wife, and died without **c**. Lk 20:29
likewise all seven left no **c** and died. Lk 20:31
but weep for yourselves and for your **c**. Lk 23:28
he gave the right to become **c** of God, Jn 1:12
said to them, "If you were Abraham's **c**, Jn 8:39
to gather into one the **c** of God who are Jn 11:52
Little **c**, yet a little while I am with you. Jn 13:33
"**C**, do you have any fish?" They Jn 21:5
for you and for your **c** and for all who Acts 2:39
to visit his brothers, the **c** of Israel. Acts 7:23
Gentiles and kings and the **c** of Israel. Acts 9:15
fulfilled to us their **c** by raising Jesus, Acts 13:33
journey, and they all, with wives and **c**, Acts 21:5
to circumcise their **c** or walk Acts 21:21
instructor of the foolish, a teacher of **c**, Rom 2:20
with our spirit that we are **c** of God, Rom 8:16
and if **c**, then heirs—heirs of God and Rom 8:17
freedom of the glory of the **c** of God. Rom 8:21
and not all are **c** of Abraham because Rom 9:7
that it is not the **c** of the flesh who are Rom 9:8
of the flesh who are the **c** of God, Rom 9:8
but the **c** of the promise are counted as Rom 9:8
Rebecca had conceived **c** by one man, Rom 9:10
to admonish you as my beloved **c**. 1 Cor 4:14
Otherwise your **c** would be unclean, 1 Cor 7:14
do not be **c** in your thinking. 1 Cor 14:20
(I speak as to **c**) widen your hearts 2 Cor 6:13
For **c** are not obligated to save up for 2 Cor 12:14
their parents, but parents for their **c**. 2 Cor 12:14
In the same way we also, when we were **c**, Gal 4:3
my little **c**, for whom I am again in the Gal 4:19
Mount Sinai, bearing **c** for slavery; Gal 4:24
for she is in slavery with her **c**. Gal 4:25
For the **c** of the desolate one will be Gal 4:27
brothers, like Isaac, are **c** of promise. Gal 4:28
we are not **c** of the slave but of the free Gal 4:31
the mind, and were by nature **c** of wrath, Eph 2:3
so that we may no longer be **c**, tossed to Eph 4:14
be imitators of God, as beloved **c**. Eph 5:1
are light in the Lord. Walk as **c** of light Eph 5:8
C, obey your parents in the Lord, for this Eph 6:1
Fathers, do not provoke your **c** to anger, Eph 6:4
c of God without blemish in the midst Phil 2:15
C, obey your parents in everything, for Col 3:20
Fathers, do not provoke your **c**, lest they Col 3:21
mother taking care of her own **c**. 1 Thes 2:7
know how, like a father with his **c**, 1 Thes 2:11
For you are all **c** of light, children of 1 Thes 5:5
are all children of light, **c** of the day. 1 Thes 5:5
all dignity keeping his **c** submissive, 1 Tm 3:4
managing their **c** and their own 1 Tm 3:12
But if a widow has **c** or grandchildren, 1 Tm 5:4
if she has brought up **c**, has shown 1 Tm 5:10
have younger widows marry, bear **c**, 1 Tm 5:14
and his **c** are believers and not open to the Ti 1:6
women to love their husbands and **c**, Ti 2:4
"Behold, I and the **c** God has given me." Heb 2:13
Since therefore the **c** share in flesh and Heb 2:14
you are illegitimate **c** and not sons. Heb 12:8
As obedient **c**, do not be conformed to 1 Pt 1:14
And you are her **c**, if you do good and do 1 Pt 3:6
hearts trained in greed. Accursed **c**! 2 Pt 2:14
My little **c**, I am writing these things to 1 Jn 2:1
I am writing to you, little **c**, because 1 Jn 2:12
you, **c**, because you know the Father. 1 Jn 2:13
C, it is the last hour, and as you have 1 Jn 2:18
And now, little **c**, abide in him, so that 1 Jn 2:28
to us, that we should be called **c** of God; 1 Jn 3:1
Beloved, we are God's **c** now, and what 1 Jn 3:2
Little **c**, let no one deceive you. Whoever 1 Jn 3:7

this it is evident who are the **c** of God, 1 Jn 3:10
of God, and who are the **c** of the devil: 1 Jn 3:10
Little **c**, let us not love in word or talk 1 Jn 3:18
Little **c**, you are from God and have 1 Jn 4:4
this we know that we love the **c** of God, 1 Jn 5:2
Little **c**, keep yourselves from idols. 1 Jn 5:21
The elder to the elect lady and her **c**, 2 Jn 1:1
find some of your **c** walking in the 2 Jn 1:4
The **c** of your elect sister greet you. 2 Jn 1:13
to hear that my **c** are walking in the 3 Jn 1:4
and I will strike her **c** dead. And all the Rv 2:23

CHILDREN'S (16)
your children and your **c** children, Gn 45:10
on the children and the **c** children, Ex 34:7
to your children and your **c** children— Dt 4:9
you father children and **c** children, Dt 4:25
and their **c** children—as their 2 Kgs 17:41
and his righteousness to **c** children, Ps 103:17
May you see your **c** children! Peace be Ps 128:6
an inheritance to his **c** children, Prv 13:22
the mouth of your **c** offspring," says the Is 59:21
and with your **c** children I will contend. Jer 2:9
grapes, and the **c** teeth are set on edge.' Jer 31:29
grapes, and the **c** teeth are set on edge'? Ezk 18:2
children and their **c** children shall Ezk 37:25
right to take the **c** bread and throw it Mt 15:26
right to take the **c** bread and throw it Mk 7:27
dogs under the table eat the **c** crumbs." Mk 7:28

CHILEAB (1)
C, of Abigail the widow of Nabal of 2 Sm 3:3

CHILION (3)
of his two sons were Mahlon and **C**. Ru 1:2
and both Mahlon and **C** died, so that the Ru 1:5
and all that belonged to **C** and to Mahlon. Ru 4:9

CHILMAD (1)
Sheba, Asshur, and **C** traded with you. Ezk 27:23

CHIMHAM (4)
mother. But here is your servant **C**. 2 Sm 19:37
answered, "**C** shall go over with me, 2 Sm 19:38
to Gilgal, and **C** went on with him. 2 Sm 19:40
stayed at Geruth **C** near Bethlehem, Jer 41:17

CHINNERETH (4)
shoulder of the Sea of **C** on the east. Nm 34:11
from **C** as far as the Sea of the Arabah, Dt 3:17
to the lower end of the Sea of **C**, Jos 13:27
Ziddim, Zer, Hammath, Rakkath, **C**, Jos 19:35

CHINNEROTH (3)
country, and in the Arabah south of **C**, Jos 11:2
and the Arabah to the Sea of **C** eastward, Jos 12:3
Dan, Abel-beth-maacah, and all **C**, 1 Kgs 15:20

CHIOS (1)
came the following day opposite **C**; Acts 20:15

CHIRP (2)
the necromancers who **c** and mutter," Is 8:19
Like a swallow or a crane I **c**; I moan Is 38:14

CHIRPED (1)
a wing or opened the mouth or **c**." Is 10:14

CHISLEV (2)
Now it happened in the month of **C**, in Neh 1:1
day of the ninth month, which is **C**. Zec 7:1

CHISLON (1)
tribe of Benjamin, Elidad the son of **C**. Nm 34:21

CHISLOTH-TABOR (1)
the sunrise to the boundary of **C**. Jos 19:12

CHITLISH (1)
Cabbon, Lahmam, **C**, Jos 15:40

CHLOE'S (1)
reported to me by **C** people that there 1 Cor 1:11

CHOICE (20)
taking all sorts of **c** gifts from his Gn 24:10
take some of the **c** fruits of the land in Gn 43:11
vine and his donkey's colt to the **c** vine, Gn 49:11
every fortified city and every **c** city, 2 Kgs 3:19
found that they were 300,000 **c** men, 2 Chr 25:5
was one ox and six **c** sheep and birds, Neh 5:18
and knowledge rather than **c** gold, Prv 8:10
fine gold, and my yield than **c** silver. Prv 8:19
The tongue of the righteous is **c** silver; Prv 10:20
is like Lebanon, **c** as the cedars. Sg 5:15
and beside our doors are all **c** fruits, Sg 7:13
it of stones, and planted it with **c** vines; Is 5:2
Yet I planted you a **c** vine, wholly of pure Jer 2:21
come, and you shall fall like a **c** vessel. Jer 25:34
and the shoulder; fill it with **c** bones. Ezk 24:4
after piece, without making any **c**. Ezk 24:6
these traded with you in **c** garments, Ezk 27:24
of Eden, the **c** and best of Lebanon, Ezk 31:16
shall not alienate this **c** portion of the Ezk 48:14

early days God made a **c** among you, Acts 15:7

CHOICEST (15)

Bury your dead in the **c** of our tombs. Gn 23:6
land, with the **c** gifts of heaven above, Dt 33:13
with the **c** fruits of the sun and the rich Dt 33:14
yourselves on the **c** parts of every 1 Sm 2:29
its tallest cedars, its **c** cypresses; 2 Kgs 19:23
bread, and his appetite the **c** food. Jb 33:20
of pomegranates with all **c** fruits, Sg 4:13
come to his garden, and eat its **c** fruits. Sg 4:16
Your **c** valleys were full of chariots, and Is 22:7
down its tallest cedars, its **c** cypresses, Is 37:24
shall cut down your **c** cedars and cast Jer 22:7
and the **c** of his young men have gone Jer 48:15
contributions and the **c** of your gifts, Ezk 20:40
them, the **c** men of Assyria all of them, Ezk 23:7
Take the **c** one of the flock; pile the logs Ezk 24:5

CHOIR (1)

The other **c** of those who gave thanks Neh 12:38

CHOIRMASTER (56)

To the **c**: with stringed instruments. A Ps 4:T
To the **c**: for the flutes. A Psalm of David. Ps 5:T
To the **c**: with stringed instruments; Ps 6:T
To the **c**: according to The Gittith. A Ps 8:T
To the **c**: according to Muth-labben. A Ps 9:T
To the **c**. Of David. Ps 11:T
To the **c**: according to The Sheminith. A Ps 12:T
To the **c**. A Psalm of David. Ps 13:T
To the **c**. Of David. Ps 14:T
To the **c**. A Psalm of David, the servant Ps 18:T
To the **c**. A Psalm of David. Ps 19:T
To the **c**. A Psalm of David. Ps 20:T
To the **c**. A Psalm of David. Ps 21:T
To the **c**: according to The Doe of the Ps 22:T
To the **c**. A Psalm of David. Ps 31:T
To the **c**. Of David, the servant of the Ps 36:T
To the **c**: to Jeduthun. A Psalm of David. Ps 39:T
To the **c**. A Psalm of David. Ps 40:T
To the **c**. A Psalm of David. Ps 41:T
To the **c**. A Maskil of the Sons of Korah. Ps 42:T
To the **c**. A Maskil of the Sons of Korah. Ps 44:T
To the **c**: according to Lilies. A Maskil Ps 45:T
To the **c**. Of the Sons of Korah. Ps 46:T
To the **c**. A Psalm of the Sons of Korah. Ps 47:T
To the **c**. A Psalm of the Sons of Korah. Ps 49:T
To the **c**. A Psalm of David, when Ps 51:T
To the **c**. A Maskil of David, when Doeg, Ps 52:T
To the **c**: according to Mahalath. A Ps 53:T
To the **c**: with stringed instruments. A Ps 54:T
To the **c**: with stringed instruments. A Ps 55:T
To the **c**: according to The Dove on Ps 56:T
To the **c**: according to Do Not Destroy. A Ps 57:T
To the **c**: according to Do Not Destroy. A Ps 58:T
To the **c**: according to Do Not Destroy. A Ps 59:T
To the **c**: according to Shushan Eduth. Ps 60:T
To the **c**: with stringed instruments. Of Ps 61:T
To the **c**: according to Jeduthun. A Ps 62:T
To the **c**. A Psalm of David. Ps 64:T
To the **c**. A Psalm of David. A Song. Ps 65:T
To the **c**. A Song. A Psalm. Ps 66:T
To the **c**: with stringed instruments. A Ps 67:T
To the **c**. A Psalm of David. A Song. Ps 68:T
To the **c**: according to Lilies. Of David. Ps 69:T
To the **c**. Of David, for the memorial Ps 70:T
To the **c**: according to Do Not Destroy. A Ps 75:T
To the **c**: with stringed instruments. A Ps 76:T
To the **c**: according to Jeduthun. A Ps 77:T
To the **c**: according to Lilies. A Ps 80:T
To the **c**: according to The Gittith. Of Ps 81:T
To the **c**: according to The Gittith. A Ps 84:T
To the **c**. A Psalm of the Sons of Korah. Ps 85:T
To the **c**: according to Mahalath Ps 88:T
To the **c**. A Psalm of David. Ps 109:T
To the **c**. A Psalm of David. Ps 139:T
To the **c**. A Psalm of David. Ps 140:T
To the **c**: with stringed instruments. Hab 3:19

CHOIRS (2)

appointed two great **c** that gave Neh 12:31
So both **c** of those who gave thanks Neh 12:40

CHOKE (3)

the deceitfulness of riches **c** the word, Mt 13:22
and seizing him, he began to **c** him, Mt 18:28
for other things enter in and **c** the word, Mk 4:19

CHOKED (4)

and the thorns grew up and **c** them. Mt 13:7
thorns, and the thorns grew up and **c** it, Mk 4:7
and the thorns grew up with it and **c** it. Lk 8:7
on their way they are **c** by the cares and Lk 8:14

CHOOSE (64)

So Moses said to Joshua, "**C** for us men, Ex 17:9
"Let us **c** a leader and go back to Nm 14:4
staff of the man whom I **c** shall sprout. Nm 17:5
C for your tribes wise, understanding, Dt 1:13
the LORD your God will **c** out of all your Dt 12:5
the place that the LORD your God will **c**, Dt 12:11
place that the LORD will **c** in one of your Dt 12:14
the place that the LORD your God will **c**, Dt 12:18
LORD your God will **c** to put his name Dt 12:21
shall go to the place that the LORD will **c**, Dt 12:26
your God, in the place that he will **c**, Dt 14:23
by year at the place that the LORD will **c**. Dt 15:20
the herd, at the place that the LORD will **c**, Dt 16:2
the place that the LORD your God will **c**, Dt 16:6
the place that the LORD your God will **c**. Dt 16:7
the place that the LORD your God will **c**, Dt 16:11
God at the place that the LORD will **c**, Dt 16:15
your God at the place that he will **c**: Dt 16:16
the place that the LORD your God will **c**. Dt 17:8
you from that place that the LORD will **c**. Dt 17:10
you whom the LORD your God will **c**. Dt 17:15
desires—to the place that the LORD will **c**, Dt 18:6
place that he shall **c** within one of your Dt 23:16
the place that the LORD your God will **c**, Dt 26:2
blessing and curse. Therefore **c** life, Dt 30:19
your God at the place that he will **c**, Dt 31:11
to this day, in the place that he should **c**. Jos 9:27
LORD, **c** this day whom you will serve, Jos 24:15
Did I **c** him out of all the tribes of 1 Sm 2:28
C a man for yourselves, and let him 1 Sm 17:8
"Let me **c** twelve thousand men, 2 Sm 17:1
C one of them, that I may do it to 2 Sm 24:12
and let them **c** one bull for 1 Kgs 18:23
"**C** for yourselves one bull and 1 Kgs 18:25
c one of them, that I may do it to 1 Chr 21:10
says the LORD, '**C** what you will: 1 Chr 21:11
so that I would **c** strangling and death Jb 7:15
and you **c** the tongue of the crafty. Jb 15:5
Let us **c** what is right; let us know among Jb 34:4
For you must **c**, and not I; therefore Jb 34:33
he instruct in the way that he should **c**. Ps 25:12
Blessed is the one you **c** and bring near, Ps 65:4
he did not **c** the tribe of Ephraim, Ps 78:67
knowledge and did not **c** the fear of the Prv 1:29
violence and do not **c** any of his ways, Prv 3:31
how to refuse the evil and **c** the good. Is 7:15
how to refuse the evil and **c** the good, Is 7:16
on Jacob and will again **c** Israel, Is 14:1
who **c** the things that please me and hold Is 56:4
Is such the fast that I **c**, a day for a person Is 58:5
"Is not this the fast that I **c**: to loose the Is 58:6
I also will **c** harsh treatment for them and Is 66:4
servant and will not **c** one of his Jer 33:26
I will appoint over her whomever I **c**. Jer 49:19
I will appoint over her whomever I **c**. Jer 50:44
comfort Zion and again **c** Jerusalem.'" Zec 1:17
holy land, and will again **c** Jerusalem." Zec 2:12
I **c** to give to this last worker as I give to Mt 20:14
to do what I **c** with what belongs to Mt 20:15
Jesus answered them, "Did I not **c** you, Jn 6:70
You did not **c** me, but I chose you and Jn 15:16
to **c** men from among them and send Acts 15:22
to **c** men and send them to you with Acts 15:25
me. Yet which I shall **c** I cannot tell. Phil 1:22

CHOOSES (9)

The one whom he **c** he will bring near Nm 16:5
man whom the LORD **c** shall be the Nm 16:7
from you, which the LORD your God **c**, Dt 14:24
go to the place that the LORD your God **c** Dt 14:25
for an offering **c** wood that will Is 40:20
an abomination is he who **c** you. Is 41:24
or he **c** a cypress tree or an oak and lets Is 44:14
to whom the Son **c** to reveal him. Mt 11:27
to whom the Son **c** to reveal him." Lk 10:22

CHOOSING (2)

can I answer him, **c** my words with him? Jb 9:14
c rather to be mistreated with the Heb 11:25

CHOP (5)

their pillars and **c** down their Asherim Dt 7:5
You shall **c** down the carved images of Dt 12:3
'**C** down the tree and lop off its Dn 4:14
saying, '**C** down the tree and destroy it, Dn 4:23
bones in pieces and **c** them up like meat Mi 3:3

CHOPPED (1)

And they **c** down the altars of the 2 Chr 34:4

CHOPS (1)

from the one who **c** your wood to the Dt 29:11

CHORAZIN (2)

"Woe to you, **C**! Woe to you, Mt 11:21
"Woe to you, **C**! Woe to you, Lk 10:13

CHOSE (44)

And they took as their wives any they **c**. Gn 6:2
So Lot **c** for himself all the Jordan Gn 13:11
Moses **c** able men out of all Israel and Ex 18:25
your fathers and **c** their offspring after Dt 4:37
the LORD set his love on you and **c** you, Dt 7:7
your fathers and **c** their offspring after Dt 10:15
He **c** the best of the land for himself, for Dt 33:21
And Joshua **c** 30,000 mighty men of valor Jos 8:3
Saul **c** three thousand men of Israel. 1 Sm 13:2
in his hand and **c** five smooth stones 1 Sm 17:40
who **c** me above your father and 2 Sm 6:21
he **c** some of the best men of Israel 2 Sm 10:9
I **c** no city out of all the tribes of Israel 1 Kgs 8:16
But I **c** David to be over my people 1 Kgs 8:16
sake of David my servant whom I **c**, 1 Kgs 11:34
he **c** some of the best men of Israel 1 Chr 19:10
LORD God of Israel **c** me from all my 1 Chr 28:4
For he **c** Judah as leader, and in the 1 Chr 28:4
I **c** no city out of all the tribes of Israel 2 Chr 6:5
and I **c** no man as prince over my 2 Chr 6:5
the God who **c** Abram and brought him Neh 9:7
I **c** their way and sat as chief, and I lived Jb 29:25
He **c** our heritage for us, the pride of Ps 47:4
but he **c** the tribe of Judah, Mount Zion, Ps 78:68
He **c** David his servant and took him Ps 78:70
evil in my eyes and **c** what I did not Is 65:12
evil in my eyes and **c** that in which I did Is 66:4
has rejected the two clans that he **c**? Jer 33:24
On the day when I **c** Israel, I swore to Ezk 20:5
for the sake of the elect, whom he **c**, Mk 13:20
his disciples and **c** from them twelve, Lk 6:13
he noticed how they **c** the places of Lk 14:7
but I **c** you and appointed you that you Jn 15:16
the world, but I **c** you out of the world, Jn 15:19
whole gathering, and they **c** Stephen, Acts 6:5
of this people Israel **c** our fathers and Acts 13:17
but Paul **c** Silas and departed, having Acts 15:40
But God **c** what is foolish in the world 1 Cor 1:27
God **c** what is weak in the world to 1 Cor 1:27
God **c** what is low and despised in the 1 Cor 1:28
the body, each one of them, as he **c**. 1 Cor 12:18
even as he **c** us in him before the Eph 1:4
To them God **c** to make known how Col 1:27
because God **c** you as the firstfruits 2 Thes 2:13

CHOSEN (118)

For I have **c** him, that he may Gn 18:19
and took six hundred **c** chariots and all Ex 14:7
and his **c** officers were sunk in the Red Ex 15:4
were the ones **c** from the congregation, Nm 1:16
the congregation, **c** from the assembly, Nm 16:2
and Abiram, **c** from the congregation, Nm 26:9
The LORD your God has **c** you to be a Dt 7:6
and the LORD has **c** you to be a people for Dt 14:2
the LORD your God has **c** him out of all Dt 18:5
LORD your God has **c** them to minister to Dt 21:5
yourselves that you have **c** the LORD, Jos 24:22
When new gods were **c**, then war was in Jgs 5:8
cry out to the gods whom you have **c**; Jgs 10:14
of Gibeah, who mustered 700 **c** men. Jgs 20:15
all these were 700 **c** men who were Jgs 20:16
against Gibeah 10,000 **c** men out of Jgs 20:34
whom you have **c** for yourselves, 1 Sm 8:18
you see him whom the LORD has **c**? 1 Sm 10:24
behold the king whom you have **c**, 1 Sm 12:13
"Neither has the LORD **c** this one." 1 Sm 16:8
"Neither has the LORD **c** this one." 1 Sm 16:9
to Jesse, "The LORD has not **c** these." 1 Sm 16:10
know that you have **c** the son of Jesse 1 Sm 20:30
took three thousand **c** men out of 1 Sm 24:2
with three thousand **c** men of Israel 1 Sm 26:2
again gathered all the **c** men of Israel, 2 Sm 6:1
and all the men of Israel have **c**, 2 Sm 16:18
the **c** of the LORD." And the king said, 2 Sm 21:6
of your people whom you have **c**, 1 Kgs 3:8
city that you have **c** and the house 1 Kgs 8:44
their fathers, the city that you have **c**, 1 Kgs 8:48
the sake of Jerusalem that I have **c**." 1 Kgs 11:13
the city that I have **c** out of all the 1 Kgs 11:32
city where I have **c** to put my name. 1 Kgs 11:36
of Benjamin, 180,000 **c** warriors, 1 Kgs 12:21
city that the LORD had **c** out of all the 1 Kgs 14:21
which I have **c** out of all the tribes of 2 Kgs 21:7
I will cast off this city that I have **c**, 2 Kgs 23:27
who were **c** as gatekeepers at the 1 Chr 9:22
for the LORD had **c** them to carry the 1 Chr 15:2
servant, sons of Jacob, his **c** ones! 1 Chr 16:13
rest of those **c** and expressly named 1 Chr 16:41
father's house being **c** for Eleazar 1 Chr 24:6
for Eleazar and one **c** for Ithamar. 1 Chr 24:6
sons) he has **c** Solomon my son 1 Chr 28:5
courts, for I have **c** him to be my son, 1 Chr 28:6
for the LORD has **c** you to build a 1 Chr 28:10
my son, whom alone God has **c**, 1 Chr 29:1
but I have **c** Jerusalem that my name 2 Chr 6:6
and I have **c** David to be over my 2 Chr 6:6
city that you have **c** and the house 2 Chr 6:34
city that you have **c** and the house 2 Chr 6:38
your prayer and have **c** this place for 2 Chr 7:12
now I have **c** and consecrated this 2 Chr 7:16

and Benjamin, 180,000 **c** warriors, 2 Chr 11:1
that the LORD had **c** out of all the 2 Chr 12:13
of valiant men of war, 400,000 **c** men. 2 Chr 13:3
him with 800,000 **c** mighty warriors. 2 Chr 13:3
fell slain of Israel 500,000 **c** men. 2 Chr 13:17
for the LORD has **c** you to stand in 2 Chr 29:11
which I have **c** out of all the tribes of 2 Chr 33:7
bring them to the place that I have **c**, Neh 1:9
and with seven **c** young women from the Est 2:9
this you have **c** rather than affliction. Jb 36:21
The LORD is my **c** portion and my cup; Ps 16:5
people whom he has **c** as his heritage! Ps 33:12
"I have made a covenant with my **c** one; Ps 89:3
I have exalted one **c** from the people. Ps 89:19
servant, children of Jacob, his **c** ones! Ps 105:6
servant, and Aaron, whom he had **c**. Ps 105:26
out with joy, his **c** ones with singing. Ps 105:43
look upon the prosperity of your **c** ones, Ps 106:5
them—had not Moses, his **c** one, Ps 106:23
I have **c** the way of faithfulness; I set Ps 119:30
to help me, for I have **c** your precepts. Ps 119:173
For the LORD has **c** Zion; he has desired Ps 132:13
For the LORD has **c** Jacob for himself, Ps 135:4
is to be **c** rather than silver. Prv 16:16
name is to be **c** rather than great riches, Prv 22:1
blush for the gardens that you have **c**. Is 1:29
Israel, my servant, Jacob, whom I have **c**, Is 41:8
I have **c** you and not cast you off"; Is 41:9
Behold my servant, whom I uphold, my **c**, Is 42:1
LORD, "and my servant whom I have **c**, Is 43:10
the desert, to give drink to my **c** people, Is 43:20
Jacob my servant, Israel whom I have **c**! Is 44:1
my servant, Jeshurun whom I have **c**. Is 44:2
of my servant Jacob, and Israel my **c**, Is 45:4
the Holy One of Israel, who has **c** you." Is 49:7
my **c** shall possess it, and my servants Is 65:9
leave your name to my **c** for a curse, Is 65:15
and my **c** shall long enjoy the work of Is 65:22
These have **c** their own ways, and their Is 66:3
you like a signet ring, for I have **c** you, Hg 2:23
LORD who has **c** Jerusalem rebuke you! Zec 3:2
"Behold, my servant whom I have **c**, Mt 12:18
For many are called, but few are **c**." Mt 22:14
he was **c** by lot to enter the temple of the Lk 1:9
saying, "This is my Son, my **C** One; Lk 9:35
Mary has **c** the good portion, which Lk 10:42
if he is the Christ of God, his **C** One!" Lk 23:35
of all of you; I know whom I have **c**. Jn 13:18
Spirit to the apostles whom he had **c**. Acts 1:2
which one of these two you have **c** Acts 1:24
for he is a **c** instrument of mine to Acts 9:15
us who had been **c** by God as Acts 10:41
time there is a remnant, **c** by grace. Rom 11:5
Greet Rufus, **c** in the Lord; also his Rom 16:13
But God gives it a body as he has **c**, 1 Cor 15:38
Put on then, as God's **c** ones, holy and Col 3:12
loved by God, that he has **c** you, 1 Thes 1:4
every high priest **c** from among men Heb 5:1
has not God **c** those who are poor in the Jas 2:5
but in the sight of God **c** and precious, 1 Pt 2:4
a stone, a cornerstone **c** and precious, 1 Pt 2:6
But you are a **c** race, a royal priesthood, 1 Pt 2:9
who is at Babylon, who is likewise **c**, 1 Pt 5:13
with him are called and **c** and faithful." Rv 17:14

CHRIST (524)

The book of the genealogy of Jesus **C**, the Mt 1:1
whom Jesus was born, who is called **C**. Mt 1:16
Babylon to the **C** fourteen generations. Mt 1:17
the birth of Jesus **C** took place in this Mt 1:18
of them where the **C** was to be born. Mt 2:4
heard in prison about the deeds of the **C**, Mt 11:2
Simon Peter replied, "You are the **C**, the Mt 16:16
to tell no one that he was the **C**. Mt 16:20
"What do you think about the **C**? Mt 22:42
for you have one instructor, the **C**. Mt 23:10
come in my name, saying, 'I am the **C**,' Mt 24:5
says to you, 'Look, here is the **C**!' Mt 24:23
the living God, tell us if you are the **C**, Mt 26:63
saying, "Prophesy to us, you **C**! Who is Mt 26:68
Barabbas, or Jesus who is called **C**?" Mt 27:17
Jesus who is called **C**?" They all said, Mt 27:22
The beginning of the gospel of Jesus **C**, Mk 1:1
Peter answered him, "You are the **C**." Mk 8:29
because you belong to **C** will by no Mk 9:41
the scribes say that the **C** is the son of Mk 12:35
says to you, 'Look, here is the **C**!' Mk 13:21
high priest asked him, "Are you the **C**, Mk 14:61
Let the **C**, the King of Israel, come Mk 15:32
city of David a Savior, who is **C** the Lord. Lk 2:11
death before he had seen the Lord's **C**. Lk 2:26
John, whether he might be the **C**, Lk 3:15
because they knew that he was the **C**. Lk 4:41
And Peter answered, "The **C** of God." Lk 9:20
can they say that the **C** is David's son? Lk 20:41
"If you are the **C**, tell us." But he said to Lk 22:67
Caesar, and saying that he himself is **C**, Lk 23:2
him save himself, if he is the **C** of God, Lk 23:35
at him, saying, "Are you not the **C**? Lk 23:39
necessary that the **C** should suffer Lk 24:26
that the **C** should suffer and on the Lk 24:46
grace and truth came through Jesus **C**. Jn 1:17
not deny, but confessed, "I am not the **C**." Jn 1:20
you baptizing, if you are neither the **C**, Jn 1:25
found the Messiah" (which means **C**). Jn 1:41
me witness, that I said, 'I am not the **C**, Jn 3:28
Messiah is coming (he who is called **C**). Jn 4:25
me all that I ever did. Can this be the **C**?" Jn 4:29
really know that this is the **C**? Jn 7:26
comes from, and when the **C** appears, Jn 7:27
They said, "When the **C** appears, will he Jn 7:31
said, "This is the **C**." But some said, Jn 7:41
said, "Is the **C** to come from Galilee? Jn 7:41
Scripture said that the **C** comes from the Jn 7:42
if anyone should confess Jesus to be **C**, Jn 9:22
If you are the **C**, tell us plainly." Jn 10:24
I believe that you are the **C**, the Son of Jn 11:27
the Law that the **C** remains forever. Jn 12:34
God, and Jesus **C** whom you have sent. Jn 17:3
that you may believe that Jesus is the **C**, Jn 20:31
spoke about the resurrection of the **C**, Acts 2:31
God has made him both Lord and **C**, Acts 2:36
the name of Jesus **C** for the forgiveness Acts 2:38
In the name of Jesus **C** of Nazareth, rise Acts 3:6
the prophets, that his **C** would suffer, Acts 3:18
he may send the **C** appointed for you, Acts 3:20
by the name of Jesus **C** of Nazareth, Acts 4:10
teaching and preaching Jesus as the **C**. Acts 5:42
Samaria and proclaimed to them the **C**. Acts 8:5
of God and the name of Jesus **C**, Acts 8:12
by proving that Jesus was the **C**. Acts 9:22
to him, "Aeneas, Jesus **C** heals you; Acts 9:34
of peace through Jesus **C** (he is Lord Acts 10:36
to be baptized in the name of Jesus **C**. Acts 10:48
when we believed in the Lord Jesus **C**, Acts 11:17
lives for the sake of our Lord Jesus **C**. Acts 15:26
in the name of Jesus **C** to come out of Acts 16:18
was necessary for the **C** to suffer and to Acts 17:3
whom I proclaim to you, is the **C**." Acts 17:3
to the Jews that the **C** was Jesus. Acts 18:5
the Scriptures that the **C** was Jesus. Acts 18:28
God and of faith in our Lord Jesus **C**. Acts 20:21
him speak about faith in **C** Jesus. Acts 24:24
that the **C** must suffer and that, by Acts 26:23
the Lord Jesus **C** with all boldness Acts 28:31
Paul, a servant of **C** Jesus, called to be Rom 1:1
from the dead, Jesus **C** our Lord, Rom 1:4
you who are called to belong to Jesus **C**, Rom 1:6
God our Father and the Lord Jesus **C**. Rom 1:7
my God through Jesus **C** for all of you, Rom 1:8
judges the secrets of men by **C** Jesus. Rom 2:16
through faith in Jesus **C** for all who Rom 3:22
the redemption that is in **C** Jesus, Rom 3:24
with God through our Lord Jesus **C**. Rom 5:1
at the right time **C** died for the ungodly. Rom 5:6
we were still sinners, **C** died for us. Rom 5:8
in God through our Lord Jesus **C**, Rom 5:11
one man Jesus **C** abounded for many. Rom 5:15
in life through the one man Jesus **C**. Rom 5:17
eternal life through Jesus **C** our Lord. Rom 5:21
been baptized into **C** Jesus were Rom 6:3
just as **C** was raised from the dead by Rom 6:4
Now if we have died with **C**, we believe Rom 6:8
We know that **C** being raised from the Rom 6:9
dead to sin and alive to God in **C** Jesus. Rom 6:11
God is eternal life in **C** Jesus our Lord. Rom 6:23
died to the law through the body of **C**, Rom 7:4
be to God through Jesus **C** our Lord! Rom 7:25
for those who are in **C** Jesus. Rom 8:1
has set you free in **C** Jesus from the law Rom 8:2
have the Spirit of **C** does not belong to Rom 8:9
But if **C** is in you, although the body is Rom 8:10
he who raised **C** Jesus from the dead Rom 8:11
—heirs of God and fellow heirs with **C**, Rom 8:17
C Jesus is the one who died—more Rom 8:34
shall separate us from the love of **C**? Rom 8:35
the love of God in **C** Jesus our Lord. Rom 8:39
am speaking the truth in **C**—I am not Rom 9:1
and cut off from **C** for the sake of Rom 9:3
to the flesh, is the **C** who is God over all, Rom 9:5
For **C** is the end of the law for Rom 10:4
heaven?'" (that is, to bring **C** down) Rom 10:6
(that is, to bring **C** up from the dead). Rom 10:7
and hearing through the word of **C**. Rom 10:17
we, though many, are one body in **C**, Rom 12:5
But put on the Lord Jesus **C**, and Rom 13:14
For to this end **C** died and lived again, Rom 14:9
not destroy the one for whom **C** died. Rom 14:15
Whoever thus serves **C** is acceptable Rom 14:18
For **C** did not please himself, but as it Rom 15:3
one another, in accord with **C** Jesus, Rom 15:5
God and Father of our Lord Jesus **C**. Rom 15:6
one another as **C** has welcomed you, Rom 15:7
I tell you that **C** became a servant to Rom 15:8
be a minister of **C** Jesus to the Rom 15:16
In **C** Jesus, then, I have reason to be Rom 15:17
except what **C** has accomplished Rom 15:18
the ministry of the gospel of **C**; Rom 15:19
not where **C** has already been named, Rom 15:20
in the fullness of the blessing of **C**. Rom 15:29
by our Lord Jesus **C** and by the love Rom 15:30
Aquila, my fellow workers in **C** Jesus, Rom 16:3
who was the first convert to **C** in Asia. Rom 16:5
apostles, and they were in **C** before me. Rom 16:7
Urbanus, our fellow worker in **C**, Rom 16:9
Greet Apelles, who is approved in **C**. Rom 16:10
kiss. All the churches of **C** greet you. Rom 16:16
persons do not serve our Lord **C**, Rom 16:18
of our Lord Jesus **C** be with you. Rom 16:20
gospel and the preaching of Jesus **C**, Rom 16:25
glory forevermore through Jesus **C**! Rom 16:27
will of God to be an apostle of **C** Jesus, 1 Cor 1:1
Corinth, to those sanctified in **C** Jesus, 1 Cor 1:2
upon the name of our Lord Jesus **C**, 1 Cor 1:2
God our Father and the Lord Jesus **C**. 1 Cor 1:3
of God that was given you in **C** Jesus, 1 Cor 1:4
the testimony about **C** was confirmed 1 Cor 1:6
for the revealing of our Lord Jesus **C**, 1 Cor 1:7
guiltless in the day of our Lord Jesus **C**. 1 Cor 1:8
fellowship of his Son, Jesus **C** our Lord. 1 Cor 1:9
by the name of our Lord Jesus **C**, 1 Cor 1:10
or "I follow Cephas," or "I follow **C**." 1 Cor 1:12
Is **C** divided? Was Paul crucified for 1 Cor 1:13
For **C** did not send me to baptize but 1 Cor 1:17
lest the cross of **C** be emptied of its 1 Cor 1:17
but we preach **C** crucified, a 1 Cor 1:23
C the power of God and the wisdom of 1 Cor 1:24
is the source of your life in **C** Jesus, 1 Cor 1:30
you except Jesus **C** and him crucified. 1 Cor 2:2
him?" But we have the mind of **C**. 1 Cor 2:16
as people of the flesh, as infants in **C**. 1 Cor 3:1
that which is laid, which is Jesus **C**. 1 Cor 3:11
and you are Christ's, and **C** is God's. 1 Cor 3:23
as servants of **C** and stewards of the 1 Cor 4:1
Christ's sake, but you are wise in **C**. 1 Cor 4:10
you have countless guides in **C**, 1 Cor 4:15
your father in **C** Jesus through the 1 Cor 4:15
Lord, to remind you of my ways in **C**, 1 Cor 4:17
as you really are unleavened. For **C**, 1 Cor 5:7
of the Lord Jesus **C** and by the Spirit 1 Cor 6:11
that your bodies are members of **C**? 1 Cor 6:15
the members of **C** and make them 1 Cor 6:15
was free when called is a slave of **C**. 1 Cor 7:22
whom we exist, and one Lord, Jesus **C**, 1 Cor 8:6
the brother for whom **C** died. 1 Cor 8:11
when it is weak, you sin against **C**. 1 Cor 8:12
obstacle in the way of the gospel of **C**. 1 Cor 9:12
under the law of **C**) that I might win 1 Cor 9:21
followed them, and the Rock was **C**. 1 Cor 10:4
We must not put **C** to the test, as 1 Cor 10:9
a participation in the blood of **C**? 1 Cor 10:16
not a participation in the body of **C**? 1 Cor 10:16
Be imitators of me, as I am of **C**. 1 Cor 11:1
that the head of every man is **C**, 1 Cor 11:3
husband, and the head of **C** is God. 1 Cor 11:3
many, are one body, so it is with **C**. 1 Cor 12:12
the body of **C** and individually 1 Cor 12:27
that **C** died for our sins in 1 Cor 15:3
Now if **C** is proclaimed as raised 1 Cor 15:12
then not even **C** has been raised. 1 Cor 15:13
And if **C** has not been raised, then 1 Cor 15:14
testified about God that he raised **C**, 1 Cor 15:15
raised, not even **C** has been raised. 1 Cor 15:16
And if **C** has not been raised, your 1 Cor 15:17
fallen asleep in **C** have perished. 1 Cor 15:18
in this life only we have hoped in **C**, 1 Cor 15:19
But in fact **C** has been raised from 1 Cor 15:20
so also in **C** shall all be made alive. 1 Cor 15:22
C the firstfruits, then at his coming 1 Cor 15:23
his coming those who belong to **C**. 1 Cor 15:23
which I have in **C** Jesus our Lord, 1 Cor 15:31
victory through our Lord Jesus **C**. 1 Cor 15:57
My love be with you all in **C** Jesus. 1 Cor 16:24
an apostle of **C** Jesus by the will of God, 2 Cor 1:1
God our Father and the Lord Jesus **C**. 2 Cor 1:2
God and Father of our Lord Jesus **C**, 2 Cor 1:3
so through **C** we share abundantly in 2 Cor 1:5
For the Son of God, Jesus **C**, whom we 2 Cor 1:19
who establishes us with you in **C**, 2 Cor 1:21
for your sake in the presence of **C**, 2 Cor 2:10
to Troas to preach the gospel of **C**, 2 Cor 2:12
who in **C** always leads us in 2 Cor 2:14
are the aroma of **C** to God among 2 Cor 2:15
in the sight of God we speak in **C**. 2 Cor 2:17
you are a letter from **C** delivered by us, 2 Cor 3:3
that we have through **C** toward God. 2 Cor 3:4

because only through **C** is it taken 2 Cor 3:14
the light of the gospel of the glory of **C**, 2 Cor 4:4
is not ourselves, but Jesus **C** as Lord, 2 Cor 4:5
the glory of God in the face of Jesus **C**. 2 Cor 4:6
appear before the judgment seat of **C**, 2 Cor 5:10
For the love of **C** controls us, because 2 Cor 5:14
we once regarded **C** according to the 2 Cor 5:16
Therefore, if anyone is in **C**, he is a 2 Cor 5:17
who through **C** reconciled us to 2 Cor 5:18
in **C** God was reconciling the world 2 Cor 5:19
Therefore, we are ambassadors for **C**, 2 Cor 5:20
We implore you on behalf of **C**, be 2 Cor 5:20
What accord has **C** with Belial? Or 2 Cor 6:15
know the grace of our Lord Jesus **C**, 2 Cor 8:9
of the churches, the glory of **C**. 2 Cor 8:23
your confession of the gospel of **C**, 2 Cor 9:13
meekness and gentleness of **C**—I who 2 Cor 10:1
take every thought captive to obey **C**, 2 Cor 10:5
the way to you with the gospel of **C**. 2 Cor 10:14
to present you as a pure virgin to **C**. 2 Cor 11:2
a sincere and pure devotion to **C**. 2 Cor 11:3
As the truth of **C** is in me, this 2 Cor 11:10
themselves as apostles of **C**. 2 Cor 11:13
Are they servants of **C**? I am a better 2 Cor 11:23
know a man in **C** who fourteen years 2 Cor 12:2
that the power of **C** may rest upon 2 Cor 12:9
For the sake of **C**, then, I am content 2 Cor 12:10
that we have been speaking in **C**, 2 Cor 12:19
you seek proof that **C** is speaking in 2 Cor 13:3
yourselves, that Jesus **C** is in you? 2 Cor 13:5
of the Lord Jesus **C** and the love of 2 Cor 13:14
but through Jesus **C** and God the Father, Gal 1:1
God our Father and the Lord Jesus **C**, Gal 1:3
you in the grace of **C** and are turning to Gal 1:6
you and want to distort the gospel of **C**. Gal 1:7
man, I would not be a servant of **C**. Gal 1:10
it through a revelation of Jesus **C**. Gal 1:12
to the churches of Judea that are in **C**. Gal 1:22
out our freedom that we have in **C** Jesus, Gal 2:4
of the law but through faith in Jesus **C**, Gal 2:16
so we also have believed in **C** Jesus, Gal 2:16
justified by faith in **C** and not by works Gal 2:16
if, in our endeavor to be justified in **C**, Gal 2:17
to be sinners, is **C** then a servant of sin? Gal 2:17
I have been crucified with **C**. It is no Gal 2:20
I who live, but **C** who lives in me. Gal 2:20
the law, then **C** died for no purpose. Gal 2:21
eyes that Jesus **C** was publicly portrayed Gal 3:1
C redeemed us from the curse of the law Gal 3:13
so that in **C** Jesus the blessing of Gal 3:14
one, "And to your offspring," who is **C**. Gal 3:16
by faith in Jesus **C** might be given to Gal 3:22
the law was our guardian until **C** came, Gal 3:24
for in **C** Jesus you are all sons of God, Gal 3:26
as were baptized into **C** have put on Gal 3:27
baptized into Christ have put on **C**. Gal 3:27
female, for you are all one in **C** Jesus. Gal 3:28
me as an angel of God, as **C** Jesus. Gal 4:14
of childbirth until **C** is formed in Gal 4:19
For freedom **C** has set us free; stand firm Gal 5:1
C will be of no advantage to you. Gal 5:2
You are severed from **C**, you who would Gal 5:4
For in **C** Jesus neither circumcision nor Gal 5:6
who belong to **C** Jesus have crucified Gal 5:24
burdens, and so fulfill the law of **C**. Gal 6:2
not be persecuted for the cross of **C**. Gal 6:12
except in the cross of our Lord Jesus **C**, Gal 6:14
of our Lord Jesus **C** be with your spirit, Gal 6:18
an apostle of **C** Jesus by the will of God, Eph 1:1
in Ephesus, and are faithful in **C** Jesus: Eph 1:1
God our Father and the Lord Jesus **C**. Eph 1:2
the God and Father of our Lord Jesus **C**, Eph 1:3
has blessed us in **C** with every spiritual Eph 1:3
us for adoption through Jesus **C**, Eph 1:5
to his purpose, which he set forth in **C** Eph 1:9
the first to hope in **C** might be to the Eph 1:12
that the God of our Lord Jesus **C**, the Eph 1:17
that he worked in **C** when he raised Eph 1:20
us alive together with **C**—by grace you Eph 2:5
him in the heavenly places in **C** Jesus, Eph 2:6
grace in kindness toward us in **C** Jesus. Eph 2:7
created in **C** Jesus for good works, Eph 2:10
you were at that time separated from **C**, Eph 2:12
But now in **C** Jesus you who once were Eph 2:13
been brought near by the blood of **C**. Eph 2:13
C Jesus himself being the cornerstone, Eph 2:20
a prisoner for **C** Jesus on behalf of you Eph 3:1
my insight into the mystery of **C**, Eph 3:4
of the promise in **C** Jesus through the Eph 3:6
Gentiles the unsearchable riches of **C**, Eph 3:8
he has realized in **C** Jesus our Lord, Eph 3:11
so that **C** may dwell in your hearts Eph 3:17
the love of **C** that surpasses knowledge, Eph 3:19
church and in **C** Jesus throughout all Eph 3:21
for building up the body of **C**, Eph 4:12
of the stature of the fullness of **C**, Eph 4:13
way into him who is the head, into **C**, Eph 4:15
But that is not the way you learned **C**! Eph 4:20
one another, as God in **C** forgave you. Eph 4:32
as **C** loved us and gave himself up for us, Eph 5:2
in the kingdom of **C** and God. Eph 5:5
the dead, and **C** will shine on you." Eph 5:14
Father in the name of our Lord Jesus **C**, Eph 5:20
to one another out of reverence for **C**. Eph 5:21
of the wife even as **C** is the head of the Eph 5:23
Now as the church submits to **C**, so Eph 5:24
as **C** loved the church and gave Eph 5:25
cherishes it, just as **C** does the church, Eph 5:29
that it refers to **C** and the church. Eph 5:32
with a sincere heart, as you would **C**, Eph 6:5
as people-pleasers, but as servants of **C**, Eph 6:6
God the Father and the Lord Jesus **C**. Eph 6:23
our Lord Jesus **C** with love Eph 6:24
Paul and Timothy, servants of **C** Jesus, Phil 1:1
To all the saints in **C** Jesus who are at Phil 1:1
God our Father and the Lord Jesus **C**. Phil 1:2
it to completion at the day of Jesus **C**. Phil 1:6
for you all with the affection of **C** Jesus. Phil 1:8
be pure and blameless for the day of **C**, Phil 1:10
that comes through Jesus **C**, Phil 1:11
the rest that my imprisonment is for **C**. Phil 1:13
Some indeed preach **C** from envy and Phil 1:15
The former proclaim **C** out of rivalry, Phil 1:17
pretense or in truth, **C** is proclaimed, Phil 1:18
the Spirit of Jesus **C** this will turn out Phil 1:19
now as always **C** will be honored Phil 1:20
For to me to live is **C**, and to die is gain. Phil 1:21
My desire is to depart and be with **C**, Phil 1:23
have ample cause to glory in **C** Jesus, Phil 1:26
of life be worthy of the gospel of **C**, Phil 1:27
for the sake of **C** you should not only Phil 1:29
So if there is any encouragement in **C**, Phil 2:1
yourselves, which is yours in **C** Jesus, Phil 2:5
tongue confess that Jesus **C** is Lord, Phil 2:11
that in the day of **C** I may be proud Phil 2:16
own interests, not those of Jesus **C**. Phil 2:21
for he nearly died for the work of **C**, Phil 2:30
of God and glory in **C** Jesus and put no Phil 3:3
I had, I counted as loss for the sake of **C**. Phil 3:7
worth of knowing **C** Jesus my Lord. Phil 3:8
as rubbish, in order that I may gain **C** Phil 3:8
that which comes through faith in **C**, Phil 3:9
because **C** Jesus has made me his own. Phil 3:12
of the upward call of God in **C** Jesus. Phil 3:14
tears, walk as enemies of the cross of **C**. Phil 3:18
it we await a Savior, the Lord Jesus **C**, Phil 3:20
your hearts and your minds in **C** Jesus. Phil 4:7
to his riches in glory in **C** Jesus. Phil 4:19
Greet every saint in **C** Jesus. The Phil 4:21
of the Lord Jesus **C** be with your spirit. Phil 4:23
an apostle of **C** Jesus by the will of God, Col 1:1
and faithful brothers in **C** at Colossae: Col 1:2
God, the Father of our Lord Jesus **C**, Col 1:3
heard of your faith in **C** Jesus and of the Col 1:4
is a faithful minister of **C** on your behalf Col 1:7
of this mystery, which is **C** in you, Col 1:27
we may present everyone mature in **C**. Col 1:28
knowledge of God's mystery, which is **C**, Col 2:2
order and the firmness of your faith in **C**. Col 2:5
as you received **C** Jesus the Lord, Col 2:6
of the world, and not according to **C**. Col 2:8
of the flesh, by the circumcision of **C**, Col 2:11
come, but the substance belongs to **C**. Col 2:17
If with **C** you died to the elemental Col 2:20
If then you have been raised with **C**, seek Col 3:1
the things that are above, where **C** is, Col 3:1
and your life is hidden with **C** in God. Col 3:3
When **C** who is your life appears, then Col 3:4
slave, free; but **C** is all, and in all. Col 3:11
let the peace of **C** rule in your hearts, Col 3:15
Let the word of **C** dwell in you richly, Col 3:16
reward. You are serving the Lord **C**. Col 3:24
for the word, to declare the mystery of **C**, Col 4:3
who is one of you, a servant of **C** Jesus, Col 4:12
God the Father and the Lord Jesus **C**: 1 Thes 1:1
of hope in our Lord Jesus **C**. 1 Thes 1:3
have made demands as apostles of **C**. 1 Thes 2:6
churches of God in **C** Jesus that are 1 Thes 2:14
God's coworker in the gospel of **C**, 1 Thes 3:2
God. And the dead in **C** will rise first. 1 Thes 4:16
salvation through our Lord Jesus **C**, 1 Thes 5:9
is the will of God in **C** Jesus for you. 1 Thes 5:18
at the coming of our Lord Jesus **C**. 1 Thes 5:23
of our Lord Jesus **C** be with you. 1 Thes 5:28
God our Father and the Lord Jesus **C**: 2 Thes 1:1
God our Father and the Lord Jesus **C**. 2 Thes 1:2
of our God and the Lord Jesus **C**. 2 Thes 1:12
of our Lord Jesus **C** and our being 2 Thes 2:1
obtain the glory of our Lord Jesus **C**. 2 Thes 2:14
Now may our Lord Jesus **C** himself, 2 Thes 2:16
of God and to the steadfastness of **C**. 2 Thes 3:5
in the name of our Lord Jesus **C**, 2 Thes 3:6
in the Lord Jesus **C** to do their work 2 Thes 3:12
of our Lord Jesus **C** be with you all. 2 Thes 3:18
an apostle of **C** Jesus by command of 1 Tm 1:1
our Savior and of **C** Jesus our hope, 1 Tm 1:1
God the Father and **C** Jesus our Lord. 1 Tm 1:2
given me strength, **C** Jesus our Lord, 1 Tm 1:12
the faith and love that are in **C** Jesus. 1 Tm 1:14
that **C** Jesus came into the world to 1 Tm 1:15
Jesus **C** might display his perfect 1 Tm 1:16
God and men, the man **C** Jesus, 1 Tm 2:5
in the faith that is in **C** Jesus. 1 Tm 3:13
you will be a good servant of **C** Jesus, 1 Tm 4:6
passions draw them away from **C**, 1 Tm 5:11
of God and of **C** Jesus and of the 1 Tm 5:21
of our Lord Jesus **C** and the teaching 1 Tm 6:3
gives life to all things, and of **C** Jesus, 1 Tm 6:13
the appearing of our Lord Jesus **C**, 1 Tm 6:14
an apostle of **C** Jesus by the will of God 2 Tm 1:1
promise of the life that is in **C** Jesus, 2 Tm 1:1
God the Father and **C** Jesus our Lord. 2 Tm 1:2
he gave us in **C** Jesus before the ages 2 Tm 1:9
the appearing of our Savior **C** Jesus, 2 Tm 1:10
the faith and love that are in **C** Jesus. 2 Tm 1:13
by the grace that is in **C** Jesus, 2 Tm 2:1
suffering as a good soldier of **C** Jesus. 2 Tm 2:3
Remember Jesus **C**, risen from the 2 Tm 2:8
that is in **C** Jesus with eternal 2 Tm 2:10
a godly life in **C** Jesus will be 2 Tm 3:12
salvation through faith in **C** Jesus. 2 Tm 3:15
in the presence of God and of **C** Jesus, 2 Tm 4:1
a servant of God and an apostle of Jesus **C**, Ti 1:1
God the Father and **C** Jesus our Savior. Ti 1:4
of our great God and Savior Jesus **C**, Ti 2:13
on us richly through Jesus **C** our Savior, Ti 3:6
Paul, a prisoner for **C** Jesus, and Phlm 1:1
God our Father and the Lord Jesus **C**. Phlm 1:3
thing that is in us for the sake of **C**. Phlm 1:6
bold enough in **C** to command you Phlm 1:8
and now a prisoner also for **C** Jesus— Phlm 1:9
in the Lord. Refresh my heart in **C**. Phlm 1:20
my fellow prisoner in **C** Jesus, Phlm 1:23
of the Lord Jesus **C** be with your Phlm 1:25
but **C** is faithful over God's house as a Heb 3:6
For we share in **C**, if indeed we hold our Heb 3:14
So also **C** did not exalt himself to be Heb 5:5
the elementary doctrine of **C** and go on Heb 6:1
C has obtained a ministry that is as Heb 8:6
But when **C** appeared as a high priest of Heb 9:11
how much more will the blood of **C**, Heb 9:14
For **C** has entered, not into holy places Heb 9:24
so **C**, having been offered once to bear Heb 9:28
when **C** came into the world, Heb 10:5
of the body of Jesus **C** once for all. Heb 10:10
But when **C** had offered for all time a Heb 10:12
the reproach of **C** greater wealth than Heb 11:26
Jesus **C** is the same yesterday and today Heb 13:8
pleasing in his sight, through Jesus **C**, Heb 13:21
a servant of God and of the Lord Jesus **C**, Jas 1:1
as you hold the faith in our Lord Jesus **C**, Jas 2:1
Peter, an apostle of Jesus **C**, To those 1 Pt 1:1
obedience to Jesus **C** and for sprinkling 1 Pt 1:2
the God and Father of our Lord Jesus **C**! 1 Pt 1:3
resurrection of Jesus **C** from the dead, 1 Pt 1:3
and honor at the revelation of Jesus **C**. 1 Pt 1:7
time the Spirit of **C** in them was 1 Pt 1:11
the sufferings of **C** and the subsequent 1 Pt 1:11
to you at the revelation of Jesus **C**. 1 Pt 1:13
but with the precious blood of **C**, like 1 Pt 1:19
acceptable to God through Jesus **C**. 1 Pt 2:5
called, because **C** also suffered for you, 1 Pt 2:21
in your hearts regard **C** the Lord as 1 Pt 3:15
your good behavior in **C** may be put to 1 Pt 3:16
For **C** also suffered once for sins, the 1 Pt 3:18
through the resurrection of Jesus **C**, 1 Pt 3:21
Since therefore **C** suffered in the flesh, 1 Pt 4:1
God may be glorified through Jesus **C**. 1 Pt 4:11
If you are insulted for the name of **C**, 1 Pt 4:14
elder and a witness of the sufferings of **C**, 1 Pt 5:1
has called you to his eternal glory in **C**, 1 Pt 5:10
of love. Peace to all of you who are in **C**. 1 Pt 5:14
Peter, a servant and apostle of Jesus **C**, 2 Pt 1:1
of our God and Savior Jesus **C**: 2 Pt 1:1
in the knowledge of our Lord Jesus **C**. 2 Pt 1:8
of our Lord and Savior Jesus **C**. 2 Pt 1:11
as our Lord Jesus **C** made clear to me. 2 Pt 1:14
power and coming of our Lord Jesus **C**, 2 Pt 1:16
of our Lord and Savior Jesus **C**, 2 Pt 2:20
of our Lord and Savior Jesus **C**. 2 Pt 3:18
the Father and with his Son Jesus **C**. 1 Jn 1:3
with the Father, Jesus **C** the righteous. 1 Jn 2:1
but he who denies that Jesus is the **C**? 1 Jn 2:22
of his Son Jesus **C** and love one 1 Jn 3:23
that confesses that Jesus **C** has come in 1 Jn 4:2

that Jesus is the **C** has been born of 1 Jn 5:1
who came by water and blood—Jesus **C**; 1 Jn 5:6
in him who is true, in his Son Jesus **C**. 1 Jn 5:20
and from Jesus **C** the Father's Son, 2 Jn 1:3
the coming of Jesus **C** in the flesh. 2 Jn 1:7
and does not abide in the teaching of **C**, 2 Jn 1:9
a servant of Jesus **C** and brother of Jude 1:1
in God the Father and kept for Jesus **C**: Jude 1:1
deny our only Master and Lord, Jesus **C**. Jude 1:4
of the apostles of our Lord Jesus **C**. Jude 1:17
of our Lord Jesus **C** that leads to eternal Jude 1:21
our Savior, through Jesus **C** our Lord, Jude 1:25
The revelation of Jesus **C**, which God gave Rv 1:1
of God and to the testimony of Jesus **C**. Rv 1:2
and from Jesus **C** the faithful witness, the Rv 1:5
the kingdom of our Lord and of his **C**, Rv 11:15
and the authority of his **C** have come, Rv 12:10
life and reigned with **C** for a thousand Rv 20:4
but they will be priests of God and of **C**, Rv 20:6

CHRIST'S (9)
and you are **C**, and Christ is God's. 1 Cor 3:23
We are fools for **C** sake, but you are 1 Cor 4:10
we share abundantly in **C** sufferings, 2 Cor 1:5
If anyone is confident that he is **C**, let 2 Cor 10:7
remind himself that just as he is **C**, 2 Cor 10:7
And if you are **C**, then you are Gal 3:29
of us according to the measure of **C** gift. Eph 4:7
what is lacking in **C** afflictions for the Col 1:24
insofar as you share **C** sufferings, 1 Pt 4:13

CHRISTIAN (2)
would you persuade me to be a **C**?" Acts 26:28
Yet if anyone suffers as a **C**, let him not 1 Pt 4:16

CHRISTIANS (1)
the disciples were first called **C**. Acts 11:26

CHRISTS (2)
For false **c** and false prophets will arise Mt 24:24
False **c** and false prophets will arise Mk 13:22

CHRONIC (1)
it is a **c** leprous disease in the skin of Lv 13:11

CHRONICLES (45)
in the Book of the **C** of the Kings of 1 Kgs 14:19
in the Book of the **C** of the Kings of 1 Kgs 14:29
in the Book of the **C** of the Kings of 1 Kgs 15:7
in the Book of the **C** of the Kings of 1 Kgs 15:23
in the Book of the **C** of the Kings of 1 Kgs 15:31
in the Book of the **C** of the Kings of 1 Kgs 16:5
in the Book of the **C** of the Kings of 1 Kgs 16:14
in the Book of the **C** of the Kings of 1 Kgs 16:20
in the Book of the **C** of the Kings of 1 Kgs 16:27
in the Book of the **C** of the Kings of 1 Kgs 22:39
in the Book of the **C** of the Kings of 1 Kgs 22:45
in the Book of the **C** of the Kings of 2 Kgs 1:18
in the Book of the **C** of the Kings of 2 Kgs 8:23
in the Book of the **C** of the Kings of 2 Kgs 10:34
in the Book of the **C** of the Kings of 2 Kgs 12:19
in the Book of the **C** of the Kings of 2 Kgs 13:8
in the Book of the **C** of the Kings of 2 Kgs 13:12
in the Book of the **C** of the Kings of 2 Kgs 14:15
in the Book of the **C** of the Kings of 2 Kgs 14:18
in the Book of the **C** of the Kings of 2 Kgs 14:28
in the Book of the **C** of the Kings of 2 Kgs 15:6
in the Book of the **C** of the Kings of 2 Kgs 15:11
in the Book of the **C** of the Kings of 2 Kgs 15:15
in the Book of the **C** of the Kings of 2 Kgs 15:21
in the Book of the **C** of the Kings of 2 Kgs 15:26
in the Book of the **C** of the Kings of 2 Kgs 15:31
in the Book of the **C** of the Kings of 2 Kgs 15:36
in the Book of the **C** of the Kings of 2 Kgs 16:19
in the Book of the **C** of the Kings of 2 Kgs 20:20
in the Book of the **C** of the Kings of 2 Kgs 21:17
in the Book of the **C** of the Kings of 2 Kgs 21:25
in the Book of the **C** of the Kings of 2 Kgs 23:28
in the Book of the **C** of the Kings of 2 Kgs 24:5
not entered in the **c** of King David. 1 Chr 27:24
are written in the **C** of Samuel the 1 Chr 29:29
and in the **C** of Nathan the prophet, 1 Chr 29:29
and in the **C** of Gad the seer, 1 Chr 29:29
not written in the **c** of Shemaiah the 2 Chr 12:15
are written in the **c** of Jehu the son 2 Chr 20:34
they are in the **C** of the Kings of 2 Chr 33:18
they are written in the **C** of the Seers. 2 Chr 33:19
in the Book of the **C** until the days of Neh 12:23
in the book of the **c** in the presence of Est 2:23
the book of memorable deeds, the **c**, Est 6:1
in the Book of the **C** of the kings of Est 10:2

CHRYSOLITE (1)
onyx, the sixth carnelian, the seventh **c**, Rv 21:20

CHRYSOPRASE (1)
beryl, the ninth topaz, the tenth **c**, Rv 21:20

CHURCH (74)
and on this rock I will build my **c**, Mt 16:18
refuses to listen to them, tell it to the **c**. Mt 18:17
And if he refuses to listen even to the **c**, Mt 18:17
came upon the whole **c** and upon all Acts 5:11
persecution against the **c** in Jerusalem, Acts 8:1
But Saul was ravaging the **c**, and Acts 8:3
So the **c** throughout all Judea and Acts 9:31
came to the ears of the **c** in Jerusalem, Acts 11:22
they met with the **c** and taught a Acts 11:26
hands on some who belonged to the **c**. Acts 12:1
for him was made to God by the **c**. Acts 12:5
there were in the **c** at Antioch prophets Acts 13:1
appointed elders for them in every **c**, Acts 14:23
arrived and gathered the **c** together, Acts 14:27
So, being sent on their way by the **c**, Acts 15:3
welcomed by the **c** and the apostles Acts 15:4
and the elders, with the whole **c**, Acts 15:22
he went up and greeted the **c**, Acts 18:22
the elders of the **c** to come to him. Acts 20:17
you overseers, to care for the **c** of God, Acts 20:28
a servant of the **c** at Cenchreae, Rom 16:1
Greet also the **c** in their house. Greet Rom 16:5
who is host to me and to the whole **c**, Rom 16:23
To the **c** of God that is in Corinth, to 1 Cor 1:2
as I teach them everywhere in every **c**. 1 Cor 4:17
not those inside the **c** whom you are 1 Cor 5:12
those who have no standing in the **c**? 1 Cor 6:4
Jews or to Greeks or to the **c** of God, 1 Cor 10:32
when you come together as a **c**, 1 Cor 11:18
do you despise the **c** of God and 1 Cor 11:22
has appointed in the **c** first apostles, 1 Cor 12:28
one who prophesies builds up the **c**. 1 Cor 14:4
so that the **c** may be built up. 1 Cor 14:5
strive to excel in building up the **c**. 1 Cor 14:12
in **c** I would rather speak five words 1 Cor 14:19
the whole **c** comes together and all 1 Cor 14:23
them keep silent in **c** and speak to 1 Cor 14:28
shameful for a woman to speak in **c**. 1 Cor 14:35
because I persecuted the **c** of God. 1 Cor 15:9
together with the **c** in their house, 1 Cor 16:19
To the **c** of God that is at Corinth, 2 Cor 1:1
how I persecuted the **c** of God violently Gal 1:13
him as head over all things to the **c**, Eph 1:22
that through the **c** the manifold Eph 3:10
be glory in the **c** and in Christ Jesus Eph 3:21
wife even as Christ is the head of the **c**, Eph 5:23
Now as the **c** submits to Christ, so also Eph 5:24
as Christ loved the **c** and gave himself Eph 5:25
he might present the **c** to himself in Eph 5:27
cherishes it, just as Christ does the **c**, Eph 5:29
saying that it refers to Christ and the **c**. Eph 5:32
as to zeal, a persecutor of the **c**; as to Phil 3:6
no **c** entered into partnership with me Phil 4:15
And he is the head of the body, the **c**. He Col 1:18
for the sake of his body, that is, the **c**, Col 1:24
and to Nympha and the **c** in her house. Col 4:15
it also read in the **c** of the Laodiceans; Col 4:16
To the **c** of the Thessalonians in God 1 Thes 1:1
To the **c** of the Thessalonians in God 2 Thes 1:1
how will he care for God's **c**? 1 Tm 3:5
God, which is the **c** of the living God, 1 Tm 3:15
Let the **c** not be burdened, so that it 1 Tm 5:16
fellow soldier, and the **c** in your house: Phlm 1:2
Let him call for the elders of the **c**, and Jas 5:14
who testified to your love before the **c**. 3 Jn 1:6
I have written something to the **c**, but 3 Jn 1:9
who want to and puts them out of the **c**. 3 Jn 1:10
"To the angel of the **c** in Ephesus write: Rv 2:1
to the angel of the **c** in Smyrna write: Rv 2:8
to the angel of the **c** in Pergamum write: Rv 2:12
to the angel of the **c** in Thyatira write: Rv 2:18
"And to the angel of the **c** in Sardis write: Rv 3:1
to the angel of the **c** in Philadelphia write: Rv 3:7
to the angel of the **c** in Laodicea write: Rv 3:14

CHURCHES (35)
and Cilicia, strengthening the **c**. Acts 15:41
So the **c** were strengthened in the faith, Acts 16:5
thanks but all the **c** of the Gentiles Rom 16:4
kiss. All the **c** of Christ greet you. Rom 16:16
him. This is my rule in all the **c**. 1 Cor 7:17
such practice, nor do the **c** of God. 1 Cor 11:16
of peace. As in all the **c** of the saints, 1 Cor 14:33
women should keep silent in the **c**. 1 Cor 14:34
as I directed the **c** of Galatia, so you 1 Cor 16:1
The **c** of Asia send you greetings. 1 Cor 16:19
been given among the **c** of Macedonia, 2 Cor 8:1
among all the **c** for his preaching 2 Cor 8:18
been appointed by the **c** to travel with 2 Cor 8:19
they are messengers of the **c**, 2 Cor 8:23
give proof before the **c** of your love 2 Cor 8:24
I robbed other **c** by accepting support 2 Cor 11:8
on me of my anxiety for all the **c**. 2 Cor 11:28
less favored than the rest of the **c**, 2 Cor 12:13
who are with me, To the **c** of Galatia: Gal 1:2
in person to the **c** of Judea that are Gal 1:22
became imitators of the **c** of God in 1 Thes 2:14
about you in the **c** of God for your 2 Thes 1:4
John to the seven **c** that are in Asia: Grace Rv 1:4
see in a book and send it to the seven **c**, Rv 1:11
seven stars are the angels of the seven **c**, Rv 1:20
the seven lampstands are the seven **c**. Rv 1:20
let him hear what the Spirit says to the **c**. Rv 2:7
let him hear what the Spirit says to the **c**. Rv 2:11
let him hear what the Spirit says to the **c**. Rv 2:17
And all the **c** will know that I am he who Rv 2:23
him hear what the Spirit says to the **c**.' Rv 2:29
let him hear what the Spirit says to the **c**.' Rv 3:6
him hear what the Spirit says to the **c**.' Rv 3:13
him hear what the Spirit says to the **c**.'" Rv 3:22
to you about these things for the **c**. Rv 22:16

CHURNS (2)
for I am in distress; my stomach **c**; Lam 1:20
are spent with weeping; my stomach **c**; Lam 2:11

CHUZA (1)
and Joanna, the wife of **C**, Herod's Lk 8:3

CILICIA (8)
and of those from **C** and Asia, Acts 6:9
Gentiles in Antioch and Syria and **C**, Acts 15:23
And he went through Syria and **C**, Acts 15:41
"I am a Jew, from Tarsus in **C**, Acts 21:39
"I am a Jew, born in Tarsus in **C**, but Acts 22:3
when he learned that he was from **C**, Acts 23:34
along the coast of **C** and Pamphylia, Acts 27:5
I went into the regions of Syria and **C**. Gal 1:21

CINNAMON (4)
and of sweet-smelling **c** half as much, Ex 30:23
my bed with myrrh, aloes, and **c**. Prv 7:17
nard and saffron, calamus and **c**, with Sg 4:14
c, spice, incense, myrrh, frankincense, Rv 18:13

CIRCLE (4)
caused the ark of the LORD to **c** the city, Jos 6:11
He has inscribed a **c** on the face of the Jb 26:10
when he drew a **c** on the face of the deep, Prv 8:27
It is he who sits above the **c** of the earth, Is 40:22

CIRCLES (1)
And the boundary **c** west of Baalah to Jos 15:10

CIRCUIT (4)
And he went on a **c** year by year to 1 Sm 7:16
around from the Millo in complete **c**, 1 Chr 11:8
the heavens, and its **c** to the end of them, Ps 19:6
there we made a **c** and arrived at Acts 28:13

CIRCUITOUS (1)
they had made a **c** march of seven 2 Kgs 3:9

CIRCUITS (1)
the wind, and on its **c** the wind returns. Eccl 1:6

CIRCUMCISE (8)
C therefore the foreskin of your heart, Dt 10:16
LORD your God will **c** your heart and the Dt 30:6
"Make flint knives and **c** the sons of Jos 5:2
C yourselves to the LORD; remove the Jer 4:4
the eighth day they came to **c** the child. Lk 1:59
and you **c** a man on the Sabbath. Jn 7:22
"It is necessary to **c** them and to order Acts 15:5
telling them not to **c** their children or Acts 21:21

CIRCUMCISED (51)
you: Every male among you shall be **c**. Gn 17:10
You shall be **c** in the flesh of your Gn 17:11
is eight days old among you shall be **c**. Gn 17:12
with your money, shall surely be **c**. Gn 17:13
male who is not **c** in the flesh of Gn 17:14
and he **c** the flesh of their foreskins Gn 17:23
years old when he was **c** in the flesh of Gn 17:24
years old when he was **c** in the flesh of Gn 17:25
Abraham and his son Ishmael were **c**. Gn 17:26
from a foreigner, were **c** with him. Gn 17:27
And Abraham **c** his son Isaac when he Gn 21:4
are by every male among you being **c**. Gn 34:15
But if you will not listen to us and be **c**, Gn 34:17
male among us is **c** as they are Gn 34:22
among us is circumcised as they are **c**. Gn 34:22
son Shechem, and every male was **c**, Gn 34:24
may eat of it after you have **c** him. Ex 12:44
to the LORD, let all his males be **c**. Ex 12:48
day the flesh of his foreskin shall be **c**. Lv 12:3
made flint knives and **c** the sons of Israel Jos 5:3
this is the reason why Joshua **c** them: Jos 5:4
all the people who came out had been **c**, Jos 5:5
had come out of Egypt had not been **c**. Jos 5:5
he raised up in their place, that Joshua **c**. Jos 5:7
because they had not been **c** on the way. Jos 5:7
all those who are **c** merely in the flesh Jer 9:25
at the end of eight days, when he was **c**, Lk 2:21
of Isaac, and **c** him on the eighth day, Acts 7:8
from among the **c** who had come Acts 10:45
"Unless you are **c** according to the Acts 15:1
he took him and **c** him because of the Acts 16:3

He will justify the **c** by faith and the Rom 3:30
Is this blessing then only for the **c**, or Rom 4:9
Was it before or after he had been **c**? Rom 4:10
It was not after, but before he was **c**. Rom 4:10
of all who believe without being **c**, Rom 4:11
the father of the **c** who are not merely Rom 4:12
who are not merely **c** but who also Rom 4:12
father Abraham had before he was **c**. Rom 4:12
a servant to the **c** to show God's Rom 15:8
at the time of his call already **c**? 1 Cor 7:18
who was with me, was not forced to be **c**, Gal 2:3
been entrusted with the gospel to the **c** Gal 2:7
ministry to the **c** worked also through Gal 2:8
go to the Gentiles and they to the **c**. Gal 2:9
the flesh who would force you to be **c**, Gal 6:12
even those who are **c** do not themselves Gal 6:13
desire to have you **c** that they may Gal 6:13
c on the eighth day, of the people of Phil 3:5
also you were **c** with a circumcision Col 2:11
Greek and Jew, **c** and uncircumcised, Col 3:11

CIRCUMCISING (1)
When the **c** of the whole nation was Jos 5:8

CIRCUMCISION (28)
bridegroom of blood," because of the **c**. Ex 4:26
Moses gave you **c** (not that it is from Jn 7:22
If on the Sabbath a man receives **c**, so Jn 7:23
And he gave him the covenant of **c**. And Acts 7:8
Jerusalem, the **c** party criticized him, Acts 11:2
For **c** indeed is of value if you obey the Rom 2:25
law, your **c** becomes uncircumcision. Rom 2:25
his uncircumcision be regarded as **c**? Rom 2:26
the written code and **c** but break the Rom 2:27
nor is **c** outward and physical. Rom 2:28
and **c** is a matter of the heart, Rom 2:29
has the Jew? Or what is the value of **c**? Rom 3:1
He received the sign of **c** as a seal of the Rom 4:11
not seek to remove the marks of **c**. 1 Cor 7:18
uncircumcised? Let him not seek **c**. 1 Cor 7:18
For neither **c** counts for anything 1 Cor 7:19
separated himself, fearing the **c** party. Gal 2:12
I, Paul, say to you that if you accept **c**, Gal 5:2
every man who accepts **c** that he is Gal 5:3
Jesus neither **c** nor uncircumcision Gal 5:6
But if I, brothers, still preach **c**, why am Gal 5:11
For neither **c** counts for anything, nor Gal 6:15
by what is called the **c**, Eph 2:11
For we are the real **c**, who worship by Phil 3:3
circumcised with a **c** made without Col 2:11
the body of the flesh, by the **c** of Christ, Col 2:11
only men of the **c** among my fellow Col 4:11
deceivers, especially those of the **c** party. Ti 1:10

CIRCUMFERENCE (5)
a line of twelve cubits measured its **c**. 1 Kgs 7:15
a line of thirty cubits measured its **c**. 1 Kgs 7:23
a line of thirty cubits measured its **c**. 2 Chr 4:2
eighteen cubits, its **c** was twelve cubits, Jer 52:21
The **c** of the city shall be 18,000 Ezk 48:35

CIRCUMSTANCE (1)
In any and every **c**, I have learned the Phil 4:12

CIRCUMSTANCES (3)
might and of the **c** that came upon 1 Chr 29:30
In all **c** take up the shield of faith, with Eph 6:16
give thanks in all **c**; for this is the 1 Thes 5:18

CISTERN (17)
a spring or a **c** holding water shall be Lv 11:36
him back from the **c** of Sirah. 2 Sm 3:26
will drink the water of his own **c**, 2 Kgs 18:31
Drink water from your own **c**, flowing Prv 5:15
fountain, or the wheel broken at the **c**, Eccl 12:6
hearth, or to dip up water out of the **c**." Is 30:14
of you will drink the water of his own **c**, Is 36:16
and cast him into the **c** of Malchiah, Jer 38:6
And there was no water in the **c**, but Jer 38:6
put Jeremiah into the **c**—the king was Jer 38:7
the prophet by casting him into the **c**, Jer 38:9
the prophet out of the **c** before he dies." Jer 38:10
let down to Jeremiah in the **c** by ropes. Jer 38:11
with ropes and lifted him out of the **c**. Jer 38:13
slaughtered them and cast them into a **c**. Jer 41:7
Now the **c** into which Ishmael had Jer 41:9
Gedaliah was the large **c** that King Asa Jer 41:9

CISTERNS (7)
did not fill, and **c** that you did not dig, Dt 6:11
and in rocks and in tombs and in **c**, 1 Sm 13:6
the wilderness and cut out many **c**, 2 Chr 26:10
full of all good things, **c** already hewn, Neh 9:25
waters, and hewed out **c** for themselves, Jer 2:13
broken **c** that can hold no water. Jer 2:13
servants for water; they come to the **c**; Jer 14:3

CITADEL (10)
he went into the **c** of the king's 1 Kgs 16:18
in the **c** of the king's house with 2 Kgs 15:25
for all the people present in Susa, the **c**, Est 1:5
Jew in Susa the **c** whose name was Est 2:5
gathered in Susa the **c** in custody of Est 2:8
and the decree was issued in Susa the **c**. Est 3:15
And the decree was issued in Susa the **c**. Est 8:14
In Susa the **c** itself the Jews killed and Est 9:6
killed in Susa the **c** was reported to the Est 9:11
"In Susa the **c** the Jews have killed and Est 9:12

CITADELS (2)
Within her **c** God has made himself Ps 48:3
well her ramparts, go through her **c**, Ps 48:13

CITIES (422)
Lot settled among the **c** of the valley Gn 13:12
And he overthrew those **c**, and all the Gn 19:25
valley, and all the inhabitants of the **c**, Gn 19:25
when God destroyed the **c** of the valley, Gn 19:29
when he overthrew the **c** in which Lot Gn 19:29
God fell upon the **c** that were around Gn 35:5
authority of Pharaoh for food in the **c**, Gn 41:35
land of Egypt, and put the food in the **c**. Gn 41:48
They built for Pharaoh store **c**, Pithom Ex 1:11
As for the **c** of the Levites, the Levites Lv 25:32
time the houses in the **c** they possess. Lv 25:32
the houses in the **c** of the Levites are Lv 25:33
belonging to their **c** may not be Lv 25:34
And if you gather within your **c**, I will Lv 26:25
I will lay your **c** waste and will make Lv 26:31
desolation, and your **c** shall be a waste. Lv 26:33
and whether the **c** that they dwell in Nm 13:19
and the **c** are fortified and very large. Nm 13:28
I will devote their **c** to destruction." Nm 21:2
them and their **c** to destruction. Nm 21:3
And Israel took all these **c**, and Israel Nm 21:25
settled in all the **c** of the Amorites, Nm 21:25
and destroy the survivors of **c**!" Nm 24:19
All their **c** in the places where they Nm 31:10
our livestock, and **c** for our little ones, Nm 32:16
live in the fortified **c** because of the Nm 32:17
Build **c** for your little ones and folds Nm 32:24
shall remain there in the **c** of Gilead, Nm 32:26
land and its **c** with their territories, Nm 32:33
the **c** of the land throughout the Nm 32:33
and Beth-haran, fortified **c**, Nm 32:36
other names to the **c** that they built. Nm 32:38
of their possession as **c** for them to Nm 35:2
the Levites pasturelands around the **c**. Nm 35:2
The **c** shall be theirs to dwell in, and Nm 35:3
The pasturelands of the **c**, which you Nm 35:4
to them as pastureland for their **c**. Nm 35:5
The **c** that you give to the Levites shall Nm 35:6
the Levites shall be the six **c** of refuge, Nm 35:6
to them you shall give forty-two **c**. Nm 35:6
All the **c** that you give to the Levites Nm 35:7
And as for the **c** that you shall give Nm 35:8
shall give of its **c** to the Levites." Nm 35:8
then you shall select **c** to be cities of Nm 35:11
select cities to be **c** of refuge for you, Nm 35:11
The **c** shall be for you a refuge from Nm 35:12
And the **c** that you give shall be your Nm 35:13
you give shall be your six **c** of refuge. Nm 35:13
shall give three **c** beyond the Jordan, Nm 35:14
and three **c** in the land of Canaan, Nm 35:14
the land of Canaan, to be **c** of refuge. Nm 35:14
These six **c** shall be for refuge for the Nm 35:15
go up and the **c** into which we shall Dt 1:22
The **c** are great and fortified up to Dt 1:28
we captured all his **c** at that time and Dt 2:34
the plunder of the **c** that we captured. Dt 2:35
river Jabbok and the **c** of the hill Dt 2:37
And we took all his **c** at that time—there Dt 3:4
that we did not take from them—sixty **c**, Dt 3:4
All these were **c** fortified with high walls, Dt 3:5
and the spoil of the **c** we took as our Dt 3:7
all the **c** of the tableland and all Gilead Dt 3:10
Edrei, **c** of the kingdom of Og in Bashan. Dt 3:10
half the hill country of Gilead with its **c**. Dt 3:12
shall remain in the **c** that I have given Dt 3:19
Moses set apart three **c** in the east beyond Dt 4:41
flee to one of these **c** and save his life: Dt 4:42
—with great and good **c** that you did not Dt 6:10
c great and fortified up to heaven, Dt 9:1
"If you hear in one of your **c**, which the Dt 13:12
and dwell in their **c** and in their houses, Dt 19:1
shall set apart three **c** for yourselves in Dt 19:2
—he may flee to one of these **c** and live, Dt 19:5
you, You shall set apart three **c**. Dt 19:7
you shall add three other **c** to these three, Dt 19:9
he dies, and he flees into one of these **c**, Dt 19:11
shall do to all the **c** that are very far Dt 20:15
which are not **c** of the nations here. Dt 20:15
But in the **c** of these peoples that the Dt 20:16
the distance to the surrounding **c**. Dt 21:2
out and reached their **c** on the third day. Jos 9:17
the third day. Now their **c** were Gibeon, Jos 9:17
was a great city, like one of the royal **c**, Jos 10:2
Do not let them enter their **c**, for the Jos 10:19
of them had entered into the fortified **c**, Jos 10:20
And all the **c** of those kings, and all Jos 11:12
But none of the **c** that stood on mounds Jos 11:13
all the spoil of these **c** and the livestock, Jos 11:14
them to destruction with their **c**. Jos 11:21
and all the **c** of Sihon king of the Jos 13:10
and all its **c** that are in the tableland; Jos 13:17
that is, all the **c** of the tableland, and all Jos 13:21
to their clans with their **c** and villages. Jos 13:23
was Jazer, and all the **c** of Gilead, Jos 13:25
to their clans, with their **c** and villages. Jos 13:28
of Jair, which are in Bashan, sixty **c**, Jos 13:30
the **c** of the kingdom of Og in Bashan. Jos 13:31
in the land, but only **c** to dwell in, Jos 14:4
were there, with great fortified **c**. Jos 14:12
from there to the **c** of Mount Ephron. Jos 15:9
The **c** belonging to the tribe of the Jos 15:21
in all, twenty-nine **c** with their villages. Jos 15:32
fourteen **c** with their villages. Jos 15:36
sixteen **c** with their villages. Jos 15:41
Mareshah: nine **c** with their villages. Jos 15:44
and Giloh: eleven **c** with their villages. Jos 15:51
and Zior: nine **c** with their villages. Jos 15:54
and Timnah: ten **c** with their villages. Jos 15:57
and Eltekon: six **c** with their villages. Jos 15:59
and Rabbah: two **c** with their villages. Jos 15:60
and Engedi: six **c** with their villages. Jos 15:62
went down to the brook Kanah. These **c**, Jos 17:9
of the brook, among the **c** of Manasseh, Jos 17:9
could not take possession of those **c**, Jos 17:12
Now the **c** of the tribe of the people of Jos 18:21
Geba—twelve **c** with their villages: Jos 18:24
Kiriath-jearim—fourteen **c** with their Jos 18:28
Sharuhen—thirteen **c** with their Jos 19:6
and Ashan—four **c** with their villages, Jos 19:7
the villages around these **c** as far as Jos 19:8
Bethlehem—twelve **c** with their Jos 19:15
their clans—these **c** with their villages. Jos 19:16
Jordan—sixteen **c** with their villages. Jos 19:22
their clans—the **c** with their villages. Jos 19:23
Rehob—twenty-two **c** with their Jos 19:30
their clans—these **c** with their villages. Jos 19:31
The fortified **c** are Ziddim, Zer, Jos 19:35
Beth-shemesh—nineteen **c** with their Jos 19:38
their clans—the **c** with their villages. Jos 19:39
their clans—these **c** with their villages. Jos 19:48
people of Israel, 'Appoint the **c** of refuge, Jos 20:2
flee to one of these **c** and shall stand at Jos 20:4
These were the **c** designated for all the Jos 20:9
Moses that we be given **c** to dwell in, Jos 21:2
Levites the following **c** and pasturelands Jos 21:3
Simeon, and Benjamin, thirteen **c**. Jos 21:4
and the half-tribe of Manasseh, ten **c**. Jos 21:5
of Manasseh in Bashan, thirteen **c**. Jos 21:6
Gad, and the tribe of Zebulun, twelve **c**. Jos 21:7
These **c** and their pasturelands the Jos 21:8
gave the following **c** mentioned by Jos 21:9
its pasturelands—nine **c** out of these Jos 21:16
Almon with its pasturelands—four **c**. Jos 21:18
The **c** of the descendants of Aaron, the Jos 21:19
in all thirteen **c** with their Jos 21:19
the **c** allotted to them were out of the Jos 21:20
with its pasturelands—four **c**; Jos 21:22
with its pasturelands—four **c**; Jos 21:24
with its pasturelands—two **c**. Jos 21:25
The **c** of the clans of the rest of the Jos 21:26
with its pasturelands—two **c**; Jos 21:27
with its pasturelands—four **c**; Jos 21:29
Rehob with its pasturelands—four **c**; Jos 21:31
Kartan with its pasturelands—three **c**. Jos 21:32
The **c** of the several clans of the Jos 21:33
in all thirteen **c** with their Jos 21:33
Nahalal with its pasturelands—four **c**; Jos 21:35
with its pasturelands—four **c**; Jos 21:37
with its pasturelands—four **c** in all. Jos 21:39
As for the **c** of the several Merarite Jos 21:40
allotted to them were in all twelve **c**. Jos 21:40
The **c** of the Levites in the midst of the Jos 21:41
in all forty-eight **c** with their Jos 21:41
These **c** each had its pasturelands Jos 21:42
around it. So it was with all these **c**. Jos 21:42
had not labored and **c** that you had not Jos 24:13
on thirty donkeys, and they had thirty **c**, Jgs 10:4
and in all the **c** that are on the banks of Jgs 11:26
neighborhood of Minnith, twenty **c**, Jgs 11:33
together out of the **c** to Gibeah to go Jgs 20:14
mustered out of their **c** on that day Jgs 20:15
came out of the **c** were destroying them Jgs 20:42
number of all the **c** of the Philistines 1 Sm 6:18
both fortified **c** and unwalled villages. 1 Sm 6:18
The **c** that the Philistines had taken 1 Sm 7:14
women came out of all the **c** of Israel, 1 Sm 18:6
Racal, in the **c** of the Jerahmeelites, 1 Sm 30:29

Jerahmeelites, in the **c** of the Kenites, 1 Sm 30:29
dead, they abandoned their **c** and fled. 1 Sm 31:7
up into any of the **c** of Judah?" And the 2 Sm 2:1
and from Berothai, **c** of Hadadezer, 2 Sm 8:8
our people, and for the **c** of our God, 2 Sm 10:12
he did to all the **c** of the Ammonites. 2 Sm 12:31
himself to fortified **c** and escape from 2 Sm 20:6
Tyre and to all the **c** of the Hivites and 2 Sm 24:7
sixty great **c** with walls and bronze 1 Kgs 4:13
gave to Hiram twenty **c** in the land of 1 Kgs 9:11
Tyre to see the **c** that Solomon had 1 Kgs 9:12
"What kind of **c** are these that you 1 Kgs 9:13
and all the store **c** that Solomon had, 1 Kgs 9:19
had, and the **c** for his chariots, 1 Kgs 9:19
chariots, and the **c** for his horsemen, 1 Kgs 9:19
in the chariot **c** and with the 1 Kgs 10:26
of Israel who lived in the **c** of Judah. 1 Kgs 12:17
that are in the **c** of Samaria shall 1 Kgs 13:32
armies against the **c** of Israel and 1 Kgs 15:20
that he did, and the **c** that he built, 1 Kgs 15:23
"The **c** that my father took from 1 Kgs 20:34
he built and all the **c** that he built, 1 Kgs 22:39
And they overthrew the **c**, and on 2 Kgs 3:25
chariots and horses, fortified **c** also, 2 Kgs 10:2
son of Hazael the **c** that he had 2 Kgs 13:25
him and recovered the **c** of Israel. 2 Kgs 13:25
of Gozan, and in the **c** of the Medes. 2 Kgs 17:6
them in the **c** of Samaria instead 2 Kgs 17:24
of Samaria and lived in its **c**. 2 Kgs 17:24
and placed in the **c** of Samaria do 2 Kgs 17:26
every nation in the **c** in which they 2 Kgs 17:29
of Gozan, and in the **c** of the Medes, 2 Kgs 18:11
all the fortified **c** of Judah and 2 Kgs 18:13
should turn fortified **c** into heaps of 2 Kgs 19:25
high places at the **c** of Judah and 2 Kgs 23:5
all the priests out of the **c** of Judah, 2 Kgs 23:8
places that were in the **c** of Samaria, 2 Kgs 23:19
who had twenty-three **c** in the land of 1 Chr 2:22
These were their **c** until David 1 Chr 4:31
Rimmon, Tochen, and Ashan, five **c**, 1 Chr 4:32
that were around these **c** as far as 1 Chr 4:33
of Aaron they gave the **c** of refuge: 1 Chr 6:57
All their **c** throughout their clans 1 Chr 6:60
the half of Manasseh, ten **c**. 1 Chr 6:61
were allotted thirteen **c** out of the 1 Chr 6:62
clans were allotted twelve **c** out of the 1 Chr 6:63
the Levites the **c** with their 1 Chr 6:64
and Benjamin these **c** that are 1 Chr 6:65
of Kohath had **c** of their territory 1 Chr 6:66
They were given the **c** of refuge: 1 Chr 6:67
their possessions in their **c** were Israel, 1 Chr 9:2
they abandoned their **c** and fled, 1 Chr 10:7
Levites in the **c** that have 1 Chr 13:2
and from Cun, **c** of Hadadezer, 1 Chr 18:8
mustered from their **c** and came to 1 Chr 19:7
our people and for the **c** of our God, 1 Chr 19:13
did to all the **c** of the Ammonites. 1 Chr 20:3
treasuries in the country, in the **c**, 1 Chr 27:25
in the chariot **c** and with the 2 Chr 1:14
Solomon rebuilt the **c** that Hiram had 2 Chr 8:2
and all the store **c** that he built in 2 Chr 8:4
Beth-horon, fortified **c** with walls, 2 Chr 8:5
and all the store **c** that Solomon had 2 Chr 8:6
had and all the **c** for his chariots and 2 Chr 8:6
chariots and the **c** for his horsemen, 2 Chr 8:6
in the chariot **c** and with the 2 Chr 9:25
of Israel who lived in the **c** of Judah. 2 Chr 10:17
and he built **c** for defense in Judah. 2 Chr 11:5
fortified **c** that are in Judah and in 2 Chr 11:10
spears in all the **c** and made them 2 Chr 11:12
and Benjamin, in all the fortified **c**, 2 Chr 11:23
he took the fortified **c** of Judah and 2 Chr 12:4
Jeroboam and took **c** from him, 2 Chr 13:19
took out of all the **c** of Judah the high 2 Chr 14:5
He built fortified **c** in Judah, for the 2 Chr 14:6
us build these **c** and surround them 2 Chr 14:7
attacked all the **c** around Gerar, 2 Chr 14:14
They plundered all the **c**, for there 2 Chr 14:14
Benjamin and from the **c** that he had 2 Chr 15:8
of his armies against the **c** of Israel, 2 Chr 16:4
and all the store **c** of Naphtali. 2 Chr 16:4
in all the fortified **c** of Judah and set 2 Chr 17:2
and in the **c** of Ephraim that Asa his 2 Chr 17:2
Micaiah, to teach in the **c** of Judah; 2 Chr 17:7
about through all the **c** of Judah and 2 Chr 17:9
built in Judah fortresses and store **c**, 2 Chr 17:12
had large supplies in the **c** of Judah. 2 Chr 17:13
in the fortified **c** throughout all 2 Chr 17:19
the land in all the fortified **c** of Judah, 2 Chr 19:5
your brothers who live in their **c**, 2 Chr 19:10
from all the **c** of Judah they came to 2 Chr 20:4
together with fortified **c** in Judah, 2 Chr 21:3
the Levites from all the **c** of Judah, 2 Chr 23:2
"Go out to the **c** of Judah and gather 2 Chr 24:5
him to battle, raided the **c** of Judah, 2 Chr 25:13
and he built **c** in the territory of 2 Chr 26:6
he built **c** in the hill country of 2 Chr 27:4
raids on the **c** in the Shephelah 2 Chr 28:18
went out to the **c** of Judah and broke 2 Chr 31:1
the people of Israel returned to their **c**, 2 Chr 31:1
who lived in the **c** of Judah also 2 Chr 31:6
assisting him in the **c** of the priests, 2 Chr 31:15
common land belonging to their **c**, 2 Chr 31:19
in the several **c** who were designated 2 Chr 31:19
and encamped against the fortified **c**, 2 Chr 32:1
He likewise provided **c** for himself, 2 Chr 32:29
army in all the fortified **c** in Judah. 2 Chr 33:14
And in the **c** of Manasseh, Ephraim, 2 Chr 34:6
and settled in the **c** of Samaria and in Ezr 4:10
Let all in our **c** who have taken foreign Ezr 10:14
they captured fortified **c** and a rich Neh 9:25
gathered in their **c** throughout all the Est 9:2
and has lived in desolate **c**, in houses Jb 15:28
everlasting ruins; their **c** you rooted out; Ps 9:6
save Zion and build up the **c** of Judah, Ps 69:35
people blossom in the **c** like the grass of Ps 72:16
lies desolate; your **c** are burned with fire; Is 1:7
"Until **c** lie waste without inhabitant, Is 6:11
world like a desert and overthrew its **c**, Is 14:17
and fill the face of the world with **c**." Is 14:21
The **c** of Aroer are deserted; they will be Is 17:2
In that day their strong **c** will be like the Is 17:9
day there will be five **c** in the land of Is 19:18
you; **c** of ruthless nations will fear you. Is 25:3
Covenants are broken; **c** are despised; Is 33:8
against all the fortified **c** of Judah and Is 36:1
should make fortified **c** crash into heaps Is 37:26
say to the **c** of Judah, "Behold your God!" Is 40:9
Let the desert and its **c** lift up their voice, Is 42:11
be inhabited,' and of the **c** of Judah, Is 44:26
the nations and will people the desolate **c**. Is 54:3
they shall repair the ruined **c**, the Is 61:4
Your holy **c** have become a wilderness; Is 64:10
all around and against all the **c** of Judah. Jer 1:15
his **c** are in ruins, without inhabitant. Jer 2:15
for as many as your **c** are your gods, O Jer 2:28
and let us go into the fortified **c**!' Jer 4:5
your **c** will be ruins without inhabitant. Jer 4:7
land; they shout against the **c** of Judah. Jer 4:16
and all its **c** were laid in ruins before the Jer 4:26
among rocks; all the **c** are forsaken, Jer 4:29
A leopard is watching their **c**; everyone Jer 5:6
your fortified **c** in which you trust they Jer 5:17
they are doing in the **c** of Judah and in Jer 7:17
I will silence in the **c** of Judah and in the Jer 7:34
us go into the fortified **c** and perish there, Jer 8:14
I will make the **c** of Judah a desolation, Jer 9:11
country to make the **c** of Judah a Jer 10:22
all these words in the **c** of Judah and in Jer 11:6
Then the **c** of Judah and the Jer 11:12
gods have become as many as your **c**, Jer 11:13
The **c** of the Negeb are shut up, with Jer 13:19
shall come from the **c** of Judah and the Jer 17:26
man be like the **c** that the LORD Jer 20:16
Jerusalem and the **c** of Judah, its kings Jer 25:18
and speak to all the **c** of Judah that come Jer 26:2
O virgin Israel, return to these your **c**. Jer 31:21
words in the land of Judah and in its **c**, Jer 31:23
Judah and all its **c** shall dwell there Jer 31:24
about Jerusalem, and in the **c** of Judah, Jer 32:44
of Judah, in the **c** of the hill country, Jer 32:44
hill country, in the **c** of the Shephelah, Jer 32:44
Shephelah, and in the **c** of the Negeb; Jer 32:44
in the **c** of Judah and the streets of Jer 33:10
man or beast, and in all of its **c**, Jer 33:12
In the **c** of the hill country, in the cities Jer 33:13
hill country, in the **c** of the Shephelah, Jer 33:13
Shephelah, and in the **c** of the Negeb, Jer 33:13
about Jerusalem, and in the **c** of Judah, Jer 33:13
against Jerusalem and all of its **c**: Jer 34:1
and against all the **c** of Judah that were Jer 34:7
were the only fortified **c** of Judah that Jer 34:7
I will make the **c** of Judah a desolation Jer 34:22
men of Judah who come out of their **c**. Jer 36:6
who came from the **c** of Judah to Jer 36:9
appointed governor of the **c** of Judah, Jer 40:5
and dwell in your **c** that you have Jer 40:10
Jerusalem and upon all the **c** of Judah. Jer 44:2
out and kindled in the **c** of Judah and in Jer 44:6
in the **c** of Judah and in the streets of Jer 44:17
that you offered in the **c** of Judah and in Jer 44:21
I will destroy **c** and their inhabitants.' Jer 46:8
her **c** shall become a desolation, with no Jer 48:9
of Moab and his **c** has come up, Jer 48:15
and all the **c** of the land of Moab, Jer 48:24
"Leave the **c**, and dwell in the rock, O Jer 48:28
the **c** shall be taken and the Jer 48:41
Gad, and his people settled in its **c**? Jer 49:1
and all her **c** shall be perpetual wastes." Jer 49:13
their neighboring **c** were overthrown, Jer 49:18
him up, and I will kindle a fire in his **c**, Jer 50:32
Gomorrah and their neighboring **c**, Jer 50:40
Her **c** have become a horror, a land of Jer 51:43
the **c** shall be waste and the high places Ezk 6:6
And the inhabited **c** shall be laid Ezk 12:20
He laid waste their **c**, and the land was Ezk 19:7
lay open the flank of Moab from the **c**, Ezk 25:9
the cities, from its **c** on its frontier, Ezk 25:9
like the **c** that are not inhabited, Ezk 26:19
and her **c** shall be a desolation forty Ezk 29:12
forty years among **c** that are laid Ezk 29:12
and their **c** shall be in the midst of Ezk 30:7
be in the midst of **c** that are laid waste. Ezk 30:7
I will lay your **c** waste, and you shall Ezk 35:4
and your **c** shall not be inhabited. Ezk 35:9
the desolate wastes and the deserted **c**, Ezk 36:4
The **c** shall be inhabited and the Ezk 36:10
I will cause the **c** to be inhabited, Ezk 36:33
desolate and ruined **c** are now fortified Ezk 36:35
so shall the waste **c** be filled with Ezk 36:38
those who dwell in the **c** of Israel will go Ezk 39:9
as their possession for **c** to live in. Ezk 45:5
and Judah has multiplied fortified **c**; Hos 8:14
so I will send a fire upon his **c**, and it Hos 8:14
The sword shall rage against their **c**, Hos 11:6
is your king, to save you in all your **c**? Hos 13:10
gave you cleanness of teeth in all your **c**, Am 4:6
so two or three **c** would wander to Am 4:8
rebuild the ruined **c** and inhabit them; Am 9:14
shall possess the **c** of the Negeb. Ob 1:20
I will cut off the **c** of your land and Mi 5:11
from among you and destroy your **c**. Mi 5:14
to you, from Assyria and the **c** of Egypt, Mi 7:12
earth, to **c** and all who dwell in them. Hab 2:8
earth, to **c** and all who dwell in them. Hab 2:17
against the fortified **c** and against the Zep 1:16
their **c** have been made desolate, without Zep 3:6
mercy on Jerusalem and the **c** of Judah, Zec 1:12
My **c** shall again overflow with Zec 1:17
and prosperous, with her **c** around her, Zec 7:7
come, even the inhabitants of many **c**. Zec 8:20
went throughout all the **c** and villages, Mt 9:35
there to teach and preach in their **c**. Mt 11:1
began to denounce the **c** where most of Mt 11:20
he came, in villages, **c**, or countryside, Mk 6:56
While he was in one of the **c**, there came Lk 5:12
he went on through **c** and villages, Lk 8:1
you shall have authority over ten **c**.' Lk 19:17
to him, 'And you are to be over five **c**.' Lk 19:19
to Lystra and Derbe, **c** of Lycaonia, Acts 14:6
they went on their way through the **c**, Acts 16:4
I persecuted them even to foreign **c**. Acts 26:11
if by turning the **c** of Sodom and 2 Pt 2:6
and Gomorrah and the surrounding **c**, Jude 1:7
three parts, and the **c** of the nations fell, Rv 16:19

CITIZEN (7)

in Cilicia, a **c** of no obscure city. Acts 21:39
is a Roman **c** and uncondemned?" Acts 22:25
to do? For this man is a Roman **c**." Acts 22:26
me, are you a Roman **c**?" And he said, Acts 22:27
Paul said, "But I am a **c** by birth." Acts 22:28
Paul was a Roman **c** and that he had Acts 22:29
learned that he was a Roman **c**. Acts 23:27

CITIZENS (5)

out to one of the **c** of that country, Lk 15:15
But his **c** hated him and sent a Lk 19:14
men who are Roman **c**, Acts 16:37
they heard that they were Roman **c**. Acts 16:38
but you are fellow **c** with the saints and Eph 2:19

CITIZENSHIP (2)

"I bought this **c** for a large sum." Acts 22:28
But our **c** is in heaven, and from it we Phil 3:20

CITY (807)

When he built a **c**, he called the name Gn 4:17
the name of the **c** after the name of Gn 4:17
Nineveh and Calah; that is the great **c**. Gn 10:12
us build ourselves a **c** and a tower with Gn 11:4
came down to see the **c** and the tower, Gn 11:5
earth, and they left off building the **c**. Gn 11:8
there are fifty righteous within the **c**. Gn 18:24
I find at Sodom fifty righteous in the **c**, Gn 18:26
you destroy the whole **c** for lack of Gn 18:28
before they lay down, the men of the **c**, Gn 19:4
or anyone you have in the **c**, Gn 19:12
about to destroy the **c**." But he seemed Gn 19:14
away in the punishment of the **c**." Gn 19:15
him out and set him outside the **c**. Gn 19:16
Behold, this **c** is near enough to flee to, Gn 19:20
will not overthrow the **c** of which you Gn 19:21
the name of the **c** was called Zoar. Gn 19:22
of all who went in at the gate of his **c**, Gn 23:10
all who went in at the gate of his **c**. Gn 23:18
to Mesopotamia to the **c** of Nahor. Gn 24:10

kneel down outside the **c** by the well of Gn 24:11
of the men of the **c** are coming out to Gn 24:13
the name of the **c** is Beersheba to this Gn 26:33
but the name of the **c** was Luz at the Gn 28:19
Jacob came safely to the **c** of Shechem, Gn 33:18
and he camped before the **c**. Gn 33:18
to the gate of their **c** and spoke to the Gn 34:20
city and spoke to the men of their **c**, Gn 34:20
the gate of his **c** listened to Hamor and Gn 34:24
all who went out of the gate of his **c**. Gn 34:24
and came against the **c** while it felt Gn 34:25
upon the slain and plundered the **c**, Gn 34:27
whatever was in the **c** and in the field. Gn 34:28
the name of his **c** being Dinhabah. Gn 36:32
place, the name of his **c** being Avith. Gn 36:35
his place, the name of his **c** being Pau; Gn 36:39
He put in every **c** the food from the Gn 41:48
gone only a short distance from the **c**. Gn 44:4
his donkey, and they returned to the **c**. Gn 44:13
him, "As soon as I have gone out of the **c**, Ex 9:29
went out of the **c** from Pharaoh and Ex 9:33
into an unclean place outside the **c**. Lv 14:40
out in an unclean place outside the **c**. Lv 14:41
them out of the **c** to an unclean place. Lv 14:45
go out of the **c** into the open country. Lv 14:53
sells a dwelling house in a walled **c**, Lv 25:29
house in the walled **c** shall belong in Lv 25:30
was sold in a **c** they possess shall be Lv 25:33
a **c** on the edge of your territory. Nm 20:16
For Heshbon was the **c** of Sihon the Nm 21:26
built; let the **c** of Sihon be established. Nm 21:27
Heshbon, flame from the **c** of Sihon. Nm 21:28
out to meet him at the **c** of Moab, Nm 22:36
the wall of the **c** outward a thousand Nm 35:4
And you shall measure, outside the **c**, Nm 35:5
cubits, the **c** being in the middle. Nm 35:5
restore him to his **c** of refuge to which Nm 35:25
the boundaries of his **c** of refuge to Nm 35:26
the boundaries of his **c** of refuge, Nm 35:27
must remain in his **c** of refuge until Nm 35:28
for him who has fled to his **c** of refuge, Nm 35:32
time and devoted to destruction every **c**, Dt 2:34
and from the **c** that is in the valley, Dt 2:36
Gilead, there was not a **c** too high for us. Dt 2:36
—there was not a **c** that we did not take Dt 3:4
Heshbon, devoting to destruction every **c**, Dt 3:6
drawn away the inhabitants of their **c**, Dt 13:13
the inhabitants of that **c** to the sword, Dt 13:15
square and burn the **c** and all its spoil Dt 13:16
the elders of his **c** shall send and take Dt 19:12
you draw near to a **c** to fight against it, Dt 20:10
livestock, and everything else in the **c**, Dt 20:14
"When you besiege a **c** for a long time, Dt 20:19
siegeworks against the **c** that makes Dt 20:20
And the elders of the **c** that is nearest to Dt 21:3
the elders of that **c** shall bring the heifer Dt 21:4
all the elders of that **c** nearest to the slain Dt 21:6
to the elders of his **c** at the gate of the Dt 21:19
and they shall say to the elders of his **c**, Dt 21:20
all the men of the **c** shall stone him to Dt 21:21
to the elders of the **c** in the gate. Dt 22:15
the cloak before the elders of the **c**. Dt 22:17
the elders of that **c** shall take the man Dt 22:18
and the men of her **c** shall stone her to Dt 22:21
meets her in the **c** and lies with her, Dt 22:23
them both out to the gate of that **c**, Dt 22:24
cry for help though she was in the **c**, Dt 22:24
the elders of his **c** shall call him and Dt 25:8
Blessed shall you be in the **c**, and blessed Dt 28:3
Cursed shall you be in the **c**, and Dt 28:16
the Valley of Jericho the **c** of palm trees, Dt 34:3
for her house was built into the **c** wall, Jos 2:15
at Adam, the **c** that is beside Zarethan, Jos 3:16
You shall march around the **c**, all the Jos 6:3
the men of war going around the **c** once. Jos 6:3
shall march around the **c** seven times, Jos 6:4
and the wall of the **c** will fall down flat, Jos 6:5
March around the **c** and let the armed Jos 6:7
caused the ark of the LORD to circle the **c**, Jos 6:11
day they marched around the **c** once, Jos 6:14
and marched around the **c** in the same Jos 6:15
they marched around the **c** seven times. Jos 6:15
"Shout, for the LORD has given you the **c**. Jos 6:16
And the **c** and all that is within it shall Jos 6:17
flat, so that the people went up into the **c**, Jos 6:20
before him, and they captured the **c**. Jos 6:20
they devoted all in the **c** to destruction, Jos 6:21
And they burned the **c** with fire, and Jos 6:24
man who rises up and rebuilds this **c**, Jos 6:26
hand the king of Ai, and his people, his **c**, Jos 8:1
Lay an ambush against the **c**, behind it." Jos 8:2
you shall lie in ambush against the **c**, Jos 8:4
Do not go very far from the **c**, but all of Jos 8:4
who are with me will approach the **c**. Jos 8:5
we have drawn them away from the **c**. Jos 8:6
rise up from the ambush and seize the **c**, Jos 8:7
And as soon as you have taken the **c**, you Jos 8:8
taken the city, you shall set the **c** on fire. Jos 8:8
drew near before the **c** and encamped on Jos 8:11
Bethel and Ai, to the west of the **c**. Jos 8:12
was north of the **c** and its rear guard Jos 8:13
the city and its rear guard west of the **c**. Jos 8:13
he and all his people, the men of the **c**, Jos 8:14
an ambush against him behind the **c**. Jos 8:14
who were in the **c** were called together to Jos 8:16
they were drawn away from the **c**. Jos 8:16
They left the **c** open and pursued Israel. Jos 8:17
that was in his hand toward the **c**. Jos 8:18
ran and entered the **c** and captured it. Jos 8:19
it. And they hurried to set the **c** on fire. Jos 8:19
the smoke of the **c** went up to heaven, Jos 8:20
that the ambush had captured the **c**, Jos 8:21
and that the smoke of the **c** went up, Jos 8:21
came out from the **c** against them, Jos 8:22
and the spoil of that **c** Israel took as their Jos 8:27
of the gate of the **c** and raised over it a Jos 8:29
greatly, because Gibeon was a great **c**, Jos 10:2
There was not a **c** that made peace with Jos 11:19
and the **c** that is in the middle of the Jos 13:9
and the **c** that is in the middle of the Jos 13:16
Nibshan, the **C** of Salt, and Engedi: six Jos 15:62
a **c** belonging to the people of Judah. Jos 18:14
reaching to the fortified **c** of Tyre. Jos 19:29
LORD they gave him the **c** that he asked, Jos 19:50
And he rebuilt the **c** and settled in it. Jos 19:50
of the gate of the **c** and explain his case Jos 20:4
explain his case to the elders of that **c**. Jos 20:4
shall take him into the **c** and give him a Jos 20:4
shall remain in that **c** until he has stood Jos 20:6
the fields of the **c** and its villages had Jos 21:12
the **c** of refuge for the manslayer, Jos 21:13
the **c** of refuge for the manslayer, Jos 21:21
the **c** of refuge for the manslayer, Jos 21:27
the **c** of refuge for the manslayer, Jos 21:32
the **c** of refuge for the manslayer, Jos 21:38
the edge of the sword and set the **c** on fire. Jgs 1:8
of Judah from the **c** of palms into the Jgs 1:16
So the name of the **c** was called Hormah. Jgs 1:17
the name of the **c** was formerly Luz.) Jgs 1:23
the spies saw a man coming out of the **c**, Jgs 1:24
him, "Please show us the way into the **c**, Jgs 1:24
And he showed them the way into the **c**. Jgs 1:25
And they struck the **c** with the edge of Jgs 1:25
Hittites and built a **c** and called its name Jgs 1:26
they took possession of the **c** of palms. Jgs 3:13
And he took the elders of the **c**, and he Jgs 8:16
of Penuel and killed the men of the **c**. Jgs 8:17
made an ephod of it and put it in his **c**, Jgs 8:27
the ruler of the **c** heard the words of Jgs 9:30
they are stirring up the **c** against you. Jgs 9:31
sun is up, rise early and rush upon the **c**. Jgs 9:33
stood in the entrance of the gate of the **c**, Jgs 9:35
and saw the people coming out of the **c**. Jgs 9:43
stood at the entrance of the gate of the **c**, Jgs 9:44
fought against the **c** all that day. Jgs 9:45
He captured the **c** and killed the people Jgs 9:45
and he razed the **c** and sowed it with salt. Jgs 9:45
there was a strong tower within the **c**, Jgs 9:51
all the leaders of the **c** fled to it and shut Jgs 9:51
died and was buried in his **c** in Gilead. Jgs 12:7
And the men of the **c** said to him on the Jgs 14:18
for him all night at the gate of the **c**. Jgs 16:2
of the gate of the **c** and the two posts, Jgs 16:3
of the sword and burned the **c** with fire. Jgs 18:27
Then they rebuilt the **c** and lived in it. Jgs 18:28
And they named the **c** Dan, after the Jgs 18:29
but the name of the **c** was Laish at the Jgs 18:29
turn aside to this **c** of the Jebusites and Jgs 19:11
not turn aside into the **c** of foreigners, Jgs 19:12
sat down in the open square of the **c**, Jgs 19:15
the traveler in the open square of the **c**. Jgs 19:17
hearts merry, behold, the men of the **c**, Jgs 19:22
men of Israel gathered against the **c**, Jgs 20:11
and were drawn away from the **c**. Jgs 20:31
away from the **c** to the highways." Jgs 20:32
out and struck all the **c** with the edge of Jgs 20:37
cloud of smoke rise up out of the **c** Jgs 20:38
to rise out of the **c** in a column of Jgs 20:40
the whole of the **c** went up in smoke to Jgs 20:40
them with the edge of the sword, the **c**, Jgs 20:48
And she took it up and went into the **c**. Ru 2:18
put it on her. Then she went into the **c**. Ru 3:15
ten men of the elders of the **c** and said, Ru 4:2
by year from his **c** to worship and to 1 Sm 1:3
man came into the **c** and told the 1 Sm 4:13
and told the news, all the **c** cried out. 1 Sm 4:13
the hand of the LORD was against the **c**, 1 Sm 5:9
panic, and he afflicted the men of the **c**, 1 Sm 5:9
panic throughout the whole **c**. 1 Sm 5:11
and the cry of the **c** went up to heaven. 1 Sm 5:12
men of Israel, "Go every man to his **c**." 1 Sm 8:22
"Behold, there is a man of God in this **c**, 1 Sm 9:6
So they went to the **c** where the man of 1 Sm 9:10
As they went up the hill to the **c**, they 1 Sm 9:11
He has come just now to the **c**, 1 Sm 9:12
as you enter the **c** you will find him, 1 Sm 9:13
So they went up to the **c**. As they were 1 Sm 9:14
As they were entering the **c**, they saw 1 Sm 9:14
down from the high place into the **c**, 1 Sm 9:25
going down to the outskirts of the **c**, 1 Sm 9:27
there, as soon as you come to the **c**, 1 Sm 10:5
Saul came to the **c** of Amalek and lay 1 Sm 15:5
The elders of the **c** came to meet him 1 Sm 16:4
leave of me to run to Bethlehem his **c**, 1 Sm 20:6
our clan holds a sacrifice in the **c**, 1 Sm 20:29
to him, "Go and carry them to the **c**." 1 Sm 20:40
and Jonathan went into the **c**. 1 Sm 20:42
And Nob, the **c** of the priests, he put 1 Sm 22:19
to destroy the **c** on my account. 1 Sm 23:10
dwell in the royal **c** with you?" 1 Sm 27:5
and buried him in Ramah, his own **c**. 1 Sm 28:3
David and his men came to the **c**, 1 Sm 30:3
of Zion, that is, the **c** of David. 2 Sm 5:7
stronghold and called it the **c** of David. 2 Sm 5:9
And David built the **c** all around from 2 Sm 5:9
the ark of the LORD into the **c** of David. 2 Sm 6:10
of Obed-edom to the **c** of David with 2 Sm 6:12
of the LORD came into the **c** of David, 2 Sm 6:16
to you to search the **c** and to spy it out 2 Sm 10:3
fled before Abishai and entered the **c**. 2 Sm 10:14
And as Joab was besieging the **c**, he 2 Sm 11:16
the men of the **c** came out and 2 Sm 11:17
did you go so near the **c** to fight? 2 Sm 11:20
attack against the **c** and overthrow 2 Sm 11:25
"There were two men in a certain **c**, 2 Sm 12:1
the Ammonites and took the royal **c**. 2 Sm 12:26
I have taken the **c** of waters. 2 Sm 12:27
encamp against the **c** and take it, 2 Sm 12:28
lest I take the **c** and it be called by 2 Sm 12:28
he brought out the spoil of the **c**, 2 Sm 12:30
"From what **c** are you?" And when he 2 Sm 15:2
David's counselor, from his **c** Giloh. 2 Sm 15:12
us and strike the **c** with the edge of 2 Sm 15:14
the people had all passed out of the **c**. 2 Sm 15:24
the ark of God back into the **c**. 2 Sm 15:25
Go back to the **c** in peace, with your 2 Sm 15:27
you return to the **c** and say to 2 Sm 15:34
David's friend, came into the **c**, 2 Sm 15:37
If he withdraws into a **c**, then all 2 Sm 17:13
all Israel will bring ropes to that **c**, 2 Sm 17:13
were not to be seen entering the **c**. 2 Sm 17:17
and went off home to his own **c**. 2 Sm 17:23
that you send us help from the **c**." 2 Sm 18:3
people stole into the **c** that day as 2 Sm 19:3
die in my own **c** near the grave of 2 Sm 19:37
They cast up a mound against the **c**, 2 Sm 20:15
a wise woman called from the **c**, 2 Sm 20:16
seek to destroy a **c** that is a mother 2 Sm 20:19
withdraw from the **c**." And the 2 Sm 20:21
and they dispersed from the **c**, 2 Sm 20:22
and from the **c** that is in the middle of 2 Sm 24:5
does this uproar in the **c** mean?" 1 Kgs 1:41
so that the **c** is in an uproar. 1 Kgs 1:45
and was buried in the **c** of David. 1 Kgs 2:10
brought her into the **c** of David until 1 Kgs 3:1
of the LORD out of the **c** of David, 1 Kgs 8:1
I chose no **c** out of all the tribes of 1 Kgs 8:16
the LORD toward the **c** that you have 1 Kgs 8:44
fathers, the **c** that you have chosen, 1 Kgs 8:48
the Canaanites who lived in the **c**, 1 Kgs 9:16
went up from the **c** of David to her 1 Kgs 9:24
the breach of the **c** of David his 1 Kgs 11:27
the **c** that I have chosen out of all 1 Kgs 11:32
the **c** where I have chosen to put my 1 Kgs 11:36
was buried in the **c** of David his 1 Kgs 11:43
told it in the **c** where the old prophet 1 Kgs 13:25
it back to the **c** to mourn and to 1 Kgs 13:29
who dies in the **c** the dogs shall eat, 1 Kgs 14:11
When your feet enter the **c**, the child 1 Kgs 14:12
the **c** that the LORD had chosen out 1 Kgs 14:21
with his fathers in the **c** of David. 1 Kgs 14:31
they buried him in the **c** of David. 1 Kgs 15:8
his fathers in the **c** of David his 1 Kgs 15:24
who dies in the **c** the dogs shall eat, 1 Kgs 16:4
Zimri saw that the **c** was taken, 1 Kgs 16:18
the name of the **c** that he built 1 Kgs 16:24
when he came to the gate of the **c**, 1 Kgs 17:10
messengers into the **c** to Ahab king 1 Kgs 20:2
took their positions against the **c**. 1 Kgs 20:12
So these went out of the **c**, the 1 Kgs 20:19
And the rest fled into the **c** of Aphek, 1 Kgs 20:30
entered an inner chamber in the **c**. 1 Kgs 20:30
who lived with Naboth in his **c**. 1 Kgs 21:8
And the men of his **c**, the elders and 1 Kgs 21:11
and the leaders who lived in his **c**, 1 Kgs 21:11

him outside the **c** and stoned him	1 Kgs 21:13
who dies in the **c** the dogs shall eat,	1 Kgs 21:24
the governor of the **c** and to Joash	1 Kgs 22:26
the army, "Every man to his **c**,	1 Kgs 22:36
his fathers in the **c** of David his	1 Kgs 22:50
Now the men of the **c** said to Elisha,	2 Kgs 2:19
the situation of this **c** is pleasant,	2 Kgs 2:19
came out of the **c** and jeered at him,	2 Kgs 2:23
attack every fortified **c** and every	2 Kgs 3:19
every fortified city and every choice **c**,	2 Kgs 3:19
came by night and surrounded the **c**.	2 Kgs 6:14
and chariots was all around the **c**.	2 Kgs 6:15
is not the way, and this is not the **c**.	2 Kgs 6:19
If we say, 'Let us enter the **c**,' the	2 Kgs 7:4
us enter the city,' the famine is in the **c**,	2 Kgs 7:4
gatekeepers of the **c** and told them,	2 Kgs 7:10
'When they come out of the **c**,	2 Kgs 7:12
take them alive and get into the **c**.'"	2 Kgs 7:12
with his fathers in the **c** of David,	2 Kgs 8:24
one slip out of the **c** to go and tell the	2 Kgs 9:15
with his fathers in the **c** of David.	2 Kgs 9:28
to Samaria, to the rulers of the **c**,	2 Kgs 10:1
the palace, and he who was over the **c**,	2 Kgs 10:5
were with the great men of the **c**,	2 Kgs 10:6
and the **c** was quiet after Athaliah	2 Kgs 11:20
with his fathers in the **c** of David,	2 Kgs 12:21
with his fathers in the **c** of David.	2 Kgs 14:20
with his fathers in the **c** of David,	2 Kgs 15:7
his fathers in the **c** of David his	2 Kgs 15:38
with his fathers in the **c** of David,	2 Kgs 16:20
towns, from watchtower to fortified **c**.	2 Kgs 17:9
from watchtower to fortified **c**.	2 Kgs 18:8
and this **c** will not be given into the	2 Kgs 18:30
the king of the **c** of Sepharvaim,	2 Kgs 19:13
not come into this **c** or shoot an	2 Kgs 19:32
and he shall not come into this **c**,	2 Kgs 19:33
For I will defend this **c** to save it, for	2 Kgs 19:34
deliver you and this **c** out of the hand	2 Kgs 20:6
I will defend this **c** for my own sake	2 Kgs 20:6
and brought water into the **c**,	2 Kgs 20:20
gate of Joshua the governor of the **c**,	2 Kgs 23:8
were on one's left at the gate of the **c**.	2 Kgs 23:8
see?" And the men of the **c** told him,	2 Kgs 23:17
will cast off this **c** that I have	2 Kgs 23:27
to Jerusalem, and the **c** was besieged.	2 Kgs 24:10
came to the **c** while his servants	2 Kgs 24:11
So the **c** was besieged till the eleventh	2 Kgs 25:2
so severe in the **c** that there was no	2 Kgs 25:3
Then a breach was made in the **c**,	2 Kgs 25:4
the Chaldeans were around the **c**.	2 Kgs 25:4
were left in the **c** and the deserters	2 Kgs 25:11
and from the **c** he took an officer	2 Kgs 25:19
council who were found in the **c**,	2 Kgs 25:19
of the land who were found in the **c**.	2 Kgs 25:19
the name of his **c** being Dinhabah.	1 Chr 1:43
place, the name of his **c** being Avith.	1 Chr 1:46
place, the name of his **c** being Pai;	1 Chr 1:50
the fields of the **c** and its villages they	1 Chr 6:56
of Zion, that is, the **c** of David.	1 Chr 11:5
therefore it was called the **c** of David.	1 Chr 11:7
And he built the **c** all around from	1 Chr 11:8
and Joab repaired the rest of the **c**.	1 Chr 11:8
the ark home into the **c** of David,	1 Chr 13:13
houses for himself in the **c** of David.	1 Chr 15:1
of the LORD came to the **c** of David,	1 Chr 15:29
battle array at the entrance of the **c**,	1 Chr 19:9
Joab's brother, and entered the **c**.	1 Chr 19:15
And he brought out the spoil of the **c**,	1 Chr 20:2
of the LORD out of the **c** of David,	2 Chr 5:2
I chose no **c** out of all the tribes of	2 Chr 6:5
to you toward this **c** that you have	2 Chr 6:34
the **c** that you have chosen and the	2 Chr 6:38
daughter up from the **c** of David to	2 Chr 8:11
was buried in the **c** of David his	2 Chr 9:31
the **c** that the LORD had chosen out	2 Chr 12:13
and was buried in the **c** of David,	2 Chr 12:16
they buried him in the **c** of David.	2 Chr 14:1
was crushed by nation and **c** by city,	2 Chr 15:6
was crushed by nation and city by **c**,	2 Chr 15:6
cut for himself in the **c** of David.	2 Chr 16:14
the governor of the **c** and to Joash	2 Chr 18:25
the fortified cities of Judah, **c** by city,	2 Chr 19:5
the fortified cities of Judah, city by **c**,	2 Chr 19:5
with his fathers in the **c** of David,	2 Chr 21:1
They buried him in the **c** of David,	2 Chr 21:20
and the **c** was quiet after Athaliah	2 Chr 23:21
buried him in the **c** of David among	2 Chr 24:16
they buried him in the **c** of David,	2 Chr 24:25
with his fathers in the **c** of David.	2 Chr 25:28
they buried him in the **c** of David,	2 Chr 27:9
at Jericho, the **c** of palm trees.	2 Chr 28:15
In every **c** of Judah he made high	2 Chr 28:25
and they buried him in the **c**,	2 Chr 28:27
the officials of the **c** and went up to	2 Chr 29:20
couriers went from **c** to city	2 Chr 30:10
from city to **c** through the country	2 Chr 30:10
of the springs that were outside the **c**;	2 Chr 32:3
the Millo in the **c** of David.	2 Chr 32:5
gate of the **c** and spoke	2 Chr 32:6
in order that they might take the **c**.	2 Chr 32:18
to the west side of the **c** of David.	2 Chr 32:30
outer wall for the **c** of David west of	2 Chr 33:14
and he threw them outside of the **c**.	2 Chr 33:15
and Maaseiah the governor of the **c**,	2 Chr 34:8
that rebellious and wicked **c**.	Ezr 4:12
the king that if this **c** is rebuilt and the	Ezr 4:13
and learn that this **c** is a rebellious city,	Ezr 4:15
and learn that this city is a rebellious **c**,	Ezr 4:15
old. That was why this **c** was laid waste.	Ezr 4:15
the king that if this **c** is rebuilt and its	Ezr 4:16
been found that this **c** from of old has	Ezr 4:19
to cease, and that this **c** be not rebuilt,	Ezr 4:21
them the elders and judges of every **c**,	Ezr 10:14
should not my face be sad, when the **c**,	Neh 2:3
to Judah, to the **c** of my fathers' graves,	Neh 2:5
of the temple, and for the wall of the **c**,	Neh 2:8
that go down from the **C** of David.	Neh 3:15
The **c** was wide and large, but the people	Neh 7:4
of ten to live in Jerusalem the holy **c**,	Neh 11:1
of Hassenuah was second over the **c**.	Neh 11:9
All the Levites in the holy **c** were 284.	Neh 11:18
them by the stairs of the **c** of David,	Neh 12:37
Tyrians also, who lived in the **c**,	Neh 13:16
all this disaster on us and on this **c**?	Neh 13:18
but the **c** of Susa was thrown into	Est 3:15
and went out into the midst of the **c**,	Est 4:1
the open square of the **c** in front of the	Est 4:6
on the horse through the square of the **c**,	Est 6:9
and led him through the square of the **c**,	Est 6:11
who were in every **c** to gather and defend	Est 8:11
and the **c** of Susa shouted and rejoiced.	Est 8:15
And in every province and in every **c**,	Est 8:17
in every clan, province, and **c**,	Est 9:28
From out of the **c** the dying groan, and	Jb 24:12
When I went out to the gate of the **c**,	Jb 29:7
He scorns the tumult of the **c**; he hears	Jb 39:7
love to me when I was in a besieged **c**.	Ps 31:21
whose streams make glad the **c** of God,	Ps 46:4
greatly to be praised in the **c** of our God!	Ps 48:1
in the far north, the **c** of the great King.	Ps 48:2
have we seen in the **c** of the LORD of hosts,	Ps 48:8
of the LORD of hosts, in the **c** of our God,	Ps 48:8
for I see violence and strife in the **c**.	Ps 55:9
like dogs and prowling about the **c**.	Ps 59:6
like dogs and prowling about the **c**.	Ps 59:14
Who will bring me to the fortified **c**?	Ps 60:9
the holy mount stands the **c** he founded;	Ps 87:1
things of you are spoken, O **c** of God.	Ps 87:3
all the evildoers from the **c** of the LORD.	Ps 101:8
wastes, finding no way to a **c** to dwell in;	Ps 107:4
way till they reached a **c** to dwell in.	Ps 107:7
dwell, and they establish a **c** to live in;	Ps 107:36
Who will bring me to the fortified **c**?	Ps 108:10
—built as a **c** that is bound firmly	Ps 122:3
Unless the LORD watches over the **c**, the	Ps 127:1
at the entrance of the **c** gates she speaks:	Prv 1:21
A rich man's wealth is his strong **c**;	Prv 10:15
well with the righteous, the **c** rejoices,	Prv 11:10
blessing of the upright a **c** is exalted,	Prv 11:11
rules his spirit than he who takes a **c**.	Prv 16:32
A rich man's wealth is his strong **c**,	Prv 18:11
is more unyielding than a strong **c**,	Prv 18:19
wise man scales the **c** of the mighty	Prv 21:22
self-control is like a **c** broken into and	Prv 25:28
Scoffers set a **c** aflame, but the wise	Prv 29:8
more than ten rulers who are in a **c**.	Eccl 7:19
were praised in the **c** where they had	Eccl 8:10
There was a little **c** with few men in it,	Eccl 9:14
and he by his wisdom delivered the **c**.	Eccl 9:15
for he does not know the way to the **c**.	Eccl 10:15
I will rise now and go about the **c**, in the	Sg 3:2
found me as they went about in the **c**.	Sg 3:3
found me as they went about in the **c**;	Sg 5:7
in a cucumber field, like a besieged **c**.	Is 1:8
How the faithful **c** has become a whore,	Is 1:21
you shall be called the **c** of righteousness,	Is 1:26
the city of righteousness, the faithful **c**."	Is 1:26
Wail, O gate; cry out, O **c**; melt in fear, O	Is 14:31
will cease to be a **c** and will become a	Is 17:1
each against his neighbor, **c** against city,	Is 19:2
each against his neighbor, city against **c**,	Is 19:2
these will be called the **C** of Destruction.	Is 19:18
who are full of shoutings, tumultuous **c**,	Is 22:2
the breaches of the **c** of David were many.	Is 22:9
Is this your exultant **c** whose origin is	Is 23:7
go about the **c**, O forgotten prostitute!	Is 23:16
The wasted **c** is broken down; every	Is 24:10
Desolation is left in the **c**; the gates are	Is 24:12
For you have made the **c** a heap, the	Is 25:2
the city a heap, the fortified **c** a ruin;	Is 25:2
ruin; the foreigners' palace is a **c** no more;	Is 25:2
in the land of Judah: "We have a strong **c**;	Is 26:1
the inhabitants of the height, the lofty **c**.	Is 26:5
For the fortified **c** is solitary, a	Is 27:10
Ariel, Ariel, the **c** where David encamped!	Is 29:1
all the joyous houses in the exultant **c**.	Is 32:13
is forsaken, the populous **c** deserted;	Is 32:14
down, and the **c** will be utterly laid low.	Is 32:19
Zion, the **c** of our appointed feasts!	Is 33:20
This **c** will not be given into the hand of	Is 36:15
Arpad, the king of the **c** of Sepharvaim,	Is 37:13
not come into this **c** or shoot an arrow	Is 37:33
and he shall not come into this **c**,	Is 37:34
For I will defend this **c** to save it, for my	Is 37:35
will deliver you and this **c** out of the hand	Is 38:6
the king of Assyria, and will defend this **c**.	Is 38:6
he shall build my **c** and set my exiles	Is 45:13
For they call themselves after the holy **c**,	Is 48:2
garments, O Jerusalem, the holy **c**;	Is 52:1
they shall call you the **C** of the LORD, the	Is 60:14
called Sought Out, A **C** Not Forsaken.	Is 62:12
"The sound of an uproar from the **c**! A	Is 66:6
behold, I make you this day a fortified **c**,	Jer 1:18
you, one from a **c** and two from a family,	Jer 3:14
and archer every **c** takes to flight;	Jer 4:29
This is the **c** that must be punished; there	Jer 6:6
fills it, the **c** and those who dwell in it.	Jer 8:16
And if I enter the **c**, behold, the diseases	Jer 14:18
the gates of this **c** on the Sabbath day,	Jer 17:24
the gates of this **c** kings and princes	Jer 17:25
And this **c** shall be inhabited forever.	Jer 17:25
And I will make this **c** a horror, a thing	Jer 19:8
So will I break this people and this **c**, as	Jer 19:11
making this **c** like Topheth.	Jer 19:12
am bringing upon this **c** and upon all	Jer 19:15
I will give all the wealth of the **c**,	Jer 20:5
them together into the midst of this **c**.	Jer 21:4
strike down the inhabitants of this **c**,	Jer 21:6
the people in this **c** who survive the	Jer 21:7
He who stays in this **c** shall die by the	Jer 21:9
my face against this **c** for harm and	Jer 21:10
make you a desert, an uninhabited **c**.	Jer 22:6
"'And many nations will pass by this **c**,	Jer 22:8
the LORD dealt thus with this great **c**?"	Jer 22:8
you and the **c** that I gave to you and	Jer 23:39
work disaster at the **c** that is called by	Jer 25:29
and I will make this **c** a curse for all the	Jer 26:6
like Shiloh, and this **c** shall be desolate,	Jer 26:9
he has prophesied against this **c**,	Jer 26:11
this house and this **c** all the words you	Jer 26:12
and upon this **c** and its inhabitants,	Jer 26:15
prophesied against this **c** and against	Jer 26:20
Why should this **c** become a	Jer 27:17
rest of the vessels that are left in this **c**,	Jer 27:19
the welfare of the **c** where I have sent	Jer 29:7
all the people who dwell in this **c**,	Jer 29:16
the **c** shall be rebuilt on its mound, and	Jer 30:18
when the **c** shall be rebuilt for the LORD	Jer 31:38
I am giving this **c** into the hand of the	Jer 32:3
have come up to the **c** to take it,	Jer 32:24
and pestilence the **c** is given into	Jer 32:24
witnesses"—though the **c** is given into	Jer 32:25
I am giving this **c** into the hands of the	Jer 32:28
fighting against this **c** shall come and	Jer 32:29
come and set this **c** on fire and burn	Jer 32:29
This **c** has aroused my anger and	Jer 32:31
concerning this **c** of which you say,	Jer 32:36
the houses of this **c** and the houses of	Jer 33:4
my face from this **c** because of all their	Jer 33:5
And this **c** shall be to me a name of joy,	Jer 33:9
I am giving this **c** into the hand of the	Jer 34:2
and will bring them back to this **c**.	Jer 34:22
come back and fight against this **c**.	Jer 37:8
rise up and burn this **c** with fire.'"	Jer 37:10
until all the bread of the **c** was gone.	Jer 37:21
He who stays in this **c** shall die by the	Jer 38:2
This **c** shall surely be given into the	Jer 38:3
of the soldiers who are left in this **c**,	Jer 38:4
for there is no bread left in the **c**."	Jer 38:9
and this **c** shall not be burned with fire,	Jer 38:17
then this **c** shall be given into the hand	Jer 38:18
and this **c** shall be burned with fire."	Jer 38:23
the month, a breach was made in the **c**.	Jer 39:2
going out of the **c** at night by way of the	Jer 39:4
rest of the people who were left in the **c**,	Jer 39:9
my words against this **c** for harm and	Jer 39:16
When they came into the **c**, Ishmael the	Jer 41:7
fills it, the **c** and those who dwell in it.	Jer 47:2
The destroyer shall come upon every **c**,	Jer 48:8
upon every city, and no **c** shall escape;	Jer 48:8
How is the famous **c** not forsaken, the	Jer 49:25
city not forsaken, the **c** of my joy?	Jer 49:25
of Babylon that his **c** is taken on every	Jer 51:31
So the **c** was besieged till the eleventh	Jer 52:5
was so severe in the **c** that there was no	Jer 52:6

Then a breach was made in the **c**, and Jer 52:7
and went out from the **c** by night by the Jer 52:7
while the Chaldeans were around the **c**. Jer 52:7
were left in the **c** and the deserters who Jer 52:15
and from the **c** he took an officer who Jer 52:25
council, who were found in the **c**; Jer 52:25
who were found in the midst of the **c**. Jer 52:25
How lonely sits the **c** that was full of Lam 1:1
my priests and elders perished in the **c**, Lam 1:19
and babies faint in the streets of the **c**. Lam 2:11
a wounded man in the streets of the **c**, Lam 2:12
"Is this the **c** that was called the Lam 2:15
at the fate of all the daughters of my **c**. Lam 3:51
The old men have left the **c** gate, the Lam 5:14
lay it before you, and engrave on it a **c**, Ezk 4:1
it as an iron wall between you and the **c**; Ezk 4:3
and you shall prophesy against the **c**. Ezk 4:7
burn in the fire in the midst of the **c**, Ezk 5:2
strike with the sword all around the **c**. Ezk 5:2
who is in the **c** famine and pestilence Ezk 7:15
bloody crimes and the **c** is full of Ezk 7:23
"Bring near the executioners of the **c**, Ezk 9:1
LORD said to him, "Pass through the **c**, Ezk 9:4
hearing, "Pass through the **c** after him, Ezk 9:5
So they went out and struck in the **c**. Ezk 9:7
full of blood, and the **c** full of injustice. Ezk 9:9
scatter them over the **c**." And he went Ezk 10:2
and who give wicked counsel in this **c**; Ezk 11:2
This **c** is the cauldron, and we are the Ezk 11:3
your slain in this **c** and have filled its Ezk 11:6
are the meat, and this **c** is the cauldron, Ezk 11:7
This **c** shall not be your cauldron, Ezk 11:11
the midst of the **c** and stood on the Ezk 11:23
that is on the east side of the **c**. Ezk 11:23
of trade and set it in a **c** of merchants. Ezk 17:4
make it at the head of the way to a **c**. Ezk 21:19
you judge, will you judge the bloody **c**? Ezk 22:2
A **c** that sheds blood in her midst, so Ezk 22:3
Woe to the bloody **c**, to the pot whose Ezk 24:6
says the Lord GOD: Woe to the bloody **c**! Ezk 24:9
as men enter a **c** that has been Ezk 26:10
from the seas, O **c** renowned, Ezk 26:17
When I make you a **c** laid waste, like Ezk 26:19
said, "The **c** has been struck down." Ezk 33:21
(Hamonah is also the name of the **c**.) Ezk 39:16
year after the **c** was struck down, Ezk 40:1
upon me, and he brought me to the **c**. Ezk 40:1
was a structure like a **c** to the south. Ezk 40:2
had seen when he came to destroy the **c**, Ezk 43:3
the property of the **c** an area 5,000 Ezk 45:6
holy district and the property of the **c**, Ezk 45:7
holy district and the property of the **c**, Ezk 45:7
shall be for common use for the **c**, Ezk 48:15
In the midst of it shall be the **c**, Ezk 48:15
And the **c** shall have open land: on the Ezk 48:17
shall be food for the workers of the **c**. Ezk 48:18
And the workers of the **c**, from all the Ezk 48:19
together with the property of the **c**. Ezk 48:20
the property of the **c** shall belong to Ezk 48:21
of the Levites and the property of the **c**, Ezk 48:22
"These shall be the exits of the **c**: On Ezk 48:30
the gates of the **c** being named after Ezk 48:31
circumference of the **c** shall be 18,000 Ezk 48:35
the name of the **c** from that time on Ezk 48:35
turn away from your **c** Jerusalem, Dn 9:16
and the **c** that is called by your name. Dn 9:18
because your **c** and your people are Dn 9:19
about your people and your holy **c**, Dn 9:24
shall destroy the **c** and the sanctuary. Dn 9:26
siegeworks and take a well-fortified **c**. Dn 11:15
Gilead is a **c** of evildoers, tracked with Hos 6:8
They leap upon the **c**, they run upon the Jl 2:9
Is a trumpet blown in a **c**, and the people Am 3:6
Does disaster come to a **c**, unless the Am 3:6
I would send rain on one **c**, and send no Am 4:7
one city, and send no rain on another **c**; Am 4:7
wander to another **c** to drink water, Am 4:8
"The **c** that went out a thousand shall Am 5:3
I will deliver up the **c** and all that is in Am 6:8
wife shall be a prostitute in the **c**, Am 7:17
"Arise, go to Nineveh, that great **c**, and Jon 1:2
"Arise, go to Nineveh, that great **c**, and Jon 3:2
Nineveh was an exceedingly great **c**, Jon 3:3
Jonah began to go into the **c**, going a Jon 3:4
Jonah went out of the **c** and sat to the east Jon 4:5
to the east of the **c** and made a booth for Jon 4:5
should see what would become of the **c**. Jon 4:5
should not I pity Nineveh, that great **c**, Jon 4:11
shall go out from the **c** and dwell in the Mi 4:10
of the LORD cries to the **c**—and it is sound Mi 6:9
Woe to the bloody **c**, all full of lies and Na 3:1
with blood and founds a **c** on iniquity! Hab 2:12
is the exultant **c** that lived securely, Zep 2:15
rebellious and defiled, the oppressing **c**! Zep 3:1
Jerusalem shall be called the faithful **c**, Zec 8:3
And the streets of the **c** shall be full of Zec 8:5
The inhabitants of one **c** shall go to Zec 8:21
and the **c** shall be taken and the houses Zec 14:2
Half of the **c** shall go out into exile, but Zec 14:2
people shall not be cut off from the **c**. Zec 14:2
he went and lived in a **c** called Nazareth, Mt 2:23
took him to the holy **c** and set him on the Mt 4:5
A **c** set on a hill cannot be hidden. Mt 5:14
for it is the **c** of the great King. Mt 5:35
going into the **c** they told everything, Mt 8:33
behold, all the **c** came out to meet Jesus, Mt 8:34
he crossed over and came to his own **c**. Mt 9:1
and no **c** or house divided against itself Mt 12:25
Jerusalem, the whole **c** was stirred up, Mt 21:10
went out of the **c** to Bethany and lodged Mt 21:17
morning, as he was returning to the **c**, Mt 21:18
those murderers and burned their **c**. Mt 22:7
the **c** that kills the prophets and stones Mt 23:37
"Go into the **c** to a certain man and say Mt 26:18
went into the holy **c** and appeared to Mt 27:53
guard went into the **c** and told the chief Mt 28:11
And the whole **c** was gathered together Mk 1:33
and told it in the **c** and in the country. Mk 5:14
evening came they went out of the **c**. Mk 11:19
and said to them, "Go into the **c**, Mk 14:13
out and went to the **c** and found it just Mk 14:16
from God to a **c** of Galilee named Lk 1:26
of Nazareth, to Judea, to the **c** of David, Lk 2:4
born this day in the **c** of David a Savior, Lk 2:11
went down to Capernaum, a **c** of Galilee. Lk 4:31
And behold, a woman of the **c**, who was Lk 7:37
him a man from the **c** who had demons. Lk 8:27
and told it in the **c** and in the country. Lk 8:34
throughout the whole **c** how much Lk 8:39
the **c** that kills the prophets and stones Lk 13:34
quickly to the streets and lanes of the **c**, Lk 14:21
"In a certain **c** there was a judge who Lk 18:2
a widow in that **c** who kept coming to Lk 18:3
And when he drew near and saw the **c**, Lk 19:41
let those who are inside the **c** depart, Lk 21:21
"Behold, when you have entered the **c**, Lk 22:10
started in the **c** and for murder. Lk 23:19
But stay in the **c** until you are clothed Lk 24:49
Bethsaida, the **c** of Andrew and Peter. Jn 1:44
had gone away into the **c** to buy food.) Jn 4:8
Jesus was crucified was near the **c**, Jn 19:20
for truly in this **c** there were gathered Acts 4:27
cast him out of the **c** and stoned him. Acts 7:58
went down to the **c** of Samaria and Acts 8:5
So there was much joy in that **c**. Acts 8:8
magic in the **c** and amazed the Acts 8:9
But rise and enter the **c**, and you will be Acts 9:6
their journey and approaching the **c**, Acts 10:9
"I was in the **c** of Joppa praying, and in Acts 11:5
to the iron gate leading into the **c**. Acts 12:10
almost the whole **c** gathered to hear Acts 13:44
and the leading men of the **c**, Acts 13:50
But the people of the **c** were divided; Acts 14:4
temple was at the entrance to the **c**, Acts 14:13
Paul and dragged him out of the **c**, Acts 14:19
him, he rose up and entered the **c**, Acts 14:20
the gospel to that **c** and had made Acts 14:21
had in every **c** those who proclaim Acts 15:21
brothers in every **c** where we Acts 15:36
which is a leading **c** of the district of Acts 16:12
We remained in this **c** some days. Acts 16:12
named Lydia, from the **c** of Thyatira, Acts 16:14
Jews, and they are disturbing our **c**. Acts 16:20
out and asked them to leave the **c**. Acts 16:39
formed a mob, set the **c** in an uproar, Acts 17:5
of the brothers before the **c** authorities, Acts 17:6
people and the **c** authorities were Acts 17:8
as he saw that the **c** was full of idols. Acts 17:16
have many in this **c** who are my Acts 18:10
So the **c** was filled with the confusion, Acts 19:29
not know that the **c** of the Ephesians Acts 19:35
me in every **c** that imprisonment and Acts 20:23
us until we were outside the **c**. Acts 21:5
the Ephesian with him in the **c**, Acts 21:29
Then all the **c** was stirred up, and the Acts 21:30
in Cilicia, a citizen of no obscure **c**. Acts 21:39
in Cilicia, but brought up in this **c**, Acts 22:3
or in the synagogues or in the **c**. Acts 24:12
and the prominent men of the **c**. Acts 25:23
Havens, near which was the **c** of Lasea. Acts 27:8
Erastus, the **c** treasurer, and our Rom 16:23
from Gentiles, danger in the **c**, 2 Cor 11:26
was guarding the **c** of Damascus in 2 Cor 11:32
forward to the **c** that has foundations, Heb 11:10
God, for he has prepared for them a **c**. Heb 11:16
Zion and to the **c** of the living God, Heb 12:22
For here we have no lasting **c**, but we Heb 13:14
city, but we seek the **c** that is to come. Heb 13:14
God, and the name of the **c** of my God, Rv 3:12
trample the holy **c** for forty-two months. Rv 11:2
street of the great **c** that symbolically is Rv 11:8
earthquake, and a tenth of the **c** fell. Rv 11:13
the winepress was trodden outside the **c**, Rv 14:20
The great **c** was split into three parts, Rv 16:19
saw is the great **c** that has dominion Rv 17:18
You great **c**, you mighty city, Babylon! Rv 18:10
You great city, you mighty **c**, Babylon! Rv 18:10
for the great **c** that was clothed in fine Rv 18:16
"What **c** was like the great city?" Rv 18:18
"What city was like the great **c**?" Rv 18:18
for the great **c** where all who had ships Rv 18:19
Babylon the great **c** be thrown down Rv 18:21
the camp of the saints and the beloved **c**, Rv 20:9
And I saw the holy **c**, new Jerusalem, Rv 21:2
me the holy **c** Jerusalem coming down Rv 21:10
wall of the **c** had twelve foundations, Rv 21:14
gold to measure the **c** and its gates and Rv 21:15
The **c** lies foursquare; its length the Rv 21:16
And he measured the **c** with his rod, Rv 21:16
of jasper, while the **c** was pure gold, Rv 21:18
the wall of the **c** were adorned with Rv 21:19
and the street of the **c** was pure gold, Rv 21:21
And I saw no temple in the **c**, for its Rv 21:22
And the **c** has no need of sun or moon Rv 21:23
through the middle of the street of the **c**; Rv 22:2
that they may enter the **c** by the gates. Rv 22:14
in the tree of life and in the holy **c**, Rv 22:19

CIVILIAN (1)
No soldier gets entangled in **c** pursuits, 2 Tm 2:4

CLAIM (7)
no portion or right or **c** in Jerusalem." Neh 2:20
Let gloom and deep darkness **c** it. Let Jb 3:5
world is coming. He has no **c** on me, Jn 14:30
If others share this rightful **c** on you, 1 Cor 9:12
in ourselves to **c** anything as coming 2 Cor 3:5
to undermine the **c** of those who 2 Cor 11:12
who would like to **c** that in their 2 Cor 11:12

CLAIMING (2)
Theudas rose up, **c** to be somebody, Acts 5:36
C to be wise, they became fools, Rom 1:22

CLAIMS (2)
him, "See, your **c** are good and right, 2 Sm 15:3
Even though a wise man **c** to know, he Eccl 8:17

CLAMOR (5)
Do not forget the **c** of your foes, the Ps 74:23
The **c** will resound to the ends of the Jer 25:31
they raised a **c** in the house of the LORD Lam 2:7
Then a great **c** arose, and some of the Acts 23:9
wrath and anger and **c** and slander be Eph 4:31

CLAMPS (1)
for the doors of the gates and for **c**, 1 Chr 22:3

CLAN (110)
house and to my **c** and take a wife Gn 24:38
my son from my **c** and from my Gn 24:40
my oath, when you come to my **c**. Gn 24:41
man and against his **c** and will cut them Lv 20:5
and each of you shall return to his **c**. Lv 25:10
go back to his own **c** and return to the Lv 25:41
you or to a member of the stranger's **c**, Lv 25:47
relative from his **c** may redeem him. Lv 25:49
and so they set out, each one in his **c**, Nm 2:34
Gershon belonged the **c** of the Libnites Nm 3:21
the Libnites and the **c** of the Shimeites; Nm 3:21
Kohath belonged the **c** of the Nm 3:27
Amramites and the **c** of the Izharites Nm 3:27
Izharites and the **c** of the Hebronites Nm 3:27
Hebronites and the **c** of the Uzzielites; Nm 3:27
Merari belonged the **c** of the Mahlites Nm 3:33
the Mahlites and the **c** of the Mushites: Nm 3:33
of Hanoch, the **c** of the Hanochites; Nm 26:5
of Pallu, the **c** of the Palluites; Nm 26:5
of Hezron, the **c** of the Hezronites; of Nm 26:6
of Carmi, the **c** of the Carmites. Nm 26:6
of Nemuel, the **c** of the Nemuelites; Nm 26:12
of Jamin, the **c** of the Jaminites; Nm 26:12
of Jachin, the **c** of the Jachinites; Nm 26:12
of Zerah, the **c** of the Zerahites; of Nm 26:13
of Shaul, the **c** of the Shaulites. Nm 26:13
of Zephon, the **c** of the Zephonites; Nm 26:15
of Haggi, the **c** of the Haggites; Nm 26:15
of Shuni, the **c** of the Shunites; Nm 26:15
of Ozni, the **c** of the Oznites; of Eri, the Nm 26:16
the Oznites; of Eri, the **c** of the Erites; Nm 26:16
of Arod, the **c** of the Arodites; of Areli, Nm 26:17
Arodites; of Areli, the **c** of the Arelites. Nm 26:17
were: of Shelah, the **c** of the Shelanites; Nm 26:20
of Perez, the **c** of the Perezites; Nm 26:20
of Zerah, the **c** of the Zerahites. Nm 26:20
of Hezron, the **c** of the Hezronites; Nm 26:21
of Hamul, the **c** of the Hamulites. Nm 26:21
clans: of Tola, the **c** of the Tolaites; Nm 26:23
of Puvah, the **c** of the Punites; Nm 26:23

of Jashub, the **c** of the Jashubites; of Nm 26:24
of Shimron, the **c** of the Shimronites. Nm 26:24
clans: of Sered, the **c** of the Seredites; Nm 26:26
Seredites; of Elon, the **c** of the Elonites; Nm 26:26
of Jahleel, the **c** of the Jahleelites. Nm 26:26
of Machir, the **c** of the Machirites; Nm 26:29
of Gilead, the **c** of the Gileadites. Nm 26:29
of Gilead: of Iezer, the **c** of the Iezerites; Nm 26:30
of Helek, the **c** of the Helekites; Nm 26:30
and of Asriel, the **c** of the Asrielites; Nm 26:31
of Shechem, the **c** of the Shechemites; Nm 26:31
of Shemida, the **c** of the Shemidaites; Nm 26:32
and of Hepher, the **c** of the Hepherites. Nm 26:32
Shuthelah, the **c** of the Shuthelahites; Nm 26:35
of Becher, the **c** of the Becherites; Nm 26:35
of Tahan, the **c** of the Tahanites. Nm 26:35
of Eran, the **c** of the Eranites. Nm 26:36
clans: of Bela, the **c** of the Belaites; Nm 26:38
of Ashbel, the **c** of the Ashbelites; Nm 26:38
of Ahiram, the **c** of the Ahiramites; Nm 26:38
the **c** of the Shuphamites; Nm 26:39
of Hupham, the **c** of the Huphamites. Nm 26:39
Naaman: of Ard, the **c** of the Ardites; Nm 26:40
of Naaman, the **c** of the Naamites. Nm 26:40
of Shuham, the **c** of the Shuhamites. Nm 26:42
clans: of Imnah, the **c** of the Imnites; Nm 26:44
Imnites; of Ishvi, the **c** of the Ishvites; Nm 26:44
Ishvites; of Beriah, the **c** of the Beriites. Nm 26:44
of Heber, the **c** of the Heberites; Nm 26:45
of Malchiel, the **c** of the Malchielites. Nm 26:45
of Jahzeel, the **c** of the Jahzeelites; Nm 26:48
of Guni, the **c** of the Gunites; Nm 26:48
of Jezer, the **c** of the Jezerites; of Nm 26:49
of Shillem, the **c** of the Shillemites. Nm 26:49
of Gershon, the **c** of the Gershonites; Nm 26:57
of Kohath, the **c** of the Kohathites; Nm 26:57
of Merari, the **c** of the Merarites. Nm 26:57
the **c** of the Libnites, the clan of the Nm 26:58
the Libnites, the **c** of the Hebronites, Nm 26:58
the Hebronites, the **c** of the Mahlites, Nm 26:58
of the Mahlites, the **c** of the Mushites, Nm 26:58
of the Mushites, the **c** of the Korahites. Nm 26:58
taken away from his **c** because he had Nm 27:4
to the nearest kinsman of his **c**, Nm 27:11
fathers' houses of the **c** of the people of Nm 36:1
shall marry within the **c** of the tribe of Nm 36:6
be wife to one of the **c** of the tribe of her Nm 36:8
in the tribe of their father's **c**. Nm 36:12
man or woman or **c** or tribe whose Dt 29:18
And the **c** that the LORD takes shall come Jos 7:14
and the **c** of the Zerahites was taken. Jos 7:17
he brought near the **c** of the Zerahites Jos 7:17
my **c** is the weakest in Manasseh, Jgs 6:15
and to the whole **c** of his mother's family, Jgs 9:1
he gave in marriage outside his **c**, Jgs 12:9
to be priest to a tribe and **c** in Israel?" Jgs 18:19
a worthy man of the **c** of Elimelech, Ru 2:1
to Boaz, who was of the **c** of Elimelech. Ru 2:3
And is not my **c** the humblest of all 1 Sm 9:21
and the **c** of the Matrites was taken 1 Sm 10:21
my relatives, my father's **c** in Israel, 1 Sm 18:18
is a yearly sacrifice there for all the **c**.' 1 Sm 20:6
for our **c** holds a sacrifice in the city, 1 Sm 20:29
now the whole **c** has risen against 2 Sm 14:7
nor did all their **c** multiply like the 1 Chr 4:27
given by lot out of the **c** of the tribe, 1 Chr 6:61
given out of the **c** of the half-tribe of 1 Chr 6:71
throughout every generation, in every **c**, Est 9:28
The least one shall become a **c**, and the Is 60:22
it shall be like a **c** in Judah, and Ekron Zec 9:7

CLANGING (1)

I am a noisy gong or a **c** cymbal. 1 Cor 13:1

CLANS (165)

each with his own language, by their **c**, Gn 10:5
Afterward the **c** of the Canaanites Gn 10:18
These are the sons of Ham, by their **c**, Gn 10:20
These are the sons of Shem, by their **c**, Gn 10:31
These are the **c** of the sons of Noah, Gn 10:32
according to their **c** and their dwelling Gn 36:40
and Carmi; these are the **c** of Reuben. Ex 6:14
woman; these are the **c** of Simeon. Ex 6:15
Gershon: Libni and Shimei, by their **c**. Ex 6:17
These are the **c** of the Levites according Ex 6:19
these are the **c** of the Korahites. Ex 6:24
fathers' houses of the Levites by their **c**. Ex 6:25
for yourselves according to your **c**, Ex 12:21
with you and their **c** that are with you, Lv 25:45
congregation of the people of Israel, by **c**, Nm 1:2
tribes, the heads of the **c** of Israel. Nm 1:16
who registered themselves by **c**, Nm 1:18
firstborn, their generations, by their **c**, Nm 1:20
of Simeon, their generations, by their **c**, Nm 1:22
of Gad, their generations, by their **c**, Nm 1:24
of Judah, their generations, by their **c**, Nm 1:26
Issachar, their generations, by their **c**, Nm 1:28
Zebulun, their generations, by their **c**, Nm 1:30
Ephraim, their generations, by their **c**, Nm 1:32
their generations, by their **c**, Nm 1:34
Benjamin, their generations, by their **c**, Nm 1:36
of Dan, their generations, by their **c**, Nm 1:38
of Asher, their generations, by their **c**, Nm 1:40
Naphtali, their generations, by their **c**, Nm 1:42
of Levi, by fathers' houses and by **c**; Nm 3:15
of the sons of Gershon by their **c**: Nm 3:18
And the sons of Kohath by their **c**: Nm 3:19
And the sons of Merari by their **c**: Nm 3:20
Mushi. These are the **c** of the Levites, Nm 3:20
these were the **c** of the Gershonites. Nm 3:21
The **c** of the Gershonites were to camp Nm 3:23
these are the **c** of the Kohathites. Nm 3:27
The **c** of the sons of Kohath were to Nm 3:29
house of the **c** of the Kohathites. Nm 3:30
the Mushites: these are the **c** of Merari. Nm 3:33
fathers' house of the **c** of Merari was Nm 3:35
at the commandment of the LORD, by **c**, Nm 3:39
Levi, by their **c** and their fathers' houses, Nm 4:2
the tribe of the **c** of the Kohathites be Nm 4:18
by their fathers' houses and by their **c**. Nm 4:22
the service of the **c** of the Gershonites, Nm 4:24
is the service of the **c** of the sons of the Nm 4:28
list them by their **c** and their fathers' Nm 4:29
is the service of the **c** of the sons of Nm 4:33
by their **c** and their fathers' houses, Nm 4:34
and those listed by **c** were 2,750. Nm 4:36
was the list of the **c** of the Kohathites, Nm 4:37
by their **c** and their fathers' houses, Nm 4:38
those listed by their **c** and their fathers' Nm 4:40
was the list of the **c** of the sons of Nm 4:41
Those listed of the **c** of the sons of Nm 4:42
by their **c** and their fathers' houses, Nm 4:42
those listed by **c** were 3,200. Nm 4:44
was the list of the **c** of the sons of Nm 4:45
by their **c** and their fathers' houses, Nm 4:46
people weeping throughout their **c**, Nm 11:10
These are the **c** of the Reubenites, and Nm 26:7
sons of Simeon according to their **c**: Nm 26:12
These are the **c** of the Simeonites, Nm 26:14
The sons of Gad according to their **c**: Nm 26:15
These are the **c** of the sons of Gad as Nm 26:18
of Judah according to their **c** were: Nm 26:20
These are the **c** of Judah as they were Nm 26:22
sons of Issachar according to their **c**: Nm 26:23
These are the **c** of Issachar as they Nm 26:25
sons of Zebulun, according to their **c**: Nm 26:26
These are the **c** of the Zebulunites as Nm 26:27
sons of Joseph according to their **c**: Nm 26:28
These are the **c** of Manasseh, and Nm 26:34
sons of Ephraim according to their **c**: Nm 26:35
These are the **c** of the sons of Ephraim Nm 26:37
sons of Joseph according to their **c**. Nm 26:37
of Benjamin according to their **c**: Nm 26:38
of Benjamin according to their **c**, Nm 26:41
the sons of Dan according to their **c**: Nm 26:42
These are the **c** of Dan according to Nm 26:42
the clans of Dan according to their **c**. Nm 26:42
All the **c** of the Shuhamites, as they Nm 26:43
sons of Asher according to their **c**: Nm 26:44
These are the **c** of the sons of Asher as Nm 26:47
sons of Naphtali according to their **c**: Nm 26:48
These are the **c** of Naphtali according Nm 26:50
of Naphtali according to their **c**, Nm 26:50
list of the Levites according to their **c**: Nm 26:57
These are the **c** of Levi: the clan of the Nm 26:58
from the **c** of Manasseh the son of Nm 27:1
the land by lot according to your **c**. Nm 33:54
from the **c** of the people of Joseph, Nm 36:1
were married into the **c** of the people Nm 36:12
LORD takes by lot shall come near by **c**. Jos 7:14
And he brought near the **c** of Judah, and Jos 7:17
people of Reuben according to their **c**. Jos 13:15
according to their **c** with their cities Jos 13:23
the people of Gad, according to their **c**. Jos 13:24
the people of Gad according to their **c**, Jos 13:28
of Manasseh according to their **c**. Jos 13:29
people of Machir according to their **c**. Jos 13:31
according to their **c** reached southward Jos 15:1
people of Judah according to their **c**. Jos 15:12
people of Judah according to their **c**. Jos 15:20
of Ephraim by their **c** was as follows: Jos 16:5
tribe of the people of Ephraim by their **c**, Jos 16:8
rest of the people of Manasseh by their **c**, Jos 17:2
Manasseh the son of Joseph, by their **c**. Jos 17:2
Benjamin according to its **c** came up, Jos 18:11
of Benjamin, according to their **c**, Jos 18:20
according to their **c** were Jericho, Jos 18:21
people of Benjamin according to its **c**. Jos 18:28
people of Simeon, according to their **c**, Jos 19:1
people of Simeon according to their **c**. Jos 19:8
people of Zebulun, according to their **c**. Jos 19:10
according to their **c**—these cities with Jos 19:16
people of Issachar, according to their **c**. Jos 19:17
according to their **c**—the cities with Jos 19:23
people of Asher according to their **c**. Jos 19:24
according to their **c**—these cities Jos 19:31
of Naphtali, according to their **c**. Jos 19:32
according to their **c**—the cities Jos 19:39
the people of Dan, according to their **c**. Jos 19:40
according to their **c**—these cities with Jos 19:48
lot came out for the **c** of the Kohathites. Jos 21:4
received by lot from the **c** of the tribe of Jos 21:5
received by lot from the **c** of the tribe of Jos 21:6
according to their **c** received from the Jos 21:7
one of the **c** of the Kohathites who Jos 21:10
to the Kohathite **c** of the Levites, Jos 21:20
The cities of the **c** of the rest of the Jos 21:26
Gershonites, one of the **c** of the Levites, Jos 21:27
cities of the several **c** of the Gershonites Jos 21:33
to the rest of the Levites, the Merarite **c**, Jos 21:34
for the cities of the several Merarite **c**, Jos 21:40
is, the remainder of the **c** of the Levites, Jos 21:40
head of a family among the **c** of Israel. Jos 22:14
Among the **c** of Reuben there were great Jgs 5:15
Among the **c** of Reuben there were great Jgs 5:16
the humblest of all the **c** of the tribe of 1 Sm 9:21
the tribe of Benjamin near by its **c**, 1 Sm 10:21
And the **c** of Kiriath-jearim: the 1 Chr 2:53
The **c** also of the scribes who lived at 1 Chr 2:55
These were the **c** of the Zorathites. 1 Chr 4:2
Anub, Zobebah, and the **c** of Aharhel, 1 Chr 4:8
and the **c** of the house of linen 1 Chr 4:21
by name were princes in their **c**, 1 Chr 4:38
And his kinsmen by their **c**, when the 1 Chr 5:7
These are the **c** of the Levites 1 Chr 6:19
sons of Aaron of the **c** of Kohathites, 1 Chr 6:54
throughout their **c** were thirteen. 1 Chr 6:60
according to their **c** were allotted 1 Chr 6:62
according to their **c** were allotted 1 Chr 6:63
And some of the **c** of the sons of 1 Chr 6:66
for the rest of the **c** of the Kohathites. 1 Chr 6:70
belonging to all the **c** of Issachar were 1 Chr 7:5
to the LORD, O **c** of the peoples, 1 Chr 16:28
places, I stationed the people by their **c**, Neh 4:13
Jacob, and all the **c** of the house of Israel. Jer 2:4
I will be the God of all the **c** of Israel, Jer 31:1
has rejected the two **c** that he chose'? Jer 33:24
are too little to be among the **c** of Judah, Mi 5:2
Then the **c** of Judah shall say to Zec 12:5
day I will make the **c** of Judah like a Zec 12:6

CLAP (8)

C your hands, all peoples! Shout to God Ps 47:1
Let the rivers **c** their hands; let the hills Ps 98:8
the trees of the field shall **c** their hands. Is 55:12
pass along the way **c** their hands at Lam 2:15
"**C** your hands and stamp your foot Ezk 6:11
C your hands and let the sword come Ezk 21:14
I also will **c** my hands, and I will Ezk 21:17
the news about you **c** their hands over Na 3:19

CLAPPED (2)

and they **c** their hands and said, 2 Kgs 11:12
Because you have **c** your hands and Ezk 25:6

CLAPS (2)

It **c** its hands at him and hisses at him Jb 27:23
he **c** his hands among us and Jb 34:37

CLASHING (1)

praise him with loud **c** cymbals! Ps 150:5

CLASP (1)

they **c** each other and cannot be Jb 41:17

CLASPS (8)

And you shall make fifty **c** of gold, and Ex 26:6
the curtains one to the other with the **c**, Ex 26:6
"You shall make fifty **c** of bronze, and Ex 26:11
of bronze, and put the **c** into the loops, Ex 26:11
And you shall hang the veil from the **c**, Ex 26:33
And he made fifty **c** of gold, and Ex 36:13
the curtains one to the other with **c**. Ex 36:13
And he made fifty **c** of bronze to couple Ex 36:18

CLASSIFIED (1)

around them shall be **c** with the fields Lv 25:31

CLASSIFY (1)

we dare to **c** or compare ourselves 2 Cor 10:12

CLAUDIA (1)

Pudens and Linus and **C** and all the 2 Tm 4:21

CLAUDIUS (3)

(this took place in the days of **C**). Acts 11:28
because **C** had commanded all the Acts 18:2
"**C** Lysias, to his Excellency the Acts 23:26

CLAWS (2)

feathers, and his nails were like birds' **c**. Dn 4:33
with its teeth of iron and **c** of bronze, Dn 7:19

CLAY (27)
in the **c** ground between Succoth and 1 Kgs 7:46
in the **c** ground between Succoth and 2 Chr 4:17
more those who dwell in houses of **c**, Jb 4:19
that you have made me like **c**; Jb 10:9
of ashes; your defenses are defenses of **c**. Jb 13:12
like dust, and pile up clothing like **c**, Jb 27:16
I too was pinched off from a piece of **c**. Jb 33:6
It is changed like **c** under the seal, and Jb 38:14
Shall the potter be regarded as the **c**, that Is 29:16
as on mortar, as the potter treads **c**. Is 41:25
Does the **c** say to him who forms it, Is 45:9
we are the **c**, and you are our potter; Is 64:8
he was making of **c** was spoiled in the Jer 18:4
Behold, like the **c** in the potter's hand, so Jer 18:6
its feet partly of iron and partly of **c**. Dn 2:33
the image on its feet of iron and **c**, Dn 2:34
Then the iron, the **c**, the bronze, the Dn 2:35
partly of potter's **c** and partly of iron, Dn 2:41
as you saw iron mixed with the soft **c**. Dn 2:41
of the feet were partly iron and partly **c**, Dn 2:42
As you saw the iron mixed with soft **c**, Dn 2:43
just as iron does not mix with **c**. Dn 2:43
in pieces the iron, the bronze, the **c**, Dn 2:45
strengthen your forts; go into the **c**; Na 3:14
Has the potter no right over the **c**, to Rom 9:21
But we have this treasure in jars of **c**, 2 Cor 4:7
and silver but also of wood and **c**, 2 Tm 2:20

CLEAN (124)
with you seven pairs of all **c** animals, Gn 7:2
and a pair of the animals that are not **c**, Gn 7:2
Of **c** animals, and of animals that are not Gn 7:8
animals, and of animals that are not **c**, Gn 7:8
took some of every **c** animal and some Gn 8:20
and some of every **c** bird and offered Gn 8:20
shall carry outside the camp to a **c** place, Lv 4:12
the ashes outside the camp to a **c** place. Lv 6:11
up with fire. All who are **c** may eat flesh, Lv 7:19
and between the unclean and the **c**, Lv 10:10
contributed you shall eat in a **c** place, Lv 10:14
until the evening; then it shall be **c**. Lv 11:32
or a cistern holding water shall be **c**, Lv 11:36
any seed grain that is to be sown, it is **c**, Lv 11:37
the unclean and the **c** and between the Lv 11:47
Then she shall be **c** from the flow of her Lv 12:7
atonement for her, and she shall be **c**.'" Lv 12:8
then the priest shall pronounce him **c**; Lv 13:6
And he shall wash his clothes and be **c**. Lv 13:6
shall pronounce him **c** of the disease; Lv 13:13
it has all turned white, and he is **c**. Lv 13:13
shall pronounce the diseased person **c**; Lv 13:17
the diseased person clean; he is **c**. Lv 13:17
and the priest shall pronounce him **c**. Lv 13:23
and the priest shall pronounce him **c**, Lv 13:28
then the priest shall pronounce him **c**. Lv 13:34
And he shall wash his clothes and be **c**. Lv 13:34
in it, the itch is healed and he is **c**, Lv 13:37
and the priest shall pronounce him **c**. Lv 13:37
that has broken out in the skin; he is **c**. Lv 13:39
out from his head, he is bald; he is **c**. Lv 13:40
he has baldness of the forehead; he is **c**. Lv 13:41
be washed a second time, and be **c**." Lv 13:58
to determine whether it is **c** or unclean. Lv 13:59
cleansed two live **c** birds and cedarwood Lv 14:4
he shall pronounce him **c** and shall let Lv 14:7
himself in water, and he shall be **c**. Lv 14:8
his body in water, and he shall be **c**. Lv 14:9
atonement for him, and he shall be **c**. Lv 14:20
the priest shall pronounce the house **c**, Lv 14:48
for the house, and it shall be **c**." Lv 14:53
when it is unclean and when it is **c**. Lv 14:57
the discharge spits on someone who is **c**, Lv 15:8
his body in fresh water and shall be **c**. Lv 15:13
seven days, and after that she shall be **c**. Lv 15:28
You shall be **c** before the LORD from all Lv 16:30
until the evening; then he shall be **c**. Lv 17:15
therefore separate the **c** beast from the Lv 20:25
and the unclean bird from the **c**. Lv 20:25
may eat of the holy things until he is **c**. Lv 22:4
When the sun goes down he shall be **c**, Lv 22:7
woman has not defiled herself and is **c**, Nm 5:28
But if anyone who is **c** and is not on a Nm 9:13
Everyone who is **c** in your house may Nm 18:11
Everyone who is **c** in your house may Nm 18:13
And a man who is **c** shall gather up the Nm 19:9
them outside the camp in a **c** place. Nm 19:9
and on the seventh day, and so be **c**. Nm 19:12
the seventh day, he will not become **c**. Nm 19:12
Then a **c** person shall take hyssop Nm 19:18
And the **c** person shall sprinkle it on Nm 19:19
in water, and at evening he shall be **c**. Nm 19:19
pass through the fire, and it shall be **c**. Nm 31:23
the seventh day, and you shall be **c**. Nm 31:24
The unclean and the **c** may eat of it, Dt 12:15
The unclean and the **c** alike may eat of Dt 12:22
"You may eat all **c** birds. Dt 14:11
All **c** winged things you may eat. Dt 14:20
The unclean and the **c** alike may eat it, Dt 15:22
He is not **c**; surely he is not clean." 1 Sm 20:26
He is not clean; surely he is not **c**." 1 Sm 20:26
shall be restored, and you shall be **c**." 2 Kgs 5:10
in them and be **c**?" So he turned and 2 Kgs 5:12
said to you, 'Wash, and be **c**'?" 2 Kgs 5:13
the flesh of a little child, and he was **c**. 2 Kgs 5:14
lamb for everyone who was not **c**, 2 Chr 30:17
themselves together; all of them were **c**. Ezr 6:20
is pure, and I am **c** in God's eyes.' Jb 11:4
Who can bring a **c** thing out of an Jb 14:4
and he who has **c** hands grows stronger Jb 17:9
I am **c**, and there is no iniquity in me. Jb 33:9
the fear of the LORD is **c**, enduring forever; Ps 19:9
He who has **c** hands and a pure heart, Ps 24:4
Purge me with hyssop, and I shall be **c**; Ps 51:7
Create in me a **c** heart, O God, and Ps 51:10
I kept my heart **c** and washed my hands Ps 73:13
there are no oxen, the manger is **c**, Prv 14:4
my heart pure; I am **c** from my sin"? Prv 20:9
strokes make **c** the innermost parts. Prv 20:30
are those who are **c** in their own eyes Prv 30:12
and the evil, to the **c** and the unclean, Eccl 9:2
Wash yourselves; make yourselves **c**; Is 1:16
grain offering in a **c** vessel to the house Is 66:20
long will it be before you are made **c**?" Jer 13:27
And he shall **c** the land of Egypt as a Jer 43:12
between the unclean and the **c**, Ezk 22:26
I will sprinkle **c** water on you, and you Ezk 36:25
and you shall be **c** from all your Ezk 36:25
and our hope is lost; we are **c** cut off.' Ezk 37:11
between the unclean and the **c**. Ezk 44:23
After he has become **c**, they shall Ezk 44:26
"Let them put a **c** turban on his head." Zec 3:5
head." So they put a **c** turban on his head Zec 3:5
"Lord, if you will, you can make me **c**." Mt 8:2
be **c**." And immediately his leprosy was Mt 8:3
For you **c** the outside of the cup and the Mt 23:25
First **c** the inside of the cup and the Mt 23:26
plate, that the outside also may be **c**. Mt 23:26
and wrapped it in a **c** linen shroud Mt 27:59
him, "If you will, you can make me **c**." Mk 1:40
him and said to him, "I will; be **c**." Mk 1:41
the leprosy left him, and he was made **c**. Mk 1:42
(Thus he declared all foods **c**.) Mk 7:19
"Lord, if you will, you can make me **c**." Lk 5:12
be **c**." And immediately the leprosy left Lk 5:13
and behold, everything is **c** for you. Lk 11:41
except for his feet, but is completely **c**. Jn 13:10
And you are **c**, but not every one of Jn 13:10
was why he said, "Not all of you are **c**." Jn 13:11
Already you are **c** because of the word Jn 15:3
second time, "What God has made **c**, Acts 10:15
from heaven, 'What God has made **c**, Acts 11:9
Everything is indeed **c**, but it is Rom 14:20
our hearts sprinkled **c** from an evil Heb 10:22

CLEANED (2)
who steals shall be **c** out according to Zec 5:3
swears falsely shall be **c** out according to Zec 5:3

CLEANNESS (7)
according to the **c** of my hands he 2 Sm 22:21
according to my **c** in his sight. 2 Sm 22:25
to the sanctuary's rules of **c**." 2 Chr 30:19
delivered through the **c** of your hands." Jb 22:30
according to the **c** of my hands he Ps 18:20
according to the **c** of my hands in his Ps 18:24
"I gave you **c** of teeth in all your cities, Am 4:6

CLEANS (1)
Egypt as a shepherd **c** his cloak of Jer 43:12

CLEANSE (34)
Thus he shall **c** the house with the Lv 14:52
and **c** it and consecrate it from the Lv 16:19
atonement be made for you to **c** you. Lv 16:30
among the people of Israel and **c** them. Nm 8:6
Thus you shall do to them to **c** them: Nm 8:7
wash their clothes and **c** themselves. Nm 8:7
made atonement for them to **c** them. Nm 8:21
He shall **c** himself with the water on Nm 19:12
if he does not **c** himself on the third Nm 19:12
who has died, and does not **c** himself, Nm 19:13
on the seventh day he shall **c** him, Nm 19:19
who is unclean does not **c** himself, Nm 19:20
the LORD, to **c** the house of the LORD. 2 Chr 29:15
part of the house of the LORD to **c** it, 2 Chr 29:16
myself with snow and **c** my hands with Jb 9:30
my iniquity, and **c** me from my sin! Ps 51:2
Blows that wound **c** away evil; strokes Prv 20:30
of my people, not to winnow or **c**, Jer 4:11
I will **c** them from all the guilt of their Jer 33:8
were you washed with water to **c** you, Ezk 16:4
and from all your idols I will **c** you. Ezk 36:25
On the day that I **c** you from all your Ezk 36:33
they have sinned, and will **c** them; Ezk 37:23
burying them, in order to **c** the land. Ezk 39:12
on the face of the land, so as to **c** it. Ezk 39:14
the city.) Thus shall they **c** the land. Ezk 39:16
make atonement for the altar and **c** it, Ezk 43:26
to **c** them from sin and uncleanness. Zec 13:1
Heal the sick, raise the dead, **c** lepers, Mt 10:8
"Now you Pharisees **c** the outside of the Lk 11:39
C out the old leaven that you may be a 1 Cor 5:7
let us **c** ourselves from every 2 Cor 7:1
C your hands, you sinners, and purify Jas 4:8
our sins and to **c** us from all 1 Jn 1:9

CLEANSED (37)
him who is to be **c** two live clean birds Lv 14:4
him who is to be **c** of the leprous disease. Lv 14:7
he who is to be **c** shall wash his clothes Lv 14:8
who is to be **c** and these things before Lv 14:11
him who is to be **c** and on the thumb of Lv 14:14
him who is to be **c** and on the thumb of Lv 14:17
put on the head of him who is to be **c**. Lv 14:18
who is to be **c** from his uncleanness. Lv 14:19
of the right ear of him who is to be **c**, Lv 14:25
him who is to be **c** and on the thumb of Lv 14:28
put on the head of him who is to be **c**, Lv 14:29
before the LORD for him who is being **c**. Lv 14:31
with a discharge is **c** of his discharge, Lv 15:13
But if she is **c** of her discharge, she Lv 15:28
when you have **c** them and offered Nm 8:15
which even yet we have not **c** ourselves, Jos 22:17
"We have **c** all the house of the 2 Chr 29:18
and Zebulun, had not **c** themselves, 2 Chr 30:18
their altars and **c** Judah and 2 Chr 34:5
when he had **c** the land and the 2 Chr 34:8
I gave orders, and they **c** the chambers, Neh 13:9
Thus I **c** them from everything Neh 13:30
daughters of Zion and **c** the bloodstains Is 4:4
a land that is not **c** or rained upon in Ezk 22:24
because I would have **c** you and you Ezk 24:13
you were not **c** from your Ezk 24:13
you shall not be **c** anymore till I have Ezk 24:13
And immediately his leprosy was **c**. Mt 8:3
walk, lepers are **c** and the deaf hear, Mt 11:5
prophet Elisha, and none of them was **c**, Lk 4:27
their sight, the lame walk, lepers are **c**, Lk 7:22
priests." And as they went they were **c**. Lk 17:14
Then Jesus answered, "Were not ten **c**? Lk 17:17
them, having **c** their hearts by faith. Acts 15:9
having **c** her by the washing of water Eph 5:26
the worshipers, having once been **c**, Heb 10:2
forgotten that he was **c** from his former 2 Pt 1:9

CLEANSES (4)
And the priest who **c** him shall set the Lv 14:11
who hate him and **c** his people's land." Dt 32:43
if anyone **c** himself from what is 2 Tm 2:21
blood of Jesus his Son **c** us from all sin. 1 Jn 1:7

CLEANSING (11)
has shown himself to the priest for his **c**, Lv 13:7
the itch spreads in the skin after his **c**, Lv 13:35
of the leprous person for the day of his **c**. Lv 14:2
shall bring them for his **c** to the priest, Lv 14:23
cannot afford the offerings for his **c**." Lv 14:32
And for the **c** of the house he shall take Lv 14:49
count for himself seven days for his **c**, Lv 15:13
shall shave his head on the day of his **c**; Nm 6:9
chambers, the **c** of all that is holy, 1 Chr 23:28
offer for your **c** what Moses Mk 1:44
priest, and make an offering for your **c**, Lk 5:14

CLEAR (31)
we speak? Or how can we **c** ourselves? Gn 44:16
his staff, he who struck him shall be **c**; Ex 21:19
but who will by no means **c** the guilty, Ex 34:7
the will of the LORD should be **c** to them. Lv 24:12
and you shall **c** out the old to make Lv 26:10
but he will by no means **c** the guilty, Nm 14:18
had not been made **c** what should be Nm 15:34
LORD your God will **c** away these nations Dt 7:22
and there **c** ground for yourselves in Jos 17:15
you shall **c** it and possess it to its Jos 17:18
have made it **c** today that 2 Sm 19:6
All this he made **c** to me in writing 1 Chr 28:19
do you understand that is not **c** to us? Jb 15:9
my dwelling like **c** heat in sunshine, Is 18:4
up, build up the highway; **c** it of stones; Is 62:10
Then I will make their waters **c**, and Ezk 32:14
and to drink of **c** water, that you must Ezk 34:18
the LORD will by no means **c** the guilty. Na 1:3
and he will **c** his threshing floor and Mt 3:12
to **c** his threshing floor and to gather the Lk 3:17
to have a **c** conscience toward both Acts 24:16
also what eagerness to **c** yourselves, 2 Cor 7:11
This is a **c** sign to them of their Phil 1:28
that I may make it **c**, which is how I Col 4:4

of the faith with a **c** conscience. 1 Tm 3:9
did my ancestors, with a **c** conscience, 2 Tm 1:3
speak thus make it **c** that they are Heb 11:14
are sure that we have a **c** conscience, Heb 13:18
as our Lord Jesus Christ made **c** to me. 2 Pt 1:14
rare jewel, like a jasper, **c** as crystal. Rv 21:11
while the city was pure gold, **c** as glass. Rv 21:18

CLEAR-SIGHTED (1)
a bribe blinds the **c** and subverts the Ex 23:8

CLEARED (4)
when the wind has passed and **c** them. Jb 37:21
You **c** the ground for it; it took deep root Ps 80:9
He dug it and **c** it of stones, and planted it Is 5:2
you; he has **c** away your enemies. Zep 3:15

CLEARLY (9)
mouth to mouth, **c**, and not in riddles, Nm 12:8
Law of God, **c**, and they gave the sense, Neh 8:8
the latter days you will understand it **c**. Jer 23:20
and then you will see **c** to take the speck Mt 7:5
was restored, and he saw everything **c**. Mk 8:25
and then you will see **c** to take out the Lk 6:42
so that it may be **c** seen that his deeds Jn 3:21
of the day he saw **c** in a vision an angel Acts 10:3
divine nature, have been **c** perceived, Rom 1:20

CLEARNESS (1)
stone, like the very heaven for **c**. Ex 24:10

CLEARS (2)
it, and **c** away many nations before you, Dt 7:1
branches he lops off and **c** away. Is 18:5

CLEFT (6)
by I will put you in a **c** of the rock, Ex 33:22
down and stayed in the **c** of the rock of Jgs 15:8
Judah went down to the **c** of the rock of Jgs 15:11
"Who has **c** a channel for the torrents Jb 38:25
gazelle or a young stag on **c** mountains. Sg 2:17
and hide it there in a **c** of the rock." Jer 13:4

CLEFTS (7)
O my dove, in the **c** of the rock, in the Sg 2:14
of the rocks and the **c** of the cliffs, Is 2:21
steep ravines, and in the **c** of the rocks, Is 7:19
in the valleys, under the **c** of the rocks? Is 57:5
every hill, and out of the **c** of the rocks. Jer 16:16
heart, you who live in the **c** of the rock, Jer 49:16
you, you who live in the **c** of the rock, Ob 1:3

CLEMENT (1)
the gospel together with **C** and the rest of Phil 4:3

CLEOPAS (1)
Then one of them, named **C**, answered Lk 24:18

CLERK (1)
And when the town **c** had quieted the Acts 19:35

CLEVERLY (1)
we did not follow **c** devised myths when 2 Pt 1:16

CLIFF (3)
their judges are thrown over the **c**, Ps 141:6
clefts of the rock, in the crannies of the **c**, Sg 2:14
that they could throw him down the **c**. Lk 4:29

CLIFFS (3)
yet they make their homes in the **c**; Prv 30:26
of the rocks and the clefts of the **c**, Is 2:21
be thrown down, and the **c** shall fall, Ezk 38:20

CLIMB (4)
I say I will **c** the palm tree and lay hold of Sg 7:8
they enter thickets; they **c** among rocks; Jer 4:29
upon the walls, they **c** up into the houses, Jl 2:9
if they **c** up to heaven, from there I will Am 9:2

CLIMBED (2)
Then Jonathan **c** up on his hands 1 Sm 14:13
ran on ahead and **c** up into a sycamore Lk 19:4

CLIMBS (3)
and he who **c** out of the pit shall be Is 24:18
and he who **c** out of the pit shall be Jer 48:44
by the door but **c** in by another way, Jn 10:1

CLING (12)
you were afraid, and they shall **c** to you. Dt 28:60
his commandments and to **c** to him and Jos 22:5
but you shall **c** to the LORD your God Jos 23:8
you turn back and **c** to the remnant of Jos 23:12
leprosy of Naaman shall **c** to you and 2 Kgs 5:27
of the mountains and **c** to the rock for Jb 24:8
those who fall away; it shall not **c** to me. Ps 101:3
loud groaning my bones **c** to my flesh. Ps 102:5
I **c** to your testimonies, O LORD; let me Ps 119:31
and the whole house of Judah **c** to me, Jer 13:11
I will make your tongue **c** to the roof of Ezk 3:26
Jesus said to her, "Do not **c** to me, for I Jn 20:17

CLINGS (6)
to the dust; our belly **c** to the ground. Ps 44:25
My soul **c** to you; your right hand Ps 63:8
My soul **c** to the dust; give me life Ps 119:25
For as the loincloth **c** to the waist of a Jer 13:11
dust of your town that **c** to our feet we Lk 10:11
weight, and sin which **c** so closely, Heb 12:1

CLOAK (38)
out red, all his body like a hairy **c**, Gn 25:25
your hand inside your **c**." And he put his Ex 4:6
cloak." And he put his hand inside his **c**, Ex 4:6
hand back inside your **c**." So he put his Ex 4:7
So he put his hand back inside his **c**, Ex 4:7
an ox, for a donkey, for a sheep, for a **c**, Ex 22:9
you take your neighbor's **c** in pledge, Ex 22:26
covering, and it is his **c** for his body; Ex 22:27
nor shall a man put on a woman's **c**, Dt 22:5
they shall spread the **c** before the elders Dt 22:17
he may sleep in his **c** and bless you. Dt 24:13
the spoil a beautiful **c** from Shinar, Jos 7:21
and the silver and the **c** and the bar of Jos 7:24
give them." And they spread a **c**, Jgs 8:25
and put on your **c** and go down to the Ru 3:3
his face in his **c** and went out and 1 Kgs 19:13
by him and cast his **c** upon him. 1 Kgs 19:19
Then Elijah took his **c** and rolled it up 2 Kgs 2:8
he took up the **c** of Elijah that had 2 Kgs 2:13
Then he took the **c** of Elijah that had 2 Kgs 2:14
my garment and my **c** and pulled hair Ezr 9:3
fasting, with my garment and my **c** torn, Ezr 9:5
wrapped in their own shame as in a **c**! Ps 109:29
house of his father, saying: "You have a **c**; Is 3:6
in my house there is neither bread nor **c**; Is 3:7
and wrapped himself in zeal as a **c**. Is 59:17
as a shepherd cleans his **c** of vermin, Jer 43:12
not put on a hairy **c** in order to deceive, Zec 13:4
your tunic, let him have your **c** as well. Mt 5:40
in the field not turn back to take his **c**. Mt 24:18
And throwing off his **c**, he sprang up Mk 10:50
in the field not turn back to take his **c**. Mk 13:16
And they clothed him in a purple **c**, Mk 15:17
him of the purple **c** and put his own Mk 15:20
who takes away your **c** do not withhold Lk 6:29
has no sword sell his **c** and buy one. Lk 22:36
"Wrap your **c** around you and follow Acts 12:8
bring the **c** that I left with Carpus at 2 Tm 4:13

CLOAKS (11)
bound up in their **c** on their shoulders. Ex 12:34
the festal robes, the mantles, the **c**, and Is 3:22
Then these men were bound in their **c**, Dn 3:21
was not singed, their **c** were not harmed, Dn 3:27
and the colt and put on them their **c**, Mt 21:7
of the crowd spread their **c** on the road, Mt 21:8
the colt to Jesus and threw their **c** on it, Mk 11:7
And many spread their **c** on the road, Mk 11:8
Jesus, and throwing their **c** on the colt, Lk 19:35
along, they spread their **c** on the road. Lk 19:36
throwing off their **c** and flinging dust Acts 22:23

CLODS (3)
The **c** of the valley are sweet to him; all Jb 21:33
a mass and the **c** stick fast together? Jb 38:38
The seed shrivels under the **c**; the Jl 1:17

CLOGGING (1)
c their chariot wheels so that they Ex 14:25

CLOPAS (1)
his mother's sister, Mary the wife of **C**, Jn 19:25

CLOSE (46)
days and followed **c** after him into Gn 31:23
and Joseph's hand shall **c** your eyes." Gn 46:4
C to the frame the rings shall lie, as Ex 25:27
C to the frame were the rings, as Ex 37:14
whole fat tail, cut off **c** to the backbone, Lv 3:9
any one of his **c** relatives to uncover Lv 18:6
the land do at all **c** their eyes to that man Lv 20:4
or a **c** relative from his clan may Lv 25:49
the night. Behold, the day draws to its **c**. Jgs 19:9
know that disaster was **c** upon them. Jgs 20:34
saw that disaster was **c** upon them. Jgs 20:41
this one, but keep **c** to my young women. Ru 2:8
to her, "The man is a **c** relative of ours, Ru 2:20
'You shall keep **c** by my young men Ru 2:21
So she kept **c** to the young women of Ru 2:23
and the horsemen were **c** upon him. 2 Sm 1:6
"Because the king is our **c** relative. 2 Sm 19:42
'If your sons pay **c** attention to their 1 Kgs 2:4
your sons pay **c** attention to their 1 Kgs 8:25
great men and his **c** friends and his 2 Kgs 10:11
your sons pay **c** attention to their 2 Chr 6:16
Let us **c** the doors of the temple, for Neh 6:10
me, my **c** friends have forgotten me. Jb 19:14
They **c** their hearts to pity; with their Ps 17:10
Even my **c** friend in whom I trusted, who Ps 41:9
me up, or the pit **c** its mouth over me. Ps 69:15
Afflicted and **c** to death from my youth Ps 88:15
all day long; they **c** in on me together. Ps 88:17
and a whisperer separates **c** friends. Prv 16:28
repeats a matter separates **c** friends. Prv 17:9
its time is **c** at hand and its days will not Is 13:22
denounce him!" say all my **c** friends, Jer 20:10
are afraid shall follow **c** after you to Jer 42:16
'Do not **c** your ear to my cry for help!' Lam 3:56
I saw him come **c** to the ram, and he was Dn 8:7
The harvest is the **c** of the age, and the Mt 13:39
with fire, so will it be at the **c** of the age. Mt 13:40
So it will be at the **c** of the age. The Mt 13:49
of your coming and of the **c** of the age?" Mt 24:3
loved, was reclining at table **c** to Jesus, Jn 13:23
since the tomb was **c** at hand, Jn 19:42
been reclining at table **c** to him and Jn 21:20
together his relatives and **c** friends. Acts 10:24
and sailed along Crete, **c** to the shore. Acts 27:13
I want to do right, evil lies **c** at hand. Rom 7:21
Keep a **c** watch on yourself and on 1 Tm 4:16

CLOSED (24)
one of his ribs and **c** up its place with Gn 2:21
and the windows of the heavens were **c**, Gn 8:2
For the LORD had **c** all the wombs of Gn 20:18
into Sheol, and the earth **c** over them, Nm 16:33
when the gate was about to be **c** at dark, Jos 2:5
the blade, and the fat **c** over the blade, Jgs 3:22
out into the porch and **c** the doors of the Jgs 3:23
her, though the LORD had **c** her womb. 1 Sm 1:5
her, because the LORD had **c** her womb. 1 Sm 1:6
and **c** up the breach of the city of 1 Kgs 11:27
he went up and **c** in on Samaria and 1 Kgs 20:1
This same Hezekiah **c** the upper 2 Chr 32:30
the breaches were beginning to be **c**, Neh 4:7
Since you have **c** their hearts to Jb 17:4
me in the wrong and **c** his net about me. Jb 19:6
sleep, and has **c** your eyes (the prophets), Is 29:10
the eyes of those who see will not be **c**, Is 32:3
doors before him that gates may not be **c**: Is 45:1
water **c** over my head; I said, 'I am lost.' Lam 3:54
I **c** the deep over it, and restrained its Ezk 31:15
The waters **c** in over me to take my life; Jon 2:5
the land whose bars **c** upon me forever; Jon 2:6
barely hear, and their eyes they have **c**, Mt 13:15
hear, and their eyes they have **c**; Acts 28:27

CLOSELY (7)
I looked at him **c** in the morning, 1 Kgs 3:21
rows of shields, shut up **c** as with a seal. Jb 41:15
followed all things **c** for some time Lk 1:3
sat in the light and looking **c** at him, Lk 22:56
Looking at it **c**, I observed animals Acts 11:6
inquire somewhat more **c** about him. Acts 23:20
weight, and sin which clings so **c**, Heb 12:1

CLOSER (2)
is a friend who sticks **c** than a brother. Prv 18:24
we must pay much **c** attention to what Heb 2:1

CLOSES (3)
is considered wise; when he **c** his lips, Prv 17:28
Whoever **c** his ear to the cry of the Prv 21:13
in need, yet **c** his heart against him, 1 Jn 3:17

CLOSEST (1)
except for his **c** relatives, his mother, his Lv 21:2

CLOSET (1)
relieving himself in the **c** of the cool Jgs 3:24

CLOSING (1)
and his men were **c** in on David and 1 Sm 23:26

CLOTH (21)
wear a garment of **c** made of two kinds Lv 19:19
and spread on top of that a **c** all of blue, Nm 4:6
they shall spread a **c** of blue and put Nm 4:7
spread over them a **c** of scarlet and cover Nm 4:8
they shall take a **c** of blue and cover Nm 4:9
they shall spread a **c** of blue and cover Nm 4:11
and put them in a **c** of blue and cover Nm 4:12
the altar and spread a purple **c** over it. Nm 4:13
You shall not wear **c** of wool and linen Dt 22:11
here wrapped in a **c** behind the ephod. 1 Sm 21:9
day he took the bed **c** and dipped it in 2 Kgs 8:15
also with embroidered **c** and shod you Ezk 16:10
fine linen and silk and embroidered **c**. Ezk 16:13
a piece of unshrunk **c** on an old Mt 9:16
a piece of unshrunk **c** on an old Mk 2:21
nothing but a linen **c** about his body. Mk 14:51
he left the linen **c** and ran away naked. Mk 14:52
strips, and his face wrapped with a **c**. Jn 11:44
and the face **c**, which had been on Jesus' Jn 20:7
jewels, pearls, fine linen, purple **c**, Rv 18:12
fine linen, purple cloth, silk, scarlet **c**, Rv 18:12

CLOTHE (20)
She sent garments to **c** Mordecai, so that Est 4:4
might? Do you **c** his neck with a mane? Jb 39:19
c yourself with glory and splendor. Jb 40:10

the meadows **c** themselves with flocks, Ps 65:13
Her priests I will **c** with salvation, and Ps 132:16
His enemies I will **c** with shame, but Ps 132:18
and slumber will **c** them with rags. Prv 23:21
and I will **c** him with your robe, and will Is 22:21
I **c** the heavens with blackness and make Is 50:3
They will **c** themselves with Ezk 26:16
the fat, you **c** yourselves with the wool, Ezk 34:3
never have your fill. You **c** yourselves, Hg 1:6
and I will **c** you with pure vestments." Zec 3:4
the oven, will he not much more **c** you, Mt 6:30
and welcome you, or naked and **c** you? Mt 25:38
me, naked and you did not **c** me, Mt 25:43
oven, how much more will he **c** you, Lk 12:28
C yourselves, all of you, with humility 1 Pt 5:5
so that you may **c** yourself and the Rv 3:18
was granted her to **c** herself with fine Rv 19:8

CLOTHED (70)
his wife garments of skins and **c** them. Gn 3:21
and **c** him in garments of fine linen Gn 41:42
around his waist and **c** him with the robe Lv 8:7
Aaron's sons and **c** them with coats Lv 8:13
But the Spirit of the LORD **c** Gideon, and Jgs 6:34
the LORD, a boy **c** with a linen ephod. 1 Sm 2:18
Then Saul **c** David with his armor. 1 Sm 17:38
on his head and **c** him with a coat 1 Sm 17:38
who **c** you luxuriously in scarlet, 2 Sm 1:24
Then the Spirit **c** Amasai, chief of 1 Chr 12:18
David was **c** with a robe of fine 1 Chr 15:27
David and the elders, **c** in sackcloth, 1 Chr 21:16
O LORD God, be **c** with salvation, 2 Chr 6:41
Spirit of God **c** Zechariah the son 2 Chr 24:20
with the spoil they **c** all who were 2 Chr 28:15
naked among them. They **c** them, 2 Chr 28:15
to enter the king's gate **c** in sackcloth. Est 4:2
My flesh is **c** with worms and dirt; my Jb 7:5
who hate you will be **c** with shame, Jb 8:22
You **c** me with skin and flesh, and knit Jb 10:11
I put on righteousness, and it **c** me; my Jb 29:14
God is **c** with awesome majesty. Jb 37:22
my sackcloth and **c** me with gladness, Ps 30:11
Let them be **c** with shame and dishonor Ps 35:26
You are **c** with splendor and majesty, Ps 104:1
He **c** himself with cursing as his coat; Ps 109:18
May my accusers be **c** with dishonor; Ps 109:29
your priests be **c** with righteousness, Ps 132:9
for all her household are **c** in scarlet. Prv 31:21
like a loathed branch, **c** with the slain, Is 14:19
for he has **c** me with the garments of Is 61:10
and with them was a man **c** in linen, Ezk 9:2
And he called to the man **c** in linen, who Ezk 9:3
And behold, the man **c** in linen, with Ezk 9:11
And he said to the man **c** in linen, "Go Ezk 10:2
he commanded the man **c** in linen, Ezk 10:6
it into the hands of the man **c** in linen, Ezk 10:7
I **c** you also with embroidered cloth Ezk 16:10
c in purple, governors and Ezk 23:6
warriors **c** in full armor, Ezk 23:12
I **c** Lebanon in gloom for it, and all Ezk 31:15
horsemen, all of them **c** in full armor, Ezk 38:4
shall be **c** with purple and have a chain Dn 5:7
you shall be **c** with purple and have a Dn 5:16
and Daniel was **c** with purple, Dn 5:29
looked, and behold, a man **c** in linen, Dn 10:5
And someone said to the man **c** in linen, Dn 12:6
And I heard the man **c** in linen, who Dn 12:7
men is red; his soldiers are **c** in scarlet. Na 2:3
before the angel, **c** with filthy garments. Zec 3:3
on his head and **c** him with garments. Zec 3:5
I was naked and you **c** me, I was sick Mt 25:36
Now John was **c** with camel's hair and Mk 1:6
sitting there, **c** and in his right mind, Mk 5:15
And they **c** him in a purple cloak, and Mk 15:17
the feet of Jesus, **c** and in his right mind, Lk 8:35
rich man who was **c** in purple and fine Lk 16:19
city until you are **c** with power from on Lk 24:49
but that we would be further **c**, 2 Cor 5:4
or sister is poorly **c** and lacking in daily Jas 2:15
c with a long robe and with a golden Rv 1:13
who conquers will be **c** thus in white Rv 3:5
twenty-four elders, **c** in white garments, Rv 4:4
and before the Lamb, **c** in white robes, Rv 7:9
saying, "Who are these, **c** in white robes, Rv 7:13
prophesy for 1,260 days, **c** in sackcloth." Rv 11:3
a woman **c** with the sun, with the moon Rv 12:1
angels with the seven plagues, **c** in pure, Rv 15:6
the great city that was **c** in fine linen, Rv 18:16
He is **c** in a robe dipped in blood, and Rv 19:13

CLOTHES (94)
Joseph was not in the pit, he tore his **c** Gn 37:29
had shaved himself and changed his **c**, Gn 41:14
Then they tore their **c**, and every man Gn 44:13
and all of them he gave a change of **c**, Gn 45:22
shekels of silver and five changes of **c**. Gn 45:22
heads hang loose, and do not tear your **c**, Lv 10:6
shall wash his **c** and be unclean Lv 11:25
shall wash his **c** and be unclean Lv 11:28
shall wash his **c** and be unclean Lv 11:40
shall wash his **c** and be unclean Lv 11:40
And he shall wash his **c** and be clean. Lv 13:6
And he shall wash his **c** and be clean. Lv 13:34
disease shall wear torn **c** and let the Lv 13:45
cleansed shall wash his **c** and shave off Lv 14:8
he shall wash his **c** and bathe his body Lv 14:9
sleeps in the house shall wash his **c**, Lv 14:47
eats in the house shall wash his **c**. Lv 14:47
bed shall wash his **c** and bathe himself Lv 15:5
sat shall wash his **c** and bathe himself Lv 15:6
shall wash his **c** and bathe himself Lv 15:7
he shall wash his **c** and bathe himself in Lv 15:8
shall wash his **c** and bathe himself Lv 15:10
shall wash his **c** and bathe himself Lv 15:11
days for his cleansing, and wash his **c**. Lv 15:13
bed shall wash his **c** and bathe himself Lv 15:21
sits shall wash his **c** and bathe himself Lv 15:22
and shall wash his **c** and bathe himself Lv 15:27
Azazel shall wash his **c** and bathe his Lv 16:26
them shall wash his **c** and bathe his Lv 16:28
shall wash his **c** and bathe himself in Lv 17:15
of his head hang loose nor tear his **c**. Lv 21:10
and wash their **c** and cleanse Nm 8:7
from sin and washed their **c**, Nm 8:21
who had spied out the land, tore their **c** Nm 14:6
priest shall wash his **c** and bathe his Nm 19:7
heifer shall wash his **c** in water and Nm 19:8
shall wash his **c** and be unclean Nm 19:10
he shall wash his **c** and bathe himself Nm 19:19
water for impurity shall wash his **c**, Nm 19:21
You must wash your **c** on the seventh Nm 31:24
shall take off the **c** in which she was Dt 21:13
Your **c** have not worn out on you, and Dt 29:5
Then Joshua tore his **c** and fell to the Jos 7:6
sandals on their feet, and worn-out **c**. Jos 9:5
bound it on his right thigh under his **c**. Jgs 3:16
as he saw her, he tore his **c** and said, Jgs 11:35
garments and thirty changes of **c**, Jgs 14:12
and thirty changes of **c**." And they said Jgs 14:13
and a suit of **c** and your living." And Jgs 17:10
with his **c** torn and with dirt on his 1 Sm 4:12
at its head and covered it with the **c**. 1 Sm 19:13
And he too stripped off his **c**, and he 1 Sm 19:24
with his **c** torn and dirt on his head. 2 Sm 1:2
took hold of his **c** and tore them, 2 Sm 1:11
"Tear your **c** and put on sackcloth 2 Sm 3:31
anointed himself and changed his **c**. 2 Sm 12:20
trimmed his beard nor washed his **c**, 2 Sm 19:24
although they covered him with **c**, 1 Kgs 1:1
he tore his **c** and put sackcloth on 1 Kgs 21:27
hold of his own **c** and tore them in 2 Kgs 2:12
shekels of gold, and ten changes of **c**. 2 Kgs 5:5
read the letter, he tore his **c** and said, 2 Kgs 5:7
that the king of Israel had torn his **c**, 2 Kgs 5:8
saying, "Why have you torn your **c**? 2 Kgs 5:8
he tore his **c**—now he was passing by 2 Kgs 6:30
And Athaliah tore her **c** and cried, 2 Kgs 11:14
Hezekiah with their **c** torn and told 2 Kgs 18:37
he tore his **c** and covered himself 2 Kgs 19:1
of the Book of the Law, he tore his **c**. 2 Kgs 22:11
have torn your **c** and wept before 2 Kgs 22:19
And Athaliah tore her **c** and cried, 2 Chr 23:13
the words of the Law, he tore his **c**. 2 Chr 34:19
have torn your **c** and wept before 2 Chr 34:27
followed me, none of us took off our **c**; Neh 4:23
Their **c** did not wear out and their feet Neh 9:21
Mordecai tore his **c** and put on sackcloth Est 4:1
into a pit, and my own **c** will abhor me. Jb 9:31
to his chest and his **c** not be burned? Prv 6:27
eat our own bread and wear our own **c**, Is 4:1
came to Hezekiah with their **c** torn, Is 36:22
he tore his **c** and covered himself with Is 37:1
from there old rags and worn-out **c**, Jer 38:11
the rags and **c** between your armpits Jer 38:12
their beards shaved and their **c** torn, Jer 41:5
strip you of your **c** and take your Ezk 16:39
strip you of your **c** and take away Ezk 23:26
in **c** of blue and embroidered work, Ezk 27:24
But if God so **c** the grass of the field, Mt 6:30
the sun, and his **c** became white as light. Mt 17:2
robe and put his own **c** on him and led Mt 27:31
and his **c** became radiant, intensely Mk 9:3
cloak and put his own **c** on him. Mk 15:20
For a long time he had worn no **c**, and Lk 8:27
But if God so **c** the grass, which is alive Lk 12:28

CLOTHING (46)
will give me bread to eat and **c** to wear, Gn 28:20
for silver and gold jewelry, and for **c**. Ex 3:22
for silver and gold jewelry and for **c**. Ex 12:35
he shall not diminish her food, her **c**, Ex 21:10
Your **c** did not wear out on you and your Dt 8:4
the sojourner, giving him food and **c**. Dt 10:18
bronze, and iron, and with much **c**. Jos 22:8
the attendance of his servants, their **c**, 1 Kgs 10:5
silver and gold and **c** and went and hid 2 Kgs 7:8
attendance of his servants, and their **c**, 2 Chr 9:4
clothing, his cupbearers, and their **c**, 2 Chr 9:4
goods, **c**, and precious things, 2 Chr 20:25
nothing and stripped the naked of their **c**. Jb 22:6
They lie all night naked, without **c**, and Jb 24:7
They go about naked, without **c**; Jb 24:10
silver like dust, and pile up **c** like clay, Jb 27:16
I have seen anyone perish for lack of **c**, Jb 31:19
them, and for my **c** they cast lots. Ps 22:18
When I made sackcloth my **c**, I Ps 69:11
the lambs will provide your **c**, and the Prv 27:26
herself; her **c** is fine linen and purple. Prv 31:22
Strength and dignity are her **c**, and she Prv 31:25
abundant food and fine **c** for those who Is 23:18
Their webs will not serve as **c**; men will Is 59:6
he put on garments of vengeance for **c**, Is 59:17
goldsmith; their **c** is violet and purple; Jer 10:9
and your **c** was of fine linen and silk Ezk 16:13
his **c** was white as snow, and the hair of Dn 7:9
than food, and the body more than **c**? Mt 6:25
And why are you anxious about **c**? Mt 6:28
to you in sheep's **c** but inwardly are Mt 7:15
go out to see? A man dressed in soft **c**? Mt 11:8
those who wear soft **c** are in kings' Mt 11:8
like lightning, and his **c** white as snow. Mt 28:3
go out to see? A man dressed in soft **c**? Lk 7:25
are dressed in splendid **c** and live in Lk 7:25
and his **c** became dazzling white. Lk 9:29
than food, and the body more than **c**. Lk 12:23
Then, arraying him in splendid **c**, he Lk 23:11
and for my **c** they cast lots." So the Jn 19:24
a man stood before me in bright **c** Acts 10:30
But if we have food and **c**, with these 1 Tm 6:8
gold ring and fine **c** comes into your Jas 2:2
a poor man in shabby **c** also comes in, Jas 2:2
to the one who wears the fine **c** and say, Jas 2:3
wearing of gold, or the putting on of **c**— 1 Pt 3:3

CLOTHS (8)
with salt, nor wrapped in swaddling **c**. Ezk 16:4
him in swaddling **c** and laid him Lk 2:7
wrapped in swaddling **c** and lying in Lk 2:12
in, he saw the linen **c** by themselves; Lk 24:12
and bound it in linen **c** with the spices, Jn 19:40
to look in, he saw the linen **c** lying there, Jn 20:5
the tomb. He saw the linen **c** lying there, Jn 20:6
lying with the linen **c** but folded up in Jn 20:7

CLOUD (102)
I have set my bow in the **c**, and it shall Gn 9:13
day in a pillar of **c** to lead them along Ex 13:21
The pillar of **c** by day and the pillar of Ex 13:22
and the pillar of **c** moved from before Ex 14:19
And there was the **c** and the darkness. Ex 14:20
of fire and of **c** looked down on the Ex 14:24
the glory of the LORD appeared in the **c**. Ex 16:10
I am coming to you in a thick **c**, Ex 19:9
and a thick **c** on the mountain Ex 19:16
and the **c** covered the mountain. Ex 24:15
Sinai, and the **c** covered it six days. Ex 24:16
called to Moses out of the midst of the **c**. Ex 24:16
Moses entered the **c** and went up on the Ex 24:18
the pillar of **c** would descend and stand Ex 33:9
saw the pillar of **c** standing at the Ex 33:10
LORD descended in the **c** and stood with Ex 34:5
Then the **c** covered the tent of meeting, Ex 40:34
of meeting because the **c** settled on it, Ex 40:35
whenever the **c** was taken up from over Ex 40:36
But if the **c** was not taken up, then they Ex 40:37
For the **c** of the LORD was on the Ex 40:38
I will appear in the **c** over the mercy seat. Lv 16:2
that the **c** of the incense may cover the Lv 16:13
set up, the **c** covered the tabernacle, Nm 9:15
the **c** covered it by day and the Nm 9:16
And whenever the **c** lifted from over the Nm 9:17
in the place where the **c** settled down, Nm 9:17
As long as the **c** rested over the Nm 9:18
Even when the **c** continued over the Nm 9:19
Sometimes the **c** was a few days over Nm 9:20
And sometimes the **c** remained from Nm 9:21
And when the **c** lifted in the morning, Nm 9:21
a night, when the **c** lifted they set out. Nm 9:21
that the **c** continued over the Nm 9:22
the **c** lifted from over the tabernacle of Nm 10:11
And the **c** settled down in the Nm 10:12
And the **c** of the LORD was over them Nm 10:34
came down in the **c** and spoke to him, Nm 11:25
down in a pillar of **c** and stood at the Nm 12:5
When the **c** removed from over the Nm 12:10
and your **c** stands over them and you Nm 14:14
in a pillar of **c** by day and in a pillar Nm 14:14
And behold, the **c** covered it, and the Nm 16:42

tents, in fire by night and in the **c** by day, Dt 1:33
wrapped in darkness, **c**, and gloom. Dt 4:11
out of the midst of the fire, the **c**, Dt 5:22
LORD appeared in the tent in a pillar of **c**. Dt 31:15
And the pillar of **c** stood over the Dt 31:15
they made a great **c** of smoke rise up Jgs 20:38
Place, a **c** filled the house of the LORD, 1 Kgs 8:10
stand to minister because of the **c**, 1 Kgs 8:11
a little **c** like a man's hand is rising 1 Kgs 18:44
house of the LORD, was filled with a **c**, 2 Chr 5:13
stand to minister because of the **c**, 2 Chr 5:14
By a pillar of **c** you led them in the day, Neh 9:12
The pillar of **c** to lead them in the way Neh 9:19
As the **c** fades and vanishes, so he who Jb 7:9
and the **c** is not split open under them. Jb 26:8
of the full moon and spreads over it his **c**. Jb 26:9
my prosperity has passed away like a **c**. Jb 30:15
He loads the thick **c** with moisture; the Jb 37:11
causes the lightning of his **c** to shine? Jb 37:15
In the daytime he led them with a **c**, and Ps 78:14
In the pillar of the **c** he spoke to them; Ps 99:7
He spread a **c** for a covering, and fire to Ps 105:39
Zion and over her assemblies a **c** by day, Is 4:5
like a **c** of dew in the heat of harvest." Is 18:4
is riding on a swift **c** and comes to Egypt; Is 19:1
as heat by the shade of a **c**, so the song of Is 25:5
transgressions like a **c** and your sins Is 44:22
Who are these that fly like a **c**, and like Is 60:8
has set the daughter of Zion under a **c**! Lam 2:1
wrapped yourself with a **c** so that no Lam 3:44
came out of the north, and a great **c**, Ezk 1:4
bow that is in the **c** on the day of rain, Ezk 1:28
the smoke of the **c** of incense went up. Ezk 8:11
went in, and a **c** filled the inner court. Ezk 10:3
and the house was filled with the **c**, Ezk 10:4
she shall be covered by a **c**, and her Ezk 30:18
I will cover the sun with a **c**, and the Ezk 32:7
You will be like a **c** covering the land, Ezk 38:9
Israel, like a **c** covering the land. Ezk 38:16
Your love is like a morning **c**, like the Hos 6:4
behold, a bright **c** overshadowed them, Mt 17:5
them, and a voice from the **c** said, Mt 17:5
And a **c** overshadowed them, and a voice Mk 9:7
them, and a voice came out of the **c**, Mk 9:7
a **c** came and overshadowed them, Lk 9:34
they were afraid as they entered the **c**. Lk 9:34
And a voice came out of the **c**, saying, Lk 9:35
"When you see a **c** rising in the west, Lk 12:54
Man coming in a **c** with power and Lk 21:27
up, and a **c** took him out of their sight. Acts 1:9
that our fathers were all under the **c**, 1 Cor 10:1
into Moses in the **c** and in the sea, 1 Cor 10:2
surrounded by so great a **c** of witnesses, Heb 12:1
down from heaven, wrapped in a **c**, Rv 10:1
And they went up to heaven in a **c**, Rv 11:12
Then I looked, and behold, a white **c**, Rv 14:14
and seated on the **c** one like a son of Rv 14:14
a loud voice to him who sat on the **c**, Rv 14:15
who sat on the **c** swung his sickle Rv 14:16

CLOUDBURST (1)
fire, with a **c** and storm and hailstones. Is 30:30

CLOUDLESS (1)
the sun shining forth on a **c** morning, 2 Sm 23:4

CLOUDS (56)
When I bring **c** over the earth and the Gn 9:14
the earth and the bow is seen in the **c**, Gn 9:14
When the bow is in the **c**, I will see it Gn 9:16
heavens dropped, yes, the **c** dropped water. Jgs 5:4
around him his canopy, thick **c**, 2 Sm 22:12
grew black with **c** and wind, 1 Kgs 18:45
Let **c** dwell upon it; let the blackness of the Jb 3:5
the heavens, and his head reach to the **c**, Jb 20:6
Thick **c** veil him, so that he does not Jb 22:14
He binds up the waters in his thick **c**, Jb 26:8
and behold the **c**, which are higher than Jb 35:5
understand the spreading of the **c**, Jb 36:29
moisture; the **c** scatter his lightning. Jb 37:11
Do you know the balancings of the **c**, Jb 37:16
when I made **c** its garment and thick Jb 38:9
"Can you lift up your voice to the **c**, that Jb 38:34
Who can number the **c** by wisdom? Or Jb 38:37
around him, thick **c** dark with water. Ps 18:11
and coals of fire broke through his **c**. Ps 18:12
to the heavens, your faithfulness to the **c**. Ps 36:5
the heavens, your faithfulness to the **c**. Ps 57:10
The **c** poured out water; the skies gave Ps 77:17
C and thick darkness are all around Ps 97:2
the waters; he makes the **c** his chariot; Ps 104:3
your faithfulness reaches to the **c**. Ps 108:4
it is who makes the **c** rise at the end of Ps 135:7
He covers the heavens with **c**; he Ps 147:8
open, and the **c** drop down the dew. Prv 3:20
favor is like the **c** that bring the spring Prv 16:15
Like **c** and wind without rain is a man Prv 25:14
If the **c** are full of rain, they empty Eccl 11:3
and he who regards the **c** will not reap. Eccl 11:4
are darkened and the **c** return after the Eccl 12:2
will also command the **c** that they rain no Is 5:6
distress; and the light is darkened by its **c**. Is 5:30
I will ascend above the heights of the **c**; I Is 14:14
and let the **c** rain down righteousness; Is 45:8
Behold, he comes up like **c**; his chariots Jer 4:13
it will be a day of **c**, a time of doom for Ezk 30:3
of towering height, its top among the **c**. Ezk 31:3
high and set its top among the **c**, Ezk 31:10
height or set their tops among the **c**, Ezk 31:14
on a day of **c** and thick darkness. Ezk 34:12
with the **c** of heaven there came one like Dn 7:13
and gloom, a day of **c** and thick darkness! Jl 2:2
storm, and the **c** are the dust of his feet. Na 1:3
your scribes like **c** of locusts settling on Na 3:17
gloom, a day of **c** and thick darkness, Zep 1:15
from the LORD who makes the storm **c**, Zec 10:1
Man coming on the **c** of heaven with Mt 24:30
Power and coming on the **c** of heaven." Mt 26:64
of Man coming in **c** with great power Mk 13:26
and coming with the **c** of heaven." Mk 14:62
with them in the **c** to meet the Lord 1 Thes 4:17
looking after themselves; waterless **c**, Jude 1:12
Behold, he is coming with the **c**, and every Rv 1:7

CLOVEN (2)
and has the hoof **c** in two and chews Dt 14:6
cud or have the hoof **c** you shall not eat Dt 14:7

CLOVEN-FOOTED (3)
the hoof and is **c** and chews the cud, Lv 11:3
parts the hoof and is **c** but does not chew Lv 11:7
the hoof but is not **c** or does not chew Lv 11:26

CLUB (1)
against his neighbor is like a war **c**, Prv 25:18

CLUBS (7)
C are counted as stubble; he laughs at Jb 41:29
bow and arrows, **c** and spears; Ezk 39:9
him a great crowd with swords and **c**, Mt 26:47
with swords and **c** to capture me? Mt 26:55
with him a crowd with swords and **c**, Mk 14:43
with swords and **c** to capture me? Mk 14:48
as against a robber, with swords and **c**? Lk 22:52

CLUNG (5)
her mother-in-law, but Ruth **c** to her. Ru 1:14
weary, and his hand **c** to the sword. 2 Sm 23:10
their gods." Solomon **c** to these in 1 Kgs 11:2
he **c** to the sin of Jeroboam the son of 2 Kgs 3:3
While he **c** to Peter and John, all the Acts 3:11

CLUSTER (5)
a branch with a single **c** of grapes, Nm 13:23
because of the **c** that the people of Nm 13:24
is to me a **c** of henna blossoms in Sg 1:14
"As the new wine is found in the **c**, and Is 65:8
there is no **c** to eat, no first-ripe fig that Mi 7:1

CLUSTERS (8)
forth, and the **c** ripened into grapes. Gn 40:10
are grapes of poison; their **c** are bitter; Dt 32:32
grain and a hundred **c** of raisins and 1 Sm 25:18
of a cake of figs and two **c** of raisins. 1 Sm 30:12
of flour, cakes of figs, **c** of raisins, 1 Chr 12:40
a palm tree, and your breasts are like its **c**. Sg 7:7
Oh may your breasts be like **c** of the vine, Sg 7:8
sickle and gather the **c** from the vine of Rv 14:18

CNIDUS (1)
days and arrived with difficulty off **C**, Acts 27:7

COAL (3)
they would quench my **c** that is left 2 Sm 14:7
in his hand a burning **c** that he had taken Is 6:6
No **c** for warming oneself is this, no fire Is 47:14

COALS (19)
take a censer full of **c** of fire from the Lv 16:12
glowing **c** flamed forth from him. 2 Sm 22:9
brightness before him **c** of fire 2 Sm 22:13
His breath kindles **c**, and a flame comes Jb 41:21
Let him rain **c** on the wicked; fire and Ps 11:6
glowing **c** flamed forth from him. Ps 18:8
him hailstones and **c** of fire broke Ps 18:12
his voice, hailstones and **c** of fire. Ps 18:13
with glowing **c** of the broom tree! Ps 120:4
Let burning **c** fall upon them! Let Ps 140:10
can one walk on hot **c** and his feet not Prv 6:28
you will heap burning **c** on his head, Prv 25:22
a cutting tool and works it over the **c**. Is 44:12
in the fire; I also baked bread on its **c**; Is 44:19
blows the fire of **c** and produces a Is 54:16
appearance was like burning **c** of fire, Ezk 1:13
hands with burning **c** from between Ezk 10:2
Then set it empty upon the **c**, that it Ezk 24:11
will heap burning **c** on his head." Rom 12:20

COAST (7)
you shall have the Great Sea and its **c**. Nm 34:6
lowland all along the **c** of the Great Sea Jos 9:1
Asher sat still at the **c** of the sea, staying Jgs 5:17
Be still, O inhabitants of the **c**; the Is 23:2
to Tarshish; wail, O inhabitants of the **c**! Is 23:6
to sail to the ports along the **c** of Asia, Acts 27:2
open sea along the **c** of Cilicia and Acts 27:5

COASTING (1)
C along it with difficulty, we came to a Acts 27:8

COASTLAND (4)
From these the **c** peoples spread in their Gn 10:5
the inhabitants of this **c** will say in that Is 20:6
and the kings of the **c** across the sea; Jer 25:22
the remnant of the **c** of Caphtor. Jer 47:4

COASTLANDS (25)
tax on the land and on the **c** of the sea. Est 10:1
and of the **c** render him tribute; Ps 72:10
the earth rejoice; let the many **c** be glad! Ps 97:1
from Hamath, and from the **c** of the sea. Is 11:11
in the **c** of the sea, give glory to the name Is 24:15
behold, he takes up the **c** like fine dust. Is 40:15
Listen to me in silence, O **c**; let the peoples Is 41:1
The **c** have seen and are afraid; the ends Is 41:5
in the earth; and the **c** wait for his law. Is 42:4
that fills it, the **c** and their inhabitants. Is 42:10
the LORD, and declare his praise in the **c**. Is 42:12
Listen to me, O **c**, and give attention, you Is 49:1
the **c** hope for me, and for my arm they Is 51:5
to the **c** he will render repayment. Is 59:18
For the **c** shall hope for me, the ships of Is 60:9
to Tubal and Javan, to the **c** afar off, Is 66:19
and declare it in the **c** far away; Jer 31:10
Will not the **c** shake at the sound of Ezk 26:15
Now the **c** tremble on the day of your Ezk 26:18
and the **c** that are on the sea are Ezk 26:18
sea, merchant of the peoples to many **c**, Ezk 27:3
Many **c** were your own special Ezk 27:15
the inhabitants of the **c** are appalled at Ezk 27:35
on those who dwell securely in the **c**, Ezk 39:6
his face to the **c** and shall capture Dn 11:18

COASTLINE (2)
boundary was the Great Sea with its **c**. Jos 15:12
of Egypt, and the Great Sea with its **c**. Jos 15:47

COASTS (3)
For cross to the **c** of Cyprus and see, or Jer 2:10
deck of pines from the **c** of Cyprus, Ezk 27:6
and purple from the **c** of Elishah was Ezk 27:7

COAT (10)
an ephod, a robe, a **c** of checker work, Ex 28:4
shall weave the **c** in checker work Ex 28:39
and put on Aaron the **c** and the robe of Ex 29:5
And he put the **c** on him and tied the sash Lv 8:7
on the holy linen **c** and shall have the Lv 16:4
and he was armed with a **c** of mail, 1 Sm 17:5
the weight of the **c** was five thousand 1 Sm 17:5
and clothed him with a **c** of mail, 1 Sm 17:38
meet him with his **c** torn and dirt on 2 Sm 15:32
clothed himself with cursing as his **c**; Ps 109:18

COATING (1)
'Where is the **c** with which you Ezk 13:12

COATS (8)
sons you shall make **c** and sashes and Ex 28:40
shall bring his sons and put **c** on them, Ex 29:8
They also made the **c**, woven of fine Ex 39:27
bring his sons also and put **c** on them, Ex 40:14
and clothed them with **c** and tied sashes Lv 8:13
carried them in their **c** out of the camp, Lv 10:5
shields, spears, helmets, **c** of mail, 2 Chr 26:14
the spears, shields, bows, and **c** of mail. Neh 4:16

COBRA (1)
child shall play over the hole of the **c**, Is 11:8

COBRAS (2)
it is the venom of **c** within him. Jb 20:14
He will suck the poison of **c**; the tongue Jb 20:16

COCK (1)
or at midnight, or when the **c** crows, Mk 13:35

CODE (2)
have the written **c** and circumcision Rom 2:27
under the old written **c** but in the new Rom 7:6

COFFIN (1)
him, and he was put in a **c** in Egypt. Gn 50:26

COHORT (3)
of what was known as the Italian **C**, Acts 10:1
the tribune of the **c** that all Jerusalem Acts 21:31
of the Augustan **C** named Julius. Acts 27:1

COIN (3)
Show me the **c** for the tax." And they Mt 22:19
ten silver coins, if she loses one **c**, Lk 15:8

me, for I have found the **c** that I had lost.' Lk 15:9

COINCIDENCE (1)
that struck us; it happened to us by **c**." 1 Sm 6:9

COINS (4)
came and put in two small copper **c**, Mk 12:42
"Or what woman, having ten silver **c**, if Lk 15:8
a poor widow put in two small copper **c**. Lk 21:2
poured out the **c** of the money-changers Jn 2:15

COL-HOZEH (2)
And Shallum the son of **C**, ruler of the Neh 3:15
Maaseiah the son of Baruch, son of **C**, Neh 11:5

COLD (19)
seedtime and harvest, **c** and heat, Gn 8:22
heat consumed me, and the **c** by night, Gn 31:40
clothing, and have no covering in the **c**. Jb 24:7
and **c** from the scattering winds. Jb 37:9
crumbs; who can stand before his **c**? Ps 147:17
Like the **c** of snow in the time of Prv 25:13
who takes off a garment on a **c** day, Prv 25:20
Like **c** water to a thirsty soul, so is Prv 25:25
waters run dry, the **c** flowing streams? Jer 18:14
fences in a day of **c**—when the sun rises, Na 3:17
day there shall be no light, **c**, or frost. Zec 14:6
even a cup of **c** water because he is Mt 10:42
increased, the love of many will grow **c**. Mt 24:12
made a charcoal fire, because it was **c**, Jn 18:18
it had begun to rain and was **c**. Acts 28:2
without food, in **c** and exposure. 2 Cor 11:27
your works: you are neither **c** nor hot. Rv 3:15
hot. Would that you were either **c** or hot! Rv 3:15
are lukewarm, and neither hot nor **c**, Rv 3:16

COLLAPSE (2)
They **c** and fall, but we rise and stand Ps 20:8
a high wall, bulging out, and about to **c**, Is 30:13

COLLAR (3)
binds me about like the **c** of my tunic. Jb 30:18
fetters; his neck was put in a **c** of iron; Ps 105:18
running down on the **c** of his robes! Ps 133:2

COLLARS (1)
and besides the **c** that were around the Jgs 8:26

COLLECT (4)
not go into his house to **c** his pledge. Dt 24:10
it is the Levites who **c** the tithes in all Neh 10:37
road; dress for battle; **c** all your strength. Na 2:1
"**C** no more than you are authorized to Lk 3:13

COLLECTED (9)
worthless fellows **c** around Jephthah Jgs 11:3
the threshold have **c** from the people. 2 Kgs 22:4
day, and **c** money in abundance. 2 Chr 24:11
had **c** from Manasseh and Ephraim 2 Chr 34:9
nails firmly fixed are the **c** sayings; Eccl 12:11
many. You **c** the waters of the lower pool, Is 22:9
all the surrounding nations shall be **c**, Zec 14:14
coming I might have **c** it with interest?' Lk 19:23
delivered to them what has been **c**, Rom 15:28

COLLECTING (2)
given the business of gathering and **c**, Eccl 2:26
that there will be no **c** when I come. 1 Cor 16:2

COLLECTION (2)
cry out, let your **c** of idols deliver you! Is 57:13
Now concerning the **c** for the saints: 1 Cor 16:1

COLLECTOR (7)
Thomas and Matthew the tax **c**; Mt 10:3
him be to you as a Gentile and a tax **c**. Mt 18:17
he went out and saw a tax **c** named Levi, Lk 5:27
one a Pharisee and the other a tax **c**. Lk 18:10
adulterers, or even like this tax **c**. Lk 18:11
But the tax **c**, standing far off, would Lk 18:13
He was a chief tax **c** and was rich. Lk 19:2

COLLECTORS (16)
have? Do not even the tax **c** do the same? Mt 5:46
many tax **c** and sinners came and were Mt 9:10
teacher eat with tax **c** and sinners?" Mt 9:11
a friend of tax **c** and sinners!' Mt 11:19
the **c** of the half-shekel tax went up to Mt 17:24
the tax **c** and the prostitutes go into the Mt 21:31
but the tax **c** and the prostitutes Mt 21:32
many tax **c** and sinners were reclining Mk 2:15
he was eating with sinners and tax **c**, Mk 2:16
does he eat with tax **c** and sinners?" Mk 2:16
Tax **c** also came to be baptized and said Lk 3:12
company of tax **c** and others reclining Lk 5:29
eat and drink with tax **c** and sinners?" Lk 5:30
the people heard this, and the tax **c** too, Lk 7:29
drunkard, a friend of tax **c** and sinners!' Lk 7:34
Now the tax **c** and sinners were all Lk 15:1

COLLECTS (1)
himself all nations and **c** as his own all Hab 2:5

COLONNADE (3)
And for the **c** on the west there were 1 Chr 26:18
four at the road and two at the **c**. 1 Chr 26:18
in the temple, in the **c** of Solomon. Jn 10:23

COLONNADES (1)
called Bethesda, which has five roofed **c**. Jn 5:2

COLONY (1)
district of Macedonia and a Roman **c**. Acts 16:12

COLOR (5)
Then the king's **c** changed, and his Dn 5:6
was greatly alarmed, and his **c** changed, Dn 5:9
thoughts alarm you or your **c** change. Dn 5:10
greatly alarmed me, and my **c** changed, Dn 7:28
they wore breastplates the **c** of fire and of Rv 9:17

COLORED (3)
stones for setting, antimony, **c** stones, 1 Chr 29:2
c linens from Egyptian linen; Prv 7:16
work, and in carpets of **c** material, Ezk 27:24

COLORFUL (1)
and made for yourself **c** shrines, Ezk 16:16

COLORS (4)
age. And he made him a robe of many **c**. Gn 37:3
robe, the robe of many **c** that he wore. Gn 37:23
the robe of many **c** and brought it to Gn 37:32
pinions, rich in plumage of many **c**, Ezk 17:3

COLOSSAE (1)
and faithful brothers in Christ at **C**: Col 1:2

COLT (15)
vine and his donkey's **c** to the choice Gn 49:11
when a wild donkey's **c** is born a man! Jb 11:12
and mounted on a donkey, on a **c**, Zec 9:9
will find a donkey tied, and a **c** with her. Mt 21:2
and mounted on a donkey, and on a **c**, Mt 21:5
the donkey and the **c** and put on them Mt 21:7
as you enter it you will find a **c** tied, Mk 11:2
went away and found a **c** tied at a door Mk 11:4
"What are you doing, untying the **c**?" Mk 11:5
And they brought the **c** to Jesus and Mk 11:7
where on entering you will find a **c** tied, Lk 19:30
And as they were untying the **c**, its Lk 19:33
to them, "Why are you untying the **c**?" Lk 19:33
and throwing their cloaks on the **c**, Lk 19:35
is coming, sitting on a donkey's **c**!" Jn 12:15

COLUMN (2)
to rise out of the city in a **c** of smoke, Jgs 20:40
and they roll upward in a **c** of smoke. Is 9:18

COLUMNS (4)
up from the wilderness like **c** of smoke, Sg 3:6
His legs are alabaster **c**, set on bases of Sg 5:15
As Jehudi read three or four **c**, the king Jer 36:23
the earth, blood and fire and **c** of smoke. Jl 2:30

COMBAT (1)
And he set **c** commanders over the 2 Chr 32:6

COMBED (1)
The workers in **c** flax will be in despair, Is 19:9

COME (1579)
with you, and you shall **c** into the ark, Gn 6:18
two of every sort shall **c** in to you to keep Gn 6:20
to one another, "**C**, let us make bricks, Gn 11:3
"**C**, let us build ourselves a city and a Gn 11:4
C, let us go down and there confuse Gn 11:7
afterward they shall **c** out with great Gn 15:14
And they shall **c** back here in the Gn 15:16
where have you **c** from and where are Gn 16:8
nations, and kings shall **c** from you. Gn 17:6
kings of peoples shall **c** from her." Gn 17:16
—since you have **c** to your servant." So Gn 18:5
to the outcry that has **c** to me. Gn 18:21
for they have **c** under the shelter of my Gn 19:8
a man on earth to **c** in to us after the Gn 19:31
C, let us make our father drink wine, Gn 19:32
at every place to which we **c**, say of me, Gn 20:13
there and worship and **c** again to you." Gn 22:5
He said, "**C** in, O blessed of the LORD. Gn 24:31
from my oath, when you **c** to my clan. Gn 24:41
said, "The thing has **c** from the LORD; Gn 24:50
said to them, "Why have you **c** to me, Gn 26:27
Isaac said to Jacob, "Please **c** near, Gn 27:21
Isaac said to him, "**C** near and kiss me, Gn 27:26
so that I **c** again to my father's house Gn 28:21
where do you **c** from?" They said, Gn 29:4
"Good fortune has **c**!" so she called his Gn 30:11
him and said, "You must **c** in to me, Gn 30:16
when you **c** to look into my wages with Gn 30:33
C now, let us make a covenant, you Gn 31:44
fear him, that he may **c** and attack me, Gn 32:11
children, until I **c** to my lord in Seir." Gn 33:14
sons of Jacob had **c** in from the field Gn 34:7
company of nations shall **c** from you, Gn 35:11

and kings shall **c** from your own body. Gn 35:11
your brothers indeed **c** to bow Gn 37:10
C, I will send you to them." And he said Gn 37:13
C now, let us kill him and throw him Gn 37:20
C, let us sell him to the Ishmaelites, Gn 37:27
"**C**, let me come in to you," for he did Gn 38:16
let me **c** in to you," for he did not know Gn 38:16
you give me, that you may **c** in to me?" Gn 38:16
There will **c** seven years of great plenty Gn 41:29
the seven years of famine began to **c**, Gn 41:54
them. "Where do you **c** from?" he said. Gn 42:7
you have **c** to see the nakedness of the Gn 42:9
lord, your servants have **c** to buy food. Gn 42:10
of the land that you have **c** to see." Gn 42:12
is why this distress has **c** upon us." Gn 42:21
Benjamin. All this has **c** against me." Gn 42:36
as soon as I **c** to your servant my Gn 44:30
said to his brothers, "**C** near to me, Gn 45:4
of all Egypt. **C** down to me; do not tarry. Gn 45:9
there are yet five years of famine to **c**, Gn 45:11
all that you have, do not **c** to poverty.' Gn 45:11
"Joseph's brothers have **c**," it pleased Gn 45:16
and your households, and **c** to me, Gn 45:18
wives, and bring your father, and **c**. Gn 45:19
in the land of Canaan, have **c** to me. Gn 46:31
have **c** from the land of Canaan. Gn 47:1
"We have **c** to sojourn in the land, Gn 47:4
father and your brothers have **c** to you. Gn 47:5
"Your son Joseph has **c** to you." Then Gn 48:2
what shall happen to you in days to **c**. Gn 49:1
Let my soul **c** not into their council; O Gn 49:6
C, let us deal shrewdly with them, lest Ex 1:10
it that you have **c** home so soon today?" Ex 2:18
Then he said, "Do not **c** near; take your Ex 3:5
and I have **c** down to deliver them out of Ex 3:8
the cry of the people of Israel has **c** to me, Ex 3:9
C, I will send you to Pharaoh that you Ex 3:10
"If I **c** to the people of Israel and say to Ex 3:13
with frogs that shall **c** up into your house Ex 8:3
The frogs shall **c** up on you and on your Ex 8:4
and make frogs **c** up on the land of Ex 8:5
arts and made frogs **c** up on the land Ex 8:7
so that they may **c** upon the land of Ex 10:12
these your servants shall **c** down to me Ex 11:8
And when you **c** to the land that the Ex 12:25
Then he may **c** near and keep it; he Ex 12:48
when in time to **c** your son asks you, Ex 13:14
that the water may **c** back upon the Ex 14:26
people of Israel, '**C** near before the LORD, Ex 16:9
the rock, and water shall **c** out of it, Ex 17:6
the hardship that had **c** upon them in Ex 18:8
"Because the people **c** to me to inquire Ex 18:15
they **c** to me and I decide between one Ex 18:16
day the LORD will **c** down on Mount Ex 19:11
blast, they shall **c** up to the mountain." Ex 19:13
let the priests who **c** near to the LORD Ex 19:22
"The people cannot **c** up to Mount Ex 19:23
and **c** up bringing Aaron with you. Ex 19:24
people break through to **c** up to the Ex 19:24
"Do not fear, for God has **c** to test you, Ex 20:20
be remembered I will **c** to you and bless Ex 20:24
woman, so that her children **c** out, Ex 21:22
owner of the house shall **c** near to God to Ex 22:8
case of both parties shall **c** before God. Ex 22:9
the people against whom you shall **c**, Ex 23:27
Then he said to Moses, "**C** up to the LORD, Ex 24:1
Moses alone shall **c** near to the LORD, but Ex 24:2
the LORD, but the others shall not **c** near, Ex 24:2
and the people shall not **c** up with him." Ex 24:2
"**C** up to me on the mountain and wait Ex 24:12
breastpiece shall not **c** loose from the Ex 28:28
meeting or when they **c** near the altar Ex 28:43
or when they **c** near the altar to Ex 30:20
that Moses delayed to **c** down from the Ex 32:1
C to me." And all the sons of Levi Ex 32:26
and **c** up in the morning to Mount Sinai, Ex 34:2
No one shall **c** up with you, and let no Ex 34:3
and they were afraid to **c** near him. Ex 34:30
craftsman among you **c** and make all Ex 35:10
heart stirred him up to **c** to do the work. Ex 36:2
breastpiece should not **c** loose from the Ex 39:21
he has seen or **c** to know the matter, Lv 5:1
of Aaron, and said to them, "**C** near; Lv 10:4
and wrath **c** upon all the congregation; Lv 10:6
anything holy, nor **c** into the sanctuary, Lv 12:4
again, then he shall **c** to the priest, Lv 13:16
And after that he may **c** into the camp, Lv 14:8
"When you **c** into the land of Canaan, Lv 14:34
owns the house shall **c** and tell the Lv 14:35
And the priest shall **c** again on the Lv 14:39
or two pigeons and **c** before the LORD to Lv 15:14
your brother not to **c** at any time into Lv 16:2
this way Aaron shall **c** into the Holy Lv 16:3
"Then Aaron shall **c** into the tent of Lv 16:23
on his garments and **c** out and offer his Lv 16:24

and afterward he may **c** into the camp. Lv 16:26
and afterward he may **c** into the camp. Lv 16:28
"When you **c** into the land and plant Lv 19:23
has a blemish shall **c** near to offer the Lv 21:21
he shall not **c** near to offer the bread of Lv 21:21
When you **c** into the land that I give Lv 23:10
When you **c** into the land that I give Lv 25:2
nearest redeemer shall **c** and redeem Lv 25:25
year after they had **c** out of the land Nm 1:1
to fifty years old, all who can **c** on duty, Nm 4:3
sons of Kohath shall **c** to carry these, Nm 4:15
not die when they **c** near to the most Nm 4:19
list them, all who can **c** to do duty, Nm 4:23
list them, everyone who can **c** on duty, Nm 4:30
old, everyone who could **c** on duty, Nm 4:35
everyone who could **c** on duty for Nm 4:39
old, everyone who could **c** on duty, Nm 4:43
everyone who could **c** to do the service Nm 4:47
people of Israel **c** near the sanctuary." Nm 8:19
and upward they shall **c** to do duty in Nm 8:24
year after they had **c** out of the land Nm 9:1
C with us, and we will do good to you, Nm 10:29
And I will **c** down and talk with you Nm 11:17
"Why did we **c** out of Egypt?"' Nm 11:20
whether my word will **c** true for you Nm 11:23
and to Aaron and Miriam, "**C** out, Nm 12:4
of Anak, who **c** from the Nephilim), Nm 13:33
not one shall **c** into the land where I Nm 14:30
this wilderness they shall **c** to a full Nm 14:35
When you **c** into the land you are to Nm 15:2
When you **c** into the land to which I Nm 15:18
and they said, "We will not **c** up. Nm 16:12
eyes of these men? We will not **c** up." Nm 16:14
but shall not **c** near to the vessels of the Nm 18:3
tent, and no outsider shall **c** near you. Nm 18:4
of Israel do not **c** near the tent of Nm 18:22
and on which a yoke has never **c**. Nm 19:2
and afterward he may **c** into the camp. Nm 19:7
have you made us **c** up out of Egypt Nm 20:5
lest I **c** out with the sword against Nm 20:18
the ballad singers say, "**C** to Heshbon, Nm 21:27
"Behold, a people has **c** out of Egypt. Nm 22:5
C now, curse this people for me, since Nm 22:6
'Behold, a people has **c** out of Egypt, Nm 22:11
it covers the face of the earth. Now **c**, Nm 22:11
said, "Balaam refuses to **c** with us." Nm 22:14
I will do. **C**, curse this people for me.'" Nm 22:17
to him, "If the men have **c** to call you, Nm 22:20
I have **c** out to oppose you because Nm 22:32
Balak heard that Balaam had **c**, Nm 22:36
to call you? Why did you not **c** to me? Nm 22:37
said to Balak, "Behold, I have **c** to you! Nm 22:38
Perhaps the LORD will **c** to meet me, and Nm 23:3
'**C**, curse Jacob for me, and come, Nm 23:7
'Come, curse Jacob for me, and **c**, Nm 23:7
"Please **c** with me to another place, Nm 23:13
And Balak said to Balaam, "**C** now, I Nm 23:27
C, I will let you know what this people Nm 24:14
not near: a star shall **c** out of Jacob, Nm 24:17
But ships shall **c** from Kittim and Nm 24:24
he too shall **c** to utter destruction." Nm 24:24
out before them and **c** in before them, Nm 27:17
go out, and at his word they shall **c** in, Nm 27:21
who had **c** from service in the war. Nm 31:14
afterward you may **c** into the camp." Nm 31:24
our inheritance has **c** to us on Nm 32:19
people of Israel had **c** out of the land Nm 33:38
'You have **c** to the hill country of the Dt 1:20
up and the cities into which we shall **c**.' Dt 1:22
and all these things **c** upon you in the Dt 4:30
"When your son asks you in time to **c**, Dt 6:20
and **c** up to me on the mountain and Dt 10:1
land of Egypt, from which you have **c**, Dt 11:10
for you have not as yet **c** to the rest and to Dt 12:9
towns, shall **c** and eat and be filled, Dt 14:29
And you shall **c** to the Levitical priests Dt 17:9
"When you **c** to the land that the LORD Dt 17:14
lives—and he may **c** when he desires—to Dt 18:6
"When you **c** into the land that the LORD Dt 18:9
if the word does not **c** to pass or come Dt 18:22
word does not come to pass or **c** true, Dt 18:22
the priest shall **c** forward and speak to Dt 20:2
your elders and your judges shall **c** out, Dt 21:2
priests, the sons of Levi, shall **c** forward, Dt 21:5
"If you **c** across a bird's nest in any tree Dt 22:6
camp. He shall not **c** inside the camp, Dt 23:10
the sun sets, he may **c** inside the camp. Dt 23:11
between men and they **c** into court and Dt 25:1
"When you **c** into the land that the LORD Dt 26:1
your God that I have **c** into the land that Dt 26:3
all these blessings shall **c** upon you and Dt 28:2
Blessed shall you be when you **c** in, and Dt 28:6
They shall **c** out against you one way Dt 28:7
all these curses shall **c** upon you and Dt 28:15
Cursed shall you be when you **c** in, and Dt 28:19
From heaven dust shall **c** down on you Dt 28:24
and you shall **c** down lower and lower. Dt 28:43
"All these curses shall **c** upon you and Dt 28:45
c down throughout all your land. Dt 28:52
"And when all these things **c** upon you, Dt 30:1
I am no longer able to go out and **c** in. Dt 31:2
evils and troubles will **c** upon them, Dt 31:17
'Have not these evils **c** upon us because Dt 31:17
evils and troubles have **c** upon them, Dt 31:21
And in the days to **c** evil will befall you, Dt 31:29
known, to new gods that had **c** recently, Dt 32:17
Your enemies shall **c** fawning to you, Dt 33:29
men of Israel have **c** here tonight to Jos 2:2
"Bring out the men who have **c** to you, Jos 2:3
for they have **c** to search out all the land." Jos 2:3
Behold, when we **c** into the land, you Jos 2:18
2,000 cubits in length. Do not **c** near it, Jos 3:4
'When you **c** to the brink of the waters of Jos 3:8
"**C** here and listen to the words of the LORD Jos 3:9
those bearing the ark had **c** as far as the Jos 3:15
When your children ask in time to **c**, Jos 4:6
ark of the testimony to **c** up out of the Jos 4:16
the priests, "**C** up out of the Jordan." Jos 4:17
children ask their fathers in times to **c**, Jos 4:21
on the way after they had **c** out of Egypt. Jos 5:4
wilderness after they had **c** out of Egypt Jos 5:5
Now I have **c**." And Joshua fell on his Jos 5:14
LORD takes by lot shall **c** near by clans. Jos 7:14
LORD takes shall **c** near by households. Jos 7:14
the LORD takes shall **c** near man by Jos 7:14
And when they **c** out against us just as Jos 8:5
And they will **c** out after us, until we have Jos 8:6
"We have **c** from a distant country, Jos 9:6
are you? And where do you **c** from?" Jos 9:8
distant country your servants have **c**, Jos 9:9
C now, make a covenant with us."' Jos 9:11
journey on the day we set out to **c** to you, Jos 9:12
"**C** up to me and help me, and let us Jos 10:4
C up to us quickly and save us and help Jos 10:6
war who had gone with him, "**C** near; Jos 10:24
that they should **c** against Israel in Jos 11:20
to their inheritances, and then **c** to me. Jos 18:4
that in time to **c** your children might Jos 22:24
not say to our children in time to **c**, Jos 22:27
to us or to our descendants in time to **c**, Jos 22:28
All have **c** to pass for you; not one of Jos 23:14
and made the sea **c** upon them and Jos 24:7
"**C** up with me into the territory allotted Jgs 1:3
not allow them to **c** down to the plain. Jgs 1:34
"**C**, and I will show you the man whom Jgs 4:22
because they did not **c** to the help of the Jgs 5:23
of the East would **c** up against them. Jgs 6:3
For they would **c** up with their livestock Jgs 6:5
they would **c** like locusts in number— Jgs 6:5
from here until I **c** to you and bring Jgs 6:18
When I **c** to the outskirts of the camp, Jgs 7:17
"**C** down against the Midianites and Jgs 7:24
men of Penuel, "When I **c** again in peace, Jgs 8:9
to the fig tree, 'You **c** and reign over us.' Jgs 9:10
to the vine, 'You **c** and reign over us.' Jgs 9:12
the bramble, 'You **c** and reign over us.' Jgs 9:14
you, then **c** and take refuge in my shade, Jgs 9:15
let fire **c** out of the bramble and devour Jgs 9:15
let fire **c** out from Abimelech and Jgs 9:20
and let fire **c** out from the leaders of Jgs 9:20
to the seventy sons of Jerubbaal might **c**, Jgs 9:24
'Increase your army, and **c** out.'" Jgs 9:29
and his relatives have **c** to Shechem, Jgs 9:31
who are with him **c** out against you, Jgs 9:33
said to Jephthah, "**C** and be our leader, Jgs 11:6
Why have you **c** to me now when you Jgs 11:7
that you have **c** to me to fight against Jgs 11:12
Why then have you **c** up to me this day Jgs 12:3
a son. No razor shall **c** upon his head, Jgs 13:5
of God whom you sent **c** again to us and Jgs 13:8
said, "Now when your words **c** true, Jgs 13:12
name, so that, when your words **c** true, Jgs 13:17
"Why have you **c** up against us?" They Jgs 15:10
said, "We have **c** up to bind Samson, Jgs 15:10
to him, "We have **c** down to bind you, Jgs 15:12
"Samson has **c** here." And they Jgs 16:2
"A razor has never **c** upon my head, Jgs 16:17
of the Philistines, saying, "**C** up again, Jgs 16:18
"Where do you **c** from?" And he said to Jgs 17:9
you will **c** to an unsuspecting people. Jgs 18:10
on your mouth and **c** with us and be Jgs 18:19
you, that you **c** with such a company?" Jgs 18:23
the servant said to his master, "**C** now, Jgs 19:11
"**C** and let us draw near to one of these Jgs 19:13
you going? and where do you **c** from?" Jgs 19:17
country of Ephraim, from which I **c**. Jgs 19:18
since this man has **c** into my house, do Jgs 19:23
that when they **c** they may repay Jgs 20:10
of Israel did not **c** up in the assembly Jgs 21:5
him who did not **c** up to the LORD Jgs 21:5
of Israel that did not **c** up to the LORD to Jgs 21:8
no one had **c** to the camp from Jgs 21:8
the daughters of Shiloh **c** out to dance Jgs 21:21
then **c** out of the vineyards and snatch Jgs 21:21
or their brothers **c** to complain to Jgs 21:22
and she happened to **c** to the part of the Ru 2:3
whose wings you have **c** to take refuge!" Ru 2:12
"**C** here and eat some bread and dip your Ru 2:14
who has **c** back from the country of Ru 4:3
redeem it, and I **c** after you." And he said, Ru 4:4
let not arrogance **c** from your mouth; 1 Sm 2:3
sacrifice, the priest's servant would **c**, 1 Sm 2:13
the priest's servant would **c** and say to 1 Sm 2:15
And this that shall **c** upon your two 1 Sm 2:34
in your house shall **c** to implore him 1 Sm 2:36
that it may **c** among us and save us 1 Sm 4:3
the ark of the LORD had **c** to the camp, 1 Sm 4:6
"A god has **c** into the camp." And they 1 Sm 4:7
"I am he who has **c** from the battle; 1 Sm 4:16
on which there has never **c** a yoke, 1 Sm 6:7
LORD. **C** down and take it up to you." 1 Sm 6:21
who was with him, "**C**, let us go back, 1 Sm 9:5
"**C**, let us go to the seer," for today's 1 Sm 9:9
c, let us go." So they went to the city 1 Sm 9:10
He has **c** just now to the city, because 1 Sm 9:12
people, because their cry has **c** to me." 1 Sm 9:16
from there further and **c** to the oak of 1 Sm 10:3
that you shall **c** to Gibeath-elohim, 1 Sm 10:5
And there, as soon as you **c** to the city, 1 Sm 10:5
until I **c** to you and show you what 1 Sm 10:8
"What has **c** over the son of Kish? 1 Sm 10:11
a man still to **c**?" and the LORD said, 1 Sm 10:22
"Whoever does not **c** out after Saul 1 Sm 11:7
said to the messengers who had **c**, 1 Sm 11:9
"**C**, let us go to Gilgal and there 1 Sm 11:14
But Samuel did not **c** to Gilgal, and 1 Sm 13:8
that you did not **c** within the days 1 Sm 13:11
the Philistines will **c** down against 1 Sm 13:12
"**C**, let us go over to the Philistine 1 Sm 14:1
"**C**, let us go over to the garrison of 1 Sm 14:6
say to us, 'Wait until we **c** to you,' 1 Sm 14:9
But if they say, '**C** up to us,' then we 1 Sm 14:10
armor-bearer and said, "**C** up to us, 1 Sm 14:12
to his armor-bearer, "**C** up after me, 1 Sm 14:12
And Saul said, "**C** here, all you 1 Sm 14:38
say, 'I have **c** to sacrifice to the LORD.' 1 Sm 16:2
and said, "Do you **c** peaceably?" 1 Sm 16:4
I have **c** to sacrifice to the LORD. 1 Sm 16:5
and **c** with me to the sacrifice." And 1 Sm 16:5
"Why have you **c** out to draw up for 1 Sm 17:8
yourselves, and let him **c** down to me. 1 Sm 17:8
you seen this man who has **c** up? 1 Sm 17:25
up? Surely he has **c** up to defy Israel. 1 Sm 17:25
and he said, "Why have you **c** down? 1 Sm 17:28
for you have **c** down to see the 1 Sm 17:28
that you **c** to me with sticks?" And 1 Sm 17:43
Philistine said to David, "**C** to me, 1 Sm 17:44
"You **c** to me with a sword and with 1 Sm 17:45
but I **c** to you in the name of the 1 Sm 17:45
my father that harm should **c** to you, 1 Sm 20:9
"**C**, let us go out into the field." So 1 Sm 20:11
of you, take them,' then you are to **c**, 1 Sm 20:21
has not the son of Jesse **c** to the meal, 1 Sm 20:27
reason he has not **c** to the king's 1 Sm 20:29
Shall this fellow **c** into my house?" 1 Sm 21:15
he had **c** down with an ephod in his 1 Sm 23:6
told Saul that David had **c** to Keilah. 1 Sm 23:7
heard that Saul seeks to **c** to Keilah, 1 Sm 23:10
Will Saul **c** down, as your servant 1 Sm 23:11
And the LORD said, "He will **c** down." 1 Sm 23:11
saw that Saul had **c** out to seek his 1 Sm 23:15
Now **c** down, O king, according to 1 Sm 23:20
to all your heart's desire to **c** down, 1 Sm 23:20
and **c** back to me with sure 1 Sm 23:23
came to Saul, saying, "Hurry and **c**, 1 Sm 23:27
whom has the king of Israel **c** out? 1 Sm 24:14
in your eyes, for we **c** on a feast day. 1 Sm 25:8
give it to men who **c** from I do not 1 Sm 25:11
I **c** after you." But she did not tell her 1 Sm 25:19
you had hurried and **c** to meet me, 1 Sm 25:34
out spies and learned that Saul had **c**. 1 Sm 26:4
strike him, or his day will **c** to die, 1 Sm 26:10
the king of Israel has **c** out to seek a 1 Sm 26:20
of the young men **c** over and take it. 1 Sm 26:22
the garments, and **c** back to Achish. 1 Sm 27:9
no punishment shall **c** upon you for 1 Sm 28:10
lest these uncircumcised **c** and thrust 1 Sm 31:4
"Where do you **c** from?" And he said to 2 Sm 1:3
"Where do you **c** from?" And he 2 Sm 1:13
daughter, when you **c** to see my face." 2 Sm 3:13
said to David, "You will not **c** in here, 2 Sm 5:6
—thinking, "David cannot **c** in here." 2 Sm 5:6
the lame shall not **c** into the house." 2 Sm 5:8
the Philistines had **c** and spread out 2 Sm 5:18
and **c** against them opposite the 2 Sm 5:23

“How can the ark of the LORD **c** to me?” 2 Sm 6:9
you, who shall **c** from your body, 2 Sm 7:12
servant's house for a great while to **c**, 2 Sm 7:19
for you, then I will **c** and help you. 2 Sm 10:11
“Have you not **c** from a journey? 2 Sm 11:10
for the guest who had **c** to him, 2 Sm 12:4
it for the man who had **c** to him.” 2 Sm 12:4
‘Let my sister Tamar **c** and give me 2 Sm 13:5
let my sister Tamar **c** and make a 2 Sm 13:6
her and said to her, “**C**, lie with me, 2 Sm 13:11
“Behold, the king's sons have **c**; 2 Sm 13:35
your servant said, so it has **c** about.” 2 Sm 13:35
Now I have **c** to say this to my lord 2 Sm 14:15
he is not to **c** into my presence.” So 2 Sm 14:24
house and did not **c** into the king's 2 Sm 14:24
king, but Joab would not **c** to him. 2 Sm 14:29
a second time, but Joab would not **c**. 2 Sm 14:29
“Behold, I sent word to you, ‘**C** here, 2 Sm 14:32
to ask, “Why have I **c** from Geshur? 2 Sm 14:32
had a dispute to **c** before the king for 2 Sm 15:2
with a dispute or cause might **c** to me, 2 Sm 15:4
I will **c** upon him while he is weary 2 Sm 17:2
So we shall **c** upon him in some 2 Sm 17:12
said again to Joab, “**C** what may, 2 Sm 18:22
“**C** what may,” he said, “I will run.” 2 Sm 18:23
the evil that has **c** upon you from 2 Sm 19:7
word of all Israel has **c** to the king? 2 Sm 19:11
hurried to **c** down with the men of 2 Sm 19:16
Therefore, behold, I have **c** this day, 2 Sm 19:20
house of Joseph to **c** down to meet 2 Sm 19:20
my lord the king has **c** safely home.” 2 Sm 19:30
the Gileadite had **c** down from 2 Sm 19:31
said to Barzillai, “**C** over with me, 2 Sm 19:33
Tell Joab, ‘**C** here, that I may speak 2 Sm 20:16
of the air to **c** upon them by day, 2 Sm 21:10
three years of famine **c** to you in 2 Sm 24:13
my lord the king **c** to his servant?” 2 Sm 24:21
Now therefore **c**, let me give you 1 Kgs 1:12
I also will **c** in after you and confirm 1 Kgs 1:14
Otherwise it will **c** to pass, when my 1 Kgs 1:21
You shall then **c** up after him, and he 1 Kgs 1:35
and he shall **c** and sit on my throne, 1 Kgs 1:35
And Adonijah said, “**C** in, for you are 1 Kgs 1:42
said, “Do you **c** peacefully?” He said, 1 Kgs 2:13
commands, ‘**C** out.’” But he said, 1 Kgs 2:30
So shall their blood **c** back on the 1 Kgs 2:33
I do not know how to go out or **c** in. 1 Kgs 3:7
almug wood has **c** or been seen 1 Kgs 10:12
of Tarshish used to **c** bringing gold, 1 Kgs 10:22
for all Israel had **c** to Shechem to 1 Kgs 12:1
then **c** again to me.” So the people 1 Kgs 12:5
said, “**C** to me again the third day.” 1 Kgs 12:12
to the man of God, “**C** home with me, 1 Kgs 13:7
“**C** home with me and eat bread.” 1 Kgs 13:15
but have **c** back and have eaten 1 Kgs 13:22
your body shall not **c** to the tomb of 1 Kgs 13:22
of Samaria shall surely **c** to pass.” 1 Kgs 13:32
came in at the door, he said, “**C** in, 1 Kgs 14:6
of Jeroboam shall **c** to the grave, 1 Kgs 14:13
one to go out or **c** in to Asa king of 1 Kgs 15:17
You have **c** to me to bring my sin to 1 Kgs 17:18
let this child's life **c** into him again.” 1 Kgs 17:21
when I **c** and tell Ahab and he 1 Kgs 18:12
“**C** near to me.” And all the people 1 Kgs 18:30
He said, “If they have **c** out for peace, 1 Kgs 20:18
Or if they have **c** out for war, take 1 Kgs 20:18
said to him, “**C**, strengthen yourself, 1 Kgs 20:22
king of Syria will **c** up against you.” 1 Kgs 20:22
he caused him to **c** up into the 1 Kgs 20:33
And when he had **c** to the king, the 1 Kgs 22:15
and water, until I **c** in peace.”’” 1 Kgs 22:27
You shall not **c** down from the bed to 2 Kgs 1:4
you shall not **c** down from the 2 Kgs 1:6
man of God, the king says, ‘**C** down.’” 2 Kgs 1:9
let fire **c** down from heaven and 2 Kgs 1:10
is the king's order, ‘**C** down quickly!’” 2 Kgs 1:11
let fire **c** down from heaven and 2 Kgs 1:12
you shall not **c** down from the 2 Kgs 1:16
nor miscarriage shall **c** from it.” 2 Kgs 2:21
that the kings had **c** up to fight 2 Kgs 3:21
but the creditor has **c** to take my two 2 Kgs 4:1
to the man of God and **c** back again.” 2 Kgs 4:22
Let him **c** now to me, that he may 2 Kgs 5:8
that he would surely **c** out to me and 2 Kgs 5:11
‘There have just now **c** to me from 2 Kgs 5:22
the Syrians did not **c** again on raids 2 Kgs 6:23
So now **c**, let us go over to the camp of 2 Kgs 7:4
and the kings of Egypt to **c** against us.” 2 Kgs 7:6
Now therefore **c**; let us go and tell the 2 Kgs 7:9
‘When they **c** out of the city, 2 Kgs 7:12
and it will **c** upon the land for seven 2 Kgs 8:1
him, “The man of God has **c** here,” 2 Kgs 8:7
did this mad fellow **c** to you?” And he 2 Kgs 9:11
king of Judah had **c** down to visit 2 Kgs 9:16
your master's sons and **c** to me at 2 Kgs 10:6

And he said, “**C** with me, and see my 2 Kgs 10:16
was not a man left who did not **c**. 2 Kgs 10:21
and had them **c** to him in the house 2 Kgs 11:4
those who **c** off duty on the Sabbath 2 Kgs 11:5
which **c** on duty in force on the 2 Kgs 11:7
those who were to **c** on duty on the 2 Kgs 11:9
“**C**, let us look one another in the 2 Kgs 14:8
C up and rescue me from the hand of 2 Kgs 16:7
C now, make a wager with my 2 Kgs 18:23
LORD that I have **c** up against this 2 Kgs 18:25
your peace with me and **c** out to me. 2 Kgs 18:31
until I **c** and take you away to a land 2 Kgs 18:32
children have **c** to the point of birth, 2 Kgs 19:3
your complacency has **c** into my 2 Kgs 19:28
He shall not **c** into this city or shoot 2 Kgs 19:32
or **c** before it with a shield or cast up 2 Kgs 19:32
and he shall not **c** into this city, 2 Kgs 19:33
from where did they **c** to you?” And 2 Kgs 20:14
“They have **c** from a far country, 2 Kgs 20:14
high places did not **c** up to the altar 2 Kgs 23:9
of Egypt did not **c** again out of his 2 Kgs 24:7
were obligated to **c** in every seven 1 Chr 9:25
these uncircumcised **c** and mistreat 1 Chr 10:4
“You will not **c** in here.” 1 Chr 11:5
“If you have **c** to me in friendship to 1 Chr 12:17
expressly named to **c** and make 1 Chr 12:31
the Philistines had **c** and made a 1 Chr 14:9
go around and **c** against them 1 Chr 14:14
bring an offering and **c** before him! 1 Chr 16:29
house for a great while to **c**, 1 Chr 17:17
Have not his servants **c** to you to 1 Chr 19:3
kings who had **c** were by themselves 1 Chr 19:9
in their service to **c** into the house of 1 Chr 24:19
Both riches and honor **c** from you, 1 Chr 29:12
For all things **c** from you, and of 1 Chr 29:14
to go out and **c** in before this people, 2 Chr 1:10
Israel saw the fire **c** down and the 2 Chr 7:3
the ark of the LORD has **c** are holy.” 2 Chr 8:11
of Tarshish used to **c** bringing gold, 2 Chr 9:21
for all Israel had **c** to Shechem to 2 Chr 10:1
“**C** to me again in three days.” So the 2 Chr 10:5
said, “**C** to me again the third day.” 2 Chr 10:12
ambush around to **c** upon them 2 Chr 13:13
name we have **c** against this 2 Chr 14:11
no one to go out or **c** in to Asa king of 2 Chr 16:1
And when he had **c** to the king, the 2 Chr 18:14
and wrath may not **c** upon you and 2 Chr 19:10
they will **c** up by the ascent of Ziz. 2 Chr 20:16
Seir, who had **c** against Judah, 2 Chr 20:22
until your bowels **c** out because of 2 Chr 21:15
of Ahaziah should **c** about through 2 Chr 22:7
priests and Levites who **c** off duty on 2 Chr 23:4
those who were to **c** on duty on the 2 Chr 23:8
chief priest would **c** and empty the 2 Chr 24:11
of the Syrians had **c** with few men, 2 Chr 24:24
the army that had **c** to him from 2 Chr 25:10
“**C**, let us look one another in the 2 Chr 25:17
C near; bring sacrifices and thank 2 Chr 29:31
that they should **c** to the house of the 2 Chr 30:1
that the people should **c** and keep the 2 Chr 30:5
to the LORD and **c** to his sanctuary, 2 Chr 30:8
that Sennacherib had **c** and intended 2 Chr 32:2
the kings of Assyria **c** and find much 2 Chr 32:4
the LORD did not **c** upon them in the 2 Chr 32:26
and all who had **c** to Jerusalem from the Ezr 3:8
time those who had **c** from captivity, Ezr 8:35
And after all that has **c** upon us for our Ezr 9:13
if anyone did not **c** within three days, Ezr 10:8
taken foreign wives **c** at appointed Ezr 10:14
the first month they had **c** to the end of Ezr 10:17
let me pass through until I **c** to Judah, Neh 2:7
greatly that someone had **c** to seek the Neh 2:10
C, let us build the wall of Jerusalem, Neh 2:17
all plotted together to **c** and fight against Neh 4:8
or see till we **c** among them and kill Neh 4:11
“**C** and let us meet together at Neh 6:2
doing a great work and I cannot **c** down. Neh 6:3
stop while I leave it and **c** down to you?” Neh 6:3
So now **c** and let us take counsel Neh 6:7
And when the seventh month had **c**, Neh 7:73
seem little to you that has **c** upon us, Neh 9:32
righteous in all that has **c** upon us, Neh 9:33
on they did not **c** on the Sabbath. Neh 13:21
purify themselves and **c** and guard Neh 13:22
Queen Vashti refused to **c** at the king's Est 1:12
brought before him, and she did not **c**.’ Est 1:17
never again to **c** before King Ahasuerus. Est 1:19
have not been called to **c** in to the king Est 4:11
whether you have not **c** to the kingdom Est 4:14
let the king and Haman **c** today to a feast Est 5:4
let the king and Haman **c** to the feast that Est 5:8
let no one but me **c** with the king to the Est 5:12
court.” And the king said, “Let him **c** in.” Est 6:5
where have you **c**?” Satan answered the Jb 1:7
where have you **c**?” Satan answered the Jb 2:2

of all this evil that had **c** upon him, Jb 2:11
appointment together to **c** to show him Jb 2:11
let it not **c** into the number of the months. Jb 3:6
birth, **c** out from the womb and expire? Jb 3:11
But now it has **c** to you, and you are Jb 4:5
For affliction does not **c** from the dust, nor Jb 5:6
You shall **c** to your grave in ripe old age, Jb 5:26
they **c** there and are disappointed. Jb 6:20
a weaver's shuttle and **c** to their end Jb 7:6
he who goes down to Sheol does not **c** up; Jb 7:9
him, that we should **c** to trial together. Jb 9:32
I will speak, and let **c** on me what may. Jb 13:13
that the godless shall not **c** before him. Jb 13:16
I would wait, till my renewal should **c**. Jb 14:14
His sons **c** to honor, and he does not Jb 14:21
the destroyer will **c** upon him. Jb 15:21
when a few years have **c** I shall go the Jb 16:22
But you, **c** on again, all of you, and I Jb 17:10
His troops **c** on together; they have cast Jb 19:12
everyone in misery will **c** against him. Jb 20:22
of his gallbladder; terrors **c** upon him. Jb 20:25
be at peace; thereby good will **c** to you. Jb 22:21
find him, that I might **c** even to his seat! Jb 23:3
he has tried me, I shall **c** out as gold. Jb 23:10
and whose breath has **c** out from you? Jb 26:4
“From where, then, does wisdom **c**? And Jb 28:20
As through a wide breach they **c**; amid Jb 30:14
still; days of affliction **c** to meet me. Jb 30:27
caused the cry of the poor to **c** to him, Jb 34:28
and said, ‘Thus far shall you **c**, and no Jb 38:11
From whose womb did the ice **c** forth, Jb 38:29
Who would **c** near him with a bridle? Jb 41:13
another that no air can **c** between them. Jb 41:16
Oh, let the evil of the wicked **c** to an end, Ps 7:9
salvation for Israel would **c** out of Zion! Ps 14:7
your presence let my vindication **c**! Ps 17:2
off! O you my help, **c** quickly to my aid! Ps 22:19
they shall **c** and proclaim his Ps 22:31
doors, that the King of glory may **c** in. Ps 24:7
doors, that the King of glory may **c** in. Ps 24:9
C, O children, listen to me; I will teach Ps 34:11
Let destruction **c** upon him when he Ps 35:8
Let not the foot of arrogance **c** upon me, Ps 36:11
me, and your hand has **c** down on me. Ps 38:2
Then I said, “Behold, I have **c**; in the Ps 40:7
When shall I **c** and appear before God? Ps 42:2
All this has **c** upon us, though we have Ps 44:17
Rise up; **c** to our help! Redeem us for the Ps 44:26
C, behold the works of the LORD, how he Ps 46:8
“David has **c** to the house of Ps 52:T
salvation for Israel would **c** out of Zion! Ps 53:6
Fear and trembling **c** upon me, and Ps 55:5
ready. Awake, **c** to meet me, and see! Ps 59:4
Each evening they **c** back, howling like Ps 59:6
Each evening they **c** back, howling like Ps 59:14
who hears prayer, to you shall all flesh **c**. Ps 65:2
that your enemies **c** cringing to you. Ps 66:3
C and see what God has done: he is Ps 66:5
I will **c** into your house with burnt Ps 66:13
C and hear, all you who fear God, and I Ps 66:16
Nobles shall **c** from Egypt; Cush shall Ps 68:31
For the waters have **c** up to my neck. Ps 69:1
I have **c** into deep waters, and the flood Ps 69:2
of refuge, to which I may continually **c**; Ps 71:3
mighty deeds of the Lord GOD I will **c**; Ps 71:16
generation, your power to all those to **c**. Ps 71:18
He made streams **c** out of the rock and Ps 78:16
the nations have **c** into your inheritance; Ps 79:1
let your compassion **c** speedily to meet Ps 79:8
the groans of the prisoners **c** before you; Ps 79:11
stir up your might and **c** to save us! Ps 80:2
say, “**C**, let us wipe them out as a nation; Ps 83:4
have made shall **c** and worship before Ps 86:9
Let my prayer **c** before you; incline your Ps 88:2
right hand, but it will not **c** near you. Ps 91:7
befall you, no plague **c** near your tent. Ps 91:10
Oh **c**, let us sing to the LORD; let us make Ps 95:1
Let us **c** into his presence with Ps 95:2
Oh **c**, let us worship and bow down; let Ps 95:6
bring an offering, and **c** into his courts! Ps 96:8
C into his presence with singing! Ps 100:2
is blameless. Oh when will you **c** to me? Ps 101:2
my prayer, O LORD; let my cry **c** to you! Ps 102:1
to favor her; the appointed time has **c**. Ps 102:13
this be recorded for a generation to **c**, Ps 102:18
When he is tried, let him **c** forth guilty; Ps 109:7
loved to curse; let curses **c** upon him! Ps 109:17
Let your steadfast love **c** to me, O LORD, Ps 119:41
Let your mercy **c** to me, that I may Ps 119:77
Let my cry **c** before you, O LORD; give Ps 119:169
Let my plea **c** before you; deliver me Ps 119:170
the hills. From where does my help **c**? Ps 121:1
shall **c** home with shouts of joy, Ps 126:6
C, bless the LORD, all you servants of the Ps 134:1
Bow your heavens, O LORD, and **c** down! Ps 144:5

If they say, "**C** with us, let us lie in wait Prv 1:11
when distress and anguish **c** upon you. Prv 1:27
from his mouth **c** knowledge and Prv 2:6
for wisdom will **c** into your heart, and Prv 2:10
none who go to her **c** back, nor do they Prv 2:19
say to your neighbor, "Go, and **c** again, Prv 3:28
for you have **c** into the hand of your Prv 6:3
and poverty will **c** upon you like a Prv 6:11
therefore calamity will **c** upon him Prv 6:15
so now I have **c** out to meet you, to seek Prv 7:15
C, let us take our fill of love till Prv 7:18
with him; at full moon he will **c** home." Prv 7:20
and from my lips will **c** what is right, Prv 8:6
"**C**, eat of my bread and drink of the wine Prv 9:5
but a babbling fool will **c** to ruin. Prv 10:8
but a babbling fool will **c** to ruin. Prv 10:10
the wicked dreads will **c** upon him, Prv 10:24
Poverty and disgrace **c** to him who Prv 13:18
but abundant crops **c** by the strength Prv 14:4
of many companions may **c** to ruin, Prv 18:24
Love not sleep, lest you **c** to poverty; Prv 20:13
gives to the rich, will only **c** to poverty. Prv 22:16
and the glutton will **c** to poverty, Prv 23:21
the ruin that will **c** from them both? Prv 24:22
and a good blessing will **c** upon them. Prv 24:25
and poverty will **c** upon you like a Prv 24:34
"**C** up here," than to be put lower in the Prv 25:7
and a stone will **c** back on him who Prv 26:27
know that poverty will **c** upon him. Prv 28:22
has ascended to heaven and **c** down? Prv 30:4
and she laughs at the time to **c**. Prv 31:25
yet to be among those who **c** after. Eccl 1:11
I said in my heart, "**C** now, I will test Eccl 2:1
that in the days to **c** all will have been Eccl 2:16
leave it to the man who will **c** after me, Eccl 2:18
all skill in work **c** from a man's envy Eccl 4:4
Yet those who **c** later will not rejoice in Eccl 4:16
Whatever has **c** to be has already been Eccl 6:10
who fears God shall **c** out from both of Eccl 7:18
before the evil days **c** and the years Eccl 12:1
my love, my beautiful one, and **c** away, Sg 2:10
on the earth, the time of singing has **c**, Sg 2:12
my love, my beautiful one, and **c** away. Sg 2:13
shorn ewes that have **c** up from the Sg 4:2
C with me from Lebanon, my bride; come Sg 4:8
my bride; **c** with me from Lebanon. Sg 4:8
Awake, O north wind, and **c**, O south Sg 4:16
flow. Let my beloved **c** to his garden, Sg 4:16
of ewes that have **c** up from the washing; Sg 6:6
C, my beloved, let us go out into the Sg 7:11
"When you **c** to appear before me, who Is 1:12
"**C** now, let us reason together, says the Is 1:18
and the widow's cause does not **c** to them. Is 1:23
It shall **c** to pass in the latter days that the Is 2:2
and many peoples shall **c**, and say: "Come, Is 2:3
"**C**, let us go up to the mountain of the Is 2:3
c, let us walk in the light of the LORD. Is 2:5
Holy One of Israel draw near, and let it **c**, Is 5:19
and behold, quickly, speedily they **c**! Is 5:26
shall not stand, and it shall not **c** to pass. Is 7:7
such days as have not **c** since the day that Is 7:17
And they will all **c** and settle in the steep Is 7:19
With bow and arrows a man will **c** there, Is 7:24
you will not **c** there for fear of briers and Is 7:25
counsel together, but it will **c** to nothing; Is 8:10
in the ruin that will **c** from afar? Is 10:3
very little while my fury will **c** to an end, Is 10:25
He has **c** to Aiath; he has passed through Is 10:28
There shall **c** forth a shoot from the Is 11:1
They **c** from a distant land, from the end Is 13:5
destruction from the Almighty it will **c**! Is 13:6
is stirred up to meet you when you **c**; Is 14:9
the serpent's root will **c** forth an adder, Is 14:29
to Assyria, and Assyria will **c** into Egypt, Is 19:23
And behold, here **c** riders, horsemen in Is 21:9
you will inquire, inquire; **c** back again." Is 21:12
all the glory of Kedar will **c** to an end. Is 21:16
Lord GOD of hosts, "**C**, go to this steward, Is 22:15
C, my people, enter your chambers, and Is 26:20
In days to **c** Jacob shall take root, Israel Is 27:6
women **c** and make a fire of them. Is 27:11
land of Egypt will **c** and worship the Is 27:13
whip passes through it will not **c** to us, Is 28:15
your voice shall **c** from the ground like Is 29:4
For the ruthless shall **c** to nothing and Is 29:20
astray in spirit will **c** to understanding, Is 29:24
from where **c** the lioness and the lion, Is 30:6
be for the time to **c** as a witness forever. Is 30:8
the LORD of hosts will **c** down to fight on Is 31:4
harvest fails, the fruit harvest will not **c**. Is 32:10
Behold, your God will **c** with vengeance, Is 35:4
of God. He will **c** and save you." Is 35:4
nor shall any ravenous beast **c** up on it; Is 35:9
LORD shall return and **c** to Zion with Is 35:10
C now, make a wager with my master the Is 36:8

LORD that I have **c** up against this land Is 36:10
your peace with me and **c** out to me. Is 36:16
until I **c** and take you away to a land Is 36:17
children have **c** to the point of birth, and Is 37:3
cypresses, to **c** to its remotest height, Is 37:24
and your complacency has **c** to my ears, Is 37:29
He shall not **c** into this city or shoot an Is 37:33
shoot an arrow there or **c** before it with a Is 37:33
return, and he shall not **c** into this city, Is 37:34
from where did they **c** to you?" Hezekiah Is 39:3
"They have **c** to me from a far country, Is 39:3
of your own sons, who will **c** from you, Is 39:7
tremble; they have drawn near and **c**. Is 41:5
outcome; or declare to us the things to **c**. Is 41:22
Tell us what is to **c** hereafter, that we Is 41:23
up one from the north, and he has **c**, Is 41:25
Behold, the former things have **c** to pass, Is 42:9
will attend and listen for the time to **c**? Is 42:23
Let them declare what is to **c**, and what Is 44:7
who formed him: "Ask me of things to **c**; Is 45:11
stature, shall **c** over to you and be yours; Is 45:14
they shall **c** over in chains and bow Is 45:14
"Assemble yourselves and **c**; draw near Is 45:20
to him shall **c** and be ashamed all who Is 45:24
C down and sit in the dust, O virgin Is 47:1
These two things shall **c** to you in a Is 47:9
and widowhood shall **c** upon you in Is 47:9
But evil shall **c** upon you, which you Is 47:11
and ruin shall **c** upon you suddenly, Is 47:11
make known what shall **c** upon you. Is 47:13
saying to the prisoners, '**C** out,' to those Is 49:9
Behold, these shall **c** from afar, and Is 49:12
and see; they all gather, they **c** to you. Is 49:18
left alone; from where have these **c**?'" Is 49:21
is my adversary? Let him **c** near to me. Is 50:8
LORD shall return and **c** to Zion with Is 51:11
there shall no more **c** into you the Is 52:1
from terror, for it shall not **c** near you. Is 54:14
"**C**, everyone who thirsts, come to the Is 55:1
everyone who thirsts, **c** to the waters; Is 55:1
he who has no money, **c**, buy and eat! Is 55:1
C, buy wine and milk without money Is 55:1
Incline your ear, and **c** to me; hear, that Is 55:3
rain and the snow **c** down from heaven Is 55:10
of the thorn shall **c** up the cypress; Is 55:13
instead of the brier shall **c** up the myrtle; Is 55:13
for soon my salvation will **c**, Is 56:1
c to devour—all you beasts in the forest. Is 56:9
"**C**," they say, "let me get wine; let us fill Is 56:12
for he will **c** like a rushing stream, Is 59:19
"And a Redeemer will **c** to Zion, to those Is 59:20
Arise, shine, for your light has **c**, and the Is 60:1
And nations shall **c** to your light, and Is 60:3
see; they all gather together, they **c** to you; Is 60:4
your sons shall **c** from afar, and your Is 60:4
the wealth of the nations shall **c** to you. Is 60:5
and Ephah; all those from Sheba shall **c**. Is 60:6
they shall **c** up with acceptance on my Is 60:7
The glory of Lebanon shall **c** to you, the Is 60:13
who afflicted you shall **c** bending low to Is 60:14
heart, and my year of redemption had **c**. Is 63:4
you would rend the heavens and **c** down, Is 64:1
say, "Keep to yourself, do not **c** near me, Is 65:5
shall not be remembered or **c** into mind. Is 65:17
"For behold, the LORD will **c** in fire, and Is 66:15
and mice, shall **c** to an end together, Is 66:17
And they shall **c** and shall see my glory, Is 66:18
all flesh shall **c** to worship before me, Is 66:23
declares the LORD, and they shall **c**, Jer 1:15
'We are free, we will **c** no more to you'? Jer 2:31
it too you will **c** away with your hands Jer 2:37
withheld, and the spring rain has not **c**; Jer 3:3
the LORD." It shall not **c** to mind or be Jer 3:16
and together they shall **c** from the land Jer 3:18
your faithlessness." "Behold, we **c** to you, Jer 3:22
"Besiegers **c** from a distant land; Jer 4:16
no disaster will **c** upon us, nor shall we Jer 5:12
with their flocks shall **c** against her; Jer 6:3
suddenly the destroyer will **c** upon us. Jer 6:26
and then **c** and stand before me in this Jer 7:10
command, nor did it **c** into my mind. Jer 7:31
They **c** and devour the land and all that Jer 8:16
and call for the mourning women to **c**; Jer 9:17
come; send for the skillful women to **c**; Jer 9:17
For death has **c** up into our windows; it Jer 9:21
heights in the desert destroyers have **c**, Jer 12:12
And it shall **c** to pass, if they will Jer 12:16
beautiful crown has **c** down from your Jer 13:18
and see those who **c** from the north. Jer 13:20
'Why have these things **c** upon me?' Jer 13:22
servants for water; they **c** to the cisterns; Jer 14:3
and famine shall not **c** upon this land': Jer 14:15
you shall the nations **c** from the ends of Jer 16:19
the desert, and shall not see any good **c**. Jer 17:6
is the word of the LORD? Let it **c**!" Jer 17:15

And people shall **c** from the cities of Jer 17:26
"**C**, let us make plots against Jeremiah, Jer 18:18
C, let us strike him with the tongue, Jer 18:18
or decree, nor did it **c** into my mind— Jer 19:5
Why did I **c** out from the womb to see Jer 20:18
who say, 'Who shall **c** down against us, Jer 21:13
will be pitied when pangs **c** upon you, Jer 22:23
say, 'No disaster shall **c** upon you.'" Jer 23:17
day, the word of the LORD has **c** to me, Jer 25:3
your slaughter and dispersion have **c**, Jer 25:34
cities of Judah that **c** to worship in the Jer 26:2
the envoys who have **c** to Jerusalem to Jer 27:3
words that you have prophesied **c** true, Jer 28:6
will call upon me and **c** and pray to me, Jer 29:12
"And it shall **c** to pass in that day, Jer 30:8
of them shall **c** songs of thanksgiving, Jer 30:19
their ruler shall **c** out from their midst; Jer 30:21
With weeping they shall **c**, and with Jer 31:9
They shall **c** and sing aloud on the Jer 31:12
and they shall **c** back from the land of Jer 31:16
and your children shall **c** back to their Jer 31:17
And it shall **c** to pass that as I have Jer 31:28
Shallum your uncle will **c** to you and Jer 32:7
made all this disaster **c** upon them. Jer 32:23
the siege mounds have **c** up to the city Jer 32:24
What you spoke has **c** to pass, and Jer 32:24
against this city shall **c** and set this city Jer 32:29
and night will not **c** at their appointed Jer 33:20
'**C**, and let us go to Jerusalem for fear of Jer 35:11
men of Judah who **c** out of their cities. Jer 36:6
plea for mercy will **c** before the LORD, Jer 36:7
and **c**." So Baruch the son of Neriah Jer 36:14
Babylon will certainly **c** and destroy Jer 36:29
army of Pharaoh had **c** out of Egypt. Jer 37:5
the Chaldeans shall **c** back and fight Jer 37:8
When Jeremiah had **c** to the dungeon Jer 37:16
of Babylon will not **c** against you and Jer 37:19
let my humble plea **c** before you and do Jer 37:20
spoken with you and **c** to you and say Jer 38:25
his voice, this thing has **c** upon you. Jer 40:3
good to you to **c** with me to Babylon, Jer 40:4
Babylon, **c**, and I will look after you well, Jer 40:4
wrong to you to **c** with me to Babylon, Jer 40:4
to come with me to Babylon, do not **c**. Jer 40:4
before the Chaldeans who will **c** to us. Jer 40:10
"**C** in to Gedaliah the son of Ahikam." Jer 41:6
"Let our plea for mercy **c** before you, Jer 42:2
He shall **c** and strike the land of Egypt, Jer 43:11
land of Egypt where you have **c** to live, Jer 44:8
have set their faces to **c** to the land of Jer 44:12
of Judah who have **c** to live in the Jer 44:14
them? Did it not **c** into his mind? Jer 44:21
and like Carmel by the sea, shall one **c**. Jer 46:18
fly from the north has **c** upon her. Jer 46:20
day of their calamity has **c** upon them, Jer 46:21
march in force and **c** against her with Jer 46:22
Baldness has **c** upon Gaza; Ashkelon Jer 47:5
'**C**, let us cut her off from being a Jer 48:2
The destroyer shall **c** upon every city, Jer 48:8
of Moab and his cities has **c** up, Jer 48:15
"**C** down from your glory, and sit on Jer 48:18
of Moab has **c** up against you; Jer 48:18
"Judgment has **c** upon the tableland, Jer 48:21
saying, 'Who will **c** against me?' Jer 49:4
yourselves together and **c** against her, Jer 49:14
those driven out of Elam shall not **c**. Jer 49:36
the north a nation has **c** up against her, Jer 50:3
and the people of Judah shall **c** together, Jer 50:4
shall come together, weeping as they **c**, Jer 50:4
'**C**, let us join ourselves to the LORD in an Jer 50:5
C against her from every quarter; open Jer 50:26
Woe to them, for their day has **c**, the Jer 50:27
Lord GOD of hosts, for your day has **c**, Jer 50:31
when they **c** against her from every side Jer 51:2
c, let us declare in Zion the work of the Jer 51:10
rich in treasures, your end has **c**; Jer 51:13
and the time of her harvest will **c**." Jer 51:33
The sea has **c** up on Babylon; she is Jer 51:42
the destroyers shall **c** against them out Jer 51:48
and let Jerusalem **c** into your mind: Jer 51:50
for foreigners have **c** into the holy Jer 51:51
yet destroyers would **c** from me against Jer 51:53
for a destroyer has **c** upon her, upon Jer 51:56
disaster that should **c** upon Babylon, Jer 51:60
to Seraiah: "When you **c** to Babylon, Jer 51:61
Zion mourn, for none **c** to the festival; Lam 1:4
"Let all their evildoing **c** before you, Lam 1:22
ceases; his mercies never **c** to an end; Lam 3:22
of the Most High that good and bad **c**? Lam 3:38
panic and pitfall have **c** upon us, Lam 3:47
were numbered, for our end had **c**. Lam 4:18
has tainted meat **c** into my mouth." Ezk 4:14
From there a fire will **c** out into all the Ezk 5:4
The end has **c** upon the four corners of Ezk 7:2
An end has **c**; the end has come; it has Ezk 7:6

An end has come; the end has **c**; it has Ezk 7:6
Your doom has **c** to you, O inhabitant of Ezk 7:7
The time has **c**; the day is near, a day of Ezk 7:7
Your doom has **c**; the rod has Ezk 7:10
The time has **c**; the day has arrived. Let Ezk 7:12
know the things that **c** into your mind. Ezk 11:5
And when they **c** there, they will Ezk 11:18
behold, when they **c** out to you, and Ezk 14:22
bribing them to **c** to you from every Ezk 16:33
GOD, Is it to inquire of me that you **c**? Ezk 20:3
hands and let the sword **c** down twice, Ezk 21:14
the sword of the king of Babylon to **c**. Ezk 21:19
Both of them shall **c** from the same Ezk 21:19
for the sword to **c** to Rabbah of the Ezk 21:20
because you have **c** to remembrance, Ezk 21:24
one, prince of Israel, whose day has **c**, Ezk 21:25
the profane wicked, whose day has **c**, Ezk 21:29
in her midst, so that her time may **c**, Ezk 22:3
the appointed time of your years has **c**. Ezk 22:4
And they shall **c** against you from the Ezk 23:24
They even sent for men to **c** from afar, Ezk 23:40
I have spoken; it shall **c** to pass; I will Ezk 24:14
day a fugitive will **c** to you to report Ezk 24:26
from their ships **c** all who handle Ezk 27:29
you have **c** to a dreadful end and shall Ezk 27:36
you have **c** to a dreadful end and shall Ezk 28:19
A sword shall **c** upon Egypt, and Ezk 30:4
fall, and her proud might shall **c** down; Ezk 30:6
and anguish shall **c** upon them on the Ezk 30:9
her proud might shall **c** to an end in Ezk 30:18
the king of Babylon shall **c** upon you. Ezk 32:11
'They have **c** down, they lie still, the Ezk 32:21
and her proud might shall **c** to an end, Ezk 33:28
'**C**, and hear what the word is that Ezk 33:30
And they **c** to you as people come, and Ezk 33:31
And they come to you as people **c**, and Ezk 33:31
When this comes—and **c** it will!— Ezk 33:33
I will cut off from it all who **c** and go. Ezk 35:7
people Israel, for they will soon **c** home. Ezk 36:8
you, and will cause flesh to **c** upon you, Ezk 37:6
on them, and flesh had **c** upon them, Ezk 37:8
C from the four winds, O breath, and Ezk 37:9
day, thoughts will **c** into your mind, Ezk 38:10
say to you, 'Have you **c** to seize spoil? Ezk 38:13
You will **c** from your place out of the Ezk 38:15
You will **c** up against my people Ezk 38:16
day that Gog shall **c** against the land Ezk 38:18
all beasts of the field, 'Assemble and **c**, Ezk 39:17
sons of Levi may **c** near to the LORD Ezk 40:46
They shall not **c** near to me, to serve Ezk 44:13
nor **c** near any of my holy things and Ezk 44:13
shall **c** near to me to minister to me. Ezk 44:15
people of the land **c** before the LORD at Ezk 46:9
of the provinces to **c** to the dedication of Dn 3:2
servants of the Most High God, **c** out, Dn 3:26
come out, and **c** here!" Then Shadrach, Dn 3:26
and no smell of fire had **c** upon them. Dn 3:27
which has **c** upon my lord the king, Dn 4:24
I saw him **c** close to the ram, and he was Dn 8:7
Moses, all this calamity has **c** upon us; Dn 9:13
I have now **c** out to give you insight and Dn 9:22
went out, and I have **c** to tell it to you, Dn 9:23
prince who is to **c** shall destroy the city Dn 9:26
sanctuary. Its end shall **c** with a flood, Dn 9:26
of abominations shall **c** one who makes Dn 9:27
and I have **c** because of your words. Dn 10:12
days. For the vision is for days yet to **c**." Dn 10:14
of the vision pains have **c** upon me, Dn 10:16
"Do you know why I have **c** to you? Dn 10:20
out, behold, the prince of Greece will **c**. Dn 10:20
king of the south shall **c** to the king of Dn 11:6
He shall **c** against the army and enter Dn 11:7
Then the latter shall **c** into the realm of Dn 11:9
shall **c** out and fight with the king of Dn 11:11
some years he shall **c** on with a great Dn 11:13
of the north shall **c** and throw up Dn 11:15
set his face to **c** with the strength of Dn 11:17
He shall **c** in without warning and Dn 11:21
warning he shall **c** into the richest Dn 11:24
he shall return and **c** into the south, Dn 11:29
ships of Kittim shall **c** against him, Dn 11:30
And he shall **c** into countries and shall Dn 11:40
He shall **c** into the glorious land. And Dn 11:41
mountain. Yet he shall **c** to his end, Dn 11:45
and they shall **c** in fear to the LORD and Hos 3:5
without understanding shall **c** to ruin. Hos 4:14
"**C**, let us return to the LORD; for he has Hos 6:1
he will **c** to us as the showers, as the Hos 6:3
it shall not **c** to the house of the LORD. Hos 9:4
The days of punishment have **c**; the days Hos 9:7
come; the days of recompense have **c**; Hos 9:7
that he may **c** and rain righteousness Hos 10:12
in your midst, and I will not **c** in wrath. Hos 11:9
his children shall **c** trembling from Hos 11:10
they shall **c** trembling like birds from Hos 11:11

Gilead, they shall surely **c** to nothing: Hos 12:11
The pangs of childbirth **c** for him, Hos 13:13
wind, the wind of the LORD, shall **c**, Hos 13:15
For a nation has **c** up against my land, Jl 1:6
"And it shall **c** to pass afterward, that I Jl 2:28
And it shall **c** to pass that everyone who Jl 2:32
all the men of war draw near; let them **c** up. Jl 3:9
Hasten and **c**, all you surrounding Jl 3:11
stir themselves up and **c** up to the Valley Jl 3:12
and a fountain shall **c** forth from the Jl 3:18
Does disaster **c** to a city, unless the LORD Am 3:6
the great houses shall **c** to an end," Am 3:15
"**C** to Bethel, and transgress; to Gilgal, Am 4:4
into exile, and Bethel shall **c** to nothing." Am 5:5
"The end has **c** upon my people Israel; Am 8:2
it, for their evil has **c** up before me." Jon 1:2
said to one another, "**C**, let us cast lots, Jon 1:7
account this evil has **c** upon us." So they Jon 1:7
whose account this evil has **c** upon us. Jon 1:8
occupation? And where do you **c** from? Jon 1:8
that this great tempest has **c** upon you." Jon 1:12
a plant and made it **c** up over Jonah, Jon 4:6
and will **c** down and tread upon the high Mi 1:3
wound is incurable, and it has **c** to Judah; Mi 1:9
the inhabitants of Zaanan do not **c** out; Mi 1:11
because disaster has **c** down from the Mi 1:12
the glory of Israel shall **c** to Adullam. Mi 1:15
of us? No disaster shall **c** upon us." Mi 3:11
It shall **c** to pass in the latter days that the Mi 4:1
and many nations shall **c**, and say: Mi 4:2
"**C**, let us go up to the mountain of the Mi 4:2
of the daughter of Zion, to you shall it **c**, Mi 4:8
it come, the former dominion shall **c**, Mi 4:8
from you shall **c** forth for me one who is Mi 5:2
"With what shall I **c** before the LORD, and Mi 6:6
Shall I **c** before him with burnt offerings, Mi 6:6
watchmen, of your punishment, has **c**; Mi 7:4
In that day they will **c** to you, from Mi 7:12
they shall **c** trembling out of their Mi 7:17
The scatterer has **c** up against you. Man Na 2:1
The chariots **c** with flashing metal on Na 2:3
whom has not **c** your unceasing evil? Na 3:19
on. Their horsemen **c** from afar; Hab 1:8
They all **c** for violence, all their faces Hab 1:9
it seems slow, wait for it; it will surely **c**; Hab 2:3
LORD'S right hand will **c** around to you, Hab 2:16
utter shame will **c** upon your glory! Hab 2:16
day of trouble to **c** upon people who Hab 3:16
the time has not yet **c** to rebuild the house Hg 1:2
that the treasures of all nations shall **c** in, Hg 2:7
head. And these have **c** to terrify them, Zec 1:21
I **c** and I will dwell in your midst, Zec 2:10
invite his neighbor to **c** under his vine Zec 3:10
who are far off shall **c** and help to build Zec 6:15
And this shall **c** to pass, if you will Zec 6:15
Peoples shall yet **c**, even the inhabitants Zec 8:20
and strong nations shall **c** to seek the Zec 8:22
From him shall **c** the cornerstone, Zec 10:4
all the nations that **c** against Jerusalem. Zec 12:9
Then the LORD my God will **c**, and all Zec 14:5
nations that have **c** against Jerusalem Zec 14:16
all who sacrifice may **c** and take of Zec 14:21
you seek will suddenly **c** to his temple; Mal 3:1
lest I **c** and strike the land with a decree Mal 4:6
when it rose and have **c** to worship him." Mt 2:2
for from you shall **c** a ruler who will Mt 2:6
word, that I too may **c** and worship him." Mt 2:8
warned you to flee from the wrath to **c**? Mt 3:7
be baptized by you, and do you **c** to me?" Mt 3:14
think that I have **c** to abolish the Law Mt 5:17
I have not **c** to abolish them but to Mt 5:17
brother, and then **c** and offer your gift. Mt 5:24
C to terms quickly with your accuser Mt 5:25
Your kingdom **c**, your will be done, on Mt 6:10
who **c** to you in sheep's clothing but Mt 7:15
he said to him, "I will **c** and heal him." Mt 8:7
not worthy to have you **c** under my roof, Mt 8:8
he goes, and to another, '**C**,' and he comes, Mt 8:9
many will **c** from east and west and Mt 8:11
Have you **c** here to torment us before the Mt 8:29
The days will **c** when the bridegroom is Mt 9:15
died, but **c** and lay your hand on her, Mt 9:18
is worthy, let your peace **c** upon it, Mt 10:13
think that I have **c** to bring peace to Mt 10:34
to the earth. I have not **c** to bring peace, Mt 10:34
For I have **c** to set a man against his Mt 10:35
said to him, "Are you the one who is to **c**, Mt 11:3
to accept it, he is Elijah who is to **c**. Mt 11:14
C to me, all who labor and are heavy Mt 11:28
the kingdom of God has **c** upon you. Mt 12:28
either in this age or in the age to **c**. Mt 12:32
the birds of the air **c** and make nests in Mt 13:32
The angels will **c** out and separate the Mt 13:49
command me to **c** to you on the water." Mt 14:28
"**C**." So Peter got out of the boat and Mt 14:29

For out of the heart **c** evil thoughts, Mt 15:19
disciples, "If anyone would **c** after me, Mt 16:24
of Man is going to **c** with his angels in Mt 16:27
scribes say that first Elijah must **c**?" Mt 17:10
He answered, "Elijah does **c**, and he will Mt 17:11
But I tell you that Elijah has already **c**, Mt 17:12
For it is necessary that temptations **c**, Mt 18:7
"Let the little children **c** to me and do Mt 19:14
will have treasure in heaven; and **c**, Mt 19:21
"May no fruit ever **c** from you again!" Mt 21:19
baptism of John, from where did it **c**? Mt 21:25
C, let us kill him and have his Mt 21:38
the wedding feast, but they would not **c**. Mt 22:3
is ready. **C** to the wedding feast.' Mt 22:4
that on you may **c** all the righteous Mt 23:35
these things will **c** upon this Mt 23:36
For many will **c** in my name, saying, 'I Mt 24:5
to all nations, and then the end will **c**. Mt 24:14
of that servant will **c** on a day when Mt 24:50
is the bridegroom! **C** out to meet him.' Mt 25:6
'**C**, you who are blessed by my Father, Mt 25:34
"Have you **c** out as against a robber, Mt 26:55
the Son of God, **c** down from the cross." Mt 27:40
let him **c** down now from the cross, Mt 27:42
see whether Elijah will **c** to save him." Mt 27:49
as he said. **C**, see the place where he lay. Mt 28:6
of Nazareth? Have you **c** to destroy us? Mk 1:24
saying, "Be silent, and **c** out of him!" Mk 1:25
The days will **c** when the bridegroom is Mk 2:20
man with the withered hand, "**C** here." Mk 3:3
is anything secret except to **c** to light. Mk 4:22
the sickle, because the harvest has **c**." Mk 4:29
On that day, when evening had **c**, he Mk 4:35
he was saying to him, "**C** out of the man, Mk 5:8
C and lay your hands on her, so that Mk 5:23
"**C** away by yourselves to a desolate Mk 6:31
of the scribes who had **c** from Jerusalem, Mk 7:1
and when they **c** from the marketplace, Mk 7:4
but the things that **c** out of a person are Mk 7:15
out of the heart of man, **c** evil thoughts, Mk 7:21
All these evil things **c** from within, and Mk 7:23
some of them have **c** from far away." Mk 8:3
to them, "If anyone would **c** after me, Mk 8:34
of God after it has **c** with power." Mk 9:1
scribes say that first Elijah must **c**?" Mk 9:11
"Elijah does **c** first to restore all things. Mk 9:12
But I tell you that Elijah has **c**, and they Mk 9:13
c out of him and never enter him Mk 9:25
said to them, "Let the children **c** to me; Mk 10:14
will have treasure in heaven; and **c**, Mk 10:21
and in the age to **c** eternal life. Mk 10:30
that what he says will **c** to pass, Mk 11:23
C, let us kill him, and the inheritance Mk 12:7
He will **c** and destroy the tenants and Mk 12:9
Many will **c** in my name, saying, 'I am Mk 13:6
you do not know when the time will **c**. Mk 13:33
when the master of the house will **c**, Mk 13:35
lest he **c** suddenly and find you asleep. Mk 13:36
your rest? It is enough; the hour has **c**. Mk 14:41
"Have you **c** out as against a robber, Mk 14:48
yourself, and **c** down from the cross!" Mk 15:30
c down now from the cross that we Mk 15:32
And when the sixth hour had **c**, there Mk 15:33
see whether Elijah will **c** to take him Mk 15:36
And when evening had **c**, since it was Mk 15:42
her, "The Holy Spirit will **c** upon you, Lk 1:35
the mother of my Lord should **c** to me? Lk 1:43
warned you to flee from the wrath to **c**? Lk 3:7
of Nazareth? Have you **c** to destroy us? Lk 4:34
"Be silent and **c** out of him!" And when Lk 4:35
the unclean spirits, and they **c** out!" Lk 4:36
in the other boat to **c** and help them. Lk 5:7
who had **c** from every village of Galilee Lk 5:17
I have not **c** to call the righteous but Lk 5:32
The days will **c** when the bridegroom is Lk 5:35
"**C** and stand here." And he rose and stood Lk 6:8
asking him to **c** and heal his servant. Lk 7:3
not worthy to have you **c** under my roof. Lk 7:6
Therefore I did not presume to **c** to you. Lk 7:7
he goes; and to another, '**C**,' and he comes; Lk 7:8
saying, "Are you the one who is to **c**, Lk 7:19
And when the men had **c** to him, they Lk 7:20
you, saying, 'Are you the one who is to **c**, Lk 7:20
John the Baptist has **c** eating no bread Lk 7:33
Son of Man has **c** eating and drinking, Lk 7:34
that will not be known and **c** to light. Lk 8:17
the unclean spirit to **c** out of the man. Lk 8:29
feet, he implored him to **c** to his house, Lk 8:41
said to all, "If anyone would **c** after me, Lk 9:23
when they had **c** down from the Lk 9:37
us to tell fire to **c** down from heaven and Lk 9:54
'The kingdom of God has **c** near to you.' Lk 10:9
that the kingdom of God has **c** near.' Lk 10:11
spend, I will repay you when I **c** back.' Lk 10:35
be your name. Your kingdom **c**. Lk 11:2

the kingdom of God has **c** upon you.	Lk 11:20
for their master to **c** home from the	Lk 12:36
at table, and he will **c** and serve them.	Lk 12:37
of that servant will **c** on a day when	Lk 12:46
you think that I have **c** to give peace on	Lk 12:51
years now I have **c** seeking fruit on this	Lk 13:7
C on those days and be healed, and not	Lk 13:14
you, 'I do not know where you **c** from.'	Lk 13:25
you, I do not know where you **c** from.	Lk 13:27
And people will **c** from east and west,	Lk 13:29
invited you both will **c** and say to you,	Lk 14:9
invited, '**C**, for everything is now ready.'	Lk 14:17
a wife, and therefore I cannot **c**.'	Lk 14:20
and hedges and compel people to **c** in,	Lk 14:23
his own cross and **c** after me cannot be	Lk 14:27
he said to him, 'Your brother has **c**,	Lk 15:27
lest they also **c** into this place of	Lk 16:28
"Temptations to sin are sure to **c**,	Lk 17:1
woe to the one through whom they **c**!	Lk 17:1
to him when he has **c** in from the field,	Lk 17:7
the field, '**C** at once and recline at table'?	Lk 17:7
when the kingdom of God would **c**,	Lk 17:20
house, not **c** down to take them away,	Lk 17:31
him, saying, "Let the children **c** to me,	Lk 18:16
will have treasure in heaven; and **c**,	Lk 18:22
time, and in the age to **c** eternal life."	Lk 18:30
to him, "Zacchaeus, hurry and **c** down,	Lk 19:5
"Today salvation has **c** to this house,	Lk 19:9
to them, 'Engage in business until I **c**.'	Lk 19:13
For the days will **c** upon you, when	Lk 19:43
He will **c** and destroy those tenants and	Lk 20:16
the days will **c** when there will not be left	Lk 21:6
led astray. For many will **c** in my name,	Lk 21:8
know that its desolation has **c** near.	Lk 21:20
As soon as they **c** out in leaf, you see for	Lk 21:30
and that day **c** upon you suddenly like	Lk 21:34
For it will **c** upon all who dwell on the	Lk 21:35
and elders, who had **c** out against him,	Lk 22:52
"Have you **c** out as against a robber,	Lk 22:52
me when you **c** into your kingdom."	Lk 23:42
The women who had **c** with him from	Lk 23:55
"**C** and you will see." So they came and	Jn 1:39
"Can anything good **c** out of Nazareth?"	Jn 1:46
Philip said to him, "**C** and see."	Jn 1:46
to do with me? My hour has not yet **c**."	Jn 2:4
know that you are a teacher **c** from God,	Jn 3:2
judgment: the light has **c** into the world,	Jn 3:19
hates the light and does not **c** to the light,	Jn 3:20
thirsty or have to **c** here to draw water."	Jn 4:15
her, "Go, call your husband, and **c** here."	Jn 4:16
"**C**, see a man who told me all that I ever	Jn 4:29
heard that Jesus had **c** from Judea to	Jn 4:47
and asked him to **c** down and heal his	Jn 4:47
him, "Sir, **c** down before my child dies."	Jn 4:49
did when he had **c** from Judea to Galilee.	Jn 4:54
He does not **c** into judgment, but has	Jn 5:24
and **c** out, those who have done good to	Jn 5:29
yet you refuse to **c** to me that you may	Jn 5:40
I have **c** in my Father's name, and you do	Jn 5:43
the Prophet who is to **c** into the world!"	Jn 6:14
they were about to **c** and take him by	Jn 6:15
dark, and Jesus had not yet **c** to them.	Jn 6:17
to him, "Rabbi, when did you **c** here?"	Jn 6:25
All that the Father gives me will **c** to me,	Jn 6:37
For I have **c** down from heaven, not to do	Jn 6:38
now say, 'I have **c** down from heaven'?"	Jn 6:42
No one can **c** to me unless the Father	Jn 6:44
you that no one can **c** to me unless it is	Jn 6:65
we have believed, and have **c** to know,	Jn 6:69
Jesus said to them, "My time has not yet **c**,	Jn 7:6
this feast, for my time has not yet fully **c**."	Jn 7:8
know me, and you know where I **c** from?	Jn 7:28
from? But I have not **c** of my own accord.	Jn 7:28
I know him, for I **c** from him, and he sent	Jn 7:29
on him, because his hour had not yet **c**.	Jn 7:30
not find me. Where I am you cannot **c**."	Jn 7:34
me,' and, 'Where I am you cannot **c**'?"	Jn 7:36
thirsts, let him **c** to me and drink.	Jn 7:37
said, "Is the Christ to **c** from Galilee?	Jn 7:41
do not know where I **c** from or where I	Jn 8:14
him, because his hour had not yet **c**.	Jn 8:20
sin. Where I am going, you cannot **c**."	Jn 8:21
says, 'Where I am going, you cannot **c**'?"	Jn 8:22
of the Jews had **c** to Martha and Mary	Jn 11:19
Now Jesus had not yet **c** into the village,	Jn 11:30
the Jews who had **c** with her also	Jn 11:33
They said to him, "Lord, **c** and see."	Jn 11:34
out with a loud voice, "Lazarus, **c** out."	Jn 11:43
who had **c** with Mary and had seen	Jn 11:45
and the Romans will **c** and take away	Jn 11:48
That he will not **c** to the feast at all?"	Jn 11:56
large crowd that had **c** to the feast heard	Jn 12:12
"The hour has **c** for the Son of Man to	Jn 12:23
for this purpose I have **c** to this hour.	Jn 12:27
"This voice has **c** for your sake,	Jn 12:30
I have **c** into the world as light, so that	Jn 12:46
for I did not **c** to judge the world but to	Jn 12:47
knew that his hour had **c** to depart out of	Jn 13:1
and that he had **c** from God and was	Jn 13:3
you, 'Where I am going you cannot **c**.'	Jn 13:33
I will **c** again and will take you to myself,	Jn 14:3
not leave you as orphans; I will **c** to you.	Jn 14:18
and we will **c** to him and make our	Jn 14:23
'I am going away, and I will **c** to you.'	Jn 14:28
If I had not **c** and spoken to them, they	Jn 15:22
not go away, the Helper will not **c** to you.	Jn 16:7
declare to you the things that are to **c**.	Jn 16:13
she has sorrow because her hour has **c**,	Jn 16:21
the Father and have **c** into the world,	Jn 16:28
the hour is coming, indeed it has **c**,	Jn 16:32
heaven, and said, "Father, the hour has **c**;	Jn 17:1
received them and have **c** to know in	Jn 17:8
in the temple, where all Jews **c** together.	Jn 18:20
this purpose I have **c** into the world—	Jn 18:37
also, who earlier had **c** to Jesus by night,	Jn 19:39
"**C** and have breakfast." Now none of	Jn 21:12
"If it is my will that he remain until I **c**,	Jn 21:22
"If it is my will that he remain until I **c**,	Jn 21:23
So when they had **c** together, they asked	Acts 1:6
when the Holy Spirit has **c** upon you,	Acts 1:8
will **c** in the same way as you saw him	Acts 1:11
And it shall **c** to pass that everyone	Acts 2:21
of refreshing may **c** from the presence	Acts 3:20
them, wondering what this would **c** to.	Acts 5:24
after that they shall **c** out and worship	Acts 7:7
and I have **c** down to deliver them.	Acts 7:34
And now **c**, I will send you to Egypt.'	Acts 7:34
what you have said may **c** upon me."	Acts 8:24
He had **c** to Jerusalem to worship	Acts 8:27
he invited Philip to **c** up and sit with	Acts 8:31
a man named Ananias **c** in and lay	Acts 9:12
And has he not **c** here for this purpose,	Acts 9:21
And when he had **c** to Jerusalem, he	Acts 9:26
him, "Please **c** to us without delay."	Acts 9:38
vision an angel of God **c** in and say to	Acts 10:3
to send for you to **c** to his house and	Acts 10:22
and you have been kind enough to **c**.	Acts 10:33
circumcised who had **c** with Peter	Acts 10:45
to those who had **c** up with him from	Acts 13:31
said in the Prophets should **c** about:	Acts 13:40
"The gods have **c** down to us in the	Acts 14:11
good to us, having **c** to one accord,	Acts 15:25
And when they had **c** up to Mysia, they	Acts 16:7
"**C** over to Macedonia and help us."	Acts 16:9
to the women who had **c** together.	Acts 16:13
c to my house and stay." And she	Acts 16:15
of Jesus Christ to **c** out of her." And	Acts 16:18
Therefore **c** out now and go in peace."	Acts 16:36
Let them **c** themselves and take us	Acts 16:37
world upside down have **c** here also,	Acts 17:6
Silas and Timothy to **c** to him as	Acts 17:15
recently **c** from Italy with his wife	Acts 18:2
in the one who was to **c** after him,	Acts 19:4
trade of ours may **c** into disrepute but	Acts 19:27
not know why they had **c** together.	Acts 19:32
the elders of the church to **c** to him.	Acts 20:17
fierce wolves will **c** in among you,	Acts 20:29
When we had **c** in sight of Cyprus,	Acts 21:3
When we had **c** to Jerusalem, the	Acts 21:17
will certainly hear that you have **c**.	Acts 21:22
When they had **c** to Caesarea and	Acts 23:33
Jews who had **c** down from Jerusalem	Acts 25:7
and Moses said would **c** to pass:	Acts 26:22
When the fourteenth night had **c**, as	Acts 27:27
the stern and prayed for day to **c**.	Acts 27:29
time and saw no misfortune **c** to him,	Acts 28:6
have often intended to **c** to you (but	Rom 1:13
And why not do evil that good may **c**?—	Rom 3:8
the world did not **c** through the law	Rom 4:13
was a type of the one who was to **c**.	Rom 5:14
nor things present nor things to **c**,	Rom 8:38
trespass salvation has **c** to the	Rom 11:11
partial hardening has **c** upon Israel,	Rom 11:25
the fullness of the Gentiles has **c** in.	Rom 11:25
"The Deliverer will **c** from Zion,	Rom 11:26
that the hour has **c** for you to wake	Rom 13:11
Isaiah says, "The root of Jesse will **c**,	Rom 15:12
longed for many years to **c** to you,	Rom 15:23
if the Gentiles have **c** to share in their	Rom 15:27
I know that when I **c** to you I will	Rom 15:29
come to you I will **c** in the fullness of	Rom 15:29
by God's will I may **c** to you with joy	Rom 15:32
did not **c** proclaiming to you the	1 Cor 2:1
But I will **c** to you soon, if the Lord	1 Cor 4:19
Shall I **c** to you with a rod, or with	1 Cor 4:21
to prayer; but then **c** together again,	1 Cor 7:5
on whom the end of the ages has **c**.	1 Cor 10:11
because when you **c** together it is	1 Cor 11:17
when you **c** together as a church,	1 Cor 11:18
When you **c** together, it is not the	1 Cor 11:20
brothers, when you **c** together to eat,	1 Cor 11:33
so that when you **c** together it will	1 Cor 11:34
I will give directions when I **c**.	1 Cor 11:34
if I **c** to you speaking in tongues,	1 Cor 14:6
When you **c** together, each one has	1 Cor 14:26
a man has **c** also the resurrection	1 Cor 15:21
With what kind of body do they **c**?"	1 Cor 15:35
you sow does not **c** to life unless it	1 Cor 15:36
then shall **c** to pass the saying that	1 Cor 15:54
there will be no collecting when I **c**.	1 Cor 16:2
it was not at all his will to **c** now.	1 Cor 16:12
He will **c** when he has opportunity.	1 Cor 16:12
let him be accursed. Our Lord, **c**!	1 Cor 16:22
sure of this, I wanted to **c** to you first,	2 Cor 1:15
and to **c** back to you from	2 Cor 1:16
once had glory has **c** to have no glory	2 Cor 3:10
passed away; behold, the new has **c**.	2 Cor 5:17
if some Macedonians **c** with me and	2 Cor 9:4
We were the first to **c** all the way to	2 Cor 10:14
the third time I am ready to **c** to you.	2 Cor 12:14
that perhaps when I **c** I may find	2 Cor 12:20
fear that when I **c** again my God	2 Cor 12:21
that if I **c** again I will not spare them	2 Cor 13:2
that when I **c** I may not have to be	2 Cor 13:10
of Abraham might **c** to the Gentiles,	Gal 3:14
the offspring should **c** to whom the	Gal 3:19
But now that faith has **c**, we are no	Gal 3:25
But when the fullness of time had **c**, God	Gal 4:4
But now that you have **c** to know God, or	Gal 4:9
only in this age but also in the one to **c**.	Eph 1:21
Let no corrupting talk **c** out of your	Eph 4:29
so that whether I **c** and see you or am	Phil 1:27
Lord that shortly I myself will **c** also.	Phil 2:24
which has **c** to you, as indeed in the	Col 1:6
These are a shadow of the things to **c**,	Col 2:17
who delivers us from the wrath to **c**.	1 Thes 1:10
But God's wrath has **c** upon them at	1 Thes 2:16
because we wanted to **c** to you—I,	1 Thes 2:18
affliction, just as it has **c** to pass,	1 Thes 3:4
now that Timothy has **c** to us from	1 Thes 3:6
day of the Lord will **c** like a thief in	1 Thes 5:2
sudden destruction will **c** upon them	1 Thes 5:3
as labor pains **c** upon a pregnant	1 Thes 5:3
effect that the day of the Lord has **c**.	2 Thes 2:2
For that day will not **c**, unless the	2 Thes 2:3
be saved and to **c** to the knowledge of	1 Tm 2:4
I hope to **c** to you soon, but I am	1 Tm 3:14
the present life and also for the life to **c**.	1 Tm 4:8
Until I **c**, devote yourself to the public	1 Tm 4:13
days there will **c** times of difficulty.	2 Tm 3:1
and the time of my departure has **c**.	2 Tm 4:6
Do your best to **c** to me soon.	2 Tm 4:9
When you **c**, bring the cloak that I	2 Tm 4:13
Do your best to **c** before winter.	2 Tm 4:21
you, do your best to **c** to me at Nicopolis,	Ti 3:12
angels that God subjected the world to **c**,	Heb 2:5
of God and the powers of the age to **c**,	Heb 6:5
priest of the good things that have **c**,	Heb 9:11
the good things to **c** instead of the true	Heb 10:1
I said, 'Behold, I have **c** to do your will,	Heb 10:7
I have **c** to do your will." He abolishes	Heb 10:9
the coming one will **c** and will not	Heb 10:37
For you have not **c** to what may be	Heb 12:18
But you have **c** to Mount Zion and to	Heb 12:22
city, but we seek the city that is to **c**.	Heb 13:14
Those who **c** from Italy send you	Heb 13:24
the same mouth **c** blessing and cursing.	Jas 3:10
C now, you who say, "Today or	Jas 4:13
C now, you rich, weep and howl for the	Jas 5:1
As you **c** to him, a living stone rejected	1 Pt 2:4
that scoffers will **c** in the last days with	2 Pt 3:3
the day of the Lord will **c** like a thief,	2 Pt 3:10
we know that we have **c** to know him,	1 Jn 2:3
so now many antichrists have **c**.	1 Jn 2:18
that Jesus Christ has **c** in the flesh is	1 Jn 4:2
So we have **c** to know and to believe the	1 Jn 4:16
the Son of God has **c** and has given us	1 Jn 5:20
Instead I hope to **c** to you and talk face	2 Jn 1:12
So if I **c**, I will bring up what he is	3 Jn 1:10
him who is and who was and who is to **c**,	Rv 1:4
God, "who is and who was and who is to **c**,	Rv 1:8
I will **c** to you and remove your	Rv 2:5
I will **c** to you soon and war against	Rv 2:16
Only hold fast what you have until I **c**.	Rv 2:25
you will not wake up, I will **c** like a thief,	Rv 3:3
know at what hour I will **c** against you.	Rv 3:3
I will make them **c** and bow down before	Rv 3:9
door, I will **c** in to him and eat with him,	Rv 3:20
to me like a trumpet, said, "**C** up here,	Rv 4:1
Almighty, who was and is and is to **c**!"	Rv 4:8
say with a voice like thunder, "**C**!"	Rv 6:1
heard the second living creature say, "**C**!"	Rv 6:3
living creature say, "**C**!" And I looked,	Rv 6:5
of the fourth living creature say, "**C**!"	Rv 6:7
for the great day of their wrath has **c**,	Rv 6:17

robes, and from where have they **c**?" Rv 7:13
passed; behold, two woes are still to **c**. Rv 9:12
"**C** up here!" And they went up to Rv 11:12
behold, the third woe is soon to **c**. Rv 11:14
and the authority of his Christ have **c**, Rv 12:10
for the devil has **c** down to you in great Rv 12:12
even making fire **c** down from heaven Rv 13:13
because the hour of his judgment has **c**, Rv 14:7
and reap, for the hour to reap has **c**, Rv 14:15
holy. All nations will **c** and worship you, Rv 15:4
"**C**, I will show you the judgment of the Rv 17:1
because it was and is not and is to **c**. Rv 17:8
fallen, one is, the other has not yet **c**, Rv 17:10
and when he does **c** he must remain Rv 17:10
voice from heaven saying, "**C** out of her, Rv 18:4
reason her plagues will **c** in a single day, Rv 18:8
in a single hour your judgment has **c**." Rv 18:10
for the marriage of the Lamb has **c**, Rv 19:7
"**C**, gather for the great supper of God, Rv 19:17
of the dead did not **c** to life until the Rv 20:5
and will **c** out to deceive the nations that Rv 20:8
me, saying, "**C**, I will show you the Bride, Rv 21:9
say, "**C**." And let the one who hears say, Rv 22:17
"**C**." And let the one who is thirsty Rv 22:17
And let the one who is thirsty **c**; Rv 22:17
coming soon." Amen. **C**, Lord Jesus! Rv 22:20

COMES (287)

Let the virgin who **c** out to draw water, Gn 24:43
"If Esau **c** to the one camp and attacks Gn 32:8
to one another, "Here **c** this dreamer. Gn 37:19
unless your youngest brother **c** here. Gn 42:15
So now there **c** a reckoning for his Gn 42:22
your youngest brother **c** down with Gn 44:23
between his feet, until tribute **c** to him; Gn 49:10
give birth before the midwife **c** to them." Ex 1:19
If he **c** in single, he shall go out single; if Ex 21:3
he shall go out single; if he **c** in married, Ex 21:3
before the LORD, and when he **c** out, Ex 28:35
who **c** into the tent of meeting to Ex 29:30
is hidden from him, when he **c** to know it, Lv 5:3
is hidden from him, when he **c** to know it, Lv 5:4
that could be eaten, on which water **c**, Lv 11:34
of the boil there **c** a white swelling or Lv 13:19
"But if the priest **c** and looks, and if the Lv 14:48
on which the semen **c** shall be washed Lv 15:17
her menstrual impurity **c** upon him, Lv 15:24
Holy Place until he **c** out and has made Lv 16:17
And if any outsider **c** near, he shall be Nm 1:51
But if any outsider **c** near, he shall be Nm 3:10
the spirit of jealousy **c** over him and he Nm 5:14
the spirit of jealousy **c** over him and he Nm 5:14
the spirit of jealousy **c** over a man and Nm 5:30
until it **c** out at your nostrils and Nm 11:20
eaten away when he **c** out of his Nm 12:12
Everyone who **c** near, who comes Nm 17:13
who **c** near to the tabernacle of the Nm 17:13
and any outsider who **c** near shall be Nm 18:7
everyone who **c** into the tent and Nm 19:14
the day that her husband **c** to hear of it, Nm 30:8
the jubilee of the people of Israel **c**, Nm 36:4
by every word that **c** from the mouth of Dt 8:3
sign or wonder that he tells you **c** to pass, Dt 13:2
of your seed that **c** from the field year Dt 14:22
"And if a Levite **c** from any of your Dt 18:6
but when evening **c**, he shall bathe Dt 23:11
her afterbirth that **c** out from between Dt 28:57
and the foreigner who **c** from a far land, Dt 29:22
when all Israel **c** to appear before the Dt 31:11
For their vine **c** from the vine of Sodom Dt 32:32
is at hand, and their doom **c** swiftly.' Dt 32:35
of Egypt, and **c** to its end at the sea. Jos 15:4
Then the boundary **c** to an end at the Jos 15:11
the tent, and if any man **c** and asks you, Jgs 4:20
then whatever **c** out from the doors of Jgs 11:31
eat of anything that **c** from the vine, Jgs 13:14
is held in honor; all that he says **c** true. 1 Sm 9:6
For the people will not eat till he **c**, 1 Sm 9:13
we will not sit down till he **c** here." 1 Sm 16:11
'Out of the wicked **c** wickedness.' 1 Sm 24:13
And when your father **c** to see you, 2 Sm 13:5
wilderness until word **c** from you to 2 Sm 15:28
you as a bride **c** home to her 2 Sm 17:3
a good man and **c** with good news." 2 Sm 18:27
take an oath and **c** and swears his 1 Kgs 8:31
c from a far country for your name's 1 Kgs 8:41
when he **c** and prays toward this 1 Kgs 8:42
a lamp, so that whenever he **c** to us, 2 Kgs 4:10
Look, when the messenger **c**, shut the 2 Kgs 6:32
then, as soon as this letter **c** to you, 2 Kgs 10:2
when he goes out and when he **c** in." 2 Kgs 11:8
the LORD, for he **c** to judge the earth. 1 Chr 16:33
your holy name **c** from your hand 1 Chr 29:16
take an oath and **c** and swears his 2 Chr 6:22
c from a far country for the sake of 2 Chr 6:32
when he **c** and prays toward this 2 Chr 6:32

Whoever **c** for ordination with a 2 Chr 13:9
whenever a case **c** to you from your 2 Chr 19:10
'If disaster **c** upon us, the sword, 2 Chr 20:9
the king when he **c** in and when he 2 Chr 23:7
who long for death, but it **c** not, and dig Jb 3:21
For my sighing **c** instead of my bread, Jb 3:24
For the thing that I fear **c** upon me, and Jb 3:25
am I quiet; I have no rest, but trouble **c**." Jb 3:26
and shall not fear destruction when it **c**. Jb 5:21
He **c** out like a flower and withers; he Jb 14:2
It is drawn forth and **c** out of his body; Jb 20:25
the glittering point **c** out of his Jb 20:25
out? That their calamity **c** upon them? Jb 21:17
hear his cry when distress **c** upon him? Jb 27:9
As for the earth, out of it **c** bread, but Jb 28:5
the rumbling that **c** from his mouth. Jb 37:2
From its chamber **c** the whirlwind, and Jb 37:9
Out of the north **c** golden splendor; God Jb 37:22
Out of his nostrils **c** forth smoke, as Jb 41:20
and a flame **c** forth from his mouth. Jb 41:21
which **c** out like a bridegroom leaving Ps 19:5
From you **c** my praise in the great Ps 22:25
the night, but joy **c** with the morning. Ps 30:5
And when one **c** to see me, he utters Ps 41:6
Our God **c**; he does not keep silence; Ps 50:3
in silence; from him **c** my salvation. Ps 62:1
and not from the wilderness **c** lifting up, Ps 75:6
a wind that passes and **c** not again. Ps 78:39
in the morning my prayer **c** before you. Ps 88:13
before the LORD, for he **c**, for he comes to Ps 96:13
for he comes, for he **c** to judge the earth. Ps 96:13
the LORD, for he **c** to judge the earth. Ps 98:9
Blessed is he who **c** in the name of the Ps 118:26
My help **c** from the LORD, who made Ps 121:2
and your calamity **c** like a whirlwind, Prv 1:27
or of the ruin of the wicked, when it **c**, Prv 3:25
When pride **c**, then comes disgrace, but Prv 11:2
When pride comes, then **c** disgrace, but Prv 11:2
but evil **c** to him who searches for it. Prv 11:27
work of a man's hand **c** back to him. Prv 12:14
he who opens wide his lips **c** to ruin. Prv 13:3
By insolence **c** nothing but strife, but Prv 13:10
the mouth of a fool **c** a rod for his back, Prv 14:3
wisdom, and humility **c** before honor. Prv 15:33
When wickedness **c**, contempt comes Prv 18:3
wickedness comes, contempt **c** also, Prv 18:3
also, and with dishonor **c** disgrace. Prv 18:3
haughty, but humility **c** before honor. Prv 18:12
until the other **c** and examines him. Prv 18:17
everyone who is hasty **c** only to poverty. Prv 21:5
sweetness of a friend **c** from his earnest Prv 27:9
A generation goes, and a generation **c**, Eccl 1:4
can the man do who **c** after the king? Eccl 2:12
For a dream **c** with much business, and Eccl 5:3
For it **c** in vanity and goes in darkness, Eccl 6:4
the way the spirit **c** to the bones in Eccl 11:5
will be many. All that **c** is vanity. Eccl 11:8
Behold, he **c**, leaping over the mountains, Sg 2:8
Behold, the day of the LORD **c**, cruel, with Is 13:9
laid low, no woodcutter **c** up against us.' Is 14:8
For smoke **c** out of the north, and there Is 14:31
when he **c** to his sanctuary to pray, Is 16:12
is riding on a swift cloud and **c** to Egypt; Is 19:1
Negeb sweep on, it **c** from the wilderness, Is 21:1
The watchman says: "Morning **c**, and Is 21:12
When the report **c** to Egypt, they will be Is 23:5
This also **c** from the LORD of hosts; he is Is 28:29
everyone **c** to shame through a people Is 30:5
to collapse, whose breaking **c** suddenly, Is 30:13
the name of the LORD **c** from afar, Is 30:27
fills it; the world, and all that **c** from it. Is 34:1
Behold, the Lord GOD **c** with might, and Is 40:10
spread out the earth and what **c** from it, Is 42:5
of Zion, "Behold, your salvation **c**; Is 62:11
Who is this who **c** from Edom, in Is 63:1
a wind too full for this **c** for me. Now it is Jer 4:12
Behold, he **c** up like clouds; his chariots Jer 4:13
so, but what will you do when the end **c**? Jer 5:31
to me is frankincense that **c** from Sheba, Jer 6:20
A voice, a rumor! Behold, it **c**!—a great Jer 10:22
stream, and does not fear when heat **c**, Jer 17:8
until the time of his own land **c**. Jer 27:7
when the word of that prophet **c** to pass, Jer 28:9
"Behold, a people **c** from the north; a Jer 50:41
when a report **c** in one year and Jer 51:46
GOD: Disaster after disaster! Behold, it **c**. Ezk 7:5
has awakened against you. Behold, it **c**. Ezk 7:6
"Behold, the day! Behold, it **c**! Your Ezk 7:10
When anguish **c**, they will seek peace, Ezk 7:25
Disaster **c** upon disaster; rumor follows Ezk 7:26
long, and every vision **c** to nothing'? Ezk 12:22
before his face, and yet **c** to the prophet, Ezk 14:4
answer him as he **c** with the multitude Ezk 14:4
and yet **c** to a prophet to consult me Ezk 14:7
his right hand **c** the divination for Ezk 21:22

This also shall not be, until he **c**, the Ezk 21:27
When this **c**, then you will know that Ezk 24:24
day of Egypt's doom; for, behold, it **c**! Ezk 30:9
and the sword **c** and takes him away, Ezk 33:4
and the sword **c** and takes any one of Ezk 33:6
what the word is that **c** from the LORD.' Ezk 33:30
When this **c**—and come it will!— Ezk 33:33
But he who **c** against him shall do as Dn 11:16
power of the holy people **c** to an end all Dn 12:7
cypress; from me **c** your fruit. Hos 14:8
as destruction from the Almighty it **c**. Jl 1:15
the great and awesome day of the LORD **c**. Jl 2:31
so that destruction **c** upon the fortress. Am 5:9
nations, to whom the house of Israel **c**! Am 6:1
When the Assyrian **c** into our land and Mi 5:5
the Assyrian when he **c** into our land and Mi 5:6
chaff—before there **c** upon you the Zep 2:2
before there **c** upon you the day of the Zep 2:2
the great and awesome day of the LORD **c**. Mal 4:5
by every word that **c** from the mouth of Mt 4:4
anything more than this **c** from evil. Mt 5:37
he goes, and to another, 'Come,' and he **c**, Mt 8:9
towns of Israel before the Son of Man **c**. Mt 10:23
And when it **c**, it finds the house empty, Mt 12:44
the evil one **c** and snatches away what Mt 13:19
a person, but what **c** out of the mouth; Mt 15:11
But what **c** out of the mouth proceeds Mt 15:18
a hook and take the first fish that **c** up, Mt 17:27
to the one by whom the temptation **c**! Mt 18:7
Blessed is he who **c** in the name of the Mt 21:9
therefore the owner of the vineyard **c**, Mt 21:40
'Blessed is he who **c** in the name of the Mt 23:39
For as the lightning **c** from the east Mt 24:27
master will find so doing when he **c**. Mt 24:46
"When the Son of Man **c** in his glory, Mt 25:31
And if this **c** to the governor's ears, we Mt 28:14
"After me **c** he who is mightier than I, Mk 1:7
Satan immediately **c** and takes away Mk 4:15
"What **c** out of a person is what defiles Mk 7:20
be ashamed when he **c** in the glory of Mk 8:38
Blessed is he who **c** in the name of the Mk 11:9
Everyone who **c** to me and hears my Lk 6:47
he goes; and to another, 'Come,' and he **c**; Lk 7:8
Then the devil **c** and takes away the Lk 8:12
be ashamed when he **c** in his glory and Lk 9:26
And when it **c**, it finds the house swept Lk 11:25
to him at once when he **c** and knocks. Lk 12:36
the master finds awake when he **c**. Lk 12:37
If he **c** in the second watch, or in the Lk 12:38
master will find so doing when he **c**. Lk 12:43
'Blessed is he who **c** in the name of the Lk 13:35
so that when your host **c** he may say to Lk 14:10
"If anyone **c** to me and does not hate Lk 14:26
to meet him who **c** against him with Lk 14:31
And when he **c** home, he calls together Lk 15:6
Nevertheless, when the Son of Man **c**, Lk 18:8
is the King who **c** in the name of Lk 19:38
the vine until the kingdom of God **c**." Lk 22:18
said, 'He who **c** after me ranks before me, Jn 1:15
even he who **c** after me, the strap of Jn 1:27
'After me **c** a man who ranks before me, Jn 1:30
do not know where it **c** from or where it Jn 3:8
whoever does what is true **c** to the light, Jn 3:21
He who **c** from above is above all. He Jn 3:31
way. He who **c** from heaven is above all. Jn 3:31
When he **c**, he will tell us all things." Jn 4:25
are yet four months, then **c** the harvest'? Jn 4:35
If another **c** in his own name, you will Jn 5:43
seek the glory that **c** from the only God? Jn 5:44
God is he who **c** down from heaven and Jn 6:33
whoever **c** to me shall not hunger, and Jn 6:35
and whoever **c** to me I will never cast out. Jn 6:37
and learned from the Father **c** to me— Jn 6:45
is the bread that **c** down from heaven, Jn 6:50
But we know where this man **c** from, and Jn 7:27
no one will know where he **c** from." Jn 7:27
said that the Christ **c** from the offspring Jn 7:42
of David, and **c** from Bethlehem, Jn 7:42
man, we do not know where he **c** from." Jn 9:29
You do not know where he **c** from, and Jn 9:30
The thief **c** only to steal and kill and Jn 10:10
Blessed is he who **c** in the name of the Jn 12:13
loved the glory that **c** from man more Jn 12:43
more than the glory that **c** from God. Jn 12:43
No one **c** to the Father except through Jn 14:6
"But when the Helper **c**, whom I will Jn 15:26
when their hour **c** you may remember Jn 16:4
And when he **c**, he will convict the world Jn 16:8
When the Spirit of truth **c**, he will guide Jn 16:13
to blood, before the day of the Lord **c**, Acts 2:20
ready to kill him before he **c** near." Acts 23:15
"When Lysias the tribune **c** down, Acts 24:22
I have had the help that **c** from God, Acts 26:22
through the law **c** knowledge of sin. Rom 3:20
of the righteousness that **c** from God, Rom 10:3

So faith **c** from hearing, and hearing Rom 10:17
before the time, before the Lord **c**, 1 Cor 4:5
proclaim the Lord's death until he **c**. 1 Cor 11:26
but when the perfect **c**, the partial 1 Cor 13:10
the whole church **c** together and all 1 Cor 14:23
Then **c** the end, when he delivers the 1 Cor 15:24
When Timothy **c**, see that you put 1 Cor 16:10
For this **c** from the Lord who is the 2 Cor 3:18
For if someone **c** and proclaims 2 Cor 11:4
For if the inheritance **c** by the law, it no Gal 3:18
by the law, it no longer **c** by promise; Gal 3:18
the wrath of God **c** upon the sons of Eph 5:6
of righteousness that **c** through Jesus Phil 1:11
of my own that **c** from the law, Phil 3:9
but that which **c** through faith in Phil 3:9
received instructions—if he **c** to you, Col 4:10
when he **c** on that day to be glorified 2 Thes 1:10
not come, unless the rebellion **c** first, 2 Thes 2:3
to die once, and after that **c** judgment, Heb 9:27
of the righteousness that **c** by faith. Heb 11:7
whom I shall see you if he **c** soon. Heb 13:23
and fine clothing **c** into your assembly, Jas 2:2
a poor man in shabby clothing also **c** in, Jas 2:2
not the wisdom that **c** down from above, Jas 3:15
the fiery trial when it **c** upon you to test 1 Pt 4:12
of Scripture **c** from someone's 2 Pt 1:20
If anyone **c** to you and does not bring 2 Jn 1:10
which **c** down from my God out of Rv 3:12
From his mouth **c** a sharp sword with Rv 19:15

COMFORT (48)
and all his daughters rose up to **c** him, Gn 37:35
and his brothers came to **c** him. 1 Chr 7:22
come to show him sympathy and **c** him. Jb 2:11
This would be my **c**; I would even exult Jb 6:10
When I say, 'My bed will **c** me, my Jb 7:13
to my words, and let this be your **c**. Jb 21:2
How then will you **c** me with empty Jb 21:34
me; your rod and your staff, they **c** me. Ps 23:4
increase my greatness and **c** me again. Ps 71:21
This is my **c** in my affliction, that Ps 119:50
of your rules from of old, I take **c**, Ps 119:52
your steadfast love **c** me according to Ps 119:76
promise; I ask, "When will you **c** me?" Ps 119:82
and they had no one to **c** them! Eccl 4:1
power, and there was no one to **c** them. Eccl 4:1
anger turned away, that you might **c** me. Is 12:1
do not labor to **c** me concerning the Is 22:4
C, comfort my people, says your God. Is 40:1
Comfort, **c** my people, says your God. Is 40:1
famine and sword; who will **c** you? Is 51:19
lead him and restore **c** to him and his Is 57:18
of our God; to **c** all who mourn; Is 61:2
his mother comforts, so I will **c** you; Is 66:13
for the mourner, to **c** him for the dead, Jer 16:7
I will **c** them, and give them gladness Jer 31:13
all her lovers she has none to **c** her; Lam 1:2
her hands, but there is none to **c** her; Lam 1:17
groaning, yet there is no one to **c** me. Lam 1:21
can I liken to you, that I may **c** you, Lam 2:13
the LORD will again **c** Zion and again Zec 1:17
the Lord and in the **c** of the Holy Spirit, Acts 9:31
the Father of mercies and God of all **c**, 2 Cor 1:3
we may be able to **c** those who are in 2 Cor 1:4
with the **c** with which we ourselves are 2 Cor 1:4
Christ we share abundantly in **c** too. 2 Cor 1:5
afflicted, it is for your **c** and salvation; 2 Cor 1:6
and if we are comforted, it is for your **c**, 2 Cor 1:6
sufferings, you will also share in our **c**. 2 Cor 1:7
rather turn to forgive and **c** him, 2 Cor 2:7
great pride in you; I am filled with **c**. 2 Cor 7:4
but also by the **c** with which he was 2 Cor 7:7
And besides our own **c**, we rejoiced 2 Cor 7:13
Aim for restoration, **c** one another, 2 Cor 13:11
in Christ, any **c** from love, Phil 2:1
of God, and they have been a **c** to me. Col 4:11
and gave us eternal **c** and good hope 2 Thes 2:16
c your hearts and establish them in 2 Thes 2:17
much joy and **c** from your love, Phlm 1:7

COMFORTED (27)
So Isaac was **c** after his mother's death. Gn 24:67
him, but he refused to be **c** and said, Gn 37:35
When Judah was **c**, he went up to Gn 38:12
little ones." Thus he **c** them and spoke Gn 50:21
for you have **c** me and spoken kindly to Ru 2:13
Then David **c** his wife, Bathsheba, 2 Sm 12:24
because he was **c** about Amnon, 2 Sm 13:39
him sympathy and **c** him for all Jb 42:11
wearying; my soul refuses to be **c**. Ps 77:2
you, LORD, have helped me and **c** me. Ps 86:17
for the LORD has **c** his people and will Is 49:13
Jerusalem, for the LORD has **c** his people; Is 52:9
"O afflicted one, storm-tossed and not **c**, Is 54:11
you; you shall be **c** in Jerusalem. Is 66:13
she refuses to be **c** for her children, Jer 31:15
water, were **c** in the world below. Ezk 31:16
he will be **c** for all his multitude, Ezk 32:31
she refused to be **c**, because they are no Mt 2:18
are those who mourn, for they shall be **c**. Mt 5:4
but now he is **c** here, and you are in Lk 16:25
away alive, and were not a little **c**. Acts 20:12
with which we ourselves are **c** by God. 2 Cor 1:4
and if we are **c**, it is for your comfort, 2 Cor 1:6
downcast, **c** us by the coming of Titus, 2 Cor 7:6
comfort with which he was **c** by you, 2 Cor 7:7
Therefore we are **c**. And besides our 2 Cor 7:13
we have been **c** about you through 1 Thes 3:7

COMFORTER (2)
her fall is terrible; she has no **c**. Lam 1:9
for a **c** is far from me, one to revive my Lam 1:16

COMFORTERS (5)
because David has sent **c** to you, 2 Sm 10:3
because David has sent **c** to you, 1 Chr 19:3
such things; miserable **c** are you all. Jb 16:2
for pity, but there was none, and for **c**, Ps 69:20
for her? Where shall I seek **c** for you? Na 3:7

COMFORTING (1)
answered gracious and **c** words to the Zec 1:13

COMFORTS (9)
your brother Esau **c** himself about Gn 27:42
Are the **c** of God too small for you, or Jb 15:11
his troops, like one who **c** mourners. Jb 29:25
For the LORD **c** Zion; he comforts all her Is 51:3
he **c** all her waste places and makes her Is 51:3
"I, I am he who **c** you; who are you that Is 51:12
As one whom his mother **c**, so I will Is 66:13
who **c** us in all our affliction, so that 2 Cor 1:4
But God, who **c** the downcast, 2 Cor 7:6

COMING (251)
men of the city are **c** out to draw water. Gn 24:13
saw, and behold, there were camels **c**. Gn 24:63
his daughter is **c** with the sheep!" Gn 29:6
brother Esau, and he is **c** to meet you, Gn 32:6
and looked, and behold, Esau was **c**, Gn 33:1
caravan of Ishmaelites **c** from Gilead, Gn 37:25
good years that are **c** and store up Gn 41:35
the present for Joseph's **c** at noon, Gn 43:25
Behold, he is **c** out to meet you, and Ex 4:14
struck down, for they are late in **c** up.) Ex 9:32
c between the host of Egypt and the Ex 14:20
the night without one **c** near the other Ex 14:20
am **c** to you with your wife and her two Ex 18:6
"Behold, I am **c** to you in a thick cloud, Ex 19:9
heard that Israel was **c** by the way of Nm 21:1
'Let nothing hinder you from **c** to me, Nm 22:16
heard of the **c** of the people of Israel. Nm 33:40
and the waters **c** down from above shall Jos 3:13
the waters **c** down from above stood and Jos 3:16
was then, for war and for going and **c**. Jos 14:11
the spies saw a man **c** out of the city, Jgs 1:24
lattice: 'Why is his chariot so long in **c**? Jgs 5:28
people are **c** down from the Jgs 9:36
people are **c** down from the center of the Jgs 9:37
one company is **c** from the direction Jgs 9:37
and saw the people **c** out of the city. Jgs 9:43
"Because Israel on **c** up from Egypt Jgs 11:13
an old man was **c** from his work in the Jgs 19:16
the woman, who is **c** into your house, Ru 4:11
the days are **c** when I will cut off your 1 Sm 2:31
they met young women **c** out to draw 1 Sm 9:11
they saw Samuel **c** out toward them 1 Sm 9:14
a group of prophets **c** down from the 1 Sm 10:5
I am **c** to you to offer burnt offerings 1 Sm 10:8
Saul was **c** from the field behind the 1 Sm 11:5
Hebrews are **c** out of the holes where 1 Sm 14:11
As they were **c** home, when David 1 Sm 18:6
Saul, "I saw the son of Jesse **c** to Nob, 1 Sm 22:9
"I see a god **c** up out of the earth." 1 Sm 28:13
And she said, "An old man is **c** up, 1 Sm 28:14
from the day of your **c** to me to this 1 Sm 29:6
to know your going out and your **c** in, 2 Sm 3:25
many people were **c** from the road 2 Sm 13:34
without **c** into the king's presence. 2 Sm 14:28
While David was **c** to the summit, 2 Sm 15:32
and his servants **c** on toward him. 2 Sm 24:20
wife of Jeroboam is **c** to inquire of 1 Kgs 14:5
him, "Men are **c** out from Samaria." 1 Kgs 20:17
When the man of God saw her **c**, he 2 Kgs 4:25
reached them, but he is not **c** back." 2 Kgs 9:18
reached them, but he is not **c** back. 2 Kgs 9:20
the son of Rechab **c** to meet him. 2 Kgs 10:15
down and your going out and **c** in, 2 Kgs 19:27
Behold, the days are **c**, when all that 2 Kgs 20:17
great multitude is **c** against you from 2 Chr 20:2
they reward us by **c** to drive us out 2 Chr 20:11
this great horde that is **c** against us. 2 Chr 20:12
those who were **c** from the war 2 Chr 28:12
I am not **c** against you this day, but 2 Chr 35:21
second year after their **c** to the house of Ezr 3:8
of the temple, for they are **c** to kill you. Neh 6:10
you. They are **c** to kill you by night." Neh 6:10
to see the calamity that is **c** to my people? Est 8:6
be told of the Lord to the **c** generation; Ps 22:30
the wicked, for he sees that his day is **c**. Ps 37:13
but tell to the **c** generation the glorious Ps 78:4
going out and your **c** in from this time Ps 121:8
What is that **c** up from the wilderness like Sg 3:6
Who is that **c** up from the wilderness, Sg 8:5
the LORD is **c** out from his place to Is 26:21
down and your going out and **c** in, Is 37:28
Behold, the days are **c**, when all that is in Is 39:6
and the time is **c** to gather all nations Is 66:18
Warn the nations that he is **c**; announce Jer 4:16
a people is **c** from the north country, Jer 6:22
Therefore, behold, the days are **c**, Jer 7:32
and crane keep the time of their **c**, Jer 8:7
"Behold, the days are **c**, declares the Jer 9:25
"Therefore, behold, the days are **c**, Jer 16:14
therefore, behold, days are **c**, declares the Jer 19:6
"Behold, the days are **c**, declares the Jer 23:5
"Therefore, behold, the days are **c**, Jer 23:7
For behold, days are **c**, declares the LORD, Jer 30:3
"Behold, the days are **c**, declares the Jer 31:27
"Behold, the days are **c**, declares the Jer 31:31
"Behold, the days are **c**, declares the Jer 31:38
They are **c** in to fight against the Jer 33:5
"Behold, the days are **c**, declares the Jer 33:14
about the **c** of Nebuchadnezzar Jer 46:13
of the day that is **c** to destroy all the Jer 47:4
"Therefore, behold, the days are **c**, Jer 48:12
Therefore, behold, the days are **c**, Jer 49:2
like a lion **c** up from the jungle of the Jer 49:19
like a lion **c** up from the thicket of the Jer 50:44
the days are **c** when I will punish the Jer 51:47
"Therefore, behold, the days are **c**, Jer 51:52
say, 'Because of the news that it is **c**. Ezk 21:7
Behold, it is **c**, and it will be fulfilled,'" Ezk 21:7
if he sees the sword **c** upon the land and Ezk 33:3
sees the sword **c** and does not Ezk 33:6
You will advance, **c** on like a storm. Ezk 38:9
it is **c** and it will be brought about, Ezk 39:8
of the God of Israel was **c** from the east. Ezk 43:2
the sound of his **c** was like the sound Ezk 43:2
one, **c** down from heaven and saying, Dn 4:23
build Jerusalem to the **c** of an anointed Dn 9:25
which shall keep **c** and overflow and Dn 11:10
land tremble, for the day of the LORD is **c**; Jl 2:1
that, behold, the days are **c** upon you, Am 4:2
the days are **c**," declares the Lord GOD, Am 8:11
the days are **c**," declares the LORD, Am 9:13
For behold, the LORD is **c** out of his place, Mi 1:3
I said, "What are these **c** to do?" He said, Zec 1:21
saw, and behold, two women **c** forward! Zec 5:9
behold, your king is **c** to you; righteous Zec 9:9
Behold, a day is **c** for the LORD, when the Zec 14:1
in whom you delight, behold, he is **c**, Mal 3:1
But who can endure the day of his **c**, and Mal 3:2
"For behold, the day is **c**, burning like Mal 4:1
The day that is **c** shall set them ablaze, Mal 4:1
Pharisees and Sadducees **c** for baptism, Mt 3:7
but he who is **c** after me is mightier Mt 3:11
like a dove and **c** to rest on him; Mt 3:16
men met him, **c** out of the tombs, Mt 8:28
and **c** to his hometown he taught them Mt 13:54
see the Son of Man **c** in his kingdom." Mt 16:28
And as they were **c** down the mountain, Mt 17:9
of Zion, 'Behold, your king is **c** to you, Mt 21:5
be the sign of your **c** and of the close of Mt 24:3
west, so will be the **c** of the Son of Man. Mt 24:27
see the Son of Man **c** on the clouds of Mt 24:30
so will be the **c** of the Son of Man. Mt 24:37
so will be the **c** of the Son of Man. Mt 24:39
not know on what day your Lord is **c**. Mt 24:42
what part of the night the thief was **c**, Mt 24:43
the Son of Man is **c** at an hour you do Mt 24:44
and at my **c** I should have received Mt 25:27
that after two days the Passover is **c**, Mt 26:2
hand of Power and **c** on the clouds of Mt 26:64
and **c** out of the tombs after his Mt 27:53
and people were **c** to him from every Mk 1:45
the sea, and all the crowd was **c** to him, Mk 2:13
he cannot stand, but is **c** to an end. Mk 3:26
a while." For many were **c** and going, Mk 6:31
And as they were **c** down the mountain, Mk 9:9
Blessed is the **c** kingdom of our father Mk 11:10
the Son of Man **c** in clouds with great Mk 13:26
and **c** with the clouds of heaven." Mk 14:62
who was **c** in from the country, Mk 15:21
And **c** up at that very hour she began to Lk 2:38
water, but he who is mightier than I is **c**, Lk 3:16
words that were **c** from his mouth. Lk 4:22
While he was **c**, the demon threw him to Lk 9:42
known at what hour the thief was **c**, Lk 12:39

the Son of Man is **c** at an hour you do Lk 12:40
to himself, 'My master is delayed in **c**,' Lk 12:45
west, you say at once, 'A shower is **c**.' Lk 12:54
the share of property that is **c** to me.' Lk 15:12
of God is not **c** with signs to be Lk 17:20
"The days are **c** when you will desire to Lk 17:22
that city who kept **c** to him and saying, Lk 18:3
not beat me down by her continual **c**.'" Lk 18:5
and at my **c** I might have collected it Lk 19:23
foreboding of what is **c** on the world. Lk 21:26
see the Son of Man **c** in a cloud with Lk 21:27
who was **c** in from the country, Lk 23:26
the days are **c** when they will say, Lk 23:29
him, **c** up and offering him sour wine Lk 23:36
enlightens everyone, was **c** into the world. Jn 1:9
The next day he saw Jesus **c** toward him, Jn 1:29
Jesus saw Nathanael **c** toward him and Jn 1:47
and people were **c** and being baptized Jn 3:23
the hour is **c** when neither on this Jn 4:21
But the hour is **c**, and is now here, when Jn 4:23
know that Messiah is **c** (he who is called Jn 4:25
went out of the town and were **c** to him. Jn 4:30
"Truly, truly, I say to you, an hour is **c**, Jn 5:25
for an hour is **c** when all who are in the Jn 5:28
that a large crowd was **c** toward him, Jn 6:5
walking on the sea and **c** near the boat, Jn 6:19
it is day; night is **c**, when no one can work. Jn 9:4
sees the wolf **c** and leaves the sheep and Jn 10:12
So when Martha heard that Jesus was **c**, Jn 11:20
the Son of God, who is **c** into the world." Jn 11:27
heard that Jesus was **c** to Jerusalem. Jn 12:12
behold, your king is **c**, sitting on a Jn 12:15
with you, for the ruler of this world is **c**. Jn 14:30
the hour is **c** when whoever kills you will Jn 16:2
The hour is **c** when I will no longer Jn 16:25
Behold, the hour is **c**, indeed it has Jn 16:32
they are in the world, and I am **c** to you. Jn 17:11
But now I am **c** to you, and these things Jn 17:13
announced beforehand the **c** of the Acts 7:52
for. What is the reason for your **c**?" Acts 10:21
who on **c** to Antioch spoke to the Acts 11:20
Before his **c**, John had proclaimed a Acts 13:24
No, but behold, after me one is **c**, the Acts 13:25
And **c** to us, he took Paul's belt and Acts 21:11
and self-control and the **c** judgment, Acts 24:25
of the brothers **c** here has reported Acts 28:21
I may now at last succeed in **c** to you. Rom 1:10
so often been hindered from **c** to you. Rom 15:22
as though I were not **c** to you. 1 Cor 4:18
then at his **c** those who belong to 1 Cor 15:23
I rejoice at the **c** of Stephanas and 1 Cor 16:17
I refrained from **c** again to Corinth. 2 Cor 1:23
to claim anything as **c** from us, 2 Cor 3:5
comforted us by the **c** of Titus, 2 Cor 7:6
and not only by his **c** but also by the 2 Cor 7:7
This is the third time I am **c** to you. 2 Cor 13:1
imprisoned until the **c** faith would be Gal 3:23
so that in the **c** ages he might show the Eph 2:7
Jesus, because of my **c** to you again. Phil 1:26
account of these the wrath of God is **c**. Col 3:6
that our **c** to you was not in vain. 1 Thes 2:1
before our Lord Jesus at his **c**? 1 Thes 2:19
at the **c** of our Lord Jesus with all his 1 Thes 3:13
who are left until the **c** of the Lord, 1 Thes 4:15
kept blameless at the **c** of our Lord 1 Thes 5:23
Now concerning the **c** of our Lord 2 Thes 2:1
to nothing by the appearance of his **c**. 2 Thes 2:8
The **c** of the lawless one is by the 2 Thes 2:9
For the time is **c** when people will not 2 Tm 4:3
"Behold, the days are **c**, declares the Heb 8:8
and the **c** one will come and will not Heb 10:37
c down from the Father of lights with Jas 1:17
howl for the miseries that are **c** upon you. Jas 5:1
therefore, brothers, until the **c** of the Lord. Jas 5:7
hearts, for the **c** of the Lord is at hand. Jas 5:8
you the power and **c** of our Lord Jesus 2 Pt 1:16
will say, "Where is the promise of his **c**? 2 Pt 3:4
for and hastening the **c** of the day of 2 Pt 3:12
as you have heard that antichrist is **c**, 1 Jn 2:18
not shrink from him in shame at his **c**. 1 Jn 2:28
which you heard was **c** and now is in 1 Jn 4:3
do not confess the **c** of Jesus Christ in 2 Jn 1:7
Behold, he is **c** with the clouds, and every Rv 1:7
hour of trial that is **c** on the whole world, Rv 3:10
I am **c** soon. Hold fast what you have, so Rv 3:11
"These are the ones **c** out of the great Rv 7:14
and smoke and sulfur **c** out of their Rv 9:18
another mighty angel **c** down from Rv 10:1
c out of the mouth of the dragon and Rv 16:13
("Behold, I am **c** like a thief! Blessed is Rv 16:15
saw another angel **c** down from heaven, Rv 18:1
I saw an angel **c** down from heaven, Rv 20:1
c down out of heaven from God, Rv 21:2
the holy city Jerusalem **c** down out of Rv 21:10
"And behold, I am **c** soon. Blessed is the Rv 22:7
"Behold, I am **c** soon, bringing my Rv 22:12
says, "Surely I am **c** soon." Amen. Rv 22:20

COMMAND (200)

that he may **c** his children and his Gn 18:19
my son, obey my voice as I **c** you. Gn 27:8
people shall order themselves as you **c**. Gn 41:40
wagons, according to the **c** of Pharaoh, Gn 45:21
"Your father gave this **c** before he died, Gn 50:16
You shall speak all that I **c** you, and your Ex 7:2
"Be pleased to **c** me when I am to plead for Ex 8:9
"You shall **c** the people of Israel that Ex 27:20
"Observe what I **c** you this day. Behold, Ex 34:11
So Moses gave **c**, and word was Ex 36:6
"**C** Aaron and his sons, saying, This is the Lv 6:9
then the priest shall **c** that they wash Lv 13:54
the priest shall **c** them to take for him Lv 14:4
And the priest shall **c** them to kill one of Lv 14:5
Then the priest shall **c** that they empty Lv 14:36
then the priest shall **c** that they take out Lv 14:40
"**C** the people of Israel to bring you pure Lv 24:2
I will **c** my blessing on you in the sixth Lv 25:21
shall be at the **c** of Aaron and his Nm 4:27
"**C** the people of Israel that they put out Nm 5:2
what the LORD will **c** concerning you." Nm 9:8
At the **c** of the LORD the people of Israel Nm 9:18
and at the **c** of the LORD they camped. Nm 9:18
and according to the **c** of the LORD they Nm 9:20
then according to the **c** of the LORD they Nm 9:20
At the **c** of the LORD they camped, and Nm 9:23
and at the **c** of the LORD they set out. Nm 9:23
the LORD, at the **c** of the LORD by Moses. Nm 9:23
the first time at the **c** of the LORD by Nm 10:13
Paran, according to the **c** of the LORD, Nm 13:3
you transgressing the **c** of the LORD, Nm 14:41
rebelled against my **c** at the waters Nm 20:24
not go beyond the **c** of the LORD my Nm 22:18
Behold, I received a **c** to bless: he has Nm 23:20
"**C** the people of Israel and say to them, Nm 28:2
the men of war who are under our **c**, Nm 31:49
So Moses gave **c** concerning them to Nm 32:28
places, stage by stage, by **c** of the LORD, Nm 33:2
up Mount Hor at the **c** of the LORD and Nm 33:38
"**C** the people of Israel, and say to them, Nm 34:2
"**C** the people of Israel to give to the Nm 35:2
but rebelled against the **c** of the LORD Dt 1:26
you rebelled against the **c** of the LORD Dt 1:43
and **c** the people, "You are about to pass Dt 2:4
You shall not add to the word that I **c** you, Dt 4:2
of the LORD your God that I **c** you. Dt 4:2
commandments, which I **c** you today, Dt 4:40
and his commandments, which I **c** you, Dt 6:2
these words that I **c** you today shall be Dt 6:6
statutes and the rules that I **c** you today. Dt 7:11
commandment that I **c** you today you Dt 8:1
and his statutes, which I **c** you today, Dt 8:11
whole commandment that I **c** you today, Dt 11:8
my commandments that I **c** you today, Dt 11:13
this commandment that I **c** you to do, Dt 11:22
the LORD your God, which I **c** you today, Dt 11:27
there you shall bring all that I **c** you: Dt 12:11
to obey all these words that I **c** you, Dt 12:28
"Everything that I **c** you, you shall be Dt 12:32
this commandment that I **c** you today. Dt 15:5
Therefore I **c** you, 'You shall open wide Dt 15:11
you; therefore I **c** you this today. Dt 15:15
he shall speak to them all that I **c** him. Dt 18:18
Therefore I **c** you, You shall set apart Dt 19:7
commandment, which I **c** you today, Dt 19:9
from there; therefore I **c** you to do this. Dt 24:18
of Egypt; therefore I **c** you to do this. Dt 24:22
whole commandment that I **c** you today. Dt 27:1
stones, concerning which I **c** you today, Dt 27:4
and his statutes, which I **c** you today." Dt 27:10
his commandments that I **c** you today, Dt 28:1
The LORD will **c** the blessing on you in Dt 28:8
the LORD your God, which I **c** you today, Dt 28:13
any of the words that I **c** you today, Dt 28:14
and his statutes that I **c** you today, Dt 28:15
obey his voice in all that I **c** you today, Dt 30:2
his commandments that I **c** you today. Dt 30:8
commandment that I **c** you today is Dt 30:11
of the LORD your God that I **c** you today, Dt 30:16
that you may **c** them to your children, Dt 32:46
the midst of the camp and **c** the people, Jos 1:11
your words, whatever you **c** him, Jos 1:18
c the priests who bear the ark of the Jos 3:8
and **c** them, saying, 'Take twelve stones Jos 4:3
"**C** the priests bearing the ark of the Jos 4:16
By **c** of the LORD they gave him the city Jos 19:50
So by **c** of the LORD the people of Israel Jos 21:3
possessed themselves by **c** of the LORD Jos 22:9
have not kept the **c** of the LORD your 1 Sm 13:13
our lord now **c** your servants who 1 Sm 16:16
For by the **c** of Absalom this has 2 Sm 13:32
army, one third under the **c** of Joab, 2 Sm 18:2
one third under the **c** of Abishai the 2 Sm 18:2
one third under the **c** of Ittai the 2 Sm 18:2
Now Joab was in **c** of all the army of 2 Sm 20:23
Jehoiada was in **c** of the Cherethites 2 Sm 20:23
son of Jehoiada was in **c** of the army; 1 Kgs 4:4
Now therefore **c** that cedars of 1 Kgs 5:6
At the king's **c** they quarried out 1 Kgs 5:17
if you will listen to all that I **c** you, 1 Kgs 11:38
have not kept the **c** that the LORD 1 Kgs 13:21
said to his fellow at the **c** of the LORD, 1 Kgs 20:35
him not a word, for the king's **c** was, 2 Kgs 18:36
according to the **c** of Pharaoh. 2 Kgs 23:35
came upon Judah at the **c** of the LORD, 2 Kgs 24:3
who had been in **c** of the men of 2 Kgs 25:19
he did not keep the **c** of the LORD, 1 Chr 10:13
and all their kinsmen under their **c**. 1 Chr 12:32
their gods there, and David gave **c**, 1 Chr 14:12
for the king's **c** was abhorrent to 1 Chr 21:6
not I who gave **c** to number the 1 Chr 21:17
of the thirty and in **c** of the thirty; 1 Chr 27:6
the people will be wholly at your **c**." 1 Chr 28:21
or **c** the locust to devour the land, 2 Chr 7:13
and by **c** of the king they stoned 2 Chr 24:21
Under their **c** was an army of 2 Chr 26:13
As soon as the **c** was spread abroad, 2 Chr 31:5
divisions according to the king's **c**. 2 Chr 35:10
place according to the **c** of David, 2 Chr 35:15
according to the **c** of King Josiah. 2 Chr 35:16
For there was a **c** from the king Neh 11:23
according to the **c** of David and his Neh 12:45
come at the king's **c** delivered by the Est 1:12
not performed the **c** of King Ahasuerus Est 1:15
"Why do you transgress the king's **c**?" Est 3:3
wherever the king's **c** and his decree Est 4:3
and explain it to her and **c** her to go to the Est 4:8
out hurriedly, urged by the king's **c**. Est 8:14
wherever the king's **c** and his edict Est 8:17
when the king's **c** and edict were about to Est 9:1
The **c** of Queen Esther confirmed these Est 9:32
how God lays his **c** upon them and Jb 37:15
Is it at your **c** that the eagle mounts up Jb 39:27
you have given the **c** to save me, for you Ps 71:3
For he will **c** his angels concerning you Ps 91:11
He sends out his **c** to the earth; his Ps 147:15
the waters might not transgress his **c**, Prv 8:29
Keep the king's **c**, because of God's oath Eccl 8:2
Whoever keeps a **c** will know no evil Eccl 8:5
I will also **c** the clouds that they rain no Is 5:6
against the people of my wrath I **c** him, Is 10:6
LORD has given **c** concerning Canaan to Is 23:11
him not a word, for the king's **c** was, Is 36:21
will you **c** me concerning my children Is 45:11
you, you shall go, and whatever I **c** you, Jer 1:7
and say to them everything that I **c** you. Jer 1:17
your fathers or **c** them concerning Jer 7:22
But this **c** I gave them: 'Obey my voice, Jer 7:23
And walk in all the way that I **c** you, that Jer 7:23
daughters in the fire, which I did not **c**, Jer 7:31
to my voice, and do all that I **c** you. Jer 11:4
nor did I **c** them or speak to them. Jer 14:14
to Baal, which I did not **c** or decree, Jer 19:5
all the words that I **c** you to speak to Jer 26:2
name lying words that I did not **c** them. Jer 29:23
to Molech, though I did not **c** them, Jer 32:35
Behold, I will **c**, declares the LORD, and Jer 34:22
The **c** that Jonadab the son of Rechab Jer 35:14
for they have obeyed their father's **c**. Jer 35:14
Rechab have kept the **c** that their father Jer 35:16
you have obeyed the **c** of Jonadab your Jer 35:18
Babylon gave **c** concerning Jeremiah Jer 39:11
officer who had been in **c** of the men of Jer 52:25
in him, and set aside the king's **c**, Dn 3:28
Then Belshazzar gave the **c**, and Daniel Dn 5:29
of the sea, there I will **c** the serpent, Am 9:3
their enemies, there I will **c** the sword, Am 9:4
"For behold, I will **c**, and shake the Am 9:9
"And now, O priests, this **c** is for you. Mal 2:1
you know that I have sent this **c** to you, Mal 2:4
c these stones to become loaves of bread." Mt 4:3
"'He will **c** his angels concerning you,' Mt 4:6
you, **c** me to come to you on the water." Mt 14:28
"Why then did Moses **c** one to give a Mt 19:7
to it, "You mute and deaf spirit, I **c** you, Mk 9:25
them, "What did Moses **c** you?" Mk 10:3
Son of God, **c** this stone to become bread." Lk 4:3
"'He will **c** his angels concerning you, Lk 4:10
begged him not to **c** them to depart into Lk 8:31
you, and I never disobeyed your **c**, Lk 15:29
are my friends if you do what I **c** you. Jn 15:14
These things I **c** you, so that you will Jn 15:17
"I **c** you in the name of Jesus Christ to Acts 16:18
and after receiving a **c** for Silas and Acts 17:15
Then, at the **c** of Festus, Paul was Acts 25:23
according to the **c** of the eternal God, Rom 16:26
Now as a concession, not a **c**, I say 1 Cor 7:6

betrothed, I have no **c** from the Lord, 1 Cor 7:25
writing to you are a **c** of the Lord. 1 Cor 14:37
I say this not as a **c**, but to prove by the 2 Cor 8:8
descend from heaven with a cry of **c**, 1 Thes 4:16
and will do the things that we **c**. 2 Thes 3:4
Now we **c** you, brothers, in the name 2 Thes 3:6
with you, we would give you this **c**: 2 Thes 3:10
such persons we **c** and encourage in 2 Thes 3:12
of Christ Jesus by **c** of God our Savior 1 Tm 1:1
C and teach these things. 1 Tm 4:11
C these things as well, so that they 1 Tm 5:7
been entrusted by the **c** of God our Savior; Ti 1:3
enough in Christ to **c** you to do what Phlm 1:8

COMMANDED (399)
And the LORD God **c** the man, saying, Gn 2:16
of the tree of which I **c** you not to eat?" Gn 3:11
have eaten of the tree of which I **c** you, Gn 3:17
Noah did this; he did all that God **c** him. Gn 6:22
Noah did all that the LORD had **c** him. Gn 7:5
the ark with Noah, as God had **c** Noah. Gn 7:9
of all flesh, went in as God had **c** him. Gn 7:16
he was eight days old, as God had **c** him. Gn 21:4
Then he **c** the steward of his house, "Fill Gn 44:1
And you, Joseph, are **c** to say, 'Do this: Gn 45:19
the land of Rameses, as Pharaoh had **c**. Gn 47:11
Then he **c** them and said to them, "I Gn 49:29
And Joseph **c** his servants the Gn 50:2
his sons did for him as he had **c** them, Gn 50:12
did not do as the king of Egypt **c** them, Ex 1:17
Then Pharaoh **c** all his people, "Every Ex 1:22
and all the signs that he had **c** him to do. Ex 4:28
same day Pharaoh **c** the taskmasters of Ex 5:6
did so; they did just as the LORD **c** them. Ex 7:6
to Pharaoh and did just as the LORD **c**. Ex 7:10
Moses and Aaron did as the LORD **c**. In Ex 7:20
as the LORD had **c** Moses and Aaron, so Ex 12:28
did just as the LORD **c** Moses and Aaron. Ex 12:50
This is what the LORD has **c**: 'Gather of Ex 16:16
to them, "This is what the LORD has **c**: Ex 16:23
aside till the morning, as Moses **c** them, Ex 16:24
said, "This is what the LORD has **c**: Ex 16:32
As the LORD **c** Moses, so Aaron placed it Ex 16:34
all these words that the LORD had **c** him. Ex 19:7
As I **c** you, you shall eat unleavened Ex 23:15
sons, according to all that I have **c** you. Ex 29:35
they may make all that I have **c** you: Ex 31:6
According to all that I have **c** you, they Ex 31:11
quickly out of the way that I **c** them. Ex 32:8
on Mount Sinai, as the LORD had **c** him, Ex 34:4
shall eat unleavened bread, as I **c** you, Ex 34:18
and he **c** them all that the LORD had Ex 34:32
told the people of Israel what he was **c**, Ex 34:34
the things that the LORD has **c** you to do. Ex 35:1
"This is the thing that the LORD has **c**. Ex 35:4
come and make all that the LORD has **c**: Ex 35:10
that the LORD had **c** by Moses to be Ex 35:29
accordance with all that the LORD has **c**." Ex 36:1
the work that the LORD has **c** us to do." Ex 36:5
Judah, made all that the LORD **c** Moses; Ex 38:22
for Aaron, as the LORD had **c** Moses. Ex 39:1
twined linen, as the LORD had **c** Moses. Ex 39:5
sons of Israel, as the LORD had **c** Moses. Ex 39:7
the ephod, as the LORD had **c** Moses. Ex 39:21
ministering, as the LORD had **c** Moses. Ex 39:26
needlework, as the LORD had **c** Moses. Ex 39:29
turban above, as the LORD had **c** Moses. Ex 39:31
to all that the LORD had **c** Moses; Ex 39:32
to all that the LORD had **c** Moses, Ex 39:42
it; as the LORD had **c**, so had they done it. Ex 39:43
according to all that the LORD **c** him, so Ex 40:16
the tent over it, as the LORD had **c** Moses. Ex 40:19
the testimony, as the LORD had **c** Moses. Ex 40:21
the LORD, as the LORD had **c** Moses. Ex 40:23
the LORD, as the LORD had **c** Moses. Ex 40:25
incense on it, as the LORD had **c** Moses. Ex 40:27
grain offering, as the LORD had **c** Moses. Ex 40:29
altar, they washed, as the LORD **c** Moses. Ex 40:32
The LORD **c** this to be given them by the Lv 7:36
which the LORD **c** Moses on Mount Sinai, Lv 7:38
on the day that he **c** the people of Israel to Lv 7:38
And Moses did as the LORD **c** him, and the Lv 8:4
the thing that the LORD has **c** to be done." Lv 8:5
plate, the holy crown, as the LORD **c** Moses. Lv 8:9
caps on them, as the LORD **c** Moses. Lv 8:13
outside the camp, as the LORD **c** Moses. Lv 8:17
for the LORD, as the LORD **c** Moses. Lv 8:21
ram of ordination, as the LORD **c** Moses. Lv 8:29
the basket of ordination offerings, as I **c**, Lv 8:31
the LORD has **c** to be done to make Lv 8:34
that you do not die, for so I have been **c**." Lv 8:35
all the things that the LORD **c** by Moses. Lv 8:36
they brought what Moses **c** in front of the Lv 9:5
is the thing that the LORD **c** you to do, Lv 9:6
atonement for them, as the LORD has **c**." Lv 9:7
burned on the altar, as the LORD **c** Moses. Lv 9:10
offering before the LORD, as Moses **c**. Lv 9:21
the LORD, which he had not **c** them. Lv 10:1
the LORD'S food offerings, for so I am **c**. Lv 10:13
you as a due forever, as the LORD has **c**." Lv 10:15
to have eaten it in the sanctuary, as I **c**." Lv 10:18
sins." And Moses did as the LORD **c** him. Lv 16:34
This is the thing that the LORD has **c**. Lv 17:2
people of Israel did as the LORD **c** Moses. Lv 24:23
that the LORD **c** Moses for the Lv 27:34
as the LORD **c** Moses. So he listed them Nm 1:19
according to all that the LORD **c** Moses. Nm 1:54
the people of Israel, as the LORD **c** Moses. Nm 2:33
According to all that the LORD **c** Moses, Nm 2:34
to the word of the LORD, as he was **c**. Nm 3:16
the people of Israel, as the LORD **c** him. Nm 3:42
word of the LORD, as the LORD **c** Moses. Nm 3:51
were listed by him, as the LORD **c** Moses. Nm 4:49
of the lampstand, as the LORD **c** Moses. Nm 8:3
that the LORD **c** Moses concerning the Nm 8:20
the LORD had **c** Moses concerning the Nm 8:22
according to all that the LORD **c** Moses, Nm 9:5
all that the LORD has **c** you by Moses, Nm 15:23
with stones, as the LORD **c** Moses. Nm 15:36
Moses; as the LORD **c** him, so he did. Nm 17:11
statute of the law that the LORD has **c**: Nm 19:2
staff from before the LORD, as he **c** him. Nm 20:9
Moses did as the LORD **c**. And they Nm 20:27
old and upward," as the LORD **c** Moses. Nm 26:4
statute and rule, as the LORD **c** Moses.'" Nm 27:11
And Moses did as the LORD **c** him. He Nm 27:22
just as the LORD had **c** Moses. Nm 29:40
saying, "This is what the LORD has **c**. Nm 30:1
statutes that the LORD **c** Moses about a Nm 30:16
against Midian, as the LORD **c** Moses, Nm 31:7
of the law that the LORD has **c** Moses: Nm 31:21
the priest did as the LORD **c** Moses. Nm 31:31
Eleazar the priest, as the LORD **c** Moses. Nm 31:41
of the LORD, as the LORD **c** Moses. Nm 31:47
Moses **c** the people of Israel, saying, Nm 34:13
which the LORD has **c** to give to the Nm 34:13
men whom the LORD **c** to divide the Nm 34:29
"The LORD **c** my lord to give the land Nm 36:2
and my lord was **c** by the LORD to give Nm 36:2
And Moses **c** the people of Israel Nm 36:5
Zelophehad did as the LORD **c** Moses, Nm 36:10
that the LORD **c** through Moses to Nm 36:13
And I **c** you at that time all the things Dt 1:18
the Amorites, as the LORD our God **c** us. Dt 1:19
and fight, just as the LORD our God **c** us.' Dt 1:41
"And I **c** you at that time, saying, 'The Dt 3:18
And I **c** Joshua at that time, 'Your eyes Dt 3:21
and rules, as the LORD my God **c** me, Dt 4:5
his covenant, which he **c** you to perform, Dt 4:13
And the LORD **c** me at that time to teach Dt 4:14
keep it holy, as the LORD your God **c** you. Dt 5:12
the LORD your God **c** you to keep the Dt 5:15
mother, as the LORD your God **c** you, Dt 5:16
to do as the LORD your God has **c** you. Dt 5:32
way that the LORD your God has **c** you, Dt 5:33
that the LORD your God **c** me to teach you, Dt 6:1
and his statutes, which he has **c** you. Dt 6:17
rules that the LORD our God has **c** you?' Dt 6:20
And the LORD **c** us to do all these statutes, Dt 6:24
before the LORD our God, as he has **c** us.' Dt 6:25
quickly out of the way that I **c** them; Dt 9:12
from the way that the LORD had **c** you. Dt 9:16
And there they are, as the LORD **c** me." Dt 10:5
the LORD has given you, as I have **c** you, Dt 12:21
which the LORD your God **c** you to walk. Dt 13:5
name that I have not **c** him to speak, Dt 18:20
Jebusites, as the LORD your God has **c**, Dt 20:17
As I **c** them, so you shall be careful to do. Dt 24:8
commandment that you have **c** me. Dt 26:13
according to all that you have **c** me. Dt 26:14
and the elders of Israel **c** the people, Dt 27:1
and his statutes that he **c** you. Dt 28:45
covenant that the LORD **c** Moses to make Dt 29:1
whole commandment that I have **c** you. Dt 31:5
And Moses **c** them, "At the end of every Dt 31:10
Moses **c** the Levites who carried the ark Dt 31:25
aside from the way that I have **c** you. Dt 31:29
when Moses **c** us a law, as a possession Dt 33:4
him and did as the LORD had **c** Moses. Dt 34:9
all the law that Moses my servant **c** you. Jos 1:7
Have I not **c** you? Be strong and Jos 1:9
And Joshua **c** the officers of the people, Jos 1:10
that Moses the servant of the LORD **c** you, Jos 1:13
"All that you have **c** us we will do, Jos 1:16
and **c** the people, "As soon as you see the Jos 3:3
did just as Joshua **c** and took up twelve Jos 4:8
finished that the LORD **c** Joshua to tell the Jos 4:10
to all that Moses had **c** Joshua. Jos 4:10
So Joshua **c** the priests, "Come up out of Jos 4:17
And just as Joshua had **c** the people, the Jos 6:8
But Joshua **c** the people, "You shall not Jos 6:10
transgressed my covenant that I **c** them; Jos 7:11
And he **c** them, "Behold, you shall lie in Jos 8:4
to the word of the Lord. See, I have **c** you." Jos 8:8
to the word of the LORD that he **c** Joshua. Jos 8:27
And at sunset Joshua **c**, and they took Jos 8:29
of the LORD had **c** the people of Israel, Jos 8:31
the servant of the LORD had **c** at the first, Jos 8:33
of all that Moses **c** that Joshua did not Jos 8:35
LORD your God had **c** his servant Moses Jos 9:24
of the going down of the sun, Joshua **c**, Jos 10:27
just as the LORD God of Israel **c**. Jos 10:40
as Moses the servant of the LORD had **c**. Jos 11:12
as the LORD had **c** Moses his servant, Jos 11:15
Moses his servant, so Moses **c** Joshua, Jos 11:15
of all that the LORD had **c** Moses. Jos 11:15
be destroyed, just as the LORD **c** Moses. Jos 11:20
Israel for an inheritance, as I have **c** you. Jos 13:6
just as the LORD had **c** by the hand of Jos 14:2
people of Israel did as the LORD **c** Moses; Jos 14:5
"The LORD **c** Moses to give us an Jos 17:4
"The LORD **c** through Moses that we be Jos 21:2
as the LORD had **c** through Moses. Jos 21:8
servant of the LORD **c** you and have Jos 22:2
obeyed my voice in all that I have **c** you. Jos 22:2
that Moses the servant of the LORD **c** you, Jos 22:5
of the LORD your God, which he **c** you, Jos 23:16
my covenant that I **c** their fathers and Jgs 2:20
which he **c** their fathers by the hand of Jgs 3:4
message for you, O king." And he **c**, Jgs 3:19
"Has not the LORD, the God of Israel, **c** you, Jgs 4:6
thing. All that I **c** her let her observe." Jgs 13:14
of their bravest men there and **c** them, Jgs 21:10
And they **c** the people of Benjamin, Jgs 21:20
did just as her mother-in-law had **c** her. Ru 3:6
sacrifices and my offerings that I **c**, 1 Sm 2:29
LORD your God, with which he **c** you. 1 Sm 13:13
and the LORD has **c** him to be prince 1 Sm 13:14
have not kept what the LORD **c** you." 1 Sm 13:14
did what the LORD **c** and came to 1 Sm 16:4
and went, as Jesse had **c** him. 1 Sm 17:20
And Saul **c** his servants, "Speak to 1 Sm 18:22
and my brother has **c** me to be there. 1 Sm 20:29
And David **c** his young men, and they 2 Sm 4:12
And David did as the LORD **c** him, and 2 Sm 5:25
whom I **c** to shepherd my people Israel, 2 Sm 7:7
Then Absalom **c** his servants, 2 Sm 13:28
him. Do not fear; have I not **c** you? 2 Sm 13:28
did to Amnon as Absalom had **c**. 2 Sm 13:29
It was your servant Joab who **c** me; it 2 Sm 14:19
hearing the king **c** you and Abishai 2 Sm 18:12
And they did all that the king **c**. 2 Sm 21:14
went up at Gad's word, as the LORD **c**. 2 Sm 24:19
to die drew near, he **c** Solomon his son, 1 Kgs 2:1
commandment with which I **c** you?" 1 Kgs 2:43
Then the king **c** Benaiah the son of 1 Kgs 2:46
and his rules, which he **c** our fathers. 1 Kgs 8:58
according to all that I have **c** you, 1 Kgs 9:4
and had **c** him concerning this 1 Kgs 11:10
But he did not keep what the LORD **c**. 1 Kgs 11:10
and my statutes that I have **c** you, 1 Kgs 11:11
for so was it **c** me by the word of the 1 Kgs 13:9
that the LORD your God **c** you, 1 Kgs 13:21
from anything that he **c** him all the 1 Kgs 15:5
and I have **c** the ravens to feed you 1 Kgs 17:4
I have **c** a widow there to feed you." 1 Kgs 17:9
of Syria had **c** the thirty-two 1 Kgs 22:31
And he **c** them, "This is the thing 2 Kgs 11:5
to all that Jehoiada the priest **c**, 2 Kgs 11:9
Jehoiada the priest **c** the captains 2 Kgs 11:15
of the Law of Moses, where the LORD **c**, 2 Kgs 14:6
And King Ahaz **c** Uriah the priest, 2 Kgs 16:15
priest did all this, as King Ahaz **c**. 2 Kgs 16:16
all the Law that I **c** your fathers, 2 Kgs 17:13
the LORD had **c** them that they 2 Kgs 17:15
Then the king of Assyria **c**, "Send 2 Kgs 17:27
that the LORD **c** the children of 2 Kgs 17:34
a covenant with them and **c** them, 2 Kgs 17:35
that the LORD **c** Moses. 2 Kgs 18:6
that Moses the servant of the LORD **c**. 2 Kgs 18:12
according to all that I have **c** them, 2 Kgs 21:8
Law that my servant Moses **c** them." 2 Kgs 21:8
And the king **c** Hilkiah the priest, 2 Kgs 22:12
And the king **c** Hilkiah the high 2 Kgs 23:4
And the king **c** all the people, "Keep 2 Kgs 23:21
that Moses the servant of God had **c**. 1 Chr 6:49
And David did as God **c** him, and 1 Chr 14:16
as Moses had **c** according to the 1 Chr 15:15
David also **c** the chiefs of the Levites 1 Chr 15:16
covenant forever, the word that he **c**, 1 Chr 16:15
the Law of the LORD that he **c** Israel. 1 Chr 16:40
whom I **c** to shepherd my people, 1 Chr 17:6
angel of the LORD had **c** Gad to say to 1 Chr 21:18
Then the LORD **c** the angel, and he 1 Chr 21:27
David **c** to gather together the 1 Chr 22:2
that the LORD **c** Moses for Israel. 1 Chr 22:13

David also **c** all the leaders of Israel 1 Chr 22:17
as the LORD God of Israel had **c** him. 1 Chr 24:19
all that I have **c** you and keeping my 2 Chr 7:17
for so David the man of God had **c**. 2 Chr 8:14
what the king had **c** the priests and 2 Chr 8:15
and **c** Judah to seek the LORD, the God 2 Chr 14:4
king of Syria had **c** the captains of 2 Chr 18:30
to all that Jehoiada the priest **c**, 2 Chr 23:8
So the king **c**, and they made a chest 2 Chr 24:8
the Book of Moses, where the LORD **c**, 2 Chr 25:4
and went in as the king had **c**, 2 Chr 29:15
And he **c** the priests the sons of 2 Chr 29:21
For the king **c** that the burnt 2 Chr 29:24
Then Hezekiah **c** that the burnt 2 Chr 29:27
and the officials **c** the Levites to 2 Chr 29:30
and his princes, as the king had **c**, 2 Chr 30:6
king and the princes **c** by the word 2 Chr 30:12
And he **c** the people who lived in 2 Chr 31:4
Then Hezekiah **c** them to prepare 2 Chr 31:11
his altars and **c** Judah and 2 Chr 32:12
careful to do all that I have **c** them, 2 Chr 33:8
and he **c** Judah to serve the LORD, 2 Chr 33:16
And the king **c** Hilkiah, Ahikam 2 Chr 34:20
at war. And God has **c** me to hurry. 2 Chr 35:21
King Cyrus the king of Persia has **c** us." Ezr 4:3
which you **c** by your servants the Ezr 9:11
the rules that you **c** your servant Moses. Neh 1:7
the word that you **c** your servant Moses, Neh 1:8
Law of Moses that the LORD had **c** Israel. Neh 8:1
that the LORD had **c** by Moses that the Neh 8:14
Sabbath and **c** them commandments Neh 9:14
I **c** that the doors should be shut and Neh 13:19
Then I **c** the Levites that they should Neh 13:22
was merry with wine, he **c** Mehuman, Est 1:10
'King Ahasuerus **c** Queen Vashti to be Est 1:17
for Mordecai had **c** her not to make it Est 2:10
or her people, as Mordecai had **c** her, Est 2:20
for the king had so **c** concerning him. Est 3:2
an edict, according to all that Haman **c**, Est 3:12
spoke to Hathach and **c** him to go to Est 4:10
all that Mordecai **c** concerning the Jews, Est 8:9
So the king **c** this to be done. A decree Est 9:14
"Have you **c** the morning since your Jb 38:12
For he spoke, and it came to be; he **c**, and Ps 33:9
which he **c** our fathers to teach to their Ps 78:5
Yet he **c** the skies above and opened the Ps 78:23
his covenant forever, the word that he **c**, Ps 105:8
destroy the peoples, as the LORD **c** them, Ps 106:34
For he **c** and raised the stormy wind, Ps 107:25
people; he has **c** his covenant forever. Ps 111:9
You have **c** your precepts to be kept Ps 119:4
For there the LORD has **c** the blessing, Ps 133:3
LORD! For he **c** and they were created. Ps 148:5
I myself have **c** my consecrated ones, and Is 13:3
For the mouth of the LORD has **c**, and his Is 34:16
out the heavens, and I **c** all their host. Is 45:12
image and my metal image **c** them.' Is 48:5
that I **c** your fathers when I brought Jer 11:4
of this covenant, which I **c** them to do, Jer 11:8
hid it by the Euphrates, as the LORD **c** me. Jer 13:5
the loincloth that I **c** you to hide there." Jer 13:6
Sabbath day holy, as I **c** your fathers. Jer 17:22
all that the LORD had **c** him to speak to Jer 26:8
did nothing of all you **c** them to do. Jer 32:23
the son of Rechab, our father, **c** us, Jer 35:6
of Rechab, our father, in all that he **c** us, Jer 35:8
done all that Jonadab our father **c** us. Jer 35:10
his precepts and done all that he **c** you, Jer 35:18
And the king **c** Jerahmeel the king's Jer 36:26
Then the king **c** Ebed-melech the Jer 38:10
the LORD, and do all that I have **c** you. Jer 50:21
Jeremiah the prophet **c** Seraiah the son Jer 51:59
the LORD has **c** against Jacob that his Lam 1:17
out his word, which he **c** long ago; Lam 2:17
came to pass, unless the Lord has **c** it? Lam 3:37
saying, "I have done as you **c** me." Ezk 9:11
And when he **c** the man clothed in Ezk 10:6
And I did as I was **c**. I brought out my Ezk 12:7
on the next morning I did as I was **c**. Ezk 24:18
So I prophesied as I was **c**. And as I Ezk 37:7
So I prophesied as he **c** me, and the Ezk 37:10
Then the king **c** Ashpenaz, his chief Dn 1:3
when the king had **c** that they should be Dn 1:18
Then the king **c** that the magicians, the Dn 2:2
and **c** that all the wise men of Babylon Dn 2:12
and **c** that an offering and incense be Dn 2:46
the herald proclaimed aloud, "You are **c**, Dn 3:4
in furious rage **c** that Shadrach, Dn 3:13
And as it was **c** to leave the stump of the Dn 4:26
c that the vessels of gold and of silver that Dn 5:2
Then the king **c**, and Daniel was Dn 6:16
and **c** that Daniel be taken up out of the Dn 6:23
And the king **c**, and those men who had Dn 6:24
drink wine, and **c** the prophets, Am 2:12
which I **c** my servants the prophets, Zec 1:6
and rules that I **c** him at Horeb for Mal 4:4
he did as the angel of the Lord **c** him: Mt 1:24
the priest and offer the gift that Moses **c**, Mt 8:4
oaths and his guests he **c** it to be given. Mt 14:9
For God **c**, 'Honor your father and your Mt 15:4
down the mountain, Jesus **c** them, Mt 17:9
them to observe all that I have **c** you. Mt 28:20
offer for your cleansing what Moses **c**, Mk 1:44
Then he **c** them all to sit down in Mk 6:39
offering for your cleansing, as Moses **c**, Lk 5:14
For he had **c** the unclean spirit to come Lk 8:29
he strictly charged and **c** them to tell Lk 9:21
said, 'Sir, what you **c** has been done, Lk 14:22
the servant because he did what was **c**? Lk 17:9
you have done all that you were **c**, Lk 17:10
And Jesus stopped and **c** him to be Lk 18:40
Now in the Law Moses **c** us to stone such Jn 8:5
but I do as the Father has **c** me, so that Jn 14:31
But when they had **c** them to leave the Acts 4:15
And he **c** the chariot to stop, and they Acts 8:38
all that you have been **c** by the Lord." Acts 10:33
And he **c** us to preach to the people Acts 10:42
And he **c** them to be baptized in the Acts 10:48
For so the Lord has **c** us, saying, "'I Acts 13:47
because Claudius had **c** all the Jews to Acts 18:2
unbound him and **c** the chief priests Acts 22:30
high priest Ananias **c** those who stood Acts 23:2
c the soldiers to go down and take Acts 23:10
accusers arrive." And he **c** him to be Acts 23:35
the Lord **c** that those who proclaim 1 Cor 9:14
of the covenant that God **c** for you." Heb 9:20
love one another, just as he has **c** us. 1 Jn 3:23
truth, just as we were **c** by the Father. 2 Jn 1:4

COMMANDER (47)

and Phicol the **c** of his army Gn 21:22
and Phicol the **c** of his army Gn 21:32
adviser and Phicol the **c** of his army, Gn 26:26
but I am the **c** of the army of the LORD. Jos 5:14
And the **c** of the LORD'S army said to Jos 5:15
The **c** of his army was Sisera, who lived Jgs 4:2
hand of Sisera, **c** of the army of Hazor, 1 Sm 12:9
the name of the **c** of his army was 1 Sm 14:50
cheeses to the **c** of their thousand. 1 Sm 17:18
he said to Abner, the **c** of the army, 1 Sm 17:55
and made him a **c** of a thousand. 1 Sm 18:13
the son of Ner, the **c** of his army. 1 Sm 26:5
Abner the son of Ner, **c** of Saul's army, 2 Sm 2:8
with Shobach the **c** of the army of 2 Sm 10:16
wounded Shobach the **c** of their 2 Sm 10:18
if you are not **c** of my army from 2 Sm 19:13
of the thirty and became their **c**, 2 Sm 23:19
king said to Joab, the **c** of the army, 2 Sm 24:2
the priest, and Joab the **c** of the army, 1 Kgs 1:19
the son of Ner, **c** of the army of Israel, 1 Kgs 2:32
son of Jether, **c** of the army of Judah. 1 Kgs 2:32
and Joab the **c** of the army went up 1 Kgs 11:15
and that Joab the **c** of the army was 1 Kgs 11:21
servant Zimri, **c** of half his chariots, 1 Kgs 16:9
Israel made Omri, the **c** of the army, 1 Kgs 16:16
the king or to the **c** of the army?'" She 2 Kgs 4:13
c of the army of the king of Syria, 2 Kgs 5:1
a word for you, O **c**." And Jehu said, 2 Kgs 9:5
of us all?" And he said, "To you, O **c**." 2 Kgs 9:5
the secretary of the **c** of the army 2 Kgs 25:19
shall be chief and **c**." And Joab the 1 Chr 11:6
of the thirty and became their **c**, 1 Chr 11:21
with Shophach the **c** of the army of 1 Chr 19:16
also Shophach the **c** of their army. 1 Chr 19:18
The third **c**, for the third month, was 1 Chr 27:5
The fifth **c**, for the fifth month, was 1 Chr 27:8
Joab was **c** of the king's army. 1 Chr 27:34
Adnah the **c**, with 300,000 mighty 2 Chr 17:14
and next to him Jehohanan the **c**, 2 Chr 17:15
son and Azrikam the **c** of the palace 2 Chr 28:7
Rehum the **c** and Shimshai the scribe Ezr 4:8
Rehum the **c**, Shimshai the scribe, and Ezr 4:9
"To Rehum the **c** and Shimshai the Ezr 4:17
In the year that the **c** in chief, who was Is 20:1
the peoples, a leader and **c** for the peoples. Is 55:4
the secretary of the **c** of the army who Jer 52:25
but a **c** shall put an end to his Dn 11:18

COMMANDER'S (1)

for there a **c** portion was reserved; Dt 33:21

COMMANDERS (74)

the **c** of thousands and the Nm 31:14
of thousands and the **c** of hundreds, Nm 31:14
the **c** of thousands and the Nm 31:48
of thousands and the **c** of hundreds, Nm 31:48
from the **c** of thousands and the Nm 31:52
of thousands and the **c** of hundreds, Nm 31:52
the gold from the **c** of thousands and Nm 31:54
them as heads over you, **c** of thousands, Dt 1:15
of thousands, **c** of hundreds, Dt 1:15
commanders of hundreds, **c** of fifties, Dt 1:15
commanders of fifties, **c** of tens, Dt 1:15
then **c** shall be appointed at the head of Dt 20:9
goes out to the **c** of Israel who offered Jgs 5:9
from Machir marched down the **c**, and Jgs 5:14
appoint for himself **c** of thousands 1 Sm 8:12
of thousands and **c** of fifties, 1 Sm 8:12
he make you all **c** of thousands and 1 Sm 22:7
of thousands and **c** of hundreds, 1 Sm 22:7
the **c** of the Philistines said, "What 1 Sm 29:3
Achish said to the **c** of the Philistines, 1 Sm 29:3
But the **c** of the Philistines were angry 1 Sm 29:4
And the **c** of the Philistines said to 1 Sm 29:4
the **c** of the Philistines have said, 1 Sm 29:9
and set over them **c** of thousands and 2 Sm 18:1
of thousands and **c** of hundreds. 2 Sm 18:1
orders to all the **c** about Absalom. 2 Sm 18:5
it clear today that **c** and servants are 2 Sm 19:6
against Joab and the **c** of the army. 2 Sm 24:4
So Joab and the **c** of the army went 2 Sm 24:4
all the king's sons, the **c** of the army, 1 Kgs 1:25
he dealt with the two **c** of the armies of 1 Kgs 2:5
soldiers, they were his officials, his **c**, 1 Kgs 9:22
his chariot **c** and his horsemen. 1 Kgs 9:22
Asa and sent the **c** of his armies 1 Kgs 15:20
his post, and put **c** in their places, 1 Kgs 20:24
and his chariot **c** struck the 2 Kgs 8:21
the **c** of the army were in council. 2 Kgs 9:5
of valor and were **c** in the army. 1 Chr 12:21
and twenty-two **c** from his own 1 Chr 12:28
Of Naphtali 1,000 **c** with whom 1 Chr 12:34
consulted with the **c** of thousands 1 Chr 13:1
Israel and the **c** of thousands went 1 Chr 15:25
said to Joab and the **c** of the army, 1 Chr 21:2
the hundreds and the **c** of the army 1 Chr 26:26
the **c** of thousands and hundreds, 1 Chr 27:1
of Perez and was chief of all the **c**. 1 Chr 27:3
served the king, the **c** of thousands, 1 Chr 28:1
of thousands, the **c** of hundreds, 1 Chr 28:1
the **c** of thousands and of hundreds, 1 Chr 29:6
to the **c** of thousands and of hundreds, 2 Chr 1:2
and his officers, the **c** of his chariots, 2 Chr 8:9
fortresses strong, and put **c** in them, 2 Chr 11:11
Asa and sent the **c** of his armies 2 Chr 16:4
Of Judah, the **c** of thousands: 2 Chr 17:14
passed over with his **c** and all his 2 Chr 21:9
surrounded him and his chariot **c**. 2 Chr 21:9
a covenant with the **c** of hundreds, 2 Chr 23:1
fathers' houses under **c** of thousands 2 Chr 25:5
of Hananiah, one of the king's **c**. 2 Chr 26:11
And he set combat **c** over the people 2 Chr 32:6
mighty warriors and **c** and officers 2 Chr 32:21
upon them the **c** of the army 2 Chr 33:11
He also put **c** of the army in all the 2 Chr 33:14
for he says: "Are not my **c** all kings? Is 10:8
Then all the **c** of the forces, and Johanan Jer 42:1
of Kareah and all the **c** of the forces who Jer 42:8
of Kareah and all the **c** of the forces and Jer 43:4
of Kareah and all the **c** of the forces took Jer 43:5
you I break in pieces governors and **c**. Jer 51:23
and her wise men, her governors, her **c**, Jer 51:57
clothed in purple, governors and **c**, all Ezk 23:6
after the Assyrians, governors and **c**, Ezk 23:12
men, governors and **c** all of them, Ezk 23:23
nobles and military **c** and the leading Mk 6:21

COMMANDING (5)

When Jacob finished **c** his sons, he Gn 49:33
which I am **c** you today for your good? Dt 10:13
from the way that I am **c** you today, Dt 11:28
there you shall do all that I am **c** you. Dt 12:14
commandments that I am **c** you today, Dt 13:18

COMMANDMENT (90)

by stages, according to the **c** of the LORD, Ex 17:1
tablets of stone, with the law and the **c**, Ex 24:12
I will give you in **c** for the people of Ex 25:22
as they were recorded at the **c** of Moses, Ex 38:21
and Aaron listed at the **c** of the LORD, Nm 3:39
listed according to the **c** of the LORD by Nm 4:37
listed according to the **c** of the LORD. Nm 4:41
listed according to the **c** of the LORD by Nm 4:45
According to the **c** of the LORD through Nm 4:49
from the day that the LORD gave **c**, Nm 15:23
of the LORD and has broken his **c**, Nm 15:31
that the LORD had given him in **c** to them, Dt 1:3
tell you the whole **c** and the statutes and Dt 5:31
"Now this is the **c**, the statutes and the Dt 6:1
to do all this **c** before the LORD our Dt 6:25
careful to do the **c** and the statutes and Dt 7:11
"The whole **c** that I command you today Dt 8:1
you rebelled against the **c** of the LORD Dt 9:23
keep the whole **c** that I command Dt 11:8
to do all this **c** that I command you Dt 11:22
to do all this **c** that I command you Dt 15:5
that he may not turn aside from the **c**, Dt 17:20
you are careful to keep all this **c**, Dt 19:9

according to all your **c** that you have Dt 26:13
"Keep the whole **c** that I command you Dt 27:1
"For this **c** that I command you today Dt 30:11
according to the whole **c** that I have Dt 31:5
rebels against your **c** and disobeys your Jos 1:18
According to the **c** of the LORD to Jos 15:13
careful to observe the **c** and the law that Jos 22:5
not rebel against the **c** of the LORD, 1 Sm 12:14
but rebel against the **c** of the LORD, 1 Sm 12:15
I have performed the **c** of the LORD." 1 Sm 15:13
I have transgressed the **c** of the LORD 1 Sm 15:24
the LORD and the **c** with which I 1 Kgs 2:43
the law or the **c** that the LORD 2 Kgs 17:34
the law and the **c** that he wrote for 2 Kgs 17:37
according to the **c** of Moses for 2 Chr 8:13
fathers, and to keep the law and the **c**. 2 Chr 14:4
concerning bloodshed, law or **c**, 2 Chr 19:10
according to the **c** of David and of 2 Chr 29:25
for the **c** was from the LORD through 2 Chr 29:25
those who tremble at the **c** of our God, Ezr 10:3
according to the **c** of David the man Neh 12:24
which were given by **c** to the Levites, Neh 13:5
have not departed from the **c** of his lips; Jb 23:12
the **c** of the LORD is pure, enlightening the Ps 19:8
but your **c** is exceedingly broad. Ps 119:96
Your **c** makes me wiser than my Ps 119:98
My son, keep your father's **c**, and Prv 6:20
For the **c** is a lamp and the teaching a Prv 6:23
he who reveres the **c** will be rewarded. Prv 13:13
Whoever keeps the **c** keeps his life; he Prv 19:16
their fear of me is a **c** taught by men, Is 29:13
The LORD has given **c** about you: "No Na 1:14
why do you break the **c** of God for the Mt 15:3
which is the great **c** in the Law?" Mt 22:36
This is the great and first **c**. Mt 22:38
You leave the **c** of God and hold to the Mk 7:8
fine way of rejecting the **c** of God in order Mk 7:9
hardness of heart he wrote you this **c**. Mk 10:5
"Which **c** is the most important of Mk 12:28
There is no other **c** greater than these." Mk 12:31
Sabbath they rested according to the **c**. Lk 23:56
has himself given me a **c**—what to say Jn 12:49
And I know that his **c** is eternal life. Jn 12:50
A new **c** I give to you, that you love one Jn 13:34
"This is my **c**, that you love one another Jn 15:12
seizing an opportunity through the **c**, Rom 7:8
from the law, but when the **c** came, Rom 7:9
The very **c** that promised life proved to Rom 7:10
seizing an opportunity through the **c**, Rom 7:11
and the **c** is holy and righteous and Rom 7:12
and through the **c** might become Rom 7:13
You shall not covet," and any other **c**, Rom 13:9
(this is the first **c** with a promise), Eph 6:2
to keep the **c** unstained and free from 1 Tm 6:14
the priestly office have a **c** in the law to Heb 7:5
a former **c** is set aside because of its Heb 7:18
For when every **c** of the law had been Heb 9:19
back from the holy **c** delivered to them. 2 Pt 2:21
holy prophets and the **c** of the Lord and 2 Pt 3:2
Beloved, I am writing you no new **c**, but 1 Jn 2:7
but an old **c** that you had from the 1 Jn 2:7
The old **c** is the word that you have 1 Jn 2:7
it is a new **c** that I am writing to you, 1 Jn 2:8
And this is his **c**, that we believe in the 1 Jn 3:23
And this **c** we have from him: whoever 1 Jn 4:21
as though I were writing you a new **c**, 2 Jn 1:5
this is the **c**, just as you have heard from 2 Jn 1:6

COMMANDMENTS (150)
my voice and kept my charge, my **c**, Gn 26:5
and give ear to his **c** and keep all his Ex 15:26
you refuse to keep my **c** and my laws? Ex 16:28
of those who love me and keep my **c**. Ex 20:6
the words of the covenant, the Ten **C**. Ex 34:28
in any of the LORD'S **c** about things not to Lv 4:2
that by the LORD'S **c** ought not to be Lv 4:13
the things that by the **c** of the LORD his Lv 4:22
that by the LORD'S **c** ought not to be Lv 4:27
that by the LORD'S **c** ought not to be Lv 5:17
"So you shall keep my **c** and do them: I Lv 22:31
statutes and observe my **c** and do them, Lv 26:3
listen to me and will not do all these **c**, Lv 26:14
rules, so that you will not do all my **c**, Lv 26:15
These are the **c** that the LORD Lv 27:34
not observe all these **c** that the LORD Nm 15:22
at and remember all the **c** of the LORD, Nm 15:39
you shall remember and do all my **c**, Nm 15:40
These are the **c** and the rules that the Nm 36:13
that you may keep the **c** of the LORD your Dt 4:2
you to perform, that is, the Ten **C**, Dt 4:13
you shall keep his statutes and his **c**, Dt 4:40
of those who love me and keep my **c**. Dt 5:10
always, to fear me and to keep all my **c**, Dt 5:29
son, by keeping all his statutes and his **c**, Dt 6:2
shall diligently keep the **c** of the LORD Dt 6:17
with those who love him and keep his **c**, Dt 7:9
whether you would keep his **c** or not. Dt 8:2
So you shall keep the **c** of the LORD your Dt 8:6
by not keeping his **c** and his rules and Dt 8:11
the Ten **C** that the LORD had spoken to Dt 10:4
and to keep the **c** and statutes of the Dt 10:13
his statutes, his rules, and his **c** always. Dt 11:1
will indeed obey my **c** that I command Dt 11:13
if you obey the **c** of the LORD your God, Dt 11:27
you do not obey the **c** of the LORD your Dt 11:28
him and keep his **c** and obey his voice, Dt 13:4
keeping all his **c** that I am Dt 13:18
I have not transgressed any of your **c**, Dt 26:13
his statutes and his **c** and his rules, Dt 26:17
you, and that you are to keep all his **c**, Dt 26:18
God, keeping his **c** and his statutes, Dt 27:10
to do all his **c** that I command you Dt 28:1
if you keep the **c** of the LORD your God Dt 28:9
if you obey the **c** of the LORD your God, Dt 28:13
to do all his **c** and his statutes that Dt 28:15
to keep his **c** and his statutes that he Dt 28:45
and keep all his **c** that I command you Dt 30:8
to keep his **c** and his statutes that are Dt 30:10
If you obey the **c** of the LORD your God Dt 30:16
and by keeping his **c** and his statutes Dt 30:16
ways and to keep his **c** and to cling to Jos 22:5
who had obeyed the **c** of the LORD, Jgs 2:17
Israel would obey the **c** of the LORD, Jgs 3:4
not performed my **c**." And Samuel 1 Sm 15:11
ways and keeping his statutes, his **c**, 1 Kgs 2:3
ways, keeping my statutes and my **c**, 1 Kgs 3:14
and keep all my **c** and walk in them, 1 Kgs 6:12
walk in all his ways and to keep his **c**, 1 Kgs 8:58
in his statutes and keeping his **c**, 1 Kgs 8:61
do not keep my **c** and my statutes that 1 Kgs 9:6
who kept my **c** and my statutes. 1 Kgs 11:34
by keeping my statutes and my **c**, 1 Kgs 11:38
who kept my **c** and followed me with 1 Kgs 14:8
have abandoned the **c** of the LORD 1 Kgs 18:18
and keep my **c** and my statutes, 2 Kgs 17:13
they abandoned all the **c** of the LORD 2 Kgs 17:16
did not keep the **c** of the LORD their 2 Kgs 17:19
but kept the **c** that the LORD 2 Kgs 18:6
and to keep his **c** and his testimonies 2 Kgs 23:3
strong in keeping my **c** and my rules, 1 Chr 28:7
seek out all the **c** of the LORD your 1 Chr 28:8
heart that he may keep your **c**, 1 Chr 29:19
my statutes and my **c** that I have set 2 Chr 7:19
God of his father and walked in his **c**, 2 Chr 17:4
do you break the **c** of the LORD, 2 Chr 24:20
accordance with the law and the **c**, 2 Chr 31:21
to keep his **c** and his testimonies 2 Chr 34:31
in matters of the **c** of the LORD and Ezr 7:11
after this? For we have forsaken your **c**, Ezr 9:10
we break your **c** again and intermarry Ezr 9:14
with those who love him and keep his **c**, Neh 1:5
against you and have not kept the **c**, Neh 1:7
to me and keep my **c** and do them, Neh 1:9
and true laws, good statutes and **c**, Neh 9:13
and commanded them **c** and statutes Neh 9:14
their neck and did not obey your **c**. Neh 9:16
and did not obey your **c**, Neh 9:29
attention to your **c** and your warnings Neh 9:34
and do all the **c** of the LORD our Neh 10:29
forget the works of God, but keep his **c**; Ps 78:7
my statutes and do not keep my **c**, Ps 89:31
covenant and remember to do his **c**. Ps 103:18
the LORD, who greatly delights in his **c**! Ps 112:1
having my eyes fixed on all your **c**. Ps 119:6
you; let me not wander from your **c**! Ps 119:10
on the earth; hide not your **c** from me! Ps 119:19
ones, who wander from your **c**. Ps 119:21
the way of your **c** when you enlarge Ps 119:32
Lead me in the path of your **c**, for I Ps 119:35
for I find my delight in your **c**, which I Ps 119:47
I will lift up my hands toward your **c**, Ps 119:48
hasten and do not delay to keep your **c**. Ps 119:60
and knowledge, for I believe in your **c**. Ps 119:66
that I may learn your **c**. Ps 119:73
All your **c** are sure; they persecute me Ps 119:86
that I may keep the **c** of my God. Ps 119:115
Therefore I love your **c** above gold, Ps 119:127
and pant, because I long for your **c**. Ps 119:131
me out, but your **c** are my delight. Ps 119:143
near, O LORD, and all your **c** are true. Ps 119:151
salvation, O LORD, and I do your **c**. Ps 119:166
of your word, for all your **c** are right. Ps 119:172
servant, for I do not forget your **c**. Ps 119:176
words and treasure up my **c** with you, Prv 2:1
teaching, but let your heart keep my **c**, Prv 3:1
hold fast my words; keep my **c**, and live. Prv 4:4
words and treasure up my **c** with you; Prv 7:1
keep my **c** and live; keep my teaching as Prv 7:2
The wise of heart will receive **c**, but a Prv 10:8
Fear God and keep his **c**, for this is Eccl 12:13
Oh that you had paid attention to my **c**! Is 48:18
with those who love him and keep his **c**, Dn 9:4
turning aside from your **c** and rules. Dn 9:5
the least of these **c** and teaches others to Mt 5:19
me, teaching as doctrines the **c** of men.'" Mt 15:9
If you would enter life, keep the **c**." Mt 19:17
On these two **c** depend all the Law and Mt 22:40
me, teaching as doctrines the **c** of men.' Mk 7:7
You know the **c**: 'Do not murder, Do Mk 10:19
blamelessly in all the **c** and statutes of the Lk 1:6
You know the **c**: 'Do not commit Lk 18:20
"If you love me, you will keep my **c**. Jn 14:15
Whoever has my **c** and keeps them, he Jn 14:21
If you keep my **c**, you will abide in my Jn 15:10
have kept my Father's **c** and abide in Jn 15:10
person who does the **c** shall live by Rom 10:5
The **c**, "You shall not commit Rom 13:9
but keeping the **c** of God. 1 Cor 7:19
the law of **c** and ordinances, Eph 2:15
come to know him, if we keep his **c**. 1 Jn 2:3
him" but does not keep his **c** is a liar, 1 Jn 2:4
because we keep his **c** and do what 1 Jn 3:22
Whoever keeps his **c** abides in him, 1 Jn 3:24
God, when we love God and obey his **c**. 1 Jn 5:2
this is the love of God, that we keep his **c**. 1 Jn 5:3
And his **c** are not burdensome. 1 Jn 5:3
is love, that we walk according to his **c**; 2 Jn 1:6
those who keep the **c** of God and hold Rv 12:17
those who keep the **c** of God and their Rv 14:12

COMMANDS (20)
"Your servants will do as my lord **c**. Nm 32:25
what the LORD **c** concerning the Nm 36:6
day the LORD your God **c** you to do these Dt 26:16
that my lord the king **c** his servant, 2 Sm 9:11
LORD and said to him, "The king **c**, 1 Kgs 2:30
who **c** the sun, and it does not rise; who Jb 9:7
to instruction and **c** that they return Jb 36:10
with the lightning and **c** it to strike the Jb 36:32
accomplish all that he **c** them on the Jb 37:12
By day the LORD **c** his steadfast love, and Ps 42:8
because they do not keep your **c**. Ps 119:158
For behold, the LORD **c**, and the great Am 6:11
humble of the land, who do his just **c**; Zep 2:3
He **c** even the unclean spirits, and they Mk 1:27
and **c** the doorkeeper to stay awake. Mk 13:34
and power he **c** the unclean spirits, Lk 4:36
is this, that he **c** even winds and water, Lk 8:25
after he had given **c** through the Holy Acts 1:2
but now he **c** all people everywhere to Acts 17:30
Jewish myths and the **c** of people who Ti 1:14

COMMEMORATION (1)
nor should the **c** of these days cease Est 9:28

COMMEND (11)
One generation shall **c** your works to Ps 145:4
And I **c** joy, for man has no good thing Eccl 8:15
And now I **c** you to God and to the Acts 20:32
I **c** to you our sister Phoebe, a servant Rom 16:1
Food will not **c** us to God. We are no 1 Cor 8:8
Now I **c** you because you remember 1 Cor 11:2
instructions I do not **c** you, 1 Cor 11:17
I say to you? Shall I **c** you in this? 1 Cor 11:22
we beginning to **c** ourselves again? 2 Cor 3:1
truth we would **c** ourselves to 2 Cor 4:2
servants of God we **c** ourselves in every 2 Cor 6:4

COMMENDABLE (1)
is pure, whatever is lovely, whatever is **c**, Phil 4:8

COMMENDATION (2)
each one will receive his **c** from God. 1 Cor 4:5
by it the people of old received their **c**. Heb 11:2

COMMENDED (8)
A man is **c** according to his good sense, Prv 12:8
The master **c** the dishonest manager for Lk 16:8
where they had been **c** to the grace of Acts 14:26
having been **c** by the brothers to the Acts 15:40
it, for I ought to have been **c** by you. 2 Cor 12:11
through which he was **c** as righteous, Heb 11:4
was taken he was **c** as having pleased Heb 11:5
these, though **c** through their faith, Heb 11:39

COMMENDING (3)
We are not **c** ourselves to you again 2 Cor 5:12
some of those who are **c** themselves. 2 Cor 10:12
God **c** him by accepting his gifts. Heb 11:4

COMMENDS (3)
The tongue of the wise **c** knowledge, Prv 15:2
not the one who **c** himself who is 2 Cor 10:18
but the one whom the Lord **c**. 2 Cor 10:18

COMMISSION (3)
and you shall **c** him in their sight. Nm 27:19
that I may **c** him." And Moses and Dt 31:14
with the authority and **c** of the chief Acts 26:12

COMMISSIONED (3)
hands on him and **c** him as the LORD Nm 27:23

And the LORD **c** Joshua the son of Nun Dt 31:23
but as men of sincerity, as **c** by God, 2 Cor 2:17

COMMISSIONS (1)
also delivered the king's **c** to the king's Ezr 8:36

COMMIT (38)
"You shall not **c** adultery. Ex 20:14
the sins that people **c** by breaking faith Nm 5:6
"'And you shall not **c** adultery. Dt 5:18
and shall never again **c** any such evil Dt 19:20
the LORD and made them **c** great sin. 2 Kgs 17:21
seek God, and to God would I **c** my cause, Jb 5:8
Into your hand I **c** my spirit; you have Ps 31:5
C your way to the LORD; trust in him, and Ps 37:5
C your work to the LORD, and your Prv 16:3
and will **c** your authority to his hand. Is 22:21
Will you steal, murder, **c** adultery, swear Jer 7:9
thing: they **c** adultery and walk in lies; Jer 23:14
Why do you **c** this great evil against Jer 44:7
still greater abominations that they **c**." Ezk 8:13
of Judah to **c** the abominations that Ezk 8:17
the abominations that they **c** here, Ezk 8:17
as women who **c** adultery and shed Ezk 16:38
they **c** lewdness in your midst. Ezk 22:9
and I will **c** the judgment to them, and Ezk 23:24
warning and not **c** lewdness as you Ezk 23:48
on the sword, you **c** abominations, Ezk 33:26
the whore, and your brides **c** adultery. Hos 4:13
nor your brides when they **c** adultery; Hos 4:14
on the way to Shechem; they **c** villainy. Hos 6:9
it was said, 'You shall not **c** adultery.' Mt 5:27
immorality, makes her **c** adultery. Mt 5:32
not murder, You shall not **c** adultery, Mt 19:18
'Do not murder, Do not **c** adultery, Do Mk 10:19
'Do not **c** adultery, Do not murder, Do Lk 18:20
into your hands I **c** my spirit!" And Lk 23:46
who say that one must not **c** adultery, Rom 2:22
commit adultery, do you **c** adultery? Rom 2:22
"You shall not **c** adultery, Rom 13:9
Or did I **c** a sin in humbling myself 2 Cor 11:7
who said, "Do not **c** adultery," also said, Jas 2:11
If you do not **c** adultery but do murder, Jas 2:11
life—to those who **c** sins that do not 1 Jn 5:16
and those who **c** adultery with her I will Rv 2:22

COMMITS (22)
"If anyone **c** a breach of faith and sins Lv 5:15
"If anyone sins and **c** a breach of faith Lv 6:2
"If a man **c** adultery with the wife of his Lv 20:10
a man or woman **c** any of the sins Nm 5:6
When he **c** iniquity, I will discipline 2 Sm 7:14
hands; to you the helpless **c** himself; Ps 10:14
He who **c** adultery lacks sense; he who Prv 6:32
from his righteousness and **c** injustice, Ezk 3:20
to the debtor his pledge, **c** no robbery, Ezk 18:7
the poor and needy, **c** robbery, Ezk 18:12
his eyes to the idols, **c** abomination, Ezk 18:12
exacts no pledge, **c** no robbery, Ezk 18:16
One **c** abomination with his Ezk 22:11
for the land **c** great whoredom by Hos 1:2
marries a divorced woman **c** adultery. Mt 5:32
and marries another, **c** adultery." Mt 19:9
marries another **c** adultery against Mk 10:11
and marries another, she **c** adultery." Mk 10:12
wife and marries another **c** adultery, Lk 16:18
divorced from her husband **c** adultery. Lk 16:18
you, everyone who **c** sin is a slave to sin. Jn 8:34
other sin a person **c** is outside the 1 Cor 6:18

COMMITTED (95)
and his baker **c** an offense against Gn 40:1
the sin that he has **c** a bull from the herd Lv 4:3
sin which they have **c** becomes known, Lv 4:14
the sin which he has **c** is made known to Lv 4:23
the sin which he has **c** is made known to Lv 4:28
blemish, for his sin which he has **c**. Lv 4:28
for him for the sin which he has **c**, Lv 4:35
of these and confesses the sin he has **c**, Lv 5:5
compensation for the sin that he has **c**, Lv 5:6
sin that he has **c** two turtledoves or two Lv 5:7
for him for the sin that he has **c**, Lv 5:10
the sin that he has **c** a tenth of an ephah Lv 5:11
the sin which he has **c** in any one of Lv 5:13
or the deposit that was **c** to him or the lost Lv 6:4
before the LORD for his sin that he has **c**, Lv 19:22
be forgiven for the sin that he has **c**. Lv 19:22
be put to death; they have **c** perversion; Lv 20:12
both of them have **c** an abomination; Lv 20:13
their treachery that they **c** against me, Lv 26:40
he shall confess his sin that he has **c**. Nm 5:7
because of all the sin that you had **c**, Dt 9:18
with any offense that he has **c**. Dt 19:15
if a man has **c** a crime punishable by Dt 21:22
she has **c** no offense punishable by Dt 22:26
faith that you have **c** against the God of Jos 22:16
because you have not **c** this breach of Jos 22:31
which he **c** against his father in killing Jgs 9:56
for they have **c** abomination and Jgs 20:6
the outrage that they have **c** in Israel." Jgs 20:10
that they have **c** against you, 1 Kgs 8:50
jealousy with their sins that they **c**, 1 Kgs 14:22
and **c** them to the hands of the 1 Kgs 14:27
because of his sins that he **c**, doing 1 Kgs 16:19
and for his sin which he **c**, 1 Kgs 16:19
of Judah has **c** these abominations 2 Kgs 21:11
all that he did, and the sin that he **c**, 2 Kgs 21:17
shields of bronze and **c** them to the 2 Chr 12:10
"All that was **c** to your servants they 2 Chr 34:16
of Egypt,' and had **c** great blasphemies, Neh 9:18
to you, and they **c** great blasphemies. Neh 9:26
fathers have sinned; we have **c** iniquity; Ps 106:6
every way: a king **c** to cultivated fields. Eccl 5:9
for my people have **c** two evils: they have Jer 2:13
they **c** adultery and trooped to the houses Jer 5:7
ashamed when they **c** abomination? Jer 6:15
ashamed when they **c** abomination? Jer 8:12
them, for to you have I **c** my cause. Jer 11:20
sin that we have **c** against the LORD our Jer 16:10
them, for to you have I **c** my cause. Jer 20:12
they have **c** adultery with their Jer 29:23
and they **c** Jeremiah to the court of the Jer 37:21
in the land and had **c** to him men, Jer 40:7
had **c** to Gedaliah the son of Ahikam. Jer 41:10
because of the evil that they **c**, Jer 44:3
which they **c** in the land of Judah and in Jer 44:9
deeds and the abominations that you **c**. Jer 44:22
own sight for the evils that they have **c**, Ezk 6:9
all the abominations that are **c** in it." Ezk 9:4
"Have you not **c** lewdness in addition Ezk 16:43
Samaria has not **c** half your sins. You Ezk 16:51
You have **c** more abominations than Ezk 16:51
all the abominations that you have **c**. Ezk 16:51
for the treachery he has **c** against me. Ezk 17:20
his sins that he has **c** and keeps all my Ezk 18:21
that he has **c** shall be remembered Ezk 18:22
he is guilty and the sin he has **c**, Ezk 18:24
wickedness he has **c** and does what Ezk 18:27
all the transgressions that he had **c**, Ezk 18:28
all the transgressions that you have **c**, Ezk 18:31
for all the evils that you have **c**. Ezk 20:43
practiced extortion and **c** robbery. Ezk 22:29
For they have **c** adultery, and blood is Ezk 23:37
With their idols they have **c** adultery, Ezk 23:37
that he has **c** shall be remembered Ezk 33:16
their abominations that they have **c**. Ezk 33:29
their abominations that they have **c**, Ezk 43:8
the abominations that they have **c**. Ezk 44:13
treachery that they have **c** against you. Dn 9:7
abomination has been **c** in Israel and Mal 2:11
intent has already **c** adultery with her Mt 5:28
who had **c** murder in the insurrection, Mk 15:7
men and women and **c** them to prison. Acts 8:3
prayer and fasting they **c** them to the Acts 14:23
against Caesar have I **c** any offense." Acts 25:8
wrongdoer and have **c** anything for Acts 25:11
of teaching to which you were **c**, Rom 6:17
from the transgressions **c** under the Heb 9:15
And if he has **c** sins, he will be forgiven. Jas 5:15
He **c** no sin, neither was deceit found in 1 Pt 2:22
them into hell and **c** them to chains of 2 Pt 2:4
that they have **c** in such an Jude 1:15
of the earth have **c** sexual immorality, Rv 17:2
of the earth have **c** immorality with her, Rv 18:3
who **c** sexual immorality and lived in Rv 18:9
to whom the authority to judge was **c**. Rv 20:4

COMMITTING (8)
the land, **c** adultery with stone and tree. Jer 3:9
lies; they weary themselves **c** iniquity. Jer 9:5
that the house of Israel are **c** here, Ezk 8:6
vile abominations that they are **c** here." Ezk 8:9
lying, murder, stealing, and **c** adultery; Hos 4:2
men **c** shameless acts with men and Rom 1:27
you are **c** sin and are convicted by the Jas 2:9
anyone sees his brother **c** a sin not 1 Jn 5:16

COMMON (30)
anyone of the **c** people sins Lv 4:27
distinguish between the holy and the **c**, Lv 10:10
its breadth, according to the **c** cubit.) Dt 3:11
David, "I have no **c** bread on hand, 1 Sm 21:4
made silver as **c** in Jerusalem as 1 Kgs 10:27
of it upon the graves of the **c** people. 2 Kgs 23:6
silver and gold as **c** in Jerusalem as 2 Chr 1:15
king made silver as **c** in Jerusalem as 2 Chr 9:27
Levites left their **c** lands and their 2 Chr 11:14
in the fields of **c** land belonging to 2 Chr 31:19
large tablet and write on it in **c** characters, Is 8:1
What has straw in **c** with wheat? Jer 23:28
into the burial place of the **c** people. Jer 26:23
between the holy and the **c**, Ezk 22:26
with men of the **c** sort drunkards were Ezk 23:42
separation between the holy and the **c**. Ezk 42:20
difference between the holy and the **c**, Ezk 44:23
length, shall be for **c** use for the city, Ezk 48:15
were together and had all things in **c**. Acts 2:44
that they were uneducated, **c** men, Acts 4:13
his own, but they had everything in **c**. Acts 4:32
eaten anything that is **c** or unclean." Acts 10:14
God has made clean, do not call **c**." Acts 10:15
not call any person **c** or unclean. Acts 10:28
for nothing **c** or unclean has ever Acts 11:8
God has made clean, do not call **c**.' Acts 11:9
overtaken you that is not **c** to man. 1 Cor 10:13
of the Spirit for the **c** good. 1 Cor 12:7
To Titus, my true child in a **c** faith: Grace Ti 1:4
to write to you about our **c** salvation, Jude 1:3

COMMONWEALTH (1)
alienated from the **c** of Israel and Eph 2:12

COMMOTION (6)
servant, your servant, I saw a great **c**, 2 Sm 18:29
a great **c** out of the north country to Jer 10:22
flute players and the crowd making a **c**, Mt 9:23
of the synagogue, and Jesus saw a **c**, Mk 5:38
are you making a **c** and weeping? Mk 5:39
that we can give to justify this **c**." Acts 19:40

COMMUNICATE (2)
lest they **c** holiness to the people with Ezk 44:19
outer court and so **c** holiness to the Ezk 46:20

COMPANIES (22)
Israel shall pitch their tents by their **c**, Nm 1:52
of the camp of Judah by their **c**, Nm 2:3
listed of the camp of Judah, by their **c**, Nm 2:9
of the camp of Reuben by their **c**, Nm 2:10
listed of the camp of Reuben, by their **c**, Nm 2:16
of the camp of Ephraim by their **c**, Nm 2:18
of the camp of Ephraim, by their **c**, Nm 2:24
standard of the camp of Dan by their **c**, Nm 2:25
in the camps by their **c** were 603,550. Nm 2:32
people of Judah set out first by their **c**, Nm 10:14
the camp of Reuben set out by their **c**, Nm 10:18
people of Ephraim set out by their **c**, Nm 10:22
of all the camps, set out by their **c**, Nm 10:25
of the people of Israel by their **c**, Nm 10:28
of Egypt by their **c** under the leadership Nm 33:1
300 men into three **c** and put trumpets Jgs 7:16
Then the three **c** blew the trumpets and Jgs 7:20
an ambush against Shechem in four **c**. Jgs 9:34
divided them into three **c** and set an Jgs 9:43
while the two **c** rushed upon all who Jgs 9:44
day Saul put the people in three **c**. 1 Sm 11:11
camp of the Philistines in three **c**. 1 Sm 13:17

COMPANION (16)
the wrong, "Why do you strike your **c**?" Ex 2:13
brother and his **c** and his neighbor.'" Ex 32:27
And Samson's wife was given to his **c**, Jgs 14:20
utterly hated her, so I gave her to your **c**. Jgs 15:2
given her to his **c**." And the Philistines Jgs 15:6
a brother of jackals and a **c** of ostriches. Jb 30:29
But it is you, a man, my equal, my **c**, Ps 55:13
My **c** stretched out his hand against his Ps 55:20
I am a **c** of all who fear you, of those Ps 119:63
who forsakes the **c** of her youth and Prv 2:17
but the **c** of fools will suffer harm. Prv 13:20
but a **c** of gluttons shames his father. Prv 28:7
no transgression," is a **c** to a man who Prv 28:24
but a **c** of prostitutes squanders his Prv 29:3
though she is your **c** and your wife by Mal 2:14
Yes, I ask you also, true **c**, help these Phil 4:3

COMPANIONS (21)
and weep for my virginity, I and my **c**." Jgs 11:37
and she departed, she and her **c**, Jgs 11:38
they brought thirty **c** to be with him. Jgs 14:11
My friends and **c** stand aloof from my Ps 38:11
with the oil of gladness beyond your **c**; Ps 45:7
with her virgin **c** following behind her. Ps 45:14
You have caused my **c** to shun me; you Ps 88:8
shun me; my **c** have become darkness. Ps 88:18
A man of many **c** may come to ruin, Prv 18:24
veils herself beside the flocks of your **c**? Sg 1:7
gardens, with **c** listening for your voice; Sg 8:13
Your princes are rebels and **c** of thieves. Is 1:23
Behold, all his **c** shall be put to shame, Is 44:11
did not put them to death with their **c**. Jer 41:8
and they sought Daniel and his **c**, to kill Dn 2:13
Hananiah, Mishael, and Azariah, his **c**, Dn 2:17
that Daniel and his **c** might not be Dn 2:18
and that seemed greater than its **c**. Dn 7:20
Now Paul and his **c** set sail from Acts 13:13
who were Paul's **c** in travel. Acts 19:29
with the oil of gladness beyond your **c**." Heb 1:9

COMPANIONS' (1)
For my brothers and **c** sake I will say, Ps 122:8

COMPANY (76)
that you may become a **c** of peoples. Gn 28:3
mean by all this **c** that I met?" Jacob Gn 33:8
A nation and a **c** of nations shall come Gn 35:11
will make of you a **c** of peoples and will Gn 48:4
O my glory, be not joined to their **c**. Gn 49:6
and horsemen. It was a very great **c**. Gn 50:9
Aaron shall list them, **c** by company. Nm 1:3
Aaron shall list them, company by **c**. Nm 1:3
his **c** as listed being 74,600. Nm 2:4
his **c** as listed being 54,400. Nm 2:6
his **c** as listed being 57,400. Nm 2:8
his **c** as listed being 46,500. Nm 2:11
his **c** as listed being 59,300. Nm 2:13
his **c** as listed being 45,650. Nm 2:15
his **c** as listed being 40,500. Nm 2:19
his **c** as listed being 32,200. Nm 2:21
his **c** as listed being 35,400. Nm 2:23
his **c** as listed being 62,700. Nm 2:26
his **c** as listed being 41,500. Nm 2:28
his **c** as listed being 53,400. Nm 2:30
and over their **c** was Nahshon the son Nm 10:14
And over the **c** of the tribe of the Nm 10:15
And over the **c** of the tribe of the Nm 10:16
and over their **c** was Elizur the son of Nm 10:18
And over the **c** of the tribe of the Nm 10:19
And over the **c** of the tribe of the Nm 10:20
and over their **c** was Elishama the son Nm 10:22
And over the **c** of the tribe of the Nm 10:23
And over the **c** of the tribe of the Nm 10:24
and over their **c** was Ahiezer the son Nm 10:25
And over the **c** of the tribe of the Nm 10:26
And over the **c** of the tribe of the Nm 10:27
and he said to Korah and all his **c**, "In Nm 16:5
this: take censers, Korah and all his **c**; Nm 16:6
and all your **c** have gathered together. Nm 16:11
"Be present, you and all your **c**, Nm 16:16
like Korah and his **c**—as the LORD Nm 16:40
Moses and Aaron in the **c** of Korah, Nm 26:9
together with Korah, when that **c** died, Nm 26:10
was not among the **c** of those who Nm 27:3
against the LORD in the **c** of Korah, Nm 27:3
and one **c** is coming from the direction Jgs 9:37
Abimelech and the **c** that was with him Jgs 9:44
you, that you come with such a **c**?" Jgs 18:23
One **c** turned toward Ophrah, to the 1 Sm 13:17
another **c** turned toward Beth-horon; 1 Sm 13:18
and another **c** turned toward the 1 Sm 13:18
when they saw the **c** of the prophets 1 Sm 19:20
to the man of God, he and all his **c**, 2 Kgs 5:15
and he saw the **c** of Jehu as he came 2 Kgs 9:17
and said, "I see a **c**." And Joram said, 2 Kgs 9:17
For the **c** of the godless is barren, and Jb 15:34
me out; he has made desolate all my **c**. Jb 16:7
They are driven out from human **c**; they Jb 30:5
who travels in **c** with evildoers and walks Jb 34:8
me; a **c** of evildoers encircles me; Ps 22:16
him, and you keep **c** with adulterers. Ps 50:18
and distress, a **c** of destroying angels. Ps 78:49
Dathan, and covered the **c** of Abiram. Ps 106:17
Fire also broke out in their **c**; the Ps 106:18
my whole heart, in the **c** of the upright, Ps 111:1
with wicked deeds in **c** with men who Ps 141:4
are all adulterers, a **c** of treacherous men. Jer 9:2
I did not sit in the **c** of revelers, nor did I Jer 15:17
together; a great **c**, they shall return here. Jer 31:8
mighty army and great **c** will not help Ezk 17:17
"Assyria is there, and all her **c**, its Ezk 32:22
and her **c** is all around her grave, all Ezk 32:23
danced before the **c** and pleased Herod, Mt 14:6
there was a large **c** of tax collectors and Lk 5:29
Then the whole **c** of them arose and Lk 23:1
some women of our **c** amazed us. Lk 24:22
the brothers (the **c** of persons was Acts 1:15
I have enjoyed your **c** for a while. Rom 15:24
with joy and be refreshed in your **c**. Rom 15:32
deceived: "Bad **c** ruins good morals." 1 Cor 15:33

COMPARE (16)
that no other king shall **c** with you, 1 Kgs 3:13
toward us; none can **c** with you! Ps 40:5
and nothing you desire can **c** with her. Prv 3:15
that you may desire cannot **c** with her. Prv 8:11
I **c** you, my love, to a mare among Sg 1:9
liken God, or what likeness **c** with him? Is 40:18
To whom then will you **c** me, that I Is 40:25
liken me and make me equal, and **c** me, Is 46:5
What can I say for you, to what **c** you, Lam 2:13
"But to what shall I **c** this generation? Mt 11:16
"With what can we **c** the kingdom of Mk 4:30
"To what then shall I **c** the people of this Lk 7:31
of God like? And to what shall I **c** it? Lk 13:18
"To what shall I **c** the kingdom of God? Lk 13:20
to classify or **c** ourselves with some 2 Cor 10:12
one another and **c** themselves with 2 Cor 10:12

COMPARED (5)
affliction is not to be **c** with the loss to the Est 7:4
who in the skies can be **c** to the LORD? Ps 89:6
of heaven may be **c** to a man who Mt 13:24
of heaven may be **c** to a king who Mt 18:23
of heaven may be **c** to a king who Mt 22:2

COMPARING (1)
time are not worth **c** with the glory Rom 8:18

COMPARISON (3)
"What have I done now in **c** with you? Jgs 8:2
able to do in **c** with you?" Then their Jgs 8:3
eternal weight of glory beyond all **c**, 2 Cor 4:17

COMPASS (1)
it with planes and marks it with a **c**. Is 44:13

COMPASSING (2)
for ten cubits, **c** the sea all around. 1 Kgs 7:24
for ten cubits, **c** the sea all around. 2 Chr 4:3

COMPASSION (53)
for his **c** grew warm for his brother, Gn 43:30
you mercy and have **c** on you and Dt 13:17
restore your fortunes and have **c** on you, Dt 30:3
his people and have **c** on his servants, Dt 32:36
people of Israel had **c** for Benjamin their Jgs 21:6
the people had **c** on Benjamin because Jgs 21:15
the LORD, for you have had **c** on me. 1 Sm 23:21
and grant them **c** in the sight of those 1 Kgs 8:50
that they may have **c** on them 1 Kgs 8:50
to them and had **c** on them, 2 Kgs 13:23
children will find **c** with their 2 Chr 30:9
because he had **c** on his people and 2 Chr 36:15
and had no **c** on young man 2 Chr 36:17
Has he in anger shut up his **c**?" Selah Ps 77:9
let your **c** come speedily to meet us, for Ps 79:8
As a father shows **c** to his children, so Ps 103:13
so the LORD shows **c** to those who fear Ps 103:13
his people and have **c** on his servants. Ps 135:14
and has no **c** on their fatherless and Is 9:17
the LORD will have **c** on Jacob and will Is 14:1
made them will not have **c** on them; Is 27:11
people and will have **c** on his afflicted. Is 49:13
that she should have no **c** on the son of Is 49:15
you, but with great **c** I will gather you. Is 54:7
love I will have **c** on you," says the Is 54:8
says the LORD, who has **c** on you. Is 54:10
to the LORD, that he may have **c** on him, Is 55:7
he has granted them according to his **c**, Is 63:7
inner parts and your **c** are held back Is 63:15
them up, I will again have **c** on them, Jer 12:15
I will not pity or spare or have **c**, that I Jer 13:14
not pity them or spare them or have **c**.' Jer 21:7
of Jacob and have **c** on his dwellings; Jer 30:18
he will have **c** according to the Lam 3:32
of these things to you out of **c** for you, Ezk 16:5
gave Daniel favor and **c** in the sight of Dn 1:9
me; my **c** grows warm and tender. Hos 11:8
your sting? **C** is hidden from my eyes. Hos 13:14
He will again have **c** on us; he will tread Mi 7:19
them back because I have **c** on them, Zec 10:6
he saw the crowds, he had **c** for them, Mt 9:36
and he had **c** on them and healed their Mt 14:14
"I have **c** on the crowd because they Mt 15:32
a great crowd, and he had **c** on them, Mk 6:34
"I have **c** on the crowd, because they Mk 8:2
do anything, have **c** on us and help us." Mk 9:22
saw her, he had **c** on her and said to her, Lk 7:13
was, and when he saw him, he had **c**. Lk 10:33
way off, his father saw him and felt **c**, Lk 15:20
and I will have **c** on whom I have Rom 9:15
have compassion on whom I have **c**." Rom 9:15
ones, holy and beloved, **c**, kindness, Col 3:12
For you had **c** on those in prison, and Heb 10:34

COMPASSIONATE (4)
if he cries to me, I will hear, for I am **c**. Ex 22:27
Yet he, being **c**, atoned for their iniquity Ps 78:38
The hands of **c** women have boiled Lam 4:10
Lord, how the Lord is **c** and merciful. Jas 5:11

COMPEL (1)
and hedges and **c** people to come Lk 14:23

COMPELLED (5)
let you go unless **c** by a mighty hand. Ex 3:19
Young men are **c** to grind at the mill, Lam 5:13
They **c** this man to carry his cross. Mt 27:32
And they **c** a passerby, Simon of Mk 15:21
I was **c** to appeal to Caesar—though I Acts 28:19

COMPELS (1)
him; with her smooth talk she **c** him. Prv 7:21

COMPENSATION (6)
to the LORD as his **c** for the sin that he Lv 5:6
to the LORD as his **c** for the sin that he Lv 5:7
LORD, he shall bring to the LORD as his **c**, Lv 5:15
to the priest as his **c** to the LORD a ram Lv 6:6
but he shall bring his **c** to the LORD, to Lv 19:21
He will accept no **c**; he will refuse Prv 6:35

COMPETE (4)
men arise and **c** before us." And 2 Sm 2:14
wearied you, how will you **c** with horses? Jer 12:5
you are a king because you **c** in cedar? Jer 22:15
know that in a race all the runners **c**, 1 Cor 9:24

COMPETENT (4)
and **c** to stand in the king's palace, Dn 1:4
an eloquent man, **c** in the Scriptures. Acts 18:24
who has made us **c** to be ministers of a 2 Cor 3:6
that the man of God may be **c**, 2 Tm 3:17

COMPETES (1)
crowned unless he **c** according to the 2 Tm 2:5

COMPILE (1)
many have undertaken to **c** a narrative of Lk 1:1

COMPLACENCY (3)
me and your **c** has come into 2 Kgs 19:28
away, and the **c** of fools destroys them; Prv 1:32
against me and your **c** has come to my Is 37:29

COMPLACENT (4)
at ease, hear my voice; you **c** daughters, Is 32:9
a year you will shudder, you **c** women; Is 32:10
who are at ease, shudder, you **c** ones; Is 32:11
and I will punish the men who are **c**, Zep 1:12

COMPLAIN (4)
or their brothers come to **c** to us, Jgs 21:22
spirit; I will **c** in the bitterness of my soul. Jb 7:11
are you, O LORD, when I **c** to you; Jer 12:1
Why should a living man **c**, a man, Lam 3:39

COMPLAINED (1)
And the people **c** in the hearing of the Nm 11:1

COMPLAINING (1)
sorrow? Who has strife? Who has **c**? Prv 23:29

COMPLAINT (19)
comfort me, my couch will ease my **c**,' Jb 7:13
If I say, 'I will forget my **c**, I will put off Jb 9:27
my life; I will give free utterance to my **c**; Jb 10:1
As for me, is my **c** against man? Why Jb 21:4
"Today also my **c** is bitter; my hand is Jb 23:2
when they brought a **c** against me, Jb 31:13
me; I am restless in my **c** and I moan, Ps 55:2
and at noon I utter my **c** and moan, Ps 55:17
Hear my voice, O God, in my **c**; preserve Ps 64:1
and pours out his **c** before the LORD. Ps 102:T
I pour out my **c** before him; I tell my Ps 142:2
find a ground for **c** against Daniel with Dn 6:4
could find no ground for **c** or any fault, Dn 6:4
find any ground for **c** against this Daniel Dn 6:5
what I will answer concerning my **c**. Hab 2:1
a **c** by the Hellenists arose against the Acts 6:1
I would have reason to accept your **c**. Acts 18:14
with him have a **c** against anyone, Acts 19:38
and, if one has a **c** against another, Col 3:13

COMPLETE (25)
iniquity of the Amorites is not yet **c**." Gn 15:16
C the week of this one, and we will give Gn 29:27
were urgent, saying, "**C** your work, Ex 5:13
you must devote them to **c** destruction. Dt 7:2
you shall devote them to **c** destruction, Dt 20:17
around from the Millo in **c** circuit, 1 Chr 11:8
so as not to make a **c** destruction. 2 Chr 12:12
For he will **c** what he appoints for me, Jb 23:14
him, they **c** their days in prosperity, Jb 36:11
I hate them with **c** hatred; I count Ps 139:22
he will make a **c** end of the adversaries, Na 1:8
He will make a **c** end; trouble will not rise Na 1:9
of this house; his hands shall also **c** it. Zec 4:9
the cost, whether he has enough to **c** it? Lk 14:28
Therefore this joy of mine is now **c**. Jn 3:29
so he should **c** among you this act of 2 Cor 8:6
when your obedience is **c**. 2 Cor 10:6
c my joy by being of the same mind, Phil 2:2
risking his life to **c** what was lacking Phil 2:30
exhort, with **c** patience and teaching. 2 Tm 4:2
full effect, that you may be perfect and **c**, Jas 1:4
these things so that our joy may be **c**. 1 Jn 1:4
face to face, so that our joy may be **c**. 2 Jn 1:12
not found your works **c** in the sight of Rv 3:2
servants and their brothers should be **c**, Rv 6:11

COMPLETED (20)
When her days to give birth were **c**, Gn 25:24
I may go in to her, for my time is **c**." Gn 29:21
Jacob did so, and **c** her week. Then Gn 29:28
until the days of your ordination are **c**, Lv 8:33
until the days of her purifying are **c**. Lv 12:4
when the days of her purifying are **c**, Lv 12:6
Until the time is **c** for which he Nm 6:5
the time of his separation has been **c**: Nm 6:13
So the house of the LORD was **c**. 2 Chr 8:16

And when these days were **c**, the king Est 1:5
Then after seventy years are **c**, I will Jer 25:12
When seventy years are **c** for Babylon, Jer 29:10
And when you have **c** these, you shall lie Ezk 4:6
till you have **c** the days of your siege. Ezk 4:8
the city, when the days of the siege are **c**. Ezk 5:2
And when they have **c** these days, then Ezk 43:27
when they had **c** their service, Acts 12:25
When the seven days were almost **c**, Acts 21:27
therefore I have **c** this and have Rom 15:28
his works, and faith was **c** by his works; Jas 2:22

COMPLETELY (8)
he lets you go, he will drive you away **c**. Ex 11:1
by its wings, but shall not sever it **c**. Lv 1:17
head from its neck but shall not sever it **c**, Lv 5:8
the Arabah, the Salt Sea, were **c** cut off. Jos 3:16
labor, but did not drive them out **c**. Jgs 1:28
who seek the LORD understand it **c**. Prv 28:5
wash, except for his feet, but is **c** clean. Jn 13:10
God of peace himself sanctify you **c**, 1 Thes 5:23

COMPLETING (1)
be matched by your **c** it out of what 2 Cor 8:11

COMPLETION (2)
bringing holiness to **c** in the fear of 2 Cor 7:1
you will bring it to **c** at the day of Jesus Phil 1:6

COMPOSED (1)
But God has so **c** the body, giving 1 Cor 12:24

COMPOSITION (2)
you shall make no other like it in **c**. Ex 30:32
that you shall make according to its **c**, Ex 30:37

COMPOUNDS (1)
Whoever **c** any like it or whoever puts Ex 30:33

COMPREHEND (3)
he does great things that we cannot **c**. Jb 37:5
of an obscure speech that you cannot **c**, Is 33:19
may have strength to **c** with all the Eph 3:18

COMPREHENDED (1)
Have you **c** the expanse of the earth? Jb 38:18

COMPREHENDS (1)
So also no one **c** the thoughts of God 1 Cor 2:11

COMPULSION (4)
"There is no **c**." For the king had given Est 1:8
his mind, not reluctantly or under **c**, 2 Cor 9:7
might not be by **c** but of your own Phlm 1:14
you, exercising oversight, not under **c**, 1 Pt 5:2

COMRADE (3)
a man was telling a dream to his **c**. Jgs 7:13
And his **c** answered, "This is no other Jgs 7:14
sword against his **c** and against all Jgs 7:22

CONANIAH (3)
in charge of them was **C** the Levite, 2 Chr 31:12
overseers assisting **C** and Shimei 2 Chr 31:13
C also, and Shemaiah and Nethanel 2 Chr 35:9

CONCEAL (9)
if we kill our brother and **c** his blood? Gn 37:26
you spare him, nor shall you **c** him. Dt 13:8
that you would **c** me until your wrath Jb 14:13
what is with the Almighty I will not **c**. Jb 27:11
from his deed and **c** pride from a man; Jb 33:17
he will **c** me under the cover of his tent; Ps 27:5
It is the glory of God to **c** things, but the Prv 25:2
places, and he is not able to **c** himself. Jer 49:10
set up a banner and proclaim, **c** it not, Jer 50:2

CONCEALED (6)
eyes of all living and **c** from the birds of Jb 28:21
if I have **c** my transgressions as others Jb 31:33
I have not **c** your steadfast love and Ps 40:10
in secret averts anger, and a **c** bribe, Prv 21:14
nor is their iniquity **c** from my eyes. Jer 16:17
this saying, and it was **c** from them, Lk 9:45

CONCEALS (5)
but the mouth of the wicked **c** violence. Prv 10:6
the mouth of the wicked **c** violence. Prv 10:11
The one who **c** hatred has lying lips, Prv 10:18
A prudent man **c** knowledge, but the Prv 12:23
Whoever **c** his transgressions will not Prv 28:13

CONCEIT (6)
regard any who are wise in their own **c**." Jb 37:24
slander, gossip, **c**, and disorder. 2 Cor 12:20
Do nothing from rivalry or **c**, but in Phil 2:3
become puffed up with **c** and fall into 1 Tm 3:6
puffed up with **c** and understands 1 Tm 6:4
treacherous, reckless, swollen with **c**, 2 Tm 3:4

CONCEITED (2)
associate with the lowly. Never be **c**. Rom 12:16
Let us not become **c**, provoking one Gal 5:26

CONCEITS (1)
Lest you be wise in your own **c**, I Rom 11:25

CONCEIVE (13)
she shall be free and shall **c** children. Nm 5:28
Did I **c** all this people? Did I give them Nm 11:12
children, but you shall **c** and bear a son. Jgs 13:3
for behold, you shall **c** and bear a son. Jgs 13:5
me, 'Behold, you shall **c** and bear a son. Jgs 13:7
They **c** trouble and give birth to evil, Jb 15:35
iniquity, and in sin did my mother **c** me. Ps 51:5
Behold, the virgin shall **c** and bear a son, Is 7:14
You **c** chaff; you give birth to stubble; Is 33:11
they **c** mischief and give birth to iniquity. Is 59:4
the virgin shall **c** and bear a son, Mt 1:23
you will **c** in your womb and bear a son, Lk 1:31
Sarah herself received power to **c**, Heb 11:11

CONCEIVED (39)
Eve his wife, and she **c** and bore Cain, Gn 4:1
his wife, and she **c** and bore Enoch. Gn 4:17
And he went in to Hagar, and she **c**. And Gn 16:4
And when she saw that she had **c**, she Gn 16:4
and when she saw that she had **c**, Gn 16:5
And Sarah **c** and bore Abraham a son Gn 21:2
his prayer, and Rebekah his wife **c**. Gn 25:21
And Leah **c** and bore a son, and she Gn 29:32
She **c** again and bore a son, and said, Gn 29:33
Again she **c** and bore a son, and said, Gn 29:34
And she **c** again and bore a son, and Gn 29:35
And Bilhah **c** and bore Jacob a son. Gn 30:5
Rachel's servant Bilhah **c** again and Gn 30:7
and she **c** and bore Jacob a fifth son. Gn 30:17
And Leah **c** again, and she bore Jacob Gn 30:19
She **c** and bore a son and said, "God Gn 30:23
and she **c** and bore a son, and he called Gn 38:3
She **c** again and bore a son, and she Gn 38:4
and went in to her, and she **c** by him. Gn 38:18
The woman **c** and bore a son, and when Ex 2:2
in due time Hannah **c** and bore a son, 1 Sm 1:20
and she **c** and bore three sons and two 1 Sm 2:21
And the woman **c**, and she sent and 2 Sm 11:5
But the woman **c**, and she bore a son 2 Kgs 4:17
and she **c** and bore Miriam, 1 Chr 4:17
to his wife, and she **c** and bore a son. 1 Chr 7:23
born, and the night that said, 'A man is **c**.' Jb 3:3
and into the chamber of her who **c** me. Sg 3:4
to the prophetess, and she **c** and bore a son. Is 8:3
Diblaim, and she **c** and bore him a son. Hos 1:3
She **c** again and bore a daughter. And Hos 1:6
weaned No Mercy, she **c** and bore a son. Hos 1:8
she who **c** them has acted shamefully. Hos 2:5
for that which is **c** in her is from the Mt 1:20
After these days his wife Elizabeth **c**, and Lk 1:24
Elizabeth in her old age has also **c** a son, Lk 1:36
the angel before he was **c** in the womb. Lk 2:21
when Rebecca had **c** children by one Rom 9:10
desire when it has **c** gives birth to sin, Jas 1:15

CONCEIVES (2)
'If a woman **c** and bears a male child, Lv 12:2
the wicked man **c** evil and is pregnant Ps 7:14

CONCEIVING (1)
c and uttering from the heart lying Is 59:13

CONCEPTION (2)
went in to her, and the LORD gave her **c**, Ru 4:13
a bird—no birth, no pregnancy, no **c**! Hos 9:11

CONCERN (6)
him he had no **c** about anything but Gn 39:6
my master has no **c** about anything in Gn 39:8
Have no **c** for your goods, for the best Gn 45:20
But I had **c** for my holy name, which Ezk 36:21
length you have revived your **c** for me. Phil 4:10
covenant, and so I showed no **c** for them, Heb 8:9

CONCERNED (4)
when called? Do not be **c** about it. 1 Cor 7:21
the grain." Is it for oxen that God is **c**? 1 Cor 9:9
will be genuinely **c** for your welfare. Phil 2:20
You were indeed **c** for me, but you had Phil 4:10

CONCERNING (210)
And Pharaoh gave men orders **c** him, Gn 12:20
master and swore to him **c** this matter. Gn 24:9
"In truth we are guilty **c** our brother, Gn 42:21
made it a statute **c** the land of Egypt, Gn 47:26
Exactly as I show you **c** the pattern of the Ex 25:9
LORD commanded Moses **c** the Levites, Nm 8:20
had commanded Moses **c** the Levites, Nm 8:22
what the LORD will command **c** you." Nm 9:8
out of her lips **c** her vows or Nm 30:12
her vows or **c** her pledge of Nm 30:12
Moses gave command **c** them to Nm 32:28
the LORD commands **c** the daughters of Nm 36:6
stones, **c** which I command you today, Dt 27:4
of God in Kadesh-barnea **c** you and me. Jos 14:6
that the LORD your God promised **c** you. Jos 23:14
your God promised **c** you have been Jos 23:15
taken a great oath **c** him who did not Jgs 21:5
times in Israel **c** redeeming and Ru 4:7
Eli all that I have spoken **c** his house, 1 Sm 3:12
you before the LORD **c** all the righteous 1 Sm 12:7
that he has spoken **c** you and has 1 Sm 25:30
me today with a fault **c** a woman. 2 Sm 3:8
you have spoken **c** your servant and 2 Sm 7:25
your servant and **c** his house, 2 Sm 7:25
servants to console him **c** his father. 2 Sm 10:2
house, and I will give orders **c** you." 2 Sm 14:8
establish his word that he spoke **c** me, 1 Kgs 2:4
that he had spoken **c** the house of Eli 1 Kgs 2:27
"**C** this house that you are building, 1 Kgs 6:12
the fame of Solomon **c** the name of 1 Kgs 10:1
from the nations **c** which the LORD 1 Kgs 11:2
had commanded him **c** this thing, 1 Kgs 11:10
is coming to inquire of you **c** her son, 1 Kgs 14:5
for he never prophesies good **c** me, 1 Kgs 22:8
he would not prophesy good **c** me, 1 Kgs 22:18
which the LORD spoke **c** the house of 2 Kgs 10:10
c whom the LORD had commanded 2 Kgs 17:15
the king heard **c** Tirhakah king of 2 Kgs 19:9
that the LORD has spoken **c** him: 2 Kgs 19:21
thus says the LORD **c** the king of 2 Kgs 19:32
c the words of this book that has 2 Kgs 22:13
according to all that is written **c** us." 2 Kgs 22:13
to the word of the LORD **c** Israel. 1 Chr 11:10
you have spoken **c** your servant and 1 Chr 17:23
your servant and **c** his house be 1 Chr 17:23
to console him **c** his father. 1 Chr 19:2
When David was told **c** the men, he 1 Chr 19:5
your God, as he has spoken **c** you. 1 Chr 22:11
in all matters **c** the divisions that 1 Chr 27:1
priests and Levites **c** any matter and 2 Chr 8:15
any matter and **c** the treasuries. 2 Chr 8:15
of Iddo the seer **c** Jeroboam the son of 2 Chr 9:29
for he never prophesies good **c** me, 2 Chr 18:7
he would not prophesy good **c** me, 2 Chr 18:17
LORD has declared disaster **c** you." 2 Chr 18:22
who live in their cities, **c** bloodshed, 2 Chr 19:10
as the LORD spoke **c** the sons of David. 2 Chr 23:3
c the words of the book that has 2 Chr 34:21
then an answer be returned by letter **c** it. Ezr 5:5
C the house of God at Jerusalem, let the Ezr 6:3
And I asked them **c** the Jews who Neh 1:2
had survived the exile, and **c** Jerusalem. Neh 1:2
prophets to proclaim **c** you in Neh 6:7
a command from the king **c** them, Neh 11:23
king's side in all matters **c** the people. Neh 11:24
Remember me, O my God, **c** this, and Neh 13:14
for the king had so commanded **c** him. Est 3:2
all that Mordecai commanded **c** the Jews, Est 8:9
I will teach you **c** the hand of God; what Jb 27:11
"I will not keep silence **c** his limbs, or Jb 41:12
he sang to the LORD **c** the words of Cush, Ps 7:T
For my enemies speak **c** me; those who Ps 71:10
command his angels **c** you to guard Ps 91:11
which he saw **c** Judah and Jerusalem in Is 1:1
son of Amoz saw **c** Judah and Jerusalem. Is 2:1
my beloved my love song **c** his vineyard: Is 5:1
The oracle **c** Babylon which Isaiah the Is 13:1
that is purposed **c** the whole earth, Is 14:26
An oracle **c** Moab. Because Ar of Moab is Is 15:1
that the LORD spoke **c** Moab in the past. Is 16:13
An oracle **c** Damascus. Behold, Is 17:1
An oracle **c** Egypt. Behold, the LORD is Is 19:1
The oracle **c** the wilderness of the sea. As Is 21:1
The oracle **c** Dumah. One is calling to Is 21:11
The oracle **c** Arabia. In the thickets in Is 21:13
The oracle **c** the valley of vision. What do Is 22:1
labor to comfort me **c** the destruction of Is 22:4
The oracle **c** Tyre. Wail, O ships of Is 23:1
has given command **c** Canaan to Is 23:11
Abraham, **c** the house of Jacob: Is 29:22
ungodliness, to utter error **c** the LORD, Is 32:6
Now the king heard **c** Tirhakah king of Is 37:9
prayed to me **c** Sennacherib king of Is 37:21
word that the LORD has spoken **c** him: Is 37:22
thus says the LORD **c** the king of Assyria: Is 37:33
you command me **c** my children and Is 45:11
or command them **c** burnt offerings Jer 7:22
thus says the LORD **c** the men of Jer 11:21
Thus says the LORD **c** all my evil Jer 12:14
that came to Jeremiah **c** the drought: Jer 14:1
Thus says the LORD **c** this people: "They Jer 14:10
thus says the LORD **c** the prophets who Jer 14:15
thus says the LORD **c** the sons and Jer 16:3
and **c** the mothers who bore them and Jer 16:3
at any time I declare **c** a nation or a Jer 18:7
if that nation, **c** which I have spoken, Jer 18:8
at any time I declare **c** a nation or a Jer 18:9
For thus says the LORD **c** the house of the Jer 22:6
thus says the LORD **c** Shallum the son of Jer 22:11
thus says the LORD **c** Jehoiakim the son Jer 22:18

c the shepherds who care for my people: Jer 23:2
C the prophets: My heart is broken Jer 23:9
says the LORD of hosts **c** the prophets: Jer 23:15
that came to Jeremiah **c** all the people of Jer 25:1
the LORD has spoken **c** any nation that Jer 27:13
thus says the LORD of hosts **c** the pillars, Jer 27:19
c the vessels that are left in the house of Jer 27:21
thus says the LORD **c** the king who sits Jer 29:16
and **c** all the people who dwell in this Jer 29:16
c Ahab the son of Kolaiah and Jer 29:21
says the LORD **c** Shemaiah of Nehelam: Jer 29:31
that the LORD spoke **c** Israel and Judah: Jer 30:4
of Israel, **c** this city of which you say, Jer 32:36
c the houses of this city and the houses Jer 33:4
Thus says the LORD **c** you: 'You shall not Jer 34:4
And **c** Jehoiakim king of Judah you Jer 36:29
thus says the LORD **c** Jehoiakim king of Jer 36:30
gave command **c** Jeremiah through Jer 39:11
that came to Jeremiah **c** all the Judeans Jer 44:1
to Jeremiah the prophet **c** the nations. Jer 46:1
C the army of Pharaoh Neco, king of Jer 46:2
to Jeremiah the prophet **c** the Philistines, Jer 47:1
C Moab. Thus says the LORD of hosts, the Jer 48:1
C the Ammonites. Thus says the LORD: Jer 49:1
C Edom. Thus says the LORD of hosts: "Is Jer 49:7
C Damascus: "Hamath and Arpad are Jer 49:23
C Kedar and the kingdoms of Hazor Jer 49:28
came to Jeremiah the prophet **c** Elam, Jer 49:34
The word that the LORD spoke **c** Babylon, Jer 50:1
Babylon, **c** the land of the Chaldeans, Jer 50:1
because his purpose **c** Babylon is to Jer 51:11
what he spoke **c** the inhabitants of Jer 51:12
these words that are written **c** Babylon. Jer 51:60
you have said **c** this place that you will Jer 51:62
says the Lord GOD **c** the inhabitants of Ezk 12:19
Israel who prophesied **c** Jerusalem and Ezk 13:16
by repeating this proverb **c** the land of Ezk 18:2
the Lord GOD **c** the Ammonites and Ezk 21:28
the Ammonites and **c** their reproach; Ezk 21:28
of man, because Tyre said **c** Jerusalem, Ezk 26:2
Therefore prophesy **c** the land of Israel, Ezk 36:6
that I shall tell you **c** all the statutes of Ezk 44:5
Israel, therefore I have sworn **c** them, Ezk 44:12
from the God of heaven **c** this mystery, Dn 2:18
said before the king, **c** the injunction, Dn 6:12
nothing might be changed **c** Daniel. Dn 6:17
there and asked him the truth **c** all this. Dn 7:16
long is the vision **c** the regular burnt Dn 8:13
which he saw **c** Israel in the days of Am 1:1
The LORD relented **c** this; "It shall not Am 7:3
The LORD relented **c** this; "This also shall Am 7:6
Thus says the Lord GOD **c** Edom: We Ob 1:1
which he saw **c** Samaria and Jerusalem. Mi 1:1
Thus says the LORD **c** the prophets who Mi 3:5
An oracle **c** Nineveh. The book of the Na 1:1
and what I will answer **c** my complaint. Hab 2:1
burden of the word of the LORD **c** Israel: Zec 12:1
"'He will command his angels **c** you,' Mt 4:6
began to speak to the crowds **c** John: Mt 11:7
"But **c** that day and hour no one Mt 24:36
"But **c** that day or that hour, no one Mk 13:32
you may have certainty **c** the things you Lk 1:4
that had been told them **c** this child. Lk 2:17
were questioning in their hearts **c** John, Lk 3:15
"'He will command his angels **c** you, Lk 4:10
began to speak to the crowds **c** John: Lk 7:24
they said to him, "**C** Jesus of Nazareth, Lk 24:19
all the Scriptures the things **c** himself. Lk 24:27
Mary to console them **c** their brother. Jn 11:19
convict the world **c** sin and Jn 16:8
c sin, because they do not believe in me; Jn 16:9
c righteousness, because I go to the Jn 16:10
c judgment, because the ruler of this Jn 16:11
by the mouth of David **c** Judas, Acts 1:16
For David says **c** him, "'I saw the Lord Acts 2:25
are being examined today **c** a good deed Acts 4:9
taught accurately the things **c** Jesus, Acts 18:25
arose no little disturbance **c** the Way. Acts 19:23
to make his defense **c** the charge laid Acts 25:16
c his Son, who was descended from Rom 1:3
made him waver **c** the promise of Rom 4:20
And Isaiah cries out **c** Israel: "Though Rom 9:27
Now **c** the matters about which you 1 Cor 7:1
Now **c** the betrothed, I have no 1 Cor 7:25
Now **c** food offered to idols: we know 1 Cor 8:1
Now **c** spiritual gifts, brothers, I do 1 Cor 12:1
Now **c** the collection for the saints: as 1 Cor 16:1
Now **c** our brother Apollos, I 1 Cor 16:12
cousin of Barnabas (**c** whom you have Col 4:10
they themselves report **c** us the kind 1 Thes 1:9
Now **c** brotherly love you have no 1 Thes 4:9
Now **c** the times and the seasons, 1 Thes 5:1
Now **c** the coming of our Lord Jesus 2 Thes 2:1
of a legal requirement **c** bodily descent, Heb 7:16
being warned by God **c** events as yet Heb 11:7
and gave directions **c** his bones. Heb 11:22
C this salvation, the prophets who 1 Pt 1:10
with our hands, **c** the word of life— 1 Jn 1:1
of God that he has borne **c** his Son. 1 Jn 5:9
that God has borne **c** his Son. 1 Jn 5:10

CONCERNS (4)
priesthood for all that **c** the altar and Nm 18:7
Your wickedness **c** a man like yourself, Jb 35:8
For the vision **c** all their multitude; Ezk 7:13
This oracle **c** the prince in Jerusalem Ezk 12:10

CONCESSION (1)
Now as a **c**, not a command, I say this. 1 Cor 7:6

CONCLUDED (1)
controls us, because we have **c** this: 2 Cor 5:14

CONCLUDING (1)
c that God had called us to preach the Acts 16:10

CONCUBINE (22)
Moreover, his **c**, whose name was Gn 22:24
went and lay with Bilhah his father's **c**. Gn 35:22
(Timna was a **c** of Eliphaz, Esau's son; Gn 36:12
And his **c** who was in Shechem also Jgs 8:31
took to himself a **c** from Bethlehem in Jgs 19:1
And his **c** was unfaithful to him, and Jgs 19:2
the man and his **c** and his servant rose Jgs 19:9
donkeys, and his **c** was with him. Jgs 19:10
here are my virgin daughter and his **c**. Jgs 19:24
the man seized his **c** and made her go Jgs 19:25
there was his **c** lying at the door of the Jgs 19:27
and taking hold of his **c** he divided her, Jgs 19:29
that belongs to Benjamin, I and my **c**, Jgs 20:4
to kill me, and they violated my **c**, Jgs 20:5
I took hold of my **c** and cut her in pieces Jgs 20:6
Now Saul had a **c** whose name was 2 Sm 3:7
have you gone in to my father's **c**?" 2 Sm 3:7
the daughter of Aiah, the **c** of Saul, 2 Sm 21:11
The sons of Keturah, Abraham's **c**: 1 Chr 1:32
Ephah also, Caleb's **c**, bore Haran, 1 Chr 2:46
Maacah, Caleb's **c**, bore Sheber and 1 Chr 2:48
Asriel, whom his Aramean **c** bore; 1 Chr 7:14

CONCUBINES (18)
to the sons of his **c** Abraham gave gifts, Gn 25:6
David took more **c** and wives from 2 Sm 5:13
the king left ten **c** to keep the house. 2 Sm 15:16
Absalom, "Go in to your father's **c**, 2 Sm 16:21
in to his father's **c** in the sight of 2 Sm 16:22
and the lives of your wives and your **c**, 2 Sm 19:5
king took the ten **c** whom he had left 2 Sm 20:3
had 700 wives, princesses, and 300 **c**. 1 Kgs 11:3
David's sons, besides the sons of the **c**, 1 Chr 3:9
all his wives and **c** (he took eighteen 2 Chr 11:21
(he took eighteen wives and sixty **c**, 2 Chr 11:21
eunuch, who was in charge of the **c**. Est 2:14
both men and women, and many **c**, Eccl 2:8
There are sixty queens and eighty **c**, and Sg 6:8
the queens and **c** also, and they praised Sg 6:9
wives, and his **c** might drink from them. Dn 5:2
his wives, and his **c** drank from them. Dn 5:3
and your **c** have drunk wine from them. Dn 5:23

CONDEMN (22)
in the right, my own mouth would **c** me; Jb 9:20
I will say to God, Do not **c** me; let me Jb 10:2
Will you **c** him who is righteous and Jb 34:17
When he is quiet, who can **c**? When he Jb 34:29
Will you **c** me that you may be in the Jb 40:8
of the righteous and **c** the innocent to Ps 94:21
him from those who **c** his soul to Ps 109:31
judgment with this generation and **c** it, Mt 12:41
judgment with this generation and **c** it, Mt 12:42
scribes, and they will **c** him to death Mt 20:18
and they will **c** him to death and Mk 10:33
c not, and you will not be condemned; Lk 6:37
the men of this generation and **c** them, Lk 11:31
judgment with this generation and **c** it, Lk 11:32
him, 'I will **c** you with your own words, Lk 19:22
his Son into the world to **c** the world, Jn 3:17
And Jesus said, "Neither do I **c** you; Jn 8:11
judgment on another you **c** yourself, Rom 2:1
keeps the law will **c** you who have the Rom 2:27
Who is to **c**? Christ Jesus is the one Rom 8:34
I do not say this to **c** you, for I said 2 Cor 7:3
Beloved, if our heart does not **c** us, we 1 Jn 3:21

CONDEMNATION (15)
C is ready for scoffers, and beating for Prv 19:29
They will receive the greater **c**." Mk 12:40
They will receive the greater **c**." Lk 20:47
you are under the same sentence of **c**? Lk 23:40
for a sentence of **c** against him. Acts 25:15
charge us with saying. Their **c** is just. Rom 3:8
following one trespass brought **c**, Rom 5:16
as one trespass led to **c** for all men, Rom 5:18
is therefore now no **c** for those who are Rom 8:1
if there was glory in the ministry of **c**, 2 Cor 3:9
conceit and fall into the **c** of the devil. 1 Tm 3:6
and so incur **c** for having abandoned 1 Tm 5:12
be no, so that you may not fall under **c**. Jas 5:12
Their **c** from long ago is not idle, and 2 Pt 2:3
who long ago were designated for this **c**, Jude 1:4

CONDEMNED (24)
I shall be **c**; why then do I labor in vain? Jb 9:29
those who hate the righteous will be **c**. Ps 34:21
those who take refuge in him will be **c**. Ps 34:22
or let him be **c** when he is brought Ps 37:33
you would not have **c** the guiltless. Mt 12:7
and by your words you will be **c**." Mt 12:37
Judas, his betrayer, saw that Jesus was **c**, Mt 27:3
And they all **c** him as deserving Mk 14:64
but whoever does not believe will be **c**. Mk 16:16
condemn not, and you will not be **c**; Lk 6:37
rulers delivered him up to be **c** to death, Lk 24:20
Whoever believes in him is not **c**, but Jn 3:18
but whoever does not believe is **c** already, Jn 3:18
where are they? Has no one **c** you?" Jn 8:10
why am I still being **c** as a sinner? Rom 3:7
flesh and for sin, he **c** sin in the flesh, Rom 8:3
whoever has doubts is **c** if he eats, Rom 14:23
we may not be **c** along with the 1 Cor 11:32
him to his face, because he stood **c**. Gal 2:11
that all may be **c** who did not 2 Thes 2:12
and sound speech that cannot be **c**, so Ti 2:8
By this he **c** the world and became an Heb 11:7
You have **c**; you have murdered the Jas 5:6
to ashes he **c** them to extinction, 2 Pt 2:6

CONDEMNING (3)
acquitting the innocent and **c** the guilty, Dt 25:1
c the guilty by bringing his conduct 1 Kgs 8:32
Sabbath, fulfilled them by **c** him. Acts 13:27

CONDEMNS (5)
The one whom God **c** shall pay double Ex 22:9
Your own mouth **c** you, and not I; your Jb 15:6
the LORD, but a man of evil devices he **c**. Prv 12:2
wicked and he who **c** the righteous are Prv 17:15
for whenever our heart **c** us, God is 1 Jn 3:20

CONDITION (9)
Only on this **c** will we agree with you— Gn 34:15
Only on this **c** will the men agree to Gn 34:22
"On this **c** I will make a treaty with 1 Sm 11:2
to its proper **c** and strengthened it. 2 Chr 24:13
Know well the **c** of your flocks, and Prv 27:23
you were in worse **c** than the youths Dn 1:10
should remain in the **c** in which he 1 Cor 7:20
in whatever **c** each was called, 1 Cor 7:24
and though my **c** was a trial to you, you Gal 4:14

CONDITIONS (2)
Moreover, **c** were good in Judah. 2 Chr 12:12
the terms and **c** and the open Jer 32:11

CONDUCT (18)
guilty by bringing his **c** on his own 1 Kgs 8:32
guilty by bringing his **c** on his own 2 Chr 6:23
by whether his **c** is pure and upright. Prv 20:11
but the **c** of the pure is upright. Prv 21:8
who knows how to **c** himself before the Eccl 6:8
For rulers are not a terror to good **c**, Rom 13:3
when I saw that their **c** was not in step Gal 2:14
C yourselves wisely toward outsiders, Col 4:5
blameless was our **c** toward you 1 Thes 2:10
believers an example in speech, in **c**, 1 Tm 4:12
have followed my teaching, my **c**, 2 Tm 3:10
By his good **c** let him show his works in Jas 3:13
is holy, you also be holy in all your **c**, 1 Pt 1:15
c yourselves with fear throughout the 1 Pt 1:17
Keep your **c** among the Gentiles 1 Pt 2:12
without a word by the **c** of their wives— 1 Pt 3:1
they see your respectful and pure **c**. 1 Pt 3:2
distressed by the sensual **c** of the wicked 2 Pt 2:7

CONDUCTED (1)
Those who **c** Paul brought him as Acts 17:15

CONDUCTS (1)
lends; who **c** his affairs with justice. Ps 112:5

CONDUIT (4)
and stood by the **c** of the upper pool, 2 Kgs 18:17
pool and the **c** and brought water 2 Kgs 20:20
at the end of the **c** of the upper pool on the Is 7:3
And he stood by the **c** of the upper pool on Is 36:2

CONFERRED (5)
And Abner **c** with the elders of Israel, 2 Sm 3:17
He **c** with Joab the son of Zeruiah and 1 Kgs 1:7
He went away and **c** with the chief Lk 22:4
the council, they **c** with one another, Acts 4:15
when he had **c** with his council, Acts 25:12

CONFESS (18)
and **c** over it all the iniquities of the Lv 16:21
"But if they **c** their iniquity and the Lv 26:40

he shall **c** his sin that he has committed. Nm 5:7
"I will **c** my transgressions to the LORD," Ps 32:5
I **c** my iniquity; I am sorry for my sin. Ps 38:18
name of the LORD and **c** the God of Israel, Is 48:1
that if anyone should **c** Jesus to be Jn 9:22
for fear of the Pharisees they did not **c** it, Jn 12:42
But this I **c** to you, that according to Acts 24:14
if you **c** with your mouth that Jesus is Rom 10:9
me, and every tongue shall **c** to God." Rom 14:11
and every tongue **c** that Jesus Christ is Phil 2:11
Great indeed, we **c**, is the mystery of 1 Tm 3:16
c your sins to one another and pray for Jas 5:16
If we **c** our sins, he is faithful and just to 1 Jn 1:9
spirit that does not **c** Jesus is not from 1 Jn 4:3
those who do not **c** the coming of Jesus 2 Jn 1:7
I will **c** his name before my Father and Rv 3:5

CONFESSED (3)
and stood and **c** their sins and Neh 9:2
He **c**, and did not deny, but confessed, "I Jn 1:20
He confessed, and did not deny, but **c**, "I Jn 1:20

CONFESSES (6)
in any of these and **c** the sin he has Lv 5:5
but he who **c** and forsakes them will Prv 28:13
with the mouth one **c** and is saved. Rom 10:10
Whoever **c** the Son has the Father also. 1 Jn 2:23
every spirit that **c** that Jesus Christ has 1 Jn 4:2
Whoever **c** that Jesus is the Son of God, 1 Jn 4:15

CONFESSING (5)
c the sins of the people of Israel, Neh 1:6
c my sin and the sin of my people Israel, Dn 9:20
by him in the river Jordan, **c** their sins. Mt 3:6
by him in the river Jordan, **c** their sins. Mk 1:5
c and divulging their practices. Acts 19:18

CONFESSION (10)
While Ezra prayed and made **c**, weeping Ezr 10:1
Now then make **c** to the LORD, the God Ezr 10:11
of it they made **c** and worshiped the Neh 9:3
I prayed to the LORD my God and made **c**, Dn 9:4
flowing from your **c** of the gospel 2 Cor 9:13
you made the good **c** in the presence 1 Tm 6:12
Pontius Pilate made the good **c**, 1 Tm 6:13
the apostle and high priest of our **c**, Heb 3:1
the Son of God, let us hold fast our **c**. Heb 4:14
us hold fast the **c** of our hope without Heb 10:23

CONFIDENCE (34)
the leaders of Shechem put **c** in him. Jgs 9:26
And the people took **c** from the words 2 Chr 32:8
Is not your fear of God your **c**, and the Jb 4:6
His **c** is severed, and his trust is a spider's Jb 8:14
I smiled on them when they had no **c**, Jb 29:24
gold my trust or called fine gold my **c**, Jb 31:24
is the path of those who have foolish **c**; Ps 49:13
LORD will be your **c** and will keep your Prv 3:26
to the LORD, but the upright are in his **c**. Prv 3:32
the fear of the LORD one has strong **c**, Prv 14:26
of Israel was ashamed of Bethel, their **c**. Jer 48:13
trust in a neighbor; have no **c** in a friend; Mi 7:5
say to you with **c** about the patriarch Acts 2:29
Such is the **c** that we have through 2 Cor 3:4
because I have perfect **c** in you. 2 Cor 7:16
ever because of his great **c** in you. 2 Cor 8:22
show boldness with such **c** as I count 2 Cor 10:2
I am saying with this boastful **c**, 2 Cor 11:17
I have **c** in the Lord that you will take Gal 5:10
and access with **c** through our faith Eph 3:12
Christ Jesus and put no **c** in the flesh— Phil 3:3
myself have reason for **c** in the flesh Phil 3:4
thinks he has reason for **c** in the flesh, Phil 3:4
And we have **c** in the Lord about you, 2 Thes 3:4
and also great **c** in the faith 1 Tm 3:13
we hold fast our **c** and our boasting in Heb 3:6
we hold our original **c** firm to the end. Heb 3:14
Let us then with **c** draw near to the Heb 4:16
since we have **c** to enter the holy Heb 10:19
Therefore do not throw away your **c**, Heb 10:35
appears we may have **c** and not shrink 1 Jn 2:28
not condemn us, we have **c** before God; 1 Jn 3:21
so that we may have **c** for the day of 1 Jn 4:17
And this is the **c** that we have toward 1 Jn 5:14

CONFIDENT (8)
They are ashamed because they were **c**; Jb 6:20
he is **c** though Jordan rushes against Jb 40:23
war arise against me, yet I will be **c**. Ps 27:3
to say nothing of you—for being so **c**. 2 Cor 9:4
If anyone is **c** that he is Christ's, let 2 Cor 10:7
having become **c** in the Lord by my Phil 1:14
about which they make **c** assertions. 1 Tm 1:7
C of your obedience, I write to you, Phlm 1:21

CONFIDENTLY (1)
So we can **c** say, "The Lord is my Heb 13:6

CONFINED (6)
where the king's prisoners were **c**, Gn 39:20
guard, in the prison where Joseph was **c**. Gn 40:3
who were **c** in the prison—each his own Gn 40:5
your brother, while you remain **c**, Gn 42:16
your brothers remain **c** where you are Gn 42:19
of Mehetabel, who was **c** to his home, Neh 6:10

CONFIRM (15)
you and will **c** my covenant with Lv 26:9
that he may **c** his covenant that he swore Dt 8:18
and that he may **c** the word that the LORD Dt 9:5
anyone who does not **c** the words of this Dt 27:26
to **c** a transaction, the one drew off his Ru 4:7
c forever the word that you have 2 Sm 7:25
come in after you and **c** your words." 1 Kgs 1:14
might help him to **c** his hold on the 2 Kgs 15:19
but I will **c** him in my house and in 1 Chr 17:14
C to your servant your promise, that Ps 119:38
that I may **c** the oath that I swore to your Jer 11:5
Then **c** your vows and perform your Jer 44:25
I stood up to **c** and strengthen him. Dn 11:1
in order to **c** the promises given to the Rom 15:8
will himself restore, **c**, strengthen, 1 Pt 5:10

CONFIRMATION (2)
and in the defense and **c** of the gospel. Phil 1:7
all their disputes an oath is final for **c**. Heb 6:16

CONFIRMED (10)
O God of Israel, let your word be **c**, 1 Kgs 8:26
which he **c** as a statute to Jacob, as 1 Chr 16:17
God of Israel, let your word be **c**, 2 Chr 6:17
of Queen Esther **c** these practices of Est 9:32
which he **c** to Jacob as a statute, to Ps 105:10
I have sworn an oath and **c** it, to keep Ps 119:106
your kingdom shall be **c** for you from Dn 4:26
He has **c** his words, which he spoke Dn 9:12
with them and **c** the message by Mk 16:20
about Christ was **c** among you— 1 Cor 1:6

CONFIRMING (1)
c this second letter about Purim. Est 9:29

CONFIRMS (1)
who **c** the word of his servant and Is 44:26

CONFISCATION (1)
for banishment or for **c** of his goods or Ezr 7:26

CONFLICT (3)
the word was true, and it was a great **c**. Dn 10:1
engaged in the same **c** that you saw I Phil 1:30
gospel of God in the midst of much **c**. 1 Thes 2:2

CONFLICTING (1)
and their **c** thoughts accuse or even Rom 2:15

CONFORMED (3)
also predestined to be **c** to the image of Rom 8:29
Do not be **c** to this world, but be Rom 12:2
do not be **c** to the passions of your 1 Pt 1:14

CONFOUND (1)
be emptied out, and I will **c** their counsel; Is 19:3

CONFOUNDED (16)
of strength, are dismayed and **c**, 2 Kgs 19:26
the moon will be **c** and the sun Is 24:23
Lebanon is **c** and withers away; Is 33:9
shorn of strength, are dismayed and **c**, Is 37:27
against you shall be put to shame and **c**; Is 41:11
All of them are put to shame and **c**; the Is 45:16
not be put to shame or **c** to all eternity. Is 45:17
be not **c**, for you will not be disgraced; Is 54:4
they are ashamed and **c** and cover their Jer 14:3
will be ashamed and **c** because of all Jer 22:22
I was ashamed, and I was **c**, because I Jer 31:19
"Hamath and Arpad are **c**, for they Jer 49:23
that you may remember and be **c**, and Ezk 16:63
you. Be ashamed and **c** for your ways, Ezk 36:32
Ekron also, because its hopes are **c**. Zec 9:5
and **c** the Jews who lived in Damascus Acts 9:22

CONFRONT (2)
this song shall **c** them as a witness (for Dt 31:21
Arise, O LORD! **C** him, subdue him! Ps 17:13

CONFRONTED (7)
me; the snares of death **c** me. 2 Sm 22:6
They **c** me in the day of my 2 Sm 22:19
So I **c** the officials and said, "Why is Neh 13:11
Then I **c** the nobles of Judah and said Neh 13:17
And I **c** them and cursed them and Neh 13:25
entangled me; the snares of death **c** me. Ps 18:5
They **c** me in the day of my calamity, Ps 18:18

CONFUSE (1)
us go down and there **c** their language, Gn 11:7

CONFUSED (2)
because there the LORD **c** the language of Gn 11:9
Why should you be like a man **c**, like a Jer 14:9

CONFUSION (18)
and will throw into **c** all the people Ex 23:27
over to you and throw them into great **c**, Dt 7:23
c, and frustration in all that you Dt 28:20
madness and blindness and **c** of mind, Dt 28:28
the Philistines and threw them into **c**, 1 Sm 7:10
his fellow, and there was very great **c**. 1 Sm 14:20
against Jerusalem and to cause **c** in it. Neh 4:8
but the city of Susa was thrown into **c**. Est 3:15
be put to shame and **c** who seek my life! Ps 70:2
has mingled within her a spirit of **c**, Is 19:14
tumult and trampling and **c** in the valley Is 22:5
He shall stretch the line of **c** over it, and Is 34:11
the makers of idols go in **c** together. Is 45:16
has come; now their **c** is at hand. Mi 7:4
So the city was filled with the **c**, and Acts 19:29
another, for the assembly was in **c**, Acts 19:32
cohort that all Jerusalem was in **c**. Acts 21:31
God is not a God of **c** but of peace. 1 Cor 14:33

CONFUTE (1)
and you shall **c** every tongue that rises Is 54:17

CONGEALED (1)
a heap; the deeps **c** in the heart of the sea. Ex 15:8

CONGRATULATE (1)
servants came to **c** our lord King 1 Kgs 1:47

CONGREGATION (142)
Tell all the **c** of Israel that on the tenth Ex 12:3
whole assembly of the **c** of Israel shall Ex 12:6
will be cut off from the **c** of Israel, Ex 12:19
All the **c** of Israel shall keep it. Ex 12:47
and all the **c** of the people of Israel came Ex 16:1
And the whole **c** of the people of Israel Ex 16:2
"Say to the whole **c** of the people of Israel, Ex 16:9
spoke to the whole **c** of the people of Ex 16:10
the leaders of the **c** came and told Ex 16:22
All the **c** of the people of Israel moved on Ex 17:1
all the leaders of the **c** returned to him, Ex 34:31
Moses assembled all the **c** of the people Ex 35:1
Moses said to all the **c** of the people of Ex 35:4
Then all the **c** of the people of Israel Ex 35:20
from those of the **c** who were recorded Ex 38:25
"If the whole **c** of Israel sins Lv 4:13
the elders of the **c** shall lay their hands Lv 4:15
And assemble all the **c** at the entrance of Lv 8:3
and the **c** was assembled at the entrance Lv 8:4
And Moses said to the **c**, "This is the thing Lv 8:5
and all the **c** drew near and stood before Lv 9:5
you die, and wrath come upon all the **c**; Lv 10:6
that you may bear the iniquity of the **c**, Lv 10:17
he shall take from the **c** of the people of Lv 16:5
"Speak to all the **c** of the people of Israel Lv 19:2
on his head, and let all the **c** stone him. Lv 24:14
put to death. All the **c** shall stone him. Lv 24:16
a census of all the **c** of the people of Nm 1:2
These were the ones chosen from the **c**, Nm 1:16
they assembled the whole **c** together, Nm 1:18
be no wrath on the **c** of the people of Nm 1:53
and over the whole **c** before the tent of Nm 3:7
and the chiefs of the **c** listed the sons of Nm 4:34
and assemble the whole **c** of the people Nm 8:9
and Aaron and all the **c** of the people of Nm 8:20
for summoning the **c** and for breaking Nm 10:2
all the **c** shall gather themselves to you Nm 10:3
Aaron and to all the **c** of the people of Nm 13:26
back word to them and to all the **c**, Nm 13:26
Then all the **c** raised a loud cry, and Nm 14:1
The whole **c** said to them, "Would that Nm 14:2
all the assembly of the **c** of the people of Nm 14:5
and said to all the **c** of the people of Nm 14:7
Then all the **c** said to stone them with Nm 14:10
shall this wicked **c** grumble against Nm 14:27
to all this wicked **c** who are gathered Nm 14:35
made all the **c** grumble against him Nm 14:36
without the knowledge of the **c**, Nm 15:24
all the **c** shall offer one bull from the Nm 15:24
atonement for all the **c** of the people of Nm 15:25
And all the **c** of the people of Israel Nm 15:26
to Moses and Aaron and to all the **c**. Nm 15:33
all the **c** shall stone him with stones Nm 15:35
And all the **c** brought him outside the Nm 15:36
the people of Israel, 250 chiefs of the **c**, Nm 16:2
For all in the **c** are holy, every one of Nm 16:3
has separated you from the **c** of Israel, Nm 16:9
to stand before the **c** to minister to Nm 16:9
assembled all the **c** against them at Nm 16:19
glory of the LORD appeared to all the **c**. Nm 16:19
yourselves from among this **c**, Nm 16:21
and will you be angry with all the **c**?" Nm 16:22
"Say to the **c**, Get away from the Nm 16:24
And he spoke to the **c**, saying, "Depart, Nm 16:26
the next day all the **c** of the people of Nm 16:41
And when the **c** had assembled Nm 16:42
"Get away from the midst of this **c**, Nm 16:45
quickly to the **c** and make atonement Nm 16:46
for impurity for the **c** of the people of Nm 19:9

And the people of Israel, the whole **c**, Nm 20:1
Now there was no water for the **c**. And Nm 20:2
"Take the staff, and assemble the **c**, Nm 20:8
give drink to the **c** and their cattle." Nm 20:8
out abundantly, and the **c** drank, Nm 20:11
and the people of Israel, the whole **c**, Nm 20:22
up Mount Hor in the sight of all the **c**. Nm 20:27
And when all the **c** saw that Aaron Nm 20:29
the sight of the whole **c** of the people of Nm 25:6
he rose and left the **c** and took a spear Nm 25:7
a census of all the **c** of the people of Nm 26:2
and Abiram, chosen from the **c**, Nm 26:9
and before the chiefs and all the **c**, Nm 27:2
of Zin when the **c** quarreled, Nm 27:14
of all flesh, appoint a man over the **c** Nm 27:16
that the **c** of the LORD may not be as Nm 27:17
before Eleazar the priest and all the **c**, Nm 27:19
that all the **c** of the people of Israel Nm 27:20
of Israel with him, the whole **c**." Nm 27:21
Eleazar the priest and the whole **c**, Nm 27:22
and to the **c** of the people of Israel, Nm 31:12
the chiefs of the **c** went to meet them Nm 31:13
plague came among the **c** of the LORD. Nm 31:16
heads of the fathers' houses of the **c**, Nm 31:26
who went out to battle and all the **c**. Nm 31:27
the priest and to the chiefs of the **c**, Nm 32:2
LORD struck down before the **c** of Israel, Nm 32:4
he stands before the **c** for judgment. Nm 35:12
then the **c** shall judge between the Nm 35:24
And the **c** shall rescue the manslayer Nm 35:25
and the **c** shall restore him to his city Nm 35:25
and the leaders of the **c** swore to them. Jos 9:15
the leaders of the **c** had sworn to them Jos 9:18
Then all the **c** murmured against the Jos 9:18
But all the leaders said to all the **c**, "We Jos 9:19
wood and drawers of water for all the **c**, Jos 9:21
of water for the **c** and for the altar Jos 9:27
Then the whole **c** of the people of Israel Jos 18:1
he has stood before the **c** for judgment, Jos 20:6
of blood, till he stood before the **c**. Jos 20:9
"Thus says the whole **c** of the LORD, Jos 22:16
came a plague upon the **c** of the LORD, Jos 22:17
will be angry with the whole **c** of Israel. Jos 22:18
and wrath fell upon all the **c** of Israel? Jos 22:20
the priest and the chiefs of the **c**, Jos 22:30
and the **c** assembled as one man to the Jgs 20:1
So the **c** sent 12,000 of their bravest Jgs 21:10
Then the whole **c** sent word to the Jgs 21:13
Then the elders of the **c** said, "What Jgs 21:16
King Solomon and all the **c** of Israel, 1 Kgs 8:5
King Solomon and all the **c** of Israel, 2 Chr 5:6
and the **c** of Israel for the tent of 2 Chr 24:6
himself banned from the **c** of the exiles. Ezr 10:8
nor sinners in the **c** of the righteous; Ps 1:5
in the midst of the **c** I will praise you: Ps 22:22
you comes my praise in the great **c**; Ps 22:25
I will thank you in the great **c**; in the Ps 35:18
glad news of deliverance in the great **c**; Ps 40:9
and your faithfulness from the great **c**. Ps 40:10
"Bless God in the great **c**, the LORD, O Ps 68:26
Remember your **c**, which you have Ps 74:2
them extol him in the **c** of the people, Ps 107:32
in the company of the upright, in the **c**. Ps 111:1
brink of utter ruin in the assembled **c**." Prv 5:14
hear, O nations, and know, O **c**, Jer 6:18
and their **c** shall be established before Jer 30:20
whom you forbade to enter your **c**. Lam 1:10
according to the report made to their **c**. Hos 7:12
Consecrate the **c**; assemble the elders; Jl 2:16
who was in the **c** in the wilderness Acts 7:38
and having gathered the **c** together, Acts 15:30
speaking evil of the Way before the **c**, Acts 19:9
in the midst of the **c** I will sing your Heb 2:12

CONGREGATION'S (1)
now the **c** half was 337,500 sheep, Nm 31:43

CONIAH (3)
LORD, though **C** the son of Jehoiakim, Jer 22:24
Is this man **C** a despised, broken pot, a Jer 22:28
reigned instead of **C** the son of Jer 37:1

CONJUGAL (1)
should give to his wife her **c** rights, 1 Cor 7:3

CONNECTED (5)
its cords—all the service **c** with these. Nm 3:26
the screen; all the service **c** with these. Nm 3:31
accessories; all the service **c** with these; Nm 3:36
shall bear iniquity **c** with the Nm 18:1
shall bear iniquity **c** with your Nm 18:1

CONNECTING (1)
loops on the edge of the other **c** curtain. Ex 36:17

CONNECTION (4)
for any wrong in **c** with any offense Dt 19:15
unless we find it in **c** with the law of his Dn 6:5
"In this **c** I journeyed to Damascus Acts 26:12
and in **c** with that tribe Moses said Heb 7:14

CONQUER (6)
besieged Ahaz but could not **c** him. 2 Kgs 16:5
and terrify it, and let us **c** it for ourselves, Is 7:6
and he came out conquering, and to **c**. Rv 6:2
war on them and **c** them and kill them, Rv 11:7
to make war on the saints and to **c** them. Rv 13:7
the Lamb, and the Lamb will **c** them, Rv 17:14

CONQUERED (7)
against the cities of Israel and **c** Ijon, 1 Kgs 15:20
the cities of Israel, and they **c** Ijon, 2 Chr 16:4
who through faith **c** kingdoms, Heb 11:33
as I also **c** and sat down with my Father Rv 3:21
tribe of Judah, the Root of David, has **c**, Rv 5:5
And they have **c** him by the blood of Rv 12:11
also those who had **c** the beast and its Rv 15:2

CONQUERING (3)
near and far, a nation mighty and **c**, Is 18:2
near and far, a nation mighty and **c**, Is 18:7
was given to him, and he came out **c**, Rv 6:2

CONQUEROR (1)
I will again bring a **c** to you, Mi 1:15

CONQUERORS (2)
their wives to others and their fields to **c**, Jer 8:10
we are more than **c** through him who Rom 8:37

CONQUERS (8)
To the one who **c** I will grant to eat of the Rv 2:7
The one who **c** will not be hurt by the Rv 2:11
To the one who **c** I will give some of the Rv 2:17
The one who **c** and who keeps my works Rv 2:26
The one who **c** will be clothed thus in Rv 3:5
The one who **c**, I will make him a pillar Rv 3:12
The one who **c**, I will grant him to sit Rv 3:21
The one who **c** will have this heritage, Rv 21:7

CONSCIENCE (27)
grief or pangs of **c** for having shed 1 Sm 25:31
God in all good **c** up to this day." Acts 23:1
to have a clear **c** toward both God Acts 24:16
while their **c** also bears witness, Rom 2:15
my **c** bears me witness in the Holy Rom 9:1
God's wrath but also for the sake of **c**. Rom 13:5
as really offered to an idol, and their **c**, 1 Cor 8:7
he not be encouraged, if his **c** is weak, 1 Cor 8:10
and wounding their **c** when it is 1 Cor 8:12
any question on the ground of **c**. 1 Cor 10:25
any question on the ground of **c**. 1 Cor 10:27
you, and for the sake of **c**— 1 Cor 10:28
I do not mean your **c**, but his. For 1 Cor 10:29
be determined by someone else's **c**? 1 Cor 10:29
testimony of our **c** that we behaved 2 Cor 1:12
ourselves to everyone's **c** in the sight 2 Cor 4:2
and I hope it is known also to your **c**. 2 Cor 5:11
heart and a good **c** and a sincere faith. 1 Tm 1:5
holding faith and a good **c**. By 1 Tm 1:19
the mystery of the faith with a clear **c**. 1 Tm 3:9
as did my ancestors, with a clear **c**, 2 Tm 1:3
cannot perfect the **c** of the worshiper, Heb 9:9
purify our **c** from dead works to serve Heb 9:14
clean from an evil **c** and our bodies Heb 10:22
for we are sure that we have a clear **c**, Heb 13:18
and respect, having a good **c**, 1 Pt 3:16
but as an appeal to God for a good **c**, 1 Pt 3:21

CONSCIENCES (2)
insincerity of liars whose **c** are seared, 1 Tm 4:2
both their minds and their **c** are defiled. Ti 1:15

CONSCIOUSNESS (1)
would no longer have any **c** of sin? Heb 10:2

CONSECRATE (44)
"**C** to me all the firstborn. Whatever is Ex 13:2
to the people and **c** them today and Ex 19:10
come near to the LORD **c** themselves, Ex 19:22
limits around the mountain and **c** it.'" Ex 19:23
make Aaron's garments to **c** him for my Ex 28:3
the people of Israel **c** as their holy gifts. Ex 28:38
them and ordain them and **c** them, Ex 28:41
is what you shall do to them to **c** them, Ex 29:1
And you shall **c** the breast of the wave Ex 29:27
for it, and shall anoint it to **c** it. Ex 29:36
make atonement for the altar and **c** it, Ex 29:37
I will **c** the tent of meeting and the altar. Ex 29:44
and his sons I will **c** to serve me as Ex 29:44
You shall **c** them, that they may be Ex 30:29
anoint Aaron and his sons, and **c** them, Ex 30:30
that is in it, and **c** it and all its furniture, Ex 40:9
and all its utensils, and **c** the altar, Ex 40:10
anoint the basin and its stand, and **c** it. Ex 40:11
And you shall anoint him and **c** him, Ex 40:13
and the basin and its stand, to **c** them. Lv 8:11
head and anointed him to **c** him. Lv 8:12
C yourselves therefore, and be holy, for Lv 11:44
and cleanse it and **c** it from the Lv 16:19
C yourselves, therefore, and be holy, for I Lv 20:7
And you shall **c** the fiftieth year, and Lv 25:10
And he shall **c** his head that same day Nm 6:11
people, '**C** yourselves for tomorrow, Nm 11:18
Joshua said to the people, "**C** yourselves, Jos 3:5
C the people and say, 'Consecrate Jos 7:13
and say, '**C** yourselves for tomorrow; Jos 7:13
C yourselves, and come with me to 1 Sm 16:5
C yourselves, you and your 1 Chr 15:12
"Hear me, Levites! Now **c** yourselves, 2 Chr 29:5
and **c** the house of the LORD, 2 Chr 29:5
They began to **c** on the first day of 2 Chr 29:17
was not clean, to **c** it to the LORD. 2 Chr 30:17
the Passover lamb, and **c** yourselves, 2 Chr 35:6
their course, Job would send and **c** them, Jb 1:5
for the altar and cleanse it, and so **c** it. Ezk 43:26
C a fast; call a solemn assembly. Gather Jl 1:14
Blow the trumpet in Zion; **c** a fast; call a Jl 2:15
C the congregation; assemble the elders; Jl 2:16
this among the nations: **C** for war; Jl 3:9
And for their sake I **c** myself, that they Jn 17:19

CONSECRATED (45)
to the people and **c** the people; Ex 19:14
"You shall be **c** to me. Therefore you Ex 22:31
and all that was in it, and **c** them. Lv 8:10
of the altar and **c** it to make atonement Lv 8:15
So he **c** Aaron and his garments, and his Lv 8:30
who is anointed and **c** as priest in his Lv 16:32
and who has been **c** to wear the Lv 21:10
I **c** for my own all the firstborn in Nm 3:13
beside him and he defiles his **c** head, Nm 6:9
Nazirite shall shave his **c** head at the Nm 6:18
take the hair from his **c** head and put it Nm 6:18
and had anointed and **c** it with all its Nm 7:1
and had anointed and **c** the altar with Nm 7:1
in the land of Egypt I **c** them for myself, Nm 8:17
all the **c** things of the people of Israel. Nm 18:8
And they **c** his son Eleazar to have 1 Sm 7:1
the sacrifice." And he **c** Jesse and his 1 Sm 16:5
same day the king **c** the middle of the 1 Kgs 8:64
I have **c** this house that you have built, 1 Kgs 9:3
the house that I have **c** for my name I 1 Kgs 9:7
and the Levites **c** themselves to 1 Chr 15:14
who were present had **c** themselves, 2 Chr 5:11
And Solomon **c** the middle of the 2 Chr 7:7
I have chosen and **c** this house that 2 Chr 7:16
this house that I have **c** for my name, 2 Chr 7:20
Aaron, who are **c** to burn incense. 2 Chr 26:18
their brothers and **c** themselves and 2 Chr 29:15
for eight days they **c** the house of the 2 Chr 29:17
faithless, we have made ready and **c**, 2 Chr 29:19
"You have now **c** yourselves to the 2 Chr 29:31
And the **c** offerings were 600 bulls 2 Chr 29:33
until other priests had **c** themselves, 2 Chr 29:34
priests had not **c** themselves in 2 Chr 30:3
sanctuary, which he has **c** forever, 2 Chr 30:8
so that they **c** themselves and 2 Chr 30:15
who had not **c** themselves. 2 Chr 30:17
And the priests **c** themselves in 2 Chr 30:24
Sheep Gate. They **c** it and set its doors. Neh 3:1
They **c** it as far as the Tower of the Neh 3:1
I myself have commanded my **c** ones, Is 13:3
you, and before you were born I **c** you; Jer 1:5
This shall be for the **c** priests, the sons Ezk 48:11
to Baal-peor and **c** themselves to the Hos 9:10
has prepared a sacrifice and **c** his guests. Zep 1:7
him whom the Father **c** and sent into Jn 10:36

CONSECRATING (2)
c himself today to the LORD?" 1 Chr 29:5
than the priests in **c** themselves. 2 Chr 29:34

CONSECRATION (3)
was made at their ordination and **c**, Ex 29:33
for the **c** of the anointing oil of his God Lv 21:12
after he has shaved the hair of his **c**, Nm 6:19

CONSENT (7)
and without your **c** no one shall lift up Gn 41:44
the king of Moab, but he would not **c**. Jgs 11:17
said to him, "Do not listen or **c**." 1 Kgs 20:8
My son, if sinners entice you, do not **c**. Prv 1:10
are witnesses and you **c** to the deeds of Lk 11:48
they are ready, waiting for your **c**." Acts 23:21
nothing without your **c** in order that Phlm 1:14

CONSENTED (3)
to fulfill all righteousness." Then he **c**. Mt 3:15
So he **c** and sought an opportunity to Lk 22:6
who had not **c** to their decision and Lk 23:51

CONSENTS (2)
and she **c** to live with him, 1 Cor 7:12
unbeliever, and he **c** to live with her, 1 Cor 7:13

CONSEQUENCES (1)
must bear the **c** of your lewdness Ezk 23:35

CONSEQUENTLY (2)
C, he is able to save to the uttermost Heb 7:25
C, when Christ came into the world, he Heb 10:5

CONSIDER (64)
C too that this nation is your people." Ex 33:13
And **c** today (since I am not speaking to Dt 11:2
it), **c** the discipline of the LORD your God, Dt 11:2
of old; **c** the years of many generations; Dt 32:7
Now therefore **c** what you will do." Jgs 18:14
this day; **c** it, take counsel, and speak." Jgs 19:30
For **c** what great things he has done 1 Sm 12:24
know this and **c** what you should 1 Sm 25:17
days' pestilence in your land? Now **c**, 2 Sm 24:13
and **c** well what you have to do, 1 Kgs 20:22
to cure a man of his leprosy? Only **c**, 2 Kgs 5:7
said to the judges, "**C** what you do, 2 Chr 19:6
and **c** what the fathers have searched out. Jb 8:8
when he sees iniquity, will he not **c** it? Jb 11:11
for words? **C**, and then we will speak. Jb 18:2
presence; when I **c**, I am in dread of him. Jb 23:15
For God has no need to **c** a man further, Jb 34:23
stop and **c** the wondrous works of God. Jb 37:14
ear to my words, O LORD; **c** my groaning. Ps 5:1
C and answer me, O LORD my God; light Ps 13:3
C my affliction and my trouble, and Ps 25:18
C how many are my foes, and with Ps 25:19
Hear, O daughter, and **c**, and incline Ps 45:10
c well her ramparts, go through her Ps 48:13
I **c** the days of old, the years long ago. Ps 77:5
Egypt, did not **c** your wondrous works; Ps 106:7
let them **c** the steadfast love of the Ps 107:43
to destroy me, but I **c** your testimonies. Ps 119:95
Therefore I **c** all your precepts to be Ps 119:128
C how I love your precepts! Give me Ps 119:159
ant, O sluggard; **c** her ways, and be wise. Prv 6:6
So I turned to **c** wisdom and madness Eccl 2:12
C the work of God: who can make Eccl 7:13
be joyful, and in the day of adversity **c**: Eccl 7:14
know, may **c** and understand together, Is 41:20
what they are, that we may **c** them, Is 41:22
former things, nor **c** the things of old. Is 43:18
"**C**, and call for the mourning women to Jer 9:17
c well the highway, the road by which Jer 31:21
"You **c** yourself a lion of the nations, Ezk 32:2
Therefore **c** the word and understand Dn 9:23
But they do not **c** that I remember all Hos 7:2
thus says the LORD of hosts: **C** your ways. Hg 1:5
says the LORD of hosts: **C** your ways. Hg 1:7
Now then, **c** from this day onward. Hg 2:15
C from this day onward, from the Hg 2:18
of the LORD'S temple was laid, **c**: Hg 2:18
C the lilies of the field, how they grow: Mt 6:28
C the ravens: they neither sow nor reap, Lk 12:24
C the lilies, how they grow: they neither Lk 12:27
were gathered together to **c** this matter. Acts 15:6
"I **c** myself fortunate that it is before Acts 26:2
So you also must **c** yourselves dead to Rom 6:11
For I **c** that the sufferings of this Rom 8:18
For **c** your calling, brothers: not 1 Cor 1:26
C the people of Israel: are not those 1 Cor 10:18
I **c** that I am not in the least inferior 2 Cor 11:5
I do not **c** that I have made it my own. Phil 3:13
So if you **c** me your partner, receive Phlm 1:17
who share in a heavenly calling, **c** Jesus, Heb 3:1
And let us **c** how to stir up one Heb 10:24
C him who endured from sinners such Heb 12:3
C the outcome of their way of life, and Heb 13:7
we **c** those blessed who remained Jas 5:11

CONSIDERABLE (1)
and a **c** crowd from the town was with Lk 7:12

CONSIDERED (21)
silver was not **c** as anything in the 1 Kgs 10:21
Silver was not **c** as anything in the 2 Chr 9:20
of Mattaniah, for they were **c** reliable, Neh 13:13
said to Satan, "Have you **c** my servant Job, Jb 1:8
said to Satan, "Have you **c** my servant Job, Jb 2:3
Even a fool who keeps silent is **c** wise; Prv 17:28
Then I saw and **c** it; I looked and Prv 24:32
Then I **c** all that my hands had done Eccl 2:11
who **c** that he was cut off out of the land Is 53:8
Because he **c** and turned away from Ezk 18:28
I **c** the horns, and behold, there came up Dn 7:8
But as he **c** these things, behold, an Mt 1:20
that those who are **c** rulers of the Mk 10:42
but those who are **c** worthy to attain to Lk 20:35
in faith when he **c** his own body, Rom 4:19
or when he **c** the barrenness of Sarah's Rom 4:19
that you may be **c** worthy of the 2 Thes 1:5
who rule well be **c** worthy of double 1 Tm 5:17
since she **c** him faithful who had Heb 11:11
He **c** that God was able even to raise Heb 11:19
He **c** the reproach of Christ greater Heb 11:26

CONSIDERING (1)
As I was **c**, behold, a male goat came Dn 8:5

CONSIDERS (5)
Blessed is the one who **c** the poor! In the Ps 41:1
Who **c** the power of your anger, and Ps 90:11
She **c** a field and buys it; with the fruit Prv 31:16
No one **c**, nor is there knowledge or Is 44:19
since indeed God **c** it just to repay 2 Thes 1:6

CONSIGNED (2)
I am **c** to the gates of Sheol for the rest of Is 38:10
For God has **c** all to disobedience, Rom 11:32

CONSIST (3)
one's life does not **c** in the abundance Lk 12:15
of God does not **c** in talk but in 1 Cor 4:20
the body does not **c** of one member 1 Cor 12:14

CONSOLATION (6)
give him the cup of **c** to drink for his Jer 16:7
you have done, becoming a **c** to them. Ezk 16:54
they tell false dreams and give empty **c**. Zec 10:2
and devout, waiting for the **c** of Israel, Lk 2:25
are rich, for you have received your **c**. Lk 6:24
and encouragement and **c**. 1 Cor 14:3

CONSOLATIONS (1)
heart are many, your **c** cheer my soul. Ps 94:19

CONSOLE (6)
his servants to **c** him concerning his 2 Sm 10:2
sent messengers to **c** him concerning 1 Chr 19:2
the Ammonites to Hanun to **c** him. 1 Chr 19:2
have happened to you—who will **c** you? Is 51:19
They will **c** you, when you see their Ezk 14:23
and Mary to **c** them concerning their Jn 11:19

CONSOLED (1)
you will be **c** for the disaster that I Ezk 14:22

CONSOLING (2)
nurse and be satisfied from her **c** breast; Is 66:11
who were with her in the house, **c** her, Jn 11:31

CONSORT (1)
of falsehood, nor do I **c** with hypocrites. Ps 26:4

CONSPICUOUS (4)
the goat had a **c** horn between his eyes. Dn 8:5
there came up four **c** horns toward the Dn 8:8
The sins of some men are **c**, going 1 Tm 5:24
So also good works are **c**, and even 1 Tm 5:25

CONSPIRACY (12)
city Giloh. And the **c** grew strong, 2 Sm 15:12
of Zimri, and the **c** that he made, 1 Kgs 16:20
and made a **c** and struck down 2 Kgs 12:20
And they made a **c** against him in 2 Kgs 14:19
of Shallum, and the **c** that he made, 2 Kgs 15:15
of Elah made a **c** against Pekah the 2 Kgs 15:30
LORD they made a **c** against him in 2 Chr 25:27
"Do not call **c** all that this people calls Is 8:12
conspiracy all that this people calls **c**, Is 8:12
"A **c** exists among the men of Judah and Jer 11:9
The **c** of her prophets in her midst is Ezk 22:25
more than forty who made this **c**. Acts 23:13

CONSPIRATORS (1)
is among the **c** with Absalom." And 2 Sm 15:31

CONSPIRE (1)
For they **c** with one accord; against you Ps 83:5

CONSPIRED (19)
near to them they **c** against him to kill Gn 37:18
that all of you have **c** against me? No 1 Sm 22:8
him, "Why have you **c** against me, 1 Sm 22:13
house of Issachar, **c** against him. 1 Kgs 15:27
of half his chariots, **c** against him. 1 Kgs 16:9
heard it said, "Zimri has **c**, 1 Kgs 16:16
the son of Nimshi **c** against Joram. 2 Kgs 9:14
It was I who **c** against my master and 2 Kgs 10:9
the son of Jabesh **c** against him and 2 Kgs 15:10
c against him with fifty men of the 2 Kgs 15:25
servants of Amon **c** against him 2 Kgs 21:23
those who had **c** against King 2 Kgs 21:24
But they **c** against him, and by 2 Chr 24:21
his servants **c** against him because 2 Chr 24:25
Those who **c** against him were 2 Chr 24:26
And his servants **c** against him and 2 Chr 33:24
those who had **c** against King 2 Chr 33:25
"Amos has **c** against you in the midst Am 7:10
Pharisees went out and **c** against him, Mt 12:14

CONSTANT (3)
patient in tribulation, be **c** in prayer. Rom 12:12
and **c** friction among people who are 1 Tm 6:5
discernment trained by **c** practice to Heb 5:14

CONSTANTLY (3)
c mentioning you in our prayers, 1 Thes 1:2
And we also thank God **c** for this, 1 Thes 2:13
as I remember you **c** in my prayers 2 Tm 1:3

CONSTELLATIONS (2)
the moon and the **c** and all the host 2 Kgs 23:5
the heavens and their **c** will not give Is 13:10

CONSTRAINED (1)
going to Jerusalem, **c** by the Spirit, Acts 20:22

CONSTRAINS (1)
full of words; the spirit within me **c** me. Jb 32:18

CONSTRUCTED (1)
in reverent fear **c** an ark for the saving Heb 11:7

CONSTRUCTION (6)
any work in the **c** of the sanctuary shall Ex 36:1
the work, in all the **c** of the sanctuary, Ex 38:24
This was the **c** of the stands: they had 1 Kgs 7:28
on, half of my servants worked on **c**, Neh 4:16
appearance of the wheels and their **c**: Ezk 1:16
their appearance and **c** being as it were Ezk 1:16

CONSULT (8)
in those days, and you shall **c** them, Dt 17:9
be a priest to **c** Urim and Thummim. Ezr 2:63
those who watch for my life **c** together Ps 71:10
they **c** together against your treasured Ps 83:3
to the Holy One of Israel or **c** the LORD! Is 31:1
Whom did he **c**, and who made him Is 40:14
to a prophet to **c** me through him, Ezk 14:7
I did not immediately **c** with anyone; Gal 1:16

CONSULTATION (1)
chief priests held a **c** with the elders and Mk 15:1

CONSULTED (4)
gave was as if one **c** the word of God; 2 Sm 16:23
of the LORD, and also **c** a medium, 1 Chr 10:13
David **c** with the commanders of 1 Chr 13:1
I indeed let myself be **c** by them? Ezk 14:3

CONSULTS (1)
shakes the arrows; he **c** the teraphim; Ezk 21:21

CONSUME (34)
of Egypt. The famine will **c** the land, Gn 41:30
hot against them and I may **c** them, Ex 32:10
the mountains and to **c** them from the Ex 32:12
up among you, lest I **c** you on the way, Ex 33:3
should go up among you, I would **c** you. Ex 33:5
disease and fever that **c** the eyes and Lv 26:16
that I may **c** them in a moment." Nm 16:21
that I may **c** them in a moment." And Nm 16:45
so that I did not **c** the people of Israel Nm 25:11
we die? For this great fire will **c** us. Dt 5:25
And you shall **c** all the peoples that the Dt 7:16
gather in little, for the locust shall **c** it. Dt 28:38
will turn and do you harm and **c** you, Jos 24:20
from heaven and **c** you and your 2 Kgs 1:10
from heaven and **c** you and your 2 Kgs 1:12
up in his wrath, and fire will **c** them. Ps 21:9
you **c** like a moth what is dear to him; Ps 39:11
c them in wrath; consume them till Ps 59:13
c them till they are no more, that they Ps 59:13
favor, but the lips of a fool **c** him. Eccl 10:12
Let the fire for your adversaries **c** them. Is 26:11
your breath is a fire that will **c** you. Is 33:11
be burned, and the flame shall not **c** you. Is 43:2
people wood, and the fire shall **c** them. Jer 5:14
But I will **c** them by the sword, by Jer 14:12
from the fire, the fire shall yet **c** them, Ezk 15:7
It is polished to **c** and to flash like Ezk 21:28
and I will **c** your uncleanness out of Ezk 22:15
their cities, **c** the bars of their gates, Hos 11:6
they shall burn them and **c** them, and Ob 1:18
And it shall remain in his house and **c** it, Zec 5:4
come down from heaven and **c** them?" Lk 9:54
written, "Zeal for your house will **c** me." Jn 2:17
fury of fire that will **c** the adversaries. Heb 10:27

CONSUMED (65)
by day the heat **c** me, and the cold by Gn 31:40
the bush was burning, yet it was not **c**. Ex 3:2
or the standing grain or the field is **c**, Ex 22:6
before the LORD and **c** the burnt offering Lv 9:24
out from before the LORD and **c** them, Lv 10:2
among them and **c** some outlying Nm 11:1
yet between their teeth, before it was **c**, Nm 11:33
from the LORD and **c** the 250 men Nm 16:35
to you until he has **c** you off the land Dt 28:21
up from the rock and **c** the flesh and the Jgs 6:21
fight against them until they are **c**.' 1 Sm 15:18
"The man who **c** us and planned to 2 Sm 21:5
did not turn back until they were **c**. 2 Sm 22:38
I **c** them; I thrust them through, so 2 Sm 22:39
spear, and they are utterly **c** with fire." 2 Sm 23:7
LORD fell and **c** the burnt offering 1 Kgs 18:38
down from heaven and **c** him and his 2 Kgs 1:10
down from heaven and **c** him and his 2 Kgs 1:12
from heaven and **c** the two former 2 Kgs 1:14
from heaven and **c** the burnt offering 2 Chr 7:1
you not be angry with us until you **c** us, Ezr 9:14

the sheep and the servants and **c** them, Jb 1:16
and by the blast of his anger they are **c**. Jb 4:9
him; what is left in his tent will be **c**. Jb 20:26
cut off, and what they left the fire has **c**.' Jb 22:20
and did not turn back till they were **c**. Ps 18:37
Their form shall be **c** in Sheol, with no Ps 49:14
For zeal for your house has **c** me, and the Ps 69:9
my accusers be put to shame and **c**; Ps 71:13
Let sinners be **c** from the earth, and let Ps 104:35
My soul is **c** with longing for your Ps 119:20
groan, when your flesh and body are **c**, Prv 5:11
those who forsake the LORD shall be **c**. Is 1:28
you have **c** them, but they refused to take Jer 5:3
blow fiercely; the lead is **c** by the fire; Jer 6:29
sword after them, until I have **c** them." Jer 9:16
they have devoured him and **c** him, Jer 10:25
set fire to it, and its branches will be **c**. Jer 11:16
and famine those prophets shall be **c**. Jer 14:15
the LORD, until I have **c** it by his hand. Jer 27:8
the entire scroll was **c** in the fire that Jer 36:23
of Egypt to live, and they shall all be **c**. Jer 44:12
sword and by famine they shall be **c**. Jer 44:12
and have been **c** by the sword Jer 44:18
of Egypt shall be **c** by the sword and Jer 44:27
sword after them, until I have **c** them, Jer 49:37
a fire in Zion that **c** its foundations. Lam 4:11
of pestilence and be **c** with famine in Ezk 5:12
When the fire has **c** both ends of it, Ezk 15:4
when the fire has **c** it and it is charred, Ezk 15:5
As for its strong stem, fire **c** it. Ezk 19:12
the stem of its shoots, has **c** its fruit, Ezk 19:14
I have **c** them with the fire of my Ezk 22:31
may be melted in it, its corrosion **c**. Ezk 24:11
fire out from your midst; it **c** you, Ezk 28:18
shall no more be **c** with hunger in the Ezk 34:29
so I have **c** them in my anger. Ezk 43:8
away, to be **c** and destroyed to the end. Dn 7:26
drink; they are **c** like stubble fully dried. Na 1:10
of his jealousy, all the earth shall be **c**; Zep 1:18
of my jealousy all the earth shall be **c**. Zep 3:8
you, O children of Jacob, are not **c**. Mal 3:6
women and were **c** with passion for Rom 1:27
out that you are not **c** by one another. Gal 5:15
came down from heaven and **c** them, Rv 20:9

CONSUMES (10)
out your fury; it **c** them like stubble. Ex 15:7
is barren, and fire **c** the tents of bribery. Jb 15:34
It **c** the parts of his skin; the firstborn of Jb 18:13
skin; the firstborn of death **c** his limbs. Jb 18:13
would be a fire that **c** as far as Abaddon, Jb 31:12
As fire **c** the forest, as the flame sets the Ps 83:14
My zeal **c** me, because my foes forget Ps 119:139
burns like a fire; it **c** briers and thorns; Is 9:18
they are like stubble; the fire **c** them; Is 47:14
pours from their mouth and **c** their foes. Rv 11:5

CONSUMING (5)
For the LORD your God is a **c** fire, a Dt 4:24
over before you as a **c** fire is the LORD your Dt 9:3
among us can dwell with the **c** fire? Is 33:14
a flaming fire in Jacob, **c** all around. Lam 2:3
for our God is a **c** fire. Heb 12:29

CONTACT (3)
that is unclean through **c** with the dead Lv 22:4
who is unclean through **c** with the dead. Nm 5:2
who is unclean by **c** with a dead body Hg 2:13

CONTAIN (5)
and the highest heaven cannot **c** you; 1 Kgs 8:27
as great as would **c** two seahs of seed. 1 Kgs 18:32
even highest heaven, cannot **c** him? 2 Chr 2:6
and the highest heaven cannot **c** you, 2 Chr 6:18
world itself could not **c** the books that Jn 21:25

CONTAINERS (1)
sorted the good into **c** but threw away Mt 13:48

CONTAINING (2)
c the terms and conditions and the Jer 32:11
the bath **c** one tenth of a homer, Ezk 45:11

CONTAINS (3)
way her land will be stripped of all it **c**, Ezk 12:19
at and held in derision, for it **c** much; Ezk 23:32
(the cor, like the homer, **c** ten baths). Ezk 45:14

CONTEMPT (28)
she looked with **c** on her mistress. Gn 16:4
had conceived, she looked on me with **c**. Gn 16:5
treated the offering of the LORD with **c**. 1 Sm 2:17
he wrote letters to cast **c** on the LORD, 2 Chr 32:17
them to look at their husbands with **c**, Est 1:17
and there will be **c** and wrath in plenty. Est 1:18
who is at ease there is **c** for misfortune; Jb 12:5
He pours **c** on princes and loosens the Jb 12:21
and the **c** of families terrified me, Jb 31:34
against the righteous in pride and **c**. Ps 31:18
he pours **c** on princes and makes Ps 107:40
Take away from me scorn and **c**, for I Ps 119:22
for we have had more than enough of **c**. Ps 123:3
who are at ease, of the **c** of the proud. Ps 123:4
When wickedness comes, **c** comes also, Prv 18:3
time he brought into **c** the land of Is 9:1
glory of Moab will be brought into **c**, Is 16:14
and mother are treated with **c** in you; Ezk 22:7
who have treated them with **c**. Ezk 28:24
who have treated them with **c**. Ezk 28:26
with wholehearted joy and utter **c**, Ezk 36:5
and some to shame and everlasting **c**. Dn 12:2
for the son treats the father with **c**, the Mi 7:6
you and treat you with **c** and make you a Na 3:6
many things and be treated with **c**? Mk 9:12
righteous, and treated others with **c**: Lk 18:9
treated him with **c** and mocked him. Lk 23:11
own harm and holding him up to **c**. Heb 6:6

CONTEMPTIBLE (2)
make myself yet more **c** than this, 2 Sm 6:22
place shall arise a **c** person to whom Dn 11:21

CONTEMPTUOUSLY (1)
and will speak **c** against their king Is 8:21

CONTEND (30)
Do not **c** with them, for I will not give you Dt 2:5
not harass Moab or **c** with them in battle, Dt 2:9
do not harass them or **c** with them, Dt 2:19
possession, and **c** with him in battle. Dt 2:24
With your hands **c** for him, and be a Dt 33:7
stood against him, "Will you **c** for Baal? Jgs 6:31
If he is a god, let him **c** for himself, Jgs 6:31
"Let Baal **c** against him," because he Jgs 6:32
Did he ever **c** against Israel, or did he Jgs 11:25
If one wished to **c** with him, one could not Jb 9:3
me; let me know why you **c** against me. Jb 10:2
Who is there who will **c** with me? For Jb 13:19
Would he **c** with me in the greatness of Jb 23:6
Why do you **c** against him, saying, 'He Jb 33:13
"Shall a faultfinder **c** with the Almighty? Jb 40:2
C, O LORD, with those who contend with Ps 35:1
O LORD, with those who **c** with me; Ps 35:1
Do not **c** with a man for no reason, Prv 3:30
The LORD has taken his place to **c**; he Is 3:13
You shall seek those who **c** with you, Is 41:12
for I will **c** with those who contend with Is 49:25
will contend with those who **c** with you, Is 49:25
me is near. Who will **c** with me? Is 50:8
For I will not **c** forever, nor will I always Is 57:16
"Therefore I still **c** with you, declares the Jer 2:9
and with your children's children I will **c**. Jer 2:9
"Why do you **c** with me? You have all Jer 2:29
Yet let no one **c**, and let none accuse, for Hos 4:4
his people, and he will **c** with Israel. Mi 6:2
appealing to you to **c** for the faith that Jude 1:3

CONTENDED (5)
the well Esek, because they **c** with him. Gn 26:20
who **c** against Moses and Aaron in the Nm 26:9
of Korah, when they **c** against the LORD Nm 26:9
by measure, by exile you **c** with them; Is 27:8
party stood up and **c** sharply, Acts 23:9

CONTENDERS (1)
and decides between powerful **c**. Prv 18:18

CONTENDING (1)
the archangel Michael, **c** with the devil, Jude 1:9

CONTENDS (2)
Whoever **c** for him shall be put to death Jgs 6:31
there is none who **c** by my side against Dn 10:21

CONTENT (10)
And Moses was **c** to dwell with the man, Ex 2:21
that we had been **c** to dwell beyond the Jos 7:7
And the Levite was **c** to dwell with the Jgs 17:11
Be **c** with your glory, and stay at 2 Kgs 14:10
accusation, and be **c** with your wages." Lk 3:14
then, I am **c** with weaknesses, 2 Cor 12:10
in whatever situation I am to be **c**. Phil 4:11
and clothing, with these we will be **c**. 1 Tm 6:8
money, and be **c** with what you have, Heb 13:5
against us. And not **c** with that, 3 Jn 1:10

CONTENTION (5)
us an object of **c** for our neighbors, Ps 80:6
but he who is slow to anger quiets **c**. Prv 15:18
a man of strife and **c** to the whole land! Jer 15:10
let none accuse, for with you is my **c**, Hos 4:4
violence are before me; strife and **c** arise. Hab 1:3

CONTENTIOUS (1)
If anyone is inclined to be **c**, we have 1 Cor 11:16

CONTENTMENT (2)
"Because he knew no **c** in his belly, he Jb 20:20
there is great gain in godliness with **c**, 1 Tm 6:6

CONTENTS (1)
its crop with its **c** and cast it beside Lv 1:16

CONTEST (1)
If it is a **c** of strength, behold, he is Jb 9:19

CONTINUAL (7)
There were **c** wars between 2 Chr 12:15
his bed and with **c** strife in his bones, Jb 33:19
but the cheerful of heart has a **c** feast. Prv 15:15
quarreling is a **c** dripping of rain. Prv 19:13
A **c** dripping on a rainy day and a Prv 27:15
of Israel, which had been a **c** waste. Ezk 38:8
not beat me down by her **c** coming.'" Lk 18:5

CONTINUALLY (59)
the thoughts of his heart was only evil **c**. Gn 6:5
and the waters receded from the earth **c**. Gn 8:3
hail and fire flashing **c** in the midst of Ex 9:24
Fire shall be kept burning on the altar **c**; Lv 6:13
shall be only oppressed and robbed **c**, Dt 28:29
shall be only oppressed and crushed **c**, Dt 28:33
after the ark, while the trumpets blew **c**. Jos 6:9
on, and they blew the trumpets **c**. Jos 6:13
of the LORD, while the trumpets blew **c**. Jos 6:13
David. So Saul was David's enemy **c**. 1 Sm 18:29
of Gera, and as he came he cursed **c**. 2 Sm 16:5
who **c** stand before you and hear 1 Kgs 10:8
Rehoboam and Jeroboam **c**. 1 Kgs 14:30
man of God who is **c** passing our way. 2 Kgs 4:9
and he gave them **c** into the hand of 2 Kgs 13:3
his strength; seek his presence **c**! 1 Chr 16:11
who **c** stand before you and hear your 2 Chr 9:7
God in their hearts." Thus Job did **c**. Jb 1:5
times; his praise shall **c** be in my mouth. Ps 34:1
those who love your salvation say **c**, Ps 40:16
day and night, while they say to me **c**, Ps 42:3
taunt me, while they say to me **c**, Ps 42:10
In God we have boasted **c**, and we will Ps 44:8
your burnt offerings are **c** before me. Ps 50:8
see, and make their loins tremble **c**. Ps 69:23
a rock of refuge, to which I may **c** come; Ps 71:3
mother's womb. My praise is **c** of you. Ps 71:6
But I will hope **c** and will praise you yet Ps 71:14
May prayer be made for him **c**, and Ps 72:15
Nevertheless, I am **c** with you; you hold Ps 73:23
who rise against you, which goes up **c**! Ps 74:23
and his strength; seek his presence **c**! Ps 105:4
Let them be before the LORD **c**, that he Ps 109:15
I will keep your law **c**, forever and ever, Ps 119:44
I hold my life in my hand **c**, but I do Ps 119:109
and have regard for your statutes **c**! Ps 119:117
things in their heart and stir up wars **c**. Ps 140:2
Yet my prayer is **c** against their evil Ps 141:5
heart devises evil, **c** sowing discord; Prv 6:14
a watchtower I stand, O Lord, **c** by day, Is 21:8
Does he who plows for sowing plow **c**? Is 28:24
does he **c** open and harrow his ground? Is 28:24
of my hands; your walls are **c** before me. Is 49:16
and you fear **c** all the day because of the Is 51:13
"and **c** all the day my name is despised. Is 52:5
LORD will guide you **c** and satisfy your Is 58:11
Your gates shall be open **c**; day and Is 60:11
a people who provoke me to my face **c**, Is 65:3
They say **c** to those who despise the Jer 23:17
My soul **c** remembers it and is bowed Lam 3:20
around it, and fire flashing forth **c**, Ezk 1:4
"May your God, whom you serve **c**, Dn 6:16
God, has your God, whom you serve **c**, Dn 6:20
and justice, and wait **c** for your God." Hos 12:6
so all the nations shall drink **c**; Ob 1:16
and were **c** in the temple blessing God. Lk 24:53
to the people, and prayed **c** to God. Acts 10:2
sacrifices that are **c** offered every year, Heb 10:1
him then let us **c** offer up a sacrifice Heb 13:15

CONTINUE (36)
what will you give me, for I **c** childless, Gn 15:2
Then she shall **c** for thirty-three days in Lv 12:4
And she shall **c** in the blood of her Lv 12:5
discharge she shall **c** in uncleanness. Lv 15:25
not listen to me, I will **c** striking you, Lv 26:21
prophesied. But they did not **c** doing it. Nm 11:25
so that he may **c** long in his kingdom, Dt 17:20
Judah shall **c** in his territory on the Jos 18:5
house of Joseph shall **c** in their territory Jos 18:5
But now your kingdom shall not **c**. 1 Sm 13:14
so that it may **c** forever before you. 2 Sm 7:29
that it may **c** forever before you, 1 Chr 17:27
c your steadfast love to those who know Ps 36:10
forever, his fame **c** as long as the sun! Ps 72:17
who utters lies shall **c** before my eyes. Ps 101:7
but **c** in the fear of the LORD all the day. Prv 23:17
and knowledge, its stability will long **c**. Prv 28:2
be struck down? Why will you **c** to rebel? Is 1:5
Now they will **c** to use her for a whore, Ezk 23:43
sea. It shall **c** in summer as in winter. Zec 14:8
name, and I will **c** to make it known, Jn 17:26
to your servants to **c** to speak your Acts 4:29
urged them to **c** in the grace of God. Acts 13:43

encouraging them to **c** in the faith, Acts 14:22
Are we to **c** in sin that grace may Rom 6:1
that God's purpose of election might **c**, Rom 9:11
you, provided you **c** in his kindness. Rom 11:22
they, if they do not **c** in their unbelief, Rom 11:23
And what I do I will **c** to do, in order 2 Cor 11:12
that I will remain and **c** with you all, Phil 1:25
if indeed you **c** in the faith, stable and Col 1:23
C steadfastly in prayer, being watchful Col 4:2
childbearing—if they **c** in faith and 1 Tm 2:15
c in what you have learned and have 2 Tm 3:14
For they did not **c** in my covenant, and Heb 8:9
Let brotherly love **c**. Heb 13:1

CONTINUED (35)
The flood **c** forty days on the earth. The Gn 7:17
And the waters **c** to abate until the tenth Gn 8:5
them. They **c** for some time in custody. Gn 40:4
when the cloud **c** over the tabernacle Nm 9:19
set out, or if it **c** for a day and a night, Nm 9:21
that the cloud **c** over the tabernacle, Nm 9:22
And from there they **c** to Beer; that is Nm 21:16
So Moses **c** to speak these words to all Dt 31:1
and she has **c** from early morning until Ru 2:7
As she **c** praying before the LORD, Eli 1 Sm 1:12
young man Samuel **c** to grow both 1 Sm 2:26
years Syria and Israel **c** without war. 1 Kgs 22:1
And the battle **c** that day, and the 1 Kgs 22:35
the people **c** to sacrifice and make 2 Kgs 12:3
And the battle **c** that day, and the 2 Chr 18:34
All this **c** until the burnt offering 2 Chr 29:28
and I **c** fasting and praying before the Neh 1:4
And Elihu **c**, and said: Jb 36:1
therefore I have **c** my faithfulness to you. Jer 31:3
have sinned, O Israel; there they have **c**. Hos 10:9
pray, and all night he **c** in prayer to God. Lk 6:12
And as they **c** to ask him, he stood up and Jn 8:7
him from the dead **c** to bear witness. Jn 12:17
he bore witness and **c** to exhort them, Acts 2:40
the Holy Spirit and **c** to speak the word Acts 4:31
And the word of God **c** to increase, and Acts 6:7
after being baptized he **c** with Philip. Acts 8:13
But Peter **c** knocking, and when they Acts 12:16
and there they **c** to preach the gospel. Acts 14:7
became stubborn and **c** in unbelief, Acts 19:9
This **c** for two years, so that all the Acts 19:10
word of the Lord **c** to increase and Acts 19:20
day that you have **c** in suspense and Acts 27:33
but **c** entrusting himself to him who 1 Pt 2:23
been of us, they would have **c** with us. 1 Jn 2:19

CONTINUES (6)
Neiel. Then it **c** in the north to Cabul, Jos 19:27
forever if he **c** strong in keeping 1 Chr 28:7
withers; he flees like a shadow and **c** not. Jb 14:2
on God and **c** in supplications and 1 Tm 5:5
the Son of God he **c** a priest forever. Heb 7:3
permanently, because he **c** forever. Heb 7:24

CONTINUING (2)
prevented by death from **c** in office, Heb 7:23
all things are **c** as they were from the 2 Pt 3:4

CONTRADICT (3)
will be able to withstand or **c**. Lk 21:15
and began to **c** what was spoken Acts 13:45
doctrine and also to rebuke those who **c** it. Ti 1:9

CONTRADICTIONS (1)
the irreverent babble and **c** of what is 1 Tm 6:20

CONTRARY (23)
"Then if you walk **c** to me and will not Lv 26:21
are not turned to me but walk **c** to me, Lv 26:23
then I also will walk **c** to you, and I Lv 26:24
will not listen to me, but walk **c** to me, Lv 26:27
then I will walk **c** to you in fury, and I Lv 26:28
me, and also in walking **c** to me, Lv 26:40
so that I walked **c** to them and brought Lv 26:41
people to worship God **c** to the law." Acts 18:13
and yet **c** to the law you order me to be Acts 23:3
relations for those that are **c** to nature; Rom 1:26
means! On the **c**, we uphold the law. Rom 3:31
hands to a disobedient and **c** people." Rom 10:21
olive tree, and grafted, **c** to nature, Rom 11:24
To the **c**, "if your enemy is hungry, Rom 12:20
and create obstacles **c** to the doctrine Rom 16:17
On the **c**, the parts of the body that 1 Cor 12:22
On the **c**, I worked harder than any 1 Cor 15:10
preach to you a gospel **c** to the one we Gal 1:8
to you a gospel **c** to the one you Gal 1:9
On the **c**, when they saw that I had been Gal 2:7
Is the law then **c** to the promises of God? Gal 3:21
whatever else is **c** to sound doctrine, 1 Tm 1:10
evil or reviling for reviling, but on the **c**, 1 Pt 3:9

CONTRIBUTE (2)
of Israel, which they **c** to the LORD, Lv 22:15
C to the needs of the saints and seek Rom 12:13

CONTRIBUTED (10)
priests' portion that is **c** from the ram Ex 29:27
and the thigh that is **c** I have taken from Lv 7:34
and the thigh that is **c** you shall eat in a Lv 10:14
The thigh that is **c** and the breast that Lv 10:15
that is waved and the thigh that is **c**. Nm 6:20
of it, when you have **c** the best of it. Nm 18:32
Then Josiah **c** to the lay people, as 2 Chr 35:7
And his officials **c** willingly to the 2 Chr 35:8
For they all **c** out of their abundance, Mk 12:44
For they all **c** out of their abundance, Lk 21:4

CONTRIBUTES (1)
the one who **c**, in generosity; Rom 12:8

CONTRIBUTING (1)
all those who are **c** to the offering box. Mk 12:43

CONTRIBUTION (38)
people of Israel, that they take for me a **c**. Ex 25:2
him you shall receive the **c** for me. Ex 25:2
And this is the **c** that you shall receive Ex 25:3
from the people of Israel, for it is a **c**. Ex 29:28
It shall be a **c** from the people of Israel Ex 29:28
their peace offerings, their **c** to the LORD. Ex 29:28
Take from among you a **c** to the LORD. Ex 35:5
heart, let him bring the LORD'S **c**: Ex 35:5
and brought the LORD'S **c** to be used for Ex 35:21
who could make a **c** of silver or bronze Ex 35:24
or bronze brought it as the LORD'S **c**. Ex 35:24
from Moses all the **c** that the people of Ex 36:3
more for the **c** for the sanctuary." Ex 36:6
to the priest as a **c** from the sacrifice of Lv 7:32
shall not eat of the **c** of the holy things. Lv 22:12
And every **c**, all the holy donations of Nm 5:9
land, you shall present a **c** to the LORD. Nm 15:19
dough you shall present a loaf as a **c**; Nm 15:20
like a **c** from the threshing floor, so Nm 15:20
LORD as a **c** throughout your Nm 15:21
the **c** of their gift, all the wave Nm 18:11
which they present as a **c** to the LORD, Nm 18:24
you shall present a **c** from it to the Nm 18:26
And your **c** shall be counted to you as Nm 18:27
shall also present a **c** to the LORD from Nm 18:28
shall give the LORD'S **c** to Aaron the Nm 18:28
you shall present every **c** due to the Nm 18:29
to Eleazar the priest as a **c** to the LORD. Nm 31:29
tribute, which was the **c** for the LORD, Nm 31:41
the gold of the **c** that they presented to Nm 31:52
your tithes and the **c** that you present, Dt 12:6
your tithes and the **c** that you present, Dt 12:11
offerings or the **c** that you present, Dt 12:17
The **c** of the king from his own 2 Chr 31:3
to apportion the **c** reserved for the 2 Chr 31:14
sons of Levi shall bring the **c** of grain, Neh 10:39
pleased to make some **c** for the poor Rom 15:26
the generosity of your **c** for them and 2 Cor 9:13

CONTRIBUTIONS (9)
given you charge of the **c** made to me, Nm 18:8
All the holy **c** that the people of Israel Nm 18:19
began to bring the **c** into the house 2 Chr 31:10
they faithfully brought in the **c**, 2 Chr 31:12
the first of our dough, and our **c**, Neh 10:37
appointed over the storerooms, the **c**, Neh 12:44
gatekeepers, and the **c** for the priests. Neh 13:5
I will require your **c** and the choicest Ezk 20:40
we robbed you?' In your tithes and **c**. Mal 3:8

CONTRITE (4)
a broken and **c** heart, O God, you will Ps 51:17
with him who is of a **c** and lowly spirit, Is 57:15
the lowly, and to revive the heart of the **c**. Is 57:15
who is humble and **c** in spirit and Is 66:2

CONTRIVED (1)
is it that you have **c** this deed in your Acts 5:4

CONTROL (5)
Joseph could not **c** himself before all Gn 45:1
but having his desire under **c**, 1 Cor 7:37
my body and keep it under **c**, 1 Cor 9:27
you know how to **c** his own body in 1 Thes 4:4
to him, he left nothing outside his **c**. Heb 2:8

CONTROLLING (1)
And **c** himself he said, "Serve the food." Gn 43:31

CONTROLS (1)
For the love of Christ **c** us, because 2 Cor 5:14

CONTROVERSIES (3)
with all the customs and **c** of the Jews. Acts 26:3
to do with foolish, ignorant **c**; 2 Tm 2:23
But avoid foolish **c**, genealogies, Ti 3:9

CONTROVERSY (2)
the LORD has a **c** with the inhabitants of Hos 4:1
unhealthy craving for **c** and for 1 Tm 6:4

CONVERSATION (2)
him, for the **c** had not been overheard. Jer 38:27
"What is this **c** that you are holding Lk 24:17

CONVERSED (3)
Stoic philosophers also **c** with him. Acts 17:18
eaten, he **c** with them a long while, Acts 20:11
he sent for him often and **c** with him. Acts 24:26

CONVERSION (1)
in detail the **c** of the Gentiles, Acts 15:3

CONVERT (2)
who was the first **c** to Christ in Asia. Rom 16:5
He must not be a recent **c**, or he may 1 Tm 3:6

CONVERTS (2)
Jews and devout **c** to Judaism Acts 13:43
Stephanas were the first **c** in Achaia, 1 Cor 16:15

CONVICT (2)
he will **c** the world concerning sin and Jn 16:8
on all and to **c** all the ungodly of Jude 1:15

CONVICTED (2)
or outsider enters, he is **c** by all, 1 Cor 14:24
committing sin and are **c** by the law as Jas 2:9

CONVICTION (2)
and in the Holy Spirit and with full **c**. 1 Thes 1:5
hoped for, the **c** of things not seen. Heb 11:1

CONVICTS (2)
this decision the king **c** himself, 2 Sm 14:13
Which one of you **c** me of sin? If I tell the Jn 8:46

CONVINCE (1)
God and trying to **c** them about Jesus Acts 28:23

CONVINCED (8)
will they be **c** if someone should Lk 16:31
for they are **c** that John was a prophet." Lk 20:6
"I myself was **c** that I ought to do Acts 26:9
And some were **c** by what he said, but Acts 28:24
fully **c** that God was able to do what he Rom 4:21
one should be fully **c** in his own mind. Rom 14:5
C of this, I know that I will remain and Phil 1:25
and I am **c** that he is able to guard 2 Tm 1:12

CONVINCINGLY (1)
desired to show more **c** to the heirs of Heb 6:17

CONVOCATION (15)
day is a Sabbath of solemn rest, a holy **c**. Lv 23:3
On the first day you shall have a holy **c**; Lv 23:7
On the seventh day is a holy **c**; you shall Lv 23:8
the same day. You shall hold a holy **c**. Lv 23:21
with blast of trumpets, a holy **c**. Lv 23:24
It shall be for you a time of holy **c**, and Lv 23:27
On the first day shall be a holy **c**; you Lv 23:35
shall hold a holy **c** and present a food Lv 23:36
you shall proclaim as times of holy **c**, Lv 23:37
the first day there shall be a holy **c**. Nm 28:18
seventh day you shall have a holy **c**. Nm 28:25
of Weeks, you shall have a holy **c**. Nm 28:26
seventh month you shall have a holy **c**. Nm 29:1
have a holy **c** and afflict yourselves. Nm 29:7
month you shall have a holy **c**. Nm 29:12

CONVOCATIONS (3)
LORD that you shall proclaim as holy **c**; Lv 23:2
appointed feasts of the LORD, the holy **c**, Lv 23:4
and the calling of **c**—I cannot endure Is 1:13

CONVULSED (3)
bristles with horror; their faces are **c**. Ezk 27:35
saw him, immediately it **c** the boy, Mk 9:20
threw him to the ground and **c** him. Lk 9:42

CONVULSES (1)
It **c** him so that he foams at the mouth; Lk 9:39

CONVULSING (2)
c him and crying out with a loud voice, Mk 1:26
after crying out and **c** him terribly, Mk 9:26

COOK (3)
And you shall **c** it and eat it at the place Dt 16:7
And Samuel said to the **c**, "Bring the 1 Sm 9:23
So the **c** took up the leg and what was 1 Sm 9:24

COOKED (1)
offering is a grain offering **c** in a pan, Lv 2:7

COOKING (1)
Once when Jacob was **c** stew, Esau Gn 25:29

COOKS (1)
to be perfumers and **c** and bakers. 1 Sm 8:13

COOL (5)
walking in the garden in the **c** of the day, Gn 3:8
was sitting alone in his **c** roof chamber. Jgs 3:20
himself in the closet of the **c** chamber." Jgs 3:24
and he who has a **c** spirit is a man of Prv 17:27
of his finger in water and **c** my tongue, Lk 16:24

COPIED (1)
the men of Hezekiah king of Judah **c**. Prv 25:1

COPIES (2)
was necessary for the **c** of the heavenly Heb 9:23
hands, which are **c** of the true things, Heb 9:24

COPING (1)
even from the foundation to the **c**, 1 Kgs 7:9

COPPER (7)
iron, and out of whose hills you can dig **c**. Dt 8:9
the earth, and **c** is smelted from the ore. Jb 28:2
may become hot, and its **c** may burn, Ezk 24:11
no gold nor silver nor **c** for your belts, Mt 10:9
cups and pots and **c** vessels and dining Mk 7:4
came and put in two small **c** coins, Mk 12:42
a poor widow put in two small **c** coins. Lk 21:2

COPPERSMITH (1)
Alexander the **c** did me great harm; 2 Tm 4:14

COPY (12)
for himself in a book a **c** of this law, Dt 17:18
wrote on the stones a **c** of the law of Jos 8:32
'Behold, the **c** of the altar of the LORD, Jos 22:28
(This is a **c** of the letter that they sent.) Ezr 4:11
when the **c** of King Artaxerxes' letter Ezr 4:23
This is a **c** of the letter that Tattenai the Ezr 5:6
This is a **c** of the letter that King Ezr 7:11
A **c** of the document was to be issued as Est 3:14
also gave him a **c** of the written decree Est 4:8
A **c** of what was written was to be issued Est 8:13
terms and conditions and the open **c**. Jer 32:11
They serve a **c** and shadow of the Heb 8:5

COR (2)
tenth of a bath from each **c** (the cor, Ezk 45:14
tenth of a bath from each cor (the **c**, Ezk 45:14

CORAL (3)
shall be made of **c** or of crystal; Jb 28:18
their bodies were more ruddy than **c**, Lam 4:7
work, fine linen, **c**, and ruby. Ezk 27:16

CORBAN (1)
have gained from me is **C**' (that is, Mk 7:11

CORD (13)
"Your signet and your **c** and your staff Gn 38:18
are, the signet and the **c** and the staff." Gn 38:25
fasten it on the turban by a **c** of blue. Ex 28:37
And they tied to it a **c** of blue to fasten it Ex 39:31
and to put a **c** of blue on the tassel of Nm 15:38
shall tie this scarlet **c** in the window Jos 2:18
And she tied the scarlet **c** in the window. Jos 2:21
God has loosed my **c** and humbled me, Jb 30:11
or press down his tongue with a **c**? Jb 41:1
him—a threefold **c** is not quickly Eccl 4:12
before the silver **c** is snapped, or the Eccl 12:6
day you were born your **c** was not cut, Ezk 16:4
with a linen **c** and a measuring reed in Ezk 40:3

CORDED (1)
you shall attach the **c** chains to the Ex 28:14

CORDS (35)
two chains of pure gold, twisted like **c**; Ex 28:14
the breastpiece twisted chains like **c**, Ex 28:22
you shall put the two **c** of gold in the Ex 28:24
ends of the two **c** you shall attach to Ex 28:25
and the pegs of the court, and their **c**; Ex 35:18
on the breastpiece twisted chains like **c**, Ex 39:15
And they put the two **c** of gold in the Ex 39:17
two ends of the two **c** to the two settings Ex 39:18
the screen for the gate of the court, its **c**, Ex 39:40
and its **c**—all the service connected Nm 3:26
court, with their bases and pegs and **c**. Nm 3:37
and their **c** and all the equipment for Nm 4:26
the court with their bases, pegs, and **c**, Nm 4:32
the **c** of Sheol entangled me; the 2 Sm 22:6
hangings fastened with **c** of fine linen Est 1:6
chains and caught in the **c** of affliction, Jb 36:8
of the Pleiades or loose the **c** of Orion? Jb 38:31
apart and cast away their **c** from us." Ps 2:3
The **c** of death encompassed me; the Ps 18:4
the **c** of Sheol entangled me; the snares of Ps 18:5
Bind the festal sacrifice with **c**, up to Ps 118:27
Though the **c** of the wicked ensnare Ps 119:61
he has cut the **c** of the wicked. Ps 129:4
me, and with **c** they have spread a net; Ps 140:5
and he is held fast in the **c** of his sin. Prv 5:22
who draw iniquity with **c** of falsehood, Is 5:18
up, nor will any of its **c** be broken. Is 33:20
Your **c** hang loose; they cannot hold the Is 33:23
lengthen your **c** and strengthen your Is 54:2
is destroyed, and all my **c** are broken; Jer 10:20
behold, **c** will be placed upon you, Ezk 3:25
And behold, I will place **c** upon you, so Ezk 4:8
bound with **c** and made secure. Ezk 27:24
I led them with **c** of kindness, with the Hos 11:4
And making a whip of **c**, he drove them Jn 2:15

CORIANDER (2)
It was like **c** seed, white, and the taste of Ex 16:31
Now the manna was like **c** seed, and its Nm 11:7

CORINTH (6)
this Paul left Athens and went to **C**. Acts 18:1
happened that while Apollos was at **C**, Acts 19:1
To the church of God that is in **C**, to 1 Cor 1:2
To the church of God that is at **C**, 2 Cor 1:1
I refrained from coming again to **C**. 2 Cor 1:23
Erastus remained at **C**, and I left 2 Tm 4:20

CORINTHIANS (2)
many of the **C** hearing Paul believed Acts 18:8
to you, **C**; our heart is wide open. 2 Cor 6:11

CORMORANT (2)
the little owl, the **c**, the short-eared owl, Lv 11:17
owl, the carrion vulture and the **c**, Dt 14:17

CORNELIUS (8)
Caesarea there was a man named **C**, Acts 10:1
of God come in and say to him, "**C**." Acts 10:3
behold, the men who were sent by **C**, Acts 10:17
And they said, "**C**, a centurion, an Acts 10:22
C was expecting them and had called Acts 10:24
C met him and fell down at his feet Acts 10:25
And **C** said, "Four days ago, about Acts 10:30
'**C**, your prayer has been heard and Acts 10:31

CORNER (28)
a cord of blue on the tassel of each **c**. Nm 15:38
stealthily cut off a **c** of Saul's robe. 1 Sm 24:4
he had cut off a **c** of Saul's robe. 1 Sm 24:5
see the **c** of your robe in my hand. 1 Sm 24:11
that I cut off the **c** of your robe and 1 Sm 24:11
the sea at the southeast **c** of the house. 1 Kgs 7:39
the Ephraim Gate to the **C** Gate. 2 Kgs 14:13
sea at the southeast **c** of the house. 2 Chr 4:10
the Ephraim Gate to the **C** Gate. 2 Chr 25:23
in Jerusalem at the **C** Gate and at the 2 Chr 26:9
altars in every **c** of Jerusalem. 2 Chr 28:24
and to the **c**. Palal the son of Uzai Neh 3:25
and to the upper chamber of the **c**. Neh 3:31
upper chamber of the **c** and the Sheep Neh 3:32
peoples and allotted to them every **c**. Neh 9:22
our daughters like **c** pillars cut for the Ps 144:12
passing along the street near her **c**, Prv 7:8
market, and at every **c** she lies in wait. Prv 7:12
better to live in a **c** of the housetop than Prv 21:9
to live in a **c** of the housetop than Prv 25:24
the tower of Hananel to the **C** Gate. Jer 31:38
to the **c** of the Horse Gate toward the Jer 31:40
taken from you for a **c** and no stone for Jer 51:26
and I spread the **c** of my garment over Ezk 16:8
in each **c** of the court there was Ezk 46:21
with the **c** of a couch and part of a bed. Am 3:12
place of the former gate, to the **C** Gate, Zec 14:10
for this has not been done in a **c**. Acts 26:26

CORNERS (34)
the rings to the four **c** at its four legs. Ex 25:26
two frames for **c** of the tabernacle Ex 26:23
both of them; they shall form the two **c**. Ex 26:24
you shall make horns for it on its four **c**; Ex 27:2
make four bronze rings at its four **c**. Ex 27:4
made two frames for **c** of the tabernacle Ex 36:28
two of them this way for the two **c**. Ex 36:29
the rings to the four **c** at its four legs. Ex 37:13
He made horns for it on its four **c**. Its Ex 38:2
rings on the four **c** of the bronze grating Ex 38:5
tassels on the **c** of their garments Nm 15:38
tassels on the four **c** of the garment Dt 22:12
and at the four **c** were supports for a 1 Kgs 7:30
supports at the four **c** of each stand. 1 Kgs 7:34
men, to be on the towers and the **c**, 2 Chr 26:15
and struck the four **c** of the house, Jb 1:19
go, and his lightning to the **c** of the earth. Jb 37:3
of Judah from the four **c** of the earth. Is 11:12
of the earth, and called from its farthest **c**, Is 41:9
in the desert who cut the **c** of their hair, Jer 9:26
Buz, and all who cut the **c** of their hair; Jer 25:23
wind those who cut the **c** of their hair, Jer 49:32
has come upon the four **c** of the land. Ezk 7:2
long, and two cubits broad. Its **c**, Ezk 41:22
altar and on the four **c** of the ledge and Ezk 43:20
the four **c** of the ledge of the altar, Ezk 45:19
me around to the four **c** of the court. Ezk 46:21
in the four **c** of the court were small Ezk 46:22
a bowl, drenched like the **c** of the altar. Zec 9:15
pray in the synagogues and at the street **c**, Mt 6:5
let down by its four **c** upon the earth. Acts 10:11
let down from heaven by its four **c**, Acts 11:5
angels standing at the four **c** of the earth, Rv 7:1
nations that are at the four **c** of the earth, Rv 20:8

CORNERSTONE (11)
were its bases sunk, or who laid its **c**, Jb 38:6
the builders rejected has become the **c**. Ps 118:22
Zion, a stone, a tested stone, a precious **c**, Is 28:16
From him shall come the **c**, from him Zec 10:4
the builders rejected has become the **c**; Mt 21:42
the builders rejected has become the **c**; Mk 12:10
builders rejected has become the **c**'? Lk 20:17
the builders, which has become the **c**. Acts 4:11
Christ Jesus himself being the **c**, Eph 2:20
in Zion a stone, a **c** chosen and precious, 1 Pt 2:6
the builders rejected has become the **c**," 1 Pt 2:7

CORNERSTONES (1)
those who are the **c** of her tribes have Is 19:13

CORPSE (6)
and the **c** of Jezebel shall be as dung 2 Kgs 9:37
Wherever the **c** is, there the vultures Mt 24:28
it came out, and the boy was like a **c**, Mk 9:26
he was dead, he granted the **c** to Joseph. Mk 15:45
He said to them, "Where the **c** is, Lk 17:37
sea, and it became like the blood of a **c**, Rv 16:3

CORPSES (4)
among the nations, filling them with **c**; Ps 110:6
and their **c** were as refuse in the midst of Is 5:25
out, and the stench of their **c** shall rise; Is 34:3
glittering spear, hosts of slain, heaps of **c**, Na 3:3

CORRECT (2)
to do good; seek justice, **c** oppression; Is 1:17
C me, O LORD, but in justice; not in Jer 10:24

CORRECTING (1)
c his opponents with gentleness. God 2 Tm 2:25

CORRECTION (6)
Whether for **c** or for his land or for love, Jb 37:13
I struck your children; they took no **c**; Jer 2:30
them, but they refused to take **c**. Jer 5:3
She listens to no voice; she accepts no **c**. Zep 3:2
you will fear me; you will accept **c**. Zep 3:7
for teaching, for reproof, for **c**, 2 Tm 3:16

CORRECTLY (1)
he said to him, "You have answered **c**; Lk 10:28

CORRECTS (1)
Whoever **c** a scoffer gets himself abuse, Prv 9:7

CORRESPOND (1)
Their end will **c** to their deeds. 2 Cor 11:15

CORRESPONDED (1)
that goes up. Watch **c** to watch. 1 Chr 26:16

CORRESPONDING (7)
breadth, **c** to the hangings of the court. Ex 38:18
them in divisions **c** to the sons 1 Chr 23:6
the gatekeepers, **c** to their chief men, 1 Chr 26:12
length, **c** to the breadth of the house, 2 Chr 3:8
of the gates, **c** to the length of the gates. Ezk 40:18
the passage before the **c** wall on the Ezk 42:12
c in length to one of the tribal portions, Ezk 45:7

CORRESPONDS (2)
she **c** to the present Jerusalem, for she is Gal 4:25
Baptism, which **c** to this, now saves 1 Pt 3:21

CORRODED (1)
Your gold and silver have **c**, and their Jas 5:3

CORROSION (6)
bloody city, to the pot whose **c** is in it, Ezk 24:6
in it, and whose **c** has not gone out of it! Ezk 24:6
may be melted in it, its **c** consumed. Ezk 24:11
its abundant **c** does not go out of it. Ezk 24:12
not go out of it. Into the fire with its **c**! Ezk 24:12
and their **c** will be evidence against you Jas 5:3

CORRUPT (15)
Now the earth was **c** in God's sight, and Gn 6:11
God saw the earth, and behold, it was **c**, Gn 6:12
and were more **c** than their fathers, Jgs 2:19
the people still followed **c** practices. 2 Chr 27:2
less one who is abominable and **c**, Jb 15:16
his heart, "There is no God." They are **c**, Ps 14:1
aside; together they have become **c**; Ps 14:3
his heart, "There is no God." They are **c**, Ps 53:1
away; together they have become **c**; Ps 53:3
time you were more **c** than they in all Ezk 16:47
ways, nor according to your **c** deeds, Ezk 20:44
she became more **c** than her sister Ezk 23:11
to speak lying and **c** words before me till Dn 2:9
they were eager to make all their deeds **c**. Zep 3:7
life and is **c** through deceitful desires, Eph 4:22

CORRUPTED (8)
for all flesh had **c** their way on the earth. Gn 6:12
of the land of Egypt, have **c** themselves. Ex 32:7
you **c** your wisdom for the sake of Ezk 28:17
They have deeply **c** themselves as in the Hos 9:9
You have **c** the covenant of Levi, says Mal 2:8
wronged no one, we have **c** no one, 2 Cor 7:2
men **c** in mind and disqualified 2 Tm 3:8
the great prostitute who **c** the earth with Rv 19:2

CORRUPTING (1)
Let no **c** talk come out of your mouths, Eph 4:29

CORRUPTION (11)
to the south of the mount of **c**, 2 Kgs 23:13
soul to Sheol, or let your holy one see **c**. Ps 16:10
to Hades, or let your Holy One see **c**. Acts 2:27
to Hades, nor did his flesh see **c**. Acts 2:31
from the dead, no more to return to **c**, Acts 13:34
will not let your Holy One see **c**.' Acts 13:35
was laid with his fathers and saw **c**, Acts 13:36
he whom God raised up did not see **c**. Acts 13:37
his own flesh will from the flesh reap **c**, Gal 6:8
having escaped from the **c** that is in the 2 Pt 1:4
but they themselves are slaves of **c**. 2 Pt 2:19

CORRUPTLY (9)
beware lest you act **c** by making a Dt 4:16
if you act **c** by making a carved image Dt 4:25
have brought from Egypt have acted **c**. Dt 9:12
you will surely act **c** and turn aside Dt 31:29
They have dealt **c** with him; they are no Dt 32:5
We have acted very **c** against you and Neh 1:7
offspring of evildoers, children who deal **c**! Is 1:4
of uprightness he deals **c** and does not Is 26:10
are bronze and iron; all of them act **c**. Jer 6:28

CORRUPTS (1)
into madness, and a bribe **c** the heart. Eccl 7:7

CORS (8)
one day was thirty **c** of fine flour and 1 Kgs 4:22
cors of fine flour and sixty **c** of meal, 1 Kgs 4:22
gave Hiram 20,000 **c** of wheat as 1 Kgs 5:11
household, and 20,000 **c** of beaten oil. 1 Kgs 5:11
timber, 20,000 **c** of crushed wheat, 2 Chr 2:10
of crushed wheat, 20,000 **c** of barley, 2 Chr 2:10
and 10,000 **c** of wheat and 10,000 of 2 Chr 27:5
to 100 talents of silver, 100 **c** of wheat, Ezr 7:22

COS (1)
sail, we came by a straight course to **C**, Acts 21:1

COSAM (1)
of Melchi, the son of Addi, the son of **C**, Lk 3:28

COSMETICS (2)
of the women. Let their **c** be given them. Est 2:3
provided her with her **c** and her portion Est 2:9

COSMIC (1)
against the **c** powers over this present Eph 6:12

COST (16)
each one at the **c** of his son and of his Ex 32:29
the fish we ate in Egypt that **c** nothing, Nm 11:5
who have sinned at the **c** of their lives, Nm 16:38
for at half the **c** of a hired servant he Dt 15:18
"At the **c** of his firstborn shall he lay its Jos 6:26
and at the **c** of his youngest son shall he Jos 6:26
LORD my God that **c** me nothing." So 2 Sm 24:24
word does not **c** Adonijah his life! 1 Kgs 2:23
foundation at the **c** of Abiram his 1 Kgs 16:34
its gates at the **c** of his youngest son 1 Kgs 16:34
burnt offerings that **c** me nothing." 1 Chr 21:24
Let the **c** be paid from the royal treasury. Ezr 6:4
The **c** is to be paid to these men in full Ezr 6:8
does not know that it will **c** him his life. Prv 7:23
have gone astray at the **c** of your lives. Jer 42:20
does not first sit down and count the **c**, Lk 14:28

COSTLY (13)
and to her mother **c** ornaments. Gn 24:53
c stones in order to lay the 1 Kgs 5:17
All these were made of **c** stones, cut 1 Kgs 7:9
The foundation was of **c** stones, huge 1 Kgs 7:10
And above were **c** stones, cut 1 Kgs 7:11
and for all kinds of **c** vessels; 2 Chr 32:27
goods, with beasts, and with **c** wares, Ezr 1:6
of their life is **c** and can never suffice, Ps 49:8
is gold and abundance of **c** stones, Prv 20:15
silver, with precious stones and **c** gifts. Dn 11:38
flask of ointment of pure nard, very **c**, Mk 14:3
hair and gold or pearls or **c** attire, 1 Tm 2:9
of ivory, all kinds of articles of **c** wood, Rv 18:12

COTS (1)
streets and laid them on **c** and mats, Acts 5:15

COTTON (2)
There were white **c** curtains and violet Est 1:6
be in despair, and the weavers of white **c**. Is 19:9

COUCH (12)
then you defiled it—he went up to my **c**! Gn 49:4
arose from his **c** and was walking 2 Sm 11:2
to lie on his **c** with the servants of 2 Sm 11:13
but because he defiled his father's **c**, 1 Chr 5:1
was falling on the **c** where Esther was. Est 7:8
me, my **c** will ease my complaint,' Jb 7:13
tears; I drench my **c** with my weeping. Ps 6:6
I have spread my **c** with coverings, Prv 7:16
While the king was on his **c**, my nard Sg 1:12
beloved, truly delightful. Our **c** is green; Sg 1:16
You sat on a stately **c**, with a table Ezk 23:41
with the corner of a **c** and part of a bed. Am 3:12

COUCHES (3)
and also **c** of gold and silver on a mosaic Est 1:6
and stretch themselves out on their **c**, Am 6:4
pots and copper vessels and dining **c**.) Mk 7:4

COUNCIL (35)
Let my soul come not into their **c**; O my Gn 49:6
commanders of the army were in **c**. 2 Kgs 9:5
men of the king's **c** who were found 2 Kgs 25:19
Have you listened in the **c** of God? And do Jb 15:8
God has taken his place in the divine **c**; Ps 82:1
to be feared in the **c** of the holy ones, Ps 89:7
them has stood in the **c** of the LORD to Jer 23:18
But if they had stood in my **c**, then they Jer 23:22
of war, and seven men of the king's **c**, Jer 52:25
They shall not be in the **c** of my people, Ezk 13:9
insults his brother will be liable to the **c**; Mt 5:22
and the whole **C** were seeking false Mt 26:59
and the whole **C** were seeking Mk 14:55
the elders and scribes and the whole **C**. Mk 15:1
a respected member of the **C**, Mk 15:43
And they led him away to their **c**, and Lk 22:66
He was a member of the **c**, a good and Lk 23:50
the Pharisees gathered the **C** and said, Jn 11:47
had commanded them to leave the **c**, Acts 4:15
they called together the **c** and all the Acts 5:21
them, they set them before the **c**. Acts 5:27
a Pharisee in the **c** named Gamaliel, Acts 5:34
Then they left the presence of the **c**, Acts 5:41
him and brought him before the **c**, Acts 6:12
all who sat in the **c** saw that his face Acts 6:15
priest and the whole **c** of elders can Acts 22:5
the chief priests and all the **c** to meet, Acts 22:30
And looking intently at the **c**, Paul Acts 23:1
other Pharisees, he cried out in the **c**, Acts 23:6
Now therefore you, along with the **c**, Acts 23:15
bring Paul down to the **c** tomorrow, Acts 23:20
him, I brought him down to their **c**. Acts 23:28
they found when I stood before the **c**, Acts 24:20
when he had conferred with his **c**, Acts 25:12
by prophecy when the **c** of elders laid 1 Tm 4:14

COUNCILS (1)
For they will deliver you over to **c**, and Mk 13:9

COUNSEL (91)
"For they are a nation void of **c**, and Dt 32:28
but did not ask **c** from the LORD. Jos 9:14
this day; consider it, take **c**, and speak." Jgs 19:30
all of you, give your advice and **c** here." Jgs 20:7
please turn the **c** of Ahithophel into 2 Sm 15:31
defeat for me the **c** of Ahithophel. 2 Sm 15:34
said to Ahithophel, "Give your **c**. 2 Sm 16:20
those days the **c** that Ahithophel 2 Sm 16:23
was all the **c** of Ahithophel esteemed, 2 Sm 16:23
"This time the **c** that Ahithophel has 2 Sm 17:7
But my **c** is that all Israel be 2 Sm 17:11
"The **c** of Hushai the Archite is 2 Sm 17:14
better than the **c** of Ahithophel." For 2 Sm 17:14
to defeat the good **c** of Ahithophel, 2 Sm 17:14
so did Ahithophel **c** Absalom and 2 Sm 17:15
saw that his **c** was not followed, 2 Sm 17:23
times, 'Let them but ask **c** at Abel,' 2 Sm 20:18
King Rehoboam took **c** with the old 1 Kgs 12:6
But he abandoned the **c** that the old 1 Kgs 12:8
gave him and took **c** with the young 1 Kgs 12:8
and forsaking the **c** that the old men 1 Kgs 12:13
according to the **c** of the young 1 Kgs 12:14
So the king took **c** and made two 1 Kgs 12:28
Israel, he took **c** with his servants, 2 Kgs 6:8
the Philistines took **c** and sent him 1 Chr 12:19
King Rehoboam took **c** with the old 2 Chr 10:6
But he abandoned the **c** that the old 2 Chr 10:8
and took **c** with the young men who 2 Chr 10:8
and forsaking the **c** of the old men, 2 Chr 10:13
according to the **c** of the young 2 Chr 10:14
he had taken **c** with the people, 2 Chr 20:21
even followed their **c** and went with 2 Chr 22:5
this and have not listened to my **c**." 2 Chr 25:16
king of Judah took **c** and sent to 2 Chr 25:17
in Jerusalem had taken **c** to keep the 2 Chr 30:2
according to the **c** of my lord and of Ezr 10:3
I took **c** with myself, and I brought Neh 5:7
So now come and let us take **c** together." Neh 6:7
and might; he has **c** and understanding. Jb 12:13
The **c** of the wicked is far from me. Jb 21:16
good things—but the **c** of the wicked is Jb 22:18
and waited and kept silence for my **c**. Jb 29:21
is this that darkens **c** by words without Jb 38:2
is this that hides **c** without knowledge?' Jb 42:3
man who walks not in the **c** of the wicked, Ps 1:1
themselves, and the rulers take **c** together, Ps 2:2
How long must I take **c** in my soul and Ps 13:2
I bless the LORD who gives me **c**; in the Ps 16:7
go; I will **c** you with my eye upon you. Ps 32:8
The LORD brings the **c** of the nations to Ps 33:10
The **c** of the LORD stands forever, the Ps 33:11
We used to take sweet **c** together; within Ps 55:14
You guide me with your **c**, and Ps 73:24
his works; they did not wait for his **c**. Ps 106:13
and spurned the **c** of the Most High. Ps 107:11
have ignored all my **c** and would have Prv 1:25
have none of my **c** and despised all my Prv 1:30
I have **c** and sound wisdom; I have Prv 8:14
Without **c** plans fail, but with many Prv 15:22
Plans are established by **c**; by wise Prv 20:18
no **c** can avail against the LORD. Prv 21:30
you thirty sayings of **c** and knowledge, Prv 22:20
of a friend comes from his earnest **c**. Prv 27:9
let the **c** of the Holy One of Israel draw Is 5:19
Take **c** together, but it will come to Is 8:10
understanding, the Spirit of **c** and might, Is 11:2
"Give **c**; grant justice; make your shade Is 16:3
emptied out, and I will confound their **c**; Is 19:3
counselors of Pharaoh give stupid **c**. Is 19:11
he is wonderful in **c** and excellent in Is 28:29
you who hide deep from the LORD your **c**, Is 29:15
the LORD, or what man shows him his **c**? Is 40:13
and fulfills the **c** of his messengers, Is 44:26
your case; let them take **c** together! Is 45:21
not yet done, saying, 'My **c** shall stand, Is 46:10
the man of my **c** from a far country. Is 46:11
from the priest, nor **c** from the wise, Jer 18:18
great in **c** and mighty in deed, whose Jer 32:19
And if I give you **c**, you will not listen to Jer 38:15
Has **c** perished from the prudent? Jer 49:7
from the priest and **c** from the elders. Ezk 7:26
and who give wicked **c** in this city; Ezk 11:2
O king, let my **c** be acceptable to you: Dn 4:27
and the **c** of peace shall be between Zec 6:13
of the people took **c** against Jesus to put Mt 27:1
So they took **c** and bought with them Mt 27:7
assembled with the elders and taken **c**, Mt 28:12
and immediately held **c** with the Mk 3:6
declaring to you the whole **c** of God. Acts 20:27
all things according to the **c** of his will, Eph 1:11
I **c** you to buy from me gold refined by Rv 3:18

COUNSELED (3)
of Israel, and thus and so have I **c**. 2 Sm 17:15
so has Ahithophel **c** against you." 2 Sm 17:21
How you have **c** him who has no Jb 26:3

COUNSELOR (12)
Ahithophel the Gilonite, David's **c**, 2 Sm 15:12
for his son Zechariah, a shrewd **c**, 1 Chr 26:14
Jonathan, David's uncle, was a **c**, 1 Chr 27:32
Ahithophel was the king's **c**, and 1 Chr 27:33
mother was his **c** in doing wickedly. 2 Chr 22:3
him, "Have we made you a royal **c**? 2 Chr 25:16
the **c** and the skillful magician and the Is 3:3
his name shall be called Wonderful **C**, Is 9:6
among these there is no **c** who, when I Is 41:28
Has your **c** perished, that pain seized you Mi 4:9
evil against the LORD, a worthless **c**. Na 1:11
of the Lord, or who has been his **c**?" Rom 11:34

COUNSELORS (19)
the death of his father they were his **c**, 2 Chr 22:4
and bribed **c** against them to frustrate Ezr 4:5
king and his seven **c** to make inquiries Ezr 7:14
the king and his **c** have freely offered to Ezr 7:15
steadfast love before the king and his **c**, Ezr 7:28
the king and his **c** and his lords and Ezr 8:25
with kings and **c** of the earth who rebuilt Jb 3:14
He leads **c** away stripped, and judges he Jb 12:17
are my delight; they are my **c**. Ps 119:24
in an abundance of **c** there is safety. Prv 11:14
and in abundance of **c** there is victory. Prv 24:6
the first, and your **c** as at the beginning. Is 1:26
the wisest **c** of Pharaoh give stupid Is 19:11
the prefects, and the governors, the **c**, Dn 3:2
the prefects, and the governors, the **c**, Dn 3:3
He declared to his **c**, "Did we not cast Dn 3:24
and the king's **c** gathered together and Dn 3:27
My **c** and my lords sought me, and I was Dn 4:36
the **c** and the governors are agreed that Dn 6:7

COUNSELS (7)
guilt, O God; let them fall by their own **c**; Ps 5:10
stubborn hearts, to follow their own **c**. Ps 81:12
just; the **c** of the wicked are deceitful. Prv 12:5
You are wearied with your many **c**; let Is 47:13
in their own **c** and the stubbornness Jer 7:24
devour them because of their own **c**. Hos 11:6
and you have walked in their **c**, that I Mi 6:16

COUNT (34)
so that if one can **c** the dust of the Gn 13:16
eat you shall make your **c** for the lamb. Ex 12:4

then he shall **c** for himself seven days Lv 15:13
she shall **c** for herself seven days, Lv 15:28
"You shall **c** seven full weeks from the Lv 23:15
You shall **c** fifty days to the day after Lv 23:16
"You shall **c** seven weeks of years, seven Lv 25:8
Who can **c** the dust of Jacob or Nm 23:10
"Take the **c** of the plunder that was Nm 31:26
"You shall **c** seven weeks. Begin to count Dt 16:9
Begin to **c** the seven weeks from the time Dt 16:9
"**C** and see who has gone from us." 1 Sm 14:17
that he may **c** the money that has 2 Kgs 22:4
were required to **c** them when they 1 Chr 9:28
David did not **c** those below twenty 1 Chr 27:23
Joab the son of Zeruiah began to **c**, 1 Chr 27:24
hide your face and **c** me as your enemy? Jb 13:24
house and my maidservants **c** me as a Jb 19:15
I can **c** all my bones—they stare and Ps 22:17
You have kept **c** of my tossings; put my Ps 56:8
If I would **c** them, they are more than Ps 139:18
complete hatred; I **c** them my enemies. Ps 139:22
clean, they shall **c** seven days for him. Ezk 44:26
does not first sit down and **c** the cost, Lk 14:28
whom the Lord will not **c** his sin." Rom 4:8
confidence as I **c** on showing against 2 Cor 10:2
but in humility **c** others more Phil 2:3
did not **c** equality with God a thing to be Phil 2:6
I **c** everything as loss because of the Phil 3:8
loss of all things and **c** them as rubbish, Phil 3:8
C it all joy, my brothers, when you meet Jas 1:2
They **c** it pleasure to revel in the 2 Pt 2:13
to fulfill his promise as some **c** slowness, 2 Pt 3:9
And **c** the patience of our Lord as 2 Pt 3:15

COUNTED (52)
the earth, your offspring also can be **c**. Gn 13:16
and he **c** it to him as righteousness. Gn 15:6
if found with me, shall be **c** stolen." Gn 30:33
of Manasseh were **c** as Joseph's own. Gn 50:23
your contribution shall be **c** to you as Nm 18:27
the rest shall be **c** to the Levites as Nm 18:30
"Your servants have **c** the men of war Nm 31:49
the Anakim they are also **c** as Rephaim, Dt 2:11
(It is also **c** as a land of Rephaim. Dt 2:20
boundary of Ekron, it is **c** as Canaanite; Jos 13:3
their camels could not be **c**—so that they Jgs 6:5
gone from us." And when they had **c**, 1 Sm 14:17
(for Beeroth also is **c** part of Benjamin; 2 Sm 4:2
my son Solomon will be **c** offenders." 1 Kgs 1:21
to be numbered or **c** for multitude. 1 Kgs 3:8
that they could not be **c** or numbered. 1 Kgs 8:5
they bagged and **c** the money that 2 Kgs 12:10
therefore they became **c** as a single 1 Chr 23:11
Then Solomon **c** all the resident 2 Chr 2:17
that they could not be **c** or numbered. 2 Chr 5:6
who **c** them out to Sheshbazzar the Ezr 1:8
The whole was **c** and weighed, and the Ezr 8:34
Why are we **c** as cattle? Why are we Jb 18:3
in spite of my right I am **c** a liar; my Jb 34:6
Clubs are **c** as stubble; he laughs at the Jb 41:29
I am **c** among those who go down to the Ps 88:4
And that was **c** to him as Ps 106:31
forth guilty; let his prayer be **c** as sin! Ps 109:7
Let my prayer be **c** as incense before Ps 141:2
in the morning, will be **c** as cursing. Prv 27:14
and what is lacking cannot be **c**. Eccl 1:15
and you **c** the houses of Jerusalem, and Is 22:10
"Where is he who **c**, where is he who Is 33:18
tribute? Where is he who **c** the towers?" Is 33:18
that they were **c** worthy to suffer Acts 5:41
And they **c** the value of them and Acts 19:19
Artemis may be **c** as nothing, Acts 19:27
and it was **c** to him as righteousness." Rom 4:3
his wages are not **c** as a gift but as his Rom 4:4
ungodly, his faith is **c** as righteousness, Rom 4:5
say that faith was **c** to Abraham as Rom 4:9
How then was it **c** to him? Was it Rom 4:10
righteousness would be **c** to them as Rom 4:11
why his faith was "**c** to him as Rom 4:22
the words "it was **c** to him" were not Rom 4:23
It will be **c** to us who believe in him Rom 4:24
but sin is not **c** where there is no law. Rom 5:13
of the promise are **c** as offspring. Rom 9:8
and it was **c** to him as righteousness"? Gal 3:6
I had, I **c** as loss for the sake of Christ. Phil 3:7
For Jesus has been **c** worthy of more Heb 3:3
and it was **c** to him as righteousness"— Jas 2:23

COUNTENANCE (2)
the LORD lift up his **c** upon you and give Nm 6:26
you change his **c**, and send him away. Jb 14:20

COUNTING (2)
and not **c** itself among the nations! Nm 23:9
not **c** their trespasses against them, 2 Cor 5:19

COUNTLESS (3)
And all for the **c** whorings of the Na 3:4
though you have **c** guides in Christ, 1 Cor 4:15
imprisonments, with **c** beatings, 2 Cor 11:23

COUNTRIES (36)
and upon all the kingdoms of the **c**. 1 Chr 29:30
the service of the kingdoms of the **c**." 2 Chr 12:8
kingdoms of the **c** when they heard 2 Chr 20:29
and be shattered; give ear, all you far **c**; Is 8:9
and out of all the **c** where he had driven Jer 16:15
flock out of all the **c** where I have driven Jer 23:3
and out of all the **c** where he had driven Jer 23:8
pestilence against many **c** and great Jer 28:8
them from all the **c** to which I drove Jer 32:37
of the nations, with **c** all around her. Ezk 5:5
statutes more than the **c** all around her; Ezk 5:6
when you are scattered through the **c**, Ezk 6:8
though I scattered them among the **c**, Ezk 11:16
a while in the **c** where they have gone.' Ezk 11:16
you out of the **c** where you have been Ezk 11:17
and scatter them among the **c**. Ezk 12:15
and disperse them through the **c**, Ezk 20:23
the nations, like the tribes of the **c**, Ezk 20:32
you out of the **c** where you are Ezk 20:34
you out of the **c** where you have been Ezk 20:41
the nations, and a mockery to all the **c**. Ezk 22:4
and disperse you through the **c**, Ezk 22:15
and will make you perish out of the **c**; Ezk 25:7
desolation in the midst of desolated **c**, Ezk 29:12
and disperse them through the **c**. Ezk 29:12
be desolated in the midst of desolated **c**, Ezk 30:7
and disperse them through the **c**. Ezk 30:23
and disperse them throughout the **c**. Ezk 30:26
into the **c** that you have not known. Ezk 32:9
peoples and gather them from the **c**, Ezk 34:13
nations and these two **c** shall be mine, Ezk 35:10
and they were dispersed through the **c**. Ezk 36:19
you from all the **c** and bring you into Ezk 36:24
shall come into **c** and shall overflow Dn 11:40
stretch out his hand against the **c**, Dn 11:42
yet in far **c** they shall remember me, Zec 10:9

COUNTRY (227)
of Sephar to the hill **c** of the east. Gn 10:30
"Go from your **c** and your kindred and Gn 12:1
he moved to the hill **c** on the east of Gn 12:8
the Horites in their hill **c** of Seir as far as Gn 14:6
and defeated all the **c** of the Amalekites, Gn 14:7
into them, and the rest fled to the hill **c**. Gn 14:10
but will go to my **c** and to my kindred, Gn 24:4
his son Isaac, eastward to the east **c**. Gn 25:6
Laban said, "It is not so done in our **c**, Gn 29:26
that I may go to my own home and **c**. Gn 30:25
set his face toward the hill **c** of Gilead. Gn 31:21
close after him into the hill **c** of Gilead. Gn 31:23
Jacob had pitched his tent in the hill **c**, Gn 31:25
pitched tents in the hill **c** of Gilead. Gn 31:25
sacrifice in the hill **c** and called his Gn 31:54
bread and spent the night in the hill **c**. Gn 31:54
in the land of Seir, the **c** of Edom, Gn 32:3
'Return to your **c** and to your kindred, Gn 32:9
So Esau settled in the hill **c** of Seir. Gn 36:8
of the Edomites in the hill **c** of Seir. Gn 36:9
who defeated Midian in the **c** of Moab, Gn 36:35
behold, I will plague all your **c** with frogs. Ex 8:2
I will bring locusts into your **c**, Ex 10:4
and settled on the whole **c** of Egypt, Ex 10:14
locust was left in all the **c** of Egypt. Ex 10:19
depart, and he went away to his own **c**. Ex 18:27
bird go out of the city into the open **c**. Lv 14:53
And in all the **c** you possess, you shall Lv 25:24
the Negeb and go up into the hill **c**, Nm 13:17
and the Amorites dwell in the hill **c**. Nm 13:29
went up to the heights of the hill **c**, Nm 14:40
to go up to the heights of the hill **c**, Nm 14:44
lived in that hill **c** came down and Nm 14:45
the cities of the land throughout the **c**. Nm 32:33
and go to the hill **c** of the Amorites and to Dt 1:7
in the hill **c** and in the lowland and in the Dt 1:7
on the way to the hill **c** of the Amorites, Dt 1:19
have come to the hill **c** of the Amorites, Dt 1:20
they turned and went up into the hill **c**, Dt 1:24
thought it easy to go up into the hill **c**. Dt 1:41
presumptuously went up into the hill **c**. Dt 1:43
lived in that hill **c** came out against you Dt 1:44
around this mountain **c** long enough. Dt 2:3
river Jabbok and the cities of the hill **c**, Dt 2:37
and half the hill **c** of Gilead with its Dt 3:12
Jordan, that good hill **c** and Lebanon.' Dt 3:25
is found slain, lying in the open **c**, Dt 21:1
"But if in the open **c** a man meets a Dt 22:25
because he met her in the open **c**, and Dt 22:27
the Jordan in the hill **c** and in the lowland Jos 9:1
of Israel, "We have come from a distant **c**, Jos 9:6
a very distant **c** your servants have Jos 9:9
all the inhabitants of our **c** said to us, Jos 9:11
dwell in the hill **c** are gathered against Jos 10:6
the hill **c** and the Negeb and the Jos 10:40
as far as Gaza, and all the **c** of Goshen, Jos 10:41
kings who were in the northern hill **c**, Jos 11:2
Perizzites, and the Jebusites in the hill **c**, Jos 11:3
the hill **c** and all the Negeb and all the Jos 11:16
Arabah and the hill **c** of Israel and its Jos 11:16
and cut off the Anakim from the hill **c**, Jos 11:21
Anab, and from all the hill **c** of Judah, Jos 11:21
Judah, and from all the hill **c** of Israel. Jos 11:21
in the hill **c**, in the lowland, in the Jos 12:8
of the hill **c** from Lebanon to Jos 13:6
give me this hill **c** of which the LORD Jos 14:12
And in the hill **c**, Shamir, Jattir, Socoh, Jos 15:48
up from Jericho into the hill **c** to Bethel. Jos 16:1
since the hill **c** of Ephraim is too Jos 17:15
said, "The hill **c** is not enough for us. Jos 17:16
but the hill **c** shall be yours, for Jos 17:18
then up through the hill **c** westward, Jos 18:12
in the hill **c** of Ephraim. Jos 19:50
in Galilee in the hill **c** of Naphtali, Jos 20:7
and Shechem in the hill **c** of Ephraim, Jos 20:7
(that is, Hebron) in the hill **c** of Judah. Jos 20:7
that is Hebron, in the hill **c** of Judah, Jos 21:11
pasturelands in the hill **c** of Ephraim, Jos 21:21
I gave Esau the hill **c** of Seir to possess, Jos 24:4
which is in the hill **c** of Ephraim, Jos 24:30
given him in the hill **c** of Ephraim. Jos 24:33
the Canaanites who lived in the hill **c**, Jgs 1:9
and he took possession of the hill **c**, Jgs 1:19
the people of Dan back into the hill **c**, Jgs 1:34
Timnath-heres, in the hill **c** of Ephraim, Jgs 2:9
the trumpet in the hill **c** of Ephraim. Jgs 3:27
went down with him from the hill **c**, Jgs 3:27
and Bethel in the hill **c** of Ephraim, Jgs 4:5
throughout all the hill **c** of Ephraim, Jgs 7:24
lived at Shamir in the hill **c** of Ephraim. Jgs 10:1
let us pass through your land to our **c**,' Jgs 11:19
of the Amorites, who inhabited that **c**. Jgs 11:21
in the hill **c** of the Amalekites. Jgs 12:15
into our hand, the ravager of our **c**, Jgs 16:24
was a man of the hill **c** of Ephraim, Jgs 17:1
he came to the hill **c** of Ephraim to the Jgs 17:8
And they came to the hill **c** of Ephraim, Jgs 18:2
on from there to the hill **c** of Ephraim, Jgs 18:13
gone to scout out the **c** of Laish said to Jgs 18:14
the remote parts of the hill **c** of Ephraim, Jgs 19:1
man was from the hill **c** of Ephraim, Jgs 19:16
remote parts of the hill **c** of Ephraim, Jgs 19:18
throughout all the **c** of the inheritance Jgs 20:6
the other to Gibeah, and in the open **c**, Jgs 20:31
Judah went to sojourn in the **c** of Moab, Ru 1:1
They went into the **c** of Moab and Ru 1:2
to return from the **c** of Moab, Ru 1:6
her, who returned from the **c** of Moab. Ru 1:22
back with Naomi from the **c** of Moab. Ru 2:6
who has come back from the **c** of Moab, Ru 4:3
of the hill **c** of Ephraim whose 1 Sm 1:1
LORD was in the **c** of the Philistines 1 Sm 6:1
through the hill **c** of Ephraim and 1 Sm 9:4
in Michmash and the hill **c** of Bethel, 1 Sm 13:2
in the hill **c** of Ephraim heard 1 Sm 14:22
in the hill **c** of the Wilderness of 1 Sm 23:14
be given me in one of the **c** towns, 1 Sm 27:5
David lived in the **c** of the Philistines 1 Sm 27:7
he lived in the **c** of the Philistines. 1 Sm 27:11
in the open **c** and brought him 1 Sm 30:11
were by themselves in the open **c**. 2 Sm 10:8
battle spread over the face of all the **c**, 2 Sm 18:8
But a man of the hill **c** of Ephraim, 2 Sm 20:21
Ben-hur, in the hill **c** of Ephraim; 1 Kgs 4:8
the **c** of Sihon king of the Amorites 1 Kgs 4:19
and 80,000 stonecutters in the hill **c**, 1 Kgs 5:15
comes from a far **c** for your name's 1 Kgs 8:41
depart, that I may go to my own **c**." 1 Kgs 11:21
to go to your own **c**?" And he said to 1 Kgs 11:22
of them were alone in the open **c**. 1 Kgs 11:29
in the hill **c** of Ephraim and 1 Kgs 12:25
dies in the open **c** the birds of the 1 Kgs 14:11
of goats, but the Syrians filled the **c**. 1 Kgs 20:27
dies in the open **c** the birds of the 1 Kgs 21:24
to his city, and every man to his **c**!" 1 Kgs 22:36
Edom, till the **c** was filled with water. 2 Kgs 3:20
me from the hill **c** of Ephraim two 2 Kgs 5:22
to hide themselves in the open **c**, 2 Kgs 7:12
said, "They have come from a far **c**, 2 Kgs 20:14
defeated Midian in the **c** of Moab, 1 Chr 1:46
in the hill **c** of Ephraim, 1 Chr 6:67
fathered sons in the **c** of Moab after he 1 Chr 8:8
were by themselves in the open **c**. 1 Chr 19:9
and ravaged the **c** of the Ammonites 1 Chr 20:1
and over the treasuries in the **c**, in 1 Chr 27:25
and 80,000 to quarry in the hill **c**, 2 Chr 2:2
80,000 to quarry in the hill **c**, 2 Chr 2:18
comes from a far **c** for the sake of 2 Chr 6:32
is in the hill **c** of Ephraim and said, 2 Chr 13:4

had taken in the hill **c** of Ephraim, 2 Chr 15:8
Beersheba to the hill **c** of Ephraim, 2 Chr 19:4
places in the hill **c** of Judah and led 2 Chr 21:11
he built cities in the hill **c** of Judah, 2 Chr 27:4
city through the **c** of Ephraim and 2 Chr 30:10
peoples of the **c** declared themselves Est 8:17
of flies, and gnats throughout their **c**. Ps 105:31
trees, and shattered the trees of their **c**. Ps 105:33
soul, so is good news from a far **c**. Prv 25:25
Your **c** lies desolate; your cities are burned Is 1:7
said, "They have come to me from a far **c**, Is 39:3
the man of my counsel from a far **c**. Is 46:11
a people is coming from the north **c**, Jer 6:22
out of the north **c** to make the cities Jer 10:22
Israel out of the north **c** and out of all Jer 16:15
on the mountains in the open **c**. Your Jer 17:3
from the Shephelah, from the hill **c**, Jer 17:26
mother who bore you into another **c**, Jer 22:26
Israel out of the north **c** and out of all the Jer 23:8
will call in the hill **c** of Ephraim: Jer 31:6
them from the north **c** and gather them Jer 31:8
shall come back to their own **c**. Jer 31:17
cities of Judah, in the cities of the hill **c**, Jer 32:44
In the cities of the hill **c**, in the cities of Jer 33:13
forces in the open **c** and their men heard Jer 40:7
forces in the open **c** came to Gedaliah Jer 40:13
sacrifice in the north **c** by the river Jer 46:10
of great nations, from the north **c**. Jer 50:9
her, and let us go each to his own **c**, Jer 51:9
the **c** that I swore to give to your Ezk 20:42
cities on its frontier, the glory of the **c**, Ezk 25:9
in all the inhabited places of the **c**. Ezk 34:13
the city, for dwellings and for open **c**. Ezk 48:15
as his **c** improved, he improved his Hos 10:1
do you come from? What is your **c**? Jon 1:8
this what I said when I was yet in my **c**? Jon 4:2
I will make Samaria a heap in the open **c**, Mi 1:6
from the city and dwell in the open **c**; Mi 4:10
the black horses goes toward the north **c**, Zec 6:6
the dappled ones go toward the south **c**." Zec 6:6
go toward the north **c** have set my Spirit Zec 6:8
have set my Spirit at rest in the north **c**." Zec 6:8
people from the east **c** and from the west Zec 8:7
the east country and from the west **c**, Zec 8:7
laid waste his hill **c** and left his heritage Mal 1:3
and they will be called 'the wicked **c**,' Mal 1:4
departed to their own **c** by another way. Mt 2:12
the other side, to the **c** of the Gadarenes, Mt 8:28
it to tenants, and went into another **c**. Mt 21:33
And all the **c** of Judea and all Jerusalem Mk 1:5
side of the sea, to the **c** of the Gerasenes. Mk 5:1
earnestly not to send them out of the **c**. Mk 5:10
fled and told it in the city and in the **c**. Mk 5:14
it to tenants and went into another **c**. Mk 12:1
who was coming in from the **c**, Mk 15:21
them, as they were walking into the **c**. Mk 16:12
arose and went with haste into the hill **c**, Lk 1:39
about through all the hill **c** of Judea, Lk 1:65
went out through all the surrounding **c**. Lk 4:14
of Judea and all the surrounding **c**. Lk 7:17
they sailed to the **c** of the Gerasenes, Lk 8:26
fled and told it in the city and in the **c**. Lk 8:34
of the surrounding **c** of the Gerasenes Lk 8:37
not leave the ninety-nine in the open **c**, Lk 15:4
he had and took a journey into a far **c**, Lk 15:13
a severe famine arose in that **c**, Lk 15:14
out to one of the citizens of that **c**, Lk 15:15
went into a far **c** to receive for himself Lk 19:12
and went into another **c** for a long while. Lk 20:9
not those who are out in the **c** enter it, Lk 21:21
Cyrene, who was coming in from the **c**, Lk 23:26
went up from the **c** to Jerusalem before Jn 11:55
he did both in the **c** of the Jews and in Acts 10:39
because their **c** depended on the Acts 12:20
depended on the king's **c** for food. Acts 12:20
of Lycaonia, and to the surrounding **c**, Acts 14:6
through the inland **c** and came to Acts 19:1
But as it is, they desire a better **c**, that Heb 11:16

COUNTRYMEN (1)
things from your own **c** as they did 1 Thes 2:14

COUNTRYSIDE (5)
of the cry of your pilots the **c** shakes, Ezk 27:28
into the surrounding **c** and villages and Mk 6:36
he came, in villages, cities, or **c**, Mk 6:56
surrounding villages and **c** to find Lk 9:12
and his disciples went into the Judean **c**, Jn 3:22

COUNTS (11)
the sun sets (for he is poor and **c** on it), Dt 24:15
wrath against me and **c** me as his Jb 19:11
against me, he **c** me as his enemy, Jb 33:10
He **c** iron as straw, and bronze as rotten Jb 41:27
against whom the LORD **c** no iniquity, Ps 32:2
while he lives, he **c** himself blessed, Ps 49:18
under the hands of the one who **c** them, Jer 33:13
to whom God **c** righteousness apart Rom 4:6
neither circumcision **c** for anything 1 Cor 7:19
nor uncircumcision **c** for anything, Gal 5:6
neither circumcision **c** for anything, Gal 6:15

COUPLE (9)
and **c** the curtains one to the other with Ex 26:6
You shall **c** five curtains by themselves, Ex 26:9
and **c** the tent together that it may be a Ex 26:11
clasps of bronze to **c** the tent together Ex 36:18
with him his servant and a **c** of donkeys. Jgs 19:3
had with him a **c** of saddled donkeys, Jgs 19:10
come and make a **c** of cakes in my 2 Sm 13:6
met him, with a **c** of donkeys saddled, 2 Sm 16:1
I am gathering a **c** of sticks that I 1 Kgs 17:12

COUPLED (6)
Five curtains shall be **c** to one another, Ex 26:3
five curtains shall be **c** to one another. Ex 26:3
He **c** five curtains to one another, and Ex 36:10
other five curtains he **c** to one another. Ex 36:10
and **c** the curtains one to the other with Ex 36:13
He **c** five curtains by themselves, and Ex 36:16

COURAGE (24)
Be of good **c** and bring some of the Nm 13:20
But the people, the men of Israel, took **c**, Jgs 20:22
Take **c**, and be men, O Philistines, lest 1 Sm 4:9
Abner had died at Hebron, his **c** failed, 2 Sm 4:1
your servant has found **c** to pray this 2 Sm 7:27
Be of good **c**, and let us be 2 Sm 10:12
servant has found **c** to pray before 1 Chr 17:25
But you, take **c**! Do not let your 2 Chr 15:7
he took **c** and put away the detestable 2 Chr 15:8
year Jehoiada took **c** and entered into 2 Chr 23:1
But Amaziah took **c** and led out his 2 Chr 25:11
I took **c**, for the hand of the LORD my Ezr 7:28
be strong, and let your heart take **c**; Ps 27:14
Be strong, and let your heart take **c**, all Ps 31:24
their **c** melted away in their evil plight; Ps 107:26
LORD, **c** shall fail both king and officials. Jer 4:9
Can your **c** endure, or can your hands Ezk 22:14
strong and of good **c**." And as he spoke Dn 10:19
took **c** and went to Pilate and asked for Mk 15:43
Lord stood by him and said, "Take **c**, Acts 23:11
them, Paul thanked God and took **c**. Acts 28:15
So we are always of good **c**. We know 2 Cor 5:6
Yes, we are of good **c**, and we would 2 Cor 5:8
but that with full **c** now as always Phil 1:20

COURAGEOUS (14)
Be strong and **c**. Do not fear or be in Dt 31:6
in the sight of all Israel, "Be strong and **c**, Dt 31:7
son of Nun and said, "Be strong and **c**, Dt 31:23
Be strong and **c**, for you shall cause this Jos 1:6
Only be strong and very **c**, being careful Jos 1:7
I not commanded you? Be strong and **c**. Jos 1:9
be put to death. Only be strong and **c**." Jos 1:18
be afraid or dismayed; be strong and **c**. Jos 10:25
and let us be **c** for our people, 2 Sm 10:12
you? Be **c** and be valiant." 2 Sm 13:28
Moses for Israel. Be strong and **c**. 1 Chr 22:13
his son, "Be strong and **c** and do it. 1 Chr 28:20
His heart was **c** in the ways of the 2 Chr 17:6
"Be strong and **c**. Do not be afraid or 2 Chr 32:7

COURAGEOUSLY (1)
will serve you as officers. Deal **c**, 2 Chr 19:11

COURIERS (6)
So **c** went throughout all Israel and 2 Chr 30:6
So the **c** went from city to city 2 Chr 30:10
Letters were sent by **c** to all the king's Est 3:13
The **c** went out hurriedly by order of the Est 3:15
the letters by mounted **c** riding on swift Est 8:10
So the **c**, mounted on their swift horses Est 8:14

COURSE (21)
In the **c** of time Cain brought to the LORD Gn 4:3
In the **c** of time the wife of Judah, Shua's Gn 38:12
to its normal **c** when the morning Ex 14:27
order to change the **c** of things your 2 Sm 14:20
cut stone and one **c** of cedar beams. 1 Kgs 6:36
all around, and a **c** of cedar beams; 1 Kgs 7:12
In the **c** of time, at the end of two 2 Chr 21:19
when the days of the feast had run their **c**, Jb 1:5
The caravans turn aside from their **c**; Jb 6:18
like a strong man, runs its **c** with joy. Ps 19:5
have swallowed up the **c** of your paths. Is 3:12
"How well you direct your **c** to seek love! Jer 2:33
Everyone turns to his own **c**, like a horse Jer 8:6
Their **c** is evil, and their might is not Jer 23:10
and the third day I finish my **c**. Lk 13:32
And as John was finishing his **c**, he Acts 13:25
I may finish my **c** and the ministry Acts 20:24
set sail, we came by a straight **c** to Cos, Acts 21:1
We take this **c** so that no one should 2 Cor 8:20
walked, following the **c** of this world, Eph 2:2
body, setting on fire the entire **c** of life, Jas 3:6

COURSES (3)
from their **c** they fought against Sisera. Jgs 5:20
inner court with three **c** of cut stone 1 Kgs 6:36
great court had three **c** of cut stone 1 Kgs 7:12

COURT (133)
"You shall make the **c** of the tabernacle. Ex 27:9
the south side the **c** shall have hangings Ex 27:9
for the breadth of the **c** on the west side Ex 27:12
The breadth of the **c** on the front to the Ex 27:13
For the gate of the **c** there shall be a Ex 27:16
the pillars around the **c** shall be filleted Ex 27:17
The length of the **c** shall be a hundred Ex 27:18
and all its pegs and all the pegs of the **c**, Ex 27:19
the hangings of the **c**, its pillars and its Ex 35:17
and the screen for the gate of the **c**; Ex 35:17
of the tabernacle and the pegs of the **c**, Ex 35:18
And he made the **c**. For the south side Ex 38:9
the hangings of the **c** were of fine twined Ex 38:9
the gate of the **c** were hangings of Ex 38:15
the hangings around the **c** were of fine Ex 38:16
the pillars of the **c** were filleted with Ex 38:17
the gate of the **c** was embroidered with Ex 38:18
corresponding to the hangings of the **c**. Ex 38:18
and for the **c** all around were Ex 38:20
the bases around the **c**, and the bases of Ex 38:31
court, and the bases of the gate of the **c**, Ex 38:31
and all the pegs around the **c**. Ex 38:31
the hangings of the **c**, its pillars, and its Ex 39:40
and the screen for the gate of the **c**, Ex 39:40
And you shall set up the **c** all around, Ex 40:8
hang up the screen for the gate of the **c**. Ex 40:8
he erected the **c** around the tabernacle Ex 40:33
and set up the screen of the gate of the **c**. Ex 40:33
In the **c** of the tent of meeting they shall Lv 6:16
be eaten, in the **c** of the tent of meeting. Lv 6:26
"You shall do no injustice in **c**. You Lv 19:15
the hangings of the **c**, the screen for the Nm 3:26
for the door of the **c** that is around the Nm 3:26
also the pillars around the **c**, with their Nm 3:37
the hangings of the **c** and the screen for Nm 4:26
of the gate of the **c** that is around the Nm 4:26
pillars around the **c** with their bases, Nm 4:32
and they come into **c** and the judges Dt 25:1
built the inner **c** with three courses 1 Kgs 6:36
to dwell, in the other **c** back of the hall, 1 Kgs 7:8
and from the outside to the great **c**. 1 Kgs 7:9
The great **c** had three courses of cut 1 Kgs 7:12
so had the inner **c** of the house of the 1 Kgs 7:12
the middle of the **c** that was before the 1 Kgs 8:64
Isaiah had gone out of the middle **c**, 2 Kgs 20:4
He made the **c** of the priests and the 2 Chr 4:9
priests and the great **c** and doors for 2 Chr 4:9
and doors for the **c** and overlaid their 2 Chr 4:9
cubits high, and had set it in the **c**, 2 Chr 6:13
the middle of the **c** that was before the 2 Chr 7:7
house of the LORD, before the new **c**, 2 Chr 20:5
with stones in the **c** of the house of 2 Chr 24:21
of the LORD into the **c** of the house of 2 Chr 29:16
house of the king at the **c** of the guard. Neh 3:25
for seven days in the **c** of the garden of the Est 1:5
walked in front of the **c** of the harem to Est 2:11
inside the inner **c** without being called, Est 4:11
stood in the inner **c** of the king's palace, Est 5:1
king saw Queen Esther standing in the **c**, Est 5:2
"Who is in the **c**?" Now Haman had just Est 6:4
just entered the outer **c** of the king's Est 6:4
standing in the **c**." And the king said, Est 6:5
and imprisons and summons the **c**, Jb 11:10
you afraid; many will **c** your favor. Jb 11:19
do not hastily bring into **c**, for what Prv 25:8
he stood in the **c** of the LORD'S house Jer 19:14
Stand in the **c** of the LORD'S house, and Jer 26:2
was shut up in the **c** of the guard that Jer 32:2
cousin came to me in the **c** of the guard, Jer 32:8
who were sitting in the **c** of the guard. Jer 32:12
he was still shut up in the **c** of the guard: Jer 33:1
the secretary, which was in the upper **c**, Jer 36:10
So they went into the **c** to the king, Jer 36:20
Jeremiah to the **c** of the guard. Jer 37:21
remained in the **c** of the guard. Jer 37:21
son, which was in the **c** of the guard, Jer 38:6
remained in the **c** of the guard. Jer 38:13
remained in the **c** of the guard Jer 38:28
took Jeremiah from the **c** of the guard. Jer 39:14
he was shut up in the **c** of the guard: Jer 39:15
gateway of the inner **c** that faces north, Ezk 8:3
he brought me to the entrance of the **c**, Ezk 8:7
me into the inner **c** of the house of Ezk 8:16
went in, and a cloud filled the inner **c**. Ezk 10:3
and the **c** was filled with the brightness Ezk 10:4
was heard as far as the outer **c**, Ezk 10:5
the vestibule of the gateway was the **c**. Ezk 40:14
Then he brought me into the outer **c**. Ezk 40:17
and a pavement, all around the **c**. Ezk 40:17
gate to the outer front of the inner **c**, Ezk 40:19

the north, belonging to the outer **c**, Ezk 40:20
on the east, was a gate to the inner **c**. Ezk 40:23
was a gate on the south of the inner **c**. Ezk 40:27
me to the inner **c** through the south Ezk 40:28
Its vestibule faced the outer **c**, and Ezk 40:31
me to the inner **c** on the east side, Ezk 40:32
Its vestibule faced the outer **c**, and it Ezk 40:34
Its vestibule faced the outer **c**, and it Ezk 40:37
were two chambers in the inner **c**, Ezk 40:44
And he measured the **c**, a hundred Ezk 40:47
of the nave and the vestibules of the **c**, Ezk 41:15
Then he led me out into the outer **c**, Ezk 42:1
cubits that belonged to the inner **c**, Ezk 42:3
pavement that belonged to the outer **c**, Ezk 42:3
to the chambers, toward the outer **c**, Ezk 42:7
on the outer **c** were fifty cubits Ezk 42:8
as one enters them from the outer **c**. Ezk 42:9
In the thickness of the wall of the **c**, on Ezk 42:10
it into the outer **c** without laying there Ezk 42:14
me up and brought me into the inner **c**; Ezk 43:5
they enter the gates of the inner **c**, Ezk 44:17
minister at the gates of the inner **c**, Ezk 44:17
go out into the outer **c** to the people, Ezk 44:19
drink wine when he enters the inner **c**. Ezk 44:21
into the Holy Place, into the inner **c**, Ezk 44:27
and the posts of the gate of the inner **c**. Ezk 45:19
gate of the inner **c** that faces east shall Ezk 46:1
into the outer **c** and so communicate Ezk 46:20
out to the outer **c** and led me around Ezk 46:21
me around to the four corners of the **c**. Ezk 46:21
each corner of the **c** there was another Ezk 46:21
of the court there was another **c**— Ezk 46:21
corners of the **c** were small courts, Ezk 46:22
But Daniel remained at the king's **c**. Dn 2:49
the **c** sat in judgment, and the books Dn 7:10
But the **c** shall sit in judgment, and his Dn 7:26
while you are going with him to **c**, Mt 5:25
with Jesus into the **c** of the high priest, Jn 18:15
a eunuch, a **c** official of Candace, Acts 8:27
a member of the **c** of Herod the Acts 13:1
be judged by you or by any human **c**. 1 Cor 4:3
you, and the ones who drag you into **c**? Jas 2:6
do not measure the **c** outside the temple; Rv 11:2

COURTESY (1)
and to show perfect **c** toward all people. Ti 3:2

COURTS (28)
of heaven in the two **c** of the house of 2 Kgs 21:5
made in the two **c** of the house of 2 Kgs 23:12
the care of the **c** and the chambers, 1 Chr 23:28
who shall build my house and my **c**, 1 Chr 28:6
had in mind for the **c** of the house of 1 Chr 28:12
shall be in the **c** of the house of 2 Chr 23:5
of heaven in the two **c** of the house of 2 Chr 33:5
and in their **c** and in the courts of the Neh 8:16
their courts and in the **c** of the house of Neh 8:16
him a chamber in the **c** of the house of Neh 13:7
and bring near, to dwell in your **c**! Ps 65:4
longs, yes, faints for the **c** of the LORD; Ps 84:2
For a day in your **c** is better than a Ps 84:10
LORD; they flourish in the **c** of our God. Ps 92:13
bring an offering, and come into his **c**! Ps 96:8
thanksgiving, and his **c** with praise! Ps 100:4
in the **c** of the house of the LORD, in Ps 116:19
LORD, in the **c** of the house of our God! Ps 135:2
required of you this trampling of my **c**? Is 1:12
it shall drink it in the **c** of my sanctuary." Is 62:9
the house, and fill the **c** with the slain. Ezk 9:7
had no pillars like the pillars of the **c**. Ezk 42:6
four corners of the court were small **c**, Ezk 46:22
around each of the four **c** was a row of Ezk 46:23
rule my house and have charge of my **c**, Zec 3:7
deliver you over to **c** and flog you in Mt 10:17
and live in luxury are in kings' **c**. Lk 7:25
against anyone, the **c** are open, Acts 19:38

COURTYARD (6)
at Bahurim, who had a well in his **c**. 2 Sm 17:18
as far as the **c** of the high priest, Mt 26:58
Now Peter was sitting outside in the **c**. Mt 26:69
right into the **c** of the high priest. Mk 14:54
And as Peter was below in the **c**, one of Mk 14:66
the middle of the **c** and sat down Lk 22:55

COURTYARDS (1)
The frogs died out in the houses, the **c**, Ex 8:13

COUSIN (5)
or his uncle or his **c** may redeem him, Lv 25:49
Then Hanamel my **c** came to me in the Jer 32:8
field at Anathoth from Hanamel my **c**, Jer 32:9
in the presence of Hanamel my **c**, Jer 32:12
and Mark the **c** of Barnabas Col 4:10

COVENANT (319)
But I will establish my **c** with you, and Gn 6:18
I establish my **c** with you and your Gn 9:9
I establish my **c** with you, that never Gn 9:11
is the sign of the **c** that I make between Gn 9:12
be a sign of the **c** between me and the Gn 9:13
I will remember my **c** that is between Gn 9:15
the everlasting **c** between God Gn 9:16
the sign of the **c** that I have established Gn 9:17
day the LORD made a **c** with Abram, Gn 15:18
I may make my **c** between me and you, Gn 17:2
"Behold, my **c** is with you, and you shall Gn 17:4
I will establish my **c** between me and Gn 17:7
their generations for an everlasting **c**, Gn 17:7
"As for you, you shall keep my **c**, Gn 17:9
This is my **c**, which you shall keep, Gn 17:10
be a sign of the **c** between me and you. Gn 17:11
So shall my **c** be in your flesh an Gn 17:13
be in your flesh an everlasting **c**. Gn 17:13
from his people; he has broken my **c**." Gn 17:14
I will establish my **c** with him as an Gn 17:19
as an everlasting **c** for his offspring Gn 17:19
But I will establish my **c** with Isaac, Gn 17:21
Abimelech, and the two men made a **c**. Gn 21:27
So they made a **c** at Beersheba. Then Gn 21:32
and us, and let us make a **c** with you, Gn 26:28
Come now, let us make a **c**, you and I. Gn 31:44
God remembered his **c** with Abraham, Ex 2:24
I also established my **c** with them to give Ex 6:4
as slaves, and I have remembered my **c**. Ex 6:5
indeed obey my voice and keep my **c**, Ex 19:5
You shall make no **c** with them and Ex 23:32
took the Book of the **C** and read it in the Ex 24:7
the blood of the **c** that the LORD has Ex 24:8
their generations, as a **c** forever. Ex 31:16
And he said, "Behold, I am making a **c**. Ex 34:10
lest you make a **c** with the inhabitants Ex 34:12
lest you make a **c** with the inhabitants Ex 34:15
I have made a **c** with you and with Ex 34:27
wrote on the tablets the words of the **c**, Ex 34:28
let the salt of the **c** with your God be Lv 2:13
is from the people of Israel as a **c** forever. Lv 24:8
you and will confirm my **c** with you. Lv 26:9
my commandments, but break my **c**, Lv 26:15
that shall execute vengeance for the **c**. Lv 26:25
then I will remember my **c** with Jacob, Lv 26:42
I will remember my **c** with Isaac and Lv 26:42
with Isaac and my **c** with Abraham, Lv 26:42
utterly and break my **c** with them, Lv 26:44
sake remember the **c** with their Lv 26:45
And the ark of the **c** of the LORD went Nm 10:33
neither the ark of the **c** of the LORD nor Nm 14:44
It is a **c** of salt forever before the LORD Nm 18:19
'Behold, I give to him my **c** of peace, Nm 25:12
after him the **c** of a perpetual Nm 25:13
And he declared to you his **c**, which he Dt 4:13
lest you forget the **c** of the LORD your God, Dt 4:23
you or forget the **c** with your fathers that Dt 4:31
LORD our God made a **c** with us in Horeb. Dt 5:2
with our fathers did the LORD make this **c**, Dt 5:3
You shall make no **c** with them and show Dt 7:2
God who keeps **c** and steadfast love Dt 7:9
keep with you the **c** and the steadfast love Dt 7:12
he may confirm his **c** that he swore to Dt 8:18
the tablets of the **c** that the LORD made Dt 9:9
two tablets of stone, the tablets of the **c**. Dt 9:11
the two tablets of the **c** were in my two Dt 9:15
carry the ark of the **c** of the LORD to stand Dt 10:8
LORD your God, in transgressing his **c**, Dt 17:2
the words of the **c** that the LORD Dt 29:1
besides the **c** that he had made with Dt 29:1
keep the words of this **c** and do them, Dt 29:9
enter into the sworn **c** of the LORD your Dt 29:12
alone that I am making this sworn **c**, Dt 29:14
he hears the words of this sworn **c**, Dt 29:19
the curses of the **c** written in this Book Dt 29:21
they abandoned the **c** of the LORD, Dt 29:25
who carried the ark of the **c** of the LORD, Dt 31:9
me and break my **c** that I have made Dt 31:16
them, and despise me and break my **c**. Dt 31:20
who carried the ark of the **c** of the LORD, Dt 31:25
of the ark of the **c** of the LORD your God, Dt 31:26
observed your word and kept your **c**. Dt 33:9
see the ark of the **c** of the LORD your God Jos 3:3
up the ark of the **c** and pass on before the Jos 3:6
up the ark of the **c** and went before the Jos 3:6
the priests who bear the ark of the **c**, Jos 3:8
the ark of the **c** of the Lord of all the Jos 3:11
the ark of the **c** before the people, Jos 3:14
bearing the ark of the **c** of the LORD stood Jos 3:17
cut off before the ark of the **c** of the LORD. Jos 4:7
priests bearing the ark of the **c** had stood; Jos 4:9
the ark of the **c** of the LORD came Jos 4:18
up the ark of the **c** and let seven priests Jos 6:6
with the ark of the **c** of the LORD following Jos 6:8
have transgressed my **c** that I Jos 7:11
he has transgressed the **c** of the LORD, Jos 7:15
who carried the ark of the **c** of the LORD, Jos 8:33
country, so now make a **c** with us." Jos 9:6
us; then how can we make a **c** with you?" Jos 9:7
servants. Come now, make a **c** with us."' Jos 9:11
with them and made a **c** with them, Jos 9:15
days after they had made a **c** with them, Jos 9:16
if you transgress the **c** of the LORD your Jos 23:16
So Joshua made a **c** with the people that Jos 24:25
I said, 'I will never break my **c** with you, Jgs 2:1
you shall make no **c** with the inhabitants Jgs 2:2
have transgressed my **c** that I Jgs 2:20
(for the ark of the **c** of God was there in Jgs 20:27
bring the ark of the **c** of the LORD here 1 Sm 4:3
there the ark of the **c** of the LORD of 1 Sm 4:4
were there with the ark of the **c** of God. 1 Sm 4:4
as the ark of the **c** of the LORD came 1 Sm 4:5
Then Jonathan made a **c** with David, 1 Sm 18:3
your servant into a **c** of the LORD with 1 Sm 20:8
Jonathan made a **c** with the house 1 Sm 20:16
my son makes a **c** with the son of 1 Sm 22:8
of them made a **c** before the LORD. 1 Sm 23:18
land belong? Make your **c** with me, 2 Sm 3:12
said, "Good; I will make a **c** with you. 2 Sm 3:13
that they may make a **c** with you, 2 Sm 3:21
King David made a **c** with them at 2 Sm 5:3
bearing the ark of the **c** of God. 2 Sm 15:24
he has made with me an everlasting **c**, 2 Sm 23:5
before the ark of the **c** of the LORD, 1 Kgs 3:15
set there the ark of the **c** of the LORD. 1 Kgs 6:19
up the ark of the **c** of the LORD out of 1 Kgs 8:1
brought the ark of the **c** of the LORD to 1 Kgs 8:6
the LORD made a **c** with the people of 1 Kgs 8:9
in which is the **c** of the LORD that he 1 Kgs 8:21
keeping **c** and showing steadfast love 1 Kgs 8:23
have not kept my **c** and my statutes 1 Kgs 11:11
"Let there be a **c** between me and 1 Kgs 15:19
break your **c** with Baasha king of 1 Kgs 15:19
of Israel have forsaken your **c**, 1 Kgs 19:10
of Israel have forsaken your **c**, 1 Kgs 19:14
So he made a **c** with him and let 1 Kgs 20:34
And he made a **c** with them and put 2 Kgs 11:4
Jehoiada made a **c** between the LORD 2 Kgs 11:17
because of his **c** with Abraham, 2 Kgs 13:23
his statutes and his **c** that he made 2 Kgs 17:15
The LORD made a **c** with them and 2 Kgs 17:35
shall not forget the **c** that I have 2 Kgs 17:38
their God but transgressed his **c**, 2 Kgs 18:12
the Book of the **C** that had been 2 Kgs 23:2
pillar and made a **c** before the LORD, 2 Kgs 23:3
the words of this **c** that were written 2 Kgs 23:3
And all the people joined in the **c**. 2 Kgs 23:3
as it is written in this Book of the **C**." 2 Kgs 23:21
and David made a **c** with them at 1 Chr 11:3
up the ark of the **c** of the LORD from 1 Chr 15:25
carrying the ark of the **c** of the LORD, 1 Chr 15:26
up the ark of the **c** of the LORD with 1 Chr 15:28
as the ark of the **c** of the LORD came 1 Chr 15:29
before the ark of the **c** of God. 1 Chr 16:6
Remember his **c** forever, the word 1 Chr 16:15
the **c** that he made with Abraham, 1 Chr 16:16
Jacob, as an everlasting **c** to Israel, 1 Chr 16:17
before the ark of the **c** of the LORD to 1 Chr 16:37
but the ark of the **c** of the LORD is 1 Chr 17:1
that the ark of the **c** of the LORD and 1 Chr 22:19
for the ark of the **c** of the LORD and for 1 Chr 28:2
covered the ark of the **c** of the LORD. 1 Chr 28:18
up the ark of the **c** of the LORD out of 2 Chr 5:2
brought the ark of the **c** of the LORD to 2 Chr 5:7
the LORD made a **c** with the people of 2 Chr 5:10
in which is the **c** of the LORD that he 2 Chr 6:11
keeping **c** and showing steadfast love 2 Chr 6:14
to David and his sons by a **c** of salt? 2 Chr 13:5
they entered into a **c** to seek the 2 Chr 15:12
"There is a **c** between me and you, as 2 Chr 16:3
break your **c** with Baasha king of 2 Chr 16:3
because of the **c** that he had made 2 Chr 21:7
entered into a **c** with the 2 Chr 23:1
the assembly made a **c** with the king 2 Chr 23:3
Jehoiada made a **c** between himself 2 Chr 23:16
my heart to make a **c** with the LORD, 2 Chr 29:10
the Book of the **C** that had been 2 Chr 34:30
place and made a **c** before the LORD, 2 Chr 34:31
the words of the **c** that were written 2 Chr 34:31
did according to the **c** of God, 2 Chr 34:32
let us make a **c** with our God to Ezr 10:3
God who keeps **c** and steadfast love Neh 1:5
and made with him the **c** to give to his Neh 9:8
God, who keeps **c** and steadfast love, Neh 9:32
of all this we make a firm **c** in writing; Neh 9:38
priesthood and the **c** of the priesthood Neh 13:29
"I have made a **c** with my eyes; how then Jb 31:1
Will he make a **c** with you to take him Jb 41:4
who keep his **c** and his testimonies. Ps 25:10
and he makes known to them his **c**. Ps 25:14
and we have not been false to your **c**. Ps 44:17
who made a **c** with me by sacrifice!" Ps 50:5

my statutes or take my **c** on your lips? Ps 50:16
against his friends; he violated his **c**. Ps 55:20
Have regard for the **c**, for the dark Ps 74:20
They did not keep God's **c**, but refused Ps 78:10
him; they were not faithful to his **c**. Ps 78:37
one accord; against you they make a **c**— Ps 83:5
"I have made a **c** with my chosen one; Ps 89:3
and my **c** will stand firm for him. Ps 89:28
I will not violate my **c** or alter the word Ps 89:34
have renounced the **c** with your Ps 89:39
those who keep his **c** and remember to Ps 103:18
He remembers his **c** forever, the word Ps 105:8
the **c** that he made with Abraham, his Ps 105:9
a statute, to Israel as an everlasting **c**, Ps 105:10
For their sake he remembered his **c**, Ps 106:45
fear him; he remembers his **c** forever. Ps 111:5
he has commanded his **c** forever. Ps 111:9
sons keep my **c** and my testimonies Ps 132:12
her youth and forgets the **c** of her God; Prv 2:17
the statutes, broken the everlasting **c**. Is 24:5
said, "We have made a **c** with death, Is 28:15
Then your **c** with death will be Is 28:18
I will give you as a **c** for the people, a light Is 42:6
keep you and give you as a **c** to the people, Is 49:8
and my **c** of peace shall not be Is 54:10
I will make with you an everlasting **c**, Is 55:3
things that please me and hold fast my **c**, Is 56:4
does not profane it, and holds fast my **c**— Is 56:6
you have made a **c** for yourself with Is 57:8
this is my **c** with them," says the LORD: Is 59:21
I will make an everlasting **c** with them. Is 61:8
"The ark of the **c** of the LORD." It shall Jer 3:16
"Hear the words of this **c**, and speak to Jer 11:2
who does not hear the words of this **c** Jer 11:3
Hear the words of this **c** and do them. Jer 11:6
upon them all the words of this **c**, Jer 11:8
Judah have broken my **c** that I made Jer 11:10
and do not break your **c** with us. Jer 14:21
they have forsaken the **c** of the LORD Jer 22:9
I will make a new **c** with the house of Jer 31:31
not like the **c** that I made with their Jer 31:32
the land of Egypt, my **c** that they broke, Jer 31:32
But this is the **c** that I will make with Jer 31:33
I will make with them an everlasting **c**, Jer 32:40
If you can break my **c** with the day and Jer 33:20
with the day and my **c** with the night, Jer 33:20
then also my **c** with David my servant Jer 33:21
and my **c** with the Levitical priests my Jer 33:21
have not established my **c** with day and Jer 33:25
Zedekiah had made a **c** with all the Jer 34:8
entered into the **c** that everyone would Jer 34:10
I myself made a **c** with your fathers Jer 34:13
and you made a **c** before me in the Jer 34:15
who transgressed my **c** and did not Jer 34:18
the terms of the **c** that they made before Jer 34:18
LORD in an everlasting **c** that will never Jer 50:5
to you and entered into a **c** with you, Ezk 16:8
despised the oath in breaking the **c**, Ezk 16:59
I will remember my **c** with you in the Ezk 16:60
will establish for you an everlasting **c**. Ezk 16:60
but not on account of the **c** with you. Ezk 16:61
I will establish my **c** with you, and Ezk 16:62
offspring and made a **c** with him, Ezk 17:13
up, and keep his **c** that it might stand. Ezk 17:14
Can he break the **c** and yet escape? Ezk 17:15
and whose **c** with him he broke, Ezk 17:16
He despised the oath in breaking the **c**, Ezk 17:18
he despised, and my **c** that he broke. Ezk 17:19
I will bring you into the bond of the **c**. Ezk 20:37
make with them a **c** of peace and Ezk 34:25
I will make a **c** of peace with them. It Ezk 37:26
It shall be an everlasting **c** with them. Ezk 37:26
You have broken my **c**, in addition to Ezk 44:7
who keeps **c** and steadfast love with those Dn 9:4
shall make a strong **c** with many for Dn 9:27
and broken, even the prince of the **c**. Dn 11:22
heart shall be set against the holy **c**. Dn 11:28
and take action against the holy **c**. Dn 11:30
to those who forsake the holy **c**. Dn 11:30
with flattery those who violate the **c**, Dn 11:32
will make for them a **c** on that day with Hos 2:18
But like Adam they transgressed the **c**; Hos 6:7
have transgressed my **c** and rebelled Hos 8:1
they make a **c** with Assyria, and oil is Hos 12:1
did not remember the **c** of brotherhood. Am 1:9
according to the **c** that I made with you Hg 2:5
because of the blood of my **c** with you, Zec 9:11
annulling the **c** that I had made with Zec 11:10
to you, that my **c** with Levi may stand, Mal 2:4
My **c** with him was one of life and peace, Mal 2:5
him. It was a **c** of fear, and he feared me. Mal 2:5
You have corrupted the **c** of Levi, says Mal 2:8
another, profaning the **c** of our fathers? Mal 2:10
is your companion and your wife by **c**. Mal 2:14
the messenger of the **c** in whom you Mal 3:1
for this is my blood of the **c**, which is Mt 26:28
to them, "This is my blood of the **c**, Mk 14:24
our fathers and to remember his holy **c**, Lk 1:72
out for you is the new **c** in my blood. Lk 22:20
prophets and of the **c** that God made Acts 3:25
And he gave him the **c** of circumcision. Acts 7:8
this will be my **c** with them when I Rom 11:27
"This cup is the new **c** in my blood. 1 Cor 11:25
competent to be ministers of a new **c**, 2 Cor 3:6
to this day, when they read the old **c**, 2 Cor 3:14
even with a man-made **c**, no one Gal 3:15
not annul a **c** previously ratified by Gal 3:17
makes Jesus the guarantor of a better **c**. Heb 7:22
the old as the **c** he mediates is better, Heb 8:6
For if that first **c** had been faultless, Heb 8:7
I will establish a new **c** with the house of Heb 8:8
not like the **c** that I made with their Heb 8:9
For they did not continue in my **c**, and Heb 8:9
For this is the **c** that I will make with Heb 8:10
In speaking of a new **c**, he makes the Heb 8:13
Now even the first **c** had regulations for Heb 9:1
and the ark of the **c** covered on all sides Heb 9:4
that budded, and the tablets of the **c**. Heb 9:4
Therefore he is the mediator of a new **c**, Heb 9:15
committed under the first **c**. Heb 9:15
even the first **c** was inaugurated Heb 9:18
blood of the **c** that God commanded Heb 9:20
"This is the **c** that I will make with Heb 10:16
the blood of the **c** by which he was Heb 10:29
and to Jesus, the mediator of a new **c**, Heb 12:24
sheep, by the blood of the eternal **c**, Heb 13:20
and the ark of his **c** was seen within his Rv 11:19

COVENANTED (1)

throne, as I **c** with David your father, 2 Chr 7:18

COVENANTS (5)

C are broken; cities are despised; there is Is 33:8
words; with empty oaths they make **c**; Hos 10:4
belong the adoption, the glory, the **c**, Rom 9:4
allegorically: these women are two **c**. Gal 4:24
Israel and strangers to the **c** of promise, Eph 2:12

COVER (73)

ark, and **c** it inside and out with pitch. Gn 6:14
and they shall **c** the face of the land, so Ex 10:5
when a man digs a pit and does not **c** it, Ex 21:33
on this side and that side, to **c** it. Ex 26:13
linen undergarments to **c** their naked Ex 28:42
and I will **c** you with my hand until I Ex 33:22
and he shall **c** his upper lip and cry out, Lv 13:45
of the incense may **c** the mercy seat Lv 16:13
pour out its blood and **c** it with earth. Lv 17:13
veil of the screen and **c** the ark of the Nm 4:5
a cloth of scarlet and **c** the same with a Nm 4:8
cloth of blue and **c** the lampstand for Nm 4:9
a cloth of blue and **c** it with a covering Nm 4:11
cloth of blue and **c** them with a Nm 4:12
vessel that has no **c** fastened on it is Nm 19:15
They **c** the face of the earth, and they Nm 22:5
the garment with which you **c** yourself. Dt 22:12
turn back and **c** up your excrement. Dt 23:13
the sea come upon them and **c** them; Jos 24:7
came down under **c** of the 1 Sm 25:20
one latticework to **c** the capital that 1 Kgs 7:18
two latticeworks to **c** the two bowls 1 Kgs 7:41
to **c** the two bowls of the capitals that 1 Kgs 7:42
two latticeworks to **c** the two bowls 2 Chr 4:12
to **c** the two bowls of the capitals that 2 Chr 4:13
Do not **c** their guilt, and let not their sin Neh 4:5
bag, and you would **c** over my iniquity. Jb 14:17
"O earth, **c** not my blood, and let my cry Jb 16:18
alike in the dust, and the worms **c** them. Jb 21:26
that a flood of waters may **c** you? Jb 38:34
For his shade the lotus trees **c** him; the Jb 40:22
you **c** him with favor as with a shield. Ps 5:12
will conceal me under the **c** of his tent; Ps 27:5
In the **c** of your presence you hide them Ps 31:20
sin to you, and I did not **c** my iniquity; Ps 32:5
He will **c** you with his pinions, and Ps 91:4
that they might not again **c** the earth. Ps 104:9
I say, "Surely the darkness shall **c** me, Ps 139:11
of the LORD as the waters **c** the sea. Is 11:9
shed on it, and will no more **c** its slain. Is 26:21
when you see the naked, to **c** him, and not Is 58:7
men will not **c** themselves with what they Is 59:6
For behold, darkness shall **c** the earth, Is 60:2
A multitude of camels shall **c** you, the Is 60:6
in our shame, and let our dishonor **c** us. Jer 3:25
and confounded and **c** their heads. Jer 14:3
farmers are ashamed; they **c** their heads. Jer 14:4
He said, 'I will rise, I will **c** the earth, I Jer 46:8
You shall **c** your face that you may not Ezk 12:6
out through it. He shall **c** his face, Ezk 12:12
embroidered garments to **c** them, Ezk 16:18
it out on the ground to **c** it with dust. Ezk 24:7
shoes on your feet; do not **c** your lips, Ezk 24:17
you shall not **c** your lips, nor eat the Ezk 24:22
be so many that their dust will **c** you. Ezk 26:10
over you, and the great waters **c** you, Ezk 26:19
I will **c** the heavens and make their Ezk 32:7
I will **c** the sun with a cloud, and the Ezk 32:7
to come upon you, and **c** you with skin, Ezk 37:6
my flax, which were to **c** her nakedness. Hos 2:9
they shall say to the mountains, **C** us, Hos 10:8
your brother Jacob, shame shall **c** you, Ob 1:10
they shall all **c** their lips, for there is no Mi 3:7
and shame will **c** her who said to me, Mi 7:10
of the LORD as the waters **c** the sea. Hab 2:14
And behold, the leaden **c** was lifted, and Zec 5:7
You **c** the LORD'S altar with tears, with Mal 2:13
spit on him and to **c** his face and to Mk 14:65
'Fall on us,' and to the hills, '**C** us.' Lk 23:30
For if a wife will not **c** her head, then 1 Cor 11:6
or shave her head, let her **c** her head. 1 Cor 11:6
For a man ought not to **c** his head, 1 Cor 11:7
from death and will **c** a multitude of Jas 5:20

COVER-UP (1)

not using your freedom as a **c** for evil, 1 Pt 2:16

COVERED (83)

under the whole heaven were **c**. Gn 7:19
walked backward and **c** the nakedness Gn 9:23
So she took her veil and **c** herself. Gn 24:65
widow's garments and **c** herself with a Gn 38:14
was a prostitute, for she had **c** her face. Gn 38:15
the frogs came up and **c** the land of Egypt. Ex 8:6
They **c** the face of the whole land, so Ex 10:15
waters returned and **c** the chariots and Ex 14:28
The floods **c** them; they went down into Ex 15:5
blew with your wind; the sea **c** them; Ex 15:10
evening quail came up and **c** the camp, Ex 16:13
and the cloud **c** the mountain. Ex 24:15
Sinai, and the cloud **c** it six days. Ex 24:16
Then the cloud **c** the tent of meeting, Ex 40:34
if the leprous disease has **c** all his body, Lv 13:13
was set up, the cloud **c** the tabernacle, Nm 9:15
the cloud **c** it by day and the Nm 9:16
And behold, the cloud **c** it, and the Nm 16:42
into the tent, and she **c** him with a rug. Jgs 4:18
milk and gave him a drink and **c** him. Jgs 4:19
at its head and **c** it with the clothes. 1 Sm 19:13
went, barefoot and with his head **c**. 2 Sm 15:30
who were with him **c** their heads, 2 Sm 15:30
The king **c** his face, and the king 2 Sm 19:4
"You have today **c** with shame the 2 Sm 19:5
And although they **c** him with clothes, 1 Kgs 1:1
he **c** them on the inside with wood, 1 Kgs 6:15
and he **c** the floor of the house with 1 Kgs 6:15
He **c** the two doors of olivewood with 1 Kgs 6:32
And it was **c** with cedar above the 1 Kgs 7:3
man threw a stone until it was **c**. 2 Kgs 3:25
And the **c** way for the Sabbath that 2 Kgs 16:18
his clothes and **c** himself with 2 Kgs 19:1
the senior priests, **c** with sackcloth, 2 Kgs 19:2
spread their wings and **c** the ark of 1 Chr 28:18
lined with cypress and **c** it with fine 2 Chr 3:5
He rebuilt it and **c** it and set its doors, Neh 3:15
house, mourning and with his head **c**. Est 6:12
mouth of the king, they **c** Haman's face. Est 7:8
because he has **c** his face with his fat Jb 15:27
transgression is forgiven, whose sin is **c**. Ps 32:1
is before me, and shame has **c** my face Ps 44:15
place of jackals and **c** us with the Ps 44:19
the wings of a dove **c** with silver, Ps 68:13
reproach, that dishonor has **c** my face. Ps 69:7
disgrace may they be **c** who seek my Ps 71:13
The mountains were **c** with its shade, Ps 80:10
of your people; you **c** all their sin. Ps 85:2
his youth; you have **c** him with shame. Ps 89:45
You **c** it with the deep as with a Ps 104:6
And the waters **c** their adversaries; not Ps 106:11
and **c** the company of Abiram. Ps 106:17
you have **c** my head in the day of battle. Ps 140:7
is trustworthy in spirit keeps a thing **c**. Prv 11:13
the ground was **c** with nettles, and its Prv 24:31
though his hatred be **c** with deception, Prv 26:26
darkness, and in darkness its name is **c**. Eccl 6:4
with two he **c** his face, and with two he Is 6:2
covered his face, and with two he **c** his feet, Is 6:2
prophets), and **c** your heads (the seers). Is 29:10
his clothes and **c** himself with sackcloth Is 37:1
and the senior priests, **c** with sackcloth, Is 37:2
in your mouth and **c** you in the shadow Is 51:16
he has **c** me with the robe of Is 61:10
she is **c** with its tumultuous waves. Jer 51:42
reproach; dishonor has **c** our face, Jer 51:51
of another, while two **c** their bodies. Ezk 1:11
over you and **c** your nakedness; Ezk 16:8
you in fine linen and **c** you with silk. Ezk 16:10
she has shed, that it may not be **c**. Ezk 24:8
end in her; she shall be **c** by a cloud, Ezk 30:18

come upon them, and skin had **c** them. Ezk 37:8
windows (now the windows were **c**), Ezk 41:16
his robe, **c** himself with sackcloth, Jon 3:6
let man and beast be **c** with sackcloth, Jon 3:8
Paran. His splendor **c** the heavens, Hab 3:3
for nothing is **c** that will not be Mt 10:26
in a field, which a man found and **c** up. Mt 13:44
Nothing is **c** up that will not be revealed, Lk 12:2
poor man named Lazarus, **c** with sores, Lk 16:20
deeds are forgiven, and whose sins are **c**; Rom 4:7
with his head **c** dishonors his head, 1 Cor 11:4
ark of the covenant **c** on all sides with Heb 9:4

COVERING (41)
mountains, **c** them fifteen cubits deep. Gn 7:20
And Noah removed the **c** of the ark and Gn 8:13
for that is his only **c**, and it is his cloak Ex 22:27
for the tent a **c** of tanned rams' skins Ex 26:14
rams' skins and a **c** of goatskins on top. Ex 26:14
the tabernacle, its tent and its **c**, its Ex 35:11
for the tent a **c** of tanned rams' skins Ex 36:19
the **c** of tanned rams' skins and Ex 39:34
tabernacle and put the **c** of the tent over Ex 40:19
he shall offer the fat **c** the entrails and all Lv 3:3
the fat **c** the entrails and all the fat that is Lv 3:14
the tabernacle, the tent with its **c**, Nm 3:25
shall put on it a **c** of goatskin and spread Nm 4:6
and cover the same with a **c** of goatskin, Nm 4:8
its utensils in a **c** of goatskin and put Nm 4:10
blue and cover it with a **c** of goatskin, Nm 4:11
cover them with a **c** of goatskin and Nm 4:12
they shall spread on it a **c** of goatskin, Nm 4:14
sons have finished **c** the sanctuary and Nm 4:15
of meeting with its **c** and the covering Nm 4:25
its covering and the **c** of goatskin that Nm 4:25
hammered plates as a **c** for the altar, Nm 16:38
hammered out as a **c** for the altar, Nm 16:39
took and spread a **c** over the well's 2 Sm 17:19
the cherubim made a **c** above the ark 2 Chr 5:8
clothing, and have no **c** in the cold. Jb 24:7
before God, and Abaddon has no **c**. Jb 26:6
lack of clothing, or the needy without **c**, Jb 31:19
He made darkness his **c**, his canopy Ps 18:11
c yourself with light as with a garment, Ps 104:2
He spread a cloud for a **c**, and fire to Ps 105:39
Like the glaze **c** an earthen vessel are Prv 26:23
He has taken away the **c** of Judah. In that Is 22:8
on this mountain the **c** that is cast over Is 25:7
and the **c** too narrow to wrap oneself in. Is 28:20
blackness and make sackcloth their **c**." Is 50:3
each creature had two wings **c** its body. Ezk 1:23
every precious stone was your **c**, Ezk 28:13
You will be like a cloud **c** the land, you Ezk 38:9
people Israel, like a cloud **c** the land. Ezk 38:16
For her hair is given to her for a **c**. 1 Cor 11:15

COVERINGS (2)
I have spread my couch with **c**, colored Prv 7:16
She makes bed **c** for herself; her Prv 31:22

COVERS (26)
shall take all the fat that **c** the entrails, Ex 29:13
fat tail and the fat that **c** the entrails, Ex 29:22
and the fat that **c** the entrails and all the Lv 3:9
the fat that **c** the entrails and all the fat Lv 4:8
the fat tail, the fat that **c** the entrails, Lv 7:3
tail and that which **c** the entrails and the Lv 9:19
that the leprous disease **c** all the skin of Lv 13:12
of Egypt, and it **c** the face of the earth. Nm 22:11
he **c** the faces of its judges—if it is not he, Jb 9:24
cannot see, and a flood of water **c** you. Jb 22:11
nor because thick darkness **c** my face. Jb 23:17
He **c** the face of the full moon and Jb 26:9
lightning about him and **c** the roots of Jb 36:30
He **c** his hands with the lightning and Jb 36:32
necklace; violence **c** them as a garment. Ps 73:6
the early rain also **c** it with pools. Ps 84:6
He **c** the heavens with clouds; he Ps 147:8
stirs up strife, but love **c** all offenses. Prv 10:12
Whoever **c** an offense seeks love, but he Prv 17:9
bed beneath you, and worms are your **c**. Is 14:11
put on sackcloth, and horror **c** them. Ezk 7:18
to the hungry and **c** the naked with a Ezk 18:7
to the hungry and **c** the naked with a Ezk 18:16
of Israel, **c** his garment with violence, Mal 2:16
one after lighting a lamp **c** it with a jar Lk 8:16
since love **c** a multitude of sins. 1 Pt 4:8

COVET (10)
"You shall not **c** your neighbor's Ex 20:17
you shall not **c** your neighbor's wife, Ex 20:17
no one shall **c** your land, when you go Ex 34:24
you shall not **c** your neighbor's wife. Dt 5:21
You shall not **c** the silver or the gold that Dt 7:25
They **c** fields and seize them, and houses, Mi 2:2
known what it is to **c** if the law had not Rom 7:7
the law had not said, "You shall not **c**." Rom 7:7
You shall not **c**," and any other Rom 13:9
You **c** and cannot obtain, so you fight Jas 4:2

COVETED (2)
50 shekels, then I **c** them and took them. Jos 7:21
I **c** no one's silver or gold or apparel. Acts 20:33

COVETING (1)
c, wickedness, deceit, sensuality, envy, Mk 7:22

COVETOUS (1)
immoral or impure, or who is **c** (that is, Eph 5:5

COVETOUSNESS (5)
and be on your guard against all **c**, Lk 12:15
of unrighteousness, evil, **c**, malice. Rom 1:29
produced in me all kinds of **c**. Rom 7:8
and all impurity or **c** must not even be Eph 5:3
impurity, passion, evil desire, and **c**, Col 3:5

COVETS (1)
Whoever is wicked **c** the spoil of Prv 12:12

COW (5)
livestock, the firstborn of **c** and sheep. Ex 34:19
But the firstborn of a **c**, or the Nm 18:17
their **c** calves and does not miscarry. Jb 21:10
will keep alive a young **c** and two sheep, Is 7:21
The **c** and the bear shall graze; their Is 11:7

COW'S (1)
I assign to you **c** dung instead of Ezk 4:15

COWARDLY (1)
But as for the **c**, the faithless, the Rv 21:8

COWER (1)
on gravel, and made me **c** in ashes; Lam 3:16

COWORKER (1)
our brother and God's **c** in the gospel 1 Thes 3:2

COWS (18)
and their calves, forty **c** and ten bulls, Gn 32:15
of the Nile seven **c** attractive and plump, Gn 41:2
And behold, seven other **c**, ugly and Gn 41:3
and stood by the other **c** on the bank of Gn 41:3
ugly, thin **c** ate up the seven attractive, Gn 41:4
ate up the seven attractive, plump **c**. Gn 41:4
Seven **c**, plump and attractive, came Gn 41:18
Seven other **c** came up after them, poor Gn 41:19
ugly **c** ate up the first seven plump Gn 41:20
cows ate up the first seven plump **c**, Gn 41:20
The seven good **c** are seven years, and Gn 41:26
seven lean and ugly **c** that came up Gn 41:27
cart and two milk **c** on which there 1 Sm 6:7
come a yoke, and yoke the **c** to the cart, 1 Sm 6:7
and took two milk **c** and yoked them 1 Sm 6:10
And the **c** went straight in the 1 Sm 6:12
cart and offered the **c** as a burnt 1 Sm 6:14
"Hear this word, you **c** of Bashan, who Am 4:1

COZBI (2)
who was killed was **C** the daughter of Nm 25:15
matter of Peor, and in the matter of **C**, Nm 25:18

COZEBA (1)
and Jokim, and the men of **C**, and 1 Chr 4:22

CRACK (1)
The **c** of the whip, and rumble of the Na 3:2

CRACKLING (2)
For as the **c** of thorns under a pot, so is Eccl 7:6
like the **c** of a flame of fire devouring the Jl 2:5

CRAFT (4)
and in carving wood, to work in every **c**. Ex 31:5
wood, for work in every skilled **c**. Ex 35:33
Tarshish, and against all the beautiful **c**. Is 2:16
a craftsman of any **c** will be found in Rv 18:22

CRAFTED (2)
from them the gold, all **c** articles. Nm 31:51
and **c** in gold were your settings and Ezk 28:13

CRAFTILY (1)
his people, to deal **c** with his servants. Ps 105:25

CRAFTINESS (4)
He catches the wise in their own **c**, and Jb 5:13
But he perceived their **c**, and said to Lk 20:23
"He catches the wise in their **c**," 1 Cor 3:19
cunning, by **c** in deceitful schemes. Eph 4:14

CRAFTSMAN (11)
"Let every skillful **c** among you come Ex 35:10
and Oholiab and every **c** in whom the Ex 36:1
and Oholiab and every **c** in whose mind Ex 36:2
LORD, a thing made by the hands of a **c**, Dt 27:15
A **c** casts it, and a goldsmith overlays it Is 40:19
he seeks out a skillful **c** to set up an idol Is 40:20
The **c** strengthens the goldsmith, and he Is 41:7
worked with an axe by the hands of a **c**. Jer 10:3
are the work of the **c** and of the hands of Jer 10:9
For it is from Israel; a **c** made it; it is not Hos 8:6
and a **c** of any craft will be found in Rv 18:22

CRAFTSMANSHIP (2)
intelligence, with knowledge and all **c**, Ex 31:3
with knowledge, and with all **c**, Ex 35:31

CRAFTSMEN (17)
so that all the **c** who were doing every Ex 36:4
And all the **c** among the workmen made Ex 36:8
and all the **c** and the smiths. 2 Kgs 24:14
and the **c** and the metal workers, 2 Kgs 24:16
so-called because they were **c**. 1 Chr 4:14
and all kinds of **c** without number, 1 Chr 22:15
and for all the work to be done by **c**, 1 Chr 29:5
may be assigned him, with your **c**, 2 Chr 2:14
your craftsmen, the **c** of my lord, 2 Chr 2:14
Lod, and Ono, the valley of **c**. Neh 11:35
put to shame, and the **c** are only human. Is 44:11
together with the officials of Judah, the **c**, Jer 24:1
officials of Judah and Jerusalem, the **c**, Jer 29:2
of their silver, all of them the work of **c**. Hos 13:2
Then the LORD showed me four **c**. Zec 1:20
brought no little business to the **c**. Acts 19:24
Demetrius and the **c** with him have Acts 19:38

CRAFTY (6)
the serpent was more **c** than any other Gn 3:1
And Jonadab was a very **c** man. 2 Sm 13:3
He frustrates the devices of the **c**, so that Jb 5:12
and you choose the tongue of the **c**. Jb 15:5
They lay **c** plans against your people; Ps 83:3
I myself did not burden you, I was **c**, 2 Cor 12:16

CRAG (4)
there was a rocky **c** on the one side 1 Sm 14:4
side and a rocky **c** on the other side. 1 Sm 14:4
The one **c** rose on the north in front of 1 Sm 14:5
home, on the rocky **c** and stronghold. Jb 39:28

CRAGS (3)
For from the top of the **c** I see him, Nm 23:9
snow of Lebanon leave the **c** of Sirion? Jer 18:14
you, and roll you down from the **c**, Jer 51:25

CRAMPING (1)
into a broad place where there was no **c**, Jb 36:16

CRANE (2)
Like a swallow or a **c** I chirp; I moan Is 38:14
and **c** keep the time of their coming, Jer 8:7

CRANNIES (1)
the clefts of the rock, in the **c** of the cliff, Sg 2:14

CRASH (6)
they come; amid the **c** they roll on. Jb 30:14
The **c** of your thunder was in the Ps 77:18
make fortified cities **c** into heaps of Is 37:26
C follows hard on crash; the whole land Jer 4:20
Crash follows hard on **c**; the whole land Jer 4:20
Second Quarter, a loud **c** from the hills. Zep 1:10

CRASHING (2)
Its **c** declares his presence; the cattle Jb 36:33
at the **c** they are beside themselves. Jb 41:25

CRAVE (1)
'I will eat meat,' because you **c** meat, Dt 12:20

CRAVED (2)
heart by demanding the food they **c**. Ps 78:18
well filled, for he gave them what they **c**. Ps 78:29

CRAVES (4)
strong drink, whatever your appetite **c**. Dt 14:26
soul of the sluggard **c** and gets nothing, Prv 13:4
All day long he **c** and craves, but the Prv 21:26
All day long he craves and **c**, but the Prv 21:26

CRAVING (8)
that was among them had a strong **c**. Nm 11:4
they buried the people who had the **c**. Nm 11:34
But before they had satisfied their **c**, Ps 78:30
they had a wanton **c** in the wilderness, Ps 106:14
but he thwarts the **c** of the wicked. Prv 10:3
to leave the **c** of the hungry unsatisfied, Is 32:6
has an unhealthy **c** for controversy 1 Tm 6:4
It is through this **c** that some have 1 Tm 6:10

CRAWL (1)
the venom of things that **c** in the dust. Dt 32:24

CRAWLING (2)
a serpent, like the **c** things of the earth; Mi 7:17
sea, like **c** things that have no ruler. Hab 1:14

CRAWLS (2)
swarming thing that **c** on the ground. Lv 11:44
by anything with which the ground **c**, Lv 20:25

CRAZED (1)
and stagger and be **c** because of the Jer 25:16

CREATE (10)
C in me a clean heart, O God, and Ps 51:10
Then the LORD will **c** over the whole site of Is 4:5
I form light and **c** darkness, I make Is 45:7

I make well-being and **c** calamity, Is 45:7
he did not **c** it empty, he formed it to be Is 45:18
behold, I **c** new heavens and a new earth, Is 65:17
and rejoice forever in that which I **c**; Is 65:18
for behold, I **c** Jerusalem to be a joy, and Is 65:18
divisions and **c** obstacles contrary Rom 16:17
that he might **c** in himself one new Eph 2:15

CREATED (49)
God **c** the heavens and the earth. Gn 1:1
So God **c** the great sea creatures and Gn 1:21
So God **c** man in his own image, in the Gn 1:27
image, in the image of God he **c** him; Gn 1:27
him; male and female he **c** them. Gn 1:27
heavens and the earth when they were **c**, Gn 2:4
When God **c** man, he made him in the Gn 5:1
Male and female he **c** them, and he Gn 5:2
and named them Man when they were **c**. Gn 5:2
out man whom I have **c** from the face of Gn 6:7
such as have not been **c** in all the earth Ex 34:10
the day that God **c** man on the earth, Dt 4:32
Is not he your father, who **c** you, who Dt 32:6
north and the south, you have **c** them; Ps 89:12
what vanity you have **c** all the children Ps 89:47
people yet to be **c** may praise the LORD: Ps 102:18
you send forth your Spirit, they are **c**, Ps 104:30
For he commanded and they were **c**. Ps 148:5
your eyes on high and see: who **c** these? Is 40:26
done this, the Holy One of Israel has **c** it. Is 41:20
who **c** the heavens and stretched them Is 42:5
now thus says the LORD, he who **c** you, Is 43:1
by my name, whom I **c** for my glory, Is 43:7
them both to sprout; I the LORD have **c** it. Is 45:8
I made the earth and **c** man on it; it was Is 45:12
the LORD, who **c** the heavens (he is God!), Is 45:18
They are **c** now, not long ago; before Is 48:7
I have **c** the smith who blows the fire of Is 54:16
I have also **c** the ravager to destroy; Is 54:16
For the LORD has **c** a new thing on the Jer 31:22
In the place where you were **c**, in the Ezk 21:30
that you were **c** they were prepared. Ezk 28:13
in your ways from the day you were **c**, Ezk 28:15
all one Father? Has not one God **c** us? Mal 2:10
read that he who **c** them from the Mt 19:4
of the creation that God **c** until now, Mk 13:19
Neither was man **c** for woman, but 1 Cor 11:9
c in Christ Jesus for good works, Eph 2:10
hidden for ages in God who **c** all things, Eph 3:9
c after the likeness of God in true Eph 4:24
For by him all things were **c**, in heaven Col 1:16
—all things were **c** through him and for Col 1:16
from foods that God **c** to be received 1 Tm 4:3
For everything **c** by God is good, and 1 Tm 4:4
through whom also he **c** the world. Heb 1:2
that the universe was **c** by the word of Heb 11:3
honor and power, for you **c** all things, Rv 4:11
by your will they existed and were **c**." Rv 4:11
and ever, who **c** heaven and what is in it, Rv 10:6

CREATES (2)
But if the LORD **c** something new, and Nm 16:30
forms the mountains and **c** the wind, Am 4:13

CREATING (1)
c the fruit of the lips. Peace, peace, to the Is 57:19

CREATION (19)
from all his work that he had done in **c**. Gn 2:3
trusts in his own **c** when he makes Hab 2:18
But from the beginning of **c**, 'God made Mk 10:6
beginning of the **c** that God created Mk 13:19
proclaim the gospel to the whole **c**. Mk 16:15
perceived, ever since the **c** of the world, Rom 1:20
For the **c** waits with eager longing for Rom 8:19
For the **c** was subjected to futility, not Rom 8:20
that the **c** itself will be set free from its Rom 8:21
that the whole **c** has been groaning Rom 8:22
And not only the **c**, but we ourselves, Rom 8:23
nor depth, nor anything else in all **c**, Rom 8:39
if anyone is in Christ, he is a new **c**. 2 Cor 5:17
nor uncircumcision, but a new **c**. Gal 6:15
the invisible God, the firstborn of all **c**. Col 1:15
been proclaimed in all **c** under heaven, Col 1:23
made with hands, that is, not of this **c**) Heb 9:11
as they were from the beginning of **c**." 2 Pt 3:4
true witness, the beginning of God's **c**. Rv 3:14

CREATOR (6)
Remember also your **C** in the days of Eccl 12:1
God, the **C** of the ends of the earth. Is 40:28
the LORD, your Holy One, the **C** of Israel, Is 43:15
served the creature rather than the **C**, Rom 1:25
in knowledge after the image of its **c**. Col 3:10
souls to a faithful **C** while doing good. 1 Pt 4:19

CREATURE (35)
creatures and every living **c** that moves, Gn 1:21
of life, and the man became a living **c**. Gn 2:7
whatever the man called every living **c**, Gn 2:19
according to its kind, every winged **c**. Gn 7:14
strike down every living **c** as I have Gn 8:21
and with every living **c** that is with you, Gn 9:10
you and every living **c** that is with you, Gn 9:12
and you and every living **c** of all flesh. Gn 9:15
God and every living **c** of all flesh that Gn 9:16
beast or any unclean detestable **c**, Lv 7:21
and every living **c** that moves through Lv 11:46
the waters and every **c** that swarms on Lv 11:46
and between the living **c** that may be Lv 11:47
eaten and the living **c** that may not be Lv 11:47
For the life of every **c** is its blood: its Lv 17:14
You shall not eat the blood of any **c**, Lv 17:14
for the life of every **c** is its blood. Lv 17:14
there is not his like, a **c** without fear. Jb 41:33
or some winged **c** tell the matter. Eccl 10:20
Each **c** had two wings, each of which Ezk 1:11
And each **c** had two wings covering its Ezk 1:23
every living **c** that swarms will live, Ezk 47:9
people saw the **c** hanging from his Acts 28:4
shook off the **c** into the fire and Acts 28:5
and served the **c** rather than the Rom 1:25
And no **c** is hidden from his sight, but Heb 4:13
of beast and bird, of reptile and sea **c**, Jas 3:7
the first living **c** like a lion, the second Rv 4:7
like a lion, the second living **c** like an ox, Rv 4:7
the third living **c** with the face of a man, Rv 4:7
and the fourth living **c** like an eagle in Rv 4:7
And I heard every **c** in heaven and on Rv 5:13
seal, I heard the second living **c** say, Rv 6:3
third seal, I heard the third living **c** say, Rv 6:5
I heard the voice of the fourth living **c** say, Rv 6:7

CREATURES (42)
waters swarm with swarms of living **c**, Gn 1:20
created the great sea **c** and every living Gn 1:21
bring forth living **c** according to their Gn 1:24
all swarming **c** that swarm on the earth, Gn 7:21
of the swarming **c** in the waters and of Lv 11:10
waters and of the living **c** that are in the Lv 11:10
him as food for the **c** of the wilderness. Ps 74:14
them all; the earth is full of your **c**. Ps 104:24
which teems with **c** innumerable, Ps 104:25
the earth, you great sea **c** and all deeps, Ps 148:7
their houses will be full of howling **c**; Is 13:21
of it came the likeness of four living **c**. Ezk 1:5
As for the likeness of the living **c**, their Ezk 1:13
moving to and fro among the living **c**. Ezk 1:13
And the living **c** darted to and fro, like Ezk 1:14
Now as I looked at the living **c**, I saw a Ezk 1:15
a wheel on the earth beside the living **c**, Ezk 1:15
And when the living **c** went, the wheels Ezk 1:19
and when the living **c** rose from the Ezk 1:19
spirit of the living **c** was in the wheels. Ezk 1:20
spirit of the living **c** was in the wheels. Ezk 1:21
heads of the living **c** there was the Ezk 1:22
wings of the living **c** as they touched Ezk 3:13
These were the living **c** that I saw by Ezk 10:15
the spirit of the living **c** was in them. Ezk 10:17
These were the living **c** that I saw Ezk 10:20
should be a kind of firstfruits of his **c**. Jas 1:18
like irrational animals, **c** of instinct, 2 Pt 2:12
each side of the throne, are four living **c**, Rv 4:6
And the four living **c**, each of them with Rv 4:8
And whenever the living **c** give glory and Rv 4:9
and the four living **c** and among the Rv 5:6
the four living **c** and the twenty-four Rv 5:8
throne and the living **c** and the elders the Rv 5:11
And the four living **c** said, "Amen!" and Rv 5:14
one of the four living **c** say with a voice Rv 6:1
be a voice in the midst of the four living **c**, Rv 6:6
around the elders and the four living **c**, Rv 7:11
A third of the living **c** in the sea died, and Rv 8:9
before the four living **c** and before the Rv 14:3
one of the four living **c** gave to the seven Rv 15:7
and the four living **c** fell down and Rv 19:4

CREDIT (3)
expect to receive, what **c** is that to you? Lk 6:34
I seek the fruit that increases to your **c**. Phil 4:17
For what **c** is it if, when you sin and are 1 Pt 2:20

CREDITED (1)
be accepted, neither shall it be **c** to him. Lv 7:18

CREDITOR (4)
every **c** shall release what he has lent to Dt 15:2
but the **c** has come to take my two 2 Kgs 4:1
May the **c** seize all that he has; may Ps 109:11
as with the **c**, so with the debtor. Is 24:2

CREDITORS (1)
Or which of my **c** is it to whom I have Is 50:1

CREEP (3)
all the beasts of the forest **c** about. Ps 104:20
creeping things that **c** on the ground, Ezk 38:20
are those who **c** into households and 2 Tm 3:6

CREEPING (12)
—livestock and **c** things and beasts Gn 1:24
earth and over every **c** thing that creeps Gn 1:26
man and animals and **c** things and birds Gn 6:7
kinds, of every **c** thing of the ground, Gn 6:20
and every **c** thing that creeps on the Gn 7:14
and animals and **c** things and birds Gn 7:23
animals and every **c** thing that creeps Gn 8:17
Every beast, every **c** thing, and every Gn 8:19
livestock, **c** things and flying birds! Ps 148:10
every form of **c** things and loathsome Ezk 8:10
the field and all **c** things that creep on Ezk 38:20
and the **c** things of the ground. Hos 2:18

CREEPS (8)
and everything that **c** on the ground Gn 1:25
creeping thing that **c** on the earth." Gn 1:26
and to everything that **c** on the earth, Gn 1:30
and of everything that **c** on the ground, Gn 7:8
every creeping thing that **c** on the earth, Gn 7:14
every creeping thing that **c** on the earth Gn 8:17
upon everything that **c** on the ground Gn 9:2
of anything that **c** on the ground, Dt 4:18

CREPT (1)
certain people have **c** in unnoticed who Jude 1:4

CRESCENS (1)
C has gone to Galatia, Titus to 2 Tm 4:10

CRESCENT (2)
and he took the **c** ornaments that were Jgs 8:21
besides the **c** ornaments and the Jgs 8:26

CRESCENTS (1)
of the anklets, the headbands, and the **c**; Is 3:18

CRETANS (3)
C and Arabians—we hear them Acts 2:11
One of the **C**, a prophet of their own, said, Ti 1:12
of their own, said, "**C** are always liars, Ti 1:12

CRETE (5)
sailed under the lee of **C** off Salmone. Acts 27:7
could reach Phoenix, a harbor of **C**, Acts 27:12
weighed anchor and sailed along **C**, Acts 27:13
set sail from **C** and incurred this Acts 27:21
This is why I left you in **C**, so that you Ti 1:5

CREW (2)
with all your **c** that is in your midst, Ezk 27:27
and all your **c** in your midst Ezk 27:34

CRIB (1)
its owner, and the donkey its master's **c**, Is 1:3

CRICKET (2)
locust of any kind, the **c** of any kind, Lv 11:22
The **c** shall possess all your trees and Dt 28:42

CRIED (127)
he **c** out with an exceedingly great and Gn 27:34
with me, and I **c** out with a loud voice. Gn 39:14
that I lifted up my voice and **c** out, Gn 39:15
as soon as I lifted up my voice and **c**, Gn 39:18
the people **c** to Pharaoh for bread. Gn 41:55
before all those who stood by him. He **c**, Gn 45:1
of their slavery and **c** out for help. Ex 2:23
people of Israel came and **c** to Pharaoh, Ex 5:15
and Moses **c** to the LORD about the frogs, Ex 8:12
the people of Israel **c** out to the LORD. Ex 14:10
And he **c** to the LORD, and the LORD Ex 15:25
So Moses **c** to the LORD, "What shall I do Ex 17:4
Then the people **c** out to Moses, and Nm 11:2
And Moses **c** to the LORD, "O God, Nm 12:13
And when we **c** to the LORD, he heard Nm 20:16
betrothed young woman **c** for help Dt 22:27
Then we **c** to the LORD, the God of our Dt 26:7
And when they **c** to the LORD, he put Jos 24:7
when the people of Israel **c** out to the LORD, Jgs 3:9
the people of Israel **c** out to the LORD, Jgs 3:15
Then the people of Israel **c** out to the LORD Jgs 4:3
And the people of Israel **c** out for help to Jgs 6:6
the people of Israel **c** out to the LORD Jgs 6:7
And they **c** out, "A sword for the LORD Jgs 7:20
all the army ran. They **c** out and fled. Jgs 7:21
of Mount Gerizim and **c** aloud and said to Jgs 9:7
the people of Israel **c** out to the LORD, Jgs 10:10
oppressed you, and you **c** out to me, Jgs 10:12
and told the news, all the city **c** out. 1 Sm 4:13
to Ekron, the people of Ekron **c** out, 1 Sm 5:10
And Samuel **c** out to the LORD for Israel, 1 Sm 7:9
then your fathers **c** out to the LORD 1 Sm 12:8
And they **c** out to the LORD and said, 1 Sm 12:10
angry, and he **c** to the LORD all night. 1 Sm 15:11
Samuel, she **c** out with a loud voice. 1 Sm 28:12
Then Ahimaaz **c** out to the king, 2 Sm 18:28
face, and the king **c** with a loud voice, 2 Sm 19:4
they **c** to the LORD, but he did not 2 Sm 22:42
And the man **c** against the altar by 1 Kgs 13:2

which he **c** against the altar at Bethel, 1 Kgs 13:4
And he **c** to the man of God who 1 Kgs 13:21
And he **c** to the LORD, "O LORD my 1 Kgs 17:20
child three times and **c** to the LORD, 1 Kgs 17:21
And they **c** aloud and cut 1 Kgs 18:28
passed, he **c** to the king and said, 1 Kgs 20:39
him. And Jehoshaphat **c** out. 1 Kgs 22:32
And Elisha saw it and he **c**, "My 2 Kgs 2:12
of the sons of the prophets **c** to Elisha, 2 Kgs 4:1
were eating of the stew, they **c** out, 2 Kgs 4:40
head fell into the water, and he **c** out, 2 Kgs 6:5
on the wall, a woman **c** out to him, 2 Kgs 6:26
And Athaliah tore her clothes and **c**, 2 Kgs 11:14
for they **c** out to God in the battle, 1 Chr 5:20
And they **c** to the LORD, and the 2 Chr 13:14
And Asa **c** to the LORD his God, "O 2 Chr 14:11
And Jehoshaphat **c** out, and the 2 Chr 18:31
Athaliah tore her clothes and **c**, 2 Chr 23:13
because of this and **c** to heaven. 2 Chr 32:20
they **c** with a loud voice to the LORD Neh 9:4
of their suffering they **c** out to you and Neh 9:27
Yet when they turned and **c** to you, you Neh 9:28
and he **c** out with a loud and bitter cry. Est 4:1
I delivered the poor who **c** for help, Jb 29:12
"If my land has **c** out against me and its Jb 31:38
I **c** aloud to the LORD, and he answered me Ps 3:4
upon the LORD; to my God I **c** for help. Ps 18:6
They **c** for help, but there was none to Ps 18:41
they **c** to the LORD, but he did not Ps 18:41
To you they **c** and were rescued; in you Ps 22:5
him, but has heard, when he **c** to him. Ps 22:24
O LORD my God, I **c** to you for help, and Ps 30:2
pleas for mercy when I **c** to you for help. Ps 31:22
This poor man **c**, and the LORD heard Ps 34:6
I **c** to him with my mouth, and high Ps 66:17
Then they **c** to the LORD in their trouble, Ps 107:6
Then they **c** to the LORD in their Ps 107:13
Then they **c** to the LORD in their Ps 107:19
Then they **c** to the LORD in their Ps 107:28
Then he who saw **c** out: "Upon a Is 21:8
Their heart **c** to the Lord. O wall of the Lam 2:18
"Away! Unclean!" people **c** at them. Lam 4:15
Then he **c** in my ears with a loud voice, Ezk 9:1
was left alone, I fell upon my face, and **c**, Ezk 9:8
on my face and **c** out with a loud Ezk 11:13
was, he **c** out in a tone of anguish. Dn 6:20
were afraid, and each **c** out to his god. Jon 1:5
out of the belly of Sheol I **c**, and you Jon 2:2
to whom the former prophets **c** out, Zec 1:4
Then he **c** to me, "Behold, those who go Zec 6:8
And behold, they **c** out, "What have you Mt 8:29
"It is a ghost!" and they **c** out in fear. Mt 14:26
afraid, and beginning to sink he **c** out, Mt 14:30
that Jesus was passing by, they **c** out, Mt 20:30
to be silent, but they **c** out all the more, Mt 20:31
the ninth hour Jesus **c** out with a loud Mt 27:46
And Jesus **c** out again with a loud voice Mt 27:50
with an unclean spirit. And he **c** out, Mk 1:23
they fell down before him and **c** out, Mk 3:11
they thought it was a ghost, and **c** out, Mk 6:49
the father of the child **c** out and said, Mk 9:24
But he **c** out all the more, "Son of Mk 10:48
And they **c** out again, "Crucify him." Mk 15:13
the ninth hour Jesus **c** with a loud Mk 15:34
demon, and he **c** out with a loud voice, Lk 4:33
he **c** out and fell down before him and Lk 8:28
behold, a man from the crowd **c** out, Lk 9:38
And he **c** out, "Jesus, Son of David, have Lk 18:38
But he **c** out all the more, "Son of Lk 18:39
But they all **c** out together, "Away with Lk 23:18
(John bore witness about him, and **c** out, Jn 1:15
the great day, Jesus stood up and **c** out, Jn 7:37
these things, he **c** out with a loud voice, Jn 11:43
And Jesus **c** out and said, "Whoever Jn 12:44
They **c** out again, "Not this man, but Jn 18:40
and the officers saw him, they **c** out, Jn 19:6
to release him, but the Jews **c** out, Jn 19:12
They **c** out, "Away with him, away with Jn 19:15
But they **c** out with a loud voice and Acts 7:57
to his knees he **c** out with a loud Acts 7:60
But Paul **c** with a loud voice, "Do not Acts 16:28
Now some **c** out one thing, some Acts 19:32
two hours they all **c** out with one Acts 19:34
Pharisees, he **c** out in the council, Acts 23:6
one thing that I **c** out while standing Acts 24:21
They **c** out with a loud voice, "O Rv 6:10
and **c** out as they saw the smoke of her Rv 18:18
Once more they **c** out, "Hallelujah! The Rv 19:3

CRIES (17)
And if he **c** to me, I will hear, for I am Ex 22:27
and the soul of the wounded **c** for help; Jb 24:12
Wisdom **c** aloud in the street, in the Prv 1:20
at the head of the noisy streets she **c** out; Prv 1:21
at the entrance of the portals she **c** aloud: Prv 8:3
My heart **c** out for Moab; her fugitives Is 15:5
woman who writhes and **c** out in her Is 26:17
A voice **c**: "In the wilderness prepare the Is 40:3
man of war he stirs up his zeal; he **c** out, Is 42:13
cannot move from its place. If one **c** to it, Is 46:7
The voice of the LORD **c** to the city—and it Mi 6:9
is bitter; the mighty man **c** aloud there. Zep 1:14
spirit seizes him, and he suddenly **c** out. Lk 9:39
demanding with loud **c** that he should Lk 23:23
And Isaiah **c** out concerning Israel: Rom 9:27
and supplications, with loud **c** and tears, Heb 5:7
and the **c** of the harvesters have reached Jas 5:4

CRIME (5)
a person for any **c** or for any wrong Dt 19:15
has committed a **c** punishable by death Dt 21:22
For that would be a heinous **c**; that Jb 31:11
For their **c** will they escape? In wrath Ps 56:7
a matter of wrongdoing or vicious **c**, Acts 18:14

CRIMES (1)
land is full of bloody **c** and the city is Ezk 7:23

CRIMINAL (1)
suffering, bound with chains as a **c**. 2 Tm 2:9

CRIMINALS (3)
Two others, who were **c**, were led away Lk 23:32
there they crucified him, and the **c**, Lk 23:33
One of the **c** who were hanged railed at Lk 23:39

CRIMSON (4)
and in purple, **c**, and blue fabrics, 2 Chr 2:7
blue, and **c** fabrics and fine linen, 2 Chr 2:14
and purple and **c** fabrics and fine 2 Chr 3:14
though they are red like **c**, they shall Is 1:18

CRIMSONED (1)
from Edom, in **c** garments from Bozrah, Is 63:1

CRINGE (1)
who hate the LORD would **c** toward him, Ps 81:15

CRINGING (3)
Foreigners came **c** to me; as soon as 2 Sm 22:45
obeyed me; foreigners came **c** to me. Ps 18:44
power that your enemies come **c** to you. Ps 66:3

CRIPPLED (10)
of Saul, had a son who was **c** in his feet. 2 Sm 4:4
a son of Jonathan; he is **c** in his feet." 2 Sm 9:3
with them the lame, the blind, the **c**, Mt 15:30
saw the mute speaking, the **c** healthy, Mt 15:31
for you to enter life **c** or lame than with Mt 18:8
you to enter life **c** than with two hands Mk 9:43
you give a feast, invite the poor, the **c**, Lk 14:13
in the poor and **c** and blind and lame.' Lk 14:21
a good deed done to a **c** man, Acts 4:9
He was **c** from birth and had never Acts 14:8

CRISPUS (2)
C, the ruler of the synagogue, believed Acts 18:8
none of you except **C** and Gaius, 1 Cor 1:14

CRITICIZED (1)
the circumcision party **c** him, Acts 11:2

CROCUS (1)
shall rejoice and blossom like the **c**; Is 35:1

CROOKED (25)
they are a **c** and twisted generation. Dt 32:5
and with the **c** you make yourself 2 Sm 22:27
and with the **c** you make yourself seem Ps 18:26
turn aside to their **c** ways the LORD will Ps 125:5
men whose paths are **c**, and who are Prv 2:15
Put away from you **c** speech, and put Prv 4:24
wicked man, goes about with **c** speech, Prv 6:12
there is nothing twisted or **c** in them. Prv 8:8
who makes his ways **c** will be found Prv 10:9
Those of **c** heart are an abomination Prv 11:20
A man of **c** heart does not discover Prv 17:20
than one who is **c** in speech and is Prv 19:1
The way of the guilty is **c**, but the Prv 21:8
and snares are in the way of the **c**; Prv 22:5
than a rich man who is **c** in his ways. Prv 28:6
but he who is **c** in his ways will Prv 28:18
What is **c** cannot be made straight, Eccl 1:15
make straight what he has made **c**? Eccl 7:13
their paths; they have made their roads **c**; Is 59:8
of stones; he has made my paths **c**. Lam 3:9
detest justice and make **c** all that is Mi 3:9
low, and the **c** shall become straight, Lk 3:5
yourselves from this **c** generation." Acts 2:40
not stop making **c** the straight paths Acts 13:10
the midst of a **c** and twisted generation, Phil 2:15

CROOKEDNESS (1)
but the **c** of the treacherous destroys Prv 11:3

CROP (8)
He shall remove its **c** with its contents Lv 1:16
if we may not sow or gather in our **c**?' Lv 25:20
it will produce a **c** sufficient for three Lv 25:21
you will be eating some of the old **c**; Lv 25:22
until the ninth year, when its **c** arrives. Lv 25:22
the **c** that you have sown and the yield of Dt 22:9
thresh in hope of sharing in the **c**. 1 Cor 9:10
and produces a **c** useful to those for Heb 6:7

CROPS (8)
according to the number of years for **c**. Lv 25:15
is the number of the **c** that he is selling Lv 25:16
For whenever the Israelites planted **c**, the Jgs 6:3
we will forego the **c** of the seventh Neh 10:31
He gave their **c** to the destroying locust Ps 78:46
but abundant **c** come by the strength Prv 14:4
I do, for I have nowhere to store my **c**?' Lk 12:17
ought to have the first share of the **c**. 2 Tm 2:6

CROSS (50)
the ascent of Akrabbim, and **c** to Zin, Nm 34:4
When you **c** the Jordan into the land Nm 35:10
'Today you are to **c** the border of Moab Dt 2:18
men of valor shall **c** over armed before Dt 3:18
he swore that I should not **c** the Jordan, Dt 4:21
you are to **c** over the Jordan today, to go in Dt 9:1
For you are to **c** over the Jordan to go in Dt 11:31
And on the day you **c** over the Jordan to Dt 27:2
when you **c** over to enter the land that Dt 27:3
"Why did you **c** over to fight against the Jgs 12:1
"Behold, we will **c** over to the men, 1 Sm 14:8
too exhausted to **c** the brook Besor. 1 Sm 30:10
as he was about to **c** the Jordan, 2 Sm 19:18
you go out and **c** the brook Kidron, 1 Kgs 2:37
the merchants of Sidon, who **c** the sea, Is 23:2
C over to Tarshish; wail, O inhabitants of Is 23:6
C over your land like the Nile, O Is 23:10
arise, **c** over to Cyprus, even there you Is 23:12
For **c** to the coasts of Cyprus and see, or Jer 2:10
and set out to **c** over to the Ammonites. Jer 41:10
enter into Gilgal or **c** over to Beersheba; Am 5:5
does not take his **c** and follow me is Mt 10:38
and take up his **c** and follow me. Mt 16:24
compelled this man to carry his **c**. Mt 27:32
the Son of God, come down from the **c**." Mt 27:40
let him come down now from the **c**, Mt 27:42
and take up his **c** and follow me. Mk 8:34
of Alexander and Rufus, to carry his **c**. Mk 15:21
yourself, and come down from the **c**!" Mk 15:30
down now from the **c** that we may see Mk 15:32
and take up his **c** daily and follow me. Lk 9:23
not bear his own **c** and come after me Lk 14:27
able, and none may **c** from there to us.' Lk 16:26
the country, and laid on him the **c**, Lk 23:26
and he went out, bearing his own **c**, to Jn 19:17
wrote an inscription and put it on the **c**. Jn 19:19
but standing by the **c** of Jesus were his Jn 19:25
not remain on the **c** on the Sabbath (for Jn 19:31
And when he wished to **c** to Achaia, Acts 18:27
lest the **c** of Christ be emptied of its 1 Cor 1:17
For the word of the **c** is folly to those 1 Cor 1:18
the offense of the **c** has been removed. Gal 5:11
not be persecuted for the **c** of Christ. Gal 6:12
boast except in the **c** of our Lord Jesus Gal 6:14
both to God in one body through the **c**, Eph 2:16
to the point of death, even death on a **c**. Phil 2:8
walk as enemies of the **c** of Christ. Phil 3:18
making peace by the blood of his **c**. Col 1:20
This he set aside, nailing it to the **c**. Col 2:14
that was set before him endured the **c**, Heb 12:2

CROSSED (31)
he had and arose and **c** the Euphrates, Gn 31:21
for with only my staff I **c** this Jordan, Gn 32:10
children, and **c** the ford of the Jabbok. Gn 32:22
Kadesh-barnea until we **c** the brook Dt 2:14
And when you have **c** over the Jordan, Dt 27:4
"When you have **c** over the Jordan, Dt 27:12
the people of Israel until they had **c** over, Jos 5:1
and they **c** the Jordan and encamped in Jgs 6:33
Gideon came to the Jordan and **c** over, Jgs 8:4
And the Ammonites **c** the Jordan to Jgs 10:9
So Jephthah **c** over to the Ammonites Jgs 11:32
and they **c** to Zaphon and said to Jgs 12:1
in my hand and **c** over against the Jgs 12:3
and some Hebrews **c** the fords of the 1 Sm 13:7
They **c** the Jordan, and marching the 2 Sm 2:29
Israel together and **c** the Jordan and 2 Sm 10:17
by, and the king **c** the brook Kidron, 2 Sm 15:23
with him, and they **c** the Jordan. 2 Sm 17:22
was left who had not **c** the Jordan. 2 Sm 17:22
And Absalom **c** the Jordan with all 2 Sm 17:24
and they **c** the ford to bring over the 2 Sm 19:18
They **c** the Jordan and began from 2 Sm 24:5
When they had **c**, Elijah said to 2 Kgs 2:9
are the men who **c** the Jordan in the 1 Chr 12:15
Israel together and **c** the Jordan and 1 Chr 19:17
they have **c** over the pass; at Geba they Is 10:29
getting into a boat he **c** over and came to Mt 9:1
And when they had **c** over, they came Mt 14:34
And when Jesus had **c** again in the boat Mk 5:21

with loud cries that he should be **c**. Lk 23:23
is called The Skull, there they **c** him, Lk 23:33
of sinful men and be **c** and on the third Lk 24:7
to be condemned to death, and **c** him. Lk 24:20
So he delivered him over to them to be **c**. Jn 19:16
There they **c** him, and with him two Jn 19:18
place where Jesus was **c** was near the Jn 19:20
When the soldiers had **c** Jesus, they Jn 19:23
of the other who had been **c** with him. Jn 19:32
place where he was **c** there was a Jn 19:41
you **c** and killed by the hands of Acts 2:23
and Christ, this Jesus whom you **c**." Acts 2:36
Jesus Christ of Nazareth, whom you **c**, Acts 4:10
our old self was **c** with him in order Rom 6:6
Christ divided? Was Paul **c** for you? 1 Cor 1:13
but we preach Christ **c**, a stumbling 1 Cor 1:23
you except Jesus Christ and him **c**. 1 Cor 2:2
they would not have **c** the Lord of 1 Cor 2:8
For he was **c** in weakness, but lives 2 Cor 13:4
I have been **c** with Christ. It is no longer Gal 2:20
Jesus Christ was publicly portrayed as **c**. Gal 3:1
to Christ Jesus have **c** the flesh with its Gal 5:24
by which the world has been **c** to me, Gal 6:14
and Egypt, where their Lord was **c**. Rv 11:8

CRUCIFY (13)
some of whom you will kill and **c**, Mt 23:34
on him and led him away to **c** him. Mt 27:31
And they cried out again, "**C** him." Mk 15:13
they shouted all the more, "**C** him." Mk 15:14
him. And they led him out to **c** him. Mk 15:20
they kept shouting, "**C**, crucify him!" Lk 23:21
they kept shouting, "Crucify, **c** him!" Lk 23:21
officers saw him, they cried out, "**C** him, Jn 19:6
him, **c** him!" Pilate said to them, Jn 19:6
them, "Take him yourselves and **c** him, Jn 19:6
to release you and authority to **c** you?" Jn 19:10
with him, **c** him!" Pilate said to them, Jn 19:15
"Shall I **c** your King?" The chief priests Jn 19:15

CRUCIFYING (1)
since they are **c** once again the Son of Heb 6:6

CRUDE (1)
filthiness nor foolish talk nor **c** joking, Eph 5:4

CRUEL (14)
for it is fierce, and their wrath, for it is **c**! Gn 49:7
of serpents and the **c** venom of asps. Dt 32:33
You have turned **c** to me; with the Jb 30:21
from the grasp of the unjust and **c** man. Ps 71:4
David his servant from the **c** sword. Ps 144:10
himself, but a **c** man hurts himself. Prv 11:17
beast, but the mercy of the wicked is **c**. Prv 12:10
and a **c** messenger will be sent against Prv 17:11
Wrath is **c**, anger is overwhelming, but Prv 27:4
lacks understanding is a **c** oppressor, Prv 28:16
comes, **c**, with wrath and fierce anger, Is 13:9
javelin; they are **c** and have no mercy; Jer 6:23
spear; they are **c** and have no mercy. Jer 50:42
daughter of my people has become **c**, Lam 4:3

CRUELLY (3)
the people of Israel **c** for twenty years. Jgs 4:3
She deals **c** with her young, as if they Jb 39:16
over to them and they deal **c** with me." Jer 38:19

CRUELTIES (1)
And Asa inflicted **c** upon some of 2 Chr 16:10

CRUMBLES (1)
"But the mountain falls and **c** away, Jb 14:18

CRUMBLY (2)
And all their provisions were dry and **c**. Jos 9:5
to you, but now, behold, it is dry and **c**. Jos 9:12

CRUMBS (3)
hurls down his crystals of ice like **c**; Ps 147:17
the dogs eat the **c** that fall from their Mt 15:27
under the table eat the children's **c**." Mk 7:28

CRUSH (23)
it shall **c** the forehead of Moab and Nm 24:17
c the loins of his adversaries, of those Dt 33:11
is, cast lots), to **c** and to destroy them. Est 9:24
that it would please God to **c** me, that he Jb 6:9
that a foot may **c** them and that the Jb 39:15
of the needy, and **c** the oppressor! Ps 72:4
I will **c** his foes before him and strike Ps 89:23
They **c** your people, O LORD, and afflict Ps 94:5
he is poor, or **c** the afflicted at the gate, Prv 22:22
C a fool in a mortar with a pestle Prv 27:22
Does one **c** grain for bread? No, he does Is 28:28
over it with his horses, he does not **c** it. Is 28:28
shall thresh the mountains and **c** them, Is 41:15
Yet it was the will of the LORD to **c** him; Is 53:10
against me to **c** my young men; Lam 1:15
To **c** underfoot all the prisoners of the Lam 3:34
crushes, it shall break and **c** all these. Dn 2:40
who oppress the poor, who **c** the needy, Am 4:1

of his king, and they shall **c** the land, Zec 11:6
when it falls on anyone, it will **c** him." Mt 21:44
because of the crowd, lest they **c** him, Mk 3:9
when it falls on anyone, it will **c** him." Lk 20:18
of peace will soon **c** Satan under your Rom 16:20

CRUSHED (38)
fresh ears, roasted with fire, **c** new grain. Lv 2:14
portion some of the **c** grain and some of Lv 2:16
itching disease or scabs or **c** testicles. Lv 21:20
its testicles bruised or **c** or torn or cut Lv 22:24
made, and burned it with fire and **c** it, Dt 9:21
one whose testicles are **c** or whose male Dt 23:1
be only oppressed and **c** continually, Dt 28:33
mallet; she struck Sisera; she **c** his head; Jgs 5:26
on Abimelech's head and **c** his skull. Jgs 9:53
and they **c** and oppressed the people of Jgs 10:8
I **c** them and stamped them down 2 Sm 22:43
cut timber, 20,000 cors of **c** wheat, 2 Chr 2:10
Nation was **c** by nation and city by 2 Chr 15:6
Asa cut down her image, **c** it, and 2 Chr 15:16
is in the dust, who are **c** like the moth. Jb 4:19
they are **c** in the gate, and there is no one Jb 5:4
For he has **c** and abandoned the poor; Jb 20:19
and the arms of the fatherless were **c**. Jb 22:9
them in the night, and they are **c**. Jb 34:25
The helpless are **c**, sink down, and fall Ps 10:10
brokenhearted and saves the **c** in spirit. Ps 34:18
I am feeble and **c**; I groan because of the Ps 38:8
You **c** the heads of Leviathan; you gave Ps 74:14
You **c** Rahab like a carcass; you Ps 89:10
my soul; he has **c** my life to the ground; Ps 143:3
but by sorrow of heart the spirit is **c**. Prv 15:13
but a **c** spirit dries up the bones. Prv 17:22
sickness, but a **c** spirit who can bear? Prv 18:14
with a pestle along with **c** grain, Prv 27:22
who are the pillars of the land will be **c**, Is 19:10
of the altars like chalkstones **c** to pieces, Is 27:9
he was **c** for our iniquities; Is 53:5
and from one that is **c** a viper is hatched. Is 59:5
Babylon has devoured me; he has **c** me; Jer 51:34
made you desolate and **c** you from all Ezk 36:3
Ephraim is oppressed, **c** in judgment, Hos 5:11
You **c** the head of the house of the Hab 3:13
are afflicted in every way, but not **c**; 2 Cor 4:8

CRUSHES (2)
For he **c** me with a tempest and Jb 9:17
And like iron that **c**, it shall break and Dn 2:40

CRUSHING (2)
net; you laid a **c** burden on our backs; Ps 66:11
What do you mean by **c** my people, by Is 3:15

CRY (174)
great and bitter **c** and said to Gn 27:34
Their **c** for rescue from slavery came up Ex 2:23
and have heard their **c** because of their Ex 3:7
the **c** of the people of Israel has come to Ex 3:9
Therefore they **c**, 'Let us go and offer Ex 5:8
shall be a great **c** throughout all the Ex 11:6
And there was a great **c** in Egypt, for Ex 12:30
said to Moses, "Why do you **c** to me? Ex 14:15
do mistreat them, and they **c** out to me, Ex 22:23
cry out to me, I will surely hear their **c**, Ex 22:23
victory, or the sound of the **c** of defeat, Ex 32:18
he shall cover his upper lip and **c** out, Lv 13:45
all the congregation raised a loud **c**, Nm 14:1
who were around them fled at their **c**, Nm 16:34
and he **c** to the LORD against you, Dt 15:9
because she did not **c** for help though Dt 22:24
on it), lest he **c** against you to the LORD, Dt 24:15
Go and **c** out to the gods whom you Jgs 10:14
and the **c** of the city went up to 1 Sm 5:12
"Do not cease to **c** out to the LORD our 1 Sm 7:8
that day you will **c** out because of 1 Sm 8:18
because their **c** has come to me." 1 Sm 9:16
to the battle line, shouting the war **c**. 1 Sm 17:20
right have I, then, to **c** to the king?" 2 Sm 19:28
my voice, and my **c** came to his ears. 2 Sm 22:7
listening to the **c** and to the prayer 1 Kgs 8:28
mocked them, saying, "**C** aloud, 1 Kgs 18:27
about sunset a **c** went through the 1 Kgs 22:36
listening to the **c** and to the prayer 2 Chr 6:19
in this house—and **c** out to you in 2 Chr 20:9
Egypt and heard their **c** at the Red Sea, Neh 9:9
and he cried out with a loud and bitter **c**. Est 4:1
night be barren; let no joyful **c** enter it. Jb 3:7
and let my **c** find no resting place. Jb 16:18
Behold, I **c** out, 'Violence!' but I am not Jb 19:7
Will God hear his **c** when distress comes Jb 27:9
I **c** to you for help and you do not Jb 30:20
his hand, and in his disaster **c** for help? Jb 30:24
stand up in the assembly and **c** for help. Jb 30:28
so that they caused the **c** of the poor to Jb 34:28
and he heard the **c** of the afflicted— Jb 34:28
the multitude of oppressions people **c** out; Jb 35:9

There they **c** out, but he does not Jb 35:12
Surely God does not hear an empty **c**, Jb 35:13
they do not **c** for help when he binds Jb 36:13
Will your **c** for help avail to keep you Jb 36:19
when its young ones **c** to God for help, Jb 38:41
Give attention to the sound of my **c**, my Ps 5:2
he does not forget the **c** of the afflicted. Ps 9:12
Hear a just cause, O LORD; attend to my **c**! Ps 17:1
voice, and my **c** to him reached his ears. Ps 18:6
O my God, I **c** by day, but you do not Ps 22:2
Hear, O LORD, when I **c** aloud; be Ps 27:7
pleas for mercy, when I **c** to you for help, Ps 28:2
the forests bare, and in his temple all **c**, Ps 29:9
To you, O LORD, I **c**, and to the Lord I Ps 30:8
righteous and his ears toward their **c**. Ps 34:15
When the righteous **c** for help, the LORD Ps 34:17
my prayer, O LORD, and give ear to my **c**; Ps 39:12
LORD; he inclined to me and heard my **c**. Ps 40:1
I **c** out to God Most High, to God who Ps 57:2
Hear my **c**, O God, listen to my prayer; Ps 61:1
I **c** aloud to God, aloud to God, and he Ps 77:1
me, O Lord, for to you do I **c** all the day. Ps 86:3
I **c** out day and night before you. Ps 88:1
before you; incline your ear to my **c**! Ps 88:2
But I, O LORD, **c** to you; in the morning Ps 88:13
He shall **c** to me, 'You are my Father, Ps 89:26
prayer, O LORD; let my **c** come to you! Ps 102:1
their distress, when he heard their **c**. Ps 106:44
With my whole heart I **c**; answer me, Ps 119:145
I rise before dawn and **c** for help; I Ps 119:147
Let my **c** come before you, O LORD; Ps 119:169
Out of the depths I **c** to you, O LORD! Ps 130:1
With my voice I **c** out to the LORD; with Ps 142:1
I **c** to you, O LORD; I say, "You are my Ps 142:5
Attend to my **c**, for I am brought very Ps 142:6
may there be no **c** of distress in our Ps 144:14
he also hears their **c** and saves them. Ps 145:19
food, and to the young ravens that **c**. Ps 147:9
I call, and my **c** is to the children of man. Prv 8:4
closes his ear to the **c** of the poor will Prv 21:13
daughters; "Give" and "Give," they **c**. Prv 30:15
the boy knows how to **c** 'My father' or 'My Is 8:4
C aloud, O daughter of Gallim! Give Is 10:30
a bare hill raise a signal; **c** aloud to them; Is 13:2
Hyenas will **c** in its towers, and jackals Is 13:22
Wail, O gate; **c** out, O city; melt in fear, Is 14:31
Heshbon and Elealeh **c** out; their voice is Is 15:4
the armed men of Moab **c** aloud; Is 15:4
to Horonaim they raise a **c** of destruction; Is 15:5
For a **c** has gone around the land of Is 15:8
When they **c** to the LORD because of Is 19:20
gracious to you at the sound of your **c**. Is 30:19
Behold, their heroes **c** in the streets; the Is 33:7
the wild goat shall **c** to his fellow; Is 34:14
and **c** to her that her warfare is ended, Is 40:2
A voice says, "**C**!" And I said, "What shall Is 40:6
I said, "What shall I **c**?" All flesh is grass, Is 40:6
He will not **c** aloud or lift up his voice, or Is 42:2
now I will **c** out like a woman in labor; Is 42:14
break forth into singing and **c** aloud, you Is 54:1
When you **c** out, let your collection of Is 57:13
"**C** aloud; do not hold back; lift up your Is 58:1
you shall **c**, and he will say, 'Here I am.' Is 58:9
but you shall **c** out for pain of heart and Is 65:14
sound of weeping and the **c** of distress. Is 65:19
c aloud and say, 'Assemble, and let us go Jer 4:5
For I heard a **c** as of a woman in labor, Jer 4:31
the **c** of the daughter of Zion gasping for Jer 4:31
people, or lift up a **c** or prayer for them, Jer 7:16
the **c** of the daughter of my people from Jer 8:19
cannot escape. Though they **c** to me, Jer 11:11
of Jerusalem will go and **c** to the gods to Jer 11:12
or lift up a **c** or prayer on their behalf, Jer 11:14
with you; they are in full **c** after you; Jer 12:6
ground, and the **c** of Jerusalem goes up. Jer 14:2
they fast, I will not hear their **c**, Jer 14:12
May a **c** be heard from their houses, Jer 18:22
For whenever I speak, I **c** out, I shout, Jer 20:8
let him hear a **c** in the morning and an Jer 20:16
"Go up to Lebanon, and **c** out, and lift Jer 22:20
c out from Abarim, for all your lovers Jer 22:20
"Wail, you shepherds, and **c** out, and Jer 25:34
A voice—the **c** of the shepherds, and Jer 25:36
We have heard a **c** of panic, of terror, Jer 30:5
Why do you **c** out over your hurt? Jer 30:15
shame, and the earth is full of your **c**; Jer 46:12
Men shall **c** out, and every inhabitant of Jer 47:2
A **c** from Horonaim, 'Desolation and Jer 48:3
destroyed; her little ones have made a **c**. Jer 48:4
heard the distressed **c** of destruction. Jer 48:5
to shame, for it is broken; wail and **c**! Jer 48:20
I wail for Moab; I **c** out for all Moab; Jer 48:31
will cause the battle **c** to be heard Jer 49:2
waste! **C** out, O daughters of Rabbah! Jer 49:3
the sound of their **c** shall be heard at Jer 49:21

from them, and men shall **c** to them: Jer 49:29
and her **c** shall be heard among the Jer 50:46
"A voice! A **c** from Babylon! The noise Jer 51:54
They **c** to their mothers, "Where is Lam 2:12
hiss, they gnash their teeth, they **c**: Lam 2:16
"Arise, **c** out in the night, at the Lam 2:19
though I call and **c** for help, he shuts Lam 3:8
not close your ear to my **c** for help!' Lam 3:56
And though they **c** in my ears with a Ezk 8:18
C out and wail, son of man, for it is Ezk 21:12
At the sound of the **c** of your pilots the Ezk 27:28
aloud over you and **c** out bitterly. Ezk 27:30
They do not **c** to me from the heart, but Hos 7:14
To me they **c**, My God, we—Israel— Hos 8:2
the LORD your God, and **c** out to the LORD. Jl 1:14
Does a young lion **c** out from his den, Am 3:4
Then they will **c** to the LORD, but he will Mi 3:4
who **c** "Peace" when they have something Mi 3:5
Now why do you **c** aloud? Is there no Mi 4:9
"Halt! Halt!" they **c**, but none turns back. Na 2:8
O LORD, how long shall I **c** for help, and Hab 1:2
Or **c** to you "Violence!" and you will not Hab 1:2
For the stone will **c** out from the wall, Hab 2:11
"a **c** will be heard from the Fish Gate, Zep 1:10
blast and battle **c** against the fortified Zep 1:16
who talked with me said to me, '**C** out, Zec 1:14
C out again, Thus says the LORD of Zec 1:17
He will not quarrel or **c** aloud, nor will Mt 12:19
But at midnight there was a **c**, 'Here is Mt 25:6
of Nazareth, he began to **c** out and say, Mk 10:47
Jesus uttered a loud **c** and breathed his Mk 15:37
and she exclaimed with a loud **c**, Lk 1:42
to his elect, who **c** to him day and night? Lk 18:7
silent, the very stones would **c** out." Lk 19:40
of adoption as sons, by whom we **c**, Rom 8:15
break forth and **c** aloud, you who are Gal 4:27
from heaven with a **c** of command, 1 Thes 4:16

CRYING (34)
your brother's blood is **c** to me from the Gn 4:10
saw the child, and behold, the baby was **c**. Ex 2:6
and went away, **c** aloud as she went. 2 Sm 13:19
and wept before him, **c**, "My father, 2 Kgs 13:14
I am weary with my **c** out; my throat is Ps 69:3
"The voice of one **c** in the wilderness: Mt 3:3
two blind men followed him, **c** aloud, Mt 9:27
from that region came out and was **c**, Mt 15:22
her away, for she is **c** out after us." Mt 15:23
and the children **c** out in the temple, Mt 21:15
the voice of one **c** in the wilderness: Mk 1:3
convulsing him and **c** out with a loud Mk 1:26
he was always **c** out and bruising Mk 5:5
And **c** out with a loud voice, he said, Mk 5:7
And after **c** out and convulsing him Mk 9:26
"The voice of one **c** in the wilderness: Lk 3:4
c, "You are the Son of God!" But he Lk 4:41
the voice of one **c** out in the wilderness, Jn 1:23
trees and went out to meet him, **c** out, Jn 12:13
who were possessed, **c** with a loud voice, Acts 8:7
and rushed out into the crowd, **c** out, Acts 14:14
She followed Paul and us, **c** out, Acts 16:17
this they were enraged and were **c** out, Acts 19:28
c out, "Men of Israel, help! This is the Acts 21:28
the mob of the people followed, **c** out, Acts 21:36
of his Son into our hearts, **c**, "Abba! Gal 4:6
kept back by fraud, are **c** out against you, Jas 5:4
and **c** out with a loud voice, "Salvation Rv 7:10
and I heard an eagle **c** with a loud voice Rv 8:13
was pregnant and was **c** out in birth Rv 12:2
heads as they wept and mourned, **c** out, Rv 18:19
of a great multitude in heaven, **c** out, Rv 19:1
sound of mighty peals of thunder, **c** out, Rv 19:6
be mourning nor **c** nor pain anymore, Rv 21:4

CRYSTAL (5)
mention shall be made of coral or of **c**; Jb 28:18
expanse, shining like awe-inspiring **c**, Ezk 1:22
there was as it were a sea of glass, like **c**. Rv 4:6
most rare jewel, like a jasper, clear as **c**. Rv 21:11
the river of the water of life, bright as **c**, Rv 22:1

CRYSTALS (1)
He hurls down his **c** of ice like Ps 147:17

CUB (2)
Judah is a lion's **c**; from the prey, my Gn 49:9
"Dan is a lion's **c** that leaps from Dt 33:22

CUBIT (38)
for the ark, and finish it to a **c** above, Gn 6:16
be its length, a **c** and a half its breadth, Ex 25:10
breadth, and a **c** and a half its height. Ex 25:10
length, and a **c** and a half its breadth. Ex 25:17
shall be its length, a **c** its breadth, Ex 25:23
breadth, and a **c** and a half its height. Ex 25:23
of the curtains, the **c** on the one side, Ex 26:13
the one side, and the **c** on the other side, Ex 26:13
and a **c** and a half the breadth of each Ex 26:16
A **c** shall be its length, and a cubit its Ex 30:2
shall be its length, and a **c** its breadth. Ex 30:2
and a **c** and a half the breadth of each Ex 36:21
was its length, a **c** and a half its breadth, Ex 37:1
its breadth, and a **c** and a half its height. Ex 37:1
its length, and a **c** and a half its breadth. Ex 37:6
cubits was its length, a **c** its breadth, Ex 37:10
breadth, and a **c** and a half its height. Ex 37:10
Its length was a **c**, and its breadth was a Ex 37:25
was a cubit, and its breadth was a **c**. Ex 37:25
breadth, according to the common **c**.) Dt 3:11
a sword with two edges, a **c** in length, Jgs 3:16
a crown that projected upward one **c**. 1 Kgs 7:31
a pedestal is made, a **c** and a half deep. 1 Kgs 7:31
height of a wheel was a **c** and a half. 1 Kgs 7:32
there was a round band half a **c** high; 1 Kgs 7:35
each being a **c** and a handbreadth in Ezk 40:5
the side rooms, one **c** on either side. Ezk 40:12
the burnt offering, a **c** and a half long, Ezk 40:42
a half long, and a **c** and a half broad, Ezk 40:42
and a half broad, and one **c** high, Ezk 40:42
altar by cubits (the **c** being a cubit Ezk 43:13
cubit being a **c** and a handbreadth): Ezk 43:13
base shall be one **c** high and one Ezk 43:13
be one cubit high and one **c** broad, Ezk 43:13
two cubits, with a breadth of one **c**; Ezk 43:14
four cubits, with a breadth of one **c**; Ezk 43:14
with a rim around it half a **c** broad, Ezk 43:17
broad, and its base one **c** all around. Ezk 43:17

CUBITS (244)
the length of the ark 300 **c**, its breadth Gn 6:15
of the ark 300 cubits, its breadth 50 **c**, Gn 6:15
breadth 50 cubits, and its height 30 **c**. Gn 6:15
covering them fifteen **c** deep. Gn 7:20
Two **c** and a half shall be its length, a Ex 25:10
Two **c** and a half shall be its length, Ex 25:17
Two **c** shall be its length, a cubit its Ex 25:23
of each curtain shall be twenty-eight **c**, Ex 26:2
and the breadth of each curtain four **c**; Ex 26:2
length of each curtain shall be thirty **c**, Ex 26:8
and the breadth of each curtain four **c**. Ex 26:8
Ten **c** shall be the length of a frame, Ex 26:16
wood, five **c** long and five cubits broad. Ex 27:1
wood, five cubits long and five **c** broad. Ex 27:1
be square, and its height shall be three **c**. Ex 27:1
twined linen a hundred **c** long for one Ex 27:9
shall be hangings a hundred **c** long, Ex 27:11
side there shall be hangings for fifty **c**, Ex 27:12
on the front to the east shall be fifty **c**. Ex 27:13
the one side of the gate shall be fifteen **c**, Ex 27:14
side the hangings shall be fifteen **c**, Ex 27:15
there shall be a screen twenty **c** long, Ex 27:16
of the court shall be a hundred **c**, Ex 27:18
the breadth fifty, and the height five **c**, Ex 27:18
be square, and two **c** shall be its height. Ex 30:2
of each curtain was twenty-eight **c**, Ex 36:9
and the breadth of each curtain four **c**. Ex 36:9
length of each curtain was thirty **c**, Ex 36:15
and the breadth of each curtain four **c**. Ex 36:15
Ten **c** was the length of a frame, and a Ex 36:21
Two **c** and a half was its length, a cubit Ex 37:1
Two **c** and a half was its length, and a Ex 37:6
Two **c** was its length, a cubit its Ex 37:10
It was square, and two **c** was its height. Ex 37:25
Five **c** was its length, and five cubits its Ex 38:1
was its length, and five **c** its breadth. Ex 38:1
It was square, and three **c** was its height. Ex 38:1
were of fine twined linen, a hundred **c**; Ex 38:9
there were hangings of a hundred **c**, Ex 38:11
the west side were hangings of fifty **c**, Ex 38:12
And for the front to the east, fifty **c**. Ex 38:13
for one side of the gate were fifteen **c**, Ex 38:14
of the court were hangings of fifteen **c**, Ex 38:15
It was twenty **c** long and five cubits Ex 38:18
cubits long and five **c** high in its Ex 38:18
and about two **c** above the ground. Nm 11:31
city outward a thousand **c** all around. Nm 35:4
city, on the east side two thousand **c**, Nm 35:5
and on the south side two thousand **c**, Nm 35:5
and on the west side two thousand **c**, Nm 35:5
and on the north side two thousand **c**, Nm 35:5
Nine **c** was its length, and four cubits its Dt 3:11
was its length, and four **c** its breadth, Dt 3:11
you and it, about 2,000 **c** in length. Jos 3:4
whose height was six **c** and a span. 1 Sm 17:4
built for the LORD was sixty **c** long, 1 Kgs 6:2
was sixty cubits long, twenty **c** wide, 1 Kgs 6:2
twenty cubits wide, and thirty **c** high. 1 Kgs 6:2
nave of the house was twenty **c** long, 1 Kgs 6:3
and ten **c** deep in front of the house. 1 Kgs 6:3
The lowest story was five **c** broad, the 1 Kgs 6:6
broad, the middle one was six **c** broad, 1 Kgs 6:6
and the third was seven **c** broad. 1 Kgs 6:6
against the whole house, five **c** high, 1 Kgs 6:10
He built twenty **c** of the rear of the 1 Kgs 6:16
the inner sanctuary, was forty **c** long. 1 Kgs 6:17
inner sanctuary was twenty **c** long, 1 Kgs 6:20
twenty cubits long, twenty **c** wide, 1 Kgs 6:20
cubits wide, and twenty **c** high, 1 Kgs 6:20
of olivewood, each ten **c** high. 1 Kgs 6:23
Five **c** was the length of one wing of 1 Kgs 6:24
and five **c** the length of the other wing 1 Kgs 6:24
it was ten **c** from the tip of one wing 1 Kgs 6:24
other cherub also measured ten **c**; 1 Kgs 6:25
The height of one cherub was ten **c**, 1 Kgs 6:26
was a hundred **c** and its breadth 1 Kgs 7:2
and its breadth fifty **c** and its height 1 Kgs 7:2
fifty cubits and its height thirty **c**, 1 Kgs 7:2
its length was fifty **c**, and its breadth 1 Kgs 7:6
fifty cubits, and its breadth thirty **c**. 1 Kgs 7:6
huge stones, stones of eight and ten **c**. 1 Kgs 7:10
Eighteen **c** was the height of one 1 Kgs 7:15
line of twelve **c** measured its 1 Kgs 7:15
height of the one capital was five **c**, 1 Kgs 7:16
height of the other capital was five **c**. 1 Kgs 7:16
the vestibule were of lily-work, four **c**. 1 Kgs 7:19
was round, ten **c** from brim to brim, 1 Kgs 7:23
from brim to brim, and five **c** high, 1 Kgs 7:23
line of thirty **c** measured its 1 Kgs 7:23
Under its brim were gourds, for ten **c**, 1 Kgs 7:24
Each stand was four **c** long, four 1 Kgs 7:27
was four cubits long, four **c** wide, 1 Kgs 7:27
four cubits wide, and three **c** high. 1 Kgs 7:27
baths, each basin measured four **c**, 1 Kgs 7:38
of Jerusalem for four hundred **c**, 2 Kgs 14:13
of the one pillar was eighteen **c**, 2 Kgs 25:17
height of the capital was three **c**. 2 Kgs 25:17
a man of great stature, five **c** tall. 1 Chr 11:23
the length, in **c** of the old standard, 2 Chr 3:3
cubits of the old standard, was sixty **c**, 2 Chr 3:3
sixty cubits, and the breadth twenty **c**. 2 Chr 3:3
nave of the house was twenty **c** long, 2 Chr 3:4
of the house, and its height was 120 **c**. 2 Chr 3:4
the breadth of the house, was twenty **c**, 2 Chr 3:8
cubits, and its breadth was twenty **c**. 2 Chr 3:8
together extended twenty **c**: 2 Chr 3:11
one wing of the one, of five **c**, touched 2 Chr 3:11
house, and its other wing, of five **c**, 2 Chr 3:11
of this cherub, one wing, of five **c**, 2 Chr 3:12
and the other wing, also of five **c**, 2 Chr 3:12
of these cherubim extended twenty **c**. 2 Chr 3:13
made two pillars thirty-five **c** high, 2 Chr 3:15
with a capital of five **c** on the top of 2 Chr 3:15
twenty **c** long and twenty cubits wide 2 Chr 4:1
cubits long and twenty **c** wide and ten 2 Chr 4:1
and twenty cubits wide and ten **c** high. 2 Chr 4:1
It was round, ten **c** from brim to brim, 2 Chr 4:2
from brim to brim, and five **c** high, 2 Chr 4:2
line of thirty **c** measured its 2 Chr 4:2
it were figures of gourds, for ten **c**, 2 Chr 4:3
made a bronze platform five **c** long, 2 Chr 6:13
platform five cubits long, five **c** wide, 2 Chr 6:13
five cubits wide, and three **c** high, 2 Chr 6:13
the wall of Jerusalem for 400 **c**, 2 Chr 25:23
height shall be sixty **c** and its breadth Ezr 6:3
be sixty cubits and its breadth sixty **c**, Ezr 6:3
and repaired a thousand **c** of the wall, Neh 3:13
him, "Let a gallows fifty **c** high be made, Est 5:14
standing at Haman's house, fifty **c** high." Est 7:9
height of the one pillar was eighteen **c**, Jer 52:21
cubits, its circumference was twelve **c**, Jer 52:21
The height of the one capital was five **c**. Jer 52:22
reed in the man's hand was six long **c**, Ezk 40:5
the space between the side rooms, five **c**; Ezk 40:7
the vestibule of the gateway, eight **c**; Ezk 40:9
eight cubits; and its jambs, two **c**; Ezk 40:9
of the opening of the gateway, ten **c**; Ezk 40:11
the length of the gateway, thirteen **c**. Ezk 40:11
side rooms were six **c** on either side. Ezk 40:12
of the other, a breadth of twenty-five **c**; Ezk 40:13
measured also the vestibule, twenty **c**. Ezk 40:14
inner vestibule of the gate was fifty **c**. Ezk 40:15
a hundred **c** on the east side and on Ezk 40:19
Its length was fifty **c**, and its breadth Ezk 40:21
cubits, and its breadth twenty-five **c**. Ezk 40:21
from gate to gate, a hundred **c**. Ezk 40:23
Its length was fifty **c**, and its breadth Ezk 40:25
cubits, and its breadth twenty-five **c**. Ezk 40:25
to gate toward the south, a hundred **c**. Ezk 40:27
Its length was fifty **c**, and its breadth Ezk 40:29
cubits, and its breadth twenty-five **c**. Ezk 40:29
twenty-five **c** long and five cubits Ezk 40:30
cubits long and five **c** broad. Ezk 40:30
Its length was fifty **c**, and its breadth Ezk 40:33
cubits, and its breadth twenty-five **c**. Ezk 40:33
Its length was fifty **c**, and its breadth Ezk 40:36
cubits, and its breadth twenty-five **c**. Ezk 40:36
a hundred **c** long and a hundred Ezk 40:47
cubits long and a hundred **c** broad, Ezk 40:47
of the vestibule, five **c** on either side. Ezk 40:48

the breadth of the gate was fourteen **c**, Ezk 40:48
of the gate were three **c** on either side. Ezk 40:48
length of the vestibule was twenty **c**, Ezk 40:49
cubits, and the breadth twelve **c**, Ezk 40:49
On each side six **c** was the breadth of Ezk 41:1
the breadth of the entrance was ten **c**, Ezk 41:2
the entrance were five **c** on either side. Ezk 41:2
the length of the nave, forty **c**, Ezk 41:2
forty cubits, and its breadth, twenty **c**. Ezk 41:2
the jambs of the entrance, two **c**; Ezk 41:3
two cubits; and the entrance, six **c**; Ezk 41:3
on either side of the entrance, seven **c**. Ezk 41:3
the length of the room, twenty **c**, Ezk 41:4
cubits, and its breadth, twenty **c**, Ezk 41:4
the wall of the temple, six **c** thick, Ezk 41:5
breadth of the side chambers, four **c**, Ezk 41:5
measured a full reed of six long **c**. Ezk 41:8
wall of the side chambers was five **c**. Ezk 41:9
a breadth of twenty **c** all around the Ezk 41:10
of the free space was five **c** all around. Ezk 41:11
on the west side was seventy **c** broad, Ezk 41:12
building was five **c** thick all around, Ezk 41:12
all around, and its length ninety **c**. Ezk 41:12
the temple, a hundred **c** long; Ezk 41:13
with its walls, a hundred **c** long; Ezk 41:13
the temple and the yard, a hundred **c**. Ezk 41:14
galleries on either side, a hundred **c**. Ezk 41:15
an altar of wood, three **c** high, two Ezk 41:22
of wood, three cubits high, two **c** long, Ezk 41:22
two cubits long, and two **c** broad. Ezk 41:22
door faced north was a hundred **c**, Ezk 42:2
hundred cubits, and the breadth fifty **c**. Ezk 42:2
Facing the twenty **c** that belonged to Ezk 42:3
ten **c** wide and a hundred cubits long, Ezk 42:4
ten cubits wide and a hundred **c** long, Ezk 42:4
opposite the chambers, fifty **c** long. Ezk 42:7
on the outer court were fifty **c** long, Ezk 42:8
the nave were a hundred **c** long. Ezk 42:8
500 **c** by the measuring reed all Ezk 42:16
500 **c** by the measuring reed all Ezk 42:17
side, 500 **c** by the measuring reed. Ezk 42:18
500 **c** by the measuring reed. Ezk 42:19
it, 500 **c** long and 500 cubits broad, Ezk 42:20
it, 500 cubits long and 500 **c** broad, Ezk 42:20
of the altar by **c** (the cubit being a Ezk 43:13
the ground to the lower ledge, two **c**, Ezk 43:14
ledge to the larger ledge, four **c**, Ezk 43:14
and the altar hearth, four **c**; and from Ezk 43:15
square, twelve **c** long by twelve broad. Ezk 43:16
fourteen **c** long by fourteen broad, Ezk 43:17
25,000 **c** long and 20,000 cubits broad. Ezk 45:1
25,000 cubits long and 20,000 **c** broad. Ezk 45:1
plot of 500 by 500 **c** shall be for the Ezk 45:2
with fifty **c** for an open space around it. Ezk 45:2
off a section 25,000 **c** long and 10,000 Ezk 45:3
25,000 **c** long and 10,000 cubits broad, Ezk 45:5
25,000 cubits long and 10,000 **c** broad, Ezk 45:5
city an area 5,000 **c** broad and 25,000 Ezk 45:6
5,000 cubits broad and 25,000 **c** long. Ezk 45:6
courts, forty **c** long and thirty broad; Ezk 46:22
hand, the man measured a thousand **c**, Ezk 47:3
you shall set apart, 25,000 **c** in breadth, Ezk 48:8
for the LORD shall be 25,000 **c** in length, Ezk 48:9
allotment measuring 25,000 **c** on the Ezk 48:10
10,000 **c** in breadth on the western Ezk 48:10
an allotment 25,000 **c** in length and Ezk 48:13
shall be 25,000 **c** and the breadth Ezk 48:13
5,000 **c** in breadth and 25,000 in Ezk 48:15
the north side 4,500 **c**, the south side Ezk 48:16
on the north 250 **c**, on the south 250, Ezk 48:17
portion shall be 10,000 **c** to the east, Ezk 48:18
set apart shall be 25,000 **c** square, Ezk 48:20
from the 25,000 **c** of the holy Ezk 48:21
westward from the 25,000 **c** to the west Ezk 48:21
which is to be 4,500 **c** by measure, Ezk 48:30
On the east side, which is to be 4,500 **c**, Ezk 48:32
which is to be 4,500 **c** by measure, Ezk 48:33
the west side, which is to be 4,500 **c**, Ezk 48:34
of the city shall be 18,000 **c**. Ezk 48:35
whose height was sixty **c** and its breadth Dn 3:1
was sixty cubits and its breadth six **c**. Dn 3:1
Its length is twenty **c**, and its width ten Zec 5:2
is twenty cubits, and its width ten **c**." Zec 5:2
wall, 144 **c** by human measurement, Rv 21:17

CUBS (10)
like a bear robbed of her **c** in the field. 2 Sm 17:8
and the **c** of the lioness are scattered. Jb 4:11
she-bear robbed of her **c** rather than a Prv 17:12
like lions; they shall growl like lions' **c**. Jer 51:38
midst of young lions she reared her **c**. Ezk 19:2
And she brought up one of her **c**; he Ezk 19:3
took another of her **c** and made him a Ezk 19:5
upon them like a bear robbed of her **c**; Hos 13:8
lion and lioness went, where his **c** were, Na 2:11
tore enough for his **c** and strangled prey Na 2:12

CUCUMBER (2)
in a vineyard, like a lodge in a **c** field, Is 1:8
idols are like scarecrows in a **c** field, Jer 10:5

CUCUMBERS (1)
we ate in Egypt that cost nothing, the **c**, Nm 11:5

CUD (11)
and is cloven-footed and chews the **c**, Lv 11:3
those that chew the **c** or part the hoof, Lv 11:4
because it chews the **c** but does not part Lv 11:4
because it chews the **c** but does not part Lv 11:5
because it chews the **c** but does not part Lv 11:6
is cloven-footed but does not chew the **c**, Lv 11:7
does not chew the **c** is unclean to you. Lv 11:26
the hoof cloven in two and chews the **c**, Dt 14:6
of those that chew the **c** or have the hoof Dt 14:7
because they chew the **c** but do not part Dt 14:7
it parts the hoof but does not chew the **c**, Dt 14:8

CULT (11)
"Where is the **c** prostitute who was at Gn 38:21
said, "No **c** prostitute has been here." Gn 38:21
said, 'No **c** prostitute has been here.'" Gn 38:22
of Israel shall be a **c** prostitute, Dt 23:17
the sons of Israel shall be a **c** prostitute. Dt 23:17
were also male **c** prostitutes in the 1 Kgs 14:24
away the male **c** prostitutes out of 1 Kgs 15:12
of the male **c** prostitutes who 1 Kgs 22:46
of the male **c** prostitutes who were 2 Kgs 23:7
their life ends among the **c** prostitutes. Jb 36:14
and sacrifice with **c** prostitutes, Hos 4:14

CULTIVATE (1)
the livestock and plants for man to **c**, Ps 104:14

CULTIVATED (3)
every way: a king committed to **c** fields. Eccl 5:9
contrary to nature, into a **c** olive tree, Rom 11:24
useful to those for whose sake it is **c**, Heb 6:7

CUMI (1)
said to her, "Talitha **c**," which means, Mk 5:41

CUMIN (4)
its surface, does he not scatter dill, sow **c**, Is 28:25
sledge, nor is a cart wheel rolled over **c**, Is 28:27
beaten out with a stick, and **c** with a rod. Is 28:27
For you tithe mint and dill and **c**, and Mt 23:23

CUN (1)
And from Tibhath and from **C**, cities 1 Chr 18:8

CUNNING (10)
attacks another to kill him by **c**, Ex 21:14
their part acted with **c** and went and Jos 9:4
for it is told me that he is very **c**. 1 Sm 23:22
Jehu did it with **c** in order to destroy 2 Kgs 10:19
voice of charmers or of the **c** enchanter. Ps 58:5
your statutes, for their **c** is in vain. Ps 119:118
By his **c** he shall make deceit prosper Dn 8:25
We refuse to practice **c** or to tamper 2 Cor 4:2
as the serpent deceived Eve by his **c**, 2 Cor 11:3
by every wind of doctrine, by human **c**, Eph 4:14

CUP (65)
Pharaoh's **c** was in my hand, and I Gn 40:11
them into Pharaoh's **c** and placed the Gn 40:11
and placed the **c** in Pharaoh's hand." Gn 40:11
shall place Pharaoh's **c** in his hand Gn 40:13
and he placed the **c** in Pharaoh's hand. Gn 40:21
and put my **c**, the silver cup, in the Gn 44:2
and put my cup, the silver **c**, in the Gn 44:2
And the **c** was found in Benjamin's Gn 44:12
in whose hand the **c** has been found." Gn 44:16
in whose hand the **c** was found shall Gn 44:17
and drink from his **c** and lie in his 2 Sm 12:3
brim was made like the brim of a **c**, 1 Kgs 7:26
its brim was made like the brim of a **c**, 2 Chr 4:5
wind shall be the portion of their **c**. Ps 11:6
LORD is my chosen portion and my **c**; Ps 16:5
anoint my head with oil; my **c** overflows. Ps 23:5
the LORD there is a **c** with foaming wine, Ps 75:8
I will lift up the **c** of salvation and call Ps 116:13
it sparkles in the **c** and goes down Prv 23:31
the hand of the LORD the **c** of his wrath, Is 51:17
to the dregs the bowl, the **c** of staggering. Is 51:17
from your hand the **c** of staggering; Is 51:22
anyone give him the **c** of consolation to Jer 16:7
from my hand this **c** of the wine of Jer 25:15
So I took the **c** from the LORD'S hand, Jer 25:17
refuse to accept the **c** from your hand Jer 25:28
not deserve to drink the **c** must drink it, Jer 49:12
Babylon was a golden **c** in the LORD'S Jer 51:7
of Uz; but to you also the **c** shall pass; Lam 4:21
I will give her **c** into your hand. Ezk 23:31
shall drink your sister's **c** that is deep Ezk 23:32
A **c** of horror and desolation, the cup Ezk 23:33
the **c** of your sister Samaria; Ezk 23:33
The **c** in the LORD'S right hand will Hab 2:16
to make Jerusalem a **c** of staggering to Zec 12:2
little ones even a **c** of cold water Mt 10:42
you able to drink the **c** that I am to Mt 20:22
He said to them, "You will drink my **c**, Mt 20:23
clean the outside of the **c** and the plate, Mt 23:25
clean the inside of the **c** and the plate, Mt 23:26
And he took a **c**, and when he had Mt 26:27
if it be possible, let this **c** pass from me; Mt 26:39
whoever gives you a **c** of water to drink Mk 9:41
you able to drink the **c** that I drink, Mk 10:38
"The **c** that I drink you will drink, Mk 10:39
And he took a **c**, and when he had Mk 14:23
for you. Remove this **c** from me. Mk 14:36
the outside of the **c** and of the dish, Lk 11:39
And he took a **c**, and when he had Lk 22:17
And likewise the **c** after they had eaten, Lk 22:20
"This **c** that is poured out for you is the Lk 22:20
you are willing, remove this **c** from me. Lk 22:42
I not drink the **c** that the Father has Jn 18:11
The **c** of blessing that we bless, is it 1 Cor 10:16
You cannot drink the **c** of the Lord 1 Cor 10:21
cup of the Lord and the **c** of demons. 1 Cor 10:21
In the same way also he took the **c**, 1 Cor 11:25
"This **c** is the new covenant in my 1 Cor 11:25
you eat this bread and drink the **c**, 1 Cor 11:26
bread or drinks the **c** of the Lord in 1 Cor 11:27
eat of the bread and drink of the **c**. 1 Cor 11:28
full strength into the **c** of his anger, Rv 14:10
to make her drain the **c** of the wine of Rv 16:19
hand a golden **c** full of abominations Rv 17:4
portion for her in the **c** she mixed. Rv 18:6

CUPBEARER (10)
the **c** of the king of Egypt and his baker Gn 40:1
officers, the chief **c** and the chief baker, Gn 40:2
both dreamed—the **c** and the baker of Gn 40:5
So the chief **c** told his dream to Joseph Gn 40:9
hand as formerly, when you were his **c**. Gn 40:13
the head of the chief **c** and the head of Gn 40:20
He restored the chief **c** to his position, Gn 40:21
Yet the chief **c** did not remember Gn 40:23
Then the chief **c** said to Pharaoh, "I Gn 41:9
of this man." Now I was **c** to the king. Neh 1:11

CUPBEARERS (2)
of his servants, their clothing, his **c**, 1 Kgs 10:5
his servants, and their clothing, his **c**, 2 Chr 9:4

CUPS (14)
its base, its stem, its **c**, its calyxes, and Ex 25:31
three **c** made like almond blossoms, Ex 25:33
and three **c** made like almond Ex 25:33
there shall be four **c** made like almond Ex 25:34
Its base, its stem, its **c**, its calyxes, and Ex 37:17
three **c** made like almond blossoms, Ex 37:19
and three **c** made like almond Ex 37:19
itself were four **c** made like almond Ex 37:20
the **c**, snuffers, basins, dishes for 1 Kgs 7:50
for the forks, the basins and the **c**; 1 Chr 28:17
vessel, from the **c** to all the flagons. Is 22:24
for Fortune and fill **c** of mixed wine for Is 65:11
Rechabites pitchers full of wine, and **c**, Jer 35:5
as the washing of **c** and pots and copper Mk 7:4

CURBED (1)
which must be **c** with bit and bridle, Ps 32:9

CURDLE (1)
me out like milk and **c** me like cheese? Jb 10:10

CURDS (9)
Then he took **c** and milk and the calf Gn 18:8
C from the herd, and milk from the Dt 32:14
she brought him **c** in a noble's bowl. Jgs 5:25
honey and **c** and sheep and cheese 2 Sm 17:29
the streams flowing with honey and **c**. Jb 20:17
For pressing milk produces **c**, Prv 30:33
He shall eat **c** and honey when he knows Is 7:15
of milk that they give, he will eat **c**, Is 7:22
is left in the land will eat **c** and honey. Is 7:22

CURE (6)
He would **c** him of his leprosy." 2 Kgs 5:3
that you may **c** him of his leprosy." 2 Kgs 5:6
sends word to me to **c** a man of his 2 Kgs 5:7
hand over the place and **c** the leper. 2 Kgs 5:11
he is not able to **c** you or heal your Hos 5:13
over all demons and to **c** diseases, Lk 9:1

CURED (3)
troubled with unclean spirits were **c**. Lk 6:18
kingdom of God and **c** those who had Lk 9:11
had diseases also came and were **c**. Acts 28:9

CURES (1)
demons and perform **c** today and Lk 13:32

CURRENT (1)
to the weights **c** among the merchants. Gn 23:16

CURSE (97)
"I will never again **c** the ground because Gn 8:21

and him who dishonors you I will **c**, Gn 12:3
him and bring a **c** upon myself and Gn 27:12
said to him, "Let your **c** be on me, Gn 27:13
revile God, nor **c** a ruler of your people. Ex 22:28
You shall not **c** the deaf or put a Lv 19:14
water of bitterness that brings the **c**. Nm 5:18
water of bitterness that brings the **c**. Nm 5:19
make the woman take the oath of the **c**, Nm 5:21
LORD make you a **c** and an oath among Nm 5:21
water that brings the **c** pass into your Nm 5:22
water of bitterness that brings the **c**, Nm 5:24
water that brings the **c** shall enter into Nm 5:24
water that brings the **c** shall enter into Nm 5:27
shall become a **c** among her people. Nm 5:27
Come now, **c** this people for me, since Nm 22:6
blessed, and he whom you **c** is cursed." Nm 22:6
the earth. Now come, **c** them for me. Nm 22:11
You shall not **c** the people, for they are Nm 22:12
I will do. Come, **c** this people for me.'" Nm 22:17
'Come, **c** Jacob for me, and come, Nm 23:7
How can I **c** whom God has not Nm 23:8
I took you to **c** my enemies, and Nm 23:11
all. Then **c** them for me from there." Nm 23:13
said to Balaam, "Do not **c** them at all, Nm 23:25
God that you may **c** them for me from Nm 23:27
you, and cursed are those who **c** you." Nm 24:9
"I called you to **c** my enemies, Nm 24:10
before you today a blessing and a **c**: Dt 11:26
and the **c**, if you do not obey the Dt 11:28
Gerizim and the **c** on Mount Ebal. Dt 11:29
from Pethor of Mesopotamia, to **c** you. Dt 23:4
your God turned the **c** into a blessing for Dt 23:5
shall stand on Mount Ebal for the **c**: Dt 27:13
come upon you, the blessing and the **c**, Dt 30:1
you life and death, blessing and **c**. Dt 30:19
words of the law, the blessing and the **c**, Jos 8:34
invited Balaam the son of Beor to **c** you, Jos 24:9
"**C** Meroz, says the angel of the LORD, Jgs 5:23
the LORD, **c** its inhabitants thoroughly, Jgs 5:23
upon them came the **c** of Jotham the son Jgs 9:57
from you, about which you uttered a **c**, Jgs 17:2
should this dead dog **c** my lord the 2 Sm 16:9
the LORD has said to him, '**C** David,' 2 Sm 16:10
Leave him alone, and let him **c**, for 2 Sm 16:11
me with a grievous **c** on the day when 1 Kgs 2:8
should become a desolation and a **c**, 2 Kgs 22:19
and enter into a **c** and an oath to walk Neh 10:29
Balaam against them to **c** them—yet Neh 13:2
our God turned the **c** into a blessing. Neh 13:2
he has, and he will **c** you to your face." Jb 1:11
his flesh, and he will **c** you to your face." Jb 2:5
hold fast your integrity? **C** God and die." Jb 2:9
Let those **c** it who curse the day, who are Jb 3:8
Let those curse it who **c** the day, who are Jb 3:8
sin by asking for his life with a **c**), Jb 31:30
with their mouths, but inwardly they **c**. Ps 62:4
who deride me use my name for a **c**. Ps 102:8
He loved to **c**; let curses come upon Ps 109:17
Let them **c**, but you will bless! They Ps 109:28
The LORD'S **c** is on the house of the Prv 3:33
The people **c** him who holds back Prv 11:26
a **c** that is causeless does not alight. Prv 26:2
who hides his eyes will get many a **c**. Prv 28:27
he hears the **c**, but discloses nothing. Prv 29:24
lest he **c** you and you be held guilty. Prv 30:10
are those who **c** their fathers and Prv 30:11
in your thought, do not **c** the king, Eccl 10:20
king, nor in your bedroom **c** the rich, Eccl 10:20
Therefore a **c** devours the earth, and its Is 24:6
leave your name to my chosen for a **c**, Is 65:15
have I borrowed, yet all of them **c** me. Jer 15:10
because of the **c** the land mourns, Jer 23:10
and a **c** in all the places where I shall Jer 24:9
and a waste, a hissing and a **c**, Jer 25:18
will make this city a **c** for all the nations Jer 26:6
all the kingdoms of the earth, to be a **c**, Jer 29:18
Because of them this **c** shall be used by Jer 29:22
become an execration, a horror, a **c**, Jer 42:18
off and become a **c** and a taunt among Jer 44:8
shall become an oath, a horror, a **c**, Jer 44:12
a desolation and a waste and a **c**, Jer 44:22
a horror, a taunt, a waste, and a **c**, Jer 49:13
of heart; your **c** will be on them. Lam 3:65
And the **c** and oath that are written in Dn 9:11
"This is the **c** that goes out over the face Zec 5:3
then I will send the **c** upon you and I will Mal 2:2
upon you and I will **c** your blessings. Mal 2:2
You are cursed with a **c**, for you are Mal 3:9
began to invoke a **c** on himself and to Mt 26:74
began to invoke a **c** on himself and to Mk 14:71
bless those who **c** you, pray for those Lk 6:28
you; bless and do not **c** them. Rom 12:14
rely on works of the law are under a **c**; Gal 3:10
redeemed us from the **c** of the law by Gal 3:13
the law by becoming a **c** for us—for it Gal 3:13
and with it we **c** people who are made in Jas 3:9

CURSED (74)

c are you above all livestock and above Gn 3:14
eat of it,' **c** is the ground because of you; Gn 3:17
And now you are **c** from the ground, Gn 4:11
that the LORD has **c** this one shall bring Gn 5:29
he said, "**C** be Canaan; a servant of Gn 9:25
C be everyone who curses you, and Gn 27:29
C be their anger, for it is fierce, and their Gn 49:7
death; he has **c** his father or his mother; Lv 20:9
son blasphemed the Name, and **c**. Lv 24:11
"Bring out of the camp the one who **c**, Lv 24:14
the one who had **c** and stoned him with Lv 24:23
blessed, and he whom you curse is **c**." Nm 22:6
How can I curse whom God has not **c**? Nm 23:8
you, and **c** are those who curse you." Nm 24:9
day, for a hanged man is **c** by God. Dt 21:23
"'**C** be the man who makes a carved or Dt 27:15
"'**C** be anyone who dishonors his father Dt 27:16
"'**C** be anyone who moves his Dt 27:17
"'**C** be anyone who misleads a blind Dt 27:18
"'**C** be anyone who perverts the justice Dt 27:19
"'**C** be anyone who lies with his father's Dt 27:20
"'**C** be anyone who lies with any kind of Dt 27:21
"'**C** be anyone who lies with his sister, Dt 27:22
"'**C** be anyone who lies with his Dt 27:23
"'**C** be anyone who strikes down his Dt 27:24
"'**C** be anyone who takes a bribe to shed Dt 27:25
"'**C** be anyone who does not confirm Dt 27:26
C shall you be in the city, and cursed Dt 28:16
the city, and **c** shall you be in the field. Dt 28:16
C shall be your basket and your Dt 28:17
C shall be the fruit of your womb and Dt 28:18
C shall you be when you come in, and Dt 28:19
in, and **c** shall you be when you go out. Dt 28:19
"**C** before the LORD be the man who rises Jos 6:26
Now therefore you are **c**, and some of Jos 9:23
"**C** be he who gives a wife to Jgs 21:18
"**C** be the man who eats food until it 1 Sm 14:24
'**C** be the man who eats food this 1 Sm 14:28
And the Philistine **c** David by his 1 Sm 17:43
men, may they be **c** before the LORD, 1 Sm 26:19
and as he came he **c** continually. 2 Sm 16:5
And Shimei said as he **c**, "Get out, get 2 Sm 16:7
opposite him and **c** as he went 2 Sm 16:13
because he **c** the LORD'S anointed?" 2 Sm 19:21
who **c** me with a grievous curse on the 1 Kgs 2:8
'You have **c** God and the king.' 1 Kgs 21:10
"Naboth **c** God and the king." So 1 Kgs 21:13
he **c** them in the name of the LORD. 2 Kgs 2:24
"See now to this **c** woman and bury 2 Kgs 9:34
confronted them and **c** them and beat Neh 13:25
and **c** God in their hearts." Thus Job did Jb 1:5
Job opened his mouth and **c** the day of his Jb 3:1
taking root, but suddenly I **c** his dwelling. Jb 5:3
the waters; their portion is **c** in the land; Jb 24:18
but those **c** by him shall be cut off. Ps 37:22
are in the right," will be **c** by peoples, Prv 24:24
times you have yourself **c** others. Eccl 7:22
C be the man who does not hear the Jer 11:3
"**C** is the man who trusts in man and Jer 17:5
C be the day on which I was born! The Jer 20:14
C be the man who brought the news to Jer 20:15
"**C** is he who does the work of the LORD Jer 48:10
and **c** is he who keeps back his sword Jer 48:10
C be the cheat who has a male in his Mal 1:14
Indeed, I have already **c** them, because Mal 2:2
You are **c** with a curse, for you are Mal 3:9
on his left, 'Depart from me, you **c**, Mt 25:41
The fig tree that you **c** has withered." Mk 11:21
"**C** be everyone who does not abide by Gal 3:10
"**C** is everyone who is hanged on a tree" Gal 3:13
it is worthless and near to being **c**, Heb 6:8
and they **c** the name of God who had Rv 16:9
and **c** the God of heaven for their pain Rv 16:11
and they **c** God for the plague of the Rv 16:21

CURSES (17)

Cursed be everyone who **c** you, and Gn 27:29
"Whoever **c** his father or his mother Ex 21:17
For anyone who **c** his father or his Lv 20:9
Whoever **c** his God shall bear his sin. Lv 24:15
priest shall write these **c** in a book and Nm 5:23
then all these **c** shall come upon you Dt 28:15
"The LORD will send on you **c**, Dt 28:20
"All these **c** shall come upon you and Dt 28:45
and the **c** written in this book will settle Dt 29:20
with all the **c** of the covenant Dt 29:21
upon it all the **c** written in this book, Dt 29:27
God will put all these **c** on your foes and Dt 30:7
all the **c** that are written in the book 2 Chr 34:24
one greedy for gain **c** and renounces the Ps 10:3
loved to curse; let **c** come upon him! Ps 109:17
If one **c** his father or his mother, his Prv 20:20
mouth is full of **c** and bitterness." Rom 3:14

CURSING (9)

If he is **c** because the LORD has said to 2 Sm 16:10
repay me with good for his **c** today." 2 Sm 16:12
mouth is filled with **c** and deceit and Ps 10:7
pride. For the **c** and lies that they utter, Ps 59:12
He clothed himself with **c** as his coat; Ps 109:18
in the morning, will be counted as **c**. Prv 27:14
say, lest you hear your servant **c** you. Eccl 7:21
been a byword of **c** among the nations, Zec 8:13
the same mouth come blessing and **c**. Jas 3:10

CURTAIN (29)

length of each **c** shall be twenty-eight Ex 26:2
and the breadth of each **c** four cubits; Ex 26:2
edge of the outermost **c** in the first set. Ex 26:4
edge of the outermost **c** in the second set. Ex 26:4
Fifty loops you shall make on the one **c**, Ex 26:5
on the edge of the **c** that is in the second Ex 26:5
The length of each **c** shall be thirty Ex 26:8
and the breadth of each **c** four cubits. Ex 26:8
and the sixth **c** you shall double over at Ex 26:9
on the edge of the **c** that is outermost in Ex 26:10
on the edge of the **c** that is outermost in Ex 26:10
of the tent, the half **c** that remains, Ex 26:12
length of each **c** was twenty-eight cubits, Ex 36:9
and the breadth of each **c** four cubits. Ex 36:9
edge of the outermost **c** of the first set. Ex 36:11
edge of the outermost **c** of the second Ex 36:11
He made fifty loops on the one **c**, and he Ex 36:12
on the edge of the **c** that was in the Ex 36:12
The length of each **c** was thirty cubits, Ex 36:15
and the breadth of each **c** four cubits. Ex 36:15
edge of the outermost **c** of the one set, Ex 36:17
on the edge of the other connecting **c**. Ex 36:17
who stretches out the heavens like a **c**, Is 40:22
the **c** of the temple was torn in two, Mt 27:51
And the **c** of the temple was torn in Mk 15:38
And the **c** of the temple was torn in two. Lk 23:45
into the inner place behind the **c**, Heb 6:19
Behind the second **c** was a second Heb 9:3
that he opened for us through the **c**, Heb 10:20

CURTAINS (30)

the tabernacle with ten **c** of fine twined Ex 26:1
cubits; all the **c** shall be the same size. Ex 26:2
Five **c** shall be coupled to one another, Ex 26:3
and the other five **c** shall be coupled to Ex 26:3
and couple the **c** one to the other with Ex 26:6
"You shall also make **c** of goats' hair for Ex 26:7
the tabernacle; eleven **c** shall you make. Ex 26:7
The eleven **c** shall be the same size. Ex 26:8
You shall couple five **c** by themselves, Ex 26:9
by themselves, and six **c** by themselves, Ex 26:9
part that remains of the **c** of the tent, Ex 26:12
that remains in the length of the **c**, Ex 26:13
made the tabernacle with ten **c**. Ex 36:8
four cubits. All the **c** were the same size. Ex 36:9
He coupled five **c** to one another, and Ex 36:10
and the other five **c** he coupled to one Ex 36:10
and coupled the **c** one to the other with Ex 36:13
He also made **c** of goats' hair for a tent Ex 36:14
over the tabernacle. He made eleven **c**. Ex 36:14
cubits. The eleven **c** were the same size. Ex 36:15
He coupled five **c** by themselves, and Ex 36:16
by themselves, and six **c** by themselves. Ex 36:16
they shall carry the **c** of the tabernacle Nm 4:25
were white cotton **c** and violet hangings Est 1:6
the tents of Kedar, like the **c** of Solomon. Sg 1:5
and let the **c** of your habitations be Is 54:2
tents are laid waste, my **c** in a moment. Jer 4:20
my tent again and to set up my **c**. Jer 10:20
be taken, their **c** and all their goods; Jer 49:29
the **c** of the land of Midian did tremble. Hab 3:7

CUSH (26)

that flowed around the whole land of **C**. Gn 2:13
of Ham: **C**, Egypt, Put, and Canaan. Gn 10:6
The sons of **C**: Seba, Havilah, Sabtah, Gn 10:7
C fathered Nimrod; he was the first on Gn 10:8
concerning Tirhakah king of **C**, 2 Kgs 19:9
of Ham: **C**, Egypt, Put, and Canaan. 1 Chr 1:8
The sons of **C**: Seba, Havilah, Sabta, 1 Chr 1:9
C fathered Nimrod. He was the first 1 Chr 1:10
to the LORD concerning the words of **C**, Ps 7:T
C shall hasten to stretch out her hands Ps 68:31
with **C**—"This one was born there," they Ps 87:4
from Egypt, from Pathros, from **C**, Is 11:11
wings that is beyond the rivers of **C**, Is 18:1
a sign and a portent against Egypt and **C**, Is 20:3
and ashamed because of **C** their hope and Is 20:5
heard concerning Tirhakah king of **C**, Is 37:9
ransom, **C** and Seba in exchange for you. Is 43:3
of Egypt and the merchandise of **C**, Is 45:14
men of **C** and Put who handle the shield, Jer 46:9
to Syene, as far as the border of **C**. Ezk 29:10
upon Egypt, and anguish shall be in **C**, Ezk 30:4
C, and Put, and Lud, and all Arabia, Ezk 30:5

to terrify the unsuspecting people of **C**, Ezk 30:9
Persia, **C**, and Put are with them, all of Ezk 38:5
C was her strength; Egypt too, and that Na 3:9
beyond the rivers of **C** my worshipers, Zep 3:10

CUSHAN (1)
I saw the tents of **C** in affliction; the Hab 3:7

CUSHAN-RISHATHAIM (4)
into the hand of **C** king of Mesopotamia. Jgs 3:8
the people of Israel served **C** eight years. Jgs 3:8
the LORD gave **C** king of Mesopotamia Jgs 3:10
hand. And his hand prevailed over **C**. Jgs 3:10

CUSHI (2)
Nethaniah, son of Shelemiah, son of **C**, Jer 36:14
that came to Zephaniah the son of **C**, Zep 1:1

CUSHION (1)
But he was in the stern, asleep on the **c**. Mk 4:38

CUSHITE (11)
because of the **C** woman whom he Nm 12:1
for he had married a **C** woman. Nm 12:1
Then Joab said to the **C**, "Go, tell the 2 Sm 18:21
have seen." The **C** bowed before 2 Sm 18:21
also run after the **C**." And Joab said, 2 Sm 18:22
way of the plain, and outran the **C**. 2 Sm 18:23
And behold, the **C** came, and the 2 Sm 18:31
the Cushite came, and the **C** said, 2 Sm 18:31
The king said to the **C**, "Is it well 2 Sm 18:32
Absalom?" And the **C** answered, 2 Sm 18:32
the Egyptian captives and the **C** exiles, Is 20:4

CUSHITES (3)
the Libyans and the **C** shall follow in Dn 11:43
"Are you not like the **C** to me, O people of Am 9:7
You also, O **C**, shall be slain by my Zep 2:12

CUSTODY (17)
and he put them in **c** in the house of the Gn 40:3
They continued for some time in **c**. Gn 40:4
were with him in **c** in his master's Gn 40:7
and the chief baker in **c** in the house of Gn 41:10
them all together in **c** for three days. Gn 42:17
remain confined where you are in **c**, Gn 42:19
And they put him in **c**, till the will of Lv 24:12
They put him in **c**, because it had not Nm 15:34
in Susa the capital, under **c** of Hegai, Est 2:3
gathered in Susa the citadel in **c** of Hegai, Est 2:8
the king's palace and put in **c** of Hegai, Est 2:8
to the second harem in **c** of Shaashgaz, Est 2:14
they brought him into **c**, that his voice Ezk 19:9
holding Jesus in **c** were mocking him Lk 22:63
and put them in **c** until the next day, Acts 4:3
should be kept in **c** but have some Acts 24:23
to be kept in **c** for the decision of Acts 25:21

CUSTOM (20)
a man, and it became a **c** in Israel Jgs 11:39
Now this was the **c** in former times in Ru 4:7
The **c** of the priests with the people 1 Sm 2:13
done.'" Such was his **c** all the while 1 Sm 27:11
themselves after their **c** with swords 1 Kgs 18:28
by the pillar, according to the **c**, 2 Kgs 11:14
they will not pay tribute, **c**, or toll, Ezr 4:13
to whom tribute, **c**, and toll were paid. Ezr 4:20
c, or toll on anyone of the priests, Ezr 7:24
And again, as was his **c**, he taught Mk 10:1
according to the **c** of the priesthood, he Lk 1:9
do for him according to the **c** of the Law, Lk 2:27
years old, they went up according to **c**. Lk 2:42
And as was his **c**, he went to the Lk 4:16
he came out and went, as was his **c**, Lk 22:39
But you have a **c** that I should release Jn 18:39
the spices, as is the burial **c** of the Jews. Jn 19:40
according to the **c** of Moses, Acts 15:1
And Paul went in, as was his **c**, and on Acts 17:2
that it was not the **c** of the Romans to Acts 25:16

CUSTOMS (11)
of these abominable **c** that were Lv 18:30
not walk in the **c** of the nation that Lv 20:23
and walked in the **c** of the nations 2 Kgs 17:8
and in the **c** that the kings of Israel 2 Kgs 17:8
but walked in the **c** that Israel had 2 Kgs 17:19
for the **c** of the peoples are vanity. A tree Jer 10:3
will change the **c** that Moses delivered Acts 6:14
They advocate **c** that are not lawful Acts 16:21
children or walk according to our **c**. Acts 21:21
with all the **c** and controversies of Acts 26:3
our people or the **c** of our fathers, Acts 28:17

CUT (312)
shall all flesh be **c** off by the waters Gn 9:11
brought him all these, **c** them in half, Gn 15:10
other. But he did not **c** the birds in half. Gn 15:10
his foreskin shall be **c** off from his Gn 17:14
And he **c** the wood for the burnt offering Gn 22:3
took a flint and **c** off her son's foreskin Ex 4:25
that the frogs be **c** off from you and your Ex 8:9
you would have been **c** off from the Ex 9:15
that person shall be **c** off from Israel. Ex 12:15
that person will be **c** off from the Ex 12:19
Then you shall **c** the ram into pieces, Ex 29:17
an outsider shall be **c** off from his Ex 30:33
as perfume shall be **c** off from his Ex 30:38
that soul shall be **c** off from among his Ex 31:14
"**C** for yourself two tablets of stone like Ex 34:1
So Moses **c** two tablets of stone like the Ex 34:4
their pillars and **c** down their Asherim Ex 34:13
and he **c** it into threads to work into the Ex 39:3
flay the burnt offering and **c** it into pieces, Lv 1:6
And he shall **c** it into pieces, with its Lv 1:12
whole fat tail, **c** off close to the backbone, Lv 3:9
that person shall be **c** off from his Lv 7:20
that person shall be **c** off from his Lv 7:21
to the LORD shall be **c** off from his people. Lv 7:25
that person shall be **c** off from his Lv 7:27
He **c** the ram into pieces, and Moses Lv 8:20
that man shall be **c** off from among his Lv 17:4
that man shall be **c** off from his people. Lv 17:9
eats blood and will **c** him off from Lv 17:10
its blood. Whoever eats it shall be **c** off. Lv 17:14
do them shall be **c** off from among Lv 18:29
that person shall be **c** off from his Lv 19:8
that man and will **c** him off from Lv 20:3
his clan and will **c** them off from among Lv 20:5
that person and will **c** him off from Lv 20:6
and they shall be **c** off in the sight of Lv 20:17
of them shall be **c** off from among their Lv 20:18
that person shall be **c** off from my Lv 22:3
crushed or torn or **c** you shall not offer Lv 22:24
very day shall be **c** off from his people. Lv 23:29
high places and **c** down your incense Lv 26:30
that person shall be **c** off from his Nm 9:13
of Eshcol and **c** down from there Nm 13:23
the people of Israel **c** down from there. Nm 13:24
that person shall be **c** off from among Nm 15:30
that person shall be utterly **c** off; Nm 15:31
that person shall be **c** off from Israel; Nm 19:13
that person shall be **c** off from the Nm 19:20
'**C** for yourself two tablets of stone like Dt 10:1
and **c** two tablets of stone like the first, Dt 10:3
You shall not **c** yourselves or make any Dt 14:1
the forest with his neighbor to **c** wood, Dt 19:5
his hand swings the axe to **c** down a tree, Dt 19:5
them, but you shall not **c** them down. Dt 20:19
for food you may destroy and **c** down, Dt 20:20
whose male organ is **c** off shall enter the Dt 23:1
then you shall **c** off her hand. Your eye Dt 25:12
faint and weary, and **c** off your tail, Dt 25:18
have said, "I will **c** them to pieces; Dt 32:26
of the Jordan shall be **c** off from flowing, Jos 3:13
the Salt Sea, were completely **c** off. Jos 3:16
of the Jordan were **c** off before the ark Jos 4:7
Jordan, the waters of the Jordan were **c** off. Jos 4:7
will surround us and **c** off our name Jos 7:9
at that time and **c** off the Anakim from Jos 11:21
all the nations that I have already **c** off, Jos 23:4
and caught him and **c** off his thumbs Jgs 1:6
and their big toes **c** off used to pick Jgs 1:7
and **c** down the Asherah that is beside it Jgs 6:25
of the Asherah that you shall **c** down." Jgs 6:26
and the Asherah beside it was **c** down, Jgs 6:28
altar of Baal and **c** down the Asherah Jgs 6:30
axe in his hand and **c** down a bundle of Jgs 9:48
one of the people **c** down his bundle and Jgs 9:49
of my concubine and **c** her in pieces Jgs 20:6
men of them were **c** down in the Jgs 20:45
"One tribe is **c** off from Israel this day. Jgs 21:6
dead may not be **c** off from among his Ru 4:10
the wicked shall be **c** off in darkness, 1 Sm 2:9
when I will **c** off your strength 1 Sm 2:31
whom I shall not **c** off from my altar 1 Sm 2:33
his hands were lying **c** off on the 1 Sm 5:4
yoke of oxen and **c** them in pieces and 1 Sm 11:7
strike you down and **c** off your head. 1 Sm 17:46
and killed him and **c** off his head 1 Sm 17:51
and do not **c** off your steadfast love 1 Sm 20:15
arose and stealthily **c** off a corner 1 Sm 24:4
because he had **c** off a corner of Saul's 1 Sm 24:5
by the fact that I **c** off the corner of 1 Sm 24:11
that you will not **c** off my offspring 1 Sm 24:21
how he has **c** off the mediums and the 1 Sm 28:9
So they **c** off his head and stripped off 1 Sm 31:9
they killed them and **c** off their hands 2 Sm 4:12
you went and have **c** off all your 2 Sm 7:9
beard of each and **c** off their garments 2 Sm 10:4
And when he **c** the hair of his head 2 Sm 14:26
the end of every year he used to **c** it; 2 Sm 14:26
when it was heavy on him, he **c** it), 2 Sm 14:26
And they **c** off the head of Sheba the 2 Sm 20:22
that cedars of Lebanon be **c** for me. 1 Kgs 5:6
who knows how to **c** timber like the 1 Kgs 5:6
with three courses of **c** stone and one 1 Kgs 6:36
costly stones, **c** according to measure, 1 Kgs 7:9
stones, **c** according to measurement, 1 Kgs 7:11
three courses of **c** stone all around, 1 Kgs 7:12
then I will **c** off Israel from the land 1 Kgs 9:7
until he had **c** off every male in 1 Kgs 11:16
so as to **c** it off and to destroy it from 1 Kgs 13:34
Jeroboam and will **c** off from 1 Kgs 14:10
over Israel who shall **c** off the house 1 Kgs 14:14
And Asa **c** down her image and 1 Kgs 15:13
and when Jezebel **c** off the prophets of 1 Kgs 18:4
bull for themselves and **c** it in pieces 1 Kgs 18:23
cried aloud and **c** themselves after 1 Kgs 18:28
wood in order and **c** the bull in 1 Kgs 18:33
and will **c** off from Ahab every 1 Kgs 21:21
and came and **c** them up into the pot 2 Kgs 4:39
came to the Jordan, they **c** down trees. 2 Kgs 6:4
he **c** off a stick and threw it in there 2 Kgs 6:6
and I will **c** off from Ahab every male, 2 Kgs 9:8
the LORD began to **c** off parts of 2 Kgs 10:32
And King Ahaz **c** off the frames of 2 Kgs 16:17
the pillars and **c** down the Asherah. 2 Kgs 18:4
the pillars and **c** down the Asherim 2 Kgs 23:14
and **c** in pieces all the vessels of gold 2 Kgs 24:13
have gone and have **c** off all your 1 Chr 17:8
shaved them and **c** off their garments 1 Chr 19:4
know how to **c** timber in Lebanon. 2 Chr 2:8
the woodsmen who **c** timber, 2 Chr 2:10
And we will **c** whatever timber you 2 Chr 2:16
the pillars and **c** down the Asherim 2 Chr 14:3
Asa **c** down her image, crushed it, 2 Chr 15:16
tomb that he had **c** for himself in 2 Chr 16:14
the wilderness and **c** out many 2 Chr 26:10
house of God and **c** in pieces the 2 Chr 28:24
the pillars and **c** down the Asherim 2 Chr 31:1
who **c** off all the mighty warriors 2 Chr 32:21
and he **c** down the incense altars that 2 Chr 34:4
into powder and **c** down all the 2 Chr 34:7
perished? Or where were the upright **c** off? Jb 4:7
he would let loose his hand and **c** me off! Jb 6:9
While yet in flower and not **c** down, they Jb 8:12
there is hope for a tree, if it be **c** down, Jb 14:7
the number of their months is **c** off? Jb 21:21
saying, 'Surely our adversaries are **c** off, Jb 22:20
they are **c** off like the heads of grain. Jb 24:24
May the LORD **c** off all flattering lips, the Ps 12:3
"I am **c** off from your sight." But you Ps 31:22
to **c** off the memory of them from the Ps 34:16
For the evildoers shall be **c** off, but those Ps 37:9
but those cursed by him shall be **c** off. Ps 37:22
the children of the wicked shall be **c** off. Ps 37:28
will look on when the wicked are **c** off. Ps 37:34
the future of the wicked shall be **c** off. Ps 37:38
All the horns of the wicked I will **c** off, Ps 75:10
burned it with fire; they have **c** it down; Ps 80:16
more, for they are **c** off from your hand. Ps 88:5
You have **c** short the days of his youth; Ps 89:45
May his posterity be **c** off; may his Ps 109:13
that he may **c** off the memory of them Ps 109:15
in the name of the LORD I **c** them off! Ps 118:10
in the name of the LORD I **c** them off! Ps 118:11
in the name of the LORD I **c** them off! Ps 118:12
he has **c** the cords of the wicked. Ps 129:4
love you will **c** off my enemies, Ps 143:12
like corner pillars **c** for the structure Ps 144:12
the wicked will be **c** off from the land, Prv 2:22
but the perverse tongue will be **c** off. Prv 10:31
future, and your hope will not be **c** off. Prv 23:18
future, and your hope will not be **c** off. Prv 24:14
the sycamores have been **c** down, but we Is 9:10
So the LORD **c** off from Israel head and tail, Is 9:14
to destroy, and to **c** off nations not a few; Is 10:7
He will **c** down the thickets of the forest Is 10:34
those who harass Judah shall be **c** off; Is 11:13
How you are **c** down to the ground, you Is 14:12
"and will **c** off from Babylon name and Is 14:22
that you have **c** out here a tomb for Is 22:16
you who **c** out a tomb on the height and Is 22:16
give way, and it will be **c** down and fall, Is 22:25
and the load that was on it will be **c** off, Is 22:25
all who watch to do evil shall be **c** off, Is 29:20
as if burned to lime, like thorns **c** down, Is 33:12
of Lebanon, to **c** down its tallest cedars, Is 37:24
doors of bronze and **c** through the bars of Is 45:2
it for you, that I may not **c** you off. Is 48:9
name would never be **c** off or destroyed Is 48:19
Was it not you who **c** Rahab in pieces, Is 51:9
considered that he was **c** off out of the Is 53:8
everlasting sign that shall not be **c** off." Is 55:13
everlasting name that shall not be **c** off. Is 56:5
says the LORD of hosts: "**C** down her trees; Jer 6:6
has perished; it is **c** off from their lips. Jer 7:28
"**C** off your hair and cast it away; raise a Jer 7:29
in the desert who **c** the corners of their Jer 9:26
from the forest is **c** down and worked Jer 10:3
let us **c** him off from the land of the Jer 11:19

lament for them or **c** himself or make Jer 16:6
and they shall **c** down your choicest Jer 22:7
and all who **c** the corners of their hair; Jer 25:23
the calf that they **c** in two and passed Jer 34:18
the king would **c** them off with a knife Jer 36:23
and will **c** off from it man and beast?" Jer 36:29
to **c** off from you man and woman, Jer 44:7
so that you may be **c** off and become a Jer 44:8
against you for harm, to **c** off all Judah. Jer 44:11
They shall **c** down her forest, declares Jer 46:23
to **c** off from Tyre and Sidon every helper Jer 47:4
let us **c** her off from being a nation!' Jer 48:2
The horn of Moab is **c** off, and his arm Jer 48:25
head is shaved and every beard **c** off. Jer 48:37
every wind those who **c** the corners of Jer 49:32
C off from Babylon the sower, and the Jer 50:16
the whole earth is **c** down and broken! Jer 50:23
Be not **c** off in her punishment, for this Jer 51:6
has come; the thread of your life is **c**. Jer 51:13
this place that you will **c** it off, Jer 51:62
He has **c** down in fierce anger all the Lam 2:3
destroyed, your incense altars **c** down, Ezk 6:6
and a byword and **c** him off from the Ezk 14:8
it, and **c** off from it man and beast, Ezk 14:13
and I **c** off from it man and beast, Ezk 14:17
blood, to **c** off from it man and beast, Ezk 14:19
to **c** off from it man and beast! Ezk 14:21
day you were born your cord was not **c**, Ezk 16:4
shall stone you and **c** you to pieces Ezk 16:40
not pull up its roots and **c** off its fruit, Ezk 17:9
siege walls built to **c** off many lives. Ezk 17:17
its sheath and will **c** off from you both Ezk 21:3
Because I will **c** off from you both Ezk 21:4
C sharply to the right; set yourself to Ezk 21:16
They shall **c** off your nose and your Ezk 23:25
stone them and **c** them down with Ezk 23:47
And I will **c** you off from the peoples Ezk 25:7
hand against Edom and **c** off from it Ezk 25:13
and I will **c** off the Cherethites and Ezk 25:16
and will **c** off from you man and beast, Ezk 29:8
and **c** off the multitude of Thebes. Ezk 30:15
of nations, have **c** it down and left it. Ezk 31:12
and I will **c** off from it all who come Ezk 35:7
our hope is lost; we are clean **c** off.' Ezk 37:11
out of the field or **c** down any out of Ezk 39:10
a stone was **c** out by no human hand, Dn 2:34
that a stone was **c** from a mountain by Dn 2:45
anointed one shall be **c** off and shall Dn 9:26
the king of Israel shall be utterly **c** off. Hos 10:15
sweet wine, for it is **c** off from your mouth. Jl 1:5
the drink offering are **c** off from the house Jl 1:9
Is not the food **c** off before our eyes, joy Jl 1:16
and **c** off the inhabitants from the Am 1:5
I will **c** off the inhabitants from Ashdod, Am 1:8
I will **c** off the ruler from its midst, and Am 2:3
of the altar shall be **c** off and fall to the Am 3:14
Mount Esau will be **c** off by slaughter. Ob 1:9
cover you, and you shall be **c** off forever. Ob 1:10
at the crossroads to **c** off his fugitives; Ob 1:14
yourselves bald and **c** off your hair, Mi 1:16
and all your enemies shall be **c** off. Mi 5:9
I will **c** off your horses from among you Mi 5:10
and I will **c** off the cities of your land Mi 5:11
and I will **c** off sorceries from your Mi 5:12
and I will **c** off your carved images and Mi 5:13
they will be **c** down and pass away. Na 1:12
of your gods I will **c** off the carved image Na 1:14
pass through you; he is utterly **c** off. Na 1:15
I will **c** off your prey from the earth, and Na 2:13
fire devour you; the sword will **c** you off. Na 3:15
the flock be **c** off from the fold and Hab 3:17
I will **c** off mankind from the face of the Zep 1:3
and I will **c** off from this place the Zep 1:4
more; all who weigh out silver are **c** off. Zep 1:11
"I have **c** off nations; their battlements Zep 3:6
dwelling would not be **c** off according to Zep 3:7
and I will **c** off the pride of Philistia. Zec 9:6
I will **c** off the chariot from Ephraim Zec 9:10
and the battle bow shall be **c** off, and he Zec 9:10
I will **c** off the names of the idols from Zec 13:2
two thirds shall be **c** off and perish, Zec 13:8
people shall not be **c** off from the city. Zec 14:2
May the LORD **c** off from the tents of Mal 2:12
bear good fruit is **c** down and thrown Mt 3:10
you to sin, **c** it off and throw it away. Mt 5:30
bear good fruit is **c** down and thrown Mt 7:19
you to sin, **c** it off and throw it away. Mt 18:8
and others **c** branches from the trees Mt 21:8
And if those days had not been **c** short, Mt 24:22
of the elect those days will be **c** short. Mt 24:22
and will **c** him in pieces and put him Mt 24:51
of the high priest and **c** off his ear. Mt 26:51
new tomb, which he had **c** in the rock. Mt 27:60
if your hand causes you to sin, **c** it off. Mk 9:43
if your foot causes you to sin, **c** it off. Mk 9:45
that they had **c** from the fields. Mk 11:8
if the Lord had not **c** short the days, Mk 13:20
of the high priest and **c** off his ear. Mk 14:47
tomb that had been **c** out of the rock. Mk 15:46
bear good fruit is **c** down and thrown into Lk 3:9
and will **c** him in pieces and put him Lk 12:46
this fig tree, and I find none. **C** it down. Lk 13:7
and good; but if not, you can **c** it down.'" Lk 13:9
of the high priest and **c** off his right ear. Lk 22:50
and laid him in a tomb **c** in stone, Lk 23:53
high priest's servant and **c** off his right Jn 18:10
of the man whose ear Peter had **c** off, Jn 18:26
they heard this they were **c** to the heart, Acts 2:37
At Cenchreae he had **c** his hair, for Acts 18:18
Then the soldiers **c** away the ropes of Acts 27:32
were accursed and **c** off from Christ Rom 9:3
Otherwise you too will be **c** off. Rom 11:22
For if you were **c** from what is by Rom 11:24
then she should **c** her hair short. 1 Cor 11:6
for a wife to **c** off her hair or 1 Cor 11:6

CUTH (1)
the men of **C** made Nergal, 2 Kgs 17:30

CUTHAH (1)
people from Babylon, **C**, Avva, 2 Kgs 17:24

CUTS (14)
shall not make any **c** on your body for Lv 19:28
beards, nor make any **c** on their body. Lv 21:5
the LORD your God **c** off before you the Dt 12:29
the LORD your God **c** off the nations Dt 19:1
when the LORD **c** off every one of the 1 Sm 20:15
hope of the godless when God **c** him off, Jb 27:8
He **c** out channels in the rocks, and his Jb 28:10
who **c** off the spirit of princes, who is to Ps 76:12
doors of bronze and **c** in two the bars Ps 107:16
the hand of a fool **c** off his own feet and Prv 26:6
he **c** off the shoots with pruning hooks, Is 18:5
up my life; he **c** me off from the loom; Is 38:12
He **c** down cedars, or he chooses a Is 44:14
upper rooms,' who **c** out windows for it, Jer 22:14

CUTTER (1)
eaten, the hopper, the destroyer, and the **c**, Jl 2:25

CUTTERS (3)
live." So they became **c** of wood and Jos 9:21
c of wood and drawers of water for the Jos 9:23
made them that day **c** of wood and Jos 9:27

CUTTING (8)
in **c** stones for setting, and in carving Ex 31:5
in **c** stones for setting, and in carving Ex 35:33
of Gebal did the **c** and prepared the 1 Kgs 5:18
c off all the evildoers from the city of Ps 101:8
The ironsmith takes a **c** tool and works Is 44:12
c off the children from the streets and Jer 9:21
What the **c** locust left, the swarming Jl 1:4
for your house by **c** off many peoples; Hab 2:10

CYMBAL (1)
I am a noisy gong or a clanging **c**. 1 Cor 13:1

CYMBALS (16)
and tambourines and castanets and **c**. 2 Sm 6:5
tambourines and **c** and trumpets. 1 Chr 13:8
on harps and lyres and **c**, 1 Chr 15:16
and Ethan, were to sound bronze **c**; 1 Chr 15:19
sound of the horn, trumpets, and **c**, 1 Chr 15:28
and lyres; Asaph was to sound the **c**, 1 Chr 16:5
had trumpets and **c** for the music 1 Chr 16:42
with lyres, with harps, and with **c**. 1 Chr 25:1
in the house of the LORD with **c**, 1 Chr 25:6
arrayed in fine linen, with **c**, 2 Chr 5:12
with trumpets and **c** and other 2 Chr 5:13
in the house of the LORD with **c**, 2 Chr 29:25
the Levites, the sons of Asaph, with **c**, Ezr 3:10
and with singing, with **c**, Neh 12:27
Praise him with sounding **c**; praise him Ps 150:5
praise him with loud clashing **c**! Ps 150:5

CYPRESS (14)
in the matter of cedar and **c** timber. 1 Kgs 5:8
timber of cedar and **c** that he desired, 1 Kgs 5:10
floor of the house with boards of **c**. 1 Kgs 6:15
and two doors of **c** wood. The two 1 Kgs 6:34
with cedar and **c** timber and gold, 1 Kgs 9:11
c, and algum timber from Lebanon, 2 Chr 2:8
nave he lined with **c** and covered it 2 Chr 3:5
I will set in the desert the **c**, the plane and Is 41:19
or he chooses a **c** tree or an oak and lets Is 44:14
Instead of the thorn shall come up the **c**; Is 55:13
of Lebanon shall come to you, the **c**, Is 60:13
I am like an evergreen **c**; from me Hos 14:8
them; the **c** spears are brandished. Na 2:3
Wail, O **c**, for the cedar has fallen, for Zec 11:2

CYPRESSES (3)
felled its tallest cedars, its choicest **c**; 2 Kgs 19:23
The **c** rejoice at you, the cedars of Is 14:8
cut down its tallest cedars, its choicest **c**, Is 37:24

CYPRUS (12)
From the land of **C** it is revealed to them. Is 23:1
arise, cross over to **C**, even there you will Is 23:12
For cross to the coasts of **C** and see, or Jer 2:10
your deck of pines from the coasts of **C**, Ezk 27:6
a Levite, a native of **C**, Acts 4:36
far as Phoenicia and **C** and Antioch, Acts 11:19
some of them, men of **C** and Cyrene, Acts 11:20
and from there they sailed to **C**. Acts 13:4
Mark with him and sailed away to **C**, Acts 15:39
When we had come in sight of **C**, Acts 21:3
us to the house of Mnason of **C**, Acts 21:16
from there we sailed under the lee of **C**, Acts 27:4

CYRENE (6)
they went out, they found a man of **C**, Mt 27:32
compelled a passerby, Simon of **C**, Mk 15:21
him away, they seized one Simon of **C**, Lk 23:26
and the parts of Libya belonging to **C**, Acts 2:10
some of them, men of Cyprus and **C**, Acts 11:20
who was called Niger, Lucius of **C**, Acts 13:1

CYRENIANS (1)
(as it was called), and of the **C**, Acts 6:9

CYRUS (23)
in the first year of **C** king of Persia, 2 Chr 36:22
up the spirit of **C** king of Persia, 2 Chr 36:22
"Thus says **C** king of Persia, 'The 2 Chr 36:23
In the first year of **C** king of Persia, that Ezr 1:1
stirred up the spirit of **C** king of Persia, Ezr 1:1
"Thus says **C** king of Persia: The LORD, Ezr 1:2
C the king also brought out the vessels of Ezr 1:7
C king of Persia brought these out in Ezr 1:8
that they had from **C** king of Persia. Ezr 3:7
as King **C** the king of Persia has Ezr 4:3
purpose, all the days of **C** king of Persia, Ezr 4:5
in the first year of **C** king of Babylon, Ezr 5:13
C the king made a decree that this Ezr 5:13
these **C** the king took out of the temple Ezr 5:14
decree was issued by **C** the king for the Ezr 5:17
In the first year of **C** the king, Cyrus the Ezr 6:3
the king, **C** the king issued a decree: Ezr 6:3
and by decree of **C** and Darius and Ezr 6:14
who says of **C**, 'He is my shepherd, and Is 44:28
Thus says the LORD to his anointed, to **C**, Is 45:1
was there until the first year of King **C**. Dn 1:21
of Darius and the reign of **C** the Persian. Dn 6:28
In the third year of **C** king of Persia a Dn 10:1

D

DABBESHETH (1)
and on to Mareal and touches **D**, Jos 19:11

DABERATH (3)
From there it goes to **D**, then up to Jos 19:12
pasturelands, **D** with its pasturelands, Jos 21:28
D with its pasturelands, 1 Chr 6:72

DAGON (13)
a great sacrifice to **D** their god and to Jgs 16:23
it into the house of **D** and set it up 1 Sm 5:2
house of Dagon and set it up beside **D**. 1 Sm 5:2
D had fallen face downward on the 1 Sm 5:3
So they took **D** and put him back in 1 Sm 5:3
D had fallen face downward on the 1 Sm 5:4
and the head of **D** and both his hands 1 Sm 5:4
Only the trunk of **D** was left to him. 1 Sm 5:4
why the priests of **D** and all who enter 1 Sm 5:5
enter the house of **D** do not tread on 1 Sm 5:5
on the threshold of **D** in Ashdod to this 1 Sm 5:5
against us and against **D** our god." 1 Sm 5:7
fastened his head in the temple of **D**. 1 Chr 10:10

DAILY (31)
your work, your **d** task each day, Ex 5:13
of bricks, your **d** task each day." Ex 5:19
will be twice as much as they gather **d**." Ex 16:5
In the same way you shall offer **d**, for Nm 28:24
the king, according to his **d** needs, 2 Kgs 25:30
and offered the **d** burnt offerings by Ezr 3:4
them for their **d** ration forty shekels Neh 5:15
Nehemiah gave the **d** portions for the Neh 12:47
Blessed be the Lord, who **d** bears us up; Ps 68:19
workman, and I was **d** his delight, Prv 8:30
listens to me, watching **d** at my gates, Prv 8:34
Yet they seek me **d** and delight to know Is 58:2
was given him **d** from the bakers' Jer 37:21
by the king according to his **d** need, Jer 52:34
days you shall provide **d** a male goat Ezk 43:25
and a male goat **d** for a sin offering. Ezk 45:23
for a burnt offering to the LORD **d**; Ezk 46:13
king assigned them a **d** portion of the Dn 1:5

Give us this day our **d** bread, Mt 6:11
and take up his cross **d** and follow me. Lk 9:23
Give us each day our **d** bread, Lk 11:3
And he was teaching **d** in the temple. Lk 19:47
whom they laid **d** at the gate of the Acts 3:2
being neglected in the **d** distribution. Acts 6:1
and they increased in numbers **d**. Acts 16:5
examining the Scriptures **d** to see if Acts 17:11
reasoning **d** in the hall of Tyrannus. Acts 19:9
there is the **d** pressure on me of my 2 Cor 11:28
those high priests, to offer sacrifices **d**, Heb 7:27
every priest stands **d** at his service, Heb 10:11
is poorly clothed and lacking in **d** food, Jas 2:15

DALMANUTHA (1)
disciples and went to the district of **D**. Mk 8:10

DALMATIA (1)
has gone to Galatia, Titus to **D**. 2 Tm 4:10

DALPHON (1)
killed Parshandatha and **D** and Aspatha Est 9:7

DAMAGE (1)
Why should **d** grow to the hurt of the Ezr 4:22

DAMARIS (1)
a woman named **D** and others with Acts 17:34

DAMASCUS (61)
pursued them to Hobah, north of **D**. Gn 14:15
the heir of my house is Eliezer of **D**?" Gn 15:2
when the Syrians of **D** came to help 2 Sm 8:5
David put garrisons in Aram of **D**, 2 Sm 8:6
And they went to **D** and lived there 1 Kgs 11:24
lived there and made him king in **D**. 1 Kgs 11:24
king of Syria, who lived in **D**, 1 Kgs 15:18
on your way to the wilderness of **D**. 1 Kgs 19:15
establish bazaars for yourself in **D**, 1 Kgs 20:34
Abana and Pharpar, the rivers of **D**, 2 Kgs 5:12
Now Elisha came to **D**. Ben-hadad the 2 Kgs 8:7
with him, all kinds of goods of **D**, 2 Kgs 8:9
how he restored **D** and Hamath to 2 Kgs 14:28
marched up against **D** and took it, 2 Kgs 16:9
Ahaz went to **D** to meet 2 Kgs 16:10
he saw the altar that was at **D**. 2 Kgs 16:10
all that King Ahaz had sent from **D**, 2 Kgs 16:11
it, before King Ahaz arrived from **D**. 2 Kgs 16:11
And when the king came from **D**, 2 Kgs 16:12
when the Syrians of **D** came to help 1 Chr 18:5
David put garrisons in Syria of **D**, 1 Chr 18:6
king of Syria, who lived in **D**, 2 Chr 16:2
sent all their spoil to the king of **D**. 2 Chr 24:23
of his people and brought them to **D**. 2 Chr 28:5
to the gods of **D** that had defeated 2 Chr 28:23
tower of Lebanon, which looks toward **D**. Sg 7:4
For the head of Syria is **D**, and the head of Is 7:8
is Damascus, and the head of **D** is Rezin. Is 7:8
the wealth of **D** and the spoil of Samaria Is 8:4
like Arpad? Is not Samaria like **D**? Is 10:9
An oracle concerning **D**. Behold, Is 17:1
D will cease to be a city and will become Is 17:1
from Ephraim, and the kingdom from **D**; Is 17:3
Concerning **D**: "Hamath and Arpad are Jer 49:23
D has become feeble, she turned to flee, Jer 49:24
And I will kindle a fire in the wall of **D**, Jer 49:27
D did business with you for your Ezk 27:18
the border between **D** and Hamath), Ezk 47:16
which is on the northern border of **D**, Ezk 47:17
shall run between Hauran and **D**; Ezk 47:18
northern border of **D** over against Ezk 48:1
"For three transgressions of **D**, and for Am 1:3
I will break the gate-bar of **D**, and cut off Am 1:5
you into exile beyond **D**," says the LORD, Am 5:27
land of Hadrach and **D** is its resting Zec 9:1
him for letters to the synagogues at **D**, Acts 9:2
as he went on his way, he approached **D**, Acts 9:3
by the hand and brought him into **D**. Acts 9:8
was a disciple at **D** named Ananias. Acts 9:10
days he was with the disciples at **D**. Acts 9:19
Jews who lived in **D** by proving that Acts 9:22
and how at **D** he had preached boldly Acts 9:27
and I journeyed toward **D** to take those Acts 22:5
I was on my way and drew near to **D**, Acts 22:6
Lord said to me, 'Rise, and go into **D**, Acts 22:10
who were with me, and came into **D**. Acts 22:11
I journeyed to **D** with the authority Acts 26:12
but declared first to those in **D**, then Acts 26:20
At **D**, the governor under King 2 Cor 11:32
guarding the city of **D** in order to 2 Cor 11:32
into Arabia, and returned again to **D**. Gal 1:17

DAMS (1)
He **d** up the streams so that they do not Jb 28:11

DAN (73)
them, and went in pursuit as far as **D**. Gn 14:14
a son." Therefore she called his name **D**. Gn 30:6
Rachel's servant: **D** and Naphtali. Gn 35:25
The sons of **D**: Hushim. Gn 46:23
"**D** shall judge his people as one of the Gn 49:16
D shall be a serpent in the way, a viper Gn 49:17
D and Naphtali, Gad and Asher. Ex 1:4
the son of Ahisamach, of the tribe of **D**. Ex 31:6
the son of Ahisamach of the tribe of **D**. Ex 35:34
the son of Ahisamach, of the tribe of **D**, Ex 38:23
the daughter of Dibri, of the tribe of **D**. Lv 24:11
from **D**, Ahiezer the son of Nm 1:12
Of the people of **D**, their generations, by Nm 1:38
listed of the tribe of **D** were 62,700. Nm 1:39
of the camp of **D** by their companies, Nm 2:25
of the people of **D** being Ahiezer the son Nm 2:25
listed of the camp of **D** were 157,600. Nm 2:31
the chief of the people of **D**: Nm 7:66
of the camp of the people of **D**, Nm 10:25
from the tribe of **D**, Ammiel the son of Nm 13:12
are the sons of **D** according to their Nm 26:42
are the clans of **D** according to their Nm 26:42
Of the tribe of the people of **D** a chief, Nm 34:22
Gad, Asher, Zebulun, **D**, and Naphtali. Dt 27:13
And of **D** he said, "Dan is a lion's cub Dt 33:22
"**D** is a lion's cub that leaps from Dt 33:22
him all the land, Gilead as far as **D**, Dt 34:1
out for the tribe of the people of **D**, Jos 19:40
of the people of **D** was lost to them, Jos 19:47
the people of **D** went up and fought Jos 19:47
D, after the name of Dan their ancestor. Jos 19:47
Dan, after the name of **D** their ancestor. Jos 19:47
of the tribe of the people of **D**, Jos 19:48
from the tribe of **D** and the half-tribe of Jos 21:5
and out of the tribe of **D**, Elteke with its Jos 21:23
pressed the people of **D** back into the hill Jgs 1:34
Gilead stayed beyond the Jordan; and **D**, Jgs 5:17
of the people of **D** was seeking for itself Jgs 18:1
So the people of **D** sent five able men Jgs 18:2
So 600 men of the tribe of **D**, armed Jgs 18:11
out, and they overtook the people of **D**. Jgs 18:22
And they shouted to the people of **D**, Jgs 18:23
And the people of **D** said to him, "Do Jgs 18:25
Then the people of **D** went their way. Jgs 18:26
But the people of **D** took what Micah Jgs 18:27
And they named the city **D**, after the Jgs 18:29
Dan, after the name of **D** their ancestor, Jgs 18:29
And the people of **D** set up the carved Jgs 18:30
of Israel came out, from **D** to Beersheba, Jgs 20:1
all Israel from **D** to Beersheba knew 1 Sm 3:20
and over Judah, from **D** to Beersheba." 2 Sm 3:10
to you, from **D** to Beersheba, 2 Sm 17:11
tribes of Israel, from **D** to Beersheba, 2 Sm 24:2
and they came to **D**, and from Dan 2 Sm 24:6
and from **D** they went around to 2 Sm 24:6
the people from **D** to Beersheba 2 Sm 24:15
in safety, from **D** even to Beersheba, 1 Kgs 4:25
in Bethel, and the other he put in **D**. 1 Kgs 12:29
went as far as **D** to be before one. 1 Kgs 12:30
Ijon, **D**, Abel-beth-maacah, 1 Kgs 15:20
calves that were in Bethel and in **D**. 2 Kgs 10:29
D, Joseph, Benjamin, Naphtali, Gad, 1 Chr 2:2
number Israel, from Beersheba to **D**, 1 Chr 21:2
for **D**, Azarel the son of Jeroham. 1 Chr 27:22
of a woman of the daughters of **D**, 2 Chr 2:14
they conquered Ijon, **D**, Abel-maim, 2 Chr 16:4
all Israel, from Beersheba to **D**, 2 Chr 30:5
voice declares from **D** and proclaims Jer 4:15
snorting of their horses is heard from **D**; Jer 8:16
the east side to the west, **D**, one portion. Ezk 48:1
Adjoining the territory of **D**, from the Ezk 48:2
gate of Benjamin, and the gate of **D**. Ezk 48:32
and say, 'As your god lives, O **D**,' Am 8:14

DANCE (10)
of Shiloh come out to **d** in the dances, Jgs 21:21
boys like a flock, and their children **d**. Jb 21:11
Praise him with tambourine and **d**; Ps 150:4
laugh; a time to mourn, and a time to **d**; Eccl 3:4
as upon a **d** before two armies? Sg 6:13
will dwell, and there wild goats will **d**. Is 13:21
go forth in the **d** of the merrymakers. Jer 31:4
shall the young women rejoice in the **d**, Jer 31:13
the flute for you, and you did not **d**; Mt 11:17
the flute for you, and you did not **d**; Lk 7:32

DANCED (3)
And David **d** before the LORD with all 2 Sm 6:14
daughter of Herodias **d** before the Mt 14:6
Herodias's daughter came in and **d**, Mk 6:22

DANCERS (2)
from the **d** whom they carried off. Jgs 21:23
Singers and **d** alike say, "All my springs Ps 87:7

DANCES (5)
him with tambourines and with **d**. Jgs 11:34
of Shiloh come out to dance in the **d**, Jgs 21:21
not sing to one another of him in **d**, 1 Sm 21:11
whom they sing to one another in **d**, 1 Sm 29:5
strength, and terror **d** before him. Jb 41:22

DANCING (10)
out after her with tambourines and **d**. Ex 15:20
the camp and saw the calf and the **d**, Ex 32:19
of all the cities of Israel, singing and **d**, 1 Sm 18:6
the land, eating and drinking and **d**, 1 Sm 30:16
David leaping and **d** before the LORD, 2 Sm 6:16
saw King David **d** and rejoicing, 1 Chr 15:29
turned for me my mourning into **d**; Ps 30:11
Let them praise his name with **d**, Ps 149:3
our **d** has been turned to mourning. Lam 5:15
to the house, he heard music and **d**. Lk 15:25

DANGER (16)
it is safe for you and there is no **d**. 1 Sm 20:21
The prudent sees **d** and hides himself, Prv 22:3
The prudent sees **d** and hides himself, Prv 27:12
were filling with water and were in **d**. Lk 8:23
And there is **d** not only that this trade Acts 19:27
we really are in **d** of being charged Acts 19:40
or famine, or nakedness, or **d**, Rom 8:35
Why am I in **d** every hour? 1 Cor 15:30
frequent journeys, in **d** from rivers, 2 Cor 11:26
danger from rivers, **d** from robbers, 2 Cor 11:26
robbers, **d** from my own people, 2 Cor 11:26
my own people, **d** from Gentiles, 2 Cor 11:26
danger from Gentiles, **d** in the city, 2 Cor 11:26
in the city, **d** in the wilderness, 2 Cor 11:26
danger in the wilderness, **d** at sea, 2 Cor 11:26
danger at sea, **d** from false brothers; 2 Cor 11:26

DANGEROUS (1)
the voyage was now **d** because even the Acts 27:9

DANIEL (82)
second, **D**, by Abigail the Carmelite, 1 Chr 3:1
sons of Ithamar, **D**. Of the sons of David, Ezr 8:2
D, Ginnethon, Baruch, Neh 10:6
if these three men, Noah, **D**, and Job, Ezk 14:14
even if Noah, **D**, and Job were in it, as I Ezk 14:20
you are indeed wiser than **D**; no secret Ezk 28:3
Among these were **D**, Hananiah, Mishael, Dn 1:6
D he called Belteshazzar, Hananiah he Dn 1:7
But **D** resolved that he would not defile Dn 1:8
And God gave **D** favor and compassion Dn 1:9
and the chief of the eunuchs said to **D**, "I Dn 1:10
Then **D** said to the steward whom the Dn 1:11
of the eunuchs had assigned over **D**, Dn 1:11
and **D** had understanding in all visions Dn 1:17
all of them none was found like **D**, Dn 1:19
And **D** was there until the first year of Dn 1:21
and they sought **D** and his companions, Dn 2:13
Then **D** replied with prudence and Dn 2:14
Arioch made the matter known to **D**. Dn 2:15
And **D** went in and requested the king to Dn 2:16
Then **D** went to his house and made the Dn 2:17
so that **D** and his companions might Dn 2:18
mystery was revealed to **D** in a vision of Dn 2:19
Then **D** blessed the God of heaven. Dn 2:19
D answered and said: "Blessed be the Dn 2:20
Therefore **D** went in to Arioch, whom Dn 2:24
Arioch brought in **D** before the king Dn 2:25
The king said to **D**, whose name was Dn 2:26
D answered the king and said, "No wise Dn 2:27
fell upon his face and paid homage to **D**, Dn 2:46
The king answered and said to **D**, Dn 2:47
Then the king gave **D** high honors and Dn 2:48
D made a request of the king, and he Dn 2:49
But **D** remained at the king's court. Dn 2:49
At last **D** came in before me—he who Dn 4:8
Then **D**, whose name was Belteshazzar, Dn 4:19
solve problems were found in this **D**, Dn 5:12
Belteshazzar. Now let **D** be called, Dn 5:12
Then **D** was brought in before the king. Dn 5:13
The king answered and said to **D**, "You Dn 5:13
and said to Daniel, "You are that **D**, Dn 5:13
Then **D** answered and said before the Dn 5:17
and **D** was clothed with purple, Dn 5:29
three presidents, of whom **D** was one, Dn 6:2
Then this **D** became distinguished above Dn 6:3
for complaint against **D** with regard to Dn 6:4
complaint against this **D** unless we find Dn 6:5
When **D** knew that the document had Dn 6:10
and found **D** making petition Dn 6:11
"**D**, who is one of the exiles from Judah, Dn 6:13
distressed and set his mind to deliver **D**. Dn 6:14
and **D** was brought and cast into the Dn 6:16
The king declared to **D**, "May your God, Dn 6:16
might be changed concerning **D**. Dn 6:17
As he came near to the den where **D** was, Dn 6:20
The king declared to **D**, "O Daniel, Dn 6:20
The king declared to Daniel, "O **D**, Dn 6:20
Then **D** said to the king, "O king, live Dn 6:21
and commanded that **D** be taken up out Dn 6:23
So **D** was taken up out of the den, and no Dn 6:23
maliciously accused **D** were brought Dn 6:24
to tremble and fear before the God of **D**, Dn 6:26
he who has saved **D** from the power of Dn 6:27

So this **D** prospered during the reign of Dn 6:28
D saw a dream and visions of his head as Dn 7:1
D declared, "I saw in my vision by night, Dn 7:2
me, **D**, my spirit within me was anxious, Dn 7:15
me, **D**, my thoughts greatly alarmed me, Dn 7:28
D, after that which appeared to me at the Dn 8:1
When I, **D**, had seen the vision, I sought Dn 8:15
D, was overcome and lay sick for some Dn 8:27
D, perceived in the books the number of Dn 9:2
speaking with me and saying, "O **D**, Dn 9:22
king of Persia a word was revealed to **D**, Dn 10:1
days I, **D**, was mourning for three weeks. Dn 10:2
And I, **D**, alone saw the vision, for the Dn 10:7
And he said to me, "O **D**, man greatly Dn 10:11
D, for from the first day that you set Dn 10:12
D, shut up the words and seal the book, Dn 12:4
Then I, **D**, looked, and behold, two Dn 12:5
D, for the words are shut up and sealed Dn 12:9
desolation spoken of by the prophet **D**, Mt 24:15

DANITES (4)
man of Zorah, of the tribe of the **D**, Jgs 13:2
Now the 600 men of the **D**, armed with Jgs 18:16
to the tribe of the **D** until the day of the Jgs 18:30
Of the **D** 28,600 men equipped for 1 Chr 12:35

DANNAH (1)
D, Kiriath-sannah (that is, Debir), Jos 15:49

DAPPLED (2)
and the fourth chariot **d** horses—all of Zec 6:3
and the **d** ones go toward the south Zec 6:6

DARA (1)
Zimri, Ethan, Heman, Calcol, and **D**, 1 Chr 2:6

DARDA (1)
Ezrahite, and Heman, Calcol, and **D**, 1 Kgs 4:31

DARE (7)
for who would **d** of himself to approach Jer 30:21
that day did anyone **d** to ask him any Mt 22:46
Moses trembled and did not **d** to look. Acts 7:32
a good person one would **d** even to die— Rom 5:7
does he **d** go to law before the 1 Cor 6:1
Not that we **d** to classify or compare 2 Cor 10:12
as a fool—I also **d** to boast of that. 2 Cor 11:21

DARED (5)
he, and where is he, who has **d** to do this?" Est 7:5
And after that no one **d** to ask him any Mk 12:34
For they no longer **d** to ask him any Lk 20:40
Now none of the disciples **d** ask him, Jn 21:12
None of the rest **d** join them, but the Acts 5:13

DARES (3)
lion and as a lioness; who **d** rouse him? Gn 49:9
one is so fierce that he **d** to stir him up. Jb 41:10
whatever anyone else **d** to boast of 2 Cor 11:21

DARICS (6)
5,000 talents and 10,000 **d** of gold, 1 Chr 29:7
treasury of the work 61,000 **d** of gold, Ezr 2:69
20 bowls of gold worth 1,000 **d**, and two Ezr 8:27
gave to the treasury 1,000 **d** of gold, Neh 7:70
of the work 20,000 **d** of gold and 2,200 Neh 7:71
of the people gave was 20,000 **d** of gold, Neh 7:72

DARIUS (26)
even until the reign of **D** king of Persia. Ezr 4:5
year of the reign of **D** king of Persia. Ezr 4:24
the report should reach **D** and then an Ezr 5:5
Beyond the River sent to **D** the king. Ezr 5:6
as follows: "To **D** the king, all peace. Ezr 5:7
Then **D** the king made a decree, and Ezr 6:1
I **D** make a decree; let it be done with all Ezr 6:12
to the word sent by **D** the king, Ezr 6:13
with all diligence what **D** the king had Ezr 6:13
of Cyrus and **D** and Artaxerxes king Ezr 6:14
the sixth year of the reign of **D** the king. Ezr 6:15
priests in the reign of **D** the Persian. Neh 12:22
And **D** the Mede received the kingdom, Dn 5:31
It pleased **D** to set over the kingdom 120 Dn 6:1
to the king and said to him, "O King **D**, Dn 6:6
Therefore King **D** signed the document Dn 6:9
Then King **D** wrote to all the peoples, Dn 6:25
during the reign of **D** and the reign of Dn 6:28
the first year of **D** the son of Ahasuerus, Dn 9:1
as for me, in the first year of **D** the Mede, Dn 11:1
In the second year of **D** the king, in the Hg 1:1
month, in the second year of **D** the king. Hg 1:15
ninth month, in the second year of **D**, Hg 2:10
eighth month, in the second year of **D**, Zec 1:1
month of Shebat, in the second year of **D**, Zec 1:7
In the fourth year of King **D**, the word of Zec 7:1

DARK (33)
the sun had gone down and it was **d**, Gn 15:17
when the gate was about to be closed at **d**, Jos 2:5
as it began to grow **d** at the gates of Neh 13:19
Let the stars of its dawn be **d**; let it hope for Jb 3:9
which are **d** with ice, and where the snow Jb 6:16
They grope in the **d** without light, and Jb 12:25
The light is **d** in his tent, and his lamp Jb 18:6
In the **d** they dig through houses; by day Jb 24:16
string to shoot in the **d** at the upright in Ps 11:2
around him, thick clouds **d** with water. Ps 18:11
Let their way be **d** and slippery, with the Ps 35:6
for the **d** places of the land are full of the Ps 74:20
parable; I will utter **d** sayings from of old, Ps 78:2
of the pit, in the regions **d** and deep. Ps 88:6
He sent darkness, and made the land **d**; Ps 105:28
even the darkness is not **d** to you; the Ps 139:12
I am very **d**, but lovely, O daughters of Sg 1:5
Do not gaze at me because I am **d**, because Sg 1:6
the sun will be **d** at its rising, and the Is 13:10
for lack of wine; all joy has grown **d**; Is 24:11
your counsel, whose deeds are in the **d**, Is 29:15
mourn, and the heavens above be **d**; Jer 4:28
of the house of Israel are doing in the **d**, Ezk 8:12
At Tehaphnehes the day shall be **d**, Ezk 30:18
the heavens and make their stars **d**; Ezk 32:7
lights of heaven will I make **d** over you, Ezk 32:8
What I tell you in the **d**, say in the Mt 10:27
in the morning, while it was still **d**, Mk 1:35
body is full of light, having no part **d**, Lk 11:36
you have said in the **d** shall be heard in Lk 12:3
It was now **d**, and Jesus had not yet come Jn 6:17
to the tomb early, while it was still **d**, Jn 20:1
as to a lamp shining in a **d** place, 2 Pt 1:19

DARKEN (1)
down at noon and **d** the earth in broad Am 8:9

DARKENED (14)
the whole land, so that the land was **d**, Ex 10:15
I go about **d**, but not by the sun; I stand Jb 30:28
Let their eyes be **d**, so that they cannot Ps 69:23
and the stars are **d** and the clouds Eccl 12:2
distress; and the light is **d** by its clouds. Is 5:30
The sun and the moon are **d**, and the stars Jl 2:10
The sun and the moon are **d**, and the stars Jl 3:15
of those days the sun will be **d**, Mt 24:29
that tribulation, the sun will be **d**, Mk 13:24
and their foolish hearts were **d**. Rom 1:21
let their eyes be **d** so that they cannot Rom 11:10
They are **d** in their understanding, Eph 4:18
so that a third of their light might be **d**, Rv 8:12
and the air were **d** with the smoke from Rv 9:2

DARKENS (2)
"Who is this that **d** counsel by words Jb 38:2
into the morning and **d** the day into Am 5:8

DARKER (1)
His eyes are **d** than wine, and his teeth Gn 49:12

DARKNESS (174)
void, and **d** was over the face of the deep. Gn 1:2
And God separated the light from the **d**. Gn 1:4
the light Day, and the **d** he called Night. Gn 1:5
and to separate the light from the **d**. Gn 1:18
dreadful and great **d** fell upon him. Gn 15:12
that there may be **d** over the land of Ex 10:21
over the land of Egypt, a **d** to be felt." Ex 10:21
and there was pitch **d** in all the land of Ex 10:22
And there was the cloud and the **d**. Ex 14:20
drew near to the thick **d** where God was. Ex 20:21
fire to the heart of heaven, wrapped in **d**, Dt 4:11
of the fire, the cloud, and the thick **d**, Dt 5:22
heard the voice out of the midst of the **d**, Dt 5:23
at noonday, as the blind grope in **d**, Dt 28:29
he put **d** between you and the Egyptians Jos 24:7
but the wicked shall be cut off in **d**, 1 Sm 2:9
down; thick **d** was under his feet. 2 Sm 22:10
He made **d** around him his canopy, 2 Sm 22:12
O LORD, and my God lightens my **d**. 2 Sm 22:29
said that he would dwell in thick **d**. 1 Kgs 8:12
said that he would dwell in thick **d**. 2 Chr 6:1
Let that day be **d**! May God above not seek Jb 3:4
Let gloom and deep **d** claim it. Let clouds Jb 3:5
That night—let thick **d** seize it! Let it not Jb 3:6
They meet with **d** in the daytime and Jb 5:14
to the land of **d** and deep shadow, Jb 10:21
the land of gloom like thick **d**, like deep Jb 10:22
any order, where light is as thick **d**." Jb 10:22
noonday; its **d** will be like the morning. Jb 11:17
the deeps out of **d** and brings deep Jb 12:22
of darkness and brings deep **d** to light. Jb 12:22
not believe that he will return out of **d**, Jb 15:22
knows that a day of **d** is ready at his Jb 15:23
he will not depart from **d**; the flame will Jb 15:30
weeping, and on my eyelids is deep **d**, Jb 16:16
'The light,' they say, 'is near to the **d**.' Jb 17:12
as my house, if I make my bed in **d**, Jb 17:13
He is thrust from light into **d**, and Jb 18:18
pass, and he has set **d** upon my paths. Jb 19:8
Utter **d** is laid up for his treasures; a fire Jb 20:26
or **d**, so that you cannot see, and a flood Jb 22:11
Can he judge through the deep **d**? Jb 22:13
yet I am not silenced because of the **d**, Jb 23:17
nor because thick **d** covers my face. Jb 23:17
For deep **d** is morning to all of them; for Jb 24:17
are friends with the terrors of deep **d**. Jb 24:17
at the boundary between light and **d**. Jb 26:10
Man puts an end to **d** and searches out to Jb 28:3
limit the ore in gloom and deep **d**. Jb 28:3
and by his light I walked through **d**, Jb 29:3
and when I waited for light, **d** came. Jb 30:26
no gloom or deep **d** where evildoers may Jb 34:22
cannot draw up our case because of **d**. Jb 37:19
garment and thick **d** its swaddling band, Jb 38:9
or have you seen the gates of deep **d**? Jb 38:17
of light, and where is the place of **d**, Jb 38:19
came down; thick **d** was under his feet. Ps 18:9
He made **d** his covering, his canopy Ps 18:11
lamp; the LORD my God lightens my **d**. Ps 18:28
understanding, they walk about in **d**; Ps 82:5
Are your wonders known in the **d**, or Ps 88:12
me; my companions have become **d**. Ps 88:18
nor the pestilence that stalks in **d**, nor Ps 91:6
Clouds and thick **d** are all around him; Ps 97:2
You make **d**, and it is night, when all Ps 104:20
He sent **d**, and made the land dark; Ps 105:28
Some sat in **d** and in the shadow of Ps 107:10
brought them out of **d** and the shadow Ps 107:14
Light dawns in the **d** for the upright; he Ps 112:4
If I say, "Surely the **d** shall cover me, Ps 139:11
even the **d** is not dark to you; the night Ps 139:12
as the day, for **d** is as light with you. Ps 139:12
made me sit in **d** like those long dead. Ps 143:3
of uprightness to walk in the ways of **d**, Prv 2:13
The way of the wicked is like deep **d**; Prv 4:19
in the evening, at the time of night and **d**. Prv 7:9
his lamp will be put out in utter **d**. Prv 20:20
as there is more gain in light than in **d**. Eccl 2:13
in his head, but the fool walks in **d**. Eccl 2:14
days he eats in **d** in much vexation Eccl 5:17
For it comes in vanity and goes in **d**, Eccl 6:4
darkness, and in **d** its name is covered. Eccl 6:4
that the days of **d** will be many. Eccl 11:8
who put **d** for light and light for darkness, Is 5:20
who put darkness for light and light for **d**, Is 5:20
looks to the land, behold, **d** and distress; Is 5:30
to the earth, but behold, distress and **d**, Is 8:22
And they will be thrust into thick **d**. Is 8:22
people who walked in **d** have seen a great Is 9:2
those who dwelt in a land of deep **d**, on Is 9:2
out of their gloom and **d** the eyes of the Is 29:18
from the prison those who sit in **d**. Is 42:7
I will turn the **d** before them into light, Is 42:16
you the treasures of **d** and the hoards in Is 45:3
I form light and create **d**, I make Is 45:7
I did not speak in secret, in a land of **d**; I Is 45:19
Sit in silence, and go into **d**, O daughter of Is 47:5
'Come out,' to those who are in **d**, Is 49:9
Let him who walks in **d** and has no light Is 50:10
light rise in the **d** and your gloom be Is 58:10
light, and behold, **d**, and for brightness, Is 59:9
For behold, **d** shall cover the earth, and Is 60:2
cover the earth, and thick **d** the peoples; Is 60:2
and pits, in a land of drought and deep **d**, Jer 2:6
wilderness to Israel, or a land of thick **d**? Jer 2:31
the LORD your God before he brings **d**, Jer 13:16
turns it into gloom and makes it deep **d**. Jer 13:16
be to them like slippery paths in the **d**, Jer 23:12
brought me into **d** without any light; Lam 3:2
has made me dwell in **d** like the dead of Lam 3:6
dark over you, and put **d** on your land, Ezk 32:8
on a day of clouds and thick **d**. Ezk 34:12
he knows what is in the **d**, and the light Dn 2:22
a day of **d** and gloom, a day of clouds and Jl 2:2
and gloom, a day of clouds and thick **d**! Jl 2:2
The sun shall be turned to **d**, and the Jl 2:31
thought, who makes the morning **d**, Am 4:13
and turns deep **d** into the morning and Am 5:8
day of the LORD? It is **d**, and not light, Am 5:18
Is not the day of the LORD **d**, and not Am 5:20
night to you, without vision, and **d** to you, Mi 3:6
when I sit in **d**, the LORD will be a light to Mi 7:8
and will pursue his enemies into **d**. Na 1:8
and devastation, a day of **d** and gloom, Zep 1:15
and gloom, a day of clouds and thick **d**, Zep 1:15
the people dwelling in **d** have seen a Mt 4:16
is bad, your whole body will be full of **d**. Mt 6:23
If then the light in you is **d**, how great is Mt 6:23
in you is darkness, how great is the **d**! Mt 6:23
will be thrown into the outer **d**. Mt 8:12
and foot and cast him into the outer **d**. Mt 22:13
the worthless servant into the outer **d**. Mt 25:30
sixth hour there was **d** over all the land Mt 27:45
there was **d** over the whole land until Mk 15:33
to those who sit in **d** and in the shadow Lk 1:79
when it is bad, your body is full of **d**. Lk 11:34

be careful lest the light in you be **d**. Lk 11:35
this is your hour, and the power of **d**." Lk 22:53
and there was **d** over the whole land Lk 23:44
The light shines in the **d**, and the darkness Jn 1:5
darkness, and the **d** has not overcome it. Jn 1:5
and people loved the **d** rather than the Jn 3:19
Whoever follows me will not walk in **d**, Jn 8:12
you have the light, lest **d** overtake you. Jn 12:35
who walks in the **d** does not know Jn 12:35
believes in me may not remain in **d**. Jn 12:46
shall be turned to **d** and the moon to Acts 2:20
Immediately mist and **d** fell upon Acts 13:11
they may turn from **d** to light and Acts 26:18
the blind, a light to those who are in **d**, Rom 2:19
cast off the works of **d** and put on the Rom 13:12
now hidden in **d** and will disclose 1 Cor 4:5
light shine out of **d**," has shone in our 2 Cor 4:6
Or what fellowship has light with **d**? 2 Cor 6:14
for at one time you were **d**, but now you Eph 5:8
no part in the unfruitful works of **d**, Eph 5:11
the cosmic powers over this present **d**, Eph 6:12
the domain of **d** and transferred us Col 1:13
But you are not in **d**, brothers, for 1 Thes 5:4
We are not of the night or of the **d**. 1 Thes 5:5
a blazing fire and **d** and gloom and a Heb 12:18
called you out of **d** into his marvelous 1 Pt 2:9
to chains of gloomy **d** to be kept until 2 Pt 2:4
the gloom of utter **d** has been reserved. 2 Pt 2:17
God is light, and in him is no **d** at all. 1 Jn 1:5
fellowship with him while we walk in **d**, 1 Jn 1:6
because the **d** is passing away and the 1 Jn 2:8
light and hates his brother is still in **d**. 1 Jn 2:9
his brother is in the **d** and walks in the 1 Jn 2:11
is in the darkness and walks in the **d**, 1 Jn 2:11
because the **d** has blinded his eyes. 1 Jn 2:11
chains under gloomy **d** until the Jude 1:6
the gloom of utter **d** has been reserved Jude 1:13
and its kingdom was plunged into **d**. Rv 16:10

DARKON (2)

the sons of Jaalah, the sons of **D**, the Ezr 2:56
the sons of Jaala, the sons of **D**, the sons Neh 7:58

DARLING (1)

my dear son? Is he my **d** child? Jer 31:20

DART (2)

it does not avail, nor the spear, the **d**, Jb 41:26
gleam like torches; they **d** like lightning. Na 2:4

DARTED (1)

And the living creatures **d** to and fro, Ezk 1:14

DARTS (1)

extinguish all the flaming **d** of the evil Eph 6:16

DASH (5)

down their altars and **d** in pieces their Dt 7:5
down their altars and **d** in pieces their Dt 12:3
with the sword and **d** in pieces their 2 Kgs 8:12
a rod of iron and **d** them in pieces like a Ps 2:9
And I will **d** them one against another, Jer 13:14

DASHED (6)

rock, and they were all **d** to pieces. 2 Chr 25:12
me by the neck and **d** me to pieces; Jb 16:12
Their infants will be **d** in pieces before Is 13:16
mothers were **d** in pieces with their Hos 10:14
their little ones shall be **d** in pieces, Hos 13:16
her infants were **d** in pieces at the head Na 3:10

DASHES (1)

your little ones and **d** them against the Ps 137:9

DATE (1)

and managers until the **d** set by his Gal 4:2

DATHAN (10)

and **D** and Abiram the sons of Eliab, Nm 16:1
Moses sent to call **D** and Abiram the Nm 16:12
dwelling of Korah, **D**, and Abiram." Nm 16:24
rose and went to **D** and Abiram, Nm 16:25
dwelling of Korah, **D**, and Abiram. Nm 16:27
And **D** and Abiram came out and Nm 16:27
sons of Eliab: Nemuel, **D**, and Abiram. Nm 26:9
These are the **D** and Abiram, chosen Nm 26:9
what he did to **D** and Abiram the sons Dt 11:6
the earth opened and swallowed up **D**, Ps 106:17

DAUBED (1)

made of bulrushes and **d** it with bitumen Ex 2:3

DAUGHTER (294)

the **d** of Haran the father of Milcah and Gn 11:29
the **d** of my father though not the Gn 20:12
father though not the **d** of my mother, Gn 20:12
said, "Please tell me whose **d** you are. Gn 24:23
"I am the **d** of Bethuel the son of Gn 24:24
Then I asked her, 'Whose **d** are you?' Gn 24:47
She said, 'The **d** of Bethuel, Nahor's Gn 24:47
way to take the **d** of my master's Gn 24:48
the **d** of Bethuel the Aramean of Gn 25:20
he took Judith the **d** of Beeri the Hittite Gn 26:34
and Basemath the **d** of Elon the Hittite, Gn 26:34
he had, Mahalath the **d** of Ishmael, Gn 28:9
Rachel his **d** is coming with the sheep!" Gn 29:6
Jacob saw Rachel the **d** of Laban his Gn 29:10
years for your younger **d** Rachel." Gn 29:18
he took his **d** Leah and brought Gn 29:23
servant Zilpah to his **d** Leah to be her Gn 29:24
Laban gave him his **d** Rachel to be his Gn 29:28
servant Bilhah to his **d** Rachel to be Gn 29:29
Afterward she bore a **d** and called her Gn 30:21
Now Dinah the **d** of Leah, whom she Gn 34:1
soul was drawn to Dinah the **d** of Jacob. Gn 34:3
heard that he had defiled his **d** Dinah. Gn 34:5
thing in Israel by lying with Jacob's **d**, Gn 34:7
of my son Shechem longs for your **d**. Gn 34:8
circumcised, then we will take our **d**, Gn 34:17
because he delighted in Jacob's **d**. Gn 34:19
Adah the **d** of Elon the Hittite, Gn 36:2
Oholibamah the **d** of Anah the Gn 36:2
daughter of Anah the **d** of Zibeon the Gn 36:2
and Basemath, Ishmael's **d**, the sister of Gn 36:3
sons of Oholibamah the **d** of Anah the Gn 36:14
the daughter of Anah the **d** of Zibeon, Gn 36:14
born of Oholibamah the **d** of Anah, Gn 36:18
and Oholibamah the **d** of Anah. Gn 36:25
name was Mehetabel, the **d** of Matred, Gn 36:39
the daughter of Matred, **d** of Mezahab. Gn 36:39
There Judah saw the **d** of a certain Gn 38:2
of time the wife of Judah, Shua's **d**, Gn 38:12
the **d** of Potiphera priest of On. Gn 41:45
the **d** of Potiphera priest of On, Gn 41:50
together with his **d** Dinah; Gn 46:15
whom Laban gave to Leah his **d**; Gn 46:18
the **d** of Potiphera the priest of On, Gn 46:20
whom Laban gave to Rachel his **d**, Gn 46:25
a son, you shall kill him, but if it is a **d**, Ex 1:16
the Nile, but you shall let every **d** live." Ex 1:22
Now the **d** of Pharaoh came down to Ex 2:5
Then his sister said to Pharaoh's **d**, "Shall Ex 2:7
And Pharaoh's **d** said to her, "Go." So the Ex 2:8
And Pharaoh's **d** said to her, "Take this Ex 2:9
up, she brought him to Pharaoh's **d**, Ex 2:10
man, and he gave Moses his **d** Zipporah. Ex 2:21
the **d** of Amminadab and the sister of Ex 6:23
any work, you, or your son, or your **d**, Ex 20:10
"When a man sells his **d** as a slave, she Ex 21:7
son, he shall deal with her as with a **d**. Ex 21:9
If it gores a man's son or **d**, he shall be Ex 21:31
completed, whether for a son or for a **d**, Lv 12:6
your father's **d** or your mother's Lv 18:9
father's daughter or your mother's **d**, Lv 18:9
nakedness of your son's **d** or of your Lv 18:10
son's daughter or of your daughter's **d**, Lv 18:10
the nakedness of your father's wife's **d**, Lv 18:11
the nakedness of a woman and of her **d**, Lv 18:17
not take her son's **d** or her daughter's Lv 18:17
or her daughter's **d** to uncover her Lv 18:17
"Do not profane your **d** by making her Lv 19:29
a **d** of his father or a daughter of his Lv 20:17
of his father or a **d** of his mother, Lv 20:17
his mother, his father, his son, his **d**, Lv 21:2
And the **d** of any priest, if she profanes Lv 21:9
If a priest's **d** marries a layman, she Lv 22:12
But if a priest's **d** is widowed or divorced Lv 22:13
name was Shelomith, the **d** of Dibri, Lv 24:11
was killed was Cozbi the **d** of Zur, Nm 25:15
of Cozbi, the **d** of the chief of Midian, Nm 25:18
the name of the **d** of Asher was Serah. Nm 26:46
wife was Jochebed the **d** of Levi, Nm 26:59
shall transfer his inheritance to his **d**. Nm 27:8
And if he has no **d**, then you shall give Nm 27:9
a father and his **d** while she is in Nm 30:16
And every **d** who possesses an Nm 36:8
your son or your **d** or your male servant Dt 5:14
choose, you and your son and your **d**, Dt 12:18
or your son or your **d** or the wife you Dt 13:6
your God, you and your son and your **d**, Dt 16:11
feast, you and your son and your **d**, Dt 16:14
burns his son or his **d** as an offering, Dt 18:10
'I gave my **d** to this man to marry, Dt 22:16
find in your **d** evidence of virginity." Dt 22:17
whether the **d** of his father or the Dt 27:22
of his father or the **d** of his mother.' Dt 27:22
she embraces, to her son and to her **d**, Dt 28:56
him will I give Achsah my **d** as wife." Jos 15:16
And he gave him Achsah his **d** as wife. Jos 15:17
I will give him Achsah my **d** for a wife." Jgs 1:12
he gave him Achsah his **d** for a wife. Jgs 1:13
his **d** came out to meet him with Jgs 11:34
besides her he had neither son nor **d**. Jgs 11:34
tore his clothes and said, "Alas, my **d**! Jgs 11:35
year to lament the **d** of Jephthah the Jgs 11:40
are my virgin **d** and his concubine. Jgs 19:24
us shall give his **d** in marriage to Jgs 21:1
favor." And she said to her, "Go, my **d**." Ru 2:2
Boaz said to Ruth, "Now, listen, my **d**, Ru 2:8
her daughter-in-law, "It is good, my **d**, Ru 2:22
her mother-in-law said to her, "My **d**, Ru 3:1
"May you be blessed by the LORD, my **d**. Ru 3:10
And now, my **d**, do not fear. I will do for Ru 3:11
my **d**?" Then she told her all that the Ru 3:16
She replied, "Wait, my **d**, until you learn Ru 3:18
wife was Ahinoam the **d** of Ahimaaz. 1 Sm 14:50
will give him his **d** and make his 1 Sm 17:25
to David, "Here is my elder **d** Merab. 1 Sm 18:17
at the time when Merab, Saul's **d**, 1 Sm 18:19
Now Saul's **d** Michal loved David. 1 Sm 18:20
Saul gave him his **d** Michal for a 1 Sm 18:27
David, and that Michal, Saul's **d**, 1 Sm 18:28
Saul had given Michal his **d**, David's 1 Sm 25:44
son of Maacah the **d** of Talmai king of 2 Sm 3:3
whose name was Rizpah, the **d** of Aiah. 2 Sm 3:7
you first bring Michal, Saul's **d**, 2 Sm 3:13
Michal the **d** of Saul looked out of the 2 Sm 6:16
But Michal the **d** of Saul came out to 2 Sm 6:20
And Michal the **d** of Saul had no 2 Sm 6:23
"Is not this Bathsheba, the **d** of Eliam, 2 Sm 11:3
in his arms, and it was like a **d** to him. 2 Sm 12:3
and one **d** whose name was Tamar. 2 Sm 14:27
had married Abigal the **d** of Nahash, 2 Sm 17:25
the two sons of Rizpah the **d** of Aiah, 2 Sm 21:8
the five sons of Merab the **d** of Saul, 2 Sm 21:8
Then Rizpah the **d** of Aiah took 2 Sm 21:10
was told what Rizpah the **d** of Aiah, 2 Sm 21:11
He took Pharaoh's **d** and brought her 1 Kgs 3:1
(he had Taphath the **d** of Solomon as 1 Kgs 4:11
taken Basemath the **d** of Solomon as 1 Kgs 4:15
this hall for Pharaoh's **d** whom he had 1 Kgs 7:8
and had given it as dowry to his **d**, 1 Kgs 9:16
But Pharaoh's **d** went up from the 1 Kgs 9:24
women, along with the **d** of Pharaoh: 1 Kgs 11:1
was Maacah the **d** of Abishalom. 1 Kgs 15:2
was Maacah the **d** of Abishalom. 1 Kgs 15:10
wife Jezebel the **d** of Ethbaal king 1 Kgs 16:31
name was Azubah the **d** of Shilhi. 1 Kgs 22:42
done, for the **d** of Ahab was his wife. 2 Kgs 8:18
and bury her, for she is a king's **d**." 2 Kgs 9:34
But Jehosheba, the **d** of King Joram, 2 Kgs 11:2
'Give your **d** to my son for a wife,' 2 Kgs 14:9
name was Jerusha the **d** of Zadok. 2 Kgs 15:33
name was Abi the **d** of Zechariah. 2 Kgs 18:2
scorns you—the virgin **d** of Zion; 2 Kgs 19:21
behind you—the **d** of Jerusalem. 2 Kgs 19:21
was Meshullemeth the **d** of Haruz of 2 Kgs 21:19
name was Jedidah the **d** of Adaiah of 2 Kgs 22:1
his son or his **d** as an offering to 2 Kgs 23:10
was Hamutal the **d** of Jeremiah of 2 Kgs 23:31
was Zebidah the **d** of Pedaiah of 2 Kgs 23:36
was Nehushta the **d** of Elnathan of 2 Kgs 24:8
was Hamutal the **d** of Jeremiah of 2 Kgs 24:18
was Mehetabel, the **d** of Matred, 1 Chr 1:50
of Matred, the **d** of Mezahab. 1 Chr 1:50
went in to the **d** of Machir the father 1 Chr 2:21
So Sheshan gave his **d** in marriage to 1 Chr 2:35
and the **d** of Caleb was Achsah. 1 Chr 2:49
mother was Maacah, the **d** of Talmai, 1 Chr 3:2
four by Bath-shua, the **d** of Ammiel; 1 Chr 3:5
the sons of Bithiah, the **d** of Pharaoh, 1 Chr 4:17
His **d** was Sheerah, who built both 1 Chr 7:24
Michal the **d** of Saul looked out of 1 Chr 15:29
brought Pharaoh's **d** up from 2 Chr 8:11
wife Mahalath the **d** of Jerimoth the 2 Chr 11:18
and of Abihail the **d** of Eliab the son 2 Chr 11:18
he took Maacah the **d** of Absalom, 2 Chr 11:20
loved Maacah the **d** of Absalom 2 Chr 11:21
name was Micaiah the **d** of Uriel of 2 Chr 13:2
name was Azubah the **d** of Shilhi. 2 Chr 20:31
done, for the **d** of Ahab was his wife. 2 Chr 21:6
But Jehoshabeath, the **d** of the king, 2 Chr 22:11
the **d** of King Jehoram and wife of 2 Chr 22:11
'Give your **d** to my son for a wife,' 2 Chr 25:18
name was Jerushah the **d** of Zadok. 2 Chr 27:1
name was Abijah the **d** of Zechariah. 2 Chr 29:1
had taken the **d** of Meshullam the Neh 6:18
that is Esther, the **d** of his uncle, Est 2:7
died, Mordecai took her as his own **d**. Est 2:7
came for Esther the **d** of Abihail the Est 2:15
who had taken her as his own **d**, Est 2:15
Then Queen Esther, the **d** of Abihail, Est 9:29
called the name of the first **d** Jemimah, Jb 42:14
in the gates of the **d** of Zion I may rejoice Ps 9:14
Hear, O **d**, and consider, and incline Ps 45:10
O **d** of Babylon, doomed to be destroyed, Ps 137:8
are your feet in sandals, O noble **d**! Sg 7:1
And the **d** of Zion is left like a booth in a Is 1:8
Cry aloud, O **d** of Gallim! Give attention, Is 10:30
his fist at the mount of the **d** of Zion, Is 10:32
of the desert, to the mount of the **d** of Zion. Is 16:1
the destruction of the **d** of my people." Is 22:4

your land like the Nile, O **d** of Tarshish; Is 23:10
exult, O oppressed virgin **d** of Sidon; Is 23:12
she scorns you—the virgin **d** of Zion; Is 37:22
head behind you—the **d** of Jerusalem. Is 37:22
and sit in the dust, O virgin **d** of Babylon; Is 47:1
without a throne, O **d** of the Chaldeans! Is 47:1
go into darkness, O **d** of the Chaldeans; Is 47:5
from your neck, O captive **d** of Zion. Is 52:2
Say to the **d** of Zion, "Behold, your Is 62:11
in the desert toward the **d** of my people, Jer 4:11
the cry of the **d** of Zion gasping for Jer 4:31
delicately bred I will destroy, the **d** of Zion. Jer 6:2
for battle, against you, O **d** of Zion!" Jer 6:23
O **d** of my people, put on sackcloth, and Jer 6:26
the cry of the **d** of my people from the Jer 8:19
For the wound of the **d** of my people is Jer 8:21
has the health of the **d** of my people not Jer 8:22
night for the slain of the **d** of my people! Jer 9:1
for the virgin **d** of my people is Jer 14:17
How long will you waver, O faithless **d**? Jer 31:22
and take balm, O virgin **d** of Egypt! Jer 46:11
The **d** of Egypt shall be put to shame; Jer 46:24
you boast of your valleys, O faithless **d**, Jer 49:4
for battle against you, O **d** of Babylon! Jer 50:42
The **d** of Babylon is like a threshing Jer 51:33
name was Hamutal the **d** of Jeremiah of Jer 52:1
From the **d** of Zion all her majesty has Lam 1:6
as in a winepress the virgin **d** of Judah. Lam 1:15
his anger has set the **d** of Zion under a Lam 2:1
down the strongholds of the **d** of Judah; Lam 2:2
in our eyes in the tent of the **d** of Zion; Lam 2:4
multiplied in the **d** of Judah mourning Lam 2:5
to lay in ruins the wall of the **d** of Zion; Lam 2:8
The elders of the **d** of Zion sit on the Lam 2:10
the destruction of the **d** of my people, Lam 2:11
what compare you, O **d** of Jerusalem? Lam 2:13
I may comfort you, O virgin **d** of Zion? Lam 2:13
wag their heads at the **d** of Jerusalem; Lam 2:15
O wall of the **d** of Zion, let tears stream Lam 2:18
the destruction of the **d** of my people. Lam 3:48
but the **d** of my people has become Lam 4:3
the chastisement of the **d** of my people Lam 4:6
the destruction of the **d** of my people. Lam 4:10
Rejoice and be glad, O **d** of Edom, you Lam 4:21
of your iniquity, O **d** of Zion, Lam 4:22
but your iniquity, O **d** of Edom, he will Lam 4:22
they would deliver neither son nor **d**. Ezk 14:20
about you: 'Like mother, like **d**.' Ezk 16:44
You are the **d** of your mother, who Ezk 16:45
in you violates his sister, his father's **d**. Ezk 22:11
for father or mother, for son or **d**, Ezk 44:25
and the **d** of the king of the south shall Dn 11:6
shall give him the **d** of women to Dn 11:17
went and took Gomer, the **d** of Diblaim, Hos 1:3
She conceived again and bore a **d**. And Hos 1:6
was the beginning of sin to the **d** of Zion, Mi 1:13
O tower of the flock, hill of the **d** of Zion, Mi 4:8
come, kingship for the **d** of Jerusalem. Mi 4:8
Writhe and groan, O **d** of Zion, like a Mi 4:10
Arise and thresh, O **d** of Zion, for I will Mi 4:13
Now muster your troops, O **d** of troops; Mi 5:1
the **d** rises up against her mother, Mi 7:6
worshipers, the **d** of my dispersed ones, Zep 3:10
Sing aloud, O **d** of Zion; shout, O Israel! Zep 3:14
with all your heart, O **d** of Jerusalem! Zep 3:14
you who dwell with the **d** of Babylon. Zec 2:7
Sing and rejoice, O **d** of Zion, for Zec 2:10
Rejoice greatly, O **d** of Zion! Shout aloud, Zec 9:9
of Zion! Shout aloud, O **d** of Jerusalem! Zec 9:9
and has married the **d** of a foreign god. Mal 2:11
before him, saying, "My **d** has just died, Mt 9:18
d; your faith has made you well." And Mt 9:22
his father, and a **d** against her mother, Mt 10:35
whoever loves son or **d** more than me is Mt 10:37
the **d** of Herodias danced before the Mt 14:6
my **d** is severely oppressed by a Mt 15:22
desire." And her **d** was healed instantly. Mt 15:28
"Say to the **d** of Zion, 'Behold, your king Mt 21:5
"My little **d** is at the point of death. Mk 5:23
her, "**D**, your faith has made you well; Mk 5:34
house some who said, "Your **d** is dead. Mk 5:35
For when Herodias's **d** came in and Mk 6:22
woman whose little **d** was possessed by Mk 7:25
him to cast the demon out of her **d**. Mk 7:26
your way; the demon has left your **d**." Mk 7:29
a prophetess, Anna, the **d** of Phanuel, Lk 2:36
for he had an only **d**, about twelve years Lk 8:42
to her, "**D**, your faith has made you well; Lk 8:48
house came and said, "Your **d** is dead; Lk 8:49
mother against **d** and daughter against Lk 12:53
daughter and **d** against mother, Lk 12:53
a **d** of Abraham whom Satan bound Lk 13:16
"Fear not, **d** of Zion; behold, your king Jn 12:15
Pharaoh's **d** adopted him and brought Acts 7:21
to be called the son of Pharaoh's **d**, Heb 11:24

DAUGHTER'S (3)

son's daughter or of your **d** daughter, Lv 18:10
daughter or her **d** daughter to uncover Lv 18:17
this is the evidence of my **d** virginity.' Dt 22:17

DAUGHTER-IN-LAW (17)

Haran, his grandson, and Sarai his **d**, Gn 11:31
Then Judah said to Tamar his **d**, Gn 38:11
for he did not know that she was his **d**. Gn 38:16
"Tamar your **d** has been immoral. Gn 38:24
not uncover the nakedness of your **d**; Lv 18:15
If a man lies with his **d**, both of them Lv 20:12
and Ruth the Moabite her **d** with her, Ru 1:22
And Naomi said to her **d**, "May he be Ru 2:20
And Naomi said to Ruth, her **d**, "It is Ru 2:22
your old age, for your **d** who loves you, Ru 4:15
Now his **d**, the wife of Phinehas, was 1 Sm 4:19
His **d** Tamar also bore him Perez and 1 Chr 2:4
wife; another lewdly defiles his **d**; Ezk 22:11
mother, the **d** against her mother-in-law; Mi 7:6
and a **d** against her mother-in-law. Mt 10:35
against her **d** and daughter-in-law Lk 12:53
daughter-in-law and **d** against Lk 12:53

DAUGHTERS (237)

800 years; and he had other sons and **d**. Gn 5:4
807 years and had other sons and **d**. Gn 5:7
815 years and had other sons and **d**. Gn 5:10
840 years and had other sons and **d**. Gn 5:13
830 years and had other sons and **d**. Gn 5:16
800 years and had other sons and **d**. Gn 5:19
300 years and had other sons and **d**. Gn 5:22
782 years and had other sons and **d**. Gn 5:26
595 years and had other sons and **d**. Gn 5:30
face of the land and **d** were born to them, Gn 6:1
God saw that the **d** of man were Gn 6:2
God came in to the **d** of man and they Gn 6:4
500 years and had other sons and **d**. Gn 11:11
403 years and had other sons and **d**. Gn 11:13
403 years and had other sons and **d**. Gn 11:15
430 years and had other sons and **d**. Gn 11:17
209 years and had other sons and **d**. Gn 11:19
207 years and had other sons and **d**. Gn 11:21
200 years and had other sons and **d**. Gn 11:23
119 years and had other sons and **d**. Gn 11:25
I have two **d** who have not known any Gn 19:8
sons, **d**, or anyone you have in the city, Gn 19:12
sons-in-law, who were to marry his **d**, Gn 19:14
your wife and your two **d** who are here, Gn 19:15
and his wife and his two **d** by the hand, Gn 19:16
and lived in the hills with his two **d**, Gn 19:30
So he lived in a cave with his two **d**. Gn 19:30
Thus both the **d** of Lot became Gn 19:36
for my son from the **d** of the Canaanites, Gn 24:3
and the **d** of the men of the city are Gn 24:13
my son from the **d** of the Canaanites, Gn 24:37
there one of the **d** of Laban your Gn 28:2
Now Laban had two **d**. The name of Gn 29:16
and driven away my **d** like captives of Gn 31:26
me to kiss my sons and my **d** farewell? Gn 31:28
you would take your **d** from me by Gn 31:31
you fourteen years for your two **d**, Gn 31:41
said to Jacob, "The **d** are my daughters, Gn 31:43
said to Jacob, "The daughters are my **d**, Gn 31:43
day for these my **d** or for their children Gn 31:43
If you oppress my **d**, or if you take Gn 31:50
or if you take wives besides my **d**, Gn 31:50
grandchildren and his **d** and blessed Gn 31:55
marriages with us. Give your **d** to us, Gn 34:9
to us, and take our **d** for yourselves. Gn 34:9
Then we will give our **d** to you, and we Gn 34:16
and we will take your **d** to ourselves, Gn 34:16
Let us take their **d** as wives, and let us Gn 34:21
as wives, and let us give them our **d**. Gn 34:21
Esau took his wives, his sons, his **d**, Gn 36:6
sons and all his **d** rose up to comfort Gn 37:35
sons, and his sons' sons with him, his **d**, Gn 46:7
with him, his daughters, and his sons' **d**. Gn 46:7
sons and his **d** numbered thirty-three. Gn 46:15
Now the priest of Midian had seven **d**, Ex 2:16
He said to his **d**, "Then where is he? Why Ex 2:20
put them on your sons and on your **d**. Ex 3:22
took as his wife one of the **d** of Putiel, Ex 6:25
with our sons and **d** and with our flocks Ex 10:9
him a wife and she bears him sons or **d**, Ex 21:4
of your wives, your sons, and your **d**, Ex 32:2
and you take of their **d** for your sons, Ex 34:16
and their **d** whore after their gods and Ex 34:16
and your sons and your **d** with you, Lv 10:14
and you shall eat the flesh of your **d**. Lv 26:29
you, and to your sons and **d** with you, Nm 18:11
you, and to your sons and **d** with you, Nm 18:19
his sons fugitives, and his **d** captives, Nm 21:29
began to whore with the **d** of Moab. Nm 25:1
the son of Hepher had no sons, but **d**. Nm 26:33
the names of the **d** of Zelophehad were Nm 26:33
drew near the **d** of Zelophehad the Nm 27:1
The names of his **d** were: Mahlah, Nm 27:1
"The **d** of Zelophehad are right. You Nm 27:7
of Zelophehad our brother to his **d**. Nm 36:2
concerning the **d** of Zelophehad, Nm 36:6
The **d** of Zelophehad did as the LORD Nm 36:10
and Noah, the **d** of Zelophehad, Nm 36:11
giving your **d** to their sons or taking their Dt 7:3
their sons or taking their **d** for your sons, Dt 7:3
God, you and your sons and your **d**, Dt 12:12
burn their sons and their **d** in the fire to Dt 12:31
"None of the **d** of Israel shall be a cult Dt 23:17
Your sons and your **d** shall be given to Dt 28:32
You shall father sons and **d**, but they Dt 28:41
womb, the flesh of your sons and **d**, Dt 28:53
of the provocation of his sons and his **d**. Dt 32:19
and his sons and **d** and his oxen and Jos 7:24
of Manasseh, had no sons, but only **d**, Jos 17:3
and these are the names of his **d**: Jos 17:3
because the **d** of Manasseh received an Jos 17:6
And their **d** they took to themselves for Jgs 3:6
and their own **d** they gave to their sons, Jgs 3:6
that the **d** of Israel went year by year to Jgs 11:40
and thirty **d** he gave in marriage outside Jgs 12:9
and thirty **d** he brought in from outside Jgs 12:9
he saw one of the **d** of the Philistines. Jgs 14:1
"I saw one of the **d** of the Philistines at Jgs 14:2
a woman among the **d** of your relatives, Jgs 14:3
not give them any of our **d** for wives?" Jgs 21:7
them wives from our **d**." For the people Jgs 21:18
If the **d** of Shiloh come out to dance in Jgs 21:21
each man his wife from the **d** of Shiloh, Jgs 21:21
But Naomi said, "Turn back, my **d**; why Ru 1:11
Turn back, my **d**; go your way, for I am Ru 1:12
No, my **d**, for it is exceedingly bitter to Ru 1:13
his wife and to all her sons and **d**. 1 Sm 1:4
and bore three sons and two **d**. 1 Sm 2:21
He will take your **d** to be perfumers 1 Sm 8:13
the names of his two **d** were these: 1 Sm 14:49
wives and sons and **d** taken captive. 1 Sm 30:3
bitter in soul, each for his sons and **d**. 1 Sm 30:6
whether small or great, sons or **d**, 1 Sm 30:19
lest the **d** of the Philistines rejoice, 2 Sm 1:20
lest the **d** of the uncircumcised exult. 2 Sm 1:20
"You **d** of Israel, weep over Saul, who 2 Sm 1:24
and more sons and **d** were born to 2 Sm 5:13
thus were the virgin **d** of the king 2 Sm 13:18
your sons and your **d** and the lives of 2 Sm 19:5
sons and their **d** as offerings and 2 Kgs 17:17
Now Sheshan had no sons, only **d**, 1 Chr 2:34
Shimei had sixteen sons and six **d**; 1 Chr 4:27
Zelophehad, and Zelophehad had **d**. 1 Chr 7:15
and David fathered more sons and **d**. 1 Chr 14:3
died having no sons, but only **d**; 1 Chr 23:22
Heman fourteen sons and three **d**. 1 Chr 25:5
the son of a woman of the **d** of Dan, 2 Chr 2:14
twenty-eight sons and sixty **d**). 2 Chr 11:21
had twenty-two sons and sixteen **d**. 2 Chr 13:21
two wives, and he had sons and **d**. 2 Chr 24:3
of their relatives, women, sons, and **d**. 2 Chr 28:8
our sons and our **d** and our wives are 2 Chr 29:9
their wives, their sons, and their **d**, 2 Chr 31:18
a wife from the **d** of Barzillai the Ezr 2:61
have taken some of their **d** to be wives for Ezr 9:2
do not give your **d** to their sons, Ezr 9:12
sons, neither take their **d** for your sons, Ezr 9:12
of Jerusalem, repaired, he and his **d**. Neh 3:12
for your brothers, your sons, your **d**, Neh 4:14
who said, "With our sons and our **d**, Neh 5:2
forcing our sons and our **d** to be slaves, Neh 5:5
and some of our **d** have already been Neh 5:5
a wife of the **d** of Barzillai the Gileadite Neh 7:63
of God, their wives, their sons, their **d**, Neh 10:28
will not give our **d** to the peoples of Neh 10:30
the land or take their **d** for our sons. Neh 10:30
shall not give your **d** to their sons, Neh 13:25
or take their **d** for your sons or for Neh 13:25
were born to him seven sons and three **d**. Jb 1:2
when his sons and **d** were eating and Jb 1:13
"Your sons and **d** were eating and Jb 1:18
He had also seven sons and three **d**. Jb 42:13
were no women so beautiful as Job's **d**. Jb 42:15
d of kings are among your ladies of Ps 45:9
Let the **d** of Judah rejoice because of Ps 48:11
and is glad, and the **d** of Judah rejoice, Ps 97:8
their sons and their **d** to the demons; Ps 106:37
blood, the blood of their sons and **d**, Ps 106:38
our **d** like corner pillars cut for the Ps 144:12
The leech has two **d**; "Give" and Prv 30:15
and all the **d** of song are brought low— Eccl 12:4
very dark, but lovely, O **d** of Jerusalem, Sg 1:5
I adjure you, O **d** of Jerusalem, by the Sg 2:7
I adjure you, O **d** of Jerusalem, by the Sg 3:5
inlaid with love by the **d** of Jerusalem. Sg 3:10
Go out, O **d** of Zion, and look upon King Sg 3:11

I adjure you, O **d** of Jerusalem, if you find Sg 5:8
and this is my friend, O **d** of Jerusalem. Sg 5:16
I adjure you, O **d** of Jerusalem, that you Sg 8:4
Because the **d** of Zion are haughty and Is 3:16
with a scab the heads of the **d** of Zion, Is 3:17
away the filth of the **d** of Zion and cleansed Is 4:4
so are the **d** of Moab at the fords of the Is 16:2
you complacent **d**, give ear to my speech. Is 32:9
sons from afar and my **d** from the end of Is 43:6
and your **d** shall be carried on their Is 49:22
and a name better than sons and **d**; Is 56:5
and your **d** shall be carried on the hip. Is 60:4
and their herds, their sons and their **d**. Jer 3:24
they shall eat up your sons and your **d**; Jer 5:17
to burn their sons and their **d** in the fire, Jer 7:31
teach to your **d** a lament, and each to her Jer 9:20
their sons and their **d** shall die by Jer 11:22
their wives, their sons, and their **d**. Jer 14:16
shall you have sons or **d** in this place. Jer 16:2
concerning the sons and **d** who are born Jer 16:3
eat the flesh of their sons and their **d**, Jer 19:9
Take wives and have sons and **d**; take Jer 29:6
your sons, and give your **d** in marriage, Jer 29:6
that they may bear sons and **d**; Jer 29:6
to offer up their sons and **d** to Molech, Jer 32:35
ourselves, our wives, our sons, or our **d**, Jer 35:8
the king's **d** and all the people who were Jer 41:10
captive, and your **d** into captivity. Jer 48:46
Ai is laid waste! Cry out, O **d** of Rabbah! Jer 49:3
grief at the fate of all the **d** of my city. Lam 3:51
your face against the **d** of your people, Ezk 13:17
they would deliver neither sons nor **d**. Ezk 14:16
they would deliver neither sons nor **d**, Ezk 14:18
it, sons and **d** who will be brought out; Ezk 14:22
And you took your sons and your **d**, Ezk 16:20
your enemies, the **d** of the Philistines, Ezk 16:27
who lived with her **d** to the north of Ezk 16:46
the south of you, is Sodom with her **d**. Ezk 16:46
sister Sodom and her **d** have not done Ezk 16:48
not done as you and your **d** have done. Ezk 16:48
she and her **d** had pride, excess of food, Ezk 16:49
both the fortunes of Sodom and her **d**, Ezk 16:53
and the fortunes of Samaria and her **d**, Ezk 16:53
Sodom and her **d** shall return to their Ezk 16:55
and Samaria and her **d** shall return to Ezk 16:55
and you and your **d** shall return to Ezk 16:55
of reproach for the **d** of Syria and all Ezk 16:57
her, and for the **d** of the Philistines, Ezk 16:57
younger, and I give them to you as **d**, Ezk 16:61
were two women, the **d** of one mother. Ezk 23:2
mine, and they bore sons and **d**. Ezk 23:4
they seized her sons and her **d**; Ezk 23:10
They shall seize your sons and your **d**, Ezk 23:25
They shall kill their sons and their **d**, Ezk 23:47
your sons and your **d** whom you left Ezk 24:21
soul's desire, and also their sons and **d**, Ezk 24:25
and her **d** on the mainland shall be Ezk 26:6
with the sword your **d** on the mainland. Ezk 26:8
and her **d** shall go into captivity. Ezk 30:18
the **d** of the nations shall chant it; Ezk 32:16
her and the **d** of majestic nations, Ezk 32:18
Therefore your **d** play the whore, and Hos 4:13
will not punish your **d** when they play Hos 4:14
your sons and your **d** shall prophesy, Jl 2:28
sell your sons and your **d** into the hand of Jl 3:8
your sons and your **d** shall fall by the Am 7:17
And he had a wife from the **d** of Aaron, Lk 1:5
to them Jesus said, "**D** of Jerusalem, Lk 23:28
your sons and your **d** shall prophesy, Acts 2:17
He had four unmarried **d**, who Acts 21:9
and you shall be sons and **d** to me, 2 Cor 6:18

DAUGHTERS-IN-LAW (3)
she arose with her **d** to return from the Ru 1:6
the place where she was with her two **d**, Ru 1:7
But Naomi said to her two **d**, "Go, return Ru 1:8

DAUNTED (1)
by their shouting or **d** at their noise, Is 31:4

DAVID (1078)
He was the father of Jesse, the father of **D**. Ru 4:17
Obed fathered Jesse, and Jesse fathered **D**. Ru 4:22
LORD rushed upon **D** from that day 1 Sm 16:13
Jesse and said, "Send me **D** your son, 1 Sm 16:19
and sent them by **D** his son to Saul. 1 Sm 16:20
And **D** came to Saul and entered his 1 Sm 16:21
saying, "Let **D** remain in my service, 1 Sm 16:22
D took the lyre and played it with his 1 Sm 16:23
Now **D** was the son of an Ephrathite 1 Sm 17:12
D was the youngest. The three eldest 1 Sm 17:14
but **D** went back and forth from 1 Sm 17:15
And Jesse said to **D** his son, "Take for 1 Sm 17:17
And **D** rose early in the morning and 1 Sm 17:20
And **D** left the things in charge of the 1 Sm 17:22
words as before. And **D** heard him. 1 Sm 17:23
And **D** said to the men who stood by 1 Sm 17:26
Eliab's anger was kindled against **D**, 1 Sm 17:28
And **D** said, "What have I done now? 1 Sm 17:29
the words that **D** spoke were heard, 1 Sm 17:31
And **D** said to Saul, "Let no man's 1 Sm 17:32
And Saul said to **D**, "You are not 1 Sm 17:33
But **D** said to Saul, "Your servant 1 Sm 17:34
And **D** said, "The LORD who delivered 1 Sm 17:37
this Philistine." And Saul said to **D**, 1 Sm 17:37
Then Saul clothed **D** with his armor. 1 Sm 17:38
and **D** strapped his sword over his 1 Sm 17:39
Then **D** said to Saul, "I cannot go 1 Sm 17:39
not tested them." So **D** put them off. 1 Sm 17:39
moved forward and came near to **D**, 1 Sm 17:41
the Philistine looked and saw **D**, 1 Sm 17:42
And the Philistine said to **D**, "Am I a 1 Sm 17:43
the Philistine cursed **D** by his gods. 1 Sm 17:43
The Philistine said to **D**, "Come to 1 Sm 17:44
Then **D** said to the Philistine, "You 1 Sm 17:45
and came and drew near to meet **D**, 1 Sm 17:48
D ran quickly toward the battle line 1 Sm 17:48
And **D** put his hand in his bag and 1 Sm 17:49
So **D** prevailed over the Philistine 1 Sm 17:50
was no sword in the hand of **D**. 1 Sm 17:50
Then **D** ran and stood over the 1 Sm 17:51
And **D** took the head of the Philistine 1 Sm 17:54
soon as Saul saw **D** go out against 1 Sm 17:55
And as soon as **D** returned from the 1 Sm 17:57
you, young man?" And **D** answered, 1 Sm 17:58
of Jonathan was knit to the soul of **D**, 1 Sm 18:1
Jonathan made a covenant with **D**, 1 Sm 18:3
robe that was on him and gave it to **D**, 1 Sm 18:4
And **D** went out and was successful 1 Sm 18:5
when **D** returned from striking down 1 Sm 18:6
thousands, and **D** his ten thousands." 1 Sm 18:7
have ascribed to **D** ten thousands, 1 Sm 18:8
And Saul eyed **D** from that day on. 1 Sm 18:9
his house while **D** was playing the 1 Sm 18:10
"I will pin **D** to the wall." But David 1 Sm 18:11
to the wall." But **D** evaded him twice. 1 Sm 18:11
was afraid of **D** because the LORD 1 Sm 18:12
And **D** had success in all his 1 Sm 18:14
But all Israel and Judah loved **D**, for 1 Sm 18:16
Then Saul said to **D**, "Here is my 1 Sm 18:17
And **D** said to Saul, "Who am I, and 1 Sm 18:18
should have been given to **D**, 1 Sm 18:19
Saul's daughter Michal loved **D**. 1 Sm 18:20
Saul said to **D** a second time, 1 Sm 18:21
"Speak to **D** in private and say, 1 Sm 18:22
spoke those words in the ears of **D**. 1 Sm 18:23
in the ears of David. And **D** said, 1 Sm 18:23
told him, "Thus and so did **D** speak." 1 Sm 18:24
Saul said, "Thus shall you say to **D**, 1 Sm 18:25
Saul thought to make **D** fall by the 1 Sm 18:25
his servants told **D** these words, 1 Sm 18:26
it pleased **D** well to be the king's 1 Sm 18:26
D arose and went, along with his 1 Sm 18:27
And **D** brought their foreskins, 1 Sm 18:27
and knew that the LORD was with **D**, 1 Sm 18:28
Saul was even more afraid of **D**. So 1 Sm 18:29
they came out **D** had more success 1 Sm 18:30
his servants, that they should kill **D**. 1 Sm 19:1
Saul's son, delighted much in **D**. 1 Sm 19:1
And Jonathan told **D**, "Saul my father 1 Sm 19:2
Jonathan spoke well of **D** to Saul his 1 Sm 19:4
not the king sin against his servant **D**, 1 Sm 19:4
blood by killing **D** without cause?" 1 Sm 19:5
And Jonathan called **D**, and Jonathan 1 Sm 19:7
And Jonathan brought **D** to Saul, and 1 Sm 19:7
And **D** went out and fought with the 1 Sm 19:8
his hand. And **D** was playing the lyre. 1 Sm 19:9
Saul sought to pin **D** to the wall with 1 Sm 19:10
And **D** fled and escaped that night. 1 Sm 19:10
So Michal let **D** down through the 1 Sm 19:12
Saul sent messengers to take **D**, 1 Sm 19:14
Saul sent the messengers to see **D**, 1 Sm 19:15
Now **D** fled and escaped, and he 1 Sm 19:18
"Behold, **D** is at Naioth in Ramah." 1 Sm 19:19
Saul sent messengers to take **D**, 1 Sm 19:20
are Samuel and **D**?" And one said, 1 Sm 19:22
Then **D** fled from Naioth in Ramah 1 Sm 20:1
But **D** vowed again, saying, "Your 1 Sm 20:3
Then Jonathan said to **D**, "Whatever 1 Sm 20:4
D said to Jonathan, "Behold, 1 Sm 20:5
'**D** earnestly asked leave of me to run 1 Sm 20:6
Then **D** said to Jonathan, "Who will 1 Sm 20:10
And Jonathan said to **D**, "Come, let 1 Sm 20:11
And Jonathan said to **D**, "The LORD, 1 Sm 20:12
if he is well disposed toward **D**, 1 Sm 20:12
of the enemies of **D** from the face of 1 Sm 20:15
a covenant with the house of **D**, 1 Sm 20:16
And Jonathan made **D** swear again 1 Sm 20:17
So **D** hid himself in the field. And 1 Sm 20:24
"**D** earnestly asked leave of me to go 1 Sm 20:28
was determined to put **D** to death. 1 Sm 20:33
the month, for he was grieved for **D**, 1 Sm 20:34
the field to the appointment with **D**, 1 Sm 20:35
Only Jonathan and **D** knew the 1 Sm 20:39
D rose from beside the stone heap 1 Sm 20:41
one another, **D** weeping the most. 1 Sm 20:41
Then Jonathan said to **D**, "Go in 1 Sm 20:42
Then **D** came to Nob to Ahimelech 1 Sm 21:1
came to meet **D** trembling and said 1 Sm 21:1
And **D** said to Ahimelech the priest, 1 Sm 21:2
And the priest answered **D**, "I have no 1 Sm 21:4
And **D** answered the priest, "Truly 1 Sm 21:5
Then **D** said to Ahimelech, "Then 1 Sm 21:8
is none but that here." And **D** said, 1 Sm 21:9
And **D** rose and fled that day from 1 Sm 21:10
"Is not this **D** the king of the land? 1 Sm 21:11
and **D** his ten thousands'?" 1 Sm 21:11
And **D** took these words to heart and 1 Sm 21:12
D departed from there and escaped to 1 Sm 22:1
And **D** went from there to Mizpeh of 1 Sm 22:3
all the time that **D** was in the 1 Sm 22:4
Then the prophet Gad said to **D**, "Do 1 Sm 22:5
of Judah." So **D** departed and went 1 Sm 22:5
Saul heard that **D** was discovered, 1 Sm 22:6
all your servants is so faithful as **D**, 1 Sm 22:14
because their hand also is with **D**, 1 Sm 22:17
Abiathar, escaped and fled after **D**. 1 Sm 22:20
And Abiathar told **D** that Saul had 1 Sm 22:21
And **D** said to Abiathar, "I knew on 1 Sm 22:22
Now they told **D**, "Behold, the 1 Sm 23:1
Therefore **D** inquired of the LORD, 1 Sm 23:2
Philistines?" And the LORD said to **D**, 1 Sm 23:2
Then **D** inquired of the LORD again. 1 Sm 23:4
And **D** and his men went to Keilah 1 Sm 23:5
So **D** saved the inhabitants of Keilah. 1 Sm 23:5
of Ahimelech had fled to **D** to Keilah, 1 Sm 23:6
was told Saul that **D** had come to 1 Sm 23:7
to Keilah, to besiege **D** and his men. 1 Sm 23:8
D knew that Saul was plotting harm 1 Sm 23:9
Then said **D**, "O LORD, the God of 1 Sm 23:10
Then **D** said, "Will the men of 1 Sm 23:12
Then **D** and his men, who were 1 Sm 23:13
was told that **D** had escaped from 1 Sm 23:13
And **D** remained in the strongholds 1 Sm 23:14
D saw that Saul had come out to 1 Sm 23:15
D was in the Wilderness of Ziph at 1 Sm 23:15
son, rose and went to **D** at Horesh, 1 Sm 23:16
D remained at Horesh, and Jonathan 1 Sm 23:18
"Is not **D** hiding among us in the 1 Sm 23:19
Now **D** and his men were in the 1 Sm 23:24
And **D** was told, so he went down to 1 Sm 23:25
he pursued after **D** in the wilderness 1 Sm 23:25
and **D** and his men on the other side 1 Sm 23:26
And **D** was hurrying to get away 1 Sm 23:26
were closing in on **D** and his men to 1 Sm 23:26
from pursuing after **D** and went 1 Sm 23:28
And **D** went up from there and lived 1 Sm 23:29
D is in the wilderness of Engedi." 1 Sm 24:1
and went to seek **D** and his men in 1 Sm 24:2
Now **D** and his men were sitting in 1 Sm 24:3
And the men of **D** said to him, "Here is 1 Sm 24:4
to you.'" Then **D** arose and stealthily 1 Sm 24:4
So **D** persuaded his men with these 1 Sm 24:7
Afterward **D** also arose and went out 1 Sm 24:8
D bowed with his face to the earth and 1 Sm 24:8
And **D** said to Saul, "Why do you 1 Sm 24:9
who say, 'Behold, **D** seeks your harm'? 1 Sm 24:9
As soon as **D** had finished speaking 1 Sm 24:16
my son **D**?" And Saul lifted up his 1 Sm 24:16
He said to **D**, "You are more 1 Sm 24:17
And **D** swore this to Saul. Then Saul 1 Sm 24:22
but **D** and his men went up to the 1 Sm 24:22
Then **D** rose and went down to the 1 Sm 25:1
D heard in the wilderness that Nabal 1 Sm 25:4
So **D** sent ten young men. And David 1 Sm 25:5
And **D** said to the young men, "Go up 1 Sm 25:5
to your servants and to your son **D**.'" 1 Sm 25:8
all this to Nabal in the name of **D**, 1 Sm 25:9
David's servants, "Who is **D**? 1 Sm 25:10
And **D** said to his men, "Every man 1 Sm 25:13
sword. **D** also strapped on his sword. 1 Sm 25:13
four hundred men went up after **D**, 1 Sm 25:13
D sent messengers out of the 1 Sm 25:14
D and his men came down toward 1 Sm 25:20
Now **D** had said, "Surely in vain 1 Sm 25:21
so to the enemies of **D** and more also, 1 Sm 25:22
When Abigail saw **D**, she hurried 1 Sm 25:23
donkey and fell before **D** on her face 1 Sm 25:23
And **D** said to Abigail, "Blessed be 1 Sm 25:32
Then **D** received from her hand 1 Sm 25:35
When **D** heard that Nabal was dead, 1 Sm 25:39
own head." Then **D** sent and spoke 1 Sm 25:39
the servants of **D** came to Abigail 1 Sm 25:40
"**D** has sent us to you to take you to 1 Sm 25:40
the messengers of **D** and became his 1 Sm 25:42
D also took Ahinoam of Jezreel, and 1 Sm 25:43
"Is not **D** hiding himself on the hill of 1 Sm 26:1

of Israel to seek **D** in the wilderness of 1 Sm 26:2
But **D** remained in the wilderness. 1 Sm 26:3
D sent out spies and learned that Saul 1 Sm 26:4
Then **D** rose and came to the place 1 Sm 26:5
And **D** saw the place where Saul lay, 1 Sm 26:5
Then **D** said to Ahimelech the Hittite, 1 Sm 26:6
So **D** and Abishai went to the army by 1 Sm 26:7
Then said Abishai to **D**, "God has 1 Sm 26:8
But **D** said to Abishai, "Do not destroy 1 Sm 26:9
And **D** said, "As the LORD lives, the 1 Sm 26:10
So **D** took the spear and the jar of 1 Sm 26:12
Then **D** went over to the other side 1 Sm 26:13
And **D** called to the army, and to 1 Sm 26:14
And **D** said to Abner, "Are you not a 1 Sm 26:15
voice, my son **D**?" And David said, 1 Sm 26:17
voice, my son David?" And **D** said, 1 Sm 26:17
Return, my son **D**, for I will no more 1 Sm 26:21
And **D** answered and said, "Here is 1 Sm 26:22
Then Saul said to **D**, "Blessed be you, 1 Sm 26:25
to David, "Blessed be you, my son **D**! 1 Sm 26:25
succeed in them." So **D** went his way, 1 Sm 26:25
Then **D** said in his heart, "Now I shall 1 Sm 27:1
So **D** arose and went over, he and the 1 Sm 27:2
And **D** lived with Achish at Gath, he 1 Sm 27:3
household, and **D** with his two wives, 1 Sm 27:3
was told Saul that **D** had fled to Gath, 1 Sm 27:4
Then **D** said to Achish, "If I have 1 Sm 27:5
of the days that **D** lived in the country 1 Sm 27:7
Now **D** and his men went up and 1 Sm 27:8
And **D** would strike the land and 1 Sm 27:9
made a raid today?" **D** would say, 1 Sm 27:10
And **D** would leave neither man nor 1 Sm 27:11
'So **D** has done.'" Such was his 1 Sm 27:11
And Achish trusted **D**, thinking, "He 1 Sm 27:12
And Achish said to **D**, "Understand 1 Sm 28:1
D said to Achish, "Very well, you 1 Sm 28:2
can do." And Achish said to **D**, 1 Sm 28:2
and given it to your neighbor, **D**. 1 Sm 28:17
and **D** and his men were passing on in 1 Sm 29:2
of the Philistines, "Is this not **D**, 1 Sm 29:3
Is not this **D**, of whom they sing to one 1 Sm 29:5
and **D** his ten thousands'?" 1 Sm 29:5
Then Achish called **D** and said to 1 Sm 29:6
And **D** said to Achish, "But what have 1 Sm 29:8
And Achish answered **D** and said, "I 1 Sm 29:9
So **D** set out with his men early in 1 Sm 29:11
Now when **D** and his men came to 1 Sm 30:1
And when **D** and his men came to the 1 Sm 30:3
Then **D** and the people who were with 1 Sm 30:4
And **D** was greatly distressed, for the 1 Sm 30:6
But **D** strengthened himself in the 1 Sm 30:6
And **D** said to Abiathar the priest, the 1 Sm 30:7
So Abiathar brought the ephod to **D**. 1 Sm 30:7
And **D** inquired of the LORD, "Shall I 1 Sm 30:8
So **D** set out, and the six hundred men 1 Sm 30:9
But **D** pursued, he and four hundred 1 Sm 30:10
open country and brought him to **D**. 1 Sm 30:11
And **D** said to him, "To whom do 1 Sm 30:13
And **D** said to him, "Will you take 1 Sm 30:15
And **D** struck them down from 1 Sm 30:17
D recovered all that the Amalekites 1 Sm 30:18
taken, and **D** rescued his two wives. 1 Sm 30:18
had been taken. **D** brought back all. 1 Sm 30:19
D also captured all the flocks and 1 Sm 30:20
Then **D** came to the two hundred 1 Sm 30:21
had been too exhausted to follow **D**, 1 Sm 30:21
went out to meet **D** and to meet the 1 Sm 30:21
And when **D** came near to the people 1 Sm 30:21
the men who had gone with **D** said, 1 Sm 30:22
But **D** said, "You shall not do so, my 1 Sm 30:23
When **D** came to Ziklag, he sent part 1 Sm 30:26
all the places where **D** and his men 1 Sm 30:31
when **D** had returned from striking 2 Sm 1:1
D remained two days in Ziklag. 2 Sm 1:1
And when he came to **D**, he fell to the 2 Sm 1:2
D said to him, "Where do you come 2 Sm 1:3
And **D** said to him, "How did it go? Tell 2 Sm 1:4
Then **D** said to the young man who 2 Sm 1:5
Then **D** took hold of his clothes and 2 Sm 1:11
And **D** said to the young man who 2 Sm 1:13
D said to him, "How is it you were not 2 Sm 1:14
Then **D** called one of the young men 2 Sm 1:15
And **D** said to him, "Your blood be on 2 Sm 1:16
And **D** lamented with this 2 Sm 1:17
After this **D** inquired of the LORD, "Shall 2 Sm 2:1
the LORD said to him, "Go up." **D** said, 2 Sm 2:1
So **D** went up there, and his two wives 2 Sm 2:2
And **D** brought up his men who were 2 Sm 2:3
there they anointed **D** king over the 2 Sm 2:4
When they told **D**, "It was the men of 2 Sm 2:4
D sent messengers to the men of 2 Sm 2:5
But the house of Judah followed **D**. 2 Sm 2:10
And the time that **D** was king in 2 Sm 2:11
and the servants of **D** went out and 2 Sm 2:13
Saul, and twelve of the servants of **D**. 2 Sm 2:15

were beaten before the servants of **D**. 2 Sm 2:17
the servants of **D** had struck down 2 Sm 2:31
the house of Saul and the house of **D**. 2 Sm 3:1
And **D** grew stronger and stronger, 2 Sm 3:1
And sons were born to **D** at Hebron: his 2 Sm 3:2
wife. These were born to **D** in Hebron. 2 Sm 3:5
the house of Saul and the house of **D**, 2 Sm 3:6
have not given you into the hand of **D**. 2 Sm 3:8
do not accomplish for **D** what the LORD 2 Sm 3:9
up the throne of **D** over Israel and over 2 Sm 3:10
sent messengers to **D** on his behalf, 2 Sm 3:12
Then **D** sent messengers to 2 Sm 3:14
you have been seeking **D** as king over 2 Sm 3:17
it about, for the LORD has promised **D**, 2 Sm 3:18
hand of my servant **D** I will save my 2 Sm 3:18
Abner went to tell **D** at Hebron all 2 Sm 3:19
with twenty men to **D** at Hebron, 2 Sm 3:20
D made a feast for Abner and the men 2 Sm 3:20
And Abner said to **D**, "I will arise and 2 Sm 3:21
heart desires." So **D** sent Abner away, 2 Sm 3:21
the servants of **D** arrived with Joab 2 Sm 3:22
But Abner was not with **D** at Hebron, 2 Sm 3:22
of Sirah. But **D** did not know about it. 2 Sm 3:26
Afterward, when **D** heard of it, he said, 2 Sm 3:28
Then **D** said to Joab and to all the 2 Sm 3:31
Abner." And King **D** followed the bier. 2 Sm 3:31
came to persuade **D** to eat bread 2 Sm 3:35
while it was yet day. But **D** swore, 2 Sm 3:35
the head of Ish-bosheth to **D** at Hebron. 2 Sm 4:8
But **D** answered Rechab and Baanah 2 Sm 4:9
And **D** commanded his young men, 2 Sm 4:12
of Israel came to **D** at Hebron and said, 2 Sm 5:1
and King **D** made a covenant with 2 Sm 5:3
and they anointed **D** king over Israel. 2 Sm 5:3
D was thirty years old when he began 2 Sm 5:4
inhabitants of the land, who said to **D**, 2 Sm 5:6
—thinking, "**D** cannot come in here." 2 Sm 5:6
D took the stronghold of Zion, 2 Sm 5:7
of Zion, that is, the city of **D**. 2 Sm 5:7
And **D** said on that day, "Whoever 2 Sm 5:8
And **D** lived in the stronghold and 2 Sm 5:9
stronghold and called it the city of **D**. 2 Sm 5:9
And **D** built the city all around from 2 Sm 5:9
And **D** became greater and greater, for 2 Sm 5:10
king of Tyre sent messengers to **D**, 2 Sm 5:11
and masons who built **D** a house. 2 Sm 5:11
And **D** knew that the LORD had 2 Sm 5:12
And **D** took more concubines and 2 Sm 5:13
sons and daughters were born to **D**. 2 Sm 5:13
Philistines heard that **D** had been 2 Sm 5:17
Philistines went up to search for **D**. 2 Sm 5:17
But **D** heard of it and went down to the 2 Sm 5:17
And **D** inquired of the LORD, "Shall I 2 Sm 5:19
my hand?" And the LORD said to **D**, 2 Sm 5:19
And **D** came to Baal-perazim, and 2 Sm 5:20
and **D** defeated them there. 2 Sm 5:20
and **D** and his men carried them 2 Sm 5:21
And when **D** inquired of the LORD, he 2 Sm 5:23
And **D** did as the LORD commanded 2 Sm 5:25
D again gathered all the chosen men of 2 Sm 6:1
And **D** arose and went with all the 2 Sm 6:2
And **D** and all the house of Israel were 2 Sm 6:5
And **D** was angry because the LORD had 2 Sm 6:8
And **D** was afraid of the LORD that day, 2 Sm 6:9
So **D** was not willing to take the ark of 2 Sm 6:10
the ark of the LORD into the city of **D**. 2 Sm 6:10
But **D** took it aside to the house of 2 Sm 6:10
And it was told King **D**, "The LORD has 2 Sm 6:12
ark of God." So **D** went and brought 2 Sm 6:12
to the city of **D** with rejoicing. 2 Sm 6:12
And **D** danced before the LORD with all 2 Sm 6:14
And **D** was wearing a linen ephod. 2 Sm 6:14
So **D** and all the house of Israel 2 Sm 6:15
of the LORD came into the city of **D**, 2 Sm 6:16
and saw King **D** leaping and dancing 2 Sm 6:16
inside the tent that **D** had pitched for 2 Sm 6:17
And **D** offered burnt offerings and 2 Sm 6:17
And when **D** had finished offering the 2 Sm 6:18
And **D** returned to bless his 2 Sm 6:20
of Saul came out to meet **D** and said, 2 Sm 6:20
And **D** said to Michal, "It was before 2 Sm 6:21
"Go and tell my servant **D**, 'Thus says 2 Sm 7:5
thus you shall say to my servant **D**, 2 Sm 7:8
all this vision, Nathan spoke to **D**. 2 Sm 7:17
Then King **D** went in and sat before 2 Sm 7:18
And what more can **D** say to you? For 2 Sm 7:20
of your servant **D** will be established 2 Sm 7:26
After this **D** defeated the Philistines and 2 Sm 8:1
and **D** took Metheg-ammah out of the 2 Sm 8:1
became servants to **D** and brought 2 Sm 8:2
D also defeated Hadadezer the son of 2 Sm 8:3
And **D** took from him 1,700 horsemen, 2 Sm 8:4
And **D** hamstrung all the chariot 2 Sm 8:4
D struck down 22,000 men of the 2 Sm 8:5
Then **D** put garrisons in Aram of 2 Sm 8:6

became servants to **D** and brought 2 Sm 8:6
gave victory to **D** wherever he went. 2 Sm 8:6
And **D** took the shields of gold that 2 Sm 8:7
King **D** took very much bronze. 2 Sm 8:8
Hamath heard that **D** had defeated the 2 Sm 8:9
Toi sent his son Joram to King **D**, to 2 Sm 8:10
These also King **D** dedicated to the 2 Sm 8:11
And **D** made a name for himself when 2 Sm 8:13
gave victory to **D** wherever he went. 2 Sm 8:14
So **D** reigned over all Israel. And 2 Sm 8:15
And **D** administered justice and 2 Sm 8:15
And **D** said, "Is there still anyone left of 2 Sm 9:1
was Ziba, and they called him to **D**. 2 Sm 9:2
Then King **D** sent and brought him 2 Sm 9:5
came to **D** and fell on his face and paid 2 Sm 9:6
his face and paid homage. And **D** said, 2 Sm 9:6
And **D** said to him, "Do not fear, for I 2 Sm 9:7
And **D** said, "I will deal loyally with 2 Sm 10:2
loyally with me." So **D** sent by his 2 Sm 10:2
because **D** has sent comforters to you, 2 Sm 10:3
Has not **D** sent his servants to you to 2 Sm 10:3
When it was told **D**, he sent to meet 2 Sm 10:5
that they had become a stench to **D**, 2 Sm 10:6
And when **D** heard of it, he sent Joab 2 Sm 10:7
And when it was told **D**, he gathered 2 Sm 10:17
themselves against **D** and fought 2 Sm 10:17
and **D** killed of the Syrians the men 2 Sm 10:18
kings go out to battle, **D** sent Joab, 2 Sm 11:1
But **D** remained at Jerusalem. 2 Sm 11:1
when **D** arose from his couch and 2 Sm 11:2
And **D** sent and inquired about the 2 Sm 11:3
So **D** sent messengers and took her, 2 Sm 11:4
conceived, and she sent and told **D**, 2 Sm 11:5
So **D** sent word to Joab, "Send me 2 Sm 11:6
the Hittite." And Joab sent Uriah to **D**. 2 Sm 11:6
D asked how Joab was doing and how 2 Sm 11:7
Then **D** said to Uriah, "Go down to 2 Sm 11:8
When they told **D**, "Uriah did not go 2 Sm 11:10
down to his house," **D** said to Uriah, 2 Sm 11:10
Uriah said to **D**, "The ark and Israel 2 Sm 11:11
Then **D** said to Uriah, "Remain here 2 Sm 11:12
And **D** invited him, and he ate in his 2 Sm 11:13
In the morning **D** wrote a letter to 2 Sm 11:14
the servants of **D** among the people 2 Sm 11:17
Joab sent and told **D** all the news 2 Sm 11:18
and came and told **D** all that Joab 2 Sm 11:22
The messenger said to **D**, "The men 2 Sm 11:23
D said to the messenger, "Thus shall 2 Sm 11:25
D sent and brought her to his house, 2 Sm 11:27
the thing that **D** had done displeased 2 Sm 11:27
And the LORD sent Nathan to **D**. He 2 Sm 12:1
Nathan said to **D**, "You are the man! 2 Sm 12:7
D said to Nathan, "I have sinned 2 Sm 12:13
the LORD." And Nathan said to **D**, 2 Sm 12:13
the child that Uriah's wife bore to **D**, 2 Sm 12:15
D therefore sought God on behalf of 2 Sm 12:16
And **D** fasted and went in and lay all 2 Sm 12:16
And the servants of **D** were afraid to 2 Sm 12:18
But when **D** saw that his servants 2 Sm 12:19
D understood that the child was 2 Sm 12:19
And **D** said to his servants, "Is the 2 Sm 12:19
Then **D** arose from the earth and 2 Sm 12:20
Then **D** comforted his wife, 2 Sm 12:24
Joab sent messengers to **D** and said, 2 Sm 12:27
So **D** gathered all the people together 2 Sm 12:29
Then **D** and all the people returned 2 Sm 12:31
Then **D** sent home to Tamar, saying, 2 Sm 13:7
When King **D** heard of all these 2 Sm 13:21
were on the way, news came to **D**, 2 Sm 13:30
And **D** mourned for his son day after 2 Sm 13:37
And a messenger came to **D**, saying, 2 Sm 15:13
Then **D** said to all his servants who 2 Sm 15:14
And **D** said to Ittai, "Go then, pass 2 Sm 15:22
But **D** went up the ascent of the 2 Sm 15:30
And it was told **D**, "Ahithophel is 2 Sm 15:31
with Absalom." And **D** said, 2 Sm 15:31
While **D** was coming to the summit, 2 Sm 15:32
D said to him, "If you go on with me, 2 Sm 15:33
When **D** had passed a little beyond 2 Sm 16:1
When King **D** came to Bahurim, 2 Sm 16:5
he threw stones at **D** and at all the 2 Sm 16:6
and at all the servants of King **D**, 2 Sm 16:6
the LORD has said to him, 'Curse **D**,' 2 Sm 16:10
And **D** said to Abishai and to all his 2 Sm 16:11
So **D** and his men went on the road, 2 Sm 16:13
both by **D** and by Absalom. 2 Sm 16:23
and I will arise and pursue **D** tonight. 2 Sm 17:1
therefore send quickly and tell **D**, 2 Sm 17:16
and they were to go and tell King **D**, 2 Sm 17:17
the well, and went and told King **D**. 2 Sm 17:21
They said to **D**, "Arise, and go 2 Sm 17:21
Then **D** arose, and all the people who 2 Sm 17:22
Then **D** came to Mahanaim. And 2 Sm 17:24
When **D** came to Mahanaim, Shobi 2 Sm 17:27
for **D** and the people with him to eat, 2 Sm 17:29

Then **D** mustered the men who were	2 Sm 18:1
And **D** sent out the army, one third	2 Sm 18:2
defeated there by the servants of **D**,	2 Sm 18:7
happened to meet the servants of **D**.	2 Sm 18:9
Now **D** was sitting between the two	2 Sm 18:24
And King **D** sent this message to	2 Sm 19:11
the men of Judah to meet King **D**.	2 Sm 19:16
But **D** said, "What have I to do with	2 Sm 19:22
and in **D** also we have more than	2 Sm 19:43
and said, "We have no portion in **D**,	2 Sm 20:1
Israel withdrew from **D** and followed	2 Sm 20:2
And **D** came to his house at	2 Sm 20:3
And **D** said to Abishai, "Now Sheba	2 Sm 20:6
favors Joab, and whoever is for **D**,	2 Sm 20:11
lifted up his hand against King **D**.	2 Sm 20:21
in the days of **D** for three years,	2 Sm 21:1
And **D** sought the face of the LORD.	2 Sm 21:1
And **D** said to the Gibeonites, "What	2 Sm 21:3
between **D** and Jonathan the son of	2 Sm 21:7
When **D** was told what Rizpah the	2 Sm 21:11
D went and took the bones of Saul	2 Sm 21:12
and **D** went down together with his	2 Sm 21:15
the Philistines. And **D** grew weary.	2 Sm 21:15
with a new sword, thought to kill **D**.	2 Sm 21:16
by the hand of **D** and by the hand	2 Sm 21:22
And **D** spoke to the LORD the words of	2 Sm 22:1
to **D** and his offspring forever."	2 Sm 22:51
Now these are the last words of **D**: The	2 Sm 23:1
The oracle of **D**, the son of Jesse, the	2 Sm 23:1
of the mighty men whom **D** had:	2 Sm 23:8
He was with **D** when they defied the	2 Sm 23:9
about harvest time to **D** at the cave	2 Sm 23:13
D was then in the stronghold, and	2 Sm 23:14
And **D** said longingly, "Oh, that	2 Sm 23:15
gate and carried and brought it to **D**.	2 Sm 23:16
And **D** set him over his bodyguard.	2 Sm 23:23
Israel, and he incited **D** against them,	2 Sm 24:1
And **D** said to the LORD, "I have	2 Sm 24:10
And when **D** arose in the morning,	2 Sm 24:11
"Go and say to **D**, 'Thus says the	2 Sm 24:12
So Gad came to **D** and told him, and	2 Sm 24:13
Then **D** said to Gad, "I am in great	2 Sm 24:14
Then **D** spoke to the LORD when he	2 Sm 24:17
came that day to **D** and said to him,	2 Sm 24:18
So **D** went up at Gad's word, as the	2 Sm 24:19
king come to his servant?" **D** said,	2 Sm 24:21
Then Araunah said to **D**, "Let my	2 Sm 24:22
me nothing." So **D** bought the	2 Sm 24:24
And **D** built there an altar to the	2 Sm 24:25
Now King **D** was old and advanced in	1 Kgs 1:1
has become king and **D** our lord does	1 Kgs 1:11
Go in at once to King **D**, and say to	1 Kgs 1:13
Then King **D** answered, "Call	1 Kgs 1:28
"May my lord King **D** live forever!"	1 Kgs 1:31
King **D** said, "Call to me Zadok the	1 Kgs 1:32
than the throne of my lord King **D**."	1 Kgs 1:37
our lord King **D** has made Solomon	1 Kgs 1:43
to congratulate our lord King **D**,	1 Kgs 1:47
Then **D** slept with his fathers and was	1 Kgs 2:10
and was buried in the city of **D**.	1 Kgs 2:10
the time that **D** reigned over Israel	1 Kgs 2:11
sat on the throne of **D** his father,	1 Kgs 2:12
me on the throne of **D** my father,	1 Kgs 2:24
of the Lord GOD before **D** my father,	1 Kgs 2:26
the knowledge of my father **D**,	1 Kgs 2:32
But for **D** and for his descendants and	1 Kgs 2:33
the harm that you did to **D** my father.	1 Kgs 2:44
the throne of **D** shall be established	1 Kgs 2:45
into the city of **D** until he had finished	1 Kgs 3:1
walking in the statutes of **D** his father,	1 Kgs 3:3
love to your servant **D** my father,	1 Kgs 3:6
servant king in place of **D** my father,	1 Kgs 3:7
as your father **D** walked,	1 Kgs 3:14
his father, for Hiram always loved **D**.	1 Kgs 5:1
"You know that **D** my father could not	1 Kgs 5:3
God, as the LORD said to **D** my father,	1 Kgs 5:5
who has given to **D** a wise son to be	1 Kgs 5:7
you, which I spoke to **D** your father.	1 Kgs 6:12
in the things that **D** his father had	1 Kgs 7:51
of the LORD out of the city of **D**,	1 Kgs 8:1
with his mouth to **D** my father,	1 Kgs 8:15
But I chose **D** to be over my people	1 Kgs 8:16
in the heart of **D** my father to build	1 Kgs 8:17
But the LORD said to **D** my father,	1 Kgs 8:18
risen in the place of **D** my father,	1 Kgs 8:20
with your servant **D** my father what	1 Kgs 8:24
for your servant **D** my father what	1 Kgs 8:25
spoken to your servant **D** my father.	1 Kgs 8:26
LORD had shown to **D** his servant and	1 Kgs 8:66
before me, as **D** your father walked,	1 Kgs 9:4
forever, as I promised **D** your father,	1 Kgs 9:5
from the city of **D** to her own house	1 Kgs 9:24
God, as was the heart of **D** his father.	1 Kgs 11:4
the LORD, as **D** his father had done.	1 Kgs 11:6
for the sake of **D** your father I will	1 Kgs 11:12
for the sake of **D** my servant and for	1 Kgs 11:13
For when **D** was in Edom, and Joab	1 Kgs 11:15
heard in Egypt that **D** slept with his	1 Kgs 11:21
band, after the killing by **D**.	1 Kgs 11:24
the breach of the city of **D** his father.	1 Kgs 11:27
sake of my servant **D** and for the	1 Kgs 11:32
and my rules, as **D** his father did.	1 Kgs 11:33
for the sake of **D** my servant whom I	1 Kgs 11:34
that **D** my servant may always have	1 Kgs 11:36
as **D** my servant did,	1 Kgs 11:38
you a sure house, as I built for **D**,	1 Kgs 11:38
the offspring of **D** because of this,	1 Kgs 11:39
buried in the city of **D** his father.	1 Kgs 11:43
"What portion do we have in **D**?	1 Kgs 12:16
Look now to your own house, **D**."	1 Kgs 12:16
against the house of **D** to this day.	1 Kgs 12:19
followed the house of **D** but the tribe	1 Kgs 12:20
will turn back to the house of **D**.	1 Kgs 12:26
a son shall be born to the house of **D**,	1 Kgs 13:2
from the house of **D** and gave it to	1 Kgs 14:8
you have not been like my servant **D**,	1 Kgs 14:8
with his fathers in the city of **D**.	1 Kgs 14:31
his God, as the heart of **D** his father.	1 Kgs 15:3
because **D** did what was right in the	1 Kgs 15:5
and they buried him in the city of **D**.	1 Kgs 15:8
of the LORD, as **D** his father had done.	1 Kgs 15:11
his fathers in the city of **D** his father,	1 Kgs 15:24
his fathers in the city of **D** his father,	1 Kgs 22:50
Judah, for the sake of **D** his servant,	2 Kgs 8:19
with his fathers in the city of **D**,	2 Kgs 8:24
tomb with his fathers in the city of **D**.	2 Kgs 9:28
him with his fathers in the city of **D**,	2 Kgs 12:21
of the LORD, yet not like **D** his father.	2 Kgs 14:3
with his fathers in the city of **D**.	2 Kgs 14:20
him with his fathers in the city of **D**,	2 Kgs 15:7
his fathers in the city of **D** his father,	2 Kgs 15:38
his God, as his father **D** had done,	2 Kgs 16:2
with his fathers in the city of **D**,	2 Kgs 16:20
had torn Israel from the house of **D**,	2 Kgs 17:21
according to all that **D** his father had	2 Kgs 18:3
and for the sake of my servant **D**."	2 Kgs 19:34
the LORD, the God of **D** your father:	2 Kgs 20:5
the LORD said to **D** and to Solomon his	2 Kgs 21:7
walked in all the way of **D** his father,	2 Kgs 22:2
Ozem the sixth, **D** the seventh.	1 Chr 2:15
are the sons of **D** who were born to	1 Chr 3:1
were their cities until **D** reigned.	1 Chr 4:31
are the men whom **D** put in charge of	1 Chr 6:31
number in the days of **D** being 22,600.	1 Chr 7:2
D and Samuel the seer established	1 Chr 9:22
the kingdom over to **D** the son of	1 Chr 10:14
gathered together to **D** at Hebron and	1 Chr 11:1
and **D** made a covenant with them at	1 Chr 11:3
And they anointed **D** king over Israel,	1 Chr 11:3
And **D** and all Israel went to	1 Chr 11:4
The inhabitants of Jebus said to **D**,	1 Chr 11:5
D took the stronghold of Zion,	1 Chr 11:5
of Zion, that is, the city of **D**.	1 Chr 11:5
D said, "Whoever strikes the	1 Chr 11:6
And **D** lived in the stronghold;	1 Chr 11:7
therefore it was called the city of **D**.	1 Chr 11:7
And **D** became greater and greater,	1 Chr 11:9
He was with **D** at Pas-dammim	1 Chr 11:13
down to the rock to **D** at the cave of	1 Chr 11:15
D was then in the stronghold, and	1 Chr 11:16
And **D** said longingly, "Oh that	1 Chr 11:17
gate and took it and brought it to **D**.	1 Chr 11:18
to David. But **D** would not drink it.	1 Chr 11:18
And **D** set him over his bodyguard.	1 Chr 11:25
are the men who came to **D** at Ziklag,	1 Chr 12:1
there went over to **D** at the stronghold	1 Chr 12:8
Judah came to the stronghold to **D**.	1 Chr 12:16
D went out to meet them and said to	1 Chr 12:17
and he said, "We are yours, O **D**,	1 Chr 12:18
helps you." Then **D** received them	1 Chr 12:18
Manasseh deserted to **D** when he	1 Chr 12:19
They helped **D** against the band of	1 Chr 12:21
to day men came to **D** to help him,	1 Chr 12:22
troops who came to **D** in Hebron to	1 Chr 12:23
named to come and make **D** king.	1 Chr 12:31
to help **D** with singleness of purpose.	1 Chr 12:33
full intent to make **D** king over all	1 Chr 12:38
of a single mind to make **D** king.	1 Chr 12:38
were there with **D** for three days,	1 Chr 12:39
D consulted with the commanders of	1 Chr 13:1
And **D** said to all the assembly of	1 Chr 13:2
So **D** assembled all Israel from the	1 Chr 13:5
And **D** and all Israel went up to	1 Chr 13:6
And **D** and all Israel were rejoicing	1 Chr 13:8
And **D** was angry because the LORD	1 Chr 13:11
And **D** was afraid of God that day,	1 Chr 13:12
So **D** did not take the ark home into	1 Chr 13:13
take the ark home into the city of **D**,	1 Chr 13:13
king of Tyre sent messengers to **D**,	1 Chr 14:1
And **D** knew that the LORD had	1 Chr 14:2
And **D** took more wives in Jerusalem,	1 Chr 14:3
and **D** fathered more sons and	1 Chr 14:3
Philistines heard that **D** had been	1 Chr 14:8
Philistines went up to search for **D**.	1 Chr 14:8
But **D** heard of it and went out	1 Chr 14:8
And **D** inquired of God, "Shall I go	1 Chr 14:10
and **D** struck them down there.	1 Chr 14:11
them down there. And **D** said,	1 Chr 14:11
gods there, and **D** gave command,	1 Chr 14:12
And when **D** again inquired of God,	1 Chr 14:14
And **D** did as God commanded him,	1 Chr 14:16
And the fame of **D** went out into all	1 Chr 14:17
D built houses for himself in the city	1 Chr 15:1
houses for himself in the city of **D**.	1 Chr 15:1
Then **D** said that no one but the	1 Chr 15:2
And **D** assembled all Israel at	1 Chr 15:3
And **D** gathered together the sons of	1 Chr 15:4
Then **D** summoned the priests	1 Chr 15:11
D also commanded the chiefs of the	1 Chr 15:16
So **D** and the elders of Israel and the	1 Chr 15:25
D was clothed with a robe of fine	1 Chr 15:27
singers. And **D** wore a linen ephod.	1 Chr 15:27
of the LORD came to the city of **D**,	1 Chr 15:29
and saw King **D** dancing and	1 Chr 15:29
inside the tent that **D** had pitched for	1 Chr 16:1
And when **D** had finished offering	1 Chr 16:2
on that day **D** first appointed that	1 Chr 16:7
So **D** left Asaph and his brothers	1 Chr 16:37
and **D** went home to bless his	1 Chr 16:43
Now when **D** lived in his house,	1 Chr 17:1
house, **D** said to Nathan the prophet,	1 Chr 17:1
And Nathan said to **D**, "Do all that is	1 Chr 17:2
"Go and tell my servant **D**, 'Thus	1 Chr 17:4
thus shall you say to my servant **D**,	1 Chr 17:7
all this vision, Nathan spoke to **D**.	1 Chr 17:15
Then King **D** went in and sat before	1 Chr 17:16
And what more can **D** say to you for	1 Chr 17:18
of your servant **D** will be	1 Chr 17:24
After this **D** defeated the Philistines	1 Chr 18:1
became servants to **D** and brought	1 Chr 18:2
D also defeated Hadadezer king of	1 Chr 18:3
And **D** took from him 1,000 chariots,	1 Chr 18:4
And **D** hamstrung all the chariot	1 Chr 18:4
D struck down 22,000 men of the	1 Chr 18:5
Then **D** put garrisons in Syria of	1 Chr 18:6
became servants to **D** and brought	1 Chr 18:6
gave victory to **D** wherever he went.	1 Chr 18:6
And **D** took the shields of gold that	1 Chr 18:7
D took a large amount of bronze.	1 Chr 18:8
Hamath heard that **D** had defeated	1 Chr 18:9
he sent his son Hadoram to King **D**,	1 Chr 18:10
These also King **D** dedicated to the	1 Chr 18:11
gave victory to **D** wherever he went.	1 Chr 18:13
So **D** reigned over all Israel, and he	1 Chr 18:14
And **D** said, "I will deal kindly with	1 Chr 19:2
with me." So **D** sent messengers to	1 Chr 19:2
because **D** has sent comforters to	1 Chr 19:3
When **D** was told concerning the	1 Chr 19:5
that they had become a stench to **D**,	1 Chr 19:6
When **D** heard of it, he sent Joab and	1 Chr 19:8
And when it was told to **D**, he	1 Chr 19:17
And when **D** set the battle in array	1 Chr 19:17
and **D** killed of the Syrians the men	1 Chr 19:18
made peace with **D** and became	1 Chr 19:19
But **D** remained at Jerusalem.	1 Chr 20:1
And **D** took the crown of their king	1 Chr 20:2
And thus **D** did to all the cities of the	1 Chr 20:3
Then **D** and all the people returned to	1 Chr 20:3
fell by the hand of **D** and by the hand	1 Chr 20:8
Israel and incited **D** to number Israel.	1 Chr 21:1
So **D** said to Joab and the	1 Chr 21:2
of the numbering of the people to **D**.	1 Chr 21:5
And **D** said to God, "I have sinned	1 Chr 21:8
"Go and say to **D**, 'Thus says the	1 Chr 21:10
So Gad came to **D** and said to him,	1 Chr 21:11
Then **D** said to Gad, "I am in great	1 Chr 21:13
And **D** lifted his eyes and saw the	1 Chr 21:16
Then **D** and the elders, clothed in	1 Chr 21:16
And **D** said to God, "Was it not I	1 Chr 21:17
Gad to say to **D** that David should	1 Chr 21:18
say to David that **D** should go up	1 Chr 21:18
So **D** went up at Gad's word, which	1 Chr 21:19
As **D** came to Ornan, Ornan looked	1 Chr 21:21
looked and saw **D** and went out	1 Chr 21:21
and paid homage to **D** with his face	1 Chr 21:21
And **D** said to Ornan, "Give me the	1 Chr 21:22
Then Ornan said to **D**, "Take it, and	1 Chr 21:23
But King **D** said to Ornan, "No, but	1 Chr 21:24
So **D** paid Ornan 600 shekels of gold	1 Chr 21:25
And **D** built there an altar to the	1 Chr 21:26
when **D** saw that the LORD had	1 Chr 21:28
but **D** could not go before it to	1 Chr 21:30
Then **D** said, "Here shall be the house	1 Chr 22:1
D commanded to gather together the	1 Chr 22:2
D also provided great quantities of	1 Chr 22:3

great quantities of cedar to **D**. 1 Chr 22:4
For **D** said, "Solomon my son is 1 Chr 22:5
for it." So **D** provided materials in 1 Chr 22:5
D said to Solomon, "My son, I had it 1 Chr 22:7
D also commanded all the leaders of 1 Chr 22:17
When **D** was old and full of days, he 1 Chr 23:1
D assembled all the leaders of Israel 1 Chr 23:2
thousand of these," **D** said, 1 Chr 23:4
And **D** organized them in divisions 1 Chr 23:6
For **D** said, "The LORD, the God of 1 Chr 23:25
the last words of **D** the sons of Levi 1 Chr 23:27
D organized them according to the 1 Chr 24:3
of Aaron, in the presence of King **D**, 1 Chr 24:31
D and the chiefs of the service also set 1 Chr 25:1
dedicated gifts that **D** the king and 1 Chr 26:26
King **D** appointed him and his 1 Chr 26:32
D did not count those below twenty 1 Chr 27:23
entered in the chronicles of King **D**. 1 Chr 27:24
D assembled at Jerusalem all the 1 Chr 28:1
Then King **D** rose to his feet and said: 1 Chr 28:2
Then **D** gave Solomon his son the 1 Chr 28:11
Then **D** said to Solomon his son, 1 Chr 28:20
And **D** the king said to all the 1 Chr 29:1
LORD. **D** the king also rejoiced greatly. 1 Chr 29:9
Therefore **D** blessed the LORD in the 1 Chr 29:10
of all the assembly. And **D** said: 1 Chr 29:10
Then **D** said to all the assembly, 1 Chr 29:20
the son of **D** king the second 1 Chr 29:22
as king in place of **D** his father. 1 Chr 29:23
and also all the sons of King **D**, 1 Chr 29:24
Thus **D** the son of Jesse reigned over 1 Chr 29:26
Now the acts of King **D**, from first to 1 Chr 29:29
the son of **D** established himself in 2 Chr 1:1
(But **D** had brought up the ark of God 2 Chr 1:4
to the place that **D** had prepared for it, 2 Chr 1:4
great and steadfast love to **D** my father, 2 Chr 1:8
let your word to **D** my father be now 2 Chr 1:9
"As you dealt with **D** my father and 2 Chr 2:3
whom **D** my father provided. 2 Chr 2:7
who has given King **D** a wise son, 2 Chr 2:12
craftsmen of my lord, **D** your father. 2 Chr 2:14
census of them that **D** his father had 2 Chr 2:17
the LORD had appeared to **D** his father, 2 Chr 3:1
at the place that **D** had appointed, 2 Chr 3:1
in the things that **D** his father had 2 Chr 5:1
of the LORD out of the city of **D**, 2 Chr 5:2
with his mouth to **D** my father, 2 Chr 6:4
and I have chosen **D** to be over my 2 Chr 6:6
in the heart of **D** my father to build 2 Chr 6:7
But the LORD said to **D** my father, 2 Chr 6:8
in the place of **D** my father and sit 2 Chr 6:10
with your servant **D** my father what 2 Chr 6:15
for your servant **D** my father what 2 Chr 6:16
you have spoken to your servant **D**. 2 Chr 6:17
steadfast love for **D** your servant." 2 Chr 6:42
the LORD that King **D** had made for 2 Chr 7:6
forever—whenever **D** offered praises 2 Chr 7:6
had granted to **D** and to Solomon 2 Chr 7:10
before me as **D** your father walked, 2 Chr 7:17
as I covenanted with **D** your father, 2 Chr 7:18
from the city of **D** to the house that 2 Chr 8:11
live in the house of **D** king of Israel, 2 Chr 8:11
to the ruling of **D** his father, 2 Chr 8:14
for so **D** the man of God had 2 Chr 8:14
was buried in the city of **D** his father, 2 Chr 9:31
king, "What portion have we in **D**? 2 Chr 10:16
D." So all Israel went to their tents. 2 Chr 10:16
against the house of **D** to this day. 2 Chr 10:19
years in the way of **D** and Solomon. 2 Chr 11:17
daughter of Jerimoth the son of **D**, 2 Chr 11:18
and was buried in the city of **D**, 2 Chr 12:16
over Israel forever to **D** and his sons 2 Chr 13:5
a servant of Solomon the son of **D**, 2 Chr 13:6
the LORD in the hand of the sons of **D**, 2 Chr 13:8
and they buried him in the city of **D**. 2 Chr 14:1
had cut for himself in the city of **D**. 2 Chr 16:14
in the earlier ways of his father **D**. 2 Chr 17:3
with his fathers in the city of **D**, 2 Chr 21:1
not willing to destroy the house of **D**, 2 Chr 21:7
covenant that he had made with **D**, 2 Chr 21:7
the LORD, the God of **D** your father, 2 Chr 21:12
They buried him in the city of **D**, 2 Chr 21:20
LORD spoke concerning the sons of **D**. 2 Chr 23:3
the Levites whom **D** had organized 2 Chr 23:18
singing, according to the order of **D**. 2 Chr 23:18
in the city of **D** among the kings, 2 Chr 24:16
they buried him in the city of **D**, 2 Chr 24:25
with his fathers in the city of **D**. 2 Chr 25:28
and they buried him in the city of **D**, 2 Chr 27:9
of the LORD, as his father **D** had done, 2 Chr 28:1
according to all that **D** his father had 2 Chr 29:2
the commandment of **D** and of Gad 2 Chr 29:25
stood with the instruments of **D**, 2 Chr 29:26
the instruments of **D** king of Israel. 2 Chr 29:27
with the words of **D** and of Asaph 2 Chr 29:30
Solomon the son of **D** king of Israel 2 Chr 30:26
the Millo in the city of **D**. 2 Chr 32:5
down to the west side of the city of **D**. 2 Chr 32:30
part of the tombs of the sons of **D**, 2 Chr 32:33
which God said to **D** and to Solomon 2 Chr 33:7
wall for the city of **D** west of Gihon, 2 Chr 33:14
walked in the ways of **D** his father; 2 Chr 34:2
began to seek the God of **D** his father, 2 Chr 34:3
the house that Solomon the son of **D**, 2 Chr 35:3
in the writing of **D** king of Israel and 2 Chr 35:4
according to the command of **D**, 2 Chr 35:15
to the directions of **D** king of Israel. Ezr 3:10
Daniel. Of the sons of **D**, Hattush. Ezr 8:2
whom **D** and his officials had set apart Ezr 8:20
stairs that go down from the City of **D**. Neh 3:15
to a point opposite the tombs of **D**, Neh 3:16
to the commandment of **D** the man of Neh 12:24
musical instruments of **D** the man of Neh 12:36
them by the stairs of the city of **D**, Neh 12:37
of the wall, above the house of **D**, Neh 12:37
to the command of **D** and his son Neh 12:45
in the days of **D** and Asaph there were Neh 12:46
A Psalm of **D**, when he fled from Ps 3:T
with stringed instruments. A Psalm of **D**. Ps 4:T
choirmaster: for the flutes. A Psalm of **D**. Ps 5:T
to The Sheminith. A Psalm of **D**. Ps 6:T
A Shiggaion of **D**, which he sang to the Ps 7:T
according to The Gittith. A Psalm of **D**. Ps 8:T
according to Muth-labben. A Psalm of **D**. Ps 9:T
To the choirmaster. Of **D**. Ps 11:T
to The Sheminith. A Psalm of **D**. Ps 12:T
To the choirmaster. A Psalm of **D**. Ps 13:T
To the choirmaster. Of **D**. Ps 14:T
A Psalm of **D**. Ps 15:T
A Miktam of **D**. Ps 16:T
A Prayer of **D**. Ps 17:T
A Psalm of **D**, the servant of the LORD, Ps 18:T
anointed, to **D** and his offspring forever. Ps 18:50
To the choirmaster. A Psalm of **D**. Ps 19:T
To the choirmaster. A Psalm of **D**. Ps 20:T
To the choirmaster. A Psalm of **D**. Ps 21:T
to The Doe of the Dawn. A Psalm of **D**. Ps 22:T
A Psalm of **D**. Ps 23:T
A Psalm of **D**. Ps 24:T
Of **D**. Ps 25:T
Of **D**. Ps 26:T
Of **D**. Ps 27:T
Of **D**. Ps 28:T
A Psalm of **D**. Ps 29:T
A Psalm of **D**. A song at the dedication Ps 30:T
To the choirmaster. A Psalm of **D**. Ps 31:T
A Maskil of **D**. Ps 32:T
Of **D**, when he changed his behavior Ps 34:T
Of **D**. Ps 35:T
To the choirmaster. Of **D**, the servant of Ps 36:T
Of **D**. Ps 37:T
A Psalm of **D**, for the memorial offering. Ps 38:T
choirmaster: to Jeduthun. A Psalm of **D**. Ps 39:T
To the choirmaster. A Psalm of **D**. Ps 40:T
To the choirmaster. A Psalm of **D**. Ps 41:T
A Psalm of **D**, when Nathan the prophet Ps 51:T
A Maskil of **D**, when Doeg, the Edomite, Ps 52:T
"**D** has come to the house of Ps 52:T
according to Mahalath. A Maskil of **D**. Ps 53:T
A Maskil of **D**, when the Ziphites went Ps 54:T
told Saul, "Is not **D** hiding among us?" Ps 54:T
stringed instruments. A Maskil of **D**. Ps 55:T
A Miktam of **D**, when the Philistines Ps 56:T
A Miktam of **D**, when he fled from Saul, Ps 57:T
to Do Not Destroy. A Miktam of **D**. Ps 58:T
A Miktam of **D**, when Saul sent men to Ps 59:T
A Miktam of **D**; for instruction; when he Ps 60:T
with stringed instruments. Of **D**. Ps 61:T
according to Jeduthun. A Psalm of **D**. Ps 62:T
A Psalm of **D**, when he was in the Ps 63:T
To the choirmaster. A Psalm of **D**. Ps 64:T
To the choirmaster. A Psalm of **D**. A Ps 65:T
To the choirmaster. A Psalm of **D**. A Ps 68:T
choirmaster: according to Lilies. Of **D**. Ps 69:T
To the choirmaster. Of **D**, for the Ps 70:T
The prayers of **D**, the son of Jesse, are Ps 72:20
He chose **D** his servant and took him Ps 78:70
A Prayer of **D**. Ps 86:T
one; I have sworn to **D** my servant: Ps 89:3
I have found **D**, my servant; with my Ps 89:20
by my holiness; I will not lie to **D**. Ps 89:35
by your faithfulness you swore to **D**? Ps 89:49
A Psalm of **D**. Ps 101:T
Of **D**. Ps 103:T
A Song. A Psalm of **D**. Ps 108:T
To the choirmaster. A Psalm of **D**. Ps 109:T
A Psalm of **D**. Ps 110:T
A Song of Ascents. Of **D**. Ps 122:T
were set, the thrones of the house of **D**. Ps 122:5
A Song of Ascents. Of **D**. Ps 124:T
A Song of Ascents. Of **D**. Ps 131:T
For the sake of your servant **D**, do not Ps 132:10
The LORD swore to **D** a sure oath from Ps 132:11
I will make a horn to sprout for **D**; Ps 132:17
A Song of Ascents. Of **D**. Ps 133:T
Of **D**. Ps 138:T
To the choirmaster. A Psalm of **D**. Ps 139:T
To the choirmaster. A Psalm of **D**. Ps 140:T
A Psalm of **D**. Ps 141:T
A Maskil of **D**, when he was in the Ps 142:T
A Psalm of **D**. Ps 143:T
Of **D**. Ps 144:T
who rescues **D** his servant from the Ps 144:10
A Song of Praise. Of **D**. Ps 145:T
The proverbs of Solomon, son of **D**, king Prv 1:1
The words of the Preacher, the son of **D**, Eccl 1:1
Your neck is like the tower of **D**, built in Sg 4:4
When the house of **D** was told, "Syria is in Is 7:2
And he said, "Hear then, O house of **D**! Is Is 7:13
on the throne of **D** and over his kingdom, Is 9:7
in the tent of **D** one who judges and Is 16:5
the breaches of the city of **D** were many. Is 22:9
his shoulder the key of the house of **D**. Is 22:22
Ariel, Ariel, the city where **D** encamped! Is 29:1
sake and for the sake of my servant **D**." Is 37:35
says the LORD, the God of **D** your father: Is 38:5
covenant, my steadfast, sure love for **D**. Is 55:3
and princes who sit on the throne of **D**, Jer 17:25
O house of **D**! Thus says the LORD: Jer 21:12
of Judah, who sits on the throne of **D**, Jer 22:2
house kings who sit on the throne of **D**, Jer 22:4
on the throne of **D** and ruling again in Jer 22:30
I will raise up for **D** a righteous Branch, Jer 23:5
the king who sits on the throne of **D**, Jer 29:16
the LORD their God and **D** their king, Jer 30:9
a righteous Branch to spring up for **D**, Jer 33:15
D shall never lack a man to sit on the Jer 33:17
my covenant with **D** my servant may Jer 33:21
multiply the offspring of **D** my servant, Jer 33:22
of Jacob and **D** my servant and Jer 33:26
have none to sit on the throne of **D**, Jer 36:30
them one shepherd, my servant **D**, Ezk 34:23
and my servant **D** shall be prince Ezk 34:24
"My servant **D** shall be king over Ezk 37:24
and **D** my servant shall be their Ezk 37:25
the LORD their God, and **D** their king, Hos 3:5
harp and like **D** invent for themselves Am 6:5
up the booth of **D** that is fallen and Am 9:11
glory of the house of **D** and the glory of Zec 12:7
them on that day shall be like **D**, Zec 12:8
and the house of **D** shall be like God, Zec 12:8
on the house of **D** and the inhabitants Zec 12:10
the family of the house of **D** by itself, Zec 12:12
for the house of **D** and the inhabitants Zec 13:1
genealogy of Jesus Christ, the son of **D**, Mt 1:1
and Jesse the father of **D** the king. And Mt 1:6
And **D** was the father of Solomon by the Mt 1:6
from Abraham to **D** were fourteen Mt 1:17
and from **D** to the deportation to Mt 1:17
in a dream, saying, "Joseph, son of **D**, Mt 1:20
aloud, "Have mercy on us, Son of **D**." Mt 9:27
you not read what **D** did when he was Mt 12:3
and said, "Can this be the Son of **D**?" Mt 12:23
"Have mercy on me, O Lord, Son of **D**; Mt 15:22
"Lord, have mercy on us, Son of **D**!" Mt 20:30
"Lord, have mercy on us, Son of **D**!" Mt 20:31
shouting, "Hosanna to the Son of **D**! Mt 21:9
to the Son of **D**!" they were indignant, Mt 21:15
he?" They said to him, "The son of **D**." Mt 22:42
He said to them, "How is it then that **D**, Mt 22:43
If then **D** calls him Lord, how is he his Mt 22:45
them, "Have you never read what **D** did, Mk 2:25
to cry out and say, "Jesus, Son of **D**, Mk 10:47
he cried out all the more, "Son of **D**, Mk 10:48
the coming kingdom of our father **D**! Mk 11:10
say that the Christ is the son of **D**? Mk 12:35
D himself, in the Holy Spirit, declared, Mk 12:36
D himself calls him Lord. So how is he Mk 12:37
name was Joseph, of the house of **D**. Lk 1:27
give to him the throne of his father **D**, Lk 1:32
for us in the house of his servant **D**, Lk 1:69
of Nazareth, to Judea, to the city of **D**, Lk 2:4
he was of the house and lineage of **D**, Lk 2:4
is born this day in the city of **D** a Savior, Lk 2:11
the son of Nathan, the son of **D**, Lk 3:31
you not read what **D** did when he was Lk 6:3
And he cried out, "Jesus, Son of **D**, have Lk 18:38
But he cried out all the more, "Son of **D**, Lk 18:39
For **D** himself says in the Book of Lk 20:42
D thus calls him Lord, so how is he his Lk 20:44
the Christ comes from the offspring of **D**, Jn 7:42
Bethlehem, the village where **D** was?" Jn 7:42
by the mouth of **D** concerning Judas, Acts 1:16
For **D** says concerning him, "'I saw the Acts 2:25
about the patriarch **D** that he both Acts 2:29

For **D** did not ascend into the heavens, Acts 2:34
through the mouth of our father **D**, Acts 4:25
fathers. So it was until the days of **D**, Acts 7:45
him, he raised up **D** to be their king, Acts 13:22
'I have found in **D** the son of Jesse a Acts 13:22
you the holy and sure blessings of **D**.' Acts 13:34
For **D**, after he had served the purpose Acts 13:36
rebuild the tent of **D** that has fallen; Acts 15:16
was descended from **D** according to the Rom 1:3
just as **D** also speaks of the blessing of Rom 4:6
And **D** says, "Let their table become a Rom 11:9
risen from the dead, the offspring of **D**, 2 Tm 2:8
"Today," saying through **D** so long Heb 4:7
of **D** and Samuel and the prophets— Heb 11:32
one, the true one, who has the key of **D**, Rv 3:7
Lion of the tribe of Judah, the Root of **D**, Rv 5:5
I am the root and the descendant of **D**, Rv 22:16

DAVID'S (63)

So Saul was **D** enemy continually. 1 Sm 18:29
sent messengers to **D** house to watch 1 Sm 19:11
But Michal, **D** wife, told him, "If you 1 Sm 19:11
LORD take vengeance on **D** enemies." 1 Sm 20:16
Saul's side, but **D** place was empty. 1 Sm 20:25
the new moon, **D** place was empty. 1 Sm 20:27
But **D** men said to him, "Behold, we 1 Sm 23:3
And afterward **D** heart struck him, 1 Sm 24:5
When **D** young men came, they said 1 Sm 25:9
And Nabal answered **D** servants, 1 Sm 25:10
So **D** young men turned away and 1 Sm 25:12
given Michal his daughter, **D** wife, 1 Sm 25:44
Saul recognized **D** voice and said, "Is 1 Sm 26:17
D two wives also had been taken 1 Sm 30:5
him, and said, "This is **D** spoil." 1 Sm 30:20
missing from **D** servants nineteen 2 Sm 2:30
and the sixth, Ithream, of Eglah, **D** wife. 2 Sm 3:5
Joab came out from **D** presence, 2 Sm 3:26
who are hated by **D** soul." Therefore it 2 Sm 5:8
all the Edomites became **D** servants. 2 Sm 8:14
the Pelethites, and **D** sons were priests. 2 Sm 8:18
do." So Mephibosheth ate at **D** table, 2 Sm 9:11
And **D** servants came into the land of 2 Sm 10:2
So Hanun took **D** servants and shaved 2 Sm 10:4
Then **D** anger was greatly kindled 2 Sm 12:5
stone, and it was placed on **D** head. 2 Sm 12:30
Now Absalom, **D** son, had a beautiful 2 Sm 13:1
And after a time Amnon, **D** son, loved 2 Sm 13:1
the son of Shimeah, **D** brother. 2 Sm 13:3
the son of Shimeah, **D** brother, 2 Sm 13:32
the Gilonite, **D** counselor, 2 Sm 15:12
So Hushai, **D** friend, came into the 2 Sm 15:37
when Hushai the Archite, **D** friend, 2 Sm 16:16
Jordan, and all **D** men with him?" 2 Sm 19:41
and Ira the Jairite was also **D** priest. 2 Sm 20:26
Then **D** men swore to him, "You 2 Sm 21:17
the son of Shimei, **D** brother, 2 Sm 21:21
But **D** heart struck him after he had 2 Sm 24:10
came to the prophet Gad, **D** seer, 2 Sm 24:11
and Rei and **D** mighty men were 1 Kgs 1:8
ride on King **D** mule and brought 1 Kgs 1:38
When **D** time to die drew near, he 1 Kgs 2:1
for **D** sake the LORD his God gave him 1 Kgs 15:4
and shields that had been King **D**, 2 Kgs 11:10
own sake and for my servant **D** sake." 2 Kgs 20:6
All these were **D** sons, besides the sons 1 Chr 3:9
are the chiefs of **D** mighty men, 1 Chr 11:10
is an account of **D** mighty men: 1 Chr 11:11
all the Edomites became **D** servants. 1 Chr 18:13
and **D** sons were the chief officials 1 Chr 18:17
And **D** servants came to the land of 1 Chr 19:2
So Hanun took **D** servants and 1 Chr 19:4
stone. And it was placed on **D** head. 1 Chr 20:2
the son of Shimea, **D** brother, 1 Chr 20:7
And the LORD spoke to Gad, **D** seer, 1 Chr 21:9
fortieth year of **D** reign search was 1 Chr 26:31
for Judah, Elihu, one of **D** brothers; 1 Chr 27:18
were stewards of King **D** property. 1 Chr 27:31
Jonathan, **D** uncle, was a counselor, 1 Chr 27:32
small shields that had been King **D**, 2 Chr 23:9
Remember, O LORD, in **D** favor, all the Ps 132:1
the kings who sit on **D** throne, the Jer 13:13
can they say that the Christ is **D** son? Lk 20:41

DAWN (25)

day they rose early, at the **d** of day, Jos 6:15
morning. And as the **d** began to break, Jgs 19:25
at the break of **d** Samuel called to 1 Sm 9:26
from the break of **d** until the stars Neh 4:21
Let the stars of its **d** be dark; let it hope for Jb 3:9
is long, and I am full of tossing till the **d**. Jb 7:4
and caused the **d** to know its place, Jb 38:12
and his eyes are like the eyelids of the **d**. Jb 41:18
according to The Doe of the **D**. Ps 22:T
O harp and lyre! I will awake the **d**! Ps 57:8
O harp and lyre! I will awake the **d**! Ps 108:2
I rise before **d** and cry for help; I hope Ps 119:147
of the righteous is like the light of **d**, Prv 4:18
for youth and the **d** of life are vanity. Eccl 11:10
"Who is this who looks down like the **d**, Sg 6:10
to this word, it is because they have no **d**. Is 8:20
from heaven, O Day Star, son of **D**! Is 14:12
shall your light break forth like the **d**, Is 58:8
the LORD; his going out is sure as the **d**; Hos 6:3
At **d** the king of Israel shall be utterly Hos 10:15
But when **d** came up the next day, God Jon 4:7
forth his justice; each **d** he does not fail; Zep 3:5
toward the **d** of the first day of the week, Mt 28:1
on the first day of the week, at early **d**, Lk 24:1
As day was about to **d**, Paul urged Acts 27:33

DAWNED (3)

As morning **d**, the angels urged Lot, Gn 19:15
came from Sinai and **d** from Seir upon Dt 33:2
shadow of death, on them a light has **d**." Mt 4:16

DAWNS (5)

he **d** on them like the morning light, 2 Sm 23:4
God will help her when morning **d**. Ps 46:5
Light **d** in the darkness for the upright; Ps 112:4
When the morning **d**, they perform it, Mi 2:1
until the day **d** and the morning star 2 Pt 1:19

DAY (1601)

God called the light **D**, and the darkness Gn 1:5
and there was morning, the first **d**. Gn 1:5
and there was morning, the second **d**. Gn 1:8
and there was morning, the third **d**. Gn 1:13
heavens to separate the **d** from the night. Gn 1:14
light to rule the **d** and the lesser light Gn 1:16
to rule over the **d** and over the night, and Gn 1:18
and there was morning, the fourth **d**. Gn 1:19
and there was morning, the fifth **d**. Gn 1:23
and there was morning, the sixth **d**. Gn 1:31
And on the seventh **d** God finished his Gn 2:2
rested on the seventh **d** from all his work Gn 2:2
God blessed the seventh **d** and made it Gn 2:3
in the **d** that the LORD God made the earth Gn 2:4
for in the **d** that you eat of it you shall Gn 2:17
walking in the garden in the cool of the **d**, Gn 3:8
on the seventeenth **d** of the month, Gn 7:11
on that **d** all the fountains of the great Gn 7:11
On the very same **d** Noah and his sons, Gn 7:13
on the seventeenth **d** of the month, Gn 8:4
tenth month, on the first **d** of the month, Gn 8:5
the first month, the first **d** of the month, Gn 8:13
on the twenty-seventh **d** of the month, Gn 8:14
heat, summer and winter, **d** and night, Gn 8:22
On that **d** the LORD made a covenant Gn 15:18
the flesh of their foreskins that very **d**, Gn 17:23
That very **d** Abraham and his son Gn 17:26
at the door of his tent in the heat of the **d**. Gn 18:1
The next **d**, the firstborn said to the Gn 19:34
is the father of the Moabites to this **d**. Gn 19:37
the father of the Ammonites to this **d**. Gn 19:38
great feast on the **d** that Isaac was Gn 21:8
On the third **d** Abraham lifted up his Gn 22:4
as it is said to this **d**, "On the mount of Gn 22:14
That same **d** Isaac's servants came and Gn 26:32
name of the city is Beersheba to this **d**. Gn 26:33
am old; I do not know the **d** of my death. Gn 27:2
I be bereft of you both in one **d**?" Gn 27:45
He said, "Behold, it is still high **d**; it is Gn 29:7
But that **d** Laban removed the male Gn 30:35
Laban on the third **d** that Jacob had Gn 31:22
whether stolen by **d** or stolen by night. Gn 31:39
by **d** the heat consumed me, and the Gn 31:40
can I do this **d** for these my daughters Gn 31:43
with him until the breaking of the **d**. Gn 32:24
for the **d** has broken." But Jacob said, Gn 32:26
Therefore to this **d** the people of Israel Gn 32:32
If they are driven hard for one **d**, all the Gn 33:13
So Esau returned that **d** on his way to Gn 33:16
On the third **d**, when they were sore, Gn 34:25
answers me in the **d** of my distress and Gn 35:3
Rachel's tomb, which is there to this **d**. Gn 35:20
And as she spoke to Joseph **d** after day, Gn 39:10
And as she spoke to Joseph day after **d**, Gn 39:10
But one **d**, when he went into the house Gn 39:11
On the third **d**, which was Pharaoh's Gn 40:20
the youngest is this **d** with our father, Gn 42:13
On the third **d** Joseph said to them, "Do Gn 42:18
the youngest is this **d** with our father Gn 42:32
I have this **d** bought you and your land Gn 47:23
land of Egypt, and it stands to this **d**, Gn 47:26
my shepherd all my life long to this **d**, Gn 48:15
So he blessed them that **d**, saying, "By Gn 48:20
One **d**, when Moses had grown up, he Ex 2:11
When he went out the next **d**, behold, Ex 2:13
The same **d** Pharaoh commanded the Ex 5:6
your work, your daily task each **d**, Ex 5:13
of bricks, your daily task each **d**." Ex 5:19
On the **d** when the LORD spoke to Moses Ex 6:28
But on that **d** I will set apart the land of Ex 8:22
And the next **d** the LORD did this thing. All Ex 9:6
in Egypt from the **d** it was founded until Ex 9:18
from the **d** they came on earth to this Ex 10:6
on earth to this **d**.'" Then he turned and Ex 10:6
the land all that **d** and all that night. Ex 10:13
for on the **d** you see my face you shall Ex 10:28
that on the tenth **d** of this month every Ex 12:3
it until the fourteenth **d** of this month, Ex 12:6
"This **d** shall be for you a memorial Ex 12:14
day shall be for you a memorial **d**, Ex 12:14
On the first **d** you shall remove leaven Ex 12:15
from the first **d** until the seventh day, Ex 12:15
from the first day until the seventh **d**, Ex 12:15
On the first **d** you shall hold a holy Ex 12:16
and on the seventh **d** a holy assembly. Ex 12:16
for on this very **d** I brought your hosts Ex 12:17
Therefore you shall observe this **d**, Ex 12:17
from the fourteenth **d** of the month at Ex 12:18
until the twenty-first **d** of the month Ex 12:18
At the end of 430 years, on that very **d**, Ex 12:41
And on that very **d** the LORD brought Ex 12:51
"Remember this **d** in which you came Ex 13:3
and on the seventh **d** there shall be a Ex 13:6
You shall tell your son on that **d**, 'It is Ex 13:8
went before them by **d** in a pillar of Ex 13:21
they might travel by **d** and by night. Ex 13:21
pillar of cloud by **d** and the pillar of Ex 13:22
LORD saved Israel that **d** from the hand Ex 14:30
on the fifteenth **d** of the second month Ex 16:1
go out and gather a day's portion every **d**, Ex 16:4
On the sixth **d**, when they prepare what Ex 16:5
On the sixth **d** they gathered twice as Ex 16:22
'Tomorrow is a **d** of solemn rest, Ex 16:23
shall gather it, but on the seventh **d**, Ex 16:26
On the seventh **d** some of the people Ex 16:27
therefore on the sixth **d** he gives you Ex 16:29
go out of his place on the seventh **d**." Ex 16:29
So the people rested on the seventh **d**. Ex 16:30
The next **d** Moses sat to judge the Ex 18:13
on that **d** they came into the wilderness Ex 19:1
and be ready for the third **d**. For on the Ex 19:11
For on the third **d** the LORD will come Ex 19:11
to the people, "Be ready for the third **d**; Ex 19:15
of the third **d** there were thunders Ex 19:16
"Remember the Sabbath **d**, to keep it Ex 20:8
but the seventh **d** is a Sabbath to the Ex 20:10
is in them, and rested the seventh **d**. Ex 20:11
LORD blessed the Sabbath **d** and made it Ex 20:11
But if the slave survives a **d** or two, he is Ex 21:21
on the eighth **d** you shall give it to me. Ex 22:30
but on the seventh **d** you shall rest; Ex 23:12
And on the seventh **d** he called to Moses Ex 24:16
and every **d** you shall offer a bull as a Ex 29:36
lambs a year old **d** by day regularly. Ex 29:38
lambs a year old day by **d** regularly. Ex 29:38
but the seventh **d** is a Sabbath of Ex 31:15
work on the Sabbath **d** shall be put to Ex 31:15
and on the seventh **d** he rested and was Ex 31:17
up early the next **d** and offered burnt Ex 32:6
And that **d** about three thousand men Ex 32:28
bestow a blessing upon you this **d**." Ex 32:29
The next **d** Moses said to the people, Ex 32:30
Nevertheless, in the **d** when I visit, I will Ex 32:34
"Observe what I command you this **d**. Ex 34:11
but on the seventh **d** you shall rest. Ex 34:21
but on the seventh **d** you shall have a Ex 35:2
your dwelling places on the Sabbath **d**." Ex 35:3
"On the first **d** of the first month you Ex 40:2
second year, on the first **d** of the month, Ex 40:17
not set out till the **d** that it was taken Ex 40:37
of the LORD was on the tabernacle by **d**, Ex 40:38
it belongs on the **d** he realizes his guilt. Lv 6:5
to the LORD on the **d** when he is anointed: Lv 6:20
shall be eaten on the **d** of his offering. Lv 7:15
shall be eaten on the **d** that he offers his Lv 7:16
and on the next **d** what remains of it Lv 7:16
sacrifice on the third **d** shall be burned Lv 7:17
his peace offering is eaten on the third **d**, Lv 7:18
from the **d** they were presented to serve as Lv 7:35
Israel, from the **d** that he anointed them. Lv 7:36
on the **d** that he commanded the people Lv 7:38
you shall remain **d** and night for Lv 8:35
On the eighth **d** Moses called Aaron and Lv 9:1
And on the eighth **d** the flesh of his Lv 12:3
shall examine him on the seventh **d**, Lv 13:5
examine him again on the seventh **d**, Lv 13:6
priest shall examine him the seventh **d**. Lv 13:27
and on the seventh **d** the priest shall Lv 13:32
And on the seventh **d** the priest shall Lv 13:34
examine the disease on the seventh **d**. Lv 13:51
leprous person for the **d** of his cleansing. Lv 14:2
And on the seventh **d** he shall shave off Lv 14:9
"And on the eighth **d** he shall take two Lv 14:10
And on the eighth **d** he shall bring Lv 14:23
shall come again on the seventh **d**, Lv 14:39

And on the eighth **d** he shall take two Lv 15:14
And on the eighth **d** she shall take two Lv 15:29
month, on the tenth **d** of the month, Lv 16:29
For on this **d** shall atonement be made Lv 16:30
shall be eaten the same **d** you offer it or Lv 19:6
same day you offer it or on the **d** after, Lv 19:6
over until the third **d** shall be burned up Lv 19:6
If it is eaten at all on the third **d**, it is Lv 19:7
and from the eighth **d** on it shall be Lv 22:27
ox or a sheep and her young in one **d**. Lv 22:28
It shall be eaten on the same **d**; you Lv 22:30
but on the seventh **d** is a Sabbath of Lv 23:3
on the fourteenth **d** of the month at Lv 23:5
And on the fifteenth **d** of the same Lv 23:6
On the first **d** you shall have a holy Lv 23:7
On the seventh **d** is a holy convocation; Lv 23:8
On the **d** after the Sabbath the priest Lv 23:11
And on the **d** when you wave the sheaf, Lv 23:12
parched or fresh until this same **d**, Lv 23:14
full weeks from the **d** after the Sabbath, Lv 23:15
from the **d** that you brought the sheaf Lv 23:15
fifty days to the **d** after the seventh Lv 23:16
make proclamation on the same **d**. Lv 23:21
month, on the first **d** of the month, Lv 23:24
you shall observe a **d** of solemn rest, Lv 23:24
"Now on the tenth **d** of this seventh Lv 23:27
seventh month is the **D** of Atonement. Lv 23:27
shall not do any work on that very **d**, Lv 23:28
that very day, for it is a **D** of Atonement, Lv 23:28
afflicted on that very **d** shall be cut off Lv 23:29
whoever does any work on that very **d**, Lv 23:30
On the ninth **d** of the month beginning Lv 23:32
On the fifteenth **d** of this seventh Lv 23:34
On the first **d** shall be a holy Lv 23:35
On the eighth **d** you shall hold a holy Lv 23:36
drink offerings, each on its proper **d**, Lv 23:37
"On the fifteenth **d** of the seventh Lv 23:39
On the first **d** shall be a solemn rest, Lv 23:39
and on the eighth **d** shall be a solemn Lv 23:39
take on the first **d** the fruit of splendid Lv 23:40
Every Sabbath **d** Aaron shall arrange it Lv 24:8
trumpet on the tenth **d** of the seventh Lv 25:9
On the **D** of Atonement you shall sound Lv 25:9
the valuation on that **d** as a holy gift Lv 27:23
on the first **d** of the second month, Nm 1:1
and on the first **d** of the second month, Nm 1:18
On the **d** that I struck down all the Nm 3:13
shave his head on the **d** of his cleansing; Nm 6:9
on the seventh **d** he shall shave it. Nm 6:9
On the eighth **d** he shall bring two Nm 6:10
shall consecrate his head that same **d** Nm 6:11
On the **d** when Moses had finished Nm 7:1
of the altar on the **d** it was anointed; Nm 7:10
offer their offerings, one chief each **d**, Nm 7:11
offering the first **d** was Nahshon the Nm 7:12
On the second **d** Nethanel the son of Nm 7:18
On the third **d** Eliab the son of Helon, Nm 7:24
On the fourth **d** Elizur the son of Nm 7:30
On the fifth **d** Shelumiel the son of Nm 7:36
On the sixth **d** Eliasaph the son of Nm 7:42
On the seventh **d** Elishama the son of Nm 7:48
On the eighth **d** Gamaliel the son of Nm 7:54
On the ninth **d** Abidan the son of Nm 7:60
On the tenth **d** Ahiezer the son of Nm 7:66
On the eleventh **d** Pagiel the son of Nm 7:72
On the twelfth **d** Ahira the son of Enan, Nm 7:78
the altar on the **d** when it was anointed, Nm 7:84
On the **d** that I struck down all the Nm 8:17
On the fourteenth **d** of this month, at Nm 9:3
on the fourteenth **d** of the month, Nm 9:5
could not keep the Passover on that **d**, Nm 9:6
came before Moses and Aaron on that **d**. Nm 9:6
on the fourteenth **d** at twilight they Nm 9:11
On the **d** that the tabernacle was set up, Nm 9:15
covered it by **d** and the appearance Nm 9:16
or if it continued for a **d** and a night, Nm 9:21
On the **d** of your gladness also, and at Nm 10:10
on the twentieth **d** of the month, Nm 10:11
cloud of the LORD was over them by **d**, Nm 10:34
You shall not eat just one **d**, or two Nm 11:19
people rose all that **d** and all night and Nm 11:32
day and all night and all the next **d**, Nm 11:32
a pillar of cloud by **d** and in a pillar of Nm 14:14
the land, forty days, a year for each **d**, Nm 14:34
from the **d** that the LORD gave Nm 15:23
gathering sticks on the Sabbath **d**. Nm 15:32
But on the next **d** all the congregation Nm 16:41
On the next **d** Moses went into the tent Nm 17:8
water on the third **d** and on the Nm 19:12
on the third day and on the seventh **d**, Nm 19:12
himself on the third **d** and on the Nm 19:12
on the third day and on the seventh **d**, Nm 19:12
unclean on the third **d** and on the Nm 19:19
on the third day and on the seventh **d**. Nm 19:19
on the seventh **d** he shall cleanse Nm 19:19

ridden all your life long to this **d**? Nm 22:30
was killed on the **d** of the plague on Nm 25:18
a year old without blemish, **d** by day, Nm 28:3
a year old without blemish, day by **d**, Nm 28:3
"On the Sabbath **d**, two male lambs a Nm 28:9
"On the fourteenth **d** of the first Nm 28:16
and on the fifteenth **d** of this month is Nm 28:17
On the first **d** there shall be a holy Nm 28:18
And on the seventh **d** you shall have a Nm 28:25
"On the **d** of the firstfruits, when you Nm 28:26
"On the first **d** of the seventh month Nm 29:1
It is a **d** for you to blow the trumpets, Nm 29:1
"On the tenth **d** of this seventh month Nm 29:7
"On the fifteenth **d** of the seventh Nm 29:12
"On the second **d** twelve bulls from Nm 29:17
"On the third **d** eleven bulls, two Nm 29:20
"On the fourth **d** ten bulls, two rams, Nm 29:23
"On the fifth **d** nine bulls, two rams, Nm 29:26
"On the sixth **d** eight bulls, two rams, Nm 29:29
"On the seventh **d** seven bulls, two Nm 29:32
"On the eighth **d** you shall have a Nm 29:35
opposes her on the **d** that he hears of Nm 30:5
nothing to her on the **d** that he hears, Nm 30:7
on the **d** that her husband comes to Nm 30:8
and void on the **d** that he hears them, Nm 30:12
says nothing to her from **d** to day, Nm 30:14
says nothing to her from day to **d**, Nm 30:14
to her on the **d** that he heard of Nm 30:14
captives on the third **d** and on the Nm 31:19
on the third day and on the seventh **d**. Nm 31:19
wash your clothes on the seventh **d**, Nm 31:24
LORD'S anger was kindled on that **d**, Nm 32:10
on the fifteenth **d** of the first month. Nm 33:3
On the **d** after the Passover, the people Nm 33:3
Egypt, on the first **d** of the fifth month. Nm 33:38
year, on the first **d** of the eleventh month, Dt 1:3
in fire by night and in the cloud by **d**, Dt 1:33
and settled in their place even to this **d**. Dt 2:22
This **d** I will begin to put the dread and Dt 2:25
give him into your hand, as he is this **d**. Dt 2:30
name, Havvoth-jair, as it is to this **d**.) Dt 3:14
how on the **d** that you stood before the Dt 4:10
saw no form on the **d** that the LORD spoke Dt 4:15
of his own inheritance, as you are this **d**. Dt 4:20
since the **d** that God created man on the Dt 4:32
land for an inheritance, as it is this **d**, Dt 4:38
"'Observe the Sabbath **d**, to keep it holy, Dt 5:12
but the seventh **d** is a Sabbath to the Dt 5:14
commanded you to keep the Sabbath **d**. Dt 5:15
This **d** we have seen God speak with man Dt 5:24
might preserve us alive, as we are this **d**. Dt 6:24
he swore to your fathers, as it is this **d**. Dt 8:18
From the **d** you came out of the land of Dt 9:7
midst of the fire on the **d** of the assembly. Dt 9:10
the LORD from the **d** that I knew you. Dt 9:24
midst of the fire on the **d** of the assembly. Dt 10:4
to him and to bless in his name, to this **d**. Dt 10:8
you above all peoples, as you are this **d**. Dt 10:15
the LORD has destroyed them to this **d**, Dt 11:4
may remember the **d** when you came Dt 16:3
evening of the first **d** remain all night Dt 16:4
and on the seventh **d** there shall be a Dt 16:8
God at Horeb on the **d** of the assembly, Dt 18:16
then on the **d** when he assigns his Dt 21:16
but you shall bury him the same **d**, Dt 21:23
shall give him his wages on the same **d**, Dt 24:15
"This **d** the LORD your God commands Dt 26:16
And on the **d** you cross over the Jordan to Dt 27:2
this **d** you have become the people of the Dt 27:9
That **d** Moses charged the people, Dt 27:11
fail with longing for them all **d** long, Dt 28:32
Night and **d** you shall be in dread and Dt 28:66
But to this **d** the LORD has not given you a Dt 29:4
into another land, as they are this **d**.' Dt 29:28
will be kindled against them in that **d**, Dt 31:17
them, so that they will say in that **d**, Dt 31:17
hide my face in that **d** because of all the Dt 31:18
this song the same **d** and taught it to Dt 31:22
for the **d** of their calamity is at hand, Dt 32:35
That very **d** the LORD spoke to Moses, Dt 32:48
High God surrounds him all **d** long, Dt 33:12
knows the place of his burial to this **d**. Dt 34:6
but you shall meditate on it **d** and night, Jos 1:8
had stood; and they are there to this **d**. Jos 4:9
On that **d** the LORD exalted Joshua in the Jos 4:14
Jordan on the tenth **d** of the first month, Jos 4:19
of that place is called Gilgal to this **d**. Jos 5:9
on the fourteenth **d** of the month Jos 5:10
And the **d** after the Passover, on that Jos 5:11
the day after the Passover, on that very **d**, Jos 5:11
the manna ceased the **d** after they ate of Jos 5:12
On the seventh **d** you shall march Jos 6:4
mouth, until the **d** I tell you to shout. Jos 6:10
And the second **d** they marched around Jos 6:14
On the seventh **d** they rose early, at the Jos 6:15

day they rose early, at the dawn of **d**, Jos 6:15
was only on that **d** that they marched Jos 6:15
And she has lived in Israel to this **d**, Jos 6:25
heap of stones that remains to this **d**. Jos 7:26
to this **d** the name of that place is called Jos 7:26
And all who fell that **d**, both men and Jos 8:25
it forever a heap of ruins, as it is to this **d**. Jos 8:28
of stones, which stands there to this **d**. Jos 8:29
for the journey on the **d** we set out to Jos 9:12
and reached their cities on the third **d**. Jos 9:17
made them that **d** cutters of wood Jos 9:27
and for the altar of the LORD, to this **d**, Jos 9:27
to the LORD in the **d** when the LORD gave Jos 10:12
did not hurry to set for about a whole **d**. Jos 10:13
There has been no **d** like it before or Jos 10:14
the cave, which remain to this very **d**. Jos 10:27
captured it on that **d** and struck it, Jos 10:28
it on the second **d** and struck it with Jos 10:32
And they captured it on that **d**, and Jos 10:35
every person in it to destruction that **d**, Jos 10:35
dwell in the midst of Israel to this **d**. Jos 13:13
And Moses swore on that **d**, saying, Jos 14:9
I am this **d** eighty-five years old. Jos 14:10
as I was in the **d** that Moses sent me; Jos 14:11
of which the LORD spoke on that **d**, Jos 14:12
you heard on that **d** how the Anakim Jos 14:12
of Jephunneh the Kenizzite to this **d**, Jos 14:14
people of Judah at Jerusalem to this **d**. Jos 15:63
of Ephraim to this **d** but have been Jos 16:10
these many days, down to this **d**, Jos 22:3
turning away this **d** from following the Jos 22:16
an altar this **d** in rebellion against Jos 22:16
turn away this **d** from following the Jos 22:18
turn away this **d** from following the Jos 22:29
your God just as you have done to this **d**. Jos 23:8
been able to stand before you to this **d**. Jos 23:9
choose this **d** whom you will serve, Jos 24:15
made a covenant with the people that **d**, Jos 24:25
of Benjamin in Jerusalem to this **d**. Jgs 1:21
its name Luz. That is its name to this **d**. Jgs 1:26
was subdued that **d** under the hand Jgs 3:30
For this is the **d** in which the LORD has Jgs 4:14
So on that **d** God subdued Jabin the king Jgs 4:23
and Barak the son of Abinoam on that **d**: Jgs 5:1
To this **d** it still stands at Ophrah, which Jgs 6:24
and the men of the town to do it by **d**, Jgs 6:27
Therefore on that **d** Gideon was called Jgs 6:32
my father's house this **d** and have killed Jgs 9:18
Jerubbaal and with his house this **d**, Jgs 9:19
On the following **d**, the people went out Jgs 9:42
fought against the city all that **d**. Jgs 9:45
cities, called Havvoth-jair to this **d**, Jgs 10:4
to you. Only please deliver us this **d**." Jgs 10:15
decide this **d** between the people of Jgs 11:27
up to me this **d** to fight against me?" Jgs 12:3
from the womb to the **d** of his death.'" Jgs 13:7
to me the other **d** has appeared to me." Jgs 13:10
On the fourth **d** they said to Samson's Jgs 14:15
lasted, and on the seventh **d** he told her, Jgs 14:17
him on the seventh **d** before the sun Jgs 14:18
En-hakkore; it is at Lehi to this **d**. Jgs 15:19
him hard with her words **d** after day, Jgs 16:16
him hard with her words day after **d**, Jgs 16:16
place is called Mahaneh-dan to this **d**; Jgs 18:12
the Danites until the **d** of the captivity Jgs 18:30
And on the fourth **d** they arose early in Jgs 19:5
And on the fifth **d** he arose early in the Jgs 19:8
and wait until the **d** declines." So they Jgs 19:8
now the **d** has waned toward evening. Jgs 19:9
night. Behold, the **d** draws to its close. Jgs 19:9
were near Jebus, the **d** was nearly over, Jgs 19:11
been seen from the **d** that the people of Jgs 19:30
up out of the land of Egypt until this **d**; Jgs 19:30
their cities on that **d** 26,000 men who Jgs 20:15
and destroyed on that **d** 22,000 men of Jgs 20:21
where they had formed it on the first **d**. Jgs 20:22
the people of Benjamin the second **d**. Jgs 20:24
them out of Gibeah the second **d**, Jgs 20:25
LORD and fasted that **d** until evening, Jgs 20:26
on the third **d** and set themselves Jgs 20:30
25,100 men of Benjamin that **d**. Jgs 20:35
all who fell that **d** of Benjamin were Jgs 20:46
And the next **d** the people rose early and Jgs 21:4
"One tribe is cut off from Israel this **d**. Jgs 21:6
"The **d** you buy the field from the hand of Ru 4:5
"You are witnesses this **d** that I have Ru 4:9
native place. You are witnesses this **d**." Ru 4:10
not left you this **d** without a redeemer, Ru 4:14
On the **d** when Elkanah sacrificed, he 1 Sm 1:4
both of them shall die on the same **d**. 1 Sm 2:34
On that **d** I will fulfill against Eli all 1 Sm 3:12
line and came to Shiloh the same **d**, 1 Sm 4:12
people of Ashdod rose early the next **d**, 1 Sm 5:3
threshold of Dagon in Ashdod to this **d**. 1 Sm 5:5
sacrifices on that **d** to the LORD. 1 Sm 6:15

saw it, they returned that **d** to Ekron. 1 Sm 6:16
is a witness to this **d** in the field of 1 Sm 6:18
From the **d** that the ark was lodged at 1 Sm 7:2
and fasted on that **d** and said there, 1 Sm 7:6
mighty sound that **d** against the 1 Sm 7:10
from the **d** I brought them up out of 1 Sm 8:8
them up out of Egypt even to this **d**, 1 Sm 8:8
And in that **d** you will cry out 1 Sm 8:18
LORD will not answer you in that **d**." 1 Sm 8:18
Now the **d** before Saul came, the LORD 1 Sm 9:15
So Saul ate with Samuel that **d**. 1 Sm 9:24
all these signs came to pass that **d**. 1 Sm 10:9
And the next **d** Saul put the people in 1 Sm 11:11
Ammonites until the heat of the **d**. 1 Sm 11:11
a man shall be put to death this **d**, 1 Sm 11:13
you from my youth until this **d**. 1 Sm 12:2
and his anointed is witness this **d**, 1 Sm 12:5
LORD sent thunder and rain that **d**, 1 Sm 12:18
So on the **d** of the battle there was 1 Sm 13:22
One **d** Jonathan the son of Saul said to 1 Sm 14:1
So the LORD saved Israel that **d**. And 1 Sm 14:23
Israel had been hard pressed that **d**, 1 Sm 14:24
who eats food this **d**." And the people 1 Sm 14:28
Philistines that **d** from Michmash 1 Sm 14:31
But he did not answer him that **d**. 1 Sm 14:37
not answered your servant this **d**? 1 Sm 14:41
with God this **d**." So the people 1 Sm 14:45
Israel from you this **d** and has given 1 Sm 15:28
Saul again until the **d** of his death, 1 Sm 15:35
upon David from that **d** forward. 1 Sm 16:13
said, "I defy the ranks of Israel this **d**. 1 Sm 17:10
This **d** the LORD will deliver you into 1 Sm 17:46
of the Philistines this **d** to the birds 1 Sm 17:46
Saul took him that **d** and would not 1 Sm 18:2
And Saul eyed David from that **d** on. 1 Sm 18:9
The next **d** a harmful spirit from 1 Sm 18:10
playing the lyre, as he did **d** by day. 1 Sm 18:10
playing the lyre, as he did day by **d**. 1 Sm 18:10
lay naked all that **d** and all that 1 Sm 19:24
in the field till the third **d** at evening. 1 Sm 20:5
this time tomorrow, or the third **d**, 1 Sm 20:12
On the third **d** go down quickly to 1 Sm 20:19
Yet Saul did not say anything that **d**, 1 Sm 20:26
But on the second **d**, the day after the 1 Sm 20:27
day, the **d** after the new moon, 1 Sm 20:27
no food the second **d** of the month, 1 Sm 20:34
by hot bread on the **d** it is taken away. 1 Sm 21:6
the servants of Saul was there that **d**, 1 Sm 21:7
rose and fled that **d** from Saul and 1 Sm 21:10
against me, to lie in wait, as at this **d**." 1 Sm 22:8
me, to lie in wait, as at this **d**?" 1 Sm 22:13
killed on that **d** eighty-five persons 1 Sm 22:18
said to Abiathar, "I knew on that **d**, 1 Sm 22:22
And Saul sought him every **d**, but 1 Sm 23:14
"Here is the **d** of which the LORD said 1 Sm 24:4
this **d** your eyes have seen how the 1 Sm 24:10
have declared this **d** how you have 1 Sm 24:18
for what you have done to me this **d**. 1 Sm 24:19
in your eyes, for we come on a feast **d**. 1 Sm 25:8
a wall to us both by night and by **d**, 1 Sm 25:16
who sent you this **d** to meet me! 1 Sm 25:32
kept me this **d** from bloodguilt and 1 Sm 25:33
your enemy into your hand this **d**. 1 Sm 26:8
strike him, or his **d** will come to die, 1 Sm 26:10
driven me out this **d** that I should 1 Sm 26:19
life was precious in your eyes this **d**. 1 Sm 26:21
life was precious this **d** in my sight, 1 Sm 26:24
I shall perish one **d** by the hand of 1 Sm 27:1
So that **d** Achish gave him Ziklag. 1 Sm 27:6
to the kings of Judah to this **d**. 1 Sm 27:6
has done this thing to you this **d**. 1 Sm 28:18
eaten nothing all **d** and all night. 1 Sm 28:20
have found no fault in him to this **d**." 1 Sm 29:3
in you from the **d** of your coming to 1 Sm 29:6
day of your coming to me to this **d**. 1 Sm 29:6
your servant from the **d** I entered your 1 Sm 29:8
men came to Ziklag on the third **d**, 1 Sm 30:1
until the evening of the next **d**, 1 Sm 30:17
for Israel from that **d** forward to this 1 Sm 30:25
from that day forward to this **d**. 1 Sm 30:25
all his men, on the same **d** together. 1 Sm 31:6
The next **d**, when the Philistines came 1 Sm 31:8
And on the third **d**, behold, a man 2 Sm 1:2
And the battle was very fierce that **d**. 2 Sm 2:17
and the **d** broke upon them at 2 Sm 2:32
To this **d** I keep showing steadfast love 2 Sm 3:8
David to eat bread while it was yet **d**. 2 Sm 3:35
all Israel understood that **d** that it had 2 Sm 3:37
a great man has fallen this **d** in Israel? 2 Sm 3:38
have been sojourners there to this **d**). 2 Sm 4:3
about the heat of the **d** they came to the 2 Sm 4:5
my lord the king this **d** on Saul and on 2 Sm 4:8
And David said on that **d**, "Whoever 2 Sm 5:8
place is called Perez-uzzah, to this **d**. 2 Sm 6:8
David was afraid of the LORD that **d**, 2 Sm 6:9
had no child to the **d** of her death. 2 Sm 6:23
in a house since the **d** I brought up the 2 Sm 7:6
the people of Israel from Egypt to this **d**, 2 Sm 7:6
in Jerusalem that **d** and the next. 2 Sm 11:12
On the seventh **d** the child died. And 2 Sm 12:18
determined from the **d** he violated 2 Sm 13:32
mourned for his son **d** after day. 2 Sm 13:37
mourned for his son day after **d**. 2 Sm 13:37
and the loss there was great on that **d**, 2 Sm 18:7
more people that **d** than the sword. 2 Sm 18:8
Absalom's monument to this **d**. 2 Sm 18:18
You may carry news another **d**, but 2 Sm 18:20
delivered you this **d** from the hand 2 Sm 18:31
So the victory that **d** was turned into 2 Sm 19:2
the people, for the people heard that **d**, 2 Sm 19:2
into the city that **d** as people steal in 2 Sm 19:3
who have this **d** saved your life and 2 Sm 19:5
did wrong on the **d** my lord the king 2 Sm 19:19
behold, I have come this **d**, 2 Sm 19:20
that you should this **d** be as an 2 Sm 19:22
be put to death in Israel this **d**? 2 Sm 19:22
that I am this **d** king over Israel?" 2 Sm 19:22
from the **d** the king departed until 2 Sm 19:24
departed until the **d** he came back 2 Sm 19:24
I am this **d** eighty years old. Can I 2 Sm 19:35
were shut up until the **d** of their death, 2 Sm 20:3
of the air to come upon them by **d**, 2 Sm 21:10
on the **d** the Philistines killed Saul 2 Sm 21:12
this song on the **d** when the LORD 2 Sm 22:1
me in the **d** of my calamity, 2 Sm 22:19
brought about a great victory that **d**, 2 Sm 23:10
in a pit on a **d** when snow had fallen. 2 Sm 23:20
And Gad came that **d** to David and 2 Sm 24:18
gone down this **d** and has sacrificed 1 Kgs 1:25
in my place,' even so will I do this **d**." 1 Kgs 1:30
someone to sit on my throne this **d**, 1 Kgs 1:48
grievous curse on the **d** when I went to 1 Kgs 2:8
shall be put to death this **d**." 1 Kgs 2:24
For on the **d** you go out and cross the 1 Kgs 2:37
certain that on the **d** you go out and 1 Kgs 2:42
him a son to sit on his throne this **d**. 1 Kgs 3:6
Then on the third **d** after I gave birth, 1 Kgs 3:18
provision for one **d** was thirty cors 1 Kgs 4:22
and said, "Blessed be the LORD this **d**, 1 Kgs 5:7
outside. And they are there to this **d**. 1 Kgs 8:8
'Since the **d** that I brought my people 1 Kgs 8:16
your hand have fulfilled it this **d**. 1 Kgs 8:24
your servant prays before you this **d**, 1 Kgs 8:28
open night and **d** toward this house, 1 Kgs 8:29
near to the LORD our God **d** and night, 1 Kgs 8:59
of his people Israel, as each **d** requires, 1 Kgs 8:59
his commandments, as at this **d**." 1 Kgs 8:61
The same **d** the king consecrated the 1 Kgs 8:64
On the eighth **d** he sent the people 1 Kgs 8:66
are called the land of Cabul to this **d**. 1 Kgs 9:13
to be slaves, and so they are to this **d**. 1 Kgs 9:21
has come or been seen to this **d**. 1 Kgs 10:12
came to Rehoboam the third **d**, 1 Kgs 12:12
"Come to me again the third **d**." 1 Kgs 12:12
against the house of David to this **d**. 1 Kgs 12:19
feast on the fifteenth **d** of the eighth 1 Kgs 12:32
on the fifteenth **d** in the eighth 1 Kgs 12:33
And he gave a sign the same **d**, 1 Kgs 13:3
of God had done that **d** in Bethel. 1 Kgs 13:11
king over Israel that **d** in the camp. 1 Kgs 16:16
until the **d** that the LORD sends rain 1 Kgs 17:14
it be known this **d** that you are God 1 Kgs 18:36
I will give it into your hand this **d**, 1 Kgs 20:13
Then on the seventh **d** the battle was 1 Kgs 20:29
100,000 foot soldiers in one **d**. 1 Kgs 20:29
shall see on that **d** when you go into 1 Kgs 22:25
And the battle continued that **d**, and 1 Kgs 22:35
So the water has been healed to this **d**, 2 Kgs 2:22
One **d** Elisha went on to Shunem, 2 Kgs 4:8
One **d** he came there, and he turned 2 Kgs 4:11
he went out one **d** to his father among 2 Kgs 4:18
him. And on the next **d** I said to her, 2 Kgs 6:29
right. This **d** is a day of good news. 2 Kgs 7:9
right. This day is a **d** of good news. 2 Kgs 7:9
of the fields from the **d** that she left the 2 Kgs 8:6
But the next **d** he took the bed cloth 2 Kgs 8:15
from the rule of Judah to this **d**. 2 Kgs 8:22
Baal, and made it a latrine to this **d**. 2 Kgs 10:27
Joktheel, which is its name to this **d**. 2 Kgs 14:7
he was a leper to the **d** of his death, 2 Kgs 15:5
to Elath, where they dwell to this **d**. 2 Kgs 16:6
own land to Assyria until this **d**. 2 Kgs 17:23
To this **d** they do according to the 2 Kgs 17:34
their fathers did, so they do to this **d**. 2 Kgs 17:41
Hezekiah, This **d** is a day of distress, 2 Kgs 19:3
Hezekiah, This day is a **d** of distress, 2 Kgs 19:3
On the third **d** you shall go up to the 2 Kgs 20:5
the house of the LORD on the third **d**?" 2 Kgs 20:8
fathers have stored up till this **d**, 2 Kgs 20:17
since the **d** their fathers came out of 2 Kgs 21:15
came out of Egypt, even to this **d**." 2 Kgs 21:15
month, on the tenth **d** of the month, 2 Kgs 25:1
On the ninth **d** of the fourth month 2 Kgs 25:3
on the seventh **d** of the month—that 2 Kgs 25:8
on the twenty-seventh **d** of the 2 Kgs 25:27
And every **d** of his life he dined 2 Kgs 25:29
them for destruction to this **d**, 1 Chr 4:41
and they have lived there to this **d**. 1 Chr 4:43
Hara, and the river Gozan, to this **d**. 1 Chr 5:26
for they were on duty **d** and night. 1 Chr 9:33
The next **d**, when the Philistines 1 Chr 10:8
a pit on a **d** when snow had fallen. 1 Chr 11:22
For from **d** to day men came to 1 Chr 12:22
For from day to **d** men came to 1 Chr 12:22
place is called Perez-uzza to this **d**. 1 Chr 13:11
And David was afraid of God that **d**, 1 Chr 13:12
Then on that **d** David first appointed 1 Chr 16:7
Tell of his salvation from **d** to day. 1 Chr 16:23
Tell of his salvation from day to **d**. 1 Chr 16:23
before the ark as each **d** required, 1 Chr 16:37
a house since the **d** I brought up 1 Chr 17:5
the day I brought up Israel to this **d**, 1 Chr 17:5
On the east there were six each **d**, on 1 Chr 26:17
each day, on the north four each **d**, 1 Chr 26:17
each day, on the south four each **d**, 1 Chr 26:17
on the next **d** offered burnt offerings 1 Chr 29:21
LORD on that **d** with great gladness. 1 Chr 29:22
outside. And they are there to this **d**. 2 Chr 5:9
'Since the **d** that I brought my people 2 Chr 6:5
your hand have fulfilled it this **d**. 2 Chr 6:15
eyes may be open **d** and night toward 2 Chr 6:20
And on the eighth **d** they held a 2 Chr 7:9
On the twenty-third **d** of the seventh 2 Chr 7:10
forced labor, and so they are to this **d**. 2 Chr 8:8
as the duty of each **d** required, 2 Chr 8:13
priests as the duty of each **d** required, 2 Chr 8:14
Solomon from the **d** the foundation 2 Chr 8:16
came to Rehoboam the third **d**, 2 Chr 10:12
"Come to me again the third **d**." 2 Chr 10:12
against the house of David to this **d**. 2 Chr 10:19
the LORD on that **d** from the spoil 2 Chr 15:11
shall see on that **d** when you go into 2 Chr 18:24
And the battle continued that **d**, and 2 Chr 18:34
On the fourth **d** they assembled in 2 Chr 20:26
the Valley of Beracah to this **d**. 2 Chr 20:26
from the rule of Judah to this **d**. 2 Chr 21:10
because of the disease, **d** by day.'" 2 Chr 21:15
because of the disease, day by **d**.'" 2 Chr 21:15
Thus they did **d** after day, and 2 Chr 24:11
Thus they did day after **d**, and 2 Chr 24:11
was a leper to the **d** of his death, 2 Chr 26:21
killed 120,000 from Judah in one **d**, 2 Chr 28:6
consecrate on the first **d** of the first 2 Chr 29:17
and on the eighth **d** of the month 2 Chr 29:17
and on the sixteenth **d** of the first 2 Chr 29:17
on the fourteenth **d** of the second 2 Chr 30:15
the priests praised the LORD **d** by day, 2 Chr 30:21
the priests praised the LORD day by **d**, 2 Chr 30:21
the duty of each **d** required—for 2 Chr 31:16
lamb on the fourteenth **d** of the first 2 Chr 35:1
of the LORD was prepared that **d**, 2 Chr 35:16
I am not coming against you this **d**, 2 Chr 35:21
of Josiah in their laments to this **d**. 2 Chr 35:25
according to the rule, as each **d** required, Ezr 3:4
From the first **d** of the seventh month Ezr 3:6
be given to them **d** by day without fail, Ezr 6:9
be given to them day by **d** without fail, Ezr 6:9
finished on the third **d** of the month of Ezr 6:15
On the fourteenth **d** of the first month, Ezr 6:19
For on the first **d** of the first month he Ezr 7:9
and on the first **d** of the fifth month he Ezr 7:9
Ahava on the twelfth **d** of the first Ezr 8:31
On the fourth **d**, within the house of our Ezr 8:33
of our fathers to this **d** we have been in Ezr 9:7
month, on the twentieth **d** of the month. Ezr 10:9
Nor is this a task for one **d** or for two, Ezr 10:13
On the first **d** of the tenth month they Ezr 10:16
and by the first **d** of the first month Ezr 10:17
now pray before you **d** and night for the Neh 1:6
sacrifice? Will they finish up in a **d**? Neh 4:2
a protection against them **d** and night. Neh 4:9
From that **d** on, half of my servants Neh 4:16
for us by night and may labor by **d**." Neh 4:22
Return to them this very **d** their fields, Neh 5:11
my expense for each **d** was one ox and Neh 5:18
on the twenty-fifth **d** of the month Neh 6:15
on the first **d** of the seventh month. Neh 8:2
"This **d** is holy to the LORD your God; Neh 8:9
ready, for this **d** is holy to our Lord. Neh 8:10
saying, "Be quiet, for this **d** is holy; Neh 8:11
On the second **d** the heads of fathers' Neh 8:13
son of Nun to that **d** the people of Israel Neh 8:17
And **d** by day, from the first day to the Neh 8:18
And day by **d**, from the first day to the Neh 8:18
by day, from the first **d** to the last day, Neh 8:18

by day, from the first day to the last **d**, Neh 8:18
and on the eighth **d** there was a solemn Neh 8:18
on the twenty-fourth **d** of this month Neh 9:1
the LORD their God for a quarter of the **d**; Neh 9:3
a name for yourself, as it is to this **d**. Neh 9:10
a pillar of cloud you led them in the **d**, Neh 9:12
the way did not depart from them by **d**, Neh 9:19
of the kings of Assyria until this **d**. Neh 9:32
Behold, we are slaves this **d**; in the land Neh 9:36
or any grain on the Sabbath **d** to sell, Neh 10:31
them on the Sabbath or on a holy **d**. Neh 10:31
for the singers, as every **d** required. Neh 11:23
great sacrifices that **d** and rejoiced, Neh 12:43
On that **d** men were appointed over Neh 12:44
On that **d** they read from the Book of Neh 13:1
into Jerusalem on the Sabbath **d**. Neh 13:15
warned them on the **d** when they sold Neh 13:15
are doing, profaning the Sabbath **d**? Neh 13:17
be brought in on the Sabbath **d**. Neh 13:19
the gates, to keep the Sabbath **d** holy. Neh 13:22
On the seventh **d**, when the heart of the Est 1:10
This very **d** the noble women of Persia Est 1:18
And every **d** Mordecai walked in front of Est 2:11
they spoke to him **d** after day and he Est 3:4
to him day after **d** and he would not Est 3:4
they cast lots) before Haman **d** after day; Est 3:7
they cast lots) before Haman day after **d**; Est 3:7
on the thirteenth **d** of the first Est 3:12
and old, women and children, in one **d**, Est 3:13
the thirteenth **d** of the twelfth month, Est 3:13
to all the peoples to be ready for that **d**. Est 3:14
eat or drink for three days, night or **d**. Est 4:16
On the third **d** Esther put on her royal Est 5:1
Haman went out that **d** joyful and glad of Est 5:9
And on the second **d**, as they were Est 7:2
On that **d** King Ahasuerus gave to Queen Est 8:1
month of Sivan, on the twenty-third **d**. Est 8:9
on one **d** throughout all the provinces of Est 8:12
on the thirteenth **d** of the twelfth month, Est 8:12
be ready on that **d** to take vengeance on Est 8:13
of Adar, on the thirteenth **d** of the same, Est 9:1
on the very **d** when the enemies of the Est 9:1
That very **d** the number of those killed Est 9:11
also on the fourteenth **d** of the month of Est 9:15
was on the thirteenth **d** of the month of Est 9:17
and on the fourteenth **d** they rested and Est 9:17
and made that a **d** of feasting and Est 9:17
gathered on the thirteenth **d** and on the Est 9:18
fourteenth, and rested on the fifteenth **d**, Est 9:18
making that a **d** of feasting and Est 9:18
hold the fourteenth **d** of the month of Est 9:19
of Adar as a **d** for gladness and feasting, Est 9:19
and as a **d** on which they send gifts of Est 9:19
to keep the fourteenth **d** of the month Est 9:21
and also the fifteenth **d** of the same, Est 9:21
a feast in the house of each one on his **d**, Jb 1:4
Now there was a **d** when the sons of God Jb 1:6
Now there was a **d** when his sons and Jb 1:13
Again there was a **d** when the sons of God Jb 2:1
his mouth and cursed the **d** of his birth. Jb 3:1
“Let the **d** perish on which I was born, and Jb 3:3
Let that **d** be darkness! May God above Jb 3:4
upon it; let the blackness of the **d** terrify it. Jb 3:5
Let those curse it who curse the **d**, who are Jb 3:8
he may enjoy, like a hired hand, his **d**. Jb 14:6
He knows that a **d** of darkness is ready Jb 15:23
They make night into **d**; ‘The light,’ Jb 17:12
They of the west are appalled at his **d**, Jb 18:20
dragged off in the **d** of God's wrath. Jb 20:28
evil man is spared in the **d** of calamity, Jb 21:30
that he is rescued in the **d** of wrath? Jb 21:30
houses; by **d** they shut themselves up; Jb 24:16
not I weep for him whose **d** was hard? Jb 30:25
of trouble, for the **d** of battle and war? Jb 38:23
and on his law he meditates **d** and night. Ps 1:2
and a God who feels indignation every **d**. Ps 7:11
and have sorrow in my heart all the **d**? Ps 13:2
the LORD on the **d** when the LORD rescued Ps 18:T
confronted me in the **d** of my calamity, Ps 18:18
D to day pours out speech, and night to Ps 19:2
Day to **d** pours out speech, and night to Ps 19:2
the LORD answer you in the **d** of trouble! Ps 20:1
O my God, I cry by **d**, but you do not Ps 22:2
salvation; for you I wait all the **d** long. Ps 25:5
hide me in his shelter in the **d** of trouble; Ps 27:5
away through my groaning all **d** long. Ps 32:3
For **d** and night your hand was heavy Ps 32:4
and of your praise all the **d** long. Ps 35:28
wicked, for he sees that his **d** is coming. Ps 37:13
prostrate; all the **d** I go about mourning. Ps 38:6
ruin and meditate treachery all **d** long. Ps 38:12
In the **d** of trouble the LORD delivers him; Ps 41:1
My tears have been my food **d** and night, Ps 42:3
By **d** the LORD commands his steadfast Ps 42:8
All **d** long my disgrace is before me, Ps 44:15
your sake we are killed all the **d** long; Ps 44:22
and call upon me in the **d** of trouble; I Ps 50:15
steadfast love of God endures all the **d**. Ps 52:1
D and night they go around it on its Ps 55:10
me; all **d** long an attacker oppresses me; Ps 56:1
my enemies trample on me all **d** long, for Ps 56:2
All **d** long they injure my cause; all their Ps 56:5
will turn back in the **d** when I call. Ps 56:9
and a refuge in the **d** of my distress. Ps 59:16
name, as I perform my vows **d** after day. Ps 61:8
name, as I perform my vows day after **d**. Ps 61:8
praise, and with your glory all the **d**. Ps 71:8
acts, of your deeds of salvation all the **d**, Ps 71:15
of your righteous help all the **d** long, Ps 71:24
and blessings invoked for him all the **d**! Ps 72:15
For all the **d** long I have been stricken Ps 73:14
Yours is the **d**, yours also the night; you Ps 74:16
how the foolish scoff at you all the **d**! Ps 74:22
In the **d** of my trouble I seek the Lord; in Ps 77:2
the bow, turned back on the **d** of battle. Ps 78:9
his power or the **d** when he redeemed Ps 78:42
moon, at the full moon, on our feast **d**. Ps 81:3
For a **d** in your courts is better than a Ps 84:10
to me, O Lord, for to you do I cry all the **d**. Ps 86:3
In the **d** of my trouble I call upon you, Ps 86:7
I cry out **d** and night before you. Ps 88:1
Every **d** I call upon you, O LORD; I spread Ps 88:9
surround me like a flood all **d** long; Ps 88:17
your name all the **d** and in your Ps 89:16
of the night, nor the arrow that flies by **d**, Ps 91:5
as on the **d** at Massah in the wilderness, Ps 95:8
name; tell of his salvation from **d** to day. Ps 96:2
name; tell of his salvation from day to **d**. Ps 96:2
face from me in the **d** of my distress! Ps 102:2
answer me speedily in the **d** when I call! Ps 102:2
All the **d** my enemies taunt me; those Ps 102:8
like a belt that he puts on every **d**! Ps 109:19
freely on the **d** of your power, Ps 110:3
will shatter kings on the **d** of his wrath. Ps 110:5
This is the **d** that the LORD has made; Ps 118:24
your appointment they stand this **d**, Ps 119:91
your law! It is my meditation all the **d**. Ps 119:97
Seven times a **d** I praise you for your Ps 119:164
The sun shall not strike you by **d**, nor Ps 121:6
the sun to rule over the **d**, for his Ps 136:8
against the Edomites the **d** of Jerusalem, Ps 137:7
On the **d** I called, you answered me; my Ps 138:3
the night is bright as the **d**, for Ps 139:12
have covered my head in the **d** of battle. Ps 140:7
Every **d** I will bless you and praise your Ps 145:2
earth; on that very **d** his plans perish. Ps 146:4
brighter and brighter until full **d**. Prv 4:18
Riches do not profit in the **d** of wrath, Prv 11:4
even the wicked for the **d** of trouble. Prv 16:4
All **d** long he craves and craves, but Prv 21:26
horse is made ready for the **d** of battle, Prv 21:31
in the fear of the LORD all the **d**. Prv 23:17
If you faint in the **d** of adversity, your Prv 24:10
who takes off a garment on a cold **d**, Prv 25:20
you do not know what a **d** may bring. Prv 27:1
house in the **d** of your calamity. Prv 27:10
on a rainy **d** and a quarrelsome Prv 27:15
and the **d** of death than the day of birth. Eccl 7:1
and the day of death than the **d** of birth. Eccl 7:1
In the **d** of prosperity be joyful, and in Eccl 7:14
and in the **d** of adversity consider: Eccl 7:14
the spirit, or power over the **d** of death. Eccl 8:8
how neither **d** nor night do one's eyes Eccl 8:16
in the **d** when the keepers of the house Eccl 12:3
Until the **d** breathes and the shadows Sg 2:17
crowned him on the **d** of his wedding, Sg 3:11
on the **d** of the gladness of his heart. Sg 3:11
Until the **d** breathes and the shadows flee, Sg 4:6
for our sister on the **d** when she is spoken Sg 8:8
the LORD alone will be exalted in that **d**. Is 2:11
LORD of hosts has a **d** against all that is Is 2:12
the LORD alone will be exalted in that **d**. Is 2:17
In that **d** mankind will cast away their Is 2:20
in that **d** he will speak out, saying: “I will Is 3:7
In that **d** the Lord will take away the Is 3:18
shall take hold of one man in that **d**, Is 4:1
In that **d** the branch of the LORD shall be Is 4:2
Zion and over her assemblies a cloud by **d**, Is 4:5
be a booth for shade by **d** from the heat, Is 4:6
They will growl over it on that **d**, like the Is 5:30
come since the **d** that Ephraim departed Is 7:17
In that **d** the LORD will whistle for the fly Is 7:18
In that **d** the Lord will shave with a razor Is 7:20
In that **d** a man will keep alive a young Is 7:21
In that **d** every place where there used to Is 7:23
you have broken as on the **d** of Midian. Is 9:4
and tail, palm branch and reed in one **d**— Is 9:14
will you do on the **d** of punishment, Is 10:3
devour his thorns and briers in one **d**. Is 10:17
In that **d** the remnant of Israel and the Is 10:20
And in that **d** his burden will depart Is 10:27
This very **d** he will halt at Nob; he will Is 10:32
In that **d** the root of Jesse, who shall Is 11:10
In that **d** the Lord will extend his hand Is 11:11
You will say in that **d**: “I will give thanks Is 12:1
And you will say in that **d**: “Give thanks Is 12:4
Wail, for the **d** of the LORD is near; as Is 13:6
Behold, the **d** of the LORD comes, cruel, Is 13:9
LORD of hosts in the **d** of his fierce anger. Is 13:13
you are fallen from heaven, O **D** Star, Is 14:12
And in that **d** the glory of Jacob will be Is 17:4
In that **d** man will look to his Maker, and Is 17:7
In that **d** their strong cities will be like the Is 17:9
them grow on the **d** that you plant them, Is 17:11
flee away in a **d** of grief and incurable Is 17:11
In that **d** the Egyptians will be like Is 19:16
In that **d** there will be five cities in the Is 19:18
In that **d** there will be an altar to the Is 19:19
the LORD in that **d** and worship with Is 19:21
In that **d** there will be a highway from Is 19:23
In that **d** Israel will be the third with Is 19:24
of this coastland will say in that **d**, Is 20:6
I stand, O Lord, continually by **d**, Is 21:8
of hosts has a **d** of tumult and trampling Is 22:5
In that **d** you looked to the weapons of the Is 22:8
In that **d** the Lord GOD of hosts called for Is 22:12
In that **d** I will call my servant Eliakim Is 22:20
In that **d**, declares the LORD of hosts, the Is 22:25
In that **d** Tyre will be forgotten for Is 23:15
On that **d** the LORD will punish the host Is 24:21
It will be said on that **d**, “Behold, this is Is 25:9
In that **d** this song will be sung in the Is 26:1
In that **d** the LORD with his hard and great Is 27:1
In that **d**, “A pleasant vineyard, sing of it! Is 27:2
anyone punish it, I keep it night and **d**; Is 27:3
his fierce breath in the **d** of the east wind. Is 27:8
In that **d** from the river Euphrates to the Is 27:12
And in that **d** a great trumpet will be Is 27:13
In that **d** the LORD of hosts will be a crown Is 28:5
it will pass through, by **d** and by night; Is 28:19
In that **d** the deaf shall hear the words of Is 29:18
In that **d** your livestock will graze in Is 30:23
water, in the **d** of the great slaughter, Is 30:25
in the **d** when the LORD binds up the Is 30:26
For in that **d** everyone shall cast away his Is 31:7
For the LORD has a **d** of vengeance, a year Is 34:8
Night and **d** it shall not be quenched; its Is 34:10
says Hezekiah, ‘This **d** is a day of distress, Is 37:3
says Hezekiah, ‘This day is a **d** of distress, Is 37:3
from **d** to night you bring me to an end; Is 38:12
from **d** to night you bring me to an end. Is 38:13
the living, he thanks you, as I do this **d**; Is 38:19
your fathers have stored up till this **d**, Is 39:6
shall come to you in a moment, in one **d**; Is 47:9
you; in a **d** of salvation I have helped you; Is 49:8
fear continually all the **d** because of the Is 51:13
“and continually all the **d** my name is Is 52:5
Therefore in that **d** they shall know that Is 52:6
and tomorrow will be like this **d**, great Is 56:12
in the **d** of your fast you seek your own Is 58:3
Fasting like yours this **d** will not make Is 58:4
a **d** for a person to humble himself? Is 58:5
this a fast, and a **d** acceptable to the LORD? Is 58:5
from doing your pleasure on my holy **d**, Is 58:13
delight and the holy **d** of the LORD Is 58:13
d and night they shall not be shut, that Is 60:11
sun shall be no more your light by **d**, Is 60:19
favor, and the **d** of vengeance of our God; Is 61:2
all the **d** and all the night they shall never Is 62:6
For the **d** of vengeance was in my heart, Is 63:4
my hands all the **d** to a rebellious people, Is 65:2
in my nostrils, a fire that burns all the **d**. Is 65:5
things? Shall a land be born in one **d**? Is 66:8
have set you this **d** over nations and over Jer 1:10
behold, I make you this **d** a fortified city, Jer 1:18
fathers, from our youth even to this **d**, Jer 3:25
“In that **d**, declares the LORD, courage Jer 4:9
Woe to us, for the **d** declines, for the Jer 6:4
For in the **d** that I brought them out of Jer 7:22
From the **d** that your fathers came out of Jer 7:25
came out of the land of Egypt to this **d**, Jer 7:25
the prophets to them, **d** after day. Jer 7:25
the prophets to them, day after **d**. Jer 7:25
that I might weep **d** and night for the slain Jer 9:1
honey, as at this **d**.” Then I answered, Jer 11:5
them persistently, even to this **d**, Jer 11:7
and set them apart for the **d** of slaughter. Jer 12:3
eyes run down with tears night and **d**, Jer 14:17
her sun went down while it was yet **d**; Jer 15:9
you shall serve other gods **d** and night, Jer 16:13
my refuge in the **d** of trouble, Jer 16:19
nor have I desired the **d** of sickness. Jer 17:16
you are my refuge in the **d** of disaster. Jer 17:17
bring upon them the **d** of disaster; Jer 17:18
burden on the Sabbath **d** or bring it in Jer 17:21

any work, but keep the Sabbath **d** holy, Jer 17:22
the gates of this city on the Sabbath **d**, Jer 17:24
but keep the Sabbath **d** holy and do no Jer 17:24
listen to me, to keep the Sabbath **d** holy, Jer 17:27
gates of Jerusalem on the Sabbath **d**, Jer 17:27
not my face, in the **d** of their calamity." Jer 18:17
The next **d**, when Pashhur released Jer 20:3
I have become a laughingstock all the **d**; Jer 20:7
me a reproach and derision all **d** long. Jer 20:8
Cursed be the **d** on which I was born! Jer 20:14
The **d** when my mother bore me, let it Jer 20:14
the son of Amon, king of Judah, to this **d**, Jer 25:3
a hissing and a curse, as at this **d**; Jer 25:18
the LORD on that **d** shall extend from Jer 25:33
remain there until the **d** when I visit Jer 27:22
That **d** is so great there is none like it; it Jer 30:7
"And it shall come to pass in that **d**, Jer 30:8
there shall be a **d** when watchmen will Jer 31:6
their fathers on the **d** when I took them Jer 31:32
sun for light by **d** and the fixed order Jer 31:35
and to this **d** in Israel and among all Jer 32:20
made a name for yourself, as at this **d**. Jer 32:20
from the **d** it was built to this day, Jer 32:31
from the day it was built to this **d**, Jer 32:31
covenant with the **d** and my covenant Jer 33:20
so that **d** and night will not come at Jer 33:20
my covenant with **d** and night and Jer 33:25
kept, and they drink none to this **d**, Jer 35:14
all the nations, from the **d** I spoke to you, Jer 36:2
and on a **d** of fasting in the hearing of all Jer 36:6
out to the heat by **d** and the frost by Jer 36:30
guard until the **d** that Jerusalem was Jer 38:28
month, on the ninth **d** of the month, Jer 39:2
be accomplished before you on that **d**. Jer 39:16
But I will deliver you on that **d**, declares Jer 39:17
On the **d** after the murder of Gedaliah, Jer 41:4
certainty that I have warned you this **d** Jer 42:19
And I have this **d** declared it to you, but Jer 42:21
Behold, this **d** they are a desolation, and Jer 44:2
a waste and a desolation, as at this **d**. Jer 44:6
not humbled themselves even to this **d**, Jer 44:10
without inhabitant, as it is this **d**. Jer 44:22
has happened to you, as at this **d**." Jer 44:23
That **d** is the day of the Lord GOD of Jer 46:10
That day is the **d** of the Lord GOD of Jer 46:10
the Lord GOD of hosts, a **d** of vengeance, Jer 46:10
for the **d** of their calamity has come Jer 46:21
because of the **d** that is coming to Jer 47:4
Moab shall be in that **d** like the heart of Jer 48:41
Edom shall be in that **d** like the heart of Jer 49:22
her soldiers shall be destroyed in that **d**, Jer 49:26
Woe to them, for their **d** has come, the Jer 50:27
soldiers shall be destroyed on that **d**, Jer 50:30
Lord GOD of hosts, for your **d** has come, Jer 50:31
her from every side on the **d** of trouble. Jer 51:2
month, on the tenth **d** of the month, Jer 52:4
On the ninth **d** of the fourth month the Jer 52:6
put him in prison till the **d** of his death. Jer 52:11
on the tenth **d** of the month—that was Jer 52:12
on the twenty-fifth **d** of the month, Jer 52:31
And every **d** of his life he dined Jer 52:33
until the **d** of his death as long as he Jer 52:34
LORD inflicted on the **d** of his fierce Lam 1:12
left me stunned, faint all the **d** long. Lam 1:13
have brought the **d** you announced; Lam 1:21
his footstool in the **d** of his anger. Lam 2:1
house of the LORD as on the **d** of festival. Lam 2:7
Ah, this is the **d** we longed for; now we Lam 2:16
down like a torrent **d** and night! Lam 2:18
killed them in the **d** of your anger, Lam 2:21
as if to a festival **d** my terrors on every Lam 2:22
and on the **d** of the anger of the LORD Lam 2:22
hand again and again the whole **d** long. Lam 3:3
the object of their taunts all **d** long. Lam 3:14
are against me all the **d** long. Lam 3:62
month, on the fifth **d** of the month, Ezk 1:1
On the fifth **d** of the month (it was the Ezk 1:2
that is in the cloud on the **d** of rain, Ezk 1:28
transgressed against me to this very **d**. Ezk 2:3
days I assign you, a **d** for each year. Ezk 4:6
shall be by weight, twenty shekels a **d**; Ezk 4:10
a day; from **d** to day you shall eat it. Ezk 4:10
a day; from day to **d** you shall eat it. Ezk 4:10
of a hin; from **d** to day you shall drink. Ezk 4:11
of a hin; from day to **d** you shall drink. Ezk 4:11
the **d** is near, a day of tumult, and not of Ezk 7:7
the day is near, a **d** of tumult, and not of Ezk 7:7
"Behold, the **d**! Behold, it comes! Your Ezk 7:10
The time has come; the **d** has arrived. Ezk 7:12
to deliver them in the **d** of the wrath of Ezk 7:19
sixth month, on the fifth **d** of the month, Ezk 8:1
and go into exile by **d** in their sight. Ezk 12:3
out your baggage by **d** in their sight, Ezk 12:4
I brought out my baggage by **d**, as Ezk 12:7
stand in battle in the **d** of the LORD. Ezk 13:5

on the **d** you were born your cord was Ezk 16:4
abhorred, on the **d** that you were born. Ezk 16:5
in your mouth in the **d** of your pride, Ezk 16:56
month, on the tenth **d** of the month, Ezk 20:1
On the **d** when I chose Israel, I swore to Ezk 20:5
On that **d** I swore to them that I would Ezk 20:6
So its name is called Bamah to this **d**.) Ezk 20:29
yourselves with all your idols to this **d**. Ezk 20:31
prince of Israel, whose **d** has come, Ezk 21:25
profane wicked, whose **d** has come, Ezk 21:29
or rained upon in the **d** of indignation. Ezk 22:24
on the same **d** and profaned my Ezk 23:38
on the same **d** they came into my Ezk 23:39
month, on the tenth **d** of the month, Ezk 24:1
of man, write down the name of this **d**, Ezk 24:2
down the name of this day, this very **d**. Ezk 24:2
has laid siege to Jerusalem this very **d**. Ezk 24:2
surely on the **d** when I take from them Ezk 24:25
on that **d** a fugitive will come to you to Ezk 24:26
On that **d** your mouth will be opened Ezk 24:27
year, on the first **d** of the month, Ezk 26:1
tremble on the **d** of your fall, Ezk 26:18
heart of the seas on the **d** of your fall. Ezk 27:27
On the **d** that you were created they Ezk 28:13
ways from the **d** you were created, Ezk 28:15
month, on the twelfth **d** of the month, Ezk 29:1
month, on the first **d** of the month, Ezk 29:17
"On that **d** I will cause a horn to Ezk 29:21
the Lord GOD: "Wail, 'Alas for the **d**!' Ezk 30:2
For the **d** is near, the day of the LORD is Ezk 30:3
the day is near, the **d** of the LORD is near; Ezk 30:3
it will be a **d** of clouds, a time of doom Ezk 30:3
"On that **d** messengers shall go out Ezk 30:9
upon them on the **d** of Egypt's doom; Ezk 30:9
and Memphis shall face enemies by **d**. Ezk 30:16
At Tehaphnehes the **d** shall be dark, Ezk 30:18
month, on the seventh **d** of the month, Ezk 30:20
month, on the first **d** of the month, Ezk 31:1
On the **d** the cedar went down to Sheol Ezk 31:15
month, on the first **d** of the month, Ezk 32:1
his own life, on the **d** of your downfall. Ezk 32:10
on the fifteenth **d** of the month, Ezk 32:17
month, on the fifth **d** of the month, Ezk 33:21
been scattered on a **d** of clouds and Ezk 34:12
On the **d** that I cleanse you from all Ezk 36:33
On that **d**, thoughts will come into Ezk 38:10
On that **d** when my people Israel are Ezk 38:14
But on that **d**, the day that Gog shall Ezk 38:18
the **d** that Gog shall come against the Ezk 38:18
On that **d** there shall be a great Ezk 38:19
That is the **d** of which I have spoken. Ezk 39:8
"On that **d** I will give to Gog a place for Ezk 39:11
them renown on the **d** that I show my Ezk 39:13
LORD their God, from that **d** forward. Ezk 39:22
of the year, on the tenth **d** of the month, Ezk 40:1
city was struck down, on that very **d**, Ezk 40:1
On the **d** when it is erected for offering Ezk 43:18
And on the second **d** you shall offer a Ezk 43:22
from the eighth **d** onward the priests Ezk 43:27
And on the **d** that he goes into the Ezk 44:27
month, on the first **d** of the month, Ezk 45:18
same on the seventh **d** of the month Ezk 45:20
on the fourteenth **d** of the month, Ezk 45:21
On that **d** the prince shall provide for Ezk 45:22
on the fifteenth **d** of the month and for Ezk 45:25
but on the Sabbath **d** it shall be opened, Ezk 46:1
and on the **d** of the new moon it shall Ezk 46:1
LORD on the Sabbath **d** shall be six Ezk 46:4
On the **d** of the new moon he shall offer Ezk 46:6
offerings as he does on the Sabbath **d**. Ezk 46:12
knees three times a **d** and prayed and Dn 6:10
but makes his petition three times a **d**." Dn 6:13
Then, at break of **d**, the king arose and Dn 6:19
but to us open shame, as at this **d**, Dn 9:7
made a name for yourself, as at this **d**, Dn 9:15
On the twenty-fourth **d** of the first Dn 10:4
for from the first **d** that you set your Dn 10:12
And on that **d** I will break the bow of Hos 1:5
land, for great shall be the **d** of Jezreel. Hos 1:11
and make her as in the **d** she was born, Hos 2:3
"And in that **d**, declares the LORD, you Hos 2:16
a covenant on that **d** with the beasts of Hos 2:18
"And in that **d** I will answer, declares Hos 2:21
You shall stumble by **d**; the prophet also Hos 4:5
a desolation in the **d** of punishment; Hos 5:9
on the third **d** he will raise us up, that we Hos 6:2
On the **d** of our king, the princes became Hos 7:5
you do on the **d** of the appointed festival, Hos 9:5
and on the **d** of the feast of the LORD? Hos 9:5
destroyed Beth-arbel on the **d** of battle; Hos 10:14
and pursues the east wind all **d** long; Hos 12:1
Alas for the **d**! For the day of the LORD is Jl 1:15
For the **d** of the LORD is near, and as Jl 1:15
tremble, for the **d** of the LORD is coming; Jl 2:1
a **d** of darkness and gloom, a day of clouds Jl 2:2

gloom, a **d** of clouds and thick darkness! Jl 2:2
For the **d** of the LORD is great and very Jl 2:11
the great and awesome **d** of the LORD Jl 2:31
For the **d** of the LORD is near in the valley Jl 3:14
"And in that **d** the mountains shall drip Jl 3:18
with shouting on the **d** of battle, Am 1:14
a tempest in the **d** of the whirlwind; Am 1:14
naked in that **d**," declares the LORD. Am 2:16
"that on the **d** I punish Israel for his Am 3:14
morning and darkens the **d** into night, Am 5:8
to you who desire the **d** of the LORD! Am 5:18
Why would you have the **d** of the LORD? Am 5:18
Is not the **d** of the LORD darkness, and Am 5:20
put far away the **d** of disaster and bring Am 6:3
wailings in that **d**," declares the Lord Am 8:3
"And on that **d**," declares the Lord GOD, Am 8:9
only son and the end of it like a bitter **d**. Am 8:10
"In that **d** the lovely virgins and the Am 8:13
"In that **d** I will raise up the booth of Am 9:11
Will I not on that **d**, declares the LORD, Ob 1:8
On the **d** that you stood aloof, on the day Ob 1:11
on the **d** that strangers carried off his Ob 1:11
not gloat over the **d** of your brother in Ob 1:12
your brother in the **d** of his misfortune; Ob 1:12
the people of Judah in the **d** of their ruin; Ob 1:12
ruin; do not boast in the **d** of distress. Ob 1:12
of my people in the **d** of their calamity; Ob 1:13
over his disaster in the **d** of his calamity; Ob 1:13
loot his wealth in the **d** of his calamity. Ob 1:13
over his survivors in the **d** of distress. Ob 1:14
For the **d** of the LORD is near upon all the Ob 1:15
But when dawn came up the next **d**, God Jon 4:7
In that **d** they shall take up a taunt song Mi 2:4
and the **d** shall be black over them; Mi 3:6
In that **d**, declares the LORD, I will Mi 4:6
And in that **d**, declares the LORD, I will Mi 5:10
The **d** of your watchmen, of your Mi 7:4
A **d** for the building of your walls! In Mi 7:11
In that **d** the boundary shall be far Mi 7:11
In that **d** they will come to you, from Mi 7:12
is good, a stronghold in the **d** of trouble; Na 1:7
flashing metal on the **d** he musters them; Na 2:3
on the fences in a **d** of cold—when the Na 3:17
quietly wait for the **d** of trouble to Hab 3:16
For the **d** of the LORD is near; the LORD Zep 1:7
And on the **d** of the LORD'S sacrifice— Zep 1:8
On that **d** I will punish everyone who Zep 1:9
"On that **d**," declares the LORD, "a cry Zep 1:10
The great **d** of the LORD is near, near and Zep 1:14
the sound of the **d** of the LORD is bitter; Zep 1:14
A **d** of wrath is that day, a day of distress Zep 1:15
A day of wrath is that **d**, a day of distress Zep 1:15
is that day, a **d** of distress and anguish, Zep 1:15
anguish, a **d** of ruin and devastation, Zep 1:15
devastation, a **d** of darkness and gloom, Zep 1:15
a **d** of clouds and thick darkness, Zep 1:15
a **d** of trumpet blast and battle cry Zep 1:16
to deliver them on the **d** of the wrath of Zep 1:18
effect —before the **d** passes away like Zep 2:2
comes upon you the **d** of the anger of Zep 2:2
may be hidden on the **d** of the anger of Zep 2:3
"for the **d** when I rise up to seize the prey. Zep 3:8
"On that **d** you shall not be put to Zep 3:11
On that **d** it shall be said to Jerusalem: Zep 3:16
sixth month, on the first **d** of the month, Hg 1:1
on the twenty-fourth **d** of the month, in Hg 1:15
on the twenty-first **d** of the month, Hg 2:1
On the twenty-fourth **d** of the ninth Hg 2:10
Now then, consider from this **d** onward. Hg 2:15
Consider from this **d** onward, from the Hg 2:18
from the twenty-fourth **d** of the ninth Hg 2:18
Since the **d** that the foundation of the Hg 2:18
But from this **d** on I will bless you." Hg 2:19
on the twenty-fourth **d** of the month, Hg 2:20
On that **d**, declares the LORD of hosts, I Hg 2:23
On the twenty-fourth **d** of the eleventh Zec 1:7
join themselves to the LORD in that **d**, Zec 2:11
the iniquity of this land in a single **d**. Zec 3:9
In that **d**, declares the LORD of hosts, Zec 3:10
has despised the **d** of small things Zec 4:10
and go the same **d** to the house of Zec 6:10
Zechariah on the fourth **d** of the ninth Zec 7:1
were present on the **d** that the foundation Zec 8:9
On that **d** the LORD their God will save Zec 9:16
So it was annulled on that **d**, and the Zec 11:11
On that **d** I will make Jerusalem a Zec 12:3
On that **d**, declares the LORD, I will strike Zec 12:4
"On that **d** I will make the clans of Zec 12:6
On that **d** the LORD will protect the Zec 12:8
among them on that **d** shall be like Zec 12:8
And on that **d** I will seek to destroy all Zec 12:9
On that **d** the mourning in Jerusalem Zec 12:11
"On that **d** there shall be a fountain Zec 13:1
"And on that **d**, declares the LORD of Zec 13:2
"On that **d** every prophet will be Zec 13:4

Behold, a **d** is coming for the LORD, Zec 14:1
as when he fights on a **d** of battle. Zec 14:3
On that **d** his feet shall stand on the Zec 14:4
On that **d** there shall be no light, cold, Zec 14:6
And there shall be a unique **d**, which is Zec 14:7
known to the LORD, neither **d** nor night, Zec 14:7
On that **d** living waters shall flow out Zec 14:8
On that **d** the LORD will be one and his Zec 14:9
And on that **d** a great panic from the Zec 14:13
And on that **d** there shall be inscribed Zec 14:20
house of the LORD of hosts on that **d**. Zec 14:21
But who can endure the **d** of his coming, Mal 3:2
in the **d** when I make up my treasured Mal 3:17
"For behold, the **d** is coming, burning Mal 4:1
The **d** that is coming shall set them Mal 4:1
the soles of your feet, on the **d** when I act, Mal 4:3
the great and awesome **d** of the LORD Mal 4:5
Give us this **d** our daily bread, Mt 6:11
Sufficient for the **d** is its own trouble. Mt 6:34
On that **d** many will say to me, 'Lord, Mt 7:22
more bearable on the **d** of judgment for Mt 10:15
more bearable on the **d** of judgment for Mt 11:22
it would have remained until this **d**. Mt 11:23
more tolerable on the **d** of judgment for Mt 11:24
on the **d** of judgment people will give Mt 12:36
That same **d** Jesus went out of the house Mt 13:1
a desolate place, and the **d** is now over; Mt 14:15
be killed, and on the third **d** be raised. Mt 16:21
raised on the third **d**." And they were Mt 17:23
with the laborers for a denarius a **d**, Mt 20:2
them, 'Why do you stand here idle all **d**?' Mt 20:6
the burden of the **d** and the scorching Mt 20:12
and he will be raised on the third **d**." Mt 20:19
The same **d** Sadducees came to him, Mt 22:23
nor from that **d** did anyone dare to ask Mt 22:46
"But concerning that **d** and hour no Mt 24:36
until the **d** when Noah entered the ark, Mt 24:38
not know on what **d** your Lord is Mt 24:42
will come on a **d** when he does not Mt 24:50
you know neither the **d** nor the hour. Mt 25:13
Now on the first **d** of Unleavened Bread Mt 26:17
of the vine until that **d** when I drink it Mt 26:29
D after day I sat in the temple teaching, Mt 26:55
Day after **d** I sat in the temple teaching, Mt 26:55
been called the Field of Blood to this **d**. Mt 27:8
Next **d**, that is, after the day of Mt 27:62
day, that is, after the **d** of Preparation, Mt 27:62
to be made secure until the third **d**, Mt 27:64
the dawn of the first **d** of the week, Mt 28:1
been spread among the Jews to this **d**. Mt 28:15
them, and then they will fast in that **d**. Mk 2:20
He sleeps and rises night and **d**, and the Mk 4:27
On that **d**, when evening had come, he Mk 4:35
Night and **d** among the tombs and on Mk 5:5
On the following **d**, when they came Mk 11:12
"But concerning that **d** or that hour, Mk 13:32
on the first **d** of Unleavened Bread, Mk 14:12
of the vine until that **d** when I drink it Mk 14:25
D after day I was with you in the Mk 14:49
Day after **d** I was with you in the Mk 14:49
since it was the **d** of Preparation, Mk 15:42
that is, the **d** before the Sabbath, Mk 15:42
And very early on the first **d** of the week, Mk 16:2
he rose early on the first **d** of the week, Mk 16:9
to speak until the **d** that these things Lk 1:20
And on the eighth **d** they came to Lk 1:59
the wilderness until the **d** of his public Lk 1:80
unto you is born this **d** in the city of Lk 2:11
with fasting and prayer night and **d**. Lk 2:37
went to the synagogue on the Sabbath **d**, Lk 4:16
And when it was **d**, he departed and went Lk 4:42
And when **d** came, he called his Lk 6:13
Rejoice in that **d**, and leap for joy, for Lk 6:23
One **d** he got into a boat with his Lk 8:22
Now the **d** began to wear away, and the Lk 9:12
be killed, and on the third **d** be raised." Lk 9:22
On the next **d**, when they had come Lk 9:37
bearable on that **d** for Sodom than Lk 10:12
And the next **d** he took out two denarii Lk 10:35
Give us each **d** our daily bread, Lk 11:3
will come on a **d** when he does not Lk 12:46
be healed, and not on the Sabbath **d**." Lk 13:14
from this bond on the Sabbath **d**?" Lk 13:16
and the third **d** I finish my course. Lk 13:32
and tomorrow and the **d** following, Lk 13:33
has fallen into a well on a Sabbath **d**, Lk 14:5
and who feasted sumptuously every **d**. Lk 16:19
he sins against you seven times in the **d**, Lk 17:4
so will the Son of Man be in his **d**. Lk 17:24
until the **d** when Noah entered the ark, Lk 17:27
but on the **d** when Lot went out from Lk 17:29
will it be on the **d** when the Son of Man Lk 17:30
On that **d**, let the one who is on the Lk 17:31
to his elect, who cry to him **d** and night? Lk 18:7
him, and on the third **d** he will rise." Lk 18:33
had known on this **d** the things that Lk 19:42
One **d**, as Jesus was teaching the people Lk 20:1
and that **d** come upon you suddenly Lk 21:34
And every **d** he was teaching in the Lk 21:37
Then came the **d** of Unleavened Bread, Lk 22:7
Peter, the rooster will not crow this **d**, Lk 22:34
When I was with you **d** after day in the Lk 22:53
I was with you day after **d** in the temple, Lk 22:53
When **d** came, the assembly of the Lk 22:66
friends with each other that very **d**, Lk 23:12
It was the **d** of Preparation, and the Lk 23:54
But on the first **d** of the week, at early Lk 24:1
and be crucified and on the third **d** rise." Lk 24:7
That very **d** two of them were going to a Lk 24:13
is now the third **d** since these things Lk 24:21
toward evening and the **d** is now far Lk 24:29
and on the third **d** rise from the dead, Lk 24:46
The next **d** he saw Jesus coming toward Jn 1:29
The next **d** again John was standing with Jn 1:35
staying, and they stayed with him that **d**, Jn 1:39
The next **d** Jesus decided to go to Galilee. Jn 1:43
On the third **d** there was a wedding at Jn 2:1
and walked. Now that **d** was the Sabbath. Jn 5:9
On the next **d** the crowd that remained Jn 6:22
has given me, but raise it up on the last **d**. Jn 6:39
life, and I will raise him up on the last **d**." Jn 6:40
And I will raise him up on the last **d**. Jn 6:44
life, and I will raise him up on the last **d**. Jn 6:54
On the last **d** of the feast, the great day, Jn 7:37
On the last day of the feast, the great **d**, Jn 7:37
rejoiced that he would see my **d**. Jn 8:56
the works of him who sent me while it is **d**; Jn 9:4
it was a Sabbath **d** when Jesus made the Jn 9:14
"Are there not twelve hours in the **d**? Jn 11:9
If anyone walks in the **d**, he does not Jn 11:9
again in the resurrection on the last **d**." Jn 11:24
So from that **d** on they made plans to Jn 11:53
she may keep it for the **d** of my burial. Jn 12:7
The next **d** the large crowd that had Jn 12:12
spoken will judge him on the last **d**. Jn 12:48
In that **d** you will know that I am in my Jn 14:20
In that **d** you will ask nothing of me. Jn 16:23
In that **d** you will ask in my name, and I Jn 16:26
Now it was the **d** of Preparation of the Jn 19:14
Since it was the **d** of Preparation, and so Jn 19:31
(for that Sabbath was a high **d**), Jn 19:31
because of the Jewish **d** of Preparation, Jn 19:42
Now on the first **d** of the week Mary Jn 20:1
On the evening of that **d**, the first day of Jn 20:19
of that day, the first **d** of the week, Jn 20:19
Just as **d** was breaking, Jesus stood on the Jn 21:4
until the **d** when he was taken up, after Acts 1:2
of John until the **d** when he was taken Acts 1:22
When the **d** of Pentecost arrived, they Acts 2:1
since it is only the third hour of the **d**. Acts 2:15
blood, before the **d** of the Lord comes, Acts 2:20
comes, the great and magnificent **d**. Acts 2:20
and his tomb is with us to this **d**. Acts 2:29
were added that **d** about three Acts 2:41
And **d** by day, attending the temple Acts 2:46
And day by **d**, attending the temple Acts 2:46
added to their number **d** by day those Acts 2:47
their number day by **d** those who were Acts 2:47
put them in custody until the next **d**, Acts 4:3
On the next **d** their rulers and elders and Acts 4:5
And every **d**, in the temple and from Acts 5:42
and circumcised him on the eighth **d**, Acts 7:8
And on the following **d** he appeared to Acts 7:26
there arose on that **d** a great persecution Acts 8:1
were watching the gates **d** and night in Acts 9:24
ninth hour of the **d** he saw clearly in Acts 10:3
The next **d**, as they were on their Acts 10:9
The next **d** he rose and went away Acts 10:23
on the following **d** they entered Acts 10:24
him on the third **d** and made him to Acts 10:40
Now when **d** came, there was no little Acts 12:18
On an appointed **d** Herod put on his Acts 12:21
And on the Sabbath **d** they went into Acts 13:14
and on the next **d** he went on with Acts 14:20
and the following **d** to Neapolis, Acts 16:11
on the Sabbath **d** we went outside Acts 16:13
But when it was **d**, the magistrates Acts 16:35
the marketplace every **d** with those Acts 17:17
he has fixed a **d** on which he will Acts 17:31
On the first **d** of the week, when we Acts 20:7
intending to depart on the next **d**, Acts 20:7
came the following **d** opposite Chios; Acts 20:15
the next **d** we touched at Samos; Acts 20:15
and the **d** after that we went to Acts 20:15
if possible, on the **d** of Pentecost. Acts 20:16
time from the first **d** that I set foot Acts 20:18
testify to you this **d** that I am Acts 20:26
cease night or **d** to admonish Acts 20:31
to Cos, and the next **d** to Rhodes, Acts 21:1
and stayed with them for one **d**. Acts 21:7
On the next **d** we departed and came to Acts 21:8
On the following **d** Paul went in with Acts 21:18
and the next **d** he purified himself Acts 21:26
zealous for God as all of you are this **d**. Acts 22:3
But on the next **d**, desiring to know Acts 22:30
in all good conscience up to this **d**." Acts 23:1
When it was **d**, the Jews made a plot Acts 23:12
And on the next **d** they returned to the Acts 23:32
that I am on trial before you this **d**.'" Acts 24:21
And the next **d** he took his seat on the Acts 25:6
but on the next **d** took my seat on the Acts 25:17
So on the next **d** Agrippa and Bernice Acts 25:23
as they earnestly worship night and **d**. Acts 26:7
To this **d** I have had the help that Acts 26:22
hear me this **d** might become such Acts 26:29
The next **d** we put in at Sidon. And Acts 27:3
they began the next **d** to jettison the Acts 27:18
And on the third **d** they threw the Acts 27:19
the stern and prayed for **d** to come. Acts 27:29
As **d** was about to dawn, Paul urged Acts 27:33
is the fourteenth **d** that you have Acts 27:33
Now when it was **d**, they did not Acts 27:39
And after one **d** a south wind sprang Acts 28:13
and on the second **d** we came to Acts 28:13
they had appointed a **d** for him, Acts 28:23
for yourself on the **d** of wrath when Rom 2:5
on that **d** when, according to my Rom 2:16
sake we are being killed all the **d** long; Rom 8:36
"All **d** long I have held out my hands Rom 10:21
would not hear, down to this very **d**." Rom 11:8
night is far gone; the **d** is at hand. Rom 13:12
person esteems one **d** as better than Rom 14:5
The one who observes the **d**, observes Rom 14:6
guiltless in the **d** of our Lord Jesus 1 Cor 1:8
manifest, for the **D** will disclose it, 1 Cor 3:13
may be saved in the **d** of the Lord. 1 Cor 5:5
thousand fell in a single **d**. 1 Cor 10:8
on the third **d** in accordance with 1 Cor 15:4
Christ Jesus our Lord, I die every **d**! 1 Cor 15:31
On the first **d** of every week, each of 1 Cor 16:2
that on the **d** of our Lord Jesus you 2 Cor 1:14
For to this **d**, when they read the old 2 Cor 3:14
to this **d** whenever Moses is read a veil 2 Cor 3:15
nature is being renewed **d** by day. 2 Cor 4:16
nature is being renewed day by **d**. 2 Cor 4:16
and in a **d** of salvation I have helped 2 Cor 6:2
time; behold, now is the **d** of salvation. 2 Cor 6:2
a night and a **d** I was adrift at sea; 2 Cor 11:25
you were sealed for the **d** of redemption. Eph 4:30
may be able to withstand in the evil **d**, Eph 6:13
in the gospel from the first **d** until now. Phil 1:5
it to completion at the **d** of Jesus Christ. Phil 1:6
pure and blameless for the **d** of Christ, Phil 1:10
so that in the **d** of Christ I may be Phil 2:16
circumcised on the eighth **d**, of the Phil 3:5
since the **d** you heard it and understood Col 1:6
And so, from the **d** we heard, we have not Col 1:9
we worked night and **d**, that we might 1 Thes 2:9
earnestly night and **d** that we may 1 Thes 3:10
fully aware that the **d** of the Lord will 1 Thes 5:2
for that **d** to surprise you like a thief. 1 Thes 5:4
all children of light, children of the **d**. 1 Thes 5:5
But since we belong to the **d**, let us be 1 Thes 5:8
he comes on that **d** to be glorified in 2 Thes 1:10
to the effect that the **d** of the Lord has 2 Thes 2:2
For that **d** will not come, unless the 2 Thes 2:3
toil and labor we worked night and **d**, 2 Thes 3:8
supplications and prayers night and **d**, 1 Tm 5:5
constantly in my prayers night and **d**. 2 Tm 1:3
to guard until that **D** what has been 2 Tm 1:12
find mercy from the Lord on that **D**! 2 Tm 1:18
judge, will award to me on that **D**, 2 Tm 4:8
on the **d** of testing in the wilderness, Heb 3:8
But exhort one another every **d**, as long Heb 3:13
spoken of the seventh **d** in this way: Heb 4:4
rested on the seventh **d** from all his Heb 4:4
again he appoints a certain **d**, "Today," Heb 4:7
not have spoken of another **d** later on. Heb 4:8
their fathers on the **d** when I took them Heb 8:9
more as you see the **D** drawing near. Heb 10:25
fattened your hearts in a **d** of slaughter. Jas 5:5
and glorify God on the **d** of visitation. 1 Pt 2:12
until the **d** dawns and the morning star 2 Pt 1:19
man lived among them **d** after day, 2 Pt 2:8
man lived among them day after **d**, 2 Pt 2:8
punishment until the **d** of judgment, 2 Pt 2:9
being kept until the **d** of judgment and 2 Pt 3:7
that with the Lord one **d** is as a thousand 2 Pt 3:8
years, and a thousand years as one **d**. 2 Pt 3:8
But the **d** of the Lord will come like a 2 Pt 3:10
hastening the coming of the **d** of God, 2 Pt 3:12
glory both now and to the **d** of eternity. 2 Pt 3:18
have confidence for the **d** of judgment, 1 Jn 4:17
until the judgment of the great **d**— Jude 1:6
I was in the Spirit on the Lord's **d**, and I Rv 1:10

and **d** and night they never cease to say, Rv 4:8
for the great **d** of their wrath has come, Rv 6:17
and serve him **d** and night in his temple; Rv 7:15
and a third of the **d** might be kept from Rv 8:12
had been prepared for the hour, the **d**, Rv 9:15
who accuses them **d** and night before Rv 12:10
ever, and they have no rest, **d** or night, Rv 14:11
battle on the great **d** of God the Rv 16:14
her plagues will come in a single **d**, Rv 18:8
will be tormented **d** and night forever Rv 20:10
will never be shut by **d**—and there will Rv 21:25

DAY'S (8)
go out and gather a **d** portion every day, Ex 16:4
about a **d** journey on this side and a Nm 11:31
this side and a **d** journey on the other Nm 11:31
he himself went a **d** journey into the 1 Kgs 19:4
also to do according to this **d** edict. Est 9:13
to go into the city, going a **d** journey. Jon 3:4
to be in the group they went a **d** journey, Lk 2:44
Jerusalem, a Sabbath **d** journey away. Acts 1:12

DAYBREAK (3)
By **d** not one was left who had not 2 Sm 17:22
entered the temple at **d** and began to Acts 5:21
with them a long while, until **d**, Acts 20:11

DAYLIGHT (1)
at noon and darken the earth in broad **d**. Am 8:9

DAYS (816)
and for seasons, and for **d** and years, Gn 1:14
dust you shall eat all the **d** of your life. Gn 3:14
you shall eat of it all the **d** of your life; Gn 3:17
The **d** of Adam after he fathered Seth were Gn 5:4
Thus all the **d** that Adam lived were 930 Gn 5:5
Thus all the **d** of Seth were 912 years, and Gn 5:8
Thus all the **d** of Enosh were 905 years, Gn 5:11
Thus all the **d** of Kenan were 910 years, Gn 5:14
Thus all the **d** of Mahalalel were 895 Gn 5:17
Thus all the **d** of Jared were 962 years, Gn 5:20
Thus all the **d** of Enoch were 365 years. Gn 5:23
Thus all the **d** of Methuselah were 969 Gn 5:27
Thus all the **d** of Lamech were 777 Gn 5:31
for he is flesh: his **d** shall be 120 years." Gn 6:3
Nephilim were on the earth in those **d**, Gn 6:4
For in seven **d** I will send rain on the Gn 7:4
rain on the earth forty **d** and forty nights, Gn 7:4
And after seven **d** the waters of the flood Gn 7:10
upon the earth forty **d** and forty nights. Gn 7:12
flood continued forty **d** on the earth. Gn 7:17
the waters prevailed on the earth 150 **d**. Gn 7:24
At the end of 150 **d** the waters had abated, Gn 8:3
the end of forty **d** Noah opened the Gn 8:6
He waited another seven **d**, and again he Gn 8:10
he waited another seven **d** and sent forth Gn 8:12
All the **d** of Noah were 950 years, and he Gn 9:29
Peleg, for in his **d** the earth was divided, Gn 10:25
The **d** of Terah were 205 years, and Gn 11:32
In the **d** of Amraphel king of Shinar, Gn 14:1
He who is eight **d** old among you shall Gn 17:12
his son Isaac when he was eight **d** old, Gn 21:4
Abraham sojourned many **d** in the Gn 21:34
remain with us a while, at least ten **d**; Gn 24:55
These are the **d** of the years of Gn 25:7
When her **d** to give birth were Gn 25:24
famine that was in the **d** of Abraham. Gn 26:1
had dug in the **d** of Abraham his Gn 26:15
been dug in the **d** of Abraham his Gn 26:18
"The **d** of mourning for my father are Gn 27:41
to him but a few **d** because of the love Gn 29:20
In the **d** of wheat harvest Reuben went Gn 30:14
him for seven **d** and followed close Gn 31:23
Now the **d** of Isaac were 180 years. Gn 35:28
gathered to his people, old and full of **d**. Gn 35:29
loins and mourned for his son many **d**. Gn 37:34
the three branches are three **d**. Gn 40:12
In three **d** Pharaoh will lift up your Gn 40:13
the three baskets are three **d**. Gn 40:18
In three **d** Pharaoh will lift up your Gn 40:19
all together in custody for three **d**. Gn 42:17
"How many are the **d** of the years of Gn 47:8
"The **d** of the years of my sojourning are Gn 47:9
and evil have been the **d** of the years of Gn 47:9
have not attained to the **d** of the years of Gn 47:9
my fathers in the **d** of their sojourning." Gn 47:9
seventeen years. So the **d** of Jacob, Gn 47:28
what shall happen to you in **d** to come. Gn 49:1
Forty **d** were required for it, for that is Gn 50:3
the Egyptians wept for him seventy **d**. Gn 50:3
And when the **d** of weeping for him were Gn 50:4
a mourning for his father seven **d**. Gn 50:10
During those many **d** the king of Egypt Ex 2:23
Seven full **d** passed after the LORD had Ex 7:25
in all the land of Egypt three **d**. Ex 10:22
anyone rise from his place for three **d**, Ex 10:23
Seven **d** you shall eat unleavened bread. Ex 12:15
No work shall be done on those **d**. Ex 12:16
For seven **d** no leaven is to be found in Ex 12:19
Seven **d** you shall eat unleavened bread, Ex 13:6
bread shall be eaten for seven **d**; Ex 13:7
They went three **d** in the wilderness and Ex 15:22
Six **d** you shall gather it, but on the Ex 16:26
sixth day he gives you bread for two **d**. Ex 16:29
Six **d** you shall labor, and do all your Ex 20:9
For in six **d** the LORD made heaven and Ex 20:11
that your **d** may be long in the land Ex 20:12
seven **d** it shall be with its mother; Ex 22:30
"Six **d** you shall do your work, but on Ex 23:12
bread for seven **d** at the appointed Ex 23:15
land; I will fulfill the number of your **d**. Ex 23:26
Sinai, and the cloud covered it six **d**. Ex 24:16
the mountain forty **d** and forty nights. Ex 24:18
Holy Place, shall wear them seven **d**. Ex 29:30
Through seven **d** shall you ordain Ex 29:35
Seven **d** you shall make atonement for Ex 29:37
Six **d** shall work be done, but the Ex 31:15
Israel that in six **d** the LORD made Ex 31:17
Seven **d** you shall eat unleavened bread, Ex 34:18
"Six **d** you shall work, but on the Ex 34:21
with the LORD forty **d** and forty nights. Ex 34:28
Six **d** work shall be done, but on the Ex 35:2
of the tent of meeting for seven **d**, Lv 8:33
until the **d** of your ordination are Lv 8:33
for it will take seven **d** to ordain you. Lv 8:33
shall remain day and night for seven **d**, Lv 8:35
child, then she shall be unclean seven **d**. Lv 12:2
continue for thirty-three **d** in the blood Lv 12:4
until the **d** of her purifying are Lv 12:4
the blood of her purifying for sixty-six **d**. Lv 12:5
"'And when the **d** of her purifying are Lv 12:6
shut up the diseased person for seven **d**. Lv 13:4
shall shut him up for another seven **d**. Lv 13:5
the priest shall shut him up seven **d**. Lv 13:21
the priest shall shut him up seven **d**, Lv 13:26
with the itching disease for seven **d**, Lv 13:31
the itching disease for another seven **d**. Lv 13:33
that which has the disease for seven **d**. Lv 13:50
he shall shut it up for another seven **d**. Lv 13:54
camp, but live outside his tent seven **d**. Lv 14:8
house and shut up the house seven **d**. Lv 14:38
for himself seven **d** for his cleansing, Lv 15:13
in her menstrual impurity for seven **d**, Lv 15:19
upon him, he shall be unclean seven **d**, Lv 15:24
has a discharge of blood for many **d**, Lv 15:25
all the **d** of the discharge she shall Lv 15:25
As in the **d** of her impurity, Lv 15:25
she lies, all the **d** of her discharge, Lv 15:26
she shall count for herself seven **d**, Lv 15:28
it shall remain seven **d** with its mother, Lv 22:27
"Six **d** shall work be done, but on the Lv 23:3
for seven **d** you shall eat unleavened Lv 23:6
a food offering to the LORD for seven **d**. Lv 23:8
You shall count fifty **d** to the day after Lv 23:16
month and for seven **d** is the Feast of Lv 23:34
For seven **d** you shall present food Lv 23:36
celebrate the feast of the LORD seven **d**. Lv 23:39
before the LORD your God seven **d**. Lv 23:40
feast to the LORD for seven **d** in the year. Lv 23:41
You shall dwell in booths for seven **d**. Lv 23:42
All the **d** of his separation he shall eat Nm 6:4
"All the **d** of his vow of separation, no Nm 6:5
"All the **d** that he separates himself to Nm 6:6
All the **d** of his separation he is holy to Nm 6:8
the LORD for the **d** of his separation and Nm 6:12
continued over the tabernacle many **d**, Nm 9:19
cloud was a few **d** over the tabernacle, Nm 9:20
Whether it was two **d**, or a month, or a Nm 9:22
shall not eat just one day, or two **d**, Nm 11:19
eat just one day, or two days, or five **d**, Nm 11:19
day, or two days, or five days, or ten **d**, Nm 11:19
or five days, or ten days, or twenty **d**, Nm 11:19
should she not be shamed seven **d**? Nm 12:14
her be shut outside the camp seven **d**, Nm 12:14
was shut outside the camp seven **d**, Nm 12:15
the end of forty **d** they returned from Nm 13:25
the number of the **d** in which you Nm 14:34
which you spied out the land, forty **d**, Nm 14:34
any person shall be unclean seven **d**. Nm 19:11
is in the tent shall be unclean seven **d**. Nm 19:14
or a grave, shall be unclean seven **d**. Nm 19:16
of Israel wept for Aaron thirty **d**. Nm 20:29
will do to your people in the latter **d**." Nm 24:14
Seven **d** shall unleavened bread be Nm 28:17
way you shall offer daily, for seven **d**, Nm 28:24
shall keep a feast to the LORD seven **d**. Nm 29:12
Encamp outside the camp seven **d**. Nm 31:19
So you remained at Kadesh many **d**, the Dt 1:46
days, the **d** that you remained there. Dt 1:46
And for many **d** we traveled around Dt 2:1
from your heart all the **d** of your life. Dt 4:9
to fear me all the **d** that they live on the Dt 4:10
things come upon you in the latter **d**, Dt 4:30
"For ask now of the **d** that are past, Dt 4:32
you may prolong your **d** in the land that Dt 4:40
Six **d** you shall labor and do all your Dt 5:13
you, that your **d** may be long, Dt 5:16
I command you, all the **d** of your life, Dt 6:2
of your life, and that your **d** may be long. Dt 6:2
on the mountain forty **d** and forty nights. Dt 9:9
at the end of forty **d** and forty nights the Dt 9:11
LORD as before, forty **d** and forty nights. Dt 9:18
LORD for these forty **d** and forty nights, Dt 9:25
at the first time, forty **d** and forty nights, Dt 10:10
that your **d** and the days of your Dt 11:21
your days and the **d** of your children Dt 11:21
all the **d** that you live on the earth. Dt 12:1
Seven **d** you shall eat it with unleavened Dt 16:3
haste—that all the **d** of your life you may Dt 16:3
with you in all your territory for seven **d**, Dt 16:4
For six **d** you shall eat unleavened bread, Dt 16:8
shall keep the Feast of Booths seven **d**, Dt 16:13
For seven **d** you shall keep the feast to Dt 16:15
to the judge who is in office in those **d**, Dt 17:9
he shall read in it all the **d** of his life, Dt 17:19
the judges who are in office in those **d**. Dt 19:17
wife. He may not divorce her all his **d**. Dt 22:19
her. He may not divorce her all his **d**. Dt 22:29
or their prosperity all your **d** forever. Dt 23:6
that your **d** may be long in the land Dt 25:15
him, for he is your life and length of **d**, Dt 30:20
the **d** approach when you must die. Dt 31:14
And in the **d** to come evil will befall Dt 31:29
Remember the **d** of old; consider the Dt 32:7
shall be iron and bronze, and as your **d**, Dt 33:25
for Moses in the plains of Moab thirty **d**. Dt 34:8
Then the **d** of weeping and mourning for Dt 34:8
to stand before you all the **d** of your life. Jos 1:5
for within three **d** you are to pass over Jos 1:11
and hide there three **d** until the pursuers Jos 2:16
remained there three **d** until the Jos 2:22
the end of three **d** the officers went Jos 3:2
stood in awe of Moses, all the **d** of his life. Jos 4:14
the city once. Thus shall you do for six **d**. Jos 6:3
into the camp. So they did for six **d**. Jos 6:14
At the end of three **d** after they had made Jos 9:16
forsaken your brothers these many **d**, Jos 22:3
served the LORD all the **d** of Joshua, Jos 24:31
and all the **d** of the elders who outlived Jos 24:31
people served the LORD all the **d** of Joshua, Jgs 2:7
and all the **d** of the elders who outlived Jgs 2:7
of their enemies all the **d** of the judge. Jgs 2:18
"In the **d** of Shamgar, son of Anath, in the Jgs 5:6
of Shamgar, son of Anath, in the **d** of Jael, Jgs 5:6
had rest forty years in the **d** of Gideon. Jgs 8:28
the Gileadite four **d** in the year. Jgs 11:40
After some **d** he returned to take her. Jgs 14:8
it is, within the seven **d** of the feast, Jgs 14:12
sweet." And in three **d** they could not Jgs 14:14
before him the seven **d** that their feast Jgs 14:17
After some **d**, at the time of wheat Jgs 15:1
judged Israel in the **d** of the Philistines Jgs 15:20
In those **d** there was no king in Israel. Jgs 17:6
In those **d** there was no king in Israel. Jgs 18:1
And in those **d** the tribe of the people of Jgs 18:1
In those **d**, when there was no king in Jgs 19:1
stay, and he remained with him three **d**. Jgs 19:4
covenant of God was there in those **d**, Jgs 20:27
Aaron, ministered before it in those **d**), Jgs 20:28
In those **d** there was no king in Israel. Jgs 21:25
In the **d** when the judges ruled there was a Ru 1:1
him to the LORD all the **d** of his life, 1 Sm 1:11
the **d** are coming when I will cut off 1 Sm 2:31
word of the LORD was rare in those **d**; 1 Sm 3:1
the Philistines all the **d** of Samuel. 1 Sm 7:13
judged Israel all the **d** of his life. 1 Sm 7:15
donkeys that were lost three **d** ago, 1 Sm 9:20
Seven **d** you shall wait, until I come to 1 Sm 10:8
He waited seven **d**, the time appointed 1 Sm 13:8
did not come within the **d** appointed, 1 Sm 13:11
the Philistines all the **d** of Saul. 1 Sm 14:52
In the **d** of Saul the man was already 1 Sm 17:12
For forty **d** the Philistine came 1 Sm 17:16
many servants these **d** who are 1 Sm 25:10
And about ten **d** later the LORD 1 Sm 25:38
the number of the **d** that David lived 1 Sm 27:7
In those **d** the Philistines gathered 1 Sm 28:1
has been with me now for **d** and years, 1 Sm 29:3
water for three **d** and three nights. 1 Sm 30:12
because I fell sick three **d** ago. 1 Sm 30:13
tree in Jabesh and fasted seven **d**. 1 Sm 31:13
David remained two **d** in Ziklag. 2 Sm 1:1
When your **d** are fulfilled and you lie 2 Sm 7:12
been mourning many **d** for the dead. 2 Sm 14:2
Now in those **d** the counsel that 2 Sm 16:23
of Judah together to me within three **d**, 2 Sm 20:4
a famine in the **d** of David for three 2 Sm 21:1

put to death in the first **d** of harvest, 2 Sm 21:9
the end of nine months and twenty **d**. 2 Sm 24:8
So Shimei lived in Jerusalem many **d**. 1 Kgs 2:38
shall compare with you, all your **d**. 1 Kgs 3:13
walked, then I will lengthen your **d**." 1 Kgs 3:14
served Solomon all the **d** of his life. 1 Kgs 4:21
his fig tree, all the **d** of Solomon. 1 Kgs 4:25
fear you all the **d** that they live in 1 Kgs 8:40
before the LORD our God, seven **d**. 1 Kgs 8:65
as anything in the **d** of Solomon. 1 Kgs 10:21
your father I will not do it in your **d**, 1 Kgs 11:12
of Israel all the **d** of Solomon, 1 Kgs 11:25
make him ruler all the **d** of his life, 1 Kgs 11:34
He said to them, "Go away for three **d**, 1 Kgs 12:5
commanded him all the **d** of his life, 1 Kgs 15:5
and Jeroboam all the **d** of his life. 1 Kgs 15:6
was wholly true to the LORD all his **d**. 1 Kgs 15:14
and Baasha king of Israel all their **d**. 1 Kgs 15:16
and Baasha king of Israel all their **d**. 1 Kgs 15:32
Zimri reigned seven **d** in Tirzah. 1 Kgs 16:15
In his **d** Hiel of Bethel built Jericho. 1 Kgs 16:34
and her household ate for many **d**. 1 Kgs 17:15
After many **d** the word of the LORD 1 Kgs 18:1
of that food forty **d** and forty nights to 1 Kgs 19:8
opposite one another seven **d**. 1 Kgs 20:29
I will not bring the disaster in his **d**; 1 Kgs 21:29
but in his son's **d** I will bring the 1 Kgs 21:29
who remained in the **d** of his father 1 Kgs 22:46
And for three **d** they sought him but 2 Kgs 2:17
made a circuitous march of seven **d**, 2 Kgs 3:9
In his **d** Edom revolted from the rule 2 Kgs 8:20
In those **d** the LORD began to cut off 2 Kgs 10:32
right in the eyes of the LORD all his **d**, 2 Kgs 12:2
Israel all the **d** of Jehoahaz. 2 Kgs 13:22
not depart all his **d** from all the sins 2 Kgs 15:18
In the **d** of Pekah king of Israel, 2 Kgs 15:29
In those **d** the LORD began to send 2 Kgs 15:37
for until those **d** the people of Israel 2 Kgs 18:4
I planned from **d** of old what now I 2 Kgs 19:25
In those **d** Hezekiah became sick and 2 Kgs 20:1
Behold, the **d** are coming, when all 2 Kgs 20:17
will be peace and security in my **d**?" 2 Kgs 20:19
been kept since the **d** of the judges 2 Kgs 23:22
or during all the **d** of the kings of 2 Kgs 23:22
In his **d** Pharaoh Neco king of 2 Kgs 23:29
In his **d**, Nebuchadnezzar king of 2 Kgs 24:1
Peleg (for in his **d** the earth was 1 Chr 1:19
by name, came in the **d** of Hezekiah, 1 Chr 4:41
And in the **d** of Saul they waged war 1 Chr 5:10
genealogies in the **d** of Jotham king 1 Chr 5:17
and in the **d** of Jeroboam king of 1 Chr 5:17
their number in the **d** of David being 1 Chr 7:2
their father mourned many **d**, 1 Chr 7:22
obligated to come in every seven **d**, 1 Chr 9:25
the oak in Jabesh and fasted seven **d**. 1 Chr 10:12
were there with David for three **d**, 1 Chr 12:39
for we did not seek it in the **d** of Saul." 1 Chr 13:3
When your **d** are fulfilled to walk 1 Chr 17:11
or else three **d** of the sword of the 1 Chr 21:12
give peace and quiet to Israel in his **d**. 1 Chr 22:9
When David was old and full of **d**, 1 Chr 23:1
Sabbaths, new moons and feast **d**, 1 Chr 23:31
Our **d** on the earth are like a 1 Chr 29:15
Then he died at a good age, full of **d**, 1 Chr 29:28
your ways all the **d** that they live in 2 Chr 6:31
Solomon held the feast for seven **d**, 2 Chr 7:8
of the altar seven **d** and the feast seven 2 Chr 7:9
altar seven days and the feast seven **d**. 2 Chr 7:9
as anything in the **d** of Solomon. 2 Chr 9:20
me again in three **d**." So the people 2 Chr 10:5
recover his power in the **d** of Abijah. 2 Chr 13:20
In his **d** the land had rest for ten 2 Chr 14:1
of Asa was wholly true all his **d**. 2 Chr 15:17
They were three **d** in taking the 2 Chr 20:25
In his **d** Edom revolted from the rule 2 Chr 21:8
the LORD all the **d** of Jehoiada the 2 Chr 24:2
LORD regularly all the **d** of Jehoiada. 2 Chr 24:14
But Jehoiada grew old and full of **d**, 2 Chr 24:15
to seek God in the **d** of Zechariah, 2 Chr 26:5
Then for eight **d** they consecrated 2 Chr 29:17
Bread seven **d** with great gladness, 2 Chr 30:21
the food of the festival for seven **d**, 2 Chr 30:22
to keep the feast for another seven **d**. 2 Chr 30:23
it for another seven **d** with gladness. 2 Chr 30:23
In those **d** Hezekiah became sick 2 Chr 32:24
upon them in the **d** of Hezekiah. 2 Chr 32:26
All his **d** they did not turn away 2 Chr 34:33
Feast of Unleavened Bread seven **d**. 2 Chr 35:17
in Israel since the **d** of Samuel the 2 Chr 35:18
three months and ten **d** in Jerusalem. 2 Chr 36:9
All the **d** that it lay desolate it kept 2 Chr 36:21
him ever since the **d** of Esarhaddon king Ezr 4:2
purpose, all the **d** of Cyrus king of Persia, Ezr 4:5
In the **d** of Artaxerxes, Bishlam and Ezr 4:7
of Unleavened Bread seven **d** with joy, Ezr 6:22
to Ahava, and there we camped three **d**. Ezr 8:15
and there we remained three **d**. Ezr 8:32
From the **d** of our fathers to this day we Ezr 9:7
if anyone did not come within three **d**, Ezr 10:8
at Jerusalem within the three **d**. Ezr 10:9
I sat down and wept and mourned for **d**, Neh 1:4
to Jerusalem and was there three **d**. Neh 2:11
and every ten **d** all kinds of wine in Neh 5:18
day of the month Elul, in fifty-two **d**. Neh 6:15
in those **d** the nobles of Judah sent Neh 6:17
for from the **d** of Jeshua the son of Nun Neh 8:17
They kept the feast seven **d**, and on the Neh 8:18
and of their brothers in the **d** of Jeshua. Neh 12:7
And in the **d** of Joiakim were priests, Neh 12:12
In the **d** of Eliashib, Joiada, Johanan, Neh 12:22
Chronicles until the **d** of Johanan the Neh 12:23
These were in the **d** of Joiakim the son Neh 12:26
and in the **d** of Nehemiah the Neh 12:26
long ago in the **d** of David and Asaph Neh 12:46
all Israel in the **d** of Zerubbabel and Neh 12:47
and in the **d** of Nehemiah gave Neh 12:47
In those **d** I saw in Judah people Neh 13:15
In those **d** also I saw the Jews who had Neh 13:23
Now in the **d** of Ahasuerus, the Est 1:1
in those **d** when King Ahasuerus sat on Est 1:2
and pomp of his greatness for many **d**, Est 1:4
of his greatness for many days, 180 **d**. Est 1:4
And when these **d** were completed, the Est 1:5
a feast lasting for seven **d** in the court of Est 1:5
In those **d**, as Mordecai was sitting at the Est 2:21
to come in to the king these thirty **d**." Est 4:11
and do not eat or drink for three **d**, Est 4:16
as the **d** on which the Jews got relief Est 9:22
should make them **d** of feasting and Est 9:22
d for sending gifts of food to one another Est 9:22
Therefore they called these **d** Purim, Est 9:26
keep these two **d** according to what Est 9:27
that these **d** should be remembered and Est 9:28
and that these **d** of Purim should never Est 9:28
of these **d** cease among their Est 9:28
that these **d** of Purim should be Est 9:31
And when the **d** of the feast had run their Jb 1:5
on the ground seven **d** and seven nights, Jb 2:13
Let it not rejoice among the **d** of the year; Jb 3:6
and are not his **d** like the days of a hired Jb 7:1
are not his days like the **d** of a hired hand? Jb 7:1
My **d** are swifter than a weaver's shuttle Jb 7:6
Leave me alone, for my **d** are a breath. Jb 7:16
was small, your latter **d** will be very great. Jb 8:7
nothing, for our **d** on earth are a shadow. Jb 8:9
"My **d** are swifter than a runner; they flee Jb 9:25
Are your **d** as the days of man, or your Jb 10:5
Are your days as the **d** of man, or your Jb 10:5
Are not my **d** few? Then cease, and leave Jb 10:20
aged, and understanding in length of **d**. Jb 12:12
of a woman is few of **d** and full of trouble. Jb 14:1
Since his **d** are determined, and the Jb 14:5
All the **d** of my service I would wait, till Jb 14:14
wicked man writhes in pain all his **d**, Jb 15:20
My spirit is broken; my **d** are extinct; the Jb 17:1
My **d** are past; my plans are broken off, Jb 17:11
They spend their **d** in prosperity, and in Jb 21:13
do those who know him never see his **d**? Jb 24:1
does not reproach me for any of my **d**. Jb 27:6
as in the **d** when God watched over me, Jb 29:2
and I shall multiply my **d** as the sand, Jb 29:18
d of affliction have taken hold of me. Jb 30:16
still; **d** of affliction come to meet me. Jb 30:27
I said, 'Let **d** speak, and many years teach Jb 32:7
him return to the **d** of his youthful Jb 33:25
him, they complete their **d** in prosperity, Jb 36:11
the morning since your **d** began, Jb 38:12
then, and the number of your **d** is great! Jb 38:21
LORD blessed the latter **d** of Job more Jb 42:12
And Job died, an old man, and full of **d**. Jb 42:17
it to him, length of **d** forever and ever. Ps 21:4
shall follow me all the **d** of my life, Ps 23:6
the house of the LORD all the **d** of my life, Ps 27:4
there who desires life and loves many **d**, Ps 34:12
The LORD knows the **d** of the blameless, Ps 37:18
in the **d** of famine they have Ps 37:19
my end and what is the measure of my **d**; Ps 39:4
have made my **d** a few handbreadths, Ps 39:5
us, what deeds you performed in their **d**, Ps 44:1
performed in their days, in the **d** of old: Ps 44:1
treachery shall not live out half their **d**. Ps 55:23
In his **d** may the righteous flourish, and Ps 72:7
I consider the **d** of old, the years long ago. Ps 77:5
So he made their **d** vanish like a breath, Ps 78:33
and his throne as the **d** of the heavens. Ps 89:29
You have cut short the **d** of his youth; Ps 89:45
For all our **d** pass away under your Ps 90:9
us to number our **d** that we may get Ps 90:12
we may rejoice and be glad all our **d**. Ps 90:14
glad for as many **d** as you have afflicted Ps 90:15
to give him rest from **d** of trouble, until Ps 94:13
For my **d** pass away like smoke, and Ps 102:3
My **d** are like an evening shadow; Ps 102:11
in midcourse; he has shortened my **d**. Ps 102:23
the midst of my **d**—you whose years Ps 102:24
As for man, his **d** are like grass; he Ps 103:15
May his **d** be few; may another take his Ps 109:8
of Jerusalem all the **d** of your life! Ps 128:5
of them, the **d** that were formed for me, Ps 139:16
I remember the **d** of old; I meditate on Ps 143:5
breath; his **d** are like a passing shadow. Ps 144:4
for length of **d** and years of life and peace Prv 3:2
For by me your **d** will be multiplied, Prv 9:11
All the **d** of the afflicted are evil, but Prv 15:15
hates unjust gain will prolong his **d**. Prv 28:16
and not harm, all the **d** of her life. Prv 31:12
heaven during the few **d** of their life. Eccl 2:3
seeing that in the **d** to come all will Eccl 2:16
For all his **d** are full of sorrow, and his Eccl 2:23
all his **d** he eats in darkness in much Eccl 5:17
under the sun the few **d** of his life that Eccl 5:18
not much remember the **d** of his life Eccl 5:20
so that the **d** of his years are many, Eccl 6:3
while he lives the few **d** of his vain life, Eccl 6:12
were the former **d** better than these?" Eccl 7:10
will he prolong his **d** like a shadow, Eccl 8:13
in his toil through the **d** of his life that Eccl 8:15
all the **d** of your vain life that he has Eccl 9:9
for you will find it after many **d**. Eccl 11:1
remember that the **d** of darkness will Eccl 11:8
heart cheer you in the **d** of your youth. Eccl 11:9
your Creator in the **d** of your youth, Eccl 12:1
before the evil **d** come and the years Eccl 12:1
Judah and Jerusalem in the **d** of Uzziah, Is 1:1
to pass in the latter **d** that the mountain of Is 2:2
In the **d** of Ahaz the son of Jotham, son of Is 7:1
your father's house such **d** as have not Is 7:17
at hand and its **d** will not be prolonged. Is 13:22
city whose origin is from **d** of old, Is 23:7
for seventy years, like the **d** of one king. Is 23:15
and after many **d** they will be punished. Is 24:22
In **d** to come Jacob shall take root, Israel Is 27:6
will be sevenfold, as the light of seven **d**, Is 30:26
I planned from **d** of old what now I bring Is 37:26
In those **d** Hezekiah became sick and was Is 38:1
said, In the middle of my **d** I must depart; Is 38:10
instruments all the **d** of our lives, Is 38:20
Behold, the **d** are coming, when all that is Is 39:6
will be peace and security in my **d**." Is 39:8
awake, as in **d** of old, the generations of Is 51:9
see his offspring; he shall prolong his **d**; Is 53:10
"This is like the **d** of Noah to me: as I Is 54:9
and your **d** of mourning shall be ended. Is 60:20
them up and carried them all the **d** of old. Is 63:9
Then he remembered the **d** of old, of Is 63:11
be in it an infant who lives but a few **d**, Is 65:20
an old man who does not fill out his **d**, Is 65:20
for like the **d** of a tree shall the days of Is 65:22
days of a tree shall the **d** of my people be, Is 65:22
the LORD came in the **d** of Josiah the son of Jer 1:2
It came also in the **d** of Jehoiakim the son Jer 1:3
have forgotten me **d** without number. Jer 2:32
LORD said to me in the **d** of King Josiah: Jer 3:6
and increased in the land, in those **d**, Jer 3:16
In those **d** the house of Judah shall join Jer 3:18
"But even in those **d**, declares the LORD, I Jer 5:18
Therefore, behold, the **d** are coming, Jer 7:32
"Behold, the **d** are coming, declares the Jer 9:25
And after many **d** the LORD said to me, Jer 13:6
place, before your eyes and in your **d**, Jer 16:9
"Therefore, behold, the **d** are coming, Jer 16:14
the midst of his **d** they will leave him, Jer 17:11
therefore, behold, **d** are coming, declares Jer 19:6
and sorrow, and spend my **d** in shame? Jer 20:18
a man who shall not succeed in his **d**, Jer 22:30
"Behold, the **d** are coming, declares the Jer 23:5
In his **d** Judah will be saved, and Israel Jer 23:6
"Therefore, behold, the **d** are coming, Jer 23:7
In the latter **d** you will understand it Jer 23:20
for the **d** of your slaughter and Jer 25:34
prophesied in the **d** of Hezekiah king Jer 26:18
For behold, **d** are coming, declares the Jer 30:3
In the latter **d** you will understand this. Jer 30:24
"Behold, the **d** are coming, declares the Jer 31:27
In those **d** they shall no longer say: Jer 31:29
"Behold, the **d** are coming, declares the Jer 31:31
with the house of Israel after those **d**, Jer 31:33
"Behold, the **d** are coming, declares the Jer 31:38
"Behold, the **d** are coming, declares the Jer 33:14
In those **d** and at that time I will cause a Jer 33:15
In those **d** Judah will be saved and Jer 33:16
the LORD in the **d** of Jehoiakim the son Jer 35:1
but you shall live in tents all your **d**, that Jer 35:7
you may live many **d** in the land where Jer 35:7
us, to drink no wine all our **d**, Jer 35:8

to you, from the **d** of Josiah until today. Jer 36:2
cells and remained there many **d**, Jer 37:16
At the end of ten **d** the word of the LORD Jer 42:7
shall be inhabited as in the **d** of old, Jer 46:26
"Therefore, behold, the **d** are coming, Jer 48:12
the fortunes of Moab in the latter **d**, Jer 48:47
Therefore, behold, the **d** are coming, Jer 49:2
"But in the latter **d** I will restore the Jer 49:39
"In those **d** and in that time, declares the Jer 50:4
In those **d** and in that time, declares the Jer 50:20
the **d** are coming when I will punish Jer 51:47
"Therefore, behold, the **d** are coming, Jer 51:52
remembers in the **d** of her affliction Lam 1:7
things that were hers from **d** of old. Lam 1:7
our **d** were numbered, for our end had Lam 4:18
why do you forsake us for so many **d**? Lam 5:20
be restored! Renew our **d** as of old— Lam 5:21
overwhelmed among them seven **d**. Ezk 3:15
And at the end of seven **d**, the word of Ezk 3:16
For the number of the **d** that you lie on Ezk 4:4
For I assign to you a number of **d**, 390 Ezk 4:5
I assign to you a number of days, 390 **d**, Ezk 4:5
Forty **d** I assign you, a day for each year. Ezk 4:6
you have completed the **d** of your siege. Ezk 4:8
During the number of **d** that you lie on Ezk 4:9
of days that you lie on your side, 390 **d**, Ezk 4:9
when the **d** of the siege are completed. Ezk 5:2
of Israel, saying, 'The **d** grow long, Ezk 12:22
But say to them, The **d** are near, and Ezk 12:23
no longer be delayed, but in your **d**, Ezk 12:25
that he sees is for many **d** from now, Ezk 12:27
did not remember the **d** of your youth, Ezk 16:22
not remembered the **d** of your youth, Ezk 16:43
with you in the **d** of your youth, Ezk 16:60
and you have brought your **d** near, Ezk 22:4
in the **d** that I shall deal with you? Ezk 22:14
remembering the **d** of her youth, Ezk 23:19
After many **d** you will be mustered. In Ezk 38:8
In the latter **d** I will bring you against Ezk 38:16
I spoke in former **d** by my servants the Ezk 38:17
who in those **d** prophesied for years Ezk 38:17
For seven **d** you shall provide daily a Ezk 43:25
Seven **d** shall they make atonement Ezk 43:26
when they have completed these **d**, Ezk 43:27
they shall count seven **d** for him. Ezk 44:26
and for seven **d** unleavened bread Ezk 45:21
And on the seven **d** of the festival he Ezk 45:23
blemish, on each of the seven **d**; Ezk 45:23
month and for the seven **d** of the feast, Ezk 45:25
east shall be shut on the six working **d**, Ezk 46:1
"Test your servants for ten **d**; let us be Dn 1:12
in this matter, and tested them for ten **d**. Dn 1:14
At the end of ten **d** it was seen that they Dn 1:15
what will be in the latter **d**. Dn 2:28
And in the **d** of those kings the God of Dn 2:44
At the end of the **d** I, Nebuchadnezzar, Dn 4:34
In the **d** of your father, light and Dn 5:11
has numbered the **d** of your kingdom Dn 5:26
petition to any god or man for thirty **d**, Dn 6:7
or man within thirty **d** except to you, Dn 6:12
placed, and the Ancient of **d** took his seat; Dn 7:9
to the Ancient of **D** and was presented Dn 7:13
until the Ancient of **D** came, and Dn 7:22
for it refers to many **d** from now." Dn 8:26
was overcome and lay sick for some **d**. Dn 8:27
In those **d** I, Daniel, was mourning for Dn 10:2
of Persia withstood me twenty-one **d**, Dn 10:13
to happen to your people in the latter **d**. Dn 10:14
For the vision is for **d** yet to come." Dn 10:14
But within a few **d** he shall be broken, Dn 11:20
though for some **d** they shall stumble Dn 11:33
desolate is set up, there shall be 1,290 **d**. Dn 12:11
he who waits and arrives at the 1,335 **d**. Dn 12:12
your allotted place at the end of the **d**." Dn 12:13
the son of Beeri, in the **d** of Uzziah, Hos 1:1
and in the **d** of Jeroboam the son of Hos 1:1
her for the feast **d** of the Baals when Hos 2:13
shall answer as in the **d** of her youth, Hos 2:15
"You must dwell as mine for many **d**. Hos 3:3
shall dwell many **d** without king or Hos 3:4
LORD and to his goodness in the latter **d**. Hos 3:5
After two **d** he will revive us; on the third Hos 6:2
The **d** of punishment have come; the Hos 9:7
come; the **d** of recompense have come; Hos 9:7
themselves as in the **d** of Gibeah: Hos 9:9
From the **d** of Gibeah, you have sinned, Hos 10:9
tents, as in the **d** of the appointed feast. Hos 12:9
Has such a thing happened in your **d**, or in Jl 1:2
in your days, or in the **d** of your fathers? Jl 1:2
female servants in those **d** I will pour out Jl 2:29
"For behold, in those **d** and at that time, Jl 3:1
Israel in the **d** of Uzziah king Am 1:1
Judah and in the **d** of Jeroboam the son Am 1:1
that, behold, the **d** are coming upon you, Am 4:2
every morning, your tithes every three **d**; Am 4:4
the **d** are coming," declares the Lord Am 8:11
ruins and rebuild it as in the **d** of old, Am 9:11
the **d** are coming," declares the LORD, Am 9:13
belly of the fish three **d** and three nights. Jon 1:17
And he called out, "Yet forty **d**, and Jon 3:4
to Micah of Moresheth in the **d** of Jotham, Mi 1:1
pass in the latter **d** that the mountain of Mi 4:1
origin is from of old, from ancient **d**. Mi 5:2
in Bashan and Gilead as in the **d** of old. Mi 7:14
As in the **d** when you came out of the Mi 7:15
sworn to our fathers from the **d** of old. Mi 7:20
a work in your **d** that you would not Hab 1:5
in the **d** of Josiah the son of Amon, Zep 1:1
of the remnant of this people in those **d**, Zec 8:6
you who in these **d** have been hearing Zec 8:9
For before those **d** there was no wage for Zec 8:10
of this people as in the former **d**, Zec 8:11
I purposed in these **d** to bring good to Zec 8:15
In those **d** ten men from the nations of Zec 8:23
the earthquake in the **d** of Uzziah king Zec 14:5
to the LORD as in the **d** of old and as in Mal 3:4
From the **d** of your fathers you have Mal 3:7
of Judea in the **d** of Herod the king, Mt 2:1
In those **d** John the Baptist came Mt 3:1
And after fasting forty **d** and forty nights, Mt 4:2
The **d** will come when the bridegroom is Mt 9:15
From the **d** of John the Baptist until Mt 11:12
as Jonah was three **d** and three nights Mt 12:40
of Man be three **d** and three nights in Mt 12:40
with me now three **d** and have nothing Mt 15:32
And after six **d** Jesus took with him Peter Mt 17:1
'If we had lived in the **d** of our fathers, Mt 23:30
who are nursing infants in those **d**! Mt 24:19
And if those **d** had not been cut short, Mt 24:22
of the elect those **d** will be cut short. Mt 24:22
the tribulation of those **d** the sun will Mt 24:29
As were the **d** of Noah, so will be the Mt 24:37
For as in those **d** before the flood they Mt 24:38
know that after two **d** the Passover is Mt 26:2
of God, and to rebuild it in three **d**.'" Mt 26:61
the temple and rebuild it in three **d**, Mt 27:40
was still alive, 'After three **d** I will rise.' Mt 27:63
In those **d** Jesus came from Nazareth of Mk 1:9
And he was in the wilderness forty **d**, Mk 1:13
he returned to Capernaum after some **d**, Mk 2:1
The **d** will come when the bridegroom Mk 2:20
In those **d**, when again a great crowd had Mk 8:1
with me now three **d** and have nothing to Mk 8:2
be killed, and after three **d** rise again. Mk 8:31
And after six **d** Jesus took with him Peter Mk 9:2
he is killed, after three **d** he will rise." Mk 9:31
him. And after three **d** he will rise." Mk 10:34
who are nursing infants in those **d**! Mk 13:17
For in those **d** there will be such Mk 13:19
if the Lord had not cut short the **d**, Mk 13:20
whom he chose, he shortened the **d**. Mk 13:20
"But in those **d**, after that tribulation, Mk 13:24
It was now two **d** before the Passover Mk 14:1
and in three **d** I will build another, Mk 14:58
the temple and rebuild it in three **d**, Mk 15:29
In the **d** of Herod, king of Judea, there was Lk 1:5
After these **d** his wife Elizabeth Lk 1:24
done for me in the **d** when he looked on Lk 1:25
In those **d** Mary arose and went with Lk 1:39
and righteousness before him all our **d**. Lk 1:75
In those **d** a decree went out from Caesar Lk 2:1
And at the end of eight **d**, when he was Lk 2:21
After three **d** they found him in the Lk 2:46
for forty **d**, being tempted by the devil. Lk 4:2
devil. And he ate nothing during those **d**. Lk 4:2
many widows in Israel in the **d** of Elijah, Lk 4:25
On one of those **d**, as he was teaching, Lk 5:17
The **d** will come when the bridegroom is Lk 5:35
them, and then they will fast in those **d**." Lk 5:35
In these **d** he went out to the mountain Lk 6:12
Now about eight **d** after these sayings he Lk 9:28
no one in those **d** anything of what they Lk 9:36
When the **d** drew near for him to be Lk 9:51
"There are six **d** in which work ought Lk 13:14
done. Come on those **d** and be healed, Lk 13:14
Not many **d** later, the younger son Lk 15:13
"The **d** are coming when you will Lk 17:22
to see one of the **d** of the Son of Man, Lk 17:22
Just as it was in the **d** of Noah, so will it Lk 17:26
so will it be in the **d** of the Son of Man. Lk 17:26
just as it was in the **d** of Lot—they were Lk 17:28
For the **d** will come upon you, when Lk 19:43
the **d** will come when there will not be Lk 21:6
for these are **d** of vengeance, to fulfill Lk 21:22
who are nursing infants in those **d**! Lk 21:23
the **d** are coming when they will say, Lk 23:29
that have happened there in these **d**?" Lk 24:18
and they stayed there for a few **d**. Jn 2:12
temple, and in three **d** I will raise it up." Jn 2:19
and will you raise it up in three **d**?" Jn 2:20
stay with them, and he stayed there two **d**. Jn 4:40
After the two **d** he departed for Galilee. Jn 4:43
he stayed two **d** longer in the place where Jn 11:6
had already been in the tomb four **d**. Jn 11:17
be an odor, for he has been dead four **d**." Jn 11:39
Six **d** before the Passover, Jesus therefore Jn 12:1
Eight **d** later, his disciples were inside Jn 20:26
them during forty **d** and speaking Acts 1:3
the Holy Spirit not many **d** from now." Acts 1:5
In those **d** Peter stood up among the Acts 1:15
"'And in the last **d** it shall be, God Acts 2:17
female servants in those **d** I will pour Acts 2:18
after him, also proclaimed these **d**. Acts 3:24
For before these **d** Theudas rose up, Acts 5:36
rose up in the **d** of the census and Acts 5:37
Now in these **d** when the disciples were Acts 6:1
And they made a calf in those **d**, and Acts 7:41
fathers. So it was until the **d** of David, Acts 7:45
And for three **d** he was without sight, Acts 9:9
For some **d** he was with the disciples at Acts 9:19
When many **d** had passed, the Jews Acts 9:23
In those **d** she became ill and died, and Acts 9:37
in Joppa for many **d** with one Simon, Acts 9:43
And Cornelius said, "Four **d** ago, Acts 10:30
they asked him to remain for some **d**. Acts 10:48
Now in these **d** prophets came down Acts 11:27
(this took place in the **d** of Claudius). Acts 11:28
was during the **d** of Unleavened Bread. Acts 12:3
and for many **d** he appeared to those Acts 13:31
for I am doing a work in your **d**, a Acts 13:41
that in the early **d** God made a choice Acts 15:7
And after some **d** Paul said to Acts 15:36
We remained in this city some **d**. Acts 16:12
And this she kept doing for many **d**. Acts 16:18
on three Sabbath **d** he reasoned with Acts 17:2
Paul stayed many **d** longer and then Acts 18:18
Philippi after the **d** of Unleavened Acts 20:6
and in five **d** we came to them at Acts 20:6
at Troas, where we stayed for seven **d**. Acts 20:6
disciples, we stayed there for seven **d**. Acts 21:4
When our **d** there were ended, we Acts 21:5
While we were staying for many **d**, a Acts 21:10
After these **d** we got ready and went Acts 21:15
notice when the **d** of purification Acts 21:26
When the seven **d** were almost Acts 21:27
And after five **d** the high priest Acts 24:1
not more than twelve **d** since I went Acts 24:11
After some **d** Felix came with his wife Acts 24:24
Now three **d** after Festus had arrived in Acts 25:1
them not more than eight or ten **d**, Acts 25:6
Now when some **d** had passed, Acts 25:13
And as they stayed there many **d**, Acts 25:14
for a number of **d** and arrived with Acts 27:7
sun nor stars appeared for many **d**, Acts 27:20
entertained us hospitably for three **d**. Acts 28:7
Syracuse, we stayed there for three **d**. Acts 28:12
invited to stay with them for seven **d**. Acts 28:14
After three **d** he called together the Acts 28:17
while another esteems all **d** alike. Rom 14:5
written in former **d** was written for Rom 15:4
and remained with him fifteen **d**. Gal 1:18
You observe **d** and months and seasons Gal 4:10
use of the time, because the **d** are evil. Eph 5:16
that in the last **d** there will come times 2 Tm 3:1
passing our **d** in malice and envy, Ti 3:3
but in these last **d** he has spoken to us Heb 1:2
In the **d** of his flesh, Jesus offered up Heb 5:7
neither beginning of **d** nor end of Heb 7:3
"Behold, the **d** are coming, declares the Heb 8:8
with the house of Israel after those **d**, Heb 8:10
I will make with them after those **d**, Heb 10:16
But recall the former **d** when, after Heb 10:32
they had been encircled for seven **d**. Heb 11:30
You have laid up treasure in the last **d**. Jas 5:3
desires to love life and see good **d**, 1 Pt 3:10
God's patience waited in the **d** of Noah, 1 Pt 3:20
will come in the last **d** with scoffing, 2 Pt 3:3
and for ten **d** you will have tribulation. Rv 2:10
faith even in the **d** of Antipas my faithful Rv 2:13
And in those **d** people will seek death and Rv 9:6
but that in the **d** of the trumpet call to be Rv 10:7
and they will prophesy for 1,260 **d**, Rv 11:3
fall during the **d** of their prophesying, Rv 11:6
three and a half **d** some from the peoples Rv 11:9
the three and a half **d** a breath of life Rv 11:11
which she is to be nourished for 1,260 **d**. Rv 12:6

DAYS' (11)

distance of three **d** journey between Gn 30:36
us go a three **d** journey into the Ex 3:18
us go a three **d** journey into the Ex 5:3
We must go three **d** journey into the Ex 8:27
mount of the LORD three **d** journey. Nm 10:33
went before them three **d** journey, Nm 10:33
they went a three **d** journey in the Nm 33:8
It is eleven **d** journey from Horeb by the Dt 1:2

“Give us seven **d** respite that we may 1 Sm 11:3
there be three **d** pestilence in your 2 Sm 24:13
great city, three **d** journey in breadth. Jon 3:3

DAYTIME (4)
with darkness in the **d** and grope at Jb 5:14
In the **d** he led them with a cloud, and Ps 78:14
Let us walk properly as in the **d**, not Rom 13:13
They count it pleasure to revel in the **d**. 2 Pt 2:13

DAZZLING (2)
and his clothing became **d** white. Lk 9:29
two men stood by them in **d** apparel. Lk 24:4

DEACONS (5)
are at Philippi, with the overseers and **d**: Phil 1:1
D likewise must be dignified, not 1 Tm 3:8
let them serve as **d** if they prove 1 Tm 3:10
Let **d** each be the husband of one 1 Tm 3:12
who serve well as **d** gain a good 1 Tm 3:13

DEAD (306)
you are a **d** man because of the woman Gn 20:3
rose up from before his **d** and said to the Gn 23:3
that I may bury my **d** out of my sight.” Gn 23:4
Bury your **d** in the choicest of our Gn 23:6
to hinder you from burying your **d**.” Gn 23:6
that I should bury my **d** out of my sight, Gn 23:8
my people I give it to you. Bury your **d**.” Gn 23:11
from me, that I may bury my **d** there.” Gn 23:13
between you and me? Bury your **d**.” Gn 23:15
go down with you, for his brother is **d**, Gn 42:38
His brother is **d**, and he alone is left of Gn 44:20
brothers saw that their father was **d**, Gn 50:15
men who were seeking your life are **d**.” Ex 4:19
not one of the livestock of Israel was **d**. Ex 9:7
not a house where someone was not **d**. Ex 12:30
haste. For they said, “We shall all be **d**.” Ex 12:33
saw the Egyptians **d** on the seashore. Ex 14:30
its owner, and the **d** beast shall be his. Ex 21:34
and the **d** beast also they shall share. Ex 21:35
ox for ox, and the **d** beast shall be his. Ex 21:36
them when they are **d** shall be unclean Lv 11:31
falls when they are **d** shall be unclean, Lv 11:32
your body for the **d** or tattoo yourselves: Lv 19:28
unclean for the **d** among his people, Lv 21:1
go in to any **d** bodies nor make himself Lv 21:11
through contact with the **d** or a man Lv 22:4
altars and cast your **d** bodies upon the Lv 26:30
dead bodies upon the **d** bodies of your Lv 26:30
is unclean through contact with the **d**. Nm 5:2
to the LORD he shall not go near a **d** body. Nm 6:6
he sinned by reason of the **d** body. Nm 6:11
unclean through touching a **d** body, Nm 9:6
are unclean through touching a **d** body. Nm 9:7
is unclean through touching a **d** body, Nm 9:10
Let her not be as one **d**, whose flesh is Nm 12:12
your **d** bodies shall fall in this Nm 14:29
your **d** bodies shall fall in this Nm 14:32
the last of your **d** bodies lies in the Nm 14:33
he stood between the **d** and the living, Nm 16:48
“Whoever touches the **d** body of any Nm 19:11
Whoever touches a **d** person, the body Nm 19:13
bone, or the slain or the **d** or the grave. Nm 19:18
had perished and were **d** from among the Dt 2:16
any baldness on your foreheads for the **d**. Dt 14:1
the wife of the **d** man shall not be Dt 25:5
succeed to the name of his **d** brother, Dt 25:6
unclean, or offered any of it to the **d**. Dt 26:14
And your **d** body shall be food for all Dt 28:26
“Moses my servant is **d**. Now therefore Jos 1:2
and there lay their lord **d** on the floor. Jgs 3:25
in to her tent, and there lay Sisera **d**, Jgs 4:22
he fell; where he sank, there he fell—**d**. Jgs 5:27
men of Israel saw that Abimelech was **d**, Jgs 9:55
So the **d** whom he killed at his death Jgs 16:30
violated my concubine, and she is **d**. Jgs 20:5
as you have dealt with the **d** and with me. Ru 1:8
the living or the **d**!” Naomi also said to Ru 2:20
Ruth the Moabite, the widow of the **d**, Ru 4:5
the name of the **d** in his inheritance.” Ru 4:5
the name of the **d** in his inheritance, Ru 4:10
that the name of the **d** may not be cut off Ru 4:10
also, Hophni and Phinehas, are **d**, 1 Sm 4:17
and her husband were **d**, 1 Sm 4:19
I will give the **d** bodies of the host 1 Sm 17:46
saw that their champion was **d**, 1 Sm 17:51
whom do you pursue? After a **d** dog! 1 Sm 24:14
David heard that Nabal was **d**, 1 Sm 25:39
his armor-bearer saw that Saul was **d**, 1 Sm 31:5
fled and that Saul and his sons were **d**, 1 Sm 31:7
of the people have fallen and are **d**, 2 Sm 1:4
Saul and his son Jonathan are also **d**.” 2 Sm 1:4
that Saul and his son Jonathan are **d**?” 2 Sm 1:5
and be valiant, for Saul your lord is **d**, 2 Sm 2:7
when one told me, ‘Behold, Saul is **d**,’ 2 Sm 4:10
show regard for a **d** dog such as I?” 2 Sm 9:8
servant Uriah the Hittite is **d** also.’” 2 Sm 11:21
Some of the king’s servants are **d**, 2 Sm 11:24
servant Uriah the Hittite is **d** also.” 2 Sm 11:24
that Uriah her husband was **d**, 2 Sm 11:26
to tell him that the child was **d**, 2 Sm 12:18
can we say to him the child is **d**? 2 Sm 12:18
understood that the child was **d**. 2 Sm 12:19
servants, “Is the child **d**?” They said, 2 Sm 12:19
the child dead?” They said, “He is **d**.” 2 Sm 12:19
But now he is **d**. Why should I fast? 2 Sm 12:23
king’s sons, for Amnon alone is **d**. 2 Sm 13:32
suppose that all the king’s sons are **d**, 2 Sm 13:33
sons are dead, for Amnon alone is **d**.” 2 Sm 13:33
about Amnon, since he was **d**. 2 Sm 13:39
been mourning many days for the **d**. 2 Sm 14:2
“Alas, I am a widow; my husband is **d**. 2 Sm 14:5
“Why should this **d** dog curse my 2 Sm 16:9
news, because the king’s son is **d**.” 2 Sm 18:20
were alive and all of us were **d** today, 2 Sm 19:6
we anointed over us, is **d** in battle. 2 Sm 19:10
and laid her **d** son at my breast. 1 Kgs 3:20
to nurse my child, behold, he was **d**. 1 Kgs 3:21
and the **d** child is yours.” The first 1 Kgs 3:22
first said, “No, the **d** child is yours, 1 Kgs 3:22
son that is alive, and your son is **d**’; 1 Kgs 3:23
but your son is **d**, and my son is the 1 Kgs 3:23
the commander of the army was **d**, 1 Kgs 11:21
“Naboth has been stoned; he is **d**.” 1 Kgs 21:14
Naboth had been stoned and was **d**, 1 Kgs 21:15
for Naboth is not alive, but **d**.” 1 Kgs 21:15
as Ahab heard that Naboth was **d**, 1 Kgs 21:16
“Your servant my husband is **d**, 2 Kgs 4:1
he saw the child lying **d** on his bed. 2 Kgs 4:32
how Elisha had restored the **d** to life, 2 Kgs 8:5
of Ahaziah saw that her son was **d**, 2 Kgs 11:1
behold, these were all **d** bodies. 2 Kgs 19:35
servants carried him **d** in a chariot 2 Kgs 23:30
armor-bearer saw that Saul was **d**, 1 Chr 10:5
and that Saul and his sons were **d**, 1 Chr 10:7
there were **d** bodies lying on the 2 Chr 20:24
of Ahaziah saw that her son was **d**, 2 Chr 22:10
upon the young people, and they are **d**, Jb 1:19
The **d** tremble under the waters and their Jb 26:5
I have been forgotten like one who is **d**; I Ps 31:12
like one set loose among the **d**, like the Ps 88:5
Do you work wonders for the **d**? Do the Ps 88:10
Peor, and ate sacrifices offered to the **d**; Ps 106:28
The **d** do not praise the LORD, nor do Ps 115:17
me sit in darkness like those long **d**. Ps 143:3
he does not know that the **d** are there, Prv 9:18
sense will rest in the assembly of the **d**. Prv 21:16
And I thought the **d** who are already Eccl 4:2
who are already **d** more fortunate than Eccl 4:2
they live, and after that they go to the **d**. Eccl 9:3
for a living dog is better than a **d** lion. Eccl 9:4
they will die, but the **d** know nothing, Eccl 9:5
D flies make the perfumer’s ointment Eccl 10:1
they inquire of the **d** on behalf of the Is 8:19
the pit, like a **d** body trampled underfoot. Is 14:19
are not slain with the sword or **d** in battle. Is 22:2
They are **d**, they will not live; they are Is 26:14
Your **d** shall live; their bodies shall rise. Is 26:19
and the earth will give birth to the **d**. Is 26:19
morning, behold, these were all **d** bodies. Is 37:36
those in full vigor we are like **d** men. Is 59:10
out and look on the **d** bodies of the men Is 66:24
And the **d** bodies of this people will be Jer 7:33
‘The **d** bodies of men shall fall like dung Jer 9:22
and their **d** bodies shall be food for the Jer 16:4
the mourner, to comfort him for the **d**, Jer 16:7
I will give their **d** bodies for food to the Jer 19:7
Weep not for him who is **d**, nor grieve Jer 22:10
sword and dumped his **d** body into the Jer 26:23
whole valley of the **d** bodies and the Jer 31:40
fill them with the **d** bodies of men whom Jer 33:5
Their **d** bodies shall be food for the Jer 34:20
and his **d** body shall be cast out to the Jer 36:30
dwell in darkness like the **d** of long ago. Lam 3:6
And I will lay the **d** bodies of the people Ezk 6:5
aloud; make no mourning for the **d**. Ezk 24:17
whoring and by the **d** bodies of their Ezk 43:7
their whoring and the **d** bodies of their Ezk 43:9
by going near to a **d** person. Ezk 44:25
“So many **d** bodies!” “They are thrown Am 8:3
d bodies without end—they stumble over Na 3:3
by contact with a **d** body touches any of Hg 2:13
those who sought the child’s life are **d**.” Mt 2:20
and leave the **d** to bury their own dead.” Mt 8:22
and leave the dead to bury their own **d**.” Mt 8:22
the girl is not **d** but sleeping.” And they Mt 9:24
Heal the sick, raise the **d**, cleanse lepers, Mt 10:8
the deaf hear, and the **d** are raised up, Mt 11:5
He has been raised from the **d**; that is Mt 14:2
the Son of Man is raised from the **d**.” Mt 17:9
And as for the resurrection of the **d**, Mt 22:31
He is not God of the **d**, but of the Mt 22:32
within are full of **d** people’s bones and Mt 23:27
tell the people, ‘He has risen from the **d**,’ Mt 27:64
trembled and became like **d** men. Mt 28:4
disciples that he has risen from the **d**, Mt 28:7
some who said, “Your daughter is **d**. Mk 5:35
The child is not **d** but sleeping.” Mk 5:39
the Baptist has been raised from the **d**. Mk 6:14
the Son of Man had risen from the **d**. Mk 9:9
this rising from the **d** might mean. Mk 9:10
so that most of them said, “He is **d**.” Mk 9:26
For when they rise from the **d**, they Mk 12:25
And as for the **d** being raised, have you Mk 12:26
He is not God of the **d**, but of the living. Mk 12:27
asked him whether he was already **d**. Mk 15:44
from the centurion that he was **d**, Mk 15:45
And the **d** man sat up and began to Lk 7:15
and the deaf hear, the **d** are raised up, Lk 7:22
came and said, “Your daughter is **d**; Lk 8:49
not weep, for she is not **d** but sleeping.” Lk 8:52
laughed at him, knowing that she was **d**. Lk 8:53
that John had been raised from the **d**, Lk 9:7
“Leave the **d** to bury their own dead. Lk 9:60
“Leave the dead to bury their own **d**. Lk 9:60
him and departed, leaving him half **d**. Lk 10:30
For this my son was **d**, and is alive Lk 15:24
be glad, for this your brother was **d**, Lk 15:32
but if someone goes to them from the **d**, Lk 16:30
if someone should rise from the **d**.’” Lk 16:31
resurrection from the **d** neither marry Lk 20:35
But that the **d** are raised, even Moses Lk 20:37
Now he is not God of the **d**, but of the Lk 20:38
do you seek the living among the **d**? Lk 24:5
and on the third day rise from the **d**, Lk 24:46
When therefore he was raised from the **d**, Jn 2:22
the Father raises the **d** and gives them Jn 5:21
when the **d** will hear the voice of the Son Jn 5:25
stone.” Martha, the sister of the **d** man, Jn 11:39
be an odor, for he has been **d** four days.” Jn 11:39
was, whom Jesus had raised from the **d**. Jn 12:1
Lazarus, whom he had raised from the **d**. Jn 12:9
raised him from the **d** continued to bear Jn 12:17
to Jesus and saw that he was already **d**, Jn 19:33
Scripture, that he must rise from the **d**. Jn 20:9
disciples after he was raised from the **d**. Jn 21:14
of life, whom God raised from the **d**. Acts 3:15
in Jesus the resurrection from the **d**. Acts 4:2
God raised from the **d**—by him this Acts 4:10
young men came in they found her **d**, Acts 5:10
with him after he rose from the **d**. Acts 10:41
to be judge of the living and the **d**. Acts 10:42
But God raised him from the **d**, Acts 13:30
the fact that he raised him from the **d**, Acts 13:34
of the city, supposing that he was **d**. Acts 14:19
Christ to suffer and to rise from the **d**, Acts 17:3
to all by raising him from the **d**.” Acts 17:31
heard of the resurrection of the **d**, Acts 17:32
the third story and was taken up **d**. Acts 20:9
the resurrection of the **d** that I am on Acts 23:6
the resurrection of the **d** that I am on Acts 24:21
and about a certain Jesus, who was **d**, Acts 25:19
by any of you that God raises the **d**? Acts 26:8
by being the first to rise from the **d**, Acts 26:23
to swell up or suddenly fall down **d**. Acts 28:6
holiness by his resurrection from the **d**, Rom 1:4
gives life to the **d** and calls into Rom 4:17
was as good as **d** (since he was about Rom 4:19
who raised from the **d** Jesus our Lord, Rom 4:24
was raised from the **d** by the glory of Rom 6:4
being raised from the **d** will never die Rom 6:9
must consider yourselves **d** to sin and Rom 6:11
to him who has been raised from the **d**, Rom 7:4
Apart from the law, sin lies **d**. Rom 7:8
although the body is **d** because of sin, Rom 8:10
raised Jesus from the **d** dwells in you, Rom 8:11
Christ Jesus from the **d** will also give Rom 8:11
is, to bring Christ up from the **d**). Rom 10:7
heart that God raised him from the **d**, Rom 10:9
acceptance mean but life from the **d**? Rom 11:15
be Lord both of the **d** and of the living. Rom 14:9
is proclaimed as raised from the **d**, 1 Cor 15:12
there is no resurrection of the **d**? 1 Cor 15:12
if there is no resurrection of the **d**, 1 Cor 15:13
if it is true that the **d** are not raised. 1 Cor 15:15
For if the **d** are not raised, not even 1 Cor 15:16
Christ has been raised from the **d**, 1 Cor 15:20
come also the resurrection of the **d**. 1 Cor 15:21
being baptized on behalf of the **d**? 1 Cor 15:29
If the **d** are not raised at all, why are 1 Cor 15:29
If the **d** are not raised, “Let us eat and 1 Cor 15:32
will ask, “How are the **d** raised? 1 Cor 15:35
So is it with the resurrection of the **d**. 1 Cor 15:42
and the **d** will be raised 1 Cor 15:52
ourselves but on God who raises the **d**. 2 Cor 1:9
the Father, who raised him from the **d**— Gal 1:1

raised him from the **d** and seated him Eph 1:20
And you were **d** in the trespasses and Eph 2:1
even when we were **d** in our trespasses, Eph 2:5
"Awake, O sleeper, and arise from the **d**, Eph 5:14
may attain the resurrection from the **d**. Phil 3:11
the beginning, the firstborn from the **d**, Col 1:18
of God, who raised him from the **d**. Col 2:12
who were **d** in your trespasses and the Col 2:13
heaven, whom he raised from the **d**, 1 Thes 1:10
And the **d** in Christ will rise first. 1 Thes 4:16
is self-indulgent is **d** even while she 1 Tm 5:6
Jesus Christ, risen from the **d**, 2 Tm 2:8
who is to judge the living and the **d**, 2 Tm 4:1
of repentance from **d** works and of Heb 6:1
on of hands, the resurrection of the **d**, Heb 6:2
our conscience from **d** works to serve Heb 9:14
from one man, and him as good as **d**, Heb 11:12
was able even to raise him from the **d**, Heb 11:19
received back their **d** by resurrection. Heb 11:35
again from the **d** our Lord Jesus, Heb 13:20
by itself, if it does not have works, is **d**. Jas 2:17
For as the body apart from the spirit is **d**, Jas 2:26
dead, so also faith apart from works is **d**. Jas 2:26
resurrection of Jesus Christ from the **d**, 1 Pt 1:3
raised him from the **d** and gave him 1 Pt 1:21
is ready to judge the living and the **d**. 1 Pt 4:5
was preached even to those who are **d**, 1 Pt 4:6
fruitless trees in late autumn, twice **d**, Jude 1:12
the faithful witness, the firstborn of the **d**, Rv 1:5
I saw him, I fell at his feet as though **d**. Rv 1:17
and I will strike her children **d**. And all Rv 2:23
reputation of being alive, but you are **d**. Rv 3:1
and their **d** bodies will lie in the street of Rv 11:8
will gaze at their **d** bodies and refuse to Rv 11:9
and the time for the **d** to be judged, Rv 11:18
Blessed are the **d** who die in the Lord Rv 14:13
The rest of the **d** did not come to life Rv 20:5
And I saw the **d**, great and small, Rv 20:12
And the **d** were judged by what was Rv 20:12
the sea gave up the **d** who were in it, Rv 20:13
Hades gave up the **d** who were in them, Rv 20:13

DEADLY (12)

he has prepared for him his **d** weapons, Ps 7:13
my **d** enemies who surround me. Ps 17:9
say, "A **d** thing is poured out on him; Ps 41:8
As with a **d** wound in my bones, my Ps 42:10
of the fowler and from the **d** pestilence. Ps 91:3
Their tongue is a **d** arrow; it speaks Jer 9:8
They shall die of **d** diseases. They shall Jer 16:4
against you the **d** arrows of famine, Ezk 5:16
the prostitute, graceful and of **d** charms, Na 3:4
and if they drink any **d** poison, it will Mk 16:18
He delivered us from such a **d** peril, 2 Cor 1:10
tongue. It is a restless evil, full of **d** poison. Jas 3:8

DEAF (16)

Who makes him mute, or **d**, or seeing, Ex 4:11
shall not curse the **d** or put a Lv 19:14
my rock, be not **d** to me, lest, if you be Ps 28:1
But I am like a **d** man; I do not hear, Ps 38:13
serpent, like the **d** adder that stops its ear, Ps 58:4
In that day the **d** shall hear the words of Is 29:18
opened, and the ears of the **d** unstopped; Is 35:5
Hear, you **d**, and look, you blind, that Is 42:18
or **d** as my messenger whom I send? Is 42:19
who are blind, yet have eyes, who are **d**, Is 43:8
on their mouths; their ears shall be **d**; Mi 7:16
walk, lepers are cleansed and the **d** hear, Mt 11:5
him a man who was **d** and had a speech Mk 7:32
He even makes the **d** hear and the mute Mk 7:37
saying to it, "You mute and **d** spirit, Mk 9:25
walk, lepers are cleansed, and the **d** hear, Lk 7:22

DEAL (60)

Now we will **d** worse with you than with Gn 19:9
that you will not **d** falsely with me or Gn 21:23
so you will **d** with me and with the Gn 21:23
and promise to **d** kindly and truly Gn 47:29
Come, let us **d** shrewdly with them, lest Ex 1:10
he shall **d** with her as with a daughter. Ex 21:9
shall not steal; you shall not **d** falsely; Lv 19:11
but **d** thus with them, that they may Nm 4:19
But thus shall you **d** with them: you shall Dt 7:5
you also will **d** kindly with my father's Jos 2:12
the land we will **d** kindly and faithfully Jos 2:14
you, lest you **d** falsely with your God." Jos 24:27
the city, and we will **d** kindly with you." Jgs 1:24
house. May the LORD **d** kindly with you, Ru 1:8
Therefore **d** kindly with your servant, 1 Sm 20:8
"I will **d** loyally with Hanun the son of 2 Sm 10:2
"**D** gently for my sake with the young 2 Sm 18:5
with the purified you **d** purely, and 2 Sm 22:27
But **d** loyally with the sons of Barzillai 1 Kgs 2:7
into their hand, for they **d** honestly." 2 Kgs 22:7
"I will **d** kindly with Hanun the son 1 Chr 19:2
a house to dwell in, so **d** with me. 2 Chr 2:3
D courageously, and may the LORD 2 Chr 19:11
his prayer not to **d** with you according to Jb 42:8
your hands **d** out violence on earth. Ps 58:2
He does not **d** with us according to our Ps 103:10
people, to **d** craftily with his servants. Ps 105:25
d on my behalf for your name's sake; Ps 109:21
D bountifully with your servant, that I Ps 119:17
D with your servant according to Ps 119:124
me, for you will **d** bountifully with me. Ps 142:7
of evildoers, children who **d** corruptly! Is 1:4
that you would surely **d** treacherously, Is 48:8
children who will not **d** falsely." And he Is 63:8
d with them in the time of your anger. Jer 18:23
the LORD will **d** with us according Jer 21:2
and he shall reign as king and **d** wisely, Jer 23:5
to them and they **d** cruelly with me." Jer 38:19
harm, but **d** with him as he tells you." Jer 39:12
and **d** with them as you have dealt Lam 1:22
I will **d** with you as you have done, Ezk 16:59
when I **d** with you for my name's sake, Ezk 20:44
in the days that I shall **d** with you? Ezk 22:14
you, that they may **d** with you in fury. Ezk 23:25
and they shall **d** with you in hatred Ezk 23:29
He shall surely **d** with it as its Ezk 31:11
I will **d** with you according to the Ezk 35:11
it was desolate, so I will **d** with you; Ezk 35:15
and **d** with your servants according to Dn 1:13
and he shall **d** with them and shall Dn 11:7
He shall **d** with the strongest fortresses Dn 11:39
evil deeds of Samaria; for they **d** falsely; Hos 7:1
shekel great and **d** deceitfully with false Am 8:5
that time I will **d** with all your Zep 3:19
of hosts purposed to **d** with us for our Zec 1:6
now I will not **d** with the remnant of Zec 8:11
and those who **d** with the world as 1 Cor 7:31
He can **d** gently with the ignorant and Heb 5:2
but **d** only with food and drink and Heb 9:10
not to **d** with sin but to save those who Heb 9:28

DEALERS (3)

Kedar were your favored **d** in lambs, Ezk 27:21
caulkers, your **d** in merchandise, Ezk 27:27
go rather to the **d** and buy for Mt 25:9

DEALING (5)

to receive instruction in wise **d**, in Prv 1:3
me, by **d** treacherously with me. Ezk 20:27
are more shrewd in **d** with their own Lk 16:8
He is not weak in **d** with you, but is 2 Cor 13:3
but in **d** with you we will live with 2 Cor 13:4

DEALINGS (5)

Sidonians and had no **d** with anyone. Jgs 18:7
Sidon, and they had no **d** with anyone. Jgs 18:28
hear of your evil **d** from all the people. 1 Sm 2:23
(For Jews have no **d** with Samaritans.) Jn 4:9
as though they had no **d** with it. 1 Cor 7:31

DEALS (9)

you, or the word that **d** gently with you? Jb 15:11
She **d** cruelly with her young, as if they Jb 39:16
an adversary who **d** insolently with me Ps 55:12
the man who **d** generously and lends; Ps 112:5
A servant who **d** wisely has the king's Prv 14:35
A servant who **d** wisely will rule over a Prv 17:2
of uprightness he **d** corruptly and does Is 26:10
from prophet to priest, everyone **d** falsely. Jer 6:13
from prophet to priest, everyone **d** falsely. Jer 8:10

DEALT (53)

for her sake he **d** well with Abram; Gn 12:16
please." Then Sarai **d** harshly with her, Gn 16:6
but as I have **d** kindly with you, Gn 21:23
because God has **d** graciously with me, Gn 33:11
So God **d** well with the midwives. And Ex 1:20
grandson how I have **d** harshly with the Ex 10:2
in this affair they **d** arrogantly with the Ex 18:11
he shall be **d** with according to this Ex 21:31
"Why have you **d** ill with your Nm 11:11
And the Egyptians **d** harshly with us Nm 20:15
They have **d** corruptly with him; they Dt 32:5
LORD that, as I have **d** kindly with you, Jos 2:12
and if you have **d** well with Jerubbaal Jgs 9:16
leaders of Shechem **d** treacherously with Jgs 9:23
to them, "This is how Micah **d** with me: Jgs 18:4
as you have **d** with the dead and with me. Ru 1:8
for the Almighty has **d** very bitterly with Ru 1:20
After he had **d** severely with them, 1 Sm 6:6
he said, "You have **d** treacherously; 1 Sm 14:33
day how you have **d** well with me, 1 Sm 24:18
when the LORD has **d** well with my 1 Sm 25:31
as his father **d** loyally with me." So 2 Sm 10:2
if I had **d** treacherously against his 2 Sm 18:13
"The LORD **d** with me according to 2 Sm 22:21
how he **d** with the two commanders of 1 Kgs 2:5
to the workmen, for they **d** honestly. 2 Kgs 12:15
and omens and **d** with mediums and 2 Kgs 21:6
for his father **d** kindly with me." So 1 Chr 19:2
"As you **d** with David my father and 2 Chr 2:3
And he **d** wisely and distributed 2 Chr 11:23
and **d** with mediums and with 2 Chr 33:6
for you have **d** faithfully and we have Neh 9:33
because he has **d** bountifully with me. Ps 13:6
The LORD **d** with me according to my Ps 18:20
for the LORD has **d** bountifully with you. Ps 116:7
You have **d** well with your servant, O Ps 119:65
He has not **d** thus with any other Ps 147:20
what his hands have **d** out shall be done Is 3:11
even they have **d** treacherously with you; Jer 12:6
"Why has the LORD **d** thus with this Jer 22:8
for I have **d** you the blow of an enemy, Jer 30:14
her friends have **d** treacherously with Lam 1:2
them as you have **d** with me because Lam 1:22
and see! With whom have you **d** thus? Lam 2:20
because they **d** so treacherously with Ezk 39:23
I **d** with them according to their Ezk 39:24
spirit was hardened so that he **d** proudly, Dn 5:20
They have **d** faithlessly with the LORD; Hos 5:7
there they **d** faithlessly with me. Hos 6:7
God, who has **d** wondrously with you. Jl 2:26
our ways and deeds, so has he **d** with us." Zec 1:6
I have **d** with all that Jesus began to do Acts 1:1
He **d** shrewdly with our race and Acts 7:19

DEAR (5)

consume like a moth what is **d** to him; Ps 39:11
hold her stones **d** and have pity Ps 102:14
Is Ephraim my **d** son? Is he my darling Jer 31:20
because you had become very **d** to us. 1 Thes 2:8
d lady—not as though I were writing 2 Jn 1:5

DEARLY (1)

to whoring; their rulers **d** love shame. Hos 4:18

DEATH (442)

put the righteous to **d** with the wicked, Gn 18:25
me not look on the **d** of the child." And Gn 21:16
was comforted after his mother's **d**. Gn 24:67
After the **d** of Abraham, God blessed Gn 25:11
or his wife shall surely be put to **d**." Gn 26:11
had stopped after the **d** of Abraham. Gn 26:18
I am old; I do not know the day of my **d**. Gn 27:2
of the LORD, and the LORD put him to **d**. Gn 38:7
of the LORD, and he put him to **d** also. Gn 38:10
met him and sought to put him to **d**. Ex 4:24
God only to remove this **d** from me." Ex 10:17
touches the mountain shall be put to **d**. Ex 19:12
a man so that he dies shall be put to **d**. Ex 21:12
father or his mother shall be put to **d**. Ex 21:15
in possession of him, shall be put to **d**. Ex 21:16
father or his mother shall be put to **d**. Ex 21:17
an ox gores a man or a woman to **d**, Ex 21:28
and its owner also shall be put to **d**. Ex 21:29
lies with an animal shall be put to **d**. Ex 22:19
who profanes it shall be put to **d**. Ex 31:14
on the Sabbath day shall be put to **d**. Ex 31:15
does any work on it shall be put to **d**. Ex 35:2
spoke to Moses after the **d** of the two sons Lv 16:1
They shall not be put to **d**, because she Lv 19:20
to Molech shall surely be put to **d**. Lv 20:2
to Molech, and do not put him to **d**, Lv 20:4
or his mother shall surely be put to **d**; Lv 20:9
the adulteress shall surely be put to **d**. Lv 20:10
both of them shall surely be put to **d**; Lv 20:11
both of them shall surely be put to **d**; Lv 20:12
they shall surely be put to **d**; Lv 20:13
an animal, he shall surely be put to **d**, Lv 20:15
animal; they shall surely be put to **d**; Lv 20:16
or a wizard shall surely be put to **d**. Lv 20:27
of the LORD shall surely be put to **d**. Lv 24:16
the Name, shall be put to **d**. Lv 24:16
a human life shall surely be put to **d**. Lv 24:17
whoever kills a person shall be put to **d**. Lv 24:21
ransomed; he shall surely be put to **d**. Lv 27:29
comes near, he shall be put to **d**. Nm 1:51
comes near, he shall be put to **d**." Nm 3:10
who came near was to be put to **d**. Nm 3:38
to Moses, "The man shall be put to **d**; Nm 15:35
and stoned him to **d** with stones, Nm 15:36
who comes near shall be put to **d**." Nm 18:7
Let me die the **d** of the upright, and let Nm 23:10
The murderer shall be put to **d**. Nm 35:16
with a stone tool that could cause **d**, Nm 35:17
The murderer shall be put to **d**. Nm 35:17
with a wooden tool that could cause **d**, Nm 35:18
The murderer shall be put to **d**. Nm 35:18
shall himself put the murderer to **d**; Nm 35:19
he meets him, he shall put him to **d**. Nm 35:19
who struck the blow shall be put to **d**. Nm 35:21
put the murderer to **d** when he meets Nm 35:21
or used a stone that could cause **d**, Nm 35:23
live in it until the **d** of the high priest Nm 35:25
of refuge until the **d** of the high priest, Nm 35:28
but after the **d** of the high priest the Nm 35:28
shall be put to **d** on the evidence of Nm 35:30

shall be put to **d** on the testimony of Nm 35:30
life of a murderer, who is guilty of **d**, Nm 35:31
of death, but he shall be put to **d**. Nm 35:31
the land before the **d** of the high priest. Nm 35:32
out to put them to **d** in the wilderness." Dt 9:28
that dreamer of dreams shall be put to **d**, Dt 13:5
shall be first against him to put him to **d**, Dt 13:9
You shall stone him to **d** with stones, Dt 13:10
that man or woman to **d** with stones. Dt 17:5
the one who is to die shall be put to **d**; Dt 17:6
shall not be put to **d** on the evidence of Dt 17:6
shall be first against him to put him to **d**, Dt 17:7
city shall stone him to **d** with stones. Dt 21:21
a crime punishable by **d** and he is put Dt 21:22
punishable by death and he is put to **d**, Dt 21:22
her city shall stone her to **d** with stones, Dt 22:21
you shall stone them to **d** with stones, Dt 22:24
committed no offense punishable by **d**. Dt 22:26
not be put to **d** because of their Dt 24:16
children be put to **d** because of their Dt 24:16
one shall be put to **d** for his own sin. Dt 24:16
you today life and good, **d** and evil. Dt 30:15
that I have set before you life and **d**, Dt 30:19
the LORD. How much more after my **d**! Dt 31:27
know that after my **d** you will surely Dt 31:29
blessed the people of Israel before his **d**. Dt 33:1
After the **d** of Moses the servant of the Jos 1:1
you command him, shall be put to **d**. Jos 1:18
to them, and deliver our lives from **d**." Jos 2:13
said to her, "Our life for yours even to **d**! Jos 2:14
Joshua struck them and put them to **d**, Jos 10:26
and struck them and put them to **d**. Jos 11:17
until the **d** of him who is high priest at Jos 20:6
After the **d** of Joshua, the people of Israel Jgs 1:1
is a people who risked their lives to the **d**; Jgs 5:18
for him shall be put to **d** by morning. Jgs 6:31
God from the womb to the day of his **d**.'" Jgs 13:7
and urged him, his soul was vexed to **d**. Jgs 16:16
he killed at his **d** were more than those Jgs 16:30
may put them to **d** and purge evil from Jgs 20:13
saying, "He shall surely be put to **d**." Jgs 21:5
also if anything but **d** parts me from Ru 1:17
mother-in-law since the **d** of your Ru 2:11
the will of the LORD to put them to **d**. 1 Sm 2:25
the time of her **d** the women attending 1 Sm 4:20
the men, that we may put them to **d**." 1 Sm 11:12
a man shall be put to **d** this day, 1 Sm 11:13
"Surely the bitterness of **d** is past." 1 Sm 15:32
see Saul again until the day of his **d**, 1 Sm 15:35
LORD lives, he shall not be put to **d**." 1 Sm 19:6
there is but a step between me and **d**." 1 Sm 20:3
father, "Why should he be put to **d**? 1 Sm 20:32
was determined to put David to **d**. 1 Sm 20:33
I have occasioned the **d** of all the 1 Sm 22:22
trap for my life to bring about my **d**?" 1 Sm 28:9
After the **d** of Saul, when David had 2 Sm 1:1
In life and in **d** they were not divided; 2 Sm 1:23
their brother Asahel to **d** in the battle 2 Sm 3:30
king's will to put to **d** Abner the son of 2 Sm 3:37
and put him to **d** and beheaded him. 2 Sm 4:7
Saul had no child to the day of her **d**. 2 Sm 6:23
Two lines he measured to be put to **d**, 2 Sm 8:2
we may put him to **d** for the life of his 2 Sm 14:7
is guilt in me, let him put me to **d**.'" 2 Sm 14:32
shall be, whether for **d** or for life, 2 Sm 15:21
"Shall not Shimei be put to **d** for this, 2 Sm 19:21
anyone be put to **d** in Israel this day? 2 Sm 19:22
but men doomed to **d** before my lord 2 Sm 19:28
were shut up until the day of their **d**, 2 Sm 20:3
because he put the Gibeonites to **d**." 2 Sm 21:1
to put any man to **d** in Israel." And he 2 Sm 21:4
They were put to **d** in the first days of 2 Sm 21:9
"For the waves of **d** encompassed me, 2 Sm 22:5
me; the snares of **d** confronted me. 2 Sm 22:6
put his servant to **d** with the sword.'" 1 Kgs 1:51
'I will not put you to **d** with the sword.' 1 Kgs 2:8
Adonijah shall be put to **d** this day." 1 Kgs 2:24
to your estate, for you deserve **d**. 1 Kgs 2:26
But I will not at this time put you to **d**, 1 Kgs 2:26
struck him down and put him to **d**. 1 Kgs 2:34
means put him to **d**." But the other 1 Kgs 3:26
and by no means put him to **d**; 1 Kgs 3:27
was in Egypt until the **d** of Solomon. 1 Kgs 11:40
Israel stoned him to **d** with stones. 1 Kgs 12:18
and to cause the **d** of my son!" 1 Kgs 17:18
sword of Hazael shall Jehu put to **d**, 1 Kgs 19:17
sword of Jehu shall Elisha put to **d**. 1 Kgs 19:17
take him out and stone him to **d**." 1 Kgs 21:10
city and stoned him to **d** with stones. 1 Kgs 21:13
After the **d** of Ahab, Moab rebelled 2 Kgs 1:1
now on neither **d** nor miscarriage 2 Kgs 2:21
there is **d** in the pot!" And they could 2 Kgs 4:40
king's sons who were being put to **d**, 2 Kgs 11:2
Athaliah, so that he was not put to **d**. 2 Kgs 11:2
approaches the ranks is to be put to **d**. 2 Kgs 11:8

and put to **d** with the sword anyone 2 Kgs 11:15
her not be put to **d** in the house of 2 Kgs 11:15
house, and there she was put to **d**. 2 Kgs 11:16
had been put to **d** with the sword at 2 Kgs 11:20
he did not put to **d** the children of the 2 Kgs 14:6
not be put to **d** because of their 2 Kgs 14:6
children be put to **d** because of their 2 Kgs 14:6
years after the **d** of Jehoash son 2 Kgs 14:17
to Lachish and put him to **d** there. 2 Kgs 14:19
that he was a leper to the day of his **d**, 2 Kgs 15:5
and put him to **d** and reigned in his 2 Kgs 15:10
and put him to **d** and reigned in his 2 Kgs 15:14
he put him to **d** and reigned in his 2 Kgs 15:25
and put him to **d** and reigned in his 2 Kgs 15:30
sick and was at the point of **d**. 2 Kgs 20:1
and put the king to **d** in his house. 2 Kgs 21:23
and put them to **d** at Riblah in the 2 Kgs 25:21
and put him to **d** along with the Jews 2 Kgs 25:25
sight of the LORD, and he put him to **d**. 1 Chr 2:3
After the **d** of Hezron, Caleb went in 1 Chr 2:24
LORD put him to **d** and turned the 1 Chr 10:14
and put to **d** also Shophach the 1 Chr 19:18
in great quantity before his **d**. 1 Chr 22:5
of Israel stoned him to **d** with stones. 2 Chr 10:18
the God of Israel, should be put to **d**, 2 Chr 15:13
For after the **d** of his father they were 2 Chr 22:4
he was brought to Jehu and put to **d**. 2 Chr 22:9
sons who were about to be put to **d**, 2 Chr 22:11
so that she did not put him to **d**. 2 Chr 22:11
enters the house shall be put to **d**. 2 Chr 23:7
is to be put to **d** with the sword." For 2 Chr 23:14
"Do not put her to **d** in the house of 2 Chr 23:14
house, and they put her to **d** there. 2 Chr 23:15
had been put to **d** with the sword. 2 Chr 23:21
died. He was 130 years old at his **d**. 2 Chr 24:15
Now after the **d** of Jehoiada the 2 Chr 24:17
But he did not put their children to **d**, 2 Chr 25:4
fifteen years after the **d** of Joash the 2 Chr 25:25
to Lachish and put him to **d** there. 2 Chr 25:27
was a leper to the day of his **d**, 2 Chr 26:21
sick and was at the point of **d**, 2 Chr 32:24
of Jerusalem did him honor at his **d**. 2 Chr 32:33
him and put him to **d** in his house. 2 Chr 33:24
whether for **d** or for banishment or for Ezr 7:26
there is but one law—to be put to **d**, Est 4:11
who long for **d**, but it comes not, and dig Jb 3:21
In famine he will redeem you from **d**, and Jb 5:20
choose strangling and **d** rather than my Jb 7:15
When disaster brings sudden **d**, he Jb 9:23
the firstborn of **d** consumes his limbs. Jb 18:13
Abaddon and **D** say, 'We have heard a Jb 28:22
you will bring me to **d** and to the house Jb 30:23
the pit, and his life to those who bring **d**. Jb 33:22
Have the gates of **d** been revealed to you, Jb 38:17
For in **d** there is no remembrance of you; Ps 6:5
O you who lift me up from the gates of **d**, Ps 9:13
light up my eyes, lest I sleep the sleep of **d**, Ps 13:3
The cords of **d** encompassed me; the Ps 18:4
me; the snares of **d** confronted me. Ps 18:5
to my jaws; you lay me in the dust of **d**. Ps 22:15
through the valley of the shadow of **d**, Ps 23:4
"What profit is there in my **d**, if I go Ps 30:9
deliver their soul from **d** and keep them Ps 33:19
the righteous and seeks to put him to **d**. Ps 37:32
and covered us with the shadow of **d**. Ps 44:19
D shall be their shepherd, and the Ps 49:14
me; the terrors of **d** have fallen upon me. Ps 55:4
Let **d** steal over them; let them go down Ps 55:15
For you have delivered my soul from **d**, Ps 56:13
the Lord, belong deliverances from **d**. Ps 68:20
For they have no pangs until **d**; their Ps 73:4
he did not spare them from **d**, but gave Ps 78:50
Afflicted and close to **d** from my youth Ps 88:15
What man can live and never see **d**? Ps 89:48
and condemn the innocent to **d**. Ps 94:21
sat in darkness and in the shadow of **d**, Ps 107:10
out of darkness and the shadow of **d**, Ps 107:14
and they drew near to the gates of **d**. Ps 107:18
the brokenhearted, to put them to **d**. Ps 109:16
those who condemn his soul to **d**. Ps 109:31
The snares of **d** encompassed me; the Ps 116:3
For you have delivered my soul from **d**, Ps 116:8
sight of the LORD is the **d** of his saints. Ps 116:15
but he has not given me over to **d**. Ps 118:18
for her house sinks down to **d**, and her Prv 2:18
Her feet go down to **d**; her steps follow the Prv 5:5
Sheol, going down to the chambers of **d**. Prv 7:27
himself; all who hate me love **d**." Prv 8:36
but righteousness delivers from **d**. Prv 10:2
but righteousness delivers from **d**. Prv 11:4
is life, and in its pathway there is no **d**. Prv 12:28
may turn away from the snares of **d**. Prv 13:14
to a man, but its end is the way to **d**. Prv 14:12
may turn away from the snares of **d**. Prv 14:27
but the righteous finds refuge in his **d**. Prv 14:32

A king's wrath is a messenger of **d**, Prv 16:14
to a man, but its end is the way to **d**. Prv 16:25
D and life are in the power of the Prv 18:21
not set your heart on putting him to **d**. Prv 19:18
is a fleeting vapor and a snare of **d**. Prv 21:6
those who are being taken away to **d**; Prv 24:11
who throws firebrands, arrows, and **d** Prv 26:18
of another, he will be a fugitive until **d**; Prv 28:17
and the day of **d** than the day of birth. Eccl 7:1
I find something more bitter than **d**: Eccl 7:26
the spirit, or power over the day of **d**. Eccl 8:8
seal upon your arm, for love is strong as **d**, Sg 8:6
He will swallow up **d** forever; and the Lord Is 25:8
said, "We have made a covenant with **d**, Is 28:15
your covenant with **d** will be annulled, Is 28:18
became sick and was at the point of **d**. Is 38:1
not thank you; **d** does not praise you; Is 38:18
the wicked and with a rich man in his **d**, Is 53:9
out his soul to **d** and was numbered Is 53:12
and the Lord GOD will put you to **d**, Is 65:15
D shall be preferred to life by all the Jer 8:3
For **d** has come up into our windows; it Jer 9:21
May their men meet **d** by pestilence, Jer 18:21
you the way of life and the way of **d**. Jer 21:8
"This man deserves the sentence of **d**, Jer 26:11
for certain that if you put me to **d**, Jer 26:15
man does not deserve the sentence of **d**, Jer 26:16
of Judah and all Judah put him to **d**? Jer 26:19
words, the king sought to put him to **d**. Jer 26:21
given over to the people to be put to **d**. Jer 26:24
to the king, "Let this man be put to **d**, Jer 38:4
you, will you not surely put me to **d**? Jer 38:15
will not put you to **d** or deliver you into Jer 38:16
from us and we will not put you to **d**,' Jer 38:25
who said to Ishmael, "Do not put us to **d**, Jer 41:8
put them to **d** with their companions. Jer 41:8
put him in prison till the day of his **d**. Jer 52:11
and put them to **d** at Riblah in the land Jer 52:27
until the day of his **d** as long as he lived. Jer 52:34
bereaves; in the house it is like **d**. Lam 1:20
putting to **d** souls who should not die Ezk 13:19
I any pleasure in the **d** of the wicked, Ezk 18:23
I have no pleasure in the **d** of anyone, Ezk 18:32
and you shall die the **d** of the slain in Ezk 28:8
shall die the **d** of the uncircumcised Ezk 28:10
For they are all given over to **d**, to the Ezk 31:14
no pleasure in the **d** of the wicked, Ezk 33:11
I will put their beloved children to **d**. Hos 9:16
of Sheol? Shall I redeem them from **D**? Hos 13:14
Shall I redeem them from Death? O **D**, Hos 13:14
as Sheol; like **d** he has never enough. Hab 2:5
and remained there until the **d** of Herod. Mt 2:15
dwelling in the region and shadow of **d**, Mt 4:16
Brother will deliver brother over to **d**, Mt 10:21
against parents and have them put to **d**, Mt 10:21
And though he wanted to put him to **d**, Mt 14:5
who will not taste **d** until they see the Mt 16:28
and they will condemn him to **d** Mt 20:18
wretches to a miserable **d** and let out Mt 21:41
you up to tribulation and put you to **d**, Mt 24:9
"My soul is very sorrowful, even to **d**; Mt 26:38
Jesus that they might put him to **d**, Mt 26:59
They answered, "He deserves **d**." Mt 26:66
counsel against Jesus to put him to **d**. Mt 27:1
"My little daughter is at the point of **d**. Mk 5:23
him and wanted to put him to **d**. Mk 6:19
who will not taste **d** until they see the Mk 9:1
condemn him to **d** and deliver him Mk 10:33
brother will deliver brother over to **d**, Mk 13:12
parents and have them put to **d**. Mk 13:12
"My soul is very sorrowful, even to **d**. Mk 14:34
against Jesus to put him to **d**, Mk 14:55
all condemned him as deserving **d**. Mk 14:64
sit in darkness and in the shadow of **d**, Lk 1:79
he would not see **d** before he had seen Lk 2:26
who was sick and at the point of **d**, Lk 7:2
who will not taste **d** until they see the Lk 9:27
man,' all the people will stone us to **d**, Lk 20:6
and some of you they will put to **d**. Lk 21:16
were seeking how to put him to **d**, Lk 22:2
to go with you both to prison and to **d**." Lk 22:33
nothing deserving **d** has been done by Lk 23:15
found in him no guilt deserving **d**. Lk 23:22
were led away to be put to **d** with him. Lk 23:32
delivered him up to be condemned to **d**, Lk 24:20
heal his son, for he was at the point of **d**. Jn 4:47
judgment, but has passed from **d** to life. Jn 5:24
keeps my word, he will never see **d**." Jn 8:51
keeps my word, he will never taste **d**.' Jn 8:52
it he said, "This illness does not lead to **d**. Jn 11:4
Now Jesus had spoken of his **d**, but they Jn 11:13
day on they made plans to put him to **d**. Jn 11:53
made plans to put Lazarus to **d** as well, Jn 12:10
show by what kind of **d** he was going to Jn 12:33
is not lawful for us to put anyone to **d**." Jn 18:31

show by what kind of **d** he was going to Jn 18:32
by what kind of **d** he was to glorify Jn 21:19
raised him up, loosing the pangs of **d**, Acts 2:24
They put him to **d** by hanging him Acts 10:39
ordered that they should be put to **d**. Acts 12:19
found in him no guilt worthy of **d**, Acts 13:28
I persecuted this Way to the **d**, binding Acts 22:4
nothing deserving **d** or Acts 23:29
to die, I do not seek to escape **d**. Acts 25:11
that he had done nothing deserving **d**. Acts 25:25
when they were put to **d** I cast my vote Acts 26:10
to deserve **d** or imprisonment." Acts 26:31
no reason for the **d** penalty in my Acts 28:18
reconciled to God by the **d** of his Son, Rom 5:10
through one man, and **d** through sin, Rom 5:12
and so **d** spread to all men because all Rom 5:12
Yet **d** reigned from Adam to Moses, Rom 5:14
d reigned through that one man, Rom 5:17
so that, as sin reigned in **d**, grace also Rom 5:21
Christ Jesus were baptized into his **d**? Rom 6:3
therefore with him by baptism into **d**, Rom 6:4
been united with him in a **d** like his, Rom 6:5
d no longer has dominion over him. Rom 6:9
For the **d** he died he died to sin, once Rom 6:10
who have been brought from **d** to life, Rom 6:13
obey, either of sin, which leads to **d**, Rom 6:16
ashamed? The end of those things is **d**. Rom 6:21
For the wages of sin is **d**, but the free Rom 6:23
in our members to bear fruit for **d**. Rom 7:5
that promised life proved to be **d** to me. Rom 7:10
which is good, then, bring **d** to me? Rom 7:13
producing **d** in me through what is Rom 7:13
will deliver me from this body of **d**? Rom 7:24
Christ Jesus from the law of sin and **d**. Rom 8:2
To set the mind on the flesh is **d**, but to Rom 8:6
the Spirit you put to **d** the deeds of the Rom 8:13
For I am sure that neither **d** nor life, Rom 8:38
the world or life or **d** or the present or 1 Cor 3:22
as last of all, like men sentenced to **d**, 1 Cor 4:9
proclaim the Lord's **d** until he 1 Cor 11:26
For as by a man came **d**, by a man 1 Cor 15:21
The last enemy to be destroyed is **d**. 1 Cor 15:26
"**D** is swallowed up in victory." 1 Cor 15:54
"O **d**, where is your victory? O death, 1 Cor 15:55
"O death, where is your victory? O **d**, 1 Cor 15:55
The sting of **d** is sin, and the power 1 Cor 15:56
that we had received the sentence of **d**. 2 Cor 1:9
to one a fragrance from **d** to death, to 2 Cor 2:16
to one a fragrance from death to **d**, to 2 Cor 2:16
Now if the ministry of **d**, carved in 2 Cor 3:7
carrying in the body the **d** of Jesus, 2 Cor 4:10
being given over to **d** for Jesus' sake, 2 Cor 4:11
So **d** is at work in us, but life in you. 2 Cor 4:12
whereas worldly grief produces **d**. 2 Cor 7:10
countless beatings, and often near **d**. 2 Cor 11:23
in my body, whether by life or by **d**. Phil 1:20
by becoming obedient to the point of **d**, Phil 2:8
to the point of death, even **d** on a cross. Phil 2:8
Indeed he was ill, near to **d**. But God Phil 2:27
sufferings, becoming like him in his **d**, Phil 3:10
reconciled in his body of flesh by his **d**, Col 1:22
Put to **d** therefore what is earthly in you: Col 3:5
who abolished **d** and brought life and 2 Tm 1:10
and honor because of the suffering of **d**, Heb 2:9
of God he might taste **d** for everyone. Heb 2:9
that through **d** he might destroy the Heb 2:14
destroy the one who has the power of **d**, Heb 2:14
who through fear of **d** were subject to Heb 2:15
to him who was able to save him from **d**, Heb 5:7
were prevented by **d** from continuing Heb 7:23
since a **d** has occurred that redeems Heb 9:15
the **d** of the one who made it must be Heb 9:16
For a will takes effect only at **d**, since it Heb 9:17
taken up so that he should not see **d**, Heb 11:5
sin when it is fully grown brings forth **d**. Jas 1:15
save his soul from **d** and will cover a Jas 5:20
being put to **d** in the flesh but made 1 Pt 3:18
that we have passed out of **d** into life, 1 Jn 3:14
Whoever does not love abides in **d**. 1 Jn 3:14
committing a sin not leading to **d**, 1 Jn 5:16
who commit sins that do not lead to **d**. 1 Jn 5:16
There is sin that leads to **d**; I do not say 1 Jn 5:16
but there is sin that does not lead to **d**. 1 Jn 5:17
and I have the keys of **D** and Hades. Rv 1:18
Be faithful unto **d**, and I will give you the Rv 2:10
will not be hurt by the second **d**.' Rv 2:11
And its rider's name was **D**, and Hades Rv 6:8
days people will seek **d** and will not find Rv 9:6
will long to die, but **d** will flee from them. Rv 9:6
they loved not their lives even unto **d**. Rv 12:11
single day, **d** and mourning and famine, Rv 18:8
Over such the second **d** has no power, Rv 20:6
D and Hades gave up the dead who were Rv 20:13
Then **D** and Hades were thrown into Rv 20:14
This is the second **d**, the lake of fire. Rv 20:14
from their eyes, and **d** shall be no more, Rv 21:4
fire and sulfur, which is the second **d**." Rv 21:8

DEATHLY (1)
there was a **d** panic throughout the 1 Sm 5:11

DEBASED (1)
gave them up to a **d** mind to do what Rom 1:28

DEBATE (2)
no small dissension and **d** with them, Acts 15:2
And after there had been much **d**, Acts 15:7

DEBATER (1)
the scribe? Where is the **d** of this age? 1 Cor 1:20

DEBAUCHERY (3)
not get drunk with wine, for that is **d**, Eph 5:18
to the charge of **d** or insubordination. Ti 1:6
do not join them in the same flood of **d**, 1 Pt 4:4

DEBIR (14)
king of Lachish, and to **D** king of Eglon, Jos 10:3
turned back to **D** and fought against Jos 10:38
its king, so he did to **D** and to its king. Jos 10:39
the hill country, from Hebron, from **D**, Jos 11:21
the king of **D**, one; the king of Geder, Jos 12:13
from Mahanaim to the territory of **D**, Jos 13:26
boundary goes up to **D** from the Valley Jos 15:7
there against the inhabitants of **D**. Jos 15:15
the name of **D** formerly was Jos 15:15
Dannah, Kiriath-sannah (that is, **D**), Jos 15:49
pasturelands, **D** with its pasturelands, Jos 21:15
they went against the inhabitants of **D**. Jgs 1:11
The name of **D** was formerly Jgs 1:11
D with its pasturelands, 1 Chr 6:58

DEBORAH (10)
And **D**, Rebekah's nurse, died, and she Gn 35:8
Now **D**, a prophetess, the wife of Jgs 4:4
under the palm of **D** between Ramah and Jgs 4:5
of a woman." Then **D** arose and went Jgs 4:9
up at his heels, and **D** went up with him. Jgs 4:10
And **D** said to Barak, "Up! For this is the Jgs 4:14
Then sang **D** and Barak the son of Jgs 5:1
I arose; I, **D**, arose as a mother in Israel. Jgs 5:7
"Awake, awake, **D**! Awake, awake, Jgs 5:12
the princes of Issachar came with **D**, Jgs 5:15

DEBT (9)
distress, and everyone who was in **d**, 1 Sm 22:2
year and the exaction of every **d**. Neh 10:31
released him and forgave him the **d**. Mt 18:27
in prison until he should pay the **d**. Mt 18:30
you all that **d** because you pleaded Mt 18:32
the jailers, until he should pay all his **d**. Mt 18:34
not pay, he cancelled the **d** of both. Lk 7:42
he cancelled the larger **d**." And he said to Lk 7:43
the record of **d** that stood against Col 2:14

DEBTOR (2)
as with the creditor, so with the **d**. Is 24:2
anyone, but restores to the **d** his pledge, Ezk 18:7

DEBTORS (5)
Will not your **d** suddenly arise, and Hab 2:7
debts, as we also have forgiven our **d**. Mt 6:12
"A certain moneylender had two **d**. One Lk 7:41
summoning his master's **d** one by one, Lk 16:5
So then, brothers, we are **d**, not to the Rom 8:12

DEBTS (3)
he said, "Go, sell the oil and pay your **d**, 2 Kgs 4:7
give pledges, who put up security for **d**. Prv 22:26
and forgive us our **d**, as we also have Mt 6:12

DECAPOLIS (3)
followed him from Galilee and the **D**, Mt 4:25
to proclaim in the **D** how much Jesus Mk 5:20
the Sea of Galilee, in the region of the **D**. Mk 7:31

DECAY (1)
from its bondage to **d** and obtain the Rom 8:21

DECEIT (35)
to evil, and their womb prepares **d**." Jb 15:35
and my tongue will not utter **d**. Jb 27:4
falsehood and my foot has hastened to **d**; Jb 31:5
filled with cursing and **d** and oppression; Ps 10:7
Give ear to my prayer from lips free of **d**! Ps 17:1
and in whose spirit there is no **d**. Ps 32:2
evil and your lips from speaking **d**. Ps 34:13
quiet in the land they devise words of **d**. Ps 35:20
words of his mouth are trouble and **d**; Ps 36:3
rein for evil, and your tongue frames **d**. Ps 50:19
like a sharp razor, you worker of **d**. Ps 52:2
No one who practices **d** shall dwell in Ps 101:7
evidence, but a false witness utters **d**. Prv 12:17
D is in the heart of those who devise Prv 12:20
Bread gained by **d** is sweet to a man, Prv 20:17
his lips and harbors **d** in his heart; Prv 26:24
and there was no **d** in his mouth. Is 53:9
of transgression, the offspring of **d**, Is 57:4
full of birds, their houses are full of **d**; Jer 5:27
They hold fast to **d**; they refuse to return. Jer 8:5
upon oppression, and **d** upon deceit, Jer 9:6
upon oppression, and deceit upon **d**, Jer 9:6
and the **d** of their own minds. Jer 14:14
and who prophesy the **d** of their own Jer 23:26
he shall make **d** prosper under his Dn 8:25
lies, and the house of Israel with **d**, Hos 11:12
coveting, wickedness, **d**, sensuality, Mk 7:22
Israelite indeed, in whom there is no **d**!" Jn 1:47
full of all **d** and villainy, Acts 13:10
envy, murder, strife, **d**, maliciousness. Rom 1:29
say, and got the better of you by **d**. 2 Cor 12:16
you captive by philosophy and empty **d**, Col 2:8
all malice and all **d** and hypocrisy and 1 Pt 2:1
sin, neither was **d** found in his mouth. 1 Pt 2:22
from evil and his lips from speaking **d**; 1 Pt 3:10

DECEITFUL (20)
LORD abhors the bloodthirsty and **d** man. Ps 5:6
from the **d** and unjust man deliver me! Ps 43:1
love all words that devour, O **d** tongue. Ps 52:4
their fathers; they twisted like a **d** bow. Ps 78:57
For wicked and **d** mouths are opened Ps 109:2
LORD, from lying lips, from a **d** tongue. Ps 120:2
shall be done to you, you **d** tongue? Ps 120:3
just; the counsels of the wicked are **d**. Prv 12:5
but one who breathes out lies is **d**. Prv 14:25
Charm is **d**, and beauty is vain, but a Prv 31:30
Will you be to me like a **d** brook, like Jer 15:18
The heart is **d** above all things, and Jer 17:9
of Achzib shall be a **d** thing to the kings Mi 1:14
scales and with a bag of **d** weights? Mi 6:11
and their tongue is **d** in their mouth. Mi 6:12
be found in their mouth a **d** tongue. Zep 3:13
men are false apostles, **d** workmen, 2 Cor 11:13
cunning, by craftiness in **d** schemes. Eph 4:14
of life and is corrupt through **d** desires, Eph 4:22
devoting themselves to **d** spirits and 1 Tm 4:1

DECEITFULLY (7)
But he said, "Your brother came **d**, and Gn 27:35
Shechem and his father Hamor **d**, Gn 34:13
falsely for God and speak **d** for him? Jb 13:7
soul to what is false and does not swear **d**. Ps 24:4
tongue is a deadly arrow; it speaks **d**; Jer 9:8
is made with him he shall act **d**, Dn 11:23
great and deal **d** with false balances, Am 8:5

DECEITFULNESS (3)
the world and the **d** of riches choke the Mt 13:22
of the world and the **d** of riches and the Mk 4:19
of you may be hardened by the **d** of sin. Heb 3:13

DECEIVE (24)
and he said to them, "Why did you **d** us, Jos 9:22
son of Ner came to **d** you and to know 2 Sm 3:25
a son? Did I not say, 'Do not **d** me?'" 2 Kgs 4:28
'Do not let Hezekiah **d** you, for he 2 Kgs 18:29
whom you trust **d** you by promising 2 Kgs 19:10
do not let Hezekiah **d** you or mislead 2 Chr 32:15
Or can you **d** him, as one deceives a Jb 13:9
cause, and do not **d** with your lips. Prv 24:28
'Do not let Hezekiah **d** you, for he will Is 36:14
in whom you trust **d** you by promising Is 37:10
your diviners who are among you **d** you, Jer 29:8
Thus says the LORD, Do not **d** yourselves, Jer 37:9
not put on a hairy cloak in order to **d**, Zec 13:4
use their tongues to **d**." "The venom of Rom 3:13
talk and flattery they **d** the hearts of Rom 16:18
Let no one **d** himself. If anyone 1 Cor 3:18
Let no one **d** you with empty words, for Eph 5:6
error or impurity or any attempt to **d**, 1 Thes 2:3
Let no one **d** you in any way. For that 2 Thes 2:3
If we say we have no sin, we **d** ourselves, 1 Jn 1:8
about those who are trying to **d** you. 1 Jn 2:26
Little children, let no one **d** you. 1 Jn 3:7
that he might not **d** the nations any Rv 20:3
will come out to **d** the nations that are Rv 20:8

DECEIVED (31)
The woman said, "The serpent **d** me, Gn 3:13
for Rachel? Why then have you **d** me?" Gn 29:25
Take care lest your heart be **d**, and you Dt 11:16
"Why have you **d** me thus and let 1 Sm 19:17
said to Saul, "Why have you **d** me? 1 Sm 28:12
"My lord, O king, my servant **d** me, 2 Sm 19:26
wisdom; the **d** and the deceiver are his. Jb 12:16
surely you have utterly **d** this people and Jer 4:10
O LORD, you have **d** me, and I was Jer 20:7
LORD, you have deceived me, and I was **d**; Jer 20:7
"Perhaps he will be **d**; then we can Jer 20:10
trusted friends have **d** you and Jer 38:22
The horror you inspire has **d** you, and Jer 49:16
"I called to my lovers, but they **d** me; Lam 1:19
if the prophet is **d** and speaks a word, Ezk 14:9
a word, I, the LORD, have **d** that prophet, Ezk 14:9
The pride of your heart has **d** you, you Ob 1:3

those at peace with you have **d** you; Ob 1:7
answered them, "Have you also been **d**? Jn 7:47
d me and through it killed me. Rom 7:11
Do not be **d**: neither the sexually 1 Cor 6:9
Do not be **d**: "Bad company ruins 1 Cor 15:33
that as the serpent **d** Eve by his 2 Cor 11:3
Do not be **d**: God is not mocked, for Gal 6:7
and Adam was not **d**, but the woman 1 Tm 2:14
but the woman was **d** and became a 1 Tm 2:14
bad to worse, deceiving and being **d**. 2 Tm 3:13
Do not be **d**, my beloved brothers. Jas 1:16
and all nations were **d** by your sorcery. Rv 18:23
signs by which he **d** those who had Rv 19:20
the devil who had **d** them was thrown Rv 20:10

DECEIVER (4)
wisdom; the deceived and the **d** are his. Jb 12:16
in any brother, for every brother is a **d**, Jer 9:4
Such a one is the **d** and the antichrist. 2 Jn 1:7
the **d** of the whole world—he was thrown Rv 12:9

DECEIVERS (2)
are insubordinate, empty talkers and **d**, Ti 1:10
For many **d** have gone out into the 2 Jn 1:7

DECEIVES (6)
Or can you deceive him, as one **d** a man? Jb 13:9
is the man who **d** his neighbor and Prv 26:19
Everyone **d** his neighbor, and no one Jer 9:5
when he is nothing, he **d** himself. Gal 6:3
not bridle his tongue but **d** his heart, Jas 1:26
of the beast it **d** those who dwell on Rv 13:14

DECEIVING (5)
against the LORD by **d** his neighbor in a Lv 6:2
him not trust in emptiness, **d** himself, Jb 15:31
his way, but the folly of fools is **d**. Prv 14:8
bad to worse, **d** and being deceived. 2 Tm 3:13
word, and not hearers only, **d** yourselves. Jas 1:22

DECENTLY (1)
should be done **d** and in order. 1 Cor 14:40

DECEPTION (2)
though his hatred be covered with **d**, Prv 26:26
and with all wicked **d** for those who 2 Thes 2:10

DECEPTIONS (1)
and blemishes, reveling in their **d**, 2 Pt 2:13

DECEPTIVE (5)
The wicked earns **d** wages, but one Prv 11:18
desire his delicacies, for they are **d** food. Prv 23:3
Do not trust in these **d** words: 'This is the Jer 7:4
"Behold, you trust in **d** words to no avail. Jer 7:8
have seen for you false and **d** visions; Lam 2:14

DECIDE (16)
that they may **d** between us two. Gn 31:37
to me and I **d** between one person and Ex 18:16
small matter they shall **d** themselves. Ex 18:22
court and the judges **d** between them, Dt 25:1
d this day between the people of Israel Jgs 11:27
and **d** what answer I shall return to 2 Sm 24:13
Now **d** what answer I shall return to 1 Chr 21:12
for the LORD and to **d** disputed cases. 2 Chr 19:8
You will **d** on a matter, and it will be Jb 22:28
and shall **d** disputes for many peoples; Is 2:4
see, or **d** disputes by what his ears hear, Is 11:3
and **d** with equity for the meek of the Is 11:4
and shall **d** for strong nations afar off; Mi 4:3
for them, to **d** what each should take. Mk 15:24
comes down, I will **d** your case." Acts 24:22
but rather **d** never to put a stumbling Rom 14:13

DECIDED (15)
any small matter they **d** themselves. Ex 18:26
I have **d**: you and Ziba shall divide 2 Sm 19:29
be; you yourself have **d** it." 1 Kgs 20:40
After this Joash **d** to restore the house 2 Chr 24:4
I have **d** what to do, so that when I am Lk 16:4
So Pilate **d** that their demand should be Lk 23:24
The next day Jesus **d** to go to Galilee. He Jn 1:43
of Pilate, when he had **d** to release him. Acts 3:13
he **d** to return through Macedonia. Acts 20:3
For Paul had **d** to sail past Ephesus, Acts 20:16
I **d** to go ahead and send him. Acts 25:25
And when it was **d** that we should sail Acts 27:1
the majority **d** to put out to sea from Acts 27:12
For I **d** to know nothing among you 1 Cor 2:2
for I have **d** to spend the winter there. Ti 3:12

DECIDES (2)
to do whatever my lord the king **d**." 2 Sm 15:15
to quarrels and **d** between powerful Prv 18:18

DECISION (13)
case arises requiring **d** between one kind Dt 17:8
them, and they shall declare to you the **d**. Dt 17:9
according to the **d** which they Dt 17:11
in giving this **d** the king convicts 2 Sm 14:13
So Jehu said, "If this is your **d**, then let 2 Kgs 9:15
lap, but its every **d** is from the LORD. Prv 16:33
the **d** by the word of the holy ones, Dn 4:17
Multitudes, multitudes, in the valley of **d**! Jl 3:14
day of the LORD is near in the valley of **d**. Jl 3:14
For my **d** is to gather nations, to Zep 3:8
What is your **d**?" And they all Mk 14:64
not consented to their **d** and action; Lk 23:51
in custody for the **d** of the emperor, Acts 25:21

DECISIONS (1)
for observance the **d** that had been Acts 16:4

DECK (2)
the valleys **d** themselves with grain, Ps 65:13
they made your **d** of pines from the Ezk 27:6

DECKS (2)
Make it with lower, second, and third **d**. Gn 6:16
as a bridegroom **d** himself like a priest Is 61:10

DECLARATION (1)
my words, and let my **d** be in your ears. Jb 13:17

DECLARE (83)
that time, to **d** to you the word of the LORD. Dt 5:5
and they shall **d** to you the decision. Dt 17:9
according to what they **d** to you from Dt 17:10
from the verdict that they **d** to you, Dt 17:11
'I **d** today to the LORD your God that I Dt 26:3
And the Levites shall **d** to all the men of Dt 27:14
I **d** to you today, that you shall surely Dt 30:18
And I **d** to him that I am about to 1 Sm 3:13
anoint for me him whom I **d** to you." 1 Sm 16:3
D his glory among the nations, his 1 Chr 16:24
I **d** to you that the LORD will build 1 Chr 17:10
you; and the fish of the sea will **d** to you. Jb 12:8
hear me, and what I have seen I will **d** Jb 15:17
timid and afraid to **d** my opinion to you. Jb 32:6
'Listen to me; let me also **d** my opinion.' Jb 32:10
with my share; I also will **d** my opinion. Jb 32:17
My words **d** the uprightness of my heart, Jb 33:3
to **d** to man what is right for him, Jb 33:23
and not I; therefore **d** what you know. Jb 34:33
presence; the cattle also **d** that he rises. Jb 36:33
of the earth? **D**, if you know all this. Jb 38:18
The heavens **d** the glory of God, and the Ps 19:1
D me innocent from hidden faults. Ps 19:12
The heavens **d** his righteousness, for God Ps 50:6
lips, and my mouth will **d** your praise. Ps 51:15
But I will **d** it forever; I will sing praises to Ps 75:9
to **d** your steadfast love in the morning, Ps 92:2
to **d** that the LORD is upright; he is my Ps 92:15
D his glory among the nations, his Ps 96:3
that they may **d** in Zion the name of Ps 102:21
deeds of the LORD, or **d** all his praise? Ps 106:2
With my lips I **d** all the rules of your Ps 119:13
another, and shall **d** your mighty acts. Ps 145:4
deeds, and I will **d** your greatness. Ps 145:6
outcome; or **d** to us the things to come. Is 41:22
come to pass, and new things I now **d**; Is 42:9
LORD, and **d** his praise in the coastlands. Is 42:12
Who among them can **d** this, and show Is 43:9
for myself that they might **d** my praise. Is 43:21
Let him **d** and set it before me, since I Is 44:7
Let them **d** what is to come, and what will Is 44:7
LORD speak the truth; I **d** what is right. Is 45:19
D and present your case; let them take Is 45:21
now see all this; and will you not **d** it? Is 48:6
from Chaldea, **d** this with a shout of joy, Is 48:20
Lord GOD helps me; who will **d** me guilty? Is 50:9
I will **d** your righteousness and your Is 57:12
d to my people their transgression, to the Is 58:1
And they shall **d** my glory among the Is 66:19
And I will **d** my judgments against Jer 1:16
D in Judah, and proclaim in Jerusalem, Jer 4:5
D this in the house of Jacob; proclaim it Jer 5:20
of the LORD spoken, that he may **d** it? Jer 9:12
If at any time I **d** concerning a nation or Jer 18:7
if at any time I **d** concerning a nation or Jer 18:9
the LORD, who use their tongues and **d**, Jer 23:31
and **d** it in the coastlands far away; Jer 31:10
the LORD our God says **d** to us and we Jer 42:20
"**D** in Egypt, and proclaim in Migdol; Jer 46:14
"**D** among the nations and proclaim, set Jer 50:2
to **d** in Zion the vengeance of the LORD Jer 50:28
let us **d** in Zion the work of the LORD Jer 51:10
that they may **d** all their Ezk 12:16
Then **d** to her all her abominations. Ezk 22:2
D to them their abominations. Ezk 23:36
jealousy and in my blazing wrath I **d**, Ezk 38:19
D all that you see to the house of Israel." Ezk 40:4
but **d** war against him who puts nothing Mi 3:5
to **d** to Jacob his transgression and to Mi 3:8
today I **d** that I will restore to you Zec 9:12
And then will I **d** to them, 'I never knew Mt 7:23
and **d** how much God has done for you." Lk 8:39
and I **d** to the world what I have heard Jn 8:26
and he will **d** to you the things that are Jn 16:13
will take what is mine and **d** it to you. Jn 16:14
will take what is mine and **d** it to you. Jn 16:15
he will **d** to you a message by which Acts 11:14
will worship God and **d** that God is 1 Cor 14:25
in chains, that I may **d** it boldly, Eph 6:20
for the word, to **d** the mystery of Christ, Col 4:3
in our God to **d** to you the gospel 1 Thes 2:2
For this we **d** to you by a word from 1 Thes 4:15
D these things; exhort and rebuke with Ti 2:15

DECLARED (50)
all that is in the house be **d** unclean. Lv 14:36
Thus Moses **d** to the people of Israel the Lv 23:44
And he **d** to you his covenant, which he Dt 4:13
You have **d** today that the LORD is your Dt 26:17
And the LORD has **d** today that you are a Dt 26:18
And you have **d** this day how you 1 Sm 24:18
David my father what you **d** to him. 1 Kgs 8:24
as you **d** through Moses your servant, 1 Kgs 8:53
the LORD has **d** disaster for you." 1 Kgs 22:23
David my father what you **d** to him. 2 Chr 6:15
The LORD has **d** disaster concerning 2 Chr 18:22
the words that were **d** to them. Neh 8:12
of the country **d** themselves Jews, Est 8:17
and plentifully **d** sound knowledge! Jb 26:3
then he saw it and **d** it; he established it, Jb 28:27
although they had **d** Job to be in the Jb 32:3
Is your steadfast love **d** in the grave, or Ps 88:11
Who **d** it from the beginning, that we Is 41:26
There was none who **d** it, none who Is 41:26
I **d** and saved and proclaimed, when Is 43:12
have I not told you from of old and **d** it? Is 44:8
Who told this long ago? Who **d** it of old? Is 45:21
"The former things I **d** of old; they went Is 48:3
I **d** them to you from of old, before they Is 48:5
who among them has **d** these things? Is 48:14
And I have this day **d** it to you, but you Jer 42:21
your wives have **d** with your mouths, Jer 44:25
He **d** to Arioch, the king's captain, Dn 2:15
They **d** to King Nebuchadnezzar, "O Dn 3:9
He **d** to his counselors, "Did we not cast Dn 3:24
door of the burning fiery furnace; he **d**, Dn 3:26
The king **d** to the wise men of Babylon, Dn 5:7
the banqueting hall, and the queen **d**, Dn 5:10
the den of lions. The king **d** to Daniel, Dn 6:16
a tone of anguish. The king **d** to Daniel, Dn 6:20
Daniel **d**, "I saw in my vision by night, Dn 7:2
At that time Jesus **d**, "I thank you, Mt 11:25
expelled?" (Thus he **d** all foods clean.) Mk 7:19
Spirit, **d**, "'The Lord said to my Lord, Mk 12:36
the tax collectors too, they **d** God just, Lk 7:29
down before him **d** in the presence Lk 8:47
to the apostles and **d** to them how on Acts 9:27
and extolling God. Then Peter **d**, Acts 10:46
they **d** all that God had done with Acts 14:27
and they **d** all that God had done with Acts 15:4
but **d** first to those in Damascus, then Acts 26:20
and was **d** to be the Son of God in power Rom 1:4
since the message **d** by angels proved Heb 2:2
It was **d** at first by the Lord, and it was Heb 2:3
of the law had been **d** by Moses to all Heb 9:19

DECLARES (376)
"By myself I have sworn, **d** the LORD, Gn 22:16
Say to them, 'As I live, **d** the LORD, Nm 14:28
Therefore the LORD the God of Israel **d**: 1 Sm 2:30
me forever,' but now the LORD **d**: 1 Sm 2:30
the LORD **d** to you that the LORD will 2 Sm 7:11
blood of his sons—**d** the LORD—I will 2 Kgs 9:26
not come into this city, **d** the LORD. 2 Kgs 19:33
I also have heard you, **d** the LORD. 2 Kgs 22:19
I also have heard you, **d** the LORD. 2 Chr 34:27
Who **d** his way to his face, and who Jb 21:31
then he **d** to them their work and their Jb 36:9
Its crashing **d** his presence; the cattle Jb 36:33
He **d** his word to Jacob, his statutes Ps 147:19
The man **d**, I am weary, O God; I am Prv 30:1
Therefore the Lord **d**, the LORD of hosts, Is 1:24
the face of the poor?" **d** the Lord GOD of Is 3:15
rise up against them," **d** the LORD of Is 14:22
the broom of destruction," **d** the LORD of Is 14:23
the children of Israel, **d** the LORD of hosts. Is 17:3
of a fruit tree, **d** the LORD God of Israel. Is 17:6
rule over them, **d** the Lord GOD of hosts. Is 19:4
In that day, **d** the LORD of hosts, the peg Is 22:25
"Ah, stubborn children," **d** the LORD, Is 30:1
desert the standard in panic," **d** the LORD, Is 31:9
shall not come into this city, **d** the LORD. Is 37:34
I am the one who helps you, **d** the LORD; Is 41:14
"You are my witnesses," **d** the LORD, "and Is 43:10
and you are my witnesses," **d** the LORD, Is 43:12
As I live, **d** the LORD, you shall put them Is 49:18
therefore what have I here," **d** the LORD, Is 52:5
Their rulers wail," **d** the LORD, "and Is 52:5
their vindication from me, **d** the LORD." Is 54:17
are your ways my ways, **d** the LORD. Is 55:8

of Israel, **d**, "I will gather yet others to him Is 56:8
turn from transgression," **d** the LORD. Is 59:20
so all these things came to be, **d** the LORD. Is 66:2
come to an end together, **d** the LORD. Is 66:17
come to worship before me, **d** the LORD. Is 66:23
I am with you to deliver you, **d** the LORD." Jer 1:8
of the kingdoms of the north, **d** the LORD, Jer 1:15
you, for I am with you, **d** the LORD, Jer 1:19
disaster came upon them, **d** the LORD." Jer 2:3
I still contend with you, **d** the LORD, Jer 2:9
shocked, be utterly desolate, **d** the LORD, Jer 2:12
me is not in you, **d** the Lord GOD of hosts. Jer 2:19
guilt is still before me, **d** the Lord GOD. Jer 2:22
all transgressed against me, **d** the LORD. Jer 2:29
and would you return to me? **d** the LORD. Jer 3:1
whole heart, but in pretense, **d** the LORD." Jer 3:10
say, "'Return, faithless Israel, **d** the LORD. Jer 3:12
in anger, for I am merciful, **d** the LORD; Jer 3:12
have not obeyed my voice, **d** the LORD. Jer 3:13
Return, O faithless children, **d** the LORD; Jer 3:14
in the land, in those days, **d** the LORD, Jer 3:16
to me, O house of Israel, **d** the LORD.'" Jer 3:20
"If you return, O Israel, **d** the LORD, to me Jer 4:1
"In that day, **d** the LORD, courage shall fail Jer 4:9
For a voice **d** from Dan and proclaims Jer 4:15
she has rebelled against me, **d** the LORD. Jer 4:17
d the LORD; and shall I not avenge myself Jer 5:9
utterly treacherous to me, **d** the LORD. Jer 5:11
from afar, O house of Israel, **d** the LORD. Jer 5:15
"But even in those days, **d** the LORD, I will Jer 5:18
d the LORD; Do you not tremble before Jer 5:22
d the LORD, and shall I not avenge myself Jer 5:29
the inhabitants of the land," **d** the LORD. Jer 6:12
Behold, I myself have seen it, **d** the LORD. Jer 7:11
have done all these things, **d** the LORD, Jer 7:13
Is it I whom they provoke? **d** the LORD. Is Jer 7:19
have done evil in my sight, **d** the LORD. Jer 7:30
behold, the days are coming, **d** the LORD, Jer 7:32
"At that time, **d** the LORD, the bones of the Jer 8:1
I have driven them, **d** the LORD of hosts. Jer 8:3
When I would gather them, **d** the LORD, Jer 8:13
and they shall bite you," **d** the LORD. Jer 8:17
evil, and they do not know me, **d** the LORD. Jer 9:3
deceit, they refuse to know me, **d** the LORD. Jer 9:6
d the LORD, and shall I not avenge myself Jer 9:9
Speak, "Thus **d** the LORD: 'The dead Jer 9:22
For in these things I delight, **d** the LORD." Jer 9:24
"Behold, the days are coming, **d** the LORD, Jer 9:25
pluck it up and destroy it, **d** the LORD." Jer 12:17
house of Judah cling to me, **d** the LORD, Jer 13:11
fathers and sons together, **d** the LORD. Jer 13:14
I have measured out to you, **d** the LORD, Jer 13:25
four kinds of destroyers, **d** the LORD: Jer 15:3
You have rejected me, **d** the LORD; you Jer 15:6
sword before their enemies, **d** the LORD." Jer 15:9
to save you and deliver you, **d** the LORD. Jer 15:20
my steadfast love and mercy, **d** the LORD. Jer 16:5
fathers have forsaken me, **d** the LORD, Jer 16:11
the days are coming, **d** the LORD, Jer 16:14
sending for many fishers, **d** the LORD, Jer 16:16
"'But if you listen to me, **d** the LORD, and Jer 17:24
you as this potter has done? **d** the LORD. Jer 18:6
behold, days are coming, **d** the LORD, Jer 19:6
Thus will I do to this place, **d** the LORD, Jer 19:12
Afterward, **d** the LORD, I will give Jer 21:7
for harm and not for good, **d** the LORD: Jer 21:10
valley, O rock of the plain, **d** the LORD; Jer 21:13
to the fruit of your deeds, **d** the LORD; Jer 21:14
words, I swear by myself, **d** the LORD, Jer 22:5
well. Is not this to know me? **d** the LORD. Jer 22:16
"As I live, **d** the LORD, though Coniah Jer 22:24
the sheep of my pasture!" **d** the LORD. Jer 23:1
to you for your evil deeds, **d** the LORD. Jer 23:2
neither shall any be missing, **d** the LORD. Jer 23:4
"Behold, the days are coming, **d** the LORD, Jer 23:5
behold, the days are coming, **d** the LORD, Jer 23:7
I have found their evil, **d** the LORD. Jer 23:11
year of their punishment, **d** the LORD. Jer 23:12
"Am I a God at hand, **d** the LORD, and Jer 23:23
so that I cannot see him? **d** the LORD. Jer 23:24
I not fill heaven and earth? **d** the LORD. Jer 23:24
in common with wheat? **d** the LORD. Jer 23:28
Is not my word like fire, **d** the LORD, and Jer 23:29
I am against the prophets, **d** the LORD, Jer 23:30
I am against the prophets, **d** the LORD, Jer 23:31
their tongues and declare, '**d** the LORD.' Jer 23:31
who prophesy lying dreams, **d** the LORD, Jer 23:32
not profit this people at all, **d** the LORD. Jer 23:32
and I will cast you off, **d** the LORD.' Jer 23:33
you have not listened to me, **d** the LORD, Jer 25:7
for all the tribes of the north, **d** the LORD, Jer 25:9
for their iniquity, **d** the LORD, Jer 25:12
of the earth, **d** the LORD of hosts.' Jer 25:29
he will put to the sword, **d** the LORD.' Jer 25:31
famine, and with pestilence, **d** the LORD, Jer 27:8
to work it and dwell there, **d** the LORD."'" Jer 27:11
I have not sent them, **d** the LORD, but Jer 27:15
the day when I visit them, **d** the LORD. Jer 27:22
Judah who went to Babylon, **d** the LORD, Jer 28:4
name; I did not send them, **d** the LORD. Jer 29:9
the plans I have for you, **d** the LORD, Jer 29:11
I will be found by you, **d** the LORD, and I Jer 29:14
where I have driven you, **d** the LORD, Jer 29:14
pay attention to my words, **d** the LORD, Jer 29:19
but you would not listen, **d** the LORD.' Jer 29:19
knows, and I am witness, **d** the LORD.'" Jer 29:23
that I will do to my people, **d** the LORD, Jer 29:32
For behold, days are coming, **d** the LORD, Jer 30:3
to pass in that day, **d** the LORD of hosts, Jer 30:8
not, O Jacob my servant, **d** the LORD, Jer 30:10
I am with you to save you, **d** the LORD; Jer 30:11
and your wounds I will heal, **d** the LORD, Jer 30:17
of himself to approach me? **d** the LORD. Jer 30:21
"At that time, **d** the LORD, I will be the Jer 31:1
satisfied with my goodness, **d** the LORD." Jer 31:14
is a reward for your work, **d** the LORD, Jer 31:16
is hope for your future, **d** the LORD, Jer 31:17
surely have mercy on him, **d** the LORD. Jer 31:20
the days are coming, **d** the LORD, Jer 31:27
them to build and to plant, **d** the LORD. Jer 31:28
the days are coming, **d** the LORD, Jer 31:31
though I was their husband, **d** the LORD. Jer 31:32
of Israel after those days, **d** the LORD: Jer 31:33
least of them to the greatest, **d** the LORD. Jer 31:34
departs from before me, **d** the LORD, Jer 31:36
for all that they have done, **d** the LORD." Jer 31:37
the days are coming, **d** the LORD, Jer 31:38
remain until I visit him, **d** the LORD. Jer 32:5
by the work of their hands, **d** the LORD. Jer 32:30
I will restore their fortunes, **d** the LORD." Jer 32:44
the days are coming, **d** the LORD, Jer 33:14
For I have spoken the word, **d** the LORD." Jer 34:5
to pestilence, and to famine, **d** the LORD. Jer 34:17
Behold, I will command, **d** the LORD, Jer 34:22
and listen to my words? **d** the LORD. Jer 35:13
will deliver you on that day, **d** the LORD, Jer 39:17
have put your trust in me, **d** the LORD.'" Jer 39:18
Do not fear him, **d** the LORD, for I am Jer 42:11
shall be the sign to you, **d** the LORD, Jer 44:29
disaster upon all flesh, **d** the LORD. Jer 45:5
back—terror on every side! **d** the LORD. Jer 46:5
"As I live, **d** the King, whose name is the Jer 46:18
shall cut down her forest, **d** the LORD, Jer 46:23
as in the days of old, **d** the LORD. Jer 46:26
not, O Jacob my servant, **d** the LORD, Jer 46:28
the days are coming, **d** the LORD, Jer 48:12
gone down to slaughter, **d** the King, Jer 48:15
off, and his arm is broken, **d** the LORD. Jer 48:25
I know his insolence, **d** the LORD; his Jer 48:30
bring to an end in Moab, **d** the LORD, Jer 48:35
for which no one cares, **d** the LORD. Jer 48:38
you, O inhabitant of Moab! **d** the LORD. Jer 48:43
year of their punishment, **d** the LORD. Jer 48:44
d the LORD." Thus far is the judgment Jer 48:47
behold, the days are coming, **d** the LORD, Jer 49:2
terror upon you, **d** the Lord GOD of hosts, Jer 49:5
fortunes of the Ammonites, **d** the LORD." Jer 49:6
For I have sworn by myself, **d** the LORD, Jer 49:13
bring you down from there, **d** the LORD. Jer 49:16
in that day, **d** the LORD of hosts. Jer 49:26
O inhabitants of Hazor! **d** the LORD. Jer 49:30
at ease, that dwells securely, **d** the LORD, Jer 49:31
from every side of them, **d** the LORD. Jer 49:32
upon them, my fierce anger, **d** the LORD. Jer 49:37
their king and officials, **d** the LORD. Jer 49:38
the fortunes of Elam, **d** the LORD." Jer 49:39
those days and in that time, **d** the LORD, Jer 50:4
plunder her shall be sated, **d** the LORD. Jer 50:10
those days and in that time, **d** the LORD, Jer 50:20
devote them to destruction, **d** the LORD, Jer 50:21
be destroyed on that day, **d** the LORD. Jer 50:30
O proud one, **d** the Lord GOD of hosts, Jer 50:31
against the Chaldeans, **d** the LORD, Jer 50:35
their neighboring cities, **d** the LORD, Jer 50:40
that they have done in Zion, **d** the LORD. Jer 51:24
O destroying mountain, **d** the LORD, Jer 51:25
shall be a perpetual waste, **d** the LORD. Jer 51:26
sleep and not wake, **d** the LORD. Jer 51:39
them out of the north, **d** the LORD. Jer 51:48
the days are coming, **d** the LORD, Jer 51:52
come from me against her, **d** the LORD. Jer 51:53
sleep and not wake, **d** the King, Jer 51:57
Therefore, as I live, **d** the Lord GOD, Ezk 5:11
the sword upon you, **d** the Lord GOD. Ezk 11:8
their own heads, **d** the Lord GOD." Ezk 11:21
word and perform it, **d** the Lord GOD." Ezk 12:25
will be performed, **d** the Lord GOD." Ezk 12:28
They say, '**D** the LORD,' when the LORD Ezk 13:6
whenever you have said, '**D** the LORD,' Ezk 13:7
I am against you, **d** the Lord GOD. Ezk 13:8
there was no peace, **d** the Lord GOD. Ezk 13:16
I may be their God, **d** the Lord GOD." Ezk 14:11
their righteousness, **d** the Lord GOD. Ezk 14:14
were in it, as I live, **d** the Lord GOD, Ezk 14:16
were in it, as I live, **d** the Lord GOD, Ezk 14:18
Job were in it, as I live, **d** the Lord GOD, Ezk 14:20
that I have done in it, **d** the Lord GOD." Ezk 14:23
have acted faithlessly, **d** the Lord GOD." Ezk 15:8
a covenant with you, **d** the Lord GOD, Ezk 16:8
I had bestowed on you, **d** the Lord GOD. Ezk 16:14
aroma; and so it was, **d** the Lord GOD. Ezk 16:19
(woe, woe to you! **d** the Lord GOD), Ezk 16:23
lovesick is your heart, **d** the Lord GOD, Ezk 16:30
deeds upon your head, **d** the Lord GOD. Ezk 16:43
As I live, **d** the Lord GOD, your sister Ezk 16:48
and your abominations, **d** the LORD. Ezk 16:58
that you have done, **d** the Lord GOD." Ezk 16:63
"As I live, **d** the Lord GOD, surely in the Ezk 17:16
As I live, **d** the Lord GOD, this proverb Ezk 18:3
he shall surely live, **d** the Lord GOD. Ezk 18:9
death of the wicked, **d** the Lord GOD, Ezk 18:23
according to his ways, **d** the Lord GOD. Ezk 18:30
in the death of anyone, **d** the Lord GOD; Ezk 18:32
As I live, **d** the Lord GOD, I will not be Ezk 20:3
As I live, **d** the Lord GOD, I will not be Ezk 20:31
"As I live, **d** the Lord GOD, surely with Ezk 20:33
judgment with you, **d** the Lord GOD. Ezk 20:36
height of Israel, **d** the Lord GOD, Ezk 20:40
O house of Israel, **d** the Lord GOD." Ezk 20:44
and it will be fulfilled,'" **d** the Lord GOD. Ezk 21:7
if you despise the rod?" **d** the Lord GOD. Ezk 21:13
you have forgotten, **d** the Lord GOD. Ezk 22:12
upon their heads, **d** the Lord GOD." Ezk 22:31
for I have spoken, **d** the Lord GOD. Ezk 23:34
you will be judged, **d** the Lord GOD." Ezk 24:14
know my vengeance, **d** the Lord GOD. Ezk 25:14
nets, for I have spoken, **d** the Lord GOD. Ezk 26:5
LORD; I have spoken, **d** the Lord GOD. Ezk 26:14
never be found again, **d** the Lord GOD." Ezk 26:21
for I have spoken, **d** the Lord GOD." Ezk 28:10
they worked for me, **d** the Lord GOD. Ezk 29:20
her by the sword, **d** the Lord GOD. Ezk 30:6
and all his multitude, **d** the Lord GOD." Ezk 31:18
darkness on your land, **d** the Lord GOD. Ezk 32:8
rivers to run like oil, **d** the Lord GOD. Ezk 32:14
shall they chant it, **d** the Lord GOD." Ezk 32:16
slain by the sword, **d** the Lord GOD. Ezk 32:31
and all his multitude, **d** the Lord GOD." Ezk 32:32
Say to them, As I live, **d** the Lord GOD, I Ezk 33:11
As I live, **d** the Lord GOD, surely because Ezk 34:8
make them lie down, **d** the Lord GOD. Ezk 34:15
Israel, are my people, **d** the Lord GOD. Ezk 34:30
and I am your God, **d** the Lord GOD." Ezk 34:31
therefore, as I live, **d** the Lord GOD, I will Ezk 35:6
therefore, as I live, **d** the Lord GOD, I Ezk 35:11
nation of children, **d** the Lord GOD. Ezk 36:14
nation to stumble, **d** the Lord GOD." Ezk 36:15
that I am the LORD, **d** the Lord GOD, Ezk 36:23
sake that I will act, **d** the Lord GOD; Ezk 36:32
spoken, and I will do it, **d** the LORD." Ezk 37:14
the land of Israel, **d** the Lord GOD, Ezk 38:18
on all my mountains, **d** the Lord GOD. Ezk 38:21
field, for I have spoken, **d** the Lord GOD. Ezk 39:5
will be brought about, **d** the Lord GOD. Ezk 39:8
who plundered them, **d** the Lord GOD. Ezk 39:10
that I show my glory, **d** the Lord GOD. Ezk 39:13
all kinds of warriors,' **d** the Lord GOD. Ezk 39:20
the house of Israel, **d** the Lord GOD." Ezk 39:29
me to minister to me, **d** the Lord GOD, Ezk 43:19
and I will accept you, **d** the Lord GOD." Ezk 43:27
concerning them, **d** the Lord GOD, Ezk 44:12
the fat and the blood, **d** the Lord GOD. Ezk 44:15
offer his sin offering, **d** the Lord GOD. Ezk 44:27
evictions of my people, **d** the Lord GOD. Ezk 45:9
atonement for them, **d** the Lord GOD. Ezk 45:15
him his inheritance, **d** the Lord GOD. Ezk 47:23
are their portions, **d** the Lord GOD. Ezk 48:29
her lovers and forgot me, **d** the LORD. Hos 2:13
"And in that day, **d** the LORD, you will Hos 2:16
in that day I will answer, **d** the LORD, Hos 2:21
them to their homes, **d** the LORD. Hos 11:11
"Yet even now," **d** the LORD, "return to me Jl 2:12
so, O people of Israel?" **d** the LORD. Am 2:11
away naked in that day," **d** the LORD. Am 2:16
not know how to do right," **d** the LORD, Am 3:10
the house of Jacob," **d** the Lord GOD, Am 3:13
shall come to an end," **d** the LORD. Am 3:15
be cast out into Harmon," **d** the LORD. Am 4:3
to do, O people of Israel!" **d** the Lord GOD. Am 4:5
yet you did not return to me," **d** the LORD. Am 4:6
yet you did not return to me," **d** the LORD. Am 4:8
yet you did not return to me," **d** the LORD. Am 4:9
you did not return to me," **d** the LORD. Am 4:10
you did not return to me," **d** the LORD. Am 4:11
and **d** to man what is his thought, Am 4:13

GOD has sworn by himself, **d** the LORD, Am 6:8
a nation, O house of Israel," **d** the LORD, Am 6:14
wailings in that day," **d** the Lord GOD. Am 8:3
"And on that day," **d** the Lord GOD, "I will Am 8:9
the days are coming," **d** the Lord GOD, Am 8:11
to me, O people of Israel?" **d** the LORD. Am 9:7
destroy the house of Jacob," **d** the LORD. Am 9:8
called by my name," **d** the LORD who Am 9:12
the days are coming," **d** the LORD, Am 9:13
there I will bring you down, **d** the LORD. Ob 1:4
Will I not on that day, **d** the LORD, destroy Ob 1:8
In that day, **d** the LORD, I will assemble the Mi 4:6
And in that day, **d** the LORD, I will cut off Mi 5:10
I am against you, **d** the LORD of hosts, Na 2:13
I am against you, **d** the LORD of hosts, Na 3:5
from the face of the earth," **d** the LORD. Zep 1:2
from the face of the earth," **d** the LORD. Zep 1:3
"On that day," **d** the LORD, "a cry will be Zep 1:10
Therefore, as I live," **d** the LORD of hosts, Zep 2:9
"Therefore wait for me," **d** the LORD, "for Zep 3:8
I blew it away. Why? **d** the LORD of hosts. Hg 1:9
message, "I am with you, **d** the LORD." Hg 1:13
now be strong, O Zerubbabel, **d** the LORD. Hg 2:4
all you people of the land, **d** the LORD. Hg 2:4
for I am with you, **d** the LORD of hosts, Hg 2:4
and the gold is mine, **d** the LORD of hosts. Hg 2:8
I will give peace, **d** the LORD of hosts.'" Hg 2:9
with this nation before me, **d** the LORD, Hg 2:14
yet you did not turn to me, **d** the LORD. Hg 2:17
On that day, **d** the LORD of hosts, I will Hg 2:23
servant, the son of Shealtiel, **d** the LORD, Hg 2:23
I have chosen you, **d** the LORD of hosts." Hg 2:23
say to them, Thus **d** the LORD of hosts: Zec 1:3
hear or pay attention to me, **d** the LORD. Zec 1:4
shall be built in it, **d** the LORD of hosts, Zec 1:16
her a wall of fire all around, **d** the LORD, Zec 2:5
from the land of the north, **d** the LORD. Zec 2:6
the four winds of the heavens, **d** the LORD. Zec 2:6
I will dwell in your midst, **d** the LORD. Zec 2:10
its inscription, **d** the LORD of hosts, Zec 3:9
In that day, **d** the LORD of hosts, every Zec 3:10
I will send it out, **d** the LORD of hosts, and Zec 5:4
in my sight, **d** the LORD of hosts? Zec 8:6
in the former days, **d** the LORD of hosts. Zec 8:11
for all these things I hate, **d** the LORD." Zec 8:17
shall walk in his name," **d** the LORD. Zec 10:12
the inhabitants of this land, **d** the LORD. Zec 11:6
Thus **d** the LORD, who stretched out the Zec 12:1
On that day, **d** the LORD, I will strike Zec 12:4
"And on that day, **d** the LORD of hosts, I Zec 13:2
stands next to me," **d** the LORD of hosts. Zec 13:7
In the whole land, **d** the LORD, two thirds Zec 13:8
not Esau Jacob's brother?" **d** the LORD. Mal 1:2
"'And in the last days it shall be, God **d**, Acts 2:17
the days are coming, **d** the Lord, Heb 8:8
showed no concern for them, **d** the Lord. Heb 8:9
of Israel after those days, **d** the Lord: Heb 8:10
with them after those days, **d** the Lord: Heb 10:16

DECLARING (4)
d the end from the beginning and from Is 46:10
not shrink from **d** to you anything Acts 20:20
did not shrink from **d** to you the Acts 20:27
exhorting and **d** that this is the true 1 Pt 5:12

DECLINED (2)
on the dial the ten steps by which it had **d**. Is 38:8
him to stay for a longer period, he **d**. Acts 18:20

DECLINES (2)
and wait until the day **d**." So they ate, Jgs 19:8
Woe to us, for the day **d**, for the shadows Jer 6:4

DECLINING (1)
the shadow cast by the **d** sun on the dial Is 38:8

DECORATE (2)
They **d** it with silver and gold; they Jer 10:4
the prophets and **d** the monuments of Mt 23:29

DECREASE (2)
daughters; multiply there, and do not **d**. Jer 29:6
He must increase, but I must **d**." Jn 3:30

DECREE (48)
And I made a **d**, and search has been Ezr 4:19
Therefore make a **d** that these men be Ezr 4:21
be not rebuilt, until a **d** is made by me. Ezr 4:21
"Who gave you a **d** to build this house Ezr 5:3
'Who gave you a **d** to build this house Ezr 5:9
the king made a **d** that this house of Ezr 5:13
to see whether a **d** was issued by Cyrus Ezr 5:17
Then Darius the king made a **d**, and Ezr 6:1
the king, Cyrus the king issued a **d**: Ezr 6:3
I make a **d** regarding what you shall do Ezr 6:8
Also I make a **d** that if anyone alters Ezr 6:11
I Darius make a **d**; let it be done with all Ezr 6:12
finished their building by **d** of the God Ezr 6:14
of Israel and by **d** of Cyrus and Darius Ezr 6:14
I make a **d** that anyone of the people of Ezr 7:13
make a **d** to all the treasurers in the Ezr 7:21
So when the **d** made by the king is Est 1:20
to be issued as a **d** in every province by Est 3:14
and the **d** was issued in Susa the citadel. Est 3:15
the king's command and his **d** reached, Est 4:3
a copy of the written **d** issued in Susa for Est 4:8
was to be issued as a **d** in every province, Est 8:13
And the **d** was issued in Susa the citadel. Est 8:14
A **d** was issued in Susa, and the ten sons Est 9:14
when he made a **d** for the rain and a Jb 28:26
I will tell of the **d**: The LORD said to me, Ps 2:7
Do you indeed **d** what is right, you gods? Ps 58:1
He made it a **d** in Joseph when he went Ps 81:5
he gave a **d**, and it shall not pass away. Ps 148:6
kings reign, and rulers **d** what is just; Prv 8:15
Woe to those who **d** iniquitous decrees, Is 10:1
I have heard a **d** of destruction from the Is 28:22
I had sent her away with a **d** of divorce. Jer 3:8
to Baal, which I did not command or **d**, Jer 19:5
So the **d** went out, and the wise men were Dn 2:13
"Why is the **d** of the king so urgent?" Dn 2:15
You, O king, have made a **d**, that every Dn 3:10
Therefore I make a **d**: Any people, Dn 3:29
So I made a **d** that all the wise men of Dn 4:6
The sentence is by the **d** of the watchers, Dn 4:17
It is a **d** of the Most High, which has Dn 4:24
I make a **d**, that in all my royal Dn 6:26
"By the **d** of the king and his nobles: Jon 3:7
before the **d** takes effect —before the day Zep 2:2
never again be a **d** of utter destruction. Zec 14:11
the land with a **d** of utter destruction." Mal 4:6
In those days a **d** went out from Caesar Lk 2:1
they know God's **d** that those who Rom 1:32

DECREED (17)
as **d** forever throughout your Lv 6:18
shall offer it to the LORD as **d** forever. Lv 6:22
So they **d** to make a proclamation 2 Chr 30:5
Whatever is **d** by the God of heaven, let Ezr 7:23
done and what had been **d** against her. Est 2:1
the king, let it be **d** that they be destroyed, Est 3:9
God, the heritage **d** for him by God." Jb 20:29
the tribes of the LORD, as was **d** for Israel, Ps 122:4
forget what has been **d** and pervert the Prv 31:5
Destruction is **d**, overflowing with Is 10:22
GOD of hosts will make a full end, as **d**, Is 10:23
planted you, has **d** disaster against you, Jer 11:17
"Seventy weeks are **d** about your people Dn 9:24
there shall be war. Desolations are **d**. Dn 9:26
until the **d** end is poured out on the Dn 9:27
for what is **d** shall be done. Dn 11:36
which God **d** before the ages for our 1 Cor 2:7

DECREES (3)
Your **d** are very trustworthy; holiness Ps 93:5
Woe to those who decree iniquitous **d**, Is 10:1
are all acting against the **d** of Caesar, Acts 17:7

DEDAN (11)
The sons of Raamah: Sheba and **D**. Gn 10:7
Jokshan fathered Sheba and **D**. The Gn 25:3
The sons of **D** were Asshurim, Gn 25:3
The sons of Raamah: Sheba and **D**. 1 Chr 1:9
The sons of Jokshan: Sheba and **D**. 1 Chr 1:32
D, Tema, Buz, and all who cut the Jer 25:23
dwell in the depths, O inhabitants of **D**! Jer 49:8
from Teman even to **D** they shall fall Ezk 25:13
The men of **D** traded with you. Many Ezk 27:15
D traded with you in saddlecloths for Ezk 27:20
Sheba and **D** and the merchants of Ezk 38:13

DEDANITES (1)
Arabia you will lodge, O caravans of **D**. Is 21:13

DEDICATE (8)
the people of Israel, which they **d** to me, Lv 22:2
that the people of Israel **d** to the LORD, Lv 22:3
belongs to the LORD, no man may **d**; Lv 27:26
and flock you shall **d** to the LORD your Dt 15:19
he die in the battle and another man **d** it. Dt 20:5
"I **d** the silver to the LORD from my hand Jgs 17:3
was set apart to **d** the most holy 1 Chr 23:13
the LORD my God and **d** it to him for 2 Chr 2:4

DEDICATED (23)
from each its best part is to be **d**.' Nm 18:29
has built a new house and has not **d** it? Dt 20:5
These also King David **d** to the LORD, 2 Sm 8:11
and gold that he **d** from all the 2 Sm 8:11
things that David his father had **d**, 1 Kgs 7:51
the people of Israel **d** the house of the 1 Kgs 8:63
fathers, the kings of Judah, had **d**, 2 Kgs 12:18
the kings of Judah had **d** to the sun, 2 Kgs 23:11
These also King David **d** to the LORD, 1 Chr 18:11
God and the treasuries of the **d** gifts. 1 Chr 26:20
treasuries of the **d** gifts that David 1 Chr 26:26
the commanders of the army had **d**. 1 Chr 26:26
won in battles they **d** gifts for the 1 Chr 26:27
son of Zeruiah had **d**—all dedicated 1 Chr 26:28
had dedicated—all **d** gifts were in 1 Chr 26:28
of God, and the treasuries for **d** gifts; 1 Chr 28:12
the things that David his father had **d**, 2 Chr 5:1
and all the people **d** the house of God. 2 Chr 7:5
also used all the **d** things of the house 2 Chr 24:7
the tithe of the **d** things that had been 2 Chr 31:6
things that had been **d** to the LORD 2 Chr 31:6
the tithes, and the **d** things. 2 Chr 31:12
Who is blind as my **d** one, or blind as Is 42:19

DEDICATES (6)
"When a man **d** his house as a holy gift Lv 27:14
"If a man **d** to the LORD part of the land Lv 27:16
If he **d** his field from the year of jubilee, Lv 27:17
but if he **d** his field after the jubilee, Lv 27:18
And if he who **d** the field wishes to Lv 27:19
If he **d** to the LORD a field that he has Lv 27:22

DEDICATING (1)
every man **d** an offering of gold to the Ex 35:22

DEDICATION (13)
offered offerings for the **d** of the altar on Nm 7:10
chief each day, for the **d** of the altar." Nm 7:11
This was the **d** offering for the altar on Nm 7:84
This was the **d** offering for the altar Nm 7:88
they had kept the **d** of the altar seven 2 Chr 7:9
celebrated the **d** of this house of God Ezr 6:16
They offered at the **d** of this house of Ezr 6:17
And at the **d** of the wall of Jerusalem Neh 12:27
to celebrate the **d** with gladness, Neh 12:27
of David. A song at the **d** of the temple. Ps 30:T
to come to the **d** of the image that Dn 3:2
provinces gathered for the **d** of the image Dn 3:3
time the Feast of **D** took place at Jn 10:22

DEDUCTION (1)
and a **d** shall be made from the Lv 27:18

DEED (25)
"What **d** is this that you have done? Gn 44:15
because by this **d** you have utterly 2 Sm 12:14
man aside from his **d** and conceal pride Jb 33:17
LORD, and he will repay him for his **d**. Prv 19:17
against an evil **d** is not executed Eccl 8:11
God will bring every **d** into judgment, Eccl 12:14
roused; to do his **d**—strange is his deed! Is 28:21
roused; to do his deed—strange is his **d**! Is 28:21
I signed the **d**, sealed it, got witnesses, Jer 32:10
Then I took the sealed **d** of purchase, Jer 32:11
And I gave the **d** of purchase to Baruch Jer 32:12
witnesses who signed the **d** of purchase, Jer 32:12
both this sealed **d** of purchase and this Jer 32:14
sealed deed of purchase and this open **d**, Jer 32:14
I had given the **d** of purchase to Baruch Jer 32:16
great in counsel and mighty in **d**, Jer 32:19
what good **d** must I do to have eternal Mt 19:16
a prophet mighty in **d** and word before Lk 24:19
Jesus answered them, "I did one **d**, and Jn 7:21
today concerning a good **d** done to a Acts 4:9
you have contrived this **d** in your heart? Acts 5:4
to obedience—by word and **d**, Rom 15:18
And whatever you do, in word or **d**, do Col 3:17
me from every evil **d** and bring me 2 Tm 4:18
in word or talk but in **d** and in truth. 1 Jn 3:18

DEEDS (162)
least of all the **d** of steadfast love and Gn 32:10
in holiness, awesome in glorious **d**, Ex 15:11
arm, and by great **d** of terror, Dt 4:34
his signs and his **d** that he did in Egypt to Dt 11:3
outstretched arm, with great **d** of terror, Dt 26:8
on account of the evil of your **d**, Dt 28:20
and all the great **d** of terror that Moses Dt 34:12
are all his wonderful **d** that our fathers Jgs 6:13
and have done to him as his **d** deserved— Jgs 9:16
According to all the **d** that they have 1 Sm 8:8
all the righteous **d** of the LORD 1 Sm 12:7
and because his **d** have brought good 1 Sm 19:4
man of Kabzeel, a doer of great **d**. 2 Sm 23:20
bring back his bloody **d** on his own 1 Kgs 2:32
Now the rest of the **d** of Amaziah, 2 Kgs 14:18
Now the rest of the **d** of Zechariah, 2 Kgs 15:11
Now the rest of the **d** of Shallum, 2 Kgs 15:15
the rest of the **d** of Menahem and all 2 Kgs 15:21
the rest of the **d** of Pekahiah and all 2 Kgs 15:26
The rest of the **d** of Hezekiah and all 2 Kgs 20:20
the rest of the **d** of Jehoiakim and all 2 Kgs 24:5
man of Kabzeel, a doer of great **d**. 1 Chr 11:22
make known his **d** among the 1 Chr 16:8
Now the rest of the **d** of Amaziah, 2 Chr 25:26
the acts of Hezekiah and his good **d**, 2 Chr 32:32
and his good **d** according to what is 2 Chr 35:26
upon us for our evil **d** and for our great Ezr 9:13
spoke of his good **d** in my presence and Neh 6:19
wipe out my good **d** that I have done Neh 13:14

orders to bring the book of memorable **d**, Est 6:1
I will recount all of your wonderful **d**. Ps 9:1
in Zion! Tell among the peoples his **d**! Ps 9:11
LORD is righteous; he loves righteous **d**; Ps 11:7
They are corrupt, they do abominable **d**, Ps 14:1
aloud, and telling all your wondrous **d**. Ps 26:7
work and according to the evil of their **d**; Ps 28:4
of them all and observes all their **d**. Ps 33:15
your wondrous **d** and your thoughts Ps 40:5
us, what **d** you performed in their days, Ps 44:1
your right hand teach you awesome **d**! Ps 45:4
By awesome **d** you answer us with Ps 65:5
Say to God, "How awesome are your **d**! So Ps 66:3
is awesome in his **d** toward the children Ps 66:5
acts, of your **d** of salvation all the day, Ps 71:15
With the mighty **d** of the Lord GOD I Ps 71:16
and I still proclaim your wondrous **d**. Ps 71:17
is near. We recount your wondrous **d**. Ps 75:1
I will remember the **d** of the LORD; yes, I Ps 77:11
work, and meditate on your mighty **d**. Ps 77:12
generation the glorious **d** of the LORD, Ps 78:4
make known his **d** among the peoples! Ps 105:1
can utter the mighty **d** of the LORD, Ps 106:2
Ham, and awesome **d** by the Red Sea. Ps 106:22
the LORD to anger with their **d**, Ps 106:29
acts, and played the whore in their **d**. Ps 106:39
and tell of his **d** in songs of joy! Ps 107:22
they saw the **d** of the LORD, his Ps 107:24
live, and recount the **d** of the LORD. Ps 118:17
myself with wicked **d** in company with Ps 141:4
is continually against their evil **d**. Ps 141:5
speak of the might of your awesome **d**, Ps 145:6
to the children of man your mighty **d**, Ps 145:12
Praise him for his mighty **d**; praise him Ps 150:2
not seen the evil **d** that are done under Eccl 4:3
according to the **d** of the wicked, Eccl 8:14
according to the **d** of the righteous. Eccl 8:14
and the wise and their **d** are in the hand Eccl 9:1
the evil of your **d** from before my eyes; Is 1:16
their speech and their **d** are against the Is 3:8
them, for they shall eat the fruit of their **d**. Is 3:10
but they do not regard the **d** of the LORD, Is 5:12
make known his **d** among the peoples, Is 12:4
they will make Egypt stagger in all its **d**, Is 19:14
your counsel, whose **d** are in the dark, Is 29:15
declare your righteousness and your **d**, Is 57:12
and **d** of violence are in their hands. Is 59:6
According to their **d**, so will he repay, Is 59:18
and all our righteous **d** are like a polluted Is 64:6
their bosom payment for their former **d**." Is 65:7
quench it, because of the evil of your **d**." Jer 4:4
Your ways and your **d** have brought this Jer 4:18
They know no bounds in **d** of evil; they Jer 5:28
Amend your ways and your **d**, and I will Jer 7:3
if you truly amend your ways and your **d**, Jer 7:5
house, when she has done many vile **d**? Jer 11:15
I knew; then you showed me their **d**. Jer 11:18
ways, according to the fruit of his **d**." Jer 17:10
way, and amend your ways and your **d**.' Jer 18:11
to all his wonderful **d** and will make Jer 21:2
to quench it, because of your evil **d**.'" Jer 21:12
you according to the fruit of your **d**, Jer 21:14
I will attend to you for your evil **d**, Jer 23:2
evil way, and from the evil of their **d**. Jer 23:22
one of you, from his evil way and evil **d**, Jer 25:5
them according to their **d** and the work Jer 25:14
to do to them because of their evil **d**. Jer 26:3
therefore mend your ways and your **d**, Jer 26:13
Take these **d**, both this sealed deed of Jer 32:14
ways and according to the fruit of his **d**. Jer 32:19
and **d** shall be signed and sealed and Jer 32:44
from his evil way, and amend your **d**, Jer 35:15
bear your evil **d** and the abominations Jer 44:22
LORD; his boasts are false, his **d** are false. Jer 48:30
Repay her according to her **d**; do to her Jer 50:29
and his righteous **d** that he has done Ezk 3:20
I will bring their **d** upon their heads." Ezk 9:10
I will bring their **d** upon their own Ezk 11:21
and you see their ways and their **d**, Ezk 14:22
when you see their ways and their **d**, Ezk 14:23
things, the **d** of a brazen prostitute, Ezk 16:30
have returned your **d** upon your head, Ezk 16:43
None of the righteous **d** that he has Ezk 18:24
ways and all your **d** with which you Ezk 20:43
nor according to your corrupt **d**, Ezk 20:44
that in all your **d** your sins appear— Ezk 21:24
your ways and your **d** you will be Ezk 24:14
of his righteous **d** shall be Ezk 33:13
defiled it by their ways and their **d**. Ezk 36:17
their ways and their **d** I judged them. Ezk 36:19
ways, and your **d** that were not good, Ezk 36:31
for their ways and repay them for their **d**. Hos 4:9
Their **d** do not permit them to return to Hos 5:4
is revealed, and the evil **d** of Samaria; Hos 7:1
their evil. Now their **d** surround them; Hos 7:2
the wickedness of their **d** I will drive Hos 9:15
he will repay him according to his **d**. Hos 12:2
will repay him for his disgraceful **d**. Hos 12:14
"Surely I will never forget any of their **d**. Am 8:7
your **d** shall return on your own head. Ob 1:15
LORD grown impatient? Are these his **d**? Mi 2:7
time, because they have made their **d** evil. Mi 3:4
of its inhabitants, for the fruit of their **d**. Mi 7:13
were eager to make all their **d** corrupt. Zep 3:7
shame because of the **d** by which you Zep 3:11
your evil ways and from your evil **d**.' Zec 1:4
to deal with us for our ways and **d**, Zec 1:6
in prison about the **d** of the Christ, Mt 11:2
Yet wisdom is justified by her **d**." Mt 11:19
They do all their **d** to be seen by others. Mt 23:5
you consent to the **d** of your fathers, Lk 11:48
are receiving the due reward of our **d**; Lk 23:41
than the light because their **d** were evil. Jn 3:19
to the light, lest his **d** should be exposed. Jn 3:20
clearly seen that his **d** have been carried Jn 3:21
and he was mighty in his words and **d**. Acts 7:22
performing **d** in keeping with their Acts 26:20
are those whose lawless **d** are forgiven, Rom 4:7
you put to death the **d** of the body, Rom 8:13
Their end will correspond to their **d**. 2 Cor 11:15
and hostile in mind, doing evil **d**, Col 1:21
will repay him according to his **d**. 2 Tm 4:14
sins and their lawless **d** no more." Heb 10:17
impartially according to each one's **d**, 1 Pt 1:17
may see your good **d** and glorify God 1 Pt 2:12
soul over their lawless **d** that he saw and 2 Pt 2:8
Because his own **d** were evil and his 1 Jn 3:12
of all their **d** of ungodliness that Jude 1:15
their labors, for their **d** follow them!" Rv 14:13
saying, "Great and amazing are your **d**, Rv 15:3
sores. They did not repent of their **d**. Rv 16:11
others, and repay her double for her **d**; Rv 18:6
fine linen is the righteous **d** of the saints. Rv 19:8

DEEMED (3)
he closes his lips, he is **d** intelligent. Prv 17:28
field, and the fruitful field is **d** a forest. Is 32:15
about myself, my testimony is not **d** true. Jn 5:31

DEEP (87)
and darkness was over the face of the **d**. Gn 1:2
LORD God caused a **d** sleep to fall upon Gn 2:21
the fountains of the great **d** burst forth, Gn 7:11
covering them fifteen cubits **d**. Gn 7:20
The fountains of the **d** and the windows Gn 8:2
going down, a **d** sleep fell on Abram. Gn 15:12
blessings of the **d** that crouches Gn 49:25
and of the **d** that crouches beneath, Dt 33:13
because a **d** sleep from the LORD had 1 Sm 26:12
and ten cubits **d** in front of the house. 1 Kgs 6:3
pedestal is made, a cubit and a half **d**. 1 Kgs 7:31
Let gloom and **d** darkness claim it. Let Jb 3:5
of the night, when **d** sleep falls on men, Jb 4:13
to the land of darkness and **d** shadow, Jb 10:21
like **d** shadow without any order, Jb 10:22
"Can you find out the **d** things of God? Jb 11:7
darkness and brings **d** darkness to Jb 12:22
and on my eyelids is **d** darkness, Jb 16:16
Can he judge through the **d** darkness? Jb 22:13
For **d** darkness is morning to all of Jb 24:17
friends with the terrors of **d** darkness. Jb 24:17
limit the ore in gloom and **d** darkness. Jb 28:3
The **d** says, 'It is not in me,' and the sea Jb 28:14
of the night, when **d** sleep falls on men, Jb 33:15
no gloom or **d** darkness where evildoers Jb 34:22
sea, or walked in the recesses of the **d**? Jb 38:16
have you seen the gates of **d** darkness? Jb 38:17
like stone, and the face of the **d** is frozen. Jb 38:30
He makes the **d** boil like a pot; he makes Jb 41:31
would think the **d** to be white-haired. Jb 41:32
speaks to the wicked **d** in his heart; Ps 36:1
God; your judgments are like the great **d**; Ps 36:6
D calls to deep at the roar of your Ps 42:7
Deep calls to **d** at the roar of your Ps 42:7
inward mind and heart of a man are **d**! Ps 64:6
I sink in **d** mire, where there is no Ps 69:2
I have come into **d** waters, and the flood Ps 69:2
my enemies and from the **d** waters. Ps 69:14
sweep over me, or the **d** swallow me up, Ps 69:15
they were afraid; indeed, the **d** trembled. Ps 77:16
them drink abundantly as from the **d**. Ps 78:15
for it; it took **d** root and filled the land. Ps 80:9
of the pit, in the regions dark and **d**. Ps 88:6
O LORD! Your thoughts are very **d**! Ps 92:5
covered it with the **d** as with a garment; Ps 104:6
led them through the **d** as through a Ps 106:9
the LORD, his wondrous works in the **d**. Ps 107:24
way of the wicked is like **d** darkness; Prv 4:19
he drew a circle on the face of the **d**, Prv 8:27
he established the fountains of the **d**, Prv 8:28
words of a man's mouth are **d** waters; Prv 18:4
Slothfulness casts into a **d** sleep, and Prv 19:15
purpose in a man's heart is like **d** water, Prv 20:5
mouth of forbidden women is a **d** pit; Prv 22:14
For a prostitute is a **d** pit; an adulteress Prv 23:27
That which has been is far off, and **d**, Eccl 7:24
has been is far off, and deep, very **d**; Eccl 7:24
let it be **d** as Sheol or high as heaven." Is 7:11
those who dwelt in a land of **d** darkness, on Is 9:2
poured out upon you a spirit of **d** sleep, Is 29:10
you who hide **d** from the LORD your Is 29:15
is made ready, its pyre made **d** and wide, Is 30:33
who says to the **d**, 'Be dry; I will dry up Is 44:27
dried up the sea, the waters of the great **d**, Is 51:10
pits, in a land of drought and **d** darkness, Jer 2:6
it into gloom and makes it **d** darkness. Jer 13:16
your sister's cup that is **d** and large; Ezk 23:32
when I bring up the **d** over you, Ezk 26:19
the **d** made it grow tall, making its Ezk 31:4
I closed the **d** over it, and restrained its Ezk 31:15
the threshold of the gate, one reed **d**. Ezk 40:6
It was **d** enough to swim in, a river that Ezk 47:5
he reveals **d** and hidden things; he Dn 2:22
I fell into a **d** sleep with my face to the Dn 8:18
fell on my face in **d** sleep with my face to Dn 10:9
the revolters have gone **d** into slaughter, Hos 5:2
and turns **d** darkness into the morning Am 5:8
it devoured the great **d** and was eating up Am 7:4
For you cast me into the **d**, into the heart Jon 2:3
me to take my life; the **d** surrounded me; Jon 2:5
swept on; the **d** gave forth its voice; Hab 3:10
"Put out into the **d** and let down your nets Lk 5:4
who dug **d** and laid the foundation on Lk 6:48
to draw water with, and the well is **d**. Jn 4:11
sank into a **d** sleep as Paul talked still Acts 20:9
for us with groanings too **d** for words. Rom 8:26
what some call the **d** things of Satan, Rv 2:24

DEEPER (13)
disease appears to be **d** than the skin of Lv 13:3
his body and appears no **d** than the skin, Lv 13:4
and if it appears **d** than the skin and its Lv 13:20
hair in it and it is not **d** than the skin, Lv 13:21
white and it appears **d** than the skin, Lv 13:25
in the spot and it is no **d** than the skin, Lv 13:26
And if it appears **d** than the skin, and Lv 13:30
and it appears no **d** than the skin and Lv 13:31
itch appears to be no **d** than the skin, Lv 13:32
and it appears to be no **d** than the skin, Lv 13:34
if it appears to be **d** than the surface, Lv 14:37
do? **D** than Sheol—what can you know? Jb 11:8
A rebuke goes **d** into a man of Prv 17:10

DEEPLY (10)
She was **d** distressed and prayed to the 1 Sm 1:10
And the king was **d** moved and went 2 Sm 18:33
and told her, the queen was **d** distressed. Est 4:4
him from whom people have **d** revolted, Is 31:6
Israel and his Holy One, to one **d** despised, Is 49:7
that you may drink **d** with delight from Is 66:11
They have **d** corrupted themselves as in Hos 9:9
And he sighed **d** in his spirit and said, Mk 8:12
he was **d** moved in his spirit and greatly Jn 11:33
Then Jesus, **d** moved again, came to the Jn 11:38

DEEPS (6)
the **d** congealed in the heart of the sea. Ex 15:8
He uncovers the **d** out of darkness and Jb 12:22
as a heap; he puts the **d** in storehouses. Ps 33:7
and on earth, in the seas and all **d**. Ps 135:6
earth, you great sea creatures and all **d**, Ps 148:7
by his knowledge the **d** broke open, and Prv 3:20

DEER (12)
eat of it, as of the gazelle and as of the **d**. Dt 12:15
Just as the gazelle or the **d** is eaten, so Dt 12:22
the **d**, the gazelle, the roebuck, the wild Dt 14:5
eat it, as though it were a gazelle or a **d**. Dt 15:22
like the feet of a **d** and set me secure 2 Sm 22:34
cattle, a hundred sheep, besides **d**, 1 Kgs 4:23
like the feet of a **d** and set me secure on Ps 18:33
the LORD makes the **d** give birth and Ps 29:9
As a **d** pants for flowing streams, so Ps 42:1
a lovely **d**, a graceful doe. Let her Prv 5:19
then shall the lame man leap like a **d**, and Is 35:6
princes have become like **d** that find no Lam 1:6

DEER'S (1)
strength; he makes my feet like the **d**; Hab 3:19

DEFEAT (10)
return from the **d** of Chedorlaomer Gn 14:17
for victory, or the sound of the cry of **d**, Ex 32:18
shall be able to **d** them and drive them Nm 22:6
gives them over to you, and you **d** them, Dt 7:2
also been a great **d** among the people. 1 Sm 4:17
For now the **d** among the Philistines 1 Sm 14:30
then you will **d** for me the counsel of 2 Sm 15:34
had ordained to **d** the good counsel 2 Sm 17:14

even if you should **d** the whole army of Jer 37:10
with one another is already a **d** for you. 1 Cor 6:7

DEFEATED (64)

with him came and **d** the Rephaim in Gn 14:5
Kadesh) and **d** all the country of the Gn 14:7
and **d** them and pursued them to Gn 14:15
who **d** Midian in the country of Moab, Gn 36:35
came down and **d** them and pursued Nm 14:45
And Israel **d** him with the edge of the Nm 21:24
So they **d** him and his sons and all his Nm 21:35
after he had **d** Sihon the king of the Dt 1:4
midst, lest you be **d** before your enemies.' Dt 1:42
and we **d** him and his sons and all his Dt 2:33
the people of Israel **d** when they came out Dt 4:46
who rise against you to be **d** before you. Dt 28:7
cause you to be **d** before your enemies. Dt 28:25
out against us to battle, but we **d** them. Dt 29:7
the people of Israel **d** and took possession Jos 12:1
the LORD, and the people of Israel **d** them. Jos 12:6
and the people of Israel **d** on the west side Jos 12:7
whom Moses **d** with the leaders of Jos 13:21
hand, and they **d** 10,000 of them at Bezek. Jgs 1:4
against him and **d** the Canaanites and Jgs 1:5
and they **d** Sheshai and Ahiman and Jgs 1:10
and they **d** the Canaanites who Jgs 1:17
the Amalekites, and went and **d** Israel. Jgs 3:13
the hand of Israel, and they **d** them. Jgs 11:21
And the LORD **d** Benjamin before Israel, Jgs 20:35
of Benjamin saw that they were **d**. Jgs 20:36
They said, "Surely they are **d** before us, Jgs 20:39
spread, Israel was **d** by the Philistines, 1 Sm 4:2
"Why has the LORD **d** us today before 1 Sm 4:3
Philistines fought, and Israel was **d**, 1 Sm 4:10
Jonathan **d** the garrison of the 1 Sm 13:3
said that Saul had **d** the garrison of 1 Sm 13:4
And Saul **d** the Amalekites from 1 Sm 15:7
and David **d** them there. 2 Sm 5:20
After this David **d** the Philistines and 2 Sm 8:1
And he **d** Moab and he measured them 2 Sm 8:2
David also **d** Hadadezer the son of 2 Sm 8:3
heard that David had **d** the whole army 2 Sm 8:9
fought against Hadadezer and **d** him, 2 Sm 8:10
saw that they had been **d** by Israel, 2 Sm 10:15
saw that they had been **d** by Israel, 2 Sm 10:19
men of Israel were **d** there by the 2 Sm 18:7
people Israel are **d** before the enemy 1 Kgs 8:33
Hazael **d** them throughout the 2 Kgs 10:32
Three times Joash **d** him and 2 Kgs 13:25
And Judah was **d** by Israel, and 2 Kgs 14:12
who **d** Midian in the country of 1 Chr 1:46
And they **d** the remnant of the 1 Chr 4:43
After this David **d** the Philistines and 1 Chr 18:1
And he **d** Moab, and the Moabites 1 Chr 18:2
David also **d** Hadadezer king of 1 Chr 18:3
that David had **d** the whole army 1 Chr 18:9
against Hadadezer and **d** him; 1 Chr 18:10
saw that they had been **d** by Israel, 1 Chr 19:16
saw that they had been **d** by Israel, 1 Chr 19:19
people Israel are **d** before the enemy 2 Chr 6:24
God **d** Jeroboam and all Israel 2 Chr 13:15
So the LORD **d** the Ethiopians before 2 Chr 14:12
And Judah was **d** by Israel, and 2 Chr 25:22
who **d** him and took captive a great 2 Chr 28:5
again invaded and **d** Judah and 2 Chr 28:17
Damascus that had **d** him and said, 2 Chr 28:23
king of Babylon **d** in the fourth Jer 46:2
but he was **d** and there was no longer Rv 12:8

DEFECT (3)

or a man with a **d** in his sight or an Lv 21:20
to bring you a red heifer without **d**, Nm 19:2
in which is a blemish, any **d** whatever, Dt 17:1

DEFEND (12)

For I will **d** this city to save it, for my 2 Kgs 19:34
and I will **d** this city for my own sake 2 Kgs 20:6
in every city to gather and **d** their lives, Est 8:11
provinces also gathered to **d** their lives, Est 9:16
and **d** my cause against an ungodly Ps 43:1
May he **d** the cause of the poor of the Ps 72:4
Arise, O God, **d** your cause; remember Ps 74:22
d the rights of the poor and needy. Prv 31:9
For I will **d** this city to save it, for my Is 37:35
of the king of Assyria, and will **d** this city. Is 38:6
and they do not **d** the rights of the needy. Jer 5:28
how you should **d** yourself or what Lk 12:11

DEFENDED (3)

of the plot and **d** it and struck down 2 Sm 23:12
of the plot and **d** it and killed the 1 Chr 11:14
he **d** the oppressed man and avenged Acts 7:24

DEFENDER (1)

he will send them a savior and **d**, Is 19:20

DEFENDING (1)

we have been **d** ourselves to you? 2 Cor 12:19

DEFENSE (17)

and he built cities for **d** in Judah. 2 Chr 11:5
his place of **d** will be the fortresses of Is 33:16
down to make a **d** against the siege Jer 33:4
Asa had made for **d** against Baasha king Jer 41:9
wanted to make a **d** to the crowd. Acts 19:33
hear the **d** that I now make before Acts 22:1
this nation, I cheerfully make my **d**. Acts 24:10
Paul argued in his **d**, "Neither against Acts 25:8
to make his **d** concerning the charge Acts 25:16
stretched out his hand and made his **d**: Acts 26:1
going to make my **d** today against all Acts 26:2
as he was saying these things in his **d**, Acts 26:24
This is my **d** to those who would 1 Cor 9:3
and in the **d** and confirmation of Phil 1:7
I am put here for the **d** of the gospel. Phil 1:16
At my first **d** no one came to stand by 2 Tm 4:16
prepared to make a **d** to anyone who 1 Pt 3:15

DEFENSELESS (1)

in you I seek refuge; leave me not **d**! Ps 141:8

DEFENSES (4)

of ashes; your **d** are defenses of clay. Jb 13:12
of ashes; your defenses are **d** of clay. Jb 13:12
God, you have rejected us, broken our **d**; Ps 60:1
land and bring down your **d** from you, Am 3:11

DEFER (2)

be partial to the poor or **d** to the great, Lv 19:15
"For my name's sake I **d** my anger, for the Is 48:9

DEFERRED (1)

Hope **d** makes the heart sick, but a Prv 13:12

DEFIANTLY (1)

the people of Israel were going out **d**. Ex 14:8

DEFIED (5)

for he has **d** the armies of the living 1 Sm 17:36
armies of Israel, whom you have **d**. 1 Sm 17:45
David when they **d** the Philistines 2 Sm 23:9
about him and **d** Rehoboam the son 2 Chr 13:7
For she has proudly **d** the LORD, the Jer 50:29

DEFIES (1)

hand against God and **d** the Almighty, Jb 15:25

DEFILE (32)

you shall not **d** yourselves with them, Lv 11:43
You shall not **d** yourselves with any Lv 11:44
camp, that they may not **d** their camp, Nm 5:3
You shall not **d** the land in which you Nm 35:34
You shall not **d** your land that the LORD Dt 21:23
it, to **d** the pompous pride of all glory, Is 23:9
Then you will **d** your carved idols Is 30:22
house that is called by my name, to **d** it. Jer 7:30
house that is called by my name, to **d** it. Jer 32:34
Then he said to them, "**D** the house, and Ezk 9:7
nor **d** themselves anymore with all Ezk 14:11
does not **d** his neighbor's wife or Ezk 18:6
Israel, does not **d** his neighbor's wife, Ezk 18:15
and do not **d** yourselves with the idols Ezk 20:7
nor **d** yourselves with their idols. Ezk 20:18
Will you **d** yourselves after the Ezk 20:30
you **d** yourselves with all your idols to Ezk 20:31
come, and that makes idols to **d** herself! Ezk 22:3
of your wisdom and **d** your splendor. Ezk 28:7
They shall not **d** themselves anymore Ezk 37:23
Israel shall no more **d** my holy name, Ezk 43:7
They shall not **d** themselves by going Ezk 44:25
sister they may **d** themselves. Ezk 44:25
that he would not **d** himself with the Dn 1:8
eunuchs to allow him not to **d** himself. Dn 1:8
These are what **d** a person. But to eat Mt 15:20
unwashed hands does not **d** anyone." Mt 15:20
that by going into him can **d** him, Mk 7:15
come out of a person are what **d** him." Mk 7:15
a person from outside cannot **d** him, Mk 7:18
from within, and they **d** a person." Mk 7:23
also, relying on their dreams, **d** the flesh, Jude 1:8

DEFILED (58)

heard that he had **d** his daughter Dinah. Gn 34:5
because he had **d** their sister Dinah. Gn 34:13
the city, because they had **d** their sister. Gn 34:27
then you **d** it—he went up to my couch! Gn 49:4
a prostitute or a woman who has been **d**, Lv 21:7
woman, or a woman who has been **d**, Lv 21:14
is undetected though she has **d** herself, Nm 5:13
is jealous of his wife who has **d** herself, Nm 5:14
his wife, though she has not **d** herself, Nm 5:14
authority, and if you have **d** yourself, Nm 5:20
if she has **d** herself and has broken Nm 5:27
the woman has not **d** herself and is Nm 5:28
be void, because his separation was **d**. Nm 6:12
since he has **d** the sanctuary of the Nm 19:20
again to be his wife, after she has been **d**, Dt 24:4
there the shield of the mighty was **d**, 2 Sm 1:21
and **d** the high places where the 2 Kgs 23:8
And he **d** Topheth, which is in the 2 Kgs 23:10
And the king **d** the high places that 2 Kgs 23:13
burned them on the altar and **d** it, 2 Kgs 23:16
but because he **d** his father's couch, 1 Chr 5:1
they have **d** your holy temple; Ps 79:1
you have **d** his crown in the dust. Ps 89:39
The earth lies **d** under its inhabitants; for Is 24:5
For your hands are **d** with blood and Is 59:3
you **d** my land and made my heritage an Jer 2:7
other gods—shall be **d** like the place of Jer 19:13
they were so **d** with blood that no one Lam 4:14
GOD! Behold, I have never **d** myself. Ezk 4:14
because you have **d** my sanctuary with Ezk 5:11
and I **d** them through their very gifts Ezk 20:26
with which you have **d** yourselves, Ezk 20:43
and **d** by the idols that you have made, Ezk 22:4
you will mock you; your name is **d**; Ezk 22:5
and she **d** herself with all the idols of Ezk 23:7
And I saw that she was **d**; they both Ezk 23:13
and they **d** her with their whoring Ezk 23:17
And after she was **d** by them, she Ezk 23:17
the nations and **d** yourself with their Ezk 23:30
they have **d** my sanctuary on the Ezk 23:38
they **d** it by their ways and their deeds. Ezk 36:17
for the idols with which they had **d** it. Ezk 36:18
They have **d** my holy name by their Ezk 43:8
you have played the whore; Israel is **d**. Hos 5:3
whoredom is there; Israel is **d**. Hos 6:10
bread to them; all who eat of it shall be **d**; Hos 9:4
against you, saying, "Let her be **d**, Mi 4:11
Woe to her who is rebellious and **d**, the Zep 3:1
his disciples ate with hands that were **d**, Mk 7:2
of the elders, but eat with **d** hands?" Mk 7:5
so that they would not be **d**, Jn 18:28
the temple and has **d** this holy place." Acts 21:28
and their conscience, being weak, is **d**. 1 Cor 8:7
are pure, but to the **d** and unbelieving, Ti 1:15
their minds and their consciences are **d**. Ti 1:15
if the sprinkling of **d** persons with the Heb 9:13
trouble, and by it many become **d**; Heb 12:15
who have not **d** themselves with women, Rv 14:4

DEFILEMENT (1)

ourselves from every **d** of body and 2 Cor 7:1

DEFILEMENTS (1)

they have escaped the **d** of the world 2 Pt 2:20

DEFILES (10)

authority, goes astray and **d** herself, Nm 5:29
him and he **d** his consecrated head, Nm 6:9
himself, **d** the tabernacle of the LORD, Nm 19:13
the mountains, **d** his neighbor's wife, Ezk 18:11
another lewdly **d** his daughter-in-law; Ezk 22:11
and each of you **d** his neighbor's wife; Ezk 33:26
goes into the mouth that **d** a person, Mt 15:11
out of the mouth; this **d** a person." Mt 15:11
from the heart, and this **d** a person. Mt 15:18
comes out of a person is what **d** him. Mk 7:20

DEFILING (2)

their uncleanness by **d** my tabernacle Lv 15:31
in the lust of **d** passion and despise 2 Pt 2:10

DEFINED (2)

the land of Canaan as **d** by its borders), Nm 34:2
be your land as **d** by its borders all Nm 34:12

DEFINITE (2)

according to the **d** plan and Acts 2:23
But I have nothing **d** to write to my Acts 25:26

DEFRAUD (2)

Do not bear false witness, Do not **d**, Mk 10:19
yourselves wrong and **d**—even your 1 Cor 6:8

DEFRAUDED (4)

have I taken? Or whom have I **d**? 1 Sm 12:3
"You have not **d** us or oppressed us or 1 Sm 12:4
And if I have **d** anyone of anything, I Lk 19:8
suffer wrong? Why not rather be **d**? 1 Cor 6:7

DEFY (3)

said, "I **d** the ranks of Israel this day. 1 Sm 17:10
Surely he has come up to **d** Israel. 1 Sm 17:25
that he should **d** the armies of the 1 Sm 17:26

DEFYING (1)

against the LORD, **d** his glorious presence. Is 3:8

DEGENERATE (1)

then have you turned **d** and become a Jer 2:21

DEGRADED (1)

these, your brother be **d** in your sight. Dt 25:3

DEGREE (1)

same image from one **d** of glory to 2 Cor 3:18

DEITY (1)

the whole fullness of **d** dwells bodily, Col 2:9

DEJECTEDLY (1)

lay in sackcloth and went about **d**. 1 Kgs 21:27

DELAIAH (7)
Akkub, Johanan, **D**, and Anani, 1 Chr 3:24
the twenty-third to **D**, the 1 Chr 24:18
the sons of **D**, the sons of Tobiah, and Ezr 2:60
the house of Shemaiah the son of **D**, Neh 6:10
the sons of **D**, the sons of Tobiah, the Neh 7:62
the secretary, **D** the son of Shemaiah, Jer 36:12
when Elnathan and **D** and Gemariah Jer 36:25

DELAY (21)
But he said to them, "Do not **d** me, Gn 24:56
young man did not **d** to do the thing, Gn 34:19
"You shall not **d** to offer from the Ex 22:29
your God, you shall not **d** fulfilling it, Dt 23:21
in full and without **d** from the royal Ezr 6:8
and my deliverer; do not **d**, O my God! Ps 40:17
help and my deliverer; O LORD, do not **d**! Ps 70:5
hasten and do not **d** to keep your Ps 119:60
vow a vow to God, do not **d** paying it, Eccl 5:4
not far off, and my salvation will not **d**; Is 46:13
D not, for your own sake, O my God, Dn 9:19
which **d** not for a man nor wait for the Mi 5:7
for it; it will surely come; it will not **d**. Hab 2:3
were wondering at his **d** in the temple. Lk 1:21
and night? Will he **d** long over them? Lk 18:7
him, "Please come to us without **d**." Acts 9:38
they came together here, I made no **d**, Acts 25:17
upon the earth fully and without **d**." Rom 9:28
if I **d**, you may know how one ought 1 Tm 3:15
coming one will come and will not **d**; Heb 10:37
is in it, that there would be no more **d**, Rv 10:6

DELAYED (9)
If we had not **d**, we would now have Gn 43:10
people saw that Moses **d** to come down Ex 32:1
Ehud escaped while they **d**, and he Jgs 3:26
but he **d** beyond the set time that had 2 Sm 20:5
It will no longer be **d**, but in your Ezk 12:25
of my words will be **d** any longer, Ezk 12:28
says to himself, 'My master is **d**,' Mt 24:48
As the bridegroom was **d**, they all Mt 25:5
to himself, 'My master is **d** in coming,' Lk 12:45

DELEGATION (2)
he sends a **d** and asks for terms of Lk 14:32
hated him and sent a **d** after him, Lk 19:14

DELIBERATE (1)
sit down first and **d** whether he is able Lk 14:31

DELIBERATELY (2)
we go on sinning **d** after receiving the Heb 10:26
For they **d** overlook this fact, that the 2 Pt 3:5

DELICACIES (8)
be rich, and he shall yield royal **d**. Gn 49:20
iniquity, and let me not eat of their **d**! Ps 141:4
Do not desire his **d**, for they are Prv 23:3
a man who is stingy; do not desire his **d**, Prv 23:6
he has filled his stomach with my **d**; Jer 51:34
who once feasted on **d** perish in the Lam 4:5
I ate no **d**, no meat or wine entered my Dn 10:3
and all your **d** and your splendors are Rv 18:14

DELICATE (2)
ground because she is so **d** and tender, Dt 28:56
you shall no more be called tender and **d**. Is 47:1

DELICATELY (1)
The lovely and **d** bred I will destroy, the Jer 6:2

DELICIOUS (8)
and prepare for me **d** food, such as I love, Gn 27:4
me game and prepare for me **d** food, Gn 27:7
may prepare from them **d** food for your Gn 27:9
and his mother prepared **d** food, Gn 27:14
And she put the **d** food and the bread, Gn 27:17
He also prepared **d** food and brought it Gn 27:31
words of a whisperer are like **d** morsels; Prv 18:8
of a whisperer are like **d** morsels; Prv 26:22

DELIGHT (74)
for food, and that it was a **d** to the eyes, Gn 3:6
But if you no longer **d** in her, you shall Dt 21:14
as the LORD took **d** in doing you good Dt 28:63
the LORD will take **d** in bringing ruin Dt 28:63
LORD will again take **d** in prospering you, Dt 30:9
you, as he took **d** in your fathers, Dt 30:9
the LORD as great **d** in burnt offerings 1 Sm 15:22
say, 'Behold, the king has **d** in you, 1 Sm 18:22
my lord the king **d** in this thing?" 2 Sm 24:3
of your servants who **d** to fear your Neh 1:11
"Whom would the king **d** to honor more Est 6:6
For then you will **d** yourself in the Jb 22:26
Will he take **d** in the Almighty? Will he Jb 27:10
nothing that he should take **d** in God.' Jb 34:9
but his **d** is in the law of the LORD, and on Ps 1:2
the excellent ones, in whom is all my **d**. Ps 16:3
Let those who **d** in my righteousness Ps 35:27
D yourself in the LORD, and he will give Ps 37:4
the land and **d** themselves in abundant Ps 37:11
By this I know that you **d** in me: my Ps 41:11
you **d** in truth in the inward being, Ps 51:6
For you will not **d** in sacrifice, or I Ps 51:16
then will you **d** in right sacrifices, in Ps 51:19
scatter the peoples who **d** in war. Ps 68:30
He did not **d** in blessing; may it be far Ps 109:17
the LORD, studied by all who **d** in them. Ps 111:2
of your testimonies I **d** as much as in Ps 119:14
I will **d** in your statutes; I will not Ps 119:16
Your testimonies are my **d**; they are Ps 119:24
of your commandments, for I **d** in it. Ps 119:35
I find my **d** in your commandments, Ps 119:47
unfeeling like fat, but I **d** in your law. Ps 119:70
that I may live; for your law is my **d**. Ps 119:77
If your law had not been my **d**, I would Ps 119:92
but your commandments are my **d**. Ps 119:143
O LORD, and your law is my **d**. Ps 119:174
His **d** is not in the strength of the Ps 147:10
long will scoffers **d** in their scoffing Prv 1:22
in doing evil and **d** in the perverseness Prv 2:14
her breasts fill you at all times with **d**; Prv 5:19
morning; let us **d** ourselves with love. Prv 7:18
master workman, and I was daily his **d**, Prv 8:30
to the LORD, but a just weight is his **d**. Prv 11:1
but those of blameless ways are his **d**. Prv 11:20
but those who act faithfully are his **d**. Prv 12:22
Righteous lips are the **d** of a king, and Prv 16:13
who rebuke the wicked will have **d**, Prv 24:25
you rest; he will give **d** to your heart. Prv 29:17
the **d** of the children of man. Eccl 2:8
Preacher sought to find words of **d**, Eccl 12:10
With great **d** I sat in his shadow, and his Sg 2:3
I do not **d** in the blood of bulls, or of Is 1:11
And his **d** shall be in the fear of the LORD. Is 11:3
no regard for silver and do not **d** in gold. Is 13:17
and the things they **d** in do not profit. Is 44:9
is good, and **d** yourselves in rich food. Is 55:2
seek me daily and **d** to know my ways, Is 58:2
judgments; they **d** to draw near to God. Is 58:2
call the Sabbath a **d** and the holy day Is 58:13
then you shall take **d** in the LORD, and I Is 58:14
but you shall be called My **D** Is in Her, Is 62:4
my eyes and chose what I did not **d** in." Is 65:12
eyes and chose that in which I did not **d**." Is 66:4
drink deeply with **d** from her glorious Is 66:11
For in these things I **d**, declares the Jer 9:24
to me a joy and the **d** of my heart, Jer 15:16
about to take the **d** of your eyes away Ezk 24:16
pride of your power, the **d** of your eyes, Ezk 24:21
the **d** of their eyes and their soul's Ezk 24:25
and I take no **d** in your solemn Am 5:21
off your hair, for the children of your **d**; Mi 1:16
of the covenant in whom you **d**, Mal 3:1
you blessed, for you will be a land of **d**, Mal 3:12
For I **d** in the law of God, in my inner Rom 7:22

DELIGHTED (9)
because he **d** in Jacob's daughter. Gn 34:19
Saul's son, **d** much in David. 1 Sm 19:1
he rescued me, because he **d** in me. 2 Sm 22:20
who has **d** in you and set you on the 1 Kgs 10:9
who has **d** in you and set you on his 2 Chr 9:8
became fat and **d** themselves in your Neh 9:25
unless the king **d** in her and she was Est 2:14
he rescued me, because he **d** in me. Ps 18:19
the light of your face, for you **d** in them. Ps 44:3

DELIGHTFUL (3)
you are beautiful, my beloved, truly **d**. Sg 1:16
has killed all who were **d** in our eyes in Lam 2:4
people you drive out from their **d** houses; Mi 2:9

DELIGHTING (1)
inhabited world and **d** in the children Prv 8:31

DELIGHTS (20)
If the LORD **d** in us, he will bring us into Nm 14:8
man whom the king **d** to honor?" And Est 6:6
"For the man whom the king **d** to honor, Est 6:7
dress the man whom the king **d** to honor, Est 6:9
to the man whom the king **d** to honor.'" Est 6:9
to the man whom the king **d** to honor." Est 6:11
let anything in which he **d** escape him. Jb 20:20
you are not a God who **d** in wickedness; Ps 5:4
let him rescue him, for he **d** in him!" Ps 22:8
who **d** in the welfare of his servant!" Ps 35:27
give them drink from the river of your **d**. Ps 36:8
by the LORD, when he **d** in his way; Ps 37:23
who greatly **d** in his commandments! Ps 112:1
loves, as a father the son in whom he **d**. Prv 3:12
you are, O loved one, with all your **d**! Sg 7:6
I uphold, my chosen, in whom my soul **d**; Is 42:1
for the LORD **d** in you, and your land shall Is 62:4
and their soul **d** in their abominations; Is 66:3
forever, because he **d** in steadfast love. Mi 7:18
LORD, and he **d** in them." Or by asking, Mal 2:17

DELILAH (7)
the Valley of Sorek, whose name was **D**. Jgs 16:4
So **D** said to Samson, "Please tell me Jgs 16:6
Then **D** said to Samson, "Behold, you Jgs 16:10
So **D** took new ropes and bound him Jgs 16:12
Then **D** said to Samson, "Until now Jgs 16:13
D took the seven locks of his head and Jgs 16:14
When **D** saw that he had told her all Jgs 16:18

DELIVER (158)
Please **d** me from the hand of my Gn 32:11
men, and I will **d** your brother to you, Gn 42:34
I have come down to **d** them out of the Ex 3:8
but you must still **d** the same number of Ex 5:18
and I will **d** you from slavery to them, Ex 6:6
to **d** you and to give up your enemies Dt 23:14
there is none that can **d** out of my hand. Dt 32:39
to them, and **d** our lives from death." Jos 2:13
good to you. Only please **d** us this day." Jgs 10:15
why did you not **d** them within that Jgs 11:26
Who can **d** us from the power of these 1 Sm 4:8
and he will **d** you out of the hand of the 1 Sm 7:3
But now **d** us out of the hand of our 1 Sm 12:10
empty things that cannot profit or **d**, 1 Sm 12:21
of the bear will **d** me from the hand 1 Sm 17:37
day the LORD will **d** you into my 1 Sm 17:46
plead my cause and **d** me from your 1 Sm 24:15
and may he **d** me out of all 1 Sm 26:24
not kill me or **d** me into the hands 1 Sm 30:15
will hear and **d** his servant from 2 Sm 14:16
"**D** to me your silver and your gold, 1 Kgs 20:5
and he had to **d** to the king of Israel 2 Kgs 3:4
and he will **d** you out of the hand of 2 Kgs 17:39
will not be able to **d** you out of my 2 Kgs 18:29
by saying, The LORD will surely **d** us, 2 Kgs 18:30
you by saying, The LORD will **d** us. 2 Kgs 18:32
the LORD should **d** Jerusalem out of 2 Kgs 18:35
I will **d** you and this city out of the 2 Kgs 20:6
and gather and **d** us from among 1 Chr 16:35
who did not **d** their own people 2 Chr 25:15
LORD our God will **d** us from the 2 Chr 32:11
at all able to **d** their lands out of 2 Chr 32:13
was able to **d** his people from 2 Chr 32:14
should be able to **d** you from my 2 Chr 32:14
has been able to **d** his people from 2 Chr 32:15
less will your God **d** you out of my 2 Chr 32:15
Hezekiah will not **d** his people from 2 Chr 32:17
you shall **d** before the God of Jerusalem. Ezr 7:19
in the gate, and there is no one to **d** them. Jb 5:4
He will **d** you from six troubles; in seven Jb 5:19
Or, '**D** me from the adversary's hand'? Or, Jb 6:23
and there is none to **d** out of your hand? Jb 10:7
'**D** him from going down into the pit; Jb 33:24
Turn, O LORD, **d** my life; save me for the Ps 6:4
save me from all my pursuers and **d** me, Ps 7:1
apart, rending it in pieces, with none to **d**. Ps 7:2
D my soul from the wicked by your Ps 17:13
"He trusts in the LORD; let him **d** him; let Ps 22:8
D my soul from the sword, my precious Ps 22:20
Oh, guard my soul, and **d** me! Let me Ps 25:20
to shame; in your righteousness **d** me! Ps 31:1
that he may **d** their soul from death and Ps 33:19
D me from all my transgressions. Do not Ps 39:8
Be pleased, O LORD, to **d** me! O LORD, Ps 40:13
from the deceitful and unjust man **d** me! Ps 43:1
I will **d** you, and you shall glorify me." Ps 50:15
I tear you apart, and there be none to **d**! Ps 50:22
D me from bloodguiltiness, O God, O Ps 51:14
D me from my enemies, O my God; Ps 59:1
d me from those who work evil, and save Ps 59:2
D me from sinking in the mire; let me Ps 69:14
Make haste, O God, to **d** me! O LORD, Ps 70:1
In your righteousness **d** me and rescue Ps 71:2
seize him, for there is none to **d** him." Ps 71:11
Do not **d** the soul of your dove to the Ps 74:19
d us, and atone for our sins, for your Ps 79:9
d them from the hand of the wicked." Ps 82:4
Who can **d** his soul from the power of Ps 89:48
For he will **d** you from the snare of the Ps 91:3
he holds fast to me in love, I will **d** him; Ps 91:14
your steadfast love is good, **d** me! Ps 109:21
of the LORD: "O LORD, I pray, **d** my soul!" Ps 116:4
Look on my affliction and **d** me, for I Ps 119:153
you; **d** me according to your word. Ps 119:170
D me, O LORD, from lying lips, from a Ps 120:2
D me, O LORD, from evil men; preserve Ps 140:1
D me from my persecutors, for they are Ps 142:6
D me from my enemies, O LORD! I have Ps 143:9
rescue me and **d** me from the many Ps 144:7
Rescue me and **d** me from the hand of Ps 144:11
will pay the penalty, for if you **d** him, Prv 19:19
wait for the LORD, and he will **d** you. Prv 20:22
nor will wickedness **d** those who are Eccl 8:8
them a savior and defender, and **d** them. Is 19:20
protect Jerusalem; he will protect and **d** it; Is 31:5
you, for he will not be able to **d** you. Is 36:14

by saying, "The LORD will surely **d** us. Is 36:15
"The LORD will **d** us." Has any of the gods Is 36:18
that the LORD should **d** Jerusalem out of Is 36:20
I will **d** you and this city out of the hand Is 38:6
there is none who can **d** from my hand; Is 43:13
and **d** Jacob to utter destruction and Is 43:28
He prays to it and says, "**D** me, for you Is 44:17
astray, and he cannot **d** himself or say, Is 44:20
they cannot **d** themselves from the Is 47:14
cannot redeem? Or have I no power to **d**? Is 50:2
out, let your collection of idols **d** you! Is 57:13
afraid of them, for I am with you to **d** you, Jer 1:8
with you, declares the LORD, to **d** you." Jer 1:19
I am with you to save you and **d** you, Jer 15:20
I will **d** you out of the hand of the Jer 15:21
Therefore **d** up their children to Jer 18:21
and **d** from the hand of the oppressor Jer 21:12
and **d** from the hand of the oppressor Jer 22:3
I will **d** them into the hand of Jer 29:21
put you to death or **d** you into the hand Jer 38:16
But I will **d** you on that day, declares Jer 39:17
to save you and to **d** you from his hand. Jer 42:11
to **d** us into the hand of the Chaldeans, Jer 43:3
I will **d** them into the hand of those who Jer 46:26
there is none to **d** us from their hand. Lam 5:8
gold are not able to **d** them in the day of Ezk 7:19
I will tear off and **d** my people out of Ezk 13:21
I will **d** my people out of your hand. Ezk 13:23
they would **d** but their own lives by Ezk 14:14
they would **d** neither sons nor Ezk 14:16
they would **d** neither sons nor Ezk 14:18
they would **d** neither son nor Ezk 14:20
They would **d** but their own lives by Ezk 14:20
and I will **d** you into the hands of Ezk 21:31
I will **d** you into the hands of those Ezk 23:28
the righteous shall not **d** him when he Ezk 33:12
and **d** them from the hand of those Ezk 34:27
And I will **d** you from all your Ezk 36:29
is the god who will **d** you out of my Dn 3:15
serve is able to **d** us from the burning Dn 3:17
and he will **d** us out of your hand, Dn 3:17
distressed and set his mind to **d** Daniel. Dn 6:14
whom you serve continually, **d** you!" Dn 6:16
been able to **d** you from the lions?" Dn 6:20
a whole people to **d** them up to Edom. Am 1:6
and I will **d** up the city and all that is in Am 6:8
and he shall **d** us from the Assyrian when Mi 5:6
and tears in pieces, and there is none to **d**. Mi 5:8
gold shall be able to **d** them on the day Zep 1:18
and I will **d** none from their hand." Zec 11:6
not into temptation, but **d** us from evil. Mt 6:13
for they will **d** you over to courts and Mt 10:17
When they **d** you over, do not be Mt 10:19
Brother will **d** brother over to death, Mt 10:21
and **d** him over to the Gentiles to be Mt 20:19
"Then they will **d** you up to tribulation Mt 24:9
you give me if I **d** him over to you?" Mt 26:15
He trusts in God; let God **d** him now, if Mt 27:43
him to death and **d** him over to the Mk 10:33
For they will **d** you over to councils, Mk 13:9
they bring you to trial and **d** you over, Mk 13:11
And brother will **d** brother over to Mk 13:12
so as to **d** him up to the authority and Lk 20:20
and I have come down to **d** them. Acts 7:34
owns this belt and **d** him into the Acts 21:11
Who will **d** me from this body of Rom 7:24
you are to **d** this man to Satan for the 1 Cor 5:5
and if I **d** up my body to be burned, 1 Cor 13:3
such a deadly peril, and he will **d** us. 2 Cor 1:10
set our hope that he will **d** us again. 2 Cor 1:10
for our sins to **d** us from the present Gal 1:4
and **d** all those who through fear of Heb 2:15

DELIVERANCE (10)
you shall have **d**.'" When the 1 Sm 11:9
them, but I will grant them some **d**, 2 Chr 12:7
relief and **d** will rise for the Jews from Est 4:14
you surround me with shouts of **d**. Ps 32:7
the glad news of **d** in the great Ps 40:9
not hidden your **d** within my heart; Ps 40:10
people, give **d** to the children of the needy, Ps 72:4
have accomplished no **d** in the earth, Is 26:18
will come, and my **d** be revealed. Is 56:1
Jesus Christ this will turn out for my **d**, Phil 1:19

DELIVERANCES (1)
to GOD, the Lord, belong **d** from death. Ps 68:20

DELIVERED (160)
fish of the sea. Into your hand they are **d**. Gn 9:2
who has **d** your enemies into your Gn 14:20
to face, and yet my life has been **d**." Gn 32:30
"An Egyptian **d** us out of the hand of the Ex 2:19
and you have not **d** your people at all." Ex 5:23
and **d** me from the sword of Pharaoh"). Ex 18:4
the way, and how the LORD had **d** them. Ex 18:8
in that he had **d** them out of the hand of Ex 18:9
who has **d** you out of the hand of the Ex 18:10
of Pharaoh and has **d** the people from Ex 18:10
and you shall be **d** into the hand of the Lv 26:25
did this to them and **d** them out of the Jos 9:26
Now you have **d** the people of Israel Jos 22:31
blessed you. So I **d** you out of his hand. Jos 24:10
And I **d** you from the hand of the Jgs 6:9
who had **d** them from the hand of all Jgs 8:34
risked his life and **d** you from the hand Jgs 9:17
and Israel **d** their territory from the 1 Sm 7:14
and I **d** you from the hand of the 1 Sm 10:18
and Samuel and **d** you out of 1 Sm 12:11
the Amalekites and **d** Israel out of 1 Sm 14:48
and struck him and **d** it out of his 1 Sm 17:35
"The LORD who **d** me from the paw of 1 Sm 17:37
and I **d** you out of the hand of Saul. 2 Sm 12:7
that the LORD has **d** him from the 2 Sm 18:19
who has **d** up the men who raised 2 Sm 18:28
For the LORD has **d** you this day from 2 Sm 18:31
"The king **d** us from the hand of our 2 Sm 19:9
day when the LORD **d** him from the 2 Sm 22:1
"You **d** me from strife with my 2 Sm 22:44
me; you **d** me from men of violence. 2 Sm 22:49
into the house and **d** him to his 1 Kgs 17:23
whose hand they **d** the money to 2 Kgs 12:15
of the nations ever **d** his land out of 2 Kgs 18:33
Have they **d** Samaria out of my 2 Kgs 18:34
of the lands have **d** their lands out of 2 Kgs 18:35
to destruction. And shall you be **d**? 2 Kgs 19:11
Have the gods of the nations **d** them, 2 Kgs 19:12
the money that is **d** into their hand, 2 Kgs 22:7
the house and have **d** it into the hand 2 Kgs 22:9
For he has **d** the inhabitants of the 1 Chr 22:18
the LORD **d** into their hand a very 2 Chr 24:24
who have not **d** their people from 2 Chr 32:17
and they were **d** to one whose name was Ezr 5:14
and he **d** us from the hand of the enemy Ezr 8:31
They also **d** the king's commissions to Ezr 8:36
many times you **d** them according to Neh 9:28
the king's command **d** by the eunuchs. Est 1:12
of King Ahasuerus **d** by the eunuchs?" Est 1:15
he has **d** them into the hand of their Jb 8:4
who will be **d** through the cleanness of Jb 22:30
because I **d** the poor who cried for help, Jb 29:12
their offspring, and are **d** of their young? Jb 39:3
You **d** me from strife with the people; Ps 18:43
who **d** me from my enemies; yes, you Ps 18:48
trusted; they trusted, and you **d** them. Ps 22:4
and you have not **d** me into the hand of Ps 31:8
a warrior is not **d** by his great strength. Ps 33:16
he answered me and **d** me from all my Ps 34:4
For he has **d** me from every trouble, and Ps 54:7
For you have **d** my soul from death, yes, Ps 56:13
That your beloved ones may be **d**, give Ps 60:5
let me be **d** from my enemies and from Ps 69:14
and **d** his power to captivity, his glory to Ps 78:61
In distress you called, and I **d** you; I Ps 81:7
you have **d** my soul from the depths of Ps 86:13
Many times he **d** them, but they were Ps 106:43
and he **d** them from their distress. Ps 107:6
and he **d** them from their distress. Ps 107:13
and he **d** them from their distress. Ps 107:19
and **d** them from their destruction. Ps 107:20
and he **d** them from their distress. Ps 107:28
That your beloved ones may be **d**, give Ps 108:6
For you have **d** my soul from death, my Ps 116:8
So you will be **d** from the forbidden Prv 2:16
The righteous is **d** from trouble, and Prv 11:8
but by knowledge the righteous are **d**. Prv 11:9
the offspring of the righteous will be **d**. Prv 11:21
Whoever walks in integrity will be **d**, Prv 28:18
but he who walks in wisdom will be **d**. Prv 28:26
man, and he by his wisdom **d** the city. Eccl 9:15
fled for help to be **d** from the king of Is 20:6
the gods of the nations **d** his land out of Is 36:18
Have they **d** Samaria out of my hand? Is 36:19
of these lands have **d** their lands out of Is 36:20
them to destruction. And shall you be **d**? Is 37:11
Have the gods of the nations **d** them, the Is 37:12
but in love you have **d** my life from the Is 38:17
her pain came upon her she **d** a son. Is 66:7
called by my name, and say, 'We are **d**!' Jer 7:10
For he has **d** the life of the needy from Jer 20:13
surely be captured and **d** into his hand. Jer 34:3
"You shall be **d** into the hand of the Jer 37:17
she shall be **d** into the hand of a people Jer 46:24
he has **d** into the hand of the enemy the Lam 2:7
iniquity, but you will have **d** your soul. Ezk 3:19
and you will have **d** your soul." Ezk 3:21
They alone would be **d**, but the land Ezk 14:16
daughters, but they alone would be **d**. Ezk 14:18
my children and **d** them up as Ezk 16:21
your allotted portion and **d** you to the Ezk 16:27
They are **d** over to the sword with my Ezk 21:12
Therefore I **d** her into the hands of her Ezk 23:9
Egypt is **d** to the sword; drag her away, Ezk 32:20
iniquity, but you will have **d** your soul. Ezk 33:9
has sent his angel and **d** his servants, Dn 3:28
but these shall be **d** out of his hand: Dn 11:41
But at that time your people shall be **d**, Dn 12:1
because they **d** up a whole people to Am 1:9
Man is about to be **d** into the hands of Mt 17:22
in anger his master **d** him to the jailers, Mt 18:34
Son of Man will be **d** over to the chief Mt 20:18
'Master, you **d** to me five talents; Mt 25:20
'Master, you **d** to me two talents; Mt 25:22
Son of Man will be **d** up to be crucified." Mt 26:2
led him away and **d** him over to Pilate Mt 27:2
was out of envy that they had **d** him up. Mt 27:18
scourged Jesus, **d** him to be crucified. Mt 27:26
Man is going to be **d** into the hands of Mk 9:31
Son of Man will be **d** over to the chief Mk 10:33
led him away and **d** him over to Pilate. Mk 15:1
that the chief priests had **d** him up. Mk 15:10
Jesus, he **d** him to be crucified. Mk 15:15
ministers of the word have **d** them to us, Lk 1:2
being **d** from the hand of our enemies, Lk 1:74
and their glory, for it has been **d** to me, Lk 4:6
Man is about to be **d** into the hands of Lk 9:44
For he will be **d** over to the Gentiles and Lk 18:32
You will be **d** up even by parents and Lk 21:16
asked, but he **d** Jesus over to their will. Lk 23:25
Son of Man must be **d** into the hands of Lk 24:7
chief priests and rulers **d** him up to be Lk 24:20
has come, but when she has **d** the baby, Jn 16:21
we would not have **d** him over to you." Jn 18:30
the chief priests have **d** you over to me. Jn 18:35
that I might not be **d** over to the Jews. Jn 18:36
Therefore he who **d** me over to you has Jn 19:11
So he **d** him over to them to be Jn 19:16
d up according to the definite plan and Acts 2:23
whom you **d** over and denied in the Acts 3:13
the customs that Moses **d** to us." Acts 6:14
received the law as **d** by angels and did Acts 7:53
the throne, and **d** an oration to them. Acts 12:21
together, they **d** the letter. Acts 15:30
they **d** to them for observance the Acts 16:4
come to Caesarea and **d** the letter to Acts 23:33
they **d** Paul and some other prisoners Acts 27:1
yet I was **d** as a prisoner from Acts 28:17
who was **d** up for our trespasses and Rom 4:25
this and have **d** to them what Rom 15:28
that I may be **d** from the unbelievers Rom 15:31
the traditions even as I **d** them to you. 1 Cor 11:2
from the Lord what I also **d** to you, 1 Cor 11:23
For I **d** to you as of first importance 1 Cor 15:3
He **d** us from such a deadly peril, and 2 Cor 1:10
you are a letter from Christ **d** by us, 2 Cor 3:3
He has **d** us from the domain of Col 1:13
that we may be **d** from wicked and 2 Thes 3:2
the holy commandment **d** to them. 2 Pt 2:21
faith that was once for all **d** to the saints. Jude 1:3

DELIVERER (9)
the LORD raised up a **d** for the people of Jgs 3:9
and the LORD raised up for them a **d**, Jgs 3:15
And there was no **d** because it was far Jgs 18:28
is my rock and my fortress and my **d**, 2 Sm 22:2
is my rock and my fortress and my **d**, Ps 18:2
You are my help and my **d**; do not Ps 40:17
You are my help and my **d**; O LORD, do Ps 70:5
my fortress, my stronghold and my **d**, Ps 144:2
written, "The **D** will come from Zion, Rom 11:26

DELIVERING (6)
d the poor from him who is too strong Ps 35:10
d you from the way of evil, from men of Prv 2:12
d you up to the synagogues and Lk 21:12
d him over to four squads of soldiers to Acts 12:4
binding and **d** to prison both men and Acts 22:4
d you from your people and from the Acts 26:17

DELIVERS (19)
He **d** even the one who is not innocent, Jb 22:30
He **d** the afflicted by their affliction and Jb 36:15
around those who fear him, and **d** them. Ps 34:7
the LORD hears and **d** them out of all Ps 34:17
but the LORD **d** him out of them all. Ps 34:19
The LORD helps them and **d** them; he Ps 37:40
he **d** them from the wicked and saves Ps 37:40
In the day of trouble the LORD **d** him; Ps 41:1
For he **d** the needy when he calls, the Ps 72:12
he **d** them from the hand of the wicked. Ps 97:10
my enemies, and your right hand **d** me. Ps 138:7
profit, but righteousness **d** from death. Prv 10:2
wrath, but righteousness **d** from death. Prv 11:4
righteousness of the upright **d** them, Prv 11:6
but the mouth of the upright **d** them. Prv 12:6
them; she **d** sashes to the merchant. Prv 31:24
He **d** and rescues; he works signs and Dn 6:27
when he **d** the kingdom to God the 1 Cor 15:24
Jesus who **d** us from the wrath to 1 Thes 1:10

DELUDE (1)
that no one may **d** you with plausible Col 2:4

DELUDED (2)
fools, and the princes of Memphis are **d**; Is 19:13
a **d** heart has led him astray, and he Is 44:20

DELUGE (2)
There will be a **d** of rain, and you, O Ezk 13:11
and there shall be a **d** of rain in my Ezk 13:13

DELUGED (1)
that then existed was **d** with water and 2 Pt 3:6

DELUSION (6)
but a breath; those of high estate are a **d**; Ps 62:9
Behold, they are all a **d**; their works are Is 41:29
Truly the hills are a **d**, the orgies on the Jer 3:23
They are worthless, a work of **d**; at the Jer 10:15
They are worthless, a work of **d**; at the Jer 51:18
God sends them a strong **d**, 2 Thes 2:11

DELVED (1)
dug, that the nobles of the people **d**, Nm 21:18

DEMAND (6)
all this I did not **d** the food allowance of Neh 5:18
on earth who can meet the king's **d**, Dn 2:10
away your goods do not **d** them back. Lk 6:30
entrusted much, they will **d** the more. Lk 12:48
decided that their **d** should be granted. Lk 23:24
For Jews **d** signs and Greeks seek 1 Cor 1:22

DEMANDED (2)
'All that you first **d** of your servant I 1 Kgs 20:9
Simon, behold, Satan **d** to have you, Lk 22:31

DEMANDING (3)
for a trifle, **d** no high price for them. Ps 44:12
in their heart by **d** the food they craved. Ps 78:18
d with loud cries that he should be Lk 23:23

DEMANDS (2)
that stood against us with its legal **d**. Col 2:14
we could have made **d** as apostles of 1 Thes 2:6

DEMAS (3)
beloved physician greets you, as does **D**. Col 4:14
For **D**, in love with this present world, 2 Tm 4:10
do Mark, Aristarchus, **D**, and Luke, Phlm 1:24

DEMETRIUS (3)
For a man named **D**, a silversmith, Acts 19:24
If therefore **D** and the craftsmen with Acts 19:38
D has received a good testimony from 3 Jn 1:12

DEMOLISH (1)
metal images and **d** all their high Nm 33:52

DEMOLISHED (3)
And they **d** the pillar of Baal, and 2 Kgs 10:27
of Baal, and **d** the house of Baal, 2 Kgs 10:27
your prophets, they have **d** your altars, Rom 11:3

DEMON (21)
And when the **d** had been cast out, the Mt 9:33
nor drinking, and they say, 'He has a **d**.' Mt 11:18
daughter is severely oppressed by a **d**." Mt 15:22
him, and the **d** came out of him, Mt 17:18
him to cast the **d** out of her daughter. Mk 7:26
your way; the **d** has left your daughter." Mk 7:29
the child lying in bed and the **d** gone. Mk 7:30
man who had the spirit of an unclean **d**, Lk 4:33
him!" And when the **d** had thrown him Lk 4:35
no wine, and you say, 'He has a **d**.' Lk 7:33
and be driven by the **d** into the desert.) Lk 8:29
the **d** threw him to the ground and Lk 9:42
he was casting out a **d** that was mute. Lk 11:14
When the **d** had gone out, the mute Lk 11:14
The crowd answered, "You have a **d**! Jn 7:20
that you are a Samaritan and have a **d**?" Jn 8:48
Jesus answered, "I do not have a **d**, but I Jn 8:49
to him, "Now we know that you have a **d**! Jn 8:52
Many of them said, "He has a **d**, and is Jn 10:20
words of one who is oppressed by a **d**. Jn 10:21
Can a **d** open the eyes of the blind?" Jn 10:21

DEMON-OPPRESSED (2)
a **d** man who was mute was brought to Mt 9:32
Then a **d** man who was blind and Mt 12:22

DEMON-POSSESSED (5)
of the Gadarenes, two **d** men met him, Mt 8:28
what had happened to the **d** men. Mt 8:33
they came to Jesus and saw the **d** man, Mk 5:15
had happened to the **d** man and to the Mk 5:16
told them how the **d** man had been Lk 8:36

DEMONIC (2)
above, but is earthly, unspiritual, **d**. Jas 3:15
For they are **d** spirits, performing signs, Rv 16:14

DEMONS (50)
more sacrifice their sacrifices to goat **d**, Lv 17:7
They sacrificed to **d** that were no gods, Dt 32:17
their sons and their daughters to the **d**; Ps 106:37
diseases and pains, those oppressed by **d**, Mt 4:24
name, and cast out **d** in your name, Mt 7:22
to him many who were oppressed by **d**, Mt 8:16
And the **d** begged him, saying, "If you Mt 8:31
"He casts out **d** by the prince of Mt 9:34
casts out demons by the prince of **d**." Mt 9:34
raise the dead, cleanse lepers, cast out **d**. Mt 10:8
"It is only by Beelzebul, the prince of **d**, Mt 12:24
of demons, that this man casts out **d**." Mt 12:24
And if I cast out **d** by Beelzebul, by Mt 12:27
is by the Spirit of God that I cast out **d**, Mt 12:28
all who were sick or oppressed by **d**. Mk 1:32
various diseases, and cast out many **d**. Mk 1:34
And he would not permit the **d** to speak, Mk 1:34
in their synagogues and casting out **d**. Mk 1:39
and have authority to cast out **d**. Mk 3:15
and "by the prince of **d** he casts out the Mk 3:22
prince of demons he casts out the **d**." Mk 3:22
been possessed with **d** begged him that Mk 5:18
they cast out many **d** and anointed with Mk 6:13
someone casting out **d** in your name, Mk 9:38
from whom he had cast out seven **d**. Mk 16:9
in my name they will cast out **d**; Mk 16:17
And **d** also came out of many, crying, Lk 4:41
from whom seven **d** had gone out, Lk 8:2
met him a man from the city who had **d**. Lk 8:27
"Legion," for many **d** had entered him. Lk 8:30
Then the **d** came out of the man and Lk 8:33
the man from whom the **d** had gone, Lk 8:35
man from whom the **d** had gone begged Lk 8:38
and authority over all **d** and to cure Lk 9:1
someone casting out **d** in your name, Lk 9:49
even the **d** are subject to us in your Lk 10:17
them said, "He casts out **d** by Beelzebul, Lk 11:15
demons by Beelzebul, the prince of **d**," Lk 11:15
you say that I cast out **d** by Beelzebul. Lk 11:18
And if I cast out **d** by Beelzebul, by Lk 11:19
is by the finger of God that I cast out **d**, Lk 11:20
I cast out **d** and perform cures today Lk 13:32
sacrifice they offer to **d** and not to 1 Cor 10:20
want you to be participants with **d**. 1 Cor 10:20
the cup of the Lord and the cup of **d**. 1 Cor 10:21
table of the Lord and the table of **d**. 1 Cor 10:21
to deceitful spirits and teachings of **d**, 1 Tm 4:1
well. Even the **d** believe—and shudder! Jas 2:19
nor give up worshiping **d** and idols of Rv 9:20
She has become a dwelling place for **d**, a Rv 18:2

DEMONSTRATION (1)
but in **d** of the Spirit and of power, 1 Cor 2:4

DEN (17)
child shall put his hand on the adder's **d**. Is 11:8
become a **d** of robbers in your eyes? Jer 7:11
O king, shall be cast into the **d** of lions. Dn 6:7
be cast into the **d** of lions?" The king Dn 6:12
was brought and cast into the **d** of lions. Dn 6:16
brought and laid on the mouth of the **d**, Dn 6:17
arose and went in haste to the **d** of lions. Dn 6:19
he came near to the **d** where Daniel was, Dn 6:20
that Daniel be taken up out of the **d**. Dn 6:23
So Daniel was taken up out of the **d**, and Dn 6:23
and cast into the **d** of lions—they, Dn 6:24
before they reached the bottom of the **d**, Dn 6:24
Does a young lion cry out from his **d**, if Am 3:4
Where is the lions' **d**, the feeding place Na 2:11
but you make it a **d** of robbers." Mt 21:13
But you have made it a **d** of robbers." Mk 11:17
but you have made it a **d** of robbers." Lk 19:46

DENARII (7)
servants who owed him a hundred **d**, Mt 18:28
and buy two hundred **d** worth of bread Mk 6:37
more than three hundred **d** and given to Mk 14:5
One owed five hundred **d**, and the other Lk 7:41
day he took out two **d** and gave them to Lk 10:35
"Two hundred **d** would not buy enough Jn 6:7
sold for three hundred **d** and given to the Jn 12:5

DENARIUS (9)
agreeing with the laborers for a **d** a day, Mt 20:2
hour came, each of them received a **d**. Mt 20:9
but each of them also received a **d**. Mt 20:10
Did you not agree with me for a **d**? Mt 20:13
for the tax." And they brought him a **d**. Mt 22:19
Bring me a **d** and let me look at it." Mk 12:15
"Show me a **d**. Whose likeness and Lk 20:24
saying, "A quart of wheat for a **d**, Rv 6:6
and three quarts of barley for a **d**, Rv 6:6

DENIED (18)
But Sarah **d** it, saying, "I did not Gn 18:15
for I have not **d** the words of the Holy Jb 6:10
But he **d** it before them all, saying, "I do Mt 26:70
And again he **d** it with an oath: "I do Mt 26:72
But he **d** it, saying, "I neither know nor Mk 14:68
But again he **d** it. And after a little Mk 14:70
was it that touched me?" When all **d** it, Lk 8:45
before men will be **d** before the angels of Lk 12:9
But he **d** it, saying, "Woman, I do not Lk 22:57
not crow till you have **d** me three times. Jn 13:38
his disciples, are you?" He **d** it and said, Jn 18:25
Peter again **d** it, and at once a rooster Jn 18:27
delivered over and **d** in the presence Acts 3:13
But you **d** the Holy and Righteous One, Acts 3:14
In his humiliation justice was **d** him. Acts 8:33
then that these things cannot be **d**, Acts 19:36
he has **d** the faith and is worse than an 1 Tm 5:8
kept my word and have not **d** my name. Rv 3:8

DENIES (5)
but whoever **d** me before men, I also Mt 10:33
but the one who **d** me before men will be Lk 12:9
the liar but he who **d** that Jesus is the 1 Jn 2:22
he who **d** the Father and the Son. 1 Jn 2:22
No one who **d** the Son has the Father. 1 Jn 2:23

DENOUNCE (5)
curse Jacob for me, and come, **d** Israel!' Nm 23:7
How can I **d** whom the LORD has not Nm 23:8
Terror is on every side! "**D** him! Jer 20:10
Let us **d** him!" say all my close friends, Jer 20:10
Then he began to **d** the cities where Mt 11:20

DENOUNCED (2)
I denounce whom the LORD has not **d**? Nm 23:8
why am I **d** because of that for 1 Cor 10:30

DENS (8)
made for themselves the **d** that are in the Jgs 6:2
go into their lairs, and remain in their **d**. Jb 37:8
they crouch in their **d** or lie in wait Jb 38:40
they steal away and lie down in their **d**. Ps 104:22
of Senir and Hermon, from the **d** of lions, Sg 4:8
the watchtower will become **d** forever, Is 32:14
with prey and his **d** with torn flesh. Na 2:12
and in **d** and caves of the earth. Heb 11:38

DENSE (1)
such a **d** swarm of locusts as had never Ex 10:14

DENY (25)
from his place, then it will **d** him, Jb 8:18
of you; **d** them not to me before I die: Prv 30:7
lest I be full and **d** you and say, "Who is Prv 30:9
to **d** a man justice in the presence of Lam 3:35
I also will **d** before my Father who is in Mt 10:33
let him **d** himself and take up his cross Mt 16:24
crows, you will **d** me three times." Mt 26:34
I will not **d** you!" And all the disciples Mt 26:35
you will **d** me three times." And he Mt 26:75
let him **d** himself and take up his cross Mk 8:34
twice, you will **d** me three times." Mk 14:30
I will not **d** you." And they all said the Mk 14:31
you will **d** me three times." And he Mk 14:72
let him **d** himself and take up his cross Lk 9:23
those who **d** that there is a resurrection, Lk 20:27
until you **d** three times that you know Lk 22:34
today, you will **d** me three times." Lk 22:61
He confessed, and did not **d**, but Jn 1:20
of Jerusalem, and we cannot **d** it. Acts 4:16
him; if we **d** him, he also will deny us; 2 Tm 2:12
him; if we deny him, he also will **d** us; 2 Tm 2:12
faithful—for he cannot **d** himself. 2 Tm 2:13
God, but they **d** him by their works. Ti 1:16
into sensuality and **d** our only Master Jude 1:4
and you did not **d** my faith even in the Rv 2:13

DENYING (3)
transgressing, and **d** the LORD, and Is 59:13
of godliness, but **d** its power. 2 Tm 3:5
even **d** the Master who bought them, 2 Pt 2:1

DEPART (81)
The scepter shall not **d** from Judah, Gn 49:10
the swarms of flies may **d** from Pharaoh, Ex 8:29
by night did not **d** from before the Ex 13:22
Then Moses let his father-in-law **d**, and Ex 18:27
LORD said to Moses, "**D**; go up from here, Ex 33:1
young man, would not **d** from the tent. Ex 33:11
I will **d** to my own land and to my Nm 10:30
the congregation, saying, "**D**, please, Nm 16:26
and lest they **d** from your heart all the Dt 4:9
of the Law shall not **d** from your mouth, Jos 1:8
Please do not **d** from here until I come to Jgs 6:18
day he arose early in the morning to **d**. Jgs 19:8
concubine and his servant rose up to **d**, Jgs 19:9
When you **d** from me today, you will 1 Sm 10:2
d; go down from among the 1 Sm 15:6
d, and go into the land of Judah." So 1 Sm 22:5
and **d** as soon as you have light." 1 Sm 29:10
away his wife and children, and **d**." 1 Sm 30:22
my steadfast love will not **d** from him, 2 Sm 7:15
sword shall never **d** from your 2 Sm 12:10
Hadad said to Pharaoh, "Let me **d**, 1 Kgs 11:21
And he said to him, "Only let me **d**." 1 Kgs 11:22
"**D** from here and turn eastward and 1 Kgs 17:3

made Israel to sin; he did not **d** from it. 2 Kgs 3:3
life, "Arise, and **d** with your household, 2 Kgs 8:1
Israel to sin; he did not **d** from them. 2 Kgs 13:2
they did not **d** from the sins of the 2 Kgs 13:6
He did not **d** from all the sins of 2 Kgs 13:11
He did not **d** from all the sins of 2 Kgs 14:24
He did not **d** from the sins of 2 Kgs 15:9
He did not **d** all his days from all the 2 Kgs 15:18
He did not **d** from the sins of 2 Kgs 15:28
did. They did not **d** from them, 2 Kgs 17:22
He did not **d** from following him, 2 Kgs 18:6
did not need to **d** from their service, 2 Chr 35:15
in the way did not **d** from them by day, Neh 9:19
he will not **d** from darkness; the flame Jb 15:30
by the breath of his mouth he will **d**. Jb 15:30
They say to God, '**D** from us! We do not Jb 21:14
They said to God, '**D** from us,' and Jb 22:17
D from me, all you workers of evil, for the Ps 6:8
again, before I **d** and am no more!" Ps 39:13
fraud do not **d** from its marketplace. Ps 55:11
D from me, you evildoers, that I may Ps 119:115
O God! O men of blood, **d** from me! Ps 139:19
and do not **d** from the words of my Prv 5:7
good, evil will not **d** from his house. Prv 17:13
when he is old he will not **d** from it. Prv 22:6
yet his folly will not **d** from him. Prv 27:22
D from the peak of Amana, from the peak Sg 4:8
his burden will **d** from your shoulder, Is 10:27
The jealousy of Ephraim shall **d**, and Is 11:13
and his yoke shall **d** from them, and his Is 14:25
I said, In the middle of my days I must **d**; Is 38:10
D, depart, go out from there; touch no Is 52:11
Depart, **d**, go out from there; touch no Is 52:11
For the mountains may **d** and the hills Is 54:10
my steadfast love shall not **d** from you, Is 54:10
mouth, shall not **d** out of your mouth, Is 59:21
and my jealousy shall **d** from you. Ezk 16:42
left. Woe to them when I **d** from them! Hos 9:12
low, and the scepter of Egypt shall **d**. Zec 10:11
d from me, you workers of lawlessness.' Mt 7:23
worthy in it and stay there until you **d**. Mt 10:11
will say to those on his left, '**D** from me, Mt 25:41
to beg Jesus to **d** from their region. Mk 5:17
house, stay there until you **d** from there. Mk 6:10
you are letting your servant **d** in peace, Lk 2:29
She did not **d** from the temple, Lk 2:37
down at Jesus' knees, saying, "**D** from me, Lk 5:8
to command them to **d** into the abyss. Lk 8:31
Gerasenes asked him to **d** from them, Lk 8:37
you enter, stay there, and from there **d**. Lk 9:4
D from me, all you workers of evil!' Lk 13:27
and let those who are inside the city **d**, Lk 21:21
his hour had come to **d** out of this world Jn 13:1
ordered them not to **d** from Jerusalem, Acts 1:4
them, intending to **d** on the next day, Acts 20:7
My desire is to **d** and be with Christ, Phil 1:23
later times some will **d** from the faith 1 Tm 4:1
name of the Lord **d** from iniquity." 2 Tm 2:19

DEPARTED (91)
years old when he **d** from Haran. Gn 12:4
And she **d** and wandered in the Gn 21:14
took ten of his master's camels and **d**, Gn 24:10
So Isaac **d** from there and encamped in Gn 26:17
way, and they **d** from him in peace. Gn 26:31
Then Laban **d** and returned home. Gn 31:55
their donkeys with their grain and **d**. Gn 42:26
sent his brothers away, and as they **d**, Gn 45:24
month after they had **d** from the land of Ex 16:1
the people of Israel **d** from the presence Ex 35:20
was kindled against them, and he **d**. Nm 12:9
the LORD nor Moses **d** out of the camp. Nm 14:44
the elders of Midian **d** with the fees for Nm 22:7
Then she sent them away, and they **d**. Jos 2:21
They **d** and went into the hills and Jos 2:22
was dead, everyone **d** to his home. Jgs 9:55
her away for two months, and she **d**, Jgs 11:38
And the man **d** from the town of Jgs 17:8
Then the five men **d** and came to Laish Jgs 18:7
So they turned and **d**, putting the little Jgs 18:21
He rose up and **d** and arrived opposite Jgs 19:10
the people of Israel **d** from there at that Jgs 21:24
"The glory has **d** from Israel!" 1 Sm 4:21
she said, "The glory has **d** from Israel, 1 Sm 4:22
not send the people away, and they **d**? 1 Sm 6:6
So the Kenites **d** from among the 1 Sm 15:6
the Spirit of the LORD **d** from Saul, 1 Sm 16:14
well, and the evil spirit **d** from him. 1 Sm 16:23
was with him but had **d** from Saul. 1 Sm 18:12
forever.'" And he rose and **d**, 1 Sm 20:42
David **d** from there and escaped to the 1 Sm 22:1
of Judah." So David **d** and went into 1 Sm 22:5
hundred, arose and **d** from Keilah, 1 Sm 23:13
Then all the people **d**, each to his 2 Sm 6:19
the day the king **d** until the day he 2 Sm 19:24
have not wickedly **d** from my God. 2 Sm 22:22
wife arose and **d** and came to 1 Kgs 14:17
So he **d** from there and found Elisha 1 Kgs 19:19
And the messengers **d** and brought 1 Kgs 20:9
And as soon as he had **d** from him, 1 Kgs 20:36
So the prophet **d** and waited for the 1 Kgs 20:38
and he sent the men away, and they **d**. 2 Kgs 5:24
Then he **d** from Elisha and came to 2 Kgs 8:14
And when he **d** from there, he met 2 Kgs 10:15
king of Assyria **d** and went home 2 Kgs 19:36
Then all the people **d** each to his 1 Chr 16:43
and they **d**. When David was told 1 Chr 19:5
So Joab **d** and went throughout all 1 Chr 21:4
And he **d** with no one's regret. 2 Chr 21:20
When they had **d** from him, leaving 2 Chr 24:25
Then we **d** from the river Ahava on the Ezr 8:31
I have not **d** from the commandment of Jb 23:12
and have not wickedly **d** from my God. Ps 18:21
nor have our steps **d** from your way; Ps 44:18
the dead? Do the **d** rise up to praise you? Ps 88:10
Egypt was glad when they **d**, for dread Ps 105:38
down to death, and her paths to the **d**; Prv 2:18
the day that Ephraim **d** from Judah— Is 7:17
king of Assyria **d** and returned home Is 37:37
the metal workers had **d** from Jerusalem. Jer 29:2
daughter of Zion all her majesty has **d**. Lam 1:6
whoring heart that has **d** from me and Ezk 6:9
spoken: The kingdom has **d** from you, Dn 4:31
over its glory—for it has **d** from them. Hos 10:5
they **d** to their own country by another Mt 2:12
Now when they had **d**, behold, an angel Mt 2:13
and his mother by night and **d** to Egypt Mt 2:14
the sign of Jonah." So he left them and **d**. Mt 16:4
the pieces of silver into the temple, he **d**, Mt 27:5
So they **d** quickly from the tomb with Mt 28:8
he **d** and went out to a desolate place, Mk 1:35
to your word." And the angel **d** from her. Lk 1:38
he **d** from him until an opportune time. Lk 4:13
day, he **d** and went into a desolate place. Lk 4:42
And they **d** and went through the villages, Lk 9:6
who stripped him and beat him and **d**, Lk 10:30
he left Judea and **d** again for Galilee. Jn 4:3
After the two days he **d** for Galilee. Jn 4:43
things, he **d** and hid himself from them. Jn 12:36
So Ananias **d** and entered the house. Acts 9:17
the angel who spoke to him had **d**, Acts 10:7
the brothers." Then he **d** and went to Acts 12:17
but Paul chose Silas and **d**, having Acts 15:40
they encouraged them and **d**. Acts 16:40
to him as soon as possible, they **d**. Acts 17:15
he **d** and went from one place to the Acts 18:23
he said farewell and **d** for Macedonia. Acts 20:1
long while, until daybreak, and so **d**. Acts 20:11
ended, we **d** and went on our journey, Acts 21:5
the next day we **d** and came to Acts 21:8
they **d** after Paul had made one Acts 28:25

DEPARTING (1)
as her soul was **d** (for she was dying), Gn 35:18

DEPARTS (5)
which the disease **d** when you have Lv 13:58
of his house, and she **d** out of his house, Dt 24:1
When his breath **d** he returns to the Ps 146:4
and he who **d** from evil makes himself a Is 59:15
"If this fixed order **d** from before me, Jer 31:36

DEPARTURE (4)
appeared in glory and spoke of his **d**, Lk 9:31
that after my **d** fierce wolves will Acts 20:29
and the time of my **d** has come. 2 Tm 4:6
so that after my **d** you may be able 2 Pt 1:15

DEPEND (2)
Will you **d** on him because his strength Jb 39:11
these two commandments **d** all the Mt 22:40

DEPENDED (1)
because their country **d** on the king's Acts 12:20

DEPENDENT (1)
before outsiders and be **d** on no one. 1 Thes 4:12

DEPENDENTS (1)
according to the number of their **d**. Gn 47:12

DEPENDS (4)
That is why it **d** on faith, in order that Rom 4:16
So then it **d** not on human will or Rom 9:16
If possible, so far as it **d** on you, live Rom 12:18
from God that **d** on faith— Phil 3:9

DEPORTATION (4)
brothers, at the time of the **d** to Babylon. Mt 1:11
And after the **d** to Babylon: Jechoniah Mt 1:12
from David to the **d** to Babylon fourteen Mt 1:17
and from the **d** to Babylon to the Christ Mt 1:17

DEPORTED (1)
and noble Osnappar **d** and settled in Ezr 4:10

DEPOSED (3)
And he **d** the priests whom the kings 2 Kgs 23:5
the king of Egypt **d** him in Jerusalem 2 Chr 36:3
may even be **d** from her Acts 19:27

DEPOSIT (8)
his neighbor in a matter of **d** or security, Lv 6:2
oppression or the **d** that was committed Lv 6:4
Then you shall **d** them in the tent of Nm 17:4
of the heifer and **d** them outside the Nm 19:9
You take what you did not **d**, and reap Lk 19:21
what I did not **d** and reaping what I Lk 19:22
guard the **d** entrusted to you. 1 Tm 6:20
us, guard the good **d** entrusted to you. 2 Tm 1:14

DEPOSITED (1)
And Moses **d** the staffs before the LORD Nm 17:7

DEPRAVED (1)
among people who are **d** in mind and 1 Tm 6:5

DEPRAVITY (4)
her nakedness; they are relatives; it is **d**. Lv 18:17
and the land become full of **d**. Lv 19:29
a woman and her mother also, it is **d**; Lv 20:14
fire, that there may be no **d** among you. Lv 20:14

DEPRIVE (5)
the wicked or to **d** the righteous of Prv 18:5
a bribe, and **d** the innocent of his right! Is 5:23
unsatisfied, and to **d** the thirsty of drink. Is 32:6
Do not **d** one another, except perhaps 1 Cor 7:5
die than have anyone **d** me of my 1 Cor 9:15

DEPRIVED (1)
depraved in mind and **d** of the truth, 1 Tm 6:5

DEPRIVES (1)
He **d** of speech those who are trusted and Jb 12:20

DEPRIVING (1)
am I toiling and **d** myself of pleasure?" Eccl 4:8

DEPTH (7)
heavens for height, and the earth for **d**, Prv 25:3
sprang up, since they had no **d** of soil, Mt 13:5
and to be drowned in the **d** of the sea. Mt 18:6
it sprang up, since it had no **d** of soil. Mk 4:5
nor height nor **d**, nor anything else in Rom 8:39
the **d** of the riches and wisdom and Rom 11:33
breadth and length and height and **d**, Eph 3:18

DEPTHS (24)
they went down into the **d** like a stone. Ex 15:5
my anger, and it burns to the **d** of Sheol, Dt 32:22
and you cast their pursuers into the **d**, Neh 9:11
life shall go down into the **d** of the earth; Ps 63:9
bring them back from the **d** of the sea, Ps 68:22
from the **d** of the earth you will bring Ps 71:20
delivered my soul from the **d** of Sheol. Ps 86:13
You have put me in the **d** of the pit, in the Ps 88:6
In his hand are the **d** of the earth; the Ps 95:4
up to heaven; they went down to the **d**; Ps 107:26
Out of the **d** I cry to you, O LORD! Ps 130:1
intricately woven in the **d** of the earth. Ps 139:15
When there were no **d** I was brought Prv 8:24
that her guests are in the **d** of Sheol. Prv 9:18
LORD has done it; shout, O **d** of the earth; Is 44:23
who made the **d** of the sea a way for the Is 51:10
who led them through the **d**? Like a Is 63:13
Flee, turn back, dwell in the **d**, O Jer 49:8
Flee, wander far away, dwell in the **d**, O Jer 49:30
name, O LORD, from the **d** of the pit; Lam 3:55
by the seas, in the **d** of the waters; Ezk 27:34
will cast all our sins into the **d** of the sea. Mi 7:19
and all the **d** of the Nile shall be dried Zec 10:11
everything, even the **d** of God. 1 Cor 2:10

DEPUTIES (1)
the Medes, with their governors and **d**, Jer 51:28

DEPUTY (1)
was no king in Edom; a **d** was king. 1 Kgs 22:47

DERBE (4)
learned of it and fled to Lystra and **D**, Acts 14:6
day he went on with Barnabas to **D**. Acts 14:20
Paul came also to **D** and to Lystra. A Acts 16:1
and Gaius of **D**, and Timothy; Acts 20:4

DERIDE (2)
those who **d** me use my name for a Ps 102:8
The insolent utterly **d** me, but I do not Ps 119:51

DERIDED (3)
mocked and **d** by those around us. Ps 79:4
And those who passed by **d** him, Mt 27:39
And those who passed by **d** him, Mk 15:29

DERIDES (1)
in the LORD. My mouth **d** my enemies, 1 Sm 2:1

DERISION (12)
break loose, to the **d** of their enemies), Ex 32:25
that we may no longer suffer **d**." Neh 2:17

heavens laughs; the Lord holds them in **d**. Ps 2:4
the **d** and scorn of those around us. Ps 44:13
at them; you hold all the nations in **d**. Ps 59:8
for me a reproach and **d** all day long. Jer 20:8
his vomit, and he too shall be held in **d**. Jer 48:26
Was not Israel a **d** to you? Was he Jer 48:27
Moab has become a **d** and a horror to Jer 48:39
you shall be laughed at and held in **d**, Ezk 23:32
have become a prey and **d** to the rest of Ezk 36:4
This shall be their **d** in the land of Hos 7:16

DERIVED (1)
For I have **d** much joy and comfort Phlm 1:7

DESCEND (7)
pillar of cloud would **d** and stand at the Ex 33:9
Shall we **d** together into the dust?" Jb 17:16
sent fire; into my bones he made it **d**; Lam 1:13
"I saw the Spirit **d** from heaven like a Jn 1:32
whom you see the Spirit **d** and remain, Jn 1:33
or "'Who will **d** into the abyss?'" (that Rom 10:7
Lord himself will **d** from heaven 1 Thes 4:16

DESCENDANT (4)
He was a **d** of Perez and was chief of 1 Chr 27:3
Jacob, any **d** of the man who does this, Mal 2:12
am an Israelite, a **d** of Abraham, Rom 11:1
I am the root and the **d** of David, the Rv 22:16

DESCENDANTS (56)
me or with my **d** or with my posterity, Gn 21:23
these are the names of the **d** of Israel, Gn 46:8
came into Egypt, who were his own **d**, Gn 46:26
All the **d** of Jacob were seventy persons; Ex 1:5
you or of your **d** is unclean through Nm 9:10
Sheshai, and Talmai, the **d** of Anak, Nm 13:22
besides, we saw the **d** of Anak there. Nm 13:28
he went, and his **d** shall possess it. Nm 14:24
outsider, who is not of the **d** of Aaron, Nm 16:40
him and to his **d** after him the Nm 25:13
well with them and with their **d** forever! Dt 5:29
none of his **d** may enter the assembly of Dt 23:2
Ahiman and Talmai, the **d** of Anak. Jos 15:14
These were the male **d** of Manasseh the Jos 17:2
those Levites who were **d** of Aaron the Jos 21:4
which went to the **d** of Aaron, one of Jos 21:10
And to the **d** of Aaron the priest they Jos 21:13
The cities of the **d** of Aaron, the priests, Jos 21:19
said to us or to our **d** in time to come, Jos 22:28
an inheritance of the **d** of Joseph. Jos 24:32
And the **d** of the Kenite, Moses' Jgs 1:16
the **d** of Hobab the father-in-law of Jgs 4:11
and all the **d** of your house shall die 1 Sm 2:33
one of the **d** of the giants, 2 Sm 21:16
who was one of the **d** of the giants. 2 Sm 21:18
Joab and on the head of his **d** forever. 1 Kgs 2:33
David and for his **d** and for his house 1 Kgs 2:33
their **d** who were left after them in the 1 Kgs 9:21
you and to your **d** forever." So he went 2 Kgs 5:27
LORD rejected all the **d** of Israel and 2 Kgs 17:20
All these were the **d** of Keturah. 1 Chr 1:33
All these were **d** of Machir, the father 1 Chr 2:23
Zaza. These were the **d** of Jerahmeel. 1 Chr 2:33
These were the **d** of Caleb. The sons 1 Chr 2:50
The **d** of Jehoiakim: Jeconiah his son, 1 Chr 3:16
Jezer and Shallum, the **d** of Bilhah. 1 Chr 7:13
who was one of the **d** of the giants, 1 Chr 20:4
from their **d** who were left after them 2 Chr 8:8
it forever to the **d** of Abraham your 2 Chr 20:7
So the **d** went in and possessed the land, Neh 9:24
and the **d** of Solomon's servants. Neh 11:3
of these days cease among their **d**. Est 9:28
and your **d** as the grass of the earth. Jb 5:25
presence, and their **d** before their eyes. Jb 21:8
and his **d** have not enough bread. Jb 27:14
You will destroy their **d** from the earth, Ps 21:10
remnant, **d** and posterity," says the LORD. Is 14:22
offspring, and my blessing on your **d**. Is 44:3
like the sand, and your **d** like its grains; Is 48:19
and their **d** in the midst of the peoples; Is 61:9
of the LORD, and their **d** with them. Is 65:23
Shemaiah of Nehelam and his **d**. Jer 29:32
The **d** also are impudent and stubborn: I Ezk 2:4
he would set one of his **d** on his throne, Acts 2:30
And those **d** of Levi who receive the Heb 7:5
were born **d** as many as the stars of Heb 11:12

DESCENDED (15)
because the LORD had **d** on it in fire. Ex 19:18
The LORD **d** in the cloud and stood with Ex 34:5
and he also was **d** from the giants. 2 Sm 21:20
These four were **d** from the giants in 2 Sm 21:22
and he also was **d** from the giants. 1 Chr 20:6
These were **d** from the giants in Gath, 1 Chr 20:8
angel of the Lord **d** from heaven and Mt 28:2
and the Holy Spirit **d** on him in bodily Lk 3:22
heaven except he who **d** from heaven, Jn 3:13
who was **d** from David according to the Rom 1:3
not all who are **d** from Israel belong to Rom 9:6
that he had also **d** into the lower parts Eph 4:9
He who **d** is the one who also ascended Eph 4:10
though these also are **d** from Abraham. Heb 7:5
that our Lord was **d** from Judah, Heb 7:14

DESCENDING (7)
of God were ascending and **d** on it! Gn 28:12
to be heard and the **d** blow of his arm to Is 30:30
saw the Spirit of God **d** like a dove and Mt 3:16
opening and the Spirit **d** on him like a Mk 1:10
of God ascending and **d** on the Son of Jn 1:51
and something like a great sheet **d**, Acts 10:11
vision, something like a great sheet **d**, Acts 11:5

DESCENDS (2)
and on his own skull his violence **d**. Ps 7:16
behold, it **d** for judgment upon Edom, Is 34:5

DESCENT (8)
far as Shebarim and struck them at the **d**. Jos 7:5
prove their fathers' houses or their **d**, Ezr 2:59
prove their fathers' houses nor their **d**, Neh 7:61
from Israel all those of foreign **d**. Neh 13:3
for at the **d** of Horonaim they have heard Jer 48:5
the son of Ahasuerus, by **d** a Mede, Dn 9:1
does not have his **d** from them received Heb 7:6
legal requirement concerning bodily **d**, Heb 7:16

DESCRIBE (3)
And you shall **d** the land in seven Jos 18:6
d to the house of Israel the temple, Ezk 43:10
him. Who can **d** his generation? Acts 8:33

DESCRIBED (4)
who had seen it **d** to them what had Mk 5:16
he **d** to them how the Lord had Acts 12:17
add to him the plagues **d** in this book, Rv 22:18
the holy city, which are **d** in this book. Rv 22:19

DESCRIBING (1)
d in detail the conversion of the Acts 15:3

DESCRIPTION (5)
They shall write a **d** of it with a view to Jos 18:4
divisions and bring the **d** here to me. Jos 18:6
those who went to write the **d** of the land, Jos 18:8
the land and write a **d** and return to me. Jos 18:8
and wrote in a book a **d** of it by towns in Jos 18:9

DESECRATED (1)
because they have **d** the priesthood Neh 13:29

DESERT (50)
of Pisgah that looks down on the **d**. Nm 21:20
the top of Peor, which overlooks the **d**. Nm 23:28
"He found him in a **d** land, and in the Dt 32:10
as the entrance of the **d** this side of the 1 Chr 5:9
our heads he will **d** to his master 1 Chr 12:19
like wild donkeys in the **d** the poor go out Jb 24:5
is, on the **d** in which there is no man, Jb 38:26
May **d** tribes bow down before him and Ps 72:9
against the Most High in the **d**. Ps 78:17
the wilderness and grieved him in the **d**! Ps 78:40
I am like a **d** owl of the wilderness, like Ps 102:6
it flowed through the **d** like a river. Ps 105:41
them through the deep as through a **d**. Ps 106:9
and put God to the test in the **d**; Ps 106:14
Some wandered in **d** wastes, finding no Ps 107:4
He turns rivers into a **d**, springs of Ps 107:33
He turns a **d** into pools of water, a Ps 107:35
better to live in a **d** land than with a Prv 21:19
the world like a **d** and overthrew its Is 14:17
of the land, from Sela, by way of the **d**, Is 16:1
reached to Jazer and strayed to the **d**; Is 16:8
and his officers **d** the standard in panic," Is 31:9
Sharon is like a **d**, and Bashan and Is 33:9
the **d** shall rejoice and blossom like the Is 35:1
in the wilderness, and streams in the **d**; Is 35:6
make straight in the **d** a highway for our Is 40:3
I will set in the **d** the cypress, the plane Is 41:19
Let the **d** and its cities lift up their voice, Is 42:11
way in the wilderness and rivers in the **d**. Is 43:19
water in the wilderness, rivers in the **d**, Is 43:20
I dry up the sea, I make the rivers a **d**; Is 50:2
Eden, her **d** like the garden of the LORD; Is 51:3
Like a horse in the **d**, they did not Is 63:13
heights in the **d** toward the daughter Jer 4:11
and behold, the fruitful land was a **d**, Jer 4:26
a wolf from the **d** shall devastate them. Jer 5:6
I had in the **d** a travelers' lodging place, Jer 9:2
who dwell in the **d** who cut the corners Jer 9:26
heights in the **d** destroyers have come, Jer 12:12
chaff driven by the wind from the **d**. Jer 13:24
He is like a shrub in the **d**, and shall not Jer 17:6
Lebanon, yet surely I will make you a **d**, Jer 22:6
of the mixed tribes who dwell in the **d**; Jer 25:24
You will be like a juniper in the **d**! Jer 48:6
a wilderness, a dry land, and a **d**. Jer 50:12
a horror, a land of drought and a **d**, Jer 51:43
a desolation, a dry waste like the **d**. Zep 2:13
and left his heritage to jackals of the **d**." Mal 1:3
and be driven by the demon into the **d**.) Lk 8:29
Jerusalem to Gaza." This is a **d** place. Acts 8:26

DESERTED (22)
number, so that your roads shall be **d**. Lv 26:22
and since he **d** to me I have found no 1 Sm 29:3
the deserters who had **d** to the king 2 Kgs 25:11
men of Manasseh **d** to David when 1 Chr 12:19
these men of Manasseh **d** to him: 1 Chr 12:20
for great numbers had **d** to him from 2 Chr 15:9
but a poor man is **d** by his friend. Prv 19:4
land whose two kings you dread will be **d**. Is 7:16
The cities of Aroer are **d**; they will be for Is 17:2
will be like the **d** places of the wooded Is 17:9
which they **d** because of the children of Is 17:9
is solitary, a habitation **d** and forsaken, Is 27:10
palace is forsaken, the populous city **d**; Is 32:14
you like a wife **d** and grieved in spirit, Is 54:6
For a brief moment I **d** you, but with Is 54:7
Judeans who have **d** to the Chaldeans, Jer 38:19
left in the city, those who had **d** to him, Jer 39:9
the deserters who had **d** to the king of Jer 52:15
the desolate wastes and the **d** cities, Ezk 36:4
For Gaza shall be **d**, and Ashkelon shall Zep 2:4
has **d** me and gone to Thessalonica. 2 Tm 4:10
came to stand by me, but all **d** me. 2 Tm 4:16

DESERTERS (2)
the city and the **d** who had deserted 2 Kgs 25:11
the city and the **d** who had deserted to Jer 52:15

DESERTING (4)
for, **d** me, you have uncovered your bed, Is 57:8
saying, "You are **d** to the Chaldeans." Jer 37:13
I am not **d** to the Chaldeans." But Irijah Jer 37:14
you are so quickly **d** him who called you Gal 1:6

DESERTS (5)
a song to him who rides through the **d**; Ps 68:4
thirst when he led them through the **d**; Is 48:21
in the wilderness, in a land of **d** and pits, Jer 2:6
worthless shepherd, who **d** the flock! Zec 11:17
about in **d** and mountains, Heb 11:38

DESERVE (11)
fatally, though the man did not **d** to die, Dt 19:6
As the LORD lives, you **d** to die, 1 Sm 26:16
to your estate, for you **d** death. 1 Kgs 2:26
the earth; repay to the proud what they **d**! Ps 94:2
"This man does not **d** the sentence of Jer 26:16
"If those who did not **d** to drink the cup Jer 49:12
anything for which I **d** to die, Acts 25:11
doing nothing to **d** death or Acts 26:31
who practice such things **d** to die, Rom 1:32
will give to each of you as your works **d**. Rv 2:23
them blood to drink. It is what they **d**!" Rv 16:6

DESERVED (4)
and have done to him as his deeds **d**— Jgs 9:16
than our iniquities **d** and have given Ezr 9:13
did not know, and did what **d** a beating, Lk 12:48
will be **d** by the one who has spurned Heb 10:29

DESERVES (9)
then if the guilty man **d** to be beaten, the Dt 25:2
the man who has done this **d** to die, 2 Sm 12:5
God exacts of you less than your guilt **d**. Jb 11:6
"This man **d** the sentence of death, Jer 26:11
surely deal with it as its wickedness **d**. Ezk 31:11
nor a staff, for the laborer **d** his food. Mt 10:10
They answered, "He **d** death." Mt 26:66
they provide, for the laborer **d** his wages. Lk 10:7
and, "The laborer **d** his wages." 1 Tm 5:18

DESERVING (7)
they all condemned him as **d** death. Mk 14:64
nothing **d** death has been done by him. Lk 23:15
I have found in him no guilt **d** death. Lk 23:22
charged with nothing **d** death or Acts 23:29
that he had done nothing **d** death. Acts 25:25
is trustworthy and **d** of full 1 Tm 1:15
is trustworthy and **d** of full 1 Tm 4:9

DESIGN (5)
into the fine twined linen, in skilled **d**. Ex 39:3
and execute any **d** that may be 2 Chr 2:14
known to them the **d** of the temple, Ezk 43:11
and its entrances, that is, its whole **d**; Ezk 43:11
statutes and its whole **d** and all its Ezk 43:11

DESIGNATED (7)
her master, who has **d** her for himself, Ex 21:8
These were the cities **d** for all the people Jos 20:9
but there is no man **d** by the king to 2 Sm 15:3
several cities who were **d** by name to 2 Chr 31:19
houses, each of them **d** by name. Ezr 10:16
being **d** by God a high priest after the Heb 5:10
long ago were **d** for this condemnation, Jude 1:4

DESIGNATES (1)
If he **d** her for his son, he shall deal with Ex 21:9

DESIGNER (4)
engraver or by a **d** or by an Ex 35:35
—by any sort of workman or skilled **d**. Ex 35:35
an engraver and **d** and embroiderer in Ex 38:23
whose **d** and builder is God. Heb 11:10

DESIGNS (4)
to devise artistic **d**, to work in gold, Ex 31:4
to devise artistic **d**, to work in gold and Ex 35:32
hands and favor the **d** of the wicked? Jb 10:3
for we are not ignorant of his **d**. 2 Cor 2:11

DESIRABLE (5)
And for whom is all that is **d** in Israel? 1 Sm 9:20
is most sweet, and he is altogether **d**. Sg 5:16
commanders, all of them **d** young men, Ezk 23:6
on horses, all of them **d** young men. Ezk 23:12
Assyrians with them, **d** young men, Ezk 23:23

DESIRE (91)
Your **d** shall be for your husband, and Gn 3:16
Its **d** is for you, but you must rule over it." Gn 4:7
the spoil, my **d** shall have its fill of them. Ex 15:9
you shall not **d** your neighbor's house, Dt 5:21
any of your towns, as much as you **d**, Dt 12:15
you may eat meat whenever you **d**. Dt 12:20
eat within your towns whenever you **d**. Dt 12:21
money for whatever you **d**—oxen or Dt 14:26
and you **d** to take her to be your wife, Dt 21:11
to all your heart's **d** to come down, 1 Sm 23:20
and all that you **d** of me I will do for 2 Sm 19:38
to prosper all my help and my **d**? 2 Sm 23:5
and the king said, "What do you **d**?" 1 Kgs 1:16
ready to do all you **d** in the matter of 1 Kgs 5:8
had sought him with their whole **d**, 2 Chr 15:15
and I **d** to argue my case with God. Jb 13:3
We do not **d** the knowledge of your Jb 21:14
answer me; speak, for I **d** to justify you. Jb 33:32
O LORD, you hear the **d** of the afflicted; Ps 10:17
grant you your heart's **d** and fulfill all Ps 20:4
given him his heart's **d** and have not Ps 21:2
"Aha, our heart's **d**!" Let them not say, Ps 35:25
I **d** to do your will, O my God; your law is Ps 40:8
brought to dishonor who **d** my hurt! Ps 40:14
and the king will **d** your beauty. Since Ps 45:11
and brought to dishonor who **d** my hurt! Ps 70:2
is nothing on earth that I **d** besides you. Ps 73:25
away; the **d** of the wicked will perish! Ps 112:10
you satisfy the **d** of every living thing. Ps 145:16
He fulfills the **d** of those who fear him; Ps 145:19
and nothing you **d** can compare with Prv 3:15
Do not **d** her beauty in your heart, and Prv 6:25
that you may **d** cannot compare with Prv 8:11
but the **d** of the righteous will be Prv 10:24
The **d** of the righteous ends only in Prv 11:23
but the **d** of the treacherous is for Prv 13:2
sick, but a **d** fulfilled is a tree of life. Prv 13:12
A **d** fulfilled is sweet to the soul, but to Prv 13:19
isolates himself seeks his own **d**; Prv 18:1
D without knowledge is not good, and Prv 19:2
The **d** of the sluggard kills him, for his Prv 21:25
Do not **d** his delicacies, for they are Prv 23:3
who is stingy; do not **d** his delicacies, Prv 23:6
of evil men, nor **d** to be with them, Prv 24:1
drags itself along, and **d** fails, Eccl 12:5
my **d** set me among the chariots of my Sg 6:12
I am my beloved's, and his **d** is for me. Sg 7:10
and remembrance are the **d** of our soul. Is 26:8
and no beauty that we should **d** him. Is 53:2
hungry and satisfy the **d** of the afflicted, Is 58:10
and satisfy your **d** in scorched places Is 58:11
you had set free according to their **d**, Jer 34:16
in the place where you **d** to go to live." Jer 42:22
to which they **d** to return to dwell there. Jer 44:14
and his **d** shall be satisfied on the hills Jer 50:19
delight of their eyes and their soul's **d**, Ezk 24:25
For I **d** steadfast love and not sacrifice, Hos 6:6
Woe to you who **d** the day of the LORD! Am 5:18
the great man utters the evil **d** of his soul; Mi 7:3
and learn what this means, 'I **d** mercy, Mt 9:13
had known what this means, 'I **d** mercy, Mt 12:7
for you as you **d**." And her daughter Mt 15:28
coming when you will **d** to see one of Lk 17:22
Father, I **d** that they also, whom you Jn 17:24
But we **d** to hear from you what your Acts 28:22
For I have the **d** to do what is right, but Rom 7:18
my heart's **d** and prayer to God for Rom 10:1
but having his **d** under control, 1 Cor 7:37
that we might not **d** evil as they did. 1 Cor 10:6
But earnestly **d** the higher gifts. And 1 Cor 12:31
and earnestly **d** the spiritual gifts, 1 Cor 14:1
If there is anything they **d** to learn, 1 Cor 14:35
brothers, earnestly **d** to prophesy, 1 Cor 14:39
to do this work but also to **d** to do it. 2 Cor 8:10
Tell me, you who **d** to be under the law, Gal 4:21
but they **d** to have you circumcised Gal 6:13
My **d** is to depart and be with Christ, Phil 1:23
immorality, impurity, passion, evil **d**, Col 3:5
eagerly and with great **d** to see you 1 Thes 2:17
I **d** then that in every place the men 1 Tm 2:8
away from Christ, they **d** to marry 1 Tm 5:11
But those who **d** to be rich fall into 1 Tm 6:9
all who **d** to live a godly life in Christ 2 Tm 3:12
And we **d** each one of you to show the Heb 6:11
But as it is, they **d** a better country, Heb 11:16
he is lured and enticed by his own **d**. Jas 1:14
Then **d** when it has conceived gives Jas 1:15
You **d** and do not have, so you murder. Jas 4:2
that is in the world because of sinful **d**. 2 Pt 1:4
immorality and pursued unnatural **d**, Jude 1:7
every kind of plague, as often as they **d**. Rv 11:6

DESIRED (32)
that the tree was to be **d** to make one wise, Gn 3:6
just as you **d** of the LORD your God at Dt 18:16
timber of cedar and cypress that he **d**, 1 Kgs 5:10
house and all that Solomon **d** to build, 1 Kgs 9:1
timber and gold, as much as he **d**, 1 Kgs 9:11
and whatever Solomon **d** to build in 1 Kgs 9:19
to the queen of Sheba all that she **d**, 1 Kgs 10:13
and whatever Solomon **d** to build in 2 Chr 8:6
to the queen of Sheba all that she **d**, 2 Chr 9:12
staff of his palace to do as each man **d**. Est 1:8
was given whatever she **d** to take with Est 2:13
have withheld anything that the poor **d**, Jb 31:16
More to be **d** are they than gold, even Ps 19:10
Sacrifice and offering you have not **d**, Ps 40:6
at the mount that God **d** for his abode, Ps 68:16
and he brought them to their **d** haven. Ps 107:30
Zion; he has **d** it for his dwelling place: Ps 132:13
forever; here I will dwell, for I have **d** it. Ps 132:14
What is **d** in a man is steadfast love, Prv 19:22
And whatever my eyes **d** I did not keep Eccl 2:10
shall be ashamed of the oaks that you **d**; Is 1:29
nor have I **d** the day of sickness. Jer 17:16
"Then I **d** to know the truth about the Dn 7:19
and called to him those whom he **d**, Mk 3:13
many prophets and kings **d** to see what Lk 10:24
who **d** to be fed with what fell from the Lk 16:21
"I have earnestly **d** to eat this Passover Lk 22:15
very glad, for he had long **d** to see him, Lk 23:8
So when God **d** to show more Heb 6:17
and offerings you have not **d**, Heb 10:5
"You have neither **d** nor taken pleasure Heb 10:8
when he **d** to inherit the blessing, Heb 12:17

DESIRES (34)
he may come when he **d**—to the place Dt 18:6
'The king **d** no bride-price except a 1 Sm 18:25
all that your heart **d**." So David sent 2 Sm 3:21
shall reign over all that your soul **d**, 1 Kgs 11:37
plans are broken off, the **d** of my heart. Jb 17:11
him back? What he **d**, that he does. Jb 23:13
For the wicked boasts of the **d** of his soul, Ps 10:3
man is there who **d** life and loves many Ps 34:12
and he will give you the **d** of your heart. Ps 37:4
Grant not, O LORD, the **d** of the wicked; Ps 140:8
The soul of the wicked **d** evil; his Prv 21:10
so that he lacks nothing of all that he **d**, Eccl 6:2
to eat, no first-ripe fig that my soul **d**. Mi 7:1
let God deliver him now, if he **d** him. Mt 27:43
of riches and the **d** for other things Mk 4:19
no one after drinking old wine **d** new, Lk 5:39
and your will is to do your father's **d**. Jn 8:44
provision for the flesh, to gratify its **d**. Rom 13:14
you will not gratify the **d** of the flesh. Gal 5:16
For the **d** of the flesh are against the Gal 5:17
and the **d** of the Spirit are against the Gal 5:17
the flesh with its passions and **d**. Gal 5:24
carrying out the **d** of the body and the Eph 2:3
life and is corrupt through deceitful **d**, Eph 4:22
who **d** all people to be saved and to 1 Tm 2:4
the office of overseer, he **d** a noble task. 1 Tm 3:1
senseless and harmful **d** that plunge 1 Tm 6:9
For "Whoever **d** to love life and see 1 Pt 3:10
scoffing, following their own sinful **d**. 2 Pt 3:3
in the world—the **d** of the flesh and the 1 Jn 2:16
of the flesh and the **d** of the eyes and 1 Jn 2:16
world is passing away along with its **d**, 1 Jn 2:17
following their own sinful **d**; Jude 1:16
let the one who **d** take the water of life Rv 22:17

DESIRING (11)
are standing outside, **d** to see you." Lk 8:20
But he, **d** to justify himself, said to Lk 10:29
For which of you, **d** to build a tower, Lk 14:28
them once more, **d** to release Jesus, Lk 23:20
d to know the real reason why he was Acts 22:30
And **d** to know the charge for which Acts 23:28
And **d** to do the Jews a favor, Felix left Acts 24:27
d to show his wrath and to make Rom 9:22
that your readiness in **d** it may be 2 Cor 8:11
d to be teachers of the law, without 1 Tm 1:7
d to act honorably in all things. Heb 13:18

DESIROUS (1)
So, being affectionately **d** of you, we 1 Thes 2:8

DESIST (1)
wealth; be discerning enough to **d**. Prv 23:4

DESOLATE (87)
die, and that the land may not be **d**." Gn 47:19
lest the land become **d** and the wild Ex 23:29
and will make your sanctuaries **d**, Lv 26:31
enjoy its Sabbaths as long as it lies **d**, Lv 26:34
As long as it lies **d** it shall have rest, the Lv 26:35
Sabbaths while it lies **d** without them, Lv 26:43
heart." So Tamar lived, a **d** woman, 2 Sm 13:20
days that it lay **d** it kept Sabbath, 2 Chr 36:21
and has lived in **d** cities, in houses that Jb 15:28
me out; he has made **d** all my company. Jb 16:7
to satisfy the waste and **d** land, and to Jb 38:27
Your country lies **d**; your cities are burned Is 1:7
land; it is **d**, as overthrown by foreigners. Is 1:7
"Surely many houses shall be **d**, large and Is 5:9
without people, and the land is a **d** waste, Is 6:11
LORD will empty the earth and make it **d**, Is 24:1
the land, to apportion the **d** heritages, Is 49:8
your waste and your **d** places and your Is 49:19
For the children of the **d** one will be more Is 54:1
the nations and will people the **d** cities. Is 54:3
and your land shall no more be termed **D**, Is 62:4
be shocked, be utterly **d**, declares the Jer 2:12
And you, O **d** one, what do you mean Jer 4:30
my pleasant portion a **d** wilderness. Jer 12:10
it a desolation; **d**, it mourns to me. Jer 12:11
The whole land is made **d**, but no man Jer 12:11
be like Shiloh, and this city shall be **d**, Jer 26:9
and the streets of Jerusalem that are **d**, Jer 33:10
waters of Nimrim also have become **d**. Jer 48:34
it shall become a **d** mound, and its Jer 49:2
nor beast, and it shall be **d** forever.' Jer 51:62
come to the festival; all her gates are **d**; Lam 1:4
my children are **d**, for the enemy has Lam 1:16
tore me to pieces; he has made me **d**; Lam 3:11
for Mount Zion which lies **d**; jackals Lam 5:18
Your altars shall become **d**, and your Ezk 6:4
them and make the land **d** and waste, Ezk 6:14
and they ravage it, and it be made **d**, Ezk 14:15
be delivered, but the land would be **d**. Ezk 14:16
And I will make the land **d**, because Ezk 15:8
the land of Israel when it was made **d**, Ezk 25:3
And I will make it **d**; from Teman Ezk 25:13
When I make the land of Egypt **d**, and Ezk 32:15
and when the land is **d** of all that fills Ezk 32:15
Israel shall be so **d** that none will pass Ezk 33:28
of Israel, saying, 'They are laid **d**; Ezk 35:12
earth rejoices, I will make you **d**. Ezk 35:14
of the house of Israel, because it was **d**, Ezk 35:15
you shall be **d**, Mount Seir, and all Ezk 35:15
they made you **d** and crushed you Ezk 36:3
the **d** wastes and the deserted cities, Ezk 36:4
And the land that was **d** shall be tilled, Ezk 36:34
'This land that was **d** has become like Ezk 36:35
and the waste and **d** and ruined cities Ezk 36:35
and replanted that which was **d**. Ezk 36:36
offering, the transgression that makes **d**, Dn 8:13
shine upon your sanctuary, which is **d**. Dn 9:17
shall come one who makes **d**, Dn 9:27
set up the abomination that makes **d**. Dn 11:31
abomination that makes **d** is set up, Dn 12:11
under the clods; the storehouses are **d**; Jl 1:17
them, but behind them a **d** wilderness, Jl 2:3
and drive him into a parched and **d** land, Jl 2:20
a desolation and Edom a **d** wilderness, Jl 3:19
the high places of Isaac shall be made **d**, Am 7:9
making you **d** because of your sins. Mi 6:13
the earth will be **d** because of its Mi 7:13
D! Desolation and ruin! Hearts melt and Na 2:10
their cities have been made **d**, without a Zep 3:6
Thus the land they left was **d**, so that no Zec 7:14
fro, and the pleasant land was made **d**." Zec 7:14
there in a boat to a **d** place by himself. Mt 14:13
to him and said, "This is a **d** place, Mt 14:15
bread in such a **d** place to feed so Mt 15:33
See, your house is left to you **d**. Mt 23:38
he departed and went out to a **d** place, Mk 1:35
enter a town, but was out in **d** places, Mk 1:45
by yourselves to a **d** place and rest a Mk 6:31
in the boat to a **d** place by themselves. Mk 6:32
to him and said, "This is a **d** place, Mk 6:35
people with bread here in this **d** place?" Mk 8:4
day, he departed and went into a **d** place. Lk 4:42
he would withdraw to **d** places and pray. Lk 5:16
provisions, for we are here in a **d** place." Lk 9:12
of Psalms, "'May his camp become **d**, Acts 1:20
the children of the **d** one will be more Gal 4:27

They will make her **d** and naked, and Rv 17:16

DESOLATED (3)
desolation in the midst of **d** countries, Ezk 29:12
And they shall be **d** in the midst of Ezk 30:7
be desolated in the midst of **d** countries, Ezk 30:7

DESOLATION (56)
after you, and your land shall be a **d**, Lv 26:33
they should become a **d** and a curse, 2 Kgs 22:19
fathers, so that he made them a **d**, 2 Chr 30:7
the dry ground by night in waste and **d**; Jb 30:3
May their camp be a **d**; let no one dwell Ps 69:25
to make the land a **d** and to destroy its Is 13:9
the waters of Nimrim are a **d**; the grass is Is 15:6
the children of Israel, and there will be **d**. Is 17:9
D is left in the city; the gates are battered Is 24:12
d and destruction are in their highways. Is 59:7
has become a wilderness, Jerusalem a **d**. Is 64:10
the LORD, "The whole land shall be a **d**; Jer 4:27
from you in disgust, lest I make you a **d**, Jer 6:8
and I will make the cities of Judah a **d**, Jer 9:11
country to make the cities of Judah a **d**, Jer 10:22
They have made it a **d**; desolate, it Jer 12:11
LORD, that this house shall become a **d**. Jer 22:5
a horror, a hissing, and an everlasting **d**. Jer 25:9
officials, to make them a **d** and a waste, Jer 25:18
live. Why should this city become a **d**? Jer 27:17
land of which you are saying, 'It is a **d**, Jer 32:43
cities of Judah a **d** without inhabitant." Jer 34:22
Behold, this day they are a **d**, and no one Jer 44:2
and they became a waste and a **d**, Jer 44:6
land has become a **d** and a waste and Jer 44:22
Horonaim, '**D** and great destruction!' Jer 48:3
her cities shall become a **d**, with no Jer 48:9
her, which shall make her land a **d**, Jer 50:3
be inhabited but shall be an utter **d**; Jer 50:13
stand, to make the land of Babylon a **d**, Jer 51:29
I will make you a **d** and an object of Ezk 5:14
waste, and the land shall become a **d**; Ezk 12:20
A cup of horror and **d**, the cup of your Ezk 23:33
land of Egypt shall be a **d** and a waste. Ezk 29:9
the land of Egypt an utter waste and **d**, Ezk 29:10
the land of Egypt a **d** in the midst of Ezk 29:12
cities shall be a **d** forty years among Ezk 29:12
I will bring **d** upon the land and Ezk 30:12
will make Pathros a **d** and will set fire Ezk 30:14
I will make the land a **d** and a waste, Ezk 33:28
made the land a **d** and a waste because Ezk 33:29
and I will make you a **d** and a waste. Ezk 35:3
cities waste, and you shall become a **d**, Ezk 35:4
I will make Mount Seir a waste and a **d**, Ezk 35:7
I will make you a perpetual **d**, and your Ezk 35:9
instead of being the **d** that it was in the Ezk 36:34
Ephraim shall become a **d** in the day of Hos 5:9
"Egypt shall become a **d** and Edom a Jl 3:19
their counsels, that I may make you a **d**, Mi 6:16
Desolate! **D** and ruin! Hearts melt and Na 2:10
deserted, and Ashkelon shall become a **d**; Zep 2:4
Assyria, and he will make Nineveh a **d**, Zep 2:13
no one else." What a **d** she has become, Zep 2:15
see the abomination of **d** spoken of by Mt 24:15
the abomination of **d** standing where Mk 13:14
then know that its **d** has come near. Lk 21:20

DESOLATIONS (4)
LORD, how he has brought **d** on the earth. Ps 46:8
pass before the end of the **d** of Jerusalem, Dn 9:2
Open your eyes and see our **d**, and the Dn 9:18
the end there shall be war. **D** are decreed. Dn 9:26

DESOLATOR (1)
the decreed end is poured out on the **d**." Dn 9:27

DESPAIR (7)
Then Saul will **d** of seeking me any 1 Sm 27:1
power; they rise up when they **d** of life. Jb 24:22
broken my heart, so that I am in **d**. Ps 69:20
gave my heart up to **d** over all the toil Eccl 2:20
The workers in combed flax will be in **d**, Is 19:9
mourns, the prince is wrapped in **d**, Ezk 7:27
crushed; perplexed, but not driven to **d**; 2 Cor 4:8

DESPAIRED (1)
our strength that we **d** of life itself. 2 Cor 1:8

DESPAIRING (1)
when the speech of a **d** man is wind? Jb 6:26

DESPERATELY (1)
is deceitful above all things, and **d** sick; Jer 17:9

DESPICABLE (2)
according to the **d** practices of the 2 Kgs 16:3
according to the **d** practices of the 2 Kgs 21:2

DESPISE (38)
"How long will this people **d** me? Nm 14:11
and **d** me and break my covenant. Dt 31:20
and those who **d** me shall be lightly 1 Sm 2:30
than you. Why then did you **d** us? 2 Sm 19:43
therefore **d** not the discipline of the Jb 5:17
to **d** the work of your hands and favor the Jb 10:3
Even young children **d** me; when I rise Jb 19:18
God is mighty, and does not **d** any; Jb 36:5
therefore I **d** myself, and repent in dust Jb 42:6
contrite heart, O God, you will not **d**. Ps 51:17
needy and does not **d** his own people Ps 69:33
yourself, you **d** them as phantoms. Ps 73:20
destitute and does not **d** their prayer. Ps 102:17
fools **d** wisdom and instruction. Prv 1:7
do not **d** the LORD'S discipline or be Prv 3:11
People do not **d** a thief if he steals to Prv 6:30
for he will **d** the good sense of your Prv 23:9
and do not **d** your mother when she is Prv 23:22
I would kiss you, and none would **d** me. Sg 8:1
"Because you **d** this word and trust in Is 30:12
Your lovers **d** you; they seek your life. Jer 4:30
continually to those who **d** the word of Jer 23:17
all who honored her **d** her, for they have Lam 1:8
those all around who **d** you. Ezk 16:57
it do if you **d** the rod?" declares the Ezk 21:13
"I hate, I **d** your feasts, and I take no Am 5:21
hosts to you, O priests, who **d** my name. Mal 1:6
be devoted to the one and **d** the other. Mt 6:24
"See that you do not **d** one of these little Mt 18:10
be devoted to the one and **d** the other. Lk 16:13
the one who eats **d** the one who Rom 14:3
Or you, why do you **d** your brother? Rom 14:10
Or do you **d** the church of God and 1 Cor 11:22
So let no one **d** him. Help him on his 1 Cor 16:11
a trial to you, you did not scorn or **d** me, Gal 4:14
Do not **d** prophecies, 1 Thes 5:20
Let no one **d** you for your youth, but 1 Tm 4:12
lust of defiling passion and **d** authority. 2 Pt 2:10

DESPISED (50)
his way. Thus Esau **d** his birthright. Gn 25:34
none of those who **d** me shall see it. Nm 14:23
Because he has **d** the word of the LORD Nm 15:31
that these men have **d** the LORD." Nm 16:30
Are not these the people whom you **d**? Jgs 9:38
us?" And they **d** him and brought 1 Sm 10:27
All that was **d** and worthless they 1 Sm 15:9
the LORD, and she **d** him in her heart. 2 Sm 6:16
Why have you **d** the word of the LORD, 2 Sm 12:9
because you have **d** me and have 2 Sm 12:10
They **d** his statutes and his 2 Kgs 17:15
and she **d** him in her heart. 1 Chr 15:29
of it, they jeered at us and **d** us and said, Neh 2:19
Hear, O our God, for we are **d**. Turn Neh 4:4
in whose eyes a vile person is **d**, but who Ps 15:4
by mankind and **d** by the people. Ps 22:6
For he has not **d** or abhorred the Ps 22:24
Then they **d** the pleasant land, having Ps 106:24
I am small and **d**, yet I do not forget Ps 119:141
of my counsel and **d** all my reproof, Prv 1:30
discipline, and my heart **d** reproof! Prv 5:12
good sense, but one of twisted mind is **d**. Prv 12:8
poor man's wisdom is **d** and his words Eccl 9:16
wealth of his house, he would be utterly **d**. Sg 8:7
LORD, they have **d** the Holy One of Israel, Is 1:4
to the elder, and the **d** to the honorable. Is 3:5
and have **d** the word of the Holy One of Is 5:24
Covenants are broken; cities are **d**; there Is 33:8
of Israel and his Holy One, to one deeply **d**, Is 49:7
continually all the day my name is **d**. Is 52:5
He was **d** and rejected by men; a man of Is 53:3
whom men hide their faces he was **d**, Is 53:3
and all who **d** you shall bow down at Is 60:14
Is this man Coniah a **d**, broken pot, a Jer 22:28
Thus they have **d** my people so that Jer 33:24
among the nations, **d** among mankind. Jer 49:15
"Look, O LORD, and see, for I am **d**." Lam 1:11
you who have **d** the oath in breaking Ezk 16:59
who made him king, whose oath he **d**, Ezk 17:16
He **d** the oath in breaking the Ezk 17:18
As I live, surely it is my oath that he **d**, Ezk 17:19
shall we rejoice? You have **d** the rod, Ezk 21:10
You have **d** my holy things and Ezk 22:8
the nations; you shall be utterly **d**. Ob 1:2
For whoever has **d** the day of small Zec 4:10
you say, 'How have we **d** your name?' Mal 1:6
By saying that the LORD'S table may be **d**. Mal 1:7
and its fruit, that is, its food may be **d**. Mal 1:12
so I make you **d** and abased before all Mal 2:9
chose what is low and **d** in the world, 1 Cor 1:28

DESPISES (10)
spoken concerning him: "She **d** you, 2 Kgs 19:21
Whoever **d** the word brings Prv 13:13
he who is devious in his ways **d** him. Prv 14:2
Whoever **d** his neighbor is a sinner, Prv 14:21
A fool **d** his father's instruction, but Prv 15:5
but a foolish man **d** his mother. Prv 15:20
ignores instruction **d** himself, Prv 15:32
his life; he who **d** his ways will die. Prv 19:16
uprightly, who **d** the gain of oppressions, Is 33:15
spoken concerning him: "'She **d** you, Is 37:22

DESPISING (2)
d his words and scoffing at his 2 Chr 36:16
him endured the cross, **d** the shame, Heb 12:2

DESPITE (1)
d his wonders, they did not believe. Ps 78:32

DESPOIL (1)
off its wealth and **d** it and plunder it; Ezk 29:19

DESPOILED (1)
seize the spoil of those who **d** them, Ezk 39:10

DESTINE (1)
I will **d** you to the sword, and all of you Is 65:12

DESTINED (4)
that was not; Assyria **d** it for wild beasts. Is 23:13
know that we are **d** for this. 1 Thes 3:3
For God has not **d** us for wrath, but to 1 Thes 5:9
disobey the word, as they were **d** to do. 1 Pt 2:8

DESTINY (1)
and fill cups of mixed wine for **D**, Is 65:11

DESTITUTE (4)
the right of the afflicted and the **d**. Ps 82:3
the prayer of the **d** and does not despise Ps 102:17
the mute, for the rights of all who are **d**. Prv 31:8
skins of sheep and goats, **d**, afflicted, Heb 11:37

DESTROY (214)
Behold, I will **d** them with the earth. Gn 6:13
upon the earth to **d** all flesh in which Gn 6:17
shall there be a flood to **d** the earth." Gn 9:11
again become a flood to **d** all flesh. Gn 9:15
Will you **d** the whole city for lack of Gn 18:28
"I will not **d** it if I find forty-five there." Gn 18:28
"For the sake of twenty I will not **d** it." Gn 18:31
"For the sake of ten I will not **d** it." Gn 18:32
For we are about to **d** this place, Gn 19:13
LORD, and the LORD has sent us to **d** it." Gn 19:13
the LORD is about to **d** the city." But he Gn 19:14
and no plague will befall you to **d** you, Ex 12:13
draw my sword; my hand shall **d** them.' Ex 15:9
that person I will **d** from among his Lv 23:30
your children and **d** your livestock and Lv 26:22
And I will **d** your high places and cut Lv 26:30
them so as to **d** them utterly and break Lv 26:44
dominion and **d** the survivors Nm 24:19
and you will **d** all this people." Nm 32:15
before you and **d** all their figured Nm 33:52
figured stones and **d** all their metal Nm 33:52
us into the hand of the Amorites, to **d** us. Dt 1:27
against them, to **d** them from the camp, Dt 2:15
will not leave you or **d** you or forget the Dt 4:31
and he **d** you from off the face of the Dt 6:15
against you, and he would **d** you quickly. Dt 7:4
He will **d** them and subdue them before Dt 9:3
angry with you that he was ready to **d** you. Dt 9:8
that I may **d** them and blot out their Dt 9:14
you, so that he was ready to **d** you. Dt 9:19
with Aaron that he was ready to **d** him. Dt 9:20
the LORD had said he would **d** you. Dt 9:25
GOD, **d** not your people and your heritage, Dt 9:26
also. The LORD was unwilling to **d** you. Dt 10:10
You shall surely **d** all the places where Dt 12:2
of their gods and **d** their name out of Dt 12:3
you shall not **d** its trees by wielding an Dt 20:19
trees for food you may **d** and cut down, Dt 20:20
He will **d** these nations before you, so Dt 31:3
out the enemy before you and said, **D**. Dt 33:27
us into the hands of the Amorites, to **d** us? Jos 7:7
unless you **d** the devoted things from Jos 7:12
the land and to **d** all the inhabitants of Jos 9:24
war against them to **d** the land where Jos 22:33
the Amalekites, lest I **d** you with them. 1 Sm 15:6
good, and would not utterly **d** them. 1 Sm 15:9
Keilah, to **d** the city on my account. 1 Sm 23:10
that you will not **d** my name out of 1 Sm 24:21
David said to Abishai, "Do not **d** him, 1 Sm 26:9
people came in to **d** the king your 1 Sm 26:15
your hand to **d** the LORD'S anointed?" 2 Sm 1:14
at your hand and **d** you from the 2 Sm 4:11
And so they would **d** the heir also. 2 Sm 14:7
the man who would **d** me and my 2 Sm 14:16
You seek to **d** a city that is a mother 2 Sm 20:19
be it, that I should swallow up or **d**! 2 Sm 20:20
consumed us and planned to **d** us, 2 Sm 21:5
his hand toward Jerusalem to **d** it, 2 Sm 24:16
cut it off and to **d** it from the face of 1 Kgs 13:34
the LORD was not willing to **d** Judah, 2 Kgs 8:19
in order to **d** the worshipers of 2 Kgs 10:19
and Jacob, and would not **d** them, 2 Kgs 13:23
come up against this place to **d** it? 2 Kgs 18:25
Go up against this land, and **d** it.'" 2 Kgs 18:25
and sent them against Judah to **d** it, 2 Kgs 24:2

sent the angel to Jerusalem to **d** it, 1 Chr 21:15
it, but as he was about to **d** it, 1 Chr 21:15
I will not **d** them, but I will grant 2 Chr 12:7
whom they avoided and did not **d**— 2 Chr 20:10
they all helped to **d** one another. 2 Chr 20:23
the LORD will **d** what you have 2 Chr 20:37
was not willing to **d** the house of 2 Chr 21:7
LORD had anointed to **d** the house of 2 Chr 22:7
that God has determined to **d** you, 2 Chr 25:16
God, who is with me, lest he **d** you." 2 Chr 35:21
or to **d** this house of God that is in Ezr 6:12
Haman sought to **d** all the Jews, Est 3:6
king's provinces with instruction to **d**, Est 3:13
which he wrote to **d** the Jews who are in Est 8:5
city to gather and defend their lives, to **d**, Est 8:11
had plotted against the Jews to **d** them, Est 9:24
is, cast lots), to crush and to **d** them. Est 9:24
me against him to **d** him without reason." Jb 2:3
of the earth; so you **d** the hope of man. Jb 14:19
You **d** those who speak lies; the LORD Ps 5:6
You will **d** their descendants from the Ps 21:10
D, O Lord, divide their tongues; for I see Ps 55:9
the choirmaster: according to Do Not **D**. Ps 57:T
the choirmaster: according to Do Not **D**. Ps 58:T
the choirmaster: according to Do Not **D**. Ps 59:T
But those who seek to **d** my life shall go Ps 63:9
mighty are those who would **d** me, those Ps 69:4
the fold of your garment and **d** them! Ps 74:11
the choirmaster: according to Do Not **D**. Ps 75:T
for their iniquity and did not **d** them; Ps 78:38
over me; your dreadful assaults **d** me. Ps 88:16
slanders his neighbor secretly I will **d**. Ps 101:5
by morning I will **d** all the wicked in Ps 101:8
he said he would **d** them—had not Ps 106:23
They did not **d** the peoples, as the LORD Ps 106:34
The wicked lie in wait to **d** me, but I Ps 119:95
and you will **d** all the adversaries of Ps 143:12
love him, but all the wicked he will **d**. Ps 145:20
the godless man would **d** his neighbor, Prv 11:9
your ways to those who **d** kings. Prv 31:3
at your voice and **d** the work of your Eccl 5:6
too wise. Why should you **d** yourself? Eccl 7:16
but it is in his heart to **d**, and to cut off Is 10:7
and of his fruitful land the LORD will **d**, Is 10:18
They shall not hurt or **d** in all my holy Is 11:9
the LORD will utterly **d** the tongue of the Is 11:15
of his indignation, to **d** the whole land. Is 13:5
a desolation and to **d** its sinners from it. Is 13:9
concerning Canaan to **d** its strongholds. Is 23:11
When you have ceased to **d**, you will be Is 33:1
I have come up against this land to **d** it? Is 36:10
to me, Go up against this land and **d** it.'" Is 36:10
the oppressor, when he sets himself to **d**? Is 51:13
I have also created the ravager to **d**; Is 54:16
in the cluster, and they say, 'Do not **d** it, Is 65:8
for my servants' sake, and not **d** them all. Is 65:8
They shall not hurt or **d** in all my holy Is 65:25
to break down, to **d** and to overthrow, Jer 1:10
"Go up through her vine rows and **d**, but Jer 5:10
The lovely and delicately bred I will **d**, the Jer 6:2
let us attack by night and **d** her palaces!" Jer 6:5
saying, "Let us **d** the tree with its fruit, Jer 11:19
then I will utterly pluck it up and **d** it, Jer 12:17
compassion, that I should not **d** them.'" Jer 13:14
the beasts of the earth to devour and **d**. Jer 15:3
d them with double destruction! Jer 17:18
I will pluck up and break down and **d** it, Jer 18:7
to the shepherds who **d** and scatter the Jer 23:1
down, to overthrow, **d**, and bring harm, Jer 31:28
will certainly come and **d** this land, Jer 36:29
I will **d** cities and their inhabitants.' Jer 46:8
that is coming to **d** all the Philistines, Jer 47:4
would they not **d** only enough for Jer 49:9
against Kedar! **D** the people of the east! Jer 49:28
throne in Elam and **d** their king and Jer 49:38
purpose concerning Babylon is to **d** it, Jer 51:11
in pieces; with you I **d** kingdoms; Jer 51:20
them in anger and **d** them from under Lam 3:66
destruction, which I will send to **d** you, Ezk 5:16
upon you, and I will **d** your high places. Ezk 6:3
Will you **d** all the remnant of Israel in Ezk 9:8
against him and will **d** him from the Ezk 14:9
and I did not **d** them or make a full Ezk 20:17
hands of brutish men, skillful to **d**. Ezk 21:31
me for the land, that I should not **d** it, Ezk 22:30
perish out of the countries; I will **d** you. Ezk 25:7
of soul to **d** in never-ending enmity, Ezk 25:15
off the Cherethites and **d** the rest of the Ezk 25:16
They shall **d** the walls of Tyre and Ezk 26:4
your walls and **d** your pleasant Ezk 26:12
shall be brought in to **d** the land, Ezk 30:11
"I will **d** the idols and put an end to the Ezk 30:13
I will **d** all its beasts from beside many Ezk 32:13
and the fat and the strong I will **d**. Ezk 34:16
I had seen when he came to **d** the city, Ezk 43:3
king had appointed to **d** the wise men of Dn 2:24
him, "Do not **d** the wise men of Babylon; Dn 2:24
and saying, 'Chop down the tree and **d** it, Dn 4:23
and **d** mighty men and the people who Dn 8:24
Without warning he shall **d** many. Dn 8:25
who is to come shall **d** the city and the Dn 9:26
daughter of women to **d** the kingdom, Dn 11:17
with great fury to **d** and devote many to Dn 11:44
you by night; and I will **d** your mother. Hos 4:5
down their altars and **d** their pillars. Hos 10:2
anger; I will not again **d** Ephraim; Hos 11:9
and I will **d** it from the surface of the Am 9:8
I will not utterly **d** the house of Jacob," Am 9:8
the LORD, **d** the wise men out of Edom, Ob 1:8
among you and will **d** your chariots; Mi 5:10
from among you and **d** your cities. Mi 5:14
and I will **d** you until no inhabitant is Zep 2:5
hand against the north and **d** Assyria, Zep 2:13
I am about to **d** the strength of the Hg 2:22
day I will seek to **d** all the nations that Zec 12:9
so that it will not **d** the fruits of your Mal 3:11
about to search for the child, to **d** him." Mt 2:13
moth and rust **d** and where thieves Mt 6:19
fear him who can **d** both soul and Mt 10:28
conspired against him, how to **d** him. Mt 12:14
said, 'I am able to **d** the temple of God, Mt 26:61
crowd to ask for Barabbas and **d** Jesus. Mt 27:20
"You who would **d** the temple and Mt 27:40
of Nazareth? Have you come to **d** us? Mk 1:24
Herodians against him, how to **d** him. Mk 3:6
him into fire and into water, to **d** him. Mk 9:22
it and were seeking a way to **d** him, Mk 11:18
He will come and **d** the tenants and give Mk 12:9
'I will **d** this temple that is made with Mk 14:58
You who would **d** the temple and Mk 15:29
of Nazareth? Have you come to **d** us? Lk 4:34
good or to do harm, to save life or to **d** it?" Lk 6:9
of the people were seeking to **d** him, Lk 19:47
He will come and **d** those tenants and Lk 20:16
Jesus answered them, "**D** this temple, and Jn 2:19
thief comes only to steal and kill and **d**. Jn 10:10
Jesus of Nazareth will **d** this place and Acts 6:14
do not **d** the one for whom Christ Rom 14:15
the sake of food, **d** the work of God. Rom 14:20
"I will **d** the wisdom of the wise, 1 Cor 1:19
God's temple, God will **d** him. 1 Cor 3:17
—and God will **d** both one and the 1 Cor 6:13
have divine power to **d** strongholds. 2 Cor 10:4
We **d** arguments and every lofty 2 Cor 10:5
of God violently and tried to **d** it. Gal 1:13
preaching the faith he once tried to **d**." Gal 1:23
through death he might **d** the one who Heb 2:14
judge, he who is able to save and to **d**. Jas 4:12
God appeared was to **d** the works of the 1 Jn 3:8

DESTROYED (139)

before the LORD **d** Sodom and Gn 13:10
when God **d** the cities of the valley, Gn 19:29
against me and attack me, I shall be **d**, Gn 34:30
of the Kohathites be **d** from among the Nm 4:18
dispossessed them and **d** them from Dt 2:12
but the LORD **d** them before the Dt 2:21
when he **d** the Horites before them and Dt 2:22
d them and settled in their place.) Dt 2:23
the LORD your God **d** from among you all Dt 4:3
not live long in it, but will be utterly **d**. Dt 4:26
left and hide themselves from you are **d**. Dt 7:20
into great confusion, until they are **d**. Dt 7:23
stand against you until you have **d** them. Dt 7:24
and how the LORD has **d** them to this day, Dt 11:4
them, after they have been **d** before you, Dt 12:30
until you are **d** and perish quickly on Dt 28:20
come down on you until you are **d**. Dt 28:24
you and overtake you till you are **d**, Dt 28:45
of iron on your neck until he has **d** you. Dt 28:48
fruit of your ground, until you are **d**; Dt 28:51
will bring upon you, until you are **d**. Dt 28:61
and to their land, when he **d** them. Dt 31:4
of the sword until they had **d** them, Jos 11:14
and should receive no mercy but be **d**, Jos 11:20
until he has **d** you from off this good Jos 23:15
of their land, and I **d** them before you. Jos 24:8
until they **d** Jabin king of Canaan. Jgs 4:24
out of Gibeah and **d** on that day 22,000 Jgs 20:21
and **d** 18,000 men of the people of Israel. Jgs 20:25
the people of Israel **d** 25,100 men of Jgs 20:35
the women are **d** out of Benjamin?" Jgs 21:16
more, and my son be not **d**." He said, 2 Sm 14:11
I pursued my enemies and **d** them, 2 Sm 22:38
those who hated me, and I **d** them. 2 Sm 22:41
one that breathed, until he had **d** it, 1 Kgs 15:29
of Jeroboam, and also because he **d** it. 1 Kgs 16:7
Thus Zimri **d** all the house of 1 Kgs 16:12
push the Syrians until they are **d**.'" 1 Kgs 22:11
she arose and **d** all the royal family. 2 Kgs 11:1
king of Syria had **d** them and made 2 Kgs 13:7
them, the nations that my fathers **d**, 2 Kgs 19:12
and stone. Therefore they were **d**. 2 Kgs 19:18
places that Hezekiah his father had **d**, 2 Kgs 21:3
whom the LORD **d** before the people 2 Kgs 21:9
and **d** their tents and the Meunites 1 Chr 4:41
land, whom God had **d** before them. 1 Chr 5:25
of Israel had not **d**—these Solomon 2 Chr 8:8
push the Syrians until they are **d**.'" 2 Chr 18:10
for you **d** the Asherahs out of the 2 Chr 19:3
she arose and **d** all the royal family 2 Chr 22:10
and Jerusalem and **d** all the princes 2 Chr 24:23
Manasseh, until they had **d** them all. 2 Chr 31:1
whom the LORD **d** before the people 2 Chr 33:9
with fire and **d** all its precious 2 Chr 36:19
who **d** this house and carried away the Ezr 5:12
down, and its gates are **d** by fire." Neh 1:3
ruins, and its gates have been **d** by fire?" Neh 2:3
and its gates that had been **d** by fire. Neh 2:13
the king, let it be decreed that they be **d**, Est 3:9
have been sold, I and my people, to be **d**, Est 7:4
itself the Jews killed and **d** 500 men, Est 9:6
Jews have killed and **d** 500 men and also Est 9:12
If he is **d** from his place, then it will deny Jb 8:18
me, and now you have **d** me altogether. Jb 10:8
And after my skin has been thus **d**, yet Jb 19:26
if the foundations are **d**, what can the Ps 11:3
to me, and those who hated me I **d**. Ps 18:40
But transgressors shall be altogether **d**; Ps 37:38
How they are **d** in a moment, swept Ps 73:19
the enemy has **d** everything in the Ps 74:3
them, and frogs, which **d** them. Ps 78:45
He **d** their vines with hail and their Ps 78:47
who were **d** at En-dor, who became Ps 83:10
O daughter of Babylon, doomed to be **d**, Ps 137:8
The house of the wicked will be **d**, but Prv 14:11
in burial, because you have **d** your land, Is 14:20
destroyer, who yourself have not been **d**, Is 33:1
you have ceased to destroy, you will be **d**; Is 33:1
them, the nations that my fathers **d**, Is 37:12
wood and stone. Therefore they were **d**. Is 37:19
never be cut off or **d** from before me." Is 48:19
My tent is **d**, and all my cords are Jer 10:20
Many shepherds have **d** my vineyard; Jer 12:10
my hand against you and **d** you—I am Jer 15:6
have bereaved them; I have **d** my people; Jer 15:7
from Abarim, for all your lovers are **d**. Jer 22:20
they shall be utterly **d** from the land Jer 24:10
Moab is **d**; her little ones have made a Jer 48:4
shall perish, and the plain shall be **d**, Jer 48:8
against you; he has **d** your strongholds. Jer 48:18
Moab shall be **d** and be no longer a Jer 48:42
it has **d** the forehead of Moab, the Jer 48:45
His children are **d**, and his brothers, Jer 49:10
all her soldiers shall be **d** in that day, Jer 49:26
all her soldiers shall be **d** on that day, Jer 50:30
her warriors, that they may be **d**! Jer 50:36
whom I held and raised my enemy **d**. Lam 2:22
and ruined, your idols broken and **d**, Ezk 6:6
like one **d** in the midst of the sea? Ezk 27:32
the mountain of God, and I **d** you, Ezk 28:16
that all the wise men of Babylon be **d**. Dn 2:12
might not be **d** with the rest Dn 2:18
set up a kingdom that shall never be **d**, Dn 2:44
his kingdom shall never be **d**, and his Dn 6:26
and its body **d** and given over to be Dn 7:11
his kingdom one that shall not be **d**. Dn 7:14
away, to be consumed and **d** to the end. Dn 7:26
My people are **d** for lack of knowledge; Hos 4:6
of Aven, the sin of Israel, shall be **d**. Hos 10:8
and all your fortresses shall be **d**, Hos 10:14
as Shalman **d** Beth-arbel on the day of Hos 10:14
The fields are **d**, the ground mourns, Jl 1:10
ground mourns, because the grain is **d**, Jl 1:10
it was I who **d** the Amorite before them, Am 2:9
I **d** his fruit above and his roots beneath. Am 2:9
came by night—how you have been **d**! Ob 1:5
In one month I **d** the three shepherds. Zec 11:8
it die. What is to be **d**, let it be destroyed. Zec 11:9
it die. What is to be destroyed, let it be **d**. Zec 11:9
who does not care for those being **d**, Zec 11:16
the wine is spilled and the skins are **d**. Mt 9:17
his troops and **d** those murderers and Mt 22:7
will burst the skins—and the wine is **d**, Mk 2:22
it will be spilled, and the skins will be **d**. Lk 5:37
ark, and the flood came and **d** them all. Lk 17:27
rained from heaven and **d** them all— Lk 17:29
prophet shall be **d** from the people.' Acts 3:23
knowledge this weak person is **d**, 1 Cor 8:11
of them did and were **d** by serpents, 1 Cor 10:9
did and were **d** by the Destroyer. 1 Cor 10:10
The last enemy to be **d** is death. 1 Cor 15:26
not forsaken; struck down, but not **d**; 2 Cor 4:9
tent, which is our earthly home, is **d**, 2 Cor 5:1
of those who shrink back and are **d**, Heb 10:39
of instinct, born to be caught and **d**, 2 Pt 2:12

will also be **d** in their destruction, 2 Pt 2:12
afterward **d** those who did not believe. Jude 1:5
and they are **d** by all that they, Jude 1:10
sea died, and a third of the ships were **d**. Rv 8:9

DESTROYER (17)

will not allow the **d** to enter your Ex 12:23
in prosperity the **d** will come upon him. Jb 15:21
you; be a shelter to them from the **d**. Is 16:4
me; the traitor betrays, and the **d** destroys. Is 21:2
Ah, you **d**, who yourself have not been Is 33:1
his thicket, a **d** of nations has set out; Jer 4:7
for suddenly the **d** will come upon us. Jer 6:26
mothers of young men a **d** at noonday; Jer 15:8
The **d** shall come upon every city, and Jer 48:8
The **d** of Moab and his cities has come Jer 48:15
For the **d** of Moab has come up against Jer 48:18
fruits and your grapes the **d** has fallen. Jer 48:32
stir up the spirit of a **d** against Babylon, Jer 51:1
for a **d** has come upon her, upon Jer 51:56
locust has eaten, the hopper, the **d**, Jl 2:25
did and were destroyed by the **D**. 1 Cor 10:10
so that the **D** of the firstborn might Heb 11:28

DESTROYERS (7)

your **d** and those who laid you waste go Is 49:17
bare heights in the desert **d** have come, Jer 12:12
I will appoint over them four kinds of **d**, Jer 15:3
I will prepare **d** against you, each with Jer 22:7
for the **d** shall come against them out Jer 51:48
yet **d** would come from me against her, Jer 51:53
and for destroying the **d** of the earth." Rv 11:18

DESTROYING (19)

face those who hate him, by **d** them. Dt 7:10
in bringing ruin upon you and **d** you. Dt 28:63
of the cities were **d** them in their midst. Jgs 20:42
of the LORD **d** throughout all the 1 Chr 21:12
with the sword, killing and **d** them, Est 9:5
their crops to the **d** locust and the fruit Ps 78:46
and distress, a company of **d** angels. Ps 78:49
to turn away his wrath from **d** them. Ps 106:23
like a storm of hail, a **d** tempest, like a Is 28:2
For the LORD is **d** the Philistines, the Jer 47:4
I am against you, O **d** mountain, Jer 51:25
he did not restrain his hand from **d**; Lam 2:8
each with his **d** weapon in his hand." Ezk 9:1
blood, **d** lives to get dishonest gain. Ezk 22:27
hopping locust left, the **d** locust has eaten. Jl 1:4
And after **d** seven nations in the land Acts 13:19
God the Father after **d** every rule and 1 Cor 15:24
building you up and not for **d** you, 2 Cor 10:8
and for **d** the destroyers of the earth." Rv 11:18

DESTROYS (16)

eye of his slave, male or female, and **d** it, Ex 21:26
He **d** both the blameless and the wicked. Jb 9:22
He makes nations great, and he **d** them; Jb 12:23
and the complacency of fools **d** them; Prv 1:32
lacks sense; he who does it **d** himself. Prv 6:32
crookedness of the treacherous **d** them. Prv 11:3
in his work is a brother to him who **d**. Prv 18:9
is a companion to a man who **d**. Prv 28:24
of war, but one sinner **d** much good. Eccl 9:18
the traitor betrays, and the destroyer **d**. Is 21:2
the LORD, which **d** the whole earth; Jer 51:25
He **d** you, O Israel, for you are against Hos 13:9
of uncleanness that **d** with a grievous Mi 2:10
moth nor rust **d** and where thieves Mt 6:20
no thief approaches and no moth **d**. Lk 12:33
If anyone **d** God's temple, God will 1 Cor 3:17

DESTRUCTION (145)

the LORD alone, shall be devoted to **d**. Ex 22:20
is to be devoted for **d** from mankind, Lv 27:29
then I will devote their cities to **d**." Nm 21:2
they devoted them and their cities to **d**. Nm 21:3
the nations, but its end is utter **d**." Nm 24:20
and he too shall come to utter **d**." Nm 24:24
at that time and devoted to **d** every city, Dt 2:34
And we devoted them to **d**, as we did to Dt 3:6
king of Heshbon, devoting to **d** every city, Dt 3:6
then you must devote them to complete **d**. Dt 7:2
house and become devoted to **d** like it. Dt 7:26
detest and abhor it, for it is devoted to **d**. Dt 7:26
of that city to the sword, devoting it to **d**, Dt 13:15
you shall devote them to complete **d**, Dt 20:17
to Sihon and Og, whom you devoted to **d**. Jos 2:10
it shall be devoted to the LORD for **d**. Jos 6:17
yourselves from the things devoted to **d**, Jos 6:18
Israel a thing for **d** and bring trouble Jos 6:18
Then they devoted all in the city to **d**, Jos 6:21
because they have become devoted for **d**. Jos 7:12
devoted all the inhabitants of Ai to **d**. Jos 8:26
had captured Ai and had devoted it to **d**, Jos 10:1
He devoted to **d** every person in it; he left Jos 10:28
devoted every person in it to **d** that day, Jos 10:35
and devoted it to **d** and every person in Jos 10:37
sword and devoted to **d** every person in Jos 10:39
but devoted to **d** all that breathed, Jos 10:40
all who were in it, devoting them to **d**; Jos 11:11
edge of the sword, devoting them to **d**, Jos 11:12
be devoted to **d** and should receive Jos 11:20
devoted them to **d** with their cities. Jos 11:21
inhabited Zephath and devoted it to **d**. Jgs 1:17
lain with a male you shall devote to **d**." Jgs 21:11
Amalek and devote to **d** all that they 1 Sm 15:3
alive and devoted to **d** all the people 1 Sm 15:8
and worthless they devoted to **d**. 1 Sm 15:9
and the rest we have devoted to **d**." 1 Sm 15:15
and said, 'Go, devote to **d** the sinners, 1 Sm 15:18
I have devoted the Amalekites to **d**. 1 Sm 15:20
the best of the things devoted to **d**, 1 Sm 15:21
me, the torrents of **d** assailed me; 2 Sm 22:5
who was working **d** among the 2 Sm 24:16
unable to devote to **d**—these Solomon 1 Kgs 9:21
the man whom I had devoted to **d**, 1 Kgs 20:42
done to all lands, devoting them to **d**. 2 Kgs 19:11
and marked them for **d** to this day, 1 Chr 4:41
to the angel who was working **d**, 1 Chr 21:15
him, so as not to make a complete **d**. 2 Chr 12:12
of Mount Seir, devoting them to **d**, 2 Chr 20:23
was strong, he grew proud, to his **d**. 2 Chr 26:16
my fathers devoted to **d** was able to 2 Chr 32:14
the king's treasuries for the **d** of the Jews. Est 4:7
written decree issued in Susa for their **d**, Est 4:8
can I bear to see the **d** of my kindred?" Est 8:6
and shall not fear **d** when it comes. Jb 5:21
At **d** and famine you shall laugh, and Jb 5:22
Let their own eyes see their **d**, and let Jb 21:20
they cast up against me their ways of **d**. Jb 30:12
in their mouth; their inmost self is **d**; Ps 5:9
me; the torrents of **d** assailed me; Ps 18:4
Let **d** come upon him when he does not Ps 35:8
him; let him fall into it—to his **d**! Ps 35:8
Rescue me from their **d**, my precious Ps 35:17
He drew me up from the pit of **d**, out of Ps 40:2
Your tongue plots **d**, like a sharp razor, Ps 52:2
riches and sought refuge in his own **d**!" Ps 52:7
will cast them down into the pit of **d**; Ps 55:23
take refuge, till the storms of **d** pass by. Ps 57:1
nor the **d** that wastes at noonday. Ps 91:6
flourish, they are doomed to **d** forever; Ps 92:7
them, and delivered them from their **d**. Ps 107:20
to the blameless, but **d** to evildoers. Prv 10:29
despises the word brings **d** on himself, Prv 13:13
Pride goes before **d**, and a haughty Prv 16:18
he who makes his door high seeks **d**. Prv 17:19
Before **d** a man's heart is haughty, but Prv 18:12
D is decreed, overflowing with Is 10:22
and my anger will be directed to their **d**. Is 10:25
as **d** from the Almighty it will come! Is 13:6
with the broom of **d**," declares the LORD Is 14:23
road to Horonaim they raise a cry of **d**; Is 15:5
oppressor is no more and **d** has ceased, Is 16:4
One of these will be called the City of **D**. Is 19:18
me concerning the **d** of the daughter Is 22:4
have visited them with **d** and wiped out Is 26:14
heard a decree of **d** from the Lord GOD Is 28:22
to sift the nations with the sieve of **d**, and Is 30:28
he has devoted them to **d**, has given them Is 34:2
Edom, upon the people I have devoted to **d**. Is 34:5
done to all lands, devoting them to **d**. Is 37:11
have delivered my life from the pit of **d**, Is 38:17
deliver Jacob to utter **d** and Israel to Is 43:28
devastation and **d**, famine and sword; Is 51:19
desolation and **d** are in their highways. Is 59:7
devastation or **d** within your borders; Is 60:18
bring disaster from the north, and great **d**. Jer 4:6
looms out of the north, and great **d**. Jer 6:1
evil; violence and **d** are heard within her; Jer 6:7
of disaster; destroy them with double **d**! Jer 17:18
"Violence and **d**!" For the word of the Jer 20:8
I will devote them to **d**, and make them a Jer 25:9
Horonaim, 'Desolation and great **d**!' Jer 48:3
they have heard the distressed cry of **d**. Jer 48:5
Kill, and devote them to **d**, declares the Jer 50:21
of battle is in the land, and great **d**! Jer 50:22
like heaps of grain, and devote her to **d**; Jer 50:26
her young men; devote to **d** all her army. Jer 51:3
The noise of great **d** from the land of Jer 51:54
because of the **d** of the daughter Lam 2:11
have come upon us, devastation and **d**; Lam 3:47
tears because of the **d** of the daughter Lam 3:48
their food during the **d** of the daughter Lam 4:10
deadly arrows of famine, arrows for **d**, Ezk 5:16
I bring your **d** among the nations, Ezk 32:9
shall cause fearful **d** and shall succeed Dn 8:24
the glorious land, with **d** in his hand. Dn 11:16
fury to destroy and devote many to **d**. Dn 11:44
D to them, for they have rebelled Hos 7:13
and gold they made idols for their own **d**. Hos 8:4
For behold, they are going away from **d**; Hos 9:6
and as **d** from the Almighty it comes. Jl 1:15
who makes **d** flash forth against the Am 5:9
strong, so that **d** comes upon the fortress. Am 5:9
that destroys with a grievous **d**. Mi 2:10
D and violence are before me; strife and Hab 1:3
as will the **d** of the beasts that terrified Hab 2:17
shall never again be a decree of utter **d**. Zec 14:11
strike the land with a decree of utter **d**." Mal 4:6
wide and the way is easy that leads to **d**, Mt 7:13
them has been lost except the son of **d**, Jn 17:12
vessels of wrath prepared for **d**, Rom 9:22
this man to Satan for the **d** of the flesh, 1 Cor 5:5
This is a clear sign to them of their **d**, Phil 1:28
Their end is **d**, their god is their belly, Phil 3:19
security," then sudden **d** will come 1 Thes 5:3
suffer the punishment of eternal **d**, 2 Thes 1:9
of lawlessness is revealed, the son of **d**, 2 Thes 2:3
that plunge people into ruin and **d**. 1 Tm 6:9
them, bringing upon themselves swift **d**. 2 Pt 2:1
ago is not idle, and their **d** is not asleep. 2 Pt 2:3
will also be destroyed in their **d**, 2 Pt 2:12
day of judgment and **d** of the ungodly. 2 Pt 3:7
and unstable twist to their own **d**, 2 Pt 3:16
rise from the bottomless pit and go to **d**. Rv 17:8
it belongs to the seven, and it goes to **d**. Rv 17:11

DESTRUCTIVE (1)

who will secretly bring in **d** heresies, 2 Pt 2:1

DETAIL (3)

describing in **d** the conversion of the Acts 15:3
of angels, going on in **d** about visions, Col 2:18
these things we cannot now speak in **d**. Heb 9:5

DETAILS (1)

and its pattern, exact in all its **d**. 2 Kgs 16:10

DETAIN (3)

"Please let us **d** you and prepare a Jgs 13:15
the LORD said to Manoah, "If you **d** me, Jgs 13:16
But, to **d** you no further, I beg you in Acts 24:4

DETAINED (1)

was there that day, **d** before the LORD. 1 Sm 21:7

DETERMINE (3)

him, and he shall pay as the judges **d**. Ex 21:22
to **d** whether it is clean or unclean. Lv 13:59
you were going to **d** his case more Acts 23:15

DETERMINED (20)

"I have **d** to make an end of all flesh, Gn 6:13
saw that she was **d** to go with her, Ru 1:18
then know that harm is **d** by him. 1 Sm 20:7
I knew that it was **d** by my father that 1 Sm 20:9
that his father was **d** to put David to 1 Sm 20:33
for harm is **d** against our master and 1 Sm 25:17
this has been **d** from the day 2 Sm 13:32
you not heard that I **d** it long ago? 2 Kgs 19:25
know that God has **d** to destroy you, 2 Chr 25:16
saw that harm was **d** against him by the Est 7:7
Since his days are **d**, and the number of Jb 14:5
Who **d** its measurements—surely you Jb 38:5
"Have you not heard that I **d** it long ago? Is 37:26
The LORD **d** to lay in ruins the wall of Lam 2:8
because he was **d** to go after filth. Hos 5:11
the Son of Man goes as it has been **d**, Lk 22:22
So the disciples **d**, everyone according Acts 11:29
having **d** allotted periods and the Acts 17:26
control, and has **d** this in his heart, 1 Cor 7:37
my liberty be **d** by someone else's 1 Cor 10:29

DETERMINES (1)

He **d** the number of the stars; he gives to Ps 147:4

DETEST (4)

flesh, and you shall **d** their carcasses. Lv 11:11
these you shall **d** among the birds; Lv 11:13
like it. You shall utterly **d** and abhor it, Dt 7:26
who **d** justice and make crooked all that Mi 3:9

DETESTABLE (30)

beast or any unclean **d** creature, Lv 7:21
that are in the waters, is **d** to you. Lv 11:10
You shall regard them as **d**; you shall Lv 11:11
that has not fins and scales is **d** to you. Lv 11:12
they shall not be eaten; they are **d**: Lv 11:13
insects that go on all fours are **d** to you. Lv 11:20
insects that have four feet are **d** to you. Lv 11:23
thing that swarms on the ground is **d**; Lv 11:41
ground, you shall not eat, for they are **d**. Lv 11:42
not make yourselves **d** with any Lv 11:43
shall not make yourselves **d** by beast or Lv 20:25
And you have seen their **d** things, their Dt 29:17
and put away the **d** idols from all the 2 Chr 15:8
had made a **d** image for Asherah. 2 Chr 15:16
If you remove your **d** things from my Jer 4:1
They have set their **d** things in the house Jer 7:30
land with the carcasses of their **d** idols, Jer 16:18
with all your **d** things and with Ezk 5:11
images and their **d** things of it. Ezk 7:20

from it all its **d** things and all its Ezk 11:18
goes after their **d** things and their Ezk 11:21
Cast away the **d** things your eyes feast Ezk 20:7
them cast away the **d** things their eyes Ezk 20:8
and go whoring after their **d** things? Ezk 20:30
with their idols and their **d** things, Ezk 37:23
and became **d** like the thing they loved. Hos 9:10
They are **d**, disobedient, unfit for any Ti 1:16
a haunt for every unclean and **d** beast. Rv 18:2
as for the cowardly, the faithless, the **d**, Rv 21:8
nor anyone who does what is **d** or false, Rv 21:27

DETESTED (2)
all these things, and therefore I **d** them. Lv 20:23
with them, and they also **d** me. Zec 11:8

DEUEL (4)
from Gad, Eliasaph the son of **D**; Nm 1:14
On the sixth day Eliasaph the son of **D**, Nm 7:42
the offering of Eliasaph the son of **D**. Nm 7:47
of Gad was Eliasaph the son of **D**. Nm 10:20

DEVASTATE (3)
And I myself will **d** the land, so that Lv 26:32
down; a wolf from the desert shall **d** them. Jer 5:6
their firstborn, that I might **d** them. Ezk 20:26

DEVASTATED (2)
desolate places and your **d** land—surely Is 49:19
the peaceful folds are **d** because of the Jer 25:37

DEVASTATION (6)
or three months of **d** by your foes 1 Chr 21:12
d and destruction, famine and sword; Is 51:19
d or destruction within your borders; Is 60:18
have come upon us, **d** and destruction; Lam 3:47
and anguish, a day of ruin and **d**, Zep 1:15
the window; **d** will be on the threshold; Zep 2:14

DEVASTATIONS (2)
ruins; they shall raise up the former **d**; Is 61:4
ruined cities, the **d** of many generations. Is 61:4

DEVICES (9)
He frustrates the **d** of the crafty, so that Jb 5:12
in whose hands are evil **d**, and whose Ps 26:10
way, over the man who carries out evil **d**! Ps 37:7
way, and have their fill of their own **d**. Prv 1:31
LORD, but a man of evil **d** he condemns. Prv 12:2
foolishly, and a man of evil **d** is hated. Prv 14:17
As for the scoundrel—his **d** are evil; he Is 32:7
that is not good, following their own **d**; Is 65:2
upon this people, the fruit of their **d**, Jer 6:19

DEVIL (34)
into the wilderness to be tempted by the **d**. Mt 4:1
Then the **d** took him to the holy city and Mt 4:5
the **d** took him to a very high mountain Mt 4:8
Then the **d** left him, and behold, angels Mt 4:11
the enemy who sowed them is the **d**. Mt 13:39
fire prepared for the **d** and his angels. Mt 25:41
for forty days, being tempted by the **d**. Lk 4:2
The **d** said to him, "If you are the Son of Lk 4:3
And the **d** took him up and showed him Lk 4:5
And when the **d** had ended every Lk 4:13
Then the **d** comes and takes away the Lk 8:12
the Twelve? And yet one of you is a **d**." Jn 6:70
You are of your father the **d**, and your Jn 8:44
when the **d** had already put it into the Jn 13:2
all who were oppressed by the **d**, Acts 10:38
and said, "You son of the **d**, you Acts 13:10
and give no opportunity to the **d**. Eph 4:27
to stand against the schemes of the **d**. Eph 6:11
fall into the condemnation of the **d**. 1 Tm 3:6
fall into disgrace, into a snare of the **d**. 1 Tm 3:7
may escape from the snare of the **d**, 2 Tm 2:26
has the power of death, that is, the **d**, Heb 2:14
Resist the **d**, and he will flee from you. Jas 4:7
Your adversary the **d** prowls around like 1 Pt 5:8
makes a practice of sinning is of the **d**, 1 Jn 3:8
for the **d** has been sinning from the 1 Jn 3:8
was to destroy the works of the **d**. 1 Jn 3:8
God, and who are the children of the **d**: 1 Jn 3:10
Michael, contending with the **d**, Jude 1:9
the **d** is about to throw some of you into Rv 2:10
serpent, who is called the **d** and Satan, Rv 12:9
for the **d** has come down to you in great Rv 12:12
ancient serpent, who is the **d** and Satan, Rv 20:2
and the **d** who had deceived them was Rv 20:10

DEVIOUS (4)
crooked, and who are **d** in their ways. Prv 2:15
for the **d** person is an abomination to Prv 3:32
speech, and put **d** talk far from you. Prv 4:24
but he who is **d** in his ways despises Prv 14:2

DEVISE (17)
to **d** artistic designs, to work in gold, Ex 31:4
to **d** artistic designs, to work in gold Ex 35:32
against you, though they **d** mischief, Ps 21:11
and disappointed who **d** evil against me! Ps 35:4
quiet in the land they **d** words of deceit. Ps 35:20
No, in your hearts you **d** wrongs; your Ps 58:2
is in the heart of those who **d** evil, Prv 12:20
Do they not go astray who **d** evil? Prv 14:22
Those who **d** good meet steadfast love Prv 14:22
for their hearts **d** violence, and their lips Prv 24:2
are the men who **d** iniquity and who Ezk 11:2
mind, and you will **d** an evil scheme Ezk 38:10
He shall **d** plans against strongholds, Dn 11:24
their arms, yet they **d** evil against me. Hos 7:15
Woe to those who **d** wickedness and work Mi 2:1
let none of you **d** evil against another in Zec 7:10
do not **d** evil in your hearts against one Zec 8:17

DEVISED (11)
month that he had **d** from his own 1 Kgs 12:33
the plot that he had **d** against the Jews. Est 8:3
to revoke the letters **d** by Haman the Est 8:5
plan that he had **d** against the Jews Est 9:25
caught in the schemes that they have **d**. Ps 10:2
son of Remaliah, has **d** evil against you, Is 7:5
it was against me they **d** schemes, Jer 11:19
stand, for plots shall be **d** against him. Dn 11:25
remember what Balak king of Moab **d**, Mi 6:5
You have **d** shame for your house by Hab 2:10
not follow cleverly **d** myths when we 2 Pt 1:16

DEVISES (3)
and he **d** means so that the banished 2 Sm 14:14
with perverted heart **d** evil, continually Prv 6:14
a heart that **d** wicked plans, feet that Prv 6:18

DEVISING (4)
The **d** of folly is sin, and the scoffer is Prv 24:9
yourself, or if you have been **d** evil, Prv 30:32
against you and **d** a plan against Jer 18:11
against this family I am **d** disaster, Mi 2:3

DEVOID (1)
worldly people, **d** of the Spirit. Jude 1:19

DEVOTE (20)
then I will **d** their cities to destruction." Nm 21:2
then you must **d** them to complete Dt 7:2
but you shall **d** them to complete Dt 20:17
with a male you shall **d** to destruction." Jgs 21:11
strike Amalek and **d** to destruction all 1 Sm 15:3
'Go, **d** to destruction the sinners, 1 Sm 15:18
were unable to **d** to destruction— 1 Kgs 9:21
I will **d** them to destruction, and make Jer 25:9
Kill, and **d** them to destruction, Jer 50:21
heaps of grain, and **d** her to destruction; Jer 50:26
men; **d** to destruction all her army. Jer 51:3
to destroy and **d** many to destruction. Dn 11:44
and shall **d** their gain to the LORD, their Mi 4:13
But we will **d** ourselves to prayer and to Acts 6:4
that you may **d** yourselves to prayer; 1 Cor 7:5
nor to **d** themselves to myths and 1 Tm 1:4
d yourself to the public reading of 1 Tm 4:13
these things, **d** yourself to them, 1 Tm 4:15
may be careful to **d** themselves to good Ti 3:8
our people learn to **d** themselves to good Ti 3:14

DEVOTED (55)
LORD alone, shall be **d** to destruction. Ex 22:20
to the LORD, like a field that has been **d**. Lv 27:21
"But no **d** thing that a man devotes to Lv 27:28
every **d** thing is most holy to the LORD. Lv 27:28
No one **d**, who is to be devoted for Lv 27:29
who is to be **d** for destruction from Lv 27:29
Every **d** thing in Israel shall be yours. Nm 18:14
and they **d** them and their cities to Nm 21:3
at that time and **d** to destruction every Dt 2:34
And we **d** them to destruction, as we did to Dt 3:6
house and become **d** to destruction like Dt 7:26
and abhor it, for it is **d** to destruction. Dt 7:26
None of the **d** things shall stick to your Dt 13:17
and Og, whom you **d** to destruction. Jos 2:10
is within it shall be **d** to the LORD for Jos 6:17
from the things **d** to destruction, Jos 6:18
lest when you have **d** them you take any Jos 6:18
take any of the **d** things and make the Jos 6:18
Then they **d** all in the city to Jos 6:21
broke faith in regard to the **d** things, Jos 7:1
tribe of Judah, took some of the **d** things. Jos 7:1
they have taken some of the **d** things; Jos 7:11
they have become **d** for destruction. Jos 7:12
you destroy the **d** things from among Jos 7:12
Israel, "There are **d** things in your midst, Jos 7:13
you take away the **d** things from among Jos 7:13
is taken with the **d** things shall be Jos 7:15
until he had **d** all the inhabitants Jos 8:26
captured Ai and had **d** it to destruction, Jos 10:1
He **d** to destruction every person in it; Jos 10:28
And he **d** every person in it to Jos 10:35
and **d** it to destruction and every person Jos 10:37
of the sword and **d** to destruction every Jos 10:39
but **d** to destruction all that breathed, Jos 10:40
they should be **d** to destruction and Jos 11:20
Joshua **d** them to destruction with their Jos 11:21
faith in the matter of the **d** things, Jos 22:20
inhabited Zephath and **d** it to Jgs 1:17
Amalekites alive and **d** to destruction 1 Sm 15:8
and worthless they **d** to destruction. 1 Sm 15:9
the rest we have **d** to destruction." 1 Sm 15:15
and I have **d** the Amalekites to 1 Sm 15:20
best of the things **d** to destruction, 1 Sm 15:21
man whom I had **d** to destruction, 1 Kgs 20:42
faith in the matter of the **d** thing; 1 Chr 2:7
that my fathers **d** to destruction was 2 Chr 32:14
he has **d** them to destruction, has given Is 34:2
upon the people I have **d** to destruction. Is 34:5
and every **d** thing in Israel shall be Ezk 44:29
or he will be **d** to the one and despise the Mt 6:24
or he will be **d** to the one and despise Lk 16:13
And they **d** themselves to the apostles' Acts 2:42
that they have **d** themselves to the 1 Cor 16:15
and has **d** herself to every good work. 1 Tm 5:10
have not benefited those **d** to them. Heb 13:9

DEVOTES (1)
devoted thing that a man **d** to the LORD, Lv 27:28

DEVOTING (10)
of Heshbon, **d** to destruction every city, Dt 3:6
city to the sword, **d** it to destruction, Dt 13:15
who were in it, **d** them to destruction; Jos 11:11
of the sword, **d** them to destruction, Jos 11:12
to all lands, **d** them to destruction. 2 Kgs 19:11
Mount Seir, **d** them to destruction, 2 Chr 20:23
done to all lands, **d** them to destruction. Is 37:11
one accord were **d** themselves to Acts 1:14
the faith by **d** themselves to deceitful 1 Tm 4:1
not **d** themselves to Jewish myths and the Ti 1:14

DEVOTION (4)
and because of my **d** to the house of 1 Chr 29:3
LORD, "I remember the **d** of your youth, Jer 2:2
secure your undivided **d** to the Lord. 1 Cor 7:35
from a sincere and pure **d** to Christ. 2 Cor 11:3

DEVOUR (65)
and my sword shall **d** flesh—with the Dt 32:42
against them and **d** the produce of Jgs 6:4
of the bramble and **d** the cedars of Jgs 9:15
out from Abimelech and **d** the leaders of Jgs 9:20
and from Beth-millo and **d** Abimelech." Jgs 9:20
to Joab, "Shall the sword **d** forever? 2 Sm 2:26
or command the locust to **d** the land, 2 Chr 7:13
treasures; a fire not fanned will **d** him; Jb 20:26
You love all words that **d**, O deceitful Ps 52:4
knives, to **d** the poor from off the earth, Prv 30:14
your very presence foreigners **d** your land; Is 1:7
Philistines on the west **d** Israel with open Is 9:12
are still hungry, and they **d** on the left, Is 9:20
it will burn and **d** his thorns and briers Is 10:17
and a sword, not of man, shall **d** him; Is 31:8
come to **d**—all you beasts in the forest. Is 56:9
They come and **d** the land and all that Jer 8:16
all the wild beasts; bring them to **d**. Jer 12:9
the beasts of the earth to **d** and destroy. Jer 15:3
and it shall **d** the palaces of Jerusalem Jer 17:27
and it shall **d** all that is around her." Jer 21:14
Therefore all who **d** you shall be Jer 30:16
The sword shall **d** and be sated and Jer 46:10
for the sword shall **d** around you.' Jer 46:14
and it shall **d** the strongholds of Jer 49:27
and it will **d** all that is around him. Jer 50:32
is in the city famine and pestilence **d**. Ezk 7:15
and it shall **d** every green tree in you Ezk 20:47
shall the beasts of the land **d** them. Ezk 34:28
laid desolate; they are given us to **d**.' Ezk 35:12
Because they say to you, 'You **d** people, Ezk 36:13
you shall no longer **d** people and no Ezk 36:14
and it was told, 'Arise, **d** much flesh.' Dn 7:5
and it shall **d** the whole earth, Dn 7:23
and the beasts of the field shall **d** them. Hos 2:12
the new moon shall **d** them with their Hos 5:7
hot as an oven, and they **d** their rulers. Hos 7:7
Strangers **d** his strength, and he knows it Hos 7:9
if it were to yield, strangers would **d** it. Hos 8:7
cities, and it shall **d** her strongholds. Hos 8:14
and **d** them because of their own Hos 11:6
and there I will **d** them like a lion, Hos 13:8
and it shall **d** the strongholds of Am 1:4
of Gaza, and it shall **d** her strongholds. Am 1:7
of Tyre, and it shall **d** her strongholds." Am 1:10
and it shall **d** the strongholds of Am 1:12
Rabbah, and it shall **d** her strongholds, Am 1:14
and it shall **d** the strongholds of Kerioth, Am 2:2
and it shall **d** the strongholds of Am 2:5
like fire in the house of Joseph, and it **d**, Am 5:6
and the sword shall **d** your young lions. Na 2:13
There will the fire **d** you; the sword will Na 3:15
cut you off. It will **d** you like the locust. Na 3:15

afar; they fly like an eagle swift to **d**. Hab 1:8
rejoicing as if to **d** the poor in secret. Hab 3:14
will protect them, and they shall **d**, Zec 9:15
that the fire may **d** your cedars! Zec 11:1
let those who are left **d** the flesh of one Zec 11:9
And they shall **d** to the right and to the Zec 12:6
who **d** widows' houses and for a Mk 12:40
who **d** widows' houses and for a Lk 20:47
But if you bite and **d** one another, Gal 5:15
a roaring lion, seeking someone to **d**. 1 Pt 5:8
when she bore her child he might **d** it. Rv 12:4
and **d** her flesh and burn her up with Rv 17:16

DEVOURED (42)
us, and he has indeed **d** our money. Gn 31:15
will say that a fierce animal has **d** him, Gn 37:20
son's robe. A fierce animal has **d** him. Gn 37:33
It **d** Ar of Moab, and swallowed the Nm 21:28
down until it has **d** the prey and Nm 23:24
died, when the fire **d** 250 men, Nm 26:10
my face from them, and they will be **d**. Dt 31:17
and **d** by plague and poisonous Dt 32:24
and the forest **d** more people that day 2 Sm 18:8
them swarms of flies, which **d** them, Ps 78:45
Fire **d** their young men, and their Ps 78:63
For they have **d** Jacob and laid waste his Ps 79:7
which **d** all the vegetation in their Ps 105:35
"It is you who have **d** the vineyard, the Is 3:14
I will remove its hedge, and it shall be **d**; I Is 5:5
your own sword **d** your prophets like a Jer 2:30
the shameful thing has **d** all for which Jer 3:24
on your name, for they have **d** Jacob; Jer 10:25
they have **d** him and consumed him, Jer 10:25
all who devour you shall be **d**, Jer 30:16
All who found them have **d** them, and Jer 50:7
First the king of Assyria **d** him, and Jer 50:17
the king of Babylon has **d** me; Jer 51:34
these you sacrificed to them to be **d**. Ezk 16:20
and he learned to catch prey; he **d** men. Ezk 19:3
and he learned to catch prey; he **d** men, Ezk 19:6
the prey; they have **d** human lives; Ezk 22:25
and your survivors shall be **d** by fire. Ezk 23:25
field I will give to the beasts to be **d**, Ezk 33:27
sort and to the beasts of the field to be **d**. Ezk 39:4
it **d** and broke in pieces and stamped Dn 7:7
and which **d** and broke in pieces and Dn 7:19
For fire has **d** the pastures of the Jl 1:19
and fire has **d** the pastures of the Jl 1:20
fig trees and your olive trees the locust **d**; Am 4:9
and it **d** the great deep and was eating up Am 7:4
to your enemies; fire has **d** your bars. Na 3:13
on the sea, and she shall be **d** by fire. Zec 9:4
path, and the birds came and **d** them. Mt 13:4
the path, and the birds came and **d** it. Mk 4:4
underfoot, and the birds of the air **d** it. Lk 8:5
who has **d** your property with Lk 15:30

DEVOURER (1)
I will rebuke the **d** for you, so that it Mal 3:11

DEVOURING (9)
in the morning **d** the prey and at Gn 49:27
of the LORD was like a **d** fire on the top of Ex 24:17
nostrils, and **d** fire from his mouth; 2 Sm 22:9
his nostrils, and **d** fire from his mouth; Ps 18:8
before him is a **d** fire, around him a Ps 50:3
and tempest, and the flame of a **d** fire. Is 29:6
of fury, and his tongue is like a **d** fire; Is 30:27
in furious anger and a flame of **d** fire, Is 30:30
crackling of a flame of fire **d** the stubble, Jl 2:5

DEVOURS (14)
it out, is a land that **d** its inhabitants, Nm 13:32
of Sheol, **d** the earth and its increase, Dt 32:22
for the sword **d** now one and now 2 Sm 11:25
the mouth of the wicked **d** iniquity. Prv 19:28
man's dwelling, but a foolish man **d** it. Prv 21:20
as the tongue of fire **d** the stubble, Is 5:24
satisfied; each **d** the flesh of his own arm, Is 9:20
Manasseh **d** Ephraim, and Ephraim Is 9:21
Ephraim, and Ephraim **d** Manasseh; Is 9:21
Therefore a curse **d** the earth, and its Is 24:6
the sword of the LORD **d** from one end of Jer 12:12
Fire **d** before them, and behind them a Jl 2:3
healthy, but **d** the flesh of the fat ones, Zec 11:16
makes slaves of you, or **d** you, 2 Cor 11:20

DEVOUT (11)
d men are taken away, while no one Is 57:1
and this man was righteous and **d**, Lk 2:25
d men from every nation under heaven. Acts 2:5
D men buried Stephen and made great Acts 8:2
a **d** man who feared God with all his Acts 10:2
servants and a **d** soldier from among Acts 10:7
many Jews and **d** converts to Judaism Acts 13:43
the Jews incited the **d** women of high Acts 13:50
a great many of the **d** Greeks and not a Acts 17:4
with the Jews and the **d** persons, Acts 17:17
a **d** man according to the law, Acts 22:12

DEW (35)
God give you of the **d** of heaven and of Gn 27:28
and away from the **d** of heaven on Gn 27:39
and in the morning **d** lay around the Ex 16:13
And when the **d** had gone up, there was Ex 16:14
When the **d** fell upon the camp in the Nm 11:9
as the rain, my speech distill as the **d**, Dt 32:2
and wine, whose heavens drop down **d**. Dt 33:28
If there is **d** on the fleece alone, and it is Jgs 6:37
he wrung enough **d** from the fleece to fill Jgs 6:38
and on all the ground let there be **d**." Jgs 6:39
only, and on all the ground there was **d**. Jgs 6:40
let there be no **d** or rain upon you, 2 Sm 1:21
upon him as the **d** falls on the 2 Sm 17:12
there shall be neither **d** nor rain these 1 Kgs 17:1
with the **d** all night on my branches, Jb 29:19
or who has begotten the drops of **d**? Jb 38:28
the **d** of your youth will be yours. Ps 110:3
It is like the **d** of Hermon, which falls Ps 133:3
open, and the clouds drop down the **d**. Prv 3:20
but his favor is like **d** on the grass. Prv 19:12
my perfect one, for my head is wet with **d**, Sg 5:2
like a cloud of **d** in the heat of harvest." Is 18:4
For your **d** is a dew of light, and the Is 26:19
For your dew is a **d** of light, and the Is 26:19
Let him be wet with the **d** of heaven Dn 4:15
and let him be wet with the **d** of heaven, Dn 4:23
you shall be wet with the **d** of heaven, Dn 4:25
was wet with the **d** of heaven till his Dn 4:33
his body was wet with the **d** of heaven, Dn 5:21
cloud, like the **d** that goes early away. Hos 6:4
mist or like the **d** that goes early away, Hos 13:3
I will be like the **d** to Israel; he shall Hos 14:5
of many peoples like **d** from the LORD, Mi 5:7
heavens above you have withheld the **d**, Hg 1:10
and the heavens shall give their **d**. Zec 8:12

DIADEM (2)
be a crown of glory, and a **d** of beauty, Is 28:5
and a royal **d** in the hand of your God. Is 62:3

DIADEMS (3)
and ten horns, and on his heads seven **d**. Rv 12:3
with ten **d** on its horns and Rv 13:1
of fire, and on his head are many **d**, Rv 19:12

DIAL (2)
declining sun on the **d** of Ahaz turn back Is 38:8
sun turned back on the **d** the ten steps by Is 38:8

DIAMOND (4)
row an emerald, a sapphire, and a **d**; Ex 28:18
row, an emerald, a sapphire, and a **d**; Ex 39:11
with a point of **d** it is engraved on the Jer 17:1
your covering, sardius, topaz, and **d**, Ezk 28:13

DIAMOND-HARD (1)
made their hearts **d** lest they should Zec 7:12

DIBLAIM (1)
went and took Gomer, the daughter of **D**, Hos 1:3

DIBON (11)
them; Heshbon, as far as **D**, perished; Nm 21:30
"Ataroth, **D**, Jazer, Nimrah, Heshbon, Nm 32:3
And the people of Gad built **D**, Nm 32:34
all the tableland of Medeba as far as **D**; Jos 13:9
D, and Bamoth-baal, and Jos 13:17
its villages, and in **D** and its villages, Neh 11:25
He has gone up to the temple, and to **D**, to Is 15:2
For the waters of **D** are full of blood; for I Is 15:9
for I will bring upon **D** even more, a lion Is 15:9
the parched ground, O inhabitant of **D**! Jer 48:18
and **D**, and Nebo, and Beth-diblathaim, Jer 48:22

DIBON-GAD (2)
set out from Iyim and camped at **D**. Nm 33:45
they set out from **D** and camped at Nm 33:46

DIBRI (1)
was Shelomith, the daughter of **D**, Lv 24:11

DICTATED (1)
them, "He **d** all these words to me, Jer 36:18

DICTATION (6)
on a scroll at the **d** of Jeremiah all the Jer 36:4
the scroll that you have written at my **d**. Jer 36:6
write all these words? Was it at his **d**?" Jer 36:17
that Baruch wrote at Jeremiah's **d**, Jer 36:27
wrote on it at the **d** of Jeremiah all the Jer 36:32
words in a book at the **d** of Jeremiah, Jer 45:1

DIE (294)
day that you eat of it you shall surely **d**." Gn 2:17
neither shall you touch it, lest you **d**.'" Gn 3:3
to the woman, "You will not surely **d**. Gn 3:4
Everything that is on the earth shall **d**. Gn 6:17
lest the disaster overtake me and I **d**. Gn 19:19
her, know that you shall surely **d**, Gn 20:7
Esau said, "I am about to **d**; of what use Gn 25:32
I thought, 'Lest I **d** because of her.'" Gn 26:9
that my soul may bless you before I **d**." Gn 27:4
and bless you before the LORD before I **d**.' Gn 27:7
Jacob, "Give me children, or I shall **d**!" Gn 30:1
hard for one day, all the flocks will **d**. Gn 33:13
up"—for he feared that he would **d**, Gn 38:11
for us there, that we may live and not **d**." Gn 42:2
and you shall not **d**." And they did so. Gn 42:20
arise and go, that we may live and not **d**, Gn 43:8
of your servants is found with it shall **d**, Gn 44:9
leave his father, his father would **d**.' Gn 44:22
that the boy is not with us, he will **d**, Gn 44:31
alive. I will go and see him before I **d**." Gn 45:28
Israel said to Joseph, "Now let me **d**, Gn 46:30
Why should we **d** before your eyes? Gn 47:15
Why should we **d** before your eyes, Gn 47:19
give us seed that we may live and not **d**, Gn 47:19
the time drew near that Israel must **d**, Gn 47:29
said to Joseph, "Behold, I am about to **d**, Gn 48:21
made me swear, saying, 'I am about to **d**: Gn 50:5
said to his brothers, "I am about to **d**, Gn 50:24
The fish in the Nile shall **d**, and the Nile Ex 7:18
belongs to the people of Israel shall **d**."'" Ex 9:4
not brought home will **d** when the hail Ex 9:19
on the day you see my face you shall **d**." Ex 10:28
firstborn in the land of Egypt shall **d**, Ex 11:5
taken us away to **d** in the wilderness? Ex 14:11
Egyptians than to **d** in the wilderness." Ex 14:12
do not let God speak to us, lest we **d**." Ex 20:19
take him from my altar, that he may **d**. Ex 21:14
and the man does not **d** but takes to his Ex 21:18
he comes out, so that he does not **d**. Ex 28:35
Holy Place, lest they bear guilt and **d**. Ex 28:43
with water, so that they may not **d**. Ex 30:20
and their feet, so that they may not **d**. Ex 30:21
LORD has charged, so that you do not **d**, Lv 8:35
and do not tear your clothes, lest you **d**, Lv 10:6
of the tent of meeting, lest you **d**, Lv 10:7
go into the tent of meeting, lest you **d**. Lv 10:9
lest they **d** in their uncleanness by Lv 15:31
that is on the ark, so that he may not **d**. Lv 16:2
the testimony, so that he does not **d**. Lv 16:13
bear their sin; they shall **d** childless. Lv 20:20
sin for it and **d** thereby when they Lv 22:9
not touch the holy things, lest they **d**. Nm 4:15
may live and not **d** when they come Nm 4:19
things even for a moment, lest they **d**." Nm 4:20
mother, for brother or sister, if they **d**, Nm 6:7
to a full end, and there they shall **d**." Nm 14:35
If these men **d** as all men die, or if they Nm 16:29
If these men die as all men **d**, or if they Nm 16:29
grumblings against me, lest they **d**." Nm 17:10
to the tabernacle of the LORD, shall **d**. Nm 17:13
or to the altar lest they, and you, **d**. Nm 18:3
of meeting, lest they bear sin and **d**. Nm 18:22
of the people of Israel, lest you **d**.'" Nm 18:32
this wilderness, that we should **d** here, Nm 20:4
to his people and shall **d** there." Nm 20:26
up out of Egypt to **d** in the wilderness? Nm 21:5
Let me **d** the death of the upright, and Nm 23:10
But the sons of Korah did not **d**. Nm 26:11
"They shall **d** in the wilderness." Not Nm 26:65
manslayer may not **d** until he stands Nm 35:12
For I must **d** in this land; I must not go Dt 4:22
Now therefore why should we **d**? For this Dt 5:25
of the LORD our God any more, we shall **d**. Dt 5:25
the one who is to **d** shall be put to death; Dt 17:6
God, or the judge, that man shall **d**. Dt 17:12
or see this great fire any more, lest I **d**.' Dt 18:16
other gods, that same prophet shall **d**.' Dt 18:20
though the man did not deserve to **d**, Dt 19:6
the avenger of blood, so that he may **d**. Dt 19:12
lest he **d** in the battle and another man Dt 20:5
lest he **d** in the battle and another man Dt 20:6
lest he **d** in the battle and another man Dt 20:7
of another man, both of them shall **d**, Dt 22:22
only the man who lay with her shall **d**. Dt 22:25
slave or sells him, then that thief shall **d**. Dt 24:7
the days approach when you must **d**. Dt 31:14
And **d** on the mountain which you go Dt 32:50
"Let Reuben live, and not **d**, but let his Dt 33:6
so that he might not **d** by the hand of the Jos 20:9
be to you. Do not fear; you shall not **d**." Jgs 6:23
"Bring out your son, that he may **d**, Jgs 6:30
said to his wife, "We shall surely **d**, Jgs 13:22
and shall I now **d** of thirst and fall into Jgs 15:18
"Let me **d** with the Philistines." Then Jgs 16:30
Where you **d** I will die, and there will I Ru 1:17
Where you die I will **d**, and there will I Ru 1:17
of your house shall **d** by the sword of 1 Sm 2:33
both of them shall **d** on the same day. 1 Sm 2:34
men who did not **d** were struck with 1 Sm 5:12
LORD your God, that we may not **d**, 1 Sm 12:19
he shall surely **d**." But there was not 1 Sm 14:39

was in my hand. Here I am; I will **d**." 1 Sm 14:43
also; you shall surely **d**, Jonathan." 1 Sm 14:44
said to Saul, "Shall Jonathan **d**, 1 Sm 14:45
Jonathan, so that he did not **d**. 1 Sm 14:45
to him, "Far from it! You shall not **d**. 1 Sm 20:2
love of the LORD, that I may not **d**; 1 Sm 20:14
him to me, for he shall surely **d**." 1 Sm 20:31
the king said, "You shall surely **d**, 1 Sm 22:16
strike him, or his day will come to **d**, 1 Sm 26:10
As the LORD lives, you deserve to **d**, 1 Sm 26:16
"Should Abner **d** as a fool dies? 2 Sm 3:33
that he may be struck down, and **d**." 2 Sm 11:15
man who has done this deserves to **d**, 2 Sm 12:5
put away your sin; you shall not **d**. 2 Sm 12:13
the child who is born to you shall **d**." 2 Sm 12:14
We must all **d**; we are like water 2 Sm 14:14
If half of us **d**, they will not care about 2 Sm 18:3
"You shall not **d**." And the king gave 2 Sm 19:23
that I may **d** in my own city near the 2 Sm 19:37
is found in him, he shall **d**." 1 Kgs 1:52
When David's time to **d** drew near, he 1 Kgs 2:1
I will **d** here." Then Benaiah brought 1 Kgs 2:30
know for certain that you shall **d**. 1 Kgs 2:37
to any place whatever, you shall **d**'? 1 Kgs 2:42
him, he said to his sons, "When I **d**, 1 Kgs 13:31
feet enter the city, the child shall **d**. 1 Kgs 14:12
my son, that we may eat it and **d**." 1 Kgs 17:12
And he asked that he might **d**, saying, 1 Kgs 19:4
you shall surely **d**.'" So Elijah went. 2 Kgs 1:4
have gone up, but you shall surely **d**.'" 2 Kgs 1:6
gone up, but you shall surely **d**.'" 2 Kgs 1:16
"Why are we sitting here until we **d**? 2 Kgs 7:3
is in the city, and we shall **d** there. 2 Kgs 7:4
die there. And if we sit here, we **d** also. 2 Kgs 7:4
live, and if they kill us we shall but **d**." 2 Kgs 7:4
shown me that he shall certainly **d**." 2 Kgs 8:10
with the illness of which he was to **d**, 2 Kgs 13:14
But each one shall **d** for his own sin." 2 Kgs 14:6
honey, that you may live, and not **d**. 2 Kgs 18:32
your house in order, for you shall **d**; 2 Kgs 20:1
"Fathers shall not **d** because of their 2 Chr 25:4
nor children **d** because of their 2 Chr 25:4
but each one shall **d** for his own sin." 2 Chr 25:4
give you over to **d** by famine and by 2 Chr 32:11
fast your integrity? Curse God and **d**." Jb 2:9
"Why did I not **d** at birth, come out from Jb 3:11
plucked up within them, do they not **d**, Jb 4:21
the people, and wisdom will **d** with you. Jb 12:2
me? For then I would be silent and **d**. Jb 13:19
in the earth, and its stump **d** in the soil, Jb 14:8
till I **d** I will not put away my integrity Jb 27:5
Then I thought, 'I shall **d** in my nest, Jb 29:18
In a moment they **d**; at midnight the Jb 34:20
by the sword and **d** without knowledge. Jb 36:12
They **d** in youth, and their life ends Jb 36:14
"When will he **d** and his name perish?" Ps 41:5
For he sees that even the wise **d**; the fool Ps 49:10
great power, preserve those doomed to **d**! Ps 79:11
nevertheless, like men you shall **d**, and Ps 82:7
to set free those who were doomed to **d**, Ps 102:20
breath, they **d** and return to their dust. Ps 104:29
into blood and caused their fish to **d**. Ps 105:29
I shall not **d**, but I shall live, and Ps 118:17
many, but fools **d** for lack of sense. Prv 10:21
live, but he who pursues evil will **d**. Prv 11:19
the way; whoever hates reproof will **d**. Prv 15:10
life; he who despises his ways will **d**. Prv 19:16
strike him with a rod, he will not **d**. Prv 23:13
of you; deny them not to me before I **d**: Prv 30:7
a time to be born, and a time to **d**; a time Eccl 3:2
Why should you **d** before your time? Eccl 7:17
For the living know that they will **d**, but Eccl 9:5
us eat and drink, for tomorrow we **d**." Is 22:13
for you until you **d**," says the Lord GOD Is 22:14
There you shall **d**, and there shall be Is 22:18
Set your house in order, for you shall **d**, Is 38:1
fish stink for lack of water and **d** of thirst. Is 50:2
they who dwell in it will **d** in like manner; Is 51:6
he shall not **d** and go down to the pit, Is 51:14
the young man shall **d** a hundred years Is 65:20
For their worm shall not **d**, their fire Is 66:24
the LORD, or you will **d** by our hand"— Jer 11:21
The young men shall **d** by the sword, Jer 11:22
and their daughters shall **d** by famine, Jer 11:22
They shall **d** of deadly diseases. They Jer 16:4
Both great and small shall **d** in this land. Jer 16:6
you shall go, and there you shall **d**, Jer 20:6
beast. They shall **d** of a great pestilence. Jer 21:6
stays in this city shall **d** by the sword, Jer 21:9
carried him captive, there shall he **d**, Jer 22:12
were not born, and there you shall **d**. Jer 22:26
laid hold of him, saying, "You shall **d**! Jer 26:8
you and your people **d** by the sword, Jer 27:13
This year you shall **d**, because you Jer 28:16
But everyone shall **d** for his own sin. Jer 31:30
you: 'You shall not **d** by the sword. Jer 34:4
You shall **d** in peace. And as spices were Jer 34:5
of Jonathan the secretary, lest I **d** there." Jer 37:20
stays in this city shall **d** by the sword, Jer 38:2
the cistern, and he will **d** there of hunger, Jer 38:9
of these words, and you shall not **d**. Jer 38:24
to the house of Jonathan to **d** there.'" Jer 38:26
you to Egypt, and there you shall **d**. Jer 42:16
Egypt to live there shall **d** by the sword, Jer 42:17
certainty that you shall **d** by the sword, Jer 42:22
they shall **d** by the sword and by Jer 44:12
I say to the wicked, 'You shall surely **d**,' Ezk 3:18
wicked person shall **d** for his iniquity, Ezk 3:18
wicked way, he shall **d** for his iniquity, Ezk 3:19
block before him, he shall **d**. Ezk 3:20
not warned him, he shall **d** for his sin, Ezk 3:20
part of you shall **d** of pestilence and be Ezk 5:12
He who is far off shall **d** of pestilence, Ezk 6:12
is left and is preserved shall **d** of famine. Ezk 6:12
he shall not see it, and he shall **d** there. Ezk 12:13
who should not **d** and keeping alive Ezk 13:19
him he broke, in Babylon he shall **d**. Ezk 17:16
son is mine: the soul who sins shall **d**. Ezk 18:4
these abominations; he shall surely **d**; Ezk 18:13
he shall not **d** for his father's iniquity; Ezk 18:17
behold, he shall **d** for his iniquity. Ezk 18:18
The soul who sins shall **d**. The son Ezk 18:20
he shall surely live; he shall not **d**. Ezk 18:21
he has committed, for them he shall **d**. Ezk 18:24
and does injustice, he shall **d** for it; Ezk 18:26
injustice that he has done he shall **d**. Ezk 18:26
he shall surely live; he shall not **d**. Ezk 18:28
Why will you **d**, O house of Israel? Ezk 18:31
and you shall **d** the death of the slain in Ezk 28:8
You shall **d** the death of the Ezk 28:10
O wicked one, you shall surely **d**, Ezk 33:8
wicked person shall **d** in his iniquity, Ezk 33:8
way, that person shall **d** in his iniquity, Ezk 33:9
your evil ways, for why will you **d**, Ezk 33:11
injustice that he has done he shall **d**. Ezk 33:13
say to the wicked, 'You shall surely **d**,' Ezk 33:14
he shall surely live; he shall not **d**. Ezk 33:15
and does injustice, he shall **d** for it. Ezk 33:18
and in caves shall **d** by pestilence. Ezk 33:27
Kerioth, and Moab shall **d** amid uproar, Am 2:2
men remain in one house, they shall **d**. Am 6:9
said, "'Jeroboam shall **d** by the sword, Am 7:11
you yourself shall **d** in an unclean Am 7:17
of my people shall **d** by the sword, Am 9:10
for it is better for me to **d** than to live." Jon 4:3
And he asked that he might **d** and said, Jon 4:8
said, "It is better for me to **d** than to live." Jon 4:8
I do well to be angry, angry enough to **d**." Jon 4:9
my God, my Holy One? We shall not **d**. Hab 1:12
be your shepherd. What is to **d**, let it die. Zec 11:9
be your shepherd. What is to die, let it **d**. Zec 11:9
reviles father or mother must surely **d**.' Mt 15:4
said to him, "Even if I must **d** with you, Mt 26:35
reviles father or mother must surely **d**.' Mk 7:10
their worm does not **d** and the fire is Mk 9:48
emphatically, "If I must **d** with you, Mk 14:31
for they cannot **d** anymore, because Lk 20:36
so that one may eat of it and not **d**. Jn 6:50
will seek me, and you will **d** in your sin. Jn 8:21
I told you that you would **d** in your sins, Jn 8:24
that I am he you will **d** in your sins." Jn 8:24
us also go, that we may **d** with him." Jn 11:16
Whoever believes in me, though he **d**, Jn 11:25
lives and believes in me shall never **d**. Jn 11:26
that one man should **d** for the people, Jn 11:50
that Jesus would **d** for the nation, Jn 11:51
by what kind of death he was going to **d**. Jn 12:33
that one man should **d** for the people. Jn 18:14
by what kind of death he was going to **d**. Jn 18:32
law he ought to **d** because he has made Jn 19:7
brothers that this disciple was not to **d**; Jn 21:23
did not say to him that he was not to **d**, Jn 21:23
but even to **d** in Jerusalem for Acts 21:13
anything for which I deserve to **d**, Acts 25:11
who practice such things deserve to **d**, Rom 1:32
For one will scarcely **d** for a righteous Rom 5:7
good person one would dare even to **d**— Rom 5:7
raised from the dead will never **d** again; Rom 6:9
live according to the flesh you will **d**, Rom 8:13
we live, we live to the Lord, and if we **d**, Rom 14:8
Lord, and if we die, we **d** to the Lord. Rom 14:8
then, whether we live or whether we **d**, Rom 14:8
I would rather **d** than have anyone 1 Cor 9:15
For as in Adam all **d**, so also in 1 Cor 15:22
Christ Jesus our Lord, I **d** every day! 1 Cor 15:31
eat and drink, for tomorrow we **d**." 1 Cor 15:32
to **d** together and to live together. 2 Cor 7:3
to me to live is Christ, and to **d** is gain. Phil 1:21
as it is appointed for man to **d** once, Heb 9:27
that we might **d** to sin and live to 1 Pt 2:24
what remains and is about to **d**, Rv 3:2
They will long to **d**, but death will flee Rv 9:6
are the dead who **d** in the Lord from Rv 14:13

DIED (238)

that Adam lived were 930 years, and he **d**. Gn 5:5
the days of Seth were 912 years, and he **d**. Gn 5:8
days of Enosh were 905 years, and he **d**. Gn 5:11
days of Kenan were 910 years, and he **d**. Gn 5:14
of Mahalalel were 895 years, and he **d**. Gn 5:17
days of Jared were 962 years, and he **d**. Gn 5:20
of Methuselah were 969 years, and he **d**. Gn 5:27
of Lamech were 777 years, and he **d**. Gn 5:31
And all flesh **d** that moved on the earth, Gn 7:21
whose nostrils was the breath of life **d**. Gn 7:22
days of Noah were 950 years, and he **d**. Gn 9:29
Haran **d** in the presence of his father Gn 11:28
were 205 years, and Terah **d** in Haran. Gn 11:32
And Sarah **d** at Kiriath-arba (that is, Gn 23:2
breathed his last and **d** in a good old Gn 25:8
He breathed his last and **d**, and was Gn 25:17
d, and she was buried under an oak Gn 35:8
So Rachel **d**, and she was buried on the Gn 35:19
and he **d** and was gathered to his Gn 35:29
Bela **d**, and Jobab the son of Zerah of Gn 36:33
Jobab **d**, and Husham of the land of the Gn 36:34
Husham **d**, and Hadad the son of Gn 36:35
Hadad **d**, and Samlah of Masrekah Gn 36:36
Samlah **d**, and Shaul of Rehoboth on Gn 36:37
Shaul **d**, and Baal-hanan the son of Gn 36:38
Baal-hanan the son of Achbor **d**, and Gn 36:39
the wife of Judah, Shua's daughter, **d**. Gn 38:12
(but Er and Onan **d** in the land of Gn 46:12
to my sorrow Rachel **d** in the land of Gn 48:7
father gave this command before he **d**, Gn 50:16
So Joseph **d**, being 110 years old. They Gn 50:26
Then Joseph **d**, and all his brothers and Ex 1:6
those many days the king of Egypt **d**, Ex 2:23
And the fish in the Nile **d**, and the Nile Ex 7:21
The frogs **d** out in the houses, the Ex 8:13
All the livestock of the Egyptians **d**, but Ex 9:6
of the livestock of the people of Israel **d**. Ex 9:6
"Would that we had **d** by the hand of the Ex 16:3
them, and they **d** before the LORD. Lv 10:2
they drew near before the LORD and **d**, Lv 16:1
But Nadab and Abihu **d** before the LORD Nm 3:4
prayed to the LORD, and the fire **d** down. Nm 11:2
"Would that we had **d** in the land of Nm 14:2
would that we had **d** in this wilderness! Nm 14:2
of the land—**d** by plague before the Nm 14:37
Now those who **d** in the plague were Nm 16:49
besides those who **d** in the affair of Nm 16:49
person, the body of anyone who has **d**, Nm 19:13
with a sword or who **d** naturally, Nm 19:16
And Miriam **d** there and was buried Nm 20:1
And Aaron **d** there on the top of the Nm 20:28
people, so that many people of Israel **d**. Nm 21:6
those who **d** by the plague were Nm 25:9
with Korah, when that company **d**, Nm 26:10
and Er and Onan **d** in the land of Nm 26:19
Nadab and Abihu **d** when they Nm 26:61
"Our father **d** in the wilderness. He was Nm 27:3
of Korah, but **d** for his own sin. Nm 27:3
the command of the LORD and **d** there, Nm 33:38
years old when he **d** on Mount Hor. Nm 33:39
down with an iron object, so that he **d**, Nm 35:16
tool that could cause death, and he **d**, Nm 35:17
tool that could cause death, and he **d**, Nm 35:18
at him, lying in wait, so that he **d**, Nm 35:20
him down with his hand, so that he **d**, Nm 35:21
him dropped it on him, so that he **d**, Nm 35:23
There Aaron **d**, and there he was buried. Dt 10:6
not eat anything that has **d** naturally. Dt 14:21
as Aaron your brother **d** in Mount Hor Dt 32:50
the servant of the LORD **d** there in the land Dt 34:5
Moses was 120 years old when he **d**. His Dt 34:7
had **d** in the wilderness on the way after Jos 5:4
on them as far as Azekah, and they **d**. Jos 10:11
There were more who **d** because of the Jos 10:11
of the LORD, **d**, being 110 years old. Jos 24:29
And Eleazar the son of Aaron **d**, and Jos 24:33
brought him to Jerusalem, and he **d** there. Jgs 1:7
of the LORD, **d** at the age of 110 years. Jgs 2:8
But whenever the judge **d**, they turned Jgs 2:19
of the nations that Joshua left when he **d**, Jgs 2:21
years. Then Othniel the son of Kenaz **d**. Jgs 3:11
evil in the sight of the LORD after Ehud **d**. Jgs 4:1
lying fast asleep from weariness. So he **d**. Jgs 4:21
Gideon the son of Joash **d** in a good old Jgs 8:32
As soon as Gideon **d**, the people of Israel Jgs 8:33
people of the Tower of Shechem also **d**, Jgs 9:49
man thrust him through, and he **d**. Jgs 9:54
Then he **d** and was buried at Shamir. Jgs 10:2
And Jair **d** and was buried in Kamon. Jgs 10:5
Jephthah the Gileadite **d** and was buried Jgs 12:7
Then Ibzan **d** and was buried at Jgs 12:10

Elon the Zebulunite **d** and was buried Jgs 12:12
Hillel the Pirathonite **d** and was buried Jgs 12:15
d, and she was left with her two sons. Ru 1:3
and both Mahlon and Chilion **d**, so that Ru 1:5
sons of Eli, Hophni and Phinehas, **d**. 1 Sm 4:11
and his neck was broken and he **d**, 1 Sm 4:18
Now Samuel **d**. And all Israel 1 Sm 25:1
things, and his heart **d** within him, 1 Sm 25:37
the LORD struck Nabal, and he **d**. 1 Sm 25:38
Now Samuel had **d**, and all Israel had 1 Sm 28:3
fell upon his sword and **d** with him. 1 Sm 31:5
Thus Saul **d**, and his three sons, and 1 Sm 31:6
And he struck him down so that he **d**. 2 Sm 1:15
And he fell there and **d** where he was. 2 Sm 2:23
place where Asahel had fallen and **d**, 2 Sm 2:23
him in the stomach, so that he **d**, 2 Sm 3:27
son, heard that Abner had **d** at Hebron, 2 Sm 4:1
and he **d** there beside the ark of God. 2 Sm 6:7
this the king of the Ammonites **d**, 2 Sm 10:1
of their army, so that he **d** there. 2 Sm 10:18
people fell. Uriah the Hittite also **d**. 2 Sm 11:17
the wall, so that he **d** at Thebez? 2 Sm 11:21
On the seventh day the child **d**. And 2 Sm 12:18
but when the child **d**, you arose and 2 Sm 12:21
and he **d** and was buried in the tomb 2 Sm 17:23
Would I had **d** instead of you, 2 Sm 18:33
striking a second blow, and he **d**. 2 Sm 20:10
And there **d** of the people from Dan 2 Sm 24:15
and he struck him down, and he **d**. 1 Kgs 2:25
out and struck him down, and he **d**. 1 Kgs 2:46
And this woman's son **d** in the night, 1 Kgs 3:19
threshold of the house, the child **d**. 1 Kgs 14:17
house over him with fire and **d**, 1 Kgs 16:18
So Tibni **d**, and Omri became king. 1 Kgs 16:22
the Syrians, until at evening he **d**. 1 Kgs 22:35
So the king **d**, and was brought to 1 Kgs 22:37
So he **d** according to the word of the 2 Kgs 1:17
But when Ahab **d**, the king of Moab 2 Kgs 3:5
sat on her lap till noon, and then he **d**. 2 Kgs 4:20
trampled him in the gate, so that he **d**, 2 Kgs 7:17
trampled him in the gate and he **d**. 2 Kgs 7:20
and spread it over his face, till he **d**. 2 Kgs 8:15
And he fled to Megiddo and **d** there. 2 Kgs 9:27
who struck him down, so that he **d**. 2 Kgs 12:21
So Elisha **d**, and they buried him. 2 Kgs 13:20
When Hazael king of Syria **d**, 2 Kgs 13:24
and he came to Egypt and **d** there. 2 Kgs 23:34
Bela **d**, and Jobab the son of Zerah of 1 Chr 1:44
Jobab **d**, and Husham of the land of 1 Chr 1:45
Husham **d**, and Hadad the son of 1 Chr 1:46
Hadad **d**, and Samlah of Masrekah 1 Chr 1:47
Samlah **d**, and Shaul of Rehoboth on 1 Chr 1:48
Shaul **d**, and Baal-hanan, the son of 1 Chr 1:49
Baal-hanan **d**, and Hadad reigned in 1 Chr 1:50
And Hadad **d**. The chiefs of Edom 1 Chr 1:51
When Azubah **d**, Caleb married 1 Chr 2:19
and Appaim; and Seled **d** childless. 1 Chr 2:30
and Jonathan; and Jether **d** childless. 1 Chr 2:32
he also fell upon his sword and **d**. 1 Chr 10:5
Thus Saul **d**; he and his three sons 1 Chr 10:6
sons and all his house **d** together. 1 Chr 10:6
So Saul **d** for his breach of faith. He 1 Chr 10:13
the ark, and he **d** there before God. 1 Chr 13:10
the king of the Ammonites **d**, 1 Chr 19:1
Eleazar **d** having no sons, but only 1 Chr 23:22
Nadab and Abihu **d** before their 1 Chr 24:2
Then he **d** at a good age, full of days, 1 Chr 29:28
LORD struck him down, and he **d**. 2 Chr 13:20
until evening. Then at sunset he **d**. 2 Chr 18:34
the disease, and he **d** in great agony. 2 Chr 21:19
grew old and full of days, and **d**. 2 Chr 24:15
So he **d**, and they buried him in the 2 Chr 24:25
And he **d** and was buried in the 2 Chr 35:24
and when her father and her mother **d**, Est 2:7
Would that I had **d** before any eye had Jb 10:18
And Job **d**, an old man, and full of days. Jb 42:17
the year that King Uzziah **d** I saw the Lord Is 6:1
year that King Ahaz **d** came this oracle: Is 14:28
month, the prophet Hananiah **d**. Jer 28:17
have never eaten what **d** of itself or was Ezk 4:14
that Pelatiah the son of Benaiah **d**. Ezk 11:13
morning, and at evening my wife **d**. Ezk 24:18
that has **d** of itself or is torn by wild Ezk 44:31
he incurred guilt through Baal and **d**. Hos 13:1
But when Herod **d**, behold, an angel of Mt 2:19
him, saying, "My daughter has just **d**, Mt 9:18
The first married and **d**, and having no Mt 22:25
After them all, the woman **d**. Mt 22:27
a wife, and when he **d** left no offspring. Mk 12:20
And the second took her, and **d**, Mk 12:21
offspring. Last of all the woman also **d**. Mk 12:22
to hear that he should have already **d**. Mk 15:44
a man who had **d** was being carried out, Lk 7:12
The poor man **d** and was carried by the Lk 16:22
The rich man also **d** and was buried, Lk 16:22
took a wife, and **d** without children. Lk 20:29
all seven left no children and **d**. Lk 20:31
Afterward the woman also **d**. Lk 20:32
the manna in the wilderness, and they **d**. Jn 6:49
from heaven, not as the fathers ate and **d**. Jn 6:58
that you have a demon! Abraham **d**, Jn 8:52
than our father Abraham, who **d**? Jn 8:53
Abraham, who died? And the prophets **d**! Jn 8:53
Jesus told them plainly, "Lazarus has **d**, Jn 11:14
here, my brother would not have **d**. Jn 11:21
here, my brother would not have **d**." Jn 11:32
The man who had **d** came out, his Jn 11:44
David that he both **d** and was buried, Acts 2:29
And after his father **d**, God removed Acts 7:4
Jacob went down into Egypt, and he **d**, Acts 7:15
In those days she became ill and **d**, and Acts 9:37
the right time Christ **d** for the ungodly. Rom 5:6
we were still sinners, Christ **d** for us. Rom 5:8
For if many **d** through one man's Rom 5:15
How can we who **d** to sin still live in it? Rom 6:2
For one who has **d** has been set free Rom 6:7
Now if we have **d** with Christ, we Rom 6:8
For the death he **d** he died to sin, once Rom 6:10
For the death he died he **d** to sin, once Rom 6:10
you also have **d** to the law through the Rom 7:4
having **d** to that which held us captive, Rom 7:6
came, sin came alive and I **d**. Rom 7:9
is the one who **d**—more than that, Rom 8:34
to this end Christ **d** and lived again, Rom 14:9
destroy the one for whom Christ **d**. Rom 14:15
the brother for whom Christ **d**. 1 Cor 8:11
are weak and ill, and some have **d**. 1 Cor 11:30
that Christ **d** for our sins in 1 Cor 15:3
that one has **d** for all, therefore all 2 Cor 5:14
has died for all, therefore all have **d**; 2 Cor 5:14
and he **d** for all, that those who live 2 Cor 5:15
who for their sake **d** and was raised. 2 Cor 5:15
For through the law I **d** to the law, so Gal 2:19
the law, then Christ **d** for no purpose. Gal 2:21
for he nearly **d** for the work of Christ, Phil 2:30
If with Christ you **d** to the elemental Col 2:20
For you have **d**, and your life is hidden Col 3:3
believe that Jesus **d** and rose again, 1 Thes 4:14
who **d** for us so that whether we are 1 Thes 5:10
If we have **d** with him, we will also 2 Tm 2:11
And through his faith, though he **d**, he Heb 11:4
These all **d** in faith, not having Heb 11:13
and the living one. I **d**, and behold I am Rv 1:18
first and the last, who **d** and came to life. Rv 2:8
A third of the living creatures in the sea **d**, Rv 8:9
and many people **d** from the water, Rv 8:11
and every living thing **d** that was in the Rv 16:3

DIES (51)
so that he may bless you before he **d**." Gn 27:10
a man so that he **d** shall be put to death. Ex 21:12
a rod and the slave **d** under his hand, Ex 21:20
man's ox butts another's, so that it **d**, Ex 21:35
breaking in and is struck so that he **d**, Ex 22:2
and it **d** or is injured or is driven away, Ex 22:10
of his neighbor, and it is injured or **d**, Ex 22:14
fat of an animal that **d** of itself and the Lv 7:24
if any animal which you may eat **d**, Lv 11:39
person who eats what **d** of itself or what Lv 17:15
He shall not eat what **d** of itself or is torn Lv 22:8
"And if any man **d** very suddenly beside Nm 6:9
is the law when someone **d** in a tent: Nm 19:14
saying, 'If a man **d** and has no son, Nm 27:8
his neighbor so that he **d**—he may flee to Dt 19:5
and strikes him fatally so that he **d**, Dt 19:11
out of his house, or if the latter man **d**, Dt 24:3
and one of them **d** and has no son, Dt 25:5
saying, "Should Abner die as a fool **d**? 2 Sm 3:33
to Jeroboam who **d** in the city 1 Kgs 14:11
and anyone who **d** in the open 1 Kgs 14:11
to Baasha who **d** in the city 1 Kgs 16:4
anyone of his who **d** in the field the 1 Kgs 16:4
belonging to Ahab who **d** in the city 1 Kgs 21:24
anyone of his who **d** in the open 1 Kgs 21:24
But a man **d** and is laid low; man Jb 14:10
If a man **d**, shall he live again? All the Jb 14:14
One **d** in his full vigor, being wholly at Jb 21:23
Another **d** in bitterness of soul, never Jb 21:25
For when he **d** he will carry nothing Ps 49:17
He **d** for lack of discipline, and because Prv 5:23
When the wicked **d**, his hope will Prv 11:7
How the wise **d** just like the fool! Eccl 2:16
is the same; as one **d**, so dies the other. Eccl 3:19
is the same; as one dies, so **d** the other. Eccl 3:19
you that you are afraid of man who **d**, Is 51:12
he who eats their eggs **d**, and from one Is 59:5
prophet out of the cistern before he **d**." Jer 38:10
He who is in the field **d** by the sword, Ezk 7:15
said, 'If a man **d** having no children, Mt 22:24
if a man's brother **d** and leaves a wife, Mk 12:19
wrote for us that if a man's brother **d**, Lk 20:28
him, "Sir, come down before my child **d**." Jn 4:49
grain of wheat falls into the earth and **d**, Jn 12:24
alone; but if it **d**, it bears much fruit. Jn 12:24
but if her husband **d** she is released Rom 7:2
But if her husband **d**, she is free from Rom 7:3
to himself, and none of us **d** to himself. Rom 14:7
But if her husband **d**, she is free to be 1 Cor 7:39
sow does not come to life unless it **d**. 1 Cor 15:36
the law of Moses **d** without mercy on Heb 10:28

DIFFER (1)
Having gifts that **d** according to the Rom 12:6

DIFFERENCE (3)
they taught the **d** between the unclean Ezk 22:26
my people the **d** between the holy Ezk 44:23
(what they were makes no **d** to me; Gal 2:6

DIFFERENT (20)
not let your cattle breed with a **d** kind. Lv 19:19
because he has a **d** spirit and has Nm 14:24
go limping between two **d** opinions? 1 Kgs 18:21
in golden vessels, vessels of **d** kinds, Est 1:7
Their laws are **d** from those of every other Est 3:8
So you were **d** from other women in Ezk 16:34
was given to you; therefore you were **d**. Ezk 16:34
up out of the sea, **d** from one another. Dn 7:3
It was **d** from all the beasts that were Dn 7:7
beast, which was **d** from all the rest, Dn 7:19
which shall be **d** from all the kingdoms, Dn 7:23
he shall be **d** from the former ones, and Dn 7:24
For who sees anything **d** in you? What 1 Cor 4:7
are doubtless many **d** languages in 1 Cor 14:10
if you receive a **d** spirit from the one 2 Cor 11:4
if you accept a **d** gospel from the one 2 Cor 11:4
of Christ and are turning to a **d** gospel— Gal 1:6
long as he is a child, is no **d** from a slave, Gal 4:1
persons not to teach any **d** doctrine, 1 Tm 1:3
If anyone teaches a **d** doctrine and does 1 Tm 6:3

DIFFERENTIATE (1)
One shall not **d** between good or bad, Lv 27:33

DIFFERS (1)
stars; for star **d** from star in glory. 1 Cor 15:41

DIFFICULT (6)
within your towns that is too **d** for you, Dt 17:8
The thing that the king asks is **d**, and Dn 2:11
you and that no mystery is too **d** for you, Dn 4:9
"How **d** it will be for those who have Mk 10:23
how **d** it is to enter the kingdom of Mk 10:24
"How **d** it is for those who have wealth Lk 18:24

DIFFICULTY (5)
only with **d** will a rich person enter the Mt 19:23
of days and arrived with **d** off Cnidus, Acts 27:7
Coasting along it with **d**, we came to a Acts 27:8
we managed with **d** to secure the Acts 27:16
the last days there will come times of **d**. 2 Tm 3:1

DIG (11)
not fill, and cisterns that you did not **d**, Dt 6:11
and out of whose hills you can **d** copper. Dt 8:9
you shall **d** a hole with it and turn back Dt 23:13
and **d** for it more than for hidden Jb 3:21
In the dark they **d** through houses; by Jb 24:16
man, **d** in the wall." So I dug in the wall, Ezk 8:8
In their sight **d** through the wall, and Ezk 12:5
They shall **d** through the wall to Ezk 12:12
"If they **d** into Sheol, from there shall my Am 9:2
until I **d** around it and put on manure. Lk 13:8
I am not strong enough to **d**, and I am Lk 16:3

DIGGING (1)
He makes a pit, **d** it out, and falls into the Ps 7:15

DIGNIFIED (4)
quiet life, godly and **d** in every way. 1 Tm 2:2
Deacons likewise must be **d**, not 1 Tm 3:8
Their wives likewise must be **d**, not 1 Tm 3:11
are to be sober-minded, **d**, self-controlled, Ti 2:2

DIGNITY (6)
preeminent in **d** and preeminent in Gn 49:3
"Adorn yourself with majesty and **d**; Jb 40:10
Strength and **d** are her clothing, and Prv 31:25
their justice and **d** go forth from Hab 1:7
with all **d** keeping his children 1 Tm 3:4
and in your teaching show integrity, **d**, Ti 2:7

DIGS (3)
or when a man **d** a pit and does not Ex 21:33
Whoever **d** a pit will fall into it, and a Prv 26:27
He who **d** a pit will fall into it, and a Eccl 10:8

DIKLAH (2)
Hadoram, Uzal, **D**, Gn 10:27
Hadoram, Uzal, **D**, 1 Chr 1:21

DILEAN (1)
D, Mizpeh, Joktheel, Jos 15:38

DILIGENCE (4)
make a decree; let it be done with all **d**." Ezr 6:12
did with all **d** what Darius the Ezr 6:13
then, you shall with all **d** buy bulls, Ezr 7:17
requires of you, let it be done with all **d**, Ezr 7:21

DILIGENT (10)
have accomplished a **d** search." For the Ps 64:6
heart." Then my spirit made a **d** search: Ps 77:6
but the hand of the **d** makes rich. Prv 10:4
The hand of the **d** will rule, while the Prv 12:24
but the **d** man will get precious Prv 12:27
the soul of the **d** is richly supplied. Prv 13:4
who loves him is **d** to discipline him. Prv 13:24
The plans of the **d** lead surely to Prv 21:5
be all the more **d** to make your calling 2 Pt 1:10
be **d** to be found by him without spot 2 Pt 3:14

DILIGENTLY (20)
"If you will **d** listen to the voice of the Ex 15:26
Now Moses **d** inquired about the goat Lv 10:16
"Only take care, and keep your soul **d**, lest Dt 4:9
You shall teach them **d** to your children, Dt 6:7
You shall **d** keep the commandments of Dt 6:17
inquire and make search and ask **d**. Dt 13:14
you hear of it, then you shall inquire **d**, Dt 17:4
The judges shall inquire **d**, and if the Dt 19:18
This work goes on **d** and prospers in Ezr 5:8
commanded your precepts to be kept **d**. Ps 119:4
they will seek me **d** but will not find me. Prv 1:28
me, and those who seek me **d** find me. Prv 8:17
Whoever **d** seeks good seeks favor, but Prv 11:27
riders on camels, let him listen **d**, Is 21:7
camels, let him listen diligently, very **d**." Is 21:7
Listen **d** to me, and eat what is good, and Is 55:2
if they will **d** learn the ways of my Jer 12:16
if you will **d** obey the voice of the LORD Zec 6:15
saying, "Go and search **d** for the child, Mt 2:8
the house and seek **d** until she finds it? Lk 15:8

DILL (4)
leveled its surface, does he not scatter **d**, Is 28:25
D is not threshed with a threshing Is 28:27
cumin, but **d** is beaten out with a stick, Is 28:27
For you tithe mint and **d** and cumin, Mt 23:23

DIM (9)
old and his eyes were **d** so that he could Gn 27:1
Now the eyes of Israel were **d** with age, Gn 48:10
had begun to grow **d** so that he could 1 Sm 3:2
for his eyes were **d** because of his age. 1 Kgs 14:4
My eye has grown **d** from vexation, and Jb 17:7
My eyes grow **d** with waiting for my God. Ps 69:3
my eye grows **d** through sorrow. Every Ps 88:9
How the gold has grown **d**, how the pure Lam 4:1
for these things our eyes have grown **d**, Lam 5:17

DIMINISH (3)
wife to himself, he shall not **d** her food, Ex 21:10
and he does not let their livestock **d**. Ps 107:38
of Egypt's Nile will **d** and dry up, Is 19:6

DIMINISHED (2)
When they are **d** and brought low Ps 107:39
against you and **d** your allotted Ezk 16:27

DIMLY (1)
For now we see in a mirror **d**, but 1 Cor 13:12

DIMMED (1)
who look through the windows are **d**, Eccl 12:3

DIMNAH (1)
D with its pasturelands, Nahalal with Jos 21:35

DIMONAH (1)
Kinah, **D**, Adadah, Jos 15:22

DINAH (7)
a daughter and called her name **D**. Gn 30:21
Now **D** the daughter of Leah, whom she Gn 34:1
soul was drawn to **D** the daughter of Gn 34:3
that he had defiled his daughter **D**. Gn 34:5
because he had defiled their sister **D**. Gn 34:13
the sword and took **D** out of Shechem's Gn 34:26
together with his daughter **D**; Gn 46:15

DINAH'S (1)
of Jacob, Simeon and Levi, **D** brothers, Gn 34:25

DINE (3)
for the men are to **d** with me at noon." Gn 43:16
a Pharisee asked him to **d** with him, Lk 11:37
when he went to **d** at the house of a ruler Lk 14:1

DINED (2)
of his life he **d** regularly at the king's 2 Kgs 25:29
of his life he **d** regularly at the king's Jer 52:33

DINHABAH (2)
in Edom, the name of his city being **D**. Gn 36:32
of Beor, the name of his city being **D**. 1 Chr 1:43

DINING (1)
pots and copper vessels and **d** couches.) Mk 7:4

DINNER (6)
Better is a **d** of herbs where love is than Prv 15:17
are invited, See, I have prepared my **d**, Mt 22:4
see that he did not first wash before **d**. Lk 11:38
him, "When you give a **d** or a banquet, Lk 14:12
So they gave a **d** for him there. Martha Jn 12:2
invites you to **d** and you are 1 Cor 10:27

DIONYSIUS (1)
whom also were **D** the Areopagite and Acts 17:34

DIOTREPHES (1)
written something to the church, but **D**, 3 Jn 1:9

DIP (12)
a bunch of hyssop and **d** it in the blood Ex 12:22
and the priest shall **d** his finger in the Lv 4:6
and the priest shall **d** his finger in the Lv 4:17
and **d** them and the live bird in the blood Lv 14:6
and **d** his right finger in the oil that is Lv 14:16
and **d** them in the blood of the bird that Lv 14:51
shall take hyssop and **d** it in the water Nm 19:18
brothers, and let him **d** his foot in oil. Dt 33:24
eat some bread and **d** your morsel in the Ru 2:14
or to **d** up water out of the cistern." Is 30:14
your waist, and do not **d** it in water." Jer 13:1
and send Lazarus to **d** the end of his Lk 16:24

DIPPED (10)
slaughtered a goat and **d** the robe in Gn 37:31
and he **d** his finger in the blood and put it Lv 9:9
bearing the ark were **d** in the brink of Jos 3:15
in his hand and **d** it in the 1 Sm 14:27
went down and **d** himself seven times 2 Kgs 5:14
the bed cloth and **d** it in water and 2 Kgs 8:15
"He who has **d** his hand in the dish Mt 26:23
of bread when I have **d** it." So when he Jn 13:26
dipped it." So when he had **d** the morsel, Jn 13:26
He is clothed in a robe **d** in blood, and Rv 19:13

DIPPING (1)
one who is **d** bread into the dish with Mk 14:20

DIRECT (16)
If you do this, God will **d** you, you will Ex 18:23
to do according to all that they **d** you. Dt 17:10
all that the Levitical priests shall **d** you. Dt 24:8
from among you and **d** your heart to 1 Sm 7:3
rafts to go by sea to the place you **d**. 1 Kgs 5:9
in music, should **d** the music, 1 Chr 15:22
and **d** their hearts toward you. 1 Chr 29:18
D your steps to the perpetual ruins; the Ps 74:3
be wise, and **d** your heart in the way. Prv 23:19
"How well you **d** your course to seek Jer 2:33
is not in man who walks to **d** his steps. Jer 10:23
And I will **d** my jealousy against you, Ezk 23:25
He will **d** the shock of his battering Ezk 26:9
we made a **d** voyage to Samothrace, Acts 16:11
our Lord Jesus, **d** our way to you, 1 Thes 3:11
May the Lord **d** your hearts to the 2 Thes 3:5

DIRECTED (20)
Jacob and blessed him and **d** him, Gn 28:1
and that as he blessed him he **d** him, Gn 28:6
him as the LORD **d** through Moses. Nm 27:23
waters of Gihon and **d** them down to 2 Chr 32:30
the burden-bearers and **d** all who 2 Chr 34:13
He has not **d** his words against me, and I Jb 32:14
my anger will be **d** to their destruction. Is 10:25
to the left, wherever your face is **d**. Ezk 21:16
went and did as Jesus had **d** them. Mt 21:6
the disciples did as Jesus had **d** them, Mt 26:19
for the potter's field, as the Lord **d** me." Mt 27:10
took the money and did as they were **d**. Mt 28:15
mountain to which Jesus had **d** them. Mt 28:16
And he **d** the crowd to sit down on the Mk 8:6
And he **d** that something should be Lk 8:55
And Peter **d** his gaze at him, as did John, Acts 3:4
who spoke to Moses **d** him to make it, Acts 7:44
was **d** by a holy angel to send for you Acts 10:22
as I **d** the churches of Galatia, so you 1 Cor 16:1
appoint elders in every town as I **d** you— Ti 1:5

DIRECTING (1)
And **d** the crowd to sit down on the Mt 15:35

DIRECTION (39)
from Sidon in the **d** of Gerar as far Gn 10:19
as far as Gaza, and in the **d** of Sodom, Gn 10:19
from Mesha in the **d** of Sephar to the Gn 10:30
like the land of Egypt, in the **d** of Zoar. Gn 13:10
is opposite Egypt in the **d** of Assyria. Gn 25:18
the Levites under the **d** of Ithamar the Ex 38:21
is to be under the **d** of Ithamar the son Nm 4:28
under the **d** of Ithamar the son of Nm 4:33
under the **d** of Ithamar the son of Aaron Nm 7:8
the wilderness in the **d** of the Red Sea.' Dt 1:40
into the wilderness in the **d** of the Red Sea, Dt 2:1
and went in the **d** of the wilderness of Dt 2:8
in your steps, receiving **d** from you, Dt 33:3
them and fled in the **d** of the wilderness. Jos 8:15
and in the **d** of Beth-jeshimoth, Jos 12:3
passes along southward in the **d** of Luz, Jos 18:13
Then the boundary goes in another **d**, Jos 18:14
bends in a northerly **d** going on to Jos 18:17
goes in the other **d** eastward toward the Jos 19:12
is coming from the **d** of the Diviners' Jgs 9:37
men of Israel in the **d** of the wilderness, Jgs 20:42
straight in the **d** of Beth-shemesh 1 Sm 6:12
Ahab went in one **d** by himself, and 1 Kgs 18:6
went in another **d** by himself. 1 Kgs 18:6
water came from the **d** of Edom, 2 Kgs 3:20
this, he fled in the **d** of Beth-haggan. 2 Kgs 9:27
And they went in the **d** of the Arabah. 2 Kgs 25:4
sons of Asaph, under the **d** of Asaph, 1 Chr 25:2
prophesied under the **d** of the king. 1 Chr 25:2
under the **d** of their father Jeduthun, 1 Chr 25:3
were all under the **d** of their father in 1 Chr 25:6
the LORD under the **d** of the Levitical 2 Chr 23:18
the officer, under the **d** of Hananiah, 2 Chr 26:11
down to Egypt, without asking for my **d**, Is 30:2
they wander about each in his own **d**; Is 47:15
falsely, and the priests rule at their **d**; Jer 5:31
And they went in the **d** of the Arabah. Jer 52:7
men came from the **d** of the upper gate, Ezk 9:2
but in whatever **d** the front wheel Ezk 10:11

DIRECTIONS (6)
according to the **d** of David king of Ezr 3:10
them came from all **d** and said to us Neh 4:12
any of their four **d** without turning as Ezk 1:17
any of their four **d** without turning as Ezk 10:11
things I will give **d** when I come. 1 Cor 11:34
Israelites and gave **d** concerning his Heb 11:22

DIRECTLY (5)
Let your eyes look **d** forward, and your Prv 4:25
But he looked **d** at them and said, Lk 20:17
with a loud voice as it flew **d** overhead, Rv 8:13
I saw another angel flying **d** overhead, Rv 14:6
to all the birds that fly **d** overhead, Rv 19:17

DIRECTORS (1)
and Asaph there were **d** of the singers, Neh 12:46

DIRECTS (1)
rudder wherever the will of the pilot **d**. Jas 3:4

DIRGE (3)
a lament, and each to her neighbor a **d**. Jer 9:20
we sang a **d**, and you did not mourn.' Mt 11:17
we sang a **d**, and you did not weep.' Lk 7:32

DIRT (6)
clothes torn and with **d** on his head. 1 Sm 4:12
with his clothes torn and **d** on his head. 2 Sm 1:2
with his coat torn and **d** on his head. 2 Sm 15:32
My flesh is clothed with worms and **d**; my Jb 7:5
quiet, and its waters toss up mire and **d**. Is 57:20
as a removal of **d** from the body but 1 Pt 3:21

DISABILITY (1)
"Woman, you are freed from your **d**." Lk 13:12

DISABLED (1)
Animals blind or **d** or mutilated or Lv 22:22

DISABLING (1)
who had had a **d** spirit for eighteen Lk 13:11

DISAGREEING (1)
And **d** among themselves, they Acts 28:25

DISAGREEMENT (1)
And there arose a sharp **d**, so that Acts 15:39

DISAPPEAR (2)
When they melt, they **d**; when it is hot, Jb 6:17
The fortress will **d** from Ephraim, and the Is 17:3

DISAPPOINTED (5)
confident; they come there and are **d**. Jb 6:20
be turned back and **d** who devise evil Ps 35:4
to shame and **d** altogether who rejoice Ps 35:26
put to shame and **d** altogether who seek Ps 40:14
put to shame and **d** who sought to do Ps 71:24

DISARMED (1)
He **d** the rulers and authorities and put Col 2:15

DISASTER (87)
hills, lest the **d** overtake me and I die. Gn 19:19
relent from this **d** against your people. Ex 32:12
LORD relented from the **d** that he had Ex 32:14
did not know that **d** was close upon Jgs 20:34
for they saw that **d** was close upon Jgs 20:41
LORD has brought all this **d** on them.'" 1 Kgs 9:9
Behold, I will bring **d** upon you. I 1 Kgs 21:21
me, I will not bring the **d** in his days; 1 Kgs 21:29
I will bring the **d** upon his house." 1 Kgs 21:29
the LORD has declared **d** for you." 1 Kgs 22:23
and Judah such **d** that the ears 2 Kgs 21:12

I will bring **d** upon this place and 2 Kgs 22:16
not see all the **d** that I will bring 2 Kgs 22:20
because **d** had befallen his house. 1 Chr 7:23
he has brought all this **d** on them.'" 2 Chr 7:22
has declared **d** concerning you." 2 Chr 18:22
'If **d** comes upon us, the sword, 2 Chr 20:9
I will bring **d** upon this place and 2 Chr 34:24
not see all the **d** that I will bring 2 Chr 34:28
our God bring all this **d** on us and on Neh 13:18
When **d** brings sudden death, he mocks Jb 9:23
out his hand, and in his **d** cry for help? Jb 30:24
and **d** for the workers of iniquity? Jb 31:3
and will be at ease, without dread of **d**." Prv 1:33
D pursues sinners, but the righteous Prv 13:21
for **d** from them will rise suddenly, Prv 24:22
you know not what **d** may happen on Eccl 11:2
And yet he is wise and brings **d**; he does Is 31:2
d shall fall upon you, for which you will Is 47:11
"Out of the north **d** shall be let loose Jer 1:14
d came upon them, declares the LORD." Jer 2:3
stay not, for I bring **d** from the north, Jer 4:6
no **d** will come upon us, nor shall we see Jer 5:12
for **d** looms out of the north, Jer 6:1
I am bringing **d** upon this people, Jer 6:19
I am bringing **d** upon them that they Jer 11:11
planted you, has decreed **d** against you, Jer 11:17
For I will bring **d** upon the men of Jer 11:23
to me; you are my refuge in the day of **d**. Jer 17:17
bring upon them the day of **d**; Jer 17:18
I will relent of the **d** that I intended to do Jer 18:8
I am shaping **d** against you and Jer 18:11
I am bringing such **d** upon this place Jer 19:3
its towns all the **d** that I have Jer 19:15
for I will bring **d** upon them in the year Jer 23:12
they say, 'No **d** shall come upon you.'" Jer 23:17
I begin to work **d** at the city that is Jer 25:29
d is going forth from nation to nation, Jer 25:32
I may relent of the **d** that I intend to do Jer 26:3
will relent of the **d** that he has Jer 26:13
LORD relent of the **d** that he had Jer 26:19
about to bring great **d** upon ourselves." Jer 26:19
have made all this **d** come upon them. Jer 32:23
all this great **d** upon this people, Jer 32:42
of Jerusalem all the **d** that I have Jer 35:17
Judah will hear all the **d** that I intend to Jer 36:3
of Judah all the **d** that I have Jer 36:31
God pronounced this **d** against this Jer 40:2
up; for I relent of the **d** that I did to you. Jer 42:10
or survivor from the **d** that I will bring Jer 42:17
have seen all the **d** that I brought upon Jer 44:2
of food, and prospered, and saw no **d**. Jer 44:17
testimonies that this **d** has happened to Jer 44:23
watching over them for **d** and not for Jer 44:27
behold, I am bringing **d** upon all flesh, Jer 45:5
In Heshbon they planned **d** against her: Jer 48:2
I will bring **d** upon them, my fierce Jer 49:37
a book all the **d** that should come upon Jer 51:60
because of the **d** that I am bringing Jer 51:64
says the Lord GOD: **D** after disaster! Ezk 7:5
says the Lord GOD: Disaster after **d**! Ezk 7:5
D comes upon disaster; rumor follows Ezk 7:26
Disaster comes upon **d**; rumor follows Ezk 7:26
be consoled for the **d** that I have Ezk 14:22
in steadfast love; and he relents over **d**. Jl 2:13
Does **d** come to a city, unless the LORD Am 3:6
far away the day of **d** and bring near the Am 6:3
say, '**D** shall not overtake or meet us.' Am 9:10
do not gloat over his **d** in the day of his Ob 1:13
God relented of the **d** that he had said he Jon 3:10
in steadfast love, and relenting from **d**. Jon 4:2
because **d** has come down from the LORD Mi 1:12
against this family I am devising **d**, Mi 2:3
walk haughtily, for it will be a time of **d**. Mi 2:3
midst of us? No **d** shall come upon us." Mi 3:11
angry but a little, they furthered the **d**. Zec 1:15
I purposed to bring **d** to you when your Zec 8:14

DISASTERS (2)
"'And I will heap **d** upon them; I will Dt 32:23
and will hiss because of all its **d**. Jer 49:17

DISASTROUS (2)
When the people heard this **d** word, they Ex 33:4
Jerusalem my four **d** acts of judgment, Ezk 14:21

DISBELIEVE (1)
it in my side. Do not **d**, but believe." Jn 20:27

DISBELIEVED (2)
And while they still **d** for joy and were Lk 24:41
by what he said, but others **d**. Acts 28:24

DISCARD (1)
wicked of the earth you **d** like dross, Ps 119:119

DISCARDED (1)
that King Ahaz **d** in his reign 2 Chr 29:19

DISCERN (15)
this; they would **d** their latter end! Dt 32:29
the angel of God to **d** good and evil. 2 Sm 14:17
Can I **d** what is pleasant and what is 2 Sm 19:35
that I may **d** between good and evil, 1 Kgs 3:9
yourself understanding to **d** what is 1 Kgs 3:11
still, but I could not **d** its appearance. Jb 4:16
Cannot my palate **d** the cause of Jb 6:30
and that you may **d** the paths to its Jb 38:20
Who can **d** his errors? Declare me Ps 19:12
I rise up; you **d** my thoughts from afar. Ps 139:2
wisdom of the prudent is to **d** his way, Prv 14:8
They know not, nor do they **d**, for he has Is 44:18
and tried to **d** what sort of greeting this Lk 1:29
by testing you may **d** what is the will Rom 12:2
and try to **d** what is pleasing to the Eph 5:10

DISCERNED (2)
the sanctuary of God; then I **d** their end. Ps 73:17
them because they are spiritually **d**. 1 Cor 2:14

DISCERNING (12)
let Pharaoh select a **d** and wise man, Gn 41:33
there is none so **d** and wise as you are. Gn 41:39
The woman was **d** and beautiful, but 1 Sm 25:3
Behold, I give you a wise and **d** mind, 1 Kgs 3:12
The wise of heart is called **d**, and Prv 16:21
The **d** sets his face toward wisdom, but Prv 17:24
to acquire wealth; be **d** enough to desist. Prv 23:4
the discernment of their **d** men shall be Is 29:14
whoever is **d**, let him know them; Hos 14:9
discernment of the **d** I will thwart." 1 Cor 1:19
and drinks without **d** the body eats 1 Cor 11:29
and **d** the thoughts and intentions of Heb 4:12

DISCERNMENT (7)
and takes away the **d** of the elders. Jb 12:20
For this is a people without **d**; therefore Is 27:11
and the **d** of their discerning men shall Is 29:14
nor is there knowledge or **d** to say, Is 44:19
and the **d** of the discerning I will 1 Cor 1:19
and more, with knowledge and all **d**, Phil 1:9
their powers of **d** trained by constant Heb 5:14

DISCHARGE (34)
When any man has a **d** from his body, Lv 15:2
from his body, his **d** is unclean. Lv 15:2
this is the law of his uncleanness for a **d**: Lv 15:3
whether his body runs with his **d**, or his Lv 15:3
or his body is blocked up by his **d**, Lv 15:3
the one with the **d** lies shall be unclean, Lv 15:4
the one with the **d** has sat shall wash Lv 15:6
the one with the **d** shall wash his clothes Lv 15:7
the one with the **d** spits on someone who Lv 15:8
the one with the **d** rides shall be unclean. Lv 15:9
one with the **d** touches without having Lv 15:11
the one with the **d** touches shall be Lv 15:12
when the one with a **d** is cleansed of his Lv 15:13
with a discharge is cleansed of his **d**, Lv 15:13
for him before the LORD for his **d**. Lv 15:15
"When a woman has a **d**, and the Lv 15:19
and the **d** in her body is blood, Lv 15:19
"If a woman has a **d** of blood for many Lv 15:25
or if she has a **d** beyond the time of her Lv 15:25
the days of the **d** she shall continue in Lv 15:25
on which she lies, all the days of her **d**, Lv 15:26
But if she is cleansed of her **d**, she shall Lv 15:28
her before the LORD for her unclean **d**. Lv 15:30
for him who has a **d** and for him who Lv 15:32
anyone, male or female, who has a **d**, Lv 15:33
a leprous disease or a **d** may eat of the Lv 22:4
or mutilated or having a **d** or an itch or Lv 22:22
is leprous or has a **d** and everyone who is Nm 5:2
one who has a **d** or who is leprous 2 Sm 3:29
There is no **d** from war, nor will Eccl 8:8
had suffered from a **d** of blood for twelve Mt 9:20
who had had a **d** of blood for twelve Mk 5:25
who had had a **d** of blood for twelve Lk 8:43
and immediately her **d** of blood ceased. Lk 8:44

DISCHARGED (1)
Then Amaziah **d** the army that had 2 Chr 25:10

DISCIPLE (30)
"A **d** is not above his teacher, nor a Mt 10:24
It is enough for the **d** to be like his Mt 10:25
a cup of cold water because he is a **d**, Mt 10:42
Joseph, who also was a **d** of Jesus. Mt 27:57
A **d** is not above his teacher, but Lk 6:40
even his own life, he cannot be my **d**. Lk 14:26
and come after me cannot be my **d**. Lk 14:27
all that he has cannot be my **d**. Lk 14:33
they reviled him, saying, "You are his **d**, Jn 9:28
So that **d**, leaning back against Jesus, Jn 13:25
followed Jesus, and so did another **d**. Jn 18:15
Since that **d** was known to the high Jn 18:15
So the other **d**, who was known to the Jn 18:16
his mother and the **d** whom he loved Jn 19:26
Then he said to the **d**, "Behold, your Jn 19:27
from that hour the **d** took her to his Jn 19:27
of Arimathea, who was a **d** of Jesus, Jn 19:38
and went to Simon Peter and the other **d**, Jn 20:2
So Peter went out with the other **d**, and Jn 20:3
but the other **d** outran Peter and reached Jn 20:4
Then the other **d**, who had reached the Jn 20:8
That **d** whom Jesus loved therefore said Jn 21:7
turned and saw the **d** whom Jesus loved Jn 21:20
the brothers that this **d** was not to die; Jn 21:23
This is the **d** who is bearing witness Jn 21:24
there was a **d** at Damascus named Acts 9:10
for they did not believe that he was a **d**. Acts 9:26
there was in Joppa a **d** named Tabitha, Acts 9:36
A **d** was there, named Timothy, the Acts 16:1
of Mnason of Cyprus, an early **d**, Acts 21:16

DISCIPLES (238)
testimony; seal the teaching among my **d**. Is 8:16
and when he sat down, his **d** came to him. Mt 5:1
Another of the **d** said to him, "Lord, let Mt 8:21
he got into the boat, his **d** followed him. Mt 8:23
and were reclining with Jesus and his **d**. Mt 9:10
the Pharisees saw this, they said to his **d**, Mt 9:11
Then the **d** of John came to him, saying, Mt 9:14
Pharisees fast, but your **d** do not fast?" Mt 9:14
Jesus rose and followed him, with his **d**. Mt 9:19
Then he said to his **d**, "The harvest is Mt 9:37
to him his twelve **d** and gave them Mt 10:1
had finished instructing his twelve **d**, Mt 11:1
deeds of the Christ, he sent word by his **d** Mt 11:2
His **d** were hungry, and they began to Mt 12:1
your **d** are doing what is not lawful to do Mt 12:2
stretching out his hand toward his **d**, Mt 12:49
Then the **d** came and said to him, Mt 13:10
And his **d** came to him, saying, Mt 13:36
And his **d** came and took the body and Mt 14:12
evening, the **d** came to him and said, Mt 14:15
the loaves and gave them to the **d**, Mt 14:19
and the **d** gave them to the crowds. Mt 14:19
Immediately he made the **d** get into the Mt 14:22
But when the **d** saw him walking on Mt 14:26
"Why do your **d** break the tradition of Mt 15:2
Then the **d** came and said to him, "Do Mt 15:12
And his **d** came and begged him, Mt 15:23
Then Jesus called his **d** to him and Mt 15:32
And the **d** said to him, "Where are we Mt 15:33
he broke them and gave them to the **d**, Mt 15:36
and the **d** gave them to the crowds. Mt 15:36
When the **d** reached the other side, they Mt 16:5
of Caesarea Philippi, he asked his **d**, Mt 16:13
he strictly charged the **d** to tell no one Mt 16:20
began to show his **d** that he must go Mt 16:21
Then Jesus told his **d**, "If anyone would Mt 16:24
When the **d** heard this, they fell on their Mt 17:6
And the **d** asked him, "Then why do Mt 17:10
Then the **d** understood that he was Mt 17:13
And I brought him to your **d**, and they Mt 17:16
Then the **d** came to Jesus privately and Mt 17:19
At that time the **d** came to Jesus, saying, Mt 18:1
The **d** said to him, "If such is the case Mt 19:10
and pray. The **d** rebuked the people, Mt 19:13
And Jesus said to his **d**, "Truly, I say to Mt 19:23
When the **d** heard this, they were Mt 19:25
to Jerusalem, he took the twelve **d** aside, Mt 20:17
Mount of Olives, then Jesus sent two **d**, Mt 21:1
The **d** went and did as Jesus had directed Mt 21:6
When the **d** saw it, they marveled, Mt 21:20
And they sent their **d** to him, along Mt 22:16
Jesus said to the crowds and to his **d**, Mt 23:1
when his **d** came to point out to him the Mt 24:1
of Olives, the **d** came to him privately, Mt 24:3
all these sayings, he said to his **d**, Mt 26:1
And when the **d** saw it, they were Mt 26:8
Unleavened Bread the **d** came to Jesus, Mt 26:17
the Passover at your house with my **d**.'" Mt 26:18
And the **d** did as Jesus had directed Mt 26:19
blessing it broke it and gave it to the **d**, Mt 26:26
deny you!" And all the **d** said the same. Mt 26:35
Gethsemane, and he said to his **d**, Mt 26:36
he came to the **d** and found them Mt 26:40
he came to the **d** and said to them, Mt 26:45
fulfilled." Then all the **d** left him and Mt 26:56
lest his **d** go and steal him away and Mt 27:64
quickly and tell his **d** that he has risen Mt 28:7
fear and great joy, and ran to tell his **d**. Mt 28:8
'His **d** came by night and stole him Mt 28:13
Now the eleven **d** went to Galilee, to the Mt 28:16
Go therefore and make **d** of all nations, Mt 28:19
were reclining with Jesus and his **d**, Mk 2:15
sinners and tax collectors, said to his **d**, Mk 2:16
Now John's **d** and the Pharisees were Mk 2:18
"Why do John's **d** and the disciples of Mk 2:18
disciples and the **d** of the Pharisees Mk 2:18
Pharisees fast, but your **d** do not fast?" Mk 2:18
his **d** began to pluck heads of grain. Mk 2:23

Jesus withdrew with his **d** to the sea, and Mk 3:7
And he told his **d** to have a boat ready for Mk 3:9
to his own **d** he explained everything. Mk 4:34
And his **d** said to him, "You see the Mk 5:31
his hometown, and his **d** followed him. Mk 6:1
When his **d** heard of it, they came and Mk 6:29
it grew late, his **d** came to him and said, Mk 6:35
and gave them to the **d** to set before the Mk 6:41
Immediately he made his **d** get into the Mk 6:45
that some of his **d** ate with hands that Mk 7:2
"Why do your **d** not walk according to Mk 7:5
his **d** asked him about the parable. Mk 7:17
he called his **d** to him and said to them, Mk 8:1
And his **d** answered him, "How can one Mk 8:4
and gave them to his **d** to set before the Mk 8:6
into the boat with his **d** and went to the Mk 8:10
went on with his **d** to the villages of Mk 8:27
And on the way he asked his **d**, "Who Mk 8:27
But turning and seeing his **d**, he Mk 8:33
the crowd with his **d** and said to them, Mk 8:34
And when they came to the **d**, they saw Mk 9:14
rigid. So I asked your **d** to cast it out, Mk 9:18
the house, his **d** asked him privately, Mk 9:28
for he was teaching his **d**, saying to Mk 9:31
in the house the **d** asked him again Mk 10:10
touch them, and the **d** rebuked them. Mk 10:13
Jesus looked around and said to his **d**, Mk 10:23
And the **d** were amazed at his words. Mk 10:24
leaving Jericho with his **d** and a great Mk 10:46
Mount of Olives, Jesus sent two of his **d** Mk 11:1
from you again." And his **d** heard it. Mk 11:14
And he called his **d** to him and said to Mk 12:43
of the temple, one of his **d** said to him, Mk 13:1
the Passover lamb, his **d** said to him, Mk 14:12
he sent two of his **d** and said to them, Mk 14:13
I may eat the Passover with my **d**?' Mk 14:14
And the **d** set out and went to the city Mk 14:16
And he said to his **d**, "Sit here while I Mk 14:32
tell his **d** and Peter that he is going Mk 16:7
and their scribes grumbled at his **d**, Lk 5:30
"The **d** of John fast often and offer Lk 5:33
prayers, and so do the **d** of the Pharisees, Lk 5:33
his **d** plucked and ate some heads of Lk 6:1
he called his **d** and chose from them Lk 6:13
great crowd of his **d** and a great Lk 6:17
And he lifted up his eyes on his **d**, and Lk 6:20
and his **d** and a great crowd went with Lk 7:11
The **d** of John reported all these things to Lk 7:18
calling two of his **d** to him, sent them to Lk 7:19
And when his **d** asked him what this Lk 8:9
One day he got into a boat with his **d**, Lk 8:22
And he said to his **d**, "Have them sit Lk 9:14
and gave them to the **d** to set before the Lk 9:16
was praying alone, the **d** were with him. Lk 9:18
And I begged your **d** to cast it out, but Lk 9:40
he was doing, Jesus said to his **d**, Lk 9:43
And when his **d** James and John saw it, Lk 9:54
Then turning to the **d** he said privately, Lk 10:23
he finished, one of his **d** said to him, Lk 11:1
teach us to pray, as John taught his **d**." Lk 11:1
another, he began to say to his **d** first, Lk 12:1
And he said to his **d**, "Therefore I tell Lk 12:22
He also said to the **d**, "There was a rich Lk 16:1
And he said to his **d**, "Temptations to sin Lk 17:1
And he said to the **d**, "The days are Lk 17:22
And when the **d** saw it, they rebuked Lk 18:15
is called Olivet, he sent two of the **d**, Lk 19:29
multitude of his **d** began to rejoice Lk 19:37
said to him, "Teacher, rebuke your **d**." Lk 19:39
of all the people he said to his **d**, Lk 20:45
I may eat the Passover with my **d**?' Lk 22:11
of Olives, and the **d** followed him. Lk 22:39
he came to the **d** and found them Lk 22:45
John was standing with two of his **d**, Jn 1:35
The two **d** heard him say this, and they Jn 1:37
also was invited to the wedding with his **d**. Jn 2:2
his glory. And his **d** believed in him. Jn 2:11
his mother and his brothers and his **d**, Jn 2:12
His **d** remembered that it was written, Jn 2:17
his **d** remembered that he had said this, Jn 2:22
this Jesus and his **d** went into the Judean Jn 3:22
between some of John's **d** and a Jew over Jn 3:25
making and baptizing more **d** than John Jn 4:1
himself did not baptize, but only his **d**), Jn 4:2
(For his **d** had gone away into the city to Jn 4:8
Just then his **d** came back. They Jn 4:27
Meanwhile the **d** were urging him, Jn 4:31
So the **d** said to one another, "Has anyone Jn 4:33
and there he sat down with his **d**. Jn 6:3
One of his **d**, Andrew, Simon Peter's Jn 6:8
they had eaten their fill, he told his **d**, Jn 6:12
evening came, his **d** went down to the sea, Jn 6:16
Jesus had not entered the boat with his **d**, Jn 6:22
but that his **d** had gone away alone. Jn 6:22
saw that Jesus was not there, nor his **d**, Jn 6:24
When many of his **d** heard it, they said, Jn 6:60
himself that his **d** were grumbling about Jn 6:61
this many of his **d** turned back and no Jn 6:66
that your **d** also may see the works you are Jn 7:3
abide in my word, you are truly my **d**, Jn 8:31
And his **d** asked him, "Rabbi, who sinned, Jn 9:2
Do you also want to become his **d**?" Jn 9:27
are his disciple, but we are **d** of Moses. Jn 9:28
Then after this he said to the **d**, "Let us go Jn 11:7
The **d** said to him, "Rabbi, the Jews were Jn 11:8
The **d** said to him, "Lord, if he has fallen Jn 11:12
called the Twin, said to his fellow **d**, Jn 11:16
Ephraim, and there he stayed with the **d**. Jn 11:54
one of his **d** (he who was about to betray Jn 12:4
His **d** did not understand these things at Jn 12:16
The **d** looked at one another, uncertain Jn 13:22
One of his **d**, whom Jesus loved, was Jn 13:23
all people will know that you are my **d**, Jn 13:35
bear much fruit and so prove to be my **d**. Jn 15:8
So some of his **d** said to one another, Jn 16:17
His **d** said, "Ah, now you are speaking Jn 16:29
went out with his **d** across the Kidron Jn 18:1
was a garden, which he and his **d** entered. Jn 18:1
place, for Jesus often met there with his **d**. Jn 18:2
"You also are not one of this man's **d**, Jn 18:17
Jesus about his **d** and his teaching. Jn 18:19
to him, "You also are not one of his **d**, Jn 18:25
Then the **d** went back to their homes. Jn 20:10
went and announced to the **d**, Jn 20:18
being locked where the **d** were for fear of Jn 20:19
Then the **d** were glad when they saw the Jn 20:20
So the other **d** told him, "We have seen Jn 20:25
Eight days later, his **d** were inside again, Jn 20:26
other signs in the presence of the **d**, Jn 20:30
himself again to the **d** by the Sea of Jn 21:1
and two others of his **d** were together. Jn 21:2
yet the **d** did not know that it was Jesus. Jn 21:4
The other **d** came in the boat, dragging Jn 21:8
Now none of the **d** dared ask him, Jn 21:12
was revealed to the **d** after he was raised Jn 21:14
days when the **d** were increasing in Acts 6:1
the full number of the **d** and said, Acts 6:2
number of the **d** multiplied greatly in Acts 6:7
and murder against the **d** of the Lord, Acts 9:1
days he was with the **d** at Damascus. Acts 9:19
but his **d** took him by night and let Acts 9:25
Jerusalem, he attempted to join the **d**. Acts 9:26
Since Lydda was near Joppa, the **d**, Acts 9:38
And in Antioch the **d** were first called Acts 11:26
So the **d** determined, everyone Acts 11:29
And the **d** were filled with joy and Acts 13:52
But when the **d** gathered about him, Acts 14:20
to that city and had made many **d**, Acts 14:21
strengthening the souls of the **d**, Acts 14:22
remained no little time with the **d**. Acts 14:28
the neck of the **d** that neither our Acts 15:10
and Phrygia, strengthening all the **d**. Acts 18:23
and wrote to the **d** to welcome him. Acts 18:27
to Ephesus. There he found some **d**. Acts 19:1
from them and took the **d** with him, Acts 19:9
the crowd, the **d** would not let him. Acts 19:30
the uproar ceased, Paul sent for the **d**, Acts 20:1
things, to draw away the **d** after them. Acts 20:30
And having sought out the **d**, we Acts 21:4
some of the **d** from Caesarea went Acts 21:16

DISCIPLES' (1)
and began to wash the **d** feet and to wipe Jn 13:5

DISCIPLINE (43)
then I will **d** you again sevenfold for Lv 26:18
"And if by this **d** you are not turned to Lv 26:23
and I myself will **d** you sevenfold for Lv 26:28
you hear his voice, that he might **d** you. Dt 4:36
it), consider the **d** of the LORD your God, Dt 11:2
of his mother, and, though they **d** him, Dt 21:18
I will **d** him with the rod of men, 2 Sm 7:14
but I will **d** you with scorpions.'" 1 Kgs 12:11
but I will **d** you with scorpions." 1 Kgs 12:14
but I will **d** you with scorpions.'" 2 Chr 10:11
but I will **d** you with scorpions." 2 Chr 10:14
despise not the **d** of the Almighty. Jb 5:17
in your anger, nor **d** me in your wrath. Ps 6:1
in your anger, nor **d** me in your wrath! Ps 38:1
When you **d** a man with rebukes for Ps 39:11
For you hate **d**, and you cast my words Ps 50:17
Blessed is the man whom you **d**, O LORD, Ps 94:12
not despise the LORD'S **d** or be weary of Prv 3:11
and you say, "How I hated **d**, and my Prv 5:12
He dies for lack of **d**, and because of his Prv 5:23
and the reproofs of **d** are the way of life, Prv 6:23
Whoever loves **d** loves knowledge, but Prv 12:1
he who loves him is diligent to **d** him. Prv 13:24
There is severe **d** for him who forsakes Prv 15:10
D your son, for there is hope; do not set Prv 19:18
but the rod of **d** drives it far from him. Prv 22:15
Do not withhold **d** from a child; if you Prv 23:13
D your son, and he will give you rest; Prv 29:17
prayer when your **d** was upon them. Is 26:16
the LORD their God, and did not accept **d**; Jer 7:28
I will **d** you in just measure, and I will Jer 30:11
I will **d** you in just measure, and I will Jer 46:28
into slaughter, but I will **d** all of them. Hos 5:2
I will **d** them according to the report Hos 7:12
When I please, I will **d** them, and Hos 10:10
But I **d** my body and keep it under 1 Cor 9:27
them up in the **d** and instruction of the Eph 6:4
do not regard lightly the **d** of the Lord, Heb 12:5
It is for **d** that you have to endure. God Heb 12:7
is there whom his father does not **d**? Heb 12:7
If you are left without **d**, in which all Heb 12:8
the moment all **d** seems painful Heb 12:11
Those whom I love, I reprove and **d**, so be Rv 3:19

DISCIPLINED (12)
My father **d** you with whips, but I 1 Kgs 12:11
My father **d** you with whips, but I 1 Kgs 12:14
My father **d** you with whips, but I 2 Chr 10:11
My father **d** you with whips, but I 2 Chr 10:14
The LORD has **d** me severely, but he Ps 118:18
By mere words a servant is not **d**, for Prv 29:19
Ephraim grieving, 'You have **d** me, Jer 31:18
'You have disciplined me, and I was **d**, Jer 31:18
we are **d** so that we may not be 1 Cor 11:32
good, self-controlled, upright, holy, and **d**. Ti 1:8
had earthly fathers who **d** us and we Heb 12:9
For they **d** us for a short time as it Heb 12:10

DISCIPLINES (5)
in your heart that, as a man **d** his son, Dt 8:5
his son, the LORD your God **d** you. Dt 8:5
He who **d** the nations, does he not Ps 94:10
For the Lord **d** the one he loves, and Heb 12:6
best to them, but he **d** us for our good, Heb 12:10

DISCLOSE (6)
shall I not then send and **d** it to you? 1 Sm 20:12
also if I do not **d** it to you and send 1 Sm 20:13
he fled and did not **d** it to me." But 1 Sm 22:17
and the earth will **d** the blood shed on it, Is 26:21
manifest, for the Day will **d** it, 1 Cor 3:13
in darkness and will **d** the purposes of 1 Cor 4:5

DISCLOSED (3)
And when it was **d** to me that there Acts 23:30
but has now been **d** and through the Rom 16:26
the secrets of his heart are **d**, and so, 1 Cor 14:25

DISCLOSES (3)
No one **d** to me when my son makes a 1 Sm 22:8
is sorry for me or **d** to me that my son 1 Sm 22:8
life; he hears the curse, but **d** nothing. Prv 29:24

DISCLOSING (1)
great or small without **d** it to me. 1 Sm 20:2

DISCOMFORT (1)
over his head, to save him from his **d**. Jon 4:6

DISCORD (2)
heart devises evil, continually sowing **d**; Prv 6:14
and one who sows **d** among brothers. Prv 6:19

DISCOURAGE (1)
Why will you **d** the heart of the people Nm 32:7

DISCOURAGED (5)
they **d** the heart of the people of Israel Nm 32:9
he is weary and **d** and throw him into 2 Sm 17:2
people of the land **d** the people of Judah Ezr 4:4
grow faint or be **d** till he has established Is 42:4
your children, lest they become **d**. Col 3:21

DISCOURSE (9)
And Balaam took up his **d** and said, Nm 23:7
And Balaam took up his **d** and said, Nm 23:18
and he took up his **d** and said, "The Nm 24:3
And he took up his **d** and said, "The Nm 24:15
Amalek and took up his **d** and said, Nm 24:20
the Kenite, and took up his **d** and said, Nm 24:21
And he took up his **d** and said, "Alas, Nm 24:23
And Job again took up his **d**, and said: Jb 27:1
And Job again took up his **d**, and said: Jb 29:1

DISCOVER (4)
would not God **d** this? For he knows the Ps 44:21
gives thought to the word will **d** good, Prv 16:20
man of crooked heart does not **d** good, Prv 17:20
who keeps understanding will **d** good. Prv 19:8

DISCOVERED (3)
Now Saul heard that David was **d**, and 1 Sm 22:6
wherever any need of repairs is **d**." 2 Kgs 12:5
and I then **d** the evil that Eliashib had Neh 13:7

DISCRETION (11)
Blessed be your **d**, and blessed be 1 Sm 25:33
grant you **d** and understanding, 1 Chr 22:12
son, who has **d** and understanding, 2 Chr 2:12

God on us, they brought us a man of **d**, Ezr 8:18
simple, knowledge and **d** to the youth— Prv 1:4
d will watch over you, understanding Prv 2:11
of these—keep sound wisdom and **d**, Prv 3:21
that you may keep **d**, and your lips may Prv 5:2
prudence, and I find knowledge and **d**. Prv 8:12
snout is a beautiful woman without **d**. Prv 11:22
replied with prudence and **d** to Arioch, Dn 2:14

DISCUSSED (4)
man?" And they **d** it among Mt 21:25
And they **d** it with one another, saying, Mk 11:31
filled with fury and **d** with one another Lk 6:11
And they **d** it with one another, saying, Lk 20:5

DISCUSSING (6)
And they began **d** it among themselves, Mt 16:7
why are you **d** among yourselves the Mt 16:8
And they began **d** with one another the Mk 8:16
"Why are you **d** the fact that you have Mk 8:17
them, "What were you **d** on the way?" Mk 9:33
they were talking and **d** together, Lk 24:15

DISCUSSION (2)
Now a **d** arose between some of John's Jn 3:25
these, have wandered away into vain **d**, 1 Tm 1:6

DISDAINED (3)
looked and saw David, he **d** him, 1 Sm 17:42
But he **d** to lay hands on Mordecai alone. Est 3:6
fathers I would have **d** to set with the Jb 30:1

DISEASE (83)
into a case of leprous **d** on the skin of his Lv 13:2
turned white and the **d** appears to be Lv 13:3
skin of his body, it is a case of leprous **d**. Lv 13:3
if in his eyes the **d** is checked and the Lv 13:5
is checked and the **d** has not spread in Lv 13:5
has faded and the **d** has not spread in Lv 13:6
him unclean; it is a leprous **d**. Lv 13:8
a man is afflicted with a leprous **d**, Lv 13:9
it is a chronic leprous **d** in the skin of Lv 13:11
And if the leprous **d** breaks out in the Lv 13:12
so that the leprous **d** covers all the skin Lv 13:12
and if the leprous **d** has covered all his Lv 13:13
he shall pronounce him clean of the **d**; Lv 13:13
flesh is unclean, for it is a leprous **d**. Lv 13:15
him, and if the **d** has turned white, Lv 13:17
a case of leprous **d** that has broken out Lv 13:20
shall pronounce him unclean; it is a **d**. Lv 13:22
than the skin, then it is a leprous **d**. Lv 13:25
him unclean; it is a case of leprous **d**. Lv 13:25
him unclean; it is a case of leprous **d**. Lv 13:27
man or woman has a **d** on the head or Lv 13:29
the priest shall examine the **d**. And if it Lv 13:30
a leprous **d** of the head or the beard. Lv 13:30
examines the itching **d** and it appears Lv 13:31
with the itching **d** for seven days, Lv 13:31
day the priest shall examine the **d**. Lv 13:32
with the itching **d** for another seven Lv 13:33
it is a leprous **d** breaking out on his Lv 13:42
the appearance of leprous **d** in the skin Lv 13:43
him unclean; his **d** is on his head. Lv 13:44
person who has the **d** shall wear torn Lv 13:45
remain unclean as long as he has the **d**. Lv 13:46
is a case of leprous **d** in a garment, Lv 13:47
if the **d** is greenish or reddish in the Lv 13:49
made of skin, it is a case of leprous **d**, Lv 13:49
priest shall examine the **d** and shut up Lv 13:50
up that which has the **d** for seven days. Lv 13:50
he shall examine the **d** on the seventh Lv 13:51
If the **d** has spread in the garment, in Lv 13:51
the **d** is a persistent leprous disease; Lv 13:51
the disease is a persistent leprous **d**; Lv 13:51
diseased, for it is a persistent leprous **d**. Lv 13:52
and if the **d** has not spread in the Lv 13:53
they wash the thing in which is the **d**, Lv 13:54
changed, though the **d** has not spread, Lv 13:55
shall burn with fire whatever has the **d**. Lv 13:57
from which the **d** departs when you Lv 13:58
for a case of leprous **d** in a garment of Lv 13:59
if the case of leprous **d** is healed in the Lv 14:3
who is to be cleansed of the leprous **d**. Lv 14:7
for him in whom is a case of leprous **d**, Lv 14:32
put a case of leprous **d** in a house in the Lv 14:34
to me to be some case of **d** in my house.' Lv 14:35
before the priest goes to examine the **d**, Lv 14:36
And he shall examine the **d**. And if the Lv 14:37
And if the **d** is in the walls of the house Lv 14:37
If the **d** has spread in the walls of the Lv 14:39
in which is the **d** and throw them into Lv 14:40
"If the **d** breaks out again in the house, Lv 14:43
And if the **d** has spread in the house, it Lv 14:44
it is a persistent leprous **d** in the house; Lv 14:44
and if the **d** has not spread in the house Lv 14:48
the house clean, for the **d** is healed. Lv 14:48
is the law for any case of leprous **d**: Lv 14:54
for leprous **d** in a garment or in a Lv 14:55
it is clean. This is the law for leprous **d**. Lv 14:57
sight or an itching **d** or scabs or Lv 21:20
who has a leprous **d** or a discharge may Lv 22:4
with wasting **d** and fever that consume Lv 26:16
"Take care, in a case of leprous **d**, to be Dt 24:8
you with wasting **d** and with fever, Dt 28:22
in his feet, and his **d** became severe. 2 Chr 16:12
Yet even in his **d** he did not seek the 2 Chr 16:12
sickness with a **d** of your bowels, 2 Chr 21:15
bowels come out because of the **d**, 2 Chr 21:15
in his bowels with an incurable **d**. 2 Chr 21:18
bowels came out because of the **d**, 2 Chr 21:19
but sent a wasting **d** among them. Ps 106:15
and healing every **d** and every affliction Mt 4:23
and healing every **d** and every affliction. Mt 9:35
and to heal every **d** and every affliction. Mt 10:1
in her body that she was healed of her **d**. Mk 5:29
go in peace, and be healed of your **d**." Mk 5:34

DISEASED (16)
priest shall examine the **d** area on the Lv 13:3
if the hair in the **d** area has turned white Lv 13:3
shall shut up the **d** person for seven days. Lv 13:4
and if the **d** area has faded and the Lv 13:6
all the skin of the **d** person from head to Lv 13:12
shall pronounce the **d** person clean; Lv 13:17
bald forehead a reddish-white **d** area, Lv 13:42
and if the **d** swelling is reddish-white on Lv 13:43
or any article made of skin that is **d**, Lv 13:52
priest shall examine the **d** thing after it Lv 13:55
the appearance of the **d** area has not Lv 13:55
and if the **d** area has faded after it has Lv 13:56
in his old age he was **d** in his feet. 1 Kgs 15:23
of his reign Asa was **d** in his feet, 2 Chr 16:12
good fruit, but the **d** tree bears bad fruit. Mt 7:17
fruit, nor can a **d** tree bear good fruit. Mt 7:18

DISEASES (16)
I will put none of the **d** on you that I put Ex 15:26
sickness, and none of the evil **d** of Egypt, Dt 7:15
bring upon you again all the **d** of Egypt, Dt 28:60
all your iniquity, who heals all your **d**, Ps 103:3
I enter the city, behold, the **d** of famine! Jer 14:18
They shall die of deadly **d**. They shall Jer 16:4
those afflicted with various **d** and pains, Mt 4:24
"He took our illnesses and bore our **d**." Mt 8:17
many who were sick with various **d**, Mk 1:34
that all who had **d** pressed around him Mk 3:10
sick with various **d** brought them to Lk 4:40
to hear him and to be healed of their **d**. Lk 6:18
many people of **d** and plagues and Lk 7:21
authority over all demons and to cure **d**, Lk 9:1
and their **d** left them and the evil Acts 19:12
the island who had **d** also came and Acts 28:9

DISFIGURE (1)
for they **d** their faces that their fasting Mt 6:16

DISFIGURED (1)
With great force my garment is **d**; it Jb 30:18

DISGRACE (29)
for that would be a **d** to us. Gn 34:14
and she sees his nakedness, it is a **d**, Lv 20:17
eyes, and thus bring **d** on all Israel." 1 Sm 11:2
a day of distress, of rebuke, and of **d**; 2 Kgs 19:3
for I am filled with **d** and look on my Jb 10:15
me and make my **d** an argument against Jb 19:5
All day long my **d** is before me, and Ps 44:15
with scorn and **d** may they be covered Ps 71:13
dismayed forever; let them perish in **d**, Ps 83:17
wise will inherit honor, but fools get **d**. Prv 3:35
he get, and his **d** will not be wiped away. Prv 6:33
When pride comes, then comes **d**, but Prv 11:2
but the wicked brings shame and **d**. Prv 13:5
Poverty and **d** come to him who Prv 13:18
comes also, and with dishonor comes **d**. Prv 18:3
neither help nor profit, but shame and **d**." Is 30:5
is a day of distress, of rebuke, and of **d**; Is 37:3
be uncovered, and your **d** shall be seen. Is 47:3
I hid not my face from **d** and spitting. Is 50:6
because I bore the **d** of my youth.' Jer 31:19
has befallen us; look, and see our **d**! Lam 5:1
Bear your **d**, you also, for you have Ezk 16:52
ashamed, you also, and bear your **d**, Ezk 16:52
you may bear your **d** and be ashamed Ezk 16:54
no longer bear the **d** of the peoples and Ezk 36:15
again suffer the **d** of famine among Ezk 36:30
of such things; **d** will not overtake us." Mi 2:6
wears long hair it is a **d** for him, 1 Cor 11:14
so that he may not fall into **d**, 1 Tm 3:7

DISGRACED (7)
David, because his father had **d** him. 1 Sm 20:34
have rejected us and **d** us and have not Ps 44:9
GOD helps me; therefore I have not been **d**; Is 50:7
be not confounded, for you will not be **d**; Is 54:4
was yet day; she has been shamed and **d**. Jer 15:9
and she who bore you shall be **d**. Jer 50:12
the seers shall be **d**, and the diviners put Mi 3:7

DISGRACEFUL (3)
and will repay him for his **d** deeds. Hos 12:14
But since it is **d** for a wife to cut off 1 Cor 11:6
But we have renounced **d**, 2 Cor 4:2

DISGUISE (4)
said to his wife, "Arise, and **d** yourself, 1 Kgs 14:2
"I will **d** myself and go into battle, 1 Kgs 22:30
"I will **d** myself and go into battle, 2 Chr 18:29
d themselves as servants of 2 Cor 11:15

DISGUISED (4)
So Saul **d** himself and put on other 1 Sm 28:8
the king of Israel **d** himself and went 1 Kgs 22:30
And the king of Israel **d** himself, 2 Chr 18:29
but **d** himself in order to fight with 2 Chr 35:22

DISGUISES (2)
Whoever hates **d** himself with his lips Prv 26:24
for even Satan **d** himself as an angel 2 Cor 11:14

DISGUISING (2)
d himself with a bandage over his 1 Kgs 20:38
d themselves as apostles of Christ. 2 Cor 11:13

DISGUST (7)
I look at the faithless with **d**, because Ps 119:158
O Jerusalem, lest I turn from you in **d**, Jer 6:8
by them, she turned from them in **d**. Ezk 23:17
her nakedness, I turned in **d** from her, Ezk 23:18
as I had turned in **d** from her sister. Ezk 23:18
lovers from whom you turned in **d**, Ezk 23:22
of those from whom you turned in **d**, Ezk 23:28

DISH (18)
one golden **d** of 10 shekels, full of Nm 7:14
one golden **d** of 10 shekels, full of Nm 7:20
one golden **d** of 10 shekels, full of Nm 7:26
one golden **d** of 10 shekels, full of Nm 7:32
one golden **d** of 10 shekels, full of Nm 7:38
one golden **d** of 10 shekels, full of Nm 7:44
one golden **d** of 10 shekels, full of Nm 7:50
one golden **d** of 10 shekels, full of Nm 7:56
one golden **d** of 10 shekels, full of Nm 7:62
one golden **d** of 10 shekels, full of Nm 7:68
one golden **d** of 10 shekels, full of Nm 7:74
one golden **d** of 10 shekels, full of Nm 7:80
will wipe Jerusalem as one wipes a **d**, 2 Kgs 21:13
his hand in the **d** and will not even Prv 19:24
The sluggard buries his hand in the **d**; Prv 26:15
his hand in the **d** with me will betray Mt 26:23
is dipping bread into the **d** with me. Mk 14:20
the outside of the cup and of the **d**, Lk 11:39

DISHAN (5)
Dishon, Ezer, and **D**; these are the Gn 36:21
These are the sons of **D**: Uz and Aran. Gn 36:28
Dishon, Ezer, and **D**; these are the Gn 36:30
Zibeon, Anah, Dishon, Ezer, and **D**. 1 Chr 1:38
Akan. The sons of **D**: Uz and Aran. 1 Chr 1:42

DISHEARTENED (2)
Because you have **d** the righteous Ezk 13:22
D by the saying, he went away Mk 10:22

DISHES (12)
shall make its plates and **d** for incense, Ex 25:29
on the table, its plates and **d** for incense, Ex 37:16
and put on it the plates, the **d** for incense, Nm 4:7
twelve silver basins, twelve golden **d**, Nm 7:84
the twelve golden **d**, full of incense, Nm 7:86
all the gold of the **d** being 120 shekels; Nm 7:86
cups, snuffers, basins, **d** for incense, 1 Kgs 7:50
snuffers and the **d** for incense and 2 Kgs 25:14
the snuffers, basins, **d** for incense, 2 Chr 4:22
and **d** for incense and vessels of gold 2 Chr 24:14
the basins and the **d** for incense and all Jer 52:18
lampstands and the **d** for incense and Jer 52:19

DISHON (7)
D, Ezer, and Dishan; these are the Gn 36:21
D and Oholibamah the daughter of Gn 36:25
These are the sons of **D**: Hemdan, Gn 36:26
D, Ezer, and Dishan; these are the Gn 36:30
Shobal, Zibeon, Anah, **D**, Ezer, 1 Chr 1:38
son of Anah: **D**. The sons of Dishon: 1 Chr 1:41
The sons of **D**: Hemdan, Eshban, 1 Chr 1:41

DISHONEST (10)
A **d** man spreads strife, and a Prv 16:28
winks his eyes plans **d** things; Prv 16:30
and one with a **d** tongue falls into Prv 17:20
eyes and heart only for your **d** gain, Jer 22:17
my hand at the **d** gain that you have Ezk 22:13
blood, destroying lives to get **d** gain. Ezk 22:27
master commended the **d** manager for Lk 16:8
and one who is **d** in a very little is also Lk 16:10
in a very little is also **d** in much. Lk 16:10
to much wine, not greedy for **d** gain. 1 Tm 3:8

DISHONESTLY (1)
all who do such things, all who act **d**, Dt 25:16

DISHONOR (23)
not fitting for us to witness the king's **d**, Ezr 4:14
be put to shame and **d** who seek after my Ps 35:4
with shame and **d** who magnify Ps 35:26
back and brought to **d** who desire my Ps 40:14
seek you be brought to **d** through me, Ps 69:6
reproach, that **d** has covered my face. Ps 69:7
my reproach, and my shame and my **d**; Ps 69:19
back and brought to **d** who desire my Ps 70:2
May my accusers be clothed with **d**; Ps 109:29
Wounds and **d** will he get, and his Prv 6:33
comes also, and with **d** comes disgrace. Prv 18:3
all glory, to **d** all the honored of the earth. Is 23:9
instead of **d** they shall rejoice in their lot; Is 61:7
in our shame, and let our **d** cover us. Jer 3:25
sake; do not **d** your glorious throne; Jer 14:21
Their eternal **d** will never be forgotten. Jer 20:11
d has covered our face, for foreigners Jer 51:51
to the ground in **d** the kingdom and its Lam 2:2
but I honor my Father, and you **d** me. Jn 8:49
worthy to suffer **d** for the name. Acts 5:41
boast in the law **d** God by breaking Rom 2:23
It is sown in **d**; it is raised in glory. It 1 Cor 15:43
through honor and **d**, through slander 2 Cor 6:8

DISHONORABLE (4)
God gave them up to **d** passions. Rom 1:26
for honored use and another for **d** use? Rom 9:21
some for honorable use, some for **d**. 2 Tm 2:20
cleanses himself from what is **d**, 2 Tm 2:21

DISHONORED (1)
But you have **d** the poor man. Are not the Jas 2:6

DISHONORING (1)
to the **d** of their bodies among Rom 1:24

DISHONORS (4)
you, and him who **d** you I will curse, Gn 12:3
"'Cursed be anyone who **d** his father or Dt 27:16
with his head covered **d** his head, 1 Cor 11:4
with her head uncovered **d** her head— 1 Cor 11:5

DISINHERIT (1)
them with the pestilence and **d** them, Nm 14:12

DISLIKED (1)
The poor is **d** even by his neighbor, Prv 14:20

DISMAY (5)
by them, lest I **d** you before them. Jer 1:17
I mourn, and **d** has taken hold on me. Jer 8:21
shall drink water by measure and in **d**. Ezk 4:16
and water, and look at one another in **d**, Ezk 4:17
with anxiety, and drink water in **d**. Ezk 12:19

DISMAYED (50)
him, for they were **d** at his presence. Gn 45:3
Now are the chiefs of Edom **d**; Ex 15:15
fathers, has told you. Do not fear or be **d**.' Dt 1:21
you or forsake you. Do not fear or be **d**." Dt 31:8
Do not be frightened, and do not be **d**, for Jos 1:9
to Joshua, "Do not fear and do not be **d**. Jos 8:1
said to them, "Do not be afraid or **d**; Jos 10:25
and the men of Benjamin were **d**, Jgs 20:41
they were **d** and greatly afraid. 1 Sm 17:11
his courage failed, and all Israel was **d**. 2 Sm 4:1
of strength, are **d** and confounded, 2 Kgs 19:26
courageous. Fear not; do not be **d**. 1 Chr 22:13
Do not be afraid and do not be **d**, for 1 Chr 28:20
and do not be **d** at this great horde, 2 Chr 20:15
Do not be afraid and do not be **d**. 2 Chr 20:17
not be afraid or **d** before the king of 2 Chr 32:7
impatient; it touches you, and you are **d**. Jb 4:5
When I remember I am **d**, and Jb 21:6
"They are **d**; they answer no more; they Jb 32:15
He laughs at fear and is not **d**; he does Jb 39:22
stand strong; you hid your face; I was **d**. Ps 30:7
Let them be put to shame and **d** forever; Ps 83:17
by your anger; by your wrath we are **d**. Ps 90:7
When you hide your face, they are **d**; Ps 104:29
They will be **d**: pangs and agony will seize Is 13:8
they shall be **d** and ashamed because Is 20:5
I cannot hear; I am **d** so that I cannot see. Is 21:3
shorn of strength, are **d** and confounded, Is 37:27
with you; be not **d**, for I am your God; Is 41:10
do harm, that we may be **d** and terrified. Is 41:23
and my righteousness will never be **d**. Is 51:6
of man, nor be **d** at their revilings. Is 51:7
Do not be **d** by them, lest I dismay you Jer 1:17
put to shame; they shall be **d** and taken; Jer 8:9
nor be **d** at the signs of the heavens Jer 10:2
because the nations are **d** at them, Jer 10:2
Because of the ground that is **d**, since Jer 14:4
let them be **d**, but let me not be Jer 17:18
them be dismayed, but let me not be **d**; Jer 17:18
and they shall fear no more, nor be **d**, Jer 23:4
my servant, declares the LORD, nor be **d**, Jer 30:10
They are **d** and have turned backward. Jer 46:5
fear not, O Jacob my servant, nor be **d**, Jer 46:27
Bel is put to shame, Merodach is **d**. Jer 50:2
images are put to shame, her idols are **d**.' Jer 50:2
of their words, nor be **d** at their looks, Ezk 2:6
Fear them not, nor be **d** at their looks, Ezk 3:9
are on the sea are **d** at your passing.' Ezk 26:18
was Belteshazzar, was **d** for a while, Dn 4:19
And your mighty men shall be **d**, O Ob 1:9

DISMISS (1)
the priest did not **d** the divisions. 2 Chr 23:8

DISMISSED (6)
When Joshua **d** the people, the people of Jgs 2:6
to the other side, while he **d** the crowds. Mt 14:22
And after he had **d** the crowds, he went Mt 14:23
side, to Bethsaida, while he **d** the crowd. Mk 6:45
said these things, he **d** the assembly. Acts 19:41
So the tribune **d** the young man, Acts 23:22

DISMOUNTED (2)
she saw Isaac, she **d** from the camel Gn 24:64
And she **d** from her donkey, and Caleb Jgs 1:14

DISOBEDIENCE (9)
by the one man's **d** the many were Rom 5:19
received mercy because of their **d**, Rom 11:30
For God has consigned all to **d**, that Rom 11:32
being ready to punish every **d**, when 2 Cor 10:6
that is now at work in the sons of **d**— Eph 2:2
wrath of God comes upon the sons of **d**. Eph 5:6
every transgression or **d** received a just Heb 2:2
good news failed to enter because of **d**, Heb 4:6
no one may fall by the same sort of **d**. Heb 4:11

DISOBEDIENT (13)
they were **d** and rebelled against you Neh 9:26
and the **d** to the wisdom of the just, Lk 1:17
I was not **d** to the heavenly vision, Acts 26:19
boastful, inventors of evil, **d** to parents, Rom 1:30
hands to a **d** and contrary people." Rom 10:21
were at one time **d** to God but now Rom 11:30
too have now been **d** in order that by Rom 11:31
for the just but for the lawless and **d**, 1 Tm 1:9
arrogant, abusive, **d** to their parents, 2 Tm 3:2
are detestable, **d**, unfit for any good work. Ti 1:16
ourselves were once foolish, **d**, led astray, Ti 3:3
enter his rest, but to those who were **d**? Heb 3:18
did not perish with those who were **d**, Heb 11:31

DISOBEY (1)
They stumble because they **d** the word, 1 Pt 2:8

DISOBEYED (3)
'Because you have **d** the word of the 1 Kgs 13:21
man of God who **d** the word of the 1 Kgs 13:26
you, and I never **d** your command, Lk 15:29

DISOBEYING (1)
land,' **d** the voice of the LORD your God Jer 42:13

DISOBEYS (1)
your commandment and **d** your words, Jos 1:18

DISORDER (2)
slander, gossip, conceit, and **d**. 2 Cor 12:20
there will be **d** and every vile practice. Jas 3:16

DISOWNED (2)
he **d** his brothers and ignored his Dt 33:9
has scorned his altar, **d** his sanctuary; Lam 2:7

DISPATCHED (1)
Now the king had **d** a man from his 2 Kgs 6:32

DISPERSE (7)
"**D** yourselves among the people and 1 Sm 14:34
when I **d** them among the nations and Ezk 12:15
the nations and **d** them through the Ezk 20:23
the nations and **d** you through the Ezk 22:15
and **d** them through the countries. Ezk 29:12
the nations and **d** them through the Ezk 30:23
the nations and **d** them throughout Ezk 30:26

DISPERSED (12)
the people of the whole earth were **d**. Gn 9:19
the clans of the Canaanites **d**. Gn 10:18
lest we be **d** over the face of the whole Gn 11:4
So the LORD **d** them from there over the Gn 11:8
from there the LORD **d** them over the face Gn 11:9
trumpet, and they **d** from the city, 2 Sm 20:22
though your **d** be under the farthest Neh 1:9
scattered abroad and **d** among the Est 3:8
and gather the **d** of Judah from the four Is 11:12
and they were **d** through the Ezk 36:19
worshipers, the daughter of my **d** ones, Zep 3:10
who followed him were **d** and came to Acts 5:36

DISPERSING (1)
the multitude was **d** here and there. 1 Sm 14:16

DISPERSION (4)
of your slaughter and **d** have come, Jer 25:34
to go to the **D** among the Greeks and Jn 7:35
Jesus Christ, To the twelve tribes in the **D**: Jas 1:1
who are elect exiles of the **d** in Pontus, 1 Pt 1:1

DISPLACES (1)
maidservant when she **d** her mistress. Prv 30:23

DISPLAY (2)
Jesus Christ might **d** his perfect 1 Tm 1:16
which he will **d** at the proper time— 1 Tm 6:15

DISPLAYED (2)
province, being publicly **d** to all peoples, Est 8:13
that the works of God might be **d** in him. Jn 9:3

DISPLEASE (2)
that you may not **d** the lords of the 1 Sm 29:7
and **d** God and oppose all mankind 1 Thes 2:15

DISPLEASED (12)
"Be not **d** because of the boy and Gn 21:12
hand on the head of Ephraim, it **d** him, Gn 48:17
LORD blazed hotly, and Moses was **d**. Nm 11:10
But the thing **d** Samuel when they said, 1 Sm 8:6
very angry, and this saying **d** him. 1 Sm 18:8
that David had done **d** the LORD. 2 Sm 11:27
never at any time **d** him by asking, 1 Kgs 1:6
But God was **d** with this thing, and he 1 Chr 21:7
it **d** them greatly that someone had Neh 2:10
lest the LORD see it and be **d**, and turn Prv 24:18
it, and it **d** him that there was no justice. Is 59:15
But it **d** Jonah exceedingly, and he was Jon 4:1

DISPLEASING (1)
the thing was very **d** to Abraham on Gn 21:11

DISPLEASURE (2)
forty years, and you shall know my **d**.' Nm 14:34
of the anger and hot **d** that the LORD bore Dt 9:19

DISPOSAL (1)
after it was sold, was it not at your **d**? Acts 5:4

DISPOSED (2)
behold, if he is well **d** toward David, 1 Sm 20:12
you to dinner and you are **d** to go, 1 Cor 10:27

DISPOSSESS (10)
are greater than I. How can I **d** them?' Dt 7:17
to go in to **d** nations greater and mightier Dt 9:1
and you will **d** nations greater and Dt 11:23
whom you shall **d** served their gods, Dt 12:2
you the nations whom you go in to **d**, Dt 12:29
and you **d** them and dwell in their land, Dt 12:29
these nations, which you are about to **d**, Dt 18:14
and you **d** them and dwell in their cities Dt 19:1
before you, so that you shall **d** them, Dt 31:3
then Israel shall **d** those who Jer 49:2

DISPOSSESSED (12)
its villages and **d** the Amorites who Nm 21:32
Edom shall be **d**; Seir also, his Nm 24:18
Seir also, his enemies, shall be **d**. Nm 24:18
it, and **d** the Amorites who were in it. Nm 32:39
the people of Esau **d** them and destroyed Dt 2:12
and they **d** them and settled in their Dt 2:21
before them and they **d** them and settled Dt 2:22
d the Amorites from before his people Jgs 11:23
that the LORD our God has **d** before us, Jgs 11:24
Why then has Milcom **d** Gad, and his Jer 49:1
Israel shall dispossess those who **d** him, Jer 49:2
Joshua when they **d** the nations that Acts 7:45

DISPUTE (14)
when they have a **d**, they come to me Ex 18:16
Whoever has a **d**, let him go to them." Ex 24:14
both parties to the **d** shall appear before Dt 19:17
by their word every **d** and every assault Dt 21:5
"If there is a **d** between men and they Dt 25:1
had a great **d** with the Ammonites, Jgs 12:2
any man had a **d** to come before the 2 Sm 15:2
every man with a **d** or cause might 2 Sm 15:4
is not able to **d** with one stronger than Eccl 6:10
In a **d**, they shall act as judges, and Ezk 44:24
A **d** also arose among them, as to Lk 22:24
certain points of **d** with him about Acts 25:19
to settle a **d** between the brothers, 1 Cor 6:5
It is beyond **d** that the inferior is blessed Heb 7:7

DISPUTED (4)
for the LORD and to decide **d** cases. 2 Chr 19:8
The Jews then **d** among themselves, Jn 6:52
and Asia, rose up and **d** with Stephen. Acts 6:9
he spoke and **d** against the Hellenists. Acts 9:29

DISPUTES (3)
and shall decide **d** for many peoples; Is 2:4
eyes see, or decide **d** by what his ears hear, Is 11:3
and in all their **d** an oath is final for Heb 6:16

DISPUTING (3)
and heard them **d** with one another, Mk 12:28

did not find me **d** with anyone or Acts 24:12
the devil, was **d** about the body of Moses, Jude 1:9

DISQUALIFIED (2)
to others I myself should be **d**. 1 Cor 9:27
in mind and **d** regarding the faith. 2 Tm 3:8

DISQUALIFY (1)
Let no one **d** you, insisting on Col 2:18

DISREGARD (1)
with all authority. Let no one **d** you. Ti 2:15

DISREGARDED (2)
the LORD, and my right is **d** by my God"? Is 40:27
clean, and they have **d** my Sabbaths, Ezk 22:26

DISREGARDS (2)
Therefore whoever **d** this, disregards 1 Thes 4:8
disregards this, **d** not man but God, 1 Thes 4:8

DISREPUTE (2)
ours may come into **d** but also that Acts 19:27
You are held in honor, but we in **d**. 1 Cor 4:10

DISRESPECTFUL (1)
masters must not be **d** on the ground 1 Tm 6:2

DISSENSION (4)
had no small **d** and debate with Acts 15:2
a **d** arose between the Pharisees and Acts 23:7
And when the **d** became violent, the Acts 23:10
words, which produce envy, **d**, slander, 1 Tm 6:4

DISSENSIONS (2)
fits of anger, rivalries, **d**, divisions, Gal 5:20
genealogies, **d**, and quarrels about the law, Ti 3:9

DISSIPATION (1)
weighed down with **d** and drunkenness Lk 21:34

DISSOLVED (3)
bodies will be burned up and **d**, 2 Pt 3:10
Since all these things are thus to be **d**, 2 Pt 3:11
the heavens will be set on fire and **d**, 2 Pt 3:12

DISSOLVES (1)
them be like the snail that **d** into slime, Ps 58:8

DISTAFF (1)
She puts her hands to the **d**, and her Prv 31:19

DISTANCE (22)
good way off, about the **d** of a bowshot, Gn 21:16
And he set a **d** of three days' journey Gn 30:36
they were still some **d** from Ephrath, Gn 35:16
had gone only a short **d** from the city. Gn 44:4
there was still some **d** to go to Ephrath, Gn 48:7
his sister stood at a **d** to know what would Ex 2:4
shall measure the **d** to the surrounding Dt 21:2
Yet there shall be a **d** between you and it, Jos 3:4
they had gone a **d** from the home of Jgs 18:22
went and stood at some **d** from them, 2 Kgs 2:7
had gone from him a short **d**, 2 Kgs 5:19
And when they saw him from a **d**, they Jb 2:12
he measured the **d** from the inner Ezk 40:19
pigs was feeding at some **d** from them. Mt 8:30
And Peter was following him at a **d**, as Mt 26:58
women there, looking on from a **d**, Mt 27:55
And seeing in the **d** a fig tree in leaf, he Mk 11:13
And Peter had followed him at a **d**, Mk 14:54
were also women looking on from a **d**, Mk 15:40
was met by ten lepers, who stood at a **d** Lk 17:12
house, and Peter was following at a **d**. Lk 22:54
stood at a **d** watching these things. Lk 23:49

DISTANCES (1)
You shall measure the **d** and divide into Dt 19:3

DISTANT (5)
Israel, "We have come from a **d** country, Jos 9:6
"From a very **d** country your servants Jos 9:9
They come from a **d** land, from the end of Is 13:5
"Besiegers come from a **d** land; Jer 4:16
Sheba, or sweet cane from a **d** land? Jer 6:20

DISTILL (2)
drop as the rain, my speech **d** as the dew, Dt 32:2
drops of water; they **d** his mist in rain, Jb 36:27

DISTINCT (2)
in your going with us, so that we are **d**, Ex 33:16
flute or the harp, do not give **d** notes, 1 Cor 14:7

DISTINCTION (11)
LORD will make a **d** between the livestock Ex 9:4
the LORD makes a **d** between Egypt and Ex 11:7
to make a **d** between the unclean and Lv 11:47
or given her freedom, a **d** shall be made. Lv 19:20
"What honor or **d** has been bestowed on Est 6:3
have made no **d** between the holy Ezk 22:26
shall see the **d** between the righteous Mal 3:18
me to go with them, making no **d**. Acts 11:12
and he made no **d** between us and Acts 15:9
for all who believe. For there is no **d**: Rom 3:22
For there is no **d** between Jew and Rom 10:12

DISTINCTIONS (1)
not then made **d** among yourselves and Jas 2:4

DISTINCTLY (1)
of the stammerers will hasten to speak **d**. Is 32:4

DISTINGUISH (5)
You are to **d** between the holy and the Lv 10:10
the people could not **d** the sound of the Ezr 3:13
them how to **d** between the unclean Ezk 44:23
the ability to **d** between spirits, 1 Cor 12:10
constant practice to **d** good from evil. Heb 5:14

DISTINGUISHED (3)
and ruddy, **d** among ten thousand. Sg 5:10
Then this Daniel became **d** above all the Dn 6:3
lest someone more **d** than you be invited Lk 14:8

DISTORT (1)
you and want to **d** the gospel of Christ. Gal 1:7

DISTRACTED (1)
But Martha was **d** with much serving. Lk 10:40

DISTRESS (79)
in the day of my **d** and has been with me Gn 35:3
in that we saw the **d** of his soul, Gn 42:21
That is why this **d** has come upon us." Gn 42:21
siege and in the **d** with which your Dt 28:53
with which your enemies shall **d** you. Dt 28:53
siege and in the **d** with which your Dt 28:55
which your enemy shall **d** you in all Dt 28:55
siege and in the **d** with which your Dt 28:57
which your enemy shall **d** you in your Dt 28:57
to them. And they were in terrible **d**. Jgs 2:15
them save you in the time of your **d**." Jgs 10:14
come to me now when you are in **d**?" Jgs 11:7
Then in **d** you will look with envious 1 Sm 2:32
And everyone who was in **d**, and 1 Sm 22:2
up?" Saul answered, "I am in great **d**, 1 Sm 28:15
"In my **d** I called upon the LORD; to my 2 Sm 22:7
David said to Gad, "I am in great **d**. 2 Sm 24:14
"Leave her alone, for she is in bitter **d**, 2 Kgs 4:27
says Hezekiah, This day is a day of **d**, 2 Kgs 19:3
David said to Gad, "I am in great **d**. 1 Chr 21:13
but when in their **d** they turned to the 2 Chr 15:4
troubled them with every sort of **d**. 2 Chr 15:6
the time of his **d** he became yet 2 Chr 28:22
And when he was in **d**, he entreated 2 Chr 33:12
as they please, and we are in great **d**. Neh 9:37
d and anguish terrify him; they prevail Jb 15:24
of his sufficiency he will be in **d**; Jb 20:22
hear his cry when **d** comes upon him? Jb 27:9
allured you out of **d** into a broad place Jb 36:16
cry for help avail to keep you from **d**, Jb 36:19
You have given me relief when I was in **d**. Ps 4:1
In my **d** I called upon the LORD; to my Ps 18:6
you have known the **d** of my soul, Ps 31:7
Be gracious to me, O LORD, for I am in **d**; Ps 31:9
peace to no avail, and my **d** grew worse. Ps 39:2
fortress and a refuge in the day of my **d**. Ps 59:16
face from your servant; for I am in **d**; Ps 69:17
anger, wrath, indignation, and **d**, Ps 78:49
In **d** you called, and I delivered you; I Ps 81:7
your face from me in the day of my **d**! Ps 102:2
Nevertheless, he looked upon their **d**, Ps 106:44
and he delivered them from their **d**. Ps 107:6
and he delivered them from their **d**. Ps 107:13
and he delivered them from their **d**. Ps 107:19
and he delivered them from their **d**. Ps 107:28
hold on me; I suffered **d** and anguish. Ps 116:3
Out of my **d** I called on the LORD; the Ps 118:5
In my **d** I called to the LORD, and he Ps 120:1
may there be no cry of **d** in our streets! Ps 144:14
when **d** and anguish come upon you. Prv 1:27
perishing, and wine to those in bitter **d**; Prv 31:6
looks to the land, behold, darkness and **d**; Is 5:30
to the earth, but behold, **d** and darkness, Is 8:22
poor, a stronghold to the needy in his **d**, Is 25:4
O LORD, in **d** they sought you; they Is 26:16
Yet I will **d** Ariel, and there shall be Is 29:2
against her and her stronghold and **d** her, Is 29:7
says Hezekiah, 'This day is a day of **d**, Is 37:3
it the sound of weeping and the cry of **d**. Is 65:19
at this time, and I will bring **d** on them, Jer 10:18
the time of trouble and in the time of **d**? Jer 15:11
of his neighbor in the siege and in the **d**, Jer 19:9
is none like it; it is a time of **d** for Jacob; Jer 30:7
all overtaken her in the midst of her **d**. Lam 1:3
"Look, O LORD, for I am in **d**; my Lam 1:20
face, and in their **d** earnestly seek me. Hos 5:15
their ruin; do not boast in the day of **d**. Ob 1:12
hand over his survivors in the day of **d**. Ob 1:14
"I called out to the LORD, out of my **d**, Jon 2:2
is that day, a day of **d** and anguish, Zep 1:15
I will bring **d** on mankind, so that they Zep 1:17
have been searching for you in great **d**." Lk 2:48
how great is my **d** until it is Lk 12:50
there will be great **d** upon the earth and Lk 21:23
and on the earth **d** of nations in Lk 21:25
be tribulation and **d** for every human Rom 2:9
Shall tribulation, or **d**, or persecution, Rom 8:35
in view of the present **d** it is good for a 1 Cor 7:26
in all our **d** and affliction we have 1 Thes 3:7

DISTRESSED (15)
Then Jacob was greatly afraid and **d**. He Gn 32:7
now do not be **d** or angry with Gn 45:5
of Ephraim, so that Israel was severely **d**. Jgs 10:9
She was deeply **d** and prayed to the 1 Sm 1:10
And David was greatly **d**, for the 1 Sm 30:6
I am **d** for you, my brother Jonathan; 2 Sm 1:26
and told her, the queen was deeply **d**. Est 4:4
through the land, greatly **d** and hungry. Is 8:21
they have heard the **d** cry of destruction. Jer 48:5
was much **d** and set his mind to deliver Dn 6:14
the third day." And they were greatly **d**. Mt 17:23
had taken place, they were greatly **d**, Mt 18:31
began to be greatly **d** and troubled. Mk 14:33
all and has been **d** because you heard Phil 2:26
greatly **d** by the sensual conduct of the 2 Pt 2:7

DISTRESSES (2)
from all your calamities and your **d**, 1 Sm 10:19
are enlarged; bring me out of my **d**. Ps 25:17

DISTRIBUTE (5)
to **d** the portions to their brothers, 2 Chr 31:15
by name to **d** portions to every 2 Chr 31:19
that they might **d** them according 2 Chr 35:12
their duty was to **d** to their brothers. Neh 13:13
Sell all that you have and **d** to the poor, Lk 18:22

DISTRIBUTED (11)
inheritances that Moses **d** in the plains Jos 13:32
of the people of Israel **d** by lot at Shiloh Jos 19:51
and **d** among all the people, the whole 2 Sm 6:19
and **d** to all Israel, both men and 1 Chr 16:3
he dealt wisely and **d** some of his 2 Chr 11:23
the way to the place where the light is **d**, Jb 38:24
He has **d** freely; he has given to the poor; Ps 112:9
he **d** them to those who were seated. Jn 6:11
and it was **d** to each as any had need. Acts 4:35
As it is written, "He has **d** freely, he has 2 Cor 9:9
of the Holy Spirit **d** according to his will. Heb 2:4

DISTRIBUTES (1)
them? That God **d** pains in his anger? Jb 21:17

DISTRIBUTING (2)
they had finished **d** the several Jos 19:49
and belongings and **d** the proceeds to Acts 2:45

DISTRIBUTION (1)
were being neglected in the daily **d**. Acts 6:1

DISTRICT (22)
of Hur, ruler of half the **d** of Jerusalem, Neh 3:9
ruler of half the **d** of Jerusalem, Neh 3:12
ruler of the **d** of Beth-haccherem, Neh 3:14
of Col-hozeh, ruler of the **d** of Mizpah, Neh 3:15
Azbuk, ruler of half the **d** of Beth-zur, Neh 3:16
ruler of half the **d** of Keilah, Neh 3:17
the district of Keilah, repaired for his **d**. Neh 3:17
Henadad, ruler of half the **d** of Keilah. Neh 3:18
from the **d** surrounding Jerusalem Neh 12:28
LORD a portion of the land as a holy **d**, Ezk 45:1
from this measured **d** you shall Ezk 45:3
apart as the holy **d** you shall assign for Ezk 45:6
sides of the holy **d** and the property of Ezk 45:7
alongside the holy **d** and the property of Ezk 45:7
a dream he withdrew to the **d** of Galilee. Mt 2:22
the report of this went through all that **d**. Mt 9:26
and spread his fame through all that **d**. Mt 9:31
and withdrew to the **d** of Tyre and Mt 15:21
came into the **d** of Caesarea Philippi, Mt 16:13
and went to the **d** of Dalmanutha. Mk 8:10
and drove them out of their **d**. Acts 13:50
city of the **d** of Macedonia and Acts 16:12

DISTRICTS (5)
governors of the **d**." Then he said, 1 Kgs 20:14
servants of the governors of the **d**, 1 Kgs 20:15
the governors of the **d** went out first. 1 Kgs 20:17
the governors of the **d** and the army 1 Kgs 20:19
sons through all the **d** of Judah and 2 Chr 11:23

DISTRUST (1)
No **d** made him waver concerning the Rom 4:20

DISTURB (1)
where his cubs were, with none to **d**? Na 2:11

DISTURBANCE (2)
was no little **d** among the soldiers Acts 12:18
arose no little **d** concerning the Way. Acts 19:23

DISTURBANCES (1)
for great **d** afflicted all the 2 Chr 15:5

DISTURBED (4)
“Why have you **d** me by bringing 1 Sm 28:15
in their own place and be **d** no more. 2 Sm 7:10
in their own place and be **d** no more. 1 Chr 17:9
city authorities were **d** when they Acts 17:8

DISTURBING (1)
men are Jews, and they are **d** our city. Acts 16:20

DISUSE (1)
should never fall into **d** among the Jews, Est 9:28

DIVERSE (1)
led away by **d** and strange teachings, Heb 13:9

DIVERSIONS (1)
no **d** were brought to him, and sleep fled Dn 6:18

DIVIDE (36)
I will **d** them in Jacob and scatter them Gn 49:7
out your hand over the sea and **d** it, Ex 14:16
pursue, I will overtake, I will **d** the spoil, Ex 15:9
and **d** the plunder into two parts Nm 31:27
of the men who shall **d** the land to you Nm 34:17
from every tribe to **d** the land for Nm 34:18
LORD commanded to **d** the inheritance Nm 34:29
the distances and **d** into three parts Dt 19:3
Now therefore **d** this land for an Jos 13:7
They shall **d** it into seven portions. Jos 18:5
D the spoil of your enemies with your Jos 22:8
you and Ziba shall **d** the land.” 2 Sm 19:29
king said, “**D** the living child in two, 1 Kgs 3:25
be neither mine nor yours; **d** him.” 1 Kgs 3:26
it, and the innocent will **d** the silver. Jb 27:17
Will they **d** him up among the Jb 41:6
they **d** my garments among them, and Ps 22:18
Destroy, O Lord, **d** their tongues; for I see Ps 55:9
exultation I will **d** up Shechem and Ps 60:6
flee!” The women at home **d** the spoil— Ps 68:12
exultation I will **d** up Shechem and Ps 108:7
the poor than to **d** the spoil with the Prv 16:19
as they are glad when they **d** the spoil. Is 9:3
and conquering, whose land the rivers **d**. Is 18:2
and conquering, whose land the rivers **d**, Is 18:7
and save you, those who **d** the heavens, Is 47:13
Therefore I will **d** him a portion with the Is 53:12
and he shall **d** the spoil with the strong, Is 53:12
balances for weighing and **d** the hair. Ezk 5:1
by which you shall **d** the land for Ezk 47:13
And you shall **d** equally what I swore Ezk 47:14
“So you shall **d** this land among you Ezk 47:21
over many and shall **d** the land for a Dn 11:39
my brother to **d** the inheritance with Lk 12:13
“Take this, and **d** it among yourselves. Lk 22:17
And they cast lots to **d** his garments. Lk 23:34

DIVIDED (55)
and there it **d** and became four rivers. Gn 2:10
Peleg, for in his days the earth was **d**, Gn 10:25
And he **d** his forces against them by Gn 14:15
two peoples from within you shall be **d**; Gn 25:23
He **d** the people who were with him, and Gn 32:7
So he **d** the children among Leah and Gn 33:1
the sea dry land, and the waters were **d**. Ex 14:21
land shall be **d** for inheritance Nm 26:53
But the land shall be **d** by lot. Nm 26:55
inheritance shall be **d** according to Nm 26:56
their inheritance, when he **d** mankind, Dt 32:8
‘Have they not found and **d** the spoil?— Jgs 5:30
And he **d** the 300 men into three Jgs 7:16
took his people and **d** them into three Jgs 9:43
taking hold of his concubine he **d** her, Jgs 19:29
In life and in death they were not **d**; 2 Sm 1:23
people of Israel were **d** into two parts. 1 Kgs 16:21
So they **d** the land between them to 1 Kgs 18:6
(for in his days the earth was **d**), 1 Chr 1:19
They **d** them by lot, all alike, for 1 Chr 24:5
And you **d** the sea before them, so that Neh 9:11
You **d** the sea by your might; you broke Ps 74:13
He **d** the sea and let them pass through Ps 78:13
to him who **d** the Red Sea in two, for Ps 136:13
prey and spoil in abundance will be **d**; Is 33:23
who **d** the waters before them to make Is 63:12
and no longer **d** into two kingdoms. Ezk 37:22
partly of iron, it shall be a **d** kingdom, Dn 2:41
your kingdom is **d** and given to the Dn 5:28
shall be broken and **d** toward the four Dn 11:4
among the nations and have **d** up my land, Jl 3:2
your land shall be **d** up with a Am 7:17
taken from you will be **d** in your midst. Zec 14:1
“Every kingdom **d** against itself is laid Mt 12:25
no city or house **d** against itself will Mt 12:25
casts out Satan, he is **d** against himself. Mt 12:26
they **d** his garments among them by Mt 27:35
If a kingdom is **d** against itself, that Mk 3:24
And if a house is **d** against itself, that Mk 3:25
has risen up against himself and is **d**, Mk 3:26
And he **d** the two fish among them all. Mk 6:41
crucified him and **d** his garments Mk 15:24
“Every kingdom **d** against itself is laid Lk 11:17
is laid waste, and a **d** household falls. Lk 11:17
And if Satan also is **d** against himself, Lk 11:18
on in one house there will be five **d**, Lk 12:52
They will be **d**, father against son and Lk 12:53
And he **d** his property between them. Lk 15:12
took his garments and **d** them into four Jn 19:23
“They **d** my garments among them, Jn 19:24
And **d** tongues as of fire appeared to Acts 2:3
But the people of the city were **d**; some Acts 14:4
Sadducees, and the assembly was **d**. Acts 23:7
Is Christ **d**? Was Paul crucified for 1 Cor 1:13
and his interests are **d**. And the 1 Cor 7:34

DIVIDES (1)
in which he trusted and **d** his spoil. Lk 11:22

DIVIDING (3)
the prey and at evening **d** the spoil.” Gn 49:27
of meeting. So they finished **d** the land. Jos 19:51
down in his flesh the **d** wall of hostility Eph 2:14

DIVINATION (19)
I have learned by **d** that the LORD has Gn 30:27
drinks, and by this that he practices **d**? Gn 44:5
a man like me can indeed practice **d**?” Gn 44:15
with the fees for **d** in their hand. Nm 22:7
against Jacob, no **d** against Israel; Nm 23:23
anyone who practices **d** or tells fortunes Dt 18:10
son of Beor, the one who practiced **d**, Jos 13:22
For rebellion is as the sin of **d**, and 1 Sm 15:23
offerings and used **d** and omens and 2 Kgs 17:17
to you a lying vision, worthless **d**, Jer 14:14
vision or flattering **d** within the house Ezk 12:24
seen a false vision and uttered a lying **d**, Ezk 13:7
more see false visions nor practice **d**. Ezk 13:23
at the head of the two ways, to use **d**. Ezk 21:21
right hand comes the **d** for Jerusalem, Ezk 21:22
But to them it will seem like a false **d**. Ezk 21:23
vision, and darkness to you, without **d**. Mi 3:6
price; its prophets practice **d** for money; Mi 3:11
had a spirit of **d** and brought her Acts 16:16

DIVINATIONS (2)
have seen false visions and lying **d**. Ezk 13:6
see false visions and who give lying **d**. Ezk 13:9

DIVINE (10)
“**D** for me by a spirit and bring up for 1 Sm 28:8
God has taken his place in the **d** council; Ps 82:1
while they **d** lies for you—to place you Ezk 21:29
to think that the **d** being is like gold Acts 17:29
his eternal power and **d** nature, Rom 1:20
because in his **d** forbearance he had Rom 3:25
the flesh but have **d** power to destroy 2 Cor 10:4
I feel a **d** jealousy for you, for I 2 Cor 11:2
His **d** power has granted to us all things 2 Pt 1:3
may become partakers of the **d** nature, 2 Pt 1:4

DIVINER (1)
judge and the prophet, the **d** and the elder, Is 3:2

DIVINERS (8)
listen to fortune-tellers and to **d**. Dt 18:14
called for the priests and the **d** and said, 1 Sm 6:2
the signs of liars and makes fools of **d**, Is 44:25
So do not listen to your prophets, your **d**, Jer 27:9
prophets and your **d** who are among Jer 29:8
A sword against the **d**, that they may Jer 50:36
be disgraced, and the **d** put to shame; Mi 3:7
gods utter nonsense, and the **d** see lies; Zec 10:2

DIVINERS’ (1)
from the direction of the **D** Oak.” Jgs 9:37

DIVINING (1)
false visions and **d** lies for them, Ezk 22:28

DIVINITIES (1)
a preacher of foreign **d**”—because he Acts 17:18

DIVISION (29)
I will put a **d** between my people and Ex 8:23
the year, each **d** numbering 24,000: 1 Chr 27:1
charge of the first **d** in the first 1 Chr 27:2
the first month; in his **d** were 24,000. 1 Chr 27:2
in charge of the **d** of the second 1 Chr 27:4
second month; in his **d** were 24,000. 1 Chr 27:4
the chief priest; in his **d** were 24,000. 1 Chr 27:5
his son was in charge of his **d**. 1 Chr 27:6
after him; in his **d** were 24,000. 1 Chr 27:7
the Izrahite; in his **d** were 24,000. 1 Chr 27:8
the Tekoite; in his **d** were 24,000. 1 Chr 27:9
of Ephraim; in his **d** were 24,000. 1 Chr 27:10
the Zerahites; in his **d** were 24,000. 1 Chr 27:11
a Benjaminite; in his **d** were 24,000. 1 Chr 27:12
the Zerahites; in his **d** were 24,000. 1 Chr 27:13
of Ephraim; in his **d** were 24,000. 1 Chr 27:14
of Othniel; in his **d** were 24,000. 1 Chr 27:15
and of the Levites, **d** by division, 2 Chr 31:2
and of the Levites, division by **d**, 2 Chr 31:2
and according to the **d** of the Levites 2 Chr 35:5
named Zechariah, of the **d** of Abijah. Lk 1:5
priest before God when his **d** was on duty, Lk 1:8
on earth? No, I tell you, but rather **d**. Lk 12:51
So there was a **d** among the people over Jn 7:43
signs?” And there was a **d** among them. Jn 9:16
There was again a **d** among the Jews Jn 10:19
that there may be no **d** in the body, 1 Cor 12:25
As for a person who stirs up **d**, after Ti 3:10
piercing to the **d** of soul and of spirit, Heb 4:12

DIVISIONS (32)
the land in seven **d** and bring the Jos 18:6
a description of it by towns in seven **d**. Jos 18:9
And the two **d** of you, which come on 2 Kgs 11:7
the numbers of the **d** of the armed 1 Chr 12:23
them in **d** corresponding to 1 Chr 23:6
The **d** of the sons of Aaron were these. 1 Chr 24:1
As for the **d** of the gatekeepers: of the 1 Chr 26:1
These **d** of the gatekeepers, 1 Chr 26:12
These were the **d** of the gatekeepers 1 Chr 26:19
matters concerning the **d** that came 1 Chr 27:1
the officers of the **d** that served the 1 Chr 28:1
for the **d** of the priests and of the 1 Chr 28:13
And behold the **d** of the priests and 1 Chr 28:21
themselves, without regard to their **d**, 2 Chr 5:11
he appointed the **d** of the priests for 2 Chr 8:14
gatekeepers in their **d** at each gate, 2 Chr 8:14
the priest did not dismiss the **d**. 2 Chr 23:8
in **d** according to the numbers in 2 Chr 26:11
Hezekiah appointed the **d** of the 2 Chr 31:2
brothers, old and young alike, by **d**, 2 Chr 31:15
according to their offices, by their **d**. 2 Chr 31:16
according to their offices, by their **d**. 2 Chr 31:17
to your fathers’ houses by your **d**, 2 Chr 35:4
Levites in their **d** according to the 2 Chr 35:10
the priests in their **d** and the Levites in Ezr 6:18
their divisions and the Levites in their **d**, Ezr 6:18
And certain **d** of the Levites in Judah Neh 11:36
those who cause **d** and create Rom 16:17
and that there be no **d** among you, 1 Cor 1:10
I hear that there are **d** among you. 1 Cor 11:18
fits of anger, rivalries, dissensions, **d**, Gal 5:20
It is these who cause **d**, worldly people, Jude 1:19

DIVORCE (16)
his wife. He may not **d** her all his days. Dt 22:19
her. He may not **d** her all his days. Dt 22:29
writes her a certificate of **d** and puts it in Dt 24:1
writes her a certificate of **d** and puts it in Dt 24:3
“Where is your mother’s certificate of **d**, Is 50:1
I had sent her away with a decree of **d**. Jer 3:8
her to shame, resolved to **d** her quietly. Mt 1:19
wife, let him give her a certificate of **d**.’ Mt 5:31
“Is it lawful to **d** one’s wife for any Mt 19:3
to give a certificate of **d** and to send her Mt 19:7
heart Moses allowed you to **d** your wives, Mt 19:8
“Is it lawful for a man to **d** his wife?” Mk 10:2
to write a certificate of **d** and to send her Mk 10:4
the husband should not **d** his wife. 1 Cor 7:11
to live with him, he should not **d** her. 1 Cor 7:12
to live with her, she should not **d** him. 1 Cor 7:13

DIVORCED (7)
marry a woman **d** from her husband, Lv 21:7
A widow, or a **d** woman, or a woman Lv 21:14
daughter is widowed or **d** and has no Lv 22:13
any vow of a widow or of a **d** woman, Nm 30:9
not marry a widow or a **d** woman, Ezk 44:22
whoever marries a **d** woman commits Mt 5:32
marries a woman **d** from her husband Lk 16:18

DIVORCES (8)
“If a man **d** his wife and she goes from Jer 3:1
“For the man who hates and **d**, says the Mal 2:16
“It was also said, ‘Whoever **d** his wife, let Mt 5:31
I say to you that everyone who **d** his wife, Mt 5:32
whoever **d** his wife, except for sexual Mt 19:9
“Whoever **d** his wife and marries Mk 10:11
and if she **d** her husband and marries Mk 10:12
“Everyone who **d** his wife and marries Lk 16:18

DIVULGING (1)
confessing and **d** their practices. Acts 19:18

DIZAHAB (1)
and Tophel, Laban, Hazeroth, and **D**. Dt 1:1

DOCTRINE (11)
For you say, ‘My **d** is pure, and I am Jb 11:4
contrary to the **d** that you have Rom 16:17
and carried about by every wind of **d**, Eph 4:14
persons not to teach any different **d**, 1 Tm 1:3
whatever else is contrary to sound **d**, 1 Tm 1:10
and of the good **d** that you have 1 Tm 4:6
teaches a different **d** and does not 1 Tm 6:3
give instruction in sound **d** and also to Ti 1:9
for you, teach what accords with sound **d**. Ti 2:1

they may adorn the **d** of God our Savior. Ti 2:10
us leave the elementary **d** of Christ and Heb 6:1

DOCTRINES (2)
teaching as **d** the commandments of Mt 15:9
teaching as **d** the commandments of Mk 7:7

DOCUMENT (6)
of Israel and the **d** of Solomon his 2 Chr 35:4
on the sealed **d** are the names of our Neh 9:38
A copy of the **d** was to be issued as a Est 3:14
establish the injunction and sign the **d**, Dn 6:8
King Darius signed the **d** and injunction. Dn 6:9
Daniel knew that the **d** had been signed, Dn 6:10

DOCUMENTS (1)
of the archives where the **d** were stored. Ezr 6:1

DODAI (1)
D the Ahohite was in charge of the 1 Chr 27:4

DODANIM (1)
Javan: Elishah, Tarshish, Kittim, and **D**. Gn 10:4

DODAVAHU (1)
the son of **D** of Mareshah 2 Chr 20:37

DODO (5)
Israel Tola the son of Puah, son of **D**, Jgs 10:1
mighty men was Eleazar the son of **D**, 2 Sm 23:9
Elhanan the son of **D** of Bethlehem, 2 Sm 23:24
men was Eleazar the son of **D**, 1 Chr 11:12
Elhanan the son of **D** of Bethlehem, 1 Chr 11:26

DOE (4)
"Naphtali is a **d** let loose that bears Gn 49:21
according to The **D** of the Dawn. Ps 22:T
a lovely deer, a graceful **d**. Let her Prv 5:19
Even the **d** in the field forsakes her Jer 14:5

DOEG (6)
His name was **D** the Edomite, the 1 Sm 21:7
Then answered **D** the Edomite, who 1 Sm 22:9
Then the king said to **D**, "You turn 1 Sm 22:18
the priests." And **D** the Edomite 1 Sm 22:18
day, when **D** the Edomite was there, 1 Sm 22:22
A Maskil of David, when **D**, the Edomite, Ps 52:T

DOER (5)
man of Kabzeel, a **d** of great deeds. 2 Sm 23:20
man of Kabzeel, a **d** of great deeds. 1 Chr 11:22
is a hearer of the word and not a **d**, Jas 1:23
no hearer who forgets but a **d** who acts, Jas 1:25
you are not a **d** of the law but a judge. Jas 4:11

DOERS (2)
but the **d** of the law who will be Rom 2:13
But be **d** of the word, and not hearers Jas 1:22

DOG (13)
But not a **d** shall growl against any of Ex 11:7
or the wages of a **d** into the house of the Dt 23:18
laps the water with his tongue, as a **d** laps, Jgs 7:5
Philistine said to David, "Am I a **d**, 1 Sm 17:43
whom do you pursue? After a dead **d**! 1 Sm 24:14
show regard for a dead **d** such as I?" 2 Sm 9:8
should this dead **d** curse my lord 2 Sm 16:9
is your servant, who is but a **d**, 2 Kgs 8:13
precious life from the power of the **d**! Ps 22:20
Like a **d** that returns to his vomit is a Prv 26:11
one who takes a passing **d** by the ears. Prv 26:17
for a living **d** is better than a dead lion. Eccl 9:4
"The **d** returns to its own vomit, and 2 Pt 2:22

DOG'S (2)
and said, "Am I a **d** head of Judah? 2 Sm 3:8
a lamb, like one who breaks a **d** neck; Is 66:3

DOGGED (1)
They **d** our steps so that we could not Lam 4:18

DOGS (26)
in the field; you shall throw it to the **d**. Ex 22:31
who dies in the city the **d** shall eat, 1 Kgs 14:11
who dies in the city the **d** shall eat, 1 Kgs 16:4
"In the place where **d** licked up the 1 Kgs 21:19
of Naboth shall **d** lick your own 1 Kgs 21:19
'The **d** shall eat Jezebel within the 1 Kgs 21:23
who dies in the city the **d** shall eat, 1 Kgs 21:24
and the **d** licked up his blood, 1 Kgs 22:38
And the **d** shall eat Jezebel in the 2 Kgs 9:10
territory of Jezreel the **d** shall eat the 2 Kgs 9:36
disdained to set with the **d** of my flock. Jb 30:1
For **d** encompass me; a company of Ps 22:16
howling like **d** and prowling about the Ps 59:6
howling like **d** and prowling about the Ps 59:14
the tongues of your **d** may have their Ps 68:23
without knowledge; they are all silent **d**; Is 56:10
The **d** have a mighty appetite; they never Is 56:11
the sword to kill, the **d** to tear, and the Jer 15:3
"Do not give **d** what is holy, and do not Mt 7:6
children's bread and throw it to the **d**." Mt 15:26
yet even the **d** eat the crumbs that fall Mt 15:27
children's bread and throw it to the **d**." Mk 7:27
yet even the **d** under the table eat the Mk 7:28
even the **d** came and licked his sores. Lk 16:21
Look out for the **d**, look out for the Phil 3:2
Outside are the **d** and sorcerers and the Rv 22:15

DOING (151)
the LORD by **d** righteousness and Gn 18:19
I have seen all that Laban is **d** to you. Gn 31:12
You have done evil in **d** this.'" Gn 44:5
awesome in glorious deeds, **d** wonders? Ex 15:11
saw all that he was **d** for the people, Ex 18:14
is this that you are **d** for the people? Ex 18:14
to him, "What you are **d** is not good. Ex 18:17
Israel had brought for **d** the work on the Ex 36:3
the craftsmen who were **d** every sort of Ex 36:4
came, each from the task that he was **d**, Ex 36:4
more than enough for **d** the work that Ex 36:5
d unintentionally any one of all the Lv 4:22
sins unintentionally in **d** any one of Lv 4:27
d any of the things that by the LORD'S Lv 5:17
But they did not continue **d** it. Nm 11:25
be dispossessed. Israel is **d** valiantly. Nm 24:18
and by **d** what is evil in the sight of the Dt 4:25
in **d** what was evil in the sight of the LORD Dt 9:18
according to all that we are **d** here today, Dt 12:8
everyone **d** whatever is right in his own Dt 12:8
and **d** what is right in the sight of the Dt 13:18
this law and these statutes, and **d** them, Dt 17:19
the words of this law by **d** them.' Dt 27:26
LORD took delight in **d** you good and Dt 28:63
d to Ai and its king as he had done to Jos 10:1
it was the LORD'S **d** to harden their Jos 11:20
you here? What are you **d** in this place? Jgs 18:3
priest said to them, "What are you **d**?" Jgs 18:18
all that his sons were **d** to all Israel, 1 Sm 2:22
other gods, so they are also **d** to you. 1 Sm 8:8
are these Hebrews **d** here?" And 1 Sm 29:3
in, and to know all that you are **d**." 2 Sm 3:25
himself a name and **d** for them great 2 Sm 7:23
asked how Joab was **d** and how the 2 Sm 11:7
how the people were **d** and how the 2 Sm 11:7
d according to all that I have 1 Kgs 9:4
of Solomon, **d** harm as Hadad did. 1 Kgs 11:25
d what is right in my sight and 1 Kgs 11:33
d only that which was right in my 1 Kgs 14:8
d evil in the sight of the LORD, 1 Kgs 16:19
he said to him, "What are you **d** here, 1 Kgs 19:9
him and said, "What are you **d** here, 1 Kgs 19:13
d what was right in the sight of the 1 Kgs 22:43
to one another, "We are not **d** right. 2 Kgs 7:9
d according to all that I have 2 Chr 7:17
d what was right in the sight of the 2 Chr 20:32
was his counselor in **d** wickedly. 2 Chr 22:3
to your servants they are **d**. 2 Chr 34:16
know where I had gone or what I was **d**, Neh 2:16
"What is this thing that you are **d**? Neh 2:19
Samaria, "What are these feeble Jews **d**? Neh 4:2
"The thing that you are **d** is not good. Neh 5:9
"I am **d** a great work and I cannot come Neh 6:3
is this evil thing that you are **d**, Neh 13:17
Who will say to him, 'What are you **d**?' Jb 9:12
But you are **d** away with the fear of God Jb 15:4
are corrupt, **d** abominable iniquity; Ps 53:1
ships, **d** business on the great waters; Ps 107:23
This is the LORD'S **d**; it is marvelous in Ps 118:23
who rejoice in **d** evil and delight in the Prv 2:14
D wrong is like a joke to a fool, but Prv 10:23
What are you **d**, my son? What are you Prv 31:2
son? What are you **d**, son of my womb? Prv 31:2
What are you **d**, son of my vows? Prv 31:2
done and the toil I had expended in **d** it, Eccl 2:11
for they do not know that they are **d** evil. Eccl 5:1
who may say to him, "What are you **d**?" Eccl 8:4
Behold, I am **d** a new thing; now it Is 43:19
it, and keeps his hand from **d** any evil." Is 56:2
from **d** your pleasure on my holy day, Is 58:13
They are 'wise'—in **d** evil! Jer 4:22
only to go on **d** all these abominations? Jer 7:10
not see what they are **d** in the cities of Jer 7:17
not turn away from **d** good to them. Jer 32:40
I will rejoice in **d** them good, and I will Jer 32:41
my rules by **d** wickedness more than Ezk 5:6
"Son of man, do you see what they are **d**, Ezk 8:6
of the house of Israel are **d** in the dark, Ezk 8:12
house, said to you, 'What are you **d**?' Ezk 12:9
profaned by your own **d** in the sight of Ezk 22:16
in the statutes of life, not **d** injustice, Ezk 33:15
their hearts shall be bent on **d** evil. Dn 11:27
For I am **d** a work in your days that you Hab 1:5
what more are you **d** than others? Mt 5:47
left hand know what your right hand is **d**, Mt 6:3
your disciples are **d** what is not lawful to Mt 12:2
of them, 'Friend, I am **d** you no wrong. Mt 20:13
what authority are you **d** these things, Mt 21:23
this was the Lord's **d**, and it is Mt 21:42
master will find so **d** when he comes. Mt 24:46
why are they **d** what is not lawful on the Mk 2:24
the great crowd heard all that he was **d**, Mk 3:8
says to you, 'Why are you **d** this?' Mk 11:3
there said to them, "What are you **d**, Mk 11:5
what authority are you **d** these things, Mk 11:28
this was the Lord's **d**, and it is Mk 12:11
"Why are you **d** what is not lawful to do Lk 6:2
all marveling at everything he was **d**, Lk 9:43
master will find so **d** when he comes. Lk 12:43
what they had gained by **d** business. Lk 19:15
sign do you show us for **d** these things?" Jn 2:18
when they saw the signs that he was **d**. Jn 2:23
because he was **d** these things on the Jn 5:16
but only what he sees the Father **d**. Jn 5:19
and shows him all that he himself is **d**. Jn 5:20
accomplish, the very works that I am **d**, Jn 5:36
saw the signs that he was **d** on the sick. Jn 6:2
must we do, to be **d** the works of God?" Jn 6:28
disciples also may see the works you are **d**. Jn 7:3
you would be **d** what Abraham did, Jn 8:39
You are **d** what your father did." They Jn 8:41
If I am not **d** the works of my Father, Jn 10:37
"What I am **d** you do not understand Jn 13:7
does not know what his master is **d**; Jn 15:15
him, "If this man were not **d** evil, Jn 18:30
was **d** great wonders and signs among Acts 6:8
He went about **d** good and healing all Acts 10:38
for I am **d** a work in your days, a Acts 13:41
"Men, why are you **d** these things? Acts 14:15
And this she kept **d** for many days. Acts 16:18
God was **d** extraordinary miracles Acts 19:11
high priest named Sceva were **d** this. Acts 19:14
Paul answered, "What are you **d**, Acts 21:13
While I was **d** this, they found me Acts 24:18
"This man is **d** nothing to deserve Acts 26:31
evil I do not want is what I keep on **d**. Rom 7:19
for by so **d** you will heap burning Rom 12:20
you, for he is **d** the work of the Lord, 1 Cor 16:10
So now finish **d** it as well, so that your 2 Cor 8:11
to keep you from **d** the things you want Gal 5:17
And let us not grow weary of **d** good, for Gal 6:9
And this is not your own **d**; it is the gift Eph 2:8
d honest work with his own hands, Eph 4:28
Christ, **d** the will of God from the heart, Eph 6:6
may know how I am and what I am **d**, Eph 6:21
and hostile in mind, **d** evil deeds, Col 1:21
and to please God, just as you are **d**, 1 Thes 4:1
is what you are **d** to all the brothers 1 Thes 4:10
one another up, just as you are **d**. 1 Thes 5:11
that you are **d** and will do the things 2 Thes 3:4
do not grow weary in **d** good. 2 Thes 3:13
for by so **d** you will save both 1 Tm 4:16
d nothing from partiality. 1 Tm 5:21
doer who acts, he will be blessed in his **d**. Jas 1:25
neighbor as yourself," you are **d** well. Jas 2:8
that by **d** good you should put to 1 Pt 2:15
For it is better to suffer for **d** good, if 1 Pt 3:17
should be God's will, than for **d** evil. 1 Pt 3:17
is past suffices for **d** what the Gentiles 1 Pt 4:3
souls to a faithful Creator while **d** good. 1 Pt 4:19
if I come, I will bring up what he is **d**, 3 Jn 1:10

DOLE (1)
single oven and shall **d** out your bread Lv 26:26

DOMAIN (1)
delivered us from the **d** of darkness and Col 1:13

DOMINEERING (1)
not **d** over those in your charge, but 1 Pt 5:3

DOMINION (41)
And let them have **d** over the fish of the Gn 1:26
and subdue it and have **d** over the fish of Gn 1:28
Jacob shall exercise **d** and destroy the Nm 24:19
For he had **d** over all the region west 1 Kgs 4:24
Lebanon, and in all the land of his **d**. 1 Kgs 9:19
Lebanon, and in all the land of his **d**. 2 Chr 8:6
enemies, so that they had **d** over them. Neh 9:28
"**D** and fear are with God; he makes peace Jb 25:2
You have given him **d** over the works of Ps 8:6
sins; let them not have **d** over me! Ps 19:13
May he have **d** from sea to sea, and from Ps 72:8
all his works, in all places of his **d**. Ps 103:22
became his sanctuary, Israel his **d**. Ps 114:2
and let no iniquity get **d** over me. Ps 119:133
and your **d** endures throughout all Ps 145:13
the earth under his **d** and all the peoples Jer 34:1
deputies, and every land under their **d**. Jer 51:28
and his **d** endures from generation to Dn 4:3
and your **d** to the ends of the earth. Dn 4:22
for his **d** is an everlasting dominion, Dn 4:34
for his dominion is an everlasting **d**, Dn 4:34
in all my royal **d** people are to tremble Dn 6:26
destroyed, and his **d** shall be to the end. Dn 6:26
had four heads, and **d** was given to it. Dn 7:6
of the beasts, their **d** was taken away, Dn 7:12

And to him was given **d** and glory and a Dn 7:14
his **d** is an everlasting dominion, which Dn 7:14
his dominion is an everlasting **d**, which Dn 7:14
and his **d** shall be taken away, Dn 7:26
kingdom and the **d** and the greatness Dn 7:27
who shall rule with great **d** and do as he Dn 11:3
shall it come, the former **d** shall come, Mi 4:8
again; death no longer has **d** over him. Rom 6:9
For sin will have no **d** over you, since Rom 6:14
all rule and authority and power and **d**, Eph 1:21
see. To him be honor and eternal **d**. 1 Tm 6:16
belong glory and **d** forever and ever. 1 Pt 4:11
To him be the **d** forever and ever. 1 Pt 5:11
be glory, majesty, **d**, and authority, Jude 1:25
to him be glory and **d** forever and ever. Rv 1:6
great city that has **d** over the kings of Rv 17:18

DOMINIONS (2)
and all **d** shall serve and obey them.' Dn 7:27
whether thrones or **d** or rulers or Col 1:16

DONATIONS (2)
all the holy **d** of the people of Israel, Nm 5:9
Each one shall keep his holy **d**: Nm 5:10

DONE (514)
day God finished his work that he had **d**, Gn 2:2
day from all his work that he had **d**. Gn 2:2
all his work that he had **d** in creation. Gn 2:3
this that you have **d**?" The woman said, Gn 3:13
to the serpent, "Because you have **d** this, Gn 3:14
And the LORD said, "What have you **d**? Gn 4:10
down every living creature as I have **d**. Gn 8:21
what his youngest son had **d** to him, Gn 9:24
said, "What is this you have **d** to me? Gn 12:18
"May the wrong **d** to me be on you! Gn 16:5
they have **d** altogether according Gn 18:21
innocence of my hands I have **d** this." Gn 20:5
know that you have **d** this in the Gn 20:6
said to him, "What have you **d** to us? Gn 20:9
You have **d** to me things that ought not Gn 20:9
to me things that ought not to be **d**." Gn 20:9
"I do not know who has **d** this thing; Gn 21:26
because you have **d** this and have not Gn 22:16
told Isaac all the things that he had **d**. Gn 24:66
said, "What is this you have **d** to us? Gn 26:10
you and have **d** to you nothing Gn 26:29
I have **d** as you told me; now sit up and Gn 27:19
and he forgets what you have **d** to him. Gn 27:45
you until I have **d** what I have Gn 28:15
"What is this you have **d** to me? Gn 29:25
said, "It is not so **d** in our country, Gn 29:26
said to Jacob, "What have you **d**, Gn 31:26
farewell? Now you have **d** foolishly. Gn 31:28
because he had **d** an outrageous thing Gn 34:7
for such a thing must not be **d**. Gn 34:7
Whatever was **d** there, he was the one Gn 39:22
here also I have **d** nothing that they Gn 40:15
for the journey. This was **d** for them. Gn 42:25
"What is this that God has **d** to us?" Gn 42:28
You have **d** evil in doing this.'" Gn 44:5
"What deed is this that you have **d**? Gn 44:15
and said to them, "Why have you **d** this, Ex 1:18
distance to know what would be **d** to him. Ex 2:4
and what has been **d** to you in Egypt, Ex 3:16
"Why have you not **d** all your task of Ex 5:14
LORD, why have you **d** evil to this people? Ex 5:22
your name, he has **d** evil to this people, Ex 5:23
and what signs I have **d** among them, Ex 10:2
No work shall be **d** on those days. Ex 12:16
of Israel had also **d** as Moses told them, Ex 12:35
and they said, "What is this we have **d**, Ex 14:5
What have you **d** to us in bringing us Ex 14:11
of all that God had **d** for Moses and for Ex 18:1
all that the LORD had **d** to Pharaoh and to Ex 18:8
all the good that the LORD had **d** to Israel, Ex 18:9
Six days shall work be **d**, but the Ex 31:15
Six days work shall be **d**, but on the Ex 35:2
by Moses to be **d** brought it as a Ex 35:29
every sort of work **d** by an engraver or Ex 35:35
the people of Israel had **d** all the work. Ex 39:42
all the work, and behold, they had **d** it; Ex 39:43
LORD had commanded, so had they **d** it. Ex 39:43
commandments about things not to be **d**, Lv 4:2
commandments ought not to be **d**, Lv 4:13
of the LORD his God ought not to be **d**, Lv 4:22
commandments ought not to be **d**, Lv 4:27
for what he has **d** amiss in the holy Lv 5:16
commandments ought not to be **d**, Lv 5:17
that the LORD has commanded to be **d**." Lv 8:5
As has been **d** today, the LORD has Lv 8:34
commanded to be **d** to make atonement Lv 8:34
"Six days shall work be **d**, but on the Lv 23:3
as he has **d** it shall be done to him, Lv 24:19
as he has done it shall be **d** to him, Lv 24:19
that needs to be **d** with regard to them. Nm 4:26
because we have **d** foolishly and have Nm 12:11
the signs that I have **d** among them? Nm 14:11
"Thus it shall be **d** for each bull or Nm 15:11
if it was **d** unintentionally without the Nm 15:24
made clear what should be **d** to him. Nm 15:34
all that Israel had **d** to the Amorites. Nm 22:2
to Balaam, "What have I **d** to you, Nm 22:28
to Balaam, "What have you **d** to me? Nm 23:11
you have **d** nothing but bless them." Nm 23:11
the generation that had **d** evil in the Nm 32:13
LORD your God has **d** to these two kings. Dt 3:21
who has **d** for you these great and Dt 10:21
LORD hates they have **d** for their gods, Dt 12:31
abomination has been **d** among you, Dt 13:14
an abomination has been **d** in Israel, Dt 17:4
or woman who has **d** this evil thing, Dt 17:5
practices that they have **d** for their gods, Dt 20:18
because she has **d** an outrageous thing Dt 22:21
'So shall it be **d** to the man who does not Dt 25:9
I have **d** according to all that you have Dt 26:14
'Why has the LORD **d** thus to this land? Dt 29:24
because of all the evil that they have **d**, Dt 31:18
because he has **d** an outrageous thing Jos 7:15
And tell me now what you have **d**; do not Jos 7:19
heard what Joshua had **d** to Jericho and to Jos 9:3
its king as he had **d** to Jericho and its Jos 10:1
just as he had **d** to the king of Jos 10:28
its king as he had **d** to the king of Jos 10:30
person in it, as he had **d** to Libnah. Jos 10:32
that day, as he had **d** to Lachish. Jos 10:35
none remaining, as he had **d** to Eglon, Jos 10:37
Just as he had **d** to Hebron and to Jos 10:39
LORD your God has **d** to all these nations Jos 23:3
your God just as you have **d** to this day. Jos 23:8
you, after having **d** you good." Jos 24:20
As I have **d**, so God has repaid me." And Jgs 1:7
my voice. What is this you have **d**? Jgs 2:2
great work that the LORD had **d** for Israel. Jgs 2:7
LORD or the work that he had **d** for Israel. Jgs 2:10
because they had **d** what was evil in the Jgs 3:12
"Who has **d** this thing?" And after they Jgs 6:29
the son of Joash has **d** this thing." Jgs 6:29
him, "What is this that you have **d** to us, Jgs 8:1
"What have I **d** now in comparison with Jgs 8:2
for all the good that he had **d** to Israel. Jgs 8:35
and his house and have **d** to him as his Jgs 9:16
that the violence **d** to the seventy sons of Jgs 9:24
seen me do, hurry and do as I have **d**." Jgs 9:48
her father, "Let this thing be **d** for me: Jgs 11:37
his father or his mother what he had **d**. Jgs 14:6
said, "Who has **d** this?" And they said, Jgs 15:6
is this that you have **d** to us?" And he Jgs 15:11
"As they did to me, so have I **d** to them." Jgs 15:11
that you have **d** for your mother-in-law Ru 2:11
The LORD repay you for what you have **d**, Ru 2:12
told her all that the man had **d** for her, Ru 3:16
it is he who has **d** us this great harm, 1 Sm 6:9
to all the deeds that they have **d**, 1 Sm 8:8
so shall it be **d** to his oxen!" Then the 1 Sm 11:7
which you have **d** in the sight of the 1 Sm 12:17
not be afraid; you have **d** all this evil. 1 Sm 12:20
what great things he has **d** for you. 1 Sm 12:24
"What have you **d**?" And Saul said, 1 Sm 13:11
said to Saul, "You have **d** foolishly. 1 Sm 13:13
what you have **d**." And Jonathan told 1 Sm 14:43
"What shall be **d** for the man who 1 Sm 17:26
"So shall it be **d** to the man who kills 1 Sm 17:27
David said, "What have I **d** now? 1 Sm 17:29
told him all that Saul had **d** to him. 1 Sm 19:18
said before Jonathan, "What have I **d**? 1 Sm 20:1
he be put to death? What has he **d**?" 1 Sm 20:32
for what you have **d** to me this day. 1 Sm 24:19
when the LORD has **d** to my lord 1 Sm 25:30
thing that you have **d** is not good. 1 Sm 26:16
after his servant? For what have I **d**? 1 Sm 26:18
'So David has **d**.'" Such was his 1 Sm 27:11
"Surely you know what Saul has **d**, 1 Sm 28:9
The LORD has **d** to you as he spoke by 1 Sm 28:17
therefore the LORD has **d** this thing to 1 Sm 28:18
said to Achish, "But what have I **d**? 1 Sm 29:8
what the Philistines had **d** to Saul, 1 Sm 31:11
to you because you have **d** this thing. 2 Sm 2:6
the king and said, "What have you **d**? 2 Sm 3:24
that David had **d** displeased the LORD. 2 Sm 11:27
the man who has **d** this deserves to 2 Sm 12:5
"What is this thing that you have **d**? 2 Sm 12:21
for such a thing is not **d** in Israel; 2 Sm 13:12
shall say, 'Why have you **d** so?'" 2 Sm 16:10
LORD will look on the wrong **d** to me, 2 Sm 16:12
Aiah, the concubine of Saul, had **d**, 2 Sm 21:11
have sinned greatly in what I have **d**. 2 Sm 24:10
servant, for I have **d** very foolishly." 2 Sm 24:10
I have sinned, and I have **d** wickedly. 2 Sm 24:17
But these sheep, what have they **d**? 2 Sm 24:17
"Why have you **d** thus and so?" He 1 Kgs 1:6
'Why has the LORD **d** thus to this land 1 Kgs 9:8
the LORD, as David his father had **d**. 1 Kgs 11:6
man of God had **d** that day in Bethel. 1 Kgs 13:11
but you have **d** evil above all who 1 Kgs 14:9
than all that their fathers had **d**. 1 Kgs 14:22
the LORD, as David his father had **d**. 1 Kgs 15:11
and that I have **d** all these things at 1 Kgs 18:36
told Jezebel all that Elijah had **d**, 1 Kgs 19:1
again, for what have I **d** to you?" 1 Kgs 19:20
after idols, as the Amorites had **d**, 1 Kgs 21:26
in every way that his father had **d**. 1 Kgs 22:53
trouble for us; what is to be **d** for you? 2 Kgs 4:13
then is to be **d** for her?" Gehazi 2 Kgs 4:14
tell you what the Syrians have **d** to us. 2 Kgs 7:12
all the great things that Elisha has **d**." 2 Kgs 8:4
of Israel, as the house of Ahab had **d**, 2 Kgs 8:18
the LORD, as the house of Ahab had **d**, 2 Kgs 8:27
for the LORD has **d** what he said by 2 Kgs 10:10
"Because you have **d** well in 2 Kgs 10:30
and have **d** to the house of Ahab 2 Kgs 10:30
in all things as Joash his father had **d**. 2 Kgs 14:3
to all that his father Amaziah had **d**. 2 Kgs 15:3
sight of the LORD, as his fathers had **d**. 2 Kgs 15:9
to all that his father Uzziah had **d**. 2 Kgs 15:34
his God, as his father David had **d**, 2 Kgs 16:2
of Assyria, as he had **d** year by year. 2 Kgs 17:4
to all that David his father had **d**. 2 Kgs 18:3
at Lachish, saying, "I have **d** wrong; 2 Kgs 18:14
kings of Assyria have **d** to all lands, 2 Kgs 19:11
and have **d** what is good in your 2 Kgs 20:3
as Ahab king of Israel had **d**, 2 Kgs 21:3
the nations had **d** whom the LORD 2 Kgs 21:9
and has **d** things more 2 Kgs 21:11
because they have **d** what is evil in 2 Kgs 21:15
LORD, as Manasseh his father had **d**. 2 Kgs 21:20
that you have **d** against the altar 2 Kgs 23:17
to all that he had **d** at Bethel. 2 Kgs 23:19
to all that his fathers had **d**. 2 Kgs 23:32
to all that his fathers had **d**. 2 Kgs 23:37
according to all that he had **d**, 2 Kgs 24:3
according to all that his father had **d**. 2 Kgs 24:9
to all that Jehoiakim had **d**. 2 Kgs 24:19
all that the Philistines had **d** to Saul, 1 Chr 10:11
the wondrous works that he has **d**, 1 Chr 16:12
heart, you have **d** all this greatness, 1 Chr 17:19
greatly in that I have **d** this thing. 1 Chr 21:8
I who have sinned and **d** great evil. 1 Chr 21:17
But these sheep, what have they **d**? 1 Chr 21:17
the work to be **d** according to the 1 Chr 28:19
for all the work to be **d** by craftsmen, 1 Chr 29:5
'Why has the LORD **d** thus to this land 2 Chr 7:21
You have **d** foolishly in this, for from 2 Chr 16:9
of Israel, as the house of Ahab had **d**, 2 Chr 21:6
the LORD, as the house of Ahab had **d**. 2 Chr 22:4
because he had **d** good in Israel, 2 Chr 24:16
because you have **d** this and have 2 Chr 25:16
to all that his father Amaziah had **d**. 2 Chr 26:4
sanctuary, for you have **d** wrong, 2 Chr 26:18
to all that his father Uzziah had **d**, 2 Chr 27:2
of the LORD, as his father David had **d**, 2 Chr 28:1
to all that David his father had **d**. 2 Chr 29:2
unfaithful and have **d** what was evil 2 Chr 29:6
and my fathers have **d** to all the 2 Chr 32:13
according to the benefit **d** to him, 2 Chr 32:25
the sign that had been **d** in the land, 2 Chr 32:31
LORD, as Manasseh his father had **d**. 2 Chr 33:22
a decree; let it be **d** with all diligence." Ezr 6:12
of you, let it be **d** with all diligence, Ezr 7:21
let it be **d** in full for the house of the God Ezr 7:23
After these things had been **d**, the Ezr 9:1
and let it be **d** according to the Law. Ezr 10:3
God, all that I have **d** for this people. Neh 5:19
"No such things as you say have been **d**, Neh 6:8
the work, and it will not be **d**." But now, Neh 6:9
day the people of Israel had not **d** so. Neh 8:17
the evil that Eliashib had **d** for Tobiah, Neh 13:7
deeds that I have **d** for the house of Neh 13:14
the law, what is to be **d** to Queen Vashti, Est 1:15
the king has Queen Vashti **d** wrong, Est 1:16
and what she had **d** and what had been Est 2:1
Mordecai learned all that had been **d**, Est 4:1
him said, "Nothing has been **d** for him." Est 6:3
"What should be **d** to the man whom the Est 6:6
'Thus shall it be **d** to the man whom the Est 6:9
"Thus shall it be **d** to the man whom Est 6:11
What then have they **d** in the rest of the Est 9:12
So the king commanded this to be **d**. A Est 9:14
Please turn; let no injustice be **d**. Turn Jb 6:29
that the hand of the LORD has **d** this? Jb 12:9
and who repays him for what he has **d**? Jb 21:31
if I have **d** iniquity, I will do it no more'? Jb 34:32
or who can say, 'You have **d** wrong'? Jb 36:23
O LORD my God, if I have **d** this, if there is Ps 7:3
to a people yet unborn, that he has **d** it. Ps 22:31
and all his work is **d** in faithfulness. Ps 33:4
my mouth, for it is you who have **d** it. Ps 39:9

These things you have **d**, and I have	Ps 50:21
have I sinned and **d** what is evil in your	Ps 51:4
thank you forever, because you have **d** it.	Ps 52:9
about and ponder what he has **d**.	Ps 64:9
Come and see what God has **d**: he is	Ps 66:5
and I will tell what he has **d** for my soul.	Ps 66:16
the wrongs I have **d** are not hidden from	Ps 69:5
You who have **d** great things, O God,	Ps 71:19
his might, and the wonders that he has **d**.	Ps 78:4
new song, for he has **d** marvelous things!	Ps 98:1
the wondrous works that he has **d**,	Ps 105:5
iniquity; we have **d** wickedness.	Ps 106:6
who had **d** great things in Egypt,	Ps 106:21
is your hand; you, O LORD, have **d** it!	Ps 109:27
I have **d** what is just and right; do not	Ps 119:121
to you, and what more shall be **d** to you,	Ps 120:3
"The LORD has **d** great things for them."	Ps 126:2
The LORD has **d** great things for us; we	Ps 126:3
repays you with what you have **d** to us!	Ps 137:8
of old; I meditate on all that you have **d**;	Ps 143:5
no reason, when he has **d** you no harm.	Prv 3:30
cannot sleep unless they have **d** wrong;	Prv 4:16
When justice is **d**, it is a joy to the	Prv 21:15
say, "I will do to him as he has **d** to me;	Prv 24:29
pay the man back for what he has **d**."	Prv 24:29
mouth and says, "I have **d** no wrong."	Prv 30:20
"Many women have **d** excellently, but	Prv 31:29
and what has been **d** is what will be	Eccl 1:9
what has been done is what will be **d**,	Eccl 1:9
by wisdom all that is **d** under heaven.	Eccl 1:13
everything that is **d** under the sun,	Eccl 1:14
all that my hands had **d** and the toil I	Eccl 2:11
king? Only what has already been **d**.	Eccl 2:12
because what is **d** under the sun was	Eccl 2:17
what God has **d** from the beginning	Eccl 3:11
God has **d** it, so that people fear before	Eccl 3:14
oppressions that are **d** under the sun.	Eccl 4:1
the evil deeds that are **d** under the sun.	Eccl 4:3
my heart to all that is **d** under the sun,	Eccl 8:9
the city where they had **d** such things.	Eccl 8:10
to see the business that is **d** on earth,	Eccl 8:16
out the work that is **d** under the sun.	Eccl 8:17
is an evil in all that is **d** under the sun,	Eccl 9:3
share in all that is **d** under the sun.	Eccl 9:6
hands have dealt out shall be **d** to him.	Is 3:11
do for my vineyard, that I have not **d** in it?	Is 5:4
her idols as I have **d** to Samaria and her	Is 10:11
"By the strength of my hand I have **d** it,	Is 10:13
to the LORD, for he has **d** gloriously;	Is 12:5
the gleaning when the grape harvest is **d**.	Is 24:13
name, for you have **d** wonderful things,	Is 25:1
for us; you have **d** for us all our works.	Is 26:12
Hear, you who are far off, what I have **d**;	Is 33:13
the kings of Assyria have **d** to all lands,	Is 37:11
and have **d** what is good in your sight."	Is 38:3
spoken to me, and he himself has **d** it.	Is 38:15
Who has performed and **d** this, calling	Is 41:4
that the hand of the LORD has **d** this,	Is 41:20
Sing, O heavens, for the LORD has **d** it;	Is 44:23
and from ancient times things not yet **d**,	Is 46:10
who have **d** business with you from	Is 47:15
his death, although he had **d** no violence,	Is 53:9
know what you have **d**—a restless	Jer 2:23
but you have **d** all the evil that you	Jer 3:5
'After she has **d** all this she will return to	Jer 3:7
not in them. Thus shall it be **d** to them!'"	Jer 5:13
the LORD our God **d** all these things to	Jer 5:19
because you have **d** all these things,	Jer 7:13
the sons of Judah have **d** evil in my sight,	Jer 7:30
relents of his evil, saying, 'What have I **d**?'	Jer 8:6
house, when she has **d** many vile deeds?	Jer 11:15
of Israel and the house of Judah have **d**,	Jer 11:17
because you have **d** worse than your	Jer 16:12
I not do with you as this potter has **d**?	Jer 18:6
The virgin Israel has **d** a very horrible	Jer 18:13
because they have **d** an outrageous	Jer 29:23
flagrant, I have **d** these things to you.	Jer 30:15
of Israel for all that they have **d**,	Jer 31:37
of Judah have **d** nothing but evil	Jer 32:30
of Israel have **d** nothing but provoke	Jer 32:30
and have obeyed and **d** all that Jonadab	Jer 35:10
all his precepts and **d** all that he	Jer 35:18
"What wrong have I **d** to you or your	Jer 37:18
these men have **d** evil in all that they did	Jer 38:9
brought it about, and has **d** as he said.	Jer 40:3
Ishmael the son of Nethaniah had **d**,	Jer 41:11
on her; do to her as she has **d**.	Jer 50:15
to her according to all that she has **d**.	Jer 50:29
has both planned and **d** what he spoke	Jer 51:12
for all the evil that they have **d** in Zion,	Jer 51:24
The violence **d** to me and to my	Jer 51:35
according to all that Jehoiakim had **d**.	Jer 52:2
they are glad that you have **d** it.	Lam 1:21
The LORD has **d** what he purposed; he	Lam 2:17
You have seen the wrong **d** to me, O	Lam 3:59
deeds that he has **d** shall not be	Ezk 3:20
will do with you what I have never yet **d**,	Ezk 5:9
"I have **d** as you commanded me."	Ezk 9:11
as I have **d**, so shall it be done to them.	Ezk 12:11
as I have done, so shall it be **d** to them.	Ezk 12:11
that I have not **d** without cause all	Ezk 14:23
without cause all that I have **d** in it,	Ezk 14:23
her daughters have not **d** as you and	Ezk 16:48
as you and your daughters have **d**.	Ezk 16:48
and be ashamed of all that you have **d**,	Ezk 16:54
I will deal with you as you have **d**, you	Ezk 16:59
I atone for you for all that you have **d**,	Ezk 16:63
He has **d** all these abominations; he	Ezk 18:13
sees all the sins that his father has **d**;	Ezk 18:14
When the son has **d** what is just and	Ezk 18:19
that he has **d** he shall live.	Ezk 18:22
that he has **d** shall be remembered;	Ezk 18:24
the injustice that he has **d** he shall die.	Ezk 18:26
Her priests have **d** violence to my law	Ezk 22:26
Moreover, this they have **d** to me: they	Ezk 23:38
not commit lewdness as you have **d**.	Ezk 23:48
And you shall do as I have **d**; you shall	Ezk 24:22
to all that he has **d** you shall do.	Ezk 24:24
his injustice that he has **d** he shall die.	Ezk 33:13
He has **d** what is just and right; he	Ezk 33:16
are ashamed of all that they have **d**,	Ezk 43:11
its service and all that is to be **d** in it.	Ezk 44:14
that the Most High God has **d** for me.	Dn 4:2
hand or say to him, "What have you **d**?"	Dn 4:35
before his God, as he had **d** previously.	Dn 6:10
before you, O king, I have **d** no harm."	Dn 6:22
we have sinned and **d** wrong and acted	Dn 9:5
there has not been **d** anything like what	Dn 9:12
like what has been **d** against Jerusalem.	Dn 9:12
righteous in all the works that he has **d**,	Dn 9:14
we have sinned, we have **d** wickedly.	Dn 9:15
fathers nor his fathers' fathers have **d**,	Dn 11:24
for what is decreed shall be **d**.	Dn 11:36
Thus it shall be **d** to you, O Bethel,	Hos 10:15
of him will rise, for he has **d** great things.	Jl 2:20
rejoice, for the LORD has **d** great things!	Jl 2:21
for the violence **d** to the people of Judah,	Jl 3:19
come to a city, unless the LORD has **d** it?	Am 3:6
of the violence **d** to your brother	Ob 1:10
As you have **d**, it shall be done to you;	Ob 1:15
As you have done, it shall be **d** to you;	Ob 1:15
this that you have **d**!" For the men	Jon 1:10
you, O LORD, have **d** as it pleased you."	Jon 1:14
"O my people, what have I **d** to you? How	Mi 6:3
The violence **d** to Lebanon will	Hab 2:17
month, as I have **d** for so many years?"	Zec 7:3
Your kingdom come, your will be **d**, on	Mt 6:10
let it be **d** for you as you have believed."	Mt 8:13
"According to your faith be it **d** to you."	Mt 9:29
most of his mighty works had been **d**,	Mt 11:20
if the mighty works **d** in you had been	Mt 11:21
in you had been **d** in Tyre and Sidon,	Mt 11:21
if the mighty works **d** in you had been	Mt 11:23
done in you had been **d** in Sodom,	Mt 11:23
He said to them, 'An enemy has **d** this.'	Mt 13:28
Be it **d** for you as you desire." And her	Mt 15:28
person according to what he has **d**.	Mt 16:27
it will be **d** for them by my Father in	Mt 18:19
only do what has been **d** to the fig tree,	Mt 21:21
These you ought to have **d**, without	Mt 23:23
His master said to him, 'Well **d**, good	Mt 25:21
His master said to him, 'Well **d**, good	Mt 25:23
For she has **d** a beautiful thing to me.	Mt 26:10
she has **d** it to prepare me for burial.	Mt 26:12
what she has **d** will also be told in	Mt 26:13
pass unless I drink it, your will be **d**."	Mt 26:42
what evil has he **d**?" But they shouted	Mt 27:23
them how much the Lord has **d** for you,	Mk 5:19
how much Jesus had **d** for him,	Mk 5:20
he looked around to see who had **d** it.	Mk 5:32
are such mighty works **d** by his hands?	Mk 6:2
told him all that they had **d** and taught.	Mk 6:30
saying, "He has **d** all things well.	Mk 7:37
will come to pass, it will be **d** for him.	Mk 11:23
her? She has **d** a beautiful thing to me.	Mk 14:6
She has **d** what she could; she has	Mk 14:8
what she has **d** will be told in memory	Mk 14:9
what evil has he **d**?" But they shouted	Mk 15:14
"Thus the Lord has **d** for me in the days	Lk 1:25
who is mighty has **d** great things for me,	Lk 1:49
for all the evil things that Herod had **d**,	Lk 3:19
out of him, having **d** him no harm.	Lk 4:35
And when they had **d** this, they enclosed a	Lk 5:6
how much God has **d** for you." And he	Lk 8:39
city how much Jesus had **d** for him.	Lk 8:39
the apostles told him all that they had **d**.	Lk 9:10
if the mighty works **d** in you had been	Lk 10:13
in you had been **d** in Tyre and Sidon,	Lk 10:13
These you ought to have **d**, without	Lk 11:42
six days in which work ought to be **d**.	Lk 13:14
the glorious things that were **d** by him.	Lk 13:17
'Sir, what you commanded has been **d**,	Lk 14:22
when you have **d** all that you were	Lk 17:10
we have only **d** what was our duty.'"	Lk 17:10
And he said to him, 'Well **d**, good	Lk 19:17
not my will, but yours, be **d**."	Lk 22:42
was hoping to see some sign **d** by him.	Lk 23:8
deserving death has been **d** by him.	Lk 23:15
said to them, "Why, what evil has he **d**?	Lk 23:22
but this man has **d** nothing wrong."	Lk 23:41
seen all that he had **d** in Jerusalem at the	Jn 4:45
those who have **d** good to the	Jn 5:29
and those who have **d** evil to the	Jn 5:29
the people saw the sign that he had **d**,	Jn 6:14
he do more signs than this man has **d**?"	Jn 7:31
and told them what Jesus had **d**.	Jn 11:46
about him and had been **d** to him.	Jn 12:16
was that they heard he had **d** this sign.	Jn 12:18
Though he had **d** so many signs before	Jn 12:37
you understand what I have **d** to you?	Jn 13:12
also should do just as I have **d** to you.	Jn 13:15
you wish, and it will be **d** for you.	Jn 15:7
If I had not **d** among them the works	Jn 15:24
you over to me. What have you **d**?"	Jn 18:35
signs were being **d** through the	Acts 2:43
concerning a good deed **d** to a crippled	Acts 4:9
wonders were regularly **d** among the	Acts 5:12
much evil he has **d** to your saints at	Acts 9:13
that what was being **d** by the angel	Acts 12:9
and wonders to be **d** by their hands.	Acts 14:3
the crowds saw what Paul had **d**,	Acts 14:11
all that God had **d** with them,	Acts 14:27
declared all that God had **d** with them.	Acts 15:4
wonders God had **d** through them	Acts 15:12
said, "Let the will of the Lord be **d**."	Acts 21:14
that God had **d** among the Gentiles	Acts 21:19
What then is to be **d**? They will	Acts 21:22
who he was and what he had **d**.	Acts 21:33
To the Jews I have **d** no wrong, as you	Acts 25:10
that he had **d** nothing deserving	Acts 25:25
for this has not been **d** in a corner.	Acts 26:26
though I had **d** nothing against our	Acts 28:17
mind to do what ought not to be **d**.	Rom 1:28
For God has **d** what the law, weakened	Rom 8:3
born and had **d** nothing either good	Rom 9:11
test what sort of work each one has **d**.	1 Cor 3:13
Let him who has **d** this be removed	1 Cor 5:2
Let all things be **d** for building up.	1 Cor 14:26
things should be **d** decently and in	1 Cor 14:40
Let all that you do be **d** in love.	1 Cor 16:14
is due for what he has **d** in the body,	2 Cor 5:10
of work already **d** in another's area	2 Cor 10:16
in the evil day, and having **d** all,	Eph 6:13
be paid back for the wrong he has **d**,	Col 3:25
not because of works **d** by us in	Ti 3:5
that when you have **d** the will of God	Heb 10:36
and the works that are **d** on it will be	2 Pt 3:10
from the throne, saying, "It is **d**!"	Rv 16:17
in its presence had **d** the signs by	Rv 19:20
books, according to what they had **d**.	Rv 20:12
of them, according to what they had **d**.	Rv 20:13
And he said to me, "It is **d**! I am the	Rv 21:6
me, to repay everyone for what he has **d**.	Rv 22:12

DONKEY (82)

He shall be a wild **d** of a man, his hand	Gn 16:12
rose early in the morning, saddled his **d**,	Gn 22:3
to his young men, "Stay here with the **d**;	Gn 22:5
sack to give his **d** fodder at the lodging	Gn 42:27
clothes, and every man loaded his **d**,	Gn 44:13
"Issachar is a strong **d**, crouching	Gn 49:14
and his sons and had them ride on a **d**,	Ex 4:20
Every firstborn of a **d** you shall redeem	Ex 13:13
or his female servant, or his ox, or his **d**,	Ex 20:17
cover it, and an ox or a **d** falls into it,	Ex 21:33
whether it is an ox or a **d** or a sheep,	Ex 22:4
of trust, whether it is for an ox, for a **d**,	Ex 22:9
gives to his neighbor a **d** or an ox or a	Ex 22:10
your enemy's ox or his **d** going astray,	Ex 23:4
If you see the **d** of one who hates you	Ex 23:5
that your ox and your **d** may have rest,	Ex 23:12
The firstborn of a **d** you shall redeem	Ex 34:20
I have not taken one **d** from them, and	Nm 16:15
and saddled his **d** and went with	Nm 22:21
Now he was riding on the **d**, and his	Nm 22:22
And the **d** saw the angel of the LORD	Nm 22:23
And the **d** turned aside out of the road	Nm 22:23
And Balaam struck the **d**, to turn her	Nm 22:23
And when the **d** saw the angel of the	Nm 22:25
When the **d** saw the angel of the LORD,	Nm 22:27
and he struck the **d** with his staff.	Nm 22:27
the LORD opened the mouth of the **d**,	Nm 22:28
And Balaam said to the **d**, "Because	Nm 22:29
And the **d** said to Balaam, "Am I not	Nm 22:30
said to Balaam, "Am I not your **d**,	Nm 22:30
you struck your **d** these three times?	Nm 22:32

did not open the **d** of the roof chamber, Jgs 3:25
comes out from the **d** of my house to Jgs 11:31
and took hold of the **d** of the gate of the Jgs 16:3
when he opened the **d** of the house and Jgs 19:27
then he opened the **d** of the house of 1 Sm 3:15
made marks on the **d** of the gate and 1 Sm 21:13
sanctuary he made **d** of olivewood; 1 Kgs 6:31
covered the two **d** of olivewood with 1 Kgs 6:32
and two **d** of cypress wood. The two 1 Kgs 6:34
for the **d** of the innermost part of the 1 Kgs 7:50
and for the **d** of the nave of the temple. 1 Kgs 7:50
the gold from the **d** of the temple of 2 Kgs 18:16
for nails for the **d** of the gates and 1 Chr 22:3
and its **d**—and he carved cherubim 2 Chr 3:7
the great court and **d** for the court and 2 Chr 4:9
court and overlaid their **d** with bronze. 2 Chr 4:9
for the inner **d** to the Most Holy Place 2 Chr 4:22
Place and for the **d** of the nave of 2 Chr 4:22
and he shut up the **d** of the house of 2 Chr 28:24
he opened the **d** of the house of the 2 Chr 29:3
They also shut the **d** of the vestibule 2 Chr 29:7
Gate. They consecrated it and set its **d**. Neh 3:1
They laid its beams and set its **d**, its Neh 3:3
They laid its beams and set its **d**, its Neh 3:6
They rebuilt it and set its **d**, its bolts, Neh 3:13
He rebuilt it and set its **d**, its bolts, and Neh 3:14
He rebuilt it and covered it and set its **d**, Neh 3:15
time I had not set up the **d** in the gates), Neh 6:1
Let us close the **d** of the temple, for they Neh 6:10
had been built and I had set up the **d**, Neh 7:1
guard, let them shut and bar the **d**. Neh 7:3
commanded that the **d** should be Neh 13:19
did not shut the **d** of my mother's womb, Jb 3:10
I have opened my **d** to the traveler), Jb 31:32
I kept silence, and did not go out of **d**— Jb 31:34
shut in the sea with **d** when it burst out Jb 38:8
limits for it and set bars and **d**, Jb 38:10
Who can open the **d** of his face? Jb 41:14
And be lifted up, O ancient **d**, that the Ps 24:7
And lift them up, O ancient **d**, that the Ps 24:9
skies above and opened the **d** of heaven, Ps 78:23
For he shatters the **d** of bronze and Ps 107:16
daily at my gates, waiting beside my **d**. Prv 8:34
and the **d** on the street are shut—when Eccl 12:4
and beside our **d** are all choice fruits, Sg 7:13
chambers, and shut your **d** behind you; Is 26:20
to open **d** before him that gates may not Is 45:1
break in pieces the **d** of bronze and cut Is 45:2
by the walls and at the **d** of the houses, Ezk 33:30
And the **d** of the side chambers opened Ezk 41:11
The double **d** had two leaves apiece, Ezk 41:24
And on the **d** of the nave were carved Ezk 41:25
long, and their **d** were on the north. Ezk 42:4
same exits and arrangements and **d**, Ezk 42:11
guard the **d** of your mouth from her who Mi 7:5
Open your **d**, O Lebanon, that the fire Zec 11:1
one among you who would shut the **d**, Mal 1:10
the **d** being locked where the disciples Jn 20:19
with them. Although the **d** were locked, Jn 20:26
opened the prison **d** and brought them Acts 5:19
and the guards standing at the **d**, Acts 5:23
immediately all the **d** were opened, Acts 16:26
and saw that the prison **d** were open, Acts 16:27

DOORWAY (1)
he had called her, she stood in the **d**. 2 Kgs 4:15

DOORWAYS (1)
All the **d** and windows had square 1 Kgs 7:5

DOPHKAH (2)
wilderness of Sin and camped at **D**. Nm 33:12
they set out from **D** and camped at Nm 33:13

DOR (4)
the king of **D** in Naphath-dor, one; the Jos 12:23
the inhabitants of **D** and its villages, Jos 17:11
or the inhabitants of **D** and its villages, Jgs 1:27
and its towns, **D** and its towns. 1 Chr 7:29

DORCAS (2)
Tabitha, which, translated, means **D**. Acts 9:36
other garments that **D** made while she Acts 9:39

DOT (2)
and earth pass away, not an iota, not a **d**, Mt 5:18
pass away than for one **d** of the Law to Lk 16:17

DOTHAN (3)
'Let us go to **D**.'" So Joseph went after Gn 37:17
after his brothers and found them at **D**. Gn 37:17
It was told him, "Behold, he is in **D**." 2 Kgs 6:13

DOUBLE (21)
Take **d** the money with you. Carry Gn 43:12
and they took **d** the money with them, Gn 43:15
ox or a donkey or a sheep, he shall pay **d**. Ex 22:4
then, if the thief is found, he shall pay **d**. Ex 22:7
condemns shall pay **d** to his neighbor. Ex 22:9
sixth curtain you shall **d** over at the Ex 26:9
by giving him a **d** portion of all that he Dt 21:17
But to Hannah he gave a **d** portion, 1 Sm 1:5
let there be a **d** portion of your spirit 2 Kgs 2:9
flattering lips and a **d** heart they speak. Ps 12:2
from the LORD'S hand **d** for all her sins. Is 40:2
of your shame there shall be a **d** portion; Is 61:7
their land they shall possess a **d** portion; Is 61:7
destroy them with **d** destruction! Jer 17:18
and the Holy Place had each a **d** door. Ezk 41:23
The **d** doors had two leaves apiece, two Ezk 41:24
they are bound up for their **d** iniquity. Hos 10:10
I declare that I will restore to you **d**. Zec 9:12
well be considered worthy of **d** honor, 1 Tm 5:17
others, and repay her **d** for her deeds; Rv 18:6
mix a **d** portion for her in the cup she Rv 18:6

DOUBLE-MINDED (3)
I hate the **d**, but I love your law. Ps 119:113
he is a **d** man, unstable in all his ways. Jas 1:8
sinners, and purify your hearts, you **d**. Jas 4:8

DOUBLE-TONGUED (1)
likewise must be dignified, not **d**, 1 Tm 3:8

DOUBLED (3)
It shall be square and **d**, a span its Ex 28:16
They made the breastpiece **d**, a span its Ex 39:9
its length and a span its breadth when **d**. Ex 39:9

DOUBLING (1)
And the **d** of Pharaoh's dream means Gn 41:32

DOUBLY (1)
But first I will **d** repay their iniquity Jer 16:18

DOUBT (8)
Joseph is without **d** torn to pieces." Gn 37:33
Your life shall hang in **d** before you. Dt 28:66
"No **d** you are the people, and wisdom Jb 12:2
"O you of little faith, why did you **d**?" Mt 14:31
to you, if you have faith and do not **d**, Mt 21:21
the sea,' and does not **d** in his heart, Mk 11:23
another, "No **d** this man is a murderer. Acts 28:4
And have mercy on those who **d**; Jude 1:22

DOUBTED (1)
him they worshiped him, but some **d**. Mt 28:17

DOUBTING (1)
But let him ask in faith, with no **d**, for the Jas 1:6

DOUBTLESS (2)
"**D** you will quote to me this proverb, Lk 4:23
There are **d** many different 1 Cor 14:10

DOUBTS (3)
and why do **d** arise in your hearts? Lk 24:38
But whoever has **d** is condemned if Rom 14:23
for the one who **d** is like a wave of the sea Jas 1:6

DOUGH (10)
the people took their **d** before it was Ex 12:34
unleavened cakes of the **d** that they had Ex 12:39
the first of your **d** you shall present a Nm 15:20
of the first of your **d** you shall give to Nm 15:21
And she took **d** and kneaded it and 2 Sm 13:8
and to bring the first of our **d**, and our Neh 10:37
kindle fire, and the women knead **d**, Jer 7:18
give to the priests the first of your **d**, Ezk 44:30
the kneading of the **d** until it is leavened. Hos 7:4
If the **d** offered as firstfruits is holy, so Rom 11:16

DOVE (19)
Then he sent forth a **d** from him, to see if Gn 8:8
But the **d** found no place to set her foot, Gn 8:9
again he sent forth the **d** out of the ark. Gn 8:10
And the **d** came back to him in the Gn 8:11
another seven days and sent forth the **d**, Gn 8:12
And I say, "Oh, that I had wings like a **d**! Ps 55:6
according to The **D** on Far-off Ps 56:T
the wings of a **d** covered with silver, Ps 68:13
the soul of your **d** to the wild beasts; Ps 74:19
O my **d**, in the clefts of the rock, in the Sg 2:14
"Open to me, my sister, my love, my **d**, my Sg 5:2
My **d**, my perfect one, is the only one, the Sg 6:9
or a crane I chirp; I moan like a **d**. Is 38:14
Be like the **d** that nests in the sides of Jer 48:28
Ephraim is like a **d**, silly and without Hos 7:11
God descending like a **d** and coming to Mt 3:16
the Spirit descending on him like a **d**. Mk 1:10
on him in bodily form, like a **d**; Lk 3:22
the Spirit descend from heaven like a **d**, Jn 1:32

DOVE'S (1)
of a kab of **d** dung for five shekels 2 Kgs 6:25

DOVES (9)
you are beautiful; your eyes are **d**. Sg 1:15
Your eyes are **d** behind your veil. Sg 4:1
His eyes are like **d** beside streams of Sg 5:12
like bears; we moan and moan like **d**; Is 59:11
like a cloud, and like **d** to their windows? Is 60:8
on the mountains, like **d** of the valleys, Ezk 7:16
and like **d** from the land of Assyria, Hos 11:11
moaning like **d** and beating their breasts. Na 2:7
be wise as serpents and innocent as **d**. Mt 10:16

DOWNCAST (2)
house, "Why are your faces **d** today?" Gn 40:7
But God, who comforts the **d**, 2 Cor 7:6

DOWNFALL (5)
by God that the **d** of Ahaziah should 2 Chr 22:7
My eyes have seen the **d** of my enemies; Ps 92:11
the righteous will look upon their **d**. Prv 29:16
gloated over her; they mocked at her **d**. Lam 1:7
for his own life, on the day of your **d**. Ezk 32:10

DOWNPOUR (2)
says, 'Fall on the earth,' likewise to the **d**, Jb 37:6
likewise to the downpour, his mighty **d**. Jb 37:6

DOWNTRODDEN (1)
Let not the **d** turn back in shame; let Ps 74:21

DOWNWARD (6)
of the Jebusites, and **d** to En-rogel. Jos 18:16
Dagon had fallen face **d** on the ground 1 Sm 5:3
Dagon had fallen face **d** on the ground 1 Sm 5:4
again take root **d** and bear fruit 2 Kgs 19:30
shall again take root **d** and bear fruit Is 37:31
And **d** from what had the appearance of Ezk 1:27

DOWRY (1)
and had given it as **d** to his daughter, 1 Kgs 9:16

DRAFT (2)
and the **d** numbered 30,000 men. 1 Kgs 5:13
Adoniram was in charge of the **d**. 1 Kgs 5:14

DRAFTED (4)
King Solomon **d** forced labor out of 1 Kgs 5:13
that King Solomon **d** to build the 1 Kgs 9:15
—these Solomon **d** to be slaves, 1 Kgs 9:21
—these Solomon **d** as forced labor, 2 Chr 8:8

DRAG (5)
city, and we shall **d** it into the valley, 2 Sm 17:13
Do not **d** me off with the wicked, with the Ps 28:3
d her away, and all her multitudes. Ezk 32:20
on the way, lest he **d** you to the judge, Lk 12:58
you, and the ones who **d** you into court? Jas 2:6

DRAGGED (10)
away, **d** off in the day of God's wrath. Jb 20:28
d and dumped beyond the gates of Jer 22:19
little ones of the flock shall be **d** away. Jer 49:20
little ones of their flock shall be **d** away; Jer 50:45
and you will be **d** before governors and Mt 10:18
he **d** off men and women and Acts 8:3
they stoned Paul and **d** him out of the Acts 14:19
Paul and Silas and **d** them into the Acts 16:19
they **d** Jason and some of the brothers Acts 17:6
They seized Paul and **d** him out of the Acts 21:30

DRAGGING (2)
came in the boat, **d** the net full of fish, Jn 21:8
d with them Gaius and Aristarchus, Acts 19:29

DRAGNET (3)
and they will haul you up in my **d**. Ezk 32:3
with his net; he gathers them in his **d**; Hab 1:15
to his net and makes offerings to his **d**; Hab 1:16

DRAGON (18)
Valley Gate to the **D** Spring and to the Neh 2:13
and he will slay the **d** that is in the sea. Is 27:1
cut Rahab in pieces, that pierced the **d**? Is 51:9
the great **d** that lies in the midst of his Ezk 29:3
nations, but you are like a **d** in the seas; Ezk 32:2
behold, a great red **d**, with seven heads Rv 12:3
And the **d** stood before the woman who Rv 12:4
and his angels fighting against the **d**. Rv 12:7
And the **d** and his angels fought back, Rv 12:7
And the great **d** was thrown down, that Rv 12:9
And when the **d** saw that he had been Rv 12:13
the river that the **d** had poured from his Rv 12:16
Then the **d** became furious with the Rv 12:17
And to it the **d** gave his power and his Rv 13:2
And they worshiped the **d**, for he had Rv 13:4
horns like a lamb and it spoke like a **d**. Rv 13:11
of the mouth of the **d** and out of the Rv 16:13
And he seized the **d**, that ancient serpent, Rv 20:2

DRAGS (2)
the grasshopper **d** itself along, Eccl 12:5
a hook; he **d** them out with his net; Hab 1:15

DRAIN (3)
wicked of the earth shall **d** it down to the Ps 75:8
you shall drink it and **d** it out, and Ezk 23:34
to make her **d** the cup of the wine of the Rv 16:19

DRAINED (2)
Its blood shall be **d** out on the side of the Lv 1:15
of the blood shall be **d** out at the base of Lv 5:9

DRANK (44)
He **d** of the wine and became drunk and Gn 9:21
So I **d**, and she gave the camels drink Gn 24:46
the men who were with him ate and **d**, Gn 24:54
and he ate and **d** and rose and went his Gn 25:34
made them a feast, and they ate and **d**. Gn 26:30
and he brought him wine, and he **d**. Gn 27:25
And they **d** and were merry with him. Gn 43:34
Israel; they beheld God, and ate and **d**. Ex 24:11
He neither ate bread nor **d** water. Ex 34:28
abundantly, and the congregation **d**, Nm 20:11
nights. I neither ate bread nor **d** water. Dt 9:9
I neither ate bread nor **d** water, because Dt 9:18
wheat—and you **d** foaming wine made Dt 32:14
of their sacrifices and **d** the wine of Dt 32:38
and ate and **d** and reviled Abimelech. Jgs 9:27
And when he **d**, his spirit returned, and Jgs 15:19
So they ate and **d** and spent the night Jgs 19:4
two of them sat and ate and **d** together. Jgs 19:6
they washed their feet, and ate and **d**. Jgs 19:21
and he ate in his presence and **d**, 2 Sm 11:13
sea. They ate and **d** and were happy. 1 Kgs 4:20
ate bread in his house and **d** water. 1 Kgs 13:19
the evening, and he **d** from the brook. 1 Kgs 17:6
And he ate and **d** and lay down again. 1 Kgs 19:6
And he arose and ate and **d**, and went 1 Kgs 19:8
they went into a tent and ate and **d**, 2 Kgs 7:8
Then he went in and ate and **d**. And 2 Kgs 9:34
I dug wells and **d** foreign waters, and 2 Kgs 19:24
And they ate and **d** before the LORD 1 Chr 29:22
my honey, I **d** my wine with my milk. Sg 5:1
I dug wells and **d** waters, to dry up with Is 37:25
earth drunken; the nations **d** of her wine; Jer 51:7
the king ate, and of the wine that he **d**. Dn 1:5
the king's food, or with the wine that he **d**. Dn 1:8
of his lords and **d** wine in front of Dn 5:1
wives, and his concubines **d** from them. Dn 5:3
They **d** wine and praised the gods of gold Dn 5:4
he gave it to them, and they all **d** of it. Mk 14:23
to say, 'We ate and **d** in your presence, Lk 13:26
He gave us the well and **d** from it himself, Jn 4:12
was without sight, and neither ate nor **d**. Acts 9:9
who ate and **d** with him after he rose Acts 10:41
and all **d** the same spiritual drink. 1 Cor 10:4
For they **d** from the spiritual Rock 1 Cor 10:4

DRAW (81)
time when women go out to **d** water. Gn 24:11
of the city are coming out to **d** water. Gn 24:13
"I will **d** water for your camels also, Gn 24:19
and ran again to the well to **d** water, Gn 24:20
the virgin who comes out to **d** water, Gn 24:43
and I will **d** for your camels also," let Gn 24:44
have its fill of them. I will **d** my sword; Ex 15:9
"**D** near to the altar and offer your sin Lv 9:7
no one who has a blemish shall **d** near, Lv 21:18
should **d** near to burn incense before Nm 16:40
Great Sea you shall **d** a line to Mount Nm 34:7
Mount Hor you shall **d** a line to Nm 34:8
"You shall **d** a line for your eastern Nm 34:10
the sons of Ammon you did not **d** near, Dt 2:37
because he sought to **d** you away from Dt 13:10
And when you **d** near to the battle, the Dt 20:2
"When you **d** near to a city to fight Dt 20:10
for they **d** from the abundance of the Dt 33:19
But Joshua did not **d** back his hand with Jos 8:26
And I will **d** out Sisera, the general of Jgs 4:7
But the young man did not **d** his sword, Jgs 8:20
said to him, "**D** your sword and kill me, Jgs 9:54
"Come and let us **d** near to one of these Jgs 19:13
"Shall we again **d** near to fight against Jgs 20:23
"Let us flee and **d** them away from the Jgs 20:32
coming out to **d** water and said 1 Sm 9:11
said, "Let us **d** near to God here." 1 Sm 14:36
have you come out to **d** up for battle? 1 Sm 17:8
to his armor-bearer, "**D** your sword, 1 Sm 31:4
fighting, and then **d** back from him, 2 Sm 11:15
that he could not **d** it back to himself. 1 Kgs 13:4
of Israel, "**D** the bow," and he drew it. 2 Kgs 13:16
"**D** your sword and thrust me 1 Chr 10:4
we cannot **d** up our case because of Jb 37:19
"Can you **d** out Leviathan with a Jb 41:1
D the spear and javelin against my Ps 35:3
The wicked **d** the sword and bend their Ps 37:14
D near to my soul, redeem me; ransom Ps 69:18
They **d** near who persecute me with Ps 119:150
a man of understanding will **d** it out. Prv 20:5
To **d** near to listen is better than to offer Eccl 5:1
come and the years **d** near of which Eccl 12:1
D me after you; let us run. The king has Sg 1:4
Woe to those who **d** iniquity with cords of Is 5:18
of falsehood, who **d** sin as with cart ropes, Is 5:18
counsel of the Holy One of Israel **d** near, Is 5:19
With joy you will **d** water from the wells Is 12:3
"Because this people **d** near with their Is 29:13
D near, O nations, to hear, and give Is 34:1
speak; let us together **d** near for judgment. Is 41:1
d near together, you survivors of the Is 45:20
D near to me, hear this: from the Is 48:16
But you, **d** near, sons of the sorceress, Is 57:3
judgments; they delight to **d** near to God. Is 58:2
Tarshish, Pul, and Lud, who **d** the bow, Is 66:19
I will make him **d** near, and he shall Jer 30:21
against you and will **d** my sword from Ezk 21:3
and they shall **d** their swords against Ezk 28:7
and I will **d** you up out of the midst of Ezk 29:4
and they shall **d** their swords against Ezk 30:11
who **d** near to me to minister to me, Ezk 43:19
Let all the men of war **d** near; let them Jl 3:9
D water for the siege; strengthen your Na 3:14
the LORD; she does not **d** near to her God. Zep 3:2
came to the wine vat to **d** fifty measures, Hg 2:16
"Then I will **d** near to you for judgment. Mal 3:5
"Now **d** some out and take it to the master Jn 2:8
came a woman of Samaria to **d** water. Jn 4:7
"Sir, you have nothing to **d** water with, Jn 4:11
thirsty or have to come here to **d** water." Jn 4:15
the earth, will **d** all people to myself." Jn 12:32
to **d** away the disciples after them. Acts 20:30
when their passions **d** them away 1 Tm 5:11
us then with confidence **d** near to the Heb 4:16
through which we **d** near to God. Heb 7:19
the uttermost those who **d** near to God Heb 7:25
year, make perfect those who **d** near. Heb 10:1
let us **d** near with a true heart in full Heb 10:22
for whoever would **d** near to God must Heb 11:6
D near to God, and he will draw near to Jas 4:8
near to God, and he will **d** near to you. Jas 4:8

DRAWERS (3)
cutters of wood and **d** of water for all Jos 9:21
cutters of wood and **d** of water for the Jos 9:23
cutters of wood and **d** of water for the Jos 9:27

DRAWING (5)
today you are **d** near for battle against Dt 20:3
and sinners were all **d** near to hear him. Lk 15:1
As he was **d** near—already on the way Lk 19:37
because your redemption is **d** near." Lk 21:28
all the more as you see the Day **d** near. Heb 10:25

DRAWN (25)
And his soul was **d** to Dinah the Gn 34:3
the road, with a **d** sword in his hand. Nm 22:23
the way, with his **d** sword in his hand. Nm 22:31
you shall take one **d** out of every fifty, Nm 31:30
you be **d** away and bow down to them Dt 4:19
you and have **d** away the inhabitants Dt 13:13
but are **d** away to worship other gods Dt 30:17
before him with his **d** sword in his hand. Jos 5:13
until we have **d** them away from the city. Jos 8:6
Joshua they were **d** away from the Jos 8:16
the people and were **d** away from the Jgs 20:31
and drink what the young men have **d**." Ru 2:9
called out and were **d** up at the 2 Kgs 3:21
in his hand a **d** sword stretched out 1 Chr 21:16
It is **d** forth and comes out of his body; Jb 20:25
for you have **d** me up and have not let Ps 30:1
softer than oil, yet they were **d** swords. Ps 55:21
fled from the swords, from the **d** sword, Is 21:15
tremble; they have **d** near and come. Is 41:5
my sword shall be **d** from its sheath Ezk 21:4
I have **d** my sword from its sheath; it Ezk 21:5
A sword, a sword is **d** for the slaughter. Ezk 21:28
like a powerful army **d** up for battle. Jl 2:5
the servants who had **d** the water knew), Jn 2:9
and all was **d** up again into heaven. Acts 11:10

DRAWS (9)
the wife of the one **d** near to rescue her Dt 25:11
your wood to the one who **d** your water, Dt 29:11
the night. Behold, the day **d** to its close. Jgs 19:9
His soul **d** near the pit, and his life to Jb 33:22
For he **d** up the drops of water; they Jb 36:27
the poor when he **d** him into his net. Ps 10:9
of troubles, and my life **d** near to Sheol. Ps 88:3
My righteousness **d** near, my salvation Is 51:5
me unless the Father who sent me **d** him. Jn 6:44

DREAD (30)
fear of you and the **d** of you shall be upon Gn 9:2
the Egyptians were in **d** of the people of Ex 1:12
Terror and **d** fall upon them; because Ex 15:16
And Moab was in great **d** of the people, Nm 22:3
to you, 'Do not be in **d** or afraid of them. Dt 1:29
will begin to put the **d** and fear of you on Dt 2:25
You shall not be in **d** of them, for the Dt 7:21
fear of you and the **d** of you on all the Dt 11:25
Do not fear or panic or be in **d** of them, Dt 20:3
you shall be in **d** and have no Dt 28:66
because of the **d** that your heart shall Dt 28:67
Do not fear or be in **d** of them, for it is the Dt 31:6
his oxen!" Then the **d** of the LORD fell 1 Sm 11:7
comes upon me, and what I **d** befalls me. Jb 3:25
d came upon me, and trembling, which Jb 4:14
from me, and let not **d** of him terrify me. Jb 9:34
you, and the **d** of him fall upon you? Jb 13:11
from me, and let not **d** of you terrify me. Jb 13:21
when I consider, I am in **d** of him. Jb 23:15
an object of **d** to my acquaintances; Ps 31:11
preserve my life from **d** of the enemy. Ps 64:1
for **d** of them had fallen upon it. Ps 105:38
Turn away the reproach that I **d**, for Ps 119:39
will be at ease, without **d** of disaster." Prv 1:33
whose two kings you **d** will be deserted. Is 7:16
do not fear what they fear, nor be in **d**. Is 8:12
him be your fear, and let him be your **d**. Is 8:13
Whom did you **d** and fear, so that you Is 57:11
But the LORD is with me as a **d** warrior; Jer 20:11
they shall turn in **d** to the LORD our God, Mi 7:17

DREADED (2)
whom your fathers had never **d**. Dt 32:17
They are **d** and fearsome; their justice Hab 1:7

DREADFUL (7)
d and great darkness fell upon him. Gn 15:12
D sounds are in his ears; in prosperity Jb 15:21
over me; your **d** assaults destroy me. Ps 88:16
I will bring you to a **d** end, and you Ezk 26:21
you have come to a **d** end and shall be Ezk 27:36
you have come to a **d** end and shall be Ezk 28:19
terrifying and **d** and exceedingly strong. Dn 7:7

DREADS (1)
What the wicked **d** will come upon Prv 10:24

DREAM (70)
to Abimelech in a **d** by night and said Gn 20:3
Then God said to him in the **d**, "Yes, I Gn 20:6
eyes and saw in a **d** that the goats that Gn 31:10
the angel of God said to me in the **d**, Gn 31:11
the Aramean in a **d** by night and said Gn 31:24
Now Joseph had a **d**, and when he told it Gn 37:5
them, "Hear this **d** that I have dreamed: Gn 37:6
Then he dreamed another **d** and told it Gn 37:9
said, "Behold, I have dreamed another **d**. Gn 37:9
"What is this **d** that you have Gn 37:10
confined in the prison—each his own **d**, Gn 40:5
and each **d** with its own interpretation. Gn 40:5
chief cupbearer told his **d** to Joseph and Gn 40:9
"In my **d** there was a vine before me, Gn 40:9
he said to Joseph, "I also had a **d**: Gn 40:16
Pharaoh awoke, and behold, it was a **d**. Gn 41:7
each having a **d** with its own Gn 41:11
to each man according to his **d**. Gn 41:12
Pharaoh said to Joseph, "I have had a **d**, Gn 41:15
when you hear a **d** you can interpret Gn 41:15
in my **d** I was standing on the banks of Gn 41:17
also saw in my **d** seven ears growing Gn 41:22
doubling of Pharaoh's **d** means that Gn 41:32
in a vision; I speak with him in a **d**. Nm 12:6
a man was telling a **d** to his comrade. Jgs 7:13
And he said, "Behold, I dreamed a **d**, and Jgs 7:13
the telling of the **d** and its interpretation, Jgs 7:15
appeared to Solomon in a **d** by night, 1 Kgs 3:5
awoke, and behold, it was a **d**. 1 Kgs 3:15
will fly away like a **d** and not be found; Jb 20:8
In a **d**, in a vision of the night, when Jb 33:15
Like a **d** when one awakes, O Lord, Ps 73:20
they are like a **d**, like grass that is Ps 90:5
of Zion, we were like those who **d**. Ps 126:1
For a **d** comes with much business, and Eccl 5:3
and distress her, shall be like a **d**, Is 29:7
the prophet who has a **d** tell the dream, Jer 23:28
the prophet who has a dream tell the **d**, Jer 23:28
do not listen to the dreams that they **d**, Jer 29:8
And the king said to them, "I had a **d**, and Dn 2:3
and my spirit is troubled to know the **d**." Dn 2:3
Tell your servants the **d**, and we will Dn 2:4
known to me the **d** and its interpretation, Dn 2:5
if you show the **d** and its interpretation, Dn 2:6
show me the **d** and its interpretation." Dn 2:6
said, "Let the king tell his servants the **d**, Dn 2:7
if you do not make the **d** known to me, Dn 2:9
Therefore tell me the **d**, and I shall know Dn 2:9
known to me the **d** that I have seen Dn 2:26
Your **d** and the visions of your head as Dn 2:28
"This was the **d**. Now we will tell the Dn 2:36
The **d** is certain, and its interpretation Dn 2:45
I saw a **d** that made me afraid. As I lay in Dn 4:5
known to me the interpretation of the **d**. Dn 4:6
came in, and I told them the **d**, Dn 4:7
of the holy gods—and I told him the **d**, Dn 4:8
me the visions of my **d** that I saw and Dn 4:9
This **d** I, King Nebuchadnezzar, saw. Dn 4:18
let not the **d** or the interpretation alarm Dn 4:19
may the **d** be for those who hate you and Dn 4:19
Daniel saw a **d** and visions of his head as Dn 7:1
he wrote down the **d** and told the sum Dn 7:1
prophesy, your old men shall **d** dreams, Jl 2:28

angel of the Lord appeared to him in a **d**, Mt 1:20
And being warned in a **d** not to return to Mt 2:12
Lord appeared to Joseph in a **d** and said, Mt 2:13
Lord appeared in a **d** to Joseph in Egypt, Mt 2:19
being warned in a **d** he withdrew to the Mt 2:22
much because of him today in a **d**." Mt 27:19
and your old men shall **d** dreams; Acts 2:17

DREAMED (13)
And he **d**, and behold, there was a Gn 28:12
to them, "Hear this dream that I have **d**: Gn 37:6
Then he **d** another dream and told it to Gn 37:9
said, "Behold, I have **d** another dream. Gn 37:9
"What is this dream that you have **d**? Gn 37:10
one night they both **d**—the cupbearer Gn 40:5
Pharaoh **d** that he was standing by the Gn 41:1
And he fell asleep and **d** a second time. Gn 41:5
we **d** on the same night, he and I, each Gn 41:11
the dreams that he had **d** of them. Gn 42:9
And he said, "Behold, I **d** a dream, and Jgs 7:13
lies in my name, saying, 'I have **d**, Jer 23:25
saying, 'I have dreamed, I have **d**!' Jer 23:25

DREAMER (4)
said to one another, "Here comes this **d**. Gn 37:19
a prophet or a **d** of dreams arises among Dt 13:1
words of that prophet or that **d** of dreams. Dt 13:3
that prophet or that **d** of dreams shall be Dt 13:5

DREAMERS (1)
to your prophets, your diviners, your **d**, Jer 27:9

DREAMING (1)
they cannot bark, **d**, lying down, loving Is 56:10

DREAMS (28)
even more for his **d** and for his words. Gn 37:8
we will see what will become of his **d**." Gn 37:20
They said to him, "We have had **d**, and Gn 40:8
Pharaoh told them his **d**, but there was Gn 41:8
we told him, he interpreted our **d** to us, Gn 41:12
to Pharaoh, "The **d** of Pharaoh are one; Gn 41:25
good ears are seven years; the **d** are one. Gn 41:26
Joseph remembered the **d** that he had Gn 42:9
or a dreamer of **d** arises among you and Dt 13:1
of that prophet or that dreamer of **d**. Dt 13:3
or that dreamer of **d** shall be put to Dt 13:5
LORD did not answer him, either by **d**, 1 Sm 28:6
no more, either by prophets or by **d**. 1 Sm 28:15
you scare me with **d** and terrify me with Jb 7:14
For when **d** increase and words grow Eccl 5:7
As when a hungry man **d** he is eating and Is 29:8
when a thirsty man **d** he is drinking and Is 29:8
my name by their **d** that they tell one Jer 23:27
am against those who prophesy lying **d**, Jer 23:32
do not listen to the **d** that they dream, Jer 29:8
had understanding in all visions and **d**. Dn 1:17
Nebuchadnezzar had **d**; Dn 2:1
be summoned to tell the king his **d**. Dn 2:2
and understanding to interpret **d**, Dn 5:12
prophesy, your old men shall dream **d**, Jl 2:28
they tell false **d** and give empty Zec 10:2
and your old men shall dream **d**; Acts 2:17
these people also, relying on their **d**, Jude 1:8

DREGS (3)
of the earth shall drain it down to the **d**. Ps 75:8
who have drunk to the **d** the bowl, Is 51:17
from his youth and has settled on his **d**; Jer 48:11

DRENCH (3)
with tears; I **d** my couch with my weeping. Ps 6:6
I **d** you with my tears, O Heshbon and Is 16:9
I will **d** the land even to the mountains Ezk 32:6

DRENCHED (1)
a bowl, **d** like the corners of the altar. Zec 9:15

DRESS (12)
You shall plant vineyards and **d** them, Dt 28:39
Let them **d** the man whom the king Est 6:9
D for action like a man; I will question Jb 38:3
"**D** for action like a man; I will question Jb 40:7
But you, **d** yourself for work; arise, and Jer 1:17
what do you mean that you **d** in scarlet, Jer 4:30
the ramparts; watch the road; **d** for battle; Na 2:1
he will **d** himself for service and have Lk 12:37
'Prepare supper for me, and **d** properly, Lk 17:8
you used to **d** yourself and walk Jn 21:18
and another will **d** you and carry you Jn 21:18
"**D** yourself and put on your sandals." Acts 12:8

DRESSED (13)
the virgin daughters of the king **d**. 2 Sm 13:18
of the house with **d** stones. 1 Kgs 5:17
Now Ahijah had **d** himself in a new 1 Kgs 11:29
stonecutters to prepare **d** stones for 1 Chr 22:2
and he **d** Mordecai and led him through Est 6:11
the woman meets him, **d** as a prostitute, Prv 7:10
fallen, but we will build with **d** stones; Is 9:10
go out to see? A man **d** in soft clothing? Mt 11:8
on the right side, **d** in a white robe, Mk 16:5
go out to see? A man **d** in soft clothing? Lk 7:25
those who are **d** in splendid clothing and Lk 7:25
"Stay **d** for action and keep your lamps Lk 12:35
we are poorly **d** and buffeted and 1 Cor 4:11

DRESSER (1)
a herdsman and a **d** of sycamore figs. Am 7:14

DRESSES (2)
Every morning when he **d** the lamps he Ex 30:7
She **d** herself with strength and makes Prv 31:17

DREW (94)
Then Abraham **d** near and said, "Will Gn 18:23
Lot, and **d** near to break the door down. Gn 19:9
water, and she **d** for all his camels. Gn 24:20
went down to the spring and **d** water. Gn 24:45
Then the servants **d** near, they and their Gn 33:6
and her children **d** near and bowed Gn 33:7
And last Joseph and Rachel **d** near, and Gn 33:7
And they **d** Joseph up and lifted him Gn 37:28
But as he **d** back his hand, behold, his Gn 38:29
And when the time **d** near that Israel Gn 47:29
he **d** up his feet into the bed and Gn 49:33
she said, "I **d** him out of the water." Ex 2:10
and they came and **d** water and filled the Ex 2:16
the shepherds and even **d** water for us Ex 2:19
When Pharaoh **d** near, the people of Ex 14:10
while Moses **d** near to the thick Ex 20:21
and all the congregation **d** near and stood Lv 9:5
So Aaron **d** near to the altar and killed the Lv 9:8
when they **d** near before the LORD and Lv 16:1
Then **d** near the daughters of Nm 27:1
him went up and **d** near before the city Jos 8:11
had fallen 120,000 men who **d** the sword. Jgs 8:10
fought against it and **d** near to the door Jgs 9:52
400,000 men on foot that **d** the sword. Jgs 20:2
that day 26,000 men who **d** the sword, Jgs 20:15
400,000 men who **d** the sword; Jgs 20:17
the men of Israel **d** up the battle line Jgs 20:20
All these were men who **d** the sword. Jgs 20:25
All these were men who **d** the sword. Jgs 20:35
were 25,000 men who **d** the sword, Jgs 20:46
the one **d** off his sandal and gave it to the Ru 4:7
"Buy it for yourself," he **d** off his sandal. Ru 4:8
The Philistines **d** up in line against 1 Sm 4:2
at Mizpah and **d** water and poured 1 Sm 7:6
the Philistines **d** near to attack Israel. 1 Sm 7:10
and **d** up in line of battle against the 1 Sm 17:2
and the Philistines **d** up for battle, 1 Sm 17:21
arose and came and **d** near to meet 1 Sm 17:48
and took his sword and **d** it out of its 1 Sm 17:51
came out and **d** up in battle 2 Sm 10:8
who were with him **d** near to battle 2 Sm 10:13
mouth." And he **d** nearer and nearer. 2 Sm 18:25
me; he **d** me out of many waters. 2 Sm 22:17
of the Philistines and **d** water out of 2 Sm 23:16
800,000 valiant men who **d** the sword, 2 Sm 24:9
When David's time to die **d** near, he 1 Kgs 2:1
gold, and he **d** chains of gold across, 1 Kgs 6:21
But a certain man **d** his bow at 1 Kgs 22:34
who were at Jericho **d** near to Elisha 2 Kgs 2:5
And Jehu **d** his bow with his full 2 Kgs 9:24
Israel, "Draw the bow," and he **d** it. 2 Kgs 13:16
Then the king **d** near to the altar 2 Kgs 16:12
shield and sword, and **d** the bow, 1 Chr 5:18
of the Philistines and **d** water out of 1 Chr 11:18
came out and **d** up in battle 1 Chr 19:9
were with him **d** near before the 1 Chr 19:14
came to them and **d** up his forces 1 Chr 19:17
were 1,100,000 men who **d** the sword, 1 Chr 21:5
in Judah 470,000 who **d** the sword. 1 Chr 21:5
And Jeroboam **d** up his line of battle 2 Chr 13:3
that carried shields and **d** bows. 2 Chr 14:8
and they **d** up their lines of battle in 2 Chr 14:10
him; God **d** them away from him. 2 Chr 18:31
But a certain man **d** his bow at 2 Chr 18:33
took me; he **d** me out of many waters. Ps 18:16
He **d** me up from the pit of destruction, Ps 40:2
and they **d** near to the gates of death. Ps 107:18
when he **d** a circle on the face of the Prv 8:27
Then they **d** Jeremiah up with ropes Jer 38:13
not walk in our streets; our end **d** near; Lam 4:18
men **d** it ashore and sat down and Mt 13:48
Now when they **d** near to Jerusalem and Mt 21:1
When the season for fruit **d** near, he Mt 21:34
out his hand and **d** his sword and Mt 26:51
Now when they **d** near to Jerusalem, to Mk 11:1
those who stood by **d** his sword and Mk 14:47
As he **d** near to the gate of the town, Lk 7:12
When the days **d** near for him to be Lk 9:51
as he came and **d** near to the house, Lk 15:25
As he **d** near to Jericho, a blind man Lk 18:35
When he **d** near to Bethphage and Lk 19:29
And when he **d** near and saw the city, Lk 19:41
the Feast of Unleavened Bread **d** near, Lk 22:1
them. He **d** near to Jesus to kiss him, Lk 22:47
Jesus himself **d** near and went with Lk 24:15
So they **d** near to the village to which Lk 24:28
"I am he," they **d** back and fell to the Jn 18:6
d it and struck the high priest's servant Jn 18:10
of the census and **d** away some of the Acts 5:37
"But as the time of the promise **d** near, Acts 7:17
at the sight, and as he **d** near to look, Acts 7:31
he **d** his sword and was about to kill Acts 16:27
on my way and **d** near to Damascus, Acts 22:6
they came he **d** back and separated Gal 2:12

DRIED (31)
until the waters were **d** up from the earth. Gn 8:7
the waters were **d** from off the earth. Gn 8:13
day of the month, the earth had **d** out. Gn 8:14
juice of grapes or eat grapes, fresh or **d**. Nm 6:3
But now our strength is **d** up, and there Nm 11:6
heard how the LORD **d** up the water of Jos 2:10
For the LORD your God **d** up the waters of Jos 4:23
which he **d** up for us until we passed Jos 4:23
heard that the LORD had **d** up the waters of Jos 5:1
fresh bowstrings that have not been **d**, Jgs 16:7
fresh bowstrings that had not been **d**, Jgs 16:8
he stretched out against him, **d** up, 1 Kgs 13:4
And after a while the brook **d** up, 1 Kgs 17:7
and I **d** up with the sole of my foot 2 Kgs 19:24
my strength is **d** up like a potsherd, and Ps 22:15
my strength was **d** up as by the heat of Ps 32:4
brooks; you **d** up ever-flowing streams. Ps 74:15
And the waters of the sea will be **d** up, and Is 19:5
Was it not you who **d** up the sea, the Is 51:10
the pastures of the wilderness are **d** up. Jer 23:10
her waters, that they may be **d** up! Jer 50:38
the ground; the east wind **d** up its fruit; Ezk 19:12
Behold, they say, 'Our bones are **d** up, Ezk 37:11
Ephraim is stricken; their root is **d** up; Hos 9:16
and apple, all the trees of the field are **d** up, Jl 1:12
are torn down because the grain has **d** up. Jl 1:17
you because the water brooks are **d** up, Jl 1:20
they are consumed like stubble fully **d**. Na 1:10
all the depths of the Nile shall be **d** up. Zec 10:11
immediately the flow of blood **d** up, Mk 5:29
river Euphrates, and its water was **d** up, Rv 16:12

DRIES (6)
a lake and a river wastes away and **d** up, Jb 14:11
but a crushed spirit **d** up the bones. Prv 17:22
the grain is destroyed, the wine **d** up, Jl 1:10
The vine **d** up; the fig tree languishes. Jl 1:12
and gladness **d** up from the children of Jl 1:12
and makes it dry; he **d** up all the rivers; Na 1:4

DRIFT (1)
we have heard, lest we **d** away from it. Heb 2:1

DRINK (350)
Come, let us make our father **d** wine, Gn 19:32
made their father **d** wine that night. Gn 19:33
Let us make him **d** wine tonight also. Gn 19:34
made their father **d** wine that night Gn 19:35
skin with water and gave the boy a **d**. Gn 21:19
'Please let down your jar that I may **d**,' Gn 24:14
'**D**, and I will water your camels'—let Gn 24:14
me a little water to **d** from your jar." Gn 24:17
"**D**, my lord." And she quickly let down Gn 24:18
jar upon her hand and gave him a **d**. Gn 24:18
When she had finished giving him a **d**, Gn 24:19
me a little water from your jar to **d**," Gn 24:43
"**D**, and I will draw for your camels Gn 24:44
water. I said to her, 'Please let me **d**.' Gn 24:45
'**D**, and I will give your camels drink Gn 24:46
and I will give your camels **d** also.' Gn 24:46
drank, and she gave the camels **d** also. Gn 24:46
places, where the flocks came to **d**. Gn 30:38
since they bred when they came to **d**, Gn 30:38
He poured out a **d** offering on it and Gn 35:14
the Egyptians could not **d** water from the Ex 7:21
dug along the Nile for water to **d**, Ex 7:24
for they could not **d** the water of the Nile. Ex 7:24
they could not **d** the water of Marah Ex 15:23
Moses, saying, "What shall we **d**?" Ex 15:24
there was no water for the people to **d**. Ex 17:1
"Give us water to **d**." And Moses said to Ex 17:2
and the people will **d**." And Moses did so, Ex 17:6
bowls with which to pour **d** offerings; Ex 25:29
fourth of a hin of wine for a **d** offering. Ex 29:40
it a grain offering and its **d** offering, Ex 29:41
and you shall not pour a **d** offering on it. Ex 30:9
sat down to eat and **d** and rose up to play. Ex 32:6
water and made the people of Israel **d** it. Ex 32:20
flagons with which to pour **d** offerings. Ex 37:16
"**D** no wine or strong drink, you or your Lv 10:9
"Drink no wine or strong **d**, you or your Lv 10:9
And all **d** that could be drunk from Lv 11:34
and the **d** offering with it shall be of Lv 23:13
grain offering and their **d** offerings, Lv 23:18

offerings, sacrifices and **d** offerings,	Lv 23:37
bowls, and the flagons for the **d** offering;	Nm 4:7
shall make the woman **d** the water of	Nm 5:24
shall make the woman **d** the water.	Nm 5:26
And when he has made her **d** the water,	Nm 5:27
himself from wine and strong **d**.	Nm 6:3
He shall **d** no vinegar made from wine	Nm 6:3
from wine or strong **d** and shall not	Nm 6:3
drink and shall not **d** any juice of grapes	Nm 6:3
grain offering and their **d** offerings.	Nm 6:15
also its grain offering and its **d** offering.	Nm 6:17
And after that the Nazirite may **d** wine.	Nm 6:20
of wine for the **d** offering for each	Nm 15:5
And for the **d** offering you shall offer a	Nm 15:7
shall offer for the **d** offering half a hin	Nm 15:10
its grain offering and its **d** offering,	Nm 15:24
and there is no water to **d**."	Nm 20:5
for them and give **d** to the congregation	Nm 20:8
or vineyard, or **d** water from a well.	Nm 20:17
highway, and if we **d** of your water,	Nm 20:19
We will not **d** the water of a well.	Nm 21:22
Its **d** offering shall be a quarter of a hin	Nm 28:7
shall pour out a **d** offering of strong	Nm 28:7
a drink offering of strong **d** to the LORD.	Nm 28:7
of the morning, and like its **d** offering,	Nm 28:8
mixed with oil, and its **d** offering:	Nm 28:9
burnt offering and its **d** offering.	Nm 28:10
Their **d** offerings shall be half a hin of	Nm 28:14
burnt offering and its **d** offering.	Nm 28:15
burnt offering and its **d** offering.	Nm 28:24
shall offer them and their **d** offering.	Nm 28:31
its grain offering, and their **d** offering,	Nm 29:6
grain offering, and their **d** offerings.	Nm 29:11
its grain offering and its **d** offering.	Nm 29:16
offering and the **d** offerings for the	Nm 29:18
grain offering, and their **d** offerings.	Nm 29:19
offering and the **d** offerings for the	Nm 29:21
its grain offering and its **d** offering.	Nm 29:22
offering and the **d** offerings for the	Nm 29:24
its grain offering and its **d** offering.	Nm 29:25
offering and the **d** offerings for the	Nm 29:27
its grain offering and its **d** offering.	Nm 29:28
offering and the **d** offerings for the	Nm 29:30
its grain offering, and its **d** offerings.	Nm 29:31
offering and the **d** offerings for the	Nm 29:33
its grain offering, and its **d** offering.	Nm 29:34
offering and the **d** offerings for the	Nm 29:37
its grain offering and its **d** offering.	Nm 29:38
offerings, and for your **d** offerings,	Nm 29:39
there was no water for the people to **d**.	Nm 33:14
water of them for money, that you may **d**.	Dt 2:6
give me water for money, that I may **d**.	Dt 2:28
—oxen or sheep or wine or strong **d**,	Dt 14:26
but you shall neither **d** of the wine nor	Dt 28:39
you have not drunk wine or strong **d**,	Dt 29:6
and drank the wine of their **d** offering?	Dt 32:38
to her, "Please give me a little water to **d**,	Jgs 4:19
milk and gave him a **d** and covered him.	Jgs 4:19
every one who kneels down to **d**."	Jgs 7:5
rest of the people knelt down to **d** water.	Jgs 7:6
Therefore be careful and **d** no wine or	Jgs 13:4
careful and drink no wine or strong **d**,	Jgs 13:4
So then **d** no wine or strong drink, and	Jgs 13:7
So then drink no wine or strong **d**, and	Jgs 13:7
neither let her **d** wine or strong drink,	Jgs 13:14
neither let her drink wine or strong **d**,	Jgs 13:14
to the vessels and **d** what the young men	Ru 2:9
have drunk neither wine nor strong **d**,	1 Sm 1:15
and he ate. They gave him water to **d**,	1 Sm 30:11
to eat and to **d** and to lie with my	2 Sm 11:11
of his morsel and **d** from his cup and	2 Sm 12:3
who faint in the wilderness to **d**."	2 Sm 16:2
give me water to **d** from the well of	2 Sm 23:15
it to David. But he would not **d** of it.	2 Sm 23:16
Shall I **d** the blood of the men who	2 Sm 23:17
lives?" Therefore he would not **d** it.	2 Sm 23:17
not eat bread or **d** water in this place,	1 Kgs 13:8
eat bread nor **d** water nor return	1 Kgs 13:9
I eat bread nor **d** water with you in	1 Kgs 13:16
neither eat bread nor **d** water there,	1 Kgs 13:17
may eat bread and **d** water.'" But he	1 Kgs 13:18
"Eat no bread and **d** no water," your	1 Kgs 13:22
You shall **d** from the brook, and I	1 Kgs 17:4
little water in a vessel, that I may **d**."	1 Kgs 17:10
said to Ahab, "Go up, eat and **d**,	1 Kgs 18:41
So Ahab went up to eat and to **d**.	1 Kgs 18:42
filled with water, so that you shall **d**,	2 Kgs 3:17
they may eat and **d** and go to their	2 Kgs 6:22
and poured his **d** offering and threw	2 Kgs 16:13
grain offering and their **d** offering.	2 Kgs 16:15
dung and to **d** their own urine?"	2 Kgs 18:27
one of you will **d** the water of his	2 Kgs 18:31
give me water to **d** from the well of	1 Chr 11:17
it to David. But David would not **d** it.	1 Chr 11:18
Shall I **d** the lifeblood of these men?	1 Chr 11:19
it." Therefore he would not **d** it.	1 Chr 11:19
1,000 lambs, with their **d** offerings,	1 Chr 29:21
provided them with food and **d**,	2 Chr 28:15
and there were the **d** offerings for the	2 Chr 29:35
d, and oil to the Sidonians and the	Ezr 3:7
grain offerings and their **d** offerings,	Ezr 7:17
Eat the fat and **d** sweet wine and send	Neh 8:10
way to eat and **d** and to send portions	Neh 8:12
And the king and Haman sat down to **d**,	Est 3:15
behalf, and do not eat or **d** for three days,	Est 4:16
their three sisters to eat and **d** with them.	Jb 1:4
and let them **d** of the wrath of the	Jb 21:20
have given no water to the weary to **d**,	Jb 22:7
their **d** offerings of blood I will not pour	Ps 16:4
and you give them **d** from the river of	Ps 36:8
flesh of bulls or **d** the blood of goats?	Ps 50:13
given us wine to **d** that made us stagger.	Ps 60:3
my thirst they gave me sour wine to **d**.	Ps 69:21
and gave them **d** abundantly as from	Ps 78:15
that they could not **d** of their streams.	Ps 78:44
given them tears to **d** in full measure.	Ps 80:5
like bread and mingle tears with my **d**,	Ps 102:9
they give **d** to every beast of the field;	Ps 104:11
He will **d** from the brook by the way;	Ps 110:7
bread of wickedness and **d** the wine of	Prv 4:17
D water from your own cistern, flowing	Prv 5:15
eat of my bread and **d** of the wine I have	Prv 9:5
Wine is a mocker, strong **d** a brawler,	Prv 20:1
"Eat and **d**!" he says to you, but his	Prv 23:7
shall I awake? I must have another **d**."	Prv 23:35
and if he is thirsty, give him water to **d**,	Prv 25:21
O Lemuel, it is not for kings to **d** wine,	Prv 31:4
wine, or for rulers to take strong **d**,	Prv 31:4
lest they **d** and forget what has been	Prv 31:5
Give strong **d** to the one who is	Prv 31:6
let them **d** and forget their poverty and	Prv 31:7
should eat and **d** and find enjoyment	Eccl 2:24
should eat and **d** and take pleasure	Eccl 3:13
is to eat and **d** and find enjoyment in	Eccl 5:18
the sun but to eat and **d** and be joyful,	Eccl 8:15
joy, and **d** your wine with a merry heart,	Eccl 9:7
Eat, friends, **d**, and be drunk with love!	Sg 5:1
I would give you spiced wine to **d**, the juice	Sg 8:2
that they may run after strong **d**,	Is 5:11
and valiant men in mixing strong **d**,	Is 5:22
they spread the rugs, they eat, they **d**.	Is 21:5
"Let us eat and **d**, for tomorrow we die."	Is 22:13
No more do they **d** wine with singing;	Is 24:9
strong **d** is bitter to those who drink it.	Is 24:9
strong drink is bitter to those who **d** it.	Is 24:9
reel with wine and stagger with strong **d**;	Is 28:7
priest and the prophet reel with strong **d**,	Is 28:7
by wine, they stagger with strong **d**,	Is 28:7
with wine; stagger, but not with strong **d**!	Is 29:9
unsatisfied, and to deprive the thirsty of **d**.	Is 32:6
Their land shall **d** its fill of blood, and	Is 34:7
their own dung and **d** their own urine?"	Is 36:12
each one of you will **d** the water of his	Is 36:16
the desert, to give **d** to my chosen people,	Is 43:20
bowl of my wrath you shall **d** no more;	Is 51:22
wine; let us fill ourselves with strong **d**;	Is 56:12
to them you have poured out a **d** offering,	Is 57:6
and foreigners shall not **d** your wine for	Is 62:8
those who gather it shall **d** it in the courts	Is 62:9
behold, my servants shall **d**, but you	Is 65:13
that you may **d** deeply with delight from	Is 66:11
by going to Egypt to **d** the waters of the	Jer 2:18
by going to Assyria to **d** the waters of the	Jer 2:18
And they pour out **d** offerings to other	Jer 7:18
and has given us poisoned water to **d**,	Jer 8:14
and give them poisonous water to **d**.	Jer 9:15
cup of consolation to **d** for his father or	Jer 16:7
of feasting to sit with them, to eat and **d**.	Jer 16:8
and **d** offerings have been poured out to	Jer 19:13
your father eat and **d** and do justice and	Jer 22:15
food and give them poisoned water to **d**,	Jer 23:15
all the nations to whom I send you **d** it.	Jer 25:15
They shall **d** and stagger and be crazed	Jer 25:16
nations to whom the LORD sent me **d** it:	Jer 25:17
after them the king of Babylon shall **d**.	Jer 25:26
D, be drunk and vomit, fall and rise no	Jer 25:27
to accept the cup from your hand to **d**,	Jer 25:28
says the LORD of hosts: You must **d**!	Jer 25:28
made to Baal and **d** offerings have been	Jer 32:29
chambers; then offer them wine to **d**."	Jer 35:2
and cups, and I said to them, "**D** wine."	Jer 35:5
But they answered, "We will **d** no wine,	Jer 35:6
commanded us, 'You shall not **d** wine,	Jer 35:6
us, to **d** no wine all our days,	Jer 35:8
Rechab gave to his sons, to **d** no wine,	Jer 35:14
been kept, and they **d** none to this day,	Jer 35:14
heaven and pour out **d** offerings to her,	Jer 44:17
and pouring out **d** offerings to her,	Jer 44:18
and poured out **d** offerings to her,	Jer 44:19
and poured out **d** offerings to her?"	Jer 44:19
and to pour out **d** offerings to her.'	Jer 44:25
and be sated and **d** its fill of their	Jer 46:10
did not deserve to **d** the cup must drink	Jer 49:12
not deserve to drink the cup must **d** it,	Jer 49:12
not go unpunished, but you must **d**.	Jer 49:12
incense and the bowls for **d** offerings.	Jer 52:19
We must pay for the water we **d**; the	Lam 5:4
And water you shall **d** by measure, the	Ezk 4:11
of a hin; from day to day you shall **d**.	Ezk 4:11
and they shall **d** water by measure and	Ezk 4:16
and **d** water with trembling and with	Ezk 12:18
with anxiety, and **d** water in dismay.	Ezk 12:19
there they poured out their **d** offerings.	Ezk 20:28
"You shall **d** your sister's cup that is	Ezk 23:32
you shall **d** it and drain it out, and	Ezk 23:34
your fruit, and they shall **d** your milk.	Ezk 25:4
that no trees that **d** water may reach	Ezk 31:14
and best of Lebanon, all that **d** water,	Ezk 31:16
and to **d** of clear water, that you must	Ezk 34:18
and **d** what you have muddied with	Ezk 34:19
and you shall eat flesh and **d** blood.	Ezk 39:17
and **d** the blood of the princes of the	Ezk 39:18
filled, and **d** blood till you are drunk,	Ezk 39:19
No priest shall **d** wine when he enters	Ezk 44:21
grain offerings, and **d** offerings,	Ezk 45:17
who assigned your food and your **d**;	Dn 1:10
be given vegetables to eat and water to **d**.	Dn 1:12
their food and the wine they were to **d**,	Dn 1:16
and his concubines might **d** from them.	Dn 5:2
my wool and my flax, my oil and my **d**.'	Hos 2:5
When their **d** is gone, they give	Hos 4:18
They shall not pour **d** offerings of wine	Hos 9:4
grain offering and the **d** offering are cut off	Jl 1:9
grain offering and **d** offering are withheld	Jl 1:13
grain offering and a **d** offering for the	Jl 2:14
of their God they **d** the wine of those	Am 2:8
"But you made the Nazirites **d** wine,	Am 2:12
your husbands, 'Bring, that we may **d**!'	Am 4:1
would wander to another city to **d** water,	Am 4:8
but you shall not **d** their wine.	Am 5:11
who **d** wine in bowls and anoint	Am 6:6
shall plant vineyards and **d** their wine,	Am 9:14
so all the nations shall **d** continually;	Ob 1:16
continually; they shall **d** and swallow,	Ob 1:16
anything. Let them not feed or **d** water,	Jon 3:7
of wine and strong **d**," he would be the	Mi 2:11
you shall tread grapes, but not **d** wine.	Mi 6:15
thorns, like drunkards as they **d**;	Na 1:10
makes his neighbors **d**—you pour	Hab 2:15
D, yourself, and show your	Hab 2:16
they shall not **d** wine from them."	Zep 1:13
eat, but you never have enough; you **d**,	Hg 1:6
And when you eat and when you **d**, do	Zec 7:6
eat for yourselves and **d** for yourselves?	Zec 7:6
and they shall **d** and roar as if drunk	Zec 9:15
life, what you will eat or what you will **d**,	Mt 6:25
shall we eat?' or 'What shall we **d**?'	Mt 6:31
Are you able to **d** the cup that I am to	Mt 20:22
cup that I am to **d**?" They said to him,	Mt 20:22
He said to them, "You will **d** my cup,	Mt 20:23
food, I was thirsty and you gave me **d**,	Mt 25:35
and feed you, or thirsty and give you **d**?	Mt 25:37
I was thirsty and you gave me no **d**,	Mt 25:42
he gave it to them, saying, "**D** of it,	Mt 26:27
tell you I will not **d** again of this fruit of	Mt 26:29
until that day when I **d** it new with you	Mt 26:29
Father, if this cannot pass unless I **d** it,	Mt 26:42
they offered him wine to **d**, mixed with	Mt 27:34
but when he tasted it, he would not **d** it.	Mt 27:34
put it on a reed and gave it to him to **d**.	Mt 27:48
cup of water to **d** because you belong to	Mk 9:41
Are you able to **d** the cup that I drink,	Mk 10:38
Are you able to drink the cup that I **d**,	Mk 10:38
them, "The cup that I **d** you will drink,	Mk 10:39
them, "The cup that I drink you will **d**,	Mk 10:39
I will not **d** again of the fruit of the	Mk 14:25
until that day when I **d** it new in the	Mk 14:25
put it on a reed and gave it to him to **d**,	Mk 15:36
hands; and if they **d** any deadly poison,	Mk 16:18
And he must not **d** wine or strong drink,	Lk 1:15
And he must not drink wine or strong **d**,	Lk 1:15
do you eat and **d** with tax collectors and	Lk 5:30
of the Pharisees, but yours eat and **d**."	Lk 5:33
for many years; relax, eat, **d**, be merry.'	Lk 12:19
you are to eat and what you are to **d**,	Lk 12:29
and to eat and **d** and get drunk,	Lk 12:45
properly, and serve me while I eat and **d**,	Lk 17:8
drink, and afterward you will eat and **d**'?	Lk 17:8
now on I will not **d** of the fruit of the	Lk 22:18
that you may eat and **d** at my table in	Lk 22:30
water. Jesus said to her, "Give me a **d**."	Jn 4:7
is it that you, a Jew, ask for a **d** from me,	Jn 4:9
it is that is saying to you, 'Give me a **d**,'	Jn 4:10
flesh of the Son of Man and **d** his blood,	Jn 6:53
flesh is true food, and my blood is true **d**.	Jn 6:55

anyone thirsts, let him come to me and **d**. Jn 7:37
shall I not **d** the cup that the Father has Jn 18:11
neither to eat nor **d** till they had killed Acts 23:12
neither to eat nor **d** till they have Acts 23:21
is thirsty, give him something to **d**; Rom 12:20
to eat meat or **d** wine or do anything Rom 14:21
Do we not have the right to eat and **d**? 1 Cor 9:4
and all drank the same spiritual **d**. 1 Cor 10:4
sat down to eat and **d** and rose up to 1 Cor 10:7
You cannot **d** the cup of the Lord 1 Cor 10:21
So, whether you eat or **d**, or whatever 1 Cor 10:31
you not have houses to eat and **d** in? 1 Cor 11:22
Do this, as often as you **d** it, in 1 Cor 11:25
as you eat this bread and **d** the cup, 1 Cor 11:26
so eat of the bread and **d** of the cup. 1 Cor 11:28
and all were made to **d** of one Spirit. 1 Cor 12:13
dead are not raised, "Let us eat and **d**, 1 Cor 15:32
poured out as a **d** offering upon the Phil 2:17
on you in questions of food and **d**, Col 2:16
(No longer **d** only water, but use a 1 Tm 5:23
being poured out as a **d** offering, 2 Tm 4:6
with food and **d** and various washings, Heb 9:10
who made all nations **d** the wine of the Rv 14:8
he also will **d** the wine of God's wrath, Rv 14:10
and you have given them blood to **d**. Rv 16:6

DRINKERS (1)
and weep, and wail, all you **d** of wine, Jl 1:5

DRINKING (33)
also, until they have finished **d**." Gn 24:19
When the camels had finished **d**, the Gn 24:22
will grow weary of **d** water from the Ex 7:18
man until he has finished eating and **d**. Ru 3:3
the land, eating and **d** and dancing, 1 Sm 30:16
they are eating and **d** before him, 1 Kgs 1:25
All King Solomon's **d** vessels were of 1 Kgs 10:21
d himself drunk in the house of Arza, 1 Kgs 16:9
message as he was **d** with the kings 1 Kgs 20:12
Ben-hadad was **d** himself drunk 1 Kgs 20:16
David for three days, eating and **d**, 1 Chr 12:39
All King Solomon's **d** vessels were of 2 Chr 9:20
night, neither eating bread nor **d** water, Ezr 10:6
And **d** was according to this edict: "There Est 1:8
And as they were **d** wine after the feast, Est 5:6
day, as they were **d** wine after the feast, Est 7:2
to the place where they were **d** wine, Est 7:8
daughters were eating and **d** wine in their Jb 1:13
daughters were eating and **d** wine in their Jb 1:18
Woe to those who are heroes at **d** wine, Is 5:22
sheep, eating flesh and **d** wine. Is 22:13
man dreams he is **d** and awakes faint, Is 29:8
For John came neither eating nor **d**, Mt 11:18
The Son of Man came eating and **d**, Mt 11:19
before the flood they were eating and **d**, Mt 24:38
And no one after **d** old wine desires new, Lk 5:39
come eating no bread and **d** no wine, Lk 7:33
The Son of Man has come eating and **d**, Lk 7:34
house, eating and **d** what they provide, Lk 10:7
were eating and **d** and marrying and Lk 17:27
days of Lot—they were eating and **d**, Lk 17:28
of eating and **d** but of righteousness Rom 14:17
passions, drunkenness, orgies, **d** parties, 1 Pt 4:3

DRINKS (17)
Is it not from this that my lord **d**, and by Gn 44:5
which **d** water by the rain from heaven, Dt 11:11
taste what he eats or what he **d**? 2 Sm 19:35
D were served in golden vessels, vessels of Est 1:7
are in me; my spirit **d** their poison; Jb 6:4
a man who **d** injustice like water! Jb 15:16
is like Job, who **d** up scoffing like water, Jb 34:7
fool cuts off his own feet and **d** violence. Prv 26:6
strength fails; he **d** no water and is faint. Is 44:12
and eats and **d** with drunkards, Mt 24:49
"Everyone who **d** of this water will be Jn 4:13
but whoever **d** of the water that I will give Jn 4:14
on my flesh and **d** my blood has eternal Jn 6:54
on my flesh and **d** my blood abides in Jn 6:56
eats the bread or **d** the cup of the 1 Cor 11:27
who eats and **d** without discerning 1 Cor 11:29
body eats and **d** judgment on 1 Cor 11:29

DRIP (4)
the lips of a forbidden woman **d** honey, Prv 5:3
Your lips **d** nectar, my bride; honey and Sg 4:11
day the mountains shall **d** sweet wine, Jl 3:18
the mountains shall **d** sweet wine, and Am 9:13

DRIPPED (1)
my beloved, and my hands **d** with myrrh, Sg 5:5

DRIPPING (3)
quarreling is a continual **d** of rain. Prv 19:13
A continual **d** on a rainy day and a Prv 27:15
herbs. His lips are lilies, **d** liquid myrrh. Sg 5:13

DRIPPINGS (2)
than honey and **d** of the honeycomb Ps 19:10
and the **d** of the honeycomb are sweet Prv 24:13

DRIVE (54)
a strong hand he will **d** them out of his Ex 6:1
you go, he will **d** you away completely. Ex 11:1
you, which shall **d** out the Hivites, Ex 23:28
I will not **d** them out from before you in Ex 23:29
by little I will **d** them out from before Ex 23:30
and you shall **d** them out before you. Ex 23:31
you, and I will **d** out the Canaanites, Ex 33:2
I will **d** out before you the Amorites, Ex 34:11
to defeat them and **d** them from the Nm 22:6
fight against them and **d** them out.'" Nm 22:11
then you shall **d** out all the Nm 33:52
if you do not **d** out the inhabitants of Nm 33:55
the nations where the LORD will **d** you. Dt 4:27
So you shall **d** them out and make them Dt 9:3
then the LORD will **d** out all these Dt 11:23
he will without fail **d** out from before Jos 3:10
I myself will **d** them out from before the Jos 13:6
of Israel did not **d** out the Geshurites or Jos 13:13
and I shall **d** them out just as the LORD Jos 14:12
the people of Judah could not **d** out, Jos 15:63
they did not **d** out the Canaanites who Jos 16:10
labor, but did not utterly **d** them out. Jos 17:13
For you shall **d** out the Canaanites, Jos 17:18
back before you and **d** them out of your Jos 23:5
God will no longer **d** out these nations Jos 23:13
but he could not **d** out the inhabitants Jgs 1:19
of Benjamin did not **d** out the Jebusites Jgs 1:21
Manasseh did not **d** out the inhabitants Jgs 1:27
but did not **d** them out completely. Jgs 1:28
Ephraim did not **d** out the Canaanites Jgs 1:29
Zebulun did not **d** out the inhabitants of Jgs 1:30
Asher did not **d** out the inhabitants of Jgs 1:31
of the land, for they did not **d** them out. Jgs 1:32
Naphtali did not **d** out the inhabitants Jgs 1:33
I say, I will not **d** them out before you, Jgs 2:3
I will no longer **d** out before them any of Jgs 2:21
you not hate me and **d** me out of my Jgs 11:7
d out the inhabitants of this land 2 Chr 20:7
us by coming to **d** us out of your 2 Chr 20:11
They **d** away the donkey of the fatherless; Jb 24:3
nor the hand of the wicked **d** me away. Ps 36:11
driven away, so you shall **d** them away; Ps 68:2
D out a scoffer, and strife will go out, Prv 22:10
in all the places where I shall **d** them. Jer 24:9
far from your land, and I will **d** you out, Jer 27:10
the result that I will **d** you out and you Jer 27:15
the nations where I will **d** them." Ezk 4:13
here, to **d** me far from my sanctuary? Ezk 8:6
will turn you about and **d** you forward, Ezk 39:2
of their deeds I will **d** them out of my Hos 9:15
and **d** him into a parched and desolate Jl 2:20
of my people you **d** out from their Mi 2:9
temple and began to **d** out those who Mk 11:15
temple and began to **d** out those who Lk 19:45

DRIVEN (56)
you have **d** me today away from the Gn 4:14
tricked me and **d** away my daughters Gn 31:26
If they are **d** hard for one day, all the Gn 33:13
And they were **d** out from Pharaoh's Ex 10:11
and it dies or is injured or is **d** away, Ex 22:10
The sound of a **d** leaf shall put them to Lv 26:36
until he has **d** out his enemies from Nm 32:21
so that you are **d** mad by the sights that Dt 28:34
where the LORD your God has **d** you, Dt 30:1
these Moses had struck and **d** out. Jos 13:12
For the LORD has **d** out before you great Jos 23:9
for they have **d** me out this day that I 1 Sm 26:19
Have you not **d** out the priests of the 2 Chr 13:9
help in me, when resource is **d** from me? Jb 6:13
Will you frighten a **d** leaf and pursue Jb 13:25
into darkness, and **d** out of the world. Jb 18:18
They are **d** out from human company; Jb 30:5
As smoke is **d** away, so you shall drive Ps 68:2
and God seeks what has been **d** away. Eccl 3:15
the Nile will be parched, will be **d** away, Is 19:7
and those who were **d** out to the land Is 27:13
his sword, like **d** stubble with his bow. Is 41:2
in all the places where I have **d** them, Jer 8:3
scatter you like chaff **d** by the wind Jer 13:24
all the countries where he had **d** them.' Jer 16:15
my flock and have **d** them away, Jer 23:2
of all the countries where I have **d** them, Jer 23:3
all the countries where he had **d** them.' Jer 23:8
into which they shall be **d** and fall, Jer 23:12
and all the places where I have **d** you, Jer 29:14
all the nations where I have **d** them, Jer 29:18
which they had been **d** and came to the Jer 40:12
the nations to which they had been **d**— Jer 43:5
of all the nations to which I have **d** you, Jer 46:28
are around you, and you shall be **d** out, Jer 49:5
nation to which those **d** out of Elam Jer 49:36
is a hunted sheep **d** away by lions. Jer 50:17
he has **d** and brought me into darkness Lam 3:2
that you shall be **d** from among men, Dn 4:25
and you shall be **d** from among men, Dn 4:32
He was **d** from among men and ate Dn 4:33
He was **d** from among the children of Dn 5:21
all the lands to which you have **d** them, Dn 9:7
All your allies have **d** you to your border; Ob 1:7
I said, 'I am **d** away from your sight; Jon 2:4
those who have been **d** away and those Mi 4:6
Ashdod's people shall be **d** out at noon, Zep 2:4
kind cannot be **d** out by anything Mk 9:29
the bonds and be **d** by the demon into Lk 8:29
we gave way to it and were **d** along. Acts 27:15
the gear, and thus they were **d** along. Acts 27:17
we were being **d** across the Adriatic Acts 27:27
perplexed, but not **d** to despair; 2 Cor 4:8
of the sea that is **d** and tossed by the wind. Jas 1:6
are so large and are **d** by strong winds, Jas 3:4
springs and mists **d** by a storm. 2 Pt 2:17

DRIVER (3)
he said to the **d** of his chariot, 1 Kgs 22:34
he said to the **d** of his chariot, 2 Chr 18:33
the city; he hears not the shouts of the **d**. Jb 39:7

DRIVES (7)
son of Nimshi, for he **d** furiously." 2 Kgs 9:20
so, but are like chaff that the wind **d** away. Ps 1:4
the wicked and **d** the wheel over Prv 20:26
the rod of discipline **d** it far from him. Prv 22:15
Surely oppression **d** the wise into Eccl 7:7
when he **d** his cart wheel over it with his Is 28:28
stream, which the wind of the LORD **d**. Is 59:19

DRIVING (15)
the nations I am **d** out before you have Lv 18:24
of the nation that I am **d** out before you, Lv 20:23
d out before you nations greater and Dt 4:38
that the LORD is **d** them out before you. Dt 9:4
LORD your God is **d** them out from before Dt 9:5
LORD your God is **d** them out before you. Dt 18:12
those nations, not **d** them out quickly, Jgs 2:23
sons of Abinadab, were **d** the new cart, 2 Sm 6:3
awesome things by **d** out before your 2 Sm 7:23
And the **d** is like the driving of Jehu 2 Kgs 9:20
driving is like the **d** of Jehu the son 2 Kgs 9:20
and Uzzah and Ahio were **d** the cart. 1 Chr 13:7
in **d** out nations before your people 1 Chr 17:21
with the angel of the LORD **d** them away! Ps 35:5
your great learning is **d** you out of Acts 26:24

DROMEDARIES (1)
and in litters and on mules and on **d**, Is 66:20

DROOPING (1)
Therefore lift your **d** hands and Heb 12:12

DROP (11)
with the oil, for your olives shall **d** off. Dt 28:40
May my teaching **d** as the rain, my Dt 32:2
and wine, whose heavens **d** down dew. Dt 33:28
They did not **d** any of their practices or Jgs 2:19
"Their hands will **d** from the work, Neh 6:9
and made him **d** his prey from Jb 29:17
pour down and **d** on mankind Jb 36:28
For they **d** trouble upon me, and in Ps 55:3
open, and the clouds **d** down the dew. Prv 3:20
the nations are like a **d** from a bucket, Is 40:15
will make your arrows **d** out of your Ezk 39:3

DROPPED (5)
and without seeing him **d** it on him, Nm 35:23
the earth trembled and the heavens **d**, Jgs 5:4
heavens dropped, yes, the clouds **d** water. Jgs 5:4
brought their tax and **d** it into the 2 Chr 24:10
speak again, and my word **d** upon them. Jb 29:22

DROPPING (1)
the forest, behold, the honey was **d**, 1 Sm 14:26

DROPS (4)
For he draws up the **d** of water; they Jb 36:27
or who has begotten the **d** of dew? Jb 38:28
dew, my locks with the **d** of the night." Sg 5:2
became like great **d** of blood falling Lk 22:44

DROPSY (1)
there was a man before him who had **d**. Lk 14:2

DROSS (7)
of the earth you discard like **d**, Ps 119:119
Take away the **d** from the silver, and Prv 25:4
Your silver has become **d**, your best wine Is 1:22
will smelt away your **d** as with lye and Is 1:25
house of Israel has become **d** to me; Ezk 22:18
lead in the furnace; they are **d** of silver. Ezk 22:18
Because you have all become **d**, Ezk 22:19

DROUGHT (9)
and with **d** and with blight and with Dt 28:22
D and heat snatch away the snow Jb 24:19
and pits, in a land of **d** and deep darkness, Jer 2:6

me; without cause they **d** a pit for my life. Ps 35:7
They **d** a pit in my way, but they have Ps 57:6
of trouble, until a pit is **d** for the wicked. Ps 94:13
The insolent have **d** pitfalls for me; Ps 119:85
He **d** it and cleared it of stones, and planted Is 5:2
I **d** wells and drank waters, to dry up Is 37:25
and to the quarry from which you were **d**. Is 51:1
Then I went to the Euphrates, and **d**, and Jer 13:7
evil? Yet they have **d** a pit for my life. Jer 18:20
For they have **d** a pit to take me and Jer 18:22
man, dig in the wall." So I **d** in the wall, Ezk 8:8
in the evening I **d** through the wall with Ezk 12:7
fence around it and **d** a winepress in it Mt 21:33
one talent went and **d** in the ground Mt 25:18
a fence around it and **d** a pit for the Mk 12:1
who **d** deep and laid the foundation on Lk 6:48

DULL (6)
on the skin of the body are of a **d** white, Lv 13:39
Make the heart of this people **d**, and their Is 6:10
that it cannot save, or his ear **d**, Is 59:1
For this people's heart has grown **d**, Mt 13:15
For this people's heart has grown **d**, Acts 28:27
since you have become **d** of hearing. Heb 5:11

DULLEST (1)
Understand, O **d** of the people! Fools, Ps 94:8

DULLNESS (1)
You will give them **d** of heart; your Lam 3:65

DUMAH (4)
Mishma, **D**, Massa, Gn 25:14
Arab, **D**, Eshan, Jos 15:52
Mishma, **D**, Massa, Hadad, Tema, 1 Chr 1:30
The oracle concerning **D**. One is calling Is 21:11

DUMPED (2)
dragged and **d** beyond the gates of Jer 22:19
with the sword and **d** his dead body into Jer 26:23

DUNG (27)
its skin and its **d** you shall burn with Ex 29:14
its head, its legs, its entrails, and its **d**— Lv 4:11
and its flesh and its **d** he burned up with Lv 8:17
their flesh and their **d** shall be burned Lv 16:27
skin, its flesh, and its blood, with its **d**, Nm 19:5
out of his belly; and the **d** came out. Jgs 3:22
as a man burns up **d** until it is all 1 Kgs 14:10
of a kab of dove's **d** for five shekels of 2 Kgs 6:25
of Jezebel shall be as **d** on the face of 2 Kgs 9:37
to eat their own **d** and to drink their 2 Kgs 18:27
to the Dragon Spring and to the **D** Gate, Neh 2:13
cubits of the wall, as far as the **D** Gate. Neh 3:13
Beth-haccherem, repaired the **D** Gate. Neh 3:14
to the south on the wall to the **D** Gate. Neh 12:31
he will perish forever like his own **d**; Jb 20:7
En-dor, who became **d** for the ground. Ps 83:10
to eat their own **d** and drink their own Is 36:12
They shall be as **d** on the surface of the Jer 8:2
men shall fall like **d** upon the open field, Jer 9:22
They shall be as **d** on the surface of the Jer 16:4
they shall be **d** on the surface of the Jer 25:33
baking it in their sight on human **d**." Ezk 4:12
assign to you cow's **d** instead of human Ezk 4:15
to you cow's dung instead of human **d**, Ezk 4:15
out like dust, and their flesh like **d**. Zep 1:17
offspring, and spread **d** on your faces, Mal 2:3
on your faces, the **d** of your offerings, Mal 2:3

DUNGEON (3)
of the captive who was in the **d**, Ex 12:29
to bring out the prisoners from the **d**, Is 42:7
had come to the **d** cells and remained Jer 37:16

DUNGHILL (2)
on it, and his house shall be made a **d**. Ezr 6:11
place, as straw is trampled down in a **d**. Is 25:10

DURA (1)
He set it up on the plain of **D**, in the Dn 3:1

DURING (27)
the land of Egypt **d** the seven plentiful Gn 41:34
D the seven plentiful years the earth Gn 41:47
D those many days the king of Egypt Ex 2:23
which she lies **d** her menstrual Lv 15:20
with a woman **d** her menstrual period Lv 20:18
those whom he had killed **d** his life. Jgs 16:30
or **d** all the days of the kings of Israel 2 Kgs 23:22
should dwell in booths **d** the feast of Neh 8:14
to do under heaven **d** the few days of Eccl 2:3
became their food **d** the destruction of Lam 4:10
D the number of days that you lie on Ezk 4:9
flock at Jerusalem **d** her appointed Ezk 36:38
So this Daniel prospered **d** the reign of Dn 6:28
sacrifices and offerings **d** the forty Am 5:25
But they said, "Not **d** the feast, lest there Mt 26:5
for they said, "Not **d** the feast, lest there Mk 14:2
d the high priesthood of Annas and Lk 3:2
the devil. And he ate nothing **d** those days. Lk 4:2
D supper, when the devil had already put Jn 13:2
appearing to them **d** forty days and Acts 1:3
have accompanied us **d** all the time Acts 1:21
But **d** the night an angel of the Lord Acts 5:19
d the forty years in the wilderness, Acts 7:42
This was **d** the days of Unleavened Acts 12:3
made the people great **d** their stay in Acts 13:17
on your behalf **d** my imprisonment Phlm 1:13
that no rain may fall **d** the days of their Rv 11:6

DUSK (3)
your shoulder and carry it out at **d**. Ezk 12:6
I brought out my baggage at **d**, Ezk 12:7
his baggage upon his shoulder at **d**, Ezk 12:12

DUST (109)
formed the man of **d** from the ground Gn 2:7
and **d** you shall eat all the days of your Gn 3:14
for you are **d**, and to dust you shall Gn 3:19
you are dust, and to **d** you shall return." Gn 3:19
your offspring as the **d** of the earth, Gn 13:16
that if one can count the **d** of the earth, Gn 13:16
to the Lord, I who am but **d** and ashes. Gn 18:27
shall be like the **d** of the earth, Gn 28:14
your staff and strike the **d** of the earth, Ex 8:16
his staff and struck the **d** of the earth, Ex 8:17
All the **d** of the earth became gnats in all Ex 8:17
It shall become fine **d** over all the land of Ex 9:9
and take some of the **d** that is on the Nm 5:17
Who can count the **d** of Jacob or Nm 23:10
it very small, until it was as fine as **d**. Dt 9:21
And I threw the **d** of it into the brook that Dt 9:21
From heaven **d** shall come down on Dt 28:24
the venom of things that crawl in the **d**. Dt 32:24
of Israel. And they put **d** on their heads. Jos 7:6
He raises up the poor from the **d**; he lifts 1 Sm 2:8
and threw stones at him and flung **d**. 2 Sm 16:13
I beat them fine as the **d** of the earth; 2 Sm 22:43
you out of the **d** and made you leader 1 Kgs 16:2
the wood and the stones and the **d**, 1 Kgs 18:38
if the **d** of Samaria shall suffice for 1 Kgs 20:10
made them like the **d** at threshing. 2 Kgs 13:7
and beat it to **d** and cast the dust 2 Kgs 23:6
to dust and cast the **d** of it upon the 2 Kgs 23:6
pieces and cast the **d** of them into 2 Kgs 23:12
down and burned, reducing it to **d**. 2 Kgs 23:15
as numerous as the **d** of the earth. 2 Chr 1:9
and he made **d** of them and scattered 2 Chr 34:4
robes and sprinkled **d** on their heads Jb 2:12
of clay, whose foundation is in the **d**, Jb 4:19
For affliction does not come from the **d**, Jb 5:6
clay; and will you return me to the **d**? Jb 10:9
skin and have laid my strength in the **d**. Jb 16:15
Shall we descend together into the **d**?" Jb 17:16
but it will lie down with him in the **d**. Jb 20:11
They lie down alike in the **d**, and the Jb 21:26
if you lay gold in the **d**, and gold of Jb 22:24
Though he heap up silver like **d**, and Jb 27:16
place of sapphires, and it has **d** of gold. Jb 28:6
and I have become like **d** and ashes. Jb 30:19
together, and man would return to **d**. Jb 34:15
when the **d** runs into a mass and the Jb 38:38
Hide them all in the **d** together; bind Jb 40:13
myself, and repent in **d** and ashes." Jb 42:6
to the ground and lay my glory in the **d**. Ps 7:5
I beat them fine as **d** before the wind; I Ps 18:42
to my jaws; you lay me in the **d** of death. Ps 22:15
him shall bow all who go down to the **d**, Ps 22:29
go down to the pit? Will the **d** praise you? Ps 30:9
For our soul is bowed down to the **d**; Ps 44:25
before him and his enemies lick the **d**! Ps 72:9
he rained meat on them like **d**, winged Ps 78:27
O my God, make them like whirling **d**, Ps 83:13
you have defiled his crown in the **d**. Ps 89:39
You return man to **d** and say, "Return, O Ps 90:3
her stones dear and have pity on her **d**. Ps 102:14
frame; he remembers that we are **d**. Ps 103:14
breath, they die and return to their **d**. Ps 104:29
the poor from the **d** and lifts the needy Ps 113:7
My soul clings to the **d**; give me life Ps 119:25
fields, or the first of the **d** of the world. Prv 8:26
All are from the **d**, and to dust all Eccl 3:20
are from the dust, and to **d** all return. Eccl 3:20
and the **d** returns to the earth as it was, Eccl 12:7
and hide in the **d** from before the terror Is 2:10
and their blossom go up like **d**; Is 5:24
wind and whirling **d** before the storm. Is 17:13
lay low, and cast to the ground, to the **d**. Is 25:12
lays it low to the ground, casts it to the **d**. Is 26:5
You who dwell in the **d**, awake and sing Is 26:19
and from the **d** your speech will be bowed Is 29:4
and from the **d** your speech shall whisper. Is 29:4
of your foreign foes shall be like small **d**, Is 29:5
enclosed the **d** of the earth in a measure Is 40:12
and are accounted as the **d** on the scales; Is 40:15
he takes up the coastlands like fine **d**. Is 40:15
he makes them like **d** with his sword, like Is 41:2
Come down and sit in the **d**, O virgin Is 47:1
down to you, and lick the **d** of your feet. Is 49:23
Shake yourself from the **d** and arise; be Is 52:2
the ox, and **d** shall be the serpent's food. Is 65:25
they have thrown **d** on their heads and Lam 2:10
In the **d** of the streets lie the young and Lam 2:21
put his mouth in the **d**—there may yet Lam 3:29
it out on the ground to cover it with **d**. Ezk 24:7
be so many that their **d** will cover you. Ezk 26:10
They cast **d** on their heads and wallow Ezk 27:30
who sleep in the **d** of the earth shall Dn 12:2
of the poor into the **d** of the earth and Am 2:7
Beth-le-aphrah roll yourselves in the **d**. Mi 1:10
they shall lick the **d** like a serpent, like Mi 7:17
storm, and the clouds are the **d** of his feet. Na 1:3
their blood shall be poured out like **d**, Zep 1:17
a rampart and heaped up silver like **d**, Zec 9:3
shake off the **d** from your feet when Mt 10:14
shake off the **d** that is on your feet as a Mk 6:11
town shake off the **d** from your feet as Lk 9:5
'Even the **d** of your town that clings to Lk 10:11
they shook off the **d** from their feet Acts 13:51
cloaks and flinging **d** into the air, Acts 22:23
man was from the earth, a man of **d**; 1 Cor 15:47
As was the man of **d**, so also are 1 Cor 15:48
so also are those who are of the **d**, 1 Cor 15:48
borne the image of the man of **d**, 1 Cor 15:49
And they threw **d** on their heads as they Rv 18:19

DUTIES (9)
do to the Levites in assigning their **d**." Nm 8:26
the rights and **d** of the kingship, 1 Sm 10:25
to the appointed **d** in their service. 1 Chr 24:3
who did the work and of their **d** was: 1 Chr 25:1
And they cast lots for their **d**, small 1 Chr 25:8
to their chief men, had **d**, 1 Chr 26:12
appointed to external **d** for Israel, 1 Chr 26:29
and I established the **d** of the priests Neh 13:30
first section, performing their ritual **d**, Heb 9:6

DUTY (39)
and perform the **d** of a brother-in-law Gn 38:8
And the guard **d** of the sons of Gershon Nm 3:25
And their guard **d** involved the ark, the Nm 3:31
And the appointed guard **d** of the sons Nm 3:36
to fifty years old, all who can come on **d**, Nm 4:3
list them, all who can come to do **d**, Nm 4:23
and their guard **d** is to be under the Nm 4:28
list them, everyone who can come on **d**, Nm 4:30
old, everyone who could come on **d**, Nm 4:35
who could come on **d** for service in the Nm 4:39
old, everyone who could come on **d**, Nm 4:43
they shall come to do **d** in the service of Nm 8:24
withdraw from the **d** of the service Nm 8:25
army or be liable for any other public **d**. Dt 24:5
wife and perform the **d** of a husband's Dt 25:5
will not perform the **d** of a husband's Dt 25:7
was required, each according to his **d**. 1 Kgs 4:28
those who come off **d** on the Sabbath 2 Kgs 11:5
which come on **d** in force on the 2 Kgs 11:7
who were to go off **d** on the Sabbath, 2 Kgs 11:9
were to come on **d** on the Sabbath, 2 Kgs 11:9
for on them lay the **d** of watching, 1 Chr 9:27
for they were on **d** day and night. 1 Chr 9:33
For their **d** was to assist the sons of 1 Chr 23:28
Their **d** was also to assist with the 1 Chr 23:29
as their appointed **d** in their service 1 Chr 24:19
and it was the **d** of the trumpeters and 2 Chr 5:13
as the **d** of each day required, offering 2 Chr 8:13
the priests as the **d** of each day 2 Chr 8:14
who come off **d** on the Sabbath, 2 Chr 23:4
who were to go off **d** on the Sabbath, 2 Chr 23:8
were to come on **d** on the Sabbath, 2 Chr 23:8
the LORD as the **d** of each day 2 Chr 31:16
and their **d** was to distribute to their Neh 13:13
for this is the whole **d** of man. Eccl 12:13
shall be the prince's **d** to furnish the Ezk 45:17
before God when his division was on **d**, Lk 1:8
we have only done what was our **d**.'" Lk 17:10
wisdom, whom we will appoint to this **d**. Acts 6:3

DWARF (1)
or a hunchback or a **d** or a man with a Lv 21:20

DWELL (290)
father of those who **d** in tents and have Gn 4:20
and let him **d** in the tents of Shem, Gn 9:27
so great that they could not **d** together, Gn 13:6
and he shall **d** over against all his Gn 16:12
is before you; **d** where it pleases you." Gn 20:15
of the Canaanites, among whom I **d**, Gn 24:3
of the Canaanites, in whose land I **d**, Gn 24:37
d in the land of which I shall tell you. Gn 26:2
You shall **d** with us, and the land shall Gn 34:10
D and trade in it, and get property in Gn 34:10
and we will **d** with you and become Gn 34:16

let them **d** in the land and trade in it, Gn 34:21
the men agree to **d** with us to become Gn 34:22
with them, and they will **d** with us." Gn 34:23
"Arise, go up to Bethel and **d** there. Gn 35:1
were too great for them to **d** together. Gn 36:7
You shall **d** in the land of Goshen, and Gn 45:10
in order that you may **d** in the land of Gn 46:34
please let your servants **d** in the land of Gn 47:4
"Zebulun shall **d** at the shore of the Gn 49:13
Moses was content to **d** with the man, Ex 2:21
the land of Goshen, where my people **d**, Ex 8:22
They shall not **d** in your land, lest they Ex 23:33
a sanctuary, that I may **d** in their midst. Ex 25:8
I will **d** among the people of Israel and Ex 29:45
of Egypt that I might **d** among them. Ex 29:46
You shall **d** in booths for seven days. Lv 23:42
All native Israelites shall **d** in booths, Lv 23:42
the people of Israel **d** in booths when I Lv 23:43
and then you will **d** in the land Lv 25:18
will eat your fill and **d** in it securely. Lv 25:19
to the full and **d** in your land securely. Lv 26:5
their camp, in the midst of which I **d**." Nm 5:3
whether the people who **d** in it are Nm 13:18
the land that they **d** in is good or Nm 13:19
the cities that they **d** in are camps or Nm 13:19
the people who **d** in the land are Nm 13:28
The Amalekites **d** in the land of the Nm 13:29
and the Amorites **d** in the hill Nm 13:29
And the Canaanites **d** by the sea, Nm 13:29
and the Canaanites **d** in the valleys, Nm 14:25
I swore that I would make you **d**, Nm 14:30
trouble you in the land where you **d**. Nm 33:55
possession as cities for them to **d** in. Nm 35:2
The cities shall be theirs to **d** in, and Nm 35:3
he may return to **d** in the land before Nm 35:32
you live, in the midst of which I **d**, Nm 35:34
for I the LORD **d** in the midst of the Nm 35:34
will choose, to make his name **d** there, Dt 12:11
you dispossess them and **d** in their land, Dt 12:29
LORD your God is giving you to **d** there, Dt 13:12
will choose, to make his name **d** there, Dt 14:23
will choose, to make his name **d** there. Dt 16:2
will choose, to make his name **d** in it, Dt 16:6
will choose, to make his name **d** there. Dt 16:11
and you possess it and **d** in it and then Dt 17:14
you dispossess them and **d** in their cities Dt 19:1
He shall **d** with you, in your midst, in Dt 23:16
"If brothers **d** together, and one of them Dt 25:5
will choose, to make his name to **d** there. Dt 26:2
build a house, but you shall not **d** in it. Dt 28:30
that you may **d** in the land that the Dt 30:20
had been content to **d** beyond the Jordan! Jos 7:7
far from you,' when you **d** among us? Jos 9:22
of the Amorites who **d** in the hill Jos 10:6
Geshur and Maacath **d** in the midst Jos 13:13
in the land, but only cities to **d** in, Jos 14:4
so the Jebusites **d** with the people of Jos 15:63
all the Canaanites who **d** in the plain Jos 17:16
Moses that we be given cities to **d** in, Jos 21:2
you had not built, and you **d** in them. Jos 24:13
of the Amorites in whose land you **d**. Jos 24:15
of the Amorites in whose land you **d**.' Jgs 6:10
so that they could not **d** at Shechem. Jgs 9:41
Levite was content to **d** with the man, Jgs 17:11
seeking for itself an inheritance to **d** in, Jgs 18:1
of the LORD and **d** there forever." 1 Sm 1:22
Egypt and made them **d** in this place. 1 Sm 12:8
the country towns, that I may **d** there. 1 Sm 27:5
should your servant **d** in the royal 1 Sm 27:5
"See now, I **d** in a house of cedar, 2 Sm 7:2
Would you build me a house to **d** in? 2 Sm 7:5
so that they may **d** in their own place 2 Sm 7:10
and Israel and Judah **d** in booths, 2 Sm 11:11
"Let him **d** apart in his own house; 2 Sm 14:24
a house in Jerusalem and **d** there, 1 Kgs 2:36
And I will **d** among the children of 1 Kgs 6:13
His own house where he was to **d**, in 1 Kgs 7:8
that he would **d** in thick darkness. 1 Kgs 8:12
house, a place for you to **d** in forever." 1 Kgs 8:13
"But will God indeed **d** on the earth? 1 Kgs 8:27
which belongs to Sidon, and **d** there. 1 Kgs 17:9
"I **d** among my own people." 2 Kgs 4:13
place where we **d** under your charge 2 Kgs 6:1
place for us to **d** there." And he 2 Kgs 6:2
to Elath, where they **d** to this day. 2 Kgs 16:6
let him go and **d** there and teach 2 Kgs 17:27
Now the first to **d** again in their 1 Chr 9:2
"Behold, I **d** in a house of cedar, 1 Chr 17:1
who will build me a house to **d** in. 1 Chr 17:4
that they may **d** in their own place 1 Chr 17:9
cedar to build himself a house to **d** in, 2 Chr 2:3
that he would **d** in thick darkness. 2 Chr 6:1
house, a place for you to **d** in forever." 2 Chr 6:2
"But will God indeed **d** with man on 2 Chr 6:18
his name to **d** there overthrow any Ezr 6:12
have chosen, to make my name **d** there.' Neh 1:9
of Israel should **d** in booths during Neh 8:14
darkness claim it. Let clouds **d** upon it; Jb 3:5
much more those who **d** in houses of Jb 4:19
and let not injustice **d** in your tents. Jb 11:14
In the gullies of the torrents they must **d**, Jb 30:6
you alone, O LORD, make me **d** in safety. Ps 4:8
in wickedness; evil may not **d** with you. Ps 5:4
tent? Who shall **d** on your holy hill? Ps 15:1
and I shall **d** in the house of the LORD Ps 23:6
the world and those who **d** therein, Ps 24:1
that I may **d** in the house of the LORD all Ps 27:4
d in the land and befriend faithfulness. Ps 37:3
evil and do good; so shall you **d** forever. Ps 37:27
inherit the land and **d** upon it forever. Ps 37:29
consumed in Sheol, with no place to **d**. Ps 49:14
Let me **d** in your tent forever! Let me take Ps 61:4
and bring near, to **d** in your courts! Ps 65:4
so that those who **d** at the ends of the Ps 65:8
but the rebellious **d** in a parched land. Ps 68:6
yes, where the LORD will **d** forever? Ps 68:16
that the LORD God may **d** there. Ps 68:18
the beasts that **d** among the reeds, Ps 68:30
a desolation; let no one **d** in their tents. Ps 69:25
and people shall **d** there and possess it; Ps 69:35
those who love his name shall **d** in it. Ps 69:36
Blessed are those who **d** in your house, Ps 84:4
house of my God than **d** in the tents of Ps 84:10
fear him, that glory may **d** in our land. Ps 85:9
fills it; the world and those who **d** in it! Ps 98:7
in the land, that they may **d** with me; Ps 101:6
practices deceit shall **d** in my house; Ps 101:7
of your servants shall **d** secure; Ps 102:28
Beside them the birds of the heavens **d**; Ps 104:12
wastes, finding no way to a city to **d** in; Ps 107:4
way till they reached a city to **d** in. Ps 107:7
And there he lets the hungry **d**, and Ps 107:36
that I **d** among the tents of Kedar! Ps 120:5
here I will **d**, for I have desired it. Ps 132:14
pleasant it is when brothers **d** in unity! Ps 133:1
of the morning and **d** in the uttermost Ps 139:9
the upright shall **d** in your presence. Ps 140:13
listens to me will **d** secure and will be Prv 1:33
"I, wisdom, **d** with prudence, and I find Prv 8:12
but the wicked will not **d** in the land. Prv 10:30
life-giving reproof will **d** among the Prv 15:31
O you who **d** in the gardens, with Sg 8:13
and you are made to **d** alone in the midst of Is 5:8
and I **d** in the midst of a people of unclean Is 6:5
"O my people, who **d** in Zion, be not Is 10:24
The wolf shall **d** with the lamb, and the Is 11:6
there ostriches will **d**, and there wild Is 13:21
of the world, you who **d** on the earth, Is 18:3
clothing for those who **d** before the LORD. Is 23:18
You who **d** in the dust, awake and sing Is 26:19
For a people shall **d** in Zion, in Is 30:19
Then justice will **d** in the wilderness, Is 32:16
among us can **d** with the consuming Is 33:14
among us can **d** with everlasting Is 33:14
he will **d** on the heights; his place of Is 33:16
the people who **d** there will be forgiven Is 33:24
it, the owl and the raven shall **d** in it. Is 34:11
to generation they shall **d** in it. Is 34:17
and spreads them like a tent to **d** in; Is 40:22
the beauty of a man, to **d** in a house. Is 44:13
for me; make room for me to **d** in.' Is 49:20
and they who **d** in it will die in like Is 51:6
"I **d** in the high and holy place, and also Is 57:15
the breach, the restorer of streets to **d** in. Is 58:12
possess it, and my servants shall **d** there. Is 65:9
deeds, and I will let you **d** in this place. Jer 7:3
then I will let you **d** in this place, in the Jer 7:7
Shiloh, where I made my name **d** at first, Jer 7:12
that fills it, the city and those who **d** in it. Jer 8:16
and all who **d** in the desert who cut the Jer 9:26
the ground, O you who **d** under siege! Jer 10:17
the evil of those who **d** in it the beasts Jer 12:4
He shall **d** in the parched places of the Jer 17:6
Pashhur, and all who **d** in your house, Jer 20:6
will be saved, and Israel will **d** securely. Jer 23:6
Then they shall **d** in their own land." Jer 23:8
and those who **d** in the land of Egypt. Jer 24:8
and **d** upon the land that the LORD has Jer 25:5
of the mixed tribes who **d** in the desert; Jer 25:24
on its own land, to work it and **d** there, Jer 27:11
all the people who **d** in this city, Jer 29:16
and all its cities shall **d** there together, Jer 31:24
place, and I will make them **d** in safety. Jer 32:37
be saved and Jerusalem will **d** securely. Jer 33:16
and not to build houses to **d** in. We have Jer 35:9
and then you shall **d** in the land that I Jer 35:15
and **d** with him among the people. Jer 40:5
D in the land and serve the king of Jer 40:9
As for me, I will **d** at Mizpah, to Jer 40:10
and **d** in your cities that you have Jer 40:10
hungry for bread, and we will **d** there,' Jer 42:14
I will punish those who **d** in the land of Jer 44:13
to which they desire to return to **d** there. Jer 44:14
all you of Judah who **d** in the land of Jer 44:26
that fills it, the city and those who **d** in it. Jer 47:2
"Leave the cities, and **d** in the rock, O Jer 48:28
Flee, turn back, **d** in the depths, O Jer 49:8
says the LORD, no man shall **d** there, Jer 49:18
Flee, wander far away, **d** in the depths, Jer 49:30
everlasting waste; no man shall **d** there; Jer 49:33
land a desolation, and none shall **d** in it; Jer 50:3
wild beasts shall **d** with hyenas in Jer 50:39
Babylon, and ostriches shall **d** in her. Jer 50:39
the LORD, so no man shall **d** there, Jer 50:40
O you who **d** by many waters, rich in Jer 51:13
cut it off, so that nothing shall **d** in it, Jer 51:62
he has made me **d** in darkness like the Lam 3:6
of Edom, you who **d** in the land of Uz; Lam 4:21
Wherever you **d**, the cities shall be waste Ezk 6:6
you **d** in the midst of a rebellious Ezk 12:2
of the violence of all those who **d** in it. Ezk 12:19
And under it will **d** every kind of bird; Ezk 17:23
will make you to **d** in the world below, Ezk 26:20
then they shall **d** in their own land Ezk 28:25
And they shall **d** securely in it, and Ezk 28:26
They shall **d** securely, when I execute Ezk 28:26
On its fallen trunk **d** all the birds of Ezk 31:13
it, when I strike down all who **d** in it, Ezk 32:15
so that they may **d** securely in the Ezk 34:25
They shall **d** securely, and none shall Ezk 34:28
You shall **d** in the land that I gave to Ezk 36:28
They shall **d** in the land that I gave to Ezk 37:25
children shall **d** there forever, Ezk 37:25
from the peoples and now **d** securely, Ezk 38:8
upon the quiet people who **d** securely, Ezk 38:11
goods, who **d** at the center of the earth. Ezk 38:12
and on those who **d** securely in the Ezk 39:6
"Then those who **d** in the cities of Israel Ezk 39:9
when they **d** securely in their land Ezk 39:26
where I will **d** in the midst of the people Ezk 43:7
me, and I will **d** in their midst forever. Ezk 43:9
hand he has given, wherever they **d**, Dn 2:38
and languages, that **d** in all the earth: Dn 4:1
and languages that **d** in all the earth: Dn 6:25
"You must **d** as mine for many days. Hos 3:3
of Israel shall **d** many days without Hos 3:4
mourns, and all who **d** in it languish, Hos 4:3
I will again make you **d** in tents, as in Hos 12:9
shall return and **d** beneath my shadow; Hos 14:7
people of Israel who **d** in Samaria be Am 3:12
stone, but you shall not **d** in them; Am 5:11
and it melts, and all who **d** in it mourn, Am 9:5
from the city and **d** in the open country; Mi 4:10
And they shall **d** secure, for now he shall Mi 5:4
who **d** alone in a forest in the midst of a Mi 7:14
before him, the world and all who **d** in it. Na 1:5
earth, to cities and all who **d** in them. Hab 2:8
earth, to cities and all who **d** in them. Hab 2:17
for you yourselves to **d** in your paneled Hg 1:4
you who **d** with the daughter of Babylon. Zec 2:7
I come and I will **d** in your midst, Zec 2:10
my people. And I will **d** in your midst, Zec 2:11
to Zion and will **d** in the midst of Zec 8:3
I will bring them to **d** in the midst of Zec 8:8
a mixed people shall **d** in Ashdod, and I Zec 9:6
Jerusalem shall **d** in security. Zec 14:11
than itself, and they enter and **d** there, Mt 12:45
than itself, and they enter and **d** there. Lk 11:26
will come upon all who **d** on the face of Lk 21:35
and let there be no one to **d** in it'; Acts 1:20
of Judea and all who **d** in Jerusalem, Acts 2:14
rejoiced; my flesh also will **d** in hope. Acts 2:26
Most High does not **d** in houses made Acts 7:48
so that Christ may **d** in your hearts Eph 3:17
all the fullness of God was pleased to **d**, Col 1:19
Let the word of Christ **d** in you richly, Col 3:16
the spirit that he has made to **d** in us"? Jas 4:5
"'I know where you **d**, where Satan's Rv 2:13
world, to try those who **d** on the earth. Rv 3:10
our blood on those who **d** on the earth?" Rv 6:10
woe, woe to those who **d** on the earth, Rv 8:13
and those who **d** on the earth will Rv 11:10
a torment to those who **d** on the earth. Rv 11:10
O heavens and you who **d** in them! Rv 12:12
dwelling, that is, those who **d** in heaven. Rv 13:6
and all who **d** on earth will worship it, Rv 13:8
beast it deceives those who **d** on earth, Rv 13:14
to proclaim to those who **d** on earth, Rv 14:6
of God is with man. He will **d** with them, Rv 21:3

DWELLERS (3)

the way of the tent **d** east of Nobah and Jgs 8:11
sexual immorality the **d** on earth have Rv 17:2
And the **d** on earth whose names have Rv 17:8

DWELLING (96)
not support both of them **d** together; Gn 13:6
and the Perizzites were **d** in the land. Gn 13:7
Amorites who were **d** in Hazazon-tamar. Gn 14:7
Abram's brother, who was **d** in Sodom, Gn 14:12
Beer-lahai-roi and was **d** in the Negeb. Gn 24:62
Jacob was a quiet man, **d** in tents. Gn 25:27
the fatness of the earth shall your **d** be, Gn 27:39
to their clans and their **d** places, Gn 36:40
according to their **d** places in the land Gn 36:43
in all your **d** places you shall eat Ex 12:20
fire in all your **d** places on the Sabbath Ex 35:3
your generations, in all your **d** places, Lv 3:17
or of animal, in any of your **d** places. Lv 7:26
alone. His **d** shall be outside the camp. Lv 13:46
Sabbath to the LORD in all your **d** places. Lv 23:3
bring from your **d** places two loaves Lv 23:17
in all your **d** places throughout your Lv 23:21
your generations in all your **d** places. Lv 23:31
"If a man sells a **d** house in a walled Lv 25:29
I will make my **d** among you, and my Lv 26:11
your Sabbaths when you were **d** in it. Lv 26:35
Get away from the **d** of Korah, Nm 16:24
So they got away from the **d** of Korah, Nm 16:27
of the earth, and they are **d** opposite me. Nm 22:5
behold, a people **d** alone, and not Nm 23:9
and said, "Enduring is your **d** place, Nm 24:21
your generations in all your **d** places. Nm 35:29
The eternal God is your **d** place, and Dt 33:27
Canaanites persisted in **d** in that land. Jos 17:12
Canaanites persisted in **d** in that land. Jgs 1:27
Amorites persisted in **d** in Mount Heres, Jgs 1:35
been moving about in a tent for my **d**. 2 Sm 7:6
and let me see both it and his **d** place. 2 Sm 15:25
And listen in heaven your **d** place, 1 Kgs 8:30
in heaven your **d** place and forgive 1 Kgs 8:39
hear in heaven your **d** place and do 1 Kgs 8:43
in heaven your **d** place their prayer 1 Kgs 8:49
at the beginning of their **d** there, 2 Kgs 17:25
These are their **d** places according to 1 Chr 6:54
tent to tent and from **d** to dwelling. 1 Chr 17:5
tent to tent and from dwelling to **d**. 1 Chr 17:5
And listen from heaven your **d** place, 2 Chr 6:21
from heaven your **d** place and forgive 2 Chr 6:30
from heaven your **d** place and do 2 Chr 6:33
from heaven your **d** place their 2 Chr 6:39
on his people and on his **d** place. 2 Chr 36:15
God of Israel, whose **d** is in Jerusalem, Ezr 7:15
taking root, but suddenly I cursed his **d**. Jb 5:3
"Where is the way to the **d** of light, and Jb 38:19
home and the salt land for his **d** place? Jb 39:6
bring me to your holy hill and to your **d**! Ps 43:3
forever, their **d** places to all generations, Ps 49:11
for evil is in their **d** place and in their Ps 55:15
your flock found a **d** in it; in your Ps 68:10
they profaned the **d** place of your name, Ps 74:7
established in Salem, his **d** place in Zion. Ps 76:2
He forsook his **d** at Shiloh, the tent Ps 78:60
How lovely is your **d** place, O LORD of Ps 84:1
Zion more than all the **d** places of Jacob. Ps 87:2
you have been our **d** place in all Ps 90:1
made the LORD your **d** place—the Most Ps 91:9
have I had my **d** among those who hate Ps 120:6
a **d** place for the Mighty One of Jacob." Ps 132:5
"Let us go to his **d** place; let us worship Ps 132:7
Zion; he has desired it for his **d** place: Ps 132:13
but he blesses the **d** of the righteous. Prv 3:33
treasure and oil are in a wise man's **d**, Prv 21:20
man against the **d** of the righteous; Prv 24:15
quietly look from my **d** like clear heat in Is 18:4
height and carve a **d** for yourself in the Is 22:16
My **d** is plucked up and removed from Is 38:12
who were **d** by the Chebar canal, Ezk 3:15
canal, and I sat where they were **d**. Ezk 3:15
desolate and waste, in all their **d** places, Ezk 6:14
My **d** place shall be with them, and I Ezk 37:27
securely, all of them **d** without walls, Ezk 38:11
when my people Israel are **d** securely, Ezk 38:14
the gods, whose **d** is not with flesh." Dn 2:11
and your **d** shall be with the beasts of Dn 4:25
and your **d** shall be with the beasts of Dn 4:32
and his **d** was with the wild donkeys. Dn 5:21
in the clefts of the rock, in your lofty **d**, Ob 1:3
Then your **d** would not be cut off Zep 3:7
he has roused himself from his holy **d**. Zec 2:13
the people **d** in darkness have seen a Mt 4:16
and for those **d** in the region and shadow Mt 4:16
Now there were **d** in Jerusalem Jews, Acts 2:5
and asked to find a **d** place for the God Acts 7:46
and the boundaries of their **d** place, Acts 17:26
longing to put on our heavenly **d**, 2 Cor 5:2
"I will make my **d** among them and 2 Cor 6:16
built together into a **d** place for God by Eph 2:22
of authority, but left their proper **d**, Jude 1:6
God, blaspheming his name and his **d**, Rv 13:6
She has become a **d** place for demons, a Rv 18:2
"Behold, the **d** place of God is with man. Rv 21:3

DWELLINGS (11)
your generations in all your **d**. Lv 23:14
such are the **d** of the unrighteous, Jb 18:21
midst of their camp, all around their **d**. Ps 78:28
in a peaceful habitation, in secure **d**, Is 32:18
because they have cast down our **d**.'" Jer 9:19
of Jacob and have compassion on his **d**; Jer 30:18
have become women; her **d** are on fire; Jer 51:30
you and make their **d** in your midst. Ezk 25:4
the city, for **d** and for open country. Ezk 48:15
of the earth, to seize **d** not their own. Hab 1:6
they may receive you into the eternal **d**. Lk 16:9

DWELLS (46)
which **d** with them in the midst of their Lv 16:16
"The beloved of the LORD **d** in safety. Dt 33:12
day long, and **d** between his shoulders." Dt 33:12
and the favor of him who **d** in the bush. Dt 33:16
of cedar, but the ark of God **d** in a tent." 2 Sm 7:2
and he **d** in Jerusalem forever. 1 Chr 23:25
me, and my eye **d** on their provocation. Jb 17:2
In his tent **d** that which is none of his; Jb 18:15
On the rock he **d** and makes his home, Jb 39:28
being rejoices; my flesh also **d** secure. Ps 16:9
house and the place where your glory **d**. Ps 26:8
He who **d** in the shelter of the Most High Ps 91:1
from Zion, he who **d** in Jerusalem! Ps 135:21
neighbor, who **d** trustingly beside you. Prv 3:29
the LORD of hosts, who **d** on Mount Zion. Is 8:18
The LORD is exalted, for he **d** on high; he Is 33:5
none passes through, where no man **d**?' Jer 2:6
are forsaken, and no man **d** in them. Jer 4:29
are a desolation, and no one **d** in them, Jer 44:2
against a nation at ease, that **d** securely, Jer 49:31
that has no gates or bars, that **d** alone. Jer 49:31
and a desert, a land in which no one **d**, Jer 51:43
she **d** now among the nations, but finds Lam 1:3
place where the king **d** who made him Ezk 17:16
Tyre, who **d** at the entrances to the sea, Ezk 27:3
the darkness, and the light **d** with him. Dn 2:22
I am the LORD your God, who **d** in Zion, Jl 3:17
have not avenged, for the LORD **d** in Zion." Jl 3:21
and everyone mourn who **d** in it, Am 8:8
swears by it and by him who **d** in it. Mt 23:21
but the Father who **d** in me does his Jn 14:10
for he **d** with you and will be in you. Jn 14:17
I who do it, but sin that **d** within me. Rom 7:17
For I know that nothing good **d** in me, Rom 7:18
I who do it, but sin that **d** within me. Rom 7:20
the law of sin that **d** in my members. Rom 7:23
if in fact the Spirit of God **d** in you. Rom 8:9
raised Jesus from the dead **d** in you, Rom 8:11
through his Spirit who **d** in you. Rom 8:11
temple and that God's Spirit **d** in you? 1 Cor 3:16
him the whole fullness of deity **d** bodily, Col 2:9
who **d** in unapproachable light, 1 Tm 6:16
and now, I am sure, **d** in you as well. 2 Tm 1:5
By the Holy Spirit who **d** within us, 2 Tm 1:14
a new earth in which righteousness **d**. 2 Pt 3:13
was killed among you, where Satan **d**. Rv 2:13

DWELT (6)
glory of the LORD **d** on Mount Sinai, Ex 24:16
Mount Zion, where you have **d**. Ps 74:2
the tent where he **d** among mankind, Ps 78:60
those who **d** in a land of deep darkness, on Is 9:2
the Word became flesh and **d** among us, Jn 1:14
a faith that **d** first in your 2 Tm 1:5

DWINDLE (1)
Wealth gained hastily will **d**, but Prv 13:11

DYED (3)
spoil of **d** materials for Sisera, spoil of Jgs 5:30
Sisera, spoil of **d** materials embroidered, Jgs 5:30
two pieces of **d** work embroidered for the Jgs 5:30

DYING (8)
her soul was departing (for she was **d**), Gn 35:18
d in the forty-first year of his reign. 2 Chr 16:13
And when he was **d**, he said, "May 2 Chr 24:22
From out of the city the **d** groan, and Jb 24:12
about twelve years of age, and she was **d**. Lk 8:42
man also have kept this man from **d**?" Jn 11:37
as unknown, and yet well known; as **d**, 2 Cor 6:9
By faith Jacob, when **d**, blessed each Heb 11:21

DYSENTERY (1)
of Publius lay sick with fever and **d**. Acts 28:8

E

EACH (430)
is their seed, **e** according to its kind, Gn 1:11
is their seed, **e** according to its kind. Gn 1:12
in their lands, **e** with his own language, Gn 10:5
east. Thus they separated from **e** other. Gn 13:11
and laid **e** half over against the other. Gn 15:10
in the prison—**e** his own dream, Gn 40:5
and **e** dream with its own interpretation. Gn 40:5
e having a dream with its own Gn 41:11
an interpretation to **e** man according Gn 41:12
and there was **e** man's money in the Gn 43:21
and put **e** man's money in the mouth of Gn 44:1
Then **e** man quickly lowered his sack Gn 44:11
ground, and **e** man opened his sack. Gn 44:11
To **e** and all of them he gave a change Gn 45:22
blessing **e** with the blessing suitable to Gn 49:28
to Egypt with Jacob, **e** with his household: Ex 1:1
but **e** woman shall ask of her neighbor, Ex 3:22
your work, your daily task **e** day, Ex 5:13
of bricks, your daily task **e** day." Ex 5:19
For **e** man cast down his staff, and they Ex 7:12
according to what **e** can eat you shall Ex 12:4
'Gather of it, **e** one of you, as much as Ex 16:16
You shall **e** take an omer, according to Ex 16:16
of the persons that **e** of you has in Ex 16:16
E of them gathered as much as he Ex 16:18
gathered it, **e** as much as he could eat; Ex 16:21
twice as much bread, two omers **e**. Ex 16:22
Remain **e** of you in his place; let no one Ex 16:29
And they asked **e** other of their welfare Ex 18:7
blossoms, **e** with calyx and flower, Ex 25:33
blossoms, **e** with calyx and flower, Ex 25:33
one piece with it under **e** pair of the six Ex 25:35
The length of **e** curtain shall be Ex 26:2
and the breadth of **e** curtain four cubits; Ex 26:2
The length of **e** curtain shall be thirty Ex 26:8
and the breadth of **e** curtain four cubits. Ex 26:8
cubit and a half the breadth of **e** frame. Ex 26:16
There shall be two tenons in **e** frame, Ex 26:17
like signets, **e** engraved with its name, Ex 28:21
then **e** shall give a ransom for his life to Ex 30:12
E one who is numbered in the census Ex 30:13
pure frankincense (of **e** shall there be Ex 30:34
'Put your sword on your side **e** of you, Ex 32:27
and **e** of you kill his brother and his Ex 32:27
e one at the cost of his son and of his Ex 32:29
up, and **e** would stand at his tent door, Ex 33:8
rise up and worship, **e** at his tent door. Ex 33:10
came, **e** from the task that he was doing, Ex 36:4
The length of **e** curtain was twenty-eight Ex 36:9
and the breadth of **e** curtain four cubits. Ex 36:9
The length of **e** curtain was thirty Ex 36:15
the breadth of **e** curtain four cubits. Ex 36:15
cubit and a half the breadth of **e** frame. Ex 36:21
E frame had two tenons for fitting Ex 36:22
blossoms, **e** with calyx and flower, Ex 37:19
blossoms, **e** with calyx and flower, Ex 37:19
one piece with it under **e** pair of the six Ex 37:21
like signets, **e** engraved with its name, Ex 39:14
it he shall offer one loaf from **e** offering, Lv 7:14
e took his censer and put fire in it and Lv 10:1
and drink offerings, **e** on its proper day, Lv 23:37
two tenths of an ephah shall be in **e** loaf. Lv 24:5
shall put pure frankincense on **e** pile, Lv 24:7
when **e** of you shall return to his Lv 25:10
to his property and **e** of you shall return Lv 25:10
this year of jubilee **e** of you shall return Lv 25:13
shall be with you a man from **e** tribe, Nm 1:4
e man being the head of the house of his Nm 1:4
men, **e** representing his fathers' house. Nm 1:44
e man in his own camp and each man Nm 1:52
his own camp and **e** man by his own Nm 1:52
of Israel shall camp **e** by his own Nm 2:2
so shall they set out, **e** in position, Nm 2:17
and so they set out, **e** one in his clan, Nm 2:34
in and appoint them **e** to his task and Nm 4:19
e one with his task of serving or Nm 4:49
E one shall keep his holy donations: Nm 5:10
two of the chiefs, and for **e** one an ox. Nm 7:3
to **e** man according to his service." Nm 7:5
offer their offerings, one chief **e** day, Nm 7:11
e silver plate weighing 130 shekels and Nm 7:85
weighing 130 shekels and **e** basin 70, Nm 7:85
From **e** tribe of their fathers you shall Nm 13:2
the land, forty days, a year for **e** day, Nm 14:34
wine for the drink offering for **e** lamb. Nm 15:5
it shall be done for **e** bull or ram, Nm 15:11
or ram, or for **e** lamb or young goat. Nm 15:11
you offer, so shall you do with **e** one, Nm 15:12
a cord of blue on the tassel of **e** corner. Nm 15:38
you also, and Aaron, **e** his censer." Nm 16:17

them staffs, one for **e** fathers' house, Nm 17:2
staffs. Write **e** man's name on his staff, Nm 17:2
staff for the head of **e** fathers' house. Nm 17:3
chiefs gave him staffs, one for **e** chief, Nm 17:6
they looked, and **e** man took his staff. Nm 17:9
from **e** its best part is to be dedicated.' Nm 18:29
and Balaam offered on **e** altar a bull Nm 23:2
and I have offered on **e** altar a bull and Nm 23:4
offered a bull and a ram on **e** altar. Nm 23:14
offered a bull and a ram on **e** altar. Nm 23:30
"**E** of you kill those of his men who Nm 25:5
shall be a quarter of a hin for **e** lamb. Nm 28:7
offering, mixed with oil, for **e** bull, Nm 28:12
burnt offering of **e** month throughout Nm 28:14
shall you offer for **e** of the seven Nm 28:21
oil, three tenths of an ephah for **e** bull, Nm 28:28
a tenth for **e** of the seven lambs; Nm 28:29
and one tenth for **e** of the seven lambs; Nm 29:4
a tenth for **e** of the seven lambs: Nm 29:10
of an ephah for **e** of the thirteen bulls, Nm 29:14
bulls, two tenths for **e** of the two rams, Nm 29:14
and a tenth for **e** of the fourteen Nm 29:15
send a thousand from **e** of the tribes of Nm 31:4
of Israel, a thousand from **e** tribe, Nm 31:5
to the war, a thousand from **e** tribe, Nm 31:6
the LORD'S offering, what **e** man found, Nm 31:50
in the army had **e** taken plunder for Nm 31:53
to our homes until **e** of the people of Nm 32:18
e, in proportion to the inheritance that Nm 35:8
for **e** of the tribes of the people of Israel Nm 36:9
men from you, one man from **e** tribe. Dt 1:23
Then **e** of you may return to his Dt 3:20
E one shall be put to death for his own Dt 24:16
the tribes of Israel, from **e** tribe a man. Jos 3:12
men from the people, from **e** tribe a man, Jos 4:2
he had appointed, a man from **e** tribe. Jos 4:4
and take up **e** of you a stone upon his Jos 4:5
Provide three men from **e** tribe, and I Jos 18:4
to the people of Israel, to **e** his portion. Jos 18:10
These cities **e** had its pasturelands Jos 21:42
one from **e** of the tribal families of Jos 22:14
people of Israel went **e** to his inheritance Jgs 2:6
and put a torch between **e** pair of tails. Jgs 15:4
And we will **e** give you 1,100 pieces of Jgs 16:5
vineyards and snatch **e** man his wife Jgs 21:21
we did not take for **e** man of them his Jgs 21:22
return **e** of you to her mother's house. Ru 1:8
e of you in the house of her husband!" Ru 1:9
take it to him **e** year when she went 1 Sm 2:19
the people away, **e** one to his home. 1 Sm 10:25
in soul, **e** for his sons and daughters. 1 Sm 30:6
except that **e** man may lead away his 1 Sm 30:22
And **e** caught his opponent by the 2 Sm 2:16
of meat, and a cake of raisins to **e** one. 2 Sm 6:19
all the people departed, **e** to his house. 2 Sm 6:19
off half the beard of **e** and cut off their 2 Sm 10:4
and **e** mounted his mule and fled. 2 Sm 13:29
who had six fingers on **e** hand, 2 Sm 21:20
on each hand, and six toes on **e** foot, 2 Sm 21:20
and rose, and **e** went his own way. 1 Kgs 1:49
E man had to make provision for one 1 Kgs 4:7
Solomon's table, **e** one in his month. 1 Kgs 4:27
was required, **e** according to his duty. 1 Kgs 4:28
of olivewood, **e** ten cubits high. 1 Kgs 6:23
other wings touched **e** other in the 1 Kgs 6:27
the forty-five pillars, fifteen in **e** row. 1 Kgs 7:3
E stand was four cubits long, four 1 Kgs 7:27
e stand had four bronze wheels and 1 Kgs 7:30
were cast with wreaths at the side of **e**. 1 Kgs 7:30
at the four corners of **e** stand. 1 Kgs 7:34
trees, according to the space of **e**, 1 Kgs 7:36
E basin held forty baths, each basin 1 Kgs 7:38
baths, **e** basin measured four cubits, 1 Kgs 7:38
was a basin for **e** of the ten stands. 1 Kgs 7:38
of pomegranates for **e** latticework, 1 Kgs 7:42
e knowing the affliction of his own 1 Kgs 8:38
act and render to **e** whose heart you 1 Kgs 8:39
of his people Israel, as **e** day requires, 1 Kgs 8:59
shekels of gold went into **e** shield. 1 Kgs 10:16
minas of gold went into **e** shield. 1 Kgs 10:17
and on **e** side of the seat were 1 Kgs 10:19
one on **e** end of a step on the six 1 Kgs 10:20
And **e** struck down his man. The 1 Kgs 20:20
remove the kings, **e** from his post, 1 Kgs 20:24
let **e** return to his home in peace.'" 1 Kgs 22:17
go to the Jordan and **e** of us get there a 2 Kgs 6:2
king of Judah set out, **e** in his chariot, 2 Kgs 9:21
king, **e** with his weapons in his hand. 2 Kgs 11:8
and they **e** brought his men who were 2 Kgs 11:9
money for which **e** man is assessed 2 Kgs 12:4
let the priests take, **e** from his donor, 2 Kgs 12:5
But **e** one shall die for his own sin." 2 Kgs 14:6
Then **e** one of you will eat of his own 2 Kgs 18:31
vine, and **e** one of his own fig tree, 2 Kgs 18:31
and **e** one of you will drink the water 2 Kgs 18:31

men and women, to **e** a loaf of bread, 1 Chr 16:3
before the ark as **e** day required, 1 Chr 16:37
the people departed **e** to his house, 1 Chr 16:43
had six fingers on **e** hand and six toes 1 Chr 20:6
on each hand and six toes on **e** foot, 1 Chr 20:6
the head of **e** father's house and his 1 Chr 24:31
On the east there were six **e** day, on 1 Chr 26:17
each day, on the north four **e** day, 1 Chr 26:17
each day, on the south four **e** day, 1 Chr 26:17
year, **e** division numbering 24,000: 1 Chr 27:1
for all golden vessels for **e** service, 1 Chr 28:14
weight of silver vessels for **e** service, 1 Chr 28:14
of gold for **e** lampstand and its 1 Chr 28:15
to the use of **e** lampstand in the 1 Chr 28:15
weight of gold for **e** table for the 1 Chr 28:16
golden bowls and the weight of **e**; 1 Chr 28:17
the silver bowls and the weight of **e**; 1 Chr 28:17
a capital of five cubits on the top of **e**. 2 Chr 3:15
of pomegranates for **e** latticework, 2 Chr 4:13
e knowing his own affliction and his 2 Chr 6:29
and render to **e** whose heart you 2 Chr 6:30
as the duty of **e** day required, offering 2 Chr 8:13
priests as the duty of **e** day required, 2 Chr 8:14
in their divisions at **e** gate, 2 Chr 8:14
of beaten gold went into **e** shield. 2 Chr 9:15
300 shekels of gold went into **e** shield; 2 Chr 9:16
and on **e** side of the seat were arm 2 Chr 9:18
one on **e** end of a step on the six steps. 2 Chr 9:19
Jesse. **E** of you to your tents, O Israel! 2 Chr 10:16
let **e** return to his home in peace.'" 2 Chr 18:16
king, **e** with his weapons in his hand. 2 Chr 23:7
and they **e** brought his men, 2 Chr 23:8
but **e** one shall die for his own sin." 2 Chr 25:4
division, **e** according to his service, 2 Chr 31:2
as the duty of **e** day required—for 2 Chr 31:16
and the gatekeepers were at **e** gate. 2 Chr 35:15
"What have we to do with **e** other, 2 Chr 35:21
And let **e** survivor, in whatever place he Ezr 1:4
Jerusalem and Judah, **e** to his own town. Ezr 2:1
according to the rule, as **e** day required, Ezr 3:4
temple that is in Jerusalem, **e** to its place. Ezr 6:5
houses, **e** of them designated by name. Ezr 10:16
repaired, **e** one opposite his own house. Neh 3:28
all returned to the wall, **e** to his work. Neh 4:15
such a way that **e** labored on the work Neh 4:17
And **e** of the builders had his sword Neh 4:18
e kept his weapon at his right hand. Neh 4:23
e from his brother." And I held a great Neh 5:7
at my expense for **e** day was one ox Neh 5:18
to Jerusalem and Judah, **e** to his town. Neh 7:6
booths for themselves, **e** on his roof, Neh 8:16
did the work, had fled **e** to his field. Neh 13:10
of Judah, but the language of **e** people. Neh 13:24
the priests and Levites, **e** in his work; Neh 13:30
staff of his palace to do as **e** man desired. Est 1:8
the turn came for **e** young woman to go Est 2:12
to **e** province in its own script and to each Est 8:9
its own script and to **e** people in its own Est 8:9
a feast in the house of **e** one on his day, Jb 1:4
him, they came **e** from his own place, Jb 2:11
they clasp **e** other and cannot be Jb 41:17
And **e** of them gave him a piece of Jb 42:11
E evening they come back, howling like Ps 59:6
E evening they come back, howling Ps 59:14
e one appears before God in Zion. Ps 84:7
righteousness and peace kiss **e** other. Ps 85:10
in war, **e** with his sword at his thigh, Sg 3:8
e one was to bring for its fruit a Sg 8:11
and **e** one is brought low—do not forgive Is 2:9
is humbled, and **e** one is brought low, Is 5:15
E had six wings: with two he covered his Is 6:2
e devours the flesh of his own arm, Is 9:20
them, **e** will turn to his own people, Is 13:14
people, and **e** will flee to his own land. Is 13:14
nations lie in glory, **e** in his own tomb; Is 14:18
e against another and each against his Is 19:2
against another and **e** against his Is 19:2
E will be like a hiding place from the Is 32:2
hawks are gathered, **e** one with her mate. Is 34:15
Then **e** one of you will eat of his own Is 36:16
own vine, and **e** one of his own fig tree, Is 36:16
and **e** one of you will drink the water of Is 36:16
they wander about **e** in his own Is 47:15
to their own way, **e** to his own gain, Is 56:11
e neighing for his neighbor's wife. Jer 5:8
her; they shall pasture, **e** in his place. Jer 6:3
with his mouth **e** speaks peace to his Jer 9:8
a lament, and **e** to her neighbor a dirge. Jer 9:20
will bring them again **e** to his heritage Jer 12:15
each to his heritage and **e** to his land. Jer 12:15
against you, **e** with his weapons, Jer 22:7
E man who eats sour grapes, his teeth Jer 31:30
And no longer shall **e** one teach his Jer 31:34
teach his neighbor and **e** his brother, Jer 31:34
rewarding **e** one according to his ways Jer 32:19

the end of seven years **e** of you must set Jer 34:14
proclaiming liberty, **e** to his neighbor, Jer 34:15
profaned my name when **e** of you took Jer 34:16
her, and let us go **e** to his own country, Jer 51:9
but **e** had four faces, and each of them Ezk 1:6
four faces, and **e** of them had four wings. Ezk 1:6
E one of them went straight forward, Ezk 1:9
of their faces, **e** had a human face. Ezk 1:10
E creature had two wings, each of Ezk 1:11
e of which touched the wing of another, Ezk 1:11
And **e** went straight forward. Wherever Ezk 1:12
creatures, one for **e** of the four of them. Ezk 1:15
And **e** creature had two wings covering Ezk 1:23
Forty days I assign you, a day for **e** year. Ezk 4:6
them moaning, **e** one over his iniquity. Ezk 7:16
E had his censer in his hand, and the Ezk 8:11
in the dark, **e** in his room of pictures? Ezk 8:12
e with his destroying weapon in his Ezk 9:1
e with his weapon for slaughter in his Ezk 9:2
the cherubim, one beside **e** cherub, Ezk 10:9
E had four faces, and each four wings, Ezk 10:21
Each had four faces, and **e** four wings, Ezk 10:21
E one of them went straight forward. Ezk 10:22
I will judge **e** of you according to his Ezk 33:20
and **e** of you defiles his neighbor's Ezk 33:26
say to one another, **e** to his brother, Ezk 33:30
e being a cubit and a handbreadth in Ezk 40:5
cubits; the openings faced **e** other. Ezk 40:13
On **e** side six cubits was the breadth of Ezk 41:1
one over another, thirty in **e** story. Ezk 41:6
the Holy Place had **e** a double door. Ezk 41:23
apiece, two swinging leaves for **e** door. Ezk 41:24
of an ephah from **e** homer of wheat, Ezk 45:13
of an ephah from **e** homer of barley, Ezk 45:13
tenth of a bath from **e** cor (the cor, Ezk 45:14
blemish, on **e** of the seven days; Ezk 45:23
as a grain offering an ephah for **e** bull, Ezk 45:24
for each bull, an ephah for **e** ram, Ezk 45:24
each ram, and a hin of oil to **e** ephah. Ezk 45:24
together with a hin of oil to **e** ephah. Ezk 46:5
together with a hin of oil to **e** ephah. Ezk 46:7
but **e** shall go out straight ahead. Ezk 46:9
in **e** corner of the court there was Ezk 46:21
around **e** of the four courts was a row Ezk 46:23
They march **e** on his way; they do not Jl 2:7
jostle one another; **e** marches in his path; Jl 2:8
the breaches, **e** one straight ahead; Am 4:3
were afraid, and **e** cried out to his god. Jon 1:5
For all the peoples walk **e** in the name of Mi 4:5
blood, and **e** hunts the other with a net. Mi 7:2
to him shall bow down, **e** in its place, Zep 2:11
forth his justice; **e** dawn he does not fail; Zep 3:5
while **e** of you busies himself with his Hg 1:9
with seven lips on **e** of the lamps that are Zec 4:2
e with staff in hand because of great age. Zec 8:4
I will cause **e** of them to fall into the Zec 11:6
and **e** into the hand of his king, Zec 11:6
land shall mourn, **e** family by itself: Zec 12:12
all the families that are left, **e** by itself, Zec 12:14
so that **e** will seize the hand of another, Zec 14:13
he will repay **e** person according to Mt 16:27
came, **e** of them received a denarius. Mt 20:9
but **e** of them also received a denarius. Mt 20:10
one, to **e** according to his ability. Mt 25:15
servants in charge, **e** with his work, Mk 13:34
for them, to decide what **e** should take. Mk 15:24
went to be registered, **e** to his own town. Lk 2:3
for **e** tree is known by its own fruit. For Lk 6:44
sit down in groups of about fifty **e**." Lk 9:14
Give us **e** day our daily bread, Lk 11:3
Does not **e** of you on the Sabbath untie Lk 13:15
became friends with **e** other that very Lk 23:12
they had been at enmity with **e** other. Lk 23:12
they were talking with **e** other about all Lk 24:14
you are holding with **e** other as you Lk 24:17
They said to **e** other, "Did not our Lk 24:32
e holding twenty or thirty gallons. Jn 2:6
not buy enough bread for **e** of them to get Jn 6:7
[[They went **e** to his own house, Jn 7:53
you will be scattered, **e** to his own home, Jn 16:32
into four parts, one part for **e** soldier; Jn 19:23
to them and rested on **e** one of them. Acts 2:3
because **e** one was hearing them speak Acts 2:6
e of us in his own native language? Acts 2:8
it was distributed to **e** as any had need. Acts 4:35
brothers. Why do you wrong **e** other?' Acts 7:26
so that they separated from **e** other. Acts 15:39
he is actually not far from **e** one of us, Acts 17:27
offering presented for **e** one of them. Acts 21:26
encouraged by **e** other's faith, Rom 1:12
He will render to **e** one according to his Rom 2:6
e according to the measure of faith Rom 12:3
no one anything, except to love **e** other, Rom 13:8
E one should be fully convinced in his Rom 14:5
So then **e** of us will give an account Rom 14:12

Let **e** of us please his neighbor for his Rom 15:2
I mean is that **e** one of you says, 1 Cor 1:12
you believed, as the Lord assigned to **e**. 1 Cor 3:5
and **e** will receive his wages according 1 Cor 3:8
Let **e** one take care how he builds 1 Cor 3:10
e one's work will become manifest, 1 Cor 3:13
test what sort of work **e** one has done. 1 Cor 3:13
Then **e** one will receive his 1 Cor 4:5
e man should have his own wife and 1 Cor 7:2
his own wife and **e** woman her own 1 Cor 7:2
But **e** has his own gift from God, one of 1 Cor 7:7
Only let **e** person lead the life that the 1 Cor 7:17
E one should remain in the condition 1 Cor 7:20
in whatever condition **e** was called, 1 Cor 7:24
e one goes ahead with his own meal. 1 Cor 11:21
To **e** is given the manifestation of the 1 Cor 12:7
apportions to **e** one individually 1 Cor 12:11
members in the body, **e** one of them, 1 Cor 12:18
come together, **e** one has a hymn, 1 Cor 14:26
two or at most three, and **e** in turn, 1 Cor 14:27
let **e** of them keep silent in church 1 Cor 14:28
But **e** in his own order: Christ the 1 Cor 15:23
and to **e** kind of seed its own body. 1 Cor 15:38
e of you is to put something aside and 1 Cor 16:2
so that **e** one may receive what is due 2 Cor 5:10
E one must give as he has made up his 2 Cor 9:7
flesh, for these are opposed to **e** other, Gal 5:17
But let **e** one test his own work, and then Gal 6:4
For **e** will have to bear his own load. Gal 6:5
grace was given to **e** one of us according Eph 4:7
when **e** part is working properly, Eph 4:16
let **e** one of you speak the truth with his Eph 4:25
let **e** one of you love his wife as himself, Eph 5:33
Let **e** of you look not only to his own Phil 2:4
against another, forgiving **e** other; Col 3:13
know how you ought to answer **e** person. Col 4:6
we exhorted **e** one of you and 1 Thes 2:12
that **e** one of you know how to 1 Thes 4:4
Let deacons **e** be the husband of one 1 Tm 3:12
And we desire **e** one of you to show the Heb 6:11
e one his neighbor and each one his Heb 8:11
one his neighbor and **e** one his brother, Heb 8:11
dying, blessed **e** of the sons of Joseph, Heb 11:21
But **e** person is tempted when he is lured Jas 1:14
impartially according to **e** one's deeds, 1 Pt 1:17
As **e** has received a gift, use it to serve 1 Pt 4:10
and I will give to **e** of you as your works Rv 2:23
around the throne, on **e** side of the throne, Rv 4:6
living creatures, **e** of them with six wings, Rv 4:8
down before the Lamb, **e** holding a harp, Rv 5:8
Then they were **e** given a white robe and Rv 6:11
about one hundred pounds **e**, Rv 16:21
and they were judged, **e** one of them, Rv 20:13
e of the gates made of a single pearl, Rv 21:21
kinds of fruit, yielding its fruit **e** month. Rv 22:2

EAGER (10)
He is like a lion **e** to tear, as a young Ps 17:12
all the more they were **e** to make all their Zep 3:7
So I am **e** to preach the gospel to you Rom 1:15
creation waits with **e** longing for the Rom 8:19
since you are **e** for manifestations of 1 Cor 14:12
the poor, the very thing I was **e** to do. Gal 2:10
e to maintain the unity of the Spirit in Eph 4:3
as it is my **e** expectation and hope that I Phil 1:20
I am the more **e** to send him, therefore, Phil 2:28
although I was very **e** to write to you Jude 1:3

EAGERLY (6)
come out to meet you, to seek you **e**, Prv 7:15
inwardly as we wait **e** for adoption as Rom 8:23
we ourselves **e** wait for the hope of Gal 5:5
endeavored the more **e** and with 1 Thes 2:17
to save those who are **e** waiting for him. Heb 9:28
have you; not for shameful gain, but **e**; 1 Pt 5:2

EAGERNESS (2)
they received the word with all **e**, Acts 17:11
but also what **e** to clear yourselves, 2 Cor 7:11

EAGLE (20)
they are detestable: the **e**, the bearded Lv 11:13
are the ones that you shall not eat: the **e**, Dt 14:12
of the earth, swooping down like the **e**, Dt 28:49
Like an **e** that stirs up its nest, that Dt 32:11
of reed, like an **e** swooping on the prey. Jb 9:26
command that the **e** mounts up and Jb 39:27
wings, flying like an **e** toward heaven. Prv 23:5
the way of an **e** in the sky, the way of a Prv 30:19
fly swiftly like an **e** and spread his Jer 48:40
fly swiftly like an **e** and spread his Jer 49:22
side, and the four had the face of an **e**. Ezk 1:10
a lion, and the fourth the face of an **e**. Ezk 10:14
A great **e** with great wings and long Ezk 17:3
was another great **e** with great wings Ezk 17:7
Though you soar aloft like the **e**, though Ob 1:4
make yourselves as bald as the **e**, for Mi 1:16
afar; they fly like an **e** swift to devour. Hab 1:8
fourth living creature like an **e** in flight. Rv 4:7
and I heard an **e** crying with a loud voice Rv 8:13
wings of the great **e** so that she might Rv 12:14

EAGLE'S (2)
so that your youth is renewed like the **e**. Ps 103:5
you make your nest as high as the **e**, Jer 49:16

EAGLES (4)
not divided; they were swifter than **e**; 2 Sm 1:23
they shall mount up with wings like **e**; Is 40:31
his horses are swifter than **e**—woe to us, Jer 4:13
were swifter than the **e** in the heavens; Lam 4:19

EAGLES' (3)
I bore you on **e** wings and brought you Ex 19:4
till his hair grew as long as **e** feathers, Dn 4:33
The first was like a lion and had **e** wings. Dn 7:4

EAR (115)
the barley was in the **e** and the flax was Ex 9:31
and give **e** to his commandments and Ex 15:26
master shall bore his **e** through with an Ex 21:6
the tip of the right **e** of Aaron and on Ex 29:20
lobe of Aaron's right **e** and on the Lv 8:23
the lobe of the right **e** of him who is to Lv 14:14
the lobe of the right **e** of him who is to Lv 14:17
the lobe of the right **e** of him who is to Lv 14:25
the lobe of the right **e** of him who is to Lv 14:28
hear; give **e** to me, O son of Zippor: Nm 23:18
not listen to your voice or give **e** to you. Dt 1:45
and put it through his **e** into the door, Dt 15:17
"Give **e**, O heavens, and I will speak, and Dt 32:1
"Hear, O kings; give **e**, O princes; to the Jgs 5:3
giving **e** to them whenever they call 1 Kgs 8:52
Incline your **e**, O LORD, and hear; 2 Kgs 19:16
let your **e** be attentive and your eyes Neh 1:6
let your **e** be attentive to the prayer of Neh 1:11
prophets. Yet they would not give **e**. Neh 9:30
stealthily; my **e** received the whisper of it. Jb 4:12
Does not the **e** test words as the palate Jb 12:11
this, my **e** has heard and understood it. Jb 13:1
When the **e** heard, it called me blessed, Jb 29:11
words, you wise men, and give **e** to me, Jb 34:2
for the **e** tests words as the palate tastes Jb 34:3
affliction and opens their **e** by adversity. Jb 36:15
I had heard of you by the hearing of the **e**, Jb 42:5
Give **e** to my words, O LORD; consider my Ps 5:1
their heart; you will incline your **e** Ps 10:17
Give **e** to my prayer from lips free of Ps 17:1
answer me, O God; incline your **e** to me; Ps 17:6
Incline your **e** to me; rescue me speedily! Ps 31:2
my prayer, O LORD, and give **e** to my cry; Ps 39:12
but you have given me an open **e**. Ps 40:6
and consider, and incline your **e**: Ps 45:10
Hear this, all peoples! Give **e**, all Ps 49:1
I will incline my **e** to a proverb; I will Ps 49:4
prayer; give **e** to the words of my mouth. Ps 54:2
Give **e** to my prayer, O God, and hide not Ps 55:1
God will give **e** and humble them, he Ps 55:19
like the deaf adder that stops its **e**, Ps 58:4
me and rescue me; incline your **e** to me, Ps 71:2
Give **e**, O my people, to my teaching; Ps 78:1
Give **e**, O Shepherd of Israel, you who Ps 80:1
LORD God of hosts, hear my prayer; give **e**, Ps 84:8
Incline your **e**, O LORD, and answer me, Ps 86:1
Give **e**, O LORD, to my prayer; listen to my Ps 86:6
before you; incline your **e** to my cry! Ps 88:2
He who planted the **e**, does he not hear? Ps 94:9
day of my distress! Incline your **e** to me; Ps 102:2
Because he inclined his **e** to me, Ps 116:2
give **e** to the voice of my pleas for Ps 140:6
Give **e** to my voice when I call to you! Ps 141:1
O LORD; give **e** to my pleas for mercy! Ps 143:1
making your **e** attentive to wisdom and Prv 2:2
my words; incline your **e** to my sayings. Prv 4:20
incline your **e** to my understanding, Prv 5:1
or incline my **e** to my instructors. Prv 5:13
The **e** that listens to life-giving reproof Prv 15:31
and a liar gives **e** to a mischievous Prv 17:4
and the **e** of the wise seeks knowledge. Prv 18:15
The hearing **e** and the seeing eye, the Prv 20:12
Whoever closes his **e** to the cry of the Prv 21:13
Incline your **e**, and hear the words of Prv 22:17
to instruction and your **e** to words of Prv 23:12
gold is a wise reprover to a listening **e**. Prv 25:12
one turns away his **e** from hearing the Prv 28:9
seeing, nor the **e** filled with hearing. Eccl 1:8
Hear, O heavens, and give **e**, O earth; for the Is 1:2
Give **e** to the teaching of our God, you Is 1:10
you peoples, and be shattered; give **e**, Is 8:9
Give **e**, and hear my voice; give Is 28:23
daughters, give **e** to my speech. Is 32:9
Incline your **e**, O LORD, and hear; open Is 37:17
Who among you will give **e** to this, will Is 42:23
from of old your **e** has not been opened. Is 48:8
he awakens my **e** to hear as those who are Is 50:4
The Lord GOD has opened my **e**, and I was Is 50:5
to me, my people, and give **e** to me, Is 51:4
Incline your **e**, and come to me; hear, that Is 55:3
that it cannot save, or his **e** dull, Is 59:1
no one has heard or perceived by the **e**, Is 64:4
But they did not obey or incline their **e**, Jer 7:24
did not listen to me or incline their **e**, Jer 7:26
and let your **e** receive the word of his Jer 9:20
Yet they did not obey or incline their **e**, Jer 11:8
Hear and give **e**; be not proud, for the Jer 13:15
Yet they did not listen or incline their **e**, Jer 17:23
did not incline your **e** or listen to me. Jer 35:15
But they did not listen or incline their **e**, Jer 44:5
'Do not close your **e** to my cry for Lam 3:56
O my God, incline your **e** and hear. Dn 9:18
Pay attention, O house of Israel! Give **e**, Hos 5:1
Hear this, you elders; give **e**, all inhabitants Jl 1:2
of the lion two legs, or a piece of an **e**, Am 3:12
of the high priest and cut off his **e**. Mt 26:51
by itself, first the blade, then the **e**, Mk 4:28
then the ear, then the full grain in the **e**. Mk 4:28
of the high priest and cut off his **e**. Mk 14:47
of the high priest and cut off his right **e**. Lk 22:50
And he touched his **e** and healed him. Lk 22:51
priest's servant and cut off his right **e**. Jn 18:10
of the man whose **e** Peter had cut off, Jn 18:26
known to you, and give **e** to my words. Acts 2:14
"What no eye has seen, nor **e** heard, 1 Cor 2:9
And if the **e** should say, "Because I 1 Cor 12:16
If the whole body were an **e**, where 1 Cor 12:17
He who has an **e**, let him hear what the Rv 2:7
He who has an **e**, let him hear what the Rv 2:11
He who has an **e**, let him hear what the Rv 2:17
He who has an **e**, let him hear what the Rv 2:29
He who has an **e**, let him hear what the Rv 3:6
He who has an **e**, let him hear what the Rv 3:13
He who has an **e**, let him hear what the Rv 3:22
If anyone has an **e**, let him hear: Rv 13:9

EARLIER (3)
he walked in the **e** ways of his father 2 Chr 17:3
also, who **e** had come to Jesus by night, Jn 19:39
of those who sinned **e** and have not 2 Cor 12:21

EARLY (69)
Then you may rise up **e** and go on your Gn 19:2
And Abraham went **e** in the morning Gn 19:27
So Abimelech rose **e** in the morning Gn 20:8
So Abraham rose **e** in the morning Gn 21:14
So Abraham rose **e** in the morning, Gn 22:3
morning they rose **e** and exchanged Gn 26:31
So **e** in the morning Jacob took the Gn 28:18
E in the morning Laban arose and Gn 31:55
"Rise up **e** in the morning and present Ex 8:20
"Rise up **e** in the morning and present Ex 9:13
He rose **e** in the morning and built an Ex 24:4
And they rose up **e** the next day and Ex 32:6
And he rose **e** in the morning and went Ex 34:4
And they rose **e** in the morning and Nm 14:40
its season, the **e** rain and the later rain, Dt 11:14
Then Joshua rose **e** in the morning and Jos 3:1
Then Joshua rose **e** in the morning, and Jos 6:12
On the seventh day they rose **e**, at the Jos 6:15
So Joshua rose **e** in the morning and Jos 7:16
Joshua arose **e** in the morning and Jos 8:10
hurried and went out **e** to the appointed Jos 8:14
men of the town rose **e** in the morning, Jgs 6:28
When he rose **e** next morning and Jgs 6:38
with him rose **e** and encamped beside Jgs 7:1
sun is up, rise **e** and rush upon the city. Jgs 9:33
fourth day they arose **e** in the morning, Jgs 19:5
the fifth day he arose **e** in the morning to Jgs 19:8
you shall arise **e** in the morning Jgs 19:9
day the people rose **e** and built there an Jgs 21:4
has continued from **e** morning until Ru 2:7
They rose **e** in the morning and 1 Sm 1:19
people of Ashdod rose **e** the next day, 1 Sm 5:3
But when they rose **e** on the next 1 Sm 5:4
And Samuel rose **e** to meet Saul in 1 Sm 15:12
And David rose **e** in the morning 1 Sm 17:20
Now then rise **e** in the morning with 1 Sm 29:10
with you, and start **e** in the morning, 1 Sm 29:10
out with his men **e** in the morning to 1 Sm 29:11
used to rise **e** and stand beside 2 Sm 15:2
And when they rose **e** in the morning 2 Kgs 3:22
man of God rose **e** in the morning 2 Kgs 6:15
when people arose **e** in the morning, 2 Kgs 19:35
And they rose **e** in the morning and 2 Chr 20:20
the king rose **e** and gathered the 2 Chr 29:20
Water Gate from **e** morning until Neh 8:3
and he would rise **e** in the morning and Jb 1:5
the **e** rain also covers it with pools. Ps 84:6
vain that you rise up **e** and go late to Ps 127:2
a loud voice, rising **e** in the morning, Prv 27:14
let us go out **e** to the vineyards and see Sg 7:12

Woe to those who rise **e** in the morning, Is 5:11
when people arose **e** in the morning, Is 37:36
cloud, like the dew that goes **e** away. Hos 6:4
mist or like the dew that goes **e** away, Hos 13:3
he has given the **e** rain for your Jl 2:23
abundant rain, the **e** and the latter rain, Jl 2:23
house who went out **e** in the morning to Mt 20:1
And rising very **e** in the morning, while Mk 1:35
And very **e** on the first day of the week, Mk 16:2
[[Now when he rose **e** on the first day of Mk 16:9
And **e** in the morning all the people Lk 21:38
on the first day of the week, at **e** dawn, Lk 24:1
were at the tomb **e** in the morning, Lk 24:22
E in the morning he came again to the Jn 8:2
headquarters. It was **e** morning. Jn 18:28
Mary Magdalene came to the tomb **e**, Jn 20:1
know that in the **e** days God made a Acts 15:7
of Mnason of Cyprus, an **e** disciple, Acts 21:16
it, until it receives the **e** and the late rains. Jas 5:7

EARN (1)
quietly and to **e** their own living. 2 Thes 3:12

EARNEST (6)
of a friend comes from his **e** counsel. Prv 27:9
but **e** prayer for him was made to God Acts 12:5
of Titus the same **e** care I have for 2 Cor 8:16
but being himself very **e** he is going 2 Cor 8:17
tested and found **e** in many matters, 2 Cor 8:22
who is now more **e** than ever because 2 Cor 8:22

EARNESTLY (23)
'David **e** asked leave of me to run to 1 Sm 20:6
"David **e** asked leave of me to go to 1 Sm 20:28
O God, you are my God; **e** I seek you; my Ps 63:1
him; they repented and sought God **e**. Ps 78:34
night; my spirit within me **e** seeks you. Is 26:9
my face, and in their distress **e** seek me. Hos 5:15
therefore pray **e** to the Lord of the Mt 9:38
And he begged him **e** not to send them Mk 5:10
and implored him **e**, saying, "My little Mk 5:23
came to Jesus, they pleaded with him **e**, Lk 7:4
Therefore pray **e** to the Lord of the Lk 10:2
"I have **e** desired to eat this Passover Lk 22:15
being in an agony he prayed more **e**; Lk 22:44
as they **e** worship night and day. Acts 26:7
But **e** desire the higher gifts. And I 1 Cor 12:31
love, and **e** desire the spiritual gifts, 1 Cor 14:1
my brothers, **e** desire to prophesy, 1 Cor 14:39
begging us **e** for the favor of taking 2 Cor 8:4
as we pray most **e** night and day that 1 Thes 3:10
he searched for me **e** and found me— 2 Tm 1:17
I urge you the more **e** to do this in Heb 13:19
love one another **e** from a pure heart, 1 Pt 1:22
Above all, keep loving one another **e**, 1 Pt 4:8

EARNESTNESS (5)
For see what **e** this godly grief has 2 Cor 7:11
in order that your **e** for us might be 2 Cor 7:12
faith, in speech, in knowledge, in all **e**, 2 Cor 8:7
to prove by the **e** of others that your 2 Cor 8:8
you to show the same **e** to have the full Heb 6:11

EARNS (2)
The wicked **e** deceptive wages, but one Prv 11:18
And he who **e** wages does so to put them Hg 1:6

EARRINGS (7)
brought brooches and **e** and signet Ex 35:22
bracelets, signet rings, **e**, and beads, Nm 31:50
of you give me the **e** from his spoil." (For Jgs 8:24
from his spoil." (For they had golden **e**, Jgs 8:24
every man threw in it the **e** of his spoil. Jgs 8:25
weight of the golden **e** that he requested Jgs 8:26
on your nose and **e** in your ears and Ezk 16:12

EARS (115)
had, and the rings that were in their **e**. Gn 35:4
And behold, seven **e** of grain, plump and Gn 41:5
And behold, after them sprouted seven **e**, Gn 41:6
And the thin **e** swallowed up the seven Gn 41:7
swallowed up the seven plump, full **e**. Gn 41:7
in my dream seven **e** growing on one Gn 41:22
Seven **e**, withered, thin, and blighted by Gn 41:23
and the thin **e** swallowed up the seven Gn 41:24
ears swallowed up the seven good **e**. Gn 41:24
and the seven good **e** are seven years; Gn 41:26
and the seven empty **e** blighted by the Gn 41:27
servant speak a word in my lord's **e**, Gn 44:18
eyes, please speak in the **e** of Pharaoh, Gn 50:4
a book and recite it in the **e** of Joshua, Ex 17:14
and on the tips of the right **e** of his sons, Ex 29:20
of gold that are in the **e** of your wives, Ex 32:2
that were in their **e** and brought them to Ex 32:3
grain offering of your firstfruits fresh **e**, Lv 2:14
lobes of their right **e** and on the thumbs Lv 8:24
you may pluck the **e** with your hand, Dt 23:25
to understand or eyes to see or **e** to hear. Dt 29:4
these words in their **e** and call heaven Dt 31:28
in the **e** of all the assembly of Israel: Dt 31:30
therefore proclaim in the **e** of the people, Jgs 7:3
"Say in the **e** of all the leaders of Shechem, Jgs 9:2
on his behalf in the **e** of all the leaders of Jgs 9:3
a curse, and also spoke it in my **e**, Jgs 17:2
and glean among the **e** of grain after him Ru 2:2
at which the two **e** of everyone who 1 Sm 3:11
he repeated them in the **e** of the LORD. 1 Sm 8:21
the matter in the **e** of the people, 1 Sm 11:4
the sheep in my **e** and the lowing of 1 Sm 15:14
spoke those words in the **e** of David. 1 Sm 18:23
let your servant speak in your **e**, 1 Sm 25:24
to all that we have heard with our **e**. 2 Sm 7:22
my voice, and my cry came to his **e**. 2 Sm 22:7
of barley and fresh **e** of grain in his 2 Kgs 4:42
complacency has come into my **e**, 2 Kgs 19:28
disaster that the **e** of everyone who 2 Kgs 21:12
to all that we have heard with our **e**. 1 Chr 17:20
be open and your **e** attentive to the 2 Chr 6:40
be open and my **e** attentive to the 2 Chr 7:15
And the **e** of all the people were attentive Neh 8:3
and let my declaration be in your **e**. Jb 13:17
Dreadful sounds are in his **e**; in Jb 15:21
have heard a rumor of it with our **e**.' Jb 28:22
"Surely you have spoken in my **e**, and I Jb 33:8
then he opens the **e** of men and terrifies Jb 33:16
He opens their **e** to instruction and Jb 36:10
voice, and my cry to him reached his **e**. Ps 18:6
the righteous and his **e** toward their cry. Ps 34:15
O God, we have heard with our **e**, our Ps 44:1
incline your **e** to the words of my mouth! Ps 78:1
my **e** have heard the doom of my evil Ps 92:11
They have **e**, but do not hear; noses, but Ps 115:6
Let your **e** be attentive to the voice of Ps 130:2
they have **e**, but do not hear, nor is Ps 135:17
one who takes a passing dog by the **e**. Prv 26:17
of this people dull, and their **e** heavy, Is 6:10
see with their eyes, and hear with their **e**, Is 6:10
see, or decide disputes by what his **e** hear, Is 11:3
grain and his arm harvests the **e**, Is 17:5
as when one gleans the **e** of grain in the Is 17:5
of hosts has revealed himself in my **e**: Is 22:14
And your **e** shall hear a word behind Is 30:21
and the **e** of those who hear will give Is 32:3
who stops his **e** from hearing of Is 33:15
be opened, and the **e** of the deaf unstopped; Is 35:5
your complacency has come to my **e**, Is 37:29
his **e** are open, but he does not hear. Is 42:20
yet have eyes, who are deaf, yet have **e**! Is 43:8
your bereavement will yet say in your **e**: Is 49:20
who have eyes, but see not, who have **e**, Jer 5:21
Behold, their **e** are uncircumcised, they Jer 6:10
this place that the **e** of everyone who Jer 19:3
listened nor inclined your **e** to hear, Jer 25:4
as you have heard with your own **e**." Jer 26:11
you to speak all these words in your **e**." Jer 26:15
not listen to me or incline their **e** to me. Jer 34:14
in your heart, and hear with your **e**. Ezk 3:10
they cry in my **e** with a loud voice, Ezk 8:18
Then he cried in my **e** with a loud voice, Ezk 9:1
to see, but see not, who have **e** to hear, Ezk 12:2
and earrings in your **e** and a beautiful Ezk 16:12
shall cut off your nose and your **e**, Ezk 23:25
with your eyes, and hear with your **e**, Ezk 40:4
and hear with your **e** all that I shall tell Ezk 44:5
on their mouths; their **e** shall be deaf; Mi 7:16
and stopped their **e** that they might Zec 7:11
He who has **e** to hear, let him hear. Mt 11:15
He who has **e**, let him hear." Mt 13:9
and with their **e** they can barely hear, Mt 13:15
hear with their **e** and understand with Mt 13:15
are your eyes, for they see, and your **e**, Mt 13:16
Father. He who has **e**, let him hear. Mt 13:43
And if this comes to the governor's **e**, Mt 28:14
And he said, "He who has **e** to hear, let Mk 4:9
If anyone has **e** to hear, let him hear." Mk 4:23
privately, he put his fingers into his **e**, Mk 7:33
And his **e** were opened, his tongue was Mk 7:35
not see, and having **e** do you not hear? Mk 8:18
the sound of your greeting came to my **e**, Lk 1:44
he called out, "He who has **e** to hear, Lk 8:8
"Let these words sink into your **e**: The Lk 9:44
He who has **e** to hear, let him hear." Lk 14:35
people, uncircumcised in heart and **e**, Acts 7:51
and stopped their **e** and rushed Acts 7:57
of this came to the **e** of the church in Acts 11:22
bring some strange things to our **e**. Acts 17:20
and with their **e** they can barely hear, Acts 28:27
hear with their **e** and understand Acts 28:27
would not see and **e** that would not Rom 11:8
but having itching **e** they will 2 Tm 4:3
harvesters have reached the **e** of the Lord Jas 5:4
and his **e** are open to their prayer. 1 Pt 3:12

EARTH (877)
God created the heavens and the **e**. Gn 1:1
The **e** was without form and void, and Gn 1:2
God called the dry land **E**, and the Gn 1:10
God said, "Let the **e** sprout vegetation, Gn 1:11
to its kind, on the **e**." And it was so. Gn 1:11
The **e** brought forth vegetation, plants Gn 1:12
to give light upon the **e**." And it was so. Gn 1:15
of the heavens to give light on the **e**, Gn 1:17
birds fly above the **e** across the expanse Gn 1:20
the seas, and let birds multiply on the **e**." Gn 1:22
"Let the **e** bring forth living creatures Gn 1:24
and beasts of the **e** according to their Gn 1:24
the beasts of the **e** according to their Gn 1:25
and over all the **e** and over every Gn 1:26
creeping thing that creeps on the **e**." Gn 1:26
multiply and fill the **e** and subdue it and Gn 1:28
every living thing that moves on the **e**." Gn 1:28
seed that is on the face of all the **e**, Gn 1:29
to every beast of the **e** and to every bird Gn 1:30
and to everything that creeps on the **e**, Gn 1:30
Thus the heavens and the **e** were finished, Gn 2:1
the heavens and the **e** when they were Gn 2:4
the LORD God made the **e** and the heavens. Gn 2:4
be a fugitive and a wanderer on the **e**." Gn 4:12
be a fugitive and a wanderer on the **e**, Gn 4:14
Nephilim were on the **e** in those days, Gn 6:4
the wickedness of man was great in the **e**, Gn 6:5
was sorry that he had made man on the **e**, Gn 6:6
Now the **e** was corrupt in God's sight, Gn 6:11
sight, and the **e** was filled with violence. Gn 6:11
And God saw the **e**, and behold, it was Gn 6:12
flesh had corrupted their way on the **e**. Gn 6:12
for the **e** is filled with violence through Gn 6:13
Behold, I will destroy them with the **e**. Gn 6:13
of waters upon the **e** to destroy all flesh Gn 6:17
Everything that is on the **e** shall die. Gn 6:17
offspring alive on the face of all the **e**. Gn 7:3
send rain on the **e** forty days and forty Gn 7:4
when the flood of waters came upon the **e**. Gn 7:6
the waters of the flood came upon the **e**. Gn 7:10
rain fell upon the **e** forty days and forty Gn 7:12
creeping thing that creeps on the **e**, Gn 7:14
The flood continued forty days on the **e**. Gn 7:17
up the ark, and it rose high above the **e**. Gn 7:17
prevailed and increased greatly on the **e**, Gn 7:18
so mightily on the **e** that all the high Gn 7:19
And all flesh died that moved on the **e**, Gn 7:21
creatures that swarm on the **e**, Gn 7:21
They were blotted out from the **e**. Gn 7:23
the waters prevailed on the **e** 150 days. Gn 7:24
And God made a wind blow over the **e**, Gn 8:1
waters receded from the **e** continually. Gn 8:3
until the waters were dried up from the **e**. Gn 8:7
were still on the face of the whole **e**. Gn 8:9
that the waters had subsided from the **e**. Gn 8:11
the waters were dried from off the **e**. Gn 8:13
day of the month, the **e** had dried out. Gn 8:14
that creeps on the **e**—that they may Gn 8:17
earth—that they may swarm on the **e**, Gn 8:17
and be fruitful and multiply on the **e**." Gn 8:17
bird, everything that moves on the **e**, Gn 8:19
While the **e** remains, seedtime and Gn 8:22
"Be fruitful and multiply and fill the **e**. Gn 9:1
every beast of the **e** and upon every bird Gn 9:2
teem on the **e** and multiply in it." Gn 9:7
and every beast of the **e** with you, Gn 9:10
of the ark; it is for every beast of the **e**. Gn 9:10
shall there be a flood to destroy the **e**." Gn 9:11
of the covenant between me and the **e**. Gn 9:13
I bring clouds over the **e** and the bow is Gn 9:14
creature of all flesh that is on the **e**." Gn 9:16
me and all flesh that is on the **e**." Gn 9:17
the people of the whole **e** were dispersed. Gn 9:19
he was the first on **e** to be a mighty man. Gn 10:8
Peleg, for in his days the **e** was divided, Gn 10:25
spread abroad on the **e** after the flood. Gn 10:32
Now the whole **e** had one language and Gn 11:1
dispersed over the face of the whole **e**." Gn 11:4
from there over the face of all the **e**, Gn 11:8
LORD confused the language of all the **e**. Gn 11:9
dispersed them over the face of all the **e**. Gn 11:9
all the families of the **e** shall be blessed." Gn 12:3
your offspring as the dust of the **e**, Gn 13:16
that if one can count the dust of the **e**, Gn 13:16
Most High, Possessor of heaven and **e**; Gn 14:19
Most High, Possessor of heaven and **e**, Gn 14:22
to meet them and bowed himself to the **e** Gn 18:2
the nations of the **e** shall be blessed in Gn 18:18
the Judge of all the **e** do what is just?" Gn 18:25
and bowed himself with his face to the **e** Gn 19:1
had risen on the **e** when Lot came to Gn 19:23
there is not a man on **e** to come in to us Gn 19:31
in to us after the manner of all the **e**. Gn 19:31
shall all the nations of the **e** be blessed, Gn 22:18
the God of heaven and God of the **e**, Gn 24:3
bowed himself to the **e** before the LORD. Gn 24:52

all the nations of the **e** shall be blessed, Gn 26:4
stopped and filled with **e** all the wells Gn 26:15
the fatness of the **e** and plenty of grain Gn 27:28
the fatness of the **e** shall your dwelling Gn 27:39
there was a ladder set up on the **e**, Gn 28:12
offspring shall be like the dust of the **e**, Gn 28:14
shall all the families of the **e** be blessed. Gn 28:14
years the **e** produced abundantly, Gn 41:47
all the **e** came to Egypt to Joseph to buy Gn 41:57
the famine was severe over all the **e**. Gn 41:57
you to preserve for you a remnant on **e**, Gn 45:7
he bowed himself with his face to the **e**. Gn 48:12
into a multitude in the midst of the **e**." Gn 48:16
out your staff and strike the dust of the **e**, Ex 8:16
his staff and struck the dust of the **e**, Ex 8:17
All the dust of the **e** became gnats in all Ex 8:17
that I am the LORD in the midst of the **e**. Ex 8:22
that there is none like me in all the **e**. Ex 9:14
you would have been cut off from the **e**. Ex 9:15
name may be proclaimed in all the **e**. Ex 9:16
and hail, and fire ran down to the **e**. Ex 9:23
you may know that the **e** is the LORD'S. Ex 9:29
the rain no longer poured upon the **e**. Ex 9:33
day they came on **e** to this day.'" Then Ex 10:6
your right hand; the **e** swallowed them. Ex 15:12
among all peoples, for all the **e** is mine; Ex 19:5
heaven above, or that is in the **e** beneath, Ex 20:4
or that is in the water under the **e**. Ex 20:4
in six days the LORD made heaven and **e**, Ex 20:11
An altar of **e** you shall make for me Ex 20:24
in six days the LORD made heaven and **e**, Ex 31:17
consume them from the face of the **e**'? Ex 32:12
every other people on the face of the **e**?" Ex 33:16
his head toward the **e** and worshiped. Ex 34:8
created in all the **e** or in any nation. Ex 34:10
among all the animals that are on the **e**. Lv 11:2
pour out its blood and cover it with **e**. Lv 17:13
like iron and your **e** like bronze. Lv 26:19
all people who were on the face of the **e**. Nm 12:3
and as all the **e** shall be filled with the Nm 14:21
And the **e** opened its mouth and Nm 16:32
into Sheol, and the **e** closed over them, Nm 16:33
they said, "Lest the **e** swallow us up!" Nm 16:34
They cover the face of the **e**, and they Nm 22:5
of Egypt, and it covers the face of the **e**. Nm 22:11
and the **e** opened its mouth and Nm 26:10
there in heaven or on **e** who can do such Dt 3:24
me all the days that they live on the **e**, Dt 4:10
likeness of any animal that is on the **e**, Dt 4:17
any fish that is in the water under the **e**. Dt 4:18
I call heaven and **e** to witness against Dt 4:26
the day that God created man on the **e**, Dt 4:32
And on **e** he let you see his great fire, and Dt 4:36
in heaven above and on the **e** beneath; Dt 4:39
heaven above, or that is on the **e** beneath, Dt 5:8
or that is in the water under the **e**. Dt 5:8
he destroy you from off the face of the **e**. Dt 6:15
all the peoples who are on the face of the **e**. Dt 7:6
of heavens, the **e** with all that is in it. Dt 10:14
how the **e** opened its mouth and Dt 11:6
as long as the heavens are above the **e**. Dt 11:21
all the days that you live on the **e**. Dt 12:1
you shall pour it out on the **e** like water. Dt 12:16
you shall pour it out on the **e** like water. Dt 12:24
from the one end of the **e** to the other, Dt 13:7
the peoples who are on the face of the **e**. Dt 14:2
you high above all the nations of the **e**. Dt 28:1
all the peoples of the **e** shall see that you Dt 28:10
and the **e** under you shall be iron. Dt 28:23
be a horror to all the kingdoms of the **e**. Dt 28:25
of the air and for the beasts of the **e**, Dt 28:26
from far away, from the end of the **e**, Dt 28:49
from one end of the **e** to the other, Dt 28:64
I call heaven and **e** to witness against Dt 30:19
call heaven and **e** to witness against Dt 31:28
and let the **e** hear the words of my Dt 32:1
of Sheol, devours the **e** and its increase, Dt 32:22
best gifts of the **e** and its fullness and Dt 33:16
peoples, all of them, to the ends of the **e**; Dt 33:17
the heavens above and on the **e** beneath. Jos 2:11
Lord of all the **e** is passing over before Jos 3:11
the ark of the LORD, the Lord of all the **e**, Jos 3:13
the peoples of the **e** may know that the Jos 4:24
his face to the **e** and worshiped and said Jos 5:14
clothes and fell to the **e** on his face before Jos 7:6
us and cut off our name from the **e**. Jos 7:9
they are hidden in the **e** inside my tent, Jos 7:21
I am about to go the way of all the **e**, Jos 23:14
the **e** trembled and the heavens dropped, Jgs 5:4
that is in the **e** and possessing wealth, Jgs 18:7
is no lack of anything that is in the **e**." Jgs 18:10
For the pillars of the **e** are the LORD'S, 1 Sm 2:8
The LORD will judge the ends of the **e**; 1 Sm 2:10
mighty shout, so that the **e** resounded. 1 Sm 4:5
the raiders trembled, the **e** quaked, 1 Sm 14:15
the air and to the wild beasts of the **e**, 1 Sm 17:46
that all the **e** may know that there is 1 Sm 17:46
of David from the face of the **e**." 1 Sm 20:15
long as the son of Jesse lives on the **e**, 1 Sm 20:31
his face to the **e** and paid homage. 1 Sm 24:8
me pin him to the **e** with one stroke of 1 Sm 26:8
blood fall to the **e** away from the 1 Sm 26:20
"I see a god coming up out of the **e**." 1 Sm 28:13
So he arose from the **e** and sat on the 1 Sm 28:23
hand and destroy you from the **e**?" 2 Sm 4:11
like the name of the great ones of the **e**. 2 Sm 7:9
the one nation on **e** whom God went 2 Sm 7:23
arose from the **e** and washed and 2 Sm 12:20
tore his garments and lay on the **e**. 2 Sm 13:31
nor remnant on the face of the **e**." 2 Sm 14:7
to know all things that are on the **e**." 2 Sm 14:20
was suspended between heaven and **e**, 2 Sm 18:9
king with his face to the **e** and said, 2 Sm 18:28
"Then the **e** reeled and rocked; the 2 Sm 22:8
I beat them fine as the dust of the **e**; I 2 Sm 22:43
that makes grass to sprout from the **e**. 2 Sm 23:4
so that the **e** was split by their noise. 1 Kgs 1:40
not one of his hairs shall fall to the **e**, 1 Kgs 1:52
"I am about to go the way of all the **e**. 1 Kgs 2:2
and from all the kings of the **e**, 1 Kgs 4:34
you, in heaven above or on **e** beneath, 1 Kgs 8:23
"But will God indeed dwell on the **e**? 1 Kgs 8:27
the peoples of the **e** may know your 1 Kgs 8:43
the peoples of the **e** to be your 1 Kgs 8:53
the peoples of the **e** may know that 1 Kgs 8:60
all the kings of the **e** in riches and in 1 Kgs 10:23
And the whole **e** sought the presence 1 Kgs 10:24
to destroy it from the face of the **e**. 1 Kgs 13:34
the LORD sends rain upon the **e**.'" 1 Kgs 17:14
and I will send rain upon the **e**." 1 Kgs 18:1
himself down on the **e** and put his 1 Kgs 18:42
is no God in all the **e** but in Israel; 2 Kgs 5:15
to your servant two mules' load of **e**, 2 Kgs 5:17
shall fall to the **e** nothing of the 2 Kgs 10:10
alone, of all the kingdoms of the **e**; 2 Kgs 19:15
earth; you have made heaven and **e**. 2 Kgs 19:15
kingdoms of the **e** may know that 2 Kgs 19:19
He was the first on **e** to be a mighty 1 Chr 1:10
(for in his days the **e** was divided), 1 Chr 1:19
God; his judgments are in all the **e**. 1 Chr 16:14
Sing to the LORD, all the **e**! Tell of his 1 Chr 16:23
tremble before him, all the **e**; yes, 1 Chr 16:30
be glad, and let the **e** rejoice, 1 Chr 16:31
the LORD, for he comes to judge the **e**. 1 Chr 16:33
the name of the great ones of the **e**. 1 Chr 17:8
the one nation on **e** whom God went 1 Chr 17:21
standing between **e** and heaven, 1 Chr 21:16
so much blood before me on the **e**. 1 Chr 22:8
in the heavens and in the **e** is yours. 1 Chr 29:11
Our days on the **e** are like a shadow, 1 Chr 29:15
as numerous as the dust of the **e**. 2 Chr 1:9
of Israel, who made heaven and **e**, 2 Chr 2:12
is no God like you, in heaven or on **e**, 2 Chr 6:14
God indeed dwell with man on the **e**? 2 Chr 6:18
the peoples of the **e** may know your 2 Chr 6:33
all the kings of the **e** in riches and in 2 Chr 9:22
the kings of the **e** sought the presence 2 Chr 9:23
to and fro throughout the whole **e**, 2 Chr 16:9
of the gods of the peoples of the **e**, 2 Chr 32:19
given me all the kingdoms of the **e**, 2 Chr 36:23
has given me all the kingdoms of the **e**, Ezr 1:2
the servants of the God of heaven and **e**, Ezr 5:11
in sackcloth, and with **e** on their heads. Neh 9:1
all their host, the **e** and all that is on it, Neh 9:6
and said, "From going to and fro on the **e**, Jb 1:7
Job, that there is none like him on the **e**, Jb 1:8
and said, "From going to and fro on the **e**, Jb 2:2
Job, that there is none like him on the **e**, Jb 2:3
and counselors of the **e** who rebuilt ruins Jb 3:14
gives rain on the **e** and sends waters on Jb 5:10
and shall not fear the beasts of the **e**. Jb 5:22
your descendants as the grass of the **e**. Jb 5:25
"Has not man a hard service on **e**, and are Jb 7:1
For now I shall lie in the **e**; you will seek Jb 7:21
nothing, for our days on **e** are a shadow. Jb 8:9
who shakes the **e** out of its place, and its Jb 9:6
The **e** is given into the hand of the Jb 9:24
is longer than the **e** and broader than the Jb 11:9
or the bushes of the **e**, and they will teach Jb 12:8
the people of the **e** and makes them Jb 12:24
Though its root grow old in the **e**, and its Jb 14:8
the torrents wash away the soil of the **e**; Jb 14:19
will his possessions spread over the **e**; Jb 15:29
"O **e**, cover not my blood, and let my cry Jb 16:18
anger, shall the **e** be forsaken for you, Jb 18:4
His memory perishes from the **e**, and he Jb 18:17
and at the last he will stand upon the **e**. Jb 19:25
from of old, since man was placed on **e**, Jb 20:4
and the **e** will rise up against him. Jb 20:27
road; the poor of the **e** all hide themselves. Jb 24:4
over the void and hangs the **e** on nothing. Jb 26:7
Iron is taken out of the **e**, and copper is Jb 28:2
As for the **e**, out of it comes bread, but Jb 28:5
the ends of the **e** and sees everything Jb 28:24
dwell, in holes of the **e** and of the rocks. Jb 30:6
Who gave him charge over the **e**, and Jb 34:13
the beasts of the **e** and makes us wiser Jb 35:11
and his lightning to the corners of the **e**. Jb 37:3
For to the snow he says, 'Fall on the **e**,' Jb 37:6
are hot when the **e** is still because of Jb 37:17
you when I laid the foundation of the **e**? Jb 38:4
it might take hold of the skirts of the **e**, Jb 38:13
you comprehended the expanse of the **e**? Jb 38:18
the east wind is scattered upon the **e**? Jb 38:24
Can you establish their rule on the **e**? Jb 38:33
leaves her eggs to the **e** and lets them be Jb 39:14
On **e** there is not his like, a creature Jb 41:33
The kings of the **e** set themselves, and the Ps 2:2
and the ends of the **e** your possession. Ps 2:8
be wise; be warned, O rulers of the **e**. Ps 2:10
how majestic is your name in all the **e**! Ps 8:1
how majestic is your name in all the **e**! Ps 8:9
who is of the **e** may strike terror no Ps 10:18
Then the **e** reeled and rocked; the Ps 18:7
line goes out through all the **e**, Ps 19:4
destroy their descendants from the **e**, Ps 21:10
the ends of the **e** shall remember and Ps 22:27
the prosperous of the **e** eat and worship; Ps 22:29
The **e** is the LORD'S and the fullness Ps 24:1
the **e** is full of the steadfast love of the Ps 33:5
Let all the **e** fear the LORD; let all the Ps 33:8
looks out on all the inhabitants of the **e**, Ps 33:14
cut off the memory of them from the **e**. Ps 34:16
you will make them princes in all the **e**. Ps 45:16
we will not fear though the **e** gives way, Ps 46:2
totter; he utters his voice, the **e** melts. Ps 46:6
how he has brought desolations on the **e**. Ps 46:8
He makes wars cease to the end of the **e**; Ps 46:9
the nations, I will be exalted in the **e**!" Ps 46:10
is to be feared, a great king over all the **e**. Ps 47:2
For God is the King of all the **e**; sing Ps 47:7
For the shields of the **e** belong to God; he Ps 47:9
in elevation, is the joy of all the **e**, Ps 48:2
your praise reaches to the ends of the **e**. Ps 48:10
and summons the **e** from the rising Ps 50:1
calls to the heavens above and to the **e**, Ps 50:4
heavens! Let your glory be over all the **e**! Ps 57:5
Let your glory be over all the **e**! Ps 57:11
your hands deal out violence on **e**. Ps 58:2
surely there is a God who judges on **e**." Ps 58:11
God rules over Jacob to the ends of the **e**. Ps 59:13
from the end of the **e** I call to you when Ps 61:2
life shall go down into the depths of the **e**; Ps 63:9
all the ends of the **e** and of the farthest Ps 65:5
at the ends of the **e** are in awe at your Ps 65:8
You visit the **e** and water it; you greatly Ps 65:9
Shout for joy to God, all the **e**; Ps 66:1
All the **e** worships you and sings praises Ps 66:4
that your way may be known on **e**, your Ps 67:2
equity and guide the nations upon **e**. Ps 67:4
The **e** has yielded its increase; God, our Ps 67:6
bless us; let all the ends of the **e** fear him! Ps 67:7
the **e** quaked, the heavens poured down Ps 68:8
O kingdoms of the **e**, sing to God; sing Ps 68:32
Let heaven and **e** praise him, the seas Ps 69:34
the depths of the **e** you will bring me Ps 71:20
grass, like showers that water the **e**! Ps 72:6
and from the River to the ends of the **e**! Ps 72:8
may the whole **e** be filled with his glory! Ps 72:19
and their tongue struts through the **e**. Ps 73:9
there is nothing on **e** that I desire Ps 73:25
working salvation in the midst of the **e**. Ps 74:12
have fixed all the boundaries of the **e**; Ps 74:17
When the **e** totters, and all its Ps 75:3
all the wicked of the **e** shall drain it down Ps 75:8
judgment; the **e** feared and was still, Ps 76:8
judgment, to save all the humble of the **e**. Ps 76:9
who is to be feared by the kings of the **e**. Ps 76:12
up the world; the **e** trembled and shook. Ps 77:18
like the high heavens, like the **e**, Ps 78:69
of your faithful to the beasts of the **e**. Ps 79:2
all the foundations of the **e** are shaken. Ps 82:5
Arise, O God, judge the **e**; for you shall Ps 82:8
LORD, are the Most High over all the **e**. Ps 83:18
heavens are yours; the **e** also is yours; Ps 89:11
the highest of the kings of the **e**. Ps 89:27
ever you had formed the **e** and the world, Ps 90:2
Rise up, O judge of the **e**; repay to the Ps 94:2
In his hand are the depths of the **e**; the Ps 95:4
a new song; sing to the LORD, all the **e**! Ps 96:1
of holiness; tremble before him, all the **e**! Ps 96:9
heavens be glad, and let the **e** rejoice; Ps 96:11
he comes, for he comes to judge the **e**. Ps 96:13
The LORD reigns, let the **e** rejoice; let the Ps 97:1
up the world; the **e** sees and trembles. Ps 97:4

the LORD, before the Lord of all the **e**.	Ps 97:5
you, O LORD, are most high over all the **e**;	Ps 97:9
the ends of the **e** have seen the salvation	Ps 98:3
Make a joyful noise to the LORD, all the **e**;	Ps 98:4
the LORD, for he comes to judge the **e**.	Ps 98:9
upon the cherubim; let the **e** quake!	Ps 99:1
a joyful noise to the LORD, all the **e**!	Ps 100:1
the kings of the **e** will fear your glory.	Ps 102:15
from heaven the LORD looked at the **e**,	Ps 102:19
Of old you laid the foundation of the **e**,	Ps 102:25
as high as the heavens are above the **e**,	Ps 103:11
He set the **e** on its foundations, so that it	Ps 104:5
that they might not again cover the **e**.	Ps 104:9
the **e** is satisfied with the fruit of your	Ps 104:13
he may bring forth food from the **e**	Ps 104:14
them all; the **e** is full of your creatures.	Ps 104:24
who looks on the **e** and it trembles,	Ps 104:32
Let sinners be consumed from the **e**,	Ps 104:35
our God; his judgments are in all the **e**.	Ps 105:7
the **e** opened and swallowed up	Ps 106:17
Let your glory be over all the **e**!	Ps 108:5
off the memory of them from the **e**!	Ps 109:15
he will shatter chiefs over the wide **e**.	Ps 110:6
far down on the heavens and the **e**?	Ps 113:6
Tremble, O **e**, at the presence of the	Ps 114:7
by the LORD, who made heaven and **e**!	Ps 115:15
but the **e** he has given to the children	Ps 115:16
I am a sojourner on the **e**; hide not	Ps 119:19
The **e**, O LORD, is full of your steadfast	Ps 119:64
have almost made an end of me on **e**,	Ps 119:87
you have established the **e**, and it	Ps 119:90
the wicked of the **e** you discard like	Ps 119:119
from the LORD, who made heaven and **e**.	Ps 121:2
of the LORD, who made heaven and **e**.	Ps 124:8
from Zion, he who made heaven and **e**!	Ps 134:3
pleases, he does, in heaven and on **e**,	Ps 135:6
makes the clouds rise at the end of the **e**,	Ps 135:7
who spread out the **e** above the waters,	Ps 136:6
the kings of the **e** shall give you thanks,	Ps 138:4
woven in the depths of the **e**.	Ps 139:15
As when one plows and breaks up the **e**,	Ps 141:7
his breath departs he returns to the **e**;	Ps 146:4
who made heaven and **e**, the sea, and all	Ps 146:6
with clouds; he prepares rain for the **e**;	Ps 147:8
He sends out his command to the **e**;	Ps 147:15
Praise the LORD from the **e**, you great sea	Ps 148:7
Kings of the **e** and all peoples, princes	Ps 148:11
peoples, princes and all rulers of the **e**!	Ps 148:11
his majesty is above **e** and heaven.	Ps 148:13
The LORD by wisdom founded the **e**; by	Prv 3:19
the first, before the beginning of the **e**.	Prv 8:23
before he had made the **e** with its fields,	Prv 8:26
he marked out the foundations of the **e**,	Prv 8:29
If the righteous is repaid on **e**, how	Prv 11:31
eyes of a fool are on the ends of the **e**.	Prv 17:24
heavens for height, and the **e** for depth,	Prv 25:3
has established all the ends of the **e**?	Prv 30:4
to devour the poor from off the **e**,	Prv 30:14
Under three things the **e** trembles;	Prv 30:21
Four things on **e** are small, but they	Prv 30:24
comes, but the **e** remains forever.	Eccl 1:4
spirit of the beast goes down into the **e**?	Eccl 3:21
for God is in heaven and you are on **e**.	Eccl 5:2
a righteous man on **e** who does good	Eccl 7:20
There is a vanity that takes place on **e**,	Eccl 8:14
to see the business that is done on **e**,	Eccl 8:16
not what disaster may happen on **e**.	Eccl 11:2
rain, they empty themselves on the **e**,	Eccl 11:3
and the dust returns to the **e** as it was,	Eccl 12:7
The flowers appear on the **e**, the time of	Sg 2:12
Hear, O heavens, and give ear, O **e**; for the	Is 1:2
his majesty, when he rises to terrify the **e**.	Is 2:19
his majesty, when he rises to terrify the **e**.	Is 2:21
whistle for them from the ends of the **e**;	Is 5:26
of hosts; the whole **e** is full of his glory!"	Is 6:3
And they will look to the **e**, but behold,	Is 8:22
forsaken, so I have gathered all the **e**;	Is 10:14
end, as decreed, in the midst of all the **e**.	Is 10:23
decide with equity for the meek of the **e**;	Is 11:4
and he shall strike the **e** with the rod of	Is 11:4
for the **e** shall be full of the knowledge of	Is 11:9
of Judah from the four corners of the **e**.	Is 11:12
let this be made known in all the **e**.	Is 12:5
and the **e** will be shaken out of its place,	Is 13:13
The whole **e** is at rest and quiet; they	Is 14:7
to greet you, all who were leaders of the **e**;	Is 14:9
'Is this the man who made the **e** tremble,	Is 14:16
fathers, lest they rise and possess the **e**,	Is 14:21
that is purposed concerning the whole **e**,	Is 14:26
of the world, you who dwell on the **e**,	Is 18:3
the mountains and to the beasts of the **e**.	Is 18:6
all the beasts of the **e** will winter on them.	Is 18:6
Assyria, a blessing in the midst of the **e**,	Is 19:24
whose traders were the honored of the **e**?	Is 23:8
glory, to dishonor all the honored of the **e**.	Is 23:9
of the world on the face of the **e**.	Is 23:17
LORD will empty the **e** and make it	Is 24:1
The **e** shall be utterly empty and utterly	Is 24:3
The **e** mourns and withers; the world	Is 24:4
the highest people of the **e** languish.	Is 24:4
The **e** lies defiled under its inhabitants;	Is 24:5
Therefore a curse devours the **e**, and its	Is 24:6
the inhabitants of the **e** are scorched,	Is 24:6
dark; the gladness of the **e** is banished.	Is 24:11
in the midst of the **e** among the nations,	Is 24:13
From the ends of the **e** we hear songs of	Is 24:16
are upon you, O inhabitant of the **e**!	Is 24:17
and the foundations of the **e** tremble.	Is 24:18
The **e** is utterly broken, the earth is split	Is 24:19
is utterly broken, the **e** is split apart,	Is 24:19
is split apart, the **e** is violently shaken.	Is 24:19
The **e** staggers like a drunken man; it	Is 24:20
in heaven, and the kings of the **e**,	Is 24:21
and the kings of the earth, on the **e**.	Is 24:21
people he will take away from all the **e**,	Is 25:8
For when your judgments are in the **e**, the	Is 26:9
accomplished no deliverance in the **e**,	Is 26:18
and the **e** will give birth to the dead.	Is 26:19
inhabitants of the **e** for their iniquity,	Is 26:21
and the **e** will disclose the blood shed on	Is 26:21
he casts down to the **e** with his hand.	Is 28:2
from the **e** you shall speak, and from the	Is 29:4
Let the **e** hear, and all that fills it; the	Is 34:1
you alone, of all the kingdoms of the **e**;	Is 37:16
the earth; you have made heaven and **e**.	Is 37:16
the kingdoms of the **e** may know that	Is 37:20
the dust of the **e** in a measure and	Is 40:12
from the foundations of the **e**?	Is 40:21
It is he who sits above the circle of the **e**,	Is 40:22
makes the rulers of the **e** as emptiness.	Is 40:23
has their stem taken root in the **e**,	Is 40:24
God, the Creator of the ends of the **e**.	Is 40:28
and are afraid; the ends of the **e** tremble;	Is 41:5
you whom I took from the ends of the **e**,	Is 41:9
till he has established justice in the **e**;	Is 42:4
who spread out the **e** and what comes	Is 42:5
song, his praise from the end of the **e**,	Is 42:10
and my daughters from the end of the **e**,	Is 43:6
LORD has done it; shout, O depths of the **e**;	Is 44:23
heavens, who spread out the **e** by myself,	Is 44:24
let the **e** open, that salvation and	Is 45:8
fruit; let the **e** cause them both to sprout;	Is 45:8
I made the **e** and created man on it; it	Is 45:12
who formed the **e** and made it (he	Is 45:18
to me and be saved, all the ends of the **e**!	Is 45:22
My hand laid the foundation of the **e**,	Is 48:13
it, send it out to the end of the **e**;	Is 48:20
salvation may reach to the end of the **e**."	Is 49:6
Sing for joy, O heavens, and exult, O **e**;	Is 49:13
to the heavens, and look at the **e** beneath;	Is 51:6
smoke, the **e** will wear out like a garment,	Is 51:6
and laid the foundations of the **e**,	Is 51:13
and laying the foundations of the **e**,	Is 51:16
the ends of the **e** shall see the salvation	Is 52:10
the God of the whole **e** he is called.	Is 54:5
of Noah should no more go over the **e**,	Is 54:9
For as the heavens are higher than the **e**,	Is 55:9
and do not return there but water the **e**,	Is 55:10
make you ride on the heights of the **e**;	Is 58:14
For behold, darkness shall cover the **e**,	Is 60:2
For as the **e** brings forth its sprouts, and	Is 61:11
Jerusalem and makes it a praise in the **e**.	Is 62:7
LORD has proclaimed to the end of the **e**:	Is 62:11
and I poured out their lifeblood on the **e**."	Is 63:6
I create new heavens and a new **e**,	Is 65:17
is my throne, and the **e** is my footstool;	Is 66:1
heavens and the new **e** that I make shall	Is 66:22
I looked on the **e**, and behold, it was	Jer 4:23
"For this the **e** shall mourn, and the	Jer 4:28
Hear, O **e**; behold, I am bringing disaster	Jer 6:19
is stirring from the farthest parts of the **e**.	Jer 6:22
of the air, and for the beasts of the **e**,	Jer 7:33
love, justice, and righteousness in the **e**.	Jer 9:24
At his wrath the **e** quakes, and the	Jer 10:10
the heavens and the **e** shall perish from	Jer 10:11
shall perish from the **e** and from under	Jer 10:11
It is he who made the **e** by his power,	Jer 10:12
the mist rise from the ends of the **e**.	Jer 10:13
the beasts of the **e** to devour and destroy.	Jer 15:3
the kingdoms of the **e** because of what	Jer 15:4
birds of the air and for the beasts of the **e**.	Jer 16:4
come from the ends of the **e** and say:	Jer 16:19
away from you shall be written in the **e**,	Jer 17:13
birds of the air and to the beasts of the **e**.	Jer 19:7
the LORD. Do I not fill heaven and **e**?	Jer 23:24
a horror to all the kingdoms of the **e**,	Jer 24:9
of the world that are on the face of the **e**.	Jer 25:26
against all the inhabitants of the **e**,	Jer 25:29
against all the inhabitants of the **e**.	Jer 25:30
clamor will resound to the ends of the **e**,	Jer 25:31
stirring from the farthest parts of the **e**!	Jer 25:32
from one end of the **e** to the other.	Jer 25:33
city a curse for all the nations of the **e**.'"	Jer 26:6
my outstretched arm have made the **e**,	Jer 27:5
the men and animals that are on the **e**,	Jer 27:5
I will remove you from the face of the **e**.	Jer 28:16
a horror to all the kingdoms of the **e**,	Jer 29:18
them from the farthest parts of the **e**,	Jer 31:8
LORD has created a new thing on the **e**:	Jer 31:22
the foundations of the **e** below can be	Jer 31:37
the heavens and the **e** by your great	Jer 32:17
"Thus says the LORD who made the **e**, the	Jer 33:2
all the nations of the **e** who shall hear of	Jer 33:9
and the fixed order of heaven and **e**,	Jer 33:25
kingdoms of the **e** under his dominion	Jer 34:1
a horror to all the kingdoms of the **e**.	Jer 34:17
birds of the air and the beasts of the **e**.	Jer 34:20
a taunt among all the nations of the **e**?	Jer 44:8
He said, 'I will rise, I will cover the **e**, I	Jer 46:8
shame, and the **e** is full of your cry;	Jer 46:12
sound of their fall the **e** shall tremble;	Jer 49:21
hammer of the whole **e** is cut down and	Jer 50:23
cause, that he may give rest to the **e**,	Jer 50:34
stirring from the farthest parts of the **e**.	Jer 50:41
capture of Babylon the **e** shall tremble,	Jer 50:46
LORD'S hand, making all the **e** drunken;	Jer 51:7
"It is he who made the **e** by his power,	Jer 51:15
the mist rise from the ends of the **e**.	Jer 51:16
the LORD, which destroys the whole **e**;	Jer 51:25
"Set up a standard on the **e**; blow the	Jer 51:27
is taken, the praise of the whole **e** seized!	Jer 51:41
Then the heavens and the **e**, and all	Jer 51:48
have fallen the slain of all the **e**.	Jer 51:49
down from heaven to **e** the splendor of	Lam 2:1
of beauty, the joy of all the **e**?"	Lam 2:15
underfoot all the prisoners of the **e**,	Lam 3:34
The kings of the **e** did not believe, nor	Lam 4:12
a wheel on the **e** beside the living	Ezk 1:15
the living creatures rose from the **e**,	Ezk 1:19
and when those rose from the **e**, the	Ezk 1:21
prey, and to the wicked of the **e** for spoil,	Ezk 7:21
lifted me up between **e** and heaven and	Ezk 8:3
their wings to mount up from the **e**,	Ezk 10:16
mounted up from the **e** before my eyes	Ezk 10:19
you enriched the kings of the **e**.	Ezk 27:33
you to ashes on the **e** in the sight of all	Ezk 28:18
To the beasts of the **e** and to the birds of	Ezk 29:5
the peoples of the **e** have gone away	Ezk 31:12
the beasts of the whole **e** with you.	Ezk 32:4
were scattered over all the face of the **e**,	Ezk 34:6
fruit, and the **e** shall yield its increase,	Ezk 34:27
While the whole **e** rejoices, I will	Ezk 35:14
goods, who dwell at the center of the **e**.	Ezk 38:12
the people who are on the face of the **e**,	Ezk 38:20
blood of the princes of the **e**—of rams,	Ezk 39:18
waters, and the **e** shone with his glory.	Ezk 43:2
is not a man on **e** who can meet the	Dn 2:10
a great mountain and filled the whole **e**.	Dn 2:35
bronze, which shall rule over all the **e**.	Dn 2:39
and languages, that dwell in all the **e**:	Dn 4:1
and behold, a tree in the midst of the **e**,	Dn 4:10
it was visible to the end of the whole **e**.	Dn 4:11
But leave the stump of its roots in the **e**,	Dn 4:15
be with the beasts in the grass of the **e**.	Dn 4:15
it was visible to the end of the whole **e**,	Dn 4:20
and your dominion to the ends of the **e**.	Dn 4:22
but leave the stump of its roots in the **e**,	Dn 4:23
inhabitants of the **e** are accounted as	Dn 4:35
and among the inhabitants of the **e**;	Dn 4:35
and languages that dwell in all the **e**:	Dn 6:25
signs and wonders in heaven and on **e**,	Dn 6:27
four kings who shall arise out of the **e**.	Dn 7:17
there shall be a fourth kingdom on **e**,	Dn 7:23
and it shall devour the whole **e**,	Dn 7:23
the west across the face of the whole **e**,	Dn 8:5
sleep in the dust of the **e** shall awake,	Dn 12:2
heavens, and they shall answer the **e**,	Hos 2:21
and the **e** shall answer the grain, the	Hos 2:22
as the spring rains that water the **e**."	Hos 6:3
The **e** quakes before them; the heavens	Jl 2:10
wonders in the heavens and on the **e**,	Jl 2:30
and the heavens and the **e** quake.	Jl 3:16
into the dust of the **e** and turn aside the	Am 2:7
have I known of all the families of the **e**;	Am 3:2
Does a bird fall in a snare on the **e**, when	Am 3:5
treads on the heights of the **e**—the LORD,	Am 4:13
and cast down righteousness to the **e**!	Am 5:7
pours them out on the surface of the **e**,	Am 5:8
and darken the **e** in broad daylight.	Am 8:9
hosts, he who touches the **e** and it melts,	Am 9:5
heavens and founds his vault upon the **e**;	Am 9:6
upon the surface of the **e**—the LORD is	Am 9:6
a sieve, but no pebble shall fall to the **e**.	Am 9:9
pay attention, O **e**, and all that is in it, and	Mi 1:2
and tread upon the high places of the **e**.	Mi 1:3

their wealth to the Lord of the whole **e**. Mi 4:13
now he shall be great to the ends of the **e**. Mi 5:4
and you enduring foundations of the **e**, Mi 6:2
The godly has perished from the **e**, and Mi 7:2
But the **e** will be desolate because of its Mi 7:13
serpent, like the crawling things of the **e**; Mi 7:17
the **e** heaves before him, the world and all Na 1:5
I will cut off your prey from the **e**, and Na 2:13
march through the breadth of the **e**, Hab 1:6
fortress, for they pile up **e** and take it. Hab 1:10
the blood of man and violence to the **e**, Hab 2:8
For the **e** will be filled with the Hab 2:14
the blood of man and violence to the **e**, Hab 2:17
let all the **e** keep silence before him." Hab 2:20
heavens, and the **e** was full of his praise. Hab 3:3
He stood and measured the **e**; he looked Hab 3:6
arrows. Selah You split the **e** with rivers. Hab 3:9
You marched through the **e** in fury; Hab 3:12
from the face of the **e**," declares the LORD. Zep 1:2
from the face of the **e**," declares the LORD. Zep 1:3
jealousy, all the **e** shall be consumed; Zep 1:18
will make of all the inhabitants of the **e**. Zep 1:18
for he will famish all the gods of the **e**, Zep 2:11
my jealousy all the **e** shall be consumed. Zep 3:8
into praise and renown in all the **e**. Zep 3:19
praised among all the peoples of the **e**, Zep 3:20
dew, and the **e** has withheld its produce. Hg 1:10
the heavens and the **e** and the sea and Hg 2:6
about to shake the heavens and the **e**, Hg 2:21
whom the LORD has sent to patrol the **e**.' Zec 1:10
trees, and said, 'We have patrolled the **e**, Zec 1:11
and behold, all the **e** remains at rest.' Zec 1:11
which range through the whole **e**." Zec 4:10
who stand by the Lord of the whole **e**." Zec 4:14
up the basket between **e** and heaven. Zec 5:9
themselves before the LORD of all the **e**. Zec 6:5
were impatient to go and patrol the **e**. Zec 6:7
patrol the **e**." So they patrolled the earth. Zec 6:7
patrol the earth." So they patrolled the **e**. Zec 6:7
and from the River to the ends of the **e**. Zec 9:10
and founded the **e** and formed the Zec 12:1
the nations of the **e** will gather against Zec 12:3
And the LORD will be king over all the **e**. Zec 14:9
of the families of the **e** do not go up to Zec 14:17
are the meek, for they shall inherit the **e**. Mt 5:5
"You are the salt of the **e**, but if salt has Mt 5:13
to you, until heaven and **e** pass away, Mt 5:18
or by the **e**, for it is his footstool, or by Mt 5:35
your will be done, on **e** as it is in heaven. Mt 6:10
not lay up for yourselves treasures on **e**, Mt 6:19
Man has authority on **e** to forgive sins"— Mt 9:6
that I have come to bring peace to the **e**. Mt 10:34
you, Father, Lord of heaven and **e**, Mt 11:25
and three nights in the heart of the **e**. Mt 12:40
the ends of the **e** to hear the wisdom Mt 12:42
whatever you bind on **e** shall be bound Mt 16:19
whatever you loose on **e** shall be loosed Mt 16:19
whom do kings of the **e** take toll or tax? Mt 17:25
whatever you bind on **e** shall be bound Mt 18:18
whatever you loose on **e** shall be loosed Mt 18:18
of you agree on **e** about anything they Mt 18:19
And call no man your father on **e**, for Mt 23:9
come all the righteous blood shed on **e**, Mt 23:35
then all the tribes of the **e** will mourn, Mt 24:30
Heaven and **e** will pass away, but my Mt 24:35
And the **e** shook, and the rocks were Mt 27:51
in heaven and on **e** has been given to Mt 28:18
Man has authority on **e** to forgive sins" Mk 2:10
The **e** produces by itself, first the blade, Mk 4:28
is the smallest of all the seeds on **e**, Mk 4:31
white, as no one on **e** could bleach them. Mk 9:3
from the ends of the **e** to the ends of Mk 13:27
Heaven and **e** will pass away, but my Mk 13:31
and on **e** peace among those with whom Lk 2:14
Man has authority on **e** to forgive sins" Lk 5:24
you, Father, Lord of heaven and **e**, Lk 10:21
the ends of the **e** to hear the wisdom Lk 11:31
"I came to cast fire on the **e**, and would Lk 12:49
that I have come to give peace on **e**? Lk 12:51
interpret the appearance of **e** and sky, Lk 12:56
easier for heaven and **e** to pass away Lk 16:17
of Man comes, will he find faith on **e**?" Lk 18:8
distress upon the **e** and wrath against Lk 21:23
and on the **e** distress of nations in Lk 21:25
Heaven and **e** will pass away, but my Lk 21:33
all who dwell on the face of the whole **e**. Lk 21:35
He who is of the **e** belongs to the earth Jn 3:31
earth belongs to the **e** and speaks in an Jn 3:31
a grain of wheat falls into the **e** and dies, Jn 12:24
And I, when I am lifted up from the **e**, Jn 12:32
I glorified you on **e**, having Jn 17:4
and Samaria, and to the end of the **e**." Acts 1:8
above and signs on the **e** below, Acts 2:19
all the families of the **e** be blessed.' Acts 3:25
the heaven and the **e** and the sea and Acts 4:24
The kings of the **e** set themselves, and Acts 4:26
is my throne, and the **e** is my footstool. Acts 7:49
For his life is taken away from the **e**." Acts 8:33
down by its four corners upon the **e**. Acts 10:11
bring salvation to the ends of the **e**.'" Acts 13:47
the heaven and the **e** and the sea and Acts 14:15
in it, being Lord of heaven and **e**, Acts 17:24
to live on all the face of the **e**, Acts 17:26
"Away with such a fellow from the **e**! Acts 22:22
might be proclaimed in all the **e**." Rom 9:17
sentence upon the **e** fully and without Rom 9:28
"Their voice has gone out to all the **e**, Rom 10:18
in heaven or on **e**—as indeed there 1 Cor 8:5
For "the **e** is the Lord's, and the 1 Cor 10:26
The first man was from the **e**, a man 1 Cor 15:47
him, things in heaven and things on **e**. Eph 1:10
family in heaven and on **e** is named, Eph 3:15
descended into the lower parts of the **e**? Eph 4:9
in heaven and on **e** and under the Phil 2:10
heaven and on earth and under the **e**, Phil 2:10
things were created, in heaven and on **e**, Col 1:16
all things, whether on **e** or in heaven, Col 1:20
are above, not on things that are on **e**. Col 3:2
foundation of the **e** in the beginning, Heb 1:10
Now if he were on **e**, he would not be a Heb 8:4
were strangers and exiles on the **e**. Heb 11:13
and in dens and caves of the **e**. Heb 11:38
refused him who warned them on **e**, Heb 12:25
At that time his voice shook the **e**, but Heb 12:26
shake not only the **e** but also the Heb 12:26
You have lived on the **e** in luxury and in Jas 5:5
waits for the precious fruit of the **e**, Jas 5:7
either by heaven or by **e** or by any other Jas 5:12
and six months it did not rain on the **e**. Jas 5:17
heaven gave rain, and the **e** bore its fruit. Jas 5:18
and the **e** was formed out of water and 2 Pt 3:5
word the heavens and **e** that now exist 2 Pt 3:7
and the **e** and the works that are done 2 Pt 3:10
and a new **e** in which righteousness 2 Pt 3:13
of the dead, and the ruler of kings on **e**. Rv 1:5
and all tribes of the **e** will wail on account Rv 1:7
world, to try those who dwell on the **e**. Rv 3:10
one in heaven or on **e** or under the earth Rv 5:3
on earth or under the **e** was able to open Rv 5:3
seven spirits of God sent out into all the **e**. Rv 5:6
our God, and they shall reign on the **e**." Rv 5:10
in heaven and on **e** and under the earth Rv 5:13
on earth and under the **e** and in the sea, Rv 5:13
was permitted to take peace from the **e**, Rv 6:4
given authority over a fourth of the **e**, Rv 6:8
with pestilence and by wild beasts of the **e**. Rv 6:8
our blood on those who dwell on the **e**?" Rv 6:10
of the sky fell to the **e** as the fig tree sheds Rv 6:13
the kings of the **e** and the great ones Rv 6:15
standing at the four corners of the **e**, Rv 7:1
holding back the four winds of the **e**, Rv 7:1
no wind might blow on **e** or sea or against Rv 7:1
had been given power to harm **e** and sea, Rv 7:2
"Do not harm the **e** or the sea or the trees, Rv 7:3
fire from the altar and threw it on the **e**, Rv 8:5
blood, and these were thrown upon the **e**. Rv 8:7
And a third of the **e** was burned up, and a Rv 8:7
woe, woe to those who dwell on the **e**, Rv 8:13
and I saw a star fallen from heaven to **e**, Rv 9:1
from the smoke came locusts on the **e**, Rv 9:3
power like the power of scorpions of the **e**. Rv 9:3
harm the grass of the **e** or any green plant Rv 9:4
and what is in it, the **e** and what is in it, Rv 10:6
that stand before the Lord of the **e**. Rv 11:4
and to strike the **e** with every kind of Rv 11:6
who dwell on the **e** will rejoice over Rv 11:10
a torment to those who dwell on the **e**. Rv 11:10
for destroying the destroyers of the **e**." Rv 11:18
stars of heaven and cast them to the **e**. Rv 12:4
world—he was thrown down to the **e**, Rv 12:9
But woe to you, O **e** and sea, for the devil Rv 12:12
that he had been thrown down to the **e**, Rv 12:13
But the **e** came to the help of the Rv 12:16
and the **e** opened its mouth and Rv 12:16
and the whole **e** marveled as they Rv 13:3
and all who dwell on **e** will worship it, Rv 13:8
I saw another beast rising out of the **e**. Rv 13:11
and makes the **e** and its inhabitants Rv 13:12
down from heaven to **e** in front of Rv 13:13
beast it deceives those who dwell on **e**, Rv 13:14
who had been redeemed from the **e**. Rv 14:3
to proclaim to those who dwell on **e**, Rv 14:6
worship him who made heaven and **e**, Rv 14:7
for the harvest of the **e** is fully ripe." Rv 14:15
the cloud swung his sickle across the **e**, Rv 14:16
across the earth, and the **e** was reaped. Rv 14:16
the clusters from the vine of the **e**, Rv 14:18
his sickle across the **e** and gathered the Rv 14:19
grape harvest of the **e** and threw it into Rv 14:19
and pour out on the **e** the seven bowls of Rv 16:1
went and poured out his bowl on the **e**, Rv 16:2
had never been since man was on the **e**, Rv 16:18
the kings of the **e** have committed sexual Rv 17:2
the dwellers on **e** have become drunk." Rv 17:2
And the dwellers on **e** whose names have Rv 17:8
has dominion over the kings of the **e**." Rv 17:18
and the **e** was made bright with his Rv 18:1
kings of the **e** have committed Rv 18:3
the merchants of the **e** have grown rich Rv 18:3
And the kings of the **e**, who committed Rv 18:9
the merchants of the **e** weep and mourn Rv 18:11
merchants were the great ones of the **e**, Rv 18:23
and of all who have been slain on **e**." Rv 18:24
who corrupted the **e** with her Rv 19:2
the kings of the **e** with their armies Rv 19:19
that are at the four corners of the **e**, Rv 20:8
broad plain of the **e** and surrounded the Rv 20:9
From his presence **e** and sky fled away, Rv 20:11
Then I saw a new heaven and a new **e**, Rv 21:1
heaven and the first **e** had passed away, Rv 21:1
the kings of the **e** will bring their glory Rv 21:24

EARTH'S (1)
of prostitutes and of **e** abominations." Rv 17:5

EARTHEN (5)
brought beds, basins, and **e** vessels, 2 Sm 17:28
glaze covering an **e** vessel are fervent Prv 26:23
who formed him, a pot among **e** pots! Is 45:9
gold, how they are regarded as **e** pots, Lam 4:2
iron, as when **e** pots are broken in pieces, Rv 2:27

EARTHENWARE (8)
And the **e** vessel in which it is boiled Lv 6:28
if any of them falls into any **e** vessel, Lv 11:33
the birds in an **e** vessel over fresh water. Lv 14:5
the birds in an **e** vessel over fresh water Lv 14:50
And an **e** vessel that the one with the Lv 15:12
holy water in an **e** vessel and take some Nm 5:17
says the LORD, "Go, buy a potter's **e** flask, Jer 19:1
open deed, and put them in an **e** vessel, Jer 32:14

EARTHLY (13)
If I have told you **e** things and you do not Jn 3:12
to the earth and speaks in an **e** way. Jn 3:31
are heavenly bodies and **e** bodies, 1 Cor 15:40
and the glory of the **e** is of another. 1 Cor 15:40
not by **e** wisdom but by the grace of 2 Cor 1:12
that if the tent, which is our **e** home, 2 Cor 5:1
obey your **e** masters with fear and Eph 6:5
shame, with minds set on **e** things. Phil 3:19
Put to death therefore what is **e** in you: Col 3:5
those who are your **e** masters, Col 3:22
for worship and an **e** place of holiness. Heb 9:1
we have had **e** fathers who disciplined Heb 12:9
that comes down from above, but is **e**, Jas 3:15

EARTHQUAKE (19)
And after the wind an **e**, but the 1 Kgs 19:11
but the LORD was not in the **e**. 1 Kgs 19:11
And after the **e** a fire, but the LORD 1 Kgs 19:12
with thunder and with **e** and great noise, Is 29:6
I heard behind me the voice of a great **e**: Ezk 3:12
beside them, and the sound of a great **e**. Ezk 3:13
there shall be a great **e** in the land of Ezk 38:19
king of Israel, two years before the **e**. Am 1:1
as you fled from the **e** in the days of Zec 14:5
Jesus, saw the **e** and what took place, Mt 27:54
And behold, there was a great **e**, for an Mt 28:2
and suddenly there was a great **e**, so Acts 16:26
I looked, and behold, there was a great **e**, Rv 6:12
rumblings, flashes of lightning, and an **e**. Rv 8:5
And at that hour there was a great **e**, Rv 11:13
thousand people were killed in the **e**, Rv 11:13
rumblings, peals of thunder, an **e**, Rv 11:19
and a great **e** such as there had never Rv 16:18
was on the earth, so great was that **e**. Rv 16:18

EARTHQUAKES (3)
will be famines and **e** in various places. Mt 24:7
There will be **e** in various places; Mk 13:8
There will be great **e**, and in various Lk 21:11

EASE (20)
There the prisoners are at **e** together; they Jb 3:18
I am not at **e**, nor am I quiet; I have no Jb 3:26
me, my couch will **e** my complaint,' Jb 7:13
of one who is at **e** there is contempt for Jb 12:5
I was at **e**, and he broke me apart; he Jb 16:12
full vigor, being wholly at **e** and secure, Jb 21:23
always at **e**, they increase in riches. Ps 73:12
of the scorn of those who are at **e**, Ps 123:4
to me will dwell secure and will be at **e**, Prv 1:33
Rise up, you women who are at **e**, hear my Is 32:9
Tremble, you women who are at **e**, Is 32:11
shall return and have quiet and **e**, Jer 30:10
shall return and have quiet and **e**, Jer 46:27
"Moab has been at **e** from his youth Jer 48:11
"Rise up, advance against a nation at **e**, Jer 49:31

pride, excess of food, and prosperous **e**, Ezk 16:49
was at **e** in my house and prospering in Dn 4:4
"Woe to those who are at **e** in Zion, and Am 6:1
angry with the nations that are at **e**; Zec 1:15
that you put him at **e** among you, 1 Cor 16:10

EASED (1)
others should be **e** and you burdened, 2 Cor 8:13

EASES (1)
to them as one who **e** the yoke on their Hos 11:4

EASIER (8)
So it will be **e** for you, and they will Ex 18:22
For which is **e**, to say, 'Your sins are Mt 9:5
it is **e** for a camel to go through the eye Mt 19:24
Which is **e**, to say to the paralytic, 'Your Mk 2:9
It is **e** for a camel to go through the eye Mk 10:25
Which is **e**, to say, 'Your sins are Lk 5:23
But it is **e** for heaven and earth to pass Lk 16:17
For it is **e** for a camel to go through the Lk 18:25

EASILY (1)
of the people might **e** have lain with Gn 26:10

EASING (1)
There is no **e** your hurt; your wound is Na 3:19

EAST (186)
God planted a garden in Eden, in the **e**, Gn 2:8
is the Tigris, which flows **e** of Assyria. Gn 2:14
and at the **e** of the garden of Eden he Gn 3:24
and settled in the land of Nod, **e** of Eden. Gn 4:16
of Sephar to the hill country of the **e**. Gn 10:30
And as people migrated from the **e**, they Gn 11:2
hill country on the **e** of Bethel and Gn 12:8
with Bethel on the west and Ai on the **e**. Gn 12:8
the Jordan Valley, and Lot journeyed **e**. Gn 13:11
which was to the **e** of Mamre, Gn 23:17
field of Machpelah **e** of Mamre (that Gn 23:19
his son Isaac, eastward to the **e** country. Gn 25:6
the son of Zohar the Hittite, **e** of Mamre, Gn 25:9
the west and to the **e** and to the north Gn 28:14
came to the land of the people of the **e**. Gn 29:1
ears, thin and blighted by the **e** wind. Gn 41:6
thin, and blighted by the **e** wind, Gn 41:23
ears blighted by the **e** wind are also Gn 41:27
field at Machpelah, to the **e** of Mamre, Gn 49:30
field at Machpelah, to the **e** of Mamre, Gn 50:13
the LORD brought an **e** wind upon the Ex 10:13
the **e** wind had brought the locusts. Ex 10:13
back by a strong **e** wind all night and Ex 14:21
the front to the **e** shall be fifty cubits. Ex 27:13
And for the front to the **e**, fifty cubits. Ex 38:13
and cast it beside the altar on the **e** side, Lv 1:16
the front of the mercy seat on the **e** side, Lv 16:14
to camp on the **e** side toward the sunrise Nm 2:3
to camp before the tabernacle on the **e**, Nm 3:38
that are on the **e** side shall set out. Nm 10:5
us on this side of the Jordan to the **e**." Nm 32:19
Pi-hahiroth, which is **e** of Baal-zephon, Nm 33:7
from the end of the Salt Sea on the **e**. Nm 34:3
to Riblah on the **e** side of Ain. Nm 34:11
of the Sea of Chinnereth on the **e**. Nm 34:11
beyond the Jordan **e** of Jericho, Nm 34:15
city, on the **e** side two thousand cubits, Nm 35:5
Sea, under the slopes of Pisgah on the **e**. Dt 3:17
three cities in the **e** beyond the Jordan, Dt 4:41
who lived to the **e** beyond the Jordan; Dt 4:47
all the Arabah on the **e** side of the Jordan Dt 4:49
at Gilgal on the **e** border of Jericho. Jos 4:19
to Ai, which is near Beth-aven, **e** of Bethel, Jos 7:2
to the Canaanites in the **e** and the west, Jos 11:3
(from the Shihor, which is **e** of Egypt, Jos 13:3
to Aroer, which is **e** of Rabbah, Jos 13:25
Moab, beyond the Jordan **e** of Jericho. Jos 13:32
And the **e** boundary is the Salt Sea, to the Jos 15:5
by Jericho, **e** of the waters of Jericho, Jos 16:1
inheritance on the **e** was Ataroth-addar Jos 16:5
Then on the **e** the boundary turns Jos 16:6
along beyond it on the **e** to Janoah, Jos 16:6
to Michmethath, which is **e** of Shechem. Jos 17:7
Asher is reached, and on the **e** Issachar. Jos 17:10
then the brook that is **e** of Jokneam. Jos 19:11
along on the **e** toward the sunrise Jos 19:13
west and Judah on the **e** at the Jordan. Jos 19:34
And beyond the Jordan **e** of Jericho, they Jos 20:8
the people of the **E** would come up against Jgs 6:3
and the people of the **E** came together, Jgs 6:33
the people of the **E** lay along the valley Jgs 7:12
left of all the army of the people of the **E**, Jgs 8:10
of the tent dwellers **e** of Nobah and Jgs 8:11
and arrived on the **e** side of the land Jgs 11:18
as far as opposite Gibeah on the **e**. Jgs 20:43
on the **e** of the highway that goes up Jgs 21:19
in Michmash, to the **e** of Beth-aven. 1 Sm 13:5
as far as Shur, which is **e** of Egypt. 1 Sm 15:7
which is on the **e** of Jeshimon?" 1 Sm 26:1
beside the road on the **e** of Jeshimon. 1 Sm 26:3
the people of the **e** and all the wisdom 1 Kgs 4:30
three facing south, and three facing **e**. 1 Kgs 7:25
on the mountain **e** of Jerusalem. 1 Kgs 11:7
Cherith, which is **e** of the Jordan. 1 Kgs 17:3
brook Cherith that is **e** of the Jordan. 1 Kgs 17:5
high places that were **e** of Jerusalem, 2 Kgs 23:13
of Gedor, to the **e** side of the valley, 1 Chr 4:39
He also lived to the **e** as far as the 1 Chr 5:9
throughout all the region **e** of Gilead. 1 Chr 5:10
at Jericho, on the **e** side of the Jordan, 1 Chr 6:78
and its towns, and to the **e** Naaran, 1 Chr 7:28
king's gate on the **e** side as the 1 Chr 9:18
were on the four sides, **e**, west, 1 Chr 9:24
the valleys, to the **e** and to the west. 1 Chr 12:15
The lot for the **e** fell to Shelemiah. 1 Chr 26:14
On the **e** there were six each day, on 1 Chr 26:17
three facing south, and three facing **e**. 2 Chr 4:4
stood **e** of the altar with 120 priests 2 Chr 5:12
valley, **e** of the wilderness of Jeruel. 2 Chr 20:16
them in the square on the **e** 2 Chr 29:4
the Levite, keeper of the **e** gate, 2 Chr 31:14
Water Gate on the **e** and the projecting Neh 3:26
of Shecaniah, the keeper of the **E** Gate, Neh 3:29
of David, to the Water Gate on the **e**. Neh 12:37
was the greatest of all the people of the **e**. Jb 1:3
and fill his belly with the **e** wind? Jb 15:2
his day, and horror seizes them of the **e**. Jb 18:20
The **e** wind lifts him up and he is gone; Jb 27:21
or where the **e** wind is scattered upon Jb 38:24
By the **e** wind you shattered the ships of Ps 48:7
For not from the **e** or from the west and Ps 75:6
He caused the **e** wind to blow in the Ps 78:26
as far as the **e** is from the west, so far Ps 103:12
the lands, from the **e** and from the west, Ps 107:3
of things from the **e** and of fortune-tellers Is 2:6
The Syrians on the **e** and the Philistines Is 9:12
they shall plunder the people of the **e**. Is 11:14
Therefore in the **e** give glory to the LORD; Is 24:15
his fierce breath in the day of the **e** wind. Is 27:8
up one from the **e** whom victory meets at Is 41:2
I will bring your offspring from the **e**, and Is 43:5
calling a bird of prey from the **e**, the Is 46:11
Like the **e** wind I will scatter them Jer 18:17
corner of the Horse Gate toward the **e**, Jer 31:40
Kedar! Destroy the people of the **e**! Jer 49:28
of the LORD, and their faces toward the **e**, Ezk 8:16
east, worshiping the sun toward the **e**. Ezk 8:16
the entrance of the **e** gate of the house Ezk 10:19
brought me to the **e** gate of the house Ezk 11:1
of the house of the LORD, which faces **e**. Ezk 11:1
that is on the **e** side of the city. Ezk 11:23
wither when the **e** wind strikes it Ezk 17:10
ground; the **e** wind dried up its fruit; Ezk 19:12
to the people of the **E** for a possession, Ezk 25:4
to the people of the **E** as a possession, Ezk 25:10
The **e** wind has wrecked you in the Ezk 27:26
the Valley of the Travelers, **e** of the sea. Ezk 39:11
Then he went into the gateway facing **e**, Ezk 40:6
side rooms on either side of the **e** gate. Ezk 40:10
hundred cubits on the **e** side and on Ezk 40:19
of the gate that faced toward the **e**. Ezk 40:22
the gate on the north, as on the **e**, Ezk 40:23
me to the inner court on the **e** side, Ezk 40:32
the breadth of the **e** front of the temple Ezk 41:14
was an entrance on the **e** side, Ezk 42:9
wall on the **e** as one enters Ezk 42:12
he led me out by the gate that faced **e**, Ezk 42:15
He measured the **e** side with the Ezk 42:16
he led me to the gate, the gate facing **e**. Ezk 43:1
God of Israel was coming from the **e**. Ezk 43:2
entered the temple by the gate facing **e**, Ezk 43:4
The steps of the altar shall face **e**." Ezk 43:17
gate of the sanctuary, which faces **e**. Ezk 44:1
of the city, on the west and on the **e**, Ezk 45:7
inner court that faces **e** shall be shut Ezk 46:1
the gate facing **e** shall be opened for Ezk 46:12
the temple toward the **e** (for the temple Ezk 47:1
toward the east (for the temple faced **e**). Ezk 47:1
to the outer gate that faces toward the **e**; Ezk 47:2
"On the **e** side, the boundary shall run Ezk 47:18
far as Tamar. This shall be the **e** side. Ezk 47:18
and extending from the **e** side to the Ezk 48:1
of Dan, from the **e** side to the west, Ezk 48:2
of Asher, from the **e** side to the west, Ezk 48:3
of Naphtali, from the **e** side to the west, Ezk 48:4
of Manasseh, from the **e** side to the west, Ezk 48:5
of Ephraim, from the **e** side to the west, Ezk 48:6
of Reuben, from the **e** side to the west, Ezk 48:7
of Judah, from the **e** side to the west, Ezk 48:8
portions, from the **e** side to the west, Ezk 48:8
the south side 4,500, the **e** side 4,500, Ezk 48:16
cubits, on the south 250, on the **e** 250, Ezk 48:17
portion shall be 10,000 cubits to the **e**, Ezk 48:18
of the holy portion to the **e** border, Ezk 48:21
from the **e** side to the west, Benjamin, Ezk 48:23
Benjamin, from the **e** side to the west, Ezk 48:24
of Simeon, from the **e** side to the west, Ezk 48:25
of Issachar, from the **e** side to the west, Ezk 48:26
of Zebulun, from the **e** side to the west, Ezk 48:27
On the **e** side, which is to be 4,500 Ezk 48:32
great toward the south, toward the **e**, Dn 8:9
But news from the **e** and the north Dn 11:44
wind and pursues the **e** wind all day Hos 12:1
among his brothers, the **e** wind, Hos 13:15
from sea to sea, and from north to **e**; Am 8:12
city and sat to the **e** of the city and made Jon 4:5
rose, God appointed a scorching **e** wind, Jon 4:8
my people from the **e** country and from Zec 8:7
that lies before Jerusalem on the **e**, Zec 14:4
be split in two from **e** to west by a very Zec 14:4
wise men from the **e** came to Jerusalem, Mt 2:1
many will come from **e** and west and Mt 8:11
comes from the **e** and shines as Mt 24:27
And people will come from **e** and west, Lk 13:29
the way for the kings from the **e**. Rv 16:12
on the **e** three gates, on the north three Rv 21:13

EASTERN (9)
king of Moab from the **e** mountains: Nm 23:7
line for your **e** border from Nm 34:10
forms its boundary on the **e** side. Jos 18:20
from the western to the **e** boundary Ezk 45:7
flows toward the **e** region and goes Ezk 47:8
Israel; to the **e** sea and as far as Tamar. Ezk 47:18
side, 10,000 in breadth on the **e** side, Ezk 48:10
desolate land, his vanguard into the **e** sea, Jl 2:20
half of them to the **e** sea and half of Zec 14:8

EASTWARD (15)
and southward and **e** and westward, Gn 13:14
from his son Isaac, **e** to the east country. Gn 25:6
and northward and southward and **e**, Dt 3:27
and **e** as far as the Valley of Mizpeh. Jos 11:8
Mount Hermon, with all the Arabah **e**: Jos 12:1
the Arabah to the Sea of Chinneroth **e**, Jos 12:3
Moses gave them, beyond the Jordan **e**, Jos 13:8
Sea of Chinnereth, **e** beyond the Jordan. Jos 13:27
their inheritance beyond the Jordan **e**, Jos 18:7
the other direction **e** toward the sunrise Jos 19:12
then it turns **e**, it goes to Beth-dagon, Jos 19:27
here and turn **e** and hide yourself 1 Kgs 17:3
from the Jordan **e**, all the land of 2 Kgs 10:33
"Open the window **e**," and he opened 2 Kgs 13:17
Going on **e** with a measuring line in Ezk 47:3

EASY (5)
of war and thought it **e** to go up into the Dt 1:41
"It is an **e** thing for the shadow to 2 Kgs 20:10
but knowledge is **e** for a man of Prv 14:6
and the way is **e** that leads to Mt 7:13
For my yoke is **e**, and my burden is Mt 11:30

EAT (519)
"You may surely **e** of every tree of the Gn 2:16
of good and evil you shall not **e**, Gn 2:17
in the day that you **e** of it you shall Gn 2:17
'You shall not **e** of any tree in the Gn 3:1
"We may **e** of the fruit of the trees in the Gn 3:2
'You shall not **e** of the fruit of the tree that Gn 3:3
knows that when you **e** of it your eyes Gn 3:5
of which I commanded you not to **e**?" Gn 3:11
and dust you shall **e** all the days of your Gn 3:14
I commanded you, 'You shall not **e** of it,' Gn 3:17
in pain you shall **e** of it all the days of Gn 3:17
and you shall **e** the plants of the field. Gn 3:18
the sweat of your face you shall **e** bread, Gn 3:19
and take also of the tree of life and **e**, Gn 3:22
But you shall not **e** flesh with its life, that Gn 9:4
Then food was set before him to **e**. But Gn 24:33
"I will not **e** until I have said what I Gn 24:33
Jacob, "Let me **e** some of that red stew, Gn 25:30
I love, and bring it to me so that I may **e**, Gn 27:4
that I may **e** it and bless you before the Gn 27:7
you shall bring it to your father to **e**, Gn 27:10
now sit up and **e** of my game, that your Gn 27:19
that I may **e** of my son's game and Gn 27:25
my father arise and **e** of his son's game, Gn 27:31
give me bread to **e** and clothing to Gn 28:20
and called his kinsmen to **e** bread. Gn 31:54
people of Israel do not **e** the sinew of the Gn 32:32
Then they sat down to **e**. And looking Gn 37:25
And the birds will **e** the flesh from Gn 40:19
heard that they should **e** bread there. Gn 43:25
Egyptians could not **e** with the Gn 43:32
and you shall **e** the fat of the land.' Gn 45:18
man? Call him, that he may **e** bread." Ex 2:20
And they shall **e** what is left to you after Ex 10:5
and they shall **e** every tree of yours that Ex 10:5
land of Egypt and **e** every plant in the Ex 10:12
to what each can **e** you shall make your Ex 12:4
the lintel of the houses in which they **e** it. Ex 12:7

They shall **e** the flesh that night, roasted	Ex 12:8
bread and bitter herbs they shall **e** it.	Ex 12:8
Do not **e** any of it raw or boiled in water,	Ex 12:9
In this manner you shall **e** it: with your	Ex 12:11
your hand. And you shall **e** it in haste.	Ex 12:11
days you shall **e** unleavened bread.	Ex 12:15
But what everyone needs to **e**, that alone	Ex 12:16
you shall **e** unleavened bread until the	Ex 12:18
You shall **e** nothing leavened; in all	Ex 12:20
places you shall **e** unleavened bread."	Ex 12:20
the Passover: no foreigner shall **e** of it,	Ex 12:43
bought for money may **e** of it after you	Ex 12:44
foreigner or hired servant may **e** of it.	Ex 12:45
no uncircumcised person shall **e** of it.	Ex 12:48
days you shall **e** unleavened bread,	Ex 13:6
the evening meat to **e** and in the	Ex 16:8
to them, 'At twilight you shall **e** meat,	Ex 16:12
bread that the LORD has given you to **e**.	Ex 16:15
each one of you, as much as he can **e**.	Ex 16:16
them gathered as much as he could **e**.	Ex 16:18
gathered it, each as much as he could **e**;	Ex 16:21
Moses said, "**E** it today, for today is a	Ex 16:25
elders of Israel to **e** bread with Moses'	Ex 18:12
Therefore you shall not **e** any flesh that	Ex 22:31
that the poor of your people may **e**;	Ex 23:11
they leave the beasts of the field may **e**.	Ex 23:11
you shall **e** unleavened bread for seven	Ex 23:15
and his sons shall **e** the flesh of the	Ex 29:32
They shall **e** those things with which	Ex 29:33
but an outsider shall not **e** of them,	Ex 29:33
people sat down to **e** and drink and rose	Ex 32:6
you are invited, you **e** of his sacrifice,	Ex 34:15
days you shall **e** unleavened bread,	Ex 34:18
places, that you **e** neither fat nor blood."	Lv 3:17
the rest of it Aaron and his sons shall **e**.	Lv 6:16
of the tent of meeting they shall **e** it.	Lv 6:16
among the children of Aaron may **e** of it,	Lv 6:18
The priest who offers it for sin shall **e** it.	Lv 6:26
male among the priests may **e** of it;	Lv 6:29
Every male among the priests may **e** of it.	Lv 7:6
with fire. All who are clean may **e** flesh,	Lv 7:19
of Israel, saying, You shall **e** no fat,	Lv 7:23
use, but on no account shall you **e** it.	Lv 7:24
you shall **e** no blood whatever,	Lv 7:26
and there **e** it and the bread that is in the	Lv 8:31
saying, 'Aaron and his sons shall **e** it.'	Lv 8:31
and **e** it unleavened beside the altar,	Lv 10:12
You shall **e** it in a holy place, because it	Lv 10:13
is contributed you shall **e** in a clean	Lv 10:14
things that you may **e** among all the	Lv 11:2
the cud, among the animals, you may **e**.	Lv 11:3
or part the hoof, you shall not **e** these:	Lv 11:4
You shall not **e** any of their flesh, and	Lv 11:8
"These you may **e**, of all that are in the	Lv 11:9
in the seas or in the rivers, you may **e**.	Lv 11:9
you shall not **e** any of their flesh, and	Lv 11:11
all fours you may **e** those that have	Lv 11:21
Of them you may **e**: the locust of any	Lv 11:22
if any animal which you may **e** dies,	Lv 11:39
swarms on the ground, you shall not **e**,	Lv 11:42
No person among you shall **e** blood,	Lv 17:12
who sojourns among you **e** blood.	Lv 17:12
You shall not **e** the blood of any	Lv 17:14
in the fifth year you may **e** of its fruit,	Lv 19:25
"You shall not **e** any flesh with the	Lv 19:26
He may **e** the bread of his God, both of	Lv 21:22
or a discharge may **e** of the holy things	Lv 22:4
evening and shall not **e** of the holy	Lv 22:6
and afterward he may **e** of the holy	Lv 22:7
He shall not **e** what dies of itself or is torn	Lv 22:8
lay person shall not **e** of a holy thing;	Lv 22:10
or hired servant shall **e** of a holy thing,	Lv 22:10
for money, the slave may **e** of it,	Lv 22:11
born in his house may **e** of his food.	Lv 22:11
she shall not **e** of the contribution of	Lv 22:12
youth, she may **e** of her father's food;	Lv 22:13
food; yet no lay person shall **e** of it.	Lv 22:13
seven days you shall **e** unleavened bread.	Lv 23:6
And you shall **e** neither bread nor	Lv 23:14
sons, and they shall **e** it in a holy place,	Lv 24:9
you. You may **e** the produce of the field.	Lv 25:12
and you will **e** your fill and dwell in it	Lv 25:19
'What shall we **e** in the seventh year,	Lv 25:20
you shall **e** the old until the ninth year,	Lv 25:22
And you shall **e** your bread to the full	Lv 26:5
You shall **e** old store long kept, and you	Lv 26:10
seed in vain, for your enemies shall **e** it.	Lv 26:16
and you shall **e** and not be satisfied.	Lv 26:26
You shall **e** the flesh of your sons, and	Lv 26:29
and you shall **e** the flesh of your	Lv 26:29
the land of your enemies shall **e** you up.	Lv 26:38
not drink any juice of grapes or **e** grapes,	Nm 6:3
his separation he shall **e** nothing that is	Nm 6:4
They shall **e** it with unleavened bread	Nm 9:11
and said, "Oh that we had meat to **e**!	Nm 11:4
and say, 'Give us meat, that we may **e**.'	Nm 11:13
for tomorrow, and you shall **e** meat,	Nm 11:18
saying, "Who will give us meat to **e**?	Nm 11:18
will give you meat, and you shall **e**.	Nm 11:18
You shall not **e** just one day, or two	Nm 11:19
that they may **e** a whole month!'	Nm 11:21
and when you **e** of the bread of the	Nm 15:19
In a most holy place shall you **e** it.	Nm 18:10
Every male may **e** it; it is holy to you.	Nm 18:10
who is clean in your house may **e** it.	Nm 18:11
who is clean in your house may **e** it.	Nm 18:13
And you may **e** it in any place, you	Nm 18:31
he shall **e** up the nations, his	Nm 24:8
from them for money, that you may **e**,	Dt 2:6
sell me food for money, that I may **e**,	Dt 2:28
hands, that neither see, nor hear, nor **e**,	Dt 4:28
not plant—and when you **e** and are full,	Dt 6:11
which you will **e** bread without scarcity,	Dt 8:9
And you shall **e** and be full, and you	Dt 8:10
livestock, and you shall **e** and be full.	Dt 11:15
And there you shall **e** before the LORD	Dt 12:7
may slaughter and **e** meat within any	Dt 12:15
The unclean and the clean may **e** of it,	Dt 12:15
Only you shall not **e** the blood; you	Dt 12:16
You may not **e** within your towns the	Dt 12:17
but you shall **e** them before the LORD	Dt 12:18
you, and you say, 'I will **e** meat,'	Dt 12:20
you may **e** meat whenever you desire.	Dt 12:20
and you may **e** within your towns	Dt 12:21
or the deer is eaten, so you may **e** of it.	Dt 12:22
unclean and the clean alike may **e** of it.	Dt 12:22
be sure that you do not **e** the blood,	Dt 12:23
and you shall not **e** the life with the	Dt 12:23
You shall not **e** it; you shall pour it out	Dt 12:24
You shall not **e** it, that all may go well	Dt 12:25
LORD your God, but the flesh you may **e**.	Dt 12:27
"You shall not **e** any abomination.	Dt 14:3
These are the animals you may **e**: the ox,	Dt 14:4
the cud, among the animals, you may **e**.	Dt 14:6
the hoof cloven you shall not **e** these:	Dt 14:7
Their flesh you shall not **e**, and their	Dt 14:8
all that are in the waters you may **e** these:	Dt 14:9
whatever has fins and scales you may **e**.	Dt 14:9
not have fins and scales you shall not **e**;	Dt 14:10
"You may **e** all clean birds.	Dt 14:11
these are the ones that you shall not **e**:	Dt 14:12
All clean winged things you may **e**.	Dt 14:20
"You shall not **e** anything that has died	Dt 14:21
is within your towns, that he may **e** it,	Dt 14:21
there, you shall **e** the tithe of your grain,	Dt 14:23
And you shall **e** there before the LORD	Dt 14:26
towns, shall come and **e** and be filled,	Dt 14:29
You shall **e** it, you and your household,	Dt 15:20
You shall **e** it within your towns. The	Dt 15:22
unclean and the clean alike may **e** it,	Dt 15:22
Only you shall not **e** its blood; you shall	Dt 15:23
You shall **e** no leavened bread with it.	Dt 16:3
days you shall **e** it with unleavened	Dt 16:3
you shall cook it and **e** it at the place that	Dt 16:7
six days you shall **e** unleavened bread,	Dt 16:8
They shall **e** the LORD'S food offerings as	Dt 18:1
then he may have equal portions to **e**,	Dt 18:8
against them. You may **e** from them,	Dt 20:19
vineyard, you may **e** your fill of grapes,	Dt 23:24
so that they may **e** within your towns	Dt 26:12
peace offerings and shall **e** there,	Dt 27:7
your eyes, but you shall not **e** any of it.	Dt 28:31
have not known shall **e** up the fruit of	Dt 28:33
the grapes, for the worm shall **e** them.	Dt 28:39
It shall **e** the offspring of your cattle and	Dt 28:51
And you shall **e** the fruit of your womb,	Dt 28:53
everything she will **e** them secretly,	Dt 28:57
You **e** the fruit of vineyards and olive	Jos 24:13
or strong drink, and **e** nothing unclean,	Jgs 13:4
or strong drink, and **e** nothing unclean,	Jgs 13:7
She may not **e** of anything that comes	Jgs 13:14
strong drink, or **e** any unclean thing.	Jgs 13:14
you detain me, I will not **e** of your food.	Jgs 13:16
"Out of the eater came something to **e**.	Jgs 14:14
"Come here and **e** some bread and dip	Ru 2:14
Hannah wept and would not **e**.	1 Sm 1:7
do you weep? And why do you not **e**?	1 Sm 1:8
that I may **e** a morsel of bread.""	1 Sm 2:36
he goes up to the high place to **e**.	1 Sm 9:13
For the people will not **e** till he comes,	1 Sm 9:13
afterward those who are invited will **e**.	1 Sm 9:13
place, for today you shall **e** with me,	1 Sm 9:19
E, because it was kept for you until	1 Sm 9:24
that you might **e** with the guests." So	1 Sm 9:24
sheep and slaughter them here and **e**,	1 Sm 14:34
came, the king sat down to **e** food.	1 Sm 20:24
a morsel of bread before you; and **e**,	1 Sm 28:22
said, "I will not **e**." But his servants,	1 Sm 28:23
to persuade David to **e** bread while it	2 Sm 3:35
and you shall **e** at my table always."	2 Sm 9:7
grandson may have bread to **e**.	2 Sm 9:10
grandson shall always **e** at my table."	2 Sm 9:10
to **e** and to drink and to lie with my	2 Sm 11:11
It used to **e** of his morsel and drink	2 Sm 12:3
not, nor did he **e** food with them.	2 Sm 12:17
Tamar come and give me bread to **e**,	2 Sm 13:5
I may see it and **e** it from her hand."'	2 Sm 13:5
sight, that I may **e** from her hand."	2 Sm 13:6
it out before him, but he refused to **e**.	2 Sm 13:9
that I may **e** from your hand." And	2 Sm 13:10
she brought them near him to **e**,	2 Sm 13:11
summer fruit for the young men to **e**,	2 Sm 16:2
David and the people with him to **e**,	2 Sm 17:29
among those who **e** at your table.	2 Sm 19:28
be among those who **e** at your table,	1 Kgs 2:7
And I will not **e** bread or drink water	1 Kgs 13:8
'You shall neither **e** bread nor drink	1 Kgs 13:9
"Come home with me and **e** bread."	1 Kgs 13:15
neither will I **e** bread nor drink	1 Kgs 13:16
'You shall neither **e** bread nor drink	1 Kgs 13:17
that he may **e** bread and drink	1 Kgs 13:18
"**E** no bread and drink no water,"	1 Kgs 13:22
who dies in the city the dogs shall **e**,	1 Kgs 14:11
the birds of the heavens shall **e**,	1 Kgs 14:11
who dies in the city the dogs shall **e**,	1 Kgs 16:4
field the birds of the heavens shall **e**."	1 Kgs 16:4
my son, that we may **e** it and die."	1 Kgs 17:12
of Asherah, who **e** at Jezebel's table."	1 Kgs 18:19
said to Ahab, "Go up, **e** and drink,	1 Kgs 18:41
So Ahab went up to **e** and to drink.	1 Kgs 18:42
him and said to him, "Arise and **e**."	1 Kgs 19:5
touched him and said, "Arise and **e**,	1 Kgs 19:7
away his face and would **e** no food.	1 Kgs 21:4
spirit so vexed that you **e** no food?"	1 Kgs 21:5
Arise and **e** bread and let your heart	1 Kgs 21:7
'The dogs shall **e** Jezebel within the	1 Kgs 21:23
who dies in the city the dogs shall **e**,	1 Kgs 21:24
the birds of the heavens shall **e**."	1 Kgs 21:24
lived, who urged him to **e** some food.	2 Kgs 4:8
way, he would turn in there to **e** food.	2 Kgs 4:8
poured out some for the men to **e**.	2 Kgs 4:40
in the pot!" And they could not **e** it.	2 Kgs 4:40
that they may **e**." And there was no	2 Kgs 4:41
"Give to the men, that they may **e**."	2 Kgs 4:42
them to the men, that they may **e**,	2 Kgs 4:43
'They shall **e** and have some left.'"	2 Kgs 4:43
that they may **e** and drink and go to	2 Kgs 6:22
your son, that we may **e** him today,	2 Kgs 6:28
and we will **e** my son tomorrow.'	2 Kgs 6:28
'Give your son, that we may **e** him.'	2 Kgs 6:29
own eyes, but you shall not **e** of it."	2 Kgs 7:2
own eyes, but you shall not **e** of it."	2 Kgs 7:19
And the dogs shall **e** Jezebel in the	2 Kgs 9:10
Jezreel the dogs shall **e** the flesh of	2 Kgs 9:36
with you to **e** their own dung	2 Kgs 18:27
one of you will **e** of his own vine,	2 Kgs 18:31
this year **e** what grows of itself, and	2 Kgs 19:29
plant vineyards, and **e** their fruit.	2 Kgs 19:29
Now because we **e** the salt of the palace	Ezr 4:14
you may be strong and **e** the good of the	Ezr 9:12
get grain, that we may **e** and keep alive."	Neh 5:2
E the fat and drink sweet wine and	Neh 8:10
went their way to **e** and drink and to	Neh 8:12
and do not **e** or drink for three days,	Est 4:16
their three sisters to **e** and drink with	Jb 1:4
The hungry **e** his harvest, and he takes it	Jb 5:5
then let me sow, and another **e**, and let	Jb 31:8
all the evildoers who **e** up my people as	Ps 14:4
up my people as they **e** bread and do not	Ps 14:4
The afflicted shall **e** and be satisfied;	Ps 22:26
prosperous of the earth **e** and worship;	Ps 22:29
evildoers assail me to **e** up my flesh,	Ps 27:2
Do I **e** the flesh of bulls or drink the	Ps 50:13
who **e** up my people as they eat bread,	Ps 53:4
who eat up my people as they **e** bread,	Ps 53:4
on them manna to **e** and gave them the	Ps 78:24
and has withered; I forget to **e** my bread.	Ps 102:4
For I **e** ashes like bread and mingle	Ps 102:9
You shall **e** the fruit of the labor of your	Ps 128:2
and let me not **e** of their delicacies!	Ps 141:4
therefore they shall **e** the fruit of their	Prv 1:31
For they **e** the bread of wickedness and	Prv 4:17
e of my bread and drink of the wine I	Prv 9:5
and those who love it will **e** its fruits.	Prv 18:21
When you sit down to **e** with a ruler,	Prv 23:1
Do not **e** the bread of a man who is	Prv 23:6
"**E** and drink!" he says to you, but his	Prv 23:7
My son, **e** honey, for it is good, and the	Prv 24:13
found honey, **e** only enough for you,	Prv 25:16
enemy is hungry, give him bread to **e**,	Prv 25:21
It is not good to **e** much honey, nor is	Prv 25:27
Whoever tends a fig tree will **e** its fruit,	Prv 27:18
household and does not **e** the bread of	Prv 31:27
than that he should **e** and drink and	Eccl 2:24
from him who can **e** or who can have	Eccl 2:25

that everyone should **e** and drink and Eccl 3:13
increase, they increase who **e** them, Eccl 5:11
and fitting is to **e** and drink and find Eccl 5:18
the sun but to **e** and drink and be Eccl 8:15
Go, **e** your bread in joy, and drink your Eccl 9:7
to his garden, and **e** its choicest fruits. Sg 4:16
E, friends, drink, and be drunk with love! Sg 5:1
obedient, you shall **e** the good of the land; Is 1:19
for they shall **e** the fruit of their deeds. Is 3:10
"We will **e** our own bread and wear our Is 4:1
and nomads shall **e** among the ruins of Is 5:17
He shall **e** curds and honey when he Is 7:15
of milk that they give, he will **e** curds, Is 7:22
is left in the land will **e** curds and honey. Is 7:22
and the lion shall **e** straw like the ox. Is 11:7
the table, they spread the rugs, they **e**, Is 21:5
and drinking wine. "Let us **e** and drink, Is 22:13
work the ground will **e** seasoned fodder, Is 30:24
doomed with you to **e** their own dung Is 36:12
each one of you will **e** of his own vine, Is 36:16
this year you shall **e** what grows of itself, Is 37:30
and plant vineyards, and **e** their fruit. Is 37:30
make your oppressors **e** their own flesh, Is 49:26
like a garment; the moth will **e** them up. Is 50:9
For the moth will **e** them up like a Is 51:8
and the worm will **e** them like wool; Is 51:8
he who has no money, come, buy and **e**! Is 55:1
diligently to me, and **e** what is good, Is 55:2
you shall **e** the wealth of the nations, and Is 61:6
who garner it shall **e** it and praise the Is 62:9
who **e** pig's flesh, and broth of tainted Is 65:4
"Behold, my servants shall **e**, but you Is 65:13
shall plant vineyards and **e** their fruit. Is 65:21
they shall not plant and another **e**; Is 65:22
the lion shall **e** straw like the ox, and Is 65:25
They shall **e** up your harvest and your Jer 5:17
they shall **e** up your sons and your Jer 5:17
they shall **e** up your flocks and your Jer 5:17
they shall **e** up your vines and your fig Jer 5:17
to your sacrifices, and **e** the flesh. Jer 7:21
feasting to sit with them, to **e** and drink. Jer 16:8
And I will make them **e** the flesh of their Jer 19:9
and everyone shall **e** the flesh of his Jer 19:9
Did not your father **e** and drink and do Jer 22:15
them; plant gardens and **e** their produce. Jer 29:5
plant gardens and **e** their produce."'" Jer 29:28
Should women **e** the fruit of their Lam 2:20
open your mouth and **e** what I give you." Ezk 2:8
"Son of man, **e** whatever you find here. Ezk 3:1
E this scroll, and go, speak to the house Ezk 3:1
mouth, and he gave me this scroll to **e**. Ezk 3:2
lie on your side, 390 days, you shall **e** it. Ezk 4:9
your food that you **e** shall be by weight, Ezk 4:10
a day; from day to day you shall **e** it. Ezk 4:10
And you shall **e** it as a barley cake, Ezk 4:12
people of Israel **e** their bread unclean, Ezk 4:13
They shall **e** bread by weight and with Ezk 4:16
Therefore fathers shall **e** their sons in Ezk 5:10
midst, and sons shall **e** their fathers. Ezk 5:10
of man, **e** your bread with quaking, Ezk 12:18
They shall **e** their bread with anxiety, Ezk 12:19
if he does not **e** upon the mountains or Ezk 18:6
he does not **e** upon the mountains or Ezk 18:15
people in you who **e** on the mountains; Ezk 22:9
your lips, nor **e** the bread of men." Ezk 24:17
your lips, nor **e** the bread of men. Ezk 24:22
in your midst. They shall **e** your fruit, Ezk 25:4
You **e** flesh with the blood and lift up Ezk 33:25
You **e** the fat, you clothe yourselves Ezk 34:3
And must my sheep **e** what you have Ezk 34:19
and you shall **e** flesh and drink blood. Ezk 39:17
You shall **e** the flesh of the mighty, Ezk 39:18
And you shall **e** fat till you are filled, Ezk 39:19
the LORD shall **e** the most holy Ezk 42:13
may sit in it to **e** bread before the LORD. Ezk 44:3
They shall **e** the grain offering, the sin Ezk 44:29
The priests shall not **e** of anything, Ezk 44:31
be given vegetables to **e** and water to Dn 1:12
of the youths who **e** the king's food be Dn 1:13
You shall be made to **e** grass like an ox, Dn 4:25
you shall be made to **e** grass like an ox, Dn 4:32
Even those who **e** his food shall break Dn 11:26
They shall **e**, but not be satisfied; they Hos 4:10
offerings, they sacrifice meat and **e** it, Hos 8:13
and they shall **e** unclean food in Assyria. Hos 9:3
to them; all who **e** of it shall be defiled; Hos 9:4
"You shall **e** in plenty and be satisfied, Jl 2:26
and **e** lambs from the flock and calves Am 6:4
to the land of Judah, and **e** bread there, Am 7:12
shall make gardens and **e** their fruit. Am 9:14
those who **e** your bread have set a trap Ob 1:7
who **e** the flesh of my people, and flay Mi 3:3
"Peace" when they have something to **e**, Mi 3:5
You shall **e**, but not be satisfied, and Mi 6:14
there is no cluster to **e**, no first-ripe fig Mi 7:1
sown much, and harvested little. You **e**, Hg 1:6
And when you **e** and when you drink, do Zec 7:6
do you not **e** for yourselves and drink for Zec 7:6
what you will **e** or what you will drink, Mt 6:25
be anxious, saying, 'What shall we **e**?' Mt 6:31
does your teacher **e** with tax collectors Mt 9:11
began to pluck heads of grain and to **e**. Mt 12:1
not lawful for him to **e** nor for those who Mt 12:4
away; you give them something to **e**." Mt 14:16
do not wash their hands when they **e**." Mt 15:2
But to **e** with unwashed hands does not Mt 15:20
yet even the dogs **e** the crumbs that fall Mt 15:27
now three days and have nothing to **e**. Mt 15:32
us prepare for you to **e** the Passover?" Mt 26:17
and said, "Take, **e**; this is my body." Mt 26:26
"Why does he **e** with tax collectors and Mk 2:16
is not lawful for any but the priests to **e**, Mk 2:26
again, so that they could not even **e**. Mk 3:20
told them to give her something to **e**. Mk 5:43
going, and they had no leisure even to **e**. Mk 6:31
and buy themselves something to **e**." Mk 6:36
them something to **e**." And they said Mk 6:37
worth of bread and give it to them to **e**?" Mk 6:37
the Jews do not **e** unless they wash their Mk 7:3
they do not **e** unless they wash. Mk 7:4
of the elders, but **e** with defiled hands?" Mk 7:5
under the table **e** the children's Mk 7:28
had gathered, and they had nothing to **e**, Mk 8:1
now three days and have nothing to **e**. Mk 8:2
"May no one ever **e** fruit from you Mk 11:14
and prepare for you to **e** the Passover?" Mk 14:12
where I may **e** the Passover with my Mk 14:14
"Why do you **e** and drink with tax Lk 5:30
of the Pharisees, but yours **e** and drink." Lk 5:33
is not lawful for any but the priests to **e**, Lk 6:4
the Pharisees asked him to **e** with him, Lk 7:36
that something should be given her to **e**. Lk 8:55
give them something to **e**." They said, Lk 9:13
they receive you, **e** what is set before you. Lk 10:8
many years; relax, **e**, drink, be merry.' Lk 12:19
about your life, what you will **e**, Lk 12:22
what you are to **e** and what you are Lk 12:29
and to **e** and drink and get drunk, Lk 12:45
is everyone who will **e** bread in the Lk 14:15
and kill it, and let us **e** and celebrate. Lk 15:23
and serve me while I **e** and drink, Lk 17:8
and afterward you will **e** and drink'? Lk 17:8
the Passover for us, that we may **e** it." Lk 22:8
where I may **e** the Passover with my Lk 22:11
earnestly desired to **e** this Passover with Lk 22:15
tell you I will not **e** it until it is fulfilled Lk 22:16
that you may **e** and drink at my table Lk 22:30
them, "Have you anything here to **e**?" Lk 24:41
were urging him, saying, "Rabbi, **e**." Jn 4:31
"I have food to **e** that you do not know Jn 4:32
anyone brought him something to **e**?" Jn 4:33
to buy bread, so that these people may **e**?" Jn 6:5
'He gave them bread from heaven to **e**.'" Jn 6:31
so that one may **e** of it and not die. Jn 6:50
can this man give us his flesh to **e**?" Jn 6:52
unless you **e** the flesh of the Son of Man Jn 6:53
not be defiled, but could **e** the Passover. Jn 18:28
hungry and wanted something to **e**, Acts 10:10
voice to him: "Rise, Peter; kill and **e**." Acts 10:13
saying to me, 'Rise, Peter; kill and **e**.' Acts 11:7
an oath neither to **e** nor drink till Acts 23:12
an oath neither to **e** nor drink till Acts 23:21
of all he broke it and began to **e**. Acts 27:35
person believes he may **e** anything, Rom 14:2
brother is grieved by what you **e**, Rom 14:15
By what you **e**, do not destroy the one Rom 14:15
It is good not to **e** meat or drink wine Rom 14:21
—not even to **e** with such a one. 1 Cor 5:11
idols, **e** food as really offered to an idol, 1 Cor 8:7
We are no worse off if we do not **e**, and 1 Cor 8:8
is weak, to **e** food offered to idols? 1 Cor 8:10
brother stumble, I will never **e** meat, 1 Cor 8:13
we not have the right to **e** and drink? 1 Cor 9:4
people sat down to **e** and drink and 1 Cor 10:7
not those who **e** the sacrifices 1 Cor 10:18
E whatever is sold in the meat 1 Cor 10:25
e whatever is set before you without 1 Cor 10:27
offered in sacrifice," then do not **e** it, 1 Cor 10:28
So, whether you **e** or drink, or 1 Cor 10:31
it is not the Lord's supper that you **e**. 1 Cor 11:20
not have houses to **e** and drink in? 1 Cor 11:22
as often as you **e** this bread and 1 Cor 11:26
and so **e** of the bread and drink of 1 Cor 11:28
when you come together to **e**, 1 Cor 11:33
let him **e** at home—so that when 1 Cor 11:34
are not raised, "Let us **e** and drink, 1 Cor 15:32
nor did we **e** anyone's bread without 2 Thes 3:8
is not willing to work, let him not **e**. 2 Thes 3:10
who serve the tent have no right to **e**. Heb 13:10
against you and will **e** your flesh like fire. Jas 5:3
conquers I will grant to **e** of the tree of life, Rv 2:7
so that they might **e** food sacrificed to Rv 2:14
immorality and to **e** food sacrificed to Rv 2:20
I will come in to him and **e** with him, Rv 3:20
And he said to me, "Take and **e** it; it will Rv 10:9
to **e** the flesh of kings, the flesh of Rv 19:18

EATEN (89)

Have you **e** of the tree of which I Gn 3:11
of your wife and have **e** of the tree of Gn 3:17
take with you every sort of food that is **e**, Gn 6:21
but what the young men have **e**, Gn 14:24
and I have not **e** the rams of your Gn 31:38
but when they had **e** them no one Gn 41:21
have known that they had **e** them, Gn 41:21
And when they had **e** the grain that they Gn 43:2
It shall be **e** in one house; you shall not Ex 12:46
this place. No leavened bread shall be **e**. Ex 13:3
bread shall be **e** for seven days; Ex 13:7
be stoned, and its flesh shall not be **e**, Ex 21:28
fire. It shall not be **e**, because it is holy. Ex 29:34
It shall be **e** unleavened in a holy place. Lv 6:16
be wholly burned. It shall not be **e**." Lv 6:23
In a holy place it shall be **e**, in the court Lv 6:26
sin offering shall be **e** from which any Lv 6:30
may eat of it. It shall be **e** in a holy place. Lv 7:6
for thanksgiving shall be **e** on the day of Lv 7:15
it shall be **e** on the day that he offers his Lv 7:16
next day what remains of it shall be **e**. Lv 7:16
of his peace offering is **e** on the third day, Lv 7:18
any unclean thing shall not be **e**. Lv 7:19
"Why have you not **e** the sin offering in Lv 10:17
certainly ought to have **e** it in the Lv 10:18
If I had **e** the sin offering today, would Lv 10:19
among the birds; they shall not be **e**; Lv 11:13
Any food in it that could be **e**, on which Lv 11:34
ground is detestable; it shall not be **e**. Lv 11:41
creature that may be **e** and the living Lv 11:47
the living creature that may not be **e**. Lv 11:47
or bird that may be **e** shall pour out its Lv 17:13
It shall be **e** the same day you offer it or Lv 19:6
If it is **e** at all on the third day, it is Lv 19:7
be forbidden to you; it must not be **e**. Lv 19:23
It shall be **e** on the same day; you shall Lv 22:30
whose flesh is half **e** away when he Nm 12:12
days shall unleavened bread be **e**. Nm 28:17
when you have **e** and are full and have Dt 8:12
Just as the gazelle or the deer is **e**, so you Dt 12:22
are unclean for you; they shall not be **e**. Dt 14:19
I have not **e** of the tithe while I was Dt 26:14
You have not **e** bread, and you have not Dt 29:6
and they have **e** and are full and grown Dt 31:20
And when Boaz had **e** and drunk, and his Ru 3:7
After they had **e** and drunk in Shiloh, 1 Sm 1:9
if the people had **e** freely today of the 1 Sm 14:30
for he had **e** nothing all day and all 1 Sm 28:20
And when he had **e**, his spirit 1 Sm 30:12
for he had not **e** bread or drunk 1 Sm 30:12
Have we **e** at all at the king's 2 Sm 19:42
back and have **e** bread and drunk 1 Kgs 13:22
And after he had **e** bread and drunk, 1 Kgs 13:23
The lion had not **e** the body or torn 1 Kgs 13:28
and when they had **e** and drunk, 2 Kgs 6:23
we have **e** and had enough and have 2 Chr 31:10
It was **e** by the people of Israel who had Ezr 6:21
that which is tasteless be **e** without salt, Jb 6:6
There was nothing left after he had **e**; Jb 20:21
or have **e** my morsel alone, and the Jb 31:17
alone, and the fatherless has not **e** of it Jb 31:17
if I have **e** its yield without payment and Jb 31:39
sweet, and bread **e** in secret is pleasant." Prv 9:17
vomit up the morsels that you have **e**, Prv 23:8
of the valley and **e** by the vultures. Prv 30:17
and rebel, you shall be **e** by the sword; Is 1:20
on its coals; I roasted meat and have **e**. Is 44:19
bad figs, so bad that they could not be **e**. Jer 24:2
very bad, so bad that they cannot be **e**." Jer 24:3
bad figs that are so bad they cannot be **e**, Jer 24:8
figs that are so rotten they cannot be **e**. Jer 29:17
"'The fathers have **e** sour grapes, and Jer 31:29
till now I have never **e** what died of itself Ezk 4:14
Israel, 'The fathers have **e** sour grapes, Ezk 18:2
days unleavened bread shall be **e**. Ezk 45:21
injustice; you have **e** the fruit of lies. Hos 10:13
locust left, the swarming locust has **e**. Jl 1:4
locust left, the hopping locust has **e**, Jl 1:4
locust left, the destroying locust has **e**. Jl 1:4
the years that the swarming locust has **e**, Jl 2:25
And likewise the cup after they had **e**, Lk 22:20
And when they had **e** their fill, he told his Jn 6:12
barley loaves, left by those who had **e**. Jn 6:13
place where they had **e** the bread after the Jn 6:23
for I have never **e** anything that is Acts 10:14
and he was **e** by worms and breathed Acts 12:23
gone up and had broken bread and **e**, Acts 20:11
And when they had **e** enough, they Acts 27:38

but when I had **e** it my stomach was Rv 10:10

EATER (3)
"Out of the **e** came something to eat. Jgs 14:14
seed to the sower and bread to the **e**, Is 55:10
shaken they fall into the mouth of the **e**. Na 3:12

EATERS (1)
or among gluttonous **e** of meat, Prv 23:20

EATING (42)
but the birds were **e** it out of the basket Gn 40:17
and guilt, by **e** their holy things: Lv 22:16
year, you will be **e** some of the old crop; Lv 25:22
the flesh of his children whom he is **e**, Dt 28:55
into his hands and went on, **e** as he went. Jgs 14:9
until he has finished **e** and drinking. Ru 3:3
the LORD by **e** with the blood." 1 Sm 14:33
the LORD by **e** with the blood.'" 1 Sm 14:34
land, **e** and drinking and dancing, 1 Sm 30:16
they are **e** and drinking before him, 1 Kgs 1:25
But while they were **e** of the stew, they 2 Kgs 4:40
for three days, **e** and drinking, 1 Chr 12:39
neither **e** bread nor drinking water, Ezr 10:6
and daughters were **e** and drinking wine Jb 1:13
and daughters were **e** and drinking wine Jb 1:18
late to rest, **e** the bread of anxious toil; Ps 127:2
sheep, **e** flesh and drinking wine. Is 22:13
man dreams he is **e** and awakes with his Is 29:8
e pig's flesh and the abomination and Is 66:17
When they had finished **e** the grass of Am 7:2
the great deep and was **e** up the land. Am 7:4
For John came neither **e** nor drinking, Mt 11:18
The Son of Man came **e** and drinking, Mt 11:19
the flood they were **e** and drinking, Mt 24:38
And as they were **e**, he said, "Truly, I Mt 26:21
Now as they were **e**, Jesus took bread, Mt 26:26
saw that he was **e** with sinners and tax Mk 2:16
as they were reclining at table and **e**, Mk 14:18
will betray me, one who is **e** with me." Mk 14:18
And as they were **e**, he took bread, and Mk 14:22
the Baptist has come **e** no bread and Lk 7:33
Son of Man has come **e** and drinking, Lk 7:34
e and drinking what they provide, Lk 10:7
They were **e** and drinking and Lk 17:27
days of Lot—they were **e** and drinking, Lk 17:28
not a matter of **e** and drinking but of Rom 14:17
eats, because the **e** is not from faith. Rom 14:23
as to the **e** of food offered to idols, 1 Cor 8:4
who have knowledge **e** in an idol's 1 Cor 8:10
plants a vineyard without **e** any of its 1 Cor 9:7
For in **e**, each one goes ahead with 1 Cor 11:21
from James, he was **e** with the Gentiles; Gal 2:12

EATS (42)
houses, for if anyone **e** what is leavened, Ex 12:15
If anyone **e** what is leavened, that Ex 12:19
and he who **e** of it shall bear his iniquity. Lv 7:18
but the person who **e** of the flesh of the Lv 7:20
and then **e** some flesh from the sacrifice Lv 7:21
For every person who **e** of the fat of an Lv 7:25
Whoever **e** any blood, that person shall Lv 7:27
and whoever **e** of its carcass shall wash Lv 11:40
and whoever **e** in the house shall wash Lv 14:47
who sojourn among them **e** any blood, Lv 17:10
that person who **e** blood and will Lv 17:10
its blood. Whoever **e** it shall be cut off. Lv 17:14
And every person who **e** what dies of Lv 17:15
and everyone who **e** it shall bear his Lv 19:8
And if anyone **e** of a holy thing Lv 22:14
be the man who **e** food until it is 1 Sm 14:24
be the man who **e** food this day.'" 1 Sm 14:28
servant taste what he **e** or what he 2 Sm 19:35
as I made you; he **e** grass like an ox. Jb 40:15
God for the image of an ox that **e** grass. Ps 106:20
of his mouth a man **e** what is good, Prv 13:2
she **e** and wipes her mouth and says, "I Prv 30:20
fool folds his hands and **e** his own flesh. Eccl 4:5
a laborer, whether he **e** little or much, Eccl 5:12
all his days he **e** in darkness in much Eccl 5:17
Over the half he **e** meat; he roasts it and Is 44:16
he who **e** their eggs dies, and from one Is 59:5
Each man who **e** sour grapes, his teeth Jer 31:30
who even **e** upon the mountains, Ezk 18:11
fellow servants and **e** and drinks with Mt 24:49
man receives sinners and **e** with them." Lk 15:2
If anyone **e** of this bread, he will live Jn 6:51
the weak person **e** only vegetables. Rom 14:2
not the one who **e** despise the one who Rom 14:3
pass judgment on the one who **e**, Rom 14:3
The one who **e**, eats in honor of the Rom 14:6
one who eats, **e** in honor of the Lord, Rom 14:6
make another stumble by what he **e**. Rom 14:20
has doubts is condemned if he **e**, Rom 14:23
e the bread or drinks the cup of the 1 Cor 11:27
For anyone who **e** and drinks 1 Cor 11:29
discerning the body **e** and drinks 1 Cor 11:29

EBAL (7)
Alvan, Manahath, **E**, Shepho, and Gn 36:23
Gerizim and the curse on Mount **E**. Dt 11:29
I command you today, on Mount **E**, Dt 27:4
shall stand on Mount **E** for the curse: Dt 27:13
the LORD, the God of Israel, on Mount **E**, Jos 8:30
and half of them in front of Mount **E**, Jos 8:33
Alvan, Manahath, **E**, Shepho, and 1 Chr 1:40

EBED (6)
Gaal the son of **E** moved into Shechem Jgs 9:26
And Gaal the son of **E** said, "Who is Jgs 9:28
city heard the words of Gaal the son of **E**, Jgs 9:30
Gaal the son of **E** and his relatives have Jgs 9:31
Gaal the son of **E** went out and stood Jgs 9:35
the sons of Adin, **E** the son of Jonathan, Ezr 8:6

EBED-MELECH (6)
When **E** the Ethiopian, a eunuch who Jer 38:7
E went from the king's house and said to Jer 38:8
the king commanded **E** the Ethiopian, Jer 38:10
So **E** took the men with him and went Jer 38:11
Then **E** the Ethiopian said to Jeremiah, Jer 38:12
"Go, and say to **E** the Ethiopian, 'Thus Jer 39:16

EBENEZER (3)
They encamped at **E**, and the 1 Sm 4:1
God, they brought it from **E** to Ashdod. 1 Sm 5:1
and Shen and called its name **E**; 1 Sm 7:12

EBER (16)
also, the father of all the children of **E**, Gn 10:21
fathered Shelah; and Shelah fathered **E**. Gn 10:24
To **E** were born two sons: the name of Gn 10:25
had lived 30 years, he fathered **E**. Gn 11:14
lived after he fathered **E** 403 years and Gn 11:15
When **E** had lived 34 years, he fathered Gn 11:16
And **E** lived after he fathered Peleg 430 Gn 11:17
Kittim and shall afflict Asshur and **E**; Nm 24:24
Shelah, and Shelah fathered **E**. 1 Chr 1:18
To **E** were born two sons: the name of 1 Chr 1:19
E, Peleg, Reu; 1 Chr 1:25
Sheba, Jorai, Jacan, Zia and **E**, 1 Chr 5:13
E, Misham, and Shemed, who built 1 Chr 8:12
Ishpan, **E**, Eliel, 1 Chr 8:22
of Sallai, Kallai; of Amok, **E**; Neh 12:20
son of Reu, the son of Peleg, the son of **E**, Lk 3:35

EBEZ (1)
Rabbith, Kishion, **E**, Jos 19:20

EBIASAPH (3)
Elkanah his son, **E** his son, Assir his 1 Chr 6:23
son of Tahath, son of Assir, son of **E**, 1 Chr 6:37
Shallum the son of Kore, son of **E**, 1 Chr 9:19

EBONY (1)
you in payment ivory tusks and **e**. Ezk 27:15

EBRON (1)
E, Rehob, Hammon, Kanah, as far as Jos 19:28

ECBATANA (1)
And in **E**, the capital that is in the Ezr 6:2

EDEN (19)
And the LORD God planted a garden in **E**, Gn 2:8
river flowed out of **E** to water the garden, Gn 2:10
him in the garden of **E** to work it and Gn 2:15
from the garden of **E** to work the ground Gn 3:23
of the garden of **E** he placed the Gn 3:24
and settled in the land of Nod, east of **E**. Gn 4:16
and the people of **E** who were in 2 Kgs 19:12
of Zimmah, and **E** the son of Joah; 2 Chr 29:12
E, Miniamin, Jeshua, Shemaiah, 2 Chr 31:15
and the people of **E** who were in Is 37:12
places and makes her wilderness like **E**, Is 51:3
Haran, Canneh, **E**, traders of Sheba, Ezk 27:23
You were in **E**, the garden of God; Ezk 28:13
and all the trees of **E** envied it, Ezk 31:9
And all the trees of **E**, the choice and Ezk 31:16
and in greatness among the trees of **E**? Ezk 31:18
with the trees of **E** to the world below. Ezk 31:18
has become like the garden of **E**, Ezk 36:35
land is like the garden of **E** before them, Jl 2:3

EDER (5)
pitched his tent beyond the tower of **E**. Gn 35:21
of Edom, were Kabzeel, **E**, Jagur, Jos 15:21
Zebadiah, Arad, **E**, 1 Chr 8:15
Mahli, **E**, and Jeremoth, three. 1 Chr 23:23
of Mushi: Mahli, **E**, and Jerimoth. 1 Chr 24:30

EDGE (61)
at Etham, on the **e** of the wilderness. Ex 13:20
into the mountain or touch the **e** of it. Ex 19:12
of blue on the **e** of the outermost curtain Ex 26:4
make loops on the **e** of the outermost Ex 26:4
shall make on the **e** of the curtain that Ex 26:5
fifty loops on the **e** of the curtain that Ex 26:10
fifty loops on the **e** of the curtain that Ex 26:10
on its inside **e** next to the ephod. Ex 28:26
of blue on the **e** of the outermost Ex 36:11
made them on the **e** of the outermost Ex 36:11
fifty loops on the **e** of the curtain that Ex 36:12
fifty loops on the **e** of the outermost Ex 36:17
fifty loops on the **e** of the other Ex 36:17
on its inside **e** next to the ephod. Ex 39:19
shall not reap your field right up to its **e**, Lv 19:9
not reap your field right up to its **e**, Lv 23:22
a city on the **e** of your territory. Nm 20:16
defeated him with the **e** of the sword Nm 21:24
which is on the **e** of the wilderness. Nm 33:6
Hor, on the **e** of the land of Edom. Nm 33:37
which is on the **e** of the Valley of the Dt 2:36
which is on the **e** of the Valley of the Dt 3:12
which is on the **e** of the Valley of the Dt 4:48
it and its cattle, with the **e** of the sword. Dt 13:15
and donkeys, with the **e** of the sword. Jos 6:21
very last had fallen by the **e** of the sword, Jos 8:24
struck it down with the **e** of the sword. Jos 8:24
it, and its king, with the **e** of the sword. Jos 10:28
he struck it with the **e** of the sword, Jos 10:30
and struck it with the **e** of the sword, Jos 10:32
and struck it with the **e** of the sword. Jos 10:35
it and struck it with the **e** of the sword, Jos 10:37
struck them with the **e** of the sword Jos 10:39
struck them with the **e** of the sword, Jos 11:12
they struck with the **e** of the sword Jos 11:14
which is on the **e** of the Valley of the Jos 12:2
which is on the **e** of the Valley of the Jos 13:9
which is on the **e** of the Valley of the Jos 13:16
and struck it with the **e** of the sword and Jgs 1:8
struck the city with the **e** of the sword, Jgs 1:25
army before Barak by the **e** of the sword. Jgs 4:15
army of Sisera fell by the **e** of the sword; Jgs 4:16
struck them with the **e** of the sword Jgs 18:27
all the city with the **e** of the sword. Jgs 20:37
struck them with the **e** of the sword, Jgs 20:48
of Jabesh-gilead with the **e** of the sword; Jgs 21:10
all the people with the **e** of the sword. 1 Sm 15:8
the city with the **e** of the sword." 2 Sm 15:14
when they came to the **e** of the camp of 2 Kgs 7:5
these lepers came to the **e** of the camp, 2 Kgs 7:8
down the servants with the **e** of the sword, Jb 1:15
down the servants with the **e** of the sword, Jb 1:17
also turned back the **e** of his sword, Ps 89:43
blunt, and one does not sharpen the **e**, Eccl 10:10
strike them down with the **e** of the sword. Jer 21:7
and the children's teeth are set on **e**.' Jer 31:29
sour grapes, his teeth shall be set on **e**. Jer 31:30
and the children's teeth are set on **e**'? Ezk 18:2
with a rim of one span around its **e**. Ezk 43:13
They will fall by the **e** of the sword and Lk 21:24
of fire, escaped the **e** of the sword, Heb 11:34

EDGES (9)
two shoulder pieces attached to its two **e**, Ex 28:7
rings on the two **e** of the breastpiece. Ex 28:23
the two rings at the **e** of the breastpiece. Ex 28:24
shoulder pieces, joined to it at its two **e**. Ex 39:4
rings on the two **e** of the breastpiece. Ex 39:16
the two rings at the **e** of the breastpiece. Ex 39:17
temples or mar the **e** of your beard. Lv 19:27
heads, nor shave off the **e** of their beards, Lv 21:5
made for himself a sword with two **e**, Jgs 3:16

EDICT (10)
a decree that if anyone alters this **e**, Ezr 6:11
And drinking was according to this **e**: Est 1:8
king's order and his **e** were proclaimed, Est 2:8
day of the first month, and an **e**, Est 3:12
for an **e** written in the name of the king Est 8:8
twenty-third day. And an **e** was written, Est 8:9
the king's command and his **e** reached, Est 8:17
the king's command and **e** were about to Est 9:1
also to do according to this day's **e**. Est 9:13
they were not afraid of the king's **e**. Heb 11:23

EDOM (95)
(Therefore his name was called **E**.) Gn 25:30
in the land of Seir, the country of **E**, Gn 32:3
are the generations of Esau (that is, **E**). Gn 36:1
in the hill country of Seir. (Esau is **E**.) Gn 36:8
the chiefs of Eliphaz in the land of **E**; Gn 36:16
are the chiefs of Reuel in the land of **E**; Gn 36:17
(that is, **E**), and these are their chiefs. Gn 36:19
the sons of Seir in the land of **E**. Gn 36:21
the kings who reigned in the land of **E**, Gn 36:31
Bela the son of Beor reigned in **E**, the Gn 36:32
these are the chiefs of **E** (that is, Esau, Gn 36:43
of Edom (that is, Esau, the father of **E**), Gn 36:43
Now are the chiefs of **E** dismayed; Ex 15:15
from Kadesh to the king of **E**: Nm 20:14
But **E** said to him, "You shall not pass Nm 20:18
pass through." And **E** came out Nm 20:20
Thus **E** refused to give Israel passage Nm 20:21
Hor, on the border of the land of **E**, Nm 20:23
the Red Sea, to go around the land of **E**. Nm 21:4

E shall be dispossessed; Seir also, his Nm 24:18
Hor, on the edge of the land of **E**. Nm 33:37
from the wilderness of Zin alongside **E**, Nm 34:3
southward to the boundary of **E**, Jos 15:1
south, toward the boundary of **E**, Jos 15:21
when you marched from the region of **E**, Jgs 5:4
then sent messengers to the king of **E**, Jgs 11:17
but the king of **E** would not listen. Jgs 11:17
around the land of **E** and the land of Jgs 11:18
against the Ammonites, against **E**, 1 Sm 14:47
from **E**, Moab, the Ammonites, the 2 Sm 8:12
Then he put garrisons in **E**; 2 Sm 8:14
throughout all **E** he put garrisons, 2 Sm 8:14
shore of the Red Sea, in the land of **E**. 1 Kgs 9:26
He was of the royal house in **E**. 1 Kgs 11:14
For when David was in **E**, and Joab 1 Kgs 11:15
he struck down every male in **E** 1 Kgs 11:15
he had cut off every male in **E**). 1 Kgs 11:16
There was no king in **E**; a deputy 1 Kgs 22:47
"By the way of the wilderness of **E**." 2 Kgs 3:8
the king of Judah and the king of **E**. 2 Kgs 3:9
and the king of **E** went down to him. 2 Kgs 3:12
water came from the direction of **E**, 2 Kgs 3:20
through, opposite the king of **E**, 2 Kgs 3:26
In his days **E** revolted from the rule of 2 Kgs 8:20
So **E** revolted from the rule of Judah 2 Kgs 8:22
You have indeed struck down **E**, 2 Kgs 14:10
in the land of **E** before any king 1 Chr 1:43
The chiefs of **E** were: chiefs Timna, 1 Chr 1:51
and Iram; these are the chiefs of **E**. 1 Chr 1:54
off from all the nations, from **E**, 1 Chr 18:11
Then he put garrisons in **E**, and all 1 Chr 18:13
the shore of the sea, in the land of **E**. 2 Chr 8:17
is coming against you from **E**, 2 Chr 20:2
In his days **E** revolted from the rule of 2 Chr 21:8
So **E** revolted from the rule of Judah 2 Chr 21:10
You say, 'See, I have struck down **E**,' 2 Chr 25:19
they had sought the gods of **E**. 2 Chr 25:20
down twelve thousand of **E** in the Valley Ps 60:T
is my washbasin; upon **E** I cast my shoe; Ps 60:8
the fortified city? Who will lead me to **E**? Ps 60:9
the tents of **E** and the Ishmaelites, Moab Ps 83:6
my washbasin; upon **E** I cast my shoe; Ps 108:9
fortified city? Who will lead me to **E**? Ps 108:10
put out their hand against **E** and Moab, Is 11:14
behold, it descends for judgment upon **E**, Is 34:5
Bozrah, a great slaughter in the land of **E**. Is 34:6
And the streams of **E** shall be turned into Is 34:9
Who is this who comes from **E**, in Is 63:1
Egypt, Judah, **E**, the sons of Ammon, Jer 9:26
E, Moab, and the sons of Ammon; Jer 25:21
Send word to the king of **E**, the king of Jer 27:3
the Ammonites and in **E** and in other Jer 40:11
Concerning **E**. Thus says the LORD of Jer 49:7
"**E** shall become a horror. Everyone Jer 49:17
has made against **E** and the purposes Jer 49:20
of the warriors of **E** shall be in that Jer 49:22
Rejoice and be glad, O daughter of **E**, Lam 4:21
but your iniquity, O daughter of **E**, he Lam 4:22
Because **E** acted revengefully against Ezk 25:12
out my hand against **E** and cut off Ezk 25:13
lay my vengeance upon **E** by the hand Ezk 25:14
they shall do in **E** according to my Ezk 25:14
"**E** is there, her kings and all her Ezk 32:29
be desolate, Mount Seir, and all **E**, Ezk 35:15
the rest of the nations and against all **E**, Ezk 36:5
E and Moab and the main part of the Dn 11:41
a desolation and **E** a desolate wilderness, Jl 3:19
a whole people to deliver them up to **E**. Am 1:6
they delivered up a whole people to **E**, Am 1:9
"For three transgressions of **E**, and for Am 1:11
to lime the bones of the king of **E**. Am 2:1
possess the remnant of **E** and all the Am 9:12
Thus says the Lord GOD concerning **E**: Ob 1:1
the LORD, destroy the wise men out of **E**, Ob 1:8
If **E** says, "We are shattered but we will Mal 1:4

EDOMITE (8)
"You shall not abhor an **E**, for he is your Dt 23:7
His name was Doeg the **E**, the chief of 1 Sm 21:7
Then answered Doeg the **E**, who stood 1 Sm 22:9
And Doeg the **E** turned and struck 1 Sm 22:18
that day, when Doeg the **E** was there, 1 Sm 22:22
Moabite, Ammonite, **E**, Sidonian, 1 Kgs 11:1
against Solomon, Hadad the **E**. 1 Kgs 11:14
A Maskil of David, when Doeg, the **E**, Ps 52:T

EDOMITES (13)
the father of the **E** in the hill country Gn 36:9
striking down 18,000 **E** in the Valley 2 Sm 8:13
and all the **E** became David's 2 Sm 8:14
together with certain **E** of his 1 Kgs 11:17
commanders struck the **E** who had 2 Kgs 8:21
down ten thousand **E** in the Valley 2 Kgs 14:7
from Elath, and the **E** came to Elath, 2 Kgs 16:6
killed 18,000 **E** in the Valley of Salt. 1 Chr 18:12
and all the **E** became David's 1 Chr 18:13
and struck the **E** who had 2 Chr 21:9
came from striking down the **E**, 2 Chr 25:14
For the **E** had again invaded and 2 Chr 28:17
against the **E** the day of Jerusalem, Ps 137:7

EDREI (8)
he and all his people, to battle at **E**. Nm 21:33
Bashan, who lived in Ashtaroth and in **E**. Dt 1:4
us, he and all his people, to battle at **E**. Dt 3:1
and all Bashan, as far as Salecah and **E**, Dt 3:10
who lived at Ashtaroth and at **E** Jos 12:4
in Ashtaroth and in **E** (he alone was Jos 13:12
and half Gilead, and Ashtaroth, and **E**, Jos 13:31
Kedesh, **E**, En-hazor, Jos 19:37

EDUCATED (2)
They were to be **e** for three years, and at Dn 1:5
e at the feet of Gamaliel according to Acts 22:3

EDUTH (1)
choirmaster: according to Shushan **E**. Ps 60:T

EFFECT (9)
Quarter) and spoke to her to that **e**. 2 Chr 34:22
And the **e** of righteousness will be peace, Is 32:17
before the decree takes **e** —before the day Zep 2:2
a parable to the **e** that they ought always Lk 18:1
God spoke to this **e**—that his offspring Acts 7:6
And he wrote a letter to this **e**: Acts 23:25
to the **e** that the day of the Lord has 2 Thes 2:2
For a will takes **e** only at death, since it Heb 9:17
And let steadfastness have its full **e**, that Jas 1:4

EFFECTIVE (2)
a wide door for **e** work has opened to 1 Cor 16:9
your faith may become **e** for the full Phlm 1:6

EFFORT (3)
make an **e** to settle with him on the Lk 12:58
make every **e** to supplement your faith 2 Pt 1:5
I will make every **e** so that after my 2 Pt 1:15

EFFORTS (1)
you do in all your **e** for these brothers, 3 Jn 1:5

EGG (1)
or if he asks for an **e**, will give him a Lk 11:12

EGGS (6)
with young ones or **e** and the mother Dt 22:6
mother sitting on the young or on the **e**, Dt 22:6
For she leaves her **e** to the earth and lets Jb 39:14
and as one gathers **e** that have been Is 10:14
They hatch adders' **e**; they weave the Is 59:5
he who eats their **e** dies, and from one that Is 59:5

EGLAH (2)
and the sixth, Ithream, of **E**, David's 2 Sm 3:5
the sixth, Ithream, by his wife **E**; 1 Chr 3:3

EGLAIM (1)
land of Moab; her wailing reaches to **E**; Is 15:8

EGLATH-SHELISHIYAH (2)
for Moab; her fugitives flee to Zoar, to **E**. Is 15:5
voice, from Zoar to Horonaim and **E**. Jer 48:34

EGLON (13)
king of Lachish, and to Debir king of **E**, Jos 10:3
the king of Lachish, and the king of **E**, Jos 10:5
the king of Lachish, and the king of **E**. Jos 10:23
with him passed on from Lachish to **E**. Jos 10:34
with him went up from **E** to Hebron. Jos 10:36
none remaining, as he had done to **E**, Jos 10:37
the king of **E**, one; the king of Gezer, Jos 12:12
Lachish, Bozkath, **E**, Jos 15:39
and the LORD strengthened **E** the king of Jgs 3:12
people of Israel served **E** the king of Jgs 3:14
tribute by him to **E** the king of Moab. Jgs 3:15
presented the tribute to **E** king of Moab. Jgs 3:17
of Moab. Now **E** was a very fat man. Jgs 3:17

EGYPT (621)
sons of Ham: Cush, **E**, Put, and Canaan. Gn 10:6
E fathered Ludim, Anamim, Lehabim, Gn 10:13
went down to **E** to sojourn there, Gn 12:10
When he was about to enter **E**, he said Gn 12:11
When Abram entered **E**, the Egyptians Gn 12:14
So Abram went up from **E**, he and his Gn 13:1
garden of the LORD, like the land of **E**, Gn 13:10
from the river of **E** to the great river, Gn 15:18
took a wife for him from the land of **E**. Gn 21:21
which is opposite **E** in the direction of Gn 25:18
to him and said, "Do not go down to **E**; Gn 26:2
on their way to carry it down to **E**. Gn 37:25
shekels of silver. They took Joseph to **E**. Gn 37:28
had sold him in **E** to Potiphar, Gn 37:36
Joseph had been brought down to **E**, Gn 39:1
of the king of **E** and his baker Gn 40:1
offense against their lord the king of **E**. Gn 40:1
and the baker of the king of **E**, Gn 40:5
all the magicians of **E** and all its wise Gn 41:8
as I had never seen in all the land of **E**. Gn 41:19
plenty throughout all the land of **E**, Gn 41:29
will be forgotten in the land of **E**. Gn 41:30
man, and set him over the land of **E**. Gn 41:33
of the land of **E** during the seven Gn 41:34
that are to occur in the land of **E**, Gn 41:36
I have set you over all the land of **E**." Gn 41:41
Thus he set him over all the land of **E**. Gn 41:43
lift up hand or foot in all the land of **E**." Gn 41:44
So Joseph went out over the land of **E**. Gn 41:45
the service of Pharaoh king of **E**. Gn 41:46
and went through all the land of **E**. Gn 41:46
years, which occurred in the land of **E**, Gn 41:48
in the land of **E** came to an end, Gn 41:53
but in all the land of **E** there was bread. Gn 41:54
When all the land of **E** was famished, Gn 41:55
the famine was severe in the land of **E**. Gn 41:56
all the earth came to **E** to Joseph to buy Gn 41:57
that there was grain for sale in **E**, Gn 42:1
heard that there is grain for sale in **E**. Gn 42:2
brothers went down to buy grain in **E**. Gn 42:3
the grain that they had brought from **E**, Gn 43:2
and went down to **E** and stood before Gn 43:15
brother, Joseph, whom you sold into **E**. Gn 45:4
house and ruler over all the land of **E**. Gn 45:8
Joseph, God has made me lord of all **E**. Gn 45:9
tell my father of all my honor in **E**, Gn 45:13
I will give you the best of the land of **E**, Gn 45:18
from the land of **E** for your little ones Gn 45:19
the best of all the land of **E** is yours.'" Gn 45:20
loaded with the good things of **E**, Gn 45:23
they went up out of **E** and came to the Gn 45:25
all the land of **E**." And his heart Gn 45:26
Do not be afraid to go down to **E**, for Gn 46:3
I myself will go down with you to **E**, and Gn 46:4
in the land of Canaan, and came into **E**, Gn 46:6
offspring he brought with him into **E**. Gn 46:7
descendants of Israel, who came into **E**, Gn 46:8
in the land of **E** were born Manasseh Gn 46:20
belonging to Jacob who came into **E**, Gn 46:26
of Joseph, who were born to him in **E**, Gn 46:27
of Jacob who came into **E** were seventy. Gn 46:27
The land of **E** is before you. Settle your Gn 47:6
them a possession in the land of **E**, Gn 47:11
so that the land of **E** and the land of Gn 47:13
found in the land of **E** and in the land Gn 47:14
spent in the land of **E** and in the land of Gn 47:15
bought all the land of **E** for Pharaoh, Gn 47:20
of them from one end of **E** to the other. Gn 47:21
it a statute concerning the land of **E**, Gn 47:26
Thus Israel settled in the land of **E**, in Gn 47:27
lived in the land of **E** seventeen years. Gn 47:28
truly with me. Do not bury me in **E**, Gn 47:29
Carry me out of **E** and bury me in Gn 47:30
you in the land of **E** before I came to you Gn 48:5
land of Egypt before I came to you in **E**, Gn 48:5
and all the elders of the land of **E**, Gn 50:7
Joseph returned to **E** with his brothers Gn 50:14
So Joseph remained in **E**, he and his Gn 50:22
him, and he was put in a coffin in **E**. Gn 50:26
sons of Israel who came to **E** with Jacob, Ex 1:1
seventy persons; Joseph was already in **E**. Ex 1:5
Now there arose a new king over **E**, who Ex 1:8
Then the king of **E** said to the Hebrew Ex 1:15
do as the king of **E** commanded them, Ex 1:17
So the king of **E** called the midwives and Ex 1:18
those many days the king of **E** died, Ex 2:23
people who are in **E** and have heard their Ex 3:7
people, the children of Israel, out of **E**." Ex 3:10
bring the children of Israel out of **E**?" Ex 3:11
you have brought the people out of **E**, Ex 3:12
you and what has been done to you in **E**, Ex 3:16
out of the affliction of **E** to the land of the Ex 3:17
shall go to the king of **E** and say to him, Ex 3:18
know that the king of **E** will not let you Ex 3:19
my hand and strike **E** with all the Ex 3:20
to my brothers in **E** to see whether they Ex 4:18
said to Moses in Midian, "Go back to **E**, Ex 4:19
donkey, and went back to the land of **E**. Ex 4:20
said to Moses, "When you go back to **E**, Ex 4:21
But the king of **E** said to them, "Moses Ex 5:4
all the land of **E** to gather stubble for Ex 5:12
tell Pharaoh king of **E** to let the people of Ex 6:11
of Israel and about Pharaoh king of **E**: Ex 6:13
the people of Israel out of the land of **E**. Ex 6:13
Israel from the land of **E** by their hosts." Ex 6:26
Pharaoh king of **E** about bringing out Ex 6:27
bringing out the people of Israel from **E**, Ex 6:27
the LORD spoke to Moses in the land of **E**, Ex 6:28
tell Pharaoh king of **E** all that I say to Ex 6:29
my signs and wonders in the land of **E**, Ex 7:3
lay my hand on **E** and bring my hosts, Ex 7:4
out of the land of **E** by great acts of Ex 7:4
out my hand against **E** and bring out the Ex 7:5
sorcerers, and they, the magicians of **E**, Ex 7:11

out your hand over the waters of **E**, Ex 7:19
be blood throughout all the land of **E**, Ex 7:19
was blood throughout all the land of **E**. Ex 7:21
But the magicians of **E** did the same by Ex 7:22
make frogs come up on the land of **E**!'" Ex 8:5
out his hand over the waters of **E**, Ex 8:6
frogs came up and covered the land of **E**. Ex 8:6
and made frogs come up on the land of **E**. Ex 8:7
may become gnats in all the land of **E**.'" Ex 8:16
earth became gnats in all the land of **E**. Ex 8:17
all the land of **E** the land was ruined Ex 8:24
livestock of Israel and the livestock of **E**, Ex 9:4
become fine dust over all the land of **E**, Ex 9:9
and beast throughout all the land of **E**." Ex 9:9
as never has been in **E** from the day it Ex 9:18
there may be hail in all the land of **E**, Ex 9:22
every plant of the field, in the land of **E**." Ex 9:22
the LORD rained hail upon the land of **E**. Ex 9:23
in all the land of **E** since it became a Ex 9:24
that was in the field in all the land of **E**, Ex 9:25
not yet understand that **E** is ruined?" Ex 10:7
hand over the land of **E** for the locusts, Ex 10:12
upon the land of **E** and eat every plant Ex 10:12
out his staff over the land of **E**, Ex 10:13
over all the land of **E** and settled on the Ex 10:14
and settled on the whole country of **E**, Ex 10:14
of the field, through all the land of **E**. Ex 10:15
locust was left in all the country of **E**. Ex 10:19
may be darkness over the land of **E**, Ex 10:21
darkness in all the land of **E** three days. Ex 10:22
I will bring upon Pharaoh and upon **E**. Ex 11:1
Moses was very great in the land of **E**, Ex 11:3
midnight I will go out in the midst of **E**, Ex 11:4
every firstborn in the land of **E** shall die, Ex 11:5
a great cry throughout all the land of **E**, Ex 11:6
a distinction between **E** and Israel. Ex 11:7
may be multiplied in the land of **E**." Ex 11:9
said to Moses and Aaron in the land of **E**, Ex 12:1
pass through the land of **E** that night, Ex 12:12
strike all the firstborn in the land of **E**, Ex 12:12
all the gods of **E** I will execute Ex 12:12
destroy you, when I strike the land of **E**. Ex 12:13
brought your hosts out of the land of **E**. Ex 12:17
the houses of the people of Israel in **E**, Ex 12:27
down all the firstborn in the land of **E**, Ex 12:29
And there was a great cry in **E**, for there Ex 12:30
dough that they had brought out of **E**, Ex 12:39
were thrust out of **E** and could not wait, Ex 12:39
people of Israel lived in **E** was 430 years. Ex 12:40
of the LORD went out from the land of **E**. Ex 12:41
LORD, to bring them out of the land of **E**; Ex 12:42
Israel out of the land of **E** by their hosts. Ex 12:51
this day in which you came out from **E**, Ex 13:3
LORD did for me when I came out of **E**.' Ex 13:8
hand the LORD has brought you out of **E**. Ex 13:9
hand the LORD brought us out of **E**, Ex 13:14
killed all the firstborn in the land of **E**, Ex 13:15
hand the LORD brought us out of **E**." Ex 13:16
when they see war and return to **E**." Ex 13:17
out of the land of **E** equipped for battle. Ex 13:18
When the king of **E** was told that the Ex 14:5
the other chariots of **E** with officers over Ex 14:7
hardened the heart of Pharaoh king of **E**, Ex 14:8
are no graves in **E** that you have taken Ex 14:11
you done to us in bringing us out of **E**? Ex 14:11
Is not this what we said to you in **E**, Ex 14:12
between the host of **E** and the host of Ex 14:20
they had departed from the land of **E**. Ex 16:1
by the hand of the LORD in the land of **E**, Ex 16:3
who brought you out of the land of **E**, Ex 16:6
I brought you out of the land of **E**.'" Ex 16:32
said, "Why did you bring us up out of **E**, Ex 17:3
the LORD had brought Israel out of **E**. Ex 18:1
of Israel had gone out of the land of **E**, Ex 19:1
who brought you out of the land of **E**, Ex 20:2
you were sojourners in the land of **E**. Ex 22:21
for you were sojourners in the land of **E**. Ex 23:9
of Abib, for in it you came out of **E**. Ex 23:15
out of the land of **E** that I might dwell Ex 29:46
who brought us up out of the land of **E**, Ex 32:1
brought you up out of the land of **E**!" Ex 32:4
you brought up out of the land of **E**, Ex 32:7
brought you up out of the land of **E**!'" Ex 32:8
of the land of **E** with great power and Ex 32:11
who brought us up out of the land of **E**, Ex 32:23
have brought up out of the land of **E**, Ex 33:1
the month Abib you came out from **E**. Ex 34:18
up out of the land of **E** to be your God. Lv 11:45
shall not do as they do in the land of **E**, Lv 18:3
for you were strangers in the land of **E**: Lv 19:34
who brought you out of the land of **E**. Lv 19:36
you out of the land of **E** to be your God: Lv 22:33
I brought them out of the land of **E**: Lv 23:43
out of the land of **E** to give you the land Lv 25:38
whom I brought out of the land of **E**; Lv 25:42
whom I brought out of the land of **E**: Lv 25:55
who brought you out of the land of **E**, Lv 26:13
out of the land of **E** in the sight of the Lv 26:45
after they had come out of the land of **E**, Nm 1:1
down all the firstborn in the land of **E**, Nm 3:13
in the land of **E** I consecrated them for Nm 8:17
after they had come out of the land of **E**, Nm 9:1
the fish we ate in **E** that cost nothing, Nm 11:5
better for us in **E**." Therefore the LORD Nm 11:18
saying, "Why did we come out of **E**?"'" Nm 11:20
built seven years before Zoan in **E**.) Nm 13:22
that we had died in the land of **E**! Nm 14:2
it not be better for us to go back to **E**?" Nm 14:3
us choose a leader and go back to **E**." Nm 14:4
this people, from **E** until now." Nm 14:19
that I did in **E** and in the wilderness, Nm 14:22
out of the land of **E** to be your God: Nm 15:41
us come up out of **E** to bring us to this Nm 20:5
how our fathers went down to **E**, and Nm 20:15
Egypt, and we lived in **E** a long time. Nm 20:15
sent an angel and brought us out of **E**. Nm 20:16
brought us up out of **E** to die in the Nm 21:5
"Behold, a people has come out of **E**. Nm 22:5
'Behold, a people has come out of **E**, Nm 22:11
brings them out of **E** and is for them Nm 23:22
God brings him out of **E** and is for him Nm 24:8
who came out of the land of **E** were: Nm 26:4
of Levi, who was born to Levi in **E**. Nm 26:59
of the men who came up out of **E**, Nm 32:11
of the land of **E** by their companies Nm 33:1
of Israel had come out of the land of **E**, Nm 33:38
turn from Azmon to the Brook of **E**, Nm 34:5
us he has brought us out of the land of **E**, Dt 1:27
as he did for you in **E** before your eyes, Dt 1:30
you out of the iron furnace, out of **E**, Dt 4:20
God did for you in **E** before your eyes? Dt 4:34
brought you out of **E** with his own Dt 4:37
people of Israel when they came out of **E**, Dt 4:45
Israel defeated when they came out of **E**. Dt 4:46
who brought you out of the land of **E**, Dt 5:6
that you were a slave in the land of **E**, Dt 5:15
who brought you out of the land of **E**, Dt 6:12
son, 'We were Pharaoh's slaves in **E**. Dt 6:21
brought us out of **E** with a mighty hand. Dt 6:21
against **E** and against Pharaoh and all Dt 6:22
from the hand of Pharaoh king of **E**. Dt 7:8
and none of the evil diseases of **E**, Dt 7:15
your God did to Pharaoh and to all **E**, Dt 7:18
who brought you out of the land of **E**, Dt 8:14
out of the land of **E** until you came to this Dt 9:7
have brought from **E** have acted Dt 9:12
have brought out of **E** with a mighty Dt 9:26
for you were sojourners in the land of **E**. Dt 10:19
fathers went down to **E** seventy persons, Dt 10:22
that he did in **E** to Pharaoh the king Dt 11:3
to Pharaoh the king of **E** and to all his Dt 11:3
and what he did to the army of **E**, to their Dt 11:4
possession of it is not like the land of **E**, Dt 11:10
of the land of **E** and redeemed you out Dt 13:5
who brought you out of the land of **E**, Dt 13:10
that you were a slave in the land of **E**, Dt 15:15
your God brought you out of **E** by night. Dt 16:1
out of the land of **E** in haste—that all Dt 16:3
day when you came out of the land of **E**. Dt 16:3
at sunset, at the time you came out of **E**. Dt 16:6
remember that you were a slave in **E**; Dt 16:12
people to return to **E** in order to acquire Dt 17:16
who brought you up out of the land of **E**. Dt 20:1
on the way, when you came out of **E**, Dt 23:4
Miriam on the way as you came out of **E**. Dt 24:9
you were a slave in **E** and the LORD your Dt 24:18
that you were a slave in the land of **E**; Dt 24:22
to you on the way as you came out of **E**, Dt 25:17
went down into **E** and sojourned there, Dt 26:5
brought us out of **E** with a mighty hand Dt 26:8
LORD will strike you with the boils of **E**, Dt 28:27
upon you again all the diseases of **E**, Dt 28:60
LORD will bring you back in ships to **E**, Dt 28:68
did before your eyes in the land of **E**, Dt 29:2
know how we lived in the land of **E**, Dt 29:16
he brought them out of the land of **E**, Dt 29:25
the LORD sent him to do in the land of **E**, Dt 34:11
Sea before you when you came out of **E**, Jos 2:10
males of the people who came out of **E**, Jos 5:4
on the way after they had come out of **E**. Jos 5:4
had come out of **E** had not been Jos 5:5
the men of war who came out of **E**, Jos 5:6
away the reproach of **E** from you." And so Jos 5:9
a report of him, and all that he did in **E**, Jos 9:9
(from the Shihor, which is east of **E**, Jos 13:3
to Azmon, goes out by the Brook of **E**, Jos 15:4
to the Brook of **E**, and the Great Sea Jos 15:47
Jacob and his children went down to **E**. Jos 24:4
and I plagued **E** with what I did in the Jos 24:5
"'Then I brought your fathers out of **E**, Jos 24:6
them; and your eyes saw what I did in **E**. Jos 24:7
served beyond the River and in **E**, Jos 24:14
and our fathers up from the land of **E**, Jos 24:17
the people of Israel brought up from **E**, Jos 24:32
brought you up from **E** and brought you Jgs 2:1
had brought them out of the land of **E**. Jgs 2:12
I led you up from **E** and brought you out Jgs 6:8
'Did not the LORD bring us up from **E**?' Jgs 6:13
on coming up from **E** took away my Jgs 11:13
but when they came up from **E**, Israel Jgs 11:16
up out of the land of **E** until this day; Jgs 19:30
when they were in **E** subject to the 1 Sm 2:27
them up out of **E** even to this day, 1 Sm 8:8
of Israel, 'I brought up Israel out of **E**, 1 Sm 10:18
your fathers up out of the land of **E**. 1 Sm 12:6
When Jacob went into **E**, and the 1 Sm 12:8
your fathers out of **E** and made them 1 Sm 12:8
the way when they came up out of **E**. 1 Sm 15:2
came up out of **E**." So the Kenites 1 Sm 15:6
as far as Shur, which is east of **E**. 1 Sm 15:7
of old, as far as Shur, to the land of **E**. 1 Sm 27:8
He said, "I am a young man of **E**, 1 Sm 30:13
the people of Israel from **E** to this day, 2 Sm 7:6
you redeemed for yourself from **E**, 2 Sm 7:23
alliance with Pharaoh king of **E**. 1 Kgs 3:1
the Philistines and to the border of **E**. 1 Kgs 4:21
of the east and all the wisdom of **E**. 1 Kgs 4:30
of Israel came out of the land of **E**, 1 Kgs 6:1
when they came out of the land of **E**. 1 Kgs 8:9
I brought my people Israel out of **E**, 1 Kgs 8:16
brought them out of the land of **E**." 1 Kgs 8:21
heritage, which you brought out of **E**, 1 Kgs 8:51
you brought our fathers out of **E**, 1 Kgs 8:53
from Lebo-hamath to the Brook of **E**, 1 Kgs 8:65
out of the land of **E** and laid hold on 1 Kgs 9:9
(Pharaoh king of **E** had gone up and 1 Kgs 9:16
of horses was from **E** and Kue, 1 Kgs 10:28
be imported from **E** for 600 shekels 1 Kgs 10:29
But Hadad fled to **E**, together with 1 Kgs 11:17
them from Paran and came to **E**, 1 Kgs 11:18
to Egypt, to Pharaoh king of **E**, 1 Kgs 11:18
Hadad heard in **E** that David slept 1 Kgs 11:21
But Jeroboam arose and fled into **E**, 1 Kgs 11:40
fled into Egypt, to Shishak king of **E**, 1 Kgs 11:40
and was in **E** until the death of 1 Kgs 11:40
heard of it (for he was still in **E**, 1 Kgs 12:2
then Jeroboam returned from **E**. 1 Kgs 12:2
you up out of the land of **E**." 1 Kgs 12:28
Shishak king of **E** came up against 1 Kgs 14:25
and the kings of **E** to come against us." 2 Kgs 7:6
had sent messengers to So, king of **E**, 2 Kgs 17:4
of the land of **E** from under the hand 2 Kgs 17:7
under the hand of Pharaoh king of **E**, 2 Kgs 17:7
of the land of **E** with great power and 2 Kgs 17:36
Behold, you are trusting now in **E**, 2 Kgs 18:21
is Pharaoh king of **E** to all who trust 2 Kgs 18:21
when you trust in **E** for chariots and 2 Kgs 18:24
sole of my foot all the streams of **E**.' 2 Kgs 19:24
the day their fathers came out of **E**, 2 Kgs 21:15
Pharaoh Neco king of **E** went up to 2 Kgs 23:29
and he came to **E** and died there. 2 Kgs 23:34
And the king of **E** did not come again 2 Kgs 24:7
to the king of **E** from the Brook of 2 Kgs 24:7
from the Brook of **E** to the river 2 Kgs 24:7
of the forces arose and went to **E**, 2 Kgs 25:26
of Ham: Cush, **E**, Put, and Canaan. 1 Chr 1:8
E fathered Ludim, Anamim, 1 Chr 1:11
from the Nile of **E** to Lebo-hamath, 1 Chr 13:5
people whom you redeemed from **E**? 1 Chr 17:21
of horses was from **E** and Kue, 2 Chr 1:16
a chariot from **E** for 600 shekels 2 Chr 1:17
of Israel, when they came out of **E**. 2 Chr 5:10
my people out of the land of **E**, 2 Chr 6:5
from Lebo-hamath to the Brook of **E**. 2 Chr 7:8
out of the land of **E** and laid hold on 2 Chr 7:22
the Philistines and to the border of **E**. 2 Chr 9:26
for Solomon from **E** and from all 2 Chr 9:28
of Nebat heard of it (for he was in **E**, 2 Chr 10:2
then Jeroboam returned from **E**. 2 Chr 10:2
Shishak king of **E** came up against 2 Chr 12:2
came with him from **E**—Libyans, 2 Chr 12:3
Shishak king of **E** came up against 2 Chr 12:9
when they came from the land of **E**, 2 Chr 20:10
fame spread even to the border of **E**, 2 Chr 26:8
Neco king of **E** went up to fight at 2 Chr 35:20
Then the king of **E** deposed him in 2 Chr 36:3
And the king of **E** made Eliakim his 2 Chr 36:4
his brother and carried him to **E**. 2 Chr 36:4
of our fathers in **E** and heard their cry Neh 9:9
a leader to return to their slavery in **E**. Neh 9:17
God who brought you up out of **E**,' Neh 9:18
Nobles shall come from **E**; Cush shall Ps 68:31
he performed wonders in the land of **E**, Ps 78:12
his signs in **E** and his marvels Ps 78:43
He struck down every firstborn in **E**, Ps 78:51

You brought a vine out of **E**; you drove Ps 80:8
when he went out over the land of **E**. Ps 81:5
brought you up out of the land of **E**. Ps 81:10
Then Israel came to **E**; Jacob Ps 105:23
E was glad when they departed, for Ps 105:38
Our fathers, when they were in **E**, did Ps 106:7
who had done great things in **E**, Ps 106:21
When Israel went out from **E**, the house Ps 114:1
who struck down the firstborn of **E**, Ps 135:8
who in your midst, O **E**, sent signs and Ps 135:9
who struck down the firstborn of **E**, Ps 136:10
fly that is at the end of the streams of **E**, Is 7:18
the sea, and he will lift it as he did in **E**. Is 10:26
of his people, from Assyria, from **E**, Is 11:11
utterly destroy the tongue of the Sea of **E**, Is 11:15
when they came up from the land of **E**. Is 11:16
An oracle concerning **E**. Behold, the LORD Is 19:1
is riding on a swift cloud and comes to **E**; Is 19:1
and the idols of **E** will tremble at his Is 19:1
LORD of hosts has purposed against **E**. Is 19:12
of her tribes have made **E** stagger. Is 19:13
and they will make **E** stagger in all its Is 19:14
will be nothing for **E** that head or tail, Is 19:15
in the land of **E** that speak the language Is 19:18
to the LORD in the midst of the land of **E**, Is 19:19
to the LORD of hosts in the land of **E**. Is 19:20
And the LORD will strike **E**, striking and Is 19:22
will be a highway from **E** to Assyria, Is 19:23
to Assyria, and Assyria will come into **E**, Is 19:23
come into Egypt, and **E** into Assyria, Is 19:23
will be the third with **E** and Assyria, Is 19:24
blessed, saying, "Blessed be **E** my people, Is 19:25
a sign and a portent against **E** and Cush, Is 20:3
buttocks uncovered, the nakedness of **E**. Is 20:4
of Cush their hope and of **E** their boast. Is 20:5
When the report comes to **E**, they will be Is 23:5
to the Brook of **E** the LORD will thresh Is 27:12
to the land of **E** will come and worship Is 27:13
who set out to go down to **E**, without Is 30:2
and to seek shelter in the shadow of **E**! Is 30:2
in the shadow of **E** to your humiliation. Is 30:3
those who go down to **E** for help and rely Is 31:1
Behold, you are trusting in **E**, that broken Is 36:6
is Pharaoh king of **E** to all who trust Is 36:6
when you trust in **E** for chariots and for Is 36:9
the sole of my foot all the streams of **E**. Is 37:25
I give **E** as your ransom, Cush and Seba Is 43:3
"The wealth of **E** and the merchandise Is 45:14
down at the first into **E** to sojourn there, Is 52:4
who brought us up from the land of **E**, Jer 2:6
gain by going to **E** to drink the waters Jer 2:18
be put to shame by **E** as you were put to Jer 2:36
that I brought them out of the land of **E**, Jer 7:22
came out of the land of **E** to this day, Jer 7:25
E, Judah, Edom, the sons of Ammon, Jer 9:26
I brought them out of the land of **E**, Jer 11:4
I brought them up out of the land of **E**, Jer 11:7
the people of Israel out of the land of **E**,' Jer 16:14
the people of Israel out of the land of **E**,' Jer 23:7
and those who dwell in the land of **E**. Jer 24:8
Pharaoh king of **E**, his servants, his Jer 25:19
he was afraid and fled and escaped to **E**. Jer 26:21
King Jehoiakim sent to **E** certain men, Jer 26:22
took Uriah from **E** and brought him Jer 26:23
hand to bring them out of the land of **E**, Jer 31:32
signs and wonders in the land of **E**, Jer 32:20
of the land of **E** with signs and wonders, Jer 32:21
I brought them out of the land of **E**, Jer 34:13
army of Pharaoh had come out of **E**. Jer 37:5
came to help you is about to return to **E**, Jer 37:7
near Bethlehem, intending to go to **E** Jer 41:17
saying, 'No, we will go to the land of **E**, Jer 42:14
set your faces to enter **E** and go to live Jer 42:15
overtake you there in the land of **E**, Jer 42:16
afraid shall follow close after you to **E**, Jer 42:16
their faces to go to **E** to live there shall Jer 42:17
be poured out on you when you go to **E**. Jer 42:18
O remnant of Judah, 'Do not go to **E**.' Jer 42:19
you to say, 'Do not go to **E** to live there,' Jer 43:2
And they came into the land of **E**, for Jer 43:7
He shall come and strike the land of **E**, Jer 43:11
a fire in the temples of the gods of **E**, Jer 43:12
clean the land of **E** as a shepherd cleans Jer 43:12
of Heliopolis, which is in the land of **E**, Jer 43:13
of the gods of **E** he shall burn with Jer 43:13
the Judeans who lived in the land of **E**, Jer 44:1
in the land of **E** where you have come Jer 44:8
faces to come to the land of **E** to live, Jer 44:12
In the land of **E** they shall fall; by the Jer 44:12
those who dwell in the land of **E**, Jer 44:13
in the land of **E** shall escape or survive Jer 44:14
who lived in Pathros in the land of **E**, Jer 44:15
you of Judah who are in the land of **E**. Jer 44:24
you of Judah who dwell in the land of **E**: Jer 44:26
any man of Judah in all the land of **E**, Jer 44:26
in the land of **E** shall be consumed by Jer 44:27
return from the land of **E** to the land of Jer 44:28
who came to the land of **E** to live, Jer 44:28
Hophra king of **E** into the hand Jer 44:30
About **E**. Concerning the army of Jer 46:2
the army of Pharaoh Neco, king of **E**, Jer 46:2
E rises like the Nile, like rivers whose Jer 46:8
and take balm, O virgin daughter of **E**! Jer 46:11
king of Babylon to strike the land of **E**: Jer 46:13
"Declare in **E**, and proclaim in Migdol; Jer 46:14
Call the name of Pharaoh, king of **E**, Jer 46:17
baggage for exile, O inhabitants of **E**! Jer 46:19
"A beautiful heifer is **E**, but a biting fly Jer 46:20
The daughter of **E** shall be put to Jer 46:24
and Pharaoh and **E** and her gods and Jer 46:25
Afterward **E** shall be inhabited as in Jer 46:26
We have given the hand to **E**, and to Lam 5:6
him by sending his ambassadors to **E**, Ezk 17:15
him with hooks to the land of **E**. Ezk 19:4
myself known to them in the land of **E**; Ezk 20:5
out of the land of **E** into a land that I Ezk 20:6
not defile yourselves with the idols of **E**; Ezk 20:7
on, nor did they forsake the idols of **E**. Ezk 20:8
them in the midst of the land of **E**. Ezk 20:8
in bringing them out of the land of **E**. Ezk 20:9
of the land of **E** and brought them Ezk 20:10
in the wilderness of the land of **E**, Ezk 20:36
They played the whore in **E**; they played Ezk 23:3
her whoring that she had begun in **E**; Ezk 23:8
she played the whore in the land of **E** Ezk 23:19
your whoring begun in the land of **E**, Ezk 23:27
eyes to them or remember **E** anymore. Ezk 23:27
embroidered linen from **E** was your Ezk 27:7
your face against Pharaoh king of **E**, Ezk 29:2
against him and against all **E**; Ezk 29:2
I am against you, Pharaoh king of **E**, Ezk 29:3
all the inhabitants of **E** shall know that Ezk 29:6
and the land of **E** shall be a desolation Ezk 29:9
make the land of **E** an utter waste and Ezk 29:10
make the land of **E** a desolation in the Ezk 29:12
the fortunes of **E** and bring them Ezk 29:14
the land of **E** to Nebuchadnezzar king Ezk 29:19
him the land of **E** as his payment for Ezk 29:20
A sword shall come upon **E**, and Ezk 30:4
be in Cush, when the slain fall in **E**, Ezk 30:4
Those who support **E** shall fall, and her Ezk 30:6
I am the LORD, when I have set fire to **E**, Ezk 30:8
"I will put an end to the wealth of **E**, by Ezk 30:10
their swords against **E** and fill the Ezk 30:11
longer be a prince from the land of **E**; Ezk 30:13
so I will put fear in the land of **E**. Ezk 30:13
on Pelusium, the stronghold of **E**, Ezk 30:15
And I will set fire to **E**; Pelusium shall Ezk 30:16
when I break there the yoke bars of **E**, Ezk 30:18
Thus I will execute judgments on **E**. Ezk 30:19
broken the arm of Pharaoh king of **E**, Ezk 30:21
Pharaoh king of **E** and will break Ezk 30:22
stretches it out against the land of **E**. Ezk 30:25
to Pharaoh king of **E** and to his Ezk 31:2
over Pharaoh king of **E** and say to him: Ezk 32:2
shall bring to ruin the pride of **E**, Ezk 32:12
When I make the land of **E** desolate, Ezk 32:15
of the nations shall chant it; over **E**, Ezk 32:16
of man, wail over the multitude of **E**, Ezk 32:18
E is delivered to the sword; drag her Ezk 32:20
along the Brook of **E** to the Great Sea. Ezk 47:19
along the Brook of **E** to the Great Sea. Ezk 48:28
out of the land of **E** with a mighty hand, Dn 9:15
also carry off to **E** their gods with their Dn 11:8
and the land of **E** shall not escape. Dn 11:42
silver, and all the precious things of **E**, Dn 11:43
when she came out of the land of **E**. Hos 2:15
silly and without sense, calling to **E**, Hos 7:11
shall be their derision in the land of **E**. Hos 7:16
their sins; they shall return to **E**. Hos 8:13
the LORD, but Ephraim shall return to **E**, Hos 9:3
destruction; but **E** shall gather them; Hos 9:6
loved him, and out of **E** I called my son. Hos 11:1
They shall not return to the land of **E**, Hos 11:5
come trembling like birds from **E**, Hos 11:11
with Assyria, and oil is carried to **E**. Hos 12:1
the LORD your God from the land of **E**; Hos 12:9
the LORD brought Israel up from **E**, Hos 12:13
the LORD your God from the land of **E**; Hos 13:4
"**E** shall become a desolation and Edom a Jl 3:19
out of the land of **E** and led you forty Am 2:10
that I brought up out of the land of **E**: Am 3:1
and to the strongholds in the land of **E**, Am 3:9
you a pestilence after the manner of **E**; Am 4:10
and sink again, like the Nile of **E**?" Am 8:8
Nile, and sinks again, like the Nile of **E**; Am 9:5
I not bring up Israel from the land of **E**, Am 9:7
from the land of **E** and redeemed you Mi 6:4
to you, from Assyria and the cities of **E**, Mi 7:12
cities of Egypt, and from **E** to the River, Mi 7:12
when you came out of the land of **E**, Mi 7:15
strength; **E** too, and that without limit; Na 3:9
I made with you when you came out of **E**. Hg 2:5
bring them home from the land of **E**, Zec 10:10
low, and the scepter of **E** shall depart. Zec 10:11
And if the family of **E** does not go up Zec 14:18
the punishment to **E** and the Zec 14:19
the child and his mother, and flee to **E**, Mt 2:13
his mother by night and departed to **E** Mt 2:14
the prophet, "Out of **E** I called my son." Mt 2:15
Lord appeared in a dream to Joseph in **E**, Mt 2:19
E and the parts of Libya belonging to Acts 2:10
jealous of Joseph, sold him into **E**; Acts 7:9
wisdom before Pharaoh, king of **E**, Acts 7:10
made him ruler over **E** and over all his Acts 7:10
famine throughout all **E** and Canaan, Acts 7:11
Jacob heard that there was grain in **E**, Acts 7:12
And Jacob went down into **E**, and he Acts 7:15
people increased and multiplied in **E** Acts 7:17
there arose over **E** another king who Acts 7:18
affliction of my people who are in **E**, Acts 7:34
And now come, I will send you to **E**.' Acts 7:34
wonders and signs in **E** and at the Red Acts 7:36
and in their hearts they turned to **E**, Acts 7:39
who led us out from the land of **E**, Acts 7:40
during their stay in the land of **E**, Acts 13:17
it not all those who left **E** led by Moses? Heb 3:16
hand to bring them out of the land of **E**. Heb 8:9
greater wealth than the treasures of **E**, Heb 11:26
By faith he left **E**, not being afraid of Heb 11:27
who saved a people out of the land of **E**, Jude 1:5
symbolically is called Sodom and **E**, Rv 11:8

EGYPT'S (3)

and the branches of **E** Nile will diminish Is 19:6
E help is worthless and empty; therefore I Is 30:7
come upon them on the day of **E** doom; Ezk 30:9

EGYPTIAN (26)

She had a female **E** servant whose name Gn 16:1
Sarai, Abram's wife, took Hagar the **E**, Gn 16:3
But Sarah saw the son of Hagar the **E**, Gn 21:9
Abraham's son, whom Hagar the **E**, Gn 25:12
Pharaoh, the captain of the guard, an **E**, Gn 39:1
and he was in the house of his **E** master. Gn 39:2
women are not like the **E** women, Ex 1:19
and he saw an **E** beating a Hebrew, Ex 2:11
he struck down the **E** and hid him in the Ex 2:12
as you killed the **E**?" Then Moses was Ex 2:14
"An **E** delivered us out of the hand of the Ex 2:19
looked down on the **E** forces and threw Ex 14:24
forces and threw the **E** forces into a Ex 14:24
woman's son, whose father was an **E**, Lv 24:10
You shall not abhor an **E**, because you Dt 23:7
They found an **E** in the open 1 Sm 30:11
And he struck down an **E**, a 2 Sm 23:21
The **E** had a spear in his hand, but 2 Sm 23:21
Sheshan had an **E** slave whose name 1 Chr 2:34
And he struck down an **E**, a man of 1 Chr 11:23
The **E** had in his hand a spear like a 1 Chr 11:23
coverings, colored linens from **E** linen; Prv 7:16
Assyria lead away the **E** captives and the Is 20:4
avenged him by striking down the **E**. Acts 7:24
kill me as you killed the **E** yesterday?' Acts 7:28
Are you not the **E**, then, who recently Acts 21:38

EGYPTIAN'S (3)

the LORD blessed the **E** house for Joseph's Gn 39:5
spear out of the **E** hand and killed 2 Sm 23:21
spear out of the **E** hand and killed 1 Chr 11:23

EGYPTIANS (98)

and when the **E** see you, they will say, Gn 12:12
the **E** saw that the woman was very Gn 12:14
Pharaoh said to all the **E**, "Go to Gn 41:55
all the storehouses and sold to the **E**, Gn 41:56
and the **E** who ate with him by Gn 43:32
because the **E** could not eat with the Gn 43:32
for that is an abomination to the **E**. Gn 43:32
he wept aloud, so that the **E** heard it, Gn 45:2
shepherd is an abomination to the **E**." Gn 46:34
all the **E** came to Joseph and said, Gn 47:15
Pharaoh, for all the **E** sold their fields, Gn 47:20
And the **E** wept for him seventy days. Gn 50:3
mourning by the **E**." Therefore the Gn 50:11
And the **E** were in dread of the people of Ex 1:12
of the hand of the **E** and to bring them up Ex 3:8
with which the **E** oppress them. Ex 3:9
this people favor in the sight of the **E**; Ex 3:21
daughters. So you shall plunder the **E**." Ex 3:22
people of Israel whom the **E** hold as slaves, Ex 6:5
you out from under the burdens of the **E**, Ex 6:6
you out from under the burdens of the **E**. Ex 6:7
The **E** shall know that I am the LORD, Ex 7:5
and the **E** will grow weary of drinking Ex 7:18
so that the **E** could not drink water from Ex 7:21
And all the **E** dug along the Nile for Ex 7:24

the houses of the **E** shall be filled with Ex 8:21
our God are an abomination to the **E**. Ex 8:26
abominable to the **E** before their eyes, Ex 8:26
All the livestock of the **E** died, but not one Ex 9:6
upon the magicians and upon all the **E**. Ex 9:11
dealt harshly with the **E** and what signs I Ex 10:2
of all your servants and of all the **E**, Ex 10:6
the people favor in the sight of the **E**. Ex 11:3
LORD will pass through to strike the **E**, Ex 12:23
when he struck the **E** but spared our Ex 12:27
he and all his servants and all the **E**. Ex 12:30
The **E** were urgent with the people to Ex 12:33
they had asked the **E** for silver and gold Ex 12:35
the people favor in the sight of the **E**, Ex 12:36
they asked. Thus they plundered the **E**. Ex 12:36
and the **E** shall know that I am the Ex 14:4
The **E** pursued them, all Pharaoh's Ex 14:9
the **E** were marching after them, Ex 14:10
us alone that we may serve the **E**'? Ex 14:12
for us to serve the **E** than to die in the Ex 14:12
For the **E** whom you see today, you Ex 14:13
the hearts of the **E** so that they shall Ex 14:17
And the **E** shall know that I am the Ex 14:18
The **E** pursued and went in after them Ex 14:23
And the **E** said, "Let us flee from before Ex 14:25
the LORD fights for them against the **E**." Ex 14:25
the water may come back upon the **E**, Ex 14:26
appeared. And as the **E** fled into it, Ex 14:27
the LORD threw the **E** into the midst of Ex 14:27
Israel that day from the hand of the **E**, Ex 14:30
and Israel saw the **E** dead on the Ex 14:30
power that the LORD used against the **E**, Ex 14:31
the diseases on you that I put on the **E**, Ex 15:26
to Pharaoh and to the **E** for Israel's sake, Ex 18:8
delivered them out of the hand of the **E**. Ex 18:9
of the hand of the **E** and out of the hand Ex 18:10
people from under the hand of the **E**. Ex 18:10
yourselves have seen what I did to the **E**, Ex 19:4
Why should the **E** say, 'With evil Ex 32:12
to the LORD, "Then the **E** will hear of it, Nm 14:13
And the **E** dealt harshly with us and Nm 20:15
triumphantly in the sight of all the **E**, Nm 33:3
while the **E** were burying all their Nm 33:4
And the **E** treated us harshly and Dt 26:6
And the **E** pursued your fathers with Jos 24:6
between you and the **E** and made the sea Jos 24:7
from the hand of the **E** and from the hand Jgs 6:9
save you from the **E** and from the Jgs 10:11
gods who struck the **E** with every sort 1 Sm 4:8
hearts as the **E** and Pharaoh hardened 1 Sm 6:6
the hand of the **E** and from the hand 1 Sm 10:18
into Egypt, and the **E** oppressed them, 1 Sm 12:8
the Ammonites, the Moabites, the **E**, Ezr 9:1
up their staff against you as the **E** did. Is 10:24
the heart of the **E** will melt within them. Is 19:1
And I will stir up **E** against Egyptians, Is 19:2
And I will stir up Egyptians against **E**, Is 19:2
and the spirit of the **E** within them will be Is 19:3
I will give over the **E** into the hand of a Is 19:4
In that day the **E** will be like women, Is 19:16
of Judah will become a terror to the **E**. Is 19:17
LORD will make himself known to the **E**, Is 19:21
and the **E** will know the LORD in that day Is 19:21
and the **E** will worship with the Is 19:23
The **E** are man, and not God, and their Is 31:3
You also played the whore with the **E**, Ezk 16:26
when the **E** handled your bosom and Ezk 23:21
I will scatter the **E** among the nations, Ezk 29:12
I will gather the **E** from the peoples Ezk 29:13
I will scatter the **E** among the nations Ezk 30:23
I will scatter the **E** among the nations Ezk 30:26
instructed in all the wisdom of the **E**, Acts 7:22
Red Sea as if on dry land, but the **E**, Heb 11:29

EHI (1)
Ashbel, Gera, Naaman, **E**, Rosh, Gn 46:21

EHUD (11)
for them a deliverer, **E**, the son of Gera, Jgs 3:15
And **E** made for himself a sword with Jgs 3:16
And when **E** had finished presenting the Jgs 3:18
And **E** came to him as he was sitting Jgs 3:20
in his cool roof chamber. And **E** said, Jgs 3:20
And **E** reached with his left hand, took Jgs 3:21
Then **E** went out into the porch and Jgs 3:23
E escaped while they delayed, and he Jgs 3:26
evil in the sight of the LORD after **E** died. Jgs 4:1
Jeush, Benjamin, **E**, Chenaanah, 1 Chr 7:10
are the sons of **E** (they were heads of 1 Chr 8:6

EIGHT (34)
He who is **e** days old among you shall Gn 17:12
his son Isaac when he was **e** days old, Gn 21:4
These **e** Milcah bore to Nahor, Gn 22:23
And there shall be **e** frames, with their Ex 26:25
There were **e** frames with their bases of Ex 36:30
And four wagons and **e** oxen he gave to Nm 7:8
"On the sixth day **e** bulls, two rams, Nm 29:29
Israel served Cushan-rishathaim **e** years. Jgs 3:8
donkeys, and he judged Israel **e** years. Jgs 12:14
Judah, named Jesse, who had **e** sons. 1 Sm 17:12
his spear against **e** hundred whom he 2 Sm 23:8
stones, stones of **e** and ten cubits. 1 Kgs 7:10
and he reigned **e** years in Jerusalem. 2 Kgs 8:17
Josiah was **e** years old when he began 2 Kgs 22:1
Eleazar, and **e** of the sons of Ithamar. 1 Chr 24:4
and he reigned **e** years in Jerusalem. 2 Chr 21:5
and he reigned **e** years in Jerusalem. 2 Chr 21:20
Then for **e** days they consecrated 2 Chr 29:17
Josiah was **e** years old when he began 2 Chr 34:1
Jehoiachin was **e** years old when he 2 Chr 36:9
Give a portion to seven, or even to **e**, for Eccl 11:2
escaped from Johanan with **e** men, Jer 41:15
the vestibule of the gateway, **e** cubits; Ezk 40:9
its jambs, and its stairway had **e** steps. Ezk 40:31
side, and its stairway had **e** steps. Ezk 40:34
side, and its stairway had **e** steps. Ezk 40:37
were on either side of the gate, **e** tables, Ezk 40:41
seven shepherds and **e** princes of men; Mi 5:5
And at the end of **e** days, when he was Lk 2:21
Now about **e** days after these sayings he Lk 9:28
E days later, his disciples were inside Jn 20:26
named Aeneas, bedridden for **e** years, Acts 9:33
them not more than **e** or ten days, Acts 25:6
in which a few, that is, **e** persons, 1 Pt 3:20

EIGHTEEN (12)
served Eglon the king of Moab **e** years. Jgs 3:14
For **e** years they oppressed all the people Jgs 10:8
E thousand men of Benjamin fell, all of Jgs 20:44
E cubits was the height of one pillar, 1 Kgs 7:15
Jehoiachin was **e** years old when he 2 Kgs 24:8
height of the one pillar was **e** cubits, 2 Kgs 25:17
had sons and brothers, able men, **e**. 1 Chr 26:9
concubines (he took **e** wives and 2 Chr 11:21
the height of the one pillar was **e** cubits, Jer 52:21
Or those **e** on whom the tower in Siloam Lk 13:4
had had a disabling spirit for **e** years. Lk 13:11
whom Satan bound for **e** years, Lk 13:16

EIGHTEENTH (11)
Now in the **e** year of King Jeroboam 1 Kgs 15:1
In the **e** year of Jehoshaphat king of 2 Kgs 3:1
In the **e** year of King Josiah, the king 2 Kgs 22:3
But in the **e** year of King Josiah this 2 Kgs 23:23
to Hezir, the **e** to Happizzez, 1 Chr 24:15
to the **e**, to Hanani, his sons and his 1 Chr 25:25
In the **e** year of King Jeroboam, 2 Chr 13:1
Now in the **e** year of his reign, when 2 Chr 34:8
In the **e** year of the reign of Josiah 2 Chr 35:19
which was the **e** year of Jer 32:1
in the **e** year of Nebuchadnezzar he Jer 52:29

EIGHTH (36)
on the **e** day you shall give it to me. Ex 22:30
On the **e** day Moses called Aaron and his Lv 9:1
And on the **e** day the flesh of his foreskin Lv 12:3
"And on the **e** day he shall take two Lv 14:10
And on the **e** day he shall bring them Lv 14:23
And on the **e** day he shall take two Lv 15:14
And on the **e** day she shall take two Lv 15:29
and from the **e** day on it shall be Lv 22:27
On the **e** day you shall hold a holy Lv 23:36
and on the **e** day shall be a solemn rest. Lv 23:39
When you sow in the **e** year, you will Lv 25:22
On the **e** day he shall bring two Nm 6:10
On the **e** day Gamaliel the son of Nm 7:54
"On the **e** day you shall have a solemn Nm 29:35
month of Bul, which is the **e** month, 1 Kgs 6:38
On the **e** day he sent the people away, 1 Kgs 8:66
fifteenth day of the **e** month like the 1 Kgs 12:32
on the fifteenth day in the **e** month, 1 Kgs 12:33
him prisoner in the **e** year of his 2 Kgs 24:12
Johanan **e**, Elzabad ninth, 1 Chr 12:12
seventh to Hakkoz, the **e** to Abijah, 1 Chr 24:10
the **e** to Jeshaiah, his sons and his 1 Chr 25:15
Issachar the seventh, Peullethai the **e**, 1 Chr 26:5
E, for the eighth month, was 1 Chr 27:11
Eighth, for the **e** month, was 1 Chr 27:11
And on the **e** day they held a solemn 2 Chr 7:9
and on the **e** day of the month they 2 Chr 29:17
For in the **e** year of his reign, while he 2 Chr 34:3
and on the **e** day there was a solemn Neh 8:18
then from the **e** day onward the priests Ezk 43:27
In the **e** month, in the second year of Zec 1:1
And on the **e** day they came to Lk 1:59
and circumcised him on the **e** day, Acts 7:8
circumcised on the **e** day, of the people Phil 3:5
not, it is an **e** but it belongs to the seven, Rv 17:11
the seventh chrysolite, the **e** beryl, Rv 21:20

EIGHTIETH (1)
the four hundred and **e** year after the 1 Kgs 6:1

EIGHTY (11)
Now Moses was **e** years old, and Aaron Ex 7:7
Israel. And the land had rest for **e** years. Jgs 3:30
was a very aged man, **e** years old. 2 Sm 19:32
I am this day **e** years old. Can I 2 Sm 19:35
head was sold for **e** shekels of silver, 2 Kgs 6:25
Jehu had stationed **e** men outside 2 Kgs 10:24
with **e** priests of the LORD who were 2 Chr 26:17
seventy, or even by reason of strength **e**; Ps 90:10
There are sixty queens and **e** concubines, Sg 6:8
e men arrived from Shechem and Shiloh Jer 41:5
said to him, 'Take your bill, and write **e**.' Lk 16:7

EIGHTY-FIVE (3)
now, behold, I am this day **e** years old. Jos 14:10
on that day **e** persons who wore 1 Sm 22:18
down a hundred and **e** thousand in the Is 37:36

EIGHTY-FOUR (1)
and then as a widow until she was **e**. She Lk 2:37

EIGHTY-SIX (1)
Abram was **e** years old when Hagar Gn 16:16

EIGHTY-THREE (1)
eighty years old, and Aaron **e** years old, Ex 7:7

EITHER (61)
say anything to Jacob, **e** good or bad." Gn 31:24
say anything to Jacob, **e** good or bad.' Gn 31:29
e in the past or since you have spoken to Ex 4:10
of the people of Israel, **e** man or beast, Ex 11:7
her who bears a child, **e** male or female. Lv 12:7
wool or linen, **e** in the warp or the woof, Lv 13:59
e the native or the stranger who Lv 16:29
e the native or the stranger who Lv 18:26
the priest shall value it as **e** good or bad; Lv 27:12
the priest shall value it as **e** good or bad; Lv 27:14
When **e** a man or a woman makes a Nm 6:2
the vineyards, with a wall on **e** side. Nm 22:24
was no way to turn **e** to the right or to Nm 22:26
to do **e** good or bad of my own will. Nm 24:13
to you, **e** to the right hand or to the left. Dt 17:11
e to the right hand or to the left, Dt 17:20
father does nothing **e** great or small 1 Sm 20:2
to the meal, **e** yesterday or today?" 1 Sm 20:27
did not answer him, **e** by dreams, 1 Sm 28:6
no more, **e** by prophets or by dreams. 1 Sm 28:15
E he is musing, or he is relieving 1 Kgs 18:27
and sling stones with **e** the right or 1 Chr 12:2
e three years of famine, or three 1 Chr 21:12
who has no other, **e** son or brother, Eccl 4:8
e the Asherim or the altars of incense. Is 17:8
three side rooms on **e** side of the east Ezk 40:10
and the jambs on **e** side were of the Ezk 40:10
the side rooms, one cubit on **e** side. Ezk 40:12
side rooms were six cubits on **e** side. Ezk 40:12
Its side rooms, three on **e** side, and its Ezk 40:21
palm trees on its jambs, one on **e** side. Ezk 40:26
had palm trees on its jambs, on **e** side, Ezk 40:34
had palm trees on its jambs, on **e** side, Ezk 40:37
of the gate were two tables on **e** side, Ezk 40:39
Four tables were on **e** side of the gate, Ezk 40:41
of the vestibule, five cubits on **e** side. Ezk 40:48
of the gate were three cubits on **e** side. Ezk 40:48
pillars beside the jambs, one on **e** side. Ezk 40:49
the entrance were five cubits on **e** side. Ezk 41:2
and the sidewalls on **e** side of the Ezk 41:3
at the back and its galleries on **e** side, Ezk 41:15
windows and palm trees on **e** side, Ezk 41:26
e a burnt offering or peace offerings as Ezk 46:12
Do not take an oath at all, **e** by heaven, Mt 5:34
for **e** he will hate the one and love the Mt 6:24
e in this age or in the age to come. Mt 12:32
"**E** make the tree good and its fruit Mt 12:33
cloak do not withhold your tunic **e**. Lk 6:29
It is of no use **e** for the soil or for the Lk 14:35
for **e** he will hate the one and love the Lk 16:13
and with him two others, one on **e** side, Jn 19:18
e in the temple or in the synagogues Acts 24:12
of the one whom you obey, **e** of sin, Rom 6:16
and had done nothing **e** good or bad— Rom 9:11
e by a spirit or a spoken word, 2 Thes 2:2
e by our spoken word or by our 2 Thes 2:15
without understanding **e** what they are 1 Tm 1:7
e by heaven or by earth or by any other Jas 5:12
keeps on sinning has **e** seen him or 1 Jn 3:6
hot. Would that you were **e** cold or hot! Rv 3:15
also, on **e** side of the river, the tree of life Rv 22:2

EKER (1)
of Jerahmeel: Maaz, Jamin, and **E**. 1 Chr 2:27

EKRON (24)
Egypt, northward to the boundary of **E**, Jos 13:3
Gaza, Ashdod, Ashkelon, Gath, and **E**), Jos 13:3
to the shoulder of the hill north of **E**, Jos 15:11
E, with its towns and its villages; Jos 15:45
from **E** to the sea, all that were by the Jos 15:46

Elon, Timnah, **E**, Jos 19:43
with its territory, and **E** with its territory. Jgs 1:18
So they sent the ark of God to **E**. But as 1 Sm 5:10
as soon as the ark of God came to **E**, 1 Sm 5:10
to Ekron, the people of **E** cried out, 1 Sm 5:10
saw it, they returned that day to **E**. 1 Sm 6:16
for Ashkelon, one for Gath, one for **E**, 1 Sm 6:17
were restored to Israel, from **E** to Gath, 1 Sm 7:14
as far as Gath and the gates of **E**, 1 Sm 17:52
from Shaaraim as far as Gath and **E**. 1 Sm 17:52
inquire of Baal-zebub, the god of **E**, 2 Kgs 1:2
to inquire of Baal-zebub, the god of **E**? 2 Kgs 1:3
to inquire of Baal-zebub, the god of **E**? 2 Kgs 1:6
the god of **E**—is it because there is no 2 Kgs 1:16
Gaza, **E**, and the remnant of Ashdod); Jer 25:20
I will turn my hand against **E**, and the Am 1:8
out at noon, and **E** shall be uprooted. Zep 2:4
E also, because its hopes are confounded. Zec 9:5
Judah, and **E** shall be like the Jebusites. Zec 9:7

EL-BERITH (1)
entered the stronghold of the house of **E**. Jgs 9:46

EL-BETHEL (1)
he built an altar and called the place **E**, Gn 35:7

EL-ELOHE-ISRAEL (1)
he erected an altar and called it **E**. Gn 33:20

EL-PARAN (1)
of Seir as far as **E** on the border of the Gn 14:6

ELA (1)
Shimei the son of **E**, in Benjamin; 1 Kgs 4:18

ELAH (16)
Oholibamah, **E**, Pinon, Gn 36:41
and encamped in the Valley of **E**, 1 Sm 17:2
men of Israel were in the valley of **E**, 1 Sm 17:19
you struck down in the valley of **E**, 1 Sm 21:9
and **E** his son reigned in his place. 1 Kgs 16:6
E the son of Baasha began to reign 1 Kgs 16:8
of Baasha and the sins of **E** his son, 1 Kgs 16:13
rest of the acts of **E** and all that he 1 Kgs 16:14
the son of **E** made a conspiracy 2 Kgs 15:30
Hoshea the son of **E** began to reign in 2 Kgs 17:1
In the third year of Hoshea son of **E**, 2 Kgs 18:1
the seventh year of Hoshea son of **E**, 2 Kgs 18:9
Oholibamah, **E**, Pinon, 1 Chr 1:52
son of Jephunneh: Iru, **E**, and Naam; 1 Chr 4:15
Elah, and Naam; and the son of **E**: 1 Chr 4:15
the son of Jeroham, **E** the son of Uzzi, 1 Chr 9:8

ELAM (28)
E, Asshur, Arpachshad, Lud, and Gn 10:22
of Ellasar, Chedorlaomer king of **E**, Gn 14:1
with Chedorlaomer king of **E**, Tidal Gn 14:9
E, Asshur, Arpachshad, Lud, and 1 Chr 1:17
Hananiah, **E**, Anthothijah, 1 Chr 8:24
E the fifth, Jehohanan the sixth, 1 Chr 26:3
The sons of **E**, 1,254. Ezr 2:7
The sons of the other **E**, 1,254. Ezr 2:31
Of the sons of **E**, Jeshaiah the son of Ezr 8:7
the son of Jehiel, of the sons of **E**, Ezr 10:2
Of the sons of **E**: Mattaniah, Ezr 10:26
The sons of **E**, 1,254. Neh 7:12
The sons of the other **E**, 1,254. Neh 7:34
Parosh, Pahath-moab, **E**, Zattu, Bani, Neh 10:14
Jehohanan, Malchijah, **E**, and Ezer. Neh 12:42
from Pathros, from Cush, from **E**, Is 11:11
Go up, O **E**; lay siege, O Media; all the Is 21:2
And **E** bore the quiver with chariots and Is 22:6
the kings of Zimri, all the kings of **E**, Jer 25:25
to Jeremiah the prophet concerning **E**, Jer 49:34
"Behold, I will break the bow of **E**, the Jer 49:35
I will bring upon **E** the four winds from Jer 49:36
those driven out of **E** shall not come. Jer 49:36
I will terrify **E** before their enemies and Jer 49:37
set my throne in **E** and destroy their Jer 49:38
days I will restore the fortunes of **E**, Jer 49:39
"**E** is there, and all her multitude Ezk 32:24
the capital, which is in the province of **E**. Dn 8:2

ELAMITES (2)
the men of Susa, that is, the **E**, Ezr 4:9
and Medes and **E** and residents of Acts 2:9

ELAPSED (1)
When two years had **e**, Felix was Acts 24:27

ELASAH (2)
Ishmael, Nethanel, Jozabad, and **E**. Ezr 10:22
sent by the hand of **E** the son of Shaphan Jer 29:3

ELATED (2)
from being too **e** by the surpassing 2 Cor 12:7
me, to keep me from being too **e**. 2 Cor 12:7

ELATH (5)
the Arabah road from **E** and Ezion-geber. Dt 2:8
He built **E** and restored it to Judah, 2 Kgs 14:22
of Syria recovered **E** for Syria and 2 Kgs 16:6
and drove the men of Judah from **E**, 2 Kgs 16:6
Elath, and the Edomites came to **E**, 2 Kgs 16:6

ELDAAH (2)
Ephah, Epher, Hanoch, Abida, and **E**. Gn 25:4
Ephah, Epher, Hanoch, Abida, and **E**. 1 Chr 1:33

ELDAD (2)
remained in the camp, one named **E**, Nm 11:26
"**E** and Medad are prophesying in the Nm 11:27

ELDER (12)
of Eber, the **e** brother of Japheth, Gn 10:21
"Here is my **e** daughter Merab. 1 Sm 18:17
and the prophet, the diviner and the **e**, Is 3:2
the youth will be insolent to the **e**, and the Is 3:5
the **e** and honored man is the head, and Is 9:15
And your **e** sister is Samaria, who Ezk 16:46
sisters, both your **e** and your younger, Ezk 16:61
the name of the **e** and Oholibah the Ezk 23:4
a charge against an **e** except on the 1 Tm 5:19
as a fellow **e** and a witness of the 1 Pt 5:1
The **e** to the elect lady and her children, 2 Jn 1:1
The **e** to the beloved Gaius, whom I love 3 Jn 1:1

ELDERLY (1)
shall be taken, the **e** and the very aged. Jer 6:11

ELDERS (188)
of Pharaoh, the **e** of his household, Gn 50:7
and all the **e** of the land of Egypt, Gn 50:7
Go and gather the **e** of Israel together and Ex 3:16
and you and the **e** of Israel shall go to the Ex 3:18
gathered together all the **e** of the people of Ex 4:29
Moses called all the **e** of Israel and said Ex 12:21
taking with you some of the **e** of Israel, Ex 17:5
did so, in the sight of the **e** of Israel. Ex 17:6
came with all the **e** of Israel to eat Ex 18:12
came and called the **e** of the people and Ex 19:7
and Abihu, and seventy of the **e** of Israel, Ex 24:1
and seventy of the **e** of Israel went up, Ex 24:9
And he said to the **e**, "Wait here for us Ex 24:14
And the **e** of the congregation shall lay Lv 4:15
Aaron and his sons and the **e** of Israel, Lv 9:1
for me seventy men of the **e** of Israel, Nm 11:16
you know to be the **e** of the people and Nm 11:16
seventy men of the **e** of the people and Nm 11:24
on him and put it on the seventy **e**. Nm 11:25
And Moses and the **e** of Israel returned Nm 11:30
and the **e** of Israel followed him. Nm 16:25
And Moab said to the **e** of Midian, Nm 22:4
So the **e** of Moab and the elders of Nm 22:7
of Moab and the **e** of Midian departed Nm 22:7
all the heads of your tribes, and your **e**. Dt 5:23
then the **e** of his city shall send and take Dt 19:12
then your **e** and your judges shall come Dt 21:2
And the **e** of the city that is nearest to the Dt 21:3
And the **e** of that city shall bring the Dt 21:4
And all the **e** of that city nearest to the Dt 21:6
bring him out to the **e** of his city at the Dt 21:19
and they shall say to the **e** of his city, Dt 21:20
of her virginity to the **e** of the city in the Dt 22:15
of the young woman shall say to the **e**, Dt 22:16
spread the cloak before the **e** of the city. Dt 22:17
Then the **e** of that city shall take the Dt 22:18
shall go up to the gate to the **e** and say, Dt 25:7
Then the **e** of his city shall call him and Dt 25:8
the presence of the **e** and pull his sandal Dt 25:9
Moses and the **e** of Israel commanded Dt 27:1
the heads of your tribes, your **e**, and Dt 29:10
of the LORD, and to all the **e** of Israel. Dt 31:9
to me all the **e** of your tribes and Dt 31:28
father, and he will show you, your **e**, Dt 32:7
until the evening, he and the **e** of Israel. Jos 7:6
and went up, he and the **e** of Israel, Jos 8:10
with their **e** and officers and their Jos 8:33
So our **e** and all the inhabitants of our Jos 9:11
and explain his case to the **e** of that city. Jos 20:4
summoned all Israel, its **e** and heads, Jos 23:2
Israel to Shechem and summoned the **e**, Jos 24:1
the days of the **e** who outlived Joshua Jos 24:31
all the days of the **e** who outlived Joshua, Jgs 2:7
for him the officials and **e** of Succoth, Jgs 8:14
And he took the **e** of the city, and he took Jgs 8:16
the **e** of Gilead went to bring Jephthah Jgs 11:5
But Jephthah said to the **e** of Gilead, "Did Jgs 11:7
And the **e** of Gilead said to Jephthah, Jgs 11:8
Jephthah said to the **e** of Gilead, "If you Jgs 11:9
And the **e** of Gilead said to Jephthah, Jgs 11:10
So Jephthah went with the **e** of Gilead, Jgs 11:11
Then the **e** of the congregation said, Jgs 21:16
took ten men of the **e** of the city and said, Ru 4:2
and in the presence of the **e** of my people.' Ru 4:4
Then Boaz said to the **e** and all the people, Ru 4:9
who were at the gate and the **e** said, Ru 4:11
came to the camp, the **e** of Israel said, 1 Sm 4:3
Then all the **e** of Israel gathered 1 Sm 8:4
The **e** of Jabesh said to him, "Give us 1 Sm 11:3
me now before the **e** of my people 1 Sm 15:30
The **e** of the city came to meet him 1 Sm 16:4
the spoil to his friends, the **e** of Judah, 1 Sm 30:26
Abner conferred with the **e** of Israel, 2 Sm 3:17
So all the **e** of Israel came to the king at 2 Sm 5:3
And the **e** of his house stood beside 2 Sm 12:17
eyes of Absalom and all the **e** of Israel. 2 Sm 17:4
counsel Absalom and the **e** of Israel, 2 Sm 17:15
the priests, "Say to the **e** of Judah, 2 Sm 19:11
Solomon assembled the **e** of Israel and 1 Kgs 8:1
And all the **e** of Israel came, and the 1 Kgs 8:3
Israel called all the **e** of the land and 1 Kgs 20:7
And all the **e** and all the people said to 1 Kgs 20:8
the letters to the **e** and the leaders who 1 Kgs 21:8
the **e** and the leaders who lived in his 1 Kgs 21:11
and the **e** were sitting with him. 2 Kgs 6:32
arrived Elisha said to the **e**, 2 Kgs 6:32
to the rulers of the city, to the **e**, 2 Kgs 10:1
together with the **e** and the guardians, 2 Kgs 10:5
and all the **e** of Judah and Jerusalem 2 Kgs 23:1
So all the **e** of Israel came to the king 1 Chr 11:3
So David and the **e** of Israel and the 1 Chr 15:25
Then David and the **e**, clothed in 1 Chr 21:16
Solomon assembled the **e** of Israel and 2 Chr 5:2
And all the **e** of Israel came, and the 2 Chr 5:4
together all the **e** of Judah and 2 Chr 34:29
eye of their God was on the **e** of the Jews, Ezr 5:5
Then we asked those **e** and spoke to them Ezr 5:9
of the Jews and the **e** of the Jews rebuild Ezr 6:7
you shall do for these **e** of the Jews for the Ezr 6:8
And the **e** of the Jews built and Ezr 6:14
the officials and the **e** all his property Ezr 10:8
and with them the **e** and judges of Ezr 10:14
takes away the discernment of the **e**. Jb 12:20
pleasure and to teach his **e** wisdom. Ps 105:22
praise him in the assembly of the **e**. Ps 107:32
when he sits among the **e** of the land. Prv 31:23
into judgment with the **e** and princes of Is 3:14
and his glory will be before his **e**. Is 24:23
and take some of the **e** of the people and Jer 19:1
people and some of the **e** of the priests, Jer 19:1
And certain of the **e** of the land arose Jer 26:17
Jerusalem to the surviving **e** of the exiles, Jer 29:1
my priests and **e** perished in the city, Lam 1:19
The **e** of the daughter of Zion sit on the Lam 2:10
shown to the priests, no favor to the **e**. Lam 4:16
hands; no respect is shown to the **e**. Lam 5:12
from the priest and counsel from the **e**. Ezk 7:26
with the **e** of Judah sitting before me, Ezk 8:1
seventy men of the **e** of the house of Ezk 8:11
have you seen what the **e** of the house of Ezk 8:12
they began with the **e** who were before Ezk 9:6
Then certain of the **e** of Israel came to Ezk 14:1
certain of the **e** of Israel came to inquire Ezk 20:1
"Son of man, speak to the **e** of Israel, Ezk 20:3
The **e** of Gebal and her skilled men Ezk 27:9
Hear this, you **e**; give ear, all inhabitants of Jl 1:2
Gather the **e** and all the inhabitants of the Jl 1:14
the congregation; assemble the **e**; Jl 2:16
disciples break the tradition of the **e**? Mt 15:2
things from the **e** and chief priests Mt 16:21
chief priests and the **e** of the people Mt 21:23
chief priests and the **e** of the people Mt 26:3
the chief priests and the **e** of the people. Mt 26:47
the scribes and the **e** had gathered. Mt 26:57
chief priests and the **e** of the people took Mt 27:1
of silver to the chief priests and the **e**, Mt 27:3
was accused by the chief priests and **e**, Mt 27:12
priests and the **e** persuaded the crowd Mt 27:20
the chief priests, with the scribes and **e**, Mt 27:41
assembled with the **e** and taken Mt 28:12
hands, holding to the tradition of the **e**, Mk 7:3
walk according to the tradition of the **e**, Mk 7:5
be rejected by the **e** and the chief priests Mk 8:31
and the scribes and the **e** came to him, Mk 11:27
chief priests and the scribes and the **e**. Mk 14:43
chief priests and the **e** and the scribes Mk 14:53
consultation with the **e** and scribes and Mk 15:1
about Jesus, he sent to him **e** of the Jews, Lk 7:3
be rejected by the **e** and chief priests and Lk 9:22
and the scribes with the **e** came up Lk 20:1
priests and officers of the temple and **e**, Lk 22:52
the assembly of the **e** of the people Lk 22:66
their rulers and **e** and scribes gathered Acts 4:5
said to them, "Rulers of the people and **e**, Acts 4:8
chief priests and the **e** had said to Acts 4:23
up the people and the **e** and the scribes, Acts 6:12
sending it to the **e** by the hand of Acts 11:30
they had appointed **e** for them in Acts 14:23
apostles and the **e** about this question. Acts 15:2
the church and the apostles and the **e**, Acts 15:4
apostles and the **e** were gathered Acts 15:6
seemed good to the apostles and the **e**, Acts 15:22
brothers, both the apostles and the **e**, Acts 15:23
by the apostles and **e** who were in Acts 16:4

and called the **e** of the church — Acts 20:17
us to James, and all the **e** were present. — Acts 21:18
the whole council of **e** can bear me — Acts 22:5
to the chief priests and **e** and said, — Acts 23:14
down with some **e** and a spokesman, — Acts 24:1
chief priests and the **e** of the Jews laid — Acts 25:15
the council of **e** laid their hands — 1 Tm 4:14
Let the **e** who rule well be considered — 1 Tm 5:17
and appoint **e** in every town as I directed — Ti 1:5
Let him call for the **e** of the church, and — Jas 5:14
So I exhort the **e** among you, as a fellow — 1 Pt 5:1
you who are younger, be subject to the **e**. — 1 Pt 5:5
seated on the thrones were twenty-four **e**, — Rv 4:4
the twenty-four **e** fall down before him — Rv 4:10
And one of the **e** said to me, "Weep no — Rv 5:5
creatures and among the **e** I saw a Lamb — Rv 5:6
and the twenty-four **e** fell down before — Rv 5:8
living creatures and the **e** the voice of — Rv 5:11
"Amen!" and the **e** fell down and — Rv 5:14
throne and around the **e** and the four — Rv 7:11
Then one of the **e** addressed me, saying, — Rv 7:13
And the twenty-four **e** who sit on their — Rv 11:16
four living creatures and before the **e**. — Rv 14:3
And the twenty-four **e** and the four — Rv 19:4

ELDEST (3)
beginning with the **e** and ending with — Gn 44:12
youngest. The three **e** followed Saul, — 1 Sm 17:14
Now Eliab his **e** brother heard when — 1 Sm 17:28

ELEAD (1)
Shuthelah his son, and Ezer and **E**, — 1 Chr 7:21

ELEADAH (1)
his son, Tahath his son, **E** his son, — 1 Chr 7:20

ELEALEH (5)
Jazer, Nimrah, Heshbon, **E**, Sebam, — Nm 32:3
built Heshbon, **E**, Kiriathaim, — Nm 32:37
Heshbon and **E** cry out; their voice is — Is 15:4
you with my tears, O Heshbon and **E**; — Is 16:9
"From the outcry at Heshbon even to **E**, — Jer 48:34

ELEASAH (4)
fathered Helez, and Helez fathered **E**. — 1 Chr 2:39
E fathered Sismai, and Sismai — 1 Chr 2:40
Raphah was his son, **E** his son, Azel — 1 Chr 8:37
and Rephaiah was his son, **E** his son, — 1 Chr 9:43

ELEAZAR (74)
him Nadab, Abihu, **E**, and Ithamar. — Ex 6:23
E, Aaron's son, took as his wife one of — Ex 6:25
sons, Nadab and Abihu, **E** and Ithamar. — Ex 28:1
to Aaron and to **E** and Ithamar his sons, — Lv 10:6
spoke to Aaron and to **E** and Ithamar, — Lv 10:12
And he was angry with **E** and Ithamar, — Lv 10:16
firstborn, and Abihu, **E**, and Ithamar. — Nm 3:2
So **E** and Ithamar served as priests in the — Nm 3:4
And **E** the son of Aaron the priest was — Nm 3:32
"And **E** the son of Aaron the priest — Nm 4:16
"Tell **E** the son of Aaron the priest to — Nm 16:37
So **E** the priest took the bronze — Nm 16:39
And you shall give it to **E** the priest, — Nm 19:3
And **E** the priest shall take some of its — Nm 19:4
Take Aaron and **E** his son and bring — Nm 20:25
garments and put them on **E** his son. — Nm 20:26
garments and put them on **E** his son. — Nm 20:28
Then Moses and **E** came down from — Nm 20:28
When Phinehas the son of **E**, son of — Nm 25:7
"Phinehas the son of **E**, son of Aaron — Nm 25:11
to Moses and to **E** the son of Aaron, — Nm 26:1
And Moses and **E** the priest spoke with — Nm 26:3
born Nadab, Abihu, **E**, and Ithamar. — Nm 26:60
those listed by Moses and **E** the priest, — Nm 26:63
Moses and before **E** the priest and — Nm 27:2
him stand before **E** the priest and — Nm 27:19
And he shall stand before **E** the priest, — Nm 27:21
him stand before **E** the priest and — Nm 27:22
with Phinehas the son of **E** the priest, — Nm 31:6
the spoil to Moses, and to **E** the priest, — Nm 31:12
Moses and **E** the priest and all the — Nm 31:13
Then **E** the priest said to the men in — Nm 31:21
you and **E** the priest and the heads of — Nm 31:26
half and give it to **E** the priest as a — Nm 31:29
And Moses and **E** the priest did as the — Nm 31:31
for the LORD, to **E** the priest, — Nm 31:41
And Moses and **E** the priest received — Nm 31:51
And Moses and **E** the priest received — Nm 31:54
said to Moses and to **E** the priest and to — Nm 32:2
concerning them to **E** the priest and — Nm 32:28
E the priest and Joshua the son of — Nm 34:17
And his son **E** ministered as priest in his — Dt 10:6
which **E** the priest and Joshua the son of — Jos 14:1
They approached **E** the priest and — Jos 17:4
the inheritances that **E** the priest and — Jos 19:51
of the Levites came to **E** the priest and to — Jos 21:1
Gilead, Phinehas the son of **E** the priest, — Jos 22:13
Phinehas the son of **E** the priest said to — Jos 22:31
Then Phinehas the son of **E** the priest, — Jos 22:32
And **E** the son of Aaron died, and they — Jos 24:33
and Phinehas the son of **E**, son of — Jgs 20:28
consecrated his son **E** to have charge — 1 Sm 7:1
three mighty men was **E** the son of — 2 Sm 23:9
Nadab, Abihu, **E**, and Ithamar. — 1 Chr 6:3
E fathered Phinehas, Phinehas — 1 Chr 6:4
E his son, Phinehas his son, Abishua — 1 Chr 6:50
Phinehas the son of **E** was the chief — 1 Chr 9:20
three mighty men was **E** the son of — 1 Chr 11:12
The sons of Mahli: **E** and Kish. — 1 Chr 23:21
E died having no sons, but only — 1 Chr 23:22
Nadab, Abihu, **E**, and Ithamar. — 1 Chr 24:1
so **E** and Ithamar became the priests. — 1 Chr 24:2
the help of Zadok of the sons of **E**, — 1 Chr 24:3
among the sons of **E** than among the — 1 Chr 24:4
of fathers' houses of the sons of **E**, — 1 Chr 24:4
both the sons of **E** and the sons of — 1 Chr 24:5
being chosen for **E** and one chosen — 1 Chr 24:6
Of Mahli: **E**, who had no sons. — 1 Chr 24:28
of Abishua, son of Phinehas, son of **E**, — Ezr 7:5
and with him was **E** the son of — Ezr 8:33
Malchijah, Mijamin, **E**, Hashabiah, — Ezr 10:25
and Maaseiah, Shemaiah, **E**, Uzzi, — Neh 12:42
and Eliud the father of **E**, and Eleazar — Mt 1:15
of Eleazar, and **E** the father of Matthan, — Mt 1:15

ELECT (13)
for the sake of the **e** those days will be — Mt 24:22
as to lead astray, if possible, even the **e**. — Mt 24:24
they will gather his **e** from the four — Mt 24:31
But for the sake of the **e**, whom he — Mk 13:20
to lead astray, if possible, the **e**. — Mk 13:22
angels and gather his **e** from the four — Mk 13:27
And will not God give justice to his **e**, — Lk 18:7
bring any charge against God's **e**? — Rom 8:33
The **e** obtained it, but the rest were — Rom 11:7
Jesus and of the **e** angels I charge you — 1 Tm 5:21
everything for the sake of the **e**, — 2 Tm 2:10
the faith of God's **e** and their knowledge of — Ti 1:1
To those who are **e** exiles of the — 1 Pt 1:1
The elder to the **e** lady and her children, — 2 Jn 1:1
The children of your **e** sister greet you. — 2 Jn 1:13

ELECTION (3)
God's purpose of **e** might continue, — Rom 9:11
But as regards **e**, they are beloved for — Rom 11:28
to make your calling and **e** sure, — 2 Pt 1:10

ELEMENTAL (2)
according to the **e** spirits of the world, — Col 2:8
you died to the **e** spirits of the world, — Col 2:20

ELEMENTARY (3)
were enslaved to the **e** principles of the — Gal 4:3
weak and worthless **e** principles of the — Gal 4:9
let us leave the **e** doctrine of Christ and — Heb 6:1

ELEVATION (1)
beautiful in **e**, is the joy of all the earth, — Ps 48:2

ELEVEN (20)
female servants, and his **e** children, — Gn 32:22
and **e** stars were bowing down to me." — Gn 37:9
tabernacle; **e** curtains shall you make. — Ex 26:7
The **e** curtains shall be the same size. — Ex 26:8
the tabernacle. He made **e** curtains. — Ex 36:14
The **e** curtains were the same size. — Ex 36:15
"On the third day **e** bulls, two rams, — Nm 29:20
It is **e** days' journey from Horeb by the — Dt 1:2
and Giloh: **e** cities with their villages. — Jos 15:51
and he reigned **e** years in Jerusalem. — 2 Kgs 23:36
and he reigned **e** years in Jerusalem. — 2 Kgs 24:18
and he reigned **e** years in Jerusalem. — 2 Chr 36:5
and he reigned **e** years in Jerusalem. — 2 Chr 36:11
and he reigned **e** years in Jerusalem. — Jer 52:1
Now the **e** disciples went to Galilee, to — Mt 28:16
he appeared to the **e** themselves as they — Mk 16:14
all these things to the **e** and to all the — Lk 24:9
And they found the **e** and those who — Lk 24:33
he was numbered with the **e** apostles. — Acts 1:26
But Peter, standing with the **e**, lifted up — Acts 2:14

ELEVENTH (20)
On the **e** day Pagiel the son of Ochran, — Nm 7:72
year, on the first day of the **e** month, — Dt 1:3
And in the **e** year, in the month of — 1 Kgs 6:38
In the **e** year of Joram the son of — 2 Kgs 9:29
was besieged till the **e** year of King — 2 Kgs 25:2
Jeremiah tenth, Machbannai **e**. — 1 Chr 12:13
the **e** to Eliashib, the twelfth to — 1 Chr 24:12
the **e** to Azarel, his sons and his — 1 Chr 25:18
E, for the eleventh month, was — 1 Chr 27:14
Eleventh, for the **e** month, was — 1 Chr 27:14
until the end of the **e** year of Zedekiah, — Jer 1:3
In the **e** year of Zedekiah, in the fourth — Jer 39:2
was besieged till the **e** year of King — Jer 52:5
In the **e** year, on the first day of the — Ezk 26:1
In the **e** year, in the first month, on the — Ezk 30:20
In the **e** year, in the third month, on the — Ezk 31:1
On the twenty-fourth day of the **e** month, — Zec 1:7
And about the **e** hour he went out and — Mt 20:6
those hired about the **e** hour came, — Mt 20:9
the tenth chrysoprase, the **e** jacinth, — Rv 21:20

ELHANAN (4)
Gob, and **E** the son of Jaare-oregim, — 2 Sm 21:19
E the son of Dodo of Bethlehem, — 2 Sm 23:24
E the son of Dodo of Bethlehem, — 1 Chr 11:26
and **E** the son of Jair struck down — 1 Chr 20:5

ELI (36)
at Shiloh, where the two sons of **E**, — 1 Sm 1:3
Now **E** the priest was sitting on the seat — 1 Sm 1:9
the LORD, **E** observed her mouth. — 1 Sm 1:12
Therefore **E** took her to be a drunken — 1 Sm 1:13
And **E** said to her, "How long will you — 1 Sm 1:14
Then **E** answered, "Go in peace, and — 1 Sm 1:17
bull, and they brought the child to **E**. — 1 Sm 1:25
LORD in the presence of **E** the priest. — 1 Sm 2:11
the sons of **E** were worthless men. — 1 Sm 2:12
Then **E** would bless Elkanah and his — 1 Sm 2:20
Now **E** was very old, and he kept — 1 Sm 2:22
a man of God to **E** and said to him, — 1 Sm 2:27
was ministering to the LORD under **E**. — 1 Sm 3:1
At that time **E**, whose eyesight had — 1 Sm 3:2
and ran to **E** and said, "Here I am, for — 1 Sm 3:5
Samuel arose and went to **E** and said, — 1 Sm 3:6
And he arose and went to **E** and said, — 1 Sm 3:8
called me." Then **E** perceived that the — 1 Sm 3:8
Therefore **E** said to Samuel, "Go, lie — 1 Sm 3:9
I will fulfill against **E** all that I have — 1 Sm 3:12
to the house of **E** that the iniquity of — 1 Sm 3:14
was afraid to tell the vision to **E**. — 1 Sm 3:15
But **E** called Samuel and said, — 1 Sm 3:16
And **E** said, "What was it that he told — 1 Sm 3:17
And the two sons of **E**, Hophni and — 1 Sm 4:4
was captured, and the two sons of **E**, — 1 Sm 4:11
E was sitting on his seat by the road — 1 Sm 4:13
When **E** heard the sound of the — 1 Sm 4:14
the man hurried and came and told **E**. — 1 Sm 4:14
Now **E** was ninety-eight years old and — 1 Sm 4:15
And the man said to **E**, "I am he who — 1 Sm 4:16
E fell over backward from his seat by — 1 Sm 4:18
brother, son of Phinehas, son of **E**, — 1 Sm 14:3
concerning the house of **E** in Shiloh. — 1 Kgs 2:27
out with a loud voice, saying, "**E**, Eli, — Mt 27:46
"Eli, **E**, lema sabachthani?" that is, — Mt 27:46

ELI'S (1)
that the iniquity of **E** house shall not — 1 Sm 3:14

ELIAB (20)
from Zebulun, **E** the son of Helon; — Nm 1:9
people of Zebulun being **E** the son of — Nm 2:7
On the third day **E** the son of Helon, the — Nm 7:24
was the offering of **E** the son of Helon. — Nm 7:29
people of Zebulun was **E** the son of — Nm 10:16
and Dathan and Abiram the sons of **E**, — Nm 16:1
Dathan and Abiram the sons of **E**, — Nm 16:12
And the sons of Pallu: **E**. — Nm 26:8
The sons of **E**: Nemuel, Dathan, and — Nm 26:9
did to Dathan and Abiram the sons of **E**, — Dt 11:6
came, he looked on **E** and thought, — 1 Sm 16:6
to the battle were **E** the firstborn, — 1 Sm 17:13
Now **E** his eldest brother heard when — 1 Sm 17:28
Jesse fathered **E** his firstborn, — 1 Chr 2:13
E his son, Jeroham his son, Elkanah — 1 Chr 6:27
the chief, Obadiah second, **E** third, — 1 Chr 12:9
Jehiel, Unni, **E**, Benaiah, — 1 Chr 15:18
Jehiel, Unni, **E**, Maaseiah, — 1 Chr 15:20
Jehiel, Mattithiah, **E**, Benaiah, — 1 Chr 16:5
Abihail the daughter of **E** the son of — 2 Chr 11:18

ELIAB'S (1)
And **E** anger was kindled against — 1 Sm 17:28

ELIADA (4)
Elishama, **E**, and Eliphelet. — 2 Sm 5:16
to him, Rezon the son of **E**, — 1 Kgs 11:23
Elishama, **E**, and Eliphelet, nine. — 1 Chr 3:8
E, a mighty man of valor, with — 2 Chr 17:17

ELIAHBA (2)
E the Shaalbonite, the sons of — 2 Sm 23:32
of Baharum, **E** the Shaalbonite, — 1 Chr 11:33

ELIAKIM (15)
came out to them **E** the son of — 2 Kgs 18:18
Then **E** the son of Hilkiah, and — 2 Kgs 18:26
Then **E** the son of Hilkiah, who was — 2 Kgs 18:37
And he sent **E**, who was over the — 2 Kgs 19:2
Pharaoh Neco made **E** the son of — 2 Kgs 23:34
of Egypt made **E** his brother king — 2 Chr 36:4
and the priests **E**, Maaseiah, — Neh 12:41
will call my servant **E** the son of — Is 22:20
came out to him **E** the son of Hilkiah, — Is 36:3
Then **E**, Shebna, and Joah said to the — Is 36:11
Then **E** the son of Hilkiah, who was over — Is 36:22

And he sent **E**, who was over the Is 37:2
of Abiud, and Abiud the father of **E**, Mt 1:13
of Eliakim, and **E** the father of Azor, Mt 1:13
of Joseph, the son of Jonam, the son of **E**, Lk 3:30

ELIAM (2)
not this Bathsheba, the daughter of **E**, 2 Sm 11:3
E the son of Ahithophel of Gilo, 2 Sm 23:34

ELIASAPH (6)
from Gad, **E** the son of Deuel; Nm 1:14
people of Gad being **E** the son of Reuel, Nm 2:14
with **E**, the son of Lael as chief of the Nm 3:24
On the sixth day **E** the son of Deuel, the Nm 7:42
was the offering of **E** the son of Deuel. Nm 7:47
people of Gad was **E** the son of Deuel. Nm 10:20

ELIASHIB (17)
Hodaviah, **E**, Pelaiah, Akkub, 1 Chr 3:24
the eleventh to **E**, the twelfth to 1 Chr 24:12
the chamber of Jehohanan the son of **E**, Ezr 10:6
Of the singers: **E**. Of the gatekeepers: Ezr 10:24
Elioenai, **E**, Mattaniah, Jeremoth, Ezr 10:27
Vaniah, Meremoth, **E**, Ezr 10:36
Then **E** the high priest rose up with his Neh 3:1
door of the house of **E** the high priest. Neh 3:20
door of the house of **E** to the end of the Neh 3:21
of Eliashib to the end of the house of **E**. Neh 3:21
of Joiakim, Joiakim the father of **E**, Neh 12:10
of Eliashib, **E** the father of Joiada, Neh 12:10
In the days of **E**, Joiada, Johanan, and Neh 12:22
until the days of Johanan the son of **E**. Neh 12:23
Now before this, **E** the priest, who was Neh 13:4
discovered the evil that **E** had done for Neh 13:7
Jehoiada, the son of **E** the high priest, Neh 13:28

ELIATHAH (2)
Hananiah, Hanani, **E**, Giddalti, 1 Chr 25:4
to the twentieth, to **E**, his sons and 1 Chr 25:27

ELIDAD (1)
of Benjamin, **E** the son of Chislon. Nm 34:21

ELIEHOENAI (2)
Jehohanan the sixth, **E** the seventh. 1 Chr 26:3
of Pahath-moab, **E** the son of Zerahiah, Ezr 8:4

ELIEL (10)
Epher, Ishi, **E**, Azriel, Jeremiah, 1 Chr 5:24
of Elkanah, son of Jeroham, son of **E**, 1 Chr 6:34
Elienai, Zillethai, **E**, 1 Chr 8:20
Ishpan, Eber, **E**, 1 Chr 8:22
E the Mahavite, and Jeribai, and 1 Chr 11:46
E, and Obed, and Jaasiel the 1 Chr 11:47
Attai sixth, **E** seventh, 1 Chr 12:11
of the sons of Hebron, **E** the chief, 1 Chr 15:9
Shemaiah, **E**, and Amminadab, 1 Chr 15:11
Jerimoth, Jozabad, **E**, Ismachiah, 2 Chr 31:13

ELIENAI (1)
E, Zillethai, Eliel, 1 Chr 8:20

ELIEZER (15)
the heir of my house is **E** of Damascus?" Gn 15:2
and the name of the other, **E** (for he said, Ex 18:4
Zemirah, Joash, **E**, Elioenai, Omri, 1 Chr 7:8
Amasai, Zechariah, Benaiah, and **E**, 1 Chr 15:24
The sons of Moses: Gershom and **E**. 1 Chr 23:15
The sons of **E**: Rehabiah the chief. 1 Chr 23:17
E had no other sons, but the sons of 1 Chr 23:17
from **E** were his son Rehabiah, and 1 Chr 26:25
E the son of Zichri was chief officer; 1 Chr 27:16
Then **E** the son of Dodavahu of 2 Chr 20:37
Then I sent for **E**, Ariel, Shemaiah, Ezr 8:16
Maaseiah, **E**, Jarib, and Gedaliah, Ezr 10:18
is, Kelita), Pethahiah, Judah, and **E**. Ezr 10:23
E, Isshijah, Malchijah, Shemaiah, Ezr 10:31
the son of Joshua, the son of **E**, the son of Lk 3:29

ELIHOREPH (1)
E and Ahijah the sons of Shisha were 1 Kgs 4:3

ELIHU (11)
Elkanah the son of Jeroham, son of **E**, 1 Sm 1:1
Michael, Jozabad, **E**, and Zillethai, 1 Chr 12:20
were able men, **E** and Semachiah. 1 Chr 26:7
Judah, **E**, one of David's brothers; 1 Chr 27:18
Then **E** the son of Barachel the Buzite, of Jb 32:2
Now **E** had waited to speak to Job Jb 32:4
And when **E** saw that there was no Jb 32:5
And **E** the son of Barachel the Buzite Jb 32:6
Then **E** answered and said: Jb 34:1
And **E** answered and said: Jb 35:1
And **E** continued, and said: Jb 36:1

ELIJAH (101)
Now **E** the Tishbite, of Tishbe in 1 Kgs 17:1
And **E** said to her, "Do not fear; go 1 Kgs 17:13
And she went and did as **E** said. And 1 Kgs 17:15
word of the LORD that he spoke by **E**. 1 Kgs 17:16
And she said to **E**, "What have you 1 Kgs 17:18
the LORD listened to the voice of **E**. 1 Kgs 17:22
And **E** took the child and brought 1 Kgs 17:23
him to his mother. And **E** said, 1 Kgs 17:23
And the woman said to **E**, "Now I 1 Kgs 17:24
days the word of the LORD came to **E**, 1 Kgs 18:1
So **E** went to show himself to Ahab. 1 Kgs 18:2
was on the way, behold, **E** met him. 1 Kgs 18:7
face and said, "Is it you, my lord **E**?" 1 Kgs 18:7
Go, tell your lord, 'Behold, **E** is here.'" 1 Kgs 18:8
tell your lord, "Behold, **E** is here."' 1 Kgs 18:11
tell your lord, "Behold, **E** is here"'; 1 Kgs 18:14
And **E** said, "As the LORD of hosts 1 Kgs 18:15
told him. And Ahab went to meet **E**. 1 Kgs 18:16
When Ahab saw **E**, Ahab said to 1 Kgs 18:17
And **E** came near to all the people 1 Kgs 18:21
Then **E** said to the people, "I, even I 1 Kgs 18:22
Then **E** said to the prophets of Baal, 1 Kgs 18:25
And at noon **E** mocked them, 1 Kgs 18:27
Then **E** said to all the people, "Come 1 Kgs 18:30
E took twelve stones, according to 1 Kgs 18:31
E the prophet came near and said, 1 Kgs 18:36
And **E** said to them, "Seize the 1 Kgs 18:40
And **E** brought them down to the 1 Kgs 18:40
And **E** said to Ahab, "Go up, eat and 1 Kgs 18:41
And **E** went up to the top of Mount 1 Kgs 18:42
And the hand of the LORD was on **E**, 1 Kgs 18:46
Ahab told Jezebel all that **E** had done, 1 Kgs 19:1
Then Jezebel sent a messenger to **E**, 1 Kgs 19:2
him, "What are you doing here, **E**?" 1 Kgs 19:9
And when **E** heard it, he wrapped his 1 Kgs 19:13
said, "What are you doing here, **E**?" 1 Kgs 19:13
E passed by him and cast his cloak 1 Kgs 19:19
the oxen and ran after **E** and said, 1 Kgs 19:20
and went after **E** and assisted him. 1 Kgs 19:21
of the LORD came to **E** the Tishbite, 1 Kgs 21:17
Ahab said to **E**, "Have you found 1 Kgs 21:20
of the LORD came to **E** the Tishbite, 1 Kgs 21:28
of the LORD said to **E** the Tishbite, 2 Kgs 1:3
but you shall surely die.'" So **E** went. 2 Kgs 1:4
And he said, "It is **E** the Tishbite." 2 Kgs 1:8
He went up to **E**, who was sitting on the 2 Kgs 1:9
But **E** answered the captain of fifty, "If 2 Kgs 1:10
But **E** answered them, "If I am a man 2 Kgs 1:12
his knees before **E** and entreated him, 2 Kgs 1:13
Then the angel of the LORD said to **E**, 2 Kgs 1:15
word of the LORD that **E** had spoken. 2 Kgs 1:17
was about to take **E** up to heaven by 2 Kgs 2:1
E and Elisha were on their way from 2 Kgs 2:1
And **E** said to Elisha, "Please stay here, 2 Kgs 2:2
E said to him, "Elisha, please stay here, 2 Kgs 2:4
Then **E** said to him, "Please stay here, 2 Kgs 2:6
Then **E** took his cloak and rolled it up 2 Kgs 2:8
they had crossed, **E** said to Elisha, 2 Kgs 2:9
And **E** went up by a whirlwind into 2 Kgs 2:11
up the cloak of **E** that had fallen from 2 Kgs 2:13
took the cloak of **E** that had fallen 2 Kgs 2:14
the God of **E**?" And when he had 2 Kgs 2:14
"The spirit of **E** rests on Elisha." And 2 Kgs 2:15
who poured water on the hands of **E**." 2 Kgs 3:11
spoke by his servant **E** the Tishbite, 2 Kgs 9:36
done what he said by his servant **E**." 2 Kgs 10:10
word of the LORD that he spoke to **E**. 2 Kgs 10:17
E, and Zichri were the sons of 1 Chr 8:27
came to him from **E** the prophet, 2 Chr 21:12
Maaseiah, **E**, Shemaiah, Jehiel, and Ezr 10:21
Jehiel, Abdi, Jeremoth, and **E**. Ezr 10:26
I will send you **E** the prophet before the Mal 4:5
to accept it, he is **E** who is to come. Mt 11:14
say John the Baptist, others say **E**, Mt 16:14
there appeared to them Moses and **E**, Mt 17:3
you and one for Moses and one for **E**." Mt 17:4
scribes say that first **E** must come?" Mt 17:10
He answered, "**E** does come, and he will Mt 17:11
But I tell you that **E** has already come, Mt 17:12
it, said, "This man is calling **E**." Mt 27:47
let us see whether **E** will come to save Mt 27:49
others said, "He is **E**." And others said, Mk 6:15
and others say, **E**; and others, one of the Mk 8:28
there appeared to them **E** with Moses, Mk 9:4
for you and one for Moses and one for **E**." Mk 9:5
the scribes say that first **E** must come?" Mk 9:11
"**E** does come first to restore all things. Mk 9:12
But I tell you that **E** has come, and they Mk 9:13
it said, "Behold, he is calling **E**." Mk 15:35
let us see whether **E** will come to take Mk 15:36
before him in the spirit and power of **E**, Lk 1:17
many widows in Israel in the days of **E**, Lk 4:25
and **E** was sent to none of them but only Lk 4:26
by some that **E** had appeared, and by Lk 9:8
But others say, **E**, and others, that one of Lk 9:19
were talking with him, Moses and **E**, Lk 9:30
Moses and one for **E**"—not knowing Lk 9:33
him, "What then? Are you **E**?" He said, Jn 1:21
if you are neither the Christ, nor **E**, Jn 1:25
not know what the Scripture says of **E**, Rom 11:2
E was a man with a nature like ours, Jas 5:17

ELIKA (1)
Shammah of Harod, **E** of Harod, 2 Sm 23:25

ELIM (6)
Then they came to **E**, where there were Ex 15:27
They set out from **E**, and all the Ex 16:1
of Sin, which is between **E** and Sinai, Ex 16:1
set out from Marah and came to **E**; Nm 33:9
at **E** there were twelve springs of water Nm 33:9
they set out from **E** and camped by Nm 33:10

ELIMELECH (6)
name of the man was **E** and the name of Ru 1:2
But **E**, the husband of Naomi, died, and Ru 1:3
husband's, a worthy man of the clan of **E**, Ru 2:1
to Boaz, who was of the clan of **E**. Ru 2:3
of land that belonged to our relative **E**. Ru 4:3
all that belonged to **E** and all that Ru 4:9

ELIOENAI (7)
E, Hizkiah, and Azrikam, three. 1 Chr 3:23
The sons of **E**: Hodaviah, Eliashib, 1 Chr 3:24
E, Jaakobah, Jeshohaiah, Asaiah, 1 Chr 4:36
Zemirah, Joash, Eliezer, **E**, Omri, 1 Chr 7:8
E, Maaseiah, Ishmael, Nethanel, Ezr 10:22
E, Eliashib, Mattaniah, Jeremoth, Ezr 10:27
Miniamin, Micaiah, **E**, Zechariah, Neh 12:41

ELIPHAL (1)
Sachar the Hararite, **E** the son of Ur, 1 Chr 11:35

ELIPHAZ (15)
bore to Esau, **E**; Basemath bore Reuel; Gn 36:4
E the son of Adah the wife of Esau, Gn 36:10
The sons of **E** were Teman, Omar, Gn 36:11
(Timna was a concubine of **E**, Esau's Gn 36:12
Esau's son; she bore Amalek to **E**.) Gn 36:12
The sons of **E** the firstborn of Esau: the Gn 36:15
these are the chiefs of **E** in the land of Gn 36:16
E, Reuel, Jeush, Jalam, and Korah. 1 Chr 1:35
The sons of **E**: Teman, Omar, Zepho, 1 Chr 1:36
from his own place, **E** the Temanite, Jb 2:11
Then **E** the Temanite answered and said: Jb 4:1
Then **E** the Temanite answered and said: Jb 15:1
Then **E** the Temanite answered and said: Jb 22:1
to Job, the LORD said to **E** the Temanite: Jb 42:7
So **E** the Temanite and Bildad the Jb 42:9

ELIPHELEHU (2)
Mattithiah, **E**, and Mikneiah, 1 Chr 15:18
but Mattithiah, **E**, Mikneiah, 1 Chr 15:21

ELIPHELET (8)
Elishama, Eliada, and **E**. 2 Sm 5:16
E the son of Ahasbai of Maacah, 2 Sm 23:34
then Ibhar, Elishama, **E**, 1 Chr 3:6
Elishama, Eliada, and **E**, nine. 1 Chr 3:8
Jeush the second, and **E** the third. 1 Chr 8:39
Elishama, Beeliada and **E**. 1 Chr 14:7
who came later, their names being **E**, Ezr 8:13
Mattattah, Zabad, **E**, Jeremai, Ezr 10:33

ELISHA (61)
and **E** the son of Shaphat of 1 Kgs 19:16
sword of Jehu shall **E** put to death. 1 Kgs 19:17
from there and found **E** the son of 1 Kgs 19:19
Elijah and **E** were on their way from 2 Kgs 2:1
And Elijah said to **E**, "Please stay here, 2 Kgs 2:2
sent me as far as Bethel." But **E** said, 2 Kgs 2:2
Bethel came out to **E** and said to him, 2 Kgs 2:3
Elijah said to him, "**E**, please stay here, 2 Kgs 2:4
Jericho drew near to **E** and said to him, 2 Kgs 2:5
they had crossed, Elijah said to **E**, 2 Kgs 2:9
I am taken from you." And **E** said, 2 Kgs 2:9
And **E** saw it and he cried, "My father, 2 Kgs 2:12
side and to the other, and **E** went over. 2 Kgs 2:14
of Elijah rests on **E**." And they came 2 Kgs 2:15
Now the men of the city said to **E**, 2 Kgs 2:19
according to the word that **E** spoke. 2 Kgs 2:22
"**E** the son of Shaphat is here, 2 Kgs 3:11
And **E** said to the king of Israel, 2 Kgs 3:13
And **E** said, "As the LORD of hosts 2 Kgs 3:14
of the sons of the prophets cried to **E**, 2 Kgs 4:1
And **E** said to her, "What shall I do for 2 Kgs 4:2
One day **E** went on to Shunem, where a 2 Kgs 4:8
following spring, as **E** had said to her. 2 Kgs 4:17
When **E** came into the house, he saw 2 Kgs 4:32
And **E** came again to Gilgal when 2 Kgs 4:38
ears of grain in his sack. And **E** said, 2 Kgs 4:42
But when **E** the man of God heard that 2 Kgs 5:8
And **E** sent a messenger to him, 2 Kgs 5:10
the servant of **E** the man of God, 2 Kgs 5:20
before his master, and **E** said to him, 2 Kgs 5:25
Now the sons of the prophets said to **E**, 2 Kgs 6:1
said, "None, my lord, O king; but **E**, 2 Kgs 6:12
Then **E** prayed and said, "O LORD, 2 Kgs 6:17
and chariots of fire all around **E**. 2 Kgs 6:17
him, **E** prayed to the LORD and said, 2 Kgs 6:18
in accordance with the prayer of **E**. 2 Kgs 6:18
And **E** said to them, "This is not the 2 Kgs 6:19

soon as they entered Samaria, **E** said, 2 Kgs 6:20
king of Israel saw them, he said to **E**, 2 Kgs 6:21
if the head of **E** the son of Shaphat 2 Kgs 6:31
E was sitting in his house, and the 2 Kgs 6:32
the messenger arrived **E** said to the 2 Kgs 6:32
But **E** said, "Hear the word of the LORD: 2 Kgs 7:1
Now **E** had said to the woman whose 2 Kgs 8:1
all the great things that **E** has done." 2 Kgs 8:4
telling the king how **E** had restored the 2 Kgs 8:5
is her son whom **E** restored to life." 2 Kgs 8:5
Now **E** came to Damascus. Ben-hadad 2 Kgs 8:7
And **E** said to him, "Go, say to him, 2 Kgs 8:10
do this great thing?" **E** answered, 2 Kgs 8:13
Then he departed from **E** and came to 2 Kgs 8:14
"What did **E** say to you?" And he 2 Kgs 8:14
Then **E** the prophet called one of the 2 Kgs 9:1
Now when **E** had fallen sick with 2 Kgs 13:14
And **E** said to him, "Take a bow and 2 Kgs 13:15
And **E** laid his hands on the king's 2 Kgs 13:16
and he opened it. Then **E** said, 2 Kgs 13:17
So **E** died, and they buried him. Now 2 Kgs 13:20
man was thrown into the grave of **E**, 2 Kgs 13:21
as the man touched the bones of **E**, 2 Kgs 13:21
in Israel in the time of the prophet **E**, Lk 4:27

ELISHA'S (1)
and stood at the door of **E** house. 2 Kgs 5:9

ELISHAH (3)
E, Tarshish, Kittim, and Dodanim. Gn 10:4
E, Tarshish, Kittim, and Rodanim. 1 Chr 1:7
from the coasts of **E** was your awning. Ezk 27:7

ELISHAMA (17)
from Ephraim, **E** the son of Ammihud, Nm 1:10
people of Ephraim being **E** the son of Nm 2:18
On the seventh day **E** the son of Nm 7:48
was the offering of **E** the son of Nm 7:53
over their company was **E** the son of Nm 10:22
E, Eliada, and Eliphelet. 2 Sm 5:16
the son of Nethaniah, son of **E**, 2 Kgs 25:25
Jekamiah, and Jekamiah fathered **E**. 1 Chr 2:41
then Ibhar, **E**, Eliphelet, 1 Chr 3:6
E, Eliada, and Eliphelet, nine. 1 Chr 3:8
his son, Ammihud his son, **E** his son, 1 Chr 7:26
E, Beeliada and Eliphelet. 1 Chr 14:7
Levites, the priests **E** and Jehoram. 2 Chr 17:8
E the secretary, Delaiah the son of Jer 36:12
in the chamber of **E** the secretary, Jer 36:20
it from the chamber of **E** the secretary. Jer 36:21
Ishmael the son of Nethaniah, son of **E**, Jer 41:1

ELISHAPHAT (1)
of Adaiah, and **E** the son of Zichri. 2 Chr 23:1

ELISHEBA (1)
Aaron took as his wife **E**, the daughter of Ex 6:23

ELISHUA (2)
Ibhar, **E**, Nepheg, Japhia, 2 Sm 5:15
Ibhar, **E**, Elpelet, 1 Chr 14:5

ELIUD (2)
of Achim, and Achim the father of **E**, Mt 1:14
and **E** the father of Eleazar, and Eleazar Mt 1:15

ELIZABETH (9)
daughters of Aaron, and her name was **E**. Lk 1:5
they had no child, because **E** was barren, Lk 1:7
and your wife **E** will bear you a son, Lk 1:13
After these days his wife **E** conceived, Lk 1:24
your relative **E** in her old age has also Lk 1:36
the house of Zechariah and greeted **E**. Lk 1:40
And when **E** heard the greeting of Mary, Lk 1:41
And **E** was filled with the Holy Spirit, Lk 1:41
Now the time came for **E** to give birth, Lk 1:57

ELIZAPHAN (4)
with **E** the son of Uzziel as chief of the Nm 3:30
a chief, **E** the son of Parnach. Nm 34:25
of the sons of **E**, Shemaiah the chief, 1 Chr 15:8
and of the sons of **E**, Shimri and 2 Chr 29:13

ELIZUR (5)
you. From Reuben, **E** the son of Shedeur; Nm 1:5
people of Reuben being **E** the son of Nm 2:10
On the fourth day **E** the son of Shedeur, Nm 7:30
was the offering of **E** the son of Nm 7:35
over their company was **E** the son of Nm 10:18

ELKANAH (20)
sons of Korah: Assir, **E**, and Abiasaph; Ex 6:24
Ephraim whose name was **E** the son of 1 Sm 1:1
On the day when **E** sacrificed, he would 1 Sm 1:4
And **E**, her husband, said to her, 1 Sm 1:8
And **E** knew Hannah his wife, and the 1 Sm 1:19
The man **E** and all his house went up 1 Sm 1:21
E her husband said to her, "Do what 1 Sm 1:23
Then **E** went home to Ramah. And 1 Sm 2:11
Then Eli would bless **E** and his wife, 1 Sm 2:20
E his son, Ebiasaph his son, Assir his 1 Chr 6:23
The sons of **E**: Amasai and Ahimoth, 1 Chr 6:25
E his son, Zophai his son, Nahath 1 Chr 6:26
his son, Jeroham his son, **E** his son. 1 Chr 6:27
son of **E**, son of Jeroham, son of Eliel, 1 Chr 6:34
son of Zuph, son of **E**, son of Mahath, 1 Chr 6:35
son of **E**, son of Joel, son of Azariah, 1 Chr 6:36
Berechiah the son of Asa, son of **E**, 1 Chr 9:16
E, Isshiah, Azarel, Joezer, and 1 Chr 12:6
Berechiah and **E** were to be 1 Chr 15:23
of the palace and **E** the next in 2 Chr 28:7

ELKOSH (1)
The book of the vision of Nahum of **E**. Na 1:1

ELLASAR (2)
king of Shinar, Arioch king of **E**, Gn 14:1
king of Shinar, and Arioch king of **E**, Gn 14:9

ELMADAM (1)
of Addi, the son of Cosam, the son of **E**, Lk 3:28

ELNAAM (1)
Jeribai, and Joshaviah, the sons of **E**, 1 Chr 11:46

ELNATHAN (7)
the daughter of **E** of Jerusalem. 2 Kgs 24:8
for Eliezer, Ariel, Shemaiah, **E**, Jarib, Ezr 8:16
Shemaiah, Elnathan, Jarib, **E**, Nathan, Ezr 8:16
leading men, and for Joiarib and **E**, Ezr 8:16
E the son of Achbor and others with Jer 26:22
son of Shemaiah, **E** the son of Achbor, Jer 36:12
Even when **E** and Delaiah and Jer 36:25

ELOI (2)
Jesus cried with a loud voice, "**E**, Eloi, Mk 15:34
E, lema sabachthani?" which means, Mk 15:34

ELON (7)
Basemath the daughter of **E** the Hittite, Gn 26:34
Adah the daughter of **E** the Hittite, Gn 36:2
sons of Zebulun: Sered, **E**, and Jahleel. Gn 46:14
of Sered, the clan of the Seredites; of **E**, Nm 26:26
E, Timnah, Ekron, Jos 19:43
After him **E** the Zebulunite judged Jgs 12:11
Then **E** the Zebulunite died and was Jgs 12:12

ELONBETH-HANAN (1)
Shaalbim, Beth-shemesh, and **E**; 1 Kgs 4:9

ELONITES (1)
the Seredites; of Elon, the clan of the **E**; Nm 26:26

ELOQUENT (3)
to the LORD, "Oh, my Lord, I am not **e**, Ex 4:10
He was an **e** man, competent in the Acts 18:24
and not with words of **e** wisdom, 1 Cor 1:17

ELOTH (3)
which is near **E** on the shore of the 1 Kgs 9:26
to Ezion-geber and **E** on the shore 2 Chr 8:17
He built **E** and restored it to Judah, 2 Chr 26:2

ELPAAL (3)
sons by Hushim: Abitub and **E**. 1 Chr 8:11
The sons of **E**: Eber, Misham, and 1 Chr 8:12
Izliah, and Jobab were the sons of **E**. 1 Chr 8:18

ELPELET (1)
Ibhar, Elishua, **E**, 1 Chr 14:5

ELSE (34)
said to Lot, "Have you anyone **e** here? Gn 19:12
stream, and everything **e** that he had. Gn 32:23
whether there is truth in you. Or **e**, Gn 42:16
"Oh, my Lord, please send someone **e**." Ex 4:13
Or **e**, if you will not let my people go, Ex 8:21
for his body; in what **e** shall he sleep? Ex 22:27
livestock, and everything **e** in the city, Dt 20:14
is eating, because he has nothing **e** left, Dt 28:55
to them, **e** you would now be guilty.'" Jgs 21:22
taste bread or anything **e** till the sun 2 Sm 3:35
or **e** there will be no escape for us 2 Sm 15:14
There was no one **e** with us in the 1 Kgs 3:18
or **e** you shall pay a talent of silver.' 1 Kgs 20:39
me your vineyard for money, or **e**, 1 Kgs 21:6
or **e** three days of the sword of the 1 Chr 21:12
And whatever **e** is required for the house Ezr 7:20
e my Maker would soon take me away. Jb 32:22
them and test them, for what **e** can I do, Jer 9:7
there will be no place **e** to bury. Jer 19:11
am the LORD your God and there is none **e**. Jl 2:27
there is no one **e**." What a desolation Zep 2:15
a little later someone **e** saw him and Lk 22:58
or **e** believe on account of the works Jn 14:11
them the works that no one **e** did, Jn 15:24
And there is salvation in no one **e**, for Acts 4:12
about himself or about someone **e**?" Acts 8:34
Or **e** let these men themselves say Acts 24:20
depth, nor anything **e** in all creation, Rom 8:39
know whether I baptized anyone **e**.) 1 Cor 1:16
and someone **e** is building upon it. 1 Cor 3:10
remain unmarried or **e** be reconciled 1 Cor 7:11
But whatever anyone **e** dares to 2 Cor 11:21
If anyone **e** thinks he has reason for Phil 3:4
and whatever **e** is contrary to sound 1 Tm 1:10

ELSE'S (2)
lest I build on someone **e** foundation, Rom 15:20
by someone **e** conscience? 1 Cor 10:29

ELSEWHERE (3)
of Ashdod and **e** among the 2 Chr 26:6
your courts is better than a thousand **e**. Ps 84:10
in Topheth, because there is no room **e**. Jer 7:32

ELTEKE (1)
tribe of Dan, **E** with its pasturelands, Jos 21:23

ELTEKEH (1)
E, Gibbethon, Baalath, Jos 19:44

ELTEKON (1)
Maarath, Beth-anoth, and **E**: six cities Jos 15:59

ELTOLAD (2)
E, Chesil, Hormah, Jos 15:30
E, Bethul, Hormah, Jos 19:4

ELUDED (1)
the wall with the spear, but he **e** Saul, 1 Sm 19:10

ELUL (1)
on the twenty-fifth day of the month **E**, Neh 6:15

ELUZAI (1)
E, Jerimoth, Bealiah, Shemariah, 1 Chr 12:5

ELYMAS (1)
But **E** the magician (for that is the Acts 13:8

ELZABAD (2)
Johanan eighth, **E** ninth, 1 Chr 12:12
Othni, Rephael, Obed and **E**, whose 1 Chr 26:7

ELZAPHAN (2)
sons of Uzziel: Mishael, **E**, and Sithri. Ex 6:22
And Moses called Mishael and **E**, the Lv 10:4

EMASCULATE (1)
who unsettle you would **e** themselves! Gal 5:12

EMBALM (1)
servants the physicians to **e** his father. Gn 50:2

EMBALMED (2)
his father. So the physicians **e** Israel. Gn 50:2
died, being 110 years old. They **e** him, Gn 50:26

EMBALMING (1)
for that is how many are required for **e**. Gn 50:3

EMBARKING (1)
And **e** in a ship of Adramyttium, Acts 27:2

EMBARRASSED (2)
And they waited till they were **e**. But Jgs 3:25
gaze and stared at him, until he was **e**. 2 Kgs 8:11

EMBERS (1)
As charcoal to hot **e** and wood to fire, Prv 26:21

EMBITTERED (1)
When my soul was **e**, when I was Ps 73:21

EMBODIMENT (1)
in the law the **e** of knowledge and Rom 2:20

EMBRACE (7)
I gave my servant to your **e**, and when Gn 16:5
or the wife you **e** or your friend who Dt 13:6
year, you shall **e** a son." And she said, 2 Kgs 4:16
exalt you; she will honor you if you **e** her. Prv 4:8
a forbidden woman and **e** the bosom of Prv 5:20
a time to **e**, and a time to refrain from Eccl 3:5
were brought up in purple **e** ash heaps. Lam 4:5

EMBRACED (5)
to meet him and **e** him and kissed him Gn 29:13
ran to meet him and **e** him and fell on Gn 33:4
him, and he kissed them and **e** them. Gn 48:10
and ran and **e** him and kissed him. Lk 15:20
of all; they **e** Paul and kissed him, Acts 20:37

EMBRACES (4)
food to his brother, to the wife he **e**, Dt 28:54
will begrudge to the husband she **e**, Dt 28:56
under my head, and his right hand **e** me! Sg 2:6
under my head, and his right hand **e** me! Sg 8:3

EMBRACING (1)
embrace, and a time to refrain from **e**; Eccl 3:5

EMBROIDERED (15)
fine twined linen, **e** with needlework. Ex 26:36
fine twined linen, **e** with needlework. Ex 27:16
shall make a sash **e** with needlework. Ex 28:39
fine twined linen, **e** with needlework, Ex 36:37
of the court was **e** with needlework in Ex 38:18
and scarlet yarns, **e** with needlework, Ex 39:29
for Sisera, spoil of dyed materials **e**, Jgs 5:30
two pieces of dyed work **e** for the neck as Jgs 5:30
clothed you also with **e** cloth and shod Ezk 16:10
was of fine linen and silk and **e** cloth. Ezk 16:13

you took your **e** garments to cover Ezk 16:18
robes and strip off their **e** garments. Ezk 26:16
Of fine **e** linen from Egypt was your Ezk 27:7
your wares emeralds, purple, **e** work, Ezk 27:16
in clothes of blue and **e** work, Ezk 27:24

EMBROIDERER (2)
a designer or by an **e** in blue and purple Ex 35:35
and designer and **e** in blue and Ex 38:23

EMEK-KEZIZ (1)
clans were Jericho, Beth-hoglah, **E**, Jos 18:21

EMERALD (5)
and the second row an **e**, a sapphire, Ex 28:18
and the second row, an **e**, a sapphire, Ex 39:11
and jasper, sapphire, **e**, and carbuncle; Ezk 28:13
rainbow that had the appearance of an **e**. Rv 4:3
sapphire, the third agate, the fourth **e**, Rv 21:19

EMERALDS (1)
they exchanged for your wares **e**, Ezk 27:16

EMERY (1)
Like **e** harder than flint have I made Ezk 3:9

EMIM (3)
in Ham, the **E** in Shaveh-kiriathaim, Gn 14:5
(The **E** formerly lived there, a people Dt 2:10
Rephaim, but the Moabites call them **E**. Dt 2:11

EMISSION (5)
"If a man has an **e** of semen, he shall Lv 15:16
with a woman and has an **e** of semen, Lv 15:18
and for him who has an **e** of semen, Lv 15:32
or a man who has had an **e** of semen, Lv 22:4
unclean because of a nocturnal **e**, Dt 23:10

EMMAUS (1)
them were going to a village named **E**, Lk 24:13

EMMER (3)
the wheat and the **e** were not struck Ex 9:32
in its proper place, and **e** as the border? Is 28:25
barley, beans and lentils, millet and **e**, Ezk 4:9

EMPEROR (4)
in custody for the decision of the **e**, Acts 25:21
And as he himself appealed to the **e**, I Acts 25:25
whether it be to the **e** as supreme, 1 Pt 2:13
brotherhood. Fear God. Honor the **e**. 1 Pt 2:17

EMPHATICALLY (1)
But he said **e**, "If I must die with you, I Mk 14:31

EMPLOYED (1)
that those who are **e** in the temple 1 Cor 9:13

EMPOWERED (1)
All these are **e** by one and the same 1 Cor 12:11

EMPOWERS (1)
the same God who **e** them all in 1 Cor 12:6

EMPTIED (9)
So she quickly **e** her jar into the trough Gn 24:20
As they **e** their sacks, behold, every Gn 42:35
took the pan and **e** it out before him, 2 Sm 13:9
"Your servants have **e** out the money 2 Kgs 22:9
They have **e** out the money that was 2 Chr 34:17
be shaken out and **e**." And all the Neh 5:13
the Egyptians within them will be **e** out, Is 19:3
he has not been **e** from vessel to vessel, Jer 48:11
the cross of Christ be **e** of its power. 1 Cor 1:17

EMPTINESS (6)
so I am allotted months of **e**, and nights of Jb 7:3
Let him not trust in **e**, deceiving Jb 15:31
himself, for **e** will be his payment. Jb 15:31
over it, and the plumb line of **e**. Is 34:11
by him as less than nothing and **e**. Is 40:17
and makes the rulers of the earth as **e**. Is 40:23

EMPTY (46)
The pit was **e**; there was no water in it. Gn 37:24
and the seven **e** ears blighted by the Gn 41:27
and when you go, you shall not go **e**, Ex 3:21
command that they **e** the house before Lv 14:36
For it is no **e** word for you, but your Dt 32:47
into the hands of all of them and **e** jars, Jgs 7:16
and the LORD has brought me back **e**. Ru 1:21
ark of the God of Israel, do not send it **e**, 1 Sm 6:3
turn aside after **e** things that cannot 1 Sm 12:21
profit or deliver, for they are **e**. 1 Sm 12:21
missed, because your seat will be **e**. 1 Sm 20:18
Saul's side, but David's place was **e**. 1 Sm 20:25
the new moon, David's place was **e**. 1 Sm 20:27
and the sword of Saul returned not **e**. 2 Sm 1:22
and the jug of oil shall not be **e**, 1 Kgs 17:14
neither did the jug of oil become **e**, 1 Kgs 17:16
neighbors, **e** vessels and not too few. 2 Kgs 4:3
would come and **e** the chest and 2 Chr 24:11
will you comfort me with **e** nothings? Jb 21:34
You have sent widows away **e**, and the Jb 22:9
Surely God does not hear an **e** cry, nor Jb 35:13
Job opens his mouth in **e** talk; he Jb 35:16
one comes to see me, he utters **e** words, Ps 41:6
of rain, they **e** themselves on the earth, Eccl 11:3
and mourn; **e**, she shall sit on the ground. Is 3:26
the LORD will **e** the earth and make it Is 24:1
shall be utterly **e** and utterly plundered; Is 24:3
and with an **e** plea turn aside him who is Is 29:21
Egypt's help is worthless and **e**; therefore I Is 30:7
nothing; their metal images are **e** wind. Is 41:29
he did not create it **e**, he formed it to be Is 45:18
it shall not return to me **e**, but it shall Is 55:11
they rely on **e** pleas, they speak lies, they Is 59:4
no water; they return with their vessels **e**; Jer 14:3
and **e** his vessels and break his jars in Jer 48:12
winnow her, and they shall **e** her land, Jer 51:2
me; he has made me an **e** vessel; Jer 51:34
Then set it **e** upon the coals, that it Ezk 24:11
with **e** oaths they make covenants; Hos 10:4
tell false dreams and give **e** consolation. Zec 10:2
do not heap up **e** phrases as the Gentiles Mt 6:7
And when it comes, it finds the house **e**, Mt 12:44
things, and the rich he has sent **e** away. Lk 1:53
Let no one deceive you with **e** words, for Eph 5:6
you captive by philosophy and **e** deceit, Col 2:8
insubordinate, **e** talkers and deceivers, Ti 1:10

EMPTY-HANDED (10)
now you would have sent me away **e**. Gn 31:42
Egypt. None shall appear before me **e**. Ex 23:15
And none shall appear before me **e**. Ex 34:20
from you, you shall not let him go **e**. Dt 15:13
They shall not appear before the LORD **e**. Dt 16:16
not go back **e** to your mother-in-law.'" Ru 3:17
a skilled warrior who does not return **e**. Jer 50:9
him and beat him and sent him away **e**. Mk 12:3
tenants beat him and sent him away **e**. Lk 20:10
him shamefully, and sent him away **e**. Lk 20:11

EMPTYING (1)
then to keep on **e** his net and Hab 1:17

EN-DOR (3)
the inhabitants of **E** and its villages, Jos 17:11
him, "Behold, there is a medium at **E**." 1 Sm 28:7
who were destroyed at **E**, who became Ps 83:10

EN-GANNIM (3)
Zanoah, **E**, Tappuah, Enam, Jos 15:34
Remeth, **E**, En-haddah, Beth-pazzez. Jos 19:21
E with its pasturelands—four cities; Jos 21:29

EN-HADDAH (1)
Remeth, En-gannim, **E**, Beth-pazzez. Jos 19:21

EN-HAKKORE (1)
Therefore the name of it was called **E**; it Jgs 15:19

EN-HAZOR (1)
Kedesh, Edrei, **E**, Jos 19:37

EN-MISHPAT (1)
they turned back and came to **E** (that is, Gn 14:7

EN-RIMMON (1)
in **E**, in Zorah, in Jarmuth, Neh 11:29

EN-ROGEL (4)
the waters of En-shemesh and ends at **E**. Jos 15:7
of the Jebusites, and downward to **E**. Jos 18:16
and Ahimaaz were waiting at **E**. 2 Sm 17:17
the Serpent's Stone, which is beside **E**, 1 Kgs 1:9

EN-SHEMESH (2)
to the waters of **E** and ends at En-rogel. Jos 15:7
in a northerly direction going on to **E**, Jos 18:17

EN-TAPPUAH (1)
along southward to the inhabitants of **E**. Jos 17:7

ENABLES (1)
by the power that **e** him even to subject Phil 3:21

ENACTED (1)
is better, since it is **e** on better promises. Heb 8:6

ENAIM (2)
herself up, and sat at the entrance to **E**, Gn 38:14
who was at **E** at the roadside?" Gn 38:21

ENAM (1)
Zanoah, En-gannim, Tappuah, **E**, Jos 15:34

ENAN (5)
from Naphtali, Ahira the son of **E**." Nm 1:15
of Naphtali being Ahira the son of **E**, Nm 2:29
On the twelfth day Ahira the son of **E**, Nm 7:78
was the offering of Ahira the son of **E**. Nm 7:83
of Naphtali was Ahira the son of **E**. Nm 10:27

ENCAMP (10)
to turn back and **e** in front of Ex 14:2
of Baal-zephon; you shall **e** facing it, Ex 14:2
E outside the camp seven days. Nm 31:19
They would **e** against them and devour Jgs 6:4
people together and **e** against the city 2 Sm 12:28
ramp against me and **e** around my tent. Jb 19:12
Though an army **e** against me, my heart Ps 27:3
And I will **e** against you all around, and Is 29:3
bow. **E** around her; let no one escape. Jer 50:29
Then I will **e** at my house as a guard, so Zec 9:8

ENCAMPED (45)
departed from there and **e** in the valley Gn 26:17
on from Succoth and **e** at Etham, Ex 13:20
his army, and overtook them **e** at the sea, Ex 14:9
trees, and they **e** there by the water. Ex 15:27
where he was **e** at the mountain Ex 18:5
of Sinai, and they **e** in the wilderness. Ex 19:2
There Israel **e** before the mountain, Ex 19:2
"When you are **e** against your enemies, Dt 23:9
and they **e** at Gilgal on the east border of Jos 4:19
the people of Israel were **e** at Gilgal, Jos 5:10
before the city and **e** on the north side Jos 8:11
their armies and **e** against Gibeon and Jos 10:5
forces and came and **e** together at the Jos 11:5
crossed the Jordan and **e** in the Valley of Jgs 6:33
him rose early and **e** beside the spring of Jgs 7:1
to Thebez and **e** against Thebez and Jgs 9:50
called to arms, and they **e** in Gilead. Jgs 10:17
came together, and they **e** at Mizpah. Jgs 10:17
his people together and **e** at Jahaz and Jgs 11:20
Philistines came up and **e** in Judah and Jgs 15:9
and went up and **e** at Kiriath-jearim in Jgs 18:12
in the morning and **e** against Gibeah. Jgs 20:19
They **e** at Ebenezer, and the Philistines 1 Sm 4:1
and the Philistines **e** at Aphek. 1 Sm 4:1
They came up and **e** in Michmash, to 1 Sm 13:5
but the Philistines **e** in Michmash. 1 Sm 13:16
and **e** between Socoh and Azekah, 1 Sm 17:1
gathered, and **e** in the Valley of Elah, 1 Sm 17:2
And Saul **e** on the hill of Hachilah, 1 Sm 26:3
came to the place where Saul had **e**. 1 Sm 26:5
while the army was **e** around him. 1 Sm 26:5
and came and **e** at Shunem. 1 Sm 28:4
all Israel, and they **e** at Gilboa. 1 Sm 28:4
And the Israelites were **e** by the spring 1 Sm 29:1
Israel and Absalom **e** in the land 2 Sm 17:26
of Philistines was **e** in the Valley 2 Sm 23:13
the troops were **e** against Gibbethon, 1 Kgs 16:15
the troops who were **e** heard it said, 1 Kgs 16:16
people of Israel **e** before them like 1 Kgs 20:27
And they **e** opposite one another 1 Kgs 20:29
of Philistines was **e** in the Valley 1 Chr 11:15
who came and **e** before Medeba. 1 Chr 19:7
invaded Judah and **e** against the 2 Chr 32:1
So they **e** from Beersheba to the valley Neh 11:30
Ah, Ariel, Ariel, the city where David **e**! Is 29:1

ENCAMPMENT (4)
the main **e** that was north of the city and Jos 8:13
And he came to the **e** as the host was 1 Sm 17:20
Saul was lying within the **e**, while the 1 Sm 26:5
there lay Saul sleeping within the **e**, 1 Sm 26:7

ENCAMPMENTS (4)
names, by their villages and by their **e**, Gn 25:16
lovely are your tents, O Jacob, your **e**, Nm 24:5
places where they lived, and all their **e**, Nm 31:10
they shall set their **e** among you and Ezk 25:4

ENCAMPS (2)
angel of the LORD **e** around those who Ps 34:7
the bones of him who **e** against you; Ps 53:5

ENCHANTER (2)
voice of charmers or of the cunning **e**. Ps 58:5
thing of any magician or **e** or Chaldean. Dn 2:10

ENCHANTERS (7)
all the magicians and **e** that were in all Dn 1:20
commanded that the magicians, the **e**, Dn 2:2
and said, "No wise men, **e**, magicians, Dn 2:27
Then the magicians, the **e**, the Dn 4:7
The king called loudly to bring in the **e**, Dn 5:7
chief of the magicians, **e**, Chaldeans, Dn 5:11
Now the wise men, the **e**, have been Dn 5:15

ENCHANTMENT (1)
For there is no **e** against Jacob, no Nm 23:23

ENCHANTMENTS (2)
sorceries and the great power of your **e**. Is 47:9
Stand fast in your **e** and your many Is 47:12

ENCIRCLE (1)
They **e** me with words of hate, and Ps 109:3

ENCIRCLED (3)
waste of the wilderness; he **e** him, Dt 32:10
Your belly is a heap of wheat, **e** with lilies. Sg 7:2
after they had been **e** for seven days. Heb 11:30

ENCIRCLES (2)
me; a company of evildoers **e** me; Ps 22:16
thing on the earth: a woman **e** a man." Jer 31:22

ENCLOSE (2)
You shall **e** them in settings of gold Ex 28:11
a door, we will **e** her with boards of cedar. Sg 8:9

ENCLOSED (6)
onyx stones, **e** in settings of gold filigree, Ex 39:6
They were **e** in settings of gold filigree. Ex 39:13
e the dust of the earth in a measure and Is 40:12
like the appearance of fire **e** all around. Ezk 1:27
the temple was **e** upward all around Ezk 41:7
done this, they **e** a large number of fish, Lk 5:6

ENCOMPASS (2)
Many bulls **e** me; strong bulls of Ps 22:12
For dogs **e** me; a company of evildoers Ps 22:16

ENCOMPASSED (4)
"For the waves of death **e** me, the 2 Sm 22:5
The cords of death **e** me; the torrents of Ps 18:4
For evils have **e** me beyond number; Ps 40:12
The snares of death **e** me; the pangs of Ps 116:3

ENCOUNTER (2)
into the hills, or the pursuers will **e** you, Jos 2:16
going out to **e** another king in war, Lk 14:31

ENCOURAGE (10)
E him, for he shall cause Israel to inherit Dt 1:38
Joshua, and **e** and strengthen him, Dt 3:28
city and overthrow it.' And **e** him." 2 Sm 11:25
we are, and that he may **e** your hearts. Eph 6:22
we are and that he may **e** your hearts, Col 4:8
Therefore **e** one another with these 1 Thes 4:18
Therefore **e** one another and build 1 Thes 5:11
the idle, **e** the fainthearted, 1 Thes 5:14
we command and **e** in the Lord 2 Thes 3:12
an older man but **e** him as you would 1 Tm 5:1

ENCOURAGED (11)
to their offices and **e** them in the 2 Chr 35:2
him, and you have **e** the wicked, Ezk 13:22
e and strengthened the brothers with Acts 15:32
brothers, they **e** them and departed. Acts 16:40
the brothers **e** him and wrote to the Acts 18:27
Then they all were **e** and ate some Acts 27:36
we may be mutually **e** by each other's Rom 1:12
in an idol's temple, will he not be **e**, 1 Cor 8:10
so that all may learn and all be **e**, 1 Cor 14:31
that their hearts may be **e**, being knit Col 2:2
one of you and **e** you and charged 1 Thes 2:12

ENCOURAGEMENT (8)
Barnabas (which means son of **e**), Acts 4:36
read it, they rejoiced because of its **e**. Acts 15:31
regions and had given them much **e**, Acts 20:2
and through the **e** of the Scriptures Rom 15:4
God of endurance and **e** grant you to Rom 15:5
upbuilding and **e** and consolation. 1 Cor 14:3
So if there is any **e** in Christ, any Phil 2:1
refuge might have strong **e** to hold fast Heb 6:18

ENCOURAGING (3)
e them to continue in the faith, Acts 14:22
sent for the disciples, and after **e** them, Acts 20:1
the habit of some, but **e** one another, Heb 10:25

ENCOURAGINGLY (2)
And Hezekiah spoke **e** to all the 2 Chr 30:22
gate of the city and spoke **e** to them, 2 Chr 32:6

END (286)
determined to make an **e** of all flesh, Gn 6:13
At the **e** of 150 days the waters had Gn 8:3
At the **e** of forty days Noah opened the Gn 8:6
which he owns; it is at the **e** of his field. Gn 23:9
in the land of Egypt came to an **e**, Gn 41:53
of them from one **e** of Egypt to the Gn 47:21
At the **e** of 430 years, on that very day, Ex 12:41
Feast of Ingathering at the **e** of the year, Ex 23:16
Make one cherub on the one **e**, and one Ex 25:19
one end, and one cherub on the other **e**. Ex 25:19
up the frames, shall run from **e** to end. Ex 26:28
up the frames, shall run from end to **e**. Ex 26:28
the Feast of Ingathering at the year's **e**. Ex 34:22
bar to run from **e** to end halfway up Ex 36:33
run from end to **e** halfway up the Ex 36:33
one cherub on the one **e**, and one cherub Ex 37:8
one end, and one cherub on the other **e**. Ex 37:8
he has made an **e** of atoning for the Lv 16:20
This is to the **e** that the people of Israel Lv 17:5
At the **e** of forty days they returned Nm 13:25
wilderness they shall come to a full **e**, Nm 14:35
may make an **e** of their grumblings Nm 17:10
the upright, and let my **e** be like his!" Nm 23:10
nations, but its **e** is utter destruction." Nm 24:20
shall run from the **e** of the Salt Sea Nm 34:3
and ask from one **e** of heaven to the Dt 4:32
You may not make an **e** of them at once, Dt 7:22
you and test you, to do you good in the **e**. Dt 8:16
And at the **e** of forty days and forty Dt 9:11
of the year to the **e** of the year. Dt 11:12
from the one **e** of the earth to the other, Dt 13:7
"At the **e** of every three years you shall Dt 14:28
"At the **e** of every seven years you shall Dt 15:1
from far away, from the **e** of the earth, Dt 28:49
from one **e** of the earth to the other, Dt 28:64
them, "At the **e** of every seven years, Dt 31:10
words of this law in a book to the very **e**, Dt 31:24
I will see what their **e** will be, For they Dt 32:20
this; they would discern their latter **e**! Dt 32:29
At the **e** of three days the officers went Jos 3:2
At the **e** of three days after they had Jos 9:16
to the lower **e** of the Sea of Chinnereth, Jos 13:27
boundary ran from the **e** of the Salt Sea, Jos 15:2
of Egypt, and comes to its **e** at the sea. Jos 15:4
at the northern **e** of the Valley of Jos 15:8
the boundary comes to an **e** at the sea. Jos 15:11
which is at the north **e** of the Valley of Jos 18:16
the Salt Sea, at the south **e** of the Jordan: Jos 18:19
And at the **e** of two months, she Jgs 11:39
gleaning until the **e** of the barley and Ru 2:23
to lie down at the **e** of the heap of grain. Ru 3:7
his house, from beginning to **e**. 1 Sm 3:12
you not know that the **e** will be bitter? 2 Sm 2:26
his head (for at the **e** of every year he 2 Sm 14:26
And at the **e** of four years Absalom 2 Sm 15:7
to Jerusalem at the **e** of nine months 2 Sm 24:8
it happened at the **e** of three years that 1 Kgs 2:39
At the **e** of twenty years, in which 1 Kgs 9:10
one on each **e** of a step on the six 1 Kgs 10:20
And at the **e** of the seven years, when 2 Kgs 8:3
was filled from one **e** to the other. 2 Kgs 10:21
he had made an **e** of offering the 2 Kgs 10:25
until you have made an **e** of them." 2 Kgs 13:17
Syria until you had made an **e** of it, 2 Kgs 13:19
and at the **e** of three years he took it. 2 Kgs 18:10
Jerusalem from one **e** to another, 2 Kgs 21:16
At the **e** of twenty years, in which 2 Chr 8:1
one on each **e** of a step on the six 2 Chr 9:19
will find them at the **e** of the valley, 2 Chr 20:16
had made an **e** of the inhabitants 2 Chr 20:23
course of time, at the **e** of two years, 2 Chr 21:19
At the **e** of the year the army of the 2 Chr 24:23
have filled it from **e** to end with their Ezr 9:11
it from end to **e** with their uncleanness. Ezr 9:11
they had come to the **e** of all the men Ezr 10:17
of Eliashib to the **e** of the house of Neh 3:21
did not make an **e** of them or forsake Neh 9:31
of the wily are brought to a quick **e**. Jb 5:13
And what is my **e**, that I should be Jb 6:11
shuttle and come to their **e** without hope. Jb 7:6
Shall windy words have an **e**? Or what Jb 16:3
There is no **e** to your iniquities. Jb 22:5
Man puts an **e** to darkness and searches Jb 28:3
Would that Job were tried to the **e**, Jb 34:36
Oh, let the evil of the wicked come to an **e**, Ps 7:9
enemy came to an **e** in everlasting ruins; Ps 9:6
and their words to the **e** of the world. Ps 19:4
Its rising is from the **e** of the heavens, Ps 19:6
heavens, and its circuit to the **e** of them, Ps 19:6
make me know my **e** and what is the Ps 39:4
He makes wars cease to the **e** of the earth; Ps 46:9
in your faithfulness put an **e** to them. Ps 54:5
from the **e** of the earth I call to you when Ps 61:2
of God; then I discerned their **e**. Ps 73:17
you put an **e** to everyone who is Ps 73:27
Are his promises at an **e** for all time? Ps 77:8
we are brought to an **e** by your anger; Ps 90:7
we bring our years to an **e** like a sigh. Ps 90:9
the same, and your years have no **e**. Ps 102:27
drunken men and were at their wits' **e**. Ps 107:27
your statutes; and I will keep it to the **e**. Ps 119:33
have almost made an **e** of me on earth, Ps 119:87
your statutes forever, to the **e**. Ps 119:112
the clouds rise at the **e** of the earth, Ps 135:7
but in the **e** she is bitter as wormwood, Prv 5:4
and at the **e** of your life you groan, Prv 5:11
to a man, but its **e** is the way to death. Prv 14:12
ache, and the **e** of joy may be grief. Prv 14:13
to a man, but its **e** is the way to death. Prv 16:25
The lot puts an **e** to quarrels and Prv 18:18
beginning will not be blessed in the **e**. Prv 20:21
In the **e** it bites like a serpent and Prv 23:32
into court, for what will you do in the **e**, Prv 25:8
you, and your ill repute have no **e**. Prv 25:10
childhood will in the **e** find him his Prv 29:21
has done from the beginning to the **e**. Eccl 3:11
or brother, yet there is no **e** to all his toil, Eccl 4:8
There was no **e** of all the people, all of Eccl 4:16
feasting, for this is the **e** of all mankind, Eccl 7:2
Better is the **e** of a thing than its Eccl 7:8
and the **e** of his talk is evil madness. Eccl 10:13
Of making many books there is no **e**, Eccl 12:12
The **e** of the matter; all has been Eccl 12:13
gold, and there is no **e** to their treasures; Is 2:7
horses, and there is no **e** to their chariots. Is 2:7
at the **e** of the conduit of the upper pool on Is 7:3
fly that is at the **e** of the streams of Egypt, Is 7:18
government and of peace there will be no **e**, Is 9:7
the Lord GOD of hosts will make a full **e**, Is 10:23
little while my fury will come to an **e**, Is 10:25
a distant land, from the **e** of the heavens, Is 13:5
I will put an **e** to the pomp of the Is 13:11
presses; I have put an **e** to the shouting. Is 16:10
the sighing she has caused I bring to an **e**. Is 21:2
all the glory of Kedar will come to an **e**. Is 21:16
At the **e** of seventy years, it will happen Is 23:15
At the **e** of seventy years, the LORD will Is 23:17
to that **e** you have visited them with Is 26:14
from day to night you bring me to an **e**; Is 38:12
from day to night you bring me to an **e**. Is 38:13
song, his praise from the **e** of the earth, Is 42:10
and my daughters from the **e** of the earth, Is 43:6
declaring the **e** from the beginning and Is 46:10
these things to heart or remember their **e**. Is 47:7
it, send it out to the **e** of the earth; Is 48:20
salvation may reach to the **e** of the earth." Is 49:6
has proclaimed to the **e** of the earth: Is 62:11
and mice, shall come to an **e** together, Is 66:17
and until the **e** of the eleventh year of Jer 1:3
forever, will he be indignant to the **e**?' Jer 3:5
a desolation; yet I will not make a full **e**. Jer 4:27
rows and destroy, but make not a full **e**; Jer 5:10
the LORD, I will not make a full **e** of you Jer 5:18
but what will you do when the **e** comes? Jer 5:31
they said, "He will not see our latter **e**." Jer 12:4
LORD devours from one **e** of the land to Jer 12:12
leave him, and at his **e** he will be a fool. Jer 17:11
shall extend from one **e** of the earth to Jer 25:33
I will make a full **e** of all the nations Jer 30:11
you, but of you I will not make a full **e**. Jer 30:11
'At the **e** of seven years each of you Jer 34:14
At the **e** of ten days the word of the LORD Jer 42:7
by famine, until there is an **e** of them. Jer 44:27
I will make a full **e** of all the nations to Jer 46:28
you, but of you I will not make a full **e**. Jer 46:28
And I will bring to an **e** in Moab, Jer 48:35
rich in treasures, your **e** has come; Jer 51:13
ceases; his mercies never come to an **e**; Lam 3:22
walk in our streets; our **e** drew near; Lam 4:18
were numbered, for our **e** had come. Lam 4:18
And at the **e** of seven days, the word of Ezk 3:16
the Lord GOD to the land of Israel: An **e**! Ezk 7:2
The **e** has come upon the four corners of Ezk 7:2
Now the **e** is upon you, and I will send Ezk 7:3
An **e** has come; the end has come; it has Ezk 7:6
An end has come; the **e** has come; it has Ezk 7:6
I will put an **e** to the pride of the strong, Ezk 7:24
you make a full **e** of the remnant of Ezk 11:13
I will put an **e** to this proverb, and they Ezk 12:23
hailstones in wrath to make a full **e**. Ezk 13:13
wilderness, to make a full **e** of them. Ezk 20:13
them or make a full **e** of them in the Ezk 20:17
I will put an **e** to your lewdness and Ezk 23:27
Thus will I put an **e** to lewdness in the Ezk 23:48
I will bring you to a dreadful **e**, and Ezk 26:21
come to a dreadful **e** and shall be no Ezk 27:36
come to a dreadful **e** and shall be no Ezk 28:19
At the **e** of forty years I will gather the Ezk 29:13
"I will put an **e** to the wealth of Egypt, Ezk 30:10
the idols and put an **e** to the images in Ezk 30:13
proud might shall come to an **e** in her; Ezk 30:18
her proud might shall come to an **e**, Ezk 33:28
At the **e** of seven months they will Ezk 39:14
the vestibule of the gate at the inner **e**, Ezk 40:7
vestibule of the gate was at the inner **e**. Ezk 40:9
there at the extreme western **e** of them. Ezk 46:19
from below the south **e** of the threshold Ezk 47:1
and at the **e** of that time they were to Dn 1:5
At the **e** of ten days it was seen that they Dn 1:15
At the **e** of the time, when the king had Dn 1:18
these kingdoms and bring them to an **e**, Dn 2:44
it was visible to the **e** of the whole earth. Dn 4:11
to the **e** that the living may know that Dn 4:17
it was visible to the **e** of the whole earth, Dn 4:20
At the **e** of twelve months he was Dn 4:29
At the **e** of the days I, Nebuchadnezzar, Dn 4:34
of your kingdom and brought it to an **e**; Dn 5:26
and his dominion shall be to the **e**. Dn 6:26
to be consumed and destroyed to the **e**. Dn 7:26
"Here is the **e** of the matter. As for me, Dn 7:28
that the vision is for the time of the **e**." Dn 8:17
shall be at the latter **e** of the indignation, Dn 8:19
for it refers to the appointed time of the **e**. Dn 8:19
And at the latter **e** of their kingdom, Dn 8:23
must pass before the **e** of the desolations Dn 9:2
the transgression, to put an **e** to sin, Dn 9:24
Its **e** shall come with a flood, and to the Dn 9:26
a flood, and to the **e** there shall be war. Dn 9:26
he shall put an **e** to sacrifice and Dn 9:27
until the decreed **e** is poured out on the Dn 9:27

shall put an **e** to his insolence. Dn 11:18
for the **e** is yet to be at the time Dn 11:27
and made white, until the time of the **e**, Dn 11:35
"At the time of the **e**, the king of the Dn 11:40
Yet he shall come to his **e**, with none to Dn 11:45
and seal the book, until the time of the **e**. Dn 12:4
shall it be till the **e** of these wonders?" Dn 12:6
people comes to an **e** all these things Dn 12:7
up and sealed until the time of the **e**. Dn 12:9
But go your way till the **e**. And you Dn 12:13
your allotted place at the **e** of the days." Dn 12:13
and I will put an **e** to the kingdom of the Hos 1:4
And I will put an **e** to all her mirth, her Hos 2:11
shall come to an **e**," declares the LORD. Am 3:15
"The **e** has come upon my people Israel; Am 8:2
and bring the poor of the land to an **e**, Am 8:4
an only son and the **e** of it like a bitter Am 8:10
will make a complete **e** of the adversaries, Na 1:8
He will make a complete **e**; trouble will Na 1:9
There is no **e** of the treasure or of the Na 2:9
full of lies and plunder—no **e** to the prey! Na 3:1
dead bodies without **e**—they stumble Na 3:3
time; it hastens to the **e**—it will not lie. Hab 2:3
for a full and sudden **e** he will make of Zep 1:18
one who endures to the **e** will be saved. Mt 10:22
this must take place, but the **e** is not yet. Mt 24:6
one who endures to the **e** will be saved. Mt 24:13
to all nations, and then the **e** will come. Mt 24:14
from one **e** of heaven to the other. Mt 24:31
he sat with the guards to see the **e**. Mt 26:58
with you always, to the **e** of the age." Mt 28:20
he cannot stand, but is coming to an **e**. Mk 3:26
must take place, but the **e** is not yet. Mk 13:7
one who endures to the **e** will be saved. Mk 13:13
and of his kingdom there will be no **e**." Lk 1:33
And at the **e** of eight days, when he was Lk 2:21
Lazarus to dip the **e** of his finger in Lk 16:24
take place, but the **e** will not be at once." Lk 21:9
were in the world, he loved them to the **e**. Jn 13:1
and Samaria, and to the **e** of the earth." Acts 1:8
The **e** of those things is death. Rom 6:21
get leads to sanctification and its **e**, Rom 6:22
For Christ is the **e** of the law for Rom 10:4
For to this **e** Christ died and lived Rom 14:9
who will sustain you to the **e**, guiltless 1 Cor 1:8
on whom the **e** of the ages has come. 1 Cor 10:11
Then comes the **e**, when he delivers 1 Cor 15:24
which was being brought to an **e**, 2 Cor 3:7
brought to an **e** came with glory, 2 Cor 3:11
of what was being brought to an **e**. 2 Cor 3:13
Their **e** will correspond to their 2 Cor 11:15
To that **e** keep alert with all Eph 6:18
Their **e** is destruction, their god is their Phil 3:19
To this **e** we always pray for you, 2 Thes 1:11
For to this **e** we toil and strive, 1 Tm 4:10
same, and your years will have no **e**." Heb 1:12
our original confidence firm to the **e**. Heb 3:14
to being cursed, and its **e** is to be burned. Heb 6:8
the full assurance of hope until the **e**, Heb 6:11
neither beginning of days nor **e** of life, Heb 7:3
once for all at the **e** of the ages to put Heb 9:26
By faith Joseph, at the **e** of his life, Heb 11:22
The **e** of all things is at hand; therefore 1 Pt 4:7
and who keeps my works until the **e**, Rv 2:26
and the Omega, the beginning and the **e**. Rv 21:6
and the last, the beginning and the **e**." Rv 22:13

ENDANGER (1)
So you would **e** my head with the king." Dn 1:10

ENDANGERED (1)
and he who splits logs is **e** by them. Eccl 10:9

ENDEAVOR (1)
But if, in our **e** to be justified in Christ, Gal 2:17

ENDEAVORED (1)
we **e** the more eagerly and with great 1 Thes 2:17

ENDED (16)
And when that year was **e**, they came Gn 47:18
weeping and mourning for Moses were **e**. Dt 34:8
far as Lakkum, and it **e** at the Jordan. Jos 19:33
of barley." The words of Job are **e**. Jb 31:40
prayers of David, the son of Jesse, are **e**. Ps 72:20
and cry to her that her warfare is **e**, Is 40:2
and your days of mourning shall be **e**. Is 60:20
"The harvest is past, the summer is **e**, Jer 8:20
And when his time of service was **e**, he Lk 1:23
And when the feast was **e**, as they were Lk 2:43
And when they were **e**, he was hungry. Lk 4:2
when the devil had **e** every temptation, Lk 4:13
When our days there were **e**, we Acts 21:5
longer, until the thousand years were **e**. Rv 20:3
to life until the thousand years were **e**. Rv 20:5
And when the thousand years are **e**, Rv 20:7

ENDING (2)
with the eldest and **e** with the youngest. Gn 44:12
and touches Jericho, **e** at the Jordan. Jos 16:7

ENDLESS (1)
themselves to myths and **e** genealogies, 1 Tm 1:4

ENDOWED (2)
"God has **e** me with a good endowment; Gn 30:20
skillful in all wisdom, **e** with knowledge, Dn 1:4

ENDOWMENT (1)
"God has endowed me with a good **e**; Gn 30:20

ENDS (58)
them, on the two **e** of the mercy seat. Ex 25:18
you make the cherubim on its two **e**. Ex 25:19
The two **e** of the two cords you shall Ex 28:25
put them at the two **e** of the breastpiece, Ex 28:26
work on the two **e** of the mercy seat, Ex 37:7
seat he made the cherubim on its two **e**. Ex 37:8
They attached the two **e** of the two Ex 39:18
put them at the two **e** of the breastpiece, Ex 39:19
peoples, all of them, to the **e** of the earth; Dt 33:17
waters of En-shemesh and **e** at En-rogel. Jos 15:7
then to Gezer, and it **e** at the sea. Jos 16:3
to the brook Kanah and **e** at the sea. Jos 16:8
north side of the brook and **e** at the sea, Jos 17:9
and it **e** at the wilderness of Beth-aven. Jos 18:12
and it **e** at Kiriath-baal (that is, Jos 18:14
And the boundary **e** at the northern Jos 18:19
and it **e** at the Valley of Iphtahel; Jos 19:14
and its boundary **e** at the Jordan— Jos 19:22
turns to Hosah, and it **e** at the sea; Jos 19:29
The LORD will judge the **e** of the earth; 1 Sm 2:10
were so long that the **e** of the poles were 1 Kgs 8:8
were so long that the **e** of the poles were 2 Chr 5:9
For he looks to the **e** of the earth and Jb 28:24
and their life **e** among the cult Jb 36:14
and the **e** of the earth your possession. Ps 2:8
All the **e** of the earth shall remember Ps 22:27
your praise reaches to the **e** of the earth. Ps 48:10
rules over Jacob to the **e** of the earth. Ps 59:13
the hope of all the **e** of the earth and of Ps 65:5
those who dwell at the **e** of the earth are Ps 65:8
us; let all the **e** of the earth fear him! Ps 67:7
and from the River to the **e** of the earth! Ps 72:8
All the **e** of the earth have seen the Ps 98:3
desire of the righteous **e** only in good; Prv 11:23
eyes of a fool are on the **e** of the earth. Prv 17:24
has established all the **e** of the earth? Prv 30:4
whistle for them from the **e** of the earth; Is 5:26
From the **e** of the earth we hear songs of Is 24:16
God, the Creator of the **e** of the earth. Is 40:28
and are afraid; the **e** of the earth tremble; Is 41:5
you whom I took from the **e** of the earth, Is 41:9
to me and be saved, all the **e** of the earth! Is 45:22
and all the **e** of the earth shall see the Is 52:10
the mist rise from the **e** of the earth. Jer 10:13
nations come from the **e** of the earth Jer 16:19
will resound to the **e** of the earth, Jer 25:31
the mist rise from the **e** of the earth. Jer 51:16
the fire has consumed both **e** of it, Ezk 15:4
and your dominion to the **e** of the earth. Dn 4:22
now he shall be great to the **e** of the earth. Mi 5:4
and from the River to the **e** of the earth. Zec 9:10
for she came from the **e** of the earth to Mt 12:42
from the **e** of the earth to the ends of Mk 13:27
the ends of the earth to the **e** of heaven. Mk 13:27
for she came from the **e** of the earth to Lk 11:31
bring salvation to the **e** of the earth.'" Acts 13:47
and their words to the **e** of the world." Rom 10:18
Love never **e**. As for prophecies, they 1 Cor 13:8

ENDURANCE (16)
so I say, "My **e** has perished; so has my Lam 3:18
By your **e** you will gain your lives. Lk 21:19
knowing that suffering produces **e**, Rom 5:3
and **e** produces character, and Rom 5:4
that through **e** and through the Rom 15:4
the God of **e** and encouragement grant Rom 15:5
by great **e**, in afflictions, hardships, 2 Cor 6:4
might, for all **e** and patience with joy, Col 1:11
For you have need of **e**, so that when Heb 10:36
and let us run with **e** the race that is set Heb 12:1
kingdom and the patient **e** that are in Rv 1:9
your works, your toil and your patient **e**, Rv 2:2
love and faith and service and patient **e**, Rv 2:19
you have kept my word about patient **e**, Rv 3:10
is a call for the **e** and faith of the saints. Rv 13:10
Here is a call for the **e** of the saints, Rv 14:12

ENDURE (36)
will direct you, you will be able to **e**, Ex 18:23
that you **e** the siege in Jerusalem? 2 Chr 32:10
stand; he lays hold of it, but it does not **e**. Jb 8:15
not be rich, and his wealth will not **e**, Jb 15:29
eaten; therefore his prosperity will not **e**. Jb 20:21
king; may his years **e** to all generations! Ps 61:6
May his name **e** forever, his fame Ps 72:17
His offspring shall **e** forever, his throne Ps 89:36
look and an arrogant heart I will not **e**. Ps 101:5
you whose years **e** throughout all Ps 102:24
May the glory of the LORD **e** forever; Ps 104:31
How long must your servant **e**? When Ps 119:84
Truthful lips **e** forever, but a lying Prv 12:19
A man's spirit will **e** sickness, but a Prv 18:14
the word of a man who hears will **e**. Prv 21:28
and does a crown **e** to all generations? Prv 27:24
I cannot **e** iniquity and solemn assembly. Is 1:13
the nations cannot **e** his indignation. Jer 10:10
Can your courage **e**, or can your Ezk 22:14
her arm, and he and his arm shall not **e**, Dn 11:6
is great and very awesome; who can **e** it? Jl 2:11
Who can **e** the heat of his anger? Na 1:6
But who can **e** the day of his coming, Mal 3:2
no root in themselves, but **e** for a while; Mk 4:17
we bless; when persecuted, we **e**; 1 Cor 4:12
but we **e** anything rather than put an 1 Cor 9:12
escape, that you may be able to **e** it. 1 Cor 10:13
when you patiently **e** the same 2 Cor 1:6
Therefore I **e** everything for the sake 2 Tm 2:10
if we **e**, we will also reign with him; if 2 Tm 2:12
when people will not **e** sound teaching, 2 Tm 4:3
always be sober-minded, **e** suffering, 2 Tm 4:5
It is for discipline that you have to **e**. Heb 12:7
For they could not **e** the order that Heb 12:20
you sin and are beaten for it, you **e**? 1 Pt 2:20
you do good and suffer for it you **e**, 1 Pt 2:20

ENDURED (8)
in David's favor, all the hardships he **e**, Ps 132:1
has **e** with much patience vessels of Rom 9:22
at Lystra—which persecutions I **e**; 2 Tm 3:11
you **e** a hard struggle with sufferings, Heb 10:32
for he **e** as seeing him who is Heb 11:27
joy that was set before him **e** the cross, Heb 12:2
Consider him who **e** from sinners such Heb 12:3
the camp and bear the reproach he **e**. Heb 13:13

ENDURES (66)
good; for his steadfast love **e** forever! 1 Chr 16:34
LORD, for his steadfast love **e** forever. 1 Chr 16:41
his steadfast love **e** forever," the 2 Chr 5:13
is good, for his steadfast love **e** forever." 2 Chr 7:3
his steadfast love **e** forever—whenever 2 Chr 7:6
for his steadfast love **e** forever." 2 Chr 20:21
his steadfast love **e** forever toward Ezr 3:11
The steadfast love of God **e** all the day. Ps 52:1
May they fear you while the sun **e**, and as Ps 72:5
his steadfast love **e** forever, and his Ps 100:5
is good, for his steadfast love **e** forever! Ps 106:1
is good, for his steadfast love **e** forever! Ps 107:1
work, and his righteousness **e** forever. Ps 111:3
understanding. His praise **e** forever! Ps 111:10
house, and his righteousness **e** forever. Ps 112:3
to the poor; his righteousness **e** forever; Ps 112:9
the faithfulness of the LORD **e** forever. Ps 117:2
is good; for his steadfast love **e** forever! Ps 118:1
Israel say, "His steadfast love **e** forever." Ps 118:2
Aaron say, "His steadfast love **e** forever." Ps 118:3
LORD say, "His steadfast love **e** forever." Ps 118:4
is good; for his steadfast love **e** forever! Ps 118:29
Your faithfulness **e** to all generations; Ps 119:90
one of your righteous rules **e** forever. Ps 119:160
Your name, O LORD, **e** forever, your Ps 135:13
is good, for his steadfast love **e** forever. Ps 136:1
of gods, for his steadfast love **e** forever. Ps 136:2
of lords, for his steadfast love **e** forever; Ps 136:3
wonders, for his steadfast love **e** forever; Ps 136:4
heavens, for his steadfast love **e** forever; Ps 136:5
waters, for his steadfast love **e** forever; Ps 136:6
lights, for his steadfast love **e** forever; Ps 136:7
the day, for his steadfast love **e** forever; Ps 136:8
the night, for his steadfast love **e** forever; Ps 136:9
Egypt, for his steadfast love **e** forever; Ps 136:10
them, for his steadfast love **e** forever; Ps 136:11
arm, for his steadfast love **e** forever; Ps 136:12
in two, for his steadfast love **e** forever; Ps 136:13
of it, for his steadfast love **e** forever; Ps 136:14
Red Sea, for his steadfast love **e** forever; Ps 136:15
for his steadfast love **e** forever; Ps 136:16
kings, for his steadfast love **e** forever; Ps 136:17
kings, for his steadfast love **e** forever; Ps 136:18
for his steadfast love **e** forever; Ps 136:19
Bashan, for his steadfast love **e** forever; Ps 136:20
for his steadfast love **e** forever; Ps 136:21
servant, for his steadfast love **e** forever. Ps 136:22
estate, for his steadfast love **e** forever; Ps 136:23
our foes, for his steadfast love **e** forever; Ps 136:24
all flesh, for his steadfast love **e** forever. Ps 136:25
heaven, for his steadfast love **e** forever. Ps 136:26
your steadfast love, O LORD, **e** forever. Ps 138:8
and your dominion **e** throughout all Ps 145:13

that whatever God does **e** forever; Eccl 3:14
is good, for his steadfast love **e** forever!' Jer 33:11
your throne **e** to all generations. Lam 5:19
and his dominion **e** from generation to Dn 4:3
and his kingdom **e** from generation to Dn 4:34
But the one who **e** to the end will be Mt 10:22
no root in himself, but **e** for a while, Mt 13:21
But the one who **e** to the end will be Mt 24:13
But the one who **e** to the end will be Mk 13:13
but for the food that **e** to eternal life, Jn 6:27
things, hopes all things, **e** all things. 1 Cor 13:7
the poor; his righteousness **e** forever." 2 Cor 9:9
one **e** sorrows while suffering unjustly. 1 Pt 2:19

ENDURING (10)
and said, "**E** is your dwelling place, Nm 24:21
the fear of the LORD is clean, **e** forever; the Ps 19:9
with me, **e** wealth and righteousness. Prv 8:18
of the fool there is no **e** remembrance, Eccl 2:16
It is an **e** nation; it is an ancient nation, a Jer 5:15
Daniel, for he is the living God, **e** forever; Dn 6:26
LORD, and you **e** foundations of the earth, Mi 6:2
and in the afflictions that you are **e**. 2 Thes 1:4
able to teach, patiently **e** evil, 2 Tm 2:24
I know you are **e** patiently and bearing up Rv 2:3

ENEGLAIM (1)
From Engedi to **E** it will be a place for Ezk 47:10

ENEMIES (235)
has delivered your **e** into your hand!" Gn 14:20
offspring shall possess the gate of his **e**, Gn 22:17
hand shall be on the neck of your **e**; Gn 49:8
they join our **e** and fight against us and Ex 1:10
an enemy to your **e** and an adversary to Ex 23:22
will make all your **e** turn their backs to Ex 23:27
break loose, to the derision of their **e**), Ex 32:25
You shall chase your **e**, and they shall Lv 26:7
and your **e** shall fall before you by the Lv 26:8
your seed in vain, for your **e** shall eat it. Lv 26:16
you shall be struck down before your **e**. Lv 26:17
so that your **e** who settle in it shall be Lv 26:32
into their hearts in the lands of their **e**. Lv 26:36
have no power to stand before your **e**. Lv 26:37
and the land of your **e** shall eat you up. Lv 26:38
into the land of their **e**—if then their Lv 26:41
when they are in the land of their **e**, Lv 26:44
and you shall be saved from your **e**. Nm 10:9
O LORD, and let your **e** be scattered, Nm 10:35
lest you be struck down before your **e**. Nm 14:42
I took you to curse my **e**, and behold, Nm 23:11
to Balaam, "I called you to curse my **e**, Nm 24:10
Seir also, his **e**, shall be dispossessed. Nm 24:18
has driven out his **e** from before him Nm 32:21
midst, lest you be defeated before your **e**.' Dt 1:42
thrusting out all your **e** from before you, Dt 6:19
gives you rest from all your **e** around, Dt 12:10
"When you go out to war against your **e**, Dt 20:1
drawing near for battle against your **e**: Dt 20:3
with you to fight for you against your **e**, Dt 20:4
And you shall enjoy the spoil of your **e**, Dt 20:14
you go out to war against your **e**, Dt 21:10
you are encamped against your **e**, Dt 23:9
you and to give up your **e** before you, Dt 23:14
you rest from all your **e** around you, Dt 25:19
LORD will cause your **e** who rise against Dt 28:7
cause you to be defeated before your **e**. Dt 28:25
Your sheep shall be given to your **e**, but Dt 28:31
you shall serve your **e** whom the LORD Dt 28:48
with which your **e** shall distress you. Dt 28:53
for sale to your **e** as male and female Dt 28:68
on your foes and **e** who persecuted you. Dt 30:7
as our Rock; our **e** are by themselves. Dt 32:31
Your **e** shall come fawning to you, and Dt 33:29
has turned their backs before their **e**! Jos 7:8
of Israel cannot stand before their **e**. Jos 7:12
They turn their backs before their **e**, Jos 7:12
stand before your **e** until you take Jos 7:13
the nation took vengeance on their **e**. Jos 10:13
Pursue your **e**; attack their rear guard. Jos 10:19
do to all your **e** against whom you Jos 10:25
one of all their **e** had withstood them, Jos 21:44
had given all their **e** into their hands. Jos 21:44
the spoil of your **e** with your brothers." Jos 22:8
to Israel from all their surrounding **e**, Jos 23:1
into the hand of their surrounding **e**, Jgs 2:14
they could no longer withstand their **e**. Jgs 2:14
from the hand of their **e** all the days of Jgs 2:18
LORD has given your **e** the Moabites into Jgs 3:28
"So may all your **e** perish, O LORD! But Jgs 5:31
from the hand of all their **e** on every side, Jgs 8:34
the LORD has avenged you on your **e**, Jgs 11:36
My mouth derides my **e**, because I 1 Sm 2:1
and save us from the power of our **e**." 1 Sm 4:3
from the hand of their surrounding **e**. 1 Sm 10:1
deliver us out of the hand of our **e**, 1 Sm 12:10
of the hand of your **e** on every side, 1 Sm 12:11
am avenged on my **e**." So none of the 1 Sm 14:24
of the spoil of their **e** that they found. 1 Sm 14:30
fought against all his **e** on every side, 1 Sm 14:47
of the king's **e**.'" Now Saul thought 1 Sm 18:25
every one of the **e** of David from the 1 Sm 20:15
LORD take vengeance on David's **e**." 1 Sm 20:16
God do so to the **e** of David and more 1 Sm 25:22
now then let your **e** and those who 1 Sm 25:26
the lives of your **e** he shall sling out 1 Sm 25:29
and fight against the **e** of my lord the 1 Sm 29:8
from the spoil of the **e** of the LORD." 1 Sm 30:26
and from the hand of all their **e**.'" 2 Sm 3:18
burst through my **e** before me like 2 Sm 5:20
him rest from all his surrounding **e**, 2 Sm 7:1
have cut off all your **e** from before you. 2 Sm 7:9
I will give you rest from all your **e**. 2 Sm 7:11
him from the hand of his **e**." 2 Sm 18:19
"May the **e** of my lord the king and 2 Sm 18:32
the hand of our **e** and saved us from 2 Sm 19:9
him from the hand of all his **e**, 2 Sm 22:1
be praised, and I am saved from my **e**. 2 Sm 22:4
I pursued my **e** and destroyed them, 2 Sm 22:38
You made my **e** turn their backs to 2 Sm 22:41
who brought me out from my **e**; you 2 Sm 22:49
long life or riches or the life of your **e**, 1 Kgs 3:11
with which his **e** surrounded him, 1 Kgs 5:3
all their heart in the land of their **e**, 1 Kgs 8:48
you out of the hand of all your **e**." 2 Kgs 17:39
give them into the hand of their **e**, 2 Kgs 21:14
a prey and a spoil to all their **e**, 2 Kgs 21:14
broken through my **e** by my hand, 1 Chr 14:11
cut off all your **e** from before you. 1 Chr 17:8
Israel. And I will subdue all your **e**. 1 Chr 17:10
the sword of your **e** overtakes you, 1 Chr 21:12
him rest from all his surrounding **e**. 1 Chr 22:9
if their **e** besiege them in the land at 2 Chr 6:28
people go out to battle against their **e**, 2 Chr 6:34
had made them rejoice over their **e**. 2 Chr 20:27
had fought against the **e** of Israel. 2 Chr 20:29
give them into the hand of their **e**, 2 Chr 25:20
and from the hand of all his **e**, 2 Chr 32:22
And our **e** said, "They will not know or Neh 4:11
When our **e** heard that it was known Neh 4:15
prevent the taunts of the nations our **e**? Neh 5:9
and the rest of our **e** heard that I had Neh 6:1
And when all our **e** heard of it, all the Neh 6:16
you gave them into the hand of their **e**, Neh 9:27
saved them from the hand of their **e**. Neh 9:27
abandoned them to the hand of their **e**, Neh 9:28
on that day to take vengeance on their **e**. Est 8:13
the very day when the **e** of the Jews hoped Est 9:1
Jews struck all their **e** with the sword, Est 9:5
got relief from their **e** and killed 75,000 Est 9:16
on which the Jews got relief from their **e**, Est 9:22
For you strike all my **e** on the cheek; you Ps 3:7
in your righteousness because of my **e**; Ps 5:8
All my **e** shall be ashamed and greatly Ps 6:10
lift yourself up against the fury of my **e**; Ps 7:6
When my **e** turn back, they stumble and Ps 9:3
violence, my deadly **e** who surround me. Ps 17:9
rescued him from the hand of all his **e**, Ps 18:T
to be praised, and I am saved from my **e**. Ps 18:3
I pursued my **e** and overtook them, and Ps 18:37
You made my **e** turn their backs to me, Ps 18:40
who delivered me from my **e**; yes, you Ps 18:48
Your hand will find out all your **e**; your Ps 21:8
a table before me in the presence of my **e**; Ps 23:5
put to shame; let not my **e** exult over me. Ps 25:2
be lifted up above my **e** all around me, Ps 27:6
lead me on a level path because of my **e**. Ps 27:11
the hand of my **e** and from my Ps 31:15
the **e** of the LORD are like the glory of the Ps 37:20
do not give him up to the will of his **e**. Ps 41:2
My **e** say of me in malice, "When will he Ps 41:5
are sharp in the heart of the king's **e**; Ps 45:5
He will return the evil to my **e**; in your Ps 54:5
my eye has looked in triumph on my **e**. Ps 54:7
my **e** trample on me all day long, for Ps 56:2
Then my **e** will turn back in the day Ps 56:9
Deliver me from my **e**, O my God; protect Ps 59:1
will let me look in triumph on my **e**. Ps 59:10
your power that your **e** come cringing to Ps 66:3
God shall arise, his **e** shall be scattered; Ps 68:1
But God will strike the heads of his **e**, Ps 68:21
be delivered from my **e** and from the Ps 69:14
me; ransom me because of my **e**! Ps 69:18
For my **e** speak concerning me; those Ps 71:10
down before him and his **e** lick the dust! Ps 72:9
afraid, but the sea overwhelmed their **e**. Ps 78:53
and our **e** laugh among themselves. Ps 80:6
would soon subdue their **e** and turn my Ps 81:14
For behold, your **e** make an uproar; Ps 83:2
you scattered your **e** with your mighty Ps 89:10
his foes; you have made all his **e** rejoice. Ps 89:42
with which your **e** mock, O LORD, with Ps 89:51
For behold, your **e**, O LORD, for behold, Ps 92:9
O LORD, for behold, your **e** shall perish; Ps 92:9
My eyes have seen the downfall of my **e**; Ps 92:11
All the day my **e** taunt me; those who Ps 102:8
Their **e** oppressed them, and they were Ps 106:42
until I make your **e** your footstool." Ps 110:1
scepter. Rule in the midst of your **e**! Ps 110:2
makes me wiser than my **e**, Ps 119:98
when he speaks with his **e** in the gate. Ps 127:5
His **e** I will clothe with shame, but on Ps 132:18
your hand against the wrath of my **e**, Ps 138:7
intent; your **e** take your name in vain! Ps 139:20
complete hatred; I count them my **e**. Ps 139:22
Deliver me from my **e**, O LORD! I have Ps 143:9
steadfast love you will cut off my **e**, Ps 143:12
he makes even his **e** to be at peace with Prv 16:7
get relief from my **e** and avenge myself on Is 1:24
of Rezin against him, and stirs up his **e**. Is 9:11
to his adversaries, repayment to his **e**; Is 59:18
give your grain to be food for your **e**, Is 62:8
the LORD, rendering recompense to his **e**! Is 66:6
shall show his indignation against his **e**. Is 66:14
of my soul into the hands of her **e**. Jer 12:7
I will give to the sword before their **e**, Jer 15:9
make you serve your **e** in a land that Jer 15:14
will make you serve your **e** in a land that Jer 17:4
people to fall by the sword before their **e**, Jer 19:7
with which their **e** and those who seek Jer 19:9
the sword of their **e** while you look on. Jer 20:4
kings of Judah into the hand of their **e**, Jer 20:5
of Babylon and into the hand of their **e**, Jer 21:7
the hand of their **e** and into the hand Jer 34:20
the hand of their **e** and into the hand Jer 34:21
into the hand of his **e** and into the hand Jer 44:30
for her **e** march in force and come Jer 46:22
Elam before their **e** and before those Jer 49:37
devoured them, and their **e** have said, Jer 50:7
with her; they have become her **e**. Lam 1:2
have become the head; her **e** prosper, Lam 1:5
All my **e** have heard of my trouble; Lam 1:21
All your **e** rail against you; they hiss, Lam 2:16
"All our **e** open their mouths against Lam 3:46
those who were my **e** without cause; Lam 3:52
delivered you to the greed of your **e**, Ezk 16:27
and Memphis shall face **e** by day. Ezk 30:16
you and its interpretation for your **e**! Dn 4:19
if they go into captivity before their **e**, Am 9:4
will redeem you from the hand of your **e**. Mi 4:10
and all your **e** shall be cut off. Mi 5:9
a man's **e** are the men of his own house. Mi 7:6
his adversaries and keeps wrath for his **e**. Na 1:2
and will pursue his **e** into darkness. Na 1:8
of your land are wide open to your **e**; Na 3:13
you; he has cleared away your **e**. Zep 3:15
Love your **e** and pray for those who Mt 5:44
And a person's **e** will be those of his Mt 10:36
until I put your **e** under your feet'? Mt 22:44
until I put your **e** under your feet.' Mk 12:36
be saved from our **e** and from the hand Lk 1:71
being delivered from the hand of our **e**, Lk 1:74
"But I say to you who hear, Love your **e**, Lk 6:27
But love your **e**, and do good, and lend, Lk 6:35
But as for these **e** of mine, who did not Lk 19:27
when your **e** will set up a barricade Lk 19:43
until I make your **e** your footstool.' Lk 20:43
until I make your **e** your footstool.' Acts 2:35
if while we were **e** we were reconciled Rom 5:10
they are **e** of God for your sake. Rom 11:28
he has put all his **e** under his feet. 1 Cor 15:25
tears, walk as **e** of the cross of Christ. Phil 3:18
until I make your **e** a footstool for your Heb 1:13
that time until his **e** should be made a Heb 10:13
in a cloud, and their **e** watched them. Rv 11:12

ENEMIES' (3)
desolate, while you are in your **e** land; Lv 26:34
rot away in your **e** lands because of Lv 26:39
and gathered them from their **e** lands, Ezk 39:27

ENEMY (100)
So the **e** took all the possessions of Gn 14:11
your right hand, O LORD, shatters the **e**. Ex 15:6
The **e** said, 'I will pursue, I will overtake, Ex 15:9
then I will be an **e** to your enemies and Ex 23:22
shall be delivered into the hand of the **e**. Lv 26:25
he was not his **e** and did not seek Nm 35:23
with which your **e** shall distress you Dt 28:55
with which your **e** shall distress you Dt 28:57
had I not feared provocation by the **e**, Dt 32:27
from the long-haired heads of the **e**.' Dt 32:42
he thrust out the **e** before you and said, Dt 33:27
given Samson our **e** into our hand." Jgs 16:23
god has given our **e** into our hand, Jgs 16:24
So Saul was David's **e** continually. 1 Sm 18:29
deceived me thus and let my **e** go, 1 Sm 19:17
I will give your **e** into your hand, 1 Sm 24:4

For if a man finds his **e**, will he let 1 Sm 24:19
"God has given your **e** into your hand 1 Sm 26:8
from you and become your **e**? 1 Sm 28:16
of Ish-bosheth, the son of Saul, your **e**, 2 Sm 4:8
He rescued me from my strong **e**, 2 Sm 22:18
defeated before the **e** because they 1 Kgs 8:33
if their **e** besieges them in the land at 1 Kgs 8:37
people go out to battle against their **e**, 1 Kgs 8:44
with them and give them to an **e**, 1 Kgs 8:46
away captive to the land of the **e**, 1 Kgs 8:46
found me, O my **e**?" He answered, 1 Kgs 21:20
defeated before the **e** because they 2 Chr 6:24
with them and give them to an **e**, 2 Chr 6:36
God will cast you down before the **e**? 2 Chr 25:8
power, to help the king against the **e**. 2 Chr 26:13
to protect us against the **e** on our way, Ezr 8:22
the hand of the **e** and from ambushes Ezr 8:31
son of Hammedatha, the **e** of the Jews. Est 3:10
And Esther said, "A foe and **e**! This Est 7:6
the house of Haman, the **e** of the Jews. Est 8:1
son of Hammedatha, the **e** of the Jews, Est 9:10
of Hammedatha, the **e** of all the Jews, Est 9:24
hide your face and count me as your **e**? Jb 13:24
"Let my **e** be as the wicked, and let him Jb 27:7
against me, he counts me as his **e**, Jb 33:10
evil or plundered my **e** without cause, Ps 7:4
let the **e** pursue my soul and overtake it, Ps 7:5
of your foes, to still the **e** and the avenger. Ps 8:2
The **e** came to an end in everlasting ruins; Ps 9:6
How long shall my **e** be exalted over me? Ps 13:2
lest my **e** say, "I have prevailed over Ps 13:4
me from my strong **e** and from those Ps 18:17
not delivered me into the hand of the **e**; Ps 31:8
my **e** will not shout in triumph over Ps 41:11
because of the oppression of the **e**?" Ps 42:9
because of the oppression of the **e**? Ps 43:2
at the sight of the **e** and the avenger. Ps 44:16
because of the noise of the **e**, because of Ps 55:3
For it is not an **e** who taunts me—then I Ps 55:12
my refuge, a strong tower against the **e**. Ps 61:3
preserve my life from dread of the **e**. Ps 64:1
the **e** has destroyed everything in the Ps 74:3
Is the **e** to revile your name forever? Ps 74:10
this, O LORD, how the **e** scoffs, Ps 74:18
The **e** shall not outwit him; the wicked Ps 89:22
them from the power of the **e**. Ps 106:10
For the **e** has pursued my soul; he has Ps 143:3
Do not rejoice when your **e** falls, and Prv 24:17
If your **e** is hungry, give him bread to Prv 25:21
of a friend; profuse are the kisses of an **e**. Prv 27:6
therefore he turned to be their **e**, and Is 63:10
walk on the road, for the **e** has a sword; Jer 6:25
for you before the **e** in the time of Jer 15:11
wind I will scatter them before the **e**. Jer 18:17
for I have dealt you the blow of an **e**, the Jer 30:14
shall come back from the land of the **e**. Jer 31:16
who was his **e** and sought his life." Jer 44:30
my affliction, for the **e** has triumphed!" Lam 1:9
The **e** has stretched out his hands over Lam 1:10
are desolate, for the **e** has prevailed." Lam 1:16
them his right hand in the face of the **e**; Lam 2:3
He has bent his bow like an **e**, with his Lam 2:4
The Lord has become like an **e**; he has Lam 2:5
into the hand of the **e** the walls of her Lam 2:7
he has made the **e** rejoice over you and Lam 2:17
I held and raised my **e** destroyed. Lam 2:22
that foe or **e** could enter the gates of Lam 4:12
GOD: Because the **e** said of you, 'Aha!' Ezk 36:2
the good; the **e** shall pursue him. Hos 8:3
lately my people have risen up as an **e**; Mi 2:8
Rejoice not over me, O my **e**; when I fall, I Mi 7:8
Then my **e** will see, and shame will Mi 7:10
hiding; you will seek a refuge from the **e**. Na 3:11
love your neighbor and hate your **e**.' Mt 5:43
his **e** came and sowed weeds among the Mt 13:25
He said to them, 'An **e** has done this.' So Mt 13:28
and the **e** who sowed them is the devil. Mt 13:39
and over all the power of the **e**, Lk 10:19
of the devil, you **e** of all righteousness, Acts 13:10
To the contrary, "if your **e** is hungry, Rom 12:20
The last **e** to be destroyed is death. 1 Cor 15:26
I then become your **e** by telling you the Gal 4:16
Do not regard him as an **e**, but warn 2 Thes 3:15
of the world makes himself an **e** of God. Jas 4:4

ENEMY'S (1)
"If you meet your **e** ox or his donkey Ex 23:4

ENERGY (1)
with all his **e** that he powerfully Col 1:29

ENFORCE (1)
an ordinance and **e** an injunction, Dn 6:7

ENFORCED (1)
faith conquered kingdoms, **e** justice, Heb 11:33

ENGAGE (1)
to them, '**E** in business until I come.' Lk 19:13

ENGAGED (3)
a virgin who is not **e** to be married and Ex 22:16
So those who were **e** in the work 2 Chr 24:13
e in the same conflict that you saw I Phil 1:30

ENGEDI (6)
Nibshan, the City of Salt, and **E**: six Jos 15:62
and lived in the strongholds of **E**. 1 Sm 23:29
David is in the wilderness of **E**." 1 Sm 24:1
are in Hazazon-tamar" (that is, **E**). 2 Chr 20:2
of henna blossoms in the vineyards of **E**. Sg 1:14
From **E** to Eneglaim it will be a place Ezk 47:10

ENGINES (1)
In Jerusalem he made **e**, invented by 2 Chr 26:15

ENGRAVE (5)
and **e** on them the names of the sons of Ex 28:9
so shall you **e** the two stones with the Ex 28:11
make a plate of pure gold and **e** on it, Ex 28:36
and lay it before you, and **e** on it a city, Ezk 4:1
with seven eyes, I will **e** its inscription, Zec 3:9

ENGRAVED (9)
be like signets, each **e** with its name, Ex 28:21
was the writing of God, **e** on the tablets. Ex 32:16
and **e** like the engravings of a signet, Ex 39:6
were like signets, each **e** with its name, Ex 39:14
house he carved **e** figures of 1 Kgs 6:29
and lead they were **e** in the rock forever! Jb 19:24
I have **e** you on the palms of my hands; Is 49:16
point of diamond it is **e** on the tablet of Jer 17:1
And there, **e** on the wall all around, was Ezk 8:10

ENGRAVER (2)
of work done by an **e** or by a designer Ex 35:35
an **e** and designer and embroiderer in Ex 38:23

ENGRAVES (1)
As a jeweler **e** signets, so shall you Ex 28:11

ENGRAVING (4)
and engrave on it, like the **e** of a signet, Ex 28:36
it an inscription, like the **e** of a signet, Ex 39:30
and blue fabrics, trained also in **e**, 2 Chr 2:7
do all sorts of **e** and execute any 2 Chr 2:14

ENGRAVINGS (2)
and engraved like the **e** of a signet, Ex 39:6
in gold were your settings and your **e**. Ezk 28:13

ENHANCES (1)
and a man of knowledge **e** his might, Prv 24:5

ENJOY (20)
"Then the land shall **e** its Sabbaths as Lv 26:34
the land shall rest, and **e** its Sabbaths. Lv 26:34
by them and **e** its Sabbaths while Lv 26:43
in the battle and another man **e** its fruit. Dt 20:6
And you shall **e** the spoil of your Dt 20:14
a vineyard, but you shall not **e** its fruit. Dt 28:30
gave to our fathers to **e** its fruit and its Neh 9:36
him and leave him alone, that he may **e**, Jb 14:6
offering, but the upright **e** acceptance. Prv 14:9
e yourself." But behold, this also was Eccl 2:1
and possessions and power to **e** them, Eccl 5:19
God does not give him power to **e** them, Eccl 6:2
yet **e** no good—do not all go to the one Eccl 6:6
E life with the wife whom you love, all Eccl 9:9
my chosen shall long **e** the work of their Is 65:22
into a plentiful land to **e** its fruits and its Jer 2:7
planters shall plant and shall **e** the fruit. Jer 31:5
"Since through you we **e** much peace, Acts 24:2
provides us with everything to **e**. 1 Tm 6:17
of God than to **e** the fleeting pleasures Heb 11:25

ENJOYED (4)
a vineyard and has not **e** its fruit? Dt 20:6
until the land had **e** its Sabbaths. 2 Chr 36:21
everything to be **e** by someone who Eccl 2:21
once I have **e** your company for a Rom 15:24

ENJOYING (1)
e your great goodness that you gave Neh 9:35

ENJOYMENT (4)
the profit of his trading he will get no **e**. Jb 20:18
eat and drink and find **e** in his toil. Eccl 2:24
him who can eat or who can have **e**? Eccl 2:25
eat and drink and find **e** in all the toil Eccl 5:18

ENJOYS (1)
to enjoy them, but a stranger **e** them. Eccl 6:2

ENLARGE (7)
May God **e** Japheth, and let him dwell in Gn 9:27
nations before you and **e** your borders; Ex 34:24
you would bless me and **e** my border, 1 Chr 4:10
when you **e** my heart! Ps 119:32
"**E** the place of your tent, and let the Is 54:2
of gold, that you **e** your eyes with paint? Jer 4:30
Gilead, that they might **e** their border. Am 1:13

ENLARGED (4)
The troubles of my heart are **e**; bring Ps 25:17
Therefore Sheol has **e** its appetite and Is 5:14
you have **e** all the borders of the land. Is 26:15
among you may be greatly **e**, 2 Cor 10:15

ENLARGES (4)
the LORD your God **e** your territory, Dt 12:20
if the LORD your God **e** your territory, Dt 19:8
Gad he said, "Blessed be he who **e** Gad! Dt 33:20
and he destroys them; he **e** nations, Jb 12:23

ENLIGHTENED (3)
having the eyes of your hearts **e**, that Eph 1:18
repentance those who have once been **e**, Heb 6:4
former days when, after you were **e**, Heb 10:32

ENLIGHTENING (1)
of the LORD is pure, **e** the eyes; Ps 19:8

ENLIGHTENS (1)
The true light, which **e** everyone, was Jn 1:9

ENLISTED (1)
his aim is to please the one who **e** him. 2 Tm 2:4

ENMITY (9)
I will put **e** between you and the woman, Gn 3:15
or in **e** struck him down with his Nm 35:21
if he pushed him suddenly without **e**, Nm 35:22
without being at **e** with him in time past; Dt 4:42
of soul to destroy in never-ending **e**, Ezk 25:15
you cherished perpetual **e** and gave Ezk 35:5
this they had been at **e** with each other. Lk 23:12
idolatry, sorcery, **e**, strife, jealousy, fits Gal 5:20
friendship with the world is **e** with God? Jas 4:4

ENOCH (13)
his wife, and she conceived and bore **E**. Gn 4:17
of the city after the name of his son, **E**. Gn 4:17
To **E** was born Irad, and Irad fathered Gn 4:18
Jared had lived 162 years he fathered **E**. Gn 5:18
lived after he fathered **E** 800 years and Gn 5:19
When **E** had lived 65 years, he fathered Gn 5:21
E walked with God after he fathered Gn 5:22
Thus all the days of **E** were 365 years. Gn 5:23
E walked with God, and he was not, for Gn 5:24
E, Methuselah, Lamech; 1 Chr 1:3
the son of Methuselah, the son of **E**, the Lk 3:37
By faith **E** was taken up so that he Heb 11:5
It was also about these that **E**, the Jude 1:14

ENOS (1)
the son of **E**, the son of Seth, the son of Lk 3:38

ENOSH (7)
son was born, and he called his name **E**. Gn 4:26
Seth had lived 105 years, he fathered **E**. Gn 5:6
lived after he fathered **E** 807 years and Gn 5:7
When **E** had lived 90 years, he fathered Gn 5:9
E lived after he fathered Kenan 815 Gn 5:10
Thus all the days of **E** were 905 years, Gn 5:11
Adam, Seth, **E**; 1 Chr 1:1

ENOUGH (63)
Behold, this city is near **e** to flee to, and Gn 19:20
But Esau said, "I have **e**, my brother; Gn 33:9
and because I have **e**." Thus he urged Gn 33:11
for behold, the land is large **e** for them. Gn 34:21
And Israel said, "It is **e**; Joseph my son Gn 45:28
for there has been **e** of God's thunder and Ex 9:28
bring much more than **e** for doing the Ex 36:5
for them, and be **e** for them? Nm 11:22
together for them, and be **e** for them?" Nm 11:22
'You have stayed long **e** at this mountain. Dt 1:6
around this mountain country long **e**. Dt 2:3
And the LORD said to me, '**E** from you; do Dt 3:26
said, "The hill country is not **e** for us. Jos 17:16
Have we not had **e** of the sin at Peor Jos 22:17
he wrung **e** dew from the fleece to fill a Jgs 6:38
but they were not **e** for them. Jgs 21:14
chariot horses but left **e** for a hundred 2 Sm 8:4
among the people, "It is **e**; 2 Sm 24:16
have gone up to Jerusalem long **e**. 1 Kgs 12:28
that he might die, saying, "It is **e**; 1 Kgs 19:4
horses, but left **e** for 100 chariots. 1 Chr 18:4
was working destruction, "It is **e**; 1 Chr 21:15
eaten and had **e** and have plenty 2 Chr 31:10
and his descendants have not **e** bread. Jb 27:14
we have had more than **e** of contempt. Ps 123:3
has had more than **e** of the scorn of Ps 123:4
The righteous has **e** to satisfy his Prv 13:25
wealth; be discerning **e** to desist. Prv 23:4
have found honey, eat only **e** for you, Prv 25:16
There will be **e** goats' milk for your Prv 27:27
are never satisfied; four never say, "**E**": Prv 30:15
water, and the fire that never says, "**E**." Prv 30:16
I have had **e** of burnt offerings of rams Is 1:11
nor are its beasts **e** for a burnt offering. Is 40:16

a mighty appetite; they never have **e**. Is 56:11
they not destroy only **e** for themselves? Jer 49:9
to Egypt, and to Assyria, to get bread **e**. Lam 5:6
Is it not **e** for you to feed on the good Ezk 34:18
of Israel, **e** of all your abominations, Ezk 44:6
the Lord GOD: **E**, O princes of Israel! Ezk 45:9
had risen. It was deep **e** to swim in, Ezk 47:5
they not steal only **e** for themselves? Ob 1:5
"Yes, I do well to be angry, angry **e** to die." Jon 4:9
The lion tore **e** for his cubs and Na 2:12
wide as Sheol; like death he has never **e**. Hab 2:5
You eat, but you never have **e**; you drink, Hg 1:6
It is **e** for the disciple to be like his Mt 10:25
"Where are we to get **e** bread in such a Mt 15:33
'Since there will not be **e** for us and for Mt 25:9
your rest? It is **e**; the hour has come. Mk 14:41
cost, whether he has **e** to complete it? Lk 14:28
hired servants have more than **e** bread, Lk 15:17
I am not strong **e** to dig, and I am Lk 16:3
swords." And he said to them, "It is **e**." Lk 22:38
denarii would not buy **e** bread for each of Jn 6:7
show us the Father, and it is **e** for us." Jn 14:8
and you have been kind **e** to come. Acts 10:33
And when they had eaten **e**, they Acts 27:38
one among you wise **e** to settle a 1 Cor 6:5
you may be giving thanks well **e**, 1 Cor 14:17
this punishment by the majority is **e**, 2 Cor 2:6
accepted, you put up with it readily **e**. 2 Cor 11:4
though I am bold **e** in Christ to Phlm 1:8

ENRAGED (12)
are mighty men, and that they are **e**, 2 Sm 17:8
the wall, he was angry and greatly **e**, Neh 4:1
At this the king became **e**, and his anger Est 1:12
they will be **e** and will speak Is 8:21
For the LORD is **e** against all the nations, Is 34:2
And the officials were **e** at Jeremiah, Jer 37:15
but have **e** me with all these things, Ezk 16:43
and he was **e** against him and struck the Dn 8:7
turn back and be **e** and take action Dn 11:30
they were **e** and wanted to kill them. Acts 5:33
they heard these things they were **e**, Acts 7:54
this they were **e** and were crying Acts 19:28

ENRICH (2)
And the king will **e** the man who 1 Sm 17:25
the earth and water it; you greatly **e** it; Ps 65:9

ENRICHED (5)
Whoever brings blessing will be **e**, Prv 11:25
one who trusts in the LORD will be **e**. Prv 28:25
and merchandise you **e** the kings of Ezk 27:33
in every way you were **e** in him in all 1 Cor 1:5
You will be **e** in every way for all 2 Cor 9:11

ENROLL (1)
But refuse to **e** younger widows, for 1 Tm 5:11

ENROLLED (14)
that he could not be **e** as the oldest son; 1 Chr 5:1
mighty warriors, **e** by genealogy. 1 Chr 7:5
Their number **e** by genealogies, 1 Chr 7:40
They were **e** by genealogies in their 1 Chr 9:22
except those **e** by genealogy, males 2 Chr 31:16
They were **e** with all their little 2 Chr 31:18
among the Levites who was **e**. 2 Chr 31:19
registration among those **e** in the Ezr 2:62
and the people to be **e** by genealogy. Neh 7:5
registration among those **e** in the Neh 7:64
let them not be **e** among the righteous. Ps 69:28
nor be **e** in the register of the house of Ezk 13:9
Let a widow be **e** if she is not less than 1 Tm 5:9
of the firstborn who are **e** in heaven, Heb 12:23

ENROLLMENT (3)
And their **e** by genealogies was 22,034. 1 Chr 7:7
And their **e** by genealogies, according 1 Chr 7:9
The **e** of the priests was according to 2 Chr 31:17

ENSLAVE (2)
female, so that no one should **e** a Jew, Jer 34:9
who would **e** them and afflict them four Acts 7:6

ENSLAVED (10)
of our daughters have already been **e**, Neh 5:5
so that they would not be **e** again. Jer 34:10
from the hand of those who **e** them. Ezk 34:27
and have never been **e** to anyone. Jn 8:33
so that we would no longer be **e** to sin. Rom 6:6
me," but I will not be **e** by anything. 1 Cor 6:12
cases the brother or sister is not **e**. 1 Cor 7:15
were **e** to the elementary principles of the Gal 4:3
you were **e** to those that by nature are not Gal 4:8
overcomes a person, to that he is **e**. 2 Pt 2:19

ENSLAVERS (1)
who practice homosexuality, **e**, liars, 1 Tm 1:10

ENSNARE (4)
reign, that he should not **e** the people. Jb 34:30
And let the net that he hid **e** him; let him Ps 35:8
Though the cords of the wicked **e** me, I Ps 119:61
The iniquities of the wicked **e** him, and Prv 5:22

ENSNARED (4)
take it for yourselves, lest you be **e** by it, Dt 7:25
care that you be not **e** to follow them, Dt 12:30
An evil man is **e** by the transgression Prv 12:13
An evil man is **e** in his transgression, Prv 29:6

ENTANGLE (2)
learn his ways and **e** yourself in a Prv 22:25
and plotted how to **e** him in his talk. Mt 22:15

ENTANGLED (5)
the cords of Sheol **e** me; the snares of 2 Sm 22:6
the cords of Sheol **e** me; the snares of Ps 18:5
For they are like **e** thorns, like Na 1:10
No soldier gets **e** in civilian pursuits, 2 Tm 2:4
they are again **e** in them and overcome, 2 Pt 2:20

ENTER (177)
When he was about to **e** Egypt, he said Gn 12:11
allow the destroyer to **e** your houses to Ex 12:23
was not able to **e** the tent of meeting Ex 40:35
brings the curse shall **e** into her and Nm 5:24
brings the curse shall **e** into her and Nm 5:27
for he shall not **e** the land that I have Nm 20:24
When you **e** the land of Canaan (this Nm 34:2
Nun, who stands before you, he shall **e**. Dt 1:38
and that I should not **e** the good land that Dt 4:21
is cut off shall **e** the assembly of the Dt 23:1
a forbidden union may **e** the assembly of Dt 23:2
of his descendants may **e** the assembly of Dt 23:2
or Moabite may **e** the assembly of Dt 23:3
none of them may **e** the assembly of the Dt 23:3
third generation may **e** the assembly of Dt 23:8
you cross over to **e** the land that the Dt 27:3
so that you may **e** into the sworn Dt 29:12
going over the Jordan to **e** and possess. Dt 30:18
Do not let them **e** their cities, for the Jos 10:19
But they did not **e** the territory of Moab, Jgs 11:18
slow to go, to **e** in and possess the land. Jgs 18:9
Dagon and all who **e** the house of 1 Sm 5:5
and did not again **e** the territory of 1 Sm 7:13
As soon as you **e** the city you will find 1 Sm 9:13
"You shall not **e** into marriage with 1 Kgs 11:2
When your feet **e** the city, the child 1 Kgs 14:12
If we say, 'Let us **e** the city,' the famine 2 Kgs 7:4
the priests could not **e** the house of the 2 Chr 7:2
Let no one **e** the house of the LORD 2 Chr 23:6
They may **e**, for they are holy, but all 2 Chr 23:6
that no one should **e** who was in 2 Chr 23:19
except he did not **e** the temple of the 2 Chr 27:2
had told their fathers to **e** and possess. Neh 9:23
and **e** into a curse and an oath to Neh 10:29
Moabite should ever **e** the assembly of Neh 13:1
one was allowed to **e** the king's gate Est 4:2
that night be barren; let no joyful cry **e** it. Jb 3:7
of your steadfast love, will **e** your house. Ps 5:7
their sword shall **e** their own heart, and Ps 37:15
are led along as they **e** the palace of the Ps 45:15
my wrath, "They shall not **e** my rest." Ps 95:11
E his gates with thanksgiving, and his Ps 100:4
that I may **e** through them and give Ps 118:19
LORD; the righteous shall **e** through it. Ps 118:20
"I will not **e** my house or get into my Ps 132:3
E not into judgment with your servant, Ps 143:2
Do not **e** the path of the wicked, and do Prv 4:14
an ancient landmark or **e** the fields of Prv 23:10
E into the rock and hide in the dust from Is 2:10
And people shall **e** the caves of the rocks Is 2:19
to **e** the caverns of the rocks and the clefts Is 2:21
The LORD will **e** into judgment with the Is 3:14
the hand for them to **e** the gates of the Is 13:2
house is shut up so that none can **e**. Is 24:10
nation that keeps faith may **e** in. Is 26:2
Come, my people, **e** your chambers, and Is 26:20
squares, and uprightness cannot **e**. Is 59:14
by fire will the LORD **e** into judgment, Is 66:16
every city takes to flight; they **e** thickets; Jer 4:29
men of Judah who **e** these gates to worship Jer 7:2
And if I **e** the city, behold, the diseases Jer 14:18
Do not **e** the house of mourning, or go to Jer 16:5
the kings of Judah **e** and by which they Jer 17:19
of Jerusalem, who **e** by these gates. Jer 17:20
then there shall **e** by the gates of this Jer 17:25
to bear a burden and **e** by the gates of Jer 17:27
us, or who shall **e** our habitations?' Jer 21:13
and your people who **e** these gates. Jer 22:2
then there shall **e** the gates of this house Jer 22:4
them, nor did it **e** into my mind, Jer 32:35
you set your faces to **e** Egypt and go to Jer 42:15
has seen the nations **e** her sanctuary, Lam 1:10
you forbade to **e** your congregation. Lam 1:10
foe or enemy could **e** the gates of Lam 4:12
place. Robbers shall **e** and profane it. Ezk 7:22
Israel, nor shall they **e** the land of Israel. Ezk 13:9
to Babylon and **e** into judgment with Ezk 17:20
and there I will **e** into judgment with Ezk 20:35
so I will **e** into judgment with you, Ezk 20:36
but they shall not **e** the land of Israel. Ezk 20:38
your gates as men **e** a city that has Ezk 26:10
Behold, I will cause breath to **e** you, and Ezk 37:5
bloodshed I will **e** into judgment with Ezk 38:22
When the priests **e** the Holy Place, Ezk 42:14
not be opened, and no one shall **e** by it, Ezk 44:2
He shall **e** by way of the vestibule of the Ezk 44:3
people of Israel, shall **e** my sanctuary. Ezk 44:9
They shall **e** my sanctuary, and they Ezk 44:16
When they **e** the gates of the inner Ezk 44:17
The prince shall **e** by the vestibule of Ezk 46:2
he shall **e** by the vestibule of the gate, Ezk 46:8
When they **e**, the prince shall enter Ezk 46:10
enter, the prince shall **e** with them, Ezk 46:10
against the army and **e** the fortress of Dn 11:7
E not into Gilgal, nor go up to Hos 4:15
they **e** through the windows like a thief. Jl 2:9
And I will **e** into judgment with them there, Jl 3:2
and do not **e** into Gilgal or cross over to Am 5:5
Do not **e** the gate of my people in the day Ob 1:13
hosts, and it shall **e** the house of the thief, Zec 5:4
you will never **e** the kingdom of heaven. Mt 5:20
"**E** by the narrow gate. For the gate is Mt 7:13
and those who **e** by it are many. Mt 7:13
Lord,' will **e** the kingdom of heaven, Mt 7:21
among the Gentiles and **e** no town of the Mt 10:5
And whatever town or village you **e**, Mt 10:11
As you **e** the house, greet it. Mt 10:12
Or how can someone **e** a strong man's Mt 12:29
than itself, and they **e** and dwell there, Mt 12:45
you will never **e** the kingdom of heaven. Mt 18:3
is better for you to **e** life crippled or lame Mt 18:8
is better for you to **e** life with one eye Mt 18:9
If you would **e** life, keep the Mt 19:17
will a rich person **e** the kingdom of Mt 19:23
a rich person to **e** the kingdom of God." Mt 19:24
For you neither **e** yourselves nor allow Mt 23:13
nor allow those who would **e** to go in. Mt 23:13
much. **E** into the joy of your master.' Mt 25:21
much. **E** into the joy of your master.' Mt 25:23
that you may not **e** into temptation. Mt 26:41
Jesus could no longer openly **e** a town, Mk 1:45
But no one can **e** a strong man's house Mk 3:27
desires for other things **e** in and choke Mk 4:19
"Send us to the pigs; let us **e** them." Mk 5:12
said to them, "Whenever you **e** a house, Mk 6:10
saying, "Do not even **e** the village." Mk 8:26
out of him and never **e** him again." Mk 9:25
better for you to **e** life crippled than Mk 9:43
is better for you to **e** life lame than with Mk 9:45
better for you to **e** the kingdom of God Mk 9:47
of God like a child shall not **e** it." Mk 10:15
who have wealth to **e** the kingdom of Mk 10:23
difficult it is to **e** the kingdom of God! Mk 10:24
a rich person to **e** the kingdom of Mk 10:25
and immediately as you **e** it you will Mk 11:2
housetop not go down, nor **e** his house, Mk 13:15
that you may not **e** into temptation. Mk 14:38
was chosen by lot to **e** the temple of the Lk 1:9
so that those who **e** may see the light. Lk 8:16
and they begged him to let them **e** these. Lk 8:32
house, he allowed no one to **e** with him, Lk 8:51
And whatever house you **e**, stay there, and Lk 9:4
Whatever house you **e**, first say, 'Peace Lk 10:5
Whenever you **e** a town and they receive Lk 10:8
But whenever you **e** a town and they do Lk 10:10
than itself, and they **e** and dwell there. Lk 11:26
so that those who **e** may see the light. Lk 11:33
You did not **e** yourselves, and you Lk 11:52
"Strive to **e** through the narrow door. Lk 13:24
you, will seek to **e** and will not be able. Lk 13:24
of God like a child shall not **e** it." Lk 18:17
who have wealth to **e** the kingdom of Lk 18:24
a rich person to **e** the kingdom of God." Lk 18:25
those who are out in the country **e** it, Lk 21:21
that you may not **e** into temptation." Lk 22:40
that you may not **e** into temptation." Lk 22:46
these things and **e** into his glory?" Lk 24:26
Can he **e** a second time into his mother's Jn 3:4
Spirit, he cannot **e** the kingdom of God. Jn 3:5
he who does not **e** the sheepfold by the Jn 10:1
themselves did not **e** the governor's Jn 18:28
But rise and **e** the city, and you will be Acts 9:6
tribulations we must **e** the kingdom Acts 14:22
and outsiders or unbelievers **e**, 1 Cor 14:23
my wrath, 'They shall not **e** my rest.'" Heb 3:11
he swear that they would not **e** his rest, Heb 3:18
were unable to **e** because of unbelief. Heb 3:19
For we who have believed **e** that rest, as Heb 4:3
'They shall not **e** my rest,'" although his Heb 4:3
he said, "They shall not **e** my rest." Heb 4:5
therefore it remains for some to **e** it, Heb 4:6

news failed to **e** because of disobedience, Heb 4:6
Let us therefore strive to **e** that rest, so Heb 4:11
have confidence to **e** the holy places Heb 10:19
and no one could **e** the sanctuary until Rv 15:8
But nothing unclean will ever **e** it, nor Rv 21:27
life and that they may **e** the city by the Rv 22:14

ENTERED (113)
wives of his sons with them **e** the ark, Gn 7:13
And those that **e**, male and female of all Gn 7:16
When Abram **e** Egypt, the Egyptians Gn 12:14
turned aside to him and **e** his house. Gn 19:3
went out of Leah's tent and **e** Rachel's. Gn 31:33
years old when he **e** the service of Gn 41:46
And he **e** his chamber and wept there. Gn 43:30
Moses **e** the cloud and went up on the Ex 24:18
When Moses **e** the tent, the pillar of Ex 33:9
who have come to you, who **e** your house, Jos 2:3
they ran and **e** the city and captured it. Jos 8:19
of them had **e** into the fortified Jos 10:20
they **e** the stronghold of the house of Jgs 9:46
land went up and **e** and took the carved Jgs 18:17
And when he **e** his house, he took a Jgs 19:29
And when the people **e** the forest, 1 Sm 14:26
David came to Saul and **e** his service. 1 Sm 16:21
from the day I **e** your service until 1 Sm 29:8
fled before Abishai and **e** the city. 2 Sm 10:14
also fled and **e** an inner chamber 1 Kgs 20:30
As soon as they **e** Samaria, Elisha 2 Kgs 6:20
came back and **e** another tent and 2 Kgs 7:8
And as Jehu **e** the gate, she said, "Is it 2 Kgs 9:31
And they **e** the house of Baal, and 2 Kgs 10:21
the right side as one **e** the house of the 2 Kgs 12:9
I **e** its farthest lodging place, its most 2 Kgs 19:23
Joab's brother, and **e** the city. 1 Chr 19:15
number was not **e** in the chronicles 1 Chr 27:24
And they **e** into a covenant to seek 2 Chr 15:12
took courage and **e** into a covenant 2 Chr 23:1
LORD his God and **e** the temple of the 2 Chr 26:16
upward—all who **e** the house of the 2 Chr 31:16
I turned back and **e** by the Valley Gate, Neh 2:15
Now Haman had just **e** the outer court of Est 6:4
"Have you **e** into the springs of the sea, Jb 38:16
"Have you **e** the storehouses of the snow, Jb 38:22
into our windows; it has **e** our palaces, Jer 9:21
And they **e** and took possession of it. Jer 32:23
the people who had **e** into the covenant Jer 34:10
the king of Babylon, **e** Jerusalem. Jer 52:12
the Spirit **e** into me and set me on my Ezk 2:2
But the Spirit **e** into me and set me on Ezk 3:24
vow to you and **e** into a covenant with Ezk 16:8
As I **e** into judgment with your fathers Ezk 20:36
the glory of the LORD **e** the temple by the Ezk 43:4
the LORD, the God of Israel, has **e** by it. Ezk 44:2
by way of the gate by which he **e**, Ezk 46:9
delicacies, no meat or wine **e** my mouth, Dn 10:3
his wealth and foreigners **e** his gates and Ob 1:11
When he **e** Capernaum, a centurion Mt 8:5
And when Jesus **e** Peter's house, he saw Mt 8:14
When he **e** the house, the blind men Mt 9:28
how he **e** the house of God and ate the Mt 12:4
on from there and **e** their synagogue. Mt 12:9
away from Galilee and **e** the region of Mt 19:1
And when he **e** Jerusalem, the whole Mt 21:10
And Jesus **e** the temple and drove out Mt 21:12
And when he **e** the temple, the chief Mt 21:23
until the day when Noah **e** the ark, Mt 24:38
on the Sabbath he **e** the synagogue and Mk 1:21
left the synagogue and **e** the house of Mk 1:29
how he **e** the house of God, in the time Mk 2:26
Again he **e** the synagogue, and a man Mk 3:1
spirits came out, and **e** the pigs, Mk 5:13
And when he had **e**, he said to them, Mk 5:39
And when he had **e** the house and left Mk 7:17
And he **e** a house and did not want Mk 7:24
And when he had **e** the house, his Mk 9:28
And he **e** Jerusalem and went into the Mk 11:11
And he **e** the temple and began to drive Mk 11:15
and she **e** the house of Zechariah and Lk 1:40
left the synagogue and **e** Simon's house. Lk 4:38
how he **e** the house of God and took and Lk 6:4
he **e** the synagogue and was teaching, Lk 6:6
hearing of the people, he **e** Capernaum. Lk 7:1
I **e** your house; you gave me no water for Lk 7:44
"Legion," for many demons had **e** him. Lk 8:30
came out of the man and **e** the pigs, Lk 8:33
and they were afraid as they **e** the cloud. Lk 9:34
who went and **e** a village of the Lk 9:52
went on their way, Jesus **e** a village. Lk 10:38
And as he **e** a village, he was met by ten Lk 17:12
until the day when Noah **e** the ark, Lk 17:27
He **e** Jericho and was passing through. Lk 19:1
And he **e** the temple and began to drive Lk 19:45
Then Satan **e** into Judas called Iscariot, Lk 22:3
"Behold, when you have **e** the city, Lk 22:10
labored, and you have **e** into their labor." Jn 4:38
and that Jesus had not **e** the boat with his Jn 6:22
had taken the morsel, Satan **e** into him. Jn 13:27
a garden, which he and his disciples **e**. Jn 18:1
he **e** with Jesus into the court of the high Jn 18:15
So Pilate **e** his headquarters again and Jn 18:33
He **e** his headquarters again and said to Jn 19:9
And when they had **e**, they went up to Acts 1:13
to walk, and **e** the temple with them, Acts 3:8
they **e** the temple at daybreak and Acts 5:21
So Ananias departed and **e** the house. Acts 9:17
on the following day they **e** Caesarea. Acts 10:24
When Peter **e**, Cornelius met him Acts 10:25
or unclean has ever **e** my mouth.' Acts 11:8
me, and we **e** the man's house. Acts 11:12
at Iconium they **e** together into the Acts 14:1
about him, he rose up and **e** the city, Acts 14:20
And he **e** the synagogue and for three Acts 19:8
and we **e** the house of Philip the Acts 21:8
so he went and **e** the barracks and Acts 23:16
and they **e** the audience hall with the Acts 25:23
no church **e** into partnership with me Phil 4:15
for whoever has **e** God's rest has also Heb 4:10
he **e** once for all into the holy places, Heb 9:12
For Christ has **e**, not into holy places Heb 9:24
days a breath of life from God **e** them, Rv 11:11

ENTERING (21)
land that you are **e** to take possession of Dt 4:5
land that you are **e** to take possession of Dt 7:1
land that you are **e** to take possession of Dt 11:10
land that you are **e** to take possession of Dt 11:29
land that you are **e** to take possession of Dt 23:20
land that you are **e** to take possession of Dt 28:21
land that you are **e** to take possession of Dt 28:63
land that you are **e** to take possession of Dt 30:16
among them in the land that they are **e**, Dt 31:16
As they were **e** the city, they saw 1 Sm 9:14
shut himself in by **e** a town that has 1 Sm 23:7
just as Absalom was **e** Jerusalem. 2 Sm 15:37
for they were not to be seen **e** the city. 2 Sm 17:17
saying, 'The land that you are **e**, Ezr 9:11
he is **e** into judgment with all flesh, and Jer 25:31
And **e** the tomb, they saw a young man Mk 16:5
and you hindered those who were **e**." Lk 11:52
you, where on **e** you will find a colt tied, Lk 19:30
Gate to ask alms of those **e** the temple. Acts 3:2
the church, and **e** house after house, Acts 8:3
while the promise of **e** his rest still Heb 4:1

ENTERS (23)
whoever **e** the house while it is shut up Lv 14:46
from the time he **e** to make atonement Lv 16:17
And whoever **e** the house shall be put 2 Chr 23:7
reproves you and **e** into judgment with Jb 22:4
he **e** into peace; they rest in their beds who Is 57:2
No one **e** suit justly; no one goes to law Is 59:4
when he **e** your gates as men enter a Ezk 26:10
as one **e** them from the outer court. Ezk 42:9
wall on the east as one **e** them. Ezk 42:12
drink wine when he **e** the inner court. Ezk 44:21
When the prince **e**, he shall enter by Ezk 46:8
he who **e** by the north gate to worship Ezk 46:9
and he who **e** by the south gate shall go Ezk 46:9
down into the Arabah, and **e** the sea; Ezk 47:8
the sound; rottenness **e** into my bones; Hab 3:16
since it **e** not his heart but his stomach, Mk 7:19
and wherever he **e**, say to the master of Mk 14:14
Follow him into the house that he **e** Lk 22:10
But he who **e** by the door is the shepherd Jn 10:2
I am the door. If anyone **e** by me, he will Jn 10:9
and an unbeliever or outsider **e**, 1 Cor 14:24
a hope that **e** into the inner place Heb 6:19
as the high priest **e** the holy places Heb 9:25

ENTERTAIN (1)
that he may **e** us." So they called Jgs 16:25

ENTERTAINED (4)
out of the prison, and he **e** them. Jgs 16:25
who looked on while Samson **e**. Jgs 16:27
received us and **e** us hospitably for Acts 28:7
thereby some have **e** angels unawares. Heb 13:2

ENTHRONED (17)
of hosts, who is **e** on the cherubim. 1 Sm 4:4
of hosts who sits **e** on the cherubim. 2 Sm 6:2
Israel, who is **e** above the cherubim, 2 Kgs 19:15
LORD who sits **e** above the cherubim. 1 Chr 13:6
But the LORD sits **e** forever; he has Ps 9:7
praises to the LORD, who sits **e** in Zion! Ps 9:11
you are holy, **e** on the praises of Israel. Ps 22:3
The LORD sits **e** over the flood; the LORD Ps 29:10
the flood; the LORD sits **e** as king forever. Ps 29:10
from where he sits **e** he looks out on all Ps 33:14
humble them, he who is **e** from of old, Ps 55:19
May he be **e** forever before God; appoint Ps 61:7
You who are **e** upon the cherubim, Ps 80:1
He sits **e** upon the cherubim; let the earth Ps 99:1
But you, O LORD, are **e** forever; you are Ps 102:12
eyes, O you who are **e** in the heavens! Ps 123:1
of Israel, who is **e** above the cherubim, Is 37:16

ENTICE (11)
"**E** your husband to tell us what the Jgs 14:15
the LORD said, 'Who will **e** Ahab, 1 Kgs 22:20
the LORD, saying, 'I will **e** him.' 1 Kgs 22:21
And he said, 'You are to **e** him, and 1 Kgs 22:22
'Who will **e** Ahab the king of Israel, 2 Chr 18:19
the LORD, saying, 'I will **e** him.' 2 Chr 18:20
And he said, 'You are to **e** him, and 2 Chr 18:21
Beware lest wrath **e** you into scoffing, Jb 36:18
My son, if sinners **e** you, do not consent. Prv 1:10
for sin. They **e** unsteady souls. 2 Pt 2:14
they **e** by sensual passions of the flesh 2 Pt 2:18

ENTICED (4)
of Israel and have **e** Judah and the 2 Chr 21:13
"If my heart has been **e** toward a woman, Jb 31:9
and my heart has been secretly **e**, and Jb 31:27
when he is lured and **e** by his own desire. Jas 1:14

ENTICES (2)
who is as your own soul **e** you secretly, Dt 13:6
A man of violence **e** his neighbor and Prv 16:29

ENTIRE (8)
thirty-eight years, until the **e** generation, Dt 2:14
years, and he finished his **e** house. 1 Kgs 7:1
Syria mustered his **e** army and went 2 Kgs 6:24
until the **e** scroll was consumed in the Jer 36:23
and it filled the **e** house where they were Acts 2:2
along with his **e** household that he Acts 16:34
Lord, together with his **e** household. Acts 18:8
body, setting on fire the **e** course of life, Jas 3:6

ENTIRELY (1)
Does he not speak **e** for our sake? It 1 Cor 9:10

ENTRAILS (21)
shall take all the fat that covers the **e**, Ex 29:13
into pieces, and wash its **e** and its legs, Ex 29:17
the fat tail and the fat that covers the **e**, Ex 29:22
but its **e** and its legs he shall wash with Lv 1:9
but the **e** and the legs he shall wash with Lv 1:13
offer the fat covering the **e** and all the fat Lv 3:3
the entrails and all the fat that is on the **e**, Lv 3:3
the fat that covers the **e** and all the fat that Lv 3:9
the entrails and all the fat that is on the **e** Lv 3:9
the fat covering the **e** and all the fat that Lv 3:14
the entrails and all the fat that is on the **e** Lv 3:14
the fat that covers the **e** and all the fat that Lv 4:8
the entrails and all the fat that is on the **e** Lv 4:8
all its flesh, with its head, its legs, its **e**, Lv 4:11
the fat tail, the fat that covers the **e**, Lv 7:3
fat that was on the **e** and the long lobe of Lv 8:16
He washed the **e** and the legs with water, Lv 8:21
fat that was on the **e** and the long lobe of Lv 8:25
And he washed the **e** and the legs and Lv 9:14
that which covers the **e** and the kidneys Lv 9:19
and spilled his **e** to the ground 2 Sm 20:10

ENTRANCE (119)
Lot went out to the men at the **e**, shut the Gn 19:6
the men who were at the **e** of the house, Gn 19:11
herself up, and sat at the **e** to Enaim, Gn 38:14
shall make a screen for the **e** of the tent, Ex 26:36
and his sons to the **e** of the tent of Ex 29:4
before the LORD at the **e** of the tent of Ex 29:11
in the basket in the **e** of the tent of Ex 29:32
your generations at the **e** of the tent of Ex 29:42
descend and stand at the **e** of the tent, Ex 33:9
of cloud standing at the **e** of the tent, Ex 33:10
also made a screen for the **e** of the tent, Ex 36:37
who ministered in the **e** of the tent of Ex 38:8
made the bases for the **e** of the tent of Ex 38:30
and the screen for the **e** of the tent; Ex 39:38
and his sons to the **e** of the tent of Ex 40:12
burnt offering at the **e** of the tabernacle Ex 40:29
shall bring it to the **e** of the tent of Lv 1:3
altar that is at the **e** of the tent of meeting. Lv 1:5
and kill it at the **e** of the tent of meeting, Lv 3:2
bring the bull to the **e** of the tent of Lv 4:4
offering that is at the **e** of the tent of Lv 4:7
offering that is at the **e** of the tent of Lv 4:18
all the congregation at the **e** of the tent of Lv 8:3
was assembled at the **e** of the tent of Lv 8:4
"Boil the flesh at the **e** of the tent of Lv 8:31
shall not go outside the **e** of the tent of Lv 8:33
At the **e** of the tent of meeting you shall Lv 8:35
do not go outside the **e** of the tent of Lv 10:7
to the priest at the **e** of the tent of meeting Lv 12:6
the LORD, at the **e** of the tent of meeting. Lv 14:11
the priest, to the **e** of the tent of meeting, Lv 14:23
before the LORD to the **e** of the tent of Lv 15:14
the priest, to the **e** of the tent of meeting. Lv 15:29
before the LORD at the **e** of the tent of Lv 16:7
not bring it to the **e** of the tent of meeting Lv 17:4

to the priest at the **e** of the tent of Lv 17:5
of the LORD at the **e** of the tent of meeting Lv 17:6
not bring it to the **e** of the tent of meeting Lv 17:9
the LORD, to the **e** of the tent of meeting, Lv 19:21
the screen for the **e** of the tent of Nm 3:25
and the screen for the **e** of the tent of Nm 4:25
and the screen for the **e** of the gate of Nm 4:26
to the priest to the **e** of the tent of Nm 6:10
shall be brought to the **e** of the tent of Nm 6:13
consecrated head at the **e** of the tent of Nm 6:18
themselves to you at the **e** of the tent of Nm 10:3
cloud and stood at the **e** of the tent and Nm 12:5
them and stood at the **e** of the tent of Nm 16:18
against them at the **e** of the tent of Nm 16:19
returned to Moses at the **e** of the tent of Nm 16:50
of the assembly to the **e** of the tent of Nm 20:6
they were weeping in the **e** of the tent of Nm 25:6
at the **e** of the tent of meeting, Nm 27:2
of cloud stood over the **e** of the tent. Dt 31:15
tree and threw it at the **e** of the gate of the Jos 8:29
the LORD, at the **e** of the tent of meeting. Jos 19:51
and shall stand at the **e** of the gate of the Jos 20:4
out and stood in the **e** of the gate of the Jgs 9:35
fell wounded, up to the **e** of the gate. Jgs 9:40
forward and stood at the **e** of the gate of Jgs 9:44
of war, stood by the **e** of the gate. Jgs 18:16
the priest stood by the **e** of the gate with Jgs 18:17
who were serving at the **e** to the tent of 1 Sm 2:22
up in battle array at the **e** of the gate, 2 Sm 10:8
drove them back to the **e** of the gate. 2 Sm 11:23
The **e** for the lowest story was on the 1 Kgs 6:8
For the **e** to the inner sanctuary he 1 Kgs 6:31
he made for the **e** to the nave 1 Kgs 6:33
ran before Ahab to the **e** of Jezreel. 1 Kgs 18:46
out and stood at the **e** of the cave. 1 Kgs 19:13
threshing floor at the **e** of the gate of 1 Kgs 22:10
who were lepers at the **e** to the gate. 2 Kgs 7:3
in two heaps at the **e** of the gate until 2 Kgs 10:8
through the horses' **e** to the king's 2 Kgs 11:16
house and the outer **e** for the king he 2 Kgs 16:18
gates that were at the **e** of the gate of 2 Kgs 23:8
sun, at the **e** to the house of the LORD, 2 Kgs 23:11
They journeyed to the **e** of Gedor, to 1 Chr 4:39
east as far as the **e** of the desert this side 1 Chr 5:9
the camp of the LORD, keepers of the **e**. 1 Chr 9:19
was gatekeeper at the **e** of the tent of 1 Chr 9:21
up in battle array at the **e** of the city, 1 Chr 19:9
threshing floor at the **e** of the gate of 2 Chr 18:9
king standing by his pillar at the **e**, 2 Chr 23:13
she went into the **e** of the horse gate 2 Chr 23:15
and for the **e** into the Fish Gate, 2 Chr 33:14
He went up to the **e** of the king's gate, for Est 4:2
throne room opposite the **e** to the palace. Est 5:1
out; at the **e** of the city gates she speaks: Prv 1:21
at the **e** of the portals she cries aloud: Prv 8:3
set his throne at the **e** of the gates of Jer 1:15
him at the third **e** of the temple of Jer 38:14
that is at the **e** to Pharaoh's palace in Jer 43:9
to the **e** of the gateway of the inner court Ezk 8:3
behold, north of the altar gate, in the **e**, Ezk 8:5
And he brought me to the **e** of the court, Ezk 8:7
in the wall, and behold, there was an **e**. Ezk 8:8
he brought me to the **e** of the north gate Ezk 8:14
at the **e** of the temple of the LORD, Ezk 8:16
And they stood at the **e** of the east gate Ezk 10:19
at the **e** of the gateway there were Ezk 11:1
of the gate at the **e** to the front of the Ezk 40:15
one goes up to the **e** of the north gate, Ezk 40:40
And the breadth of the **e** was ten cubits, Ezk 41:2
the sidewalls of the **e** were five cubits on Ezk 41:2
room and measured the jambs of the **e**, Ezk 41:3
two cubits; and the **e**, six cubits; Ezk 41:3
and the sidewalls on either side of the **e**, Ezk 41:3
these chambers was an **e** on the east Ezk 42:9
There was an **e** at the beginning of the Ezk 42:12
And mark well the **e** to the temple and Ezk 44:5
bow down at the **e** of that gate before Ezk 46:3
Then he brought me through the **e**, Ezk 46:19
And when he went out to the **e**, another Mt 26:71
a great stone to the **e** of the tomb and Mt 27:60
a stone against the **e** of the tomb. Mk 15:46
the stone for us from the **e** of the tomb?" Mk 16:3
whose temple was at the **e** to the city, Acts 14:13
provided for you an **e** into the eternal 2 Pt 1:11

ENTRANCES (4)
to Tyre, who dwells at the **e** to the sea, Ezk 27:3
as were the **e** of the chambers on the Ezk 42:12
its arrangement, its exits and its **e**, Ezk 43:11
the sword, and the land of Nimrod at its **e**; Mi 5:6

ENTREAT (13)
hear me and **e** for me Ephron the son of Gn 23:8
"**E** now the favor of the LORD your 1 Kgs 13:6
I **e** your favor with all my heart; be Ps 119:58
not fear the LORD and **e** the favor of the Jer 26:19
and their men to **e** the favor of the Zec 7:2
us go at once to **e** the favor of the LORD Zec 8:21
in Jerusalem and to **e** the favor of the Zec 8:22
And now **e** the favor of God, that he may Mal 1:9
when slandered, we **e**. We have 1 Cor 4:13
I, Paul, myself **e** you, by the meekness 2 Cor 10:1
Brothers, I **e** you, become as I am, for I Gal 4:12
I **e** Euodia and I entreat Syntyche to Phil 4:2
entreat Euodia and I **e** Syntyche to agree Phil 4:2

ENTREATED (5)
me." And the man of God **e** the LORD, 1 Kgs 13:6
on his knees before Elijah and **e** him, 2 Kgs 1:13
he **e** the favor of the LORD his God 2 Chr 33:12
yet we have not **e** the favor of the LORD Dn 9:13
to go in. His father came out and **e** him, Lk 15:28

ENTREATIES (1)
The poor use **e**, but the rich answer Prv 18:23

ENTREATY (3)
was moved by his **e** and heard his 2 Chr 33:13
and how God was moved by his **e**, 2 Chr 33:19
God for this, and he listened to our **e**. Ezr 8:23

ENTRUST (5)
who will **e** to you the true riches? Lk 16:11
on his part did not **e** himself to them, Jn 2:24
This charge I **e** to you, Timothy, my 1 Tm 1:18
of many witnesses **e** to faithful men 2 Tm 2:2
according to God's will **e** their souls to 1 Pt 4:19

ENTRUSTED (15)
were **e** to be over the chambers and 1 Chr 9:26
was **e** with making the flat cakes. 1 Chr 9:31
They **e** him to Gedaliah the son of Jer 39:14
called his servants and **e** to them his Mt 25:14
and from him to whom they **e** much, Lk 12:48
the Jews were **e** with the oracles of God. Rom 3:2
will, I am still **e** with a stewardship. 1 Cor 9:17
saw that I had been **e** with the gospel to Gal 2:7
just as Peter had been **e** with the gospel to Gal 2:7
by God to be **e** with the gospel, 1 Thes 2:4
blessed God with which I have been **e**. 1 Tm 1:11
Timothy, guard the deposit **e** to you. 1 Tm 6:20
until that Day what has been **e** to me. 2 Tm 1:12
us, guard the good deposit **e** to you. 2 Tm 1:14
which I have been **e** by the command of Ti 1:3

ENTRUSTING (2)
and **e** to us the message of 2 Cor 5:19
but continued **e** himself to him who 1 Pt 2:23

ENTRY (3)
of Hinnom at the **e** of the Potsherd Gate, Jer 19:2
took their seat in the **e** of the New Gate Jer 26:10
at the **e** of the New Gate of the LORD'S Jer 36:10

ENTWINE (1)
His roots **e** the stone heap; he looks upon Jb 8:17

ENVELOPED (1)
has besieged and **e** me with bitterness Lam 3:5

ENVIED (3)
servants, so that the Philistines **e** him. Gn 26:14
bore Jacob no children, she **e** her sister. Gn 30:1
branches, and all the trees of Eden **e** it, Ezk 31:9

ENVIOUS (5)
you will look with **e** eye on all the 1 Sm 2:32
of evildoers; be not **e** of wrongdoers! Ps 37:1
For I was **e** of the arrogant when I saw Ps 73:3
Be not **e** of evil men, nor desire to be Prv 24:1
of evildoers, and be not **e** of the wicked, Prv 24:19

ENVOY (2)
but a faithful **e** brings healing. Prv 13:17
and an **e** has been sent among the Jer 49:14

ENVOYS (8)
sent **e** with letters and a present to 2 Kgs 20:12
the matter of the **e** of the princes of 2 Chr 32:31
But he sent **e** to him, saying, "What 2 Chr 35:21
are at Zoan and his **e** reach Hanes, Is 30:4
in the streets; the **e** of peace weep bitterly. Is 33:7
sent **e** with letters and a present to Is 39:1
you sent your **e** far off, and sent down Is 57:9
by the hand of the **e** who have come to Jer 27:3

ENVY (16)
Do not **e** a man of violence and do not Prv 3:31
to the flesh, but **e** makes the bones rot. Prv 14:30
Let not your heart **e** sinners, but Prv 23:17
come from a man's **e** of his neighbor. Eccl 4:4
hate and their **e** have already perished, Eccl 9:6
to the anger and **e** that you showed Ezk 35:11
it was out of **e** that they had delivered Mt 27:18
deceit, sensuality, **e**, slander, Mk 7:22
it was out of **e** that the chief priests Mk 15:10
They are full of **e**, murder, strife, Rom 1:29
and kind; love does not **e** or boast; 1 Cor 13:4
e, drunkenness, orgies, and things like Gal 5:21
preach Christ from **e** and rivalry, Phil 1:15
about words, which produce **e**, 1 Tm 6:4
passing our days in malice and **e**, Ti 3:3
and hypocrisy and **e** and all slander. 1 Pt 2:1

ENVYING (1)
provoking one another, **e** one another. Gal 5:26

EPAENETUS (1)
Greet my beloved **E**, who was the first Rom 16:5

EPAPHRAS (3)
you learned it from **E** our beloved fellow Col 1:7
E, who is one of you, a servant of Christ Col 4:12
E, my fellow prisoner in Christ Jesus, Phlm 1:23

EPAPHRODITUS (2)
to send to you **E** my brother and fellow Phil 2:25
having received from **E** the gifts you Phil 4:18

EPHAH (49)
The sons of Midian were **E**, Epher, Gn 25:4
(An omer is the tenth part of an **e**.) Ex 16:36
a tenth of an **e** of fine flour for Lv 5:11
a tenth of an **e** of fine flour as a regular Lv 6:20
three tenths of an **e** of fine flour mixed Lv 14:10
and a tenth of an **e** of fine flour mixed Lv 14:21
just balances, just weights, a just **e**, Lv 19:36
be two tenths of an **e** of fine flour mixed Lv 23:13
to be waved, made of two tenths of an **e**. Lv 23:17
two tenths of an **e** shall be in each loaf. Lv 24:5
of her, a tenth of an **e** of barley flour. Nm 5:15
offering of a tenth of an **e** of fine flour, Nm 15:4
two tenths of an **e** of fine flour mixed Nm 15:6
of three tenths of an **e** of fine flour, Nm 15:9
also a tenth of an **e** of fine flour for a Nm 28:5
and two tenths of an **e** of fine flour for a Nm 28:9
three tenths of an **e** of fine flour for Nm 28:12
three tenths of an **e** shall you offer for Nm 28:20
oil, three tenths of an **e** for each bull, Nm 28:28
oil, three tenths of an **e** for the bull, Nm 29:3
oil, three tenths of an **e** for the bull, Nm 29:9
three tenths of an **e** for each of the Nm 29:14
unleavened cakes from an **e** of flour. Jgs 6:19
gleaned, and it was about an **e** of barley. Ru 2:17
a three-year-old bull, an **e** of flour, 1 Sm 1:24
your brothers an **e** of this parched 1 Sm 17:17
E, Epher, Hanoch, Abida, and 1 Chr 1:33
E also, Caleb's concubine, bore 1 Chr 2:46
Geshan, Pelet, **E**, and Shaaph. 1 Chr 2:47
and a homer of seed shall yield but an **e**." Is 5:10
you, the young camels of Midian and **E**; Is 60:6
shall have just balances, a just **e**, Ezk 45:10
The **e** and the bath shall be of the Ezk 45:11
homer, and the **e** one tenth of a homer; Ezk 45:11
one sixth of an **e** from each homer of Ezk 45:13
one sixth of an **e** from each homer of Ezk 45:13
as a grain offering an **e** for each bull, Ezk 45:24
for each bull, an **e** for each ram, Ezk 45:24
each ram, and a hin of oil to each **e**. Ezk 45:24
offering with the ram shall be an **e**, Ezk 46:5
able, together with a hin of oil to each **e**. Ezk 46:5
he shall provide an **e** with the bull and Ezk 46:7
with the bull and an **e** with the ram, Ezk 46:7
able, together with a hin of oil to each **e**. Ezk 46:7
with a young bull shall be an **e**, Ezk 46:11
be an ephah, and with a ram an **e**, Ezk 46:11
give, together with a hin of oil to an **e**. Ezk 46:11
by morning, one sixth of an **e**, Ezk 46:14
we may make the **e** small and the shekel Am 8:5

EPHAI (1)
the sons of **E** the Netophathite, Jer 40:8

EPHER (4)
sons of Midian were Ephah, **E**, Hanoch, Gn 25:4
Ephah, **E**, Hanoch, Abida, and 1 Chr 1:33
of Ezrah: Jether, Mered, **E**, and Jalon. 1 Chr 4:17
E, Ishi, Eliel, Azriel, Jeremiah, 1 Chr 5:24

EPHES-DAMMIM (1)
between Socoh and Azekah, in **E**. 1 Sm 17:1

EPHESIAN (1)
seen Trophimus the **E** with him in Acts 21:29

EPHESIANS (3)
out, "Great is Artemis of the **E**!" Acts 19:28
one voice, "Great is Artemis of the **E**!" Acts 19:34
the city of the **E** is temple keeper of Acts 19:35

EPHESUS (17)
And they came to **E**, and he left them Acts 18:19
if God wills," and he set sail from **E**. Acts 18:21
a native of Alexandria, came to **E**. Acts 18:24
the inland country and came to **E**. Acts 19:1
known to all the residents of **E**, Acts 19:17
that not only in **E** but in almost all Acts 19:26
quieted the crowd, he said, "Men of **E**, Acts 19:35
For Paul had decided to sail past **E**, so Acts 20:16
Miletus he sent to **E** and called the Acts 20:17

speaking, I fought with beasts at **E**? 1 Cor 15:32
But I will stay in **E** until Pentecost, 1 Cor 16:8
will of God, To the saints who are in **E**, Eph 1:1
remain at **E** that you may charge 1 Tm 1:3
know all the service he rendered at **E**. 2 Tm 1:18
Tychicus I have sent to **E**. 2 Tm 4:12
to **E** and to Smyrna and to Pergamum Rv 1:11
"To the angel of the church in **E** write: Rv 2:1

EPHLAL (2)
Zabad fathered **E**, and Ephlal 1 Chr 2:37
fathered Ephlal, and **E** fathered Obed. 1 Chr 2:37

EPHOD (51)
setting, for the **e** and for the breastpiece. Ex 25:7
a breastpiece, an **e**, a robe, a coat of Ex 28:4
"And they shall make the **e** of gold, of Ex 28:6
stones on the shoulder pieces of the **e**, Ex 28:12
In the style of the **e** you shall make it— Ex 28:15
it in front to the shoulder pieces of the **e**. Ex 28:25
on its inside edge next to the **e**. Ex 28:26
part of the two shoulder pieces of the **e**, Ex 28:27
the skillfully woven band of the **e**. Ex 28:27
to the rings of the **e** with a lace of blue, Ex 28:28
on the skillfully woven band of the **e**, Ex 28:28
shall not come loose from the **e**. Ex 28:28
shall make the robe of the **e** all of blue. Ex 28:31
on Aaron the coat and the robe of the **e**, Ex 29:5
coat and the robe of the ephod, and the **e**, Ex 29:5
with the skillfully woven band of the **e**. Ex 29:5
setting, for the **e** and for the breastpiece. Ex 35:9
be set, for the **e** and for the breastpiece, Ex 35:27
He made the **e** of gold, blue and purple Ex 39:2
made for the **e** attaching shoulder pieces, Ex 39:4
shoulder pieces of the **e** to be stones of Ex 39:7
in skilled work, in the style of the **e**, Ex 39:8
it in front to the shoulder pieces of the **e**. Ex 39:18
on its inside edge next to the **e**. Ex 39:19
part of the two shoulder pieces of the **e**, Ex 39:20
the skillfully woven band of the **e**. Ex 39:20
to the rings of the **e** with a lace of blue, Ex 39:21
on the skillfully woven band of the **e**, Ex 39:21
should not come loose from the **e**, Ex 39:21
the robe of the **e** woven all of blue, Ex 39:22
the robe and put the **e** on him and tied the Lv 8:7
woven band of the **e** around him, Lv 8:7
a chief, Hanniel the son of **E**. Nm 34:23
And Gideon made an **e** of it and put it in Jgs 8:27
and he made an **e** and household gods, Jgs 17:5
that in these houses there are an **e**, Jgs 18:14
and took the carved image, the **e**, Jgs 18:17
house and took the carved image, the **e**, Jgs 18:18
He took the **e** and the household gods Jgs 18:20
the LORD, a boy clothed with a linen **e**. 1 Sm 2:18
burn incense, to wear an **e** before me? 1 Sm 2:28
of the LORD in Shiloh, wearing an **e**. 1 Sm 14:3
here wrapped in a cloth behind the **e**. 1 Sm 21:9
persons who wore the linen **e**. 1 Sm 22:18
had come down with an **e** in his hand. 1 Sm 23:6
Abiathar the priest, "Bring the **e** here." 1 Sm 23:9
"Bring me the **e**." So Abiathar 1 Sm 30:7
So Abiathar brought the **e** to David. 1 Sm 30:7
And David was wearing a linen **e**. 2 Sm 6:14
singers. And David wore a linen **e**. 1 Chr 15:27
or pillar, without **e** or household gods. Hos 3:4

EPHPHATHA (1)
he sighed and said to him, "**E**," that is, Mk 7:34

EPHRAIM (171)
The name of the second he called **E**, Gn 41:52
of Egypt were born Manasseh and **E**, Gn 46:20
with him his two sons, Manasseh and **E**. Gn 48:1
E and Manasseh shall be mine, as Gn 48:5
E in his right hand toward Israel's left Gn 48:13
right hand and laid it on the head of **E**, Gn 48:14
laid his right hand on the head of **E**, Gn 48:17
make you as **E** and as Manasseh.'" Gn 48:20
Thus he put **E** before Manasseh. Gn 48:20
from the sons of Joseph, from **E**, Nm 1:10
of Joseph, namely, of the people of **E**, Nm 1:32
those listed of the tribe of **E** were 40,500. Nm 1:33
of the camp of **E** by their companies, Nm 2:18
of the people of **E** being Elishama the Nm 2:18
All those listed of the camp of **E**, by Nm 2:24
Ammihud, the chief of the people of **E**: Nm 7:48
of the people of **E** set out by their Nm 10:22
from the tribe of **E**, Hoshea the son of Nm 13:8
to their clans: Manasseh and **E**. Nm 26:28
are the sons of **E** according to their Nm 26:35
of the sons of **E** as they were listed, Nm 26:37
of the tribe of the people of **E** a chief, Nm 34:24
they are the ten thousands of **E**, and Dt 33:17
Naphtali, the land of **E** and Manasseh, Dt 34:2
Joseph were two tribes, Manasseh and **E**. Jos 14:4
The people of Joseph, Manasseh and **E**, Jos 16:4
of the people of **E** by their clans was Jos 16:5
the tribe of the people of **E** by their clans, Jos 16:8
the people of **E** within the inheritance Jos 16:9
lived in the midst of **E** to this day but Jos 16:10
of Manasseh belonged to the people of **E**. Jos 17:8
the cities of Manasseh, belong to **E**. Jos 17:9
the hill country of **E** is too narrow for Jos 17:15
house of Joseph, to **E** and Manasseh, Jos 17:17
in the hill country of **E**. Jos 19:50
and Shechem in the hill country of **E**, Jos 20:7
by lot from the clans of the tribe of **E**, Jos 21:5
to them were out of the tribe of **E**. Jos 21:20
pasturelands in the hill country of **E**, Jos 21:21
which is in the hill country of **E**, Jos 24:30
given him in the hill country of **E**. Jos 24:33
And **E** did not drive out the Canaanites Jgs 1:29
Timnath-heres, in the hill country of **E**, Jgs 2:9
the trumpet in the hill country of **E**. Jgs 3:27
and Bethel in the hill country of **E**, Jgs 4:5
From **E** their root they marched down Jgs 5:14
throughout all the hill country of **E**, Jgs 7:24
So all the men of **E** were called out, Jgs 7:24
Then the men of **E** said to him, "What is Jgs 8:1
of the grapes of **E** better than the grape Jgs 8:2
lived at Shamir in the hill country of **E**. Jgs 10:1
Benjamin and against the house of **E**, Jgs 10:9
The men of **E** were called to arms, and Jgs 12:1
all the men of Gilead and fought with **E**. Jgs 12:4
And the men of Gilead struck **E**, Jgs 12:4
they said, "You are fugitives of **E**, Jgs 12:4
in the midst of **E** and Manasseh." Jgs 12:4
And when any of the fugitives of **E** said, Jgs 12:5
was buried at Pirathon in the land of **E**, Jgs 12:15
was a man of the hill country of **E**, Jgs 17:1
to the hill country of **E** to the house of Jgs 17:8
And they came to the hill country of **E**, Jgs 18:2
on from there to the hill country of **E**, Jgs 18:13
the remote parts of the hill country of **E**, Jgs 19:1
man was from the hill country of **E**, Jgs 19:16
remote parts of the hill country of **E**, Jgs 19:18
the hill country of **E** whose name was 1 Sm 1:1
hill country of **E** and passed through 1 Sm 9:4
the hill country of **E** heard that the 1 Sm 14:22
and Jezreel and **E** and Benjamin and 2 Sm 2:9
at Baal-hazor, which is near **E**, 2 Sm 13:23
the battle was fought in the forest of **E**. 2 Sm 18:6
But a man of the hill country of **E**, 2 Sm 20:21
Ben-hur, in the hill country of **E**; 1 Kgs 4:8
the hill country of **E** and lived there. 1 Kgs 12:25
the hill country of **E** two young men 2 Kgs 5:22
from the **E** Gate to the Corner Gate. 2 Kgs 14:13
of their territory out of the tribe of **E**. 1 Chr 6:66
pasturelands in the hill country of **E**, 1 Chr 6:67
The sons of **E**: Shuthelah, and Bered 1 Chr 7:20
And **E** their father mourned many 1 Chr 7:22
And **E** went in to his wife, and she 1 Chr 7:23
E, and Manasseh lived in Jerusalem: 1 Chr 9:3
Helez the Pelonite, of the sons of **E**; 1 Chr 27:10
of Pirathon, of the sons of **E**; 1 Chr 27:14
is in the hill country of **E** and said, 2 Chr 13:4
he had taken in the hill country of **E**, 2 Chr 15:8
and Benjamin, and those from **E**, 2 Chr 15:9
in the cities of **E** that Asa his father 2 Chr 17:2
Beersheba to the hill country of **E**, 2 Chr 19:4
come to him from **E** to go home 2 Chr 25:10
from the **E** Gate to the Corner Gate. 2 Chr 25:23
And Zichri, a mighty man of **E**, 2 Chr 28:7
Certain chiefs also of the men of **E**, 2 Chr 28:12
wrote letters also to **E** and Manasseh, 2 Chr 30:1
the country of **E** and Manasseh, 2 Chr 30:10
of the people, many of them from **E**, 2 Chr 30:18
Benjamin, and in **E** and Manasseh, 2 Chr 31:1
cities of Manasseh, **E**, and Simeon, 2 Chr 34:6
from Manasseh and **E** and from all 2 Chr 34:9
Gate and in the square at the Gate of **E**. Neh 8:16
and above the Gate of **E**, and by the Neh 12:39
mine; Manasseh is mine; **E** is my helmet; Ps 60:7
Joseph; he did not choose the tribe of **E**, Ps 78:67
Before **E** and Benjamin and Manasseh, Ps 80:2
E is my helmet, Judah my scepter. Ps 108:8
is in league with **E**," the heart of Ahaz Is 7:2
Syria, with **E** and the son of Remaliah, Is 7:5
(Within sixty-five years **E** will be broken Is 7:8
"'And the head of **E** is Samaria, and the Is 7:9
since the day that **E** departed from Judah Is 7:17
know, **E** and the inhabitants of Samaria, Is 9:9
Manasseh devours **E**, and Ephraim Is 9:21
Ephraim, and **E** devours Manasseh; Is 9:21
The jealousy of **E** shall depart, and those Is 11:13
E shall not be jealous of Judah, and Is 11:13
of Judah, and Judah shall not harass **E**. Is 11:13
The fortress will disappear from **E**, and Is 17:3
the proud crown of the drunkards of **E**, Is 28:1
of the drunkards of **E** will be trodden Is 28:3
and proclaims trouble from Mount **E**. Jer 4:15
all your kinsmen, all the offspring of **E**. Jer 7:15
will call in the hill country of **E**: Jer 31:6
a father to Israel, and **E** is my firstborn. Jer 31:9
I have heard **E** grieving, 'You have Jer 31:18
Is **E** my dear son? Is he my darling Jer 31:20
satisfied on the hills of **E** and in Gilead. Jer 50:19
Joseph (the stick of **E**) and all the Ezk 37:16
is in the hand of **E**) and the tribes of Ezk 37:19
the east side to the west, **E**, one portion. Ezk 48:5
Adjoining the territory of **E**, from the Ezk 48:6
E is joined to idols; leave him alone. Hos 4:17
I know **E**, and Israel is not hidden from Hos 5:3
for now, O **E**, you have played the whore; Hos 5:3
Israel and **E** shall stumble in his guilt; Hos 5:5
E shall become a desolation in the day of Hos 5:9
E is oppressed, crushed in judgment, Hos 5:11
But I am like a moth to **E**, and like dry Hos 5:12
When **E** saw his sickness, and Judah Hos 5:13
his wound, then **E** went to Assyria, Hos 5:13
For I will be like a lion to **E**, and like a Hos 5:14
What shall I do with you, O **E**? What Hos 6:4
heal Israel, the iniquity of **E** is revealed, Hos 7:1
E mixes himself with the peoples; Hos 7:8
with the peoples; **E** is a cake not turned. Hos 7:8
E is like a dove, silly and without sense, Hos 7:11
wandering alone; **E** has hired lovers. Hos 8:9
Because **E** has multiplied altars for Hos 8:11
of the LORD, but **E** shall return to Egypt, Hos 9:3
is the watchman of **E** with my God; Hos 9:8
E, as I have seen, was like a young palm Hos 9:13
but **E** must lead his children out to Hos 9:13
E is stricken; their root is dried up; they Hos 9:16
E shall be put to shame, and Israel Hos 10:6
E was a trained calf that loved to Hos 10:11
fair neck; but I will put **E** to the yoke; Hos 10:11
Yet it was I who taught **E** to walk; I took Hos 11:3
How can I give you up, O **E**? How can I Hos 11:8
anger; I will not again destroy **E**; Hos 11:9
E has surrounded me with lies, and Hos 11:12
E feeds on the wind and pursues the Hos 12:1
E has said, "Ah, but I am rich; I have Hos 12:8
E has given bitter provocation; so his Hos 12:14
When **E** spoke, there was trembling; he Hos 13:1
The iniquity of **E** is bound up; his sin Hos 13:12
O **E**, what have I to do with idols? It is I Hos 14:8
possess the land of **E** and the land of Ob 1:19
off the chariot from **E** and the war Zec 9:10
as my bow; I have made **E** its arrow. Zec 9:13
Then **E** shall become like a mighty Zec 10:7
near the wilderness, to a town called **E**, Jn 11:54

EPHRAIM'S (5)
to move it from **E** head to Manasseh's Gn 48:17
And Joseph saw **E** children of the third Gn 50:23
to the south being **E** and that to the Jos 17:10
a horrible thing; **E** whoredom is there; Hos 6:10
E glory shall fly away like a bird— Hos 9:11

EPHRAIMITE (2)
to him, "Are you an **E**?" When he said, Jgs 12:5
the son of Nebat, an **E** of Zeredah, 1 Kgs 11:26

EPHRAIMITES (6)
the fords of the Jordan against the **E**. Jgs 12:5
Jordan. At that time 42,000 of the **E** fell. Jgs 12:6
Of the **E** 20,800, mighty men of 1 Chr 12:30
for the **E**, Hoshea the son of Azaziah; 1 Chr 27:20
is not with Israel, with all these **E**. 2 Chr 25:7
The **E**, armed with the bow, turned back Ps 78:9

EPHRATH (5)
they were still some distance from **E**, Gn 35:16
she was buried on the way to **E** (that is, Gn 35:19
there was still some distance to go to **E**, Gn 48:7
buried her there on the way to **E** (that is, Gn 48:7
Azubah died, Caleb married **E**, 1 Chr 2:19

EPHRATHAH (6)
you act worthily in **E** and be renowned Ru 4:11
death of Hezron, Caleb went in to **E**, 1 Chr 2:24
The sons of Hur the firstborn of **E**: 1 Chr 2:50
the sons of Hur, the firstborn of **E**, 1 Chr 4:4
Behold, we heard of it in **E**; we found it Ps 132:6
But you, O Bethlehem **E**, who are too little Mi 5:2

EPHRATHITE (2)
Elihu, son of Tohu, son of Zuph, an **E**. 1 Sm 1:1
the son of an **E** of Bethlehem in 1 Sm 17:12

EPHRATHITES (1)
They were **E** from Bethlehem in Judah. Ru 1:2

EPHRON (15)
and entreat for me **E** the son of Zohar, Gn 23:8
Now **E** was sitting among the Hittites, Gn 23:10
and **E** the Hittite answered Abraham Gn 23:10
And he said to **E** in the hearing of the Gn 23:13
E answered Abraham, Gn 23:14
Abraham listened to **E**, and Abraham Gn 23:16
weighed out for **E** the silver that Gn 23:16
So the field of **E** in Machpelah, which Gn 23:17

in the field of **E** the son of Zohar the Gn 25:9
cave that is in the field of **E** the Hittite, Gn 49:29
with the field from **E** the Hittite to Gn 49:30
with the field from **E** the Hittite to Gn 50:13
and from there to the cities of Mount **E**. Jos 15:9
And the boundary goes from there to **E**, Jos 18:15
its villages and **E** with its villages. 2 Chr 13:19

EPICUREAN (1)
Some of the **E** and Stoic philosophers Acts 17:18

EPILEPTIC (1)
for he is an **e** and he suffers terribly. Mt 17:15

EPILEPTICS (1)
oppressed by demons, **e**, and paralytics, Mt 4:24

EQUAL (18)
he shall pay money **e** to the bride-price Ex 22:17
(of each shall there be an **e** part), Ex 30:34
then he may have **e** portions to eat, Dt 18:8
cubits long, **e** to the width of the house, 1 Kgs 6:3
long, **e** to the width of the house, 2 Chr 3:4
Gold and glass cannot **e** it, nor can it be Jb 28:17
The topaz of Ethiopia cannot **e** it, nor Jb 28:19
But it is you, a man, my **e**, my Ps 55:13
whom will you liken me and make me **e**, Is 46:5
e to the number of the years of their Ezk 4:5
rival it, nor the fir trees **e** its boughs; Ezk 31:8
in the garden of God was its **e** in beauty. Ezk 31:8
and in length **e** to one of the tribal Ezk 48:8
you have made them **e** to us who have Mt 20:12
because they are **e** to angels and are Lk 20:36
own Father, making himself **e** with God. Jn 5:18
obtained a faith of **e** standing with ours 2 Pt 1:1
Its length and width and height are **e**. Rv 21:16

EQUALITY (1)
did not count **e** with God a thing to be Phil 2:6

EQUALLY (2)
shall be shared **e** among all the sons of Lv 7:10
And you shall divide **e** what I swore to Ezk 47:14

EQUIP (4)
other, besides me there is no God; I **e** you, Is 45:5
who **e** yourselves with burning torches! Is 50:11
to **e** the saints for the work of ministry, Eph 4:12
e you with everything good that you Heb 13:21

EQUIPMENT (6)
cords and all the **e** for their service. Nm 4:26
with all their **e** and all their Nm 4:32
of war and the **e** of his chariots. 1 Sm 8:12
with garments and **e** that the Syrians 2 Kgs 7:15
and all the **e** for these Huram-abi 2 Chr 4:16
"Take once more the **e** of a foolish Zec 11:15

EQUIPPED (8)
up out of the land of Egypt **e** for battle. Ex 13:18
For you **e** me with strength for the 2 Sm 22:40
e for battle with all the weapons of 1 Chr 12:33
the Danites 28,600 men **e** for battle. 1 Chr 12:35
the God who **e** me with strength and Ps 18:32
For you **e** me with strength for the Ps 18:39
by every joint with which it is **e**, Eph 4:16
be competent, **e** for every good work. 2 Tm 3:17

EQUITY (10)
administered justice and **e** to all his 2 Sm 8:15
administered justice and **e** to all his 1 Chr 18:14
judge the peoples with **e** and guide the Ps 67:4
set time that I appoint I will judge with **e**. Ps 75:2
moved; he will judge the peoples with **e**." Ps 96:10
righteousness, and the peoples with **e**. Ps 98:9
You have established **e**; you have Ps 99:4
dealing, in righteousness, justice, and **e**; Prv 1:3
righteousness and justice and **e**, Prv 2:9
and decide with **e** for the meek of the Is 11:4

EQUIVALENT (2)
of the flock, or its **e** for a guilt offering, Lv 5:18
out of the flock, or its **e** for a guilt offering. Lv 6:6

ER (11)
bore a son, and he called his name **E**. Gn 38:3
Judah took a wife for **E** his firstborn, Gn 38:6
But **E**, Judah's firstborn, was wicked in Gn 38:7
E, Onan, Shelah, Perez, and Zerah (but Gn 46:12
and Zerah (but **E** and Onan died in the Gn 46:12
The sons of Judah were **E** and Onan; Nm 26:19
and **E** and Onan died in the land of Nm 26:19
sons of Judah: **E**, Onan and Shelah; 1 Chr 2:3
the Canaanite bore to him. Now **E**, 1 Chr 2:3
E the father of Lecah, Laadah the 1 Chr 4:21
the son of Elmadam, the son of **E**, Lk 3:28

ERAN (1)
these are the sons of Shuthelah: of **E**, Nm 26:36

ERANITES (1)
Shuthelah: of Eran, the clan of the **E**. Nm 26:36

ERASTUS (3)
two of his helpers, Timothy and **E**, Acts 19:22
E, the city treasurer, and our brother Rom 16:23
E remained at Corinth, and I left 2 Tm 4:20

ERECH (2)
of his kingdom was Babel, **E**, Accad, Gn 10:10
the officials, the Persians, the men of **E**, Ezr 4:9

ERECT (6)
Then you shall **e** the tabernacle Ex 26:30
first month you shall **e** the tabernacle of Ex 40:2
idols for yourselves or **e** an image or Lv 26:1
of your yoke and made you walk **e**. Lv 26:13
for the house of God, to **e** it on its site. Ezr 2:68
For when Moses was about to **e** the tent, Heb 8:5

ERECTED (10)
There he **e** an altar and called it Gn 33:20
day of the month, the tabernacle was **e**. Ex 40:17
Moses **e** the tabernacle. He laid its Ex 40:18
And he **e** the court around the Ex 40:33
He **e** an altar for Baal in the house of 1 Kgs 16:32
and he **e** altars for Baal and made an 2 Kgs 21:3
the high place **e** by Jeroboam the 2 Kgs 23:15
down, and he **e** altars to the Baals, 2 Chr 33:3
They **e** their siege towers, they stripped Is 23:13
day when it is **e** for offering burnt Ezk 43:18

ERI (2)
Haggi, Shuni, Ezbon, **E**, Arodi, Gn 46:16
of Ozni, the clan of the Oznites; of **E**, Nm 26:16

ERITES (1)
of the Oznites; of Eri, the clan of the **E**; Nm 26:16

ERRED (1)
And even if it be true that I have **e**, my Jb 19:4

ERROR (13)
him down there because of his **e**, 2 Sm 6:7
trust, and his angels he charges with **e**; Jb 4:18
I have erred, my **e** remains with myself. Jb 19:4
as it were an **e** proceeding from the Eccl 10:5
to utter **e** concerning the LORD, Is 32:6
has sinned through **e** or ignorance; Ezk 45:20
and no **e** or fault was found in him. Dn 6:4
themselves the due penalty for their **e**. Rom 1:27
does not spring from **e** or impurity or 1 Thes 2:3
escaping from those who live in **e**. 2 Pt 2:18
away with the **e** of lawless people 2 Pt 3:17
the Spirit of truth and the spirit of **e**. 1 Jn 4:6
of gain to Balaam's **e** and perished in Jude 1:11

ERRORS (1)
Who can discern his **e**? Declare me Ps 19:12

ERUPTION (5)
of his body a swelling or an **e** or a spot, Lv 13:2
pronounce him clean; it is only an **e**. Lv 13:6
But if the **e** spreads in the skin, after he Lv 13:7
look, and if the **e** has spread in the skin, Lv 13:8
and for a swelling or an **e** or a spot, Lv 14:56

ESARHADDON (3)
And **E** his son reigned in his place. 2 Kgs 19:37
since the days of **E** king of Assyria who Ezr 4:2
of Ararat, **E** his son reigned in his place. Is 37:38

ESAU (92)
hairy cloak, so they called his name **E**. Gn 25:25
boys grew up, **E** was a skillful hunter, Gn 25:27
Isaac loved **E** because he ate of his Gn 25:28
cooking stew, **E** came in from the field, Gn 25:29
And **E** said to Jacob, "Let me eat some Gn 25:30
E said, "I am about to die; of what use Gn 25:32
Then Jacob gave **E** bread and lentil Gn 25:34
way. Thus **E** despised his birthright. Gn 25:34
When **E** was forty years old, he took Gn 26:34
he called **E** his older son and said to Gn 27:1
listening when Isaac spoke to his son **E**. Gn 27:5
So when **E** went to the field to hunt for Gn 27:5
your father speak to your brother **E**, Gn 27:6
"Behold, my brother **E** is a hairy man, Gn 27:11
the best garments of **E** her older son, Gn 27:15
to his father, "I am **E** your firstborn. Gn 27:19
you are really my son **E** or not." Gn 27:21
but the hands are the hands of **E**." Gn 27:22
you really my son **E**?" He answered, Gn 27:24
E his brother came in from his Gn 27:30
"I am your son, your firstborn, **E**." Gn 27:32
As soon as **E** heard the words of his Gn 27:34
E said, "Is he not rightly named Jacob? Gn 27:36
Isaac answered and said to **E**, "Behold, I Gn 27:37
E said to his father, "Have you but one Gn 27:38
O my father." And **E** lifted up his voice Gn 27:38
Now **E** hated Jacob because of the Gn 27:41
had blessed him, and **E** said to himself, Gn 27:41
But the words of **E** her older son were Gn 27:42
your brother **E** comforts himself Gn 27:42
Now **E** saw that Isaac had blessed Jacob Gn 28:6
So when **E** saw that the Canaanite Gn 28:8
E went to Ishmael and took as his wife, Gn 28:9
before him to **E** his brother in Gn 32:3
them, "Thus you shall say to my lord **E**: Gn 32:4
saying, "We came to your brother **E**, Gn 32:6
"If **E** comes to the one camp and attacks Gn 32:8
of my brother, from the hand of **E**, Gn 32:11
he took a present for his brother **E**, Gn 32:13
"When **E** my brother meets you and Gn 32:17
They are a present sent to my lord **E**. Gn 32:18
the same thing to **E** when you find Gn 32:19
and looked, and behold, **E** was coming, Gn 33:1
But **E** ran to meet him and embraced Gn 33:4
And when **E** lifted up his eyes and saw Gn 33:5
E said, "What do you mean by all this Gn 33:8
But **E** said, "I have enough, my brother; Gn 33:9
Then **E** said, "Let us journey on our Gn 33:12
So **E** said, "Let me leave with you some Gn 33:15
So **E** returned that day on his way to Gn 33:16
when you fled from your brother **E**." Gn 35:1
And his sons **E** and Jacob buried him. Gn 35:29
These are the generations of **E** (that is, Gn 36:1
E took his wives from the Canaanites: Gn 36:2
And Adah bore to **E**, Eliphaz; Basemath Gn 36:4
are the sons of **E** who were born to Gn 36:5
Then **E** took his wives, his sons, his Gn 36:6
So **E** settled in the hill country of Seir. Gn 36:8
in the hill country of Seir. (**E** is Edom.) Gn 36:8
are the generations of **E** the father of the Gn 36:9
Eliphaz the son of Adah the wife of **E**, Gn 36:10
the son of Basemath the wife of **E**. Gn 36:10
she bore to **E** Jeush, Jalam, and Korah. Gn 36:14
These are the chiefs of the sons of **E**. Gn 36:15
The sons of Eliphaz the firstborn of **E**: Gn 36:15
These are the sons of **E** (that is, Edom), Gn 36:19
These are the names of the chiefs of **E**, Gn 36:40
Edom (that is, **E**, the father of Edom), Gn 36:43
territory of your brothers, the people of **E**, Dt 2:4
given Mount Seir to **E** as a possession. Dt 2:5
away from our brothers, the people of **E**, Dt 2:8
the people of **E** dispossessed them and Dt 2:12
as he did for the people of **E**, who live in Dt 2:22
as the sons of **E** who live in Seir and the Dt 2:29
And to Isaac I gave Jacob and **E**. And I Jos 24:4
And I gave **E** the hill country of Seir to Jos 24:4
Isaac. The sons of Isaac: **E** and Israel. 1 Chr 1:34
The sons of **E**: Eliphaz, Reuel, Jeush, 1 Chr 1:35
I will bring the calamity of **E** upon him, Jer 49:8
But I have stripped **E** bare; I have Jer 49:10
How **E** has been pillaged, his treasures Ob 1:6
and understanding out of Mount **E**? Ob 1:8
every man from Mount **E** will be cut off Ob 1:9
a flame, and the house of **E** stubble; Ob 1:18
shall be no survivor for the house of **E**, Ob 1:18
of the Negeb shall possess Mount **E**, Ob 1:19
go up to Mount Zion to rule Mount **E**, Ob 1:21
us?" "Is not **E** Jacob's brother?" declares Mal 1:2
but **E** I have hated. I have laid waste his Mal 1:3
written, "Jacob I loved, but **E** I hated." Rom 9:13
future blessings on Jacob and **E**. Heb 11:20
is sexually immoral or unholy like **E**, Heb 12:16

ESAU'S (12)
out with his hand holding **E** heel, Gn 25:26
were hairy like his brother **E** hands. Gn 27:23
of Rebekah, Jacob's and **E** mother. Gn 28:5
These are the names of **E** sons: Eliphaz Gn 36:10
was a concubine of Eliphaz, **E** son; Gn 36:12
These are the sons of Adah, **E** wife. Gn 36:12
These are the sons of Basemath, **E** wife. Gn 36:13
of Anah the daughter of Zibeon, **E** wife: Gn 36:14
These are the sons of Reuel, **E** son: the Gn 36:17
these are the sons of Basemath, **E** wife. Gn 36:17
are the sons of Oholibamah, **E** wife: Gn 36:18
the daughter of Anah, **E** wife. Gn 36:18

ESCAPE (67)
went into the ark to **e** the waters of the Gn 7:7
them out, one said, "**E** for your life. Gn 19:17
E to the hills, lest you be swept away." Gn 19:17
my life. But I cannot **e** to the hills, Gn 19:19
Let me **e** there—is it not a little one? Gn 19:20
E there quickly, for I can do nothing Gn 19:22
it, then the camp that is left will **e**." Gn 32:8
fight against us and **e** from the land." Ex 1:10
over one another, as if to **e** a sword, Lv 26:37
"If you do not **e** with your life 1 Sm 19:11
that place was called the Rock of **E**. 1 Sm 23:28
me than that I should **e** to the land of 1 Sm 27:1
of Israel, and I shall **e** out of his hand." 1 Sm 27:1
there will be no **e** for us from 2 Sm 15:14
to fortified cities and **e** from us." 2 Sm 20:6
not one of them **e**." And they seized 1 Kgs 18:40
into your hands to **e** shall forfeit his 2 Kgs 10:24
let not a man **e**." So when they put 2 Kgs 10:25
should be no remnant, nor any to **e**? Ezr 9:14

king's palace you will **e** any more than Est 4:13
all way of **e** will be lost to them, and Jb 11:20
let anything in which he delights **e** him. Jb 20:20
For their crime will they **e**? In wrath cast Ps 56:7
to them. I am shut in so that I cannot **e**; Ps 88:8
Let them not **e** from your sight; keep Prv 4:21
and he who breathes out lies will not **e**. Prv 19:5
more, a lion for those of Moab who **e**, Is 15:9
of Assyria! And we, how shall we **e**?'" Is 20:6
disaster upon them that they cannot **e**. Jer 11:11
nor **e** for the lords of the flock. Jer 25:35
king of Judah shall not **e** out of the hand Jer 32:4
You shall not **e** from his hand but shall Jer 34:3
and you shall not **e** from their hand." Jer 38:18
yourself shall not **e** from their hand, Jer 38:23
land of Egypt shall **e** or survive or Jer 44:14
And those who **e** the sword shall return Jer 44:28
swift cannot flee away, nor the warrior **e**; Jer 46:6
upon every city, and no city shall **e**; Jer 48:8
They flee and **e** from the land of Jer 50:28
bow. Encamp around her; let no one **e**. Jer 50:29
has walled me about so that I cannot **e**; Lam 3:7
the nations some who **e** the sword, Ezk 6:8
those of you who **e** will remember me Ezk 6:9
And if any survivors **e**, they will be on Ezk 7:16
will let a few of them **e** from the sword, Ezk 12:16
Though they **e** from the fire, the fire Ezk 15:7
Can one **e** who does such things? Ezk 17:15
Can he break the covenant and yet **e**? Ezk 17:15
and did all these things; he shall not **e**. Ezk 17:18
and the land of Egypt shall not **e**. Dn 11:42
in Jerusalem there shall be those who **e**, Jl 2:32
shall flee away; not one of them shall **e**. Am 9:1
Mount Zion there shall be those who **e**, Ob 1:17
E to Zion, you who dwell with the Zec 2:7
but they put God to the test and they **e**.'" Mal 3:15
how are you to **e** being sentenced to Mt 23:33
may have strength to **e** all these things Lk 21:36
deserve to die, I do not seek to **e** death. Acts 25:11
were seeking to **e** from the ship, Acts 27:30
lest any should swim away and **e**. Acts 27:42
—that you will **e** the judgment of God? Rom 2:3
he will also provide the way of **e**, 1 Cor 10:13
pregnant woman, and they will not **e**. 1 Thes 5:3
and they may **e** from the snare of the 2 Tm 2:26
how shall we **e** if we neglect such a great Heb 2:3
if they did not **e** when they refused Heb 12:25
much less will we **e** if we reject him Heb 12:25

ESCAPED (47)
Then one who had **e** came and told Gn 14:13
a slave who has **e** from his master to Dt 23:15
there was left none that survived or **e**. Jos 8:22
Ehud **e** while they delayed, and he passed Jgs 3:26
passed beyond the idols and **e** to Seirah. Jgs 3:26
strong, able-bodied men; not a man **e**. Jgs 3:29
Saul were taken, but the people **e**. 1 Sm 14:41
And David fled and **e** that night. 1 Sm 19:10
the window, and he fled away and **e**. 1 Sm 19:12
that he has **e**?" And Michal 1 Sm 19:17
Now David fled and **e**, and he came 1 Sm 19:18
departed from there and **e** to the cave 1 Sm 22:1
Abiathar, **e** and fled after David. 1 Sm 22:20
told that David had **e** from Keilah, 1 Sm 23:13
next day, and not a man of them **e**, 1 Sm 30:17
him, "I have **e** from the camp of Israel." 2 Sm 1:3
Rechab and Baanah his brother **e**. 2 Sm 4:6
king of Syria **e** on a horse 1 Kgs 20:20
so that they **e** from the hand of the 2 Kgs 13:5
with the sword and **e** into the land of 2 Kgs 19:37
of the Amalekites who had **e**, 1 Chr 4:43
army of the king of Syria has **e** you. 2 Chr 16:7
lying on the ground; none had **e**. 2 Chr 20:24
of you who have **e** from the hand of 2 Chr 30:6
those who had **e** from the sword, 2 Chr 36:20
just, for we are left a remnant that has **e**, Ezr 9:15
I asked them concerning the Jews who **e**, Neh 1:2
the sword, and I alone have **e** to tell you." Jb 1:15
them, and I alone have **e** to tell you." Jb 1:16
the sword, and I alone have **e** to tell you." Jb 1:17
are dead, and I alone have **e** to tell you." Jb 1:19
and I have **e** by the skin of my teeth. Jb 19:20
We have **e** like a bird from the snare of Ps 124:7
the snare is broken, and we have **e**! Ps 124:7
And after they **e** into the land of Ararat, Is 37:38
it, he was afraid and fled and **e** to Egypt. Jer 26:21
son of Nethaniah **e** from Johanan with Jer 41:15
"You who have **e** from the sword, go, do Jer 51:50
anger of the LORD no one **e** or survived; Lam 2:22
to arrest him, but he **e** from their hands. Jn 10:39
supposing that the prisoners had **e**. Acts 16:27
none of these things has **e** his notice, Acts 26:26
Though he has **e** from the sea, Acts 28:4
window in the wall and **e** his hands. 2 Cor 11:33
power of fire, **e** the edge of the sword, Heb 11:34
having **e** from the corruption that is in 2 Pt 1:4
after they have **e** the defilements of the 2 Pt 2:20

ESCAPES (6)
And the one who **e** from the sword of 1 Kgs 19:17
and the one who **e** from the sword of 1 Kgs 19:17
lips, but the righteous **e** from trouble. Prv 12:13
He who pleases God **e** her, but the Eccl 7:26
Ask him who flees and her who **e**; say, Jer 48:19
a desolate wilderness, and nothing **e** them. Jl 2:3

ESCAPING (1)
those who are barely **e** from those who 2 Pt 2:18

ESCORT (1)
the Jordan, to **e** him over the Jordan. 2 Sm 19:31

ESEK (1)
So he called the name of the well **E**, Gn 26:20

ESHAN (1)
Arab, Dumah, **E**, Jos 15:52

ESHBAAL (2)
Malchi-shua, Abinadab and **E**; 1 Chr 8:33
Malchi-shua, Abinadab, and **E**. 1 Chr 9:39

ESHBAN (2)
Hemdan, **E**, Ithran, and Cheran. Gn 36:26
Hemdan, **E**, Ithran, and Cheran. 1 Chr 1:41

ESHCOL (6)
the Amorite, brother of **E** and of Aner. Gn 14:13
Aner, **E**, and Mamre take their share." Gn 14:24
to the Valley of **E** and cut down from Nm 13:23
That place was called the Valley of **E**, Nm 13:24
up to the Valley of **E** and saw the land, Nm 32:9
came to the Valley of **E** and spied it out. Dt 1:24

ESHEK (1)
The sons of **E** his brother: Ulam his 1 Chr 8:39

ESHTAOL (7)
And in the lowland, **E**, Zorah, Ashnah, Jos 15:33
included Zorah, **E**, Ir-shemesh, Jos 19:41
Mahaneh-dan, between Zorah and **E**. Jgs 13:25
him between Zorah and **E** in the tomb Jgs 16:31
of their tribe, from Zorah and from **E**, Jgs 18:2
came to their brothers at Zorah and **E**, Jgs 18:8
of war, set out from Zorah and **E**, Jgs 18:11

ESHTAOLITES (1)
these came the Zorathites and the **E**. 1 Chr 2:53

ESHTEMOA (5)
pasturelands, **E** with its pasturelands, Jos 21:14
in Aroer, in Siphmoth, in **E**, 1 Sm 30:28
and Ishbah, the father of **E**. 1 Chr 4:17
the Garmite and **E** the Maacathite. 1 Chr 4:19
Jattir, **E** with its pasturelands, 1 Chr 6:57

ESHTEMOH (1)
Anab, **E**, Anim, Jos 15:50

ESHTON (2)
fathered Mehir, who fathered **E**. 1 Chr 4:11
E fathered Beth-rapha, Paseah, and 1 Chr 4:12

ESLI (1)
Amos, the son of Nahum, the son of **E**, Lk 3:25

ESPECIALLY (14)
e Jericho." And they went and came into Jos 2:1
become a reproach, **e** to my neighbors, Ps 31:11
e what had happened to the Mt 8:33
him before you all, and **e** before you, Acts 25:26
e because you are familiar with all the Acts 26:3
gifts, **e** that you may prophesy. 1 Cor 14:1
and **e** to those who are of the household Gal 6:10
you, **e** those of Caesar's household. Phil 4:22
of all people, **e** of those who believe. 1 Tm 4:10
and **e** for members of his household, 1 Tm 5:8
e those who labor in preaching and 1 Tm 5:17
e those of the circumcision party. Ti 1:10
slave, as a beloved brother—**e** to me, Phlm 1:16
and **e** those who indulge in the lust of 2 Pt 2:10

ESTABLISH (53)
But I will **e** my covenant with you, and Gn 6:18
I **e** my covenant with you and your Gn 9:9
I **e** my covenant with you, that never Gn 9:11
And I will **e** my covenant between me Gn 17:7
I will **e** my covenant with him as an Gn 17:19
But I will **e** my covenant with Isaac, Gn 17:21
and I will **e** the oath that I swore to Gn 26:3
to afflict herself, her husband may **e**, Nm 30:13
The LORD will **e** you as a people holy to Dt 28:9
that he may **e** you today as his people, Dt 29:13
may the LORD **e** his word." So the 1 Sm 1:23
your body, and I will **e** his kingdom. 2 Sm 7:12
and I will **e** the throne of his kingdom 2 Sm 7:13
that the LORD may **e** his word that he 1 Kgs 2:4
them, then I will **e** my word with you, 1 Kgs 6:12
then I will **e** your royal throne over 1 Kgs 9:5
and you may **e** bazaars for yourself 1 Kgs 20:34
that he might **e** the words of the law 2 Kgs 23:24
own sons, and I will **e** his kingdom. 1 Chr 17:11
me, and I will **e** his throne forever. 1 Chr 17:12
and I will **e** his royal throne in Israel 1 Chr 22:10
I will **e** his kingdom forever if he 1 Chr 28:7
then I will **e** your royal throne, as I 2 Chr 7:18
loved Israel and would **e** them forever, 2 Chr 9:8
Can you **e** their rule on the earth? Jb 38:33
and may you **e** the righteous—you who Ps 7:9
city of our God, which God will **e** forever. Ps 48:8
when God arose to **e** judgment, to save all Ps 76:9
for the Most High himself will **e** her. Ps 87:5
heavens you will **e** your faithfulness." Ps 89:2
'I will **e** your offspring forever, and build Ps 89:4
I will **e** his offspring forever and his Ps 89:29
and **e** the work of our hands upon us; Ps 90:17
upon us; yes, **e** the work of our hands! Ps 90:17
dwell, and they **e** a city to live in; Ps 107:36
to **e** it and to uphold it with justice and Is 9:7
as a covenant to the people, to **e** the land, Is 49:8
LORD who formed it to **e** it—the LORD is Jer 33:2
and I will **e** for you an everlasting Ezk 16:60
I will **e** my covenant with you, and Ezk 16:62
that the king should **e** an ordinance and Dn 6:7
e the injunction and sign the document, Dn 6:8
and love good, and **e** justice in the gate; Am 5:15
of God in order to **e** your tradition! Mk 7:9
from God, and seeking to **e** their own, Rom 10:3
to **e** and exhort you in your faith, 1 Thes 3:2
that he may **e** your hearts blameless 1 Thes 3:13
your hearts and **e** them in every 2 Thes 2:17
He will **e** you and guard you against 2 Thes 3:3
when I will **e** a new covenant with the Heb 8:8
the first in order to **e** the second. Heb 10:9
E your hearts, for the coming of the Lord Jas 5:8
restore, confirm, strengthen, and **e** you. 1 Pt 5:10

ESTABLISHED (86)
covenant that I have **e** between me and Gn 9:17
I also **e** my covenant with them to give Ex 6:4
O Lord, which your hands have **e**. Ex 15:17
let it be built; let the city of Sihon be **e**. Nm 21:27
He has **e** them, because he said Nm 30:14
or of three witnesses shall a charge be **e**. Dt 19:15
created you, who made you and **e** you? Dt 32:6
knew that Samuel was **e** as a prophet 1 Sm 3:20
LORD would have **e** your kingdom 1 Sm 13:13
you nor your kingdom shall be **e**. 1 Sm 20:31
of Israel shall be **e** in your hand. 1 Sm 24:20
that the LORD had **e** him king over 2 Sm 5:12
me. Your throne shall be **e** forever.'" 2 Sm 7:16
And you **e** for yourself your people 2 Sm 7:24
servant David will be **e** before you. 2 Sm 7:26
father, and his kingdom was firmly **e**. 1 Kgs 2:12
who has **e** me and placed me on the 1 Kgs 2:24
of David shall be **e** before the LORD 1 Kgs 2:45
So the kingdom was **e** in the hand of 1 Kgs 2:46
and Samuel the seer **e** them in their 1 Chr 9:22
that the LORD had **e** him as king over 1 Chr 14:2
him, all the earth; yes, the world is **e**; 1 Chr 16:30
and his throne shall be **e** forever.'" 1 Chr 17:14
concerning his house be **e** forever, 1 Chr 17:23
name will be **e** and magnified 1 Chr 17:24
servant David will be **e** before you. 1 Chr 17:24
to the procedure **e** for them by 1 Chr 24:19
the son of David **e** himself in his 2 Chr 1:1
rule of Rehoboam was **e** and he was 2 Chr 12:1
Therefore the LORD **e** the kingdom in 2 Chr 17:5
LORD your God, and you will be **e**; 2 Chr 20:20
the throne of his father and was **e**, 2 Chr 21:4
and I **e** the duties of the priests and Neh 13:30
Their offspring are **e** in their presence, Jb 21:8
on a matter, and it will be **e** for you, Jb 22:28
then he saw it and declared it; he **e** it, Jb 28:27
you have **e** strength because of your foes, Ps 8:2
forever; he has **e** his throne for justice, Ps 9:7
it upon the seas and **e** it upon the rivers. Ps 24:2
The steps of a man are **e** by the LORD, Ps 37:23
who by his strength **e** the mountains, Ps 65:6
you have **e** the heavenly lights and the Ps 74:16
His abode has been **e** in Salem, his Ps 76:2
He **e** a testimony in Jacob and appointed Ps 78:5
so that my hand shall be **e** with him; Ps 89:21
Like the moon it shall be **e** forever, a Ps 89:37
Yes, the world is **e**; it shall never be Ps 93:1
Your throne is **e** from of old; you are Ps 93:2
Yes, the world is **e**; it shall never be Ps 96:10
You have **e** equity; you have executed Ps 99:4
their offspring shall be **e** before you. Ps 102:28
The LORD has **e** his throne in the Ps 103:19
they are **e** forever and ever, to be Ps 111:8
all generations; you have **e** the earth, Ps 119:90
Let not the slanderer be **e** in the land; Ps 140:11
And he **e** them forever and ever; he gave Ps 148:6
by understanding he **e** the heavens; Prv 3:19
When he **e** the heavens, I was there; Prv 8:27
when he **e** the fountains of the deep, Prv 8:28

no more, but the righteous is **e** forever. Prv 10:25
No one is **e** by wickedness, but the root Prv 12:3
to the LORD, and your plans will be **e**. Prv 16:3
for the throne is **e** by righteousness. Prv 16:12
Plans are **e** by counsel; by wise Prv 20:18
is built, and by understanding it is **e**; Prv 24:3
his throne will be **e** in righteousness. Prv 25:5
the poor, his throne will be **e** forever. Prv 29:14
Who has **e** all the ends of the earth? Prv 30:4
of the LORD shall be **e** as the highest of the Is 2:2
then a throne will be **e** in steadfast love, Is 16:5
discouraged till he has **e** justice in the Is 42:4
formed the earth and made it (he **e** it; Is 45:18
In righteousness you shall be **e**; you Is 54:14
power, who **e** the world by his wisdom, Jer 10:12
their congregation shall be **e** before me, Jer 30:20
If I have not **e** my covenant with day Jer 33:25
power, who **e** the world by his wisdom, Jer 51:15
sought me, and I was **e** in my kingdom, Dn 4:36
of the LORD shall be **e** as the highest of the Mi 4:1
you, O Rock, have **e** them for reproof. Hab 1:12
every charge may be **e** by the evidence Mt 18:16
But whoever is firmly **e** in his heart, 1 Cor 7:37
charge must be **e** by the evidence 2 Cor 13:1
and built up in him and **e** in the faith, Col 2:7
death of the one who made it must be **e**. Heb 9:16
know them and are **e** in the truth that 2 Pt 1:12

ESTABLISHES (5)
then he **e** all her vows or all her Nm 30:14
plans his way, but the LORD **e** his steps. Prv 16:9
no rest until he **e** Jerusalem and makes it Is 62:7
that the king **e** can be changed." Dn 6:15
And it is God who **e** us with you in 2 Cor 1:21

ESTABLISHING (2)
up his son after him, and **e** Jerusalem, 1 Kgs 15:4
e the heavens and laying the Is 51:16

ESTABLISHMENT (1)
his sons until the **e** of the kingdom 2 Chr 36:20

ESTATE (6)
king said, "Go to Anathoth, to your **e**, 1 Kgs 2:26
Those of low **e** are but a breath; those of Ps 62:9
a breath; those of high **e** are a delusion; Ps 62:9
is he who remembered us in our low **e**, Ps 136:23
looked on the humble **e** of his servant. Lk 1:48
thrones and exalted those of humble **e**; Lk 1:52

ESTEEM (3)
afraid and fell greatly in their own **e**, Neh 6:16
but the people held them in high **e**. Acts 5:13
and to **e** them very highly in love 1 Thes 5:13

ESTEEMED (6)
who despise me shall be lightly **e**. 1 Sm 2:30
Saul, so that his name was highly **e**. 1 Sm 18:30
was all the counsel of Ahithophel **e**, 2 Sm 16:23
faces he was despised, and we **e** him not. Is 53:3
our sorrows; yet we **e** him stricken, Is 53:4
who feared the LORD and **e** his name. Mal 3:16

ESTEEMS (2)
One person **e** one day as better than Rom 14:5
another, while another **e** all days alike. Rom 14:5

ESTHER (53)
He was bringing up Hadassah, that is **E**, Est 2:7
E also was taken into the king's palace Est 2:8
E had not made known her people or Est 2:10
harem to learn how **E** was and what was Est 2:11
the turn came for **E** the daughter of Est 2:15
Now **E** was winning favor in the eyes of Est 2:15
And when **E** was taken to King Est 2:16
the king loved **E** more than all the Est 2:17
E had not made known her kindred or Est 2:20
for **E** obeyed Mordecai just as when she Est 2:20
of Mordecai, and he told it to Queen **E**, Est 2:22
and **E** told the king in the name of Est 2:22
Then **E** called for Hathach, one of the Est 4:5
he might show it to **E** and explain it to Est 4:8
went and told **E** what Mordecai had Est 4:9
Then **E** spoke to Hathach and Est 4:10
they told Mordecai what **E** had said. Est 4:12
Then Mordecai told them to reply to **E**, Est 4:13
Then **E** told them to reply to Mordecai, Est 4:15
did everything as **E** had ordered him. Est 4:17
On the third day **E** put on her royal robes Est 5:1
the king saw Queen **E** standing in the Est 5:2
he held out to **E** the golden scepter that Est 5:2
Then **E** approached and touched the tip Est 5:2
king said to her, "What is it, Queen **E**? Est 5:3
And **E** said, "If it please the king, let the Est 5:4
that we may do as **E** has asked." So the Est 5:5
came to the feast that **E** had prepared. Est 5:5
wine after the feast, the king said to **E**, Est 5:6
Then **E** answered, "My wish and my Est 5:7
"Even Queen **E** let no one but me come Est 5:12
Haman to the feast that **E** had prepared. Est 6:14
Haman went in to feast with Queen **E**. Est 7:1
after the feast, the king again said to **E**, Est 7:2
to Esther, "What is your wish, Queen **E**? Est 7:2
Then Queen **E** answered, "If I have found Est 7:3
Then King Ahasuerus said to Queen **E**, Est 7:5
And **E** said, "A foe and enemy! This Est 7:6
stayed to beg for his life from Queen **E**, Est 7:7
was falling on the couch where **E** was. Est 7:8
Ahasuerus gave to Queen **E** the house of Est 8:1
king, for **E** had told what he was to her. Est 8:1
And **E** set Mordecai over the house of Est 8:2
Then **E** spoke again to the king. She fell Est 8:3
the king held out the golden scepter to **E**, Est 8:4
E rose and stood before the king. And she Est 8:5
said to Queen **E** and to Mordecai Est 8:7
I have given **E** the house of Haman, Est 8:7
And the king said to Queen **E**, "In Susa Est 9:12
And **E** said, "If it please the king, let the Est 9:13
Then Queen **E**, the daughter of Abihail, Est 9:29
the Jew and Queen **E** obligated them, Est 9:31
command of Queen **E** confirmed these Est 9:32

ESTHER'S (2)
his officials and servants; it was **E** feast. Est 2:18
When **E** young women and her eunuchs Est 4:4

ESTRANGED (4)
who knew me are wholly **e** from me. Jb 19:13
The wicked are **e** from the womb; they Ps 58:3
the Holy One of Israel, they are utterly **e**. Is 1:4
who are all **e** from me through their Ezk 14:5

ETAM (5)
and stayed in the cleft of the rock of **E**. Jgs 15:8
went down to the cleft of the rock of **E**, Jgs 15:11
These were the sons of **E**: Jezreel, 1 Chr 4:3
And their villages were **E**, Ain, 1 Chr 4:32
He built Bethlehem, **E**, Tekoa, 2 Chr 11:6

ETERNAL (73)
The **e** God is your dwelling place, and Dt 33:27
because man is going to his **e** home, Eccl 12:5
Their **e** dishonor will never be Jer 20:11
then the **e** mountains were scattered; Hab 3:6
or two feet to be thrown into the **e** fire. Mt 18:8
good deed must I do to have **e** life?" Mt 19:16
a hundredfold and will inherit **e** life. Mt 19:29
into the **e** fire prepared for the devil and Mt 25:41
these will go away into **e** punishment, Mt 25:46
but the righteous into **e** life." Mt 25:46
forgiveness, but is guilty of an **e** sin"— Mk 3:29
what must I do to inherit **e** life?" Mk 10:17
and in the age to come **e** life. Mk 10:30
what shall I do to inherit **e** life?" Lk 10:25
may receive you into the **e** dwellings. Lk 16:9
what must I do to inherit **e** life?" Lk 18:18
this time, and in the age to come **e** life." Lk 18:30
whoever believes in him may have **e** life. Jn 3:15
in him should not perish but have **e** life. Jn 3:16
Whoever believes in the Son has **e** life; Jn 3:36
a spring of water welling up to **e** life." Jn 4:14
wages and gathering fruit for **e** life, Jn 4:36
and believes him who sent me has **e** life. Jn 5:24
you think that in them you have **e** life; Jn 5:39
but for the food that endures to **e** life, Jn 6:27
and believes in him should have **e** life, Jn 6:40
I say to you, whoever believes has **e** life. Jn 6:47
my flesh and drinks my blood has **e** life, Jn 6:54
shall we go? You have the words of **e** life, Jn 6:68
I give them **e** life, and they will never Jn 10:28
life in this world will keep it for **e** life. Jn 12:25
I know that his commandment is **e** life. Jn 12:50
to give **e** life to all whom you have given Jn 17:2
And this is **e** life, that they know you the Jn 17:3
judge yourselves unworthy of **e** life, Acts 13:46
as were appointed to **e** life believed. Acts 13:48
namely, his **e** power and divine nature, Rom 1:20
and immortality, he will give **e** life; Rom 2:7
righteousness leading to **e** life through Rom 5:21
to sanctification and its end, **e** life. Rom 6:22
free gift of God is **e** life in Christ Jesus Rom 6:23
to the command of the **e** God, Rom 16:26
preparing for us an **e** weight of glory 2 Cor 4:17
but the things that are unseen are **e**. 2 Cor 4:18
not made with hands, **e** in the heavens. 2 Cor 5:1
the Spirit will from the Spirit reap **e** life. Gal 6:8
was according to the **e** purpose that he Eph 3:11
the punishment of **e** destruction, 2 Thes 1:9
us and gave us **e** comfort and good 2 Thes 2:16
who were to believe in him for **e** life. 1 Tm 1:16
Take hold of the **e** life to which you 1 Tm 6:12
To him be honor and **e** dominion. 1 Tm 6:16
that is in Christ Jesus with **e** glory. 2 Tm 2:10
in hope of **e** life, which God, who never Ti 1:2
heirs according to the hope of **e** life. Ti 3:7
became the source of **e** salvation to all Heb 5:9
of the dead, and **e** judgment. Heb 6:2
blood, thus securing an **e** redemption. Heb 9:12
who through the **e** Spirit offered Heb 9:14
receive the promised **e** inheritance, Heb 9:15
sheep, by the blood of the **e** covenant, Heb 13:20
has called you to his **e** glory in Christ, 1 Pt 5:10
an entrance into the **e** kingdom of our 2 Pt 1:11
testify to it and proclaim to you the **e** life, 1 Jn 1:2
the promise that he made to us—**e** life. 1 Jn 2:25
that no murderer has **e** life abiding in 1 Jn 3:15
is the testimony, that God gave us **e** life, 1 Jn 5:11
you may know that you have **e** life. 1 Jn 5:13
Christ. He is the true God and **e** life. 1 Jn 5:20
he has kept in **e** chains under gloomy Jude 1:6
by undergoing a punishment of **e** fire. Jude 1:7
Lord Jesus Christ that leads to **e** life. Jude 1:21
with an **e** gospel to proclaim to those Rv 14:6

ETERNITY (4)
Also, he has put **e** into man's heart, yet Eccl 3:11
be put to shame or confounded to all **e**. Is 45:17
is high and lifted up, who inhabits **e**, Is 57:15
the glory both now and to the day of **e**. 2 Pt 3:18

ETH-KAZIN (1)
the sunrise to Gath-hepher, to **E**, Jos 19:13

ETHAM (4)
on from Succoth and encamped at **E**, Ex 13:20
set out from Succoth and camped at **E**, Nm 33:6
they set out from **E** and turned back to Nm 33:7
in the wilderness of **E** and camped at Nm 33:8

ETHAN (7)
other men, wiser than **E** the Ezrahite, 1 Kgs 4:31
Zimri, **E**, Heman, Calcol, and Dara, 1 Chr 2:6
son of **E**, son of Zimmah, son of 1 Chr 6:42
E the son of Kishi, son of Abdi, son of 1 Chr 6:44
brothers, **E** the son of Kushaiah; 1 Chr 15:17
The singers, Heman, Asaph, and **E**, 1 Chr 15:19
A Maskil of **E** the Ezrahite. Ps 89:T

ETHAN'S (1)
and **E** son was Azariah. 1 Chr 2:8

ETHANIM (1)
Solomon at the feast in the month **E**, 1 Kgs 8:2

ETHBAAL (1)
Jezebel the daughter of **E** king of the 1 Kgs 16:31

ETHER (2)
Libnah, **E**, Ashan, Jos 15:42
E, and Ashan—four cities with their Jos 19:7

ETHIOPIA (3)
from India to **E** over 127 provinces, Est 1:1
officials of the provinces from India to **E**, Est 8:9
The topaz of **E** cannot equal it, nor can Jb 28:19

ETHIOPIAN (7)
Zerah the **E** came out against them 2 Chr 14:9
Can the **E** change his skin or the Jer 13:23
When Ebed-melech the **E**, a eunuch Jer 38:7
king commanded Ebed-melech the **E**, Jer 38:10
Then Ebed-melech the **E** said to Jer 38:12
"Go, and say to Ebed-melech the **E**, Jer 39:16
And there was an **E**, a eunuch, a court Acts 8:27

ETHIOPIANS (7)
Egypt—Libyans, Sukkiim, and **E**. 2 Chr 12:3
LORD defeated the **E** before Asa and 2 Chr 14:12
and before Judah, and the **E** fled. 2 Chr 14:12
and the **E** fell until none remained 2 Chr 14:13
Were not the **E** and the Libyans a 2 Chr 16:8
of the Arabians who are near the **E**. 2 Chr 21:16
official of Candace, queen of the **E**, Acts 8:27

ETHNAN (1)
sons of Helah: Zereth, Izhar, and **E**. 1 Chr 4:7

ETHNI (1)
son of **E**, son of Zerah, son of Adaiah, 1 Chr 6:41

EUBULUS (1)
E sends greetings to you, as do 2 Tm 4:21

EUNICE (1)
Lois and your mother **E** and now, 2 Tm 1:5

EUNUCH (11)
under custody of Hegai, the king's **e**, Est 2:3
in custody of Shaashgaz, the king's **e**, Est 2:14
nothing except what Hegai the king's **e**, Est 2:15
and let not the **e** say, "Behold, I am a dry Is 56:3
a **e** who was in the king's house, Jer 38:7
king commanded Ashpenaz, his chief **e**, Dn 1:3
And there was an Ethiopian, a **e**, a Acts 8:27
And the **e** said to Philip, "About Acts 8:34
came to some water, and the **e** said, Acts 8:36
down into the water, Philip and the **e**, Acts 8:38
away, and the **e** saw him no more, Acts 8:39

EUNUCHS (27)
Who?" Two or three **e** looked out at 2 Kgs 9:32
and they shall be **e** in the palace of 2 Kgs 20:18

the seven **e** who served in the presence of Est 1:10
the king's command delivered by the **e**. Est 1:12
of King Ahasuerus delivered by the **e**?" Est 1:15
Bigthan and Teresh, two of the king's **e**, Est 2:21
young women and her **e** came and told Est 4:4
called for Hathach, one of the king's **e**, Est 4:5
Bigthana and Teresh, two of the king's **e**, Est 6:2
the king's **e** arrived and hurried to bring Est 6:14
one of the **e** in attendance on the king, Est 7:9
and they shall be **e** in the palace of the Is 39:7
"To the **e** who keep my Sabbaths, who Is 56:4
Jeconiah and the queen mother, the **e**, Jer 29:2
Judah, the officials of Jerusalem, the **e**, Jer 34:19
—soldiers, women, children, and **e**, Jer 41:16
And the chief of the **e** gave them names: Dn 1:7
asked the chief of the **e** to allow him not Dn 1:8
in the sight of the chief of the **e**, Dn 1:9
and the chief of the **e** said to Daniel, "I Dn 1:10
the chief of the **e** had assigned over Dn 1:11
the chief of the **e** brought them in before Dn 1:18
For there are **e** who have been so from Mt 19:12
and there are **e** who have been made Mt 19:12
who have been made **e** by men, Mt 19:12
and there are **e** who have made Mt 19:12
have made themselves **e** for the sake Mt 19:12

EUODIA (1)
I entreat **E** and I entreat Syntyche to Phil 4:2

EUPHRATES (35)
of Assyria. And the fourth river is the **E**. Gn 2:14
of Egypt to the great river, the river **E**, Gn 15:18
he had and arose and crossed the **E**, Gn 31:21
of Rehoboth on the **E** reigned in his Gn 36:37
and from the wilderness to the **E**, Ex 23:31
as far as the great river, the river **E**. Dt 1:7
and from the River, the river **E**, Dt 11:24
as far as the great river, the river **E**, Jos 1:4
ago, your fathers lived beyond the **E**, Jos 24:2
went to restore his power at the river **E**. 2 Sm 8:3
the Syrians who were beyond the **E**. 2 Sm 10:16
the kingdoms from the **E** to the land 1 Kgs 4:21
region west of the **E** from Tiphsah to 1 Kgs 4:24
Gaza, over all the kings west of the **E**. 1 Kgs 4:24
and scatter them beyond the **E**, 1 Kgs 14:15
to the king of Assyria to the river **E**. 2 Kgs 23:29
the Brook of Egypt to the river **E**. 2 Kgs 24:7
of Rehoboth on the **E** reigned in his 1 Chr 1:48
entrance of the desert this side of the **E**, 1 Chr 5:9
set up his monument at the river **E**. 1 Chr 18:3
the Syrians who were beyond the **E**, 1 Chr 19:16
all the kings from the **E** to the land of 2 Chr 9:26
Carchemish on the **E** and Josiah 2 Chr 35:20
that day from the river **E** to the Brook of Is 27:12
to Assyria to drink the waters of the **E**? Jer 2:18
go to the **E** and hide it there in a cleft of Jer 13:4
So I went and hid it by the **E**, as the LORD Jer 13:5
the LORD said to me, "Arise, go to the **E**, Jer 13:6
Then I went to the **E**, and dug, and I took Jer 13:7
was by the river **E** at Carchemish and Jer 46:2
north by the river **E** they have stumbled Jer 46:6
in the north country by the river **E**. Jer 46:10
to it and cast it into the midst of the **E**, Jer 51:63
who are bound at the great river **E**." Rv 9:14
out his bowl on the great river **E**, Rv 16:12

EUTYCHUS (1)
And a young man named **E**, sitting at Acts 20:9

EVADED (1)
to the wall." But David **e** him twice. 1 Sm 18:11

EVANGELIST (2)
we entered the house of Philip the **e**, Acts 21:8
endure suffering, do the work of an **e**, 2 Tm 4:5

EVANGELISTS (1)
he gave the apostles, the prophets, the **e**, Eph 4:11

EVE (4)
The man called his wife's name **E**, Gn 3:20
Now Adam knew **E** his wife, and she Gn 4:1
the serpent deceived **E** by his 2 Cor 11:3
For Adam was formed first, then **E**; 1 Tm 2:13

EVEN (396)
said to his father, "Bless me, **e** me also, Gn 27:34
Bless me, **e** me also, O my father." And Gn 27:38
that **e** I may have children through Gn 30:3
it to his brothers they hated him **e** more. Gn 37:5
So they hated him **e** more for his dreams Gn 37:8
livestock from our youth **e** until now, Gn 46:34
of the shepherds and **e** drew water for us Ex 2:19
If they will not believe **e** these two signs or Ex 4:9
e in vessels of wood and in vessels of Ex 7:19
house, and he did not take **e** this to heart. Ex 7:23
e to the firstborn of the slave girl who is Ex 11:5
e to him and to his offspring Ex 30:21
e for his father or for his mother. Lv 21:11
on the holy things **e** for a moment, Nm 4:20
grapevine, not **e** the seeds or the skins. Nm 6:4
Not **e** for his father or for his mother, for Nm 6:7
E when the cloud continued over the Nm 9:19
them and pursued them, **e** to Hormah. Nm 14:45
E with me the LORD was angry on your Dt 1:37
and settled in their place **e** to this day. Dt 2:22
E at Horeb you provoked the LORD to Dt 9:8
for they **e** burn their sons and their Dt 12:31
E to the tenth generation, none of his Dt 23:2
E to the tenth generation, none of them Dt 23:3
what they are inclined to do **e** today, Dt 31:21
e today while I am yet alive with you, Dt 31:27
"'See now that I, **e** I, am he, and there is Dt 32:39
said to her, "Our life for yours **e** to death! Jos 2:14
Misrephoth-maim, **e** all the Sidonians. Jos 13:6
at Peor from which **e** yet we have not Jos 22:17
before the LORD, **e** Sinai before the LORD, Jgs 5:5
e if I should have a husband this night Ru 1:12
"Let her glean **e** among the sheaves, Ru 2:15
them up out of Egypt **e** to this day, 1 Sm 8:8
The garrison and **e** the raiders 1 Sm 14:15
e they also turned to be with the 1 Sm 14:21
and **e** his sword and his bow and his 1 Sm 18:4
Saul was **e** more afraid of David. So 1 Sm 18:29
young men are holy **e** when it is an 1 Sm 21:5
e now he has hidden himself in one of 2 Sm 17:9
Then **e** the valiant man, whose heart 2 Sm 17:10
until not **e** a pebble is to be found 2 Sm 17:13
"**E** if I felt in my hand the weight of a 2 Sm 18:12
in my place,' **e** so will I do this day." 1 Kgs 1:30
king, **e** so may he be with Solomon, 1 Kgs 1:37
in safety, from Dan **e** to Beersheba, 1 Kgs 4:25
judgment, **e** the Hall of Judgment. 1 Kgs 7:7
e from the foundation to the coping, 1 Kgs 7:9
you brought calamity **e** upon the 1 Kgs 17:20
Elijah said to the people, "I, **e** I only, 1 Kgs 18:22
with the sword, and I, **e** I only, 1 Kgs 19:10
with the sword, and I, **e** I only, 1 Kgs 19:14
He **e** burned his son as an offering, 2 Kgs 16:3
e all that Moses the servant of the 2 Kgs 18:12
came out of Egypt, **e** to this day." 2 Kgs 21:15
In times past, **e** when Saul was king, 1 Chr 11:2
for the LORD God, **e** my God, 1 Chr 28:20
you, and have not **e** asked long life, 2 Chr 1:11
house, since heaven, **e** highest heaven, 2 Chr 2:6
E Maacah, his mother, King Asa 2 Chr 15:16
Yet **e** in his disease he did not seek 2 Chr 16:12
He **e** followed their counsel and went 2 Chr 22:5
and his fame spread **e** to the border of 2 Chr 26:8
He **e** made metal images for the 2 Chr 28:2
e though not according to the 2 Chr 30:19
e until the reign of Darius king of Persia. Ezr 4:5
but **e** now there is hope for Israel in spite Ezr 10:2
of the women had **e** borne children. Ezr 10:44
E I and my father's house have sinned. Neh 1:6
but you **e** sell your brothers that they Neh 5:8
E their servants lorded it over the Neh 5:15
E when they had made for themselves Neh 9:18
E in their own kingdom, enjoying Neh 9:35
foreign women made **e** him to sin. Neh 13:26
given you, **e** to the half of my kingdom." Est 5:3
E to the half of my kingdom, it shall be Est 5:6
"**E** Queen Esther let no one but me come Est 5:12
E to the half of my kingdom, it shall be Est 7:2
"Will he **e** assault the queen in my Est 7:8
E in his servants he puts no trust, and his Jb 4:18
his harvest, and he takes it **e** out of thorns, Jb 5:5
I would **e** exult in pain unsparing, for I Jb 6:10
You would **e** cast lots over the fatherless, Jb 6:27
E now, behold, my witness is in heaven, Jb 16:19
And **e** if it be true that I have erred, my Jb 19:4
E young children despise me; when I Jb 19:18
He delivers **e** the one who is not Jb 22:30
find him, that I might come **e** to his seat! Jb 23:3
Behold, **e** the moon is not bright, and the Jb 25:5
Will you **e** put me in the wrong? Will Jb 40:8
false; he is laid low **e** at the sight of him. Jb 41:9
there is none who does good, not **e** one. Ps 14:3
are they than gold, **e** much fine gold; Ps 19:10
e the one who could not keep himself Ps 22:29
E though I walk through the valley of Ps 23:4
O LORD, be upon us, **e** as we hope in you. Ps 33:22
E my close friend in whom I trusted, who Ps 41:9
For he sees that **e** the wise die; the fool Ps 49:10
there is none who does good, not **e** one. Ps 53:3
among men, **e** among the rebellious, Ps 68:18
So **e** to old age and gray hairs, O God, do Ps 71:18
E the sparrow finds a home, and the Ps 84:3
or **e** by reason of strength eighty; Ps 90:10
frogs, **e** in the chambers of their kings. Ps 105:30
I believed, **e** when I spoke, "I am Ps 116:10
E though princes sit plotting against Ps 119:23
E before a word is on my tongue, Ps 139:4
e there your hand shall lead me, and Ps 139:10
e the darkness is not dark to you; the Ps 139:12
My fruit is better than gold, **e** fine gold, Prv 8:19
E in laughter the heart may ache, and Prv 14:13
The poor is disliked **e** by his neighbor, Prv 14:20
it makes itself known **e** in the midst of Prv 14:33
e the wicked for the day of trouble. Prv 16:4
he makes **e** his enemies to be at peace Prv 16:7
E a fool who keeps silent is considered Prv 17:28
the dish and will not **e** bring it back to Prv 19:24
E a child makes himself known by Prv 20:11
e when he is old he will not depart from Prv 22:6
them known to you today, **e** to you. Prv 22:19
the law, **e** his prayer is an abomination. Prv 28:9
E in the night his heart does not rest. Eccl 2:23
of justice, **e** there was wickedness, Eccl 3:16
righteousness, **e** there was wickedness. Eccl 3:16
E though he should live a thousand Eccl 6:6
E though a wise man claims to know, Eccl 8:17
E when the fool walks on the road, he Eccl 10:3
E in your thought, do not curse the Eccl 10:20
Give a portion to seven, or **e** to eight, Eccl 11:2
From the sole of the foot **e** to the head, there Is 1:6
e though you make many prayers, I will Is 1:15
and pass on, reaching **e** to the neck, Is 8:8
for I will bring upon Dibon **e** more, a lion Is 15:9
to Cyprus, **e** there you will have no rest." Is 23:12
e when the plea of the needy is right. Is 32:7
be divided; **e** the lame will take the prey. Is 33:23
e if they are fools, they shall not go astray. Is 35:8
E youths shall faint and be weary, and Is 40:30
all down as fugitives, **e** the Chaldeans, Is 43:14
e to your old age I am he, and to gray Is 46:4
I, **e** I, have spoken and called him; I have Is 48:15
E these may forget, yet I will not forget Is 49:15
"**E** the captives of the mighty shall be Is 49:25
envoys far off, and sent down **e** to Sheol. Is 57:9
I not held my peace, **e** for a long time, Is 57:11
its gods, **e** though they are no gods? Jer 2:11
So that **e** to wicked women you have Jer 2:33
our fathers, from our youth **e** to this day, Jer 3:25
"But **e** in those days, declares the LORD, I Jer 5:18
E the stork in the heavens knows her Jer 8:7
e the leaves are withered, and what I gave Jer 8:13
warning them persistently, **e** to this day, Jer 11:7
Can **e** sacrificial flesh avert your Jer 11:15
For **e** your brothers and the house of Jer 12:6
e they have dealt treacherously with you; Jer 12:6
e as they taught my people to swear by Jer 12:16
E so will I spoil the pride of Judah and Jer 13:9
E the doe in the field forsakes her Jer 14:5
e into the hand of Nebuchadnezzar Jer 22:25
e in my house I have found their evil, Jer 23:11
e as their fathers forgot my name for Jer 23:27
kings shall make slaves **e** of them, Jer 25:14
E so will I break the yoke of Jer 28:11
I have given to him **e** the beasts of the Jer 28:14
E when Elnathan and Delaiah and Jer 36:25
For **e** if you should defeat the whole Jer 37:10
not humbled themselves **e** to this day, Jer 44:10
E her hired soldiers in her midst are Jer 46:21
the outcry at Heshbon **e** to Elealeh, Jer 48:34
E the little ones of the flock shall be Jer 49:20
and has been lifted up **e** to the skies. Jer 51:9
E jackals offer the breast; they nurse Lam 4:3
and engrave on it a city, **e** Jerusalem. Ezk 4:1
and have not **e** acted according to the Ezk 5:7
Lord GOD: Behold, I, **e** I, am against you. Ezk 5:8
Behold, I, **e** I, will bring a sword upon Ezk 6:3
man, your brothers, **e** your brothers, Ezk 11:15
e if these three men, Noah, Daniel, and Ezk 14:14
e if these three men were in it, as I live, Ezk 14:16
e if Noah, Daniel, and Job were in it, as Ezk 14:20
and **e** with this you were not satisfied. Ezk 16:29
who **e** eats upon the mountains, Ezk 18:11
and they have **e** offered up to them for Ezk 23:37
They **e** sent for men to come from Ezk 23:40
continue to use her for a whore, **e** her! Ezk 23:43
from Teman **e** to Dedan they shall fall Ezk 25:13
will drench the land **e** to the mountains Ezk 32:6
and say to them, **e** to the shepherds, Ezk 34:2
people walk on you, **e** my people Israel. Ezk 36:12
above the door, **e** to the inner room, Ezk 41:17
It grew great, **e** to the host of heaven. Dn 8:10
great, **e** as great as the Prince of the host. Dn 8:11
And he shall **e** rise up against the Prince Dn 8:25
shall not stand, or **e** his best troops, Dn 11:15
broken, **e** the prince of the covenant. Dn 11:22
E those who eat his food shall break Dn 11:26
e as the LORD loves the children of Israel, Hos 3:1
and **e** the fish of the sea are taken away. Hos 4:3
I, **e** I, will tear and go away; I will carry Hos 5:14
E if they bring up children, I will Hos 9:12
E though they give birth, I will put Hos 9:16
for them; **e** the flocks of sheep suffer. Jl 1:18
E the beasts of the field pant for you Jl 1:20
"Yet **e** now," declares the LORD, "return to Jl 2:12

gather the children, **e** nursing infants. Jl 2:16
E on the male and female servants in Jl 2:29
hooks, **e** the last of you with fishhooks. Am 4:2
E though you offer me your burnt Am 5:22
e the owl and the hedgehog shall lodge Zep 2:14
come, **e** the inhabitants of many cities. Zec 8:20
of the fat ones, tearing off **e** their hoofs. Zec 11:16
E Judah will fight against Jerusalem. Zec 14:14
E now the axe is laid to the root of the Mt 3:10
Do not **e** the tax collectors do the same? Mt 5:46
Do not **e** the Gentiles do the same? Mt 5:47
e Solomon in all his glory was not Mt 6:29
is this, that **e** winds and sea obey him?" Mt 8:27
But **e** the hairs of your head are all Mt 10:30
one of these little ones **e** a cup of cold Mt 10:42
not, **e** what he has will be taken away. Mt 13:12
yet **e** the dogs eat the crumbs that fall Mt 15:27
if he refuses to listen **e** to the church, Mt 18:17
e as the Son of Man came not to be Mt 20:28
tree, but **e** if you say to this mountain, Mt 21:21
And **e** when you saw it, you did not Mt 21:32
as to lead astray, if possible, **e** the elect. Mt 24:24
one knows, not **e** the angels of heaven, Mt 24:36
not, **e** what he has will be taken away. Mt 25:29
said to him, "**E** if I must die with you, Mt 26:35
"My soul is very sorrowful, **e** to death; Mt 26:38
no answer, not **e** to a single charge, Mt 27:14
He commands **e** the unclean spirits, Mk 1:27
was no more room, not **e** at the door. Mk 2:2
Son of Man is lord **e** of the Sabbath." Mk 2:28
again, so that they could not **e** eat. Mk 3:20
not, **e** what he has will be taken away." Mk 4:25
is this, that **e** wind and sea obey him?" Mk 4:41
bind him anymore, not **e** with a chain, Mk 5:3
For she said, "If I touch **e** his garments, Mk 5:28
going, and they had no leisure **e** to eat. Mk 6:31
that they might touch **e** the fringe of his Mk 6:56
yet **e** the dogs under the table eat the Mk 7:28
He **e** makes the deaf hear and the mute Mk 7:37
saying, "Do not **e** enter the village." Mk 8:26
For **e** the Son of Man came not to be Mk 10:45
one knows, not **e** the angels in heaven, Mk 13:32
to him, "**E** though they all fall away, Mk 14:29
"My soul is very sorrowful, **e** to death. Mk 14:34
Yet **e** about this their testimony did Mk 14:59
Holy Spirit, **e** from his mother's womb. Lk 1:15
E now the axe is laid to the root of the Lk 3:9
But now **e** more the report about him Lk 5:15
For **e** sinners love those who love them. Lk 6:32
is that to you? For **e** sinners do the same. Lk 6:33
E sinners lend to sinners, to get back the Lk 6:34
merciful, **e** as your Father is merciful. Lk 6:36
not **e** in Israel have I found such faith." Lk 7:9
"Who is this, who **e** forgives sins?" Lk 7:49
e what he thinks that he has will be Lk 8:18
that he commands **e** winds and water, Lk 8:25
'**E** the dust of your town that clings to Lk 10:11
e the demons are subject to us in your Lk 10:17
e the hairs of your head are all Lk 12:7
e Solomon in all his glory was not Lk 12:27
and sisters, yes, and **e** his own life, Lk 14:26
e the dogs came and licked his sores. Lk 16:21
adulterers, or **e** like this tax collector. Lk 18:11
would not **e** lift up his eyes to heaven, Lk 18:13
they were bringing **e** infants to him Lk 18:15
not, **e** what he has will be taken away. Lk 19:26
saying, "Would that you, **e** you, had Lk 19:42
the dead are raised, **e** Moses showed, Lk 20:37
will be delivered up **e** by parents and Lk 21:16
all Judea, from Galilee **e** to this place." Lk 23:5
saying that they had **e** seen a vision of Lk 24:23
e he who comes after me, the strap of Jn 1:27
person cannot receive **e** one thing unless Jn 3:27
but he was **e** calling God his own Father, Jn 5:18
For not **e** his brothers believed in him. Jn 7:5
"**E** if I do bear witness about myself, Jn 8:14
Yet **e** if I do judge, my judgment is true, Jn 8:16
We have one Father—**e** God." Jn 8:41
them, **e** though you do not believe me, Jn 10:38
But **e** now I know that whatever you ask Jn 11:22
name of the Lord, **e** the King of Israel!" Jn 12:13
many **e** of the authorities believed in Jn 12:42
e the Spirit of truth, whom the world Jn 14:17
that they may be one, **e** as we are one. Jn 17:11
that they may be one **e** as we are one, Jn 17:22
me and loved them **e** as you loved me. Jn 17:23
e though the world does not know you, Jn 17:25
this statement, he was **e** more afraid. Jn 19:8
has sent me, **e** so I am sending you." Jn 20:21
e on my male servants and female Acts 2:18
so that they **e** carried out the sick into Acts 5:15
You might **e** be found opposing God!" Acts 5:39
inheritance in it, not **e** a foot's length, Acts 7:5
E Simon himself believed, and after Acts 8:13
was poured out **e** on the Gentiles. Acts 10:45
not believe, **e** if one tells it to you.'" Acts 13:41
E with these words they scarcely Acts 14:18
as **e** some of your own poets have Acts 17:28
we have not **e** heard that there is a Holy Acts 19:2
so that **e** handkerchiefs or aprons Acts 19:12
and that she may **e** be deposed from Acts 19:27
And **e** some of the Asiarchs, who were Acts 19:31
to be imprisoned but **e** to die in Acts 21:13
he **e** brought Greeks into the temple Acts 21:28
language, they became **e** more quiet. Acts 22:2
He **e** tried to profane the temple, but we Acts 24:6
I persecuted them **e** to foreign cities. Acts 26:11
now dangerous because **e** the Fast was Acts 27:9
e though they do not have the law. Rom 2:14
thoughts accuse or **e** excuse them Rom 2:15
no one does good, not **e** one." Rom 3:12
a good person one would dare **e** to die— Rom 5:7
e over those whose sinning was not Rom 5:14
e us whom he has called, not from the Rom 9:24
And **e** they, if they do not continue in Rom 11:23
e he who arises to rule the Gentiles; Rom 15:12
e as the testimony about Christ was 1 Cor 1:6
in the world, **e** things that are not, 1 Cor 1:28
everything, **e** the depths of God. 1 Cor 2:10
for it. And **e** now you are not yet ready, 1 Cor 3:2
court. In fact, I do not **e** judge myself. 1 Cor 4:3
that is not tolerated **e** among pagans, 1 Cor 5:1
or swindler—not **e** to eat with such a 1 Cor 5:11
and defraud—**e** your own brothers! 1 Cor 6:8
from marriage will do **e** better. 1 Cor 7:38
claim on you, do not we **e** more? 1 Cor 9:12
maintain the traditions **e** as I 1 Cor 11:2
fully, **e** as I have been fully known. 1 Cor 13:12
in tongues, but **e** more to prophesy. 1 Cor 14:5
If **e** lifeless instruments, such as the 1 Cor 14:7
and **e** then they will not listen to me, 1 Cor 14:21
then not **e** Christ has been raised. 1 Cor 15:13
We are **e** found to be 1 Cor 15:15
raised, not **e** Christ has been raised. 1 Cor 15:16
stay with you or **e** spend the winter, 1 Cor 16:6
e though a door was opened for me in 2 Cor 2:12
of the Spirit have **e** more glory? 2 Cor 3:8
And **e** if our gospel is veiled, it is veiled 2 Cor 4:3
E though we once regarded Christ 2 Cor 5:16
For **e** when we came into Macedonia, 2 Cor 7:5
For **e** if I made you grieve with my 2 Cor 7:8
And his affection for you is **e** greater, 2 Cor 7:15
For **e** if I boast a little too much of 2 Cor 10:8
God assigned to us, to reach **e** to you. 2 Cor 10:13
E if I am unskilled in speaking, I am 2 Cor 11:6
for **e** Satan disguises himself as an 2 Cor 11:14
But **e** if you do, accept me as a fool, 2 Cor 11:16
e though I am nothing. 2 Cor 12:11
But **e** if we or an angel from heaven Gal 1:8
But **e** Titus, who was with me, was not Gal 2:3
not yield in submission **e** for a moment, Gal 2:5
so that **e** Barnabas was led astray by Gal 2:13
e with a man-made covenant, no one Gal 3:15
For **e** those who are circumcised do not Gal 6:13
e as he chose us in him before the Eph 1:4
e when we were dead in our trespasses, Eph 2:5
covetousness must not **e** be named Eph 5:3
For it is shameful **e** to speak of the Eph 5:12
the head of the wife **e** as Christ is the Eph 5:23
to the point of death, **e** death on a cross. Phil 2:8
E if I am to be poured out as a drink Phil 2:17
told you and now tell you **e** with tears, Phil 3:18
power that enables him **e** to subject all Phil 3:21
E in Thessalonica you sent me help for Phil 4:16
that Jesus died and rose again, **e** so, 1 Thes 4:14
For **e** when we were with you, we 2 Thes 3:10
self-indulgent is dead **e** while she lives. 1 Tm 5:6
and **e** those that are not cannot 1 Tm 5:25
of your owing me **e** your own self. Phlm 1:19
that you will do **e** more than I say. Phlm 1:21
One might **e** say that Levi himself, who Heb 7:9
This becomes **e** more evident when Heb 7:15
Now **e** the first covenant had Heb 9:1
Therefore not **e** the first covenant was Heb 9:18
conceive, **e** when she was past the age, Heb 11:11
that God was able **e** to raise him from Heb 11:19
and **e** chains and imprisonment. Heb 11:36
"If **e** a beast touches the mountain, Heb 12:20
E the demons believe—and shudder! Jas 2:19
so that **e** if some do not obey the word, 1 Pt 3:1
But **e** if you should suffer for 1 Pt 3:14
the gospel was preached **e** to those who 1 Pt 4:6
e denying the Master who bought them, 2 Pt 2:1
hating **e** the garment stained by the Jude 1:23
of Jesus Christ, **e** to all that he saw. Rv 1:2
eye will see him, **e** those who pierced him, Rv 1:7
earth will wail on account of him. **E** so. Rv 1:7
did not deny my faith **e** in the days of Rv 2:13
e as I myself have received authority Rv 2:27
they loved not their lives **e** unto death Rv 12:11
e making fire come down from heaven Rv 13:13
of the beast might **e** speak and might Rv 13:15

EVENING (140)

And there was **e** and there was morning, Gn 1:5
And there was **e** and there was morning, Gn 1:8
And there was **e** and there was morning, Gn 1:13
And there was **e** and there was morning, Gn 1:19
And there was **e** and there was morning, Gn 1:23
And there was **e** and there was morning, Gn 1:31
And the dove came back to him in the **e**, Gn 8:11
The two angels came to Sodom in the **e**, Gn 19:1
city by the well of water at the time of **e**, Gn 24:11
out to meditate in the field toward **e**. Gn 24:63
But in the **e** he took his daughter Leah Gn 29:23
Jacob came from the field in the **e**, Gn 30:16
the prey and at **e** dividing the spoil." Gn 49:27
the fourteenth day of the month at **e**, Ex 12:18
the twenty-first day of the month at **e**. Ex 12:18
"At **e** you shall know that it was the LORD Ex 16:6
LORD gives you in the **e** meat to eat and in Ex 16:8
In the **e** quail came up and covered the Ex 16:13
around Moses from morning till **e**. Ex 18:13
around you from morning till **e**?" Ex 18:14
shall tend it from **e** to morning before Ex 27:21
of it in the morning and half in the **e**. Lv 6:20
carcass shall be unclean until the **e**, Lv 11:24
his clothes and be unclean until the **e** Lv 11:25
carcass shall be unclean until the **e**, Lv 11:27
his clothes and be unclean until the **e**; Lv 11:28
are dead shall be unclean until the **e**. Lv 11:31
and it shall be unclean until the **e**; Lv 11:32
its carcass shall be unclean until the **e**, Lv 11:39
his clothes and be unclean until the **e**. Lv 11:40
his clothes and be unclean until the **e**. Lv 11:40
is shut up shall be unclean until the **e**, Lv 14:46
in water and be unclean until the **e**. Lv 15:5
in water and be unclean until the **e**. Lv 15:6
in water and be unclean until the **e**. Lv 15:7
in water and be unclean until the **e**. Lv 15:8
under him shall be unclean until the **e**. Lv 15:10
in water and be unclean until the **e**. Lv 15:10
in water and be unclean until the **e**. Lv 15:11
in water and be unclean until the **e**. Lv 15:16
with water and be unclean until the **e**. Lv 15:17
in water and be unclean until the **e**. Lv 15:18
her shall be unclean until the **e**. Lv 15:19
in water and be unclean until the **e**. Lv 15:21
in water and be unclean until the **e**. Lv 15:22
it he shall be unclean until the **e**. Lv 15:23
in water and be unclean until the **e**. Lv 15:27
in water and be unclean until the **e**; Lv 17:15
be unclean until the **e** and shall not eat Lv 22:6
ninth day of the month beginning at **e**, Lv 23:32
from **e** to evening shall you keep your Lv 23:32
from evening to **e** shall you keep your Lv 23:32
arrange it from **e** to morning before Lv 24:3
And at **e** it was over the tabernacle like Nm 9:15
cloud remained from **e** until morning. Nm 9:21
But the priest shall be unclean until **e**. Nm 19:7
in water and shall be unclean until **e**. Nm 19:8
his clothes and be unclean until **e**. Nm 19:10
in water, and at **e** he shall be clean. Nm 19:19
for impurity shall be unclean until **e**. Nm 19:21
touches it shall be unclean until **e**." Nm 19:22
that you sacrifice on the **e** of the first day Dt 16:4
the Passover sacrifice, in the **e** at sunset, Dt 16:6
but when **e** comes, he shall bathe Dt 23:11
you shall say, 'If only it were **e**!' Dt 28:67
and at **e** you shall say, 'If only it were Dt 28:67
of the month in the **e** on the plains of Jos 5:10
face before the ark of the LORD until the **e**, Jos 7:6
hanged the king of Ai on a tree until **e**. Jos 8:29
And they hung on the trees until **e**. Jos 10:26
now the day has waned toward **e**. Jgs 19:9
coming from his work in the field at **e**. Jgs 19:16
up and wept before the LORD until the **e**. Jgs 20:23
the LORD and fasted that day until **e**, Jgs 20:26
to Bethel and sat there till **e** before God, Jgs 21:2
So she gleaned in the field until **e**. Then Ru 2:17
food until it is **e** and I am avenged 1 Sm 14:24
and took his stand, morning and **e**. 1 Sm 17:16
in the field till the third day at **e**. 1 Sm 20:5
from twilight until the **e** of the next 1 Sm 30:17
wept and fasted until **e** for Saul and 2 Sm 1:12
And in the **e** he went out to lie on his 2 Sm 11:13
and bread and meat in the **e**, 1 Kgs 17:6
facing the Syrians, until at **e** he died. 1 Kgs 22:35
offering and the **e** grain offering and 2 Kgs 16:15
offering regularly morning and **e**, 1 Chr 16:40
praising the LORD, and likewise at **e**, 1 Chr 23:30
for burnt offerings morning and **e**, 2 Chr 2:4
and every **e** burnt offerings 2 Chr 13:11
that its lamps may burn every **e**. 2 Chr 13:11
chariot facing the Syrians until **e**. 2 Chr 18:34
the burnt offerings of morning and **e**, 2 Chr 31:3

the LORD, burnt offerings morning and **e**. Ezr 3:3
while I sat appalled until the **e** sacrifice. Ezr 9:4
And at the **e** sacrifice I rose from my Ezr 9:5
In the **e** she would go in, and in the Est 2:14
Between morning and **e** they are beaten Jb 4:20
E and morning and at noon I utter my Ps 55:17
Each **e** they come back, howling like Ps 59:6
Each **e** they come back, howling like Ps 59:14
of the morning and the **e** to shout for joy. Ps 65:8
is renewed; in the **e** it fades and withers. Ps 90:6
My days are like an **e** shadow; I wither Ps 102:11
his work and to his labor until the **e**. Ps 104:23
I am gone like a shadow at **e**; I am Ps 109:23
up of my hands as the **e** sacrifice! Ps 141:2
in the twilight, in the **e**, at the time of Prv 7:9
seed, and at **e** withhold not your hand, Eccl 11:6
tarry late into the **e** as wine inflames Is 5:11
At **e** time, behold, terror! Before Is 17:14
declines, for the shadows of **e** lengthen! Jer 6:4
shall go out yourself at **e** in their sight, Ezk 12:4
and in the **e** I dug through the wall with Ezk 12:7
in the morning, and at **e** my wife died. Ezk 24:18
been upon me the **e** before the fugitive Ezk 33:22
but the gate shall not be shut until **e**. Ezk 46:2
swift flight at the time of the **e** sacrifice. Dn 9:21
leopards, more fierce than the **e** wolves; Hab 1:8
of Ashkelon they shall lie down at **e**. Zep 2:7
her judges are **e** wolves that leave Zep 3:3
night, but at **e** time there shall be light. Zec 14:7
That **e** they brought to him many who Mt 8:16
Now when it was **e**, the disciples came Mt 14:15
by himself to pray. When **e** came, Mt 14:23
He answered them, "When it is **e**, you Mt 16:2
And when **e** came, the owner of the Mt 20:8
When it was **e**, he reclined at table with Mt 26:20
When it was **e**, there came a rich man Mt 27:57
That **e** at sundown they brought to him Mk 1:32
On that day, when **e** had come, he said Mk 4:35
And when **e** came, the boat was out on Mk 6:47
And when **e** came they went out of the Mk 11:19
master of the house will come, in the **e**, Mk 13:35
And when it was **e**, he came with the Mk 14:17
And when **e** had come, since it was the Mk 15:42
for it is toward **e** and the day is now far Lk 24:29
When **e** came, his disciples went down to Jn 6:16
On the **e** of that day, the first day of the Jn 20:19
until the next day, for it was already **e**. Acts 4:3
From morning till **e** he expounded to Acts 28:23

EVENINGS (2)
said to me, "For 2,300 **e** and mornings. Dn 8:14
The vision of the **e** and the mornings Dn 8:26

EVENLY (1)
them with gold **e** applied on the 1 Kgs 6:35

EVENT (3)
that the same **e** happens to all Eccl 2:14
since the same **e** happens to the Eccl 9:2
the sun, that the same **e** happens to all. Eccl 9:3

EVENTS (2)
Now after these **e** Paul resolved in the Acts 19:21
by God concerning **e** as yet unseen, Heb 11:7

EVER (101)
Neither will I **e** again strike down every Gn 8:21
to this people? Why did you **e** send me? Ex 5:22
you, if **e** I let you and your little ones go! Ex 10:10
never been before, nor **e** will be again. Ex 10:14
there has never been, nor **e** will be again. Ex 11:6
The LORD will reign forever and **e**." Ex 15:18
If **e** you take your neighbor's cloak in Ex 22:26
thing as this has **e** happened or was ever Dt 4:32
this has ever happened or was **e** heard of. Dt 4:32
Did any people **e** hear the voice of a god Dt 4:33
Or has any god **e** attempted to go and Dt 4:34
your God and by walking **e** in his ways— Dt 19:9
Did he **e** contend against Israel, or did Jgs 11:25
Israel, or did he **e** go to war with them? Jgs 11:25
let me **e** find favor in your sight, my 2 Sm 16:4
of the nations **e** delivered his land 2 Kgs 18:33
of Israel our father, forever and **e**. 1 Chr 29:10
Nothing like it was **e** made for any 2 Chr 9:19
been sacrificing to him **e** since the days Ezr 4:2
or Moabite should **e** enter the Neh 13:1
who that was innocent **e** perished? Jb 4:7
me, and my bow **e** new in my hand.' Jb 29:20
Did a man **e** wish that he would be Jb 37:20
let them **e** sing for joy, and spread your Ps 5:11
have blotted out their name forever and **e**. Ps 9:5
The LORD is king forever and **e**; the Ps 10:16
it to him, length of days forever and **e**. Ps 21:4
My eyes are **e** toward the LORD, for he Ps 25:15
He is **e** lending generously, and his Ps 37:26
to fall, and my pain is **e** before me. Ps 38:17
your faithfulness will **e** preserve me! Ps 40:11
Your throne, O God, is forever and **e**. The Ps 45:6
nations will praise you forever and **e**. Ps 45:17
that this is God, our God forever and **e**. Ps 48:14
and my sin is **e** before me. Ps 51:3
in the steadfast love of God forever and **e**. Ps 52:8
So will I **e** sing praises to your name, as I Ps 61:8
in your house, **e** singing your praise! Ps 84:4
or **e** you had formed the earth and the Ps 90:2
old age; they are **e** full of sap and green, Ps 92:14
they are established forever and **e**, to be Ps 111:8
your law continually, forever and **e**, Ps 119:44
than my enemies, for it is **e** with me. Ps 119:98
and bless your name forever and **e**. Ps 145:1
and praise your name forever and **e**. Ps 145:2
bless his holy name forever and **e**. Ps 145:21
And he established them forever and **e**; Ps 148:6
none shall pass through it forever and **e**. Is 34:10
her; sickness and wounds are **e** before me. Jer 6:7
eyes failed, **e** watching vainly for help; Lam 4:17
charred, can it **e** be used for anything! Ezk 15:5
like has never been, nor **e** shall be. Ezk 16:16
do more good to you than **e** before. Ezk 36:11
be the name of God forever and **e**, Dn 2:20
the kingdom forever, forever and **e**.' Dn 7:18
like the stars forever and **e**. Dn 12:3
name of the LORD our God forever and **e**. Mi 4:5
"May no fruit **e** come from you again!" Mt 21:19
a colt tied, on which no one has **e** sat. Mk 11:2
"May no one **e** eat fruit from you Mk 11:14
colt tied, on which no one has **e** yet sat. Lk 19:30
stone, where no one had **e** yet been laid. Lk 23:53
No one has **e** seen God; the only God, who Jn 1:18
see a man who told me all that I **e** did. Jn 4:29
testimony, "He told me all that I **e** did." Jn 4:39
"No one **e** spoke like this man!" Jn 7:46
And more than **e** believers were added Acts 5:14
or unclean has **e** entered my mouth.' Acts 11:8
e since the creation of the world, Rom 1:20
the Spirit of God **e** says "Jesus is 1 Cor 12:3
more earnest than **e** because of his 2 Cor 8:22
to whom be the glory forever and **e**. Gal 1:5
all generations, forever and **e**. Eph 3:21
For no one **e** hated his own flesh, but Eph 5:29
God and Father be glory forever and **e**. Phil 4:20
be honor and glory forever and **e**. 1 Tm 1:17
whom no one has **e** seen or can see. 1 Tm 6:16
To him be the glory forever and **e**. 2 Tm 4:18
For to which of the angels did God **e** say, Heb 1:5
"Your throne, O God, is forever and **e**, Heb 1:8
to which of the angels has he **e** said, Heb 1:13
which no one has **e** served at the altar. Heb 7:13
to whom be glory forever and **e**. Heb 13:21
glory and dominion forever and **e**. 1 Pt 4:11
To him be the dominion forever and **e**. 1 Pt 5:11
For no prophecy was **e** produced by the 2 Pt 1:21
For **e** since the fathers fell asleep, all 2 Pt 3:4
No one has **e** seen God; if we love one 1 Jn 4:12
him be glory and dominion forever and **e**. Rv 1:6
on the throne, who lives forever and **e**, Rv 4:9
worship him who lives forever and **e**. Rv 4:10
and glory and might forever and **e**!" Rv 5:13
and might be to our God forever and **e**! Rv 7:12
swore by him who lives forever and **e**, Rv 10:6
and he shall reign forever and **e**." Rv 11:15
of their torment goes up forever and **e**, Rv 14:11
the wrath of God who lives forever and **e**, Rv 15:7
smoke from her goes up forever and **e**." Rv 19:3
tormented day and night forever and **e**. Rv 20:10
But nothing unclean will **e** enter it, nor Rv 21:27
light, and they will reign forever and **e**. Rv 22:5

EVER-FLOWING (2)
and brooks; you dried up **e** streams. Ps 74:15
and righteousness like an **e** stream. Am 5:24

EVERGREEN (1)
I am like an **e** cypress; from me comes Hos 14:8

EVERLASTING (67)
and remember the **e** covenant between Gn 9:16
their generations for an **e** covenant, Gn 17:7
the land of Canaan, for an **e** possession, Gn 17:8
be in your flesh an **e** covenant. Gn 17:13
with him as an **e** covenant for his Gn 17:19
on the name of the LORD, the **E** God. Gn 21:33
offspring after you for an **e** possession.' Gn 48:4
up to the bounties of the **e** hills. Gn 49:26
and the abundance of the **e** hills, Dt 33:15
place, and underneath are the **e** arms. Dt 33:27
he has made with me an **e** covenant, 2 Sm 23:5
to Jacob, as an **e** covenant to Israel, 1 Chr 16:17
from **e** to everlasting!" Then all the 1 Chr 16:36
from everlasting to **e**!" Then all the 1 Chr 16:36
the LORD your God from **e** to everlasting. Neh 9:5
the LORD your God from everlasting to **e**. Neh 9:5
The enemy came to an end in **e** ruins; Ps 9:6
the God of Israel, from **e** to everlasting! Ps 41:13
the God of Israel, from everlasting to **e**! Ps 41:13
to rout; he put them to **e** shame. Ps 78:66
world, from **e** to everlasting you are God. Ps 90:2
world, from everlasting to **e** you are God. Ps 90:2
is established from of old; you are from **e**. Ps 93:2
the LORD is from **e** to everlasting on Ps 103:17
is from everlasting to **e** on those who Ps 103:17
as a statute, to Israel as an **e** covenant, Ps 105:10
the God of Israel, from **e** to everlasting! Ps 106:48
the God of Israel, from everlasting to **e**! Ps 106:48
way in me, and lead me in the way **e**! Ps 139:24
Your kingdom is an **e** kingdom, and Ps 145:13
Counselor, Mighty God, **E** Father, Is 9:6
the statutes, broken the **e** covenant. Is 24:5
forever, for the LORD GOD is an **e** rock. Is 26:4
among us can dwell with **e** burnings?" Is 33:14
singing; **e** joy shall be upon their heads; Is 35:10
The LORD is the **e** God, the Creator of the Is 40:28
is saved by the LORD with **e** salvation; Is 45:17
singing; **e** joy shall be upon their heads; Is 51:11
but with **e** love I will have compassion on Is 54:8
and I will make with you an **e** covenant, Is 55:3
LORD, an **e** sign that shall not be cut off." Is 55:13
I will give them an **e** name that shall not Is 56:5
but the LORD will be your **e** light, and Is 60:19
for the LORD will be your **e** light, and Is 60:20
a double portion; they shall have **e** joy. Is 61:7
and I will make an **e** covenant with them. Is 61:8
them to make for himself an **e** name, Is 63:12
he is the living God and the **e** King. Jer 10:10
bring upon you **e** reproach and Jer 23:40
a horror, a hissing, and an **e** desolation. Jer 25:9
the LORD, making the land an **e** waste. Jer 25:12
I have loved you with an **e** love; therefore Jer 31:3
I will make with them an **e** covenant, Jer 32:40
become a haunt of jackals, an **e** waste; Jer 49:33
the LORD in an **e** covenant that will never Jer 50:5
I will establish for you an **e** covenant. Ezk 16:60
It shall be an **e** covenant with them. Ezk 37:26
His kingdom is an **e** kingdom, and his Dn 4:3
for his dominion is an **e** dominion, Dn 4:34
his dominion is an **e** dominion, which Dn 7:14
their kingdom shall be an **e** kingdom, Dn 7:27
for iniquity, to bring in **e** righteousness, Dn 9:24
of the earth shall awake, some to **e** life, Dn 12:2
life, and some to shame and **e** contempt. Dn 12:2
Are you not from **e**, O LORD my God, Hab 1:12
were scattered; the **e** hills sank low. Hab 3:6
hills sank low. His were the **e** ways. Hab 3:6

EVERMORE (2)
shout for joy and be glad and say **e**, Ps 35:27
May those who love your salvation say **e**, Ps 70:4

EVERY (739)
sea creatures and **e** living creature that Gn 1:21
and **e** winged bird according to its kind. Gn 1:21
the earth and over **e** creeping thing that Gn 1:26
the heavens and over **e** living thing that Gn 1:28
I have given you **e** plant yielding seed Gn 1:29
the earth, and **e** tree with seed in its fruit. Gn 1:29
And to **e** beast of the earth and to every Gn 1:30
of the earth and to **e** bird of the heavens Gn 1:30
I have given **e** green plant for food." And Gn 1:30
made to spring up **e** tree that is pleasant Gn 2:9
may surely eat of **e** tree of the garden, Gn 2:16
the LORD God formed **e** beast of the field Gn 2:19
of the field and **e** bird of the heavens Gn 2:19
the man called **e** living creature, Gn 2:19
of the heavens and to **e** beast of the field. Gn 2:20
sword that turned **e** way to guard Gn 3:24
and that **e** intention of the thoughts of his Gn 6:5
And of **e** living thing of all flesh, you Gn 6:19
you shall bring two of **e** sort into the ark Gn 6:19
kinds, of **e** creeping thing of the ground, Gn 6:20
two of **e** sort shall come in to you to keep Gn 6:20
Also take with you **e** sort of food that is Gn 6:21
and **e** living thing that I have made I will Gn 7:4
they and **e** beast, according to its kind, Gn 7:14
and **e** creeping thing that creeps on the Gn 7:14
earth, according to its kind, and **e** bird, Gn 7:14
according to its kind, **e** winged creature. Gn 7:14
He blotted out **e** living thing that was on Gn 7:23
Bring out with you **e** living thing that is Gn 8:17
and animals and **e** creeping thing that Gn 8:17
E beast, every creeping thing, and every Gn 8:19
Every beast, **e** creeping thing, and every Gn 8:19
beast, every creeping thing, and **e** bird, Gn 8:19
and took some of **e** clean animal and Gn 8:20
animal and some of **e** clean bird and Gn 8:20
again strike down **e** living creature as Gn 8:21
of you shall be upon **e** beast of the earth Gn 9:2
the earth and upon **e** bird of the heavens, Gn 9:2
E moving thing that lives shall be food Gn 9:3
from **e** beast I will require it and from Gn 9:5
and with **e** living creature that is with Gn 9:10
and **e** beast of the earth with you, Gn 9:10

of the ark; it is for **e** beast of the earth. Gn 9:10
me and you and **e** living creature that is Gn 9:12
me and you and **e** living creature of all Gn 9:15
between God and **e** living creature of Gn 9:16
E male among you shall be Gn 17:10
E male throughout your generations, Gn 17:12
e male among the men of Abraham's Gn 17:23
at **e** place to which we come, say of me, Gn 20:13
removing from it **e** speckled and Gn 30:32
and spotted sheep and **e** black lamb, Gn 30:32
E one that is not speckled and spotted Gn 30:33
and spotted, **e** one that had white on it, Gn 30:35
white on it, and **e** lamb that was black, Gn 30:35
over to his servants, **e** drove by itself, Gn 32:16
as we are by **e** male among you being Gn 34:15
one people—when **e** male among us is Gn 34:22
and **e** male was circumcised, Gn 34:24
He put in **e** city the food from the fields Gn 41:48
and to replace **e** man's money in his Gn 42:25
e man's bundle of money was in his Gn 42:35
clothes, and **e** man loaded his donkey, Gn 44:13
for **e** shepherd is an abomination to Gn 46:34
"**E** son that is born to the Hebrews you Ex 1:22
Nile, but you shall let **e** daughter live." Ex 1:22
for **e** man and beast that is in the field Ex 9:19
man and beast and **e** plant of the field, Ex 9:22
the hail struck down **e** plant of the field Ex 9:25
of the field and broke **e** tree of the field. Ex 9:25
and they shall eat **e** tree of yours that Ex 10:5
of Egypt and eat **e** plant in the land, Ex 10:12
e man of his neighbor and every woman Ex 11:2
of his neighbor and **e** woman of her Ex 11:2
and **e** firstborn in the land of Egypt shall Ex 11:5
day of this month **e** man shall take a Ex 12:3
but **e** slave that is bought for money Ex 12:44
E firstborn of a donkey you shall Ex 13:13
E firstborn of man among your sons Ex 13:13
go out and gather a day's portion **e** day, Ex 16:4
E great matter they shall bring to you, Ex 18:22
In **e** place where I cause my name to be Ex 20:24
For **e** breach of trust, whether it is for an Ex 22:9
From **e** man whose heart moves him Ex 25:2
the utensils of the tabernacle for **e** use, Ex 27:19
and **e** day you shall offer a bull as a sin Ex 29:36
E morning when he dresses the lamps he Ex 30:7
and in carving wood, to work in **e** craft. Ex 31:5
from **e** other people on the face of the Ex 33:16
"Let **e** skillful craftsman among you Ex 35:10
e man dedicating an offering of gold to Ex 35:22
And **e** one who possessed blue or purple Ex 35:23
And **e** one who possessed acacia wood Ex 35:24
And **e** skillful woman spun with her Ex 35:25
wood, for work in **e** skilled craft. Ex 35:33
with skill to do **e** sort of work done Ex 35:35
and Oholiab and **e** craftsman in whom Ex 36:1
and Oholiab and **e** craftsman in whose Ex 36:2
him freewill offerings **e** morning, Ex 36:3
craftsmen who were doing **e** sort of task Ex 36:4
sixteen bases, under **e** frame two bases. Ex 36:30
priest shall burn wood on it **e** morning, Lv 6:12
E male among the children of Aaron Lv 6:18
E grain offering of a priest shall be Lv 6:23
E male among the priests may eat of it; it Lv 6:29
E male among the priests may eat of it. It Lv 7:6
And **e** grain offering baked in the oven Lv 7:9
And **e** grain offering, mixed with oil or Lv 7:10
For **e** person who eats of the fat of an Lv 7:25
e raven of any kind, Lv 11:15
E animal that parts the hoof but is not Lv 11:26
be drunk from **e** such vessel shall Lv 11:34
"**E** swarming thing that swarms on the Lv 11:41
and bird and **e** living creature that Lv 11:46
the waters and **e** creature that swarms Lv 11:46
E bed on which the one with the Lv 15:4
and **e** vessel of wood shall be rinsed in Lv 15:12
And **e** garment and every skin on Lv 15:17
every garment and **e** skin on which Lv 15:17
and **e** bed on which he lies shall be Lv 15:24
E bed on which she lies, all the days of Lv 15:26
For the life of **e** creature is its blood: its Lv 17:14
for the life of **e** creature is its blood. Lv 17:14
And **e** person who eats what dies of Lv 17:15
E one of you shall revere his mother and Lv 19:3
E Sabbath day Aaron shall arrange it Lv 24:8
E valuation shall be according to the Lv 27:25
e devoted thing is most holy to the LORD. Lv 27:28
"**E** tithe of the land, whether of the seed Lv 27:30
And **e** tithe of herds and flocks, every Lv 27:32
e tenth animal of all that pass under Lv 27:32
to the number of names, **e** male, Nm 1:2
e male from twenty years old and Nm 1:20
e male from twenty years old and Nm 1:22
and upward, **e** man able to go to war: Nm 1:26
and upward, **e** man able to go to war: Nm 1:28
and upward, **e** man able to go to war: Nm 1:30
and upward, **e** man able to go to war: Nm 1:32
and upward, **e** man able to go to war: Nm 1:34
and upward, **e** man able to go to war: Nm 1:36
and upward, **e** man able to go to war: Nm 1:38
and upward, **e** man able to go to war: Nm 1:40
and upward, **e** man able to go to war: Nm 1:42
e man able to go to war in Israel— Nm 1:45
facing the tent of meeting on **e** side. Nm 2:2
Israel instead of **e** firstborn who opens Nm 3:12
e male from a month old and upward Nm 3:15
And **e** contribution, all the holy Nm 5:9
oxen, a wagon for **e** two of the chiefs, Nm 7:3
a man, **e** one a chief among them." Nm 13:2
E native Israelite shall do these things Nm 15:13
congregation are holy, **e** one of them, Nm 16:3
And let **e** one of you take his censer Nm 16:17
and **e** one of you bring before the LORD Nm 16:17
So **e** man took his censer and put fire Nm 16:18
e offering of theirs, every grain offering Nm 18:9
e grain offering of theirs and every sin Nm 18:9
offering of theirs and **e** sin offering of Nm 18:9
offering of theirs and **e** guilt offering of Nm 18:9
it. **E** male may eat it; it is holy to you. Nm 18:10
E devoted thing in Israel shall be Nm 18:14
Levites I have given **e** tithe in Israel for Nm 18:21
you shall present **e** contribution due Nm 18:29
And **e** open vessel that has no cover Nm 19:15
e tribe shall be given its inheritance Nm 26:54
e male from a month old and upward. Nm 26:62
this is the burnt offering of **e** Sabbath, Nm 28:10
with oil as a grain offering for **e** lamb; Nm 28:13
and **e** pledge by which she has bound Nm 30:4
and **e** pledge by which she bound Nm 30:11
commanded Moses, and killed **e** male. Nm 31:7
kill **e** male among the little ones, Nm 31:17
and kill **e** woman who has known Nm 31:17
You shall purify **e** garment, every Nm 31:20
purify every garment, **e** article of skin, Nm 31:20
of goats' hair, and **e** article of wood." Nm 31:20
you shall take one drawn out of **e** fifty, Nm 31:30
of Israel's half Moses took one of **e** 50, Nm 31:47
and **e** armed man of you will pass Nm 32:21
over, **e** man who is armed for war, Nm 32:27
e man who is armed to battle before Nm 32:29
take one chief from **e** tribe to divide Nm 34:18
for **e** one of the people of Israel shall Nm 36:7
And **e** daughter who possesses an Nm 36:8
so that **e** one of the people of Israel may Nm 36:8
And **e** one of you fastened on his Dt 1:41
time and devoted to destruction **e** city, Dt 2:34
of Heshbon, devoting to destruction **e** city, Dt 3:6
but man lives by **e** word that comes from Dt 8:3
and **e** living thing that followed them, Dt 11:6
E place on which the sole of your foot Dt 11:24
and on the hills and under **e** green tree. Dt 12:2
for **e** abominable thing that the LORD Dt 12:31
E animal that parts the hoof and has the Dt 14:6
e raven of any kind; Dt 14:14
"At the end of **e** three years you shall Dt 14:28
"At the end of **e** seven years you shall Dt 15:1
e creditor shall release what he has lent Dt 15:2
E man shall give as he is able, Dt 16:17
and by their word **e** dispute and every Dt 21:5
word every dispute and **e** assault shall be Dt 21:5
you shall keep yourself from **e** evil thing. Dt 23:9
E sickness also and every affliction that Dt 28:61
sickness also and **e** affliction that is Dt 28:61
them, "At the end of **e** seven years, Dt 31:10
E place that the sole of your foot will tread Jos 1:3
gold, and **e** vessel of bronze and iron, Jos 6:19
into the city, **e** man straight before him, Jos 6:20
He devoted to destruction **e** person in it; Jos 10:28
the edge of the sword, and **e** person in it; Jos 10:30
the edge of the sword, and **e** person in it, Jos 10:32
And he devoted **e** person in it to Jos 10:35
king and its towns, and **e** person in it. Jos 10:37
it to destruction and **e** person in it. Jos 10:37
devoted to destruction **e** person in it; Jos 10:39
But **e** man they struck with the edge of Jos 11:14
LORD gave them rest on **e** side just as he Jos 21:44
e one of them the head of a family Jos 22:14
people away, **e** man to his inheritance. Jos 24:28
A womb or two for **e** man; spoil of Jgs 5:30
"**E** one who laps the water with his Jgs 7:5
e one who kneels down to drink." Jgs 7:5
let all the others go **e** man to his home." Jgs 7:7
sent all the rest of Israel **e** man to his tent, Jgs 7:8
the trumpets also on **e** side of all the Jgs 7:18
E man stood in his place around the Jgs 7:21
the LORD set **e** man's sword against his Jgs 7:22
E one of them resembled the son of a Jgs 8:18
e one of you give me the earrings from Jgs 8:24
and **e** man threw in it the earrings of his Jgs 8:25
the hand of all their enemies on **e** side, Jgs 8:34
So **e** one of the people cut down his Jgs 9:49
e one could sling a stone at a hair and Jgs 20:16
e male and every woman that has lain Jgs 21:11
every male and **e** woman that has lain Jgs 21:11
time, **e** man to his tribe and family, Jgs 21:24
went out from there **e** man to his Jgs 21:24
the choicest parts of **e** offering of my 1 Sm 2:29
the Egyptians with **e** sort of plague 1 Sm 4:8
and they fled, **e** man to his home. 1 Sm 4:10
men of Israel, "Go **e** man to his city." 1 Sm 8:22
the hand of your enemies on **e** side, 1 Sm 12:11
people he sent home, **e** man to his tent. 1 Sm 13:2
But **e** one of the Israelites went down 1 Sm 13:20
e Philistine's sword was against his 1 Sm 14:20
'Let **e** man bring his ox or his sheep 1 Sm 14:34
with the blood.'" So **e** one of the 1 Sm 14:34
against all his enemies on **e** side, 1 Sm 14:47
the LORD cuts off **e** one of the enemies 1 Sm 20:15
the son of Jesse give **e** one of you fields 1 Sm 22:7
And Saul sought him **e** day, but God 1 Sm 23:14
"**E** man strap on his sword!" And 1 Sm 25:13
on his sword!" And **e** man of them 1 Sm 25:13
The LORD rewards **e** man for his 1 Sm 26:23
his men, **e** man with his household, 1 Sm 27:3
has redeemed my life out of **e** adversity, 2 Sm 4:9
(for at the end of **e** year he used to cut 2 Sm 14:26
Then **e** man with a dispute or cause 2 Sm 15:4
And all Israel fled **e** one to his own 2 Sm 18:17
Now Israel had fled **e** man to his own 2 Sm 19:8
of Jesse; **e** man to his tents, O Israel!" 2 Sm 20:1
from the city, **e** man to his home. 2 Sm 20:22
redeemed my soul out of **e** adversity, 1 Kgs 1:29
e man under his vine and under his 1 Kgs 4:25
my God has given me rest on **e** side. 1 Kgs 5:4
Once **e** three years the fleet of ships 1 Kgs 10:22
E one of them brought his present, 1 Kgs 10:25
he struck down **e** male in Edom 1 Kgs 11:15
he had cut off **e** male in Edom). 1 Kgs 11:16
E man return to his home, for this 1 Kgs 12:24
will cut off from Jeroboam **e** male, 1 Kgs 14:10
and Asherim on **e** high hill and 1 Kgs 14:23
high hill and under **e** green tree, 1 Kgs 14:23
and **e** mouth that has not kissed 1 Kgs 19:18
and will cut off from Ahab **e** male, 1 Kgs 21:21
the army, "**E** man to his city, 1 Kgs 22:36
his city, and **e** man to his country!" 1 Kgs 22:36
to anger in **e** way that his father had 1 Kgs 22:53
you shall attack **e** fortified city and 2 Kgs 3:19
every fortified city and **e** choice city, 2 Kgs 3:19
and shall fell **e** good tree and stop up 2 Kgs 3:19
of water and ruin **e** good piece of land 2 Kgs 3:19
and on **e** good piece of land every 2 Kgs 3:25
good piece of land **e** man threw a 2 Kgs 3:25
They stopped **e** spring of water and 2 Kgs 3:25
and I will cut off from Ahab **e** male, 2 Kgs 9:8
Then in haste **e** man of them took his 2 Kgs 9:13
e man with his weapons in his 2 Kgs 11:11
Israel, and **e** man fled to his home. 2 Kgs 14:12
fifty shekels of silver from **e** man, 2 Kgs 15:20
on the hills and under **e** green tree. 2 Kgs 16:4
and Asherim on **e** high hill and 2 Kgs 17:10
high hill and under **e** green tree, 2 Kgs 17:10
and Judah by **e** prophet and every 2 Kgs 17:13
Judah by every prophet and **e** seer, 2 Kgs 17:13
But **e** nation still made gods of its 2 Kgs 17:29
e nation in the cities in which they 2 Kgs 17:29
e great house he burned down. 2 Kgs 25:9
And **e** day of his life he dined 2 Kgs 25:29
obligated to come in **e** seven days, 1 Chr 9:25
had charge of opening it **e** morning. 1 Chr 9:27
showbread, to prepare it **e** Sabbath. 1 Chr 9:32
and of hundreds, with **e** leader. 1 Chr 13:1
he not given you peace on **e** side? 1 Chr 22:18
And they were to stand **e** morning, 1 Chr 23:30
hearts and understands **e** plan and 1 Chr 28:9
the work will be **e** willing man who 1 Chr 28:21
Once **e** three years the ships of 2 Chr 9:21
E one of them brought his present, 2 Chr 9:24
Return **e** man to his home, for this 2 Chr 11:4
to the LORD **e** morning and every 2 Chr 13:11
every morning and **e** evening burnt 2 Chr 13:11
that its lamps may burn **e** evening. 2 Chr 13:11
given us peace on **e** side." So they 2 Chr 14:7
troubled them with **e** sort of distress. 2 Chr 15:6
e man of Judah and Jerusalem, 2 Chr 20:27
e man with his weapon in his hand, 2 Chr 23:10
Israel, and **e** man fled to his home. 2 Chr 25:22
on the hills and under **e** green tree. 2 Chr 28:4
himself altars in **e** corner of 2 Chr 28:24
In **e** city of Judah he made high 2 Chr 28:25
their cities, **e** man to his possession. 2 Chr 31:1
distribute portions to **e** male among 2 Chr 31:19
And **e** work that he undertook in 2 Chr 31:21
and he provided for them on **e** side. 2 Chr 32:22
who did work in **e** kind of service, 2 Chr 34:13
them the elders and judges of **e** city, Ezr 10:14

"Let **e** man and his servant pass the Neh 4:22
may God shake out **e** man from his Neh 5:13
and **e** ten days all kinds of wine in Neh 5:18
peoples and allotted to them **e** corner. Neh 9:22
year and the exaction of **e** debt. Neh 10:31
and the firstfruits of all fruit of **e** tree, Neh 10:35
our contributions, the fruit of **e** tree, Neh 10:37
of Judah, **e** one in his inheritance. Neh 11:20
for the singers, as **e** day required. Neh 11:23
to **e** province in its own script and to Est 1:22
its own script and to **e** people in its own Est 1:22
that **e** man be master in his own Est 1:22
And **e** day Mordecai walked in front of Est 2:11
are different from those of **e** other people, Est 3:8
to **e** province in its own script and every Est 3:12
in its own script and **e** people in its own Est 3:12
a decree in **e** province by proclamation Est 3:14
And in **e** province, wherever the king's Est 4:3
the Jews who were in **e** city to gather and Est 8:11
to be issued as a decree in **e** province, Est 8:13
And in **e** province and in every city, Est 8:17
And in every province and in **e** city, Est 8:17
written and at the time appointed **e** year, Est 9:27
and kept throughout **e** generation, Est 9:28
throughout every generation, in **e** clan, Est 9:28
his house and all that he has, on **e** side? Jb 1:10
visit him **e** morning and test him every Jb 7:18
every morning and test him **e** moment? Jb 7:18
hand is the life of **e** living thing and the Jb 12:10
Terrors frighten him on **e** side, and Jb 18:11
He breaks me down on **e** side, and I am Jb 19:10
rocks, and his eye sees **e** precious thing. Jb 28:10
He seals up the hand of **e** man, that all Jb 37:7
and he searches after **e** green thing. Jb 39:8
e night I flood my bed with tears; Ps 6:6
and a God who feels indignation **e** day. Ps 7:11
On **e** side the wicked prowl, as vileness is Ps 12:8
whispering of many—terror on **e** side! Ps 31:13
For **e** beast of the forest is mine, the Ps 50:10
For he has delivered me from **e** trouble, Ps 54:7
been stricken and rebuked **e** morning. Ps 73:14
thunder; your arrows flashed on **e** side. Ps 77:17
He struck down **e** firstborn in Egypt, Ps 78:51
E day I call upon you, O LORD; I spread Ps 88:9
they give drink to **e** beast of the field; Ps 104:11
him, like a belt that he puts on **e** day! Ps 109:19
me, surrounded me on **e** side; Ps 118:11
I hold back my feet from **e** evil way, Ps 119:101
therefore I hate **e** false way. Ps 119:104
precepts to be right; I hate **e** false way. Ps 119:128
and **e** one of your righteous rules Ps 119:160
your book were written, **e** one of them, Ps 139:16
E day I will bless you and praise your Ps 145:2
you satisfy the desire of **e** living thing. Ps 145:16
and justice and equity, **e** good path; Prv 2:9
market, and at **e** corner she lies in wait. Prv 7:12
The eyes of the LORD are in **e** place, Prv 15:3
lap, but its **e** decision is from the LORD. Prv 16:33
strife, but **e** fool will be quarreling. Prv 20:3
E way of a man is right in his own eyes, Prv 21:2
E word of God proves true; he is a shield Prv 30:5
and a time for **e** matter under heaven: Eccl 3:1
is a time for **e** matter and for every Eccl 3:17
a time for every matter and for **e** work. Eccl 3:17
But this is gain for a land in **e** way: a Eccl 5:9
God will bring **e** deed into judgment, Eccl 12:14
into judgment, with **e** secret thing, Eccl 12:14
against **e** high tower, and against every Is 2:15
high tower, and against **e** fortified wall; Is 2:15
e one his fellow and every one his Is 3:5
one his fellow and **e** one his neighbor; Is 3:5
In that day **e** place where there used to be Is 7:23
For **e** boot of the tramping warrior in Is 9:5
in battle tumult and **e** garment rolled in Is 9:5
an evildoer, and **e** mouth speaks folly. Is 9:17
be feeble, and **e** human heart will melt. Is 13:7
On **e** head is baldness; every beard is Is 15:2
every head is baldness; **e** beard is shorn; Is 15:2
the offspring and issue, **e** small vessel, Is 22:24
e house is shut up so that none can Is 24:10
LORD, am its keeper; **e** moment I water it. Is 27:3
And on **e** lofty mountain and every high Is 30:25
lofty mountain and **e** high hill there Is 30:25
And **e** stroke of the appointed staff that Is 30:32
Be our arm **e** morning, our salvation in Is 33:2
E valley shall be lifted up, and every Is 40:4
up, and **e** mountain and hill be made low; Is 40:4
the east whom victory meets at **e** step? Is 41:2
O mountains, O forest, and **e** tree in it! Is 44:23
'To me **e** knee shall bow, every tongue Is 45:23
bow, **e** tongue shall swear allegiance.' Is 45:23
lie at the head of **e** street like an antelope Is 51:20
we have turned **e** one to his own way; Is 53:6
and you shall confute **e** tongue that rises Is 54:17
lust among the oaks, under **e** green tree, Is 57:5
remove **e** obstruction from my people's Is 57:14
the oppressed go free, and to break **e** yoke? Is 58:6
and **e** one shall set his throne at the Jer 1:15
on **e** high hill and under every green tree Jer 2:20
high hill and under **e** green tree you Jer 2:20
how she went up on **e** high hill and under Jer 3:6
on every high hill and under **e** green tree, Jer 3:6
among foreigners under **e** green tree, Jer 3:13
of horseman and archer **e** city takes to Jer 4:29
enemy has a sword; terror is on **e** side. Jer 6:25
in any brother, for **e** brother is a deceiver, Jer 9:4
and **e** neighbor goes about as a slanderer. Jer 9:4
E man is stupid and without Jer 10:14
e goldsmith is put to shame by his Jer 10:14
mourn and the grass of **e** field wither? Jer 12:4
"**E** jar shall be filled with wine."' And Jer 13:12
not indeed know that **e** jar will be filled Jer 13:12
e one of you follows his stubborn, Jer 16:12
hunt them from **e** mountain and every Jer 16:16
them from every mountain and **e** hill, Jer 16:16
beside **e** green tree and on the high hills, Jer 17:2
to give **e** man according to his ways, Jer 17:10
Return, **e** one from his evil way, and Jer 18:11
and will **e** one act according to the Jer 18:12
name Pashhur, but Terror On **E** Side. Jer 20:3
many whispering. Terror is on **e** side! Jer 20:10
city, and **e** man will say to his neighbor, Jer 22:8
e one to his neighbor and every one to Jer 23:35
to his neighbor and **e** one to his Jer 23:35
for the burden is **e** man's own word, Jer 23:36
saying, 'Turn now, **e** one of you, from Jer 25:5
listen, and **e** one turn from his evil way, Jer 26:3
the LORD over **e** madman who Jer 29:26
Why then do I see **e** man with his hands Jer 30:6
in labor? Why has **e** face turned pale? Jer 30:6
and all your foes, **e** one of them, Jer 30:16
and **e** languishing soul I will Jer 31:25
e one to his brother and to his Jer 34:17
'Turn now **e** one of you from his evil Jer 35:15
so that **e** one may turn from his evil way, Jer 36:3
and that **e** one will turn from his evil Jer 36:7
only wounded men, **e** man in his tent, Jer 37:10
and **e** person whom Nebuzaradan the Jer 43:6
they look not back—terror on **e** side! Jer 46:5
and **e** inhabitant of the land shall wail. Jer 47:2
Tyre and Sidon **e** helper that remains. Jer 47:4
The destroyer shall come upon **e** city, Jer 48:8
"For **e** head is shaved and every beard Jer 48:37
head is shaved and **e** beard cut off. Jer 48:37
driven out, **e** man straight before him, Jer 49:5
shall cry to them: 'Terror on **e** side!' Jer 49:29
I will scatter to **e** wind those who cut Jer 49:32
their calamity from **e** side of them, Jer 49:32
e one shall turn to his own people, Jer 50:16
and **e** one shall flee to his own land. Jer 50:16
Come against her from **e** quarter; open Jer 50:26
come against her from **e** side on the day Jer 51:2
midst of Babylon; let **e** one save his life! Jer 51:6
E man is stupid and without Jer 51:17
e goldsmith is put to shame by his Jer 51:17
and **e** land under their dominion. Jer 51:28
Babylon that his city is taken on **e** side; Jer 51:31
Let **e** one save his life from the fierce Jer 51:45
e great house he burned down. Jer 52:13
And **e** day of his life he dined regularly Jer 52:33
faint for hunger at the head of **e** street." Lam 2:19
if to a festival day my terrors on **e** side, Lam 2:22
they are new **e** morning; great is your Lam 3:23
lie scattered at the head of **e** street. Lam 4:1
idols around their altars, on **e** high hill, Ezk 6:13
the mountaintops, under **e** green tree, Ezk 6:13
every green tree, and under **e** leafy oak, Ezk 6:13
was **e** form of creeping things and Ezk 8:10
And **e** one had four faces: the first face Ezk 10:14
I will scatter toward **e** wind all who are Ezk 12:14
long, and **e** vision comes to nothing'? Ezk 12:22
near, and the fulfillment of **e** vision. Ezk 12:23
for the heads of persons of **e** stature, Ezk 13:18
yourself a lofty place in **e** square. Ezk 16:24
At the head of **e** street you built your Ezk 16:25
chamber at the head of **e** street, Ezk 16:31
making your lofty place in **e** square. Ezk 16:31
come to you from **e** side with your Ezk 16:33
them against you from **e** side and will Ezk 16:37
survivors shall be scattered to **e** wind, Ezk 17:21
And under it will dwell **e** kind of bird; Ezk 17:23
of its branches birds of **e** sort will nest. Ezk 17:23
of Israel, **e** one according to his ways, Ezk 18:30
against him from provinces on **e** side; Ezk 19:8
things your eyes feast on, **e** one of you, Ezk 20:7
Go serve **e** one of you his idols, now Ezk 20:39
and it shall devour **e** green tree in you Ezk 20:47
every green tree in you and **e** dry tree. Ezk 20:47
E heart will melt, and all hands will be Ezk 21:7
e spirit will faint, and all knees will be Ezk 21:7
in you, **e** one according to his power, Ezk 22:6
bring them against you from **e** side: Ezk 23:22
against you on **e** side with buckler, Ezk 23:24
ground and tremble **e** moment and be Ezk 26:16
because of your great wealth of **e** kind; Ezk 27:12
because of your great wealth of **e** kind; Ezk 27:18
e precious stone was your covering, Ezk 28:13
the sword that is against her on **e** side. Ezk 28:23
E head was made bald, and every Ezk 29:18
bald, and **e** shoulder was rubbed bare, Ezk 29:18
They shall tremble **e** moment, every Ezk 32:10
every moment, **e** one for his own life, Ezk 32:10
all the mountains and on **e** high hill. Ezk 34:6
and **e** wall shall tumble to the ground. Ezk 38:20
E man's sword will be against his Ezk 38:21
to birds of prey of **e** sort and to the Ezk 39:4
Speak to the birds of **e** sort and to all Ezk 39:17
cubits all around the temple on **e** side. Ezk 41:10
and cherub. **E** cherub had two faces: Ezk 41:18
and **e** devoted thing in Israel shall be Ezk 44:29
and **e** offering of all kinds from all Ezk 44:30
And one sheep from **e** flock of two Ezk 45:15
e living creature that swarms will live, Ezk 47:9
but they will bear fresh fruit **e** month, Ezk 47:12
And in **e** matter of wisdom and Dn 1:20
harp, bagpipe, and **e** kind of music, Dn 3:5
harp, bagpipe, and **e** kind of music, Dn 3:7
that **e** man who hears the sound of the Dn 3:10
harp, bagpipe, and **e** kind of music, Dn 3:10
harp, bagpipe, and **e** kind of music, Dn 3:15
and magnify himself above **e** god, Dn 11:36
E evil of theirs is in Gilgal; there I Hos 9:15
strip his treasury of **e** precious thing. Hos 13:15
themselves down beside **e** altar on Am 2:8
bring your sacrifices **e** morning, your Am 4:4
every morning, your tithes **e** three days; Am 4:4
bring sackcloth on **e** waist and Am 8:10
on every waist and baldness on **e** head; Am 8:10
so that **e** man from Mount Esau will be Ob 1:9
but they shall sit **e** man under his vine Mi 4:4
dashed in pieces at the head of **e** street; Na 3:10
They laugh at **e** fortress, for they pile Hab 1:10
e morning he shows forth his justice; Zep 3:5
LORD, and so with **e** work of their hands. Hg 2:14
down, **e** one by the sword of his brother. Hg 2:22
e one of you will invite his neighbor to Zec 3:10
in, for I set **e** man against his neighbor. Zec 8:10
from the nations of **e** tongue shall take Zec 8:23
from him **e** ruler—all of them together. Zec 10:4
LORD, I will strike **e** horse with panic, Zec 12:4
when I strike **e** horse of the peoples with Zec 12:4
"On that day **e** prophet will be ashamed Zec 13:4
And **e** pot in Jerusalem and Judah Zec 14:21
and in **e** place incense will be offered to Mal 1:11
E tree therefore that does not bear good Mt 3:10
but by **e** word that comes from the Mt 4:4
kingdom and healing **e** disease and Mt 4:23
every disease and **e** affliction among the Mt 4:23
So, **e** healthy tree bears good fruit, but Mt 7:17
E tree that does not bear good fruit is cut Mt 7:19
kingdom and healing **e** disease and Mt 9:35
healing every disease and **e** affliction. Mt 9:35
and to heal **e** disease and every affliction. Mt 10:1
and to heal every disease and **e** affliction. Mt 10:1
"**E** kingdom divided against itself is Mt 12:25
e sin and blasphemy will be forgiven Mt 12:31
give account for **e** careless word they Mt 12:36
into the sea and gathered fish of **e** kind. Mt 13:47
"Therefore **e** scribe who has been Mt 13:52
"**E** plant that my heavenly Father has Mt 15:13
that **e** charge may be established by Mt 18:16
heavenly Father will do to **e** one of you, Mt 18:35
were coming to him from **e** quarter. Mk 1:45
"**E** male who first opens the womb shall Lk 2:23
parents went to Jerusalem **e** year at the Lk 2:41
E valley shall be filled, and every Lk 3:5
and **e** mountain and hill shall be made Lk 3:5
E tree therefore that does not bear good Lk 3:9
when the devil had ended **e** temptation, Lk 4:13
him went out into **e** place in the Lk 4:37
he laid his hands on **e** one of them and Lk 4:40
who had come from **e** village of Galilee Lk 5:17
into **e** town and place where he himself Lk 10:1
"**E** kingdom divided against itself is Lk 11:17
For you tithe mint and rue and **e** herb, Lk 11:42
and who feasted sumptuously **e** day. Lk 16:19
surround you and hem you in on **e** side Lk 19:43
And **e** day he was teaching in the Lk 21:37
you are clean, but not **e** one of you." Jn 13:10
E branch of mine that does not bear fruit Jn 15:2
and **e** branch that does bear fruit he Jn 15:2
Were **e** one of them to be written, I Jn 21:25
devout men from **e** nation under Acts 2:5
"Repent and be baptized **e** one of you in Acts 2:38
And awe came upon **e** soul, and many Acts 2:43

it shall be that **e** soul who does not Acts 3:23
bless you by turning **e** one of you from Acts 3:26
And **e** day, in the temple and from Acts 5:42
but in **e** nation anyone who fears Acts 10:35
prophets, which are read **e** Sabbath, Acts 13:27
elders for them in **e** church, Acts 14:23
Moses has had in **e** city those who Acts 15:21
for he is read **e** Sabbath in the Acts 15:21
visit the brothers in **e** city where we Acts 15:36
in the marketplace **e** day with those Acts 17:17
I perceive that in **e** way you are very Acts 17:22
from one man **e** nation of mankind Acts 17:26
reasoned in the synagogue **e** Sabbath, Acts 18:4
to me in **e** city that imprisonment Acts 20:23
in **e** way and everywhere we accept this Acts 24:3
excuse, O man, **e** one of you who judges. Rom 2:1
and distress for **e** human being who Rom 2:9
Much in **e** way. To begin with, the Jews Rom 3:2
God be true though **e** one were a liar, Rom 3:4
law, so that **e** mouth may be stopped, Rom 3:19
Let **e** person be subject to the Rom 13:1
says the Lord, **e** knee shall bow to me, Rom 14:11
and **e** tongue shall confess to God." Rom 14:11
all those who in **e** place call upon the 1 Cor 1:2
that in **e** way you were enriched in 1 Cor 1:5
I teach them everywhere in **e** church. 1 Cor 4:17
E other sin a person commits is 1 Cor 6:18
E athlete exercises self-control in all 1 Cor 9:25
that the head of **e** man is Christ, 1 Cor 11:3
E man who prays or prophesies with 1 Cor 11:4
but **e** wife who prays or prophesies 1 Cor 11:5
Father after destroying **e** rule and 1 Cor 15:24
every rule and **e** authority and 1 Cor 15:24
Why am I in danger **e** hour? 1 Cor 15:30
in Christ Jesus our Lord, I die **e** day! 1 Cor 15:31
On the first day of **e** week, each of you 1 Cor 16:2
and to **e** fellow worker and laborer. 1 Cor 16:16
We are afflicted in **e** way, but not 2 Cor 4:8
God we commend ourselves in **e** way: 2 Cor 6:4
cleanse ourselves from **e** defilement of 2 Cor 7:1
we were afflicted at **e** turn—fighting 2 Cor 7:5
At **e** point you have proved yourselves 2 Cor 7:11
you may abound in **e** good work. 2 Cor 9:8
will be enriched in **e** way for all your 2 Cor 9:11
arguments and **e** lofty opinion 2 Cor 10:5
and take **e** thought captive to obey 2 Cor 10:5
being ready to punish **e** disobedience, 2 Cor 10:6
in **e** way we have made this plain to 2 Cor 11:6
E charge must be established by the 2 Cor 13:1
I testify again to **e** man who accepts Gal 5:3
us in Christ with **e** spiritual blessing in Eph 1:3
and above **e** name that is named, Eph 1:21
from whom **e** family in heaven and on Eph 3:15
carried about by **e** wind of doctrine, Eph 4:14
are to grow up in **e** way into him who is Eph 4:15
and held together by **e** joint with which Eph 4:16
greedy to practice **e** kind of impurity. Eph 4:19
always in **e** prayer of mine for you all Phil 1:4
Only that in **e** way, whether in pretense Phil 1:18
on him the name that is above **e** name, Phil 2:9
the name of Jesus **e** knee should bow, Phil 2:10
and **e** tongue confess that Jesus Christ Phil 2:11
In any and **e** circumstance, I have Phil 4:12
my God will supply **e** need of yours Phil 4:19
Greet **e** saint in Christ Jesus. The Phil 4:21
bearing fruit in **e** good work and Col 1:10
Abstain from **e** form of evil. 1 Thes 5:22
and the love of **e** one of you for one 2 Thes 1:3
and may fulfill **e** resolve for good 2 Thes 1:11
resolve for good and **e** work of faith 2 Thes 1:11
exalts himself against **e** so-called god 2 Thes 2:4
establish them in **e** good work and 2 Thes 2:17
give you peace at all times in **e** way. 2 Thes 3:16
of genuineness in **e** letter of mine; 2 Thes 3:17
quiet life, godly and dignified in **e** way. 1 Tm 2:2
desire then that in **e** place the men 1 Tm 2:8
value, godliness is of value in **e** way, 1 Tm 4:8
has devoted herself to **e** good work. 1 Tm 5:10
of the house, ready for **e** good work. 2 Tm 2:21
competent, equipped for **e** good work. 2 Tm 3:17
will rescue me from **e** evil deed and 2 Tm 4:18
and appoint elders in **e** town as I directed Ti 1:5
to be obedient, to be ready for **e** good work, Ti 3:1
the full knowledge of **e** good thing that Phlm 1:6
be reliable and **e** transgression or Heb 2:2
be made like his brothers in **e** respect, Heb 2:17
(For **e** house is built by someone, but Heb 3:4
But exhort one another **e** day, as long Heb 3:13
but one who in **e** respect has been Heb 4:15
For **e** high priest chosen from among Heb 5:1
For **e** high priest is appointed to offer Heb 8:3
For when **e** commandment of the law Heb 9:19
enters the holy places **e** year with blood Heb 9:25
that are continually offered **e** year, Heb 10:1
there is a reminder of sin **e** year. Heb 10:3
And **e** priest stands daily at his Heb 10:11
witnesses, let us also lay aside **e** weight, Heb 12:1
and chastises **e** son whom he receives." Heb 12:6
E good gift and every perfect gift is from Jas 1:17
Every good gift and **e** perfect gift is from Jas 1:17
let **e** person be quick to hear, slow to Jas 1:19
For **e** kind of beast and bird, of reptile and Jas 3:7
there will be disorder and **e** vile practice. Jas 3:16
the Lord's sake to **e** human institution, 1 Pt 2:13
make **e** effort to supplement your faith 2 Pt 1:5
And I will make **e** effort so that after 2 Pt 1:15
Beloved, do not believe **e** spirit, but test 1 Jn 4:1
e spirit that confesses that Jesus Christ 1 Jn 4:2
and **e** spirit that does not confess Jesus is 1 Jn 4:3
you. Greet the friends, **e** one of them. 3 Jn 1:15
with the clouds, and **e** eye will see him, Rv 1:7
people for God from **e** tribe and language Rv 5:9
And I heard **e** creature in heaven and on Rv 5:13
and **e** mountain and island was removed Rv 6:14
sealed from **e** tribe of the sons of Israel: Rv 7:4
that no one could number, from **e** nation, Rv 7:9
God will wipe away **e** tear from their Rv 7:17
to strike the earth with **e** kind of plague, Rv 11:6
was given it over **e** tribe and people and Rv 13:7
to **e** nation and tribe and language and Rv 14:6
and **e** living thing died that was in the Rv 16:3
And **e** island fled away, and no Rv 16:20
for demons, a haunt for **e** unclean spirit, Rv 18:2
spirit, a haunt for **e** unclean bird, Rv 18:2
a haunt for **e** unclean and detestable Rv 18:2
He will wipe away **e** tear from their eyes, Rv 21:4
city were adorned with **e** kind of jewel. Rv 21:19

EVERYONE (205)

his hand against **e** and everyone's Gn 16:12
you, and before **e** you are vindicated." Gn 20:16
for me; **e** who hears will laugh over me." Gn 21:6
Cursed be **e** who curses you, and Gn 27:29
you, and blessed be **e** who blesses you!" Gn 27:29
"Make **e** go out from me." So no one Gn 45:1
But what **e** needs to eat, that alone may Ex 12:16
E who is numbered in the census, from Ex 30:14
E who profanes it shall be put to death. Ex 31:14
And **e** who sought the LORD would go out Ex 33:7
they came, **e** whose heart stirred him, Ex 35:21
him, and **e** whose spirit moved him, Ex 35:21
E who could make a contribution of Ex 35:24
e whose heart stirred him up to come to Ex 36:2
for **e** who was listed in the records, Ex 38:26
E who touches them shall be unclean. Lv 11:26
For **e** who does any of these Lv 18:29
and **e** who eats it shall bear his iniquity, Lv 19:8
list them, **e** who can come on duty, Nm 4:30
years old, **e** who could come on duty, Nm 4:35
e who could come on duty for service Nm 4:39
years old, **e** who could come on duty, Nm 4:43
e who could come to do the service of Nm 4:47
put out of the camp **e** who is leprous or Nm 5:2
has a discharge and **e** who is unclean Nm 5:2
their clans, **e** at the door of his tent. Nm 11:10
E who comes near, who comes near to Nm 17:13
E who is clean in your house may eat Nm 18:11
E who is clean in your house may eat Nm 18:13
e who comes into the tent and Nm 19:14
comes into the tent and **e** who is in the Nm 19:14
and set it on a pole, and **e** who is bitten, Nm 21:8
e doing whatever is right in his own eyes, Dt 12:8
people shall go up, **e** straight before him." Jos 6:5
was dead, **e** departed to his home. Jgs 9:55
E did what was right in his own eyes. Jgs 17:6
E did what was right in his own eyes. Jgs 21:25
And **e** who is left in your house shall 1 Sm 2:36
the two ears of **e** who hears it will 1 Sm 3:11
And **e** who was in distress, and 1 Sm 22:2
was in distress, and **e** who was in debt, 1 Sm 22:2
in debt, and **e** who was bitter in soul, 1 Sm 22:2
were with him, **e** with his household, 2 Sm 2:3
"Send out **e** from me." So everyone 2 Sm 13:9
from me." So **e** went out from 2 Sm 13:9
E passing by it will be astonished and 1 Kgs 9:8
that the ears of **e** who hears of it 2 Kgs 21:12
from **e** according to his assessment, 2 Kgs 23:35
e passing by will be astonished and 2 Chr 7:21
Passover lamb for **e** who was not 2 Chr 30:17
"May the good LORD pardon **e** 2 Chr 30:18
priests and to **e** among the Levites 2 Chr 31:19
e whose spirit God had stirred to go up to Ezr 1:5
and the offerings of **e** who made a freewill Ezr 3:5
and also by **e** who had joined them and Ezr 6:21
the towns of Judah **e** lived on his Neh 11:3
the hand of **e** in misery will come Jb 20:22
and look on **e** who is proud and abase Jb 40:11
Look on **e** who is proud and bring him Jb 40:12
E utters lies to his neighbor; with Ps 12:2
Therefore let **e** who is godly offer prayer Ps 32:6
you put an end to **e** who is unfaithful to Ps 73:27
Blessed is **e** who fears the LORD, who Ps 128:1
Such are the ways of **e** who is greedy for Prv 1:19
E who is arrogant in heart is an Prv 16:5
and **e** is a friend to a man who gives Prv 19:6
but **e** who is hasty comes only to Prv 21:5
an archer who wounds **e** is one who Prv 26:10
also that **e** should eat and drink and Eccl 3:13
E also to whom God has given wealth Eccl 5:19
sense, and he says to **e** that he is a fool. Eccl 10:3
E loves a bribe and runs after gifts. Is 1:23
e who has been recorded for life in Is 4:3
for **e** who is left in the land will eat curds Is 7:22
for **e** is godless and an evildoer, and every Is 9:17
and in the squares **e** wails and melts in Is 15:3
let Moab wail for Moab, let **e** wail. Is 16:7
E to whom it is mentioned will fear Is 19:17
e comes to shame through a people that Is 30:5
For in that day **e** shall cast away his idols Is 31:7
E helps his neighbor and says to his Is 41:6
e who is called by my name, whom I Is 43:7
"Come, **e** who thirsts, come to the waters; Is 55:1
e who keeps the Sabbath and does not Is 56:6
e who goes out of them shall be torn in Jer 5:6
of them, **e** is greedy for unjust gain; Jer 6:13
from prophet to priest, **e** deals falsely. Jer 6:13
E turns to his own course, like a horse Jer 8:6
least to the greatest **e** is greedy for unjust Jer 8:10
from prophet to priest, **e** deals falsely. Jer 8:10
Let **e** beware of his neighbor, and put no Jer 9:4
E deceives his neighbor, and no one Jer 9:5
but **e** walked in the stubbornness of his Jer 11:8
E who passes by it is horrified and Jer 18:16
place that the ears of **e** who hears of it Jer 19:3
E who passes by it will be horrified and Jer 19:8
and **e** shall eat the flesh of his neighbor Jer 19:9
laughingstock all the day; **e** mocks me. Jer 20:7
and to **e** who stubbornly follows his Jer 23:17
But **e** shall die for his own sin. Each Jer 31:30
that **e** should set free his Hebrew slaves, Jer 34:9
into the covenant that **e** would set free Jer 34:10
E who passes by it will be horrified and Jer 49:17
e who passes by Babylon shall be Jer 50:13
e who uses proverbs will use this Ezk 16:44
all the idols of **e** after whom she lusted. Ezk 23:7
e whose name shall be found written in Dn 12:1
shall come to pass that **e** who calls on the Jl 2:32
account, and **e** mourn who dwells in it, Am 8:8
Let **e** turn from his evil way and from the Jon 3:8
day I will punish **e** who leaps over the Zep 1:9
E who passes by her hisses and shakes Zep 2:15
For **e** who steals shall be cleaned out Zec 5:3
and **e** who swears falsely shall be cleaned Zec 5:3
of rain, to **e** the vegetation in the field. Zec 10:1
Then **e** who survives of all the nations Zec 14:16
"**E** who does evil is good in the sight of Mal 2:17
I say to you that **e** who is angry with his Mt 5:22
I say to you that **e** who looks at a woman Mt 5:28
I say to you that **e** who divorces his wife, Mt 5:32
For **e** who asks receives, and the one who Mt 7:8
"Not **e** who says to me, 'Lord, Lord,' will Mt 7:21
"**E** then who hears these words of mine Mt 7:24
And **e** who hears these words of mine Mt 7:26
So **e** who acknowledges me before men, Mt 10:32
to them, "Not **e** can receive this saying, Mt 19:11
And **e** who has left houses or brothers Mt 19:29
For to **e** who has will more be given, Mt 25:29
and said to him, "**E** is looking for you." Mk 1:37
Jesus had done for him, and **e** marveled. Mk 5:20
For **e** will be salted with fire. Mk 9:49
Give to **e** who begs from you, and from Lk 6:30
but **e** when he is fully trained will be Lk 6:40
E who comes to me and hears my words Lk 6:47
we ourselves forgive **e** who is indebted Lk 11:4
For **e** who asks receives, and the one Lk 11:10
e who acknowledges me before men, Lk 12:8
And **e** who speaks a word against the Lk 12:10
E to whom much was given, of him Lk 12:48
For **e** who exalts himself will be Lk 14:11
"Blessed is **e** who will eat bread in the Lk 14:15
is preached, and **e** forces his way into it. Lk 16:16
"**E** who divorces his wife and marries Lk 16:18
For **e** who exalts himself will be Lk 18:14
'I tell you that to **e** who has, more will Lk 19:26
E who falls on that stone will be Lk 20:18
The true light, which enlightens **e**, was Jn 1:9
said to him, "**E** serves the good wine first, Jn 2:10
So it is with **e** who is born of the Spirit." Jn 3:8
For **e** who does wicked things hates the Jn 3:20
"**E** who drinks of this water will be Jn 4:13
that **e** who looks on the Son and believes Jn 6:40
E who has heard and learned from the Jn 6:45
you, **e** who commits sin is a slave to sin. Jn 8:34
and **e** who lives and believes in me shall Jn 11:26
go on like this, **e** will believe in him, Jn 11:48
E who is of the truth listens to my Jn 18:37

E who makes himself a king opposes Jn 19:12
come to pass that **e** who calls upon the Acts 2:21
e whom the Lord our God calls to Acts 2:39
bear witness that **e** who believes in Acts 10:43
e according to his ability, Acts 11:29
and by him **e** who believes is freed Acts 13:38
or day to admonish **e** with tears. Acts 20:31
who is teaching **e** everywhere against Acts 21:28
witness for him to **e** of what you have Acts 22:15
of God for salvation to **e** who believes, Rom 1:16
honor and peace for **e** who does good, Rom 2:10
for righteousness to **e** who believes. Rom 10:4
"**E** who believes in him will not be Rom 10:11
For "**e** who calls on the name of the Rom 10:13
to me I say to **e** among you not to Rom 12:3
as I try to please **e** in everything I do, 1 Cor 10:33
God who empowers them all in **e**. 1 Cor 12:6
"Cursed be **e** who does not abide by all Gal 3:10
"Cursed is **e** who is hanged on a tree"— Gal 3:13
we have opportunity, let us do good to **e**, Gal 6:10
to bring to light for **e** what is the plan of Eph 3:9
that **e** who is sexually immoral or Eph 5:5
Let your reasonableness be known to **e**. Phil 4:5
warning **e** and teaching everyone with Col 1:28
everyone and teaching **e** with all Col 1:28
that we may present **e** mature in Christ. Col 1:28
to do good to one another and to **e**. 1 Thes 5:15
"Let **e** who names the name of the 2 Tm 2:19
not be quarrelsome but kind to **e**, 2 Tm 2:24
grace of God he might taste death for **e**. Heb 2:9
for **e** who lives on milk is unskilled in Heb 5:13
Strive for peace with **e**, and for the Heb 12:14
Honor **e**. Love the brotherhood. Fear 1 Pt 2:17
be sure that **e** who practices 1 Jn 2:29
And **e** who thus hopes in him purifies 1 Jn 3:3
E who makes a practice of sinning also 1 Jn 3:4
E who hates his brother is a murderer, 1 Jn 3:15
E who believes that Jesus is the Christ 1 Jn 5:1
and **e** who loves the Father loves 1 Jn 5:1
For **e** who has been born of God 1 Jn 5:4
We know that **e** who has been born of 1 Jn 5:18
E who goes on ahead and does not abide 2 Jn 1:9
has received a good testimony from **e**, 3 Jn 1:12
and the rich and the powerful, and **e**, Rv 6:15
e whose name has not been written Rv 13:8
me, to repay **e** for what he has done. Rv 22:12
and **e** who loves and practices Rv 22:15
I warn **e** who hears the words of the Rv 22:18

EVERYONE'S (3)
against everyone and **e** hand against Gn 16:12
opened, and **e** bonds were unfastened. Acts 16:26
commend ourselves to **e** conscience in 2 Cor 4:2

EVERYTHING (139)
and **e** that creeps on the ground Gn 1:25
the heavens and to **e** that creeps on the Gn 1:30
on the earth, **e** that has the breath of life, Gn 1:30
And God saw **e** that he had made, and Gn 1:31
heaven. **E** that is on the earth shall die. Gn 6:17
birds, and of **e** that creeps on the ground, Gn 7:8
E on the dry land in whose nostrils was Gn 7:22
every bird, **e** that moves on the earth, Gn 8:19
upon **e** that creeps on the ground and all Gn 9:2
I gave you the green plants, I give you **e**. Gn 9:3
And Abram gave him a tenth of **e**. Gn 14:20
the stream, and **e** else that he had. Gn 32:23
and he has put **e** that he has in my Gn 39:8
The hail struck down **e** that was in the Ex 9:25
E in the waters that has fins and scales, Lv 11:9
E in the waters that has not fins and Lv 11:12
And **e** on which any part of their Lv 11:35
and **e** on which he sits shall be unclean. Lv 15:4
And **e** on which she lies during her Lv 15:20
E also on which she sits shall be Lv 15:20
And **e** on which she sits shall be Lv 15:26
E that opens the womb of all flesh, Nm 18:15
the people of Israel **e** just as the LORD Nm 29:40
e that can stand the fire, you shall Nm 31:23
"**E** that I command you, you shall be Dt 12:32
ones, the livestock, and **e** else in the city, Dt 20:14
and thirst, in nakedness, and lacking **e**. Dt 28:48
because lacking **e** she will eat them Dt 28:57
of the Jordan until **e** was finished that Jos 4:10
they burned the city with fire, and **e** in it. Jos 6:24
So Samuel told him **e** and hid nothing 1 Sm 3:18
as **e** that the king did pleased all the 2 Sm 3:36
you shall send to me **e** you hear." 2 Sm 15:36
of the king's house. He took away **e**. 1 Kgs 14:26
fills it; let the field exult, and **e** in it! 1 Chr 16:32
the Manassites for **e** pertaining to 1 Chr 26:32
of the king's house. He took away **e**. 2 Chr 12:9
brought in abundantly the tithe of **e**. 2 Chr 31:5
and the weight of **e** was recorded. Ezr 8:34
Thus I cleansed them from **e** foreign, Neh 13:30
went away and did **e** as Esther had Est 4:17
and all his friends **e** that had happened Est 6:13
the earth and sees **e** under the heavens. Jb 28:24
He sees **e** that is high; he is king over all Jb 41:34
him, the seas and **e** that moves in them. Ps 69:34
enemy has destroyed **e** in the sanctuary! Ps 74:3
let the field exult, and **e** in it! Then shall Ps 96:12
Let **e** that has breath praise the LORD! Ps 150:6
In **e** the prudent acts with knowledge, Prv 13:16
The simple believes **e**, but the prudent Prv 14:15
The LORD has made **e** for its purpose, Prv 16:4
get **e** ready for yourself in the field, and Prv 24:27
to one who is hungry **e** bitter is sweet. Prv 27:7
I have seen **e** that is done under the Eccl 1:14
and skill must leave **e** to be enjoyed by Eccl 2:21
For **e** there is a season, and a time for Eccl 3:1
He has made **e** beautiful in its time. Eccl 3:11
In my vain life I have seen **e**. There is a Eccl 7:15
For there is a time and a way for **e**, Eccl 8:6
gladdens life, and money answers **e**. Eccl 10:19
know the work of God who makes **e**. Eccl 11:5
and say to them **e** that I command you. Jer 1:17
against it, **e** written in this book, Jer 25:13
But we will do **e** that we have vowed, Jer 44:17
we have lacked **e** and have been Jer 44:18
blown the trumpet and made **e** ready, Ezk 7:14
the rod, my son, with **e** of wood.) Ezk 21:10
desolation upon the land and **e** in it, Ezk 30:12
fresh; so **e** will live where the river goes. Ezk 47:9
will utterly sweep away **e** from the face of Zep 1:2
fled, and going into the city they told **e**, Mt 8:33
patience with me, and I will pay you **e**.' Mt 18:26
"See, we have left **e** and followed you. Mt 19:27
have been slaughtered, and **e** is ready. Mt 22:4
by the altar swears by it and by **e** on it. Mt 23:20
but for those outside **e** is in parables, Mk 4:11
to his own disciples he explained **e**. Mk 4:34
sight was restored, and he saw **e** clearly. Mk 8:25
"See, we have left **e** and followed you." Mk 10:28
And when he had looked around at **e**, Mk 11:11
out of her poverty has put in **e** she had, Mk 12:44
they had performed **e** according to the Lk 2:39
to land, they left **e** and followed him. Lk 5:11
And leaving **e**, he rose and followed him. Lk 5:28
were all marveling at **e** he was doing, Lk 9:43
within, and behold, **e** is clean for you. Lk 11:41
been invited, 'Come, for **e** is now ready.' Lk 14:17
And when he had spent **e**, a severe Lk 15:14
and **e** that is written about the Son of Lk 18:31
that **e** written about me in the Law of Lk 24:44
but **e** that John said about this man was Jn 10:41
Now they know that **e** that you have Jn 17:7
and he said to him, "Lord, you know **e**; Jn 21:17
the earth and the sea and **e** in them, Acts 4:24
his own, but they had **e** in common. Acts 4:32
and having related **e** to them, he sent Acts 10:8
everyone who believes is freed from **e** Acts 13:38
God who made the world and **e** in it, Acts 17:24
to all mankind life and breath and **e**. Acts 17:25
out from him about **e** of which we Acts 24:8
believing **e** laid down by the Law and Acts 24:14
E is indeed clean, but it is wrong for Rom 14:20
For the Spirit searches **e**, even the 1 Cor 2:10
as I try to please everyone in **e** I do, 1 Cor 10:33
remember me in **e** and maintain the 1 Cor 11:2
know whether you are obedient in **e**. 2 Cor 2:9
as having nothing, yet possessing **e**. 2 Cor 6:10
But just as **e** we said to you was true, 2 Cor 7:14
But as you excel in **e**—in faith, in 2 Cor 8:7
the Scripture imprisoned **e** under sin, Gal 3:22
from a slave, though he is the owner of **e**, Gal 4:1
thanks always and for **e** to God the Eph 5:20
should submit in **e** to their husbands. Eph 5:24
minister in the Lord will tell you **e**. Eph 6:21
I count **e** as loss because of the Phil 3:8
but in **e** by prayer and supplication Phil 4:6
dead, that in **e** he might be preeminent. Col 1:18
which binds **e** together in perfect Col 3:14
deed, do **e** in the name of the Lord Jesus, Col 3:17
Children, obey your parents in **e**, for Col 3:20
obey in **e** those who are your earthly Col 3:22
will tell you of **e** that has taken place Col 4:9
but test **e**; hold fast what is good. 1 Thes 5:21
For **e** created by God is good, and 1 Tm 4:4
richly provides us with **e** to enjoy. 1 Tm 6:17
Lord will give you understanding in **e**. 2 Tm 2:7
Therefore I endure **e** for the sake of 2 Tm 2:10
be submissive to their own masters in **e**; Ti 2:9
so that in **e** they may adorn the doctrine Ti 2:10
putting **e** in subjection under his feet." Heb 2:8
feet." Now in putting **e** in subjection to Heb 2:8
we do not yet see **e** in subjection to him. Heb 2:8
Abraham apportioned a tenth part of **e**. Heb 7:2
"See that you make **e** according to the Heb 8:5
under the law almost **e** is purified with Heb 9:22
equip you with **e** good that you may Heb 13:21
in order that in **e** God may be glorified 1 Pt 4:11
anointing teaches you about **e**—and is 1 Jn 2:27
greater than our heart, and he knows **e**. 1 Jn 3:20

EVERYWHERE (12)
was well watered **e** like the garden Gn 13:10
bodies!" "They are thrown **e**!" "Silence!" Am 8:3
his fame spread **e** throughout all the Mk 1:28
And they went out and preached **e**, Mk 16:20
preaching the gospel and healing **e**. Lk 9:6
he commands all people **e** to repent, Acts 17:30
is teaching everyone **e** against the Acts 21:28
in every way and **e** we accept this with Acts 24:3
sect we know that **e** it is spoken Acts 28:22
as I teach them **e** in every church. 1 Cor 4:17
fragrance of the knowledge of him **e**. 2 Cor 2:14
your faith in God has gone forth **e**, 1 Thes 1:8

EVI (2)
with the rest of their slain, **E**, Rekem, Nm 31:8
E and Rekem and Zur and Hur and Jos 13:21

EVICTIONS (1)
Cease your **e** of my people, declares the Ezk 45:9

EVIDENCE (17)
it is torn by beasts, let him bring it as **e**. Ex 22:13
be put to death on the **e** of witnesses. Nm 35:30
On the **e** of two witnesses or of three Dt 17:6
be put to death on the **e** of one witness. Dt 17:6
Only on the **e** of two witnesses or of Dt 19:15
her, I did not find in her **e** of virginity,' Dt 22:14
and bring out the **e** of her virginity to Dt 22:15
in your daughter **e** of virginity." And Dt 22:17
yet this is the **e** of my daughter's Dt 22:17
that **e** of virginity was not found in the Dt 22:20
speaks the truth gives honest **e**, Prv 12:17
be established by the **e** of two or three Mt 18:16
be established by the **e** of two or three 2 Cor 13:1
This is **e** of the righteous judgment of 2 Thes 1:5
an elder except on the **e** of two or three 1 Tm 5:19
without mercy on the **e** of two or three Heb 10:28
their corrosion will be **e** against you and Jas 5:3

EVIDENT (6)
performed through them is **e** to all the Acts 4:16
Now it is **e** that no one is justified before Gal 3:11
Now the works of the flesh are **e**: sexual Gal 5:19
For it is **e** that our Lord was descended Heb 7:14
becomes even more **e** when another Heb 7:15
By this it is **e** who are the children of 1 Jn 3:10

EVIL (525)
the tree of the knowledge of good and **e**. Gn 2:9
knowledge of good and **e** you shall not Gn 2:17
will be like God, knowing good and **e**." Gn 3:5
like one of us in knowing good and **e**. Gn 3:22
of his heart was only **e** continually. Gn 6:5
of man's heart is **e** from his youth. Gn 8:21
them, 'Why have you repaid **e** for good? Gn 44:4
You have done **e** in doing this.'" Gn 44:5
down my gray hairs in **e** to Sheol.' Gn 44:29
I fear to see the **e** that would find my Gn 44:34
Few and **e** have been the days of the Gn 47:9
angel who has redeemed me from all **e**, Gn 48:16
us back for all the **e** that we did to Gn 50:15
their sin, because they did **e** to you.' Gn 50:17
As for you, you meant **e** against me, Gn 50:20
why have you done **e** to this people? Ex 5:22
your name, he has done **e** to this people, Ex 5:23
you have some **e** purpose in mind. Ex 10:10
shall not fall in with the many to do **e**, Ex 23:2
'With **e** intent did he bring them out, Ex 32:12
know the people, that they are set on **e**. Ex 32:22
his lips a rash oath to do **e** or to do good, Lv 5:4
out of Egypt to bring us to this **e** place? Nm 20:5
Now therefore, if it is **e** in your sight, I Nm 22:34
that had done **e** in the sight Nm 32:13
these men of this **e** generation shall see Dt 1:35
today have no knowledge of good or **e**, Dt 1:39
and by doing what is **e** in the sight of the Dt 4:25
and none of the **e** diseases of Egypt, Dt 7:15
in doing what was **e** in the sight of the Dt 9:18
you shall purge the **e** from your midst. Dt 13:5
woman who does what is **e** in the sight of Dt 17:2
or woman who has done this **e** thing, Dt 17:5
you shall purge the **e** from your midst. Dt 17:7
die. So you shall purge the **e** from Israel. Dt 17:12
you shall purge the **e** from your midst. Dt 19:19
again commit any such **e** among you. Dt 19:20
you shall purge the **e** from your midst, Dt 21:21
you shall purge the **e** from your midst. Dt 22:21
So you shall purge the **e** from Israel. Dt 22:22
you shall purge the **e** from your midst. Dt 22:24
shall keep yourself from every **e** thing. Dt 23:9
you shall purge the **e** from your midst. Dt 24:7
on account of the **e** of your deeds, Dt 28:20
you today life and good, death and **e**. Dt 30:15

because of all the **e** that they have done, Dt 31:18
in the days to come **e** will befall you, Dt 31:29
you will do what is **e** in the sight of the Dt 31:29
will bring upon you all the **e** things, Jos 23:15
And if it is **e** in your eyes to serve the Jos 24:15
of Israel did what was **e** in the sight of Jgs 2:11
of Israel did what was **e** in the sight of the Jgs 3:7
again did what was **e** in the sight of Jgs 3:12
they had done what was **e** in the sight of Jgs 3:12
Israel again did what was **e** in the sight of Jgs 4:1
of Israel did what was **e** in the sight of the Jgs 6:1
God sent an **e** spirit between Abimelech Jgs 9:23
Thus God returned the **e** of Abimelech, Jgs 9:56
God also made all the **e** of the men of Jgs 9:57
again did what was **e** in the sight of Jgs 10:6
again did what was **e** in the sight of Jgs 13:1
said, "Tell us, how did this **e** happen?" Jgs 20:3
"What **e** is this that has taken place Jgs 20:12
to death and purge **e** from Israel." But Jgs 20:13
I hear of your **e** dealings from all the 1 Sm 2:23
we have added to all our sins this **e**, 1 Sm 12:19
be afraid; you have done all this **e**. 1 Sm 12:20
and do what was **e** in the sight of 1 Sm 15:19
and an **e** spirit from the LORD 1 Sm 16:14
an **e** spirit from God is tormenting 1 Sm 16:15
and when the **e** spirit from God is 1 Sm 16:16
And whenever the **e** spirit from God 1 Sm 16:23
and the **e** spirit departed from him. 1 Sm 16:23
presumption and the **e** of your heart, 1 Sm 17:28
good, whereas I have repaid you **e**. 1 Sm 24:17
and he has returned me **e** for good. 1 Sm 25:21
those who seek to do **e** to my lord be 1 Sm 25:26
and **e** shall not be found in you so 1 Sm 25:28
LORD has returned the **e** of Nabal on 1 Sm 25:39
I done? What **e** is on my hands? 1 Sm 26:18
the LORD, to do what is **e** in his sight? 2 Sm 12:9
I will raise up **e** against you out of 2 Sm 12:11
angel of God to discern good and **e**. 2 Sm 14:17
See, your **e** is on you, for you are a 2 Sm 16:8
up against you for **e** be like that 2 Sm 18:32
you than all the **e** that has come upon 2 Sm 19:7
that I may discern between good and **e**, 1 Kgs 3:9
Solomon did what was **e** in the sight 1 Kgs 11:6
did not turn from his **e** way, 1 Kgs 13:33
but you have done **e** above all who 1 Kgs 14:9
Judah did what was **e** in the sight of 1 Kgs 14:22
He did what was **e** in the sight of the 1 Kgs 15:26
He did what was **e** in the sight of the 1 Kgs 15:34
because of all the **e** that he did in 1 Kgs 16:7
doing **e** in the sight of the LORD, 1 Kgs 16:19
Omri did what was **e** in the sight of 1 Kgs 16:25
and did more **e** than all who were 1 Kgs 16:25
the son of Omri did **e** in the sight of 1 Kgs 16:30
to do what is **e** in the sight of 1 Kgs 21:20
to do what was **e** in the sight of 1 Kgs 21:25
me, but **e**." And Jehoshaphat said, 1 Kgs 22:8
good concerning me, but **e**?" 1 Kgs 22:18
He did what was **e** in the sight of the 1 Kgs 22:52
He did what was **e** in the sight of the 2 Kgs 3:2
"Because I know the **e** that you will 2 Kgs 8:12
And he did what was **e** in the sight of 2 Kgs 8:18
and did what was **e** in the sight of 2 Kgs 8:27
He did what was **e** in the sight of the 2 Kgs 13:2
He also did what was **e** in the sight of 2 Kgs 13:11
And he did what was **e** in the sight of 2 Kgs 14:24
And he did what was **e** in the sight of 2 Kgs 15:9
And he did what was **e** in the sight of 2 Kgs 15:18
And he did what was **e** in the sight of 2 Kgs 15:24
And he did what was **e** in the sight of 2 Kgs 15:28
And he did what was **e** in the sight of 2 Kgs 17:2
"Turn from your **e** ways and keep 2 Kgs 17:13
sold themselves to do **e** in the sight 2 Kgs 17:17
And he did what was **e** in the sight of 2 Kgs 21:2
He did much **e** in the sight of the 2 Kgs 21:6
astray to do more **e** than the nations 2 Kgs 21:9
has done things more **e** than all that 2 Kgs 21:11
have done what is **e** in my sight and 2 Kgs 21:15
they did what was **e** in the sight of 2 Kgs 21:16
And he did what was **e** in the sight of 2 Kgs 21:20
And he did what was **e** in the sight of 2 Kgs 23:32
And he did what was **e** in the sight of 2 Kgs 23:37
And he did what was **e** in the sight of 2 Kgs 24:9
And he did what was **e** in the sight of 2 Kgs 24:19
was **e** in the sight of the LORD, 1 Chr 2:3
I who have sinned and done great **e**. 1 Chr 21:17
And he did **e**, for he did not set his 2 Chr 12:14
but always **e**." And Jehoshaphat said, 2 Chr 18:7
good concerning me, but **e**?" 2 Chr 18:17
And he did what was **e** in the sight of 2 Chr 21:6
He did what was **e** in the sight of the 2 Chr 22:4
have done what was **e** in the sight of 2 Chr 29:6
And he did what was **e** in the sight of 2 Chr 33:2
He did much **e** in the sight of the 2 Chr 33:6
to do more **e** than the nations whom 2 Chr 33:9
he did what was **e** in the sight of 2 Chr 33:22
He did what was **e** in the sight of the 2 Chr 36:5
He did what was **e** in the sight of the 2 Chr 36:9
He did what was **e** in the sight of the 2 Chr 36:12
upon us for our **e** deeds and for our Ezr 9:13
had rest they did **e** again before you, Neh 9:28
then discovered the **e** that Eliashib had Neh 13:7
"What is this **e** thing that you are Neh 13:17
all this great **e** and act treacherously Neh 13:27
him to avert the **e** plan of Haman the Est 8:3
in writing that his **e** plan that he had Est 9:25
who feared God and turned away from **e**. Jb 1:1
who fears God and turns away from **e**?" Jb 1:8
who fears God and turns away from **e**? Jb 2:3
and shall we not receive **e**?" In all this Job Jb 2:10
heard of all this **e** that had come upon Jb 2:11
troubles; in seven no **e** shall touch you. Jb 5:19
conceive trouble and give birth to **e**, Jb 15:35
"Though **e** is sweet in his mouth, Jb 20:12
that the **e** man is spared in the day of Jb 21:30
Is not your **e** abundant? There is no end Jb 22:5
to turn away from **e** is understanding.'" Jb 28:28
But when I hoped for good, **e** came, and Jb 30:26
me, or exulted when **e** overtook him Jb 31:29
answer, because of the pride of **e** men. Jb 35:12
him for all the **e** that the LORD had Jb 42:11
in wickedness; **e** may not dwell with you. Ps 5:4
Depart from me, all you workers of **e**, for Ps 6:8
repaid my friend with **e** or plundered my Ps 7:4
Oh, let the **e** of the wicked come to an end, Ps 7:9
wicked man conceives **e** and is pregnant Ps 7:14
his tongue and does no **e** to his neighbor, Ps 15:3
Though they plan **e** against you, Ps 21:11
of the shadow of death, I will fear no **e**, Ps 23:4
in whose hands are **e** devices, and Ps 26:10
with the wicked, with the workers of **e**, Ps 28:3
with their neighbors while **e** is in their Ps 28:3
and according to the **e** of their deeds; Ps 28:4
Keep your tongue from **e** and your lips Ps 34:13
Turn away from **e** and do good; seek Ps 34:14
of the LORD is against those who do **e**, Ps 34:16
disappointed who devise **e** against me! Ps 35:4
They repay me **e** for good; my soul is Ps 35:12
way that is not good; he does not reject **e**. Ps 36:4
over the man who carries out **e** devices! Ps 37:7
Fret not yourself; it tends only to **e**. Ps 37:8
they are not put to shame in **e** times; in Ps 37:19
Turn away from **e** and do good; so shall Ps 37:27
Those who render me **e** for good accuse Ps 38:20
"You give your mouth free rein for **e**, Ps 50:19
I sinned and done what is **e** in your sight, Ps 51:4
Why do you boast of **e**, O mighty man? Ps 52:1
You love **e** more than good, and lying Ps 52:3
Have those who work **e** no knowledge, Ps 53:4
He will return the **e** to my enemies; in Ps 54:5
for **e** is in their dwelling place and in Ps 55:15
all their thoughts are against me for **e**. Ps 56:5
deliver me from those who work **e**, and Ps 59:2
none of those who treacherously plot **e**. Ps 59:5
They hold fast to their **e** purpose; they Ps 64:5
for as many years as we have seen **e**. Ps 90:15
no **e** shall be allowed to befall you, no Ps 91:10
have heard the doom of my **e** assailants. Ps 92:11
O you who love the LORD, hate **e**! He Ps 97:10
far from me; I will know nothing of **e**. Ps 101:4
courage melted away in their **e** plight; Ps 107:26
because of the **e** of its inhabitants. Ps 107:34
low through oppression, **e**, and sorrow, Ps 107:39
So they reward me **e** for good, and Ps 109:5
of those who speak **e** against my life! Ps 109:20
I hold back my feet from every **e** way, Ps 119:101
who persecute me with **e** purpose; Ps 119:150
The LORD will keep you from all **e**; he Ps 121:7
Deliver me, O LORD, from **e** men; Ps 140:1
who plan **e** things in their heart and stir Ps 140:2
do not further their **e** plot or they will be Ps 140:8
let **e** hunt down the violent man Ps 140:11
Do not let my heart incline to any **e**, to Ps 141:4
is continually against their **e** deeds. Ps 141:5
for their feet run to **e**, and they make Prv 1:16
delivering you from the way of **e**, from Prv 2:12
who rejoice in doing **e** and delight in Prv 2:14
evil and delight in the perverseness of **e**, Prv 2:14
eyes; fear the LORD, and turn away from **e**. Prv 3:7
Do not plan **e** against your neighbor, Prv 3:29
and do not walk in the way of the **e**. Prv 4:14
to the left; turn your foot away from **e**. Prv 4:27
with perverted heart devises **e**, Prv 6:14
plans, feet that make haste to run to **e**, Prv 6:18
to preserve you from the **e** woman, from Prv 6:24
The fear of the LORD is hatred of **e**. Pride Prv 8:13
and the way of **e** and perverted speech I Prv 8:13
will live, but he who pursues **e** will die. Prv 11:19
an **e** person will not go unpunished, Prv 11:21
but **e** comes to him who searches for Prv 11:27
but a man of **e** devices he condemns. Prv 12:2
An **e** man is ensnared by the Prv 12:13
is in the heart of those who devise **e**, Prv 12:20
turn away from **e** is an abomination Prv 13:19
is cautious and turns away from **e**, Prv 14:16
and a man of **e** devices is hated. Prv 14:17
The **e** bow down before the good, the Prv 14:19
Do they not go astray who devise **e**? Prv 14:22
keeping watch on the **e** and the good. Prv 15:3
All the days of the afflicted are **e**, but Prv 15:15
of the wicked pours out **e** things. Prv 15:28
fear of the LORD one turns away from **e**. Prv 16:6
It is an abomination to kings to do **e**, Prv 16:12
of the upright turns aside from **e**; Prv 16:17
A worthless man plots **e**, and his Prv 16:27
he who purses his lips brings **e** to pass. Prv 16:30
An **e** man seeks only rebellion, and a Prv 17:11
If anyone returns **e** for good, evil will Prv 17:13
good, **e** will not depart from his house. Prv 17:13
judgment winnows all **e** with his eyes. Prv 20:8
Do not say, "I will repay **e**"; wait for the Prv 20:22
Blows that wound cleanse away **e**; Prv 20:30
The soul of the wicked desires **e**; his Prv 21:10
more when he brings it with **e** intent. Prv 21:27
Be not envious of **e** men, nor desire to be Prv 24:1
Whoever plans to do **e** will be called a Prv 24:8
for the **e** man has no future; the lamp Prv 24:20
vessel are fervent lips with an **e** heart. Prv 26:23
E men do not understand justice, but Prv 28:5
the upright into an **e** way will fall into Prv 28:10
An **e** man is ensnared in his Prv 29:6
or if you have been devising **e**, Prv 30:32
for it. This also is vanity and a great **e**. Eccl 2:21
has not seen the **e** deeds that are done Eccl 4:3
they do not know that they are doing **e**. Eccl 5:1
There is a grievous **e** that I have seen Eccl 5:13
This also is a grievous **e**: just as he Eccl 5:16
There is an **e** that I have seen under the Eccl 6:1
them. This is vanity; it is a grievous **e**. Eccl 6:2
Do not take your stand in an **e** cause, Eccl 8:3
keeps a command will know no **e** thing, Eccl 8:5
the sentence against an **e** deed is not Eccl 8:11
the children of man is fully set to do **e**. Eccl 8:11
a sinner does **e** a hundred times Eccl 8:12
and the wicked, to the good and the **e**, Eccl 9:2
This is an **e** in all that is done under the Eccl 9:3
of the children of man are full of **e**, Eccl 9:3
Like fish that are taken in an **e** net, Eccl 9:12
of man are snared at an **e** time, Eccl 9:12
There is an **e** that I have seen under the Eccl 10:5
and the end of his talk is **e** madness. Eccl 10:13
before the **e** days come and the years Eccl 12:1
every secret thing, whether good or **e**. Eccl 12:14
remove the **e** of your deeds from before Is 1:16
deeds from before my eyes; cease to do **e**, Is 1:16
For they have brought **e** on themselves. Is 3:9
to those who call **e** good and good evil, Is 5:20
to those who call evil good and good **e**, Is 5:20
son of Remaliah, has devised **e** against you, Is 7:5
how to refuse the **e** and choose the good. Is 7:15
how to refuse the **e** and choose the good, Is 7:16
I will punish the world for its **e**, and the Is 13:11
all who watch to do **e** shall be cut off, Is 29:20
As for the scoundrel—his devices are **e**; Is 32:7
and shuts his eyes from looking on **e**, Is 33:15
But **e** shall come upon you, which you Is 47:11
it, and keeps his hand from doing any **e**." Is 56:2
Their feet run to **e**, and they are swift to Is 59:7
he who departs from **e** makes himself a Is 59:15
but you did what was **e** in my eyes and Is 65:12
but they did what was **e** in my eyes and Is 66:4
them, for all their **e** in forsaking me. Jer 1:16
Your **e** will chastise you, and your Jer 2:19
and see that it is **e** and bitter for you to Jer 2:19
you have done all the **e** that you could." Jer 3:5
stubbornly follow their own **e** heart. Jer 3:17
quench it, because of the **e** of your deeds." Jer 4:4
O Jerusalem, wash your heart from **e**, Jer 4:14
They are 'wise'—in doing **e**! Jer 4:22
They know no bounds in deeds of **e**; they Jer 5:28
its water fresh, so she keeps fresh her **e**; Jer 6:7
to it because of the **e** of my people Israel. Jer 7:12
and the stubbornness of their **e** hearts, Jer 7:24
sons of Judah have done **e** in my sight, Jer 7:30
that remains of this **e** family in all the Jer 8:3
no man relents of his **e**, saying, 'What Jer 8:6
for they proceed from **e** to evil, and they do Jer 9:3
for they proceed from evil to **e**, and they do Jer 9:3
be afraid of them, for they cannot do **e**, Jer 10:5
in the stubbornness of his **e** heart. Jer 11:8
because of the **e** that the house of Israel Jer 11:17
For the **e** of those who dwell in it the Jer 12:4
concerning all my **e** neighbors who Jer 12:14
This **e** people, who refuse to hear my Jer 13:10
do good who are accustomed to do **e**. Jer 13:23
For I will pour out their **e** upon them. Jer 14:16

pronounced all this great **e** against us? Jer 16:10
one of you follows his stubborn, **e** will, Jer 16:12
which I have spoken, turns from its **e**, Jer 18:8
and if it does **e** in my sight, not Jer 18:10
Return, every one from his **e** way, and Jer 18:11
to the stubbornness of his **e** heart.' Jer 18:12
Should good be repaid with **e**? Yet they Jer 18:20
to quench it, because of your **e** deeds.'" Jer 21:12
and confounded because of all your **e**. Jer 22:22
I will attend to you for your **e** deeds, Jer 23:2
Their course is **e**, and their might is not Jer 23:10
even in my house I have found their **e**, Jer 23:11
so that no one turns from his **e**; Jer 23:14
have turned them from their **e** way, Jer 23:22
evil way, and from the **e** of their deeds. Jer 23:22
one of you, from his **e** way and evil deeds, Jer 25:5
one of you, from his evil way and **e** deeds, Jer 25:5
and every one turn from his **e** way, Jer 26:3
to do to them because of their **e** deeds. Jer 26:3
LORD, plans for wholeness and not for **e**, Jer 29:11
have done nothing but **e** in my sight Jer 32:30
because of all the **e** of the children of Jer 32:32
face from this city because of all their **e**. Jer 33:5
now every one of you from his **e** way, Jer 35:15
that every one may turn from his **e** way, Jer 36:3
that every one will turn from his **e** way, Jer 36:7
these men have done **e** in all that they Jer 38:9
heard of all the **e** that Ishmael the son Jer 41:11
because of the **e** that they committed, Jer 44:3
to turn from their **e** and make no Jer 44:5
commit this great **e** against yourselves, Jer 44:7
Have you forgotten the **e** of your fathers, Jer 44:9
your fathers, the **e** of the kings of Judah, Jer 44:9
of the kings of Judah, the **e** of their wives, Jer 44:9
Judah, the evil of their wives, your own **e**, Jer 44:9
your own evil, and the **e** of your wives, Jer 44:9
no longer bear your **e** deeds and the Jer 44:22
eyes for all the **e** that they have done Jer 51:24
And he did what was **e** in the sight of the Jer 52:2
in vain that I would do this **e** to them." Ezk 6:10
of all the **e** abominations of the Ezk 6:11
not turn from his **e** way to save his Ezk 13:22
sake, not according to your **e** ways, Ezk 20:44
back, turn back from your **e** ways, Ezk 33:11
became the talk and **e** gossip of the Ezk 36:3
Then you will remember your **e** ways, Ezk 36:31
mind, and you will devise an **e** scheme Ezk 38:10
their hearts shall be bent on doing **e**. Dn 11:27
is revealed, and the **e** deeds of Samaria; Hos 7:1
not consider that I remember all their **e**. Hos 7:2
By their **e** they make the king glad, and Hos 7:3
their arms, yet they devise **e** against me. Hos 7:15
Every **e** of theirs is in Gilgal; there I Hos 9:15
you, O Bethel, because of your great **e**. Hos 10:15
full. The vats overflow, for their **e** is great. Jl 3:13
silent in such a time, for it is an **e** time. Am 5:13
Seek good, and not **e**, that you may live; Am 5:14
Hate **e**, and love good, and establish Am 5:15
eyes upon them for **e** and not for good." Am 9:4
it, for their **e** has come up before me." Jon 1:2
on whose account this **e** has come upon Jon 1:7
on whose account this **e** has come upon Jon 1:8
everyone turn from his **e** way and from Jon 3:8
did, how they turned from their **e** way, Jon 3:10
wickedness and work **e** on their beds! Mi 2:1
you who hate the good and love the **e**, who Mi 3:2
because they have made their deeds **e**. Mi 3:4
Their hands are on what is **e**, to do it well; Mi 7:3
great man utters the **e** desire of his soul; Mi 7:3
one who plotted **e** against the LORD, Na 1:11
whom has not come your unceasing **e**? Na 3:19
eyes than to see **e** and cannot look at Hab 1:13
to him who gets **e** gain for his house, Hab 2:9
midst; you shall never again fear **e**. Zep 3:15
Return from your **e** ways and from your Zec 1:4
your evil ways and from your **e** deeds.' Zec 1:4
none of you devise **e** against another in Zec 7:10
do not devise **e** in your hearts against Zec 8:17
blind animals in sacrifice, is that not **e**? Mal 1:8
those that are lame or sick, is that not **e**? Mal 1:8
"Everyone who does **e** is good in the Mal 2:17
utter all kinds of **e** against you falsely on Mt 5:11
anything more than this comes from **e**. Mt 5:37
say to you, Do not resist the one who is **e**. Mt 5:39
his sun rise on the **e** and on the good, Mt 5:45
into temptation, but deliver us from **e**. Mt 6:13
If you then, who are **e**, know how to give Mt 7:11
"Why do you think **e** in your hearts? Mt 9:4
can you speak good, when you are **e**? Mt 12:34
and the **e** person out of his evil treasure Mt 12:35
out of his **e** treasure brings forth Mt 12:35
out of his evil treasure brings forth **e**. Mt 12:35
"An **e** and adulterous generation seeks Mt 12:39
it seven other spirits more **e** than itself, Mt 12:45
also will it be with this **e** generation." Mt 12:45
the **e** one comes and snatches away Mt 13:19
The weeds are the sons of the **e** one, Mt 13:38
and separate the **e** from the righteous Mt 13:49
For out of the heart come **e** thoughts, Mt 15:19
An **e** and adulterous generation seeks Mt 16:4
what **e** has he done?" But they shouted Mt 27:23
of the heart of man, come **e** thoughts, Mk 7:21
All these **e** things come from within, Mk 7:23
be able soon afterward to speak **e** of me. Mk 9:39
what **e** has he done?" But they shouted Mk 15:14
and for all the **e** things that Herod had Lk 3:19
revile you and spurn your name as **e**, Lk 6:22
for he is kind to the ungrateful and the **e**. Lk 6:35
and the **e** person out of his evil treasure Lk 6:45
out of his **e** treasure produces evil, Lk 6:45
out of his evil treasure produces **e**, Lk 6:45
of diseases and plagues and **e** spirits, Lk 7:21
been healed of **e** spirits and infirmities: Lk 8:2
If you then, who are **e**, know how to Lk 11:13
seven other spirits more **e** than itself, Lk 11:26
"This generation is an **e** generation. Lk 11:29
Depart from me, all you workers of **e**!' Lk 13:27
to them, "Why, what **e** has he done? Lk 23:22
than the light because their deeds were **e**. Jn 3:19
those who have done **e** to the resurrection Jn 5:29
I testify about it that its works are **e**. Jn 7:7
but that you keep them from the **e** one. Jn 17:15
him, "If this man were not doing **e**, Jn 18:30
how much **e** he has done to your Acts 9:13
speaking **e** of the Way before the Acts 19:9
left them and the **e** spirits came out of Acts 19:12
Jesus over those who had **e** spirits, Acts 19:13
But the **e** spirit answered them, "Jesus Acts 19:15
in whom was the **e** spirit leaped on Acts 19:16
'You shall not speak **e** of a ruler of Acts 23:5
reported or spoken any **e** about you. Acts 28:21
of unrighteousness, **e**, covetousness, Rom 1:29
haughty, boastful, inventors of **e**, Rom 1:30
for every human being who does **e**, Rom 2:9
And why not do **e** that good may come? Rom 3:8
but the **e** I do not want is what I keep Rom 7:19
I want to do right, **e** lies close at hand. Rom 7:21
Abhor what is **e**; hold fast to what is Rom 12:9
Repay no one **e** for evil, but give Rom 12:17
Repay no one evil for **e**, but give Rom 12:17
Do not be overcome by **e**, but Rom 12:21
by evil, but overcome **e** with good. Rom 12:21
you regard as good be spoken of as **e**. Rom 14:16
is good and innocent as to what is **e**. Rom 16:19
old leaven, the leaven of malice and **e**, 1 Cor 5:8
"Purge the **e** person from among 1 Cor 5:13
that we might not desire **e** as they did. 1 Cor 10:6
Be infants in **e**, but in your thinking 1 Cor 14:20
done in the body, whether good or **e**. 2 Cor 5:10
sins to deliver us from the present **e** age, Gal 1:4
use of the time, because the days are **e**. Eph 5:16
the spiritual forces of **e** in the heavenly Eph 6:12
may be able to withstand in the **e** day, Eph 6:13
all the flaming darts of the **e** one; Eph 6:16
and hostile in mind, doing **e** deeds, Col 1:21
immorality, impurity, passion, **e** desire, Col 3:5
that no one repays anyone **e** for evil, 1 Thes 5:15
that no one repays anyone evil for **e**, 1 Thes 5:15
Abstain from every form of **e**. 1 Thes 5:22
be delivered from wicked and **e** men. 2 Thes 3:2
you and guard you against the **e** one. 2 Thes 3:3
envy, dissension, slander, **e** suspicions, 1 Tm 6:4
able to teach, patiently enduring **e**, 2 Tm 2:24
while **e** people and impostors will go 2 Tm 3:13
me from every **e** deed and bring 2 Tm 4:18
said, "Cretans are always liars, **e** beasts, Ti 1:12
shame, having nothing **e** to say about us. Ti 2:8
to speak **e** of no one, to avoid quarreling, Ti 3:2
lest there be in any of you an **e**, Heb 3:12
practice to distinguish good from **e**. Heb 5:14
clean from an **e** conscience and our Heb 10:22
God," for God cannot be tempted with **e**, Jas 1:13
and become judges with **e** thoughts? Jas 2:4
It is a restless **e**, full of deadly poison. Jas 3:8
Do not speak **e** against one another, Jas 4:11
speaks **e** against the law and judges the Jas 4:11
your arrogance. All such boasting is **e**. Jas 4:16
punish those who do **e** and to praise 1 Pt 2:14
using your freedom as a cover-up for **e**, 1 Pt 2:16
Do not repay **e** for evil or reviling for 1 Pt 3:9
not repay evil for **e** or reviling for 1 Pt 3:9
keep his tongue from **e** and his lips 1 Pt 3:10
let him turn away from **e** and do good; 1 Pt 3:11
of the Lord is against those who do **e**." 1 Pt 3:12
should be God's will, than for doing **e**. 1 Pt 3:17
because you have overcome the **e** one. 1 Jn 2:13
you, and you have overcome the **e** one. 1 Jn 2:14
who was of the **e** one and murdered his 1 Jn 3:12
his own deeds were **e** and his brother's 1 Jn 3:12
him, and the **e** one does not touch him. 1 Jn 5:18
world lies in the power of the **e** one. 1 Jn 5:19
do not imitate **e** but imitate good. 3 Jn 1:11
God; whoever does **e** has not seen God. 3 Jn 1:11
you cannot bear with those who are **e**, Rv 2:2
Let the evildoer still do **e**, and the filthy Rv 22:11

EVIL-MERODACH (2)
of the month, **E** king of Babylon, 2 Kgs 25:27
day of the month, **E** king of Babylon, Jer 52:31

EVILDOER (6)
The LORD repay the **e** according to his 2 Sm 3:39
Break the arm of the wicked and **e**; call Ps 10:15
An **e** listens to wicked lips, and a liar Prv 17:4
for everyone is godless and an **e**, and every Is 9:17
or a thief or an **e** or as a meddler. 1 Pt 4:15
Let the **e** still do evil, and the filthy still Rv 22:11

EVILDOERS (35)
a blameless man, nor take the hand of **e**. Jb 8:20
in company with **e** and walks with Jb 34:8
deep darkness where **e** may hide Jb 34:22
not stand before your eyes; you hate all **e**. Ps 5:5
all the **e** who eat up my people as they eat Ps 14:4
me; a company of **e** encircles me; Ps 22:16
I hate the assembly of **e**, and I will not sit Ps 26:5
When **e** assail me to eat up my flesh, my Ps 27:2
There the **e** lie fallen; they are thrust Ps 36:12
Fret not yourself because of **e**; be not Ps 37:1
For the **e** shall be cut off, but those who Ps 37:9
plots of the wicked, from the throng of **e**, Ps 64:2
sprout like grass and all **e** flourish, Ps 92:7
shall perish; all **e** shall be scattered. Ps 92:9
out their arrogant words; all the **e** boast. Ps 94:4
Who stands up for me against **e**? Ps 94:16
cutting off all the **e** from the city of the Ps 101:8
Depart from me, you **e**, that I may Ps 119:115
ways the LORD will lead away with **e**! Ps 125:5
laid for me and from the snares of **e**! Ps 141:9
to the blameless, but destruction to **e**. Prv 10:29
is wicked covets the spoil of **e**, Prv 12:12
is a joy to the righteous but terror to **e**. Prv 21:15
Fret not yourself because of **e**, and be Prv 24:19
a people laden with iniquity, offspring of **e**, Is 1:4
the offspring of **e** nevermore be named! Is 14:20
the house of the **e** and against the helpers Is 31:2
the life of the needy from the hand of **e**. Jer 20:13
they strengthen the hands of **e**, so that Jer 23:14
will sell the land into the hand of **e**; Ezk 30:12
Gilead is a city of **e**, tracked with blood. Hos 6:8
E not only prosper but they put God to Mal 3:15
all the arrogant and all **e** will be stubble. Mal 4:1
Look out for the dogs, look out for the **e**, Phil 3:2
that when they speak against you as **e**, 1 Pt 2:12

EVILDOING (3)
wicked is overthrown through his **e**, Prv 14:32
man who prolongs his life in his **e**. Eccl 7:15
"Let all their **e** come before you, and Lam 1:22

EVILS (9)
And many **e** and troubles will come Dt 31:17
'Have not these **e** come upon us because Dt 31:17
And when many **e** and troubles have Dt 31:21
For **e** have encompassed me beyond Ps 40:12
for my people have committed two **e**: Jer 2:13
own sight for the **e** that they have Ezk 6:9
yourselves for all the **e** that you have Ezk 20:43
in his case of such **e** as I supposed. Acts 25:18
of money is a root of all kinds of **e**. 1 Tm 6:10

EWE (6)
Abraham set seven **e** lambs of the Gn 21:28
of these seven **e** lambs that you Gn 21:29
"These seven **e** lambs you will take Gn 21:30
and one **e** lamb a year old without Lv 14:10
and one **e** lamb a year old without Nm 6:14
had nothing but one little **e** lamb, 2 Sm 12:3

EWES (5)
Your **e** and your female goats have not Gn 31:38
goats, two hundred **e** and twenty rams, Gn 32:14
following the nursing **e** he brought Ps 78:71
like a flock of shorn **e** that have come up Sg 4:2
are like a flock of **e** that have come up Sg 6:6

EXACT (8)
and you shall not **e** interest from him. Ex 22:25
in **e** accordance with the vow that he Nm 6:21
He shall not **e** it of his neighbor, his Dt 15:2
Of a foreigner you may **e** it, but whatever Dt 15:3
and its pattern, **e** in all its details. 2 Kgs 16:10
and the **e** sum of money that Haman had Est 4:7
the poor and you **e** taxes of grain from Am 5:11
of God and the **e** imprint of his nature, Heb 1:3

EXACTED (3)
Menahem **e** the money from Israel, 2 Kgs 15:20
He **e** the silver and the gold of the 2 Kgs 23:35
For you have **e** pledges of your brothers Jb 22:6

EXACTING (3)
I said to them, "You are **e** interest, each — Neh 5:7
grain. Let us abandon this **e** of interest. — Neh 5:10
oil that you have been **e** from them." — Neh 5:11

EXACTION (2)
seventh year and the **e** of every debt. — Neh 10:31
be ready as a willing gift, not as an **e**. — 2 Cor 9:5

EXACTLY (3)
E as I show you concerning the pattern — Ex 25:9
going to determine his case more **e**. — Acts 23:15
God that it will be **e** as I have been — Acts 27:25

EXACTOR (1)
who shall send an **e** of tribute for the — Dn 11:20

EXACTS (3)
Know then that God **e** of you less than — Jb 11:6
land, but he who **e** gifts tears it down. — Prv 29:4
does not oppress anyone, **e** no pledge, — Ezk 18:16

EXALT (18)
him, my father's God, and I will **e** him. — Ex 15:2
then do you **e** yourselves above the — Nm 16:3
"Today I will begin to **e** you in the sight of — Jos 3:7
to his king and **e** the power of his — 1 Sm 2:10
to the promise of God to **e** him, — 1 Chr 25:5
with me, and let us **e** his name together! — Ps 34:3
and he will **e** you to inherit the land; — Ps 37:34
let not the rebellious **e** themselves. — Ps 66:7
E the LORD our God; worship at his — Ps 99:5
E the LORD our God, and worship at his — Ps 99:9
Prize her highly, and she will **e** you; she — Prv 4:8
O LORD, you are my God; I will **e** you; I will — Is 25:1
E that which is low, and bring low — Ezk 21:26
and never again **e** itself above the — Ezk 29:15
He shall **e** himself and magnify — Dn 11:36
also Christ did not **e** himself to be made — Heb 5:5
before the Lord, and he will **e** you. — Jas 4:10
so that at the proper time he may **e** you, — 1 Pt 5:6

EXALTATION (1)
Let the lowly brother boast in his **e**, — Jas 1:9

EXALTED (67)
than Agag, and his kingdom shall be **e**. — Nm 24:7
that day the LORD **e** Joshua in the sight — Jos 4:14
the LORD; my strength is **e** in the LORD. — 1 Sm 2:1
and that he had **e** his kingdom for the — 2 Sm 5:12
be my rock, and **e** be my God, — 2 Sm 22:47
you **e** me above those who rose — 2 Sm 22:49
Adonijah the son of Haggith **e** himself, — 1 Kgs 1:5
I have indeed built you an **e** house, a — 1 Kgs 8:13
"Because I **e** you from among the — 1 Kgs 14:7
"Since I **e** you out of the dust and — 1 Kgs 16:2
kingdom was highly **e** for the sake — 1 Chr 14:2
and you are **e** as head above all. — 1 Chr 29:11
But I have built you an **e** house, a — 2 Chr 6:2
And at this house, which was **e**, — 2 Chr 7:21
so that he was **e** in the sight of all — 2 Chr 32:23
which is **e** above all blessing and praise. — Neh 9:5
They are **e** a little while, and then are — Jb 24:24
he sets them forever, and they are **e**. — Jb 36:7
Behold, God is **e** in his power; who is a — Jb 36:22
as vileness is **e** among the children of — Ps 12:8
How long shall my enemy be **e** over me? — Ps 13:2
and **e** be the God of my salvation— — Ps 18:46
you **e** me above those who rose against — Ps 18:48
Be **e**, O LORD, in your strength! We will — Ps 21:13
I am God. I will be **e** among the nations, — Ps 46:10
the nations, I will be **e** in the earth!" — Ps 46:10
of the earth belong to God; he is highly **e**! — Ps 47:9
Be **e**, O God, above the heavens! Let your — Ps 57:5
Be **e**, O God, above the heavens! Let — Ps 57:11
the day and in your righteousness are **e**. — Ps 89:16
strength; by your favor our horn is **e**. — Ps 89:17
I have **e** one chosen from the people. — Ps 89:19
and in my name shall his horn be **e**. — Ps 89:24
You have **e** the right hand of his foes; — Ps 89:42
But you have **e** my horn like that of the — Ps 92:10
all the earth; you are **e** far above all gods. — Ps 97:9
great in Zion; he is **e** over all the peoples. — Ps 99:2
Be **e**, O God, above the heavens! Let — Ps 108:5
endures forever; his horn is **e** in honor. — Ps 112:9
for you have **e** above all things your — Ps 138:2
further their evil plot or they will be **e**! — Ps 140:8
of the LORD, for his name alone is **e**; — Ps 148:13
the blessing of the upright a city is **e**, — Prv 11:11
and the LORD alone will be **e** in that day. — Is 2:11
and the LORD alone will be **e** in that day. — Is 2:17
But the LORD of hosts is **e** in justice, and — Is 5:16
the peoples, proclaim that his name is **e**. — Is 12:4
The LORD is **e**, for he dwells on high; he — Is 33:5
"now I will lift myself up; now I will be **e**. — Is 33:10
"I will go before you and level the **e** places, — Is 45:2
be high and lifted up, and shall be **e**. — Is 52:13
rejoice over you and **e** the might of — Lam 2:17
is low, and bring low that which is **e**. — Ezk 21:26
is taken away, his heart shall be **e**, — Dn 11:12
there was trembling; he was **e** in Israel, — Hos 13:1
Capernaum, will you be **e** to heaven? — Mt 11:23
whoever humbles himself will be **e**. — Mt 23:12
their thrones and **e** those of humble — Lk 1:52
Capernaum, will you be **e** to heaven? — Lk 10:15
he who humbles himself will be **e**." — Lk 14:11
For what is **e** among men is an — Lk 16:15
one who humbles himself will be **e**." — Lk 18:14
Being therefore **e** at the right hand of — Acts 2:33
God **e** him at his right hand as Leader — Acts 5:31
myself so that you might be **e**, — 2 Cor 11:7
God has highly **e** him and bestowed — Phil 2:9
from sinners, and **e** above the heavens. — Heb 7:26

EXALTING (2)
You are still **e** yourself against my — Ex 9:17
If you have been foolish, **e** yourself, or — Prv 30:32

EXALTS (9)
makes rich; he brings low and he **e**. — 1 Sm 2:7
the right hand of the LORD **e**, the right — Ps 118:16
but he who has a hasty temper **e** folly. — Prv 14:29
Righteousness **e** a nation, but sin is a — Prv 14:34
and therefore he **e** himself to show — Is 30:18
Whoever **e** himself will be humbled, — Mt 23:12
For everyone who **e** himself will be — Lk 14:11
For everyone who **e** himself will be — Lk 18:14
who opposes and **e** himself against — 2 Thes 2:4

EXAMINE (25)
and the priest shall **e** the diseased area on — Lv 13:3
And the priest shall **e** him on the seventh — Lv 13:5
And the priest shall **e** him again on the — Lv 13:6
And the priest shall **e** the raw flesh and — Lv 13:15
and the priest shall **e** him, and if the — Lv 13:17
the priest shall **e** it, and if the hair in the — Lv 13:25
and the priest shall **e** him the seventh — Lv 13:27
the priest shall **e** the disease. And if it — Lv 13:30
day the priest shall **e** the disease. — Lv 13:32
seventh day the priest shall **e** the itch, — Lv 13:34
then the priest shall **e** him, and if the — Lv 13:36
Then the priest shall **e** him, and if the — Lv 13:43
And the priest shall **e** the disease and — Lv 13:50
Then he shall **e** the disease on the — Lv 13:51
And the priest shall **e** the diseased thing — Lv 13:55
before the priest goes to **e** the disease, — Lv 14:36
And he shall **e** the disease. And if the — Lv 14:37
month they sat down to **e** the matter; — Ezr 10:16
and see, or send to Kedar and **e** with care; — Jer 2:10
Let us test and **e** our ways, and return — Lam 3:40
five yoke of oxen, and I go to **e** them. — Lk 14:19
were about to **e** him withdrew from — Acts 22:29
is my defense to those who would **e** me. — 1 Cor 9:3
Let a person **e** himself, then, and so — 1 Cor 11:28
E yourselves, to see whether you are — 2 Cor 13:5

EXAMINED (6)
When the priest has **e** him, he shall — Lv 13:3
if we are being **e** today concerning a — Acts 4:9
he **e** the sentries and ordered that they — Acts 12:19
that he should be **e** by flogging, — Acts 22:24
Agrippa, so that, after we have **e** him, — Acts 25:26
When they had **e** me, they wished to — Acts 28:18

EXAMINES (6)
But if the priest **e** it and there is no — Lv 13:21
But if the priest **e** it and there is no — Lv 13:26
And if the priest **e** the itching disease — Lv 13:31
"And if the priest **e**, and if the disease — Lv 13:53
"But if the priest **e**, and if the diseased — Lv 13:56
right, until the other comes and **e** him. — Prv 18:17

EXAMINING (4)
But all this I laid to heart, **e** it all, how — Eccl 9:1
And after **e** him before you, behold, I — Lk 23:14
e the Scriptures daily to see if these — Acts 17:11
By **e** him yourself you will be able to — Acts 24:8

EXAMPLE (13)
have also seen this **e** of wisdom under — Eccl 9:13
For I have given you an **e**, that you also — Jn 13:15
things happened to them as an **e**, — 1 Cor 10:11
To give a human **e**, brothers: even with — Gal 3:15
walk according to the **e** you have in us. — Phil 3:17
that you became an **e** to all the — 1 Thes 1:7
give you in ourselves an **e** to imitate. — 2 Thes 3:9
perfect patience as an **e** to those who — 1 Tm 1:16
but set the believers an **e** in speech, — 1 Tm 4:12
As an **e** of suffering and patience, — Jas 5:10
also suffered for you, leaving you an **e**, — 1 Pt 2:21
making them an **e** of what is going to — 2 Pt 2:6
serve as an **e** by undergoing a — Jude 1:7

EXAMPLES (2)
these things took place as **e** for us, — 1 Cor 10:6
in your charge, but being **e** to the flock. — 1 Pt 5:3

EXCEED (2)
of righteousness must far **e** it in glory. — 2 Cor 3:9
and that your latter works **e** the first. — Rv 2:19

EXCEEDING (2)
go to the altar of God, to God my **e** joy, — Ps 43:4
This image, mighty and of **e** brightness, — Dn 2:31

EXCEEDINGLY (35)
I will make you **e** fruitful, and I will — Gn 17:6
cried out with an **e** great and bitter cry — Gn 27:34
they multiplied and grew **e** strong, so that — Ex 1:7
through to spy it out, is an **e** good land. — Nm 14:7
for it is **e** bitter to me for your sake that — Ru 1:13
But they were **e** afraid and said, — 2 Kgs 10:4
for the LORD must be **e** magnificent, — 1 Chr 22:5
was with him and made him **e** great. — 2 Chr 1:1
people likewise were **e** unfaithful, — 2 Chr 36:14
who rejoice **e** and are glad when they find — Jb 3:22
but your commandment is **e** broad. — Ps 119:96
keeps your testimonies; I love them **e**. — Ps 119:167
on earth are small, but they are **e** wise: — Prv 30:24
on the aged you made your yoke **e** heavy. — Is 47:6
us, and you remain **e** angry with us. — Lam 5:22
the house of Israel and Judah is **e** great. — Ezk 9:9
You grew **e** beautiful and advanced to — Ezk 16:13
stood on their feet, an **e** great army. — Ezk 37:10
Then the king was **e** glad, and — Dn 6:23
terrifying and dreadful and **e** strong. — Dn 7:7
different from all the rest, **e** terrifying, — Dn 7:19
Then the goat became **e** great, but when — Dn 8:8
which grew **e** great toward the south, — Dn 8:9
wage war with an **e** great and mighty — Dn 11:25
before his army, for his camp is **e** great; — Jl 2:11
Then the men were **e** afraid and said to — Jon 1:10
Then the men feared the LORD **e**, and — Jon 1:16
Now Nineveh was an **e** great city, three — Jon 3:3
But it displeased Jonah **e**, and he was — Jon 4:1
So Jonah was **e** glad because of the plant. — Jon 4:6
I am **e** jealous for Jerusalem and for — Zec 1:14
And I am **e** angry with the nations that — Zec 1:15
the star, they rejoiced **e** with great joy. — Mt 2:10
And the king was **e** sorry, but because — Mk 6:26
And they were **e** astonished, and said — Mk 10:26

EXCEEDS (1)
unless your righteousness **e** that of the — Mt 5:20

EXCEL (3)
strive to **e** in building up the — 1 Cor 14:12
But as you **e** in everything—in faith, — 2 Cor 8:7
you—see that you **e** in this act of grace — 2 Cor 8:7

EXCELLED (2)
Thus King Solomon **e** all the kings — 1 Kgs 10:23
Thus King Solomon **e** all the kings — 2 Chr 9:22

EXCELLENCE (2)
is commendable, if there is any **e**, — Phil 4:8
who called us to his own glory and **e**, — 2 Pt 1:3

EXCELLENCIES (1)
you may proclaim the **e** of him who — 1 Pt 2:9

EXCELLENCY (1)
Lysias, to his **E** the governor Felix, — Acts 23:26

EXCELLENT (17)
the saints in the land, they are the **e** ones, — Ps 16:3
praise him according to his **e** greatness! — Ps 150:2
An **e** wife is the crown of her husband, — Prv 12:4
An **e** wife who can find? She is far — Prv 31:10
wonderful in counsel and **e** in wisdom. — Is 28:29
because an **e** spirit, knowledge, and — Dn 5:12
and understanding and **e** wisdom are — Dn 5:14
satraps, because an **e** spirit was in him. — Dn 6:3
account for you, most **e** Theophilus, — Lk 1:3
since by your foresight, most **e** Felix, — Acts 24:2
not out of my mind, most **e** Festus, — Acts 26:25
know his will and approve what is **e**, — Rom 2:18
I will show you a still more **e** way. — 1 Cor 12:31
so that you may approve what is **e**, and — Phil 1:10
These things are **e** and profitable for — Ti 3:8
he has inherited is more **e** than theirs. — Heb 1:4
that is as much more **e** than the old as — Heb 8:6

EXCELLENTLY (1)
"Many women have done **e**, but you — Prv 31:29

EXCEPT (84)
kept back anything from me **e** yourself, — Gn 39:9
e for his closest relatives, his mother, his — Lv 21:2
e Caleb the son of Jephunneh and — Nm 14:30
e Caleb the son of Jephunneh and — Nm 26:65
none **e** Caleb the son of Jephunneh — Nm 32:12
e by the blood of the one who shed it. — Nm 35:33
e Caleb the son of Jephunneh. He shall — Dt 1:36
mounds did Israel burn, **e** Hazor alone; — Jos 11:13
with the people of Israel **e** the Hivites, — Jos 11:19
morning until now, **e** for a short rest." — Ru 2:7
desires no bride-price **e** a hundred — 1 Sm 18:25
escaped, **e** four hundred young men, — 1 Sm 30:17
e that each man may lead away his — 1 Sm 30:22

LORD? And who is a rock, **e** our God? 2 Sm 22:32
nothing in the ark **e** the two tablets of 1 Kgs 8:9
e in the matter of Uriah the Hittite. 1 Kgs 15:5
nor rain these years, **e** by my word." 1 Kgs 17:1
has nothing in the house **e** a jar of oil." 2 Kgs 4:2
e the poorest people of the land. 2 Kgs 24:14
e as a place to make offerings before 2 Chr 2:6
nothing in the ark **e** the two tablets 2 Chr 5:10
no son was left to him **e** Jehoahaz, 2 Chr 21:17
house of the LORD **e** the priests and 2 Chr 23:6
e he did not enter the temple of the 2 Chr 27:2
e those enrolled by genealogy, males 2 Chr 31:16
she asked for nothing **e** what Hegai the Est 2:15
e the one to whom the king holds out Est 4:11
the LORD? And who is a rock, **e** our God? Ps 18:31
they shall not return, **e** some fugitives." Jer 44:14
one can show it to the king **e** the gods, Dn 2:11
and worship any god **e** their own God. Dn 3:28
any god or man for thirty days, **e** to you, Dn 6:7
god or man within thirty days **e** to you, Dn 6:12
by my side against these **e** Michael, Dn 10:21
e that I will not utterly destroy the house Am 9:8
longer good for anything **e** to be thrown Mt 5:13
e on the ground of sexual immorality, Mt 5:32
and no one knows the Son **e** the Father, Mt 11:27
one knows the Father **e** the Son and Mt 11:27
will be given to it **e** the sign of the Mt 12:39
not without honor **e** in his hometown Mt 13:57
will be given to it **e** the sign of Jonah." So Mt 16:4
his wife, **e** for sexual immorality, Mt 19:9
For nothing is hidden **e** to be made Mk 4:22
nor is anything secret **e** to come to Mk 4:22
one to follow him **e** Peter and James and Mk 5:37
e in his hometown and among his Mk 6:4
e that he laid his hands on a few sick Mk 6:5
nothing for their journey **e** a staff—no Mk 6:8
me good? No one is good **e** God alone. Mk 10:18
with him, **e** Peter and John and James, Lk 8:51
one knows who the Son is **e** the Father, Lk 10:22
who the Father is **e** the Son and anyone Lk 10:22
will be given to it **e** the sign of Jonah. Lk 11:29
and give praise to God **e** this foreigner?" Lk 17:18
me good? No one is good **e** God alone. Lk 18:19
ascended into heaven **e** he who descended Jn 3:13
has seen the Father **e** he who is from Jn 6:46
does not need to wash, **e** for his feet, Jn 13:10
one comes to the Father **e** through me. Jn 14:6
them has been lost **e** the son of Jn 17:12
of Judea and Samaria, **e** the apostles. Acts 8:1
speaking the word to no one **e** Jews. Acts 11:19
time in nothing **e** telling or hearing Acts 17:21
e that the Holy Spirit testifies to me in Acts 20:23
such as I am—**e** for these chains." Acts 26:29
For there is no authority **e** from God, Rom 13:1
no one anything, **e** to love each other, Rom 13:8
speak of anything **e** what Christ has Rom 15:18
none of you **e** Crispus and Gaius, 1 Cor 1:14
nothing among you **e** Jesus Christ and 1 Cor 2:2
a person's thoughts **e** the spirit of 1 Cor 2:11
the thoughts of God **e** the Spirit of 1 Cor 2:11
e perhaps by agreement for a limited 1 Cor 7:5
say "Jesus is Lord" **e** in the Holy 1 Cor 12:3
I will not boast, **e** of my weaknesses. 2 Cor 12:5
e that I myself did not burden you? 2 Cor 12:13
of the other apostles **e** James the Lord's Gal 1:19
it from me to boast **e** in the cross of our Gal 6:14
me in giving and receiving, **e** you only. Phil 4:15
against an elder **e** on the evidence 1 Tm 5:19
that overcomes the world **e** the one who 1 Jn 5:5
that no one knows **e** the one who Rv 2:17
could learn that song **e** the 144,000 who Rv 14:3

EXCEPTED (1)
plain that he is **e** who put all things 1 Cor 15:27

EXCESS (1)
and her daughters had pride, **e** of food, Ezk 16:49

EXCESSIVE (2)
he acquire for himself **e** silver and gold. Dt 17:17
he may be overwhelmed by **e** sorrow. 2 Cor 2:7

EXCHANGE (10)
with you tonight in **e** for your son's Gn 30:15
in **e** for the grain that they bought. Gn 47:14
give you food in **e** for your livestock, Gn 47:16
gave them food in **e** for the horses, Gn 47:17
them with food in **e** for all their Gn 47:17
He shall not **e** it or make a substitute Lv 27:10
your ransom, Cush and Seba in **e** for you. Is 43:3
return for you, peoples in **e** for your life. Is 43:4
They shall not sell or **e** any of it. They Ezk 48:14
them and make merry and **e** presents, Rv 11:10

EXCHANGED (13)
morning they rose early and **e** oaths. Gn 26:31
it, nor can it be **e** for jewels of fine gold. Jb 28:17
They **e** the glory of God for the image Ps 106:20
tin, and lead they **e** for your wares. Ezk 27:12
they **e** human beings and vessels of Ezk 27:13
From Beth-togarmah they **e** horses, Ezk 27:14
they **e** for your wares emeralds, purple, Ezk 27:16
they **e** for your merchandise wheat of Ezk 27:17
wine from Uzal they **e** for your wares; Ezk 27:19
they **e** for your wares the best of all Ezk 27:22
and **e** the glory of the immortal God Rom 1:23
because they **e** the truth about God for Rom 1:25
For their women **e** natural relations Rom 1:26

EXCHANGING (1)
in Israel concerning redeeming and **e**: Ru 4:7

EXCLAIMED (1)
and she **e** with a loud cry, "Blessed are Lk 1:42

EXCLUDE (1)
you and when they **e** you and revile you Lk 6:22

EXCLUDED (4)
for he was **e** from the house of the 2 Chr 26:21
and so they were **e** from the priesthood Ezr 2:62
so they were **e** from the priesthood as Neh 7:64
what becomes of our boasting? It is **e**. Rom 3:27

EXCREMENT (1)
it and turn back and cover up your **e**. Dt 23:13

EXCUSE (4)
sin, but now they have no **e** for their sin. Jn 15:22
have been made. So they are without **e**. Rom 1:20
Therefore you have no **e**, O man, every Rom 2:1
thoughts accuse or even **e** them Rom 2:15

EXCUSED (2)
go out and see it. Please have me **e**.' Lk 14:18
go to examine them. Please have me **e**.' Lk 14:19

EXCUSES (1)
But they all alike began to make **e**. The Lk 14:18

EXECRATION (1)
You shall become an **e**, a horror, a Jer 42:18

EXECUTE (34)
all the gods of Egypt I will **e** judgments: Ex 12:12
that shall **e** vengeance for the covenant. Lv 26:25
against Midian to **e** the LORD'S Nm 31:3
e him." And he struck him down so 2 Sm 1:15
that you may **e** justice and 1 Kgs 10:9
of engraving and **e** any design that 2 Chr 2:14
that you may **e** justice and 2 Chr 9:8
will you not **e** judgment on them? 2 Chr 20:12
He will **e** judgment among the nations, Ps 110:6
and will **e** justice for the needy. Ps 140:12
to **e** vengeance on the nations and Ps 149:7
to **e** on them the judgment written! Ps 149:9
my mighty men to **e** my anger, Is 13:3
if you truly **e** justice one with another, Jer 7:5
"'**E** justice in the morning, and deliver Jer 21:12
and shall **e** justice and righteousness in Jer 23:5
and he shall **e** justice and Jer 33:15
when I will **e** judgment upon her Jer 51:52
And I will **e** judgments in your midst in Ezk 5:8
fathers. And I will **e** judgments on you, Ezk 5:10
when I **e** judgments on you in anger Ezk 5:15
foreigners, and **e** judgments upon you. Ezk 11:9
your houses and **e** judgments upon Ezk 16:41
and I will **e** judgments upon Moab. Ezk 25:11
I will **e** great vengeance on them with Ezk 25:17
the LORD when I **e** judgments in her Ezk 28:22
when I **e** judgments upon all their Ezk 28:26
Zoan and will **e** judgments on Thebes. Ezk 30:14
Thus I will **e** judgments on Egypt. Ezk 30:19
and **e** justice and righteousness. Ezk 45:9
I will not **e** my burning anger; I will not Hos 11:9
and wrath I will **e** vengeance on the Mi 5:15
has given him authority to **e** judgment, Jn 5:27
to **e** judgment on all and to convict all Jude 1:15

EXECUTED (12)
their gods also the LORD **e** judgments. Nm 33:4
with Israel he **e** the justice of the LORD, Dt 33:21
Thus they **e** judgment on Joash. 2 Chr 24:24
king, let judgment be strictly **e** on him, Ezr 7:26
himself known; he has **e** judgment; Ps 9:16
you have **e** justice and righteousness in Ps 99:4
against an evil deed is not **e** speedily, Eccl 8:11
until he has **e** and accomplished the Jer 23:20
until he has **e** and accomplished the Jer 30:24
when judgment had been **e** on her. Ezk 23:10
shall see my judgment that I have **e**, Ezk 39:21
they asked Pilate to have him **e**. Acts 13:28

EXECUTES (6)
He **e** justice for the fatherless and the Dt 10:18
but it is God who **e** judgment, putting Ps 75:7
who **e** justice for the oppressed, who Ps 146:7
e true justice between man and man, Ezk 18:8
great; he who **e** his word is powerful. Jl 2:11
pleads my cause and **e** judgment for me. Mi 7:9

EXECUTING (1)
when Jehu was **e** judgment on the 2 Chr 22:8

EXECUTION (1)
And Saul approved of his **e**. And there Acts 8:1

EXECUTIONER (1)
the king sent an **e** with orders to bring Mk 6:27

EXECUTIONERS (1)
saying, "Bring near the **e** of the city, Ezk 9:1

EXEMPT (1)
to all Judah, none was **e**, 1 Kgs 15:22

EXERCISE (7)
from Jacob shall **e** dominion and Nm 24:19
their great ones **e** authority over them. Mt 20:25
their great ones **e** authority over them. Mk 10:42
of the Gentiles **e** lordship over them, Lk 22:25
But if they cannot **e** self-control, they 1 Cor 7:9
to teach or to **e** authority over a man; 1 Tm 2:12
was allowed to **e** authority for forty-two Rv 13:5

EXERCISED (1)
250, who **e** authority over the people. 2 Chr 8:10

EXERCISES (3)
one of the Levites **e** his right of Lv 25:33
Every athlete **e** self-control in all 1 Cor 9:25
It **e** all the authority of the first beast in Rv 13:12

EXERCISING (1)
of God that is among you, **e** oversight, 1 Pt 5:2

EXERTION (1)
it depends not on human will or **e**, Rom 9:16

EXHAUSTED (9)
came in from the field, and he was **e**. Gn 25:29
for I am **e**!" (Therefore his name was Gn 25:30
men who were with him, **e** yet pursuing. Jgs 8:4
to the people who follow me, for they are **e**, Jgs 8:5
give bread to your men who are **e**?'" Jgs 8:15
who were too **e** to cross the brook 1 Sm 30:10
who had been too **e** to follow David, 1 Sm 30:21
be weary, and young men shall fall **e**; Is 40:30
and they shall become **e**.'" Thus far are Jer 51:64

EXHIBITED (1)
think that God has **e** us apostles as last 1 Cor 4:9

EXHORT (6)
bore witness and continued to **e** them, Acts 2:40
to establish and **e** you in your faith, 1 Thes 3:2
reprove, rebuke, and **e**, with complete 2 Tm 4:2
things; **e** and rebuke with all authority. Ti 2:15
But **e** one another every day, as long as Heb 3:13
So I **e** the elders among you, as a fellow 1 Pt 5:1

EXHORTATION (5)
you have any word of **e** for the people, Acts 13:15
the one who exhorts, in his **e**; the one Rom 12:8
the public reading of Scripture, to **e**, 1 Tm 4:13
you forgotten the **e** that addresses you Heb 12:5
you, brothers, bear with my word of **e**, Heb 13:22

EXHORTATIONS (1)
So with many other **e** he preached good Lk 3:18

EXHORTED (2)
and he **e** them all to remain faithful Acts 11:23
we **e** each one of you and 1 Thes 2:12

EXHORTING (1)
e and declaring that this is the true 1 Pt 5:12

EXHORTS (1)
the one who **e**, in his exhortation; the Rom 12:8

EXILE (64)
and also an **e** from your home. 2 Sm 15:19
captain of the guard carried into **e**. 2 Kgs 25:11
Judah was taken into **e** out of its 2 Kgs 25:21
year of the **e** of Jehoiachin king 2 Kgs 25:27
king of Assyria carried away into **e**; 1 Chr 5:6
they lived in their place until the **e**. 1 Chr 5:22
of Assyria, and he took them into **e**, 1 Chr 5:26
Jehozadak went into **e** when the LORD 1 Chr 6:15
and Jerusalem into **e** by the hand 1 Chr 6:15
they were carried into **e** to Manahath): 1 Chr 8:6
was taken into **e** in Babylon because 1 Chr 9:1
He took into **e** in Babylon those who 2 Chr 36:20
of Israel who had returned from **e**, Ezr 6:21
who escaped, who had survived the **e**, Neh 1:2
who had survived the **e** is in great Neh 1:3
the king of Babylon had carried into **e**. Neh 7:6
my people go into **e** for lack of knowledge; Is 5:13
measure, by **e** you contended with them; Is 27:8
all Judah is taken into **e**, wholly taken Jer 13:19
is taken into exile, wholly taken into **e**. Jer 13:19
had taken into **e** from Jerusalem Jer 24:1
when he took into **e** from Jerusalem to Jer 27:20
had taken into **e** from Jerusalem to Jer 29:1
I have sent into **e** from Jerusalem to Jer 29:4

of the city where I have sent you into **e**, Jer 29:7
the place from which I sent you into **e**. Jer 29:14
who did not go out with you into **e**: Jer 29:16
Babylon, saying, "Your **e** will be long; Jer 29:28
carried into **e** to Babylon the rest of the Jer 39:9
had not been taken into **e** to Babylon, Jer 40:7
kill us or take us into **e** in Babylon." Jer 43:3
Prepare yourselves baggage for **e**, O Jer 46:19
Chemosh shall go into **e** with his priests Jer 48:7
vessel to vessel, nor has he gone into **e**; Jer 48:11
For Milcom shall go into **e**, with his Jer 49:3
Judah was taken into **e** out of its land. Jer 52:27
year of the **e** of Jehoiachin king Jer 52:31
has gone into **e** because of affliction Lam 1:3
he will keep you in **e** no longer; Lam 4:22
fifth year of the **e** of King Jehoiachin), Ezk 1:2
and go into **e** by day in their sight. Ezk 12:3
shall go like an **e** from your place to Ezk 12:3
by day in their sight, as baggage for **e**, Ezk 12:4
sight, as those do who must go into **e**. Ezk 12:4
my baggage by day, as baggage for **e**, Ezk 12:7
They shall go into **e**, into captivity.' Ezk 12:11
house of Judah when they went into **e**, Ezk 25:3
In the twelfth year of our **e**, in the Ezk 33:21
I sent them into **e** among the nations Ezk 39:28
In the twenty-fifth year of our **e**, at the Ezk 40:1
of Syria shall go into **e** to Kir," says the Am 1:5
they carried into **e** a whole people Am 1:6
and their king shall go into **e**, he and Am 1:15
for Gilgal shall surely go into **e**, and Am 5:5
send you into **e** beyond Damascus," Am 5:27
now be the first of those who go into **e**, Am 6:7
Israel must go into **e** away from his Am 7:11
shall surely go into **e** away from its Am 7:17
eagle, for they shall go from you into **e**. Mi 1:16
Yet she became an **e**; she went into Na 3:10
Half of the city shall go out into **e**, but Zec 14:2
fled and became an **e** in the land of Acts 7:29
I will send you into **e** beyond Babylon.' Acts 7:43
fear throughout the time of your **e**, 1 Pt 1:17

EXILE'S (1)
man, prepare for yourself an **e** baggage, Ezk 12:3

EXILED (3)
So Israel was **e** from their own land 2 Kgs 17:23
bereaved and barren, **e** and put away, Is 49:21
and Judah who were being **e** to Babylon. Jer 40:1

EXILES (37)
when the **e** were brought up from Ezr 1:11
of those **e** whom Nebuchadnezzar Ezr 2:1
heard that the returned **e** were building a Ezr 4:1
Levites, and the rest of the returned **e**, Ezr 6:16
month, the returned **e** kept the Passover. Ezr 6:19
the Passover lamb for all the returned **e**, Ezr 6:20
had come from captivity, the returned **e**, Ezr 8:35
of the faithlessness of the returned **e**, Ezr 9:4
over the faithlessness of the **e**. Ezr 10:6
to all the returned **e** that they should Ezr 10:7
banned from the congregation of the **e**. Ezr 10:8
Then the returned **e** did so. Ezra the Ezr 10:16
of those **e** whom Nebuchadnezzar Neh 7:6
the Egyptian captives and the Cushite **e**, Is 20:4
he shall build my city and set my **e** free, Is 45:13
so I will regard as good the **e** from Judah, Jer 24:5
and all the **e** from Judah who went to Jer 28:4
of the house of the LORD, and all the **e**. Jer 28:6
Jerusalem to the surviving elders of the **e**, Jer 29:1
to all the **e** whom I have sent into exile Jer 29:4
all you **e** whom I sent away from Jer 29:20
used by all the **e** from Judah in Jer 29:22
"Send to all the **e**, saying, 'Thus says the Jer 29:31
I was among the **e** by the Chebar canal, Ezk 1:1
And go to the **e**, to your people, and Ezk 3:11
And I came to the **e** at Tel-abib, who Ezk 3:15
the Spirit of God into Chaldea, to the **e**. Ezk 11:24
And I told the **e** all the things that the Ezk 11:25
have found among the **e** from Judah a Dn 2:25
are that Daniel, one of the **e** of Judah, Dn 5:13
"Daniel, who is one of the **e** from Judah, Dn 6:13
The **e** of this host of the people of Israel Ob 1:20
and the **e** of Jerusalem who are in Ob 1:20
"Take from the **e** Heldai, Tobijah, and Zec 6:10
they were strangers and **e** on the earth. Heb 11:13
those who are elect **e** of the dispersion in 1 Pt 1:1
as sojourners and **e** to abstain from 1 Pt 2:11

EXIST (7)
into existence the things that do not **e**. Rom 4:17
and those that **e** have been instituted Rom 13:1
are all things and for whom we **e**, 1 Cor 8:6
are all things and through whom we **e**. 1 Cor 8:6
for whom and by whom all things **e**, Heb 2:10
where jealousy and selfish ambition **e**, Jas 3:16
and earth that now **e** are stored up for 2 Pt 3:7

EXISTED (4)
that I had with you before the world **e**. Jn 17:5
this fact, that the heavens **e** long ago, 2 Pt 3:5
the world that then **e** was deluged with 2 Pt 3:6
by your will they **e** and were created." Rv 4:11

EXISTENCE (2)
dead and calls into **e** the things that do Rom 4:17
idol has no real **e**," and that "there is 1 Cor 8:4

EXISTS (2)
"A conspiracy **e** among the men of Jer 11:9
must believe that he **e** and that he Heb 11:6

EXITS (4)
with the same **e** and arrangements Ezk 42:11
arrangement, its **e** and its entrances, Ezk 43:11
and all the **e** from the sanctuary. Ezk 44:5
"These shall be the **e** of the city: On Ezk 48:30

EXODUS (1)
made mention of the **e** of the Israelites Heb 11:22

EXORCISTS (1)
the itinerant Jewish **e** undertook to Acts 19:13

EXPANSE (15)
"Let there be an **e** in the midst of the Gn 1:6
And God made the **e** and separated the Gn 1:7
that were under the **e** from the waters that Gn 1:7
from the waters that were above the **e**. Gn 1:7
And God called the **e** Heaven. And there Gn 1:8
there be lights in the **e** of the heavens to Gn 1:14
them be lights in the **e** of the heavens to Gn 1:15
God set them in the **e** of the heavens to Gn 1:17
the earth across the **e** of the heavens." Gn 1:20
you comprehended the **e** of the earth? Jb 38:18
creatures there was the likeness of an **e**, Ezk 1:22
And under the **e** their wings were Ezk 1:23
voice from above the **e** over their heads. Ezk 1:25
And above the **e** over their heads there Ezk 1:26
on the **e** that was over the heads of the Ezk 10:1

EXPECT (6)
and yet they **e** him to fulfill their word. Ezk 13:6
is coming at an hour you do not **e**. Mt 24:44
day when he does not **e** him and at an Mt 24:50
to those from whom you **e** to receive, Lk 6:34
is coming at an hour you do not **e**." Lk 12:40
day when he does not **e** him and at an Lk 12:46

EXPECTATION (6)
joy, but the **e** of the wicked will perish. Prv 10:28
perish, and the **e** of wealth perishes too. Prv 11:7
in good; the **e** of the wicked in wrath. Prv 11:23
As the people were in **e**, and all were Lk 3:15
as it is my eager **e** and hope that I will Phil 1:20
but a fearful **e** of judgment, and a fury Heb 10:27

EXPECTED (3)
to Joseph, "I never **e** to see your face; Gn 48:11
and that all Israel fully **e** me to reign. 1 Kgs 2:15
and this, not as we **e**, but they gave 2 Cor 8:5

EXPECTING (5)
do good, and lend, **e** nothing in return, Lk 6:35
e to receive something from them. Acts 3:5
Cornelius was **e** them and had called Acts 10:24
all that the Jewish people were **e**." Acts 12:11
for I am **e** him with the brothers. 1 Cor 16:11

EXPEDIENT (1)
that it would be **e** that one man should Jn 18:14

EXPEDITION (2)
from us as always when I go on an **e**. 1 Sm 21:5
from Keilah, he gave up the **e**. 1 Sm 23:13

EXPELLED (3)
So Solomon **e** Abiathar from being 1 Kgs 2:27
passes into the stomach and is **e**? Mt 15:17
and is **e**?" (Thus he declared all foods Mk 7:19

EXPENDED (1)
done and the toil I had **e** in doing it, Eccl 2:11

EXPENSE (4)
Have we eaten at all at the king's **e**? 2 Sm 19:42
was prepared at my **e** for each day was Neh 5:18
there two whole years at his own **e**, Acts 28:30
Who serves as a soldier at his own **e**? 1 Cor 9:7

EXPENSES (1)
along with them and pay their **e**, Acts 21:24

EXPENSIVE (2)
an alabaster flask of very **e** ointment, Mt 26:7
took a pound of **e** ointment made from Jn 12:3

EXPERIENCE (3)
heart has had great **e** of wisdom and Eccl 1:16
which you **e** when you patiently 2 Cor 1:6
you might have a second **e** of grace. 2 Cor 1:15

EXPERIENCED (6)
tribes wise, understanding, and **e** men, Dt 1:13
the heads of your tribes, wise and **e** men, Dt 1:15
in Israel who had not **e** all the wars in Jgs 3:1
wilderness mighty and **e** warriors, 1 Chr 12:8
brothers, of the affliction we **e** in Asia. 2 Cor 1:8
suffering are being **e** by your 1 Pt 5:9

EXPERT (6)
and became an **e** with the bow. Gn 21:20
Besides, your father is **e** in war; he will 2 Sm 17:8
sword, and drew the bow, **e** in war, 1 Chr 5:18
warriors, **e** with shield and spear, 1 Chr 12:8
all of them wearing swords and **e** in war, Sg 3:8
the skillful magician and the **e** in charms. Is 3:3

EXPIRE (1)
at birth, come out from the womb and **e**? Jb 3:11

EXPIRED (1)
son-in-law. Before the time had **e**, 1 Sm 18:26

EXPLAIN (11)
there was no one who could **e** it to me." Gn 41:24
of Moab, Moses undertook to **e** this law, Dt 1:5
gate of the city and **e** his case to the Jos 20:4
the king that he could not **e** to her. 1 Kgs 10:3
Solomon that he could not **e** to her. 2 Chr 9:2
show it to Esther and **e** it to her and Est 4:8
and to whom will he **e** the message? Is 28:9
to interpret dreams, **e** riddles, Dn 5:12
"**E** to us the parable of the weeds of the Mt 13:36
Peter said to him, "**E** the parable to us." Mt 15:15
have much to say, and it is hard to **e**, Heb 5:11

EXPLAINED (3)
to his own disciples he **e** everything. Mk 4:34
But Peter began and **e** it to them in Acts 11:4
they took him and **e** to him the way Acts 18:26

EXPLAINING (1)
e and proving that it was necessary for Acts 17:3

EXPLOIT (1)
their greed they will **e** you with false 2 Pt 2:3

EXPLORE (3)
that they may **e** the land for us and bring Dt 1:22
Eshtaol, to spy out the land and to **e** it. Jgs 18:2
"Go and **e** the land." And they came to Jgs 18:2

EXPLORED (1)
of the earth below can be **e**, Jer 31:37

EXPLORERS (2)
came from the **e** and from the 1 Kgs 10:15
that which the **e** and merchants 2 Chr 9:14

EXPORTED (2)
king's traders they were **e** to all the 1 Kgs 10:29
through them these were **e** to all the 2 Chr 1:17

EXPOSE (2)
forced our fathers to **e** their infants, Acts 7:19
works of darkness, but instead **e** them. Eph 5:11

EXPOSED (11)
that your nakedness be not **e** on it.' Ex 20:26
wickedness will be **e** in the assembly. Prv 26:26
they have not **e** your iniquity to restore Lam 2:14
I **e** you before kings, to feast their eyes Ezk 28:17
to the light, lest his deeds should be **e**. Jn 3:20
and when he was **e**, Pharaoh's Acts 7:21
But when anything is **e** by the light, it Eph 5:13
but all are naked and **e** to the eyes of Heb 4:13
being publicly **e** to reproach Heb 10:33
the works that are done on it will be **e**. 2 Pt 3:10
not go about naked and be seen **e**!") Rv 16:15

EXPOSING (1)
in them, **e** the white of the sticks. Gn 30:37

EXPOSURE (1)
often without food, in cold and **e**. 2 Cor 11:27

EXPOUNDED (1)
morning till evening he **e** to them, Acts 28:23

EXPRESSING (1)
but only in **e** his opinion. Prv 18:2

EXPRESSION (1)
and the **e** of his face was changed Dn 3:19

EXPRESSLY (3)
who were **e** named to come and 1 Chr 12:31
of those chosen and **e** named to give 1 Chr 16:41
Now the Spirit **e** says that in later 1 Tm 4:1

EXTEND (5)
Then the border shall **e** to Ziphron, Nm 34:9
Let there be none to **e** kindness to him, Ps 109:12
that day the Lord will **e** his hand yet a Is 11:11
"Behold, I will **e** peace to her like a river, Is 66:12
on that day shall **e** from one end of Jer 25:33

EXTENDED (8)
of the Canaanites **e** from Sidon in Gn 10:19
in which they lived **e** from Mesha in Gn 10:30

Their region **e** from Mahanaim, Jos 13:30
cherubim together **e** twenty cubits: 2 Chr 3:11
of these cherubim **e** twenty cubits. 2 Chr 3:13
and who **e** to me his steadfast love Ezr 7:28
but has **e** to us his steadfast love before Ezr 9:9
In that day the boundary shall be far **e**. Mi 7:11

EXTENDING (4)
bronze, under its ledge, **e** halfway down. Ex 38:4
and **e** from the western to the eastern Ezk 45:7
and **e** from the east side to the west, Ezk 48:1
E from the 25,000 cubits of the holy Ezk 48:21

EXTENDS (6)
so that the net **e** halfway down the altar. Ex 27:5
the wilderness that **e** from the border Nm 21:13
slope of the valleys that **e** to the seat of Nm 21:15
Then the boundary **e** from the top of the Jos 15:9
steadfast love, O LORD, **e** to the heavens, Ps 36:5
so that as grace **e** to more and more 2 Cor 4:15

EXTENT (1)
It shall be holy throughout its whole **e**. Ezk 45:1

EXTERMINATED (1)
from the land he **e** the remnant of 1 Kgs 22:46

EXTERNAL (2)
were appointed to **e** duties for Israel, 1 Chr 26:29
let your adorning be **e**—the braiding of 1 Pt 3:3

EXTINCT (1)
My spirit is broken; my days are **e**; the Jb 17:1

EXTINCTION (1)
to ashes he condemned them to **e**, 2 Pt 2:6

EXTINGUISH (1)
with which you can **e** all the flaming Eph 6:16

EXTINGUISHED (1)
lie down, they cannot rise, they are **e**, Is 43:17

EXTOL (9)
"Remember to **e** his work, of which Jb 36:24
I will **e** you, O LORD, for you have drawn Ps 30:1
Let them **e** him in the congregation of Ps 107:32
the LORD, all nations! **E** him, all peoples! Ps 117:1
to you; you are my God; I will **e** you. Ps 118:28
I will **e** you, my God and King, and Ps 145:1
you; we will **e** your love more than wine; Sg 1:4
praise and **e** and honor the King of Dn 4:37
and let all the peoples **e** him." Rom 15:11

EXTOLLED (1)
and the name of the Lord Jesus was **e**. Acts 19:17

EXTOLLING (1)
them speaking in tongues and **e** God. Acts 10:46

EXTORT (1)
"Do not **e** money from anyone by Lk 3:14

EXTORTED (1)
and have **e** from the sojourner Ezk 22:29

EXTORTION (5)
Put no trust in **e**; set no vain hopes on Ps 62:10
for his father, because he practiced **e**, Ezk 18:18
the sojourner suffers **e** in your midst; Ezk 22:7
make gain of your neighbors by **e**; Ezk 22:12
land have practiced **e** and committed Ezk 22:29

EXTORTIONERS (1)
that I am not like other men, **e**, unjust, Lk 18:11

EXTRA (1)
And the **e** that remains in the length of Ex 26:13

EXTRAORDINARY (4)
on you and your offspring **e** afflictions, Dt 28:59
your love to me was **e**, surpassing the 2 Sm 1:26
saying, "We have seen **e** things today." Lk 5:26
And God was doing **e** miracles by the Acts 19:11

EXTREME (4)
of the people of Judah in the **e** south, Jos 15:21
was there at the **e** western end of them. Ezk 46:19
Beginning at the northern **e**, beside the Ezk 48:1
joy and their **e** poverty have overflowed 2 Cor 8:2

EXTREMELY (2)
he became very sad, for he was **e** rich. Lk 18:23
so **e** zealous was I for the traditions of Gal 1:14

EXTREMITY (1)
by the Arnon, at the **e** of the border. Nm 22:36

EXULT (27)
the daughters of the uncircumcised **e**. 2 Sm 1:20
it; let the field **e**, and everything in it! 1 Chr 16:32
I would even **e** in pain unsparing, Jb 6:10
those who love your name may **e** in you. Ps 5:11
I will be glad and **e** in you; I will sing Ps 9:2
to shame; let not my enemies **e** over me. Ps 25:2
all who swear by him shall **e**, for the Ps 63:11
in him! Let all the upright in heart **e**! Ps 64:10
shall be glad; they shall **e** before God; Ps 68:3
his name is the LORD; **e** before him! Ps 68:4
who **e** in your name all the day and in Ps 89:16
the wicked, how long shall the wicked **e**? Ps 94:3
let the field **e**, and everything in it! Then Ps 96:12
Let the godly **e** in glory; let them sing Ps 149:5
My inmost being will **e** when your lips Prv 23:16
We will **e** and rejoice in you; we will extol Sg 1:4
"You will no more **e**, O oppressed virgin Is 23:12
among mankind shall **e** in the Holy Is 29:19
Sing for joy, O heavens, and **e**, O earth; Is 49:13
your heart shall thrill and **e**, because the Is 60:5
in the LORD; my soul shall **e** in my God, Is 61:10
flesh avert your doom? Can you then **e**? Jer 11:15
"Though you rejoice, though you **e**, O Jer 50:11
E not like the peoples; for you have Hos 9:1
Rejoice and **e** with all your heart, O Zep 3:14
he will **e** over you with loud singing. Zep 3:17
Let us rejoice and **e** and give him the Rv 19:7

EXULTANT (5)
of shoutings, tumultuous city, **e** town? Is 22:2
Is this your **e** city whose origin is from Is 23:7
for all the joyous houses in the **e** city. Is 32:13
This is the **e** city that lived securely, Zep 2:15
from your midst your proudly **e** ones, Zep 3:11

EXULTATION (2)
"With **e** I will divide up Shechem and Ps 60:6
"With **e** I will divide up Shechem and Ps 108:7

EXULTED (1)
hated me, or **e** when evil overtook him Jb 31:29

EXULTING (3)
that the **e** of the wicked is short, and the Jb 20:5
rejoice in the LORD, **e** in his salvation. Ps 35:9
to execute my anger, my proudly **e** ones. Is 13:3

EXULTS (5)
and said, "My heart **e** in the LORD; 1 Sm 2:1
paws in the valley and **e** in his strength; Jb 39:21
and in your salvation how greatly he **e**! Ps 21:1
my heart **e**, and with my song I give Ps 28:7
go down, her revelers and he who **e** in her. Is 5:14

EYE (102)
e for eye, tooth for tooth, hand for hand, Ex 21:24
eye for **e**, tooth for tooth, hand for hand, Ex 21:24
"When a man strikes the **e** of his slave, Ex 21:26
let the slave go free because of his **e**. Ex 21:26
fracture for fracture, **e** for eye, tooth for Lv 24:20
fracture for fracture, eye for **e**, tooth for Lv 24:20
oracle of the man whose **e** is opened, Nm 24:3
oracle of the man whose **e** is opened, Nm 24:15
Your **e** shall not pity them, neither shall Dt 7:16
listen to him, nor shall your **e** pity him, Dt 13:8
and your **e** look grudgingly on your poor Dt 15:9
Your **e** shall not pity him, but you shall Dt 19:13
Your **e** shall not pity. It shall be life for Dt 19:21
It shall be life for life, **e** for eye, tooth for Dt 19:21
It shall be life for life, eye for **e**, tooth for Dt 19:21
off her hand. Your **e** shall have no pity. Dt 25:12
him, he kept him as the apple of his **e**. Dt 32:10
His **e** was undimmed, and his vigor Dt 34:7
which you go is under the **e** of the LORD." Jgs 18:6
will look with envious **e** on all the 1 Sm 2:32
But the **e** of their God was on the elders of Ezr 5:5
is a breath; my **e** will never again see good. Jb 7:7
The **e** of him who sees me will behold me Jb 7:8
that I had died before any **e** had seen me Jb 10:18
"Behold, my **e** has seen all this, my ear Jb 13:1
scorn me; my **e** pours out tears to God, Jb 16:20
and my **e** dwells on their provocation. Jb 17:2
My **e** has grown dim from vexation, and Jb 17:7
The **e** that saw him will see him no more, Jb 20:9
The **e** of the adulterer also waits for the Jb 24:15
the twilight, saying, 'No **e** will see me'; Jb 24:15
knows, and the falcon's **e** has not seen it. Jb 28:7
and his **e** sees every precious thing. Jb 28:10
it called me blessed, and when the **e** saw, Jb 29:11
of the ear, but now my **e** sees you; Jb 42:5
My **e** wastes away because of grief; it Ps 6:7
Keep me as the apple of your **e**; hide me Ps 17:8
am in distress; my **e** is wasted from grief; Ps 31:9
I will counsel you with my **e** upon you. Ps 32:8
the **e** of the LORD is on those who fear Ps 33:18
not those wink the **e** who hate me Ps 35:19
and my **e** has looked in triumph on my Ps 54:7
my **e** grows dim through sorrow. Every Ps 88:9
He who formed the **e**, does he not see? Ps 94:9
keep my teaching as the apple of your **e**; Prv 7:2
Whoever winks the **e** causes trouble, Prv 10:10
The hearing ear and the seeing **e**, the Prv 20:12
has a bountiful **e** will be blessed, Prv 22:9
The **e** that mocks a father and scorns Prv 30:17
the **e** is not satisfied with seeing, nor the Eccl 1:8
for **e** to eye they see the return of the LORD Is 52:8
for eye to **e** they see the return of the LORD Is 52:8
the ear, no **e** has seen a God besides you, Is 64:4
him face to face and see him **e** to eye. Jer 32:4
him face to face and see him eye to **e**. Jer 32:4
the king of Babylon **e** to eye and speak Jer 34:3
of Babylon eye to **e** and speak with him Jer 34:3
My **e** will not spare, and I will have no Ezk 5:11
And my **e** will not spare you, nor will I Ezk 7:4
And my **e** will not spare, nor will I have Ezk 7:9
My **e** will not spare, nor will I have pity. Ezk 8:18
Your **e** shall not spare, and you shall Ezk 9:5
As for me, my **e** will not spare, nor will I Ezk 9:10
No **e** pitied you, to do any of these Ezk 16:5
Nevertheless, my **e** spared them, and I Ezk 20:17
touches you touches the apple of his **e**: Zec 2:8
the LORD has an **e** on mankind and on Zec 9:1
sword strike his arm and his right **e**! Zec 11:17
withered, his right **e** utterly blinded!" Zec 11:17
If your right **e** causes you to sin, tear it Mt 5:29
'An **e** for an eye and a tooth for a tooth.' Mt 5:38
'An eye for an **e** and a tooth for a tooth.' Mt 5:38
"The **e** is the lamp of the body. So, if Mt 6:22
So, if your **e** is healthy, your whole body Mt 6:22
but if your **e** is bad, your whole body Mt 6:23
see the speck that is in your brother's **e**, Mt 7:3
not notice the log that is in your own **e**? Mt 7:3
'Let me take the speck out of your **e**,' Mt 7:4
eye,' when there is the log in your own **e**? Mt 7:4
first take the log out of your own **e**, Mt 7:5
to take the speck out of your brother's **e**. Mt 7:5
And if your **e** causes you to sin, tear it Mt 18:9
enter life with one **e** than with two eyes Mt 18:9
to go through the **e** of a needle than Mt 19:24
And if your **e** causes you to sin, tear it Mk 9:47
of God with one **e** than with two eyes Mk 9:47
to go through the **e** of a needle than Mk 10:25
see the speck that is in your brother's **e**, Lk 6:41
not notice the log that is in your own **e**? Lk 6:41
me take out the speck that is in your **e**,' Lk 6:42
do not see the log that is in your own **e**? Lk 6:42
first take the log out of your own **e**, Lk 6:42
out the speck that is in your brother's **e**. Lk 6:42
Your **e** is the lamp of your body. When Lk 11:34
of your body. When your **e** is healthy, Lk 11:34
to go through the **e** of a needle than Lk 18:25
as it is written, "What no **e** has seen, 1 Cor 2:9
should say, "Because I am not an **e**, 1 Cor 12:16
If the whole body were an **e**, where 1 Cor 12:17
The **e** cannot say to the hand, "I 1 Cor 12:21
a moment, in the twinkling of an **e**, 1 Cor 15:52
with the clouds, and every **e** will see him, Rv 1:7

EYE-SERVICE (2)
not by the way of **e**, as people-pleasers, Eph 6:6
your earthly masters, not by way of **e**, Col 3:22

EYEBROWS (1)
hair from his head, his beard, and his **e**. Lv 14:9

EYED (1)
And Saul **e** David from that day on. 1 Sm 18:9

EYELASHES (1)
do not let her capture you with her **e**; Prv 6:25

EYELIDS (9)
have none, nor see the **e** of the morning, Jb 3:9
weeping, and on my **e** is deep darkness, Jb 16:16
and his eyes are like the **e** of the dawn. Jb 41:18
his eyes see, his **e** test, the children of Ps 11:4
You hold my **e** open; I am so troubled Ps 77:4
sleep to my eyes or slumber to my **e**, Ps 132:4
eyes no sleep and your **e** no slumber; Prv 6:4
are their eyes, how high their **e** lift! Prv 30:13
with tears and our **e** flow with water. Jer 9:18

EYES (522)
when you eat of it your **e** will be opened, Gn 3:5
for food, and that it was a delight to the **e**, Gn 3:6
Then the **e** of both were opened, and they Gn 3:7
Noah found favor in the **e** of the LORD. Gn 6:8
And Lot lifted up his **e** and saw that the Gn 13:10
"Lift up your **e** and look from the place Gn 13:14
He lifted up his **e** and looked, and Gn 18:2
your innocence in the **e** of all who are Gn 20:16
Then God opened her **e**, and she saw a Gn 21:19
Abraham lifted up his **e** and saw the Gn 22:4
Abraham lifted up his **e** and looked, Gn 22:13
And he lifted up his **e** and saw, and Gn 24:63
And Rebekah lifted up her **e**, and when Gn 24:64
Isaac was old and his **e** were dim so that Gn 27:1
Leah's **e** were weak, but Rachel was Gn 29:17
in the troughs before the **e** of the flock, Gn 30:41
flock I lifted up my **e** and saw in a Gn 31:10
And he said, 'Lift up your **e** and see, all Gn 31:12
by night, and my sleep fled from my **e**. Gn 31:40
And Jacob lifted up his **e** and looked, Gn 33:1
Esau lifted up his **e** and saw the women Gn 33:5
brothers, "Let me find favor in your **e**, Gn 34:11

master's wife cast her **e** on Joseph and Gn 39:7
them and bound him before their **e**. Gn 42:24
he lifted up his **e** and saw his brother Gn 43:29
to me, that I may set my **e** on him.' Gn 44:21
And now your **e** see, and the eyes of my Gn 45:12
and the **e** of my brother Benjamin see, Gn 45:12
and Joseph's hand shall close your **e**." Gn 46:4
food. Why should we die before your **e**? Gn 47:15
Why should we die before your **e**, both Gn 47:19
Now the **e** of Israel were dim with age, Gn 48:10
His **e** are darker than wine, and his Gn 49:12
"If now I have found favor in your **e**, Gn 50:4
to the Egyptians before their **e**, Ex 8:26
hand and as a memorial between your **e**, Ex 13:9
your hand or frontlets between your **e**, Ex 13:16
the people of Israel lifted up their **e**, Ex 14:10
God, and do that which is right in his **e**, Ex 15:26
is hidden from the **e** of the assembly, Lv 4:13
and if in his **e** the disease is checked and Lv 13:5
But if in his **e** the itch is unchanged Lv 13:37
do at all close their **e** to that man when Lv 20:4
fever that consume the **e** and make the Lv 26:16
it is hidden from the **e** of her husband, Nm 5:13
and you will serve as **e** for us. Nm 10:31
after your own heart and your own **e**, Nm 15:39
Will you put out the **e** of these men? Nm 16:14
the rock before their **e** to yield its water. Nm 20:8
me as holy in the **e** of the people of Nm 20:12
the LORD opened the **e** of Balaam, Nm 22:31
Balaam lifted up his **e** and saw Israel Nm 24:2
falling down with his **e** uncovered: Nm 24:4
falling down with his **e** uncovered: Nm 24:16
waters before their **e**." (These are the Nm 27:14
as barbs in your **e** and thorns in your Nm 33:55
as he did for you in Egypt before your **e**, Dt 1:30
'Your **e** have seen all that the LORD your Dt 3:21
lift up your **e** westward and northward Dt 3:27
and eastward, and look at it with your **e**, Dt 3:27
Your **e** have seen what the LORD did at Dt 4:3
forget the things that your **e** have seen, Dt 4:9
beware lest you raise your **e** to heaven, Dt 4:19
God did for you in Egypt before your **e**? Dt 4:34
they shall be as frontlets between your **e**. Dt 6:8
and all his household, before our **e**. Dt 6:22
the great trials that your **e** saw, the signs, Dt 7:19
two hands and broke them before your **e**. Dt 9:17
terrifying things that your **e** have seen. Dt 10:21
For your **e** have seen all the great work of Dt 11:7
The **e** of the LORD your God are always Dt 11:12
shall be as frontlets between your **e**. Dt 11:18
doing whatever is right in his own **e**, Dt 12:8
for a bribe blinds the **e** of the wise and Dt 16:19
shed this blood, nor did our **e** see it shed. Dt 21:7
no favor in his **e** because he has found Dt 24:1
ox shall be slaughtered before your **e**, Dt 28:31
while your **e** look on and fail with Dt 28:32
mad by the sights that your **e** see. Dt 28:34
heart and failing **e** and a languishing Dt 28:65
feel, and the sights that your **e** shall see. Dt 28:67
the LORD did before your **e** in the land of Dt 29:2
the great trials that your **e** saw, the signs, Dt 29:3
a heart to understand or **e** to see or ears to Dt 29:4
I have let you see it with your **e**, but you Dt 34:4
by Jericho, he lifted up his **e** and looked, Jos 5:13
Manasseh spoke, it was good in their **e**. Jos 22:30
report was good in the **e** of the people of Jos 22:33
on your sides and thorns in your **e**, Jos 23:13
and your **e** saw what I did in Egypt. Jos 24:7
if it is evil in your **e** to serve the LORD, Jos 24:15
"If now I have found favor in your **e**, Jgs 6:17
"Get her for me, for she is right in my **e**." Jgs 14:3
and she was right in Samson's **e**. Jgs 14:7
and gouged out his **e** and brought him Jgs 16:21
on the Philistines for my two **e**." Jgs 16:28
did what was right in his own **e**. Jgs 17:6
he lifted up his **e** and saw the traveler Jgs 19:17
did what was right in his own **e**. Jgs 21:25
Let your **e** be on the field that they are Ru 2:9
him, "Why have I found favor in your **e**, Ru 2:10
she said, "I have found favor in your **e**, Ru 2:13
favor in your **e**." Then the woman 1 Sm 1:18
spared to weep his **e** out to grieve his 1 Sm 2:33
years old and his **e** were set so that 1 Sm 4:15
they lifted up their **e** and saw the ark, 1 Sm 6:13
you, that I gouge out all your right **e**, 1 Sm 11:2
I taken a bribe to blind my **e** with it? 1 Sm 12:3
that the LORD will do before your **e**. 1 Sm 12:16
his mouth, and his **e** became bright. 1 Sm 14:27
See how my **e** have become bright 1 Sm 14:29
you are little in your own **e**, 1 Sm 15:17
and had beautiful **e** and was 1 Sm 16:12
well that I have found favor in your **e**, 1 Sm 20:3
now, if I have found favor in your **e**, 1 Sm 20:29
this day your **e** have seen how the 1 Sm 24:10
my young men find favor in your **e**, 1 Sm 25:8

life was precious in your **e** this day. 1 Sm 26:21
"If I have found favor in your **e**, 1 Sm 27:5
today before the **e** of his servants' 2 Sm 6:20
this, and I will be abased in your **e**. 2 Sm 6:22
yet this was a small thing in your **e**, 2 Sm 7:19
wives before your **e** and give them 2 Sm 12:11
the watch lifted up his **e** and looked, 2 Sm 13:34
If I find favor in the **e** of the LORD, he 2 Sm 15:25
seemed right in the **e** of Absalom and 2 Sm 17:4
when he lifted up his **e** and looked, 2 Sm 18:24
but your **e** are on the haughty to 2 Sm 22:28
while the **e** of my lord the king still see 2 Sm 24:3
the king, the **e** of all Israel are on you, 1 Kgs 1:20
throne this day, my own **e** seeing it.'" 1 Kgs 1:48
that your **e** may be open night and 1 Kgs 8:29
Let your **e** be open to the plea of your 1 Kgs 8:52
My **e** and my heart will be there for all 1 Kgs 9:3
I came and my own **e** had seen it. 1 Kgs 10:7
is right in my **e** by keeping my 1 Kgs 11:38
for his **e** were dim because of his age. 1 Kgs 14:4
only that which was right in my **e**, 1 Kgs 14:8
was right in the **e** of the LORD and 1 Kgs 15:5
what was right in the **e** of the LORD, 1 Kgs 15:11
himself with a bandage over his **e**. 1 Kgs 20:38
to take the bandage away from his **e**, 1 Kgs 20:41
on his mouth, his **e** on his eyes, 2 Kgs 4:34
on his mouth, his eyes on his **e**, 2 Kgs 4:34
times, and the child opened his **e**. 2 Kgs 4:35
please open his **e** that he may see." So 2 Kgs 6:17
the LORD opened the **e** of the young 2 Kgs 6:17
said, "O LORD, open the **e** of these men, 2 Kgs 6:20
the LORD opened their **e** and they saw, 2 Kgs 6:20
said, "You shall see it with your own **e**, 2 Kgs 7:2
"You shall see it with your own **e**, 2 Kgs 7:19
she painted her **e** and adorned her 2 Kgs 9:30
king. Do whatever is good in your **e**." 2 Kgs 10:5
carrying out what is right in my **e**, 2 Kgs 10:30
what was right in the **e** of the LORD all 2 Kgs 12:2
what was right in the **e** of the LORD, 2 Kgs 14:3
what was right in the **e** of the LORD, 2 Kgs 15:3
what was right in the **e** of the LORD, 2 Kgs 15:34
what was right in the **e** of the LORD his 2 Kgs 16:2
what was right in the **e** of the LORD, 2 Kgs 18:3
hear; open your **e**, O LORD, and see; 2 Kgs 19:16
and lifted your **e** to the heights? 2 Kgs 19:22
was right in the **e** of the LORD and 2 Kgs 22:2
and your **e** shall not see all the 2 Kgs 22:20
the sons of Zedekiah before his **e**, 2 Kgs 25:7
and put out the **e** of Zedekiah and 2 Kgs 25:7
was right in the **e** of all the people. 1 Chr 13:4
this was a small thing in your **e**, 1 Chr 17:17
And David lifted his **e** and saw the 1 Chr 21:16
that your **e** may be open day and 2 Chr 6:20
let your **e** be open and your ears 2 Chr 6:40
Now my **e** will be open and my ears 2 Chr 7:15
My **e** and my heart will be there for 2 Chr 7:16
until I came and my own **e** had seen it. 2 Chr 9:6
good and right in the **e** of the LORD his 2 Chr 14:2
For the **e** of the LORD run to and fro 2 Chr 16:9
what to do, but our **e** are on you." 2 Chr 20:12
what was right in the **e** of the LORD all 2 Chr 24:2
what was right in the **e** of the LORD, 2 Chr 25:2
what was right in the **e** of the LORD, 2 Chr 26:4
was right in the **e** of the LORD 2 Chr 27:2
do what was right in the **e** of the LORD, 2 Chr 28:1
what was right in the **e** of the LORD, 2 Chr 29:2
hissing, as you see with your own **e**. 2 Chr 29:8
what was right in the **e** of the LORD, 2 Chr 34:2
and your **e** shall not see all the 2 Chr 34:28
God may brighten our **e** and grant us a Ezr 9:8
let your ear be attentive and your **e** open, Neh 1:6
winning favor in the **e** of all who saw Est 2:15
the king, and I am pleasing in his **e**, Est 8:5
womb, nor hide trouble from my **e**. Jb 3:10
A form was before my **e**; there was Jb 4:16
while your **e** are on me, I shall be gone. Jb 7:8
Have you **e** of flesh? Do you see as man Jb 10:4
is pure, and I am clean in God's **e**.' Jb 11:4
But the **e** of the wicked will fail; all way Jb 11:20
And do you open your **e** on such a one Jb 14:3
you away, and why do your **e** flash, Jb 15:12
my adversary sharpens his **e** against me. Jb 16:9
their property—the **e** of his children will Jb 17:5
I have become a foreigner in their **e**. Jb 19:15
see for myself, and my **e** shall behold, Jb 19:27
and their descendants before their **e**. Jb 21:8
Let their own **e** see their destruction, Jb 21:20
and his **e** are upon their ways. Jb 24:23
bright, and the stars are not pure in his **e**; Jb 25:5
he opens his **e**, and his wealth is gone. Jb 27:19
It is hidden from the **e** of all living and Jb 28:21
I was **e** to the blind and feet to the lame. Jb 29:15
"I have made a covenant with my **e**; how Jb 31:1
way and my heart has gone after my **e**, Jb 31:7
or have caused the **e** of the widow to fail, Jb 31:16

because he was righteous in his own **e**. Jb 32:1
"For his **e** are on the ways of a man, and Jb 34:21
not withdraw his **e** from the righteous, Jb 36:7
out the prey; his **e** behold it afar off. Jb 39:29
Can one take him by his **e**, or pierce his Jb 40:24
and his **e** are like the eyelids of the Jb 41:18
boastful shall not stand before your **e**; Ps 5:5
His **e** stealthily watch for the helpless; Ps 10:8
the LORD'S throne is in heaven; his **e** see, Ps 11:4
light up my **e**, lest I sleep the sleep of Ps 13:3
in whose **e** a vile person is despised, but Ps 15:4
come! Let your **e** behold the right! Ps 17:2
they set their **e** to cast us to the ground. Ps 17:11
but the haughty **e** you bring down. Ps 18:27
of the LORD is pure, enlightening the **e**; Ps 19:8
My **e** are ever toward the LORD, for he Ps 25:15
For your steadfast love is before my **e**, Ps 26:3
The **e** of the LORD are toward the Ps 34:15
they say, "Aha, Aha! our **e** have seen it!" Ps 35:21
heart; there is no fear of God before his **e**. Ps 36:1
himself in his own **e** that his iniquity Ps 36:2
and the light of my **e**—it also has gone Ps 38:10
whose **e** keep watch on the nations— Ps 66:7
My **e** grow dim with waiting for my God. Ps 69:3
Let their **e** be darkened, so that they Ps 69:23
Their **e** swell out through fatness; their Ps 73:7
known among the nations before our **e**! Ps 79:10
only look with your **e** and see the Ps 91:8
My **e** have seen the downfall of my Ps 92:11
not set before my **e** anything that is Ps 101:3
utters lies shall continue before my **e**. Ps 101:7
but do not speak; **e**, but do not see. Ps 115:5
my soul from death, my **e** from tears, Ps 116:8
LORD'S doing; it is marvelous in our **e**. Ps 118:23
having my **e** fixed on all your Ps 119:6
precepts and fix my **e** on your ways. Ps 119:15
Open my **e**, that I may behold Ps 119:18
Turn my **e** from looking at worthless Ps 119:37
My **e** long for your promise; I ask, Ps 119:82
My **e** long for your salvation and for Ps 119:123
My **e** shed streams of tears, because Ps 119:136
My **e** are awake before the watches of Ps 119:148
I lift up my **e** to the hills. From where Ps 121:1
To you I lift up my **e**, O you who are Ps 123:1
as the **e** of servants look to the hand of Ps 123:2
as the **e** of a maidservant to the hand of Ps 123:2
so our **e** look to the LORD our God, Ps 123:2
lifted up; my **e** are not raised too high; Ps 131:1
not give sleep to my **e** or slumber to my Ps 132:4
not speak; they have **e**, but do not see; Ps 135:16
Your **e** saw my unformed substance; Ps 139:16
But my **e** are toward you, O GOD, my Ps 141:8
The **e** of all look to you, and you give Ps 145:15
the LORD opens the **e** of the blind. The Ps 146:8
Be not wise in your own **e**; fear the LORD, Prv 3:7
Let your **e** look directly forward, and Prv 4:25
man's ways are before the **e** of the LORD, Prv 5:21
Give your **e** no sleep and your eyelids no Prv 6:4
winks with his **e**, signals with his feet, Prv 6:13
haughty **e**, a lying tongue, and hands Prv 6:17
vinegar to the teeth and smoke to the **e**, Prv 10:26
The way of a fool is right in his own **e**, Prv 12:15
The **e** of the LORD are in every place, Prv 15:3
The light of the **e** rejoices the heart, Prv 15:30
the ways of a man are pure in his own **e**, Prv 16:2
Whoever winks his **e** plans dishonest Prv 16:30
a magic stone in the **e** of the one who Prv 17:8
but the **e** of a fool are on the ends of the Prv 17:24
of judgment winnows all evil with his **e**. Prv 20:8
open your **e**, and you will have plenty Prv 20:13
way of a man is right in his own **e**, Prv 21:2
Haughty **e** and a proud heart, the lamp Prv 21:4
his neighbor finds no mercy in his **e**. Prv 21:10
The **e** of the LORD keep watch over Prv 22:12
When your **e** light on it, it is gone, for Prv 23:5
heart, and let your **e** observe my ways. Prv 23:26
without cause? Who has redness of **e**? Prv 23:29
Your **e** will see strange things, and Prv 23:33
of a noble. What your **e** have seen Prv 25:7
to his folly, lest he be wise in his own **e**. Prv 26:5
see a man who is wise in his own **e**? Prv 26:12
wiser in his own **e** than seven men Prv 26:16
and never satisfied are the **e** of man. Prv 27:20
A rich man is wise in his own **e**, but a Prv 28:11
but he who hides his **e** will get many a Prv 28:27
the LORD gives light to the **e** of both. Prv 29:13
clean in their own **e** but are not Prv 30:12
There are those—how lofty are their **e**, Prv 30:13
And whatever my **e** desired I did not Eccl 2:10
The wise person has his **e** in his head, Eccl 2:14
and his **e** are never satisfied with riches, Eccl 4:8
their owner but to see them with his **e**? Eccl 5:11
the sight of the **e** than the wandering of Eccl 6:9
day nor night do one's **e** see sleep, Eccl 8:16
it is pleasant for the **e** to see the sun. Eccl 11:7

of your heart and the sight of your **e**. Eccl 11:9
you are beautiful; your **e** are doves. Sg 1:15
Your **e** are doves behind your veil. Sg 4:1
my heart with one glance of your **e**, Sg 4:9
His **e** are like doves beside streams of Sg 5:12
Turn away your **e** from me, for they Sg 6:5
Your **e** are pools in Heshbon, by the gate Sg 7:4
then I was in his **e** as one who finds Sg 8:10
your hands, I will hide my **e** from you; Is 1:15
the evil of your deeds from before my **e**; Is 1:16
necks, glancing wantonly with their **e**, Is 3:16
and the **e** of the haughty are brought low. Is 5:15
Woe to those who are wise in their own **e**, Is 5:21
for my **e** have seen the King, the LORD of Is 6:5
and their ears heavy, and blind their **e**; Is 6:10
lest they see with their **e**, and hear with Is 6:10
of Assyria and the boastful look in his **e**. Is 10:12
He shall not judge by what his **e** see, or Is 11:3
will be dashed in pieces before their **e**; Is 13:16
the womb; their **e** will not pity children. Is 13:18
and his **e** will look on the Holy One of Is 17:7
and has closed your **e** (the prophets), Is 29:10
gloom and darkness the **e** of the blind Is 29:18
but your **e** shall see your Teacher. Is 30:20
Then the **e** of those who see will not be Is 32:3
and shuts his **e** from looking on Is 33:15
Your **e** will behold the king in his Is 33:17
Your **e** will see Jerusalem, an Is 33:20
Then the **e** of the blind shall be opened, Is 35:5
and hear; open your **e**, O LORD, and see; Is 37:17
voice and lifted your **e** to the heights? Is 37:23
My **e** are weary with looking upward. Is 38:14
Lift up your **e** on high and see: who Is 40:26
to open the **e** that are blind, to bring out Is 42:7
Because you are precious in my **e**, and Is 43:4
out the people who are blind, yet have **e**, Is 43:8
do they discern, for he has shut their **e**, Is 44:18
for I am honored in the **e** of the LORD, Is 49:5
Lift up your **e** around and see; they all Is 49:18
Lift up your **e** to the heavens, and look at Is 51:6
holy arm before the **e** of all the nations, Is 52:10
blind; we grope like those who have no **e**; Is 59:10
Lift up your **e** all around, and see; they all Is 60:4
what was evil in my **e** and chose what I Is 65:12
are forgotten and are hidden from my **e**. Is 65:16
what was evil in my **e** and chose that in Is 66:4
Lift up your **e** to the bare heights, and see! Jer 3:2
gold, that you enlarge your **e** with paint? Jer 4:30
O LORD, do not your **e** look for truth? You Jer 5:3
foolish and senseless people, who have **e**, Jer 5:21
become a den of robbers in your **e**? Jer 7:11
were waters, and my **e** a fountain of tears, Jer 9:1
that our **e** may run down with tears and Jer 9:18
my **e** will weep bitterly and run down Jer 13:17
"Lift up your **e** and see those who come Jer 13:20
their **e** fail because there is no Jer 14:6
'Let my **e** run down with tears night Jer 14:17
place, before your **e** and in your days, Jer 16:9
For my **e** are on all their ways. They are Jer 16:17
is their iniquity concealed from my **e**. Jer 16:17
But you have **e** and heart only for your Jer 22:17
I will set my **e** on them for good, and I Jer 24:6
shall strike them down before your **e**. Jer 29:21
from weeping, and your **e** from tears, Jer 31:16
whose **e** are open to all the ways of the Jer 32:19
right in my **e** by proclaiming liberty, Jer 34:15
sons of Zedekiah at Riblah before his **e**, Jer 39:6
He put out the **e** of Zedekiah and bound Jer 39:7
are left with but a few, as your **e** see us— Jer 42:2
Chaldea before your very **e** for all the Jer 51:24
the sons of Zedekiah before his **e**, Jer 52:10
He put out the **e** of Zedekiah, and Jer 52:11
things I weep; my **e** flow with tears; Lam 1:16
were delightful in our **e** in the tent of Lam 2:4
My **e** are spent with weeping; my Lam 2:11
Give yourself no rest, your **e** no respite! Lam 2:18
my **e** flow with rivers of tears because Lam 3:48
"My **e** will flow without ceasing, Lam 3:49
my **e** cause me grief at the fate of all Lam 3:51
Our **e** failed, ever watching vainly for Lam 4:17
for these things our **e** have grown dim, Lam 5:17
of all four were full of **e** all around. Ezk 1:18
me and over their **e** that go whoring after Ezk 6:9
lift up your **e** now toward the north." So I Ezk 8:5
So I lifted up my **e** toward the north, Ezk 8:5
the city." And he went in before my **e**. Ezk 10:2
wheels were full of **e** all around—the Ezk 10:12
the earth before my **e** as they went out, Ezk 10:19
of a rebellious house, who have **e** to see, Ezk 12:2
he may not see the land with his **e**. Ezk 12:12
mountains or lift up his **e** to the idols of Ezk 18:6
the pledge, lifts up his **e** to the idols, Ezk 18:12
or lift up his **e** to the idols of Ezk 18:15
the detestable things your **e** feast on, Ezk 20:7
the detestable things their **e** feasted on, Ezk 20:8
and their **e** were set on their fathers' Ezk 20:24
and bitter grief, groan before their **e**. Ezk 21:6
not lift up your **e** to them or Ezk 23:27
you bathed yourself, painted your **e**, Ezk 23:40
the delight of your **e** away from you at Ezk 24:16
of your power, the delight of your **e**, Ezk 24:21
the delight of their **e** and their soul's Ezk 24:25
before kings, to feast their **e** on you. Ezk 28:17
and lift up your **e** to your idols and Ezk 33:25
I vindicate my holiness before their **e**. Ezk 36:23
write are in your hand before their **e**, Ezk 37:20
I vindicate my holiness before their **e**. Ezk 38:16
known in the **e** of many nations. Ezk 38:23
to me, "Son of man, look with your **e**, Ezk 40:4
of man, mark well, see with your **e**, Ezk 44:5
Nebuchadnezzar, lifted my **e** to heaven, Dn 4:34
in this horn were **e** like the eyes of a man, Dn 7:8
in this horn were eyes like the **e** of a man, Dn 7:8
the horn that had **e** and a mouth that Dn 7:20
I raised my **e** and saw, and behold, a ram Dn 8:3
had a conspicuous horn between his **e**. Dn 8:5
great horn between his **e** is the first Dn 8:21
Open your **e** and see our desolations, Dn 9:18
I lifted up my **e** and looked, and behold, Dn 10:5
of lightning, his **e** like flaming torches, Dn 10:6
Compassion is hidden from my **e**. Hos 13:14
Is not the food cut off before our **e**, joy and Jl 1:16
and I will fix my **e** upon them for evil Am 9:4
the **e** of the Lord GOD are upon the sinful Am 9:8
be defiled, and let our **e** gaze upon Zion." Mi 4:11
LORD your God?" My **e** will look upon Mi 7:10
You who are of purer **e** than to see evil Hab 1:13
fortunes before your **e**," says the LORD. Zep 3:20
see it now? Is it not as nothing in your **e**? Hg 2:3
And I lifted my **e** and saw, and behold, Zec 1:18
And I lifted my **e** and saw, and behold, a Zec 2:1
Joshua, on a single stone with seven **e**, Zec 3:9
"These seven are the **e** of the LORD, Zec 4:10
Again I lifted my **e** and saw, and behold, Zec 5:1
"Lift your **e** and see what this is that is Zec 5:5
Then I lifted my **e** and saw, and behold, Zec 5:9
Again I lifted my **e** and saw, and behold, Zec 6:1
over them, for now I see with my own **e**. Zec 9:8
house of Judah I will keep my **e** open, Zec 12:4
feet, their **e** will rot in their sockets, Zec 14:12
Your own **e** shall see this, and you shall Mal 1:5
Then he touched their **e**, saying, Mt 9:29
And their **e** were opened. And Jesus Mt 9:30
hear, and their **e** they have closed, Mt 13:15
should see with their **e** and hear with Mt 13:15
But blessed are your **e**, for they see, and Mt 13:16
And when they lifted up their **e**, they saw Mt 17:8
eye than with two **e** to be thrown into Mt 18:9
said to him, "Lord, let our **e** be opened." Mt 20:33
And Jesus in pity touched their **e**, and Mt 20:34
doing, and it is marvelous in our **e**'? Mt 21:42
them sleeping, for their **e** were heavy. Mt 26:43
Having **e** do you not see, and having Mk 8:18
he had spit on his **e** and laid his hands Mk 8:23
Jesus laid his hands on his **e** again; Mk 8:25
and he opened his **e**, his sight was Mk 8:25
eye than with two **e** to be thrown into Mk 9:47
doing, and it is marvelous in our **e**'?" Mk 12:11
sleeping, for their **e** were very heavy, Mk 14:40
for my **e** have seen your salvation Lk 2:30
And the **e** of all in the synagogue were Lk 4:20
And he lifted up his **e** on his disciples, Lk 6:20
"Blessed are the **e** that see what you see! Lk 10:23
he lifted up his **e** and saw Abraham far Lk 16:23
would not even lift up his **e** to heaven, Lk 18:13
But now they are hidden from your **e**. Lk 19:42
But their **e** were kept from recognizing Lk 24:16
And their **e** were opened, and they Lk 24:31
Look, I tell you, lift up your **e**, and see Jn 4:35
Lifting up his **e**, then, and seeing that a Jn 6:5
he anointed the man's **e** with the mud Jn 9:6
to him, "Then how were your **e** opened?" Jn 9:10
mud and anointed my **e** and said to me, Jn 9:11
Jesus made the mud and opened his **e**. Jn 9:14
he said to them, "He put mud on my **e**, Jn 9:15
since he has opened your **e**?" He said, Jn 9:17
know, nor do we know who opened his **e**. Jn 9:21
he do to you? How did he open your **e**?" Jn 9:26
he comes from, and yet he opened my **e**. Jn 9:30
that anyone opened the **e** of a man born Jn 9:32
Can a demon open the **e** of the blind?" Jn 10:21
he who opened the **e** of the blind man Jn 11:37
And Jesus lifted up his **e** and said, Jn 11:41
has blinded their **e** and hardened their Jn 12:40
their heart, lest they see with their **e**, Jn 12:40
these words, he lifted up his **e** to heaven, Jn 17:1
and although his **e** were opened, Acts 9:8
something like scales fell from his **e**, Acts 9:18
"Tabitha, arise." And she opened her **e**, Acts 9:40
to open their **e**, so that they may turn Acts 26:18
hear, and their **e** they have closed; Acts 28:27
should see with their **e** and hear with Acts 28:27
"There is no fear of God before their **e**." Rom 3:18
e that would not see and ears that Rom 11:8
let their **e** be darkened so that they Rom 11:10
Look at what is before your **e**. If 2 Cor 10:7
It was before your **e** that Jesus Christ was Gal 3:1
have gouged out your **e** and given them Gal 4:15
having the **e** of your hearts Eph 1:18
and keep your **e** on those who walk Phil 3:17
and exposed to the **e** of him to whom Heb 4:13
For the **e** of the Lord are on the 1 Pt 3:12
They have **e** full of adultery, insatiable 2 Pt 2:14
heard, which we have seen with our **e**, 1 Jn 1:1
because the darkness has blinded his **e**. 1 Jn 2:11
the desires of the **e** and pride in 1 Jn 2:16
as snow. His **e** were like a flame of fire, Rv 1:14
Son of God, who has **e** like a flame of fire, Rv 2:18
not be seen, and salve to anoint your **e**, Rv 3:18
creatures, full of **e** in front and behind: Rv 4:6
wings, are full of **e** all around and within, Rv 4:8
slain, with seven horns and with seven **e**, Rv 5:6
will wipe away every tear from their **e**." Rv 7:17
His **e** are like a flame of fire, and on his Rv 19:12
He will wipe away every tear from their **e**, Rv 21:4

EYESIGHT (1)
whose **e** had begun to grow dim so that 1 Sm 3:2

EYEWITNESSES (2)
the beginning were **e** and ministers of Lk 1:2
Christ, but we were **e** of his majesty. 2 Pt 1:16

EZBAI (1)
of Carmel, Naarai the son of **E**, 1 Chr 11:37

EZBON (2)
Ziphion, Haggi, Shuni, **E**, Eri, Arodi, Gn 46:16
E, Uzzi, Uzziel, Jerimoth, and Iri, five, 1 Chr 7:7

EZEKIEL (2)
the word of the LORD came to **E** the priest, Ezk 1:3
Thus shall **E** be to you a sign; Ezk 24:24

EZEM (3)
Baalah, Iim, **E**, Jos 15:29
Hazar-shual, Balah, **E**, Jos 19:3
Bilhah, **E**, Tolad, 1 Chr 4:29

EZER (10)
Dishon, **E**, and Dishan; these are the Gn 36:21
These are the sons of **E**: Bilhan, Gn 36:27
Dishon, **E**, and Dishan; these are the Gn 36:30
Anah, Dishon, **E**, and Dishan. 1 Chr 1:38
The sons of **E**: Bilhan, Zaavan, and 1 Chr 1:42
Gedor, and **E** fathered Hushah. 1 Chr 4:4
Shuthelah his son, and **E** and Elead, 1 Chr 7:21
E the chief, Obadiah second, Eliab 1 Chr 12:9
Next to him **E** the son of Jeshua, ruler Neh 3:19
Jehohanan, Malchijah, Elam, and **E**. Neh 12:42

EZION-GEBER (7)
out from Abronah and camped at **E**. Nm 33:35
they set out from **E** and camped in the Nm 33:36
from the Arabah road from Elath and **E**. Dt 2:8
Solomon built a fleet of ships at **E**, 1 Kgs 9:26
go, for the ships were wrecked at **E**. 1 Kgs 22:48
Solomon went to **E** and Eloth on 2 Chr 8:17
and they built the ships in **E**. 2 Chr 20:36

EZRA (25)
king of Persia, **E** the son of Seraiah, Ezr 7:1
this **E** went up from Babylonia. He was a Ezr 7:6
For **E** had set his heart to study the Law Ezr 7:10
King Artaxerxes gave to **E** the priest, Ezr 7:11
king of kings, to **E** the priest, Ezr 7:12
Whatever **E** the priest, the scribe of the Ezr 7:21
E, according to the wisdom of your God Ezr 7:25
While **E** prayed and made confession, Ezr 10:1
Jehiel, of the sons of Elam, addressed **E**: Ezr 10:2
Then **E** arose and made the leading Ezr 10:5
Then **E** withdrew from before the house Ezr 10:6
And **E** the priest stood up and said to Ezr 10:10
E the priest selected men, heads of Ezr 10:16
And they told **E** the scribe to bring the Neh 8:1
So **E** the priest brought the Law before Neh 8:2
And **E** the scribe stood on a wooden Neh 8:4
And **E** opened the book in the sight of Neh 8:5
And **E** blessed the LORD, the great God, Neh 8:6
governor, and **E** the priest and scribe, Neh 8:9
came together to **E** the scribe in order Neh 8:13
and Jeshua: Seraiah, Jeremiah, **E**, Neh 12:1
of **E**, Meshullam; of Amariah, Neh 12:13
of Nehemiah the governor and of **E**, Neh 12:26
and Azariah, **E**, Meshullam, Neh 12:33
And **E** the scribe went before them. Neh 12:36

EZRAH (1)
The sons of **E**: Jether, Mered, Epher, 1 Chr 4:17

EZRAHITE (3)
other men, wiser than Ethan the **E**, 1 Kgs 4:31
Leannoth. A Maskil of Heman the **E**. Ps 88:T
A Maskil of Ethan the **E**. Ps 89:T

EZRI (1)
tilling the soil was **E** the son of 1 Chr 27:26

F

FABRICS (3)
and in purple, crimson, and blue **f**, 2 Chr 2:7
blue, and crimson **f** and fine linen, 2 Chr 2:14
purple and crimson **f** and fine linen, 2 Chr 3:14

FACE (382)
and darkness was over the **f** of the deep. Gn 1:2
God was hovering over the **f** of the waters. Gn 1:2
seed that is on the **f** of all the earth, Gn 1:29
was watering the whole **f** of the ground— Gn 2:6
the sweat of your **f** you shall eat bread, Gn 3:19
So Cain was very angry, and his **f** fell. Gn 4:5
are you angry, and why has your **f** fallen? Gn 4:6
and from your **f** I shall be hidden. Gn 4:14
began to multiply on the **f** of the land and Gn 6:1
I have created from the **f** of the land, Gn 6:7
offspring alive on the **f** of all the earth. Gn 7:3
I will blot out from the **f** of the ground." Gn 7:4
and the ark floated on the **f** of the waters. Gn 7:18
thing that was on the **f** of the ground, Gn 7:23
had subsided from the **f** of the ground. Gn 8:8
were still on the **f** of the whole earth. Gn 8:9
and behold, the **f** of the ground was dry. Gn 8:13
be dispersed over the **f** of the whole Gn 11:4
from there over the **f** of all the earth, Gn 11:8
dispersed them over the **f** of all the earth. Gn 11:9
Then Abram fell on his **f**. And God said Gn 17:3
Abraham fell on his **f** and laughed and Gn 17:17
bowed himself with his **f** to the earth Gn 19:1
and set his **f** toward the hill country of Gn 31:21
of me, and afterward I shall see his **f**. Gn 32:20
saying, "For I have seen God **f** to face, Gn 32:30
saying, "For I have seen God face to **f**, Gn 32:30
For I have seen your **f**, which is like Gn 33:10
face, which is like seeing the **f** of God, Gn 33:10
a prostitute, for she had covered her **f**. Gn 38:15
shall not see my **f** unless your brother is Gn 43:3
man said to us, 'You shall not see my **f**, Gn 43:5
Then he washed his **f** and came out. Gn 43:31
with you, you shall not see my **f** again.' Gn 44:23
see the man's **f** unless our youngest Gn 44:26
I have seen your **f** and know that you Gn 46:30
Joseph, "I never expected to see your **f**; Gn 48:11
bowed himself with his **f** to the earth. Gn 48:12
fell on his father's **f** and wept over him Gn 50:1
the God of Jacob." And Moses hid his **f**, Ex 3:6
and they shall cover the **f** of the land, so Ex 10:5
They covered the **f** of the whole land, so Ex 10:15
take care never to see my **f** again, for on Ex 10:28
on the day you see my **f** you shall die." Ex 10:28
"As you say! I will not see your **f** again." Ex 10:29
there was on the **f** of the wilderness a Ex 16:14
consume them from the **f** of the earth'? Ex 32:12
LORD used to speak to Moses **f** to face, Ex 33:11
LORD used to speak to Moses face to **f**, Ex 33:11
every other people on the **f** of the earth?" Ex 33:16
But," he said, "you cannot see my **f**, for Ex 33:20
my back, but my **f** shall not be seen." Ex 33:23
the skin of his **f** shone because he had Ex 34:29
and behold, the skin of his **f** shone, Ex 34:30
with them, he put a veil over his **f**. Ex 34:33
people of Israel would see the **f** of Moses, Ex 34:35
that the skin of Moses' **f** was shining. Ex 34:35
would put the veil over his **f** again, Ex 34:35
I will set my **f** against that person who Lv 17:10
head and honor the **f** of an old man, Lv 19:32
myself will set my **f** against that man Lv 20:3
then I will set my **f** against that man and Lv 20:5
I will set my **f** against that person and Lv 20:6
one who has a mutilated **f** or a limb too Lv 21:18
I will set my **f** against you, and you Lv 26:17
the LORD make his **f** to shine upon you Nm 6:25
people who were on the **f** of the earth. Nm 12:3
"If her father had but spit in her **f**, Nm 12:14
For you, O LORD, are seen **f** to face, and Nm 14:14
For you, O LORD, are seen face to **f**, and Nm 14:14
When Moses heard it, he fell on his **f**, Nm 16:4
of Egypt. They cover the **f** of the earth, Nm 22:5
Egypt, and it covers the **f** of the earth. Nm 22:11
And he bowed down and fell on his **f**. Nm 22:31
but set his **f** toward the wilderness. Nm 24:1
The LORD spoke with you **f** to face at the Dt 5:4
spoke with you face to **f** at the mountain, Dt 5:4
he destroy you from off the **f** of the earth. Dt 6:15
the peoples who are on the **f** of the earth. Dt 7:6
and repays to their **f** those who hate him, Dt 7:10
hates him. He will repay him to his **f**. Dt 7:10
the peoples who are on the **f** of the earth. Dt 14:2
his sandal off his foot and spit in his **f**. Dt 25:9
donkey shall be seized before your **f**, Dt 28:31
forsake them and hide my **f** from them, Dt 31:17
will surely hide my **f** in that day Dt 31:18
he said, 'I will hide my **f** from them; Dt 32:20
Moses, whom the LORD knew **f** to face, Dt 34:10
Moses, whom the LORD knew face to **f**, Dt 34:10
And Joshua fell on his **f** to the earth and Jos 5:14
to the earth on his **f** before the ark of the Jos 7:6
"Get up! Why have you fallen on your **f**? Jos 7:10
have seen the angel of the LORD **f** to face." Jgs 6:22
have seen the angel of the LORD face to **f**." Jgs 6:22
Then she fell on her **f**, bowing to the Ru 2:10
and ate, and her **f** was no longer sad. 1 Sm 1:18
Dagon had fallen **f** downward on the 1 Sm 5:3
Dagon had fallen **f** downward on the 1 Sm 5:4
and he fell on his **f** to the ground. 1 Sm 17:49
of David from the **f** of the earth." 1 Sm 20:15
and fell on his **f** to the ground and 1 Sm 20:41
David bowed with his **f** to the earth 1 Sm 24:8
before David on her **f** and bowed to 1 Sm 25:23
and bowed with her **f** to the ground 1 Sm 25:41
he bowed with his **f** to the ground 1 Sm 28:14
I lift up my **f** to your brother Joab?" 2 Sm 2:22
shall not see my **f** unless you first 2 Sm 3:13
when you come to see my **f**." 2 Sm 3:13
and fell on his **f** and paid homage. 2 Sm 9:6
she fell on her **f** to the ground and 2 Sm 14:4
nor remnant on the **f** of the earth." 2 Sm 14:7
Joab fell on his **f** to the ground and 2 Sm 14:22
bowed himself on his **f** to the ground 2 Sm 14:33
battle spread over the **f** of all the 2 Sm 18:8
the king with his **f** to the earth and 2 Sm 18:28
The king covered his **f**, and the king 2 Sm 19:4
And David sought the **f** of the LORD. 2 Sm 21:1
to the king with his **f** to the ground. 2 Sm 24:20
the king, with his **f** to the ground. 1 Kgs 1:23
bowed with her **f** to the ground 1 Kgs 1:31
to destroy it from the **f** of the earth. 1 Kgs 13:34
him and fell on his **f** and said, 1 Kgs 18:7
and put his **f** between his knees. 1 Kgs 18:42
he wrapped his **f** in his cloak and 1 Kgs 19:13
and turned away his **f** and would eat 1 Kgs 21:4
lay my staff on the **f** of the child." 2 Kgs 4:29
and laid the staff on the **f** of the child, 2 Kgs 4:31
it in water and spread it over his **f**, 2 Kgs 8:15
he lifted up his **f** to the window and 2 Kgs 9:32
be as dung on the **f** of the field in the 2 Kgs 9:37
when Hazael set his **f** to go up 2 Kgs 12:17
let us look one another in the **f**." 2 Kgs 14:8
Hezekiah turned his **f** to the wall 2 Kgs 20:2
to David with his **f** to the ground. 1 Chr 21:21
not turn away the **f** of your anointed 2 Chr 6:42
pray and seek my **f** and turn from 2 Chr 7:14
afraid and set his **f** to seek the LORD, 2 Chr 20:3
his head with his **f** to the ground, 2 Chr 20:18
let us look one another in the **f**." 2 Chr 25:17
will not turn away his **f** from you, 2 Chr 30:9
returned with shame of **f** to his own 2 Chr 32:21
ashamed and blush to lift my **f** to you, Ezr 9:6
the king said to me, "Why is your **f** sad, Neh 2:2
Why should not my **f** be sad, when the Neh 2:3
Persia and Media, who saw the king's **f**, Est 1:14
of the king, they covered Haman's **f**. Est 7:8
he has, and he will curse you to your **f**." Jb 1:11
his flesh, and he will curse you to your **f**." Jb 2:5
A spirit glided past my **f**; the hair of my Jb 4:15
to look at me, for I will not lie to your **f**. Jb 6:28
my complaint, I will put off my sad **f**, Jb 9:27
you will lift up your **f** without blemish; Jb 11:15
in him; yet I will argue my ways to his **f**. Jb 13:15
then I will not hide myself from your **f**: Jb 13:20
do you hide your **f** and count me as Jb 13:24
he has covered his **f** with his fat and Jb 15:27
risen up against me; it testifies to my **f**. Jb 16:8
My **f** is red with weeping, and on my Jb 16:16
Who declares his way to his **f**, and who Jb 21:31
the Almighty and lift up your **f** to God. Jb 22:26
because thick darkness covers my **f**. Jb 23:17
'No eye will see me'; and he veils his **f**. Jb 24:15
say, 'Swift are they on the **f** of the waters; Jb 24:18
He covers the **f** of the full moon and Jb 26:9
a circle on the **f** of the waters at Jb 26:10
and the light of my **f** they did not cast Jb 29:24
he sees his **f** with a shout of joy, and he Jb 33:26
When he hides his **f**, who can behold Jb 34:29
them on the **f** of the habitable Jb 37:12
like stone, and the **f** of the deep is frozen. Jb 38:30
Who can open the doors of his **f**? Jb 41:14
Lift up the light of your **f** upon us, O Ps 4:6
In the pride of his **f** the wicked does not Ps 10:4
"God has forgotten, he has hidden his **f**, Ps 10:11
deeds; the upright shall behold his **f**. Ps 11:7
How long will you hide your **f** from me? Ps 13:1
I shall behold your **f** in righteousness; Ps 17:15
and he has not hidden his **f** from him, Ps 22:24
him, who seek the **f** of the God of Jacob. Ps 24:6
said, "Seek my **f**." My heart says to you, Ps 27:8
my face." My heart says to you, "Your **f**, Ps 27:8
Hide not your **f** from me. Turn not your Ps 27:9
mountain stand strong; you hid your **f**; Ps 30:7
Make your **f** shine on your servant; Ps 31:16
The **f** of the LORD is against those who Ps 34:16
and your arm, and the light of your **f**, Ps 44:3
before me, and shame has covered my **f** Ps 44:15
Why do you hide your **f**? Why do you Ps 44:24
Hide your **f** from my sins, and blot out Ps 51:9
bless us and make his **f** to shine upon us, Ps 67:1
that dishonor has covered my **f**. Ps 69:7
Hide not your **f** from your servant; for I Ps 69:17
let your **f** shine, that we may be saved! Ps 80:3
let your **f** shine, that we may be saved! Ps 80:7
may they perish at the rebuke of your **f**! Ps 80:16
let your **f** shine, that we may be saved! Ps 80:19
O God; look on the **f** of your anointed! Ps 84:9
Why do you hide your **f** from me? Ps 88:14
who walk, O LORD, in the light of your **f**, Ps 89:15
Do not hide your **f** from me in the day Ps 102:2
oil to make his **f** shine and bread to Ps 104:15
When you hide your **f**, they are Ps 104:29
and you renew the **f** of the ground. Ps 104:30
Make your **f** shine upon your Ps 119:135
not turn away the **f** of your anointed Ps 132:10
Hide not your **f** from me, lest I be like Ps 143:7
him, and with bold **f** she says to him, Prv 7:13
he drew a circle on the **f** of the deep, Prv 8:27
A glad heart makes a cheerful **f**, but Prv 15:13
In the light of a king's **f** there is life, Prv 16:15
discerning sets his **f** toward wisdom, Prv 17:24
A wicked man puts on a bold **f**, but Prv 21:29
As in water **f** reflects face, so the heart Prv 27:19
As in water face reflects **f**, so the heart Prv 27:19
Many seek the **f** of a ruler, but it is Prv 29:26
for by sadness of **f** the heart is made Eccl 7:3
A man's wisdom makes his **f** shine, and Eccl 8:1
and the hardness of his **f** is changed. Eccl 8:1
the crannies of the cliff, let me see your **f**, Sg 2:14
your voice is sweet, and your **f** is lovely. Sg 2:14
by grinding the **f** of the poor?" declares Is 3:15
with two he covered his **f**, and with two he Is 6:2
who is hiding his **f** from the house of Is 8:17
and fill the **f** of the world with cities." Is 14:21
of the world on the **f** of the earth. Is 23:17
ashamed, no more shall his **f** grow pale. Is 29:22
Then Hezekiah turned his **f** to the wall Is 38:2
I hid not my **f** from disgrace and spitting. Is 50:6
therefore I have set my **f** like a flint, and I Is 50:7
anger for a moment I hid my **f** from you, Is 54:8
I struck him; I hid my **f** and was angry, Is 57:17
sins have hidden his **f** from you so that Is 59:2
for you have hidden your **f** from us, and Is 64:7
who provoke me to my **f** continually, Is 65:3
turned their back to me, and not their **f**. Jer 2:27
will lift up your skirts over your **f**, Jer 13:26
out of my lips; it was before your **f**. Jer 17:16
I will show them my back, not my **f**, in Jer 18:17
For I have set my **f** against this city for Jer 21:10
the world that are on the **f** of the earth. Jer 25:26
will remove you from the **f** of the earth. Jer 28:16
in labor? Why has every **f** turned pale? Jer 30:6
shall speak with him **f** to face and see Jer 32:4
speak with him face to **f** and see him eye Jer 32:4
turned to me their back and not their **f**. Jer 32:33
I have hidden my **f** from this city Jer 33:5
eye to eye and speak with him **f** to face. Jer 34:3
eye to eye and speak with him face to **f**. Jer 34:3
I will set my **f** against you for harm, Jer 44:11
Why are your mighty ones **f** down? Jer 46:15
dishonor has covered our **f**, for Jer 51:51
she herself groans and turns her **f** away. Lam 1:8
his right hand in the **f** of the enemy; Lam 2:3
Now their **f** is blacker than soot; they Lam 4:8
of their faces, each had a human **f**. Ezk 1:10
The four had the **f** of a lion on the right Ezk 1:10
the four had the **f** of an ox on the left Ezk 1:10
side, and the four had the **f** of an eagle. Ezk 1:10
And when I saw it, I fell on my **f**, and I Ezk 1:28
I have made your **f** as hard as their faces, Ezk 3:8
by the Chebar canal, and I fell on my **f**. Ezk 3:23
and set your **f** toward it, and let it be in a Ezk 4:3
you shall set your **f** toward the siege of Ezk 4:7
set your **f** toward the mountains of Ezk 6:2
I will turn my **f** from them, and they Ezk 7:22
and I was left alone, I fell upon my **f**, Ezk 9:8
the first **f** was the face of the cherub, Ezk 10:14
the first face was the **f** of the cherub, Ezk 10:14

FACED (15)

FACES (75)

FACING (29)

FACT (11)

FACTIONS (1)

FACTS (2)

FADE (3)

FADED (5)

FADES (4)

FADING (2)

FAIL (31)

in order that we might be justified by **f**. Gal 3:24
But now that **f** has come, we are no Gal 3:25
Jesus you are all sons of God, through **f**. Gal 3:26
For through the Spirit, by **f**, we ourselves Gal 5:5
but only **f** working through love. Gal 5:6
to those who are of the household of **f**. Gal 6:10
I have heard of your **f** in the Lord Jesus Eph 1:15
by grace you have been saved through **f**. Eph 2:8
with confidence through our **f** in him. Eph 3:12
in your hearts through **f**—that you, Eph 3:17
one Lord, one **f**, one baptism, Eph 4:5
the unity of the **f** and of the knowledge Eph 4:13
circumstances take up the shield of **f**, Eph 6:16
be to the brothers, and love with **f**, Eph 6:23
all, for your progress and joy in the **f**, Phil 1:25
side by side for the **f** of the gospel, Phil 1:27
upon the sacrificial offering of your **f**, Phil 2:17
that which comes through **f** in Christ, Phil 3:9
from God that depends on **f**— Phil 3:9
we heard of your **f** in Christ Jesus and Col 1:4
if indeed you continue in the **f**, stable Col 1:23
and the firmness of your **f** in Christ. Col 2:5
built up in him and established in the **f**, Col 2:7
with him through **f** in the powerful Col 2:12
Father your work of **f** and labor of 1 Thes 1:3
but your **f** in God has gone forth 1 Thes 1:8
to establish and exhort you in your **f**, 1 Thes 3:2
no longer, I sent to learn about your **f**, 1 Thes 3:5
good news of your **f** and love and 1 Thes 3:6
comforted about you through your **f**. 1 Thes 3:7
supply what is lacking in your **f**? 1 Thes 3:10
put on the breastplate of **f** and love, 1 Thes 5:8
because your **f** is growing 2 Thes 1:3
your steadfastness and **f** in all your 2 Thes 1:4
and every work of **f** by his power, 2 Thes 1:11
and evil men. For not all have **f**. 2 Thes 3:2
To Timothy, my true child in the **f**: 1 Tm 1:2
the stewardship from God that is by **f**. 1 Tm 1:4
and a good conscience and a sincere **f**. 1 Tm 1:5
for me with the **f** and love that are 1 Tm 1:14
holding **f** and a good conscience. By 1 Tm 1:19
some have made shipwreck of their **f**, 1 Tm 1:19
a teacher of the Gentiles in **f** and truth. 1 Tm 2:7
if they continue in **f** and love and 1 Tm 2:15
the mystery of the **f** with a clear 1 Tm 3:9
great confidence in the **f** that is in 1 Tm 3:13
depart from the **f** by devoting 1 Tm 4:1
in the words of the **f** and of the good 1 Tm 4:6
in speech, in conduct, in love, in **f**, 1 Tm 4:12
he has denied the **f** and is worse than 1 Tm 5:8
for having abandoned their former **f**. 1 Tm 5:12
away from the **f** and pierced 1 Tm 6:10
righteousness, godliness, **f**, love, 1 Tm 6:11
Fight the good fight of the **f**. Take 1 Tm 6:12
it some have swerved from the **f**. 1 Tm 6:21
I am reminded of your sincere **f**, a faith 2 Tm 1:5
a **f** that dwelt first in your 2 Tm 1:5
in the **f** and love that are in Christ 2 Tm 1:13
They are upsetting the **f** of some. 2 Tm 2:18
and pursue righteousness, **f**, love, 2 Tm 2:22
mind and disqualified regarding the **f**. 2 Tm 3:8
my conduct, my aim in life, my **f**, 2 Tm 3:10
for salvation through **f** in Christ 2 Tm 3:15
finished the race, I have kept the **f**. 2 Tm 4:7
for the sake of the **f** of God's elect and their Ti 1:1
To Titus, my true child in a common **f**: Ti 1:4
sharply, that they may be sound in the **f**, Ti 1:13
dignified, self-controlled, sound in **f**, Ti 2:2
not pilfering, but showing all good **f**, so Ti 2:10
to you. Greet those who love us in the **f**. Ti 3:15
love and of the **f** that you have toward Phlm 1:5
sharing of your **f** may become Phlm 1:6
were not united by **f** with those who Heb 4:2
from dead works and of **f** toward God, Heb 6:1
those who through **f** and patience Heb 6:12
a true heart in full assurance of **f**, Heb 10:22
but my righteous one shall live by **f**, Heb 10:38
of those who have **f** and preserve their Heb 10:39
Now **f** is the assurance of things hoped Heb 11:1
By **f** we understand that the universe Heb 11:3
By **f** Abel offered to God a more Heb 11:4
And through his **f**, though he died, he Heb 11:4
By **f** Enoch was taken up so that he Heb 11:5
And without **f** it is impossible to please Heb 11:6
By **f** Noah, being warned by God Heb 11:7
of the righteousness that comes by **f**. Heb 11:7
By **f** Abraham obeyed when he was Heb 11:8
By **f** he went to live in the land of Heb 11:9
By **f** Sarah herself received power to Heb 11:11
These all died in **f**, not having Heb 11:13
By **f** Abraham, when he was tested, Heb 11:17
By **f** Isaac invoked future blessings on Heb 11:20
By **f** Jacob, when dying, blessed each Heb 11:21
By **f** Joseph, at the end of his life, made Heb 11:22
By **f** Moses, when he was born, was Heb 11:23
By **f** Moses, when he was grown up, Heb 11:24
By **f** he left Egypt, not being afraid of Heb 11:27
By **f** he kept the Passover and Heb 11:28
By **f** the people crossed the Red Sea as Heb 11:29
By **f** the walls of Jericho fell down after Heb 11:30
By **f** Rahab the prostitute did not Heb 11:31
who through **f** conquered kingdoms, Heb 11:33
though commended through their **f**, Heb 11:39
Jesus, the founder and perfecter of our **f**, Heb 12:2
of their way of life, and imitate their **f**. Heb 13:7
testing of your **f** produces steadfastness. Jas 1:3
But let him ask in **f**, with no doubting, for Jas 1:6
as you hold the **f** in our Lord Jesus Jas 2:1
world to be rich in **f** and heirs of the Jas 2:5
someone says he has **f** but does not have Jas 2:14
not have works? Can that **f** save him? Jas 2:14
So also **f** by itself, if it does not have Jas 2:17
"You have **f** and I have works." Show me Jas 2:18
works." Show me your **f** apart from your Jas 2:18
and I will show you my **f** by my works. Jas 2:18
that **f** apart from works is useless? Jas 2:20
You see that **f** was active along with his Jas 2:22
and **f** was completed by his works; Jas 2:22
is justified by works and not by **f** alone. Jas 2:24
dead, so also **f** apart from works is dead. Jas 2:26
And the prayer of **f** will save the one who Jas 5:15
being guarded through **f** for a salvation 1 Pt 1:5
genuineness of your **f**—more precious 1 Pt 1:7
obtaining the outcome of your **f**, the 1 Pt 1:9
so that your **f** and hope are in God. 1 Pt 1:21
Resist him, firm in your **f**, knowing that 1 Pt 5:9
who have obtained a **f** of equal standing 2 Pt 1:1
effort to supplement your **f** with virtue, 2 Pt 1:5
that has overcome the world—our **f**. 1 Jn 5:4
to contend for the **f** that was once for Jude 1:3
yourselves up in your most holy **f**; Jude 1:20
you did not deny my **f** even in the days of Rv 2:13
your love and **f** and service and patient Rv 2:19
for the endurance and **f** of the saints. Rv 13:10
of God and their **f** in Jesus. Rv 14:12

FAITHFUL (82)

servant Moses. He is **f** in all my house. Nm 12:7
the **f** God who keeps covenant and Dt 7:9
with Deborah, and Issachar **f** to Barak; Jgs 5:15
"He will guard the feet of his **f** ones, but 1 Sm 2:9
I will raise up for myself a **f** priest, 1 Sm 2:35
all your servants is so **f** as David, 1 Sm 22:14
who are peaceable and **f** in Israel. 2 Sm 20:19
for they were **f** in keeping 2 Chr 31:18
good and right and **f** before the LORD 2 Chr 31:20
he was a more **f** and God-fearing man Neh 7:2
You found his heart **f** before you, and Neh 9:8
for the **f** have vanished from among the Ps 12:1
you have redeemed me, O LORD, **f** God. Ps 31:5
LORD preserves the **f** but abundantly Ps 31:23
"Gather to me my **f** ones, who made a Ps 50:5
steadfast, whose spirit was not **f** to God. Ps 78:8
him; they were not **f** to his covenant. Ps 78:37
the flesh of your **f** to the beasts of the Ps 79:2
forever, a **f** witness in the skies." Selah Ps 89:37
will look with favor on the **f** in the land, Ps 101:6
The works of his hands are **f** and just; Ps 111:7
[The LORD is **f** in all his words and Ps 145:13
trouble, but a **f** envoy brings healing. Prv 13:17
A **f** witness does not lie, but a false Prv 14:5
love, but a **f** man who can find? Prv 20:6
of harvest is a **f** messenger to those Prv 25:13
F are the wounds of a friend; profuse are Prv 27:6
A **f** man will abound with blessings, Prv 28:20
How the **f** city has become a whore, she Is 1:21
the city of righteousness, the **f** city." Is 1:26
things, plans formed of old, **f** and sure. Is 25:1
because of the LORD, who is **f**, the Holy Is 49:7
LORD be a true and **f** witness against us if Jer 42:5
complaint or any fault, because he was **f**, Dn 6:4
with God and is **f** to the Holy One. Hos 11:12
and Jerusalem shall be called the **f** city, Zec 8:3
"Who then is the **f** and wise servant, Mt 24:45
to him, 'Well done, good and **f** servant. Mt 25:21
servant. You have been **f** over a little; Mt 25:21
to him, 'Well done, good and **f** servant. Mt 25:23
servant. You have been **f** over a little; Mt 25:23
"Who then is the **f** and wise manager, Lk 12:42
"One who is **f** in a very little is also Lk 16:10
in a very little is also **f** in much, Lk 16:10
you have not been **f** in the unrighteous Lk 16:11
if you have not been **f** in that which is Lk 16:12
Because you have been **f** in a very little, Lk 19:17
them all to remain **f** to the Lord with Acts 11:23
have judged me to be **f** to the Lord, Acts 16:15
God is **f**, by whom you were called into 1 Cor 1:9
my beloved and **f** child in the Lord, 1 Cor 4:17
God is **f**, and he will not let you be 1 Cor 10:13
As surely as God is **f**, our word to you 2 Cor 1:18
are in Ephesus, and are **f** in Christ Jesus: Eph 1:1
beloved brother and **f** minister in the Eph 6:21
To the saints and **f** brothers in Christ at Col 1:2
He is a **f** minister of Christ on your Col 1:7
beloved brother and **f** minister and Col 4:7
Onesimus, our **f** and beloved brother, Col 4:9
He who calls you is **f**; he will surely 1 Thes 5:24
But the Lord is **f**. He will establish 2 Thes 3:3
our Lord, because he judged me **f**, 1 Tm 1:12
but sober-minded, **f** in all things. 1 Tm 3:11
witnesses entrust to **f** men who will 2 Tm 2:2
he remains **f**—for he cannot deny 2 Tm 2:13
become a merciful and **f** high priest in Heb 2:17
who was **f** to him who appointed him, Heb 3:2
as Moses also was **f** in all God's house. Heb 3:2
Now Moses was **f** in all God's house as a Heb 3:5
but Christ is **f** over God's house as a son. Heb 3:6
wavering, for he who promised is **f**. Heb 10:23
she considered him **f** who had Heb 11:11
their souls to a **f** Creator while doing 1 Pt 4:19
Silvanus, a **f** brother as I regard him, 1 Pt 5:12
he is **f** and just to forgive us our sins and 1 Jn 1:9
it is a **f** thing you do in all your efforts 3 Jn 1:5
and from Jesus Christ the **f** witness, the Rv 1:5
Be **f** unto death, and I will give you the Rv 2:10
even in the days of Antipas my **f** witness, Rv 2:13
of the Amen, the **f** and true witness, Rv 3:14
with him are called and chosen and **f**." Rv 17:14
one sitting on it is called **F** and True, Rv 19:11

FAITHFULLY (13)

"And if you **f** obey the voice of the LORD Dt 28:1
land we will deal kindly and **f** with you." Jos 2:14
LORD and serve him **f** with all your 1 Sm 12:24
And they **f** brought in the 2 Chr 31:12
and Shecaniah were **f** assisting him 2 Chr 31:15
And the men did the work **f**. Over 2 Chr 34:12
for you have dealt **f** and we have acted Neh 9:33
but those who act **f** are his delight. Prv 12:22
If a king **f** judges the poor, his throne Prv 29:14
not quench; he will **f** bring forth justice. Is 42:3
I will **f** give them their recompense, and I Is 61:8
who has my word speak my word **f**. Jer 23:28
my rules by acting **f**—he is righteous; Ezk 18:9

FAITHFULNESS (76)

love and his **f** toward my master. Gn 24:27
show steadfast love and **f** to my master, Gn 24:49
love and all the **f** that you have shown Gn 32:10
and abounding in steadfast love and **f**, Ex 34:6
justice. A God of **f** and without iniquity, Dt 32:4
generation, children in whom is no **f**. Dt 32:20
and serve him in sincerity and in **f**. Jos 24:14
man for his righteousness and his **f**, 1 Sm 26:23
LORD show steadfast love and **f** to you. 2 Sm 2:6
show steadfast love and **f** to you." 2 Sm 15:20
walk before me in **f** with all their heart 1 Kgs 2:4
because he walked before you in **f**, 1 Kgs 3:6
walked before you in **f** and with a 2 Kgs 20:3
shall do in the fear of the LORD, in **f**, 2 Chr 19:9
After these things and these acts of **f**, 2 Chr 32:1
of the LORD are steadfast love and **f**, Ps 25:10
is before my eyes, and I walk in your **f**. Ps 26:3
the dust praise you? Will it tell of your **f**? Ps 30:9
is upright, and all his work is done in **f**. Ps 33:4
to the heavens, your **f** to the clouds. Ps 36:5
do good; dwell in the land and befriend **f**. Ps 37:3
spoken of your **f** and your salvation; Ps 40:10
steadfast love and your **f** from the great Ps 40:10
love and your **f** will ever preserve Ps 40:11
enemies; in your **f** put an end to them. Ps 54:5
will send out his steadfast love and his **f**! Ps 57:3
to the heavens, your **f** to the clouds. Ps 57:10
appoint steadfast love and **f** to watch over Ps 61:7
love answer me in your saving **f**. Ps 69:13
also praise you with the harp for your **f**, Ps 71:22
Steadfast love and **f** meet; righteousness Ps 85:10
F springs up from the ground, and Ps 85:11
and abounding in steadfast love and **f**. Ps 86:15
in the grave, or your **f** in Abaddon? Ps 88:11
make known your **f** to all generations. Ps 89:1
in the heavens you will establish your **f**." Ps 89:2
your **f** in the assembly of the holy ones! Ps 89:5
are, O LORD, with your **f** all around you? Ps 89:8
steadfast love and **f** go before you. Ps 89:14
My **f** and my steadfast love shall be Ps 89:24
my steadfast love or be false to my **f**. Ps 89:33
which by your **f** you swore to David? Ps 89:49
find refuge; his **f** is a shield and buckler. Ps 91:4
love in the morning, and your **f** by night, Ps 92:2
righteousness, and the peoples in his **f**. Ps 96:13
his steadfast love and **f** to the house of Ps 98:3
forever, and his **f** to all generations. Ps 100:5
heavens; your **f** reaches to the clouds. Ps 108:4
to be performed with **f** and uprightness. Ps 111:8
sake of your steadfast love and your **f**! Ps 115:1
us, and the **f** of the LORD endures forever. Ps 117:2

I have chosen the way of **f**; I set your Ps 119:30
and that in **f** you have afflicted me. Ps 119:75
Your **f** endures to all generations; you Ps 119:90
in righteousness and in all **f**. Ps 119:138
name for your steadfast love and your **f**, Ps 138:2
pleas for mercy! In your **f** answer me, Ps 143:1
Let not steadfast love and **f** forsake you; Prv 3:3
devise good meet steadfast love and **f**. Prv 14:22
steadfast love and **f** iniquity is atoned Prv 16:6
Steadfast love and **f** preserve the king, Prv 20:28
belt of his waist, and **f** the belt of his loins. Is 11:5
and on it will sit in **f** in the tent of David Is 16:5
walked before you in **f** and with a whole Is 38:3
go down to the pit do not hope for your **f**. Is 38:18
makes known to the children your **f**. Is 38:19
therefore I have continued my **f** to you. Jer 31:3
and I will plant them in this land in **f**, Jer 32:41
are new every morning; great is your **f**. Lam 3:23
I will betroth you to me in **f**. And you Hos 2:20
the land. There is no **f** or steadfast love, Hos 4:1
You will show **f** to Jacob and steadfast Mi 7:20
be their God, in **f** and in righteousness." Zec 8:8
of the law: justice and mercy and **f**. Mt 23:23
their faithlessness nullify the **f** of God? Rom 3:3
peace, patience, kindness, goodness, **f**, Gal 5:22

FAITHLESS (23)
he became yet more **f** to the LORD— 2 Chr 28:22
in his reign when he was **f**, 2 Chr 29:19
who were **f** to the LORD God of their 2 Chr 30:7
I look at the **f** with disgust, because Ps 119:158
"Have you seen what she did, that **f** one, Jer 3:6
saw that for all the adulteries of that **f** one, Jer 3:8
"**F** Israel has shown herself more Jer 3:11
the north, and say, "'Return, **f** Israel, Jer 3:12
Return, O **f** children, declares the LORD; Jer 3:14
"Return, O **f** sons; I will heal your Jer 3:22
How long will you waver, O **f** daughter? Jer 31:22
you boast of your valleys, O **f** daughter, Jer 49:4
Why then are we **f** to one another, Mal 2:10
Judah has been **f**, and abomination Mal 2:11
your youth, to whom you have been **f**, Mal 2:14
let none of you be **f** to the wife of your Mal 2:15
in your spirit, and do not be **f**." Mal 2:16
answered, "O **f** and twisted generation, Mt 17:17
And he answered them, "O **f** generation, Mk 9:19
answered, "O **f** and twisted generation, Lk 9:41
foolish, **f**, heartless, ruthless. Rom 1:31
if we are **f**, he remains faithful—for 2 Tm 2:13
But as for the cowardly, the **f**, the Rv 21:8

FAITHLESSLY (4)
a land sins against me by acting **f**, Ezk 14:13
desolate, because they have acted **f**, Ezk 15:8
They have dealt **f** with the LORD; for they Hos 5:7
the covenant; there they dealt **f** with me. Hos 6:7

FAITHLESSNESS (7)
forty years and shall suffer for your **f**, Nm 14:33
entreaty, and all his sin and his **f**, 2 Chr 33:19
And in this **f** the hand of the officials and Ezr 9:2
because of the **f** of the returned exiles, Ezr 9:4
he was mourning over the **f** of the exiles. Ezr 10:6
I will heal your **f**." "Behold, we come to Jer 3:22
Does their **f** nullify the faithfulness of Rom 3:3

FALCON (2)
the kite, the **f** of any kind, Lv 11:14
the kite, the **f** of any kind; Dt 14:13

FALCON'S (1)
prey knows, and the **f** eye has not seen it. Jb 28:7

FALL (221)
caused a deep sleep to **f** upon the man, Gn 2:21
may assault us and **f** upon us to make Gn 43:18
lest he **f** upon us with pestilence or with Ex 5:3
hand of the LORD will **f** with a very severe Ex 9:3
I will cause very heavy hail to **f**, Ex 9:18
Terror and dread **f** upon them; because Ex 15:16
him, but God let him **f** into his hand, Ex 21:13
You shall not **f** in with the many to do Ex 23:2
lest the land **f** into prostitution and the Lv 19:29
and they shall **f** before you by the sword. Lv 26:7
and your enemies shall **f** before you by Lv 26:8
and they shall **f** when none pursues. Lv 26:36
makes your thigh **f** away and your Nm 5:21
womb swell and your thigh **f** away.' Nm 5:22
shall swell, and her thigh shall **f** away, Nm 5:27
the sea and let them **f** beside the camp, Nm 11:31
us into this land, to **f** by the sword? Nm 14:3
dead bodies shall **f** in this wilderness, Nm 14:29
dead bodies shall **f** in this wilderness. Nm 14:32
you, and you shall **f** by the sword. Nm 14:43
is the land that shall **f** to you for an Nm 34:2
your house, if anyone should **f** from it. Dt 22:8
and the wall of the city will **f** down flat, Jos 6:5
said, "Rise yourself and **f** upon us, Jgs 8:21
now die of thirst and **f** into the hands of Jgs 15:18
us, lest angry fellows **f** upon you, Jgs 18:25
let none of his words **f** to the ground. 1 Sm 3:19
one hair of his head **f** to the ground, 1 Sm 14:45
to make David **f** by the hand 1 Sm 18:25
let not my blood **f** to the earth away 1 Sm 26:20
May it **f** upon the head of Joab and 2 Sm 3:29
of your son shall **f** to the ground." 2 Sm 14:11
some of the people **f** at the first attack, 2 Sm 17:9
Let us **f** into the hand of the LORD, for 2 Sm 24:14
but let me not **f** into the hand of 2 Sm 24:14
one of his hairs shall **f** to the earth, 1 Kgs 1:52
may go up and **f** at Ramoth-gilead?' 1 Kgs 22:20
"Where did it **f**?" When he showed 2 Kgs 6:6
then that there shall **f** to the earth 2 Kgs 10:10
you provoke trouble so that you **f**, 2 Kgs 14:10
and I will make him **f** by the sword in 2 Kgs 19:7
Let me **f** into the hand of the LORD, 1 Chr 21:13
but do not let me **f** into the hand of 1 Chr 21:13
may go up and **f** at Ramoth-gilead?' 2 Chr 18:19
you provoke trouble so that you **f**, 2 Chr 25:19
before whom you have begun to **f**, Est 6:13
him but will surely **f** before him." Est 6:13
Purim should never **f** into disuse Est 9:28
you, and the dread of him **f** upon you? Jb 13:11
my shoulder blade **f** from my shoulder, Jb 31:22
For to the snow he says, '**F** on the earth,' Jb 37:6
O God; let them **f** by their own counsels; Ps 5:10
crushed, sink down, and **f** by his might. Ps 10:10
They collapse and **f**, but we rise and Ps 20:8
and foes, it is they who stumble and **f**. Ps 27:2
him; let him **f** into it—to his destruction! Ps 35:8
though he **f**, he shall not be cast Ps 37:24
For I am ready to **f**, and my pain is ever Ps 38:17
king's enemies; the peoples **f** under you. Ps 45:5
kings there, let snow **f** on Zalmon. Ps 68:14
May all kings **f** down before him, all Ps 72:11
places; you make them **f** to ruin. Ps 73:18
he let them **f** in the midst of their camp, Ps 78:28
men you shall die, and **f** like any prince." Ps 82:7
A thousand may **f** at your side, ten Ps 91:7
I hate the work of those who **f** away; it Ps 101:3
would make them **f** in the wilderness, Ps 106:26
make their offspring **f** among the Ps 106:27
Let burning coals **f** upon them! Let Ps 140:10
Let the wicked **f** into their own nets, Ps 141:10
the people to whom such blessings **f**! Ps 144:15
Whoever trusts in his riches will **f**, Prv 11:28
and a haughty spirit before a **f**. Prv 16:18
whom the LORD is angry will **f** into it. Prv 22:14
Whoever digs a pit will **f** into it, and a Prv 26:27
into an evil way will **f** into his own pit, Prv 28:10
hardens his heart will **f** into calamity. Prv 28:14
is crooked in his ways will suddenly **f**. Prv 28:18
For if they **f**, one will lift up his fellow. Eccl 4:10
He who digs a pit will **f** into it, and a Eccl 10:8
Your men shall **f** by the sword and your Is 3:25
They shall **f** and be broken; they shall be Is 8:15
a word against Jacob, and it will **f** on Israel; Is 9:8
the prisoners or **f** among the slain. Is 10:4
and Lebanon will **f** by the Majestic One. Is 10:34
whoever is caught will **f** by the sword. Is 13:15
give way, and it will be cut down and **f**, Is 22:25
sound of the terror shall **f** into the pit, Is 24:18
little, that they may go, and **f** backward, Is 28:13
of the great slaughter, when the towers **f**. Is 30:25
will stumble, and he who is helped will **f**, Is 31:3
"And the Assyrian shall **f** by a sword, not Is 31:8
All their host shall **f**, as leaves fall from Is 34:4
host shall fall, as leaves **f** from the vine, Is 34:4
Wild oxen shall **f** with them, and young Is 34:7
and I will make him **f** by the sword in his Is 37:7
and young men shall **f** exhausted; Is 40:30
Shall I **f** down before a block of wood?" Is 44:19
into a god; then they **f** down and worship! Is 46:6
charm away; disaster shall **f** upon you, Is 47:11
up strife with you shall **f** because of you. Is 54:15
Therefore they shall **f** among those who Jer 6:15
they shall fall among those who **f**; Jer 6:15
the report of it; our hands **f** helpless; Jer 6:24
LORD: When men **f**, do they not rise again? Jer 8:4
Therefore they shall **f** among the fallen; Jer 8:12
bodies of men shall **f** like dung upon the Jer 9:22
anguish and terror **f** upon them Jer 15:8
cause their people to **f** by the sword Jer 19:7
They shall **f** by the sword of their Jer 20:4
all my close friends, watching for my **f**. Jer 20:10
into which they shall be driven and **f**, Jer 23:12
drunk and vomit, **f** and rise no more, Jer 25:27
and you shall **f** like a choice vessel. Jer 25:34
you, and you shall not **f** by the sword, Jer 39:18
In the land of Egypt they shall **f**; by the Jer 44:12
flees from the terror shall **f** into the pit, Jer 48:44
the sound of their **f** the earth shall Jer 49:21
her young men shall **f** in her squares, Jer 49:26
her young men shall **f** in her squares, Jer 50:30
The proud one shall stumble and **f**, Jer 50:32
They shall **f** down slain in the land of Jer 51:4
and all her slain shall **f** in the midst of Jer 51:47
Babylon must **f** for the slain of Israel, Jer 51:49
of her future; therefore her **f** is terrible; Lam 1:9
a third part shall **f** by the sword all Ezk 5:12
And the slain shall **f** in your midst, and Ezk 6:7
of Israel, for they shall **f** by the sword, Ezk 6:11
and he who is near shall **f** by the sword, Ezk 6:12
You shall **f** by the sword. I will judge Ezk 11:10
it with whitewash that it shall **f**! Ezk 13:11
and you, O great hailstones, will **f**, Ezk 13:11
pick of his troops shall **f** by the sword, Ezk 17:21
your survivors shall **f** by the sword. Ezk 23:25
you left behind shall **f** by the sword. Ezk 24:21
to Dedan they shall **f** by the sword. Ezk 25:13
mighty pillars will **f** to the ground. Ezk 26:11
shake at the sound of your **f**, Ezk 26:15
tremble on the day of your **f**, Ezk 26:18
heart of the seas on the day of your **f**. Ezk 27:27
and the slain shall **f** in her midst, by Ezk 28:23
you shall **f** on the open field, and not be Ezk 29:5
be in Cush, when the slain **f** in Egypt, Ezk 30:4
league, shall **f** with them by the sword. Ezk 30:5
Those who support Egypt shall **f**, and Ezk 30:6
to Syene they shall **f** within her by the Ezk 30:6
and of Pi-beseth shall **f** by the sword, Ezk 30:17
I will make the sword **f** from his hand. Ezk 30:22
but the arms of Pharaoh shall **f**. Ezk 30:25
the nations quake at the sound of its **f**, Ezk 31:16
your multitude to **f** by the swords Ezk 32:12
They shall **f** amid those who are slain Ezk 32:20
he shall not **f** by it when he turns Ezk 33:12
the waste places shall **f** by the sword, Ezk 33:27
those slain with the sword shall **f**. Ezk 35:8
I will **f** upon the quiet people who Ezk 38:11
be thrown down, and the cliffs shall **f**, Ezk 38:20
You shall **f** on the mountains of Israel, Ezk 39:4
You shall **f** in the open field, for I have Ezk 39:5
This land shall **f** to you as your Ezk 47:14
you are to **f** down and worship the golden Dn 3:5
whoever does not **f** down and worship Dn 3:6
shall **f** down and worship the golden Dn 3:10
whoever does not **f** down and worship Dn 3:11
to **f** down and worship the image that I Dn 3:15
own land, but he shall stumble and **f**, Dn 11:19
away, and many shall **f** down slain. Dn 11:26
And tens of thousands shall **f**, but Dn 11:41
their princes shall **f** by the sword Hos 7:16
Cover us, and to the hills, **F** on us. Hos 10:8
I will **f** upon them like a bear robbed of Hos 13:8
her God; they shall **f** by the sword; Hos 13:16
Does a bird **f** in a snare on the earth, Am 3:5
shall be cut off and **f** to the ground. Am 3:14
your daughters shall **f** by the sword, Am 7:17
Way of Beersheba lives,' they shall **f**, Am 8:14
a sieve, but no pebble shall **f** to the earth. Am 9:9
me, O my enemy; when I **f**, I shall rise; Mi 7:8
figs—if shaken they **f** into the mouth of Na 3:12
cause each of them to **f** into the hand of Zec 11:6
panic from the LORD shall **f** on them, Zec 14:13
like this plague shall **f** on the horses, Zec 14:15
you, if you will **f** down and worship me." Mt 4:9
and beat on that house, but it did not **f**, Mt 7:25
and it fell, and great was the **f** of it." Mt 7:27
one of them will **f** to the ground apart Mt 10:29
lead the blind, both will **f** into a pit." Mt 15:14
the crumbs that **f** from their masters' Mt 15:27
And then many will **f** away and betray Mt 24:10
light, and the stars will **f** from heaven, Mt 24:29
"You will all **f** away because of me this Mt 26:31
"Though they all **f** away because of Mt 26:33
because of you, I will never **f** away." Mt 26:33
of the word, immediately they **f** away. Mk 4:17
said to them, "You will all **f** away, Mk 14:27
to him, "Even though they all **f** away, Mk 14:29
is appointed for the **f** and rising of many Lk 2:34
man? Will they not both **f** into a pit? Lk 6:39
for a while, and in time of testing **f** away. Lk 8:13
"I saw Satan **f** like lightning from Lk 10:18
They will **f** by the edge of the sword and Lk 21:24
to say to the mountains, '**F** on us,' Lk 23:30
least his shadow might **f** on some of Acts 5:15
to swell up or suddenly **f** down dead. Acts 28:6
all have sinned and **f** short of the glory Rom 3:23
the spirit of slavery to **f** back into fear, Rom 8:15
stumble in order that they might **f**? Rom 11:11
that he stands take heed lest he **f**. 1 Cor 10:12
Who is made to **f**, and I am not 2 Cor 11:29
with conceit and **f** into the 1 Tm 3:6
so that he may not **f** into disgrace, 1 Tm 3:7
who desire to be rich **f** into temptation, 1 Tm 6:9
leading you to **f** away from the living Heb 3:12
so that no one may **f** by the same sort Heb 4:11

if they then **f** away, since they are Heb 6:6
is a fearful thing to **f** into the hands of Heb 10:31
you may not **f** under condemnation. Jas 5:12
practice these qualities you will never **f**. 2 Pt 1:10
the twenty-four elders **f** down before him Rv 4:10
"**F** on us and hide us from the face of Rv 6:16
that no rain may **f** during the days of Rv 11:6

FALLEN (86)
are you angry, and why has your face **f**? Gn 4:6
shall you gather the **f** grapes of your Lv 19:10
donkey or his ox **f** down by the way Dt 22:4
and that the fear of you has **f** upon us, Jos 2:9
"Get up! Why have you **f** on your face? Jos 7:10
to the very last had **f** by the edge of the Jos 8:24
for there had **f** 120,000 men who drew Jgs 8:10
among the tribes of Israel had **f** to them. Jgs 18:1
Dagon had **f** face downward on the 1 Sm 5:3
Dagon had **f** face downward on the 1 Sm 5:4
sleep from the LORD had **f** upon them. 1 Sm 26:12
and his three sons **f** on Mount Gilboa. 1 Sm 31:8
many of the people have **f** and are dead, 2 Sm 1:4
that he could not live after he had **f**. 2 Sm 1:10
because they had **f** by the sword. 2 Sm 1:12
high places! How the mighty have **f**! 2 Sm 1:19
"How the mighty have **f** in the midst 2 Sm 1:25
"How the mighty have **f**, and the 2 Sm 1:27
the place where Asahel had **f** and died, 2 Sm 2:23
the wicked you have **f**." And all the 2 Sm 3:34
a great man has **f** this day in Israel? 2 Sm 3:38
in a pit on a day when snow had **f**. 2 Sm 23:20
of Elijah that had **f** from him and 2 Kgs 2:13
of Elijah that had **f** from him and 2 Kgs 2:14
when Elisha had **f** sick with the 2 Kgs 13:14
Saul and his sons **f** on Mount Gilboa. 1 Chr 10:8
in a pit on a day when snow had **f**. 1 Chr 11:22
our fathers have **f** by the sword, 2 Chr 29:9
Jews, for fear of the Jews had **f** on them. Est 8:17
for the fear of them had **f** on all peoples. Est 9:2
for the fear of Mordecai had **f** on them. Est 9:3
The lines have **f** for me in pleasant Ps 16:6
There the evildoers lie **f**; they are thrust Ps 36:12
They have all **f** away; together they have Ps 53:3
me; the terrors of death have **f** upon me. Ps 55:4
way, but they have **f** into it themselves. Ps 57:6
of those who reproach you have **f** on me. Ps 69:9
for dread of them had **f** upon it. Ps 105:38
This blessing has **f** to me, that I have Ps 119:56
Jerusalem has stumbled, and Judah has **f**, Is 3:8
"The bricks have **f**, but we will build Is 9:10
"How you are **f** from heaven, O Day Star, Is 14:12
And he answered, "**F**, fallen is Babylon; Is 21:9
And he answered, "Fallen, **f** is Babylon; Is 21:9
the inhabitants of the world have not **f**. Is 26:18
Therefore they shall fall among the **f**; Jer 8:12
Euphrates they have stumbled and **f**. Jer 46:6
warrior; they have both **f** together." Jer 46:12
and your grapes the destroyer has **f**. Jer 48:32
has surrendered; her bulwarks have **f**; Jer 50:15
Suddenly Babylon has **f** and been Jer 51:8
flow to him; the wall of Babylon has **f**. Jer 51:44
as for Babylon have **f** the slain of all Jer 51:49
my young men have **f** by the sword; Lam 2:21
The crown has **f** from our head; woe to Lam 5:16
in all the valleys its branches have **f**, Ezk 31:12
On its **f** trunk dwell all the birds of the Ezk 31:13
it, all of them slain, **f** by the sword, Ezk 32:22
grave, all of them slain, **f** by the sword, Ezk 32:23
all of them slain, **f** by the sword, who Ezk 32:24
the **f** from among the uncircumcised, Ezk 32:27
All their kings have **f**, and none of them Hos 7:7
"**F**, no more to rise, is the virgin Israel; Am 5:2
of David that is **f** and repair its Am 9:11
Wail, O cypress, for the cedar has **f**, for Zec 11:2
the saints who had **f** asleep were raised, Mt 27:52
son or an ox that has **f** into a well on a Lk 14:5
them, "Our friend Lazarus has **f** asleep, Jn 11:11
said to him, "Lord, if he has **f** asleep, Jn 11:12
for he had not yet **f** on any of them, but Acts 8:16
rebuild the tent of David that has **f**; Acts 15:16
And when we had all **f** to the ground, Acts 26:14
severity toward those who have **f**, but Rom 11:22
still alive, though some have **f** asleep. 1 Cor 15:6
also who have **f** asleep in Christ 1 Cor 15:18
firstfruits of those who have **f** asleep. 1 Cor 15:20
by the law; you have **f** away from grace. Gal 5:4
with him those who have **f** asleep. 1 Thes 4:14
not precede those who have **f** asleep. 1 Thes 4:15
therefore from where you have **f**; Rv 2:5
and I saw a star **f** from heaven to earth, Rv 9:1
saying, "**F**, fallen is Babylon the great, Rv 14:8
saying, "Fallen, **f** is Babylon the great, Rv 14:8
also seven kings, five of whom have **f**, Rv 17:10
voice, "**F**, fallen is Babylon the great! Rv 18:2
voice, "Fallen, **f** is Babylon the great! Rv 18:2

FALLING (16)
f down with his eyes uncovered: Nm 24:4
f down with his eyes uncovered: Nm 24:16
as Haman was **f** on the couch where Est 7:8
my soul from death, yes, my feet from **f**, Ps 56:13
I was pushed hard, so that I was **f**, but Ps 118:13
upholds all who are **f** and raises up all Ps 145:14
the vine, like leaves **f** from the fig tree. Is 34:4
and the stars will be **f** from heaven, Mk 13:25
And **f** at Jesus' feet, he implored him to Lk 8:41
and **f** down before him declared in the Lk 8:47
great drops of blood **f** down to the Lk 22:44
things to you to keep you from **f** away. Jn 16:1
and **f** headlong he burst open in the Acts 1:18
And **f** to his knees he cried out with a Acts 7:60
And **f** to the ground he heard a voice Acts 9:4
are disclosed, and so, **f** on his face, 1 Cor 14:25

FALLOW (4)
year you shall let it rest and lie **f**, Ex 23:11
The **f** ground of the poor would yield Prv 13:23
"Break up your **f** ground, and sow not Jer 4:3
break up your **f** ground, for it is the Hos 10:12

FALLS (54)
heels so that his rider **f** backward. Gn 49:17
home will die when the hail **f** on them.""" Ex 9:19
cover it, and an ox or a donkey **f** into it, Ex 21:33
which any of them **f** when they are Lv 11:32
if any of them **f** into any earthenware Lv 11:33
part of their carcass **f** shall be unclean. Lv 11:35
part of their carcass **f** upon any seed Lv 11:37
and any part of their carcass **f** on it, Lv 11:38
"If a man's hair **f** out from his head, he Lv 13:40
if a man's hair **f** out from his forehead, Lv 13:41
Wherever the lot **f** for anyone, that Nm 33:54
city that makes war with you, until it **f**. Dt 20:20
a spindle or who **f** by the sword or 2 Sm 3:29
as one **f** before the wicked you have 2 Sm 3:34
him as the dew **f** on the ground, 2 Sm 17:12
of your God, which it **f** to you to provide, Ezr 7:20
of the night, when deep sleep **f** on men, Jb 4:13
"But the mountain **f** and crumbles Jb 14:18
My skin turns black and **f** from me, Jb 30:30
of the night, when deep sleep **f** on men, Jb 33:15
out, and **f** into the hole that he has made. Ps 7:15
he be like rain that **f** on the mown grass, Ps 72:6
which **f** on the mountains of Zion! Ps 133:3
but the wicked **f** by his own Prv 11:5
Where there is no guidance, a people **f**, Prv 11:14
A wicked messenger **f** into trouble, Prv 13:17
but his wrath **f** on one who acts Prv 14:35
a dishonest tongue **f** into calamity. Prv 17:20
for the righteous **f** seven times and Prv 24:16
Do not rejoice when your enemy **f**, and Prv 24:17
is alone when he **f** and has not another Eccl 4:10
time, when it suddenly **f** upon them. Eccl 9:12
and if a tree **f** to the south or to the Eccl 11:3
the north, in the place where the tree **f**, Eccl 11:3
transgression lies heavy upon it, and it **f**, Is 24:20
And it will hail when the forest **f** down, Is 32:19
he makes it an idol and **f** down before it. Is 44:15
his idol, and **f** down to it and worships it. Is 44:17
And when the wall **f**, will it not be said Ezk 13:12
When it **f**, you shall perish in the Ezk 13:14
a sheep, if it **f** into a pit on the Sabbath, Mt 12:11
of the word, immediately he **f** away. Mt 13:21
terribly. For often he **f** into the fire, Mt 17:15
And the one who **f** on this stone will be Mt 21:44
and when it **f** on anyone, it will crush Mt 21:44
is laid waste, and a divided household **f**. Lk 11:17
Everyone who **f** on that stone will be Lk 20:18
to pieces, and when it **f** on anyone, Lk 20:18
a grain of wheat **f** into the earth and Jn 12:24
judgment of God rightly **f** on those who Rom 2:2
his own master that he stands or **f**. Rom 14:4
that has drunk the rain that often **f** on it, Heb 6:7
its flower **f**, and its beauty perishes. Jas 1:11
The grass withers, and the flower **f**, 1 Pt 1:24

FALSE (82)
shall not bear **f** witness against your Ex 20:16
"You shall not spread a **f** report. You Ex 23:1
Keep far from a **f** charge, and do not kill Ex 23:7
you shall not bear **f** witness against your Dt 5:20
the witness is a **f** witness and has Dt 19:18
They went after **f** idols and became 2 Kgs 17:15
went after false idols and became **f**, 2 Kgs 17:15
for I would have been **f** to God above. Jb 31:28
For truly my words are not **f**; one who is Jb 36:4
Behold, the hope of a man is **f**; he is laid Jb 41:9
his soul to what is **f** and does not swear Ps 24:4
for **f** witnesses have risen against me, Ps 27:12
The war horse is a **f** hope for salvation, Ps 33:17
we have not been **f** to your covenant. Ps 44:17
steadfast love or be **f** to my faithfulness. Ps 89:33
Put **f** ways far from me and graciously Ps 119:29
therefore I hate every **f** way. Ps 119:104
to be right; I hate every **f** way. Ps 119:128
a **f** witness who breathes out lies, and Prv 6:19
A **f** balance is an abomination to the Prv 11:1
evidence, but a **f** witness utters deceit. Prv 12:17
not lie, but a **f** witness breathes out lies. Prv 14:5
to a fool; still less is **f** speech to a prince. Prv 17:7
A **f** witness will not go unpunished, and Prv 19:5
A **f** witness will not go unpunished, and Prv 19:9
to the LORD, and **f** scales are not good. Prv 20:23
A **f** witness will perish, but the word of Prv 21:28
A man who bears **f** witness against his Prv 25:18
shame by his idols, for his images are **f**, Jer 10:14
there any among the **f** gods of the Jer 14:22
me; they make offerings to **f** gods; Jer 18:15
his boasts are **f**, his deeds are false. Jer 48:30
his boasts are false, his deeds are **f**. Jer 48:30
shame by his idols, for his images are **f**, Jer 51:17
seen for you **f** and deceptive visions; Lam 2:14
you oracles that are **f** and misleading. Lam 2:14
be no more any **f** vision or flattering Ezk 12:24
They have seen **f** visions and lying Ezk 13:6
you not seen a **f** vision and uttered a Ezk 13:7
the prophets who see **f** visions and who Ezk 13:9
no more see **f** visions nor practice Ezk 13:23
to them it will seem like a **f** divination. Ezk 21:23
while they see for you **f** visions, while Ezk 21:29
seeing **f** visions and divining lies for Ezk 22:28
Their heart is **f**; now they must bear Hos 10:2
in whose hands are **f** balances, Hos 12:7
and deal deceitfully with **f** balances, Am 8:5
against one another, and love no **f** oath, Zec 8:17
they tell **f** dreams and give empty Zec 10:2
"Beware of **f** prophets, who come to you Mt 7:15
sexual immorality, theft, **f** witness, Mt 15:19
not steal, You shall not bear **f** witness, Mt 19:18
And many **f** prophets will arise and Mt 24:11
For **f** christs and false prophets will Mt 24:24
false christs and **f** prophets will arise Mt 24:24
were seeking **f** testimony against Mt 26:59
though many **f** witnesses came Mt 26:60
Do not steal, Do not bear **f** witness, Mk 10:19
F christs and false prophets will arise Mk 13:22
False christs and **f** prophets will arise Mk 13:22
For many bore **f** witness against him, Mk 14:56
up and bore **f** witness against him, Mk 14:57
anyone by threats or by **f** accusation, Lk 3:14
for so their fathers did to the **f** prophets. Lk 6:26
Do not steal, Do not bear **f** witness, Lk 18:20
and they set up **f** witnesses who said, Acts 6:13
a Jewish **f** prophet named Bar-Jesus. Acts 13:6
For such men are **f** apostles, 2 Cor 11:13
at sea, danger from **f** brothers; 2 Cor 11:26
Yet because of **f** brothers secretly Gal 2:4
all power and **f** signs and wonders, 2 Thes 2:9
so that they may believe what is **f**, 2 Thes 2:11
hearts, do not boast and be **f** to the truth. Jas 3:14
But **f** prophets also arose among the 2 Pt 2:1
as there will be **f** teachers among you, 2 Pt 2:1
greed they will exploit you with **f** words. 2 Pt 2:3
for many **f** prophets have gone out into 1 Jn 4:1
and are not, and found them to be **f**. Rv 2:2
and out of the mouth of the **f** prophet, Rv 16:13
and with it the **f** prophet who in its Rv 19:20
where the beast and the **f** prophet were, Rv 20:10
anyone who does what is detestable or **f**, Rv 21:27

FALSEHOOD (21)
is nothing left of your answers but **f**." Jb 21:34
my lips will not speak **f**, and my tongue Jb 27:4
"If I have walked with **f** and my foot has Jb 31:5
I do not sit with men of **f**, nor do I consort Ps 26:4
high position. They take pleasure in **f**. Ps 62:4
because they have wronged me with **f**; Ps 119:78
are sure; they persecute me with **f**; Ps 119:86
I hate and abhor **f**, but I love your Ps 119:163
whose right hand is a right hand of **f**. Ps 144:8
whose right hand is a right hand of **f**. Ps 144:11
The righteous hates **f**, but the wicked Prv 13:5
If a ruler listens to **f**, all his officials Prv 29:12
Remove far from me **f** and lying; give Prv 30:8
those who draw iniquity with cords of **f**, Is 5:18
refuge, and in **f** we have taken shelter"; Is 28:15
f and not truth has grown strong in the Jer 9:3
you have uttered **f** and seen lying Ezk 13:8
day long; they multiply **f** and violence; Hos 12:1
sent him is true, and in him there is no **f**. Jn 7:18
Therefore, having put away **f**, let each Eph 4:25
and everyone who loves and practices **f**. Rv 22:15

FALSELY (26)
that you will not deal **f** with me or with Gn 21:23
swearing **f**—in any of all the things that Lv 6:3
or anything about which he has sworn **f**, Lv 6:5
shall not steal; you shall not deal **f**; Lv 19:11
You shall not swear by my name **f**, and Lv 19:12

witness and has accused his brother **f**, Dt 19:18
you, lest you deal **f** with your God." Jos 24:27
Will you speak **f** for God and speak Jb 13:7
who will not deal **f**." And he became their Is 63:8
say, "As the LORD lives," yet they swear **f**. Jer 5:2
They have spoken **f** of the LORD and have Jer 5:12
the prophets prophesy **f**, and the priests Jer 5:31
from prophet to priest, everyone deals **f**. Jer 6:13
steal, murder, commit adultery, swear **f**, Jer 7:9
from prophet to priest, everyone deals **f**. Jer 8:10
friends, to whom you have prophesied **f**." Jer 20:6
but they are prophesying **f** in my name, Jer 27:15
for you are speaking **f** of Ishmael." Jer 40:16
you have disheartened the righteous **f**, Ezk 13:22
the evil deeds of Samaria; for they deal **f**; Hos 7:1
everyone who swears **f** shall be cleaned Zec 5:3
house of him who swears **f** by my name. Zec 5:4
adulterers, against those who swear **f**, Mal 3:5
of evil against you **f** on my account. Mt 5:11
to those of old, 'You shall not swear **f**, Mt 5:33
of what is **f** called "knowledge," 1 Tm 6:20

FAME (19)
who have heard your **f** will say, Nm 14:15
in praise and in **f** and in honor high Dt 26:19
Joshua, and his **f** was in all the land. Jos 6:27
and his **f** was in all the surrounding 1 Kgs 4:31
heard of the **f** of Solomon concerning 1 Kgs 10:1
And the **f** of David went out into all 1 Chr 14:17
of **f** and glory throughout all lands. 1 Chr 22:5
of Sheba heard of the **f** of Solomon, 2 Chr 9:1
and his **f** spread even to the border of 2 Chr 26:8
great stones. And his **f** spread far, 2 Chr 26:15
and his **f** spread throughout all the Est 9:4
his **f** continue as long as the sun! Ps 72:17
shall pour forth the **f** of your abundant Ps 145:7
have not heard my **f** or seen my glory. Is 66:19
their **f** shall be like the wine of Hos 14:7
So his **f** spread throughout all Syria, and Mt 4:24
away and spread his **f** through all that Mt 9:31
the tetrarch heard about the **f** of Jesus, Mt 14:1
at once his **f** spread everywhere Mk 1:28

FAMILIAR (4)
seamen who were **f** with the sea, 1 Kgs 9:27
ships and servants **f** with the sea, 2 Chr 8:18
my equal, my companion, my **f** friend. Ps 55:13
because you are **f** with all the Acts 26:3

FAMILIES (18)
on the earth, went out by **f** from the ark. Gn 8:19
and in you all the **f** of the earth shall be Gn 12:3
offspring shall all the **f** of the earth be Gn 28:14
the midwives feared God, he gave them **f**. Ex 1:21
one from each of the tribal **f** of Israel, Jos 22:14
in answer to the heads of the **f** of Israel, Jos 22:21
the heads of the **f** of Israel who were Jos 22:30
and priests and heads of **f** of Israel, 2 Chr 19:8
Some of the heads of **f**, when they came Ezr 2:68
and the contempt of **f** terrified me, Jb 31:34
and all the **f** of the nations shall Ps 22:27
Ascribe to the LORD, O **f** of the peoples, Ps 96:7
and makes their **f** like flocks. Ps 107:41
have I known of all the **f** of the earth; Am 3:2
and all the **f** that are left, each by itself, Zec 12:14
And if any of the **f** of the earth do not Zec 14:17
offspring shall all the **f** of the earth be Acts 3:25
are upsetting whole **f** by teaching for Ti 1:11

FAMILY (39)
brought up in the **f** or in another home. Lv 18:9
daughter, brought up in your father's **f**, Lv 18:11
brought a Midianite woman to his **f**, Nm 25:6
not be married outside the **f** to a stranger. Dt 25:5
them the head of a **f** among the clans of Jos 22:14
but they let the man and all his **f** go. Jgs 1:25
was too afraid of his **f** and the men of the Jgs 6:27
it became a snare to Gideon and to his **f**. Jgs 8:27
steadfast love to the **f** of Jerubbaal (that Jgs 8:35
and to the whole clan of his mother's **f**, Jgs 9:1
brothers and all his **f** came down and Jgs 16:31
of Bethlehem in Judah, of the **f** of Judah, Jgs 17:7
that time, every man to his tribe and **f**, Jgs 21:24
out a man of the **f** of the house of Saul, 2 Sm 16:5
she arose and destroyed all the royal **f**. 2 Kgs 11:1
son of Elishama, of the royal **f**, 2 Kgs 25:25
destroyed all the royal **f** of the house 2 Chr 22:10
of Barachel the Buzite, of the **f** of Ram, Jb 32:2
you, one from a city and two from a **f**, Jer 3:14
that remains of this evil **f** in all the places Jer 8:3
son of Elishama, of the royal **f**, Jer 41:1
the Levitical priests of the **f** of Zadok, Ezk 43:19
both of the royal **f** and of the nobility, Dn 1:3
against the whole **f** that I brought up out Am 3:1
against this **f** I am devising disaster, Mi 2:3
The land shall mourn, each **f** by itself: Zec 12:12
the **f** of the house of David by itself, Zec 12:12
the **f** of the house of Nathan by itself, Zec 12:12
the **f** of the house of Levi by itself, and Zec 12:13
the **f** of the Shimeites by itself, and Zec 12:13
And if the **f** of Egypt does not go up Zec 14:18
And when his **f** heard it, they went out Mk 3:21
and all who were of the high-priestly **f**. Acts 4:6
and Joseph's **f** became known to Acts 7:13
"Brothers, sons of the **f** of Abraham, Acts 13:26
was baptized at once, he and all his **f**. Acts 16:33
who belong to the **f** of Aristobulus. Rom 16:10
who belong to the **f** of Narcissus. Rom 16:11
from whom every **f** in heaven and on Eph 3:15

FAMINE (104)
Now there was a **f** in the land. So Gn 12:10
there, for the **f** was severe in the land. Gn 12:10
Now there was a **f** in the land, besides Gn 26:1
besides the former **f** that was in the days Gn 26:1
the east wind are also seven years of **f**. Gn 41:27
them there will arise seven years of **f**, Gn 41:30
of Egypt. The **f** will consume the land, Gn 41:30
land by reason of the **f** that will follow, Gn 41:31
the seven years of **f** that are to occur Gn 41:36
the land may not perish through the **f**." Gn 41:36
Before the year of **f** came, two sons were Gn 41:50
and the seven years of **f** began to come, Gn 41:54
There was **f** in all lands, but in all the Gn 41:54
So when the **f** had spread over all the Gn 41:56
for the **f** was severe in the land of Egypt. Gn 41:56
because the **f** was severe over all the Gn 41:57
for the **f** was in the land of Canaan. Gn 42:5
grain for the **f** of your households, Gn 42:19
take grain for the **f** of your households, Gn 42:33
Now the **f** was severe in the land. Gn 43:1
For the **f** has been in the land these two Gn 45:6
for there are yet five years of **f** to come, Gn 45:11
for the **f** is severe in the land of Canaan. Gn 47:4
in all the land, for the **f** was very severe, Gn 47:13
Canaan languished by reason of the **f**. Gn 47:13
because the **f** was severe on them. Gn 47:20
the judges ruled there was a **f** in the land, Ru 1:1
Now there was a **f** in the days of David 2 Sm 21:1
"Shall three years of **f** come to you in 2 Sm 24:13
"If there is **f** in the land, if there is 1 Kgs 8:37
Now the **f** was severe in Samaria. 1 Kgs 18:2
Gilgal when there was a **f** in the land. 2 Kgs 4:38
And there was a great **f** in Samaria, as 2 Kgs 6:25
us enter the city,' the **f** is in the city, 2 Kgs 7:4
you can, for the LORD has called for a **f**, 2 Kgs 8:1
the fourth month the **f** was so severe 2 Kgs 25:3
either three years of **f**, or three 1 Chr 21:12
"If there is **f** in the land, if there is 2 Chr 6:28
sword, judgment, or pestilence, or **f**, 2 Chr 20:9
you over to die by **f** and by thirst, 2 Chr 32:11
our houses to get grain because of the **f**." Neh 5:3
In **f** he will redeem you from death, and Jb 5:20
At destruction and **f** you shall laugh, and Jb 5:22
from death and keep them alive in **f**. Ps 33:19
in the days of **f** they have abundance. Ps 37:19
When he summoned a **f** on the land Ps 105:16
but I will kill your root with **f**, and your Is 14:30
and destruction, **f** and sword; Is 51:19
upon us, nor shall we see sword or **f**. Jer 5:12
sons and their daughters shall die by **f**, Jer 11:22
I will consume them by the sword, by **f**, Jer 14:12
not see the sword, nor shall you have **f**, Jer 14:13
'Sword and **f** shall not come upon this Jer 14:15
By sword and **f** those prophets shall be Jer 14:15
of Jerusalem, victims of **f** and sword, Jer 14:16
I enter the city, behold, the diseases of **f**! Jer 14:18
those who are for **f**, to famine, and those Jer 15:2
those who are for famine, to **f**, and those Jer 15:2
They shall perish by the sword and by **f**, Jer 16:4
Therefore deliver up their children to **f**; Jer 18:21
and **f** into the hand of Nebuchadnezzar Jer 21:7
in this city shall die by the sword, by **f**, Jer 21:9
sword, **f**, and pestilence upon them, Jer 24:10
that nation with the sword, with **f**, Jer 27:8
and your people die by the sword, by **f**, Jer 27:13
f, and pestilence against many countries Jer 28:8
on them sword, **f**, and pestilence, Jer 29:17
them with sword, **f**, and pestilence, Jer 29:18
of sword and **f** and pestilence the Jer 32:24
of the king of Babylon by sword, by **f**, Jer 32:36
to the sword, to pestilence, and to **f**, Jer 34:17
in this city shall die by the sword, by **f**, Jer 38:2
and the **f** of which you are afraid shall Jer 42:16
to live there shall die by the sword, by **f**, Jer 42:17
that you shall die by the sword, by **f**, Jer 42:22
the sword and by **f** they shall be Jer 44:12
they shall die by the sword and by **f**, Jer 44:12
Jerusalem, with the sword, with **f**, Jer 44:13
been consumed by the sword and by **f**." Jer 44:18
be consumed by the sword and by **f**, Jer 44:27
the fourth month the **f** was so severe in Jer 52:6
as an oven with the burning heat of **f**. Lam 5:10
and be consumed with **f** in your midst; Ezk 5:12
send against you the deadly arrows of **f**, Ezk 5:16
bring more and more **f** upon you and Ezk 5:16
I will send **f** and wild beasts against Ezk 5:17
for they shall fall by the sword, by **f**, Ezk 6:11
who is left and is preserved shall die of **f**. Ezk 6:12
is without; pestilence and **f** are within. Ezk 7:15
is in the city **f** and pestilence devour. Ezk 7:15
from the sword, from **f** and pestilence, Ezk 12:16
its supply of bread and send **f** upon it, Ezk 14:13
acts of judgment, sword, **f**, wild beasts, Ezk 14:21
it abundant and lay no **f** upon you. Ezk 36:29
the disgrace of **f** among the nations. Ezk 36:30
"when I will send a **f** on the land—not a Am 8:11
a famine on the land—not a **f** of bread, Am 8:11
and a great **f** came over all the land, Lk 4:25
a severe **f** arose in that country, Lk 15:14
there came a **f** throughout all Egypt Acts 7:11
would be a great **f** over all the world Acts 11:28
or distress, or persecution, or **f**, Rom 8:35
with sword and with **f** and with pestilence Rv 6:8
a single day, death and mourning and **f**, Rv 18:8

FAMINES (3)
and there will be **f** and earthquakes in Mt 24:7
in various places; there will be **f**. Mk 13:8
and in various places **f** and pestilences. Lk 21:11

FAMISH (1)
for he will **f** all the gods of the earth, and Zep 2:11

FAMISHED (2)
When all the land of Egypt was **f**, the Gn 41:55
His strength is **f**, and calamity is ready Jb 18:12

FAMOUS (5)
name of Solomon more **f** than yours, 1 Kgs 1:47
and Jahdiel, mighty warriors, **f** men, 1 Chr 5:24
valor, **f** men in their fathers' houses. 1 Chr 12:30
How is the **f** city not forsaken, the city Jer 49:25
the brother who is **f** among all the 2 Cor 8:18

FAN (1)
I remind you to **f** into flame the gift 2 Tm 1:6

FANCIES (1)
As I lay in bed the **f** and the visions of my Dn 4:5

FANGS (4)
I broke the **f** of the unrighteous and Jb 29:17
tear out the **f** of the young lions, O LORD! Ps 58:6
teeth are swords, whose **f** are knives, Prv 30:14
are lions' teeth, and it has the **f** of a lioness. Jl 1:6

FANNED (1)
treasures; a fire not **f** will devour him; Jb 20:26

FAR (287)
in the direction of Gerar as **f** as Gaza, Gn 10:19
Admah, and Zeboiim, as **f** as Lasha. Gn 10:19
on from the Negeb as **f** as Bethel to the Gn 13:3
and moved his tent as **f** as Sodom. Gn 13:12
country of Seir as **f** as El-paran on the Gn 14:6
them, and went in pursuit as **f** as Dan. Gn 14:14
F be it from you to do such a thing, to Gn 18:25
fare as the wicked! **F** be that from you! Gn 18:25
F be it from your servants to do such a Gn 44:7
"**F** be it from me that I should do so! Gn 44:17
But so **f**, you have not obeyed." Ex 7:16
only you must not go very **f** away. Ex 8:28
and trembled, and they stood **f** off Ex 20:18
The people stood **f** off, while Moses drew Ex 20:21
Keep **f** from a false charge, and do not Ex 23:7
it outside the camp, **f** off from the camp, Ex 33:7
head to foot, so **f** as the priest can see, Lv 13:12
and said to them, "You have gone too **f**! Nm 16:3
one. You have gone too **f**, sons of Levi!" Nm 16:7
Then scatter the fire **f** and wide, for Nm 16:37
the Jabbok, as **f** as to the Ammonites, Nm 21:24
out of his hand, as **f** as the Arnon. Nm 21:26
Heshbon, as **f** as Dibon, perished; Nm 21:30
and we laid waste as **f** as Nophah; Nm 21:30
Nophah; fire spread as **f** as Medeba." Nm 21:30
Beth-jeshimoth as **f** as Abel-shittim Nm 33:49
and Lebanon, as **f** as the great river, Dt 1:7
beat you down in Seir as **f** as Hormah. Dt 1:44
Avvim, who lived in villages as **f** as Gaza, Dt 2:23
city that is in the valley, as **f** as Gilead, Dt 2:36
all Bashan, as **f** as Salecah and Edrei, Dt 3:10
as **f** as the border of the Geshurites and Dt 3:14
territory from Gilead as **f** as the Valley of Dt 3:16
as a border, as **f** over as the river Jabbok, Dt 3:16
from Chinnereth as **f** as the Sea of the Dt 3:17
the Arnon, as **f** as Mount Sirion (that is, Dt 4:48
side of the Jordan as **f** as the Sea of the Dt 4:49
to put his name there is too **f** from you, Dt 12:21
you, whether near you or **f** off from you, Dt 13:7
you, because the place is too **f** from you, Dt 14:24
to all the cities that are very **f** from you, Dt 20:15
a nation against you from **f** away, Dt 28:49

the foreigner who comes from a **f** land, Dt 29:22
is not too hard for you, neither is it **f** off. Dt 30:11
him all the land, Gilead as **f** as Dan, Dt 34:1
the land of Judah as **f** as the western sea, Dt 34:2
the city of palm trees, as **f** as Zoar. Dt 34:3
and this Lebanon as **f** as the great river, Jos 1:4
on the way to the Jordan as **f** as the fords. Jos 2:7
the ark had come as **f** as the Jordan, Jos 3:15
stood and rose up in a heap very **f** away, Jos 3:16
before the gate as **f** as Shebarim and Jos 7:5
Do not go very **f** from the city, but all of Jos 8:4
us, saying, 'We are very **f** from you,' Jos 9:22
and struck them as **f** as Azekah and Jos 10:10
from heaven on them as **f** as Azekah, Jos 10:11
them from Kadesh-barnea as **f** as Gaza, Jos 10:41
the country of Goshen, as **f** as Gibeon. Jos 10:41
and chased them as **f** as Great Sidon and Jos 11:8
and eastward as **f** as the Valley of Jos 11:8
as **f** as Baal-gad in the Valley of Jos 11:17
of the valley as **f** as the river Jabbok, Jos 12:2
the tableland of Medeba as **f** as Dibon; Jos 13:9
as **f** as the boundary of the Ammonites; Jos 13:10
as **f** as the territory of Lower Beth-horon, Jos 16:3
was Ataroth-addar as **f** as Upper Jos 16:5
around these cities as **f** as Baalath-beer, Jos 19:8
their inheritance reached as **f** as Sarid. Jos 19:10
Kanah, as **f** as Sidon the Great. Jos 19:28
and Jabneel, as **f** as Lakkum, Jos 19:33
F be it from us that we should rebel Jos 22:29
"**F** be it from us that we should forsake Jos 24:16
Baal-hermon as **f** as Lebo-hamath. Jgs 3:3
had pitched his tent as **f** away as the oak Jgs 4:11
the produce of the land, as **f** as Gaza, Jgs 6:4
the army fled as **f** as Beth-shittah toward Jgs 7:22
as **f** as the border of Abel-meholah, Jgs 7:22
waters against them, as **f** as Beth-barah, Jgs 7:24
captured the waters as **f** as Beth-barah, Jgs 7:24
cities, and as **f** as Abel-keramim, Jgs 11:33
and how they were **f** from the Sidonians Jgs 18:7
deliverer because it was **f** from Sidon, Jgs 18:28
from Nohah as **f** as opposite Gibeah Jgs 20:43
'**F** be it from me, for those who honor 1 Sm 2:30
went after them as **f** as the border of 1 Sm 6:12
struck them, as **f** as below Beth-car. 1 Sm 7:11
f be it from me that I should sin 1 Sm 12:23
great salvation in Israel? **F** from it! 1 Sm 14:45
from Havilah as **f** as Shur, 1 Sm 15:7
the Philistines as **f** as Gath and 1 Sm 17:52
way from Shaaraim as **f** as Gath and 1 Sm 17:52
And he said to him, "**F** from it! You 1 Sm 20:2
And Jonathan said, "**F** be it from you! 1 Sm 20:9
other side and stood **f** off on the top 1 Sm 26:13
of the land from of old, as **f** as Shur, 1 Sm 27:8
that you have brought me thus **f**? 2 Sm 7:18
Joab answered, "**F** be it from me, far 2 Sm 20:20
answered, "Far be it from me, **f** be it, 2 Sm 20:20
and said, "**F** be it from me, O LORD, 2 Sm 23:17
as **f** as the other side of Jokmeam; 1 Kgs 4:12
comes from a **f** country for your 1 Kgs 8:41
to the land of the enemy, **f** off or near, 1 Kgs 8:46
for the people went as **f** as Dan to be 1 Kgs 12:30
has sent me as **f** as Bethel." But Elisha 2 Kgs 2:2
went after them as **f** as the Jordan, 2 Kgs 7:15
from Lebo-hamath as **f** as the Sea 2 Kgs 14:25
down the Philistines as **f** as Gaza and 2 Kgs 18:8
to the **f** recesses of Lebanon; 2 Kgs 19:23
"They have come from a **f** country, 2 Kgs 20:14
were around these cities as **f** as Baal. 1 Chr 4:33
in Aroer, as **f** as Nebo and Baal-meon. 1 Chr 5:8
lived to the east as **f** as the entrance of 1 Chr 5:9
in the land of Bashan as **f** as Salecah: 1 Chr 5:11
"**F** be it from me before my God that 1 Chr 11:19
from as **f** as Issachar and Zebulun 1 Chr 12:40
that you have brought me thus **f**? 1 Chr 17:16
house of my God, so **f** as I was able, 1 Chr 29:2
comes from a **f** country for the sake 2 Chr 6:32
away captive to a land **f** or near, 2 Chr 6:36
of Judah and came as **f** as Jerusalem. 2 Chr 12:4
chariots, and came as **f** as Mareshah. 2 Chr 14:9
him pursued them as **f** as Gerar, 2 Chr 14:13
And his fame spread **f**, for he was 2 Chr 26:15
and Manasseh, and as **f** as Zebulun, 2 Chr 30:10
and Simeon, and as **f** as Naphtali, 2 Chr 34:6
shout, and the sound was heard **f** away. Ezr 3:13
They consecrated it as **f** as the Tower of Neh 3:1
Hundred, as **f** as the Tower of Hananel. Neh 3:1
they restored Jerusalem as **f** as the Broad Neh 3:8
of the wall, as **f** as the Dung Gate. Neh 3:13
as **f** as the stairs that go down from the Neh 3:15
of David, as **f** as the artificial pool, Neh 3:16
and as **f** as the house of the mighty Neh 3:16
great projecting tower as **f** as the wall Neh 3:27
repaired as **f** as the house of the temple Neh 3:31
on the wall, **f** from one another. Neh 4:19
said to them, "We, as **f** as we are able, Neh 5:8
the joy of Jerusalem was heard **f** away. Neh 12:43
of King Ahasuerus, both near and **f**, Est 9:20
His children are **f** from safety; they are Jb 5:4
If iniquity is in your hand, put it **f** away, Jb 11:14
withdraw your hand **f** from me, and let Jb 13:21
"He has put my brothers **f** from me, and Jb 19:13
The counsel of the wicked is **f** from me. Jb 21:16
the counsel of the wicked is **f** from me. Jb 22:18
you remove injustice **f** from your tents, Jb 22:23
F be it from me to say that you are right; Jb 27:5
hang in the air, **f** away from mankind; Jb 28:4
a fire that consumes as **f** as Abaddon, Jb 31:12
f be it from God that he should do Jb 34:10
and said, 'Thus **f** shall you come, and Jb 38:11
Why are you so **f** from saving me, from Ps 22:1
Be not **f** from me, for trouble is near, Ps 22:11
But you, O LORD, do not be **f** off! O you Ps 22:19
be not silent! O Lord, be not **f** from me! Ps 35:22
plague, and my nearest kin stand **f** off. Ps 38:11
O LORD! O my God, be not **f** from me! Ps 38:21
all the earth, Mount Zion, in the **f** north, Ps 48:2
yes, I would wander **f** away; I would lodge Ps 55:7
O God, be not **f** from me; O my God, Ps 71:12
those who are **f** from you shall perish; Ps 73:27
earth; you are exalted **f** above all gods. Ps 97:9
A perverse heart shall be **f** from me; I Ps 101:4
as **f** as the east is from the west, so far Ps 103:12
so **f** does he remove our transgressions Ps 103:12
seeking food **f** from the ruins they Ps 109:10
in blessing; may it be **f** from him! Ps 109:17
who looks **f** down on the heavens and Ps 113:6
Put false ways **f** from me and Ps 119:29
purpose; they are **f** from your law. Ps 119:150
Salvation is **f** from the wicked, for Ps 119:155
speech, and put devious talk **f** from you. Prv 4:24
Keep your way **f** from her, and do not go Prv 5:8
The LORD is **f** from the wicked, but he Prv 15:29
more do his friends go **f** from him! Prv 19:7
guards his soul will keep **f** from them. Prv 22:5
rod of discipline drives it **f** from him. Prv 22:15
soul, so is good news from a **f** country. Prv 25:25
is near than a brother who is **f** away. Prv 27:10
Remove **f** from me falsehood and lying; Prv 30:8
She is **f** more precious than jewels. Prv 31:10
"I will be wise," but it was **f** from me. Eccl 7:23
That which has been is **f** off, and deep, Eccl 7:24
and the LORD removes people **f** away, and Is 6:12
be shattered; give ear, all you **f** countries; Is 8:9
of assembly in the **f** reaches of the north; Is 14:13
down to Sheol, to the **f** reaches of the pit. Is 14:15
cry out; their voice is heard as **f** as Jahaz; Is 15:4
rebuke them, and they will flee **f** away, Is 17:13
and smooth, to a people feared near and **f**, Is 18:2
smooth, from a people feared near and **f**, Is 18:7
captured, though they had fled **f** away. Is 22:3
old, whose feet carried her to settle **f** away? Is 23:7
lips, while their hearts are **f** from me, Is 29:13
Hear, you who are **f** off, what I have Is 33:13
mountains, to the **f** recesses of Lebanon, Is 37:24
"They have come to me from a **f** country, Is 39:3
man of my counsel from a **f** country. Is 46:11
heart, you who are **f** from righteousness: Is 46:12
it is not **f** off, and my salvation will not Is 46:13
who swallowed you up will be **f** away. Is 49:19
you shall be **f** from oppression, for you Is 54:14
you sent your envoys **f** off, and sent down Is 57:9
to the **f** and to the near," says the LORD, Is 57:19
Therefore justice is **f** from us, and Is 59:9
is none; for salvation, but it is **f** from us. Is 59:11
find in me that they went **f** from me, Jer 2:5
in their mouth and **f** from their heart. Jer 12:2
all the kings of the north, **f** and near, Jer 25:26
you will be removed **f** from your land, Jer 27:10
for behold, I will save you from **f** away, Jer 30:10
the LORD appeared to him from **f** away. I Jer 31:3
and declare it in the coastlands **f** away; Jer 31:10
all the fields as **f** as the brook Kidron, Jer 31:40
for behold, I will save you from **f** away, Jer 46:27
cities of the land of Moab, **f** and near. Jer 48:24
as **f** as Jahaz they utter their voice, Jer 48:34
the LORD." Thus **f** is the judgment Jer 48:47
Flee, wander **f** away, dwell in the depths, Jer 49:30
Remember the LORD from **f** away, and Jer 51:50
become exhausted.'" Thus **f** are the Jer 51:64
for a comforter is **f** from me, one to Lam 1:16
He who is **f** off shall die of pestilence, Ezk 6:12
here, to drive me **f** from my sanctuary? Ezk 8:6
cherubim was heard as **f** as the outer Ezk 10:5
have said, 'Go **f** from the LORD; Ezk 11:15
I removed them **f** off among the Ezk 11:16
now, and he prophesies of times **f** off.' Ezk 12:27
and those who are **f** from you will Ezk 22:5
to Syene, as **f** as the border of Cush. Ezk 29:10
dead bodies of their kings **f** from me, Ezk 43:9
But the Levites who went **f** from me, Ezk 44:10
and Hamath), as **f** as Hazer-hatticon, Ezk 47:16
to the eastern sea and as **f** as Tamar. Ezk 47:18
run from Tamar as **f** as the waters of Ezk 47:19
as **f** as Hazar-enan (which is on the Ezk 48:1
who are near and those who are **f** away, Dn 9:7
and a fourth shall be **f** richer than all of Dn 11:2
shall carry the war as **f** as his fortress. Dn 11:10
"I will remove the northerner **f** from you, Jl 2:20
order to remove them **f** from their own Jl 3:6
them to the Sabeans, to a nation **f** away, Jl 3:8
O you who put **f** away the day of disaster Am 6:3
of the Canaanites as **f** as Zarephath, Ob 1:20
day the boundary shall be **f** extended. Mi 7:11
"And those who are **f** off shall come and Zec 6:15
yet in **f** countries they shall remember Zec 10:9
their lips, but their heart is **f** from me; Mt 15:8
rebuke him, saying, "**F** be it from you, Mt 16:22
the east and shines as **f** as the west, Mt 24:27
as **f** as the courtyard of the high priest, Mt 26:58
their lips, but their heart is **f** from me; Mk 7:6
some of them have come from **f** away." Mk 8:3
"You are not **f** from the kingdom of Mk 12:34
When he was not **f** from the house, the Lk 7:6
and took a journey into a **f** country, Lk 15:13
and saw Abraham **f** off and Lazarus Lk 16:23
But the tax collector, standing **f** off, Lk 18:13
went into a **f** country to receive Lk 19:12
and the day is now **f** spent." So he went Lk 24:29
Then he led them out as **f** as Bethany, Lk 24:50
of fish, for they were not **f** from the land, Jn 21:8
your children and for all who are **f** off, Acts 2:39
Stephen traveled as **f** as Phoenicia Acts 11:19
the whole island as **f** as Paphos, Acts 13:6
Paul brought him as **f** as Athens, Acts 17:15
he is actually not **f** from each one of Acts 17:27
I will send you **f** away to the Acts 22:21
spearmen to go as **f** as Caesarea at the Acts 23:23
came as **f** as the Forum of Appius Acts 28:15
you (but thus **f** have been prevented), Rom 1:13
If possible, so **f** as it depends on you, Rom 12:18
The night is **f** gone; the day is at Rom 13:12
of righteousness must **f** exceed it in 2 Cor 3:9
a madman—with **f** greater labors, 2 Cor 11:23
labors, **f** more imprisonments, 2 Cor 11:23
But **f** be it from me to boast except in Gal 6:14
f above all rule and authority and Eph 1:21
you who once were **f** off have been Eph 2:13
peace to you who were **f** off and peace to Eph 2:17
is able to do **f** more abundantly than Eph 3:20
one who also ascended **f** above all the Eph 4:10
and be with Christ, for that is **f** better. Phil 1:23
But they will not get very **f**, for their 2 Tm 3:9
They will stand **f** off, in fear of her Rv 18:10
gained wealth from her, will stand **f** off, Rv 18:15
all whose trade is on the sea, stood **f** off Rv 18:17

FAR-OFF (1)
according to The Dove on **F** Terebinths. Ps 56:T

FARE (5)
so that the righteous **f** as the wicked! Gn 18:25
mother-in-law, she said, "How did you **f**, Ru 3:16
are left here will **f** like the whole 2 Kgs 7:13
So he paid the **f** and went on board, Jon 1:3
how did you **f**? When one came to a Hg 2:16

FARED (1)
and how your livestock has **f** with me. Gn 30:29

FAREWELL (5)
to kiss my sons and my daughters **f**? Gn 31:28
but let me first say **f** to those at my Lk 9:61
from these, you will do well. **F**." Acts 15:29
he said **f** and departed for Macedonia. Acts 20:1
and said **f** to one another. Then we Acts 21:6

FARM (1)
no attention and went off, one to his **f**, Mt 22:5

FARMER (3)
you I break in pieces the **f** and his team; Jer 51:23
It is the hard-working **f** who ought to 2 Tm 2:6
See how the **f** waits for the precious fruit Jas 5:7

FARMERS (4)
and he had **f** and vinedressers in the 2 Chr 26:10
is no rain on the land, the **f** are ashamed; Jer 14:4
and the **f** and those who wander with Jer 31:24
They shall call the **f** to mourning and Am 5:16

FARTHER (8)
said, 'Thus far shall you come, and no **f**, Jb 38:11
And the measuring line shall go out **f**, Jer 31:39
And going a little **f** he fell on his face Mt 26:39
And going on a little **f**, he saw James the Mk 1:19
And going a little **f**, he fell on the Mk 14:35
going. He acted as if he were going **f**, Lk 24:28
as the wind did not allow us to go **f**, Acts 27:7
A little **f** on they took a sounding Acts 27:28

FARTHEST (11)
to the wilderness of Zin at the **f** south. Jos 15:1
clear it and possess it to its **f** borders. Jos 17:18
I entered its **f** lodging place, its most 2 Kgs 19:23
your dispersed be under the **f** skies, Neh 1:9
and searches out to the **f** limit the ore in Jb 28:3
all the ends of the earth and of the **f** seas; Ps 65:5
of the earth, and called from its **f** corners, Is 41:9
is stirring from the **f** parts of the earth. Jer 6:22
is stirring from the **f** parts of the earth! Jer 25:32
gather them from the **f** parts of the earth, Jer 31:8
are stirring from the **f** parts of the earth. Jer 50:41

FASHION (3)
deceive you or mislead you in this **f**, 2 Chr 32:15
him? And did not one **f** us in the womb? Jb 31:15
All who **f** idols are nothing, and the Is 44:9

FASHIONED (4)
from their hand and **f** it with a graving Ex 32:4
Your hands **f** and made me, and now you Jb 10:8
Your hands have made and **f** me; give Ps 119:73
no weapon that is **f** against you shall Is 54:17

FASHIONS (3)
he who **f** the hearts of them all and Ps 33:15
Who **f** a god or casts an idol that is Is 44:10
He **f** it with hammers and works it with Is 44:12

FAST (89)
and his mother and hold **f** to his wife, Gn 2:24
boy, and hold him **f** with your hand, Gn 21:18
But you who held **f** to the LORD your God Dt 4:4
You shall serve him and hold **f** to him, Dt 10:20
in all his ways, and holding **f** to him, Dt 11:22
you shall serve him and hold **f** to him. Dt 13:4
obeying his voice and holding **f** to him, Dt 30:20
he was lying **f** asleep from weariness. Jgs 4:21
But now he is dead. Why should I **f**? 2 Sm 12:23
and his head caught **f** in the oak, 2 Sm 18:9
she wrote in the letters, "Proclaim a **f**, 1 Kgs 21:9
they proclaimed a **f** and set Naboth 1 Kgs 21:12
door and hold the door **f** against him. 2 Kgs 6:32
For he held **f** to the LORD. He did not 2 Kgs 18:6
and proclaimed a **f** throughout all 2 Chr 20:3
Then I proclaimed a **f** there, at the river Ezr 8:21
in Susa, and hold a **f** on my behalf, Est 4:16
my young women will also **f** as you do. Est 4:16
He still holds **f** his integrity, although you Jb 2:3
to him, "Do you still hold **f** your integrity? Jb 2:9
My foot has held **f** to his steps; I have Jb 23:11
I hold **f** my righteousness and will not let Jb 27:6
given, and the broad waters are frozen **f**. Jb 37:10
a mass and the clods stick **f** together? Jb 38:38
My steps have held **f** to your paths; my Ps 17:5
They hold **f** to their evil purpose; they Ps 64:5
"Because he holds **f** to me in love, I will Ps 91:14
established the earth, and it stands **f**. Ps 119:90
those who hold her **f** are called blessed. Prv 3:18
to me, "Let your heart hold **f** my words; Prv 4:4
and he is held **f** in the cords of his sin. Prv 5:22
to the slaughter, or as a stag is caught **f** Prv 7:22
Stand **f** in your enchantments and your Is 47:12
this, and the son of man who holds it **f**, Is 56:2
that please me and hold **f** my covenant, Is 56:4
not profane it, and holds **f** my covenant— Is 56:6
in the day of your **f** you seek your own Is 58:3
you **f** only to quarrel and to fight and to Is 58:4
Is such the **f** that I choose, a day for a Is 58:5
Will you call this a **f**, and a day Is 58:5
"Is not this the **f** that I choose: to loose the Is 58:6
backsliding? They hold **f** to deceit; Jer 8:5
Though they **f**, I will not hear their cry, Jer 14:12
Jerusalem proclaimed a **f** before the Jer 36:9
took them captive have held them **f**; Jer 50:33
answered and said, "The thing stands **f**, Dn 6:12
God, return, hold **f** to love and justice, Hos 12:6
Consecrate a **f**; call a solemn assembly. Jl 1:14
Blow the trumpet in Zion; consecrate a **f**; Jl 2:15
ship and had lain down and was **f** asleep. Jon 1:5
They called for a **f** and put on sackcloth, Jon 3:5
the LORD is near, near and hastening **f**; Zep 1:14
The **f** of the fourth month and the fast Zec 8:19
fourth month and the **f** of the fifth and Zec 8:19
of the fifth and the **f** of the seventh and Zec 8:19
the seventh and the **f** of the tenth shall Zec 8:19
"And when you **f**, do not look gloomy Mt 6:16
But when you **f**, anoint your head and Mt 6:17
saying, "Why do we and the Pharisees **f**, Mt 9:14
fast, but your disciples do not **f**?" Mt 9:14
away from them, and then they will **f**. Mt 9:15
and his mother and hold **f** to his wife, Mt 19:5
and the disciples of the Pharisees **f**, Mk 2:18
fast, but your disciples do not **f**?" Mk 2:18
the wedding guests **f** while the Mk 2:19
bridegroom with them, they cannot **f**. Mk 2:19
them, and then they will **f** in that day. Mk 2:20
and mother and hold **f** to his wife, Mk 10:7
"The disciples of John **f** often and offer Lk 5:33
make wedding guests **f** while the Lk 5:34
them, and then they will **f** in those days." Lk 5:35
hold it **f** in an honest and good heart, Lk 8:15
I **f** twice a week; I give tithes of all that I Lk 18:12
because even the **F** was already over, Acts 27:9
but you stand **f** through faith. Rom 11:20
what is evil; hold **f** to what is good. Rom 12:9
if you hold **f** to the word I preached to 1 Cor 15:2
and mother and hold **f** to his wife, Eph 5:31
holding **f** to the word of life, so that in Phil 2:16
and not holding **f** to the Head, from Col 2:19
live, if you are standing **f** in the Lord. 1 Thes 3:8
test everything; hold **f** what is good. 1 Thes 5:21
if indeed we hold **f** our confidence and Heb 3:6
Son of God, let us hold **f** our confession. Heb 4:14
encouragement to hold **f** to the hope Heb 6:18
Let us hold **f** the confession of our Heb 10:23
Yet you hold **f** my name, and you did not Rv 2:13
Only hold **f** what you have until I come. Rv 2:25
Hold **f** what you have, so that no one Rv 3:11

FASTED (13)
before the LORD and **f** that day until Jgs 20:26
before the LORD and **f** on that day and 1 Sm 7:6
tree in Jabesh and **f** seven days. 1 Sm 31:13
and wept and **f** until evening for 2 Sm 1:12
And David **f** and went in and lay all 2 Sm 12:16
You **f** and wept for the child while he 2 Sm 12:21
the child was still alive, I **f** and wept, 2 Sm 12:22
on his flesh and **f** and lay in 1 Kgs 21:27
the oak in Jabesh and **f** seven days. 1 Chr 10:12
So we **f** and implored our God for this, Ezr 8:23
'Why have we **f**, and you see it not? Why Is 58:3
When you **f** and mourned in the fifth Zec 7:5
seventy years, was it for me that you **f**? Zec 7:5

FASTEN (6)
and **f** the rings to the four corners at its Ex 25:26
And you shall **f** it on the turban by a Ex 28:37
a cord of blue to **f** it on the turban Ex 39:31
with the web and **f** it tight with the Jgs 16:13
And I will **f** him like a peg in a secure Is 22:23
they **f** it with hammer and nails so that Jer 10:4

FASTENED (15)
with your belt **f**, your sandals on your Ex 12:11
four rings of gold and **f** the rings to the Ex 37:13
that has no cover **f** on it is unclean. Nm 19:15
And every one of you **f** on his weapons of Dt 1:41
and they **f** his body to the wall of 1 Sm 31:10
a sword in its sheath **f** on his thigh, 2 Sm 20:8
of their gods and **f** his head in the 1 Chr 10:10
and violet hangings **f** with cords of Est 1:6
the peg that was **f** in a secure place will Is 22:25
yoke; by his hand they were **f** together; Lam 1:14
long, were **f** all around within. Ezk 40:43
have a great millstone **f** around his neck Mt 18:6
the inner prison and **f** their feet in the Acts 16:24
because of the heat and **f** on his hand. Acts 28:3
therefore, having **f** on the belt of truth, Eph 6:14

FASTING (20)
at the evening sacrifice I rose from my **f**, Ezr 9:5
and I continued **f** and praying before the Neh 1:4
were assembled with **f** and in sackcloth, Neh 9:1
Jews, with **f** and weeping and lamenting, Est 4:3
wore sackcloth; I afflicted myself with **f**; Ps 35:13
I wept and humbled my soul with **f**, Ps 69:10
My knees are weak through **f**; my Ps 109:24
F like yours this day will not make your Is 58:4
and on a day of **f** in the hearing of all the Jer 36:6
went to his palace and spent the night **f**; Dn 6:18
pleas for mercy with **f** and sackcloth and Dn 9:3
"return to me with all your heart, with **f**, Jl 2:12
And after **f** forty days and forty nights, he Mt 4:2
their faces that their **f** may be seen by Mt 6:16
that your **f** may not be seen by others Mt 6:18
disciples and the Pharisees were **f**. Mk 2:18
worshiping with **f** and prayer night and Lk 2:37
they were worshiping the Lord and **f**, Acts 13:2
Then after **f** and praying they laid Acts 13:3
with prayer and **f** they committed Acts 14:23

FASTS (1)
regard to their **f** and their lamenting. Est 9:31

FAT (109)
of his flock and of their **f** portions. Gn 4:4
and you shall eat the **f** of the land.' Gn 45:18
or let the **f** of my feast remain until the Ex 23:18
shall take all the **f** that covers the Ex 29:13
two kidneys with the **f** that is on them, Ex 29:13
shall also take the **f** from the ram and Ex 29:22
from the ram and the **f** tail and the fat Ex 29:22
fat tail and the **f** that covers the entrails, Ex 29:22
two kidneys with the **f** that is on them, Ex 29:22
arrange the pieces, the head, and the **f**, Lv 1:8
cut it into pieces, with its head and its **f**, Lv 1:12
he shall offer the **f** covering the entrails Lv 3:3
the entrails and all the **f** that is on the Lv 3:3
the two kidneys with the **f** that is on them Lv 3:4
offer as a food offering to the LORD its **f**; Lv 3:9
he shall remove the whole **f** tail, cut off Lv 3:9
and the **f** that covers the entrails and all Lv 3:9
the entrails and all the **f** that is on the Lv 3:9
two kidneys with the **f** that is on them Lv 3:10
the **f** covering the entrails and all the fat Lv 3:14
the entrails and all the **f** that is on the Lv 3:14
two kidneys with the **f** that is on them Lv 3:15
with a pleasing aroma. All **f** is the LORD'S. Lv 3:16
places, that you eat neither **f** nor blood." Lv 3:17
And all the **f** of the bull of the sin offering Lv 4:8
the **f** that covers the entrails and all the fat Lv 4:8
the entrails and all the **f** that is on the Lv 4:8
the two kidneys with the **f** that is on them Lv 4:9
And all its **f** he shall take from it and Lv 4:19
And all its **f** he shall burn on the altar, Lv 4:26
like the **f** of the sacrifice of peace Lv 4:26
And all its **f** he shall remove, as the fat is Lv 4:31
as the **f** is removed from the peace Lv 4:31
And all its **f** he shall remove as the fat of Lv 4:35
he shall remove as the **f** of the lamb is Lv 4:35
burn on it the **f** of the peace offerings. Lv 6:12
And all its **f** shall be offered, the fat tail, Lv 7:3
And all its fat shall be offered, the **f** tail, Lv 7:3
the fat tail, the **f** that covers the entrails, Lv 7:3
the two kidneys with the **f** that is on them Lv 7:4
of Israel, saying, You shall eat no **f**, Lv 7:23
The **f** of an animal that dies of itself and Lv 7:24
dies of itself and the **f** of one that is torn Lv 7:24
person who eats of the **f** of an animal of Lv 7:25
He shall bring the **f** with the breast, that Lv 7:30
The priest shall burn the **f** on the altar, Lv 7:31
peace offerings and the **f** shall have the Lv 7:33
And he took all the **f** that was on the Lv 8:16
the liver and the two kidneys with their **f**, Lv 8:16
burned the head and the pieces and the **f**. Lv 8:20
Then he took the **f** and the fat tail and all Lv 8:25
took the fat and the **f** tail and all the fat Lv 8:25
fat tail and all the **f** that was on the Lv 8:25
two kidneys with their **f** and the right Lv 8:25
them on the pieces of **f** and on the right Lv 8:26
But the **f** and the kidneys and the long Lv 9:10
But the **f** pieces of the ox and of the ram, Lv 9:19
the **f** tail and that which covers the Lv 9:19
they put the **f** pieces on the breasts, and Lv 9:20
and he burned the **f** pieces on the altar, Lv 9:20
offering and the pieces of **f** on the altar, Lv 9:24
food offerings of the **f** pieces to wave for Lv 10:15
And the **f** of the sin offering he shall Lv 16:25
meeting and burn the **f** for a pleasing Lv 17:6
and shall burn their **f** as a food Nm 18:17
have eaten and are full and grown **f**, Dt 31:20
milk from the flock, with **f** of lambs, Dt 32:14
"But Jeshurun grew **f**, and kicked; you Dt 32:15
and kicked; you grew **f**, stout, and sleek; Dt 32:15
who ate the **f** of their sacrifices and Dt 32:38
of Moab. Now Eglon was a very **f** man. Jgs 3:17
the blade, and the **f** closed over the blade, Jgs 3:22
Moreover, before the **f** was burned, the 1 Sm 2:15
said to him, "Let them burn the **f** first, 1 Sm 2:16
and to listen than the **f** of rams. 1 Sm 15:22
of the slain, from the **f** of the mighty, 2 Sm 1:22
ten **f** oxen, and twenty pasture-fed 1 Kgs 4:23
grain offering and the **f** pieces of the 1 Kgs 8:64
grain offering and the **f** pieces of the 1 Kgs 8:64
burnt offering and the **f** of the peace 2 Chr 7:7
and the grain offering and the **f**. 2 Chr 7:7
there was the **f** of the peace offerings, 2 Chr 29:35
offerings and the **f** parts until night; 2 Chr 35:14
Eat the **f** and drink sweet wine and Neh 8:10
filled and became **f** and delighted Neh 9:25
his face with his **f** and gathered fat upon Jb 15:27
his fat and gathered **f** upon his waist Jb 15:27
will be satisfied as with **f** and rich food, Ps 63:5
until death; their bodies are **f** and sleek. Ps 73:4
my body has become gaunt, with no **f**. Ps 109:24
their heart is unfeeling like **f**, but I Ps 119:70
of rams and the **f** of well-fed beasts; Is 1:11
yoke will be broken because of the **f**." Is 10:27
low, and the **f** of his flesh will grow lean. Is 17:4
it is gorged with **f**, with the blood of Is 34:6
goats, with the **f** of the kidneys of rams. Is 34:6
and their soil shall be gorged with **f**. Is 34:7
satisfied me with the **f** of your sacrifices. Is 43:24
they have grown **f** and sleek. They know Jer 5:28
You eat the **f**, you clothe yourselves Ezk 34:3
with the wool, you slaughter the **f** ones, Ezk 34:3
and the **f** and the strong I will destroy. Ezk 34:16
will judge between the **f** sheep and the Ezk 34:20
bulls, all of them **f** beasts of Bashan. Ezk 39:18

And you shall eat **f** till you are filled, Ezk 39:19
offer to me my food, the **f** and the blood. Ezk 44:7
me to offer me the **f** and the blood, Ezk 44:15
but devours the flesh of the **f** ones, Zec 11:16
my oxen and my **f** calves have been Mt 22:4

FATALLY (2)
the way is long, and strike him **f**, Dt 19:6
him and strikes him **f** so that he dies, Dt 19:11

FATE (5)
are visited by the **f** of all mankind, Nm 16:29
him, and their **f** would last forever. Ps 81:15
their fold shall be appalled at their **f**. Jer 49:20
their fold shall be appalled at their **f**. Jer 50:45
me grief at the **f** of all the daughters Lam 3:51

FATHER (977)
man shall leave his **f** and his mother Gn 2:24
he was the **f** of those who dwell in tents Gn 4:20
he was the **f** of all those who play the Gn 4:21
Japheth. (Ham was the **f** of Canaan.) Gn 9:18
And Ham, the **f** of Canaan, saw the Gn 9:22
the nakedness of his **f** and told his two Gn 9:22
and covered the nakedness of their **f**. Gn 9:23
also, the **f** of all the children of Eber, Gn 10:21
the presence of his **f** Terah in the land Gn 11:28
daughter of Haran the **f** of Milcah and Gn 11:29
and you shall be the **f** of a multitude of Gn 17:4
I have made you the **f** of a multitude of Gn 17:5
him greatly. He shall **f** twelve princes, Gn 17:20
said to the younger, "Our **f** is old, Gn 19:31
Come, let us make our **f** drink wine, Gn 19:32
we may preserve offspring from our **f**." Gn 19:32
So they made their **f** drink wine that Gn 19:33
firstborn went in and lay with her **f**. Gn 19:33
"Behold, I lay last night with my **f**. Gn 19:34
we may preserve offspring from our **f**." Gn 19:34
So they made their **f** drink wine that Gn 19:35
of Lot became pregnant by their **f**. Gn 19:36
He is the **f** of the Moabites to this day. Gn 19:37
He is the **f** of the Ammonites to this Gn 19:38
the daughter of my **f** though not the Gn 20:12
And Isaac said to his **f** Abraham, "My Gn 22:7
father Abraham, "My **f**!" And he said, Gn 22:7
Buz his brother, Kemuel the **f** of Aram, Gn 22:21
the oath that I swore to Abraham your **f**. Gn 26:3
had dug in the days of Abraham his **f**.) Gn 26:15
been dug in the days of Abraham his **f**, Gn 26:18
the names that his **f** had given them. Gn 26:18
said, "I am the God of Abraham your **f**. Gn 26:24
"I heard your **f** speak to your brother Gn 27:6
from them delicious food for your **f**, Gn 27:9
And you shall bring it to your **f** to eat, Gn 27:10
Perhaps my **f** will feel me, and I shall Gn 27:12
delicious food, such as his **f** loved. Gn 27:14
So he went in to his **f** and said, "My Gn 27:18
father and said, "My **f**." And he said, Gn 27:18
Jacob said to his **f**, "I am Esau your Gn 27:19
So Jacob went near to Isaac his **f**, who Gn 27:22
Then his **f** Isaac said to him, "Come Gn 27:26
out from the presence of Isaac his **f**, Gn 27:30
delicious food and brought it to his **f**. Gn 27:31
And he said to his **f**, "Let my father Gn 27:31
"Let my **f** arise and eat of his son's Gn 27:31
His **f** Isaac said to him, "Who are Gn 27:32
soon as Esau heard the words of his **f**, Gn 27:34
great and bitter cry and said to his **f**, Gn 27:34
"Bless me, even me also, O my **f**!" Gn 27:34
Esau said to his **f**, "Have you but one Gn 27:38
"Have you but one blessing, my **f**? Gn 27:38
O my **f**." And Esau lifted up his voice Gn 27:38
Then Isaac his **f** answered and said to Gn 27:39
with which his **f** had blessed him, Gn 27:41
of mourning for my **f** are approaching; Gn 27:41
to the house of Bethuel your mother's **f**, Gn 28:2
Jacob had obeyed his **f** and his mother Gn 28:7
women did not please Isaac his **f**, Gn 28:8
God of Abraham your **f** and the God of Gn 28:13
son, and she ran and told her **f**. Gn 29:12
"I see that your **f** does not regard me Gn 31:5
But the God of my **f** has been with me. Gn 31:5
I have served your **f** with all my Gn 31:6
yet your **f** has cheated me and changed Gn 31:7
the livestock of your **f** and given them to Gn 31:9
taken away from our **f** belongs to us Gn 31:16
go to the land of Canaan to his **f** Isaac. Gn 31:18
But the God of your **f** spoke to me last Gn 31:29
And she said to her **f**, "Let not my lord Gn 31:35
If the God of my **f**, the God of Abraham Gn 31:42
the God of Nahor, the God of their **f**, Gn 31:53
Jacob swore by the Fear of his **f** Isaac, Gn 31:53
"O God of my **f** Abraham and God of Gn 32:9
father Abraham and God of my **f** Isaac, Gn 32:9
from the sons of Hamor, Shechem's **f**, Gn 33:19
So Shechem spoke to his **f** Hamor, Gn 34:4
And Hamor the **f** of Shechem went out Gn 34:6
also said to her **f** and to her brothers, Gn 34:11
Shechem and his **f** Hamor deceitfully, Gn 34:13
but his **f** called him Benjamin. Gn 35:18
Jacob came to his **f** Isaac at Mamre, Gn 35:27
of Esau the **f** of the Edomites Gn 36:9
pastured the donkeys of Zibeon his **f**. Gn 36:24
of Edom (that is, Esau, the **f** of Edom), Gn 36:43
brought a bad report of them to their **f**. Gn 37:2
saw that their **f** loved him more Gn 37:4
he told it to his **f** and to his brothers, Gn 37:10
his **f** rebuked him and said to him, Gn 37:10
him, but his **f** kept the saying in mind. Gn 37:11
out of their hand to restore him to his **f**. Gn 37:22
and brought it to their **f** and said, Gn 37:32
mourning." Thus his **f** wept for him. Gn 37:35
the youngest is this day with our **f**, Gn 42:13
came to Jacob their **f** in the land of Gn 42:29
We are twelve brothers, sons of our **f**. Gn 42:32
is this day with our **f** in the land of Gn 42:32
they and their **f** saw their bundles Gn 42:35
And Jacob their **f** said to them, "You Gn 42:36
Then Reuben said to his **f**, "Kill my Gn 42:37
from Egypt, their **f** said to them, Gn 43:2
our kindred, saying, 'Is your **f** still alive? Gn 43:7
And Judah said to Israel his **f**, "Send the Gn 43:8
Then their **f** Israel said to them, "If it Gn 43:11
the God of your **f** has put treasure in Gn 43:23
their welfare and said, "Is your **f** well, Gn 43:27
They said, "Your servant our **f** is well; Gn 43:28
as for you, go up in peace to your **f**." Gn 44:17
his servants, saying, 'Have you a **f**, Gn 44:19
And we said to my lord, 'We have a **f**, Gn 44:20
mother's children, and his **f** loves him.' Gn 44:20
to my lord, 'The boy cannot leave his **f**, Gn 44:22
his father, for if he should leave his **f**, Gn 44:22
should leave his father, his **f** would die.' Gn 44:22
we went back to your servant my **f**, Gn 44:24
And when our **f** said, 'Go again, buy us Gn 44:25
Then your servant my **f** said to us, Gn 44:27
as soon as I come to your servant my **f**, Gn 44:30
of your servant our **f** with sorrow to Gn 44:31
a pledge of safety for the boy to my **f**, Gn 44:32
bear the blame before my **f** all my life.' Gn 44:32
can I go back to my **f** if the boy is not Gn 44:34
to see the evil that would find my **f**." Gn 44:34
Is my **f** still alive?" But his brothers Gn 45:3
He has made me a **f** to Pharaoh, and Gn 45:8
Hurry and go up to my **f** and say to him, Gn 45:9
You must tell my **f** of all my honor in Gn 45:13
Hurry and bring my **f** down here." Gn 45:13
and take your **f** and your households, Gn 45:18
and for your wives, and bring your **f**, Gn 45:19
To his **f** he sent as follows: ten donkeys Gn 45:23
and provision for his **f** on the journey. Gn 45:23
to the land of Canaan to their **f** Jacob. Gn 45:25
him, the spirit of their **f** Jacob revived. Gn 45:27
sacrifices to the God of his **f** Isaac. Gn 46:1
he said, "I am God, the God of your **f**. Gn 46:3
The sons of Israel carried Jacob their **f**, Gn 46:5
went up to meet Israel his **f** in Goshen. Gn 46:29
told Pharaoh, "My **f** and my brothers, Gn 47:1
"Your **f** and your brothers have come to Gn 47:5
Settle your **f** and your brothers in the Gn 47:6
brought in Jacob his **f** and stood him Gn 47:7
Joseph settled his **f** and his brothers Gn 47:11
And Joseph provided his **f**, his brothers, Gn 47:12
your **f** is ill." So he took with him his Gn 48:1
Joseph said to his **f**, "They are my sons, Gn 48:9
Joseph saw that his **f** laid his right Gn 48:17
And Joseph said to his **f**, "Not this way, Gn 48:18
said to his father, "Not this way, my **f**; Gn 48:18
But his **f** refused and said, "I know, my Gn 48:19
O sons of Jacob, listen to Israel your **f**. Gn 49:2
by the God of your **f** who will help you, Gn 49:25
blessings of your **f** are mighty beyond Gn 49:26
This is what their **f** said to them as he Gn 49:28
the physicians to embalm his **f**. Gn 50:2
My **f** made me swear, saying, 'I am Gn 50:5
let me please go up and bury my **f**, Gn 50:5
answered, "Go up, and bury your **f**, Gn 50:6
So Joseph went up to bury his **f**. With Gn 50:7
made a mourning for his **f** seven days. Gn 50:10
After he had buried his **f**, Joseph Gn 50:14
had gone up with him to bury his **f**. Gn 50:14
brothers saw that their **f** was dead, Gn 50:15
"Your **f** gave this command before he Gn 50:16
the God of your **f**." Joseph wept when Gn 50:17
When they came home to their **f** Reuel, Ex 2:18
And he said, "I am the God of your **f**, the Ex 3:6
he said, "The God of my **f** was my help, Ex 18:4
"Honor your **f** and your mother, that Ex 20:12
"Whoever strikes his **f** or his mother Ex 21:15
"Whoever curses his **f** or his mother Ex 21:17
If her **f** utterly refuses to give her to Ex 22:17
anoint them, as you anointed their **f**, Ex 40:15
not uncover the nakedness of your **f**, Lv 18:7
of you shall revere his mother and his **f**, Lv 19:3
anyone who curses his **f** or his mother Lv 20:9
death; he has cursed his **f** or his mother; Lv 20:9
a daughter of his **f** or a daughter of his Lv 20:17
for his closest relatives, his mother, his **f**, Lv 21:2
herself by whoring, profanes her **f**; Lv 21:9
even for his **f** or for his mother. Lv 21:11
woman's son, whose **f** was an Egyptian, Lv 24:10
as priests in the lifetime of Aaron their **f**. Nm 3:4
Not even for his **f** or for his mother, for Nm 6:7
"If her **f** had but spit in her face, Nm 12:14
the tribe of Levi, the tribe of your **f**, Nm 18:2
and Machir was the **f** of Gilead; Nm 26:29
And Kohath was the **f** of Amram. Nm 26:58
"Our **f** died in the wilderness. He was Nm 27:3
the name of our **f** be taken away from Nm 27:4
the inheritance of their **f** to them. Nm 27:7
And if his **f** has no brothers, then you Nm 27:11
and her **f** hears of her vow and of her Nm 30:4
But if her **f** opposes her on the day that Nm 30:5
forgive her, because her **f** opposed her. Nm 30:5
wife and about a **f** and his daughter Nm 30:16
within the clan of the tribe of their **f**. Nm 36:6
to one of the clan of the tribe of her **f**, Nm 36:8
"When you **f** children and children's Dt 4:25
"'Honor your **f** and your mother, as the Dt 5:16
house and lament her **f** and her mother Dt 21:13
obey the voice of his **f** or the voice of his Dt 21:18
then his **f** and his mother shall take Dt 21:19
then the **f** of the young woman and her Dt 22:15
And the **f** of the young woman shall say Dt 22:16
give them to the **f** of the young woman, Dt 22:19
shall give to the **f** of the young woman Dt 22:29
God, 'A wandering Aramean was my **f**. Dt 26:5
who dishonors his **f** or his mother.' Dt 27:16
the daughter of his **f** or the daughter of Dt 27:22
You shall **f** sons and daughters, but Dt 28:41
Is not he your **f**, who created you, who Dt 32:6
ask your **f**, and he will show you, your Dt 32:7
who said of his **f** and mother, 'I regard Dt 33:9
you will save alive my **f** and mother, Jos 2:13
into your house your **f** and mother, Jos 2:18
out Rahab and her **f** and mother and Jos 6:23
is, Hebron (Arba was the **f** of Anak). Jos 15:13
she urged him to ask her **f** for a field. Jos 15:18
firstborn of Manasseh, the **f** of Gilead, Jos 17:1
among the brothers of their **f**. Jos 17:4
(Arba being the **f** of Anak), Jos 21:11
Terah, the **f** of Abraham and of Nahor; Jos 24:2
I took your **f** Abraham from beyond Jos 24:3
sons of Hamor the **f** of Shechem for a Jos 24:32
she urged him to ask her **f** for a field. Jgs 1:14
down the altar of Baal that your **f** has, Jgs 6:25
was buried in the tomb of Joash his **f**, Jgs 8:32
for my **f** fought for you and risked his Jgs 9:17
the men of Hamor the **f** of Shechem; Jgs 9:28
he committed against his **f** in killing his Jgs 9:56
a prostitute. Gilead was the **f** of Jephthah. Jgs 11:1
And she said to him, "My **f**, you have Jgs 11:36
So she said to her **f**, "Let this thing be Jgs 11:37
of two months, she returned to her **f**, Jgs 11:39
he came up and told his **f** and mother, Jgs 14:2
But his **f** and mother said to him, "Is Jgs 14:3
Philistines?" But Samson said to his **f**, Jgs 14:3
His **f** and mother did not know that it Jgs 14:4
went down with his **f** and mother to Jgs 14:5
he did not tell his **f** or his mother what Jgs 14:6
he came to his **f** and mother and gave Jgs 14:9
His **f** went down to the woman, and Jgs 14:10
I have not told my **f** nor my mother, Jgs 14:16
the chamber." But her **f** would not allow Jgs 15:1
And her **f** said, "I really thought that you Jgs 15:2
up and burned her and her **f** with fire. Jgs 15:6
Eshtaol in the tomb of Manoah his **f**. Jgs 16:31
with me, and be to me a **f** and a priest, Jgs 17:10
with us and be to us a **f** and a priest. Jgs 18:19
And when the girl's **f** saw him, he came Jgs 19:3
And his father-in-law, the girl's **f**, made Jgs 19:4
go, but the girl's **f** said to his son-in-law, Jgs 19:5
And the girl's **f** said to the man, "Be Jgs 19:6
And the girl's **f** said, "Strengthen your Jgs 19:8
to depart, his father-in-law, the girl's **f**, Jgs 19:9
how you left your **f** and mother and Ru 2:11
He was the **f** of Jesse, the father of David. Ru 4:17
He was the father of Jesse, the **f** of David. Ru 4:17
would not listen to the voice of their **f**, 1 Sm 2:25
the house of your **f** when they were in 1 Sm 2:27
the house of your **f** all my offerings by 1 Sm 2:28
the house of your **f** should go in and 1 Sm 2:30
Now the donkeys of Kish, Saul's **f**, were 1 Sm 9:3
lest my **f** cease to care about the 1 Sm 9:5
and now your **f** has ceased to care 1 Sm 10:2
who is their **f**?" Therefore it became 1 Sm 10:12
the other side." But he did not tell his **f**. 1 Sm 14:1

had not heard his **f** charge the people	1 Sm 14:27
"Your **f** strictly charged the people	1 Sm 14:28
said, "My **f** has troubled the land.	1 Sm 14:29
Kish was the **f** of Saul, and Ner the	1 Sm 14:51
and Ner the **f** of Abner was the son of	1 Sm 14:51
servant used to keep sheep for his **f**.	1 Sm 17:34
David, "Saul my **f** seeks to kill you.	1 Sm 19:2
and stand beside my **f** in the field	1 Sm 19:3
and I will speak to my **f** about you.	1 Sm 19:3
of David to Saul his **f** and said to him,	1 Sm 19:4
And what is my sin before your **f**, that	1 Sm 20:1
my **f** does nothing either great or	1 Sm 20:2
And why should my **f** hide this from	1 Sm 20:2
"Your **f** knows well that I have found	1 Sm 20:3
If your **f** misses me at all, then say,	1 Sm 20:6
why should you bring me to your **f**?"	1 Sm 20:8
determined by my **f** that harm should	1 Sm 20:9
me if your **f** answers you roughly?"	1 Sm 20:10
When I have sounded out my **f**,	1 Sm 20:12
should it please my **f** to do you harm,	1 Sm 20:13
with you, as he has been with my **f**.	1 Sm 20:13
Then Jonathan answered Saul his **f**,	1 Sm 20:32
knew that his **f** was determined to	1 Sm 20:33
because his **f** had disgraced him.	1 Sm 20:34
"Please let my **f** and my mother stay	1 Sm 22:3
servant or to all the house of my **f**,	1 Sm 22:15
hand of Saul my **f** shall not find you.	1 Sm 23:17
to you. Saul my **f** also knows this."	1 Sm 23:17
See, my **f**, see the corner of your robe	1 Sm 24:11
and buried him in the tomb of his **f**,	2 Sm 2:32
love to the house of Saul your **f**,	2 Sm 3:8
chose me above your **f** and above all	2 Sm 6:21
I will be to him a **f**, and he shall be to	2 Sm 7:14
for the sake of your **f** Jonathan,	2 Sm 9:7
to you all the land of Saul your **f**,	2 Sm 9:7
as his **f** dealt loyally with me." So	2 Sm 10:2
to console him concerning his **f**.	2 Sm 10:2
to you, that he is honoring your **f**?	2 Sm 10:3
And when your **f** comes to see you,	2 Sm 13:5
give me back the kingdom of my **f**.'"	2 Sm 16:3
As I have served your **f**, so I will serve	2 Sm 16:19
made yourself a stench to your **f**,	2 Sm 16:21
"You know that your **f** and his men	2 Sm 17:8
Besides, your **f** is expert in war; he will	2 Sm 17:8
Israel knows that your **f** is a mighty	2 Sm 17:10
and was buried in the tomb of his **f**.	2 Sm 17:23
the grave of my **f** and my mother.	2 Sm 19:37
in Zela, in the tomb of Kish his **f**.	2 Sm 21:14
His **f** had never at any time displeased	1 Kgs 1:6
sat on the throne of David his **f**,	1 Kgs 2:12
me on the throne of David my **f**,	1 Kgs 2:24
of the Lord GOD before David my **f**,	1 Kgs 2:26
without the knowledge of my **f** David,	1 Kgs 2:32
the harm that you did to David my **f**.	1 Kgs 2:44
walking in the statutes of David his **f**,	1 Kgs 3:3
love to your servant David my **f**,	1 Kgs 3:6
servant king in place of David my **f**,	1 Kgs 3:7
as your **f** David walked,	1 Kgs 3:14
anointed him king in place of his **f**,	1 Kgs 5:1
know that David my **f** could not build	1 Kgs 5:3
God, as the LORD said to David my **f**,	1 Kgs 5:5
you, which I spoke to David your **f**.	1 Kgs 6:12
and his **f** was a man of Tyre,	1 Kgs 7:14
things that David his **f** had dedicated,	1 Kgs 7:51
with his mouth to David my **f**,	1 Kgs 8:15
heart of David my **f** to build a house	1 Kgs 8:17
But the LORD said to David my **f**,	1 Kgs 8:18
have risen in the place of David my **f**,	1 Kgs 8:20
servant David my **f** what you	1 Kgs 8:24
servant David my **f** what you have	1 Kgs 8:25
spoken to your servant David my **f**.	1 Kgs 8:26
before me, as David your **f** walked,	1 Kgs 9:4
forever, as I promised David your **f**,	1 Kgs 9:5
God, as was the heart of David his **f**.	1 Kgs 11:4
the LORD, as David his **f** had done.	1 Kgs 11:6
the sake of David your **f** I will not do	1 Kgs 11:12
the breach of the city of David his **f**.	1 Kgs 11:27
and my rules, as David his **f** did.	1 Kgs 11:33
was buried in the city of David his **f**.	1 Kgs 11:43
"Your **f** made our yoke heavy. Now	1 Kgs 12:4
hard service of your **f** and his heavy	1 Kgs 12:4
before Solomon his **f** while he was	1 Kgs 12:6
the yoke that your **f** put on us'?"	1 Kgs 12:9
you, 'Your **f** made our yoke heavy,	1 Kgs 12:10
whereas my **f** laid on you a heavy	1 Kgs 12:11
My **f** disciplined you with whips,	1 Kgs 12:11
"My **f** made your yoke heavy,	1 Kgs 12:14
My **f** disciplined you with whips,	1 Kgs 12:14
also told to their **f** the words that he	1 Kgs 13:11
And their **f** said to them, "Which	1 Kgs 13:12
all the sins that his **f** did before him,	1 Kgs 15:3
his God, as the heart of David his **f**.	1 Kgs 15:3
of the LORD, as David his **f** had done.	1 Kgs 15:11
sacred gifts of his **f** and his own	1 Kgs 15:15
was between my **f** and your father.	1 Kgs 15:19
was between my father and your **f**.	1 Kgs 15:19
his fathers in the city of David his **f**,	1 Kgs 15:24
LORD and walked in the way of his **f**,	1 Kgs 15:26
"Let me kiss my **f** and my mother,	1 Kgs 19:20
"The cities that my **f** took from your	1 Kgs 20:34
father took from your **f** I will restore,	1 Kgs 20:34
as my **f** did in Samaria." And Ahab	1 Kgs 20:34
He walked in all the way of Asa his **f**.	1 Kgs 22:43
remained in the days of his **f** Asa.	1 Kgs 22:46
his fathers in the city of David his **f**,	1 Kgs 22:50
in the way of his **f** and in the way of	1 Kgs 22:52
in every way that his **f** had done.	1 Kgs 22:53
And Elisha saw it and he cried, "My **f**,	2 Kgs 2:12
saw it and he cried, "My father, my **f**!	2 Kgs 2:12
though not like his **f** and mother,	2 Kgs 3:2
the pillar of Baal that his **f** had made.	2 Kgs 3:2
the prophets of your **f** and to the	2 Kgs 3:13
one day to his **f** among the reapers.	2 Kgs 4:18
And he said to his **f**, "Oh, my head,	2 Kgs 4:19
my head!" The **f** said to his servant,	2 Kgs 4:19
came near and said to him, "My **f**,	2 Kgs 5:13
saw them, he said to Elisha, "My **f**,	2 Kgs 6:21
I rode side by side behind Ahab his **f**,	2 Kgs 9:25
and wept before him, crying, "My **f**,	2 Kgs 13:14
him, crying, "My father, my **f**!	2 Kgs 13:14
taken from Jehoahaz his **f** in war.	2 Kgs 13:25
of the LORD, yet not like David his **f**.	2 Kgs 14:3
in all things as Joash his **f** had done.	2 Kgs 14:3
who had struck down the king his **f**.	2 Kgs 14:5
him king instead of his **f** Amaziah.	2 Kgs 14:21
to all that his **f** Amaziah had done.	2 Kgs 15:3
to all that his **f** Uzziah had done.	2 Kgs 15:34
his fathers in the city of David his **f**,	2 Kgs 15:38
LORD his God, as his **f** David had done,	2 Kgs 16:2
to all that David his **f** had done.	2 Kgs 18:3
the LORD, the God of David your **f**:	2 Kgs 20:5
that Hezekiah his **f** had destroyed,	2 Kgs 21:3
LORD, as Manasseh his **f** had done.	2 Kgs 21:20
in which his **f** walked and served	2 Kgs 21:21
idols that his **f** served and worshiped	2 Kgs 21:21
walked in all the way of David his **f**,	2 Kgs 22:2
king in the place of Josiah his **f**,	2 Kgs 23:34
according to all that his **f** had done.	2 Kgs 24:9
and the **f** of Amasa was Jether the	1 Chr 2:17
daughter of Machir the **f** of Gilead,	1 Chr 2:21
of Machir, the **f** of Gilead.	1 Chr 2:23
Ephrathah, the wife of Hezron his **f**,	1 Chr 2:24
she bore him Ashhur, the **f** of Tekoa.	1 Chr 2:24
fathered Raham, the **f** of Jorkeam;	1 Chr 2:44
bore Shaaph the **f** of Madmannah,	1 Chr 2:49
Sheva the **f** of Machbenah and the	1 Chr 2:49
of Machbenah and the **f** of Gibea;	1 Chr 2:49
Shobal the **f** of Kiriath-jearim,	1 Chr 2:50
Salma, the **f** of Bethlehem, and	1 Chr 2:51
and Hareph the **f** of Beth-gader.	1 Chr 2:51
Shobal the **f** of Kiriath-jearim had	1 Chr 2:52
the **f** of the house of Rechab.	1 Chr 2:55
of Ephrathah, the **f** of Bethlehem.	1 Chr 4:4
Ashhur, the **f** of Tekoa, had two wives,	1 Chr 4:5
and Tehinnah, the **f** of Ir-nahash.	1 Chr 4:12
fathered Joab, the **f** of Ge-harashim,	1 Chr 4:14
and Ishbah, the **f** of Eshtemoa.	1 Chr 4:17
wife bore Jered the **f** of Gedor,	1 Chr 4:18
father of Gedor, Heber the **f** of Soco,	1 Chr 4:18
Soco, and Jekuthiel the **f** of Zanoah.	1 Chr 4:18
the son of Judah: Er the **f** of Lecah,	1 Chr 4:21
of Lecah, Laadah the **f** of Mareshah,	1 Chr 4:21
bore; she bore Machir the **f** of Gilead.	1 Chr 7:14
And Ephraim their **f** mourned many	1 Chr 7:22
Jeiel the **f** of Gibeon lived in Gibeon,	1 Chr 8:29
Ner was the **f** of Kish, Kish of Saul,	1 Chr 8:33
and Merib-baal was the **f** of Micah.	1 Chr 8:34
In Gibeon lived the **f** of Gibeon, Jeiel,	1 Chr 9:35
and Mikloth was the **f** of Shimeam;	1 Chr 9:38
I will be to him a **f**, and he shall be	1 Chr 17:13
for his **f** dealt kindly with me." So	1 Chr 19:2
to console him concerning his **f**.	1 Chr 19:2
to you, that he is honoring your **f**?	1 Chr 19:3
shall be my son, and I will be his **f**,	1 Chr 22:10
Abihu died before their **f** and had no	1 Chr 24:2
for them by Aaron their **f**,	1 Chr 24:19
the direction of their **f** Jeduthun,	1 Chr 25:3
the direction of their **f** in the music	1 Chr 25:6
the firstborn, his **f** made him chief),	1 Chr 26:10
him to be my son, and I will be his **f**.	1 Chr 28:6
the God of your **f** and serve him with	1 Chr 28:9
you, O LORD, the God of Israel our **f**,	1 Chr 29:10
LORD as king in place of David his **f**.	1 Chr 29:23
great and steadfast love to David my **f**,	2 Chr 1:8
word to David my **f** be now fulfilled,	2 Chr 1:9
dealt with David my **f** and sent him	2 Chr 2:3
whom David my **f** provided.	2 Chr 2:7
of Dan, and his **f** was a man of Tyre.	2 Chr 2:14
craftsmen of my lord, David your **f**.	2 Chr 2:14
of them that David his **f** had taken,	2 Chr 2:17
the LORD had appeared to David his **f**,	2 Chr 3:1
things that David his **f** had dedicated,	2 Chr 5:1
with his mouth to David my **f**,	2 Chr 6:4
heart of David my **f** to build a house	2 Chr 6:7
But the LORD said to David my **f**,	2 Chr 6:8
the place of David my **f** and sit on the	2 Chr 6:10
servant David my **f** what you	2 Chr 6:15
servant David my **f** what you have	2 Chr 6:16
before me as David your **f** walked,	2 Chr 7:17
as I covenanted with David your **f**,	2 Chr 7:18
to the ruling of David his **f**,	2 Chr 8:14
was buried in the city of David his **f**,	2 Chr 9:31
"Your **f** made our yoke heavy. Now	2 Chr 10:4
hard service of your **f** and his heavy	2 Chr 10:4
before Solomon his **f** while he was	2 Chr 10:6
the yoke that your **f** put on us'?"	2 Chr 10:9
you, 'Your **f** made our yoke heavy,	2 Chr 10:10
whereas my **f** laid on you a heavy	2 Chr 10:11
My **f** disciplined you with whips,	2 Chr 10:11
"My **f** made your yoke heavy,	2 Chr 10:14
My **f** disciplined you with whips,	2 Chr 10:14
sacred gifts of his **f** and his own	2 Chr 15:18
was between my **f** and your father.	2 Chr 16:3
was between my father and your **f**.	2 Chr 16:3
Ephraim that Asa his **f** had captured.	2 Chr 17:2
in the earlier ways of his **f** David.	2 Chr 17:3
the God of his **f** and walked in his	2 Chr 17:4
the way of Asa his **f** and did not turn	2 Chr 20:32
Their **f** gave them great gifts of silver,	2 Chr 21:3
throne of his **f** and was established,	2 Chr 21:4
the LORD, the God of David your **f**,	2 Chr 21:12
in the ways of Jehoshaphat your **f**,	2 Chr 21:12
the death of his **f** they were his	2 Chr 22:4
that Jehoiada, Zechariah's **f**,	2 Chr 24:22
who had struck down the king his **f**.	2 Chr 25:3
him king instead of his **f** Amaziah.	2 Chr 26:1
to all that his **f** Amaziah had done.	2 Chr 26:4
to all that his **f** Uzziah had done,	2 Chr 27:2
of the LORD, as his **f** David had done,	2 Chr 28:1
to all that David his **f** had done.	2 Chr 29:2
places that his **f** Hezekiah had	2 Chr 33:3
LORD, as Manasseh his **f** had done.	2 Chr 33:22
that Manasseh his **f** had made,	2 Chr 33:22
as Manasseh his **f** had humbled	2 Chr 33:23
walked in the ways of David his **f**;	2 Chr 34:2
began to seek the God of David his **f**,	2 Chr 34:3
And Jeshua was the **f** of Joiakim,	Neh 12:10
of Joiakim, Joiakim the **f** of Eliashib,	Neh 12:10
of Eliashib, Eliashib the **f** of Joiada,	Neh 12:10
Joiada the **f** of Jonathan, and	Neh 12:11
and Jonathan the **f** of Jaddua.	Neh 12:11
uncle, for she had neither **f** nor mother.	Est 2:7
at, and when her **f** and her mother died,	Est 2:7
aged are among us, older than your **f**.	Jb 15:10
if I say to the pit, 'You are my **f**,' and to	Jb 17:14
I was a **f** to the needy, and I searched out	Jb 29:16
fatherless grew up with me as with a **f**,	Jb 31:18
"Has the rain a **f**, or who has begotten	Jb 38:28
And their **f** gave them an inheritance	Jb 42:15
For my **f** and my mother have forsaken	Ps 27:10
F of the fatherless and protector of	Ps 68:5
He shall cry to me, 'You are my **F**, my	Ps 89:26
As a **f** shows compassion to his	Ps 103:13
as a **f** the son in whom he delights.	Prv 3:12
When I was a son with my **f**, tender, the	Prv 4:3
A wise son makes a glad **f**, but a foolish	Prv 10:1
A wise son makes a glad **f**, but a	Prv 15:20
sorrow, and the **f** of a fool has no joy.	Prv 17:21
is a grief to his **f** and bitterness to her	Prv 17:25
A foolish son is ruin to his **f**, and a	Prv 19:13
does violence to his **f** and chases away	Prv 19:26
If one curses his **f** or his mother, his	Prv 20:20
Listen to your **f** who gave you life, and	Prv 23:22
The **f** of the righteous will greatly	Prv 23:24
Let your **f** and mother be glad; let her	Prv 23:25
a companion of gluttons shames his **f**.	Prv 28:7
Whoever robs his **f** or his mother and	Prv 28:24
He who loves wisdom makes his **f** glad,	Prv 29:3
eye that mocks a **f** and scorns to obey	Prv 30:17
in a bad venture. And he is **f** of a son,	Eccl 5:14
hold of his brother in the house of his **f**,	Is 3:6
knows how to cry 'My **f**' or 'My mother,'	Is 8:4
Counselor, Mighty God, Everlasting **F**,	Is 9:6
And he shall be a **f** to the inhabitants of	Is 22:21
says the LORD, the God of David your **f**:	Is 38:5
the **f** makes known to the children your	Is 38:19
will come from you, whom you will **f**,	Is 39:7
Your first **f** sinned, and your mediators	Is 43:27
Woe to him who says to a **f**, 'What are	Is 45:10
Look to Abraham your **f** and to Sarah	Is 51:2
you with the heritage of Jacob your **f**,	Is 58:14
For you are our **F**, though Abraham	Is 63:16
you, O LORD, are our **F**, our Redeemer	Is 63:16
But now, O LORD, you are our **F**; we are the	Is 64:8
who say to a tree, 'You are my **f**,' and to a	Jer 2:27

Have you not just now called to me, 'My **f**, Jer 3:4
And I thought you would call me, My **F**, Jer 3:19
your brothers and the house of your **f**, Jer 12:6
to drink for his **f** or his mother. Jer 16:7
the man who brought the news to my **f**, Jer 20:15
who reigned instead of Josiah his **f**, Jer 22:11
Did not your **f** eat and drink and do Jer 22:15
shall not stumble, for I am a **f** to Israel, Jer 31:9
for Jonadab the son of Rechab, our **f**, Jer 35:6
of Jonadab the son of Rechab, our **f**, Jer 35:8
all that Jonadab our **f** commanded us. Jer 35:10
the command that their **f** gave them, Jer 35:16
of Jonadab your **f** and kept all Jer 35:18
your **f** was an Amorite and your Ezk 16:3
was a Hittite and your **f** an Amorite. Ezk 16:45
the soul of the **f** as well as the soul of the Ezk 18:4
sees all the sins that his **f** has done; Ezk 18:14
As for his **f**, because he practiced Ezk 18:18
the son suffer for the iniquity of the **f**?' Ezk 18:19
not suffer for the iniquity of the **f**, Ezk 18:20
nor the **f** suffer for the iniquity of the Ezk 18:20
F and mother are treated with Ezk 22:7
However, for **f** or mother, for son or Ezk 44:25
that Nebuchadnezzar his **f** had taken out Dn 5:2
In the days of your **f**, light and Dn 5:11
your **f**—your father the king—made Dn 5:11
your father—your **f** the king—made Dn 5:11
the king my **f** brought from Judah. Dn 5:13
Nebuchadnezzar your **f** kingship and Dn 5:18
a man and his **f** go in to the same girl, so Am 2:7
for the son treats the **f** with contempt, the Mi 7:6
his **f** and mother who bore him will say Zec 13:3
And his **f** and mother who bore him Zec 13:3
"A son honors his **f**, and a servant his Mal 1:6
If then I am a **f**, where is my honor? Mal 1:6
Have we not all one **F**? Has not one God Mal 2:10
Abraham was the **f** of Isaac, and Isaac the Mt 1:2
father of Isaac, and Isaac the **f** of Jacob, Mt 1:2
and Jacob the **f** of Judah and his brothers, Mt 1:2
and Judah the **f** of Perez and Zerah by Mt 1:3
by Tamar, and Perez the **f** of Hezron, Mt 1:3
father of Hezron, and Hezron the **f** of Ram, Mt 1:3
and Ram the **f** of Amminadab, and Mt 1:4
and Amminadab the **f** of Nahshon, Mt 1:4
Nahshon, and Nahshon the **f** of Salmon, Mt 1:4
and Salmon the **f** of Boaz by Rahab, and Mt 1:5
Rahab, and Boaz the **f** of Obed by Ruth, Mt 1:5
of Obed by Ruth, and Obed the **f** of Jesse, Mt 1:5
and Jesse the **f** of David the king. And Mt 1:6
And David was the **f** of Solomon by the Mt 1:6
and Solomon the **f** of Rehoboam, and Mt 1:7
and Rehoboam the **f** of Abijah, Mt 1:7
of Abijah, and Abijah the **f** of Asaph, Mt 1:7
and Asaph the **f** of Jehoshaphat, and Mt 1:8
and Jehoshaphat the **f** of Joram, Mt 1:8
of Joram, and Joram the **f** of Uzziah, Mt 1:8
and Uzziah the **f** of Jotham, and Jotham Mt 1:9
of Jotham, and Jotham the **f** of Ahaz, Mt 1:9
of Ahaz, and Ahaz the **f** of Hezekiah, Mt 1:9
and Hezekiah the **f** of Manasseh, and Mt 1:10
Manasseh, and Manasseh the **f** of Amos, Mt 1:10
of Amos, and Amos the **f** of Josiah, Mt 1:10
and Josiah the **f** of Jechoniah and his Mt 1:11
Jechoniah was the **f** of Shealtiel, and Mt 1:12
and Shealtiel the **f** of Zerubbabel, Mt 1:12
and Zerubbabel the **f** of Abiud, and Mt 1:13
of Abiud, and Abiud the **f** of Eliakim, Mt 1:13
of Eliakim, and Eliakim the **f** of Azor, Mt 1:13
and Azor the **f** of Zadok, and Zadok the Mt 1:14
of Zadok, and Zadok the **f** of Achim, Mt 1:14
of Achim, and Achim the **f** of Eliud, Mt 1:14
and Eliud the **f** of Eleazar, and Eleazar Mt 1:15
of Eleazar, and Eleazar the **f** of Matthan, Mt 1:15
of Matthan, and Matthan the **f** of Jacob, Mt 1:15
and Jacob the **f** of Joseph the husband of Mt 1:16
over Judea in place of his **f** Herod, Mt 2:22
yourselves, 'We have Abraham as our **f**,' Mt 3:9
brother, in the boat with Zebedee their **f**, Mt 4:21
the boat and their **f** and followed him. Mt 4:22
give glory to your **F** who is in heaven. Mt 5:16
may be sons of your **F** who is in heaven. Mt 5:45
be perfect, as your heavenly **F** is perfect. Mt 5:48
no reward from your **F** who is in heaven. Mt 6:1
And your **F** who sees in secret will reward Mt 6:4
door and pray to your **F** who is in secret. Mt 6:6
And your **F** who sees in secret will reward Mt 6:6
for your **F** knows what you need before Mt 6:8
"Our **F** in heaven, hallowed be your Mt 6:9
your heavenly **F** will also forgive you, Mt 6:14
neither will your **F** forgive your Mt 6:15
by others but by your **F** who is in secret. Mt 6:18
And your **F** who sees in secret will Mt 6:18
and yet your heavenly **F** feeds them. Mt 6:26
and your heavenly **F** knows that you Mt 6:32
much more will your **F** who is in Mt 7:11
does the will of my **F** who is in heaven. Mt 7:21
"Lord, let me first go and bury my **f**." Mt 8:21
Spirit of your **F** speaking through you. Mt 10:20
over to death, and the **f** his child, Mt 10:21
fall to the ground apart from your **F**. Mt 10:29
acknowledge before my **F** who is in Mt 10:32
will deny before my **F** who is in Mt 10:33
I have come to set a man against his **f**, Mt 10:35
Whoever loves **f** or mother more than Mt 10:37
you, **F**, Lord of heaven and earth, Mt 11:25
yes, **F**, for such was your gracious will. Mt 11:26
have been handed over to me by my **F**, Mt 11:27
and no one knows the Son except the **F**, Mt 11:27
no one knows the **F** except the Son and Mt 11:27
does the will of my **F** in heaven is my Mt 12:50
like the sun in the kingdom of their **F**. Mt 13:43
'Honor your **f** and your mother,' Mt 15:4
'Whoever reviles **f** or mother must Mt 15:4
say, 'If anyone tells his **f** or his mother, Mt 15:5
he need not honor his **f**.' So for the sake Mt 15:6
that my heavenly **F** has not planted Mt 15:13
this to you, but my **F** who is in heaven. Mt 16:17
with his angels in the glory of his **F**, Mt 16:27
see the face of my **F** who is in heaven. Mt 18:10
not the will of my **F** who is in heaven Mt 18:14
be done for them by my **F** in heaven. Mt 18:19
So also my heavenly **F** will do to every Mt 18:35
man shall leave his **f** and his mother Mt 19:5
Honor your **f** and mother, and, You Mt 19:19
brothers or sisters or **f** or mother or Mt 19:29
whom it has been prepared by my **F**." Mt 20:23
the two did the will of his **f**?" They said, Mt 21:31
And call no man your **f** on earth, for Mt 23:9
your father on earth, for you have one **F**, Mt 23:9
of heaven, nor the Son, but the **F** only. Mt 24:36
'Come, you who are blessed by my **F**, Mt 25:34
on his face and prayed, saying, "My **F**, Mt 26:39
time, he went away and prayed, "My **F**, Mt 26:42
you think that I cannot appeal to my **F**, Mt 26:53
in the name of the **F** and of the Son and Mt 28:19
and they left their **f** Zebedee in the boat Mk 1:20
and took the child's **f** and mother and Mk 5:40
said, 'Honor your **f** and your mother'; Mk 7:10
'Whoever reviles **f** or mother must Mk 7:10
say, 'If a man tells his **f** or his mother, Mk 7:11
him to do anything for his **f** or mother, Mk 7:12
the glory of his **F** with the holy angels." Mk 8:38
And Jesus asked his **f**, "How long has Mk 9:21
Immediately the **f** of the child cried out Mk 9:24
man shall leave his **f** and mother and Mk 10:7
defraud, Honor your **f** and mother.'" Mk 10:19
sisters or mother or **f** or children or Mk 10:29
is the coming kingdom of our **f** David! Mk 11:10
so that your **F** also who is in heaven Mk 11:25
over to death, and the **f** his child, Mk 13:12
in heaven, nor the Son, but only the **F**. Mk 13:32
F, all things are possible for you. Mk 14:36
country, the **f** of Alexander and Rufus, Mk 15:21
give to him the throne of his **f** David, Lk 1:32
have called him Zechariah after his **f**, Lk 1:59
And they made signs to his **f**, inquiring Lk 1:62
And his **f** Zechariah was filled with the Lk 1:67
oath that he swore to our **f** Abraham, Lk 1:73
And his **f** and his mother marveled at Lk 2:33
your **f** and I have been searching for you Lk 2:48
yourselves, 'We have Abraham as our **f**.' Lk 3:8
Be merciful, even as your **F** is merciful. Lk 6:36
James, and the **f** and mother of the child. Lk 8:51
and the glory of the **F** and of the holy Lk 9:26
the boy, and gave him back to his **f**. Lk 9:42
"Lord, let me first go and bury my **f**." Lk 9:59
you, **F**, Lord of heaven and earth, Lk 10:21
yes, **F**, for such was your gracious will. Lk 10:21
have been handed over to me by my **F**, Lk 10:22
one knows who the Son is except the **F**, Lk 10:22
or who the **F** is except the Son and Lk 10:22
pray, say: "**F**, hallowed be your name. Lk 11:2
What **f** among you, if his son asks for Lk 11:11
more will the heavenly **F** give the Holy Lk 11:13
and your **F** knows that you need them. Lk 12:30
f against son and son against father, Lk 12:53
father against son and son against **f**, Lk 12:53
not hate his own **f** and mother and wife Lk 14:26
And the younger of them said to his **f**, Lk 15:12
'**F**, give me the share of property that is Lk 15:12
I will arise and go to my **f**, and I will say Lk 15:18
"**F**, I have sinned against heaven and Lk 15:18
And he arose and came to his **f**. But Lk 15:20
off, his **f** saw him and felt compassion, Lk 15:20
'**F**, I have sinned against heaven and Lk 15:21
But the **f** said to his servants, 'Bring Lk 15:22
and your **f** has killed the fattened calf, Lk 15:27
in. His **f** came out and entreated him, Lk 15:28
but he answered his **f**, 'Look, these Lk 15:29
And he called out, '**F** Abraham, have Lk 16:24
f, to send him to my father's house— Lk 16:27
And he said, 'No, **f** Abraham, but if Lk 16:30
witness, Honor your **f** and mother.'" Lk 18:20
I assign to you, as my **F** assigned to me, Lk 22:29
saying, "**F**, if you are willing, remove Lk 22:42
And Jesus said, "**F**, forgive them, for Lk 23:34
"**F**, into your hands I commit my Lk 23:46
sending the promise of my **F** upon you. Lk 24:49
glory, glory as of the only Son from the **F**, Jn 1:14
The **F** loves the Son and has given all Jn 3:35
Are you greater than our **f** Jacob? He Jn 4:12
nor in Jerusalem will you worship the **F**. Jn 4:21
will worship the **F** in spirit and Jn 4:23
for the **F** is seeking such people to Jn 4:23
The **f** knew that was the hour when Jesus Jn 4:53
them, "My **F** is working until now, Jn 5:17
but he was even calling God his own **F**, Jn 5:18
but only what he sees the **F** doing. Jn 5:19
For whatever the **F** does, that the Son Jn 5:19
For the **F** loves the Son and shows him Jn 5:20
For as the **F** raises the dead and gives Jn 5:21
The **F** judges no one, but has given all Jn 5:22
honor the Son, just as they honor the **F**. Jn 5:23
Son does not honor the **F** who sent him. Jn 5:23
For as the **F** has life in himself, so he has Jn 5:26
For the works that the **F** has given me to Jn 5:36
witness about me that the **F** has sent me. Jn 5:36
And the **F** who sent me has himself Jn 5:37
not think that I will accuse you to the **F**. Jn 5:45
For on him God the **F** has set his seal." Jn 6:27
but my **F** gives you the true bread from Jn 6:32
All that the **F** gives me will come to me, Jn 6:37
For this is the will of my **F**, that everyone Jn 6:40
of Joseph, whose **f** and mother we know? Jn 6:42
to me unless the **F** who sent me draws Jn 6:44
and learned from the **F** comes to me— Jn 6:45
anyone has seen the **F** except he who is Jn 6:46
he who is from God; he has seen the **F**. Jn 6:46
As the living **F** sent me, and I live Jn 6:57
sent me, and I live because of the **F**, Jn 6:57
to me unless it is granted him by the **F**." Jn 6:65
who judge, but I and the **F** who sent me. Jn 8:16
and the **F** who sent me bears witness Jn 8:18
"Where is your **F**?" Jesus answered, Jn 8:19
"You know neither me nor my **F**. Jn 8:19
knew me, you would know my **F** also." Jn 8:19
had been speaking to them about the **F**. Jn 8:27
but speak just as the **F** taught me. Jn 8:28
I speak of what I have seen with my **F**, Jn 8:38
do what you have heard from your **f**." Jn 8:38
"Abraham is our **f**." Jesus said to them, Jn 8:39
are doing what your **f** did." They said to Jn 8:41
immorality. We have one **F**—even God." Jn 8:41
Jesus said to them, "If God were your **F**, Jn 8:42
You are of your **f** the devil, and your will Jn 8:44
character, for he is a liar and the **f** of lies. Jn 8:44
do not have a demon, but I honor my **F**, Jn 8:49
Are you greater than our **f** Abraham, Jn 8:53
is nothing. It is my **F** who glorifies me, Jn 8:54
Your **f** Abraham rejoiced that he would Jn 8:56
just as the **F** knows me and I know the Jn 10:15
the Father knows me and I know the **F**; Jn 10:15
For this reason the **F** loves me, because Jn 10:17
charge I have received from my **F**." Jn 10:18
My **F**, who has given them to me, is Jn 10:29
I and the **F** are one." Jn 10:30
you many good works from the **F**; Jn 10:32
him whom the **F** consecrated and sent Jn 10:36
If I am not doing the works of my **F**, Jn 10:37
and understand that the **F** is in me and Jn 10:38
the Father is in me and I am in the **F**." Jn 10:38
"**F**, I thank you that you have heard me. Jn 11:41
anyone serves me, the **F** will honor him. Jn 12:26
shall I say? '**F**, save me from this hour'? Jn 12:27
F, glorify your name." Then a voice Jn 12:28
but the **F** who sent me has himself Jn 12:49
therefore, I say as the **F** has told me." Jn 12:50
come to depart out of this world to the **F**, Jn 13:1
knowing that the **F** had given all things Jn 13:3
one comes to the **F** except through me. Jn 14:6
me, you would have known my **F** also. Jn 14:7
Philip said to him, "Lord, show us the **F**, Jn 14:8
Whoever has seen me has seen the **F**. Jn 14:9
How can you say, 'Show us the **F**'? Jn 14:9
that I am in the **F** and the Father is in Jn 14:10
I am in the Father and the **F** is in me? Jn 14:10
but the **F** who dwells in me does his Jn 14:10
that I am in the **F** and the Father is in Jn 14:11
I am in the Father and the **F** is in me, Jn 14:11
will he do, because I am going to the **F**. Jn 14:12
that the **F** may be glorified in the Son. Jn 14:13
And I will ask the **F**, and he will give Jn 14:16
day you will know that I am in my **F**, Jn 14:20
he who loves me will be loved by my **F**, Jn 14:21
keep my word, and my **F** will love him, Jn 14:23

whom the **F** will send in my name, Jn 14:26
rejoiced, because I am going to the **F**, Jn 14:28
to the Father, for the **F** is greater than I. Jn 14:28
but I do as the **F** has commanded me, so Jn 14:31
the world may know that I love the **F**. Jn 14:31
the true vine, and my **F** is the vinedresser. Jn 15:1
By this my **F** is glorified, that you bear Jn 15:8
As the **F** has loved me, so have I loved Jn 15:9
have heard from my **F** I have made Jn 15:15
whatever you ask the **F** in my name, Jn 15:16
Whoever hates me hates my **F** also. Jn 15:23
have seen and hated both me and my **F**. Jn 15:24
whom I will send to you from the **F**, Jn 15:26
Spirit of truth, who proceeds from the **F**, Jn 15:26
because they have not known the **F**, Jn 16:3
righteousness, because I go to the **F**, Jn 16:10
All that the **F** has is mine; therefore I Jn 16:15
me'; and, 'because I am going to the **F**?" Jn 16:17
whatever you ask of the **F** in my name, Jn 16:23
but will tell you plainly about the **F**. Jn 16:25
you that I will ask the **F** on your behalf; Jn 16:26
for the **F** himself loves you, because you Jn 16:27
I came from the **F** and have come into Jn 16:28
leaving the world and going to the **F**." Jn 16:28
Yet I am not alone, for the **F** is with me. Jn 16:32
heaven, and said, "**F**, the hour has come; Jn 17:1
F, glorify me in your own presence with Jn 17:5
world, and I am coming to you. Holy **F**, Jn 17:11
may all be one, just as you, **F**, are in me, Jn 17:21
F, I desire that they also, whom you Jn 17:24
O righteous **F**, even though the world Jn 17:25
drink the cup that the **F** has given me?" Jn 18:11
me, for I have not yet ascended to the **F**; Jn 20:17
am ascending to my **F** and your Father, Jn 20:17
am ascending to my Father and your **F**, Jn 20:17
As the **F** has sent me, even so I am Jn 20:21
but to wait for the promise of the **F**, Acts 1:4
or seasons that the **F** has fixed by his Acts 1:7
received from the **F** the promise of Acts 2:33
through the mouth of our **f** David, Acts 4:25
appeared to our **f** Abraham when he Acts 7:2
And after his **f** died, God removed him Acts 7:4
And so Abraham became the **f** of Isaac, Acts 7:8
day, and Isaac became the **f** of Jacob, Acts 7:8
and summoned Jacob his **f** and all his Acts 7:14
where he became the **f** of two sons. Acts 7:29
was a believer, but his **f** was a Greek. Acts 16:1
they all knew that his **f** was a Greek. Acts 16:3
It happened that the **f** of Publius lay Acts 28:8
peace from God our **F** and the Lord Rom 1:7
to make him the **f** of all who believe Rom 4:11
to make him the **f** of the circumcised Rom 4:12
faith that our **f** Abraham had before Rom 4:12
of Abraham, who is the **f** of us all, Rom 4:16
have made you the **f** of many nations" Rom 4:17
should become the **f** of many nations, Rom 4:18
from the dead by the glory of the **F**, Rom 6:4
as sons, by whom we cry, "Abba! **F**!" Rom 8:15
glorify the God and **F** of our Lord Jesus Rom 15:6
peace from God our **F** and the Lord 1 Cor 1:3
For I became your **f** in Christ Jesus 1 Cor 4:15
yet for us there is one God, the **F**, from 1 Cor 8:6
to God the **F** after destroying every 1 Cor 15:24
peace from God our **F** and the Lord 2 Cor 1:2
be the God and **F** of our Lord Jesus 2 Cor 1:3
the **F** of mercies and God of all 2 Cor 1:3
and I will be a **f** to you, and you shall 2 Cor 6:18
The God and **F** of the Lord Jesus, he 2 Cor 11:31
but through Jesus Christ and God the **F**, Gal 1:1
peace from God our **F** and the Lord Jesus Gal 1:3
according to the will of our God and **F**, Gal 1:4
and managers until the date set by his **f**. Gal 4:2
Son into our hearts, crying, "Abba! **F**!" Gal 4:6
peace from God our **F** and the Lord Jesus Eph 1:2
be the God and **F** of our Lord Jesus Eph 1:3
of our Lord Jesus Christ, the **F** of glory, Eph 1:17
both have access in one Spirit to the **F**. Eph 2:18
reason I bow my knees before the **F**, Eph 3:14
one God and **F** of all, who is over all and Eph 4:6
everything to God the **F** in the name of Eph 5:20
man shall leave his **f** and mother and Eph 5:31
"Honor your **f** and mother" (this is the Eph 6:2
from God the **F** and the Lord Jesus Eph 6:23
peace from God our **F** and the Lord Phil 1:2
is Lord, to the glory of God the **F**. Phil 2:11
as a son with a **f** he has served with me Phil 2:22
To our God and **F** be glory forever and Phil 4:20
Grace to you and peace from God our **F**. Col 1:2
God, the **F** of our Lord Jesus Christ, Col 1:3
giving thanks to the **F**, who has Col 1:12
thanks to God the **F** through him. Col 3:17
in God the **F** and the Lord 1 Thes 1:1
before our God and **F** your work of 1 Thes 1:3
how, like a **f** with his children, 1 Thes 2:11
Now may our God and **F** himself, 1 Thes 3:11
in holiness before our God and **F**, 1 Thes 3:13
in God our **F** and the Lord 2 Thes 1:1
peace from God our **F** and the Lord 2 Thes 1:2
Jesus Christ himself, and God our **F**, 2 Thes 2:16
peace from God the **F** and Christ Jesus 1 Tm 1:2
but encourage him as you would a **f**. 1 Tm 5:1
peace from God the **F** and Christ Jesus 2 Tm 1:2
peace from God the **F** and Christ Jesus our Ti 1:4
peace from God our **F** and the Lord Phlm 1:3
whose **f** I became in my Phlm 1:10
Or again, "I will be to him a **f**, and he Heb 1:5
He is without **f** or mother or genealogy, Heb 7:3
is there whom his **f** does not discipline? Heb 12:7
be subject to the **F** of spirits and live? Heb 12:9
coming down from the **F** of lights with Jas 1:17
is pure and undefiled before God, the **F**, Jas 1:27
not Abraham our **f** justified by works Jas 2:21
With it we bless our Lord and **F**, and with Jas 3:9
to the foreknowledge of God the **F**, 1 Pt 1:2
be the God and **F** of our Lord Jesus 1 Pt 1:3
on him as **F** who judges impartially 1 Pt 1:17
honor and glory from God the **F**, 2 Pt 1:17
which was with the **F** and was made 1 Jn 1:2
fellowship is with the **F** and with his Son 1 Jn 1:3
does sin, we have an advocate with the **F**, 1 Jn 2:1
you, children, because you know the **F**. 1 Jn 2:13
world, the love of the **F** is not in him. 1 Jn 2:15
—is not from the **F** but is from the 1 Jn 2:16
he who denies the **F** and the Son. 1 Jn 2:22
No one who denies the Son has the **F**. 1 Jn 2:23
confesses the Son has the **F** also. 1 Jn 2:23
too will abide in the Son and in the **F**. 1 Jn 2:24
what kind of love the **F** has given to us, 1 Jn 3:1
and testify that the **F** has sent his Son 1 Jn 4:14
who loves the **F** loves whoever has 1 Jn 5:1
from God the **F** and from Jesus Christ 2 Jn 1:3
just as we were commanded by the **F**. 2 Jn 1:4
the teaching has both the **F** and the Son. 2 Jn 1:9
beloved in God the **F** and kept for Jesus Jude 1:1
us a kingdom, priests to his God and **F**, Rv 1:6
have received authority from my **F**. Rv 2:27
his name before my **F** and before his Rv 3:5
and sat down with my **F** on his throne. Rv 3:21

FATHER'S (149)

and they did not see their **f** nakedness. Gn 9:23
your kindred and your **f** house to the Gn 12:1
caused me to wander from my **f** house, Gn 20:13
took me from my **f** house and from the Gn 24:7
Is there room in your **f** house for us to Gn 24:23
you shall go to my **f** house and to my Gn 24:38
from my clan and from my **f** house. Gn 24:40
the wells that his **f** servants had dug in Gn 26:15
I come again to my **f** house in peace, Gn 28:21
them, Rachel came with her **f** sheep, Gn 29:9
told Rachel that he was her **f** kinsman, Gn 29:12
"Jacob has taken all that was our **f**, Gn 31:1
from what was our **f** he has gained all Gn 31:1
or inheritance left to us in our **f** house? Gn 31:14
and Rachel stole her **f** household gods. Gn 31:19
you longed greatly for your **f** house, Gn 31:30
the most honored of all his **f** house. Gn 34:19
and lay with Bilhah his **f** concubine. Gn 35:22
lived in the land of his **f** sojournings, Gn 37:1
sons of Bilhah and Zilpah, his **f** wives. Gn 37:2
to pasture their **f** flock near Shechem. Gn 37:12
"Remain a widow in your **f** house, Gn 38:11
went and remained in her **f** house. Gn 38:11
all my hardship and all my **f** house." Gn 41:51
to his brothers and to his **f** household, Gn 46:31
'My brothers and my **f** household, Gn 46:31
and all his **f** household with food, Gn 47:12
and he took his **f** hand to move it from Gn 48:17
because you went up to your **f** bed; Gn 49:4
your **f** sons shall bow down before you. Gn 49:8
Joseph fell on his **f** face and wept over Gn 50:1
his brothers, and his **f** household. Gn 50:8
remained in Egypt, he and his **f** house. Gn 50:22
filled the troughs to water their **f** flock. Ex 2:16
took as his wife Jochebed his **f** sister, Ex 6:20
my God, and I will praise him, my **f** God, Ex 15:2
as priest in his **f** place shall make Lv 16:32
uncover the nakedness of your **f** wife; Lv 18:8
your father's wife; it is your **f** nakedness. Lv 18:8
your **f** daughter or your mother's Lv 18:9
the nakedness of your **f** wife's daughter, Lv 18:11
daughter, brought up in your **f** family, Lv 18:11
uncover the nakedness of your **f** sister; Lv 18:12
father's sister; she is your **f** relative. Lv 18:12
the nakedness of your **f** brother, Lv 18:14
If a man lies with his **f** wife, he has Lv 20:11
wife, he has uncovered his **f** nakedness; Lv 20:11
your mother's sister or of your **f** sister, Lv 20:19
has no child and returns to her **f** house, Lv 22:13
in her youth, she may eat of her **f** food; Lv 22:13
your sons and your **f** house with you Nm 18:1
chief of a **f** house belonging to the Nm 25:14
the tribal head of a **f** house in Midian. Nm 25:15
us a possession among our **f** brothers." Nm 27:4
among their **f** brothers and Nm 27:7
give his inheritance to his **f** brothers. Nm 27:10
while within her **f** house in her youth, Nm 30:3
she is in her youth within her **f** house. Nm 30:16
married to sons of their **f** brothers. Nm 36:11
remained in the tribe of their **f** clan. Nm 36:12
woman to the door of her **f** house, Dt 22:21
in Israel by whoring in her **f** house. Dt 22:21
"A man shall not take his **f** wife, so that Dt 22:30
he does not uncover his **f** nakedness. Dt 22:30
be anyone who lies with his **f** wife, Dt 27:20
he has uncovered his **f** nakedness.' Dt 27:20
also will deal kindly with my **f** house, Jos 2:12
your brothers, and all your **f** household. Jos 2:18
prostitute and her **f** household and all Jos 6:25
and I am the least in my **f** house." Jgs 6:15
the LORD said to him, "Take your **f** bull, Jgs 6:25
And he went to his **f** house at Ophrah and Jgs 9:5
risen up against my **f** house this day and Jgs 9:18
not have an inheritance in our **f** house, Jgs 11:2
hate me and drive me out of my **f** house? Jgs 11:7
burn you and your **f** house with fire. Jgs 14:15
hot anger he went back to his **f** house. Jgs 14:19
from him to her **f** house at Bethlehem in Jgs 19:2
And she brought him into her **f** house. Jgs 19:3
and the strength of your **f** house, 1 Sm 2:31
not for you and for all your **f** house?" 1 Sm 9:20
Saul to feed his **f** sheep at Bethlehem. 1 Sm 17:15
and make his **f** house free in 1 Sm 17:25
not let him return to his **f** house. 1 Sm 18:2
are my relatives, my **f** clan in Israel, 1 Sm 18:18
brothers and all his **f** house heard it, 1 Sm 22:1
son of Ahitub, and all his **f** house, 1 Sm 22:11
you and all your **f** house." 1 Sm 22:16
of all the persons of your **f** house. 1 Sm 22:22
destroy my name out of my **f** house." 1 Sm 24:21
have you gone in to my **f** concubine?" 2 Sm 3:7
head of Joab and upon all his **f** house, 2 Sm 3:29
my lord the king, and on my **f** house; 2 Sm 14:9
I have been your **f** servant in time 2 Sm 15:34
"Go in to your **f** concubines, 2 Sm 16:21
went in to his **f** concubines in the 2 Sm 16:22
For all my **f** house were but men 2 Sm 19:28
against me and against my **f** house." 2 Sm 24:17
you shared in all my **f** affliction." 1 Kgs 2:26
me and from my **f** house the guilt for 1 Kgs 2:31
certain Edomites of his **f** servants, 1 Kgs 11:17
finger is thicker than my **f** thighs. 1 Kgs 12:10
but you have, and your **f** house, 1 Kgs 18:18
set him on his **f** throne and fight for 2 Kgs 10:3
and made him king in his **f** place. 2 Kgs 23:30
but because he defiled his **f** couch, 1 Chr 5:1
against me and against my **f** house. 1 Chr 21:17
became counted as a single **f** house. 1 Chr 23:11
one **f** house being chosen for Eleazar 1 Chr 24:6
the head of each **f** house and his 1 Chr 24:31
me from all my **f** house to be king 1 Chr 28:4
in the house of Judah my **f** house, 1 Chr 28:4
and among my **f** sons he took 1 Chr 28:4
finger is thicker than my **f** thighs. 2 Chr 10:10
your brothers, of your **f** house, 2 Chr 21:13
him king in his **f** place in Jerusalem. 2 Chr 36:1
you. Even I and my **f** house have sinned. Neh 1:6
but you and your **f** house will perish. Est 4:14
ear: forget your people and your **f** house, Ps 45:10
Hear, my son, your **f** instruction, and Prv 1:8
Hear, O sons, a **f** instruction, and be Prv 4:1
My son, keep your **f** commandment, Prv 6:20
A wise son hears his **f** instruction, but a Prv 13:1
A fool despises his **f** instruction, but Prv 15:5
forsake your friend and your **f** friend, Prv 27:10
people and upon your **f** house such days Is 7:17
become a throne of honor to his **f** house. Is 22:23
on him the whole honor of his **f** house, Is 22:24
for they have obeyed their **f** command. Jer 35:14
he shall not die for his **f** iniquity; Ezk 18:17
you violates his sister, his **f** daughter. Ezk 22:11
it new with you in my **F** kingdom." Mt 26:29
know that I must be in my **F** house?" Lk 2:49
for it is your **F** good pleasure to give Lk 12:32
'How many of my **f** hired servants have Lk 15:17
father, to send him to my **f** house— Lk 16:27
the only God, who is at the **F** side, he has Jn 1:18
do not make my **F** house a house of Jn 2:16
I have come in my **F** name, and you do Jn 5:43
devil, and your will is to do your **f** desires. Jn 8:44
I do in my **F** name bear witness about Jn 10:25
able to snatch them out of the **F** hand. Jn 10:29
In my **F** house are many rooms. If it were Jn 14:2
hear is not mine but the **F** who sent me. Jn 14:24
have kept my **F** commandments and Jn 15:10
up for three months in his **f** house, Acts 7:20

pagans, for a man has his **f** wife. 1 Cor 5:1
Father and from Jesus Christ the **F** Son, 2 Jn 1:3
his name and his **F** name written on Rv 14:1

FATHER-IN-LAW (26)
"Your **f** is going up to Timnah to shear Gn 38:13
brought out, she sent word to her **f**, Gn 38:25
Now Moses was keeping the flock of his **f**, Ex 3:1
back to Jethro his **f** and said to him, Ex 4:18
Jethro, the priest of Midian, Moses' **f**, Ex 18:1
Now Jethro, Moses' **f**, had taken Ex 18:2
Jethro, Moses' **f**, came with his sons and Ex 18:5
he sent word to Moses, "I, your **f** Jethro, Ex 18:6
out to meet his **f** and bowed down and Ex 18:7
Then Moses told his **f** all that the LORD Ex 18:8
And Jethro, Moses' **f**, brought a burnt Ex 18:12
to eat bread with Moses' **f** before God. Ex 18:12
When Moses' **f** saw all that he was Ex 18:14
And Moses said to his **f**, "Because the Ex 18:15
Moses' **f** said to him, "What you are Ex 18:17
to the voice of his **f** and did all that he Ex 18:24
Then Moses let his **f** depart, and he Ex 18:27
son of Reuel the Midianite, Moses' **f**, Nm 10:29
the descendants of the Kenite, Moses' **f**, Jgs 1:16
the descendants of Hobab the **f** of Moses, Jgs 4:11
And his **f**, the girl's father, made him Jgs 19:4
the man rose up to go, his **f** pressed him, Jgs 19:7
and his servant rose up to depart, his **f**, Jgs 19:9
and that her **f** and her husband were 1 Sm 4:19
because of her **f** and her husband. 1 Sm 4:21
to Annas, for he was the **f** of Caiaphas, Jn 18:13

FATHERED (150)
was born Irad, and Irad **f** Mehujael, Gn 4:18
Mehujael, and Mehujael **f** Methushael, Gn 4:18
Methushael, and Methushael **f** Lamech. Gn 4:18
130 years, he **f** a son in his own likeness, Gn 5:3
of Adam after he **f** Seth were 800 years; Gn 5:4
Seth had lived 105 years, he **f** Enosh. Gn 5:6
Seth lived after he **f** Enosh 807 years and Gn 5:7
Enosh had lived 90 years, he **f** Kenan. Gn 5:9
Enosh lived after he **f** Kenan 815 years Gn 5:10
had lived 70 years, he **f** Mahalalel. Gn 5:12
lived after he **f** Mahalalel 840 years Gn 5:13
Mahalalel had lived 65 years, he **f** Jared. Gn 5:15
Mahalalel lived after he **f** Jared 830 years Gn 5:16
Jared had lived 162 years he **f** Enoch. Gn 5:18
Jared lived after he **f** Enoch 800 years Gn 5:19
had lived 65 years, he **f** Methuselah. Gn 5:21
God after he **f** Methuselah 300 years Gn 5:22
had lived 187 years, he **f** Lamech. Gn 5:25
lived after he **f** Lamech 782 years Gn 5:26
Lamech had lived 182 years, he **f** a son Gn 5:28
Lamech lived after he **f** Noah 595 years Gn 5:30
Noah was 500 years old, Noah **f** Shem, Gn 5:32
Cush **f** Nimrod; he was the first on earth Gn 10:8
Egypt **f** Ludim, Anamim, Lehabim, Gn 10:13
Canaan **f** Sidon his firstborn and Heth, Gn 10:15
Arpachshad **f** Shelah; and Shelah Gn 10:24
fathered Shelah; and Shelah **f** Eber. Gn 10:24
Joktan **f** Almodad, Sheleph, Gn 10:26
he **f** Arpachshad two years after the Gn 11:10
lived after he **f** Arpachshad 500 years Gn 11:11
had lived 35 years, he **f** Shelah. Gn 11:12
lived after he **f** Shelah 403 years Gn 11:13
Shelah had lived 30 years, he **f** Eber. Gn 11:14
Shelah lived after he **f** Eber 403 years Gn 11:15
Eber had lived 34 years, he **f** Peleg. Gn 11:16
Eber lived after he **f** Peleg 430 years Gn 11:17
Peleg had lived 30 years, he **f** Reu. Gn 11:18
Peleg lived after he **f** Reu 209 years and Gn 11:19
Reu had lived 32 years, he **f** Serug. Gn 11:20
Reu lived after he **f** Serug 207 years and Gn 11:21
Serug had lived 30 years, he **f** Nahor. Gn 11:22
Serug lived after he **f** Nahor 200 years Gn 11:23
Nahor had lived 29 years, he **f** Terah. Gn 11:24
Nahor lived after he **f** Terah 119 years Gn 11:25
Terah had lived 70 years, he **f** Abram, Gn 11:26
generations of Terah. Terah **f** Abram, Gn 11:27
Nahor, and Haran; and Haran **f** Lot. Gn 11:27
(Bethuel **f** Rebekah.) These eight Gn 22:23
Jokshan **f** Sheba and Dedan. The sons of Gn 25:3
Abraham's son: Abraham **f** Isaac, Gn 25:19
the children that you **f** after them shall Gn 48:6
the generations of Perez: Perez **f** Hezron, Ru 4:18
Hezron **f** Ram, Ram fathered Ru 4:19
fathered Ram, Ram **f** Amminadab, Ru 4:19
Amminadab **f** Nahshon, Nahshon Ru 4:20
fathered Nahshon, Nahshon **f** Salmon, Ru 4:20
Salmon **f** Boaz, Boaz fathered Obed, Ru 4:21
Salmon fathered Boaz, Boaz **f** Obed, Ru 4:21
Obed **f** Jesse, and Jesse fathered David. Ru 4:22
Obed fathered Jesse, and Jesse **f** David. Ru 4:22
Cush **f** Nimrod. He was the first on 1 Chr 1:10
Egypt **f** Ludim, Anamim, Lehabim, 1 Chr 1:11
Canaan **f** Sidon his firstborn and 1 Chr 1:13
Arpachshad **f** Shelah, and Shelah 1 Chr 1:18
fathered Shelah, and Shelah **f** Eber. 1 Chr 1:18
Joktan **f** Almodad, Sheleph, 1 Chr 1:20
Abraham **f** Isaac. The sons of Isaac: 1 Chr 1:34
Ram **f** Amminadab, and 1 Chr 2:10
and Amminadab **f** Nahshon, 1 Chr 2:10
Nahshon **f** Salmon, Salmon fathered 1 Chr 2:11
fathered Salmon, Salmon **f** Boaz, 1 Chr 2:11
Boaz **f** Obed, Obed fathered Jesse. 1 Chr 2:12
Boaz fathered Obed, Obed **f** Jesse. 1 Chr 2:12
Jesse **f** Eliab his firstborn, Abinadab 1 Chr 2:13
the son of Hezron **f** children by his 1 Chr 2:18
Hur **f** Uri, and Uri fathered Bezalel. 1 Chr 2:20
Hur fathered Uri, and Uri **f** Bezalel. 1 Chr 2:20
And Segub **f** Jair, who had 1 Chr 2:22
Attai **f** Nathan, and Nathan fathered 1 Chr 2:36
Nathan, and Nathan **f** Zabad. 1 Chr 2:36
Zabad **f** Ephlal, and Ephlal fathered 1 Chr 2:37
fathered Ephlal, and Ephlal **f** Obed. 1 Chr 2:37
Obed **f** Jehu, and Jehu fathered 1 Chr 2:38
fathered Jehu, and Jehu **f** Azariah. 1 Chr 2:38
Azariah **f** Helez, and Helez fathered 1 Chr 2:39
fathered Helez, and Helez **f** Eleasah. 1 Chr 2:39
Eleasah **f** Sismai, and Sismai 1 Chr 2:40
Sismai, and Sismai **f** Shallum. 1 Chr 2:40
Shallum **f** Jekamiah, and Jekamiah 1 Chr 2:41
Jekamiah, and Jekamiah **f** Elishama. 1 Chr 2:41
Mareshah his firstborn, who **f** Ziph. 1 Chr 2:42
Shema **f** Raham, the father of 1 Chr 2:44
of Jorkeam; and Rekem **f** Shammai. 1 Chr 2:44
Maon; and Maon **f** Beth-zur. 1 Chr 2:45
Moza, and Gazez; and Haran **f** Gazez. 1 Chr 2:46
Reaiah the son of Shobal **f** Jahath, and 1 Chr 4:2
and Jahath **f** Ahumai and Lahad. 1 Chr 4:2
and Penuel **f** Gedor, and Ezer fathered 1 Chr 4:4
fathered Gedor, and Ezer **f** Hushah. 1 Chr 4:4
Koz **f** Anub, Zobebah, and the clans of 1 Chr 4:8
the brother of Shuhah, **f** Mehir, 1 Chr 4:11
fathered Mehir, who **f** Eshton. 1 Chr 4:11
Eshton **f** Beth-rapha, Paseah, and 1 Chr 4:12
Meonothai **f** Ophrah; and Seraiah 1 Chr 4:14
and Seraiah **f** Joab, the father of 1 Chr 4:14
Eleazar **f** Phinehas, Phinehas fathered 1 Chr 6:4
Phinehas, Phinehas **f** Abishua, 1 Chr 6:4
Abishua **f** Bukki, Bukki fathered 1 Chr 6:5
fathered Bukki, Bukki **f** Uzzi, 1 Chr 6:5
Uzzi **f** Zerahiah, Zerahiah fathered 1 Chr 6:6
Zerahiah, Zerahiah **f** Meraioth, 1 Chr 6:6
Meraioth **f** Amariah, Amariah 1 Chr 6:7
fathered Amariah, Amariah **f** Ahitub, 1 Chr 6:7
Ahitub **f** Zadok, Zadok fathered 1 Chr 6:8
fathered Zadok, Zadok **f** Ahimaaz, 1 Chr 6:8
Ahimaaz **f** Azariah, Azariah fathered 1 Chr 6:9
fathered Azariah, Azariah **f** Johanan, 1 Chr 6:9
and Johanan **f** Azariah (it was he 1 Chr 6:10
Azariah **f** Amariah, Amariah 1 Chr 6:11
Amariah, Amariah **f** Ahitub, 1 Chr 6:11
Ahitub **f** Zadok, Zadok fathered 1 Chr 6:12
fathered Zadok, Zadok **f** Shallum, 1 Chr 6:12
Shallum **f** Hilkiah, Hilkiah fathered 1 Chr 6:13
fathered Hilkiah, Hilkiah **f** Azariah, 1 Chr 6:13
Azariah **f** Seraiah, Seraiah fathered 1 Chr 6:14
Seraiah, Seraiah **f** Jehozadak; 1 Chr 6:14
Heber, and Malchiel, who **f** Birzaith. 1 Chr 7:31
Heber **f** Japhlet, Shomer, Hotham, 1 Chr 7:32
Benjamin **f** Bela his firstborn, Ashbel 1 Chr 8:1
is, Heglam, who **f** Uzza and Ahihud. 1 Chr 8:7
And Shaharaim **f** sons in the country 1 Chr 8:8
He **f** sons by Hodesh his wife: Jobab, 1 Chr 8:9
He also **f** sons by Hushim: Abitub 1 Chr 8:11
and Mikloth (he **f** Shimeah). Now 1 Chr 8:32
Ahaz **f** Jehoaddah, and Jehoaddah 1 Chr 8:36
Jehoaddah, and Jehoaddah **f** Alemeth, 1 Chr 8:36
Azmaveth, and Zimri. Zimri **f** Moza. 1 Chr 8:36
Moza **f** Binea; Raphah was his son, 1 Chr 8:37
Ner **f** Kish, Kish fathered Saul, Saul 1 Chr 9:39
Ner fathered Kish, Kish **f** Saul, Saul 1 Chr 9:39
Kish fathered Saul, Saul **f** Jonathan, 1 Chr 9:39
Merib-baal, and Merib-baal **f** Micah. 1 Chr 9:40
And Ahaz **f** Jarah, and Jarah fathered 1 Chr 9:42
fathered Jarah, and Jarah **f** Alemeth, 1 Chr 9:42
and Zimri. And Zimri **f** Moza. 1 Chr 9:42
Moza **f** Binea, and Rephaiah was his 1 Chr 9:43
and David **f** more sons and 1 Chr 14:3
and **f** twenty-eight sons and sixty 2 Chr 11:21
and the fathers who **f** them in this land: Jer 16:3
up, and her attendants, he who **f** her, Dn 11:6

FATHERLESS (42)
shall not mistreat any widow or **f** child. Ex 22:22
become widows and your children **f**. Ex 22:24
executes justice for the **f** and the widow, Dt 10:18
with you, and the sojourner, the **f**, Dt 14:29
within your towns, the sojourner, the **f**, Dt 16:11
servant, the Levite, the sojourner, the **f**, Dt 16:14
justice due to the sojourner or to the **f**, Dt 24:17
It shall be for the sojourner, the **f**, and Dt 24:19
It shall be for the sojourner, the **f**, and Dt 24:20
It shall be for the sojourner, the **f**, and Dt 24:21
it to the Levite, the sojourner, the **f**, Dt 26:12
it to the Levite, the sojourner, the **f**, Dt 26:13
the justice due to the sojourner, the **f**, Dt 27:19
You would even cast lots over the **f**, and Jb 6:27
and the arms of the **f** were crushed. Jb 22:9
They drive away the donkey of the **f**; they Jb 24:3
those who snatch the **f** child from the Jb 24:9
and the **f** who had none to help him. Jb 29:12
alone, and the **f** has not eaten of it Jb 31:17
from my youth the **f** grew up with me Jb 31:18
if I have raised my hand against the **f**, Jb 31:21
you have been the helper of the **f**. Ps 10:14
to do justice to the **f** and the oppressed, Ps 10:18
Father of the **f** and protector of widows is Ps 68:5
Give justice to the weak and the **f**; Ps 82:3
and the sojourner, and murder the **f**; Ps 94:6
May his children be **f** and his wife a Ps 109:9
to him, nor any to pity his **f** children! Ps 109:12
he upholds the widow and the **f**, but the Ps 146:9
landmark or enter the fields of the **f**, Prv 23:10
bring justice to the **f**, plead the widow's Is 1:17
They do not bring justice to the **f**, and the Is 1:23
no compassion on their **f** and widows; Is 9:17
and that they may make the **f** their prey! Is 10:2
judge not with justice the cause of the **f**, Jer 5:28
if you do not oppress the sojourner, the **f**, Jer 7:6
or violence to the resident alien, the **f**, Jer 22:3
Leave your **f** children; I will keep them Jer 49:11
f; our mothers are like widows. Lam 5:3
the **f** and the widow are wronged in you. Ezk 22:7
do not oppress the widow, the **f**, the Zec 7:10
in his wages, the widow and the **f**, Mal 3:5

FATHERS (426)
you shall go to your **f** in peace; Gn 15:15
the land of your **f** and to your kindred, Gn 31:3
even until now, both we and our **f**,' Gn 46:34
servants are shepherds, as our **f** were." Gn 47:3
of the life of my **f** in the days of their Gn 47:9
but let me lie with my **f**. Carry me out Gn 47:30
before whom my **f** Abraham and Isaac Gn 48:15
the name of my **f** Abraham and Isaac; Gn 48:16
bring you again to the land of your **f**. Gn 48:21
bury me with my **f** in the cave that is Gn 49:29
'The God of your **f** has sent me to you,' Ex 3:13
of Israel, 'The LORD, the God of your **f**, Ex 3:15
say to them, 'The LORD, the God of your **f**, Ex 3:16
believe that the LORD, the God of their **f**, Ex 4:5
as neither your **f** nor your grandfathers Ex 10:6
which he swore to your **f** to give you, Ex 13:5
as he swore to you and your **f**, Ex 13:11
the iniquity of the **f** on the children to Ex 20:5
the iniquity of the **f** on the children and Ex 34:7
and return to the possession of his **f**. Lv 25:41
the iniquities of their **f** they shall rot Lv 26:39
the iniquity of their **f** in their treachery Lv 26:40
man being the head of the house of his **f**. Nm 1:4
the land that you swore to give their **f**? Nm 11:12
each tribe of their **f** you shall send a Nm 13:2
the iniquity of the **f** on the children, Nm 14:18
the land that I swore to give to their **f**. Nm 14:23
how our **f** went down to Egypt, and we Nm 20:15
dealt harshly with us and our **f**. Nm 20:15
the tribes of their **f** they shall inherit. Nm 26:55
Your **f** did this, when I sent them from Nm 32:8
the tribes of your **f** you shall inherit. Nm 33:54
the inheritance of our **f** and added to Nm 36:3
the inheritance of the tribe of our **f**." Nm 36:4
to the inheritance of the tribe of his **f**. Nm 36:7
may possess the inheritance of his **f**. Nm 36:8
of the land that the LORD swore to your **f**, Dt 1:8
May the LORD, the God of your **f**, make Dt 1:11
possession, as the LORD, the God of your **f**, Dt 1:21
good land that I swore to give to your **f**, Dt 1:35
of the land that the LORD, the God of your **f**, Dt 4:1
the covenant with your **f** that he swore to Dt 4:31
because he loved your **f** and chose their Dt 4:37
Not with our **f** did the LORD make this Dt 5:3
the iniquity of the **f** on the children to Dt 5:9
greatly, as the LORD, the God of your **f**, Dt 6:3
you into the land that he swore to your **f**, Dt 6:10
land that the LORD swore to give to your **f** Dt 6:18
us the land that he swore to give to our **f**. Dt 6:23
is keeping the oath that he swore to your **f**, Dt 7:8
the steadfast love that he swore to your **f**. Dt 7:12
land that he swore to your **f** to give you. Dt 7:13
land that the LORD swore to give to your **f**. Dt 8:1
you did not know, nor did your **f** know, Dt 8:3
with manna that your **f** did not know, Dt 8:16
his covenant that he swore to your **f**, Dt 8:18
the word that the LORD swore to your **f**, Dt 9:5
which I swore to their **f** to give them.' Dt 10:11
in love on your **f** and chose their Dt 10:15

Your **f** went down to Egypt seventy Dt 10:22
the LORD swore to your **f** to give to them Dt 11:9
the LORD swore to your **f** to give them, Dt 11:21
the land that the LORD, the God of your **f**, Dt 12:1
neither you nor your **f** have known, Dt 13:6
and multiply you, as he swore to your **f**, Dt 13:17
your territory, as he has sworn to your **f**, Dt 19:8
land that he promised to give to your **f**— Dt 19:8
"**F** shall not be put to death because of Dt 24:16
be put to death because of their **f**. Dt 24:16
that the LORD swore to our **f** to give us.' Dt 26:3
we cried to the LORD, the God of our **f**, Dt 26:7
have given us, as you swore to our **f**, Dt 26:15
and honey, as the LORD, the God of your **f**, Dt 27:3
the LORD swore to your **f** to give you. Dt 28:11
neither you nor your **f** have known. Dt 28:36
neither you nor your **f** have known. Dt 28:64
promised you, and as he swore to your **f**, Dt 29:13
covenant of the LORD, the God of their **f**, Dt 29:25
you into the land that your **f** possessed, Dt 30:5
prosperous and numerous than your **f**. Dt 30:5
you, as he took delight in your **f**, Dt 30:9
the land that the LORD swore to your **f**, Dt 30:20
LORD has sworn to their **f** to give them, Dt 31:7
you are about to lie down with your **f**. Dt 31:16
honey, which I swore to give to their **f**, Dt 31:20
whom your **f** had never dreaded. Dt 32:17
land that I swore to their **f** to give them. Jos 1:6
your children ask their **f** in times to Jos 4:21
the LORD had sworn to their **f** to give to us, Jos 5:6
land, which the LORD, the God of your **f**, Jos 18:3
the land that he swore to give to their **f**. Jos 21:43
side just as he had sworn to their **f**. Jos 21:44
the altar of the LORD, which our **f** made, Jos 22:28
ago, your **f** lived beyond the Euphrates, Jos 24:2
"'Then I brought your **f** out of Egypt, Jos 24:6
Egyptians pursued your **f** with chariots Jos 24:6
the gods that your **f** served beyond the Jos 24:14
whether the gods your **f** served in the Jos 24:15
brought us and our **f** up from the land Jos 24:17
into the land that I swore to give to your **f**. Jgs 2:1
generation also were gathered to their **f**. Jgs 2:10
abandoned the LORD, the God of their **f**, Jgs 2:12
the way in which their **f** had walked, Jgs 2:17
and were more corrupt than their **f**, Jgs 2:19
that I commanded their **f** and have not Jgs 2:20
walk in the way of the LORD as their **f** did, Jgs 2:22
which he commanded their **f** by the hand Jgs 3:4
deeds that our **f** recounted to us, Jgs 6:13
And when their **f** or their brothers Jgs 21:22
Aaron and brought your **f** up out of 1 Sm 12:6
he performed for you and for your **f**. 1 Sm 12:7
then your **f** cried out to the LORD and 1 Sm 12:8
who brought your **f** out of Egypt and 1 Sm 12:8
fulfilled and you lie down with your **f**, 2 Sm 7:12
my lord the king sleeps with his **f**, 1 Kgs 1:21
David slept with his **f** and was buried 1 Kgs 2:10
of the LORD that he made with our **f**, 1 Kgs 8:21
to the land that you gave to their **f**. 1 Kgs 8:34
live in the land that you gave to our **f**. 1 Kgs 8:40
their land, which you gave to their **f**, 1 Kgs 8:48
when you brought our **f** out of Egypt, 1 Kgs 8:53
God be with us, as he was with our **f**. 1 Kgs 8:57
rules, which he commanded our **f**. 1 Kgs 8:58
God who brought their **f** out of the 1 Kgs 9:9
David slept with his **f** and that Joab 1 Kgs 11:21
slept with his **f** and was buried 1 Kgs 11:43
not come to the tomb of your **f**.'" 1 Kgs 13:22
he gave to their **f** and scatter them 1 Kgs 14:15
And he slept with his **f**, and Nadab 1 Kgs 14:20
more than all that their **f** had done. 1 Kgs 14:22
slept with his **f** and was buried 1 Kgs 14:31
was buried with his **f** in the city of 1 Kgs 14:31
And Abijam slept with his **f**, and they 1 Kgs 15:8
all the idols that his **f** had made. 1 Kgs 15:12
Asa slept with his **f** and was buried 1 Kgs 15:24
was buried with his **f** in the city of 1 Kgs 15:24
slept with his **f** and was buried 1 Kgs 16:6
Omri slept with his **f** and was buried 1 Kgs 16:28
my life, for I am no better than my **f**." 1 Kgs 19:4
give you the inheritance of my **f**." 1 Kgs 21:3
the inheritance of my **f**." And he lay 1 Kgs 21:4
So Ahab slept with his **f**, and 1 Kgs 22:40
slept with his **f** and was buried 1 Kgs 22:50
was buried with his **f** in the city of 1 Kgs 22:50
Joram slept with his **f** and was buried 2 Kgs 8:24
was buried with his **f** in the city of 2 Kgs 8:24
in his tomb with his **f** in the city of 2 Kgs 9:28
So Jehu slept with his **f**, and they 2 Kgs 10:35
and Jehoram and Ahaziah his **f**, 2 Kgs 12:18
buried him with his **f** in the city of 2 Kgs 12:21
So Jehoahaz slept with his **f**, and they 2 Kgs 13:9
So Joash slept with his **f**, and 2 Kgs 13:13
"**F** shall not be put to death because 2 Kgs 14:6
be put to death because of their **f**. 2 Kgs 14:6

slept with his **f** and was buried 2 Kgs 14:16
in Jerusalem with his **f** in the city of 2 Kgs 14:20
Judah, after the king slept with his **f**. 2 Kgs 14:22
And Jeroboam slept with his **f**, the 2 Kgs 14:29
And Azariah slept with his **f**, and they 2 Kgs 15:7
buried him with his **f** in the city of 2 Kgs 15:7
sight of the LORD, as his **f** had done. 2 Kgs 15:9
And Menahem slept with his **f**, and 2 Kgs 15:22
slept with his **f** and was buried 2 Kgs 15:38
was buried with his **f** in the city of 2 Kgs 15:38
Ahaz slept with his **f** and was buried 2 Kgs 16:20
was buried with his **f** in the city of 2 Kgs 16:20
the Law that I commanded your **f**, 2 Kgs 17:13
were stubborn, as their **f** had been, 2 Kgs 17:14
made with their **f** and the warnings 2 Kgs 17:15
children's children—as their **f** did, 2 Kgs 17:41
the nations that my **f** destroyed, 2 Kgs 19:12
that which your **f** have stored up 2 Kgs 20:17
And Hezekiah slept with his **f**, and 2 Kgs 20:21
out of the land that I gave to their **f**, 2 Kgs 21:8
since the day their **f** came out of 2 Kgs 21:15
slept with his **f** and was buried 2 Kgs 21:18
the LORD, the God of his **f**, 2 Kgs 21:22
because our **f** have not obeyed the 2 Kgs 22:13
behold, I will gather you to your **f**, 2 Kgs 22:20
according to all that his **f** had done. 2 Kgs 23:32
according to all that his **f** had done. 2 Kgs 23:37
So Jehoiakim slept with his **f**, and 2 Kgs 24:6
were the **f** of Keilah the Garmite and 1 Chr 4:19
broke faith with the God of their **f**, 1 Chr 5:25
of the Levites according to their **f**. 1 Chr 6:19
as their **f** had been in charge of the 1 Chr 9:19
the God of our **f** see and rebuke 1 Chr 12:17
are fulfilled to walk with your **f**, 1 Chr 17:11
and sojourners, as all our **f** were. 1 Chr 29:15
of Abraham, Isaac, and Israel, our **f**, 1 Chr 29:18
blessed the LORD, the God of their **f**, 1 Chr 29:20
that you gave to them and to their **f**. 2 Chr 6:25
live in the land that you gave to our **f**. 2 Chr 6:31
their land, which you gave to their **f**, 2 Chr 6:38
the God of their **f** who brought them 2 Chr 7:22
slept with his **f** and was buried 2 Chr 9:31
to the LORD, the God of their **f**. 2 Chr 11:16
slept with his **f** and was buried 2 Chr 12:16
against the LORD, the God of your **f**, 2 Chr 13:12
relied on the LORD, the God of their **f**. 2 Chr 13:18
Abijah slept with his **f**, and they 2 Chr 14:1
to seek the LORD, the God of their **f**, 2 Chr 14:4
to seek the LORD, the God of their **f**, 2 Chr 15:12
And Asa slept with his **f**, dying in 2 Chr 16:13
back to the LORD, the God of their **f**. 2 Chr 19:4
and said, "O LORD, God of our **f**, are 2 Chr 20:6
their hearts upon the God of their **f**. 2 Chr 20:33
slept with his **f** and was buried 2 Chr 21:1
was buried with his **f** in the city of 2 Chr 21:1
forsaken the LORD, the God of his **f**. 2 Chr 21:10
honor, like the fires made for his **f**. 2 Chr 21:19
house of the LORD, the God of their **f**, 2 Chr 24:18
forsaken the LORD, the God of their **f**. 2 Chr 24:24
"**F** shall not die because of their 2 Chr 25:4
nor children die because of their **f**, 2 Chr 25:4
was buried with his **f** in the city of 2 Chr 25:28
Judah, after the king slept with his **f**. 2 Chr 26:2
And Uzziah slept with his **f**, and 2 Chr 26:23
buried him with his **f** in the burial 2 Chr 26:23
And Jotham slept with his **f**, and they 2 Chr 27:9
forsaken the LORD, the God of their **f**. 2 Chr 28:6
because the LORD, the God of your **f**, 2 Chr 28:9
to anger the LORD, the God of his **f**. 2 Chr 28:25
And Ahaz slept with his **f**, and they 2 Chr 28:27
house of the LORD, the God of your **f**, 2 Chr 29:5
For our **f** have been unfaithful and 2 Chr 29:6
our **f** have fallen by the sword, 2 Chr 29:9
not be like your **f** and your brothers, 2 Chr 30:7
faithless to the LORD God of their **f**, 2 Chr 30:7
now be stiff-necked as your **f** were, 2 Chr 30:8
seek God, the LORD, the God of his **f**, 2 Chr 30:19
to the LORD, the God of their **f**. 2 Chr 30:22
what I and my **f** have done to all 2 Chr 32:13
nations that my **f** devoted to 2 Chr 32:14
my hand or from the hand of my **f**. 2 Chr 32:15
And Hezekiah slept with his **f**, and 2 Chr 32:33
the land that I appointed for your **f**, 2 Chr 33:8
greatly before the God of his **f**. 2 Chr 33:12
So Manasseh slept with his **f**, and 2 Chr 33:20
because our **f** have not kept the 2 Chr 34:21
Behold, I will gather you to your **f**, 2 Chr 34:28
covenant of God, the God of their **f**. 2 Chr 34:32
the LORD, the God of their **f**. 2 Chr 34:33
was buried in the tombs of his **f**. 2 Chr 35:24
The LORD, the God of their **f**, sent 2 Chr 36:15
in the book of the records of your **f**. Ezr 4:15
But because our **f** had angered the God Ezr 5:12
Blessed be the LORD, the God of our **f**, Ezr 7:27
offering to the LORD, the God of your **f**. Ezr 8:28

From the days of our **f** to this day we Ezr 9:7
LORD, the God of your **f** and do his will. Ezr 10:11
their sins and the iniquities of their **f**. Neh 9:2
the affliction of our **f** in Egypt and heard Neh 9:9
they acted arrogantly against our **f**. Neh 9:10
they and our **f** acted presumptuously Neh 9:16
you had told their **f** to enter and Neh 9:23
princes, our priests, our prophets, our **f**, Neh 9:32
and our **f** have not kept your law or Neh 9:34
that you gave to our **f** to enjoy its fruit Neh 9:36
Did not your **f** act in this way, and did Neh 13:18
and consider what the **f** have searched out. Jb 8:8
have told, without hiding it from their **f**, Jb 15:18
whose **f** I would have disdained to set Jb 30:1
In you our **f** trusted; they trusted, and Ps 22:4
with you, a guest, like all my **f**. Ps 39:12
heard with our ears, our **f** have told us, Ps 44:1
In place of your **f** shall be your sons; Ps 45:16
soul will go to the generation of his **f**, Ps 49:19
and known, that our **f** have told us. Ps 78:3
which he commanded our **f** to teach to Ps 78:5
and that they should not be like their **f**, a Ps 78:8
sight of their **f** he performed wonders Ps 78:12
and acted treacherously like their **f**; Ps 78:57
when your **f** put me to the test and put Ps 95:9
Both we and our **f** have sinned; we have Ps 106:6
Our **f**, when they were in Egypt, did not Ps 106:7
iniquity of his **f** be remembered before Ps 109:14
aged, and the glory of children is their **f**. Prv 17:6
House and wealth are inherited from **f**, Prv 19:14
ancient landmark that your **f** have set. Prv 22:28
he who **f** a wise son will be glad in Prv 23:24
those who curse their **f** and do not Prv 30:11
If a man **f** a hundred children and lives Eccl 6:3
his sons because of the guilt of their **f**, Is 14:21
them, the nations that my **f** destroyed, Is 37:12
and that which your **f** have stored up till Is 39:6
Kings shall be your foster **f**, and their Is 49:23
house, where our **f** praised you, Is 64:11
"What wrong did your **f** find in me that Jer 2:5
the land that I gave your **f** for a heritage. Jer 3:18
has devoured all for which our **f** labored, Jer 3:24
against the LORD our God, we and our **f**, Jer 3:25
f and sons together, neighbor and friend Jer 6:21
the land that I gave of old to your **f** forever. Jer 7:7
the place that I gave to you and to your **f**, Jer 7:14
children gather wood, the **f** kindle fire, Jer 7:18
not speak to your **f** or command them Jer 7:22
From the day that your **f** came out of the Jer 7:25
their neck. They did worse than their **f**. Jer 7:26
after the Baals, as their **f** taught them. Jer 9:14
neither they nor their **f** have known, Jer 9:16
I commanded your **f** when I brought Jer 11:4
confirm the oath that I swore to your **f**, Jer 11:5
solemnly warned your **f** when I brought Jer 11:7
my covenant that I made with their **f**. Jer 11:10
against another, **f** and sons together, Jer 13:14
O LORD, and the iniquity of our **f**, Jer 14:20
bore them and the **f** who fathered them Jer 16:3
'Because your **f** have forsaken me, Jer 16:11
you have done worse than your **f**, Jer 16:12
neither you nor your **f** have known, Jer 16:13
to their own land that I gave to their **f**. Jer 16:15
"Our **f** have inherited nothing but lies, Jer 16:19
day holy, as I commanded your **f**. Jer 17:22
neither they nor their **f** nor the kings of Jer 19:4
even as their **f** forgot my name for Jer 23:27
the city that I gave to you and your **f**. Jer 23:39
the land that I gave to them and their **f**." Jer 24:10
given to you and your **f** from of old and Jer 25:5
back to the land that I gave to their **f**, Jer 30:3
"'The **f** have eaten sour grapes, and the Jer 31:29
I made with their **f** on the day when Jer 31:32
repay the guilt of **f** to their children Jer 32:18
which you swore to their **f** to give them, Jer 32:22
And as spices were burned for your **f**, the Jer 34:5
a covenant with your **f** when I brought Jer 34:13
But your **f** did not listen to me or Jer 34:14
the land that I gave to you and your **f**.' Jer 35:15
not, neither they, nor you, nor your **f**. Jer 44:3
Have you forgotten the evil of your **f**, the Jer 44:9
that I set before you and before your **f**. Jer 44:10
to her, as we did, both we and our **f**, Jer 44:17
the streets of Jerusalem, you and your **f**, Jer 44:21
the **f** look not back to their children, Jer 47:3
the LORD, the hope of their **f**.' Jer 50:7
Our **f** sinned, and are no more; and we Lam 5:7
They and their **f** have transgressed Ezk 2:3
Therefore **f** shall eat their sons in your Ezk 5:10
in your midst, and sons shall eat their **f**. Ezk 5:10
of Israel, 'The **f** have eaten sour grapes, Ezk 18:2
"If he **f** a son who is violent, a shedder Ezk 18:10
"Now suppose this man **f** a son who Ezk 18:14
them know the abominations of their **f**, Ezk 20:4
Do not walk in the statutes of your **f**, Ezk 20:18

In this also your **f** blasphemed me, by Ezk 20:27
the manner of your **f** and go whoring Ezk 20:30
judgment with your **f** in the Ezk 20:36
country that I swore to give to your **f**. Ezk 20:42
dwell in the land that I gave to your **f**, Ezk 36:28
my servant Jacob, where your **f** lived. Ezk 37:25
equally what I swore to give to your **f**. Ezk 47:14
To you, O God of my **f**, I give thanks and Dn 2:23
to our kings, our princes, and our **f**, Dn 9:6
to our kings, to our princes, and to our **f**, Dn 9:8
our sins, and for the iniquities of our **f**, Dn 9:16
do what neither his **f** nor his fathers' Dn 11:24
his fathers nor his fathers' **f** have done, Dn 11:24
pay no attention to the gods of his **f**, Dn 11:37
A god whom his **f** did not know he Dn 11:38
fig tree in its first season, I saw your **f**. Hos 9:10
in your days, or in the days of your **f**? Jl 1:2
astray, those after which their **f** walked. Am 2:4
you have sworn to our **f** from the days of Mi 7:20
"The LORD was very angry with your **f**. Zec 1:2
Do not be like your **f**, to whom the Zec 1:4
Your **f**, where are they? And the prophets, Zec 1:5
prophets, did they not overtake your **f**? Zec 1:6
to you when your **f** provoked me to Zec 8:14
profaning the covenant of our **f**? Mal 2:10
the days of your **f** you have turned aside Mal 3:7
turn the hearts of **f** to their children and Mal 4:6
and the hearts of children to their **f**, Mal 4:6
'If we had lived in the days of our **f**, Mt 23:30
Fill up, then, the measure of your **f**. Mt 23:32
to turn the hearts of the **f** to the children, Lk 1:17
as he spoke to our **f**, to Abraham and to Lk 1:55
promised to our **f** and to remember Lk 1:72
heaven; for so their **f** did to the prophets. Lk 6:23
for so their **f** did to the false prophets. Lk 6:26
of the prophets whom your **f** killed. Lk 11:47
and you consent to the deeds of your **f**, Lk 11:48
Our **f** worshiped on this mountain, but Jn 4:20
Our **f** ate the manna in the wilderness; as Jn 6:31
Your **f** ate the manna in the wilderness, Jn 6:49
from heaven, not as the **f** ate and died. Jn 6:58
that it is from Moses, but from the **f**), Jn 7:22
and the God of Jacob, the God of our **f**, Acts 3:13
covenant that God made with your **f**, Acts 3:25
The God of our **f** raised Jesus, whom Acts 5:30
Stephen said: "Brothers and **f**, hear me. Acts 7:2
affliction, and our **f** could find no food. Acts 7:11
he sent out our **f** on their first visit. Acts 7:12
into Egypt, and he died, he and our **f**, Acts 7:15
race and forced our **f** to expose their Acts 7:19
'I am the God of your **f**, the God of Acts 7:32
to him at Mount Sinai, and with our **f**. Acts 7:38
Our **f** refused to obey him, but thrust Acts 7:39
"Our **f** had the tent of witness in the Acts 7:44
Our **f** in turn brought it in with Acts 7:45
that God drove out before our **f**. Acts 7:45
Holy Spirit. As your **f** did, so do you. Acts 7:51
the prophets did not your **f** persecute? Acts 7:52
Israel chose our **f** and made the Acts 13:17
news that what God promised to the **f**, Acts 13:32
laid with his **f** and saw corruption, Acts 13:36
that neither our **f** nor we have Acts 15:10
"Brothers and **f**, hear the defense that I Acts 22:1
to the strict manner of the law of our **f**, Acts 22:3
'The God of our **f** appointed you to Acts 22:14
call a sect, I worship the God of our **f**, Acts 24:14
in the promise made by God to our **f**, Acts 26:6
our people or the customs of our **f**, Acts 28:17
in saying to your **f** through Isaiah the Acts 28:25
in Christ, you do not have many **f**. 1 Cor 4:15
that our **f** were all under the cloud, 1 Cor 10:1
zealous was I for the traditions of my **f**. Gal 1:14
F, do not provoke your children to Eph 6:4
F, do not provoke your children, lest Col 3:21
those who strike their **f** and mothers, 1 Tm 1:9
ways, God spoke to our **f** by the prophets, Heb 1:1
where your **f** put me to the test and saw Heb 3:9
that I made with their **f** on the day when Heb 8:9
have had earthly **f** who disciplined us Heb 12:9
For ever since the **f** fell asleep, all things 2 Pt 3:4
f, because you know him who is from 1 Jn 2:13
f, because you know him who is from 1 Jn 2:14

FATHERS' (127)
These are the heads of their **f** houses: the Ex 6:14
the heads of the **f** houses of the Levites Ex 6:25
take a lamb according to their **f** houses, Ex 12:3
people of Israel, by clans, by **f** houses, Nm 1:2
themselves by clans, by **f** houses, Nm 1:18
by their clans, by their **f** houses, Nm 1:20
by their clans, by their **f** houses, Nm 1:22
by their clans, by their **f** houses, Nm 1:24
by their clans, by their **f** houses, Nm 1:26
by their clans, by their **f** houses, Nm 1:28
by their clans, by their **f** houses, Nm 1:30
by their clans, by their **f** houses, Nm 1:32
by their clans, by their **f** houses, Nm 1:34
by their clans, by their **f** houses, Nm 1:36
by their clans, by their **f** houses, Nm 1:38
by their clans, by their **f** houses, Nm 1:40
by their clans, by their **f** houses, Nm 1:42
men, each representing his **f** house. Nm 1:44
of the people of Israel, by their **f** houses, Nm 1:45
with the banners of their **f** houses. Nm 2:2
of Israel as listed by their **f** houses. Nm 2:32
in his clan, according to his **f** house. Nm 2:34
sons of Levi, by **f** houses and by clans; Nm 3:15
clans of the Levites, by their **f** houses. Nm 3:20
as chief of the **f** house of the Nm 3:24
as chief of the **f** house of the clans Nm 3:30
the chief of the **f** house of the clans Nm 3:35
Levi, by their clans and their **f** houses, Nm 4:2
by their **f** houses and by their clans. Nm 4:22
them by their clans and their **f** houses. Nm 4:29
by their clans and their **f** houses, Nm 4:34
by their clans and their **f** houses, Nm 4:38
clans and their **f** houses were 2,630. Nm 4:40
by their clans and their **f** houses, Nm 4:42
by their clans and their **f** houses, Nm 4:46
chiefs of Israel, heads of their **f** houses, Nm 7:2
from them staffs, one for each **f** house, Nm 17:2
chiefs according to their **f** houses, Nm 17:2
one staff for the head of each **f** house. Nm 17:3
each chief, according to their **f** houses, Nm 17:6
old and upward, by their **f** houses, Nm 26:2
the heads of the **f** houses of the Nm 31:26
you have risen in your **f** place, Nm 32:14
the heads of the **f** houses of the tribes Nm 32:28
people of Reuben by **f** houses and the Nm 34:14
of Gad by their **f** houses have received Nm 34:14
The heads of the **f** houses of the clan of Nm 36:1
the heads of the **f** houses of the people Nm 36:1
the heads of the **f** houses of the tribes Jos 14:1
the heads of the **f** houses of the tribes Jos 19:51
the heads of the **f** houses of the Levites Jos 21:1
to the heads of the **f** houses of the tribes Jos 21:1
the leaders of the **f** houses of the people 1 Kgs 8:1
and their **f** houses increased greatly. 1 Chr 4:38
kinsmen according to their **f** houses: 1 Chr 5:13
of Guni, was chief in their **f** houses, 1 Chr 5:15
were the heads of their **f** houses: 1 Chr 5:24
famous men, heads of their **f** houses. 1 Chr 5:24
and Shemuel, heads of their **f** houses, 1 Chr 7:2
according to their **f** houses, 1 Chr 7:4
and Iri, five, heads of **f** houses, 1 Chr 7:7
generations, as heads of their **f** houses, 1 Chr 7:9
to the heads of their **f** houses, 1 Chr 7:11
were men of Asher, heads of **f** houses, 1 Chr 7:40
(they were heads of **f** houses of the 1 Chr 8:6
were his sons, heads of **f** houses. 1 Chr 8:10
(they were heads of **f** houses of the 1 Chr 8:13
These were the heads of **f** houses, 1 Chr 8:28
were heads of **f** houses according to 1 Chr 9:9
houses according to their **f** houses. 1 Chr 9:9
kinsmen, heads of their **f** houses, 1 Chr 9:13
and his kinsmen of his **f** house, 1 Chr 9:19
the heads of **f** houses of the Levites, 1 Chr 9:33
These were heads of **f** houses of the 1 Chr 9:34
commanders from his own **f** house. 1 Chr 12:28
famous men in their **f** houses. 1 Chr 12:30
the heads of the **f** houses of the 1 Chr 15:12
the heads of the **f** houses of Ladan. 1 Chr 23:9
the sons of Levi by their **f** houses, 1 Chr 23:24
the heads of **f** houses as they were 1 Chr 23:24
under sixteen heads of **f** houses of the 1 Chr 24:4
the heads of the **f** houses of the 1 Chr 24:6
Levites according to their **f** houses. 1 Chr 24:30
and the heads of **f** houses of the 1 Chr 24:31
who were rulers in their **f** houses, 1 Chr 26:6
And they cast lots by **f** houses, 1 Chr 26:13
heads of the **f** houses belonging to 1 Chr 26:21
the heads of the **f** houses and the 1 Chr 26:26
of whatever genealogy or **f** houses. 1 Chr 26:31
men of ability, heads of **f** houses, 1 Chr 26:32
people of Israel, the heads of **f** houses, 1 Chr 27:1
the leaders of **f** houses made their 1 Chr 29:6
in all Israel, the heads of **f** houses. 2 Chr 1:2
the leaders of the **f** houses of the people 2 Chr 5:2
was the muster of them by **f** houses: 2 Chr 17:14
and the heads of **f** houses of Israel, 2 Chr 23:2
set them by **f** houses under 2 Chr 25:5
of the heads of **f** houses of mighty 2 Chr 26:12
was according to their **f** houses; 2 Chr 31:17
according to your **f** houses by your 2 Chr 35:4
the groupings of the **f** houses of your 2 Chr 35:5
of the Levites by **f** household. 2 Chr 35:5
the groupings of the **f** houses of the 2 Chr 35:12
up the heads of the **f** houses of Judah Ezr 1:5
could not prove their **f** houses or their Ezr 2:59
and Levites and heads of **f** houses, Ezr 3:12
and the heads of **f** houses and said to Ezr 4:2
rest of the heads of **f** houses in Israel said Ezr 4:3
These are the heads of their **f** houses, and Ezr 8:1
and the heads of **f** houses in Israel at Ezr 8:29
priest selected men, heads of **f** houses, Ezr 10:16
houses, according to their **f** houses, Ezr 10:16
when the city, the place of my **f** graves, Neh 2:3
me to Judah, to the city of my **f** graves, Neh 2:5
not prove their **f** houses nor their Neh 7:61
of the heads of **f** houses gave to the Neh 7:70
of the heads of **f** houses gave into the Neh 7:71
day the heads of **f** houses of all the Neh 8:13
our God, according to our **f** houses, Neh 10:34
and his brothers, heads of **f** houses, Neh 11:13
were priests, heads of **f** houses: Neh 12:12
were recorded as heads of **f** houses; Neh 12:22
their heads of **f** houses were written Neh 12:23
iniquities and your **f** iniquities together, Is 65:7
and their eyes were set on their **f** idols. Ezk 20:24
you men uncover their **f** nakedness; Ezk 22:10
his fathers nor his **f** fathers have done, Dn 11:24

FATHOMS (2)
took a sounding and found twenty **f**. Acts 27:28
a sounding again and found fifteen **f**. Acts 27:28

FATNESS (4)
of heaven and of the **f** of the earth and Gn 27:28
away from the **f** of the earth shall your Gn 27:39
what was set on your table was full of **f**. Jb 36:16
Their eyes swell out through **f**; their Ps 73:7

FATTENED (16)
oxen and of the **f** calves and the 1 Sm 15:9
the woman had a **f** calf in the house, 1 Sm 28:24
he sacrificed an ox and a **f** animal. 2 Sm 6:13
and **f** cattle by the Serpent's Stone, 1 Kgs 1:9
He has sacrificed oxen, **f** cattle, and 1 Kgs 1:19
day and has sacrificed oxen, **f** cattle, 1 Kgs 1:25
deer, gazelles, roebucks, and **f** fowl. 1 Kgs 4:23
to you burnt offerings of **f** animals, Ps 66:15
love is than a **f** ox and hatred with Prv 15:17
calf and the lion and the **f** calf together; Is 11:6
soldiers in her midst are like **f** calves; Jer 46:21
the peace offerings of your **f** animals, Am 5:22
And bring the **f** calf and kill it, and let Lk 15:23
and your father has killed the **f** calf, Lk 15:27
you killed the **f** calf for him!' Lk 15:30
You have **f** your hearts in a day of Jas 5:5

FATTENING (1)
sons above me by **f** yourselves on the 1 Sm 2:29

FATTER (1)
better in appearance and **f** in flesh than Dn 1:15

FAULT (11)
beaten; but the **f** is in your own people." Ex 5:16
me I have found no **f** in him to this 1 Sm 29:3
today with a **f** concerning a woman. 2 Sm 3:8
for no **f** of mine, they run and make Ps 59:4
back to them, and find no **f** in them. Ps 73:10
find no ground for complaint or any **f**, Dn 6:4
and no error or **f** was found in him. Dn 6:4
sins against you, go and tell him his **f**, Mt 18:15
to me then, "Why does he still find **f**? Rom 9:19
so that no **f** may be found with our 2 Cor 6:3
For he finds **f** with them when he says: Heb 8:8

FAULTFINDER (1)
"Shall a **f** contend with the Almighty? He Jb 40:2

FAULTLESS (1)
For if that first covenant had been **f**, Heb 8:7

FAULTS (1)
Declare me innocent from hidden **f**. Ps 19:12

FAVOR (126)
But Noah found **f** in the eyes of the LORD. Gn 6:8
"O Lord, if I have found **f** in your sight, Gn 18:3
your servant has found **f** in your sight, Gn 19:19
to him, "Behold, I grant you this **f** also, Gn 19:21
to him, "If I have found **f** in your sight, Gn 30:27
did not regard him with **f** as before. Gn 31:2
not regard me with **f** as he did before. Gn 31:5
in order that I may find **f** in your sight.'" Gn 32:5
"To find **f** in the sight of my lord." Gn 33:8
please, if I have found **f** in your sight, Gn 33:10
Let me find **f** in the sight of my lord." Gn 33:15
brothers, "Let me find **f** in your eyes, Gn 34:11
So Joseph found **f** in his sight and Gn 39:4
love and gave him **f** in the sight of Gn 39:21
"If now I have found **f** in your sight, Gn 47:29
"If now I have found **f** in your eyes, Gn 50:4
I will give this people **f** in the sight of the Ex 3:21
the LORD gave the people **f** in the sight of Ex 11:3
had given the people **f** in the sight of Ex 12:36
and you have also found **f** in my sight.' Ex 33:12
therefore, if I have found **f** in your sight, Ex 33:13
you in order to find **f** in your sight. Ex 33:13
that I have found **f** in your sight, Ex 33:16

do, for you have found **f** in my sight, Ex 33:17
said, "If now I have found **f** in your sight, Ex 34:9
why have I not found **f** in your sight, Nm 11:11
me at once, if I find **f** in your sight, Nm 11:15
said, "If we have found **f** in your sight, Nm 32:5
if then she finds no **f** in his eyes because Dt 24:1
its fullness and the **f** of him who dwells Dt 33:16
he said, "O Naphtali, sated with **f**, Dt 33:23
him, "If now I have found **f** in your eyes, Jgs 6:17
whose sight I shall find **f**." And she said to Ru 2:2
him, "Why have I found **f** in your eyes, Ru 2:10
she said, "I have found **f** in your eyes, Ru 2:13
"Let your servant find **f** in your eyes." 1 Sm 1:18
in stature and in **f** with the LORD and 1 Sm 2:26
I have not sought the **f** of the LORD.' 1 Sm 13:12
for he has found **f** in my sight." 1 Sm 16:22
well that I have found **f** in your eyes, 1 Sm 20:3
So now, if I have found **f** in your eyes, 1 Sm 20:29
let my young men find **f** in your eyes, 1 Sm 25:8
Achish, "If I have found **f** in your eyes, 1 Sm 27:5
that I have found **f** in your sight, 2 Sm 14:22
If I find **f** in the eyes of the LORD, he 2 Sm 15:25
let me ever find **f** in your sight, my 2 Sm 16:4
And Hadad found great **f** in the sight 1 Kgs 11:19
"Entreat now the **f** of the LORD your 1 Kgs 13:6
man with his master and in high **f**, 2 Kgs 5:1
Jehoahaz sought the **f** of the LORD, 2 Kgs 13:4
he entreated the **f** of the LORD his 2 Chr 33:12
for a brief moment **f** has been shown by Ezr 9:8
your servant has found **f** in your sight, Neh 2:5
Remember this also in my **f**, O my Neh 13:22
woman pleased him and won his **f**. Est 2:9
Now Esther was winning **f** in the eyes of Est 2:15
she won grace and **f** in his sight more Est 2:17
the king to beg his **f** and plead with him Est 4:8
in the court, she won **f** in his sight, Est 5:2
If I have found **f** in the sight of the king, Est 5:8
answered, "If I have found **f** in your sight, Est 7:3
king, and if I have found **f** in his sight, Est 8:5
of your hands and **f** the designs of the Jb 10:3
you afraid; many will court your **f**. Jb 11:19
His children will seek the **f** of the poor, Jb 20:10
you cover him with **f** as with a shield. Ps 5:12
and regard with **f** your burnt sacrifices! Ps 20:3
for a moment, and his **f** is for a lifetime. Ps 30:5
By your **f**, O LORD, you made my Ps 30:7
of Tyre will seek your **f** with gifts, Ps 45:12
shield; the LORD bestows **f** and honor. Ps 84:11
Show me a sign of your **f**, that those Ps 86:17
strength; by your **f** our horn is exalted. Ps 89:17
Let the **f** of the Lord our God be upon Ps 90:17
I will look with **f** on the faithful in the Ps 101:6
pity on Zion; it is the time to **f** her; Ps 102:13
O LORD, when you show **f** to your people; Ps 106:4
I entreat your **f** with all my heart; be Ps 119:58
Remember, O LORD, in David's **f**, all the Ps 132:1
So you will find **f** and good success in the Prv 3:4
scornful, but to the humble he gives **f**. Prv 3:34
finds life and obtains **f** from the LORD, Prv 8:35
Whoever diligently seeks good seeks **f**, Prv 11:27
A good man obtains **f** from the LORD, Prv 12:2
Good sense wins **f**, but the way of the Prv 13:15
who deals wisely has the king's **f**, Prv 14:35
and his **f** is like the clouds that bring Prv 16:15
thing and obtains **f** from the LORD. Prv 18:22
Many seek the **f** of a generous man, and Prv 19:6
lion, but his **f** is like dew on the grass. Prv 19:12
and **f** is better than silver or gold. Prv 22:1
will afterward find more **f** than he who Prv 28:23
nor **f** to those with knowledge, Eccl 9:11
of a wise man's mouth win him **f**, Eccl 10:12
If **f** is shown to the wicked, he does not Is 26:10
who formed them will show them no **f**. Is 27:11
LORD: "In a time of **f** I have answered you; Is 49:8
but in my **f** I have had mercy on you. Is 60:10
to proclaim the year of the LORD'S **f**, and Is 61:2
day and night, for I will show you no **f**.' Jer 16:13
the LORD and entreat the **f** of the LORD, Jer 26:19
shown to the priests, no **f** to the elders. Lam 4:16
God gave Daniel **f** and compassion in Dn 1:9
have not entreated the **f** of the LORD our Dn 9:13
and prevailed; he wept and sought his **f**. Hos 12:4
and their men to entreat the **f** of the LORD, Zec 7:2
at once to entreat the **f** of the LORD and Zec 8:21
and to entreat the **f** of the LORD. Zec 8:22
And I took two staffs, one I named **F**, the Zec 11:7
And I took my staff **F**, and I broke it, Zec 11:10
will he accept you or show you **f**? Mal 1:8
And now entreat the **f** of God, that he Mal 1:9
your hand, will he show **f** to any of you? Mal 1:9
or accepts it with **f** from your hand. Mal 2:13
Mary, for you have found **f** with God. Lk 1:30
wisdom. And the **f** of God was upon him. Lk 2:40
in stature and in **f** with God and man. Lk 2:52
to proclaim the year of the Lord's **f**." Lk 4:19
praising God and having **f** with all the Acts 2:47
and gave him **f** and wisdom before Acts 7:10
who found **f** in the sight of God and Acts 7:46
And desiring to do the Jews a **f**, Felix Acts 24:27
asking as a **f** against Paul that he Acts 25:3
But Festus, wishing to do the Jews a **f**, Acts 25:9
be puffed up in **f** of one against 1 Cor 4:6
us earnestly for the **f** of taking part in 2 Cor 8:4

FAVORABLE (8)
baker saw that the interpretation was **f**, Gn 40:16
me; God will give Pharaoh a **f** answer." Gn 41:16
with one accord are **f** to the king. 1 Kgs 22:13
with one accord are **f** to the king. 2 Chr 18:12
Lord spurn forever, and never again be **f**? Ps 77:7
LORD, you were **f** to your land; you Ps 85:1
he says, "In a **f** time I listened to you, 2 Cor 6:2
helped you." Behold, now is the **f** time; 2 Cor 6:2

FAVORABLY (2)
word of one of them, and speak **f**." 1 Kgs 22:13
word of one of them, and speak **f**." 2 Chr 18:12

FAVORED (4)
the land, and the **f** man lived in it. Jb 22:8
of Kedar were your **f** dealers in lambs, Ezk 27:21
to her and said, "Greetings, O **f** one, Lk 1:28
what were you less **f** than the rest of 2 Cor 12:13

FAVORITE (1)
let him be the **f** of his brothers, and let Dt 33:24

FAVORITISM (1)
boasters, showing **f** to gain advantage. Jude 1:16

FAVORS (2)
Amasa and said, "Whoever **f** Joab, 2 Sm 20:11
and scattered your **f** among foreigners Jer 3:13

FAWN (1)
forsakes her newborn **f** because there is Jer 14:5

FAWNING (1)
Your enemies shall come **f** to you, and Dt 33:29

FAWNS (3)
is a doe let loose that bears beautiful **f**. Gn 49:21
Your two breasts are like two **f**, twins of a Sg 4:5
Your two breasts are like two **f**, twins of a Sg 7:3

FEAR (352)
The **f** of you and the dread of you shall be Gn 9:2
vision: "**F** not, Abram, I am your shield; Gn 15:1
There is no **f** of God at all in this place, Gn 20:11
F not, for God has heard the voice of Gn 21:17
to him, for now I know that you **f** God, Gn 22:12
F not, for I am with you and will bless Gn 26:24
God of Abraham and the **F** of Isaac, Gn 31:42
Jacob swore by the **F** of his father Gn 31:53
from the hand of Esau, for I **f** him, Gn 32:11
the midwife said to her, "Do not **f**, Gn 35:17
"Do this and you will live, for I **f** God: Gn 42:18
I **f** to see the evil that would find my Gn 44:34
But Joseph said to them, "Do not **f**, for Gn 50:19
So do not **f**; I will provide for you and Gn 50:21
that you do not yet **f** the LORD God." Ex 9:30
And Moses said to the people, "**F** not, Ex 14:13
from all the people, men who **f** God, Ex 18:21
Moses said to the people, "Do not **f**, for Ex 20:20
that the **f** of him may be before you, Ex 20:20
the blind, but you shall **f** your God: Lv 19:14
an old man, and you shall **f** your God: Lv 19:32
one another, but you shall **f** your God, Lv 25:17
from him or profit, but **f** your God, Lv 25:36
him ruthlessly but shall **f** your God. Lv 25:43
And do not **f** the people of the land, for Nm 14:9
and the LORD is with us; do not **f** them." Nm 14:9
the LORD said to Moses, "Do not **f** him, Nm 21:34
was overcome with **f** of the people Nm 22:3
has told you. Do not **f** or be dismayed.' Dt 1:21
to put the dread and **f** of you on the Dt 2:25
But the LORD said to me, 'Do not **f** him, for Dt 3:2
You shall not **f** them, for it is the LORD Dt 3:22
that they may learn to **f** me all the days Dt 4:10
to **f** me and to keep all my Dt 5:29
that you may **f** the LORD your God, you Dt 6:2
It is the LORD your God you shall **f**. Him Dt 6:13
all these statutes, to **f** the LORD our God, Dt 6:24
of you, but to **f** the LORD your God, Dt 10:12
You shall **f** the LORD your God. You Dt 10:20
your God will lay the **f** of you and the Dt 11:25
LORD your God and **f** him and keep his Dt 13:4
Israel shall hear and **f** and never again Dt 13:11
you may learn to **f** the LORD your God Dt 14:23
people shall hear and **f** and not act Dt 17:13
that he may learn to **f** the LORD his God Dt 17:19
And the rest shall hear and **f**, and shall Dt 19:20
Do not **f** or panic or be in dread of them, Dt 20:3
midst, and all Israel shall hear, and **f**. Dt 21:21
behind you, and he did not **f** God. Dt 25:18
that you may **f** this glorious and Dt 28:58
Do not **f** or be in dread of them, for it is Dt 31:6
or forsake you. Do not **f** or be dismayed." Dt 31:8
hear and learn to **f** the LORD your God, Dt 31:12
hear and learn to **f** the LORD your God, Dt 31:13
and that the **f** of you has fallen upon us, Jos 2:9
that you may **f** the LORD your God Jos 4:24
Joshua, "Do not **f** and do not be dismayed. Jos 8:1
the LORD said to Joshua, "Do not **f** them, Jos 10:8
but we did it from **f** that in time to Jos 22:24
"Now therefore **f** the LORD and serve Jos 24:14
you shall not **f** the gods of the Amorites Jgs 6:10
be to you. Do not **f**; you shall not die." Jgs 6:23
And now, my daughter, do not **f**. I will do Ru 3:11
If you will **f** the LORD and serve him 1 Sm 12:14
Only **f** the LORD and serve him 1 Sm 12:24
And he said to him, "Do not **f**, for the 1 Sm 23:17
filled with **f** because of the words of 1 Sm 28:20
And David said to him, "Do not **f**, for I 2 Sm 9:7
Do not **f**; have I not commanded 2 Sm 13:28
of a lion, will utterly melt with **f**, 2 Sm 17:10
justly over men, ruling in the **f** of God, 2 Sm 23:3
that they may **f** you all the days that 1 Kgs 8:40
may know your name and **f** you, 1 Kgs 8:43
And Elijah said to her, "Do not **f**; go 1 Kgs 17:13
there, they did not **f** the LORD. 2 Kgs 17:25
them how they should **f** the LORD. 2 Kgs 17:28
They do not **f** the LORD, and they do 2 Kgs 17:34
"You shall not **f** other gods or bow 2 Kgs 17:35
but you shall **f** the LORD, who 2 Kgs 17:36
to do. You shall not **f** other gods, 2 Kgs 17:37
with you. You shall not **f** other gods, 2 Kgs 17:38
but you shall **f** the LORD your God, 2 Kgs 17:39
the LORD brought the **f** of him upon 1 Chr 14:17
F not; do not be dismayed. 1 Chr 22:13
that they may **f** you and walk in your 2 Chr 6:31
may know your name and **f** you, 2 Chr 6:33
for the **f** of the LORD was upon them. 2 Chr 14:14
And the **f** of the LORD fell upon all 2 Chr 17:10
let the **f** of the LORD be upon you. 2 Chr 19:7
you shall do in the **f** of the LORD, 2 Chr 19:9
And the **f** of God came on all the 2 Chr 20:29
who instructed him in the **f** of God, 2 Chr 26:5
for **f** was on them because of the peoples Ezr 3:3
servants who delight to **f** your name, Neh 1:11
not to walk in the **f** of our God to prevent Neh 5:9
I did not do so, because of the **f** of God. Neh 5:15
Jews, for **f** of the Jews had fallen on them. Est 8:17
for the **f** of them had fallen on all peoples. Est 9:2
for the **f** of Mordecai had fallen on them. Est 9:3
and said, "Does Job **f** God for no reason? Jb 1:9
For the thing that I **f** comes upon me, Jb 3:25
Is not your **f** of God your confidence, and Jb 4:6
and shall not **f** destruction when it Jb 5:21
and shall not **f** the beasts of the earth. Jb 5:22
a friend forsakes the **f** of the Almighty. Jb 6:14
Then I would speak without **f** of him, for Jb 9:35
you will be secure and will not **f**. Jb 11:15
doing away with the **f** of God and Jb 15:4
Their houses are safe from **f**, and no rod Jb 21:9
Is it for your **f** of him that he reproves Jb 22:4
"Dominion and **f** are with God; he makes Jb 25:2
said to man, 'Behold, the **f** of the Lord, Jb 28:28
I stood in great **f** of the multitude, Jb 31:34
Behold, no **f** of me need terrify you; my Jb 33:7
Therefore men **f** him; he does not regard Jb 37:24
her labor be in vain, yet she has no **f**, Jb 39:16
He laughs at **f** and is not dismayed; he Jb 39:22
is not his like, a creature without **f**. Jb 41:33
Serve the LORD with **f**, and rejoice with Ps 2:11
toward your holy temple in the **f** of you. Ps 5:7
Put them in **f**, O LORD! Let the nations Ps 9:20
but who honors those who **f** the LORD; Ps 15:4
the **f** of the LORD is clean, enduring Ps 19:9
You who **f** the LORD, praise him! All you Ps 22:23
I will perform before those who **f** him. Ps 22:25
of the shadow of death, I will **f** no evil, Ps 23:4
of the LORD is for those who **f** him, Ps 25:14
light and my salvation; whom shall I **f**? Ps 27:1
encamp against me, my heart shall not **f**; Ps 27:3
up for those who **f** you and worked for Ps 31:19
Let all the earth **f** the LORD; let all the Ps 33:8
eye of the LORD is on those who **f** him, Ps 33:18
LORD encamps around those who **f** him, Ps 34:7
Oh, **f** the LORD, you his saints, for those Ps 34:9
saints, for those who **f** him have no lack! Ps 34:9
to me; I will teach you the **f** of the LORD. Ps 34:11
heart; there is no **f** of God before his eyes. Ps 36:1
Many will see and **f**, and put their trust Ps 40:3
Therefore we will not **f** though the earth Ps 46:2
Why should I **f** in times of trouble, when Ps 49:5
The righteous shall see and **f**, and shall Ps 52:6
F and trembling come upon me, and Ps 55:5
they do not change and do not **f** God. Ps 55:19
have set up a banner for those who **f** you, Ps 60:4
the heritage of those who **f** your name. Ps 61:5

shooting at him suddenly and without **f**. Ps 64:4
Come and hear, all you who **f** God, and Ps 66:16
us; let all the ends of the earth **f** him! Ps 67:7
May they **f** you while the sun endures, Ps 72:5
his salvation is near to those who **f** him, Ps 85:9
truth; unite my heart to **f** your name. Ps 86:11
your wrath according to the **f** of you? Ps 90:11
You will not **f** the terror of the night, nor Ps 91:5
Nations will **f** the name of the LORD, Ps 102:15
the kings of the earth will **f** your glory. Ps 102:15
steadfast love toward those who **f** him; Ps 103:11
shows compassion to those who **f** him. Ps 103:13
to everlasting on those who **f** him, Ps 103:17
He provides food for those who **f** him; he Ps 111:5
The **f** of the LORD is the beginning of Ps 111:10
You who **f** the LORD, trust in the LORD! Ps 115:11
he will bless those who **f** the LORD, Ps 115:13
Let those who **f** the LORD say, "His Ps 118:4
The LORD is on my side; I will not **f**. Ps 118:6
I am a companion of all who **f** you, of Ps 119:63
Those who **f** you shall see me and Ps 119:74
Let those who **f** you turn to me, that Ps 119:79
My flesh trembles for **f** of you, and I Ps 119:120
bless the LORD! You who **f** the LORD, Ps 135:20
fulfills the desire of those who **f** him; Ps 145:19
takes pleasure in those who **f** him, Ps 147:11
The **f** of the LORD is the beginning of Prv 1:7
and did not choose the **f** of the LORD, Prv 1:29
you will understand the **f** of the LORD and Prv 2:5
eyes; **f** the LORD, and turn away from evil. Prv 3:7
The **f** of the LORD is hatred of evil. Pride Prv 8:13
The **f** of the LORD is the beginning of Prv 9:10
The **f** of the LORD prolongs life, but the Prv 10:27
In the **f** of the LORD one has strong Prv 14:26
The **f** of the LORD is a fountain of life, Prv 14:27
is a little with the **f** of the LORD than Prv 15:16
The **f** of the LORD is instruction in Prv 15:33
and by the **f** of the LORD one turns away Prv 16:6
The **f** of the LORD leads to life, and Prv 19:23
reward for humility and **f** of the LORD is Prv 22:4
but continue in the **f** of the LORD all Prv 23:17
My son, **f** the LORD and the king, and Prv 24:21
The **f** of man lays a snare, but Prv 29:25
has done it, so that people **f** before him. Eccl 3:14
is vanity; but God is the one you must **f**. Eccl 5:7
it will be well with those who **f** God, Eccl 8:12
fear God, because they **f** before him. Eccl 8:12
because he does not **f** before God. Eccl 8:13
F God and keep his commandments, Eccl 12:13
say to him, 'Be careful, be quiet, do not **f**, Is 7:4
not come there for **f** of briers and thorns, Is 7:25
conspiracy, and do not **f** what they fear, Is 8:12
conspiracy, and do not fear what they **f**, Is 8:12
Let him be your **f**, and let him be your Is 8:13
Spirit of knowledge and the **f** of the LORD. Is 11:2
his delight shall be in the **f** of the LORD. Is 11:3
O city; melt in **f**, O Philistia, all of you! Is 14:31
and tremble with **f** before the hand that Is 19:16
it is mentioned will **f** because of the Is 19:17
you; cities of ruthless nations will **f** you. Is 25:3
and their **f** of me is a commandment Is 29:13
the **f** of the LORD is Zion's treasure. Is 33:6
have an anxious heart, "Be strong; **f** not! Is 35:4
herald of good news; lift it up, **f** not; Is 40:9
f not, for I am with you; be not Is 41:10
it is I who say to you, "**F** not, I am the Is 41:13
F not, you worm Jacob, you men of Is 41:14
O Israel: "**F** not, for I have redeemed you; Is 43:1
F not, for I am with you; I will bring your Is 43:5
F not, O Jacob my servant, Jeshurun Is 44:2
F not, nor be afraid; have I not told you Is 44:8
f not the reproach of man, nor be Is 51:7
and you **f** continually all the day Is 51:13
"**F** not, for you will not be ashamed; be Is 54:4
far from oppression, for you shall not **f**; Is 54:14
Whom did you dread and **f**, so that you Is 57:11
for a long time, and you do not **f** me? Is 57:11
So they shall **f** the name of the LORD Is 59:19
harden our heart, so that we **f** you not? Is 63:17
the **f** of me is not in you, declares the Jer 2:19
Yet her treacherous sister Judah did not **f**, Jer 3:8
Do you not **f** me? declares the LORD; Do Jer 5:22
their hearts, 'Let us **f** the LORD our God, Jer 5:24
Who would not **f** you, O King of the Jer 10:7
stream, and does not **f** when heat comes, Jer 17:8
care for them, and they shall **f** no more, Jer 23:4
Did he not **f** the LORD and entreat the Jer 26:19
"Then **f** not, O Jacob my servant, Jer 30:10
one way, that they may **f** me forever, Jer 32:39
And I will put the **f** of me in their Jer 32:40
They shall **f** and tremble because of all Jer 33:9
us go to Jerusalem for **f** of the army of Jer 35:11
words, they turned one to another in **f**. Jer 36:16
Do not **f** the king of Babylon, of whom Jer 42:11
Do not **f** him, declares the LORD, for I Jer 42:11
the sword that you **f** shall overtake you Jer 42:16
"But **f** not, O Jacob my servant, nor be Jer 46:27
F not, O Jacob my servant, declares the Jer 46:28
they melt in **f**, they are troubled like the Jer 49:23
I called on you; you said, 'Do not **f**!' Lam 3:57
F them not, nor be dismayed at their Ezk 3:9
so I will put **f** in the land of Egypt. Ezk 30:13
said to Daniel, "I **f** my lord the king, Dn 1:10
are to tremble and **f** before the God of Dn 6:26
Then he said to me, "**F** not, Daniel, for Dn 10:12
he said, "O man greatly loved, **f** not, Dn 10:19
and they shall come in **f** to the LORD and Hos 3:5
have no king, for we do not **f** the LORD; Hos 10:3
"**F** not, O land; be glad and rejoice, for the Jl 2:21
F not, you beasts of the field, for the Jl 2:22
The lion has roared; who will not **f**? The Am 3:8
to them, "I am a Hebrew, and I **f** the LORD, Jon 1:9
and it is sound wisdom to **f** your name: Mi 6:9
our God, and they shall be in **f** of you. Mi 7:17
of you, and your work, O LORD, do I **f**. Hab 3:2
I said, 'Surely you will **f** me; you will Zep 3:7
your midst; you shall never again **f** evil. Zep 3:15
be said to Jerusalem: "**F** not, O Zion; Zep 3:16
My Spirit remains in your midst. **F** not. Hg 2:5
F not, but let your hands be strong." Zec 8:13
and to the house of Judah; **f** not. Zec 8:15
And if I am a master, where is my **f**? Mal 1:6
It was a covenant of **f**, and he feared me. Mal 2:5
aside the sojourner, and do not **f** me, Mal 3:5
But for you who **f** my name, the sun of Mal 4:2
do not **f** to take Mary as your wife, Mt 1:20
"So have no **f** of them, for nothing is Mt 10:26
And do not **f** those who kill the body Mt 10:28
Rather **f** him who can destroy both Mt 10:28
F not, therefore; you are of more value Mt 10:31
"It is a ghost!" and they cried out in **f**. Mt 14:26
them, saying, "Rise, and have no **f**." Mt 17:7
And for **f** of him the guards trembled Mt 28:4
from the tomb with **f** and great joy, Mt 28:8
were filled with great **f** and said to one Mk 4:41
came in **f** and trembling and fell down Mk 5:33
to the ruler of the synagogue, "Do not **f**, Mk 5:36
when he saw him, and **f** fell upon him. Lk 1:12
is for those who **f** him from generation Lk 1:50
And **f** came on all their neighbors. And Lk 1:65
our enemies, might serve him without **f**, Lk 1:74
around them, and they were filled with **f**. Lk 2:9
And the angel said to them, "**F** not, for Lk 2:10
F seized them all, and they glorified God, Lk 7:16
them, for they were seized with great **f**. Lk 8:37
on hearing this answered him, "Do not **f**; Lk 8:50
friends, do not **f** those who kill the body, Lk 12:4
But I will warn you whom to **f**: fear him Lk 12:5
f him who, after he has killed, has Lk 12:5
to cast into hell. Yes, I tell you, **f** him! Lk 12:5
F not; you are of more value than many Lk 12:7
"**F** not, little flock, for it is your Lk 12:32
'Though I neither **f** God nor respect Lk 18:4
people fainting with **f** and with Lk 21:26
him, saying, "Do you not **f** God, Lk 23:40
Yet for **f** of the Jews no one spoke openly Jn 7:13
"**F** not, daughter of Zion; behold, your Jn 12:15
but for **f** of the Pharisees they did not Jn 12:42
of Jesus, but secretly for **f** of the Jews, Jn 19:38
where the disciples were for **f** of the Jews, Jn 20:19
And great **f** came upon all who heard of Acts 5:5
And great **f** came upon the whole Acts 5:11
And walking in the **f** of the Lord and Acts 9:31
"Men of Israel and you who **f** God, Acts 13:16
and those among you who **f** God, Acts 13:26
and trembling with **f** he fell down Acts 16:29
And **f** fell upon them all, and the Acts 19:17
"There is no **f** of God before their eyes." Rom 3:18
the spirit of slavery to fall back into **f**, Rom 8:15
Would you have no **f** of the one who is Rom 13:3
weakness and in **f** and much 1 Cor 2:3
Therefore, knowing the **f** of the Lord, 2 Cor 5:11
holiness to completion in the **f** of God. 2 Cor 7:1
turn—fighting without and **f** within. 2 Cor 7:5
yourselves, what indignation, what **f**, 2 Cor 7:11
received him with **f** and trembling. 2 Cor 7:15
For I **f** that perhaps when I come I 2 Cor 12:20
I **f** that when I come again my God 2 Cor 12:21
earthly masters with **f** and trembling, Eph 6:5
more bold to speak the word without **f**. Phil 1:14
own salvation with **f** and trembling, Phil 2:12
for **f** that somehow the tempter had 1 Thes 3:5
of all, so that the rest may stand in **f**. 1 Tm 5:20
us a spirit not of **f** but of power and 2 Tm 1:7
all those who through **f** of death were Heb 2:15
let us **f** lest any of you should seem to Heb 4:1
in reverent **f** constructed an ark for the Heb 11:7
that Moses said, "I tremble with **f**." Heb 12:21
say, "The Lord is my helper; I will not **f**; Heb 13:6
yourselves with **f** throughout the 1 Pt 1:17
everyone. Love the brotherhood. **F** God. 1 Pt 2:17
good and do not **f** anything that is 1 Pt 3:6
you will be blessed. Have no **f** of them, 1 Pt 3:14
There is no **f** in love, but perfect love 1 Jn 4:18
fear in love, but perfect love casts out **f**. 1 Jn 4:18
For **f** has to do with punishment, and 1 Jn 4:18
feasts, as they feast with you without **f**, Jude 1:12
to others show mercy with **f**, hating Jude 1:23
his right hand on me, saying, "**F** not, Rv 1:17
Do not **f** what you are about to suffer. Rv 2:10
and great **f** fell on those who saw them. Rv 11:11
and saints, and those who **f** your name, Rv 11:18
a loud voice, "**F** God and give him glory, Rv 14:7
Who will not **f**, O Lord, and glorify your Rv 15:4
will stand far off, in **f** of her torment, Rv 18:10
will stand far off, in **f** of her torment, Rv 18:15
God, all you his servants, you who **f** him, Rv 19:5

FEARED (56)

he said, "She is my sister," for he **f** to say, Gn 26:7
grows up"—for he **f** that he would die, Gn 38:11
for he **f** that harm might happen to him. Gn 42:4
But the midwives **f** God and did not do as Ex 1:17
And because the midwives **f** God, he Ex 1:21
Then whoever **f** the word of the LORD Ex 9:20
after them, and they **f** greatly. Ex 14:10
the Egyptians, so the people **f** the LORD, Ex 14:31
had I not **f** provocation by the enemy, Dt 32:27
before you—so we **f** greatly for our lives Jos 9:24
he **f** greatly, because Gibeon was a great Jos 10:2
all the people greatly **f** the LORD and 1 Sm 12:18
his mouth, for the people **f** the oath. 1 Sm 14:26
because I **f** the people and obeyed 1 Sm 15:24
would not, for he **f** greatly. 1 Sm 31:4
another word, because he **f** him. 2 Sm 3:11
And Adonijah **f** Solomon. So he arose 1 Kgs 1:50
(Now Obadiah **f** the LORD greatly, 1 Kgs 18:3
I your servant have **f** the LORD from 1 Kgs 18:12
you know that your servant **f** the LORD, 2 Kgs 4:1
king of Egypt, and had **f** other gods 2 Kgs 17:7
They also **f** the LORD and appointed 2 Kgs 17:32
So they **f** the LORD but also served 2 Kgs 17:33
So these nations **f** the LORD and also 2 Kgs 17:41
would not, for he **f** greatly. 1 Chr 10:4
one who **f** God and turned away from evil. Jb 1:1
For the LORD, the Most High, is to be **f**, a Ps 47:2
But you, you are to be **f**! Who can stand Ps 76:7
judgment; the earth **f** and was still, Ps 76:8
him bring gifts to him who is to be **f**, Ps 76:11
who is to be **f** by the kings of the earth. Ps 76:12
a God greatly to be **f** in the council of the Ps 89:7
to be praised; he is to be **f** above all gods. Ps 96:4
your promise, that you may be **f**. Ps 119:38
there is forgiveness, that you may be **f**. Ps 130:4
tall and smooth, to a people **f** near and far, Is 18:2
and smooth, from a people **f** near and far, Is 18:7
even to this day, nor have they **f**, Jer 44:10
You have **f** the sword, and I will bring Ezk 11:8
languages trembled and **f** before him. Dn 5:19
Then the men **f** the LORD exceedingly, Jon 1:16
had sent him. And the people **f** the LORD. Hg 1:12
my name will be **f** among the nations. Mal 1:14
It was a covenant of fear, and he **f** me. Mal 2:5
Then those who **f** the LORD spoke with Mal 3:16
him of those who **f** the LORD and Mal 3:16
to put him to death, he **f** the people, Mt 14:5
to arrest him, they **f** the crowds, Mt 21:46
for Herod **f** John, knowing that he was a Mk 6:20
a way to destroy him, for they **f** him, Mk 11:18
seeking to arrest him but **f** the people, Mk 12:12
a judge who neither **f** God nor respected Lk 18:2
against them, but they **f** the people. Lk 20:19
to put him to death, for they **f** the people. Lk 22:2
said these things because they **f** the Jews, Jn 9:22
a devout man who **f** God with all his Acts 10:2

FEARFUL (7)

there any man who is **f** and fainthearted? Dt 20:8
saying, 'Whoever is **f** and trembling, Jgs 7:3
success, he stood in **f** awe of him. 1 Sm 18:15
and be not **f** at the report heard in the Jer 51:46
he shall cause **f** destruction and shall Dn 8:24
but a **f** expectation of judgment, and a Heb 10:27
It is a **f** thing to fall into the hands of Heb 10:31

FEARFULLY (2)

you, for I am **f** and wonderfully made. Ps 139:14
My radiant appearance was **f** changed, Dn 10:8

FEARING (5)

God by walking in his ways and by **f** him. Dt 8:6
f that they would run aground on the Acts 27:17
And **f** that we might run on the Acts 27:29
himself, **f** the circumcision party. Gal 2:12
but with sincerity of heart, **f** the Lord. Col 3:22

FEARS (17)

"Behold, Adonijah **f** King Solomon, 1 Kgs 1:51

who **f** God and turns away from evil?" Jb 1:8
who **f** God and turns away from evil?" Jb 2:3
Who is the man who **f** the LORD? Him Ps 25:12
me and delivered me from all my **f**. Ps 34:4
Then all mankind **f**; they tell what God Ps 64:9
Blessed is the man who **f** the LORD, who Ps 112:1
Blessed is everyone who **f** the LORD, who Ps 128:1
the man be blessed who **f** the LORD. Ps 128:4
walks in uprightness **f** the LORD, Prv 14:2
is the one who **f** the LORD always, Prv 28:14
but a woman who **f** the LORD is to be Prv 31:30
for the one who **f** God shall come out Eccl 7:18
Who among you **f** the LORD and obeys Is 50:10
for them and bring their **f** upon them, Is 66:4
nation anyone who **f** him and does Acts 10:35
and whoever **f** has not been perfected in 1 Jn 4:18

FEARSOME (1)
They are dreaded and **f**; their justice and Hab 1:7

FEAST (149)
he made them a **f** and baked unleavened Gn 19:3
Abraham made a great **f** on the day that Gn 21:8
So he made them a **f**, and they ate and Gn 26:30
all the people of the place and made a **f**. Gn 29:22
he made a **f** for all his servants and Gn 40:20
that they may hold a **f** to me in the Ex 5:1
herds, for we must hold a **f** to the LORD." Ex 10:9
and you shall keep it as a **f** to the LORD; Ex 12:14
a statute forever, you shall keep it as a **f**. Ex 12:14
shall observe the **F** of Unleavened Ex 12:17
seventh day there shall be a **f** to the LORD. Ex 13:6
in the year you shall keep a **f** to me. Ex 23:14
shall keep the **F** of Unleavened Bread. Ex 23:15
You shall keep the **F** of Harvest, of the Ex 23:16
You shall keep the **F** of Ingathering at Ex 23:16
the fat of my **f** remain until the Ex 23:18
"Tomorrow shall be a **f** to the LORD." Ex 32:5
shall keep the **F** of Unleavened Bread. Ex 34:18
You shall observe the **F** of Weeks, the Ex 34:22
and the **F** of Ingathering at the year's Ex 34:22
the sacrifice of the **F** of the Passover Ex 34:25
month is the **F** of Unleavened bread Lv 23:6
for seven days is the **F** of Booths to the Lv 23:34
you shall celebrate the **f** of the LORD Lv 23:39
shall celebrate it as a **f** to the LORD for Lv 23:41
the fifteenth day of this month is a **f**. Nm 28:17
grain to the LORD at your **F** of Weeks, Nm 28:26
you shall keep a **f** to the LORD seven Nm 29:12
you shall keep the **F** of Weeks to the Dt 16:10
"You shall keep the **F** of Booths seven Dt 16:13
You shall rejoice in your **f**, you and Dt 16:14
you shall keep the **f** to the LORD your Dt 16:15
at the **F** of Unleavened Bread, at the Dt 16:16
of Unleavened Bread, at the **F** of Weeks, Dt 16:16
Feast of Weeks, and at the **F** of Booths. Dt 16:16
in the year of release, at the **F** of Booths, Dt 31:10
woman, and Samson prepared a **f** there, Jgs 14:10
what it is, within the seven days of the **f**, Jgs 14:12
him the seven days that their **f** lasted, Jgs 14:17
there is the yearly **f** of the LORD at Jgs 21:19
in your eyes, for we come on a **f** day. 1 Sm 25:8
he was holding a **f** in his house, 1 Sm 25:36
feast in his house, like the **f** of a king. 1 Sm 25:36
David made a **f** for Abner and the 2 Sm 3:20
and made a **f** for all his servants. 1 Kgs 3:15
King Solomon at the **f** in the month 1 Kgs 8:2
So Solomon held the **f** at that time, 1 Kgs 8:65
Jeroboam appointed a **f** on the 1 Kgs 12:32
eighth month like the **f** that was in 1 Kgs 12:32
And he instituted a **f** for the people of 1 Kgs 12:33
So he prepared for them a great **f**, and 2 Kgs 6:23
Sabbaths, new moons and **f** days, 1 Chr 23:31
before the king at the **f** that is in the 2 Chr 5:3
Solomon held the **f** for seven days, 2 Chr 7:8
altar seven days and the **f** seven days. 2 Chr 7:9
feasts—the **F** of Unleavened Bread, 2 Chr 8:13
of Unleavened Bread, the **F** of Weeks, 2 Chr 8:13
Feast of Weeks, and the **F** of Booths. 2 Chr 8:13
to keep the **F** of Unleavened Bread 2 Chr 30:13
Jerusalem kept the **F** of Unleavened 2 Chr 30:21
to keep the **f** for another seven 2 Chr 30:23
and the **F** of Unleavened Bread 2 Chr 35:17
And they kept the **F** of Booths, as it is Ezr 3:4
they kept the **F** of Unleavened Bread Ezr 6:22
in booths during the **f** of the seventh Neh 8:14
They kept the **f** seven days, and on the Neh 8:18
his reign he gave a **f** for all his officials Est 1:3
a **f** lasting for seven days in the court of Est 1:5
Vashti also gave a **f** for the women in Est 1:9
king gave a great **f** for all his officials Est 2:18
officials and servants; it was Esther's **f**. Est 2:18
come today to a **f** that I have prepared Est 5:4
Haman came to the **f** that Esther had Est 5:5
as they were drinking wine after the **f**, Est 5:6
Haman come to the **f** that I will prepare Est 5:8
come with the king to the **f** she prepared. Est 5:12
the king to the **f**." This idea pleased Est 5:14
bring Haman to the **f** that Esther had Est 6:14
Haman went in to **f** with Queen Esther. Est 7:1
as they were drinking wine after the **f**, Est 7:2
joy among the Jews, a **f** and a holiday. Est 8:17
to go and hold a **f** in the house of each Jb 1:4
the days of the **f** had run their course, Jb 1:5
like profane mockers at a **f**, they gnash Ps 35:16
They **f** on the abundance of your house, Ps 36:8
moon, at the full moon, on our **f** day. Ps 81:3
the cheerful of heart has a continual **f**. Prv 15:15
and your princes **f** in the morning! Eccl 10:16
and your princes **f** at the proper time, Eccl 10:17
will make for all peoples a **f** of rich food, Is 25:6
a feast of rich food, a **f** of well-aged wine, Is 25:6
as in the night when a holy **f** is kept, Is 30:29
I will **f** the soul of the priests with Jer 31:14
will prepare them a **f** and make them Jer 51:39
the detestable things your eyes **f** on, Ezk 20:7
before kings, to **f** their eyes on you. Ezk 28:17
around to the sacrificial **f** that I am Ezk 39:17
a great sacrificial **f** on the mountains Ezk 39:17
at the sacrificial **f** that I am preparing Ezk 39:19
shall celebrate the **F** of the Passover, Ezk 45:21
month and for the seven days of the **f**, Ezk 45:25
Belshazzar made a great **f** for a thousand Dn 5:1
punish her for the **f** days of the Baals Hos 2:13
and on the day of the **f** of the LORD? Hos 9:5
tents, as in the days of the appointed **f**. Hos 12:9
of hosts, and to keep the **F** of Booths. Zec 14:16
do not go up to keep the **F** of Booths. Zec 14:18
do not go up to keep the **F** of Booths. Zec 14:19
a king who gave a wedding **f** for his son, Mt 22:2
those who were invited to the wedding **f**, Mt 22:3
is ready. Come to the wedding **f**.' Mt 22:4
to his servants, 'The wedding **f** is ready, Mt 22:8
invite to the wedding **f** as many as you Mt 22:9
went in with him to the marriage **f**, Mt 25:10
But they said, "Not during the **f**, lest Mt 26:5
Now at the **f** the governor was Mt 27:15
Passover and the **F** of Unleavened Mk 14:1
for they said, "Not during the **f**, lest Mk 14:2
Now at the **f** he used to release for them Mk 15:6
every year at the **F** of the Passover. Lk 2:41
And when the **f** was ended, as they were Lk 2:43
Levi made him a great **f** in his house, Lk 5:29
to come home from the wedding **f**, Lk 12:36
are invited by someone to a wedding **f**, Lk 14:8
But when you give a **f**, invite the poor, Lk 14:13
Now the **F** of Unleavened Bread drew Lk 22:1
it to the master of the **f**." So they took it. Jn 2:8
the master of the **f** tasted the water now Jn 2:9
the master of the **f** called the bridegroom Jn 2:9
he was in Jerusalem at the Passover **F**, Jn 2:23
all that he had done in Jerusalem at the **f**. Jn 4:45
at the feast. For they too had gone to the **f**. Jn 4:45
After this there was a **f** of the Jews, and Jn 5:1
Now the Passover, the **f** of the Jews, was at Jn 6:4
Now the Jews' **F** of Booths was at hand. Jn 7:2
You go up to the **f**. I am not going up to Jn 7:8
I am not going up to this **f**, for my time Jn 7:8
after his brothers had gone up to the **f**, Jn 7:10
The Jews were looking for him at the **f**, Jn 7:11
the middle of the **f** Jesus went up into Jn 7:14
On the last day of the **f**, the great day, Jn 7:37
At that time the **F** of Dedication took Jn 10:22
That he will not come to the **f** at all?" Jn 11:56
had come to the **f** heard that Jesus was Jn 12:12
up to worship at the **f** were some Greeks. Jn 12:20
Now before the **F** of the Passover, when Jn 13:1
we need for the **f**," or that he should Jn 13:29
their deceptions, while they **f** with you. 2 Pt 2:13
feasts, as they **f** with you without fear, Jude 1:12

FEASTED (3)
Those who once **f** on delicacies perish Lam 4:5
the detestable things their eyes **f** on, Ezk 20:8
linen and who **f** sumptuously every Lk 16:19

FEASTING (8)
with him heard it as they finished **f**. 1 Kgs 1:41
and made that a day of **f** and gladness. Est 9:17
making that a day of **f** and gladness. Est 9:18
of Adar as a day for gladness and **f**, Est 9:19
make them days of **f** and gladness, Est 9:22
quiet than a house full of **f** with strife. Prv 17:1
mourning than to go to the house of **f**, Eccl 7:2
go into the house of **f** to sit with them, Jer 16:8

FEASTS (33)
These are the appointed **f** of the LORD that Lv 23:2
convocations; they are my appointed **f**. Lv 23:2
"These are the appointed **f** of the LORD, Lv 23:4
"These are the appointed **f** of the LORD, Lv 23:37
of Israel the appointed **f** of the LORD. Lv 23:44
and at your appointed **f** and at the Nm 10:10
freewill offering or at your appointed **f**, Nm 15:3
offer to the LORD at your appointed **f**, Nm 29:39
moons and the appointed **f** of the LORD 2 Chr 2:4
and the three annual **f**—the Feast of 2 Chr 8:13
the new moons, and the appointed **f**, 2 Chr 31:3
and at all the appointed **f** of the LORD, Ezr 3:5
the new moons, the appointed **f**, Neh 10:33
and your appointed **f** my soul hates; Is 1:14
tambourine and flute and wine at their **f**, Is 5:12
Add year to year; let the **f** run their round. Is 29:1
Behold Zion, the city of our appointed **f**! Is 33:20
at Jerusalem during her appointed **f**, Ezk 36:38
and my statutes in all my appointed **f**, Ezk 44:24
offerings, and drink offerings, at the **f**, Ezk 45:17
all the appointed **f** of the house of Ezk 45:17
come before the LORD at the appointed **f**, Ezk 46:9
"At the **f** and the appointed festivals, Ezk 46:11
I will put an end to all her mirth, her **f**, Hos 2:11
her Sabbaths, and all her appointed **f**. Hos 2:11
"I hate, I despise your **f**, and I take no Am 5:21
I will turn your **f** into mourning and Am 8:10
Keep your **f**, O Judah; fulfill your vows, Na 1:15
of joy and gladness and cheerful **f**. Zec 8:19
the place of honor at **f** and the best seats Mt 23:6
and the places of honor at **f**, Mk 12:39
and the places of honor at **f**, Lk 20:46
These are blemishes on your love **f**, as Jude 1:12

FEATHERS (1)
till his hair grew as long as eagles' **f**, Dn 4:33

FEATURES (1)
seal, and its **f** stand out like a garment. Jb 38:14

FED (19)
and plump, and they **f** in the reed grass. Gn 41:2
out of the Nile and **f** in the reed grass. Gn 41:18
bread with which I **f** you in the Ex 16:32
let you hunger and **f** you with manna, Dt 8:3
who **f** you in the wilderness with manna Dt 8:16
in a cave and **f** them with bread and 1 Kgs 18:4
in a cave and **f** them with bread and 1 Kgs 18:13
You have **f** them with the bread of tears Ps 80:5
When I **f** them to the full, they committed Jer 5:7
I gave you—I **f** you with fine flour and Ezk 16:19
but the shepherds have **f** themselves, Ezk 34:8
themselves, and have not **f** my sheep, Ezk 34:8
its branches, and all flesh was **f** from it. Dn 4:12
He was **f** grass like an ox, and his body Dn 5:21
and I bent down to them and **f** them. Hos 11:4
said to her, "Let the children be **f** first, Mk 7:27
was longing to be **f** with the pods that Lk 15:16
who desired to be **f** with what fell from Lk 16:21
I **f** you with milk, not solid food, for 1 Cor 3:2

FEE (4)
if it was hired, it came for its hiring **f**. Ex 22:15
shall not bring the **f** of a prostitute or Dt 23:18
for from the **f** of a prostitute she gathered Mi 1:7
and to the **f** of a prostitute they shall Mi 1:7

FEEBLE (13)
are broken, but the **f** bind on strength. 1 Sm 2:4
carrying all the **f** among them on 2 Chr 28:15
Samaria, "What are these **f** Jews doing? Neh 4:2
and you have made firm the **f** knees. Jb 4:4
I am **f** and crushed; I groan because of Ps 38:8
Therefore all hands will be **f**, and every Is 13:7
who remain will be very few and **f**." Is 16:14
weak hands, and make firm the **f** knees. Is 35:3
She who bore seven has grown **f**; she has Jer 15:9
to their children, so **f** are their hands, Jer 47:3
Damascus has become **f**, she turned to Jer 49:24
All hands are **f**, and all knees turn to Ezk 7:17
heart will melt, and all hands will be **f**; Ezk 21:7

FEEBLER (2)
but for the **f** of the flock he would not Gn 30:42
So the **f** would be Laban's, and the Gn 30:42

FEEBLEST (1)
so that the **f** among them on that day Zec 12:8

FEED (40)
We have straw and **f** for our donkeys, Jgs 19:19
into his house and gave the donkeys **f**. Jgs 19:21
forth from Saul to **f** his father's sheep 1 Sm 17:15
the ravens to **f** you there." 1 Kgs 17:4
commanded a widow there to **f** you." 1 Kgs 17:9
in prison and **f** him meager rations 1 Kgs 22:27
in prison and **f** him with meager 2 Chr 18:26
it, and all that move in the field **f** on it. Ps 80:13
But he would **f** you with the finest of the Ps 81:16
The lips of the righteous **f** many, but Prv 10:21
but the mouths of fools **f** on folly. Prv 15:14
f me with the food that is needful for Prv 30:8
They shall **f** along the ways; on all bare Is 49:9
I will **f** you with the heritage of Jacob Is 58:14
who will **f** you with knowledge and Jer 3:15
I will **f** this people with bitter food, Jer 9:15

I will **f** them with bitter food and give Jer 23:15
and he shall **f** on Carmel and in Jer 50:19
f your belly with this scroll that I give Ezk 3:3
Should not shepherds **f** the sheep? Ezk 34:2
the fat ones, but you do not **f** the sheep. Ezk 34:3
shall the shepherds **f** themselves. Ezk 34:10
And I will **f** them on the mountains of Ezk 34:13
I will **f** them with good pasture, and on Ezk 34:14
pasture they shall **f** on the mountains Ezk 34:14
I will destroy. I will **f** them in justice. Ezk 34:16
enough for you to **f** on the good Ezk 34:18
servant David, and he shall **f** them: Ezk 34:23
he shall **f** them and be their shepherd. Ezk 34:23
They **f** on the sin of my people; they are Hos 4:8
can the LORD now **f** them like a lamb in Hos 4:16
floor and wine vat shall not **f** them, Hos 9:2
anything. Let them not **f** or drink water, Jon 3:7
a desolate place to **f** so great a crowd?" Mt 15:33
when did we see you hungry and **f** you, Mt 25:37
"How can one **f** these people with bread Mk 8:4
who sent him into his fields to **f** pigs. Lk 15:15
you." He said to him, "**F** my lambs." Jn 21:15
you." Jesus said to him, "**F** my sheep. Jn 21:17
"if your enemy is hungry, **f** him; Rom 12:20

FEEDING (7)
plowing and the donkeys **f** beside them, Jb 1:14
of Israel who have been **f** yourselves! Ezk 34:2
and put a stop to their **f** the sheep. Ezk 34:10
lions' den, the **f** place of the young lions, Na 2:11
of many pigs was **f** at some distance Mt 8:30
herd of pigs was **f** there on the hillside, Mk 5:11
herd of pigs was **f** there on the hillside, Lk 8:32

FEEDS (9)
beast loose and it **f** in another man's Ex 22:5
He **f** on ashes; a deluded heart has led Is 44:20
Ephraim **f** on the wind and pursues the Hos 12:1
and yet your heavenly Father **f** them. Mt 6:26
nor barn, and yet God **f** them. Lk 12:24
Whoever **f** on my flesh and drinks my Jn 6:54
Whoever **f** on my flesh and drinks my Jn 6:56
of the Father, so whoever **f** on me, Jn 6:57
Whoever **f** on this bread will live Jn 6:58

FEEL (15)
Perhaps my father will **f** me, and I Gn 27:12
"Please come near, that I may **f** you, Gn 27:21
of the dread that your heart shall **f**, Dt 28:67
"Let me **f** the pillars on which the Jgs 16:26
And you will **f** secure, because there is Jb 11:18
than your pots can **f** the heat of thorns, Ps 58:9
They have hands, but do not **f**; feet, but Ps 115:7
hurt; they beat me, but I did not **f** it. Prv 23:35
distress on them, that they may **f** it." Jer 10:18
and to those who **f** secure on the Am 6:1
that they might **f** their way toward Acts 17:27
I **f** a divine jealousy for you, for I 2 Cor 11:2
is right for me to **f** this way about you Phil 1:7
the joy that we **f** for your sake before 1 Thes 3:9
we **f** sure of better things—things that Heb 6:9

FEELS (2)
He **f** only the pain of his own body, and Jb 14:22
and a God who **f** indignation every day. Ps 7:11

FEES (1)
departed with the **f** for divination in Nm 22:7

FEET (243)
little water be brought, and wash your **f**, Gn 18:4
and spend the night and wash your **f**. Gn 19:2
was water to wash his **f** and the feet of Gn 24:32
wash his feet and the **f** of the men who Gn 24:32
water, and they had washed their **f**, Gn 43:24
nor the ruler's staff from between his **f**, Gn 49:10
he drew up his **f** into the bed and Gn 49:33
take your sandals off your **f**, for the place Ex 3:5
and touched Moses' **f** with it and Ex 4:25
belt fastened, your sandals on your **f**, Ex 12:11
There was under his **f** as it were a Ex 24:10
of gold for it and put them on its four **f**, Ex 25:12
and on the great toes of their right **f**, Ex 29:20
sons shall wash their hands and their **f**. Ex 30:19
shall wash their hands and their **f**, Ex 30:21
cast for it four rings of gold for its four **f**, Ex 37:3
his sons washed their hands and their **f**. Ex 40:31
hands and on the big toes of their right **f**. Lv 8:24
that have jointed legs above their **f**, Lv 11:21
insects that have four **f** are detestable to Lv 11:23
on all fours, or whatever has many **f**, Lv 11:42
from between her **f** and her children Dt 28:57
your sandals have not worn off your **f**. Dt 29:5
the soles of the **f** of the priests bearing Jos 3:13
and the **f** of the priests bearing the ark Jos 3:15
place where the priests' **f** stood firmly, Jos 4:3
the place where the **f** of the priests bearing Jos 4:9
the soles of the priests' **f** were lifted up on Jos 4:18
"Take off your sandals from your **f**, Jos 5:15
with worn-out, patched sandals on their **f**, Jos 9:5
put your **f** on the necks of these kings." Jos 10:24
near and put their **f** on their necks. Jos 10:24
Between her **f** he sank, he fell, he lay still; Jgs 5:27
he fell, he lay still; between her **f** he sank, Jgs 5:27
And they washed their **f**, and ate and Jgs 19:21
Then go and uncover his **f** and lie down, Ru 3:4
softly and uncovered his **f** and lay down. Ru 3:7
over, and behold, a woman lay at his **f**! Ru 3:8
So she lay at his **f** until the morning, but Ru 3:14
"He will guard the **f** of his faithful ones, 1 Sm 2:9
climbed up on his hands and **f**, 1 Sm 14:13
She fell at his **f** and said, "On me 1 Sm 25:24
servant to wash the **f** of the servants 1 Sm 25:41
not bound; your **f** were not fettered; 2 Sm 3:34
had a son who was crippled in his **f**. 2 Sm 4:4
their hands and **f** and hanged them 2 Sm 4:12
son of Jonathan; he is crippled in his **f**." 2 Sm 9:3
table. Now he was lame in both his **f**. 2 Sm 9:13
and wash your **f**." And Uriah went 2 Sm 11:8
taken care of his **f** nor trimmed his 2 Sm 19:24
thick darkness was under his **f**. 2 Sm 22:10
He made my **f** like the feet of a deer 2 Sm 22:34
made my feet like the **f** of a deer and 2 Sm 22:34
steps under me, and my **f** did not slip; 2 Sm 22:37
they did not rise; they fell under my **f**. 2 Sm 22:39
his waist and on the sandals on his **f**. 1 Kgs 2:5
LORD put them under the soles of his **f**. 1 Kgs 5:3
Ahijah heard the sound of her **f**, 1 Kgs 14:6
When your **f** enter the city, the child 1 Kgs 14:12
his old age he was diseased in his **f**. 1 Kgs 15:23
man of God, she caught hold of his **f**. 2 Kgs 4:27
She came and fell at his **f**, bowing to 2 Kgs 4:37
sound of his master's **f** behind him?" 2 Kgs 6:32
the skull and the **f** and the palms of 2 Kgs 9:35
Elisha, he revived and stood on his **f**. 2 Kgs 13:21
will not cause the **f** of Israel to wander 2 Kgs 21:8
King David rose to his **f** and said: 1 Chr 28:2
The cherubim stood on their **f**, 2 Chr 3:13
his reign Asa was diseased in his **f**, 2 Chr 16:12
not wear out and their **f** did not swell. Neh 9:21
She fell at his **f** and wept and pleaded with Est 8:3
it is ready for those whose **f** slip. Jb 12:5
You put my **f** in the stocks and watch Jb 13:27
you set a limit for the soles of my **f**. Jb 13:27
For he is cast into a net by his own **f**, and Jb 18:8
I was eyes to the blind and **f** to the lame. Jb 29:15
the rabble rise; they push away my **f**; Jb 30:12
he puts my **f** in the stocks and watches Jb 33:11
hands; you have put all things under his **f**, Ps 8:6
fast to your paths; my **f** have not slipped. Ps 17:5
down; thick darkness was under his **f**. Ps 18:9
He made my **f** like the feet of a deer and Ps 18:33
made my feet like the **f** of a deer and set Ps 18:33
steps under me, and my **f** did not slip. Ps 18:36
not able to rise; they fell under my **f**. Ps 18:38
me; they have pierced my hands and **f**— Ps 22:16
for he will pluck my **f** out of the net. Ps 25:15
you have set my **f** in a broad place. Ps 31:8
the miry bog, and set my **f** upon a rock, Ps 40:2
under us, and nations under our **f**. Ps 47:3
soul from death, yes, my **f** from falling, Ps 56:13
he will bathe his **f** in the blood of the Ps 58:10
the living and has not let our **f** slip. Ps 66:9
you may strike your **f** in their blood, Ps 68:23
as for me, my **f** had almost stumbled, Ps 73:2
His **f** were hurt with fetters; his neck Ps 105:18
but do not feel; **f**, but do not walk; Ps 115:7
eyes from tears, my **f** from stumbling; Ps 116:8
ways, I turn my **f** to your testimonies; Ps 119:59
I hold back my **f** from every evil way, Ps 119:101
is a lamp to my **f** and a light to my Ps 119:105
Our **f** have been standing within your Ps 122:2
men, who have planned to trip up my **f**. Ps 140:4
for their **f** run to evil, and they make Prv 1:16
Ponder the path of your **f**; then all your Prv 4:26
Her **f** go down to death; her steps follow Prv 5:5
winks with his eyes, signals with his **f**, Prv 6:13
plans, **f** that make haste to run to evil, Prv 6:18
on hot coals and his **f** not be scorched? Prv 6:28
and wayward; her **f** do not stay at home; Prv 7:11
makes haste with his **f** misses his way. Prv 19:2
cuts off his own **f** and drinks violence. Prv 26:6
his neighbor spreads a net for his **f**. Prv 29:5
I had bathed my **f**; how could I soil them? Sg 5:3
How beautiful are your **f** in sandals, O Sg 7:1
along as they go, tinkling with their **f**, Is 3:16
his face, and with two he covered his **f**, Is 6:2
of Assyria—the head and the hair of the **f**, Is 7:20
your sandals from your **f**," and he did so, Is 20:2
old, whose **f** carried her to settle far away? Is 23:7
The foot tramples it, the **f** of the poor, the Is 26:6
who let the **f** of the ox and the donkey Is 32:20
on safely, by paths his **f** have not trod. Is 41:3
down to you, and lick the dust of your **f**. Is 49:23
the mountains are the **f** of him who Is 52:7
Their **f** run to evil, and they are swift to Is 59:7
I will make the place of my **f** glorious. Is 60:13
despised you shall bow down at your **f**; Is 60:14
Keep your **f** from going unshod and Jer 2:25
before your **f** stumble on the twilight Jer 13:16
thus; they have not restrained their **f**; Jer 14:10
pit to take me and laid snares for my **f**. Jer 18:22
now that your **f** are sunk in the mud, Jer 38:22
it descend; he spread a net for my **f**; Lam 1:13
and the soles of their **f** were like the sole Ezk 1:7
said to me, "Son of man, stand on your **f**, Ezk 2:1
entered into me and set me on my **f**, Ezk 2:2
entered into me and set me on my **f**, Ezk 3:24
turban, and put your shoes on your **f**; Ezk 24:17
your heads and your shoes on your **f**; Ezk 24:23
and stamped your **f** and rejoiced with Ezk 25:6
rivers, trouble the waters with your **f**, Ezk 32:2
tread down with your **f** the rest of your Ezk 34:18
the rest of the water with your **f**? Ezk 34:18
eat what you have trodden with your **f**, Ezk 34:19
what you have muddied with your **f**? Ezk 34:19
and they lived and stood on their **f**, Ezk 37:10
and the place of the soles of my **f**, Ezk 43:7
its **f** partly of iron and partly of clay. Dn 2:33
the image on its **f** of iron and clay, Dn 2:34
And as you saw the **f** and toes, partly of Dn 2:41
as the toes of the **f** were partly iron and Dn 2:42
and made to stand on two **f** like a man, Dn 7:4
and stamped what was left with its **f**. Dn 7:7
and stamped what was left with its **f**, Dn 7:19
storm, and the clouds are the dust of his **f**. Na 1:3
the **f** of him who brings good news, Na 1:15
strength; he makes my **f** like the deer's; Hab 3:19
On that day his **f** shall stand on the Zec 14:4
while they are still standing on their **f**, Zec 14:12
will be ashes under the soles of your **f**, Mal 4:3
out and trampled under people's **f**. Mt 5:13
the dust from your **f** when you leave Mt 10:14
others, and they put them at his **f**, Mt 15:30
two hands or two **f** to be thrown into Mt 18:8
until I put your enemies under your **f**? Mt 22:44
took hold of his **f** and worshiped him. Mt 28:9
by name, and seeing him, he fell at his **f** Mk 5:22
that is on your **f** as a testimony against Mk 6:11
of him and came and fell down at his **f**. Mk 7:25
lame than with two **f** to be thrown into Mk 9:45
until I put your enemies under your **f**.' Mk 12:36
to guide our **f** into the way of peace." Lk 1:79
and standing behind him at his **f**, Lk 7:38
she began to wet his **f** with her tears and Lk 7:38
head and kissed his **f** and anointed them Lk 7:38
you gave me no water for my **f**, but she Lk 7:44
but she has wet my **f** with her tears and Lk 7:44
came in she has not ceased to kiss my **f**. Lk 7:45
she has anointed my **f** with ointment. Lk 7:46
had gone, sitting at the **f** of Jesus, Lk 8:35
And falling at Jesus' **f**, he implored him Lk 8:41
the dust from your **f** as a testimony Lk 9:5
that clings to our **f** we wipe off against Lk 10:11
sat at the Lord's **f** and listened to his Lk 10:39
a ring on his hand, and shoes on his **f**. Lk 15:22
and he fell on his face at Jesus' **f**, giving Lk 17:16
See my hands and my **f**, that it is I Lk 24:39
he showed them his hands and his **f**. Lk 24:40
ointment and wiped his **f** with her hair, Jn 11:2
Jesus was and saw him, she fell at his **f**, Jn 11:32
his hands and **f** bound with linen strips, Jn 11:44
and anointed the **f** of Jesus and wiped his Jn 12:3
feet of Jesus and wiped his **f** with her hair. Jn 12:3
to wash the disciples' **f** and to wipe them Jn 13:5
said to him, "Lord, do you wash my **f**?" Jn 13:6
never wash my **f**." Jesus answered him, Jn 13:8
not my **f** only but also my hands and my Jn 13:9
does not need to wash, except for his **f**, Jn 13:10
he had washed their **f** and put on his Jn 13:12
Lord and Teacher, have washed your **f**, Jn 13:14
you also ought to wash one another's **f**. Jn 13:14
lain, one at the head and one at the **f**. Jn 20:12
and immediately his **f** and ankles were Acts 3:7
and laid it at the apostles' **f**, and it was Acts 4:35
the money and laid it at the apostles' **f**. Acts 4:37
a part of it and laid it at the apostles' **f**. Acts 5:2
the **f** of those who have buried your Acts 5:9
fell down at his **f** and breathed her last. Acts 5:10
him, 'Take off the sandals from your **f**, Acts 7:33
their garments at the **f** of a young man Acts 7:58
fell down at his **f** and worshiped him. Acts 10:25
the sandals of whose **f** I am not Acts 13:25
dust from their **f** against them and Acts 13:51
a man sitting who could not use his **f**. Acts 14:8
upright on your **f**." And he sprang Acts 14:10
and fastened their **f** in the stocks. Acts 16:24
and bound his own **f** and hands and Acts 21:11

educated at the **f** of Gamaliel Acts 22:3
But rise and stand upon your **f**, for I Acts 26:16
"Their **f** are swift to shed blood; Rom 3:15
"How beautiful are the **f** of those who Rom 10:15
will soon crush Satan under your **f**. Rom 16:20
of you," nor again the head to the **f**, 1 Cor 12:21
has put all his enemies under his **f**. 1 Cor 15:25
subjection under his **f**." But when it 1 Cor 15:27
all things under his **f** and gave him as Eph 1:22
and, as shoes for your **f**, having put on Eph 6:15
has washed the **f** of the saints, 1 Tm 5:10
your enemies a footstool for your **f**"? Heb 1:13
subjection under his **f**." Now in putting Heb 2:8
should be made a footstool for his **f**. Heb 10:13
and make straight paths for your **f**, so Heb 12:13
stand over there," or, "Sit down at my **f**," Jas 2:3
his **f** were like burnished bronze, refined Rv 1:15
I saw him, I fell at his **f** as though dead. Rv 1:17
and whose **f** are like burnished bronze. Rv 2:18
bow down before your **f** and they will Rv 3:9
them, and they stood up on their **f**, Rv 11:11
with the sun, with the moon under her **f**, Rv 12:1
its **f** were like a bear's, and its mouth was Rv 13:2
I fell down at his **f** to worship him, Rv 19:10
down to worship at the **f** of the angel who Rv 22:8

FELIX (9)

bring him safely to **F** the governor." Acts 23:24
to his Excellency the governor **F**, Acts 23:26
by your foresight, most excellent **F**, Acts 24:2
But **F**, having a rather accurate Acts 24:22
After some days **F** came with his wife Acts 24:24
judgment, **F** was alarmed and said, Acts 24:25
F was succeeded by Porcius Festus. Acts 24:27
the Jews a favor, **F** left Paul in prison. Acts 24:27
"There is a man left prisoner by **F**, Acts 25:14

FELL (215)

So Cain was very angry, and his face **f**. Gn 4:5
And rain **f** upon the earth forty days and Gn 7:12
and Gomorrah fled, some **f** into them, Gn 14:10
going down, a deep sleep **f** on Abram. Gn 15:12
and great darkness **f** upon him. Gn 15:12
Then Abram **f** on his face. And God Gn 17:3
Then Abraham **f** on his face and Gn 17:17
and embraced him and **f** on his neck Gn 33:4
a terror from God **f** upon the cities that Gn 35:5
And he **f** asleep and dreamed a second Gn 41:5
there. They **f** before him to the ground. Gn 44:14
Then he **f** upon his brother Gn 45:14
himself to him and **f** on his neck and Gn 46:29
Then Joseph **f** on his father's face and Gn 50:1
also came and **f** down before him Gn 50:18
three thousand men of the people **f**. Ex 32:28
saw it, they shouted and **f** on their faces. Lv 9:24
goat on which the lot **f** for the LORD and Lv 16:9
on which the lot **f** for Azazel shall be Lv 16:10
When the dew **f** upon the camp in the Nm 11:9
camp in the night, the manna **f** with it. Nm 11:9
Then Moses and Aaron **f** on their faces Nm 14:5
When Moses heard it, he **f** on his face, Nm 16:4
And they **f** on their faces and said, "O Nm 16:22
a moment." And they **f** on their faces. Nm 16:45
the tent of meeting and **f** on their faces. Nm 20:6
And he bowed down and **f** on his face. Nm 22:31
have come." And Joshua **f** on his face to Jos 5:14
a great shout, and the wall **f** down flat, Jos 6:20
tore his clothes and **f** to the earth on Jos 7:6
And all who **f** that day, both men and Jos 8:25
the waters of Merom and **f** upon them. Jos 11:7
Thus there **f** to Manasseh ten portions, Jos 17:5
allotted to it **f** between the people Jos 18:11
of Levi; since the lot **f** to them first. Jos 21:10
and wrath **f** upon all the congregation Jos 22:20
all the army of Sisera **f** by the edge of the Jgs 4:16
Between her feet he sank, he **f**, he lay Jgs 5:27
lay still; between her feet he sank, he **f**; Jgs 5:27
he fell; where he sank, there he **f**—dead. Jgs 5:27
struck it so that it **f** and turned it upside Jgs 7:13
And many **f** wounded, up to the Jgs 9:40
At that time 42,000 of the Ephraimites **f**. Jgs 12:6
and they **f** on their faces to the ground. Jgs 13:20
and the house **f** upon the lords and Jgs 16:30
the woman came and **f** down at the Jgs 19:26
Eighteen thousand men of Benjamin **f**, Jgs 20:44
So all who **f** that day of Benjamin were Jgs 20:46
Then she **f** on her face, bowing to the Ru 2:10
for there **f** of Israel thirty thousand 1 Sm 4:10
Eli **f** over backward from his seat by 1 Sm 4:18
dread of the LORD **f** upon the people, 1 Sm 11:7
him. And they **f** before Jonathan, 1 Sm 14:13
and he **f** on his face to the ground. 1 Sm 17:49
the wounded Philistines **f** on the way 1 Sm 17:52
the stone heap and **f** on his face to 1 Sm 20:41
the donkey and **f** before David on 1 Sm 25:23
She **f** at his feet and said, "On me 1 Sm 25:24
Then Saul **f** at once full length on 1 Sm 28:20
behind because I **f** sick three days 1 Sm 30:13
the Philistines and **f** slain on Mount 1 Sm 31:1
took his own sword and **f** upon it. 1 Sm 31:4
he also **f** upon his sword and died with 1 Sm 31:5
he **f** to the ground and paid homage. 2 Sm 1:2
side, so they **f** down together. 2 Sm 2:16
And he **f** there and died where he was. 2 Sm 2:23
fled in her haste, he **f** and became lame. 2 Sm 4:4
came to David and **f** on his face and 2 Sm 9:6
of David among the people **f**. 2 Sm 11:17
she **f** on her face to the ground and 2 Sm 14:4
And Joab **f** on his face to the ground 2 Sm 14:22
the son of Gera **f** down before the 2 Sm 19:18
thigh, and as he went forward it **f** out. 2 Sm 20:8
harvest until rain **f** upon them from 2 Sm 21:10
and they **f** by the hand of David and 2 Sm 21:22
did not rise; they **f** under my feet. 2 Sm 22:39
Abijah the son of Jeroboam **f** sick. 1 Kgs 14:1
recognized him and **f** on his face 1 Kgs 18:7
fire of the LORD **f** and consumed the 1 Kgs 18:38
saw it, they **f** on their faces and said, 1 Kgs 18:39
and the wall **f** upon 27,000 men who 1 Kgs 20:30
Now Ahaziah **f** through the lattice in 2 Kgs 1:2
up and came and **f** on his knees 2 Kgs 1:13
and shall **f** every good tree and stop 2 Kgs 3:19
She came and **f** at his feet, bowing to 2 Kgs 4:37
a log, his axe head **f** into the water, 2 Kgs 6:5
the Hagrites, who **f** into their hand. 1 Chr 5:10
For many **f**, because the war was of 1 Chr 5:22
the Philistines and **f** slain on Mount 1 Chr 10:1
took his own sword and **f** upon it. 1 Chr 10:4
he also **f** upon his sword and died. 1 Chr 10:5
and they **f** by the hand of David and 1 Chr 20:8
on Israel, and 70,000 men of Israel **f**. 1 Chr 21:14
in sackcloth, **f** upon their faces. 1 Chr 21:16
The first lot **f** to Jehoiarib, the second 1 Chr 24:7
The first lot **f** for Asaph to Joseph; the 1 Chr 25:9
The lot for the east **f** to Shelemiah. 1 Chr 26:14
so there **f** slain of Israel 500,000 2 Chr 13:17
and the Ethiopians **f** until none 2 Chr 14:13
fear of the LORD **f** upon all the 2 Chr 17:10
of Jerusalem **f** down before 2 Chr 20:18
and **f** upon my knees and spread out my Ezr 9:5
us were afraid and **f** greatly in their Neh 6:16
She **f** at his feet and wept and pleaded with Est 8:3
and the Sabeans **f** upon them and took Jb 1:15
"The fire of God **f** from heaven and Jb 1:16
the house, and it **f** upon the young people, Jb 1:19
shaved his head and **f** on the ground and Jb 1:20
not able to rise; they **f** under my feet. Ps 18:38
Their priests **f** by the sword, and their Ps 78:64
down with hard labor; they **f** down, Ps 107:12
He made many stumble, and they **f**, Jer 46:16
her with axes like those who **f** trees. Jer 46:22
report of them, and his hands **f** helpless; Jer 50:43
When her people **f** into the hand of the Lam 1:7
And when I saw it, I **f** on my face, and I Ezk 1:28
the Chebar canal, and I **f** on my face. Ezk 3:23
hand of the Lord GOD **f** upon me there. Ezk 8:1
and I was left alone, I **f** upon my face, Ezk 9:8
And the Spirit of the LORD **f** upon me, Ezk 11:5
Then I **f** down on my face and cried Ezk 11:13
and they all **f** by the sword. Ezk 39:23
the Chebar canal. And I **f** on my face. Ezk 43:3
temple of the LORD. And I **f** on my face. Ezk 44:4
Then King Nebuchadnezzar **f** upon his Dn 2:46
and languages **f** down and worshiped the Dn 3:7
f bound into the burning fiery furnace. Dn 3:23
mouth, there **f** a voice from heaven, Dn 4:31
up and before which three of them **f**, Dn 7:20
came, I was frightened and **f** on my face. Dn 8:17
I **f** into a deep sleep with my face to the Dn 8:18
but a great trembling **f** upon them, Dn 10:7
I **f** on my face in deep sleep with my face Dn 10:9
So they cast lots, and the lot **f** on Jonah. Jon 1:7
and they **f** down and worshiped him. Mt 2:11
And the rain **f**, and the floods came, and Mt 7:25
And the rain **f**, and the floods came, and Mt 7:27
and beat against that house, and it **f**, Mt 7:27
as he sowed, some seeds **f** along the path, Mt 13:4
Other seeds **f** on rocky ground, where Mt 13:5
Other seeds **f** among thorns, and the Mt 13:7
Other seeds **f** on good soil and produced Mt 13:8
they **f** on their faces and were terrified. Mt 17:6
So the servant **f** on his knees, Mt 18:26
his fellow servant **f** down and pleaded Mt 18:29
a little farther he **f** on his face and Mt 26:39
they **f** down before him and cried out, Mk 3:11
as he sowed, some seed **f** along the path, Mk 4:4
Other seed **f** on rocky ground, where it Mk 4:5
Other seed **f** among thorns, and the Mk 4:7
And other seeds **f** into good soil and Mk 4:8
from afar, he ran and **f** down before him. Mk 5:6
by name, and seeing him, he **f** at his feet Mk 5:22
and trembling and **f** down before him Mk 5:33
of him and came and **f** down at his feet. Mk 7:25
and he **f** on the ground and rolled Mk 9:20
he **f** on the ground and prayed that, Mk 14:35
when he saw him, and fear **f** upon him. Lk 1:12
Peter saw it, he **f** down at Jesus' knees, Lk 5:8
Jesus, he **f** on his face and begged him, Lk 5:12
broke against it, immediately it **f**, Lk 6:49
some **f** along the path and was trampled Lk 8:5
And some **f** on the rock, and as it grew up, Lk 8:6
And some **f** among thorns, and the Lk 8:7
And some **f** into good soil and grew and Lk 8:8
And as for what **f** among the thorns, Lk 8:14
and as they sailed he **f** asleep. And a Lk 8:23
he cried out and **f** down before him and Lk 8:28
to Jericho, and he **f** among robbers, Lk 10:30
to the man who **f** among the robbers?" Lk 10:36
the tower in Siloam **f** and killed them: Lk 13:4
be fed with what **f** from the rich man's Lk 16:21
and he **f** on his face at Jesus' feet, giving Lk 17:16
Jesus was and saw him, she **f** at his feet, Jn 11:32
he," they drew back and **f** to the ground. Jn 18:6
lots for them, and the lot **f** on Matthias, Acts 1:26
words, he **f** down and breathed his last. Acts 5:5
Immediately she **f** down at his feet and Acts 5:10
And when he had said this, he **f** asleep. Acts 7:60
something like scales **f** from his eyes, Acts 9:18
were preparing it, he **f** into a trance Acts 10:10
Cornelius met him and **f** down at his Acts 10:25
the Holy Spirit **f** on all who heard the Acts 10:44
the Holy Spirit **f** on them just as on us Acts 11:15
they heard these things they **f** silent. Acts 11:18
And the chains **f** off his hands. Acts 12:7
mist and darkness **f** upon him, Acts 13:11
f asleep and was laid with his fathers Acts 13:36
And all the assembly **f** silent, and Acts 15:12
with fear he **f** down before Paul Acts 16:29
And fear **f** upon them all, and the Acts 19:17
the sacred stone that **f** from the sky? Acts 19:35
he **f** down from the third story and was Acts 20:9
And I **f** to the ground and heard a voice Acts 22:7
praying in the temple, I **f** into a trance Acts 22:17
of those who reproached you **f** on me." Rom 15:3
and twenty-three thousand **f** in a 1 Cor 10:8
whose bodies **f** in the wilderness? Heb 3:17
the walls of Jericho **f** down after they Heb 11:30
For ever since the fathers **f** asleep, all 2 Pt 3:4
I saw him, I **f** at his feet as though dead. Rv 1:17
the twenty-four elders **f** down before the Rv 5:8
and the elders **f** down and worshiped. Rv 5:14
the stars of the sky **f** to the earth as the Rv 6:13
and they **f** on their faces before the Rv 7:11
trumpet, and a great star **f** from heaven, Rv 8:10
and it **f** on a third of the rivers and on the Rv 8:10
and great fear **f** on those who saw them. Rv 11:11
earthquake, and a tenth of the city **f**. Rv 11:13
their thrones before God **f** on their faces Rv 11:16
parts, and the cities of the nations **f**, Rv 16:19
pounds each, **f** from heaven on people; Rv 16:21
four living creatures **f** down and Rv 19:4
Then I **f** down at his feet to worship Rv 19:10
I **f** down to worship at the feet of the Rv 22:8

FELLED (4)

spring of water and **f** all the good 2 Kgs 3:25
I **f** its tallest cedars, its choicest 2 Kgs 19:23
remains when it is **f**." The holy seed is Is 6:13
Bashan, for the thick forest has been **f**! Zec 11:2

FELLING (1)

But as one was **f** a log, his axe head fell 2 Kgs 6:5

FELLOW (55)

From his **f** man I will require a Gn 9:5
And they said, "This **f** came to sojourn, Gn 19:9
like all his **f** Levites who stand to Dt 18:7
for all my **f** townsmen know that you Ru 3:11
Philistine's sword was against his **f**, 1 Sm 14:20
you have brought this **f** to behave as 1 Sm 21:15
Shall this **f** come into my house?" 1 Sm 21:15
guarded all that this **f** has in the 1 Sm 25:21
not my lord regard this worthless **f**, 1 Sm 25:25
how could this **f** reconcile himself to 1 Sm 29:4
said to his **f** at the command 1 Kgs 20:35
"Put this **f** in prison and feed him 1 Kgs 22:27
Why did this mad **f** come to you?" 2 Kgs 9:11
them, "You know the **f** and his talk." 2 Kgs 9:11
Put this **f** in prison and feed him 2 Chr 18:26
the son of Jozadak, with his **f** priests, Ezr 3:2
all the returned exiles, for their **f** priests, Ezr 6:20
For if they fall, one will lift up his **f**. Eccl 4:10
every one his **f** and every one his neighbor; Is 3:5
hyenas; the wild goat shall cry to his **f**; Is 34:14
must set free the **f** Hebrew who has Jer 34:14
found one of his **f** servants who owed Mt 18:28
So his **f** servant fell down and pleaded Mt 18:29
When his **f** servants saw what had Mt 18:31

his hands on a **f** sick people and healed Mk 6:5
And they had a **f** small fish. And having Mk 8:7
is plentiful, but the laborers are **f**. Lk 10:2
who are saved be **f**?" And he said to Lk 13:23
and they stayed there for a **f** days. Jn 2:12
Greeks and not a **f** of the leading Acts 17:4
with not a **f** Greek women of high Acts 17:12
ark was being prepared, in which a **f**, 1 Pt 3:20
But I have a **f** things against you: you Rv 2:14
Yet you have still a **f** names in Sardis, Rv 3:4

FEWEST (1)
chose you, for you were the **f** of all peoples, Dt 7:7

FICKLE (1)
Her prophets are **f**, treacherous men; her Zep 3:4

FIELD (263)
When no bush of the **f** was yet in the Gn 2:5
no small plant of the **f** had yet sprung up Gn 2:5
every beast of the **f** and every bird of Gn 2:19
of the heavens and to every beast of the **f**. Gn 2:20
any other beast of the **f** that the LORD God Gn 3:1
livestock and above all beasts of the **f**; Gn 3:14
you; and you shall eat the plants of the **f**. Gn 3:18
And when they were in the **f**, Cain rose up Gn 4:8
which he owns; it is at the end of his **f**. Gn 23:9
I give you the **f**, and I give you the cave Gn 23:11
will, hear me: I give the price of the **f**. Gn 23:13
So the **f** of Ephron in Machpelah, Gn 23:17
the **f** with the cave that was in it and all Gn 23:17
in it and all the trees that were in the **f**, Gn 23:17
the cave of the **f** of Machpelah east of Gn 23:19
The **f** and the cave that is in it were Gn 23:20
out to meditate in the **f** toward evening. Gn 24:63
walking in the **f** to meet us?" The Gn 24:65
in the **f** of Ephron the son of Zohar the Gn 25:9
the **f** that Abraham purchased from Gn 25:10
was a skillful hunter, a man of the **f**, Gn 25:27
cooking stew, Esau came in from the **f**, Gn 25:29
and go out to the **f** and hunt game for Gn 27:3
Esau went to the **f** to hunt for game Gn 27:5
as the smell of a **f** that the LORD has Gn 27:27
As he looked, he saw a well in the **f**, and Gn 29:2
mandrakes in the **f** and brought them Gn 30:14
Jacob came from the **f** in the evening, Gn 30:16
and Leah into the **f** where his flock was Gn 31:4
his sons were with his livestock in the **f**, Gn 34:5
had come in from the **f** as soon as they Gn 34:7
whatever was in the city and in the **f**. Gn 34:28
we were binding sheaves in the **f**, Gn 37:7
was on all that he had, in house and **f**. Gn 39:5
as seed for the **f** and as food for Gn 47:24
that is in the **f** of Ephron the Hittite, Gn 49:29
the cave that is in the **f** at Machpelah, Gn 49:30
bought with the **f** from Ephron the Gn 49:30
the **f** and the cave that is in it were Gn 49:32
him in the cave of the **f** at Machpelah, Gn 50:13
bought with the **f** from Ephron the Gn 50:13
brick, and in all kinds of work in the **f**. Ex 1:14
upon your livestock that are in the **f**, Ex 9:3
that you have in the **f** into safe shelter, Ex 9:19
beast that is in the **f** and is not brought Ex 9:19
left his slaves and his livestock in the **f**. Ex 9:21
man and beast and every plant of the **f**, Ex 9:22
that was in the **f** in all the land Ex 9:25
every plant of the **f** and broke every tree Ex 9:25
of the field and broke every tree of the **f**. Ex 9:25
eat every tree of yours that grows in the **f**, Ex 10:5
remained, neither tree nor plant of the **f**, Ex 10:15
LORD; today you will not find it in the **f**. Ex 16:25
"If a man causes a **f** or vineyard to be Ex 22:5
loose and it feeds in another man's **f**, Ex 22:5
the best in his own **f** and in his own Ex 22:5
the standing grain or the **f** is consumed, Ex 22:6
any flesh that is torn by beasts in the **f**; Ex 22:31
they leave the beasts of the **f** may eat. Ex 23:11
of your labor, of what you sow in the **f**. Ex 23:16
gather in from the **f** the fruit of your Ex 23:16
let the living bird go into the open **f**. Lv 14:7
that they sacrifice in the open **f**, Lv 17:5
you shall not reap your **f** right up to its Lv 19:9
shall not sow your **f** with two kinds of Lv 19:19
you shall not reap your **f** right up to its Lv 23:22
For six years you shall sow your **f**, and Lv 25:3
shall not sow your **f** or prune your Lv 25:4
you. You may eat the produce of the **f**. Lv 25:12
the trees of the **f** shall yield their fruit. Lv 26:4
If he dedicates his **f** from the year of Lv 27:17
but if he dedicates his **f** after the jubilee, Lv 27:18
he who dedicates the **f** wishes to redeem Lv 27:19
But if he does not wish to redeem the **f**, Lv 27:20
or if he has sold the **f** to another man, Lv 27:20
But the **f**, when it is released in the Lv 27:21
the LORD, like a **f** that has been devoted. Lv 27:21
to the LORD a **f** that he has bought, Lv 27:22
year of jubilee the **f** shall return to him Lv 27:24
man or beast, or of his inherited **f**, Lv 27:28
in the open **f** touches someone who Nm 19:16
will not pass through **f** or vineyard, Nm 20:17
will not turn aside into **f** or vineyard. Nm 21:22
up the grass of the **f**." So Balak the son Nm 22:4
out of the road and went into the **f**. Nm 22:23
And he took him to the **f** of Zophim, Nm 23:14
not desire your neighbor's house, his **f**, Dt 5:21
seed that comes from the **f** year by year. Dt 14:22
Are the trees in the **f** human, that they Dt 20:19
your harvest in your **f** and forget a Dt 24:19
in your field and forget a sheaf in the **f**, Dt 24:19
the city, and blessed shall you be in the **f**. Dt 28:3
city, and cursed shall you be in the **f**. Dt 28:16
much seed into the **f** and shall gather in Dt 28:38
the land, and he ate the produce of the **f**, Dt 32:13
she urged him to ask her father for a **f**. Jos 15:18
she urged him to ask her father for a **f**. Jgs 1:14
Naphtali, too, on the heights of the **f**. Jgs 5:18
went out into the **f** and gathered the Jgs 9:27
with you, and set an ambush in the **f**. Jgs 9:32
day, the people went out into the **f**, Jgs 9:42
all who were in the **f** and killed them. Jgs 9:44
again to the woman as she sat in the **f**. Jgs 13:9
from his work in the **f** at evening. Jgs 19:16
"Let me go to the **f** and glean among the Ru 2:2
went and gleaned in the **f** after the reapers, Ru 2:3
to the part of the **f** belonging to Boaz, Ru 2:3
go to glean in another **f** or leave this one, Ru 2:8
eyes be on the **f** that they are reaping, Ru 2:9
So she gleaned in the **f** until evening. Ru 2:17
lest in another **f** you be assaulted." Ru 2:22
"The day you buy the **f** from the hand of Ru 4:5
four thousand men on the **f** of battle. 1 Sm 4:2
cart came into the **f** of Joshua of 1 Sm 6:14
this day in the **f** of Joshua of 1 Sm 6:18
coming from the **f** behind the oxen. 1 Sm 11:5
was a panic in the camp, in the **f**, 1 Sm 14:15
of the air and to the beasts of the **f**." 1 Sm 17:44
my father in the **f** where you are, 1 Sm 19:3
hide myself in the **f** till the third day 1 Sm 20:5
go out into the **f**." So they both went 1 Sm 20:11
So they both went out into the **f**. 1 Sm 20:11
So David hid himself in the **f**. And 1 Sm 20:24
out into the **f** to the appointment 1 Sm 20:35
of my lord are camping in the open **f**. 2 Sm 11:11
us and came out against us in the **f**, 2 Sm 11:23
quarreled with one another in the **f**. 2 Sm 14:6
"See, Joab's **f** is next to mine, 2 Sm 14:30
Absalom's servants set the **f** on fire. 2 Sm 14:30
have your servants set my **f** on fire?" 2 Sm 14:31
like a bear robbed of her cubs in the **f**. 2 Sm 17:8
went out into the **f** against Israel, 2 Sm 18:6
the highway into the **f** and threw a 2 Sm 20:12
day, or the beasts of the **f** by night. 2 Sm 21:10
his who dies in the **f** the birds of the 1 Kgs 16:4
went out into the **f** to gather herbs, 2 Kgs 4:39
on the face of the **f** in the territory of 2 Kgs 9:37
is on the highway to the Washer's **F**. 2 Kgs 18:17
like plants of the **f** and like tender 2 Kgs 19:26
let the **f** exult, and everything in it! 1 Chr 16:32
the work of the **f** for tilling the soil 1 Chr 27:26
in the burial **f** that belonged to 2 Chr 26:23
honey, and of all the produce of the **f**. 2 Chr 31:5
did the work, had fled each to his **f**. Neh 13:10
shall be in league with the stones of the **f**, Jb 5:23
and the beasts of the **f** shall be at peace Jb 5:23
They gather their fodder in the **f**, and Jb 24:6
and oxen, and also the beasts of the **f**, Ps 8:7
and all that moves in the **f** is mine. Ps 50:11
in the cities like the grass of the **f**! Ps 72:16
it, and all that move in the **f** feed on it. Ps 80:13
let the **f** exult, and everything in it! Ps 96:12
he flourishes like a flower of the **f**; Ps 103:15
they give drink to every beast of the **f**; Ps 104:11
everything ready for yourself in the **f**, Prv 24:27
I passed by the **f** of a sluggard, by the Prv 24:30
clothing, and the goats the price of a **f**. Prv 27:26
She considers a **f** and buys it; with the Prv 31:16
by the gazelles or the does of the **f**, Sg 2:7
by the gazelles or the does of the **f**, Sg 3:5
in a vineyard, like a lodge in a cucumber **f**, Is 1:8
who join house to house, who add **f** to field, Is 5:8
who join house to house, who add field to **f**, Is 5:8
pool on the highway to the Washer's **F**. Is 7:3
are taken away from the fruitful **f**, Is 16:10
shall be turned into a fruitful **f**, Is 29:17
and the fruitful **f** shall be regarded as a Is 29:17
and the wilderness becomes a fruitful **f**, Is 32:15
field, and the fruitful **f** is deemed a forest. Is 32:15
and righteousness abide in the fruitful **f**. Is 32:16
pool on the highway to the Washer's **F**. Is 36:2
like plants of the **f** and like tender grass, Is 37:27
all its beauty is like the flower of the **f**. Is 40:6
the trees of the **f** shall clap their hands. Is 55:12
All you beasts of the **f**, come to devour— Is 56:9
Like keepers of a **f** are they against her Jer 4:17
Go not out into the **f**, nor walk on the Jer 6:25
upon the trees of the **f** and the fruit of the Jer 7:20
men shall fall like dung upon the open **f**, Jer 9:22
are like scarecrows in a cucumber **f**, Jer 10:5
mourn and the grass of every **f** wither? Jer 12:4
lewd whorings, on the hills in the **f**. Jer 13:27
the doe in the **f** forsakes her newborn Jer 14:5
If I go out into the **f**, behold, those Jer 14:18
of hosts, "'Zion shall be plowed as a **f**; Jer 26:18
him also the beasts of the **f** to serve him. Jer 27:6
given to him even the beasts of the **f**.'" Jer 28:14
and say, 'Buy my **f** that is at Anathoth, Jer 32:7
'Buy my **f** that is at Anathoth in the land Jer 32:8
"And I bought the **f** at Anathoth from Jer 32:9
"Buy the **f** for money and get witnesses" Jer 32:25
in. We have no vineyard or **f** or seed, Jer 35:9
pierced by lack of the fruits of the **f**. Lam 4:9
He who is in the **f** dies by the sword, and Ezk 7:15
but you were cast out on the open **f**, Ezk 16:5
I made you flourish like a plant of the **f**. Ezk 16:7
all the trees of the **f** shall know that I Ezk 17:24
you shall fall on the open **f**, and not be Ezk 29:5
forth its streams to all the trees of the **f**. Ezk 31:4
towered high above all the trees of the **f**; Ezk 31:5
all the beasts of the **f** gave birth to their Ezk 31:6
its branches are all the beasts of the **f**. Ezk 31:13
the trees of the **f** fainted because of it. Ezk 31:15
on the open **f** I will fling you, and will Ezk 32:4
whoever is in the open **f** I will give to Ezk 33:27
the trees of the **f** shall yield their fruit, Ezk 34:27
and the increase of the **f** abundant, Ezk 36:30
the beasts of the **f** and all creeping Ezk 38:20
and to the beasts of the **f** to be devoured. Ezk 39:4
You shall fall in the open **f**, for I have Ezk 39:5
take wood out of the **f** or cut down any Ezk 39:10
of every sort and to all beasts of the **f**, Ezk 39:17
the children of man, the beasts of the **f**, Dn 2:38
The beasts of the **f** found shade under it, Dn 4:12
bronze, amid the tender grass of the **f**. Dn 4:15
under which beasts of the **f** found shade, Dn 4:21
and bronze, in the tender grass of the **f**, Dn 4:23
let his portion be with the beasts of the **f**, Dn 4:23
dwelling shall be with the beasts of the **f**. Dn 4:25
dwelling shall be with the beasts of the **f**. Dn 4:32
the beasts of the **f** shall devour them. Hos 2:12
on that day with the beasts of the **f**, Hos 2:18
also the beasts of the **f** and the birds of Hos 4:3
poisonous weeds in the furrows of the **f**. Hos 10:4
stone heaps on the furrows of the **f**. Hos 12:11
because the harvest of the **f** has perished. Jl 1:11
and apple, all the trees of the **f** are dried up, Jl 1:12
and flame has burned all the trees of the **f**. Jl 1:19
the beasts of the **f** pant for you because Jl 1:20
Fear not, you beasts of the **f**, for the Jl 2:22
one **f** would have rain, and the field on Am 4:7
and the **f** on which it did not rain would Am 4:7
of you Zion shall be plowed as a **f**; Mi 3:12
rain, to everyone the vegetation in the **f**. Zec 10:1
and your vine in the **f** shall not fail to Mal 3:11
Consider the lilies of the **f**, how they Mt 6:28
But if God so clothes the grass of the **f**, Mt 6:30
to a man who sowed good seed in his **f**, Mt 13:24
did you not sow good seed in your **f**? Mt 13:27
that a man took and sowed in his **f**. Mt 13:31
to us the parable of the weeds of the **f**." Mt 13:36
The **f** is the world, and the good seed is Mt 13:38
of heaven is like treasure hidden in a **f**, Mt 13:44
sells all that he has and buys that **f**. Mt 13:44
one who is in the **f** not turn back to Mt 24:18
Then two men will be in the **f**; one will Mt 24:40
with them the potter's **f** as a burial place Mt 27:7
Therefore that **f** has been called the Mt 27:8
has been called the **F** of Blood to this Mt 27:8
and they gave them for the potter's **f**, as Mt 27:10
one who is in the **f** not turn back to Mk 13:16
region there were shepherds out in the **f**, Lk 2:8
the grass, which is alive in the **f** today, Lk 12:28
The first said to him, 'I have bought a **f**, Lk 14:18
"Now his older son was in the **f**, and as Lk 15:25
to him when he has come in from the **f**, Lk 17:7
the one who is in the **f** not turn back. Lk 17:31
near the **f** that Jacob had given to his son Jn 4:5
this man bought a **f** with the reward of Acts 1:18
so that the **f** was called in their own Acts 1:19
Akeldama, that is, **F** of Blood.) Acts 1:19
sold a **f** that belonged to him and Acts 4:37
You are God's **f**, God's building. 1 Cor 3:9

FIELDS (56)
a man found him wandering in the **f**. Gn 37:15
every city the food from the **f** around it. Gn 41:48
for all the Egyptians sold their **f**, Gn 47:20
in the houses, the courtyards, and the **f**. Ex 8:13
shall be classified with the **f** of the land. Lv 25:31

But the **f** of pastureland belonging to Lv 25:34
us inheritance of **f** and vineyards. Nm 16:14
give grass in your **f** for your livestock, Dt 11:15
of Sodom and from the **f** of Gomorrah; Dt 32:32
But the **f** of the city and its villages had Jos 21:12
companies and set an ambush in the **f**. Jgs 9:43
she had heard in the **f** of Moab that the Ru 1:6
the best of your **f** and vineyards and 1 Sm 8:14
give every one of you **f** and vineyards, 1 Sm 22:7
miss anything when we were in the **f**, 1 Sm 25:15
or rain upon you, nor **f** of offerings! 2 Sm 1:21
the produce of the **f** from the day that 2 Kgs 8:6
Jerusalem in the **f** of the Kidron 2 Kgs 23:4
but the **f** of the city and its villages 1 Chr 6:56
who were in the **f** of common land 2 Chr 31:19
who said, "We are mortgaging our **f**, Neh 5:3
king's tax on our **f** and our vineyards. Neh 5:4
men have our **f** and our vineyards." Neh 5:5
Return to them this very day their **f**, Neh 5:11
And as for the villages, with their **f**, Neh 11:25
and their villages, Lachish and its **f**, Neh 11:30
according to the **f** of the towns, Neh 12:44
on the earth and sends waters on the **f**; Jb 5:10
in the land of Egypt, in the **f** of Zoan. Ps 78:12
Egypt and his marvels in the **f** of Zoan. Ps 78:43
they sow **f** and plant vineyards and get Ps 107:37
Ephrathah; we found it in the **f** of Jaar. Ps 132:6
thousands and ten thousands in our **f**; Ps 144:13
before he had made the earth with its **f**, Prv 8:26
or enter the **f** of the fatherless, Prv 23:10
way: a king committed to cultivated **f**. Eccl 5:9
us go out into the **f** and lodge in the Sg 7:11
For the **f** of Heshbon languish, and the Is 16:8
Beat your breasts for the pleasant **f**, for Is 32:12
over to others, their **f** and wives together, Jer 6:12
wives to others and their **f** to conquerors, Jer 8:10
and all the **f** as far as the brook Kidron, Jer 31:40
Houses and **f** and vineyards shall again Jer 32:15
F shall be bought in this land of which Jer 32:43
F shall be bought for money, and deeds Jer 32:44
gave them vineyards and **f** at the same Jer 39:10
honey hidden in the **f**." So he refrained Jer 41:8
moon shall devour them with their **f**. Hos 5:7
The **f** are destroyed, the ground mourns, Jl 1:10
They covet **f** and seize them, and houses, Mi 2:2
from me! To an apostate he allots our **f**." Mi 2:4
of the olive fail and the **f** yield no food, Hab 3:17
branches that they had cut from the **f**. Mk 11:8
who sent him into his **f** to feed pigs. Lk 15:15
and see that the **f** are white for harvest. Jn 4:35
wages of the laborers who mowed your **f**, Jas 5:4

FIERCE (39)
will say that a **f** animal has devoured Gn 37:20
robe. A **f** animal has devoured him. Gn 37:33
Cursed be their anger, for it is **f**, and Gn 49:7
that the **f** anger of the LORD may turn Nm 25:4
increase still more the **f** anger of the Nm 32:14
from the table in **f** anger and ate no 1 Sm 20:34
carry out his **f** wrath against 1 Sm 28:18
And the battle was very **f** that day. 2 Sm 2:17
and returned home in **f** anger. 2 Chr 25:10
for the **f** wrath of the LORD is upon 2 Chr 28:11
and there is **f** wrath against Israel." 2 Chr 28:13
in order that his **f** anger may turn 2 Chr 29:10
that his **f** anger may turn away from 2 Chr 30:8
until the **f** wrath of our God over this Ezr 10:14
roar of the lion, the voice of the **f** lion, Jb 4:10
No one is so **f** that he dares to stir him Jb 41:10
my life; **f** men stir up strife against me. Ps 59:3
strong as death, jealousy is **f** as the grave. Sg 8:6
at the **f** anger of Rezin and Syria and the Is 7:4
comes, cruel, with wrath and **f** anger, Is 13:9
LORD of hosts in the day of his **f** anger. Is 13:13
master, and a **f** king will rule over them, Is 19:4
removed them with his **f** breath in the Is 27:8
for the **f** anger of the LORD has not turned Jer 4:8
ruins before the LORD, before his **f** anger. Jer 4:26
harvests because of the **f** anger of the Jer 12:13
devastated because of the **f** anger of the Jer 25:37
oppressor, and because of his **f** anger." Jer 25:38
The **f** anger of the LORD will not turn Jer 30:24
bring disaster upon them, my **f** anger, Jer 49:37
his life from the **f** anger of the LORD! Jer 51:45
LORD inflicted on the day of his **f** anger. Lam 1:12
has cut down in **f** anger all the might Lam 2:3
and in his **f** indignation has spurned Lam 2:6
and relent and turn from his **f** anger, Jon 3:9
more **f** than the evening wolves; Hab 1:8
so **f** that no one could pass that way. Mt 8:28
after my departure **f** wolves will come Acts 20:29
They were scorched by the **f** heat, and Rv 16:9

FIERCELY (2)
with Midian?" And they accused him **f**. Jgs 8:1
The bellows blow **f**; the lead is Jer 6:29

FIERCENESS (2)
may turn from the **f** of his anger and Dt 13:17
With **f** and rage he swallows the Jb 39:24

FIERCER (1)
men of Judah were **f** than the words 2 Sm 19:43

FIERY (22)
the LORD sent **f** serpents among the Nm 21:6
"Make a **f** serpent and set it on a pole, Nm 21:8
with its **f** serpents and scorpions and Dt 8:15
with fever, inflammation and **f** heat, Dt 28:22
weapons, making his arrows **f** shafts. Ps 7:13
I lie down amid **f** beasts—the children of Ps 57:4
a cloud, and all the night with a **f** light. Ps 78:14
and **f** lightning bolts through their Ps 105:32
and its fruit will be a flying **f** serpent. Is 14:29
the lion, the adder and the flying **f** serpent, Is 30:6
be cast into a burning **f** furnace." Dn 3:6
shall be cast into a burning **f** furnace. Dn 3:11
be cast into a burning **f** furnace. Dn 3:15
deliver us from the burning **f** furnace, Dn 3:17
to cast them into the burning **f** furnace. Dn 3:20
were thrown into the burning **f** furnace. Dn 3:21
fell bound into the burning **f** furnace. Dn 3:23
to the door of the burning **f** furnace; Dn 3:26
like pure wool; his throne was **f** flames; Dn 7:9
and throw them into the **f** furnace. In Mt 13:42
and throw them into the **f** furnace. In Mt 13:50
be surprised at the **f** trial when it comes 1 Pt 4:12

FIFTEEN (17)
covering them **f** cubits deep. Gn 7:20
the one side of the gate shall be **f** cubits, Ex 27:14
side the hangings shall be **f** cubits, Ex 27:15
for one side of the gate were **f** cubits, Ex 38:14
of the court were hangings of **f** cubits, Ex 38:15
valuation for a male shall be **f** shekels, Lv 27:7
Now Ziba had **f** sons and twenty 2 Sm 9:10
with his **f** sons and his twenty 2 Sm 19:17
on the forty-five pillars, **f** in each row. 1 Kgs 7:3
lived **f** years after the death of 2 Kgs 14:17
and I will add **f** years to your life. I 2 Kgs 20:6
lived **f** years after the death of Joash 2 Chr 25:25
tears. Behold, I will add **f** years to your life. Is 38:5
shekels plus **f** shekels shall Ezk 45:12
So I bought her for **f** shekels of silver and Hos 3:2
sounding again and found **f** fathoms. Acts 27:28
Cephas and remained with him **f** days. Gal 1:18

FIFTEENTH (18)
on the **f** day of the second month after Ex 16:1
And on the **f** day of the same month is Lv 23:6
On the **f** day of this seventh month and Lv 23:34
"On the **f** day of the seventh month, Lv 23:39
and on the **f** day of this month is a Nm 28:17
"On the **f** day of the seventh month Nm 29:12
month, on the **f** day of the first month. Nm 33:3
a feast on the **f** day of the eighth 1 Kgs 12:32
in Bethel on the **f** day in the eighth 1 Kgs 12:33
In the **f** year of Amaziah the son of 2 Kgs 14:23
the **f** to Bilgah, the sixteenth to 1 Chr 24:14
to the **f**, to Jeremoth, his sons and 1 Chr 25:22
third month of the **f** year of the 2 Chr 15:10
the fourteenth, and rested on the **f** day, Est 9:18
Adar and also the **f** day of the same, Est 9:21
month, on the **f** day of the month, Ezk 32:17
on the **f** day of the month and for the Ezk 45:25
In the **f** year of the reign of Tiberius Lk 3:1

FIFTH (54)
and there was morning, the **f** day. Gn 1:23
she conceived and bore Jacob a **f** son. Gn 30:17
harvests you shall give a **f** to Pharaoh, Gn 47:24
day, that Pharaoh should have the **f**; Gn 47:26
thing and shall add a **f** to it and give it Lv 5:16
restore it in full and shall add a **f** to it, Lv 6:5
But in the **f** year you may eat of its fruit, Lv 19:25
he shall add the **f** of its value to it and Lv 22:14
it, he shall add a **f** to the valuation. Lv 27:13
he shall add a **f** to the valuation price, Lv 27:15
he shall add a **f** to its valuation price, Lv 27:19
back at the valuation, and add a **f** to it; Lv 27:27
some of his tithe, he shall add a **f** to it. Lv 27:31
adding a **f** to it and giving it to him to Nm 5:7
On the **f** day Shelumiel the son of Nm 7:36
"On the **f** day nine bulls, two rams, Nm 29:26
Egypt, on the first day of the **f** month. Nm 33:38
The **f** lot came out for the tribe of the Jos 19:24
And on the **f** day he arose early in the Jgs 19:8
and the **f**, Shephatiah the son of Abital; 2 Sm 3:4
In the **f** year of King Rehoboam, 1 Kgs 14:25
In the **f** year of Joram the son of 2 Kgs 8:16
In the **f** month, on the seventh day of 2 Kgs 25:8
Nethanel the fourth, Raddai the **f**, 1 Chr 2:14
the **f**, Shephatiah, by Abital; the sixth, 1 Chr 3:3
Nohah the fourth, and Rapha the **f**. 1 Chr 8:2
Mishmannah fourth, Jeremiah **f**, 1 Chr 12:10
the **f** to Malchijah, the sixth to 1 Chr 24:9
the **f** to Nethaniah, his sons and his 1 Chr 25:12
Elam the **f**, Jehohanan the sixth, 1 Chr 26:3
Sachar the fourth, Nethanel the **f**, 1 Chr 26:4
The **f** commander, for the fifth 1 Chr 27:8
fifth commander, for the **f** month, 1 Chr 27:8
In the **f** year of King Rehoboam, 2 Chr 12:2
he came to Jerusalem in the **f** month, Ezr 7:8
the first day of the **f** month he came to Ezr 7:9
way Sanballat for the **f** time sent his Neh 6:5
the captivity of Jerusalem in the **f** month. Jer 1:3
Judah, in the **f** month of the fourth year, Jer 28:1
In the **f** year of Jehoiakim the son of Jer 36:9
In the **f** month, on the tenth day of the Jer 52:12
fourth month, on the **f** day of the month, Ezk 1:1
On the **f** day of the month (it was the Ezk 1:2
the month (it was the **f** year of the exile Ezk 1:2
sixth month, on the **f** day of the month, Ezk 8:1
In the seventh year, in the **f** month, on Ezk 20:1
month, on the **f** day of the month, Ezk 33:21
I weep and abstain in the **f** month, Zec 7:3
and mourned in the **f** month and in the Zec 7:5
and the fast of the **f** and the fast of the Zec 8:19
When he opened the **f** seal, I saw under Rv 6:9
And the **f** angel blew his trumpet, and I Rv 9:1
The **f** angel poured out his bowl on the Rv 16:10
the **f** onyx, the sixth carnelian, the Rv 21:20

FIFTHS (1)
Pharaoh, and four **f** shall be your own, Gn 47:24

FIFTIES (8)
chiefs of thousands, of hundreds, of **f**, Ex 18:21
chiefs of thousands, of hundreds, of **f**, Ex 18:25
of hundreds, commanders of **f**, Dt 1:15
of thousands and commanders of **f**, 1 Sm 8:12
and hid them by **f** in a cave and 1 Kgs 18:4
the LORD'S prophets by **f** in a cave 1 Kgs 18:13
captains of fifty men with their **f**, 2 Kgs 1:14
down in groups, by hundreds and by **f**. Mk 6:40

FIFTIETH (3)
And you shall consecrate the **f** year, Lv 25:10
That **f** year shall be a jubilee for you; in Lv 25:11
In the **f** year of Azariah king of 2 Kgs 15:23

FIFTY (79)
Suppose there are **f** righteous within Gn 18:24
spare it for the **f** righteous who are in Gn 18:24
I find at Sodom **f** righteous in the city, Gn 18:26
five of the **f** righteous are lacking. Gn 18:28
F loops you shall make on the one Ex 26:5
and **f** loops you shall make on the edge Ex 26:5
And you shall make **f** clasps of gold, and Ex 26:6
You shall make **f** loops on the edge of Ex 26:10
and **f** loops on the edge of the curtain Ex 26:10
"You shall make **f** clasps of bronze, Ex 26:11
there shall be hangings for **f** cubits, Ex 27:12
on the front to the east shall be **f** cubits. Ex 27:13
be a hundred cubits, the breadth **f**, Ex 27:18
He made **f** loops on the one curtain, and Ex 36:12
and he made **f** loops on the edge of the Ex 36:12
And he made **f** clasps of gold, and Ex 36:13
And he made **f** loops on the edge of the Ex 36:17
and **f** loops on the edge of the other Ex 36:17
And he made **f** clasps of bronze to Ex 36:18
the west side were hangings of **f** cubits, Ex 38:12
And for the front to the east, **f** cubits. Ex 38:13
You shall count **f** days to the day after Lv 23:16
sixty years old shall be **f** shekels of silver, Lv 27:3
shall be valued at **f** shekels of silver. Lv 27:16
from thirty years old up to **f** years old, all Nm 4:3
From thirty years old up to **f** years old, Nm 4:23
From thirty years old up to **f** years old, Nm 4:30
from thirty years old up to **f** years old, Nm 4:35
from thirty years old up to **f** years old, Nm 4:39
from thirty years old up to **f** years old, Nm 4:43
from thirty years old up to **f** years old, Nm 4:47
from the age of **f** years they shall Nm 8:25
shall take one drawn out of every **f**, Nm 31:30
of the young woman **f** shekels of silver, Dt 22:29
horses, and **f** men to run before him. 2 Sm 15:1
and the oxen for **f** shekels of silver. 2 Sm 24:24
and **f** men to run before him. 1 Kgs 1:5
cubits and its breadth **f** cubits and its 1 Kgs 7:2
its length was **f** cubits, and its breadth 1 Kgs 7:6
him a captain of **f** men with his fifty. 2 Kgs 1:9
him a captain of fifty men with his **f**. 2 Kgs 1:9
But Elijah answered the captain of **f**, 2 Kgs 1:10
you and your **f**." Then fire came 2 Kgs 1:10
heaven and consumed him and his **f**. 2 Kgs 1:10
another captain of **f** men with his 2 Kgs 1:11
captain of fifty men with his **f**. 2 Kgs 1:11
you and your **f**." Then the fire 2 Kgs 1:12
heaven and consumed him and his **f**. 2 Kgs 1:12
the captain of a third **f** with his fifty. 2 Kgs 1:13
the captain of a third fifty with his **f**. 2 Kgs 1:13

the third captain of **f** went up and 2 Kgs 1:13
the life of these **f** servants of yours, 2 Kgs 1:13
former captains of **f** men with their 2 Kgs 1:14
F men of the sons of the prophets also 2 Kgs 2:7
are with your servants **f** strong men. 2 Kgs 2:16
"Send." They sent therefore **f** men. 2 Kgs 2:17
of more than **f** horsemen and ten 2 Kgs 13:7
f shekels of silver from every man, 2 Kgs 15:20
against him with **f** men of the 2 Kgs 15:25
of gold for the nails was **f** shekels. 2 Chr 3:9
"Let a gallows **f** cubits high be made, Est 5:14
at Haman's house, **f** cubits high." Est 7:9
the captain of **f** and the man of rank, the Is 3:3
vestibule of the gate was **f** cubits. Ezk 40:15
Its length was **f** cubits, and its breadth Ezk 40:21
Its length was **f** cubits, and its breadth Ezk 40:25
Its length was **f** cubits, and its breadth Ezk 40:29
Its length was **f** cubits, and its breadth Ezk 40:33
Its length was **f** cubits, and its breadth Ezk 40:36
cubits, and the breadth **f** cubits. Ezk 42:2
opposite the chambers, **f** cubits long. Ezk 42:7
on the outer court were **f** cubits long, Ezk 42:8
with **f** cubits for an open space around Ezk 45:2
came to the wine vat to draw **f** measures, Hg 2:16
five hundred denarii, and the other **f**. Lk 7:41
sit down in groups of about **f** each." Lk 9:14
bill, and sit down quickly and write **f**.' Lk 16:6
said to him, "You are not yet **f** years old, Jn 8:57
found it came to **f** thousand pieces of Acts 19:19

FIFTY-FIVE (2)
and he reigned **f** years in Jerusalem. 2 Kgs 21:1
and he reigned **f** years in Jerusalem. 2 Chr 33:1

FIFTY-SECOND (1)
In the **f** year of Azariah king of 2 Kgs 15:27

FIFTY-TWO (3)
and he reigned **f** years in Jerusalem. 2 Kgs 15:2
and he reigned **f** years in Jerusalem. 2 Chr 26:3
day of the month Elul, in **f** days. Neh 6:15

FIG (42)
And they sewed **f** leaves together and Gn 3:7
of vines and **f** trees and pomegranates, Dt 8:8
And the trees said to the **f** tree, 'You Jgs 9:10
But the **f** tree said to them, 'Shall I leave Jgs 9:11
under his vine and under his **f** tree, 1 Kgs 4:25
vine, and each one of his own **f** tree, 2 Kgs 18:31
He struck down their vines and **f** trees, Ps 105:33
Whoever tends a **f** tree will eat its fruit, Prv 27:18
The **f** tree ripens its figs, and the vines are Sg 2:13
be like a first-ripe **f** before the summer: Is 28:4
the vine, like leaves falling from the **f** tree. Is 34:4
own vine, and each one of his own **f** tree, Is 36:16
shall eat up your vines and your **f** trees; Jer 5:17
grapes on the vine, nor figs on the **f** tree; Jer 8:13
I will lay waste her vines and her **f** trees, Hos 2:12
the first fruit on the **f** tree in its first Hos 9:10
laid waste my vine and splintered my **f** tree; Jl 1:7
The vine dries up; the **f** tree languishes. Jl 1:12
the **f** tree and vine give their full yield. Jl 2:22
your **f** trees and your olive trees the Am 4:9
man under his vine and under his **f** tree, Mi 4:4
to eat, no first-ripe **f** that my soul desires. Mi 7:1
fortresses are like **f** trees with first-ripe Na 3:12
Though the **f** tree should not blossom, Hab 3:17
Indeed, the vine, the **f** tree, the Hg 2:19
under his vine and under his **f** tree." Zec 3:10
And seeing a **f** tree by the wayside, he Mt 21:19
you again!" And the **f** tree withered at Mt 21:19
"How did the **f** tree wither at once?" Mt 21:20
do what has been done to the **f** tree, Mt 21:21
"From the **f** tree learn its lesson: as Mt 24:32
seeing in the distance a **f** tree in leaf, Mk 11:13
they saw the **f** tree withered away to its Mk 11:20
The **f** tree that you cursed has Mk 11:21
"From the **f** tree learn its lesson: as Mk 13:28
"A man had a **f** tree planted in his Lk 13:6
I have come seeking fruit on this **f** tree, Lk 13:7
"Look at the **f** tree, and all the trees. Lk 21:29
you, when you were under the **f** tree, Jn 1:48
I said to you, 'I saw you under the **f** tree,' Jn 1:50
Can a **f** tree, my brothers, bear olives, or Jas 3:12
to the earth as the **f** tree sheds its winter Rv 6:13

FIGHT (97)
join our enemies and **f** against us and Ex 1:10
The LORD will **f** for you, and you have Ex 14:14
us men, and go out and **f** with Amalek. Ex 17:9
shall be able to **f** against them and Nm 22:11
goes before you will himself **f** for you, Dt 1:30
We ourselves will go up and **f**, just as the Dt 1:41
to me, 'Say to them, Do not go up or **f**, Dt 1:42
goes with you to **f** for you against your Dt 20:4
you draw near to a city to **f** against it, Dt 20:10
"When men **f** with one another and the Dt 25:11
together as one to **f** against Joshua and Jos 9:2
all your enemies against whom you **f**." Jos 10:25
at the waters of Merom to **f** with Israel. Jos 11:5
the Canaanites, to **f** against them?" Jgs 1:1
me, that we may **f** against the Canaanites. Jgs 1:3
went down to **f** against the Canaanites Jgs 1:9
when you went to **f** with Midian?" And Jgs 8:1
despised? Go out now and **f** with them." Jgs 9:38
the Jordan to **f** also against Judah Jgs 10:9
will begin to **f** against the Ammonites? Jgs 10:18
that we may **f** with the Ammonites." Jgs 11:6
go with us and **f** with the Ammonites Jgs 11:8
home again to **f** with the Ammonites, Jgs 11:9
have come to me to **f** against my land?" Jgs 11:12
to the Ammonites to **f** against them, Jgs 11:32
cross over to **f** against the Ammonites Jgs 12:1
come up to me this day to **f** against me?" Jgs 12:3
up first for us to **f** against the people of Jgs 20:18
Israel went out to **f** against Benjamin, Jgs 20:20
draw near to **f** against our brothers, Jgs 20:23
they have been to you; be men and **f**." 1 Sm 4:9
go out before us and **f** our battles." 1 Sm 8:20
Philistines mustered to **f** with Israel, 1 Sm 13:5
and **f** against them until they are 1 Sm 15:18
If he is able to **f** with me and kill me, 1 Sm 17:9
me a man, that we may **f** together." 1 Sm 17:10
will go and **f** with this Philistine." 1 Sm 17:32
against this Philistine to **f** with him, 1 Sm 17:33
for me and **f** the LORD'S battles." 1 Sm 18:17
their forces for war, to **f** against Israel. 1 Sm 28:1
may not go and **f** against the enemies 1 Sm 29:8
no more, nor did they **f** anymore. 2 Sm 2:28
'Why did you go so near the city to **f**? 2 Sm 11:20
to **f** against the house of Israel, 1 Kgs 12:21
not go up or **f** against your relatives 1 Kgs 12:24
But let us **f** against them in the 1 Kgs 20:23
Then we will **f** against them in the 1 Kgs 20:25
went up to Aphek to **f** against Israel. 1 Kgs 20:26
"**F** with neither small nor great, 1 Kgs 22:31
So they turned to **f** against him. 1 Kgs 22:32
kings had come up to **f** against them, 2 Kgs 3:21
father's throne and **f** for your 2 Kgs 10:3
For you shall **f** the Syrians in Aphek 2 Kgs 13:17
he has set out to **f** against you." So he 2 Kgs 19:9
chosen warriors, to **f** against Israel, 2 Chr 11:1
not go up or **f** against your relatives. 2 Chr 11:4
of Israel, do not **f** against the LORD, 2 Chr 13:12
"**F** with neither small nor great, 2 Chr 18:30
So they turned to **f** against him. 2 Chr 18:31
You will not need to **f** in this battle. 2 Chr 20:17
and intended to **f** against Jerusalem, 2 Chr 32:2
help us and to **f** our battles." And the 2 Chr 32:8
went up to **f** at Carchemish on 2 Chr 35:20
himself in order to **f** with him. 2 Chr 35:22
but came to **f** in the plain of 2 Chr 35:22
to come and **f** against Jerusalem and Neh 4:8
and awesome, and **f** for your brothers, Neh 4:14
rally to us there. Our God will **f** for us." Neh 4:20
me; **f** against those who fight against me! Ps 35:1
me; fight against those who **f** against me! Ps 35:1
A fool's lips walk into a **f**, and his Prv 18:6
against Egyptians, and they will **f**, Is 19:2
of all the nations that **f** against Ariel, Is 29:7
all that **f** against her and her stronghold Is 29:7
the nations be that **f** against Mount Zion. Is 29:8
brandished arm, he will **f** with them. Is 30:32
will come down to **f** on Mount Zion and Is 31:4
has set out to **f** against you." And when Is 37:9
only to quarrel and to **f** and to hit with a Is 58:4
They will **f** against you, but they shall Jer 1:19
wall of bronze; they will **f** against you, Jer 15:20
I myself will **f** against you with Jer 21:5
Though you **f** against the Chaldeans, Jer 32:5
are coming in to **f** against the Chaldeans Jer 33:5
And they will **f** against it and take it Jer 34:22
shall come back and **f** against this city. Jer 37:8
men and went to **f** against Ishmael the Jer 41:12
I will return to **f** against the prince of Dn 10:20
shall come out and **f** with the king of Dn 11:11
they shall **f** because the LORD is with Zec 10:5
will go out and **f** against those nations Zec 14:3
Even Judah will **f** against Jerusalem. Zec 14:14
F the good fight of the faith. Take 1 Tm 6:12
Fight the good **f** of the faith. Take 1 Tm 6:12
I have fought the good **f**, I have 2 Tm 4:7
and cannot obtain, so you **f** and quarrel. Jas 4:2
like the beast, and who can **f** against it?" Rv 13:4

FIGHTING (23)
be dismayed. Take all the **f** men with you, Jos 8:1
So Joshua and all the **f** men arose to go up Jos 8:3
And all the **f** men who were with him Jos 8:11
There was hard **f** against the 1 Sm 14:52
valley of Elah, **f** with the Philistines. 1 Sm 17:19
the Philistines are **f** against Keilah 1 Sm 23:1
because my lord is **f** the battles of the 1 Sm 25:28
Joab returned from **f** against the 2 Sm 10:14
in the forefront of the hardest **f**, 2 Sm 11:15
told David all the news about the **f**. 2 Sm 11:18
all the news about the **f** to the king, 2 Sm 11:19
the king of Assyria **f** against Libnah, 2 Kgs 19:8
the king of Assyria **f** against Libnah, Is 37:8
with which you are **f** against the king of Jer 21:4
of the Chaldeans who are **f** against it. Jer 32:24
Chaldeans who are **f** against this city Jer 32:29
the peoples were **f** against Jerusalem and Jer 34:1
of Babylon was **f** against Jerusalem and Jer 34:7
of Chaldeans who are **f** against you, Jer 37:10
The warriors of Babylon have ceased **f**; Jer 51:30
world, my servants would have been **f**, Jn 18:36
at every turn—**f** without and fear 2 Cor 7:5
and his angels **f** against the dragon. Rv 12:7

FIGHTS (5)
for the LORD **f** for them against the Ex 14:25
for it is the LORD your God who **f** for you.' Dt 3:22
it is the LORD your God who **f** for you, Jos 23:10
those nations as when he **f** on a day of Zec 14:3
quarrels and what causes **f** among you? Jas 4:1

FIGS (26)
brought some pomegranates and **f**. Nm 13:23
place for grain or **f** or vines or Nm 20:5
raisins and two hundred cakes of **f**, 1 Sm 25:18
of a cake of **f** and two clusters of 1 Sm 30:12
And Isaiah said, "Bring a cake of **f**. 2 Kgs 20:7
provisions of flour, cakes of **f**, 1 Chr 12:40
wine, grapes, **f**, and all kinds of loads, Neh 13:15
The fig tree ripens its **f**, and the vines are Sg 2:13
them take a cake of **f** and apply it to the Is 38:21
grapes on the vine, nor **f** on the fig tree; Jer 8:13
two baskets of **f** placed before the temple Jer 24:1
One basket had very good **f**, like Jer 24:2
had very good figs, like first-ripe **f**, Jer 24:2
figs, but the other basket had very bad **f**, Jer 24:2
I said, "**F**, the good figs very good, Jer 24:3
I said, "Figs, the good **f** very good, Jer 24:3
figs very good, and the bad **f** very bad, Jer 24:3
Like these good **f**, so I will regard as good Jer 24:5
Like the bad **f** that are so bad they Jer 24:8
make them like vile **f** that are so rotten Jer 29:17
herdsman and a dresser of sycamore **f**. Am 7:14
fig trees with first-ripe **f**—if shaken they Na 3:12
from thornbushes, or **f** from thistles? Mt 7:16
leaves, for it was not the season for **f**. Mk 11:13
For **f** are not gathered from Lk 6:44
bear olives, or a grapevine produce **f**? Jas 3:12

FIGURATIVE (1)
plainly and not using **f** speech! Jn 16:29

FIGURATIVELY (1)
the dead, from which, **f** speaking, Heb 11:19

FIGURE (4)
for yourselves, in the form of any **f**, Dt 4:16
woman had a beautiful **f** and was lovely Est 2:7
He shapes it into the **f** of a man, with the Is 44:13
This **f** of speech Jesus used with them, Jn 10:6

FIGURED (2)
shall not set up a **f** stone in your land to Lv 26:1
destroy all their **f** stones and destroy Nm 33:52

FIGUREHEAD (1)
Alexandria, with the twin gods as a **f**. Acts 28:11

FIGURES (6)
and put in a box at its side the **f** of gold, 1 Sm 6:8
beside it, in which were the golden **f**, 1 Sm 6:15
he carved engraved **f** of cherubim 1 Kgs 6:29
Under it were **f** of gourds, for ten 2 Chr 4:3
said these things to you in **f** of speech. Jn 16:25
speak to you in **f** of speech but will Jn 16:25

FILIGREE (8)
shall enclose them in settings of gold **f**. Ex 28:11
You shall make settings of gold **f**, Ex 28:13
and a jasper. They shall be set in gold **f**. Ex 28:20
you shall attach to the two settings of **f**, Ex 28:25
stones, enclosed in settings of gold **f**, Ex 39:6
They were enclosed in settings of gold **f**. Ex 39:13
two settings of gold **f** and two gold Ex 39:16
of the two cords to the two settings of **f**. Ex 39:18

FILL (64)
fruitful and multiply and **f** the waters in Gn 1:22
and multiply and **f** the earth and Gn 1:28
"Be fruitful and multiply and **f** the earth. Gn 9:1
Joseph gave orders to **f** their bags with Gn 42:25
his house, "**F** the men's sacks with food, Gn 44:1
and they shall **f** your houses and the Ex 10:6
spoil, my desire shall have its **f** of them. Ex 15:9
and you will eat your **f** and dwell in it Lv 25:19
full of all good things that you did not **f**, Dt 6:11
vineyard, you may eat your **f** of grapes, Dt 23:24
from the fleece to **f** a bowl with water. Jgs 6:38
Israel? **F** your horn with oil, and go. 1 Sm 16:1

"**F** four jars with water and pour it 1 Kgs 18:33
He will yet **f** your mouth with laughter, Jb 8:21
and **f** his belly with the east wind? Jb 15:2
To **f** his belly to the full God will send Jb 20:23
case before him and **f** my mouth with Jb 23:4
Can you **f** his skin with harpoons or his Jb 41:7
You **f** their womb with treasure; they Ps 17:14
food and growl if they do not get their **f**. Ps 59:15
Open your mouth wide, and I will **f** it. Ps 81:10
F their faces with shame, that they may Ps 83:16
the reaper does not **f** his hand nor the Ps 129:7
we shall **f** our houses with plunder; Prv 1:13
and have their **f** of their own devices. Prv 1:31
strangers take their **f** of your strength, Prv 5:10
Let her breasts **f** you at all times with Prv 5:19
let us take our **f** of love till morning; Prv 7:18
lest you have your **f** of it and vomit it. Prv 25:16
lest he have his **f** of you and hate you. Prv 25:17
its outspread wings will **f** the breadth of Is 8:8
and **f** the face of the world with cities." Is 14:21
put forth shoots and **f** the whole world Is 27:6
he will **f** Zion with justice and Is 33:5
my sword has drunk its **f** in the heavens; Is 34:5
Their land shall drink its **f** of blood, and Is 34:7
let us **f** ourselves with strong drink; Is 56:12
table for Fortune and **f** cups of mixed Is 65:11
an old man who does not **f** out his days, Is 65:20
I will **f** with drunkenness all the Jer 13:13
the LORD. Do I not **f** heaven and earth? Jer 23:24
the Chaldeans and to **f** them with the Jer 33:5
be sated and drink its **f** of their blood. Jer 46:10
himself: Surely I will **f** you with men, Jer 51:14
I give you and **f** your stomach with it." Ezk 3:3
their hunger or **f** their stomachs with Ezk 7:19
that they should **f** the land with Ezk 8:17
house, and **f** the courts with the slain. Ezk 9:7
F your hands with burning coals from Ezk 10:2
the shoulder; **f** it with choice bones. Ezk 24:4
against Egypt and **f** the land with Ezk 30:11
the mountains and **f** the valleys with Ezk 32:5
And I will **f** its mountains with the Ezk 35:8
You will have your **f** of shame instead Hab 2:16
and those who **f** their master's house Zep 1:9
you drink, but you never have your **f**. Hg 1:6
in, and I will **f** this house with glory, Hg 2:7
F up, then, the measure of your fathers. Mt 23:32
"**F** the jars with water." And they filled Jn 2:7
And when they had eaten their **f**, he told Jn 6:12
but because you ate your **f** of the loaves. Jn 6:26
the God of hope **f** you with all joy Rom 15:13
the heavens, that he might **f** all things.) Eph 4:10
—so as always to **f** up the measure of 1 Thes 2:16

FILLED (141)
sight, and the earth was **f** with violence. Gn 6:11
for the earth is **f** with violence through Gn 6:13
And she went and **f** the skin with water Gn 21:19
to the spring and **f** her jar and came Gn 24:16
had stopped and **f** with earth all Gn 26:15
strong, so that the land was **f** with them. Ex 1:7
and drew water and **f** the troughs to Ex 2:16
the Egyptians shall be **f** with swarms of Ex 8:21
the morning you shall be **f** with bread. Ex 16:12
whom I have **f** with a spirit of skill, Ex 28:3
and I have **f** him with the Spirit of God, Ex 31:3
and he has **f** him with the Spirit of God, Ex 35:31
He has **f** them with skill to do every sort Ex 35:35
the glory of the LORD **f** the tabernacle. Ex 40:34
the glory of the LORD **f** the tabernacle. Ex 40:35
the earth shall be **f** with the glory of Nm 14:21
towns, shall come and eat and be **f**, Dt 14:29
may eat within your towns and be **f**, Dt 26:12
wineskins were new when we **f** them, Jos 9:13
f with fear because of the words of 1 Sm 28:20
Place, a cloud **f** the house of the LORD, 1 Kgs 8:10
the glory of the LORD **f** the house of the 1 Kgs 8:11
the altar and **f** the trench also 1 Kgs 18:35
goats, but the Syrians **f** the country. 1 Kgs 20:27
that streambed shall be **f** with water, 2 Kgs 3:17
till the country was **f** with water. 2 Kgs 3:20
house of Baal was **f** from one end to 2 Kgs 10:21
till he had **f** Jerusalem from one end 2 Kgs 21:16
the Asherim and **f** their places with 2 Kgs 23:14
For he **f** Jerusalem with innocent 2 Kgs 24:4
house of the LORD, was **f** with a cloud, 2 Chr 5:13
glory of the LORD **f** the house of God. 2 Chr 5:14
and the glory of the LORD **f** the temple. 2 Chr 7:1
glory of the LORD **f** the LORD'S house. 2 Chr 7:2
that had been **f** with various kinds 2 Chr 16:14
abominations that have **f** it from end Ezr 9:11
they ate and were **f** and became fat and Neh 9:25
homage to him, Haman was **f** with fury. Est 3:5
he was **f** with wrath against Mordecai. Est 5:9
had gold, who **f** their houses with silver. Jb 3:15
for I am **f** with disgrace and look on my Jb 10:15
Yet he **f** their houses with good things— Jb 22:18
there that has not been **f** with his meat?' Jb 31:31
His mouth is **f** with cursing and deceit Ps 10:7
For my sides are **f** with burning, and Ps 38:7
right hand is **f** with righteousness. Ps 48:10
My mouth is **f** with your praise, and with Ps 71:8
may the whole earth be **f** with his glory! Ps 72:19
And they ate and were well **f**, for he gave Ps 78:29
for it; it took deep root and **f** the land. Ps 80:9
your hand, they are **f** with good things. Ps 104:28
Then our mouth was **f** with laughter, Ps 126:2
then your barns will be **f** with plenty, Prv 3:10
but the wicked are **f** with trouble. Prv 12:21
in heart will be **f** with the fruit of Prv 14:14
a good man will be **f** with the fruit of Prv 14:14
the rooms are **f** with all precious Prv 24:4
king, and a fool when he is **f** with food; Prv 30:22
with seeing, nor the ear **f** with hearing. Eccl 1:8
Their land is **f** with silver and gold, and Is 2:7
their land is **f** with horses, and there is no Is 2:7
Their land is **f** with idols; they bow down Is 2:8
up; and the train of his robe **f** the temple. Is 6:1
called, and the house was **f** with smoke. Is 6:4
Therefore my loins are **f** with anguish; Is 21:3
of Sidon, who cross the sea, have **f** you. Is 23:2
"Every jar shall be **f** with wine."' And Jer 13:12
that every jar will be **f** with wine?' Jer 13:12
me, for you had **f** me with indignation. Jer 15:17
and have **f** my inheritance with their Jer 16:18
and because they have **f** this place with Jer 19:4
the son of Nethaniah **f** it with the slain. Jer 41:9
he has **f** his stomach with my Jer 51:34
He has **f** me with bitterness; he has Lam 3:15
strikes, and let him be **f** with insults. Lam 3:30
went in, and a cloud **f** the inner court. Ezk 10:3
and the house was **f** with the cloud, Ezk 10:4
and the court was **f** with the brightness Ezk 10:4
this city and have **f** its streets with the Ezk 11:6
you will be **f** with drunkenness and Ezk 23:33
So you were **f** and heavily laden in the Ezk 27:25
your trade you were **f** with violence in Ezk 28:16
the waste cities be **f** with flocks of Ezk 36:38
And you shall eat fat till you are **f**, and Ezk 39:19
And you shall be **f** at my table with Ezk 39:20
the glory of the LORD **f** the temple. Ezk 43:5
the glory of the LORD **f** the temple of the Ezk 44:4
a great mountain and **f** the whole earth. Dn 2:35
Then Nebuchadnezzar was **f** with fury, Dn 3:19
grazed, they became full, they were **f**, Hos 13:6
But as for me, I am **f** with power, with the Mi 3:8
he **f** his caves with prey and his dens Na 2:12
the earth will be **f** with the knowledge Hab 2:14
So the wedding hall was **f** with guests. Mt 22:10
and took a sponge, **f** it with sour wine, Mt 27:48
place, they were **f** with awe and said, Mt 27:54
And they were **f** with great fear and said Mk 4:41
And someone ran and **f** a sponge with Mk 15:36
and he will be **f** with the Holy Spirit, Lk 1:15
And Elizabeth was **f** with the Holy Spirit, Lk 1:41
he has **f** the hungry with good things, Lk 1:53
his father Zechariah was **f** with the Holy Lk 1:67
around them, and they were **f** with fear. Lk 2:9
grew and became strong, **f** with wisdom. Lk 2:40
Every valley shall be **f**, and every Lk 3:5
all in the synagogue were **f** with wrath. Lk 4:28
And they came and **f** both the boats, so Lk 5:7
they glorified God and were **f** with awe, Lk 5:26
But they were **f** with fury and discussed Lk 6:11
to come in, that my house may be **f**. Lk 14:23
jars with water." And they **f** them up to the Jn 2:7
them up and **f** twelve baskets with Jn 6:13
The house was **f** with the fragrance of the Jn 12:3
things to you, sorrow has **f** your heart. Jn 16:6
and it **f** the entire house where they were Acts 2:2
And they were all **f** with the Holy Spirit Acts 2:4
said, "They are **f** with new wine." Acts 2:13
And they were **f** with wonder and Acts 3:10
Then Peter, **f** with the Holy Spirit, said Acts 4:8
and they were all **f** with the Holy Spirit Acts 4:31
why has Satan **f** your heart to lie to the Acts 5:3
of the Sadducees), and **f** with jealousy Acts 5:17
here you have **f** Jerusalem with your Acts 5:28
your sight and be **f** with the Holy Acts 9:17
also called Paul, **f** with the Holy Spirit, Acts 13:9
they were **f** with jealousy and began Acts 13:45
And the disciples were **f** with joy and Acts 13:52
So the city was **f** with the confusion, Acts 19:29
They were **f** with all manner of Rom 1:29
f with all knowledge and able to Rom 15:14
great pride in you; I am **f** with comfort. 2 Cor 7:4
that you may be **f** with all the fullness Eph 3:19
is debauchery, but be **f** with the Spirit, Eph 5:18
f with the fruit of righteousness that Phil 1:11
that you may be **f** with the knowledge of Col 1:9
and you have been **f** in him, who is the Col 2:10
to see you, that I may be **f** with joy. 2 Tm 1:4
be warmed and **f**," without giving them Jas 2:16
joy that is inexpressible and **f** with glory, 1 Pt 1:8
took the censer and **f** it with fire from Rv 8:5
the sanctuary was **f** with smoke from Rv 15:8

FILLETED (2)
around the court shall be **f** with silver. Ex 27:17
pillars of the court were **f** with silver. Ex 38:17

FILLETS (9)
the pillars and their **f** shall be of silver. Ex 27:10
the pillars and their **f** shall be of silver. Ex 27:11
their capitals, and their **f** were of gold, Ex 36:38
of the pillars and their **f** were of silver. Ex 38:10
of the pillars and their **f** were of silver. Ex 38:11
of the pillars and their **f** were of silver. Ex 38:12
of the pillars and their **f** were of silver. Ex 38:17
of their capitals and their **f** of silver. Ex 38:19
their capitals and made **f** for them. Ex 38:28

FILLING (6)
the nations, **f** them with corpses; Ps 110:6
who love me, and **f** their treasuries. Prv 8:21
prophesy to you, **f** you with vain hopes. Jer 23:16
the boat, so that the boat was already **f**. Mk 4:37
and they were **f** with water and were in Lk 8:23
in my flesh I am **f** up what is lacking in Col 1:24

FILLS (13)
Let the sea roar, and all that **f** it; let 1 Chr 16:32
get my breath, but **f** me with bitterness. Jb 9:18
rejoice; let the sea roar, and all that **f** it; Ps 96:11
Let the sea roar, and all that **f** it; the Ps 98:7
the hungry soul he **f** with good things. Ps 107:9
is the man who **f** his quiver with them! Ps 127:5
he **f** you with the finest of the wheat. Ps 147:14
Let the earth hear, and all that **f** it; the Is 34:1
who go down to the sea, and all that **f** it, Is 42:10
and devour the land and all that **f** it, Jer 8:16
shall overflow the land and all that **f** it, Jer 47:2
the land is desolate of all that **f** it, Ezk 32:15
the fullness of him who **f** all in all. Eph 1:23

FILTH (5)
and carry out the **f** from the Holy 2 Chr 29:5
own eyes but are not washed of their **f**. Prv 30:12
have washed away the **f** of the daughters of Is 4:4
because he was determined to go after **f**. Hos 5:11
I will throw **f** at you and treat you with Na 3:6

FILTHINESS (2)
Let there be no **f** nor foolish talk nor Eph 5:4
put away all **f** and rampant wickedness Jas 1:21

FILTHY (7)
For all tables are full of **f** vomit, with no Is 28:8
grievously; therefore she became **f**; Lam 1:8
has become a **f** thing among them. Lam 1:17
the angel, clothed with **f** garments. Zec 3:3
"Remove the **f** garments from him." And Zec 3:4
still do evil, and the **f** still be filthy, Rv 22:11
still do evil, and the filthy still be **f**, Rv 22:11

FINAL (4)
come, the time of your **f** punishment, Ezk 21:25
come, the time of their **f** punishment, Ezk 21:29
at the time of their **f** punishment, Ezk 35:5
disputes an oath is **f** for confirmation. Heb 6:16

FINALLY (9)
F he sent his son to them, saying, 'They Mt 21:37
F he sent him to them, saying, 'They Mk 12:6
F, brothers, rejoice. Aim for 2 Cor 13:11
F, be strong in the Lord and in the Eph 6:10
F, my brothers, rejoice in the Lord. To Phil 3:1
F, brothers, whatever is true, whatever is Phil 4:8
F, then, brothers, we ask and urge 1 Thes 4:1
F, brothers, pray for us, that the word 2 Thes 3:1
F, all of you, have unity of mind, 1 Pt 3:8

FIND (181)
"If I **f** at Sodom fifty righteous in the Gn 18:26
will not destroy it if I **f** forty-five there." Gn 18:28
"I will not do it, if I **f** thirty there." Gn 18:30
with whom you **f** your gods shall Gn 31:32
female servants, but he did not **f** them. Gn 31:33
all about the tent, but did not **f** them. Gn 31:34
but did not **f** the household gods. Gn 31:35
order that I may **f** favor in your sight."' Gn 32:5
same thing to Esau when you **f** him, Gn 32:19
"To **f** favor in the sight of my lord." Gn 33:8
Let me **f** favor in the sight of my lord." Gn 33:15
brothers, "Let me **f** favor in your eyes, Gn 34:11
the woman's hand, he did not **f** her. Gn 38:20
this young goat, and you did not **f** her." Gn 38:23
his servants, "Can we **f** a man like this, Gn 41:38
to see the evil that would **f** my father." Gn 44:34
straw yourselves wherever you can **f** it, Ex 5:11
LORD; today you will not **f** it in the field. Ex 16:25
you in order to **f** favor in your sight. Ex 33:13
me at once, if I **f** favor in your sight, Nm 11:15

and be sure your sin will **f** you out. Nm 32:23
the LORD your God and you will **f** him, Dt 4:29
your brother's, which he loses and you **f**; Dt 22:3
I did not **f** in her evidence of virginity,' Dt 22:14
"I did not **f** in your daughter evidence of Dt 22:17
these nations you shall **f** no respite, Dt 28:65
the seven days of the feast, and **f** it out, Jgs 14:12
to sojourn where he could **f** a place. Jgs 17:8
going to sojourn where I may **f** a place." Jgs 17:9
The LORD grant that you may **f** rest, each Ru 1:9
whose sight I shall **f** favor." And she said Ru 2:2
"Let your servant **f** favor in your 1 Sm 1:18
of Shalishah, but they did not **f** them. 1 Sm 9:4
land of Benjamin, but did not **f** them. 1 Sm 9:4
as you enter the city you will **f** him, 1 Sm 9:13
man, saying, 'Go, **f** the arrows.' 1 Sm 20:21
"Run and **f** the arrows that I shoot." 1 Sm 20:36
of Saul my father shall not **f** you. 1 Sm 23:17
let my young men **f** favor in your 1 Sm 25:8
If I **f** favor in the eyes of the LORD, he 2 Sm 15:25
let me ever **f** favor in your sight, my 2 Sm 16:4
had sought and could not **f** them, 2 Sm 17:20
Perhaps we may **f** grass and save the 1 Kgs 18:5
and tell Ahab and he cannot **f** you, 1 Kgs 18:12
they sought him but did not **f** him. 2 Kgs 2:17
You will **f** them at the end of the 2 Chr 20:16
your children will **f** compassion with 2 Chr 30:9
of Assyria come and **f** much water?" 2 Chr 32:4
You will **f** in the book of the records Ezr 4:15
gold that you shall **f** in the whole Ezr 7:16
were silent and could not **f** a word to say. Neh 5:8
and are glad when they **f** the grave? Jb 3:22
leave me alone, that I may **f** a little cheer Jb 10:20
"Can you **f** out the deep things of God? Jb 11:7
Can you **f** out the limit of the Almighty? Jb 11:7
blood, and let my cry **f** no resting place. Jb 16:18
and I shall not **f** a wise man among you. Jb 17:10
Oh, that I knew where I might **f** him, that Jb 23:3
I must speak, that I may **f** relief; I must Jb 32:20
The Almighty—we cannot **f** him; he is Jb 37:23
wickedness to account till you **f** none. Ps 10:15
have tested me, and you will **f** nothing; Ps 17:3
Your hand will **f** out all your enemies; Ps 21:8
your right hand will **f** out those who hate Ps 21:8
not answer, and by night, but I **f** no rest. Ps 22:2
I would hurry to **f** a shelter from the Ps 55:8
back to them, and **f** no fault in them. Ps 73:10
and under his wings you will **f** refuge; Ps 91:4
for I **f** my delight in your Ps 119:47
until I **f** a place for the LORD, a dwelling Ps 132:5
we shall **f** all precious goods, we shall Prv 1:13
seek me diligently but will not **f** me. Prv 1:28
of the LORD and **f** the knowledge of God. Prv 2:5
So you will **f** favor and good success in Prv 3:4
For they are life to those who **f** them, Prv 4:22
and right to those who **f** knowledge. Prv 8:9
and I **f** knowledge and discretion. Prv 8:12
and those who seek me diligently **f** me. Prv 8:17
but he who fails to **f** me injures himself; Prv 8:36
love, but a faithful man who can **f**? Prv 20:6
righteousness and kindness will **f** life, Prv 21:21
if you **f** it, there will be a future, and Prv 24:14
who has understanding will **f** him out. Prv 28:11
man will afterward **f** more favor than Prv 28:23
will in the end **f** him his heir. Prv 29:21
An excellent wife who can **f**? She is far Prv 31:10
eat and drink and **f** enjoyment in his Eccl 2:24
so that he cannot **f** out what God has Eccl 3:11
eat and drink and **f** enjoyment in all Eccl 5:18
that man may not **f** out anything that Eccl 7:14
and deep, very deep; who can **f** it out? Eccl 7:24
And I **f** something more bitter than Eccl 7:26
thing to another to **f** the scheme of Eccl 7:27
that man cannot **f** out the work that is Eccl 8:17
may toil in seeking, he will not **f** it out. Eccl 8:17
claims to know, he cannot **f** it out. Eccl 8:17
for you will **f** it after many days. Eccl 11:1
Preacher sought to **f** words of delight, Eccl 12:10
of Jerusalem, if you **f** my beloved, Sg 5:8
in her the afflicted of his people **f** refuge." Is 14:32
with you, but you shall not **f** them; Is 41:12
wrong did your fathers **f** in me that they Jer 2:5
themselves; in her month they will **f** her. Jer 2:24
poor; you did not **f** them breaking in. Jer 2:34
her squares to see if you can **f** a man, Jer 5:1
and walk in it, and **f** rest for your souls. Jer 6:16
come to the cisterns; they **f** no water; Jer 14:3
for in its welfare you will **f** your welfare. Jer 29:7
You will seek me and **f** me. When you Jer 29:13
weary with my groaning, and I **f** no rest.' Jer 45:3
have become like deer that **f** no pasture; Lam 1:6
and her prophets **f** no vision from the Lam 2:9
"Son of man, eat whatever you **f** here. Ezk 3:1
to it, and **f** its vestibule before them. Ezk 40:22
the satraps sought to **f** a ground for Dn 6:4
but they could **f** no ground for complaint Dn 6:4
"We shall not **f** any ground for Dn 6:5
this Daniel unless we **f** it in connection Dn 6:5
her, so that she cannot **f** her paths. Hos 2:6
she shall seek them but shall not **f** them. Hos 2:7
to seek the LORD, but they will not **f** him; Hos 5:6
my labors they cannot **f** in me iniquity Hos 12:8
word of the LORD, but they shall not **f** it. Am 8:12
will be given to you; seek, and you will **f**; Mt 7:7
leads to life, and those who **f** it are few. Mt 7:14
f out who is worthy in it and stay there Mt 10:11
loses his life for my sake will **f** it. Mt 10:39
heart, and you will **f** rest for your souls. Mt 11:29
loses his life for my sake will **f** it. Mt 16:25
you open its mouth you will **f** a shekel. Mt 17:27
immediately you will **f** a donkey tied, Mt 21:2
to the wedding feast as many as you **f**.' Mt 22:9
whom his master will **f** so doing when Mt 24:46
as you enter it you will **f** a colt tied, Mk 11:2
went to see if he could **f** anything on it. Mk 11:13
he come suddenly and **f** you asleep. Mk 13:36
you will **f** a baby wrapped in swaddling Lk 2:12
and when they did not **f** him, they Lk 2:45
so that they might **f** a reason to accuse Lk 6:7
and countryside to **f** lodging and get Lk 9:12
will be given to you; seek, and you will **f**; Lk 11:9
whom his master will **f** so doing when Lk 12:43
fruit on this fig tree, and I **f** none. Lk 13:7
of Man comes, will he **f** faith on earth?" Lk 18:8
where on entering you will **f** a colt tied, Lk 19:30
but they did not **f** anything they could Lk 19:48
the crowds, "I **f** no guilt in this man." Lk 23:4
I did not **f** this man guilty of any of Lk 23:14
went in they did not **f** the body of the Lk 24:3
and when they did not **f** his body, they Lk 24:23
You will seek me and you will not **f** me. Jn 7:34
man intend to go that we will not **f** him? Jn 7:35
'You will seek me and you will not **f** me,' Jn 7:36
and will go in and out and **f** pasture. Jn 10:9
Jews and told them, "I **f** no guilt in him. Jn 18:38
you may know that I **f** no guilt in him." Jn 19:4
and crucify him, for I **f** no guilt in him." Jn 19:6
boat, and you will **f** some." So they cast it, Jn 21:6
they did not **f** them in the prison, Acts 5:22
and our fathers could **f** no food. Acts 7:11
God and asked to **f** a dwelling place for Acts 7:46
searched for him and did not **f** him, Acts 12:19
And when they could not **f** them, they Acts 17:6
feel their way toward him and **f** him. Acts 17:27
to **f** out why they were shouting Acts 22:24
"We **f** nothing wrong in this man. Acts 23:9
will be able to **f** out from him about Acts 24:8
and they did not **f** me disputing with Acts 24:12
So I **f** it to be a law that when I want to Rom 7:21
to me then, "Why does he still **f** fault? Rom 9:19
and I will **f** out not the talk of these 1 Cor 4:19
the promises of God **f** their Yes in 2 Cor 1:20
because I did not **f** my brother Titus 2 Cor 2:13
come with me and **f** that you are not 2 Cor 9:4
when I come I may **f** you not as I 2 Cor 12:20
and that you may **f** me not as you 2 Cor 12:20
I hope you will **f** out that we have not 2 Cor 13:6
Lord grant him to **f** mercy from the 2 Tm 1:18
may receive mercy and **f** grace to help Heb 4:16
I rejoiced greatly to **f** some of your 2 Jn 1:4
people will seek death and will not **f** it. Rv 9:6

FINDING (5)

wastes, **f** no way to a city to dwell in; Ps 107:4
who, on **f** one pearl of great value, went Mt 13:46
but **f** no way to bring him in, because of Lk 5:19
places seeking rest, and **f** none it says, Lk 11:24
let them go, **f** no way to punish them, Acts 4:21

FINDS (37)

earth, and whoever **f** me will kill me." Gn 4:14
prosperous and **f** sufficient means Lv 25:26
the avenger of blood **f** him outside the Nm 35:27
if then she **f** no favor in his eyes because Dt 24:1
may do to them as your hand **f** to do." Jgs 9:33
meet you, do what your hand **f** to do, 1 Sm 10:7
For if a man **f** his enemy, will he let 1 Sm 24:19
forgets them; the worm **f** them sweet; Jb 24:20
Behold, he **f** occasions against me, he Jb 33:10
Even the sparrow **f** a home, and the Ps 84:3
your word like one who **f** great spoil. Ps 119:162
Blessed is the one who **f** wisdom, and Prv 3:13
For whoever **f** me finds life and obtains Prv 8:35
For whoever finds me **f** life and obtains Prv 8:35
but the righteous **f** refuge in his death. Prv 14:32
He who **f** a wife finds a good thing and Prv 18:22
He who finds a wife **f** a good thing and Prv 18:22
his neighbor **f** no mercy in his eyes. Prv 21:10
anything, yet it **f** rest rather than he. Eccl 6:5
Whatever your hand **f** to do, do it with Eccl 9:10
then I was in his eyes as one who **f** peace. Sg 8:10
night bird settles and **f** for herself a Is 34:14
the nations, but **f** no resting place; Lam 1:3
our hands. In you the orphan **f** mercy." Hos 14:3
asks receives, and the one who seeks **f**, Mt 7:8
Whoever **f** his life will lose it, and Mt 10:39
places seeking rest, but **f** none. Mt 12:43
when it comes, it **f** the house empty, Mt 12:44
And if he **f** it, truly, I say to you, he Mt 18:13
asks receives, and the one who seeks **f**, Lk 11:10
it **f** the house swept and put in order. Lk 11:25
whom the master **f** awake when he Lk 12:37
or in the third, and **f** them awake, Lk 12:38
go after the one that is lost, until he **f** it? Lk 15:4
house and seek diligently until she **f** it? Lk 15:8
me because my word **f** no place in you. Jn 8:37
For he **f** fault with them when he says: Heb 8:8

FINE (135)

and said, "Quick! Three seahs of **f** flour! Gn 18:6
him in garments of **f** linen and put a Gn 41:42
and when she saw that he was a **f** child, Ex 2:2
It shall become **f** dust over all the land of Ex 9:9
was on the face of the wilderness a **f**, Ex 16:14
thing, **f** as frost on the ground. Ex 16:14
and scarlet yarns and **f** twined linen, Ex 25:4
with ten curtains of **f** twined linen and Ex 26:1
and scarlet yarns and **f** twined linen. Ex 26:31
and scarlet yarns and **f** twined linen, Ex 26:36
shall have hangings of **f** twined linen a Ex 27:9
and scarlet yarns and **f** twined linen, Ex 27:16
with hangings of **f** twined linen and Ex 27:18
and scarlet yarns, and **f** twined linen. Ex 28:5
and scarlet yarns, and of **f** twined linen, Ex 28:6
and scarlet yarns, and **f** twined linen. Ex 28:8
and **f** twined linen shall you make it. Ex 28:15
the coat in checker work of **f** linen, Ex 28:39
and you shall make a turban of **f** linen, Ex 28:39
You shall make them of **f** wheat flour. Ex 29:2
a tenth seah of **f** flour mingled with a Ex 29:40
and scarlet yarns and **f** twined linen; Ex 35:6
or scarlet yarns or **f** linen or goats' hair Ex 35:23
and scarlet yarns and **f** twined linen. Ex 35:25
and scarlet yarns and **f** twined linen, Ex 35:35
They were made of **f** twined linen and Ex 36:8
and scarlet yarns and **f** twined linen; Ex 36:35
and scarlet yarns and **f** twined linen, Ex 36:37
of the court were of **f** twined linen, Ex 38:9
around the court were of **f** twined linen. Ex 38:16
and scarlet yarns and **f** twined linen. Ex 38:18
and scarlet yarns and **f** twined linen. Ex 38:23
and scarlet yarns, and **f** twined linen. Ex 39:2
scarlet yarns, and into the **f** twined linen, Ex 39:3
and scarlet yarns, and **f** twined linen, Ex 39:5
and scarlet yarns, and **f** twined linen. Ex 39:8
and scarlet yarns and **f** twined linen. Ex 39:24
also made the coats, woven of **f** linen, Ex 39:27
and the turban of **f** linen, and the caps Ex 39:28
of fine linen, and the caps of **f** linen, Ex 39:28
linen undergarments of **f** twined linen, Ex 39:28
and the sash of **f** twined linen and of Ex 39:29
to the LORD, his offering shall be of **f** flour. Lv 2:1
from it a handful of the **f** flour and oil, Lv 2:2
unleavened loaves of **f** flour mixed with Lv 2:4
a griddle, it shall be of **f** flour unleavened, Lv 2:5
a pan, it shall be made of **f** flour with oil. Lv 2:7
tenth of an ephah of **f** flour for a sin Lv 5:11
it a handful of the **f** flour of the grain Lv 6:15
tenth of an ephah of **f** flour as a regular Lv 6:20
and loaves of **f** flour well mixed with oil. Lv 7:12
of an ephah of **f** flour mixed with oil, Lv 14:10
of an ephah of **f** flour mixed with oil Lv 14:21
of an ephah of **f** flour mixed with oil, Lv 23:13
They shall be of **f** flour, and they shall Lv 23:17
"You shall take **f** flour and bake twelve Lv 24:5
bread, loaves of **f** flour mixed with oil, Nm 6:15
of them full of **f** flour mixed with oil Nm 7:13
of them full of **f** flour mixed with oil Nm 7:19
of them full of **f** flour mixed with oil Nm 7:25
of them full of **f** flour mixed with oil Nm 7:31
of them full of **f** flour mixed with oil Nm 7:37
of them full of **f** flour mixed with oil Nm 7:43
of them full of **f** flour mixed with oil Nm 7:49
of them full of **f** flour mixed with oil Nm 7:55
of them full of **f** flour mixed with oil Nm 7:61
of them full of **f** flour mixed with oil Nm 7:67
of them full of **f** flour mixed with oil Nm 7:73
of them full of **f** flour mixed with oil Nm 7:79
its grain offering of **f** flour mixed with Nm 8:8
of a tenth of an ephah of **f** flour, Nm 15:4
of an ephah of **f** flour mixed with a Nm 15:6
of three tenths of an ephah of **f** flour, Nm 15:9
tenth of an ephah of **f** flour for a grain Nm 28:5
tenths of an ephah of **f** flour for a grain Nm 28:9
of an ephah of **f** flour for a grain Nm 28:12
and two tenths of **f** flour for a grain Nm 28:12
and a tenth of **f** flour mixed with oil as Nm 28:13

grain offering of **f** flour mixed with Nm 28:20
grain offering of **f** flour mixed with Nm 28:28
grain offering of **f** flour mixed with Nm 29:3
offering shall be of **f** flour mixed with Nm 29:9
grain offering of **f** flour mixed with Nm 29:14
it very small, until it was as **f** as dust. Dt 9:21
and they shall **f** him a hundred shekels Dt 22:19
I beat them **f** as the dust of the earth; 2 Sm 22:43
was thirty cors of **f** flour and sixty 1 Kgs 4:22
this time a seah of **f** flour shall be sold 2 Kgs 7:1
So a seah of **f** flour was sold for a 2 Kgs 7:16
and a seah of **f** flour for a shekel, 2 Kgs 7:18
the holy utensils, also over the **f** flour, 1 Chr 9:29
was clothed with a robe of **f** linen, 1 Chr 15:27
and crimson fabrics and **f** linen, 2 Chr 2:14
and covered it with **f** gold and made 2 Chr 3:5
He overlaid it with 600 talents of **f** gold. 2 Chr 3:8
and crimson fabrics and **f** linen, 2 Chr 3:14
sons and kinsmen, arrayed in **f** linen, 2 Chr 5:12
and two vessels of **f** bright bronze as Ezr 8:27
fastened with cords of **f** linen and purple Est 1:6
crown and a robe of **f** linen and purple, Est 8:15
can it be exchanged for jewels of **f** gold. Jb 28:17
my trust or called **f** gold my confidence, Jb 31:24
I beat them **f** as dust before the wind; I Ps 18:42
are they than gold, even much **f** gold; Ps 19:10
you set a crown of **f** gold upon his head. Ps 21:3
above gold, above **f** gold. Ps 119:127
My fruit is better than gold, even **f** gold, Prv 8:19
F speech is not becoming to a fool; still Prv 17:7
To impose a **f** on a righteous man is Prv 17:26
her clothing is **f** linen and purple. Prv 31:22
I will make people more rare than **f** gold, Is 13:12
abundant food and **f** clothing for those Is 23:18
he takes up the coastlands like **f** dust. Is 40:15
of Zion, worth their weight in **f** gold, Lam 4:2
cloth and shod you with **f** leather. Ezk 16:10
I wrapped you in **f** linen and covered Ezk 16:10
your clothing was of **f** linen and silk Ezk 16:13
You ate **f** flour and honey and oil. Ezk 16:13
—I fed you with **f** flour and oil and Ezk 16:19
Of **f** embroidered linen from Egypt was Ezk 27:7
purple, embroidered work, **f** linen, Ezk 27:16
The head of this image was of **f** gold, its Dn 2:32
with a belt of **f** gold from Uphaz around Dn 10:5
and **f** gold like the mud of the streets. Zec 9:3
is like a merchant in search of **f** pearls, Mt 13:45
"You have a **f** way of rejecting the Mk 7:9
clothed in purple and **f** linen and who Lk 16:19
a gold ring and **f** clothing comes into Jas 2:2
the one who wears the **f** clothing and say, Jas 2:3
of gold, silver, jewels, pearls, **f** linen, Rv 18:12
myrrh, frankincense, wine, oil, **f** flour, Rv 18:13
great city that was clothed in **f** linen, Rv 18:16
granted her to clothe herself with **f** linen, Rv 19:8
pure"—for the **f** linen is the righteous Rv 19:8
the armies of heaven, arrayed in **f** linen, Rv 19:14

FINED (2)
the one who hit her shall surely be **f**, Ex 21:22
drink the wine of those who have been **f**. Am 2:8

FINELY (4)
and the **f** worked garments, the holy Ex 31:10
the **f** worked garments for ministering Ex 35:19
yarns they made **f** woven garments, Ex 39:1
the **f** worked garments for ministering Ex 39:41

FINERY (1)
Lord will take away the **f** of the anklets, Is 3:18

FINEST (9)
"Take the **f** spices: of liquid myrrh 500 Ex 30:23
and all your **f** vow offerings that you Dt 12:11
with the very **f** of the wheat—and you Dt 32:14
with the **f** produce of the ancient Dt 33:15
and overlaid it with the **f** gold. 1 Kgs 10:18
would feed you with the **f** of the wheat, Ps 81:16
he fills you with the **f** of the wheat. Ps 147:14
His head is the **f** gold; his locks are wavy, Sg 5:11
and anoint themselves with the **f** oils, Am 6:6

FINGER (28)
"This is the **f** of God." But Pharaoh's Ex 8:19
it on the horns of the altar with your **f**, Ex 29:12
of stone, written with the **f** of God. Ex 31:18
the priest shall dip his **f** in the blood and Lv 4:6
the priest shall dip his **f** in the blood and Lv 4:17
the sin offering with his **f** and put it on Lv 4:25
of its blood with his **f** and put it on the Lv 4:30
the sin offering with his **f** and put it on Lv 4:34
and with his **f** put it on the horns of the Lv 8:15
and he dipped his **f** in the blood and put it Lv 9:9
and dip his right **f** in the oil that is in Lv 14:16
some oil with his **f** seven times before Lv 14:16
sprinkle with his right **f** some of the oil Lv 14:27
and sprinkle it with his **f** on the front of Lv 16:14
of the blood with his **f** seven times. Lv 16:14
of the blood on it with his **f** seven times, Lv 16:19
shall take some of its blood with his **f**, Nm 19:4
tablets of stone written with the **f** of God, Dt 9:10
'My little **f** is thicker than my 1 Kgs 12:10
'My little **f** is thicker than my 2 Chr 10:10
signals with his feet, points with his **f**, Prv 6:13
from your midst, the pointing of the **f**, Is 58:9
not willing to move them with their **f**. Mt 23:4
But if it is by the **f** of God that I cast out Lk 11:20
dip the end of his **f** in water and cool Lk 16:24
down and wrote with his **f** on the ground. Jn 8:6
and place my **f** into the mark of the Jn 20:25
he said to Thomas, "Put your **f** here, Jn 20:27

FINGERS (14)
stature, who had six **f** on each hand, 2 Sm 21:20
hollow, and its thickness was four **f**. 1 Kgs 7:15
who had six **f** on each hand and six 1 Chr 20:6
I look at your heavens, the work of your **f**, Ps 8:3
my hands for war, and my **f** for battle; Ps 144:1
bind them on your **f**; write them on the Prv 7:3
with myrrh, my **f** with liquid myrrh, Sg 5:5
hands, to what their own **f** have made. Is 2:8
not look on what his own **f** have made, Is 17:8
with blood and your **f** with iniquity; Is 59:3
cubits, and its thickness was four **f**, Jer 52:21
Immediately the **f** of a human hand Dn 5:5
privately, he put his **f** into his ears, Mk 7:33
touch the burdens with one of your **f**. Lk 11:46

FINISH (12)
roof for the ark, and **f** it to a cubit above, Gn 6:16
began to count, but did not **f**. 1 Chr 27:24
build this house and to **f** this structure?" Ezr 5:3
build this house and to **f** this structure?' Ezr 5:9
they sacrifice? Will they **f** up in a day? Neh 4:2
When you **f** reading this book, tie a Jer 51:63
your holy city, to **f** the transgression, Dn 9:24
and the third day I **f** my course. Lk 13:32
laid a foundation and is not able to **f**, Lk 14:29
began to build and was not able to **f**.' Lk 14:30
if only I may **f** my course and the Acts 20:24
So now **f** doing it as well, so that your 2 Cor 8:11

FINISHED (105)
Thus the heavens and the earth were **f**, Gn 2:1
on the seventh day God **f** his work that he Gn 2:2
When he had **f** talking with him, God Gn 17:22
when he had **f** speaking to Abraham, Gn 18:33
Before he had **f** speaking, behold, Gn 24:15
When she had **f** giving him a drink, Gn 24:19
also, until they have **f** drinking." Gn 24:19
When the camels had **f** drinking, the Gn 24:22
"Before I had **f** speaking in my heart, Gn 24:45
As soon as Isaac had **f** blessing Jacob, Gn 27:30
When Jacob **f** commanding his sons, Gn 49:33
when he had **f** speaking with him on Ex 31:18
when Moses had **f** speaking with them, Ex 34:33
tabernacle of the tent of meeting was **f**, Ex 39:32
gate of the court. So Moses **f** the work. Ex 40:33
his sons have **f** covering the sanctuary Nm 4:15
day when Moses had **f** setting up the Nm 7:1
soon as he had **f** speaking all these Nm 16:31
when the officers have **f** speaking to the Dt 20:9
"When you have **f** paying all the tithe Dt 26:12
When Moses had **f** writing the words of Dt 31:24
the words of this song until they were **f**, Dt 31:30
when Moses had **f** speaking all these Dt 32:45
until all the nation **f** passing over the Jos 3:17
all the nation had **f** passing over the Jos 4:1
until everything was **f** that the LORD Jos 4:10
when all the people had **f** passing over, Jos 4:11
circumcising of the whole nation was **f**, Jos 5:8
When Israel had **f** killing all the Jos 8:24
sons of Israel had **f** striking them with Jos 10:20
When they had **f** distributing the Jos 19:49
of meeting. So they **f** dividing the land. Jos 19:51
when Ehud had **f** presenting the tribute, Jgs 3:18
As soon as he had **f** speaking, he threw Jgs 15:17
men until they have **f** all my harvest.'" Ru 2:21
man until he has **f** eating and drinking. Ru 3:3
When he had **f** prophesying, he 1 Sm 10:13
soon as he had **f** offering the burnt 1 Sm 13:10
As soon as he had **f** speaking to Saul, 1 Sm 18:1
as David had **f** speaking these words 1 Sm 24:16
when David had **f** offering the burnt 2 Sm 6:18
"When you have **f** telling all the 2 Sm 11:19
And as soon as he had **f** speaking, 2 Sm 13:36
with him heard it as they **f** feasting. 1 Kgs 1:41
David until he had **f** building his own 1 Kgs 3:1
So he built the house and **f** it, and he 1 Kgs 6:9
So Solomon built the house and **f** it. 1 Kgs 6:14
with gold, until all the house was **f**. 1 Kgs 6:22
the house was **f** in all its parts, 1 Kgs 6:38
years, and he **f** his entire house. 1 Kgs 7:1
It was **f** with cedar from floor to rafters. 1 Kgs 7:7
Thus the work of the pillars was **f**. 1 Kgs 7:22
So Hiram **f** all the work that he did 1 Kgs 7:40
did on the house of the LORD was **f**. 1 Kgs 7:51
Now as Solomon **f** offering all this 1 Kgs 8:54
as Solomon had **f** building the house 1 Kgs 9:1
it before the LORD. So he **f** the house. 1 Kgs 9:25
when David had **f** offering the burnt 1 Chr 16:2
service of the house of the LORD is **f**. 1 Chr 28:20
So Hiram **f** the work that he did for 2 Chr 4:11
did for the house of the LORD was **f**. 2 Chr 5:1
As soon as Solomon **f** his prayer, fire 2 Chr 7:1
Thus Solomon **f** the house of the 2 Chr 7:11
of the LORD was laid until it was **f**. 2 Chr 8:16
it into the chest until they had **f**. 2 Chr 24:10
And when they had **f**, they brought 2 Chr 24:14
day of the first month they **f**. 2 Chr 29:17
until the burnt offering was **f**. 2 Chr 29:28
When the offering was **f**, the king 2 Chr 29:29
until the work was **f**—for the 2 Chr 29:34
Now when all this was **f**, all Israel 2 Chr 31:1
and **f** them in the seventh month. 2 Chr 31:7
that if this city is rebuilt and the walls **f**, Ezr 4:13
that if this city is rebuilt and its walls **f**, Ezr 4:16
which a great king of Israel built and **f**. Ezr 5:11
has been in building, and it is not yet **f**.' Ezr 5:16
They **f** their building by decree of the Ezr 6:14
and this house was **f** on the third day of Ezr 6:15
So the wall was **f** on the twenty-fifth Neh 6:15
When the Lord has **f** all his work on Is 10:12
and when you have **f** betraying, they will Is 33:1
when Jeremiah had **f** speaking all that Jer 26:8
When Jeremiah **f** speaking to all the Jer 43:1
when he had **f** measuring the interior Ezk 42:15
When you have **f** purifying it, you Ezk 43:23
to an end all these things would be **f**. Dn 12:7
When they had **f** eating the grass of the Am 7:2
And when Jesus **f** these sayings, the Mt 7:28
When Jesus had **f** instructing his twelve Mt 11:1
And when Jesus had **f** these parables, Mt 13:53
Now when Jesus had **f** these sayings, he Mt 19:1
When Jesus had **f** all these sayings, he Mt 26:1
And when he had **f** speaking, he said to Lk 5:4
After he had **f** all his sayings in the Lk 7:1
in a certain place, and when he **f**, Lk 11:1
this, Jesus, knowing that all was now **f**, Jn 19:28
"It is **f**," and he bowed his head and gave Jn 19:30
When they had **f** breakfast, Jesus said to Jn 21:15
After they **f** speaking, James replied, Acts 15:13
When we had **f** the voyage from Tyre, Acts 21:7
fought the good fight, I have **f** the race, 2 Tm 4:7
his works were **f** from the foundation Heb 4:3
And when they have **f** their testimony, Rv 11:7
last, for with them the wrath of God is **f**. Rv 15:1
seven plagues of the seven angels were **f**. Rv 15:8

FINISHING (2)
They are **f** the walls and repairing the Ezr 4:12
And as John was **f** his course, he said, Acts 13:25

FINS (5)
in the waters that has **f** and scales, Lv 11:9
or the rivers that has not **f** and scales, Lv 11:10
waters that has not **f** and scales is Lv 11:12
whatever has **f** and scales you may eat. Dt 14:9
whatever does not have **f** and scales you Dt 14:10

FIR (3)
the stork has her home in the **f** trees. Ps 104:17
all your planks of **f** trees from Senir; Ezk 27:5
rival it, nor the **f** trees equal its boughs; Ezk 31:8

FIRE (465)
a smoking **f** pot and a flaming torch Gn 15:17
Gomorrah sulfur and **f** from the LORD Gn 19:24
he took in his hand the **f** and the knife. Gn 22:6
He said, "Behold, the **f** and the wood, Gn 22:7
to him in a flame of **f** out of the midst of a Ex 3:2
and hail, and **f** ran down to the earth. Ex 9:23
was hail and **f** flashing continually in Ex 9:24
eat the flesh that night, roasted on the **f**; Ex 12:8
night in a pillar of **f** to give them light, Ex 13:21
day and the pillar of **f** by night did not Ex 13:22
in the pillar of **f** and of cloud looked Ex 14:24
the LORD had descended on it in **f**. Ex 19:18
"If **f** breaks out and catches in thorns so Ex 22:6
he who started the **f** shall make full Ex 22:6
was like a devouring **f** on the top of Ex 24:17
shovels and basins and forks and **f** pans. Ex 27:3
you shall burn with **f** outside the camp; Ex 29:14
you shall burn the remainder with **f**. Ex 29:34
and burned it with **f** and ground it to Ex 32:20
gave it to me, and I threw it into the **f**, Ex 32:24
You shall kindle no **f** in all your Ex 35:3
the basins, the forks, and the **f** pans. Ex 38:3
by day, and **f** was in it by night, Ex 40:38
the priest shall put **f** on the altar and Lv 1:7
on the altar and arrange wood on the **f**. Lv 1:7
on the wood that is on the **f** on the altar; Lv 1:8

on the wood that is on the **f** on the altar, Lv 1:12
on the altar, on the wood that is on the **f**. Lv 1:17
your firstfruits fresh ears, roasted with **f**, Lv 2:14
offering, which is on the wood on the **f**; Lv 3:5
heap, and shall burn it up on a **f** of wood. Lv 4:12
and the **f** of the altar shall be kept Lv 6:9
ashes to which the **f** has reduced the Lv 6:10
The **f** on the altar shall be kept burning Lv 6:12
F shall be kept burning on the altar Lv 6:13
Holy Place; it shall be burned up with **f**. Lv 6:30
the third day shall be burned up with **f**. Lv 7:17
not be eaten. It shall be burned up with **f**. Lv 7:19
he burned up with **f** outside the camp, Lv 8:17
and the bread you shall burn up with **f**. Lv 8:32
he burned up with **f** outside the camp. Lv 9:11
And **f** came out from before the LORD Lv 9:24
took his censer and put **f** in it and laid Lv 10:1
and offered unauthorized **f** before the Lv 10:1
And **f** came out from before the LORD Lv 10:2
disease. It shall be burned in the **f**. Lv 13:52
You shall burn it in the **f**, whether the Lv 13:55
You shall burn with **f** whatever has the Lv 13:57
full of coals of **f** from the altar before Lv 16:12
put the incense on the **f** before the LORD, Lv 16:13
their dung shall be burned up with **f**. Lv 16:27
the third day shall be burned up with **f**. Lv 19:6
he and they shall be burned with **f**, that Lv 20:14
her father; she shall be burned with **f**. Lv 21:9
they offered unauthorized **f** before the Nm 3:4
are used for the service there, the **f** pans, Nm 4:14
and put it on the **f** that is under the Nm 6:18
like the appearance of **f** until morning. Nm 9:15
day and the appearance of **f** by night. Nm 9:16
and the **f** of the LORD burned among Nm 11:1
prayed to the LORD, and the **f** died down. Nm 11:2
because the **f** of the LORD burned Nm 11:3
by day and in a pillar of **f** by night. Nm 14:14
put **f** in them and put incense on them Nm 16:7
his censer and put **f** in them and laid Nm 16:18
And **f** came out from the LORD and Nm 16:35
blaze. Then scatter the **f** far and wide, Nm 16:37
and put **f** on it from off the altar and Nm 16:46
most holy things, reserved from the **f**: Nm 18:9
them into the **f** burning the heifer. Nm 19:6
For **f** came out from Heshbon, flame Nm 21:28
Nophah; **f** spread as far as Medeba." Nm 21:30
died, when the **f** devoured 250 men, Nm 26:10
they offered unauthorized **f** before the Nm 26:61
encampments, they burned with **f**, Nm 31:10
everything that can stand the **f**, you Nm 31:23
the fire, you shall pass through the **f**, Nm 31:23
And whatever cannot stand the **f**, you Nm 31:23
in **f** by night and in the cloud by day, Dt 1:33
the mountain burned with **f** to the heart Dt 4:11
spoke to you out of the midst of the **f**. Dt 4:12
to you at Horeb out of the midst of the **f**, Dt 4:15
For the LORD your God is a consuming **f**, Dt 4:24
a god speaking out of the midst of the **f**, Dt 4:33
And on earth he let you see his great **f**, Dt 4:36
heard his words out of the midst of the **f**. Dt 4:36
at the mountain, out of the midst of the **f**, Dt 5:4
For you were afraid because of the **f**, and Dt 5:5
at the mountain out of the midst of the **f**, Dt 5:22
while the mountain was burning with **f**, Dt 5:23
heard his voice out of the midst of the **f**. Dt 5:24
we die? For this great **f** will consume us. Dt 5:25
speaking out of the midst of **f** as we have, Dt 5:26
and burn their carved images with **f**. Dt 7:5
of their gods you shall burn with **f**. Dt 7:25
you as a consuming **f** is the LORD your Dt 9:3
out of the midst of the **f** on the day of the Dt 9:10
and the mountain was burning with **f**. Dt 9:15
and burned it with **f** and crushed it, Dt 9:21
out of the midst of the **f** on the day of the Dt 10:4
pillars and burn their Asherim with **f**. Dt 12:3
their daughters in the **f** to their gods. Dt 12:31
burn the city and all its spoil with **f**, Dt 13:16
my God or see this great **f** any more, Dt 18:16
For a **f** is kindled by my anger, and it Dt 32:22
and sets on **f** the foundations of the Dt 32:22
ones, with flaming **f** at his right hand. Dt 33:2
And they burned the city with **f**, and Jos 6:24
devoted things shall be burned with **f**, Jos 7:15
burned them with **f** and stoned them Jos 7:25
taken the city, you shall set the city on **f**. Jos 8:8
it. And they hurried to set the city on **f**. Jos 8:19
horses and burn their chariots with **f**." Jos 11:6
horses and burned their chariots with **f**. Jos 11:9
breathed. And he burned Hazor with **f**. Jos 11:11
The offerings by **f** to the LORD God of Jos 13:14
the edge of the sword and set the city on **f**. Jgs 1:8
And **f** sprang up from the rock and Jgs 6:21
let **f** come out of the bramble and Jgs 9:15
let **f** come out from Abimelech and Jgs 9:20
and let **f** come out from the leaders of Jgs 9:20

they set the stronghold on **f** over them, Jgs 9:49
to the door of the tower to burn it with **f**. Jgs 9:52
will burn your house over you with **f**." Jgs 12:1
you and your father's house with **f**. Jgs 14:15
And when he had set **f** to the torches, he Jgs 15:5
the Philistines and set **f** to the stacked Jgs 15:5
up and burned her and her father with **f**. Jgs 15:6
arms became as flax that has caught **f**, Jgs 15:14
of flax snaps when it touches the **f**. Jgs 16:9
of the sword and burned the city with **f**. Jgs 18:27
the towns that they found they set on **f**. Jgs 20:48
all my offerings by **f** from the people 1 Sm 2:28
overcome Ziklag and burned it with **f** 1 Sm 30:1
the city, they found it burned with **f**, 1 Sm 30:3
Caleb, and we burned Ziklag with **f**." 1 Sm 30:14
set it on **f**." So Absalom's servants 2 Sm 14:30
Absalom's servants set the field on **f**. 2 Sm 14:30
your servants set my field on **f**?" 2 Sm 14:31
and devouring **f** from his mouth; 2 Sm 22:9
before him coals of **f** flamed forth. 2 Sm 22:13
they are utterly consumed with **f**." 2 Sm 23:7
basins, dishes for incense, and **f** pans, 1 Kgs 7:50
captured Gezer and burned it with **f**, 1 Kgs 9:16
house over him with **f** and died, 1 Kgs 16:18
lay it on the wood, but put no **f** to it. 1 Kgs 18:23
lay it on the wood and put no **f** to it. 1 Kgs 18:23
LORD, and the God who answers by **f**, 1 Kgs 18:24
name of your god, but put no **f** to it." 1 Kgs 18:25
Then the **f** of the LORD fell and 1 Kgs 18:38
And after the earthquake a **f**, but the 1 Kgs 19:12
a fire, but the LORD was not in the **f**. 1 Kgs 19:12
And after the **f** the sound of a low 1 Kgs 19:12
let **f** come down from heaven and 2 Kgs 1:10
your fifty." Then **f** came down from 2 Kgs 1:10
let **f** come down from heaven and 2 Kgs 1:12
your fifty." Then the **f** of God came 2 Kgs 1:12
f came down from heaven and 2 Kgs 1:14
chariots of **f** and horses of fire 2 Kgs 2:11
fire and horses of **f** separated the two 2 Kgs 2:11
and chariots of **f** all around Elisha. 2 Kgs 6:17
You will set on **f** their fortresses, and 2 Kgs 8:12
children in the **f** to Adrammelech 2 Kgs 17:31
and have cast their gods into the **f**, 2 Kgs 19:18
the chariots of the sun with **f**. 2 Kgs 23:11
the **f** pans also and the bowls. What 2 Kgs 25:15
answered him with **f** from heaven 1 Chr 21:26
basins, dishes for incense, and **f** pans, 2 Chr 4:22
f came down from heaven and 2 Chr 7:1
of Israel saw the **f** come down and the 2 Chr 7:3
made a very great **f** in his honor. 2 Chr 16:14
His people made no **f** in his honor, 2 Chr 21:19
Passover lamb with **f** according to 2 Chr 35:13
its palaces with **f** and destroyed all 2 Chr 36:19
down, and its gates are destroyed by **f**." Neh 1:3
and its gates have been destroyed by **f**?" Neh 2:3
its gates that had been destroyed by **f**. Neh 2:13
and by a pillar of **f** in the night to light Neh 9:12
nor the pillar of **f** by night to light for Neh 9:19
"The **f** of God fell from heaven and Jb 1:16
and **f** consumes the tents of bribery. Jb 15:34
out, and the flame of his **f** does not shine. Jb 18:5
a **f** not fanned will devour him; Jb 20:26
and what they left the **f** has consumed.' Jb 22:20
but underneath it is turned up as by **f**. Jb 28:5
that would be a **f** that consumes as far Jb 31:12
flaming torches; sparks of **f** leap forth. Jb 41:19
f and sulfur and a scorching wind shall Ps 11:6
and devouring **f** from his mouth; Ps 18:8
and coals of **f** broke through his Ps 18:12
his voice, hailstones and coals of **f**. Ps 18:13
in his wrath, and **f** will consume them. Ps 21:9
voice of the LORD flashes forth flames of **f**. Ps 29:7
As I mused, the **f** burned; then I spoke Ps 39:3
the spear; he burns the chariots with **f**. Ps 46:9
before him is a devouring **f**, around him Ps 50:3
we went through **f** and through water; Ps 66:12
as wax melts before **f**, so the wicked shall Ps 68:2
They set your sanctuary on **f**; they Ps 74:7
of wrath; a **f** was kindled against Jacob; Ps 78:21
F devoured their young men, and their Ps 78:63
forever? Will your jealousy burn like **f**? Ps 79:5
They have burned it with **f**; they have Ps 80:16
As **f** consumes the forest, as the flame Ps 83:14
How long will your wrath burn like **f**? Ps 89:46
F goes before him and burns up his Ps 97:3
winds, his ministers a flaming **f**. Ps 104:4
a covering, and **f** to give light by night. Ps 105:39
F also broke out in their company; the Ps 106:18
they went out like a **f** among thorns; Ps 118:12
Let them be cast into **f**, into miry pits, Ps 140:10
f and hail, snow and mist, stormy wind Ps 148:8
Can a man carry **f** next to his chest and Prv 6:27
and his speech is like a scorching **f**. Prv 16:27
For lack of wood the **f** goes out, and Prv 26:20
charcoal to hot embers and wood to **f**, Prv 26:21

with water, and the **f** that never says, Prv 30:16
Its flashes are flashes of **f**, the very flame of Sg 8:6
lies desolate; your cities are burned with **f**; Is 1:7
and the shining of a flaming **f** by night; Is 4:5
as the tongue of **f** devours the stubble, Is 5:24
in blood will be burned as fuel for the **f**. Is 9:5
For wickedness burns like a **f**; it Is 9:18
and the people are like fuel for the **f**; Is 9:19
will be kindled, like the burning of **f**. Is 10:16
The light of Israel will become a **f**, and Is 10:17
Let the **f** for your adversaries consume Is 26:11
women come and make a **f** of them. Is 27:11
tempest, and the flame of a devouring **f**. Is 29:6
with which to take **f** from the hearth, Is 30:14
and his tongue is like a devouring **f**; Is 30:27
anger and a flame of devouring **f**, Is 30:30
wide, with **f** and wood in abundance; Is 30:33
declares the LORD, whose **f** is in Zion, Is 31:9
your breath is a **f** that will consume Is 33:11
cut down, that are burned in the **f**." Is 33:12
us can dwell with the consuming **f**? Is 33:14
and have cast their gods into the **f**. For Is 37:19
it set him on **f** all around, but he did not Is 42:25
when you walk through **f** you shall not Is 43:2
himself; he kindles a **f** and bakes bread. Is 44:15
Half of it he burns in the **f**. Over the half Is 44:16
"Aha, I am warm, I have seen the **f**!" Is 44:16
to say, "Half of it I burned in the **f**; Is 44:19
are like stubble; the **f** consumes them; Is 47:14
oneself is this, no **f** to sit before! Is 47:14
Behold, all you who kindle a **f**, who Is 50:11
Walk by the light of your **f**, and by the Is 50:11
smith who blows the **f** of coals and Is 54:16
as when **f** kindles brushwood and the fire Is 64:2
brushwood and the **f** causes water to Is 64:2
praised you, has been burned by **f**, Is 64:11
in my nostrils, a **f** that burns all the day. Is 65:5
"For behold, the LORD will come in **f**, and Is 66:15
in fury, and his rebuke with flames of **f**. Is 66:15
For by **f** will the LORD enter into Is 66:16
not die, their **f** shall not be quenched, Is 66:24
lest my wrath go forth like **f**, and burn Jer 4:4
making my words in your mouth a **f**, Jer 5:14
wood, and the **f** shall consume them. Jer 5:14
fiercely; the lead is consumed by the **f**; Jer 6:29
gather wood, the fathers kindle **f**, Jer 7:18
their sons and their daughters in the **f**, Jer 7:31
roar of a great tempest he will set **f** to it, Jer 11:16
for in my anger a **f** is kindled that shall Jer 15:14
for in my anger a **f** is kindled that shall Jer 17:4
day, then I will kindle a **f** in its gates, Jer 17:27
their sons in the **f** as burnt offerings to Jer 19:5
as it were a burning **f** shut up in my Jer 20:9
of Babylon, and he shall burn it with **f**.' Jer 21:10
robbed, lest my wrath go forth like **f**, Jer 21:12
I will kindle a **f** in her forest, and it Jer 21:14
choicest cedars and cast them into the **f**. Jer 22:7
Is not my word like **f**, declares the LORD, Jer 23:29
the king of Babylon roasted in the **f**," Jer 29:22
come and set this city on **f** and burn it, Jer 32:29
of Babylon, and he shall burn it with **f**. Jer 34:2
against it and take it and burn it with **f**. Jer 34:22
and there was a **f** burning in the fire pot Jer 36:22
a fire burning in the **f** pot before him. Jer 36:22
throw them into the **f** in the fire pot, Jer 36:23
throw them into the fire in the **f** pot, Jer 36:23
was consumed in the **f** that was in the Jer 36:23
in the fire that was in the **f** pot. Jer 36:23
king of Judah had burned in the **f**. Jer 36:32
They shall capture it and burn it with **f**. Jer 37:8
rise up and burn this city with **f**.'" Jer 37:10
and this city shall not be burned with **f**, Jer 38:17
and they shall burn it with **f**, Jer 38:18
and this city shall be burned with **f**." Jer 38:23
I shall kindle a **f** in the temples of the Jer 43:12
the gods of Egypt he shall burn with **f**.'" Jer 43:13
strength, for **f** came out from Heshbon, Jer 48:45
and its villages shall be burned with **f**; Jer 49:2
And I will kindle a **f** in the wall of Jer 49:27
up, and I will kindle a **f** in his cities, Jer 50:32
become women; her dwellings are on **f**; Jer 51:30
seized, the marshes are burned with **f**, Jer 51:32
her high gates shall be burned with **f**. Jer 51:58
nations weary themselves only for **f**." Jer 51:58
small bowls and the **f** pans and the Jer 52:19
"From on high he sent **f**; into my Lam 1:13
he has burned like a flaming **f** in Jacob, Lam 2:3
Zion; he has poured out his fury like **f**. Lam 2:4
and he kindled a **f** in Zion that Lam 4:11
it, and **f** flashing forth continually, Ezk 1:4
continually, and in the midst of the **f**, Ezk 1:4
appearance was like burning coals of **f**, Ezk 1:13
living creatures. And the **f** was bright, Ezk 1:13
and out of the **f** went forth lightning. Ezk 1:13
the appearance of **f** enclosed all around. Ezk 1:27

I saw as it were the appearance of **f**, Ezk 1:27
you shall burn in the **f** in the midst of Ezk 5:2
into the midst of the **f** and burn them in Ezk 5:4
midst of the fire and burn them in the **f**. Ezk 5:4
From there a **f** will come out into all the Ezk 5:4
what appeared to be his waist was **f**, Ezk 8:2
"Take **f** from between the whirling Ezk 10:6
the cherubim to the **f** that was between Ezk 10:7
Behold, it is given to the **f** for fuel. Ezk 15:4
When the **f** has consumed both ends of Ezk 15:4
when the **f** has consumed it and it is Ezk 15:5
which I have given to the **f** for fuel, Ezk 15:6
Though they escape from the **f**, the fire Ezk 15:7
the fire, the **f** shall yet consume them, Ezk 15:7
them up as an offering by **f** to them? Ezk 16:21
As for its strong stem, **f** consumed it. Ezk 19:12
And **f** has gone out from the stem of Ezk 19:14
gifts and offer up your children in **f**, Ezk 20:31
GOD, Behold, I will kindle a **f** in you, Ezk 20:47
blow upon you with the **f** of my wrath, Ezk 21:31
You shall be fuel for the **f**. Your blood Ezk 21:32
to blow the **f** on it in order to melt it, Ezk 22:20
blow on you with the **f** of my wrath, Ezk 22:21
them with the **f** of my wrath. Ezk 22:31
your survivors shall be devoured by **f**. Ezk 23:25
Heap on the logs, kindle the **f**, boil the Ezk 24:10
out of it. Into the **f** with its corrosion! Ezk 24:12
the midst of the stones of **f** you walked. Ezk 28:14
from the midst of the stones of **f**. Ezk 28:16
so I brought **f** out from your midst; Ezk 28:18
am the LORD, when I have set **f** to Egypt, Ezk 30:8
desolation and will set **f** to Zoan and Ezk 30:14
And I will set **f** to Egypt; Pelusium Ezk 30:16
rains and hailstones, **f** and sulfur. Ezk 38:22
I will send **f** on Magog and on those Ezk 39:6
the flame of the **f** killed those men who Dn 3:22
bound into the **f**?" They answered and Dn 3:24
unbound, walking in the midst of the **f**, Dn 3:25
and Abednego came out from the **f**. Dn 3:26
and saw that the **f** had not had any Dn 3:27
and no smell of **f** had come upon them. Dn 3:27
fiery flames; its wheels were burning **f**. Dn 7:9
A stream of **f** issued and came out from Dn 7:10
and given over to be burned with **f**. Dn 7:11
oven whose baker ceases to stir the **f**, Hos 7:4
in the morning it blazes like a flaming **f**. Hos 7:6
so I will send a **f** upon his cities, and it Hos 8:14
For **f** has devoured the pastures of the Jl 1:19
and **f** has devoured the pastures of the Jl 1:20
F devours before them, and behind them a Jl 2:3
of a flame of **f** devouring the stubble, Jl 2:5
earth, blood and **f** and columns of smoke. Jl 2:30
So I will send a **f** upon the house of Am 1:4
So I will send a **f** upon the wall of Gaza, Am 1:7
So I will send a **f** upon the wall of Tyre, Am 1:10
So I will send a **f** upon Teman, and it Am 1:12
So I will kindle a **f** in the wall of Am 1:14
So I will send a **f** upon Moab, and it shall Am 2:2
So I will send a **f** upon Judah, and it shall Am 2:5
lest he break out like **f** in the house of Am 5:6
GOD was calling for a judgment by **f**, Am 7:4
The house of Jacob shall be a **f**, and the Ob 1:18
will split open, like wax before the **f**, Mi 1:4
all her wages shall be burned with **f**, Mi 1:7
His wrath is poured out like **f**, and the Na 1:6
your enemies; **f** has devoured your bars. Na 3:13
There will the **f** devour you; the sword Na 3:15
of hosts that peoples labor merely for **f**, Hab 2:13
In the **f** of his jealousy, all the earth Zep 1:18
for in the **f** of my jealousy all the earth Zep 3:8
And I will be to her a wall of **f** all around, Zec 2:5
Is not this a brand plucked from the **f**?" Zec 3:2
the sea, and she shall be devoured by **f**. Zec 9:4
that the **f** may devour your cedars! Zec 11:1
And I will put this third into the **f**, and Zec 13:9
you might not kindle **f** on my altar in Mal 1:10
is like a refiner's **f** and like fullers' soap. Mal 3:2
fruit is cut down and thrown into the **f**. Mt 3:10
you with the Holy Spirit and with **f**. Mt 3:11
he will burn with unquenchable **f**." Mt 3:12
'You fool!' will be liable to the hell of **f**. Mt 5:22
fruit is cut down and thrown into the **f**. Mt 7:19
weeds are gathered and burned with **f**, Mt 13:40
For often he falls into the **f**, and often Mt 17:15
two feet to be thrown into the eternal **f**. Mt 18:8
two eyes to be thrown into the hell of **f**. Mt 18:9
into the eternal **f** prepared for the devil Mt 25:41
has often cast him into **f** and into water, Mk 9:22
to go to hell, to the unquenchable **f**. Mk 9:43
does not die and the **f** is not quenched.' Mk 9:48
For everyone will be salted with **f**. Mk 9:49
guards and warming himself at the **f**. Mk 14:54
fruit is cut down and thrown into the **f**." Lk 3:9
you with the Holy Spirit and with **f**. Lk 3:16
he will burn with unquenchable **f**." Lk 3:17
you want us to tell **f** to come down from Lk 9:54
"I came to cast **f** on the earth, and Lk 12:49
f and sulfur rained from heaven and Lk 17:29
they had kindled a **f** in the middle of Lk 22:55
branches are gathered, thrown into the **f**, Jn 15:6
and officers had made a charcoal **f**, Jn 18:18
on land, they saw a charcoal **f** in place, Jn 21:9
divided tongues as of **f** appeared to them Acts 2:3
signs on the earth below, blood, and **f**, Acts 2:19
Mount Sinai, in a flame of **f** in a bush. Acts 7:30
for they kindled a **f** and welcomed us Acts 28:2
bundle of sticks and put them on the **f**, Acts 28:3
the creature into the **f** and suffered no Acts 28:5
it, because it will be revealed by **f**, 1 Cor 3:13
and the **f** will test what sort of work 1 Cor 3:13
will be saved, but only as through **f**. 1 Cor 3:15
in flaming **f**, inflicting vengeance on 2 Thes 1:8
winds, and his ministers a flame of **f**." Heb 1:7
and a fury of **f** that will consume the Heb 10:27
quenched the power of **f**, escaped the Heb 11:34
a blazing **f** and darkness and gloom Heb 12:18
for our God is a consuming **f**. Heb 12:29
a forest is set ablaze by such a small **f**! Jas 3:5
And the tongue is a **f**, a world of Jas 3:6
body, setting on **f** the entire course of life, Jas 3:6
entire course of life, and set on **f** by hell. Jas 3:6
against you and will eat your flesh like **f**. Jas 5:3
though it is tested by **f**—may be found 1 Pt 1:7
earth that now exist are stored up for **f**, 2 Pt 3:7
heavens will be set on **f** and dissolved, 2 Pt 3:12
undergoing a punishment of eternal **f**. Jude 1:7
others by snatching them out of the **f**; Jude 1:23
as snow. His eyes were like a flame of **f**, Rv 1:14
of God, who has eyes like a flame of **f**, Rv 2:18
you to buy from me gold refined by **f**, Rv 3:18
throne were burning seven torches of **f**, Rv 4:5
and filled it with **f** from the altar and Rv 8:5
his trumpet, and there followed hail and **f**, Rv 8:7
like a great mountain, burning with **f**, Rv 8:8
the color of **f** and of sapphire Rv 9:17
and **f** and smoke and sulfur came out of Rv 9:17
by the **f** and smoke and sulfur coming Rv 9:18
like the sun, and his legs like pillars of **f**. Rv 10:1
f pours from their mouth and consumes Rv 11:5
even making **f** come down from Rv 13:13
will be tormented with **f** and sulfur in Rv 14:10
the angel who has authority over the **f**, Rv 14:18
of glass mingled with **f**—and also those Rv 15:2
it was allowed to scorch people with **f**. Rv 16:8
her flesh and burn her up with **f**, Rv 17:16
and she will be burned up with **f**; Rv 18:8
His eyes are like a flame of **f**, and on his Rv 19:12
into the lake of **f** that burns with Rv 19:20
but **f** came down from heaven and Rv 20:9
into the lake of **f** and sulfur where the Rv 20:10
Hades were thrown into the lake of **f**. Rv 20:14
This is the second death, the lake of **f**. Rv 20:14
of life, he was thrown into the lake of **f**. Rv 20:15
in the lake that burns with **f** and sulfur, Rv 21:8

FIREBRANDS (2)
Like a madman who throws **f**, arrows, Prv 26:18
of these two smoldering stumps of **f**, Is 7:4

FIRES (4)
like the **f** made for his fathers. 2 Chr 21:19
go out and make **f** of the weapons and Ezk 39:9
and they will make **f** of them for seven Ezk 39:9
they will make their **f** of the weapons. Ezk 39:10

FIRM (29)
said to the people, "Fear not, stand **f**, Ex 14:13
need to fight in this battle. Stand **f**, 2 Chr 20:17
this we make a **f** covenant in writing; Neh 9:38
and you have made **f** the feeble knees. Jb 4:4
to be; he commanded, and it stood **f**. Ps 33:9
and my covenant will stand **f** for him. Ps 89:28
news; his heart is **f**, trusting in the LORD. Ps 112:7
when he made **f** the skies above, when Prv 8:28
If you are not **f** in faith, you will not be Is 7:9
not firm in faith, you will not be **f** at all.'" Is 7:9
strong man. He will seize **f** hold on you Is 22:17
cannot hold the mast **f** in its place or Is 33:23
weak hands, and make **f** the feeble knees. Is 35:3
"Remember this and stand **f**, recall it to Is 46:8
to the Chaldeans, "The word from me is **f**: Dn 2:5
you see that the word from me is **f**— Dn 2:8
their God shall stand **f** and take action. Dn 11:32
Be watchful, stand **f** in the faith, act 1 Cor 16:13
your joy, for you stand **f** in your faith. 2 Cor 1:24
Christ has set us free; stand **f** therefore, Gal 5:1
evil day, and having done all, to stand **f**. Eph 6:13
that you are standing **f** in one spirit, Phil 1:27
joy and crown, stand **f** thus in the Lord, Phil 4:1
stand **f** and hold to the traditions 2 Thes 2:15
But God's **f** foundation stands, 2 Tm 2:19
He must hold **f** to the trustworthy word as Ti 1:9
our original confidence **f** to the end. Heb 3:14
Resist him, **f** in your faith, knowing that 1 Pt 5:9
is the true grace of God. Stand **f** in it. 1 Pt 5:12

FIRMLY (12)
of the LORD stood **f** on dry ground in Jos 3:17
very place where the priests' feet stood **f**, Jos 4:3
and his kingdom was **f** established. 1 Kgs 2:12
as the royal power was **f** in his hand, 2 Kgs 14:5
as soon as the royal power was **f** his, 2 Chr 25:3
the Jews **f** obligated themselves and their Est 9:27
together, **f** cast on him and immovable. Jb 41:23
your word is **f** fixed in the heavens. Ps 119:89
built as a city that is bound **f** together, Ps 122:3
and like nails **f** fixed are the collected Eccl 12:11
But whoever is **f** established in his 1 Cor 7:37
you have learned and have **f** believed, 2 Tm 3:14

FIRMNESS (2)
but some of the **f** of iron shall be in it, Dn 2:41
your good order and the **f** of your faith in Col 2:5

FIRST (374)
and there was morning, the **f** day. Gn 1:5
The name of the **f** is the Pishon. It is the Gn 2:11
tenth month, on the **f** day of the month, Gn 8:5
In the six hundred and **f** year, in the first Gn 8:13
hundred and first year, in the **f** month, Gn 8:13
the first month, the **f** day of the month, Gn 8:13
he was the **f** on earth to be a mighty Gn 10:8
where he had made an altar at the **f**. Gn 13:4
The **f** came out red, all his body like a Gn 25:25
the name of the city was Luz at the **f**. Gn 28:19
He instructed the **f**, "When Esau my Gn 32:17
hand, saying, "This one came out **f**." Gn 38:28
cows ate up the **f** seven plump cows, Gn 41:20
was replaced in our sacks the **f** time, Gn 43:18
we came down the **f** time to buy food. Gn 43:20
you," God said, "or listen to the **f** sign, Ex 4:8
It shall be the **f** month of the year for Ex 12:2
On the **f** day you shall remove leaven Ex 12:15
from the **f** day until the seventh day, Ex 12:15
On the **f** day you shall hold a holy Ex 12:16
In the **f** month, from the fourteenth day Ex 12:18
Whatever is the **f** to open the womb Ex 13:2
to the LORD all that **f** opens the womb. Ex 13:12
all the males that **f** open the womb, Ex 13:15
edge of the outermost curtain in the **f** set. Ex 26:4
but joined at the top, at the **f** ring. Ex 26:24
topaz, and carbuncle shall be the **f** row; Ex 28:17
And with the **f** lamb a tenth seah of fine Ex 29:40
for yourself two tablets of stone like the **f**, Ex 34:1
the words that were on the **f** tablets, Ex 34:1
Moses cut two tablets of stone like the **f**. Ex 34:4
of the outermost curtain of the **f** set. Ex 36:11
but joined at the top, at the **f** ring. Ex 36:29
topaz, and carbuncle was the **f** row; Ex 39:10
"On the **f** day of the first month you Ex 40:2
first day of the **f** month you shall erect Ex 40:2
In the **f** month in the second year, on Ex 40:17
second year, on the **f** day of the month, Ex 40:17
and burn it up as he burned the **f** bull; Lv 4:21
who shall offer **f** the one for the sin Lv 5:8
offered it as a sin offering, like the **f** one. Lv 9:15
In the **f** month, on the fourteenth day of Lv 23:5
On the **f** day you shall have a holy Lv 23:7
month, on the **f** day of the month, Lv 23:24
On the **f** day shall be a holy Lv 23:35
On the **f** day shall be a solemn rest, and Lv 23:39
you shall take on the **f** day the fruit of Lv 23:40
on the **f** day of the second month, Nm 1:1
and on the **f** day of the second month, Nm 1:18
They shall set out **f** on the march. Nm 2:9
his offering the **f** day was Nahshon Nm 7:12
in the **f** month of the second year after Nm 9:1
they kept the Passover in the **f** month, Nm 9:5
set out for the **f** time at the command Nm 10:13
of Judah set out **f** by their companies, Nm 10:14
was the season of the **f** ripe grapes. Nm 13:20
Of the **f** of your dough you shall Nm 15:20
Some of the **f** of your dough you shall Nm 15:21
The **f** ripe fruits of all that is in their Nm 18:13
the wilderness of Zin in the **f** month, Nm 20:1
"Amalek was the **f** among the Nm 24:20
fourteenth day of the **f** month is the Nm 28:16
On the **f** day there shall be a holy Nm 28:18
"On the **f** day of the seventh month you Nm 29:1
set out from Rameses in the **f** month, Nm 33:3
on the fifteenth day of the **f** month. Nm 33:3
Egypt, on the **f** day of the fifth month. Nm 33:38
year, on the **f** day of the eleventh month, Dt 1:3
for yourself two tablets of stone like the **f**, Dt 10:1
that were on the **f** tablets that you broke, Dt 10:2
and cut two tablets of stone like the **f**, Dt 10:3
stayed on the mountain, as at the **f** time, Dt 10:10
Your hand shall be **f** against him to put Dt 13:9
the evening of the **f** day remain all night Dt 16:4

the time the sickle is **f** put to the standing Dt 16:9
the witnesses shall be **f** against him to Dt 17:7
of your oil, and the **f** fleece of your sheep, Dt 18:4
And the **f** son whom she bears shall Dt 25:6
shall take some of the **f** of all the fruit of Dt 26:2
now I bring the **f** of the fruit of the Dt 26:10
Jordan on the tenth day of the **f** month, Jos 4:19
of the LORD had commanded at the **f**, Jos 8:33
of Levi; since the lot fell to them **f**. Jos 21:10
"Who shall go up **f** for us against the Jgs 1:1
the name of the city was Laish at the **f**. Jgs 18:29
"Who shall go up **f** for us to fight Jgs 20:18
the LORD said, "Judah shall go up **f**." Jgs 20:18
where they had formed it on the **f** day. Jgs 20:22
as at the **f**." But the people of Israel said, Jgs 20:32
defeated before us, as in the **f** battle." Jgs 20:39
kindness greater than the **f** in that you Ru 3:10
said to him, "Let them burn the fat **f**, 1 Sm 2:16
And that **f** strike, which Jonathan 1 Sm 14:14
it was the **f** altar that he built to the 1 Sm 14:35
Is today the **f** time that I have 1 Sm 22:15
my face unless you **f** bring Michal, 2 Sm 3:13
some of the people fall at the **f** attack, 2 Sm 17:9
the running of the **f** is like the 2 Sm 18:27
the **f** of all the house of Joseph to 2 Sm 19:20
Were we not the **f** to speak of 2 Sm 19:43
put to death in the **f** days of harvest, 2 Sm 21:9
Solomon swear to me **f** that he will 1 Kgs 1:51
the dead child is yours." The **f** said, 1 Kgs 3:22
"Give the living child to the **f** woman, 1 Kgs 3:27
But **f** make me a little cake of it and 1 Kgs 17:13
yourselves one bull and prepare it **f**, 1 Kgs 18:25
'All that you **f** demanded of your 1 Kgs 20:9
governors of the districts went out **f**. 1 Kgs 20:17
"Inquire **f** for the word of the LORD." 1 Kgs 22:5
He was the **f** on earth to be a mighty 1 Chr 1:10
of Kohathites, for theirs was the **f** lot, 1 Chr 6:54
Now the **f** to dwell again in their 1 Chr 9:2
strikes the Jebusites **f** shall be chief 1 Chr 11:6
Joab the son of Zeruiah went up **f**, 1 Chr 11:6
crossed the Jordan in the **f** month, 1 Chr 12:15
you did not carry it the **f** time, 1 Chr 15:13
that day David **f** appointed that 1 Chr 16:7
The **f** lot fell to Jehoiarib, the second 1 Chr 24:7
The **f** lot fell for Asaph to Joseph; the 1 Chr 25:9
in charge of the **f** division in the first 1 Chr 27:2
of the first division in the **f** month; 1 Chr 27:2
He served for the **f** month. 1 Chr 27:3
acts of King David, from **f** to last, 1 Chr 29:29
joined to the wing of the **f** cherub. 2 Chr 3:12
of the acts of Solomon, from **f** to last, 2 Chr 9:29
the acts of Rehoboam, from **f** to last, 2 Chr 12:15
The acts of Asa, from **f** to last, are 2 Chr 16:11
"Inquire **f** for the word of the LORD." 2 Chr 18:4
acts of Jehoshaphat, from **f** to last, 2 Chr 20:34
the deeds of Amaziah, from **f** to last, 2 Chr 25:26
of the acts of Uzziah, from **f** to last, 2 Chr 26:22
acts and all his ways, from **f** to last, 2 Chr 28:26
In the **f** year of his reign, in the first 2 Chr 29:3
first year of his reign, in the **f** month, 2 Chr 29:3
to consecrate on the **f** day of the first 2 Chr 29:17
on the first day of the **f** month, 2 Chr 29:17
day of the **f** month they finished. 2 Chr 29:17
on the fourteenth day of the **f** month. 2 Chr 35:1
and his acts, **f** and last, behold, they 2 Chr 35:27
Now in the **f** year of Cyrus king of 2 Chr 36:22
In the **f** year of Cyrus king of Persia, that Ezr 1:1
From the **f** day of the seventh month they Ezr 3:6
old men who had seen the **f** house, Ezr 3:12
in the **f** year of Cyrus king of Babylon, Ezr 5:13
In the **f** year of Cyrus the king, Cyrus the Ezr 6:3
On the fourteenth day of the **f** month, Ezr 6:19
For on the **f** day of the first month he Ezr 7:9
the first day of the **f** month he began to Ezr 7:9
and on the **f** day of the fifth month he Ezr 7:9
on the twelfth day of the **f** month, Ezr 8:31
On the **f** day of the tenth month they Ezr 10:16
and by the **f** day of the first month they Ezr 10:17
first day of the **f** month they had come Ezr 10:17
genealogy of those who came up at the **f**, Neh 7:5
on the **f** day of the seventh month. Neh 8:2
by day, from the **f** day to the last day, Neh 8:18
and to bring the **f** of our dough, and Neh 10:37
king's face, and sat **f** in the kingdom): Est 1:14
In the **f** month, which is the month of Est 3:7
on the thirteenth day of the **f** month, Est 3:12
"Are you the **f** man who was born? Or Jb 15:7
"He is the **f** of the works of God; let him Jb 40:19
Who has **f** given to me, that I should Jb 41:11
the name of the **f** daughter Jemimah, Jb 42:14
of his work, the **f** of his acts of old. Prv 8:22
Ages ago I was set up, at the **f**, before the Prv 8:23
its fields, or the **f** of the dust of the world. Prv 8:26
one who states his case **f** seems right, Prv 18:17
And I will restore your judges as at the **f**, Is 1:26

I, the LORD, the **f**, and with the last; I am Is 41:4
I was the **f** to say to Zion, "Behold, here Is 41:27
Your **f** father sinned, and your Is 43:27
of hosts: "I am the **f** and I am the last; Is 44:6
I am he; I am the **f**, and I am the last. Is 48:12
went down at the **f** into Egypt to sojourn Is 52:4
shall hope for me, the ships of Tarshish **f**, Is 60:9
as of one giving birth to her **f** child, Jer 4:31
where I made my name dwell at **f**, Jer 7:12
But **f** I will doubly repay their iniquity Jer 16:18
(that was the **f** year of Nebuchadnezzar Jer 25:1
Israel, and rebuild them as they were at **f**. Jer 33:7
restore the fortunes of the land as at **f**, Jer 33:11
former words that were in the **f** scroll, Jer 36:28
F the king of Assyria devoured him, Jer 50:17
the **f** face was the face of the cherub, Ezk 10:14
year, on the **f** day of the month, Ezk 26:1
twenty-seventh year, in the **f** month, Ezk 29:17
first month, on the **f** day of the month, Ezk 29:17
In the eleventh year, in the **f** month, Ezk 30:20
third month, on the **f** day of the month, Ezk 31:1
month, on the **f** day of the month, Ezk 32:1
of the same size as those of the **f** gate. Ezk 40:21
And the **f** of all the firstfruits of all Ezk 44:30
give to the priests the **f** of your dough, Ezk 44:30
In the **f** month, on the first day of the Ezk 45:18
first month, on the **f** day of the month, Ezk 45:18
"In the **f** month, on the fourteenth day Ezk 45:21
was there until the **f** year of King Cyrus. Dn 1:21
In the **f** year of Belshazzar king of Dn 7:1
The **f** was like a lion and had eagles' Dn 7:4
which three of the **f** horns were plucked Dn 7:8
after that which appeared to me at the **f**. Dn 8:1
great horn between his eyes is the **f** king. Dn 8:21
In the **f** year of Darius the son of Dn 9:1
in the **f** year of his reign, I, Daniel, Dn 9:2
whom I had seen in the vision at the **f**, Dn 9:21
the twenty-fourth day of the **f** month, Dn 10:4
for from the **f** day that you set your Dn 10:12
for me, in the **f** year of Darius the Mede, Dn 11:1
raise a multitude, greater than the **f**. Dn 11:13
When the LORD **f** spoke through Hosea, Hos 1:2
'I will go and return to my **f** husband, Hos 2:7
Like the **f** fruit on the fig tree in its first Hos 9:10
first fruit on the fig tree in its **f** season, Hos 9:10
the notable men of the **f** of the nations, Am 6:1
they shall now be the **f** of those who go Am 6:7
sixth month, on the **f** day of the month, Hg 1:1
The **f** chariot had red horses, the second Zec 6:2
give salvation to the tents of Judah **f**, Zec 12:7
F be reconciled to your brother, and Mt 5:24
But seek **f** the kingdom of God and his Mt 6:33
f take the log out of your own eye, Mt 7:5
"Lord, let me **f** go and bury my father." Mt 8:21
f, Simon, who is called Peter, and Mt 10:2
unless he **f** binds the strong man? Mt 12:29
state of that person is worse than the **f**. Mt 12:45
Gather the weeds **f** and bind them in Mt 13:30
scribes say that **f** Elijah must come?" Mt 17:10
into the house, Jesus spoke to him **f**, Mt 17:25
hook and take the **f** fish that comes up, Mt 17:27
But many who are **f** will be last, and Mt 19:30
who are first will be last, and the last **f**. Mt 19:30
beginning with the last, up to the **f**.' Mt 20:8
Now when those hired **f** came, they Mt 20:10
So the last will be **f**, and the first last." Mt 20:16
So the last will be first, and the **f** last." Mt 20:16
whoever would be **f** among you must Mt 20:27
And he went to the **f** and said, 'Son, go Mt 21:28
They said, "The **f**." Jesus said to them, Mt 21:31
he sent other servants, more than the **f**. Mt 21:36
The **f** married and died, and having no Mt 22:25
This is the great and **f** commandment. Mt 22:38
F clean the inside of the cup and the Mt 23:26
Now on the **f** day of Unleavened Bread Mt 26:17
the last fraud will be worse than the **f**." Mt 27:64
toward the dawn of the **f** day of the week, Mt 28:1
unless he **f** binds the strong man. Mk 3:27
The earth produces by itself, **f** the blade, Mk 4:28
he said to her, "Let the children be fed **f**, Mk 7:27
scribes say that **f** Elijah must come?" Mk 9:11
"Elijah does come **f** to restore all things. Mk 9:12
he said to them, "If anyone would be **f**, Mk 9:35
But many who are **f** will be last, and Mk 10:31
are first will be last, and the last **f**." Mk 10:31
whoever would be **f** among you must Mk 10:44
the **f** took a wife, and when he died left Mk 12:20
the gospel must **f** be proclaimed to Mk 13:10
And on the **f** day of Unleavened Bread, Mk 14:12
And very early on the **f** day of the week, Mk 16:2
he rose early on the **f** day of the week, Mk 16:9
week, he appeared **f** to Mary Magdalene, Mk 16:9
This was the **f** registration when Lk 2:2
"Every male who **f** opens the womb Lk 2:23
f take the log out of your own eye, Lk 6:42

"Lord, let me **f** go and bury my father." Lk 9:59
but let me **f** say farewell to those at my Lk 9:61
Whatever house you enter, **f** say, 'Peace Lk 10:5
state of that person is worse than the **f**." Lk 11:26
see that he did not **f** wash before dinner. Lk 11:38
he began to say to his disciples **f**, Lk 12:1
behold, some are last who will be **f**, Lk 13:30
first, and some are **f** who will be last." Lk 13:30
The **f** said to him, 'I have bought a Lk 14:18
does not **f** sit down and count the cost, Lk 14:28
not sit down **f** and deliberate whether Lk 14:31
debtors one by one, he said to the **f**, Lk 16:5
But **f** he must suffer many things and Lk 17:25
The **f** came before him, saying, 'Lord, Lk 19:16
The **f** took a wife, and died without Lk 20:29
for these things must **f** take place, Lk 21:9
But on the **f** day of the week, at early Lk 24:1
He **f** found his own brother Simon and Jn 1:41
to him, "Everyone serves the good wine **f**, Jn 2:10
This, the **f** of his signs, Jesus did at Cana Jn 2:11
judge a man without **f** giving him a Jn 7:51
sin among you be the **f** to throw a stone at Jn 8:7
where John had been baptizing at **f**, Jn 10:40
did not understand these things at **f**, Jn 12:16
F they led him to Annas, for he was the Jn 18:13
came and broke the legs of the **f**, Jn 19:32
Now on the **f** day of the week Mary Jn 20:1
outran Peter and reached the tomb **f**. Jn 20:4
disciple, who had reached the tomb **f**, Jn 20:8
of that day, the **f** day of the week, Jn 20:19
In the **f** book, O Theophilus, I have dealt Acts 1:1
up his servant, sent him to you **f**, Acts 3:26
he sent out our fathers on their **f** visit. Acts 7:12
the disciples were **f** called Christians. Acts 11:26
they had passed the **f** and the second Acts 12:10
the word of God be spoken **f** to you. Acts 13:46
related how God **f** visited the Gentiles, Acts 15:14
On the **f** day of the week, when we were Acts 20:7
whole time from the **f** day that I set Acts 20:18
but declared **f** to those in Damascus, Acts 26:20
by being the **f** to rise from the dead, Acts 26:23
to jump overboard **f** and make for Acts 27:43
F, I thank my God through Jesus Christ Rom 1:8
to the Jew **f** and also to the Greek. Rom 1:16
does evil, the Jew **f** and also the Greek, Rom 2:9
does good, the Jew **f** and also the Greek. Rom 2:10
F Moses says, "I will make you Rom 10:19
to us now than when we **f** believed. Rom 13:11
who was the **f** convert to Christ in Rom 16:5
For, in the **f** place, when you come 1 Cor 11:18
appointed in the church **f** apostles, 1 Cor 12:28
sitting there, let the **f** be silent. 1 Cor 14:30
to you as of **f** importance what I also 1 Cor 15:3
"The **f** man Adam became a living 1 Cor 15:45
spiritual that is **f** but the natural, 1 Cor 15:46
The **f** man was from the earth, a 1 Cor 15:47
On the **f** day of every week, each of 1 Cor 16:2
Stephanas were the **f** converts in 1 Cor 16:15
sure of this, I wanted to come to you **f**, 2 Cor 1:15
but they gave themselves **f** to the Lord 2 Cor 8:5
We were the **f** to come all the way to 2 Cor 10:14
that I preached the gospel to you at **f**, Gal 4:13
that we who were the **f** to hope in Christ Eph 1:12
(this is the **f** commandment with a Eph 6:2
in the gospel from the **f** day until now. Phil 1:5
And the dead in Christ will rise **f**. 1 Thes 4:16
come, unless the rebellion comes **f**, 2 Thes 2:3
F of all, then, I urge that supplications, 1 Tm 2:1
For Adam was formed **f**, then Eve; 1 Tm 2:13
And let them also be tested **f**; then let 1 Tm 3:10
let them **f** learn to show godliness to 1 Tm 5:4
faith that dwelt **f** in your grandmother 2 Tm 1:5
ought to have the **f** share of the crops. 2 Tm 2:6
At my **f** defense no one came to stand 2 Tm 4:16
It was declared at **f** by the Lord, and it Heb 2:3
He is **f**, by translation of his name, king Heb 7:2
f for his own sins and then for those of Heb 7:27
For if that **f** covenant had been faultless, Heb 8:7
covenant, he makes the **f** one obsolete. Heb 8:13
Now even the **f** covenant had Heb 9:1
For a tent was prepared, the **f** section, in Heb 9:2
the priests go regularly into the **f** section, Heb 9:6
as long as the **f** section is still standing Heb 9:8
committed under the **f** covenant. Heb 9:15
not even the **f** covenant was Heb 9:18
will." He abolishes the **f** in order to Heb 10:9
But the wisdom from above is **f** pure, Jas 3:17
knowing this **f** of all, that no prophecy 2 Pt 1:20
has become worse for them than the **f**. 2 Pt 2:20
knowing this **f** of all, that scoffers will 2 Pt 3:3
We love because he **f** loved us. 1 Jn 4:19
Diotrephes, who likes to put himself **f**, 3 Jn 1:9
saying, "Fear not, I am the **f** and the last, Rv 1:17
you have abandoned the love you had at **f**. Rv 2:4
repent, and do the works you did at **f**. Rv 2:5

‘The words of the **f** and the last, who died Rv 2:8
and that your latter works exceed the **f**. Rv 2:19
And the **f** voice, which I had heard Rv 4:1
the **f** living creature like a lion, the second Rv 4:7
The **f** angel blew his trumpet, and there Rv 8:7
The **f** woe has passed; behold, two woes Rv 9:12
the authority of the **f** beast in its Rv 13:12
and its inhabitants worship the **f** beast, Rv 13:12
So the **f** angel went and poured out his Rv 16:2
were ended. This is the **f** resurrection. Rv 20:5
the one who shares in the **f** resurrection! Rv 20:6
for the **f** heaven and the first earth had Rv 21:1
first heaven and the **f** earth had passed Rv 21:1
The **f** was jasper, the second sapphire, Rv 21:19
and the Omega, the **f** and the last, Rv 22:13

FIRST-RIPE (4)
will be like a **f** fig before the summer: Is 28:4
One basket had very good figs, like **f** figs, Jer 24:2
cluster to eat, no **f** fig that my soul desires. Mi 7:1
are like fig trees with **f** figs—if shaken Na 3:12

FIRSTBORN (140)
also brought of the **f** of his flock and Gn 4:4
Canaan fathered Sidon his **f** and Heth, Gn 10:15
And the **f** said to the younger, “Our Gn 19:31
And the **f** went in and lay with her Gn 19:33
The next day, the **f** said to the younger, Gn 19:34
The **f** bore a son and called his name Gn 19:37
Uz his **f**, Buz his brother, Kemuel the Gn 22:21
their birth: Nebaioth, the **f** of Ishmael; Gn 25:13
said to his father, “I am Esau your **f**. Gn 27:19
He answered, “I am your son, your **f**, Gn 27:32
to give the younger before the **f**. Gn 29:26
Reuben (Jacob’s **f**), Simeon, Levi, Gn 35:23
The sons of Eliphaz the **f** of Esau: the Gn 36:15
And Judah took a wife for Er his **f**, and Gn 38:6
But Er, Judah’s **f**, was wicked in the Gn 38:7
called the name of the **f** Manasseh. Gn 41:51
the **f** according to his birthright and Gn 43:33
Jacob and his sons. Reuben, Jacob’s **f**, Gn 46:8
his hands (for Manasseh was the **f**). Gn 48:14
since this one is the **f**, put your right Gn 48:18
“Reuben, you are my **f**, my might, and Gn 49:3
‘Thus says the LORD, Israel is my **f** son, Ex 4:22
let him go, behold, I will kill your **f** son.’” Ex 4:23
the sons of Reuben, the **f** of Israel: Ex 6:14
and every **f** in the land of Egypt shall die, Ex 11:5
from the **f** of Pharaoh who sits on his Ex 11:5
even to the **f** of the slave girl who is Ex 11:5
the handmill, and all the **f** of the cattle. Ex 11:5
I will strike all the **f** in the land of Ex 12:12
struck down all the **f** in the land of Ex 12:29
from the **f** of Pharaoh who sat on his Ex 12:29
on his throne to the **f** of the captive who Ex 12:29
dungeon, and all the **f** of the livestock. Ex 12:29
“Consecrate to me all the **f**. Whatever is Ex 13:2
All the **f** of your animals that are males Ex 13:12
Every **f** of a donkey you shall redeem Ex 13:13
Every **f** of man among your sons you Ex 13:13
the LORD killed all the **f** in the land of Ex 13:15
both the **f** of man and the firstborn of Ex 13:15
firstborn of man and the **f** of animals. Ex 13:15
but all the **f** of my sons I redeem.’ Ex 13:15
The **f** of your sons you shall give to me. Ex 22:29
male livestock, the **f** of cow and sheep. Ex 34:19
The **f** of a donkey you shall redeem Ex 34:20
All the **f** of your sons you shall redeem. Ex 34:20
“But a **f** of animals, which as a Lv 27:26
which as a **f** belongs to the LORD, Lv 27:26
The people of Reuben, Israel’s **f**, their Nm 1:20
Nadab the **f**, and Abihu, Eleazar, and Nm 3:2
Israel instead of every **f** who opens the Nm 3:12
for all the **f** are mine. On the day that I Nm 3:13
I struck down all the **f** in the land of Nm 3:13
for my own all the **f** in Israel, Nm 3:13
“List all the **f** males of the people of Nm 3:40
instead of all the **f** among the people of Nm 3:41
instead of all the **f** among the cattle of Nm 3:41
Moses listed all the **f** among the people Nm 3:42
And all the **f** males, according to the Nm 3:43
instead of all the **f** among the people of Nm 3:45
for the 273 of the **f** of the people of Nm 3:46
From the **f** of the people of Israel he Nm 3:50
womb, the **f** of all the people of Israel, Nm 8:16
For all the **f** among the people of Israel Nm 8:17
I struck down all the **f** in the land of Nm 8:17
instead of all the **f** among the people of Nm 8:18
the **f** of man you shall redeem, Nm 18:15
and the **f** of unclean animals you Nm 18:15
But the **f** of a cow, or the firstborn of a Nm 18:17
firstborn of a cow, or the **f** of a sheep, Nm 18:17
firstborn of a sheep, or the **f** of a goat, Nm 18:17
Reuben, the **f** of Israel; the sons of Nm 26:5
the Egyptians were burying all their **f**, Nm 33:4
and the **f** of your herd and of your flock. Dt 12:6
or the **f** of your herd or of your flock, Dt 12:17
oil, and the **f** of your herd and flock, Dt 14:23
“All the **f** males that are born of your Dt 15:19
do no work with the **f** of your herd, Dt 15:19
your herd, nor shear the **f** of your flock. Dt 15:19
and if the **f** son belongs to the unloved, Dt 21:15
of the loved as the **f** in preference to the Dt 21:16
to the son of the unloved, who is the **f**, Dt 21:16
but he shall acknowledge the **f**, the son Dt 21:17
of his strength. The right of the **f** is his. Dt 21:17
A **f** bull—he has majesty, and his Dt 33:17
“At the cost of his **f** shall he lay its Jos 6:26
of Manasseh, for he was the **f** of Joseph. Jos 17:1
To Machir the **f** of Manasseh, the father Jos 17:1
So he said to Jether his **f**, “Rise and kill Jgs 8:20
The name of his **f** son was Joel, and the 1 Sm 8:2
the name of the **f** was Merab, and the 1 Sm 14:49
went to the battle were Eliab the **f**, 1 Sm 17:13
his **f** was Amnon, of Ahinoam of 2 Sm 3:2
at the cost of Abiram his **f**, 1 Kgs 16:34
fathered Sidon his **f** and Heth, 1 Chr 1:13
the **f** of Ishmael, Nebaioth, and 1 Chr 1:29
Now Er, Judah’s **f**, was evil in the sight 1 Chr 2:3
Jesse fathered Eliab his **f**, Abinadab 1 Chr 2:13
sons of Jerahmeel, the **f** of Hezron: 1 Chr 2:25
Ram, his **f**, Bunah, Oren, Ozem, and 1 Chr 2:25
The sons of Ram, the **f** of Jerahmeel: 1 Chr 2:27
Mareshah his **f**, who fathered Ziph. 1 Chr 2:42
The sons of Hur the **f** of Ephrathah: 1 Chr 2:50
were born to him in Hebron: the **f**, 1 Chr 3:1
Johanan the **f**, the second Jehoiakim, 1 Chr 3:15
the sons of Hur, the **f** of Ephrathah, 1 Chr 4:4
sons of Reuben the **f** of Israel (for he 1 Chr 5:1
the firstborn of Israel (for he was the **f**, 1 Chr 5:1
the sons of Reuben, the **f** of Israel: 1 Chr 5:3
Samuel: Joel his **f**, the second Abijah. 1 Chr 6:28
Benjamin fathered Bela his **f**, Ashbel 1 Chr 8:1
His **f** son: Abdon, then Zur, Kish, 1 Chr 8:30
Ulam his **f**, Jeush the second, and 1 Chr 8:39
Shilonites: Asaiah the **f**, and his sons. 1 Chr 9:5
the **f** of Shallum the Korahite, 1 Chr 9:31
and his **f** son Abdon, then Zur, Kish, 1 Chr 9:36
Zechariah the **f**, Jediael the second, 1 Chr 26:2
Shemaiah the **f**, Jehozabad the 1 Chr 26:4
chief (for though he was not the **f**, 1 Chr 26:10
to Jehoram, because he was the **f**. 2 Chr 21:3
the **f** of our sons and of our cattle, Neh 10:36
and the **f** of our herds and of our Neh 10:36
skin; the **f** of death consumes his limbs. Jb 18:13
He struck down every **f** in Egypt, the Ps 78:51
And I will make him the **f**, the highest Ps 89:27
He struck down all the **f** in their land, Ps 105:36
it was who struck down the **f** of Egypt, Ps 135:8
him who struck down the **f** of Egypt, Ps 136:10
And the **f** of the poor will graze, and the Is 14:30
a father to Israel, and Ephraim is my **f**. Jer 31:9
gifts in their offering up all their **f**, Ezk 20:26
Shall I give my **f** for my transgression, the Mi 6:7
over him, as one weeps over a **f**. Zec 12:10
gave birth to her **f** son and wrapped him Lk 2:7
might be the **f** among many brothers. Rom 8:29
of the invisible God, the **f** of all creation. Col 1:15
He is the beginning, the **f** from the dead, Col 1:18
when he brings the **f** into the world, Heb 1:6
the Destroyer of the **f** might not touch Heb 11:28
the assembly of the **f** who are enrolled Heb 12:23
the faithful witness, the **f** of the dead, Rv 1:5

FIRSTFRUITS (33)
my might, and the **f** of my strength, Gn 49:3
Feast of Harvest, of the **f** of your labor, Ex 23:16
“The best of the **f** of your ground you Ex 23:19
Feast of Weeks, the **f** of wheat harvest, Ex 34:22
The best of the **f** of your ground you Ex 34:26
As an offering of **f** you may bring them Lv 2:12
you offer a grain offering of **f** to the LORD, Lv 2:14
for the grain offering of your **f** fresh ears, Lv 2:14
the sheaf of the **f** of your harvest to Lv 23:10
be baked with leaven, as **f** to the LORD. Lv 23:17
the bread of the **f** as a wave offering Lv 23:20
the **f** of what they give to the LORD, Nm 18:12
“On the day of the **f**, when you offer a Nm 28:26
The **f** of your grain, of your wine and of Dt 18:4
he has, for he is the **f** of his strength. Dt 21:17
the man of God bread of the **f**, 2 Kgs 4:42
gave in abundance the **f** of grain, 2 Chr 31:5
ourselves to bring the **f** of our ground Neh 10:35
of our ground and the **f** of all fruit of Neh 10:35
storerooms, the contributions, the **f**, Neh 12:44
at appointed times, and for the **f**. Neh 13:31
the **f** of their strength in the tents of Ps 78:51
in their land, the **f** of all their strength. Ps 105:36
wealth and with the **f** of all your produce; Prv 3:9
was holy to the LORD, the **f** of his harvest. Jer 2:3
And the first of all the **f** of all kinds, Ezk 44:30
ourselves, who have the **f** of the Spirit, Rom 8:23
If the dough offered as **f** is holy, so is Rom 11:16
the **f** of those who have fallen asleep. 1 Cor 15:20
Christ the **f**, then at his coming 1 Cor 15:23
God chose you as the **f** to be saved, 2 Thes 2:13
we should be a kind of **f** of his creatures. Jas 1:18
from mankind as **f** for God and Rv 14:4

FISH (63)
have dominion over the **f** of the sea and Gn 1:26
have dominion over the **f** of the sea and Gn 1:28
on the ground and all the **f** of the sea. Gn 9:2
The **f** in the Nile shall die, and the Nile Ex 7:18
And the **f** in the Nile died, and the Nile Ex 7:21
We remember the **f** we ate in Egypt Nm 11:5
Or shall all the **f** of the sea be gathered Nm 11:22
the likeness of any **f** that is in the water Dt 4:18
and of birds, and of reptiles, and of **f**. 1 Kgs 4:33
and for the entrance into the **F** Gate, 2 Chr 33:14
The sons of Hassenaah built the **F** Gate. Neh 3:3
and by the **F** Gate and the Tower of Neh 12:39
brought in **f** and all kinds of goods Neh 13:16
and the **f** of the sea will declare to you. Jb 12:8
birds of the heavens, and the **f** of the sea, Ps 8:8
into blood and caused their **f** to die. Ps 105:29
Like **f** that are taken in an evil net, and Eccl 9:12
their **f** stink for lack of water and die of Is 50:2
and make the **f** of your streams stick to Ezk 29:4
with all the **f** of your streams that stick Ezk 29:4
you and all the **f** of your streams; Ezk 29:5
The **f** of the sea and the birds of the Ezk 38:20
will live, and there will be very many **f**. Ezk 47:9
Its **f** will be of very many kinds, like Ezk 47:10
many kinds, like the **f** of the Great Sea. Ezk 47:10
and even the **f** of the sea are taken away. Hos 4:3
LORD appointed a great **f** to swallow up Jon 1:17
in the belly of the **f** three days and three Jon 1:17
the LORD his God from the belly of the **f**, Jon 2:1
And the LORD spoke to the **f**, and it Jon 2:10
make mankind like the **f** of the sea, Hab 1:14
birds of the heavens and the **f** of the sea, Zep 1:3
“a cry will be heard from the **F** Gate, Zep 1:10
Or if he asks for a **f**, will give him a Mt 7:10
three nights in the belly of the great **f**, Mt 12:40
the sea and gathered **f** of every kind. Mt 13:47
have only five loaves here and two **f**.” Mt 14:17
and taking the five loaves and the two **f**, Mt 14:19
They said, “Seven, and a few small **f**.” Mt 15:34
he took the seven loaves and the **f**, and Mt 15:36
hook and take the first **f** that comes up, Mt 17:27
found out, they said, “Five, and two **f**.” Mk 6:38
five loaves and the two **f** he looked up to Mk 6:41
he divided the two **f** among them all. Mk 6:41
full of broken pieces and of the **f**. Mk 6:43
And they had a few small **f**. And having Mk 8:7
this, they enclosed a large number of **f**, Lk 5:6
at the catch of **f** that they had taken, Lk 5:9
five loaves and two **f**—unless we are Lk 9:13
And taking the five loaves and the two **f**, Lk 9:16
among you, if his son asks for a **f**, Lk 11:11
will instead of a **f** give him a serpent; Lk 11:11
They gave him a piece of broiled **f**, Lk 24:42
here who has five barley loaves and two **f**, Jn 6:9
So also the **f**, as much as they wanted. Jn 6:11
do you have any **f**?” They answered him, Jn 21:5
to haul it in, because of the quantity of **f**. Jn 21:6
in the boat, dragging the net full of **f**, Jn 21:8
fire in place, with **f** laid out on it, Jn 21:9
“Bring some of the **f** that you have just Jn 21:10
and hauled the net ashore, full of large **f**, Jn 21:11
and gave it to them, and so with the **f**. Jn 21:13
another for birds, and another for **f**. 1 Cor 15:39

FISHERMEN (5)
The **f** will mourn and lament, all who Is 19:8
F will stand beside the sea. From Ezk 47:10
casting a net into the sea, for they were **f**. Mt 4:18
a net into the sea, for they were **f**. Mk 1:16
but the **f** had gone out of them and were Lk 5:2

FISHERS (3)
“Behold, I am sending for many **f**, Jer 16:16
me, and I will make you **f** of men.” Mt 4:19
and I will make you become **f** of men.” Mk 1:17

FISHHOOK (1)
out Leviathan with a **f** or press down his Jb 41:1

FISHHOOKS (1)
with hooks, even the last of you with **f**. Am 4:2

FISHING (2)
with harpoons or his head with **f** spears? Jb 41:7
to them, “I am going **f**.” They said to him, Jn 21:3

FIST (4)
a stone or with his **f** and the man does Ex 21:18
he will shake his **f** at the mount of the Is 10:32
and to fight and to hit with a wicked **f**. Is 58:4
passes by her hisses and shakes his **f**. Zep 2:15

FISTS (1)
Who has gathered the wind in his **f**? Prv 30:4

FIT (7)
I will make him a helper **f** for him." Gn 2:18
there was not found a helper **f** for him. Gn 2:20
all of them strong and **f** for war. 2 Kgs 24:16
were 300,000 choice men, **f** for war, 2 Chr 25:5
had an army of soldiers, **f** for war, 2 Chr 26:11
and looks back is **f** for the kingdom of Lk 9:62
they did not see **f** to acknowledge God, Rom 1:28

FITLY (1)
A word **f** spoken is like apples of gold Prv 25:11

FITS (2)
enmity, strife, jealousy, **f** of anger, Gal 5:20
good for building up, as **f** the occasion, Eph 4:29

FITTED (1)
they have **f** their arrow to the string to Ps 11:2

FITTEST (1)
select the best and **f** of your master's 2 Kgs 10:3

FITTING (12)
two tenons in each frame, for **f** together. Ex 26:17
frame had two tenons for **f** together. Ex 36:22
palace and it is not **f** for us to witness Ezr 4:14
it is pleasant, and a song of praise is **f**. Ps 147:1
It is not **f** for a fool to live in luxury, Prv 19:10
in harvest, so honor is not **f** for a fool. Prv 26:1
seen to be good and **f** is to eat and Eccl 5:18
for thus it is **f** for us to fulfill all Mt 3:15
It was **f** to celebrate and be glad, for this Lk 15:32
to your husbands, as is **f** in the Lord. Col 3:18
For it was **f** that he, for whom and by Heb 2:10
For it was indeed **f** that we should have Heb 7:26

FIVE (193)
king of Ellasar, four kings against **f**. Gn 14:9
Suppose **f** of the fifty righteous are Gn 18:28
whole city for lack of **f**?" And he said, Gn 18:28
Benjamin's portion was **f** times as Gn 43:34
and there are yet **f** years in which there Gn 45:6
for there are yet **f** years of famine to Gn 45:11
of silver and **f** changes of clothes. Gn 45:22
brothers he took **f** men and presented Gn 47:2
or sells it, he shall repay **f** oxen for an ox, Ex 22:1
F curtains shall be coupled to one Ex 26:3
and the other **f** curtains shall be coupled Ex 26:3
You shall couple **f** curtains by Ex 26:9
f for the frames of the one side of the Ex 26:26
and **f** bars for the frames of the other Ex 26:27
and **f** bars for the frames of the side of Ex 26:27
make for the screen **f** pillars of acacia, Ex 26:37
and you shall cast **f** bases of bronze for Ex 26:37
f cubits long and five cubits broad. Ex 27:1
five cubits long and **f** cubits broad. Ex 27:1
breadth fifty, and the height **f** cubits, Ex 27:18
He coupled **f** curtains to one another, Ex 36:10
and the other **f** curtains he coupled to Ex 36:10
He coupled **f** curtains by themselves, Ex 36:16
f for the frames of the one side of the Ex 36:31
and **f** bars for the frames of the other Ex 36:32
and **f** bars for the frames of the Ex 36:32
and its **f** pillars with their hooks. He Ex 36:38
of gold, but their **f** bases were of bronze. Ex 36:38
F cubits was its length, and five cubits Ex 38:1
was its length, and **f** cubits its breadth. Ex 38:1
twenty cubits long and **f** cubits high in Ex 38:18
F of you shall chase a hundred, and a Lv 26:8
If the person is from **f** years old up to Lv 27:5
is from a month old up to **f** years old, Lv 27:6
shall be for a male **f** shekels of silver, Lv 27:6
you shall take **f** shekels per head; you Nm 3:47
of peace offerings, two oxen, **f** rams, Nm 7:17
two oxen, five rams, **f** male goats, Nm 7:17
goats, and **f** male lambs a year old. Nm 7:17
of peace offerings, two oxen, **f** rams, Nm 7:23
two oxen, five rams, **f** male goats, Nm 7:23
goats, and **f** male lambs a year old. Nm 7:23
of peace offerings, two oxen, **f** rams, Nm 7:29
two oxen, five rams, **f** male goats, Nm 7:29
goats, and **f** male lambs a year old. Nm 7:29
of peace offerings, two oxen, **f** rams, Nm 7:35
two oxen, five rams, **f** male goats, Nm 7:35
goats, and **f** male lambs a year old. Nm 7:35
of peace offerings, two oxen, **f** rams, Nm 7:41
two oxen, five rams, **f** male goats, Nm 7:41
goats, and **f** male lambs a year old. Nm 7:41
of peace offerings, two oxen, **f** rams, Nm 7:47
two oxen, five rams, **f** male goats, Nm 7:47
goats, and **f** male lambs a year old. Nm 7:47
of peace offerings, two oxen, **f** rams, Nm 7:53
two oxen, five rams, **f** male goats, Nm 7:53
goats, and **f** male lambs a year old. Nm 7:53
of peace offerings, two oxen, **f** rams, Nm 7:59
two oxen, five rams, **f** male goats, Nm 7:59
goats, and **f** male lambs a year old. Nm 7:59
of peace offerings, two oxen, **f** rams, Nm 7:65
two oxen, five rams, **f** male goats, Nm 7:65
goats, and **f** male lambs a year old. Nm 7:65
of peace offerings, two oxen, **f** rams, Nm 7:71
two oxen, five rams, **f** male goats, Nm 7:71
goats, and **f** male lambs a year old. Nm 7:71
of peace offerings, two oxen, **f** rams, Nm 7:77
two oxen, five rams, **f** male goats, Nm 7:77
goats, and **f** male lambs a year old. Nm 7:77
of peace offerings, two oxen, **f** rams, Nm 7:83
two oxen, five rams, **f** male goats, Nm 7:83
goats, and **f** male lambs a year old. Nm 7:83
eat just one day, or two days, or **f** days, Nm 11:19
you shall fix at **f** shekels in silver, Nm 18:16
Hur, and Reba, the **f** kings of Midian. Nm 31:8
out to battle, one out of **f** hundred, Nm 31:28
Then the **f** kings of the Amorites, the Jos 10:5
These **f** kings fled and hid themselves Jos 10:16
Joshua, "The **f** kings have been found, Jos 10:17
cave and bring those **f** kings out to me Jos 10:22
and brought those **f** kings out to him Jos 10:23
to death, and he hanged them on **f** trees. Jos 10:26
there are **f** rulers of the Philistines, those Jos 13:3
the **f** lords of the Philistines and all the Jgs 3:3
people of Dan sent **f** able men from the Jgs 18:2
Then the **f** men departed and came to Jgs 18:7
Then the **f** men who had gone to scout Jgs 18:14
And the **f** men who had gone to scout Jgs 18:17
F thousand men of them were cut Jgs 20:45
"**F** golden tumors and five golden mice, 1 Sm 6:4
"Five golden tumors and **f** golden mice, 1 Sm 6:4
And when the **f** lords of the Philistines 1 Sm 6:16
Philistines belonging to the **f** lords, 1 Sm 6:18
of the coat was **f** thousand shekels of 1 Sm 17:5
hand and chose **f** smooth stones 1 Sm 17:40
Give me **f** loaves of bread, or whatever 1 Sm 21:3
of wine and **f** sheep already prepared 1 Sm 25:18
already prepared and **f** seahs of 1 Sm 25:18
and her **f** young women attended 1 Sm 25:42
He was **f** years old when the news about 2 Sm 4:4
and the **f** sons of Merab the daughter 2 Sm 21:8
The lowest story was **f** cubits broad, 1 Kgs 6:6
the whole house, **f** cubits high, 1 Kgs 6:10
F cubits was the length of one wing 1 Kgs 6:24
and **f** cubits the length of the other 1 Kgs 6:24
height of the one capital was **f** cubits, 1 Kgs 7:16
of the other capital was **f** cubits. 1 Kgs 7:16
brim to brim, and **f** cubits high, 1 Kgs 7:23
f on the south side of the house, 1 Kgs 7:39
and **f** on the north side of the house. 1 Kgs 7:39
f on the south side and five on the 1 Kgs 7:49
on the south side and **f** on the north, 1 Kgs 7:49
of dove's dung for **f** shekels of silver. 2 Kgs 6:25
some men take **f** of the remaining 2 Kgs 7:13
should have struck **f** or six times; 2 Kgs 13:19
and **f** men of the king's council who 2 Kgs 25:19
and Zerah. Judah had **f** sons in all. 1 Chr 2:4
Heman, Calcol, and Dara, **f** in all. 1 Chr 2:6
Hasadiah, and Jushab-hesed, **f**. 1 Chr 3:20
Tochen, and Ashan, **f** cities, 1 Chr 4:32
f hundred men of the Simeonites, 1 Chr 4:42
Isshiah, all **f** of them were chief men. 1 Chr 7:3
and Iri, **f**, heads of fathers' houses, 1 Chr 7:7
a man of great stature, **f** cubits tall. 1 Chr 11:23
one wing of the one, of **f** cubits, 2 Chr 3:11
house, and its other wing, of **f** cubits, 2 Chr 3:11
of this cherub, one wing, of **f** cubits, 2 Chr 3:12
and the other wing, also of **f** cubits, 2 Chr 3:12
with a capital of **f** cubits on the top of 2 Chr 3:15
from brim to brim, and **f** cubits high, 2 Chr 4:2
to wash, and set **f** on the south side, 2 Chr 4:6
the south side, and **f** on the north side. 2 Chr 4:6
f on the south side and five on the 2 Chr 4:7
on the south side and **f** on the north. 2 Chr 4:7
f on the south side and five on the 2 Chr 4:8
on the south side and **f** on the north. 2 Chr 4:8
a bronze platform **f** cubits long, 2 Chr 6:13
five cubits long, **f** cubits wide, 2 Chr 6:13
four or **f** on the branches of a fruit tree, Is 17:6
that day there will be **f** cities in the land Is 19:18
at the threat of **f** you shall flee, till you Is 30:17
height of the one capital was **f** cubits. Jer 52:22
space between the side rooms, **f** cubits; Ezk 40:7
cubits long and **f** cubits broad. Ezk 40:30
of the vestibule, **f** cubits on either side. Ezk 40:48
of the entrance were **f** cubits on either Ezk 41:2
wall of the side chambers was **f** cubits. Ezk 41:9
the free space was **f** cubits all around. Ezk 41:11
of the building was **f** cubits thick all Ezk 41:12
"We have only **f** loaves here and two Mt 14:17
and taking the **f** loaves and the two Mt 14:19
who ate were about **f** thousand men, Mt 14:21
you not remember the **f** loaves for the Mt 16:9
the five loaves for the **f** thousand, Mt 16:9
F of them were foolish, and five were Mt 25:2
of them were foolish, and **f** were wise. Mt 25:2
To one he gave **f** talents, to another two, Mt 25:15
who had received the **f** talents went at Mt 25:16
with them, and he made **f** talents more. Mt 25:16
had received the **f** talents came Mt 25:20
came forward, bringing **f** talents more, Mt 25:20
'Master, you delivered to me **f** talents; Mt 25:20
here I have made **f** talents more.' Mt 25:20
found out, they said, "**F**, and two fish." Mk 6:38
And taking the **f** loaves and the two fish Mk 6:41
ate the loaves were **f** thousand men. Mk 6:44
When I broke the **f** loaves for the five Mk 8:19
broke the five loaves for the **f** thousand, Mk 8:19
and for **f** months she kept herself Lk 1:24
debtors. One owed **f** hundred denarii, Lk 7:41
have no more than **f** loaves and two fish Lk 9:13
For there were about **f** thousand men. Lk 9:14
And taking the **f** loaves and the two fish, Lk 9:16
Are not **f** sparrows sold for two pennies? Lk 12:6
on in one house there will be **f** divided, Lk 12:52
said, 'I have bought **f** yoke of oxen, Lk 14:19
for I have **f** brothers—so that he may Lk 16:28
'Lord, your mina has made **f** minas.' Lk 19:18
to him, 'And you are to be over **f** cities.' Lk 19:19
for you have had **f** husbands, and the one Jn 4:18
Bethesda, which has **f** roofed colonnades. Jn 5:2
boy here who has **f** barley loaves and two Jn 6:9
sat down, about **f** thousand in number. Jn 6:10
with fragments from the **f** barley loaves, Jn 6:13
of the men came to about **f** thousand. Acts 4:4
and in **f** days we came to them at Acts 20:6
And after **f** days the high priest Acts 24:1
would rather speak **f** words with my 1 Cor 14:19
to more than **f** hundred brothers at 1 Cor 15:6
F times I received at the hands of the 2 Cor 11:24
allowed to torment them for **f** months, Rv 9:5
to hurt people for **f** months is in their Rv 9:10
also seven kings, **f** of whom have fallen, Rv 17:10

FIVE-SIDED (1)
the lintel and the doorposts were **f**. 1 Kgs 6:31

FIX (3)
them) you shall **f** at five shekels Nm 18:16
on your precepts and **f** my eyes on Ps 119:15
and I will **f** my eyes upon them for evil Am 9:4

FIXED (18)
means that the thing is **f** by God, Gn 41:32
priests had a **f** allowance from Gn 47:22
he **f** the borders of the peoples according Dt 32:8
And he **f** his gaze and stared at him, 2 Kgs 8:11
and a **f** provision for the singers, Neh 11:23
You have **f** all the boundaries of the Ps 74:17
having my eyes **f** on all your Ps 119:6
your word is firmly **f** in the heavens. Ps 119:89
like nails firmly **f** are the collected Eccl 12:11
light by day and the **f** order of the moon Jer 31:35
"If this **f** order departs from before me, Jer 31:36
and night and the **f** order of heaven and Jer 33:25
and as the **f** portion of oil, measured in Ezk 45:14
of all in the synagogue were **f** on him. Lk 4:20
us and you a great chasm has been **f**, Lk 16:26
that the Father has **f** by his own Acts 1:7
And he **f** his attention on them, Acts 3:5
because he has **f** a day on which he Acts 17:31

FLAGONS (4)
and its **f** and bowls with which to pour Ex 25:29
and its bowls and **f** with which to pour Ex 37:16
bowls, and the **f** for the drink offering; Nm 4:7
small vessel, from the cups to all the **f**. Is 22:24

FLAGRANT (2)
guilt is great, because your sins are **f**. Jer 30:14
guilt is great, because your sins are **f**, Jer 30:15

FLAGSTAFF (1)
till you are left like a **f** on the top of a Is 30:17

FLAIL (1)
I will **f** your flesh with the thorns of the Jgs 8:7

FLAKE-LIKE (1)
the face of the wilderness a fine, **f** thing, Ex 16:14

FLAME (31)
appeared to him in a **f** of fire out of the Ex 3:2
Heshbon, **f** from the city of Sihon. Nm 21:28
And when the **f** went up toward heaven Jgs 13:20
of the LORD went up in the **f** of the altar. Jgs 13:20
the **f** will dry up his shoots, and by the Jb 15:30
out, and the **f** of his fire does not shine. Jb 18:5
and a **f** comes forth from his mouth. Jb 41:21
as the **f** sets the mountains ablaze, Ps 83:14
company; the **f** burned up the wicked. Ps 106:18
are flashes of fire, the very **f** of the LORD. Sg 8:6
and as dry grass sinks down in the **f**, Is 5:24
will become a fire, and his Holy One a **f**, Is 10:17

and tempest, and the **f** of a devouring fire. Is 29:6
furious anger and a **f** of devouring fire, Is 30:30
burned, and the **f** shall not consume you. Is 43:2
themselves from the power of the **f**. Is 47:14
Heshbon, **f** from the house of Sihon; Jer 48:45
The blazing **f** shall not be quenched, Ezk 20:47
the **f** of the fire killed those men who Dn 3:22
they shall stumble by sword and **f**, Dn 11:33
and **f** has burned all the trees of the field. Jl 1:19
before them, and behind them a **f** burns. Jl 2:3
the crackling of a **f** of fire devouring the Jl 2:5
be a fire, and the house of Joseph a **f**, Ob 1:18
tongue, for I am in anguish in this **f**.' Lk 16:24
of Mount Sinai, in a **f** of fire in a bush. Acts 7:30
remind you to fan into **f** the gift of God, 2 Tm 1:6
winds, and his ministers a **f** of fire." Heb 1:7
as snow. His eyes were like a **f** of fire, Rv 1:14
Son of God, who has eyes like a **f** of fire, Rv 2:18
His eyes are like a **f** of fire, and on his Rv 19:12

FLAMED (3)
glowing coals **f** forth from him. 2 Sm 22:9
before him coals of fire **f** forth. 2 Sm 22:13
mouth; glowing coals **f** forth from him. Ps 18:8

FLAMES (3)
voice of the LORD flashes forth **f** of fire. Ps 29:7
in fury, and his rebuke with **f** of fire. Is 66:15
like pure wool; his throne was fiery **f**; Dn 7:9

FLAMING (12)
the cherubim and a **f** sword that turned Gn 3:24
fire pot and a **f** torch passed between Gn 15:17
of holy ones, with **f** fire at his right hand. Dt 33:2
Out of his mouth go **f** torches; sparks of Jb 41:19
messengers winds, his ministers a **f** fire. Ps 104:4
smoke and the shining of a **f** fire by night; Is 4:5
he has burned like a **f** fire in Jacob, Lam 2:3
of lightning, his eyes like **f** torches, Dn 10:6
in the morning it blazes like a **f** fire. Hos 7:6
of wood, like a **f** torch among sheaves. Zec 12:6
can extinguish all the **f** darts of the evil Eph 6:16
in **f** fire, inflicting vengeance on 2 Thes 1:8

FLANK (1)
I will lay open the **f** of Moab from the Ezk 25:9

FLASH (8)
carry you away, and why do your eyes **f**, Jb 15:12
His sneezings **f** forth light, and his eyes Jb 41:18
F forth the lightning and scatter them; Ps 144:6
like the appearance of a **f** of lightning. Ezk 1:14
slaughter, polished to **f** like lightning! Ezk 21:10
to consume and to **f** like lightning— Ezk 21:28
who makes destruction **f** forth against Am 5:9
sped, at the **f** of your glittering spear. Hab 3:11

FLASHED (4)
he **f** forth lightnings and routed them. Ps 18:14
thunder; your arrows **f** on every side. Ps 77:17
was like the light; rays **f** from his hand; Hab 3:4
a light from heaven **f** around him. Acts 9:3

FLASHES (9)
the thunder and the **f** of lightning and Ex 20:18
voice of the LORD **f** forth flames of fire. Ps 29:7
Its **f** are flashes of fire, the very flame of the Sg 8:6
Its flashes are **f** of fire, the very flame of the Sg 8:6
For as the lightning **f** and lights up the Lk 17:24
From the throne came **f** of lightning, and Rv 4:5
of thunder, rumblings, **f** of lightning, Rv 8:5
his temple. There were **f** of lightning, Rv 11:19
And there were **f** of lightning, Rv 16:18

FLASHING (7)
was hail and fire **f** continually in the Ex 9:24
if I sharpen my **f** sword and my hand Dt 32:41
the quiver, the **f** spear and the javelin. Jb 39:23
There he broke the **f** arrows, the shield, Ps 76:3
around it, and fire **f** forth continually, Ezk 1:4
The chariots come with **f** metal on the Na 2:3
charging, **f** sword and glittering spear, Na 3:3

FLASK (9)
Then Samuel took a **f** of oil and 1 Sm 10:1
and take this **f** of oil in your hand, 2 Kgs 9:1
Then take the **f** of oil and pour it on 2 Kgs 9:3
LORD, "Go, buy a potter's earthenware **f**, Jer 19:1
you shall break the **f** in the sight of Jer 19:10
with an alabaster **f** of very expensive Mt 26:7
came with an alabaster **f** of ointment of Mk 14:3
and she broke the **f** and poured it over Mk 14:3
brought an alabaster **f** of ointment, Lk 7:37

FLASKS (1)
but the wise took **f** of oil with their Mt 25:4

FLAT (4)
and the wall of the city will fall down **f**, Jos 6:5
a great shout, and the wall fell down **f**, Jos 6:20
it upside down, so that the tent lay **f**." Jgs 7:13
entrusted with making the **f** cakes. 1 Chr 9:31

FLATTER (2)
For I do not know how to **f**, else my Jb 32:22
is an open grave; they **f** with their tongue. Ps 5:9

FLATTERED (1)
But they **f** him with their mouths; they Ps 78:36

FLATTERIES (1)
warning and obtain the kingdom by **f**. Dn 11:21

FLATTERING (4)
with **f** lips and a double heart they speak. Ps 12:2
May the LORD cut off all **f** lips, the tongue Ps 12:3
its victims, and a **f** mouth works ruin. Prv 26:28
false vision or **f** divination within the Ezk 12:24

FLATTERS (3)
For he **f** himself in his own eyes that his Ps 36:2
favor than he who **f** with his tongue. Prv 28:23
A man who **f** his neighbor spreads a net Prv 29:5

FLATTERY (5)
to any man or use **f** toward any person. Jb 32:21
shall seduce with **f** those who violate Dn 11:32
shall join themselves to them with **f**, Dn 11:34
by smooth talk and **f** they deceive the Rom 16:18
For we never came with words of **f**, as 1 Thes 2:5

FLAUNTED (1)
so openly and **f** her nakedness, Ezk 23:18

FLAUNTS (1)
with knowledge, but a fool **f** his folly. Prv 13:16

FLAW (1)
beautiful, my love; there is no **f** in you. Sg 4:7

FLAX (9)
(The **f** and the barley were struck down, Ex 9:31
was in the ear and the **f** was in bud. Ex 9:31
them with the stalks of **f** that she had laid Jos 2:6
his arms became as **f** that has caught Jgs 15:14
as a thread of **f** snaps when it touches Jgs 16:9
She seeks wool and **f**, and works with Prv 31:13
The workers in combed **f** will be in Is 19:9
bread and my water, my wool and my **f**, Hos 2:5
and I will take away my wool and my **f**, Hos 2:9

FLAY (3)
Then he shall **f** the burnt offering and cut Lv 1:6
few and could not **f** all the burnt 2 Chr 29:34
my people, and **f** their skin from off them, Mi 3:3

FLAYED (1)
while the Levites **f** the sacrifices. 2 Chr 35:11

FLEA (2)
pursue? After a dead dog! After a **f**! 1 Sm 24:14
to seek a single **f** like one who hunts 1 Sm 26:20

FLED (143)
the kings of Sodom and Gomorrah **f**, Gn 14:10
them, and the rest **f** to the hill country. Gn 14:10
harshly with her, and she **f** from her. Gn 16:6
He **f** with all that he had and arose and Gn 31:21
on the third day that Jacob had **f**, Gn 31:22
by night, and my sleep **f** from my eyes. Gn 31:40
to you when you **f** from your brother Gn 35:1
to him when he **f** from his brother. Gn 35:7
in her hand and **f** and got out of Gn 39:12
in her hand and had **f** out of the house, Gn 39:13
garment beside me and **f** and got out of Gn 39:15
garment beside me and **f** out of the Gn 39:18
But Moses **f** from Pharaoh and stayed in Ex 2:15
of Egypt was told that the people had **f**, Ex 14:5
And as the Egyptians **f** into it, the LORD Ex 14:27
who were around them **f** at their cry, Nm 16:34
to his city of refuge to which he had **f**, Nm 35:25
of his city of refuge to which he **f**, Nm 35:26
for him who has **f** to his city of Nm 35:32
people. And they **f** before the men of Ai, Jos 7:4
before them and **f** in the direction Jos 8:15
for the people who **f** to the wilderness Jos 8:20
And as they **f** before Israel, while they Jos 10:11
These five kings **f** and hid themselves Jos 10:16
home, to the town from which he **f**.'" Jos 20:6
Adoni-bezek **f**, but they pursued him and Jgs 1:6
from his chariot and **f** away on foot. Jgs 4:15
But Sisera **f** away on foot to the tent of Jgs 4:17
all the army ran. They cried out and **f**. Jgs 7:21
And the army **f** as far as Beth-shittah Jgs 7:22
And Zebah and Zalmunna **f**, and he Jgs 8:12
Jotham ran away and **f** and went to Beer Jgs 9:21
chased him, and he **f** before him. Jgs 9:40
the leaders of the city **f** to it and shut Jgs 9:51
Then Jephthah **f** from his brothers and Jgs 11:3
they turned and **f** toward the wilderness Jgs 20:45
men turned and **f** toward the Jgs 20:47
and Israel was defeated, and they **f**, 1 Sm 4:10
I **f** from the battle today." And he said, 1 Sm 4:16
"Israel has **f** before the Philistines, 1 Sm 4:17
f from him and were much afraid. 1 Sm 17:24
that their champion was dead, they **f**. 1 Sm 17:51
a great blow, so that they **f** before him. 1 Sm 19:8
And David **f** and escaped that night. 1 Sm 19:10
window, and he **f** away and escaped. 1 Sm 19:12
Now David **f** and escaped, and he 1 Sm 19:18
Then David **f** from Naioth in Ramah 1 Sm 20:1
And David rose and **f** that day from 1 Sm 21:10
they knew that he **f** and did not 1 Sm 22:17
Abiathar, escaped and **f** after David. 1 Sm 22:20
son of Ahimelech had **f** to David to 1 Sm 23:6
told Saul that David had **f** to Gath, 1 Sm 27:4
men, who mounted camels and **f**. 1 Sm 30:17
men of Israel **f** before the Philistines 1 Sm 31:1
men of Israel had **f** and that Saul and 1 Sm 31:7
they abandoned their cities and **f**. 1 Sm 31:7
answered, "The people **f** from the battle, 2 Sm 1:4
the Beerothites **f** to Gittaim and have 2 Sm 4:3
and his nurse took him up and **f**, 2 Sm 4:4
up and fled, and as she **f** in her haste, 2 Sm 4:4
the Syrians, and they **f** before him. 2 Sm 10:13
Ammonites saw that the Syrians **f**, 2 Sm 10:14
they likewise **f** before Abishai and 2 Sm 10:14
And the Syrians **f** before Israel, and 2 Sm 10:18
and each mounted his mule and **f**. 2 Sm 13:29
But Absalom **f**. And the young man 2 Sm 13:34
But Absalom **f** and went to Talmai 2 Sm 13:37
So Absalom **f** and went to Geshur, 2 Sm 13:38
And all Israel **f** every one to his own 2 Sm 18:17
Now Israel had **f** every man to his 2 Sm 19:8
and now he has **f** out of the land from 2 Sm 19:9
and the men **f** from the Philistines. 2 Sm 23:11
met me when I **f** from Absalom your 1 Kgs 2:7
Absalom—Joab **f** to the tent 1 Kgs 2:28
"Joab has **f** to the tent of the LORD, 1 Kgs 2:29
But Hadad **f** to Egypt, together with 1 Kgs 11:17
who had **f** from his master 1 Kgs 11:23
Jeroboam arose and **f** into Egypt, 1 Kgs 11:40
where he had **f** from King Solomon), 1 Kgs 12:2
The Syrians **f**, and Israel pursued 1 Kgs 20:20
And the rest **f** into the city of Aphek, 1 Kgs 20:30
Ben-hadad also **f** and entered an 1 Kgs 20:30
the Moabites, till they **f** before them. 2 Kgs 3:24
So they **f** away in the twilight and 2 Kgs 7:7
the camp as it was, and **f** for their lives. 2 Kgs 7:7
him, but his army **f** home. 2 Kgs 8:21
her." Then he opened the door and **f**. 2 Kgs 9:10
Then Joram reined about and **f**, 2 Kgs 9:23
he **f** in the direction of Beth-haggan. 2 Kgs 9:27
And he **f** to Megiddo and died there. 2 Kgs 9:27
Israel, and every man **f** to his home. 2 Kgs 14:12
in Jerusalem, and he **f** to Lachish. 2 Kgs 14:19
all the men of war **f** by night by the 2 Kgs 25:4
men of Israel **f** before the Philistines 1 Chr 10:1
that the army had **f** and that Saul 1 Chr 10:7
they abandoned their cities and **f**, 1 Chr 10:7
and the men **f** from the Philistines. 1 Chr 11:13
for battle, and they **f** before him. 1 Chr 19:14
Ammonites saw that the Syrians **f**, 1 Chr 19:15
fled, they likewise **f** before Abishai, 1 Chr 19:15
And the Syrians **f** before Israel, and 1 Chr 19:18
where he had **f** from King Solomon), 2 Chr 10:2
The men of Israel **f** before Judah, 2 Chr 13:16
before Judah, and the Ethiopians **f**. 2 Chr 14:12
Israel, and every man **f** to his home. 2 Chr 25:22
in Jerusalem, and he **f** to Lachish. 2 Chr 25:27
did the work, had **f** each to his field. Neh 13:10
David, when he **f** from Absalom his son. Ps 3:T
Miktam of David, when he **f** from Saul, Ps 57:T
At your rebuke they **f**; at the sound of Ps 104:7
The sea looked and **f**; Jordan turned Ps 114:3
O LORD! I have **f** to you for refuge! Ps 143:9
Ramah trembles; Gibeah of Saul has **f**. Is 10:29
hoped and to whom we **f** for help to be Is 20:6
For they have **f** from the swords, from Is 21:15
All your leaders have **f** together; without Is 22:3
captured, though they had **f** far away. Is 22:3
no man, and all the birds of the air had **f**. Jer 4:25
air and the beasts have **f** and are gone. Jer 9:10
he was afraid and **f** and escaped to Jer 26:21
and all the soldiers saw them, they **f**, Jer 39:4
are beaten down and have **f** in haste; Jer 46:5
yes, they have turned and **f** together; Jer 46:21
all the men of war **f** and went out from Jer 52:7
they **f** without strength before the Lam 1:6
brought to him, and sleep **f** from him. Dn 6:18
them, and they **f** to hide themselves. Dn 10:7
Jacob **f** to the land of Aram; there Hos 12:12
as if a man **f** from a lion, and a bear Am 5:19
shall flee as you **f** from the earthquake Zec 14:5
The herdsmen **f**, and going into the city Mt 8:33
Then all the disciples left him and **f**. Mt 26:56
The herdsmen **f** and told it in the city Mk 5:14
And they all left him and **f**. Mk 14:50
And they went out and **f** from the tomb, Mk 16:8

they **f** and told it in the city and in the Lk 8:34
At this retort Moses **f** and became an Acts 7:29
learned of it and **f** to Lystra and Derbe, Acts 14:6
so that they **f** out of that house naked Acts 19:16
we who have **f** for refuge might have Heb 6:18
and the woman **f** into the wilderness, Rv 12:6
And every island **f** away, and no Rv 16:20
his presence earth and sky **f** away, Rv 20:11

FLEE (100)

Behold, this city is near enough to **f** to, Gn 19:20
Arise, **f** to Laban my brother in Haran Gn 27:43
by not telling him that he intended to **f**. Gn 31:20
Why did you **f** secretly and trick me, Gn 31:27
said, "Let us **f** from before Israel, Ex 14:25
for you a place to which he may **f**. Ex 21:13
and you shall **f** when none pursues Lv 26:17
and they shall **f** as one flees from the Lv 26:36
let those who hate you **f** before you." Nm 10:35
Therefore now **f** to your own place. I Nm 24:11
you shall permit the manslayer to **f**, Nm 35:6
person without intent may **f** there. Nm 35:11
person without intent may **f** there. Nm 35:15
that the manslayer might **f** there, anyone Dt 4:42
he may **f** to one of these cities and save Dt 4:42
so that any manslayer can **f** to them. Dt 19:3
he dies—he may **f** to one of these cities Dt 19:5
you one way and **f** before you seven Dt 28:7
against them and **f** seven ways before Dt 28:25
us just as before, we shall **f** before them. Jos 8:5
just as before.' So we will **f** before them. Jos 8:6
they had no power to **f** this way or that, Jos 8:20
intent or unknowingly may **f** there. Jos 20:3
He shall **f** to one of these cities and shall Jos 20:4
a person without intent could **f** there, Jos 20:9
"Let us **f** and draw them away from the Jgs 20:32
him at Jerusalem, "Arise, and let us **f**, 2 Sm 15:14
all the people who are with him will **f**. 2 Sm 17:2
For if we **f**, they will not care about us. 2 Sm 18:3
are ashamed when they **f** in battle. 2 Sm 19:3
Or will you **f** three months before 2 Sm 24:13
mount his chariot to **f** to Jerusalem. 1 Kgs 12:18
Then open the door and **f**; do not 2 Kgs 9:3
caused the inhabitants of Gath to **f**); 1 Chr 8:13
his chariot to **f** to Jerusalem. 2 Chr 10:18
are swifter than a runner; they **f** away; Jb 9:25
He will **f** from an iron weapon; a bronze Jb 20:24
When she rouses herself to **f**, she laughs Jb 39:18
The arrow cannot make him **f**; for him Jb 41:28
soul, "**F** like a bird to your mountain, Ps 11:1
who see me in the street **f** from me. Ps 31:11
you, that they may **f** to it from the bow. Ps 60:4
those who hate him shall **f** before him! Ps 68:1
"The kings of the armies—they **f**, they Ps 68:12
they **f**!" The women at home divide the Ps 68:12
What ails you, O sea, that you **f**? O Ps 114:5
Or where shall I **f** from your presence? Ps 139:7
The wicked **f** when no one pursues, but Prv 28:1
the day breathes and the shadows **f**, Sg 2:17
Until the day breathes and the shadows **f**, Sg 4:6
To whom will you **f** for help, and where Is 10:3
the inhabitants of Gebim **f** for safety. Is 10:31
people, and each will **f** to his own land. Is 13:14
cries out for Moab; her fugitives **f** to Zoar, Is 15:5
yet the harvest will **f** away in a day of Is 17:11
rebuke them, and they will **f** far away, Is 17:13
you said, "No! We will **f** upon horses"; Is 30:16
upon horses"; therefore you shall **f** away; Is 30:16
A thousand shall **f** at the threat of one; at Is 30:17
at the threat of five you shall **f**, till you Is 30:17
him; and he shall **f** from the sword, Is 31:8
At the tumultuous noise peoples **f**; when Is 33:3
and sorrow and sighing shall **f** away. Is 35:10
Go out from Babylon, **f** from Chaldea, Is 48:20
and sorrow and sighing shall **f** away. Is 51:11
Raise a standard toward Zion, **f** for safety, Jer 4:6
F for safety, O people of Benjamin, from Jer 6:1
The swift cannot **f** away, nor the warrior Jer 46:6
F! Save yourselves! You will be like a Jer 48:6
F, turn back, dwell in the depths, O Jer 49:8
has become feeble, she turned to **f**, Jer 49:24
F, wander far away, dwell in the depths, Jer 49:30
in it; both man and beast shall **f** away. Jer 50:3
"**F** from the midst of Babylon, and go Jer 50:8
and every one shall **f** to his own land. Jer 50:16
They **f** and escape from the land of Jer 50:28
"**F** from the midst of Babylon; let every Jer 51:6
Let the beasts **f** from under it and the Dn 4:14
the mighty shall **f** away naked in Am 2:16
"O seer, go, **f** away to the land of Judah, Am 7:12
the sword; not one of them shall **f** away; Am 9:1
But Jonah rose to **f** to Tarshish from the Jon 1:3
is why I made haste to **f** to Tarshish; Jon 4:2
F from the land of the north, declares the Zec 2:6
And you shall **f** to the valley of my Zec 14:5
And you shall **f** as you fled from the Zec 14:5
the child and his mother, and **f** to Egypt, Mt 2:13
Who warned you to **f** from the wrath to Mt 3:7
persecute you in one town, **f** to the next, Mt 10:23
who are in Judea **f** to the mountains. Mt 24:16
who are in Judea **f** to the mountains. Mk 13:14
Who warned you to **f** from the wrath to Lk 3:7
who are in Judea **f** to the mountains, Lk 21:21
will not follow, but they will **f** from him, Jn 10:5
F from sexual immorality. Every 1 Cor 6:18
my beloved, **f** from idolatry. 1 Cor 10:14
for you, O man of God, **f** these things. 1 Tm 6:11
So **f** youthful passions and pursue 2 Tm 2:22
Resist the devil, and he will **f** from you. Jas 4:7
long to die, but death will **f** from them. Rv 9:6

FLEECE (9)

of your oil, and the first **f** of your sheep, Dt 18:4
I am laying a **f** of wool on the threshing Jgs 6:37
If there is dew on the **f** alone, and it is dry Jgs 6:37
early next morning and squeezed the **f**, Jgs 6:38
enough dew from the **f** to fill a bowl Jgs 6:38
let me test just once more with the **f**. Jgs 6:39
Please let it be dry on the **f** only, and on Jgs 6:39
and it was dry on the **f** only, and on all Jgs 6:40
was not warmed with the **f** of my sheep, Jb 31:20

FLEEING (8)

said, "I am **f** from my mistress Sarai." Gn 16:8
who by **f** there may save his life. Dt 19:4
For they will say, 'They are **f** from us, just Jos 8:6
heard that the Philistines were **f**, 1 Sm 14:22
fair; his hand pierced the **f** serpent. Jb 26:13
Like **f** birds, like a scattered nest, so are Is 16:2
will punish Leviathan the **f** serpent, Is 27:1
knew that he was **f** from the presence of Jon 1:10

FLEES (9)

they shall flee as one **f** from the sword, Lv 26:36
he dies, and he **f** into one of these cities, Dt 19:11
he **f** like a shadow and continues not. Jb 14:2
he **f** from its power in headlong flight. Jb 27:22
He who **f** at the sound of the terror shall Is 24:18
Ask him who **f** and her who escapes; Jer 48:19
He who **f** from the terror shall fall into Jer 48:44
wolf coming and leaves the sheep and **f**, Jn 10:12
He **f** because he is a hired hand and Jn 10:13

FLEET (6)

King Solomon built a **f** of ships at 1 Kgs 9:26
Hiram sent with the **f** his servants, 1 Kgs 9:27
Moreover, the **f** of Hiram, which 1 Kgs 10:11
the king had a **f** of ships of Tarshish 1 Kgs 10:22
Tarshish at sea with the **f** of Hiram. 1 Kgs 10:22
every three years the **f** of ships of 1 Kgs 10:22

FLEETING (3)

of my days; let me know how **f** I am! Ps 39:4
a lying tongue is a **f** vapor and a snare Prv 21:6
than to enjoy the **f** pleasures of sin. Heb 11:25

FLESH (315)

of his ribs and closed up its place with **f**. Gn 2:21
is bone of my bones and **f** of my flesh; Gn 2:23
is bone of my bones and flesh of my **f**; Gn 2:23
to his wife, and they shall become one **f**. Gn 2:24
shall not abide in man forever, for he is **f**: Gn 6:3
for all **f** had corrupted their way on the Gn 6:12
have determined to make an end of all **f**, Gn 6:13
the earth to destroy all **f** in which is the Gn 6:17
And of every living thing of all **f**, you Gn 6:19
two and two of all **f** in which there was Gn 7:15
that entered, male and female of all **f**, Gn 7:16
And all **f** died that moved on the earth, Gn 7:21
is with you of all **f**—birds and animals Gn 8:17
But you shall not eat **f** with its life, that is, Gn 9:4
that never again shall all **f** be cut off by Gn 9:11
you and every living creature of all **f**. Gn 9:15
again become a flood to destroy all **f**. Gn 9:15
living creature of all **f** that is on the Gn 9:16
between me and all **f** that is on the Gn 9:17
circumcised in the **f** of your foreskins, Gn 17:11
be in your **f** an everlasting covenant. Gn 17:13
not circumcised in the **f** of his foreskin Gn 17:14
he circumcised the **f** of their foreskins Gn 17:23
circumcised in the **f** of his foreskin. Gn 17:24
circumcised in the **f** of his foreskin. Gn 17:25
my bone and my **f**!" And he stayed Gn 29:14
our own **f**." And his brothers listened Gn 37:27
And the birds will eat the **f** from you." Gn 40:19
behold, it was restored like the rest of his **f**. Ex 4:7
They shall eat the **f** that night, roasted Ex 12:8
not take any of the **f** outside the house, Ex 12:46
be stoned, and its **f** shall not be eaten, Ex 21:28
you shall not eat any **f** that is torn by Ex 22:31
undergarments to cover their naked **f**. Ex 28:42
But the **f** of the bull and its skin and its Ex 29:14
ordination and boil its **f** in a holy place. Ex 29:31
his sons shall eat the **f** of the ram and Ex 29:32
And if any of the **f** for the ordination or Ex 29:34
But the skin of the bull and all its **f**, with Lv 4:11
Whatever touches its **f** shall be holy, Lv 6:27
And the **f** of the sacrifice of his peace Lv 7:15
what remains of the **f** of the sacrifice on Lv 7:17
If any of the **f** of the sacrifice of his peace Lv 7:18
"**F** that touches any unclean thing shall Lv 7:19
up with fire. All who are clean may eat **f**, Lv 7:19
person who eats of the **f** of the sacrifice of Lv 7:20
and then eats some **f** from the sacrifice Lv 7:21
and its skin and its **f** and its dung he Lv 8:17
"Boil the **f** at the entrance of the tent of Lv 8:31
what remains of the **f** and the bread you Lv 8:32
The **f** and the skin he burned up with Lv 9:11
You shall not eat any of their **f**, and you Lv 11:8
you shall not eat any of their **f**, and you Lv 11:11
the eighth day the **f** of his foreskin shall Lv 12:3
white, and there is raw **f** in the swelling, Lv 13:10
But when raw **f** appears on him, he Lv 13:14
examine the raw **f** and pronounce him Lv 13:15
Raw **f** is unclean, for it is a leprous Lv 13:15
But if the raw **f** recovers and turns Lv 13:16
skin and the raw **f** of the burn becomes Lv 13:24
Their skin and their **f** and their dung Lv 16:27
For the life of the **f** is in the blood, and I Lv 17:11
if he does not wash them or bathe his **f**, Lv 17:16
shall not eat any **f** with the blood in Lv 19:26
You shall eat the **f** of your sons, and Lv 26:29
you shall eat the **f** of your daughters. Lv 26:29
whose **f** is half eaten away when he Nm 12:12
"O God, the God of the spirits of all **f**, Nm 16:22
that opens the womb of all **f**, Nm 18:15
But their **f** shall be yours, as the Nm 18:18
Its skin, its **f**, and its blood, with its Nm 19:5
the LORD, the God of the spirits of all **f**, Nm 27:16
For who is there of all **f**, that has heard Dt 5:26
and you shall not eat the life with the **f**. Dt 12:23
burnt offerings, the **f** and the blood, Dt 12:27
LORD your God, but the **f** you may eat. Dt 12:27
Their **f** you shall not eat, and their Dt 14:8
shall any of the **f** that you sacrifice on Dt 16:4
the **f** of your sons and daughters, Dt 28:53
them any of the **f** of his children whom Dt 28:55
my sword shall devour **f**—with the Dt 32:42
and consumed the **f** and the unleavened Jgs 6:21
I will flail your **f** with the thorns of the Jgs 8:7
also that I am your bone and your **f**." Jgs 9:2
and I will give your **f** to the birds of 1 Sm 17:44
said, "Behold, we are your bone and **f**. 2 Sm 5:1
brothers; you are my bone and my **f**. 2 Sm 19:12
'Are you not my bone and my **f**? 2 Sm 19:13
and boiled their **f** with the yokes 1 Kgs 19:21
sackcloth on his **f** and fasted and 1 Kgs 21:27
him, the **f** of the child became warm. 2 Kgs 4:34
times, and your **f** shall be restored, 2 Kgs 5:10
and his **f** was restored like the flesh of 2 Kgs 5:14
was restored like the **f** of a little child, 2 Kgs 5:14
the dogs shall eat the **f** of Jezebel, 2 Kgs 9:36
said, "Behold, we are your bone and **f**. 1 Chr 11:1
With him is an arm of **f**, but with us 2 Chr 32:8
Now our **f** is as the flesh of our brothers, Neh 5:5
Now our flesh is as the **f** of our brothers, Neh 5:5
your hand and touch his bone and his **f**, Jb 2:5
past my face; the hair of my **f** stood up. Jb 4:15
the strength of stones, or is my **f** bronze? Jb 6:12
My **f** is clothed with worms and dirt; my Jb 7:5
Have you eyes of **f**? Do you see as man Jb 10:4
You clothed me with skin and **f**, and Jb 10:11
Why should I take my **f** in my teeth and Jb 13:14
My bones stick to my skin and to my **f**, Jb 19:20
Why are you not satisfied with my **f**? Jb 19:22
destroyed, yet in my **f** I shall see God, Jb 19:26
dismayed, and shuddering seizes my **f**. Jb 21:6
His **f** is so wasted away that it cannot be Jb 33:21
let his **f** become fresh with youth; let Jb 33:25
all **f** would perish together, and man Jb 34:15
The folds of his **f** stick together, firmly Jb 41:23
being rejoices; my **f** also dwells secure. Ps 16:9
When evildoers assail me to eat up my **f**, Ps 27:2
no soundness in my **f** because of your Ps 38:3
and there is no soundness in my **f**. Ps 38:7
Do I eat the **f** of bulls or drink the blood Ps 50:13
shall not be afraid. What can **f** do to me? Ps 56:4
my **f** faints for you, as in a dry and weary Ps 63:1
who hears prayer, to you shall all **f** come. Ps 65:2
My **f** and my heart may fail, but God is Ps 73:26
He remembered that they were but **f**, a Ps 78:39
the **f** of your faithful to the beasts of the Ps 79:2
my heart and **f** sing for joy to the living Ps 84:2
loud groaning my bones cling to my **f**. Ps 102:5
My **f** trembles for fear of you, and I Ps 119:120
he who gives food to all **f**, for his Ps 136:25
and let all **f** bless his holy name Ps 145:21
be healing to your **f** and refreshment to Prv 3:8
find them, and healing to all their **f**. Prv 4:22

when your **f** and body are consumed, Prv 5:11
A tranquil heart gives life to the **f**, but Prv 14:30
fool folds his hands and eats his own **f**. Eccl 4:5
much study is a weariness of the **f**. Eccl 12:12
each devours the **f** of his own arm, Is 9:20
low, and the fat of his **f** will grow lean. Is 17:4
sheep, eating **f** and drinking wine. Is 22:13
man, and not God, and their horses are **f**, Is 31:3
be revealed, and all **f** shall see it together, Is 40:5
I said, "What shall I cry?" All **f** is grass, Is 40:6
make your oppressors eat their own **f**, Is 49:26
Then all **f** shall know that I am the LORD Is 49:26
and not to hide yourself from your own **f**? Is 58:7
who eat pig's **f**, and broth of tainted meat Is 65:4
judgment, and by his sword, with all **f**; Is 66:16
eating pig's **f** and the abomination and Is 66:17
all **f** shall come to worship before me, Is 66:23
they shall be an abhorrence to all **f**." Is 66:24
offerings to your sacrifices, and eat the **f**. Jer 7:21
who are circumcised merely in the **f**— Jer 9:25
Can even sacrificial **f** avert your doom? Jer 11:15
of the land to the other; no **f** has peace. Jer 12:12
trusts in man and makes **f** his strength, Jer 17:5
make them eat the **f** of their sons and Jer 19:9
everyone shall eat the **f** of his neighbor Jer 19:9
he is entering into judgment with all **f**, Jer 25:31
"Behold, I am the LORD, the God of all **f**. Jer 32:27
I am bringing disaster upon all **f**, Jer 45:5
He has made my **f** and my skin waste Lam 3:4
of stone from their **f** and give them a Ezk 11:19
their flesh and give them a heart of **f**, Ezk 11:19
All **f** shall see that I the LORD have Ezk 20:48
its sheath against all **f** from south to Ezk 21:4
And all **f** shall know that I am the LORD. Ezk 21:5
I will strew your **f** upon the mountains Ezk 32:5
You eat **f** with the blood and lift up Ezk 33:25
of stone from your **f** and give you a Ezk 36:26
your flesh and give you a heart of **f**. Ezk 36:26
you, and will cause **f** to come upon you, Ezk 37:6
on them, and **f** had come upon them, Ezk 37:8
and you shall eat **f** and drink blood. Ezk 39:17
You shall eat the **f** of the mighty, and Ezk 39:18
on the tables the **f** of the offering was Ezk 40:43
uncircumcised in heart and **f**, Ezk 44:7
uncircumcised in heart and **f**, Ezk 44:9
appearance and fatter in **f** than all the Dn 1:15
the gods, whose dwelling is not with **f**." Dn 2:11
in its branches, and all **f** was fed from it. Dn 4:12
and it was told, 'Arise, devour much **f**.' Dn 7:5
that I will pour out my Spirit on all **f**; Jl 2:28
my people and their **f** from off their Mi 3:2
who eat the **f** of my people, and flay their Mi 3:3
up like meat in a pot, like **f** in a cauldron. Mi 3:3
caves with prey and his dens with torn **f**. Na 2:12
out like dust, and their **f** like dung. Zep 1:17
Be silent, all **f**, before the LORD, for he Zec 2:13
are left devour the **f** of one another." Zec 11:9
but devours the **f** of the fat ones, Zec 11:16
their **f** will rot while they are still Zec 14:12
For **f** and blood has not revealed this to Mt 16:17
to his wife, and they shall become one **f**? Mt 19:5
So they are no longer two but one **f**. Mt 19:6
indeed is willing, but the **f** is weak." Mt 26:41
and they shall become one **f**.' So they Mk 10:8
So they are no longer two but one **f**. Mk 10:8
indeed is willing, but the **f** is weak." Mk 14:38
and all **f** shall see the salvation of God.'" Lk 3:6
spirit does not have **f** and bones as you Lk 24:39
nor of the will of the **f** nor of the will of Jn 1:13
the Word became **f** and dwelt among Jn 1:14
That which is born of the **f** is flesh, and Jn 3:6
That which is born of the flesh is **f**, and Jn 3:6
I will give for the life of the world is my **f**." Jn 6:51
"How can this man give us his **f** to eat?" Jn 6:52
unless you eat the **f** of the Son of Man Jn 6:53
Whoever feeds on my **f** and drinks my Jn 6:54
For my **f** is true food, and my blood is Jn 6:55
Whoever feeds on my **f** and drinks my Jn 6:56
Spirit who gives life; the **f** is of no avail. Jn 6:63
You judge according to the **f**; I judge no Jn 8:15
you have given him authority over all **f**, Jn 17:2
that I will pour out my Spirit on all **f**, Acts 2:17
rejoiced; my **f** also will dwell in hope. Acts 2:26
to Hades, nor did his **f** see corruption. Acts 2:31
from David according to the **f** Rom 1:3
our forefather according to the **f**? Rom 4:1
For while we were living in the **f**, our Rom 7:5
the law is spiritual, but I am of the **f**, Rom 7:14
good dwells in me, that is, in my **f**. Rom 7:18
but with my **f** I serve the law of sin. Rom 7:25
done what the law, weakened by the **f**, Rom 8:3
in the likeness of sinful **f** and for sin, Rom 8:3
and for sin, he condemned sin in the **f**, Rom 8:3
not according to the **f** but according to Rom 8:4
live according to the **f** set their minds Rom 8:5
set their minds on the things of the **f**, Rom 8:5
To set the mind on the **f** is death, but to Rom 8:6
that is set on the **f** is hostile to God, Rom 8:7
who are in the **f** cannot please God. Rom 8:8
are not in the **f** but in the Spirit, Rom 8:9
brothers, we are debtors, not to the **f**, Rom 8:12
to the flesh, to live according to the **f**. Rom 8:12
you live according to the **f** you will die, Rom 8:13
my kinsmen according to the **f**. Rom 9:3
and from their race, according to the **f**, Rom 9:5
the children of the **f** who are the Rom 9:8
and make no provision for the **f**, Rom 13:14
spiritual people, but as people of the **f**, 1 Cor 3:1
for you are still of the **f**. For while there 1 Cor 3:3
you not of the **f** and behaving only in 1 Cor 3:3
to Satan for the destruction of the **f**, 1 Cor 5:5
written, "The two will become one **f**." 1 Cor 6:16
For not all **f** is the same, but there is 1 Cor 15:39
f and blood cannot inherit the 1 Cor 15:50
I make my plans according to the **f**, 2 Cor 1:17
may be manifested in our mortal **f**. 2 Cor 4:11
we regard no one according to the **f**. 2 Cor 5:16
regarded Christ according to the **f**, 2 Cor 5:16
us of walking according to the **f**. 2 Cor 10:2
For though we walk in the **f**, we are 2 Cor 10:3
not waging war according to the **f**. 2 Cor 10:3
are not of the **f** but have divine power 2 Cor 10:4
many boast according to the **f**, 2 Cor 11:18
a thorn was given me in the **f**, 2 Cor 12:7
life I now live in the **f** I live by faith in Gal 2:20
are you now being perfected by the **f**? Gal 3:3
of the slave was born according to the **f**, Gal 4:23
according to the **f** persecuted him who Gal 4:29
freedom as an opportunity for the **f**, Gal 5:13
you will not gratify the desires of the **f**. Gal 5:16
the desires of the **f** are against the Spirit, Gal 5:17
the desires of the Spirit are against the **f**, Gal 5:17
Now the works of the **f** are evident: Gal 5:19
have crucified the **f** with its passions Gal 5:24
who sows to his own **f** will from the flesh Gal 6:8
flesh will from the **f** reap corruption, Gal 6:8
good showing in the **f** who would force Gal 6:12
that they may boast in your **f**. Gal 6:13
we all once lived in the passions of our **f**, Eph 2:3
that at one time you Gentiles in the **f**, Eph 2:11
which is made in the **f** by hands— Eph 2:11
broken down in his **f** the dividing wall Eph 2:14
For no one ever hated his own **f**, but Eph 5:29
wife, and the two shall become one **f**." Eph 5:31
we do not wrestle against **f** and blood, Eph 6:12
If I am to live in the **f**, that means Phil 1:22
to remain in the **f** is more necessary on Phil 1:24
look out for those who mutilate the **f**. Phil 3:2
Jesus and put no confidence in the **f**— Phil 3:3
have reason for confidence in the **f** also. Phil 3:4
he has reason for confidence in the **f**, Phil 3:4
reconciled in his body of **f** by his death, Col 1:22
and in my **f** I am filling up what is Col 1:24
hands, by putting off the body of the **f**, Col 2:11
and the uncircumcision of your **f**, Col 2:13
in stopping the indulgence of the **f**. Col 2:23
He was manifested in the **f**, vindicated 1 Tm 3:16
to you, both in the **f** and in the Lord. Phlm 1:16
the children share in **f** and blood, Heb 2:14
In the days of his **f**, Jesus offered up Heb 5:7
sanctifies for the purification of the **f**, Heb 9:13
the curtain, that is, through his **f**, Heb 10:20
against you and will eat your **f** like fire. Jas 5:3
for "All **f** is like grass and all its glory 1 Pt 1:24
to abstain from the passions of the **f**, 1 Pt 2:11
put to death in the **f** but made alive in 1 Pt 3:18
Since therefore Christ suffered in the **f**, 1 Pt 4:1
has suffered in the **f** has ceased from sin, 1 Pt 4:1
of the time in the **f** no longer for human 1 Pt 4:2
though judged in the **f** the way people 1 Pt 4:6
sensual passions of the **f** those who are 2 Pt 2:18
—the desires of the **f** and the desires of 1 Jn 2:16
Christ has come in the **f** is from God, 1 Jn 4:2
the coming of Jesus Christ in the **f**. 2 Jn 1:7
also, relying on their dreams, defile the **f**, Jude 1:8
even the garment stained by the **f**. Jude 1:23
and devour her **f** and burn her up with Rv 17:16
to eat the **f** of kings, the flesh of Rv 19:18
eat the flesh of kings, the **f** of captains, Rv 19:18
flesh of captains, the **f** of mighty men, Rv 19:18
men, the **f** of horses and their riders, Rv 19:18
and their riders, and the **f** of all men, Rv 19:18
all the birds were gorged with their **f**. Rv 19:21

FLEW (5)
He rode on a cherub and **f**; he was 2 Sm 22:11
He rode on a cherub and **f**; he came Ps 18:10
two he covered his feet, and with two he **f**. Is 6:2
Then one of the seraphim **f** to me, having Is 6:6
a loud voice as it **f** directly overhead, Rv 8:13

FLIES (13)
I will send swarms of **f** on you and your Ex 8:21
shall be filled with swarms of **f**, Ex 8:21
so that no swarms of **f** shall be there, Ex 8:22
came great swarms of **f** into the house of Ex 8:24
the land was ruined by the swarms of **f**. Ex 8:24
that the swarms of **f** may depart from Ex 8:29
removed the swarms of **f** from Pharaoh, Ex 8:31
of any winged bird that **f** in the air, Dt 4:17
He sent among them swarms of **f**, Ps 78:45
of the night, nor the arrow that **f** by day, Ps 91:5
He spoke, and there came swarms of **f**, Ps 105:31
Dead **f** make the perfumer's ointment Eccl 10:1
The locust spreads its wings and **f** away. Na 3:16

FLIGHT (16)
of a driven leaf shall put them to **f**, Lv 26:36
and two have put ten thousand to **f**, Dt 32:30
One man of you puts to **f** a thousand, Jos 23:10
and put to **f** all those in the valleys, 1 Chr 12:15
he flees from its power in headlong **f**. Jb 27:22
For you will put them to **f**; you will aim Ps 21:12
they were in panic; they took to **f**. Ps 48:5
sound of your thunder they took to **f**. Ps 104:7
Madmenah is in **f**; the inhabitants of Is 10:31
go out in haste, and you shall not go in **f**, Is 52:12
and archer every city takes to **f**; Jer 4:29
came to me in swift **f** at the time of the Dn 9:21
F shall perish from the swift, and the Am 2:14
Pray that your **f** may not be in winter Mt 24:20
mighty in war, put foreign armies to **f**. Heb 11:34
fourth living creature like an eagle in **f**. Rv 4:7

FLING (1)
on the open field I will **f** you, and will Ezk 32:4

FLINGING (1)
off their cloaks and **f** dust into the air, Acts 22:23

FLINT (7)
Then Zipporah took a **f** and cut off her Ex 4:25
"Make **f** knives and circumcise the sons Jos 5:2
So Joshua made **f** knives and Jos 5:3
of water, the **f** into a spring of water. Ps 114:8
bows bent, their horses' hoofs seem like **f**, Is 5:28
therefore I have set my face like a **f**, and I Is 50:7
Like emery harder than **f** have I made Ezk 3:9

FLINTY (3)
who brought you water out of the **f** rock, Dt 8:15
out of the rock, and oil out of the **f** rock. Dt 32:13
his hand to the **f** rock and overturns Jb 28:9

FLITTING (1)
Like a sparrow in its **f**, like a swallow in Prv 26:2

FLOAT (1)
threw it in there and made the iron **f**. 2 Kgs 6:6

FLOATED (1)
and the ark **f** on the face of the waters. Gn 7:18

FLOCK (119)
of the firstborn of his **f** and of their fat Gn 4:4
set seven ewe lambs of the **f** apart. Gn 21:28
Go to the **f** and bring me two good Gn 27:9
mouth and watered the **f** of Laban his Gn 29:10
I will again pasture your **f** and keep it: Gn 30:31
let me pass through all your **f** today, Gn 30:32
Jacob pastured the rest of Laban's **f**. Gn 30:36
and all the black in the **f** of Laban. Gn 30:40
and did not put them with Laban's **f**. Gn 30:40
the stronger of the **f** were breeding, Gn 30:41
in the troughs before the eyes of the **f**, Gn 30:41
for the feebler of the **f** he would not lay Gn 30:42
and Leah into the field where his **f** was Gn 31:4
your wages,' then all the **f** bore spotted; Gn 31:8
your wages,' then all the **f** bore striped. Gn 31:8
breeding season of the **f** I lifted up my Gn 31:10
that mated with the **f** were striped, Gn 31:10
goats that mate with the **f** are striped, Gn 31:12
two daughters, and six years for your **f**, Gn 31:41
was pasturing the **f** with his brothers. Gn 37:2
pasture their father's **f** near Shechem. Gn 37:12
brothers pasturing the **f** at Shechem? Gn 37:13
well with your brothers and with the **f**, Gn 37:14
please, where they are pasturing the **f**." Gn 37:16
a young goat from the **f**." And she said, Gn 38:17
filled the troughs to water their father's **f**. Ex 2:16
up and saved them, and watered their **f**. Ex 2:17
drew water for us and watered the **f**." Ex 2:19
was keeping the **f** of his father-in-law, Ex 3:1
and he led his **f** to the west side of the Ex 3:1
of livestock from the herd or from the **f**. Lv 1:2
his gift for a burnt offering is from the **f**, Lv 1:10
to the LORD is an animal from the **f**, Lv 3:6
he has committed, a female from the **f**, Lv 5:6
a ram without blemish out of the **f**, Lv 5:15
a ram without blemish out of the **f**, Lv 5:18
LORD a ram without blemish out of the **f**, Lv 6:6

offering from the herd or from the **f**, Lv 22:21
the herd or from the **f** a food offering or Nm 15:3
of your herds and the young of your **f**, Dt 7:13
the firstborn of your herd and of your **f**. Dt 12:6
the firstborn of your herd or of your **f**, Dt 12:17
you may kill any of your herd or your **f**, Dt 12:21
oil, and the firstborn of your herd and **f**, Dt 14:23
furnish him liberally out of your **f**, Dt 15:14
of your herd and **f** you shall dedicate to Dt 15:19
herd, nor shear the firstborn of your **f**. Dt 15:19
the LORD your God, from the **f** or the herd, Dt 16:2
of your herds and the young of your **f**. Dt 28:4
of your herds and the young of your **f**. Dt 28:18
of your herds or the young of your **f**, Dt 28:51
from the herd, and milk from the **f**, Dt 32:14
a bear, and took a lamb from the **f**, 1 Sm 17:34
one of his own **f** or herd to prepare 2 Sm 12:4
goats from the **f** to the number 2 Chr 35:7
was a ram of the **f** for their guilt. Ezr 10:19
They send out their little boys like a **f**, Jb 21:11
disdained to set with the dogs of my **f**. Jb 30:1
your **f** found a dwelling in it; in your Ps 68:10
led your people like a **f** by the hand of Ps 77:20
guided them in the wilderness like a **f**. Ps 78:52
of Israel, you who lead Joseph like a **f**! Ps 80:1
my soul loves, where you pasture your **f**, Sg 1:7
women, follow in the tracks of the **f**, Sg 1:8
Your hair is like a **f** of goats leaping down Sg 4:1
Your teeth are like a **f** of shorn ewes that Sg 4:2
Your hair is like a **f** of goats leaping down Sg 6:5
Your teeth are like a **f** of ewes that have Sg 6:6
He will tend his **f** like a shepherd; he will Is 40:11
out of the sea with the shepherds of his **f**? Is 63:11
prospered, and all their **f** is scattered. Jer 10:21
because the LORD'S **f** has been taken Jer 13:17
Where is the **f** that was given you, your Jer 13:20
that was given you, your beautiful **f**? Jer 13:20
have scattered my **f** and have driven Jer 23:2
gather the remnant of my **f** out of all the Jer 23:3
out, and roll in ashes, you lords of the **f**, Jer 25:34
nor escape for the lords of the **f**. Jer 25:35
and the wail of the lords of the **f**! Jer 25:36
will keep him as a shepherd keeps his **f**.' Jer 31:10
over the young of the **f** and the herd; Jer 31:12
little ones of the **f** shall be dragged Jer 49:20
and be as male goats before the **f**. Jer 50:8
little ones of their **f** shall be dragged Jer 50:45
I break in pieces the shepherd and his **f**; Jer 51:23
Take the choicest one of the **f**; pile the Ezk 24:5
shepherd seeks out his **f** when he is Ezk 34:12
"As for you, my **f**, thus says the Lord Ezk 34:17
I will rescue my **f**; they shall no longer Ezk 34:22
them: to increase their people like a **f**. Ezk 36:37
Like the **f** for sacrifices, like the flock Ezk 36:38
like the **f** at Jerusalem during her Ezk 36:38
a ram from the **f** without blemish. Ezk 43:23
from the herd and a ram from the **f**, Ezk 43:25
one sheep from every **f** of two hundred, Ezk 45:15
eat lambs from the **f** and calves from the Am 6:4
the LORD took me from following the **f**, Am 7:15
Let neither man nor beast, herd nor **f**, Jon 3:7
like sheep in a fold, like a **f** in its pasture, Mi 2:12
And you, O tower of the **f**, hill of the Mi 4:8
stand and shepherd his **f** in the strength Mi 5:4
with your staff, the **f** of your inheritance, Mi 7:14
the **f** be cut off from the fold and there Hab 3:17
will save them, as the **f** of his people; Zec 9:16
for the LORD of hosts cares for his **f**, the Zec 10:3
shepherd of the **f** doomed to slaughter. Zec 11:4
the shepherd of the **f** doomed to be Zec 11:7
worthless shepherd, who deserts the **f**! Zec 11:17
be the cheat who has a male in his **f**, Mal 1:14
and the sheep of the **f** will be scattered.' Mt 26:31
field, keeping watch over their **f** by night. Lk 2:8
"Fear not, little **f**, for it is your Father's Lk 12:32
So there will be one **f**, one shepherd. Jn 10:16
believe because you are not part of my **f**. Jn 10:26
to yourselves and to all the **f**, Acts 20:28
in among you, not sparing the **f**; Acts 20:29
Or who tends a **f** without getting some 1 Cor 9:7
shepherd the **f** of God that is among you, 1 Pt 5:2
charge, but being examples to the **f**. 1 Pt 5:3

FLOCKS (75)
Abram, also had **f** and herds and tents, Gn 13:5
He has given him **f** and herds, silver Gn 24:35
He had possessions of **f** and herds and Gn 26:14
behold, three **f** of sheep lying beside it, Gn 29:2
it, for out of that well the **f** were watered. Gn 29:2
and when all the **f** were gathered there, Gn 29:3
until all the **f** are gathered together Gn 29:8
peeled in front of the **f** in the troughs, Gn 30:38
places, where the **f** came to drink. Gn 30:38
the **f** bred in front of the sticks and so Gn 30:39
and so the **f** brought forth striped, Gn 30:39
the faces of the **f** toward the striped and Gn 30:40
man increased greatly and had large **f**, Gn 30:43
and I have not eaten the rams of your **f**. Gn 31:38
are my children, the **f** are my flocks, Gn 31:43
are my children, the flocks are my **f**, Gn 31:43
I have oxen, donkeys, **f**, male servants, Gn 32:5
him, and the **f** and herds and camels, Gn 32:7
and that the nursing **f** and herds are a Gn 33:13
hard for one day, all the **f** will die. Gn 33:13
They took their **f** and their herds, their Gn 34:28
your children's children, and your **f**, Gn 45:10
have brought their **f** and their herds Gn 46:32
with their **f** and herds and all that they Gn 47:1
there is no pasture for your servants' **f**, Gn 47:4
food in exchange for the horses, the **f**, Gn 47:17
Only their children, their **f**, and their Gn 50:8
donkeys, the camels, the herds, and the **f**. Ex 9:3
and daughters and with our **f** and herds, Ex 10:9
only let your **f** and your herds remain Ex 10:24
Take your **f** and your herds, as you Ex 12:32
very much livestock, both **f** and herds. Ex 12:38
Let no **f** or herds graze opposite that Ex 34:3
And every tithe of herds and **f**, every Lv 27:32
Shall **f** and herds be slaughtered for Nm 11:22
took as plunder all their cattle, their **f**, Nm 31:9
oxen and of the donkeys and of the **f**. Nm 31:28
the oxen, of the donkeys, and of the **f**, Nm 31:30
your herds and **f** multiply and your Dt 8:13
to hear the whistling for the **f**? Jgs 5:16
He will take the tenth of your **f**, and 1 Sm 8:17
also captured all the **f** and herds, 1 Sm 30:20
rich man had very many **f** and herds, 2 Sm 12:2
before them like two little **f** of goats, 1 Kgs 20:27
the valley, to seek pasture for their **f**, 1 Chr 4:39
there was pasture there for their **f**. 1 Chr 4:41
Over the **f** was Jaziz the Hagrite. 1 Chr 27:30
and **f** and herds in abundance, 2 Chr 32:29
the firstborn of our herds and of our **f**; Neh 10:36
they seize **f** and pasture them. Jb 24:2
the meadows clothe themselves with **f**, Ps 65:13
to the hail and their **f** to thunderbolts. Ps 78:48
and makes their families like **f**. Ps 107:41
Know well the condition of your **f**, and Prv 27:23
also great possessions of herds and **f**, Eccl 2:7
herself beside the **f** of your companions? Sg 1:7
will make their **f** lie down there. Is 13:20
they will be for **f**, which will lie down, and Is 17:2
a joy of wild donkeys, a pasture of **f**; Is 32:14
All the **f** of Kedar shall be gathered to you; Is 60:7
Strangers shall stand and tend your **f**; Is 61:5
Sharon shall become a pasture for **f**, and Is 65:10
fathers labored, their **f** and their herds, Jer 3:24
they shall eat up your **f** and your herds; Jer 5:17
Shepherds with their **f** shall come against Jer 6:3
and those who wander with their **f**. Jer 31:24
habitations of shepherds resting their **f**. Jer 33:12
f shall again pass under the hands of Jer 33:13
Their tents and their **f** shall be taken, Jer 49:29
for camels and Ammon a fold for **f**. Ezk 25:5
waste cities be filled with **f** of people. Ezk 36:38
With their **f** and herds they shall go to Hos 5:6
for them; even the **f** of sheep suffer. Jl 1:18
like a young lion among the **f** of sheep, Mi 5:8
meadows for shepherds and folds for **f**. Zep 2:6

FLOG (4)
over to courts and **f** you in their Mt 10:17
some you will **f** in your synagogues Mt 23:34
spit on him, and **f** him and kill him. Mk 10:34
it lawful for you to **f** a man who is a Acts 22:25

FLOGGED (2)
to be mocked and **f** and crucified, Mt 20:19
Then Pilate took Jesus and **f** him. Jn 19:1

FLOGGING (3)
And after **f** him, they will kill him, and Lk 18:33
that he should be examined by **f**, Acts 22:24
Others suffered mocking and **f**, and Heb 11:36

FLOOD (34)
I will bring a **f** of waters upon the earth Gn 6:17
years old when the **f** of waters came upon Gn 7:6
into the ark to escape the waters of the **f**. Gn 7:7
the waters of the **f** came upon the earth. Gn 7:10
The **f** continued forty days on the earth. Gn 7:17
all flesh be cut off by the waters of the **f**, Gn 9:11
shall there be a **f** to destroy the earth." Gn 9:11
never again become a **f** to destroy all Gn 9:15
After the **f** Noah lived 350 years. Gn 9:28
Sons were born to them after the **f**. Gn 10:1
spread abroad on the earth after the **f**. Gn 10:32
Arpachshad two years after the **f**. Gn 11:10
like a bursting **f**." Therefore the name 2 Sm 5:20
like a bursting **f**." Therefore the 1 Chr 14:11
cannot see, and a **f** of water covers you. Jb 22:11
Terrors overtake him like a **f**; in the Jb 27:20
that a **f** of waters may cover you? Jb 38:34
every night I **f** my bed with tears; Ps 6:6
The LORD sits enthroned over the **f**; the Ps 29:10
deep waters, and the **f** sweeps over me. Ps 69:2
Let not the **f** sweep over me, or the deep Ps 69:15
They surround me like a **f** all day long; Ps 88:17
You sweep them away as with a **f**; they Ps 90:5
then the **f** would have swept us away, Ps 124:4
Its end shall come with a **f**, and to the Dn 9:26
of the seas, and the **f** surrounded me; Jon 2:3
But with an overflowing **f** he will make a Na 1:8
those days before the **f** they were eating Mt 24:38
unaware until the **f** came and swept Mt 24:39
And when a **f** arose, the stream broke Lk 6:48
and the **f** came and destroyed them all. Lk 17:27
join them in the same **f** of debauchery, 1 Pt 4:4
when he brought a **f** upon the world of 2 Pt 2:5
the woman, to sweep her away with a **f**. Rv 12:15

FLOODS (8)
The **f** covered them; they went down into Ex 15:5
waters piled up; the **f** stood up in a heap; Ex 15:8
The **f** have lifted up, O LORD, the floods Ps 93:3
O LORD, the **f** have lifted up their voice; Ps 93:3
up their voice; the **f** lift up their roaring. Ps 93:3
quench love, neither can **f** drown it. Sg 8:7
And the rain fell, and the **f** came, and the Mt 7:25
And the rain fell, and the **f** came, and the Mt 7:27

FLOOR (43)
they came to the threshing **f** of Atad, Gn 50:10
mourning on the threshing **f** of Atad, Gn 50:11
that is on the **f** of the tabernacle and Nm 5:17
a contribution from the threshing **f**, Nm 15:20
it were the grain of the threshing **f**, Nm 18:27
Levites as produce of the threshing **f**, Nm 18:30
of your flock, out of your threshing **f**, Dt 15:14
from your threshing **f** and your Dt 16:13
and there lay their lord dead on the **f**. Jgs 3:25
a fleece of wool on the threshing **f**. Jgs 6:37
barley tonight at the threshing **f**. Ru 3:2
cloak and go down to the threshing **f**, Ru 3:3
down to the threshing **f** and did just as Ru 3:6
the woman came to the threshing **f**." Ru 3:14
they came to the threshing **f** of Nacon, 2 Sm 6:6
by the threshing **f** of Araunah the 2 Sm 24:16
on the threshing **f** of Araunah the 2 Sm 24:18
"To buy the threshing **f** from you, 2 Sm 24:21
bought the threshing **f** and the oxen 2 Sm 24:24
From the **f** of the house to the walls of 1 Kgs 6:15
and he covered the **f** of the house with 1 Kgs 6:15
of cedar from the **f** to the walls, 1 Kgs 6:16
The **f** of the house he overlaid with 1 Kgs 6:30
finished with cedar from **f** to rafters. 1 Kgs 7:7
at the threshing **f** at the entrance of 1 Kgs 22:10
From the threshing **f**, or from the 2 Kgs 6:27
came to the threshing **f** of Chidon, 1 Chr 13:9
by the threshing **f** of Ornan the 1 Chr 21:15
on the threshing **f** of Ornan the 1 Chr 21:18
from the threshing **f** and paid 1 Chr 21:21
site of the threshing **f** that I may 1 Chr 21:22
him at the threshing **f** of Ornan the 1 Chr 21:28
on the threshing **f** of Ornan the 2 Chr 3:1
at the threshing **f** at the entrance 2 Chr 18:9
grain and gather it to your threshing **f**? Jb 39:12
is like a threshing **f** at the time when Jer 51:33
from the **f** up to the windows (now the Ezk 41:16
From the **f** to above the door, Ezk 41:20
Threshing **f** and wine vat shall not feed Hos 9:2
from the threshing **f** or like smoke Hos 13:3
them as sheaves to the threshing **f**. Mi 4:12
will clear his threshing **f** and gather his Mt 3:12
to clear his threshing **f** and to gather the Lk 3:17

FLOORS (4)
and are robbing the threshing **f**." 1 Sm 23:1
the chaff of the summer threshing **f**; Dn 2:35
a prostitute's wages on all threshing **f**. Hos 9:1
"The threshing **f** shall be full of grain; the Jl 2:24

FLOUR (68)
and said, "Quick! Three seahs of fine **f**! Gn 18:6
oil. You shall make them of fine wheat **f**. Ex 29:2
tenth seah of fine **f** mingled with a Ex 29:40
to the LORD, his offering shall be of fine **f**. Lv 2:1
take from it a handful of the fine **f** and oil, Lv 2:2
unleavened loaves of fine **f** mixed with oil Lv 2:4
a griddle, it shall be of fine **f** unleavened, Lv 2:5
in a pan, it shall be made of fine **f** with oil. Lv 2:7
of an ephah of fine **f** for a sin offering. Lv 5:11
handful of the fine **f** of the grain offering Lv 6:15
of an ephah of fine **f** as a regular grain Lv 6:20
and loaves of fine **f** well mixed with oil. Lv 7:12
of an ephah of fine **f** mixed with oil, Lv 14:10
of an ephah of fine **f** mixed with oil for Lv 14:21
of an ephah of fine **f** mixed with oil, Lv 23:13
They shall be of fine **f**, and they shall Lv 23:17
"You shall take fine **f** and bake twelve Lv 24:5

of her, a tenth of an ephah of barley **f**. Nm 5:15
bread, loaves of fine **f** mixed with oil, Nm 6:15
of them full of fine **f** mixed with oil for Nm 7:13
of them full of fine **f** mixed with oil for Nm 7:19
of them full of fine **f** mixed with oil for Nm 7:25
of them full of fine **f** mixed with oil for Nm 7:31
of them full of fine **f** mixed with oil for Nm 7:37
of them full of fine **f** mixed with oil for Nm 7:43
of them full of fine **f** mixed with oil for Nm 7:49
of them full of fine **f** mixed with oil for Nm 7:55
of them full of fine **f** mixed with oil for Nm 7:61
of them full of fine **f** mixed with oil for Nm 7:67
of them full of fine **f** mixed with oil for Nm 7:73
of them full of fine **f** mixed with oil for Nm 7:79
its grain offering of fine **f** mixed with oil, Nm 8:8
offering of a tenth of an ephah of fine **f**, Nm 15:4
of an ephah of fine **f** mixed with a third Nm 15:6
of three tenths of an ephah of fine **f**, Nm 15:9
an ephah of fine **f** for a grain offering, Nm 28:5
an ephah of fine **f** for a grain offering, Nm 28:9
an ephah of fine **f** for a grain offering, Nm 28:12
two tenths of fine **f** for a grain Nm 28:12
and a tenth of fine **f** mixed with oil as Nm 28:13
grain offering of fine **f** mixed with oil; Nm 28:20
grain offering of fine **f** mixed with oil, Nm 28:28
grain offering of fine **f** mixed with oil, Nm 29:3
shall be of fine **f** mixed with oil, Nm 29:9
grain offering of fine **f** mixed with oil, Nm 29:14
unleavened cakes from an ephah of **f**. Jgs 6:19
a three-year-old bull, an ephah of **f**, 1 Sm 1:24
and she took **f** and kneaded it and 1 Sm 28:24
wheat, barley, **f**, parched grain, 2 Sm 17:28
thirty cors of fine **f** and sixty cors of 1 Kgs 4:22
only a handful of **f** in a jar and a 1 Kgs 17:12
'The jar of **f** shall not be spent, 1 Kgs 17:14
The jar of **f** was not spent, neither 1 Kgs 17:16
"Then bring **f**." And he threw it into 2 Kgs 4:41
time a seah of fine **f** shall be sold for a 2 Kgs 7:1
So a seah of fine **f** was sold for a 2 Kgs 7:16
and a seah of fine **f** for a shekel, 2 Kgs 7:18
the holy utensils, also over the fine **f**, 1 Chr 9:29
on oxen, abundant provisions of **f**, 1 Chr 12:40
the **f** for the grain offering, 1 Chr 23:29
Take the millstones and grind **f**, put off Is 47:2
You ate fine **f** and honey and oil. Ezk 16:13
I fed you with fine **f** and oil and honey Ezk 16:19
third of a hin of oil to moisten the **f**, Ezk 46:14
grain has no heads; it shall yield no **f**; Hos 8:7
took and hid in three measures of **f**, Mt 13:33
took and hid in three measures of **f**, Lk 13:21
myrrh, frankincense, wine, oil, fine **f**, Rv 18:13

FLOURISH (13)
Can reeds **f** where there is no water? Jb 8:11
In his days may the righteous **f**, and Ps 72:7
sprout like grass and all evildoers **f**, Ps 92:7
The righteous **f** like the palm tree and Ps 92:12
the LORD; they **f** in the courts of our God. Ps 92:13
but the righteous will **f** like a green Prv 11:28
but the tent of the upright will **f**. Prv 14:11
rejoice; your bones shall **f** like the grass; Is 66:14
I made you **f** like a plant of the field. Ezk 16:7
the green tree, and make the dry tree **f**. Ezk 17:24
Though he may **f** among his Hos 13:15
my shadow; they shall **f** like the grain; Hos 14:7
Grain shall make the young men **f**, and Zec 9:17

FLOURISHES (2)
in the morning it **f** and is renewed; in the Ps 90:6
like grass; he **f** like a flower of the field; Ps 103:15

FLOW (27)
shall be clean from the **f** of her blood. Lv 12:7
Water shall **f** from his buckets, and Nm 24:7
water of the Red Sea **f** over them as they Dt 11:4
and caused waters to **f** down like rivers. Ps 78:16
in the valleys; they **f** between the hills; Ps 104:10
makes his wind blow and the waters **f**. Ps 147:18
for from it **f** the springs of life. Prv 4:23
to the place where the streams **f**, there Eccl 1:7
the streams flow, there they **f** again. Eccl 1:7
Blow upon my garden, let its spices **f**. Sg 4:16
the hills; and all the nations shall **f** to it, Is 2:2
refused the waters of Shiloah that **f** gently, Is 8:6
the mountains shall **f** with their blood. Is 34:3
he made water **f** for them from the rock; Is 48:21
with tears and our eyelids **f** with water. Jer 9:18
The nations shall no longer **f** to him; Jer 51:44
things I weep; my eyes **f** with tears; Lam 1:16
my eyes **f** with rivers of tears because Lam 3:48
"My eyes will **f** without ceasing, Lam 3:49
making its rivers **f** around the place of Ezk 31:4
sweet wine, and the hills shall **f** with milk, Jl 3:18
streambeds of Judah shall **f** with water; Jl 3:18
wine, and all the hills shall **f** with it. Am 9:13
above the hills; and peoples shall **f** to it, Mi 4:1
living waters shall **f** out from Zec 14:8
And immediately the **f** of blood dried Mk 5:29
of his heart will **f** rivers of living water.'" Jn 7:38

FLOWED (7)
A river **f** out of Eden to water the garden, Gn 2:10
It is the one that **f** around the whole land Gn 2:11
It is the one that **f** around the whole land Gn 2:13
of the wound **f** into the bottom 1 Kgs 22:35
the brook that **f** through the land, 2 Chr 32:4
out; it **f** through the desert like a river. Ps 105:41
city, and blood **f** from the winepress, Rv 14:20

FLOWER (19)
blossoms, each with calyx and **f**, Ex 25:33
blossoms, each with calyx and **f**, Ex 25:33
blossoms, each with calyx and **f**, Ex 37:19
blossoms, each with calyx and **f**, Ex 37:19
the brim of a cup, like the **f** of a lily. 1 Kgs 7:26
the brim of a cup, like the **f** of a lily. 2 Chr 4:5
While yet in **f** and not cut down, they Jb 8:12
He comes out like a **f** and withers; he flees Jb 14:2
grass; he flourishes like a **f** of the field; Ps 103:15
over, and the **f** becomes a ripening grape, Is 18:5
and the fading **f** of its glorious beauty, Is 28:1
and the fading **f** of its glorious beauty, Is 28:4
and all its beauty is like the **f** of the field. Is 40:6
the **f** fades when the breath of the LORD Is 40:7
The grass withers, the **f** fades, but the Is 40:8
because like a **f** of the grass he will pass Jas 1:10
heat and withers the grass; its **f** falls, Jas 1:11
grass and all its glory like the **f** of grass. 1 Pt 1:24
grass. The grass withers, and the **f** falls, 1 Pt 1:24

FLOWERS (12)
and its **f** shall be of one piece with it. Ex 25:31
blossoms, with their calyxes and **f**, Ex 25:34
and its **f** were of one piece with it. Ex 37:17
blossoms, with their calyxes and **f**, Ex 37:20
From its base to its **f**, it was hammered Nm 8:4
in the form of gourds and open **f**. 1 Kgs 6:18
cherubim and palm trees and open **f**, 1 Kgs 6:29
of cherubim, palm trees, and open **f**. 1 Kgs 6:32
cherubim and palm trees and open **f**, 1 Kgs 6:35
before the inner sanctuary; the **f**, 1 Kgs 7:49
the **f**, the lamps, and the tongs, of 2 Chr 4:21
The **f** appear on the earth, the time of Sg 2:12

FLOWING (34)
broad land, a land **f** with milk and honey, Ex 3:8
a land **f** with milk and honey.'" Ex 3:17
give you, a land **f** with milk and honey, Ex 13:5
Go up to a land **f** with milk and honey; Ex 33:3
possess, a land **f** with milk and honey.' Lv 20:24
out of a land **f** with milk and honey, Nm 16:13
us into a land **f** with milk and honey, Nm 16:14
you, in a land **f** with milk and honey. Dt 6:3
and springs, **f** out in the valleys and hills, Dt 8:7
offspring, a land **f** with milk and honey. Dt 11:9
this land, a land **f** with milk and honey. Dt 26:9
fathers, a land **f** with milk and honey.' Dt 26:15
you, a land **f** with milk and honey, Dt 27:3
them into the land **f** with milk and Dt 31:20
of the Jordan shall be cut off from **f**, Jos 3:13
and those **f** down toward the Sea of the Jos 3:16
give to us, a land **f** with milk and honey. Jos 5:6
is not another." Then the oil stopped **f**. 2 Kgs 4:6
the streams **f** with honey and curds. Jb 20:17
As a deer pants for **f** streams, so pants my Ps 42:1
cistern, **f** water from your own well. Prv 5:15
water, and **f** streams from Lebanon. Sg 4:15
Carmel, and your **f** locks are like purple; Sg 7:5
the grass like willows by **f** streams. Is 44:4
give them a land **f** with milk and honey, Jer 11:5
waters run dry, the cold **f** streams? Jer 18:14
them, a land **f** with milk and honey. Jer 32:22
for them, a land **f** with milk and honey, Ezk 20:6
them, a land **f** with milk and honey, Ezk 20:15
waists, with **f** turbans on their heads, Ezk 23:15
to the mountains with your **f** blood, Ezk 32:6
The water was **f** down from below the Ezk 47:1
of your submission **f** from your 2 Cor 9:13
f from the throne of God and of the Rv 22:1

FLOWS (6)
is the Tigris, which **f** east of Assyria. Gn 2:14
It **f** with milk and honey, and this is Nm 13:27
us, a land that **f** with milk and honey. Nm 14:8
"This water **f** toward the eastern region Ezk 47:8
the sea; when the water **f** into the sea, Ezk 47:8
water for them **f** from the sanctuary. Ezk 47:12

FLUNG (2)
and threw stones at him and **f** dust. 2 Sm 16:13
they **f** me alive into the pit and cast Lam 3:53

FLUTE (10)
tambourine, **f**, and lyre before them, 1 Sm 10:5
tambourine and **f** and wine at their feasts, Is 5:12
to the sound of the **f** to go to the Is 30:29
my heart moans for Moab like a **f**, Jer 48:36
my heart moans like a **f** for the men of Jer 48:36
house and saw the **f** players and the Mt 9:23
"'We played the **f** for you, and you did Mt 11:17
to one another, "'We played the **f** for you, Lk 7:32
such as the **f** or the harp, 1 Cor 14:7
musicians, of **f** players and trumpeters, Rv 18:22

FLUTES (1)
To the choirmaster: for the **f**. A Psalm of Ps 5:T

FLUTTERS (1)
stirs up its nest, that **f** over its young, Dt 32:11

FLY (16)
and let birds **f** above the earth across the Gn 1:20
is born to trouble as the sparks **f** upward. Jb 5:7
He will **f** away like a dream and not be Jb 20:8
like a dove! I would **f** away and be at rest; Ps 55:6
they are soon gone, and we **f** away. Ps 90:10
LORD will whistle for the **f** that is at the Is 7:18
Who are these that **f** like a cloud, and like Is 60:8
but a biting **f** from the north has come Jer 46:20
wings to Moab, for she would **f** away; Jer 48:9
one shall **f** swiftly like an eagle and Jer 48:40
shall mount up and **f** swiftly like an Jer 49:22
Ephraim's glory shall **f** away like a Hos 9:11
cold—when the sun rises, they **f** away; Na 3:17
afar; they **f** like an eagle swift to devour. Hab 1:8
so that she might **f** from the serpent Rv 12:14
to all the birds that **f** directly overhead, Rv 19:17

FLYING (8)
livestock, creeping things and **f** birds! Ps 148:10
wings, **f** like an eagle toward heaven. Prv 23:5
in its flitting, like a swallow in its **f**, Prv 26:2
and its fruit will be a **f** fiery serpent. Is 14:29
the lion, the adder and the **f** fiery serpent, Is 30:6
my eyes and saw, and behold, a **f** scroll! Zec 5:1
do you see?" I answered, "I see a **f** scroll. Zec 5:2
I saw another angel **f** directly overhead, Rv 14:6

FOAL (3)
Binding his **f** to the vine and his Gn 49:11
on a donkey, on a colt, the **f** of a donkey. Zec 9:9
and on a colt, the **f** of a beast of burden.'" Mt 21:5

FOAM (2)
though its waters roar and **f**, though the Ps 46:3
casting up the **f** of their own shame; Jude 1:13

FOAMING (3)
—and you drank **f** wine made from the Dt 32:14
of the LORD there is a cup with **f** wine, Ps 75:8
and rolled about, **f** at the mouth. Mk 9:20

FOAMS (2)
and he **f** and grinds his teeth and Mk 9:18
convulses him so that he **f** at the mouth; Lk 9:39

FODDER (7)
"We have plenty of both straw and **f**, Gn 24:25
and gave straw and **f** to the camels, Gn 24:32
to give his donkey **f** at the lodging Gn 42:27
and when he had given their donkeys **f**, Gn 43:24
he has grass, or the ox low over his **f**? Jb 6:5
They gather their **f** in the field, and they Jb 24:6
that work the ground will eat seasoned **f**, Is 30:24

FOE (16)
And Esther said, "A **f** and enemy! This Est 7:6
have made us turn back from the **f**, Ps 44:10
Oh, grant us help against the **f**, for vain Ps 60:11
may have their portion from the **f**." Ps 68:23
How long, O God, is the **f** to scoff? Is the Ps 74:10
day when he redeemed them from the **f**, Ps 78:42
captivity, his glory to the hand of the **f**. Ps 78:61
the hand of the **f** and redeemed them Ps 106:10
Oh grant us help against the **f**, for vain Ps 108:12
the punishment of a merciless **f**, Jer 30:14
have gone away, captives before the **f**. Lam 1:5
her people fell into the hand of the **f**, Lam 1:7
enemy, with his right hand set like a **f**; Lam 2:4
that **f** or enemy could enter the gates of Lam 4:12
any safety from the **f** for him who went Zec 8:10
trampling the **f** in the mud of the Zec 10:5

FOES (36)
these curses on your **f** and enemies who Dt 30:7
months before your **f** while they 2 Sm 24:13
devastation by your **f** while the 1 Chr 21:12
O LORD, how many are my **f**! Many are Ps 3:1
of grief; it grows weak because of all my **f**. Ps 6:7
established strength because of your **f**, Ps 8:2
his sight; as for all his **f**, he puffs at them. Ps 10:5
over him," lest my **f** rejoice because I am Ps 13:4
Consider how many are my **f**, and with Ps 25:19
to eat up my flesh, my adversaries and **f**, Ps 27:2
up and have not let my **f** rejoice over me. Ps 30:1
over me who are wrongfully my **f**, Ps 35:19
But my **f** are vigorous, they are mighty, Ps 38:19

Through you we push down our **f**; Ps 44:5
have saved us from our **f** and have put to Ps 44:7
it is he who will tread down our **f**. Ps 60:12
dishonor; my **f** are all known to you. Ps 69:19
Your **f** have roared in the midst of your Ps 74:4
Do not forget the clamor of your **f**, the Ps 74:23
and turn my hand against their **f**. Ps 81:14
I will crush his **f** before him and strike Ps 89:23
You have exalted the right hand of his **f**; Ps 89:42
and made them stronger than their **f**. Ps 105:24
it is he who will tread down our **f**. Ps 108:13
me, because my **f** forget your words. Ps 119:139
and rescued us from our **f**, for his Ps 136:24
my enemies and avenge myself on my **f**. Is 1:24
multitude of your foreign **f** shall be like Is 29:5
he shows himself mighty against his **f**. Is 42:13
you shall be devoured, and all your **f**, Jer 30:16
vengeance, to avenge himself on his **f**. Jer 46:10
Her **f** have become the head; her Lam 1:5
none to help her, her **f** gloated over her; Lam 1:7
that his neighbors should be his **f**; Lam 1:17
you and exalted the might of your **f**. Lam 2:17
from their mouth and consumes their **f**. Rv 11:5

FOLD (14)

also shook out the **f** of my garment Neh 5:13
shall inspect your **f** and miss nothing. Jb 5:24
Take it from the **f** of your garment and Ps 74:11
and I will bring them back to their **f**, Jer 23:3
he will roar mightily against his **f**, and Jer 25:30
Surely their **f** shall be appalled at their Jer 49:20
have gone. They have forgotten their **f**. Jer 50:6
surely their **f** shall be appalled at their Jer 50:45
for camels and Ammon a **f** for flocks. Ezk 25:5
I will set them together like sheep in a **f**, Mi 2:12
be cut off from the **f** and there be no Hab 3:17
holy meat in the **f** of his garment and Hg 2:12
and touches with his **f** bread or stew or Hg 2:12
I have other sheep that are not of this **f**. Jn 10:16

FOLDED (1)

with the linen cloths but **f** up in a place Jn 20:7

FOLDING (4)

The two leaves of the one door were **f**, 1 Kgs 6:34
the two leaves of the other door were **f**. 1 Kgs 6:34
slumber, a little **f** of the hands to rest, Prv 6:10
slumber, a little **f** of the hands to rest, Prv 24:33

FOLDS (7)

your little ones and **f** for your sheep, Nm 32:24
fortified cities, and **f** for sheep. Nm 32:36
The **f** of his flesh stick together, firmly Jb 41:23
from your house or goats from your **f**. Ps 50:9
The fool **f** his hands and eats his own Eccl 4:5
and the peaceful **f** are devastated Jer 25:37
meadows for shepherds and **f** for flocks. Zep 2:6

FOLLIES (1)

fatness; their hearts overflow with **f**. Ps 73:7

FOLLOW (90)

may not be willing to **f** me to this land. Gn 24:5
But if the woman is not willing to **f** you, Gn 24:8
'Perhaps the woman will not **f** me.' Gn 24:39
by reason of the famine that will **f**, Gn 41:31
said to his steward, "Up, **f** after the men, Gn 44:4
out, you and all the people who **f** you.' Ex 11:8
You shall **f** my rules and keep my Lv 18:4
him and all who **f** him in whoring after Lv 20:5
not to **f** after your own heart and your Nm 15:39
care that you be not ensnared to **f** them, Dt 12:30
Justice, and only justice, you shall **f**, Dt 16:20
not learn to **f** the abominable practices Dt 18:9
you shall set out from your place and **f** it. Jos 3:3
And he said to them, "**F** after me, for the Jgs 3:28
the Abiezrites were called out to **f** him. Jgs 6:34
and they too were called out to **f** him. Jgs 6:35
loaves of bread to the people who **f** me, Jgs 8:5
and their hearts inclined to **f** Abimelech, Jgs 9:3
reigns over you will **f** the LORD your 1 Sm 12:14
to the young men who **f** my lord. 1 Sm 25:27
had been too exhausted to **f** David, 1 Sm 30:21
among the people who **f** Absalom.' 2 Sm 17:9
whoever is for David, let him **f** Joab." 2 Sm 20:11
LORD and did not wholly **f** the LORD, 1 Kgs 11:6
If the LORD is God, **f** him; but if Baal, 1 Kgs 18:21
then **f** him." And the people did not 1 Kgs 18:21
and then I will **f** you." And he said to 1 Kgs 19:20
for all the people who **f** me." 1 Kgs 20:10
F me, and I will bring you to the man 2 Kgs 6:19
and they do not **f** the statutes or the 2 Kgs 17:34
goodness and mercy shall **f** me all the Ps 23:6
good accuse me because I **f** after good. Ps 38:20
hearts, to **f** their own counsels. Ps 81:12
and all the upright in heart will **f** it. Ps 94:15
to death; her steps **f** the path to Sheol; Prv 5:5
women, **f** in the tracks of the flock, Sg 1:8
to you and be yours; they shall **f** you; Is 45:14
no more stubbornly **f** their own evil Jer 3:17
who stubbornly **f** their own heart and Jer 13:10
We will **f** our own plans, and will every Jer 18:12
you are afraid shall **f** close after you to Jer 42:16
foolish prophets who **f** their own spirit, Ezk 13:3
and the Cushites shall **f** in his train. Dn 11:43
Sound the alarm at Beth-aven; we **f** you, Hos 5:8
And he said to them, "**F** me, and I will Mt 4:19
"Teacher, I will **f** you wherever you go." Mt 8:19
And Jesus said to him, "**F** me, and leave Mt 8:22
"**F** me." And he rose and followed him. Mt 9:9
take his cross and **f** me is not worthy Mt 10:38
himself and take up his cross and **f** me. Mt 16:24
treasure in heaven; and come, **f** me." Mt 19:21
And Jesus said to them, "**F** me, and I Mk 1:17
"**F** me." And he rose and followed him. Mk 2:14
allowed no one to **f** him except Peter Mk 5:37
himself and take up his cross and **f** me. Mk 8:34
treasure in heaven; and come, **f** me." Mk 10:21
a jar of water will meet you. **F** him, Mk 14:13
tax booth. And he said to him, "**F** me." Lk 5:27
and take up his cross daily and **f** me. Lk 9:23
stop him, because he does not **f** with us." Lk 9:49
to him, "I will **f** you wherever you go." Lk 9:57
To another he said, "**F** me." But he said, Lk 9:59
Yet another said, "I will **f** you, Lord, but Lk 9:61
or 'Look, here!' Do not go out or **f** them. Lk 17:23
treasure in heaven; and come, **f** me." Lk 18:22
F him into the house that he enters Lk 22:10
were around him saw what would **f**, Lk 22:49
He found Philip and said to him, "**F** me." Jn 1:43
he goes before them, and the sheep **f** him, Jn 10:4
A stranger they will not **f**, but they will Jn 10:5
voice, and I know them, and they **f** me. Jn 10:27
If anyone serves me, he must **f** me; and Jn 12:26
I am going you cannot **f** me now, Jn 13:36
me now, but you will **f** afterward." Jn 13:36
to him, "Lord, why can I not **f** you now? Jn 13:37
after saying this he said to him, "**F** me." Jn 21:19
I come, what is that to you? You **f** me!" Jn 21:22
your cloak around you and **f** me." Acts 12:8
"I **f** Paul," or "I follow Apollos," or "I 1 Cor 1:12
follow Paul," or "I **f** Apollos," or "I 1 Cor 1:12
follow Apollos," or "I **f** Cephas," or "I 1 Cor 1:12
or "I follow Cephas," or "I **f** Christ." 1 Cor 1:12
when one says, "I **f** Paul," and another, 1 Cor 3:4
"I **f** Apollos," are you not being merely 1 Cor 3:4
F the pattern of the sound words that 2 Tm 1:13
so that you might **f** in his steps. 1 Pt 2:21
For we did not **f** cleverly devised myths 2 Pt 1:16
And many will **f** their sensuality, and 2 Pt 2:2
It is these who **f** the Lamb wherever he Rv 14:4
their labors, for their deeds **f** them!" Rv 14:13

FOLLOWED (113)

and rode on the camels and **f** the man. Gn 24:61
for seven days and **f** close after him Gn 31:23
and the third and all who **f** the droves, Gn 32:19
of Pharaoh that had **f** them into the sea, Ex 14:28
a different spirit and has **f** me fully, Nm 14:24
Abiram, and the elders of Israel **f** him. Nm 16:25
because they have not wholly **f** me, Nm 32:11
Nun, for they have wholly **f** the LORD.' Nm 32:12
because he has wholly **f** the LORD!' Dt 1:36
you all the men who **f** the Baal of Peor. Dt 4:3
tents, and every living thing that **f** them, Dt 11:6
so they **f** in your steps, receiving Dt 33:3
melt; yet I wholly **f** the LORD my God. Jos 14:8
because you have wholly **f** the LORD my Jos 14:9
this day, because he wholly **f** the LORD, Jos 14:14
and reckless fellows, who **f** him. Jgs 9:4
and all the people **f** him trembling. 1 Sm 13:7
they too **f** hard after them in the 1 Sm 14:22
sons of Jesse had **f** Saul to the battle. 1 Sm 17:13
the youngest. The three eldest **f** Saul, 1 Sm 17:14
She **f** the messengers of David and 1 Sm 25:42
years. But the house of Judah **f** David. 2 Sm 2:10
Abner." And King David **f** the bier. 2 Sm 3:31
and there **f** him a present from the 2 Sm 11:8
Gittites who had **f** him from Gath, 2 Sm 15:18
saw that his counsel was not **f**, 2 Sm 17:23
from David and **f** Sheba the son 2 Sm 20:2
men of Judah **f** their king steadfastly 2 Sm 20:2
Bichrites assembled and **f** him in. 2 Sm 20:14
And they **f** Adonijah and helped him. 1 Kgs 1:7
There was none that **f** the house of 1 Kgs 12:20
my commandments and **f** me with 1 Kgs 14:8
Half of the people **f** Tibni the son of 1 Kgs 16:21
to make him king, and half **f** Omri. 1 Kgs 16:21
the people who **f** Omri overcame the 1 Kgs 16:22
the people who **f** Tibni the son 1 Kgs 16:22
of the LORD and **f** the Baals. 1 Kgs 18:18
districts and the army that **f** them. 1 Kgs 20:19
army or for the animals that **f** them. 2 Kgs 3:9
not leave you." So he arose and **f** her. 2 Kgs 4:30
So Gehazi **f** Naaman. And when 2 Kgs 5:21
of the LORD and **f** the sins of Jeroboam 2 Kgs 13:2
and they **f** the nations that were 2 Kgs 17:15
He even **f** their counsel and went with 2 Chr 22:5
the people still **f** corrupt practices. 2 Chr 27:2
nor the men of the guard who **f** me, Neh 4:23
and I **f** them with half of the people, Neh 12:38
as a bride, how you **f** me in the wilderness, Jer 2:2
but have stubbornly **f** their own hearts Jer 9:14
the others **f** without turning as they Ezk 10:11
pestilence, and plague **f** at his heels. Hab 3:5
they left their nets and **f** him. Mt 4:20
left the boat and their father and **f** him. Mt 4:22
And great crowds **f** him from Galilee Mt 4:25
from the mountain, great crowds **f** him. Mt 8:1
marveled and said to those who **f** him, Mt 8:10
he got into the boat, his disciples **f** him. Mt 8:23
him, "Follow me." And he rose and **f** him. Mt 9:9
And Jesus rose and **f** him, with his Mt 9:19
on from there, two blind men **f** him, Mt 9:27
And many **f** him, and he healed them Mt 12:15
it, they **f** him on foot from the towns. Mt 14:13
And large crowds **f** him, and he healed Mt 19:2
"See, we have left everything and **f** you. Mt 19:27
you who have **f** me will also sit on Mt 19:28
out of Jericho, a great crowd **f** him. Mt 20:29
they recovered their sight and **f** him. Mt 20:34
him and that **f** him were shouting, Mt 21:9
distance, who had **f** Jesus from Galilee, Mt 27:55
they left their nets and **f** him. Mk 1:18
boat with the hired servants and **f** him. Mk 1:20
"Follow me." And he rose and **f** him. Mk 2:14
for there were many who **f** him. Mk 2:15
disciples to the sea, and a great crowd **f**, Mk 3:7
And a great crowd **f** him and thronged Mk 5:24
to his hometown, and his disciples **f** him. Mk 6:1
we have left everything and **f** you." Mk 10:28
amazed, and those who **f** were afraid. Mk 10:32
recovered his sight and **f** him on the Mk 10:52
before and those who **f** were shouting, Mk 11:9
And a young man **f** him, with nothing Mk 14:51
And Peter had **f** him at a distance, Mk 14:54
they **f** him and ministered to him, Mk 15:41
having **f** all things closely for some time Lk 1:3
to land, they left everything and **f** him. Lk 5:11
leaving everything, he rose and **f** him. Lk 5:28
him, and turning to the crowd that **f** him, Lk 7:9
When the crowds learned it, they **f** him, Lk 9:11
"See, we have left our homes and **f** you." Lk 18:28
he recovered his sight and **f** him, Lk 18:43
of Olives, and the disciples **f** him. Lk 22:39
And there **f** him a great multitude of Lk 23:27
the women who had **f** him from Galilee Lk 23:49
with him from Galilee **f** and saw the Lk 23:55
heard him say this, and they **f** Jesus. Jn 1:37
John speak and **f** Jesus was Andrew, Jn 1:40
Mary rise quickly and go out, they **f** her, Jn 11:31
Simon Peter **f** Jesus, and so did another Jn 18:15
and all who **f** him were dispersed and Acts 5:36
and all who **f** him were scattered. Acts 5:37
And he went out and **f** him. He did not Acts 12:9
converts to Judaism **f** Paul and Acts 13:43
She **f** Paul and us, crying out, "These Acts 16:17
for the mob of the people **f**, crying Acts 21:36
from the spiritual Rock that **f** them, 1 Cor 10:4
of the good doctrine that you have **f**. 1 Tm 4:6
You, however, have **f** my teaching, 2 Tm 3:10
They have **f** the way of Balaam, the son 2 Pt 2:15
rider's name was Death, and Hades **f** him. Rv 6:8
blew his trumpet, and there **f** hail and fire, Rv 8:7
whole earth marveled as they **f** the beast. Rv 13:3
Another angel, a second, **f**, saying, Rv 14:8
And another angel, a third, **f** them, Rv 14:9

FOLLOWING (67)

they came to him the **f** year and said to Gn 47:18
have turned back from **f** the LORD, Nm 14:43
For if you turn away from **f** him, he Nm 32:15
would turn away your sons from **f** me, Dt 7:4
ark of the covenant of the LORD **f** them. Jos 6:8
the Levites the **f** cities and pasturelands Jos 21:3
they gave the **f** cities mentioned by Jos 21:9
away this day from **f** the LORD by Jos 22:16
turn away this day from **f** the LORD? Jos 22:18
an altar to turn away from **f** the LORD. Jos 22:23
away this day from **f** the LORD by Jos 22:29
Mount Tabor with 10,000 men **f** him. Jgs 4:14
marched down into the valley, **f** you, Jgs 5:14
On the **f** day, the people went out into the Jgs 9:42
down his bundle and **f** Abimelech put it Jgs 9:49
me to leave you or to return from **f** you. Ru 1:16
Yet do not turn aside from **f** the LORD, 1 Sm 12:20
has turned back from **f** me and has 1 Sm 15:11
Saul returned from **f** the Philistines, 1 Sm 24:1
hand nor to the left from **f** Abner. 2 Sm 2:19
would not turn aside from **f** him. 2 Sm 2:21

to Asahel, “Turn aside from **f** me. 2 Sm 2:22
you from the pasture, from **f** the sheep, 2 Sm 7:8
But if you turn aside from **f** me, you or 1 Kgs 9:6
he returned from **f** him and took 1 Kgs 19:21
a son about that time the **f** spring, 2 Kgs 4:17
drove Israel from **f** the LORD and 2 Kgs 17:21
He did not depart from **f** him, but 2 Kgs 18:6
from the pasture, from **f** the sheep, 1 Chr 17:7
did not turn away from **f** the LORD, 2 Chr 34:33
f all the abominations of the 2 Chr 36:14
The **f** were those who came up from Ezr 2:59
The **f** were those who came up from Neh 7:61
they turned aside from **f** him and had Jb 34:27
her virgin companions **f** behind her. Ps 45:14
from **f** the nursing ewes he brought Ps 78:71
LORD, and turning back from **f** our God, Is 59:13
a way that is not good, **f** their own devices; Is 65:2
to go into the gardens, **f** one in the midst, Is 66:17
Father, and would not turn from **f** me. Jer 3:19
But the LORD took me from **f** the flock, Am 7:15
who have turned back from **f** the LORD, Zep 1:6
And Peter was **f** him at a distance, as Mt 26:58
to stop him, because he was not **f** us.” Mk 9:38
On the **f** day, when they came from Mk 11:12
way today and tomorrow and the day **f**, Lk 13:33
house, and Peter was **f** at a distance. Lk 22:54
turned and saw them **f** and said to them, Jn 1:38
And a large crowd was **f** him, because Jn 6:2
Then Simon Peter came, **f** him, and went Jn 20:6
the disciple whom Jesus loved **f** them, Jn 21:20
And on the **f** day he appeared to them Acts 7:26
And on the **f** day they entered Acts 10:24
with the **f** letter: “The brothers, both Acts 15:23
and the **f** day to Neapolis, Acts 16:11
we came the **f** day opposite Chios; Acts 20:15
On the **f** day Paul went in with us to Acts 21:18
The **f** night the Lord stood by him Acts 23:11
For the judgment **f** one trespass Rom 5:16
the free gift **f** many trespasses brought Rom 5:16
But in the **f** instructions I do not 1 Cor 11:17
once walked, **f** the course of this world, Eph 2:2
world, **f** the prince of the power of the air, Eph 2:2
with scoffing, **f** their own sinful desires. 2 Pt 3:3
malcontents, **f** their own sinful desires; Jude 1:16
scoffers, **f** their own ungodly passions.” Jude 1:18
and pure, were **f** him on white horses. Rv 19:14

FOLLOWS (16)

To his father he sent as **f**: ten donkeys Gn 45:23
of Ephraim by their clans was as **f**: Jos 16:5
sword anyone who **f** her.” For the 2 Kgs 11:15
and anyone who **f** her is to be put to 2 Chr 23:14
Jerusalem to Artaxerxes the king as **f**: Ezr 4:8
him a report, in which was written as **f**: Ezr 5:7
sweet to him; all mankind **f** after him, Jb 21:33
All at once he **f** her, as an ox goes to the Prv 7:22
but he who **f** worthless pursuits lacks Prv 12:11
but he who **f** worthless pursuits will Prv 28:19
Crash **f** hard on crash; the whole land is Jer 4:20
behold, every one of you **f** his stubborn, Jer 16:12
everyone who stubbornly **f** his own Jer 23:17
comes upon disaster; rumor **f** rumor. Ezk 7:26
all bounds, and bloodshed **f** bloodshed. Hos 4:2
Whoever **f** me will not walk in darkness, Jn 8:12

FOLLY (43)

is his name, and **f** is with him. 1 Sm 25:25
not to deal with you according to your **f**. Jb 42:8
O God, you know my **f**; the wrongs I have Ps 69:5
saints; but let them not turn back to **f**. Ps 85:8
because of his great **f** he is led astray. Prv 5:23
The woman **F** is loud; she is seductive Prv 9:13
but the heart of fools proclaims **f**. Prv 12:23
knowledge, but a fool flaunts his **f**. Prv 13:16
but **f** with her own hands tears it down. Prv 14:1
his way, but the **f** of fools is deceiving. Prv 14:8
The simple inherit **f**, but the prudent Prv 14:18
wealth, but the **f** of fools brings folly. Prv 14:24
wealth, but the folly of fools brings **f**. Prv 14:24
but he who has a hasty temper exalts **f**. Prv 14:29
but the mouths of fools pour out **f**. Prv 15:2
but the mouths of fools feed on **f**. Prv 15:14
F is a joy to him who lacks sense, but Prv 15:21
has it, but the instruction of fools is **f**. Prv 16:22
of her cubs rather than a fool in his **f**. Prv 17:12
before he hears, it is his **f** and shame. Prv 18:13
When a man's **f** brings his way to ruin, Prv 19:3
F is bound up in the heart of a child, Prv 22:15
The devising of **f** is sin, and the scoffer Prv 24:9
Answer not a fool according to his **f**, Prv 26:4
Answer a fool according to his **f**, lest he Prv 26:5
to his vomit is a fool who repeats his **f**. Prv 26:11
yet his **f** will not depart from him. Prv 27:22
wisdom and to know madness and **f**. Eccl 1:17
with wisdom—and how to lay hold on **f**, Eccl 2:3
consider wisdom and madness and **f**. Eccl 2:12
there is more gain in wisdom than in **f**, Eccl 2:13
the wickedness of **f** and the foolishness Eccl 7:25
so a little **f** outweighs wisdom and Eccl 10:1
f is set in many high places, and the Eccl 10:6
an evildoer, and every mouth speaks **f**. Is 9:17
For the fool speaks **f**, and his heart is Is 32:6
word of the cross is **f** to those who are 1 Cor 1:18
pleased God through the **f** of what we 1 Cor 1:21
block to Jews and **f** to Gentiles, 1 Cor 1:23
the Spirit of God, for they are **f** to him, 1 Cor 2:14
wisdom of this world is **f** with God. 1 Cor 3:19
very far, for their **f** will be plain to all, 2 Tm 3:9
For, speaking loud boasts of **f**, they 2 Pt 2:18

FOOD (306)

in its fruit. You shall have them for **f**. Gn 1:29
every green plant for **f**.” And it was so. Gn 1:30
that is pleasant to the sight and good for **f**. Gn 2:9
woman saw that the tree was good for **f**, Gn 3:6
with you every sort of **f** that is eaten, Gn 6:21
It shall serve as **f** for you and for them.” Gn 6:21
moving thing that lives shall be **f** for you. Gn 9:3
Then **f** was set before him to eat. But he Gn 24:33
and prepare for me delicious **f**, such as I Gn 27:4
me game and prepare for me delicious **f**, Gn 27:7
from them delicious **f** for your father, Gn 27:9
and his mother prepared delicious **f**, Gn 27:14
she put the delicious **f** and the bread, Gn 27:17
also prepared delicious **f** and brought Gn 27:31
about anything but the **f** he ate. Gn 39:6
were all sorts of baked **f** for Pharaoh, Gn 40:17
them gather all the **f** of these good Gn 41:35
authority of Pharaoh for **f** in the cities, Gn 41:35
That **f** shall be a reserve for the land Gn 41:36
gathered up all the **f** of these seven Gn 41:48
of Egypt, and put the **f** in the cities. Gn 41:48
in every city the **f** from the fields Gn 41:48
“From the land of Canaan, to buy **f**.” Gn 42:7
lord, your servants have come to buy **f**. Gn 42:10
to them, “Go again, buy us a little **f**.” Gn 43:2
with us, we will go down and buy you **f**. Gn 43:4
we came down the first time to buy **f**. Gn 43:20
other money down with us to buy **f**. Gn 43:22
himself he said, “Serve the **f**.” Gn 43:31
his house, “Fill the men's sacks with **f**, Gn 44:1
father said, ‘Go again, buy us a little **f**,’ Gn 44:25
and all his father's household with **f**, Gn 47:12
Now there was no **f** in all the land, for Gn 47:13
came to Joseph and said, “Give us **f**. Gn 47:15
I will give you **f** in exchange for your Gn 47:16
and Joseph gave them **f** in exchange for Gn 47:17
supplied them with **f** in exchange for Gn 47:17
Buy us and our land for **f**, and we with Gn 47:19
the field and as **f** for yourselves and Gn 47:24
and as **f** for your little ones.” Gn 47:24
“Asher's **f** shall be rich, and he shall Gn 49:20
to himself, he shall not diminish her **f**, Ex 21:10
pleasing aroma, a **f** offering to the LORD. Ex 29:18
the LORD. It is a **f** offering to the LORD. Ex 29:25
pleasing aroma, a **f** offering to the LORD. Ex 29:41
to burn a **f** offering to the LORD, Ex 30:20
a **f** offering with a pleasing aroma to the Lv 1:9
a **f** offering with a pleasing aroma to the Lv 1:13
a **f** offering with a pleasing aroma to the Lv 1:17
a **f** offering with a pleasing aroma to the Lv 2:2
a most holy part of the LORD'S **f** offerings. Lv 2:3
a **f** offering with a pleasing aroma to the Lv 2:9
a most holy part of the LORD'S **f** offerings. Lv 2:10
nor any honey as a **f** offering to the LORD. Lv 2:11
it is a **f** offering to the LORD. Lv 2:16
peace offering, as a **f** offering to the LORD, Lv 3:3
it is a **f** offering with a pleasing aroma to Lv 3:5
he shall offer as a **f** offering to the LORD its Lv 3:9
it on the altar as a **f** offering to the LORD. Lv 3:11
as his offering for a **f** offering to the LORD, Lv 3:14
the altar as a **f** offering with a pleasing Lv 3:16
the altar, on top of the LORD'S **f** offerings. Lv 4:35
on the altar, on the LORD'S **f** offerings; Lv 5:12
given it as their portion of my **f** offerings. Lv 6:17
generations, from the LORD'S **f** offerings. Lv 6:18
on the altar as a **f** offering to the LORD; Lv 7:5
animal of which a **f** offering may be Lv 7:25
hands shall bring the LORD'S **f** offerings. Lv 7:30
of his sons from the LORD'S **f** offerings, Lv 7:35
pleasing aroma, a **f** offering for the LORD, Lv 8:21
pleasing aroma, a **f** offering to the LORD. Lv 8:28
that is left of the LORD'S **f** offerings, Lv 10:12
sons' due, from the LORD'S **f** offerings, Lv 10:13
shall bring with the **f** offerings of the Lv 10:15
Any **f** in it that could be eaten, on Lv 11:34
the land and plant any kind of tree for **f**, Lv 19:23
For they offer the LORD'S **f** offerings, the Lv 21:6
come near to offer the LORD'S **f** offerings; Lv 21:21
of the holy things, because they are his **f**. Lv 22:7
born in his house may eat of his **f**. Lv 22:11
her youth, she may eat of her father's **f**; Lv 22:13
to the LORD as a **f** offering on the altar. Lv 22:22
be acceptable as a **f** offering to the LORD. Lv 22:27
you shall present a **f** offering to the LORD Lv 23:8
a **f** offering to the LORD with a pleasing Lv 23:13
a **f** offering with a pleasing aroma to Lv 23:18
you shall present a **f** offering to the Lv 23:25
and present a **f** offering to the Lv 23:27
days you shall present **f** offerings to the Lv 23:36
and present a **f** offering to the Lv 23:36
for presenting to the LORD **f** offerings, Lv 23:37
memorial portion as a **f** offering to the Lv 24:7
holy portion out of the LORD'S **f** offerings, Lv 24:9
of the land shall provide **f** for you, Lv 25:6
in your land: all its yield shall be for **f**. Lv 25:7
interest, nor give him your **f** for profit. Lv 25:37
or from the flock a **f** offering or a burnt Nm 15:3
half a hin of wine, as a **f** offering, Nm 15:10
in this way, in offering a **f** offering, Nm 15:13
you, and he wishes to offer a **f** offering, Nm 15:14
their offering, a **f** offering to the LORD, Nm 15:25
and shall burn their fat as a **f** offering, Nm 18:17
For there is no **f** and no water, and we Nm 21:5
water, and we loathe this worthless **f**.” Nm 21:5
offering, my **f** for my food offerings, Nm 28:2
offering, my food for my **f** offerings, Nm 28:2
This is the **f** offering that you shall Nm 28:3
pleasing aroma, a **f** offering to the LORD. Nm 28:6
you shall offer it as a **f** offering, Nm 28:8
aroma, a **f** offering to the LORD. Nm 28:13
but offer a **f** offering, a burnt offering Nm 28:19
for seven days, the **f** of a food offering, Nm 28:24
for seven days, the food of a **f** offering, Nm 28:24
pleasing aroma, a **f** offering to the LORD. Nm 29:6
offer a burnt offering, a **f** offering, Nm 29:13
offer a burnt offering, a **f** offering, Nm 29:36
You shall purchase **f** from them for Dt 2:6
You shall sell me **f** for money, that I may Dt 2:28
sojourner, giving him **f** and clothing. Dt 10:18
shall eat the LORD'S **f** offerings as their Dt 18:1
are not trees for **f** you may destroy and Dt 20:20
interest on money, interest on **f**, Dt 23:19
your dead body shall be **f** for all birds of Dt 28:26
you will begrudge **f** to his brother, Dt 28:54
our houses as our **f** for the journey on Jos 9:12
you detain me, I will not eat of your **f**. Jgs 13:16
had visited his people and given them **f**. Ru 1:6
out and gave her what **f** she had left over Ru 2:18
the man who eats **f** until it is evening 1 Sm 14:24
So none of the people had tasted **f**. 1 Sm 14:24
the man who eats **f** this day.’” And 1 Sm 14:28
came, the king sat down to eat **f**. 1 Sm 20:24
anger and ate no **f** the second day of 1 Sm 20:34
not, nor did he eat **f** with them. 2 Sm 12:17
when he asked, they set **f** before him, 2 Sm 12:20
the child died, you arose and ate **f**.” 2 Sm 12:21
to eat, and prepare the **f** in my sight, 2 Sm 13:5
house and prepare **f** for him.” 2 Sm 13:7
“Bring the **f** into the chamber, 2 Sm 13:10
the king with **f** while he stayed 2 Sm 19:32
who provided **f** for the king and his 1 Kgs 4:7
wishes by providing **f** for my 1 Kgs 5:9
cors of wheat as **f** for his household, 1 Kgs 5:11
the **f** of his table, the seating of his 1 Kgs 10:5
him an allowance of **f** and gave him 1 Kgs 11:18
the strength of that **f** forty days and 1 Kgs 19:8
away his face and would eat no **f**. 1 Kgs 21:4
spirit so vexed that you eat no **f**?” 1 Kgs 21:5
lived, who urged him to eat some **f**. 2 Kgs 4:8
way, he would turn in there to eat **f**. 2 Kgs 4:8
that there was no **f** for the people of 2 Kgs 25:3
came bringing **f** on donkeys and on 1 Chr 12:40
the **f** of his table, the seating of his 2 Chr 9:4
in them, and stores of **f**, 2 Chr 11:11
provided them with **f** and drink, 2 Chr 28:15
So they ate the **f** of the festival for 2 Chr 30:22
were not to partake of the most holy **f**, Ezr 2:63
to the masons and the carpenters, and **f**, Ezr 3:7
my brothers ate the **f** allowance of the Neh 5:14
did not demand the **f** allowance of the Neh 5:18
of the most holy **f** until a priest with Neh 7:65
them on the day when they sold **f**. Neh 13:15
with her cosmetics and her portion of **f**, Est 2:9
which they send gifts of **f** to one another. Est 9:19
for sending gifts of **f** to one another and Est 9:22
them; they are as **f** that is loathsome to me. Jb 6:7
the ear test words as the palate tastes **f**? Jb 12:11
yet his **f** is turned in his stomach; it is Jb 20:14
of his mouth more than my portion of **f**. Jb 23:12
the wasteland yields **f** for their children. Jb 24:5
and the roots of the broom tree for their **f**. Jb 30:4
bread, and his appetite the choicest **f**. Jb 33:20
the ear tests words as the palate tastes **f**. Jb 34:3
judges peoples; he gives **f** in abundance. Jb 36:31
for help, and wander about for lack of **f**? Jb 38:41
the mountains yield **f** for him where Jb 40:20

My tears have been my **f** day and night, Ps 42:3
They wander about for **f** and growl if Ps 59:15
will be satisfied as with fat and rich **f**, Ps 63:5
They gave me poison for **f**, and for my Ps 69:21
you gave him as **f** for the creatures of Ps 74:14
heart by demanding the **f** they craved. Ps 78:18
angels; he sent them **f** in abundance. Ps 78:25
while the **f** was still in their mouths, Ps 78:30
servants to the birds of the heavens for **f**, Ps 79:2
he may bring forth **f** from the earth Ps 104:14
their prey, seeking their **f** from God. Ps 104:21
you, to give them their **f** in due season. Ps 104:27
they loathed any kind of **f**, and they Ps 107:18
seeking **f** far from the ruins they Ps 109:10
He provides **f** for those who fear him; he Ps 111:5
he who gives **f** to all flesh, for his Ps 136:25
you give them their **f** in due season. Ps 145:15
oppressed, who gives **f** to the hungry. Ps 146:7
He gives to the beasts their **f**, and to the Ps 147:9
in summer and gathers her **f** in harvest. Prv 6:8
of the poor would yield much **f**, Prv 13:23
his delicacies, for they are deceptive **f**. Prv 23:3
will be enough goats' milk for your **f**, Prv 27:27
for the **f** of your household and Prv 27:27
poor is a beating rain that leaves no **f**. Prv 28:3
feed me with the **f** that is needful for me, Prv 30:8
and a fool when he is filled with **f**; Prv 30:22
yet they provide their **f** in the summer; Prv 30:25
merchant; she brings her **f** from afar. Prv 31:14
night and provides **f** for her household Prv 31:15
will supply abundant **f** and fine Is 23:18
will make for all peoples a feast of rich **f**, Is 25:6
of well-aged wine, of rich **f** full of marrow, Is 25:6
is good, and delight yourselves in rich **f**. Is 55:2
give your grain to be **f** for your enemies, Is 62:8
the ox, and dust shall be the serpent's **f**. Is 65:25
shall eat up your harvest and your **f**; Jer 5:17
of this people will be **f** for the birds of the Jer 7:33
I will feed this people with bitter **f**, Jer 9:15
dead bodies shall be **f** for the birds of Jer 16:4
give their dead bodies for **f** to the birds of Jer 19:7
feed them with bitter **f** and give them Jer 23:15
dead bodies shall be **f** for the birds of Jer 34:20
him an allowance of **f** and a present, Jer 40:5
For then we had plenty of **f**, and Jer 44:17
city that there was no **f** for the people of Jer 52:6
their treasures for **f** to revive their Lam 1:11
while they sought **f** to revive their Lam 1:19
the children beg for **f**, but no one gives Lam 4:4
they became their **f** during the Lam 4:10
And your **f** that you eat shall be by Ezk 4:10
her daughters had pride, excess of **f**, Ezk 16:49
up to them for **f** the children whom Ezk 23:37
the birds of the heavens I give you as **f**. Ezk 29:5
and they became **f** for all the wild Ezk 34:5
my sheep have become **f** for all the wild Ezk 34:8
that they may not be **f** for them. Ezk 34:10
my temple, when you offer to me my **f**, Ezk 44:7
there will grow all kinds of trees for **f**. Ezk 47:12
Their fruit will be for **f**, and their Ezk 47:12
Its produce shall be **f** for the workers Ezk 48:18
a daily portion of the **f** that the king ate, Dn 1:5
would not defile himself with the king's **f**, Dn 1:8
who assigned your **f** and your drink; Dn 1:10
who eat the king's **f** be observed by you, Dn 1:13
than all the youths who ate the king's **f**. Dn 1:15
steward took away their **f** and the wine Dn 1:16
its fruit abundant, and in it was **f** for all. Dn 4:12
abundant, and in which was **f** for all, Dn 4:21
those who eat his **f** shall break him. Dn 11:26
and they shall eat unclean **f** in Assyria. Hos 9:3
Is not the **f** cut off before our eyes, joy and Jl 1:16
he lives in luxury, and his **f** is rich. Hab 1:16
of the olive fail and the fields yield no **f**, Hab 3:17
or stew or wine or oil or any kind of **f**, Hg 2:12
By offering polluted **f** upon my altar. But Mal 1:7
its fruit, that is, its **f** may be despised. Mal 1:12
that there may be **f** in my house. Mal 3:10
and his **f** was locusts and wild honey. Mt 3:4
Is not life more than **f**, and the body Mt 6:25
a staff, for the laborer deserves his **f**. Mt 10:10
the villages and buy **f** for themselves." Mt 14:15
to give them their **f** at the proper time? Mt 24:45
For I was hungry and you gave me **f**, I Mt 25:35
I was hungry and you gave me no **f**, Mt 25:42
and whoever has **f** is to do likewise." Lk 3:11
are to go and buy **f** for all these people." Lk 9:13
For life is more than **f**, and the body Lk 12:23
them their portion of **f** at the proper Lk 12:42
had gone away into the city to buy **f**.) Jn 4:8
"I have **f** to eat that you do not know Jn 4:32
"My **f** is to do the will of him who sent me Jn 4:34
Do not labor for the **f** that perishes, but Jn 6:27
but for the **f** that endures to eternal life, Jn 6:27
For my flesh is true **f**, and my blood is Jn 6:55
they received their **f** with glad and Acts 2:46
and our fathers could find no **f**. Acts 7:11
and taking **f**, he was strengthened. For Acts 9:19
depended on the king's country for **f**. Acts 12:20
your hearts with **f** and gladness." Acts 14:17
into his house and set **f** before them. Acts 16:34
an oath to taste no **f** till we have killed Acts 23:14
they had been without **f** for a long Acts 27:21
Paul urged them all to take some **f**, Acts 27:33
continued in suspense and without **f**, Acts 27:33
Therefore I urge you to take some **f**. It Acts 27:34
and ate some **f** themselves. Acts 27:36
Do not, for the sake of **f**, destroy the Rom 14:20
I fed you with milk, not solid **f**, for you 1 Cor 3:2
"**F** is meant for the stomach and the 1 Cor 6:13
and the stomach for **f**"—and God will 1 Cor 6:13
Now concerning **f** offered to idols: we 1 Cor 8:1
as to the eating of **f** offered to idols, 1 Cor 8:4
idols, eat **f** as really offered to an idol, 1 Cor 8:7
F will not commend us to God. We are 1 Cor 8:8
is weak, to eat **f** offered to idols? 1 Cor 8:10
if **f** makes my brother stumble, 1 Cor 8:13
service get their **f** from the temple, 1 Cor 9:13
and all ate the same spiritual **f**, 1 Cor 10:3
That **f** offered to idols is anything, or 1 Cor 10:19
sower and bread for **f** will supply and 2 Cor 9:10
hunger and thirst, often without **f**, 2 Cor 11:27
on you in questions of **f** and drink, Col 2:16
But if we have **f** and clothing, with 1 Tm 6:8
of God. You need milk, not solid **f**, Heb 5:12
But solid **f** is for the mature, for those Heb 5:14
but deal only with **f** and drink and Heb 9:10
is poorly clothed and lacking in daily **f**, Jas 2:15
that they might eat **f** sacrificed to idols Rv 2:14
and to eat **f** sacrificed to idols. Rv 2:20

FOODS (3)

(Thus he declared all **f** clean.) Mk 7:19
require abstinence from **f** that God 1 Tm 4:3
to be strengthened by grace, not by **f**, Heb 13:9

FOOL (76)

"Because you have made a **f** of me. Nm 22:29
saying, "Should Abner die as a **f** dies? 2 Sm 3:33
Surely vexation kills the **f**, and jealousy Jb 5:2
I have seen the **f** taking root, but suddenly Jb 5:3
The **f** says in his heart, "There is no Ps 14:1
Do not make me the scorn of the **f**! Ps 39:8
the **f** and the stupid alike must perish Ps 49:10
The **f** says in his heart, "There is no Ps 53:1
know; the **f** cannot understand this: Ps 92:6
but a babbling **f** will come to ruin. Prv 10:8
but a babbling **f** will come to ruin. Prv 10:10
but the mouth of a **f** brings ruin near. Prv 10:14
lips, and whoever utters slander is a **f**. Prv 10:18
Doing wrong is like a joke to a **f**, but Prv 10:23
and the **f** will be servant to the wise of Prv 11:29
The way of a **f** is right in his own eyes, Prv 12:15
The vexation of a **f** is known at once, Prv 12:16
knowledge, but a **f** flaunts his folly. Prv 13:16
By the mouth of a **f** comes a rod for his Prv 14:3
Leave the presence of a **f**, for there you Prv 14:7
evil, but a **f** is reckless and careless. Prv 14:16
A **f** despises his father's instruction, but Prv 15:5
Fine speech is not becoming to a **f**; still Prv 17:7
than a hundred blows into a **f**. Prv 17:10
of her cubs rather than a **f** in his folly. Prv 17:12
Why should a **f** have money in his Prv 17:16
He who sires a **f** gets himself sorrow, Prv 17:21
sorrow, and the father of a **f** has no joy. Prv 17:21
but the eyes of a **f** are on the ends of the Prv 17:24
Even a **f** who keeps silent is considered Prv 17:28
A **f** takes no pleasure in understanding, Prv 18:2
one who is crooked in speech and is a **f**. Prv 19:1
It is not fitting for a **f** to live in luxury, Prv 19:10
strife, but every **f** will be quarreling. Prv 20:3
Do not speak in the hearing of a **f**, for he Prv 23:9
Wisdom is too high for a **f**; in the gate Prv 24:7
in harvest, so honor is not fitting for a **f**. Prv 26:1
Answer not a **f** according to his folly, Prv 26:4
Answer a **f** according to his folly, lest he Prv 26:5
by the hand of a **f** cuts off his own feet Prv 26:6
the sling is one who gives honor to a **f**. Prv 26:8
one who hires a passing **f** or drunkard. Prv 26:10
to his vomit is a **f** who repeats his folly. Prv 26:11
is more hope for a **f** than for him. Prv 26:12
Crush a **f** in a mortar with a pestle Prv 27:22
Whoever trusts in his own mind is a **f**, Prv 28:26
If a wise man has an argument with a **f**, Prv 29:9
with a fool, the **f** only rages and laughs, Prv 29:9
A **f** gives full vent to his spirit, but a Prv 29:11
is more hope for a **f** than for him. Prv 29:20
and a **f** when he is filled with food; Prv 30:22
his head, but the **f** walks in darkness. Eccl 2:14
"What happens to the **f** will happen to Eccl 2:15
the wise as of the **f** there is no enduring Eccl 2:16
How the wise dies just like the **f**! Eccl 2:16
knows whether he will be wise or a **f**? Eccl 2:19
The **f** folds his hands and eats his own Eccl 4:5
advantage has the wise man over the **f**? Eccl 6:8
Be not overly wicked, neither be a **f**. Eccl 7:17
Even when the **f** walks on the road, he Eccl 10:3
and he says to everyone that he is a **f**. Eccl 10:3
but the lips of a **f** consume him. Eccl 10:12
A **f** multiplies words, though no man Eccl 10:14
The toil of a **f** wearies him, for he does Eccl 10:15
The **f** will no more be called noble, nor Is 32:5
For the **f** speaks folly, and his heart is Is 32:6
leave him, and at his end he will be a **f**. Jer 17:11
The prophet is a **f**; the man of the spirit is Hos 9:7
the council; and whoever says, 'You **f**!' Mt 5:22
'**F**! This night your soul is required of Lk 12:20
let him become a **f** that he may 1 Cor 3:18
But even if you do, accept me as a **f**, 2 Cor 11:16
with the Lord's authority but as a **f**. 2 Cor 11:17
I am speaking as a **f**—I also dare to 2 Cor 11:21
wish to boast, I would not be a **f**, 2 Cor 12:6
I have been a **f**! You forced me to it, 2 Cor 12:11

FOOL'S (5)

A **f** lips walk into a fight, and his Prv 18:6
A **f** mouth is his ruin, and his lips are a Prv 18:7
but a **f** provocation is heavier than Prv 27:3
and a **f** voice with many words. Eccl 5:3
to the right, but a **f** heart to the left. Eccl 10:2

FOOLISH (43)

the LORD, you **f** and senseless people? Dt 32:6
provoke them to anger with a **f** nation. Dt 32:21
speak as one of the **f** women would speak. Jb 2:10
the path of those who have **f** confidence; Ps 49:13
scoffs, and a **f** people reviles your name. Ps 74:18
remember how the **f** scoff at you all the Ps 74:22
but a **f** son is a sorrow to his mother. Prv 10:1
but a **f** man despises his mother. Prv 15:20
A **f** son is a grief to his father and Prv 17:25
A **f** son is ruin to his father, and a Prv 19:13
dwelling, but a **f** man devours it. Prv 21:20
If you have been **f**, exalting yourself, or Prv 30:32
than an old and **f** king who no longer Eccl 4:13
The princes of Zoan are utterly **f**; the Is 19:11
men back and makes their knowledge **f**, Is 44:25
"For my people are **f**; they know me not; Jer 4:22
"Hear this, O **f** and senseless people, who Jer 5:21
They are both stupid and **f**; the Jer 10:8
Woe to the **f** prophets who follow their Ezk 13:3
more the equipment of a **f** shepherd. Zec 11:15
them will be like a **f** man who built his Mt 7:26
Five of them were **f**, and five were wise. Mt 25:2
For when the **f** took their lamps, they Mt 25:3
And the **f** said to the wise, 'Give us some Mt 25:8
And he said to them, "O **f** ones, and Lk 24:25
both to the wise and to the **f**. Rom 1:14
and their **f** hearts were darkened. Rom 1:21
f, faithless, heartless, ruthless. Rom 1:31
an instructor of the **f**, a teacher of Rom 2:20
with a **f** nation I will make you Rom 10:19
Has not God made **f** the wisdom of the 1 Cor 1:20
God chose what is **f** in the world to 1 Cor 1:27
You **f** person! What you sow does 1 Cor 15:36
I repeat, let no one think me **f**. But 2 Cor 11:16
O **f** Galatians! Who has bewitched you? Gal 3:1
Are you so **f**? Having begun by the Spirit, Gal 3:3
be no filthiness nor **f** talk nor crude Eph 5:4
Therefore do not be **f**, but understand Eph 5:17
Have nothing to do with **f**, ignorant 2 Tm 2:23
For we ourselves were once **f**, disobedient, Ti 3:3
But avoid **f** controversies, genealogies, Ti 3:9
Do you want to be shown, you **f** person, Jas 2:20
put to silence the ignorance of **f** people. 1 Pt 2:15

FOOLISHLY (8)

farewell? Now you have done **f**. Gn 31:28
we have done **f** and have sinned. Nm 12:11
said to Saul, "You have done **f**. 1 Sm 13:13
Behold, I have acted **f**, and have 1 Sm 26:21
your servant, for I have done very **f**." 2 Sm 24:10
your servant, for I have acted very **f**." 1 Chr 21:8
You have done **f** in this, for from now 2 Chr 16:9
A man of quick temper acts **f**, and a Prv 14:17

FOOLISHNESS (7)

the counsel of Ahithophel into **f**." 2 Sm 15:31
wounds stink and fester because of my **f**, Ps 38:5
of folly and the **f** that is madness. Eccl 7:25
of the words of his mouth is **f**, Eccl 10:13
deceit, sensuality, envy, slander, pride, **f**. Mk 7:22
For the **f** of God is wiser than men, 1 Cor 1:25
you would bear with me in a little **f**. 2 Cor 11:1

FOOLS (41)

as one of the outrageous **f** in Israel. 2 Sm 13:13
away stripped, and judges he makes **f**. Jb 12:17
of the people! **F**, when will you be wise? Ps 94:8

Some were **f** through their sinful ways, Ps 107:17
f despise wisdom and instruction. Prv 1:7
in their scoffing and **f** hate knowledge? Prv 1:22
the complacency of **f** destroys them; Prv 1:32
will inherit honor, but **f** get disgrace. Prv 3:35
O simple ones, learn prudence; O **f**, learn Prv 8:5
feed many, but **f** die for lack of sense. Prv 10:21
but the heart of **f** proclaims folly. Prv 12:23
away from evil is an abomination to **f**. Prv 13:19
the companion of **f** will suffer harm. Prv 13:20
his way, but the folly of **f** is deceiving. Prv 14:8
F mock at the guilt offering, but the Prv 14:9
wealth, but the folly of **f** brings folly. Prv 14:24
itself known even in the midst of **f**. Prv 14:33
but the mouths of **f** pour out folly. Prv 15:2
spread knowledge; not so the hearts of **f**. Prv 15:7
but the mouths of **f** feed on folly. Prv 15:14
has it, but the instruction of **f** is folly. Prv 16:22
scoffers, and beating for the backs of **f**. Prv 19:29
the donkey, and a rod for the back of **f**. Prv 26:3
useless, is a proverb in the mouth of **f**. Prv 26:7
is a proverb in the mouth of **f**. Prv 26:9
is better than to offer the sacrifice of **f**, Eccl 5:1
paying it, for he has no pleasure in **f**. Eccl 5:4
but the heart of **f** is in the house of Eccl 7:4
of the wise than to hear the song of **f**. Eccl 7:5
under a pot, so is the laughter of the **f**; Eccl 7:6
for anger lodges in the bosom of **f**. Eccl 7:9
than the shouting of a ruler among **f**. Eccl 9:17
The princes of Zoan have become **f**, and Is 19:13
even if they are **f**, they shall not go astray. Is 35:8
signs of liars and makes **f** of diviners, Is 44:25
the diviners, that they may become **f**! Jer 50:36
You blind **f**! For which is greater, the Mt 23:17
You **f**! Did not he who made the outside Lk 11:40
Claiming to be wise, they became **f**, Rom 1:22
We are **f** for Christ's sake, but you 1 Cor 4:10
For you gladly bear with **f**, being 2 Cor 11:19

FOOT (92)
But the dove found no place to set her **f**, Gn 8:9
shall lift up hand or **f** in all the land of Gn 41:44
about six hundred thousand men on **f**, Ex 12:37
their stand at the **f** of the mountain. Ex 19:17
for tooth, hand for hand, **f** for foot, Ex 21:24
for tooth, hand for hand, foot for **f**, Ex 21:24
built an altar at the **f** of the mountain, Ex 24:4
broke them at the **f** of the mountain. Ex 32:19
hand and on the big toe of his right **f**. Lv 8:23
of the diseased person from head to **f**, Lv 13:12
hand and on the big toe of his right **f**. Lv 14:14
hand and on the big toe of his right **f**, Lv 14:17
hand and on the big toe of his right **f**. Lv 14:25
hand and on the big toe of his right **f**, Lv 14:28
who has an injured **f** or an injured Lv 21:19
number six hundred thousand on **f**, Nm 11:21
Let me only pass through on **f**, Nm 20:19
and pressed Balaam's **f** against the Nm 22:25
so much as for the sole of the **f** to tread on, Dt 2:5
drink. Only let me pass through on **f**, Dt 2:28
near and stood at the **f** of the mountain, Dt 4:11
out on you and your **f** did not swell these Dt 8:4
the sole of your **f** treads shall be yours. Dt 11:24
tooth for tooth, hand for hand, **f** for foot. Dt 19:21
tooth for tooth, hand for hand, foot for **f**. Dt 19:21
pull his sandal off his **f** and spit in his Dt 25:9
from the sole of your **f** to the crown of Dt 28:35
the sole of her **f** on the ground because Dt 28:56
be no resting place for the sole of your **f**, Dt 28:65
for the time when their **f** shall slip; Dt 32:35
his brothers, and let him dip his **f** in oil. Dt 33:24
that the sole of your **f** will tread upon I Jos 1:3
southward to the **f** of the slopes of Jos 12:3
land on which your **f** has trodden shall Jos 14:9
from his chariot and fled away on **f**. Jgs 4:15
But Sisera fled away on **f** to the tent of Jgs 4:17
400,000 men on **f** that drew the sword. Jgs 20:2
fell of Israel thirty thousand **f** soldiers. 1 Sm 4:10
two hundred thousand men on **f**, 1 Sm 15:4
and see the place where his **f** is, 1 Sm 23:22
was as swift of **f** as a wild gazelle. 2 Sm 2:18
1,700 horsemen, and 20,000 **f** soldiers. 2 Sm 8:4
Syrians of Zobah, 20,000 **f** soldiers, 2 Sm 10:6
From the sole of his **f** to the crown of 2 Sm 14:25
on each hand, and six toes on each **f**, 2 Sm 21:20
the Syrians 100,000 **f** soldiers in one 1 Kgs 20:29
the sole of my **f** all the streams of 2 Kgs 19:24
7,000 horsemen, and 20,000 **f** soldiers. 1 Chr 18:4
7,000 chariots and 40,000 **f** soldiers, 1 Chr 19:18
on each hand and six toes on each **f**, 1 Chr 20:6
no more remove the **f** of Israel from 2 Chr 33:8
from the sole of his **f** to the crown of his Jb 2:7
My **f** has held fast to his steps; I have Jb 23:11
with falsehood and my **f** has hastened to Jb 31:5
forgetting that a **f** may crush them and Jb 39:15
they hid their own **f** has been caught. Ps 9:15
My **f** stands on level ground; in the Ps 26:12
Let not the **f** of arrogance come upon Ps 36:11
who boast against me when my **f** slips!" Ps 38:16
land; they passed through the river on **f**. Ps 66:6
lest you strike your **f** against a stone. Ps 91:12
"My **f** slips," your steadfast love, Ps 94:18
He will not let your **f** be moved; he who Ps 121:3
hold back your **f** from their paths, Prv 1:15
securely, and your **f** will not stumble. Prv 3:23
and will keep your **f** from being caught. Prv 3:26
or to the left; turn your **f** away from evil. Prv 4:27
Let your **f** be seldom in your Prv 25:17
is like a bad tooth or a **f** that slips. Prv 25:19
From the sole of the **f** even to the head, Is 1:6
The **f** tramples it, the feet of the poor, the Is 26:6
with the sole of my **f** all the streams of Is 37:25
you turn back your **f** from the Sabbath, Is 58:13
"If you have raced with men on **f**, and Jer 12:5
of their feet were like the sole of a calf's **f**. Ezk 1:7
your hands and stamp your **f** and say, Ezk 6:11
No **f** of man shall pass through it, and Ezk 29:11
and no **f** of beast shall pass through it; Ezk 29:11
and no **f** of man shall trouble them Ezk 32:13
who is swift of **f** shall not save himself, Am 2:15
us; he will tread our iniquities under **f**. Mi 7:19
up, lest you strike your **f** against a stone.'" Mt 4:6
they followed him on **f** from the towns. Mt 14:13
if your hand or your **f** causes you to sin, Mt 18:8
'Bind him hand and **f** and cast him Mt 22:13
they ran there on **f** from all the towns Mk 6:33
And if your **f** causes you to sin, cut it Mk 9:45
lest you strike your **f** against a stone.'" Lk 4:11
from the first day that I set **f** in Asia, Acts 20:18
If the **f** should say, "Because I am 1 Cor 12:15
And he set his right **f** on the sea, and his Rv 10:2
foot on the sea, and his left **f** on the land, Rv 10:2

FOOT'S (1)
no inheritance in it, not even a **f** length, Acts 7:5

FOOTHOLD (1)
I sink in deep mire, where there is no **f**; I Ps 69:2

FOOTMEN (1)
and ten chariots and ten thousand **f**, 2 Kgs 13:7

FOOTPRINTS (1)
the great waters; yet your **f** were unseen. Ps 77:19

FOOTSTEPS (3)
go before him and make his **f** a way. Ps 85:13
they mock the **f** of your anointed. Ps 89:51
who also walk in the **f** of the faith that Rom 4:12

FOOTSTOOL (13)
of the LORD and for the **f** of our God, 1 Chr 28:2
throne had six steps and a **f** of gold, 2 Chr 9:18
Exalt the LORD our God; worship at his **f**! Ps 99:5
until I make your enemies your **f**." Ps 110:1
dwelling place; let us worship at his **f**!" Ps 132:7
is my throne, and the earth is my **f**; Is 66:1
has not remembered his **f** in the day of Lam 2:1
or by the earth, for it is his **f**, or by Mt 5:35
until I make your enemies your **f**.' Lk 20:43
until I make your enemies your **f**.' Acts 2:35
is my throne, and the earth is my **f**. Acts 7:49
I make your enemies a **f** for your feet"? Heb 1:13
should be made a **f** for his feet. Heb 10:13

FORBADE (1)
those whom you **f** to enter your Lam 1:10

FORBEAR (1)
speak, my pain is not assuaged, and if I **f**, Jb 16:6

FORBEARANCE (3)
In your **f** take me not away; know that Jer 15:15
of his kindness and **f** and patience, Rom 2:4
because in his divine **f** he had passed Rom 3:25

FORBID (5)
"The LORD **f** that I should do this thing 1 Sm 24:6
The LORD **f** that I should put out my 1 Sm 26:11
"The LORD **f** that I should give you the 1 Kgs 21:3
and do not **f** speaking in tongues. 1 Cor 14:39
who **f** marriage and require 1 Tm 4:3

FORBIDDEN (12)
food, then you shall regard its fruit as **f**. Lv 19:23
Three years it shall be **f** to you; it must Lv 19:23
whatever the LORD our God had **f** us. Dt 2:37
that the LORD your God has **f** you. Dt 4:23
any of the host of heaven, which I have **f**, Dt 17:3
"No one born of a **f** union may enter the Dt 23:2
you will be delivered from the **f** woman, Prv 2:16
For the lips of a **f** woman drip honey, and Prv 5:3
with a **f** woman and embrace the Prv 5:20
to keep you from the **f** woman, from the Prv 7:5
The mouth of **f** women is a deep pit; he Prv 22:14
having been **f** by the Holy Spirit to Acts 16:6

FORBIDDING (1)
misleading our nation and **f** us to give Lk 23:2

FORCE (19)
take your daughters from me by **f**. Gn 31:31
with a large army and with a strong **f**. Nm 20:20
it now, and if not, I will take it by **f**." 1 Sm 2:16
come on duty in **f** on the Sabbath 2 Kgs 11:7
his people struck them with great **f**, 2 Chr 13:17
Israel, who struck him with great **f**. 2 Chr 28:5
at Jerusalem and by **f** and power made Ezr 4:23
to annihilate any armed **f** of any people Est 8:11
With great **f** my garment is disfigured; Jb 30:18
distress, or all the **f** of your strength? Jb 36:19
enemies march in **f** and come against Jer 46:22
and with **f** and harshness you have Ezk 34:4
violence, and the violent take it by **f**. Mt 11:12
and take him by **f** to make him king, Jn 6:15
went and brought them, but not by **f**, Acts 5:26
among them by **f** and bring him Acts 23:10
how can you **f** the Gentiles to live like Gal 2:14
the flesh who would **f** you to be Gal 6:12
since it is not in **f** as long as the one Heb 9:17

FORCED (22)
bear, and became a servant at **f** labor. Gn 49:15
found in it shall do **f** labor for you and Dt 20:11
day but have been made to do **f** labor. Jos 16:10
they put the Canaanites to **f** labor, Jos 17:13
they put the Canaanites to **f** labor, Jgs 1:28
them, but became subject to **f** labor. Jgs 1:30
became subject to **f** labor for them. Jgs 1:33
and they became subject to **f** labor. Jgs 1:35
So I **f** myself, and offered the burnt 1 Sm 13:12
Adoram was in charge of the **f** labor; 2 Sm 20:24
of Abda was in charge of the **f** labor. 1 Kgs 4:6
King Solomon drafted **f** labor out of 1 Kgs 5:13
the account of the **f** labor that King 1 Kgs 9:15
charge over all the **f** labor of the 1 Kgs 11:28
was taskmaster over the **f** labor, 1 Kgs 12:18
—these Solomon drafted as **f** labor, 2 Chr 8:8
was taskmaster over the **f** labor, 2 Chr 10:18
the slothful will be put to **f** labor. Prv 12:24
his young men shall be put to **f** labor. Is 31:8
with our race and **f** our fathers to Acts 7:19
You **f** me to it, for I ought to have 2 Cor 12:11
with me, was not **f** to be circumcised, Gal 2:3

FORCEFUL (1)
How **f** are upright words! But what does Jb 6:25

FORCES (28)
And all these joined **f** in the Valley of Gn 14:3
And he divided his **f** against them by Gn 14:15
down on the Egyptian **f** and threw the Ex 14:24
and threw the Egyptian **f** into a panic, Ex 14:24
So they stationed the **f**, the main Jos 8:13
gathered their **f** and went up with all Jos 10:5
these kings joined their **f** and came and Jos 11:5
Philistines gathered their **f** for war, 1 Sm 28:1
had gathered all their **f** at Aphek. 1 Sm 29:1
the captains of the **f** arose and went 2 Kgs 25:26
and drew up his **f** against them. 1 Chr 19:17
He placed **f** in all the fortified cities of 2 Chr 17:2
was besieging Lachish with all his **f**, 2 Chr 32:9
the captains of the **f** in the open country Jer 40:7
the leaders of the **f** in the open country Jer 40:13
all the leaders of the **f** with him heard of Jer 41:11
and all the leaders of the **f** with him, Jer 41:13
the leaders of the **f** with him took from Jer 41:16
Then all the commanders of the **f**, and Jer 42:1
the commanders of the **f** who were with Jer 42:8
the commanders of the **f** and all the Jer 43:4
the commanders of the **f** took all the Jer 43:5
and assemble a multitude of great **f**, Dn 11:10
And the **f** of the south shall not stand, Dn 11:15
F from him shall appear and profane Dn 11:31
And if anyone **f** you to go one mile, go Mt 5:41
and everyone **f** his way into it. Lk 16:16
against the spiritual **f** of evil in the Eph 6:12

FORCING (1)
Yet we are **f** our sons and our daughters Neh 5:5

FORD (2)
and crossed the **f** of the Jabbok. Gn 32:22
and they crossed the **f** to bring over 2 Sm 19:18

FORDS (9)
on the way to the Jordan as far as the **f**. Jos 2:7
him and seized the **f** of the Jordan Jgs 3:28
Gileadites captured the **f** of the Jordan Jgs 12:5
slaughtered him at the **f** of the Jordan. Jgs 12:6
Hebrews crossed the **f** of the Jordan 1 Sm 13:7
will wait at the **f** of the wilderness 2 Sm 15:28
stay tonight at the **f** of the wilderness, 2 Sm 17:16
daughters of Moab at the **f** of the Arnon. Is 16:2
the **f** have been seized, the marshes are Jer 51:32

FOREBODING (1)
with fear and with **f** of what is coming Lk 21:26

FOREFATHER (2)
Abraham, our **f** according to the flesh? Rom 4:1
children by one man, our **f** Isaac, Rom 9:10

FOREFATHERS (4)
remember the covenant with their **f**, Lv 26:45
turned back to the iniquities of their **f**, Jer 11:10
are beloved for the sake of their **f**. Rom 11:28
the futile ways inherited from your **f**, 1 Pt 1:18

FOREFRONT (1)
"Set Uriah in the **f** of the hardest 2 Sm 11:15

FOREGO (1)
And we will **f** the crops of the seventh Neh 10:31

FOREHEAD (21)
It shall be on Aaron's **f**, and Aaron Ex 28:38
It shall regularly be on his **f**, that they Ex 28:38
And if a man's hair falls out from his **f**, Lv 13:41
his forehead, he has baldness of the **f**; Lv 13:41
or the bald **f** a reddish-white diseased Lv 13:42
out on his bald head or his bald **f**. Lv 13:42
on his bald head or on his bald **f**, Lv 13:43
it shall crush the **f** of Moab and break Nm 24:17
it and struck the Philistine on his **f**. 1 Sm 17:49
The stone sank into his **f**, and he fell 1 Sm 17:49
broke out on his **f** in the presence of 2 Chr 26:19
and behold, he was leprous in his **f**! 2 Chr 26:20
neck is an iron sinew and your **f** brass, Is 48:4
not come; yet you have the **f** of a whore; Jer 3:3
it has destroyed the **f** of Moab, the Jer 48:45
Israel have a hard **f** and a stubborn Ezk 3:7
and your **f** as hard as their foreheads. Ezk 3:8
harder than flint have I made your **f**. Ezk 3:9
to be marked on the right hand or the **f**, Rv 13:16
receives a mark on his **f** or on his hand, Rv 14:9
And on her **f** was written a name of Rv 17:5

FOREHEADS (8)
any baldness on your **f** for the dead. Dt 14:1
and your forehead as hard as their **f**. Ezk 3:8
put a mark on the **f** of the men who sigh Ezk 9:4
sealed the servants of our God on their **f**." Rv 7:3
who do not have the seal of God on their **f**. Rv 9:4
and his Father's name written on their **f**. Rv 14:1
its mark on their **f** or their hands. Rv 20:4
his face, and his name will be on their **f**. Rv 22:4

FOREIGN (45)
"Put away the **f** gods that are among Gn 35:2
to Jacob all the **f** gods that they had, Gn 35:4
"I have been a sojourner in a **f** land." Ex 2:22
"I have been a sojourner in a **f** land"), Ex 18:3
have no right to sell her to a **f** people, Ex 21:8
no **f** guest of the priest or hired servant Lv 22:10
and whore after the **f** gods among them Dt 31:16
guided him, no **f** god was with him. Dt 32:12
If you forsake the LORD and serve **f** gods, Jos 24:20
"Then put away the **f** gods that are Jos 24:23
they put away the **f** gods from among Jgs 10:16
then put away the **f** gods and the 1 Sm 7:3
King Solomon loved many **f** women, 1 Kgs 11:1
And so he did for all his **f** wives, who 1 Kgs 11:8
I dug wells and drank **f** waters, and I 2 Kgs 19:24
He took away the **f** altars and the 2 Chr 14:3
he took away the **f** gods and the idol 2 Chr 33:15
and have married **f** women from the Ezr 10:2
broken faith and married **f** women, Ezr 10:10
of the land and from the **f** wives." Ezr 10:11
cities who have taken **f** wives come at Ezr 10:14
all the men who had married **f** women. Ezr 10:17
the priests who had married **f** women: Ezr 10:18
All these had married **f** women, and Ezr 10:44
from Israel all those of **f** descent. Neh 13:3
f women made even him to sin. Neh 13:26
our God by marrying **f** women?" Neh 13:27
I cleansed them from everything **f**, Neh 13:30
God or spread out our hands to a **f** god, Ps 44:20
you; you shall not bow down to a **f** god. Ps 81:9
we sing the LORD'S song in a **f** land? Ps 137:4
lips and with a **f** tongue the LORD will Is 28:11
the multitude of your **f** foes shall be like Is 29:5
forsaken me and served **f** gods in your Jer 5:19
carved images and with their **f** idols?" Jer 8:19
and against all the **f** troops in her Jer 50:37
sent to a people of **f** speech and a hard Ezk 3:5
to many peoples of **f** speech and a hard Ezk 3:6
fortresses with the help of a **f** god. Dn 11:39
and all who array themselves in **f** attire. Zep 1:8
has married the daughter of a **f** god. Mal 2:11
a preacher of **f** divinities"—because Acts 17:18
I persecuted them even to **f** cities. Acts 26:11
in the land of promise, as in a **f** land, Heb 11:9
mighty in war, put **f** armies to flight. Heb 11:34

FOREIGNER (24)
your money from any **f** who is not of Gn 17:12
and those bought with money from a **f**, Gn 17:27
"I am a sojourner and **f** among you; give Gn 23:4
of the Passover: no **f** shall eat of it, Ex 12:43
No **f** or hired servant may eat of it. Ex 12:45
God any such animals gotten from a **f**. Lv 22:25
he may eat it, or you may sell it to a **f**. Dt 14:21
Of a **f** you may exact it, but whatever of Dt 15:3
You may not put a **f** over you, who is Dt 17:15
You may charge a **f** interest, but you Dt 23:20
and the **f** who comes from a far land, Dt 29:22
take notice of me, since I am a **f**?" Ru 2:10
for you are a **f** and also an exile from 2 Sm 15:19
"Likewise, when a **f**, who is not of 1 Kgs 8:41
to all for which the **f** calls to you, 1 Kgs 8:43
"Likewise, when a **f**, who is not of 2 Chr 6:32
to all for which the **f** calls to you, 2 Chr 6:33
stranger; I have become a **f** in their eyes. Jb 19:15
and your labors go to the house of a **f**, Prv 5:10
Let not the **f** who has joined himself to the Is 56:3
"Thus says the Lord GOD: No **f**, Ezk 44:9
and give praise to God except this **f**?" Lk 17:18
I will be a **f** to the speaker and the 1 Cor 14:11
speaker and the speaker a **f** to me. 1 Cor 14:11

FOREIGNERS (35)
Are we not regarded by him as **f**? For Gn 31:15
will not turn aside into the city of **f**, Jgs 19:12
F came cringing to me; as soon as 2 Sm 22:45
F lost heart and came trembling out 2 Sm 22:46
themselves from all **f** and stood and Neh 9:2
they obeyed me; **f** came cringing to me. Ps 18:44
F lost heart and came trembling out of Ps 18:45
the many waters, from the hand of **f**, Ps 144:7
me and deliver me from the hand of **f**, Ps 144:11
pledge when he puts up security for **f**. Prv 20:16
in your very presence **f** devour your land; Is 1:7
land; it is desolate, as overthrown by **f**. Is 1:7
they strike hands with the children of **f**. Is 2:6
You subdue the noise of the **f**; as heat by Is 25:5
"And the **f** who join themselves to the Is 56:6
F shall build up your walls, and their Is 60:10
f shall be your plowmen and Is 61:5
and **f** shall not drink your wine for which Is 62:8
you said, 'It is hopeless, for I have loved **f**, Jer 2:25
your favors among **f** under every green Jer 3:13
so you shall serve **f** in a land that is not Jer 5:19
and **f** shall no more make a servant of Jer 30:8
for **f** have come into the holy places of Jer 51:51
turned over to strangers, our homes to **f**. Lam 5:2
I will give it into the hands of **f** for prey, Ezk 7:21
of it, and give you into the hands of **f**, Ezk 11:9
behold, I will bring **f** upon you, Ezk 28:7
of the uncircumcised by the hand of **f**; Ezk 28:10
and everything in it, by the hand of **f**; Ezk 30:12
F, the most ruthless of nations, have Ezk 31:12
in admitting **f**, uncircumcised in heart Ezk 44:7
of all the **f** who are among the people of Ezk 44:9
off his wealth and **f** entered his gates and Ob 1:11
Athenians and the **f** who lived there Acts 17:21
and by the lips of **f** will I speak to 1 Cor 14:21

FOREIGNERS' (1)
city a ruin; the **f** palace is a city no more; Is 25:2

FOREKNEW (2)
those whom he **f** he also predestined Rom 8:29
has not rejected his people whom he **f**. Rom 11:2

FOREKNOWLEDGE (2)
to the definite plan and **f** of God, Acts 2:23
according to the **f** of God the Father, in 1 Pt 1:2

FOREKNOWN (1)
He was **f** before the foundation of the 1 Pt 1:20

FOREMAN (1)
the owner of the vineyard said to his **f**, Mt 20:8

FOREMEN (5)
the taskmasters of the people and their **f**, Ex 5:6
the taskmasters and the **f** of the people Ex 5:10
And the **f** of the people of Israel, whom Ex 5:14
Then the **f** of the people of Israel came Ex 5:15
The **f** of the people of Israel saw that they Ex 5:19

FOREMOST (3)
of the officials and chief men has been **f**." Ezr 9:2
to save sinners, of whom I am the **f**. 1 Tm 1:15
for this reason, that in me, as the **f**, 1 Tm 1:16

FORERUNNER (1)
Jesus has gone as a **f** on our behalf, Heb 6:20

FORESAIL (1)
Then hoisting the **f** to the wind they Acts 27:40

FORESAW (1)
he **f** and spoke about the resurrection Acts 2:31

FORESEEING (1)
f that God would justify the Gentiles by Gal 3:8

FORESIGHT (1)
much peace, and since by your **f**, Acts 24:2

FORESKIN (7)
in the flesh of his **f** shall be cut off Gn 17:14
was circumcised in the flesh of his **f**. Gn 17:24
was circumcised in the flesh of his **f**. Gn 17:25
cut off her son's **f** and touched Moses' Ex 4:25
the flesh of his **f** shall be circumcised. Lv 12:3
Circumcise therefore the **f** of your Dt 10:16
remove the **f** of your hearts, O men of Jer 4:4

FORESKINS (5)
be circumcised in the flesh of your **f**, Gn 17:11
the flesh of their **f** that very day, Gn 17:23
except a hundred **f** of the Philistines, 1 Sm 18:25
And David brought their **f**, which 1 Sm 18:27
of a hundred **f** of the Philistines." 2 Sm 3:14

FOREST (54)
goes into the **f** with his neighbor Dt 19:5
people, go up by yourselves to the **f**, Jos 17:15
shall be yours, for though it is a **f**, Jos 17:18
when all the people came to the **f**, 1 Sm 14:25
And when the people entered the **f**, 1 Sm 14:26
departed and went into the **f** of Hereth. 1 Sm 22:5
battle was fought in the **f** of Ephraim. 2 Sm 18:6
and the **f** devoured more people that 2 Sm 18:8
great pit in the **f** and raised over him 2 Sm 18:17
built the House of the **F** of Lebanon. 1 Kgs 7:2
in the House of the **F** of Lebanon. 1 Kgs 10:17
the House of the **F** of Lebanon were 1 Kgs 10:21
lodging place, its most fruitful **f**. 2 Kgs 19:23
the trees of the **f** sing for joy before 1 Chr 16:33
in the House of the **F** of Lebanon. 2 Chr 9:16
the House of the **F** of Lebanon were of 2 Chr 9:20
letter to Asaph, the keeper of the king's **f**, Neh 2:8
For every beast of the **f** is mine, the Ps 50:10
like those who swing axes in a **f** of trees. Ps 74:5
The boar from the **f** ravages it, and all Ps 80:13
As fire consumes the **f**, as the flame sets Ps 83:14
shall all the trees of the **f** sing for joy Ps 96:12
all the beasts of the **f** creep about. Ps 104:20
which to water the **f** of growing trees. Eccl 2:6
As an apple tree among the trees of the **f**, Sg 2:3
as the trees of the **f** shake before the wind. Is 7:2
it kindles the thickets of the **f**, and they Is 9:18
The glory of his **f** and of his fruitful land Is 10:18
of the trees of his **f** will be so few that Is 10:19
down the thickets of the **f** with an axe, Is 10:34
to the weapons of the House of the **F**, Is 22:8
the fruitful field shall be regarded as a **f**? Is 29:17
field, and the fruitful field is deemed a **f**. Is 32:15
And it will hail when the **f** falls down, Is 32:19
to its remotest height, its most fruitful **f**. Is 37:24
it grow strong among the trees of the **f**. Is 44:14
forth into singing, O mountains, O **f**, Is 44:23
come to devour—all you beasts in the **f**. Is 56:9
a lion from the **f** shall strike them down; Jer 5:6
A tree from the **f** is cut down and worked Jer 10:3
has become to me like a lion in the **f**; Jer 12:8
I will kindle a fire in her **f**, and it shall Jer 21:14
They shall cut down her **f**, declares the Jer 46:23
branch that is among the trees of the **f**? Ezk 15:2
of the vine among the trees of the **f**, Ezk 15:6
and prophesy against the **f** land in the Ezk 20:46
Say to the **f** of the Negeb, Hear the Ezk 20:47
with beautiful branches and **f** shade, Ezk 31:3
I will make them a **f**, and the beasts of Hos 2:12
Does a lion roar in the **f**, when he has no Am 3:4
like a lion among the beasts of the **f**, Mi 5:8
who dwell alone in a **f** in the midst of a Mi 7:14
Bashan, for the thick **f** has been felled! Zec 11:2
How great a **f** is set ablaze by such a Jas 3:5

FORESTS (2)
the deer give birth and strips the **f** bare, Ps 29:9
the field or cut down any out of the **f**, Ezk 39:10

FORETOLD (3)
of Israel had made, as the LORD had **f**. 2 Kgs 24:13
But what God **f** by the mouth of all the Acts 3:18
Agabus stood up and **f** by the Spirit Acts 11:28

FOREVER (390)
of the tree of life and eat, and live **f**—" Gn 3:22
said, "My Spirit shall not abide in man **f**, Gn 6:3
will give to you and to your offspring **f**. Gn 13:15
before you, then let me bear the blame **f**. Gn 43:9
This is my name **f**, and thus I am to be Ex 3:15
your generations, as a statute **f**, Ex 12:14
your generations, as a statute **f**. Ex 12:17
as a statute for you and for your sons **f**. Ex 12:24
The LORD will reign **f** and ever." Ex 15:18
also believe you **f**." When Moses told Ex 19:9
with an awl, and he shall be his slave **f**. Ex 21:6

shall be a statute **f** to be observed Ex 27:21
This shall be a statute **f** for him and for Ex 28:43
priesthood shall be theirs by a statute **f**. Ex 29:9
It shall be a statute **f** to them, even to Ex 30:21
their generations, as a covenant **f**. Ex 31:16
It is a sign **f** between me and the people Ex 31:17
offspring, and they shall inherit it **f**.'" Ex 32:13
be a statute **f** throughout your Lv 3:17
as decreed **f** throughout your Lv 6:18
shall offer it to the LORD as decreed **f**. Lv 6:22
be a statute **f** throughout your Lv 10:9
and your sons' with you as a due **f**, Lv 10:15
be a statute to you **f** that in the seventh Lv 16:29
shall afflict yourselves; it is a statute **f**. Lv 16:31
And this shall be a statute **f** for you, Lv 16:34
shall be a statute **f** for them throughout Lv 17:7
is a statute **f** throughout your Lv 23:14
It is a statute **f** in all your dwelling Lv 23:21
is a statute **f** throughout your Lv 23:31
is a statute **f** throughout your Lv 23:41
be a statute **f** throughout your Lv 24:3
from the people of Israel as a covenant **f**. Lv 24:8
not be sold, for that is their possession **f**. Lv 25:34
after you to inherit as a possession **f**. Lv 25:46
a statute **f** throughout your Nm 15:15
a covenant of salt **f** before the LORD for Nm 18:19
And it shall be a statute **f** for them. Nm 19:21
with them and with their descendants **f**! Dt 5:29
you and with your children after you **f**, Dt 12:28
the LORD your God. It shall be a heap **f**. Dt 13:16
the door, and he shall be your slave **f**. Dt 15:17
may enter the assembly of the LORD **f**, Dt 23:3
peace or their prosperity all your days **f**. Dt 23:6
against you and your offspring **f**. Dt 28:46
belong to us and to our children **f**, Dt 29:29
hand to heaven and swear, As I live **f**, Dt 32:40
be to the people of Israel a memorial **f**." Jos 4:7
that you may fear the LORD your God **f**." Jos 4:24
burned Ai and made it **f** a heap of ruins, Jos 8:28
inheritance for you and your children **f**, Jos 14:9
of the LORD and dwell there **f**." 1 Sm 1:22
should go in and out before me **f**,' 1 Sm 2:30
not be an old man in your house **f**. 1 Sm 2:32
go in and out before my anointed **f**. 1 Sm 2:35
that I am about to punish his house **f**, 1 Sm 3:13
atoned for by sacrifice or offering **f**." 1 Sm 3:14
your kingdom over Israel **f**. 1 Sm 13:13
your steadfast love from my house **f**, 1 Sm 20:15
the LORD is between you and me **f**." 1 Sm 20:23
my offspring and your offspring, **f**.'" 1 Sm 20:42
to Joab, "Shall the sword devour **f**? 2 Sm 2:26
my kingdom are **f** guiltless before the 2 Sm 3:28
establish the throne of his kingdom **f**. 2 Sm 7:13
shall be made sure **f** before me. 2 Sm 7:16
Your throne shall be established **f**.'" 2 Sm 7:16
your people Israel to be your people **f**. 2 Sm 7:24
confirm **f** the word that you have 2 Sm 7:25
And your name will be magnified **f**, 2 Sm 7:26
so that it may continue **f** before you. 2 Sm 7:29
house of your servant be blessed **f**." 2 Sm 7:29
to David and his offspring **f**." 2 Sm 22:51
"May my lord King David live **f**!" 1 Kgs 1:31
and on the head of his descendants **f**. 1 Kgs 2:33
be established before the LORD **f**." 1 Kgs 2:45
house, a place for you to dwell in **f**." 1 Kgs 8:13
built, by putting my name there **f**. 1 Kgs 9:3
your royal throne over Israel **f**, 1 Kgs 9:5
Because the LORD loved Israel **f**, he has 1 Kgs 10:9
of David because of this, but not **f**.'" 1 Kgs 11:39
then they will be your servants **f**." 1 Kgs 12:7
to your descendants **f**." So he went 2 Kgs 5:27
give a lamp to him and to his sons **f**. 2 Kgs 8:19
tribes of Israel, I will put my name **f**. 2 Kgs 21:7
of the LORD and to minister to him **f**. 1 Chr 15:2
Remember his covenant **f**, the word 1 Chr 16:15
for his steadfast love endures **f**! 1 Chr 16:34
LORD, for his steadfast love endures **f**. 1 Chr 16:41
me, and I will establish his throne **f**. 1 Chr 17:12
in my house and in my kingdom **f**, 1 Chr 17:14
his throne shall be established **f**.'" 1 Chr 17:14
people Israel to be your people **f**, 1 Chr 17:22
his house be established **f**, 1 Chr 17:23
will be established and magnified **f**, 1 Chr 17:24
that it may continue **f** before you, 1 Chr 17:27
have blessed, and it is blessed **f**." 1 Chr 17:27
his royal throne in Israel **f**.' 1 Chr 22:10
and his sons **f** should make 1 Chr 23:13
pronounce blessings in his name **f**. 1 Chr 23:13
people, and he dwells in Jerusalem **f**. 1 Chr 23:25
father's house to be king over Israel **f**. 1 Chr 28:4
establish his kingdom **f** if he 1 Chr 28:7
to your children after you **f**. 1 Chr 28:8
forsake him, he will cast you off **f**. 1 Chr 28:9
God of Israel our father, **f** and ever. 1 Chr 29:10
keep **f** such purposes and thoughts 1 Chr 29:18
LORD our God, as ordained **f** for Israel. 2 Chr 2:4
steadfast love endures **f**," the house, 2 Chr 5:13
house, a place for you to dwell in **f**." 2 Chr 6:2
good, for his steadfast love endures **f**." 2 Chr 7:3
steadfast love endures **f**—whenever 2 Chr 7:6
house that my name may be there **f**. 2 Chr 7:16
Israel and would establish them **f**, 2 Chr 9:8
then they will be your servants **f**." 2 Chr 10:7
kingship over Israel **f** to David and 2 Chr 13:5
and give it **f** to the descendants of 2 Chr 20:7
for his steadfast love endures **f**." 2 Chr 20:21
give a lamp to him and to his sons **f**. 2 Chr 21:7
which he has consecrated **f**, 2 Chr 30:8
"In Jerusalem shall my name be **f**." 2 Chr 33:4
tribes of Israel, I will put my name **f**, 2 Chr 33:7
steadfast love endures **f** toward Israel." Ezr 3:11
it for an inheritance to your children **f**.' Ezr 9:12
I said to the king, "Let the king live **f**! Neh 2:3
they perish **f** without anyone regarding Jb 4:20
I loathe my life; I would not live **f**. Leave Jb 7:16
You prevail **f** against him, and he Jb 14:20
lead they were engraved in the rock **f**! Jb 19:24
he will perish **f** like his own dung; those Jb 20:7
and I would be acquitted **f** by my judge. Jb 23:7
with kings on the throne he sets them **f**, Jb 36:7
with you to take him for your servant **f**? Jb 41:4
have blotted out their name **f** and ever. Ps 9:5
But the LORD sits enthroned **f**; he has Ps 9:7
the hope of the poor shall not perish **f**. Ps 9:18
The LORD is king **f** and ever; the nations Ps 10:16
you will guard us from this generation **f**. Ps 12:7
How long, O LORD? Will you forget me **f**? Ps 13:1
anointed, to David and his offspring **f**. Ps 18:50
the fear of the LORD is clean, enduring **f**; Ps 19:9
gave it to him, length of days **f** and ever. Ps 21:4
For you make him most blessed **f**; you Ps 21:6
praise the LORD! May your hearts live **f**! Ps 22:26
I shall dwell in the house of the LORD **f**. Ps 23:6
Be their shepherd and carry them **f**. Ps 28:9
flood; the LORD sits enthroned as king **f**. Ps 29:10
my God, I will give thanks to you **f**! Ps 30:12
The counsel of the LORD stands **f**, the Ps 33:11
and their heritage will remain **f**; Ps 37:18
evil and do good; so shall you dwell **f**. Ps 37:27
They are preserved **f**, but the children of Ps 37:28
inherit the land and dwell upon it **f**. Ps 37:29
integrity, and set me in your presence **f**. Ps 41:12
and we will give thanks to your name **f**. Ps 44:8
Lord? Rouse yourself! Do not reject us **f**! Ps 44:23
lips; therefore God has blessed you **f**. Ps 45:2
Your throne, O God, is **f** and ever. The Ps 45:6
nations will praise you **f** and ever. Ps 45:17
of our God, which God will establish **f**. Ps 48:8
that this is God, our God **f** and ever. He Ps 48:14
God forever and ever. He will guide us **f**. Ps 48:14
that he should live on **f** and never see the Ps 49:9
Their graves are their homes **f**, their Ps 49:11
But God will break you down **f**; he will Ps 52:5
in the steadfast love of God **f** and ever. Ps 52:8
I will thank you **f**, because you have Ps 52:9
Let me dwell in your tent **f**! Let me take Ps 61:4
May he be enthroned **f** before God; Ps 61:7
who rules by his might **f**, whose eyes Ps 66:7
abode, yes, where the LORD will dwell **f**? Ps 68:16
May his name endure **f**, his fame Ps 72:17
Blessed be his glorious name **f**; may the Ps 72:19
strength of my heart and my portion **f**. Ps 73:26
O God, why do you cast us off **f**? Why Ps 74:1
Is the enemy to revile your name **f**? Ps 74:10
do not forget the life of your poor **f**. Ps 74:19
But I will declare it **f**; I will sing praises to Ps 75:9
"Will the Lord spurn **f**, and never again Ps 77:7
Has his steadfast love **f** ceased? Are his Ps 77:8
like the earth, which he has founded **f**. Ps 78:69
How long, O LORD? Will you be angry **f**? Ps 79:5
your pasture, will give thanks to you **f**; Ps 79:13
toward him, and their fate would last **f**. Ps 81:15
them be put to shame and dismayed **f**; Ps 83:17
Will you be angry with us **f**? Will you Ps 85:5
heart, and I will glorify your name **f**. Ps 86:12
f; with my mouth I will make known Ps 89:1
I said, "Steadfast love will be built up **f**; Ps 89:2
'I will establish your offspring **f**, and Ps 89:4
My steadfast love I will keep for him **f**, Ps 89:28
establish his offspring **f** and his throne Ps 89:29
His offspring shall endure **f**, his throne Ps 89:36
Like the moon it shall be established **f**, Ps 89:37
long, O LORD? Will you hide yourself **f**? Ps 89:46
Blessed be the LORD **f**! Amen and Amen. Ps 89:52
they are doomed to destruction **f**; Ps 92:7
but you, O LORD, are on high **f**. Ps 92:8
his steadfast love endures **f**, and his Ps 100:5
But you, O LORD, are enthroned **f**; you Ps 102:12
chide, nor will he keep his anger **f**. Ps 103:9
May the glory of the LORD endure **f**; Ps 104:31
He remembers his covenant **f**, the word Ps 105:8
is good, for his steadfast love endures **f**! Ps 106:1
from generation to generation **f**. Ps 106:31
is good, for his steadfast love endures **f**! Ps 107:1
"You are a priest **f** after the order of Ps 110:4
work, and his righteousness endures **f**. Ps 111:3
fear him; he remembers his covenant **f**. Ps 111:5
they are established **f** and ever, to be Ps 111:8
he has commanded his covenant **f**. Ps 111:9
understanding. His praise endures **f**! Ps 111:10
house, and his righteousness endures **f**. Ps 112:3
be moved; he will be remembered **f**. Ps 112:6
to the poor; his righteousness endures **f**; Ps 112:9
the faithfulness of the LORD endures **f**. Ps 117:2
is good; for his steadfast love endures **f**! Ps 118:1
Israel say, "His steadfast love endures **f**." Ps 118:2
say, "His steadfast love endures **f**." Ps 118:3
LORD say, "His steadfast love endures **f**." Ps 118:4
is good; for his steadfast love endures **f**! Ps 118:29
keep your law continually, **f** and ever, Ps 119:44
F, O LORD, your word is firmly fixed in Ps 119:89
Your testimonies are my heritage **f**, Ps 119:111
my heart to perform your statutes **f**, Ps 119:112
Your righteousness is righteous **f**, Ps 119:142
Your testimonies are righteous **f**; give Ps 119:144
that you have founded them **f**. Ps 119:152
one of your righteous rules endures **f**. Ps 119:160
which cannot be moved, but abides **f**. Ps 125:1
their sons also **f** shall sit on your Ps 132:12
"This is my resting place **f**; here I will Ps 132:14
Your name, O LORD, endures **f**, your Ps 135:13
is good, for his steadfast love endures **f**. Ps 136:1
of gods, for his steadfast love endures **f**. Ps 136:2
of lords, for his steadfast love endures **f**; Ps 136:3
wonders, for his steadfast love endures **f**; Ps 136:4
heavens, for his steadfast love endures **f**; Ps 136:5
waters, for his steadfast love endures **f**; Ps 136:6
lights, for his steadfast love endures **f**; Ps 136:7
the day, for his steadfast love endures **f**; Ps 136:8
night, for his steadfast love endures **f**; Ps 136:9
Egypt, for his steadfast love endures **f**; Ps 136:10
them, for his steadfast love endures **f**; Ps 136:11
arm, for his steadfast love endures **f**; Ps 136:12
in two, for his steadfast love endures **f**; Ps 136:13
of it, for his steadfast love endures **f**; Ps 136:14
Sea, for his steadfast love endures **f**; Ps 136:15
for his steadfast love endures **f**; Ps 136:16
kings, for his steadfast love endures **f**; Ps 136:17
kings, for his steadfast love endures **f**; Ps 136:18
for his steadfast love endures **f**; Ps 136:19
for his steadfast love endures **f**; Ps 136:20
for his steadfast love endures **f**; Ps 136:21
for his steadfast love endures **f**. Ps 136:22
estate, for his steadfast love endures **f**; Ps 136:23
foes, for his steadfast love endures **f**; Ps 136:24
flesh, for his steadfast love endures **f**. Ps 136:25
heaven, for his steadfast love endures **f**. Ps 136:26
your steadfast love, O LORD, endures **f**. Ps 138:8
King, and bless your name **f** and ever. Ps 145:1
you and praise your name **f** and ever. Ps 145:2
flesh bless his holy name **f** and ever. Ps 145:21
all that is in them, who keeps faith **f**; Ps 146:6
The LORD will reign **f**, your God, O Ps 146:10
And he established them **f** and ever; he Ps 148:6
but the righteous is established **f**. Prv 10:25
Truthful lips endure **f**, but a lying Prv 12:19
for riches do not last **f**; and does a Prv 27:24
poor, his throne will be established **f**. Prv 29:14
comes, but the earth remains **f**. Eccl 1:4
that whatever God does endures **f**; Eccl 3:14
and **f** they have no more share in all Eccl 9:6
He will swallow up death **f**; and the Lord Is 25:8
Trust in the LORD **f**, for the LORD GOD is an Is 26:4
No, he does not thresh it **f**; when he Is 28:28
be for the time to come as a witness **f**. Is 30:8
and the watchtower will become dens **f**, Is 32:14
of righteousness, quietness and trust **f**. Is 32:17
not be quenched; its smoke shall go up **f**. Is 34:10
none shall pass through it **f** and ever. Is 34:10
them with the line; they shall possess it **f**; Is 34:17
but the word of our God will stand **f**. Is 40:8
"I shall be mistress **f**," so that you did not Is 47:7
but my salvation will be **f**, and my Is 51:6
but my righteousness will be **f**, and my Is 51:8
For I will not contend **f**, nor will I always Is 57:16
through, I will make you majestic **f**, Is 60:15
they shall possess the land **f**, the branch Is 60:21
O LORD, and remember not iniquity **f**. Is 64:9
But be glad and rejoice **f** in that which I Is 65:18
will he be angry **f**, will he be indignant to Jer 3:5
declares the LORD; I will not be angry **f**. Jer 3:12
the land that I gave of old to your fathers **f**. Jer 7:7
a fire is kindled that shall burn **f**." Jer 15:14
anger a fire is kindled that shall burn **f**." Jer 17:4
And this city shall be inhabited **f**. Jer 17:25

land a horror, a thing to be hissed at **f**. Jer 18:16
been my grave, and her womb **f** great. Jer 20:17
you and your fathers from of old and **f**. Jer 25:5
cease from being a nation before me **f**." Jer 31:36
be uprooted or overthrown anymore **f**." Jer 31:40
and one way, that they may fear me **f**, Jer 32:39
is good, for his steadfast love endures **f**!' Jer 33:11
offerings, and to make sacrifices **f**." Jer 33:18
drink wine, neither you nor your sons **f**. Jer 35:6
nor beast, and it shall be desolate **f**.' Jer 51:62
For the Lord will not cast off **f**, Lam 3:31
But you, O LORD, reign **f**; your throne Lam 5:19
Why do you forget us **f**, why do you Lam 5:20
dreadful end and shall be no more **f**.'" Ezk 27:36
dreadful end and shall be no more **f**." Ezk 28:19
children's children shall dwell there **f**, Ezk 37:25
my servant shall be their prince **f**. Ezk 37:25
in the midst of the people of Israel **f**. Ezk 43:7
me, and I will dwell in their midst **f**. Ezk 43:9
to the king in Aramaic, "O king, live **f**! Dn 2:4
"Blessed be the name of God **f** and ever, Dn 2:20
them to an end, and it shall stand **f**, Dn 2:44
to King Nebuchadnezzar, "O king, live **f**! Dn 3:9
praised and honored him who lives **f**, Dn 4:34
and the queen declared, "O king, live **f**! Dn 5:10
and said to him, "O King Darius, live **f**! Dn 6:6
Daniel said to the king, "O king, live **f**! Dn 6:21
for he is the living God, enduring **f**; Dn 6:26
the kingdom and possess the kingdom **f**, Dn 7:18
possess the kingdom forever, **f** and ever.' Dn 7:18
righteousness, like the stars **f** and ever. Dn 12:3
by him who lives **f** that it would be Dn 12:7
And I will betroth you to me **f**. I will Hos 2:19
But Judah shall be inhabited **f**, and Jl 3:20
perpetually, and he kept his wrath **f**. Am 1:11
cover you, and you shall be cut off **f**. Ob 1:10
to the land whose bars closed upon me **f**; Jon 2:6
children you take away my splendor **f**. Mi 2:9
the name of the LORD our God **f** and ever. Mi 4:5
He does not retain his anger **f**, because Mi 7:18
net and mercilessly killing nations **f**? Hab 1:17
by nettles and salt pits, and a waste **f**. Zep 2:9
are they? And the prophets, do they live **f**? Zec 1:5
people with whom the LORD is angry **f**.'" Mal 1:4
he will reign over the house of Jacob **f**, Lk 1:33
to Abraham and to his offspring **f**." Lk 1:55
that I will give him will never be thirsty **f**. Jn 4:14
If anyone eats of this bread, he will live **f**. Jn 6:51
Whoever feeds on this bread will live **f**." Jn 6:58
The slave does not remain in the house **f**; Jn 8:35
in the house forever; the son remains **f**. Jn 8:35
from the Law that the Christ remains **f**. Jn 12:34
you another Helper, to be with you **f**, Jn 14:16
than the Creator, who is blessed **f**! Rom 1:25
the Christ who is God over all, blessed **f**. Rom 9:5
cannot see, and bend their backs **f**." Rom 11:10
him are all things. To him be glory **f**. Rom 11:36
the poor; his righteousness endures **f**." 2 Cor 9:9
of the Lord Jesus, he who is blessed **f**, 2 Cor 11:31
to whom be the glory **f** and ever. Amen. Gal 1:5
throughout all generations, **f** and ever. Eph 3:21
our God and Father be glory **f** and ever. Phil 4:20
God, be honor and glory **f** and ever. 1 Tm 1:17
To him be the glory **f** and ever. 2 Tm 4:18
that you might have him back **f**, Phlm 1:15
says, "Your throne, O God, is **f** and ever, Heb 1:8
also in another place, "You are a priest **f**, Heb 5:6
become a high priest **f** after the order of Heb 6:20
the Son of God he continues a priest **f**. Heb 7:3
is witnessed of him, "You are a priest **f**, Heb 7:17
change his mind, 'You are a priest **f**.'" Heb 7:21
permanently, because he continues **f**. Heb 7:24
a Son who has been made perfect **f**. Heb 7:28
is the same yesterday and today and **f**. Heb 13:8
Christ, to whom be glory **f** and ever. Heb 13:21
of the Lord remains **f**." And this word is 1 Pt 1:25
belong glory and dominion **f** and ever. 1 Pt 4:11
To him be the dominion **f** and ever. 1 Pt 5:11
whoever does the will of God abides **f**. 1 Jn 2:17
that abides in us and will be with us **f**: 2 Jn 1:2
of utter darkness has been reserved **f**. Jude 1:13
before all time and now and **f**. Jude 1:25
to him be glory and dominion **f** and ever. Rv 1:6
seated on the throne, who lives **f** and ever, Rv 4:9
and worship him who lives **f** and ever. Rv 4:10
honor and glory and might **f** and ever!" Rv 5:13
and might be to our God **f** and ever! Rv 7:12
and swore by him who lives **f** and ever, Rv 10:6
Christ, and he shall reign **f** and ever." Rv 11:15
of their torment goes up **f** and ever, Rv 14:11
of the wrath of God who lives **f** and ever, Rv 15:7
The smoke from her goes up **f** and ever." Rv 19:3
be tormented day and night **f** and ever. Rv 20:10
their light, and they will reign **f** and ever. Rv 22:5

FOREVERMORE (16)
there shall be peace from the LORD **f**." 1 Kgs 2:33
joy; at your right hand are pleasures **f**. Ps 16:11
holiness befits your house, O LORD, **f**. Ps 93:5
of the LORD from this time forth and **f**! Ps 113:2
the LORD from this time forth and **f**. Ps 115:18
coming in from this time forth and **f**. Ps 121:8
his people, from this time forth and **f**. Ps 125:2
in the LORD from this time forth and **f**. Ps 131:3
has commanded the blessing, life **f**. Ps 133:3
righteousness from this time forth and **f**. Is 9:7
the LORD, "from this time forth and **f**." Is 59:21
will set my sanctuary in their midst **f**. Ezk 37:26
my sanctuary is in their midst **f**." Ezk 37:28
in Mount Zion from this time forth and **f**. Mi 4:7
God be glory **f** through Jesus Christ! Rom 16:27
I died, and behold I am alive **f**, and I have Rv 1:18

FORFEIT (2)
your hands to escape shall **f** his life." 2 Kgs 10:24
to gain the whole world and **f** his life? Mk 8:36

FORFEITED (3)
kinds of seed, lest the whole yield be **f**, Dt 22:9
the elders all his property should be **f**, Ezr 10:8
off many peoples; you have **f** your life. Hab 2:10

FORFEITS (3)
provokes him to anger **f** his life. Prv 20:2
he gains the whole world and **f** his life? Mt 16:26
the whole world and loses or **f** himself? Lk 9:25

FORGAVE (5)
to the LORD," and you **f** the iniquity of my Ps 32:5
You **f** the iniquity of your people; you Ps 85:2
released him and **f** him the debt. Mt 18:27
I **f** you all that debt because you Mt 18:32
one another, as God in Christ **f** you. Eph 4:32

FORGE (1)
"**F** a chain! For the land is full of Ezk 7:23

FORGER (1)
he was the **f** of all instruments of bronze Gn 4:22

FORGET (57)
"God has made me **f** all my hardship Gn 41:51
lest you **f** the things that your eyes have Dt 4:9
lest you **f** the covenant of the LORD your Dt 4:23
or destroy you or **f** the covenant with Dt 4:31
then take care lest you **f** the LORD, who Dt 6:12
"Take care lest you **f** the LORD your God Dt 8:11
be lifted up, and you **f** the LORD your God, Dt 8:14
And if you **f** the LORD your God and go Dt 8:19
and do not **f** how you provoked Dt 9:7
harvest in your field and **f** a sheaf in the Dt 24:19
from under heaven; you shall not **f**. Dt 25:19
remember me and not **f** your servant, 1 Sm 1:11
you shall not **f** the covenant that 2 Kgs 17:38
Such are the paths of all who **f** God; the Jb 8:13
If I say, 'I will **f** my complaint, I will put Jb 9:27
You will **f** your misery; you will Jb 11:16
God has made her **f** wisdom and given Jb 39:17
he does not **f** the cry of the afflicted. Ps 9:12
to Sheol, all the nations that **f** God. Ps 9:17
lift up your hand; **f** not the afflicted. Ps 10:12
long, O LORD? Will you **f** me forever? Ps 13:1
Why do you **f** our affliction and Ps 44:24
f your people and your father's house, Ps 45:10
"Mark this, then, you who **f** God, lest I Ps 50:22
Kill them not, lest my people **f**; make Ps 59:11
do not **f** the life of your poor forever. Ps 74:19
Do not **f** the clamor of your foes, the Ps 74:23
hope in God and not **f** the works of God, Ps 78:7
and has withered; I **f** to eat my bread. Ps 102:4
O my soul, and **f** not all his benefits, Ps 103:2
in your statutes; I will not **f** your word. Ps 119:16
ensnare me, I do not **f** your law. Ps 119:61
I will never **f** your precepts, for by Ps 119:93
continually, but I do not **f** your law. Ps 119:109
me, because my foes **f** your words. Ps 119:139
despised, yet I do not **f** your precepts. Ps 119:141
deliver me, for I do not **f** your law. Ps 119:153
for I do not **f** your commandments. Ps 119:176
If I **f** you, O Jerusalem, let my right Ps 137:5
Jerusalem, let my right hand **f** its skill! Ps 137:5
My son, do not **f** my teaching, but let Prv 3:1
do not **f**, and do not turn away from the Prv 4:5
lest they drink and **f** what has been Prv 31:5
let them drink and **f** their poverty and Prv 31:7
"Can a woman **f** her nursing child, that Is 49:15
Even these may **f**, yet I will not forget Is 49:15
these may forget, yet I will not **f** you. Is 49:15
for you will **f** the shame of your youth, Is 54:4
the LORD, who **f** my holy mountain, Is 65:11
Can a virgin **f** her ornaments, or a bride Jer 2:32
to make my people **f** my name by their Jer 23:27
has made Zion **f** festival and Sabbath, Lam 2:6
Why do you **f** us forever, why do you Lam 5:20
They shall **f** their shame and all the Ezk 39:26
of your God, I also will **f** your children. Hos 4:6
"Surely I will never **f** any of their deeds. Am 8:7
Can I **f** any longer the treasures of Mi 6:10

FORGETFULNESS (1)
or your righteousness in the land of **f**? Ps 88:12

FORGETS (5)
and he **f** what you have done to him. Gn 27:45
The womb **f** them; the worm finds them Jb 24:20
of her youth and **f** the covenant of her Prv 2:17
away and at once **f** what he was like. Jas 1:24
being no hearer who **f** but a doer who Jas 1:25

FORGETTING (2)
f that a foot may crush them and that Jb 39:15
f what lies behind and straining Phil 3:13

FORGIVE (58)
Please **f** the transgression of your Gn 50:17
please **f** the transgression of the Gn 50:17
Now therefore, **f** my sin, please, only Ex 10:17
now, if you will **f** their sin—but if not, Ex 32:32
And the LORD will **f** her, because her Nm 30:5
bound herself. And the LORD will **f** her. Nm 30:8
them void, and the LORD will **f** her. Nm 30:12
The LORD will not be willing to **f** him, Dt 29:20
he will not **f** your transgressions or Jos 24:19
Please **f** the trespass of your servant. 1 Sm 25:28
dwelling place, and when you hear, **f**. 1 Kgs 8:30
hear in heaven and **f** the sin of your 1 Kgs 8:34
hear in heaven and **f** the sin of your 1 Kgs 8:36
your dwelling place and **f** and act and 1 Kgs 8:39
and **f** your people who have sinned 1 Kgs 8:50
dwelling place, and when you hear, **f**. 2 Chr 6:21
hear from heaven and **f** the sin of 2 Chr 6:25
hear in heaven and **f** the sin of your 2 Chr 6:27
dwelling place and **f** and render to 2 Chr 6:30
their cause and **f** your people who 2 Chr 6:39
from heaven and will **f** their sin and 2 Chr 7:14
But you are a God ready to **f**, gracious Neh 9:17
and my trouble, and **f** all my sins. Ps 25:18
each one is brought low—do not **f** them! Is 2:9
F not their iniquity, nor blot out their Jer 18:23
For I will **f** their iniquity, and I will Jer 31:34
and I will **f** all the guilt of their sin and Jer 33:8
and that I may **f** their iniquity and their Jer 36:3
O Lord, **f**. O Lord, pay attention and act. Dn 9:19
on the house of Israel, to **f** them at all. Hos 1:6
of the land, I said, "O Lord GOD, please **f**! Am 7:2
and **f** us our debts, as we also have Mt 6:12
For if you **f** others their trespasses, your Mt 6:14
your heavenly Father will also **f** you, Mt 6:14
if you do not **f** others their trespasses, Mt 6:15
will your Father **f** your trespasses. Mt 6:15
has authority on earth to **f** sins"—he then Mt 9:6
brother sin against me, and I **f** him? Mt 18:21
if you do not **f** your brother from your Mt 18:35
Who can **f** sins but God alone?" Mk 2:7
authority on earth to **f** sins"—he said Mk 2:10
f, if you have anything against Mk 11:25
in heaven may **f** you your trespasses." Mk 11:25
Who can **f** sins but God alone?" Lk 5:21
authority on earth to **f** sins"—he said Lk 5:24
condemned; **f**, and you will be forgiven; Lk 6:37
and **f** us our sins, for we ourselves Lk 11:4
for we ourselves **f** everyone who is Lk 11:4
rebuke him, and if he repents, **f** him, Lk 17:3
saying, 'I repent,' you must **f** him." Lk 17:4
And Jesus said, "Father, **f** them, for they Lk 23:34
If you **f** the sins of anyone, they are Jn 20:23
rather turn to **f** and comfort him, 2 Cor 2:7
Anyone whom you **f**, I also forgive. 2 Cor 2:10
Anyone whom you forgive, I also **f**. 2 Cor 2:10
not burden you? **F** me this wrong! 2 Cor 12:13
has forgiven you, so you also must **f**. Col 3:13
is faithful and just to **f** us our sins and to 1 Jn 1:9

FORGIVEN (45)
atonement for them, and they shall be **f**. Lv 4:20
for him for his sin, and he shall be **f**. Lv 4:26
atonement for him, and he shall be **f**. Lv 4:31
he has committed, and he shall be **f**. Lv 4:35
that he has committed, and he shall be **f**. Lv 5:10
any one of these things, and he shall be **f**. Lv 5:13
of the guilt offering, and he shall be **f**. Lv 5:16
made unintentionally, and he shall be **f**. Lv 5:18
and he shall be **f** for any of the things that Lv 6:7
and he shall be **f** for the sin that he has Lv 19:22
love, just as you have **f** this people, Nm 14:19
the people of Israel, and they shall be **f**, Nm 15:25
of the people of Israel shall be **f**, Nm 15:26
atonement for him, and he shall be **f**. Nm 15:28
is the one whose transgression is **f**, Ps 32:1
who dwell there will be **f** their iniquity. Is 33:24
and rebelled, and you have not **f**. Lam 3:42
our debts, as we also have **f** our debtors. Mt 6:12

“Take heart, my son; your sins are **f**.” Mt 9:2
which is easier, to say, ‘Your sins are **f**,’ Mt 9:5
sin and blasphemy will be **f** people, Mt 12:31
against the Spirit will not be **f**. Mt 12:31
a word against the Son of Man will be **f**, Mt 12:32
against the Holy Spirit will not be **f**, Mt 12:32
the paralytic, “My son, your sins are **f**.” Mk 2:5
to say to the paralytic, ‘Your sins are **f**,’ Mk 2:9
all sins will be **f** the children of man, Mk 3:28
lest they should turn and be **f**.” Mk 4:12
faith, he said, “Man, your sins are **f** you.” Lk 5:20
is easier, to say, ‘Your sins are **f** you,’ Lk 5:23
condemned; forgive, and you will be **f**; Lk 6:37
are many, are **f**—for she loved much. Lk 7:47
much. But he who is **f** little, loves little.” Lk 7:47
And he said to her, “Your sins are **f**.” Lk 7:48
a word against the Son of Man will be **f**, Lk 12:10
against the Holy Spirit will not be **f**. Lk 12:10
forgive the sins of anyone, they are **f**; Jn 20:23
the intent of your heart may be **f** you. Acts 8:22
are those whose lawless deeds are **f**, Rom 4:7
What I have **f**, if I have forgiven 2 Cor 2:10
I have forgiven, if I have **f** anything, 2 Cor 2:10
with him, having **f** us all our trespasses, Col 2:13
as the Lord has **f** you, so you also must Col 3:13
if he has committed sins, he will be **f**. Jas 5:15
because your sins are **f** for his name’s 1 Jn 2:12

FORGIVENESS (18)
But with you there is **f**, that you may be Ps 130:4
To the Lord our God belong mercy and **f**, Dn 9:9
is poured out for many for the **f** of sins. Mt 26:28
a baptism of repentance for the **f** of sins. Mk 1:4
against the Holy Spirit never has **f**, Mk 3:29
to his people in the **f** of their sins, Lk 1:77
a baptism of repentance for the **f** of sins. Lk 3:3
that repentance and **f** of sins should Lk 24:47
if you withhold **f** from anyone, it is Jn 20:23
of Jesus Christ for the **f** of your sins, Acts 2:38
give repentance to Israel and **f** of sins. Acts 5:31
in him receives **f** of sins through Acts 10:43
that through this man **f** of sins is Acts 13:38
that they may receive **f** of sins and a Acts 26:18
his blood, the **f** of our trespasses, Eph 1:7
whom we have redemption, the **f** of sins. Col 1:14
shedding of blood there is no **f** of sins. Heb 9:22
Where there is **f** of these, there is no Heb 10:18

FORGIVES (2)
who **f** all your iniquity, who heals all Ps 103:3
“Who is this, who even **f** sins?” Lk 7:49

FORGIVING (6)
f iniquity and transgression and sin, Ex 34:7
love, **f** iniquity and transgression, Nm 14:18
For you, O Lord, are good and **f**, Ps 86:5
them; you were a **f** God to them, Ps 99:8
another, tenderhearted, **f** one another, Eph 4:32
against another, **f** each other; Col 3:13

FORGOT (10)
did not remember Joseph, but **f** him. Gn 40:23
and you **f** the God who gave you birth. Dt 32:18
They **f** the LORD their God and served the Jgs 3:7
But they **f** the LORD their God. And he 1 Sm 12:9
They **f** his works and the wonders that Ps 78:11
But they soon **f** his works; they did not Ps 106:13
They **f** God, their Savior, who had Ps 106:21
even as their fathers **f** my name for Jer 23:27
and went after her lovers and **f** me, Hos 2:13
heart was lifted up; therefore they **f** me. Hos 13:6

FORGOTTEN (41)
all the plenty will be **f** in the land of Gn 41:30
commandments, nor have I **f** them. Dt 26:13
failed me, my close friends have **f** me. Jb 19:14
anyone lives; they are **f** by travelers; Jb 28:4
For the needy shall not always be **f**, and Ps 9:18
He says in his heart, “God has **f**, he has Ps 10:11
I have been **f** like one who is dead; I Ps 31:12
to God, my rock: “Why have you **f** me? Ps 42:9
upon us, though we have not **f** you, Ps 44:17
If we had **f** the name of our God or Ps 44:20
Has God **f** to be gracious? Has he in Ps 77:9
smoke, yet I have not **f** your statutes. Ps 119:83
days to come all will have been long **f**. Eccl 2:16
reward, for the memory of them is **f**. Eccl 9:5
For you have **f** the God of your salvation Is 17:10
that day Tyre will be **f** for seventy years, Is 23:15
a harp; go about the city, O **f** prostitute! Is 23:16
servant; O Israel, you will not be **f** by me. Is 44:21
has forsaken me; my Lord has **f** me.” Is 49:14
and have **f** the LORD, your Maker, who Is 51:13
the former troubles are **f** and are hidden Is 65:16
Yet my people have **f** me days without Jer 2:32
their way; they have **f** the LORD their God. Jer 3:21
because you have **f** me and trusted in Jer 13:25
But my people have **f** me; they make Jer 18:15
Their eternal dishonor will never be **f**. Jer 20:11
perpetual shame, which shall not be **f**.’” Jer 23:40
All your lovers have **f** you; they care Jer 30:14
Have you **f** the evil of your fathers, the Jer 44:9
covenant that will never be **f**.’ Jer 50:5
they have gone. They have **f** their fold. Jer 50:6
of peace; I have **f** what happiness is; Lam 3:17
but me you have **f**, declares the Lord Ezk 22:12
Because you have **f** me and cast me Ezk 23:35
And since you have **f** the law of your Hos 4:6
For Israel has **f** his Maker and built Hos 8:14
other side, they had **f** to bring any bread. Mt 16:5
Now they had **f** to bring bread, and they Mk 8:14
And not one of them is **f** before God. Lk 12:6
And have you **f** the exhortation that Heb 12:5
having **f** that he was cleansed from his 2 Pt 1:9

FORK (6)
with a three-pronged **f** in his hand, 1 Sm 2:13
All that the **f** brought up the priest 1 Sm 2:14
has been winnowed with shovel and **f**. Is 30:24
them with a winnowing **f** in the gates of Jer 15:7
His winnowing **f** is in his hand, and he Mt 3:12
His winnowing **f** is in his hand, to clear Lk 3:17

FORKS (5)
shovels and basins and **f** and fire pans. Ex 27:3
the pots, the shovels, the basins, the **f**, Ex 38:3
for the service there, the fire pans, the **f**, Nm 4:14
and pure gold for the **f**, the basins 1 Chr 28:17
The pots, the shovels, the **f**, and all 2 Chr 4:16

FORLORN (1)
but she who has many children is **f**. 1 Sm 2:5

FORM (34)
The earth was without **f** and void, and Gn 1:2
was beautiful in **f** and appearance. Gn 29:17
was handsome in **f** and appearance. Gn 39:6
of them; they shall **f** the two corners. Ex 26:24
and he beholds the **f** of the LORD. Nm 12:8
heard the sound of words, but saw no **f**; Dt 4:12
Since you saw no **f** on the day that the Dt 4:15
for yourselves, in the **f** of any figure, Dt 4:16
the **f** of anything that the LORD your God Dt 4:23
a carved image in the **f** of anything, Dt 4:25
was carved in the **f** of gourds and 1 Kgs 6:18
the same measure and the same **f**. 1 Kgs 6:25
of olivewood, in the **f** of a square, 1 Kgs 6:33
of the same measure and the same **f**. 1 Kgs 7:37
A **f** was before my eyes; there was silence, Jb 4:16
Their **f** shall be consumed in Sheol, Ps 49:14
I **f** light and create darkness, I make Is 45:7
and his **f** beyond that of the children of Is 52:14
he had no **f** or majesty that we should Is 53:2
and behold, it was without **f** and void; Jer 4:23
the beauty of their **f** was like sapphire. Lam 4:7
a **f** that had the appearance of a man. Ezk 8:2
He put out the **f** of a hand and took me Ezk 8:3
was every **f** of creeping things and Ezk 8:10
appeared to have the **f** of a human hand Ezk 10:8
he appeared in another **f** to two of Mk 16:12
Spirit descended on him in bodily **f**, Lk 3:22
never heard, his **f** you have never seen, Jn 5:37
For the present **f** of this world is 1 Cor 7:31
who, though he was in the **f** of God, did Phil 2:6
nothing, taking the **f** of a servant, Phil 2:7
And being found in human **f**, he Phil 2:8
Abstain from every **f** of evil. 1 Thes 5:22
instead of the true **f** of these realities, Heb 10:1

FORMED (44)
then the LORD God **f** the man of dust from Gn 2:7
and there he put the man whom he had **f**. Gn 2:8
ground the LORD God **f** every beast of the Gn 2:19
Moab, on the border **f** by the Arnon, Nm 22:36
the people of Simeon **f** part of the Jos 19:9
and again **f** the battle line in the same Jgs 20:22
place where they had **f** it on the first Jgs 20:22
“The Chaldeans **f** three groups and made Jb 1:17
or ever you had **f** the earth and the world, Ps 90:2
ear, does he not hear? He who **f** the eye, Ps 94:9
he made it, and his hands **f** the dry land. Ps 95:5
Leviathan, which you **f** to play in it. Ps 104:26
For you **f** my inward parts; you Ps 139:13
of them, the days that were **f** for me, Ps 139:16
done wonderful things, plans **f** of old, Is 25:1
he who **f** them will show them no favor. Is 27:11
or the thing **f** say of him who formed it, Is 29:16
or the thing formed say of him who **f** it, Is 29:16
who created you, O Jacob, he who **f** you, Is 43:1
for my glory, whom I **f** and made.” Is 43:7
Before me no god was **f**, nor shall there Is 43:10
the people whom I **f** for myself that they Is 43:21
who **f** you from the womb and will help Is 44:2
Israel, for you are my servant; I **f** you; Is 44:21
Redeemer, who **f** you from the womb: Is 44:24
to him who strives with him who **f** him, Is 45:9
One of Israel, and the one who **f** him: Is 45:11
who **f** the earth and made it (he Is 45:18
create it empty, he **f** it to be inhabited!): Is 45:18
he who **f** me from the womb to be his Is 49:5
“Before I **f** you in the womb I knew you, Jer 1:5
Jacob, for he is the one who **f** all things, Jer 10:16
the LORD who **f** it to establish it—the Jer 33:2
that he has **f** against the inhabitants Jer 49:20
against you and **f** a purpose against Jer 49:30
purposes that he has **f** against the land Jer 50:45
Jacob, for he is the one who **f** all things, Jer 51:19
Your breasts were **f**, and your hair had Ezk 16:7
founded the earth and **f** the spirit of Zec 12:1
men of the rabble, they **f** a mob, Acts 17:5
an image **f** by the art and Acts 17:29
of childbirth until Christ is **f** in you! Gal 4:19
For Adam was **f** first, then Eve; 1 Tm 2:13
and the earth was **f** out of water and 2 Pt 3:5

FORMER (54)
besides the **f** famine that was in the days Gn 26:1
had fought against the **f** king of Moab Nm 21:26
then her **f** husband, who sent her away, Dt 24:4
was the custom in **f** times in Israel Ru 4:7
she said, “They used to say in **f** times, 2 Sm 20:18
consumed the two **f** captains of fifty 2 Kgs 1:14
they do according to the **f** manner. 2 Kgs 17:34
did according to their **f** manner. 2 Kgs 17:40
for the **f** inhabitants there belonged 1 Chr 4:40
The **f** governors who were before me Neh 5:15
remember against us our **f** iniquities; Ps 79:8
There is no remembrance of **f** things, Eccl 1:11
“Why were the **f** days better than Eccl 7:10
In the **f** time he brought into contempt the Is 9:1
Tell us the **f** things, what they are, that Is 41:22
Behold, the **f** things have come to pass, Is 42:9
declare this, and show us the **f** things? Is 43:9
“Remember not the **f** things, nor Is 43:18
remember the **f** things of old; for I am Is 46:9
“The **f** things I declared of old; they went Is 48:3
they shall raise up the **f** devastations; Is 61:4
their bosom payment for their **f** deeds.” Is 65:7
because the **f** troubles are forgotten and Is 65:16
and the **f** things shall not be Is 65:17
fathers, the **f** kings who were before you, Jer 34:5
write on it all the **f** words that were in Jer 36:28
daughters shall return to their **f** state, Ezk 16:55
daughters shall return to their **f** state, Ezk 16:55
daughters shall return to your **f** state. Ezk 16:55
you to be inhabited as in your **f** times, Ezk 36:11
whom I spoke in **f** days by my Ezk 38:17
he shall be different from the **f** ones, and Dn 7:24
shall it come, the **f** dominion shall come, Mi 4:8
you who saw this house in its **f** glory? Hg 2:3
of this house shall be greater than the **f**, Hg 2:9
fathers, to whom the **f** prophets cried out, Zec 1:4
the LORD proclaimed by the **f** prophets, Zec 7:7
by his Spirit through the **f** prophets. Zec 7:12
remnant of this people as in the **f** days, Zec 8:11
of Benjamin to the place of the **f** gate, Zec 14:10
as in the days of old and as in **f** years. Mal 3:4
forbearance he had passed over **f** sins. Rom 3:25
was written in **f** days was written Rom 15:4
some, through **f** association with idols, 1 Cor 8:7
you have heard of my **f** life in Judaism, Gal 1:13
which belongs to your **f** manner of life Eph 4:22
The **f** proclaim Christ out of rivalry, Phil 1:17
for having abandoned their **f** faith. 1 Tm 5:12
a **f** commandment is set aside because Heb 7:18
The **f** priests were many in number, Heb 7:23
But recall the **f** days when, after you Heb 10:32
to the passions of your **f** ignorance, 1 Pt 1:14
that he was cleansed from his **f** sins. 2 Pt 1:9
for the **f** things have passed away.” Rv 21:4

FORMERLY (22)
place Pharaoh’s cup in his hand as **f**, Gn 40:13
(The Emim **f** lived there, a people great Dt 2:10
The Horites also lived in Seir **f**, but the Dt 2:12
Rephaim **f** lived there—but the Dt 2:20
for Hazor **f** was the head of all those Jos 11:10
name of Hebron **f** was Kiriath-arba. Jos 14:15
the name of Debir **f** was Kiriath-sepher. Jos 15:15
the name of Hebron was **f** Kiriath-arba), Jgs 1:10
The name of Debir was **f** Kiriath-sepher. Jgs 1:11
(Now the name of the city was **f** Luz.) Jgs 1:23
(**F** in Israel, when a man went to 1 Sm 9:9
today’s “prophet” was **f** called a seer.) 1 Sm 9:9
men shall afflict them no more, as **f**, 2 Sm 7:10
of Israel lived in their homes as **f**. 2 Kgs 13:5
men shall waste them no more, as **f**, 1 Chr 17:9
Pharisees the man who had **f** been blind. Jn 9:13
F, when you did not know God, you were Gal 4:8
though **f** I was a blasphemer, 1 Tm 1:13
(**F** he was useless to you, but now he Phlm 1:11
and those who **f** received the good news Heb 4:6

For those who **f** became priests were Heb 7:20
because they **f** did not obey, when 1 Pt 3:20

FORMING (2)
with the sea **f** its boundary. Jos 17:10
he was **f** locusts when the latter growth Am 7:1

FORMS (4)
people of Judah. This **f** the western side. Jos 18:14
The Jordan **f** its boundary on the Jos 18:20
Does the clay say to him who **f** it, 'What Is 45:9
he who **f** the mountains and creates the Am 4:13

FORSAKE (54)
with you. He will not leave you or **f** you." Dt 31:6
with you; he will not leave you or **f** you. Dt 31:8
and they will **f** me and break my Dt 31:16
and I will **f** them and hide my face from Dt 31:17
be with you. I will not leave you or **f** you. Jos 1:5
us that we should **f** the LORD to serve Jos 24:16
If you **f** the LORD and serve foreign gods, Jos 24:20
For the LORD will not **f** his people, for 1 Sm 12:22
Israel and will not **f** my people Israel." 1 Kgs 6:13
fathers. May he not leave us or **f** us, 1 Kgs 8:57
And I will **f** the remnant of my 2 Kgs 21:14
be found by you, but if you **f** him, 1 Chr 28:9
He will not leave you or **f** you, until 1 Chr 28:20
you turn aside and **f** my statutes and 2 Chr 7:19
be found by you, but if you **f** him, 2 Chr 15:2
but if you forsake him, he will **f** you. 2 Chr 15:2
of his wrath is against all who **f** him." Ezr 8:22
in steadfast love, and did not **f** them. Neh 9:17
great mercies did not **f** them in the Neh 9:19
did not make an end of them or **f** them, Neh 9:31
not off; **f** me not, O God of my salvation! Ps 27:9
Refrain from anger, and **f** wrath! Fret not Ps 37:8
loves justice; he will not **f** his saints. Ps 37:28
Do not **f** me, O LORD! O my God, be not Ps 38:21
age; **f** me not when my strength is spent. Ps 71:9
age and gray hairs, O God, do not **f** me, Ps 71:18
If his children **f** my law and do not Ps 89:30
For the LORD will not **f** his people; he Ps 94:14
keep your statutes; do not utterly **f** me! Ps 119:8
because of the wicked, who **f** your law. Ps 119:53
Do not **f** the work of your hands. Ps 138:8
and **f** not your mother's teaching, Prv 1:8
who **f** the paths of uprightness to walk Prv 2:13
not steadfast love and faithfulness **f** you; Prv 3:3
you good precepts; do not **f** my teaching. Prv 4:2
Do not **f** her, and she will keep you; love Prv 4:6
and **f** not your mother's teaching. Prv 6:20
Do not **f** your friend and your father's Prv 27:10
Those who **f** the law praise the wicked, Prv 28:4
and those who **f** the LORD shall be Is 1:28
them; I the God of Israel will not **f** them. Is 41:17
are the things I do, and I do not **f** them. Is 42:16
let the wicked **f** his way, and the Is 55:7
and did not **f** the judgment of Is 58:2
But you who **f** the LORD, who forget my Is 65:11
and bitter for you to **f** the LORD your God; Jer 2:19
all who **f** you shall be put to shame; Jer 17:13
F her, and let us go each to his own Jer 51:9
why do you **f** us for so many days? Lam 5:20
on, nor did they **f** the idols of Egypt. Ezk 20:8
to those who **f** the holy covenant. Dn 11:30
regard to vain idols **f** their hope of Jon 2:8
are among the Gentiles to **f** Moses, Acts 21:21
said, "I will never leave you nor **f** you." Heb 13:5

FORSAKEN (62)
who has not **f** his steadfast love and his Gn 24:27
of your deeds, because you have **f** me. Dt 28:20
You have not **f** your brothers these Jos 22:3
But now the LORD has **f** us and given us Jgs 6:13
because we have **f** our God and have Jgs 10:10
Yet you have **f** me and served other Jgs 10:13
whose kindness has not **f** the living or Ru 2:20
because we have **f** the LORD and have 1 Sm 12:10
because they have **f** me and 1 Kgs 11:33
of Israel have **f** your covenant, 1 Kgs 19:10
of Israel have **f** your covenant, 1 Kgs 19:14
Because they have **f** me and have 2 Kgs 22:17
is our God, and we have not **f** him. 2 Chr 13:10
LORD our God, but you have **f** him. 2 Chr 13:11
his rule, because he had **f** the LORD, 2 Chr 21:10
Because you have **f** the LORD, he has 2 Chr 24:20
forsaken the LORD, he has **f** you.'" 2 Chr 24:20
army, because Judah had **f** the LORD, 2 Chr 24:24
of valor, because they had **f** the LORD, 2 Chr 28:6
They have **f** him and have turned 2 Chr 29:6
Because they have **f** me and have 2 Chr 34:25
Yet our God has not **f** us in our slavery, Ezr 9:9
For we have **f** your commandments, Ezr 9:10
the house of God **f**?" And I gathered Neh 13:11
your anger, shall the earth be **f** for you, Jb 18:4
O LORD, have not **f** those who seek you. Ps 9:10
My God, my God, why have you **f** me? Ps 22:1
my father and my mother have **f** me, Ps 27:10
not seen the righteous **f** or his children Ps 37:25
and say, "God has **f** him; pursue and Ps 71:11
earth, but I have not **f** your precepts. Ps 119:87
who deal corruptly! They have **f** the LORD, Is 1:4
and the **f** places are many in the midst of Is 6:12
and as one gathers eggs that have been **f**, Is 10:14
is solitary, a habitation deserted and **f**, Is 27:10
For the palace is **f**, the populous city Is 32:14
But Zion said, "The LORD has **f** me; my Is 49:14
Whereas you have been **f** and hated, Is 60:15
You shall no more be termed **F**, and your Is 62:4
be called Sought Out, A City Not **F**. Is 62:12
they have **f** me, the fountain of living Jer 2:13
all the cities are **f**, and no man dwells in Jer 4:29
Your children have **f** me and have sworn Jer 5:7
'As you have **f** me and served foreign Jer 5:19
LORD has rejected and **f** the generation of Jer 7:29
"Because they have **f** my law that I set Jer 9:13
"I have **f** my house; I have abandoned Jer 12:7
'Because your fathers have **f** me, Jer 16:11
and have **f** me and have not kept my Jer 16:11
in the earth, for they have **f** the LORD, Jer 17:13
Because the people have **f** me and have Jer 19:4
"Because they have **f** the covenant of the Jer 22:9
How is the famous city not **f**, the city of Jer 49:25
and Judah have not been **f** by their God, Jer 51:5
not see us, the LORD has **f** the land.'" Ezk 8:12
For they say, 'The LORD has **f** the land, Ezk 9:9
because they have **f** the LORD to cherish Hos 4:10
f on her land, with none to raise her up." Am 5:2
God, my God, why have you **f** me?" Mt 27:46
God, my God, why have you **f** me?" Mk 15:34
Behold, your house is **f**. And I tell you, Lk 13:35
persecuted, but not **f**; struck down, but 2 Cor 4:9

FORSAKES (5)
kindness from a friend **f** the fear of the Jb 6:14
who **f** the companion of her youth and Prv 2:17
discipline for him who **f** the way; Prv 15:10
who confesses and **f** them will obtain Prv 28:13
doe in the field **f** her newborn fawn Jer 14:5

FORSAKING (8)
to this day, **f** me and serving other gods, 1 Sm 8:8
and **f** the counsel that the old men 1 Kgs 12:13
and **f** the counsel of the old men, 2 Chr 10:13
against them, for all their evil in **f** me. Jer 1:16
this upon yourself by **f** the LORD your Jer 2:17
commits great whoredom by **f** the LORD." Hos 1:2
you have played the whore, **f** your God. Hos 9:1
F the right way, they have gone astray. 2 Pt 2:15

FORSOOK (3)
then he **f** God who made him and Dt 32:15
And they **f** the LORD and did not serve Jgs 10:6
He **f** his dwelling at Shiloh, the tent Ps 78:60

FORTH (141)
The earth brought **f** vegetation, plants Gn 1:12
the earth bring **f** living creatures Gn 1:24
in pain you shall bring **f** children. Gn 3:16
and thistles it shall bring **f** for you; Gn 3:18
the fountains of the great deep burst **f**, Gn 7:11
and sent **f** a raven. It went to and fro until Gn 8:7
Then he sent **f** a dove from him, to see if Gn 8:8
and again he sent **f** the dove out of the Gn 8:10
another seven days and sent **f** the dove, Gn 8:12
of Noah who went **f** from the ark were Gn 9:18
and they went **f** together from Ur of the Gn 11:31
taken captive, he led **f** his trained men, Gn 14:14
and so the flocks brought **f** striped, Gn 30:39
soon as it budded, its blossoms shot **f**, Gn 40:10
sprouted and put **f** buds and produced Nm 17:8
upon us; he shone **f** from Mount Paran; Dt 33:2
David went back and **f** from Saul to 1 Sm 17:15
the LORD had burst **f** against Uzzah. 2 Sm 6:8
glowing coals flamed **f** from him. 2 Sm 22:9
before him coals of fire flamed **f**. 2 Sm 22:13
like the sun shining **f** on a cloudless 2 Sm 23:4
walked once back and **f** in the house, 2 Kgs 4:35
there is no strength to bring them **f**. 2 Kgs 19:3
Or were you brought **f** before the hills? Jb 15:7
It is drawn **f** and comes out of his body; Jb 20:25
From whose womb did the ice come **f**, Jb 38:29
Can you lead **f** the Mazzaroth in their Jb 38:32
Can you send **f** lightnings, that they Jb 38:35
they crouch, bring **f** their offspring, Jb 39:3
His sneezings flash **f** light, and his eyes Jb 41:18
go flaming torches; sparks of fire leap **f**. Jb 41:19
Out of his nostrils comes **f** smoke, as Jb 41:20
and a flame comes **f** from his mouth. Jb 41:21
glowing coals flamed **f** from him. Ps 18:8
he flashed **f** lightnings and routed Ps 18:14
voice of the LORD flashes **f** flames of fire. Ps 29:7
He will bring **f** your righteousness as the Ps 37:6
the perfection of beauty, God shines **f**. Ps 50:2
Behold, I was brought **f** in iniquity, and Ps 51:5
You do not go **f**, O God, with our Ps 60:10
out water; the skies gave **f** thunder; Ps 77:17
enthroned upon the cherubim, shine **f**. Ps 80:1
alter the word that went **f** from my lips. Ps 89:34
Before the mountains were brought **f**, or Ps 90:2
vengeance, O God of vengeance, shine **f**! Ps 94:1
break **f** into joyous song and sing Ps 98:4
make springs gush **f** in the valleys; Ps 104:10
that he may bring **f** food from the Ps 104:14
When you send **f** your Spirit, they are Ps 104:30
When he is tried, let him come **f** guilty; Ps 109:7
The LORD sends **f** from Zion your Ps 110:2
LORD from this time **f** and forevermore! Ps 113:2
LORD from this time **f** and forevermore. Ps 115:18
My lips will pour **f** praise, for you Ps 119:171
in from this time **f** and forevermore. Ps 121:8
from this time **f** and forevermore. Ps 125:2
LORD from this time **f** and forevermore. Ps 131:3
the rain and brings **f** the wind from his Ps 135:7
Flash **f** the lightning and scatter them; Ps 144:6
our sheep bring **f** thousands and ten Ps 144:13
They shall pour **f** the fame of your Ps 145:7
there were no depths I was brought **f**, Prv 8:24
shaped, before the hills, I was brought **f**, Prv 8:25
of the righteous brings **f** wisdom, Prv 10:31
The north wind brings **f** rain, and a Prv 25:23
his couch, my nard gave **f** its fragrance. Sg 1:12
are in blossom; they give **f** fragrance. Sg 2:13
The mandrakes give **f** fragrance, and Sg 7:13
from this time **f** and forevermore. Is 9:7
There shall come **f** a shoot from the Is 11:1
rest and quiet; they break **f** into singing. Is 14:7
the serpent's root will come **f** an adder, Is 14:29
shall blossom and put **f** shoots and fill Is 27:6
joy. For waters break **f** in the wilderness, Is 35:6
and there is no strength to bring them **f**. Is 37:3
Set **f** your case, says the LORD; bring your Is 41:21
him; he will bring **f** justice to the nations. Is 42:1
quench; he will faithfully bring **f** justice. Is 42:3
before they spring **f** I tell you of them." Is 42:9
who brings **f** chariot and horse, army Is 43:17
now it springs **f**, do you not perceive it? Is 43:19
set **f** your case, that you may be proved Is 43:26
Let them all assemble, let them stand **f**. Is 44:11
break **f** into singing, O mountains, O Is 44:23
counsels; let them stand **f** and save you, Is 47:13
From this time **f** I announce to you new Is 48:6
I call to them, they stand **f** together. Is 48:13
O heavens, and exult, O earth; break **f**, Is 49:13
Break **f** together into singing, you waste Is 52:9
break **f** into singing and cry aloud, you Is 54:1
the earth, making it bring **f** and sprout, Is 55:10
shall go out in joy and be led **f** in peace; Is 55:12
before you shall break **f** into singing, Is 55:12
shall your light break **f** like the dawn, Is 58:8
"from this time **f** and forevermore." Is 59:21
For as the earth brings **f** its sprouts, and Is 61:11
her righteousness goes **f** as brightness, Is 62:1
I will bring **f** offspring from Jacob, and Is 65:9
a nation be brought **f** in one moment? Is 66:8
was in labor she brought **f** her children. Is 66:8
and not cause to bring **f**?" says the LORD; Is 66:9
"shall I, who cause to bring **f**, shut the Is 66:9
lest my wrath go **f** like fire, and burn with Jer 4:4
and he brings **f** the wind from his Jer 10:13
robbed, lest my wrath go **f** like fire, Jer 21:12
Wrath has gone **f**, a whirling tempest; Jer 23:19
disaster is going **f** from nation to Jer 25:32
Wrath has gone **f**, a whirling tempest; Jer 30:23
tambourines and shall go **f** in the dance Jer 31:4
and he brings **f** the wind from his Jer 51:16
it, and fire flashing **f** continually, Ezk 1:4
and out of the fire went **f** lightning. Ezk 1:13
your renown went **f** among the Ezk 16:14
him and shot **f** its branches toward Ezk 17:7
sending **f** its streams to all the trees of Ezk 31:4
you burst **f** in your rivers, trouble the Ezk 32:2
shall shoot **f** your branches and yield Ezk 36:8
and my judgment goes **f** as the light. Hos 6:5
a fountain shall come **f** from the house of Jl 3:18
makes destruction flash **f** against the Am 5:9
paths." For out of Zion shall go **f** the law, Mi 4:2
Zion from this time **f** and forevermore. Mi 4:7
from you shall come **f** for me one who is Mi 5:2
is paralyzed, and justice never goes **f**. Hab 1:4
the righteous; so justice goes **f** perverted. Hab 1:4
and dignity go **f** from themselves. Hab 1:7
swept on; the deep gave **f** its voice; Hab 3:10
every morning he shows **f** his justice; Zep 3:5
the oil, on what the ground brings **f**, Hg 1:11
and his arrow will go **f** like lightning; Zec 9:14
and will march **f** in the whirlwinds Zec 9:14
out of his good treasure brings **f** good, Mt 12:35
out of his evil treasure brings **f** evil. Mt 12:35

of time had come, God sent **f** his Son, Gal 4:4
break **f** and cry aloud, you who are not Gal 4:27
to his purpose, which he set **f** in Christ Eph 1:9
of the Lord sounded **f** from you in 1 Thes 1:8
faith in God has gone **f** everywhere, 1 Thes 1:8
sin when it is fully grown brings **f** death. Jas 1:15
own will he brought us **f** by the word of Jas 1:18
Does a spring pour **f** from the same Jas 3:11

FORTIETH (3)
in the **f** year after the people of Israel Nm 33:38
In the **f** year, on the first day of the Dt 1:3
(In the **f** year of David's reign search 1 Chr 26:31

FORTIFICATIONS (1)
And the high **f** of his walls he will bring Is 25:12

FORTIFIED (50)
and the cities are **f** and very large. Nm 13:28
shall live in the **f** cities because of the Nm 32:17
Beth-nimrah and Beth-haran, **f** cities, Nm 32:36
The cities are great and **f** up to heaven. Dt 1:28
All these were cities **f** with high walls, Dt 3:5
yourselves, cities great and **f** up to heaven, Dt 9:1
your towns, until your high and **f** walls, Dt 28:52
of them had entered into the **f** cities, Jos 10:20
Anakim were there, with great **f** cities. Jos 14:12
Ramah, reaching to the **f** city of Tyre. Jos 19:29
The **f** cities are Ziddim, Zer, Hammath, Jos 19:35
both **f** cities and unwalled villages. 1 Sm 6:18
he get himself to **f** cities and escape 2 Sm 20:6
and he **f** the hill and called the name 1 Kgs 16:24
shall attack every **f** city and every 2 Kgs 3:19
you chariots and horses, **f** cities also, 2 Kgs 10:2
towns, from watchtower to **f** city. 2 Kgs 17:9
territory, from watchtower to **f** city. 2 Kgs 18:8
up against all the **f** cities of Judah 2 Kgs 18:13
you should turn **f** cities into heaps 2 Kgs 19:25
Lower Beth-horon, **f** cities with walls, 2 Chr 8:5
f cities that are in Judah and in 2 Chr 11:10
and Benjamin, in all the **f** cities, 2 Chr 11:23
And he took the **f** cities of Judah and 2 Chr 12:4
He built **f** cities in Judah, for the land 2 Chr 14:6
forces in all the **f** cities of Judah and 2 Chr 17:2
placed in the **f** cities throughout all 2 Chr 17:19
in the land in all the **f** cities of Judah, 2 Chr 19:5
together with **f** cities in Judah, 2 Chr 21:3
Gate and at the Angle, and **f** them. 2 Chr 26:9
and encamped against the **f** cities, 2 Chr 32:1
the army in all the **f** cities in Judah. 2 Chr 33:14
And they captured **f** cities and a rich Neh 9:25
Who will bring me to the **f** city? Who Ps 60:9
Who will bring me to the **f** city? Who Ps 108:10
every high tower, and against every **f** wall; Is 2:15
made the city a heap, the **f** city a ruin; Is 25:2
For the **f** city is solitary, a habitation Is 27:10
up against all the **f** cities of Judah and Is 36:1
that you should make **f** cities crash into Is 37:26
I, behold, I make you this day a **f** city, Jer 1:18
'Assemble, and let us go into the **f** cities!' Jer 4:5
your **f** cities in which you trust they Jer 5:17
let us go into the **f** cities and perish there, Jer 8:14
you to this people a **f** wall of bronze; Jer 15:20
these were the only **f** cities of Judah that Jer 34:7
and to Judah, into Jerusalem the **f**. Ezk 21:20
ruined cities are now **f** and inhabited.' Ezk 36:35
and Judah has multiplied **f** cities; Hos 8:14
cry against the **f** cities and against Zep 1:16

FORTIFY (2)
you broke down the houses to **f** the wall. Is 22:10
though she should **f** her strong height, Jer 51:53

FORTRESS (24)
is my rock and my **f** and my deliverer, 2 Sm 22:2
and came to the **f** of Tyre and to all 2 Sm 24:7
beams for the gates of the **f** of the temple, Neh 2:8
is my rock and my **f** and my deliverer, Ps 18:2
of refuge for me, a strong **f** to save me! Ps 31:2
For you are my rock and my **f**; and for Ps 31:3
hosts is with us; the God of Jacob is our **f**. Ps 46:7
is with us; the God of Jacob is our **f**. Ps 46:11
God has made himself known as a **f**. Ps 48:3
watch for you, for you, O God, are my **f**. Ps 59:9
have been to me a **f** and a refuge in the Ps 59:16
praises to you, for you, O God, are my **f**, Ps 59:17
only is my rock and my salvation, my **f**; Ps 62:2
only is my rock and my salvation, my **f**; Ps 62:6
save me, for you are my rock and my **f**. Ps 71:3
will say to the LORD, "My refuge and my **f**, Ps 91:2
he is my steadfast love and my **f**, my Ps 144:2
The **f** will disappear from Ephraim, and Is 17:3
the **f** is put to shame and broken down; Jer 48:1
the army and enter the **f** of the king of Dn 11:7
shall carry the war as far as his **f**. Dn 11:10
appear and profane the temple and **f**, Dn 11:31
so that destruction comes upon the **f**. Am 5:9
They laugh at every **f**, for they pile up Hab 1:10

FORTRESSES (12)
and came trembling out of their **f**. 2 Sm 22:46
You will set on fire their **f**, and you 2 Kgs 8:12
He made the **f** strong, and put 2 Chr 11:11
He built in Judah **f** and store cities, 2 Chr 17:12
heart and came trembling out of their **f**. Ps 18:45
his place of defense will be the **f** of rocks; Is 33:16
strongholds, nettles and thistles in its **f**. Is 34:13
face back toward the **f** of his own land, Dn 11:19
honor the god of **f** instead of these. Dn 11:38
deal with the strongest **f** with the help Dn 11:39
and all your **f** shall be destroyed, Hos 10:14
All your **f** are like fig trees with first-ripe Na 3:12

FORTS (2)
and **f** and towers on the wooded hills. 2 Chr 27:4
water for the siege; strengthen your **f**; Na 3:14

FORTUNATE (2)
are already dead more **f** than the living Eccl 4:2
"I consider myself **f** that it is before Acts 26:2

FORTUNATUS (1)
of Stephanas and **F** and Achaicus, 1 Cor 16:17

FORTUNE (2)
"Good **f** has come!" so she called his Gn 30:11
who set a table for **F** and fill cups of Is 65:11

FORTUNE-TELLERS (3)
to dispossess, listen to **f** and to diviners. Dt 18:14
from the east and of **f** like the Philistines, Is 2:6
your diviners, your dreamers, your **f**, Jer 27:9

FORTUNE-TELLING (3)
an offering and used **f** and omens and 2 Kgs 21:6
and used **f** and omens and sorcery, 2 Chr 33:6
brought her owners much gain by **f**. Acts 16:16

FORTUNES (34)
You shall not interpret omens or tell **f**. Lv 19:26
divination or tells **f** or interprets omens, Dt 18:10
will restore your **f** and have compassion Dt 30:3
And the LORD restored the **f** of Job, when Jb 42:10
the LORD restores the **f** of his people, Ps 14:7
When God restores the **f** of his people, Let Ps 53:6
to your land; you restored the **f** of Jacob. Ps 85:1
When the LORD restored the **f** of Zion, Ps 126:1
Restore our **f**, O LORD, like streams in Ps 126:4
I will restore your **f** and gather you Jer 29:14
when I will restore the **f** of my people, Jer 30:3
I will restore the **f** of the tents of Jacob Jer 30:18
and in its cities, when I restore their **f**: Jer 31:23
for I will restore their **f**, declares the Jer 32:44
I will restore the **f** of Judah and the Jer 33:7
the fortunes of Judah and the **f** of Israel, Jer 33:7
For I will restore the **f** of the land as at Jer 33:11
I will restore their **f** and will have Jer 33:26
Yet I will restore the **f** of Moab in the Jer 48:47
I will restore the **f** of the Ammonites, Jer 49:6
latter days I will restore the **f** of Elam, Jer 49:39
exposed your iniquity to restore your **f**, Lam 2:14
"I will restore their **f**, both the fortunes Ezk 16:53
both the **f** of Sodom and her Ezk 16:53
and the **f** of Samaria and her Ezk 16:53
I will restore your own **f** in their midst, Ezk 16:53
I will restore the **f** of Egypt and bring Ezk 29:14
I will restore the **f** of Jacob and have Ezk 39:25
when I restore the **f** of my people. Hos 6:11
when I restore the **f** of Judah and Jerusalem, Jl 3:1
I will restore the **f** of my people Israel, Am 9:14
and you shall have no more tellers of **f**; Mi 5:12
be mindful of them and restore their **f**. Zep 2:7
when I restore your **f** before your eyes," Zep 3:20

FORTY (93)
rain on the earth **f** days and forty nights, Gn 7:4
rain on the earth forty days and **f** nights, Gn 7:4
fell upon the earth **f** days and forty Gn 7:12
upon the earth forty days and **f** nights. Gn 7:12
The flood continued **f** days on the earth. Gn 7:17
At the end of **f** days Noah opened the Gn 8:6
"Suppose **f** are found there." He Gn 18:29
"For the sake of **f** I will not do it." Gn 18:29
and Isaac was **f** years old when he took Gn 25:20
When Esau was **f** years old, he took Gn 26:34
and their calves, **f** cows and ten bulls, Gn 32:15
F days were required for it, for that is Gn 50:3
people of Israel ate the manna **f** years, Ex 16:35
was on the mountain **f** days and forty Ex 24:18
the mountain forty days and **f** nights. Ex 24:18
and **f** bases of silver you shall make Ex 26:19
and their **f** bases of silver, two bases Ex 26:21
there with the LORD **f** days and forty Ex 34:28
with the LORD forty days and **f** nights. Ex 34:28
And he made **f** bases of silver under the Ex 36:24
and their **f** bases of silver, two bases Ex 36:26
At the end of **f** days they returned Nm 13:25
in the wilderness **f** years and shall Nm 14:33
which you spied out the land, **f** days, Nm 14:34
you shall bear your iniquity **f** years, Nm 14:34
them wander in the wilderness **f** years, Nm 32:13
These **f** years the LORD your God has been Dt 2:7
has led you these **f** years in the wilderness, Dt 8:2
and your foot did not swell these **f** years. Dt 8:4
on the mountain **f** days and forty Dt 9:9
on the mountain forty days and **f** nights. Dt 9:9
And at the end of **f** days and forty nights Dt 9:11
of forty days and **f** nights the LORD gave Dt 9:11
LORD as before, **f** days and forty nights. Dt 9:18
LORD as before, forty days and **f** nights. Dt 9:18
the LORD for these **f** days and forty nights, Dt 9:25
the LORD for these forty days and **f** nights, Dt 9:25
at the first time, **f** days and forty nights, Dt 10:10
at the first time, forty days and **f** nights, Dt 10:10
F stripes may be given him, but not Dt 25:3
I have led you **f** years in the wilderness. Dt 29:5
people of Israel walked **f** years in the Jos 5:6
I was **f** years old when Moses the servant Jos 14:7
So the land had rest **f** years. Then Jgs 3:11
to be seen among **f** thousand in Israel? Jgs 5:8
might." And the land had rest for **f** years. Jgs 5:31
And the land had rest **f** years in the days Jgs 8:28
He had **f** sons and thirty grandsons, Jgs 12:14
the hand of the Philistines for **f** years. Jgs 13:1
heavy. He had judged Israel **f** years. 1 Sm 4:18
For **f** days the Philistine came 1 Sm 17:16
was **f** years old when he began to 2 Sm 2:10
began to reign, and he reigned **f** years. 2 Sm 5:4
David reigned over Israel was **f** years. 1 Kgs 2:11
inner sanctuary, was **f** cubits long. 1 Kgs 6:17
Each basin held **f** baths, each basin 1 Kgs 7:38
Jerusalem over all Israel was **f** years. 1 Kgs 11:42
strength of that food **f** days and forty 1 Kgs 19:8
food forty days and **f** nights to Horeb, 1 Kgs 19:8
of goods of Damascus, **f** camel loads. 2 Kgs 8:9
and he reigned **f** years in Jerusalem. 2 Kgs 12:1
he reigned over Israel was **f** years. 1 Chr 29:27
in Jerusalem over all Israel **f** years. 2 Chr 9:30
and he reigned **f** years in Jerusalem. 2 Chr 24:1
for their daily ration **f** shekels of silver. Neh 5:15
F years you sustained them in the Neh 9:21
For **f** years I loathed that generation Ps 95:10
F days I assign you, a day for each year. Ezk 4:6
it; it shall be uninhabited **f** years. Ezk 29:11
be a desolation **f** years among cities Ezk 29:12
At the end of **f** years I will gather the Ezk 29:13
the length of the nave, **f** cubits, Ezk 41:2
courts, **f** cubits long and thirty broad; Ezk 46:22
Egypt and led you **f** years in the Am 2:10
and offerings during the **f** years in the Am 5:25
And he called out, "Yet **f** days, and Jon 3:4
And after fasting **f** days and forty nights, Mt 4:2
And after fasting forty days and **f** nights, Mt 4:2
And he was in the wilderness **f** days, Mk 1:13
for **f** days, being tempted by the devil. And Lk 4:2
to them during **f** days and speaking Acts 1:3
performed was more than **f** years old. Acts 4:22
"When he was **f** years old, it came into Acts 7:23
"Now when **f** years had passed, an Acts 7:30
Sea and in the wilderness for **f** years. Acts 7:36
during the **f** years in the wilderness, Acts 7:42
And for about **f** years he put up with Acts 13:18
of the tribe of Benjamin, for **f** years. Acts 13:21
were more than **f** who made this Acts 23:13
for more than **f** of their men are lying Acts 23:21
of the Jews the **f** lashes less one. 2 Cor 11:24
for **f** years. Therefore I was provoked Heb 3:10
whom was he provoked for **f** years? Heb 3:17

FORTY-EIGHT (2)
that you give to the Levites shall be **f**, Nm 35:7
Israel were in all **f** cities with their Jos 21:41

FORTY-FIRST (1)
dying in the **f** year of his reign. 2 Chr 16:13

FORTY-FIVE (3)
"I will not destroy it if I find **f** there." Gn 18:28
these **f** years since the time that the Jos 14:10
chambers that were on the **f** pillars, 1 Kgs 7:3

FORTY-NINE (1)
weeks of years shall give you **f** years. Lv 25:8

FORTY-ONE (4)
Rehoboam was **f** years old when he 1 Kgs 14:21
and he reigned **f** years in Jerusalem. 1 Kgs 15:10
in Samaria, and he reigned **f** years. 2 Kgs 14:23
Rehoboam was **f** years old when he 2 Chr 12:13

FORTY-SIX (1)
"It has taken **f** years to build this temple, Jn 2:20

FORTY-TWO (5)
addition to them you shall give **f** cities. Nm 35:6
of the woods and tore **f** of the boys. 2 Kgs 2:24
at the pit of Beth-eked, **f** persons, 2 Kgs 10:14
will trample the holy city for **f** months. Rv 11:2

to exercise authority for **f** months. Rv 13:5

FORUM (1)
as far as the **F** of Appius and Three Acts 28:15

FORWARD (47)
to me? Tell the people of Israel to go **f**. Ex 14:15
and Miriam, and they both came **f**. Nm 12:5
the priest shall come **f** and speak to the Dt 20:2
the priests, the sons of Levi, shall come **f**, Dt 21:5
And he said to the people, "Go **f**. March Jos 6:7
of rams' horns before the LORD went **f**, Jos 6:8
was with him rushed **f** and stood at the Jgs 9:44
rushed upon David from that day **f**. 1 Sm 16:13
the Philistine came **f** and took his 1 Sm 17:16
the Philistine moved **f** and came 1 Sm 17:41
for Israel from that day **f** to this day. 1 Sm 30:25
his thigh, and as he went **f** it fell out. 2 Sm 20:8
a spirit came **f** and stood before 1 Kgs 22:21
And they went **f**, striking the 2 Kgs 3:24
shall the shadow go **f** ten steps, or go 2 Kgs 20:9
a spirit came **f** and stood before 2 Chr 18:20
the repairing went **f** in their hands, 2 Chr 24:13
their vestments came **f** with trumpets, Ezr 3:10
of Jerusalem was going **f** and that the Neh 4:7
"Behold, I go **f**, but he is not there, and Jb 23:8
Let your eyes look directly **f**, and your Prv 4:25
Do not put yourself **f** in the king's Prv 25:6
hearts, and went backward and not **f**. Jer 7:24
Each one of them went straight **f**, Ezk 1:9
And each went straight **f**. Wherever the Ezk 1:12
Each one of them went straight **f**. Ezk 10:22
I will turn you about and drive you **f**, Ezk 39:2
the LORD their God, from that day **f**. Ezk 39:22
Chaldeans came **f** and maliciously Dn 3:8
all come for violence, all their faces **f**. Hab 1:9
the angel who talked with me came **f**, Zec 2:3
and another angel came **f** to meet him Zec 2:3
And he shall bring **f** the top stone amid Zec 4:7
talked with me came **f** and said to me, Zec 5:5
saw, and behold, two women coming **f**! Zec 5:9
Capernaum, a centurion came **f** to him, Mt 8:5
had received the five talents came **f**, Mt 25:20
he also who had the two talents came **f**, Mt 25:22
who had received the one talent came **f**, Mt 25:24
though many false witnesses came **f**. Mt 26:60
came forward. At last two came **f** Mt 26:60
happen to him, came **f** and said to them, Jn 18:4
And they put **f** two, Joseph called Acts 1:23
Alexander, whom the Jews had put **f**. Acts 19:33
whom God put **f** as a propitiation by Rom 3:25
lies behind and straining **f** to what lies Phil 3:13
For he was looking **f** to the city that Heb 11:10

FOSTER (1)
Kings shall be your **f** fathers, and their Is 49:23

FOUGHT (63)
Then Amalek came and **f** with Israel at Ex 17:8
as Moses told him, and **f** with Amalek, Ex 17:10
son and a man of Israel **f** in the camp, Lv 24:10
the way of Atharim, he **f** against Israel, Nm 21:1
came to Jahaz and **f** against Israel. Nm 21:23
who had **f** against the former king of Nm 21:26
voice of a man, for the LORD **f** for Israel. Jos 10:14
to Libnah and **f** against Libnah. Jos 10:29
and laid siege to it and **f** against it. Jos 10:31
And they laid siege to it and **f** against it. Jos 10:34
Eglon to Hebron. And they **f** against it Jos 10:36
turned back to Debir and **f** against it Jos 10:38
the LORD God of Israel **f** for Israel. Jos 10:42
of Dan went up and **f** against Leshem, Jos 19:47
is the LORD your God who has **f** for you. Jos 23:3
They **f** with you, and I gave them into Jos 24:8
king of Moab, arose and **f** against Israel. Jos 24:9
and the leaders of Jericho **f** against you, Jos 24:11
at Bezek and **f** against him and Jgs 1:5
the men of Judah **f** against Jerusalem and Jgs 1:8
"The kings came, they **f**; then fought the Jgs 5:19
then **f** the kings of Canaan, at Taanach, Jgs 5:19
From heaven the stars **f**, from their Jgs 5:20
from their courses they **f** against Sisera. Jgs 5:20
for my father **f** for you and risked his life Jgs 9:17
of Shechem and **f** with Abimelech. Jgs 9:39
And Abimelech **f** against the city all Jgs 9:45
to the tower and **f** against it and drew Jgs 9:52
encamped at Jahaz and **f** with Israel. Jgs 11:20
the men of Gilead and **f** with Ephraim. Jgs 12:4
So the Philistines **f**, and Israel was 1 Sm 4:10
of Moab. And they **f** against them. 1 Sm 12:9
he **f** against all his enemies on every 1 Sm 14:47
went out and **f** with the Philistines 1 Sm 19:8
to Keilah and **f** with the Philistines 1 Sm 23:5
Now the Philistines **f** against Israel, 1 Sm 31:1
because he had **f** against Hadadezer 2 Sm 8:10
against David and **f** with him. 2 Sm 10:17
of the city came out and **f** with Joab, 2 Sm 11:17
Now Joab **f** against Rabbah of the 2 Sm 12:26
and said, "I have **f** against Rabbah; 2 Sm 12:27
went to Rabbah and **f** against it and 2 Sm 12:29
and the battle was **f** in the forest of 2 Sm 18:6
and they **f** against the Philistines. 2 Sm 21:15
closed in on Samaria and **f** against it. 1 Kgs 20:1
kings have surely **f** together and 2 Kgs 3:23
when he **f** against Hazael king of 2 Kgs 8:29
when he **f** with Hazael king of Syria.) 2 Kgs 9:15
went up and **f** against Gath and 2 Kgs 12:17
with which he **f** against Amaziah 2 Kgs 13:12
and how he **f** with Amaziah king of 2 Kgs 14:15
that he did, and his might, how he **f**, 2 Kgs 14:28
Now the Philistines **f** against Israel, 1 Chr 10:1
because he had **f** against Hadadezer 1 Chr 18:10
against the Syrians, they **f** with him. 1 Chr 19:17
the LORD had **f** against the enemies 2 Chr 20:29
when he **f** against Hazael king of 2 Chr 22:6
He **f** with the king of the Ammonites 2 Chr 27:5
came to Ashdod and **f** against it and Is 20:1
their enemy, and himself **f** against them. Is 63:10
speaking, I **f** with beasts at Ephesus? 1 Cor 15:32
I have **f** the good fight, I have finished 2 Tm 4:7
And the dragon and his angels **f** back, Rv 12:7

FOUL (4)
and **f** weeds instead of barley." The Jb 31:40
and its canals will become **f**, and the Is 19:6
waters with your feet, and **f** their rivers. Ezk 32:2
the stench and **f** smell of him will rise, for Jl 2:20

FOUND (370)
for Adam there was not **f** a helper fit for Gn 2:20
lest any who **f** him should attack him. Gn 4:15
But Noah **f** favor in the eyes of the LORD. Gn 6:8
But the dove **f** no place to set her foot, and Gn 8:9
they **f** a plain in the land of Shinar and Gn 11:2
The angel of the LORD **f** her by a spring Gn 16:7
"O Lord, if I have **f** favor in your sight, Gn 18:3
"Suppose forty are **f** there." He Gn 18:29
Suppose thirty are **f** there." He Gn 18:30
Suppose twenty are **f** there." He Gn 18:31
Suppose ten are **f** there." He answered, Gn 18:32
your servant has **f** favor in your sight, Gn 19:19
dug in the valley and **f** there a well of Gn 26:19
and said to him, "We have **f** water." Gn 26:32
"How is it that you have **f** it so quickly, Gn 27:20
Reuben went and **f** mandrakes in the Gn 30:14
to him, "If I have **f** favor in your sight, Gn 30:27
black among the lambs, if **f** with me, Gn 30:33
what have you **f** of all your household Gn 31:37
please, if I have **f** favor in your sight, Gn 33:10
he is the Anah who **f** the hot springs in Gn 36:24
And a man **f** him wandering in the Gn 37:15
his brothers and **f** them at Dothan. Gn 37:17
their father and said, "This we have **f**; Gn 37:32
to Judah and said, "I have not **f** her. Gn 38:22
So Joseph **f** favor in his sight and Gn 39:4
the money that we **f** in the mouths of Gn 44:8
of your servants is **f** with it shall die, Gn 44:9
he who is **f** with it shall be my servant, Gn 44:10
And the cup was **f** in Benjamin's sack. Gn 44:12
God has **f** out the guilt of your Gn 44:16
in whose hand the cup has been **f**." Gn 44:16
hand the cup was **f** shall be my Gn 44:17
all the money that was **f** in the land of Gn 47:14
"If now I have **f** favor in your sight, Gn 47:29
"If now I have **f** favor in your eyes, Gn 50:4
days no leaven is to be **f** in your houses. Ex 12:19
days in the wilderness and **f** no water. Ex 15:22
went out to gather, but they **f** none. Ex 16:27
and anyone **f** in possession of him, Ex 21:16
"If a thief is **f** breaking in and is struck Ex 22:2
the stolen beast is **f** alive in his Ex 22:4
the man's house, then, if the thief is **f**, Ex 22:7
If the thief is not **f**, the owner of the house Ex 22:8
and you have also **f** favor in my sight.' Ex 33:12
therefore, if I have **f** favor in your sight, Ex 33:13
known that I have **f** favor in your sight, Ex 33:16
do, for you have **f** favor in my sight, Ex 33:17
said, "If now I have **f** favor in your sight, Ex 34:9
or has **f** something lost and lied about it, Lv 6:3
to him or the lost thing that he **f** Lv 6:4
why have I not **f** favor in your sight, Nm 11:11
they **f** a man gathering sticks on the Nm 15:32
And those who **f** him gathering sticks Nm 15:33
the LORD'S offering, what each man **f**, Nm 31:50
said, "If we have **f** favor in your sight, Nm 32:5
"If there is **f** among you, within any of Dt 17:2
There shall not be **f** among you anyone Dt 18:10
all the people who are **f** in it shall do Dt 20:11
giving you to possess someone is **f** slain, Dt 21:1
of virginity was not **f** in the young Dt 22:20
"If a man is **f** lying with the wife of Dt 22:22
her and lies with her, and they are **f**, Dt 22:28
eyes because he has **f** some indecency in Dt 24:1
"If a man is **f** stealing one of his brothers, Dt 24:7
"He **f** him in a desert land, and in the Dt 32:10
all along the way and **f** nothing. Jos 2:22
to Joshua, "The five kings have been **f**, Jos 10:17
They **f** Adoni-bezek at Bezek and fought Jgs 1:5
'Have they not **f** and divided the spoil?— Jgs 5:30
him, "If now I have **f** favor in your eyes, Jgs 6:17
you would not have **f** out my riddle." Jgs 14:18
And he **f** a fresh jawbone of a donkey, Jgs 15:15
city, men and beasts and all that they **f**. Jgs 20:48
all the towns that they **f** they set on fire. Jgs 20:48
And they **f** among the inhabitants of Jgs 21:12
to him, "Why have I **f** favor in your eyes, Ru 2:10
she said, "I have **f** favor in your eyes, Ru 2:13
mind on them, for they have been **f**. 1 Sm 9:20
donkeys that you went to seek are **f**, 1 Sm 10:2
when we saw they were not to be **f**, 1 Sm 10:14
donkeys had been **f**." But about the 1 Sm 10:16
they sought him, he could not be **f**. 1 Sm 10:21
that you have not **f** anything in my 1 Sm 12:5
blacksmith to be **f** throughout all 1 Sm 13:19
neither sword nor spear **f** in the hand 1 Sm 13:22
the spoil of their enemies that they **f**. 1 Sm 14:30
for he has **f** favor in my sight." 1 Sm 16:22
well that I have **f** favor in your eyes, 1 Sm 20:3
So now, if I have **f** favor in your eyes, 1 Sm 20:29
and evil shall not be **f** in you so long 1 Sm 25:28
Achish, "If I have **f** favor in your eyes, 1 Sm 27:5
deserted to me I have **f** no fault in him 1 Sm 29:3
For I have **f** nothing wrong in you 1 Sm 29:6
What have you **f** in your servant 1 Sm 29:8
to the city, they **f** it burned with fire, 1 Sm 30:3
They **f** an Egyptian in the open 1 Sm 30:11
against Saul, and the archers **f** him, 1 Sm 31:3
they **f** Saul and his three sons fallen 1 Sm 31:8
your servant has **f** courage to pray 2 Sm 7:27
knows that I have **f** favor in your 2 Sm 14:22
in some place where he is to be **f**, 2 Sm 17:12
not even a pebble is to be **f** there." 2 Sm 17:13
Israel, and **f** Abishag the Shunammite, 1 Kgs 1:3
earth, but if wickedness is **f** in him, 1 Kgs 1:52
And Hadad **f** great favor in the sight 1 Kgs 11:19
Ahijah the Shilonite **f** him on the 1 Kgs 11:29
man of God and **f** him sitting under 1 Kgs 13:14
And he went and **f** his body thrown 1 Kgs 13:28
him there is **f** something pleasing to 1 Kgs 14:13
or nation, that they had not **f** you. 1 Kgs 18:10
from there and **f** Elisha the son 1 Kgs 19:19
Then he **f** another man and said, 1 Kgs 20:37
Ahab said to Elijah, "Have you **f** me, 1 Kgs 21:20
enemy?" He answered, "I have **f** you, 1 Kgs 21:20
and **f** a wild vine and gathered from it 2 Kgs 4:39
they **f** no more of her than the skull 2 Kgs 9:35
the money that was **f** in the house of 2 Kgs 12:10
the gold that was **f** in the treasuries 2 Kgs 12:18
the vessels that were **f** in the house of 2 Kgs 14:14
and gold that was **f** in the house of 2 Kgs 16:8
king of Assyria **f** treachery in 2 Kgs 17:4
the silver that was **f** in the house of 2 Kgs 18:15
and **f** the king of Assyria fighting 2 Kgs 19:8
all that was **f** in his storehouses. 2 Kgs 20:13
"I have **f** the Book of the Law in the 2 Kgs 22:8
the money that was **f** in the house 2 Kgs 22:9
words of this book that has been **f**. 2 Kgs 22:13
that had been **f** in the house 2 Kgs 23:2
that Hilkiah the priest **f** in the house 2 Kgs 23:24
council who were **f** in the city, 2 Kgs 25:19
of the land who were **f** in the city. 2 Kgs 25:19
where they **f** rich, good pasture, and 1 Chr 4:40
and the Meunites who were **f** there, 1 Chr 4:41
against Saul, and the archers **f** him, 1 Chr 10:3
they **f** Saul and his sons fallen on 1 Chr 10:8
your servant has **f** courage to pray 1 Chr 17:25
He **f** that it weighed a talent of gold, 1 Chr 20:2
chief men were **f** among the sons 1 Chr 24:4
among them were **f** at Jazer in 1 Chr 26:31
If you seek him, he will be **f** by you, 1 Chr 28:9
had taken, and there were **f** 153,600. 2 Chr 2:17
If you seek him, he will be **f** by you, 2 Chr 15:2
and sought him, he was **f** by them. 2 Chr 15:4
whole desire, and he was **f** by them, 2 Chr 15:15
Nevertheless, some good is **f** in you, 2 Chr 19:3
take their spoil, they **f** among them, 2 Chr 20:25
the possessions they **f** that belonged 2 Chr 21:17
and **f** that they were 300,000 choice 2 Chr 25:5
the vessels that were **f** in the house 2 Chr 25:24
uncleanness that they **f** in the 2 Chr 29:16
Hilkiah the priest **f** the Book of the 2 Chr 34:14
"I have **f** the Book of the Law in the 2 Chr 34:15
the money that was **f** in the house of 2 Chr 34:17
words of the book that has been **f**. 2 Chr 34:21
that had been **f** in the house 2 Chr 34:30
he did, and what was **f** against him, 2 Chr 36:8
genealogies, but they were not **f** there, Ezr 2:62
and it has been **f** that this city from of Ezr 4:19

a scroll was **f** on which this was written: Ezr 6:2
priests, I **f** there none of the sons of Levi. Ezr 8:15
Now there were **f** some of the sons of Ezr 10:18
if your servant has **f** favor in your sight, Neh 2:5
And I **f** the book of the genealogy of Neh 7:5
came up at the first, and I **f** written in it: Neh 7:5
the genealogies, but it was not **f** there, Neh 7:64
And they **f** it written in the Law that Neh 8:14
You **f** his heart faithful before you, and Neh 9:8
And in it was **f** written that no Neh 13:1
I also **f** out that the portions of the Neh 13:10
the affair was investigated and **f** to be so, Est 2:23
"Go, gather all the Jews to be **f** in Susa, Est 4:16
If I have **f** favor in the sight of the king, Est 5:8
And it was **f** written how Mordecai had Est 6:2
answered, "If I have **f** favor in your sight, Est 7:3
the king, and if I have **f** favor in his sight, Est 8:5
and, 'The root of the matter is **f** in him,' Jb 19:28
will fly away like a dream and not be **f**; Jb 20:8
"But where shall wisdom be **f**? And Jb 28:12
and it is not **f** in the land of the living. Jb 28:13
or because my hand had **f** much, Jb 31:25
friends because they had **f** no answer, Jb 32:3
Beware lest you say, 'We have **f** wisdom; Jb 32:13
down into the pit; I have **f** a ransom; Jb 33:24
to you at a time when you may be **f**; Ps 32:6
his iniquity cannot be **f** out and hated. Ps 36:2
though I sought him, he could not be **f**. Ps 37:36
your flock **f** a dwelling in it; in your Ps 68:10
none, and for comforters, but I **f** none. Ps 69:20
I have **f** David, my servant; with my Ps 89:20
Trouble and anguish have **f** me out, Ps 119:143
Ephrathah; we **f** it in the fields of Jaar. Ps 132:6
to seek you eagerly, and I have **f** you. Prv 7:15
makes his ways crooked will be **f** out. Prv 10:9
who has understanding, wisdom is **f**, Prv 10:13
If you have **f** honey, eat only enough Prv 25:16
lest he rebuke you and you be **f** a liar. Prv 30:6
for my heart **f** pleasure in all my toil, Eccl 2:10
Behold, this is what I **f**, says the Eccl 7:27
has sought repeatedly, but I have not **f**. Eccl 7:28
One man among a thousand I **f**, but a Eccl 7:28
a woman among all these I have not **f**. Eccl 7:28
See, this alone I **f**, that God made man Eccl 7:29
But there was **f** in it a poor, wise man, Eccl 9:15
soul loves; I sought him, but **f** him not. Sg 3:1
soul loves. I sought him, but **f** him not. Sg 3:2
The watchmen **f** me as they went about in Sg 3:3
passed them when I **f** him whom my soul Sg 3:4
I sought him, but **f** him not; I called him, Sg 5:6
The watchmen **f** me as they went about in Sg 5:7
at my mother's breasts! If I **f** you outside, Sg 8:1
My hand has **f** like a nest the wealth of Is 10:14
Whoever is **f** will be thrust through, and Is 13:15
All of you who were **f** were captured, Is 22:3
not a shard is **f** with which to take Is 30:14
they shall not be **f** there, but the redeemed Is 35:9
and **f** the king of Assyria fighting against Is 37:8
armory, all that was **f** in his storehouses. Is 39:2
joy and gladness will be **f** in her, Is 51:3
"Seek the LORD while he may be **f**; call Is 55:6
you **f** new life for your strength, and so Is 57:10
I was ready to be **f** by those who did not Is 65:1
"As the new wine is **f** in the cluster, and Is 65:8
on your skirts is **f** the lifeblood of the Jer 2:34
For wicked men are **f** among my people; Jer 5:26
Your words were **f**, and I ate them, and Jer 15:16
even in my house I have **f** their evil, Jer 23:11
I will be **f** by you, declares the LORD, and Jer 29:14
who survived the sword **f** grace in the Jer 31:2
to you? Was he **f** among thieves, Jer 48:27
All who **f** them have devoured them, and Jer 50:7
And sin in Judah, and none shall be **f**, Jer 50:20
did not know it; you were **f** and caught, Jer 50:24
king's council, who were **f** in the city; Jer 52:25
land, who were **f** in the midst of the city. Jer 52:25
I should not destroy it, but I **f** none. Ezk 22:30
sought for, you will never be **f** again, Ezk 26:21
till unrighteousness was **f** in you. Ezk 28:15
all of them none was **f** like Daniel, Dn 1:19
he **f** them ten times better than all the Dn 1:20
"I have **f** among the exiles from Judah a Dn 2:25
so that not a trace of them could be **f**. Dn 2:35
The beasts of the field **f** shade under it, Dn 4:12
under which beasts of the field **f** shade, Dn 4:21
the wisdom of the gods were **f** in him, Dn 5:11
solve problems were **f** in this Daniel, Dn 5:12
and excellent wisdom are **f** in you. Dn 5:14
weighed in the balances and **f** wanting; Dn 5:27
and no error or fault was **f** in him. Dn 6:4
by agreement and **f** Daniel making Dn 6:11
because I was **f** blameless before him; Dn 6:22
den, and no kind of harm was **f** on him, Dn 6:23
stumble and fall, and shall not be **f**. Dn 11:19
whose name shall be **f** written in the Dn 12:1

Like grapes in the wilderness, I **f** Israel. Hos 9:10
I am rich; I have **f** wealth for myself; Hos 12:8
went down to Joppa and **f** a ship going to Jon 1:3
for in you were **f** the transgressions of Mi 1:13
nor shall there be **f** in their mouth a Zep 3:13
mouth, and no wrong was **f** on his lips. Mal 2:6
came together she was **f** to be with child Mt 1:18
for the child, and when you have **f** him, Mt 2:8
with no one in Israel have I **f** such faith. Mt 8:10
a field, which a man **f** and covered up. Mt 13:44
he **f** one of his fellow servants who Mt 18:28
hour he went out and **f** others standing. Mt 20:6
he went to it and **f** nothing on it but Mt 21:19
the roads and gathered all whom they **f**, Mt 22:10
to the disciples and **f** them sleeping. Mt 26:40
again he came and **f** them sleeping, Mt 26:43
but they **f** none, though many false Mt 26:60
they went out, they **f** a man of Cyrene, Mt 27:32
and they **f** him and said to him, Mk 1:37
Go and see." And when they had **f** out, Mk 6:38
she went home and **f** the child lying in Mk 7:30
And they went away and **f** a colt tied at Mk 11:4
he came to it, he **f** nothing but leaves, Mk 11:13
went to the city and **f** it just as he had Mk 14:16
And he came and **f** them sleeping, and Mk 14:37
again he came and **f** them sleeping, Mk 14:40
to put him to death, but they **f** none. Mk 14:55
Mary, for you have **f** favor with God. Lk 1:30
went with haste and **f** Mary and Joseph, Lk 2:16
After three days they **f** him in the temple, Lk 2:46
unrolled the scroll and **f** the place where Lk 4:17
not even in Israel have I **f** such faith." Lk 7:9
to the house, they **f** the servant well. Lk 7:10
came to Jesus and **f** the man from whom Lk 8:35
the voice had spoken, Jesus was **f** alone. Lk 9:36
he came seeking fruit on it and **f** none. Lk 13:6
And when he has **f** it, he lays it on his Lk 15:5
me, for I have **f** my sheep that was lost.' Lk 15:6
And when she has **f** it, she calls together Lk 15:9
me, for I have **f** the coin that I had lost.' Lk 15:9
and is alive again; he was lost, and is **f**.' Lk 15:24
dead, and is alive; he was lost, and is **f**.'" Lk 15:32
Was no one **f** to return and give praise Lk 17:18
were sent went away and **f** it just as he Lk 19:32
And they went and **f** it just as he had Lk 22:13
to the disciples and **f** them sleeping for Lk 22:45
"We **f** this man misleading our nation Lk 23:2
I have **f** in him no guilt deserving Lk 23:22
And they **f** the stone rolled away from Lk 24:2
went to the tomb and **f** it just as the Lk 24:24
And they **f** the eleven and those who Lk 24:33
He first **f** his own brother Simon and said Jn 1:41
"We have **f** the Messiah" (which means Jn 1:41
He **f** Philip and said to him, "Follow me." Jn 1:43
Philip **f** Nathanael and said to him, "We Jn 1:45
"We have **f** him of whom Moses in the Jn 1:45
In the temple he **f** those who were selling Jn 2:14
Afterward Jesus **f** him in the temple and Jn 5:14
When they **f** him on the other side of the Jn 6:25
cast him out, and having **f** him he said, Jn 9:35
he **f** that Lazarus had already been in Jn 11:17
And Jesus **f** a young donkey and sat on Jn 12:14
young men came in they **f** her dead, Acts 5:10
"We **f** the prison securely locked and Acts 5:23
we opened them we **f** no one inside." Acts 5:23
might even be **f** opposing God!" So Acts 5:39
who **f** favor in the sight of God and Acts 7:46
But Philip **f** himself at Azotus, and as Acts 8:40
so that if he **f** any belonging to the Way, Acts 9:2
There he **f** a man named Aeneas, Acts 9:33
went in and **f** many persons gathered. Acts 10:27
and when he had **f** him, he brought Acts 11:26
'I have **f** in David the son of Jesse a Acts 13:22
And though they **f** in him no guilt Acts 13:28
I **f** also an altar with this inscription, Acts 17:23
And he **f** a Jew named Aquila, a native Acts 18:2
to Ephesus. There he **f** some disciples. Acts 19:1
value of them and **f** it came to fifty Acts 19:19
And having **f** a ship crossing to Acts 21:2
I **f** that he was being accused about Acts 23:29
For we have **f** this man a plague, one Acts 24:5
this, they **f** me purified in the temple, Acts 24:18
what wrongdoing they **f** when I stood Acts 24:20
But I **f** that he had done nothing Acts 25:25
There the centurion **f** a ship of Acts 27:6
a sounding and **f** twenty fathoms. Acts 27:28
sounding again and **f** fifteen fathoms. Acts 27:28
There we **f** brothers and were invited Acts 28:14
"I have been **f** by those who did not Rom 10:20
of stewards that they be **f** trustworthy. 1 Cor 4:2
We are even **f** to be misrepresenting 1 Cor 15:15
putting it on we may not be **f** naked. 2 Cor 5:3
no fault may be **f** with our ministry, 2 Cor 6:3
often tested and **f** earnest in many 2 Cor 8:22
in Christ, we too were **f** to be sinners, Gal 2:17

the fruit of light is **f** in all that is good Eph 5:9
And being **f** in human form, he Phil 2:8
and be **f** in him, not having a Phil 3:9
searched for me earnestly and **f** me— 2 Tm 1:17
should not see death, and he was not **f**, Heb 11:5
rejected, for he **f** no chance to repent, Heb 12:17
by fire—may be **f** to result in praise and 1 Pt 1:7
sin, neither was deceit **f** in his mouth. 1 Pt 2:22
be diligent to be **f** by him without spot 2 Pt 3:14
I **f** it necessary to write appealing to you Jude 1:3
and are not, and **f** them to be false. Rv 2:2
for I have not **f** your works complete in Rv 3:2
because no one was **f** worthy to open the Rv 5:4
and in their mouth no lie was **f**, for they Rv 14:5
away, and no mountains were to be **f**. Rv 16:20
are lost to you, never to be **f** again!" Rv 18:14
with violence, and will be **f** no more; Rv 18:21
of any craft will be **f** in you no more, Rv 18:22
And in her was **f** the blood of prophets Rv 18:24
fled away, and no place was **f** for them. Rv 20:11
anyone's name was not **f** written in the Rv 20:15

FOUNDATION (50)

the cost of his firstborn shall he lay its **f**, Jos 6:26
in order to lay the **f** of the house with 1 Kgs 5:17
In the fourth year the **f** of the house of 1 Kgs 6:37
front, even from the **f** to the coping, 1 Kgs 7:9
The **f** was of costly stones, huge 1 Kgs 7:10
He laid its **f** at the cost of Abiram his 1 Kgs 16:34
from the day the **f** of the house of 2 Chr 8:16
and one third at the Gate of the **F**. 2 Chr 23:5
But the **f** of the temple of the LORD was not Ezr 3:6
the builders laid the **f** of the temple of Ezr 3:10
because the **f** of the house of the LORD Ezr 3:11
when they saw the **f** of this house being Ezr 3:12
in houses of clay, whose **f** is in the dust, Jb 4:19
their time; their **f** was washed away. Jb 22:16
were you when I laid the **f** of the earth? Jb 38:4
and justice are the **f** of your throne; Ps 89:14
and justice are the **f** of his throne. Ps 97:2
Of old you laid the **f** of the earth, and Ps 102:25
I am the one who has laid as a **f** in Zion, Is 28:16
stone, a precious cornerstone, of a sure **f**: Is 28:16
and of the temple, 'Your **f** shall be laid.'" Is 44:28
My hand laid the **f** of the earth, and my Is 48:13
you for a corner and no stone for a **f**, Jer 51:26
ground, so that its **f** will be laid bare. Ezk 13:14
the day that the **f** of the LORD'S temple Hg 2:18
Zerubbabel have laid the **f** of this house; Zec 4:9
on the day that the **f** of the house of the Zec 8:9
been hidden since the **f** of the world." Mt 13:35
for you from the **f** of the world. Mt 25:34
who dug deep and laid the **f** on the rock. Lk 6:48
built a house on the ground without a **f**. Lk 6:49
prophets, shed from the **f** of the world, Lk 11:50
when he has laid a **f** and is not able to Lk 14:29
you loved me before the **f** of the world. Jn 17:24
lest I build on someone else's **f**, Rom 15:20
like a skilled master builder I laid a **f**, 1 Cor 3:10
one can lay a **f** other than that which 1 Cor 3:11
if anyone builds on the **f** with gold, 1 Cor 3:12
anyone has built on the **f** survives, 1 Cor 3:14
chose us in him before the **f** of the world, Eph 1:4
built on the **f** of the apostles and Eph 2:20
themselves as a good **f** for the future, 1 Tm 6:19
But God's firm **f** stands, bearing this 2 Tm 2:19
laid the **f** of the earth in the beginning, Heb 1:10
were finished from the **f** of the world. Heb 4:3
not laying again a **f** of repentance from Heb 6:1
repeatedly since the **f** of the world. Heb 9:26
was foreknown before the **f** of the world 1 Pt 1:20
been written before the **f** of the world in Rv 13:8
book of life from the **f** of the world will Rv 17:8

FOUNDATIONS (30)

and sets on fire the **f** of the mountains. Dt 32:22
the **f** of the heavens trembled and 2 Sm 22:8
the **f** of the world were laid bare, at 2 Sm 22:16
finishing the walls and repairing the **f**. Ezr 4:12
came and laid the **f** of the house of Ezr 5:16
were offered, and let its **f** be retained. Ezr 6:3
if the **f** are destroyed, what can the Ps 11:3
the **f** also of the mountains trembled and Ps 18:7
and the **f** of the world were laid bare at Ps 18:15
all the **f** of the earth are shaken. Ps 82:5
He set the earth on its **f**, so that it should Ps 104:5
"Lay it bare, lay it bare, down to its **f**!" Ps 137:7
when he marked out the **f** of the earth, Prv 8:29
And the **f** of the thresholds shook at the Is 6:4
opened, and the **f** of the earth tremble. Is 24:18
not understood from the **f** of the earth? Is 40:21
the heavens and laid the **f** of the earth, Is 51:13
the heavens and laying the **f** of the earth, Is 51:16
and lay your **f** with sapphires. Is 54:11
shall raise up the **f** of many generations; Is 58:12
and the **f** of the earth below can be Jer 31:37

a fire in Zion that consumed its **f**. Lam 4:11
carried away, and her **f** are torn down. Ezk 30:4
the **f** of the side chambers measured a Ezk 41:8
stones into the valley and uncover her **f**. Mi 1:6
the LORD, and you enduring **f** of the earth, Mi 6:2
so that the **f** of the prison were Acts 16:26
looking forward to the city that has **f**, Heb 11:10
And the wall of the city had twelve **f**, Rv 21:14
The **f** of the wall of the city were Rv 21:19

FOUNDED (10)
in Egypt from the day it was **f** until now. Ex 9:18
for he has **f** it upon the seas and Ps 24:2
like the earth, which he has **f** forever. Ps 78:69
On the holy mount stands the city he **f**; Ps 87:1
and all that is in it, you have **f** them. Ps 89:11
that you have **f** them forever. Ps 119:152
The LORD by wisdom **f** the earth; by Prv 3:19
"The LORD has **f** Zion, and in her the Is 14:32
out the heavens and **f** the earth and Zec 12:1
fall, because it had been **f** on the rock. Mt 7:25

FOUNDER (2)
should make the **f** of their salvation Heb 2:10
to Jesus, the **f** and perfecter of our faith, Heb 12:2

FOUNDS (2)
in the heavens and **f** his vault upon the Am 9:6
town with blood and **f** a city on Hab 2:12

FOUNTAIN (24)
nakedness, he has made naked her **f**, Lv 20:18
she has uncovered the **f** of her blood. Lv 20:18
I went on to the **F** Gate and to the Neh 2:14
district of Mizpah, repaired the **F** Gate. Neh 3:15
At the **F** Gate they went up straight Neh 12:37
For with you is the **f** of life; in your light Ps 36:9
the LORD, O you who are of Israel's **f**!" Ps 68:26
Let your **f** be blessed, and rejoice in the Prv 5:18
mouth of the righteous is a **f** of life, Prv 10:11
The teaching of the wise is a **f** of life, Prv 13:14
The fear of the LORD is a **f** of life, that Prv 14:27
Good sense is a **f** of life to him who has Prv 16:22
the **f** of wisdom is a bubbling brook. Prv 18:4
spring or a polluted **f** is a righteous Prv 25:26
or the pitcher is shattered at the **f**, Eccl 12:6
my bride, a spring locked, a **f** sealed. Sg 4:12
a garden **f**, a well of living water, and Sg 4:15
have forsaken me, the **f** of living waters, Jer 2:13
head were waters, and my eyes a **f** of tears, Jer 9:1
forsaken the LORD, the **f** of living water. Jer 17:13
I will dry up her sea and make her **f** dry, Jer 51:36
the wilderness, and his **f** shall dry up; Hos 13:15
and a **f** shall come forth from the house of Jl 3:18
there shall be a **f** opened for the house Zec 13:1

FOUNTAINS (5)
on that day all the **f** of the great deep Gn 7:11
The **f** of the deep and the windows of the Gn 8:2
a land of brooks of water, of **f** and springs, Dt 8:7
when he established the **f** of the deep, Prv 8:28
heights, and **f** in the midst of the valleys. Is 41:18

FOUR (213)
and there it divided and became **f** rivers. Gn 2:10
king of Ellasar, **f** kings against five. Gn 14:9
will be afflicted for **f** hundred years. Gn 15:13
of land worth **f** hundred shekels of Gn 23:15
the Hittites, **f** hundred shekels of silver, Gn 23:16
and there are **f** hundred men with him." Gn 32:6
coming, and **f** hundred men with him. Gn 33:1
and **f** fifths shall be your own, Gn 47:24
oxen for an ox, and **f** sheep for a sheep. Ex 22:1
You shall cast **f** rings of gold for it and Ex 25:12
of gold for it and put them on its **f** feet, Ex 25:12
you shall make for it **f** rings of gold, Ex 25:26
the rings to the **f** corners at its four Ex 25:26
the rings to the four corners at its **f** legs. Ex 25:26
itself there shall be **f** cups made like Ex 25:34
and the breadth of each curtain **f** cubits; Ex 26:2
and the breadth of each curtain **f** cubits. Ex 26:8
shall hang it on **f** pillars of acacia Ex 26:32
with hooks of gold, on **f** bases of silver. Ex 26:32
shall make horns for it on its **f** corners; Ex 27:2
net you shall make **f** bronze rings at its Ex 27:4
make four bronze rings at its **f** corners. Ex 27:4
It shall have **f** pillars and with them Ex 27:16
have four pillars and with them **f** bases. Ex 27:16
You shall set in it **f** rows of stones. A Ex 28:17
and the breadth of each curtain **f** cubits. Ex 36:9
the breadth of each curtain **f** cubits. Ex 36:15
for it he made **f** pillars of acacia and Ex 36:36
and he cast for them **f** bases of silver. Ex 36:36
And he cast for it **f** rings of gold for its Ex 37:3
cast for it four rings of gold for its **f** feet, Ex 37:3
He cast for it **f** rings of gold and Ex 37:13
the rings to the **f** corners at its four Ex 37:13
the rings to the four corners at its **f** legs. Ex 37:13
lampstand itself were **f** cups made like Ex 37:20
He made horns for it on its **f** corners. Its Ex 38:2
He cast **f** rings on the four corners of the Ex 38:5
four rings on the **f** corners of the bronze Ex 38:5
And their pillars were **f** in number. Ex 38:19
Their **f** bases were of bronze, their Ex 38:19
And they set in it **f** rows of stones. A row Ex 39:10
insects that have **f** feet are detestable Lv 11:23
Two wagons and **f** oxen he gave to the Nm 7:7
And **f** wagons and eight oxen he gave to Nm 7:8
was its length, and **f** cubits its breadth, Dt 3:11
yourself tassels on the **f** corners of the Dt 22:12
and Ashan—**f** cities with their villages, Jos 19:7
Almon with its pasturelands—**f** cities. Jos 21:18
with its pasturelands—**f** cities; Jos 21:22
with its pasturelands—**f** cities; Jos 21:24
with its pasturelands—**f** cities; Jos 21:29
Rehob with its pasturelands—**f** cities; Jos 21:31
Nahalal with its pasturelands—**f** cities; Jos 21:35
with its pasturelands—**f** cities; Jos 21:37
with its pasturelands—**f** cities in all. Jos 21:39
against Shechem in **f** companies. Jgs 9:34
of Jephthah the Gileadite **f** days in the Jgs 11:40
in Judah, and was there some **f** months. Jgs 19:2
at the rock of Rimmon **f** months. Jgs 20:47
who killed about **f** thousand men on 1 Sm 4:2
were with him about **f** hundred men. 1 Sm 22:2
And about **f** hundred men went up 1 Sm 25:13
Philistines was a year and **f** months. 1 Sm 27:7
pursued, he and **f** hundred men. 1 Sm 30:10
except **f** hundred young men, 1 Sm 30:17
at the end of **f** years Absalom said to 2 Sm 15:7
These **f** were descended from the 2 Sm 21:22
In the **f** hundred and eightieth year 1 Kgs 6:1
it was built on **f** rows of cedar pillars, 1 Kgs 7:2
and its thickness was **f** fingers. 1 Kgs 7:15
vestibule were of lily-work, **f** cubits. 1 Kgs 7:19
Each stand was **f** cubits long, four 1 Kgs 7:27
was four cubits long, **f** cubits wide, 1 Kgs 7:27
each stand had **f** bronze wheels and 1 Kgs 7:30
and at the **f** corners were supports for 1 Kgs 7:30
And the **f** wheels were underneath the 1 Kgs 7:32
There were **f** supports at the four 1 Kgs 7:34
four supports at the **f** corners of each 1 Kgs 7:34
baths, each basin measured **f** cubits, 1 Kgs 7:38
and the **f** hundred pomegranates for 1 Kgs 7:42
"Fill **f** jars with water and pour it on 1 Kgs 18:33
together, about **f** hundred men, 1 Kgs 22:6
Now there were **f** men who were lepers 2 Kgs 7:3
of Jerusalem for **f** hundred cubits, 2 Kgs 14:13
Nathan and Solomon, **f** by Bath-shua, 1 Chr 3:5
Tola, Puah, Jashub, and Shimron, **f**. 1 Chr 7:1
The gatekeepers were on the **f** sides, 1 Chr 9:24
for the **f** chief gatekeepers, who were 1 Chr 9:26
and his **f** sons who were with him 1 Chr 21:20
These **f** were the sons of Shimei. 1 Chr 23:10
Izhar, Hebron, and Uzziel, **f**. 1 Chr 23:12
each day, on the north **f** each day, 1 Chr 26:17
each day, on the south **f** each day, 1 Chr 26:17
the west there were **f** at the road and 1 Chr 26:18
the prophets together, **f** hundred men, 2 Chr 18:5
And they sent to me **f** times in this way, Neh 6:4
wilderness and struck the **f** corners of the Jb 1:19
sons, and his sons' sons, **f** generations. Jb 42:16
never satisfied; **f** never say, "Enough": Prv 30:15
for me; **f** I do not understand: Prv 30:18
trembles; under **f** it cannot bear up: Prv 30:21
F things on earth are small, but they Prv 30:24
their tread; **f** are stately in their stride: Prv 30:29
of Judah from the **f** corners of the earth. Is 11:12
f or five on the branches of a fruit tree, Is 17:6
appoint over them **f** kinds of destroyers, Jer 15:3
As Jehudi read three or **f** columns, the Jer 36:23
bring upon Elam the **f** winds from the Jer 49:36
winds from the **f** quarters of heaven. Jer 49:36
cubits, and its thickness was **f** fingers, Jer 52:21
it came the likeness of **f** living creatures. Ezk 1:5
but each had **f** faces, and each of them Ezk 1:6
four faces, and each of them had **f** wings. Ezk 1:6
their wings on their **f** sides they had Ezk 1:8
And the **f** had their faces and their wings Ezk 1:8
The **f** had the face of a lion on the right Ezk 1:10
the **f** had the face of an ox on the left Ezk 1:10
side, and the **f** had the face of an eagle. Ezk 1:10
creatures, one for each of the **f** of them. Ezk 1:15
And the **f** had the same likeness, their Ezk 1:16
any of their **f** directions without Ezk 1:17
and the rims of all **f** were full of eyes all Ezk 1:18
has come upon the **f** corners of the land. Ezk 7:2
there were **f** wheels beside the Ezk 10:9
the **f** had the same likeness, Ezk 10:10
any of their **f** directions without Ezk 10:11
—the wheels that the **f** of them had. Ezk 10:12
And every one had **f** faces: the first Ezk 10:14
Each had **f** faces, and each four wings, Ezk 10:21
Each had four faces, and each **f** wings, Ezk 10:21
upon Jerusalem my **f** disastrous acts Ezk 14:21
Come from the **f** winds, O breath, and Ezk 37:9
F tables were on either side of the gate, Ezk 40:41
And there were **f** tables of hewn stone Ezk 40:42
breadth of the side chambers, **f** cubits, Ezk 41:5
He measured it on the **f** sides. It had a Ezk 42:20
ledge to the larger ledge, **f** cubits, Ezk 43:14
and the altar hearth, **f** cubits; and Ezk 43:15
hearth projecting upward, **f** horns. Ezk 43:15
and put it on the **f** horns of the altar Ezk 43:20
altar and on the **f** corners of the ledge Ezk 43:20
the **f** corners of the ledge of the altar, Ezk 45:19
me around to the **f** corners of the Ezk 46:21
in the **f** corners of the court were Ezk 46:22
broad; the **f** were of the same size. Ezk 46:22
around each of the **f** courts was a row Ezk 46:23
As for these **f** youths, God gave them Dn 1:17
and said, "But I see **f** men unbound, Dn 3:25
the **f** winds of heaven were stirring up the Dn 7:2
And **f** great beasts came up out of the sea, Dn 7:3
with **f** wings of a bird on its back. Dn 7:6
And the beast had **f** heads, and dominion Dn 7:6
'These **f** great beasts are four kings who Dn 7:17
four great beasts are **f** kings who shall Dn 7:17
there came up **f** conspicuous horns Dn 8:8
horns toward the **f** winds of heaven. Dn 8:8
broken, in place of which **f** others arose, Dn 8:22
f kingdoms shall arise from his nation, Dn 8:22
divided toward the **f** winds of heaven, Dn 11:4
transgressions of Damascus, and for **f**, Am 1:3
three transgressions of Gaza, and for **f**, Am 1:6
three transgressions of Tyre, and for **f**, Am 1:9
three transgressions of Edom, and for **f**, Am 1:11
of the Ammonites, and for **f**, Am 1:13
three transgressions of Moab, and for **f**, Am 2:1
three transgressions of Judah, and for **f**, Am 2:4
three transgressions of Israel, and for **f**, Am 2:6
my eyes and saw, and behold, **f** horns! Zec 1:18
Then the LORD showed me **f** craftsmen. Zec 1:20
you abroad as the **f** winds of the heavens, Zec 2:6
f chariots came out from between two Zec 6:1
are going out to the **f** winds of heaven, Zec 6:5
Those who ate were **f** thousand men, Mt 15:38
Or the seven loaves for the **f** thousand, Mt 16:10
will gather his elect from the **f** winds, Mt 24:31
to him a paralytic carried by **f** men. Mk 2:3
And there were about **f** thousand people. Mk 8:9
"And the seven for the **f** thousand, how Mk 8:20
and gather his elect from the **f** winds, Mk 13:27
Do you not say, 'There are yet **f** months, Jn 4:35
they had rowed about three or **f** miles, Jn 6:19
had already been in the tomb **f** days. Jn 11:17
be an odor, for he has been dead **f** days." Jn 11:39
garments and divided them into **f** parts, Jn 19:23
a number of men, about **f** hundred, Acts 5:36
them and afflict them **f** hundred years. Acts 7:6
let down by its **f** corners upon the Acts 10:11
And Cornelius said, "**F** days ago, Acts 10:30
let down from heaven by its **f** corners, Acts 11:5
him over to **f** squads of soldiers Acts 12:4
He had **f** unmarried daughters, who Acts 21:9
We have **f** men who are under a vow; Acts 21:23
revolt and led the **f** thousand men of Acts 21:38
they let down **f** anchors from the Acts 27:29
side of the throne, are **f** living creatures, Rv 4:6
And the **f** living creatures, each of them Rv 4:8
the throne and the **f** living creatures and Rv 5:6
the **f** living creatures and the twenty-four Rv 5:8
And the **f** living creatures said, "Amen!" Rv 5:14
heard one of the **f** living creatures say Rv 6:1
voice in the midst of the **f** living creatures, Rv 6:6
After this I saw **f** angels standing at the Rv 7:1
angels standing at the **f** corners of the Rv 7:1
holding back the **f** winds of the earth, Rv 7:1
a loud voice to the **f** angels who had been Rv 7:2
the elders and the **f** living creatures, Rv 7:11
a voice from the **f** horns of the golden Rv 9:13
"Release the **f** angels who are bound at Rv 9:14
So the **f** angels, who had been prepared Rv 9:15
and before the **f** living creatures and Rv 14:3
And one of the **f** living creatures gave to Rv 15:7
elders and the **f** living creatures fell Rv 19:4
that are at the **f** corners of the earth, Rv 20:8

FOURFOLD (2)
and he shall restore the lamb **f**, 2 Sm 12:6
anyone of anything, I restore it **f**." Lk 19:8

FOURS (4)
that go on all **f** are detestable to you. Lv 11:20
that go on all **f** you may eat those Lv 11:21
among the animals that go on all **f**, Lv 11:27
on its belly, and whatever goes on all **f**, Lv 11:42

FOURSQUARE (1)
The city lies **f**; its length the same as its Rv 21:16

FOURTEEN (22)
I served you **f** years for your two Gn 31:41
were born to Jacob—**f** persons in all. Gn 46:22
two rams, **f** male lambs a year old; Nm 29:13
and a tenth for each of the **f** lambs; Nm 29:15
f male lambs a year old without Nm 29:17
f male lambs a year old without Nm 29:20
f male lambs a year old without Nm 29:23
f male lambs a year old without Nm 29:26
f male lambs a year old without Nm 29:29
f male lambs a year old without Nm 29:32
f cities with their villages. Jos 15:36
and Kiriath-jearim—**f** cities with their Jos 18:28
had given Heman **f** sons and three 1 Chr 25:5
And he took **f** wives and had 2 Chr 13:21
the breadth of the gate was **f** cubits, Ezk 40:48
f cubits long by fourteen broad, Ezk 43:17
fourteen cubits long by **f** broad, Ezk 43:17
Abraham to David were **f** generations, Mt 1:17
deportation to Babylon **f** generations, Mt 1:17
to Babylon to the Christ **f** generations. Mt 1:17
man in Christ who **f** years ago was 2 Cor 12:2
Then after **f** years I went up again to Gal 2:1

FOURTEENTH (25)
In the **f** year Chedorlaomer and the Gn 14:5
keep it until the **f** day of this month, Ex 12:6
from the **f** day of the month at evening, Ex 12:18
on the **f** day of the month at twilight, Lv 23:5
On the **f** day of this month, at twilight, Nm 9:3
first month, on the **f** day of the month, Nm 9:5
second month on the **f** day at twilight Nm 9:11
"On the **f** day of the first month is the Nm 28:16
the Passover on the **f** day of the month Jos 5:10
In the **f** year of King Hezekiah, 2 Kgs 18:13
to Huppah, the **f** to Jeshebeab, 1 Chr 24:13
to the **f**, Mattithiah, his sons and his 1 Chr 25:21
Passover lamb on the **f** day of the 2 Chr 30:15
Passover lamb on the **f** day of the 2 Chr 35:1
On the **f** day of the first month, the Ezr 6:19
gathered also on the **f** day of the month Est 9:15
and on the **f** day they rested and made Est 9:17
on the thirteenth day and on the **f**, Est 9:18
hold the **f** day of the month of Adar as a Est 9:19
them to keep the **f** day of the month Est 9:21
In the **f** year of King Hezekiah, Is 36:1
in the **f** year after the city was struck Ezk 40:1
first month, on the **f** day of the month, Ezk 45:21
When the **f** night had come, as we Acts 27:27
"Today is the **f** day that you have Acts 27:33

FOURTH (75)
and there was morning, the **f** day. Gn 1:19
Assyria. And the **f** river is the Euphrates. Gn 2:14
come back here in the **f** generation, Gn 15:16
the third and the **f** generation of those Ex 20:5
and the **f** row a beryl, an onyx, and a Ex 28:20
fine flour mingled with a **f** of a hin of Ex 29:40
and a **f** of a hin of wine for a drink Ex 29:40
to the third and the **f** generation." Ex 34:7
and the **f** row, a beryl, an onyx, and a Ex 39:13
And in the **f** year all its fruit shall be Lv 19:24
with it shall be of wine, a **f** of a hin. Lv 23:13
On the **f** day Elizur the son of Shedeur, Nm 7:30
to the third and the **f** generation.' Nm 14:18
Jacob or number the **f** part of Israel? Nm 23:10
"On the **f** day ten bulls, two rams, Nm 29:23
to the third and **f** generation of those who Dt 5:9
The **f** lot came out for Issachar, for the Jos 19:17
On the **f** day they said to Samson's wife, Jgs 14:15
And on the **f** day they arose early in the Jgs 19:5
and the **f**, Adonijah the son of Haggith; 2 Sm 3:4
in the **f** year of Solomon's reign over 1 Kgs 6:1
In the **f** year the foundation of the 1 Kgs 6:37
over Judah in the **f** year of Ahab 1 Kgs 22:41
and the **f** part of a kab of dove's dung 2 Kgs 6:25
sons of the **f** generation shall sit 2 Kgs 10:30
of Israel to the **f** generation." And so 2 Kgs 15:12
In the **f** year of King Hezekiah, which 2 Kgs 18:9
ninth day of the **f** month the famine 2 Kgs 25:3
Nethanel the **f**, Raddai the fifth, 1 Chr 2:14
of Talmai, king of Geshur; the **f**, 1 Chr 3:2
the third Zedekiah, the **f** Shallum. 1 Chr 3:15
Nohah the **f**, and Rapha the fifth. 1 Chr 8:2
Mishmannah **f**, Jeremiah fifth, 1 Chr 12:10
the third, and Jekameam the **f**. 1 Chr 23:19
the third to Harim, the **f** to Seorim, 1 Chr 24:8
Jahaziel the third, Jekameam the **f**. 1 Chr 24:23
the **f** to Izri, his sons and his 1 Chr 25:11
Zebadiah the third, Jathniel the **f**, 1 Chr 26:2
second, Joah the third, Sachar the **f**, 1 Chr 26:4
Tebaliah the third, Zechariah the **f**: 1 Chr 26:11
Asahel the brother of Joab was **f**, for 1 Chr 27:7
of Joab was fourth, for the **f** month, 1 Chr 27:7
second month of the **f** year of his 2 Chr 3:2
On the **f** day they assembled in the 2 Chr 20:26
On the **f** day, within the house of our Ezr 8:33
in the **f** year of Jehoiakim the son of Jer 25:1
of Judah, in the fifth month of the **f** year, Jer 28:1
In the **f** year of Jehoiakim the son of Jer 36:1
year of Zedekiah, in the **f** month, Jer 39:2
in the **f** year of Jehoiakim the son of Jer 45:1
defeated in the **f** year of Jehoiakim Jer 46:2
to Babylon, in the **f** year of his reign. Jer 51:59
ninth day of the **f** month the famine was Jer 52:6
In the thirtieth year, in the **f** month, on Ezk 1:1
of a lion, and the **f** the face of an eagle. Ezk 10:14
And there shall be a **f** kingdom, strong Dn 2:40
and the appearance of the **f** is like a son Dn 3:25
in the night visions, and behold, a **f** beast, Dn 7:7
to know the truth about the **f** beast, Dn 7:19
'As for the **f** beast, there shall be a fourth Dn 7:23
there shall be a **f** kingdom on earth, Dn 7:23
and a **f** shall be far richer than all of Dn 11:2
and the **f** chariot dappled horses—all of Zec 6:3
In the **f** year of King Darius, the word of Zec 7:1
to Zechariah on the **f** day of the ninth Zec 7:1
The fast of the **f** month and the fast of Zec 8:19
And in the **f** watch of the night he Mt 14:25
And about the **f** watch of the night he Mk 6:48
and the **f** living creature like an eagle in Rv 4:7
When he opened the **f** seal, I heard the Rv 6:7
the voice of the **f** living creature say, Rv 6:7
were given authority over a **f** of the earth, Rv 6:8
The **f** angel blew his trumpet, and a Rv 8:12
The **f** angel poured out his bowl on the Rv 16:8
sapphire, the third agate, the **f** emerald, Rv 21:19

FOWL (2)
whatever, whether of **f** or of animal, Lv 7:26
gazelles, roebucks, and fattened **f**. 1 Kgs 4:23

FOWLER (2)
the snare of the **f** and from the deadly Ps 91:3
hunter, like a bird from the hand of the **f**. Prv 6:5

FOWLER'S (1)
yet a **f** snare is on all his ways, and Hos 9:8

FOWLERS (2)
like a bird from the snare of the **f**; Ps 124:7
my people; they lurk like **f** lying in wait. Jer 5:26

FOX (2)
they are building—if a **f** goes up on it he Neh 4:3
And he said to them, "Go and tell that **f**, Lk 13:32

FOXES (6)
went and caught 300 **f** and took torches. Jgs 15:4
he let the **f** go into the standing grain of Jgs 15:5
Catch the **f** for us, the little foxes that Sg 2:15
for us, the little **f** that spoil the vineyards, Sg 2:15
And Jesus said to him, "**F** have holes, Mt 8:20
And Jesus said to him, "**F** have holes, Lk 9:58

FRACTION (2)
from there he saw a **f** of the people. Nm 22:41
shall see only a **f** of them and shall Nm 23:13

FRACTURE (2)
f for fracture, eye for eye, tooth for Lv 24:20
fracture for **f**, eye for eye, tooth for Lv 24:20

FRAGMENTS (4)
ruthlessly that among its **f** not a shard is Is 30:14
great house shall be struck down into **f**, Am 6:11
his disciples, "Gather up the leftover **f**, Jn 6:12
filled twelve baskets with **f** from the five Jn 6:13

FRAGRANCE (11)
on his couch, my nard gave forth its **f**. Sg 1:12
vines are in blossom; they give forth **f**. Sg 2:13
and the **f** of your oils than any spice! Sg 4:10
the **f** of your garments is like the Sg 4:11
your garments is like the **f** of Lebanon. Sg 4:11
The mandrakes give forth **f**, and beside Sg 7:13
like the olive, and his **f** like Lebanon. Hos 14:6
house was filled with the **f** of the perfume. Jn 12:3
us spreads the **f** of the knowledge 2 Cor 2:14
to one a **f** from death to death, to the 2 Cor 2:16
death, to the other a **f** from life to life. 2 Cor 2:16

FRAGRANT (16)
the anointing oil and for the **f** incense, Ex 25:6
And Aaron shall burn **f** incense on it. Ex 30:7
anointing oil and the **f** incense for the Ex 31:11
the anointing oil and for the **f** incense, Ex 35:8
and the anointing oil and the **f** incense, Ex 35:15
the anointing oil, and for the **f** incense. Ex 35:28
oil also, and the pure **f** incense, Ex 37:29
the anointing oil and the **f** incense, Ex 39:38
and burned **f** incense on it, as the LORD Ex 40:27
of the altar of **f** incense before the LORD Lv 4:7
of the oil for the light, the **f** incense, Nm 4:16
your robes are all **f** with myrrh and aloes Ps 45:8
your anointing oils are **f**; your name is oil Sg 1:3
with all the **f** powders of a merchant? Sg 3:6
for us, a **f** offering and sacrifice to God. Eph 5:2
the gifts you sent, a **f** offering, Phil 4:18

FRAIL (1)
"My lord knows that the children are **f**, Gn 33:13

FRAME (25)
Close to the **f** the rings shall lie, as Ex 25:27
Ten cubits shall be the length of a **f**, Ex 26:16
a cubit and a half the breadth of each **f**. Ex 26:16
There shall be two tenons in each **f**, for Ex 26:17
two bases under one **f** for its two tenons, Ex 26:19
bases under the next **f** for its two Ex 26:19
bases of silver, two bases under one **f**, Ex 26:21
frame, and two bases under the next **f**. Ex 26:21
two bases under one **f**, and two bases Ex 26:25
frame, and two bases under another **f**. Ex 26:25
Ten cubits was the length of a **f**, and a Ex 36:21
a cubit and a half the breadth of each **f**. Ex 36:21
Each **f** had two tenons for fitting Ex 36:22
two bases under one **f** for its two tenons, Ex 36:24
bases under the next **f** for its two Ex 36:24
two bases under one **f** and two bases Ex 36:26
frame and two bases under the next **f**. Ex 36:26
sixteen bases, under every **f** two bases. Ex 36:30
Close to the **f** were the rings, as holders Ex 37:14
of goatskin and put it on the carrying **f**. Nm 4:10
and put them on the carrying **f**. Nm 4:12
or his mighty strength, or his goodly **f**. Jb 41:12
you, those who **f** injustice by statute? Ps 94:20
For he knows our **f**; he remembers Ps 103:14
My **f** was not hidden from you, when I Ps 139:15

FRAMES (41)
shall make upright **f** for the tabernacle Ex 26:15
you do for all the **f** of the tabernacle. Ex 26:17
shall make the **f** for the tabernacle: Ex 26:18
tabernacle: twenty **f** for the south side; Ex 26:18
you shall make under the twenty **f**, Ex 26:19
tabernacle, on the north side twenty **f**, Ex 26:20
westward you shall make six **f**. Ex 26:22
you shall make two **f** for corners of the Ex 26:23
And there shall be eight **f**, with their Ex 26:25
five for the **f** of the one side of the Ex 26:26
and five bars for the **f** of the other side Ex 26:27
and five bars for the **f** of the side of the Ex 26:27
The middle bar, halfway up the **f**, shall Ex 26:28
You shall overlay the **f** with gold and Ex 26:29
tent and its covering, its hooks and its **f**, Ex 35:11
made the upright **f** for the tabernacle Ex 36:20
did this for all the **f** of the tabernacle. Ex 36:22
The **f** for the tabernacle he made thus: Ex 36:23
made thus: twenty **f** for the south side. Ex 36:23
forty bases of silver under the twenty **f**, Ex 36:24
on the north side, he made twenty **f** Ex 36:25
the tabernacle westward he made six **f**. Ex 36:27
He made two **f** for corners of the Ex 36:28
There were eight **f** with their bases of Ex 36:30
five for the **f** of the one side of the Ex 36:31
and five bars for the **f** of the other side Ex 36:32
five bars for the **f** of the tabernacle at Ex 36:32
to run from end to end halfway up the **f**. Ex 36:33
And he overlaid the **f** with gold, and Ex 36:34
tent and all its utensils, its hooks, its **f**, Ex 39:33
He laid its bases, and set up its **f**, and Ex 40:18
Merari involved the **f** of the tabernacle, Nm 3:36
the **f** of the tabernacle, with its bars, Nm 4:31
for the house windows with recessed **f**. 1 Kgs 6:4
There were window **f** in three rows, 1 Kgs 7:4
doorways and windows had square **f**, 1 Kgs 7:5
and the panels were set in the **f**, 1 Kgs 7:28
that were set in the **f** were lions, 1 Kgs 7:29
On the **f**, both above and below the 1 Kgs 7:29
Ahaz cut off the **f** of the stands and 2 Kgs 16:17
rein for evil, and your tongue **f** deceit. Ps 50:19

FRANKINCENSE (21)
sweet spices with pure **f** (of each shall Ex 30:34
He shall pour oil on it and put **f** on it Lv 2:1
of the fine flour and oil, with all of its **f**, Lv 2:2
you shall put oil on it and lay **f** on it; Lv 2:15
grain and some of the oil with all of its **f**; Lv 2:16
put no oil on it and shall put no **f** on it, Lv 5:11
its oil and all the **f** that is on the grain Lv 6:15
And you shall put pure **f** on each pile, Lv 24:7
pour no oil on it and put no **f** on it, Nm 5:15
previously put the grain offering, the **f**, Neh 13:5
God, with the grain offering and the **f**. Neh 13:9
of smoke, perfumed with myrrh and **f**, Sg 3:6
to the mountain of myrrh and the hill of **f**. Sg 4:6
and cinnamon, with all trees of **f**, Sg 4:14
with offerings, or wearied you with **f**. Is 43:23
They shall bring gold and **f**, and shall Is 60:6
he who makes a memorial offering of **f**, Is 66:3
use to me is **f** that comes from Sheba, Jer 6:20
and sacrifices, grain offerings and **f**, Jer 17:26
offered him gifts, gold and **f** and myrrh. Mt 2:11

spice, incense, myrrh, **f**, wine, Rv 18:13

FRANKLY (1)

you shall reason **f** with your neighbor, Lv 19:17

FRAUD (4)

oppression and **f** do not depart from its Ps 55:11
their master's house with violence and **f**. Zep 1:9
and the last **f** will be worse than the Mt 27:64
your fields, which you kept back by **f**, Jas 5:4

FREE (98)

then you will be **f** from this oath of Gn 24:8
Then you will be **f** from my oath, Gn 24:41
her to you, you will be **f** from my oath.' Gn 24:41
and in the seventh he shall go out **f**, Ex 21:2
wife, and my children; I will not go out **f**,' Ex 21:5
let the slave go **f** because of his eye. Ex 21:26
let the slave go **f** because of his tooth. Ex 21:27
shall let the goat go **f** in the wilderness. Lv 16:22
be put to death, because she was not **f**; Lv 19:20
be **f** from this water of bitterness that Nm 5:19
then she shall be **f** and shall conceive Nm 5:28
The man shall be **f** from iniquity, but Nm 5:31
shall return and be **f** of obligation to Nm 32:22
year you shall let him go **f** from you. Dt 15:12
And when you let him go **f** from you, Dt 15:13
to you when you let him go **f** from you, Dt 15:18
He shall be **f** at home one year to be Dt 24:5
and there is none remaining, bond or **f**. Dt 32:36
times and shake myself **f**." But he did Jgs 16:20
make his father's house **f** in Israel." 1 Sm 17:25
male, both bond and **f** in Israel, 1 Kgs 14:10
off from Ahab every male, bond or **f**, 1 Kgs 21:21
off from Ahab every male, bond or **f**, 2 Kgs 9:8
for there was none left, bond or **f**, 2 Kgs 14:26
of the temple **f** from other service, 1 Chr 9:33
there, and the slave is **f** from his master. Jb 3:19
I will give **f** utterance to my complaint; Jb 10:1
"Who has let the wild donkey go **f**? Who Jb 39:5
ear to my prayer from lips **f** of deceit! Ps 17:1
afflicted the peoples, but them you set **f**; Ps 44:2
"You give your mouth **f** rein for evil, Ps 50:19
to set **f** those who were doomed to die, Ps 102:20
him; the ruler of the peoples set him **f**; Ps 105:20
the LORD answered me and set me **f**. Ps 118:5
hungry. The LORD sets the prisoners **f**; Ps 146:7
the feet of the ox and the donkey range **f**. Is 32:20
shall build my city and set my exiles **f**, Is 45:13
straps of the yoke, to let the oppressed go **f**, Is 58:6
Why then do my people say, 'We are **f**, Jer 2:31
"Have I not set you **f** for their good? Jer 15:11
everyone should set **f** his Hebrew slaves, Jer 34:9
that everyone would set **f** his slave, Jer 34:10
again. They obeyed and set them **f**. Jer 34:10
male and female slaves they had set **f**, Jer 34:11
of you must set **f** the fellow Hebrew who Jer 34:14
you must set him **f** from your service.' Jer 34:14
whom you had set **f** according to their Jer 34:16
will let the souls whom you hunt go **f**, Ezk 13:20
The **f** space between the side chambers Ezk 41:9
side chambers opened on the **f** space, Ezk 41:11
the breadth of the **f** space was five Ezk 41:11
set your prisoners **f** from the waterless Zec 9:11
Jesus said to him, "Then the sons are **f**. Mt 17:26
and the truth, and the truth will set you **f**." Jn 8:32
is it that you say, 'You will become **f**?" Jn 8:33
So if the Son sets you **f**, you will be free Jn 8:36
the Son sets you free, you will be **f** indeed. Jn 8:36
could have been set **f** if he had not Acts 26:32
But the **f** gift is not like the trespass. Rom 5:15
grace of God and the **f** gift by the grace Rom 5:15
And the **f** gift is not like the result of Rom 5:16
but the **f** gift following many Rom 5:16
of grace and the **f** gift of righteousness Rom 5:17
who has died has been set **f** from sin. Rom 6:7
and, having been set **f** from sin, have Rom 6:18
you were **f** in regard to righteousness. Rom 6:20
you have been set **f** from sin and have Rom 6:22
but the **f** gift of God is eternal life in Rom 6:23
her husband dies, she is **f** from that law, Rom 7:3
of life has set you **f** in Christ Jesus from Rom 8:2
itself will be set **f** from its bondage to Rom 8:21
Likewise he who was **f** when called is 1 Cor 7:22
bound to a wife? Do not seek to be **f**. 1 Cor 7:27
seek to be free. Are you **f** from a wife? 1 Cor 7:27
I want you to be **f** from anxieties. The 1 Cor 7:32
she is **f** to be married to whom she 1 Cor 7:39
Am I not **f**? Am I not an apostle? Have I 1 Cor 9:1
I may present the gospel **f** of charge, 1 Cor 9:18
For though I am **f** from all, I have 1 Cor 9:19
slaves or **f**—and all were made to 1 Cor 12:13
their means, of their own **f** will, 2 Cor 8:3
God's gospel to you **f** of charge? 2 Cor 11:7
nor Greek, there is neither slave nor **f**, Gal 3:28
a slave woman and one by a **f** woman. Gal 4:22
the son of the **f** woman was born Gal 4:23
But the Jerusalem above is **f**, and she is Gal 4:26
inherit with the son of the **f** woman." Gal 4:30
of the slave but of the **f** woman. Gal 4:31
For freedom Christ has set us **f**; stand Gal 5:1
from the Lord, whether he is a slave or **f**. Eph 6:8
Scythian, slave, **f**; but Christ is all, Col 3:11
unstained and **f** from reproach 1 Tm 6:14
compulsion but of your own **f** will. Phlm 1:14
Keep your life **f** from love of money, Heb 13:5
Live as people who are **f**, not using your 1 Pt 2:16
the powerful, and everyone, slave and **f**, Rv 6:15
both rich and poor, both **f** and slave, Rv 13:16
the flesh of all men, both **f** and slave, Rv 19:18

FREED (6)

graciously **f** Jehoiachin king of 2 Kgs 25:27
your hands were **f** from the basket. Ps 81:6
you are **f** from your disability." Lk 13:12
who believes is **f** from everything Acts 13:38
you could not be **f** by the law of Acts 13:39
who loves us and has **f** us from our sins Rv 1:5

FREEDMAN (1)

the Lord as a slave is a **f** of the Lord. 1 Cor 7:22

FREEDMEN (1)

the synagogue of the **F** (as it was Acts 6:9

FREEDOM (10)

and not yet ransomed or given her **f**, Lv 19:20
decay and obtain the **f** of the glory of Rom 8:21
But if you can gain your **f**, avail 1 Cor 7:21
the Spirit of the Lord is, there is **f**. 2 Cor 3:17
in to spy out our **f** that we have in Christ Gal 2:4
For **f** Christ has set us free; stand firm Gal 5:1
For you were called to **f**, brothers. Only Gal 5:13
do not use your **f** as an opportunity for Gal 5:13
not using your **f** as a cover-up for evil, 1 Pt 2:16
They promise them **f**, but they 2 Pt 2:19

FREELY (18)

You shall give to him **f**, and your heart Dt 15:10
the people had eaten **f** today of the 1 Sm 14:30
not move about **f** because of Saul 1 Chr 12:1
heart they had offered **f** to the LORD. 1 Chr 29:9
my heart I have **f** offered all these 1 Chr 29:17
here, offering **f** and joyously to you. 1 Chr 29:17
wares, besides all that was **f** offered. Ezr 1:6
who **f** offers to go to Jerusalem, Ezr 7:13
and his counselors have **f** offered to the Ezr 7:15
people will offer themselves **f** on the day Ps 110:3
He has distributed **f**; he has given to the Ps 112:9
One gives **f**, yet grows all the richer; Prv 11:24
I will love them **f**, for my anger has Hos 14:4
he went out and began to talk **f** about it, Mk 1:45
wine first, and when people have drunk **f**, Jn 2:10
understand the things **f** given us by 1 Cor 2:12
We have spoken **f** to you, 2 Cor 6:11
As it is written, "He has distributed **f**, 2 Cor 9:9

FREEWILL (24)

brought it as a **f** offering to the LORD. Ex 35:29
kept bringing him **f** offerings every Ex 36:3
offering is a vow offering or a **f** offering, Lv 7:16
of their vows or **f** offerings that they Lv 22:18
a vow or as a **f** offering from the herd or Lv 22:21
too long or too short for a **f** offering, Lv 22:23
and besides all your **f** offerings, Lv 23:38
a vow or as a **f** offering or at your Nm 15:3
vow offerings and your **f** offerings, Nm 29:39
your vow offerings, your **f** offerings, Dt 12:6
or your **f** offerings or the contribution Dt 12:17
the tribute of a **f** offering from your Dt 16:10
fathers' houses made their **f** offerings, 1 Chr 29:6
gate, was over the **f** offerings to God, 2 Chr 31:14
besides **f** offerings for the house of God Ezr 1:4
made **f** offerings for the house of God, Ezr 2:68
everyone who made a **f** offering to the Ezr 3:5
and with the **f** offerings of the people Ezr 7:16
and the gold are a **f** offering to the LORD, Ezr 8:28
With a **f** offering I will sacrifice to you; I Ps 54:6
Accept my **f** offerings of praise, O Ps 119:108
When the prince provides a **f** offering, Ezk 46:12
peace offerings as a **f** offering to the Ezk 46:12
is leavened, and proclaim **f** offerings, Am 4:5

FREQUENT (3)

in those days; there was no **f** vision. 1 Sm 3:1
on **f** journeys, in danger from rivers, 2 Cor 11:26
your stomach and your **f** ailments.) 1 Tm 5:23

FRESH (32)

Then Jacob took **f** sticks of poplar and Gn 30:37
grain offering of your firstfruits **f** ears, Lv 2:14
in an earthenware vessel over **f** water. Lv 14:5
the bird that was killed over the **f** water. Lv 14:6
in an earthenware vessel over **f** water Lv 14:50
killed and in the **f** water and sprinkle Lv 14:51
bird and with the **f** water and with the Lv 14:52
bathe his body in **f** water and shall be Lv 15:13
nor grain parched or **f** until this same Lv 23:14
juice of grapes or eat grapes, **f** or dried. Nm 6:3
and **f** water shall be added in a vessel. Nm 19:17
And he found a **f** jawbone of a donkey, Jgs 15:15
me with seven **f** bowstrings that have Jgs 16:7
up to her seven **f** bowstrings that had Jgs 16:8
loaves of barley and **f** ears of grain in 2 Kgs 4:42
me; you bring **f** troops against me. Jb 10:17
my glory **f** with me, and my bow ever Jb 29:20
let his flesh become **f** with youth; let Jb 33:25
wild ox; you have poured over me **f** oil. Ps 92:10
The meek shall obtain **f** joy in the LORD, Is 29:19
As a well keeps its water **f**, so she keeps Jer 6:7
its water fresh, so she keeps **f** her evil; Jer 6:7
so that all its **f** sprouting leaves wither? Ezk 17:9
into the sea, the water will become **f**. Ezk 47:8
that the waters of the sea may become **f**; Ezk 47:9
and marshes will not become **f**; Ezk 47:11
but they will bear **f** fruit every month, Ezk 47:12
But new wine is put into **f** wineskins, Mt 9:17
skins. But new wine is for **f** wineskins." Mk 2:22
new wine must be put into **f** wineskins. Lk 5:38
the same opening both **f** and salt water? Jas 3:11
Neither can a salt pond yield **f** water. Jas 3:12

FRESHLY (1)

in her mouth was a **f** plucked olive leaf. Gn 8:11

FRET (4)

F not yourself because of evildoers; be Ps 37:1
f not yourself over the one who prospers Ps 37:7
F not yourself; it tends only to evil. Ps 37:8
F not yourself because of evildoers, Prv 24:19

FRETFUL (1)

with a quarrelsome and **f** woman. Prv 21:19

FRICTION (1)

and constant **f** among people who are 1 Tm 6:5

FRIEND (51)

he and his **f** Hirah the Adullamite. Gn 38:12
young goat by his **f** the Adullamite to Gn 38:20
face to face, as a man speaks to his **f**. Ex 33:11
you embrace or your **f** who is as your Dt 13:6
f; sit down here." And he turned aside and Ru 4:1
But Amnon had a **f**, whose name was 2 Sm 13:3
So Hushai, David's **f**, came into the 2 Sm 15:37
when Hushai the Archite, David's **f**, 2 Sm 16:16
"Is this your loyalty to your **f**? 2 Sm 16:17
Why did you not go with your **f**?" 2 Sm 16:17
son of Nathan was priest and king's **f**; 1 Kgs 4:5
Hushai the Archite was the king's **f**. 1 Chr 27:33
the descendants of Abraham your **f**? 2 Chr 20:7
kindness from a **f** forsakes the fear Jb 6:14
the fatherless, and bargain over your **f**. Jb 6:27
if I have repaid my **f** with evil or plundered Ps 7:4
nor takes up a reproach against his **f**; Ps 15:3
I grieved for my **f** or my brother; Ps 35:14
Even my close **f** in whom I trusted, who Ps 41:9
equal, my companion, my familiar **f**. Ps 55:13
my beloved and my **f** to shun me; Ps 88:18
sister," and call insight your intimate **f**, Prv 7:4
A **f** loves at all times, and a brother is Prv 17:17
but there is a **f** who sticks closer than Prv 18:24
but a poor man is deserted by his **f**. Prv 19:4
and everyone is a **f** to a man who gives Prv 19:6
is gracious, will have the king as his **f**. Prv 22:11
Faithful are the wounds of a **f**; profuse Prv 27:6
the sweetness of a **f** comes from his Prv 27:9
not forsake your **f** and your father's Prv 27:10
forsake your friend and your father's **f**, Prv 27:10
This is my beloved and this is my **f**, O Sg 5:16
chosen, the offspring of Abraham, my **f**; Is 41:8
'My father, you are the **f** of my youth— Jer 3:4
together, neighbor and **f** shall perish.'" Jer 6:21
in a neighbor; have no confidence in a **f**; Mi 7:5
a **f** of tax collectors and sinners!' Mt 11:19
of them, '**F**, I am doing you no wrong. Mt 20:13
'**F**, how did you get in here without a Mt 22:12
"**F**, do what you came to do." Then they Mt 26:50
a **f** of tax collectors and sinners!' Lk 7:34
of you who has a **f** will go to him at Lk 11:5
and say to him, '**F**, lend me three loaves, Lk 11:5
for a **f** of mine has arrived on a journey, Lk 11:6
give him anything because he is his **f**, Lk 11:8
he may say to you, '**F**, move up higher.' Lk 14:10
The **f** of the bridegroom, who stands and Jn 3:29
them, "Our **f** Lazarus has fallen asleep, Jn 11:11
release this man, you are not Caesar's **f**. Jn 19:12
—and he was called a **f** of God. Jas 2:23
wishes to be a **f** of the world makes Jas 4:4

FRIENDLY (2)

them, though they speak **f** words to you." Jer 12:6
she had given a **f** welcome to the spies. Heb 11:31

FRIENDS (56)

But your **f** be like the sun as he rises in Jgs 5:31

he sent part of the spoil to his **f**, 1 Sm 30:26
father, to his brothers, and to his **f**, 2 Sm 3:8
a single male of his relatives or his **f**. 1 Kgs 16:11
men and his close **f** and his priests, 2 Kgs 10:11
sent and brought his **f** and his wife Est 5:10
his wife Zeresh and all his **f** said to him, Est 5:14
Zeresh and all his **f** everything that had Est 6:13
Now when Job's three **f** heard of all this Jb 2:11
I am a laughingstock to my **f**; I, who Jb 12:4
My **f** scorn me; my eye pours out tears Jb 16:20
who informs against his **f** to get a share Jb 17:5
failed me, my close **f** have forgotten me. Jb 19:14
All my intimate **f** abhor me, and those Jb 19:19
on me, have mercy on me, O you my **f**, Jb 19:21
for they are **f** with the terrors of deep Jb 24:17
also at Job's three **f** because they had Jb 32:3
I will answer you and your **f** with you. Jb 35:4
against you and against your two **f**, Jb 42:7
of Job, when he had prayed for his **f**. Jb 42:10
My **f** and companions stand aloof from Ps 38:11
stretched out his hand against his **f**; Ps 55:20
his neighbor, but the rich has many **f**. Prv 14:20
and a whisperer separates close **f**. Prv 16:28
who repeats a matter separates close **f**. Prv 17:9
Wealth brings many new **f**, but a poor Prv 19:4
much more do his **f** go far from him! Prv 19:7
Eat, **f**, drink, and be drunk with love! Sg 5:1
you yourself have taught to be **f** to you? Jer 13:21
you a terror to yourself and to all your **f**. Jer 20:4
you shall be buried, you and all your **f**, Jer 20:6
us denounce him!" say all my close **f**, Jer 20:10
"'Your trusted **f** have deceived you and Jer 38:22
all her **f** have dealt treacherously with Lam 1:2
priest, you and your **f** who sit before you, Zec 3:8
wounds I received in the house of my **f**.' Zec 13:6
"Go home to your **f** and tell them how Mk 5:19
far from the house, the centurion sent **f**, Lk 7:6
"I tell you, my **f**, do not fear those who Lk 12:4
do not invite your **f** or your brothers or Lk 14:12
he calls together his **f** and his neighbors, Lk 15:6
it, she calls together her **f** and neighbors, Lk 15:9
goat, that I might celebrate with my **f**. Lk 15:29
make **f** for yourselves by means of Lk 16:9
and brothers and relatives and **f**, Lk 21:16
and Pilate became **f** with each other Lk 23:12
that someone lays down his life for his **f**. Jn 15:13
You are my **f** if you do what I command Jn 15:14
but I have called you **f**, for all that I Jn 15:15
they went to their **f** and reported what Acts 4:23
together his relatives and close **f**. Acts 10:24
of the Asiarchs, who were **f** of his, Acts 19:31
that none of his **f** should be prevented Acts 24:23
leave to go to his **f** and be cared for. Acts 27:3
Peace be to you. The **f** greet you. Greet 3 Jn 1:15
greet you. Greet the **f**, every one of them. 3 Jn 1:15

FRIENDSHIP (5)
have come to me in **f** to help me, 1 Chr 12:17
when the **f** of God was upon my tent, Jb 29:4
The **f** of the LORD is for those who fear Ps 25:14
Make no **f** with a man given to anger, Prv 22:24
Do you not know that **f** with the world is Jas 4:4

FRIGHTEN (6)
there shall be no one to **f** them away. Dt 28:26
on the wall, to **f** and terrify them, 2 Chr 32:18
For they all wanted to **f** us, thinking, Neh 6:9
Will you **f** a driven leaf and pursue dry Jb 13:25
Terrors **f** him on every side, and chase Jb 18:11
of the earth, and none will **f** them away. Jer 7:33

FRIGHTENED (7)
Do not be **f**, and do not be dismayed, for Jos 1:9
if the river is turbulent he is not **f**; Jb 40:23
he came, I was **f** and fell on my face. Dn 8:17
And as they were **f** and bowed their faces Lk 24:5
were startled and **f** and thought they Lk 24:37
coming near the boat, and they were **f**. Jn 6:19
and not **f** in anything by your Phil 1:28

FRIGHTENING (3)
before you, and its appearance was **f**. Dn 2:31
to appear to be **f** you with my letters. 2 Cor 10:9
good and do not fear anything that is **f**. 1 Pt 3:6

FRINGE (4)
him and touched the **f** of his garment, Mt 9:20
might only touch the **f** of his garment. Mt 14:36
might touch even the **f** of his garment. Mk 6:56
him and touched the **f** of his garment, Lk 8:44

FRINGES (1)
their phylacteries broad and their **f** long, Mt 23:5

FRO (17)
It went to and **f** until the waters were dried Gn 8:7
and go to and **f** from gate to gate Ex 32:27
run to and **f** throughout the whole 2 Chr 16:9
said, "From going to and **f** on the earth, Jb 1:7
said, "From going to and **f** on the earth, Jb 2:2
away from mankind; they swing to and **f**. Jb 28:4
and all the hills moved to and **f**. Jer 4:24
Run to and **f** through the streets of Jer 5:1
and run to and **f** among the hedges! Jer 49:3
moving to and **f** among the living Ezk 1:13
And the living creatures darted to and **f**, Ezk 1:14
Many shall run to and **f**, and knowledge Dn 12:4
they shall run to and **f**, to seek the word Am 8:12
they rush to and **f** through the squares; Na 2:4
desolate, so that no one went to and **f**, Zec 7:14
guard, so that none shall march to and **f**; Zec 9:8
tossed to and **f** by the waves and carried Eph 4:14

FROGS (14)
I will plague all your country with **f**. Ex 8:2
Nile shall swarm with **f** that shall come Ex 8:3
The **f** shall come up on you and on your Ex 8:4
and make **f** come up on the land of Ex 8:5
and the **f** came up and covered the land of Ex 8:6
secret arts and made **f** come up on the Ex 8:7
LORD to take away the **f** from me and from Ex 8:8
that the **f** be cut off from you and your Ex 8:9
The **f** shall go away from you and your Ex 8:11
and Moses cried to the LORD about the **f**, Ex 8:12
The **f** died out in the houses, the Ex 8:13
of flies, which devoured them, and **f**, Ps 78:45
Their land swarmed with **f**, even in the Ps 105:30
prophet, three unclean spirits like **f**. Rv 16:13

FROLIC (1)
though you **f** like a heifer in the Jer 50:11

FRONT (88)
three men were standing in **f** of him. Gn 18:2
that he had peeled in **f** of the flocks in Gn 30:38
the flocks bred in **f** of the sticks and so Gn 30:39
put the servants with their children in **f**, Gn 33:2
back and encamp in **f** of Pi-hahiroth, Ex 14:2
Migdol and the sea, in **f** of Baal-zephon; Ex 14:2
sea, by Pi-hahiroth, in **f** of Baal-zephon. Ex 14:9
so as to give light on the space in **f** of it. Ex 25:37
you shall double over at the **f** of the tent. Ex 26:9
of the court on the **f** to the east shall be Ex 27:13
so attach it in **f** to the shoulder pieces Ex 28:25
and attach them in **f** to the lower part of Ex 28:27
blue. It shall be on the **f** of the turban. Ex 28:37
And you shall put it in **f** of the veil that is Ex 30:6
in **f** of the mercy seat that is above the Ex 30:6
on the **f** and on the back they were Ex 32:15
And for the **f** to the east, fifty cubits. Ex 38:13
they attached it in **f** to the shoulder Ex 39:18
and attached them in **f** to the lower part Ex 39:20
and kill it in **f** of the tent of meeting; Lv 3:8
head and kill it in **f** of the tent of Lv 3:13
times before the LORD in **f** of the veil of the Lv 4:6
offering and bring it in **f** of the tent of Lv 4:14
times before the LORD in **f** of the veil. Lv 4:17
offer it before the LORD in **f** of the altar. Lv 6:14
on his head, and on the turban, in **f**, Lv 8:9
what Moses commanded in **f** of the tent of Lv 9:5
away from the **f** of the sanctuary Lv 10:4
the rot is on the back or on the **f**. Lv 13:55
his finger on the **f** of the mercy seat Lv 16:14
and in **f** of the mercy seat he shall Lv 16:14
mercy seat and in **f** of the mercy seat. Lv 16:15
gift to the LORD in **f** of the tabernacle of Lv 17:4
shall give light in **f** of the lampstand." Nm 8:2
he set up its lamps in **f** of the lampstand, Nm 8:3
and Aaron came to the **f** of the tent of Nm 16:43
of its blood toward the **f** of the tent of Nm 19:4
half of them in **f** of Mount Gerizim and Jos 8:33
and half of them in **f** of Mount Ebal, Jos 8:33
the top of the hill that is in **f** of Hebron. Jgs 16:3
livestock and the goods in **f** of them. Jgs 18:21
rose on the north in **f** of Michmash, 1 Sm 14:5
the other on the south in **f** of Geba. 1 Sm 14:5
with his shield-bearer in **f** of him. 1 Sm 17:41
and his men in **f** of the Wildgoats' 1 Sm 24:2
against him both in **f** and in the rear, 2 Sm 10:9
The vestibule in **f** of the nave of the 1 Kgs 6:3
and ten cubits deep in **f** of the house. 1 Kgs 6:3
the nave in **f** of the inner sanctuary, 1 Kgs 6:17
across, in **f** of the inner sanctuary, 1 Kgs 6:21
There was a porch in **f** with pillars, 1 Kgs 7:6
with pillars, and a canopy in **f** of them. 1 Kgs 7:6
measure, sawed with saws, back and **f**, 1 Kgs 7:9
with twelve yoke of oxen in **f** of him, 1 Kgs 19:19
he removed from the **f** of the house, 2 Kgs 16:14
against him both in **f** and in the 1 Chr 19:10
The vestibule in **f** of the nave of the 2 Chr 3:4
In **f** of the house he made two pillars 2 Chr 3:15
He set up the pillars in **f** of the temple, 2 Chr 3:17
Thus his troops were in **f** of Judah, 2 Chr 13:13
the battle was in **f** of and behind 2 Chr 13:14
LORD that was in **f** of the vestibule of 2 Chr 15:8
posts and some in **f** of their own homes." Neh 7:3
day Mordecai walked in **f** of the court of Est 2:11
square of the city in **f** of the king's gate, Est 4:6
king's palace, in **f** of the king's quarters, Est 5:1
the singers in **f**, the musicians last, Ps 68:25
beside the gates in **f** of the town, at the Prv 8:3
it had writing on the **f** and on the back, Ezk 2:10
whatever direction the **f** wheel faced, Ezk 10:11
From the **f** of the gate at the entrance Ezk 40:15
the entrance to the **f** of the inner Ezk 40:15
distance from the inner **f** of the lower Ezk 40:19
gate to the outer **f** of the inner court, Ezk 40:19
And the altar was in **f** of the temple. Ezk 40:47
breadth of the east **f** of the temple and Ezk 41:14
and in **f** of the Holy Place was Ezk 41:21
canopy of wood in **f** of the vestibule Ezk 41:25
with a passage in **f** of them. They were Ezk 42:11
of the north gate to the **f** of the temple, Ezk 44:4
and drank wine in **f** of the thousand. Dn 5:1
to them, "Go into the village in **f** of you, Mt 21:2
to them, "Go into the village in **f** of you, Mk 11:2
And those who were in **f** rebuked him, Lk 18:39
saying, "Go into the village in **f** of you, Lk 19:30
and beat him in **f** of the tribunal. Acts 18:17
creatures, full of eyes in **f** and behind: Rv 4:6
from heaven to earth in **f** of people, Rv 13:13

FRONTIER (2)
built the altar at the **f** of the land of Jos 22:11
from the cities, from its cities on its **f**, Ezk 25:9

FRONTLETS (3)
on your hand or **f** between your eyes, Ex 13:16
and they shall be as **f** between your eyes. Dt 6:8
they shall be as **f** between your eyes. Dt 11:18

FROST (5)
flake-like thing, fine as **f** on the ground. Ex 16:14
who has given birth to the **f** of heaven? Jb 38:29
with hail and their sycamores with **f**. Ps 78:47
to the heat by day and the **f** by night. Jer 36:30
day there shall be no light, cold, or **f**. Zec 14:6

FROZEN (2)
is given, and the broad waters are **f** fast. Jb 37:10
like stone, and the face of the deep is **f**. Jb 38:30

FRUIT (207)
and **f** trees bearing fruit in which is Gn 1:11
and fruit trees bearing **f** in which is Gn 1:11
and trees bearing **f** in which is their Gn 1:12
earth, and every tree with seed in its **f**. Gn 1:29
"We may eat of the **f** of the trees in the Gn 3:2
shall not eat of the **f** of the tree that is Gn 3:3
to make one wise, she took of its **f** and ate, Gn 3:6
to be with me, she gave me **f** of the tree, Gn 3:12
LORD an offering of the **f** of the ground, Gn 4:3
withheld from you the **f** of the womb?" Gn 30:2
the land and all the **f** of the trees that Ex 10:15
in from the field the **f** of your labor. Ex 23:16
then you shall regard its **f** as forbidden. Lv 19:23
in the fourth year all its **f** shall be holy, Lv 19:24
But in the fifth year you may eat of its **f**, Lv 19:25
on the first day the **f** of splendid trees, Lv 23:40
The land will yield its **f**, and you will Lv 25:19
the trees of the field shall yield their **f**. Lv 26:4
trees of the land shall not yield their **f**. Lv 26:20
seed of the land or of the **f** of the trees, Lv 27:30
bring some of the **f** of the land." Now Nm 13:20
and showed them the **f** of the land. Nm 13:26
with milk and honey, and this is its **f**. Nm 13:27
their hands some of the **f** of the land and Dt 1:25
He will also bless the **f** of your womb and Dt 7:13
of your womb and the **f** of your ground, Dt 7:13
be no rain, and the land will yield no **f**, Dt 11:17
a vineyard and has not enjoyed its **f**? Dt 20:6
in the battle and another man enjoy its **f**. Dt 20:6
some of the first of all the **f** of the ground, Dt 26:2
I bring the first of the **f** of the ground, Dt 26:10
Blessed shall be the **f** of your womb and Dt 28:4
your womb and the **f** of your ground and Dt 28:4
of your ground and the **f** of your cattle, Dt 28:4
in the **f** of your womb and in the fruit of Dt 28:11
womb and in the **f** of your livestock Dt 28:11
livestock and in the **f** of your ground, Dt 28:11
Cursed shall be the **f** of your womb and Dt 28:18
of your womb and the **f** of your ground, Dt 28:18
a vineyard, but you shall not enjoy its **f**. Dt 28:30
shall eat up the **f** of your ground and Dt 28:33
all your trees and the **f** of your ground. Dt 28:42
of your cattle and the **f** of your ground, Dt 28:51
And you shall eat the **f** of your womb, Dt 28:53
a root bearing poisonous and bitter **f**, Dt 29:18
in the **f** of your womb and in the fruit of Dt 30:9
womb and in the **f** of your cattle and Dt 30:9
your cattle and in the **f** of your ground. Dt 30:9
but they ate of the **f** of the land of Jos 5:12
You eat the **f** of vineyards and olive Jos 24:13
sweetness and my good **f** and go hold Jgs 9:11

the bread and summer **f** for the young 2 Sm 16:2
and plant vineyards, and eat their **f**. 2 Kgs 19:29
root downward and bear **f** upward. 2 Kgs 19:30
olive orchards and **f** trees in Neh 9:25
fathers to enjoy its **f** and its good gifts, Neh 9:36
and the firstfruits of all **f** of every tree, Neh 10:35
our contributions, the **f** of every tree, Neh 10:37
He will give back the **f** of his toil and Jb 20:18
of water that yields its **f** in its season, Ps 1:3
may it wave; may its **f** be like Lebanon; Ps 72:16
locust and the **f** of their labor Ps 78:46
all who pass along the way pluck its **f**? Ps 80:12
They still bear **f** in old age; they are ever Ps 92:14
is satisfied with the **f** of your work. Ps 104:13
land and ate up the **f** of their ground. Ps 105:35
took possession of the **f** of the peoples' Ps 105:44
the LORD, the **f** of the womb a reward. Ps 127:3
You shall eat the **f** of the labor of your Ps 128:2
and all hills, **f** trees and all cedars! Ps 148:9
they shall eat the **f** of their way, Prv 1:31
My **f** is better than gold, even fine gold, Prv 8:19
The **f** of the righteous is a tree of life, Prv 11:30
but the root of the righteous bears **f**. Prv 12:12
From the **f** of his mouth a man is Prv 12:14
From the **f** of his mouth a man eats Prv 13:2
will be filled with the **f** of his ways, Prv 14:14
will be filled with the **f** of his ways. Prv 14:14
From the **f** of a man's mouth his Prv 18:20
Whoever tends a fig tree will eat its **f**, Prv 27:18
with the **f** of her hands she plants a Prv 31:16
Give her of the **f** of her hands, and let Prv 31:31
and planted in them all kinds of **f** trees. Eccl 2:5
shadow, and his **f** was sweet to my taste. Sg 2:3
climb the palm tree and lay hold of its **f**. Sg 7:8
was to bring for its **f** a thousand pieces of Sg 8:11
and the keepers of the **f** two hundred. Sg 8:12
them, for they shall eat the **f** of their deeds. Is 3:10
and the **f** of the land shall be the pride and Is 4:2
and a branch from his roots shall bear **f**. Is 11:1
have no mercy on the **f** of the womb; Is 13:18
and its **f** will be a flying fiery serpent. Is 14:29
for over your summer **f** and your harvest Is 16:9
four or five on the branches of a **f** tree, Is 17:6
shoots and fill the whole world with **f**. Is 27:6
this will be the full **f** of the removal of his Is 27:9
harvest fails, the **f** harvest will not come. Is 32:10
reap, and plant vineyards, and eat their **f**. Is 37:30
take root downward and bear **f** upward. Is 37:31
salvation and righteousness may bear **f**; Is 45:8
creating the **f** of the lips. Peace, peace, to Is 57:19
shall plant vineyards and eat their **f**. Is 65:21
upon this people, the **f** of their devices, Jer 6:19
trees of the field and the **f** of the ground; Jer 7:20
green olive tree, beautiful with good **f**.' Jer 11:16
"Let us destroy the tree with its **f**, Jer 11:19
they take root; they grow and produce **f**; Jer 12:2
drought, for it does not cease to bear **f**." Jer 17:8
ways, according to the **f** of his deeds." Jer 17:10
you according to the **f** of your deeds, Jer 21:14
planters shall plant and shall enjoy the **f**. Jer 31:5
and according to the **f** of his deeds. Jer 32:19
Should women eat the **f** of their womb, Lam 2:20
branches and bear **f** and become a Ezk 17:8
he not pull up its roots and cut off its **f**, Ezk 17:9
branches and produce **f** and become a Ezk 17:23
the ground; the east wind dried up its **f**; Ezk 19:12
stem of its shoots, has consumed its **f**, Ezk 19:14
take away all the **f** of your labor and Ezk 23:29
They shall eat your **f**, and they shall Ezk 25:4
the trees of the field shall yield their **f**, Ezk 34:27
branches and yield your **f** to my people Ezk 36:8
I will make the **f** of the tree and the Ezk 36:30
leaves will not wither, nor their **f** fail, Ezk 47:12
but they will bear fresh **f** every month, Ezk 47:12
Their **f** will be for food, and their Ezk 47:12
were beautiful and its **f** abundant, Dn 4:12
strip off its leaves and scatter its **f**. Dn 4:14
were beautiful and its **f** abundant, Dn 4:21
Like the first **f** on the fig tree in its first Hos 9:10
root is dried up; they shall bear no **f**. Hos 9:16
is a luxuriant vine that yields its **f**. Hos 10:1
The more his **f** increased, the more Hos 10:1
injustice; you have eaten the **f** of lies. Hos 10:13
cypress; from me comes your **f**. Hos 14:8
wilderness are green; the tree bears its **f**; Jl 2:22
I destroyed his **f** above and his roots Am 2:9
poison and the **f** of righteousness into Am 6:12
me: behold, a basket of summer **f**. Am 8:1
"A basket of summer **f**." Then the LORD Am 8:2
they shall make gardens and eat their **f**. Am 9:14
the **f** of my body for the sin of my soul?" Mi 6:7
as when the summer **f** has been gathered, Mi 7:1
of its inhabitants, for the **f** of their deeds. Mi 7:13
not blossom, nor **f** be on the vines, Hab 3:17
The vine shall give its **f**, and the ground Zec 8:12
the Lord's table is polluted, and its **f**, Mal 1:12
Bear **f** in keeping with repentance. Mt 3:8
does not bear good **f** is cut down and Mt 3:10
So, every healthy tree bears good **f**, but Mt 7:17
fruit, but the diseased tree bears bad **f**. Mt 7:17
A healthy tree cannot bear bad **f**, nor Mt 7:18
fruit, nor can a diseased tree bear good **f**. Mt 7:18
does not bear good **f** is cut down and Mt 7:19
make the tree good and its **f** good, Mt 12:33
or make the tree bad and its **f** bad, Mt 12:33
fruit bad, for the tree is known by its **f**. Mt 12:33
He indeed bears **f** and yields, in one Mt 13:23
"May no **f** ever come from you again!" Mt 21:19
When the season for **f** drew near, he Mt 21:34
his servants to the tenants to get his **f**. Mt 21:34
drink again of this **f** of the vine until Mt 26:29
hear the word and accept it and bear **f**, Mk 4:20
no one ever eat **f** from you again." And Mk 11:14
from them some of the **f** of the vineyard. Mk 12:2
drink again of the **f** of the vine until Mk 14:25
and blessed is the **f** of your womb! Lk 1:42
that does not bear good **f** is cut down and Lk 3:9
"For no good tree bears bad **f**, nor again Lk 6:43
nor again does a bad tree bear good **f**, Lk 6:43
for each tree is known by its own **f**. For Lk 6:44
of life, and their **f** does not mature. Lk 8:14
and good heart, and bear **f** with patience. Lk 8:15
and he came seeking **f** on it and found Lk 13:6
I have come seeking **f** on this fig tree, Lk 13:7
Then if it should bear **f** next year, well Lk 13:9
give him some of the **f** of the vineyard. Lk 20:10
will not drink of the **f** of the vine until Lk 22:18
wages and gathering **f** for eternal life, Jn 4:36
alone; but if it dies, it bears much **f**. Jn 12:24
mine that does not bear **f** he takes away, Jn 15:2
every branch that does bear **f** he prunes, Jn 15:2
fruit he prunes, that it may bear more **f**. Jn 15:2
As the branch cannot bear **f** by itself, Jn 15:4
and I in him, he it is that bears much **f**, Jn 15:5
that you bear much **f** and so prove to be Jn 15:8
should go and bear **f** and that your fruit Jn 15:16
bear fruit and that your **f** should abide, Jn 15:16
But what **f** were you getting at that Rom 6:21
the **f** you get leads to sanctification Rom 6:22
in order that we may bear **f** for God. Rom 7:4
in our members to bear **f** for death. Rom 7:5
a vineyard without eating any of its **f**? 1 Cor 9:7
But the **f** of the Spirit is love, joy, peace, Gal 5:22
(for the **f** of light is found in all that is Eph 5:9
filled with the **f** of righteousness that Phil 1:11
but I seek the **f** that increases to your Phil 4:17
world it is bearing **f** and growing—as Col 1:6
bearing **f** in every good work and Col 1:10
yields the peaceful **f** of righteousness Heb 12:11
the **f** of lips that acknowledge his Heb 13:15
waits for the precious **f** of the earth, Jas 5:7
gave rain, and the earth bore its **f**. Jas 5:18
tree sheds its winter **f** when shaken by a Rv 6:13
"The **f** for which your soul longed has Rv 18:14
the tree of life with its twelve kinds of **f**, Rv 22:2
kinds of fruit, yielding its **f** each month. Rv 22:2

FRUITFUL (38)
"Be **f** and multiply and fill the waters in Gn 1:22
"Be **f** and multiply and fill the earth and Gn 1:28
and be **f** and multiply on the earth." Gn 8:17
"Be **f** and multiply and fill the earth. Gn 9:1
And you, be **f** and multiply, teem on the Gn 9:7
I will make you exceedingly **f**, and I will Gn 17:6
and will make him **f** and multiply him Gn 17:20
for us, and we shall be **f** in the land." Gn 26:22
you and make you **f** and multiply you, Gn 28:3
am God Almighty: be **f** and multiply. Gn 35:11
"For God has made me **f** in the land of Gn 41:52
in it, and were **f** and multiplied greatly. Gn 47:27
I will make you **f** and multiply you, Gn 48:4
"Joseph is a **f** bough, a fruitful bough Gn 49:22
fruitful bough, a **f** bough by a spring; Gn 49:22
of Israel were **f** and increased greatly; Ex 1:7
you and make you **f** and multiply you Lv 26:9
lodging place, its most **f** forest. 2 Kgs 19:23
made his people very **f** and made them Ps 105:24
a **f** land into a salty waste, because of Ps 107:34
and plant vineyards and get a **f** yield. Ps 107:37
will be like a **f** vine within your house; Ps 128:3
his forest and of his **f** land the LORD will Is 10:18
gladness are taken away from the **f** field, Is 16:10
Lebanon shall be turned into a **f** field, Is 29:17
and the **f** field shall be regarded as a Is 29:17
for the pleasant fields, for the **f** vine, Is 32:12
and the wilderness becomes a **f** field, Is 32:15
field, and the **f** field is deemed a forest. Is 32:15
and righteousness abide in the **f** field. Is 32:16
to its remotest height, its most **f** forest. Is 37:24
and behold, the **f** land was a desert, Jer 4:26
fold, and they shall be **f** and multiply. Jer 23:3
taken away from the **f** land of Moab; Jer 48:33
f and full of branches by reason of Ezk 19:10
and they shall multiply and be **f**. Ezk 36:11
you rains from heaven and **f** seasons, Acts 14:17
in the flesh, that means **f** labor for me. Phil 1:22

FRUITLESS (1)
f trees in late autumn, twice dead, Jude 1:12

FRUITS (22)
take some of the choice **f** of the land in Gn 43:11
prune your vineyard and gather in its **f**, Lv 25:3
The first ripe **f** of all that is in their Nm 18:13
with the choicest **f** of the sun and the Dt 33:14
of raisins, a hundred of summer **f**, 2 Sm 16:1
may strangers plunder the **f** of his toil! Ps 109:11
and those who love it will eat its **f**. Prv 18:21
of pomegranates with all choicest **f**, Sg 4:13
come to his garden, and eat its choicest **f**. Sg 4:16
and beside our doors are all choice **f**, Sg 7:13
land to enjoy its **f** and its good things. Jer 2:7
you, gather wine and summer **f** and oil, Jer 40:10
wine and summer **f** in great Jer 40:12
on your summer **f** and your grapes the Jer 48:32
pierced by lack of the **f** of the field. Lam 4:9
that it will not destroy the **f** of your soil, Mal 3:11
You will recognize them by their **f**. Are Mt 7:16
Thus you will recognize them by their **f**. Mt 7:20
will give him the **f** in their seasons." Mt 21:41
and given to a people producing its **f**. Mt 21:43
Bear **f** in keeping with repentance. And do Lk 3:8
open to reason, full of mercy and good **f**, Jas 3:17

FRUSTRATE (1)
against them to **f** their purpose, Ezr 4:5

FRUSTRATED (1)
to us and that God had **f** their plan, Neh 4:15

FRUSTRATES (3)
He **f** the devices of the crafty, so that their Jb 5:12
to nothing; he **f** the plans of the peoples. Ps 33:10
who **f** the signs of liars and makes fools Is 44:25

FRUSTRATION (1)
and **f** in all that you undertake to do, Dt 28:20

FUEL (7)
in blood will be burned as **f** for the fire. Is 9:5
and the people are like **f** for the fire; Is 9:19
Lebanon would not suffice for **f**, nor are Is 40:16
Then it becomes **f** for a man. He takes a Is 44:15
Behold, it is given to the fire for **f**. When Ezk 15:4
which I have given to the fire for **f**, Ezk 15:6
You shall be **f** for the fire. Your blood Ezk 21:32

FUGITIVE (9)
You shall be a **f** and a wanderer on the Gn 4:12
I shall be a **f** and a wanderer on the Gn 4:14
of another, he will be a **f** until death; Prv 28:17
shelter the outcasts; do not reveal the **f**; Is 16:3
bring water; meet the **f** with bread, Is 21:14
on that day a **f** will come to you to Ezk 24:26
your mouth will be opened to the **f**, Ezk 24:27
a **f** from Jerusalem came to me and Ezk 33:21
me the evening before the **f** came; Ezk 33:22

FUGITIVES (10)
He has made his sons **f**, and his Nm 21:29
they said, "You are **f** of Ephraim, Jgs 12:4
And when any of the **f** of Ephraim said, Jgs 12:5
her **f** flee to Zoar, to Eglath-shelishiyah. Is 15:5
Babylon and bring them all down as **f**, Is 43:14
they shall not return, except some **f**." Jer 44:14
shadow of Heshbon **f** stop without Jer 48:45
before him, with none to gather the **f**. Jer 49:5
So they became **f** and wanderers; Lam 4:15
stand at the crossroads to cut off his **f**; Ob 1:14

FULFILL (42)
land; I will **f** the number of your days. Ex 23:26
offerings to the LORD to **f** a vow or as a Lv 22:21
to **f** a vow or as a freewill offering or at Nm 15:3
to **f** a vow or for peace offerings to the Nm 15:8
Or has he spoken, and will he not **f** it? Nm 23:19
On that day I will **f** against Eli all that 1 Sm 3:12
the LORD that he might **f** his word, 1 Kgs 12:15
God that the LORD might **f** his word, 2 Chr 10:15
to **f** the word of the LORD by the 2 Chr 36:21
it kept Sabbath, to **f** seventy years. 2 Chr 36:21
king to grant my wish and **f** my request, Est 5:8
request, and that God would **f** my hope, Jb 6:8
Can you number the months that they **f**, Jb 39:2
your heart's desire and **f** all your plans! Ps 20:4
May the LORD **f** all your petitions! Ps 20:5
The LORD will **f** his purpose for me; your Ps 138:8
shepherd, and he shall **f** all my purpose'; Is 44:28
and I will **f** to you my promise and Jer 29:10
when I will **f** the promise I made to the Jer 33:14
I will **f** my words against this city for Jer 39:16
and yet they expect him to **f** their word. Ezk 13:6

themselves up in order to **f** the vision, Dn 11:14
f your vows, for never again shall the Na 1:15
this took place to **f** what the Lord had Mt 1:22
This was to **f** what the Lord had spoken Mt 2:15
for us to **f** all righteousness." Then Mt 3:15
not come to abolish them but to **f** them. Mt 5:17
This was to **f** what was spoken by the Mt 8:17
This was to **f** what was spoken by the Mt 12:17
This was to **f** what was spoken by the Mt 13:35
This took place to **f** what was spoken by Mt 21:4
of vengeance, to **f** all that is written. Lk 21:22
This was to **f** the word that he had Jn 18:9
This was to **f** the word that Jesus had Jn 18:32
be." This was to **f** the Scripture which Jn 19:24
now finished, said (to **f** the Scripture), Jn 19:28
burdens, and so **f** the law of Christ. Gal 6:2
"See that you **f** the ministry that you Col 4:17
calling and may **f** every resolve for 2 Thes 1:11
work of an evangelist, **f** your ministry. 2 Tm 4:5
If you really **f** the royal law according to Jas 2:8
Lord is not slow to **f** his promise as some 2 Pt 3:9

FULFILLED (54)
concerning you have been **f** for you, Jos 23:15
When your days are **f** and you lie 2 Sm 7:12
with his hand has **f** what he promised 1 Kgs 8:15
Now the LORD has **f** his promise that 1 Kgs 8:20
and with your hand have **f** it this day. 1 Kgs 8:24
When your days are **f** to walk with 1 Chr 17:11
word to David my father be now **f**, 2 Chr 1:9
with his hand has **f** what he promised 2 Chr 6:4
Now the LORD has **f** his promise that 2 Chr 6:10
and with your hand have **f** it this day. 2 Chr 6:15
the mouth of Jeremiah might be **f**, 2 Chr 36:22
by the mouth of Jeremiah might be **f**, Ezr 1:1
to the half of my kingdom, it shall be **f**." Est 5:6
to the half of my kingdom, it shall be **f**." Est 7:2
further is your request? It shall be **f**." Est 9:12
heart sick, but a desire **f** is a tree of life. Prv 13:12
A desire **f** is sweet to the soul, but to Prv 13:19
mouths, and have **f** it with your hands, Jer 44:25
and it will be **f**,'" declares the Lord GOD. Ezk 21:7
word was **f** against Nebuchadnezzar. Dn 4:33
Then was **f** what was spoken by the Mt 2:17
was spoken by the prophets might be **f**: Mt 2:23
spoken by the prophet Isaiah might be **f**: Mt 4:14
the prophecy of Isaiah is **f** that says: Mt 13:14
how then should the Scriptures be **f**, Mt 26:54
the prophets might be **f**." Then all the Mt 26:56
Then was **f** what had been spoken by Mt 27:9
and saying, "The time is **f**, and the Mk 1:15
seize me. But let the Scriptures be **f**." Mk 14:49
my words, which will be **f** in their time." Lk 1:20
Scripture has been **f** in your hearing." Lk 4:21
until the times of the Gentiles are **f**. Lk 21:24
eat it until it is **f** in the kingdom of Lk 22:16
you that this Scripture must be **f** in me: Lk 22:37
Prophets and the Psalms must be **f**." Lk 24:44
by the prophet Isaiah might be **f**: Jn 12:38
But the Scripture will be **f**, 'He who ate Jn 13:18
that is written in their Law must be **f**: Jn 15:25
that the Scripture might be **f**. Jn 17:12
they may have my joy **f** in themselves. Jn 17:13
took place that the Scripture might be **f**: Jn 19:36
"Brothers, the Scripture had to be **f**, Acts 1:16
that his Christ would suffer, he thus **f**. Acts 3:18
f them by condemning him. Acts 13:27
this he has **f** to us their children by Acts 13:33
of God for the work that they had **f**. Acts 14:26
purification would be **f** and the Acts 21:26
requirement of the law might be **f** in us, Rom 8:4
one who loves another has **f** the law. Rom 13:8
to Illyricum I have **f** the ministry of Rom 15:19
For the whole law is **f** in one word: "You Gal 5:14
and the Scripture was **f** that says, Jas 2:23
angel, the mystery of God would be **f**, Rv 10:7
the beast, until the words of God are **f**. Rv 17:17

FULFILLING (4)
LORD your God, you shall not delay **f** it, Dt 23:21
thus **f** the word of the LORD that he 1 Kgs 2:27
snow and mist, stormy wind **f** his word! Ps 148:8
therefore love is the **f** of the law. Rom 13:10

FULFILLMENT (4)
and for the **f** of your righteous Ps 119:123
days are near, and the **f** of every vision. Ezk 12:23
there would be a **f** of what was spoken Lk 1:45
For what is written about me has its **f**." Lk 22:37

FULFILLS (3)
High, to God who **f** his purpose for me. Ps 57:2
He **f** the desire of those who fear him; Ps 145:19
of his servant and **f** the counsel of his Is 44:26

FULL (273)
Valley of Siddim was **f** of bitumen pits, Gn 14:10
For the **f** price let him give it to me in Gn 23:9
good old age, an old man and **f** of years, Gn 25:8
you give me I will give a **f** tenth to you." Gn 28:22
gathered to his people, old and **f** of days. Gn 35:29
swallowed up the seven plump, **f** ears. Gn 41:7
ears growing on one stalk, **f** and good. Gn 41:22
of his sack, our money in **f** weight. Gn 43:21
Seven **f** days passed after the LORD had Ex 7:25
by the meat pots and ate bread to the **f**, Ex 16:3
to eat and in the morning bread to the **f**, Ex 16:8
started the fire shall make **f** restitution. Ex 22:6
with it, he shall make **f** restitution. Ex 22:14
he shall restore it in **f** and shall add a fifth Lv 6:5
he shall take a censer **f** of coals of fire Lv 16:12
and the land become **f** of depravity. Lv 19:29
shall count seven **f** weeks from the Lv 23:15
For a **f** year he shall have the right of Lv 25:29
If it is not redeemed within a **f** year, Lv 25:30
eat your bread to the **f** and dwell in your Lv 26:5
And he shall make **f** restitution for his Nm 5:7
both of them **f** of fine flour mixed with Nm 7:13
golden dish of 10 shekels, **f** of incense; Nm 7:14
both of them **f** of fine flour mixed with Nm 7:19
golden dish of 10 shekels, **f** of incense; Nm 7:20
both of them **f** of fine flour mixed with Nm 7:25
golden dish of 10 shekels, **f** of incense; Nm 7:26
both of them **f** of fine flour mixed with Nm 7:31
golden dish of 10 shekels, **f** of incense; Nm 7:32
both of them **f** of fine flour mixed with Nm 7:37
golden dish of 10 shekels, **f** of incense; Nm 7:38
both of them **f** of fine flour mixed with Nm 7:43
golden dish of 10 shekels, **f** of incense; Nm 7:44
both of them **f** of fine flour mixed with Nm 7:49
golden dish of 10 shekels, **f** of incense; Nm 7:50
both of them **f** of fine flour mixed with Nm 7:55
golden dish of 10 shekels, **f** of incense; Nm 7:56
both of them **f** of fine flour mixed with Nm 7:61
golden dish of 10 shekels, **f** of incense; Nm 7:62
both of them **f** of fine flour mixed with Nm 7:67
golden dish of 10 shekels, **f** of incense; Nm 7:68
both of them **f** of fine flour mixed with Nm 7:73
golden dish of 10 shekels, **f** of incense; Nm 7:74
both of them **f** of fine flour mixed with Nm 7:79
golden dish of 10 shekels, **f** of incense; Nm 7:80
the twelve golden dishes, **f** of incense, Nm 7:86
wilderness they shall come to a **f** end, Nm 14:35
give me his house **f** of silver and gold, Nm 22:18
give me his house **f** of silver and gold, Nm 24:13
and houses **f** of all good things that you Dt 6:11
not plant—and when you eat and are **f**, Dt 6:11
And you shall eat and be **f**, and you shall Dt 8:10
have eaten and are **f** and have built good Dt 8:12
livestock, and you shall eat and be **f**. Dt 11:15
her father and her mother a **f** month. Dt 21:13
A **f** and fair weight you shall have, Dt 25:15
a **f** and fair measure you shall have, Dt 25:15
they have eaten and are **f** and grown fat, Dt 31:20
favor, and **f** of the blessing of the LORD, Dt 33:23
the son of Nun was **f** of the spirit of Dt 34:9
Now the house was **f** of men and Jgs 16:27
I went away **f**, and the LORD has brought Ru 1:21
and a **f** reward be given you by the LORD, Ru 2:12
Those who were **f** have hired 1 Sm 2:5
which were given in **f** number to the 1 Sm 18:27
Saul fell at once **f** length on the 1 Sm 28:20
put to death, and one **f** line to be spared. 2 Sm 8:2
After two **f** years Absalom had 2 Sm 13:23
Absalom lived two **f** years in 2 Sm 14:28
there was a plot of ground **f** of lentils, 2 Sm 23:11
And he was **f** of wisdom, 1 Kgs 7:14
make this dry streambed **f** of pools.' 2 Kgs 3:16
vessels. And when one is **f**, set it aside." 2 Kgs 4:4
When the vessels were **f**, she said to her 2 Kgs 4:6
from it his lap **f** of wild gourds, 2 Kgs 4:39
the mountain was **f** of horses and 2 Kgs 6:17
Jehu drew his bow with his **f** strength, 2 Kgs 9:24
was a plot of ground **f** of barley, 1 Chr 11:13
to Hebron with **f** intent to make 1 Chr 12:38
it to me at its **f** price—that the 1 Chr 21:22
but I will buy them for the **f** price. 1 Chr 21:24
When David was old and **f** of days, he 1 Chr 23:1
Then he died at a good age, **f** of days, 1 Chr 29:28
But Jehoiada grew old and **f** of days, 2 Chr 24:15
to these men in **f** and without delay from Ezr 6:8
let it be done in **f** for the house of the Ezr 7:23
took possession of houses **f** of all good Neh 9:25
the Jew gave **f** written authority, Est 9:29
and the **f** account of the high honor of Est 10:2
is long, and I am **f** of tossing till the dawn. Jb 7:4
and a man **f** of talk be judged right? Jb 11:2
a woman is few of days and **f** of trouble. Jb 14:1
It will be paid in **f** before his time, and Jb 15:32
His bones are **f** of his youthful vigor, Jb 20:11
fill his belly to the **f** God will send his Jb 20:23
One dies in his **f** vigor, being wholly at Jb 21:23
his pails **f** of milk and the marrow of Jb 21:24
the face of the **f** moon and spreads over Jb 26:9
For I am **f** of words; the spirit within me Jb 32:18
was set on your table was **f** of fatness. Jb 36:16
"But you are **f** of the judgment on the Jb 36:17
And Job died, an old man, and **f** of days. Jb 42:17
and whose right hands are **f** of bribes. Ps 26:10
the voice of the LORD is **f** of majesty. Ps 29:4
the earth is **f** of the steadfast love of the Ps 33:5
in his illness you restore him to **f** health. Ps 41:3
enrich it; the river of God is **f** of water; Ps 65:9
of the land are **f** of the habitations of Ps 74:20
when the LORD heard, he was **f** of wrath; Ps 78:21
When God heard, he was **f** of wrath, Ps 78:59
given them tears to drink in **f** measure. Ps 80:5
trumpet at the new moon, at the **f** moon, Ps 81:3
For my soul is **f** of troubles, and my life Ps 88:3
you are **f** of wrath against your Ps 89:38
old age; they are ever **f** of sap and green, Ps 92:14
all; the earth is **f** of your creatures. Ps 104:24
F of splendor and majesty is his work, Ps 111:3
O LORD, is **f** of your steadfast love; Ps 119:64
in their youth be like plants **f** grown, Ps 144:12
may our granaries be **f**, providing all Ps 144:13
brighter and brighter until **f** day. Prv 4:18
him; at **f** moon he will come home." Prv 7:20
quiet than a house **f** of feasting with Prv 17:1
his mouth will be **f** of gravel. Prv 20:17
A wise man is **f** of strength, and a man Prv 24:5
One who is **f** loathes honey, but to one Prv 27:7
A fool gives **f** vent to his spirit, but a Prv 29:11
lest I be **f** and deny you and say, "Who Prv 30:9
run to the sea, but the sea is not **f**; Eccl 1:7
All things are **f** of weariness; a man Eccl 1:8
For all his days are **f** of sorrow, and his Eccl 2:23
quietness than two hands **f** of toil and a Eccl 4:6
but the **f** stomach of the rich will not Eccl 5:12
of the children of man are **f** of evil, Eccl 9:3
If the clouds are **f** of rain, they empty Eccl 11:3
bathed in milk, sitting beside a **f** pool. Sg 5:12
I will not listen; your hands are **f** of blood. Is 1:15
become a whore, she who was **f** of justice! Is 1:21
because they are **f** of things from the east Is 2:6
of hosts; the whole earth is **f** of his glory!" Is 6:3
the Lord GOD of hosts will make a **f** end, Is 10:23
for the earth shall be **f** of the knowledge of Is 11:9
houses will be **f** of howling creatures; Is 13:21
For the waters of Dibon are **f** of blood; for Is 15:9
you who are **f** of shoutings, tumultuous Is 22:2
Your choicest valleys were **f** of chariots, Is 22:7
well-aged wine, of rich food **f** of marrow, Is 25:6
and this will be the **f** fruit of the removal Is 27:9
For all tables are **f** of filthy vomit, with no Is 28:8
his lips are **f** of fury, and his tongue is Is 30:27
shall come upon you in **f** measure, Is 47:9
they are **f** of the wrath of the LORD, the Is 51:20
among those in **f** vigor we are like dead Is 59:10
a wind too **f** for this comes for me. Now Jer 4:12
a desolation; yet I will not make a **f** end. Jer 4:27
When I fed them to the **f**, they committed Jer 5:7
rows and destroy, but make not a **f** end; Jer 5:10
the LORD, I will not make a **f** end of you. Jer 5:18
Like a cage **f** of birds, their houses are Jer 5:27
full of birds, their houses are **f** of deceit; Jer 5:27
Therefore I am **f** of the wrath of the LORD; Jer 6:11
with you; they are in **f** cry after you; Jer 12:6
For the land is **f** of adulterers; because Jer 23:10
I will make a **f** end of all the nations Jer 30:11
you, but of you I will not make a **f** end. Jer 30:11
before the Rechabites pitchers **f** of wine, Jer 35:5
shame, and the earth is **f** of your cry; Jer 46:12
I will make a **f** end of all the nations to Jer 46:28
you, but of you I will not make a **f** end. Jer 46:28
of the Chaldeans is **f** of guilt against the Jer 51:5
lonely sits the city that was **f** of people! Lam 1:1
The LORD gave **f** vent to his wrath; he Lam 4:11
of all four were **f** of eyes all around. Ezk 1:18
For the land is **f** of bloody crimes and Ezk 7:23
crimes and the city is **f** of violence. Ezk 7:23
The land is **f** of blood, and the city full of Ezk 9:9
is full of blood, and the city **f** of injustice. Ezk 9:9
and the wheels were **f** of eyes all Ezk 10:12
Will you make a **f** end of the remnant Ezk 11:13
hailstones in wrath to make a **f** end. Ezk 13:13
tall and arrived at **f** adornment. Ezk 16:7
fruitful and **f** of branches by reason of Ezk 19:10
wilderness, to make a **f** end of them. Ezk 20:13
them or make a **f** end of them in Ezk 20:17
name is defiled; you are **f** of tumult. Ezk 22:5
warriors clothed in **f** armor, Ezk 23:12
f of wisdom and perfect in beauty. Ezk 28:12
blood, and the ravines will be **f** of you. Ezk 32:6
middle of the valley; it was **f** of bones. Ezk 37:1
all of them clothed in **f** armor, Ezk 38:4
side chambers measured a **f** reed of six Ezk 41:8
myself at all, for the **f** three weeks. Dn 10:3

when they had grazed, they became **f**, Hos 13:6
fruit; the fig tree and vine give their **f** yield. Jl 2:22
"The threshing floors shall be **f** of grain; Jl 2:24
is ripe. Go in, tread, for the winepress is **f**. Jl 3:13
as a cart **f** of sheaves presses down. Am 2:13
Your rich men are **f** of violence; your Mi 6:12
they are at **f** strength and many, Na 1:12
all **f** of lies and plunder—no end to the Na 3:1
and the earth was **f** of his praise. Hab 3:3
for a **f** and sudden end he will make of Zep 1:18
of the city shall be **f** of boys and girls Zec 8:5
if drunk with wine, and be **f** like a bowl, Zec 9:15
Bring the **f** tithes into the storehouse, Mal 3:10
your whole body will be **f** of light, Mt 6:22
your whole body will be **f** of darkness. Mt 6:23
When it was **f**, men drew it ashore and Mt 13:48
took up twelve baskets **f** of the broken Mt 14:20
took up seven baskets **f** of the broken Mt 15:37
but inside they are **f** of greed and Mt 23:25
but within are **f** of dead people's bones Mt 23:27
but within you are **f** of hypocrisy and Mt 23:28
then the ear, then the **f** grain in the ear. Mk 4:28
up twelve baskets **f** of broken pieces Mk 6:43
broken pieces left over, seven baskets **f**. Mk 8:8
how many baskets **f** of broken pieces Mk 8:19
how many baskets **f** of broken pieces Mk 8:20
And Jesus, **f** of the Holy Spirit, returned Lk 4:1
the cities, there came a man **f** of leprosy. Lk 5:12
"Woe to you who are **f** now, for you Lk 6:25
is healthy, your whole body is **f** of light, Lk 11:34
it is bad, your body is **f** of darkness. Lk 11:34
If then your whole body is **f** of light, Lk 11:36
but inside you are **f** of greed and Lk 11:39
Son from the Father, **f** of grace and truth. Jn 1:14
be in you, and that your joy may be **f**. Jn 15:11
you will receive, that your joy may be **f**. Jn 16:24
A jar **f** of sour wine stood there, so they Jn 19:29
so they put a sponge **f** of the sour wine Jn 19:29
in the boat, dragging the net **f** of fish, Jn 21:8
hauled the net ashore, **f** of large fish, Jn 21:11
you will make me **f** of gladness with Acts 2:28
Now the **f** number of those who Acts 4:32
twelve summoned the **f** number of the Acts 6:2
repute, **f** of the Spirit and of wisdom, Acts 6:3
a man **f** of faith and of the Holy Spirit, Acts 6:5
And Stephen, **f** of grace and power, was Acts 6:8
But he, **f** of the Holy Spirit, gazed into Acts 7:55
She was **f** of good works and acts of Acts 9:36
man, **f** of the Holy Spirit and of faith. Acts 11:24
f of all deceit and villainy, Acts 13:10
as he saw that the city was **f** of idols. Acts 17:16
malice. They are **f** of envy, Rom 1:29
"Their mouth is **f** of curses and Rom 3:14
more will their **f** inclusion mean! Rom 11:12
that you yourselves are **f** of goodness, Rom 15:14
so as not to make **f** use of my right in 1 Cor 9:18
but that with **f** courage now as always Phil 1:20
love, being in **f** accord and of one mind. Phil 2:2
I have received **f** payment, and more. I Phil 4:18
the riches of **f** assurance of Col 2:2
the Holy Spirit and with **f** conviction. 1 Thes 1:5
and deserving of **f** acceptance, 1 Tm 1:15
and deserving of **f** acceptance. 1 Tm 4:9
effective for the **f** knowledge of every Phlm 1:6
to have the **f** assurance of hope Heb 6:11
a true heart in **f** assurance of faith, Heb 10:22
And let steadfastness have its **f** effect, that Jas 1:4
It is a restless evil, **f** of deadly poison. Jas 3:8
to reason, **f** of mercy and good fruits, Jas 3:17
They have eyes **f** of adultery, insatiable 2 Pt 2:14
worked for, but may win a **f** reward. 2 Jn 1:8
was like the sun shining in **f** strength. Rv 1:16
creatures, **f** of eyes in front and behind: Rv 4:6
wings, are **f** of eyes all around and within, Rv 4:8
a harp, and golden bowls **f** of incense, Rv 5:8
the **f** moon became like blood, Rv 6:12
poured **f** strength into the cup of his Rv 14:10
angels seven golden bowls **f** of the wrath Rv 15:7
beast that was **f** of blasphemous names, Rv 17:3
a golden cup **f** of abominations and Rv 17:4
had the seven bowls **f** of the seven last Rv 21:9

FULLERS' (1)
he is like a refiner's fire and like **f** soap. Mal 3:2

FULLNESS (18)
to offer from the **f** of your harvest and Ex 22:29
floor, and as the **f** of the winepress. Nm 18:27
of the earth and its **f** and the favor of Dt 33:16
In the **f** of his sufficiency he will be in Jb 20:22
of life; in your presence there is **f** of joy; Ps 16:11
The earth is the LORD'S and the **f** thereof, Ps 24:1
tell you, for the world and its **f** are mine. Ps 50:12
And from his **f** we have all received, Jn 1:16
until the **f** of the Gentiles has come Rom 11:25
I will come in the **f** of the blessing of Rom 15:29
earth is the Lord's, and the **f** thereof." 1 Cor 10:26
But when the **f** of time had come, God Gal 4:4
as a plan for the **f** of time, to unite all Eph 1:10
body, the **f** of him who fills all in all. Eph 1:23
you may be filled with all the **f** of God. Eph 3:19
measure of the stature of the **f** of Christ, Eph 4:13
For in him all the **f** of God was pleased Col 1:19
in him the whole **f** of deity dwells bodily, Col 2:9

FULLY (25)
different spirit and has followed me **f**, Nm 14:24
of your husband has been **f** told to me, Ru 2:11
and that all Israel **f** expected me to 1 Kgs 2:15
of the children of man is **f** set to do evil. Eccl 8:11
they are consumed like stubble **f** dried. Na 1:10
everyone when he is **f** trained will be like Lk 6:40
but when they became **f** awake they saw Lk 9:32
When a strong man, **f** armed, guards Lk 11:21
over and could not **f** straighten herself. Lk 13:11
this feast, for my time has not yet **f** come." Jn 7:8
f convinced that God was able to do Rom 4:21
upon the earth **f** and without delay." Rom 9:28
Each one should be **f** convinced in his Rom 14:5
then I shall know **f**, even as I have 1 Cor 13:12
fully, even as I have been **f** known. 1 Cor 13:12
and I hope you will **f** acknowledge— 2 Cor 1:13
worthy of the Lord, **f** pleasing to him, Col 1:10
you, to make the word of God **f** known, Col 1:25
may stand mature and **f** assured in all Col 4:12
you yourselves are **f** aware that the 1 Thes 5:2
message might be **f** proclaimed and 2 Tm 4:17
sin when it is **f** grown brings forth Jas 1:15
set your hope **f** on the grace that will be 1 Pt 1:13
you, although you once **f** knew it, Jude 1:5
for the harvest of the earth is **f** ripe." Rv 14:15

FUNCTION (1)
members do not all have the same **f**, Rom 12:4

FURIOUS (8)
For jealousy makes a man **f**, and he Prv 6:34
in **f** anger and a flame of devouring fire, Is 30:30
the nations, and **f** against all their host; Is 34:2
and with **f** rebukes—I am the LORD, Ezk 5:15
of this the king was angry and very **f**, Dn 2:12
Nebuchadnezzar in **f** rage commanded Dn 3:13
been tricked by the wise men, became **f**, Mt 2:16
the dragon became **f** with the woman Rv 12:17

FURIOUSLY (1)
the son of Nimshi, for he drives **f**." 2 Kgs 9:20

FURNACE (27)
the land went up like the smoke of a **f**. Gn 19:28
you and brought you out of the iron **f**, Dt 4:20
of Egypt, from the midst of the iron **f**). 1 Kgs 8:51
like silver refined in a **f** on the ground, Ps 12:6
like smoke, and my bones burn like a **f**. Ps 102:3
is for silver, and the **f** is for gold, Prv 17:3
is for silver, and the **f** is for gold, Prv 27:21
is in Zion, and whose **f** is in Jerusalem. Is 31:9
I have tried you in the **f** of affliction. Is 48:10
out of the land of Egypt, from the iron **f**, Jer 11:4
and tin and iron and lead in the **f**; Ezk 22:18
and iron and lead and tin into a **f**, Ezk 22:20
As silver is melted in a **f**, so you shall Ezk 22:22
be cast into a burning fiery **f**." Dn 3:6
shall be cast into a burning fiery **f**. Dn 3:11
be cast into a burning fiery **f**. Dn 3:15
to deliver us from the burning fiery **f**, Dn 3:17
He ordered the **f** heated seven times more Dn 3:19
to cast them into the burning fiery **f**. Dn 3:20
were thrown into the burning fiery **f**. Dn 3:21
order was urgent and the **f** overheated, Dn 3:22
fell bound into the burning fiery **f**. Dn 3:23
near to the door of the burning fiery **f**; Dn 3:26
and throw them into the fiery **f**. In that Mt 13:42
and throw them into the fiery **f**. In that Mt 13:50
like burnished bronze, refined in a **f**, Rv 1:15
rose smoke like the smoke of a great **f**, Rv 9:2

FURNISH (2)
You shall **f** him liberally out of your Dt 15:14
prince's duty to **f** the burnt offerings, Ezk 45:17

FURNISHED (2)
you a large upper room **f** and ready; Mk 14:15
he will show you a large upper room **f**; Lk 22:12

FURNISHINGS (7)
seat that is on it, and all the **f** of the tent, Ex 31:7
of the testimony, and over all its **f**, Nm 1:50
are to carry the tabernacle and all its **f**, Nm 1:50
They shall guard all the **f** of the tent of Nm 3:8
and all the **f** of the sanctuary, Nm 4:15
it with all its **f** and had anointed and Nm 7:1
and on all the **f** and on the persons Nm 19:18

FURNITURE (4)
pattern of the tabernacle, and of all its **f**, Ex 25:9
is in it, and consecrate it and all its **f**, Ex 40:9
were appointed over the **f** and over all 1 Chr 9:29
all the household **f** of Tobiah out Neh 13:8

FURROW (1)
Can you bind him in the **f** with ropes, Jb 39:10

FURROW'S (1)
as it were half a **f** length in an acre of 1 Sm 14:14

FURROWS (5)
against me and its **f** have wept together, Jb 31:38
You water its **f** abundantly, settling its Ps 65:10
upon my back; they made long their **f**." Ps 129:3
poisonous weeds in the **f** of the field. Hos 10:4
like stone heaps on the **f** of the field. Hos 12:11

FURTHER (22)
the officers shall speak **f** to the people, Dt 20:8
go on from there **f** and come to the 1 Sm 10:3
What **f** right have I, then, to cry to 2 Sm 19:28
the king, and **f** reported to the king, 2 Chr 34:16
granted you. And what **f** is your request? Est 9:12
God has no need to consider a man **f**, Jb 34:23
answer; twice, but I will proceed no **f**." Jb 40:5
do not **f** their evil plot or they will be Ps 140:8
and provoke me still **f** to anger? Ezk 8:17
But she carried her whoring **f**. She saw Ezk 23:14
What **f** witnesses do we need? Mt 26:65
dead. Why trouble the Teacher any **f**?" Mk 5:35
said, "What **f** witnesses do we need? Mk 14:63
But Jesus made no **f** answer, so that Mk 15:5
said, "What **f** testimony do we need? Lk 22:71
it may spread no **f** among the people, Acts 4:17
And when they had **f** threatened them, Acts 4:21
But if you seek anything **f**, it shall be Acts 19:39
But, to detain you no **f**, I beg you in Acts 24:4
but that we would be **f** clothed, 2 Cor 5:4
what **f** need would there have been for Heb 7:11
beg that no **f** messages be spoken Heb 12:19

FURTHERED (1)
angry but a little, they **f** the disaster. Zec 1:15

FURTHERMORE (3)
F, the LORD was angry with me because Dt 4:21
"**F**, the LORD said to me, 'I have seen this Dt 9:13
in the ways of the LORD. And **f**, 2 Chr 17:6

FURY (33)
until your brother's **f** turns away— Gn 27:44
your adversaries; you send out your **f**; Ex 15:7
then I will walk contrary to you in **f**, Lv 26:28
land in anger and **f** and great wrath, Dt 29:28
homage to him, Haman was filled with **f**. Est 3:5
in his wrath, and terrify them in his **f**, Ps 2:5
yourself up against the **f** of my enemies; Ps 7:6
calamity, and the rod of his **f** will fail. Prv 22:8
my anger; the staff in their hands is my **f**! Is 10:5
a very little while my **f** will come to an Is 10:25
has ceased, the insolent **f** ceased! Is 14:4
a little while until the **f** has passed by. Is 26:20
his lips are full of **f**, and his tongue is Is 30:27
the whirlwind, to render his anger in **f**, Is 66:15
in anger and in **f** and in great wrath. Jer 21:5
of Zion; he has poured out his **f** like fire. Lam 2:4
I will vent my **f** upon them and satisfy Ezk 5:13
—when I spend my **f** upon them. Ezk 5:13
judgments on you in anger and **f**, Ezk 5:15
Thus I will spend my **f** upon them. Ezk 6:12
But the vine was plucked up in **f**, cast Ezk 19:12
clap my hands, and I will satisfy my **f**; Ezk 21:17
you, that they may deal with you in **f**. Ezk 23:25
till I have satisfied my **f** upon you. Ezk 24:13
Then Nebuchadnezzar was filled with **f**, Dn 3:19
go out with great **f** to destroy and Dn 11:44
You marched through the earth in **f**; Hab 3:12
were filled with **f** and discussed with Lk 6:11
and in raging **f** against them I Acts 26:11
there will be wrath and **f**. Rom 2:8
and a **f** of fire that will consume the Heb 10:27
the cup of the wine of the **f** of his wrath. Rv 16:19
the winepress of the **f** of the wrath of Rv 19:15

FUTILE (4)
but they became **f** in their thinking, Rom 1:21
thoughts of the wise, that they are **f**." 1 Cor 3:20
your faith is **f** and you are still in 1 Cor 15:17
ransomed from the **f** ways inherited 1 Pt 1:18

FUTILITY (2)
For the creation was subjected to **f**, not Rom 8:20
the Gentiles do, in the **f** of their minds. Eph 4:17

FUTURE (14)
that is with you, for all **f** generations: Gn 9:12
and have shown me **f** generations, 1 Chr 17:17
for there is a **f** for the man of peace. Ps 37:37
the **f** of the wicked shall be cut off. Ps 37:38
that you may gain wisdom in the **f**. Prv 19:20
Surely there is a **f**, and your hope will Prv 23:18

if you find it, there will be a **f**, and your Prv 24:14
for the evil man has no **f**; the lamp of Prv 24:20
not for evil, to give you a **f** and a hope. Jer 29:11
There is hope for your **f**, declares the Jer 31:17
her skirts; she took no thought of her **f**; Lam 1:9
or the present or the **f**—all are yours, 1 Cor 3:22
as a good foundation for the **f**, 1 Tm 6:19
faith Isaac invoked **f** blessings on Heb 11:20

G

GAAL (9)
And **G** the son of Ebed moved into Jgs 9:26
And **G** the son of Ebed said, "Who is Jgs 9:28
heard the words of **G** the son of Ebed, Jgs 9:30
G the son of Ebed and his relatives have Jgs 9:31
And **G** the son of Ebed went out and Jgs 9:35
And when **G** saw the people, he said to Jgs 9:36
G spoke again and said, "Look, people Jgs 9:37
And **G** went out at the head of the leaders Jgs 9:39
and Zebul drove out **G** and his relatives, Jgs 9:41

GAASH (4)
Ephraim, north of the mountain of **G**. Jos 24:30
of Ephraim, north of the mountain of **G**. Jgs 2:9
Pirathon, Hiddai of the brooks of **G**, 2 Sm 23:30
Hurai of the brooks of **G**, Abiel the 1 Chr 11:32

GABBATHA (1)
Stone Pavement, and in Aramaic **G**. Jn 19:13

GABRIEL (4)
"**G**, make this man understand the Dn 8:16
I was speaking in prayer, the man **G**, Dn 9:21
And the angel answered him, "I am **G**, Lk 1:19
sixth month the angel **G** was sent from Lk 1:26

GAD (70)
has come!" so she called his name **G**. Gn 30:11
of Zilpah, Leah's servant: **G** and Asher. Gn 35:26
The sons of **G**: Ziphion, Haggi, Shuni, Gn 46:16
"Raiders shall raid **G**, but he shall raid Gn 49:19
Dan and Naphtali, **G** and Asher. Ex 1:4
from **G**, Eliasaph the son of Deuel; Nm 1:14
Of the people of **G**, their generations, by Nm 1:24
listed of the tribe of **G** were 45,650. Nm 1:25
Then the tribe of **G**, the chief of the Nm 2:14
of the people of **G** being Eliasaph the Nm 2:14
of Deuel, the chief of the people of **G**: Nm 7:42
of the people of **G** was Eliasaph the Nm 10:20
from the tribe of **G**, Geuel the son of Nm 13:15
The sons of **G** according to their Nm 26:15
of the sons of **G** as they were listed, Nm 26:18
and the people of **G** had a very great Nm 32:1
So the people of **G** and the people of Nm 32:2
said to the people of **G** and to the people Nm 32:6
And the people of **G** and the people of Nm 32:25
"If the people of **G** and the people of Nm 32:29
And the people of **G** and the people of Nm 32:31
to the people of **G** and to the people of Nm 32:33
And the people of **G** built Dibon, Nm 32:34
of the people of **G** by their fathers' Nm 34:14
Reuben, **G**, Asher, Zebulun, Dan, and Dt 27:13
And of **G** he said, "Blessed be he who Dt 33:20
he said, "Blessed be he who enlarges **G**! Dt 33:20
G crouches like a lion; he tears off arm Dt 33:20
and the sons of **G** and the half-tribe of Jos 4:12
an inheritance also to the tribe of **G**, Jos 13:24
to the tribe of Gad, to the people of **G**, Jos 13:24
of the people of **G** according to their Jos 13:28
And **G** and Reuben and half the tribe of Jos 18:7
Ramoth in Gilead, from the tribe of **G**, Jos 20:8
from the tribe of Reuben, the tribe of **G**, Jos 21:7
and out of the tribe of **G**, Ramoth in Jos 21:38
and the people of **G** and the half-tribe of Jos 22:9
and the people of **G** and the half-tribe of Jos 22:10
and the people of **G** and the half-tribe of Jos 22:11
and the people of **G** and the half-tribe of Jos 22:13
to the people of Reuben, the people of **G**, Jos 22:15
the people of Reuben, the people of **G**, Jos 22:21
you people of Reuben and people of **G**. Jos 22:25
and the people of **G** and the people of Jos 22:30
and the people of **G** and the people of Jos 22:31
and the people of **G** in the land of Jos 22:32
Reuben and the people of **G** were settled. Jos 22:33
and the people of **G** called the altar Jos 22:34
the Jordan to the land of **G** and Gilead. 1 Sm 13:7
Then the prophet **G** said to David, "Do 1 Sm 22:5
of the valley, toward **G** and on to Jazer. 2 Sm 24:5
of the LORD came to the prophet **G**, 2 Sm 24:11
So **G** came to David and told him, 2 Sm 24:13
Then David said to **G**, "I am in great 2 Sm 24:14
And **G** came that day to David and 2 Sm 24:18
Benjamin, Naphtali, **G**, and Asher. 1 Chr 2:2
The sons of **G** lived over against 1 Chr 5:11
the tribes of Reuben, **G** and Zebulun. 1 Chr 6:63
and out of the tribe of **G**: Ramoth in 1 Chr 6:80
And the LORD spoke to **G**, David's seer, 1 Chr 21:9
So **G** came to David and said to him, 1 Chr 21:11
Then David said to **G**, "I am in great 1 Chr 21:13
LORD had commanded **G** to say to 1 Chr 21:18
and in the Chronicles of **G** the seer, 1 Chr 29:29
of David and of **G** the king's seer 2 Chr 29:25
Why then has Milcom dispossessed **G**, Jer 49:1
the east side to the west, **G**, one portion. Ezk 48:27
the territory of **G** to the south, Ezk 48:28
4,500 cubits, three gates, the gate of **G**, Ezk 48:34
of Reuben, 12,000 from the tribe of **G**, Rv 7:5

GAD'S (2)
So David went up at **G** word, as the 2 Sm 24:19
So David went up at **G** word, which 1 Chr 21:19

GADARENES (1)
to the other side, to the country of the **G**, Mt 8:28

GADDI (1)
tribe of Manasseh), **G** the son of Susi; Nm 13:11

GADDIEL (1)
tribe of Zebulun, **G** the son of Sodi; Nm 13:10

GADI (2)
the son of **G** came up from 2 Kgs 15:14
the son of **G** began to reign 2 Kgs 15:17

GADITE (1)
son of Nathan of Zobah, Bani the **G**, 2 Sm 23:36

GADITES (15)
Reubenites and the **G** the territory Dt 3:12
the Reubenites and the **G** I gave the Dt 3:16
Reubenites, Ramoth in Gilead for the **G**, Dt 4:43
an inheritance to the Reubenites, the **G**, Dt 29:8
And to the Reubenites, the **G**, and the Jos 1:12
Reubenites and the **G** and the half-tribe Jos 12:6
Reubenites and the **G** received their Jos 13:8
Reubenites and the **G** and the half-tribe Jos 22:1
all the land of Gilead, the **G**, 2 Kgs 10:33
The Reubenites, the **G**, and the 1 Chr 5:18
exile, namely, the Reubenites, the **G**, 1 Chr 5:26
From the **G** there went over to David 1 Chr 12:8
These **G** were officers of the army; 1 Chr 12:14
the Reubenites and **G** and the 1 Chr 12:37
the **G** and the half-tribe of the 1 Chr 26:32

GAHAM (1)
was Reumah, bore Tebah, **G**, Tahash, Gn 22:24

GAHAR (2)
the sons of Giddel, the sons of **G**, the Ezr 2:47
the sons of Giddel, the sons of **G**, Neh 7:49

GAIN (57)
in his ways but turned aside after **g**. 1 Sm 8:3
the Jews hoped to **g** the mastery over Est 9:1
or is it **g** to him if you make your ways Jb 22:3
What could I **g** from the strength of their Jb 30:2
one greedy for **g** curses and renounces Ps 10:3
your testimonies, and not to selfish **g**! Ps 119:36
of everyone who is greedy for unjust **g**; Prv 1:19
for the **g** from her is better than gain Prv 3:14
her is better than **g** from silver and her Prv 3:14
and be attentive, that you may **g** insight, Prv 4:1
leads to life, the **g** of the wicked to sin. Prv 10:16
is greedy for unjust **g** troubles his own Prv 15:27
that you may **g** wisdom in the future. Prv 19:20
and he will **g** knowledge. Prv 19:25
he who hates unjust **g** will prolong his Prv 28:16
in her, and he will have no lack of **g**. Prv 31:11
What does man **g** by all the toil at Eccl 1:3
that there is more **g** in wisdom than in Eccl 2:13
as there is more **g** in light than in Eccl 2:13
What **g** has the worker from his toil? Eccl 3:9
But this is **g** for a land in every way: a Eccl 5:9
and what **g** is there to him who toils Eccl 5:16
who despises the **g** of oppressions, Is 33:15
to their own way, each to his own **g**, Is 56:11
the iniquity of his unjust **g** I was angry, Is 57:17
now what do you **g** by going to Egypt Jer 2:18
Or what do you **g** by going to Assyria to Jer 2:18
of them, everyone is greedy for unjust **g**; Jer 6:13
greatest everyone is greedy for unjust **g**; Jer 8:10
and heart only for your dishonest **g**, Jer 22:17
profit and make **g** of your neighbors Ezk 22:12
hand at the dishonest **g** that you have Ezk 22:13
destroying lives to get dishonest **g**. Ezk 22:27
they act; their heart is set on their **g**. Ezk 33:31
certainty that you are trying to **g** time, Dn 2:8
and shall devote their **g** to the LORD, their Mi 4:13
to him who gets evil **g** for his house, Hab 2:9
it profit a man to **g** the whole world and Mk 8:36
your endurance you will **g** your lives. Lk 21:19
owners much **g** by fortune-telling. Acts 16:16
saw that their hope of **g** was gone, Acts 16:19
But if you can **g** your freedom, avail 1 Cor 7:21
but have not love, I **g** nothing. 1 Cor 13:3
What do I **g** if, humanly speaking, I 1 Cor 15:32
to me to live is Christ, and to die is **g**. Phil 1:21
But whatever **g** I had, I counted as loss Phil 3:7
as rubbish, in order that I may **g** Christ Phil 3:8
much wine, not greedy for dishonest **g**. 1 Tm 3:8
well as deacons **g** a good standing 1 Tm 3:13
that godliness is a means of **g**. 1 Tm 6:5
Now there is great **g** in godliness with 1 Tm 6:6
or a drunkard or violent or greedy for **g**, Ti 1:7
teaching for shameful **g** what they ought Ti 1:11
you; not for shameful **g**, but eagerly; 1 Pt 5:2
of Beor, who loved **g** from wrongdoing, 2 Pt 2:15
for the sake of **g** to Balaam's error and Jude 1:11
showing favoritism to **g** advantage. Jude 1:16

GAINED (23)
and **g** more and more until he became Gn 26:13
our father's he has **g** all this wealth." Gn 31:1
all his property that he had **g**, Gn 31:18
which they had **g** in the land of Canaan, Gn 46:6
And they **g** possessions in it, and were Gn 47:27
people of Israel has **g** his inheritance. Nm 32:18
"The men **g** an advantage over us 2 Sm 11:23
the Jews **g** mastery over those who hated Est 9:1
Treasures **g** by wickedness do not Prv 10:2
Wealth **g** hastily will dwindle, but Prv 13:11
of glory; it is **g** in a righteous life. Prv 16:31
Bread **g** by deceit is sweet to a man, Prv 20:17
An inheritance **g** hastily in the Prv 20:21
was nothing to be **g** under the sun. Eccl 2:11
the abundance they have **g** and what they Is 15:7
the riches they **g** have perished. Jer 48:36
What you would have **g** from me is Mt 15:5
listens to you, you have **g** your brother. Mt 18:15
Whatever you would have **g** from me is Mk 7:11
what they had **g** by doing business. Lk 19:15
then shall we say was **g** by Abraham, Rom 4:1
Though there is nothing to be **g** by it, 2 Cor 12:1
of these wares, who **g** wealth from her, Rv 18:15

GAINING (3)
our iniquities and **g** insight by your Dn 9:13
when Pilate saw that he was **g** nothing, Mt 27:24
"You see that you are **g** nothing. Jn 12:19

GAINS (5)
who listens to reproof **g** intelligence. Prv 15:32
man is instructed, he **g** knowledge. Prv 21:11
give all the wealth of the city, all its **g**, Jer 20:5
a man if he **g** the whole world and Mt 16:26
profit a man if he **g** the whole world and Lk 9:25

GAIUS (5)
with them **G** and Aristarchus, Acts 19:29
and **G** of Derbe, and Timothy; Acts 20:4
G, who is host to me and to the whole Rom 16:23
none of you except Crispus and **G**, 1 Cor 1:14
The elder to the beloved **G**, whom I love 3 Jn 1:1

GALAL (3)
G and Mattaniah the son of Mica, 1 Chr 9:15
the son of Shemaiah, son of **G**, 1 Chr 9:16
Abda the son of Shammua, son of **G**, Neh 11:17

GALATIA (6)
through the region of Phrygia and **G**, Acts 16:6
through the region of **G** and Phrygia, Acts 18:23
as I directed the churches of **G**, so you 1 Cor 16:1
who are with me, To the churches of **G**: Gal 1:2
Crescens has gone to **G**, Titus to 2 Tm 4:10
the dispersion in Pontus, **G**, Cappadocia, 1 Pt 1:1

GALATIANS (1)
O foolish **G**! Who has bewitched you? It Gal 3:1

GALBANUM (1)
sweet spices, stacte, and onycha, and **g**, Ex 30:34

GALE (1)
its winter fruit when shaken by a **g**. Rv 6:13

GALEED (2)
Jegar-sahadutha, but Jacob called it **G**. Gn 31:47
me today." Therefore he named it **G**, Gn 31:48

GALILEAN (5)
said, "You also were with Jesus the **G**." Mt 26:69
you are one of them, for you are a **G**." Mk 14:70
also was with him, for he too is a **G**." Lk 22:59
this, he asked whether the man was a **G**. Lk 23:6
After him Judas the **G** rose up in the Acts 5:37

GALILEANS (5)
told him about the **G** whose blood Pilate Lk 13:1
think that these **G** were worse sinners Lk 13:2
were worse sinners than all the other **G**, Lk 13:2
he came to Galilee, the **G** welcomed him, Jn 4:45
"Are not all these who are speaking **G**? Acts 2:7

GALILEE (69)
one; the king of Goiim in **G**, one; Jos 12:23

set apart Kedesh in **G** in the hill country Jos 20:7
Kedesh in **G** with its pasturelands, Jos 21:32
Hiram twenty cities in the land of **G**. 1 Kgs 9:11
Kedesh, Hazor, Gilead, and **G**, 2 Kgs 15:29
Kedesh in **G** with its pasturelands, 1 Chr 6:76
land beyond the Jordan, **G** of the nations. Is 9:1
a dream he withdrew to the district of **G**. Mt 2:22
Then Jesus came from **G** to the Jordan to Mt 3:13
had been arrested, he withdrew into **G**. Mt 4:12
beyond the Jordan, **G** of the Gentiles— Mt 4:15
While walking by the Sea of **G**, he saw Mt 4:18
And he went throughout all **G**, teaching Mt 4:23
followed him from **G** and the Decapolis, Mt 4:25
there and walked beside the Sea of **G**. Mt 15:29
As they were gathering in **G**, Jesus said Mt 17:22
he went away from **G** and entered the Mt 19:1
the prophet Jesus, from Nazareth of **G**." Mt 21:11
am raised up, I will go before you to **G**." Mt 26:32
who had followed Jesus from **G**, Mt 27:55
and behold, he is going before you to **G**; Mt 28:7
go and tell my brothers to go to **G**, and Mt 28:10
Now the eleven disciples went to **G**, to Mt 28:16
from Nazareth of **G** and was baptized Mk 1:9
John was arrested, Jesus came into **G**, Mk 1:14
Passing alongside the Sea of **G**, he saw Mk 1:16
all the surrounding region of **G**. Mk 1:28
And he went throughout all **G**, Mk 1:39
a great crowd followed, from **G** and Judea Mk 3:7
commanders and the leading men of **G**. Mk 6:21
and went through Sidon to the Sea of **G**, Mk 7:31
on from there and passed through **G**. Mk 9:30
raised up, I will go before you to **G**." Mk 14:28
When he was in **G**, they followed him Mk 15:41
Peter that he is going before you to **G**. Mk 16:7
from God to a city of **G** named Nazareth, Lk 1:26
And Joseph also went up from **G**, from the Lk 2:4
Law of the Lord, they returned into **G**, Lk 2:39
of Judea, and Herod being tetrarch of **G**, Lk 3:1
returned in the power of the Spirit to **G**, Lk 4:14
he went down to Capernaum, a city of **G**. Lk 4:31
from every village of **G** and Judea and Lk 5:17
of the Gerasenes, which is opposite **G**. Lk 8:26
passing along between Samaria and **G**. Lk 17:11
all Judea, from **G** even to this place." Lk 23:5
had followed him from **G** stood at a Lk 23:49
with him from **G** followed and saw Lk 23:55
how he told you, while he was still in **G**, Lk 24:6
The next day Jesus decided to go to **G**. He Jn 1:43
day there was a wedding at Cana in **G**, Jn 2:1
first of his signs, Jesus did at Cana in **G**, Jn 2:11
he left Judea and departed again for **G**. Jn 4:3
After the two days he departed for **G**. Jn 4:43
So when he came to **G**, the Galileans Jn 4:45
So he came again to Cana in **G**, where he Jn 4:46
that Jesus had come from Judea to **G**, Jn 4:47
did when he had come from Judea to **G**. Jn 4:54
went away to the other side of the Sea of **G**, Jn 6:1
After this Jesus went about in **G**. He would Jn 7:1
After saying this, he remained in **G**. Jn 7:9
some said, "Is the Christ to come from **G**? Jn 7:41
They replied, "Are you from **G** too? Jn 7:52
and see that no prophet arises from **G**." Jn 7:52
to Philip, who was from Bethsaida in **G**, Jn 12:21
the Twin), Nathanael of Cana in **G**, Jn 21:2
and said, "Men of **G**, why do you stand Acts 1:11
all Judea and **G** and Samaria had Acts 9:31
beginning from **G** after the baptism Acts 10:37
up with him from **G** to Jerusalem, Acts 13:31

GALL (4)
spare; he pours out my **g** on the ground. Jb 16:13
wanderings, the wormwood and the **g**! Lam 3:19
him wine to drink, mixed with **g**, Mt 27:34
you are in the **g** of bitterness and in Acts 8:23

GALLBLADDER (1)
the glittering point comes out of his **g**; Jb 20:25

GALLERIES (3)
at the back and its **g** on either side, Ezk 41:15
windows and the **g** all around the Ezk 41:16
for the **g** took more away from them Ezk 42:5

GALLERY (2)
was **g** against gallery in three stories. Ezk 42:3
was gallery against **g** in three stories. Ezk 42:3

GALLEY (1)
streams, where no **g** with oars can go, Is 33:21

GALLIM (2)
Palti the son of Laish, who was of **G**. 1 Sm 25:44
Cry aloud, O daughter of **G**! Give Is 10:30

GALLIO (3)
But when **G** was proconsul of Acts 18:12
to open his mouth, **G** said to the Jews, Acts 18:14
But **G** paid no attention to any of this. Acts 18:17

GALLONS (1)
each holding twenty or thirty **g**. Jn 2:6

GALLOPING (3)
loud beat the horses' hoofs with the **g**, Jgs 5:22
hoofs with the galloping, **g** of his steeds. Jgs 5:22
the wheel, **g** horse and bounding chariot! Na 3:2

GALLOWS (9)
so, the men were both hanged on the **g**. Est 2:23
him, "Let a **g** fifty cubits high be made, Est 5:14
pleased Haman, and he had the **g** made. Est 5:14
Mordecai hanged on the **g** that he had Est 6:4
the **g** that Haman has prepared for Est 7:9
hanged Haman on the **g** that he had Est 7:10
and they have hanged him on the **g**, Est 8:7
ten sons of Haman be hanged on the **g**." Est 9:13
and his sons should be hanged on the **g**. Est 9:25

GAMAD (1)
and men of **G** were in your towers. Ezk 27:11

GAMALIEL (7)
from Manasseh, **G** the son of Pedahzur; Nm 1:10
people of Manasseh being **G** the son of Nm 2:20
On the eighth day **G** the son of Nm 7:54
was the offering of **G** the son of Nm 7:59
people of Manasseh was **G** the son of Nm 10:23
a Pharisee in the council named **G**, Acts 5:34
at the feet of **G** according to the strict Acts 22:3

GAME (10)
loved Esau because he ate of his **g**, Gn 25:28
go out to the field and hunt **g** for me, Gn 27:3
to the field to hunt for **g** and bring it, Gn 27:5
'Bring me **g** and prepare for me Gn 27:7
now sit up and eat of my **g**, that your Gn 27:19
eat of my son's **g** and bless you." So Gn 27:25
my father arise and eat of his son's **g**, Gn 27:31
it then that hunted **g** and brought it to Gn 27:33
the poor go out to their toil, seeking **g**; Jb 24:5
is slothful will not roast his **g**, Prv 12:27

GAMUL (1)
to Jachin, the twenty-second to **G**, 1 Chr 24:17

GANGRENE (1)
and their talk will spread like **g**. 2 Tm 2:17

GAPED (1)
Men have **g** at me with their mouth; Jb 16:10

GARBAGE (1)
us scum and **g** among the peoples. Lam 3:45

GARDEN (53)
And the LORD God planted a **g** in Eden, in Gn 2:8
The tree of life was in the midst of the **g**, Gn 2:9
A river flowed out of Eden to water the **g**, Gn 2:10
and put him in the **g** of Eden to work it Gn 2:15
may surely eat of every tree of the **g**, Gn 2:16
'You shall not eat of any tree in the **g**'?" Gn 3:1
may eat of the fruit of the trees in the **g**, Gn 3:2
of the tree that is in the midst of the **g**, Gn 3:3
LORD God walking in the **g** in the cool of Gn 3:8
of the LORD God among the trees of the **g**. Gn 3:8
said, "I heard the sound of you in the **g**, Gn 3:10
sent him out from the **g** of Eden to work Gn 3:23
at the east of the **g** of Eden he placed the Gn 3:24
everywhere like the **g** of the LORD, Gn 13:10
and irrigated it, like a **g** of vegetables. Dt 11:10
that I may have it for a vegetable **g**, 1 Kgs 21:2
and was buried in the **g** of his house, 2 Kgs 21:18
garden of his house, in the **g** of Uzza, 2 Kgs 21:18
buried in his tomb in the **g** of Uzza, 2 Kgs 21:26
the two walls, by the king's **g**, 2 Kgs 25:4
of the Pool of Shelah of the king's **g**, Neh 3:15
in the court of the **g** of the king's palace. Est 1:5
and went into the palace **g**, Est 7:7
returned from the palace **g** to the place Est 7:8
the sun, and his shoots spread over his **g**. Jb 8:16
A **g** locked is my sister, my bride, a Sg 4:12
a **g** fountain, a well of living water, and Sg 4:15
wind! Blow upon my **g**, let its spices flow. Sg 4:16
Let my beloved come to his **g**, and eat its Sg 4:16
I came to my **g**, my sister, my bride, I Sg 5:1
has gone down to his **g** to the beds of Sg 6:2
leaf withers, and like a **g** without water. Is 1:30
like Eden, her desert like the **g** of the LORD; Is 51:3
and you shall be like a watered **g**, like a Is 58:11
and as a **g** causes what is sown in it to Is 61:11
their life shall be like a watered **g**, and Jer 31:12
way of the king's **g** through the gate Jer 39:4
between the two walls, by the king's **g**, Jer 52:7
He has laid waste his booth like a **g**, laid Lam 2:6
You were in Eden, the **g** of God; every Ezk 28:13
The cedars in the **g** of God could not Ezk 31:8
no tree in the **g** of God was its equal in Ezk 31:8
Eden envied it, that were in the **g** of God. Ezk 31:9
has become like the **g** of Eden, Ezk 36:35
The land is like the **g** of Eden before them, Jl 2:3
alone in a forest in the midst of a **g** land; Mi 7:14
than all the **g** plants and becomes Mt 13:32
larger than all the **g** plants and puts out Mk 4:32
that a man took and sowed in his **g**, Lk 13:19
the Kidron Valley, where there was a **g**, Jn 18:1
"Did I not see you in the **g** with him?" Jn 18:26
where he was crucified there was a **g**, Jn 19:41
and in the **g** a new tomb in which no Jn 19:41

GARDENER (1)
seeking?" Supposing him to be the **g**, Jn 20:15

GARDENS (11)
that stretch afar, like **g** beside a river, Nm 24:6
I made myself **g** and parks, and planted Eccl 2:5
spices, to graze in the **g** and to gather lilies. Sg 6:2
O you who dwell in the **g**, with Sg 8:13
shall blush for the **g** that you have Is 1:29
sacrificing in **g** and making offerings on Is 65:3
and purify themselves to go into the **g**, Is 66:17
in them; plant **g** and eat their produce. Jer 29:5
and plant **g** and eat their produce.''" Jer 29:28
your many **g** and your vineyards, your Am 4:9
and they shall make **g** and eat their Am 9:14

GAREB (3)
Ira the Ithrite, **G** the Ithrite, 2 Sm 23:38
Ira the Ithrite, **G** the Ithrite, 1 Chr 11:40
go out farther, straight to the hill **G**, Jer 31:39

GARLAND (2)
they are a graceful **g** for your head and Prv 1:9
She will place on your head a graceful **g**; Prv 4:9

GARLANDS (1)
brought oxen and **g** to the gates and Acts 14:13

GARLIC (1)
melons, the leeks, the onions, and the **g**. Nm 11:5

GARMENT (87)
Then Shem and Japheth took a **g**, laid it Gn 9:23
she caught him by his **g**, saying, "Lie Gn 39:12
me." But he left his **g** in her hand and Gn 39:12
that he had left his **g** in her hand and Gn 39:13
he left his **g** beside me and fled and got Gn 39:15
Then she laid up his **g** by her until his Gn 39:16
he left his **g** beside me and fled out of Gn 39:18
the opening, like the opening in a **g**, Ex 28:32
robe in it was like the opening in a **g**, Ex 39:23
shall put on his linen **g** and put his linen Lv 6:10
when any of its blood is splashed on a **g**, Lv 6:27
an article of wood or a **g** or a skin or a Lv 11:32
there is a case of leprous disease in a **g**, Lv 13:47
garment, whether a woolen or a linen **g**, Lv 13:47
disease is greenish or reddish in the **g**, Lv 13:49
If the disease has spread in the **g**, in the Lv 13:51
And he shall burn the **g**, or the warp or Lv 13:52
if the disease has not spread in the **g**, Lv 13:53
tear it out of the **g** or the skin or the Lv 13:56
Then if it appears again in the **g**, in the Lv 13:57
But the **g**, or the warp or the woof, or Lv 13:58
leprous disease in a **g** of wool or linen, Lv 13:59
for leprous disease in a **g** or in a house, Lv 14:55
And every **g** and every skin on which Lv 15:17
nor shall you wear a **g** of cloth made of Lv 19:19
You shall purify every **g**, every article Nm 31:20
the same with his donkey or with his **g**, Dt 22:3
"A woman shall not wear a man's **g**, nor Dt 22:5
four corners of the **g** with which you Dt 22:12
fatherless, or take a widow's **g** in pledge, Dt 24:17
"Bring the **g** you are wearing and hold it Ru 3:15
Now Joab was wearing a soldier's **g**, 2 Sm 20:8
into the field and threw a **g** over him. 2 Sm 20:12
had dressed himself in a new **g**, 1 Kgs 11:29
hold of the new **g** that was on him, 1 Kgs 11:30
he gathered up his **g** and ran before 1 Kgs 18:46
answered him, "He wore a **g** of hair, 2 Kgs 1:8
"Tie up your **g** and take my staff in 2 Kgs 4:29
of them took his **g** and put it under 2 Kgs 9:13
I tore my **g** and my cloak and pulled hair Ezr 9:3
fasting, with my **g** and my cloak torn, Ezr 9:5
shook out the fold of my **g** and said, Neh 5:13
rotten thing, like a **g** that is moth-eaten. Jb 13:28
With great force my **g** is disfigured; it Jb 30:18
I made clouds its **g** and thick darkness Jb 38:9
seal, and its features stand out like a **g**. Jb 38:14
Who can strip off his outer **g**? Who Jb 41:13
necklace; violence covers them as a **g**. Ps 73:6
the fold of your **g** and destroy them! Ps 74:11
remain; they will all wear out like a **g**. Ps 102:26
covering yourself with light as with a **g**, Ps 104:2
You covered it with the deep as with a **g**; Ps 104:6
it be like a **g** that he wraps around Ps 109:19
Take a man's **g** when he has put up Prv 20:16
one who takes off a **g** on a cold day, Prv 25:20
Take a man's **g** when he has put up Prv 27:13
Who has wrapped up the waters in a **g**? Prv 30:4
I had put off my **g**; how could I put it on? I Sg 5:3

battle tumult and every **g** rolled in blood Is 9:5
Behold, all of them will wear out like a **g**; Is 50:9
smoke, the earth will wear out like a **g**, Is 51:6
For the moth will eat them up like a **g**, Is 51:8
the **g** of praise instead of a faint spirit; Is 61:3
our righteous deeds are like a polluted **g**. Is 64:6
the corner of my **g** over you and Ezk 16:8
hungry and covers the naked with a **g**, Ezk 18:7
hungry and covers the naked with a **g**, Ezk 18:16
in the fold of his **g** and touches with his Hg 2:12
of Israel, covers his **g** with violence, Mal 2:16
Now John wore a **g** of camel's hair and a Mt 3:4
a piece of unshrunk cloth on an old **g**, Mt 9:16
for the patch tears away from the **g**, Mt 9:16
him and touched the fringe of his **g**, Mt 9:20
she said to herself, "If I only touch his **g**, Mt 9:21
might only touch the fringe of his **g**. Mt 14:36
there a man who had no wedding **g**. Mt 22:11
you get in here without a wedding **g**?' Mt 22:12
a piece of unshrunk cloth on an old **g**. Mk 2:21
him in the crowd and touched his **g**. Mk 5:27
might touch even the fringe of his **g**. Mk 6:56
a piece from a new **g** and puts it on an Lk 5:36
a new garment and puts it on an old **g**. Lk 5:36
him and touched the fringe of his **g**, Lk 8:44
that it was the Lord, he put on his outer **g**, Jn 21:7
remain; they will all wear out like a **g**, Heb 1:11
them up, like a **g** they will be changed. Heb 1:12
hating even the **g** stained by the flesh. Jude 1:23

GARMENTS (129)
and for his wife **g** of skins and clothed Gn 3:21
out jewelry of silver and of gold, and **g**, Gn 24:53
Rebekah took the best **g** of Esau her Gn 27:15
the smell of his **g** and blessed him and Gn 27:27
purify yourselves and change your **g**. Gn 35:2
Jacob tore his **g** and put sackcloth Gn 37:34
off her widow's **g** and covered herself Gn 38:14
veil she put on the **g** of her widowhood. Gn 38:19
and clothed him in **g** of fine linen and Gn 41:42
he has washed his **g** in wine and his Gn 49:11
tomorrow, and let them wash their **g** Ex 19:10
the people; and they washed their **g**. Ex 19:14
you shall make holy **g** for Aaron your Ex 28:2
they make Aaron's **g** to consecrate him Ex 28:3
These are the **g** that they shall make: a Ex 28:4
They shall make holy **g** for Aaron your Ex 28:4
Then you shall take the **g**, and put on Ex 29:5
oil, and sprinkle it on Aaron and his **g**, Ex 29:21
on his sons and his sons' **g** with him. Ex 29:21
with him. He and his **g** shall be holy, Ex 29:21
and his sons and his sons' **g** with him. Ex 29:21
"The holy **g** of Aaron shall be for his Ex 29:29
and the finely worked **g**, the holy Ex 31:10
the holy **g** for Aaron the priest and the Ex 31:10
Aaron the priest and the **g** of his sons, Ex 31:10
the finely worked **g** for ministering in Ex 35:19
Place, the holy **g** for Aaron the priest, Ex 35:19
Aaron the priest, and the **g** of his sons, Ex 35:19
for all its service, and for the holy **g**. Ex 35:21
scarlet yarns they made finely woven **g**, Ex 39:1
They made the holy **g** for Aaron, as the Ex 39:1
the finely worked **g** for ministering in Ex 39:41
Place, the holy **g** for Aaron the priest, Ex 39:41
and the **g** of his sons for their service as Ex 39:41
and put on Aaron the holy **g**. And you Ex 40:13
he shall take off his **g** and put on other Lv 6:11
and put on other **g** and carry the ashes Lv 6:11
and the **g** and the anointing oil and the Lv 8:2
and sprinkled it on Aaron and his **g**, Lv 8:30
and also on his sons and his sons' **g**. Lv 8:30
So he consecrated Aaron and his **g**, and Lv 8:30
and his sons and his sons' **g** with him. Lv 8:30
the linen turban; these are the holy **g**. Lv 16:4
shall take off the linen **g** that he put on Lv 16:23
and put on his **g** and come out and Lv 16:24
atonement, wearing the holy linen **g**. Lv 16:32
has been consecrated to wear the **g**, Lv 21:10
corners of their **g** throughout their Nm 15:38
strip Aaron of his **g** and put them on Nm 20:26
stripped Aaron of his **g** and put them Nm 20:28
And these **g** and sandals of ours are Jos 9:13
pendants and the purple **g** worn by the Jgs 8:26
you thirty linen **g** and thirty changes Jgs 14:12
me thirty linen **g** and thirty changes Jgs 14:13
spoil and gave the **g** to those who had Jgs 14:19
the donkeys, the camels, and the **g**, 1 Sm 27:9
himself and put on other **g** and went, 1 Sm 28:8
each and cut off their **g** in the middle, 2 Sm 10:4
arose and tore his **g** and lay on the 2 Sm 13:31
who were standing by tore their **g**. 2 Sm 13:31
a mourner and put on mourning **g**. 2 Sm 14:2
articles of silver and gold, **g**, myrrh, 1 Kgs 10:25
a talent of silver and two festal **g**.'" 2 Kgs 5:22
of silver in two bags, with two festal **g**, 2 Kgs 5:23
Was it a time to accept money and **g**, 2 Kgs 5:26
was littered with **g** and equipment 2 Kgs 7:15
and said to him, "Tie up your **g**, 2 Kgs 9:1
So Jehoiachin put off his prison **g**. 2 Kgs 25:29
and cut off their **g** in the middle, 1 Chr 19:4
of silver and of gold, **g**, myrrh, 2 Chr 9:24
5,000 minas of silver, and 100 priests' **g**. Ezr 2:69
30 priests' **g** and 500 minas of silver. Neh 7:70
2,000 minas of silver, and 67 priests' **g**. Neh 7:72
She sent **g** to clothe Mordecai, so that he Est 4:4
you whose **g** are hot when the earth is Jb 37:17
they divide my **g** among them, and for Ps 22:18
on the day of your power, in holy **g**; Ps 110:3
She makes linen **g** and sells them; she Prv 31:24
Let your **g** be always white. Let not oil Eccl 9:8
the fragrance of your **g** is like the Sg 4:11
the mirrors, the linen **g**, the turbans, and Is 3:23
put on your beautiful **g**, O Jerusalem, the Is 52:1
he put on **g** of vengeance for clothing, Is 59:17
has clothed me with the **g** of salvation; Is 61:10
from Edom, in crimsoned **g** from Bozrah, Is 63:1
and your **g** like his who treads in the Is 63:2
their lifeblood spattered on my **g**, and Is 63:3
was afraid, nor did they tear their **g**. Jer 36:24
So Jehoiachin put off his prison **g**. And Jer 52:33
that no one was able to touch their **g**. Lam 4:14
took some of your **g** and made for Ezk 16:16
took your embroidered **g** to cover Ezk 16:18
and strip off their embroidered **g**. Ezk 26:16
these traded with you in choice **g**, Ezk 27:24
laying there the **g** in which they Ezk 42:14
shall put on other **g** before they go Ezk 42:14
inner court, they shall wear linen **g**. Ezk 44:17
shall put off the **g** in which they have Ezk 44:19
And they shall put on other **g**, lest they Ezk 44:19
holiness to the people with their **g**. Ezk 44:19
tunics, their hats, and their other **g**, Dn 3:21
hearts and not your **g**." Return to the Jl 2:13
beside every altar on **g** taken in pledge, Am 2:8
before the angel, clothed with filthy **g**. Zec 3:3
"Remove the filthy **g** from him." And to Zec 3:4
on his head and clothed him with **g**. Zec 3:5
gold, silver, and **g** in great abundance. Zec 14:14
they divided his **g** among them by Mt 27:35
For she said, "If I touch even his **g**, I will Mk 5:28
crowd and said, "Who touched my **g**?" Mk 5:30
And the high priest tore his **g** and said, Mk 14:63
him and divided his **g** among them, Mk 15:24
do." And they cast lots to divide his **g**. Lk 23:34
He laid aside his outer **g**, and taking a Jn 13:4
put on his outer **g** and resumed his Jn 13:12
they took his **g** and divided them into Jn 19:23
says, "They divided my **g** among them, Jn 19:24
witnesses laid down their **g** at the feet Acts 7:58
tunics and other **g** that Dorcas made Acts 9:39
they tore their **g** and rushed out into Acts 14:14
magistrates tore the **g** off them and Acts 16:22
he shook out his **g** and said to them, Acts 18:6
and watching over the **g** of those who Acts 22:20
have rotted and your **g** are moth-eaten. Jas 5:2
Sardis, people who have not soiled their **g**, Rv 3:4
conquers will be clothed thus in white **g**, Rv 3:5
and white **g** so that you may clothe Rv 3:18
twenty-four elders, clothed in white **g**, Rv 4:4
one who stays awake, keeping his **g** on, Rv 16:15

GARMITE (1)
of Keilah the **G** and Eshtemoa the 1 Chr 4:19

GARNER (1)
but those who **g** it shall eat it and praise Is 62:9

GARRISON (12)
where there is a **g** of the Philistines. 1 Sm 10:5
Jonathan defeated the **g** of the 1 Sm 13:3
had defeated the **g** of the Philistines, 1 Sm 13:4
And the **g** of the Philistines went out 1 Sm 13:23
over to the Philistine **g** on the other 1 Sm 14:1
sought to go over to the Philistine **g**, 1 Sm 14:4
over to the **g** of these uncircumcised. 1 Sm 14:6
themselves to the **g** of the Philistines. 1 Sm 14:11
the men of the **g** hailed Jonathan and 1 Sm 14:12
The **g** and even the raiders trembled, 1 Sm 14:15
and the **g** of the Philistines was then 2 Sm 23:14
and the **g** of the Philistines was then 1 Chr 11:16

GARRISONS (6)
Then David put **g** in Aram of 2 Sm 8:6
Then he put **g** in Edom; throughout 2 Sm 8:14
throughout all Edom he put **g**, and all 2 Sm 8:14
Then David put **g** in Syria of 1 Chr 18:6
Then he put **g** in Edom, and all the 1 Chr 18:13
cities of Judah and set **g** in the land of 2 Chr 17:2

GASH (2)
valley, how long will you **g** yourselves? Jer 47:5
for grain and wine they **g** themselves; Hos 7:14

GASHED (1)
their clothes torn, and their bodies **g**, Jer 41:5

GASHES (1)
On all the hands are **g**, and around the Jer 48:37

GASP (1)
like a woman in labor; I will **g** and pant. Is 42:14

GASPING (1)
cry of the daughter of Zion **g** for breath, Jer 4:31

GATAM (3)
Teman, Omar, Zepho, **G**, and Kenaz. Gn 36:11
Korah, **G**, and Amalek; these are the Gn 36:16
Teman, Omar, Zepho, **G**, Kenaz, and 1 Chr 1:36

GATE (264)
and Lot was sitting in the **g** of Sodom. Gn 19:1
shall possess the **g** of his enemies, Gn 22:17
of all who went in at the **g** of his city, Gn 23:10
all who went in at the **g** of his city. Gn 23:18
offspring possess the **g** of those who Gn 24:60
of God, and this is the **g** of heaven." Gn 28:17
Shechem came to the **g** of their city Gn 34:20
went out of the **g** of his city listened Gn 34:24
all who went out of the **g** of his city. Gn 34:24
one side of the **g** shall be fifteen cubits, Ex 27:14
For the **g** of the court there shall be a Ex 27:16
Moses stood in the **g** of the camp and Ex 32:26
to and fro from **g** to gate throughout Ex 32:27
from gate to **g** throughout the camp, Ex 32:27
and the screen for the **g** of the court; Ex 35:17
for one side of the **g** were fifteen cubits, Ex 38:14
On both sides of the **g** of the court were Ex 38:15
the screen for the **g** of the court was Ex 38:18
and the bases of the **g** of the court, Ex 38:31
and the screen for the **g** of the court, Ex 39:40
hang up the screen for the **g** of the court. Ex 40:8
set up the screen of the **g** of the court. Ex 40:33
the entrance of the **g** of the court that Nm 4:26
of his city at the **g** of the place where he Dt 21:19
to the elders of the city in the **g**. Dt 22:15
them both out to the **g** of that city, Dt 22:24
shall go up to the **g** to the elders and say, Dt 25:7
And when the **g** was about to be closed at Jos 2:5
And the **g** was shut as soon as the Jos 2:7
chased them before the **g** as far as Jos 7:5
at the entrance of the **g** of the city and Jos 8:29
at the entrance of the **g** of the city and Jos 20:4
stood in the entrance of the **g** of the city, Jgs 9:35
fell wounded, up to the entrance of the **g**. Jgs 9:40
stood at the entrance of the **g** of the city, Jgs 9:44
for him all night at the **g** of the city. Jgs 16:2
of the doors of the **g** of the city and the Jgs 16:3
of war, stood by the entrance of the **g**. Jgs 18:16
the entrance of the **g** with the 600 men Jgs 18:17
had gone up to the **g** and sat down there. Ru 4:1
brothers and from the **g** of his native Ru 4:10
who were at the **g** and the elders said, Ru 4:11
from his seat by the side of the **g**, 1 Sm 4:18
approached Samuel in the **g** and said, 1 Sm 9:18
the doors of the **g** and let his spittle 1 Sm 21:13
the midst of the **g** to speak with him 2 Sm 3:27
in battle array at the entrance of the **g**, 2 Sm 10:8
them back to the entrance of the **g**. 2 Sm 11:23
and stand beside the way of the **g**. 2 Sm 15:2
So the king stood at the side of the **g**, 2 Sm 18:4
up to the roof of the **g** by the wall, 2 Sm 18:24
watchman called to the **g** and said, 2 Sm 18:26
to the chamber over the **g** and wept. 2 Sm 18:33
king arose and took his seat in the **g**. 2 Sm 19:8
is sitting in the **g**." And all the people 2 Sm 19:8
well of Bethlehem that is by the **g**!" 2 Sm 23:15
that was by the **g** and carried and 2 Sm 23:16
when he came to the **g** of the city, 1 Kgs 17:10
at the entrance of the **g** of Samaria, 1 Kgs 22:10
for a shekel, at the **g** of Samaria." 2 Kgs 7:1
were lepers at the entrance to the **g**. 2 Kgs 7:3
he leaned to have charge of the **g**. 2 Kgs 7:17
And the people trampled him in the **g**, 2 Kgs 7:17
time tomorrow in the **g** of Samaria," 2 Kgs 7:18
trampled him in the **g** and he died. 2 Kgs 7:20
And as Jehu entered the **g**, she said, "Is 2 Kgs 9:31
entrance of the **g** until the morning." 2 Kgs 10:8
third being at the **g** Sur and a third 2 Kgs 11:6
a third at the **g** behind the guards) 2 Kgs 11:6
marching through the **g** of the 2 Kgs 11:19
from the Ephraim **G** to the Corner 2 Kgs 14:13
the Ephraim Gate to the Corner **G**. 2 Kgs 14:13
He built the upper **g** of the house of 2 Kgs 15:35
the entrance of the **g** of Joshua the 2 Kgs 23:8
were on one's left at the **g** of the city. 2 Kgs 23:8
the way of the **g** between the two 2 Kgs 25:4
were in the king's **g** on the east side 1 Chr 9:18
well of Bethlehem that is by the **g**!" 1 Chr 11:17
that was by the **g** and took it and 1 Chr 11:18
of Jeduthun were appointed to the **g**. 1 Chr 16:42

at the **g** of Shallecheth on the road 1 Chr 26:16
in their divisions at each **g**, 2 Chr 8:14
at the entrance of the **g** of Samaria, 2 Chr 18:9
one third at the **G** of the Foundation. 2 Chr 23:5
entrance of the horse **g** of the king's 2 Chr 23:15
through the upper **g** to the king's 2 Chr 23:20
and set it outside the **g** of the house of 2 Chr 24:8
from the Ephraim **G** to the Corner 2 Chr 25:23
the Ephraim Gate to the Corner **G**. 2 Chr 25:23
Jerusalem at the Corner **G** and at the 2 Chr 26:9
and at the Valley **G** and at the Angle, 2 Chr 26:9
He built the upper **g** of the house of 2 Chr 27:3
the Levite, keeper of the east **g**, 2 Chr 31:14
in the square at the **g** of the city and 2 Chr 32:6
and for the entrance into the Fish **G**, 2 Chr 33:14
and the gatekeepers were at each **g**. 2 Chr 35:15
night by the Valley **G** to the Dragon Neh 2:13
the Dragon Spring and to the Dung **G**, Neh 2:13
on to the Fountain **G** and to the King's Neh 2:14
back and entered by the Valley **G**, Neh 2:15
the priests, and they built the Sheep **G**. Neh 3:1
The sons of Hassenaah built the Fish **G**. Neh 3:3
Besodeiah repaired the **G** of Yeshanah. Neh 3:6
of Zanoah repaired the Valley **G**. Neh 3:13
cubits of the wall, as far as the Dung **G**. Neh 3:13
Beth-haccherem, repaired the Dung **G**. Neh 3:14
of Mizpah, repaired the Fountain **G**. Neh 3:15
point opposite the Water **G** on the east Neh 3:26
Above the Horse **G** the priests repaired, Neh 3:28
of Shecaniah, the keeper of the East **G**, Neh 3:29
the merchants, opposite the Muster **G**, Neh 3:31
and the Sheep **G** the goldsmiths and Neh 3:32
man into the square before the Water **G**. Neh 8:1
before the Water **G** from early morning Neh 8:3
square at the Water **G** and in the Neh 8:16
and in the square at the **G** of Ephraim. Neh 8:16
the south on the wall to the Dung **G**. Neh 12:31
At the Fountain **G** they went up Neh 12:37
of David, to the Water **G** on the east. Neh 12:37
and above the **G** of Ephraim, and by Neh 12:39
Ephraim, and by the **G** of Yeshanah, Neh 12:39
and by the Fish **G** and the Tower of Neh 12:39
Tower of the Hundred, to the Sheep **G**; Neh 12:39
came to a halt at the **G** of the Guard. Neh 12:39
Mordecai was sitting at the king's **g**. Est 2:19
as Mordecai was sitting at the king's **g**, Est 2:21
were at the king's **g** bowed down and paid Est 3:2
who were at the king's **g** said to Mordecai, Est 3:3
He went up to the entrance of the king's **g**, Est 4:2
to enter the king's **g** clothed in sackcloth. Est 4:2
square of the city in front of the king's **g**, Est 4:6
Haman saw Mordecai in the king's **g**, Est 5:9
Mordecai the Jew sitting at the king's **g**." Est 5:13
the Jew who sits at the king's **g**. Est 6:10
Then Mordecai returned to the king's **g**. Est 6:12
they are crushed in the **g**, and there is no Jb 5:4
When I went out to the **g** of the city, Jb 29:7
because I saw my help in the **g**, Jb 31:21
I am the talk of those who sit in the **g**, Ps 69:12
This is the **g** of the LORD; the righteous Ps 118:20
he speaks with his enemies in the **g**. Ps 127:5
is poor, or crush the afflicted at the **g**, Prv 22:22
in the **g** he does not open his mouth. Prv 24:7
in Heshbon, by the **g** of Bath-rabbim. Sg 7:4
Wail, O **g**; cry out, O city; melt in fear, O Is 14:31
to those who turn back the battle at the **g**. Is 28:6
a snare for him who reproves in the **g**, Is 29:21
"Stand in the **g** of the LORD'S house, and Jer 7:2
"Go and stand in the People's **G**, by Jer 17:19
Hinnom at the entry of the Potsherd **G**, Jer 19:2
in the upper Benjamin **G** of the house of Jer 20:2
the entry of the New **G** of the house of Jer 26:10
the tower of Hananel to the Corner **G**. Jer 31:38
corner of the Horse **G** toward the east, Jer 31:40
entry of the New **G** of the LORD'S house. Jer 36:10
When he was at the Benjamin **G**, a Jer 37:13
the king was sitting in the Benjamin **G**— Jer 38:7
of Babylon came and sat in the middle **g**: Jer 39:3
garden through the **g** between the two Jer 39:4
by the way of a **g** between the two walls, Jer 52:7
The old men have left the city **g**, the Lam 5:14
north, and behold, north of the altar **g**, Ezk 8:5
entrance of the north **g** of the house of Ezk 8:14
came from the direction of the upper **g**, Ezk 9:2
entrance of the east **g** of the house of Ezk 10:19
brought me to the east **g** of the house of Ezk 11:1
'Aha, the **g** of the peoples is broken; Ezk 26:2
and measured the threshold of the **g**, Ezk 40:6
the threshold of the **g** by the vestibule Ezk 40:7
the vestibule of the **g** at the inner end, Ezk 40:7
the vestibule of the **g** was at the inner Ezk 40:9
side rooms on either side of the east **g**. Ezk 40:10
he measured the **g** from the ceiling Ezk 40:13
the front of the **g** at the entrance to Ezk 40:15
vestibule of the **g** was fifty cubits. Ezk 40:15
front of the lower **g** to the outer front Ezk 40:19
As for the **g** that faced toward the Ezk 40:20
of the same size as those of the first **g**. Ezk 40:21
as those of the **g** that faced toward the Ezk 40:22
And opposite the **g** on the north, as on Ezk 40:23
on the east, was a **g** to the inner court. Ezk 40:23
And he measured from **g** to gate, a Ezk 40:23
And he measured from gate to **g**, a Ezk 40:23
behold, there was a **g** on the south. Ezk 40:24
And there was a **g** on the south of the Ezk 40:27
he measured from **g** to gate toward Ezk 40:27
from gate to **g** toward the south, Ezk 40:27
the inner court through the south **g**, Ezk 40:28
gate, and he measured the south **g**. Ezk 40:28
the east side, and he measured the **g**. Ezk 40:32
Then he brought me to the north **g**, Ezk 40:35
with its door in the vestibule of the **g**, Ezk 40:38
the vestibule of the **g** were two tables Ezk 40:39
goes up to the entrance of the north **g**, Ezk 40:40
the vestibule of the **g** were two tables. Ezk 40:40
tables were on either side of the **g**, Ezk 40:41
at the side of the north **g** facing south, Ezk 40:44
at the side of the south **g** facing north. Ezk 40:44
breadth of the **g** was fourteen cubits, Ezk 40:48
the sidewalls of the **g** were three cubits Ezk 40:48
he led me out by the **g** that faced east, Ezk 42:15
Then he led me to the **g**, the gate facing Ezk 43:1
he led me to the gate, the **g** facing east. Ezk 43:1
entered the temple by the **g** facing east, Ezk 43:4
back to the outer **g** of the sanctuary, Ezk 44:1
said to me, "This **g** shall remain shut; Ezk 44:2
enter by way of the vestibule of the **g**, Ezk 44:3
by way of the north **g** to the front of the Ezk 44:4
the posts of the **g** of the inner court. Ezk 45:19
The **g** of the inner court that faces east Ezk 46:1
by the vestibule of the **g** from outside, Ezk 46:2
shall take his stand by the post of the **g**. Ezk 46:2
shall worship at the threshold of the **g**. Ezk 46:2
but the **g** shall not be shut until Ezk 46:2
the entrance of that **g** before the LORD Ezk 46:3
he shall enter by the vestibule of the **g**, Ezk 46:8
enters by the north **g** to worship shall Ezk 46:9
to worship shall go out by the south **g**, Ezk 46:9
enters by the south **g** shall go out by Ezk 46:9
south gate shall go out by the north **g**: Ezk 46:9
by way of the **g** by which he entered, Ezk 46:9
the **g** facing east shall be opened for Ezk 46:12
he has gone out the **g** shall be shut. Ezk 46:12
which was at the side of the **g**, Ezk 46:19
way of the north **g** and led me around Ezk 47:2
outside to the outer **g** that faces toward Ezk 47:2
three gates, the **g** of Reuben, the gate of Ezk 48:31
the gate of Reuben, the **g** of Judah, Ezk 48:31
the gate of Judah, and the **g** of Levi, Ezk 48:31
cubits, three gates, the **g** of Joseph, Ezk 48:32
the gate of Joseph, the **g** of Benjamin, Ezk 48:32
gate of Benjamin, and the **g** of Dan. Ezk 48:32
measure, three gates, the **g** of Simeon, Ezk 48:33
the gate of Simeon, the **g** of Issachar, Ezk 48:33
gate of Issachar, and the **g** of Zebulun. Ezk 48:33
4,500 cubits, three gates, the **g** of Gad, Ezk 48:34
gates, the gate of Gad, the **g** of Asher, Ezk 48:34
gate of Asher, and the **g** of Naphtali. Ezk 48:34
They hate him who reproves in the **g**, Am 5:10
bribe, and turn aside the needy in the **g**. Am 5:12
love good, and establish justice in the **g**; Am 5:15
Do not enter the **g** of my people in the Ob 1:13
it has reached to the **g** of my people, to Mi 1:9
from the LORD to the **g** of Jerusalem. Mi 1:12
they break through and pass the **g**, Mi 2:13
"a cry will be heard from the Fish **G**, Zep 1:10
its site from the **G** of Benjamin to the Zec 14:10
Benjamin to the place of the former **g**, Zec 14:10
of the former gate, to the Corner **G**, Zec 14:10
"Enter by the narrow **g**. For the gate is Mt 7:13
For the **g** is wide and the way is easy that Mt 7:13
For the **g** is narrow and the way is hard Mt 7:14
As he drew near to the **g** of the town, Lk 7:12
And at his **g** was laid a poor man Lk 16:20
is in Jerusalem by the Sheep **G** a pool, Jn 5:2
they laid daily at the **g** of the temple that Acts 3:2
is called the Beautiful **G** to ask alms of Acts 3:2
sat at the Beautiful **G** of the temple, Acts 3:10
for Simon's house, stood at the **g** Acts 10:17
came to the iron **g** leading into the Acts 12:10
she did not open the **g** but ran in and Acts 12:14
that Peter was standing at the **g**. Acts 12:14
we went outside the **g** to the riverside, Acts 16:13
also suffered outside the **g** in order to Heb 13:12

GATE-BAR (1)
I will break the **g** of Damascus, and cut Am 1:5

GATEHOUSE (2)
and to his sons was allotted the **g**. 1 Chr 26:15
day, as well as two and two at the **g**. 1 Chr 26:17

GATEKEEPER (2)
of Meshelemiah was **g** at the 1 Chr 9:21
To him the **g** opens. The sheep hear his Jn 10:3

GATEKEEPERS (34)
and called to the **g** of the city and 2 Kgs 7:10
Then the **g** called out, and it was told 2 Kgs 7:11
The **g** were Shallum, Akkub, 1 Chr 9:17
the east side as the **g** of the camps of 1 Chr 9:18
were chosen as **g** at the thresholds, 1 Chr 9:22
The **g** were on the four sides, east, 1 Chr 9:24
for the four chief **g**, who were Levites, 1 Chr 9:26
and the **g** Obed-edom and Jeiel. 1 Chr 15:18
Elkanah were to be **g** for the ark. 1 Chr 15:23
and Jehiah were to be **g** for the ark. 1 Chr 15:24
of Jeduthun, and Hosah were to be **g**. 1 Chr 16:38
4,000 **g**, and 4,000 shall offer praises 1 Chr 23:5
As for the divisions of the **g**: of the 1 Chr 26:1
These divisions of the **g**, 1 Chr 26:12
divisions of the **g** among the 1 Chr 26:19
and the **g** in their divisions at each 2 Chr 8:14
on the Sabbath, one third shall be **g**, 2 Chr 23:4
He stationed the **g** at the gates of the 2 Chr 23:19
were scribes and officials and **g**. 2 Chr 34:13
seer; and the **g** were at each gate. 2 Chr 35:15
The sons of the **g**: the sons of Shallum, Ezr 2:42
some of the people, the singers, the **g**, Ezr 2:70
the priests and Levites, the singers and **g**, Ezr 7:7
Of the **g**: Shallum, Telem, and Uri. Ezr 10:24
and I had set up the doors, and the **g**, Neh 7:1
The **g**: the sons of Shallum, the sons of Neh 7:45
So the priests, the Levites, the **g**, the Neh 7:73
people, the priests, the Levites, the **g**, Neh 10:28
minister, and the **g** and the singers. Neh 10:39
The **g**, Akkub, Talmon and their Neh 11:19
and Akkub were **g** standing guard at Neh 12:25
as did the singers and the **g**, Neh 12:45
portions for the singers and the **g**; Neh 12:47
to the Levites, singers, and **g**, Neh 13:5

GATES (121)
or the sojourner who is within your **g**. Ex 20:10
fortified with high walls, **g**, and bars, Dt 3:5
or the sojourner who is within your **g**, Dt 5:14
doorposts of your house and on your **g**. Dt 6:9
doorposts of your house and on your **g**, Dt 11:20
bring out to your **g** that man or woman Dt 17:5
of his youngest son shall he set up its **g**." Jos 6:26
gods were chosen, then war was in the **g**. Jgs 5:8
"Then down to the **g** marched the people Jgs 5:11
as far as Gath and the **g** of Ekron, 1 Sm 17:52
entering a town that has **g** and bars." 1 Sm 23:7
David was sitting between the two **g**, 2 Sm 18:24
besieges them in the land at their **g**, 1 Kgs 8:37
and set up its **g** at the cost of his 1 Kgs 16:34
high places of the **g** that were at the 2 Kgs 23:8
were in charge of the **g** of the house of 1 Chr 9:23
for the doors of the **g** and for clamps, 1 Chr 22:3
small and great alike, for their **g**. 1 Chr 26:13
besiege them in the land at their **g**, 2 Chr 6:28
fortified cities with walls, **g**, and bars, 2 Chr 8:5
with walls and towers, **g** and bars. 2 Chr 14:7
the gatekeepers at the **g** of the house 2 Chr 23:19
to minister in the **g** of the camp of the 2 Chr 31:2
down, and its **g** are destroyed by fire." Neh 1:3
and its **g** have been destroyed by fire?" Neh 2:3
make beams for the **g** of the fortress of Neh 2:8
broken down and its **g** that had been Neh 2:13
lies in ruins with its **g** burned. Neh 2:17
time I had not set up the doors in the **g**), Neh 6:1
"Let not the **g** of Jerusalem be opened Neh 7:3
brothers, who kept watch at the **g**, Neh 11:19
guard at the storehouses of the **g**. Neh 12:25
the people and the **g** and the wall. Neh 12:30
grow dark at the **g** of Jerusalem before Neh 13:19
some of my servants at the **g**, Neh 13:19
and come and guard the **g**, Neh 13:22
Have the **g** of death been revealed to you, Jb 38:17
or have you seen the **g** of deep darkness? Jb 38:17
O you who lift me up from the **g** of death, Ps 9:13
that in the **g** of the daughter of Zion I Ps 9:14
Lift up your heads, O **g**! And be lifted up, Ps 24:7
Lift up your heads, O **g**! And lift them up, Ps 24:9
the LORD loves the **g** of Zion more than Ps 87:2
Enter his **g** with thanksgiving, and his Ps 100:4
and they drew near to the **g** of death. Ps 107:18
Open to me the **g** of righteousness, that Ps 118:19
feet have been standing within your **g**, Ps 122:2
For he strengthens the bars of your **g**; Ps 147:13
at the entrance of the city **g** she speaks: Prv 1:21
beside the **g** in front of the town, at the Prv 8:3
listens to me, watching daily at my **g**, Prv 8:34
the wicked at the **g** of the righteous. Prv 14:19
is known in the **g** when he sits among Prv 31:23
and let her works praise her in the **g**. Prv 31:31
And her **g** shall lament and mourn; Is 3:26

hand for them to enter the **g** of the nobles. Is 13:2
the horsemen took their stand at the **g**. Is 22:7
in the city; the **g** are battered into ruins. Is 24:12
Open the **g**, that the righteous nation that Is 26:2
I am consigned to the **g** of Sheol for the Is 38:10
doors before him that **g** may not be Is 45:1
pinnacles of agate, your **g** of carbuncles, Is 54:12
Your **g** shall be open continually; day Is 60:11
your walls Salvation, and your **g** Praise. Is 60:18
Go through, go through the **g**; prepare Is 62:10
at the entrance of the **g** of Jerusalem, Jer 1:15
Judah who enter these **g** to worship the Jer 7:2
"Judah mourns and her **g** languish; her Jer 14:2
a winnowing fork in the **g** of the land; Jer 15:7
go out, and in all the **g** of Jerusalem, Jer 17:19
of Jerusalem, who enter by these **g**. Jer 17:20
day or bring it in by the **g** of Jerusalem. Jer 17:21
in no burden by the **g** of this city on the Jer 17:24
shall enter by the **g** of this city kings Jer 17:25
and enter by the **g** of Jerusalem on the Jer 17:27
day, then I will kindle a fire in its **g**, Jer 17:27
and your people who enter these **g**. Jer 22:2
there shall enter the **g** of this house Jer 22:4
dumped beyond the **g** of Jerusalem." Jer 22:19
declares the LORD, that has no **g** or bars, Jer 49:31
and her high **g** shall be burned with Jer 51:58
to the festival; all her **g** are desolate; Lam 1:4
Her **g** have sunk into the ground; he Lam 2:9
enemy could enter the **g** of Jerusalem. Lam 4:12
At all their **g** I have given the Ezk 21:15
to set battering rams against the **g**, Ezk 21:22
when he enters your **g** as men enter a Ezk 26:10
walls, and having no bars or **g**,' Ezk 38:11
pavement ran along the side of the **g**, Ezk 40:18
corresponding to the length of the **g**. Ezk 40:18
having oversight at the **g** of the temple Ezk 44:11
When they enter the **g** of the inner Ezk 44:17
they minister at the **g** of the inner Ezk 44:17
three **g**, the gate of Reuben, the gate of Ezk 48:31
the **g** of the city being named after the Ezk 48:31
which is to be 4,500 cubits, three **g**, Ezk 48:32
to be 4,500 cubits by measure, three **g**, Ezk 48:33
which is to be 4,500 cubits, three **g**, Ezk 48:34
their cities, consume the bars of their **g**, Hos 11:6
foreigners entered his **g** and cast lots Ob 1:11
The river **g** are opened; the palace melts Na 2:6
The **g** of your land are wide open to your Na 3:13
render in your **g** judgments that are Zec 8:16
and the **g** of hell shall not prevail Mt 16:18
you know that he is near, at the very **g**. Mt 24:33
you know that he is near, at the very **g**. Mk 13:29
were watching the **g** day and night Acts 9:24
and garlands to the **g** and wanted to Acts 14:13
temple, and at once the **g** were shut. Acts 21:30
It had a great, high wall, with twelve **g**, Rv 21:12
twelve gates, and at the **g** twelve angels, Rv 21:12
and on the **g** the names of the twelve Rv 21:12
on the east three **g**, on the north three Rv 21:13
east three gates, on the north three **g**, Rv 21:13
north three gates, on the south three **g**, Rv 21:13
three gates, and on the west three **g**. Rv 21:13
to measure the city and its **g** and walls. Rv 21:15
And the twelve **g** were twelve pearls, Rv 21:21
each of the **g** made of a single pearl, Rv 21:21
and its **g** will never be shut by day— Rv 21:25
that they may enter the city by the **g**. Rv 22:14

GATEWAY (13)
to the entrance of the **g** of the inner court Ezk 8:3
entrance of the **g** there were twenty-five Ezk 11:1
his hand. And he was standing in the **g**. Ezk 40:3
Then he went into the **g** facing east, Ezk 40:6
he measured the vestibule of the **g**, Ezk 40:8
he measured the vestibule of the **g**, Ezk 40:9
the width of the opening of the **g**, Ezk 40:11
and the length of the **g**, thirteen Ezk 40:11
the vestibule of the **g** was the court. Ezk 40:14
And the **g** had windows all around, Ezk 40:16
outside of the inner **g** there were two Ezk 40:44
went out into the **g** and the rooster Mk 14:68
when he knocked at the door of the **g**, Acts 12:13

GATH (35)
Only in Gaza, in **G**, and in Ashdod did Jos 11:22
Gaza, Ashdod, Ashkelon, **G**, and Ekron), Jos 13:3
brought around to **G**." So they brought 1 Sm 5:8
for Gaza, one for Ashkelon, one for **G**, 1 Sm 6:17
restored to Israel, from Ekron to **G**, 1 Sm 7:14
a champion named Goliath of **G**, 1 Sm 17:4
the champion, the Philistine of **G**, 1 Sm 17:23
Philistines as far as **G** and the gates 1 Sm 17:52
Shaaraim as far as **G** and Ekron. 1 Sm 17:52
and went to Achish the king of **G**. 1 Sm 21:10
afraid of Achish the king of **G**. 1 Sm 21:12
Achish the son of Maoch, king of **G**. 1 Sm 27:2
And David lived with Achish at **G**, he 1 Sm 27:3
was told Saul that David had fled to **G**, 1 Sm 27:4
nor woman alive to bring news to **G**, 1 Sm 27:11
Tell it not in **G**, publish it not in the 2 Sm 1:20
who had followed him from **G**, 2 Sm 15:18
And there was again war at **G**, where 2 Sm 21:20
were descended from the giants in **G**, 2 Sm 21:22
to Achish, son of Maacah, king of **G**. 1 Kgs 2:39
"Behold, your servants are in **G**," 1 Kgs 2:39
donkey and went to **G** to Achish to 1 Kgs 2:40
and brought his servants from **G**. 1 Kgs 2:40
from Jerusalem to **G** and returned, 1 Kgs 2:41
up and fought against **G** and took it. 2 Kgs 12:17
whom the men of **G** who were born 1 Chr 7:21
caused the inhabitants of **G** to flee); 1 Chr 8:13
and he took **G** and its villages out of 1 Chr 18:1
And there was again war at **G**, where 1 Chr 20:6
were descended from the giants in **G**, 1 Chr 20:8
G, Mareshah, Ziph, 2 Chr 11:8
through the wall of **G** and the wall of 2 Chr 26:6
when the Philistines seized him in **G**. Ps 56:T
then go down to **G** of the Philistines. Am 6:2
Tell it not in **G**; weep not at all; in Mi 1:10

GATH-HEPHER (2)
on the east toward the sunrise to **G**, Jos 19:13
the prophet, who was from **G**. 2 Kgs 14:25

GATH-RIMMON (4)
Jehud, Bene-berak, **G**, Jos 19:45
G with its pasturelands—four cities; Jos 21:24
and **G** with its pasturelands—two Jos 21:25
G with its pasturelands, 1 Chr 6:69

GATHER (144)
"**G** stones." And they took stones and Gn 31:46
and if they **g** themselves against me Gn 34:30
And let them **g** all the food of these Gn 41:35
sons and said, "**G** yourselves together, Gn 49:1
Go and **g** the elders of Israel together and Ex 3:16
let them go and **g** straw for themselves. Ex 5:7
the land of Egypt to **g** stubble for straw. Ex 5:12
shall go out and **g** a day's portion every Ex 16:4
it will be twice as much as they **g** daily." Ex 16:5
'**G** of it, each one of you, as much as he Ex 16:16
Six days you shall **g** it, but on the Ex 16:26
day some of the people went out to **g**, Ex 16:27
shall sow your land and **g** in its yield, Ex 23:10
when you **g** in from the field the fruit of Ex 23:16
neither shall you **g** the gleanings after Lv 19:9
neither shall you **g** the fallen grapes of Lv 19:10
nor shall you **g** the gleanings after your Lv 23:22
prune your vineyard and **g** in its fruits, Lv 25:3
or **g** the grapes of your undressed vine. Lv 25:5
grows of itself nor **g** the grapes from the Lv 25:11
if we may not sow or **g** in our crop?' Lv 25:20
And if you **g** within your cities, Lv 26:25
the congregation shall **g** themselves to Nm 10:3
of Israel, shall **g** themselves to you. Nm 10:4
"**G** for me seventy men of the elders of Nm 11:16
who is clean shall **g** up the ashes of Nm 19:9
said to Moses, "**G** the people together, Nm 21:16
the LORD said to me, '**G** the people to me, Dt 4:10
that you may **g** in your grain and your Dt 11:14
You shall **g** all its spoil into the midst of Dt 13:16
When you **g** the grapes of your Dt 24:21
seed into the field and shall **g** in little, Dt 28:38
drink of the wine nor **g** the grapes, Dt 28:39
and he will **g** you again from all the Dt 30:3
from there the LORD your God will **g** you, Dt 30:4
and you shall **g** into your house your Jos 2:18
you, 'Go, **g** your men at Mount Tabor, Jgs 4:6
let me glean and **g** among the sheaves Ru 2:7
Samuel said, "**G** all Israel at Mizpah, 1 Sm 7:5
arise and go and will **g** all Israel to my 2 Sm 3:21
Now then **g** the rest of the people 2 Sm 12:28
therefore send and **g** all Israel to 1 Kgs 18:19
went out into the field to **g** herbs, 2 Kgs 4:39
behold, I will **g** you to your fathers, 2 Kgs 22:20
and **g** and deliver us from among 1 Chr 16:35
David commanded to **g** together the 1 Chr 22:2
cities of Judah and **g** from all Israel 2 Chr 24:5
Behold, I will **g** you to your fathers, 2 Chr 34:28
I will **g** them from there and bring them Neh 1:9
to **g** into them the portions required Neh 12:44
of his kingdom to **g** all the beautiful Est 2:3
"Go, **g** all the Jews to be found in Susa, Est 4:16
in every city to **g** and defend their lives, Est 8:11
They **g** their fodder in the field, and they Jb 24:6
his heart to it and **g** to himself his spirit Jb 34:14
return your grain and **g** it to your Jb 39:12
up wealth and does not know who will **g**! Ps 39:6
princes of the peoples **g** as the people of Ps 47:9
"**G** to me my faithful ones, who made a Ps 50:5
when peoples **g** together, and Ps 102:22
When you give it to them, they **g** it up; Ps 104:28
and **g** us from among the nations, Ps 106:47
stones, and a time to **g** stones together; Eccl 3:5
to graze in the gardens and to **g** lilies. Sg 6:2
and **g** the dispersed of Judah from the Is 11:12
or like sheep with none to **g** them, Is 13:14
he will **g** the lambs in his arms; Is 40:11
the east, and from the west I will **g** you. Is 43:5
All the nations **g** together, and the peoples Is 43:9
and see; they all **g**, they come to you. Is 49:18
but with great compassion I will **g** you. Is 54:7
"I will **g** yet others to him besides those Is 56:8
see; they all **g** together, they come to you; Is 60:4
and those who **g** it shall drink it in the Is 62:9
time is coming to **g** all nations and Is 66:18
of the LORD, and all nations shall **g** to it, Jer 3:17
The children **g** wood, the fathers kindle Jer 7:18
When I would **g** them, declares the LORD, Jer 8:13
G together; let us go into the fortified Jer 8:14
after the reaper, and none shall **g** them.'" Jer 9:22
G up your bundle from the ground, O Jer 10:17
Then I will **g** the remnant of my flock Jer 23:3
your fortunes and **g** you from all Jer 29:14
the north country and **g** them from the Jer 31:8
say, 'He who scattered Israel will **g** him, Jer 31:10
I will **g** them from all the countries to Jer 32:37
you, **g** wine and summer fruits and oil, Jer 40:10
before him, with none to **g** the fugitives. Jer 49:5
"**G** yourselves together and come Jer 49:14
I will **g** you from the peoples and Ezk 11:17
I will **g** all your lovers with whom you Ezk 16:37
I will **g** them against you from every Ezk 16:37
from the peoples and **g** you out of the Ezk 20:34
from the peoples and **g** you out of the Ezk 20:41
I will **g** you into the midst of Ezk 22:19
so I will **g** you in my anger and in my Ezk 22:20
I will **g** you and blow on you with the Ezk 22:21
When I **g** the house of Israel from the Ezk 28:25
forty years I will **g** the Egyptians from Ezk 29:13
from the peoples and **g** them from the Ezk 34:13
from the nations and **g** you from all Ezk 36:24
and will **g** them from all around, Ezk 37:21
g from all around to the sacrificial Ezk 39:17
Nebuchadnezzar sent to **g** the satraps, Dn 3:2
the nations, I will soon **g** them up. Hos 8:10
destruction; but Egypt shall **g** them; Hos 9:6
G the elders and all the inhabitants of the Jl 1:14
g the people. Consecrate the congregation; Jl 2:16
g the children, even nursing infants. Jl 2:16
I will **g** all the nations and bring them Jl 3:2
nations, and **g** yourselves there. Jl 3:11
O Jacob; I will **g** the remnant of Israel; Mi 2:12
assemble the lame and **g** those who have Mi 4:6
on the mountains with none to **g** them. Na 3:18
faces forward. They **g** captives like sand. Hab 1:9
G together, yes, gather, O shameless Zep 2:1
together, yes, **g**, O shameless nation, Zep 2:1
For my decision is to **g** nations, to Zep 3:8
I will **g** those of you who mourn for the Zep 3:18
I will save the lame and **g** the outcast, Zep 3:19
in, at the time when I **g** you together; Zep 3:20
"I will whistle for them and **g** them in, Zec 10:8
of Egypt, and **g** them from Assyria, Zec 10:10
the nations of the earth will **g** against it. Zec 12:3
For I will **g** all the nations against Zec 14:2
his threshing floor and **g** his wheat into Mt 3:12
neither sow nor reap nor **g** into barns, Mt 6:26
whoever does not **g** with me scatters. Mt 12:30
do you want us to go and **g** them?' Mt 13:28
G the weeds first and bind them in Mt 13:30
but **g** the wheat into my barn.'" Mt 13:30
and they will **g** out of his kingdom all Mt 13:41
the corpse is, there the vultures will **g**. Mt 24:28
and they will **g** his elect from the four Mt 24:31
have not sowed and **g** where I scattered Mt 25:26
out the angels and **g** his elect from the Mk 13:27
threshing floor and to **g** the wheat into Lk 3:17
whoever does not **g** with me scatters. Lk 11:23
the corpse is, there the vultures will **g**." Lk 17:37
disciples, "**G** up the leftover fragments, Jn 6:12
but also to **g** into one the children of Jn 11:52
in your sickle and **g** the clusters from Rv 14:18
"Come, **g** for the great supper of God, Rv 19:17
Gog and Magog, to **g** them for battle; Rv 20:8

GATHERED (221)
under the heavens be **g** together into one Gn 1:9
the waters that were **g** together he called Gn 1:10
and all their possessions that they had **g**, Gn 12:5
and full of years, and was **g** to his people. Gn 25:8
last and died, and was **g** to his people.) Gn 25:17
and when all the flocks were **g** there, the Gn 29:3
time for the livestock to be **g** together. Gn 29:7
all the flocks are **g** together and the Gn 29:8
So Laban **g** together all the people of Gn 29:22
and he died and was **g** to his people, Gn 35:29
your sheaves **g** around it and bowed Gn 37:7
and he **g** up all the food of these seven Gn 41:48
And Joseph **g** up all the money that Gn 47:14

to them, "I am to be **g** to my people; Gn 49:29
his last and was **g** to his people. Gn 49:33
and Aaron went and **g** together all the Ex 4:29
And they **g** them together in heaps, and Ex 8:14
And the people of Israel did so. They **g**, Ex 16:17
whoever **g** much had nothing left over, Ex 16:18
over, and whoever **g** little had no lack. Ex 16:18
Each of them **g** as much as he could Ex 16:18
Morning by morning they **g** it, each as Ex 16:21
the sixth day they **g** twice as much Ex 16:22
the people **g** themselves together to Ex 32:1
And all the sons of Levi **g** around him. Ex 32:26
when you have **g** in the produce of the Lv 23:39
when the assembly is to be **g** together, Nm 10:7
people went about and **g** it and ground Nm 11:8
fish of the sea be **g** together for them, Nm 11:22
And he **g** seventy men of the elders of Nm 11:24
and all the next day, and **g** the quail. Nm 11:32
Those who **g** least gathered ten Nm 11:32
who gathered least **g** ten homers. Nm 11:32
who are **g** together against Nm 14:35
all your company have **g** together. Nm 16:11
Moses and Aaron **g** the assembly Nm 20:10
"Let Aaron be **g** to his people, for he Nm 20:24
And Aaron shall be **g** to his people Nm 20:26
He **g** all his people together and went Nm 21:23
of those who **g** themselves together Nm 27:3
it, you also shall be **g** to your people, Nm 27:13
you shall be **g** to your people." Nm 31:2
when you have **g** in the produce from Dt 16:13
you go up, and be **g** to your people, Dt 32:50
in Mount Hor and was **g** to his people, Dt 32:50
when the heads of the people were **g**, Dt 33:5
they **g** together as one to fight against Jos 9:2
g their forces and went up with all their Jos 10:5
in the hill country are **g** against us." Jos 10:6
the people of Israel **g** at Shiloh to make Jos 22:12
Joshua **g** all the tribes of Israel to Jos 24:1
generation also were **g** to their fathers. Jgs 2:10
He **g** to himself the Ammonites and the Jgs 3:13
into the field and **g** the grapes from their Jgs 9:27
the Tower of Shechem were **g** together. Jgs 9:47
so Sihon **g** all his people together and Jgs 11:20
Then Jephthah **g** all the men of Gilead Jgs 12:4
lords of the Philistines **g** to offer a great Jgs 16:23
all the men of Israel **g** against the city, Jgs 20:11
So they sent and **g** together all the lords 1 Sm 5:8
sent therefore and **g** together all the 1 Sm 5:11
So they **g** at Mizpah and drew water 1 Sm 7:6
the people of Israel had **g** at Mizpah, 1 Sm 7:7
the elders of Israel **g** together and came 1 Sm 8:4
Now the Philistines **g** their armies for 1 Sm 17:1
And they were **g** at Socoh, which 1 Sm 17:1
And Saul and the men of Israel were **g**, 1 Sm 17:2
So Jonathan's boy **g** up the arrows 1 Sm 20:38
who was bitter in soul, **g** to him. 1 Sm 22:2
days the Philistines **g** their forces for 1 Sm 28:1
at Shunem. And Saul **g** all Israel, 1 Sm 28:4
the Philistines had **g** all their forces 1 Sm 29:1
of Benjamin **g** themselves together 2 Sm 2:25
And when he had **g** all the people 2 Sm 2:30
David again **g** all the chosen men of 2 Sm 6:1
by Israel, they **g** themselves together. 2 Sm 10:15
he **g** all Israel together and crossed 2 Sm 10:17
So David **g** all the people together 2 Sm 12:29
which cannot be **g** up again. 2 Sm 14:14
counsel is that all Israel be **g** to you, 2 Sm 17:11
and they **g** the bones of those who 2 Sm 21:13
Philistines who were **g** there for battle, 2 Sm 23:9
The Philistines **g** together at Lehi, 2 Sm 23:11
And Solomon **g** together chariots 1 Kgs 10:26
And he **g** men about him and 1 Kgs 11:24
of Israel and **g** the prophets together 1 Kgs 18:20
and he **g** up his garment and ran 1 Kgs 18:46
the king of Syria **g** all his army 1 Kgs 20:1
king of Israel **g** the prophets together, 1 Kgs 22:6
a wild vine and **g** from it his lap 2 Kgs 4:39
and you shall be **g** to your grave in 2 Kgs 22:20
Judah and Jerusalem were **g** to him. 2 Kgs 23:1
Then all Israel **g** together to David at 1 Chr 11:1
the Philistines were **g** there for 1 Chr 11:13
that they may be **g** to us. 1 Chr 13:2
And David **g** together the sons of 1 Chr 15:4
he **g** all Israel together and crossed 1 Chr 19:17
Solomon **g** together chariots and 2 Chr 1:14
who had **g** at Jerusalem because of 2 Chr 12:5
worthless scoundrels **g** about him 2 Chr 13:7
And he **g** all Judah and Benjamin, 2 Chr 15:9
They were **g** at Jerusalem in the 2 Chr 15:10
king of Israel **g** the prophets together, 2 Chr 18:5
through Judah and **g** the Levites 2 Chr 23:2
And he **g** the priests and the Levites 2 Chr 24:5
And Ahaz **g** together the vessels of 2 Chr 28:24
They **g** their brothers and 2 Chr 29:15
king rose early and **g** the officials of 2 Chr 29:20
A great many people were **g**, and they 2 Chr 32:4
the people and **g** them together to 2 Chr 32:6
and you shall be **g** to your grave in 2 Chr 34:28
the king sent and **g** together all the 2 Chr 34:29
the people **g** as one man to Jerusalem. Ezr 3:1
and I **g** leading men from Israel to go up Ezr 7:28
I **g** them to the river that runs to Ahava, Ezr 8:15
g around me while I sat appalled until Ezr 9:4
and children, **g** to him out of Israel, Ezr 10:1
all my servants were **g** there for the Neh 5:16
And all the people **g** as one man into the Neh 8:1
sons of the singers **g** together from the Neh 12:28
forsaken?" And I **g** them together and Neh 13:11
many young women were **g** in Susa the Est 2:8
the virgins were **g** together the second Est 2:19
The Jews **g** in their cities throughout all Est 9:2
who were in Susa **g** also on the Est 9:15
king's provinces also **g** to defend their Est 9:16
who were in Susa **g** on the thirteenth Est 9:18
old age, like a sheaf **g** up in its season. Jb 5:26
with his fat and **g** fat upon his waist Jb 15:27
are brought low and **g** up like all others; Jb 24:24
assembly of the peoples be **g** about you; Ps 7:7
at my stumbling they rejoiced and **g**; Ps 35:15
gathered; they **g** together against me; Ps 35:15
and **g** in from the lands, from the east Ps 107:3
the vegetation of the mountains is **g**, Prv 27:25
down? Who has **g** the wind in his fists? Prv 30:4
I also **g** for myself silver and gold and Eccl 2:8
my bride, I **g** my myrrh with my spice, Sg 5:1
been forsaken, so I have **g** all the earth; Is 10:14
They will be **g** together as prisoners in a Is 24:22
and your spoil is **g** as the caterpillar Is 33:4
indeed, there the hawks are **g**, each one Is 34:15
commanded, and his Spirit has **g** them. Is 34:16
and that Israel might be **g** to him—for I Is 49:5
yet others to him besides those already **g**." Is 56:8
All the flocks of Kedar shall be **g** to you; Is 60:7
And they shall not be **g** or buried. Jer 8:2
They shall not be lamented, or **g**, or Jer 25:33
And all the people **g** around Jeremiah in Jer 26:9
And they **g** wine and summer fruits in Jer 40:12
the Judeans who are **g** about you would Jer 40:15
and have **g** gold and silver into your Ezk 28:4
field, and not be brought together or **g**. Ezk 29:5
whose people were **g** from many peoples Ezk 38:8
people who were **g** from the nations, Ezk 38:12
the peoples and **g** them from their Ezk 39:27
of the provinces **g** for the dedication Dn 3:3
the king's counselors **g** together and Dn 3:27
children of Israel shall be **g** together, Hos 1:11
nations shall be **g** against them when Hos 10:10
for from the fee of a prostitute she **g** them, Mi 1:7
that he has **g** them as sheaves to the Mi 4:12
as when the summer fruit has been **g**, Mi 7:1
fruits. Are grapes **g** from thornbushes, Mt 7:16
And great crowds **g** about him, so that Mt 13:2
as the weeds are **g** and burned with fire, Mt 13:40
into the sea and **g** fish of every kind. Mt 13:47
and how many baskets you **g**? Mt 16:9
and how many baskets you **g**? Mt 16:10
where two or three are **g** in my name, Mt 18:20
into the roads and **g** all whom they Mt 22:10
silenced the Sadducees, they **g** together. Mt 22:34
while the Pharisees were **g** together, Mt 22:41
would I have **g** your children together Mt 23:37
Before him will be **g** all the nations, Mt 25:32
the elders of the people **g** in the palace of Mt 26:3
where the scribes and the elders had **g**. Mt 26:57
So when they had **g**, Pilate said to them, Mt 27:17
and they **g** the whole battalion before Mt 27:27
priests and the Pharisees **g** before Pilate Mt 27:62
the whole city was **g** together at the Mk 1:33
And many were **g** together, so that there Mk 2:2
he went home, and the crowd **g** again, Mk 3:20
And a very large crowd **g** about him, so Mk 4:1
other side, a great crowd **g** about him, Mk 5:21
Now when the Pharisees **g** to him, with Mk 7:1
days, when again a great crowd had **g**, Mk 8:1
the Jordan, and crowds **g** to him again. Mk 10:1
and great crowds **g** to hear him and to Lk 5:15
For figs are not **g** from thornbushes, nor Lk 6:44
of the people had **g** together that they Lk 12:1
would I have **g** your children together Lk 13:34
the younger son **g** all he had and took a Lk 15:13
of the elders of the people **g** together, Lk 22:66
those who were with them **g** together, Lk 24:33
So they **g** them up and filled twelve Jn 6:13
So the Jews **g** around him and said to Jn 10:24
and the Pharisees **g** the Council and Jn 11:47
and the branches are **g**, thrown into the Jn 15:6
elders and scribes **g** together in Acts 4:5
and the rulers were **g** together, Acts 4:26
city there were **g** together against your Acts 4:27
which they were **g** together was Acts 4:31
The people also **g** from the towns Acts 5:16
went in and found many persons **g**. Acts 10:27
where many were **g** together and were Acts 12:12
almost the whole city **g** to hear the Acts 13:44
But when the disciples **g** about him, Acts 14:20
they arrived and **g** the church Acts 14:27
the elders were **g** together to consider Acts 15:6
and having **g** the congregation Acts 15:30
These he **g** together, with the Acts 19:25
when we were **g** together to break Acts 20:7
in the upper room where we were **g**. Acts 20:8
When Paul had **g** a bundle of sticks Acts 28:3
of the Jews, and when they had **g**, Acts 28:17
"Whoever **g** much had nothing left 2 Cor 8:15
and whoever **g** little had no lack." 2 Cor 8:15
and our being **g** together to him, 2 Thes 2:1
across the earth and **g** the grape harvest Rv 14:19
earth with their armies **g** to make war Rv 19:19

GATHERERS (1)
If grape **g** came to you, would they not Ob 1:5

GATHERING (15)
they found a man **g** sticks on the Nm 15:32
who found him **g** sticks brought him Nm 15:33
canopy, thick clouds, a **g** of water. 2 Sm 22:12
behold, a widow was there **g** sticks. 1 Kgs 17:10
And now I am **g** a couple of sticks 1 Kgs 17:12
given the business of **g** and collecting, Eccl 2:26
of kingdoms, of nations **g** together! Is 13:4
against Babylon a **g** of great nations, Jer 50:9
lest in **g** the weeds you root up the Mt 13:29
As they were **g** in Galilee, Jesus said to Mt 17:22
sow, and **g** where you scattered no seed, Mt 25:24
a great crowd was **g** and people from town Lk 8:4
is receiving wages and **g** fruit for eternal Jn 4:36
And what they said pleased the whole **g**, Acts 6:5
and to innumerable angels in festal **g**, Heb 12:22

GATHERINGS (1)
the street, and upon the **g** of young men, Jer 6:11

GATHERS (19)
And the one who **g** the ashes of the Nm 19:10
He **g** the waters of the sea as a heap; he Ps 33:7
empty words, while his heart **g** iniquity; Ps 41:6
up Jerusalem; he **g** the outcasts of Israel. Ps 147:2
bread in summer and **g** her food in Prv 6:8
He who **g** in summer is a prudent son, Prv 10:5
but whoever **g** little by little will Prv 13:11
by interest and profit **g** it for him who Prv 28:8
and as one **g** eggs that have been Is 10:14
as when the reaper **g** standing grain and Is 17:5
your spoil is gathered as the caterpillar **g**; Is 33:4
lays and hatches and **g** her young in her Is 34:15
Lord GOD, who **g** the outcasts of Israel, Is 56:8
Like the partridge that **g** a brood that Jer 17:11
As one **g** silver and bronze and iron Ezk 22:20
with his net; he **g** them in his dragnet; Hab 1:15
He **g** for himself all nations and collects Hab 2:5
together as a hen **g** her brood under her Mt 23:37
together as a hen **g** her brood under her Lk 13:34

GAUNT (1)
my body has become **g**, with no fat. Ps 109:24

GAVE (557)
The man **g** names to all livestock and to Gn 2:20
and she also **g** some to her husband who Gn 3:6
"The woman whom you **g** to be with Gn 3:12
to be with me, she **g** me fruit of the tree, Gn 3:12
And as I **g** you the green plants, I give you Gn 9:3
And Pharaoh **g** men orders Gn 12:20
your hand!" And Abram **g** him a tenth Gn 14:20
and **g** her to Abram her husband as a Gn 16:3
I **g** my servant to your embrace, and Gn 16:5
and good, and **g** it to a young man, Gn 18:7
servants, and **g** them to Abraham, Gn 20:14
and a skin of water and **g** it to Hagar, Gn 21:14
skin with water and **g** the boy a drink. Gn 21:19
and oxen and **g** them to Abimelech, Gn 21:27
jar upon her hand and **g** him a drink. Gn 24:18
and **g** straw and fodder to the camels, Gn 24:32
and she **g** the camels drink also. Gn 24:46
and garments, and **g** them to Rebekah. Gn 24:53
He also **g** to her brother and to her Gn 24:53
Abraham **g** all he had to Isaac. Gn 25:5
of his concubines Abraham **g** gifts, Gn 25:6
Then Jacob **g** Esau bread and lentil Gn 25:34
And he **g** them the names that his Gn 26:18
sojournings that God **g** to Abraham!" Gn 28:4
(Laban **g** his female servant Zilpah to Gn 29:24
Then Laban **g** him his daughter Gn 29:28
(Laban **g** his female servant Bilhah to Gn 29:29
So she **g** him her servant Bilhah as a Gn 30:4
her servant Zilpah and **g** her to Jacob as Gn 30:9
my wages because I **g** my servant to Gn 30:18
So they **g** to Jacob all the foreign gods Gn 35:4

The land that I **g** to Abraham and Gn 35:12
in your hand." So he **g** them to her and Gn 38:18
him steadfast love and **g** him favor in Gn 39:21
And he **g** him in marriage Asenath, Gn 41:45
And Joseph **g** orders to fill their bags Gn 42:25
did so: and Joseph **g** them wagons, Gn 45:21
and **g** them provisions for the journey. Gn 45:21
all of them he **g** a change of clothes, Gn 45:22
to Benjamin he **g** three hundred Gn 45:22
whom Laban **g** to Leah his daughter; Gn 46:18
whom Laban **g** to Rachel his daughter, Gn 46:25
his brothers and **g** them a possession Gn 47:11
and Joseph **g** them food in exchange Gn 47:17
on the allowance that Pharaoh **g** them; Gn 47:22
"Your father **g** this command before Gn 50:16
midwives feared God, he **g** them families. Ex 1:21
and he **g** Moses his daughter Zipporah. Ex 2:21
She **g** birth to a son, and he called his Ex 2:22
Moses and Aaron and **g** them a charge Ex 6:13
And the LORD **g** the people favor in the Ex 11:3
And he **g** to Moses, when he had Ex 31:18
So they **g** it to me, and I threw it into the Ex 32:24
So Moses **g** command, and word was Ex 36:6
And Moses **g** the redemption money to Nm 3:51
and the oxen and **g** them to the Levites. Nm 7:6
wagons and four oxen he **g** to the sons of Nm 7:7
and eight oxen he **g** to the sons of Nm 7:8
But to the sons of Kohath he **g** none, Nm 7:9
day that the LORD **g** commandment, Nm 15:23
And all their chiefs **g** him staffs, one Nm 17:6
of Israel and **g** over the Canaanites, Nm 21:3
to Balaam and **g** him Balak's message. Nm 22:7
And Moses **g** the tribute, which was Nm 31:41
and **g** them to the Levites who kept Nm 31:47
So Moses **g** command concerning Nm 32:28
And Moses **g** to them, to the people of Nm 32:33
And they **g** other names to the cities Nm 32:38
And Moses **g** Gilead to Machir the son Nm 32:40
possession, which the LORD **g** to them.) Dt 2:12
And the LORD our God **g** him over to us, Dt 2:33
The LORD our God **g** all into our hands. Dt 2:36
So the LORD our God **g** into our hand Og Dt 3:3
I **g** to the Reubenites and the Gadites the Dt 3:12
Argob, I **g** to the half-tribe of Manasseh. Dt 3:13
To Machir I **g** Gilead, Dt 3:15
and the Gadites I **g** the territory from Dt 3:16
on two tablets of stone and **g** them to me. Dt 5:22
And the LORD **g** me the two tablets of Dt 9:10
forty nights the LORD **g** me the two tablets Dt 9:11
assembly. And the LORD **g** them to me. Dt 10:4
'I **g** my daughter to this man to marry, Dt 22:16
us into this place and **g** us this land, Dt 26:9
took their land and **g** it for an Dt 29:8
wrote this law and **g** it to the priests, Dt 31:9
When the Most High **g** to the nations Dt 32:8
you forgot the God who **g** you birth. Dt 32:18
the land that Moses **g** you beyond the Jos 1:14
servant of the LORD **g** you beyond the Jos 1:15
day when the LORD **g** the Amorites over Jos 10:12
And the LORD **g** it also and its king into Jos 10:30
And the LORD **g** Lachish into the hand Jos 10:32
And the LORD **g** them into the hand of Jos 11:8
And Joshua **g** it for an inheritance to Jos 11:23
the servant of the LORD **g** their land for a Jos 12:6
toward Seir (and Joshua **g** their land to Jos 12:7
their inheritance, which Moses **g** them, Jos 13:8
as Moses the servant of the LORD **g** them: Jos 13:8
of Levi alone Moses **g** no inheritance. Jos 13:14
And Moses **g** an inheritance to the Jos 13:15
Moses **g** an inheritance also to the tribe Jos 13:24
And Moses **g** an inheritance to the Jos 13:29
tribe of Levi Moses **g** no inheritance; Jos 13:33
of the people of Israel **g** them to inherit. Jos 14:1
the Levites he **g** no inheritance among Jos 14:3
and he **g** Hebron to Caleb the son of Jos 14:13
he **g** to Caleb the son of Jephunneh a Jos 15:13
And he **g** him Achsah his daughter as Jos 15:17
of water." And he **g** her the upper Jos 15:19
of the LORD he **g** them an inheritance Jos 17:4
Moses the servant of the LORD **g** them." Jos 18:7
people of Israel **g** an inheritance Jos 19:49
of the LORD they **g** him the city that Jos 19:50
the people of Israel **g** to the Levites the Jos 21:3
the people of Israel **g** by lot to the Jos 21:8
of Simeon they **g** the following cities Jos 21:9
They **g** them Kiriath-arba (Arba being Jos 21:11
of Aaron the priest they **g** Hebron, Jos 21:13
Thus the LORD **g** to Israel all the land Jos 21:43
And the LORD **g** them rest on every side Jos 21:44
servant of the LORD **g** you on the other Jos 22:4
made his offspring many. I **g** him Isaac. Jos 24:3
And to Isaac I **g** Jacob and Esau. And I Jos 24:4
And I **g** Esau the hill country of Seir to Jos 24:4
with you, and I **g** them into your hand, Jos 24:8
Jebusites. And I **g** them into your hand. Jos 24:11
I **g** you a land on which you had not Jos 24:13
up and the LORD **g** the Canaanites and the Jgs 1:4
And he **g** him Achsah his daughter for a Jgs 1:13
of water." And Caleb **g** her the upper Jgs 1:15
Israel, and he **g** them over to plunderers, Jgs 2:14
their own daughters they **g** to their sons, Jgs 3:6
the LORD **g** Cushan-rishathaim king Jgs 3:10
a skin of milk and **g** him a drink and Jgs 4:19
He asked water and she **g** him milk; she Jgs 5:25
and the LORD **g** them into the hand of Jgs 6:1
them out before you and **g** you their land. Jgs 6:9
And they **g** him seventy pieces of silver Jgs 9:4
g Sihon and all his people into the Jgs 11:21
and the LORD **g** them into his hand. Jgs 11:32
and the LORD **g** them into my hand. Jgs 12:3
thirty daughters he **g** in marriage Jgs 12:9
so the LORD **g** them into the hand of the Jgs 13:1
father and mother and **g** some to them, Jgs 14:9
took their spoil and **g** the garments to Jgs 14:19
hated her, so I **g** her to your companion. Jgs 15:2
pieces of silver and **g** it to the Jgs 17:4
into his house and **g** the donkeys feed. Jgs 19:21
men of Israel **g** ground to Benjamin, Jgs 20:36
And they **g** them the women whom Jgs 21:14
also brought out and **g** her what food Ru 2:18
six measures of barley he **g** to me, Ru 3:17
drew off his sandal and **g** it to the other, Ru 4:7
in to her, and the LORD **g** her conception, Ru 4:13
of the neighborhood **g** him a name, Ru 4:17
But to Hannah he **g** a double portion, 1 Sm 1:5
I **g** to the house of your father all my 1 Sm 2:28
the camp, all Israel **g** a mighty shout, 1 Sm 4:5
were dead, she bowed and **g** birth, 1 Sm 4:19
into the hall and **g** them a place at 1 Sm 9:22
to the cook, "Bring the portion I **g** you, 1 Sm 9:23
Samuel, God **g** him another heart. 1 Sm 10:9
that was on him and **g** it to David, 1 Sm 18:4
And Saul **g** him his daughter 1 Sm 18:27
And Jonathan **g** his weapons to his 1 Sm 20:40
So the priest **g** him the holy bread, for 1 Sm 21:6
for him and **g** him provisions and 1 Sm 22:10
him provisions and **g** him the sword 1 Sm 22:10
from Keilah, he **g** up the expedition. 1 Sm 23:13
seen how the LORD **g** you today into 1 Sm 24:10
for the LORD **g** you into my hand 1 Sm 26:23
So that day Achish **g** him Ziklag. 1 Sm 27:6
And they **g** him bread and he ate. 1 Sm 30:11
he ate. They **g** him water to drink, 1 Sm 30:11
and they **g** him a piece of a cake of 1 Sm 30:12
was the reward I **g** him for his news. 2 Sm 4:10
And the LORD **g** victory to David 2 Sm 8:6
And the LORD **g** victory to David 2 Sm 8:14
And I **g** you your master's house and 2 Sm 12:8
into your arms and **g** you the house of 2 Sm 12:8
would not go but **g** him his blessing. 2 Sm 13:25
counsel that Ahithophel **g** was as if 2 Sm 16:23
heard when the king **g** orders to all 2 Sm 18:5
die." And the king **g** him his oath. 2 Sm 19:23
and he **g** them into the hands of the 2 Sm 21:9
You **g** a wide place for my steps 2 Sm 22:37
the God who **g** me vengeance and 2 Sm 22:48
And Joab **g** the sum of the numbering 2 Sm 24:9
and I **g** birth to a child while she was 1 Kgs 3:17
Then on the third day after I **g** birth, 1 Kgs 3:18
I gave birth, this woman also **g** birth. 1 Kgs 3:18
And God **g** Solomon wisdom and 1 Kgs 4:29
while Solomon **g** Hiram 20,000 cors 1 Kgs 5:11
Solomon **g** this to Hiram year by 1 Kgs 5:11
And the LORD **g** Solomon wisdom, as 1 Kgs 5:12
to the land that you **g** to their fathers. 1 Kgs 8:34
in the land that you **g** to our fathers. 1 Kgs 8:40
land, which you **g** to their fathers, 1 Kgs 8:48
King Solomon **g** to Hiram twenty 1 Kgs 9:11
Then she **g** the king 120 talents of 1 Kgs 10:10
queen of Sheba **g** to King Solomon. 1 Kgs 10:10
And King Solomon **g** to the queen of 1 Kgs 10:13
who **g** him a house and assigned 1 Kgs 11:18
allowance of food and **g** him land. 1 Kgs 11:18
so that he **g** him in marriage the 1 Kgs 11:19
was industrious he **g** him charge 1 Kgs 11:28
that the old men **g** him and took 1 Kgs 12:8
And he **g** a sign the same day, saying, 1 Kgs 13:3
the house of David and **g** it to you, 1 Kgs 14:8
good land that he **g** to their fathers 1 Kgs 14:15
the LORD his God **g** him a lamp in 1 Kgs 15:4
the king's house and **g** them into the 1 Kgs 15:18
of the oxen and **g** it to the people, 1 Kgs 19:21
your hand." So he **g** him his hand. 2 Kgs 10:15
And the priest **g** to the captains the 2 Kgs 11:10
on him and **g** him the testimony. 2 Kgs 11:12
and he **g** them continually into the 2 Kgs 13:3
(Therefore the LORD **g** Israel a savior, 2 Kgs 13:5
of the LORD that he **g** to Jehu, 2 Kgs 15:12
and Menahem **g** Pul a thousand 2 Kgs 15:19
and the warnings that he **g** them. 2 Kgs 17:15
afflicted them and **g** them into the 2 Kgs 17:20
And Hezekiah **g** him all the silver 2 Kgs 18:15
Judah had overlaid and **g** it to the 2 Kgs 18:16
out of the land that I **g** to their fathers, 2 Kgs 21:8
the LORD." And Hilkiah **g** the book to 2 Kgs 22:8
And Jehoiakim **g** the silver and the 2 Kgs 23:35
the king of Judah **g** himself up to the 2 Kgs 24:12
kindly to him and **g** him a seat 2 Kgs 25:28
So Sheshan **g** his daughter in 1 Chr 2:35
to them they **g** Hebron in the land of 1 Chr 6:55
and its villages they **g** to Caleb the 1 Chr 6:56
sons of Aaron they **g** the cities of 1 Chr 6:57
the people of Israel **g** the Levites the 1 Chr 6:64
They **g** by lot out of the tribes of 1 Chr 6:65
who **g** him strong support in his 1 Chr 11:10
gods there, and David **g** command, 1 Chr 14:12
And the LORD **g** victory to David 1 Chr 18:6
And the LORD **g** victory to David 1 Chr 18:13
And Joab **g** the sum of the 1 Chr 21:5
it not I who **g** command to number 1 Chr 21:17
Then David **g** Solomon his son the 1 Chr 28:11
They **g** for the service of the house of 1 Chr 29:7
had precious stones **g** them to the 1 Chr 29:8
to the land that you **g** to them and to 2 Chr 6:25
in the land that you **g** to our fathers. 2 Chr 6:31
land, which you **g** to their fathers, 2 Chr 6:38
and worshiped and **g** thanks to the 2 Chr 7:3
Then she **g** the king 120 talents of 2 Chr 9:9
the queen of Sheba **g** to King Solomon. 2 Chr 9:9
And King Solomon **g** to the queen of 2 Chr 9:12
the counsel that the old men **g** him, 2 Chr 10:8
and he **g** them abundant provisions 2 Chr 11:23
God of Israel **g** the kingship over 2 Chr 13:5
and God **g** them into their hand. 2 Chr 13:16
those years, for the LORD **g** him peace. 2 Chr 14:6
and the LORD **g** them rest all around. 2 Chr 15:15
the LORD, he **g** them into your hand. 2 Chr 16:8
for his God **g** him rest all around. 2 Chr 20:30
Their father **g** them great gifts of 2 Chr 21:3
but he **g** the kingdom to Jehoram, 2 Chr 21:3
Jehoiada the priest **g** to the captains 2 Chr 23:9
on him and **g** him the testimony. 2 Chr 23:11
the king and Jehoiada **g** it to those 2 Chr 24:12
And the Ammonites **g** him that year 2 Chr 27:5
the LORD his God **g** him into the hand 2 Chr 28:5
Judah, he **g** them into your hand, 2 Chr 28:9
They clothed them, **g** them sandals, 2 Chr 28:15
and **g** tribute to the king of Assyria, 2 Chr 28:21
king of Judah **g** the assembly 1,000 2 Chr 30:24
and the princes **g** the assembly 2 Chr 30:24
people of Israel **g** in abundance the 2 Chr 31:5
he answered him and **g** him a sign. 2 Chr 32:24
the high priest and **g** him the money 2 Chr 34:9
And they **g** it to the workmen who 2 Chr 34:10
house of the LORD **g** it for repairing 2 Chr 34:10
They **g** it to the carpenters and the 2 Chr 34:11
LORD." And Hilkiah **g** the book to 2 Chr 34:15
g to the priests for the Passover 2 Chr 35:8
g to the Levites for the Passover 2 Chr 35:9
or aged. He **g** them all into his hand. 2 Chr 36:17
to their ability they **g** to the treasury of Ezr 2:69
So they **g** money to the masons and the Ezr 3:7
"Who **g** you a decree to build this house Ezr 5:3
'Who **g** you a decree to build this house Ezr 5:9
he **g** them into the hand of Ezr 5:12
letter that King Artaxerxes **g** to Ezra the Ezr 7:11
I took up the wine and **g** it to the king. Neh 2:1
Beyond the River and **g** them the king's Neh 2:9
I **g** my brother Hanani and Hananiah Neh 7:2
heads of fathers' houses **g** to the work. Neh 7:70
The governor **g** to the treasury 1,000 Neh 7:70
of fathers' houses **g** into the treasury Neh 7:71
rest of the people **g** was 20,000 darics of Neh 7:72
of God, clearly, and they **g** the sense, Neh 8:8
of the Chaldeans and **g** him the name Neh 9:7
from heaven and **g** them right rules Neh 9:13
You **g** them bread from heaven for Neh 9:15
You **g** your good Spirit to instruct Neh 9:20
from their mouth and **g** them water for Neh 9:20
"And you **g** them kingdoms and Neh 9:22
and **g** them into their hand, Neh 9:24
Therefore you **g** them into the hand of Neh 9:27
great mercies you **g** them saviors who Neh 9:27
Therefore you **g** them into the hand of Neh 9:30
and your warnings that you **g** them. Neh 9:34
your great goodness that you **g** them, Neh 9:35
in the land that you **g** to our fathers to Neh 9:36
the leader of the praise, who **g** thanks, Neh 11:17
two great choirs that **g** thanks. Neh 12:31
choir of those who **g** thanks went to Neh 12:38
choirs of those who **g** thanks stood in Neh 12:40
days of Nehemiah **g** the daily Neh 12:47
Then I **g** orders, and they cleansed the Neh 13:9
should be shut and **g** orders that they Neh 13:19
year of his reign he **g** a feast for all his Est 1:3

the king **g** for all the people present in Est 1:5
Queen Vashti also **g** a feast for the Est 1:9
Then the king **g** a great feast for all his Est 2:18
to the provinces and **g** gifts with royal Est 2:18
from his hand and **g** it to Haman the Est 3:10
Mordecai also **g** him a copy of the written Est 4:8
And he **g** orders to bring the book of Est 6:1
day King Ahasuerus **g** to Queen Esther Est 8:1
taken from Haman, and **g** it to Mordecai. Est 8:2
he **g** orders in writing that his evil plan Est 9:25
Mordecai the Jew **g** full written Est 9:29
The LORD **g**, and the LORD has taken Jb 1:21
When he **g** to the wind its weight and Jb 28:25
I **g** you my attention, and, behold, there Jb 32:12
Who **g** him charge over the earth, and Jb 34:13
And the LORD **g** Job twice as much as he Jb 42:10
And each of them **g** him a piece of Jb 42:11
And their father **g** them an inheritance Jb 42:15
You **g** a wide place for my steps under Ps 18:36
the God who **g** me vengeance and Ps 18:47
you **g** it to him, length of days forever Ps 21:4
They **g** me poison for food, and for my Ps 69:21
for my thirst they **g** me sour wine to Ps 69:21
you **g** him as food for the creatures of Ps 74:14
out water; the skies **g** forth thunder; Ps 77:17
the wilderness and **g** them drink Ps 78:15
manna to eat and **g** them the grain of Ps 78:24
filled, for he **g** them what they craved. Ps 78:29
He **g** their crops to the destroying locust Ps 78:46
He **g** over their cattle to the hail and Ps 78:48
but **g** their lives over to the plague. Ps 78:50
He **g** his people over to the sword and Ps 78:62
So I **g** them over to their stubborn Ps 81:12
and the statute that he **g** them. Ps 99:7
He **g** them hail for rain, and fiery Ps 105:32
and **g** them bread from heaven in Ps 105:40
And he **g** them the lands of the Ps 105:44
he **g** them what they asked, but sent a Ps 106:15
he **g** them into the hand of the nations, Ps 106:41
and **g** their land as a heritage, a Ps 135:12
and **g** their land as a heritage, for his Ps 136:21
he **g** a decree, and it shall not pass away. Ps 148:6
Listen to your father who **g** you life, Prv 23:22
So I turned about and **g** my heart up to Eccl 2:20
and the spirit returns to God who **g** it. Eccl 12:7
his couch, my nard **g** forth its fragrance. Sg 1:12
him not; I called him, but he **g** no answer. Sg 5:6
Who **g** up Jacob to the looter, and Israel Is 42:24
my heritage; I **g** them into your hand; Is 47:6
I **g** my back to those who strike, and my Is 50:6
valley, the Spirit of the LORD **g** them rest. Is 63:14
"Before she was in labor she **g** birth; Is 66:7
father,' and to a stone, 'You **g** me birth.' Jer 2:27
to the land that I **g** your fathers for a Jer 3:18
in the land that I **g** of old to your fathers Jer 7:7
to the place that I **g** to you and to your Jer 7:14
But this command I **g** them: 'Obey my Jer 7:23
and what I **g** them has passed away from Jer 8:13
their own land that I **g** to their fathers. Jer 16:15
hand from your heritage that I **g** to you, Jer 17:4
and the city that I **g** to you and your Jer 23:39
from the land that I **g** to them and their Jer 24:10
back to the land that I **g** to their fathers, Jer 30:3
And I **g** the deed of purchase to Baruch Jer 32:12
And you **g** them this land, which you Jer 32:22
the son of Rechab **g** to his sons, Jer 35:14
in the land that I **g** to you and your Jer 35:15
the command that their father **g** them, Jer 35:16
took another scroll and **g** it to Baruch Jer 36:32
So King Zedekiah **g** orders, and they Jer 37:21
and **g** them vineyards and fields at the Jer 39:10
of Babylon **g** command concerning Jer 39:11
captain of the guard **g** him an allowance Jer 40:5
as I **g** Zedekiah king of Judah into the Jer 44:30
and **g** him a seat above the seats of the Jer 52:32
the Lord **g** me into the hands of those Lam 1:14
The LORD **g** full vent to his wrath; he Lam 4:11
my mouth, and he **g** me this scroll to eat. Ezk 3:2
Also my bread that I **g** you—I fed you Ezk 16:19
but you **g** your gifts to all your lovers, Ezk 16:33
to play the whore, and you **g** payment, Ezk 16:34
of your children that you **g** to them, Ezk 16:36
he **g** his hand and did all these things; Ezk 17:18
I **g** them my statutes and made known Ezk 20:11
Moreover, I **g** them my Sabbaths, as a Ezk 20:12
I **g** them statutes that were not good Ezk 20:25
helmet in you; they **g** you splendor. Ezk 27:10
own land that I **g** to my servant Jacob. Ezk 28:25
beasts of the field **g** birth to their Ezk 31:6
perpetual enmity and **g** over the people Ezk 35:5
who **g** my land to themselves as a Ezk 36:5
in the land that I **g** to your fathers, Ezk 36:28
the land that I **g** to my servant Jacob, Ezk 37:25
face from them and **g** them into the Ezk 39:23
And the Lord **g** Jehoiakim king of Judah Dn 1:2
the chief of the eunuchs **g** them names: Dn 1:7
And God **g** Daniel favor and compassion Dn 1:9
were to drink, and **g** them vegetables. Dn 1:16
God **g** them learning and skill in all Dn 1:17
Then the king **g** Daniel high honors Dn 2:48
his limbs **g** way, and his knees knocked Dn 5:6
Most High God **g** Nebuchadnezzar your Dn 5:18
because of the greatness that he **g** him, Dn 5:19
Then Belshazzar **g** the command, and Dn 5:29
day and prayed and **g** thanks before his Dn 6:10
know that it was I who **g** her the grain, Hos 2:8
and through the prophets **g** parables. Hos 12:10
I **g** you a king in my anger, and I took Hos 13:11
"I **g** you cleanness of teeth in all your Am 4:6
swept on; the deep **g** forth its voice; Hab 3:10
of life and peace, and I **g** them to him. Mal 2:5
he **g** orders to go over to the other side. Mt 8:18
twelve disciples and **g** them authority Mt 10:1
broke the loaves and **g** them to the Mt 14:19
and the disciples **g** them to the crowds. Mt 14:19
he broke them and **g** them to the Mt 15:36
and the disciples **g** them to the crowds. Mt 15:36
things, and who **g** you this authority?" Mt 21:23
to a king who **g** a wedding feast for Mt 22:2
To one he **g** five talents, to another two, Mt 25:15
For I was hungry and you **g** me food, I Mt 25:35
food, I was thirsty and you **g** me drink, Mt 25:35
I was hungry and you **g** me no food, Mt 25:42
I was thirsty and you **g** me no drink, Mt 25:42
it broke it and **g** it to the disciples, Mt 26:26
he had given thanks he **g** it to them, Mt 26:27
and they **g** them for the potter's field, as Mt 27:10
chief priests and elders, he **g** no answer. Mt 27:12
But he **g** him no answer, not even to a Mt 27:14
put it on a reed and **g** it to him to drink. Mt 27:48
they **g** a sufficient sum of money to the Mt 28:12
and also **g** it to those who were with Mk 2:26
Simon (to whom he **g** the name Peter); Mk 3:16
(to whom he **g** the name Boanerges, Mk 3:17
So he **g** them permission. And the Mk 5:13
and **g** them authority over the unclean Mk 6:7
Herod on his birthday **g** a banquet for Mk 6:21
his head on a platter and **g** it to the girl, Mk 6:28
the girl, and the girl **g** it to her mother. Mk 6:28
broke the loaves and **g** them to the Mk 6:41
he broke them and **g** them to his Mk 8:6
or who **g** you this authority to do Mk 11:28
blessing it broke it and **g** it to them, Mk 14:22
he had given thanks he **g** it to them, Mk 14:23
it on a reed and **g** it to him to drink, Mk 15:36
And she **g** birth to her firstborn son and Lk 2:7
rolled up the scroll and **g** it back to the Lk 4:20
to eat, and also **g** it to those with him?" Lk 6:4
to speak, and Jesus **g** him to his mother. Lk 7:15
you **g** me no water for my feet, but she Lk 7:44
You **g** me no kiss, but from the time I Lk 7:45
enter these. So he **g** them permission. Lk 8:32
the twelve together and **g** them power and Lk 9:1
broke the loaves and **g** them to the Lk 9:16
the boy, and **g** him back to his father. Lk 9:42
out two denarii and **g** them to the Lk 10:35
"A man once **g** a great banquet and Lk 14:16
pigs ate, and no one **g** him anything. Lk 15:16
yet you never **g** me a young goat, Lk 15:29
when they saw it, **g** praise to God. Lk 18:43
of his servants, he **g** them ten minas, Lk 19:13
or who it is that **g** you this authority." Lk 20:2
thanks, he broke it and **g** it to them, Lk 22:19
blessed and broke it and **g** it to them. Lk 24:30
They **g** him a piece of broiled fish, Lk 24:42
he **g** the right to become children of God, Jn 1:12
so loved the world, that he **g** his only Son, Jn 3:16
He **g** us the well and drank from it Jn 4:12
'He **g** them bread from heaven to eat.'" Jn 6:31
was not Moses who **g** you the bread from Jn 6:32
Moses **g** you circumcision (not that it is Jn 7:22
So they **g** a dinner for him there. Martha Jn 12:2
had dipped the morsel, he **g** it to Judas, Jn 13:26
the work that you **g** me to do. Jn 17:4
to the people whom you **g** me out of the Jn 17:6
Yours they were, and you **g** them to me, Jn 17:6
given them the words that you **g** me, Jn 17:8
"Of those whom you **g** me I have lost not Jn 18:9
you from?" But Jesus **g** him no answer. Jn 19:9
he bowed his head and **g** up his spirit. Jn 19:30
of Jesus, and Pilate **g** him permission. Jn 19:38
and took the bread and **g** it to them, Jn 21:13
tongues as the Spirit **g** them utterance. Acts 2:4
stood up and **g** orders to put the men Acts 5:34
Yet he **g** him no inheritance in it, not Acts 7:5
And he **g** him the covenant of Acts 7:8
all his afflictions and **g** him favor and Acts 7:10
God turned away and **g** them over to Acts 7:42
And he **g** her his hand and raised her Acts 9:41
g alms generously to the people, Acts 10:2
If then God **g** the same gift to them as Acts 11:17
gift to them as he **g** to us when we Acts 11:17
he **g** them their land as an Acts 13:19
And after that he **g** them judges until Acts 13:20
and God **g** them Saul the son of Kish, Acts 13:21
although we **g** them no instructions, Acts 15:24
off them and **g** orders to beat Acts 16:22
Then he **g** orders to the centurion Acts 24:23
treated Paul kindly and **g** him leave to Acts 27:3
we **g** way to it and were driven along. Acts 27:15
Therefore God **g** them up in the lusts Rom 1:24
For this reason God **g** them up to Rom 1:26
the men likewise **g** up natural Rom 1:27
God **g** them up to a debased mind to do Rom 1:28
strong in his faith as he **g** glory to God, Rom 4:20
spare his own Son but **g** him up for us Rom 8:32
written, "God **g** them a spirit of stupor, Rom 11:8
Apollos watered, but God **g** the growth. 1 Cor 3:6
became a man, I **g** up childish ways. 1 Cor 13:11
us to himself and **g** us the ministry of 2 Cor 5:18
For they **g** according to their means, 2 Cor 8:3
but they **g** themselves first to the Lord 2 Cor 8:5
which the Lord **g** for building you up 2 Cor 10:8
who **g** himself for our sins to deliver us Gal 1:4
they **g** the right hand of fellowship to Gal 2:9
who loved me and **g** himself for me. Gal 2:20
but God **g** it to Abraham by a promise. Gal 3:18
under his feet and **g** him as head over Eph 1:22
a host of captives, and he **g** gifts to men." Eph 4:8
And he **g** the apostles, the prophets, the Eph 4:11
Christ loved us and **g** himself up for us, Eph 5:2
loved the church and **g** himself up for Eph 5:25
what instructions we **g** you through 1 Thes 4:2
loved us and **g** us eternal comfort 2 Thes 2:16
who **g** himself as a ransom for all, 1 Tm 2:6
for God **g** us a spirit not of fear but of 2 Tm 1:7
which he **g** us in Christ Jesus before 2 Tm 1:9
who **g** himself for us to redeem us from Ti 2:14
Abraham the patriarch **g** a tenth of Heb 7:4
Israelites and **g** directions concerning Heb 11:22
he prayed again, and heaven **g** rain, Jas 5:18
him from the dead and **g** him glory, 1 Pt 1:21
testimony, that God **g** us eternal life, 1 Jn 5:11
which God **g** him to show to his servants Rv 1:1
I **g** her time to repent, but she refuses to Rv 2:21
rest were terrified and **g** glory to the God Rv 11:13
She **g** birth to a male child, one who is to Rv 12:5
And to it the dragon **g** his power and his Rv 13:2
the four living creatures **g** to the seven Rv 15:7
And the sea **g** up the dead who were in Rv 20:13
Death and Hades **g** up the dead who Rv 20:13

GAZA (22)

in the direction of Gerar as far as **G**, Gn 10:19
Avvim, who lived in villages as far as **G**, Dt 2:23
them from Kadesh-barnea as far as **G**, Jos 10:41
Only in **G**, in Gath, and in Ashdod did Jos 11:22
five rulers of the Philistines, those of **G**, Jos 13:3
its villages; **G**, its towns and its villages; Jos 15:47
Judah also captured **G** with its territory, Jgs 1:18
the produce of the land, as far as **G**, Jgs 6:4
Samson went to **G**, and there he saw a Jgs 16:1
him down to **G** and bound him Jgs 16:21
one for Ashdod, one for **G**, one for 1 Sm 6:17
of the Euphrates from Tiphsah to **G**, 1 Kgs 4:24
as far as **G** and its territory, 2 Kgs 18:8
of the Philistines (Ashkelon, **G**, Ekron, Jer 25:20
before Pharaoh struck down **G**. Jer 47:1
Baldness has come upon **G**; Ashkelon Jer 47:5
"For three transgressions of **G**, and for Am 1:6
So I will send a fire upon the wall of **G**, Am 1:7
For **G** shall be deserted, and Ashkelon Zep 2:4
G too, and shall writhe in anguish; Zec 9:5
The king shall perish from **G**; Ashkelon Zec 9:5
down from Jerusalem to **G**." This is a Acts 8:26

GAZE (12)

And he fixed his **g** and stared at him, 2 Kgs 8:11
my eyes; how then could I **g** at a virgin? Jb 31:1
to **g** upon the beauty of the LORD and to Ps 27:4
and your **g** be straight before you. Prv 4:25
Do not **g** at me because I am dark, Sg 1:6
divide the heavens, who **g** at the stars, Is 47:13
be defiled, and let our eyes **g** upon Zion." Mi 4:11
drunk, in order to **g** at their nakedness! Hab 2:15
And Peter directed his **g** at him, as did Acts 3:4
the Israelites could not **g** at Moses' face 2 Cor 3:7
Israelites might not **g** at the outcome 2 Cor 3:13
and nations will **g** at their dead Rv 11:9

GAZED (2)

The man **g** at her in silence to learn Gn 24:21
g into heaven and saw the glory of Acts 7:55

GAZELLE (12)

eat of it, as of the **g** and as of the deer. Dt 12:15
Just as the **g** or the deer is eaten, so you Dt 12:22

the deer, the **g**, the roebuck, the wild goat, Dt 14:5
eat it, as though it were a **g** or a deer. Dt 15:22
Asahel was as swift of foot as a wild **g**. 2 Sm 2:18
save yourself like a **g** from the hand of Prv 6:5
My beloved is like a **g** or a young stag. Sg 2:9
be like a **g** or a young stag on cleft Sg 2:17
breasts are like two fawns, twins of a **g**, Sg 4:5
breasts are like two fawns, twins of a **g**. Sg 7:3
and be like a **g** or a young stag on the Sg 8:14
And like a hunted **g**, or like sheep with Is 13:14

GAZELLES (4)
sheep, besides deer, **g**, roebucks, 1 Kgs 4:23
were swift as **g** upon the mountains: 1 Chr 12:8
Jerusalem, by the **g** or the does of the field, Sg 2:7
Jerusalem, by the **g** or the does of the field, Sg 3:5

GAZEZ (2)
bore Haran, Moza, and **G**; 1 Chr 2:46
and Gazez; and Haran fathered **G**. 1 Chr 2:46

GAZING (3)
behind our wall, **g** through the windows, Sg 2:9
And while they were **g** into heaven as Acts 1:10
And **g** at him, all who sat in the Acts 6:15

GAZITES (1)
The **G** were told, "Samson has come Jgs 16:2

GAZZAM (2)
Rezin, the sons of Nekoda, the sons of **G**, Ezr 2:48
the sons of **G**, the sons of Uzza, the sons Neh 7:51

GE-HARASHIM (1)
Seraiah fathered Joab, the father of **G**, 1 Chr 4:14

GEAR (1)
on the Syrtis, they lowered the **g**, Acts 27:17

GEBA (17)
G—twelve cities with their villages: Jos 18:24
pasturelands, **G** with its pasturelands, Jos 21:17
of the Philistines that was at **G**, 1 Sm 13:3
with them stayed in **G** of Benjamin, 1 Sm 13:16
the other on the south in front of **G**. 1 Sm 14:5
down the Philistines from **G** to Gezer. 2 Sm 5:25
King Asa built **G** of Benjamin and 1 Kgs 15:22
made offerings, from **G** to Beersheba. 2 Kgs 23:8
Gibeon, **G** with its pasturelands, 1 Chr 6:60
fathers' houses of the inhabitants of **G**, 1 Chr 8:6
with them he built **G** and Mizpah. 2 Chr 16:6
The sons of Ramah and **G**, 621. Ezr 2:26
The men of Ramah and **G**, 621. Neh 7:30
Benjamin also lived from **G** onward, Neh 11:31
from the region of **G** and Azmaveth, Neh 12:29
the pass; at **G** they lodge for the night; Is 10:29
into a plain from **G** to Rimmon south Zec 14:10

GEBAL (3)
and the men of **G** did the cutting and 1 Kgs 5:18
G and Ammon and Amalek, Philistia Ps 83:7
The elders of **G** and her skilled men Ezk 27:9

GEBALITES (1)
and the land of the **G**, and all Lebanon, Jos 13:5

GEBER (1)
G the son of Uri, in the land of Gilead, 1 Kgs 4:19

GEBIM (1)
the inhabitants of **G** flee for safety. Is 10:31

GECKO (1)
the **g**, the monitor lizard, the lizard, the Lv 11:30

GEDALIAH (32)
he appointed **G** the son of Ahikam, 2 Kgs 25:22
Babylon had appointed **G** governor, 2 Kgs 25:23
with their men to **G** at Mizpah, 2 Kgs 25:23
And **G** swore to them and their men, 2 Kgs 25:24
and struck down **G** and put him 2 Kgs 25:25
G, Zeri, Jeshaiah, Shimei, Hashabiah, 1 Chr 25:3
the second to **G**, to him and his 1 Chr 25:9
Maaseiah, Eliezer, Jarib, and **G**, some Ezr 10:18
the son of Mattan, **G** the son of Pashhur, Jer 38:1
They entrusted him to **G** the son of Jer 39:14
then return to **G** the son of Ahikam, Jer 40:5
Then Jeremiah went to **G** the son of Jer 40:6
of Babylon had appointed **G** the son of Jer 40:7
they went to **G** at Mizpah—Ishmael the Jer 40:8
G the son of Ahikam, son of Shaphan, Jer 40:9
Judah and had appointed **G** the son of Jer 40:11
to the land of Judah, to **G** at Mizpah. Jer 40:12
the open country came to **G** at Mizpah Jer 40:13
take your life?" But **G** the son of Jer 40:14
Kareah spoke secretly to **G** at Mizpah, Jer 40:15
But **G** the son of Ahikam said to Jer 40:16
with ten men to **G** the son of Ahikam, Jer 41:1
up and struck down **G** the son of Jer 41:2
the Judeans who were with **G** at Mizpah, Jer 41:3
On the day after the murder of **G**, before Jer 41:4
"Come in to **G** the son of Ahikam." Jer 41:6
struck down along with **G** was the large Jer 41:9
had committed to **G** the son of Jer 41:10
he had struck down **G** the son of Jer 41:16
had struck down **G** the son of Jer 41:18
guard had left with **G** the son of Jer 43:6
to Zephaniah the son of Cushi, son of **G**, Zep 1:1

GEDER (1)
king of Debir, one; the king of **G**, one; Jos 12:13

GEDERAH (3)
Shaaraim, Adithaim, **G**, Gederothaim: Jos 15:36
were inhabitants of Netaim and **G**. 1 Chr 4:23
Jahaziel, Johanan, Jozabad of **G**, 1 Chr 12:4

GEDERITE (1)
Shephelah was Baal-hanan the **G**; 1 Chr 27:28

GEDEROTH (2)
G, Beth-dagon, Naamah, and Jos 15:41
Aijalon, **G**, Soco with its villages, 2 Chr 28:18

GEDEROTHAIM (1)
G: fourteen cities with their villages. Jos 15:36

GEDOR (7)
Halhul, Beth-zur, **G**, Jos 15:58
and Penuel fathered **G**, and Ezer 1 Chr 4:4
wife bore Jered the father of **G**, 1 Chr 4:18
They journeyed to the entrance of **G**, 1 Chr 4:39
G, Ahio, Zecher, 1 Chr 8:31
G, Ahio, Zechariah, and Mikloth; 1 Chr 9:37
Zebadiah, the sons of Jeroham of **G**. 1 Chr 12:7

GEHAZI (13)
And he said to **G** his servant, "Call 2 Kgs 4:12
is to be done for her?" **G** answered, 2 Kgs 4:14
her coming, he said to **G** his servant, 2 Kgs 4:25
feet. And **G** came to push her away. 2 Kgs 4:27
He said to **G**, "Tie up your garment 2 Kgs 4:29
G went on ahead and laid the staff on 2 Kgs 4:31
Then he summoned **G** and said, 2 Kgs 4:36
G, the servant of Elisha the man of 2 Kgs 5:20
So **G** followed Naaman. And when 2 Kgs 5:21
And they carried them before **G**. 2 Kgs 5:23
have you been, **G**?" And he said, 2 Kgs 5:25
king was talking with **G** the servant of 2 Kgs 8:4
her house and her land. And **G** said, 2 Kgs 8:5

GELILOTH (1)
En-shemesh, and from there goes to **G**, Jos 18:17

GEMALLI (1)
the tribe of Dan, Ammiel the son of **G**; Nm 13:12

GEMARIAH (5)
son of Shaphan and **G** the son of Jer 29:3
in the chamber of **G** the son of Jer 36:10
When Micaiah the son of **G**, son of Jer 36:11
son of Achbor, **G** the son of Shaphan, Jer 36:12
and Delaiah and **G** urged the king Jer 36:25

GENEALOGICAL (1)
settlements, and they kept a **g** record. 1 Chr 4:33

GENEALOGIES (12)
the sons of Noah, according to their **g**, Gn 10:32
These are their **g**: the firstborn of 1 Chr 1:29
these were recorded in **g** in the days of 1 Chr 5:17
And their enrollment by **g** was 22,034. 1 Chr 7:7
And their enrollment by **g**, according 1 Chr 7:9
Their number enrolled by **g**, for 1 Chr 7:40
So all Israel was recorded in **g**, and 1 Chr 9:1
were enrolled by **g** in their villages. 1 Chr 9:22
among those enrolled in the **g**, Ezr 2:62
among those enrolled in the **g**, Neh 7:64
themselves to myths and endless **g**, 1 Tm 1:4
avoid foolish controversies, **g**, dissensions, Ti 3:9

GENEALOGY (9)
when the **g** of their generations was 1 Chr 5:7
87,000 mighty warriors, enrolled by **g**. 1 Chr 7:5
Hebronites of whatever **g** or fathers' 1 Chr 26:31
except those enrolled by **g**, males 2 Chr 31:16
and this is the **g** of those who went up Ezr 8:1
and the people to be enrolled by **g**. Neh 7:5
the book of the **g** of those who came Neh 7:5
The book of the **g** of Jesus Christ, the son Mt 1:1
He is without father or mother or **g**, Heb 7:3

GENERAL (1)
draw out Sisera, the **g** of Jabin's army, Jgs 4:7

GENERALS (1)
the great ones and the **g** and the rich and Rv 6:15

GENERATION (93)
was a righteous man, blameless in his **g**. Gn 6:9
you are righteous before me in this **g**. Gn 7:1
shall come back here in the fourth **g**, Gn 15:16
saw Ephraim's children of the third **g**. Gn 50:23
died, and all his brothers and all that **g**. Ex 1:6
with Amalek from **g** to generation." Ex 17:16
with Amalek from generation to **g**." Ex 17:16
third and the fourth **g** of those who hate Ex 20:5
children, to the third and the fourth **g**." Ex 34:7
to the third and the fourth **g**.' Nm 14:18
until all the **g** that had done evil in the Nm 32:13
these men of this evil **g** shall see the good Dt 1:35
was thirty-eight years, until the entire **g**, Dt 2:14
to the third and fourth **g** of those who hate Dt 5:9
Even to the tenth **g**, none of his Dt 23:2
Even to the tenth **g**, none of them may Dt 23:3
them in the third **g** may enter the Dt 23:8
And the next **g**, your children who rise Dt 29:22
they are a crooked and twisted **g**. Dt 32:5
end will be, For they are a perverse **g**, Dt 32:20
And all that **g** also were gathered to their Jgs 2:10
there arose another **g** after them who Jgs 2:10
sons of the fourth **g** shall sit on the 2 Kgs 10:30
Israel to the fourth **g**." And so it 2 Kgs 15:12
and kept throughout every **g**, Est 9:28
you will guard us from this **g** forever. Ps 12:7
for God is with the **g** of the righteous. Ps 14:5
be told of the Lord to the coming **g**; Ps 22:30
Such is the **g** of those who seek him, who Ps 24:6
her citadels, that you may tell the next **g** Ps 48:13
his soul will go to the **g** of his fathers, Ps 49:19
I proclaim your might to another **g**, Ps 71:18
have betrayed the **g** of your children. Ps 73:15
tell to the coming **g** the glorious deeds of Ps 78:4
that the next **g** might know them, the Ps 78:6
fathers, a stubborn and rebellious **g**, Ps 78:8
a **g** whose heart was not steadfast, Ps 78:8
from **g** to generation we will recount Ps 79:13
from generation to **g** we will recount Ps 79:13
For forty years I loathed that **g** and said, Ps 95:10
Let this be recorded for a **g** to come, so Ps 102:18
as righteousness from **g** to generation Ps 106:31
from generation to **g** forever. Ps 106:31
name be blotted out in the second **g**! Ps 109:13
the **g** of the upright will be blessed. Ps 112:2
One **g** shall commend your works to Ps 145:4
A **g** goes, and a generation comes, but Eccl 1:4
A generation goes, and a **g** comes, but Eccl 1:4
From **g** to generation it shall lie waste; Is 34:10
From generation to **g** it shall lie waste; Is 34:10
from **g** to generation they shall dwell in Is 34:17
from generation to **g** they shall dwell in Is 34:17
and as for his **g**, who considered that he Is 53:8
And you, O **g**, behold the word of the Jer 2:31
rejected and forsaken the **g** of his wrath.' Jer 7:29
dominion endures from **g** to generation. Dn 4:3
dominion endures from generation to **g**. Dn 4:3
kingdom endures from **g** to generation; Dn 4:34
kingdom endures from generation to **g**; Dn 4:34
children, and their children to another **g**. Jl 1:3
"But to what shall I compare this **g**? It Mt 11:16
"An evil and adulterous **g** seeks for a Mt 12:39
judgment with this **g** and condemn it, Mt 12:41
judgment with this **g** and condemn it, Mt 12:42
first. So also will it be with this evil **g**." Mt 12:45
An evil and adulterous **g** seeks for a Mt 16:4
answered, "O faithless and twisted **g**, Mt 17:17
all these things will come upon this **g**. Mt 23:36
this **g** will not pass away until all these Mt 24:34
and said, "Why does this **g** seek a sign? Mk 8:12
to you, no sign will be given to this **g**." Mk 8:12
words in this adulterous and sinful **g**, Mk 8:38
And he answered them, "O faithless **g**, Mk 9:19
this **g** will not pass away until all these Mk 13:30
who fear him from **g** to generation. Lk 1:50
who fear him from generation to **g**. Lk 1:50
then shall I compare the people of this **g**, Lk 7:31
answered, "O faithless and twisted **g**, Lk 9:41
to say, "This **g** is an evil generation. Lk 11:29
to say, "This generation is an evil **g**. Lk 11:29
so will the Son of Man be to this **g**. Lk 11:30
the men of this **g** and condemn them, Lk 11:31
judgment with this **g** and condemn it, Lk 11:32
world, may be charged against this **g**, Lk 11:50
I tell you, it will be required of this **g**. Lk 11:51
dealing with their own **g** than the sons Lk 16:8
many things and be rejected by this **g**. Lk 17:25
this **g** will not pass away until all has Lk 21:32
"Save yourselves from this crooked **g**." Acts 2:40
denied him. Who can describe his **g**? Acts 8:33
the purpose of God in his own **g**, Acts 13:36
in the midst of a crooked and twisted **g**, Phil 2:15
Therefore I was provoked with that **g**, Heb 3:10

GENERATIONS (119)
These are the **g** of the heavens and the Gn 2:4
This is the book of the **g** of Adam. When Gn 5:1
These are the **g** of Noah. Noah was a Gn 6:9
that is with you, for all future **g**: Gn 9:12
These are the **g** of the sons of Noah, Gn 10:1
These are the **g** of Shem. When Shem Gn 11:10
Now these are the **g** of Terah. Terah Gn 11:27
you throughout their **g** for an Gn 17:7
offspring after you throughout their **g**. Gn 17:9

Every male throughout your **g**, Gn 17:12
These are the **g** of Ishmael, Abraham's Gn 25:12
These are the **g** of Isaac, Abraham's Gn 25:19
These are the **g** of Esau (that is, Edom). Gn 36:1
These are the **g** of Esau the father of the Gn 36:9
These are the **g** of Jacob. Joseph, being Gn 37:2
I am to be remembered throughout all **g**. Ex 3:15
of the sons of Levi according to their **g**: Ex 6:16
clans of the Levites according to their **g**. Ex 6:19
throughout your **g**, as a statute forever, Ex 12:14
observe this day, throughout your **g**, Ex 12:17
the people of Israel throughout their **g**. Ex 12:42
omer of it be kept throughout your **g**, Ex 16:32
the LORD to be kept throughout your **g**." Ex 16:33
observed throughout their **g** by the Ex 27:21
offering throughout your **g** at the Ex 29:42
before the LORD throughout your **g**. Ex 30:8
it once in the year throughout your **g**. Ex 30:10
to his offspring throughout their **g**." Ex 30:21
holy anointing oil throughout your **g**. Ex 30:31
me and you throughout your **g**, Ex 31:13
the Sabbath throughout their **g**, Ex 31:16
priesthood throughout their **g**." Ex 40:15
be a statute forever throughout your **g**, Lv 3:17
it, as decreed forever throughout your **g**, Lv 6:18
It is a perpetual due throughout their **g**." Lv 7:36
be a statute forever throughout your **g**. Lv 10:9
forever for them throughout their **g**. Lv 17:7
offspring throughout their **g** who has a Lv 21:17
throughout your **g** approaches the Lv 22:3
forever throughout your **g** in all your Lv 23:14
dwelling places throughout your **g**. Lv 23:21
forever throughout your **g** in all your Lv 23:31
is a statute forever throughout your **g**; Lv 23:41
that your **g** may know that I made the Lv 23:43
be a statute forever throughout your **g**. Lv 24:3
to the buyer, throughout his **g**; Lv 25:30
of Reuben, Israel's firstborn, their **g**, Nm 1:20
Of the people of Simeon, their **g**, by Nm 1:22
Of the people of Gad, their **g**, by their Nm 1:24
Of the people of Judah, their **g**, by their Nm 1:26
Of the people of Issachar, their **g**, by Nm 1:28
Of the people of Zebulun, their **g**, by Nm 1:30
of the people of Ephraim, their **g**, Nm 1:32
Of the people of Manasseh, their **g**, by Nm 1:34
Of the people of Benjamin, their **g**, by Nm 1:36
Of the people of Dan, their **g**, by their Nm 1:38
Of the people of Asher, their **g**, by their Nm 1:40
Of the people of Naphtali, their **g**, by Nm 1:42
These are the **g** of Aaron and Moses at Nm 3:1
a perpetual statute throughout your **g**. Nm 10:8
a statute forever throughout your **g**. Nm 15:15
as a contribution throughout your **g**. Nm 15:21
and onward throughout your **g**, Nm 15:23
of their garments throughout their **g**, Nm 15:38
a perpetual statute throughout your **g**, Nm 18:23
for you throughout your **g** in all your Nm 35:29
his commandments, to a thousand **g**, Dt 7:9
days of old; consider the years of many **g**; Dt 32:7
us and you, and between our **g** after us, Jos 22:27
only in order that the **g** of the people of Jgs 3:2
Now these are the **g** of Perez: Perez Ru 4:18
the genealogy of their **g** was recorded: 1 Chr 5:7
of Tola, mighty warriors of their **g**, 1 Chr 7:2
And along with them, by their **g**, 1 Chr 7:4
by genealogies, according to their **g**, 1 Chr 7:9
fathers' houses, according to their **g**, 1 Chr 8:28
their kinsmen according to their **g**, 1 Chr 9:9
of the Levites, according to their **g**, 1 Chr 9:34
he commanded, for a thousand **g**, 1 Chr 16:15
come, and have shown me future **g**, 1 Chr 17:17
saw his sons, and his sons' sons, four **g**. Jb 42:16
throughout all **g** I shall not meet Ps 10:6
forever, the plans of his heart to all **g**. Ps 33:11
your name to be remembered in all **g**; Ps 45:17
forever, their dwelling places to all **g**, Ps 49:11
the king; may his years endure to all **g**! Ps 61:6
as long as the moon, throughout all **g**! Ps 72:5
Will you prolong your anger to all **g**? Ps 85:5
make known your faithfulness to all **g**. Ps 89:1
and build your throne for all **g**.'" Selah Ps 89:4
have been our dwelling place in all **g**. Ps 90:1
forever, and his faithfulness to all **g**. Ps 100:5
you are remembered throughout all **g**. Ps 102:12
whose years endure throughout all **g**!" Ps 102:24
that he commanded, for a thousand **g**, Ps 105:8
Your faithfulness endures to all **g**; you Ps 119:90
dominion endures throughout all **g**. Ps 145:13
forever, your God, O Zion, to all **g**. Ps 146:10
and does a crown endure to all **g**? Prv 27:24
never be inhabited or lived in for all **g**; Is 13:20
this, calling the **g** from the beginning? Is 41:4
will be forever, and my salvation to all **g**." Is 51:8
awake, as in days of old, the **g** of long ago. Is 51:9
raise up the foundations of many **g**; Is 58:12
ruined cities, the devastations of many **g**. Is 61:4
have people, nor be inhabited for all **g**. Jer 50:39
forever; your throne endures to all **g**. Lam 5:19
again after them through the years of all **g**. Jl 2:2
inhabited forever, and Jerusalem to all **g**. Jl 3:20
So all the **g** from Abraham to David Mt 1:17
Abraham to David were fourteen **g**, Mt 1:17
to the deportation to Babylon fourteen **g**, Mt 1:17
to Babylon to the Christ fourteen **g**. Mt 1:17
from now on all **g** will call me blessed; Lk 1:48
In past **g** he allowed all the nations to Acts 14:16
For from ancient **g** Moses has had in Acts 15:21
sons of men in other **g** as it has now Eph 3:5
and in Christ Jesus throughout all **g**, Eph 3:21
hidden for ages and **g** but now revealed Col 1:26

GENEROSITY (6)
provinces and gave gifts with royal **g**. Est 2:18
to me? Or do you begrudge my **g**?' Mt 20:15
the one who contributes, in **g**; Rom 12:8
in a wealth of **g** on their part. 2 Cor 8:2
enriched in every way for all your **g**, 2 Cor 9:11
and the **g** of your contribution for 2 Cor 9:13

GENEROUS (10)
Whoever is of a **g** heart, let him bring Ex 35:5
back, but the righteous is **g** and gives; Ps 37:21
but blessed is he who is **g** to the poor. Prv 14:21
but he who is **g** to the needy honors Prv 14:31
Many seek the favor of a **g** man, and Prv 19:6
Whoever is **g** to the poor lends to the Prv 19:17
gathers it for him who is **g** to the poor. Prv 28:8
their food with glad and **g** hearts, Acts 2:46
blame us about this **g** gift that is 2 Cor 8:20
works, to be **g** and ready to share, 1 Tm 6:18

GENEROUSLY (4)
He is ever lending **g**, and his children Ps 37:26
with the man who deals **g** and lends; Ps 112:5
household, gave alms **g** to the people, Acts 10:2
God, who gives **g** to all without reproach, Jas 1:5

GENNESARET (3)
crossed over, they came to land at **G**. Mt 14:34
came to land at **G** and moored to the Mk 6:53
of God, he was standing by the lake of **G**, Lk 5:1

GENTILE (4)
be to you as a **G** and a tax collector. Mt 18:17
Now the woman was a **G**, a Mk 7:26
a Jew, live like a **G** and not like a Jew, Gal 2:14
are Jews by birth and not **G** sinners; Gal 2:15

GENTILES (92)
sea, beyond the Jordan, Galilee of the **G**— Mt 4:15
others? Do not even the **G** do the same? Mt 5:47
do not heap up empty phrases as the **G** do, Mt 6:7
For the **G** seek after all these things, and Mt 6:32
"Go nowhere among the **G** and enter no Mt 10:5
to bear witness before them and the **G**. Mt 10:18
and he will proclaim justice to the **G**. Mt 12:18
and in his name the **G** will hope." Mt 12:21
him over to the **G** to be mocked and Mt 20:19
the rulers of the **G** lord it over them, Mt 20:25
to death and deliver him over to the **G**. Mk 10:33
considered rulers of the **G** lord it over Mk 10:42
a light for revelation to the **G**, and for Lk 2:32
delivered over to the **G** and will be Lk 18:32
will be trampled underfoot by the **G**, Lk 21:24
until the times of the **G** are fulfilled. Lk 21:24
kings of the **G** exercise lordship over Lk 22:25
the Holy Spirit, "'Why did the **G** rage, Acts 4:25
along with the **G** and the peoples of Acts 4:27
my name before the **G** and kings and Acts 9:15
Spirit was poured out even on the **G**. Acts 10:45
heard that the **G** also had received Acts 11:1
"Then to the **G** also God has granted Acts 11:18
life, behold, we are turning to the **G**. Acts 13:46
"'I have made you a light for the **G**, Acts 13:47
And when the **G** heard this, they Acts 13:48
stirred up the **G** and poisoned their Acts 14:2
attempt was made by both **G** and Jews, Acts 14:5
he had opened a door of faith to the **G**. Acts 14:27
in detail the conversion of the **G**, Acts 15:3
by my mouth the **G** should hear the Acts 15:7
done through them among the **G**. Acts 15:12
related how God first visited the **G**, Acts 15:14
and all the **G** who are called by my Acts 15:17
trouble those of the **G** who turn to Acts 15:19
who are of the **G** in Antioch and Acts 15:23
From now on I will go to the **G**." Acts 18:6
deliver him into the hands of the **G**.'" Acts 21:11
done among the **G** through his Acts 21:19
are among the **G** to forsake Moses, Acts 21:21
But as for the **G** who have believed, Acts 21:25
for I will send you far away to the **G**.'" Acts 22:21
people and from the **G**—to whom I Acts 26:17
the region of Judea, and also to the **G**, Acts 26:20
light both to our people and to the **G**." Acts 26:23
of God has been sent to the **G**; Acts 28:28
you as well as among the rest of the **G**. Rom 1:13
For when **G**, who do not have the law, Rom 2:14
blasphemed among the **G** because of Rom 2:24
Jews only? Is he not the God of **G** also? Rom 3:29
the God of Gentiles also? Yes, of **G** also, Rom 3:29
the Jews only but also from the **G**? Rom 9:24
That **G** who did not pursue Rom 9:30
trespass salvation has come to the **G**, Rom 11:11
their failure means riches for the **G**, Rom 11:12
Now I am speaking to you **G**. Rom 11:13
then as I am an apostle to the **G**, Rom 11:13
the fullness of the **G** has come in. Rom 11:25
in order that the **G** might glorify God Rom 15:9
I will praise you among the **G**, Rom 15:9
And again it is said, "Rejoice, O **G**, Rom 15:10
again, "Praise the Lord, all you **G**, Rom 15:11
even he who arises to rule the **G**; Rom 15:12
the Gentiles; in him will the **G** hope." Rom 15:12
Christ Jesus to the **G** in the priestly Rom 15:16
offering of the **G** may be acceptable, Rom 15:16
me to bring the **G** to obedience—by Rom 15:18
For if the **G** have come to share in Rom 15:27
the churches of the **G** give thanks as Rom 16:4
block to Jews and folly to **G**, 1 Cor 1:23
my own people, danger from **G**, 2 Cor 11:26
that I might preach him among the **G**, Gal 1:16
the gospel that I proclaim among the **G**, Gal 2:2
also through me for mine to the **G**), Gal 2:8
we should go to the **G** and they to the Gal 2:9
from James, he was eating with the **G**; Gal 2:12
can you force the **G** to live like Jews?" Gal 2:14
that God would justify the **G** by faith, Gal 3:8
of Abraham might come to the **G**, Gal 3:14
that at one time you **G** in the flesh, Eph 2:11
for Christ Jesus on behalf of you **G**— Eph 3:1
mystery is that the **G** are fellow heirs, Eph 3:6
preach to the **G** the unsearchable riches Eph 3:8
you must no longer walk as the **G** do, Eph 4:17
how great among the **G** are the riches of Col 1:27
speaking to the **G** that they might 1 Thes 2:16
of lust like the **G** who do not know 1 Thes 4:5
a teacher of the **G** in faith and truth. 1 Tm 2:7
and all the **G** might hear it. 2 Tm 4:17
your conduct among the **G** honorable, 1 Pt 2:12
suffices for doing what the **G** want to do, 1 Pt 4:3
name, accepting nothing from the **G**. 3 Jn 1:7

GENTLE (11)
dew, like **g** rain upon the tender grass, Dt 32:2
And I was **g** today, though anointed 2 Sm 3:39
A **g** tongue is a tree of life, but Prv 15:4
But I was like a **g** lamb led to the Jer 11:19
from me, for I am **g** and lowly in heart, Mt 11:29
But we were **g** among you, like a 1 Thes 2:7
not a drunkard, not violent but **g**, not 1 Tm 3:3
evil of no one, to avoid quarreling, to be **g**, Ti 3:2
pure, then peaceable, **g**, open to reason, Jas 3:17
only to the good and **g** but also to the 1 Pt 2:18
beauty of a **g** and quiet spirit, 1 Pt 3:4

GENTLENESS (10)
salvation, and your **g** made me great. 2 Sm 22:36
me, and your **g** made me great. Ps 18:35
a rod, or with love in a spirit of **g**? 1 Cor 4:21
by the meekness and **g** of Christ—I 2 Cor 10:1
g, self-control; against such things Gal 5:23
should restore him in a spirit of **g**. Gal 6:1
with all humility and **g**, with patience, Eph 4:2
godliness, faith, love, steadfastness, **g**. 1 Tm 6:11
correcting his opponents with **g**. God 2 Tm 2:25
yet do it with **g** and respect, having a 1 Pt 3:16

GENTLY (6)
"Deal **g** for my sake with the young 2 Sm 18:5
you, or the word that deals **g** with you? Jb 15:11
refused the waters of Shiloah that flow **g**, Is 8:6
and **g** lead those that are with young. Is 40:11
Now when the south wind blew **g**, Acts 27:13
He can deal **g** with the ignorant and Heb 5:2

GENUBATH (2)
of Tahpenes bore him **G** his son, 1 Kgs 11:20
And **G** was in Pharaoh's house 1 Kgs 11:20

GENUINE (4)
Let love be **g**. Abhor what is evil; hold Rom 12:9
those who are **g** among you may 1 Cor 11:19
kindness, the Holy Spirit, **g** love; 2 Cor 6:6
of others that your love also is **g**. 2 Cor 8:8

GENUINELY (1)
who will be **g** concerned for your Phil 2:20

GENUINENESS (2)
This is the sign of **g** in every letter of 2 Thes 3:17
so that the tested **g** of your faith—more 1 Pt 1:7

GERA (9)
Bela, Becher, Ashbel, **G**, Naaman, Ehi, Gn 46:21
for them a deliverer, Ehud, the son of **G**, Jgs 3:15
whose name was Shimei, the son of **G**, 2 Sm 16:5
And Shimei the son of **G**, the 2 Sm 19:16
Shimei the son of **G** fell down before 2 Sm 19:18
is also with you Shimei the son of **G**, 1 Kgs 2:8
And Bela had sons: Addar, **G**, Abihud, 1 Chr 8:3
G, Shephuphan, and Huram. 1 Chr 8:5
Naaman, Ahijah, and **G**, that is, 1 Chr 8:7

GERAHS (5)
the sanctuary (the shekel is twenty **g**), Ex 30:13
twenty **g** shall make a shekel. Lv 27:25
the sanctuary (the shekel of twenty **g**), Nm 3:47
of the sanctuary, which is twenty **g**. Nm 18:16
The shekel shall be twenty **g**; twenty Ezk 45:12

GERAR (10)
in the direction of **G** as far as Gaza, Gn 10:19
and Shur; and he sojourned in **G**. Gn 20:1
And Abimelech king of **G** sent and took Gn 20:2
And Isaac went to **G** to Abimelech king Gn 26:1
So Isaac settled in **G**. Gn 26:6
in the valley of **G** and settled there. Gn 26:17
the herdsmen of **G** quarreled with Gn 26:20
went to him from **G** with Ahuzzath his Gn 26:26
with him pursued them as far as **G**, 2 Chr 14:13
attacked all the cities around **G**, 2 Chr 14:14

GERASENES (3)
side of the sea, to the country of the **G**. Mk 5:1
Then they sailed to the country of the **G**, Lk 8:26
country of the **G** asked him to Lk 8:37

GERIZIM (4)
the blessing on Mount **G** and the curse Dt 11:29
shall stand on Mount **G** to bless the Dt 27:12
in front of Mount **G** and half of them Jos 8:33
on top of Mount **G** and cried aloud and Jgs 9:7

GERSHOM (12)
birth to a son, and he called his name **G**, Ex 2:22
The name of the one was **G** (for he said, Ex 18:3
themselves, and Jonathan the son of **G**, Jgs 18:30
sons of Levi: **G**, Kohath, and Merari. 1 Chr 6:16
these are the names of the sons of **G**: 1 Chr 6:17
Of **G**: Libni his son, Jahath his son, 1 Chr 6:20
son of Jahath, son of **G**, son of Levi. 1 Chr 6:43
of the sons of **G**, Joel the chief, with 1 Chr 15:7
The sons of Moses: **G** and Eliezer. 1 Chr 23:15
The sons of **G**: Shebuel the chief. 1 Chr 23:16
and Shebuel the son of **G**, son of 1 Chr 26:24
of Phinehas, **G**. Of the sons of Ithamar, Ezr 8:2

GERSHOMITES (2)
To the **G** according to their clans 1 Chr 6:62
To the **G** were given out of the clan of 1 Chr 6:71

GERSHON (16)
sons of Levi: **G**, Kohath, and Merari. Gn 46:11
G, Kohath, and Merari, the years of the Ex 6:16
The sons of **G**: Libni and Shimei, by Ex 6:17
names: **G** and Kohath and Merari. Nm 3:17
names of the sons of **G** by their clans: Nm 3:18
To **G** belonged the clan of the Libnites Nm 3:21
duty of the sons of **G** in the tent of Nm 3:25
"Take a census of the sons of **G** also, by Nm 4:22
Those listed of the sons of **G**, by their Nm 4:38
was the list of the clans of the sons of **G**, Nm 4:41
and four oxen he gave to the sons of **G**, Nm 7:7
the sons of **G** and the sons of Merari, Nm 10:17
Levites according to their clans: of **G**, Nm 26:57
sons of Levi: **G**, Kohath, and Merari. 1 Chr 6:1
sons of Levi: **G**, Kohath, and Merari. 1 Chr 23:6
The sons of **G** were Ladan and 1 Chr 23:7

GERSHONITE (2)
houses belonging to Ladan the **G**: 1 Chr 26:21
of the LORD, in the care of Jehiel the **G**. 1 Chr 29:8

GERSHONITES (12)
Shimeites; these were the clans of the **G**. Nm 3:21
The clans of the **G** were to camp Nm 3:23
as chief of the fathers' house of the **G**. Nm 3:24
This is the service of the clans of the **G**, Nm 4:24
of the sons of the **G** shall be at the Nm 4:27
of the sons of the **G** in the tent of Nm 4:28
clans: of Gershon, the clan of the **G**; Nm 26:57
The **G** received by lot from the clans of Jos 21:6
And to the **G**, one of the clans of the Jos 21:27
several clans of the **G** were in all Jos 21:33
sons of the **G** belonging to Ladan, 1 Chr 26:21
and of the **G**, Joah the son of 2 Chr 29:12

GERUTH (1)
and stayed at **G** Chimham near Jer 41:17

GESHAN (1)
Regem, Jotham, **G**, Pelet, Ephah, and 1 Chr 2:47

GESHEM (4)
Ammonite servant and **G** the Arab Neh 2:19
and Tobiah and **G** the Arab and Neh 6:1
Sanballat and **G** sent to me, saying, Neh 6:2
among the nations, and **G** also says it, Neh 6:6

GESHUR (9)
but **G** and Maacath dwell in the midst Jos 13:13
the daughter of Talmai king of **G**; 2 Sm 3:3
the son of Ammihud, king of **G**. 2 Sm 13:37
So Absalom fled and went to **G**, and 2 Sm 13:38
and went to **G** and brought Absalom 2 Sm 14:23
to ask, "Why have I come from **G**? 2 Sm 14:32
a vow while I lived at **G** in Aram, 2 Sm 15:8
But **G** and Aram took from them 1 Chr 2:23
the daughter of Talmai, king of **G**; 1 Chr 3:2

GESHURITES (6)
the border of the **G** and the Maacathites, Dt 3:14
boundary of the **G** and the Maacathites, Jos 12:5
of the Philistines, and all those of the **G** Jos 13:2
the region of the **G** and Maacathites, Jos 13:11
not drive out the **G** or the Maacathites, Jos 13:13
went up and made raids against the **G**, 1 Sm 27:8

GET (113)
G out of this place, for the LORD is Gn 19:14
saying, "**G** me this girl for my wife." Gn 34:4
and trade in it, and **g** property in it." Gn 34:10
and so **g** me out of this house. Gn 40:14
their work? **G** back to your burdens." Ex 5:4
Go and **g** your straw yourselves Ex 5:11
g your livestock and all that you have in Ex 9:19
said to him, "**G** away from me; Ex 10:28
me and bow down to me, saying, '**G** out, Ex 11:8
and I will **g** glory over Pharaoh and all Ex 14:4
and I will **g** glory over Pharaoh and all Ex 14:17
Where am I to **g** meat to give to all Nm 11:13
G away from the dwelling of Korah, Nm 16:24
"**G** away from the midst of this Nm 16:45
people of Israel, and **g** from them staffs, Nm 17:2
it is he who gives you power to **g** wealth, Dt 8:18
the field, you shall not go back to **g** it. Dt 24:19
The LORD said to Joshua, "**G** up! Why Jos 7:10
G up! Consecrate the people and say, Jos 7:13
Timnah. Now **g** her for me as my wife." Jgs 14:2
Samson said to his father, "**G** her for me, Jgs 14:3
He said to her, "**G** up, let us be going." Jgs 19:28
said to Jesse, "Send and **g** him, 1 Sm 16:11
let me **g** away and see my brothers.' 1 Sm 20:29
was hurrying to **g** away from Saul. 1 Sm 23:26
the midst of the house as if to **g** wheat, 2 Sm 4:6
let him **g** up the water shaft to attack 2 Sm 5:8
her. And Amnon said to her, "**G** up! 2 Sm 13:15
And Shimei said as he cursed, "**G** out, 2 Sm 16:7
said as he cursed, "Get out, **g** out, 2 Sm 16:7
lest he **g** himself to fortified cities and 2 Sm 20:6
with clothes, he could not **g** warm. 1 Kgs 1:1
after him and **g** something from 2 Kgs 5:20
the Jordan and each of us **g** there a log, 2 Kgs 6:2
take them alive and **g** into the city.'" 2 Kgs 7:12
So let us **g** grain, that we may eat and Neh 5:2
and our houses to **g** grain because of the Neh 5:3
he will not let me **g** my breath, but fills Jb 9:18
stupid man will **g** understanding when Jb 11:12
against his friends to **g** a share of their Jb 17:5
of his trading he will **g** no enjoyment. Jb 20:18
And what profit do we **g** if we pray to Jb 21:15
I will **g** my knowledge from afar and Jb 36:3
—and though you **g** praise when you do Ps 49:18
food and growl if they do not **g** their fill. Ps 59:15
days that we may **g** a heart of wisdom. Ps 90:12
plant vineyards and **g** a fruitful yield. Ps 107:37
your precepts I **g** understanding; Ps 119:104
let no iniquity **g** dominion over me. Ps 119:133
not enter my house or **g** into my bed, Ps 132:3
will inherit honor, but fools **g** disgrace. Prv 3:35
G wisdom; get insight; do not forget, and Prv 4:5
Get wisdom; **g** insight; do not forget, and Prv 4:5
G wisdom, and whatever you get, get Prv 4:7
Get wisdom, and whatever you **g**, get Prv 4:7
wisdom, and whatever you get, **g** insight. Prv 4:7
Wounds and dishonor will he **g**, and Prv 6:33
gets honor, and violent men **g** riches. Prv 11:16
diligent man will **g** precious wealth. Prv 12:27
much better to **g** wisdom than gold! Prv 16:16
To **g** understanding is to be chosen Prv 16:16
g everything ready for yourself in the Prv 24:27
hides his eyes will **g** many a curse. Prv 28:27
I will **g** relief from my enemies and Is 1:24
And I will **g** reliable witnesses, Uriah the Is 8:2
G you up to a high mountain, O Zion, Is 40:9
"Come," they say, "let me **g** wine; let us Is 56:12
for money and **g** witnesses"—though Jer 32:25
the king sent Jehudi to **g** the scroll, Jer 36:21
drink; the wood we **g** must be bought. Lam 5:4
and to Assyria, to **g** bread enough. Lam 5:6
We **g** our bread at the peril of our lives, Lam 5:9
destroying lives to **g** dishonest gain. Ezk 22:27
men rowed hard to **g** back to dry land, Jon 1:13
you will never **g** out until you have paid Mt 5:26
did this man **g** this wisdom and Mt 13:54
then did this man **g** all these things?" Mt 13:56
he made the disciples **g** into the boat Mt 14:22
"Where are we to **g** enough bread in Mt 15:33
turned and said to Peter, "**G** behind me, Mt 16:23
his servants to the tenants to **g** his fruit. Mt 21:34
how did you **g** in here without a Mt 22:12
when they could not **g** near him because Mk 2:4
"Where did this man **g** these things? Mk 6:2
he made his disciples **g** into the boat Mk 6:45
rebuked Peter and said, "**G** behind me, Mk 8:33
"Take heart. **G** up; he is calling you." Mk 10:49
to the tenants to **g** from them some of Mk 12:2
to sinners, to **g** back the same amount. Lk 6:34
to find lodging and **g** provisions, Lk 9:12
I cannot **g** up and give you anything'? Lk 11:7
though he will not **g** up and give him Lk 11:8
and to eat and drink and **g** drunk, Lk 12:45
will but did not **g** ready or act Lk 12:47
you will never **g** out until you have Lk 12:59
and said to him, "**G** away from here, Lk 13:31
twice a week; I give tithes of all that I **g**.' Lk 18:12
deep. Where do you **g** that living water? Jn 4:11
them the hour when he began to **g** better, Jn 4:52
Jesus said to him, "**G** up, take up your bed, Jn 5:8
bread for each of them to **g** a little." Jn 6:7
"**G** up quickly." And the chains fell off Acts 12:7
'Make haste and **g** out of Jerusalem Acts 22:18
said, "**G** ready two hundred soldiers, Acts 23:23
When I **g** an opportunity I will Acts 24:25
the fruit you **g** leads to sanctification Rom 6:22
the temple service **g** their food from 1 Cor 9:13
the gospel should **g** their living by 1 Cor 9:14
sound, who will **g** ready for battle? 1 Cor 14:8
And do not **g** drunk with wine, for that Eph 5:18
at night, and those who **g** drunk, 1 Thes 5:7
But they will not **g** very far, for their 2 Tm 3:9
G Mark and bring him with you, for 2 Tm 4:11

GETHER (2)
sons of Aram: Uz, Hul, **G**, and Mash. Gn 10:23
of Aram: Uz, Hul, **G**, and Meshech. 1 Chr 1:17

GETHSEMANE (2)
went with them to a place called **G**, Mt 26:36
And they went to a place called **G**. And Mk 14:32

GETS (13)
and the one who **g** understanding, Prv 3:13
corrects a scoffer **g** himself abuse, Prv 9:7
A gracious woman **g** honor, and Prv 11:16
who sows righteousness **g** a sure Prv 11:18
of the sluggard craves and **g** nothing, Prv 13:4
He who sires a fool **g** himself sorrow, Prv 17:21
Whoever **g** sense loves his own soul; he Prv 19:8
is from the LORD that a man **g** justice. Prv 29:26
woman when she **g** a husband, Prv 30:23
so is he who **g** riches but not by justice; Jer 17:11
"Woe to him who **g** evil gain for his Hab 2:9
One goes hungry, another **g** drunk. 1 Cor 11:21
No soldier **g** entangled in civilian 2 Tm 2:4

GETTING (6)
The **g** of treasures by a lying tongue is a Prv 21:6
And **g** into a boat he crossed over and Mt 9:1
As he was **g** into the boat, the man who Mk 5:18
G into one of the boats, which was Lk 5:3
what fruit were you **g** at that time Rom 6:21
tends a flock without **g** some of the 1 Cor 9:7

GEUEL (1)
the tribe of Gad, **G** the son of Machi. Nm 13:15

GEZER (15)
Then Horam king of **G** came up to Jos 10:33
king of Eglon, one; the king of **G**, one; Jos 12:12
territory of Lower Beth-horon, then to **G**, Jos 16:3
out the Canaanites who lived in **G**, Jos 16:10
of Ephraim, **G** with its pasturelands, Jos 21:21
drive out the Canaanites who lived in **G**, Jgs 1:29
the Canaanites lived in **G** among them. Jgs 1:29
down the Philistines from Geba to **G**. 2 Sm 5:25
and Hazor and Megiddo and **G** 1 Kgs 9:15
up and captured **G** and burned it 1 Kgs 9:16
so Solomon rebuilt **G**) and Lower 1 Kgs 9:17
of Ephraim, **G** with its pasturelands, 1 Chr 6:67
and to the west **G** and its towns, 1 Chr 7:28
Philistine army from Gibeon to **G**. 1 Chr 14:16
arose war with the Philistines at **G**. 1 Chr 20:4

GHOST (3)
from the ground like the voice of a **g**, Is 29:4
"It is a **g**!" and they cried out in fear. Mt 14:26
on the sea they thought it was a **g**, Mk 6:49

GIAH (1)
which lies before **G** on the way to the 2 Sm 2:24

GIANTS (7)
one of the descendants of the **g**, 2 Sm 21:16
was one of the descendants of the **g**. 2 Sm 21:18
he also was descended from the **g**. 2 Sm 21:20
were descended from the **g** in Gath, 2 Sm 21:22
was one of the descendants of the **g**, 1 Chr 20:4
he also was descended from the **g**. 1 Chr 20:6
were descended from the **g** in Gath, 1 Chr 20:8

GIBBAR (1)
The sons of **G**, 95. Ezr 2:20

GIBBETHON (6)
Eltekeh, **G**, Baalath, Jos 19:44
pasturelands, **G** with its pasturelands, Jos 21:23
And Baasha struck him down at **G**, 1 Kgs 15:27
and all Israel were laying siege to **G**. 1 Kgs 15:27
the troops were encamped against **G**, 1 Kgs 16:15
So Omri went up from **G**, and all 1 Kgs 16:17

GIBEA (1)
of Machbenah and the father of **G**; 1 Chr 2:49

GIBEAH (47)
Kain, **G**, and Timnah: ten cities with Jos 15:57
G and Kiriath-jearim—fourteen cities Jos 18:28
Aaron died, and they buried him at **G**, Jos 24:33
of Israel, but we will pass on to **G**." Jgs 19:12
and spend the night at **G** or at Ramah." Jgs 19:13
the sun went down on them near **G**, Jgs 19:14
there, to go in and spend the night at **G**. Jgs 19:15
Ephraim, and he was sojourning in **G**. Jgs 19:16
"I came to **G** that belongs to Benjamin, Jgs 20:4
And the leaders of **G** rose against me and Jgs 20:5
But now this is what we will do to **G**: we Jgs 20:9
come they may repay **G** of Benjamin, Jgs 20:10
up the men, the worthless fellows in **G**, Jgs 20:13
out of the cities to **G** to go out to battle Jgs 20:14
the sword, besides the inhabitants of **G**, Jgs 20:15
the morning and encamped against **G**. Jgs 20:19
up the battle line against them at **G**. Jgs 20:20
came out of **G** and destroyed on Jgs 20:21
against them out of **G** the second day, Jgs 20:25
So Israel set men in ambush around **G**. Jgs 20:29
and set themselves in array against **G**, Jgs 20:30
goes up to Bethel and the other to **G**, Jgs 20:31
there came against **G** 10,000 chosen Jgs 20:34
ambush whom they had set against **G**. Jgs 20:36
ambush hurried and rushed against **G**; Jgs 20:37
Nohah as far as opposite **G** on the east. Jgs 20:43
When they came to **G**, behold, a 1 Sm 10:10
Saul also went to his home at **G**, and 1 Sm 10:26
the messengers came to **G** of Saul, 1 Sm 11:4
were with Jonathan in **G** of Benjamin. 1 Sm 13:2
up from Gilgal to **G** of Benjamin. 1 Sm 13:15
the outskirts of **G** in the pomegranate 1 Sm 14:2
of Saul in **G** of Benjamin looked, 1 Sm 14:16
went up to his house in **G** of Saul. 1 Sm 15:34
was sitting at **G** under the tamarisk 1 Sm 22:6
the Ziphites went up to Saul at **G**, 1 Sm 23:19
Then the Ziphites came to Saul at **G**, 1 Sm 26:1
them before the LORD at **G** of Saul, 2 Sm 21:6
the son of Ribai of **G** of the people of 2 Sm 23:29
the son of Ribai of **G** of the people of 1 Chr 11:31
Joash, both sons of Shemaah of **G**; 1 Chr 12:3
Micaiah the daughter of Uriel of **G**. 2 Chr 13:2
Ramah trembles; **G** of Saul has fled. Is 10:29
Blow the horn in **G**, the trumpet in Hos 5:8
corrupted themselves as in the days of **G**: Hos 9:9
From the days of **G**, you have sinned, O Hos 10:9
against the unjust overtake them in **G**? Hos 10:9

GIBEATH-ELOHIM (1)
After that you shall come to **G**, where 1 Sm 10:5

GIBEATH-HAARALOTH (1)
and circumcised the sons of Israel at **G**. Jos 5:3

GIBEON (39)
the inhabitants of **G** heard what Joshua Jos 9:3
Now their cities were **G**, Chephirah, Jos 9:17
the inhabitants of **G** had made peace Jos 10:1
greatly, because **G** was a great city, Jos 10:2
to me and help me, and let us strike **G**. Jos 10:4
and encamped against **G** and made war Jos 10:5
And the men of **G** sent to Joshua at the Jos 10:6
a great blow at **G** and chased them by Jos 10:10
the sight of Israel, "Sun, stand still at **G**, Jos 10:12
all the country of Goshen, as far as **G**. Jos 10:41
except the Hivites, the inhabitants of **G**. Jos 11:19
G, Ramah, Beeroth, Jos 18:25
of Benjamin, **G** with its pasturelands, Jos 21:17
Saul, went out from Mahanaim to **G**. 2 Sm 2:12
out and met them at the pool of **G**. 2 Sm 2:13
Helkath-hazzurim, which is at **G**. 2 Sm 2:16
on the way to the wilderness of **G**. 2 Sm 2:24
Asahel to death in the battle at **G**. 2 Sm 3:30
were at the great stone that is in **G**, 2 Sm 20:8
the king went to **G** to sacrifice there, 1 Kgs 3:4
At **G** the LORD appeared to Solomon in 1 Kgs 3:5
time, as he had appeared to him at **G**. 1 Kgs 9:2
G, Geba with its pasturelands, 1 Chr 6:60
Jeiel the father of **G** lived in Gibeon, 1 Chr 8:29
Jeiel the father of Gibeon lived in **G**, 1 Chr 8:29
In **G** lived the father of Gibeon, Jeiel, 1 Chr 9:35
In Gibeon lived the father of **G**, Jeiel, 1 Chr 9:35
Ishmaiah of **G**, a mighty man 1 Chr 12:4
the Philistine army from **G** to Gezer. 1 Chr 14:16
LORD in the high place that was at **G** 1 Chr 16:39
at that time in the high place at **G**, 1 Chr 21:29
went to the high place that was at **G**, 2 Chr 1:3
came from the high place at **G**, 2 Chr 1:13
the men of **G** and of Mizpah, Neh 3:7
The sons of **G**, 95. Neh 7:25
as in the Valley of **G** he will be roused; Is 28:21
the son of Azzur, the prophet from **G**, Jer 28:1
upon him at the great pool that is in **G**. Jer 41:12
whom Johanan brought back from **G**. Jer 41:16

GIBEONITE (1)
repaired Melatiah the **G** and Jadon the Neh 3:7

GIBEONITES (6)
house, because he put the **G** to death." 2 Sm 21:1
the king called the **G** and spoke to 2 Sm 21:2
Now the **G** were not of the people of 2 Sm 21:2
And David said to the **G**, "What shall 2 Sm 21:3
The **G** said to him, "It is not a matter 2 Sm 21:4
he gave them into the hands of the **G**, 2 Sm 21:9

GIDDALTI (2)
Eliathah, **G**, and Romamti-ezer, 1 Chr 25:4
to the twenty-second, to **G**, his sons 1 Chr 25:29

GIDDEL (4)
the sons of **G**, the sons of Gahar, the Ezr 2:47
the sons of Darkon, the sons of **G**, Ezr 2:56
the sons of Hanan, the sons of **G**, the Neh 7:49
the sons of Darkon, the sons of **G**, Neh 7:58

GIDEON (41)
while his son **G** was beating out wheat Jgs 6:11
And **G** said to him, "Please, sir, if the Jgs 6:13
So **G** went into his house and prepared a Jgs 6:19
Then **G** perceived that he was the angel Jgs 6:22
he was the angel of the LORD. And **G** said, Jgs 6:22
Then **G** built an altar there to the LORD Jgs 6:24
So **G** took ten men of his servants and Jgs 6:27
"**G** the son of Joash has done this thing." Jgs 6:29
on that day **G** was called Jerubbaal, Jgs 6:32
But the Spirit of the LORD clothed **G**, and Jgs 6:34
Then **G** said to God, "If you will save Jgs 6:36
Then **G** said to God, "Let not your anger Jgs 6:39
G) and all the people who were with him Jgs 7:1
The LORD said to **G**, "The people with you Jgs 7:2
And the LORD said to **G**, "The people are Jgs 7:4
And the LORD said to **G**, "Every one who Jgs 7:5
And the LORD said to **G**, "With the 300 Jgs 7:7
When **G** came, behold, a man was Jgs 7:13
than the sword of **G** the son of Joash, Jgs 7:14
As soon as **G** heard the telling of the Jgs 7:15
and shout, 'For the LORD and for **G**.'" Jgs 7:18
So **G** and the hundred men who were Jgs 7:19
out, "A sword for the LORD and for **G**!" Jgs 7:20
G sent messengers throughout all the Jgs 7:24
of Oreb and Zeeb to **G** across the Jordan. Jgs 7:25
And **G** came to the Jordan and crossed Jgs 8:4
So **G** said, "Well then, when the LORD has Jgs 8:7
And **G** went up by the way of the tent Jgs 8:11
Then **G** the son of Joash returned from Jgs 8:13
is his strength." And **G** arose and killed Jgs 8:21
Then the men of Israel said to **G**, "Rule Jgs 8:22
G said to them, "I will not rule over you, Jgs 8:23
And **G** said to them, "Let me make a Jgs 8:24
And **G** made an ephod of it and put it in Jgs 8:27
it became a snare to **G** and to his family. Jgs 8:27
land had rest forty years in the days of **G**. Jgs 8:28
Now **G** had seventy sons, his own Jgs 8:30
And **G** the son of Joash died in a good old Jgs 8:32
As soon as **G** died, the people of Israel Jgs 8:33
G) in return for all the good that he had Jgs 8:35
For time would fail me to tell of **G**, Heb 11:32

GIDEONI (5)
from Benjamin, Abidan the son of **G**; Nm 1:11
Benjamin being Abidan the son of **G**, Nm 2:22
On the ninth day Abidan the son of **G**, Nm 7:60
was the offering of Abidan the son of **G**. Nm 7:65
of Benjamin was Abidan the son of **G**. Nm 10:24

GIDOM (1)
And they were pursued hard to **G**, and Jgs 20:45

GIFT (61)
as great a bride price and **g** as you will, Gn 34:12
"If his **g** for a burnt offering is from the Lv 1:10
from each offering, as a **g** to the LORD. Lv 7:14
to offer it as a **g** to the LORD in front Lv 17:4
his house as a holy **g** to the LORD, Lv 27:14
jubilee, shall be a holy **g** to the LORD, Lv 27:21
on that day as a holy **g** to the LORD. Lv 27:23
and he shall bring his **g** to the LORD, Nm 6:14
the Levites as a **g** to Aaron and his Nm 8:19
They are a **g** to you, given to the LORD, Nm 18:6
I give your priesthood as a **g**, and any Nm 18:7
the contribution of their **g**, all the Nm 18:11
expense? Or has he given us any **g**?" 2 Sm 19:42
Have I said, 'Make me a **g**'? Or, 'From Jb 6:22
A man's **g** makes room for him and Prv 18:16
A **g** in secret averts anger, and a Prv 21:14
who boasts of a **g** he does not give. Prv 25:14
in all his toil—this is God's **g** to man. Eccl 3:13
rejoice in his toil—this is the **g** of God. Eccl 5:19
If the prince makes a **g** to any of his Ezk 46:16
if he makes a **g** out of his inheritance Ezk 46:17
to us. With such a **g** from your hand, Mal 1:9
if you are offering your **g** at the altar and Mt 5:23
leave your **g** there before the altar and Mt 5:24
brother, and then come and offer your **g**. Mt 5:24
and offer the **g** that Moses commanded, Mt 8:4
if anyone swears by the **g** that is on the Mt 23:18
the **g** or the altar that makes the gift Mt 23:19
or the altar that makes the **g** sacred? Mt 23:19
answered her, "If you knew the **g** of God, Jn 4:10
you will receive the **g** of the Holy Spirit. Acts 2:38
you could obtain the **g** of God with Acts 8:20
because the **g** of the Holy Spirit was Acts 10:45
God gave the same **g** to them as he Acts 11:17
you some spiritual **g** to strengthen you Rom 1:11
and are justified by his grace as a **g**, Rom 3:24
are not counted as a **g** but as his due. Rom 4:4
But the free **g** is not like the trespass. Rom 5:15
of God and the free **g** by the grace of Rom 5:15
And the free **g** is not like the result of Rom 5:16
but the free **g** following many Rom 5:16
and the free **g** of righteousness reign Rom 5:17
but the free **g** of God is eternal life in Rom 6:23
"Or who has given a **g** to him that he Rom 11:35
you are not lacking in any spiritual **g**, 1 Cor 1:7
But each has his own **g** from God, one 1 Cor 7:7
by letter to carry your **g** to Jerusalem. 1 Cor 16:3
us about this generous **g** that is being 2 Cor 8:20
advance for the **g** you have promised, 2 Cor 9:5
so that it may be ready as a willing **g**, 2 Cor 9:5
be to God for his inexpressible **g**! 2 Cor 9:15
is not your own doing; it is the **g** of God, Eph 2:8
according to the **g** of God's grace, Eph 3:7
according to the measure of Christ's **g**. Eph 4:7
Not that I seek the **g**, but I seek the fruit Phil 4:17
Do not neglect the **g** you have, which 1 Tm 4:14
you to fan into flame the **g** of God, 2 Tm 1:6
who have tasted the heavenly **g**, Heb 6:4
Every good **g** and every perfect gift is Jas 1:17
gift and every perfect **g** is from above, Jas 1:17
As each has received a **g**, use it to serve 1 Pt 4:10

GIFTS (66)
all sorts of choice **g** from his master; Gn 24:10
of his concubines Abraham gave **g**, Gn 25:6
of Israel consecrate as their holy **g**. Ex 28:38
and besides your **g** and besides all Lv 23:38
Out of all the **g** to you, you shall Nm 18:29
with the choicest **g** of heaven above, Dt 33:13
with the best **g** of the earth and its Dt 33:16
the LORD the sacred **g** of his father 1 Kgs 15:15
of his father and his own sacred **g**, 1 Kgs 15:15
all the sacred **g** that Jehoshaphat 2 Kgs 12:18
had dedicated, and his own sacred **g**, 2 Kgs 12:18
and the treasuries of the dedicated **g**. 1 Chr 26:20
of the dedicated **g** that David the 1 Chr 26:26
battles they dedicated **g** for the 1 Chr 26:27
—all dedicated **g** were in the 1 Chr 26:28
and the treasuries for dedicated **g**; 1 Chr 28:12
of God the sacred **g** of his father and 2 Chr 15:18
of his father and his own sacred **g**, 2 Chr 15:18
father gave them great **g** of silver, 2 Chr 21:3
And many brought **g** to the LORD to 2 Chr 32:23
fathers to enjoy its fruit and its good **g**, Neh 9:36
provinces and gave **g** with royal Est 2:18
day on which they send **g** of food to one Est 9:19
days for sending **g** of food to one another Est 9:22
of food to one another and **g** to the poor. Est 9:22
of Tyre will seek your favor with **g**, Ps 45:12
your train and receiving **g** among men, Ps 68:18
at Jerusalem kings shall bear **g** to you. Ps 68:29
the kings of Sheba and Seba bring **g**! Ps 72:10
all around him bring **g** to him who is Ps 76:11
he will refuse though you multiply **g**. Prv 6:35
is a friend to a man who gives **g**. Prv 19:6
land, but he who exacts **g** tears it down. Prv 29:4
Everyone loves a bribe and runs after **g**. Is 1:23
Men give **g** to all prostitutes, but you Ezk 16:33
but you gave your **g** to all your lovers, Ezk 16:33

through their very **g** in their offering Ezk 20:26
When you present your **g** and offer up Ezk 20:31
profane with your **g** and your idols. Ezk 20:39
and the choicest of your **g**, Ezk 20:40
shall receive from me **g** and rewards and Dn 2:6
Daniel high honors and many great **g**, Dn 2:48
the king, "Let your **g** be for yourself, Dn 5:17
with precious stones and costly **g**. Dn 11:38
shall give parting **g** to Moresheth-gath; Mi 1:14
their treasures, they offered him **g**, Mt 2:11
how to give good **g** to your children, Mt 7:11
how to give good **g** to your children, Lk 11:13
the rich putting their **g** into the offering Lk 21:1
For the **g** and the calling of God are Rom 11:29
Having **g** that differ according to the Rom 12:6
Now concerning spiritual **g**, 1 Cor 12:1
Now there are varieties of **g**, but the 1 Cor 12:4
to another **g** of healing by the one 1 Cor 12:9
then miracles, then **g** of healing, 1 Cor 12:28
Do all possess **g** of healing? Do all 1 Cor 12:30
But earnestly desire the higher **g**. 1 Cor 12:31
and earnestly desire the spiritual **g**, 1 Cor 14:1
a host of captives, and he gave **g** to men." Eph 4:8
from Epaphroditus the **g** you sent, Phil 4:18
various miracles and by **g** of the Holy Heb 2:4
to God, to offer **g** and sacrifices for sins. Heb 5:1
is appointed to offer **g** and sacrifices; Heb 8:3
are priests who offer **g** according to the Heb 8:4
g and sacrifices are offered that cannot Heb 9:9
commending him by accepting his **g**. Heb 11:4

GIHON (6)
The name of the second river is the **G**. It Gn 2:13
own mule, and bring him down to **G**. 1 Kgs 1:33
David's mule and brought him to **G**. 1 Kgs 1:38
prophet have anointed him king at **G**, 1 Kgs 1:45
of the waters of **G** and directed them 2 Chr 32:30
wall for the city of David west of **G**, 2 Chr 33:14

GILALAI (1)
Shemaiah, Azarel, Milalai, **G**, Maai, Neh 12:36

GILBOA (8)
all Israel, and they encamped at **G**. 1 Sm 28:4
Philistines and fell slain on Mount **G**. 1 Sm 31:1
and his three sons fallen on Mount **G**. 1 Sm 31:8
chance I happened to be on Mount **G**, 2 Sm 1:6
"You mountains of **G**, let there be no 2 Sm 1:21
day the Philistines killed Saul on **G**. 2 Sm 21:12
and fell slain on Mount **G**. 1 Chr 10:1
Saul and his sons fallen on Mount **G**. 1 Chr 10:8

GILEAD (100)
his face toward the hill country of **G**. Gn 31:21
after him into the hill country of **G**. Gn 31:23
pitched tents in the hill country of **G**. Gn 31:25
of Ishmaelites coming from **G**, Gn 37:25
and Machir was the father of **G**; Nm 26:29
Machir was the father of Gilead; of **G**, Nm 26:29
These are the sons of **G**: of Iezer, the Nm 26:30
Zelophehad the son of Hepher, son of **G**, Nm 27:1
saw the land of Jazer and the land of **G**, Nm 32:1
shall remain there in the cities of **G**, Nm 32:26
them the land of **G** for a possession. Nm 32:29
Manasseh went to **G** and captured it, Nm 32:39
And Moses gave **G** to Machir the son Nm 32:40
of the people of **G** the son of Machir, Nm 36:1
the city that is in the valley, as far as **G**, Dt 2:36
the tableland and all **G** and all Bashan, Dt 3:10
half the hill country of **G** with its cities. Dt 3:12
The rest of **G**, and all Bashan, the Dt 3:13
To Machir I gave **G**, Dt 3:15
I gave the territory from **G** as far as the Dt 3:16
Reubenites, Ramoth in **G** for the Gadites, Dt 4:43
showed him all the land, **G** as far as Dan, Dt 34:1
of the Ammonites, that is, half of **G**, Jos 12:2
and over half of **G** to the boundary of Jos 12:5
and **G**, and the region of the Geshurites Jos 13:11
was Jazer, and all the cities of **G**, Jos 13:25
and half **G**, and Ashtaroth, and Edrei, Jos 13:31
firstborn of Manasseh, the father of **G**, Jos 17:1
of Gilead, were allotted **G** and Bashan, Jos 17:1
Zelophehad the son of Hepher, son of **G**, Jos 17:3
besides the land of **G** and Bashan, Jos 17:5
The land of **G** was allotted to the rest of Jos 17:6
the tribe of Reuben, and Ramoth in **G**, Jos 20:8
Ramoth in **G** with its pasturelands, Jos 21:38
land of Canaan, to go to the land of **G**, Jos 22:9
of Manasseh, in the land of **G**, Jos 22:13
of Manasseh, in the land of **G**, Jos 22:15
Gad in the land of **G** to the land of Jos 22:32
G stayed beyond the Jordan; and Dan, Jgs 5:17
away from Mount **G**.'" Then 22,000 of Jgs 7:3
to this day, which are in the land of **G**. Jgs 10:4
the land of the Amorites, which is in **G**. Jgs 10:8
to arms, and they encamped in **G**. Jgs 10:17
And the people, the leaders of **G**, said Jgs 10:18
be head over all the inhabitants of **G**." Jgs 10:18
prostitute. **G** was the father of Jephthah. Jgs 11:1
the elders of **G** went to bring Jephthah Jgs 11:5
But Jephthah said to the elders of **G**, "Did Jgs 11:7
And the elders of **G** said to Jephthah, Jgs 11:8
our head over all the inhabitants of **G**." Jgs 11:8
Jephthah said to the elders of **G**, "If you Jgs 11:9
And the elders of **G** said to Jephthah, Jgs 11:10
So Jephthah went with the elders of **G**, Jgs 11:11
he passed through **G** and Manasseh Jgs 11:29
and passed on to Mizpah of **G**, Jgs 11:29
and from Mizpah of **G** he passed on to Jgs 11:29
all the men of **G** and fought with Jgs 12:4
And the men of **G** struck Ephraim, Jgs 12:4
me go over," the men of **G** said to him, Jgs 12:5
died and was buried in his city in **G**. Jgs 12:7
to Beersheba, including the land of **G**, Jgs 20:1
of the Jordan to the land of Gad and **G**. 1 Sm 13:7
him king over **G** and the Ashurites 2 Sm 2:9
Absalom encamped in the land of **G**. 2 Sm 17:26
Then they came to **G**, and to Kadesh 2 Sm 24:6
the son of Manasseh, which are in **G**, 1 Kgs 4:13
Geber the son of Uri, in the land of **G**, 1 Kgs 4:19
Elijah the Tishbite, of Tishbe in **G**, 1 Kgs 17:1
Jordan eastward, all the land of **G**, 2 Kgs 10:33
of the Arnon, that is, **G** and Bashan. 2 Kgs 10:33
with fifty men of the people of **G**, 2 Kgs 15:25
Kedesh, Hazor, **G**, and Galilee, 2 Kgs 15:29
daughter of Machir the father of **G**, 1 Chr 2:21
twenty-three cities in the land of **G**. 1 Chr 2:22
of Machir, the father of **G**. 1 Chr 2:23
had multiplied in the land of **G**. 1 Chr 5:9
throughout all the region east of **G**. 1 Chr 5:10
son of Huri, son of Jaroah, son of **G**, 1 Chr 5:14
and they lived in **G**, in Bashan and in 1 Chr 5:16
Ramoth in **G** with its pasturelands, 1 Chr 6:80
bore; she bore Machir the father of **G**. 1 Chr 7:14
were the sons of **G** the son of Machir, 1 Chr 7:17
them were found at Jazer in **G**.) 1 Chr 26:31
for the half-tribe of Manasseh in **G**, 1 Chr 27:21
G is mine; Manasseh is mine; Ephraim Ps 60:7
G is mine; Manasseh is mine; Ephraim Ps 108:8
of goats leaping down the slopes of **G**. Sg 4:1
of goats leaping down the slopes of **G**. Sg 6:5
Is there no balm in **G**? Is there no Jer 8:22
"'You are like **G** to me, like the summit Jer 22:6
Go up to **G**, and take balm, O virgin Jer 46:11
on the hills of Ephraim and in **G**. Jer 50:19
the Jordan between **G** and the land Ezk 47:18
G is a city of evildoers, tracked with Hos 6:8
If there is iniquity in **G**, they shall Hos 12:11
they have threshed **G** with threshing Am 1:3
ripped open pregnant women in **G**, Am 1:13
Samaria, and Benjamin shall possess **G**. Ob 1:19
graze in Bashan and **G** as in the days Mi 7:14
them to the land of **G** and to Lebanon, Zec 10:10

GILEAD'S (1)
And **G** wife also bore him sons. And Jgs 11:2

GILEADITE (9)
After him arose Jair the **G**, who judged Jgs 10:3
Now Jephthah the **G** was a mighty Jgs 11:1
of Jephthah the **G** four days in Jgs 11:40
Then Jephthah the **G** died and was Jgs 12:7
and Barzillai the **G** from Rogelim, 2 Sm 17:27
Now Barzillai the **G** had come down 2 Sm 19:31
loyally with the sons of Barzillai the **G**, 1 Kgs 2:7
from the daughters of Barzillai the **G**, Ezr 2:61
of Barzillai the **G** and was called Neh 7:63

GILEADITES (3)
of Gilead; of Gilead, the clan of the **G**. Nm 26:29
"You are fugitives of Ephraim, you **G**, Jgs 12:4
And the **G** captured the fords of the Jgs 12:5

GILGAL (40)
who live in the Arabah, opposite **G**, Dt 11:30
and they encamped at **G** on the east Jos 4:19
out of the Jordan, Joshua set up at **G**. Jos 4:20
name of that place is called **G** to this day. Jos 5:9
the people of Israel were encamped at **G**, Jos 5:10
Joshua in the camp at **G** and said to him Jos 9:6
Gibeon sent to Joshua at the camp in **G**, Jos 10:6
So Joshua went up from **G**, he and all the Jos 10:7
having marched up all night from **G**. Jos 10:9
all Israel with him, to the camp at **G**. Jos 10:15
all Israel with him, to the camp at **G**. Jos 10:43
the people of Judah came to Joshua at **G**. Jos 14:6
and so northward, turning toward **G**, Jos 15:7
of the LORD went up from **G** to Bochim. Jgs 2:1
turned back at the idols near **G** and said, Jgs 3:19
year by year to Bethel, **G**, and Mizpah. 1 Sm 7:16
Then go down before me to **G**. And 1 Sm 10:8
let us go to **G** and there renew the 1 Sm 11:14
So all the people went to **G**, and there 1 Sm 11:15
made Saul king before the LORD in **G**. 1 Sm 11:15
were called out to join Saul at **G**. 1 Sm 13:4
Saul was still at **G**, and all the people 1 Sm 13:7
But Samuel did not come to **G**, and 1 Sm 13:8
will come down against me at **G**, 1 Sm 13:12
Samuel arose and went up from **G**. 1 Sm 13:15
they went up from **G** to Gibeah of 1 Sm 13:15
and passed on and went down to **G**." 1 Sm 15:12
sacrifice to the LORD your God in **G**." 1 Sm 15:21
Agag to pieces before the LORD in **G**. 1 Sm 15:33
and Judah came to **G** to meet the 2 Sm 19:15
The king went on to **G**, and 2 Sm 19:40
and Elisha were on their way from **G**. 2 Kgs 2:1
came again to **G** when there was 2 Kgs 4:38
Enter not into **G**, nor go up to Hos 4:15
Every evil of theirs is in **G**; there I began Hos 9:15
to nothing: in **G** they sacrifice bulls; Hos 12:11
"Come to Bethel, and transgress; to **G**, Am 4:4
and do not enter into **G** or cross over to Am 5:5
for **G** shall surely go into exile, and Am 5:5
and what happened from Shittim to **G**, Mi 6:5

GILO (1)
Eliam the son of Ahithophel of **G**, 2 Sm 23:34

GILOH (2)
Goshen, Holon, and **G**: eleven cities Jos 15:51
David's counselor, from his city **G**. 2 Sm 15:12

GILONITE (1)
he sent for Ahithophel the **G**, 2 Sm 15:12

GIMZO (1)
its villages, and **G** with its villages. 2 Chr 28:18

GINATH (2)
people followed Tibni the son of **G**, 1 Kgs 16:21
who followed Tibni the son of **G**. 1 Kgs 16:22

GINNETHOI (1)
Iddo, **G**, Abijah, Neh 12:4

GINNETHON (2)
Daniel, **G**, Baruch, Neh 10:6
of Iddo, Zechariah; of **G**, Meshullam; Neh 12:16

GIRD (4)
and **g** him with the skillfully woven Ex 29:5
and you shall **g** Aaron and his sons with Ex 29:9
G your sword on your thigh, O mighty Ps 45:3
the hills **g** themselves with joy, Ps 65:12

GIRDED (1)
the mountains, being **g** with might; Ps 65:6

GIRGASHITE (1)
the Perizzite, the Jebusite, and the **G**. Neh 9:8

GIRGASHITES (6)
and the Jebusites, the Amorites, the **G**, Gn 10:16
Canaanites, the **G** and the Jebusites." Gn 15:21
nations before you, the Hittites, the **G**, Dt 7:1
Hittites, the Hivites, the Perizzites, the **G**, Jos 3:10
the Canaanites, the Hittites, the **G**, Jos 24:11
the Jebusites, the Amorites, the **G**, 1 Chr 1:14

GIRL (23)
saying, "Get me this **g** for my wife." Gn 34:4
"Go." So the **g** went and called the child's Ex 2:8
firstborn of the slave **g** who is behind the Ex 11:5
carried off a little **g** from the land of 2 Kgs 5:2
and so spoke the **g** from the land of 2 Kgs 5:4
and have sold a **g** for wine and have drunk Jl 3:3
a man and his father go in to the same **g**, Am 2:7
for the **g** is not dead but sleeping." And Mt 9:24
took her by the hand, and the **g** arose. Mt 9:25
brought on a platter and given to the **g**, Mt 14:11
And a servant **g** came up to him and Mt 26:69
entrance, another servant **g** saw him, Mt 26:71
"Talitha cumi," which means, "Little **g**, Mk 5:41
And immediately the **g** got up and Mk 5:42
And the king said to the **g**, "Ask me for Mk 6:22
his head on a platter and gave it to the **g**, Mk 6:28
the girl, and the **g** gave it to her mother. Mk 6:28
And the servant **g** saw him and began Mk 14:69
Then a servant **g**, seeing him as he sat Lk 22:56
spoke to the servant **g** who kept watch Jn 18:16
The servant **g** at the door said to Peter, Jn 18:17
a servant **g** named Rhoda came to Acts 12:13
were met by a slave **g** who had a spirit Acts 16:16

GIRL'S (6)
house. And when the **g** father saw him, Jgs 19:3
And his father-in-law, the **g** father, made Jgs 19:4
but the **g** father said to his son-in-law, Jgs 19:5
And the **g** father said to the man, "Be Jgs 19:6
morning to depart. And the **g** father said, Jgs 19:8
to depart, his father-in-law, the **g** father, Jgs 19:9

GIRLS (6)
But all the young **g** who have not Nm 31:18
will you put him on a leash for your **g**? Jb 41:5
and maintenance for your **g**. Prv 27:27
she is carried off, her slave **g** lamenting, Na 2:7

full of boys and **g** playing in its streets. Zec 8:5
one of the servant **g** of the high priest Mk 14:66

GIRZITES (1)
raids against the Geshurites, the **G**, 1 Sm 27:8

GISHPA (1)
and Ziha and **G** were over the temple Neh 11:21

GITTAIM (2)
the Beerothites fled to **G** and have been 2 Sm 4:3
Hazor, Ramah, **G**, Neh 11:33

GITTITE (8)
to the house of Obed-edom the **G**. 2 Sm 6:10
of Obed-edom the **G** three months, 2 Sm 6:11
Then the king said to Ittai the **G**, 2 Sm 15:19
on." So Ittai the **G** passed on with all 2 Sm 15:22
under the command of Ittai the **G**. 2 Sm 18:2
struck down Goliath the **G**, 2 Sm 21:19
to the house of Obed-edom the **G**. 1 Chr 13:13
Lahmi the brother of Goliath the **G**, 1 Chr 20:5

GITTITES (1)
the six hundred **G** who had followed 2 Sm 15:18

GITTITH (3)
To the choirmaster: according to The **G**. Ps 8:T
To the choirmaster: according to The **G**. Ps 81:T
To the choirmaster: according to The **G**. Ps 84:T

GIVE (963)
of the heavens to **g** light upon the earth." Gn 1:15
of the heavens to **g** light on the earth, Gn 1:17
you the green plants, I **g** you everything. Gn 9:3
your offspring I will **g** this land." So he Gn 12:7
that you see I will **g** to you and to your Gn 13:15
of the land, for I will **g** it to you." Gn 13:17
said to Abram, "**G** me the persons, Gn 14:21
said, "O Lord GOD, what will you **g** me, Gn 15:2
of the Chaldeans to **g** you this land to Gn 15:7
"To your offspring I **g** this land, Gn 15:18
And I will **g** to you and to your offspring Gn 17:8
moreover, I will **g** you a son by her. Gn 17:16
g me property among you for a burying Gn 23:4
that he may **g** me the cave of Gn 23:9
the full price let him **g** it to me in your Gn 23:9
I **g** you the field, and I give you the cave Gn 23:11
field, and I **g** you the cave that is in it. Gn 23:11
of the sons of my people I **g** it to you. Gn 23:11
will, hear me: I **g** the price of the field. Gn 23:13
me, 'To your offspring I will **g** this land,' Gn 24:7
"Please **g** me a little water to drink Gn 24:17
And if they will not **g** her to you, you Gn 24:41
"Please **g** me a little water from your Gn 24:43
and I will **g** your camels drink also.' Gn 24:46
her days to **g** birth were completed, Gn 25:24
to your offspring I will **g** all these lands, Gn 26:3
of heaven and will **g** to your offspring Gn 26:4
May God **g** you of the dew of heaven Gn 27:28
May he **g** the blessing of Abraham to Gn 28:4
which you lie I will **g** to you and to Gn 28:13
and will **g** me bread to eat and clothing Gn 28:20
And of all that you **g** me I will give a Gn 28:22
you give me I will **g** a full tenth to you." Gn 28:22
"It is better that I **g** her to you than that Gn 29:19
than that I should **g** her to any other Gn 29:19
"**G** me my wife that I may go in to her, Gn 29:21
to **g** the younger before the firstborn. Gn 29:26
and we will **g** you the other also in Gn 29:27
She said to Jacob, "**G** me children, or I Gn 30:1
so that she may **g** birth on my behalf, Gn 30:3
"Please **g** me some of your son's Gn 30:14
G me my wives and my children for Gn 30:26
Name your wages, and I will **g** it." Gn 30:28
said, "What shall I **g** you?" Jacob said, Gn 30:31
said, "You shall not **g** me anything. Gn 30:31
Please **g** her to him to be his wife. Gn 34:8
G your daughters to us, and take our Gn 34:9
and whatever you say to me I will **g**. Gn 34:11
and I will **g** whatever you say to me. Gn 34:12
Only **g** me the young woman to be my Gn 34:12
to **g** our sister to one who is Gn 34:14
Then we will **g** our daughters to you, Gn 34:16
wives, and let us **g** them our daughters. Gn 34:21
to Abraham and Isaac I will **g** to you, Gn 35:12
and I will **g** the land to your offspring Gn 35:12
so as not to **g** offspring to his brother. Gn 38:9
She said, "What will you **g** me, that Gn 38:16
And she said, "If you **g** me a pledge, Gn 38:17
pledge shall I **g** you?" She replied, Gn 38:18
since I did not **g** her to my son Shelah." Gn 38:26
God will **g** Pharaoh a favorable Gn 41:16
and to **g** them provisions for the Gn 42:25
opened his sack to **g** his donkey fodder Gn 42:27
and I will **g** you the best of the land of Gn 45:18
came to Joseph and said, "**G** us food. Gn 47:15
Joseph answered, "**G** your livestock, Gn 47:16
and I will **g** you food in exchange for Gn 47:16
And **g** us seed that we may live and not Gn 47:19
the harvests you shall **g** a fifth to Gn 47:24
of peoples and will **g** this land to your Gn 48:4
they are vigorous and **g** birth before the Ex 1:19
and I will **g** you your wages." So the Ex 2:9
And I will **g** this people favor in the sight Ex 3:21
"You shall no longer **g** the people straw to Ex 5:7
says Pharaoh, 'I will not **g** you straw. Ex 5:10
covenant with them to **g** them the land of Ex 6:4
the land that I swore to **g** to Abraham, Ex 6:8
to Jacob. I will **g** it to you for a possession. Ex 6:8
to the land that the LORD will **g** you, Ex 12:25
which he swore to your fathers to **g** you, Ex 13:5
and your fathers, and shall **g** it to you, Ex 13:11
night in a pillar of fire to **g** them light, Ex 13:21
and **g** ear to his commandments and Ex 15:26
"**G** us water to drink." And Moses said to Ex 17:2
Now obey my voice; I will **g** you advice, Ex 18:19
then he shall **g** for the redemption of Ex 21:30
the owner shall **g** to their master thirty Ex 21:32
He shall **g** money to its owner, and the Ex 21:34
he shall **g** the bride-price for her and Ex 22:16
father utterly refuses to **g** her to him, Ex 22:17
of your sons you shall **g** to me. Ex 22:29
on the eighth day you shall **g** it to me. Ex 22:30
for I will **g** the inhabitants of the land Ex 23:31
that I may **g** you the tablets of stone, Ex 24:12
the ark the testimony that I shall **g** you. Ex 25:16
put the testimony that I shall **g** you. Ex 25:21
all that I will **g** you in commandment Ex 25:22
be set up so as to **g** light on the space in Ex 25:37
then each shall **g** a ransom for his life Ex 30:12
is numbered in the census shall **g** this: Ex 30:13
and upward, shall **g** the LORD'S offering. Ex 30:14
The rich shall not **g** more, and the poor Ex 30:15
give more, and the poor shall not **g** less, Ex 30:15
when you **g** the LORD'S offering to make Ex 30:15
of Israel and shall **g** it for the service Ex 30:16
promised I will **g** to your offspring, Ex 32:13
saying, 'To your offspring I will **g** it.' Ex 33:1
will go with you, and I will **g** you rest." Ex 33:14
shall add a fifth to it and **g** it to the priest. Lv 5:16
and **g** it to him to whom it belongs on the Lv 6:5
right thigh you shall **g** to the priest as Lv 7:32
Canaan, which I **g** you for a possession, Lv 14:34
tent of meeting and **g** them to the priest. Lv 15:14
You shall not **g** any of your children to Lv 18:21
shall any woman **g** herself to an Lv 18:23
land, and I will **g** it to you to possess, Lv 20:24
its value to it and **g** the holy thing to the Lv 22:14
offer to the LORD or **g** them to the LORD Lv 22:22
into the land that I **g** you and reap its Lv 23:10
offerings, which you **g** to the LORD. Lv 23:38
you come into the land that I **g** you, Lv 25:2
of years shall **g** you forty-nine years. Lv 25:8
interest, nor **g** him your food for profit. Lv 25:37
the land of Egypt to **g** you the land of Lv 25:38
then I will **g** you your rains in their Lv 26:4
I will **g** peace in the land, and you shall Lv 26:6
and the man shall **g** the valuation on Lv 27:23
And you shall **g** the Levites to Aaron Nm 3:9
and **g** the money to Aaron and his sons Nm 3:48
upon you and **g** you peace. Nm 6:26
of meeting, and **g** them to the Levites, Nm 7:5
the seven lamps shall **g** light in front of Nm 8:2
which the LORD said, 'I will **g** it to you.' Nm 10:29
all this people? Did I **g** them birth, Nm 11:12
land that you swore to **g** their fathers? Nm 11:12
am I to get meat to **g** to all this people? Nm 11:13
weep before me and say, '**G** us meat, Nm 11:13
saying, "Who will **g** us meat to eat? Nm 11:18
Therefore the LORD will **g** you meat, Nm 11:18
and you have said, 'I will **g** them meat, Nm 11:21
bring us into this land and **g** it to us, Nm 14:8
land that he swore to **g** to them that he Nm 14:16
land that I swore to **g** to their fathers. Nm 14:23
your dough you shall **g** to the LORD as Nm 15:21
I **g** your priesthood as a gift, and any Nm 18:7
firstfruits of what they **g** to the LORD, Nm 18:12
what they give to the LORD, I **g** to you. Nm 18:12
of Israel present to the LORD I **g** to you, Nm 18:19
it you shall **g** the LORD'S contribution Nm 18:28
And you shall **g** it to Eleazar the priest, Nm 19:3
rock for them and **g** drink to the Nm 20:8
Edom refused to **g** Israel passage Nm 20:21
"If you will indeed **g** this people into my Nm 21:2
together, so that I may **g** them water." Nm 21:16
Balak were to **g** me his house Nm 22:18
and hear; **g** ear to me, O son of Zippor: Nm 23:18
'If Balak should **g** me his house full of Nm 24:13
I **g** to him my covenant of peace, Nm 25:12
tribe you shall **g** a large inheritance, Nm 26:54
tribe you shall **g** a small inheritance; Nm 26:54
G to us a possession among our Nm 27:4
You shall **g** them possession of an Nm 27:7
then you shall **g** his inheritance to his Nm 27:9
then you shall **g** his inheritance to his Nm 27:10
then you shall **g** his inheritance to the Nm 27:11
from their half and **g** it to Eleazar the Nm 31:29
and **g** them to the Levites who keep Nm 31:30
the land that I swore to **g** to Abraham, Nm 32:11
then you shall **g** them the land of Nm 32:29
tribe you shall **g** a large inheritance, Nm 33:54
tribe you shall **g** a small inheritance. Nm 33:54
LORD has commanded to **g** to the nine Nm 34:13
people of Israel to **g** to the Levites some Nm 35:2
And you shall **g** to the Levites Nm 35:2
cities, which you shall **g** to the Levites, Nm 35:4
The cities that you **g** to the Levites Nm 35:6
to them you shall **g** forty-two cities. Nm 35:6
the cities that you **g** to the Levites shall Nm 35:7
that you shall **g** from the possession Nm 35:8
shall **g** of its cities to the Levites." Nm 35:8
the cities that you **g** shall be your six Nm 35:13
You shall **g** three cities beyond the Nm 35:14
commanded my lord to **g** the land for Nm 36:2
by the LORD to **g** the inheritance of Nm 36:2
to **g** to them and to their offspring after Dt 1:8
to **g** us into the hand of the Amorites, Dt 1:27
land that I swore to **g** to your fathers, Dt 1:35
to his children I will **g** the land on which Dt 1:36
And to them I will **g** it, and they shall Dt 1:39
not listen to your voice or **g** ear to you. Dt 1:45
them, for I will not **g** you any of their land, Dt 2:5
for I will not **g** you any of their land for a Dt 2:9
for I will not **g** you any of the land of the Dt 2:19
I may eat, and **g** me water for money, Dt 2:28
that he might **g** him into your hand, Dt 2:30
I have begun to **g** Sihon and his land Dt 2:31
in, to **g** you their land for an inheritance, Dt 4:38
to **g** you—with great and good cities that Dt 6:10
that the LORD swore to **g** to your fathers Dt 6:18
might bring us in and **g** us the land that Dt 6:23
the land that he swore to **g** to our fathers. Dt 6:23
that he swore to your fathers to **g** you. Dt 7:13
that the LORD your God will **g** over to you. Dt 7:16
LORD your God will **g** them over to you Dt 7:23
And he will **g** their kings into your hand, Dt 7:24
that the LORD swore to **g** to your fathers. Dt 8:1
I swore to their fathers to **g** them.' Dt 10:11
swore to your fathers to **g** to them and to Dt 11:9
he will **g** the rain for your land in its Dt 11:14
And he will **g** grass in your fields for Dt 11:15
LORD swore to your fathers to **g** them, Dt 11:21
You may **g** it to the sojourner who is Dt 14:21
poor brother, and you **g** him nothing, Dt 15:9
You shall **g** to him freely, and your Dt 15:10
not be grudging when you **g** to him, Dt 15:10
has blessed you, you shall **g** to him. Dt 15:14
which you shall **g** as the LORD your God Dt 16:10
Every man shall **g** as he is able, Dt 16:17
to the instructions that they **g** you, Dt 17:11
they shall **g** to the priest the shoulder and Dt 18:3
fleece of your sheep, you shall **g** him. Dt 18:4
that he promised to **g** to your fathers— Dt 19:8
your enemies, to **g** you the victory.' Dt 20:4
shekels of silver and **g** them to the Dt 22:19
who lay with her shall **g** to the father of Dt 22:29
deliver you and to **g** up your enemies Dt 23:14
"You shall not **g** up to his master a Dt 23:15
You shall **g** him his wages on the same Dt 24:15
the LORD swore to our fathers to **g** us.' Dt 26:3
the LORD swore to your fathers to **g** you. Dt 28:11
to **g** the rain to your land in its season Dt 28:12
so that he will not **g** to any of them any Dt 28:55
but the LORD will **g** you there a Dt 28:65
to Isaac, and to Jacob, to **g** them." Dt 30:20
And the LORD will **g** them over to you, Dt 31:5
has sworn to their fathers to **g** them, Dt 31:7
which I swore to **g** to their fathers, Dt 31:20
them into the land that I swore to **g**." Dt 31:21
into the land that I swore to **g** them. Dt 31:23
"**G** ear, O heavens, and I will speak, and Dt 32:1
Levi he said, "**G** to Levi your Thummim, Dt 33:8
and to Jacob, 'I will **g** it to your offspring.' Dt 34:4
that I swore to their fathers to **g** them. Jos 1:6
a place of rest and will **g** you this land.' Jos 1:13
my father's house, and **g** me a sure sign Jos 2:12
LORD had sworn to their fathers to **g** to us, Jos 5:6
all, to **g** us into the hands of the Amorites, Jos 7:7
g glory to the LORD God of Israel and give Jos 7:19
LORD God of Israel and **g** praise to him. Jos 7:19
LORD your God will **g** it into your hand. Jos 8:7
for I will **g** it into your hand." And Jos 8:18
his servant Moses to **g** you all the land Jos 9:24
at this time I will **g** over all of them, Jos 11:6
So now **g** me this hill country of which Jos 14:12
to him will I **g** Achsah my daughter as Jos 15:16
She said to him, "**G** me a blessing. Jos 15:19
g me also springs of water." And he Jos 15:19

commanded Moses to **g** us an Jos 17:4
take him into the city and **g** him a place, Jos 20:4
they shall not **g** up the manslayer into Jos 20:5
land that he swore to **g** to their fathers. Jos 21:43
I will **g** him Achsah my daughter for a Jgs 1:12
She said to him, "**G** me a blessing. Since Jgs 1:15
g me also springs of water." And Caleb Jgs 1:15
the land that I swore to **g** to your fathers. Jgs 2:1
and he did not **g** them into the hand of Jgs 2:23
troops, and I will **g** him into your hand'?" Jgs 4:7
her, "Please **g** me a little water to drink, Jgs 4:19
"Hear, O kings; **g** ear, O princes; to the Jgs 5:3
many for me to **g** the Midianites into Jgs 7:2
will save you and **g** the Midianites into Jgs 7:7
"Please **g** loaves of bread to the people Jgs 8:5
that we should **g** bread to your army?" Jgs 8:6
that we should **g** bread to your men who Jgs 8:15
every one of you **g** me the earrings from Jgs 8:24
"We will willingly **g** them." And they Jgs 8:25
"If you will **g** the Ammonites into my Jgs 11:30
then I will **g** you thirty linen garments Jgs 14:12
then you shall **g** me thirty linen Jgs 14:13
that we may **g** you into the hands of the Jgs 15:12
only bind you and **g** you into their Jgs 15:13
And we will each **g** you 1,100 pieces of Jgs 16:5
and I will **g** you ten pieces of silver a Jgs 17:10
of you, **g** your advice and counsel here." Jgs 20:7
Now therefore **g** up the men, the Jgs 20:13
for tomorrow I will **g** them into your Jgs 20:28
one of us shall **g** his daughter in Jgs 21:1
LORD that we will not **g** them any of our Jgs 21:7
Yet we cannot **g** them wives from our Jgs 21:18
battle, neither did you **g** them to them, Jgs 21:22
that the LORD will **g** you by this young Ru 4:12
he would **g** portions to Peninnah his 1 Sm 1:4
but will **g** to your servant a son, 1 Sm 1:11
then I will **g** him to the LORD all the 1 Sm 1:11
he will **g** strength to his king and 1 Sm 2:10
"**G** meat for the priest to roast, 1 Sm 2:15
he would say, "No, you must **g** it now, 1 Sm 2:16
"May the LORD **g** you children by this 1 Sm 2:20
was pregnant, about to **g** birth. 1 Sm 4:19
land, and **g** glory to the God of Israel. 1 Sm 6:5
"**G** us a king to judge us." And Samuel 1 Sm 8:6
and olive orchards and **g** them to his 1 Sm 8:14
of your vineyards and **g** it to his 1 Sm 8:15
and I will **g** it to the man of God to tell 1 Sm 9:8
will greet you and **g** you two loaves of 1 Sm 10:4
"**G** us seven days respite that we may 1 Sm 11:3
save us, we will **g** ourselves up to you." 1 Sm 11:3
"Tomorrow we will **g** ourselves up to 1 Sm 11:10
Will you **g** them into the hand of 1 Sm 14:37
son, O LORD, God of Israel, **g** Urim. 1 Sm 14:41
g Thummim." And Jonathan and 1 Sm 14:41
G me a man, that we may fight 1 Sm 17:10
riches and will **g** him his daughter 1 Sm 17:25
and I will **g** your flesh to the birds of 1 Sm 17:44
And I will **g** the dead bodies of the 1 Sm 17:46
and he will **g** you into our hand." 1 Sm 17:47
Merab. I will **g** her to you for a wife. 1 Sm 18:17
Saul thought, "Let me **g** her to him, 1 Sm 18:21
G me five loaves of bread, or whatever 1 Sm 21:3
"There is none like that; **g** it to me." 1 Sm 21:9
will the son of Jesse **g** every one of you 1 Sm 22:7
for I will **g** the Philistines into your 1 Sm 23:4
but God did not **g** him into his hand. 1 Sm 23:14
I will **g** your enemy into your hand, 1 Sm 24:4
be judge and **g** sentence between me 1 Sm 24:15
Please **g** whatever you have at hand to 1 Sm 25:8
for my shearers and **g** it to men who 1 Sm 25:11
the LORD will **g** Israel also with you 1 Sm 28:19
The LORD will **g** the army of Israel 1 Sm 28:19
we will not **g** them any of the spoil 1 Sm 30:22
son, saying, "**G** me my wife Michal, 2 Sm 3:14
Will you **g** them into my hand?" And 2 Sm 5:19
I will certainly **g** the Philistines into 2 Sm 5:19
And I will **g** you rest from all your 2 Sm 7:11
before your eyes and **g** them to your 2 Sm 12:11
sister Tamar come and **g** me bread to 2 Sm 13:5
'**G** up the man who struck his 2 Sm 14:7
and I will **g** orders concerning you." 2 Sm 14:8
to me, and I would **g** him justice." 2 Sm 15:4
house of Israel will **g** me back the 2 Sm 16:3
said to Ahithophel, "**G** your counsel. 2 Sm 16:20
have been glad to **g** you ten pieces of 2 Sm 18:11
G up him alone, and I will withdraw 2 Sm 20:21
And the king said, "I will **g** them." 2 Sm 21:6
that someone would **g** me water to 2 Sm 23:15
therefore come, let me **g** you advice, 1 Kgs 1:12
refuse you—to **g** me Abishag the 1 Kgs 2:17
and God said, "Ask what I shall **g** you." 1 Kgs 3:5
G your servant therefore an 1 Kgs 3:9
I **g** you a wise and discerning mind, 1 Kgs 3:12
I **g** you also what you have not asked, 1 Kgs 3:13
and **g** half to the one and half to the 1 Kgs 3:25

"Oh, my lord, **g** her the living child, 1 Kgs 3:26
"**G** the living child to the first 1 Kgs 3:27
angry with them and **g** them to an 1 Kgs 8:46
from you and will **g** it to your 1 Kgs 11:11
but I will **g** one tribe to your son, 1 Kgs 11:13
of Solomon and will **g** you ten tribes 1 Kgs 11:31
of his son's hand and will **g** it to you, 1 Kgs 11:35
Yet to his son I will **g** one tribe, that 1 Kgs 11:36
for David, and I will **g** Israel to you. 1 Kgs 11:38
yourself, and I will **g** you a reward." 1 Kgs 13:7
king, "If you **g** me half your house, 1 Kgs 13:8
And he will **g** Israel up because of 1 Kgs 14:16
"**G** me your son." And he took him 1 Kgs 17:19
that you would **g** your servant into 1 Kgs 18:9
I will **g** it into your hand this day, 1 Kgs 20:13
therefore I will **g** all this great 1 Kgs 20:28
said to Naboth, "**G** me your vineyard, 1 Kgs 21:2
and I will **g** you a better vineyard for 1 Kgs 21:2
you, I will **g** you its value in money." 1 Kgs 21:2
that I should **g** you the inheritance 1 Kgs 21:3
"I will not **g** you the inheritance of 1 Kgs 21:4
him, '**G** me your vineyard for money, 1 Kgs 21:6
I will **g** you another vineyard for it.' 1 Kgs 21:6
'I will not **g** you my vineyard.'" 1 Kgs 21:6
I will **g** you the vineyard of Naboth 1 Kgs 21:7
he refused to **g** you for money, 1 Kgs 21:15
for the Lord will **g** it into the hand of 1 Kgs 22:6
the LORD will **g** it into the hand of the 1 Kgs 22:12
the LORD will **g** it into the hand of the 1 Kgs 22:15
these three kings to **g** them into the 2 Kgs 3:10
these three kings to **g** them into the 2 Kgs 3:13
He will also **g** the Moabites into your 2 Kgs 3:18
And Elisha said, "**G** to the men, that 2 Kgs 4:42
So he repeated, "**G** them to the men, 2 Kgs 4:43
Please **g** them a talent of silver and 2 Kgs 5:22
"This woman said to me, '**G** your son, 2 Kgs 6:28
the next day I said to her, '**G** your son, 2 Kgs 6:29
since he promised to **g** a lamp to him 2 Kgs 8:19
g me your hand." So he gave him 2 Kgs 10:15
of those whom I **g** into your hands 2 Kgs 10:24
Then they would **g** the money that 2 Kgs 12:11
'**G** your daughter to my son for a 2 Kgs 14:9
man, to **g** to the king of Assyria. 2 Kgs 15:20
I will **g** you two thousand horses, if 2 Kgs 18:23
of my heritage and **g** them into the 2 Kgs 21:14
and let them **g** it to the workmen who 2 Kgs 22:5
the land to **g** the money according 2 Kgs 23:35
assessment, to **g** it to Pharaoh Neco. 2 Kgs 23:35
that someone would **g** me water to 1 Chr 11:17
Will you **g** them into my hand?" 1 Chr 14:10
and I will **g** them into your hand." 1 Chr 14:10
Oh **g** thanks to the LORD; call upon 1 Chr 16:8
"To you I will **g** the land of Canaan, 1 Chr 16:18
Oh **g** thanks to the LORD, for he is 1 Chr 16:34
that we may **g** thanks to your holy 1 Chr 16:35
expressly named to **g** thanks to the 1 Chr 16:41
"**G** me the site of the threshing floor 1 Chr 21:22
an altar to the LORD—**g** it to me at its 1 Chr 21:22
I **g** the oxen for burnt offerings and 1 Chr 21:23
wheat for a grain offering; I **g** it all." 1 Chr 21:23
I will **g** him rest from all his 1 Chr 22:9
and I will **g** peace and quiet to Israel 1 Chr 22:9
house of my God I **g** it to the house of 1 Chr 29:3
make great and to **g** strength to all. 1 Chr 29:12
said to him, "Ask what I shall **g** you." 2 Chr 1:7
G me now wisdom and knowledge to 2 Chr 1:10
I will also **g** you riches, possessions, 2 Chr 1:12
I will **g** for your servants, the 2 Chr 2:10
angry with them and **g** them to an 2 Chr 6:36
to **g** strong support to those whose 2 Chr 16:9
for God will **g** it into the hand of the 2 Chr 18:5
The LORD will **g** it into the hand of 2 Chr 18:11
to **g** judgment for the LORD and to 2 Chr 19:8
and **g** it forever to the descendants of 2 Chr 20:7
and say, "**G** thanks to the LORD, 2 Chr 20:21
he had promised to **g** a lamp to him 2 Chr 21:7
LORD is able to **g** you much more 2 Chr 25:9
'**G** your daughter to my son for a 2 Chr 25:18
order that he might **g** them into the 2 Chr 25:20
also on Judah to **g** them one heart to 2 Chr 30:12
the LORD and to **g** thanks and praise. 2 Chr 31:2
in Jerusalem to **g** the portion due 2 Chr 31:4
that they might **g** themselves to the 2 Chr 31:4
that he may **g** you over to die by 2 Chr 32:11
us a remnant and to **g** us a secure hold Ezr 9:8
and to **g** us protection in Judea and Ezr 9:9
Therefore do not **g** your daughters to Ezr 9:12
and **g** success to your servant today, Neh 1:11
that he may **g** me timber to make Neh 2:8
on their own heads and **g** them up to be Neh 4:4
and so they could **g** me a bad name in Neh 6:13
him the covenant to **g** to his offspring Neh 9:8
the land that you had sworn to **g** them. Neh 9:15
prophets. Yet they would not **g** ear. Neh 9:30
"We will not **g** our daughters to the Neh 10:30

the obligation to **g** yearly a third Neh 10:32
them, to praise and to **g** thanks, Neh 12:24
"You shall not **g** your daughters to Neh 13:25
And let the king **g** her royal position to Est 1:19
all women will **g** honor to their Est 1:20
All that a man has he will **g** for his life. Jb 2:4
I will **g** free utterance to my complaint; Jb 10:1
conceive trouble and **g** birth to evil, Jb 15:35
and his hands will **g** back his wealth. Jb 20:10
He will **g** back the fruit of his toil and Jb 20:18
I would **g** him an account of all my Jb 31:37
my words, you wise men, and **g** ear to me, Jb 34:2
you are righteous, what do you **g** to him? Jb 35:7
know when the mountain goats **g** birth? Jb 39:1
do you know the time when they **g** birth, Jb 39:2
"Do you **g** the horse his might? Do you Jb 39:19
G ear to my words, O LORD; consider my Ps 5:1
G attention to the sound of my cry, my Ps 5:2
of you; in Sheol who will **g** you praise? Ps 6:5
I will **g** to the LORD the thanks due to his Ps 7:17
I will **g** thanks to the LORD with my whole Ps 9:1
G ear to my prayer from lips free of Ps 17:1
the sanctuary and **g** you support from Ps 20:2
G me not up to the will of my Ps 27:12
G to them according to their work and Ps 28:4
g to them according to the work of their Ps 28:4
and with my song I **g** thanks to him. Ps 28:7
LORD makes the deer **g** birth and strips Ps 29:9
May the LORD **g** strength to his people! Ps 29:11
saints, and **g** thanks to his holy name. Ps 30:4
my God, I will **g** thanks to you forever! Ps 30:12
G thanks to the LORD with the lyre; make Ps 33:2
and you **g** them drink from the river of Ps 36:8
and he will **g** you the desires of your Ps 37:4
my prayer, O LORD, and **g** ear to my cry; Ps 39:12
you do not **g** him up to the will of his Ps 41:2
and we will **g** thanks to your name Ps 44:8
G ear, all inhabitants of the world, Ps 49:1
another, or **g** to God the price of his life, Ps 49:7
"You **g** your mouth free rein for evil, Ps 50:19
not delight in sacrifice, or I would **g** it; Ps 51:16
prayer; **g** ear to the words of my mouth. Ps 54:2
I will **g** thanks to your name, O LORD, for Ps 54:6
G ear to my prayer, O God, and hide not Ps 55:1
God will **g** ear and humble them, he Ps 55:19
I will **g** thanks to you, O Lord, among the Ps 57:9
g salvation by your right hand and Ps 60:5
of his name; **g** to him glorious praise! Ps 66:2
G the king your justice, O God, and your Ps 72:1
g deliverance to the children of the Ps 72:4
We **g** thanks to you, O God; we give Ps 75:1
give thanks to you, O God; we **g** thanks, Ps 75:1
G ear, O my people, to my teaching; Ps 78:1
Can he also **g** bread or provide meat for Ps 78:20
pasture, will **g** thanks to you forever; Ps 79:13
G ear, O Shepherd of Israel, you who lead Ps 80:1
g us life, and we will call upon your Ps 80:18
G justice to the weak and the fatherless; Ps 82:3
hear my prayer; **g** ear, O God of Jacob! Ps 84:8
Yes, the LORD will **g** what is good, and Ps 85:12
G ear, O LORD, to my prayer; listen to my Ps 86:6
I **g** thanks to you, O Lord my God, with Ps 86:12
g your strength to your servant, and Ps 86:16
It is good to **g** thanks to the LORD, to sing Ps 92:1
to **g** him rest from days of trouble, until Ps 94:13
and **g** thanks to his holy name! Ps 97:12
G thanks to him; bless his name! Ps 100:4
they **g** drink to every beast of the field; Ps 104:11
to **g** them their food in due season. Ps 104:27
When you **g** it to them, they gather it Ps 104:28
Oh **g** thanks to the LORD; call upon his Ps 105:1
"To you I will **g** the land of Canaan as Ps 105:11
a covering, and fire to **g** light by night. Ps 105:39
Oh **g** thanks to the LORD, for he is good, Ps 106:1
that we may **g** thanks to your holy Ps 106:47
Oh **g** thanks to the LORD, for he is good, Ps 107:1
I will **g** thanks to you, O LORD, among Ps 108:3
g salvation by your right hand and Ps 108:6
accuse me, but I **g** myself to prayer. Ps 109:4
my mouth I will **g** great thanks to the Ps 109:30
I will **g** thanks to the LORD with my Ps 111:1
not to us, but to your name **g** glory, Ps 115:1
May the LORD **g** you increase, you and Ps 115:14
Oh **g** thanks to the LORD, for he is good; Ps 118:1
through them and **g** thanks to the Ps 118:19
O LORD! O LORD, we pray, **g** us success! Ps 118:25
are my God, and I will **g** thanks to you; Ps 118:28
Oh **g** thanks to the LORD, for he is good; Ps 118:29
dust; **g** me life according to your word! Ps 119:25
G me understanding, that I may keep Ps 119:34
things; and **g** me life in your ways. Ps 119:37
in your righteousness **g** me life! Ps 119:40
g me understanding that I may learn Ps 119:73
In your steadfast love **g** me life, that I Ps 119:88
g me life, O LORD, according to your Ps 119:107

G your servant a pledge of good; let Ps 119:122
g me understanding, that I may Ps 119:125
g me understanding that I may live. Ps 119:144
according to your justice **g** me life. Ps 119:149
g me life according to your promise! Ps 119:154
g me life according to your rules. Ps 119:156
G me life according to your steadfast Ps 119:159
g me understanding according to Ps 119:169
to **g** thanks to the name of the LORD. Ps 122:4
I will not **g** sleep to my eyes or slumber Ps 132:4
Praise the name of the LORD, **g** praise, O Ps 135:1
G thanks to the LORD, for he is good, for Ps 136:1
G thanks to the God of gods, for his Ps 136:2
G thanks to the Lord of lords, for his Ps 136:3
G thanks to the God of heaven, for his Ps 136:26
I **g** you thanks, O LORD, with my whole Ps 138:1
your holy temple and **g** thanks to your Ps 138:2
kings of the earth shall **g** you thanks, Ps 138:4
g ear to the voice of my pleas for mercy, Ps 140:6
the righteous shall **g** thanks to your Ps 140:13
G ear to my voice when I call to you! Ps 141:1
that I may **g** thanks to your name! Ps 142:7
O LORD; **g** ear to my pleas for mercy! Ps 143:1
All your works shall **g** thanks to you, Ps 145:10
and you **g** them their food in due Ps 145:15
to **g** prudence to the simple, knowledge Prv 1:4
tomorrow I will **g** it"—when you have it Prv 3:28
for I **g** you good precepts; do not forsake Prv 4:2
lest you **g** your honor to others and your Prv 5:9
G your eyes no sleep and your eyelids no Prv 6:4
he will **g** all the goods of his house. Prv 6:31
G instruction to a wise man, and he will Prv 9:9
another withholds what he should **g**, Prv 11:24
that you may **g** a true answer to those Prv 22:21
Be not one of those who **g** pledges, who Prv 22:26
My son, **g** me your heart, and let your Prv 23:26
man who boasts of a gift he does not **g**. Prv 25:14
enemy is hungry, **g** him bread to eat, Prv 25:21
if he is thirsty, **g** him water to drink, Prv 25:21
flocks, and **g** attention to your herds, Prv 27:23
The rod and reproof **g** wisdom, but a Prv 29:15
your son, and he will **g** you rest; Prv 29:17
rest; he will **g** delight to your heart. Prv 29:17
lying; **g** me neither poverty nor riches; Prv 30:8
daughters; "**G**" and "Give," they cry. Prv 30:15
daughters; "Give" and "**G**," they cry. Prv 30:15
Do not **g** your strength to women, your Prv 31:3
G strong drink to the one who is Prv 31:6
G her of the fruit of her hands, and let Prv 31:31
only to **g** to one who pleases God. Eccl 2:26
yet God does not **g** him power to enjoy Eccl 6:2
the perfumer's ointment **g** off a stench; Eccl 10:1
G a portion to seven, or even to eight, Eccl 11:2
are in blossom; they **g** forth fragrance. Sg 2:13
are in bloom. There I will **g** you my love. Sg 7:12
The mandrakes **g** forth fragrance, and Sg 7:13
I would **g** you spiced wine to drink, the Sg 8:2
Hear, O heavens, and **g** ear, O earth; for the Is 1:2
G ear to the teaching of our God, you Is 1:10
the Lord himself will **g** you a sign. Is 7:14
of the abundance of milk that they **g**, Is 7:22
be shattered; **g** ear, all you far countries; Is 8:9
of Gallim! **G** attention, O Laishah! Is 10:30
"I will **g** thanks to you, O LORD, for Is 12:1
"**G** thanks to the LORD, call upon his Is 12:4
their constellations will not **g** their light; Is 13:10
"**G** counsel; grant justice; make your Is 16:3
and I will **g** over the Egyptians into the Is 19:4
counselors of Pharaoh **g** stupid counsel. Is 19:11
fastened in a secure place will **g** way, Is 22:25
Therefore in the east **g** glory to the LORD; Is 24:15
the sea, **g** glory to the name of the LORD, Is 24:15
and the earth will **g** birth to the dead. Is 26:19
has said, "This is rest; **g** rest to the weary; Is 28:12
G ear, and hear my voice; give attention, Is 28:23
voice; **g** attention, and hear my speech. Is 28:23
When men **g** it to one who can read, Is 29:11
And when they **g** the book to one who Is 29:12
And though the Lord **g** you the bread of Is 30:20
And he will **g** rain for the seed with Is 30:23
ears of those who hear will **g** attention. Is 32:3
daughters, **g** ear to my speech. Is 32:9
conceive chaff; you **g** birth to stubble; Is 33:11
near, O nations, to hear, and **g** attention, Is 34:1
I will **g** you two thousand horses, if you Is 36:8
they are!" and I **g** to Jerusalem a herald Is 41:27
I will **g** you as a covenant for the people, a Is 42:6
that is my name; my glory I **g** to no other, Is 42:8
Let them **g** glory to the LORD, and declare Is 42:12
Who among you will **g** ear to this, will Is 42:23
I **g** Egypt as your ransom, Cush and Seba Is 43:3
and I love you, I **g** men in return for you, Is 43:4
I will say to the north, **G** up, and to the Is 43:6
ostriches, for I **g** water in the wilderness, Is 43:20
desert, to **g** drink to my chosen people, Is 43:20

I will **g** you the treasures of darkness and Is 45:3
My glory I will not **g** to another. Is 48:11
to me, O coastlands, and **g** attention, Is 49:1
I will keep you and **g** you as a covenant to Is 49:8
"**G** attention to me, my people, and give Is 51:4
to me, my people, and **g** ear to me, Is 51:4
I will **g** in my house and within my walls Is 56:5
I will **g** them an everlasting name that Is 56:5
conceive mischief and **g** birth to iniquity. Is 59:4
brightness shall the moon **g** you light; Is 60:19
in Zion—to **g** them a beautiful headdress Is 61:3
I will faithfully **g** them their recompense, Is 61:8
name that the mouth of the LORD will **g**. Is 62:2
and **g** him no rest until he establishes Is 62:7
"I will not again **g** your grain to be food Is 62:8
"'And I will **g** you shepherds after my Jer 3:15
my sons, and **g** you a pleasant land, Jer 3:19
To whom shall I speak and **g** warning, Jer 6:10
Therefore I will **g** their wives to others Jer 8:10
and **g** them poisonous water to drink. Jer 9:15
to **g** them a land flowing with milk and Jer 11:5
Hear and **g** ear; be not proud, for the Jer 13:15
G glory to the LORD your God before he Jer 13:16
but I will **g** you assured peace in this Jer 14:13
rain? Or can the heavens **g** showers? Jer 14:22
rest of them I will **g** to the sword before Jer 15:9
and your treasures I will **g** as spoil, Jer 15:13
nor shall anyone **g** him the cup of Jer 16:7
all your treasures I will **g** for spoil as the Jer 17:3
to **g** every man according to his ways, Jer 17:10
g them over to the power of the sword; Jer 18:21
I will **g** their dead bodies for food to the Jer 19:7
And I will **g** all Judah into the hand of Jer 20:4
I will **g** all the wealth of the city, Jer 20:5
I will **g** Zedekiah king of Judah and his Jer 21:7
nothing and does not **g** him his wages, Jer 22:13
and **g** you into the hand of those who Jer 22:25
bitter food and **g** them poisoned water Jer 23:15
I will **g** them a heart to know that I am Jer 24:7
G them this charge for their masters: Jer 27:4
and I **g** it to whomever it seems right to Jer 27:5
sons, and **g** your daughters in marriage, Jer 29:6
for evil, to **g** you a future and a hope. Jer 29:11
proclaim, **g** praise, and say, 'O LORD, save Jer 31:7
them, and **g** them gladness for sorrow. Jer 31:13
you swore to their fathers to **g** them, Jer 32:22
I will **g** them one heart and one way, Jer 32:39
"'**G** thanks to the LORD of hosts, for the Jer 33:11
And I will **g** them into the hand of their Jer 34:20
his officials I will **g** into the hand of Jer 34:21
And if I **g** you counsel, you will not Jer 38:15
I will **g** Pharaoh Hophra king of Egypt Jer 44:30
But I will **g** you your life as a prize of war Jer 45:5
"**G** wings to Moab, for she would fly Jer 48:9
cause, that he may **g** rest to the earth, Jer 50:34
G yourself no rest, your eyes no Lam 2:18
let him **g** his cheek to the one who Lam 3:30
You will **g** them dullness of heart; Lam 3:65
open your mouth and eat what I **g** you." Ezk 2:8
with this scroll that I **g** you and fill your Ezk 3:3
you shall **g** them warning from me. Ezk 3:17
surely die,' and you **g** him no warning, Ezk 3:18
And I will **g** it into the hands of Ezk 7:21
iniquity and who **g** wicked counsel in Ezk 11:2
and **g** you into the hands of foreigners, Ezk 11:9
and I will **g** you the land of Israel.' Ezk 11:17
And I will **g** them one heart, and a new Ezk 11:19
from their flesh and **g** them a heart of Ezk 11:19
visions and who **g** lying divinations. Ezk 13:9
Men **g** gifts to all prostitutes, but you Ezk 16:33
And I will **g** you into their hands, and Ezk 16:39
you shall also **g** payment no more. Ezk 16:41
and I **g** them to you as daughters, Ezk 16:61
that they might **g** him horses and a Ezk 17:15
into the land that I swore to **g** them, Ezk 20:28
that I swore to **g** to your fathers. Ezk 20:42
belongs, and I will **g** it to him. Ezk 21:27
She did not **g** up her whoring that she Ezk 23:8
therefore I will **g** her cup into your Ezk 23:31
I will **g** it along with the Ammonites Ezk 25:10
the birds of the heavens I **g** you as food. Ezk 29:5
I will **g** the land of Egypt to Ezk 29:19
I will **g** it into the hand of a mighty Ezk 31:11
and the moon shall not **g** its light. Ezk 32:7
you shall **g** them warning from me. Ezk 33:7
the open field I will **g** to the beasts to Ezk 33:27
And I will **g** you a new heart, and a Ezk 36:26
from your flesh and **g** you a heart of Ezk 36:26
I will **g** you to birds of prey of every sort Ezk 39:4
"On that day I will **g** to Gog a place for Ezk 39:11
you shall **g** to the Levitical priests of Ezk 43:19
and you shall **g** them no possession in Ezk 44:28
You shall also **g** to the priests the first Ezk 44:30
shall be obliged to **g** this offering to Ezk 45:16
the lambs as much as one is able to **g**, Ezk 46:11

He shall **g** his sons their inheritance Ezk 46:18
what I swore to **g** to your fathers. Ezk 47:14
God of my fathers, I **g** thanks and praise, Dn 2:23
that you can **g** interpretations and solve Dn 5:16
yourself, and **g** your rewards to another. Dn 5:17
to whom these satraps should **g** account, Dn 6:2
now come out to **g** you insight and Dn 9:22
He shall **g** him the daughter of women Dn 11:17
who **g** me my bread and my water, Hos 2:5
And there I will **g** her her vineyards and Hos 2:15
is gone, they **g** themselves to whoring; Hos 4:18
of Israel! **G** ear, O house of the king! Hos 5:1
G them, O LORD—what will you give? Hos 9:14
Give them, O LORD—what will you **g**? Hos 9:14
G them a miscarrying womb and dry Hos 9:14
Even though they **g** birth, I will put Hos 9:16
How can I **g** you up, O Ephraim? How Hos 11:8
you said, "**G** me a king and princes"? Hos 13:10
elders; **g** ear, all inhabitants of the land! Jl 1:2
fruit; the fig tree and vine **g** their full yield. Jl 2:22
Perhaps the god will **g** a thought to us, Jon 1:6
Therefore you shall **g** parting gifts to Mi 1:14
Its heads **g** judgment for a bribe; its Mi 3:11
Therefore he shall **g** them up until the Mi 5:3
Shall I **g** my firstborn for my Mi 6:7
what you preserve I will **g** to the sword. Mi 6:14
And in this place I will **g** peace, declares Hg 2:9
and I will **g** you the right of access Zec 3:7
The vine shall **g** its fruit, and the Zec 8:12
and the ground shall **g** its produce, Zec 8:12
and the heavens shall **g** their dew. Zec 8:12
and he will **g** them showers of rain, Zec 10:1
false dreams and **g** empty consolation. Zec 10:2
it seems good to you, **g** me my wages; Zec 11:12
"And the LORD will **g** salvation to the Zec 12:7
take it to heart to **g** honor to my name, Mal 2:2
And he said to him, "All these I will **g** you, Mt 4:9
your good works and **g** glory to your Mt 5:16
let him **g** her a certificate of divorce.' Mt 5:31
G to the one who begs from you, and do Mt 5:42
"Thus, when you **g** to the needy, sound no Mt 6:2
But when you **g** to the needy, do not let Mt 6:3
G us this day our daily bread, Mt 6:11
"Do not **g** dogs what is holy, and do not Mt 7:6
asks him for bread, will **g** him a stone? Mt 7:9
if he asks for a fish, will **g** him a serpent? Mt 7:10
know how to **g** good gifts to your Mt 7:11
who is in heaven **g** good things to those Mt 7:11
received without paying; **g** without pay. Mt 10:8
are heavy laden, and I will **g** you rest. Mt 11:28
judgment people will **g** account for Mt 12:36
with an oath to **g** her whatever she Mt 14:7
"**G** me the head of John the Baptist here Mt 14:8
go away; you **g** them something to eat." Mt 14:16
I will **g** you the keys of the kingdom of Mt 16:19
Or what shall a man **g** in return for his Mt 16:26
However, not to **g** offense to them, go to Mt 17:27
Take that and **g** it to them for me and Mt 17:27
Moses command one to **g** a certificate of Mt 19:7
sell what you possess and **g** to the poor, Mt 19:21
too, and whatever is right I will **g** you.' Mt 20:4
I choose to **g** to this last worker as I give Mt 20:14
to give to this last worker as I **g** to you. Mt 20:14
and to **g** his life as a ransom for many." Mt 20:28
other tenants who will **g** him the fruits Mt 21:41
and the moon will not **g** its light, Mt 24:29
to **g** them their food at the proper time? Mt 24:45
said to the wise, '**G** us some of your oil, Mt 25:8
talent from him and **g** it to him who Mt 25:28
feed you, or thirsty and **g** you drink? Mt 25:37
"What will you **g** me if I deliver him Mt 26:15
and told them to **g** her something to eat. Mk 5:43
you wish, and I will **g** it to you." Mk 6:22
"Whatever you ask me, I will **g** you, Mk 6:23
"I want you to **g** me at once the head of Mk 6:25
"You **g** them something to eat." And Mk 6:37
worth of bread and **g** it to them to Mk 6:37
For what can a man **g** in return for his Mk 8:37
sell all that you have and **g** to the poor, Mk 10:21
and to **g** his life as a ransom for Mk 10:45
the tenants and **g** the vineyard to Mk 12:9
and the moon will not **g** its light, Mk 13:24
glad and promised to **g** him money. Mk 14:11
the Lord God will **g** to him the throne Lk 1:32
the time came for Elizabeth to **g** birth, Lk 1:57
to **g** knowledge of salvation to his people Lk 1:77
to **g** light to those who sit in darkness Lk 1:79
there, the time came for her to **g** birth. Lk 2:6
hour she began to **g** thanks to God and Lk 2:38
"To you I will **g** all this authority and Lk 4:6
delivered to me, and I **g** it to whom I will. Lk 4:6
G to everyone who begs from you, and Lk 6:30
g, and it will be given to you. Good Lk 6:38
"You **g** them something to eat." They Lk 9:13
G us each day our daily bread, Lk 11:3

I cannot get up and **g** you anything'? Lk 11:7
not get up and **g** him anything because Lk 11:8
he will rise and **g** him whatever he Lk 11:8
will instead of a fish **g** him a serpent; Lk 11:11
asks for an egg, will **g** him a scorpion? Lk 11:12
know how to **g** good gifts to your Lk 11:13
the heavenly Father **g** the Holy Spirit Lk 11:13
But **g** as alms those things that are Lk 11:41
good pleasure to **g** you the kingdom. Lk 12:32
your possessions, and **g** to the needy. Lk 12:33
to **g** them their portion of food at the Lk 12:42
that I have come to **g** peace on earth? Lk 12:51
say to you, '**G** your place to this person,' Lk 14:9
"When you **g** a dinner or a banquet, Lk 14:12
But when you **g** a feast, invite the poor, Lk 14:13
g me the share of property that is Lk 15:12
who will **g** you that which is your Lk 16:12
found to return and **g** praise to God Lk 17:18
'**G** me justice against my adversary.' Lk 18:3
keeps bothering me, I will **g** her justice, Lk 18:5
And will not God **g** justice to his elect, Lk 18:7
you, he will **g** justice to them speedily. Lk 18:8
twice a week; I **g** tithes of all that I get.' Lk 18:12
Lord, the half of my goods I **g** to the poor. Lk 19:8
and **g** it to the one who has the ten Lk 19:24
so that they would **g** him some of the Lk 20:10
those tenants and **g** the vineyard to Lk 20:16
Is it lawful for us to **g** tribute to Caesar, Lk 20:22
for I will **g** you a mouth and wisdom, Lk 21:15
were glad, and agreed to **g** him money. Lk 22:5
and forbidding us to **g** tribute to Caesar, Lk 23:2
We need to **g** an answer to those who sent Jn 1:22
water. Jesus said to her, "**G** me a drink." Jn 4:7
it is that is saying to you, '**G** me a drink,' Jn 4:10
the water that I will **g** him will never be Jn 4:14
water that I will **g** him will become in Jn 4:14
woman said to him, "Sir, **g** me this water, Jn 4:15
life, which the Son of Man will **g** to you. Jn 6:27
said to him, "Sir, **g** us this bread always." Jn 6:34
the bread that I will **g** for the life of the Jn 6:51
"How can this man **g** us his flesh to eat?" Jn 6:52
blind and said to him, "**G** glory to God. Jn 9:24
I **g** them eternal life, and they will never Jn 10:28
you ask from God, God will **g** you." Jn 11:22
he to whom I will **g** this morsel of bread Jn 13:26
or that he should **g** something to the Jn 13:29
A new commandment I **g** to you, that Jn 13:34
and he will **g** you another Helper, Jn 14:16
I leave with you; my peace I **g** to you. Jn 14:27
you. Not as the world gives do I **g** to you. Jn 14:27
Father in my name, he may **g** it to you. Jn 15:16
Father in my name, he will **g** it to you. Jn 16:23
to **g** eternal life to all whom you have Jn 17:2
known to you, and **g** ear to my words. Acts 2:14
and gold, but what I do have I **g** to you. Acts 3:6
to **g** repentance to Israel and Acts 5:31
right that we should **g** up preaching the Acts 6:2
but promised to **g** it to him as a Acts 7:5
He received living oracles to **g** to us. Acts 7:38
saying, "**G** me this power also, so that Acts 8:19
because he did not **g** God the glory, Acts 12:23
"'I will **g** you the holy and sure Acts 13:34
cause that we can **g** to justify this Acts 19:40
you up and to **g** you the inheritance Acts 20:32
is more blessed to **g** than to receive.'" Acts 20:35
g notice to the tribune to bring him Acts 23:15
"I will **g** you a hearing when your Acts 23:35
me, no one can **g** me up to them. Acts 25:11
of the Romans to **g** up anyone before Acts 25:16
take some food. It will **g** you strength, Acts 27:34
honor him as God or **g** thanks to him, Rom 1:21
only do them but **g** approval to those Rom 1:32
and immortality, he will **g** eternal life; Rom 2:7
the dead will also **g** life to your mortal Rom 8:11
with him graciously **g** us all things? Rom 8:32
but **g** thought to do what is Rom 12:17
is thirsty, **g** him something to drink; Rom 12:20
each of us will **g** an account of Rom 14:12
whom not only I **g** thanks but all the Rom 16:4
of the Gentiles **g** thanks as well. Rom 16:4
I **g** thanks to my God always for you 1 Cor 1:4
The husband should **g** to his wife her 1 Cor 7:3
To the married I **g** this charge (not I, 1 Cor 7:10
but I **g** my judgment as one who by 1 Cor 7:25
of that for which I **g** thanks? 1 Cor 10:30
G no offense to Jews or to Greeks or 1 Cor 10:32
things I will **g** directions when I 1 Cor 11:34
If I **g** away all I have, and if I deliver 1 Cor 13:3
or the harp, do not **g** distinct notes, 1 Cor 14:7
if you **g** thanks with your spirit, 1 Cor 14:16
yours. **G** recognition to such men. 1 Cor 16:18
so that many will **g** thanks on our 2 Cor 1:11
shone in our hearts to **g** the light of the 2 Cor 4:6
And in this matter I **g** my judgment: 2 Cor 8:10
So **g** proof before the churches of 2 Cor 8:24
Each one must **g** as he has made up 2 Cor 9:7
To **g** a human example, brothers: even Gal 3:15
if a law had been given that could **g** life, Gal 3:21
due season we will reap, if we do not **g** up. Gal 6:9
I do not cease to **g** thanks for you, Eph 1:16
may **g** you a spirit of wisdom and of Eph 1:17
and **g** no opportunity to the devil. Eph 4:27
that it may **g** grace to those who hear. Eph 4:29
G my greetings to the brothers at Col 4:15
We **g** thanks to God always for all of 1 Thes 1:2
g thanks in all circumstances; for 1 Thes 5:18
We ought always to **g** thanks to God 2 Thes 1:3
we ought always to **g** thanks to God 2 Thes 2:13
but to **g** you in ourselves an example 2 Thes 3:9
you, we would **g** you this command: 2 Thes 3:10
Lord of peace himself **g** you peace at 2 Thes 3:16
and **g** the adversary no occasion for 1 Tm 5:14
the Lord will **g** you understanding in 2 Tm 2:7
may be able to **g** instruction in sound Ti 1:9
of him to whom we must **g** account. Heb 4:13
those who will have to **g** an account. Heb 13:17
but they will **g** account to him who is 1 Pt 4:5
and God will **g** him life—to those who 1 Jn 5:16
into your house or **g** him any greeting, 2 Jn 1:10
death, and I will **g** you the crown of life. Rv 2:10
who conquers I will **g** some of the hidden Rv 2:17
manna, and I will **g** him a white stone, Rv 2:17
and I will **g** to each of you as your works Rv 2:23
to him I will **g** authority over the Rv 2:26
And I will **g** him the morning star. Rv 2:28
the living creatures **g** glory and honor Rv 4:9
their hands nor **g** up worshiping Rv 9:20
and told him to **g** me the little scroll. Rv 10:9
saying, "We **g** thanks to you, Lord God Rv 11:17
the woman who was about to **g** birth, Rv 12:4
it was allowed to **g** breath to the image Rv 13:15
a loud voice, "Fear God and **g** him glory, Rv 14:7
They did not repent and **g** him glory. Rv 16:9
so **g** her a like measure of torment and Rv 18:7
us rejoice and exult and **g** him the glory, Rv 19:7
To the thirsty I will **g** from the spring of Rv 21:6

GIVEN (498)
I have **g** you every plant yielding seed Gn 1:29
I have **g** every green plant for food." And Gn 1:30
"Behold, you have **g** me no offspring, Gn 15:3
I have **g** your brother a thousand Gn 20:16
He has **g** him flocks and herds, silver Gn 24:35
old, and to him he has **g** all that he has. Gn 24:36
the names that his father had **g** them. Gn 26:18
his brothers I have **g** to him for Gn 27:37
he has **g** me this son also." And she Gn 29:33
heard my voice and **g** me a son." Gn 30:6
"God has **g** me my wages because I Gn 30:18
know the service that I have **g** you." Gn 30:26
of your father and **g** them to me. Gn 31:9
God has graciously **g** your servant." Gn 33:5
she had not been **g** to him in marriage. Gn 38:14
into Joseph's house and **g** them water, Gn 43:24
when he had **g** their donkeys fodder, Gn 43:24
whom God has **g** me here." And he said, Gn 48:9
I have **g** to you rather than to your Gn 48:22
No straw is **g** to your servants, yet they Ex 5:16
No straw will be **g** you, but you must Ex 5:18
And the LORD had **g** the people favor in Ex 12:36
the bread that the LORD has **g** you to eat. Ex 16:15
See! The LORD has **g** you the Sabbath; Ex 16:29
And I have **g** to all able men ability, that Ex 31:6
I have **g** it as their portion of my food Lv 6:17
and have **g** them to Aaron the priest and Lv 7:34
commanded this to be **g** them by the Lv 7:36
for they are **g** as your due and your Lv 10:14
holy and has been **g** to you that you Lv 10:17
and I have **g** it for you on the altar to Lv 17:11
and not yet ransomed or **g** her freedom, Lv 19:20
because he has **g** one of his children to Lv 20:3
whatever injury he has **g** a person shall Lv 24:20
he has given a person shall be **g** to him. Lv 24:20
they are wholly **g** to him from among Nm 3:9
For they are wholly **g** to me from Nm 8:16
And I have **g** the Levites as a gift to Nm 8:19
nor **g** us inheritance of fields and Nm 16:14
They are a gift to you, **g** to the LORD, to Nm 18:6
I have **g** you charge of the Nm 18:8
I have **g** them to you as a portion and to Nm 18:8
I have **g** them to you, and to your sons Nm 18:11
the Levites I have **g** every tithe in Nm 18:21
I have **g** to the Levites for an Nm 18:24
tithe that I have **g** you from them for Nm 18:26
into the land that I have **g** them." Nm 20:12
the land that I have **g** to the people of Nm 20:24
him, for I have **g** him into your hand, Nm 21:34
tribe shall be **g** its inheritance in Nm 26:54
was no inheritance **g** to them among Nm 26:62
the land that I have **g** to the people of Nm 27:12
let this land be **g** to your servants for a Nm 32:5
into the land that the LORD has **g** them? Nm 32:7
into the land that the LORD had **g** them. Nm 32:9
for I have **g** the land to you to possess Nm 33:53
the LORD had **g** him in commandment Dt 1:3
because I have **g** Mount Seir to Esau as a Dt 2:5
because I have **g** Ar to the people of Lot for Dt 2:9
because I have **g** it to the sons of Lot for a Dt 2:19
I have **g** into your hand Sihon the Dt 2:24
for I have **g** him and all his people and his Dt 3:2
LORD your God has **g** you this land to Dt 3:18
remain in the cities that I have **g** you, Dt 3:19
to his possession which I have **g** you.' Dt 3:20
your God for the good land he has **g** you. Dt 8:10
possession of the land that I have **g** you,' Dt 9:23
God of your fathers, has **g** you to possess, Dt 12:1
of the LORD your God that he has **g** you. Dt 12:15
your flock, which the LORD has **g** you, Dt 12:21
of the LORD your God that he has **g** you. Dt 16:17
which the LORD your God has **g** you. Dt 20:14
Forty stripes may be **g** him, but not Dt 25:3
LORD your God has **g** you rest from all Dt 25:19
ground, which you, O LORD, have **g** me.' Dt 26:10
the LORD your God has **g** to you and to Dt 26:11
and moreover, I have **g** it to the Levite, Dt 26:13
and the ground that you have **g** us, Dt 26:15
Your sheep shall be **g** to your enemies, Dt 28:31
daughters shall be **g** to another people, Dt 28:32
which the LORD your God has **g** you. Dt 28:52
whom the LORD your God has **g** you, Dt 28:53
day the LORD has not **g** you a heart to Dt 29:4
sold them, and the LORD had **g** them up? Dt 32:30
your foot will tread upon I have **g** to you, Jos 1:3
"I know that the LORD has **g** you the land, Jos 2:9
"Truly the LORD has **g** all the land into Jos 2:24
"See, I have **g** Jericho into your hand, Jos 6:2
"Shout, for the LORD has **g** you the city. Jos 6:16
I have **g** into your hand the king of Ai, Jos 8:1
them, for I have **g** them into your hands. Jos 10:8
LORD your God has **g** them into your Jos 10:19
For Moses had **g** an inheritance to the Jos 14:3
And no portion was **g** to the Levites in Jos 14:4
Since you have **g** me the land of the Jos 15:19
"Why have you **g** me but one lot and Jos 17:14
LORD, the God of your fathers, has **g** you? Jos 18:3
Moses that we be **g** cities to dwell in, Jos 21:2
its villages had been **g** to Caleb the son Jos 21:12
To them were **g** Shechem, the city of Jos 21:21
were **g** out of the half-tribe of Jos 21:27
were **g** out of the tribe of Zebulun, Jos 21:34
for the LORD had **g** all their enemies Jos 21:44
LORD your God has **g** rest to your Jos 22:4
Manasseh Moses had **g** a possession in Jos 22:7
half Joshua had **g** a possession beside Jos 22:7
when the LORD had **g** rest to Israel from Jos 23:1
that the LORD your God has **g** you. Jos 23:13
land that the LORD your God has **g** you, Jos 23:15
off the good land that he has **g** to you." Jos 23:16
which had been **g** him in the hill Jos 24:33
behold, I have **g** the land into his hand." Jgs 1:2
And Hebron was **g** to Caleb, as Moses Jgs 1:20
for the LORD has **g** your enemies the Jgs 3:28
which the LORD has **g** Sisera into your Jgs 4:14
has forsaken us and **g** us into the hand Jgs 6:13
the camp, for I have **g** it into your hand Jgs 7:9
God has **g** into his hand Midian and all Jgs 7:14
for the LORD has **g** the host of Midian Jgs 7:15
God has **g** into your hands the princes of Jgs 8:3
the LORD has **g** Zebah and Zalmunna Jgs 8:7
Samson's wife was **g** to his companion, Jgs 14:20
taken his wife and **g** her to his Jgs 15:6
"Our god has **g** Samson our enemy Jgs 16:23
"Our god has **g** our enemy into our Jgs 16:24
for God has **g** it into your hands, Jgs 18:10
had visited his people and **g** them food. Ru 1:6
and a full reward be **g** you by the LORD, Ru 2:12
than seven sons, has **g** birth to him." Ru 4:15
for the LORD has **g** them into our 1 Sm 14:10
for the LORD has **g** them into the 1 Sm 14:12
this day and has **g** it to a neighbor 1 Sm 15:28
should have been **g** to David, 1 Sm 18:19
she was **g** to Adriel the Meholathite 1 Sm 18:19
which were **g** in full number to the 1 Sm 18:27
in that you have **g** him bread and a 1 Sm 22:13
said, "God has **g** him into my hand, 1 Sm 23:7
to my lord be **g** to the young men 1 Sm 25:27
Saul had **g** Michal his daughter, 1 Sm 25:44
"God has **g** your enemy into your 1 Sm 26:8
let a place be **g** me in one of the 1 Sm 27:5
of your hand and **g** it to your 1 Sm 28:17
with what the LORD has **g** us. 1 Sm 30:23
has preserved us and **g** into our hand 1 Sm 30:23
men would not have **g** up the pursuit 2 Sm 2:27
and have not **g** you into the hand of 2 Sm 3:8
and the LORD had **g** him rest from all 2 Sm 7:1
his house I have **g** to your master's 2 Sm 9:9

and the LORD has **g** the kingdom into 2 Sm 16:8
that Ahithophel has **g** is not good." 2 Sm 17:7
expense? Or has he **g** us any gift?" 2 Sm 19:42
let seven of his sons be **g** to us, so that 2 Sm 21:6
You have **g** me the shield of your 2 Sm 22:36
the Shunammite be **g** to Adonijah 1 Kgs 2:21
steadfast love and have **g** him a son to 1 Kgs 3:6
LORD my God has **g** me rest on every 1 Kgs 5:4
who has **g** to David a wise son to be 1 Kgs 5:7
which you have **g** to your people as 1 Kgs 8:36
the LORD who has **g** rest to his people 1 Kgs 8:56
Israel from the land that I have **g** them, 1 Kgs 9:7
the cities that Solomon had **g** him, 1 Kgs 9:12
of cities are these that you have **g** me, 1 Kgs 9:13
and had **g** it as dowry to his daughter, 1 Kgs 9:16
asked besides what was **g** her by the 1 Kgs 10:13
counsel that the old men had **g** him, 1 Kgs 12:13
the man of God had **g** by the word of 1 Kgs 13:5
therefore the LORD has **g** him to the 1 Kgs 13:26
Let two bulls be **g** to us, and let them 1 Kgs 18:23
they took the bull that was **g** them, 1 Kgs 18:26
by him the LORD had **g** victory to Syria. 2 Kgs 5:1
please let there be **g** to your servant 2 Kgs 5:17
that the Syrians had **g** him at Ramah, 2 Kgs 8:29
wounds that the Syrians had **g** him, 2 Kgs 9:15
for that was **g** to the workmen who 2 Kgs 12:14
city will not be **g** into the hand of 2 Kgs 18:30
will not be **g** into the hand 2 Kgs 19:10
And let it be **g** into the hand of the 2 Kgs 22:5
the priest has **g** me a book." 2 Kgs 22:10
regular allowance was **g** him by the 2 Kgs 25:30
his birthright was **g** to the sons of 1 Chr 5:1
with them were **g** into their hands, 1 Chr 5:20
of the Kohathites were **g** by lot out of 1 Chr 6:61
They were **g** the cities of refuge: 1 Chr 6:67
To the Gershomites were **g** out of the 1 Chr 6:71
And has he not **g** you peace on every 1 Chr 22:18
God of Israel, has **g** rest to his people, 1 Chr 23:25
for God had **g** Heman fourteen sons 1 Chr 25:5
(for the LORD has **g** me many sons) 1 Chr 28:5
because they had **g** willingly, 1 Chr 29:9
you, and of your own have we **g** you. 1 Chr 29:14
who has **g** King David a wise son, 2 Chr 2:12
which you have **g** to your people as 2 Chr 6:27
up from my land that I have **g** you, 2 Chr 7:20
the cities that Hiram had **g** to him, 2 Chr 8:2
and he has **g** us peace on every side." 2 Chr 14:7
they will be **g** into your hand." 2 Chr 18:14
which you have **g** us to inherit. 2 Chr 20:11
talents that I have **g** to the army of 2 Chr 25:9
He was also **g** into the hand of the 2 Chr 28:5
for God had **g** him very great 2 Chr 32:29
and the rules **g** through Moses." 2 Chr 33:8
Law of the LORD **g** through Moses. 2 Chr 34:14
the LORD and have **g** it into the hand 2 Chr 34:17
the priest has **g** me a book." 2 Chr 34:18
has **g** me all the kingdoms of the 2 Chr 36:23
has **g** me all the kingdoms of the earth, Ezr 1:2
require—let that be **g** to them day by day Ezr 6:9
that the LORD the God of Israel had **g**, Ezr 7:6
vessels that have been **g** you for the Ezr 7:19
our priests have been **g** into the hand of Ezr 9:7
iniquities deserved and have **g** us such a Ezr 9:13
to send me when I had **g** him a time. Neh 2:6
let letters be **g** me to the governors of the Neh 2:7
God's Law that was **g** by Moses the Neh 10:29
which were **g** by commandment to the Neh 13:5
of the Levites had not been **g** to them, Neh 13:10
For the king had **g** orders to all the Est 1:8
women. Let their cosmetics be **g** them. Est 2:3
she was **g** whatever she desired to take Est 2:13
said to Haman, "The money is **g** to you, Est 3:11
It shall be **g** you, even to the half of my Est 5:3
I have **g** Esther the house of Haman, Est 8:7
"Why is light **g** to him who is in misery, Jb 3:20
Why is light **g** to a man whose way is Jb 3:23
The earth is **g** into the hand of the Jb 9:24
to whom alone the land was **g**, and no Jb 15:19
You have **g** no water to the weary to Jb 22:7
By the breath of God ice is **g**, and the Jb 37:10
and who has **g** birth to the frost of Jb 38:29
inward parts or **g** understanding to the Jb 38:36
to whom I have **g** the arid plain for his Jb 39:6
her forget wisdom and **g** her no share in Jb 39:17
Who has first **g** to me, that I should Jb 41:11
You have **g** me relief when I was in Ps 4:1
You have **g** him dominion over the works Ps 8:6
You have **g** me the shield of your Ps 18:35
You have **g** him his heart's desire and Ps 21:2
desired, but you have **g** me an open ear. Ps 40:6
you have **g** us wine to drink that made Ps 60:3
you have **g** me the heritage of those who Ps 61:5
they shall be **g** over to the power of the Ps 63:10
you have **g** the command to save me, for Ps 71:3
he live; may gold of Sheba be **g** to him! Ps 72:15

They have **g** the bodies of your servants Ps 79:2
bread of tears and **g** them tears to drink Ps 80:5
distributed freely; he has **g** to the poor; Ps 112:9
the earth he has **g** to the children of Ps 115:16
but he has not **g** me over to death. Ps 118:18
for by them you have **g** me life. Ps 119:93
What shall be **g** to you, and what more Ps 120:3
who has not **g** us as prey to their teeth! Ps 124:6
have **g** your pledge for a stranger, Prv 6:1
no friendship with a man **g** to anger, Prv 22:24
to your throat if you are **g** to appetite. Prv 23:2
and one **g** to anger causes much Prv 29:22
that God has **g** to the children Eccl 1:13
him God has **g** wisdom and knowledge Eccl 2:26
the sinner he has **g** the business of Eccl 2:26
that God has **g** to the children Eccl 3:10
few days of his life that God has **g** him, Eccl 5:18
whom God has **g** wealth and Eccl 5:19
wickedness deliver those who are **g** to it. Eccl 8:8
life that God has **g** him under the sun. Eccl 8:15
life that he has **g** you under the sun, Eccl 9:9
sayings; they are **g** by one Shepherd. Eccl 12:11
whom the LORD has **g** me are signs and Is 8:18
For to us a child is born, to us a son is **g**; Is 9:6
When the LORD has **g** you rest from your Is 14:3
"I have neither labored nor **g** birth, I have Is 23:4
the LORD has **g** command concerning Is 23:11
we writhed, but we have **g** birth to wind. Is 26:18
of rocks; his bread will be **g** him; Is 33:16
has **g** them over for slaughter. Is 34:2
The glory of Lebanon shall be **g** to it, the Is 35:2
This city will not be **g** into the hand of Is 36:15
Jerusalem will not be **g** into the hand of Is 37:10
The Lord GOD has **g** me the tongue of Is 50:4
to perish and has **g** us poisoned water to Jer 8:14
I have **g** the beloved of my soul into the Jer 12:7
heritage that I have **g** my people Israel Jer 12:14
Where is the flock that was **g** you, your Jer 13:20
it shall be **g** into the hand of the king of Jer 21:10
land that the LORD has **g** to you and your Jer 25:5
so that he was not **g** over to the people to Jer 26:24
Now I have **g** all these lands into the Jer 27:6
and I have **g** him also the beasts of the Jer 27:6
for I have **g** to him even the beasts of Jer 28:14
but shall surely be **g** into the hand of the Jer 32:4
"After I had **g** the deed of purchase to Jer 32:16
pestilence the city is **g** into the hands of Jer 32:24
—though the city is **g** into the hands of Jer 32:25
'It is **g** into the hand of the king of Jer 32:36
it is **g** into the hand of the Chaldeans.' Jer 32:43
loaf of bread was **g** him daily from the Jer 37:21
city shall surely be **g** into the hand of Jer 38:3
this city shall be **g** into the hand of Jer 38:18
said, "You shall not be **g** to them. Jer 38:20
and you shall not be **g** into the hand of Jer 39:17
the people who had **g** him this answer: Jer 44:20
be quiet when the LORD has **g** it a charge? Jer 47:7
a regular allowance was **g** him by the Jer 52:34
necks; we are weary; we are **g** no rest. Lam 5:5
We have **g** the hand to Egypt, and to Lam 5:6
to us this land is **g** for a possession.' Ezk 11:15
Behold, it is **g** to the fire for fuel. When Ezk 15:4
forest, which I have **g** to the fire for fuel, Ezk 15:6
so have I **g** up the inhabitants of Ezk 15:6
and of my silver, which I had **g** you, Ezk 16:17
while no payment was **g** to you; Ezk 16:34
them into the land that I had **g** them, Ezk 20:15
So the sword is **g** to be polished, that it Ezk 21:11
and polished to be **g** into the hand of Ezk 21:11
gates I have **g** the glittering sword. Ezk 21:15
I have **g** him the land of Egypt as his Ezk 29:20
For they are all **g** over to death, to the Ezk 31:14
the land is surely **g** us to possess.' Ezk 33:24
laid desolate; they are **g** us to devour.' Ezk 35:12
let us be **g** vegetables to eat and water to Dn 1:12
for you have **g** me wisdom and might, Dn 2:23
the God of heaven has **g** the kingdom, Dn 2:37
and into whose hand he has **g**, wherever Dn 2:38
and let a beast's mind be **g** to him; Dn 4:16
kingdom is divided and **g** to the Medes Dn 5:28
a man, and the mind of a man was **g** to it. Dn 7:4
had four heads, and dominion was **g** to it. Dn 7:6
its body destroyed and **g** over to be Dn 7:11
And to him was **g** dominion and glory Dn 7:14
and judgment was **g** for the saints of the Dn 7:22
and they shall be **g** into his hand for a Dn 7:25
whole heaven shall be **g** to the people of Dn 7:27
And a host will be **g** over to it together Dn 8:12
shall not endure, but she shall be **g** up, Dn 11:6
but it shall be **g** into his hand. Dn 11:11
to whom royal majesty has not been **g**. Dn 11:21
my wages, which my lovers have **g** me.' Hos 2:12
Ephraim has **g** bitter provocation; so Hos 12:14
for he has **g** the early rain for your Jl 2:23
land that I have **g** them," says the LORD Am 9:15

when she who is in labor has **g** birth; Mi 5:3
The LORD has **g** commandment about Na 1:14
her not until she had **g** birth to a son. Mt 1:25
"Ask, and it will be **g** to you; seek, and Mt 7:7
God, who had **g** such authority to men. Mt 9:8
are to say will be **g** to you in that hour. Mt 10:19
but no sign will be **g** to it except the Mt 12:39
you it has been **g** to know the secrets Mt 13:11
heaven, but to them it has not been **g**. Mt 13:11
For to the one who has, more will be **g**, Mt 13:12
and his guests he commanded it to be **g**. Mt 14:9
brought on a platter and **g** to the girl, Mt 14:11
would have gained from me is **g** to God, Mt 15:5
and having **g** thanks he broke them Mt 15:36
but no sign will be **g** to it except the sign Mt 16:4
saying, but only those to whom it is **g**. Mt 19:11
away from you and **g** to a people Mt 21:43
neither marry nor are **g** in marriage, Mt 22:30
to everyone who has will more be **g**, Mt 25:29
sold for a large sum and **g** to the poor." Mt 26:9
and when he had **g** thanks he gave it to Mt 26:27
Now the betrayer had **g** them a sign, Mt 26:48
Then Pilate ordered it to be **g** to him. Mt 27:58
heaven and on earth has been **g** to me. Mt 28:18
"To you has been **g** the secret of the Mk 4:11
For to the one who has, more will be **g**, Mk 4:25
things? What is the wisdom **g** to him? Mk 6:2
from me is Corban' (that is, **g** to God)— Mk 7:11
the seven loaves, and having **g** thanks, Mk 8:6
no sign will be **g** to this generation." Mk 8:12
neither marry nor are **g** in marriage, Mk 12:25
but say whatever is **g** you in that hour, Mk 13:11
hundred denarii and **g** to the poor." Mk 14:5
and when he had **g** thanks he gave it Mk 14:23
Now the betrayer had **g** them a sign, Mk 14:44
the name **g** by the angel before he was Lk 2:21
scroll of the prophet Isaiah was **g** to him. Lk 4:17
give, and it will be **g** to you. Good Lk 6:38
you it has been **g** to know the secrets Lk 8:10
for to the one who has, more will be **g**, Lk 8:18
that something should be **g** her to eat. Lk 8:55
I have **g** you authority to tread on Lk 10:19
I tell you, ask, and it will be **g** to you; Lk 11:9
but no sign will be **g** to it except the Lk 11:29
Everyone to whom much was **g**, of him Lk 12:48
marrying and being **g** in marriage, Lk 17:27
to whom he had **g** the money to be Lk 19:15
to everyone who has, more will be **g**, Lk 19:26
this age marry and are **g** in marriage, Lk 20:34
neither marry nor are **g** in marriage, Lk 20:35
cup, and when he had **g** thanks he said, Lk 22:17
took bread, and when he had **g** thanks, Lk 22:19
"This is my body, which is **g** for you. Lk 22:19
For the law was **g** through Moses; grace Jn 1:17
one thing unless it is **g** him from heaven. Jn 3:27
the Son and has **g** all things into his Jn 3:35
the field that Jacob had **g** to his son Joseph. Jn 4:5
and he would have **g** you living water." Jn 4:10
one, but has **g** all judgment to the Son, Jn 5:22
And he has **g** him authority to execute Jn 5:27
that the Father has **g** me to accomplish, Jn 5:36
the loaves, and when he had **g** thanks, Jn 6:11
the bread after the Lord had **g** thanks. Jn 6:23
lose nothing of all that he has **g** me, Jn 6:39
Has not Moses **g** you the law? Yet none of Jn 7:19
for as yet the Spirit had not been **g**, Jn 7:39
My Father, who has **g** them to me, is Jn 10:29
and the Pharisees had **g** orders that if Jn 11:57
three hundred denarii and **g** to the poor?" Jn 12:5
me has himself **g** me a commandment Jn 12:49
that the Father had **g** all things into his Jn 13:3
For I have **g** you an example, that you Jn 13:15
since you have **g** him authority over all Jn 17:2
eternal life to all whom you have **g** him. Jn 17:2
everything that you have **g** me is from Jn 17:7
For I have **g** them the words that you Jn 17:8
but for those whom you have **g** me, Jn 17:9
in your name, which you have **g** me, Jn 17:11
in your name, which you have **g** me. Jn 17:12
I have **g** them your word, and the world Jn 17:14
glory that you have **g** me I have given Jn 17:22
you have given me I have **g** to them, Jn 17:22
that they also, whom you have **g** me, Jn 17:24
glory that you have **g** me because you Jn 17:24
the cup that the Father has **g** me?" Jn 18:11
all unless it had been **g** you from above. Jn 19:11
after he had **g** commands through the Acts 1:2
is through Jesus has **g** the man this Acts 3:16
name under heaven **g** among men by Acts 4:12
whom God has **g** to those who obey Acts 5:32
the Spirit was **g** through the laying Acts 8:18
of this he has **g** assurance to all by Acts 17:31
regions and had **g** them much Acts 20:2
And when he had **g** him permission, Acts 21:40
that money would be **g** him by Paul. Acts 24:26

the Holy Spirit who has been **g** to us. Rom 5:5
was in the world before the law was **g**, Rom 5:13
"Or who has **g** a gift to him that he Rom 11:35
For by the grace **g** to me I say to Rom 12:3
differ according to the grace **g** to us, Rom 12:6
confirm the promises **g** to the Rom 15:8
because of the grace **g** me by God Rom 15:15
of God that was **g** you in Christ Jesus, 1 Cor 1:4
the things freely **g** us by God. 1 Cor 2:12
to the grace of God **g** to me, 1 Cor 3:10
For her hair is **g** to her for a 1 Cor 11:15
and when he had **g** thanks, he broke 1 Cor 11:24
To each is **g** the manifestation of the 1 Cor 12:7
To one is **g** through the Spirit the 1 Cor 12:8
his seal on us and **g** us his Spirit in 2 Cor 1:22
live are always being **g** over to death 2 Cor 4:11
who has **g** us the Spirit as a guarantee. 2 Cor 5:5
that has been **g** among the churches 2 Cor 8:1
distributed freely, he has **g** to the poor; 2 Cor 9:9
a thorn was **g** me in the flesh, 2 Cor 12:7
that the Lord has **g** me for building 2 Cor 13:10
perceived the grace that was **g** to me, Gal 2:9
if a law had been **g** that could give life, Gal 3:21
Jesus Christ might be **g** to those who Gal 3:22
gouged out your eyes and **g** them to me. Gal 4:15
of God's grace that was **g** to me for you, Eph 3:2
which was **g** me by the working of his Eph 3:7
least of all the saints, this grace was **g**, Eph 3:8
But grace was **g** to each one of us Eph 4:7
callous and have **g** themselves up to Eph 4:19
put on the readiness **g** by the gospel of Eph 6:15
that words may be **g** to me in opening Eph 6:19
from God that was **g** to me for you, Col 1:25
I thank him who has **g** me strength, 1 Tm 1:12
which is the testimony **g** at the proper 1 Tm 2:6
which was **g** you by prophecy when 1 Tm 4:14
prayers I will be graciously **g** to you. Phlm 1:22
I and the children God has **g** me." Heb 2:13
For if Joshua had **g** them rest, God Heb 4:8
because she had **g** a friendly welcome Heb 11:31
could not endure the order that was **g**, Heb 12:20
all without reproach, and it will be **g** him. Jas 1:5
to you according to the wisdom **g** him, 2 Pt 3:15
what kind of love the Father has **g** to us, 1 Jn 3:1
in us, by the Spirit whom he has **g** us. 1 Jn 3:24
in us, because he has **g** us of his Spirit. 1 Jn 4:13
has come and has **g** us understanding, 1 Jn 5:20
had a bow, and a crown was **g** to him, Rv 6:2
one another, and he was **g** a great sword. Rv 6:4
And they were **g** authority over a fourth of Rv 6:8
Then they were each **g** a white robe and Rv 6:11
angels who had been **g** power to harm Rv 7:2
God, and seven trumpets were **g** to them. Rv 8:2
and he was **g** much incense to offer with Rv 8:3
and he was **g** the key to the shaft of the Rv 9:1
and they were **g** power like the power of Rv 9:3
Then I was **g** a measuring rod like a Rv 11:1
that out, for it is **g** over to the nations, Rv 11:2
the woman who had **g** birth to the male Rv 12:13
But the woman was **g** the two wings of Rv 12:14
for he had **g** his authority to the beast, Rv 13:4
And the beast was **g** a mouth uttering Rv 13:5
And authority was **g** it over every tribe Rv 13:7
and you have **g** them blood to drink. Rv 16:6
for God has **g** judgment for you against Rv 18:20

GIVER (1)
for God loves a cheerful **g**. 2 Cor 9:7

GIVES (118)
"When the LORD **g** you in the evening Ex 16:8
on the sixth day he **g** you bread for two Ex 16:29
If his master **g** him a wife and she bears Ex 21:4
"If a man **g** to his neighbor money or Ex 22:7
"If a man **g** to his neighbor a donkey or Ex 22:10
sojourn in Israel who **g** any of his Lv 20:2
that man when he **g** one of his children Lv 20:4
all of it that he **g** to the LORD is holy. Lv 27:9
whatever anyone **g** to the priest shall be Nm 5:10
until the LORD **g** rest to your brothers, as Dt 3:20
the LORD your God **g** them beyond the Dt 3:20
the LORD your God **g** them over to you, Dt 7:2
for it is he who **g** you power to get wealth, Dt 8:18
and when he **g** you rest from all your Dt 12:10
arises among you and **g** you a sign or Dt 13:1
the LORD your God **g** you as a possession, Dt 19:3
and **g** you all the land that he promised Dt 19:8
the LORD your God **g** it into your hand, Dt 20:13
the LORD your God **g** them into your Dt 21:10
until the LORD **g** rest to your brothers as Jos 1:15
then when the LORD **g** us the land we will Jos 2:14
and the LORD **g** them over to me, Jgs 11:9
Chemosh your god **g** you to possess? Jgs 11:24
"Cursed be he who **g** a wife to Jgs 21:18
Araunah **g** to the king." And 2 Sm 24:23
that when he **g** you charge over 1 Chr 22:12
he **g** rain on the earth and sends waters Jb 5:10
God **g** me up to the ungodly and casts Jb 16:11
to my servant, but he **g** me no answer; Jb 19:16
He **g** them security, and they are Jb 24:23
and the breath of the Almighty **g** me life. Jb 33:4
my Maker, who **g** songs in the night, Jb 35:10
alive, but **g** the afflicted their right. Jb 36:6
judges peoples; he **g** food in abundance. Jb 36:31
with mischief and **g** birth to lies. Ps 7:14
I bless the LORD who **g** me counsel; in the Ps 16:7
but the righteous is generous and **g**; Ps 37:21
we will not fear though the earth **g** way, Ps 46:2
The Lord **g** the word; the women who Ps 68:11
is the one who **g** power and strength to Ps 68:35
He **g** the barren woman a home, Ps 113:9
affliction, that your promise **g** me life. Ps 119:50
The unfolding of your words **g** light; Ps 119:130
toil; for he **g** to his beloved sleep. Ps 127:2
he who **g** food to all flesh, for his Ps 136:25
who **g** victory to kings, who rescues Ps 144:10
the oppressed, who **g** food to the hungry. Ps 146:7
stars; he **g** to all of them their names. Ps 147:4
He **g** to the beasts their food, and to the Ps 147:9
He **g** snow like wool; he scatters Ps 147:16
For the LORD **g** wisdom; from his mouth Prv 2:6
scornful, but to the humble he **g** favor. Prv 3:34
One **g** freely, yet grows all the richer; Prv 11:24
speaks the truth **g** honest evidence, Prv 12:17
but the prudent **g** thought to his steps. Prv 14:15
A tranquil heart **g** life to the flesh, but Prv 14:30
Whoever **g** thought to the word will Prv 16:20
and a liar **g** ear to a mischievous Prv 17:4
stone in the eyes of the one who **g** it; Prv 17:8
One who lacks sense **g** a pledge and Prv 17:18
If one **g** an answer before he hears, it is Prv 18:13
is a friend to a man who **g** gifts. Prv 19:6
but the righteous **g** and does not hold Prv 21:26
but the upright **g** thought to his ways. Prv 21:29
his own wealth, or **g** to the rich, Prv 22:16
Whoever **g** an honest answer kisses Prv 24:26
a righteous man who **g** way before the Prv 25:26
in the sling is one who **g** honor to a fool. Prv 26:8
Whoever **g** to the poor will not want, Prv 28:27
A fool **g** full vent to his spirit, but a Prv 29:11
the LORD **g** light to the eyes of both. Prv 29:13
a man to whom God **g** wealth, Eccl 6:2
Wisdom **g** strength to the wise man Eccl 7:19
He **g** power to the faint, and to him who Is 40:29
He **g** up nations before him, so that he Is 41:2
counselor who, when I ask, **g** an answer. Is 41:28
who **g** breath to the people on it and spirit Is 42:5
our God, who **g** the rain in its season, Jer 5:24
who **g** the sun for light by day and the Jer 31:35
beg for food, but no one **g** to them. Lam 4:4
g his bread to the hungry and covers Ezk 18:7
but **g** his bread to the hungry and Ezk 18:16
g back what he has taken by robbery, Ezk 33:15
he **g** wisdom to the wise and knowledge Dn 2:21
kingdom of men and **g** it to whom he Dn 4:17
kingdom of men and **g** it to whom he Dn 4:25
kingdom of men and **g** it to whom he Dn 4:32
and their walking staff **g** them oracles. Hos 4:12
a stand, and it **g** light to all in the house. Mt 5:15
And whoever **g** one of these little ones Mt 10:42
whoever **g** you a cup of water to drink Mk 9:41
when a lamp with its rays **g** you light." Lk 11:36
God, for he **g** the Spirit without measure. Jn 3:34
the Father raises the dead and **g** them life, Jn 5:21
life, so also the Son **g** life to whom he will. Jn 5:21
but my Father **g** you the true bread from Jn 6:32
down from heaven and **g** life to the Jn 6:33
All that the Father **g** me will come to me, Jn 6:37
It is the Spirit who **g** life; the flesh is of no Jn 6:63
you. Not as the world **g** do I give to you. Jn 14:27
since he himself **g** to all mankind life Acts 17:25
who **g** life to the dead and calls into Rom 4:17
of the Lord, since he **g** thanks to God, Rom 14:6
of the Lord and **g** thanks to God. Rom 14:6
but only God who **g** the growth. 1 Cor 3:7
that **g** me no ground for boasting. 1 Cor 9:16
if the bugle **g** an indistinct sound, 1 Cor 14:8
But God **g** it a body as he has 1 Cor 15:38
who **g** us the victory through our 1 Cor 15:57
For the letter kills, but the Spirit **g** life. 2 Cor 3:6
but God, who **g** his Holy Spirit to you. 1 Thes 4:8
of God, who **g** life to all things, 1 Tm 6:13
who **g** generously to all without reproach, Jas 1:5
when it has conceived **g** birth to sin, Jas 1:15
But he **g** more grace. Therefore it says, Jas 4:6
the proud, but **g** grace to the humble." Jas 4:6
opposes the proud but **g** grace to the 1 Pt 5:5
on it, for the glory of God **g** it light, Rv 21:23

GIVING (91)
When she had finished **g** him a drink, Gn 24:19
g an interpretation to each man Gn 41:12
land that the LORD your God is **g** you. Ex 20:12
a fifth to it and **g** it to him to whom Nm 5:7
which I am **g** to the people of Israel. Nm 13:2
you are to inhabit, which I am **g** you, Nm 15:2
which the LORD our God is **g** us. Dt 1:20
good land that the LORD our God is **g** us.' Dt 1:25
the land that the LORD our God is **g** to us.' Dt 2:29
the LORD, the God of your fathers, is **g** you. Dt 4:1
LORD your God is **g** you for an Dt 4:21
the LORD your God is **g** you for all time." Dt 4:40
the land that the LORD your God is **g** you. Dt 5:16
in the land that I am **g** them to possess.' Dt 5:31
g your daughters to their sons or taking Dt 7:3
LORD your God is not **g** you this good land Dt 9:6
the sojourner, **g** him food and clothing. Dt 10:18
off the good land that the LORD is **g** you. Dt 11:17
land that the LORD your God is **g** you. Dt 11:31
that the LORD your God is **g** you. Dt 12:9
the LORD your God is **g** you to inherit, Dt 12:10
LORD your God is **g** you to dwell there, Dt 13:12
LORD your God is **g** you for an Dt 15:4
land that the LORD your God is **g** you, Dt 15:7
towns that the LORD your God is **g** you, Dt 16:5
towns that the LORD your God is **g** you, Dt 16:18
land that the LORD your God is **g** you. Dt 16:20
towns that the LORD your God is **g** you, Dt 17:2
land that the LORD your God is **g** you, Dt 17:14
the land that the LORD your God is **g** you, Dt 18:9
whose land the LORD your God is **g** you, Dt 19:1
the LORD your God is **g** you to possess. Dt 19:2
LORD your God is **g** you for an Dt 19:10
the LORD your God is **g** you to possess. Dt 19:14
LORD your God is **g** you for an Dt 20:16
LORD your God is **g** you to possess Dt 21:1
by **g** him a double portion of all that he Dt 21:17
LORD your God is **g** you for an Dt 21:23
LORD your God is **g** you for an Dt 24:4
land that the LORD your God is **g** you. Dt 25:15
LORD your God is **g** you for an Dt 25:19
LORD your God is **g** you for an Dt 26:1
land that the LORD your God is **g** you, Dt 26:2
is the year of tithing, **g** it to the Levite, Dt 26:12
the land that the LORD your God is **g** you, Dt 27:2
the land that the LORD your God is **g** you, Dt 27:3
the land that the LORD your God is **g** you. Dt 28:8
which I am **g** to the people of Israel for a Dt 32:49
the land that I am **g** to the people of Dt 32:52
people, into the land that I am **g** to them, Jos 1:2
the LORD your God is **g** you to possess.'" Jos 1:11
land that the LORD your God is **g** them. Jos 1:15
For in **g** this decision the king 2 Sm 14:13
g ear to them whenever they call to 1 Kgs 8:52
David had made for **g** thanks to the 2 Chr 7:6
LORD. He is with you in **g** judgment. 2 Chr 19:6
peace offerings and **g** thanks to the 2 Chr 30:22
praising and **g** thanks to the LORD, Ezr 3:11
sat on the throne, **g** righteous judgment. Ps 9:4
A Psalm for **g** thanks. Ps 100:T
in **g** them the inheritance of the Ps 111:6
in her pangs when she is near to **g** birth, Is 26:17
in vision, they stumble in **g** judgment. Is 28:7
g seed to the sower and bread to the eater, Is 55:10
anguish as of one **g** birth to her first Jer 4:31
I am **g** this city into the hand of the king Jer 32:3
I am **g** this city into the hands of the Jer 32:28
I am **g** this city into the hand of the king Jer 34:2
g over to the pestilence those who are Jer 43:11
and the **g** over of the sanctuary and host Dn 8:13
so that your **g** may be in secret. And your Mt 6:4
drinking, marrying and **g** in marriage, Mt 24:38
on his face at Jesus' feet, **g** him thanks. Lk 17:16
a man without first **g** him a hearing and Jn 7:51
When a woman is **g** birth, she has Jn 16:21
the apostles were **g** their testimony to Acts 4:33
that God was **g** them salvation by Acts 7:25
he did good by **g** you rains from Acts 14:17
by **g** them the Holy Spirit just as he did Acts 15:8
g notice when the days of Acts 21:26
and **g** thanks to God in the presence Acts 27:35
glory, the covenants, the **g** of the law, Rom 9:4
g greater honor to the part that 1 Cor 12:24
you may be **g** thanks well enough, 1 Cor 14:17
to you again but **g** you cause to boast 2 Cor 5:12
g thanks always and for everything to Eph 5:20
with me in **g** and receiving, Phil 4:15
g thanks to the Father, who has Col 1:12
g thanks to God the Father through Col 3:17
and filled," without **g** them the things Jas 2:16
in birth pains and the agony of **g** birth. Rv 12:2

GIZONITE (1)
Hashem the **G**, Jonathan the son of 1 Chr 11:34

GLAD (93)
he sees you, he will be **g** in his heart. Ex 4:14
And the priest's heart was **g**. He took Jgs 18:20

told the men of Jabesh, they were **g**. 1 Sm 11:9
I would have been **g** to give you ten 2 Sm 18:11
their homes joyful and **g** of heart for 1 Kgs 8:66
Let the heavens be **g**, and let the 1 Chr 16:31
joyful and **g** of heart for the 2 Chr 7:10
went out that day joyful and **g** of heart. Est 5:9
exceedingly and are **g** when they find Jb 3:22
The righteous see it and are **g**; the Jb 22:19
I will be **g** and exult in you; I will sing Ps 9:2
people, let Jacob rejoice, let Israel be **g**. Ps 14:7
Therefore my heart is **g**, and my whole Ps 16:9
you make him **g** with the joy of your Ps 21:6
will rejoice and be **g** in your steadfast Ps 31:7
Be **g** in the LORD, and rejoice, O Ps 32:11
For our heart is **g** in him, because we Ps 33:21
the LORD; let the humble hear and be **g**. Ps 34:2
for joy and be **g** and say evermore, Ps 35:27
I have told the **g** news of deliverance in Ps 40:9
who seek you rejoice and be **g** in you; Ps 40:16
house of God with **g** shouts and songs of Ps 42:4
stringed instruments make you **g**; Ps 45:8
river whose streams make **g** the city of Ps 46:4
Let Mount Zion be **g**! Let the daughters Ps 48:11
people, Let Jacob rejoice, let Israel be **g**. Ps 53:6
Let the nations be **g** and sing for joy, for Ps 67:4
But the righteous shall be **g**; they shall Ps 68:3
When the humble see it they will be **g**; Ps 69:32
all who seek you rejoice and be **g** in you! Ps 70:4
we may rejoice and be **g** all our days. Ps 90:14
Make us **g** for as many days as you Ps 90:15
O LORD, have made me **g** by your work; Ps 92:4
Let the heavens be **g**, and let the earth Ps 96:11
rejoice; let the many coastlands be **g**! Ps 97:1
Zion hears and is **g**, and the daughters of Ps 97:8
Egypt was **g** when they departed, for Ps 105:38
Then they were **g** that the waters were Ps 107:30
The upright see it and are **g**, and all Ps 107:42
to shame, but your servant will be **g**! Ps 109:28
G songs of salvation are in the tents of Ps 118:15
has made; let us rejoice and be **g** in it. Ps 118:24
I was **g** when they said to me, "Let us go Ps 122:1
has done great things for us; we are **g**. Ps 126:3
Let Israel be **g** in his Maker; let the Ps 149:2
A wise son makes a **g** father, but a Prv 10:1
down, but a good word makes him **g**. Prv 12:25
A **g** heart makes a cheerful face, but Prv 15:13
A wise son makes a **g** father, but a Prv 15:20
he who is **g** at calamity will not go Prv 17:5
heart is wise, my heart too will be **g**. Prv 23:15
fathers a wise son will be **g** in him. Prv 23:24
Let your father and mother be **g**; let Prv 23:25
not your heart be **g** when he stumbles, Prv 24:17
Oil and perfume make the heart **g**, and Prv 27:9
Be wise, my son, and make my heart **g**, Prv 27:11
who loves wisdom makes his father **g**, Prv 29:3
by sadness of face the heart is made **g**. Eccl 7:3
as they are **g** when they divide the spoil. Is 9:3
let us be **g** and rejoice in his salvation." Is 25:9
wilderness and the dry land shall be **g**; Is 35:1
But be **g** and rejoice forever in that Is 65:18
in Jerusalem and be **g** in my people; Is 65:19
with Jerusalem, and be **g** for her, Is 66:10
is born to you," making him very **g**. Jer 20:15
they are **g** that you have done it. Lam 1:21
Rejoice and be **g**, O daughter of Edom, Lam 4:21
Then the king was exceedingly **g**, and Dn 6:23
By their evil they make the king **g**, and Hos 7:3
be **g** and rejoice, for the LORD has done Jl 2:21
"Be **g**, O children of Zion, and rejoice in Jl 2:23
Jonah was exceedingly **g** because of the Jon 4:6
in his dragnet; so he rejoices and is **g**. Hab 1:15
and their hearts shall be **g** as with wine. Zec 10:7
Their children shall see it and be **g**; Zec 10:7
Rejoice and be **g**, for your reward is great Mt 5:12
they were **g** and promised to give him Mk 14:11
It was fitting to celebrate and be **g**, for Lk 15:32
And they were **g**, and agreed to give him Lk 22:5
When Herod saw Jesus, he was very **g**, Lk 23:8
Then they were **g** to take him into the Jn 6:21
would see my day. He saw it and was **g**." Jn 8:56
for your sake I am **g** that I was not there, Jn 11:15
the disciples were **g** when they saw Jn 20:20
therefore my heart was **g**, and my Acts 2:26
their food with **g** and generous hearts, Acts 2:46
and saw the grace of God, he was **g**, Acts 11:23
there to make me **g** but the one whom 2 Cor 2:2
For we are **g** when we are weak and 2 Cor 13:9
faith, I am **g** and rejoice with you all. Phil 2:17
you also should be **g** and rejoice with Phil 2:18
I would have been **g** to keep him with Phlm 1:13
also rejoice and be **g** when his glory is 1 Pt 4:13

GLADDEN (2)
G the soul of your servant, for to you, O Ps 86:4
and wine to **g** the heart of man, oil to Ps 104:15

GLADDENS (1)
is made for laughter, and wine **g** life, Eccl 10:19

GLADLY (7)
And Hezekiah welcomed them **g**. And he Is 39:2
perplexed, and yet he heard him **g**. Mk 6:20
And the great throng heard him **g**. Mk 12:37
Jerusalem, the brothers received us **g**. Acts 21:17
For you **g** bear with fools, being 2 Cor 11:19
all the more **g** of my weaknesses, 2 Cor 12:9
I will most **g** spend and be spent for 2 Cor 12:15

GLADNESS (47)
On the day of your **g** also, and at your Nm 10:10
God with joyfulness and **g** of heart, Dt 28:47
the LORD on that day with great **g**. 1 Chr 29:22
And they sang praises with **g**, and 2 Chr 29:30
Bread seven days with great **g**, 2 Chr 30:21
it for another seven days with **g**. 2 Chr 30:23
to celebrate the dedication with **g**, Neh 12:27
Jews had light and **g** and joy and honor. Est 8:16
there was **g** and joy among the Jews, Est 8:17
and made that a day of feasting and **g**. Est 9:17
making that a day of feasting and **g**. Est 9:18
of Adar as a day for **g** and feasting, Est 9:19
from sorrow into **g** and from mourning Est 9:22
make them days of feasting and **g**, Est 9:22
my sackcloth and clothed me with **g**, Ps 30:11
the oil of **g** beyond your companions; Ps 45:7
With joy and **g** they are led along as Ps 45:15
Let me hear joy and **g**; let the bones that Ps 51:8
Serve the LORD with **g**! Come into his Ps 100:2
I may rejoice in the **g** of your nation, Ps 106:5
the wicked perish there are shouts of **g**. Prv 11:10
wedding, on the day of the **g** of his heart. Sg 3:11
And joy and **g** are taken away from the Is 16:10
and behold, joy and **g**, killing oxen and Is 22:13
dark; the **g** of the earth is banished. Is 24:11
when a holy feast is kept, and **g** of heart, Is 30:29
they shall obtain **g** and joy, and sorrow Is 35:10
joy and **g** will be found in her, Is 51:3
they shall obtain **g** and joy, and sorrow Is 51:11
of ashes, the oil of **g** instead of mourning, Is 61:3
my servants shall sing for **g** of heart, Is 65:14
to be a joy, and her people to be a **g**. Is 65:18
the voice of mirth and the voice of **g**, Jer 7:34
the voice of mirth and the voice of **g**, Jer 16:9
the voice of mirth and the voice of **g**, Jer 25:10
"Sing aloud with **g** for Jacob, and raise Jer 31:7
them, and give them **g** for sorrow. Jer 31:13
the voice of mirth and the voice of **g**, Jer 33:11
G and joy have been taken away from Jer 48:33
and **g** dries up from the children of man. Jl 1:12
eyes, joy and **g** from the house of our God? Jl 1:16
save; he will rejoice over you with **g**; Zep 3:17
seasons of joy and **g** and cheerful feasts. Zec 8:19
And you will have joy and **g**, and many Lk 1:14
make me full of **g** with your presence.' Acts 2:28
your hearts with food and **g**." Acts 14:17
the oil of **g** beyond your companions." Heb 1:9

GLANCE (1)
my heart with one **g** of your eyes, Sg 4:9

GLANCING (1)
necks, **g** wantonly with their eyes, Is 3:16

GLASS (6)
Gold and **g** cannot equal it, nor can it Jb 28:17
the throne there was as it were a sea of **g**, Rv 4:6
to be a sea of **g** mingled with fire—and Rv 15:2
beside the sea of **g** with harps of God Rv 15:2
while the city was pure gold, clear as **g**. Rv 21:18
the city was pure gold, transparent as **g**. Rv 21:21

GLAZE (1)
Like the **g** covering an earthen vessel Prv 26:23

GLEAM (2)
and legs like the **g** of burnished bronze, Dn 10:6
through the squares; they **g** like torches; Na 2:4

GLEAMING (4)
in the midst of the fire, as it were **g** metal. Ezk 1:4
their appearance was like the **g** of beryl. Ezk 1:16
of his waist I saw as it were **g** metal, Ezk 1:27
appearance of brightness, like **g** metal. Ezk 8:2

GLEAN (9)
go to the field and **g** among the ears of Ru 2:2
'Please let me **g** and gather among the Ru 2:7
do not go to **g** in another field or leave this Ru 2:8
When she rose to **g**, Boaz instructed his Ru 2:15
"Let her **g** even among the sheaves, Ru 2:15
bundles for her and leave it for her to **g**, Ru 2:16
said to her, "Where did you **g** today? Ru 2:19
and they **g** the vineyard of the wicked Jb 24:6
"They shall **g** thoroughly as a vine the Jer 6:9

GLEANED (6)
set out and went and **g** in the field after Ru 2:3
So she **g** in the field until evening. Then Ru 2:17
Then she beat out what she had **g**, and it Ru 2:17
Her mother-in-law saw what she had **g**. Ru 2:18
the grain, and you will be **g** one by one, Is 27:12
gathered, as when the grapes have been **g**: Mi 7:1

GLEANING (3)
Is not the **g** of the grapes of Ephraim Jgs 8:2
g until the end of the barley and wheat Ru 2:23
as at the **g** when the grape harvest is Is 24:13

GLEANINGS (5)
shall you gather the **g** after your harvest. Lv 19:9
you gather the **g** after your harvest. Lv 23:22
G will be left in it, as when an olive tree is Is 17:6
came to you, would they not leave **g**? Jer 49:9
came to you, would they not leave **g**? Ob 1:5

GLEANS (1)
and as when one **g** the ears of grain in the Is 17:5

GLEN (1)
standing among the myrtle trees in the **g**, Zec 1:8

GLIDED (1)
A spirit **g** past my face; the hair of my Jb 4:15

GLIDING (2)
for my beloved, **g** over lips and teeth. Sg 7:9
makes a sound like a serpent **g** away; Jer 46:22

GLITTERING (4)
the **g** point comes out of his gallbladder; Jb 20:25
all their gates I have given the **g** sword. Ezk 21:15
charging, flashing sword and **g** spear, Na 3:3
they sped, at the flash of your **g** spear. Hab 3:11

GLOAT (3)
my bones—they stare and **g** over me; Ps 22:17
But do not **g** over the day of your Ob 1:12
do not **g** over his disaster in the day of Ob 1:13

GLOATED (1)
none to help her, her foes **g** over her; Lam 1:7

GLOOM (19)
wrapped in darkness, cloud, and **g**. Dt 4:11
Let **g** and deep darkness claim it. Let Jb 3:5
the land of **g** like thick darkness, like Jb 10:22
limit the ore in **g** and deep darkness. Jb 28:3
There is no **g** or deep darkness where Jb 34:22
distress and darkness, the **g** of anguish. Is 8:22
But there will be no **g** for her who was in Is 9:1
and out of their **g** and darkness the eyes Is 29:18
the darkness and your **g** be as the Is 58:10
and for brightness, but we walk in **g**. Is 59:9
he turns it into **g** and makes it deep Jer 13:16
I clothed Lebanon in **g** for it, and all Ezk 31:15
a day of darkness and **g**, a day of clouds Jl 2:2
light, and **g** with no brightness in it? Am 5:20
devastation, a day of darkness and **g**, Zep 1:15
fire and darkness and **g** and a tempest Heb 12:18
be turned to mourning and your joy to **g**. Jas 4:9
For them the **g** of utter darkness has 2 Pt 2:17
for whom the **g** of utter darkness has Jude 1:13

GLOOMY (3)
fast, do not look **g** like the hypocrites, Mt 6:16
them to chains of **g** darkness to be kept 2 Pt 2:4
eternal chains under **g** darkness until Jude 1:6

GLORIES (1)
of Christ and the subsequent **g**. 1 Pt 1:11

GLORIFIED (38)
people I will be **g**.'" And Aaron held his Lv 10:3
have increased the nation; you are **g**; Is 26:15
redeemed Jacob, and will be **g** in Israel. Is 44:23
my servant, Israel, in whom I will be **g**." Is 49:3
of the Holy One of Israel, for he has **g** you. Is 55:5
the work of my hands, that I might be **g**. Is 60:21
the planting of the LORD, that he may be **g**. Is 61:3
name's sake have said, 'Let the LORD be **g**, Is 66:5
take pleasure in it and that I may be **g**, Hg 1:8
saw it, they were afraid, and they **g** God, Mt 9:8
seeing. And they **g** the God of Israel. Mt 15:31
so that they were all amazed and **g** God, Mk 2:12
in their synagogues, being **g** by all. Lk 4:15
and they **g** God and were filled with awe, Lk 5:26
Fear seized them all, and they **g** God, Lk 7:16
she was made straight, and she **g** God. Lk 13:13
been given, because Jesus was not yet **g**. Jn 7:39
that the Son of God may be **g** through it." Jn 11:4
things at first, but when Jesus was **g**, Jn 12:16
has come for the Son of Man to be **g**. Jn 12:23
"I have **g** it, and I will glorify it again." Jn 12:28
Jesus said, "Now is the Son of Man **g**, Jn 13:31
of Man glorified, and God is **g** in him. Jn 13:31
If God is **g** in him, God will also glorify Jn 13:32
do, that the Father may be **g** in the Son. Jn 14:13
By this my Father is **g**, that you bear Jn 15:8
I **g** you on earth, having accomplished Jn 17:4

and yours are mine, and I am **g** in them. Jn 17:10
God of our fathers, **g** his servant Jesus, Acts 3:13
And they **g** God, saying, "Then to the Acts 11:18
And when they heard it, they **g** God. Acts 21:20
order that we may also be **g** with him. Rom 8:17
and those whom he justified he also **g**. Rom 8:30
And they **g** God because of me. Gal 1:24
on that day to be **g** in his saints, 2 Thes 1:10
of our Lord Jesus may be **g** in you, 2 Thes 1:12
God may be **g** through Jesus Christ. 1 Pt 4:11
As she **g** herself and lived in luxury, so Rv 18:7

GLORIFIES (2)

thanksgiving as his sacrifice **g** me; Ps 50:23
It is my Father who **g** me, of whom you Jn 8:54

GLORIFY (22)

All you offspring of Jacob, **g** him, and Ps 22:23
I will deliver you, and you shall **g** me." Ps 50:15
you, O Lord, and shall **g** your name. Ps 86:9
heart, and I will **g** your name forever. Ps 86:12
Therefore strong peoples will **g** you; cities Is 25:3
Jesus answered, "If I **g** myself, my glory is Jn 8:54
g your name." Then a voice came from Jn 12:28
"I have glorified it, and I will **g** it again." Jn 12:28
in him, God will also **g** him in himself, Jn 13:32
him in himself, and **g** him at once. Jn 13:32
He will **g** me, for he will take what is Jn 16:14
g your Son that the Son may glorify you, Jn 17:1
glorify your Son that the Son may **g** you, Jn 17:1
g me in your own presence with the glory Jn 17:5
by what kind of death he was to **g** God.) Jn 21:19
may with one voice **g** the God and Rom 15:6
that the Gentiles might **g** God for his Rom 15:9
with a price. So **g** God in your body. 1 Cor 6:20
they will **g** God because of your 2 Cor 9:13
your good deeds and **g** God on the day 1 Pt 2:12
but let him **g** God in that name. 1 Pt 4:16
will not fear, O Lord, and **g** your name? Rv 15:4

GLORIFYING (4)

g and praising God for all they had Lk 2:20
been lying on and went home, **g** God. Lk 5:25
his sight and followed him, **g** God. Lk 18:43
began rejoicing and **g** the word of Acts 13:48

GLORIOUS (47)

Your right hand, O LORD, **g** in power, Ex 15:6
in holiness, awesome in **g** deeds, Ex 15:11
may fear this **g** and awesome name, Dt 28:58
our God, and praise your **g** name. 1 Chr 29:13
Blessed be your **g** name, which is Neh 9:5
All **g** is the princess in her chamber, Ps 45:13
glory of his name; give to him **g** praise! Ps 66:2
Blessed be his **g** name forever; may the Ps 72:19
G are you, more majestic than the Ps 76:4
the coming generation the **g** deeds of the Ps 78:4
G things of you are spoken, O city of Ps 87:3
and your **g** power to their children. Ps 90:16
On the **g** splendor of your majesty, and Ps 145:5
and the **g** splendor of your kingdom. Ps 145:12
nor is it **g** to seek one's own glory. Prv 25:27
against the LORD, defying his **g** presence. Is 3:8
of the LORD shall be beautiful and **g**, Is 4:2
latter time he has made **g** the way of the Is 9:1
inquire, and his resting place shall be **g**. Is 11:10
die, and there shall be your **g** chariots, Is 22:18
and the fading flower of its **g** beauty, Is 28:1
and the fading flower of its **g** beauty, Is 28:4
sake, to magnify his law and make it **g**. Is 42:21
and I will make the place of my feet **g**. Is 60:13
who caused his **g** arm to go at the right Is 63:12
people, to make for yourself a **g** name. Is 63:14
with delight from her **g** abundance." Is 66:11
sake; do not dishonor your **g** throne; Jer 14:21
A **g** throne set on high from the Jer 17:12
mighty scepter is broken, the **g** staff.' Jer 48:17
milk and honey, the most **g** of all lands. Ezk 20:6
and honey, the most **g** of all lands, Ezk 20:15
toward the east, and toward the **g** land. Dn 8:9
And he shall stand in the **g** land, with Dn 11:16
He shall come into the **g** land. And tens Dn 11:41
the sea and the **g** holy mountain. Dn 11:45
has fallen, for the **g** trees are ruined! Zec 11:2
the Son of Man will sit on his **g** throne, Mt 19:28
him, then he will sit on his **g** throne. Mt 25:31
rejoiced at all the **g** things that were Lk 13:17
to the praise of his **g** grace, with which Eph 1:6
the riches of his **g** inheritance in the Eph 1:18
our lowly body to be like his **g** body, Phil 3:21
all power, according to his **g** might, Col 1:11
in accordance with the **g** gospel of the 1 Tm 1:11
tremble as they blaspheme the **g** ones, 2 Pt 2:10
authority, and blaspheme the **g** ones. Jude 1:8

GLORIOUSLY (3)

sing to the LORD, for he has triumphed **g**; Ex 15:1
to the LORD, for he has triumphed **g**; Ex 15:21
praises to the LORD, for he has done **g**; Is 12:5

GLORY (357)

O my **g**, be not joined to their company. Gn 49:6
and I will get **g** over Pharaoh and all his Ex 14:4
and I will get **g** over Pharaoh and all Ex 14:17
when I have gotten **g** over Pharaoh, Ex 14:18
morning you shall see the **g** of the LORD, Ex 16:7
the **g** of the LORD appeared in the cloud. Ex 16:10
The **g** of the LORD dwelt on Mount Ex 24:16
the appearance of the **g** of the LORD was Ex 24:17
your brother, for **g** and for beauty. Ex 28:2
You shall make them for **g** and beauty. Ex 28:40
and it shall be sanctified by my **g**. Ex 29:43
Moses said, "Please show me your **g**." Ex 33:18
and while my **g** passes by I will put you Ex 33:22
and the **g** of the LORD filled the Ex 40:34
and the **g** of the LORD filled the Ex 40:35
that the **g** of the LORD may appear to you." Lv 9:6
and the **g** of the LORD appeared to all the Lv 9:23
But the **g** of the LORD appeared at the Nm 14:10
shall be filled with the **g** of the LORD, Nm 14:21
who have seen my **g** and my signs Nm 14:22
And the **g** of the LORD appeared to all Nm 16:19
it, and the **g** of the LORD appeared. Nm 16:42
And the **g** of the LORD appeared to them, Nm 20:6
God has shown us his **g** and greatness, Dt 5:24
give **g** to the LORD God of Israel and give Jos 7:19
you are going will not lead to your **g**, Jgs 4:9
"The **g** has departed from Israel!" 1 Sm 4:21
said, "The **g** has departed from Israel, 1 Sm 4:22
the land, and give **g** to the God of Israel. 1 Sm 6:5
And also the **G** of Israel will not lie or 1 Sm 15:29
"Your **g**, O Israel, is slain on your 2 Sm 1:19
for the **g** of the LORD filled the house of 1 Kgs 8:11
Be content with your **g**, and stay at 2 Kgs 14:10
G in his holy name; let the hearts of 1 Chr 16:10
Declare his **g** among the nations, 1 Chr 16:24
ascribe to the LORD **g** and strength! 1 Chr 16:28
to the LORD the **g** due his name; 1 Chr 16:29
holy name, and **g** in your praise. 1 Chr 16:35
of fame and **g** throughout all lands. 1 Chr 22:5
the power and the **g** and the victory 1 Chr 29:11
for the **g** of the LORD filled the house 2 Chr 5:14
and the **g** of the LORD filled the temple. 2 Chr 7:1
because the **g** of the LORD filled the 2 Chr 7:2
come down and the **g** of the LORD on 2 Chr 7:3
riches of his royal **g** and the splendor and Est 1:4
stripped from me my **g** and taken the Jb 19:9
my **g** fresh with me, and my bow ever Jb 29:20
clothe yourself with **g** and splendor. Jb 40:10
you, O LORD, are a shield about me, my **g**, Ps 3:3
life to the ground and lay my **g** in the dust. Ps 7:5
You have set your **g** above the heavens. Ps 8:1
and crowned him with **g** and honor. Ps 8:5
The heavens declare the **g** of God, and Ps 19:1
His **g** is great through your salvation; Ps 21:5
doors, that the King of **g** may come in. Ps 24:7
Who is this King of **g**? The LORD, strong Ps 24:8
doors, that the King of **g** may come in. Ps 24:9
Who is this King of **g**? The LORD of Ps 24:10
The LORD of hosts, he is the King of **g**! Ps 24:10
house and the place where your **g** dwells. Ps 26:8
ascribe to the LORD **g** and strength. Ps 29:1
Ascribe to the LORD the **g** due his name; Ps 29:2
the God of **g** thunders, the LORD, over Ps 29:3
bare, and in his temple all cry, "**G**!" Ps 29:9
that my **g** may sing your praise and not Ps 30:12
of the LORD are like the **g** of the pastures; Ps 37:20
rich, when the **g** of his house increases. Ps 49:16
away; his **g** will not go down after him. Ps 49:17
heavens! Let your **g** be over all the earth! Ps 57:5
Awake, my **g**! Awake, O harp and lyre! I Ps 57:8
Let your **g** be over all the earth! Ps 57:11
On God rests my salvation and my **g**; my Ps 62:7
sanctuary, beholding your power and **g**. Ps 63:2
sing the **g** of his name; give to him Ps 66:2
your praise, and with your **g** all the day. Ps 71:8
the whole earth be filled with his **g**! Ps 72:19
and afterward you will receive me to **g**. Ps 73:24
to captivity, his **g** to the hand of the foe. Ps 78:61
of our salvation, for the **g** of your name; Ps 79:9
fear him, that **g** may dwell in our land. Ps 85:9
For you are the **g** of their strength; by Ps 89:17
Declare his **g** among the nations, his Ps 96:3
ascribe to the LORD **g** and strength! Ps 96:7
Ascribe to the LORD the **g** due his name; Ps 96:8
and all the peoples see his **g**. Ps 97:6
the kings of the earth will fear your **g**. Ps 102:15
builds up Zion; he appears in his **g**; Ps 102:16
May the **g** of the LORD endure forever; Ps 104:31
G in his holy name; let the hearts of Ps 105:3
that I may **g** with your inheritance. Ps 106:5
They exchanged the **g** of God for the Ps 106:20
your holy name and **g** in your praise. Ps 106:47
Let your **g** be over all the earth! Ps 108:5
nations, and his **g** above the heavens! Ps 113:4
LORD, not to us, but to your name give **g**, Ps 115:1
of the LORD, for great is the **g** of the LORD. Ps 138:5
shall speak of the **g** of your kingdom Ps 145:11
Let the godly exult in **g**; let them sing Ps 149:5
a multitude of people is the **g** of a king, Prv 14:28
Gray hair is a crown of **g**; it is gained Prv 16:31
and the **g** of children is their fathers. Prv 17:6
and it is his **g** to overlook an offense. Prv 19:11
The **g** of young men is their strength, Prv 20:29
It is the **g** of God to conceal things, but Prv 25:2
but the **g** of kings is to search things Prv 25:2
nor is it glorious to seek one's own **g**. Prv 25:27
the righteous triumph, there is great **g**, Prv 28:12
for over all the **g** there will be a canopy. Is 4:5
of hosts; the whole earth is full of his **g**!" Is 6:3
many, the king of Assyria and all his **g**. Is 8:7
and under his **g** a burning will be Is 10:16
The **g** of his forest and of his fruitful Is 10:18
And Babylon, the **g** of kingdoms, the Is 13:19
All the kings of the nations lie in **g**, each Is 14:18
the **g** of Moab will be brought into Is 16:14
Syria will be like the **g** of the children of Is 17:3
And in that day the **g** of Jacob will be Is 17:4
all the **g** of Kedar will come to an end. Is 21:16
it, to defile the pompous pride of all **g**, Is 23:9
Therefore in the east give **g** to the LORD; Is 24:15
of the sea, give **g** to the name of the LORD, Is 24:15
of praise, of **g** to the Righteous One. Is 24:16
and his **g** will be before his elders. Is 24:23
day the LORD of hosts will be a crown of **g**, Is 28:5
The **g** of Lebanon shall be given to it, the Is 35:2
They shall see the **g** of the LORD, the Is 35:2
And the **g** of the LORD shall be revealed, Is 40:5
in the Holy One of Israel you shall **g**. Is 41:16
my **g** I give to no other, nor my praise to Is 42:8
Let them give **g** to the LORD, and declare Is 42:12
by my name, whom I created for my **g**, Is 43:7
of Israel shall be justified and shall **g**." Is 45:25
put salvation in Zion, for Israel my **g**." Is 46:13
My **g** I will not give to another. Is 48:11
the **g** of the LORD shall be your rear guard. Is 58:8
and his **g** from the rising of the sun; Is 59:19
and the **g** of the LORD has risen upon you. Is 60:1
you, and his **g** will be seen upon you. Is 60:2
The **g** of Lebanon shall come to you, the Is 60:13
light, and your God will be your **g**. Is 60:19
nations, and in their **g** you shall boast. Is 61:6
righteousness, and all the kings your **g**, Is 62:2
and the **g** of the nations like an Is 66:12
And they shall come and shall see my **g**, Is 66:18
have not heard my fame or seen my **g**. Is 66:19
shall declare my **g** among the nations. Is 66:19
have changed their **g** for that which Jer 2:11
in him, and in him shall they **g**." Jer 4:2
me a people, a name, a praise, and a **g**, Jer 13:11
Give **g** to the LORD your God before he Jer 13:16
a praise and a **g** before all the nations of Jer 33:9
"Come down from your **g**, and sit on Jer 48:18
of the likeness of the **g** of the LORD. Ezk 1:28
"Blessed be the **g** of the LORD from its Ezk 3:12
behold, the **g** of the LORD stood there, Ezk 3:23
like the **g** that I had seen by the Chebar Ezk 3:23
the **g** of the God of Israel was there, Ezk 8:4
Now the **g** of the God of Israel had gone Ezk 9:3
And the **g** of the LORD went up from the Ezk 10:4
with the brightness of the **g** of the LORD. Ezk 10:4
Then the **g** of the LORD went out from Ezk 10:18
and the **g** of the God of Israel was over Ezk 10:19
and the **g** of the God of Israel was over Ezk 11:22
And the **g** of the LORD went up from Ezk 11:23
them their stronghold, their joy and **g**, Ezk 24:25
on its frontier, the **g** of the country, Ezk 25:9
I will manifest my **g** in your midst. Ezk 28:22
you thus like in **g** and in greatness Ezk 31:18
renown on the day that I show my **g**, Ezk 39:13
I will set my **g** among the nations, Ezk 39:21
the **g** of the God of Israel was coming Ezk 43:2
waters, and the earth shone with his **g**. Ezk 43:2
As the **g** of the LORD entered the temple Ezk 43:4
the **g** of the LORD filled the temple. Ezk 43:5
the **g** of the LORD filled the temple of the Ezk 44:4
the power, and the might, and the **g**, Dn 2:37
residence and for the **g** of my majesty?" Dn 4:30
to me, and for the **g** of my kingdom, Dn 4:36
and greatness and **g** and majesty. Dn 5:18
throne, and his **g** was taken from him. Dn 5:20
given dominion and **g** and a kingdom, Dn 7:14
of tribute for the **g** of the kingdom. Dn 11:20
me; I will change their **g** into shame. Hos 4:7
Ephraim's **g** shall fly away like a bird— Hos 9:11
over it and over its **g**—for it has Hos 10:5
the **g** of Israel shall come to Adullam. Mi 1:15
the knowledge of the **g** of the LORD as Hab 2:14
have your fill of shame instead of **g**. Hab 2:16

utter shame will come upon your **g**! Hab 2:16
you who saw this house in its former **g**? Hg 2:3
come in, and I will fill this house with **g**, Hg 2:7
The latter **g** of this house shall be greater Hg 2:9
LORD, and I will be the **g** in her midst.'" Zec 2:5
after his **g** sent me to the nations who Zec 2:8
of the shepherds, for their **g** is ruined! Zec 11:3
that the **g** of the house of David and the Zec 12:7
of David and the **g** of the inhabitants of Zec 12:7
all the kingdoms of the world and their **g**. Mt 4:8
good works and give **g** to your Father Mt 5:16
Solomon in all his **g** was not arrayed Mt 6:29
with his angels in the **g** of his Father, Mt 16:27
of heaven with power and great **g**. Mt 24:30
"When the Son of Man comes in his **g**, Mt 25:31
he comes in the **g** of his Father with Mk 8:38
hand and one at your left, in your **g**." Mk 10:37
in clouds with great power and **g**. Mk 13:26
and the **g** of the Lord shone around them, Lk 2:9
"**G** to God in the highest, and on earth Lk 2:14
Gentiles, and for **g** to your people Israel." Lk 2:32
I will give all this authority and their **g**, Lk 4:6
when he comes in his **g** and the glory of Lk 9:26
in his glory and the **g** of the Father and Lk 9:26
who appeared in **g** and spoke of his Lk 9:31
awake they saw his **g** and the two men Lk 9:32
Solomon in all his **g** was not arrayed Lk 12:27
Peace in heaven and **g** in the highest!" Lk 19:38
in a cloud with power and great **g**. Lk 21:27
these things and enter into his **g**?" Lk 24:26
dwelt among us, and we have seen his **g**, Jn 1:14
g as of the only Son from the Father, Jn 1:14
at Cana in Galilee, and manifested his **g**. Jn 2:11
I do not receive **g** from people. Jn 5:41
when you receive **g** from one another Jn 5:44
do not seek the **g** that comes from the Jn 5:44
on his own authority seeks his own **g**, Jn 7:18
the one who seeks the **g** of him who sent Jn 7:18
Yet I do not seek my own **g**; there is One Jn 8:50
"If I glorify myself, my **g** is nothing. Jn 8:54
blind and said to him, "Give **g** to God. Jn 9:24
It is for the **g** of God, so that the Son of Jn 11:4
believed you would see the **g** of God?" Jn 11:40
because he saw his **g** and spoke of him. Jn 12:41
for they loved the **g** that comes from Jn 12:43
man more than the **g** that comes from Jn 12:43
own presence with the **g** that I had with Jn 17:5
The **g** that you have given me I have Jn 17:22
to see my **g** that you have given me Jn 17:24
The God of **g** appeared to our father Acts 7:2
into heaven and saw the **g** of God, Acts 7:55
because he did not give God the **g**, Acts 12:23
and exchanged the **g** of the immortal Rom 1:23
in well-doing seek for **g** and honor and Rom 2:7
but **g** and honor and peace for Rom 2:10
my lie God's truth abounds to his **g**, Rom 3:7
sinned and fall short of the **g** of God, Rom 3:23
strong in his faith as he gave **g** to God, Rom 4:20
and we rejoice in hope of the **g** of God. Rom 5:2
from the dead by the **g** of the Father, Rom 6:4
worth comparing with the **g** that is to Rom 8:18
the freedom of the **g** of the children of Rom 8:21
and to them belong the adoption, the **g**, Rom 9:4
the riches of his **g** for vessels of mercy, Rom 9:23
he has prepared beforehand for **g**— Rom 9:23
are all things. To him be **g** forever. Rom 11:36
has welcomed you, for the **g** of God. Rom 15:7
wise God be **g** forevermore through Rom 16:27
God decreed before the ages for our **g**. 1 Cor 2:7
would not have crucified the Lord of **g**. 1 Cor 2:8
you do, do all to the **g** of God. 1 Cor 10:31
since he is the image and **g** of God, 1 Cor 11:7
of God, but woman is the **g** of man. 1 Cor 11:7
if a woman has long hair, it is her **g**? 1 Cor 11:15
but the **g** of the heavenly is of one 1 Cor 15:40
and the **g** of the earthly is of another. 1 Cor 15:40
There is one **g** of the sun, and 1 Cor 15:41
the sun, and another **g** of the moon, 1 Cor 15:41
the moon, and another **g** of the stars; 1 Cor 15:41
stars; for star differs from star in **g**. 1 Cor 15:41
is sown in dishonor; it is raised in **g**. 1 Cor 15:43
we utter our Amen to God for his **g**. 2 Cor 1:20
came with such **g** that the Israelites 2 Cor 3:7
not gaze at Moses' face because of its **g**, 2 Cor 3:7
of the Spirit have even more **g**? 2 Cor 3:8
For if there was **g** in the ministry of 2 Cor 3:9
righteousness must far exceed it in **g**. 2 Cor 3:9
what once had **g** has come to have no 2 Cor 3:10
glory has come to have no **g** at all, 2 Cor 3:10
all, because of the **g** that surpasses it. 2 Cor 3:10
being brought to an end came with **g**, 2 Cor 3:11
more will what is permanent have **g**. 2 Cor 3:11
face, beholding the **g** of the Lord, 2 Cor 3:18
from one degree of **g** to another. 2 Cor 3:18
the light of the gospel of the **g** of Christ, 2 Cor 4:4
of the knowledge of the **g** of God in the 2 Cor 4:6
thanksgiving, to the **g** of God. 2 Cor 4:15
eternal weight of **g** beyond all 2 Cor 4:17
for the **g** of the Lord himself and to 2 Cor 8:19
of the churches, the **g** of Christ. 2 Cor 8:23
to whom be the **g** forever and ever. Gal 1:5
Christ might be to the praise of his **g**. Eph 1:12
possession of it, to the praise of his **g**. Eph 1:14
our Lord Jesus Christ, the Father of **g**, Eph 1:17
I am suffering for you, which is your **g**. Eph 3:13
to the riches of his **g** he may grant you Eph 3:16
to him be **g** in the church and in Eph 3:21
Jesus Christ, to the **g** and praise of God. Phil 1:11
have ample cause to **g** in Christ Jesus, Phil 1:26
is Lord, to the **g** of God the Father. Phil 2:11
Spirit of God and **g** in Christ Jesus and Phil 3:3
their belly, and they **g** in their shame, Phil 3:19
to his riches in **g** in Christ Jesus. Phil 4:19
God and Father be **g** forever and ever. Phil 4:20
are the riches of the **g** of this mystery, Col 1:27
which is Christ in you, the hope of **g**. Col 1:27
then you also will appear with him in **g**. Col 3:4
Nor did we seek **g** from people, 1 Thes 2:6
you into his own kingdom and **g**. 1 Thes 2:12
For you are our **g** and joy. 1 Thes 2:20
the Lord and from the **g** of his might, 2 Thes 1:9
you may obtain the **g** of our Lord 2 Thes 2:14
God, be honor and **g** forever and ever. 1 Tm 1:17
on in the world, taken up in **g**. 1 Tm 3:16
that is in Christ Jesus with eternal **g**. 2 Tm 2:10
To him be the **g** forever and ever. 2 Tm 4:18
the appearing of the **g** of our great God Ti 2:13
is the radiance of the **g** of God and the Heb 1:3
have crowned him with **g** and honor, Heb 2:7
crowned with **g** and honor because of Heb 2:9
exist, in bringing many sons to **g**, Heb 2:10
counted worthy of more **g** than Moses— Heb 3:3
—as much more **g** as the builder of Heb 3:3
the cherubim of **g** overshadowing the Heb 9:5
Christ, to whom be **g** forever and ever. Heb 13:21
in our Lord Jesus Christ, the Lord of **g**. Jas 2:1
to result in praise and **g** and honor at the 1 Pt 1:7
that is inexpressible and filled with **g**, 1 Pt 1:8
him from the dead and gave him **g**, 1 Pt 1:21
like grass and all its **g** like the flower of 1 Pt 1:24
To him belong **g** and dominion forever 1 Pt 4:11
and be glad when his **g** is revealed. 1 Pt 4:13
because the Spirit of **g** and of God rests 1 Pt 4:14
as a partaker in the **g** that is going to be 1 Pt 5:1
will receive the unfading crown of **g**. 1 Pt 5:4
called you to his eternal **g** in Christ, 1 Pt 5:10
called us to his own **g** and excellence, 2 Pt 1:3
he received honor and **g** from God the 2 Pt 1:17
was borne to him by the Majestic **G**, 2 Pt 1:17
To him be the **g** both now and to the 2 Pt 3:18
the presence of his **g** with great joy, Jude 1:24
through Jesus Christ our Lord, be **g**, Jude 1:25
to him be **g** and dominion forever and Rv 1:6
the living creatures give **g** and honor and Rv 4:9
God, to receive **g** and honor and power, Rv 4:11
might and honor and **g** and blessing!" Rv 5:12
and honor and **g** and might forever Rv 5:13
Blessing and **g** and wisdom and Rv 7:12
were terrified and gave **g** to the God of Rv 11:13
a loud voice, "Fear God and give him **g**, Rv 14:7
with smoke from the **g** of God and from Rv 15:8
They did not repent and give him **g**. Rv 16:9
the earth was made bright with his **g**. Rv 18:1
Salvation and **g** and power belong to our Rv 19:1
us rejoice and exult and give him the **g**, Rv 19:7
having the **g** of God, its radiance like a Rv 21:11
on it, for the **g** of God gives it light, Rv 21:23
of the earth will bring their **g** into it, Rv 21:24
will bring into it the **g** and the honor of Rv 21:26

GLOWING (3)
g coals flamed forth from him. 2 Sm 22:9
mouth; **g** coals flamed forth from him. Ps 18:8
arrows, with **g** coals of the broom tree! Ps 120:4

GLUTTON (4)
our voice; he is a **g** and a drunkard.' Dt 21:20
the drunkard and the **g** will come to Prv 23:21
A **g** and a drunkard, a friend of tax Mt 11:19
A **g** and a drunkard, a friend of tax Lk 7:34

GLUTTONOUS (1)
drunkards or among **g** eaters of meat, Prv 23:20

GLUTTONS (2)
a companion of **g** shames his father. Prv 28:7
are always liars, evil beasts, lazy **g**." Ti 1:12

GNASH (2)
at a feast, they **g** at me with their teeth. Ps 35:16
they hiss, they **g** their teeth, they cry: Lam 2:16

GNASHED (1)
and hated me; he has **g** his teeth at me; Jb 16:9

GNASHES (2)
against the righteous and **g** his teeth at Ps 37:12
angry; he **g** his teeth and melts away; Ps 112:10

GNASHING (7)
there will be weeping and **g** of teeth." Mt 8:12
there will be weeping and **g** of teeth. Mt 13:42
there will be weeping and **g** of teeth. Mt 13:50
there will be weeping and **g** of teeth.' Mt 22:13
there will be weeping and **g** of teeth. Mt 24:51
there will be weeping and **g** of teeth.' Mt 25:30
there will be weeping and **g** of teeth, Lk 13:28

GNAT (1)
straining out a **g** and swallowing a Mt 23:24

GNATS (6)
so that it may become **g** in all the land of Ex 8:16
and there were **g** on man and beast. Ex 8:17
dust of the earth became **g** in all the land Ex 8:17
tried by their secret arts to produce **g**, Ex 8:18
not. So there were **g** on man and beast. Ex 8:18
flies, and **g** throughout their country. Ps 105:31

GNAW (2)
and hard hunger they **g** the dry ground Jb 30:3
it and drain it out, and **g** its shards, Ezk 23:34

GNAWED (2)
king of Babylon has **g** his bones. Jer 50:17
People **g** their tongues in anguish Rv 16:10

GNAWS (1)
and the pain that **g** me takes no rest. Jb 30:17

GO (1504)
on your belly you shall **g**, and dust you Gn 3:14
the LORD said to Noah, "**G** into the ark, Gn 7:1
"**G** out from the ark, you and your wife, Gn 8:16
let us **g** down and there confuse their Gn 11:7
of the Chaldeans to **g** into the land of Gn 11:31
"**G** from your country and your kindred Gn 12:1
and they set out to **g** to the land of Gn 12:5
that it may **g** well with me because of Gn 12:13
then, here is your wife; take her, and **g**." Gn 12:19
the left hand, then I will **g** to the right, Gn 13:9
the right hand, then I will **g** to the left." Gn 13:9
you shall **g** to your fathers in peace; Gn 15:15
G in to my servant; it may be that I shall Gn 16:2
I will **g** down to see whether they have Gn 18:21
rise up early and **g** on your way." They Gn 19:2
Then you **g** in and lie with him, that Gn 19:34
you love, and **g** to the land of Moriah, Gn 22:2
and the boy will **g** over there and Gn 22:5
but will **g** to my country and to my Gn 24:4
the time when women **g** out to draw Gn 24:11
but you shall **g** to my father's house Gn 24:38
you are prospering the way that I **g**, Gn 24:42
take her and **g**, and let her be the wife Gn 24:51
at least ten days; after that she may **g**." Gn 24:55
me away that I may **g** to my master." Gn 24:56
"Will you **g** with this man?" She said, Gn 24:58
go with this man?" She said, "I will **g**." Gn 24:58
him and said, "Do not **g** down to Egypt; Gn 26:2
said to Isaac, "**G** away from us, Gn 26:16
and **g** out to the field and hunt game for Gn 27:3
G to the flock and bring me two good Gn 27:9
only obey my voice, and **g**, bring them Gn 27:13
g to Paddan-aram to the house of Gn 28:2
you and will keep you wherever you **g**, Gn 28:15
and will keep me in this way that I **g**, Gn 28:20
Water the sheep and **g**, pasture them." Gn 29:7
me my wife that I may **g** in to her, Gn 29:21
g in to her, so that she may give birth on Gn 30:3
that I may **g** to my own home and Gn 30:25
whom I have served you, that I may **g**, Gn 30:26
g out from this land and return to the Gn 31:13
to **g** to the land of Canaan to his father Gn 31:18
Then he said, "Let me **g**, for the day has Gn 32:26
will not let you **g** unless you bless me." Gn 32:26
on our way, and I will **g** ahead of you." Gn 33:12
"Arise, **g** up to Bethel and dwell there. Gn 35:1
Then let us arise and **g** up to Bethel, so Gn 35:3
So he said to him, "**G** now, see if it is Gn 37:14
'Let us **g** to Dothan.'" So Joseph went Gn 37:17
boy is gone, and I, where shall I **g**?" Gn 37:30
"No, I shall **g** down to Sheol to my son, Gn 37:35
"**G** in to your brother's wife and perform Gn 38:8
said to all the Egyptians, "**G** to Joseph. Gn 41:55
G down and buy grain for us there, that Gn 42:2
you shall not **g** from this place unless Gn 42:15
and let the rest **g** and carry grain for Gn 42:19
of your households, and **g** your way. Gn 42:33
"My son shall not **g** down with you, Gn 42:38
their father said to them, "**G** again, Gn 43:2
us, we will **g** down and buy you food. Gn 43:4
will not send him, we will not **g** down, Gn 43:5

the boy with me, and we will arise and **g**, Gn 43:8
brother, and arise, **g** again to the man. Gn 43:13
for you, **g** up in peace to your father." Gn 44:17
And when our father said, '**G** again, Gn 44:25
we said, 'We cannot **g** down. If our Gn 44:26
goes with us, then we will **g** down. Gn 44:26
and let the boy **g** back with his Gn 44:33
For how can I **g** back to my father if Gn 44:34
"Make everyone **g** out from me." So no Gn 45:1
Hurry and **g** up to my father and say to Gn 45:9
load your beasts and **g** back to the Gn 45:17
alive. I will **g** and see him before I die." Gn 45:28
Do not be afraid to **g** down to Egypt, for Gn 46:3
I myself will **g** down with you to Egypt, Gn 46:4
"I will **g** up and tell Pharaoh and will Gn 46:31
was still some distance to **g** to Ephrath, Gn 48:7
let me please **g** up and bury my father. Gn 50:5
And Pharaoh answered, "**G** up, and Gn 50:6
"Shall I **g** and call you a nurse from the Ex 2:7
"**G**." So the girl went and called the child's Ex 2:8
I that I should **g** to Pharaoh and bring Ex 3:11
G and gather the elders of Israel together Ex 3:16
the elders of Israel shall **g** to the king of Ex 3:18
please let us **g** a three days' journey into Ex 3:18
will not let you **g** unless compelled by a Ex 3:19
I will do in it; after that he will let you **g**. Ex 3:20
and when you **g**, you shall not go empty, Ex 3:21
and when you go, you shall not **g** empty, Ex 3:21
Now therefore **g**, and I will be with your Ex 4:12
"Please let me **g** back to my brothers in Ex 4:18
And Jethro said to Moses, "**G** in peace." Ex 4:18
to Moses in Midian, "**G** back to Egypt, Ex 4:19
to Moses, "When you **g** back to Egypt, Ex 4:21
heart, so that he will not let the people **g**. Ex 4:21
"Let my son **g** that he may serve me." If Ex 4:23
may serve me." If you refuse to let him **g**, Ex 4:23
"**G** into the wilderness to meet Moses." So Ex 4:27
LORD, the God of Israel, 'Let my people **g**, Ex 5:1
I should obey his voice and let Israel **g**? Ex 5:2
LORD, and moreover, I will not let Israel **g**." Ex 5:2
Please let us **g** a three days' journey into Ex 5:3
let them **g** and gather straw for Ex 5:7
'Let us **g** and offer sacrifice to our God.' Ex 5:8
G and get your straw yourselves Ex 5:11
say, 'Let us **g** and sacrifice to the LORD.' Ex 5:17
G now and work. No straw will be given Ex 5:18
"**G** in, tell Pharaoh king of Egypt to let Ex 6:11
let the people of Israel **g** out of his land." Ex 6:11
to let the people of Israel **g** out of his land. Ex 7:2
is hardened; he refuses to let the people **g**. Ex 7:14
G to Pharaoh in the morning, as he is Ex 7:15
sent me to you, saying, "Let my people **g**, Ex 7:16
Moses, "**G** in to Pharaoh and say to him, Ex 8:1
'Thus says the LORD, "Let my people **g**, Ex 8:1
But if you refuse to let them **g**, behold, I Ex 8:2
I will let the people **g** to sacrifice to the Ex 8:8
The frogs shall **g** away from you and Ex 8:11
'Thus says the LORD, "Let my people **g**, Ex 8:20
Or else, if you will not let my people **g**, Ex 8:21
"**G**, sacrifice to your God within the Ex 8:25
We must **g** three days' journey into the Ex 8:27
"I will let you **g** to sacrifice to the LORD Ex 8:28
only you must not **g** very far away. Ex 8:28
not letting the people **g** to sacrifice to the Ex 8:29
time also, and did not let the people **g**. Ex 8:32
Moses, "**G** in to Pharaoh and say to him, Ex 9:1
the God of the Hebrews, "Let my people **g**, Ex 9:1
refuse to let them **g** and still hold them, Ex 9:2
hardened, and he did not let the people **g**. Ex 9:7
the God of the Hebrews, "Let my people **g**, Ex 9:13
my people and will not let them **g**. Ex 9:17
I will let you **g**, and you shall stay no Ex 9:28
and he did not let the people of Israel **g**, Ex 9:35
the LORD said to Moses, "**G** in to Pharaoh, Ex 10:1
Let my people **g**, that they may serve me. Ex 10:3
For if you refuse to let my people **g**, Ex 10:4
Let the men **g**, that they may serve the Ex 10:7
to them, "**G**, serve the LORD your God. Ex 10:8
your God. But which ones are to **g**?" Ex 10:8
"We will **g** with our young and our old. Ex 10:9
We will **g** with our sons and daughters Ex 10:9
if ever I let you and your little ones **g**! Ex 10:10
G, the men among you, and serve the Ex 10:11
and he did not let the people of Israel **g**. Ex 10:20
Moses and said, "**G**, serve the LORD; Ex 10:24
your little ones also may **g** with you; Ex 10:24
Our livestock also must **g** with us; not Ex 10:26
heart, and he would not let them **g**. Ex 10:27
Afterward he will let you **g** from here. Ex 11:1
When he lets you **g**, he will drive you Ex 11:1
About midnight I will **g** out in the midst Ex 11:4
And after that I will **g** out." And he went Ex 11:8
let the people of Israel **g** out of his land. Ex 11:10
"**G** and select lambs for yourselves Ex 12:21
None of you shall **g** out of the door of Ex 12:22

said, "Up, **g** out from among my people, Ex 12:31
both you and the people of Israel; and **g**, Ex 12:31
Pharaoh stubbornly refused to let us **g**, Ex 13:15
When Pharaoh let the people **g**, God did Ex 13:17
we have let Israel **g** from serving us?" Ex 14:5
Tell the people of Israel to **g** forward. Ex 14:15
people of Israel may **g** through the sea Ex 14:16
so that they shall **g** in after them, Ex 14:17
and the people shall **g** out and gather a Ex 16:4
let no one **g** out of his place on the Ex 16:29
with which you struck the Nile, and **g**. Ex 17:5
men, and **g** out and fight with Amalek. Ex 17:9
this people also will **g** to their place in Ex 18:23
"**G** to the people and consecrate them Ex 19:10
'Take care not to **g** up into the Ex 19:12
the third day; do not **g** near a woman." Ex 19:15
to Moses, "**G** down and warn the people, Ex 19:21
And the LORD said to him, "**G** down, and Ex 19:24
And you shall not **g** up by steps to my Ex 20:26
and in the seventh he shall **g** out free, Ex 21:2
he comes in single, he shall **g** out single; Ex 21:3
then his wife shall **g** out with him. Ex 21:3
be her master's, and he shall **g** out alone. Ex 21:4
and my children; I will not **g** out free,' Ex 21:5
she shall not **g** out as the male slaves do. Ex 21:7
for her, she shall **g** out for nothing, Ex 21:11
shall let the slave **g** free because of his Ex 21:26
shall let the slave **g** free because of his Ex 21:27
has a dispute, let him **g** to them." Ex 24:14
on his sons when they **g** into the tent of Ex 28:43
When they **g** into the tent of meeting, Ex 30:20
make us gods who shall **g** before us. Ex 32:1
And the LORD said to Moses, "**G** down, for Ex 32:7
'Make us gods who shall **g** before us. Ex 32:23
and **g** to and fro from gate to gate Ex 32:27
sin. And now I will **g** up to the LORD; Ex 32:30
But now **g**, lead the people to the place Ex 32:34
behold, my angel shall **g** before you. Ex 32:34
g up from here, you and the people Ex 33:1
G up to a land flowing with milk and Ex 33:3
but I will not **g** up among you, lest I Ex 33:3
moment I should **g** up among you, Ex 33:5
sought the LORD would **g** out to the tent Ex 33:7
he said, "My presence will **g** with you, Ex 33:14
"If your presence will not **g** with me, Ex 33:15
please let the Lord **g** in the midst of us, Ex 34:9
inhabitants of the land to which you **g**, Ex 34:12
when you **g** up to appear before the Ex 34:24
be kept burning on it; it shall not **g** out. Lv 6:12
the altar continually; it shall not **g** out. Lv 6:13
And you shall not **g** outside the entrance Lv 8:33
And do not **g** outside the entrance of the Lv 10:7
you, when you **g** into the tent of meeting, Lv 10:9
"All winged insects that **g** on all fours Lv 11:20
the winged insects that **g** on all fours Lv 11:21
among the animals that **g** on all fours, Lv 11:27
and the priest shall **g** out of the camp, Lv 14:3
let the living bird **g** into the open field. Lv 14:7
afterward the priest shall **g** in to see the Lv 14:36
then the priest shall **g** out of the house Lv 14:38
then the priest shall **g** and look. And if Lv 14:44
shall let the live bird **g** out of the city Lv 14:53
Then he shall **g** out to the altar that is Lv 16:18
shall let the goat **g** free in the Lv 16:22
who lets the goat **g** to Azazel shall wash Lv 16:26
You shall not **g** around as a slanderer Lv 19:16
He shall not **g** in to any dead bodies nor Lv 21:11
He shall not **g** out of the sanctuary, lest Lv 21:12
but he shall not **g** through the veil or Lv 21:23
that it may **g** with the bread as a Lv 24:7
Then he shall **g** out from you, he and Lv 25:41
and **g** back to his own clan and return Lv 25:41
the sword shall not **g** through your land. Lv 26:6
all in Israel who are able to **g** to war, Nm 1:3
upward, all who were able to **g** to war: Nm 1:20
upward, all who were able to **g** to war: Nm 1:22
upward, all who were able to **g** to war: Nm 1:24
upward, every man able to **g** to war: Nm 1:26
upward, every man able to **g** to war: Nm 1:28
upward, every man able to **g** to war: Nm 1:30
upward, every man able to **g** to war: Nm 1:32
upward, every man able to **g** to war: Nm 1:34
upward, every man able to **g** to war: Nm 1:36
upward, every man able to **g** to war: Nm 1:38
upward, every man able to **g** to war: Nm 1:40
upward, every man able to **g** to war: Nm 1:42
every man able to **g** to war in Israel— Nm 1:45
and his sons shall **g** in and take down Nm 4:5
and his sons shall **g** in and appoint Nm 4:19
but they shall not **g** in to look on the Nm 4:20
restitution for wrong shall **g** to the LORD Nm 5:8
the LORD he shall not **g** near a dead body. Nm 6:6
and let them **g** with a razor over all their Nm 8:7
that the Levites shall **g** in to serve at Nm 8:15
And when you **g** to war in your land Nm 10:9

But he said to him, "I will not **g**. I will Nm 10:30
And if you do **g** with us, whatever Nm 10:32
"**G** up into the Negeb and go up into Nm 13:17
into the Negeb and **g** up into the hill Nm 13:17
"Let us **g** up at once and occupy it, Nm 13:30
are not able to **g** up against the people, Nm 13:31
not be better for us to **g** back to Egypt?" Nm 14:3
choose a leader and **g** back to Egypt." Nm 14:4
over them and you **g** before them, Nm 14:14
We will **g** up to the place that the LORD Nm 14:40
Do not **g** up, for the Lord is not among Nm 14:42
But they presumed to **g** up to the Nm 14:44
and they **g** down alive into Sheol, Nm 16:30
We will **g** along the King's Highway. Nm 20:17
to him, "We will **g** up by the highway, Nm 20:19
Red Sea, to **g** around the land of Edom. Nm 21:4
We will **g** by the King's Highway Nm 21:22
Balaam, "You shall not **g** with them. Nm 22:12
princes of Balak, "**G** to your own land, Nm 22:13
LORD has refused to let me **g** with you." Nm 22:13
I could not **g** beyond the command of Nm 22:18
come to call you, rise, **g** with them; Nm 22:20
LORD said to Balaam, "**G** with the men, Nm 22:35
beside your burnt offering, and I will **g**. Nm 23:3
the LORD to bless Israel, he did not **g**, Nm 24:1
not be able to **g** beyond the word of Nm 24:13
all in Israel who are able to **g** to war." Nm 26:2
"**G** up into this mountain of Abarim Nm 27:12
who shall **g** out before them and Nm 27:17
At his word they shall **g** out, and at Nm 27:21
that they may **g** against Midian to Nm 31:3
"Shall your brothers **g** to the war while Nm 32:6
ready to **g** before the people of Israel, Nm 32:17
take up arms to **g** before the LORD for Nm 32:20
Then it shall **g** on to Hazar-addar, Nm 34:4
the border shall **g** down from Nm 34:11
the border shall **g** down and reach Nm 34:11
And the border shall **g** down to the Nm 34:12
at any time **g** beyond the boundaries Nm 35:26
and **g** to the hill country of the Amorites Dt 1:7
G in and take possession of the land that Dt 1:8
G up, take possession, as the LORD, the Dt 1:21
by which we must **g** up and the cities Dt 1:22
"Yet you would not **g** up, but rebelled Dt 1:26
to show you by what way you should **g**. Dt 1:33
and said, 'You also shall not **g** in there. Dt 1:37
of good or evil, they shall **g** in there. Dt 1:39
LORD. We ourselves will **g** up and fight, Dt 1:41
and thought it easy to **g** up into the hill Dt 1:41
to me, 'Say to them, Do not **g** up or fight, Dt 1:42
'Now rise up and **g** over the brook Zered.' Dt 2:13
on your journey and **g** over the Valley of Dt 2:24
I will **g** only by the road; I will turn aside Dt 2:27
until I **g** over the Jordan into the land Dt 2:29
Please let me **g** over and see the good land Dt 3:25
G up to the top of Pisgah and lift up your Dt 3:27
eyes, for you shall not **g** over this Jordan. Dt 3:27
for he shall **g** over at the head of this Dt 3:28
and **g** in and take possession of the land Dt 4:1
in this land; I must not **g** over the Jordan. Dt 4:22
But you shall **g** over and take possession Dt 4:22
god ever attempted to **g** and take a nation Dt 4:34
that it may **g** well with you and with Dt 4:40
and you did not **g** up into the mountain. Dt 5:5
and that it may **g** well with you in the Dt 5:16
G near and hear all that the LORD our Dt 5:27
that it might **g** well with them and with Dt 5:29
G and say to them, "Return to your Dt 5:30
live, and that it may **g** well with you, Dt 5:33
to do them, that it may **g** well with you, Dt 6:3
You shall not **g** after other gods, the gods Dt 6:14
of the LORD, that it may **g** well with you, Dt 6:18
and that you may **g** in and take Dt 6:18
and **g** in and possess the land that the Dt 8:1
LORD your God and **g** after other gods and Dt 8:19
to **g** in to dispossess nations greater and Dt 9:1
to me, 'Arise, **g** down quickly from here, Dt 9:12
'**G** up and take possession of the land Dt 9:23
g on your journey at the head of the Dt 10:11
so that they may **g** in and possess the Dt 10:11
and **g** in and take possession of the land Dt 11:8
to **g** after other gods that you have not Dt 11:28
over the Jordan to **g** in to take Dt 11:31
his habitation there. There you shall **g**, Dt 12:5
But when you **g** over the Jordan and live Dt 12:10
that all may **g** well with you and with Dt 12:25
and you shall **g** to the place that the Dt 12:26
that it may **g** well with you and with Dt 12:28
nations whom you **g** in to dispossess, Dt 12:29
and if he says, 'Let us **g** after other gods,' Dt 13:2
saying, 'Let us **g** and serve other gods,' Dt 13:6
saying, 'Let us **g** and serve other gods,' Dt 13:13
in your hand and **g** to the place that Dt 14:25
year you shall let him **g** free from you. Dt 15:12
And when you let him **g** free from you, Dt 15:13

you shall not let him **g** empty-handed.	Dt 15:13
says to you, 'I will not **g** out from you,'	Dt 15:16
you when you let him **g** free from you,	Dt 15:18
you shall turn and **g** to your tents.	Dt 16:7
then you shall arise and **g** up to the place	Dt 17:8
"When you **g** out to war against your	Dt 20:1
Let him **g** back to his house, lest he die	Dt 20:5
Let him **g** back to his house, lest he die	Dt 20:6
Let him **g** back to his house, lest he die	Dt 20:7
Let him **g** back to his house, lest he	Dt 20:8
"When you **g** out to war against your	Dt 21:10
After that you may **g** in to her and be	Dt 21:13
her, you shall let her **g** where she wants.	Dt 21:14
You shall let the mother **g**, but the	Dt 22:7
for yourself, that it may **g** well with you,	Dt 22:7
then he shall **g** outside the camp.	Dt 23:10
the camp, and you shall **g** out to it.	Dt 23:12
"If you **g** into your neighbor's vineyard,	Dt 23:24
If you **g** into your neighbor's standing	Dt 23:25
he shall not **g** out with the army or be	Dt 24:5
you shall not **g** into his house to collect	Dt 24:10
the field, you shall not **g** back to get it.	Dt 24:19
trees, you shall not **g** over them again.	Dt 24:20
if one should **g** on to beat him with more	Dt 25:3
Her husband's brother shall **g** in to her	Dt 25:5
his brother's wife shall **g** up to the gate	Dt 25:7
his brother's wife shall **g** up to him in	Dt 25:9
and you shall **g** to the place that the LORD	Dt 26:2
And you shall **g** to the priest who is in	Dt 26:3
and blessed shall you be when you **g** out.	Dt 28:6
and you shall only **g** up and not down,	Dt 28:13
left, to **g** after other gods to serve them.	Dt 28:14
cursed shall you be when you **g** out.	Dt 28:19
You shall **g** out one way against them	Dt 28:25
be yours, for they shall **g** into captivity.	Dt 28:41
the LORD our God to **g** and serve the gods	Dt 29:18
'Who will **g** over the sea for us and	Dt 30:13
I am no longer able to **g** out and come in.	Dt 31:2
to me, 'You shall not **g** over this Jordan.'	Dt 31:2
your God himself will **g** over before you.	Dt 31:3
and Joshua will **g** over at your head,	Dt 31:3
for you shall **g** with this people into the	Dt 31:7
"**G** up this mountain of the Abarim,	Dt 32:49
die on the mountain which you **g** up,	Dt 32:50
before you, but you shall not **g** there,	Dt 32:52
eyes, but you shall not **g** over there."	Dt 34:4
Now therefore arise, **g** over this Jordan,	Jos 1:2
may have good success wherever you **g**.	Jos 1:7
your God is with you wherever you **g**."	Jos 1:9
over this Jordan to **g** in to take	Jos 1:11
do, and wherever you send us we will **g**.	Jos 1:16
Shittim as spies, saying, "**G**, view the land,	Jos 2:1
And she said to them, "**G** into the hills,	Jos 2:16
Then afterward you may **g** your way."	Jos 2:16
that you may know the way you shall **g**,	Jos 3:4
fall down flat, and the people shall **g** up,	Jos 6:5
And he said to the people, "**G** forward.	Jos 6:7
neither shall any word **g** out of your	Jos 6:10
they shall **g** into the treasury of the	Jos 6:19
"**G** into the prostitute's house and bring	Jos 6:22
"**G** up and spy out the land." And the men	Jos 7:2
to him, "Do not have all the people **g** up,	Jos 7:3
or three thousand men **g** up and attack	Jos 7:3
men with you, and arise, **g** up to Ai.	Jos 8:1
all the fighting men arose to **g** up to Ai.	Jos 8:3
Do not **g** very far from the city, but all of	Jos 8:4
or Bethel who did not **g** out after Israel.	Jos 8:17
for the journey and **g** to meet them and	Jos 9:11
people, **g** up by yourselves to the forest,	Jos 17:15
they may set out and **g** up and down the	Jos 18:4
"**G** up and down in the land and write a	Jos 18:8
Therefore turn and **g** to your tents in the	Jos 22:4
"**G** back to your tents with much wealth	Jos 22:8
of Canaan, to **g** to the land of Gilead,	Jos 22:9
now I am about to **g** the way of all the	Jos 23:14
and **g** and serve other gods and bow	Jos 23:16
"Who shall **g** up first for us against the	Jgs 1:1
The LORD said, "Judah shall **g** up; behold,	Jgs 1:2
And I likewise will **g** with you into the	Jgs 1:3
they let the man and all his family **g**.	Jgs 1:25
'**G**, gather your men at Mount Tabor,	Jgs 4:6
Barak said to her, "If you will **g** with me, I	Jgs 4:8
to her, "If you will go with me, I will **g**,	Jgs 4:8
I will go, but if you will not **g** with me,	Jgs 4:8
if you will not go with me, I will not **g**."	Jgs 4:8
And she said, "I will surely **g** with you.	Jgs 4:9
Does not the LORD **g** out before you?" So	Jgs 4:14
"**G** in this might of yours and save Israel	Jgs 6:14
I say to you, 'This one shall **g** with you,'	Jgs 7:4
one shall go with you,' shall **g** with you,	Jgs 7:4
to you, 'This one shall not **g** with you,'	Jgs 7:4
one shall not go with you,' shall not **g**."	Jgs 7:4
and let all the others **g** every man to his	Jgs 7:7
to him, "Arise, **g** down against the camp,	Jgs 7:9
But if you are afraid to **g** down, go down	Jgs 7:10
g down to the camp with Purah your	Jgs 7:10
be strengthened to **g** down against the	Jgs 7:11
honored, and **g** hold sway over the trees?'	Jgs 9:9
my good fruit and **g** hold sway over the	Jgs 9:11
God and men and **g** hold sway over the	Jgs 9:13
Now therefore, **g** by night, you and the	Jgs 9:32
G out now and fight with them."	Jgs 9:38
G and cry out to the gods whom you	Jgs 10:14
that you may **g** with us and fight with	Jgs 11:8
or did he ever **g** to war with them?	Jgs 11:25
that I may **g** up and down on the	Jgs 11:37
"**G**." Then he sent her away for two	Jgs 11:38
and did not call us to **g** with you?	Jgs 12:1
"Let me **g** over," the men of Gilead said	Jgs 12:5
that you must **g** to take a wife from the	Jgs 14:3
"I will **g** in to my wife in the chamber."	Jgs 15:1
her father would not allow him to **g** in.	Jgs 15:1
he let the foxes **g** into the standing grain	Jgs 15:5
"I will **g** out as at other times and shake	Jgs 16:20
"**G** and explore the land." And they came	Jgs 18:2
And the priest said to them, "**G** in peace.	Jgs 18:6
journey on which you **g** is under the eye	Jgs 18:6
"Arise, and let us **g** up against them,	Jgs 18:9
Do not be slow to **g**, to enter in and	Jgs 18:9
As soon as you **g**, you will come to an	Jgs 18:10
that I made and the priest, and **g** away,	Jgs 18:24
in the morning, and he prepared to **g**,	Jgs 19:5
of bread, and after that you may **g**."	Jgs 19:5
And when the man rose up to **g**, his	Jgs 19:7
morning for your journey, and **g** home."	Jgs 19:9
to **g** in and spend the night at Gibeah.	Jgs 19:15
and made her **g** out to them.	Jgs 19:25
the dawn began to break, they let her **g**.	Jgs 19:25
the house and went out to **g** on his way,	Jgs 19:27
saying, "None of us will **g** to his tent,	Jgs 20:8
to Gibeah: we will **g** up against it by lot,	Jgs 20:9
cities to Gibeah to **g** out to battle	Jgs 20:14
"Who shall **g** up first for us to fight	Jgs 20:18
the LORD said, "Judah shall **g** up first."	Jgs 20:18
the LORD said, "**G** up against them."	Jgs 20:23
"Shall we **g** out once more to battle	Jgs 20:28
we cease?" And the LORD said, "**G** up,	Jgs 20:28
"**G** and strike the inhabitants of	Jgs 21:10
"**G** and lie in ambush in the vineyards	Jgs 21:20
Shiloh, and **g** to the land of Benjamin.	Jgs 21:21
"**G**, return each of you to her mother's	Ru 1:8
my daughters; why will you **g** with me?	Ru 1:11
g your way, for I am too old to have a	Ru 1:12
following you. For where you **g** I will go,	Ru 1:16
For where you go I will **g**, and where you	Ru 1:16
that she was determined to **g** with her,	Ru 1:18
"Let me **g** to the field and glean among	Ru 2:2
And she said to her, "**G**, my daughter."	Ru 2:2
do not **g** to glean in another field or leave	Ru 2:8
that they are reaping, and **g** after them.	Ru 2:9
g to the vessels and drink what the young	Ru 2:9
that you **g** out with his young women,	Ru 2:22
on your cloak and **g** down to the	Ru 3:3
Then **g** and uncover his feet and lie down,	Ru 3:4
'You must not **g** back empty-handed to	Ru 3:17
this man used to **g** up year by year	1 Sm 1:3
long will you **g** on being drunk?	1 Sm 1:14
Then Eli answered, "**G** in peace, and	1 Sm 1:17
But Hannah did not **g** up, for she said	1 Sm 1:22
to be my priest, to **g** up to my altar,	1 Sm 2:28
of your father should **g** in and out	1 Sm 2:30
and he shall **g** in and out before my	1 Sm 2:35
Eli said to Samuel, "**G**, lie down,	1 Sm 3:9
today." And he said, "How did it **g**,	1 Sm 4:16
Then send it off and let it **g** its way	1 Sm 6:8
to whom shall he **g** up away from	1 Sm 6:20
may judge us and **g** out before us and	1 Sm 8:20
of Israel, "**G** every man to his city."	1 Sm 8:22
and arise, **g** and look for the donkeys."	1 Sm 9:3
was with him, "Come, let us **g** back,	1 Sm 9:5
says comes true. So now let us **g** there.	1 Sm 9:6
he can tell us the way we should **g**."	1 Sm 9:6
Saul said to his servant, "But if we **g**,	1 Sm 9:7
let us **g** to the seer," for today's	1 Sm 9:9
let us **g**." So they went to the city	1 Sm 9:10
who are invited will eat. Now **g** up,	1 Sm 9:13
G up before me to the high place, for	1 Sm 9:19
I will let you **g** and will tell you	1 Sm 9:19
Then you shall **g** on from there	1 Sm 10:3
Then **g** down before me to Gilgal. And	1 Sm 10:8
"Where did you **g**?" And he said,	1 Sm 10:14
let us **g** to Gilgal and there renew the	1 Sm 11:14
let us **g** over to the Philistine garrison	1 Sm 14:1
Jonathan sought to **g** over to the	1 Sm 14:4
let us **g** over to the garrison of these	1 Sm 14:6
place, and we will not **g** up to them.	1 Sm 14:9
'Come up to us,' then we will **g** up,	1 Sm 14:10
"Let us **g** down after the Philistines	1 Sm 14:36
"Shall I **g** down after the Philistines?	1 Sm 14:37
Now **g** and strike Amalek and devote	1 Sm 15:3
Saul said to the Kenites, "**G**, depart;	1 Sm 15:6
g down from among the Amalekites,	1 Sm 15:6
'**G**, devote to destruction the sinners,	1 Sm 15:18
As Samuel turned to **g** away, Saul	1 Sm 15:27
Israel? Fill your horn with oil, and **g**.	1 Sm 16:1
And Samuel said, "How can I **g**? If	1 Sm 16:2
Your servant will **g** and fight with	1 Sm 17:32
not able to **g** against this Philistine	1 Sm 17:33
"**G**, and the LORD be with you!"	1 Sm 17:37
And he tried in vain to **g**, for he had	1 Sm 17:39
said to Saul, "I cannot **g** with these,	1 Sm 17:39
as Saul saw David **g** out against the	1 Sm 17:55
And I will **g** out and stand beside my	1 Sm 19:3
me thus and let my enemy **g**,	1 Sm 19:17
Saul, "He said to me, 'Let me **g**.	1 Sm 19:17
But let me **g**, that I may hide myself in	1 Sm 20:5
let us **g** out into the field." So they	1 Sm 20:11
you away, that you may **g** in safety.	1 Sm 20:13
On the third day **g** down quickly to	1 Sm 20:19
man, saying, '**G**, find the arrows.'	1 Sm 20:21
the arrows are beyond you,' then **g**,	1 Sm 20:22
asked leave of me to **g** to Bethlehem.	1 Sm 20:28
He said, 'Let me **g**, for our clan holds	1 Sm 20:29
him, "**G** and carry them to the city."	1 Sm 20:40
Jonathan said to David, "**G** in peace,	1 Sm 20:42
as always when I **g** on an expedition.	1 Sm 21:5
and **g** into the land of Judah." So	1 Sm 22:5
"Shall I **g** and attack these	1 Sm 23:2
"**G** and attack the Philistines and save	1 Sm 23:2
more then if we **g** to Keilah against	1 Sm 23:3
him, "Arise, **g** down to Keilah,	1 Sm 23:4
the people to war, to **g** down to Keilah,	1 Sm 23:8
and they went wherever they could **g**.	1 Sm 23:13
G, make yet more sure. Know and	1 Sm 23:22
information. Then I will **g** with you.	1 Sm 23:23
enemy, will he let him **g** away safe?	1 Sm 24:19
to the young men, "**G** up to Carmel,	1 Sm 25:5
and **g** to Nabal and greet him in my	1 Sm 25:5
to her young men, "**G** on before me;	1 Sm 25:19
to her, "**G** up in peace to your house.	1 Sm 25:35
"Who will **g** down with me into the	1 Sm 26:6
said, "I will **g** down with you."	1 Sm 26:6
or he will **g** down into battle and	1 Sm 26:10
and the jar of water, and let us **g**."	1 Sm 26:11
LORD, saying, '**G**, serve other gods.'	1 Sm 26:19
and your men are to **g** out with me in	1 Sm 28:1
that I may **g** to her and inquire of	1 Sm 28:7
strength when you **g** on your way."	1 Sm 28:22
He shall not **g** down with us to battle,	1 Sm 29:4
So **g** back now; and go peaceably, that	1 Sm 29:7
So go back now; and **g** peaceably, that	1 Sm 29:7
that I may not **g** and fight against the	1 Sm 29:8
'He shall not **g** up with us to the	1 Sm 29:9
said, "Because they did not **g** with us,	1 Sm 30:22
And David said to him, "How did it **g**?	2 Sm 1:4
"**G**, execute him." And he struck him	2 Sm 1:15
"Shall I **g** up into any of the cities of	2 Sm 2:1
LORD said to him, "**G** up." David said,	2 Sm 2:1
"To which shall I **g** up?" And he said,	2 Sm 2:1
to him, "**G**, return." And he returned.	2 Sm 3:16
"I will arise and **g** and will gather all	2 Sm 3:21
to the king, and he has let him **g**,	2 Sm 3:23
"Shall I **g** up against the Philistines?	2 Sm 5:19
And the LORD said to David, "**G** up,	2 Sm 5:19
the LORD, he said, "You shall not **g** up;	2 Sm 5:23
g around to their rear, and come	2 Sm 5:23
king, "**G**, do all that is in your heart,	2 Sm 7:3
"**G** and tell my servant David, 'Thus	2 Sm 7:5
the time when kings **g** out to battle,	2 Sm 11:1
"**G** down to your house and wash	2 Sm 11:8
lord, and did not **g** down to his house.	2 Sm 11:9
"Uriah did not **g** down to his house,"	2 Sm 11:10
Why did you not **g** down to your	2 Sm 11:10
field. Shall I then **g** to my house,	2 Sm 11:11
but he did not **g** down to his house.	2 Sm 11:13
'Why did you **g** so near the city to	2 Sm 11:20
Why did you **g** so near the wall?'	2 Sm 11:21
him back again? I shall **g** to him,	2 Sm 12:23
"**G** to your brother Amnon's house	2 Sm 13:7
And Amnon said to her, "Get up! **G**!"	2 Sm 13:15
and his servants **g** with your	2 Sm 13:24
"No, my son, let us not all **g**,	2 Sm 13:25
but he would not **g** but gave him his	2 Sm 13:25
my brother Amnon **g** with us." And	2 Sm 13:26
him, "Why should he **g** with you?"	2 Sm 13:26
and all the king's sons **g** with him.	2 Sm 13:27
the king longed to **g** out to Absalom,	2 Sm 13:39
G to the king and speak thus to him."	2 Sm 14:3
said to the woman, "**G** to your house,	2 Sm 14:8
g, bring back the young man	2 Sm 14:21
g and set it on fire." So Absalom's	2 Sm 14:30
therefore let me **g** into the presence	2 Sm 14:32
"Please let me **g** and pay my vow,	2 Sm 15:7
"**G** in peace." So he arose and went to	2 Sm 15:9
G quickly, lest he overtake us	2 Sm 15:14

Gittite, "Why do you also **g** with us? 2 Sm 15:19
G back and stay with the king, for 2 Sm 15:19
with us, since I **g** I know not where? 2 Sm 15:20
G back and take your brothers with 2 Sm 15:20
And David said to Ittai, "**G** then, pass 2 Sm 15:22
G back to the city in peace, with 2 Sm 15:27
said to him, "If you **g** on with me, 2 Sm 15:33
Let me **g** over and take off his head." 2 Sm 16:9
did you not **g** with your friend?" 2 Sm 16:17
"**G** in to your father's concubines, 2 Sm 16:21
and that you **g** to battle in person. 2 Sm 17:11
servant was to **g** and tell them, 2 Sm 17:17
and they were to **g** and tell King 2 Sm 17:17
"Arise, and **g** quickly over the water, 2 Sm 17:21
"I myself will also **g** out with you." 2 Sm 18:2
the men said, "You shall not **g** out. 2 Sm 18:3
"**G**, tell the king what you have 2 Sm 18:21
g out and speak kindly to your 2 Sm 19:7
for I swear by the LORD, if you do not **g**, 2 Sm 19:7
to him, "Why did you not **g** with me, 2 Sm 19:25
I may ride on it and **g** with the king.' 2 Sm 19:26
that I should **g** up with the king to 2 Sm 19:34
Your servant will **g** a little way over 2 Sm 19:36
Let him **g** over with my lord the 2 Sm 19:37
"Chimham shall **g** over with me, 2 Sm 19:38
for them, but did not **g** in to them. 2 Sm 20:3
"You shall no longer **g** out with us to 2 Sm 21:17
saying, "**G**, number Israel and Judah." 2 Sm 24:1
"**G** through all the tribes of Israel, 2 Sm 24:2
"**G** and say to David, 'Thus says the 2 Sm 24:12
day to David and said to him, "**G** up, 2 Sm 24:18
G in at once to King David, and say to 1 Kgs 1:13
said to him, "**G** to your house." 1 Kgs 1:53
"I am about to **g** the way of all the 1 Kgs 2:2
let his gray head **g** down to Sheol in 1 Kgs 2:6
priest the king said, "**G** to Anathoth, 1 Kgs 2:26
saying, "**G**, strike him down." 1 Kgs 2:29
and do not **g** out from there to any 1 Kgs 2:36
on the day you **g** out and cross the 1 Kgs 2:37
that on the day you **g** out and go to 1 Kgs 2:42
you go out and **g** to any place 1 Kgs 2:42
I do not know how to **g** out or come in. 1 Kgs 3:7
make it into rafts to **g** by sea to the 1 Kgs 5:9
"If your people **g** out to battle against 1 Kgs 8:44
but **g** and serve other gods and 1 Kgs 9:6
that he should not **g** after other gods. 1 Kgs 11:10
that I may **g** to my own country." 1 Kgs 11:21
are now seeking to **g** to your own 1 Kgs 11:22
said to them, "**G** away for three days, 1 Kgs 12:5
You shall not **g** up or fight against 1 Kgs 12:24
If this people **g** up to offer sacrifices 1 Kgs 12:27
your house, I will not **g** in with you. 1 Kgs 13:8
way did he **g**?" And his sons 1 Kgs 13:12
return with you, or **g** in with you, 1 Kgs 13:16
the wife of Jeroboam, and **g** to Shiloh. 1 Kgs 14:2
and a jar of honey, and **g** to him. 1 Kgs 14:3
G, tell Jeroboam, 'Thus says the LORD, 1 Kgs 14:7
Arise therefore, **g** to your house. 1 Kgs 14:12
permit no one to **g** out or come in 1 Kgs 15:17
G, break your covenant with 1 Kgs 15:19
"Arise, **g** to Zarephath, which 1 Kgs 17:9
sticks that I may **g** in and prepare it 1 Kgs 17:12
not fear; **g** and do as you have said. 1 Kgs 17:13
saying, "**G**, show yourself to Ahab, 1 Kgs 18:1
"**G** through the land to all the springs 1 Kgs 18:5
G, tell your lord, 'Behold, Elijah is 1 Kgs 18:8
And now you say, '**G**, tell your lord, 1 Kgs 18:11
And now you say, '**G**, tell your lord, 1 Kgs 18:14
long will you **g** limping between two 1 Kgs 18:21
And Elijah said to Ahab, "**G** up, eat 1 Kgs 18:41
he said to his servant, "**G** up now, 1 Kgs 18:43
And he said, "**G** again," seven times. 1 Kgs 18:43
from the sea." And he said, "**G** up, 1 Kgs 18:44
'Prepare your chariot and **g** down, 1 Kgs 18:44
"**G** out and stand on the mount 1 Kgs 19:11
"**G**, return on your way to the 1 Kgs 19:15
And he said to him, "**G** back again, 1 Kgs 19:20
on our heads and **g** out to the king 1 Kgs 20:31
"**G** and bring him." Then 1 Kgs 20:33
"I will let you **g** on these terms." So 1 Kgs 20:34
a covenant with him and let him **g**. 1 Kgs 20:34
'Because you have let **g** out of your 1 Kgs 20:42
Ahab arose to **g** down to the 1 Kgs 21:16
g down to meet Ahab king of Israel, 1 Kgs 21:18
"Will you **g** with me to battle at 1 Kgs 22:4
"Shall I **g** to battle against 1 Kgs 22:6
shall I refrain?" And they said, "**G** up, 1 Kgs 22:6
"**G** up to Ramoth-gilead and 1 Kgs 22:12
shall we **g** to Ramoth-gilead to 1 Kgs 22:15
answered him, "**G** up and triumph; 1 Kgs 22:15
that he may **g** up and fall at 1 Kgs 22:20
And he said, 'I will **g** out, and will be 1 Kgs 22:22
you shall succeed; **g** out and do so.' 1 Kgs 22:22
Spirit of the LORD **g** from me to speak 1 Kgs 22:24
that day when you **g** into an inner 1 Kgs 22:25
disguise myself and **g** into battle, 1 Kgs 22:30
ships of Tarshish to **g** to Ophir for 1 Kgs 22:48
to Ophir for gold, but they did not **g**, 1 Kgs 22:48
"Let my servants **g** with your 1 Kgs 22:49
them, "**G**, inquire of Baal-zebub, 2 Kgs 1:2
g up to meet the messengers of the 2 Kgs 1:3
us, '**G** back to the king who sent you, 2 Kgs 1:6
said to Elijah, "**G** down with him; 2 Kgs 1:15
two of them could **g** over on dry 2 Kgs 2:8
Please let them **g** and seek your 2 Kgs 2:16
"Did I not say to you, 'Do not **g**'?" 2 Kgs 2:18
city and jeered at him, saying, "**G** up, 2 Kgs 2:23
you baldhead! **G** up, you baldhead!" 2 Kgs 2:23
Will you **g** with me to battle against 2 Kgs 3:7
against Moab?" And he said, "I will **g**. 2 Kgs 3:7
G to the prophets of your father and 2 Kgs 3:13
Then he said, "**G** outside, borrow 2 Kgs 4:3
Then **g** in and shut the door behind 2 Kgs 4:4
said, "**G**, sell the oil and pay your debts, 2 Kgs 4:7
he comes to us, he can **g** in there." 2 Kgs 4:10
that I may quickly **g** to the man of 2 Kgs 4:22
said, "Why will you **g** to him today? 2 Kgs 4:23
and take my staff in your hand and **g**. 2 Kgs 4:29
And the king of Syria said, "**G** now, 2 Kgs 5:5
"**G** and wash in the Jordan seven 2 Kgs 5:10
"**G** in peace." But when Naaman had 2 Kgs 5:19
"Did not my heart **g** when the man 2 Kgs 5:26
Let us **g** to the Jordan and each of us 2 Kgs 6:2
to dwell there." And he answered, "**G**." 2 Kgs 6:2
"Be pleased to **g** with your servants." 2 Kgs 6:3
servants." And he answered, "I will **g**." 2 Kgs 6:3
And he said, "**G** and see where he is, 2 Kgs 6:13
eat and drink and **g** to their master." 2 Kgs 6:22
let us **g** over to the camp of the Syrians. 2 Kgs 7:4
arose at twilight to **g** to the camp of 2 Kgs 7:5
let us **g** and tell the king's household." 2 Kgs 7:9
of the Syrians, saying, "**G** and see." 2 Kgs 7:14
present with you and **g** to meet the 2 Kgs 8:8
Elisha said to him, "**G**, say to him, 2 Kgs 8:10
in your hand, and **g** to Ramoth-gilead. 2 Kgs 9:1
And **g** in and have him rise from 2 Kgs 9:2
out of the city to **g** and tell the news in 2 Kgs 9:15
"**G** in and strike them down; 2 Kgs 10:25
his men who were to **g** off duty on the 2 Kgs 11:9
his face to **g** up against Jerusalem, 2 Kgs 12:17
he caused to **g** around the house 2 Kgs 16:18
and let him **g** and dwell there and 2 Kgs 17:27
said to me, **G** up against this land, 2 Kgs 18:25
out of Jerusalem shall **g** a remnant, 2 Kgs 19:31
third day you shall **g** up to the house 2 Kgs 20:5
and that I shall **g** up to the house of 2 Kgs 20:8
shall the shadow **g** forward ten steps, 2 Kgs 20:9
ten steps, or **g** back ten steps?" 2 Kgs 20:9
let the shadow **g** back ten steps." 2 Kgs 20:10
"**G** up to Hilkiah the high priest, that 2 Kgs 22:4
"**G**, inquire of the LORD for me, and 2 Kgs 22:13
expert in war, 44,760, able to **g** to war. 1 Chr 5:18
warriors, 17,200, able to **g** to war. 1 Chr 7:11
"Shall I **g** up against the Philistines? 1 Chr 14:10
And the LORD said to him, "**G** up, 1 Chr 14:10
him, "You shall not **g** up after them; 1 Chr 14:14
g around and come against them 1 Chr 14:14
balsam trees, then **g** out to battle, 1 Chr 14:15
"**G** and tell my servant David, 'Thus 1 Chr 17:4
the time when kings **g** out to battle, 1 Chr 20:1
of the army, "**G**, number Israel, 1 Chr 21:2
"**G** and say to David, 'Thus says the 1 Chr 21:10
that David should **g** up and raise 1 Chr 21:18
but David could not **g** before it to 1 Chr 21:30
and knowledge to **g** out and come 2 Chr 1:10
"If your people **g** out to battle against 2 Chr 6:34
LORD God, and **g** to your resting place, 2 Chr 6:41
and **g** and serve other gods and 2 Chr 7:19
You shall not **g** up or fight against 2 Chr 11:4
and did not **g** against Jeroboam. 2 Chr 11:4
permit no one to **g** out or come in 2 Chr 16:1
G, break your covenant with Baasha 2 Chr 16:3
induced him to **g** up against 2 Chr 18:2
"Will you **g** with me to 2 Chr 18:3
"Shall we **g** to battle against 2 Chr 18:5
shall I refrain?" And they said, "**G** up, 2 Chr 18:5
"**G** up to Ramoth-gilead and 2 Chr 18:11
shall we **g** to Ramoth-gilead to 2 Chr 18:14
he answered, "**G** up and triumph; 2 Chr 18:14
that he may **g** up and fall at 2 Chr 18:19
And he said, 'I will **g** out, and will be 2 Chr 18:21
you shall succeed; **g** out and do so.' 2 Chr 18:21
Spirit of the LORD **g** from me to 2 Chr 18:23
that day when you **g** into an inner 2 Chr 18:24
disguise myself and **g** into battle, 2 Chr 18:29
Tomorrow **g** down against them. 2 Chr 20:16
Tomorrow **g** out against them, and 2 Chr 20:17
in building ships to **g** to Tarshish, 2 Chr 20:36
and were not able to **g** to Tarshish. 2 Chr 20:37
and made Judah **g** astray. 2 Chr 21:11
who were to **g** off duty on the 2 Chr 23:8
"**G** out to the cities of Judah and 2 Chr 24:5
not let the army of Israel **g** with you, 2 Chr 25:7
But **g**, act, be strong for the battle. 2 Chr 25:8
from Ephraim to **g** home again. 2 Chr 25:10
not letting them **g** with him to 2 Chr 25:13
G out of the sanctuary, for you have 2 Chr 26:18
and he himself hurried to **g** out, 2 Chr 26:20
the kings of Judah had let **g** to ruin. 2 Chr 34:11
"**G**, inquire of the LORD for me and 2 Chr 34:21
his God be with him. Let him **g** up.'" 2 Chr 36:23
with him, and let him **g** up to Jerusalem, Ezr 1:3
God had stirred to **g** up to rebuild the Ezr 1:5
g and put them in the temple that is in Ezr 5:15
month he began to **g** up from Babylonia, Ezr 7:9
who freely offers to **g** to Jerusalem, Ezr 7:13
to go to Jerusalem, may **g** with you. Ezr 7:13
men from Israel to **g** up with me. Ezr 7:28
day of the first month, to **g** to Jerusalem. Ezr 8:31
as the stairs that **g** down from the City Neh 3:15
such as I could **g** into the temple and Neh 6:11
the temple and live? I will not **g** in." Neh 6:11
Then he said to them, "**G** your way. Eat Neh 8:10
"**G** out to the hills and bring branches Neh 8:15
them the way in which they should **g**. Neh 9:12
and you told them to **g** in to possess the Neh 9:15
them the way by which they should **g**. Neh 9:19
king, let a royal order **g** out from him, Est 1:19
each young woman to **g** in to King Est 2:12
In the evening she would **g** in, and in the Est 2:14
She would not **g** in to the king again, Est 2:14
as his own daughter, to **g** in to the king, Est 2:15
and ordered him to **g** to Mordecai to learn Est 4:5
her and command her to **g** to the king to Est 4:8
commanded him to **g** to Mordecai and Est 4:10
"**G**, gather all the Jews to be found in Est 4:16
fast as you do. Then I will **g** to the king, Est 4:16
Then **g** joyfully with the king to the Est 5:14
His sons used to **g** and hold a feast in the Jb 1:4
they **g** up into the waste and perish. Jb 6:18
They **g** by like skiffs of reed, like an eagle Jb 9:26
before I **g**—and I shall not return— Jb 10:21
a multitude of words **g** unanswered, Jb 11:2
have come I shall **g** the way from which Jb 16:22
Will it **g** down to the bars of Sheol? Jb 17:16
he is loath to let it **g** and holds it in his Jb 20:13
and in peace they **g** down to Sheol. Jb 21:13
and those who **g** before him are Jb 21:33
"Behold, I **g** forward, but he is not there, Jb 23:8
in the desert the poor **g** out to their toil, Jb 24:5
They **g** about naked, without clothing; Jb 24:10
my righteousness and will not let it **g**; Jb 27:6
I **g** about darkened, but not by the sun; I Jb 30:28
kept silence, and did not **g** out of doors— Jb 31:34
that he should **g** before God in Jb 34:23
Under the whole heaven he lets it **g**, and Jb 37:3
Then the beasts **g** into their lairs, and Jb 37:8
that they may **g** and say to you, Jb 38:35
they **g** out and do not return to them. Jb 39:4
"Who has let the wild donkey **g** free? Jb 39:5
Out of his mouth **g** flaming torches; Jb 41:19
and seven rams and **g** to my servant Job Jb 42:8
shall bow all who **g** down to the dust, Ps 22:29
in innocence and **g** around your altar, Ps 26:6
become like those who **g** down to the pit. Ps 28:1
from among those who **g** down to the pit. Ps 30:3
there in my death, if I **g** down to the pit? Ps 30:9
to shame; let them **g** silently to Sheol. Ps 31:17
and teach you in the way you should **g**; Ps 32:8
all the day I **g** about mourning. Ps 38:6
proud, to those who **g** astray after a lie! Ps 40:4
how I would **g** with the throng and lead Ps 42:4
Why do I **g** mourning because of the Ps 42:9
Why do I **g** about mourning because of Ps 43:2
Then I will **g** to the altar of God, to God Ps 43:4
Walk about Zion, **g** around her, Ps 48:12
her ramparts, **g** through her citadels, Ps 48:13
his glory will not **g** down after him. Ps 49:17
his soul will **g** to the generation of his Ps 49:19
Day and night they **g** around it on its Ps 55:10
them; let them **g** down to Sheol alive; Ps 55:15
they **g** astray from birth, speaking lies. Ps 58:3
You do not **g** forth, O God, with our Ps 60:10
are a delusion; in the balances they **g** up; Ps 62:9
destroy my life shall **g** down into the Ps 63:9
As they **g** through the Valley of Baca Ps 84:6
They **g** from strength to strength; each Ps 84:7
Righteousness will **g** before him and Ps 85:13
counted among those who **g** down to the Ps 88:4
love and faithfulness **g** before you. Ps 89:14
are a people who **g** astray in their heart, Ps 95:10
There **g** the ships, and Leviathan, Ps 104:26
You do not **g** out, O God, with our Ps 108:11
nor do any who **g** down into silence. Ps 115:17
spurn all who **g** astray from your Ps 119:118

me, "Let us **g** to the house of the LORD!" Ps 122:1
to which the tribes **g** up, the tribes of Ps 122:4
that you rise up early and **g** late to rest, Ps 127:2
"Let us **g** to his dwelling place; let us Ps 132:7
O LORD, and **g** to your resting place, Ps 132:8
Where shall I **g** from your Spirit? Or Ps 139:7
lest I be like those who **g** down to the pit. Ps 143:7
Make me know the way I should **g**, for Ps 143:8
whole, like those who **g** down to the pit; Prv 1:12
none who **g** to her come back, nor do Prv 2:19
to your neighbor, "**G**, and come again, Prv 3:28
Keep hold of instruction; do not let **g**; Prv 4:13
Avoid it; do not **g** on it; turn away from Prv 4:15
Her feet **g** down to death; her steps follow Prv 5:5
and do not **g** near the door of her house, Prv 5:8
and your labors **g** to the house of a Prv 5:10
g, hasten, and plead urgently with your Prv 6:3
G to the ant, O sluggard; consider her Prv 6:6
who touches her will **g** unpunished. Prv 6:29
does not let the righteous **g** hungry, Prv 10:3
an evil person will not **g** unpunished, Prv 11:21
Do they not **g** astray who devise evil? Prv 14:22
to be reproved; he will not **g** to the wise. Prv 15:12
be assured, he will not **g** unpunished. Prv 16:5
glad at calamity will not **g** unpunished. Prv 17:5
they **g** down into the inner parts of the Prv 18:8
A false witness will not **g** unpunished, Prv 19:5
more do his friends **g** far from him! Prv 19:7
A false witness will not **g** unpunished, Prv 19:9
but the simple **g** on and suffer for it. Prv 22:3
up a child in the way he should **g**; Prv 22:6
out a scoffer, and strife will **g** out, Prv 22:10
to anger, nor **g** with a wrathful man, Prv 22:24
wine; those who **g** to try mixed wine. Prv 23:30
they **g** down into the inner parts of the Prv 26:22
and do not **g** to your brother's house Prv 27:10
but the simple **g** on and suffer for it. Prv 27:12
to be rich will not **g** unpunished. Prv 28:20
Her lamp does not **g** out at night. Prv 31:18
All **g** to one place. All are from the Eccl 3:20
your steps when you **g** to the house of Eccl 5:1
his mother's womb he shall **g** again, Eccl 5:15
just as he came, so shall he **g**, and Eccl 5:16
no good—do not all **g** to the one place? Eccl 6:6
It is better to **g** to the house of mourning Eccl 7:2
of mourning than to **g** to the house of Eccl 7:2
Be not hasty to **g** from his presence. Do Eccl 8:3
They used to **g** in and out of the holy Eccl 8:10
for this will **g** with him in his toil Eccl 8:15
live, and after that they **g** to the dead. Eccl 9:3
G, eat your bread in joy, and drink your Eccl 9:7
and the mourners **g** about the streets— Eccl 12:5
I will rise now and **g** about the city, in the Sg 3:2
would not let him **g** until I had brought Sg 3:4
G out, O daughters of Zion, and look Sg 3:11
I will **g** away to the mountain of myrrh Sg 4:6
let us **g** out into the fields and lodge in Sg 7:11
let us **g** out early to the vineyards and see Sg 7:12
let us **g** up to the mountain of the LORD, Is 2:3
his paths." For out of Zion shall **g** the law, Is 2:3
with their eyes, mincing along as they **g**, Is 3:16
Therefore my people **g** into exile for lack Is 5:13
their honored men **g** hungry, and their Is 5:13
Jerusalem and her multitude will **g** down, Is 5:14
and their blossom **g** up like dust; Is 5:24
I send, and who will **g** for us?" Then I said, Is 6:8
And he said, "**G**, and say to this people: Is 6:9
LORD said to Isaiah, "**G** out to meet Ahaz, Is 7:3
"Let us **g** up against Judah and terrify it, Is 7:6
all its channels and **g** over all its banks, Is 8:7
who did not let his prisoners **g** home?' Is 14:17
who **g** down to the stones of the pit, Is 14:19
at the ascent of Luhith they **g** up weeping; Is 15:5
G, you swift messengers, to a nation, tall Is 18:2
"**G**, and loose the sackcloth from your Is 20:2
G up, O Elam; lay siege, O Media; all the Is 21:2
the Lord said to me: "**G**, set a watchman; Is 21:6
GOD of hosts, "Come, **g** to this steward, Is 22:15
g about the city, O forgotten prostitute! Is 23:16
a little, there a little, that they may **g**, Is 28:13
And those who **g** astray in spirit will Is 29:24
who set out to **g** down to Egypt, without Is 30:2
g, write it before them on a tablet and Is 30:8
of the flute to **g** to the mountain of Is 30:29
Woe to those who **g** down to Egypt for Is 31:1
where no galley with oars can **g**, Is 33:21
quenched; its smoke shall **g** up forever. Is 34:10
if they are fools, they shall not **g** astray. Is 35:8
G up against this land and destroy it.'" Is 36:10
For out of Jerusalem shall **g** a remnant, Is 37:32
"**G** and say to Hezekiah, Thus says the Is 38:5
those who **g** down to the pit do not hope Is 38:18
the sign that I shall **g** up to the house of Is 38:22
of the earth, you who **g** down to the sea, Is 42:10
"I will **g** before you and level the exalted Is 45:2
makers of idols **g** in confusion together. Is 45:16
burden, but themselves **g** into captivity. Is 46:2
Sit in silence, and **g** into darkness, O Is 47:5
who leads you in the way you should **g**. Is 48:17
G out from Babylon, flee from Chaldea, Is 48:20
who laid you waste **g** out from you. Is 49:17
for a law will **g** out from me, and I will set Is 51:4
he shall not die and **g** down to the pit, Is 51:14
Depart, depart, **g** out from there; touch Is 52:11
thing; **g** out from the midst of her; Is 52:11
For you shall not **g** out in haste, and you Is 52:12
in haste, and you shall not **g** in flight, Is 52:12
in flight, for the LORD will **g** before you, Is 52:12
of Noah should no more **g** over the earth, Is 54:9
"For you shall **g** out in joy and be led Is 55:12
of the yoke, to let the oppressed **g** free, Is 58:6
your righteousness shall **g** before you; Is 58:8
Your sun shall no more **g** down, nor Is 60:20
G through, go through the gates; prepare Is 62:10
Go through, **g** through the gates; prepare Is 62:10
his glorious arm to **g** at the right hand Is 63:12
Like livestock that **g** down into the Is 63:14
purify themselves to **g** into the gardens, Is 66:17
"And they shall **g** out and look on the Is 66:24
for to all to whom I send you, you shall **g**, Jer 1:7
"**G** and proclaim in the hearing of Jer 2:2
loved foreigners, and after them I will **g**.' Jer 2:25
How much you **g** about, changing your Jer 2:36
G, and proclaim these words toward the Jer 3:12
Jerusalem; lest my wrath **g** forth like fire, Jer 4:4
and let us **g** into the fortified cities!' Jer 4:5
I will **g** to the great and will speak to them, Jer 5:5
"**G** up through her vine rows and Jer 5:10
G not out into the field, nor walk on the Jer 6:25
and if you do not **g** after other gods to Jer 7:6
and **g** after other gods that you have not Jer 7:9
to **g** on doing all these abominations? Jer 7:10
G now to my place that was in Shiloh, Jer 7:12
let us **g** into the fortified cities and perish Jer 8:14
leave my people and **g** away from them! Jer 9:2
of Jerusalem will **g** and cry to Jer 11:12
G, assemble all the wild beasts; bring Jer 12:9
"**G** and buy a linen loincloth and put it Jer 13:1
g to the Euphrates and hide it there in a Jer 13:4
said to me, "Arise, **g** to the Euphrates, Jer 13:6
If I **g** out into the field, behold, those Jer 14:18
them out of my sight, and let them **g**! Jer 15:1
when they ask you, 'Where shall we **g**?' Jer 15:2
or **g** to lament or grieve for them, Jer 16:5
You shall not **g** into the house of Jer 16:8
"**G** and stand in the People's Gate, by Jer 17:19
of Judah enter and by which they **g** out, Jer 17:19
"Arise, and **g** down to the potter's house, Jer 18:2
"**G**, buy a potter's earthenware flask, Jer 19:1
and **g** out to the Valley of the Son of Jer 19:2
in the sight of the men who **g** with you, Jer 19:10
in your house, shall **g** into captivity. Jer 20:6
To Babylon you shall **g**, and there you Jer 20:6
robbed, lest my wrath **g** forth like fire, Jer 21:12
"**G** down to the house of the king of Jer 22:1
"**G** up to Lebanon, and cry out, and lift Jer 22:20
and your lovers shall **g** into captivity; Jer 22:22
Do not **g** after other gods to serve and Jer 25:6
name, and shall you **g** unpunished? Jer 25:29
You shall not **g** unpunished, for I am Jer 25:29
in Jerusalem may not **g** to Babylon. Jer 27:18
"**G**, tell Hananiah, 'Thus says the LORD: Jer 28:13
kinsmen who did not **g** out with you Jer 29:16
one of them, shall **g** into captivity; Jer 30:16
tambourines and shall **g** forth in the Jer 31:4
'Arise, and let us **g** up to Zion, to the LORD Jer 31:6
the measuring line shall **g** out farther, Jer 31:39
G and speak to Zedekiah king of Judah Jer 34:2
face to face. And you shall **g** to Babylon.' Jer 34:3
"**G** to the house of the Rechabites and Jer 35:2
and let us **g** to Jerusalem for fear of the Jer 35:11
G and say to the people of Judah and the Jer 35:13
and do not **g** after other gods to serve Jer 35:15
so you are to **g**, and on a day of fasting in Jer 36:6
officials said to Baruch, "**G** and hide, Jer 36:19
Chaldeans will surely **g** away from us," Jer 37:9
away from us," for they will not **g** away. Jer 37:9
out from Jerusalem to **g** to the land of Jer 37:12
"**G**, and say to Ebed-melech the Jer 39:16
of the guard had let him **g** from Ramah, Jer 40:1
g wherever you think it good and right Jer 40:4
you think it good and right to **g**. Jer 40:4
Or **g** wherever you think it right to go." Jer 40:5
you think it right to **g**." So the captain of Jer 40:5
of food and a present, and let him **g**. Jer 40:5
"Please let me **g** and strike down Jer 40:15
near Bethlehem, intending to **g** to Egypt Jer 41:17
God may show us the way we should **g**, Jer 42:3
'No, we will **g** to the land of Egypt, Jer 42:14
faces to enter Egypt and **g** to live there, Jer 42:15
who set their faces to **g** to Egypt to live Jer 42:17
poured out on you when you **g** to Egypt. Jer 42:18
O remnant of Judah, 'Do not **g** to Egypt.' Jer 42:19
the place where you desire to **g** to live." Jer 42:22
to say, 'Do not **g** to Egypt to live there,' Jer 43:2
and he shall **g** away from there in Jer 43:12
of war in all places to which you may **g**." Jer 45:5
Let the warriors **g** out: men of Cush and Jer 46:9
G up to Gilead, and take balm, O virgin Jer 46:11
and let us **g** back to our own people and Jer 46:16
'Noisy one who lets the hour **g** by.' Jer 46:17
the ascent of Luhith they **g** up weeping; Jer 48:5
and Chemosh shall **g** into exile with his Jer 48:7
For Milcom shall **g** into exile, with his Jer 49:3
must drink it, will you **g** unpunished? Jer 49:12
You shall not **g** unpunished, but you Jer 49:12
and **g** out of the land of the Chaldeans, Jer 50:8
"**G** up against the land of Merathaim, Jer 50:21
bulls; let them **g** down to the slaughter. Jer 50:27
held them fast; they refuse to let them **g**. Jer 50:33
and let us **g** each to his own country, Jer 51:9
"**G** out of the midst of her, my people! Jer 51:45
from the sword, **g**, do not stand still! Jer 51:50
Wherever the spirit would **g**, they went, Ezk 1:12
Wherever the spirit wanted to **g**, they Ezk 1:20
Eat this scroll, and **g**, speak to the house Ezk 3:1
g to the house of Israel and speak with Ezk 3:4
And **g** to the exiles, to your people, and Ezk 3:11
said to me, "Arise, **g** out into the valley, Ezk 3:22
"**G**, shut yourself within your house. Ezk 3:24
so that you cannot **g** out among the Ezk 3:25
over their eyes that **g** whoring after their Ezk 6:9
And he said to me, "**G** in, and see the vile Ezk 8:9
G out." So they went out and struck in Ezk 9:7
"**G** in among the whirling wheels Ezk 10:2
have said, '**G** far from the LORD; Ezk 11:15
and **g** into exile by day in their sight. Ezk 12:3
You shall **g** like an exile from your Ezk 12:3
and you shall **g** out yourself at evening Ezk 12:4
sight, as those do who must **g** into exile. Ezk 12:4
done to them. They shall **g** into exile, Ezk 12:11
his shoulder at dusk, and shall **g** out. Ezk 12:12
among the nations where they **g**, Ezk 12:16
let the souls whom you hunt **g** free, Ezk 13:20
Israel may no more **g** astray from me, Ezk 14:11
is the high place to which you **g**? Ezk 20:29
your fathers and **g** whoring after their Ezk 20:30
G serve every one of you his idols, now Ezk 20:39
in to her, as men **g** in to a prostitute. Ezk 23:44
corrosion does not **g** out of it. Ezk 24:12
I will not **g** back; I will not spare; I will Ezk 24:14
I will make you **g** down with those Ezk 26:20
down with those who **g** down to the Ezk 26:20
old, with those who **g** down to the pit, Ezk 26:20
day messengers shall **g** out from me Ezk 30:9
and the women shall **g** into captivity. Ezk 30:17
her daughters shall **g** into captivity. Ezk 30:18
man, with those who **g** down to the pit. Ezk 31:14
Sheol with those who **g** down to the Ezk 31:16
G down and be laid to rest with the Ezk 32:19
shame with those who **g** down to the Ezk 32:24
shame with those who **g** down to the Ezk 32:25
with those who **g** down to the pit. Ezk 32:29
shame with those who **g** down to the Ezk 32:30
will cut off from it all who come and **g**. Ezk 35:7
and yet they had to **g** out of his land.' Ezk 36:20
latter years you will **g** against the land Ezk 38:8
'I will **g** up against the land of Ezk 38:11
cities of Israel will **g** out and make fires Ezk 39:9
by seven steps people would **g** up to it, Ezk 40:22
and people would **g** up to it by ten Ezk 40:49
they shall not **g** out of it into the outer Ezk 42:14
garments before they **g** near to that Ezk 42:14
gate, and shall **g** out by the same way." Ezk 44:3
And when they **g** out into the outer Ezk 44:19
Then he shall **g** out, but the gate shall Ezk 46:2
and he shall **g** out by the same way. Ezk 46:8
gate to worship shall **g** out by the south Ezk 46:9
the south gate shall **g** out by the north Ezk 46:9
but each shall **g** out straight ahead. Ezk 46:9
enter with them, and when they **g** out, Ezk 46:10
and when they go out, he shall **g** out. Ezk 46:10
Then he shall **g** out, and after he has Ezk 46:12
who did not **g** astray when the people Ezk 48:11
and when I **g** out, behold, the prince of Dn 10:20
be plucked up and **g** to others besides Dn 11:4
and he shall **g** out with great fury to Dn 11:44
He said, "**G** your way, Daniel, for the Dn 12:9
But **g** your way till the end. And you Dn 12:13
"**G**, take to yourself a wife of whoredom Hos 1:2
And they shall **g** up from the land, for Hos 1:11
For she said, 'I will **g** after my lovers, Hos 2:5
'I will **g** and return to my first husband, Hos 2:7
And the LORD said to me, "**G** again, love a Hos 3:1
the men themselves **g** aside with Hos 4:14

not into Gilgal, nor **g** up to Beth-aven, Hos 4:15
and herds they shall **g** to seek the LORD, Hos 5:6
he was determined to **g** after filth. Hos 5:11
I, even I, will tear and **g** away; I will Hos 5:14
As they **g**, I will spread over them my Hos 7:12
They shall **g** after the LORD; he will Hos 11:10
G in, pass the night in sackcloth, O Jl 1:13
is ripe. **G** in, tread, for the winepress is full. Jl 3:13
people of Syria shall **g** into exile to Kir," Am 1:5
and their king shall **g** into exile, he and Am 1:15
a man and his father **g** in to the same Am 2:7
And you shall **g** out through the Am 4:3
stench of your camp **g** up into your Am 4:10
for Gilgal shall surely **g** into exile, and Am 5:5
and from there **g** to Hamath the great; Am 6:2
then **g** down to Gath of the Philistines. Am 6:2
now be the first of those who **g** into exile, Am 6:7
and Israel must **g** into exile away from Am 7:11
seer, **g**, flee away to the land of Judah, Am 7:12
to me, '**G**, prophesy to my people Israel.' Am 7:15
and Israel shall surely **g** into exile away Am 7:17
"I will make the sun **g** down at noon and Am 8:9
And if they **g** into captivity before their Am 9:4
Saviors shall **g** up to Mount Zion to rule Ob 1:21
"Arise, **g** to Nineveh, that great city, and Jon 1:2
on board, to **g** with them to Tarshish, Jon 1:3
"Arise, **g** to Nineveh, that great city, and Jon 3:2
Jonah began to **g** into the city, going a Jon 3:4
and wail; I will **g** stripped and naked; Mi 1:8
for they shall **g** from you into exile. Mi 1:16
Arise and **g**, for this is no place to rest, Mi 2:10
If a man should **g** about and utter wind Mi 2:11
The sun shall **g** down on the prophets, Mi 3:6
let us **g** up to the mountain of the LORD, Mi 4:2
For out of Zion shall **g** forth the law, Mi 4:2
for now you shall **g** out from the city Mi 4:10
open country; you shall **g** to Babylon. Mi 4:10
they stumble as they **g**, they hasten to the Na 2:5
will be drunken; you will **g** into hiding; Na 3:11
strengthen your forts; **g** into the clay; Na 3:14
justice and dignity **g** forth from Hab 1:7
they sweep by like the wind and **g** on, Hab 1:11
G up to the hills and bring wood and Hg 1:8
the horses and their riders shall **g** down, Hg 2:22
country, the white ones **g** after them, Zec 6:6
and the dappled ones **g** toward the south Zec 6:6
they were impatient to **g** and patrol the Zec 6:7
"**G**, patrol the earth." So they patrolled Zec 6:7
those who **g** toward the north country Zec 6:8
and **g** the same day to the house of Zec 6:10
of one city shall **g** to another, Zec 8:21
'Let us **g** at once to entreat the favor of Zec 8:21
robe of a Jew, saying, 'Let us **g** with you, Zec 8:23
his arrow will **g** forth like lightning; Zec 9:14
slaughter them and **g** unpunished, Zec 11:5
Half of the city shall **g** out into exile, Zec 14:2
Then the LORD will **g** out and fight Zec 14:3
against Jerusalem shall **g** up year after Zec 14:16
of the earth do not **g** up to Jerusalem to Zec 14:17
of Egypt does not **g** up and present Zec 14:18
the nations that do not **g** up to keep the Zec 14:18
the nations that do not **g** up to keep the Zec 14:19
You shall **g** out leaping like calves from Mal 4:2
"**G** and search diligently for the child, Mt 2:8
and his mother and **g** to the land of Mt 2:20
his father Herod, he was afraid to **g** there, Mt 2:22
your gift there before the altar and **g**. Mt 5:24
than that your whole body **g** into hell. Mt 5:30
And if anyone forces you to **g** one mile, Mt 5:41
to go one mile, **g** with him two miles. Mt 5:41
g into your room and shut the door and Mt 6:6
that you say nothing to anyone, but **g**, Mt 8:4
And I say to one, '**G**,' and he goes, and to Mt 8:9
"**G**; let it be done for you as you have Mt 8:13
he gave orders to **g** over to the other side. Mt 8:18
I will follow you wherever you **g**." Mt 8:19
let me first **g** and bury my father." Mt 8:21
"**G**." So they came out and went into the Mt 8:32
—"Rise, pick up your bed and **g** home." Mt 9:6
G and learn what this means, 'I desire Mt 9:13
he said, "**G** away, for the girl is not dead Mt 9:24
"**G** nowhere among the Gentiles and Mt 10:5
but **g** rather to the lost sheep of the Mt 10:6
And proclaim as you **g**, saying, 'The Mt 10:7
"**G** and tell John what you hear and see: Mt 11:4
"What did you **g** out into the wilderness Mt 11:7
What then did you **g** out to see? A man Mt 11:8
What then did you **g** out to see? A Mt 11:9
do you want us to **g** and gather them?' Mt 13:28
the crowds away to **g** into the villages Mt 14:15
But Jesus said, "They need not **g** away; Mt 14:16
into the boat and **g** before him to the Mt 14:22
that he must **g** to Jerusalem and Mt 16:21
g to the sea and cast a hook and take Mt 17:27
on the mountains and **g** in search of Mt 18:12
against you, **g** and tell him his fault, Mt 18:15
g, sell what you possess and give to the Mt 19:21
for a camel to **g** through the eye of Mt 19:24
he said, 'You **g** into the vineyard too, Mt 20:4
to them, 'You **g** into the vineyard too.' Mt 20:7
Take what belongs to you and **g**. I Mt 20:14
them, "**G** into the village in front of you, Mt 21:2
'Son, **g** and work in the vineyard today.' Mt 21:28
And he answered, 'I **g**, sir,' but did not Mt 21:30
he answered, 'I go, sir,' but did not **g**. Mt 21:30
and the prostitutes **g** into the kingdom Mt 21:31
G therefore to the main roads and invite Mt 22:9
allow those who would enter to **g** in. Mt 23:13
on the housetop not **g** down to take Mt 24:17
he is in the wilderness,' do not **g** out. Mt 24:26
g rather to the dealers and buy for Mt 25:9
And these will **g** away into eternal Mt 25:46
"**G** into the city to a certain man and Mt 26:18
raised up, I will **g** before you to Galilee." Mt 26:32
"Sit here, while I **g** over there and pray." Mt 26:36
lest his disciples **g** and steal him away Mt 27:64
G, make it as secure as you can." Mt 27:65
Then **g** quickly and tell his disciples Mt 28:7
g and tell my brothers to go to Galilee, Mt 28:10
go and tell my brothers to **g** to Galilee, Mt 28:10
G therefore and make disciples of all Mt 28:19
to them, "Let us **g** on to the next towns, Mk 1:38
that you say nothing to anyone, but **g**, Mk 1:44
rise, pick up your bed, and **g** home." Mk 2:11
them, "Let us **g** across to the other side." Mk 4:35
"**G** home to your friends and tell them Mk 5:19
g in peace, and be healed of your Mk 5:34
them away to **g** into the surrounding Mk 6:36
"Shall we **g** and buy two hundred Mk 6:37
G and see." And when they had found Mk 6:38
get into the boat and **g** before him to the Mk 6:45
this statement you may **g** your way; Mk 7:29
than with two hands to **g** to hell, Mk 9:43
g, sell all that you have and give to the Mk 10:21
for a camel to **g** through the eye of Mk 10:25
And Jesus said to him, "**G** your way; Mk 10:52
them, "**G** into the village in front of you, Mk 11:2
Jesus had said, and they let them **g**. Mk 11:6
who is on the housetop not **g** down, Mk 13:15
will you have us **g** and prepare for you Mk 14:12
and said to them, "**G** into the city, Mk 14:13
up, I will **g** before you to Galilee." Mk 14:28
so that they might **g** and anoint him. Mk 16:1
But **g**, tell his disciples and Peter that he Mk 16:7
"**G** into all the world and proclaim the Mk 16:15
and he will **g** before him in the spirit Lk 1:17
for you will **g** before the Lord to prepare Lk 1:76
"Let us **g** over to Bethlehem and see this Lk 2:15
but "**g** and show yourself to the priest, Lk 5:14
you, rise, pick up your bed and **g** home." Lk 5:24
me: and I say to one, '**G**,' and he goes; Lk 7:8
"**G** and tell John what you have seen and Lk 7:22
"What did you **g** out into the wilderness Lk 7:24
What then did you **g** out to see? A man Lk 7:25
What then did you **g** out to see? A Lk 7:26
"Your faith has saved you; **g** in peace." Lk 7:50
but as they **g** on their way they are Lk 8:14
"Let us **g** across to the other side of the Lk 8:22
faith has made you well; **g** in peace." Lk 8:48
crowd away to **g** into the surrounding Lk 9:12
—unless we are to **g** and buy food for all Lk 9:13
up, he set his face to **g** to Jerusalem. Lk 9:51
him, "I will follow you wherever you **g**." Lk 9:57
let me first **g** and bury my father." Lk 9:59
g and proclaim the kingdom of God." Lk 9:60
place where he himself was about to **g**. Lk 10:1
G your way; behold, I am sending you Lk 10:3
his wages. Do not **g** from house to house. Lk 10:7
receive you, **g** into its streets and say, Lk 10:10
mercy." And Jesus said to him, "You **g**, Lk 10:37
has a friend will **g** to him at midnight Lk 11:5
As you **g** with your accuser before the Lk 12:58
he said to them, "**G** and tell that fox, Lk 13:32
I must **g** on my way today and Lk 13:33
are invited, **g** and sit in the lowest place, Lk 14:10
a field, and I must **g** out and see it. Lk 14:18
yoke of oxen, and I **g** to examine them. Lk 14:19
'**G** out quickly to the streets and lanes Lk 14:21
'**G** out to the highways and hedges and Lk 14:23
country, and **g** after the one that is lost, Lk 15:4
I will arise and **g** to my father, and I Lk 15:18
But he was angry and refused to **g** in. Lk 15:28
"**G** and show yourselves to the priests." Lk 17:14
he said to him, "Rise and **g** your way; Lk 17:19
here!' Do not **g** out or follow them. Lk 17:23
for a camel to **g** through the eye of Lk 18:25
"**G** into the village in front of you, Lk 19:30
time is at hand!' Do not **g** after them. Lk 21:8
"**G** and prepare the Passover for us, Lk 22:8
I am ready to **g** with you both to prison Lk 22:33
The next day Jesus decided to **g** to Galilee. Jn 1:43
Jesus said to her, "**G**, call your husband, Jn 4:16
"**G**; your son will live." The man believed Jn 4:50
Twelve, "Do you want to **g** away as well?" Jn 6:67
him, "Lord, to whom shall we **g**? Jn 6:68
in Galilee. He would not **g** about in Judea, Jn 7:1
said to him, "Leave here and **g** to Judea, Jn 7:3
You **g** up to the feast. I am not going up to Jn 7:8
does this man intend to **g** that we will not Jn 7:35
Does he intend to **g** to the Dispersion Jn 7:35
you; **g**, and from now on sin no more."]] Jn 8:11
"**G**, wash in the pool of Siloam" (which Jn 9:7
and said to me, '**G** to Siloam and wash.' Jn 9:11
will be saved and will **g** in and out and Jn 10:9
to the disciples, "Let us **g** to Judea again." Jn 11:7
fallen asleep, but I **g** to awaken him." Jn 11:11
you may believe. But let us **g** to him." Jn 11:15
to his fellow disciples, "Let us also **g**, Jn 11:16
her, saw Mary rise quickly and **g** out, Jn 11:31
to them, "Unbind him, and let him **g**." Jn 11:44
If we let him **g** on like this, everyone will Jn 11:48
have told you that I **g** to prepare a place Jn 14:2
And if I **g** and prepare a place for you, I Jn 14:3
I love the Father. Rise, let us **g** from here. Jn 14:31
you that you should **g** and bear fruit Jn 15:16
it is to your advantage that I **g** away, for if Jn 16:7
that I go away, for if I do not **g** away, Jn 16:7
to you. But if I **g**, I will send him to you. Jn 16:7
righteousness, because I **g** to the Father, Jn 16:10
he. So, if you seek me, let these men **g**." Jn 18:8
cloths lying there, but he did not **g** in. Jn 20:5
but **g** to my brothers and say to them, 'I Jn 20:17
"We will **g** with you." They went out and Jn 21:3
carry you where you do not want to **g**." Jn 21:18
way as you saw him **g** into heaven." Acts 1:11
Judas turned aside to **g** to his own Acts 1:25
and John about to **g** into the temple, Acts 3:3
threatened them, they let them **g**, Acts 4:21
"**G** and stand in the temple and speak Acts 5:20
in the name of Jesus, and let them **g**. Acts 5:40
'**G** out from your land and from your Acts 7:3
from your kindred and **g** into the land Acts 7:3
'Make for us gods who will **g** before us. Acts 7:40
"Rise and **g** toward the south to the Acts 8:26
Philip, "**G** over and join this chariot." Acts 8:29
"Rise and **g** to the street called Straight, Acts 9:11
"**G**, for he is a chosen instrument of Acts 9:15
Rise and **g** down and accompany Acts 10:20
And the Spirit told me to **g** with them, Acts 11:12
were appointed to **g** up to Jerusalem Acts 15:2
they attempted to **g** into Bithynia, Acts 16:7
we sought to **g** on into Macedonia, Acts 16:10
the police, saying, "Let those men **g**." Acts 16:35
magistrates have sent to let you **g**. Acts 16:36
come out now and **g** in peace." Acts 16:36
Jason and the rest, they let them **g**. Acts 17:9
From now on I will **g** to the Gentiles." Acts 18:6
but **g** on speaking and do not be silent, Acts 18:9
and Achaia and **g** to Jerusalem, Acts 19:21
when Paul wished to **g** in among the Acts 19:30
intending himself to **g** by land. Acts 20:13
telling Paul not to **g** on to Jerusalem. Acts 21:4
urged him not to **g** up to Jerusalem. Acts 21:12
to me, 'Rise, and **g** into Damascus, Acts 22:10
'**G**, for I will send you far away to the Acts 22:21
the soldiers to **g** down and take Acts 23:10
two hundred spearmen to **g** as far as Acts 23:23
letting the horsemen **g** on with him. Acts 23:32
and said, "**G** away for the present. Acts 24:25
he himself intended to **g** there shortly. Acts 25:4
authority among you **g** down with me, Acts 25:5
"Do you wish to **g** up to Jerusalem and Acts 25:9
have appealed; to Caesar you shall **g**." Acts 25:12
he wanted to **g** to Jerusalem and Acts 25:20
I decided to **g** ahead and send him. Acts 25:25
gave him leave to **g** to his friends and Acts 27:3
the wind did not allow us to **g** farther, Acts 27:7
the ropes of the ship's boat and let it **g**. Acts 27:32
"'**G** to this people, and say, You will Acts 28:26
to see you in passing as I **g** to Spain, Rom 15:24
by us not to **g** beyond what is written, 1 Cor 4:6
you would need to **g** out of the world. 1 Cor 5:10
does he dare **g** to law before the 1 Cor 6:1
to dinner and you are disposed to **g**, 1 Cor 10:27
as is right, and do not **g** on sinning. 1 Cor 15:34
seems advisable that I should **g** also, 1 Cor 16:4
help me on my journey, wherever I **g**. 1 Cor 16:6
Therefore **g** out from their midst, and 2 Cor 6:17
urge the brothers to **g** on ahead to you 2 Cor 9:5
I must **g** on boasting. Though there 2 Cor 12:1
I will **g** on to visions and revelations 2 Cor 12:1
I urged Titus to **g**, and sent the 2 Cor 12:18
nor did I **g** up to Jerusalem to those who Gal 1:17
that we should **g** to the Gentiles and they Gal 2:9
not let the sun **g** down on your anger, Eph 4:26

Then **G** said to Noah and to his sons with	Gn 9:8
And **G** said, "This is the sign of the	Gn 9:12
covenant between **G** and every	Gn 9:16
G said to Noah, "This is the sign of the	Gn 9:17
"Blessed be the LORD, the **G** of Shem;	Gn 9:26
May **G** enlarge Japheth, and let him	Gn 9:27
wine. (He was priest of **G** Most High.)	Gn 14:18
"Blessed be Abram by **G** Most High,	Gn 14:19
and blessed be **G** Most High, who has	Gn 14:20
my hand to the LORD, **G** Most High,	Gn 14:22
But Abram said, "O Lord **G**, what will	Gn 15:2
But he said, "O Lord **G**, how am I to	Gn 15:8
"You are a **G** of seeing," for she said,	Gn 16:13
and said to him, "I am **G** Almighty;	Gn 17:1
fell on his face. And **G** said to him,	Gn 17:3
to be **G** to you and to your offspring	Gn 17:7
possession, and I will be their **G**."	Gn 17:8
And **G** said to Abraham, "As for you,	Gn 17:9
And **G** said to Abraham, "As for Sarai	Gn 17:15
And Abraham said to **G**, "Oh that	Gn 17:18
G said, "No, but Sarah your wife shall	Gn 17:19
with him, **G** went up from Abraham.	Gn 17:22
that very day, as **G** had said to him.	Gn 17:23
when **G** destroyed the cities of the	Gn 19:29
G remembered Abraham and sent Lot	Gn 19:29
But **G** came to Abimelech in a dream	Gn 20:3
Then **G** said to him in the dream, "Yes, I	Gn 20:6
There is no fear of **G** at all in this place,	Gn 20:11
And when **G** caused me to wander	Gn 20:13
Then Abraham prayed to **G**, and God	Gn 20:17
to God, and **G** healed Abimelech,	Gn 20:17
the time of which **G** had spoken to him.	Gn 21:2
days old, as **G** had commanded him.	Gn 21:4
said, "**G** has made laughter for me;	Gn 21:6
But **G** said to Abraham, "Be not	Gn 21:12
And **G** heard the voice of the boy, and	Gn 21:17
and the angel of **G** called to Hagar	Gn 21:17
for **G** has heard the voice of the boy	Gn 21:17
Then **G** opened her eyes, and she saw a	Gn 21:19
And **G** was with the boy, and he grew	Gn 21:20
"**G** is with you in all that you do.	Gn 21:22
swear to me here by **G** that you will not	Gn 21:23
name of the LORD, the Everlasting **G**.	Gn 21:33
After these things **G** tested Abraham	Gn 22:1
to the place of which **G** had told him.	Gn 22:3
"**G** will provide for himself the lamb for	Gn 22:8
to the place of which **G** had told him,	Gn 22:9
to him, for now I know that you fear **G**,	Gn 22:12
lord; you are a prince of **G** among us.	Gn 23:6
the **G** of heaven and God of the earth,	Gn 24:3
the God of heaven and **G** of the earth,	Gn 24:3
The LORD, the **G** of heaven, who took me	Gn 24:7
"O LORD, **G** of my master Abraham,	Gn 24:12
LORD, the **G** of my master Abraham,	Gn 24:27
'O LORD, the **G** of my master Abraham,	Gn 24:42
LORD, the **G** of my master Abraham,	Gn 24:48
of Abraham, **G** blessed Isaac his son.	Gn 25:11
"I am the **G** of Abraham your father.	Gn 26:24
the LORD your **G** granted me success."	Gn 27:20
May **G** give you of the dew of heaven	Gn 27:28
G Almighty bless you and make you	Gn 28:3
your sojournings that **G** gave to	Gn 28:4
the angels of **G** were ascending and	Gn 28:12
the **G** of Abraham your father and the	Gn 28:13
your father and the **G** of Isaac.	Gn 28:13
This is none other than the house of **G**,	Gn 28:17
"If **G** will be with me and will keep me	Gn 28:20
in peace, then the LORD shall be my **G**,	Gn 28:21
and he said, "Am I in the place of **G**,	Gn 30:2
Then Rachel said, "**G** has judged me,	Gn 30:6
And **G** listened to Leah, and she	Gn 30:17
"**G** has given me my wages because I	Gn 30:18
"**G** has endowed me with a good	Gn 30:20
Then **G** remembered Rachel, and God	Gn 30:22
and **G** listened to her and opened her	Gn 30:22
said, "**G** has taken away my reproach."	Gn 30:23
But the **G** of my father has been with	Gn 31:5
But **G** did not permit him to harm me.	Gn 31:7
Thus **G** has taken away the livestock of	Gn 31:9
Then the angel of **G** said to me in the	Gn 31:11
I am the **G** of Bethel, where you	Gn 31:13
All the wealth that **G** has taken away	Gn 31:16
Now then, whatever **G** has said to you,	Gn 31:16
But **G** came to Laban the Aramean in	Gn 31:24
But the **G** of your father spoke to me	Gn 31:29
If the **G** of my father, the God of	Gn 31:42
the **G** of Abraham and the Fear of	Gn 31:42
G saw my affliction and the labor of	Gn 31:42
see, **G** is witness between you and me."	Gn 31:50
The **G** of Abraham and the God of	Gn 31:53
God of Abraham and the **G** of Nahor,	Gn 31:53
the God of Nahor, the **G** of their father,	Gn 31:53
his way, and the angels of **G** met him.	Gn 32:1
"O **G** of my father Abraham and God of	Gn 32:9
my father Abraham and **G** of my father	Gn 32:9
you have striven with **G** and with men,	Gn 32:28
saying, "For I have seen **G** face to face,	Gn 32:30
"The children whom **G** has graciously	Gn 33:5
face, which is like seeing the face of **G**,	Gn 33:10
because **G** has dealt graciously with	Gn 33:11
G said to Jacob, "Arise, go up to Bethel	Gn 35:1
altar there to the **G** who appeared to you	Gn 35:1
an altar to the **G** who answers me in	Gn 35:3
a terror from **G** fell upon the cities that	Gn 35:5
because there **G** had revealed himself to	Gn 35:7
G appeared to Jacob again, when he	Gn 35:9
And **G** said to him, "Your name is	Gn 35:10
And **G** said to him, "I am God	Gn 35:11
God said to him, "I am **G** Almighty:	Gn 35:11
Then **G** went up from him in the place	Gn 35:13
of the place where **G** had spoken with	Gn 35:15
great wickedness and sin against **G**?"	Gn 39:9
"Do not interpretations belong to **G**?	Gn 40:8
G will give Pharaoh a favorable	Gn 41:16
G has revealed to Pharaoh what he is	Gn 41:25
G has shown to Pharaoh what he is	Gn 41:28
means that the thing is fixed by **G**,	Gn 41:32
God, and **G** will shortly bring it about.	Gn 41:32
like this, in whom is the Spirit of **G**?"	Gn 41:38
"Since **G** has shown you all this,	Gn 41:39
"**G** has made me forget all my	Gn 41:51
"For **G** has made me fruitful in the	Gn 41:52
"Do this and you will live, for I fear **G**:	Gn 42:18
"What is this that **G** has done to us?"	Gn 42:28
May **G** Almighty grant you mercy	Gn 43:14
Your **G** and the God of your father has	Gn 43:23
Your God and the **G** of your father has	Gn 43:23
to me? **G** be gracious to you, my son!"	Gn 43:29
G has found out the guilt of your	Gn 44:16
for **G** sent me before you to preserve life.	Gn 45:5
And **G** sent me before you to preserve for	Gn 45:7
it was not you who sent me here, but **G**.	Gn 45:8
Joseph, **G** has made me lord of all Egypt.	Gn 45:9
offered sacrifices to the **G** of his father	Gn 46:1
And **G** spoke to Israel in visions of the	Gn 46:2
Then he said, "I am **G**, the God of your	Gn 46:3
he said, "I am God, the **G** of your father.	Gn 46:3
"**G** Almighty appeared to me at Luz in	Gn 48:3
whom **G** has given me here." And he	Gn 48:9
G has let me see your offspring also."	Gn 48:11
"The **G** before whom my fathers	Gn 48:15
the **G** who has been my shepherd all	Gn 48:15
'**G** make you as Ephraim and as	Gn 48:20
but **G** will be with you and will bring	Gn 48:21
by the **G** of your father who will help	Gn 49:25
the servants of the **G** of your father."	Gn 50:17
"Do not fear, for am I in the place of **G**?	Gn 50:19
against me, but **G** meant it for good,	Gn 50:20
but **G** will visit you and bring you up	Gn 50:24
swear, saying, "**G** will surely visit you,	Gn 50:25
But the midwives feared **G** and did not do	Ex 1:17
So **G** dealt well with the midwives. And	Ex 1:20
And because the midwives feared **G**, he	Ex 1:21
for rescue from slavery came up to **G**.	Ex 2:23
And **G** heard their groaning, and God	Ex 2:24
and **G** remembered his covenant with	Ex 2:24
G saw the people of Israel—and God	Ex 2:25
saw the people of Israel—and **G** knew.	Ex 2:25
and came to Horeb, the mountain of **G**.	Ex 3:1
to see, **G** called to him out of the bush,	Ex 3:4
And he said, "I am the **G** of your father,	Ex 3:6
the God of your father, the **G** of Abraham,	Ex 3:6
the God of Abraham, the **G** of Isaac,	Ex 3:6
and the **G** of Jacob." And Moses hid his	Ex 3:6
hid his face, for he was afraid to look at **G**.	Ex 3:6
But Moses said to **G**, "Who am I that I	Ex 3:11
you shall serve **G** on this mountain."	Ex 3:12
Then Moses said to **G**, "If I come to the	Ex 3:13
'The **G** of your fathers has sent me to	Ex 3:13
G said to Moses, "I AM WHO I AM." And	Ex 3:14
G also said to Moses, "Say this to the	Ex 3:15
of Israel, 'The LORD, the **G** of your fathers,	Ex 3:15
God of your fathers, the **G** of Abraham,	Ex 3:15
the God of Abraham, the **G** of Isaac,	Ex 3:15
the God of Isaac, and the **G** of Jacob,	Ex 3:15
to them, 'The LORD, the **G** of your fathers,	Ex 3:16
God of your fathers, the **G** of Abraham,	Ex 3:16
to him, 'The LORD, the **G** of the Hebrews,	Ex 3:18
that we may sacrifice to the LORD our **G**.'	Ex 3:18
that the LORD, the **G** of their fathers,	Ex 4:5
God of their fathers, the **G** of Abraham,	Ex 4:5
the God of Abraham, the **G** of Isaac,	Ex 4:5
the God of Isaac, and the **G** of Jacob,	Ex 4:5
Then **G** said, "Put your hand back inside	Ex 4:7
"If they will not believe you," **G** said, "or	Ex 4:8
mouth, and you shall be as **G** to him.	Ex 4:16
Moses took the staff of **G** in his hand.	Ex 4:20
at the mountain of **G** and kissed him.	Ex 4:27
"Thus says the LORD, the **G** of Israel,	Ex 5:1
"The **G** of the Hebrews has met with us.	Ex 5:3
that we may sacrifice to the LORD our **G**,	Ex 5:3
cry, 'Let us go and offer sacrifice to our **G**.'	Ex 5:8
G spoke to Moses and said to him, "I am	Ex 6:2
to Isaac, and to Jacob, as **G** Almighty,	Ex 6:3
you to be my people, and I will be your **G**,	Ex 6:7
shall know that I am the LORD your **G**,	Ex 6:7
"See, I have made you like **G** to Pharaoh,	Ex 7:1
to him, 'The LORD, the **G** of the Hebrews,	Ex 7:16
that there is no one like the LORD our **G**.	Ex 8:10
is the finger of **G**." But Pharaoh's heart	Ex 8:19
"Go, sacrifice to your **G** within the land."	Ex 8:25
to the LORD our **G** are an abomination to	Ex 8:26
sacrifice to the LORD our **G** as he tells us."	Ex 8:27
to the LORD your **G** in the wilderness;	Ex 8:28
'Thus says the LORD, the **G** of the Hebrews,	Ex 9:1
says the LORD, the **G** of the Hebrews,	Ex 9:13
that you do not yet fear the LORD **G**."	Ex 9:30
says the LORD, the **G** of the Hebrews,	Ex 10:3
go, that they may serve the LORD their **G**.	Ex 10:7
said to them, "Go, serve the LORD your **G**.	Ex 10:8
"I have sinned against the LORD your **G**,	Ex 10:16
with the LORD your **G** only to remove	Ex 10:17
that we may sacrifice to the LORD our **G**.	Ex 10:25
take of them to serve the LORD our **G**,	Ex 10:26
G did not lead them by way of the land	Ex 13:17
although that was near. For **G** said,	Ex 13:17
But **G** led the people around by the way	Ex 13:18
swear, saying, "**G** will surely visit you,	Ex 13:19
Then the angel of **G** who was going	Ex 14:19
this is my **G**, and I will praise him, my	Ex 15:2
God, and I will praise him, my father's **G**,	Ex 15:2
listen to the voice of the LORD your **G**,	Ex 15:26
shall know that I am the LORD your **G**.'"	Ex 16:12
the hill with the staff of **G** in my hand."	Ex 17:9
heard of all that **G** had done for Moses	Ex 18:1
said, "The **G** of my father was my help,	Ex 18:4
he was encamped at the mountain of **G**.	Ex 18:5
a burnt offering and sacrifices to **G**;	Ex 18:12
with Moses' father-in-law before **G**.	Ex 18:12
the people come to me to inquire of **G**;	Ex 18:15
know the statutes of **G** and his laws."	Ex 18:16
give you advice, and **G** be with you!	Ex 18:19
the people before **G** and bring their	Ex 18:19
before God and bring their cases to **G**,	Ex 18:19
from all the people, men who fear **G**,	Ex 18:21
If you do this, **G** will direct you, you	Ex 18:23
while Moses went up to **G**. The LORD	Ex 19:3
the people out of the camp to meet **G**,	Ex 19:17
spoke, and **G** answered him in thunder.	Ex 19:19
And **G** spoke all these words, saying,	Ex 20:1
"I am the LORD your **G**, who brought you	Ex 20:2
for I the LORD your **G** am a jealous God,	Ex 20:5
for I the LORD your God am a jealous **G**,	Ex 20:5
the name of the LORD your **G** in vain,	Ex 20:7
day is a Sabbath to the LORD your **G**.	Ex 20:10
land that the LORD your **G** is giving you.	Ex 20:12
but do not let **G** speak to us, lest we die."	Ex 20:19
"Do not fear, for **G** has come to test you,	Ex 20:20
to the thick darkness where **G** was.	Ex 20:21
then his master shall bring him to **G**,	Ex 21:6
him, but **G** let him fall into his hand,	Ex 21:13
shall come near to **G** to show whether or	Ex 22:8
case of both parties shall come before **G**.	Ex 22:9
The one whom **G** condemns shall pay	Ex 22:9
"Whoever sacrifices to any **g**, other	Ex 22:20
"You shall not revile **G**, nor curse a	Ex 22:28
your males appear before the Lord **G**.	Ex 23:17
into the house of the LORD your **G**.	Ex 23:19
You shall serve the LORD your **G**, and he	Ex 23:25
and they saw the **G** of Israel. There was	Ex 24:10
they beheld **G**, and ate and drank.	Ex 24:11
Moses went up into the mountain of **G**.	Ex 24:13
the people of Israel and will be their **G**.	Ex 29:45
shall know that I am the LORD their **G**,	Ex 29:46
among them. I am the LORD their **G**.	Ex 29:46
and I have filled him with the Spirit of **G**,	Ex 31:3
of stone, written with the finger of **G**.	Ex 31:18
implored the LORD his **G** and said,	Ex 32:11
The tablets were the work of **G**, and the	Ex 32:16
and the writing was the writing of **G**,	Ex 32:16
them, "Thus says the LORD **G** of Israel,	Ex 32:27
the LORD, a **G** merciful and gracious,	Ex 34:6
(for you shall worship no other **g**, for	Ex 34:14
whose name is Jealous, is a jealous **G**),	Ex 34:14
your males appear before the LORD **G**,	Ex 34:23
before the LORD God, the **G** of Israel.	Ex 34:23
before the LORD your **G** three times in	Ex 34:24
bring to the house of the LORD your **G**.	Ex 34:26
because he had been talking with **G**.	Ex 34:29
he has filled him with the Spirit of **G**,	Ex 35:31
covenant with your **G** be missing from	Lv 2:13
of the LORD his **G** ought not to be	Lv 4:22
For I am the LORD your **G**. Consecrate	Lv 11:44
up out of the land of Egypt to be your **G**.	Lv 11:45
and say to them, I am the LORD your **G**.	Lv 18:2

and walk in them. I am the LORD your **G**. Lv 18:4
and so profane the name of your **G**: Lv 18:21
by them: I am the LORD your **G**." Lv 18:30
be holy, for I the LORD your **G** am holy. Lv 19:2
my Sabbaths: I am the LORD your **G**. Lv 19:3
gods of cast metal: I am the LORD your **G**. Lv 19:4
for the sojourner: I am the LORD your **G**. Lv 19:10
and so profane the name of your **G**: Lv 19:12
the blind, but you shall fear your **G**: Lv 19:14
its yield for you: I am the LORD your **G**. Lv 19:25
by them: I am the LORD your **G**. Lv 19:31
an old man, and you shall fear your **G**: Lv 19:32
the land of Egypt: I am the LORD your **G**. Lv 19:34
I am the LORD your **G**, who brought you Lv 19:36
and be holy, for I am the LORD your **G**. Lv 20:7
I am the LORD your **G**, who have Lv 20:24
be holy to their **G** and not profane the Lv 21:6
God and not profane the name of their **G**. Lv 21:6
food offerings, the bread of their **G**; Lv 21:6
husband, for the priest is holy to his **G**. Lv 21:7
him, for he offers the bread of your **G**. Lv 21:8
lest he profane the sanctuary of his **G**, Lv 21:12
of the anointing oil of his **G** is on him: Lv 21:12
approach to offer the bread of his **G**. Lv 21:17
come near to offer the bread of his **G**. Lv 21:21
He may eat the bread of his **G**, both of Lv 21:22
the bread of your **G** any such animals Lv 22:25
out of the land of Egypt to be your **G**: Lv 22:33
have brought the offering of your **G**: Lv 23:14
the sojourner: I am the LORD your **G**." Lv 23:22
for you before the LORD your **G**. Lv 23:28
before the LORD your **G** seven days. Lv 23:40
land of Egypt: I am the LORD your **G**." Lv 23:43
Whoever curses his **G** shall bear his Lv 24:15
the native, for I am the LORD your **G**." Lv 24:22
one another, but you shall fear your **G**, Lv 25:17
fear your God, for I am the LORD your **G**. Lv 25:17
from him or profit, but fear your **G**, Lv 25:36
I am the LORD your **G**, who brought you Lv 25:38
the land of Canaan, and to be your **G**. Lv 25:38
him ruthlessly but shall fear your **G**. Lv 25:43
the land of Egypt: I am the LORD your **G**. Lv 25:55
bow down to it, for I am the LORD your **G**. Lv 26:1
walk among you and will be your **G**, Lv 26:12
I am the LORD your **G**, who brought you Lv 26:13
with them, for I am the LORD their **G**. Lv 26:44
of the nations, that I might be their **G**: Lv 26:45
because his separation to **G** is on his Nm 6:7
be remembered before the LORD your **G**, Nm 10:9
be a reminder of you before your **G**: Nm 10:10
your God: I am the LORD your **G**." Nm 10:10
And Moses cried to the LORD, "O **G**, Nm 12:13
and be holy to your **G**. Nm 15:40
I am the LORD your **G**, who brought Nm 15:41
out of the land of Egypt to be your **G**: Nm 15:41
to be your God: I am the LORD your **G**." Nm 15:41
for you that the **G** of Israel has Nm 16:9
they fell on their faces and said, "O **G**, Nm 16:22
"O God, the **G** of the spirits of all flesh, Nm 16:22
people spoke against **G** and against Nm 21:5
And **G** came to Balaam and said, Nm 22:9
And Balaam said to **G**, "Balak the son Nm 22:10
G said to Balaam, "You shall not go Nm 22:12
of the LORD my **G** to do less or Nm 22:18
And **G** came to Balaam at night and Nm 22:20
The word that **G** puts in my mouth, Nm 22:38
and **G** met Balaam. And Balaam said Nm 23:4
can I curse whom **G** has not cursed? Nm 23:8
G is not man, that he should lie, or a Nm 23:19
Israel. The LORD their **G** is with them, Nm 23:21
G brings them out of Egypt and is for Nm 23:22
and Israel, 'What has **G** wrought!' Nm 23:23
Perhaps it will please **G** that you may Nm 23:27
And the Spirit of **G** came upon him, Nm 24:2
of him who hears the words of **G**, Nm 24:4
G brings him out of Egypt and is for Nm 24:8
of him who hears the words of **G**, Nm 24:16
who shall live when **G** does this? Nm 24:23
jealous for his **G** and made atonement Nm 25:13
LORD, the **G** of the spirits of all flesh, Nm 27:16
"The LORD our **G** said to us in Horeb, 'You Dt 1:6
The LORD your **G** has multiplied you, Dt 1:10
May the LORD, the **G** of your fathers, Dt 1:11
as the LORD our **G** commanded us. Dt 1:19
which the LORD our **G** is giving us. Dt 1:20
the LORD your **G** has set the land before Dt 1:21
as the LORD, the **G** of your fathers, Dt 1:21
land that the LORD our **G** is giving us.' Dt 1:25
the command of the LORD your **G**. Dt 1:26
The LORD your **G** who goes before you Dt 1:30
seen how the LORD your **G** carried you, Dt 1:31
you did not believe the LORD your **G**, Dt 1:32
just as the LORD our **G** commanded us.' Dt 1:41
For the LORD your **G** has blessed you in all Dt 2:7
years the LORD your **G** has been with you. Dt 2:7
land that the LORD our **G** is giving to us.' Dt 2:29
for the LORD your **G** hardened his spirit Dt 2:30
And the LORD our **G** gave him over to us, Dt 2:33
The LORD our **G** gave all into our hands. Dt 2:36
the LORD our **G** had forbidden us. Dt 2:37
So the LORD our **G** gave into our hand Og Dt 3:3
'The LORD your **G** has given you this Dt 3:18
that the LORD your **G** gives them beyond Dt 3:20
all that the LORD your **G** has done to these Dt 3:21
it is the LORD your **G** who fights for you.' Dt 3:22
'O Lord **G**, you have only begun to show Dt 3:24
For what **g** is there in heaven or on earth Dt 3:24
land that the LORD, the **G** of your fathers, Dt 4:1
of the LORD your **G** that I command you. Dt 4:2
the LORD your **G** destroyed from among Dt 4:3
fast to the LORD your **G** are all alive today. Dt 4:4
rules, as the LORD my **G** commanded me, Dt 4:5
nation is there that has a **g** so near to it as Dt 4:7
god so near to it as the LORD our **G** is to us, Dt 4:7
stood before the LORD your **G** at Horeb, Dt 4:10
that the LORD your **G** has allotted to all Dt 4:19
that the LORD your **G** is giving you for Dt 4:21
forget the covenant of the LORD your **G**, Dt 4:23
that the LORD your **G** has forbidden you. Dt 4:23
For the LORD your **G** is a consuming fire, Dt 4:24
God is a consuming fire, a jealous **G**. Dt 4:24
is evil in the sight of the LORD your **G**, Dt 4:25
seek the LORD your **G** and you will find Dt 4:29
to the LORD your **G** and obey his voice. Dt 4:30
For the LORD your **G** is a merciful God. Dt 4:31
For the LORD your God is a merciful **G**. Dt 4:31
since the day that **G** created man on the Dt 4:32
hear the voice of a **g** speaking out of the Dt 4:33
Or has any **g** ever attempted to go and Dt 4:34
of which the LORD your **G** did for you in Dt 4:34
that you might know that the LORD is **G**; Dt 4:35
that the LORD is **G** in heaven above and Dt 4:39
that the LORD your **G** is giving you for Dt 4:40
The LORD our **G** made a covenant with us Dt 5:2
"'I am the LORD your **G**, who brought you Dt 5:6
for I the LORD your **G** am a jealous God, Dt 5:9
for I the LORD your God am a jealous **G**, Dt 5:9
the name of the LORD your **G** in vain, Dt 5:11
as the LORD your **G** commanded you. Dt 5:12
day is a Sabbath to the LORD your **G**. Dt 5:14
and the LORD your **G** brought you out Dt 5:15
the LORD your **G** commanded you to Dt 5:15
as the LORD your **G** commanded you, Dt 5:16
land that the LORD your **G** is giving you. Dt 5:16
the LORD our **G** has shown us his glory Dt 5:24
day we have seen **G** speak with man and Dt 5:24
the voice of the LORD our **G** any more, Dt 5:25
voice of the living **G** speaking out of the Dt 5:26
that the LORD our **G** will say and speak Dt 5:27
all that the LORD our **G** will speak to you, Dt 5:27
as the LORD your **G** has commanded you. Dt 5:32
the LORD your **G** has commanded you, Dt 5:33
that the LORD your **G** commanded me to Dt 6:1
that you may fear the LORD your **G**, you Dt 6:2
greatly, as the LORD, the **G** of your fathers, Dt 6:3
O Israel: The LORD our **G**, the LORD is one. Dt 6:4
love the LORD your **G** with all your heart Dt 6:5
when the LORD your **G** brings you into Dt 6:10
It is the LORD your **G** you shall fear. Him Dt 6:13
for the LORD your **G** in your midst is a Dt 6:15
your God in your midst is a jealous **G**, Dt 6:15
of the LORD your **G** be kindled against Dt 6:15
shall not put the LORD your **G** to the test, Dt 6:16
the commandments of the LORD your **G**, Dt 6:17
the LORD our **G** has commanded you?' Dt 6:20
all these statutes, to fear the LORD our **G**, Dt 6:24
commandment before the LORD our **G**, Dt 6:25
"When the LORD your **G** brings you into Dt 7:1
when the LORD your **G** gives them over to Dt 7:2
you are a people holy to the LORD your **G**. Dt 7:6
The LORD your **G** has chosen you to be a Dt 7:6
therefore that the LORD your **G** is God, Dt 7:9
therefore that the LORD your God is **G**, Dt 7:9
the faithful **G** who keeps covenant and Dt 7:9
the LORD your **G** will keep with you the Dt 7:12
that the LORD your **G** will give over to Dt 7:16
what the LORD your **G** did to Pharaoh Dt 7:18
which the LORD your **G** brought you out. Dt 7:19
So will the LORD your **G** do to all the Dt 7:19
the LORD your **G** will send hornets Dt 7:20
for the LORD your **G** is in your midst, Dt 7:21
is in your midst, a great and awesome **G**. Dt 7:21
The LORD your **G** will clear away these Dt 7:22
But the LORD your **G** will give them over Dt 7:23
it is an abomination to the LORD your **G**. Dt 7:25
that the LORD your **G** has led you these Dt 8:2
his son, the LORD your **G** disciplines you. Dt 8:5
of the LORD your **G** by walking in his Dt 8:6
For the LORD your **G** is bringing you into Dt 8:7
bless the LORD your **G** for the good land Dt 8:10
forget the LORD your **G** by not keeping Dt 8:11
lifted up, and you forget the LORD your **G**, Dt 8:14
You shall remember the LORD your **G**, Dt 8:18
forget the LORD your **G** and go after other Dt 8:19
not obey the voice of the LORD your **G**. Dt 8:20
as a consuming fire is the LORD your **G**. Dt 9:3
after the LORD your **G** has thrust them out Dt 9:4
nations the LORD your **G** is driving them Dt 9:5
that the LORD your **G** is not giving you this Dt 9:6
provoked the LORD your **G** to wrath in the Dt 9:7
of stone written with the finger of **G**, Dt 9:10
you had sinned against the LORD your **G**. Dt 9:16
of the LORD your **G** and did not believe Dt 9:23
And I prayed to the LORD, 'O Lord **G**, Dt 9:26
as the LORD your **G** said to him.) Dt 10:9
does the LORD your **G** require of you, Dt 10:12
of you, but to fear the LORD your **G**, Dt 10:12
serve the LORD your **G** with all your Dt 10:12
to the LORD your **G** belong heaven and Dt 10:14
For the LORD your **G** is God of gods and Dt 10:17
the LORD your God is **G** of gods and Lord Dt 10:17
great, the mighty, and the awesome **G**, Dt 10:17
You shall fear the LORD your **G**. You Dt 10:20
He is your **G**, who has done for you Dt 10:21
now the LORD your **G** has made you as Dt 10:22
love the LORD your **G** and keep his Dt 11:1
the discipline of the LORD your **G**, Dt 11:2
a land that the LORD your **G** cares for. Dt 11:12
of the LORD your **G** are always upon it, Dt 11:12
you today, to love the LORD your **G**, Dt 11:13
you to do, loving the LORD your **G**, Dt 11:22
The LORD your **G** will lay the fear of you Dt 11:25
the commandments of the LORD your **G**, Dt 11:27
the commandments of the LORD your **G**, Dt 11:28
when the LORD your **G** brings you into Dt 11:29
land that the LORD your **G** is giving you. Dt 11:31
land that the LORD, the **G** of your fathers, Dt 12:1
not worship the LORD your **G** in that way. Dt 12:4
that the LORD your **G** will choose out of Dt 12:5
you shall eat before the LORD your **G**, Dt 12:7
which the LORD your **G** has blessed you. Dt 12:7
that the LORD your **G** is giving you. Dt 12:9
that the LORD your **G** is giving you to Dt 12:10
place that the LORD your **G** will choose, Dt 12:11
shall rejoice before the LORD your **G**, Dt 12:12
of the LORD your **G** that he has given Dt 12:15
before the LORD your **G** in the place that Dt 12:18
place that the LORD your **G** will choose, Dt 12:18
before the LORD your **G** in all that you Dt 12:18
the LORD your **G** enlarges your territory, Dt 12:20
that the LORD your **G** will choose to put Dt 12:21
blood, on the altar of the LORD your **G**. Dt 12:27
out on the altar of the LORD your **G**, Dt 12:27
right in the sight of the LORD your **G**. Dt 12:28
"When the LORD your **G** cuts off before Dt 12:29
worship the LORD your **G** in that way, Dt 12:31
For the LORD your **G** is testing you, to Dt 13:3
love the LORD your **G** with all your heart Dt 13:3
after the LORD your **G** and fear him and Dt 13:4
rebellion against the LORD your **G**, Dt 13:5
the LORD your **G** commanded you to Dt 13:5
draw you away from the LORD your **G**, Dt 13:10
which the LORD your **G** is giving you to Dt 13:12
burnt offering to the LORD your **G**. Dt 13:16
if you obey the voice of the LORD your **G**, Dt 13:18
is right in the sight of the LORD your **G**. Dt 13:18
"You are the sons of the LORD your **G**. Dt 14:1
you are a people holy to the LORD your **G**, Dt 14:2
are a people holy to the LORD your **G**. Dt 14:21
And before the LORD your **G**, in the Dt 14:23
learn to fear the LORD your **G** always. Dt 14:23
tithe, when the LORD your **G** blesses you, Dt 14:24
you, which the LORD your **G** chooses, Dt 14:24
the place that the LORD your **G** chooses Dt 14:25
before the LORD your **G** and rejoice, Dt 14:26
that the LORD your **G** may bless you in Dt 14:29
that the LORD your **G** is giving you for Dt 15:4
obey the voice of the LORD your **G**, Dt 15:5
For the LORD your **G** will bless you, as he Dt 15:6
land that the LORD your **G** is giving you, Dt 15:7
this the LORD your **G** will bless you in Dt 15:10
As the LORD your **G** has blessed you, Dt 15:14
and the LORD your **G** redeemed you; Dt 15:15
So the LORD your **G** will bless you in all Dt 15:18
you shall dedicate to the LORD your **G**. Dt 15:19
before the LORD your **G** year by year at Dt 15:20
shall not sacrifice it to the LORD your **G**. Dt 15:21
keep the Passover to the LORD your **G**, Dt 16:1
Abib the LORD your **G** brought you out Dt 16:1
the Passover sacrifice to the LORD your **G**, Dt 16:2
towns that the LORD your **G** is giving you, Dt 16:5
place that the LORD your **G** will choose, Dt 16:6
place that the LORD your **G** will choose. Dt 16:7
a solemn assembly to the LORD your **G**. Dt 16:8
to the LORD your **G** with the tribute of Dt 16:10

give as the LORD your **G** blesses you. Dt 16:10
shall rejoice before the LORD your **G**, Dt 16:11
place that the LORD your **G** will choose, Dt 16:11
feast to the LORD your **G** at the place that Dt 16:15
because the LORD your **G** will bless you Dt 16:15
before the LORD your **G** at the place that Dt 16:16
of the LORD your **G** that he has given Dt 16:17
that the LORD your **G** is giving you, Dt 16:18
land that the LORD your **G** is giving you. Dt 16:20
of the LORD your **G** that you shall make. Dt 16:21
a pillar, which the LORD your **G** hates. Dt 16:22
sacrifice to the LORD your **G** an ox or a Dt 17:1
is an abomination to the LORD your **G**. Dt 17:1
towns that the LORD your **G** is giving you, Dt 17:2
is evil in the sight of the LORD your **G**, Dt 17:2
place that the LORD your **G** will choose. Dt 17:8
minister there before the LORD your **G**, Dt 17:12
land that the LORD your **G** is giving you, Dt 17:14
you whom the LORD your **G** will choose. Dt 17:15
to fear the LORD his **G** by keeping all the Dt 17:19
For the LORD your **G** has chosen him out Dt 18:5
ministers in the name of the LORD his **G**, Dt 18:7
land that the LORD your **G** is giving you, Dt 18:9
the LORD your **G** is driving them Dt 18:12
be blameless before the LORD your **G**, Dt 18:13
the LORD your **G** has not allowed you to Dt 18:14
"The LORD your **G** will raise up for you Dt 18:15
of the LORD your **G** at Horeb on the Dt 18:16
voice of the LORD my **G** or see this great Dt 18:16
"When the LORD your **G** cuts off the Dt 19:1
land the LORD your **G** is giving you, Dt 19:1
that the LORD your **G** is giving you to Dt 19:2
land that the LORD your **G** gives you as a Dt 19:3
the LORD your **G** enlarges your territory, Dt 19:8
loving the LORD your **G** and by walking Dt 19:9
that the LORD your **G** is giving you for Dt 19:10
that the LORD your **G** is giving you to Dt 19:14
of them, for the LORD your **G** is with you, Dt 20:1
for the LORD your **G** is he who goes with Dt 20:4
when the LORD your **G** gives it into your Dt 20:13
which the LORD your **G** has given you. Dt 20:14
that the LORD your **G** is giving you for Dt 20:16
as the LORD your **G** has commanded, Dt 20:17
and so you sin against the LORD your **G**. Dt 20:18
that the LORD your **G** is giving you to Dt 21:1
for the LORD your **G** has chosen them to Dt 21:5
and the LORD your **G** gives them into Dt 21:10
day, for a hanged man is cursed by **G**. Dt 21:23
that the LORD your **G** is giving you for Dt 21:23
is an abomination to the LORD your **G**. Dt 22:5
But the LORD your **G** would not listen to Dt 23:5
instead the LORD your **G** turned the curse Dt 23:5
you, because the LORD your **G** loved you. Dt 23:5
Because the LORD your **G** walks in the Dt 23:14
of the LORD your **G** in payment for any Dt 23:18
are an abomination to the LORD your **G**. Dt 23:18
that the LORD your **G** may bless you in Dt 23:20
"If you make a vow to the LORD your **G**, Dt 23:21
for the LORD your **G** will surely require Dt 23:21
to the LORD your **G** what you have Dt 23:23
that the LORD your **G** is giving you for Dt 24:4
what the LORD your **G** did to Miriam on Dt 24:9
for you before the LORD your **G**. Dt 24:13
the LORD your **G** redeemed you from Dt 24:18
that the LORD your **G** may bless you in Dt 24:19
land that the LORD your **G** is giving you. Dt 25:15
are an abomination to the LORD your **G**. Dt 25:16
behind you, and he did not fear **G**. Dt 25:18
when the LORD your **G** has given you Dt 25:19
that the LORD your **G** is giving you for Dt 25:19
that the LORD your **G** is giving you for Dt 26:1
land that the LORD your **G** is giving you, Dt 26:2
place that the LORD your **G** will choose, Dt 26:2
to the LORD your **G** that I have come Dt 26:3
down before the altar of the LORD your **G**. Dt 26:4
make response before the LORD your **G**, Dt 26:5
we cried to the LORD, the **G** of our fathers, Dt 26:7
the LORD your **G** and worship before Dt 26:10
and worship before the LORD your **G**. Dt 26:10
that the LORD your **G** has given to you Dt 26:11
you shall say before the LORD your **G**, Dt 26:13
have obeyed the voice of the LORD my **G**. Dt 26:14
day the LORD your **G** commands you to Dt 26:16
declared today that the LORD is your **G**, Dt 26:17
be a people holy to the LORD your **G**, Dt 26:19
land that the LORD your **G** is giving you, Dt 27:2
land that the LORD your **G** is giving you, Dt 27:3
honey, as the LORD, the **G** of your fathers, Dt 27:3
shall build an altar to the LORD your **G**, Dt 27:5
altar to the LORD your **G** of uncut stones. Dt 27:6
burnt offerings on it to the LORD your **G**, Dt 27:6
you shall rejoice before the LORD your **G**. Dt 27:7
become the people of the LORD your **G**. Dt 27:9
obey the voice of the LORD your **G**, Dt 27:10
obey the voice of the LORD your **G**, Dt 28:1

the LORD your **G** will set you high above Dt 28:1
if you obey the voice of the LORD your **G**. Dt 28:2
land that the LORD your **G** is giving you. Dt 28:8
of the LORD your **G** and walk in his Dt 28:9
the commandments of the LORD your **G**, Dt 28:13
voice of the LORD your **G** or be careful to Dt 28:15
not obey the voice of the LORD your **G**, Dt 28:45
the LORD your **G** with joyfulness and Dt 28:47
which the LORD your **G** has given you. Dt 28:52
whom the LORD your **G** has given you, Dt 28:53
and awesome name, the LORD your **G**, Dt 28:58
not obey the voice of the LORD your **G**. Dt 28:62
may know that I am the LORD your **G**. Dt 29:6
today all of you before the LORD your **G**: Dt 29:10
the sworn covenant of the LORD your **G**, Dt 29:12
which the LORD your **G** is making with Dt 29:12
his people, and that he may be your **G**, Dt 29:13
with us today before the LORD our **G**, Dt 29:15
from the LORD our **G** to go and serve Dt 29:18
of the LORD, the **G** of their fathers, Dt 29:25
secret things belong to the LORD our **G**, Dt 29:29
where the LORD your **G** has driven you, Dt 30:1
and return to the LORD your **G**, you and Dt 30:2
then the LORD your **G** will restore your Dt 30:3
where the LORD your **G** has scattered you. Dt 30:3
there the LORD your **G** will gather you, Dt 30:4
And the LORD your **G** will bring you into Dt 30:5
the LORD your **G** will circumcise your Dt 30:6
love the LORD your **G** with all your heart Dt 30:6
And the LORD your **G** will put all these Dt 30:7
The LORD your **G** will make you Dt 30:9
you obey the voice of the LORD your **G**, Dt 30:10
to the LORD your **G** with all your heart Dt 30:10
of the LORD your **G** that I command you Dt 30:16
you today, by loving the LORD your **G**, Dt 30:16
and the LORD your **G** will bless you in Dt 30:16
loving the LORD your **G**, obeying his Dt 30:20
The LORD your **G** himself will go over Dt 31:3
it is the LORD your **G** who goes with you. Dt 31:6
before the LORD your **G** at the place that Dt 31:11
hear and learn to fear the LORD your **G**, Dt 31:12
hear and learn to fear the LORD your **G**, Dt 31:13
upon us because our **G** is not among Dt 31:17
ark of the covenant of the LORD your **G**, Dt 31:26
of the LORD; ascribe greatness to our **G**! Dt 32:3
A **G** of faithfulness and without iniquity, Dt 32:4
to the number of the sons of **G**. Dt 32:8
guided him, no foreign **g** was with him. Dt 32:12
then he forsook **G** who made him and Dt 32:15
and you forgot the **G** who gave you Dt 32:18
made me jealous with what is no **g**; Dt 32:21
I, am he, and there is no **g** besides me; Dt 32:39
Moses the man of **G** blessed the people of Dt 33:1
The High **G** surrounds him all day Dt 33:12
"There is none like **G**, O Jeshurun, who Dt 33:26
The eternal **G** is your dwelling place, Dt 33:27
for the LORD your **G** is with you wherever Jos 1:9
that the LORD your **G** is giving you to Jos 1:11
'The LORD your **G** is providing you a Jos 1:13
that the LORD your **G** is giving them. Jos 1:15
Only may the LORD your **G** be with you, Jos 1:17
because of you, for the LORD your **G**, Jos 2:11
he is **G** in the heavens above and on the Jos 2:11
of the LORD your **G** being carried by the Jos 3:3
listen to the words of the LORD your **G**." Jos 3:9
know that the living **G** is among you Jos 3:10
ark of the LORD your **G** into the midst of Jos 4:5
For the LORD your **G** dried up the waters Jos 4:23
as the LORD your **G** did to the Red Sea, Jos 4:23
you may fear the LORD your **G** forever." Jos 4:24
And Joshua said, "Alas, O Lord **G**, why Jos 7:7
for thus says the LORD, **G** of Israel, Jos 7:13
glory to the LORD **G** of Israel and give Jos 7:19
have sinned against the LORD **G** of Israel, Jos 7:20
for the LORD your **G** will give it into your Jos 8:7
built an altar to the LORD, the **G** of Israel, Jos 8:30
because of the name of the LORD your **G**. Jos 9:9
to them by the LORD, the **G** of Israel. Jos 9:18
to them by the LORD, the **G** of Israel, Jos 9:19
drawers of water for the house of my **G**." Jos 9:23
the LORD your **G** had commanded his Jos 9:24
for the LORD your **G** has given them Jos 10:19
as the LORD **G** of Israel commanded. Jos 10:40
because the LORD **G** of Israel fought for Jos 10:42
by fire to the LORD **G** of Israel are their Jos 13:14
the LORD **G** of Israel is their inheritance, Jos 13:33
the man of **G** in Kadesh-barnea Jos 14:6
yet I wholly followed the LORD my **G**. Jos 14:8
have wholly followed the LORD my **G**.' Jos 14:9
followed the LORD, the **G** of Israel. Jos 14:14
which the LORD, the **G** of your fathers, Jos 18:3
lots for you here before the LORD our **G**. Jos 18:6
to keep the charge of the LORD your **G**. Jos 22:3
now the LORD your **G** has given rest to Jos 22:4
you, to love the LORD your **G**, Jos 22:5

committed against the **G** of Israel in Jos 22:16
other than the altar of the LORD our **G**. Jos 22:19
"The Mighty One, **G**, the LORD! The Jos 22:22
the LORD! The Mighty One, **G**, the LORD! Jos 22:22
you to do with the LORD, the **G** of Israel? Jos 22:24
of the LORD our **G** that stands before his Jos 22:29
people of Israel blessed **G** and spoke no Jos 22:33
witness between us that the LORD is **G**." Jos 22:34
all that the LORD your **G** has done to all Jos 23:3
it is the LORD your **G** who has fought for Jos 23:3
The LORD your **G** will push them back Jos 23:5
just as the LORD your **G** promised you. Jos 23:5
to the LORD your **G** just as you have Jos 23:8
it is the LORD your **G** who fights for you, Jos 23:10
therefore, to love the LORD your **G**. Jos 23:11
that the LORD your **G** will no longer Jos 23:13
that the LORD your **G** has given you. Jos 23:13
the LORD your **G** promised concerning Jos 23:14
the LORD your **G** promised concerning Jos 23:15
that the LORD your **G** has given you, Jos 23:15
the covenant of the LORD your **G**, Jos 23:16
And they presented themselves before **G**. Jos 24:1
"Thus says the LORD, the **G** of Israel, Jos 24:2
is the LORD our **G** who brought us and Jos 24:17
will serve the LORD, for he is our **G**." Jos 24:18
to serve the LORD, for he is a holy **G**. Jos 24:19
He is a jealous **G**; he will not forgive Jos 24:19
your heart to the LORD, the **G** of Israel." Jos 24:23
Joshua, "The LORD our **G** we will serve, Jos 24:24
words in the Book of the Law of **G**. Jos 24:26
you, lest you deal falsely with your **G**." Jos 24:27
so **G** has repaid me." And they brought Jgs 1:7
the LORD, the **G** of their fathers, Jgs 2:12
forgot the LORD their **G** and served the Jgs 3:7
have a message from **G** for you." And he Jgs 3:20
to him, "Has not the LORD, the **G** of Israel, Jgs 4:6
So on that day **G** subdued Jabin the king Jgs 4:23
make melody to the LORD, the **G** of Israel. Jgs 5:3
even Sinai before the LORD, the **G** of Israel. Jgs 5:5
them, "Thus says the LORD, the **G** of Israel: Jgs 6:8
And I said to you, 'I am the LORD your **G**; Jgs 6:10
And the angel of **G** said to him, "Take Jgs 6:20
LORD. And Gideon said, "Alas, O Lord **G**! Jgs 6:22
altar to the LORD your **G** on the top of the Jgs 6:26
If he is a **g**, let him contend for himself, Jgs 6:31
Then Gideon said to **G**, "If you will save Jgs 6:36
Then Gideon said to **G**, "Let not your Jgs 6:39
And **G** did so that night; and it was dry Jgs 6:40
G has given into his hand Midian and Jgs 7:14
G has given into your hands the princes Jgs 8:3
the Baals and made Baal-berith their **g**. Jgs 8:33
did not remember the LORD their **G**, Jgs 8:34
of Shechem, that **G** may listen to you. Jgs 9:7
my wine that cheers **G** and men and go Jgs 9:13
And **G** sent an evil spirit between Jgs 9:23
the house of their **g** and ate and drank Jgs 9:27
Thus **G** returned the evil of Abimelech, Jgs 9:56
And **G** also made all the evil of the men Jgs 9:57
have forsaken our **G** and have served Jgs 10:10
And the LORD, the **G** of Israel, gave Jgs 11:21
So then the LORD, the **G** of Israel, Jgs 11:23
what Chemosh your **g** gives you to Jgs 11:24
the LORD our **G** has dispossessed before Jgs 11:24
shall be a Nazirite to **G** from the womb, Jgs 13:5
her husband, "A man of **G** came to me, Jgs 13:6
like the appearance of the angel of **G**, Jgs 13:6
be a Nazirite to **G** from the womb to Jgs 13:7
let the man of **G** whom you sent come Jgs 13:8
And **G** listened to the voice of Manoah, Jgs 13:9
and the angel of **G** came again to the Jgs 13:9
shall surely die, for we have seen **G**." Jgs 13:22
And **G** split open the hollow place that Jgs 15:19
been a Nazirite to **G** from my mother's Jgs 16:17
to Dagon their **g** and to rejoice, Jgs 16:23
"Our **g** has given Samson our enemy Jgs 16:23
people saw him, they praised their **g**. Jgs 16:24
"Our **g** has given our enemy into our Jgs 16:24
called to the LORD and said, "O Lord **G**, Jgs 16:28
strengthen me only this once, O **G**, Jgs 16:28
And they said to him, "Inquire of **G**, Jgs 18:5
for **G** has given it into your hands, Jgs 18:10
as long as the house of **G** was at Shiloh. Jgs 18:31
in the assembly of the people of **G**, Jgs 20:2
went up to Bethel and inquired of **G**, Jgs 20:18
of the covenant of **G** was there in those Jgs 20:27
and sat there till evening before **G**, Jgs 21:2
And they said, "O LORD, the **G** of Israel, Jgs 21:3
shall be my people, and your **G** my God. Ru 1:16
shall be my people, and your God my **G**. Ru 1:16
be given you by the LORD, the **G** of Israel, Ru 2:12
and the **G** of Israel grant your petition 1 Sm 1:17
besides you; there is no rock like our **G**. 1 Sm 2:2
for the LORD is a **G** of knowledge, and 1 Sm 2:3
a man, **G** will mediate for him, 1 Sm 2:25
there came a man of **G** to Eli and said 1 Sm 2:27

the LORD the **G** of Israel declares: 1 Sm 2:30
The lamp of **G** had not yet gone out, 1 Sm 3:3
of the LORD, where the ark of **G** was. 1 Sm 3:3
his sons were blaspheming **G**, 1 Sm 3:13
May **G** do so to you and more also if 1 Sm 3:17
there with the ark of the covenant of **G**. 1 Sm 4:4
"A **g** has come into the camp." And 1 Sm 4:7
And the ark of **G** was captured, and 1 Sm 4:11
for his heart trembled for the ark of **G**. 1 Sm 4:13
and the ark of **G** has been captured." 1 Sm 4:17
As soon as he mentioned the ark of **G**, 1 Sm 4:18
news that the ark of **G** was captured, 1 Sm 4:19
the ark of **G** had been captured 1 Sm 4:21
for the ark of **G** has been captured." 1 Sm 4:22
the Philistines captured the ark of **G**, 1 Sm 5:1
took the ark of **G** and brought it into 1 Sm 5:2
"The ark of the **G** of Israel must not 1 Sm 5:7
against us and against Dagon our **g**." 1 Sm 5:7
the ark of the **G** of Israel?" They 1 Sm 5:8
the ark of the **G** of Israel be brought 1 Sm 5:8
brought the ark of the **G** of Israel there. 1 Sm 5:8
So they sent the ark of **G** to Ekron. But 1 Sm 5:10
soon as the ark of **G** came to Ekron, 1 Sm 5:10
us the ark of the **G** of Israel to kill us 1 Sm 5:10
"Send away the ark of the **G** of Israel, 1 Sm 5:11
The hand of **G** was very heavy there. 1 Sm 5:11
send away the ark of the **G** of Israel, 1 Sm 6:3
land, and give glory to the **G** of Israel. 1 Sm 6:5
to stand before the LORD, this holy **G**? 1 Sm 6:20
to cry out to the LORD our **G** for us, 1 Sm 7:8
there is a man of **G** in this city, 1 Sm 9:6
is no present to bring to the man of **G**. 1 Sm 9:7
it to the man of **G** to tell us our way." 1 Sm 9:8
when a man went to inquire of **G**, 1 Sm 9:9
to the city where the man of **G** was. 1 Sm 9:10
make known to you the word of **G**." 1 Sm 9:27
men going up to **G** at Bethel will meet 1 Sm 10:3
hand finds to do, for **G** is with you. 1 Sm 10:7
Samuel, **G** gave him another heart. 1 Sm 10:9
and the Spirit of **G** rushed upon him, 1 Sm 10:10
"Thus says the LORD, the **G** of Israel, 1 Sm 10:18
But today you have rejected your **G**, 1 Sm 10:19
of valor whose hearts **G** had touched. 1 Sm 10:26
And the Spirit of **G** rushed upon Saul 1 Sm 11:6
But they forgot the LORD their **G**. And 1 Sm 12:9
the LORD your **G** was your king. 1 Sm 12:12
over you will follow the LORD your **G**, 1 Sm 12:14
for your servants to the LORD your **G**, 1 Sm 12:19
the command of the LORD your **G**, 1 Sm 13:13
"Bring the ark of **G** here." For the 1 Sm 14:18
For the ark of **G** went at that time 1 Sm 14:18
said, "Let us draw near to **G** here." 1 Sm 14:36
And Saul inquired of **G**, "Shall I go 1 Sm 14:37
Saul said, "O LORD **G** of Israel, 1 Sm 14:41
Jonathan my son, O LORD, **G** of Israel, 1 Sm 14:41
said, "**G** do so to me and more also; 1 Sm 14:44
he has worked with **G** this day." So 1 Sm 14:45
oxen to sacrifice to the LORD your **G**, 1 Sm 15:15
to the LORD your **G** in Gilgal." 1 Sm 15:21
I may bow before the LORD your **G**." 1 Sm 15:30
evil spirit from **G** is tormenting you. 1 Sm 16:15
the evil spirit from **G** is upon you, 1 Sm 16:16
the evil spirit from **G** was upon Saul, 1 Sm 16:23
defy the armies of the living **G**?" 1 Sm 17:26
defied the armies of the living **G**." 1 Sm 17:36
of hosts, the **G** of the armies of Israel, 1 Sm 17:45
may know that there is a **G** in Israel, 1 Sm 17:46
harmful spirit from **G** rushed upon 1 Sm 18:10
the Spirit of **G** came upon the 1 Sm 19:20
And the Spirit of **G** came upon him 1 Sm 19:23
to David, "The LORD, the **G** of Israel, 1 Sm 20:12
till I know what **G** will do for me." 1 Sm 22:3
and have inquired of **G** for him, 1 Sm 22:13
that I have inquired of **G** for him? 1 Sm 22:15
said, "**G** has given him into my hand, 1 Sm 23:7
said David, "O LORD, the **G** of Israel, 1 Sm 23:10
O LORD, the **G** of Israel, please tell 1 Sm 23:11
but **G** did not give him into his 1 Sm 23:14
and strengthened his hand in **G**. 1 Sm 23:16
G do so to the enemies of David and 1 Sm 25:22
living in the care of the LORD your **G**. 1 Sm 25:29
"Blessed be the LORD, the **G** of Israel, 1 Sm 25:32
as the LORD the **G** of Israel lives, 1 Sm 25:34
"**G** has given your enemy into your 1 Sm 26:8
"I see a **g** coming up out of the 1 Sm 28:13
and **G** has turned away from me and 1 Sm 28:15
in my sight as an angel of **G**. 1 Sm 29:9
himself in the LORD his **G**. 1 Sm 30:6
"Swear to me by **G** that you will not 1 Sm 30:15
And Joab said, "As **G** lives, if you had 2 Sm 2:27
G do so to Abner and more also, if I do 2 Sm 3:9
saying, "**G** do so to me and more also, 2 Sm 3:35
greater, for the LORD, the **G** of hosts, 2 Sm 5:10
to bring up from there the ark of **G**, 2 Sm 6:2
they carried the ark of **G** on a new cart 2 Sm 6:3
with the ark of **G**, and Ahio went before 2 Sm 6:4
hand to the ark of **G** and took hold of it, 2 Sm 6:6
and **G** struck him down there because 2 Sm 6:7
and he died there beside the ark of **G**. 2 Sm 6:7
of the ark of **G**." So David went and 2 Sm 6:12
up the ark of **G** from the house of 2 Sm 6:12
cedar, but the ark of **G** dwells in a tent." 2 Sm 7:2
LORD and said, "Who am I, O Lord **G**, 2 Sm 7:18
a small thing in your eyes, O Lord **G**. 2 Sm 7:19
is instruction for mankind, O Lord **G**! 2 Sm 7:19
you know your servant, O Lord **G**! 2 Sm 7:20
Therefore you are great, O LORD **G**. For 2 Sm 7:22
you, and there is no **G** besides you, 2 Sm 7:22
on earth whom **G** went to redeem 2 Sm 7:23
And you, O LORD, became their **G**. 2 Sm 7:24
And now, O LORD **G**, confirm forever 2 Sm 7:25
'The LORD of hosts is **G** over Israel,' 2 Sm 7:26
you, O LORD of hosts, the **G** of Israel, 2 Sm 7:27
And now, O Lord **G**, you are God, and 2 Sm 7:28
And now, O Lord GOD, you are **G**, and 2 Sm 7:28
For you, O Lord **G**, have spoken, and 2 Sm 7:29
show the kindness of **G** to him?" Ziba 2 Sm 9:3
people, and for the cities of our **G**, 2 Sm 10:12
Thus says the LORD, the **G** of Israel, 'I 2 Sm 12:7
David therefore sought **G** on behalf 2 Sm 12:16
let the king invoke the LORD your **G**, 2 Sm 14:11
such a thing against the people of **G**? 2 Sm 14:13
But **G** will not take away life, and he 2 Sm 14:14
son together from the heritage of **G**.' 2 Sm 14:16
like the angel of **G** to discern good 2 Sm 14:17
evil. The LORD your **G** be with you!" 2 Sm 14:17
of the angel of **G** to know all things 2 Sm 14:20
bearing the ark of the covenant of **G**. 2 Sm 15:24
down the ark of **G** until the people 2 Sm 15:24
"Carry the ark of **G** back into the 2 Sm 15:25
the ark of **G** back to Jerusalem, 2 Sm 15:29
the summit, where **G** was worshiped, 2 Sm 15:32
as if one consulted the word of **G**; 2 Sm 16:23
said, "Blessed be the LORD your **G**, 2 Sm 18:28
G do so to me and more also, if you 2 Sm 19:13
lord the king is like the angel of **G**; 2 Sm 19:27
And after that **G** responded to the 2 Sm 21:14
my **G**, my rock, in whom I take 2 Sm 22:3
called upon the LORD; to my **G** I called. 2 Sm 22:7
not wickedly departed from my **G**. 2 Sm 22:22
and my **G** lightens my darkness. 2 Sm 22:29
and by my **G** I can leap over a wall. 2 Sm 22:30
This **G**—his way is perfect; the word 2 Sm 22:31
"For who is **G**, but the LORD? And 2 Sm 22:32
And who is a rock, except our **G**? 2 Sm 22:32
This **G** is my strong refuge and has 2 Sm 22:33
be my rock, and exalted be my **G**, 2 Sm 22:47
the **G** who gave me vengeance and 2 Sm 22:48
high, the anointed of the **G** of Jacob, 2 Sm 23:1
The **G** of Israel has spoken; the Rock 2 Sm 23:3
over men, ruling in the fear of **G**, 2 Sm 23:3
does not my house stand so with **G**? 2 Sm 23:5
"May the LORD your **G** add to the 2 Sm 24:3
king, "The LORD your **G** accept you." 2 Sm 24:23
to the LORD my **G** that cost me 2 Sm 24:24
to your servant by the LORD your **G**, 1 Kgs 1:17
to you by the LORD, the **G** of Israel, 1 Kgs 1:30
the LORD, the **G** of my lord the king, 1 Kgs 1:36
'May your **G** make the name of 1 Kgs 1:47
'Blessed be the LORD, the **G** of Israel, 1 Kgs 1:48
keep the charge of the LORD your **G**, 1 Kgs 2:3
"**G** do so to me and more also if this 1 Kgs 2:23
ark of the Lord **G** before David my 1 Kgs 2:26
in a dream by night, and **G** said, 1 Kgs 3:5
And now, O LORD my **G**, you have 1 Kgs 3:7
And **G** said to him, "Because you 1 Kgs 3:11
that the wisdom of **G** was in him to 1 Kgs 3:28
And **G** gave Solomon wisdom and 1 Kgs 4:29
of the LORD his **G** because of the 1 Kgs 5:3
now the LORD my **G** has given me rest 1 Kgs 5:4
a house for the name of the LORD my **G**, 1 Kgs 5:5
"Blessed be the LORD, the **G** of Israel, 1 Kgs 8:15
the name of the LORD, the **G** of Israel. 1 Kgs 8:17
the name of the LORD, the **G** of Israel. 1 Kgs 8:20
and said, "O LORD, **G** of Israel, there is 1 Kgs 8:23
God of Israel, there is no **G** like you, 1 Kgs 8:23
Now therefore, O LORD, **G** of Israel, 1 Kgs 8:25
Now therefore, O **G** of Israel, let your 1 Kgs 8:26
"But will **G** indeed dwell on the earth? 1 Kgs 8:27
servant and to his plea, O LORD my **G**, 1 Kgs 8:28
our fathers out of Egypt, O Lord **G**." 1 Kgs 8:53
The LORD our **G** be with us, as he was 1 Kgs 8:57
near to the LORD our **G** day and night, 1 Kgs 8:59
earth may know that the LORD is **G**; 1 Kgs 8:60
be wholly true to the LORD our **G**, 1 Kgs 8:61
of Egypt, before the LORD our **G**, 1 Kgs 8:65
the LORD their **G** who brought their 1 Kgs 9:9
Blessed be the LORD your **G**, who has 1 Kgs 10:9
which **G** had put into his mind. 1 Kgs 10:24
was not wholly true to the LORD his **G**, 1 Kgs 11:4
away from the LORD, the **G** of Israel, 1 Kgs 11:9
G also raised up as an adversary to 1 Kgs 11:23
thus says the LORD, the **G** of Israel, 1 Kgs 11:31
Sidonians, Chemosh the **g** of Moab, 1 Kgs 11:33
and Milcom the **g** of the 1 Kgs 11:33
the word of **G** came to Shemaiah 1 Kgs 12:22
came to Shemaiah the man of **G**: 1 Kgs 12:22
a man of **G** came out of Judah by the 1 Kgs 13:1
heard the saying of the man of **G**, 1 Kgs 13:4
that the man of **G** had given by the 1 Kgs 13:5
And the king said to the man of **G**, 1 Kgs 13:6
now the favor of the LORD your **G**, 1 Kgs 13:6
And the man of **G** entreated the LORD, 1 Kgs 13:6
And the king said to the man of **G**, 1 Kgs 13:7
And the man of **G** said to the king, "If 1 Kgs 13:8
that the man of **G** had done that day 1 Kgs 13:11
that the man of **G** who came from 1 Kgs 13:12
after the man of **G** and found him 1 Kgs 13:14
you the man of **G** who came from 1 Kgs 13:14
to the man of **G** who came from 1 Kgs 13:21
the LORD your **G** commanded you, 1 Kgs 13:21
is the man of **G** who disobeyed the 1 Kgs 13:26
body of the man of **G** and laid it on 1 Kgs 13:29
in which the man of **G** is buried; 1 Kgs 13:31
'Thus says the LORD, the **G** of Israel: 1 Kgs 14:7
pleasing to the LORD, the **G** of Israel, 1 Kgs 14:13
was not wholly true to the LORD his **G**, 1 Kgs 15:3
sake the LORD his **G** gave him a lamp 1 Kgs 15:4
he provoked the LORD, the **G** of Israel. 1 Kgs 15:30
provoking the LORD **G** of Israel to 1 Kgs 16:13
provoking the LORD, the **G** of Israel, 1 Kgs 16:26
to provoke the LORD, the **G** of Israel, 1 Kgs 16:33
"As the LORD the **G** of Israel lives, 1 Kgs 17:1
she said, "As the LORD your **G** lives, 1 Kgs 17:12
thus says the LORD the **G** of Israel, 1 Kgs 17:14
have you against me, O man of **G**? 1 Kgs 17:18
he cried to the LORD, "O LORD my **G**, 1 Kgs 17:20
and cried to the LORD, "O LORD my **G**, 1 Kgs 17:21
I know that you are a man of **G**, 1 Kgs 17:24
As the LORD your **G** lives, there is no 1 Kgs 18:10
If the LORD is **G**, follow him; but if 1 Kgs 18:21
you call upon the name of your **g**, 1 Kgs 18:24
LORD, and the **G** who answers by fire, 1 Kgs 18:24
he is **G**." And all the people 1 Kgs 18:24
and call upon the name of your **g**, 1 Kgs 18:25
saying, "Cry aloud, for he is a **g**. 1 Kgs 18:27
and said, "O LORD, **G** of Abraham, 1 Kgs 18:36
this day that you are **G** in Israel, 1 Kgs 18:36
may know that you, O LORD, are **G**, 1 Kgs 18:37
faces and said, "The LORD, he is **G**; 1 Kgs 18:39
LORD, he is God; the LORD, he is **G**." 1 Kgs 18:39
forty nights to Horeb, the mount of **G**. 1 Kgs 19:8
jealous for the LORD, the **G** of hosts. 1 Kgs 19:10
jealous for the LORD, the **G** of hosts. 1 Kgs 19:14
And a man of **G** came near and said 1 Kgs 20:28
"The LORD is a **g** of the hills but he is 1 Kgs 20:28
he is not a **g** of the valleys," therefore 1 Kgs 20:28
'You have cursed **G** and the king.' 1 Kgs 21:10
"Naboth cursed **G** and the king." So 1 Kgs 21:13
provoked the LORD, the **G** of Israel, 1 Kgs 22:53
inquire of Baal-zebub, the **g** of Ekron, 2 Kgs 1:2
because there is no **G** in Israel that you 2 Kgs 1:3
inquire of Baal-zebub, the **g** of Ekron? 2 Kgs 1:3
because there is no **G** in Israel that you 2 Kgs 1:6
inquire of Baal-zebub, the **g** of Ekron? 2 Kgs 1:6
of a hill, and said to him, "O man of **G**, 2 Kgs 1:9
captain of fifty, "If I am a man of **G**, 2 Kgs 1:10
and said to him, "O man of **G**, 2 Kgs 1:11
answered them, "If I am a man of **G**, 2 Kgs 1:12
Then the fire of **G** came down from 2 Kgs 1:12
and entreated him, "O man of **G**, 2 Kgs 1:13
the **g** of Ekron—is it because there is 2 Kgs 1:16
because there is no **G** in Israel to 2 Kgs 1:16
the **G** of Elijah?" And when he had 2 Kgs 2:14
She came and told the man of **G**, and 2 Kgs 4:7
a holy man of **G** who is continually 2 Kgs 4:9
she said, "No, my lord, O man of **G**; 2 Kgs 4:16
bed of the man of **G** and shut the door 2 Kgs 4:21
to the man of **G** and come back 2 Kgs 4:22
to the man of **G** at Mount Carmel. 2 Kgs 4:25
When the man of **G** saw her coming, 2 Kgs 4:25
to the mountain to the man of **G**, 2 Kgs 4:27
But the man of **G** said, "Leave her 2 Kgs 4:27
the stew, they cried out, "O man of **G**, 2 Kgs 4:40
bringing the man of **G** bread of the 2 Kgs 4:42
he tore his clothes and said, "Am I **G**, 2 Kgs 5:7
Elisha the man of **G** heard that the 2 Kgs 5:8
call upon the name of the LORD his **G**, 2 Kgs 5:11
to the word of the man of **G**, 2 Kgs 5:14
Then he returned to the man of **G**, he 2 Kgs 5:15
that there is no **G** in all the earth 2 Kgs 5:15
or sacrifice to any **g** but the LORD. 2 Kgs 5:17
the servant of Elisha the man of **G**, 2 Kgs 5:20
Then the man of **G** said, "Where did it 2 Kgs 6:6
But the man of **G** sent word to the king 2 Kgs 6:9

about which the man of **G** told him. 2 Kgs 6:10
of the man of **G** rose early in the 2 Kgs 6:15
"May **G** do so to me and more also, 2 Kgs 6:31
the king leaned said to the man of **G**, 2 Kgs 7:2
as the man of **G** had said when the 2 Kgs 7:17
when the man of **G** had said to the 2 Kgs 7:18
captain had answered the man of **G**, 2 Kgs 7:19
according to the word of the man of **G**. 2 Kgs 8:2
Gehazi the servant of the man of **G**, 2 Kgs 8:4
him, "The man of **G** has come here," 2 Kgs 8:7
with you and go to meet the man of **G**, 2 Kgs 8:8
embarrassed. And the man of **G** wept. 2 Kgs 8:11
"Thus says the LORD the **G** of Israel, 2 Kgs 9:6
of the LORD the **G** of Israel with all 2 Kgs 10:31
Then the man of **G** was angry with 2 Kgs 13:19
the word of the LORD, the **G** of Israel, 2 Kgs 14:25
right in the eyes of the LORD his **G**, 2 Kgs 16:2
had sinned against the LORD their **G**, 2 Kgs 17:7
the LORD their **G** things that were 2 Kgs 17:9
did not believe in the LORD their **G**. 2 Kgs 17:14
commandments of the LORD their **G**, 2 Kgs 17:16
commandments of the LORD their **G**, 2 Kgs 17:19
know the law of the **g** of the land. 2 Kgs 17:26
know the law of the **g** of the land." 2 Kgs 17:26
them the law of the **g** of the land." 2 Kgs 17:27
but you shall fear the LORD your **G**, 2 Kgs 17:39
He trusted in the LORD the **G** of Israel, 2 Kgs 18:5
the LORD their **G** but transgressed 2 Kgs 18:12
trust in the LORD our **G**," is it not he 2 Kgs 18:22
that the LORD your **G** heard all the 2 Kgs 19:4
has sent to mock the living **G**, 2 Kgs 19:4
that the LORD your **G** has heard; 2 Kgs 19:4
'Do not let your **G** in whom you 2 Kgs 19:10
"O LORD the **G** of Israel, who is 2 Kgs 19:15
above the cherubim, you are the **G**, 2 Kgs 19:15
he has sent to mock the living **G**. 2 Kgs 19:16
So now, O LORD our **G**, save us, 2 Kgs 19:19
know that you, O LORD, are **G** alone." 2 Kgs 19:19
"Thus says the LORD, the **G** of Israel: 2 Kgs 19:20
in the house of Nisroch his **g**, 2 Kgs 19:37
the LORD, the **G** of David your father: 2 Kgs 20:5
thus says the LORD, the **G** of Israel: 2 Kgs 21:12
the LORD, the **G** of his fathers, 2 Kgs 21:22
"Thus says the LORD, the **G** of Israel: 2 Kgs 22:15
Thus says the LORD, the **G** of Israel: 2 Kgs 22:18
LORD that the man of **G** proclaimed, 2 Kgs 23:16
of the man of **G** who came from 2 Kgs 23:17
the Passover to the LORD your **G**, 2 Kgs 23:21
Jabez called upon the **G** of Israel, 1 Chr 4:10
me pain!" And **G** granted what he 1 Chr 4:10
for they cried out to **G** in the battle, 1 Chr 5:20
many fell, because the war was of **G**. 1 Chr 5:22
faith with the **G** of their fathers, 1 Chr 5:25
whom **G** had destroyed before them. 1 Chr 5:25
So the **G** of Israel stirred up the spirit 1 Chr 5:26
of the tabernacle of the house of **G**. 1 Chr 6:48
the servant of **G** had commanded. 1 Chr 6:49
the chief officer of the house of **G**; 1 Chr 9:11
work of the service of the house of **G**. 1 Chr 9:13
and the treasures of the house of **G**. 1 Chr 9:26
they lodged around the house of **G**, 1 Chr 9:27
And the LORD your **G** said to you, 1 Chr 11:2
from me before my **G** that I should 1 Chr 11:19
then may the **G** of our fathers see 1 Chr 12:17
For your **G** helps you." Then David 1 Chr 12:18
was a great army, like an army of **G**. 1 Chr 12:22
good to you and from the LORD our **G**, 1 Chr 13:2
us bring again the ark of our **G** to us, 1 Chr 13:3
the ark of **G** from Kiriath-jearim. 1 Chr 13:5
to bring up from there the ark of **G**, 1 Chr 13:6
carried the ark of **G** on a new cart, 1 Chr 13:7
were rejoicing before **G** with all their 1 Chr 13:8
the ark, and he died there before **G**. 1 Chr 13:10
And David was afraid of **G** that day, 1 Chr 13:12
I bring the ark of **G** home to me?" 1 Chr 13:12
And the ark of **G** remained with the 1 Chr 13:14
And David inquired of **G**, "Shall I go 1 Chr 14:10
"**G** has broken through my enemies 1 Chr 14:11
when David again inquired of **G**, 1 Chr 14:14
inquired of God, **G** said to him, 1 Chr 14:14
for **G** has gone out before you to 1 Chr 14:15
David did as **G** commanded him, 1 Chr 14:16
for the ark of **G** and pitched a tent 1 Chr 15:1
the Levites may carry the ark of **G**, 1 Chr 15:2
the ark of the LORD, the **G** of Israel, 1 Chr 15:12
the LORD our **G** broke out against 1 Chr 15:13
the ark of the LORD, the **G** of Israel. 1 Chr 15:14
the ark of **G** on their shoulders 1 Chr 15:15
the trumpets before the ark of **G**. 1 Chr 15:24
And because **G** helped the Levites 1 Chr 15:26
in the ark of **G** and set it inside 1 Chr 16:1
and peace offerings before **G**. 1 Chr 16:1
and to praise the LORD, the **G** of Israel. 1 Chr 16:4
before the ark of the covenant of **G**. 1 Chr 16:6
He is the LORD our **G**; his judgments 1 Chr 16:14

"Save us, O **G** of our salvation, and 1 Chr 16:35
Blessed be the LORD, the **G** of Israel, 1 Chr 16:36
is in your heart, for **G** is with you." 1 Chr 17:2
and said, "Who am I, O LORD **G**, 1 Chr 17:16
was a small thing in your eyes, O **G**. 1 Chr 17:17
me future generations, O LORD **G**! 1 Chr 17:17
LORD, and there is no **G** besides you, 1 Chr 17:20
on earth whom **G** went to redeem 1 Chr 17:21
and you, O LORD, became their **G**. 1 Chr 17:22
'The LORD of hosts, the **G** of Israel, 1 Chr 17:24
hosts, the God of Israel, is Israel's **G**,' 1 Chr 17:24
For you, my **G**, have revealed to 1 Chr 17:25
And now, O LORD, you are **G**, and 1 Chr 17:26
people and for the cities of our **G**, 1 Chr 19:13
But **G** was displeased with this thing, 1 Chr 21:7
And David said to **G**, "I have sinned 1 Chr 21:8
And **G** sent the angel to Jerusalem to 1 Chr 21:15
And David said to **G**, "Was it not I 1 Chr 21:17
Please let your hand, O LORD my **G**, 1 Chr 21:17
not go before it to inquire of **G**, 1 Chr 21:30
house of the LORD **G** and here the 1 Chr 22:1
stones for building the house of **G**. 1 Chr 22:2
a house for the LORD, the **G** of Israel. 1 Chr 22:6
house to the name of the LORD my **G**. 1 Chr 22:7
the house of the LORD your **G**, 1 Chr 22:11
keep the law of the LORD your **G**. 1 Chr 22:12
"Is not the LORD your **G** with you? 1 Chr 22:18
and heart to seek the LORD your **G**. 1 Chr 22:19
build the sanctuary of the LORD **G**, 1 Chr 22:19
holy vessels of **G** may be brought 1 Chr 22:19
the man of **G** were named among 1 Chr 23:14
said, "The LORD, the **G** of Israel, 1 Chr 23:25
for the service of the house of **G**. 1 Chr 23:28
and officers of **G** among both the 1 Chr 24:5
as the LORD **G** of Israel had 1 Chr 24:19
to the promise of **G** to exalt him, 1 Chr 25:5
for **G** had given Heman fourteen sons 1 Chr 25:5
lyres for the service of the house of **G**. 1 Chr 25:6
the eighth, for **G** blessed him. 1 Chr 26:5
of the house of **G** and the treasuries 1 Chr 26:20
everything pertaining to **G** and for 1 Chr 26:32
LORD and for the footstool of our **G**, 1 Chr 28:2
But **G** said to me, 'You may not build 1 Chr 28:3
Yet the LORD **G** of Israel chose me 1 Chr 28:4
the LORD, and in the hearing of our **G**, 1 Chr 28:8
commandments of the LORD your **G**, 1 Chr 28:8
know the **G** of your father and serve 1 Chr 28:9
the treasuries of the house of **G**, 1 Chr 28:12
do not be dismayed, for the LORD **G**, 1 Chr 28:20
for the LORD God, even my **G**, 1 Chr 28:20
for all the service of the house of **G**; 1 Chr 28:21
my son, whom alone **G** has chosen, 1 Chr 29:1
not be for man but for the LORD **G**. 1 Chr 29:1
have provided for the house of my **G**, 1 Chr 29:2
to the house of my **G** I give it to the 1 Chr 29:3
my God I give it to the house of my **G**: 1 Chr 29:3
of the house of **G** 5,000 talents and 1 Chr 29:7
O LORD, the **G** of Israel our father, 1 Chr 29:10
And now we thank you, our **G**, and 1 Chr 29:13
O LORD our **G**, all this abundance 1 Chr 29:16
I know, my **G**, that you test the heart 1 Chr 29:17
O LORD, the **G** of Abraham, Isaac, 1 Chr 29:18
"Bless the LORD your **G**." And all the 1 Chr 29:20
the LORD, the **G** of their fathers, 1 Chr 29:20
and the LORD his **G** was with him and 2 Chr 1:1
at Gibeon, for the tent of meeting of **G**, 2 Chr 1:3
up the ark of **G** from Kiriath-jearim to 2 Chr 1:4
In that night **G** appeared to Solomon, 2 Chr 1:7
And Solomon said to **G**, "You have 2 Chr 1:8
O LORD **G**, let your word to David my 2 Chr 1:9
G answered Solomon, "Because this 2 Chr 1:11
of the LORD my **G** and dedicate it to 2 Chr 2:4
the appointed feasts of the LORD our **G**, 2 Chr 2:4
for our **G** is greater than all gods. 2 Chr 2:5
said, "Blessed be the LORD **G** of Israel, 2 Chr 2:12
for building the house of **G**: 2 Chr 3:3
for King Solomon on the house of **G**: 2 Chr 4:11
vessels that were in the house of **G**: 2 Chr 4:19
in the treasuries of the house of **G**. 2 Chr 5:1
glory of the LORD filled the house of **G**. 2 Chr 5:14
"Blessed be the LORD, the **G** of Israel, 2 Chr 6:4
the name of the LORD, the **G** of Israel. 2 Chr 6:7
the name of the LORD, the **G** of Israel. 2 Chr 6:10
and said, "O LORD, **G** of Israel, there is 2 Chr 6:14
God of Israel, there is no **G** like you, 2 Chr 6:14
Now therefore, O LORD, **G** of Israel, 2 Chr 6:16
Now therefore, O LORD, **G** of Israel, let 2 Chr 6:17
"But will **G** indeed dwell with man on 2 Chr 6:18
servant and to his plea, O LORD my **G**, 2 Chr 6:19
Now, O my **G**, let your eyes be open 2 Chr 6:40
"And now arise, O LORD **G**, and go to 2 Chr 6:41
Let your priests, O LORD **G**, be clothed 2 Chr 6:41
O LORD **G**, do not turn away the face 2 Chr 6:42
all the people dedicated the house of **G**. 2 Chr 7:5
the **G** of their fathers who brought 2 Chr 7:22

the man of **G** had commanded. 2 Chr 8:14
Blessed be the LORD your **G**, who has 2 Chr 9:8
throne as king for the LORD your **G**! 2 Chr 9:8
Because your **G** loved Israel and would 2 Chr 9:8
which **G** had put into his mind. 2 Chr 9:23
brought about by **G** that the LORD 2 Chr 10:15
came to Shemaiah the man of **G**: 2 Chr 11:2
to seek the LORD **G** of Israel came 2 Chr 11:16
to the LORD, the **G** of their fathers. 2 Chr 11:16
know that the LORD **G** of Israel gave 2 Chr 13:5
But as for us, the LORD is our **G**, and 2 Chr 13:10
keep the charge of the LORD our **G**, 2 Chr 13:11
Behold, **G** is with us at our head, 2 Chr 13:12
the LORD, the **G** of your fathers, 2 Chr 13:12
G defeated Jeroboam and all Israel 2 Chr 13:15
and **G** gave them into their hand. 2 Chr 13:16
on the LORD, the **G** of their fathers. 2 Chr 13:18
right in the eyes of the LORD his **G**. 2 Chr 14:2
seek the LORD, the **G** of their fathers, 2 Chr 14:4
we have sought the LORD our **G**. 2 Chr 14:7
And Asa cried to the LORD his **G**, "O 2 Chr 14:11
Help us, O LORD our **G**, for we rely on 2 Chr 14:11
O LORD, you are our **G**; let not man 2 Chr 14:11
The Spirit of **G** came upon Azariah 2 Chr 15:1
time Israel was without the true **G**, 2 Chr 15:3
turned to the LORD, the **G** of Israel, 2 Chr 15:4
for **G** troubled them with every sort 2 Chr 15:6
that the LORD his **G** was with him. 2 Chr 15:9
seek the LORD, the **G** of their fathers, 2 Chr 15:12
not seek the LORD, the **G** of Israel, 2 Chr 15:13
into the house of **G** the sacred gifts 2 Chr 15:18
and did not rely on the LORD your **G**, 2 Chr 16:7
but sought the **G** of his father and 2 Chr 17:4
for **G** will give it into the hand of the 2 Chr 18:5
"As the LORD lives, what my **G** says, 2 Chr 18:13
him; **G** drew them away from him. 2 Chr 18:31
and have set your heart to seek **G**." 2 Chr 19:3
to the LORD, the **G** of their fathers. 2 Chr 19:4
is no injustice with the LORD our **G**, 2 Chr 19:7
and said, "O LORD, **G** of our fathers, 2 Chr 20:6
our fathers, are you not **G** in heaven? 2 Chr 20:6
Did you not, our **G**, drive out the 2 Chr 20:7
O our **G**, will you not execute 2 Chr 20:12
up to praise the LORD, the **G** of Israel, 2 Chr 20:19
Believe in the LORD your **G**, and you 2 Chr 20:20
And the fear of **G** came on all the 2 Chr 20:29
for his **G** gave him rest all around. 2 Chr 20:30
hearts upon the **G** of their fathers. 2 Chr 20:33
the LORD, the **G** of his fathers. 2 Chr 21:10
the LORD, the **G** of David your father, 2 Chr 21:12
was ordained by **G** that the downfall 2 Chr 22:7
six years, hidden in the house of **G**, 2 Chr 22:12
with the king in the house of **G**. 2 Chr 23:3
which were in the house of **G**. 2 Chr 23:9
the house of your **G** from year to 2 Chr 24:5
had broken into the house of **G**, 2 Chr 24:7
Moses the servant of **G** laid on Israel 2 Chr 24:9
restored the house of **G** to its proper 2 Chr 24:13
Israel, and toward **G** and his house. 2 Chr 24:16
of the LORD, the **G** of their fathers, 2 Chr 24:18
the Spirit of **G** clothed Zechariah 2 Chr 24:20
and said to them, "Thus says **G**, 2 Chr 24:20
the LORD, the **G** of their fathers. 2 Chr 24:24
of the house of **G** are written in the 2 Chr 24:27
But a man of **G** came to him and 2 Chr 25:7
you suppose that **G** will cast you 2 Chr 25:8
For **G** has power to help or to cast 2 Chr 25:8
And Amaziah said to the man of **G**, 2 Chr 25:9
of Israel?" The man of **G** answered, 2 Chr 25:9
"I know that **G** has determined to 2 Chr 25:16
would not listen, for it was of **G**, 2 Chr 25:20
that were found in the house of **G**, 2 Chr 25:24
He set himself to seek **G** in the days of 2 Chr 26:5
who instructed him in the fear of **G**, 2 Chr 26:5
the LORD, **G** made him prosper. 2 Chr 26:5
G helped him against the Philistines 2 Chr 26:7
to the LORD his **G** and entered the 2 Chr 26:16
you no honor from the LORD **G**." 2 Chr 26:18
his ways before the LORD his **G**. 2 Chr 27:6
the LORD his **G** gave him into 2 Chr 28:5
the LORD, the **G** of their fathers. 2 Chr 28:6
the LORD, the **G** of your fathers, 2 Chr 28:9
your own against the LORD your **G**? 2 Chr 28:10
of the house of **G** and cut in pieces 2 Chr 28:24
pieces the vessels of the house of **G**, 2 Chr 28:24
anger the LORD, the **G** of his fathers. 2 Chr 28:25
of the LORD, the **G** of your fathers, 2 Chr 29:5
evil in the sight of the LORD our **G**. 2 Chr 29:6
in the Holy Place to the **G** of Israel. 2 Chr 29:7
with the LORD, the **G** of Israel, 2 Chr 29:10
rejoiced because **G** had prepared 2 Chr 29:36
Passover to the LORD, the **G** of Israel. 2 Chr 30:1
Passover to the LORD, the **G** of Israel, 2 Chr 30:5
to the LORD, the **G** of Abraham, 2 Chr 30:6
to the LORD **G** of their fathers, 2 Chr 30:7

forever, and serve the LORD your **G**, 2 Chr 30:8
For the LORD your **G** is gracious and 2 Chr 30:9
The hand of **G** was also on Judah to 2 Chr 30:12
to the Law of Moses the man of **G**. 2 Chr 30:16
who sets his heart to seek **G**, the 2 Chr 30:19
God, the LORD, the **G** of his fathers, 2 Chr 30:19
to the LORD, the **G** of their fathers. 2 Chr 30:22
been dedicated to the LORD their **G**, 2 Chr 31:6
the chief officer of the house of **G**. 2 Chr 31:13
was over the freewill offerings to **G**, 2 Chr 31:14
and faithful before the LORD his **G**. 2 Chr 31:20
of the house of **G** and in accordance 2 Chr 31:21
the commandments, seeking his **G**, 2 Chr 31:21
flesh, but with us is the LORD our **G**, 2 Chr 32:8
"The LORD our **G** will deliver us 2 Chr 32:11
that your **G** should be able to 2 Chr 32:14
for no **g** of any nation or kingdom 2 Chr 32:15
less will your **G** deliver you out 2 Chr 32:15
against the Lord **G** and against his 2 Chr 32:16
the **G** of Israel and to speak against 2 Chr 32:17
so the **G** of Hezekiah will not deliver 2 Chr 32:17
they spoke of the **G** of Jerusalem as 2 Chr 32:19
he came into the house of his **g**, 2 Chr 32:21
for **G** had given him very great 2 Chr 32:29
in the land, **G** left him to himself, 2 Chr 32:31
he had made he set in the house of **G**, 2 Chr 33:7
of which **G** said to David and to 2 Chr 33:7
the LORD his **G** and humbled 2 Chr 33:12
greatly before the **G** of his fathers. 2 Chr 33:12
and **G** was moved by his entreaty 2 Chr 33:13
knew that the LORD was **G**. 2 Chr 33:13
to serve the LORD, the **G** of Israel. 2 Chr 33:16
places, but only to the LORD their **G**. 2 Chr 33:17
Manasseh, and his prayer to his **G**, 2 Chr 33:18
the name of the LORD, the **G** of Israel, 2 Chr 33:18
and how **G** was moved by his 2 Chr 33:19
began to seek the **G** of David his 2 Chr 34:3
to repair the house of the LORD his **G**. 2 Chr 34:8
been brought into the house of **G**, 2 Chr 34:9
"Thus says the LORD, the **G** of Israel: 2 Chr 34:23
Thus says the LORD, the **G** of Israel: 2 Chr 34:26
yourself before **G** when you 2 Chr 34:27
did according to the covenant of **G**, 2 Chr 34:32
of God, the **G** of their fathers. 2 Chr 34:32
in Israel serve the LORD their **G**. 2 Chr 34:33
the LORD, the **G** of their fathers. 2 Chr 34:33
serve the LORD your **G** and his people 2 Chr 35:3
the chief officers of the house of **G**, 2 Chr 35:8
And **G** has commanded me to 2 Chr 35:21
Cease opposing **G**, who is with me, 2 Chr 35:21
words of Neco from the mouth of **G**, 2 Chr 35:22
was evil in the sight of the LORD his **G**. 2 Chr 36:5
evil in the sight of the LORD his **G**. 2 Chr 36:12
who had made him swear by **G**. 2 Chr 36:13
turning to the LORD, the **G** of Israel. 2 Chr 36:13
The LORD, the **G** of their fathers, sent 2 Chr 36:15
kept mocking the messengers of **G**, 2 Chr 36:16
And all the vessels of the house of **G**, 2 Chr 36:18
the house of **G** and broke down 2 Chr 36:19
Persia, 'The LORD, the **G** of heaven, 2 Chr 36:23
may the LORD his **G** be with him. 2 Chr 36:23
The LORD, the **G** of heaven, has given me Ezr 1:2
of all his people, may his **G** be with him, Ezr 1:3
the **G** of Israel—he is the God who is in Ezr 1:3
Israel—he is the **G** who is in Jerusalem. Ezr 1:3
for the house of **G** that is in Jerusalem." Ezr 1:4
everyone whose spirit **G** had stirred to go Ezr 1:5
freewill offerings for the house of **G**, Ezr 2:68
and they built the altar of the **G** of Israel, Ezr 3:2
in the Law of Moses the man of **G**. Ezr 3:2
coming to the house of **G** at Jerusalem, Ezr 3:8
the workmen in the house of **G**, Ezr 3:9
a temple to the LORD, the **G** of Israel, Ezr 4:1
you, for we worship your **G** as you do, Ezr 4:2
do with us in building a house to our **G**; Ezr 4:3
will build to the LORD, the **G** of Israel, Ezr 4:3
on the house of **G** that is in Jerusalem Ezr 4:24
in the name of the **G** of Israel who was Ezr 5:1
rebuild the house of **G** that is in Ezr 5:2
and the prophets of **G** were with them, Ezr 5:2
But the eye of their **G** was on the elders of Ezr 5:5
of Judah, to the house of the great **G**. Ezr 5:8
the servants of the **G** of heaven and Ezr 5:11
fathers had angered the **G** of heaven, Ezr 5:12
that this house of **G** should be rebuilt. Ezr 5:13
gold and silver vessels of the house of **G**, Ezr 5:14
and let the house of **G** be rebuilt on its Ezr 5:15
of the house of **G** that is in Jerusalem, Ezr 5:16
of this house of **G** in Jerusalem. Ezr 5:17
Concerning the house of **G** at Jerusalem, Ezr 6:3
gold and silver vessels of the house of **G**, Ezr 6:5
You shall put them in the house of **G**. Ezr 6:5
Let the work on this house of **G** alone. Let Ezr 6:7
Jews rebuild this house of **G** on its site. Ezr 6:7
Jews for the rebuilding of this house of **G**. Ezr 6:8
for burnt offerings to the **G** of heaven, Ezr 6:9
sacrifices to the **G** of heaven and Ezr 6:10
May the **G** who has caused his name to Ezr 6:12
destroy this house of **G** that is in Ezr 6:12
by decree of the **G** of Israel and by Ezr 6:14
dedication of this house of **G** with joy. Ezr 6:16
dedication of this house of **G** 100 bulls, Ezr 6:17
for the service of **G** at Jerusalem, Ezr 6:18
land to worship the LORD, the **G** of Israel. Ezr 6:21
them in the work of the house of **G**, Ezr 6:22
work of the house of God, the **G** of Israel. Ezr 6:22
that the LORD the **G** of Israel had given, Ezr 7:6
the hand of the LORD his **G** was on him. Ezr 7:6
for the good hand of his **G** was on him. Ezr 7:9
the scribe of the Law of the **G** of heaven. Ezr 7:12
according to the Law of your **G**, Ezr 7:14
have freely offered to the **G** of Israel, Ezr 7:15
the house of their **G** that is in Jerusalem. Ezr 7:16
the house of your **G** that is in Jerusalem. Ezr 7:17
may do, according to the will of your **G**. Ezr 7:18
for the service of the house of your **G**, Ezr 7:19
shall deliver before the **G** of Jerusalem. Ezr 7:19
else is required for the house of your **G**, Ezr 7:20
the scribe of the Law of the **G** of heaven, Ezr 7:21
Whatever is decreed by the **G** of heaven, Ezr 7:23
in full for the house of the **G** of heaven, Ezr 7:23
or other servants of this house of **G**. Ezr 7:24
to the wisdom of your **G** that is in your Ezr 7:25
all such as know the laws of your **G**. Ezr 7:25
obey the law of your **G** and the law of Ezr 7:26
Blessed be the LORD, the **G** of our fathers, Ezr 7:27
the hand of the LORD my **G** was on me, Ezr 7:28
us ministers for the house of our **G**. Ezr 8:17
And by the good hand of our **G** on us, Ezr 8:18
might humble ourselves before our **G**, Ezr 8:21
"The hand of our **G** is for good on all Ezr 8:22
we fasted and implored our **G** for this, Ezr 8:23
for the house of our **G** that the king and Ezr 8:25
to the LORD, the **G** of your fathers. Ezr 8:28
to Jerusalem, to the house of our **G**. Ezr 8:30
The hand of our **G** was on us, and he Ezr 8:31
fourth day, within the house of our **G**, Ezr 8:33
offered burnt offerings to the **G** of Israel, Ezr 8:35
they aided the people and the house of **G**. Ezr 8:36
trembled at the words of the **G** of Israel, Ezr 9:4
spread out my hands to the LORD my **G**, Ezr 9:5
"O my **G**, I am ashamed and blush to lift Ezr 9:6
and blush to lift my face to you, my **G**, Ezr 9:6
favor has been shown by the LORD our **G**, Ezr 9:8
that our **G** may brighten our eyes and Ezr 9:8
Yet our **G** has not forsaken us in our Ezr 9:9
reviving to set up the house of our **G**, Ezr 9:9
"And now, O our **G**, what shall we say Ezr 9:10
our great guilt, seeing that you, our **G**, Ezr 9:13
O LORD the **G** of Israel, you are just, for Ezr 9:15
himself down before the house of **G**, Ezr 10:1
faith with our **G** and have married Ezr 10:2
a covenant with our **G** to put away all Ezr 10:3
tremble at the commandment of our **G**, Ezr 10:3
before the house of **G** and went to the Ezr 10:6
the open square before the house of **G**, Ezr 10:9
the **G** of your fathers and do his will. Ezr 10:11
fierce wrath of our **G** over this matter Ezr 10:14
and praying before the **G** of heaven. Neh 1:4
And I said, "O LORD **G** of heaven, the Neh 1:5
great and awesome **G** who keeps Neh 1:5
So I prayed to the **G** of heaven. Neh 2:4
for the good hand of my **G** was upon me. Neh 2:8
no one what my **G** had put into my Neh 2:12
the hand of my **G** that had been upon Neh 2:18
"The **G** of heaven will make us Neh 2:20
Hear, O our **G**, for we are despised. Turn Neh 4:4
And we prayed to our **G** and set a guard Neh 4:9
to us and that **G** had frustrated their Neh 4:15
to us there. Our **G** will fight for us." Neh 4:20
in the fear of our **G** to prevent the taunts Neh 5:9
"So may **G** shake out every man from Neh 5:13
I did not do so, because of the fear of **G**. Neh 5:15
Remember for my good, O my **G**, all Neh 5:19
and it will not be done." But now, O **G**, Neh 6:9
"Let us meet together in the house of **G**, Neh 6:10
and saw that **G** had not sent Neh 6:12
Tobiah and Sanballat, O my **G**, Neh 6:14
accomplished with the help of our **G**. Neh 6:16
Then my **G** put it into my heart to Neh 7:5
And Ezra blessed the LORD, the great **G**, Neh 8:6
read from the book, from the Law of **G**, Neh 8:8
"This day is holy to the LORD your **G**; Neh 8:9
and in the courts of the house of **G**, Neh 8:16
he read from the Book of the Law of **G**. Neh 8:18
Law of the LORD their **G** for a quarter of Neh 9:3
and worshiped the LORD their **G**. Neh 9:3
with a loud voice to the LORD their **G**. Neh 9:4
the LORD your **G** from everlasting to Neh 9:5
the **G** who chose Abram and brought Neh 9:7
But you are a **G** ready to forgive, Neh 9:17
'This is your **G** who brought you up Neh 9:18
for you are a gracious and merciful **G**. Neh 9:31
"Now, therefore, our **G**, the great, the Neh 9:32
great, the mighty, and the awesome **G**, Neh 9:32
peoples of the lands to the Law of **G**, Neh 10:28
was given by Moses the servant of **G**, Neh 10:29
for the service of the house of our **G**: Neh 10:32
for all the work of the house of our **G**. Neh 10:33
to bring it into the house of our **G**, Neh 10:34
to burn on the altar of the LORD our **G**, Neh 10:34
also to bring to the house of our **G**, to Neh 10:36
who minister in the house of our **G**, Neh 10:36
the chambers of the house of our **G**; Neh 10:37
of the tithes to the house of our **G**, Neh 10:38
will not neglect the house of our **G**." Neh 10:39
son of Ahitub, ruler of the house of **G**, Neh 11:11
the outside work of the house of **G**; Neh 11:16
over the work of the house of **G**. Neh 11:22
of David the man of **G**, Neh 12:24
instruments of David the man of **G**. Neh 12:36
gave thanks stood in the house of **G**, Neh 12:40
for **G** had made them rejoice with Neh 12:43
the service of their **G** and the service Neh 12:45
of praise and thanksgiving to **G**. Neh 12:46
should ever enter the assembly of **G**, Neh 13:1
them—yet our **G** turned the curse into Neh 13:2
the chambers of the house of our **G**, Neh 13:4
in the courts of the house of **G**. Neh 13:7
there the vessels of the house of **G**, Neh 13:9
is the house of **G** forsaken?" And I Neh 13:11
Remember me, O my **G**, concerning Neh 13:14
the house of my **G** and for his service. Neh 13:14
and did not our **G** bring all this Neh 13:18
this also in my favor, O my **G**, Neh 13:22
them take oath in the name of **G**, Neh 13:25
him, and he was beloved by his **G**, Neh 13:26
and **G** made him king over all Israel. Neh 13:26
against our **G** by marrying Neh 13:27
Remember them, O my **G**, because Neh 13:29
Remember me, O my **G**, for good. Neh 13:31
one who feared **G** and turned away from Jb 1:1
and cursed **G** in their hearts." Thus Job Jb 1:5
when the sons of **G** came to present Jb 1:6
who fears **G** and turns away from evil?" Jb 1:8
and said, "Does Job fear **G** for no reason? Jb 1:9
"The fire of **G** fell from heaven and Jb 1:16
Job did not sin or charge **G** with wrong. Jb 1:22
when the sons of **G** came to present Jb 2:1
who fears **G** and turns away from evil? Jb 2:3
hold fast your integrity? Curse **G** and die." Jb 2:9
Shall we receive good from **G**, and shall Jb 2:10
May **G** above not seek it, nor light shine Jb 3:4
way is hidden, whom **G** has hedged in? Jb 3:23
Is not your fear of **G** your confidence, and Jb 4:6
By the breath of **G** they perish, and by the Jb 4:9
mortal man be in the right before **G**? Jb 4:17
"As for me, I would seek **G**, and to God Jb 5:8
God, and to **G** would I commit my cause, Jb 5:8
blessed is the one whom **G** reproves; Jb 5:17
the terrors of **G** are arrayed against me. Jb 6:4
request, and that **G** would fulfill my hope, Jb 6:8
that it would please **G** to crush me, that he Jb 6:9
Does **G** pervert justice? Or does the Jb 8:3
If you will seek **G** and plead with the Jb 8:5
Such are the paths of all who forget **G**; Jb 8:13
G will not reject a blameless man, Jb 8:20
how can a man be in the right before **G**? Jb 9:2
"**G** will not turn back his anger; beneath Jb 9:13
I will say to **G**, Do not condemn me; let Jb 10:2
that **G** would speak and open his lips to Jb 11:5
Know then that **G** exacts of you less than Jb 11:6
"Can you find out the deep things of **G**? Jb 11:7
I, who called to **G** and he answered me, a Jb 12:4
and those who provoke **G** are secure, Jb 12:6
secure, who bring their **g** in their hand. Jb 12:6
"With **G** are wisdom and might; he has Jb 12:13
and I desire to argue my case with **G**. Jb 13:3
speak falsely for **G** and speak deceitfully Jb 13:7
him? Will you plead the case for **G**? Jb 13:8
the fear of **G** and hindering meditation Jb 15:4
God and hindering meditation before **G**. Jb 15:4
Have you listened in the council of **G**? Jb 15:8
Are the comforts of **G** too small for you, Jb 15:11
your spirit against **G** and bring such Jb 15:13
Behold, **G** puts no trust in his holy ones, Jb 15:15
out his hand against **G** and defies the Jb 15:25
Surely now **G** has worn me out; he has Jb 16:7
G gives me up to the ungodly and casts Jb 16:11
scorn me; my eye pours out tears to **G**, Jb 16:20
would argue the case of a man with **G**, Jb 16:21
is the place of him who knows not **G**." Jb 18:21
know then that **G** has put me in the Jb 19:6
for the hand of **G** has touched me! Jb 19:21
Why do you, like **G**, pursue me? Why Jb 19:22

destroyed, yet in my flesh I shall see **G**, Jb 19:26
up again; **G** casts them out of his belly. Jb 20:15
belly to the full **G** will send his burning Jb 20:23
is the wicked man's portion from **G**, Jb 20:29
God, the heritage decreed for him by **G**." Jb 20:29
from fear, and no rod of **G** is upon them. Jb 21:9
They say to **G**, 'Depart from us! We do Jb 21:14
That **G** distributes pains in his anger? Jb 21:17
'**G** stores up their iniquity for their Jb 21:19
Will any teach **G** knowledge, seeing Jb 21:22
"Can a man be profitable to **G**? Surely he Jb 22:2
"Is not **G** high in the heavens? See the Jb 22:12
But you say, 'What does **G** know? Can Jb 22:13
They said to **G**, 'Depart from us,' and Jb 22:17
"Agree with **G**, and be at peace; thereby Jb 22:21
the Almighty and lift up your face to **G**. Jb 22:26
G has made my heart faint; the Jb 23:16
help; yet **G** charges no one with wrong. Jb 24:12
Yet **G** prolongs the life of the mighty by Jb 24:22
"Dominion and fear are with **G**; he Jb 25:2
then can man be in the right before **G**? Jb 25:4
Sheol is naked before **G**, and Abaddon Jb 26:6
"As **G** lives, who has taken away my Jb 27:2
me, and the spirit of **G** is in my nostrils, Jb 27:3
hope of the godless when **G** cuts him off, Jb 27:8
cuts him off, when **G** takes away his life? Jb 27:8
Will **G** hear his cry when distress comes Jb 27:9
Will he call upon **G** at all times? Jb 27:10
teach you concerning the hand of **G**; Jb 27:11
is the portion of a wicked man with **G**, Jb 27:13
"**G** understands the way to it, and he Jb 28:23
as in the days when **G** watched over me, Jb 29:2
when the friendship of **G** was upon my Jb 29:4
Because **G** has loosed my cord and Jb 30:11
G has cast me into the mire, and I have Jb 30:19
be my portion from **G** above and my Jb 31:2
balance, and let **G** know my integrity!) Jb 31:6
what then shall I do when **G** rises up? Jb 31:14
For I was in terror of calamity from **G**, Jb 31:23
for I would have been false to **G** above. Jb 31:28
he justified himself rather than **G**. Jb 32:2
G may vanquish him, not a man.' Jb 32:13
The Spirit of **G** has made me, and the Jb 33:4
Behold, I am toward **G** as you are; I too Jb 33:6
answer you, for **G** is greater than man. Jb 33:12
For **G** speaks in one way, and in two, Jb 33:14
then man prays to **G**, and he accepts Jb 33:26
"Behold, **G** does all these things, twice, Jb 33:29
right, and **G** has taken away my right; Jb 34:5
nothing that he should take delight in **G**.' Jb 34:9
far be it from **G** that he should do Jb 34:10
Of a truth, **G** will not do wickedly, and Jb 34:12
For **G** has no need to consider a man Jb 34:23
that he should go before **G** in judgment. Jb 34:23
"For has anyone said to **G**, 'I have borne Jb 34:31
us and multiplies his words against **G**." Jb 34:37
just? Do you say, 'It is my right before **G**,' Jb 35:2
But none says, 'Where is **G** my Maker, Jb 35:10
Surely **G** does not hear an empty cry, Jb 35:13
"Behold, **G** is mighty, and does not Jb 36:5
Behold, **G** is exalted in his power; who is Jb 36:22
Behold, **G** is great, and we know him Jb 36:26
G thunders wondrously with his voice; Jb 37:5
By the breath of **G** ice is given, and the Jb 37:10
and consider the wondrous works of **G**. Jb 37:14
Do you know how **G** lays his command Jb 37:15
G is clothed with awesome majesty. Jb 37:22
and all the sons of **G** shouted for joy? Jb 38:7
when its young ones cry to **G** for help, Jb 38:41
because **G** has made her forget wisdom Jb 39:17
He who argues with **G**, let him answer it." Jb 40:2
Have you an arm like **G**, and can you Jb 40:9
"He is the first of the works of **G**; let him Jb 40:19
soul, there is no salvation for him in **G**. Ps 3:2
Arise, O LORD! Save me, O my **G**! For you Ps 3:7
me when I call, O **G** of my righteousness! Ps 4:1
the sound of my cry, my King and my **G**, Ps 5:2
you are not a **G** who delights in Ps 5:4
Make them bear their guilt, O **G**; let Ps 5:10
O LORD my **G**, in you do I take refuge; save Ps 7:1
O LORD my **G**, if I have done this, if there is Ps 7:3
test the minds and hearts, O righteous **G**! Ps 7:9
My shield is with **G**, who saves the Ps 7:10
G is a righteous judge, and a God who Ps 7:11
and a **G** who feels indignation every day. Ps 7:11
does not repent, **G** will whet his sword; Ps 7:12
to Sheol, all the nations that forget **G**. Ps 9:17
all his thoughts are, "There is no **G**." Ps 10:4
He says in his heart, "**G** has forgotten, Ps 10:11
Arise, O LORD; O **G**, lift up your hand; Ps 10:12
does the wicked renounce **G** and say in Ps 10:13
Consider and answer me, O LORD my **G**; Ps 13:3
heart, "There is no **G**." They are corrupt, Ps 14:1
any who understand, who seek after **G**. Ps 14:2
for **G** is with the generation of the Ps 14:5
Preserve me, O **G**, for in you I take refuge. Ps 16:1
who run after another **g** shall multiply; Ps 16:4
upon you, for you will answer me, O **G**; Ps 17:6
and my fortress and my deliverer, my **G**, Ps 18:2
upon the LORD; to my **G** I cried for help. Ps 18:6
have not wickedly departed from my **G**. Ps 18:21
the LORD my **G** lightens my darkness. Ps 18:28
and by my **G** I can leap over a wall. Ps 18:29
This **G**—his way is perfect; the word of Ps 18:30
For who is **G**, but the LORD? And who is Ps 18:31
LORD? And who is a rock, except our **G**? Ps 18:31
the **G** who equipped me with strength Ps 18:32
and exalted be the **G** of my salvation— Ps 18:46
the **G** who gave me vengeance and Ps 18:47
The heavens declare the glory of **G**, and Ps 19:1
the name of the **G** of Jacob protect you! Ps 20:1
in the name of our **G** set up our banners! Ps 20:5
we trust in the name of the LORD our **G**. Ps 20:7
My **G**, my God, why have you forsaken Ps 22:1
My God, my **G**, why have you forsaken Ps 22:1
O my **G**, I cry by day, but you do not Ps 22:2
mother's womb you have been my **G**. Ps 22:10
righteousness from the **G** of his Ps 24:5
him, who seek the face of the **G** of Jacob. Ps 24:6
O my **G**, in you I trust; let me not be put Ps 25:2
me, for you are the **G** of my salvation; Ps 25:5
Redeem Israel, O **G**, out of all his Ps 25:22
off; forsake me not, O **G** of my salvation! Ps 27:9
the **G** of glory thunders, the LORD, over Ps 29:3
O LORD my **G**, I cried to you for help, and Ps 30:2
O LORD my **G**, I will give thanks to you Ps 30:12
have redeemed me, O LORD, faithful **G**. Ps 31:5
in you, O LORD; I say, "You are my **G**." Ps 31:14
is the nation whose **G** is the LORD, Ps 33:12
for my cause, my **G** and my Lord! Ps 35:23
Vindicate me, O LORD, my **G**, according Ps 35:24
heart; there is no fear of **G** before his eyes. Ps 36:1
righteousness is like the mountains of **G**; Ps 36:6
How precious is your steadfast love, O **G**! Ps 36:7
The law of his **G** is in his heart; his Ps 37:31
it is you, O Lord my **G**, who will answer. Ps 38:15
O LORD! O my **G**, be not far from me! Ps 38:21
in my mouth, a song of praise to our **G**. Ps 40:3
You have multiplied, O LORD my **G**, your Ps 40:5
I desire to do your will, O my **G**; your law Ps 40:8
and my deliverer; do not delay, O my **G**! Ps 40:17
Blessed be the LORD, the **G** of Israel, from Ps 41:13
streams, so pants my soul for you, O **G**. Ps 42:1
My soul thirsts for **G**, for the living God. Ps 42:2
My soul thirsts for God, for the living **G**. Ps 42:2
When shall I come and appear before **G**? Ps 42:2
to me continually, "Where is your **G**?" Ps 42:3
to the house of **G** with glad shouts and Ps 42:4
Hope in **G**; for I shall again praise him, Ps 42:5
and my **G**. My soul is cast down within Ps 42:6
is with me, a prayer to the **G** of my life. Ps 42:8
I say to **G**, my rock: "Why have you Ps 42:9
to me continually, "Where is your **G**?" Ps 42:10
Hope in **G**; for I shall again praise him, Ps 42:11
praise him, my salvation and my **G**. Ps 42:11
Vindicate me, O **G**, and defend my cause Ps 43:1
For you are the **G** in whom I take refuge; Ps 43:2
Then I will go to the altar of **G**, to God Ps 43:4
the altar of God, to **G** my exceeding joy, Ps 43:4
and I will praise you with the lyre, O **G**, Ps 43:4
praise you with the lyre, O God, my **G**. Ps 43:4
Hope in **G**; for I shall again praise him, Ps 43:5
praise him, my salvation and my **G**. Ps 43:5
O **G**, we have heard with our ears, our Ps 44:1
You are my King, O **G**; ordain salvation Ps 44:4
In **G** we have boasted continually, and Ps 44:8
the name of our **G** or spread out our Ps 44:20
or spread out our hands to a foreign **g**, Ps 44:20
would not **G** discover this? For he Ps 44:21
lips; therefore **G** has blessed you forever. Ps 45:2
Your throne, O **G**, is forever and ever. Ps 45:6
and hated wickedness. Therefore **G**, Ps 45:7
Therefore God, your **G**, has anointed you Ps 45:7
G is our refuge and strength, a very Ps 46:1
whose streams make glad the city of **G**, Ps 46:4
G is in the midst of her; she shall not be Ps 46:5
G will help her when morning dawns. Ps 46:5
is with us; the **G** of Jacob is our fortress. Ps 46:7
"Be still, and know that I am **G**. I will be Ps 46:10
is with us; the **G** of Jacob is our fortress. Ps 46:11
Shout to **G** with loud songs of joy! Ps 47:1
G has gone up with a shout, the LORD Ps 47:5
Sing praises to **G**, sing praises! Sing Ps 47:6
For **G** is the King of all the earth; sing Ps 47:7
G reigns over the nations; God sits on his Ps 47:8
the nations; **G** sits on his holy throne. Ps 47:8
as the people of the **G** of Abraham. Ps 47:9
For the shields of the earth belong to **G**; Ps 47:9
greatly to be praised in the city of our **G**! Ps 48:1
Within her citadels **G** has made himself Ps 48:3
of the LORD of hosts, in the city of our **G**, Ps 48:8
our God, which **G** will establish forever. Ps 48:8
have thought on your steadfast love, O **G**, Ps 48:9
As your name, O **G**, so your praise Ps 48:10
that this is **G**, our God forever and ever. Ps 48:14
that this is God, our **G** forever and ever. Ps 48:14
another, or give to **G** the price of his life, Ps 49:7
But **G** will ransom my soul from the Ps 49:15
The Mighty One, **G** the LORD, speaks and Ps 50:1
the perfection of beauty, **G** shines forth. Ps 50:2
Our **G** comes; he does not keep silence; Ps 50:3
his righteousness, for **G** himself is judge! Ps 50:6
testify against you. I am **G**, your God. Ps 50:7
testify against you. I am God, your **G**. Ps 50:7
Offer to **G** a sacrifice of thanksgiving, Ps 50:14
But to the wicked **G** says: "What right Ps 50:16
"Mark this, then, you who forget **G**, lest Ps 50:22
rightly I will show the salvation of **G**!" Ps 50:23
Have mercy on me, O **G**, according to Ps 51:1
Create in me a clean heart, O **G**, and Ps 51:10
Deliver me from bloodguiltiness, O **G**, Ps 51:14
O God, O **G** of my salvation, Ps 51:14
The sacrifices of **G** are a broken spirit; Ps 51:17
a broken and contrite heart, O **G**, you Ps 51:17
The steadfast love of **G** endures all the Ps 52:1
But **G** will break you down forever; he Ps 52:5
man who would not make **G** his refuge, Ps 52:7
like a green olive tree in the house of **G**. Ps 52:8
in the steadfast love of **G** forever and ever. Ps 52:8
heart, "There is no **G**." They are corrupt, Ps 53:1
G looks down from heaven on the Ps 53:2
any who understand, who seek after **G**. Ps 53:2
they eat bread, and do not call upon **G**? Ps 53:4
For **G** scatters the bones of him who Ps 53:5
them to shame, for **G** has rejected them. Ps 53:5
When **G** restores the fortunes of his Ps 53:6
O **G**, save me, by your name, and Ps 54:1
O **G**, hear my prayer; give ear to the Ps 54:2
life; they do not set **G** before themselves. Ps 54:3
Behold, **G** is my helper; the Lord is the Ps 54:4
Give ear to my prayer, O **G**, and hide not Ps 55:1
But I call to **G**, and the LORD will save Ps 55:16
G will give ear and humble them, he Ps 55:19
they do not change and do not fear **G**. Ps 55:19
But you, O **G**, will cast them down into Ps 55:23
Be gracious to me, O **G**, for man Ps 56:1
In **G**, whose word I praise, in God I trust; I Ps 56:4
In God, whose word I praise, in **G** I trust; I Ps 56:4
In wrath cast down the peoples, O **G**! Ps 56:7
I call. This I know, that **G** is for me. Ps 56:9
In **G**, whose word I praise, in the LORD, Ps 56:10
in **G** I trust; I shall not be afraid. What Ps 56:11
I must perform my vows to you, O **G**; I Ps 56:12
that I may walk before **G** in the light of Ps 56:13
Be merciful to me, O **G**, be merciful to Ps 57:1
I cry out to **G** Most High, to God who Ps 57:2
to **G** who fulfills his purpose for me. Ps 57:2
Selah **G** will send out his steadfast love Ps 57:3
Be exalted, O **G**, above the heavens! Let Ps 57:5
My heart is steadfast, O **G**, my heart is Ps 57:7
Be exalted, O **G**, above the heavens! Let Ps 57:11
O **G**, break the teeth in their mouths; tear Ps 58:6
surely there is a **G** who judges on Ps 58:11
Deliver me from my enemies, O my **G**; Ps 59:1
You, LORD **G** of hosts, are God of Israel. Ps 59:5
You, LORD God of hosts, are **G** of Israel. Ps 59:5
I will watch for you, for you, O **G**, Ps 59:9
My **G** in his steadfast love will meet me; Ps 59:10
G will let me look in triumph on my Ps 59:10
they may know that **G** rules over Jacob Ps 59:13
I will sing praises to you, for you, O **G**, Ps 59:17
the **G** who shows me steadfast love. Ps 59:17
O **G**, you have rejected us, broken our Ps 60:1
G has spoken in his holiness: "With Ps 60:6
Have you not rejected us, O **G**? You do Ps 60:10
You do not go forth, O **G**, with our Ps 60:10
With **G** we shall do valiantly; it is he Ps 60:12
Hear my cry, O **G**, listen to my prayer; Ps 61:1
For you, O **G**, have heard my vows; you Ps 61:5
May he be enthroned forever before **G**; Ps 61:7
For **G** alone my soul waits in silence; Ps 62:1
For **G** alone, O my soul, wait in silence, Ps 62:5
On **G** rests my salvation and my glory; Ps 62:7
glory; my mighty rock, my refuge is **G**. Ps 62:7
heart before him; **G** is a refuge for us. Ps 62:8
Once **G** has spoken; twice have I heard Ps 62:11
I heard this: that power belongs to **G**, Ps 62:11
O **G**, you are my God; earnestly I seek Ps 63:1
O God, you are my **G**; earnestly I seek Ps 63:1
But the king shall rejoice in **G**; all who Ps 63:11
Hear my voice, O **G**, in my complaint; Ps 64:1
But **G** shoots his arrow at them; they are Ps 64:7
they tell what **G** has brought about and Ps 64:9
Praise is due to you, O **G**, in Zion, and to Ps 65:1
with righteousness, O **G** of our salvation, Ps 65:5

enrich it; the river of **G** is full of water; Ps 65:9
Shout for joy to **G**, all the earth; Ps 66:1
Say to **G**, "How awesome are your deeds! Ps 66:3
Come and see what **G** has done: he is Ps 66:5
Bless our **G**, O peoples; let the sound of Ps 66:8
For you, O **G**, have tested us; you have Ps 66:10
Come and hear, all you who fear **G**, and Ps 66:16
But truly **G** has listened; he has Ps 66:19
Blessed be **G**, because he has not Ps 66:20
May **G** be gracious to us and bless us Ps 67:1
Let the peoples praise you, O **G**; let all the Ps 67:3
Let the peoples praise you, O **G**; let all the Ps 67:5
its increase; **G**, our God, shall bless us. Ps 67:6
its increase; God, our **G**, shall bless us. Ps 67:6
G shall bless us; let all the ends of the Ps 67:7
G shall arise, his enemies shall be Ps 68:1
fire, so the wicked shall perish before **G**! Ps 68:2
shall be glad; they shall exult before **G**; Ps 68:3
Sing to **G**, sing praises to his name; lift Ps 68:4
protector of widows is **G** in his holy Ps 68:5
G settles the solitary in a home; he leads Ps 68:6
O **G**, when you went out before your Ps 68:7
the heavens poured down rain, before **G**, Ps 68:8
before God, the One of Sinai, before **G**, Ps 68:8
One of Sinai, before God, the **G** of Israel. Ps 68:8
Rain in abundance, O **G**, you shed Ps 68:9
in your goodness, O **G**, you provided for Ps 68:10
O mountain of **G**, mountain of Bashan; Ps 68:15
at the mount that **G** desired for his Ps 68:16
The chariots of **G** are twice ten Ps 68:17
that the LORD **G** may dwell there. Ps 68:18
daily bears us up; **G** is our salvation. Ps 68:19
Our **G** is a God of salvation, and to GOD, Ps 68:20
Our God is a **G** of salvation, and to GOD, Ps 68:20
Our God is a God of salvation, and to **G**, Ps 68:20
But **G** will strike the heads of his Ps 68:21
Your procession is seen, O **G**, the Ps 68:24
is seen, O God, the procession of my **G**, Ps 68:24
"Bless **G** in the great congregation, the Ps 68:26
Summon your power, O **G**, the power, O Ps 68:28
your power, O God, the power, O **G**, Ps 68:28
hasten to stretch out her hands to **G**. Ps 68:31
O kingdoms of the earth, sing to **G**; sing Ps 68:32
Ascribe power to **G**, whose majesty is Ps 68:34
Awesome is **G** from his sanctuary; the Ps 68:35
the **G** of Israel—he is the one who gives Ps 68:35
and strength to his people. Blessed be **G**! Ps 68:35
Save me, O **G**! For the waters have come Ps 69:1
eyes grow dim with waiting for my **G**. Ps 69:3
O **G**, you know my folly; the wrongs I Ps 69:5
to shame through me, O Lord **G** of hosts; Ps 69:6
to dishonor through me, O **G** of Israel. Ps 69:6
At an acceptable time, O **G**, in the Ps 69:13
let your salvation, O **G**, set me on high! Ps 69:29
I will praise the name of **G** with a song; I Ps 69:30
you who seek **G**, let your hearts revive. Ps 69:32
For **G** will save Zion and build up the Ps 69:35
Make haste, O **G**, to deliver me! O LORD, Ps 70:1
salvation say evermore, "**G** is great!" Ps 70:4
I am poor and needy; hasten to me, O **G**! Ps 70:5
Rescue me, O my **G**, from the hand of the Ps 71:4
and say, "**G** has forsaken him; pursue Ps 71:11
O **G**, be not far from me; O my God, Ps 71:12
me; O my **G**, make haste to help me! Ps 71:12
mighty deeds of the Lord **G** I will come; Ps 71:16
O **G**, from my youth you have taught Ps 71:17
So even to old age and gray hairs, O **G**, Ps 71:18
Your righteousness, O **G**, reaches the Ps 71:19
You who have done great things, O **G**, Ps 71:19
the harp for your faithfulness, O my **G**; Ps 71:22
Give the king your justice, O **G**, and your Ps 72:1
Blessed be the LORD, the **G** of Israel, who Ps 72:18
Truly **G** is good to Israel, to those who Ps 73:1
And they say, "How can **G** know? Is Ps 73:11
until I went into the sanctuary of **G**; Ps 73:17
but **G** is the strength of my heart and Ps 73:26
But for me it is good to be near **G**; I have Ps 73:28
I have made the Lord **G** my refuge, that Ps 73:28
O **G**, why do you cast us off forever? Ps 74:1
all the meeting places of **G** in the land. Ps 74:8
How long, O **G**, is the foe to scoff? Is the Ps 74:10
Yet **G** my King is from of old, working Ps 74:12
Arise, O **G**, defend your cause; Ps 74:22
We give thanks to you, O **G**; we give Ps 75:1
but it is **G** who executes judgment, Ps 75:7
I will sing praises to the **G** of Jacob. Ps 75:9
In Judah **G** is known; his name is great Ps 76:1
At your rebuke, O **G** of Jacob, both rider Ps 76:6
when **G** arose to establish judgment, to Ps 76:9
to the LORD your **G** and perform them; Ps 76:11
I cry aloud to **G**, aloud to God, and he Ps 77:1
I cry aloud to God, aloud to **G**, and he Ps 77:1
When I remember **G**, I moan; when I Ps 77:3
Has **G** forgotten to be gracious? Has he Ps 77:9
Your way, O **G**, is holy. What god is Ps 77:13

is holy. What **g** is great like our God? Ps 77:13
is holy. What god is great like our **G**? Ps 77:13
You are the **G** who works wonders; you Ps 77:14
When the waters saw you, O **G**, when Ps 77:16
set their hope in **G** and not forget the Ps 78:7
in God and not forget the works of **G**, Ps 78:7
whose spirit was not faithful to **G**. Ps 78:8
They tested **G** in their heart by Ps 78:18
They spoke against **G**, saying, "Can Ps 78:19
"Can **G** spread a table in the Ps 78:19
did not believe in **G** and did not trust Ps 78:22
the anger of **G** rose against them, and Ps 78:31
they repented and sought **G** earnestly. Ps 78:34
They remembered that **G** was their Ps 78:35
rock, the Most High **G** their redeemer. Ps 78:35
They tested **G** again and again and Ps 78:41
against the Most High **G** and did not Ps 78:56
When **G** heard, he was full of wrath, Ps 78:59
O **G**, the nations have come into your Ps 79:1
Help us, O **G** of our salvation, for the Ps 79:9
"Where is their **G**?" Let the avenging of Ps 79:10
Restore us, O **G**; let your face shine, that Ps 80:3
O LORD **G** of hosts, how long will you be Ps 80:4
Restore us, O **G** of hosts; let your face Ps 80:7
Turn again, O **G** of hosts! Look down Ps 80:14
Restore us, O LORD **G** of hosts! let your Ps 80:19
Sing aloud to **G** our strength; shout for Ps 81:1
strength; shout for joy to the **G** of Jacob! Ps 81:1
statute for Israel, a rule of the **G** of Jacob. Ps 81:4
There shall be no strange **g** among you; Ps 81:9
you shall not bow down to a foreign **g**. Ps 81:9
I am the LORD your **G**, who brought you Ps 81:10
G has taken his place in the divine Ps 82:1
Arise, O **G**, judge the earth; for you shall Ps 82:8
O **G**, do not keep silence; do not hold Ps 83:1
do not hold your peace or be still, O **G**! Ps 83:1
for ourselves of the pastures of **G**." Ps 83:12
O my **G**, make them like whirling dust, Ps 83:13
and flesh sing for joy to the living **G**. Ps 84:2
O LORD of hosts, my King and my **G**. Ps 84:3
each one appears before **G** in Zion. Ps 84:7
O LORD **G** of hosts, hear my prayer; give Ps 84:8
hear my prayer; give ear, O **G** of Jacob! Ps 84:8
Behold our shield, O **G**; look on the face Ps 84:9
in the house of my **G** than dwell in the Ps 84:10
For the LORD **G** is a sun and shield; the Ps 84:11
Restore us again, O **G** of our salvation, Ps 85:4
Let me hear what **G** the LORD will speak, Ps 85:8
who trusts in you—you are my **G**. Ps 86:2
do wondrous things; you alone are **G**. Ps 86:10
I give thanks to you, O Lord my **G**, with Ps 86:12
O **G**, insolent men have risen up Ps 86:14
O Lord, are a **G** merciful and gracious, Ps 86:15
things of you are spoken, O city of **G**. Ps 87:3
O LORD, **G** of my salvation; I cry out day Ps 88:1
a **G** greatly to be feared in the council of Ps 89:7
O LORD **G** of hosts, who is mighty as you Ps 89:8
cry to me, 'You are my Father, my **G**, Ps 89:26
A Prayer of Moses, the man of **G**. Ps 90:T
everlasting to everlasting you are **G**. Ps 90:2
the favor of the Lord our **G** be upon us, Ps 90:17
LORD, "My refuge and my fortress, my **G**, Ps 91:2
they flourish in the courts of our **G**. Ps 92:13
O LORD, **G** of vengeance, O God of Ps 94:1
God of vengeance, O **G** of vengeance, Ps 94:1
not see; the **G** of Jacob does not perceive." Ps 94:7
and my **G** the rock of my refuge. Ps 94:22
the LORD our **G** will wipe them out. Ps 94:23
For the LORD is a great **G**, and a great Ps 95:3
For he is our **G**, and we are the people of Ps 95:7
earth have seen the salvation of our **G**. Ps 98:3
Exalt the LORD our **G**; worship at his Ps 99:5
O LORD our **G**, you answered them; you Ps 99:8
you were a forgiving **G** to them, but an Ps 99:8
Exalt the LORD our **G**, and worship at his Ps 99:9
mountain; for the LORD our **G** is holy! Ps 99:9
Know that the LORD, he is **G**! It is he who Ps 100:3
"O my **G**," I say, "take me not away in Ps 102:24
soul! O LORD my **G**, you are very great! Ps 104:1
their prey, seeking their food from **G**. Ps 104:21
sing praise to my **G** while I have being. Ps 104:33
He is the LORD our **G**; his judgments are Ps 105:7
and put **G** to the test in the desert; Ps 106:14
exchanged the glory of **G** for the image Ps 106:20
They forgot **G**, their Savior, who had Ps 106:21
Save us, O LORD our **G**, and gather us Ps 106:47
Blessed be the LORD, the **G** of Israel, Ps 106:48
had rebelled against the words of **G**, Ps 107:11
My heart is steadfast, O **G**! I will sing Ps 108:1
Be exalted, O **G**, above the heavens! Let Ps 108:5
G has promised in his holiness: "With Ps 108:7
Have you not rejected us, O **G**? You do Ps 108:11
You do not go out, O **G**, with our Ps 108:11
With **G** we shall do valiantly; it is he Ps 108:13
Be not silent, O **G** of my praise! Ps 109:1

But you, O **G** my Lord, deal on my Ps 109:21
Help me, O LORD my **G**! Save me Ps 109:26
Who is like the LORD our **G**, who is Ps 113:5
Lord, at the presence of the **G** of Jacob, Ps 114:7
the nations say, "Where is their **G**?" Ps 115:2
Our **G** is in the heavens; he does all that Ps 115:3
LORD, and righteous; our **G** is merciful. Ps 116:5
The LORD is **G**, and he has made his Ps 118:27
You are my **G**, and I will give thanks Ps 118:28
will give thanks to you; you are my **G**; Ps 118:28
keep the commandments of my **G**. Ps 119:115
the sake of the house of the LORD our **G**, Ps 122:9
so our eyes look to the LORD our **G**, Ps 123:2
in the courts of the house of our **G**! Ps 135:2
Give thanks to the **G** of gods, for his Ps 136:2
Give thanks to the **G** of heaven, for his Ps 136:26
to me are your thoughts, O **G**! Ps 139:17
that you would slay the wicked, O **G**! Ps 139:19
Search me, O **G**, and know my heart! Ps 139:23
I say to the LORD, You are my **G**; give ear Ps 140:6
But my eyes are toward you, O **G**, my Ps 141:8
me to do your will, for you are my **G**! Ps 143:10
I will sing a new song to you, O **G**; upon Ps 144:9
are the people whose **G** is the LORD! Ps 144:15
I will extol you, my **G** and King, and Ps 145:1
sing praises to my **G** while I have my Ps 146:2
is he whose help is the **G** of Jacob, Ps 146:5
Jacob, whose hope is in the LORD his **G**, Ps 146:5
The LORD will reign forever, your **G**, O Ps 146:10
For it is good to sing praises to our **G**; Ps 147:1
make melody to our **G** on the lyre! Ps 147:7
O Jerusalem! Praise your **G**, O Zion! Ps 147:12
the high praises of **G** be in their throats Ps 149:6
Praise **G** in his sanctuary; praise him Ps 150:1
of the LORD and find the knowledge of **G**. Prv 2:5
and forgets the covenant of her **G**; Prv 2:17
good success in the sight of **G** and man. Prv 3:4
It is the glory of **G** to conceal things, Prv 25:2
The man declares, I am weary, O **G**; I Prv 30:1
O God; I am weary, O **G**, and worn out. Prv 30:1
Every word of **G** proves true; he is a Prv 30:5
steal and profane the name of my **G**. Prv 30:9
unhappy business that **G** has given to Eccl 1:13
This also, I saw, is from the hand of **G**, Eccl 2:24
who pleases him **G** has given wisdom Eccl 2:26
only to give to one who pleases **G**. Eccl 2:26
seen the business that **G** has given to Eccl 3:10
cannot find out what **G** has done from Eccl 3:11
that whatever **G** does endures Eccl 3:14
G has done it, so that people fear before Eccl 3:14
and **G** seeks what has been driven Eccl 3:15
G will judge the righteous and the Eccl 3:17
children of man that **G** is testing them Eccl 3:18
steps when you go to the house of **G**. Eccl 5:1
heart be hasty to utter a word before **G**, Eccl 5:2
for **G** is in heaven and you are on earth. Eccl 5:2
When you vow a vow to **G**, do not delay Eccl 5:4
Why should **G** be angry at your voice Eccl 5:6
vanity; but **G** is the one you must fear. Eccl 5:7
days of his life that **G** has given him, Eccl 5:18
also to whom **G** has given wealth Eccl 5:19
rejoice in his toil—this is the gift of **G**. Eccl 5:19
his life because **G** keeps him occupied Eccl 5:20
a man to whom **G** gives wealth, Eccl 6:2
yet **G** does not give him power to enjoy Eccl 6:2
Consider the work of **G**: who can Eccl 7:13
G has made the one as well as the Eccl 7:14
the one who fears **G** shall come out Eccl 7:18
He who pleases **G** escapes her, but the Eccl 7:26
I found, that **G** made man upright, Eccl 7:29
it will be well with those who fear **G**, Eccl 8:12
because he does not fear before **G**. Eccl 8:13
of his life that **G** has given him under Eccl 8:15
then I saw all the work of **G**, that man Eccl 8:17
and their deeds are in the hand of **G**. Eccl 9:1
for **G** has already approved what you do. Eccl 9:7
the work of **G** who makes everything. Eccl 11:5
for all these things **G** will bring you Eccl 11:9
and the spirit returns to **G** who gave it. Eccl 12:7
Fear **G** and keep his commandments, Eccl 12:13
For **G** will bring every deed into Eccl 12:14
Give ear to the teaching of our **G**, you Is 1:10
of the LORD, to the house of the **G** of Jacob, Is 2:3
the Lord **G** of hosts is taking away from Is 3:1
of the poor?" declares the Lord **G** of hosts. Is 3:15
and the Holy **G** shows himself holy in Is 5:16
thus says the Lord **G**: "'It shall not stand, Is 7:7
"Ask a sign of the LORD your **G**; let it be Is 7:11
to weary men, that you weary my **G** also? Is 7:13
but it will not stand, for **G** is with us. Is 8:10
should not a people inquire of their **G**? Is 8:19
against their king and their **G**, Is 8:21
be called Wonderful Counselor, Mighty **G**, Is 9:6
Therefore the Lord **G** of hosts will send Is 10:16
the remnant of Jacob, to the mighty **G**. Is 10:21

For the Lord **G** of hosts will make a full Is 10:23
Therefore thus says the Lord **G** of hosts: Is 10:24
the Lord **G** of hosts will lop the boughs Is 10:33
"Behold, **G** is my salvation; I will trust, Is 12:2
for the LORD **G** is my strength and my Is 12:2
and Gomorrah when **G** overthrew them. Is 13:19
above the stars of **G** I will set my throne Is 14:13
a fruit tree, declares the LORD **G** of Israel. Is 17:6
have forgotten the **G** of your salvation Is 17:10
over them, declares the Lord **G** of hosts. Is 19:4
from the LORD of hosts, the **G** of Israel, Is 21:10
will be few, for the LORD, the **G** of Israel, Is 21:17
For the Lord **G** of hosts has a day of Is 22:5
In that day the Lord **G** of hosts called for Is 22:12
until you die," says the Lord **G** of hosts. Is 22:14
Thus says the Lord **G** of hosts, "Come, Is 22:15
to the name of the LORD, the **G** of Israel. Is 24:15
O LORD, you are my **G**; I will exalt you; I Is 25:1
and the Lord **G** will wipe away tears from Is 25:8
be said on that day, "Behold, this is our **G**; Is 25:9
for the LORD **G** is an everlasting rock. Is 26:4
O LORD our **G**, other lords besides you Is 26:13
therefore thus says the Lord **G**, "Behold, I Is 28:16
from the Lord **G** of hosts against Is 28:22
is rightly instructed; his **G** teaches him. Is 28:26
and will stand in awe of the **G** of Israel. Is 29:23
For thus said the Lord **G**, the Holy One Is 30:15
For the LORD is a **G** of justice; blessed are Is 30:18
The Egyptians are man, and not **G**, and Is 31:3
glory of the LORD, the majesty of our **G**. Is 35:2
your **G** will come with vengeance, Is 35:4
vengeance, with the recompense of **G**. Is 35:4
trust in the LORD our **G**," is it not he whose Is 36:7
that the LORD your **G** will hear the words Is 37:4
of Assyria has sent to mock the living **G**, Is 37:4
the words that the LORD your **G** has heard; Is 37:4
'Do not let your **G** in whom you trust Is 37:10
"O LORD of hosts, **G** of Israel, who is Is 37:16
above the cherubim, you are the **G**, Is 37:16
which he has sent to mock the living **G**. Is 37:17
So now, O LORD our **G**, save us from his Is 37:20
"Thus says the LORD, the **G** of Israel: Is 37:21
in the house of Nisroch his **g**, Is 37:38
says the LORD, the **G** of David your father: Is 38:5
Comfort, comfort my people, says your **G**. Is 40:1
straight in the desert a highway for our **G**. Is 40:3
but the word of our **G** will stand forever. Is 40:8
to the cities of Judah, "Behold your **G**!" Is 40:9
Behold, the Lord **G** comes with might, Is 40:10
To whom then will you liken **G**, or what Is 40:18
and my right is disregarded by my **G**"? Is 40:27
The LORD is the everlasting **G**, the Is 40:28
you; be not dismayed, for I am your **G**; Is 41:10
For I, the LORD your **G**, hold your right Is 41:13
I the **G** of Israel will not forsake them. Is 41:17
Thus says **G**, the LORD, who created the Is 42:5
For I am the LORD your **G**, the Holy One of Is 43:3
Before me no **g** was formed, nor shall Is 43:10
there was no strange **g** among you; Is 43:12
declares the LORD, "and I am **G**. Is 43:12
and I am the last; besides me there is no **g**. Is 44:6
are my witnesses! Is there a **G** besides me? Is 44:8
Who fashions a **g** or casts an idol that is Is 44:10
Also he makes a **g** and worships it; he Is 44:15
And the rest of it he makes into a **g**, his Is 44:17
and says, "Deliver me, for you are my **g**!" Is 44:17
know that it is I, the LORD, the **G** of Israel, Is 45:3
there is no other, besides me there is no **G**; Is 45:5
'Surely **G** is in you, and there is no other, Is 45:14
and there is no other, no **g** besides him.'" Is 45:14
Truly, you are a **G** who hides yourself, O Is 45:15
a God who hides yourself, O **G** of Israel, Is 45:15
LORD, who created the heavens (he is **G**!), Is 45:18
keep on praying to a **g** that cannot save. Is 45:20
And there is no other **g** besides me, a Is 45:21
besides me, a righteous **G** and a Savior; Is 45:21
earth! For I am **G**, and there is no other. Is 45:22
a goldsmith, and he makes it into a **g**; Is 46:6
of old; for I am **G**, and there is no other; Is 46:9
other; I am **G**, and there is none like me, Is 46:9
of the LORD and confess the **G** of Israel, Is 48:1
and stay themselves on the **G** of Israel; Is 48:2
there." And now the Lord **G** has sent me, Is 48:16
"I am the LORD your **G**, who teaches you Is 48:17
LORD, and my recompense with my **G**." Is 49:4
and my **G** has become my strength— Is 49:5
Thus says the Lord **G**: "Behold, I will lift Is 49:22
The Lord **G** has given me the tongue of Is 50:4
The Lord **G** has opened my ear, and I was Is 50:5
But the Lord **G** helps me; therefore I have Is 50:7
Behold, the Lord **G** helps me; who will Is 50:9
the name of the LORD and rely on his **G**. Is 50:10
I am the LORD your **G**, who stirs up the Is 51:15
wrath of the LORD, the rebuke of your **G**. Is 51:20
your **G** who pleads the cause of his Is 51:22

For thus says the Lord **G**: "My people Is 52:4
who says to Zion, "Your **G** reigns." Is 52:7
the earth shall see the salvation of our **G**. Is 52:10
and the **G** of Israel will be your rear Is 52:12
we esteemed him stricken, smitten by **G**, Is 53:4
the **G** of the whole earth he is called. Is 54:5
of youth when she is cast off, says your **G**. Is 54:6
run to you, because of the LORD your **G**, Is 55:5
have compassion on him, and to our **G**, Is 55:7
The Lord **G**, who gathers the outcasts of Is 56:8
There is no peace," says my **G**, "for the Is 57:21
did not forsake the judgment of their **G**; Is 58:2
judgments; they delight to draw near to **G**. Is 58:2
a separation between you and your **G**, Is 59:2
and turning back from following our **G**, Is 59:13
them, for the name of the LORD your **G**, Is 60:9
light, and your **G** will be your glory. Is 60:19
The Spirit of the Lord **G** is upon me, Is 61:1
favor, and the day of vengeance of our **G**; Is 61:2
speak of you as the ministers of our **G**; Is 61:6
my soul shall exult in my **G**, for he has Is 61:10
so the Lord **G** will cause righteousness Is 61:11
and a royal diadem in the hand of your **G**. Is 62:3
bride, so shall your **G** rejoice over you. Is 62:5
the ear, no eye has seen a **G** besides you, Is 64:4
Therefore thus says the Lord **G**: "Behold, Is 65:13
and the Lord **G** will put you to death, Is 65:15
shall bless himself by the **G** of truth, Is 65:16
in the land shall swear by the **G** of truth; Is 65:16
forth, shut the womb?" says your **G**. Is 66:9
Then I said, "Ah, Lord **G**! Behold, I do not Jer 1:6
yourself by forsaking the LORD your **G**, Jer 2:17
bitter for you to forsake the LORD your **G**; Jer 2:19
not in you, declares the Lord **G** of hosts. Jer 2:19
is still before me, declares the Lord **G**. Jer 2:22
the LORD your **G** and scattered your Jer 3:13
they have forgotten the LORD their **G**. Jer 3:21
come to you, for you are the LORD our **G**. Jer 3:22
in the LORD our **G** is the salvation of Jer 3:23
we have sinned against the LORD our **G**, Jer 3:25
not obeyed the voice of the LORD our **G**." Jer 3:25
Then I said, "Ah, Lord **G**, surely you Jer 4:10
the way of the LORD, the justice of their **G**. Jer 5:4
the justice of their **G**." But they all alike Jer 5:5
thus says the LORD, the **G** of hosts: Jer 5:14
has the LORD our **G** done all these things Jer 5:19
their hearts, 'Let us fear the LORD our **G**, Jer 5:24
says the LORD of hosts, the **G** of Israel: Jer 7:3
Therefore thus says the Lord **G**: behold, Jer 7:20
says the LORD of hosts, the **G** of Israel: Jer 7:21
'Obey my voice, and I will be your **G**, Jer 7:23
not obey the voice of the LORD their **G**, Jer 7:28
for the LORD our **G** has doomed us to Jer 8:14
says the LORD of hosts, the **G** of Israel: Jer 9:15
But the LORD is the true **G**; he is the Jer 10:10
he is the living **G** and the everlasting Jer 10:10
them, Thus says the LORD, the **G** of Israel: Jer 11:3
you be my people, and I will be your **G**, Jer 11:4
'Thus says the LORD, the **G** of Israel, Jer 13:12
to the LORD your **G** before he brings Jer 13:16
"Ah, Lord **G**, behold, the prophets say to Jer 14:13
showers? Are you not he, O LORD our **G**? Jer 14:22
by your name, O LORD, **G** of hosts. Jer 15:16
says the LORD of hosts, the **G** of Israel: Jer 16:9
committed against the LORD our **G**?' Jer 16:10
says the LORD of hosts, the **G** of Israel: Jer 19:3
says the LORD of hosts, the **G** of Israel, Jer 19:15
'Thus says the LORD, the **G** of Israel: Jer 21:4
of the LORD their **G** and worshiped other Jer 22:9
thus says the LORD, the **G** of Israel, Jer 23:2
"Am I a **G** at hand, declares the LORD, Jer 23:23
declares the LORD, and not a **G** afar off? Jer 23:23
you pervert the words of the living **G**, Jer 23:36
the living God, the LORD of hosts, our **G**. Jer 23:36
"Thus says the LORD, the **G** of Israel: Like Jer 24:5
shall be my people and I will be their **G**, Jer 24:7
Thus the LORD, the **G** of Israel, said to Jer 25:15
says the LORD of hosts, the **G** of Israel: Jer 25:27
and obey the voice of the LORD your **G**, Jer 26:13
to us in the name of the LORD our **G**." Jer 26:16
says the LORD of hosts, the **G** of Israel: Jer 27:4
says the LORD of hosts, the **G** of Israel, Jer 27:21
says the LORD of hosts, the **G** of Israel: Jer 28:2
says the LORD of hosts, the **G** of Israel: Jer 28:14
says the LORD of hosts, the **G** of Israel, Jer 29:4
says the LORD of hosts, the **G** of Israel: Jer 29:8
says the LORD of hosts, the **G** of Israel, Jer 29:21
says the LORD of hosts, the **G** of Israel: Jer 29:25
"Thus says the LORD, the **G** of Israel: Jer 30:2
serve the LORD their **G** and David their Jer 30:9
be my people, and I will be your **G**." Jer 30:22
I will be the **G** of all the clans of Israel, Jer 31:1
let us go up to Zion, to the LORD our **G**.'" Jer 31:6
be restored, for you are the LORD my **G**. Jer 31:18
says the LORD of hosts, the **G** of Israel: Jer 31:23

And I will be their **G**, and they shall be Jer 31:33
says the LORD of hosts, the **G** of Israel: Jer 32:14
says the LORD of hosts, the **G** of Israel: Jer 32:15
'Ah, Lord **G**! It is you who has made the Jer 32:17
after them, O great and mighty **G**, Jer 32:18
Yet you, O Lord **G**, have said to me, Jer 32:25
I am the LORD, the **G** of all flesh. Jer 32:27
thus says the LORD, the **G** of Israel, Jer 32:36
be my people, and I will be their **G**. Jer 32:38
For thus says the LORD, the **G** of Israel, Jer 33:4
"Thus says the LORD, the **G** of Israel: Go Jer 34:2
"Thus says the LORD, the **G** of Israel: I Jer 34:13
Hanan the son of Igdaliah, the man of **G**, Jer 35:4
says the LORD of hosts, the **G** of Israel: Jer 35:13
thus says the LORD, the **G** of hosts, Jer 35:17
LORD, the God of hosts, the **G** of Israel: Jer 35:17
says the LORD of hosts, the **G** of Israel: Jer 35:18
says the LORD of hosts, the **G** of Israel: Jer 35:19
"Please pray for us to the LORD our **G**." Jer 37:3
"Thus says the LORD, **G** of Israel: Thus Jer 37:7
"Thus says the LORD, the **G** of hosts, Jer 38:17
LORD, the God of hosts, the **G** of Israel: Jer 38:17
says the LORD of hosts, the **G** of Israel: Jer 39:16
"The LORD your **G** pronounced this Jer 40:2
you, and pray to the LORD your **G** for us, Jer 42:2
that the LORD your **G** may show us the Jer 42:3
to the LORD your **G** according to your Jer 42:4
which the LORD your **G** sends you to us. Jer 42:5
voice of the LORD our **G** to whom we are Jer 42:6
we obey the voice of the LORD our **G**." Jer 42:6
"Thus says the LORD, the **G** of Israel, Jer 42:9
disobeying the voice of the LORD your **G** Jer 42:13
says the LORD of hosts, the **G** of Israel: Jer 42:15
says the LORD of hosts, the **G** of Israel: Jer 42:18
For you sent me to the LORD your **G**, Jer 42:20
saying, 'Pray for us to the LORD our **G**, Jer 42:20
whatever the LORD our **G** says declare to Jer 42:20
of the LORD your **G** in anything that he Jer 42:21
people all these words of the LORD their **G**, Jer 43:1
which the LORD their **G** had sent him to Jer 43:1
The LORD our **G** did not send you to say, Jer 43:2
says the LORD of hosts, the **G** of Israel: Jer 43:10
says the LORD of hosts, the **G** of Israel: Jer 44:2
And now thus says the LORD **G** of hosts, Jer 44:7
the LORD God of hosts, the **G** of Israel: Jer 44:7
says the LORD of hosts, the **G** of Israel: Jer 44:11
says the LORD of hosts, the **G** of Israel: Jer 44:25
of Egypt, saying, 'As the Lord **G** lives.' Jer 44:26
"Thus says the LORD, the **G** of Israel, to Jer 45:2
day is the day of the Lord **G** of hosts, Jer 46:10
For the Lord **G** of hosts holds a Jer 46:10
The LORD of hosts, the **G** of Israel, said: Jer 46:25
says the LORD of hosts, the **G** of Israel: Jer 48:1
place and makes offerings to his **g**. Jer 48:35
upon you, declares the Lord **G** of hosts, Jer 49:5
and they shall seek the LORD their **G**. Jer 50:4
says the LORD of hosts, the **G** of Israel: Jer 50:18
for the Lord **G** of hosts has a work to do Jer 50:25
Zion the vengeance of the LORD our **G**, Jer 50:28
proud one, declares the Lord **G** of hosts, Jer 50:31
As when **G** overthrew Sodom and Jer 50:40
have not been forsaken by their **G**, Jer 51:5
in Zion the work of the LORD our **G**. Jer 51:10
says the LORD of hosts, the **G** of Israel: Jer 51:33
for the LORD is a **G** of recompense; Jer 51:56
our hearts and hands to **G** in heaven: Lam 3:41
were opened, and I saw visions of **G**. Ezk 1:1
say to them, 'Thus says the Lord **G**.' Ezk 2:4
say to them, 'Thus says the Lord **G**,' Ezk 3:11
say to them, 'Thus says the Lord **G**.' Ezk 3:27
Then I said, "Ah, Lord **G**! Behold, I have Ezk 4:14
"Thus says the Lord **G**: This is Ezk 5:5
Therefore thus says the Lord **G**: Because Ezk 5:7
therefore thus says the Lord **G**: Behold, I, Ezk 5:8
Therefore, as I live, declares the Lord **G**, Ezk 5:11
of Israel, hear the word of the Lord **G**! Ezk 6:3
Thus says the Lord **G** to the mountains Ezk 6:3
Thus says the Lord **G**: "Clap your Ezk 6:11
thus says the Lord **G** to the land of Israel: Ezk 7:2
"Thus says the Lord **G**: Disaster after Ezk 7:5
hand of the Lord **G** fell upon me there. Ezk 8:1
brought me in visions of **G** to Jerusalem, Ezk 8:3
the glory of the **G** of Israel was there, Ezk 8:4
Now the glory of the **G** of Israel had gone Ezk 9:3
upon my face, and cried, "Ah, Lord **G**! Ezk 9:8
like the voice of **G** Almighty when he Ezk 10:5
the glory of the **G** of Israel was over Ezk 10:19
I saw underneath the **G** of Israel by the Ezk 10:20
Therefore thus says the Lord **G**: Your Ezk 11:7
sword upon you, declares the Lord **G**. Ezk 11:8
a loud voice and said, "Ah, Lord **G**! Ezk 11:13
Therefore say, 'Thus says the Lord **G**: Ezk 11:16
Therefore say, 'Thus says the Lord **G**: I Ezk 11:17
be my people, and I will be their **G**. Ezk 11:20
their own heads, declares the Lord **G**." Ezk 11:21

the glory of the **G** of Israel was over Ezk 11:22
vision by the Spirit of **G** into Chaldea, Ezk 11:24
Say to them, 'Thus says the Lord **G**: Ezk 12:10
says the Lord **G** concerning the Ezk 12:19
them therefore, 'Thus says the Lord **G**: Ezk 12:23
and perform it, declares the Lord **G**." Ezk 12:25
say to them, Thus says the Lord **G**: Ezk 12:28
be performed, declares the Lord **G**." Ezk 12:28
Thus says the Lord **G**, Woe to the Ezk 13:3
Therefore thus says the Lord **G**: Ezk 13:8
I am against you, declares the Lord **G**. Ezk 13:8
you shall know that I am the Lord **G**. Ezk 13:9
Therefore thus says the Lord **G**: I will Ezk 13:13
was no peace, declares the Lord **G**. Ezk 13:16
and say, Thus says the Lord **G**: Woe to Ezk 13:18
"Therefore thus says the Lord **G**: Ezk 13:20
and say to them, Thus says the Lord **G**: Ezk 14:4
house of Israel, Thus says the Lord **G**: Ezk 14:6
be my people and I may be their **G**, Ezk 14:11
be their God, declares the Lord **G**." Ezk 14:11
righteousness, declares the Lord **G**. Ezk 14:14
were in it, as I live, declares the Lord **G**, Ezk 14:16
were in it, as I live, declares the Lord **G**, Ezk 14:18
were in it, as I live, declares the Lord **G**, Ezk 14:20
"For thus says the Lord **G**: How much Ezk 14:21
I have done in it, declares the Lord **G**." Ezk 14:23
Therefore thus says the Lord **G**: Like Ezk 15:6
acted faithlessly, declares the Lord **G**." Ezk 15:8
say, Thus says the Lord **G** to Jerusalem: Ezk 16:3
covenant with you, declares the Lord **G**, Ezk 16:8
bestowed on you, declares the Lord **G**. Ezk 16:14
and so it was, declares the Lord **G**. Ezk 16:19
(woe, woe to you! declares the Lord **G**), Ezk 16:23
is your heart, declares the Lord **G**, Ezk 16:30
Thus says the Lord **G**, Because your Ezk 16:36
upon your head, declares the Lord **G**. Ezk 16:43
As I live, declares the Lord **G**, your Ezk 16:48
"For thus says the Lord **G**: I will deal Ezk 16:59
you have done, declares the Lord **G**." Ezk 16:63
say, Thus says the Lord **G**: A great eagle Ezk 17:3
"Say, Thus says the Lord **G**: Will it Ezk 17:9
"As I live, declares the Lord **G**, surely Ezk 17:16
Therefore thus says the Lord **G**: As I Ezk 17:19
Thus says the Lord **G**: "I myself will Ezk 17:22
As I live, declares the Lord **G**, this Ezk 18:3
he shall surely live, declares the Lord **G**. Ezk 18:9
of the wicked, declares the Lord **G**, Ezk 18:23
to his ways, declares the Lord **G**. Ezk 18:30
death of anyone, declares the Lord **G**; Ezk 18:32
and say to them, Thus says the Lord **G**, Ezk 20:3
As I live, declares the Lord **G**, I will not Ezk 20:3
and say to them, Thus says the Lord **G**: Ezk 20:5
to them, saying, I am the LORD your **G**. Ezk 20:5
the idols of Egypt; I am the LORD your **G**. Ezk 20:7
I am the LORD your **G**; walk in my Ezk 20:19
may know that I am the LORD your **G**. Ezk 20:20
say to them, Thus says the Lord **G**: Ezk 20:27
house of Israel, Thus says the Lord **G**: Ezk 20:30
As I live, declares the Lord **G**, I will not Ezk 20:31
"As I live, declares the Lord **G**, surely Ezk 20:33
with you, declares the Lord **G**. Ezk 20:36
house of Israel, thus says the Lord **G**: Ezk 20:39
height of Israel, declares the Lord **G**, Ezk 20:40
O house of Israel, declares the Lord **G**." Ezk 20:44
Thus says the Lord **G**, Behold, I will Ezk 20:47
Then I said, "Ah, Lord **G**! They are Ezk 20:49
it will be fulfilled,'" declares the Lord **G**. Ezk 21:7
despise the rod?" declares the Lord **G**. Ezk 21:13
"Therefore thus says the Lord **G**: Ezk 21:24
thus says the Lord **G**: Remove the Ezk 21:26
says the Lord **G** concerning the Ezk 21:28
You shall say, Thus says the Lord **G**: A Ezk 22:3
have forgotten, declares the Lord **G**. Ezk 22:12
Therefore thus says the Lord **G**: Ezk 22:19
them, saying, 'Thus says the Lord **G**,' Ezk 22:28
their heads, declares the Lord **G**." Ezk 22:31
O Oholibah, thus says the Lord **G**: Ezk 23:22
"For thus says the Lord **G**: Behold, I Ezk 23:28
Thus says the Lord **G**: "You shall Ezk 23:32
for I have spoken, declares the Lord **G**. Ezk 23:34
Therefore thus says the Lord **G**: Ezk 23:35
For thus says the Lord **G**: "Bring up a Ezk 23:46
you shall know that I am the Lord **G**." Ezk 23:49
and say to them, Thus says the Lord **G**: Ezk 24:3
"Therefore thus says the Lord **G**: Woe Ezk 24:6
Therefore thus says the Lord **G**: Woe to Ezk 24:9
will be judged, declares the Lord **G**." Ezk 24:14
house of Israel, Thus says the Lord **G**: Ezk 24:21
you will know that I am the Lord **G**.' Ezk 24:24
Hear the word of the Lord **G**: Ezk 25:3
Thus says the Lord **G**, Because you Ezk 25:3
For thus says the Lord **G**: Because you Ezk 25:6
"Thus says the Lord **G**: Because Moab Ezk 25:8
"Thus says the Lord **G**: Because Edom Ezk 25:12
therefore thus says the Lord **G**, I will Ezk 25:13
my vengeance, declares the Lord **G**. Ezk 25:14
"Thus says the Lord **G**: Because the Ezk 25:15
therefore thus says the Lord **G**, Behold, Ezk 25:16
therefore thus says the Lord **G**: Behold, I Ezk 26:3
for I have spoken, declares the Lord **G**. Ezk 26:5
"For thus says the Lord **G**: Behold, I will Ezk 26:7
I have spoken, declares the Lord **G**. Ezk 26:14
"Thus says the Lord **G** to Tyre: Will Ezk 26:15
"For thus says the Lord **G**: When I Ezk 26:19
be found again, declares the Lord **G**." Ezk 26:21
many coastlands, thus says the Lord **G**: Ezk 27:3
prince of Tyre, Thus says the Lord **G**: Ezk 28:2
is proud, and you have said, 'I am a **g**, Ezk 28:2
seas,' yet you are but a man, and no **g**, Ezk 28:2
make your heart like the heart of a **g**— Ezk 28:2
therefore thus says the Lord **G**: Because Ezk 28:6
make your heart like the heart of a **g**, Ezk 28:6
Will you still say, 'I am a **g**,' in the Ezk 28:9
though you are but a man, and no **g**, Ezk 28:9
I have spoken, declares the Lord **G**." Ezk 28:10
and say to him, Thus says the Lord **G**: Ezk 28:12
You were in Eden, the garden of **G**; Ezk 28:13
you were on the holy mountain of **G**; Ezk 28:14
thing from the mountain of **G**, Ezk 28:16
and say, Thus says the Lord **G**: Ezk 28:22
they will know that I am the Lord **G**. Ezk 28:24
"Thus says the Lord **G**: When I gather Ezk 28:25
will know that I am the LORD their **G**." Ezk 28:26
speak, and say, Thus says the Lord **G**: Ezk 29:3
Therefore thus says the Lord **G**: Behold, Ezk 29:8
"For thus says the Lord **G**: At the end Ezk 29:13
they will know that I am the Lord **G**." Ezk 29:16
Therefore thus says the Lord **G**: Ezk 29:19
worked for me, declares the Lord **G**. Ezk 29:20
and say, Thus says the Lord **G**: Ezk 30:2
her by the sword, declares the Lord **G**. Ezk 30:6
"Thus says the Lord **G**: "I will put an Ezk 30:10
"Thus says the Lord **G**: "I will destroy Ezk 30:13
Therefore thus says the Lord **G**: Ezk 30:22
in the garden of **G** could not rival it, Ezk 31:8
tree in the garden of **G** was its equal in Ezk 31:8
envied it, that were in the garden of **G**. Ezk 31:9
"Therefore thus says the Lord **G**: Ezk 31:10
"Thus says the Lord **G**: On the day the Ezk 31:15
his multitude, declares the Lord **G**." Ezk 31:18
Thus says the Lord **G**: I will throw my Ezk 32:3
on your land, declares the Lord **G**. Ezk 32:8
"For thus says the Lord **G**: The sword Ezk 32:11
to run like oil, declares the Lord **G**. Ezk 32:14
they chant it, declares the Lord **G**." Ezk 32:16
by the sword, declares the Lord **G**. Ezk 32:31
his multitude, declares the Lord **G**." Ezk 32:32
to them, As I live, declares the Lord **G**, Ezk 33:11
say to them, Thus says the Lord **G**: Ezk 33:25
this to them, Thus says the Lord **G**: Ezk 33:27
to the shepherds, Thus says the Lord **G**: Ezk 34:2
As I live, declares the Lord **G**, surely Ezk 34:8
Thus says the Lord **G**, Behold, I am Ezk 34:10
"For thus says the Lord **G**: Behold, I, I Ezk 34:11
them lie down, declares the Lord **G**. Ezk 34:15
you, my flock, thus says the Lord **G**: Ezk 34:17
thus says the Lord **G** to them: Ezk 34:20
And I, the LORD, will be their **G**, and Ezk 34:24
that I am the LORD their **G** with them, Ezk 34:30
are my people, declares the Lord **G**. Ezk 34:30
sheep of my pasture, and I am your **G**, Ezk 34:31
I am your God, declares the Lord **G**." Ezk 34:31
and say to it, Thus says the Lord **G**: Ezk 35:3
therefore, as I live, declares the Lord **G**, I Ezk 35:6
therefore, as I live, declares the Lord **G**, Ezk 35:11
Thus says the Lord **G**: While the Ezk 35:14
Thus says the Lord **G**: Because the Ezk 36:2
and say, Thus says the Lord **G**: Ezk 36:3
of Israel, hear the word of the Lord **G**: Ezk 36:4
Thus says the Lord **G** to the mountains Ezk 36:4
therefore thus says the Lord **G**: Surely I Ezk 36:5
and valleys, Thus says the Lord **G**: Ezk 36:6
Therefore thus says the Lord **G**: I swear Ezk 36:7
Thus says the Lord **G**: Because they Ezk 36:13
of children, declares the Lord **G**. Ezk 36:14
to stumble, declares the Lord **G**." Ezk 36:15
house of Israel, Thus says the Lord **G**: Ezk 36:22
I am the LORD, declares the Lord **G**, Ezk 36:23
be my people, and I will be your **G**. Ezk 36:28
that I will act, declares the Lord **G**; Ezk 36:32
"Thus says the Lord **G**: On the day Ezk 36:33
"Thus says the Lord **G**: This also I will Ezk 36:37
bones live?" And I answered, "O Lord **G**, Ezk 37:3
Thus says the Lord **G** to these bones: Ezk 37:5
say to the breath, Thus says the Lord **G**: Ezk 37:9
say to them, Thus says the Lord **G**: Ezk 37:12
say to them, Thus says the Lord **G**: Ezk 37:19
say to them, Thus says the Lord **G**: Ezk 37:21
be my people, and I will be their **G**. Ezk 37:23
be with them, and I will be their **G**, Ezk 37:27
and say, Thus says the Lord **G**: Behold, Ezk 38:3
"Thus says the Lord **G**: On that day, Ezk 38:10
and say to Gog, Thus says the Lord **G**: Ezk 38:14
"Thus says the Lord **G**: Are you he of Ezk 38:17
the land of Israel, declares the Lord **G**, Ezk 38:18
my mountains, declares the Lord **G**. Ezk 38:21
Gog and say, Thus says the Lord **G**: Ezk 39:1
for I have spoken, declares the Lord **G**. Ezk 39:5
be brought about, declares the Lord **G**. Ezk 39:8
plundered them, declares the Lord **G**. Ezk 39:10
I show my glory, declares the Lord **G**. Ezk 39:13
you, son of man, thus says the Lord **G**: Ezk 39:17
of warriors,' declares the Lord **G**. Ezk 39:20
shall know that I am the LORD their **G**, Ezk 39:22
"Therefore thus says the Lord **G**: Now Ezk 39:25
shall know that I am the LORD their **G**, Ezk 39:28
house of Israel, declares the Lord **G**." Ezk 39:29
In visions of **G** he brought me to the Ezk 40:2
the glory of the **G** of Israel was coming Ezk 43:2
"Son of man, thus says the Lord **G**: Ezk 43:18
to minister to me, declares the Lord **G**, Ezk 43:19
I will accept you, declares the Lord **G**." Ezk 43:27
enter by it, for the LORD, the **G** of Israel, Ezk 44:2
house of Israel, Thus says the Lord **G**: Ezk 44:6
"Thus says the Lord **G**: No foreigner, Ezk 44:9
concerning them, declares the Lord **G**, Ezk 44:12
fat and the blood, declares the Lord **G**. Ezk 44:15
his sin offering, declares the Lord **G**. Ezk 44:27
"Thus says the Lord **G**: Enough, O Ezk 45:9
of my people, declares the Lord **G**. Ezk 45:9
for them, declares the Lord **G**. Ezk 45:15
"Thus says the Lord **G**: In the first Ezk 45:18
"Thus says the Lord **G**: The gate of the Ezk 46:1
"Thus says the Lord **G**: If the prince Ezk 46:16
Thus says the Lord **G**: "This is the Ezk 47:13
his inheritance, declares the Lord **G**. Ezk 47:23
are their portions, declares the Lord **G**. Ezk 48:29
with some of the vessels of the house of **G**. Dn 1:2
the land of Shinar, to the house of his **g**, Dn 1:2
placed the vessels in the treasury of his **g**. Dn 1:2
And **G** gave Daniel favor and Dn 1:9
G gave them learning and skill in all Dn 1:17
mercy from the **G** of heaven concerning Dn 2:18
Then Daniel blessed the **G** of heaven. Dn 2:19
be the name of **G** forever and ever, Dn 2:20
To you, O **G** of my fathers, I give thanks Dn 2:23
but there is a **G** in heaven who reveals Dn 2:28
to whom the **G** of heaven has given the Dn 2:37
of those kings the **G** of heaven will set Dn 2:44
A great **G** has made known to the king Dn 2:45
your **G** is God of gods and Lord of kings, Dn 2:47
your God is **G** of gods and Lord of kings, Dn 2:47
And who is the **g** who will deliver you Dn 3:15
our **G** whom we serve is able to deliver Dn 3:17
Abednego, servants of the Most High **G**, Dn 3:26
and said, "Blessed be the **G** of Shadrach, Dn 3:28
and worship any **g** except their own Dn 3:28
worship any god except their own **G**. Dn 3:28
anything against the **G** of Shadrach, Dn 3:29
for there is no other **g** who is able to Dn 3:29
that the Most High **G** has done for me. Dn 4:2
Belteshazzar after the name of my **g**, Dn 4:8
the temple, the house of **G** in Jerusalem, Dn 5:3
the Most High **G** gave Nebuchadnezzar Dn 5:18
that the Most High **G** rules the kingdom Dn 5:21
but the **G** in whose hand is your breath, Dn 5:23
G has numbered the days of your Dn 5:26
it in connection with the law of his **G**." Dn 6:5
makes petition to any **g** or man for thirty Dn 6:7
prayed and gave thanks before his **G**, Dn 6:10
making petition and plea before his **G**. Dn 6:11
makes petition to any **g** or man within Dn 6:12
king declared to Daniel, "May your **G**, Dn 6:16
"O Daniel, servant of the living **G**, Dn 6:20
servant of the living God, has your **G**, Dn 6:20
My **G** sent his angel and shut the lions' Dn 6:22
on him, because he had trusted in his **G**. Dn 6:23
tremble and fear before the **G** of Daniel, Dn 6:26
the God of Daniel, for he is the living **G**, Dn 6:26
Then I turned my face to the Lord **G**, Dn 9:3
to the LORD my **G** and made confession, Dn 9:4
"O Lord, the great and awesome **G**, Dn 9:4
To the Lord our **G** belong mercy and Dn 9:9
of the LORD our **G** by walking in his Dn 9:10
the servant of **G** have been poured Dn 9:11
entreated the favor of the LORD our **G**, Dn 9:13
for the LORD our **G** is righteous in all the Dn 9:14
And now, O Lord our **G**, who brought Dn 9:15
Now therefore, O our **G**, listen to the Dn 9:17
O my **G**, incline your ear and hear. Dn 9:18
Delay not, for your own sake, O my **G**, Dn 9:19
before the LORD my **G** for the holy hill Dn 9:20
LORD my God for the holy hill of my **G**, Dn 9:20
and humbled yourself before your **G**, Dn 10:12
who know their **G** shall stand firm Dn 11:32

and magnify himself above every **g**, Dn 11:36
things against the **G** of gods. Dn 11:36
shall not pay attention to any other **g**, Dn 11:37
shall honor the **g** of fortresses instead Dn 11:38
A **g** whom his fathers did not know he Dn 11:38
fortresses with the help of a foreign **g**. Dn 11:39
and I will save them by the LORD their **G**. Hos 1:7
are not my people, and I am not your **G**." Hos 1:9
said to them, "Children of the living **G**." Hos 1:10
and he shall say, 'You are my **G**.'" Hos 2:23
shall return and seek the LORD their **G**, Hos 3:5
love, and no knowledge of **G** in the land; Hos 4:1
you have forgotten the law of your **G**, Hos 4:6
they have left their **G** to play the whore. Hos 4:12
do not permit them to return to their **G**. Hos 5:4
the knowledge of **G** rather than burnt Hos 6:6
they do not return to the LORD their **G**, Hos 7:10
To me they cry, My **G**, we—Israel— Hos 8:2
Israel; a craftsman made it; it is not **G**. Hos 8:6
played the whore, forsaking your **G**. Hos 9:1
is the watchman of Ephraim with my **G**; Hos 9:8
ways, and hatred in the house of his **G**. Hos 9:8
My **G** will reject them because they Hos 9:17
for I am **G** and not a man, the Holy One Hos 11:9
still walks with **G** and is faithful Hos 11:12
and in his manhood he strove with **G**. Hos 12:3
sought his favor. He met **G** at Bethel, Hos 12:4
at Bethel, and there **G** spoke with us— Hos 12:4
the LORD, the **G** of hosts, the LORD is his Hos 12:5
"So you, by the help of your **G**, return, Hos 12:6
and wait continually for your **G**." Hos 12:6
I am the LORD your **G** from the land of Hos 12:9
I am the LORD your **G** from the land of Hos 13:4
you know no **G** but me, and besides me Hos 13:4
she has rebelled against her **G**; Hos 13:16
Return, O Israel, to the LORD your **G**, for Hos 14:1
and we will say no more, 'Our **G**,' to the Hos 14:3
night in sackcloth, O ministers of my **G**! Jl 1:13
are withheld from the house of your **G**. Jl 1:13
the land to the house of the LORD your **G**, Jl 1:14
joy and gladness from the house of our **G**? Jl 1:16
garments." Return to the LORD, your **G**, Jl 2:13
and a drink offering for the LORD your **G**? Jl 2:14
among the peoples, 'Where is their **G**?'" Jl 2:17
of Zion, and rejoice in the LORD your **G**, Jl 2:23
and praise the name of the LORD your **G**, Jl 2:26
I am the LORD your **G** and there is none Jl 2:27
shall know that I am the LORD your **G**, Jl 3:17
shall perish," says the Lord **G**. Am 1:8
the house of their **G** they drink the wine Am 2:8
"For the Lord **G** does nothing without Am 3:7
will not fear? The Lord **G** has spoken; Am 3:8
Therefore thus says the Lord **G**: "An Am 3:11
house of Jacob," declares the Lord **G**, Am 3:13
declares the Lord GOD, the **G** of hosts, Am 3:13
The Lord **G** has sworn by his holiness Am 4:2
O people of Israel!" declares the Lord **G**. Am 4:5
as when **G** overthrew Sodom and Am 4:11
do this to you, prepare to meet your **G**, Am 4:12
of the earth—the LORD, the **G** of hosts, Am 4:13
For thus says the Lord **G**: "The city that Am 5:3
and so the LORD, the **G** of hosts, will be Am 5:14
it may be that the LORD, the **G** of hosts, Am 5:15
thus says the LORD, the **G** of hosts, Am 5:16
the LORD, whose name is the **G** of hosts. Am 5:27
The Lord **G** has sworn by himself, Am 6:8
himself, declares the LORD, the **G** of hosts: Am 6:8
Israel," declares the LORD, the **G** of hosts; Am 6:14
This is what the Lord **G** showed me: Am 7:1
the grass of the land, I said, "O Lord **G**, Am 7:2
This is what the Lord **G** showed me: Am 7:4
the Lord **G** was calling for a judgment Am 7:4
Then I said, "O Lord **G**, please cease! Am 7:5
"This also shall not be," said the Lord **G**. Am 7:6
This is what the Lord **G** showed me: Am 8:1
in that day," declares the Lord **G**. Am 8:3
"And on that day," declares the Lord **G**, Am 8:9
days are coming," declares the Lord **G**, Am 8:11
of Samaria, and say, 'As your **g** lives, Am 8:14
The Lord **G** of hosts, he who touches the Am 9:5
the eyes of the Lord **G** are upon the sinful Am 9:8
given them," says the LORD your **G**. Am 9:15
Thus says the Lord **G** concerning Edom: Ob 1:1
were afraid, and each cried out to his **g**. Jon 1:5
you sleeper? Arise, call out to your **g**! Jon 1:6
Perhaps the **g** will give a thought to us, Jon 1:6
and I fear the LORD, the **G** of heaven, Jon 1:9
prayed to the LORD his **G** from the belly of Jon 2:1
up my life from the pit, O LORD my **G**. Jon 2:6
And the people of Nineveh believed **G**. Jon 3:5
and let them call out mightily to **G**. Jon 3:8
G may turn and relent and turn from his Jon 3:9
When **G** saw what they did, how they Jon 3:10
G relented of the disaster that he had Jon 3:10
that you are a gracious **G** and merciful, Jon 4:2
Now the LORD **G** appointed a plant and Jon 4:6
G appointed a worm that attacked the Jon 4:7
rose, **G** appointed a scorching east wind, Jon 4:8
But **G** said to Jonah, "Do you do well to be Jon 4:9
and let the Lord **G** be a witness against Mi 1:2
their lips, for there is no answer from **G**. Mi 3:7
of the LORD, to the house of the **G** of Jacob, Mi 4:2
the peoples walk each in the name of its **g**, Mi 4:5
name of the LORD our **G** forever and ever. Mi 4:5
the majesty of the name of the LORD his **G**. Mi 5:4
LORD, and bow myself before **G** on high? Mi 6:6
and to walk humbly with your **G**? Mi 6:8
LORD; I will wait for the **G** of my salvation; Mi 7:7
God of my salvation; my **G** will hear me. Mi 7:7
is the LORD your **G**?" My eyes will look Mi 7:10
shall turn in dread to the LORD our **G**, Mi 7:17
Who is a **G** like you, pardoning iniquity Mi 7:18
The LORD is a jealous and avenging **G**; the Na 1:2
men, whose own might is their **g**!" Hab 1:11
not from everlasting, O LORD my **G**, Hab 1:12
G came from Teman, and the Holy One Hab 3:3
I will take joy in the **G** of my salvation. Hab 3:18
G, the Lord, is my strength; he makes Hab 3:19
Be silent before the Lord **G**! For the day Zep 1:7
For the LORD their **G** will be mindful of Zep 2:7
declares the LORD of hosts, the **G** of Israel, Zep 2:9
the LORD; she does not draw near to her **G**. Zep 3:2
The LORD your **G** is in your midst, a Zep 3:17
obeyed the voice of the LORD their **G**, Hg 1:12
as the LORD their **G** had sent him. Hg 1:12
the house of the LORD of hosts, their **G**, Hg 1:14
obey the voice of the LORD your **G**." Zec 6:15
shall be my people, and I will be their **G**, Zec 8:8
for we have heard that **G** is with you.'" Zec 8:23
teeth; it too shall be a remnant for our **G**; Zec 9:7
the Lord **G** will sound the trumpet and Zec 9:14
day the LORD their **G** will save them, Zec 9:16
I am the LORD their **G** and I will answer Zec 10:6
Thus said the LORD my **G**: "Become Zec 11:4
through the LORD of hosts, their **G**.' Zec 12:5
and the house of David shall be like **G**, Zec 12:8
and they will say, 'The LORD is my **G**.'" Zec 13:9
Then the LORD my **G** will come, and all Zec 14:5
And now entreat the favor of **G**, that he Mal 1:9
one Father? Has not one **G** created us? Mal 2:10
married the daughter of a foreign **g**. Mal 2:11
And what was the one **G** seeking? Mal 2:15
divorces, says the LORD, the **G** of Israel, Mal 2:16
by asking, "Where is the **G** of justice?" Mal 2:17
Will man rob **G**? Yet you are robbing Mal 3:8
You have said, 'It is vain to serve **G**. Mal 3:14
prosper but they put **G** to the test and Mal 3:15
between one who serves **G** and one who Mal 3:18
Immanuel" (which means, **G** with us). Mt 1:23
G is able from these stones to raise up Mt 3:9
saw the Spirit of **G** descending like a Mt 3:16
and said to him, "If you are the Son of **G**, Mt 4:3
word that comes from the mouth of **G**.'" Mt 4:4
and said to him, "If you are the Son of **G**, Mt 4:6
shall not put the Lord your **G** to the test.'" Mt 4:7
worship the Lord your **G** and him only Mt 4:10
are the pure in heart, for they shall see **G**. Mt 5:8
for they shall be called sons of **G**. Mt 5:9
either by heaven, for it is the throne of **G**, Mt 5:34
other. You cannot serve **G** and money. Mt 6:24
But if **G** so clothes the grass of the field, Mt 6:30
the kingdom of **G** and his righteousness, Mt 6:33
have you to do with us, O Son of **G**? Mt 8:29
it, they were afraid, and they glorified **G**, Mt 9:8
entered the house of **G** and ate the bread Mt 12:4
is by the Spirit of **G** that I cast out Mt 12:28
then the kingdom of **G** has come upon Mt 12:28
saying, "Truly you are the Son of **G**." Mt 14:33
the commandment of **G** for the sake Mt 15:3
For **G** commanded, 'Honor your father Mt 15:4
have gained from me is given to **G**, Mt 15:5
you have made void the word of **G**. Mt 15:6
And they glorified the **G** of Israel. Mt 15:31
are the Christ, the Son of the living **G**." Mt 16:16
setting your mind on the things of **G**, Mt 16:23
What therefore **G** has joined together, let Mt 19:6
rich person to enter the kingdom of **G**." Mt 19:24
but with **G** all things are possible." Mt 19:26
go into the kingdom of **G** before you. Mt 21:31
the kingdom of **G** will be taken away Mt 21:43
true and teach the way of **G** truthfully, Mt 22:16
and to **G** the things that are God's." Mt 22:21
the Scriptures nor the power of **G**. Mt 22:29
not read what was said to you by **G**: Mt 22:31
'I am the **G** of Abraham, and the God of Mt 22:32
God of Abraham, and the **G** of Isaac, Mt 22:32
the God of Isaac, and the **G** of Jacob'? Mt 22:32
God of Jacob'? He is not **G** of the dead, Mt 22:32
love the Lord your **G** with all your Mt 22:37
by the throne of **G** and by him who Mt 23:22
'I am able to destroy the temple of **G**, Mt 26:61
to him, "I adjure you by the living **G**, Mt 26:63
us if you are the Christ, the Son of **G**." Mt 26:63
If you are the Son of **G**, come down Mt 27:40
He trusts in **G**; let God deliver him now, Mt 27:43
let **G** deliver him now, if he desires him. Mt 27:43
him. For he said, 'I am the Son of **G**.'" Mt 27:43
Eli, lema sabachthani?" that is, "My **G**, Mt 27:46
sabachthani?" that is, "My God, my **G**, Mt 27:46
and said, "Truly this was the Son of **G**!" Mt 27:54
of the gospel of Jesus Christ, the Son of **G**. Mk 1:1
Galilee, proclaiming the gospel of **G**, Mk 1:14
and the kingdom of **G** is at hand; Mk 1:15
who you are—the Holy One of **G**." Mk 1:24
Who can forgive sins but **G** alone?" Mk 2:7
they were all amazed and glorified **G**, Mk 2:12
how he entered the house of **G**, in the Mk 2:26
and cried out, "You are the Son of **G**." Mk 3:11
Whoever does the will of **G**, he is my Mk 3:35
given the secret of the kingdom of **G**, Mk 4:11
"The kingdom of **G** is as if a man Mk 4:26
can we compare the kingdom of **G**, Mk 4:30
with me, Jesus, Son of the Most High **G**? Mk 5:7
I adjure you by **G**, do not torment me." Mk 5:7
the commandment of **G** and hold to Mk 7:8
the commandment of **G** in order to Mk 7:9
me is Corban' (that is, given to **G**)— Mk 7:11
void the word of **G** by your tradition Mk 7:13
setting your mind on the things of **G**, Mk 8:33
see the kingdom of **G** after it has come Mk 9:1
enter the kingdom of **G** with one eye Mk 9:47
'**G** made them male and female.' Mk 10:6
What therefore **G** has joined together, Mk 10:9
for to such belongs the kingdom of **G**. Mk 10:14
receive the kingdom of **G** like a child Mk 10:15
good? No one is good except **G** alone. Mk 10:18
wealth to enter the kingdom of **G**!" Mk 10:23
it is to enter the kingdom of **G**! Mk 10:24
person to enter the kingdom of **G**." Mk 10:25
man it is impossible, but not with **G**. Mk 10:27
For all things are possible with **G**." Mk 10:27
Jesus answered them, "Have faith in **G**. Mk 11:22
but truly teach the way of **G**. Mk 12:14
and to **G** the things that are God's." Mk 12:17
the Scriptures nor the power of **G**? Mk 12:24
about the bush, how **G** spoke to him, Mk 12:26
him, saying, 'I am the **G** of Abraham, Mk 12:26
God of Abraham, and the **G** of Isaac, Mk 12:26
the God of Isaac, and the **G** of Jacob'? Mk 12:26
He is not **G** of the dead, but of the Mk 12:27
Israel: The Lord our **G**, the Lord is one. Mk 12:29
love the Lord your **G** with all your Mk 12:30
the kingdom of **G**." And after that Mk 12:34
the creation that **G** created until now, Mk 13:19
I drink it new in the kingdom of **G**." Mk 14:25
sabachthani?" which means, "My **G**, Mk 15:34
which means, "My God, my **G**, Mk 15:34
"Truly this man was the Son of **G**!" Mk 15:39
himself looking for the kingdom of **G**, Mk 15:43
and sat down at the right hand of **G**. Mk 16:19
And they were both righteous before **G**, Lk 1:6
as priest before **G** when his division Lk 1:8
the children of Israel to the Lord their **G**, Lk 1:16
Gabriel, who stands in the presence of **G**, Lk 1:19
Gabriel was sent from **G** to a city of Lk 1:26
Mary, for you have found favor with **G**. Lk 1:30
And the Lord **G** will give to him the Lk 1:32
born will be called holy—the Son of **G**. Lk 1:35
For nothing will be impossible with **G**." Lk 1:37
and my spirit rejoices in **G** my Savior, Lk 1:47
tongue loosed, and he spoke, blessing **G**. Lk 1:64
"Blessed be the Lord **G** of Israel, for he Lk 1:68
because of the tender mercy of our **G**, Lk 1:78
heavenly host praising **G** and saying, Lk 2:13
"Glory to **G** in the highest, and on earth Lk 2:14
glorifying and praising **G** for all they Lk 2:20
up in his arms and blessed **G** and said, Lk 2:28
to give thanks to **G** and to speak of Lk 2:38
And the favor of **G** was upon him. Lk 2:40
in stature and in favor with **G** and man. Lk 2:52
the word of **G** came to John the son of Lk 3:2
and all flesh shall see the salvation of **G**.'" Lk 3:6
G is able from these stones to raise up Lk 3:8
of Seth, the son of Adam, the son of **G**. Lk 3:38
devil said to him, "If you are the Son of **G**, Lk 4:3
"'You shall worship the Lord your **G**, Lk 4:8
and said to him, "If you are the Son of **G**, Lk 4:9
not put the Lord your **G** to the test.'" Lk 4:12
know who you are—the Holy One of **G**." Lk 4:34
are the Son of **G**!" But he rebuked them Lk 4:41
of the kingdom of **G** to the other towns Lk 4:43
pressing in on him to hear the word of **G**, Lk 5:1
Who can forgive sins but **G** alone?" Lk 5:21
lying on and went home, glorifying **G**. Lk 5:25
and they glorified **G** and were filled with Lk 5:26

entered the house of **G** and took and ate Lk 6:4
all night he continued in prayer to **G**. Lk 6:12
are poor, for yours is the kingdom of **G**. Lk 6:20
seized them all, and they glorified **G**, Lk 7:16
among us!" and "**G** has visited his Lk 7:16
in the kingdom of **G** is greater than he." Lk 7:28
tax collectors too, they declared **G** just, Lk 7:29
rejected the purpose of **G** for themselves, Lk 7:30
the good news of the kingdom of **G**. Lk 8:1
to know the secrets of the kingdom of **G**, Lk 8:10
parable is this: The seed is the word of **G**. Lk 8:11
those who hear the word of **G** and do it." Lk 8:21
with me, Jesus, Son of the Most High **G**? Lk 8:28
and declare how much **G** has done for Lk 8:39
proclaim the kingdom of **G** and to heal. Lk 9:2
of the kingdom of **G** and cured those Lk 9:11
And Peter answered, "The Christ of **G**." Lk 9:20
death until they see the kingdom of **G**." Lk 9:27
all were astonished at the majesty of **G**. Lk 9:43
go and proclaim the kingdom of **G**." Lk 9:60
looks back is fit for the kingdom of **G**." Lk 9:62
'The kingdom of **G** has come near to Lk 10:9
that the kingdom of **G** has come near.' Lk 10:11
love the Lord your **G** with all your Lk 10:27
is by the finger of **G** that I cast out Lk 11:20
then the kingdom of **G** has come upon Lk 11:20
who hear the word of **G** and keep it!" Lk 11:28
and neglect justice and the love of **G**. Lk 11:42
Therefore also the Wisdom of **G** said, 'I Lk 11:49
not one of them is forgotten before **G**. Lk 12:6
will acknowledge before the angels of **G**, Lk 12:8
will be denied before the angels of **G**. Lk 12:9
But **G** said to him, 'Fool! This night Lk 12:20
for himself and is not rich toward **G**." Lk 12:21
nor barn, and yet **G** feeds them. Lk 12:24
But if **G** so clothes the grass, which is Lk 12:28
was made straight, and she glorified **G**. Lk 13:13
"What is the kingdom of **G** like? Lk 13:18
shall I compare the kingdom of **G**? Lk 13:20
the kingdom of **G** but you yourselves Lk 13:28
recline at table in the kingdom of **G**. Lk 13:29
will eat bread in the kingdom of **G**!" Lk 14:15
before the angels of **G** over one sinner Lk 15:10
other. You cannot serve **G** and money." Lk 16:13
before men, but **G** knows your hearts. Lk 16:15
is an abomination in the sight of **G**. Lk 16:15
news of the kingdom of **G** is preached, Lk 16:16
back, praising **G** with a loud voice; Lk 17:15
give praise to **G** except this foreigner?" Lk 17:18
when the kingdom of **G** would come, Lk 17:20
"The kingdom of **G** is not coming with Lk 17:20
the kingdom of **G** is in the midst of Lk 17:21
who neither feared **G** nor respected man. Lk 18:2
I neither fear **G** nor respect man, Lk 18:4
And will not **G** give justice to his elect, Lk 18:7
'**G**, I thank you that I am not like other Lk 18:11
breast, saying, '**G**, be merciful to me, Lk 18:13
for to such belongs the kingdom of **G**. Lk 18:16
receive the kingdom of **G** like a child Lk 18:17
good? No one is good except **G** alone. Lk 18:19
have wealth to enter the kingdom of **G**! Lk 18:24
rich person to enter the kingdom of **G**." Lk 18:25
with men is possible with **G**." Lk 18:27
for the sake of the kingdom of **G**, Lk 18:29
sight and followed him, glorifying **G**. Lk 18:43
when they saw it, gave praise to **G**. Lk 18:43
that the kingdom of **G** was to appear Lk 19:11
to rejoice and praise **G** with a loud Lk 19:37
partiality, but truly teach the way of **G**. Lk 20:21
and to **G** the things that are God's." Lk 20:25
are equal to angels and are sons of **G**, Lk 20:36
calls the Lord the **G** of Abraham and Lk 20:37
of Abraham and the **G** of Isaac and the Lk 20:37
the God of Isaac and the **G** of Jacob. Lk 20:37
Now he is not **G** of the dead, but of the Lk 20:38
know that the kingdom of **G** is near. Lk 21:31
it is fulfilled in the kingdom of **G**." Lk 22:16
vine until the kingdom of **G** comes." Lk 22:18
at the right hand of the power of **G**." Lk 22:69
So they all said, "Are you the Son of **G**, Lk 22:70
save himself, if he is the Christ of **G**, Lk 23:35
him, saying, "Do you not fear **G**, Lk 23:40
what had taken place, he praised **G**, Lk 23:47
he was looking for the kingdom of **G**. Lk 23:51
deed and word before **G** and all the Lk 24:19
continually in the temple blessing **G**. Lk 24:53
was the Word, and the Word was with **G**, Jn 1:1
Word was with God, and the Word was **G**. Jn 1:1
He was in the beginning with **G**. Jn 1:2
There was a man sent from **G**, whose Jn 1:6
gave the right to become children of **G**, Jn 1:12
the flesh nor of the will of man, but of **G**. Jn 1:13
No one has ever seen **G**; the only God, Jn 1:18
the only **G**, who is at the Father's side, he Jn 1:18
him, and said, "Behold, the Lamb of **G**, Jn 1:29
borne witness that this is the Son of **G**." Jn 1:34
by and said, "Behold, the Lamb of **G**!" Jn 1:36
him, "Rabbi, you are the Son of **G**! Jn 1:49
the angels of **G** ascending and Jn 1:51
know that you are a teacher come from **G**, Jn 3:2
signs that you do unless **G** is with him." Jn 3:2
again he cannot see the kingdom of **G**." Jn 3:3
Spirit, he cannot enter the kingdom of **G**. Jn 3:5
"For **G** so loved the world, that he gave Jn 3:16
For **G** did not send his Son into the world Jn 3:17
believed in the name of the only Son of **G**. Jn 3:18
his deeds have been carried out in **G**." Jn 3:21
sets his seal to this, that **G** is true. Jn 3:33
For he whom **G** has sent utters the words Jn 3:34
whom God has sent utters the words of **G**, Jn 3:34
life, but the wrath of **G** remains on him. Jn 3:36
answered her, "If you knew the gift of **G**, Jn 4:10
G is spirit, and those who worship him Jn 4:24
he was even calling **G** his own Father, Jn 5:18
Father, making himself equal with **G**. Jn 5:18
dead will hear the voice of the Son of **G**, Jn 5:25
you do not have the love of **G** within you. Jn 5:42
the glory that comes from the only **G**? Jn 5:44
For on him **G** the Father has set his seal." Jn 6:27
must we do, to be doing the works of **G**?" Jn 6:28
answered them, "This is the work of **G**, Jn 6:29
For the bread of **G** is he who comes down Jn 6:33
'And they will all be taught by **G**.' Jn 6:45
seen the Father except he who is from **G**; Jn 6:46
to know, that you are the Holy One of **G**." Jn 6:69
the teaching is from **G** or whether I am Jn 7:17
told you the truth that I heard from **G**. Jn 8:40
We have one Father—even **G**." Jn 8:41
said to them, "If **G** were your Father, Jn 8:42
love me, for I came from **G** and I am here. Jn 8:42
Whoever is of **G** hears the words of God. Jn 8:47
Whoever is of God hears the words of **G**. Jn 8:47
not hear them is that you are not of **G**." Jn 8:47
me, of whom you say, 'He is our **G**.' Jn 8:54
that the works of **G** might be displayed in Jn 9:3
Pharisees said, "This man is not from **G**, Jn 9:16
blind and said to him, "Give glory to **G**. Jn 9:24
We know that **G** has spoken to Moses, Jn 9:29
We know that **G** does not listen to Jn 9:31
is a worshiper of **G** and does his will, Jn 9:31
of God and does his will, **G** listens to him. Jn 9:31
If this man were not from **G**, he could do Jn 9:33
you, being a man, make yourself **G**." Jn 10:33
whom the word of **G** came—and Jn 10:35
because I said, 'I am the Son of **G**'? Jn 10:36
It is for the glory of **G**, so that the Son of Jn 11:4
that the Son of **G** may be glorified Jn 11:4
I know that whatever you ask from **G**, Jn 11:22
you ask from God, **G** will give you." Jn 11:22
that you are the Christ, the Son of **G**, Jn 11:27
believed you would see the glory of **G**?" Jn 11:40
one the children of **G** who are scattered Jn 11:52
more than the glory that comes from **G**. Jn 12:43
he had come from **G** and was going back Jn 13:3
from God and was going back to **G**, Jn 13:3
Man glorified, and **G** is glorified in him. Jn 13:31
If **G** is glorified in him, God will also Jn 13:32
him, **G** will also glorify him in himself, Jn 13:32
troubled. Believe in **G**; believe also in me. Jn 14:1
you will think he is offering service to **G**. Jn 16:2
and have believed that I came from **G**. Jn 16:27
why we believe that you came from **G**." Jn 16:30
life, that they know you the only true **G**, Jn 17:3
he has made himself the Son of **G**." Jn 19:7
your Father, to my **G** and your God.'" Jn 20:17
your Father, to my God and your **G**.'" Jn 20:17
answered him, "My Lord and my **G**!" Jn 20:28
that Jesus is the Christ, the Son of **G**, Jn 20:31
what kind of death he was to glorify **G**.) Jn 21:19
and speaking about the kingdom of **G**. Acts 1:3
own tongues the mighty works of **G**." Acts 2:11
in the last days it shall be, **G** declares, Acts 2:17
to you by **G** with mighty works Acts 2:22
and signs that **G** did through him Acts 2:22
definite plan and foreknowledge of **G**, Acts 2:23
G raised him up, loosing the pangs of Acts 2:24
and knowing that **G** had sworn with Acts 2:30
This Jesus **G** raised up, and of that we Acts 2:32
therefore exalted at the right hand of **G**, Acts 2:33
know for certain that **G** has made him Acts 2:36
the Lord our **G** calls to himself." Acts 2:39
praising **G** and having favor with all Acts 2:47
walking and leaping and praising **G**. Acts 3:8
saw him walking and praising **G**, Acts 3:9
The **G** of Abraham, the God of Isaac, Acts 3:13
The God of Abraham, the **G** of Isaac, Acts 3:13
the God of Isaac, and the **G** of Jacob, Acts 3:13
the God of Jacob, the **G** of our fathers, Acts 3:13
of life, whom **G** raised from the dead. Acts 3:15
But what **G** foretold by the mouth of Acts 3:18
the things about which **G** spoke by the Acts 3:21
'The Lord **G** will raise up for you a Acts 3:22
of the covenant that **G** made with your Acts 3:25
G, having raised up his servant, sent Acts 3:26
whom **G** raised from the dead—by Acts 4:10
right in the sight of **G** to listen to you Acts 4:19
of God to listen to you rather than to **G**, Acts 4:19
for all were praising **G** for what had Acts 4:21
their voices together to **G** and said, Acts 4:24
to speak the word of **G** with boldness. Acts 4:31
You have not lied to men but to **G**." Acts 5:4
"We must obey **G** rather than men. Acts 5:29
The **G** of our fathers raised Jesus, Acts 5:30
G exalted him at his right hand as Acts 5:31
whom **G** has given to those who obey Acts 5:32
but if it is of **G**, you will not be able to Acts 5:39
be found opposing **G**!" So they took Acts 5:39
preaching the word of **G** to serve tables. Acts 6:2
the word of **G** continued to increase, Acts 6:7
words against Moses and **G**." Acts 6:11
The **G** of glory appeared to our father Acts 7:2
G removed him from there into this Acts 7:4
And **G** spoke to this effect—that his Acts 7:6
judge the nation that they serve,' said **G**, Acts 7:7
him into Egypt; but **G** was with him Acts 7:9
which **G** had granted to Abraham, Acts 7:17
would understand that **G** was giving Acts 7:25
'I am the **G** of your fathers, the God of Acts 7:32
the **G** of Abraham and of Isaac and of Acts 7:32
—this man **G** sent as both ruler and Acts 7:35
'**G** will raise up for you a prophet like Acts 7:37
But **G** turned away and gave them over Acts 7:42
Moloch and the star of your **g** Rephan, Acts 7:43
the nations that **G** drove out before Acts 7:45
in the sight of **G** and asked to find Acts 7:46
a dwelling place for the **G** of Jacob. Acts 7:46
into heaven and saw the glory of **G**, Acts 7:55
Jesus standing at the right hand of **G**. Acts 7:55
Man standing at the right hand of **G**." Acts 7:56
is the power of **G** that is called Great." Acts 8:10
about the kingdom of **G** and the name Acts 8:12
Samaria had received the word of **G**, Acts 8:14
could obtain the gift of **G** with money! Acts 8:20
for your heart is not right before **G**. Acts 8:21
saying, "He is the Son of **G**." Acts 9:20
devout man who feared **G** with all his Acts 10:2
people, and prayed continually to **G**. Acts 10:2
a vision an angel of **G** come in and say Acts 10:3
have ascended as a memorial before **G**. Acts 10:4
time, "What **G** has made clean, Acts 10:15
but **G** has shown me that I should Acts 10:28
have been remembered before **G**. Acts 10:31
in the presence of **G** to hear all that Acts 10:33
I understand that **G** shows no Acts 10:34
how **G** anointed Jesus of Nazareth Acts 10:38
by the devil, for **G** was with him. Acts 10:38
but **G** raised him on the third day Acts 10:40
had been chosen by **G** as witnesses, Acts 10:41
the one appointed by **G** to be judge of Acts 10:42
speaking in tongues and extolling **G**. Acts 10:46
also had received the word of **G**. Acts 11:1
heaven, 'What **G** has made clean, Acts 11:9
If then **G** gave the same gift to them Acts 11:17
And they glorified **G**, saying, "Then Acts 11:18
the Gentiles also **G** has granted Acts 11:18
he came and saw the grace of **G**, Acts 11:23
for him was made to **G** by the church. Acts 12:5
were shouting, "The voice of a **g**, Acts 12:22
because he did not give **G** the glory, Acts 12:23
the word of **G** increased and Acts 12:24
the word of **G** in the synagogues Acts 13:5
Saul and sought to hear the word of **G**. Acts 13:7
"Men of Israel and you who fear **G**, Acts 13:16
The **G** of this people Israel chose our Acts 13:17
and **G** gave them Saul the son of Acts 13:21
this man's offspring **G** has brought Acts 13:23
and those among you who fear **G**, Acts 13:26
But **G** raised him from the dead, Acts 13:30
news that what **G** promised to the Acts 13:32
served the purpose of **G** in his own Acts 13:36
but he whom **G** raised up did not see Acts 13:37
them to continue in the grace of **G**. Acts 13:43
that the word of **G** be spoken first to Acts 13:46
from these vain things to a living **G**, Acts 14:15
we must enter the kingdom of **G**. Acts 14:22
to the grace of **G** for the work that Acts 14:26
declared all that **G** had done with Acts 14:27
they declared all that **G** had done with Acts 15:4
in the early days **G** made a choice Acts 15:7
And **G**, who knows the heart, bore Acts 15:8
why are you putting **G** to the test by Acts 15:10
signs and wonders **G** had done Acts 15:12
has related how **G** first visited the Acts 15:14
those of the Gentiles who turn to **G**, Acts 15:19
concluding that **G** had called us to Acts 16:10

goods, who was a worshiper of **G**. Acts 16:14
men are servants of the Most High **G**, Acts 16:17
praying and singing hymns to **G**, Acts 16:25
household that he had believed in **G**. Acts 16:34
that the word of **G** was proclaimed by Acts 17:13
this inscription, 'To the unknown **g**.' Acts 17:23
The **G** who made the world and Acts 17:24
that they should seek **G**, in the hope Acts 17:27
The times of ignorance **G** overlooked, Acts 17:30
named Titius Justus, a worshiper of **G**. Acts 18:7
teaching the word of **G** among them. Acts 18:11
people to worship **G** contrary to the Acts 18:13
return to you if **G** wills," and he set Acts 18:21
to him the way of **G** more accurately. Acts 18:26
them about the kingdom of **G**. Acts 19:8
And **G** was doing extraordinary Acts 19:11
of repentance toward **G** and of faith Acts 20:21
testify to the gospel of the grace of **G**. Acts 20:24
to you the whole counsel of **G**. Acts 20:27
overseers, to care for the church of **G**, Acts 20:28
I commend you to **G** and to the word Acts 20:32
the things that **G** had done among Acts 21:19
when they heard it, they glorified **G**. Acts 21:20
being zealous for **G** as all of you are Acts 22:3
'The **G** of our fathers appointed you Acts 22:14
lived my life before **G** in all good Acts 23:1
said to him, "**G** is going to strike you, Acts 23:3
a sect, I worship the **G** of our fathers, Acts 24:14
having a hope in **G**, which these men Acts 24:15
conscience toward both **G** and man. Acts 24:16
the promise made by **G** to our fathers, Acts 26:6
by any of you that **G** raises the dead? Acts 26:8
and from the power of Satan to **G**, Acts 26:18
that they should repent and turn to **G**, Acts 26:20
have had the help that comes from **G**, Acts 26:22
I would to **G** that not only you but Acts 26:29
an angel of the **G** to whom I belong Acts 27:23
G has granted you all those who sail Acts 27:24
for I have faith in **G** that it will be Acts 27:25
giving thanks to **G** in the presence Acts 27:35
their minds and said that he was a **g**. Acts 28:6
Paul thanked **G** and took courage. Acts 28:15
to the kingdom of **G** and trying to Acts 28:23
that this salvation of **G** has been sent Acts 28:28
the kingdom of **G** and teaching Acts 28:31
an apostle, set apart for the gospel of **G**, Rom 1:1
to be the Son of **G** in power according to Rom 1:4
who are loved by **G** and called to be Rom 1:7
you and peace from **G** our Father and Rom 1:7
I thank my **G** through Jesus Christ for Rom 1:8
For **G** is my witness, whom I serve with Rom 1:9
is the power of **G** for salvation to Rom 1:16
the righteousness of **G** is revealed from Rom 1:17
For the wrath of **G** is revealed from Rom 1:18
can be known about **G** is plain to Rom 1:19
them, because **G** has shown it to them. Rom 1:19
For although they knew **G**, they did Rom 1:21
not honor him as **G** or give thanks to Rom 1:21
of the immortal **G** for images Rom 1:23
Therefore **G** gave them up in the lusts Rom 1:24
exchanged the truth about **G** for a lie Rom 1:25
For this reason **G** gave them up to Rom 1:26
they did not see fit to acknowledge **G**, Rom 1:28
G gave them up to a debased mind to Rom 1:28
slanderers, haters of **G**, insolent, Rom 1:30
that the judgment of **G** rightly falls on Rom 2:2
that you will escape the judgment of **G**? Rom 2:3
For **G** shows no partiality. Rom 2:11
of the law who are righteous before **G**, Rom 2:13
G judges the secrets of men by Christ Rom 2:16
Jew and rely on the law and boast in **G** Rom 2:17
in the law dishonor **G** by breaking the Rom 2:23
"The name of **G** is blasphemed among Rom 2:24
praise is not from man but from **G**. Rom 2:29
were entrusted with the oracles of **G**. Rom 3:2
nullify the faithfulness of **G**? Rom 3:3
Let **G** be true though every one were a Rom 3:4
serves to show the righteousness of **G**, Rom 3:5
That **G** is unrighteous to inflict wrath Rom 3:5
For then how could **G** judge the world? Rom 3:6
one understands; no one seeks for **G**. Rom 3:11
is no fear of **G** before their eyes." Rom 3:18
world may be held accountable to **G**. Rom 3:19
the righteousness of **G** has been Rom 3:21
the righteousness of **G** through faith Rom 3:22
sinned and fall short of the glory of **G**, Rom 3:23
whom **G** put forward as a propitiation Rom 3:25
Or is **G** the God of Jews only? Is he not Rom 3:29
Or is God the **G** of Jews only? Is he not Rom 3:29
only? Is he not the **G** of Gentiles also? Rom 3:29
since **G** is one. He will justify the Rom 3:30
to boast about, but not before **G**. Rom 4:2
"Abraham believed **G**, and it was Rom 4:3
one to whom **G** counts righteousness Rom 4:6
the presence of the **G** in whom he Rom 4:17
waver concerning the promise of **G**, Rom 4:20
in his faith as he gave glory to **G**, Rom 4:20
fully convinced that **G** was able to do Rom 4:21
we have peace with **G** through our Lord Rom 5:1
and we rejoice in hope of the glory of **G**. Rom 5:2
but **G** shows his love for us in that Rom 5:8
be saved by him from the wrath of **G**. Rom 5:9
we were reconciled to **G** by the death of Rom 5:10
we also rejoice in **G** through our Lord Rom 5:11
have the grace of **G** and the free gift Rom 5:15
all, but the life he lives he lives to **G**. Rom 6:10
to sin and alive to **G** in Christ Jesus. Rom 6:11
present yourselves to **G** as those who Rom 6:13
your members to **G** as instruments for Rom 6:13
But thanks be to **G**, that you who were Rom 6:17
from sin and have become slaves of **G**, Rom 6:22
but the free gift of **G** is eternal life in Rom 6:23
in order that we may bear fruit for **G**. Rom 7:4
For I delight in the law of **G**, in my Rom 7:22
Thanks be to **G** through Jesus Christ Rom 7:25
serve the law of **G** with my mind, Rom 7:25
For **G** has done what the law, weakened Rom 8:3
that is set on the flesh is hostile to **G**, Rom 8:7
who are in the flesh cannot please **G**. Rom 8:8
if in fact the Spirit of **G** dwells in you. Rom 8:9
led by the Spirit of **G** are sons of God. Rom 8:14
led by the Spirit of God are sons of **G**. Rom 8:14
our spirit that we are children of **G**, Rom 8:16
heirs—heirs of **G** and fellow heirs with Rom 8:17
for the revealing of the sons of **G**. Rom 8:19
of the glory of the children of **G**. Rom 8:21
the saints according to the will of **G**. Rom 8:27
for those who love **G** all things work Rom 8:28
If **G** is for us, who can be against us? Rom 8:31
God's elect? It is **G** who justifies. Rom 8:33
raised—who is at the right hand of **G**, Rom 8:34
from the love of **G** in Christ Jesus our Rom 8:39
the flesh, is the Christ who is **G** over all, Rom 9:5
not as though the word of **G** has failed. Rom 9:6
of the flesh who are the children of **G**, Rom 9:8
on human will or exertion, but on **G**, Rom 9:16
are you, O man, to answer back to **G**? Rom 9:20
What if **G**, desiring to show his wrath Rom 9:22
will be called 'sons of the living **G**.'" Rom 9:26
desire and prayer to **G** for them is that Rom 10:1
witness that they have a zeal for **G**, Rom 10:2
the righteousness that comes from **G**, Rom 10:3
in your heart that **G** raised him from Rom 10:9
I ask, then, has **G** rejected his people? Rom 11:1
G has not rejected his people whom he Rom 11:2
how he appeals to **G** against Israel? Rom 11:2
"**G** gave them a spirit of stupor, Rom 11:8
For if **G** did not spare the natural Rom 11:21
the kindness and the severity of **G**: Rom 11:22
for **G** has the power to graft them in Rom 11:23
they are enemies of **G** for your sake. Rom 11:28
and the calling of **G** are irrevocable. Rom 11:29
time disobedient to **G** but now have Rom 11:30
For **G** has consigned all to Rom 11:32
and wisdom and knowledge of **G**! Rom 11:33
brothers, by the mercies of **G**, Rom 12:1
sacrifice, holy and acceptable to **G**, Rom 12:1
you may discern what is the will of **G**, Rom 12:2
measure of faith that **G** has assigned. Rom 12:3
but leave it to the wrath of **G**, Rom 12:19
there is no authority except from **G**, Rom 13:1
that exist have been instituted by **G**. Rom 13:1
resists what **G** has appointed, Rom 13:2
For he is the servant of **G**, an avenger Rom 13:4
for the authorities are ministers of **G**, Rom 13:6
who eats, for **G** has welcomed him. Rom 14:3
of the Lord, since he gives thanks to **G**, Rom 14:6
of the Lord and gives thanks to **G**. Rom 14:6
stand before the judgment seat of **G**; Rom 14:10
and every tongue shall confess to **G**." Rom 14:11
will give an account of himself to **G**. Rom 14:12
For the kingdom of **G** is not a matter Rom 14:17
is acceptable to **G** and approved by Rom 14:18
sake of food, destroy the work of **G**. Rom 14:20
have, keep between yourself and **G**. Rom 14:22
May the **G** of endurance and Rom 15:5
one voice glorify the **G** and Father of Rom 15:6
has welcomed you, for the glory of **G**. Rom 15:7
Gentiles might glorify **G** for his Rom 15:9
May the **G** of hope fill you with all Rom 15:13
because of the grace given me by **G** Rom 15:15
the priestly service of the gospel of **G**, Rom 15:16
reason to be proud of my work for **G**. Rom 15:17
power of the Spirit of **G**—so that from Rom 15:19
in your prayers to **G** on my behalf, Rom 15:30
May the **G** of peace be with you all. Rom 15:33
The **G** of peace will soon crush Satan Rom 16:20
to the command of the eternal **G**, Rom 16:26
the only wise **G** be glory forevermore Rom 16:27
called by the will of **G** to be an apostle 1 Cor 1:1
To the church of **G** that is in Corinth, 1 Cor 1:2
you and peace from **G** our Father and 1 Cor 1:3
give thanks to my **G** always for you 1 Cor 1:4
of the grace of **G** that was given you 1 Cor 1:4
G is faithful, by whom you were called 1 Cor 1:9
I thank **G** that I baptized none of you 1 Cor 1:14
are being saved it is the power of **G**. 1 Cor 1:18
Has not **G** made foolish the wisdom 1 Cor 1:20
For since, in the wisdom of **G**, the 1 Cor 1:21
did not know **G** through wisdom, 1 Cor 1:21
it pleased **G** through the folly of what 1 Cor 1:21
Christ the power of **G** and the wisdom 1 Cor 1:24
power of God and the wisdom of **G**. 1 Cor 1:24
For the foolishness of **G** is wiser than 1 Cor 1:25
the weakness of **G** is stronger than 1 Cor 1:25
But **G** chose what is foolish in the 1 Cor 1:27
G chose what is weak in the world to 1 Cor 1:27
G chose what is low and despised in 1 Cor 1:28
might boast in the presence of **G**. 1 Cor 1:29
whom **G** made our wisdom and our 1 Cor 1:30
the testimony of **G** with lofty speech 1 Cor 2:1
wisdom of men but in the power of **G**. 1 Cor 2:5
a secret and hidden wisdom of **G**, 1 Cor 2:7
which **G** decreed before the ages for 1 Cor 2:7
what **G** has prepared for those who 1 Cor 2:9
these things **G** has revealed to us 1 Cor 2:10
everything, even the depths of **G**. 1 Cor 2:10
the thoughts of **G** except the Spirit 1 Cor 2:11
thoughts of God except the Spirit of **G**. 1 Cor 2:11
world, but the Spirit who is from **G**, 1 Cor 2:12
the things freely given us by **G**. 1 Cor 2:12
accept the things of the Spirit of **G**, 1 Cor 2:14
watered, but **G** gave the growth. 1 Cor 3:6
but only **G** who gives the growth. 1 Cor 3:7
to the grace of **G** given to me, 1 Cor 3:10
God's temple, **G** will destroy him. 1 Cor 3:17
wisdom of this world is folly with **G**. 1 Cor 3:19
and stewards of the mysteries of **G**. 1 Cor 4:1
receive his commendation from **G**. 1 Cor 4:5
For I think that **G** has exhibited us 1 Cor 4:9
the kingdom of **G** does not consist 1 Cor 4:20
G judges those outside. "Purge the 1 Cor 5:13
will not inherit the kingdom of **G**? 1 Cor 6:9
will inherit the kingdom of **G**. 1 Cor 6:10
Christ and by the Spirit of our **G**. 1 Cor 6:11
for food"—and **G** will destroy both 1 Cor 6:13
And **G** raised the Lord and will also 1 Cor 6:14
within you, whom you have from **G**? 1 Cor 6:19
a price. So glorify **G** in your body. 1 Cor 6:20
But each has his own gift from **G**, one 1 Cor 7:7
enslaved. **G** has called you to peace. 1 Cor 7:15
him, and to which **G** has called him. 1 Cor 7:17
keeping the commandments of **G**. 1 Cor 7:19
called, there let him remain with **G**. 1 Cor 7:24
I think that I too have the Spirit of **G**. 1 Cor 7:40
But if anyone loves **G**, he is known by 1 Cor 8:3
if anyone loves God, he is known by **G**. 1 Cor 8:3
and that "there is no **G** but one." 1 Cor 8:4
yet for us there is one **G**, the Father, 1 Cor 8:6
Food will not commend us to **G**. We 1 Cor 8:8
Is it for oxen that **G** is concerned? 1 Cor 9:9
outside the law of **G** but under the 1 Cor 9:21
with most of them **G** was not pleased, 1 Cor 10:5
G is faithful, and he will not let you 1 Cor 10:13
they offer to demons and not to **G**. 1 Cor 10:20
you do, do all to the glory of **G**. 1 Cor 10:31
or to Greeks or to the church of **G**, 1 Cor 10:32
husband, and the head of Christ is **G**. 1 Cor 11:3
since he is the image and glory of **G**, 1 Cor 11:7
woman. And all things are from **G**. 1 Cor 11:12
wife to pray to **G** with her head 1 Cor 11:13
practice, nor do the churches of **G**. 1 Cor 11:16
the church of **G** and humiliate 1 Cor 11:22
in the Spirit of **G** ever says "Jesus is 1 Cor 12:3
it is the same **G** who empowers them 1 Cor 12:6
G arranged the members in the 1 Cor 12:18
But **G** has so composed the body, 1 Cor 12:24
And **G** has appointed in the church 1 Cor 12:28
a tongue speaks not to men but to **G**; 1 Cor 14:2
I thank **G** that I speak in tongues 1 Cor 14:18
he will worship **G** and declare that 1 Cor 14:25
and declare that **G** is really among 1 Cor 14:25
and speak to himself and to **G**. 1 Cor 14:28
For **G** is not a God of confusion but 1 Cor 14:33
God is not a **G** of confusion but of 1 Cor 14:33
from you that the word of **G** came? 1 Cor 14:36
because I persecuted the church of **G**. 1 Cor 15:9
But by the grace of **G** I am what I 1 Cor 15:10
I, but the grace of **G** that is with me. 1 Cor 15:10
even found to be misrepresenting **G**, 1 Cor 15:15
we testified about **G** that he raised 1 Cor 15:15
the kingdom to **G** the Father after 1 Cor 15:24
For "**G** has put all things in 1 Cor 15:27
under him, that **G** may be all in all. 1 Cor 15:28
For some have no knowledge of **G**. 1 Cor 15:34

But **G** gives it a body as he has	1 Cor 15:38
cannot inherit the kingdom of **G**,	1 Cor 15:50
But thanks be to **G**, who gives us the	1 Cor 15:57
apostle of Christ Jesus by the will of **G**,	2 Cor 1:1
To the church of **G** that is at Corinth,	2 Cor 1:1
you and peace from **G** our Father and	2 Cor 1:2
Blessed be the **G** and Father of our	2 Cor 1:3
Father of mercies and **G** of all comfort,	2 Cor 1:3
we ourselves are comforted by **G**.	2 Cor 1:4
on ourselves but on **G** who raises the	2 Cor 1:9
earthly wisdom but by the grace of **G**,	2 Cor 1:12
As surely as **G** is faithful, our word to	2 Cor 1:18
For the Son of **G**, Jesus Christ, whom	2 Cor 1:19
all the promises of **G** find their Yes in	2 Cor 1:20
we utter our Amen to **G** for his glory.	2 Cor 1:20
And it is **G** who establishes us with	2 Cor 1:21
But I call **G** to witness against me—it	2 Cor 1:23
But thanks be to **G**, who in Christ	2 Cor 2:14
of Christ to **G** among those who	2 Cor 2:15
of sincerity, as commissioned by **G**,	2 Cor 2:17
in the sight of **G** we speak in Christ.	2 Cor 2:17
ink but with the Spirit of the living **G**,	2 Cor 3:3
that we have through Christ toward **G**.	2 Cor 3:4
from us, but our sufficiency is from **G**,	2 Cor 3:5
this ministry by the mercy of **G**,	2 Cor 4:1
conscience in the sight of **G**.	2 Cor 4:2
In their case the **g** of this world has	2 Cor 4:4
glory of Christ, who is the image of **G**.	2 Cor 4:4
For **G**, who said, "Let light shine out of	2 Cor 4:6
of the glory of **G** in the face of	2 Cor 4:6
power belongs to **G** and not to	2 Cor 4:7
thanksgiving, to the glory of **G**.	2 Cor 4:15
destroyed, we have a building from **G**,	2 Cor 5:1
prepared us for this very thing is **G**,	2 Cor 5:5
But what we are is known to **G**, and I	2 Cor 5:11
if we are beside ourselves, it is for **G**;	2 Cor 5:13
All this is from **G**, who through	2 Cor 5:18
in Christ **G** was reconciling the	2 Cor 5:19
G making his appeal through us.	2 Cor 5:20
behalf of Christ, be reconciled to **G**.	2 Cor 5:20
become the righteousness of **G**.	2 Cor 5:21
not to receive the grace of **G** in vain.	2 Cor 6:1
as servants of **G** we commend	2 Cor 6:4
by truthful speech, and the power of **G**;	2 Cor 6:7
has the temple of **G** with idols?	2 Cor 6:16
For we are the temple of the living **G**;	2 Cor 6:16
temple of the living God; as **G** said,	2 Cor 6:16
among them, and I will be their **G**,	2 Cor 6:16
holiness to completion in the fear of **G**.	2 Cor 7:1
But **G**, who comforts the downcast,	2 Cor 7:6
be revealed to you in the sight of **G**.	2 Cor 7:12
about the grace of **G** that has been	2 Cor 8:1
Lord and then by the will of **G** to us.	2 Cor 8:5
But thanks be to **G**, who put into the	2 Cor 8:16
for **G** loves a cheerful giver.	2 Cor 9:7
And **G** is able to make all grace	2 Cor 9:8
us will produce thanksgiving to **G**.	2 Cor 9:11
in many thanksgivings to **G**.	2 Cor 9:12
they will glorify **G** because of your	2 Cor 9:13
the surpassing grace of **G** upon you.	2 Cor 9:14
Thanks be to **G** for his inexpressible	2 Cor 9:15
raised against the knowledge of **G**,	2 Cor 10:5
area of influence **G** assigned to us,	2 Cor 10:13
I do not love you? **G** knows I do!	2 Cor 11:11
The **G** and Father of the Lord Jesus,	2 Cor 11:31
of the body I do not know, **G** knows.	2 Cor 12:2
of the body I do not know, **G** knows—	2 Cor 12:3
is in the sight of **G** that we have been	2 Cor 12:19
I come again my **G** may humble me	2 Cor 12:21
weakness, but lives by the power of **G**.	2 Cor 13:4
will live with him by the power of **G**.	2 Cor 13:4
But we pray to **G** that you may not do	2 Cor 13:7
and the **G** of love and peace will be	2 Cor 13:11
and the love of **G** and the fellowship	2 Cor 13:14
through Jesus Christ and **G** the Father,	Gal 1:1
you and peace from **G** our Father and	Gal 1:3
to the will of our **G** and Father,	Gal 1:4
seeking the approval of man, or of **G**?	Gal 1:10
the church of **G** violently and tried	Gal 1:13
(In what I am writing to you, before **G**, I	Gal 1:20
And they glorified **G** because of me.	Gal 1:24
G shows no partiality)—those, I say, who	Gal 2:6
died to the law, so that I might live to **G**.	Gal 2:19
the flesh I live by faith in the Son of **G**,	Gal 2:20
I do not nullify the grace of **G**, for if	Gal 2:21
just as Abraham "believed **G**, and it was	Gal 3:6
foreseeing that **G** would justify the	Gal 3:8
no one is justified before **G** by the law,	Gal 3:11
a covenant previously ratified by **G**,	Gal 3:17
but **G** gave it to Abraham by a promise.	Gal 3:18
implies more than one, but **G** is one.	Gal 3:20
law then contrary to the promises of **G**?	Gal 3:21
for in Christ Jesus you are all sons of **G**,	Gal 3:26
of time had come, **G** sent forth his Son,	Gal 4:4
G has sent the Spirit of his Son into our	Gal 4:6
son, and if a son, then an heir through **G**.	Gal 4:7
Formerly, when you did not know **G**,	Gal 4:8
But now that you have come to know **G**,	Gal 4:9
know God, or rather to be known by **G**,	Gal 4:9
me, but received me as an angel of **G**,	Gal 4:14
will not inherit the kingdom of **G**.	Gal 5:21
G is not mocked, for whatever one sows,	Gal 6:7
be upon them, and upon the Israel of **G**.	Gal 6:16
apostle of Christ Jesus by the will of **G**,	Eph 1:1
you and peace from **G** our Father and	Eph 1:2
Blessed be the **G** and Father of our Lord	Eph 1:3
that the **G** of our Lord Jesus Christ, the	Eph 1:17
But **G**, being rich in mercy, because of	Eph 2:4
is not your own doing; it is the gift of **G**,	Eph 2:8
works, which **G** prepared beforehand,	Eph 2:10
no hope and without **G** in the world.	Eph 2:12
reconcile us both to **G** in one body	Eph 2:16
and members of the household of **G**,	Eph 2:19
a dwelling place for **G** by the Spirit.	Eph 2:22
hidden for ages in **G** who created all	Eph 3:9
manifold wisdom of **G** might now be	Eph 3:10
may be filled with all the fullness of **G**.	Eph 3:19
one **G** and Father of all, who is over all	Eph 4:6
and of the knowledge of the Son of **G**,	Eph 4:13
from the life of **G** because of the	Eph 4:18
the likeness of **G** in true righteousness	Eph 4:24
And do not grieve the Holy Spirit of **G**,	Eph 4:30
another, as **G** in Christ forgave you.	Eph 4:32
Therefore be imitators of **G**, as beloved	Eph 5:1
us, a fragrant offering and sacrifice to **G**.	Eph 5:2
in the kingdom of Christ and **G**.	Eph 5:5
things the wrath of **G** comes upon the	Eph 5:6
and for everything to **G** the Father in	Eph 5:20
doing the will of **G** from the heart,	Eph 6:6
Put on the whole armor of **G**, that you	Eph 6:11
take up the whole armor of **G**,	Eph 6:13
of the Spirit, which is the word of **G**,	Eph 6:17
from **G** the Father and the Lord Jesus	Eph 6:23
you and peace from **G** our Father and	Phil 1:2
I thank my **G** in all my remembrance	Phil 1:3
For **G** is my witness, how I yearn for you	Phil 1:8
Christ, to the glory and praise of **G**.	Phil 1:11
but of your salvation, and that from **G**.	Phil 1:28
who, though he was in the form of **G**,	Phil 2:6
not count equality with **G** a thing to be	Phil 2:6
Therefore **G** has highly exalted him and	Phil 2:9
is Lord, to the glory of **G** the Father.	Phil 2:11
for it is **G** who works in you, both to	Phil 2:13
children of **G** without blemish in the	Phil 2:15
But **G** had mercy on him, and not only	Phil 2:27
by the Spirit of **G** and glory in Christ	Phil 3:3
the righteousness from **G** that depends	Phil 3:9
of the upward call of **G** in Christ Jesus.	Phil 3:14
G will reveal that also to you.	Phil 3:15
end is destruction, their **g** is their belly,	Phil 3:19
let your requests be made known to **G**.	Phil 4:6
And the peace of **G**, which surpasses all	Phil 4:7
and the **G** of peace will be with you.	Phil 4:9
sacrifice acceptable and pleasing to **G**.	Phil 4:18
And my **G** will supply every need of	Phil 4:19
To our **G** and Father be glory forever	Phil 4:20
apostle of Christ Jesus by the will of **G**,	Col 1:1
to you and peace from **G** our Father.	Col 1:2
We always thank **G**, the Father of our	Col 1:3
it and understood the grace of **G** in truth,	Col 1:6
and increasing in the knowledge of **G**.	Col 1:10
He is the image of the invisible **G**, the	Col 1:15
all the fullness of **G** was pleased to	Col 1:19
the stewardship from **G** that was given	Col 1:25
to make the word of **G** fully known,	Col 1:25
To them **G** chose to make known how	Col 1:27
faith in the powerful working of **G**,	Col 2:12
flesh, **G** made alive together with him,	Col 2:13
grows with a growth that is from **G**.	Col 2:19
Christ is, seated at the right hand of **G**.	Col 3:1
and your life is hidden with Christ in **G**.	Col 3:3
of these the wrath of **G** is coming.	Col 3:6
with thankfulness in your hearts to **G**.	Col 3:16
giving thanks to **G** the Father through	Col 3:17
that **G** may open to us a door for the	Col 4:3
fellow workers for the kingdom of **G**,	Col 4:11
and fully assured in all the will of **G**.	Col 4:12
the Thessalonians in **G** the Father	1 Thes 1:1
We give thanks to **G** always for all of	1 Thes 1:2
before our **G** and Father	1 Thes 1:3
For we know, brothers loved by **G**,	1 Thes 1:4
but your faith in **G** has gone forth	1 Thes 1:8
how you turned to **G** from idols to	1 Thes 1:9
idols to serve the living and true **G**,	1 Thes 1:9
had boldness in our **G** to declare to	1 Thes 2:2
to you the gospel of **G** in the midst of	1 Thes 2:2
been approved by **G** to be entrusted	1 Thes 2:4
but to please **G** who tests our hearts.	1 Thes 2:4
with a pretext for greed—**G** is witness.	1 Thes 2:5
only the gospel of **G** but also our own	1 Thes 2:8
we proclaimed to you the gospel of **G**.	1 Thes 2:9
You are witnesses, and **G** also, how	1 Thes 2:10
to walk in a manner worthy of **G**,	1 Thes 2:12
we also thank **G** constantly for this,	1 Thes 2:13
when you received the word of **G**,	1 Thes 2:13
as what it really is, the word of **G**,	1 Thes 2:13
of the churches of **G** in Christ Jesus	1 Thes 2:14
and displease **G** and oppose all	1 Thes 2:15
can we return to **G** for you,	1 Thes 3:9
we feel for your sake before our **G**,	1 Thes 3:9
Now may our **G** and Father himself,	1 Thes 3:11
in holiness before our **G** and Father,	1 Thes 3:13
how you ought to live and to please **G**,	1 Thes 4:1
For this is the will of **G**, your	1 Thes 4:3
like the Gentiles who do not know **G**;	1 Thes 4:5
For **G** has not called us for impurity,	1 Thes 4:7
this, disregards not man but **G**,	1 Thes 4:8
have been taught by **G** to love one	1 Thes 4:9
G will bring with him those who	1 Thes 4:14
with the sound of the trumpet of **G**.	1 Thes 4:16
For **G** has not destined us for wrath,	1 Thes 5:9
is the will of **G** in Christ Jesus for	1 Thes 5:18
Now may the **G** of peace himself	1 Thes 5:23
the Thessalonians in **G** our Father	2 Thes 1:1
you and peace from **G** our Father and	2 Thes 1:2
always to give thanks to **G** for you,	2 Thes 1:3
the churches of **G** for your	2 Thes 1:4
of the righteous judgment of **G**,	2 Thes 1:5
worthy of the kingdom of **G**,	2 Thes 1:5
since indeed **G** considers it just to	2 Thes 1:6
who do not know **G** and on those who	2 Thes 1:8
that our **G** may make you worthy of	2 Thes 1:11
the grace of our **G** and the Lord	2 Thes 1:12
against every so-called **g** or object of	2 Thes 2:4
he takes his seat in the temple of **G**,	2 Thes 2:4
of God, proclaiming himself to be **G**.	2 Thes 2:4
Therefore **G** sends them a strong	2 Thes 2:11
always to give thanks to **G** for you,	2 Thes 2:13
because **G** chose you as the	2 Thes 2:13
Christ himself, and **G** our Father,	2 Thes 2:16
to the love of **G** and to the	2 Thes 3:5
by command of **G** our Savior and	1 Tm 1:1
and peace from **G** the Father and	1 Tm 1:2
than the stewardship from **G** that is by	1 Tm 1:4
gospel of the blessed **G** with which I	1 Tm 1:11
ages, immortal, invisible, the only **G**,	1 Tm 1:17
is pleasing in the sight of **G** our Savior,	1 Tm 2:3
For there is one **G**, and there is one	1 Tm 2:5
is one mediator between **G** and men,	1 Tm 2:5
to behave in the household of **G**,	1 Tm 3:15
which is the church of the living **G**,	1 Tm 3:15
from foods that **G** created to be	1 Tm 4:3
For everything created by **G** is good,	1 Tm 4:4
holy by the word of **G** and prayer.	1 Tm 4:5
we have our hope set on the living **G**,	1 Tm 4:10
for this is pleasing in the sight of **G**.	1 Tm 5:4
set her hope on **G** and continues in	1 Tm 5:5
In the presence of **G** and of Christ	1 Tm 5:21
that the name of **G** and the teaching	1 Tm 6:1
But as for you, O man of **G**, flee these	1 Tm 6:11
I charge you in the presence of **G**,	1 Tm 6:13
the uncertainty of riches, but on **G**,	1 Tm 6:17
by the will of **G** according to the	2 Tm 1:1
and peace from **G** the Father and	2 Tm 1:2
I thank **G** whom I serve, as did my	2 Tm 1:3
you to fan into flame the gift of **G**,	2 Tm 1:6
for **G** gave us a spirit not of fear but of	2 Tm 1:7
for the gospel by the power of **G**,	2 Tm 1:8
But the word of **G** is not bound!	2 Tm 2:9
charge them before **G** not to quarrel	2 Tm 2:14
present yourself to **G** as one approved,	2 Tm 2:15
G may perhaps grant them	2 Tm 2:25
of pleasure rather than lovers of **G**,	2 Tm 3:4
breathed out by **G** and profitable for	2 Tm 3:16
that the man of **G** may be competent,	2 Tm 3:17
in the presence of **G** and of Christ	2 Tm 4:1
a servant of **G** and an apostle of Jesus	Ti 1:1
in hope of eternal life, which **G**, who never	Ti 1:2
by the command of **G** our Savior;	Ti 1:3
Grace and peace from **G** the Father and	Ti 1:4
They profess to know **G**, but they deny	Ti 1:16
that the word of **G** may not be reviled.	Ti 2:5
may adorn the doctrine of **G** our Savior.	Ti 2:10
For the grace of **G** has appeared,	Ti 2:11
glory of our great **G** and Savior Jesus	Ti 2:13
loving kindness of **G** our Savior appeared,	Ti 3:4
who have believed in **G** may be careful to	Ti 3:8
you and peace from **G** our Father and	Phlm 1:3
I thank my **G** always when I	Phlm 1:4
G spoke to our fathers by the prophets,	Heb 1:1
of the glory of **G** and the exact imprint	Heb 1:3
to which of the angels did **G** ever say,	Heb 1:5
of the Son he says, "Your throne, O **G**,	Heb 1:8
and hated wickedness; therefore **G**,	Heb 1:9
therefore God, your **G**, has anointed you	Heb 1:9

while **G** also bore witness by signs and Heb 2:4
not to angels that **G** subjected the world Heb 2:5
by the grace of **G** he might taste death Heb 2:9
I and the children **G** has given me." Heb 2:13
faithful high priest in the service of **G**, Heb 2:17
but the builder of all things is **G**.) Heb 3:4
you to fall away from the living **G**. Heb 3:12
"And **G** rested on the seventh day from Heb 4:4
G would not have spoken of another day Heb 4:8
a Sabbath rest for the people of **G**, Heb 4:9
from his works as **G** did from his. Heb 4:10
For the word of **G** is living and active, Heb 4:12
the heavens, Jesus, the Son of **G**, Heb 4:14
to act on behalf of men in relation to **G**, Heb 5:1
for himself, but only when called by **G**, Heb 5:4
being designated by **G** a high priest Heb 5:10
the basic principles of the oracles of **G**. Heb 5:12
from dead works and of faith toward **G**, Heb 6:1
And this we will do if **G** permits. Heb 6:3
of the word of **G** and the powers of Heb 6:5
again the Son of **G** to their own harm Heb 6:6
is cultivated, receives a blessing from **G**. Heb 6:7
For **G** is not so unjust as to overlook Heb 6:10
For when **G** made a promise to Heb 6:13
So when **G** desired to show more Heb 6:17
in which it is impossible for **G** to lie, Heb 6:18
king of Salem, priest of the Most High **G**, Heb 7:1
resembling the Son of **G** he continues a Heb 7:3
through which we draw near to **G**. Heb 7:19
who draw near to **G** through him, Heb 7:25
to erect the tent, he was instructed by **G**, Heb 8:5
on their hearts, and I will be their **G**, Heb 8:10
offered himself without blemish to **G**, Heb 9:14
from dead works to serve the living **G**. Heb 9:14
the covenant that **G** commanded for Heb 9:20
in the presence of **G** on our behalf. Heb 9:24
I have come to do your will, O **G**, Heb 10:7
he sat down at the right hand of **G**, Heb 10:12
have a great priest over the house of **G**, Heb 10:21
the one who has spurned the Son of **G**, Heb 10:29
to fall into the hands of the living **G**. Heb 10:31
done the will of **G** you may receive Heb 10:36
universe was created by the word of **G**, Heb 11:3
Abel offered to **G** a more acceptable Heb 11:4
G commending him by accepting his Heb 11:4
not found, because **G** had taken him. Heb 11:5
was commended as having pleased **G**. Heb 11:5
would draw near to **G** must believe that Heb 11:6
being warned by **G** concerning events Heb 11:7
whose designer and builder is **G**. Heb 11:10
Therefore **G** is not ashamed to be Heb 11:16
is not ashamed to be called their **G**, Heb 11:16
He considered that **G** was able even to Heb 11:19
with the people of **G** than to enjoy the Heb 11:25
since **G** had provided something Heb 11:40
at the right hand of the throne of **G**. Heb 12:2
to endure. **G** is treating you as sons. Heb 12:7
no one fails to obtain the grace of **G**; Heb 12:15
Zion and to the city of the living **G**, Heb 12:22
who are enrolled in heaven, and to **G**, Heb 12:23
let us offer to **G** acceptable worship, Heb 12:28
for our **G** is a consuming fire. Heb 12:29
for **G** will judge the sexually immoral Heb 13:4
those who spoke to you the word of **G**. Heb 13:7
offer up a sacrifice of praise to **G**, Heb 13:15
for such sacrifices are pleasing to **G**. Heb 13:16
Now may the **G** of peace who brought Heb 13:20
a servant of **G** and of the Lord Jesus Jas 1:1
any of you lacks wisdom, let him ask **G**, Jas 1:5
which **G** has promised to those who love Jas 1:12
am being tempted by **G**," for God cannot Jas 1:13
by God," for **G** cannot be tempted Jas 1:13
the righteousness that **G** requires. Jas 1:20
that is pure and undefiled before **G**, Jas 1:27
has not **G** chosen those who are poor in Jas 2:5
You believe that **G** is one; you do well. Jas 2:19
that says, "Abraham believed **G**, Jas 2:23
—and he was called a friend of **G**. Jas 2:23
people who are made in the likeness of **G**. Jas 3:9
with the world is enmity with **G**? Jas 4:4
the world makes himself an enemy of **G**. Jas 4:4
Therefore it says, "**G** opposes the proud, Jas 4:6
Submit yourselves therefore to **G**. Resist Jas 4:7
Draw near to **G**, and he will draw near to Jas 4:8
to the foreknowledge of **G** the Father, 1 Pt 1:2
Blessed be the **G** and Father of our Lord 1 Pt 1:3
who through him are believers in **G**, 1 Pt 1:21
so that your faith and hope are in **G**. 1 Pt 1:21
the living and abiding word of **G**; 1 Pt 1:23
in the sight of **G** chosen and precious, 1 Pt 2:4
sacrifices acceptable to **G** through Jesus 1 Pt 2:5
good deeds and glorify **G** on the day of 1 Pt 2:12
For this is the will of **G**, that by doing 1 Pt 2:15
for evil, but living as servants of **G**. 1 Pt 2:16
Love the brotherhood. Fear **G**. 1 Pt 2:17
a gracious thing, when, mindful of **G**, 1 Pt 2:19
is a gracious thing in the sight of **G**. 1 Pt 2:20
women who hoped in **G** used to adorn 1 Pt 3:5
that he might bring us to **G**, 1 Pt 3:18
as an appeal to **G** for a good 1 Pt 3:21
heaven and is at the right hand of **G**, 1 Pt 3:22
human passions but for the will of **G**. 1 Pt 4:2
might live in the spirit the way **G** does. 1 Pt 4:6
speaks, as one who speaks oracles of **G**; 1 Pt 4:11
by the strength that **G** supplies—in 1 Pt 4:11
that in everything **G** may be glorified 1 Pt 4:11
Spirit of glory and of **G** rests upon you. 1 Pt 4:14
but let him glorify **G** in that name. 1 Pt 4:16
to begin at the household of **G**; 1 Pt 4:17
those who do not obey the gospel of **G**? 1 Pt 4:17
shepherd the flock of **G** that is among 1 Pt 5:2
but willingly, as **G** would have you; 1 Pt 5:2
for "**G** opposes the proud but gives grace 1 Pt 5:5
the mighty hand of **G** so that at the 1 Pt 5:6
suffered a little while, the **G** of all grace, 1 Pt 5:10
that this is the true grace of **G**. 1 Pt 5:12
righteousness of our **G** and Savior Jesus 2 Pt 1:1
in the knowledge of **G** and of Jesus our 2 Pt 1:2
honor and glory from **G** the Father, 2 Pt 1:17
but men spoke from **G** as they were 2 Pt 1:21
For if **G** did not spare angels when they 2 Pt 2:4
and through water by the word of **G**, 2 Pt 3:5
hastening the coming of the day of **G**, 2 Pt 3:12
him and proclaim to you, that **G** is light, 1 Jn 1:5
in him truly the love of **G** is perfected. 1 Jn 2:5
and the word of **G** abides in you, 1 Jn 2:14
does the will of **G** abides forever. 1 Jn 2:17
that we should be called children of **G**; 1 Jn 3:1
reason the Son of **G** appeared was to 1 Jn 3:8
No one born of **G** makes a practice of 1 Jn 3:9
sinning because he has been born of **G**. 1 Jn 3:9
it is evident who are the children of **G**, 1 Jn 3:10
not practice righteousness is not of **G**, 1 Jn 3:10
us, **G** is greater than our heart, 1 Jn 3:20
us, we have confidence before **G**; 1 Jn 3:21
spirits to see whether they are from **G**, 1 Jn 4:1
By this you know the Spirit of **G**: every 1 Jn 4:2
Christ has come in the flesh is from **G**, 1 Jn 4:2
that does not confess Jesus is not from **G**. 1 Jn 4:3
you are from **G** and have overcome 1 Jn 4:4
We are from **G**. Whoever knows God 1 Jn 4:6
Whoever knows **G** listens to us; whoever 1 Jn 4:6
whoever is not from **G** does not listen to 1 Jn 4:6
us love one another, for love is from **G**, 1 Jn 4:7
has been born of **G** and knows God. 1 Jn 4:7
has been born of God and knows **G**. 1 Jn 4:7
who does not love does not know **G**, 1 Jn 4:8
does not know God, because **G** is love. 1 Jn 4:8
this the love of **G** was made manifest 1 Jn 4:9
that **G** sent his only Son into the world, 1 Jn 4:9
that we have loved **G** but that he loved 1 Jn 4:10
Beloved, if **G** so loved us, we also ought 1 Jn 4:11
No one has ever seen **G**; if we love one 1 Jn 4:12
G abides in us and his love is perfected 1 Jn 4:12
confesses that Jesus is the Son of **G**, 1 Jn 4:15
is the Son of God, **G** abides in him, 1 Jn 4:15
of God, God abides in him, and he in **G**. 1 Jn 4:15
to believe the love that **G** has for us. 1 Jn 4:16
G is love, and whoever abides in love 1 Jn 4:16
and whoever abides in love abides in **G**, 1 Jn 4:16
abides in God, and **G** abides in him. 1 Jn 4:16
says, "I love **G**," and hates his brother, 1 Jn 4:20
has seen cannot love **G** whom he has 1 Jn 4:20
whoever loves **G** must also love his 1 Jn 4:21
Jesus is the Christ has been born of **G**, 1 Jn 5:1
we know that we love the children of **G**, 1 Jn 5:2
when we love **G** and obey his 1 Jn 5:2
For this is the love of **G**, that we keep his 1 Jn 5:3
been born of **G** overcomes the world. 1 Jn 5:4
who believes that Jesus is the Son of **G**? 1 Jn 5:5
of men, the testimony of **G** is greater, 1 Jn 5:9
is the testimony of **G** that he has borne 1 Jn 5:9
in the Son of **G** has the testimony in 1 Jn 5:10
does not believe **G** has made him 1 Jn 5:10
the testimony that **G** has borne 1 Jn 5:10
testimony, that **G** gave us eternal life, 1 Jn 5:11
not have the Son of **G** does not have life. 1 Jn 5:12
of the Son of **G** that you may know 1 Jn 5:13
and **G** will give him life—to those who 1 Jn 5:16
has been born of **G** does not keep on 1 Jn 5:18
he who was born of **G** protects him, 1 Jn 5:18
We know that we are from **G**, and the 1 Jn 5:19
that the Son of **G** has come and has 1 Jn 5:20
Christ. He is the true **G** and eternal life. 1 Jn 5:20
from **G** the Father and from Jesus Christ 2 Jn 1:3
the teaching of Christ, does not have **G**. 2 Jn 1:9
their journey in a manner worthy of **G**. 3 Jn 1:6
Whoever does good is from **G**; whoever 3 Jn 1:11
God; whoever does evil has not seen **G**. 3 Jn 1:11
beloved in **G** the Father and kept for Jude 1:1
the grace of our **G** into sensuality and Jude 1:4
keep yourselves in the love of **G**, Jude 1:21
to the only **G**, our Savior, through Jude 1:25
which **G** gave him to show to his servants Rv 1:1
to the word of **G** and to the testimony Rv 1:2
us a kingdom, priests to his **G** and Father, Rv 1:6
Alpha and the Omega," says the Lord **G**, Rv 1:8
of the word of **G** and the testimony of Rv 1:9
tree of life, which is in the paradise of **G**.' Rv 2:7
'The words of the Son of **G**, who has eyes Rv 2:18
the seven spirits of **G** and the seven stars. Rv 3:1
your works complete in the sight of my **G**. Rv 3:2
make him a pillar in the temple of my **G**. Rv 3:12
I will write on him the name of my **G**, Rv 3:12
God, and the name of the city of my **G**, Rv 3:12
comes down from my **G** out of heaven, Rv 3:12
of fire, which are the seven spirits of **G**, Rv 4:5
"Holy, holy, holy, is the Lord **G** Almighty, Rv 4:8
"Worthy are you, our Lord and **G**, to Rv 4:11
are the seven spirits of **G** sent out into all Rv 5:6
ransomed people for **G** from every tribe Rv 5:9
them a kingdom and priests to our **G**, Rv 5:10
slain for the word of **G** and for the witness Rv 6:9
of the sun, with the seal of the living **G**, Rv 7:2
the servants of our **G** on their foreheads." Rv 7:3
"Salvation belongs to our **G** who sits on Rv 7:10
faces before the throne and worshiped **G**, Rv 7:11
and might be to our **G** forever and ever! Rv 7:12
they are before the throne of **G**, Rv 7:15
and **G** will wipe away every tear from Rv 7:17
I saw the seven angels who stand before **G**, Rv 8:2
rose before **G** from the hand of the angel. Rv 8:4
not have the seal of **G** on their foreheads. Rv 9:4
four horns of the golden altar before **G**, Rv 9:13
the mystery of **G** would be fulfilled, Rv 10:7
measure the temple of **G** and the altar Rv 11:1
a breath of life from **G** entered them, Rv 11:11
and gave glory to the **G** of heaven. Rv 11:13
on their thrones before **G** fell on their Rv 11:16
God fell on their faces and worshiped **G**, Rv 11:16
give thanks to you, Lord **G** Almighty, Rv 11:17
was caught up to **G** and to his throne, Rv 12:5
where she has a place prepared by **G**, Rv 12:6
kingdom of our **G** and the authority Rv 12:10
them day and night before our **G**. Rv 12:10
the commandments of **G** and hold to Rv 12:17
mouth to utter blasphemies against **G**, Rv 13:6
as firstfruits for **G** and the Lamb, Rv 14:4
a loud voice, "Fear **G** and give him glory, Rv 14:7
the commandments of **G** and their Rv 14:12
the great winepress of the wrath of **G**. Rv 14:19
for with them the wrath of **G** is finished. Rv 15:1
of glass with harps of **G** in their hands. Rv 15:2
sing the song of Moses, the servant of **G**, Rv 15:3
are your deeds, O Lord **G** the Almighty! Rv 15:3
of the wrath of **G** who lives forever and Rv 15:7
from the glory of **G** and from his power, Rv 15:8
earth the seven bowls of the wrath of **G**." Rv 16:1
altar saying, "Yes, Lord **G** the Almighty, Rv 16:7
cursed the name of **G** who had power Rv 16:9
and cursed the **G** of heaven for their Rv 16:11
on the great day of **G** the Almighty. Rv 16:14
and **G** remembered Babylon the great, Rv 16:19
and they cursed **G** for the plague of the Rv 16:21
for **G** has put it into their hearts to Rv 17:17
beast, until the words of **G** are fulfilled. Rv 17:17
and **G** has remembered her iniquities. Rv 18:5
mighty is the Lord **G** who has judged Rv 18:8
for **G** has given judgment for you Rv 18:20
and glory and power belong to our **G**, Rv 19:1
down and worshiped **G** who was seated Rv 19:4
came a voice saying, "Praise our **G**, Rv 19:5
For the Lord our **G** the Almighty reigns. Rv 19:6
to me, "These are the true words of **G**." Rv 19:9
Worship **G**." For the testimony of Jesus Rv 19:10
by which he is called is The Word of **G**. Rv 19:13
the fury of the wrath of **G** the Almighty. Rv 19:15
"Come, gather for the great supper of **G**, Rv 19:17
testimony of Jesus and for the word of **G**, Rv 20:4
they will be priests of **G** and of Christ, Rv 20:6
coming down out of heaven from **G**, Rv 21:2
the dwelling place of **G** is with man. Rv 21:3
and **G** himself will be with them as their Rv 21:3
himself will be with them as their **G**. Rv 21:3
and I will be his **G** and he will be my Rv 21:7
coming down out of heaven from **G**, Rv 21:10
having the glory of **G**, its radiance like Rv 21:11
temple is the Lord **G** the Almighty and Rv 21:22
on it, for the glory of **G** gives it light, Rv 21:23
from the throne of **G** and of the Lamb Rv 22:1
but the throne of **G** and of the Lamb will Rv 22:3
or sun, for the Lord **G** will be their light, Rv 22:5
Lord, the **G** of the spirits of the prophets, Rv 22:6
the words of this book. Worship **G**." Rv 22:9
G will add to him the plagues described Rv 22:18

G will take away his share in the tree of Rv 22:19

GOD'S (81)

Now the earth was corrupt in **G** sight, Gn 6:11
set up for a pillar, shall be **G** house. Gn 28:22
"This is **G** camp!" So he called the name Gn 32:2
has been enough of **G** thunder and hail. Ex 9:28
But **G** anger was kindled because he Nm 22:22
by anyone, for the judgment is **G**. Dt 1:17
for the battle is not yours but **G**. 2 Chr 20:15
oath to walk in **G** Law that was given Neh 10:29
is pure, and I am clean in **G** eyes.' Jb 11:4
away, dragged off in the day of **G** wrath. Jb 20:28
I have yet something to say on **G** behalf. Jb 36:2
within **G** house we walked in the Ps 55:14
They did not keep **G** covenant, but Ps 78:10
in all his toil—this is **G** gift to man. Eccl 3:13
command, because of **G** oath to him. Eccl 8:2
and to God the things that are **G**." Mt 22:21
things that are **G**." And they marveled Mk 12:17
and to God the things that are **G**." Lk 20:25
If anyone's will is to do **G** will, he will Jn 7:17
born; and he was beautiful in **G** sight. Acts 7:20
was I that I could stand in **G** way?" Acts 11:17
Being then **G** offspring, we ought not Acts 17:29
"Would you revile **G** high priest?" Acts 23:4
asking that somehow by **G** will I may Rom 1:10
Though they know **G** decree that Rom 1:32
not knowing that **G** kindness is meant Rom 2:4
of wrath when **G** righteous judgment Rom 2:5
if through my lie **G** truth abounds to Rom 3:7
This was to show **G** righteousness, Rom 3:25
because **G** love has been poured into Rom 5:5
to God, for it does not submit to **G** law; Rom 8:7
bring any charge against **G** elect? Rom 8:33
—in order that **G** purpose of election Rom 9:11
say then? Is there injustice on **G** part? Rom 9:14
did not submit to **G** righteousness. Rom 10:3
But what is **G** reply to him? "I have Rom 11:4
have fallen, but **G** kindness to you, Rom 11:22
for he is **G** servant for your good. But if Rom 13:4
who carries out **G** wrath on the Rom 13:4
not only to avoid **G** wrath but also for Rom 13:5
circumcised to show **G** truthfulness, Rom 15:8
so that by **G** will I may come to you Rom 15:32
For we are **G** fellow workers. You are 1 Cor 3:9
You are **G** field, God's building. 1 Cor 3:9
You are God's field, **G** building. 1 Cor 3:9
know that you are **G** temple and that 1 Cor 3:16
temple and that **G** Spirit dwells in 1 Cor 3:16
If anyone destroys **G** temple, God will 1 Cor 3:17
For **G** temple is holy, and you are that 1 Cor 3:17
and you are Christ's, and Christ is **G**. 1 Cor 3:23
not, like so many, peddlers of **G** word, 2 Cor 2:17
cunning or to tamper with **G** word, 2 Cor 4:2
because I preached **G** gospel to you 2 Cor 11:7
of the stewardship of **G** grace that was Eph 3:2
minister according to the gift of **G** grace, Eph 3:7
and the knowledge of **G** mystery, Col 2:2
Put on then, as **G** chosen ones, holy and Col 3:12
But **G** wrath has come upon them at 1 Thes 2:16
our brother and **G** coworker in the 1 Thes 3:2
how will he care for **G** church? 1 Tm 3:5
But **G** firm foundation stands, 2 Tm 2:19
of the faith of **G** elect and their knowledge Ti 1:1
For an overseer, as **G** steward, must be Ti 1:7
he says, "Let all **G** angels worship him." Heb 1:6
Moses also was faithful in all **G** house. Heb 3:2
was faithful in all **G** house as a servant, Heb 3:5
Christ is faithful over **G** house as a son. Heb 3:6
for whoever has entered **G** rest has also Heb 4:10
who by **G** power are being guarded 1 Pt 1:5
not a people, but now you are **G** people; 1 Pt 2:10
spirit, which in **G** sight is very precious. 1 Pt 3:4
for doing good, if that should be **G** will, 1 Pt 3:17
when **G** patience waited in the days of 1 Pt 3:20
as good stewards of **G** varied grace: 1 Pt 4:10
suffer according to **G** will entrust their 1 Pt 4:19
Beloved, we are **G** children now, and 1 Jn 3:2
of sinning, for **G** seed abides in him, 1 Jn 3:9
him, how does **G** love abide in him? 1 Jn 3:17
witness, the beginning of **G** creation. Rv 3:14
Then **G** temple in heaven was opened, Rv 11:19
he also will drink the wine of **G** wrath, Rv 14:10

GOD-FEARING (2)

a more faithful and **G** man than many. Neh 7:2
a centurion, an upright and **G** man, Acts 10:22

GODDESS (4)

after Ashtoreth the **g** of the Sidonians, 1 Kgs 11:5
worshiped Ashtoreth the **g** of the 1 Kgs 11:33
temple of the great **g** Artemis may be Acts 19:27
nor blasphemers of our **g**. Acts 19:37

GODLESS (12)

forget God; the hope of the **g** shall perish. Jb 8:13
that the **g** shall not come before him. Jb 13:16
For the company of the **g** is barren, and Jb 15:34
innocent stirs himself up against the **g**. Jb 17:8
and the joy of the **g** but for a moment? Jb 20:5
is the hope of the **g** when God cuts him Jb 27:8
that a **g** man should not reign, that he Jb 34:30
"The **g** in heart cherish anger; they do Jb 36:13
his mouth the **g** man would destroy Prv 11:9
widows; for everyone is **g** and an evildoer, Is 9:17
Against a **g** nation I send him, and Is 10:6
are afraid; trembling has seized the **g**: Is 33:14

GODLINESS (15)

for women who profess **g**—with good 1 Tm 2:10
indeed, we confess, is the mystery of **g**: 1 Tm 3:16
silly myths. Rather train yourself for **g**; 1 Tm 4:7
some value, **g** is of value in every way, 1 Tm 4:8
first learn to show **g** to their own 1 Tm 5:4
and the teaching that accords with **g**, 1 Tm 6:3
imagining that **g** is a means of gain. 1 Tm 6:5
is great gain in **g** with contentment, 1 Tm 6:6
Pursue righteousness, **g**, faith, love, 1 Tm 6:11
having the appearance of **g**, but 2 Tm 3:5
of the truth, which accords with **g**, Ti 1:1
to us all things that pertain to life and **g**, 2 Pt 1:3
steadfastness, and steadfastness with **g**, 2 Pt 1:6
and **g** with brotherly affection, and 2 Pt 1:7
you to be in lives of holiness and **g**, 2 Pt 3:11

GODLY (20)

and your Urim to your **g** one, Dt 33:8
the LORD has set apart the **g** for himself; Ps 4:3
Save, O LORD, for the **g** one is gone; for the Ps 12:1
let everyone who is **g** offer prayer to you Ps 32:6
for it is good, in the presence of the **g**. Ps 52:9
Preserve my life, for I am **g**; save your Ps 86:2
old you spoke in a vision to your **g** one, Ps 89:19
his praise in the assembly of the **g**! Ps 149:1
Let the **g** exult in glory; let them sing for Ps 149:5
written! This is honor for all his **g** ones. Ps 149:9
The **g** has perished from the earth, and Mi 7:2
was the one God seeking? **G** offspring. Mal 2:15
world with simplicity and **g** sincerity, 2 Cor 1:12
For you felt a **g** grief, so that you 2 Cor 7:9
For **g** grief produces a repentance 2 Cor 7:10
what earnestness this **g** grief has 2 Cor 7:11
quiet life, **g** and dignified in every way. 1 Tm 2:2
desire to live a **g** life in Christ Jesus 2 Tm 3:12
upright, and **g** lives in the present age, Ti 2:12
knows how to rescue the **g** from trials, 2 Pt 2:9

GODS (253)

Rachel stole her father's household **g**. Gn 31:19
house, but why did you steal my **g**?" Gn 31:30
whom you find your **g** shall not live. Gn 31:32
taken the household **g** and put them Gn 31:34
but did not find the household **g**. Gn 31:35
"Put away the foreign **g** that are among Gn 35:2
to Jacob all the foreign **g** that they had, Gn 35:4
and on all the **g** of Egypt I will execute Ex 12:12
"Who is like you, O LORD, among the **g**? Ex 15:11
know that the LORD is greater than all **g**, Ex 18:11
"You shall have no other **g** before me. Ex 20:3
You shall not make **g** of silver to be Ex 20:23
shall you make for yourselves **g** of gold. Ex 20:23
no mention of the names of other **g**, Ex 23:13
not bow down to their **g** nor serve them, Ex 23:24
no covenant with them and their **g**. Ex 23:32
for if you serve their **g**, it will surely be Ex 23:33
"Up, make us **g** who shall go before us. Ex 32:1
And they said, "These are your **g**, O Ex 32:4
to it and said, 'These are your **g**, Ex 32:8
me, 'Make us **g** who shall go before us. Ex 32:23
have made for themselves **g** of gold. Ex 32:31
they whore after their **g** and sacrifice to Ex 34:15
and sacrifice to their **g** and you are Ex 34:15
whore after their **g** and make your Ex 34:16
make your sons whore after their **g**. Ex 34:16
make for yourself any **g** of cast metal. Ex 34:17
make for yourselves any **g** of cast metal: Lv 19:4
the people to the sacrifices of their **g**, Nm 25:2
people ate and bowed down to their **g**. Nm 25:2
On their **g** also the LORD executed Nm 33:4
there you will serve **g** of wood and stone, Dt 4:28
"'You shall have no other **g** before me. Dt 5:7
You shall not go after other **g**, the gods of Dt 6:14
the **g** of the peoples who are around you, Dt 6:14
sons from following me, to serve other **g**. Dt 7:4
pity them, neither shall you serve their **g**, Dt 7:16
carved images of their **g** you shall burn Dt 7:25
and go after other **g** and serve them and Dt 8:19
your God is God of **g** and Lord of lords, Dt 10:17
and serve other **g** and worship them; Dt 11:16
to go after other **g** that you have not Dt 11:28
you shall dispossess served their **g**, Dt 12:2
images of their **g** and destroy their Dt 12:3
that you do not inquire about their **g**, Dt 12:30
'How did these nations serve their **g**? Dt 12:30
LORD hates they have done for their **g**, Dt 12:31
and their daughters in the fire to their **g**. Dt 12:31
and if he says, 'Let us go after other **g**,' Dt 13:2
saying, 'Let us go and serve other **g**,' Dt 13:6
some of the **g** of the peoples who are Dt 13:7
saying, 'Let us go and serve other **g**,' Dt 13:13
and served other **g** and worshiped them, Dt 17:3
or who speaks in the name of other **g**, Dt 18:20
that they have done for their **g**, Dt 20:18
the left, to go after other **g** to serve them. Dt 28:14
you shall serve other **g** of wood and Dt 28:36
you shall serve other **g** of wood and Dt 28:64
to go and serve the **g** of those nations. Dt 29:18
and served other **g** and worshiped them, Dt 29:26
g whom they had not known and Dt 29:26
to worship other **g** and serve them, Dt 30:17
after the foreign **g** among them in Dt 31:16
because they have turned to other **g**. Dt 31:18
they will turn to other **g** and serve them, Dt 31:20
stirred him to jealousy with strange **g**; Dt 32:16
sacrificed to demons that were no **g**, Dt 32:17
no gods, to **g** they had never known, Dt 32:17
to new **g** that had come recently, Dt 32:17
Then he will say, 'Where are their **g**, the Dt 32:37
bow down to him, all **g**, for he avenges Dt 32:43
of the names of their **g** or swear by them Jos 23:7
go and serve other **g** and bow down to Jos 23:16
and of Nahor; and they served other **g**. Jos 24:2
Put away the **g** that your fathers served Jos 24:14
whether the **g** your fathers served in the Jos 24:15
or the **g** of the Amorites in whose land Jos 24:15
forsake the LORD to serve other **g**, Jos 24:16
forsake the LORD and serve foreign **g**, Jos 24:20
put away the foreign **g** that are among Jos 24:23
sides, and their **g** shall be a snare to you." Jgs 2:3
They went after other **g**, from among the Jgs 2:12
from among the **g** of the peoples who Jgs 2:12
whored after other **g** and bowed down Jgs 2:17
than their fathers, going after other **g**, Jgs 2:19
gave to their sons, and they served their **g**. Jgs 3:6
When new **g** were chosen, then war was Jgs 5:8
shall not fear the **g** of the Amorites in Jgs 6:10
by which **g** and men are honored, Jgs 9:9
Baals and the Ashtaroth, the **g** of Syria, Jgs 10:6
the gods of Syria, the **g** of Sidon, Jgs 10:6
Syria, the gods of Sidon, the **g** of Moab, Jgs 10:6
gods of Moab, the **g** of the Ammonites, Jgs 10:6
Ammonites, and the **g** of the Philistines. Jgs 10:6
have forsaken me and served other **g**; Jgs 10:13
cry out to the **g** whom you have Jgs 10:14
away the foreign **g** from among them Jgs 10:16
and he made an ephod and household **g**, Jgs 17:5
there are an ephod, household **g**, Jgs 18:14
image, the ephod, the household **g**, Jgs 18:17
image, the ephod, the household **g**, Jgs 18:18
and the household **g** and the carved Jgs 18:20
"You take my **g** that I made and the Jgs 18:24
has gone back to her people and to her **g**; Ru 1:15
us from the power of these mighty **g**? 1 Sm 4:8
These are the **g** who struck the 1 Sm 4:8
from off you and your **g** and your land. 1 Sm 6:5
away the foreign **g** and the Ashtaroth 1 Sm 7:3
day, forsaking me and serving other **g**, 1 Sm 8:8
the Philistine cursed David by his **g**. 1 Sm 17:43
the LORD, saying, 'Go, serve other **g**.' 1 Sm 26:19
from Egypt, a nation and its **g**? 2 Sm 7:23
and serve other **g** and worship them, 1 Kgs 9:6
hold on other **g** and worshiped them 1 Kgs 9:9
heart after their **g**." Solomon clung to 1 Kgs 11:2
turned away his heart after other **g**, 1 Kgs 11:4
offerings and sacrificed to their **g**. 1 Kgs 11:8
that he should not go after other **g**. 1 Kgs 11:10
Behold your **g**, O Israel, who 1 Kgs 12:28
for yourself other **g** and metal 1 Kgs 14:9
"So may the **g** do to me and more 1 Kgs 19:2
"The **g** do so to me and more also, 1 Kgs 20:10
to him, "Their **g** are gods of the hills, 1 Kgs 20:23
to him, "Their gods are **g** of the hills, 1 Kgs 20:23
king of Egypt, and had feared other **g** 2 Kgs 17:7
every nation still made **g** of its own 2 Kgs 17:29
Anammelech, the **g** of Sepharvaim. 2 Kgs 17:31
the LORD but also served their own **g**, 2 Kgs 17:33
not fear other **g** or bow yourselves 2 Kgs 17:35
to do. You shall not fear other **g**, 2 Kgs 17:37
with you. You shall not fear other **g**, 2 Kgs 17:38
Has any of the **g** of the nations ever 2 Kgs 18:33
Where are the **g** of Hamath and 2 Kgs 18:34
Where are the **g** of Sepharvaim, 2 Kgs 18:34
Who among all the **g** of the lands 2 Kgs 18:35
Have the **g** of the nations delivered 2 Kgs 19:12
and have cast their **g** into the fire, 2 Kgs 19:18
gods into the fire, for they were not **g**, 2 Kgs 19:18
and have made offerings to other **g**, 2 Kgs 22:17
and the household **g** and the idols 2 Kgs 23:24

and whored after the **g** of the peoples 1 Chr 5:25
temple of their **g** and fastened his 1 Chr 10:10
And they left their **g** there, and 1 Chr 14:12
he is to be held in awe above all **g**. 1 Chr 16:25
For all the **g** of the peoples are idols, 1 Chr 16:26
great, for our God is greater than all **g**. 2 Chr 2:5
and serve other **g** and worship them, 2 Chr 7:19
hold on other **g** and worshiped them 2 Chr 7:22
calves that Jeroboam made you for **g**. 2 Chr 13:8
becomes a priest of what are no **g**. 2 Chr 13:9
he brought the **g** of the men of Seir 2 Chr 25:14
up as his **g** and worshiped them, 2 Chr 25:14
have you sought the **g** of a people 2 Chr 25:15
they had sought the **g** of Edom. 2 Chr 25:20
sacrificed to the **g** of Damascus that 2 Chr 28:23
"Because the **g** of the kings of Syria 2 Chr 28:23
places to make offerings to other **g**, 2 Chr 28:25
Were the **g** of the nations of those 2 Chr 32:13
among all the **g** of those nations 2 Chr 32:14
"Like the **g** of the nations of the 2 Chr 32:17
they spoke of the **g** of the peoples of 2 Chr 32:19
took away the foreign **g** and the idol 2 Chr 33:15
and have made offerings to other **g**, 2 Chr 34:25
and placed in the house of his **g**. Ezr 1:7
you indeed decree what is right, you **g**? Ps 58:1
in the midst of the **g** he holds judgment: Ps 82:1
I said, "You are **g**, sons of the Most High, Ps 82:6
There is none like you among the **g**, O Ps 86:8
a great God, and a great King above all **g**. Ps 95:3
be praised; he is to be feared above all **g**. Ps 96:4
For all the **g** of the peoples are worthless Ps 96:5
worthless idols; worship him, all you **g**! Ps 97:7
the earth; you are exalted far above all **g**. Ps 97:9
great, and that our Lord is above all **g**. Ps 135:5
Give thanks to the God of **g**, for his Ps 136:2
heart; before the **g** I sing your praise; Ps 138:1
carved images of her **g** he has shattered to Is 21:9
Has any of the **g** of the nations delivered Is 36:18
Where are the **g** of Hamath and Arpad? Is 36:19
Arpad? Where are the **g** of Sepharvaim? Is 36:19
Who among all the **g** of these lands Is 36:20
Have the **g** of the nations delivered them, Is 37:12
and have cast their **g** into the fire. For Is 37:19
For they were no **g**, but the work of Is 37:19
that we may know that you are **g**; Is 41:23
say to metal images, "You are our **g**." Is 42:17
offerings to other **g** and worshiped the Jer 1:16
Has a nation changed its **g**, even though Jer 2:11
its gods, even though they are no **g**? Jer 2:11
But where are your **g** that you made for Jer 2:28
for as many as your cities are your **g**, O Jer 2:28
and have sworn by those who are no **g**. Jer 5:7
me and served foreign **g** in your land, Jer 5:19
do not go after other **g** to your own harm, Jer 7:6
and go after other **g** that you have not Jer 7:9
they pour out drink offerings to other **g**, Jer 7:18
"The **g** who did not make the heavens Jer 10:11
have gone after other **g** to serve them. Jer 11:10
go and cry to the **g** to whom they make Jer 11:12
For your **g** have become as many as Jer 11:13
have gone after other **g** to serve them Jer 13:10
any among the false **g** of the nations Jer 14:22
have gone after other **g** and have served Jer 16:11
you shall serve other **g** day and night, Jer 16:13
Can man make for himself **g**? Such are Jer 16:20
for himself gods? Such are not **g**!" Jer 16:20
me; they make offerings to false **g**; Jer 18:15
in it to other **g** whom neither they nor Jer 19:4
poured out to other **g**—shall be defiled Jer 19:13
and worshiped other **g** and served Jer 22:9
not go after other **g** to serve and worship Jer 25:6
have been poured out to other **g**, Jer 32:29
do not go after other **g** to serve them, Jer 35:15
a fire in the temples of the **g** of Egypt, Jer 43:12
the temples of the **g** of Egypt he shall Jer 43:13
and serve other **g** that they knew Jer 44:3
evil and make no offerings to other **g**. Jer 44:5
making offerings to other **g** in the land Jer 44:8
wives had made offerings to other **g**, Jer 44:15
and Egypt and her **g** and her kings, Jer 46:25
said, 'I am a god, I sit in the seat of the **g**, Ezk 28:2
one can show it to the king except the **g**, Dn 2:11
your God is God of **g** and Lord of kings, Dn 2:47
do not serve your **g** or worship the Dn 3:12
do not serve my **g** or worship the golden Dn 3:14
will not serve your **g** or worship the Dn 3:18
of the fourth is like a son of the **g**." Dn 3:25
is the spirit of the holy **g**—and I told him Dn 4:8
the spirit of the holy **g** is in you and that Dn 4:9
for the spirit of the holy **g** is in you." Dn 4:18
wine and praised the **g** of gold and silver, Dn 5:4
in whom is the spirit of the holy **g**. Dn 5:11
the wisdom of the **g** were found in him, Dn 5:11
of you that the spirit of the **g** is in you, Dn 5:14
you have praised the **g** of silver and gold, Dn 5:23
off to Egypt their **g** with their metal Dn 11:8
things against the God of **g**. Dn 11:36
pay no attention to the **g** of his fathers, Dn 11:37
they turn to other **g** and love cakes of Hos 3:1
or pillar, without ephod or household **g**. Hos 3:4
from the house of your **g** I will cut off Na 1:14
for he will famish all the **g** of the earth, Zep 2:11
For the household **g** utter nonsense, Zec 10:2
written in your Law, 'I said, you are **g**'? Jn 10:34
If he called them **g** to whom the word of Jn 10:35
'Make for us **g** who will go before us. Acts 7:40
"The **g** have come down to us in the Acts 14:11
saying that **g** made with hands are Acts 19:26
that gods made with hands are not **g**. Acts 19:26
with the twin **g** as a figurehead. Acts 28:11
there may be so-called **g** in heaven or 1 Cor 8:5
there are many "**g**" and many "lords" 1 Cor 8:5
to those that by nature are not **g**. Gal 4:8

GOES (156)

with the present that **g** ahead of me, Gn 32:20
If our youngest brother **g** with us, then Gn 44:26
to Pharaoh, as he **g** out to the water, Ex 8:20
return it to him before the sun **g** down, Ex 22:26
"When my angel **g** before you and Ex 23:23
heart, when he **g** into the Holy Place, Ex 28:29
heart, when he **g** in before the LORD. Ex 28:30
be heard when he **g** into the Holy Place Ex 28:35
Whatever **g** on its belly, and whatever Lv 11:42
its belly, and whatever **g** on all fours, Lv 11:42
house before the priest **g** to examine the Lv 14:36
When the sun **g** down he shall be clean, Lv 22:7
If any man's wife **g** astray and breaks Nm 5:12
authority, **g** astray and defiles herself, Nm 5:29
LORD your God who **g** before you will Dt 1:30
today that he who **g** over before you as Dt 9:3
as when someone **g** into the forest with Dt 19:5
your God is he who **g** with you to fight Dt 20:4
man takes a wife and **g** in to her and Dt 22:13
and if she **g** and becomes another man's Dt 24:2
it is the LORD your God who **g** with you. Dt 31:6
It is the LORD who **g** before you. He will be Dt 31:8
Then if anyone **g** out of the doors of Jos 2:19
It **g** out southward of the ascent of Jos 15:3
Zin, and **g** up south of Kadesh-barnea, Jos 15:3
to Azmon, **g** out by the Brook of Egypt, Jos 15:4
And the boundary **g** up to Beth-hoglah Jos 15:6
And the boundary **g** up to the stone of Jos 15:6
And the boundary **g** up to Debir from Jos 15:7
Then the boundary **g** up by the Valley Jos 15:8
And the boundary **g** up to the top of the Jos 15:8
and **g** down to Beth-shemesh and Jos 15:10
The boundary **g** out to the shoulder of Jos 15:11
to Mount Baalah and **g** out to Jabneel. Jos 15:11
Then it **g** down westward to the territory Jos 16:3
and the boundary **g** from there to the Jos 16:6
then it **g** down from Janoah to Ataroth Jos 16:7
Tappuah the boundary **g** westward to Jos 16:8
Then the boundary **g** along southward Jos 17:7
boundary of Manasseh **g** on the north Jos 17:9
Then the boundary **g** up to the Jos 18:12
then the boundary **g** down to Jos 18:13
Then the boundary **g** in another Jos 18:14
And the boundary **g** from there to Jos 18:15
Then the boundary **g** down to the Jos 18:16
And it then **g** down the Valley of Jos 18:16
and from there **g** to Geliloth, Jos 18:17
Then it **g** down to the stone of Bohan Jos 18:17
of Beth-arabah it **g** down to the Jos 18:18
Then their boundary **g** up westward Jos 19:11
From Sarid it **g** in the other direction Jos 19:12
From there it **g** to Daberath, then up to Jos 19:12
it turns eastward, it **g** to Beth-dagon, Jos 19:27
to Aznoth-tabor and **g** from there to Jos 19:34
My heart **g** out to the commanders of Jgs 5:9
one of which **g** up to Bethel and the Jgs 20:31
of the highway that **g** up from Bethel to Jgs 21:19
If it **g** up on the way to its own land, to 1 Sm 6:9
before he **g** up to the high place to eat. 1 Sm 9:13
his share is who **g** down into the 1 Sm 30:24
or anything else till the sun **g** down!" 2 Sm 3:35
when my master **g** into the house of 2 Kgs 5:18
the king when he **g** out and when he 2 Kgs 11:8
on the way that **g** down to Silla. 2 Kgs 12:20
of Shallecheth on the road that **g** up. 1 Chr 26:16
he comes in and when he **g** out." 2 Chr 23:7
This work **g** on diligently and prospers Ezr 5:8
are building—if a fox **g** up on it he will Neh 4:3
And its rich yield **g** to the kings whom Neh 9:37
any man or woman **g** to the king inside Est 4:11
so he who **g** down to Sheol does not come Jb 7:9
He **g** to bed rich, but will do so no more; Jb 27:19
strength; he **g** out to meet the weapons. Jb 39:21
Their measuring line **g** out through all Ps 19:4
Surely a man **g** about as a shadow! Ps 39:6
when he **g** out, he tells it abroad. Ps 41:6
against you, which **g** up continually! Ps 74:23
Fire **g** before him and burns up his Ps 97:3
Man **g** out to his work and to his labor Ps 104:23
He who **g** out weeping, bearing the seed Ps 126:6
man, **g** about with crooked speech, Prv 6:12
So is he who **g** in to his neighbor's wife; Prv 6:29
follows her, as an ox **g** to the slaughter, Prv 7:22
When it **g** well with the righteous, the Prv 11:10
Whoever **g** about slandering reveals Prv 11:13
Pride **g** before destruction, and a Prv 16:18
A rebuke **g** deeper into a man of Prv 17:10
says the buyer, but when he **g** away, Prv 20:14
Whoever **g** about slandering reveals Prv 20:19
in the cup and **g** down smoothly. Prv 23:31
Like a thorn that **g** up into the hand of Prv 26:9
For lack of wood the fire **g** out, and Prv 26:20
A generation **g**, and a generation comes, Eccl 1:4
The sun rises, and the sun **g** down, and Eccl 1:5
to the south and **g** around to the north; Eccl 1:6
around and around **g** the wind, and on Eccl 1:6
the spirit of man **g** upward and the Eccl 3:21
spirit of the beast **g** down into the Eccl 3:21
it comes in vanity and **g** in darkness, Eccl 6:4
It **g** down smoothly for my beloved, Sg 7:9
The LORD **g** out like a mighty man, like Is 42:13
my word be that **g** out from my mouth; Is 55:11
suit justly; no one **g** to law honestly; Is 59:4
until her righteousness **g** forth as Is 62:1
his wife and she **g** from him and becomes Jer 3:1
everyone who **g** out of them shall be torn Jer 5:6
in vain the refining **g** on, for the wicked Jer 6:29
and every neighbor **g** about as a Jer 9:4
ground, and the cry of Jerusalem **g** up. Jer 14:2
but he who **g** out and surrenders to the Jer 21:9
but weep bitterly for him who **g** away, Jer 22:10
but he who **g** out to the Chaldeans shall Jer 38:2
everything ready, but none **g** to battle, Ezk 7:14
those whose heart **g** after their Ezk 11:21
the outside as one **g** up to the entrance Ezk 40:40
the day that he **g** into the Holy Place, Ezk 44:27
the eastern region and **g** down into the Ezk 47:8
And wherever the river **g**, every living Ezk 47:9
For this water **g** there, that the waters of Ezk 47:9
so everything will live where the river **g**. Ezk 47:9
cloud, like the dew that **g** early away. Hos 6:4
and my judgment **g** forth as the light. Hos 6:5
mist or like the dew that **g** early away, Hos 13:3
who opens the breach **g** up before them; Mi 2:13
flocks of sheep, which, when it **g** through, Mi 5:8
is paralyzed, and justice never **g** forth. Hab 1:4
righteous; so justice **g** forth perverted. Hab 1:4
"This is the curse that **g** out over the face Zec 5:3
with the black horses **g** toward the north Zec 6:6
And I say to one, 'Go,' and he **g**, and to Mt 8:9
Then it **g** and brings with it seven Mt 12:45
Then in his joy he **g** and sells all that Mt 13:44
it is not what **g** into the mouth that Mt 15:11
not see that whatever **g** into the mouth Mt 15:17
The Son of Man **g** as it is written of Mt 26:24
not see that whatever **g** into a person Mk 7:18
For the Son of Man **g** as it is written of Mk 14:21
under me: and I say to one, 'Go,' and he **g**; Lk 7:8
Then it **g** and brings seven other spirits Lk 11:26
but if someone **g** to them from the Lk 16:30
For the Son of Man **g** as it has been Lk 22:22
know where it comes from or where it **g**. Jn 3:8
out all his own, he **g** before them, Jn 10:4
the road that **g** down from Jerusalem Acts 8:26
but brother **g** to law against brother, 1 Cor 6:6
each one **g** ahead with his own 1 Cor 11:21
with his own meal. One **g** hungry, 1 Cor 11:21
into the second only the high priest **g**, Heb 9:7
looks at himself and **g** away and at once Jas 1:24
Everyone who **g** on ahead and does not 2 Jn 1:9
good health, as it **g** well with your soul. 3 Jn 1:2
is to be taken captive, to captivity he **g**; Rv 13:10
who follow the Lamb wherever he **g**. Rv 14:4
of their torment **g** up forever and Rv 14:11
to the seven, and it **g** to destruction. Rv 17:11
The smoke from her **g** up forever and Rv 19:3

GOG (12)

Shemaiah his son, **G** his son, Shimei 1 Chr 5:4
"Son of man, set your face toward **G**, of Ezk 38:2
Behold, I am against you, O **G**, chief Ezk 38:3
son of man, prophesy, and say to **G**, Ezk 38:14
know me, when through you, O **G**, Ezk 38:16
the day that **G** shall come against the Ezk 38:18
summon a sword against **G** on all my Ezk 38:21
of man, prophesy against **G** and say, Ezk 39:1
Behold, I am against you, O **G**, chief Ezk 39:1
day I will give to **G** a place for burial Ezk 39:11
for there **G** and all his multitude will Ezk 39:11
four corners of the earth, **G** and Magog, Rv 20:8

GOIIM (3)
king of Elam, and Tidal king of **G**, Gn 14:1
king of Elam, Tidal king of **G**, Gn 14:9
one; the king of **G** in Galilee, one; Jos 12:23

GOING (211)
and a mist was **g** up from the land and Gn 2:6
journeyed on, still **g** toward the Negeb. Gn 12:9
As the sun was **g** down, a deep sleep fell Gn 15:12
from and where are you **g**?" She said, Gn 16:8
if you are **g** to show steadfast love and Gn 24:49
do you belong? Where are you **g**? Gn 32:17
"Your father-in-law is **g** up to Timnah Gn 38:13
the morning, as he is **g** out to the water. Ex 7:15
I am **g** out from you and I will plead with Ex 8:29
in the month of Abib, you are **g** out. Ex 13:4
the people of Israel were **g** out defiantly. Ex 14:8
of God who was **g** before the host of Ex 14:19
were steady until the **g** down of the sun. Ex 17:12
your enemy's ox or his donkey **g** astray, Ex 23:4
shall be six branches **g** out of its sides, Ex 25:32
for the six branches **g** out of the Ex 25:33
of the six branches **g** out from the Ex 25:35
Is it not in your **g** with us, so that we are Ex 33:16
there were six branches **g** out of its Ex 37:18
for the six branches **g** out of the Ex 37:19
each pair of the six branches **g** out of it. Ex 37:21
And now, behold, I am **g** to my people. Nm 24:14
people of Israel from **g** over into the Nm 32:7
people of Israel from **g** into the land Nm 32:9
Where are we **g** up? Our brothers have Dt 1:28
He knows your **g** through this great Dt 2:7
in the land that you are **g** over to possess. Dt 4:14
the land that you are **g** over the Jordan to Dt 4:26
them in the land to which you are **g** over, Dt 6:1
of your heart are you **g** in to possess their Dt 9:5
of the land that you are **g** over to possess, Dt 11:8
the land that you are **g** over to possess is Dt 11:11
the road, toward the **g** down of the sun, Dt 11:30
ox or his sheep **g** astray and ignore them. Dt 22:1
land that you are **g** over the Jordan to Dt 30:18
land that you are **g** over the Jordan to Dt 31:13
land that you are **g** over the Jordan to Dt 32:47
said, "Rejoice, Zebulun, in your **g** out, Dt 33:18
Great Sea toward the **g** down of the sun Jos 1:4
all the men of war **g** around the city once. Jos 6:3
LORD to circle the city, **g** about it once. Jos 6:11
while they were **g** down the ascent of Jos 10:11
But at the time of the **g** down of the sun, Jos 10:27
then, for war and for **g** and coming. Jos 14:11
g up from Jericho into the hill country Jos 16:1
Then **g** from Bethel to Luz, it passes Jos 16:2
will you put off **g** in to take possession Jos 18:3
a northerly direction **g** on to Jos 18:17
and **g** on to Rimmon it bends toward Jos 19:13
than their fathers, **g** after other gods, Jgs 2:19
road on which you are **g** will not lead to Jgs 4:9
and I am **g** to sojourn where I may find a Jgs 17:9
the old man said, "Where are you **g**? Jgs 19:17
and I am **g** to the house of the Lord, Jgs 19:18
let us be **g**." But there was no answer. Jgs 19:28
As they were **g** down to the outskirts 1 Sm 9:27
Three men **g** up to God at Bethel will 1 Sm 10:3
as the host was **g** out to the battle 1 Sm 17:20
as the sun was **g** down they came to 2 Sm 2:24
and to know your **g** out and your 2 Sm 3:25
were doing and how the war was **g**. 2 Sm 11:7
And as she was **g** to bring it, he 1 Kgs 17:11
very abominably in **g** after idols, 1 Kgs 21:26
Israel that you are **g** to inquire of 2 Kgs 1:3
and while he was **g** up on the way, 2 Kgs 2:23
saw that the battle was **g** against him, 2 Kgs 3:26
for the Syrians are **g** down there." 2 Kgs 6:9
down and your **g** out and coming 2 Kgs 19:27
about through his **g** to visit Joram. 2 Chr 22:7
of Jerusalem was **g** forward and that Neh 4:7
and said, "From **g** to and fro on the earth, Jb 1:7
and said, "From **g** to and fro on the earth, Jb 2:2
'Deliver him from **g** down into the pit; Jb 33:24
redeemed my soul from **g** down into the Jb 33:28
You make the **g** out of the morning and Ps 65:8
LORD will keep your **g** out and your Ps 121:8
Sheol, **g** down to the chambers of death. Prv 7:27
by, who are **g** straight on their way, Prv 9:15
wisdom in Sheol, to which you are **g**. Eccl 9:10
because man is **g** to his eternal home, Eccl 12:5
sitting down and your **g** out and coming Is 37:28
if you honor it, not **g** your own ways, or Is 58:13
what do you gain by **g** to Egypt to drink Jer 2:18
do you gain by **g** to Assyria to drink Jer 2:18
Keep your feet from **g** unshod and your Jer 2:25
rebellious, **g** about with slanders; Jer 6:28
you keep **g** backward, so I have stretched Jer 15:6
disaster is **g** forth from nation to Jer 25:32
"I am banned from **g** to the house of the Jer 36:5
Now Jeremiah was still **g** in and out Jer 37:4
g out of the city at night by way of the Jer 39:4
the gateway facing east, **g** up its steps, Ezk 40:6
g astray from me after their idols Ezk 44:10
not defile themselves by **g** near to a Ezk 44:25
G on eastward with a measuring line in Ezk 47:3
understand that from the **g** out of the Dn 9:25
the LORD; his **g** out is sure as the dawn; Hos 6:3
sense, calling to Egypt, **g** to Assyria. Hos 7:11
they are **g** away from destruction; Hos 9:6
to Joppa and found a ship **g** to Tarshish. Jon 1:3
to go into the city, **g** a day's journey. Jon 3:4
through and pass the gate, **g** out by it. Mi 2:13
"Where are you **g**?" And he said to me, Zec 2:2
eyes and see what this is that is **g** out." Zec 5:5
is the basket that is **g** out." And he said, Zec 5:6
"These are **g** out to the four winds of Zec 6:5
to seek the LORD of hosts; I myself am **g**.' Zec 8:21
the angel of the LORD, **g** before them. Zec 12:8
And **g** into the house they saw the child Mt 2:11
about the Jordan were **g** out to him, Mt 3:5
And **g** on from there he saw two other Mt 4:21
accuser while you are **g** with him to Mt 5:25
and **g** into the city they told everything, Mt 8:33
As they were **g** away, behold, a Mt 9:32
the Son of Man is **g** to come with his Mt 16:27
And **g** out about the third hour he saw Mt 20:3
G out again about the sixth hour and Mt 20:5
And as Jesus was **g** up to Jerusalem, he Mt 20:17
"See, we are **g** up to Jerusalem. And the Mt 20:18
Jesus left the temple and was **g** away, Mt 24:1
of your oil, for our lamps are **g** out.' Mt 25:8
And while they were **g** to buy, the Mt 25:10
it will be like a man **g** on a journey, Mt 25:14
And **g** a little farther he fell on his face Mt 26:39
Rise, let us be **g**; see, my betrayer is at Mt 26:46
and **g** inside he sat with the guards to Mt 26:58
and behold, he is **g** before you to Galilee; Mt 28:7
While they were **g**, behold, some of the Mt 28:11
and all Jerusalem were **g** out to him and Mk 1:5
And **g** on a little farther, he saw James Mk 1:19
Sabbath he was **g** through the Mk 2:23
a while." For many were coming and **g**, Mk 6:31
many saw them **g** and recognized them, Mk 6:33
a person that by **g** into him can defile Mk 7:15
Son of Man is **g** to be delivered into Mk 9:31
were on the road, **g** up to Jerusalem, Mk 10:32
saying, "See, we are **g** up to Jerusalem, Mk 10:33
It is like a man **g** on a journey, when Mk 13:34
And **g** a little farther, he fell on the Mk 14:35
Rise, let us be **g**; see, my betrayer is at Mk 14:42
Peter that he is **g** before you to Galilee. Mk 16:7
while he was **g** through the grainfields, Lk 6:1
As they were **g** along the road, someone Lk 9:57
"A man was **g** down from Jerusalem to Lk 10:30
chance a priest was **g** down that road, Lk 10:31
g out to encounter another king in Lk 14:31
to them, "See, we are **g** up to Jerusalem, Lk 18:31
And hearing a crowd **g** by, he inquired Lk 18:36
he went on ahead, **g** up to Jerusalem. Lk 19:28
all these things that are **g** to take place, Lk 21:36
them it could be who was **g** to do this. Lk 22:23
two of them were **g** to a village named Lk 24:13
near to the village to which they were **g**. Lk 24:28
going. He acted as if he were **g** farther, Lk 24:28
he is baptizing, and all are **g** to him." Jn 3:26
As he was **g** down, his servants met him Jn 4:51
and while I am **g** another steps down Jn 5:7
was at the land to which they were **g**. Jn 6:21
one of the Twelve, was **g** to betray him. Jn 6:71
I am not **g** up to this feast, for my time has Jn 7:8
and then I am **g** to him who sent me. Jn 7:33
where I came from and where I am **g**, Jn 8:14
where I come from or where I am **g**. Jn 8:14
So he said to them again, "I am **g** away, Jn 8:21
sin. Where I am **g**, you cannot come." Jn 8:21
himself, since he says, 'Where I am **g**, Jn 8:22
which of them are you **g** to stone me?" Jn 10:32
work that we are **g** to stone you but Jn 10:33
to stone you, and are you **g** there again?" Jn 11:8
supposing that she was **g** to the tomb to Jn 11:31
of the Jews were **g** away and believing in Jn 12:11
by what kind of death he was **g** to die. Jn 12:33
darkness does not know where he is **g**. Jn 12:35
come from God and was **g** back to God, Jn 13:3
said to him, "What you are **g** to do, Jn 13:27
you, 'Where I am **g** you cannot come.' Jn 13:33
where are you **g**?" Jesus answered him, Jn 13:36
"Where I am **g** you cannot follow me Jn 13:36
And you know the way to where I am **g**." Jn 14:4
"Lord, we do not know where you are **g**. Jn 14:5
will he do, because I am **g** to the Father. Jn 14:12
You heard me say to you, 'I am **g** away, Jn 14:28
rejoiced, because I am **g** to the Father, Jn 14:28
But now I am **g** to him who sent me, and Jn 16:5
none of you asks me, 'Where are you **g**?' Jn 16:5
and, 'because I am **g** to the Father'?" Jn 16:17
leaving the world and **g** to the Father." Jn 16:28
by what kind of death he was **g** to die. Jn 18:32
and they were **g** toward the tomb. Jn 20:3
them, "I am **g** fishing." They said to him, Jn 21:3
"Lord, who is it that is **g** to betray you?" Jn 21:20
Peter and John were **g** up to the temple Acts 3:1
And as they were **g** along the road they Acts 8:36
As we were **g** to the place of prayer, we Acts 16:16
But **g** ahead to the ship, we set sail for Acts 20:13
now, behold, I am **g** to Jerusalem, Acts 20:22
said to him, "God is **g** to strike you, Acts 23:3
though you were **g** to determine his Acts 23:15
and **g** aside asked him privately, Acts 23:19
though they were **g** to inquire Acts 23:20
I am **g** to make my defense today Acts 26:2
I am **g** to Jerusalem bringing aid to Rom 15:25
very earnest he is **g** to you of his 2 Cor 8:17
of angels, **g** on in detail about visions, Col 2:18
urged you when I was **g** to Macedonia, 1 Tm 1:3
idlers, **g** about from house to house, 1 Tm 5:13
g before them to judgment, 1 Tm 5:24
went out, not knowing where he was **g**. Heb 11:8
in the glory that is **g** to be revealed: 1 Pt 5:1
an example of what is **g** to happen to the 2 Pt 2:6
and does not know where he is **g**, 1 Jn 2:11

GOLAN (4)
and **G** in Bashan for the Manassites. Dt 4:43
from the tribe of Gad, and **G** in Bashan, Jos 20:8
G in Bashan with its pasturelands, Jos 21:27
G in Bashan with its pasturelands 1 Chr 6:71

GOLD (411)
whole land of Havilah, where there is **g**. Gn 2:11
And the **g** of that land is good; bdellium Gn 2:12
very rich in livestock, in silver, and in **g**. Gn 13:2
the man took a **g** ring weighing a half Gn 24:22
for her arms weighing ten **g** shekels, Gn 24:22
him flocks and herds, silver and **g**, Gn 24:35
brought out jewelry of silver and of **g**, Gn 24:53
linen and put a **g** chain about his Gn 41:42
we steal silver or **g** from your lord's Gn 44:8
in her house, for silver and **g** jewelry, Ex 3:22
of her neighbor, for silver and **g** jewelry." Ex 11:2
for silver and **g** jewelry and for Ex 12:35
you make for yourselves gods of **g**. Ex 20:23
receive from them: **g**, silver, and bronze, Ex 25:3
You shall overlay it with pure **g**, inside Ex 25:11
make on it a molding of **g** around it. Ex 25:11
shall cast four rings of **g** for it and put Ex 25:12
acacia wood and overlay them with **g**. Ex 25:13
shall make a mercy seat of pure **g**. Ex 25:17
you shall make two cherubim of **g**; Ex 25:18
overlay it with pure **g** and make a Ex 25:24
and make a molding of **g** around it. Ex 25:24
and a molding of **g** around the rim. Ex 25:25
you shall make for it four rings of **g**, Ex 25:26
acacia wood, and overlay them with **g**, Ex 25:28
you shall make them of pure **g**. Ex 25:29
shall make a lampstand of pure **g**. Ex 25:31
piece of hammered work of pure **g**. Ex 25:36
tongs and their trays shall be of pure **g**. Ex 25:38
these utensils, out of a talent of pure **g**. Ex 25:39
And you shall make fifty clasps of **g**, and Ex 26:6
the frames with **g** and shall make Ex 26:29
make their rings of **g** for holders for the Ex 26:29
and you shall overlay the bars with **g**. Ex 26:29
four pillars of acacia overlaid with **g**, Ex 26:32
overlaid with gold, with hooks of **g**, Ex 26:32
of acacia, and overlay them with **g**. Ex 26:37
Their hooks shall be of **g**, and you Ex 26:37
They shall receive **g**, blue and purple Ex 28:5
"And they shall make the ephod of **g**, of Ex 28:6
like it and be of one piece with it, of **g**, Ex 28:8
enclose them in settings of **g** filigree. Ex 28:11
You shall make settings of **g** filigree, Ex 28:13
and two chains of pure **g**, twisted like Ex 28:14
of the ephod you shall make it—of **g**, Ex 28:15
a jasper. They shall be set in **g** filigree. Ex 28:20
twisted chains like cords, of pure **g**. Ex 28:22
make for the breastpiece two rings of **g**, Ex 28:23
put the two cords of **g** in the two rings Ex 28:24
You shall make two rings of **g**, and put Ex 28:26
And you shall make two rings of **g**, and Ex 28:27
its hem, with bells of **g** between them, Ex 28:33
a plate of pure **g** and engrave on it, Ex 28:36
You shall overlay it with pure **g**, its top Ex 30:3
shall make a molding of **g** around it. Ex 30:3
of acacia wood and overlay them with **g**. Ex 30:5
to devise artistic designs, to work in **g**, Ex 31:4
"Take off the rings of **g** that are in the Ex 32:2
took off the rings of **g** that were in their Ex 32:3
And he received the **g** from their hand Ex 32:4
to them, 'Let any who have **g** take it off.' Ex 32:24
have made for themselves gods of **g**. Ex 32:31

contribution: **g**, silver, and bronze; Ex 35:5
rings and armlets, all sorts of **g** objects, Ex 35:22
dedicating an offering of **g** to the LORD. Ex 35:22
to work in **g** and silver and bronze, Ex 35:32
And he made fifty clasps of **g**, and Ex 36:13
And he overlaid the frames with **g**, and Ex 36:34
made their rings of **g** for holders for the Ex 36:34
the bars, and overlaid the bars with **g**. Ex 36:34
of acacia and overlaid them with **g**. Ex 36:36
Their hooks were of **g**, and he cast for Ex 36:36
their capitals, and their fillets were of **g**, Ex 36:38
it with pure **g** inside and outside, Ex 37:2
and made a molding of **g** around it. Ex 37:2
cast for it four rings of **g** for its four feet, Ex 37:3
of acacia wood and overlaid them with **g** Ex 37:4
And he made a mercy seat of pure **g**. Ex 37:6
And he made two cherubim of **g**. He Ex 37:7
And he overlaid it with pure **g**, and Ex 37:11
and made a molding of **g** around it. Ex 37:11
made a molding of **g** around the rim. Ex 37:12
it four rings of **g** and fastened the rings Ex 37:13
the table, and overlaid them with **g**. Ex 37:15
the vessels of pure **g** that were to be Ex 37:16
He also made the lampstand of pure **g**. Ex 37:17
piece of hammered work of pure **g**. Ex 37:22
and its tongs and its trays of pure **g**. Ex 37:23
all its utensils out of a talent of pure **g**. Ex 37:24
He overlaid it with pure **g**, its top and Ex 37:26
And he made a molding of **g** around it, Ex 37:26
and made two rings of **g** on it under its Ex 37:27
acacia wood and overlaid them with **g**. Ex 37:28
All the **g** that was used for the work, in Ex 38:24
the sanctuary, the **g** from the offering, Ex 38:24
He made the ephod of **g**, blue and purple Ex 39:2
And they hammered out **g** leaf, and he Ex 39:3
of one piece with it and made like it, of **g**, Ex 39:5
stones, enclosed in settings of **g** filigree, Ex 39:6
work, in the style of the ephod, of **g**, Ex 39:8
were enclosed in settings of **g** filigree. Ex 39:13
twisted chains like cords, of pure **g**. Ex 39:15
made two settings of **g** filigree and two Ex 39:16
settings of gold filigree and two **g** rings, Ex 39:16
put the two cords of **g** in the two rings Ex 39:17
Then they made two rings of **g**, and put Ex 39:19
And they made two rings of **g**, and Ex 39:20
They also made bells of pure **g**, and put Ex 39:25
the plate of the holy crown of pure **g**, Ex 39:30
the lampstand of pure **g** and its lamps Ex 39:37
the lampstand of pure **g** before the LORD Lv 24:4
on the table of pure **g** before the LORD. Lv 24:6
all the **g** of the dishes being 120 Nm 7:86
of the lampstand, hammered work of **g**. Nm 8:4
give me his house full of silver and **g**, Nm 22:18
give me his house full of silver and **g**, Nm 24:13
only the **g**, the silver, the bronze, the Nm 31:22
what each man found, articles of **g**, Nm 31:50
the priest received from them the **g**, Nm 31:51
And all the **g** of the contribution that Nm 31:52
priest received the **g** from the Nm 31:54
covet the silver or the **g** that is on them Dt 7:25
and your silver and **g** is multiplied and Dt 8:13
for himself excessive silver and **g**. Dt 17:17
idols of wood and stone, of silver and **g**, Dt 29:17
But all silver and **g**, and every vessel of Jos 6:19
Only the silver and **g**, and the vessels of Jos 6:24
and a bar of **g** weighing 50 shekels, Jos 7:21
the silver and the cloak and the bar of **g**, Jos 7:24
much livestock, with silver, **g**, bronze, Jos 22:8
that he requested was 1,700 shekels of **g**, Jgs 8:26
put in a box at its side the figures of **g**, 1 Sm 6:8
put ornaments of **g** on your apparel. 2 Sm 1:24
took the shields of **g** that were carried 2 Sm 8:7
with him articles of silver, of **g**, 2 Sm 8:10
with the silver and **g** that he dedicated 2 Sm 8:11
The weight of it was a talent of **g**, and 2 Sm 12:30
matter of silver or **g** between us and 2 Sm 21:4
high, and he overlaid it with pure **g**. 1 Kgs 6:20
the inside of the house with pure **g**, 1 Kgs 6:21
gold, and he drew chains of **g** across, 1 Kgs 6:21
sanctuary, and overlaid it with **g**. 1 Kgs 6:21
he overlaid the whole house with **g**, 1 Kgs 6:22
inner sanctuary he overlaid with **g**. 1 Kgs 6:22
And he overlaid the cherubim with **g**. 1 Kgs 6:28
house he overlaid with **g** in the inner 1 Kgs 6:30
overlaid them with **g** and spread gold 1 Kgs 6:32
gold and spread **g** on the cherubim 1 Kgs 6:32
overlaid them with **g** evenly applied 1 Kgs 6:35
the lampstands of pure **g**, five on the 1 Kgs 7:49
flowers, the lamps, and the tongs, of **g**; 1 Kgs 7:49
for incense, and fire pans, of pure **g**; 1 Kgs 7:50
and the sockets of **g**, for the doors of 1 Kgs 7:50
father had dedicated, the silver, the **g**, 1 Kgs 7:51
with cedar and cypress timber and **g**, 1 Kgs 9:11
had sent to the king 120 talents of **g**. 1 Kgs 9:14
to Ophir and brought from there **g**, 1 Kgs 9:28

and very much **g** and precious 1 Kgs 10:2
she gave the king 120 talents of **g**, 1 Kgs 10:10
which brought **g** from Ophir, 1 Kgs 10:11
Now the weight of **g** that came to 1 Kgs 10:14
in one year was 666 talents of **g**, 1 Kgs 10:14
made 200 large shields of beaten **g**; 1 Kgs 10:16
600 shekels of **g** went into each 1 Kgs 10:16
he made 300 shields of beaten **g**; 1 Kgs 10:17
three minas of **g** went into each 1 Kgs 10:17
and overlaid it with the finest **g**. 1 Kgs 10:18
drinking vessels were of **g**, 1 Kgs 10:21
Forest of Lebanon were of pure **g**. 1 Kgs 10:21
Tarshish used to come bringing **g**, 1 Kgs 10:22
his present, articles of silver and **g**, 1 Kgs 10:25
counsel and made two calves of **g**. 1 Kgs 12:28
all the shields of **g** that Solomon had 1 Kgs 14:26
his own sacred gifts, silver, and **g**, 1 Kgs 15:15
the silver and the **g** that were left in 1 Kgs 15:18
to you a present of silver and **g**. 1 Kgs 15:19
'Your silver and your **g** are mine; 1 Kgs 20:3
"Deliver to me your silver and your **g**, 1 Kgs 20:5
children, and for my silver and my **g**, 1 Kgs 20:7
of Tarshish to go to Ophir for **g**, 1 Kgs 22:48
of silver, six thousand shekels of **g**, 2 Kgs 5:5
off silver and **g** and clothing and 2 Kgs 7:8
bowls, trumpets, or any vessels of **g**, 2 Kgs 12:13
and all the **g** that was found in the 2 Kgs 12:18
And he seized all the **g** and silver, 2 Kgs 14:14
took the silver and **g** that was found 2 Kgs 16:8
of silver and thirty talents of **g**. 2 Kgs 18:14
Hezekiah stripped the **g** from the 2 Kgs 18:16
his treasure house, the silver, the **g**, 2 Kgs 20:13
talents of silver and a talent of **g**. 2 Kgs 23:33
gave the silver and the **g** to Pharaoh, 2 Kgs 23:35
the silver and the **g** of the people of 2 Kgs 23:35
all the vessels of **g** in the temple of 2 Kgs 24:13
What was of **g** the captain of the 2 Kgs 25:15
captain of the guard took away as **g**, 2 Kgs 25:15
took the shields of **g** that were carried 1 Chr 18:7
And he sent all sorts of articles of **g**, 1 Chr 18:10
with the silver and **g** that he had 1 Chr 18:11
He found that it weighed a talent of **g**, 1 Chr 20:2
600 shekels of **g** by weight for 1 Chr 21:25
of the LORD 100,000 talents of **g**, 1 Chr 22:14
g, silver, bronze, and iron. Arise and 1 Chr 22:16
the weight of **g** for all golden vessels 1 Chr 28:14
the weight of **g** for each lampstand 1 Chr 28:15
the weight of **g** for each table for the 1 Chr 28:16
and pure **g** for the forks, the basins 1 Chr 28:17
altar of incense made of refined **g**, 1 Chr 28:18
I was able, the **g** for the things of gold, 1 Chr 29:2
I was able, the gold for the things of **g**, 1 Chr 29:2
a treasure of my own of **g** and silver, 1 Chr 29:3
3,000 talents of **g**, of the gold of Ophir, 1 Chr 29:4
3,000 talents of gold, of the **g** of Ophir, 1 Chr 29:4
g for the things of gold and silver for 1 Chr 29:5
for the things of **g** and silver for the 1 Chr 29:5
5,000 talents and 10,000 darics of **g**, 1 Chr 29:7
made silver and **g** as common in 2 Chr 1:15
send me a man skilled to work in **g**, 2 Chr 2:7
He is trained to work in **g**, silver, 2 Chr 2:14
overlaid it on the inside with pure **g**. 2 Chr 3:4
covered it with fine **g** and made palms 2 Chr 3:5
stones. The **g** was gold of Parvaim. 2 Chr 3:6
stones. The gold was **g** of Parvaim. 2 Chr 3:6
he lined the house with **g**—its beams, 2 Chr 3:7
He overlaid it with 600 talents of fine **g**. 2 Chr 3:8
The weight of **g** for the nails was fifty 2 Chr 3:9
overlaid the upper chambers with **g**. 2 Chr 3:9
of wood and overlaid them with **g**. 2 Chr 3:10
And he made a hundred basins of **g**. 2 Chr 4:8
their lamps of pure **g** to burn before 2 Chr 4:20
the lamps, and the tongs, of purest **g**; 2 Chr 4:21
for incense, and fire pans, of pure **g**, 2 Chr 4:22
of the nave of the temple were of **g**. 2 Chr 4:22
dedicated, and stored the silver, the **g**, 2 Chr 5:1
there 450 talents of **g** and brought it 2 Chr 8:18
and very much **g** and precious stones. 2 Chr 9:1
she gave the king 120 talents of **g**, 2 Chr 9:9
who brought **g** from Ophir, 2 Chr 9:10
Now the weight of **g** that came to 2 Chr 9:13
in one year was 666 talents of **g**, 2 Chr 9:13
of the land brought **g** and silver to 2 Chr 9:14
made 200 large shields of beaten **g**; 2 Chr 9:15
shekels of beaten **g** went into each 2 Chr 9:15
And he made 300 shields of beaten **g**; 2 Chr 9:16
300 shekels of **g** went into each 2 Chr 9:16
throne and overlaid it with pure **g**. 2 Chr 9:17
had six steps and a footstool of **g**, 2 Chr 9:18
Solomon's drinking vessels were of **g**, 2 Chr 9:20
the Forest of Lebanon were of pure **g**. 2 Chr 9:20
of Tarshish used to come bringing **g**, 2 Chr 9:21
his present, articles of silver and of **g**, 2 Chr 9:24
the shields of **g** that Solomon had 2 Chr 12:9
showbread on the table of pure **g**, 2 Chr 13:11

his own sacred gifts, silver, and **g**, 2 Chr 15:18
took silver and **g** from the treasures 2 Chr 16:2
I am sending to you silver and **g**. 2 Chr 16:3
of silver, **g**, and valuable possessions, 2 Chr 21:3
incense and vessels of **g** and silver. 2 Chr 24:14
And he seized all the **g** and silver, 2 Chr 25:24
himself treasuries for silver, for **g**, 2 Chr 32:27
talents of silver and a talent of **g**. 2 Chr 36:3
by the men of his place with silver and **g**, Ezr 1:4
aided them with vessels of silver, with **g**, Ezr 1:6
30 basins of **g**, 1,000 basins of silver, 29 Ezr 1:9
30 bowls of **g**, 410 bowls of silver, and Ezr 1:10
all the vessels of **g** and of silver were Ezr 1:11
treasury of the work 61,000 darics of **g**, Ezr 2:69
And the **g** and silver vessels of the house Ezr 5:14
And also let the **g** and silver vessels of the Ezr 6:5
carry the silver and **g** that the king and Ezr 7:15
all the silver and **g** that you shall find Ezr 7:16
to do with the rest of the silver and **g**, Ezr 7:18
the silver and the **g** and the vessels, Ezr 8:25
worth 200 talents, and 100 talents of **g**, Ezr 8:26
20 bowls of **g** worth 1,000 darics, and Ezr 8:27
of fine bright bronze as precious as **g**. Ezr 8:27
the silver and the **g** are a freewill Ezr 8:28
of the silver and the **g** and the vessels, Ezr 8:30
the silver and the **g** and the vessels were Ezr 8:33
gave to the treasury 1,000 darics of **g**, Neh 7:70
20,000 darics of **g** and 2,200 minas Neh 7:71
the people gave was 20,000 darics of **g**, Neh 7:72
and also couches of **g** and silver on a Est 1:6
or with princes who had **g**, who filled Jb 3:15
if you lay **g** in the dust, and gold of Jb 22:24
and **g** of Ophir among the stones of the Jb 22:24
will be your **g** and your precious Jb 22:25
he has tried me, I shall come out as **g**. Jb 23:10
silver, and a place for **g** that they refine. Jb 28:1
place of sapphires, and it has dust of **g**. Jb 28:6
It cannot be bought for **g**, and silver Jb 28:15
It cannot be valued in the **g** of Ophir, in Jb 28:16
G and glass cannot equal it, nor can it Jb 28:17
can it be exchanged for jewels of fine **g**. Jb 28:17
equal it, nor can it be valued in pure **g**. Jb 28:19
"If I have made **g** my trust or called fine Jb 31:24
my trust or called fine **g** my confidence, Jb 31:24
him a piece of money and a ring of **g**. Jb 42:11
More to be desired are they than **g**, even Ps 19:10
are they than gold, even much fine **g**; Ps 19:10
you set a crown of fine **g** upon his head. Ps 21:3
hand stands the queen in **g** of Ophir. Ps 45:9
with robes interwoven with **g**. Ps 45:13
silver, its pinions with shimmering **g**. Ps 68:13
he live; may **g** of Sheba be given to him! Ps 72:15
brought out Israel with silver and **g**, Ps 105:37
Their idols are silver and **g**, the work of Ps 115:4
than thousands of **g** and silver pieces. Ps 119:72
I love your commandments above **g**, Ps 119:127
above gold, above fine **g**. Ps 119:127
idols of the nations are silver and **g**, Ps 135:15
from silver and her profit better than **g**. Prv 3:14
and knowledge rather than choice **g**, Prv 8:10
My fruit is better than **g**, even fine gold, Prv 8:19
My fruit is better than gold, even fine **g**, Prv 8:19
Like a **g** ring in a pig's snout is a Prv 11:22
much better to get wisdom than **g**! Prv 16:16
is for silver, and the furnace is for **g**, Prv 17:3
There is **g** and abundance of costly Prv 20:15
and favor is better than silver or **g**. Prv 22:1
spoken is like apples of **g** in a setting of Prv 25:11
Like a **g** ring or an ornament of gold is Prv 25:12
or an ornament of **g** is a wise reprover Prv 25:12
is for silver, and the furnace is for **g**, Prv 27:21
for myself silver and **g** and the treasure Eccl 2:8
We will make for you ornaments of **g**, Sg 1:11
He made its posts of silver, its back of **g**, Sg 3:10
His head is the finest **g**; his locks are Sg 5:11
His arms are rods of **g**, set with jewels. Sg 5:14
are alabaster columns, set on bases of **g**. Sg 5:15
Their land is filled with silver and **g**, and Is 2:7
their idols of silver and their idols of **g**, Is 2:20
I will make people more rare than fine **g**, Is 13:12
gold, and mankind than the **g** of Ophir. Is 13:12
regard for silver and do not delight in **g**. Is 13:17
away his idols of silver and his idols of **g**, Is 31:7
them his treasure house, the silver, the **g**, Is 39:2
overlays it with **g** and casts for Is 40:19
Those who lavish **g** from the purse, and Is 46:6
They shall bring **g** and frankincense, Is 60:6
from afar, their silver and **g** with them, Is 60:9
Instead of bronze I will bring **g**, and Is 60:17
you adorn yourself with ornaments of **g**, Jer 4:30
They decorate it with silver and **g**; they Jer 10:4
from Tarshish, and **g** from Uphaz. Jer 10:9
What was of **g** the captain of the guard Jer 52:19
the captain of the guard took away as **g**, Jer 52:19
How the **g** has grown dim, how the pure Lam 4:1

grown dim, how the pure **g** is changed! Lam 4:1
of Zion, worth their weight in fine **g**, Lam 4:2
and their **g** is like an unclean thing. Ezk 7:19
Their silver and **g** are not able to Ezk 7:19
you were adorned with **g** and silver, Ezk 16:13
beautiful jewels of my **g** and of my Ezk 16:17
of spices and all precious stones and **g**. Ezk 27:22
and have gathered **g** and silver into Ezk 28:4
and crafted in **g** were your settings Ezk 28:13
off plunder, to carry away silver and **g**, Ezk 38:13
The head of this image was of fine **g**, its Dn 2:32
the clay, the bronze, the silver, and the **g**, Dn 2:35
over them all—you are the head of **g**. Dn 2:38
the bronze, the clay, the silver, and the **g**. Dn 2:45
Nebuchadnezzar made an image of **g**, Dn 3:1
that the vessels of **g** and of silver that Dn 5:2
wine and praised the gods of **g** and silver, Dn 5:4
have a chain of **g** around his neck and Dn 5:7
have a chain of **g** around your neck and Dn 5:16
have praised the gods of silver and **g**, Dn 5:23
a chain of **g** was put around his neck, Dn 5:29
a belt of fine **g** from Uphaz around his Dn 10:5
their precious vessels of silver and **g**, Dn 11:8
know he shall honor with **g** and silver, Dn 11:38
ruler of the treasures of **g** and of silver, Dn 11:43
oil, and who lavished on her silver and **g**, Hos 2:8
With their silver and **g** they made idols Hos 8:4
For you have taken my silver and my **g**, Jl 3:5
Plunder the silver, plunder the **g**! There is Na 2:9
Behold, it is overlaid with **g** and silver, Hab 2:19
their silver nor their **g** shall be able to Zep 1:18
The silver is mine, and the **g** is mine, Hg 2:8
"I see, and behold, a lampstand all of **g**, Zec 4:2
Take from them silver and **g**, and make Zec 6:11
and fine **g** like the mud of the streets. Zec 9:3
silver, and test them as **g** is tested. Zec 13:9
nations shall be collected, **g**, silver, Zec 14:14
of Levi and refine them like **g** and silver, Mal 3:3
gifts, **g** and frankincense and myrrh. Mt 2:11
Acquire no **g** nor silver nor copper for Mt 10:9
if anyone swears by the **g** of the temple, Mt 23:16
the **g** or the temple that has made the Mt 23:17
the temple that has made the **g** sacred? Mt 23:17
But Peter said, "I have no silver and **g**, Acts 3:6
divine being is like **g** or silver or Acts 17:29
coveted no one's silver or **g** or apparel. Acts 20:33
builds on the foundation with **g**, 1 Cor 3:12
with braided hair and **g** or pearls or 1 Tm 2:9
not only vessels of **g** and silver but 2 Tm 2:20
the covenant covered on all sides with **g**, Heb 9:4
a man wearing a **g** ring and fine clothing Jas 2:2
Your **g** and silver have corroded, and Jas 5:3
more precious than **g** that perishes 1 Pt 1:7
perishable things such as silver or **g**, 1 Pt 1:18
—the braiding of hair, the wearing of **g**, 1 Pt 3:3
you to buy from me **g** refined by fire, Rv 3:18
heads were what looked like crowns of **g**; Rv 9:7
demons and idols of **g** and silver and Rv 9:20
and adorned with **g** and jewels and Rv 17:4
cargo of **g**, silver, jewels, pearls, fine Rv 18:12
in purple and scarlet, adorned with **g**, Rv 18:16
a measuring rod of **g** to measure the Rv 21:15
of jasper, while the city was pure **g**, Rv 21:18
and the street of the city was pure **g**, Rv 21:21

GOLD-PLATED (1)
with silver and your **g** metal images. Is 30:22

GOLDEN (77)
a **g** bell and a pomegranate, a golden Ex 28:34
a **g** bell and a pomegranate, Ex 28:34
And you shall make two **g** rings for it. Ex 30:4
it with a graving tool and made a **g** calf. Ex 32:4
made for themselves a **g** calf and have Ex 32:8
the **g** altar, the anointing oil and the Ex 39:38
you shall put the **g** altar for incense Ex 40:5
He put the **g** altar in the tent of meeting Ex 40:26
on the turban, in front, he set the **g** plate, Lv 8:9
And over the **g** altar they shall spread a Nm 4:11
one **g** dish of 10 shekels, full of incense; Nm 7:14
one **g** dish of 10 shekels, full of incense; Nm 7:20
one **g** dish of 10 shekels, full of incense; Nm 7:26
one **g** dish of 10 shekels, full of incense; Nm 7:32
one **g** dish of 10 shekels, full of incense; Nm 7:38
one **g** dish of 10 shekels, full of incense; Nm 7:44
one **g** dish of 10 shekels, full of incense; Nm 7:50
one **g** dish of 10 shekels, full of incense; Nm 7:56
one **g** dish of 10 shekels, full of incense; Nm 7:62
one **g** dish of 10 shekels, full of incense; Nm 7:68
one **g** dish of 10 shekels, full of incense; Nm 7:74
one **g** dish of 10 shekels, full of incense; Nm 7:80
twelve silver basins, twelve **g** dishes, Nm 7:84
the twelve **g** dishes, full of incense, Nm 7:86
God. You had made yourselves a **g** calf. Dt 9:16
his spoil." (For they had **g** earrings, Jgs 8:24
the weight of the **g** earrings that he Jgs 8:26
"Five **g** tumors and five golden mice, 1 Sm 6:4
"Five golden tumors and five **g** mice, 1 Sm 6:4
the box with the **g** mice and the 1 Sm 6:11
beside it, in which were the **g** figures, 1 Sm 6:15
These are the **g** tumors that the 1 Sm 6:17
and the **g** mice, according to the 1 Sm 6:18
in the house of the LORD: the **g** altar, 1 Kgs 7:48
the **g** table for the bread of the 1 Kgs 7:48
the **g** calves that were in Bethel and 2 Kgs 10:29
of gold for all **g** vessels for each 1 Chr 28:14
weight of the **g** lampstands and 1 Chr 28:15
for the **g** bowls and the weight of 1 Chr 28:17
his plan for the **g** chariot of the 1 Chr 28:18
he made ten **g** lampstands as 2 Chr 4:7
were in the house of God: the **g** altar, 2 Chr 4:19
with you the **g** calves that Jeroboam 2 Chr 13:8
and care for the **g** lampstand that its 2 Chr 13:11
made for themselves a **g** calf and said, Neh 9:18
Drinks were served in **g** vessels, vessels of Est 1:7
king holds out the **g** scepter so that he Est 4:11
out to Esther the **g** scepter that was in Est 5:2
the king held out the **g** scepter to Esther, Est 8:4
with a great **g** crown and a robe of fine Est 8:15
Out of the north comes **g** splendor; God Jb 37:22
is snapped, or the **g** bowl is broken, Eccl 12:6
Babylon was a **g** cup in the LORD'S hand, Jer 51:7
down and worship the **g** image that King Dn 3:5
and worshiped the **g** image that King Dn 3:7
fall down and worship the **g** image. Dn 3:10
gods or worship the **g** image that you Dn 3:12
gods or worship the **g** image that I have Dn 3:14
gods or worship the **g** image that you Dn 3:18
they brought in the **g** vessels that had Dn 5:3
are beside the two **g** pipes from which Zec 4:12
pipes from which the **g** oil is poured Zec 4:12
having the **g** altar of incense and the ark Heb 9:4
in which was a **g** urn holding the Heb 9:4
on turning I saw seven **g** lampstands, Rv 1:12
robe and with a **g** sash around his chest. Rv 1:13
right hand, and the seven **g** lampstands, Rv 1:20
walks among the seven **g** lampstands. Rv 2:1
garments, with **g** crowns on their heads. Rv 4:4
a harp, and **g** bowls full of incense, Rv 5:8
and stood at the altar with a **g** censer, Rv 8:3
the saints on the **g** altar before the throne, Rv 8:3
the four horns of the **g** altar before God, Rv 9:13
of man, with a **g** crown on his head, Rv 14:14
linen, with **g** sashes around their chests. Rv 15:6
the seven angels seven **g** bowls full of the Rv 15:7
in her hand a **g** cup full of Rv 17:4

GOLDSMITH (6)
and a **g** overlays it with gold and casts Is 40:19
The craftsman strengthens the **g**, and he Is 41:7
weigh out silver in the scales, hire a **g**, Is 46:6
the craftsman and of the hands of the **g**; Jer 10:9
every **g** is put to shame by his idols, for Jer 10:14
every **g** is put to shame by his idols, for Jer 51:17

GOLDSMITHS (3)
Uzziel the son of Harhaiah, **g**, repaired. Neh 3:8
After him Malchijah, one of the **g**, Neh 3:31
Sheep Gate the **g** and the merchants Neh 3:32

GOLGOTHA (3)
to a place called **G** (which means Place Mt 27:33
the place called **G** (which means Mk 15:22
a skull, which in Aramaic is called **G**. Jn 19:17

GOLIATH (6)
a champion named **G** of Gath, 1 Sm 17:4
the Philistine of Gath, **G** by name, 1 Sm 17:23
said, "The sword of **G** the Philistine, 1 Sm 21:9
him the sword of **G** the Philistine." 1 Sm 22:10
struck down **G** the Gittite, 2 Sm 21:19
Lahmi the brother of **G** the Gittite, 1 Chr 20:5

GOMER (6)
G, Magog, Madai, Javan, Tubal, Gn 10:2
The sons of **G**: Ashkenaz, Riphath, and Gn 10:3
G, Magog, Madai, Javan, Tubal, 1 Chr 1:5
The sons of **G**: Ashkenaz, Riphath, 1 Chr 1:6
G and all his hordes; Beth-togarmah Ezk 38:6
So he went and took **G**, the daughter of Hos 1:3

GOMORRAH (23)
in the direction of Sodom, **G**, Admah, Gn 10:19
the LORD destroyed Sodom and **G**.) Gn 13:10
Bera king of Sodom, Birsha king of **G**, Gn 14:2
Then the king of Sodom, the king of **G**, Gn 14:8
and as the kings of Sodom and **G** fled, Gn 14:10
all the possessions of Sodom and **G**, Gn 14:11
against Sodom and **G** is great and Gn 18:20
rained on Sodom and **G** sulfur and fire Gn 19:24
toward Sodom and **G** and toward all Gn 19:28
an overthrow like that of Sodom and **G**, Dt 29:23
vine of Sodom and from the fields of **G**; Dt 32:32
have been like Sodom, and become like **G**. Is 1:9
the teaching of our God, you people of **G**! Is 1:10
like Sodom and **G** when God overthrew Is 13:19
to me, and its inhabitants like **G**." Jer 23:14
when Sodom and **G** and their Jer 49:18
overthrew Sodom and **G** and their Jer 50:40
as when God overthrew Sodom and **G**, Am 4:11
like Sodom, and the Ammonites like **G**, Zep 2:9
land of Sodom and **G** than for that Mt 10:15
been like Sodom and become like **G**." Rom 9:29
cities of Sodom and **G** to ashes he 2 Pt 2:6
as Sodom and **G** and the surrounding Jude 1:7

GONE (211)
When the sun had **g** down and it was Gn 15:17
When the water in the skin was **g**, she Gn 21:15
Jacob had scarcely **g** out from the Gn 27:30
and his mother and **g** to Paddan-aram. Gn 28:7
Laban had **g** to shear his sheep, and Gn 31:19
now you have **g** away because you Gn 31:30
take our daughter, and we will be **g**." Gn 34:17
has been with me wherever I have **g**." Gn 35:3
And the man said, "They have **g** away, Gn 37:17
to his brothers and said, "The boy is **g**, Gn 37:30
They had **g** only a short distance from Gn 44:4
before your eyes? For our money is **g**." Gn 47:15
for your livestock, if your money is **g**." Gn 47:16
from the prey, my son, you have **g** up. Gn 49:9
and all who had **g** up with him to Gn 50:14
him, "As soon as I have **g** out of the city, Ex 9:29
your herds, as you have said, and be **g**, Ex 12:32
And when the dew had **g** up, there was Ex 16:14
the people of Israel had **g** out of the land Ex 19:1
watch Moses until he had **g** into the tent. Ex 33:8
But if you have **g** astray, though you Nm 5:20
but they had not **g** out to the tent, Nm 11:26
the men who had **g** up with him said, Nm 13:31
through which we have **g** to spy it out, Nm 13:32
and said to them, "You have **g** too far! Nm 16:3
be the holy one. You have **g** too far, Nm 16:7
for wrath has **g** out from the LORD; Nm 16:46
men in the army who had **g** to battle: Nm 31:21
of those who had **g** out in the army, Nm 31:36
evil in the sight of the LORD was **g**. Nm 32:13
worthless fellows have **g** out among Dt 13:13
and has **g** and served other gods and Dt 17:3
that their power is **g** and there is none Dt 32:36
shut as soon as the pursuers had **g** out. Jos 2:7
of the men of war who had **g** with him, Jos 10:24
When he had **g**, the servants came, and Jgs 3:24
son of Abinoam had **g** up to Mount Jgs 4:12
according to what has **g** out of your Jgs 11:36
the five men who had **g** to scout out the Jgs 18:14
the five men who had **g** to scout out the Jgs 18:17
When they had **g** a distance from the Jgs 18:22
the people of Israel had **g** up to Mizpah.) Jgs 20:3
hand of the LORD has **g** out against me." Ru 1:13
your sister-in-law has **g** back to her Ru 1:15
in that you have not **g** after young men, Ru 3:10
Now Boaz had **g** up to the gate and sat Ru 4:1
The lamp of God had not yet **g** out, and 1 Sm 3:3
For the bread in our sacks is **g**, and 1 Sm 9:7
did not know that Jonathan had **g**. 1 Sm 14:3
and see who has **g** from us." And 1 Sm 14:17
time and who had **g** up with them 1 Sm 14:21
I have **g** on the mission on which the 1 Sm 15:20
And as soon as the boy had **g**, David 1 Sm 20:41
when the wine had **g** out of Nabal, 1 Sm 25:37
the men who had **g** with David said, 1 Sm 30:22
"Why have you **g** in to my father's 2 Sm 3:7
sent him away, and he had **g** in peace. 2 Sm 3:22
has let him go, and he has **g** in peace." 2 Sm 3:23
have sent him away, so that he is **g**? 2 Sm 3:24
then the LORD has **g** out before you to 2 Sm 5:24
the ark of the LORD had **g** six steps, 2 Sm 6:13
men of Israel have **g** after Absalom." 2 Sm 15:13
"They have **g** over the brook of 2 Sm 17:20
After they had **g**, the men came up 2 Sm 17:21
So when they had **g** through all the 2 Sm 24:8
For he has **g** down this day and has 1 Kgs 1:25
and they have **g** up from there 1 Kgs 1:45
that Shimei had **g** from Jerusalem to 1 Kgs 2:41
king of Egypt had **g** up and captured 1 Kgs 9:16
"You have **g** up to Jerusalem long 1 Kgs 12:28
of God who came from Judah had **g**. 1 Kgs 13:12
before you and have **g** and made for 1 Kgs 14:9
man burns up dung until it is all **g**. 1 Kgs 14:10
And as soon as I have **g** from you, 1 Kgs 18:12
as soon as you have **g** from me, 1 Kgs 20:36
he was **g**." The king of Israel said to 1 Kgs 20:40
where he has **g** to take possession. 1 Kgs 21:18
from the bed to which you have **g** up, 2 Kgs 1:4
from the bed to which you have **g** up, 2 Kgs 1:6
from the bed to which you have **g** up, 2 Kgs 1:16
But when Naaman had **g** from him a 2 Kgs 5:19
Therefore they have **g** out of the 2 Kgs 7:12
chariots I have **g** up the heights 2 Kgs 19:23

And before Isaiah had **g** out of the 2 Kgs 20:4
by which it had **g** down on the steps 2 Kgs 20:11
for God has **g** out before you to 1 Chr 14:15
but I have **g** from tent to tent and 1 Chr 17:5
wherever you have **g** and have cut 1 Chr 17:8
wrath has **g** out against you from the 2 Chr 19:2
up from you to us have **g** to Jerusalem. Ezr 4:12
beside him), "How long will you be **g**, Neh 2:6
not know where I had **g** or what I was Neh 2:16
me understand how I have **g** astray. Jb 6:24
while your eyes are on me, I shall be **g**. Jb 7:8
me down on every side, and I am **g**, Jb 19:10
are exalted a little while, and then are **g**; Jb 24:24
he opens his eyes, and his wealth is **g**. Jb 27:19
The east wind lifts him up and he is **g**; it Jb 27:21
of their hands, men whose vigor is **g**? Jb 30:2
way and my heart has **g** after my eyes, Jb 31:7
Save, O LORD, for the godly one is **g**; for Ps 12:1
For my iniquities have **g** over my head; Ps 38:4
light of my eyes—it also has **g** from me. Ps 38:10
breakers and your waves have **g** over me. Ps 42:7
us and have not **g** out with our armies. Ps 44:9
God has **g** up with a shout, the LORD with Ps 47:5
to him, after he had **g** in to Bathsheba. Ps 51:T
they are soon **g**, and we fly away. Ps 90:10
for the wind passes over it, and it is **g**, Ps 103:16
I am **g** like a shadow at evening; I am Ps 109:23
I have **g** astray like a lost sheep; seek Ps 119:176
away, the torrent would have **g** over us; Ps 124:4
over us would have **g** the raging waters. Ps 124:5
at home; he has **g** on a long journey; Prv 7:19
When your eyes light on it, it is **g**, for Prv 23:5
When the grass is **g** and the new Prv 27:25
the winter is past; the rain is over and **g**. Sg 2:11
but my beloved had turned and **g**. Sg 5:6
Where has your beloved **g**, O most Sg 6:1
My beloved has **g** down to his garden to Sg 6:2
He has **g** up to the temple, and to Dibon, Is 15:2
For a cry has **g** around the land of Moab; Is 15:8
What do you mean that you have **g** up, Is 22:1
things. You will say to them, "Be **g**!" Is 30:22
many chariots I have **g** up the heights of Is 37:24
my mouth has **g** out in righteousness Is 45:23
draws near, my salvation has **g** out, Is 51:5
All we like sheep have **g** astray; we have Is 53:6
uncovered your bed, you have **g** up to it, Is 57:8
unclean, I have not **g** after the Baals'? Jer 2:23
A lion has **g** up from his thicket, a Jer 4:7
he has **g** out from his place to make your Jer 4:7
they have turned aside and **g** away. Jer 5:23
loved and served, which they have **g** after, Jer 8:2
My joy is **g**; grief is upon me; my heart is Jer 8:18
the air and the beasts have fled and are **g**. Jer 9:10
own hearts and have **g** after the Baals, Jer 9:14
my children have **g** from me, and they Jer 10:20
They have **g** after other gods to serve Jer 11:10
own heart and have **g** after other gods Jer 13:10
and have **g** after other gods and have Jer 16:11
Jerusalem ungodliness has **g** out into Jer 23:15
Wrath has **g** forth, a whirling tempest; Jer 23:19
Wrath has **g** forth, a whirling tempest; Jer 30:23
until all the bread of the city was **g**. Jer 37:21
that you have **g** astray at the cost of Jer 42:20
vessel to vessel, nor has he **g** into exile; Jer 48:11
young men have **g** down to slaughter, Jer 48:15
From mountain to hill they have **g**. Jer 50:6
Judah has **g** into exile because of Lam 1:3
her children have **g** away, captives Lam 1:5
my young men have **g** into captivity. Lam 1:18
God of Israel had **g** up from the cherub Ezk 9:3
in the countries where they have **g**.' Ezk 11:16
You have not **g** up into the breaches, or Ezk 13:5
And fire has **g** out from the stem of its Ezk 19:14
You have **g** the way of your sister; Ezk 23:31
For they have **g** in to her, as men go in Ezk 23:44
and whose corrosion has not **g** out of it! Ezk 24:6
of the earth have **g** away from its Ezk 31:12
to those who have **g** down to the pit: Ezk 32:18
who have **g** down in shame with the Ezk 32:30
the nations among which they have **g**, Ezk 37:21
and after he has **g** out the gate shall be Ezk 46:12
who had **g** out to kill the wise men of Dn 2:14
When their drink is **g**, they give Hos 4:18
the revolters have **g** deep into slaughter, Hos 5:2
For they have **g** up to Assyria, a wild Hos 8:9
But Jonah had **g** down into the inner part Jon 1:5
Then Jesus said to him, "Be **g**, Satan! For Mt 4:10
you will not have **g** through all the Mt 10:23
the unclean spirit has **g** out of a person, Mt 12:43
sheep and one of them has **g** astray, Mt 18:12
himself that power had **g** out from him, Mk 5:30
the child lying in bed and the demon **g**. Mk 7:30
but the fishermen had **g** out of them and Lk 5:2
When John's messengers had **g**, Jesus Lk 7:24
from whom seven demons had **g** out, Lk 8:2
the man from whom the demons had **g**, Lk 8:35
whom the demons had **g** begged that he Lk 8:38
perceive that power has **g** out from me." Lk 8:46
When the demon had **g** out, the mute Lk 11:14
the unclean spirit has **g** out of a person, Lk 11:24
"He has **g** in to be the guest of a man Lk 19:7
(For his disciples had **g** away into the city Jn 4:8
at the feast. For they too had **g** to the feast. Jn 4:45
but that his disciples had **g** away alone. Jn 6:22
after his brothers had **g** up to the feast, Jn 7:10
Nicodemus, who had **g** to him before, Jn 7:50
Look, the world has **g** after him." Jn 12:19
When he had **g** out, Jesus said, "Now is Jn 13:31
When they had **g** through the whole Acts 13:6
that some persons have **g** out from us Acts 15:24
and had not **g** with them to Acts 15:38
saw that their hope of gain was **g**, Acts 16:19
When he had **g** through those regions Acts 20:2
And when Paul had **g** up and had Acts 20:11
whom I have **g** about proclaiming Acts 20:25
for "Their voice has **g** out to all the Rom 10:18
The night is far **g**; the day is at hand. Rom 13:12
faith in God has **g** forth everywhere, 1 Thes 1:8
deserted me and **g** to Thessalonica. 2 Tm 4:10
Crescens has **g** to Galatia, 2 Tm 4:10
where Jesus has **g** as a forerunner on Heb 6:20
that land from which they had **g** out, Heb 11:15
who has **g** into heaven and is at the 1 Pt 3:22
the right way, they have **g** astray. 2 Pt 2:15
many false prophets have **g** out into the 1 Jn 4:1
For many deceivers have **g** out into the 2 Jn 1:7
For they have **g** out for the sake of the 3 Jn 1:7
your soul longed has **g** from you, Rv 18:14

GONG (1)

I am a noisy **g** or a clanging cymbal. 1 Cor 13:1

GOOD (673)

And God saw that the light was **g**. And Gn 1:4
called Seas. And God saw that it was **g**. Gn 1:10
to its kind. And God saw that it was **g**. Gn 1:12
the darkness. And God saw that it was **g**. Gn 1:18
to its kind. And God saw that it was **g**. Gn 1:21
to its kind. And God saw that it was **g**. Gn 1:25
he had made, and behold, it was very **g**. Gn 1:31
that is pleasant to the sight and **g** for food. Gn 2:9
the tree of the knowledge of **g** and evil. Gn 2:9
And the gold of that land is **g**; bdellium Gn 2:12
of the knowledge of **g** and evil you shall Gn 2:17
"It is not **g** that the man should be Gn 2:18
will be like God, knowing **g** and evil." Gn 3:5
woman saw that the tree was **g** for food, Gn 3:6
like one of us in knowing **g** and evil. Gn 3:22
you shall be buried in a **g** old age. Gn 15:15
to the herd and took a calf, tender and **g**, Gn 18:7
and sat down opposite him a **g** way off, Gn 21:16
LORD; we cannot speak to you bad or **g**. Gn 24:50
breathed his last and died in a **g** old age, Gn 25:8
to you nothing but **g** and have sent Gn 26:29
flock and bring me two **g** young goats, Gn 27:9
the land, what **g** will my life be to me?" Gn 27:46
"**G** fortune has come!" so she called his Gn 30:11
has endowed me with a **g** endowment; Gn 30:20
said, "**G**! Let it be as you have said." Gn 30:34
say anything to Jacob, either **g** or bad." Gn 31:24
say anything to Jacob, either **g** or bad.' Gn 31:29
to your kindred, that I may do you **g**,' Gn 32:9
But you said, 'I will surely do you **g**, Gn 32:12
seven ears of grain, plump and **g**, Gn 41:5
ears growing on one stalk, full and **g**. Gn 41:22
ears swallowed up the seven **g** ears. Gn 41:24
The seven **g** cows are seven years, and Gn 41:26
and the seven **g** ears are seven years; Gn 41:26
the food of these **g** years that are Gn 41:35
them, 'Why have you repaid evil for **g**? Gn 44:4
loaded with the **g** things of Egypt, Gn 45:23
neck and wept on his neck a **g** while. Gn 46:29
He saw that a resting place was **g**, and Gn 49:15
evil against me, but God meant it for **g**, Gn 50:20
up out of that land to a **g** and broad land, Ex 3:8
rejoiced for all the **g** that the LORD had Ex 18:9
to him, "What you are doing is not **g**. Ex 18:17
his lips a rash oath to do evil or to do **g**, Lv 5:4
takes an animal's life shall make it **g**, Lv 24:18
kills an animal shall make it **g**, Lv 24:21
it or make a substitute for it, **g** for bad, Lv 27:10
for it, good for bad, or bad for **g**; Lv 27:10
priest shall value it as either **g** or bad; Lv 27:12
priest shall value it as either **g** or bad; Lv 27:14
shall not differentiate between **g** or bad, Lv 27:33
Come with us, and we will do **g** to you, Nm 10:29
for the LORD has promised **g** to Israel." Nm 10:29
us, whatever **g** the LORD will do to us, Nm 10:32
the land that they dwell in is **g** or bad, Nm 13:19
Be of **g** courage and bring some of the Nm 13:20
to spy it out, is an exceedingly **g** land. Nm 14:7
to do either **g** or bad of my own will. Nm 24:13
that you have spoken is **g** for us to do.' Dt 1:14
The thing seemed **g** to me, and I took Dt 1:23
'It is a **g** land that the LORD our God is Dt 1:25
generation shall see the **g** land that I Dt 1:35
today have no knowledge of **g** or evil, Dt 1:39
over and see the **g** land beyond the Dt 3:25
that **g** hill country and Lebanon.' Dt 3:25
should not enter the **g** land that the LORD Dt 4:21
over and take possession of that **g** land. Dt 4:22
you—with great and **g** cities that you did Dt 6:10
houses full of all **g** things that you did Dt 6:11
do what is right and **g** in the sight of the Dt 6:18
take possession of the **g** land that the Dt 6:18
fear the LORD our God, for our **g** always, Dt 6:24
your God is bringing you into a **g** land, Dt 8:7
your God for the **g** land he has given Dt 8:10
full and have built **g** houses and live in Dt 8:12
you and test you, to do you **g** in the end. Dt 8:16
not giving you this **g** land to possess Dt 9:6
am commanding you today for your **g**? Dt 10:13
perish quickly off the **g** land that the Dt 11:17
when you do what is **g** and right in the Dt 12:28
rejoice in all the **g** that the LORD your Dt 26:11
LORD will open to you his **g** treasury, Dt 28:12
in doing you **g** and multiplying you, Dt 28:63
I have set before you today life and **g**, Dt 30:15
you may have **g** success wherever you Jos 1:7
and then you will have **g** success. Jos 1:8
Whatever seems **g** and right in your Jos 9:25
word of all the **g** promises that the LORD Jos 21:45
Manasseh spoke, it was **g** in their eyes. Jos 22:30
And the report was **g** in the eyes of the Jos 22:33
perish from off this **g** ground that the Jos 23:13
failed of all the **g** things that the LORD Jos 23:14
just as all the **g** things that the LORD Jos 23:15
you from off this **g** land that the LORD Jos 23:15
quickly from off the **g** land that he has Jos 23:16
you, after having done you **g**." Jos 24:20
of Joash died in a **g** old age and was Jgs 8:32
in return for all the **g** that he had done to Jgs 8:35
my sweetness and my **g** fruit and go Jgs 9:11
'If in **g** faith you are anointing me king Jgs 9:15
if you acted in **g** faith and integrity Jgs 9:16
then have acted in **g** faith and integrity Jgs 9:19
do to us whatever seems **g** to you. Jgs 10:15
seen the land, and behold, it is very **g**. Jgs 18:9
and do with them what seems **g** to you, Jgs 19:24
to Ruth, her daughter-in-law, "It is **g**, Ru 2:22
if he will redeem you, **g**; let him do it. Ru 3:13
it is no **g** report that I hear the people 1 Sm 2:24
Let him do what seems **g** to him." 1 Sm 3:18
do to us whatever seems **g** to you." 1 Sm 11:10
instruct you in the **g** and the right 1 Sm 12:23
"Do whatever seems **g** to you." But 1 Sm 14:36
to Saul, "Do what seems **g** to you." 1 Sm 14:40
and the lambs, and all that was **g**, 1 Sm 15:9
in speech, and a man of **g** presence, 1 Sm 16:18
And this was **g** in the sight of all the 1 Sm 18:5
his deeds have brought **g** to you. 1 Sm 19:4
'**G**!' it will be well with your servant, 1 Sm 20:7
as it shall seem **g** to you.'" Then David 1 Sm 24:4
than I, for you have repaid me **g**, 1 Sm 24:17
LORD reward you with **g** for what you 1 Sm 24:19
Yet the men were very **g** to us, and we 1 Sm 25:15
and he has returned me evil for **g**. 1 Sm 25:21
according to all the **g** that he has 1 Sm 25:30
thing that you have done is not **g**. 1 Sm 26:16
to carry the **g** news to the house of 1 Sm 31:9
And I will do **g** to you because you 2 Sm 2:6
"**G**; I will make a covenant with you. 2 Sm 3:13
house of Benjamin thought **g** to do. 2 Sm 3:19
and thought he was bringing **g** news, 2 Sm 4:10
have promised this **g** thing to your 2 Sm 7:28
Be of **g** courage, and let us be 2 Sm 10:12
the LORD do what seems **g** to him." 2 Sm 10:12
spoke to Amnon neither **g** nor bad, 2 Sm 13:22
angel of God to discern **g** and evil. 2 Sm 14:17
"See, your claims are **g** and right, 2 Sm 15:3
him do to me what seems **g** to him." 2 Sm 15:26
will repay me with **g** for his cursing 2 Sm 16:12
that Ahithophel has given is not **g**." 2 Sm 17:7
to defeat the **g** counsel of Ahithophel, 2 Sm 17:14
"He is a **g** man and comes with good 2 Sm 18:27
a good man and comes with **g** news." 2 Sm 18:27
said, "**G** news for my lord the king! 2 Sm 18:31
do therefore what seems **g** to you. 2 Sm 19:27
do for him whatever seems **g** to you." 2 Sm 19:37
do for him whatever seems **g** to you, 2 Sm 19:38
and offer up what seems **g** to him. 2 Sm 24:22
are a worthy man and bring **g** news." 1 Kgs 1:42
said to the king, "What you say is **g**; 1 Kgs 2:38
you said to me, 'What you say is **g**; 1 Kgs 2:42
that I may discern between **g** and evil, 1 Kgs 3:9
you teach them the **g** way in which 1 Kgs 8:36

word has failed of all his **g** promise, 1 Kgs 8:56
and speak **g** words to them when you 1 Kgs 12:7
Israel out of this **g** land that he gave 1 Kgs 14:15
or, if it seems **g** to you, I will give you 1 Kgs 21:2
he never prophesies **g** concerning me, 1 Kgs 22:8
not prophesy **g** concerning me, 1 Kgs 22:18
and shall fell every **g** tree and stop up 2 Kgs 3:19
water and ruin every **g** piece of land 2 Kgs 3:19
and on every **g** piece of land every 2 Kgs 3:25
of water and felled all the **g** trees, 2 Kgs 3:25
right. This day is a day of **g** news. 2 Kgs 7:9
king. Do whatever is **g** in your eyes." 2 Kgs 10:5
have done what is **g** in your sight." 2 Kgs 20:3
have spoken is **g**." For he thought, 2 Kgs 20:19
where they found rich, **g** pasture, and 1 Chr 4:40
to carry the **g** news to their 1 Chr 10:9
"If it seems **g** to you and from the 1 Chr 13:2
give thanks to the LORD, for he is **g**; 1 Chr 16:34
have promised this **g** thing to your 1 Chr 17:26
the LORD do what seems **g** to him." 1 Chr 19:13
the king do what seems **g** to him. 1 Chr 21:23
may possess this **g** land and leave 1 Chr 28:8
Then he died at a **g** age, full of days, 1 Chr 29:28
in praise to the LORD, "For he is **g**, 2 Chr 5:13
you teach them the **g** way in which 2 Chr 6:27
to the LORD, saying, "For he is **g**, 2 Chr 7:3
"If you will be **g** to this people and 2 Chr 10:7
them and speak **g** words to them, 2 Chr 10:7
conditions were **g** in Judah. 2 Chr 12:12
Asa did what was **g** and right in the 2 Chr 14:2
never prophesies **g** concerning me, 2 Chr 18:7
not prophesy **g** concerning me, 2 Chr 18:17
Nevertheless, some **g** is found in you, 2 Chr 19:3
because he had done **g** in Israel, 2 Chr 24:16
"May the **g** LORD pardon everyone 2 Chr 30:18
Levites who showed **g** skill in the 2 Chr 30:22
he did what was **g** and right and 2 Chr 31:20
the acts of Hezekiah and his **g** deeds, 2 Chr 32:32
and his **g** deeds according to what is 2 Chr 35:26
giving thanks to the LORD, "For he is **g**, Ezr 3:11
Therefore, if it seems **g** to the king, let Ezr 5:17
for the **g** hand of his God was on him. Ezr 7:9
Whatever seems **g** to you and your Ezr 7:18
And by the **g** hand of our God on us, Ezr 8:18
of our God is for **g** on all who seek him, Ezr 8:22
be strong and eat the **g** of the land and Ezr 9:12
for the **g** hand of my God was upon me. Neh 2:8
my God that had been upon me for **g**, Neh 2:18
their hands for the **g** work. Neh 2:18
"The thing that you are doing is not **g**. Neh 5:9
Remember for my **g**, O my God, all Neh 5:19
they spoke of his **g** deeds in my Neh 6:19
laws, **g** statutes and commandments, Neh 9:13
You gave your **g** Spirit to instruct Neh 9:20
of houses full of all **g** things, Neh 9:25
fathers to enjoy its fruit and its **g** gifts, Neh 9:36
do not wipe out my **g** deeds that I have Neh 13:14
Remember me, O my God, for **g**. Neh 13:31
to do with them as it seems **g** to you." Est 3:11
Shall we receive **g** from God, and shall we Jb 2:10
it is true. Hear, and know it for your **g**." Jb 5:27
is a breath; my eye will never again see **g**. Jb 7:7
a runner; they flee away; they see no **g**. Jb 9:25
put off my sad face, and be of **g** cheer,' Jb 9:27
Does it seem **g** to you to oppress, to Jb 10:3
or in words with which he can do no **g**? Jb 15:3
filled their houses with **g** things—but Jb 22:18
be at peace; thereby **g** will come to you. Jb 22:21
woman, and do no **g** to the widow. Jb 24:21
But when I hoped for **g**, evil came, and Jb 30:26
let us know among ourselves what is **g**. Jb 34:4
who say, "Who will show us some **g**? Ps 4:6
deeds, there is none who does **g**. Ps 14:1
there is none who does **g**, not even one. Ps 14:3
my Lord; I have no **g** apart from you." Ps 16:2
G and upright is the LORD; therefore he Ps 25:8
Oh, taste and see that the LORD is **g**! Ps 34:8
who seek the LORD lack no **g** thing. Ps 34:10
loves many days, that he may see **g**? Ps 34:12
Turn away from evil and do **g**; seek Ps 34:14
They repay me evil for **g**; my soul is Ps 35:12
he has ceased to act wisely and do **g**. Ps 36:3
bed; he sets himself in a way that is not **g**; Ps 36:4
Trust in the LORD, and do **g**; dwell in the Ps 37:3
Turn away from evil and do **g**; so shall Ps 37:27
render me evil for **g** accuse me because Ps 38:20
good accuse me because I follow after **g**. Ps 38:20
Do **g** to Zion in your good pleasure; Ps 51:18
Do good to Zion in your **g** pleasure; Ps 51:18
You love evil more than **g**, and lying Ps 52:3
I will wait for your name, for it is **g**, in Ps 52:9
iniquity; there is none who does **g**. Ps 53:1
there is none who does **g**, not even one. Ps 53:3
thanks to your name, O LORD, for it is **g**. Ps 54:6
me, O LORD, for your steadfast love is **g**; Ps 69:16

Truly God is **g** to Israel, to those who are Ps 73:1
But for me it is **g** to be near God; I have Ps 73:28
No **g** thing does he withhold from those Ps 84:11
Yes, the LORD will give what is **g**, and Ps 85:12
For you, O Lord, are **g** and forgiving, Ps 86:5
It is **g** to give thanks to the LORD, to sing Ps 92:1
For the LORD is **g**; his steadfast love Ps 100:5
who satisfies you with **g** so that your Ps 103:5
hand, they are filled with **g** things. Ps 104:28
Oh give thanks to the LORD, for he is **g**, Ps 106:1
Oh give thanks to the LORD, for he is **g**, Ps 107:1
the hungry soul he fills with **g** things. Ps 107:9
So they reward me evil for **g**, and hatred Ps 109:5
because your steadfast love is **g**, Ps 109:21
practice it have a **g** understanding. Ps 111:10
Oh give thanks to the LORD, for he is **g**; Ps 118:1
Oh give thanks to the LORD, for he is **g**; Ps 118:29
that I dread, for your rules are **g**. Ps 119:39
Teach me **g** judgment and knowledge, Ps 119:66
You are **g** and do good; teach me your Ps 119:68
You are good and do **g**; teach me your Ps 119:68
It is **g** for me that I was afflicted, that I Ps 119:71
Give your servant a pledge of **g**; let Ps 119:122
of the LORD our God, I will seek your **g**. Ps 122:9
Do **g**, O LORD, to those who are good, and Ps 125:4
Do good, O LORD, to those who are **g**, and Ps 125:4
how **g** and pleasant it is when brothers Ps 133:1
Praise the LORD, for the LORD is **g**; sing to Ps 135:3
Give thanks to the LORD, for he is **g**, for Ps 136:1
Let your **g** Spirit lead me on level Ps 143:10
The LORD is **g** to all, and his mercy is Ps 145:9
For it is **g** to sing praises to our God; for Ps 147:1
and justice and equity, every **g** path; Prv 2:9
in the way of the **g** and keep to the paths Prv 2:20
will find favor and **g** success in the sight Prv 3:4
Do not withhold **g** from those to whom Prv 3:27
for I give you **g** precepts; do not forsake Prv 4:2
desire of the righteous ends only in **g**; Prv 11:23
diligently seeks **g** seeks favor, Prv 11:27
A **g** man obtains favor from the LORD, Prv 12:2
is commended according to his **g** sense, Prv 12:8
of his mouth a man is satisfied with **g**, Prv 12:14
down, but a **g** word makes him glad. Prv 12:25
fruit of his mouth a man eats what is **g**, Prv 13:2
G sense wins favor, but the way of the Prv 13:15
but the righteous are rewarded with **g**. Prv 13:21
A **g** man leaves an inheritance to his Prv 13:22
and a **g** man will be filled with the Prv 14:14
The evil bow down before the **g**, the Prv 14:19
Those who devise **g** meet steadfast love Prv 14:22
keeping watch on the evil and the **g**. Prv 15:3
man, and a word in season, how **g** it is! Prv 15:23
heart, and **g** news refreshes the bones. Prv 15:30
thought to the word will discover **g**, Prv 16:20
G sense is a fountain of life to him Prv 16:22
and leads him in a way that is not **g**. Prv 16:29
If anyone returns evil for **g**, evil will Prv 17:13
of crooked heart does not discover **g**, Prv 17:20
A joyful heart is **g** medicine, but a Prv 17:22
a fine on a righteous man is not **g**, Prv 17:26
It is not **g** to be partial to the wicked or Prv 18:5
a wife finds a **g** thing and obtains Prv 18:22
Desire without knowledge is not **g**, and Prv 19:2
keeps understanding will discover **g**. Prv 19:8
G sense makes one slow to anger, and Prv 19:11
to the LORD, and false scales are not **g**. Prv 20:23
from the way of **g** sense will rest in Prv 21:16
A **g** name is to be chosen rather than Prv 22:1
he will despise the **g** sense of your Prv 23:9
My son, eat honey, for it is **g**, and the Prv 24:13
the wise. Partiality in judging is not **g**. Prv 24:23
and a **g** blessing will come upon them. Prv 24:25
soul, so is **g** news from a far country. Prv 25:25
It is not **g** to eat much honey, nor is it Prv 25:27
To show partiality is not **g**, but for a Prv 28:21
She does him **g**, and not harm, all the Prv 31:12
might see what was **g** for the children of Eccl 2:3
be joyful and to do **g** as long as they Eccl 3:12
because they have a **g** reward for their Eccl 4:9
I have seen to be **g** and fitting is to eat Eccl 5:18
soul is not satisfied with life's **g** things, Eccl 6:3
yet enjoy no **g**—do not all go to the one Eccl 6:6
who knows what is **g** for man while he Eccl 6:12
A **g** name is better than precious Eccl 7:1
Wisdom is **g** with an inheritance, an Eccl 7:11
It is **g** that you should take hold of this, Eccl 7:18
on earth who does **g** and never sins. Eccl 7:20
for man has no **g** thing under the sun Eccl 8:15
and the wicked, to the **g** and the evil, Eccl 9:2
As is the **g**, so is the sinner, and he who Eccl 9:2
war, but one sinner destroys much **g**. Eccl 9:18
or that, or whether both alike will be **g**. Eccl 11:6
every secret thing, whether **g** or evil. Eccl 12:14
learn to do **g**; seek justice, correct Is 1:17
obedient, you shall eat the **g** of the land; Is 1:19

to those who call evil **g** and good evil, Is 5:20
to those who call evil good and **g** evil, Is 5:20
how to refuse the evil and choose the **g**. Is 7:15
how to refuse the evil and choose the **g**, Is 7:16
have done what is **g** in your sight." And Is 38:3
you have spoken is **g**." For he thought, Is 39:8
high mountain, O Zion, herald of **g** news; Is 40:9
strength, O Jerusalem, herald of **g** news; Is 40:9
the anvil, saying of the soldering, "It is **g**"; Is 41:7
we may know that you are gods; do **g**, Is 41:23
I give to Jerusalem a herald of **g** news. Is 41:27
are the feet of him who brings **g** news, Is 52:7
peace, who brings **g** news of happiness, Is 52:7
Listen diligently to me, and eat what is **g**, Is 55:2
frankincense, and shall bring **g** news, Is 60:6
anointed me to bring **g** news to the poor; Is 61:1
people, who walk in a way that is not **g**, Is 65:2
land to enjoy its fruits and its **g** things. Jer 2:7
evil! But how to do **g** they know not." Jer 4:22
and your sins have kept **g** from you. Jer 5:25
for the ancient paths, where the **g** way is; Jer 6:16
We looked for peace, but no **g** came; for Jer 8:15
do evil, neither is it in them to do **g**." Jer 10:5
green olive tree, beautiful with **g** fruit.' Jer 11:16
was spoiled; it was **g** for nothing. Jer 13:7
this loincloth, which is **g** for nothing. Jer 13:10
also you can do **g** who are accustomed Jer 13:23
We looked for peace, but no **g** came; for Jer 14:19
said, "Have I not set you free for their **g**? Jer 15:11
the desert, and shall not see any **g** come. Jer 17:6
vessel, as it seemed **g** to the potter to do. Jer 18:4
I will relent of the **g** that I had intended Jer 18:10
Should **g** be repaid with evil? Yet they Jer 18:20
I stood before you to speak **g** for them, Jer 18:20
against this city for harm and not for **g**, Jer 21:10
One basket had very **g** figs, like first-ripe Jer 24:2
I said, "Figs, the **g** figs very good, Jer 24:3
I said, "Figs, the good figs very **g**, Jer 24:3
Like these **g** figs, so I will regard as good Jer 24:5
I will regard as **g** the exiles from Judah, Jer 24:5
I will set my eyes on them for **g**, and I Jer 24:6
Do with me as seems **g** and right to you. Jer 26:14
he shall not see the **g** that I will do to Jer 29:32
for their own **g** and the good of their Jer 32:39
own good and the **g** of their children Jer 32:39
not turn away from doing **g** to them. Jer 32:40
I will rejoice in doing them **g**, and I will Jer 32:41
upon them all the **g** that I promise Jer 32:42
shall hear of all the **g** that I do for them. Jer 33:9
because of all the **g** and all the prosperity Jer 33:9
to the LORD of hosts, for the LORD is **g**, Jer 33:11
against this city for harm and not for **g**, Jer 39:16
If it seems **g** to you to come with me to Jer 40:4
wherever you think it **g** and right to go. Jer 40:4
Whether it is **g** or bad, we will obey the Jer 42:6
over them for disaster and not for **g**. Jer 44:27
The LORD is **g** to those who wait for Lam 3:25
It is **g** that one should wait quietly for Lam 3:26
It is **g** for a man that he bear the yoke Lam 3:27
of the Most High that **g** and bad come? Lam 3:38
been planted on **g** soil by abundant Ezk 17:8
did what is not **g** among his people, Ezk 18:18
statutes that were not **g** and rules by Ezk 20:25
in it the pieces of meat, all the **g** pieces, Ezk 24:4
I will feed them with **g** pasture, and on Ezk 34:14
they shall lie down in **g** grazing land, Ezk 34:14
for you to feed on the **g** pasture, Ezk 34:18
and will do more **g** to you than ever Ezk 36:11
ways, and your deeds that were not **g**, Ezk 36:31
of **g** appearance and skillful in all Dn 1:4
the image that I have made, well and **g**. Dn 3:15
It has seemed **g** to me to show the signs Dn 4:2
be strong and of **g** courage." And as he Dn 10:19
and terebinth, because their shade is **g**. Hos 4:13
Israel has spurned the **g**; the enemy shall Hos 8:3
accept what is **g**, and we will pay with Hos 14:2
Seek **g**, and not evil, that you may live; Am 5:14
Hate evil, and love **g**, and establish Am 5:15
eyes upon them for evil and not for **g**." Am 9:4
of Maroth wait anxiously for **g**, Mi 1:12
Do not my words do **g** to him who walks Mi 2:7
you who hate the **g** and love the evil, who Mi 3:2
He has told you, O man, what is **g**; and Mi 6:8
The LORD is **g**, a stronghold in the day of Na 1:7
the feet of him who brings **g** news, Na 1:15
in their hearts, 'The LORD will not do **g**, Zep 1:12
these days to bring **g** to Jerusalem and Zec 8:15
I said to them, "If it seems **g** to you, Zec 11:12
who does evil is **g** in the sight of Mal 2:17
that does not bear **g** fruit is cut down Mt 3:10
It is no longer **g** for anything except to Mt 5:13
they may see your **g** works and give Mt 5:16
his sun rise on the evil and on the **g**, Mt 5:45
know how to give **g** gifts to your Mt 7:11
is in heaven give **g** things to those who Mt 7:11

So, every healthy tree bears **g** fruit, but Mt 7:17
fruit, nor can a diseased tree bear **g** fruit. Mt 7:18
that does not bear **g** fruit is cut down Mt 7:19
and the poor have **g** news preached to Mt 11:5
So it is lawful to do **g** on the Sabbath." Mt 12:12
"Either make the tree **g** and its fruit Mt 12:33
make the tree good and its fruit **g**, Mt 12:33
How can you speak **g**, when you are Mt 12:34
The **g** person out of his good treasure Mt 12:35
out of his **g** treasure brings forth Mt 12:35
out of his good treasure brings forth **g**, Mt 12:35
Other seeds fell on **g** soil and produced Mt 13:8
As for what was sown on **g** soil, this is Mt 13:23
to a man who sowed **g** seed in his field, Mt 13:24
did you not sow **g** seed in your field? Mt 13:27
"The one who sows the **g** seed is the Son Mt 13:37
and the **g** seed is the children of the Mt 13:38
and sorted the **g** into containers but Mt 13:48
to Jesus, "Lord, it is **g** that we are here. Mt 17:4
what **g** deed must I do to have eternal Mt 19:16
"Why do you ask me about what is **g**? Mt 19:17
is good? There is only one who is **g**. Mt 19:17
all whom they found, both bad and **g**. Mt 22:10
him, 'Well done, **g** and faithful servant. Mt 25:21
him, 'Well done, **g** and faithful servant. Mt 25:23
on the Sabbath to do **g** or to do harm, Mk 3:4
other seeds fell into **g** soil and produced Mk 4:8
that were sown on the **g** soil are the ones Mk 4:20
to Jesus, "Rabbi, it is **g** that we are here. Mk 9:5
Salt is **g**, but if the salt has lost its Mk 9:50
him and asked him, "**G** Teacher, Mk 10:17
said to him, "Why do you call me **g**? Mk 10:18
good? No one is **g** except God alone. Mk 10:18
you want, you can do **g** for them. Mk 14:7
it seemed **g** to me also, having followed all Lk 1:3
to you and to bring you this **g** news. Lk 1:19
he has filled the hungry with **g** things, Lk 1:53
I bring you **g** news of a great joy that Lk 2:10
that does not bear **g** fruit is cut down Lk 3:9
exhortations he preached **g** news to the Lk 3:18
anointed me to proclaim **g** news to the Lk 4:18
"I must preach the **g** news of the Lk 4:43
desires new, for he says, 'The old is **g**.'" Lk 5:39
on the Sabbath to do **g** or to do harm, Lk 6:9
enemies, do **g** to those who hate you, Lk 6:27
And if you do **g** to those who do good to Lk 6:33
if you do good to those who do **g** to you, Lk 6:33
But love your enemies, and do **g**, and Lk 6:35
G measure, pressed down, shaken Lk 6:38
"For no **g** tree bears bad fruit, nor again Lk 6:43
nor again does a bad tree bear **g** fruit, Lk 6:43
The **g** person out of the good treasure of Lk 6:45
person out of the **g** treasure of his heart Lk 6:45
good treasure of his heart produces **g**, Lk 6:45
the poor have **g** news preached to them. Lk 7:22
and bringing the **g** news of the Lk 8:1
And some fell into **g** soil and grew and Lk 8:8
As for that in the **g** soil, they are those Lk 8:15
hold it fast in an honest and **g** heart, Lk 8:15
to Jesus, "Master, it is **g** that we are here. Lk 9:33
Mary has chosen the **g** portion, which Lk 10:42
know how to give **g** gifts to your Lk 11:13
it is your Father's **g** pleasure to give Lk 12:32
it should bear fruit next year, well and **g**; Lk 13:9
"Salt is **g**, but if salt has lost its taste, Lk 14:34
since then the **g** news of the kingdom Lk 16:16
in your lifetime received your **g** things, Lk 16:25
And a ruler asked him, "**G** Teacher, Lk 18:18
said to him, "Why do you call me **g**? Lk 18:19
me good? No one is **g** except God alone. Lk 18:19
he said to him, 'Well done, **g** servant! Lk 19:17
of the council, a **g** and righteous man, Lk 23:50
"Can anything **g** come out of Nazareth?" Jn 1:46
to him, "Everyone serves the **g** wine first, Jn 2:10
But you have kept the **g** wine until now." Jn 2:10
who have done **g** to the resurrection Jn 5:29
some said, "He is a **g** man," others said, Jn 7:12
I am the **g** shepherd. The good shepherd Jn 10:11
The **g** shepherd lays down his life for Jn 10:11
I am the **g** shepherd. I know my own Jn 10:14
shown you many **g** works from the Jn 10:32
"It is not for a **g** work that we are going Jn 10:33
today concerning a **g** deed done to Acts 4:9
from among you seven men of **g** repute, Acts 6:3
Philip as he preached **g** news about the Acts 8:12
he told him the **g** news about Jesus. Acts 8:35
She was full of **g** works and acts of Acts 9:36
preaching **g** news of peace through Acts 10:36
went about doing **g** and healing all Acts 10:38
for he was a **g** man, full of the Holy Acts 11:24
we bring you the **g** news that what Acts 13:32
with you, and we bring you **g** news, Acts 14:15
for he did **g** by giving you rains from Acts 14:17
Then it seemed **g** to the apostles and Acts 15:22
it has seemed **g** to us, having come to Acts 15:25
For it has seemed **g** to the Holy Spirit Acts 15:28
before God in all **g** conscience up to Acts 23:1
and peace for everyone who does **g**, Rom 2:10
And why not do evil that **g** may come? Rom 3:8
no one does **g**, not even one." Rom 3:12
which was as **g** as dead (since he was Rom 4:19
perhaps for a **g** person one would Rom 5:7
is holy and righteous and **g**. Rom 7:12
Did that which is **g**, then, bring death Rom 7:13
death in me through what is **g**, Rom 7:13
want, I agree with the law, that it is **g**. Rom 7:16
I know that nothing **g** dwells in me, Rom 7:18
For I do not do the **g** I want, but the Rom 7:19
God all things work together for **g**, Rom 8:28
had done nothing either **g** or bad—in Rom 9:11
feet of those who preach the **g** news!" Rom 10:15
what is **g** and acceptable and perfect. Rom 12:2
what is evil; hold fast to what is **g**. Rom 12:9
by evil, but overcome evil with **g**. Rom 12:21
rulers are not a terror to **g** conduct, Rom 13:3
Then do what is **g**, and you will Rom 13:3
for he is God's servant for your **g**. But Rom 13:4
what you regard as **g** be spoken of as Rom 14:16
It is **g** not to eat meat or drink wine or Rom 14:21
of us please his neighbor for his **g**, Rom 15:2
as to what is **g** and innocent as to Rom 16:19
Your boasting is not **g**. Do you not 1 Cor 5:6
"It is **g** for a man not to have sexual 1 Cor 7:1
I say that it is **g** for them to remain 1 Cor 7:8
present distress it is **g** for a person to 1 Cor 7:26
but to promote **g** order and to secure 1 Cor 7:35
Let no one seek his own **g**, but the 1 Cor 10:24
own good, but the **g** of his neighbor. 1 Cor 10:24
of the Spirit for the common **g**. 1 Cor 12:7
"Bad company ruins **g** morals." 1 Cor 15:33
So we are always of **g** courage. We 2 Cor 5:6
Yes, we are of **g** courage, and we would 2 Cor 5:8
done in the body, whether **g** or evil. 2 Cor 5:10
Lord himself and to show our **g** will. 2 Cor 8:19
you may abound in every **g** work. 2 Cor 9:8
much of you, but for no **g** purpose. Gal 4:17
It is always **g** to be made much of for a Gal 4:18
to be made much of for a **g** purpose, Gal 4:18
word must share all **g** things with the Gal 6:6
And let us not grow weary of doing **g**, for Gal 6:9
opportunity, let us do **g** to everyone, Gal 6:10
want to make a **g** showing in the flesh Gal 6:12
created in Christ Jesus for **g** works, Eph 2:10
but only such as is **g** for building up, Eph 4:29
found in all that is **g** and right and true), Eph 5:9
rendering service with a **g** will as to the Eph 6:7
knowing that whatever **g** anyone does, Eph 6:8
that he who began a **g** work in you will Phil 1:6
and rivalry, but others from **g** will. Phil 1:15
to will and to work for his **g** pleasure. Phil 2:13
fruit in every **g** work and increasing Col 1:10
rejoicing to see your **g** order and the Col 2:5
has brought us the **g** news of your 1 Thes 3:6
always seek to do **g** to one another 1 Thes 5:15
test everything; hold fast what is **g**. 1 Thes 5:21
every resolve for **g** and every work 2 Thes 1:11
eternal comfort and **g** hope through 2 Thes 2:16
them in every **g** work and word. 2 Thes 2:17
do not grow weary in doing **g**. 2 Thes 3:13
pure heart and a **g** conscience and a 1 Tm 1:5
Now we know that the law is **g**, if one 1 Tm 1:8
by them you may wage the **g** warfare, 1 Tm 1:18
holding faith and a **g** conscience. By 1 Tm 1:19
This is **g**, and it is pleasing in the sight 1 Tm 2:3
who profess godliness—with **g** works. 1 Tm 2:10
deacons gain a **g** standing for 1 Tm 3:13
For everything created by God is **g**, 1 Tm 4:4
you will be a **g** servant of Christ Jesus, 1 Tm 4:6
faith and of the **g** doctrine that you 1 Tm 4:6
and having a reputation for **g** works: 1 Tm 5:10
has devoted herself to every **g** work. 1 Tm 5:10
So also **g** works are conspicuous, and 1 Tm 5:25
benefit by their **g** service are believers 1 Tm 6:2
Fight the **g** fight of the faith. Take 1 Tm 6:12
you made the **g** confession in the 1 Tm 6:12
Pontius Pilate made the **g** confession, 1 Tm 6:13
They are to do **g**, to be rich in good 1 Tm 6:18
are to do good, to be rich in **g** works, 1 Tm 6:18
themselves as a **g** foundation for the 1 Tm 6:19
guard the **g** deposit entrusted to you. 2 Tm 1:14
in suffering as a **g** soldier of Christ 2 Tm 2:3
about words, which does no **g**, 2 Tm 2:14
of the house, ready for every **g** work. 2 Tm 2:21
self-control, brutal, not loving **g**, 2 Tm 3:3
competent, equipped for every **g** work. 2 Tm 3:17
I have fought the **g** fight, I have 2 Tm 4:7
but hospitable, a lover of **g**, Ti 1:8
disobedient, unfit for any **g** work. Ti 1:16
to much wine. They are to teach what is **g**, Ti 2:3
in all respects to be a model of **g** works, Ti 2:7
not pilfering, but showing all **g** faith, so Ti 2:10
possession who are zealous for **g** works. Ti 2:14
be obedient, to be ready for every **g** work, Ti 3:1
be careful to devote themselves to **g** works. Ti 3:8
learn to devote themselves to **g** works, Ti 3:14
full knowledge of every **g** thing that is Phlm 1:6
For **g** news came to us just as to them, Heb 4:2
formerly received the **g** news failed to Heb 4:6
practice to distinguish **g** from evil. Heb 5:14
high priest of the **g** things that have Heb 9:11
a shadow of the **g** things to come Heb 10:1
up one another to love and **g** works, Heb 10:24
from one man, and him as **g** as dead, Heb 11:12
them, but he disciplines us for our **g**, Heb 12:10
for it is **g** for the heart to be Heb 13:9
not neglect to do **g** and to share what Heb 13:16
you with everything **g** that you may Heb 13:21
Every **g** gift and every perfect gift is from Jas 1:17
"You sit here in a **g** place," while you say Jas 2:3
What **g** is it, my brothers, if someone Jas 2:14
needed for the body, what **g** is that? Jas 2:16
By his **g** conduct let him show his Jas 3:13
to reason, full of mercy and **g** fruits, Jas 3:17
those who preached the **g** news to you 1 Pt 1:12
this word is the **g** news that was 1 Pt 1:25
indeed you have tasted that the Lord is **g**. 1 Pt 2:3
they may see your **g** deeds and glorify 1 Pt 2:12
do evil and to praise those who do **g**. 1 Pt 2:14
that by doing **g** you should put to 1 Pt 2:15
not only to the **g** and gentle but also to 1 Pt 2:18
But if when you do **g** and suffer for it 1 Pt 2:20
if you do **g** and do not fear anything that 1 Pt 3:6
desires to love life and see **g** days, 1 Pt 3:10
let him turn away from evil and do **g**; 1 Pt 3:11
you if you are zealous for what is **g**? 1 Pt 3:13
and respect, having a **g** conscience, 1 Pt 3:16
who revile your **g** behavior in Christ 1 Pt 3:16
For it is better to suffer for doing **g**, if 1 Pt 3:17
as an appeal to God for a **g** conscience, 1 Pt 3:21
as **g** stewards of God's varied grace: 1 Pt 4:10
to a faithful Creator while doing **g**. 1 Pt 4:19
you and that you may be in **g** health, 3 Jn 1:2
do not imitate evil but imitate **g**. 3 Jn 1:11
Whoever does **g** is from God; whoever 3 Jn 1:11
has received a **g** testimony from 3 Jn 1:12

GOODLY (2)

or his mighty strength, or his **g** frame. Jb 41:12
blameless will have a **g** inheritance. Prv 28:10

GOODNESS (22)

will make all my **g** pass before you and Ex 33:19
of heart for all the **g** that the LORD had 1 Kgs 8:66
and let your saints rejoice in your **g**. 2 Chr 6:41
delighted themselves in your great **g**. Neh 9:25
enjoying your great **g** that you gave Neh 9:35
Surely **g** and mercy shall follow me all Ps 23:6
remember me, for the sake of your **g**, Ps 25:7
I shall look upon the **g** of the LORD in Ps 27:13
Oh, how abundant is your **g**, which Ps 31:19
be satisfied with the **g** of your house, Ps 65:4
in your **g**, O God, you provided for the Ps 68:10
fame of your abundant **g** and shall sing Ps 145:7
and the great **g** to the house of Israel that Is 63:7
shall be radiant over the **g** of the LORD, Jer 31:12
my people shall be satisfied with my **g**, Jer 31:14
to the LORD and to his **g** in the latter days. Hos 3:5
For how great is his **g**, and how great Zec 9:17
that you yourselves are full of **g**, Rom 15:14
patience, kindness, **g**, faithfulness, Gal 5:22
But when the **g** and loving kindness of Ti 3:4
in order that your **g** might not be by Phlm 1:14
and have tasted the **g** of the word of God Heb 6:5

GOODS (40)

persons, but take the **g** for yourself." Gn 14:21
For you have felt through all my **g**; Gn 31:37
you found of all your household **g**? Gn 31:37
Have no concern for your **g**, for the Gn 45:20
also took their livestock and their **g**, Gn 46:6
to his neighbor money or **g** to keep safe, Ex 22:7
belonged to Korah and all their **g**. Nm 16:32
their cattle, their flocks, and all their **g**. Nm 31:9
the livestock and the **g** in front of them. Jgs 18:21
with him, all kinds of **g** of Damascus, 2 Kgs 8:9
them, in great numbers, **g**, clothing, 2 Chr 20:25
silver and gold, with **g** and with beasts, Ezr 1:4
with vessels of silver, with gold, with **g**, Ezr 1:6
confiscation of his **g** or for Ezr 7:26
ourselves, our children, and all our **g**. Ezr 8:21
of the land bring in **g** or any grain on Neh 10:31
and all kinds of **g** and sold them on Neh 13:16
month of Adar, and to plunder their **g**. Est 3:13
women included, and to plunder their **g**, Est 8:11
we shall find all precious **g**, we shall fill Prv 1:13
he will give all the **g** of his house. Prv 6:31
When **g** increase, they increase who Eccl 5:11

be taken, their curtains and all their **g**; Jer 49:29
with you because of your abundant **g**; Ezk 27:16
with you for your abundant **g**, Ezk 27:18
who have acquired livestock and **g**, Ezk 38:12
and gold, to take away livestock and **g**, Ezk 38:13
among them plunder, spoil, and **g**. Dn 11:24
Their **g** shall be plundered, and their Zep 1:13
strong man's house and plunder his **g**, Mt 12:29
strong man's house and plunder his **g**, Mk 3:27
who takes away your **g** do not demand Lk 6:30
guards his own palace, his **g** are safe; Lk 11:21
there I will store all my grain and my **g**. Lk 12:18
you have ample **g** laid up for many Lk 12:19
the housetop, with his **g** in the house, Lk 17:31
Lord, the half of my **g** I give to the poor. Lk 19:8
city of Thyatira, a seller of purple **g**, Acts 16:14
who buy as though they had no **g**, 1 Cor 7:30
anyone has the world's **g** and sees his 1 Jn 3:17

GOPHER (1)
Make yourself an ark of **g** wood. Make Gn 6:14

GORE (3)
has been accustomed to **g** in the past, Ex 21:29
has been accustomed to **g** in the past, Ex 21:36
with them he shall **g** the peoples, all of Dt 33:17

GORES (3)
"When an ox **g** a man or a woman to Ex 21:28
If it **g** a man's son or daughter, he shall Ex 21:31
If the ox **g** a slave, male or female, the Ex 21:32

GORGE (2)
nests in the sides of the mouth of a **g**. Jer 48:28
and I will **g** the beasts of the whole Ezk 32:4

GORGED (3)
it is sated with blood; it is **g** with fat, with Is 34:6
of blood, and their soil shall be **g** with fat. Is 34:7
and all the birds were **g** with their flesh. Rv 19:21

GOSHEN (15)
You shall dwell in the land of **G**, and Gn 45:10
to show the way before him in **G**, Gn 46:28
and they came into the land of **G**. Gn 46:28
went up to meet Israel his father in **G**. Gn 46:29
that you may dwell in the land of **G**, Gn 46:34
Canaan. They are now in the land of **G**." Gn 47:1
let your servants dwell in the land of **G**." Gn 47:4
Let them settle in the land of **G**, and if Gn 47:6
in the land of Egypt, in the land of **G**. Gn 47:27
and their herds were left in the land of **G**. Gn 50:8
on that day I will set apart the land of **G**, Ex 8:22
Only in the land of **G**, where the people of Ex 9:26
as far as Gaza, and all the country of **G**, Jos 10:41
all the land of **G** and the lowland and Jos 11:16
G, Holon, and Giloh: eleven cities with Jos 15:51

GOSPEL (96)
and proclaiming the **g** of the kingdom Mt 4:23
and proclaiming the **g** of the kingdom Mt 9:35
And this **g** of the kingdom will be Mt 24:14
wherever this **g** is proclaimed in the Mt 26:13
The beginning of the **g** of Jesus Christ, Mk 1:1
into Galilee, proclaiming the **g** of God, Mk 1:14
is at hand; repent and believe in the **g**." Mk 1:15
or lands, for my sake and for the **g**, Mk 10:29
And the **g** must first be proclaimed to Mk 13:10
wherever the **g** is proclaimed in the Mk 14:9
world and proclaim the **g** to the whole Mk 16:15
preaching the **g** and healing everywhere. Lk 9:6
in the temple and preaching the **g**, Lk 20:1
preaching the **g** to many villages of the Acts 8:25
through he preached the **g** to all the Acts 8:40
there they continued to preach the **g**. Acts 14:7
they had preached the **g** to that city Acts 14:21
hear the word of the **g** and believe. Acts 15:7
had called us to preach the **g** to them. Acts 16:10
to testify to the **g** of the grace of God. Acts 20:24
be an apostle, set apart for the **g** of God, Rom 1:1
I serve with my spirit in the **g** of his Son, Rom 1:9
eager to preach the **g** to you also who Rom 1:15
For I am not ashamed of the **g**, for it is Rom 1:16
on that day when, according to my **g**, Rom 2:16
But they have not all obeyed the **g**. Rom 10:16
As regards the **g**, they are enemies of Rom 11:28
in the priestly service of the **g** of God, Rom 15:16
the ministry of the **g** of Christ; Rom 15:19
make it my ambition to preach the **g**, Rom 15:20
according to my **g** and the preaching Rom 16:25
me to baptize but to preach the **g**, 1 Cor 1:17
father in Christ Jesus through the **g**. 1 Cor 4:15
obstacle in the way of the **g** of Christ. 1 Cor 9:12
who proclaim the **g** should get their 1 Cor 9:14
should get their living by the **g**. 1 Cor 9:14
For if I preach the **g**, that gives me no 1 Cor 9:16
Woe to me if I do not preach the **g**! 1 Cor 9:16
I may present the **g** free of charge, 1 Cor 9:18
to make full use of my right in the **g**. 1 Cor 9:18
I do it all for the sake of the **g**, that I 1 Cor 9:23
brothers, of the **g** I preached to you, 1 Cor 15:1
to Troas to preach the **g** of Christ, 2 Cor 2:12
And even if our **g** is veiled, it is veiled 2 Cor 4:3
seeing the light of the **g** of the glory of 2 Cor 4:4
churches for his preaching of the **g**. 2 Cor 8:18
your confession of the **g** of Christ, 2 Cor 9:13
the way to you with the **g** of Christ. 2 Cor 10:14
may preach the **g** in lands beyond 2 Cor 10:16
you accept a different **g** from the one 2 Cor 11:4
because I preached God's **g** to you free 2 Cor 11:7
Christ and are turning to a different **g**— Gal 1:6
you and want to distort the **g** of Christ. Gal 1:7
preach to you a **g** contrary to the one Gal 1:8
preaching to you a **g** contrary to the one Gal 1:9
that the **g** that was preached by me is Gal 1:11
that was preached by me is not man's **g**. Gal 1:11
seemed influential) the **g** that I proclaim Gal 2:2
the truth of the **g** might be preserved for Gal 2:5
entrusted with the **g** to the Gal 2:7
entrusted with the **g** to the circumcised Gal 2:7
was not in step with the truth of the **g**, Gal 2:14
preached the **g** beforehand to Abraham, Gal 3:8
that I preached the **g** to you at first, Gal 4:13
word of truth, the **g** of your salvation, Eph 1:13
promise in Christ Jesus through the **g**. Eph 3:6
Of this **g** I was made a minister Eph 3:7
the readiness given by the **g** of peace. Eph 6:15
boldly to proclaim the mystery of the **g**, Eph 6:19
your partnership in the **g** from the first Phil 1:5
in the defense and confirmation of the **g**. Phil 1:7
me has really served to advance the **g**, Phil 1:12
I am put here for the defense of the **g**. Phil 1:16
of life be worthy of the **g** of Christ, Phil 1:27
side by side for the faith of the **g**, Phil 1:27
a father he has served with me in the **g**. Phil 2:22
with me in the **g** together with Clement Phil 4:3
know that in the beginning of the **g**, Phil 4:15
before in the word of the truth, the **g**, Col 1:5
from the hope of the **g** that you heard, Col 1:23
because our **g** came to you not only 1 Thes 1:5
to declare to you the **g** of God in the 1 Thes 2:2
by God to be entrusted with the **g**, 1 Thes 2:4
you not only the **g** of God but also 1 Thes 2:8
we proclaimed to you the **g** of God. 1 Thes 2:9
God's coworker in the **g** of Christ, 1 Thes 3:2
do not obey the **g** of our Lord Jesus. 2 Thes 1:8
To this he called you through our **g**, 2 Thes 2:14
with the glorious **g** of the blessed 1 Tm 1:11
in suffering for the **g** by the power of 2 Tm 1:8
immortality to light through the **g**, 2 Tm 1:10
of David, as preached in my **g**, 2 Tm 2:8
during my imprisonment for the **g**, Phlm 1:13
this is why the **g** was preached even to 1 Pt 4:6
for those who do not obey the **g** of God? 1 Pt 4:17
with an eternal **g** to proclaim to those Rv 14:6

GOSPEL'S (1)
life for my sake and the **g** will save it. Mk 8:35

GOSSIP (2)
became the talk and evil **g** of the people, Ezk 36:3
anger, hostility, slander, **g**, conceit, 2 Cor 12:20

GOSSIPS (2)
deceit, maliciousness. They are **g**, Rom 1:29
idlers, but also **g** and busybodies, 1 Tm 5:13

GOT (40)
hand and fled and **g** out of the house. Gn 39:12
me and fled and **g** out of the house." Gn 39:15
robbery or what he **g** by oppression or the Lv 6:4
So they **g** away from the dwelling of Nm 16:27
And she **g** off her donkey, and Caleb Jos 15:18
And Sisera **g** down from his chariot and Jgs 4:15
of Megiddo; they **g** no spoils of silver. Jgs 5:19
she hurried and **g** down from the 1 Sm 25:23
After this Absalom **g** himself a 2 Sm 15:1
Then he **g** up again and walked once 2 Kgs 4:35
he **g** down from the chariot to meet 2 Kgs 5:21
Jehoiada **g** for him two wives, and he 2 Chr 24:3
and **g** relief from their enemies and Est 9:16
on which the Jews **g** relief from their Est 9:22
of kings and provinces. I **g** singers, Eccl 2:8
I signed the deed, sealed it, **g** witnesses, Jer 32:10
nor his army **g** anything from Tyre Ezk 29:18
man, yet he **g** possession of the land; Ezk 33:24
He **g** down on his knees three times a Dn 6:10
And when he **g** into the boat, his Mt 8:23
so that he **g** into a boat and sat down. Mt 13:2
"Come." So Peter **g** out of the boat and Mt 14:29
And when they **g** into the boat, the Mt 14:32
he **g** into the boat and went to the Mt 15:39
so that he **g** into a boat and sat in it on Mk 4:1
immediately the girl **g** up and began Mk 5:42
all the towns and **g** there ahead of them. Mk 6:33
And he **g** into the boat with them, and Mk 6:51
And when they **g** out of the boat, the Mk 6:54
And immediately he **g** into the boat Mk 8:10
And he left them, **g** into the boat again, Mk 8:13
One day he **g** into a boat with his Lk 8:22
fear. So he **g** into the boat and returned. Lk 8:37
her spirit returned, and she **g** up at once. Lk 8:55
g into a boat, and started across the sea to Jn 6:17
they themselves **g** into the boats and Jn 6:24
you." They went out and **g** into the boat, Jn 21:3
When they **g** out on land, they saw a Jn 21:9
After these days we **g** ready and went Acts 21:15
say, and **g** the better of you by deceit. 2 Cor 12:16

GOTTEN (5)
"I have **g** a man with the help of the Gn 4:1
when I have **g** glory over Pharaoh, Ex 14:18
any such animals **g** from a foreigner. Lv 22:25
of my hand have **g** me this wealth.' Dt 8:17
foe, and those who hate us have **g** spoil. Ps 44:10

GOUGE (1)
you, that I **g** out all your right eyes, 1 Sm 11:2

GOUGED (2)
seized him and **g** out his eyes Jgs 16:21
you would have **g** out your eyes and Gal 4:15

GOURDS (6)
in the form of **g** and open flowers. 1 Kgs 6:18
Under its brim were **g**, for ten cubits, 1 Kgs 7:24
The **g** were in two rows, cast with it 1 Kgs 7:24
gathered from it his lap full of wild **g**, 2 Kgs 4:39
Under it were figures of **g**, for ten 2 Chr 4:3
The **g** were in two rows, cast with it 2 Chr 4:3

GOVERN (7)
understanding mind to **g** your people, 1 Kgs 3:9
who is able to **g** this your great 1 Kgs 3:9
said to him, "Do you now **g** Israel? 1 Kgs 21:7
for who can **g** this people of yours, 2 Chr 1:10
that you may **g** my people over 2 Chr 1:11
Shall one who hates justice **g**? Will you Jb 34:17
rule, and nobles, all who **g** justly. Prv 8:16

GOVERNING (3)
household, **g** the people of the land. 2 Kgs 15:5
household, **g** the people of the land. 2 Chr 26:21
person be subject to the **g** authorities. Rom 13:1

GOVERNMENT (2)
and the **g** shall be upon his shoulder, and Is 9:6
Of the increase of his **g** and of peace there Is 9:7

GOVERNOR (53)
Now Joseph was **g** over the land. He was Gn 42:6
And there was one **g** who was over the 1 Kgs 4:19
back to Amon the **g** of the city and 1 Kgs 22:26
of the gate of Joshua the **g** of the city, 2 Kgs 23:8
son of Ahikam, son of Shaphan, **g**. 2 Kgs 25:22
Babylon had appointed Gedaliah **g**, 2 Kgs 25:23
back to Amon the **g** of the city and 2 Chr 18:25
Ishmael, the **g** of the house of Judah, 2 Chr 19:11
and Maaseiah the **g** of the city, 2 Chr 34:8
The **g** told them that they were not to Ezr 2:63
same time Tattenai the **g** of the province Ezr 5:3
letter that Tattenai the **g** of the province Ezr 5:6
was Sheshbazzar, whom he had made **g**; Ezr 5:14
g of the province Beyond the River, Ezr 6:6
Let the **g** of the Jews and the elders of the Ezr 6:7
the **g** of the province Beyond the River, Ezr 6:13
the seat of the **g** of the province Beyond Neh 3:7
appointed to be their **g** in the land of Neh 5:14
ate the food allowance of the **g**. Neh 5:14
demand the food allowance of the **g**, Neh 5:18
and Hananiah the **g** of the castle Neh 7:2
The **g** told them that they were not to Neh 7:65
The **g** gave to the treasury 1,000 darics Neh 7:70
And Nehemiah, who was the **g**, and Neh 8:9
seals are the names of Nehemiah the **g**, Neh 10:1
days of Nehemiah the **g** and of Ezra, Neh 12:26
king of Babylon appointed **g** of the cities Jer 40:5
the son of Ahikam **g** in the land and Jer 40:7
son of Shaphan, as **g** over them, Jer 40:11
of Babylon had appointed **g** in the land. Jer 41:2
of Babylon had made **g** over the land. Jer 41:18
the son of Shealtiel, **g** of Judah, Hg 1:1
the son of Shealtiel, **g** of Judah, Hg 1:14
the son of Shealtiel, **g** of Judah, Hg 2:2
"Speak to Zerubbabel, **g** of Judah, Hg 2:21
Present that to your **g**; will he accept you Mal 1:8
and delivered him over to Pilate the **g**. Mt 27:2
Now Jesus stood before the **g**, and the Mt 27:11
the governor, and the **g** asked him, Mt 27:11
so that the **g** was greatly amazed. Mt 27:14
at the feast the **g** was accustomed to Mt 27:15
The **g** again said to them, "Which of Mt 27:21
the soldiers of the **g** took Jesus into the Mt 27:27
when Quirinius was **g** of Syria. Lk 2:2
Caesar, Pontius Pilate being **g** of Judea, Lk 3:1
the authority and jurisdiction of the **g**. Lk 20:20

and bring him safely to Felix the **g**." Acts 23:24
Lysias, to his Excellency the **g** Felix, Acts 23:26
and delivered the letter to the **g**, Acts 23:33
laid before the **g** their case against Acts 24:1
And when the **g** had nodded to him to Acts 24:10
and the **g** and Bernice and those who Acts 26:30
the **g** under King Aretas was 2 Cor 11:32

GOVERNOR'S (5)
took Jesus into the **g** headquarters, Mt 27:27
And if this comes to the **g** ears, we will Mt 28:14
palace (that is, the **g** headquarters), Mk 15:16
of Caiaphas to the **g** headquarters. Jn 18:28
did not enter the **g** headquarters, Jn 18:28

GOVERNORS (32)
the west and from the **g** of the land. 1 Kgs 10:15
the servants of the **g** of the districts." 1 Kgs 20:14
the servants of the **g** of the districts, 1 Kgs 20:15
The servants of the **g** of the districts 1 Kgs 20:17
the servants of the **g** of the districts 1 Kgs 20:19
of Arabia and the **g** of the land 2 Chr 9:14
the nobles, the **g** of the people, 2 Chr 23:20
rest of their associates, the judges, the **g**, Ezr 4:9
and his associates the **g** who were in the Ezr 5:6
and your associates the **g** who are in the Ezr 6:6
satraps and to the **g** of the province Ezr 8:36
given me to the **g** of the province Beyond Neh 2:7
I came to the **g** of the province Beyond Neh 2:9
The former **g** who were before me laid Neh 5:15
and the nobles and **g** of the provinces Est 1:3
satraps and to the **g** over all the Est 3:12
the satraps and the **g** and the officials of Est 8:9
the satraps and the **g** and the royal agents Est 9:3
I break in pieces **g** and commanders. Jer 51:23
of the Medes, with their **g** and deputies, Jer 51:28
her officials and her wise men, her **g**, Jer 51:57
clothed in purple, **g** and commanders, Ezk 23:6
the Assyrians, **g** and commanders, Ezk 23:12
men, **g** and commanders all of them, Ezk 23:23
gather the satraps, the prefects, and the **g**, Dn 3:2
Then the satraps, the prefects, and the **g**, Dn 3:3
And the satraps, the prefects, the **g**, and Dn 3:27
the counselors and the **g** are agreed that Dn 6:7
will be dragged before **g** and kings for Mt 10:18
you will stand before **g** and kings for Mk 13:9
before kings and **g** for my name's Lk 21:12
or to **g** as sent by him to punish those 1 Pt 2:14

GOZAN (5)
and on the Habor, the river of **G**, 2 Kgs 17:6
and on the Habor, the river of **G**, 2 Kgs 18:11
that my fathers destroyed, **G**, Haran, 2 Kgs 19:12
Halah, Habor, Hara, and the river **G**, 1 Chr 5:26
that my fathers destroyed, **G**, Haran, Is 37:12

GRACE (131)
and she won **g** and favor in his sight Est 2:17
sons of men; **g** is poured upon your lips; Ps 45:2
to my prayer; listen to my plea for **g**. Ps 86:6
the sword found **g** in the wilderness; Jer 31:2
forward the top stone amid shouts of '**G**, Zec 4:7
top stone amid shouts of 'Grace, **g** to it!'" Zec 4:7
Jerusalem a spirit of **g** and pleas for Zec 12:10
Son from the Father, full of **g** and truth. Jn 1:14
we have all received, **g** upon grace. Jn 1:16
we have all received, grace upon **g**. Jn 1:16
g and truth came through Jesus Christ. Jn 1:17
Jesus, and great **g** was upon them all. Acts 4:33
And Stephen, full of **g** and power, was Acts 6:8
When he came and saw the **g** of God, Acts 11:23
them to continue in the **g** of God. Acts 13:43
who bore witness to the word of his **g**, Acts 14:3
been commended to the **g** of God for Acts 14:26
be saved through the **g** of the Lord Acts 15:11
by the brothers to the **g** of the Lord. Acts 15:40
those who through **g** had believed, Acts 18:27
to testify to the gospel of the **g** of God. Acts 20:24
you to God and to the word of his **g**, Acts 20:32
we have received **g** and apostleship to Rom 1:5
G to you and peace from God our Rom 1:7
and are justified by his **g** as a gift, Rom 3:24
may rest on **g** and be guaranteed Rom 4:16
by faith into this **g** in which we stand, Rom 5:2
much more have the **g** of God and the Rom 5:15
the free gift by the **g** of that one man Rom 5:15
the abundance of **g** and the free Rom 5:17
increased, **g** abounded all the more, Rom 5:20
g also might reign through Rom 5:21
to continue in sin that **g** may abound? Rom 6:1
you are not under law but under **g**. Rom 6:14
we are not under law but under **g**? Rom 6:15
time there is a remnant, chosen by **g**. Rom 11:5
But if it is by **g**, it is no longer on the Rom 11:6
otherwise **g** would no longer be grace. Rom 11:6
otherwise grace would no longer be **g**. Rom 11:6
For by the **g** given to me I say to Rom 12:3
differ according to the **g** given to us, Rom 12:6
because of the **g** given me by God Rom 15:15
The **g** of our Lord Jesus Christ be Rom 16:20
G to you and peace from God our 1 Cor 1:3
you because of the **g** of God that was 1 Cor 1:4
According to the **g** of God given to 1 Cor 3:10
But by the **g** of God I am what I am, 1 Cor 15:10
and his **g** toward me was not in 1 Cor 15:10
I, but the **g** of God that is with me. 1 Cor 15:10
The **g** of the Lord Jesus be with you. 1 Cor 16:23
G to you and peace from God our 2 Cor 1:2
earthly wisdom but by the **g** of God, 2 Cor 1:12
might have a second experience of **g**. 2 Cor 1:15
so that as **g** extends to more and more 2 Cor 4:15
you not to receive the **g** of God in vain. 2 Cor 6:1
about the **g** of God that has been given 2 Cor 8:1
complete among you this act of **g**. 2 Cor 8:6
see that you excel in this act of **g** also. 2 Cor 8:7
For you know the **g** of our Lord Jesus 2 Cor 8:9
out this act of **g** that is being 2 Cor 8:19
is able to make all **g** abound to you, 2 Cor 9:8
of the surpassing **g** of God upon 2 Cor 9:14
said to me, "My **g** is sufficient for you, 2 Cor 12:9
The **g** of the Lord Jesus Christ and 2 Cor 13:14
G to you and peace from God our Father Gal 1:3
who called you in the **g** of Christ and are Gal 1:6
I was born, and who called me by his **g**, Gal 1:15
perceived the **g** that was given to me, Gal 2:9
I do not nullify the **g** of God, for if Gal 2:21
by the law; you have fallen away from **g**. Gal 5:4
The **g** of our Lord Jesus Christ be with Gal 6:18
G to you and peace from God our Father Eph 1:2
to the praise of his glorious **g**, with Eph 1:6
according to the riches of his **g**, Eph 1:7
with Christ—by **g** you have been saved Eph 2:5
riches of his **g** in kindness toward Eph 2:7
For by **g** you have been saved through Eph 2:8
stewardship of God's **g** that was given Eph 3:2
minister according to the gift of God's **g**, Eph 3:7
least of all the saints, this **g** was given, Eph 3:8
But **g** was given to each one of us Eph 4:7
that it may give **g** to those who hear. Eph 4:29
G be with all who love our Lord Jesus Eph 6:24
G to you and peace from God our Father Phil 1:2
for you are all partakers with me of **g**, Phil 1:7
The **g** of the Lord Jesus Christ be with Phil 4:23
G to you and peace from God our Father. Col 1:2
it and understood the **g** of God in truth, Col 1:6
Remember my chains. **G** be with you. Col 4:18
Lord Jesus Christ: **G** to you and peace. 1 Thes 1:1
The **g** of our Lord Jesus Christ be 1 Thes 5:28
G to you and peace from God our 2 Thes 1:2
according to the **g** of our God and 2 Thes 1:12
comfort and good hope through **g**, 2 Thes 2:16
The **g** of our Lord Jesus Christ be 2 Thes 3:18
G, mercy, and peace from God the 1 Tm 1:2
and the **g** of our Lord overflowed for 1 Tm 1:14
from the faith. **G** be with you. 1 Tm 6:21
G, mercy, and peace from God the 2 Tm 1:2
but because of his own purpose and **g**, 2 Tm 1:9
be strengthened by the **g** that is in 2 Tm 2:1
be with your spirit. **G** be with you. 2 Tm 4:22
G and peace from God the Father and Ti 1:4
For the **g** of God has appeared, bringing Ti 2:11
being justified by his **g** we might become Ti 3:7
love us in the faith. **G** be with you all. Ti 3:15
G to you and peace from God our Phlm 1:3
The **g** of the Lord Jesus Christ be with Phlm 1:25
so that by the **g** of God he might taste Heb 2:9
draw near to the throne of **g**, Heb 4:16
receive mercy and find **g** to help in Heb 4:16
and has outraged the Spirit of **g**? Heb 10:29
no one fails to obtain the **g** of God; Heb 12:15
for the heart to be strengthened by **g**, Heb 13:9
G be with all of you. Heb 13:25
But he gives more **g**. Therefore it says, Jas 4:6
the proud, but gives **g** to the humble." Jas 4:6
May **g** and peace be multiplied to you. 1 Pt 1:2
who prophesied about the **g** that was to 1 Pt 1:10
hope fully on the **g** that will be brought 1 Pt 1:13
they are heirs with you of the **g** of life, 1 Pt 3:7
as good stewards of God's varied **g**: 1 Pt 4:10
the proud but gives **g** to the humble." 1 Pt 5:5
suffered a little while, the God of all **g**, 1 Pt 5:10
declaring that this is the true **g** of God. 1 Pt 5:12
May **g** and peace be multiplied to you in 2 Pt 1:2
But grow in the **g** and knowledge of our 2 Pt 3:18
G, mercy, and peace will be with us, 2 Jn 1:3
who pervert the **g** of our God into Jude 1:4
G to you and peace from him who is and Rv 1:4
The **g** of the Lord Jesus be with all. Rv 22:21

GRACEFUL (4)
for they are a **g** garland for your head Prv 1:9
She will place on your head a **g** garland; Prv 4:9
a lovely deer, a **g** doe. Let her breasts fill Prv 5:19
of the prostitute, **g** and of deadly charms, Na 3:4

GRACIOUS (50)
you spoke to me? God be **g** to you, Gn 43:29
And I will be **g** to whom I will be Ex 33:19
I will be gracious to whom I will be **g**, Ex 33:19
LORD, the LORD, a God merciful and **g**, Ex 34:6
face to shine upon you and be **g** to you; Nm 6:25
whether the LORD will be **g** to me, 2 Sm 12:22
But the LORD was **g** to them and had 2 Kgs 13:23
LORD your God is **g** and merciful and 2 Chr 30:9
a God ready to forgive, **g** and merciful, Neh 9:17
for you are a **g** and merciful God. Neh 9:31
in distress. Be **g** to me and hear my prayer! Ps 4:1
Be **g** to me, O LORD, for I am languishing; Ps 6:2
Be **g** to me, O LORD! See my affliction Ps 9:13
Turn to me and be **g** to me, for I am Ps 25:16
integrity; redeem me, and be **g** to me. Ps 26:11
I cry aloud; be **g** to me and answer me! Ps 27:7
Be **g** to me, O LORD, for I am in distress; Ps 31:9
As for me, I said, "O LORD, be **g** to me; Ps 41:4
But you, O LORD, be **g** to me, and raise Ps 41:10
Be **g** to me, O God, for man tramples on Ps 56:1
May God be **g** to us and bless us and Ps 67:1
Has God forgotten to be **g**? Has he in Ps 77:9
Be **g** to me, O Lord, for to you do I cry all Ps 86:3
you, O Lord, are a God merciful and **g**, Ps 86:15
Turn to me and be **g** to me; give your Ps 86:16
The LORD is merciful and **g**, slow to Ps 103:8
the LORD is **g** and merciful. Ps 111:4
he is **g**, merciful, and righteous. Ps 112:4
G is the LORD, and righteous; our God is Ps 116:5
be **g** to me according to your promise. Ps 119:58
Turn to me and be **g** to me, as is your Ps 119:132
The LORD is **g** and merciful, slow to Ps 145:8
A **g** woman gets honor, and violent Prv 11:16
to the LORD, but **g** words are pure. Prv 15:26
G words are like a honeycomb, Prv 16:24
purity of heart, and whose speech is **g**, Prv 22:11
Therefore the LORD waits to be **g** to you, Is 30:18
He will surely be **g** to you at the sound of Is 30:19
O LORD, be **g** to us; we wait for you. Be our Is 33:2
LORD, your God, for he is **g** and merciful, Jl 2:13
will be **g** to the remnant of Joseph. Am 5:15
knew that you are a **g** God and merciful, Jon 4:2
the LORD answered **g** and comforting Zec 1:13
the favor of God, that he may be **g** to us. Mal 1:9
yes, Father, for such was your **g** will. Mt 11:26
and marveled at the **g** words that were Lk 4:22
yes, Father, for such was your **g** will. Lk 10:21
Let your speech always be **g**, seasoned Col 4:6
For this is a **g** thing, when, mindful of 1 Pt 2:19
this is a **g** thing in the sight of God. 1 Pt 2:20

GRACIOUSLY (8)
whom God has **g** given your servant." Gn 33:5
you, because God has dealt **g** with me, Gn 33:11
will say to them, 'Grant them **g** to us, Jgs 21:22
g freed Jehoiachin king of Judah 2 Kgs 25:27
far from me and **g** teach me your law! Ps 119:29
when he speaks **g**, believe him not, for Prv 26:25
not also with him **g** give us all things? Rom 8:32
your prayers I will be **g** given to you. Phlm 1:22

GRAFT (1)
has the power to **g** them in again. Rom 11:23

GRAFTED (5)
were **g** in among the others and now Rom 11:17
broken off so that I might be **g** in." Rom 11:19
in their unbelief, will be **g** in, Rom 11:23
is by nature a wild olive tree, and **g**, Rom 11:24
be **g** back into their own olive tree. Rom 11:24

GRAIN (260)
of the earth and plenty of **g** and wine. Gn 27:28
and with **g** and wine I have sustained Gn 27:37
And behold, seven ears of **g**, plump and Gn 41:5
and store up **g** under the authority Gn 41:35
Joseph stored up **g** in great abundance, Gn 41:49
earth came to Egypt to Joseph to buy **g**, Gn 41:57
learned that there was **g** for sale in Gn 42:1
heard that there is **g** for sale in Egypt. Gn 42:2
Go down and buy **g** for us there, that we Gn 42:2
brothers went down to buy **g** in Egypt. Gn 42:3
rest go and carry **g** for the famine of Gn 42:19
gave orders to fill their bags with **g**, Gn 42:25
donkeys with their **g** and departed. Gn 42:26
and take **g** for the famine of your Gn 42:33
they had eaten the **g** that they had Gn 43:2
with his money for the **g**." And he did as Gn 44:2
and ten female donkeys loaded with **g**, Gn 45:23
in exchange for the **g** that they bought. Gn 47:14
so that the stacked **g** or the standing Ex 22:6
grain or the standing **g** or the field is Ex 22:6
offer with it a **g** offering and its drink Ex 29:41
on it, or a burnt offering, or a **g** offering, Ex 30:9
it the burnt offering and the **g** offering, Ex 40:29

"When anyone brings a **g** offering as an Lv 2:1
But the rest of the **g** offering shall be for Lv 2:3
"When you bring a **g** offering baked in Lv 2:4
if your offering is a **g** offering baked on a Lv 2:5
pieces and pour oil on it; it is a **g** offering. Lv 2:6
if your offering is a **g** offering cooked in a Lv 2:7
you shall bring the **g** offering that is Lv 2:8
take from the **g** offering its memorial Lv 2:9
But the rest of the **g** offering shall be for Lv 2:10
"No **g** offering that you bring to the LORD Lv 2:11
season all your **g** offerings with salt. Lv 2:13
God be missing from your **g** offering; Lv 2:13
"If you offer a **g** offering of firstfruits to Lv 2:14
shall offer for the **g** offering of your Lv 2:14
ears, roasted with fire, crushed new **g**. Lv 2:14
lay frankincense on it; it is a **g** offering. Lv 2:15
some of the crushed **g** and some of the Lv 2:16
be for the priest, as in the **g** offering." Lv 5:13
"And this is the law of the **g** offering. The Lv 6:14
the fine flour of the **g** offering and its oil Lv 6:15
that is on the **g** offering and burn this Lv 6:15
of fine flour as a regular **g** offering, Lv 6:20
mixed, in baked pieces like a **g** offering, Lv 6:21
Every **g** offering of a priest shall be Lv 6:23
And every **g** offering baked in the oven Lv 7:9
And every **g** offering, mixed with oil or Lv 7:10
of the burnt offering, of the **g** offering, Lv 7:37
the LORD, and a **g** offering mixed with oil, Lv 9:4
And he presented the **g** offering, took a Lv 9:17
"Take the **g** offering that is left of the Lv 10:12
falls upon any seed **g** that is to be Lv 11:37
and a **g** offering of three tenths of an Lv 14:10
burnt offering and the **g** offering on the Lv 14:20
flour mixed with oil for a **g** offering, Lv 14:21
burnt offering, along with a **g** offering. Lv 14:31
And the **g** offering with it shall be two Lv 23:13
eat neither bread nor **g** parched or fresh Lv 23:14
you shall present a **g** offering of new Lv 23:16
a grain offering of new **g** to the LORD. Lv 23:16
with their **g** offering and their drink Lv 23:18
burnt offerings and **g** offerings, Lv 23:37
fragrant incense, the regular **g** offering, Nm 4:16
on it, for it is a **g** offering of jealousy, Nm 5:15
jealousy, a **g** offering of remembrance, Nm 5:15
her hands the **g** offering of Nm 5:18
which is the **g** offering of jealousy. Nm 5:18
shall take the **g** offering of jealousy Nm 5:25
and shall wave the **g** offering before the Nm 5:25
shall take a handful of the **g** offering, Nm 5:26
and their **g** offering and their drink Nm 6:15
shall offer also its **g** offering and its Nm 6:17
flour mixed with oil for a **g** offering; Nm 7:13
flour mixed with oil for a **g** offering; Nm 7:19
flour mixed with oil for a **g** offering; Nm 7:25
flour mixed with oil for a **g** offering; Nm 7:31
flour mixed with oil for a **g** offering; Nm 7:37
flour mixed with oil for a **g** offering; Nm 7:43
flour mixed with oil for a **g** offering; Nm 7:49
flour mixed with oil for a **g** offering; Nm 7:55
flour mixed with oil for a **g** offering; Nm 7:61
flour mixed with oil for a **g** offering; Nm 7:67
flour mixed with oil for a **g** offering; Nm 7:73
flour mixed with oil for a **g** offering; Nm 7:79
lambs a year old, with their **g** offering; Nm 7:87
the herd and its **g** offering of fine flour Nm 8:8
offer to the LORD a **g** offering of a tenth Nm 15:4
shall offer for a **g** offering two tenths of Nm 15:6
with the bull a **g** offering of three Nm 15:9
with its **g** offering and its drink Nm 15:24
every **g** offering of theirs and every sin Nm 18:9
all the best of the wine and of the **g**, Nm 18:12
though it were the **g** of the threshing Nm 18:27
It is no place for **g** or figs or vines or Nm 20:5
an ephah of fine flour for a **g** offering, Nm 28:5
Like the **g** offering of the morning, and Nm 28:8
an ephah of fine flour for a **g** offering, Nm 28:9
an ephah of fine flour for a **g** offering, Nm 28:12
tenths of fine flour for a **g** offering, Nm 28:12
with oil as a **g** offering for every lamb; Nm 28:13
also their **g** offering of fine flour Nm 28:20
when you offer a **g** offering of new Nm 28:26
a grain offering of new **g** to the LORD at Nm 28:26
also their **g** offering of fine flour Nm 28:28
burnt offering and its **g** offering, Nm 28:31
also their **g** offering of fine flour mixed Nm 29:3
of the new moon, and its **g** offering, Nm 29:6
burnt offering and its **g** offering, Nm 29:6
And their **g** offering shall be of fine Nm 29:9
burnt offering and its **g** offering, Nm 29:11
and their **g** offering of fine flour Nm 29:14
its **g** offering and its drink offering. Nm 29:16
with the **g** offering and the drink Nm 29:18
burnt offering and its **g** offering, Nm 29:19
with the **g** offering and the drink Nm 29:21
offering and its **g** offering and its Nm 29:22
with the **g** offering and the drink Nm 29:24
its **g** offering and its drink offering. Nm 29:25
with the **g** offering and the drink Nm 29:27
offering and its **g** offering and its Nm 29:28
with the **g** offering and the drink Nm 29:30
regular burnt offering, its **g** offering, Nm 29:31
with the **g** offering and the drink Nm 29:33
regular burnt offering, its **g** offering, Nm 29:34
and the **g** offering and the drink Nm 29:37
offering and its **g** offering and its Nm 29:38
offerings, and for your **g** offerings, Nm 29:39
your **g** and your wine and your oil, Dt 7:13
may gather in your **g** and your wine Dt 11:14
towns the tithe of your **g** or of your wine Dt 12:17
there, you shall eat the tithe of your **g**, Dt 14:23
the sickle is first put to the standing **g**. Dt 16:9
The firstfruits of your **g**, of your wine Dt 18:4
you go into your neighbor's standing **g**, Dt 23:25
a sickle to your neighbor's standing **g**. Dt 23:25
an ox when it is treading out the **g**. Dt 25:4
it also shall not leave you **g**, wine, or oil, Dt 28:51
lived alone, in a land of **g** and wine, Dt 33:28
land, unleavened cakes and parched **g**. Jos 5:11
burnt offerings or **g** offerings or peace Jos 22:23
an altar for burnt offering, **g** offering, Jos 22:29
took the young goat with the **g** offering, Jgs 13:19
burnt offering and a **g** offering at our Jgs 13:23
go into the standing **g** of the Philistines Jgs 15:5
fire to the stacked **g** and the standing Jgs 15:5
to the stacked grain and the standing **g**, Jgs 15:5
among the ears of **g** after him in whose Ru 2:2
reapers, and he passed to her roasted **g**. Ru 2:14
to lie down at the end of the heap of **g**. Ru 3:7
the tenth of your **g** and of your 1 Sm 8:15
brothers an ephah of this parched **g**, 1 Sm 17:17
seahs of parched **g** and a hundred 1 Sm 25:18
well's mouth and scattered **g** on it, 2 Sm 17:19
wheat, barley, flour, parched **g**, 2 Sm 17:28
offering and the **g** offering and the 1 Kgs 8:64
offering and the **g** offering and the 1 Kgs 8:64
barley and fresh ears of **g** in his sack. 2 Kgs 4:42
offering and his **g** offering and 2 Kgs 16:13
and the evening **g** offering and the 2 Kgs 16:15
burnt offering and his **g** offering, 2 Kgs 16:15
and their **g** offering and their drink 2 Kgs 16:15
your own land, a land of **g** and wine, 2 Kgs 18:32
wood and the wheat for a **g** offering; 1 Chr 21:23
the flour for the **g** offering, 1 Chr 23:29
offering and the **g** offering and the 2 Chr 7:7
in abundance the firstfruits of **g**, 2 Chr 31:5
storehouses also for the yield of **g**, 2 Chr 32:28
with their **g** offerings and their drink Ezr 7:17
So let us get **g**, that we may eat and keep Neh 5:2
our houses to get **g** because of the Neh 5:3
are lending them money and **g**. Neh 5:10
and the percentage of money, **g**, wine, Neh 5:11
in goods or any **g** on the Sabbath day Neh 10:31
the showbread, the regular **g** offering, Neh 10:33
shall bring the contribution of **g**, Neh 10:39
they had previously put the **g** offering, Neh 13:5
the vessels, and the tithes of **g**, Neh 13:5
with the **g** offering and the Neh 13:9
all Judah brought the tithe of the **g**, Neh 13:12
in heaps of **g** and loading them Neh 13:15
they are cut off like the heads of **g**. Jb 24:24
he will return your **g** and gather it to Jb 39:12
they have when their **g** and wine abound. Ps 4:7
you provide their **g**, for so you have Ps 65:9
the valleys deck themselves with **g**, Ps 65:13
there be abundance of **g** in the land; Ps 72:16
to eat and gave them the **g** of heaven. Ps 78:24
people curse him who holds back **g**, Prv 11:26
with a pestle along with crushed **g**, Prv 27:22
the reaper gathers standing **g** and his arm Is 17:5
one gleans the ears of **g** in the Valley of Is 17:5
waters your revenue was the **g** of Shihor, Is 23:3
of Egypt the LORD will thresh out the **g**, Is 27:12
Does one crush **g** for bread? No, he does Is 28:28
like your own land, a land of **g** and wine, Is 36:17
offering, you have brought a **g** offering. Is 57:6
will not again give your **g** to be food for Is 62:8
he who presents a **g** offering, like one who Is 66:3
the Israelites bring their **g** offering in a Is 66:20
they offer burnt offering and **g** offering, Jer 14:12
g offerings and frankincense, Jer 17:26
the goodness of the LORD, over the **g**, Jer 31:12
burnt offerings, to burn **g** offerings, Jer 33:18
bringing **g** offerings and incense to Jer 41:5
pile her up like heaps of **g**, and devote Jer 50:26
I will summon the **g** and make it Ezk 36:29
most holy offerings—the **g** offering, Ezk 42:13
They shall eat the **g** offering, the sin Ezk 44:29
watering places of Israel for **g** offering, Ezk 45:15
the burnt offerings, **g** offerings, Ezk 45:17
provide the sin offerings, **g** offerings, Ezk 45:17
shall provide as a **g** offering an ephah Ezk 45:24
burnt offerings, and **g** offerings, Ezk 45:25
And the **g** offering with the ram shall Ezk 46:5
and the **g** offering with the lambs shall Ezk 46:5
As a **g** offering he shall provide an Ezk 46:7
the **g** offering with a young bull shall Ezk 46:11
you shall provide a **g** offering with it Ezk 46:14
the flour, as a **g** offering to the LORD. Ezk 46:14
where they shall bake the **g** offering, Ezk 46:20
know that it was I who gave her the **g**, Hos 2:8
I will take back my **g** in its time, Hos 2:9
and the earth shall answer the **g**, the Hos 2:22
for **g** and wine they gash themselves; Hos 7:14
The standing **g** has no heads; it shall Hos 8:7
shadow; they shall flourish like the **g**; Hos 14:7
The **g** offering and the drink offering are Jl 1:9
mourns, because the **g** is destroyed, Jl 1:10
Because **g** offering and drink offering are Jl 1:13
are torn down because the **g** has dried up. Jl 1:17
a **g** offering and a drink offering for the Jl 2:14
his people, "Behold, I am sending to you **g**, Jl 2:19
"The threshing floors shall be full of **g**; Jl 2:24
poor and you exact taxes of **g** from him, Am 5:11
your burnt offerings and **g** offerings, Am 5:22
new moon be over, that we may sell **g**? Am 8:5
on the land and the hills, on the **g**, Hg 1:11
G shall make the young men flourish, Zec 9:17
began to pluck heads of **g** and to eat. Mt 12:1
seeds fell on good soil and produced **g**, Mt 13:8
when the plants came up and bore **g**, Mt 13:26
heaven is like a **g** of mustard seed that Mt 13:31
you have faith like a **g** of mustard seed, Mt 17:20
his disciples began to pluck heads of **g**. Mk 2:23
up and choked it, and it yielded no **g**. Mk 4:7
seeds fell into good soil and produced **g**, Mk 4:8
then the ear, then the full **g** in the ear. Mk 4:28
But when the **g** is ripe, at once he puts Mk 4:29
It is like a **g** of mustard seed, which, Mk 4:31
disciples plucked and ate some heads of **g**, Lk 6:1
I will store all my **g** and my goods. Lk 12:18
It is like a **g** of mustard seed that a man Lk 13:19
you had faith like a **g** of mustard seed, Lk 17:6
unless a **g** of wheat falls into the earth Jn 12:24
Jacob heard that there was **g** in Egypt, Acts 7:12
when it treads out the **g**." Is it for oxen 1 Cor 9:9
perhaps of wheat or of some other **g**. 1 Cor 15:37
an ox when it treads out the **g**," and, 1 Tm 5:18

GRAINFIELDS (3)
went through the **g** on the Sabbath. Mt 12:1
Sabbath he was going through the **g**, Mk 2:23
while he was going through the **g**, Lk 6:1

GRAINS (2)
sand, and your descendants like its **g**; Is 48:19
as the innumerable **g** of sand by Heb 11:12

GRANARIES (3)
may our **g** be full, providing all kinds Ps 144:13
her from every quarter; open her **g**; Jer 50:26
the **g** are torn down because the grain has Jl 1:17

GRANDCHILDREN (3)
and kissed his **g** and his daughters Gn 31:55
G are the crown of the aged, and the Prv 17:6
But if a widow has children or **g**, let 1 Tm 5:4

GRANDDAUGHTER (2)
she was a **g** of Omri king of Israel. 2 Kgs 8:26
name was Athaliah, the **g** of Omri. 2 Chr 22:2

GRANDFATHERS (1)
your fathers nor your **g** have seen, Ex 10:6

GRANDMOTHER (1)
dwelt first in your **g** Lois and your 2 Tm 1:5

GRANDSON (8)
his son and Lot the son of Haran, his **g**, Gn 11:31
your son and of your **g** how I have dealt Ex 10:2
us, you and your son and your **g** also, Jgs 8:22
house I have given to your master's **g**. 2 Sm 9:9
that your master's **g** may have bread 2 Sm 9:10
your master's **g** shall always 2 Sm 9:10
they said, "He is the **g** of Jehoshaphat, 2 Chr 22:9
shall serve him and his son and his **g**, Jer 27:7

GRANDSONS (2)
He had forty sons and thirty **g**, who Jgs 12:14
bowmen, having many sons and **g**, 1 Chr 8:40

GRANT (42)
to him, "Behold, I **g** you this favor also, Gn 19:21
please **g** me success today and show Gn 24:12
May God Almighty **g** you mercy Gn 43:14
of every seven years you shall **g** a release. Dt 15:1
say to them, '**G** them graciously to us, Jgs 21:22
The LORD **g** that you may find rest, each Ru 1:9
the God of Israel **g** your petition that 1 Sm 1:17
said to Joab, "Behold now, I **g** this; 2 Sm 14:21
walk, and **g** rain upon your land, 1 Kgs 8:36

and **g** them compassion in the sight 1 Kgs 8:50
may the LORD **g** you discretion and 1 Chr 22:12
G to Solomon my son a whole heart 1 Chr 29:19
walk, and **g** rain upon your land, 2 Chr 6:27
but I will **g** them some deliverance, 2 Chr 12:7
according to the **g** that they had from Ezr 3:7
brighten our eyes and **g** us a little Ezr 9:8
to **g** us some reviving to set up the house Ezr 9:9
and **g** him mercy in the sight of this Neh 1:11
it please the king to **g** my wish and fulfill Est 5:8
Only **g** me two things, then I will not Jb 13:20
May he **g** you your heart's desire and Ps 20:4
Oh, **g** us help against the foe, for vain is Ps 60:11
love, O LORD, and **g** us your salvation. Ps 85:7
Oh **g** us help against the foe, for vain is Ps 108:12
G not, O LORD, the desires of the wicked; Ps 140:8
"Give counsel; **g** justice; make your shade Is 16:3
to **g** to those who mourn in Zion—to give Is 61:3
I will **g** you mercy, that he may have Jer 42:12
hand and at my left is not mine to **g**, Mt 20:23
And they said to him, "**G** us to sit, one Mk 10:37
hand or at my left is not mine to **g**, Mk 10:40
he swore to our father Abraham, to **g** us Lk 1:73
their threats and **g** to your servants Acts 4:29
and encouragement **g** you to Rom 15:5
his glory he may **g** you to be Eph 3:16
and to **g** relief to you who are afflicted 2 Thes 1:7
May the Lord **g** mercy to the 2 Tm 1:16
may the Lord **g** him to find mercy 2 Tm 1:18
God may perhaps **g** them repentance 2 Tm 2:25
one who conquers I will **g** to eat of the tree Rv 2:7
I will **g** him to sit with me on my throne, Rv 3:21
And I will **g** authority to my two Rv 11:3

GRANTED (37)
And the LORD **g** his prayer, and Gn 25:21
the LORD your God **g** me success." Gn 27:20
"You have **g** this great salvation by the Jgs 15:18
and the LORD has **g** me my petition 1 Sm 1:27
voice, and I have **g** your petition." 1 Sm 25:35
that the king has **g** the request of his 2 Sm 14:22
who has **g** someone to sit on my 1 Kgs 1:48
me pain!" And God **g** what he asked. 1 Chr 4:10
and he **g** their urgent plea because 1 Chr 5:20
wisdom and knowledge are **g** to you. I 2 Chr 1:12
that the LORD had **g** to David and to 2 Chr 7:10
and the king **g** him all that he asked, Ezr 7:6
occupy." And the king **g** me what I Neh 2:8
He also **g** a remission of taxes to the Est 2:18
"What is your wish? It shall be **g** you. Est 5:6
wish, Queen Esther? It shall be **g** you. Est 7:2
the king, let my life be **g** me for my wish, Est 7:3
what is your wish? It shall be **g** you. Est 9:12
You have **g** me life and steadfast love, Jb 10:12
"I have **g** help to one who is mighty; Ps 89:19
the desire of the righteous will be **g**. Prv 10:24
according to all that the LORD has **g** us, Is 63:7
Israel that he has **g** them according to his Is 63:7
he was dead, he **g** the corpse to Joseph. Mk 15:45
And why is this **g** to me that the mother Lk 1:43
decided that their demand should be **g**. Lk 23:24
so he has **g** the Son also to have life in Jn 5:26
to me unless it is **g** him by the Father." Jn 6:65
asked for a murderer to be **g** to you, Acts 3:14
near, which God had **g** to Abraham, Acts 7:17
also God has **g** repentance that leads Acts 11:18
God has **g** you all those who sail with Acts 27:24
for the blessing **g** us through the 2 Cor 1:11
For it has been **g** to you that for the Phil 1:29
His divine power has **g** to us all things 2 Pt 1:3
by which he has **g** to us his precious 2 Pt 1:4
it was **g** her to clothe herself with fine Rv 19:8

GRANTING (3)
g an inheritance to those who love me, Prv 8:21
g signs and wonders to be done by Acts 14:3
But **g** that I myself did not burden 2 Cor 12:16

GRAPE (11)
shall last to the time of the **g** harvest, Lv 26:5
and the **g** harvest shall last to the time Lv 26:5
wine made from the blood of the **g**. Dt 32:14
better than the **g** harvest of Abiezer? Jgs 8:2
will shake off his unripe **g** like the vine, Jb 15:33
whether the **g** blossoms have opened and Sg 7:12
and the flower becomes a ripening **g**, Is 18:5
the gleaning when the **g** harvest is done. Is 24:13
women; for the **g** harvest fails, Is 32:10
If **g** gatherers came to you, would they Ob 1:5
earth and gathered the **g** harvest of the Rv 14:19

GRAPE-GATHERER (1)
like a **g** pass your hand again over its Jer 6:9

GRAPE-GATHERERS (1)
If **g** came to you, would they not leave Jer 49:9

GRAPES (35)
forth, and the clusters ripened into **g**. Gn 40:10
and I took the **g** and pressed them into Gn 40:11
wine and his vesture in the blood of **g**. Gn 49:11
gather the fallen **g** of your vineyard. Lv 19:10
or gather the **g** of your undressed vine. Lv 25:5
nor gather the **g** from the undressed Lv 25:11
not drink any juice of **g** or eat grapes, Nm 6:3
not drink any juice of grapes or eat **g**, Nm 6:3
time was the season of the first ripe **g**. Nm 13:20
a branch with a single cluster of **g**, Nm 13:23
vineyard, you may eat your fill of **g**, Dt 23:24
you gather the **g** of your vineyard, Dt 24:21
drink of the wine nor gather the **g**, Dt 28:39
Gomorrah; their **g** are grapes of poison; Dt 32:32
Gomorrah; their grapes are **g** of poison; Dt 32:32
the gleaning of the **g** of Ephraim better Jgs 8:2
and gathered the **g** from their vineyards Jgs 9:27
on donkeys, and also wine, **g**, figs, Neh 13:15
and he looked for it to yield **g**, but it yielded Is 5:2
for it to yield grapes, but it yielded wild **g**. Is 5:2
When I looked for it to yield **g**, why did it Is 5:4
it to yield grapes, why did it yield wild **g**? Is 5:4
the LORD, there are no **g** on the vine, Jer 8:13
fold, and shout, like those who tread **g**, Jer 25:30
"'The fathers have eaten sour **g**, and the Jer 31:29
Each man who eats sour **g**, his teeth Jer 31:30
fruits and your **g** the destroyer has Jer 48:32
of Israel, 'The fathers have eaten sour **g**, Ezk 18:2
Like **g** in the wilderness, I found Israel. Hos 9:10
and the treader of **g** him who sows the Am 9:13
you shall tread **g**, but not drink wine. Mi 6:15
as when the **g** have been gleaned: Mi 7:1
Are **g** gathered from thornbushes, or Mt 7:16
nor are **g** picked from a bramble bush. Lk 6:44
the vine of the earth, for its **g** are ripe." Rv 14:18

GRAPEVINE (2)
eat nothing that is produced by the **g**, Nm 6:4
bear olives, or a **g** produce figs? Jas 3:12

GRASP (4)
from the **g** of the unjust and cruel man. Ps 71:4
the wind or to **g** oil in one's right Prv 27:16
redeem you from the **g** of the ruthless." Jer 15:21
them, and they did not **g** what was said. Lk 18:34

GRASPED (5)
And Samson **g** the two middle pillars Jgs 16:29
to Cyrus, whose right hand I have **g**, Is 45:1
polished, that it may be **g** in the hand. Ezk 21:11
when they **g** you with the hand, you Ezk 29:7
count equality with God a thing to be **g**, Phil 2:6

GRASS (62)
and plump, and they fed in the reed **g**. Gn 41:2
up out of the Nile and fed in the reed **g**. Gn 41:18
the ox licks up the **g** of the field." So Nm 22:4
And he will give **g** in your fields for Dt 11:15
dew, like gentle rain upon the tender **g**, Dt 32:2
like rain that makes **g** to sprout from 2 Sm 23:4
Perhaps we may find **g** and save the 1 Kgs 18:5
plants of the field and like tender **g**, 2 Kgs 19:26
tender grass, like **g** on the housetops, 2 Kgs 19:26
your descendants as the **g** of the earth. Jb 5:25
Does the wild donkey bray when he has **g**, Jb 6:5
and to make the ground sprout with **g**? Jb 38:27
made as I made you; he eats **g** like an ox. Jb 40:15
soon fade like the **g** and wither like the Ps 37:2
he be like rain that falls on the mown **g**, Ps 72:6
in the cities like the **g** of the field! Ps 72:16
like **g** that is renewed in the morning: Ps 90:5
the wicked sprout like **g** and all evildoers Ps 92:7
is struck down like **g** and has withered; Ps 102:4
evening shadow; I wither away like **g**. Ps 102:11
As for man, his days are like **g**; he Ps 103:15
You cause the **g** to grow for the Ps 104:14
God for the image of an ox that eats **g**. Ps 106:20
Let them be like the **g** on the housetops, Ps 129:6
the earth; he makes **g** grow on the hills. Ps 147:8
lion, but his favor is like dew on the **g**. Prv 19:12
When the **g** is gone and the new Prv 27:25
and as dry **g** sinks down in the flame, Is 5:24
the **g** is withered, the vegetation fails, the Is 15:6
the **g** shall become reeds and rushes. Is 35:7
like plants of the field and like tender **g**, Is 37:27
tender grass, like **g** on the housetops, Is 37:27
I said, "What shall I cry?" All flesh is **g**, Is 40:6
The **g** withers, the flower fades when the Is 40:7
LORD blows on it; surely the people are **g**. Is 40:7
The **g** withers, the flower fades, but the Is 40:8
spring up among the **g** like willows by Is 44:4
of the son of man who is made like **g**, Is 51:12
your bones shall flourish like the **g**; Is 66:14
land mourn and the **g** of every field Jer 12:4
her newborn fawn because there is no **g**. Jer 14:5
bronze, amid the tender **g** of the field. Dn 4:15
be with the beasts in the **g** of the earth. Dn 4:15
and bronze, in the tender **g** of the field, Dn 4:23
You shall be made to eat **g** like an ox, Dn 4:25
you shall be made to eat **g** like an ox, Dn 4:32
from among men and ate **g** like an ox, Dn 4:33
wild donkeys. He was fed **g** like an ox, Dn 5:21
had finished eating the **g** of the land, Am 7:2
dew from the LORD, like showers on the **g**, Mi 5:7
But if God so clothes the **g** of the field, Mt 6:30
ordered the crowds to sit down on the **g**, Mt 14:19
all to sit down in groups on the green **g**. Mk 6:39
But if God so clothes the **g**, which is Lk 12:28
Now there was much **g** in the place. Jn 6:10
like a flower of the **g** he will pass away. Jas 1:10
its scorching heat and withers the **g**; Jas 1:11
for "All flesh is like **g** and all its glory 1 Pt 1:24
and all its glory like the flower of **g**. 1 Pt 1:24
like the flower of grass. The **g** withers, 1 Pt 1:24
up, and all green **g** was burned up. Rv 8:7
told not to harm the **g** of the earth or any Rv 9:4

GRASSHOPPER (3)
of any kind, and the **g** of any kind. Lv 11:22
tree blossoms, the **g** drags itself along, Eccl 12:5
like the locust; multiply like the **g**! Na 3:15

GRASSHOPPERS (3)
and we seemed to ourselves like **g**, Nm 13:33
the earth, and its inhabitants are like **g**; Is 40:22
Your princes are like **g**, your scribes Na 3:17

GRATEFUL (1)
Therefore let us be **g** for receiving a Heb 12:28

GRATIFY (2)
provision for the flesh, to **g** its desires. Rom 13:14
and you will not **g** the desires of the Gal 5:16

GRATING (6)
You shall also make for it a **g**, a network Ex 27:4
of burnt offering, with its **g** of bronze, Ex 35:16
And he made for the altar a **g**, a network Ex 38:4
corners of the bronze **g** as holders for the Ex 38:5
altar and the bronze **g** for it and all Ex 38:30
the bronze altar, and its **g** of bronze, its Ex 39:39

GRATITUDE (1)
everywhere we accept this with all **g**. Acts 24:3

GRAVE (26)
is great and their sin is very **g**, Gn 18:20
or touches a human bone or a **g**, Nm 19:16
bone, or the slain or the dead or the **g**. Nm 19:18
his voice and wept at the **g** of Abner, 2 Sm 3:32
own city near the **g** of my father and 2 Sm 19:37
And he laid the body in his own **g**. 1 Kgs 13:30
bury me in the **g** in which the man 1 Kgs 13:31
of Jeroboam shall come to the **g**, 1 Kgs 14:13
was thrown into the **g** of Elisha, 2 Kgs 13:21
shall be gathered to your **g** in peace, 2 Kgs 22:20
shall be gathered to your **g** in peace, 2 Chr 34:28
and are glad when they find the **g**? Jb 3:22
You shall come to your **g** in ripe old age, Jb 5:26
been, carried from the womb to the **g**. Jb 10:19
When he is carried to the **g**, watch is Jb 21:32
is destruction; their throat is an open **g**; Ps 5:9
the dead, like the slain that lie in the **g**, Ps 88:5
Is your steadfast love declared in the **g**, Ps 88:11
strong as death, jealousy is fierce as the **g**. Sg 8:6
but you are cast out, away from your **g**, Is 14:19
And they made his **g** with the wicked and Is 53:9
so my mother would have been my **g**, Jer 20:17
and her company is all around her **g**, Ezk 32:23
and all her multitude around her **g**; Ezk 32:24
I will make your **g**, for you are vile." Na 1:14
"Their throat is an open **g**; they use Rom 3:13

GRAVEL (2)
afterward his mouth will be full of **g**. Prv 20:17
He has made my teeth grind on **g**, and Lam 3:16

GRAVES (15)
because there are no **g** in Egypt that Ex 14:11
of it upon the **g** of the common 2 Kgs 23:6
scattered it over the **g** of those who 2 Chr 34:4
when the city, the place of my fathers' **g**, Neh 2:3
me to Judah, to the city of my fathers' **g**, Neh 2:5
Their **g** are their homes forever, their Ps 49:11
all her company, its **g** all around it, Ezk 32:22
whose **g** are set in the uttermost parts Ezk 32:23
all her multitude, her **g** all around it, Ezk 32:25
all her multitude, her **g** all around it, Ezk 32:26
I will open your **g** and raise you from Ezk 37:12
graves and raise you from your **g**, Ezk 37:12
I am the LORD, when I open your **g**, Ezk 37:13
graves, and raise you from your **g**, Ezk 37:13
For you are like unmarked **g**, and Lk 11:44

GRAVEYARD (1)
my days are extinct; the **g** is ready for me. Jb 17:1

GRAVING (1)
fashioned it with a **g** tool and made a Ex 32:4

GRAY (13)
bring down my **g** hairs with sorrow Gn 42:38
will bring down my **g** hairs in evil to Gn 44:29
will bring down the **g** hairs of your Gn 44:31
stand up before the **g** head and honor Lv 19:32
nursing child with the man of **g** hairs. Dt 32:25
walks before you, and I am old and **g**; 1 Sm 12:2
but do not let his **g** head go down to 1 Kgs 2:6
you shall bring his **g** head down with 1 Kgs 2:9
So even to old age and **g** hairs, O God, do Ps 71:18
G hair is a crown of glory; it is gained Prv 16:31
the splendor of old men is their **g** hair. Prv 20:29
I am he, and to **g** hairs I will carry you. Is 46:4
g hairs are sprinkled upon him, and he Hos 7:9

GRAY-HAIRED (1)
Both the **g** and the aged are among us, Jb 15:10

GRAZE (11)
flocks or herds **g** opposite that Ex 34:3
twins of a gazelle, that **g** among the lilies. Sg 4:5
to **g** in the gardens and to gather lilies. Sg 6:2
Then shall the lambs **g** as in their Is 5:17
The cow and the bear shall **g**; their young Is 11:7
And the firstborn of the poor will **g**, and Is 14:30
your livestock will **g** in large pastures, Is 30:23
The wolf and the lamb shall **g** together; Is 65:25
let them **g** in Bashan and Gilead as in Mi 7:14
house of Judah, on which they shall **g**, Zep 2:7
tongue. For they shall **g** and lie down, Zep 3:13

GRAZED (2)
causes a field or vineyard to be **g** over, Ex 22:5
but when they had **g**, they became full, Hos 13:6

GRAZES (3)
mine, and I am his; he **g** among the lilies. Sg 2:16
my beloved is mine; he **g** among the lilies. Sg 6:3
like the wilderness; there the calf **g**; Is 27:10

GRAZING (2)
heights of Israel shall be their **g** land. Ezk 34:14
they shall lie down in good **g** land, Ezk 34:14

GREAT (857)
God made the two **g** lights—the greater Gn 1:16
So God created the **g** sea creatures and Gn 1:21
the wickedness of man was **g** in the earth, Gn 6:5
the fountains of the **g** deep burst forth, Gn 7:11
Nineveh and Calah; that is the **g** city. Gn 10:12
And I will make of you a **g** nation, and I Gn 12:2
I will bless you and make your name **g**, Gn 12:2
his house with **g** plagues because of Gn 12:17
possessions were so **g** that they could Gn 13:6
wicked, **g** sinners against the LORD. Gn 13:13
shield; your reward shall be very **g**." Gn 15:1
dreadful and **g** darkness fell upon him. Gn 15:12
they shall come out with **g** possessions. Gn 15:14
from the river of Egypt to the **g** river, Gn 15:18
and I will make him into a **g** nation. Gn 17:20
surely become a **g** and mighty nation, Gn 18:18
and Gomorrah is **g** and their sin Gn 18:20
of the house, both small and **g**, Gn 19:11
people has become **g** before the LORD, Gn 19:13
have shown me **g** kindness in saving Gn 19:19
on me and my kingdom a **g** sin? Gn 20:9
And Abraham made a **g** feast on the day Gn 21:8
for I will make him into a **g** nation." Gn 21:18
my master, and he has become **g**. Gn 24:35
with an exceedingly **g** and bitter cry Gn 27:34
Ask me for as **g** a bride price and gift Gn 34:12
their possessions were too **g** for them to Gn 36:7
can I do this **g** wickedness and sin Gn 39:9
seven years of **g** plenty throughout all Gn 41:29
Joseph stored up grain in **g** abundance, Gn 41:49
for there I will make you into a **g** nation. Gn 46:3
a people, and he also shall be **g**. Gn 48:19
and horsemen. It was a very **g** company. Gn 50:9
with a very **g** and grievous Gn 50:10
said, "I will turn aside to see this **g** sight, Ex 3:3
arm and with **g** acts of judgment. Ex 6:6
of the land of Egypt by **g** acts of judgment. Ex 7:4
There came **g** swarms of flies into the Ex 8:24
the man Moses was very **g** in the land of Ex 11:3
There shall be a **g** cry throughout all the Ex 11:6
And there was a **g** cry in Egypt, for Ex 12:30
Israel saw the **g** power that the LORD Ex 14:31
Every **g** matter they shall bring to you, Ex 18:22
hands and on the **g** toes of their right Ex 29:20
that I may make a **g** nation of you." Ex 32:10
land of Egypt with **g** power and with a Ex 32:11
brought such a **g** sin upon them?" Ex 32:21
to the people, "You have sinned a **g** sin. Ex 32:30
"Alas, this people have sinned a **g** sin. Ex 32:31
rat, the mouse, the **g** lizard of any kind, Lv 11:29
be partial to the poor or defer to the **g**, Lv 19:15
down the people with a very **g** plague. Nm 11:33
people that we saw in it are of **g** height. Nm 13:32
of the Lord be **g** as you have promised, Nm 14:17
And Moab was in **g** dread of the people, Nm 22:3
for I will surely do you **g** honor, and Nm 22:17
Gad had a very **g** number of livestock. Nm 32:1
you shall have the **G** Sea and its coast. Nm 34:6
from the **G** Sea you shall draw a line to Nm 34:7
and Lebanon, as far as the **g** river, Dt 1:7
You shall hear the small and the **g** alike. Dt 1:17
through all that **g** and terrifying Dt 1:19
The cities are **g** and fortified up to Dt 1:28
your going through this **g** wilderness. Dt 2:7
lived there, a people **g** and many, Dt 2:10
a people **g** and many, and tall as the Dt 2:21
'Surely this **g** nation is a wise and Dt 4:6
For what **g** nation is there that has a god Dt 4:7
And what **g** nation is there, that has Dt 4:8
whether such a **g** thing as this has ever Dt 4:32
arm, and by **g** deeds of terror, Dt 4:34
And on earth he let you see his **g** fire, and Dt 4:36
with his own presence, by his **g** power, Dt 4:37
we die? For this **g** fire will consume us. Dt 5:25
to give you—with **g** and good cities that Dt 6:10
signs and wonders, **g** and grievous, Dt 6:22
the **g** trials that your eyes saw, the signs, Dt 7:19
is in your midst, a **g** and awesome God. Dt 7:21
to you and throw them into **g** confusion, Dt 7:23
you through the **g** and terrifying Dt 8:15
cities **g** and fortified up to heaven, Dt 9:1
a people **g** and tall, the sons of the Dt 9:2
brought out by your **g** power and by Dt 9:29
is God of gods and Lord of lords, the **g**, Dt 10:17
for you these **g** and terrifying things Dt 10:21
eyes have seen all the **g** work of the LORD Dt 11:7
LORD my God or see this **g** fire any more, Dt 18:16
and there he became a nation, **g**, mighty, Dt 26:5
outstretched arm, with **g** deeds of terror, Dt 26:8
the **g** trials that your eyes saw, the signs, Dt 29:3
eyes saw, the signs, and those **g** wonders. Dt 29:3
What caused the heat of this **g** anger?' Dt 29:24
land in anger and fury and **g** wrath, Dt 29:28
power and all the **g** deeds of terror that Dt 34:12
and this Lebanon as far as the **g** river, Jos 1:4
the Hittites to the **G** Sea toward the going Jos 1:4
all the people shall shout with a **g** shout, Jos 6:5
trumpet, the people shouted a **g** shout, Jos 6:20
And what will you do for your **g** name?" Jos 7:9
raised over him a **g** heap of stones that Jos 7:26
city and raised over it a **g** heap of stones, Jos 8:29
the coast of the **G** Sea toward Lebanon, Jos 9:1
greatly, because Gibeon was a **g** city, Jos 10:2
struck them with a **g** blow at Gibeon Jos 10:10
striking them with a **g** blow until they Jos 10:20
came out with all their troops, a **g** horde, Jos 11:4
chased them as far as **G** Sidon and Jos 11:8
were there, with **g** fortified cities. Jos 14:12
west boundary was the **G** Sea with its Jos 15:12
Egypt, and the **G** Sea with its coastline. Jos 15:47
a numerous people and have **g** power. Jos 17:17
Kanah, as far as Sidon the **G**. Jos 19:28
from the Jordan to the **G** Sea in the west. Jos 23:4
out before you **g** and strong nations. Jos 23:9
and who did those **g** signs in our sight Jos 24:17
who had seen all the **g** work that the LORD Jgs 2:7
Reuben there were **g** searchings of heart. Jgs 5:15
Reuben there were **g** searchings of heart. Jgs 5:16
as far as Abel-keramim, with a **g** blow. Jgs 11:33
become the cause of **g** trouble to me. Jgs 11:35
my people had a **g** dispute with the Jgs 12:2
them hip and thigh with a **g** blow, Jgs 15:8
have granted this **g** salvation by the Jgs 15:18
him, and see where his **g** strength lies, Jgs 16:5
tell me where your **g** strength lies, Jgs 16:6
not told me where your **g** strength lies." Jgs 16:15
gathered to offer a **g** sacrifice to Dagon Jgs 16:23
when they made a **g** cloud of smoke Jgs 20:38
they had taken a **g** oath concerning him Jgs 21:5
out of my **g** anxiety and vexation." 1 Sm 1:16
young men was very **g** in the sight of 1 Sm 2:17
"What does this **g** shouting in the 1 Sm 4:6
And there was a very **g** slaughter, for 1 Sm 4:10
has also been a **g** defeat among the 1 Sm 4:17
the city, causing a very **g** panic, 1 Sm 5:9
it is he who has done us this **g** harm, 1 Sm 6:9
and stopped there. A **g** stone was there. 1 Sm 6:14
figures, and set them upon the **g** stone. 1 Sm 6:15
The **g** stone beside which they set 1 Sm 6:18
had struck the people with a **g** blow. 1 Sm 6:19
still and see this **g** thing that the 1 Sm 12:16
and see that your wickedness is **g**, 1 Sm 12:17
his people, for his **g** name's sake, 1 Sm 12:22
For consider what **g** things he has 1 Sm 12:24
and it became a very **g** panic. 1 Sm 14:15
and there was very **g** confusion. 1 Sm 14:20
the Philistines has not been **g**." 1 Sm 14:30
roll a **g** stone to me here." 1 Sm 14:33
has worked this **g** salvation in 1 Sm 14:45
"Has the LORD as **g** delight in burnt 1 Sm 15:22
who kills him with **g** riches and will 1 Sm 17:25
Saul saw that he had **g** success, 1 Sm 18:15
the LORD worked a **g** salvation for all 1 Sm 19:5
and struck them with a **g** blow, 1 Sm 19:8
and came to the **g** well that is in 1 Sm 19:22
does nothing either **g** or small 1 Sm 20:2
and struck them with a **g** blow. 1 Sm 23:5
hill, with a **g** space between them. 1 Sm 26:13
and have made a **g** mistake." 1 Sm 26:21
Saul answered, "I am in **g** distress, 1 Sm 28:15
all who were in it, both small and **g**. 1 Sm 30:2
because of all the **g** spoil they had 1 Sm 30:16
was missing, whether small or **g**, 1 Sm 30:19
a prince and a **g** man has fallen this 2 Sm 3:38
And I will make for you a **g** name, like 2 Sm 7:9
like the name of the **g** ones of the earth. 2 Sm 7:9
servant's house for a **g** while to come, 2 Sm 7:19
Therefore you are **g**, O LORD God. For 2 Sm 7:22
doing for them **g** and awesome things 2 Sm 7:23
the spoil of the city, a very **g** amount. 2 Sm 12:30
Amnon hated her with very **g** hatred, 2 Sm 13:15
and the loss there was **g** on that day, 2 Sm 18:7
the thick branches of a **g** terebinth, 2 Sm 18:9
threw him into a **g** pit in the forest 2 Sm 18:17
over him a very **g** heap of stones. 2 Sm 18:17
your servant, I saw a **g** commotion, 2 Sm 18:29
they were at the **g** stone that is in 2 Sm 20:8
where there was a man of **g** stature, 2 Sm 21:20
and your gentleness made me **g**. 2 Sm 22:36
G salvation he brings to his king, 2 Sm 22:51
brought about a **g** victory that day, 2 Sm 23:10
and the LORD worked a **g** victory. 2 Sm 23:12
man of Kabzeel, a doer of **g** deeds. 2 Sm 23:20
David said to Gad, "I am in **g** distress. 2 Sm 24:14
hand of the LORD, for his mercy is **g**; 2 Sm 24:14
on pipes, and rejoicing with **g** joy, 1 Kgs 1:40
there, for that was the **g** high place. 1 Kgs 3:4
"You have shown **g** and steadfast love 1 Kgs 3:6
kept for him this **g** and steadfast love 1 Kgs 3:6
whom you have chosen, a **g** people, 1 Kgs 3:8
is able to govern this your **g** people?" 1 Kgs 3:9
sixty **g** cities with walls and bronze 1 Kgs 4:13
a wise son to be over this **g** people." 1 Kgs 5:7
king's command they quarried out **g**, 1 Kgs 5:17
and from the outside to the **g** court. 1 Kgs 7:9
The **g** court had three courses of cut 1 Kgs 7:12
shall hear of your **g** name and your 1 Kgs 8:42
and all Israel with him, a **g** assembly, 1 Kgs 8:65
to Jerusalem with a very **g** retinue, 1 Kgs 10:2
and a very **g** quantity of spices and 1 Kgs 10:10
Ophir a very **g** amount of almug 1 Kgs 10:11
king also made a **g** ivory throne and 1 Kgs 10:18
And Hadad found **g** favor in the 1 Kgs 11:19
as **g** as would contain two seahs of 1 Kgs 18:32
and wind, and there was a **g** rain. 1 Kgs 18:45
eat, for the journey is too **g** for you." 1 Kgs 19:7
and a **g** and strong wind tore the 1 Kgs 19:11
Have you seen all this **g** multitude? 1 Kgs 20:13
struck the Syrians with a **g** blow. 1 Kgs 20:21
give all this **g** multitude into your 1 Kgs 20:28
"Fight with neither small nor **g**, 1 Kgs 22:31
And there came **g** wrath against 2 Kgs 3:27
was a **g** man with his master and in 2 Kgs 5:1
it is a **g** word the prophet has spoken 2 Kgs 5:13
horses and chariots and a **g** army, 2 Kgs 6:14
So he prepared for them a **g** feast, and 2 Kgs 6:23
And there was a **g** famine in Samaria, 2 Kgs 6:25
and of horses, the sound of a **g** army, 2 Kgs 7:6
"Tell me all the **g** things that Elisha 2 Kgs 8:4
should do this **g** thing?" Elisha 2 Kgs 8:13
were with the **g** men of the city, 2 Kgs 10:6
all his **g** men and his close friends 2 Kgs 10:11
for I have a **g** sacrifice to offer to 2 Kgs 10:19
"On the **g** altar burn the morning 2 Kgs 16:15
LORD and made them commit **g** sin. 2 Kgs 17:21
land of Egypt with **g** power and with 2 Kgs 17:36
Rabshakeh with a **g** army from 2 Kgs 18:17
to Hezekiah, 'Thus says the **g** king, 2 Kgs 18:19
"Hear the word of the **g** king, the 2 Kgs 18:28
For **g** is the wrath of the LORD that is 2 Kgs 22:13
all the people, both small and **g**. 2 Kgs 23:2
from the burning of his **g** wrath, 2 Kgs 23:26
every **g** house he burned down. 2 Kgs 25:9
all the people, both small and **g**, 2 Kgs 25:26
the LORD saved them by a **g** victory. 1 Chr 11:14
man of Kabzeel, a doer of **g** deeds. 1 Chr 11:22
an Egyptian, a man of **g** stature, 1 Chr 11:23
help him, until there was a **g** army, 1 Chr 12:22
For **g** is the LORD, and greatly to be 1 Chr 16:25
the name of the **g** ones of the earth. 1 Chr 17:8
house for a **g** while to come, 1 Chr 17:17

making known all these **g** things. 1 Chr 17:19
a name for **g** and awesome things, 1 Chr 17:21
the spoil of the city, a very **g** amount. 1 Chr 20:2
where there was a man of **g** stature, 1 Chr 20:6
said to Gad, "I am in **g** distress. 1 Chr 21:13
of the LORD, for his mercy is very **g**, 1 Chr 21:13
is I who have sinned and done **g** evil. 1 Chr 21:17
David also provided **g** quantities of 1 Chr 22:3
and Tyrians brought **g** quantities of 1 Chr 22:4
materials in **g** quantity before 1 Chr 22:5
much blood and have waged **g** wars. 1 Chr 22:8
With **g** pains I have provided for the 1 Chr 22:14
cast lots for their duties, small and **g**, 1 Chr 25:8
for they were men of **g** ability. 1 Chr 26:6
fathers' houses, small and **g** alike, 1 Chr 26:13
and men of **g** ability among them 1 Chr 26:31
and inexperienced, and the work is **g**, 1 Chr 29:1
besides **g** quantities of onyx and 1 Chr 29:2
it is to make **g** and to give strength 1 Chr 29:12
LORD on that day with **g** gladness. 1 Chr 29:22
made Solomon very **g** in the sight 1 Chr 29:25
him and made him exceedingly **g**. 2 Chr 1:1
"You have shown **g** and steadfast love 2 Chr 1:8
this people of yours, which is so **g**?" 2 Chr 1:10
The house that I am to build will be **g**, 2 Chr 2:5
I am to build will be **g** and wonderful. 2 Chr 2:9
the priests and the **g** court and doors 2 Chr 4:9
made all these things in **g** quantities, 2 Chr 4:18
the sake of your **g** name and your 2 Chr 6:32
all Israel with him, a very **g** assembly, 2 Chr 7:8
having a very **g** retinue and camels 2 Chr 9:1
of gold, and a very **g** quantity of spices, 2 Chr 9:9
king also made a **g** ivory throne and 2 Chr 9:17
you are a **g** multitude and have 2 Chr 13:8
his people struck them with **g** force, 2 Chr 13:17
for **g** disturbances afflicted all the 2 Chr 15:5
for **g** numbers had deserted to him 2 Chr 15:9
they made a very **g** fire in his honor. 2 Chr 16:14
and he had **g** riches and honor. 2 Chr 17:5
Now Jehoshaphat had **g** riches and 2 Chr 18:1
"Fight with neither small nor **g**, 2 Chr 18:30
"A **g** multitude is coming against 2 Chr 20:2
powerless against this **g** horde that 2 Chr 20:12
do not be dismayed at this **g** horde, 2 Chr 20:15
found among them, in **g** numbers, 2 Chr 20:25
father gave them **g** gifts of silver, 2 Chr 21:3
LORD will bring a **g** plague on your 2 Chr 21:14
the disease, and he died in **g** agony. 2 Chr 21:19
into their hand a very **g** army, 2 Chr 24:24
to shoot arrows and **g** stones. 2 Chr 26:15
and took captive a **g** number of his 2 Chr 28:5
Israel, who struck him with **g** force. 2 Chr 28:5
For our guilt is already **g**, and there 2 Chr 28:13
Besides the **g** number of burnt 2 Chr 29:35
second month, a very **g** assembly. 2 Chr 30:13
Bread seven days with **g** gladness, 2 Chr 30:21
themselves in **g** numbers. 2 Chr 30:24
So there was **g** joy in Jerusalem, for 2 Chr 30:26
A **g** many people were gathered, and 2 Chr 32:4
Hezekiah had very **g** riches and 2 Chr 32:27
had given him very **g** possessions. 2 Chr 32:29
and raised it to a very **g** height. 2 Chr 33:14
For **g** is the wrath of the LORD that is 2 Chr 34:21
all the people both **g** and small. 2 Chr 34:30
of the house of God, **g** and small, 2 Chr 36:18
shouted with a **g** shout when they Ezr 3:11
for the people shouted with a **g** shout, Ezr 3:13
nations whom the **g** and noble Ezr 4:10
of Judah, to the house of the **g** God. Ezr 5:8
which a **g** king of Israel built and Ezr 5:11
with three layers of **g** stones and one Ezr 6:4
to this day we have been in **g** guilt. Ezr 9:7
us for our evil deeds and for our **g** guilt, Ezr 9:13
house of God, a very **g** assembly of men, Ezr 10:1
the exile is in **g** trouble and shame. Neh 1:3
the **g** and awesome God who keeps Neh 1:5
have redeemed by your **g** power and by Neh 1:10
section opposite the **g** projecting tower Neh 3:27
the Lord, who is **g** and awesome, Neh 4:14
"The work is **g** and widely spread, Neh 4:19
Now there arose a **g** outcry of the people Neh 5:1
And I held a **g** assembly against them Neh 5:7
"I am doing a **g** work and I cannot come Neh 6:3
And Ezra blessed the LORD, the **g** God, Neh 8:6
send portions and to make **g** rejoicing, Neh 8:12
so. And there was very **g** rejoicing. Neh 8:17
and had committed **g** blasphemies, Neh 9:18
you in your **g** mercies did not forsake Neh 9:19
themselves in your **g** goodness. Neh 9:25
and they committed **g** blasphemies. Neh 9:26
according to your **g** mercies you gave Neh 9:27
in your **g** mercies you did not make an Neh 9:31
"Now, therefore, our God, the **g**, the Neh 9:32
enjoying your **g** goodness that you Neh 9:35
as they please, and we are in **g** distress. Neh 9:37
and appointed two **g** choirs that gave Neh 12:31
And they offered **g** sacrifices that day Neh 12:43
had made them rejoice with **g** joy; Neh 12:43
and do all this **g** evil and act Neh 13:27
in Susa, the citadel, both **g** and small, Est 1:5
Then the king gave a **g** feast for all his Est 2:18
there was **g** mourning among the Jews, Est 4:3
with a **g** golden crown and a robe of fine Est 8:15
For Mordecai was **g** in the king's house, Est 9:4
and he was **g** among the Jews and Est 10:3
a **g** wind came across the wilderness and Jb 1:19
for they saw that his suffering was very **g**. Jb 2:13
The small and the **g** are there, and the Jb 3:19
who does **g** things and unsearchable, Jb 5:9
and the words of your mouth be a **g** wind? Jb 8:2
was small, your latter days will be very **g**. Jb 8:7
who does **g** things beyond searching out, Jb 9:10
He makes nations **g**, and he destroys Jb 12:23
With **g** force my garment is disfigured; Jb 30:18
because I stood in **g** fear of the Jb 31:34
Behold, God is **g**, and we know him not; Jb 36:26
he does **g** things that we cannot Jb 37:5
—we cannot find him; he is **g** in power; Jb 37:23
then, and the number of your days is **g**! Jb 38:21
on him because his strength is **g**, Jb 39:11
lips, the tongue that makes **g** boasts, Ps 12:3
There they are in **g** terror, for God is with Ps 14:5
me, and your gentleness made me **g**. Ps 18:35
G salvation he brings to his king, and Ps 18:50
in keeping them there is **g** reward. Ps 19:11
and innocent of **g** transgression. Ps 19:13
His glory is **g** through your salvation; Ps 21:5
comes my praise in the **g** congregation; Ps 22:25
O LORD, pardon my guilt, for it is **g**. Ps 25:11
in the **g** assembly I will bless the LORD. Ps 26:12
surely in the rush of **g** waters, they shall Ps 32:6
The king is not saved by his **g** army; a Ps 33:16
is not delivered by his **g** strength. Ps 33:16
and by its **g** might it cannot rescue. Ps 33:17
I will thank you in the **g** congregation; Ps 35:18
glad and say evermore, "**G** is the LORD, Ps 35:27
God; your judgments are like the **g** deep; Ps 36:6
of deliverance in the **g** congregation; Ps 40:9
faithfulness from the **g** congregation. Ps 40:10
say continually, "**G** is the LORD!" Ps 40:16
is to be feared, a **g** king over all the earth. Ps 47:2
G is the LORD and greatly to be praised in Ps 48:1
in the far north, the city of the **g** King. Ps 48:2
There they are, in **g** terror, where there is Ps 53:5
your steadfast love is **g** to the heavens, Ps 57:10
So **g** is your power that your enemies Ps 66:3
who announce the news are a **g** host: Ps 68:11
"Bless God in the **g** congregation, the Ps 68:26
your salvation say evermore, "God is **g**!" Ps 70:4
You who have done **g** things, O God, Ps 71:19
God is known; his name is **g** in Israel. Ps 76:1
is holy. What god is **g** like our God? Ps 77:13
the sea, your path through the **g** waters; Ps 77:19
according to your **g** power, preserve Ps 79:11
For you are **g** and do wondrous things; Ps 86:10
For **g** is your steadfast love toward me; Ps 86:13
How **g** are your works, O LORD! Your Ps 92:5
For the LORD is a **g** God, and a great King Ps 95:3
a great God, and a **g** King above all gods Ps 95:3
For **g** is the LORD, and greatly to be Ps 96:4
The LORD is **g** in Zion; he is exalted over Ps 99:2
them praise your **g** and awesome name! Ps 99:3
so **g** is his steadfast love toward those Ps 103:11
soul! O LORD my God, you are very **g**! Ps 104:1
Here is the sea, **g** and wide, which Ps 104:25
living things both small and **g**. Ps 104:25
who had done **g** things in Egypt, Ps 106:21
ships, doing business on the **g** waters; Ps 107:23
steadfast love is **g** above the heavens; Ps 108:4
mouth I will give **g** thanks to the LORD; Ps 109:30
G are the works of the LORD, studied by Ps 111:2
fear the LORD, both the small and the **g**. Ps 115:13
For **g** is his steadfast love toward us, Ps 117:2
G is your mercy, O LORD; give me life Ps 119:156
your word like one who finds **g** spoil. Ps 119:162
G peace have those who love your Ps 119:165
"The LORD has done **g** things for them." Ps 126:2
The LORD has done **g** things for us; we Ps 126:3
with things too **g** and too marvelous Ps 131:1
For I know that the LORD is **g**, and that Ps 135:5
to him who alone does **g** wonders, for Ps 136:4
to him who made the **g** lights, for his Ps 136:7
to him who struck down **g** kings, for Ps 136:17
of the LORD, for **g** is the glory of the LORD. Ps 138:5
G is the LORD, and greatly to be praised, Ps 145:3
G is our Lord, and abundant in power; Ps 147:5
earth, you **g** sea creatures and all deeps, Ps 148:7
and because of his **g** folly he is led Prv 5:23
than to play the **g** man and lack bread. Prv 12:9
pretends to be poor, yet has **g** wealth. Prv 13:7
is slow to anger has **g** understanding, Prv 14:29
the LORD than **g** treasure and trouble Prv 15:16
righteousness than **g** revenues with Prv 16:8
for him and brings him before the **g**. Prv 18:16
A man of **g** wrath will pay the penalty, Prv 19:19
is to be chosen rather than **g** riches, Prv 22:1
presence or stand in the place of the **g**, Prv 25:6
the righteous triumph, there is **g** glory, Prv 28:12
my heart, "I have acquired **g** wisdom, Eccl 1:16
heart has had **g** experience of wisdom Eccl 1:16
I made **g** works. I built houses and Eccl 2:4
I had also **g** possessions of herds and Eccl 2:7
So I became **g** and surpassed all who Eccl 2:9
for it. This also is vanity and a **g** evil. Eccl 2:21
under the sun, and it seemed **g** to me. Eccl 9:13
and a **g** king came against it and Eccl 9:14
it, building **g** siegeworks against it. Eccl 9:14
for calmness will lay **g** offenses to rest. Eccl 10:4
arranging many proverbs with **g** care. Eccl 12:9
With **g** delight I sat in his shadow, and his Sg 2:3
walked in darkness have seen a **g** light; Is 9:2
the **g** in height will be hewn down, and Is 10:33
for **g** in your midst is the Holy One of Is 12:6
is on the mountains as of a **g** multitude! Is 13:4
contempt, in spite of all his **g** multitude, Is 16:14
with his hard and **g** and strong sword will Is 27:1
in that day a **g** trumpet will be blown, Is 27:13
and with earthquake and **g** noise, Is 29:6
with water, in the day of the **g** slaughter, Is 30:25
like the shade of a **g** rock in a weary land. Is 32:2
a **g** slaughter in the land of Edom. Is 34:6
Hezekiah at Jerusalem, with a **g** army. Is 36:2
"Say to Hezekiah, 'Thus says the **g** king, Is 36:4
"Hear the words of the **g** king, the king Is 36:13
for my welfare that I had **g** bitterness; Is 38:17
many sorceries and the **g** power of your Is 47:9
dried up the sea, the waters of the **g** deep, Is 51:10
but with **g** compassion I will gather you. Is 54:7
and **g** shall be the peace of your Is 54:13
will be like this day, **g** beyond measure." Is 56:12
and the **g** goodness to the house of Israel Is 63:7
from the north, and **g** destruction. Jer 4:6
I will go to the **g** and will speak to them, Jer 5:5
are many, their apostasies are **g**. Jer 5:6
therefore they have become **g** and rich; Jer 5:27
looms out of the north, and **g** destruction. Jer 6:1
a **g** nation is stirring from the farthest Jer 6:22
you are **g**, and your name is great in Jer 10:6
are great, and your name is **g** in might. Jer 10:6
—a **g** commotion out of the north Jer 10:22
with the roar of a **g** tempest he will set Jer 11:16
of Judah and the **g** pride of Jerusalem. Jer 13:9
my people is shattered with a **g** wound, Jer 14:17
Both **g** and small shall die in this land. Jer 16:6
pronounced all this **g** evil against us? Jer 16:10
my grave, and her womb forever **g**. Jer 20:17
in anger and in fury and in **g** wrath. Jer 21:5
beast. They shall die of a **g** pestilence. Jer 21:6
has the LORD dealt thus with this **g** city?" Jer 22:8
build myself a **g** house with spacious Jer 22:14
many nations and **g** kings shall make Jer 25:14
and a **g** tempest is stirring from the Jer 25:32
about to bring **g** disaster upon Jer 26:19
I who by my **g** power and my Jer 27:5
many nations and **g** kings shall make Jer 27:7
many countries and **g** kingdoms. Jer 28:8
That day is so **g** there is none like it; it is Jer 30:7
a merciless foe, because your guilt is **g**, Jer 30:14
Because your guilt is **g**, because your Jer 30:15
who is in labor, together; a **g** company, Jer 31:8
the earth by your **g** power and by your Jer 32:17
after them, O **g** and mighty God, Jer 32:18
g in counsel and mighty in deed, whose Jer 32:19
outstretched arm, and with **g** terror. Jer 32:21
and my wrath and in **g** indignation. Jer 32:37
brought all this **g** disaster upon this Jer 32:42
and will tell you **g** and hidden things Jer 33:3
for **g** is the anger and wrath that the Jer 36:7
and summer fruits in **g** abundance. Jer 40:12
came upon him at the **g** pool that is in Jer 41:12
you commit this **g** evil against Jer 44:7
the women who stood by, a **g** assembly, Jer 44:15
Behold, I have sworn by my **g** name, Jer 44:26
And do you seek **g** things for yourself? Jer 45:5
'Desolation and **g** destruction!' Jer 48:3
Babylon a gathering of **g** nations, Jer 50:9
battle is in the land, and **g** destruction! Jer 50:22
The noise of **g** destruction from the Jer 51:54
every **g** house he burned down. Jer 52:13
she who was **g** among the nations! Lam 1:1
every morning; **g** is your faithfulness. Lam 3:23
came out of the north, and a **g** cloud, Ezk 1:4
behind me the voice of a **g** earthquake: Ezk 3:12
them, and the sound of a **g** earthquake. Ezk 3:13
the **g** abominations that the house of Ezk 8:6

of Israel and Judah is exceedingly **g**. Ezk 9:9
of rain, and you, O **g** hailstones, Ezk 13:11
and **g** hailstones in wrath to make a Ezk 13:13
A **g** eagle with great wings and long Ezk 17:3
A great eagle with **g** wings and long Ezk 17:3
there was another **g** eagle with great Ezk 17:7
great eagle with **g** wings and much Ezk 17:7
mighty army and **g** company will not Ezk 17:17
It is the sword for the **g** slaughter, Ezk 21:14
bloody city! I also will make the pile **g**. Ezk 24:9
I will execute **g** vengeance on them Ezk 25:17
over you, and the **g** waters cover you, Ezk 26:19
you because of your **g** wealth of every Ezk 27:12
because of your **g** wealth of every Ezk 27:18
by your **g** wisdom in your trade you Ezk 28:5
the **g** dragon that lies in the midst of his Ezk 29:3
Egypt; Pelusium shall be in **g** agony; Ezk 30:16
under its shadow lived all **g** nations. Ezk 31:6
vindicate the holiness of my **g** name, Ezk 36:23
on their feet, an exceedingly **g** army. Ezk 37:10
of them clothed in full armor, a **g** host, Ezk 38:4
livestock and goods, to seize **g** spoil?' Ezk 38:13
all of them riding on horses, a **g** host, Ezk 38:15
there shall be a **g** earthquake in the Ezk 38:19
a **g** sacrificial feast on the mountains Ezk 39:17
many kinds, like the fish of the **G** Sea. Ezk 47:10
from the **G** Sea by way of Hethlon to Ezk 47:15
along the Brook of Egypt to the **G** Sea. Ezk 47:19
the **G** Sea shall be the boundary to a Ezk 47:20
along the Brook of Egypt to the **G** Sea. Ezk 48:28
from me gifts and rewards and **g** honor. Dn 2:6
for no **g** and powerful king has asked Dn 2:10
saw, O king, and behold, a **g** image. Dn 2:31
image became a **g** mountain and filled Dn 2:35
A **g** God has made known to the king Dn 2:45
Daniel high honors and many **g** gifts, Dn 2:48
How **g** are his signs, how mighty his Dn 4:3
midst of the earth, and its height was **g**. Dn 4:10
and said, "Is not this **g** Babylon, Dn 4:30
King Belshazzar made a **g** feast for a Dn 5:1
of heaven were stirring up the **g** sea. Dn 7:2
And four **g** beasts came up out of the sea, Dn 7:3
exceedingly strong. It had **g** iron teeth; Dn 7:7
a man, and a mouth speaking **g** things. Dn 7:8
of the sound of the **g** words that the horn Dn 7:11
'These four **g** beasts are four kings who Dn 7:17
eyes and a mouth that spoke **g** things, Dn 7:20
power. He did as he pleased and became **g**. Dn 8:4
Then the goat became exceedingly **g**, but Dn 8:8
he was strong, the **g** horn was broken, Dn 8:8
which grew exceedingly **g** toward the Dn 8:9
It grew **g**, even to the host of heaven. And Dn 8:10
It became **g**, even as great as the Prince Dn 8:11
great, even as **g** as the Prince of the host. Dn 8:11
And the **g** horn between his eyes is the Dn 8:21
His power shall be **g**—but not by his Dn 8:24
and in his own mind he shall become **g**. Dn 8:25
saying, "O Lord, the **g** and awesome God, Dn 9:4
us, by bringing upon us a **g** calamity. Dn 9:12
but because of your **g** mercy. Dn 9:18
word was true, and it was a **g** conflict. Dn 10:1
on the bank of the **g** river (that is, Dn 10:4
but a **g** trembling fell upon them, Dn 10:7
So I was left alone and saw this **g** vision, Dn 10:8
who shall rule with **g** dominion and do Dn 11:3
and his authority shall be a **g** authority. Dn 11:5
and assemble a multitude of **g** forces, Dn 11:10
And he shall raise a **g** multitude, but it Dn 11:11
come on with a **g** army and abundant Dn 11:13
the king of the south with a **g** army. Dn 11:25
with an exceedingly **g** and mighty Dn 11:25
shall return to his land with **g** wealth, Dn 11:28
shall go out with **g** fury to destroy and Dn 11:44
the **g** prince who has charge of your Dn 12:1
the land commits **g** whoredom by Hos 1:2
the land, for **g** shall be the day of Jezreel. Hos 1:11
went to Assyria, and sent to the **g** king. Hos 5:13
because of your **g** iniquity and great Hos 9:7
of your great iniquity and **g** hatred. Hos 9:7
to Assyria as tribute to the **g** king. Hos 10:6
you, O Bethel, because of your **g** evil. Hos 10:15
the mountains a **g** and powerful people; Jl 2:2
his army, for his camp is exceedingly **g**; Jl 2:11
the day of the LORD is **g** and very awesome; Jl 2:11
of him will rise, for he has done **g** things. Jl 2:20
rejoice, for the LORD has done **g** things! Jl 2:21
the destroyer, and the cutter, my **g** army, Jl 2:25
before the **g** and awesome day of the LORD Jl 2:31
full. The vats overflow, for their evil is **g**. Jl 3:13
and see the **g** tumults within her, Am 3:9
and the **g** houses shall come to an end," Am 3:15
transgressions and how **g** are your sins Am 5:12
see, and from there go to Hamath the **g**; Am 6:2
and the **g** house shall be struck down Am 6:11
and it devoured the **g** deep and was Am 7:4

and the shekel **g** and deal deceitfully Am 8:5
"Arise, go to Nineveh, that **g** city, and Jon 1:2
the LORD hurled a **g** wind upon the sea, Jon 1:4
of me that this **g** tempest has come Jon 1:12
the LORD appointed a **g** fish to swallow Jon 1:17
"Arise, go to Nineveh, that **g** city, and Jon 3:2
Now Nineveh was an exceedingly **g** city, Jon 3:3
should not I pity Nineveh, that **g** city, Jon 4:11
for now he shall be **g** to the ends of the Mi 5:4
and the **g** man utters the evil desire of his Mi 7:3
The LORD is slow to anger and **g** in power, Na 1:3
and all her **g** men were bound in Na 3:10
The **g** day of the LORD is near, near and Zep 1:14
Who are you, O **g** mountain? Before Zec 4:7
Therefore **g** anger came from the LORD Zec 7:12
I am jealous for Zion with **g** jealousy, Zec 8:2
and I am jealous for her with **g** wrath. Zec 8:2
each with staff in hand because of **g** age. Zec 8:4
For how **g** is his goodness, and how Zec 9:17
is his goodness, and how **g** his beauty! Zec 9:17
will be as **g** as the mourning Zec 12:11
on that day a **g** panic from the LORD Zec 14:13
silver, and garments in **g** abundance. Zec 14:14
"**G** is the LORD beyond the border of Mal 1:5
my name will be **g** among the nations, Mal 1:11
my name will be **g** among the nations, Mal 1:11
For I am a **g** King, says the LORD of Mal 1:14
prophet before the **g** and awesome day Mal 4:5
they rejoiced exceedingly with **g** joy. Mt 2:10
dwelling in darkness have seen a **g** light, Mt 4:16
And **g** crowds followed him from Galilee Mt 4:25
be glad, for your reward is **g** in heaven, Mt 5:12
them will be called **g** in the kingdom of Mt 5:19
Jerusalem, for it is the city of the **g** King. Mt 5:35
you is darkness, how **g** is the darkness! Mt 6:23
house, and it fell, and **g** was the fall of it." Mt 7:27
the mountain, **g** crowds followed him. Mt 8:1
when Jesus saw a **g** crowd around him, Mt 8:18
behold, there arose a **g** storm on the sea, Mt 8:24
and the sea, and there was a **g** calm. Mt 8:26
three nights in the belly of the **g** fish, Mt 12:40
And **g** crowds gathered about him, so Mt 13:2
who, on finding one pearl of **g** value, Mt 13:46
he went ashore he saw a **g** crowd, Mt 14:14
her, "O woman, **g** is your faith! Mt 15:28
And **g** crowds came to him, bringing Mt 15:30
a desolate place to feed so **g** a crowd?" Mt 15:33
to have a **g** millstone fastened around Mt 18:6
sorrowful, for he had **g** possessions. Mt 19:22
and their **g** ones exercise authority over Mt 20:25
whoever would be **g** among you must Mt 20:26
out of Jericho, a **g** crowd followed him. Mt 20:29
which is the **g** commandment in the Mt 22:36
This is the **g** and first commandment. Mt 22:38
For then there will be **g** tribulation, Mt 24:21
arise and perform **g** signs and wonders, Mt 24:24
of heaven with power and **g** glory. Mt 24:30
and with him a **g** crowd with swords Mt 26:47
And he rolled a **g** stone to the entrance Mt 27:60
And behold, there was a **g** earthquake, Mt 28:2
from the tomb with fear and **g** joy, Mt 28:8
to the sea, and a **g** crowd followed, Mk 3:7
When the **g** crowd heard all that he was Mk 3:8
And a **g** windstorm arose, and the Mk 4:37
wind ceased, and there was a **g** calm. Mk 4:39
they were filled with **g** fear and said to Mk 4:41
Now a **g** herd of pigs was feeding there Mk 5:11
side, a **g** crowd gathered about him, Mk 5:21
And a **g** crowd followed him and Mk 5:24
When he went ashore he saw a **g** crowd, Mk 6:34
when again a **g** crowd had gathered, Mk 8:1
they saw a **g** crowd around them, Mk 9:14
for him if a **g** millstone were hung Mk 9:42
sorrowful, for he had **g** possessions. Mk 10:22
and their **g** ones exercise authority Mk 10:42
whoever would be **g** among you must Mk 10:43
with his disciples and a **g** crowd, Mk 10:46
his son?" And the **g** throng heard him Mk 12:37
to him, "Do you see these **g** buildings? Mk 13:2
in clouds with **g** power and glory. Mk 13:26
for he will be **g** before the Lord. And he Lk 1:15
He will be **g** and will be called the Son of Lk 1:32
who is mighty has done **g** things for me, Lk 1:49
that the Lord had shown **g** mercy to her, Lk 1:58
you good news of a **g** joy that will be for Lk 2:10
been searching for you in **g** distress." Lk 2:48
and a **g** famine came over all the land, Lk 4:25
and **g** crowds gathered to hear him and Lk 5:15
Levi made him a **g** feast in his house, Lk 5:29
with a **g** crowd of his disciples and a Lk 6:17
his disciples and a **g** multitude of people Lk 6:17
for behold, your reward is **g** in heaven; Lk 6:23
in return, and your reward will be **g**, Lk 6:35
it fell, and the ruin of that house was **g**." Lk 6:49
his disciples and a **g** crowd went with Lk 7:11

"A **g** prophet has arisen among us!" and Lk 7:16
And when a **g** crowd was gathering and Lk 8:4
them, for they were seized with **g** fear. Lk 8:37
from the mountain, a **g** crowd met him. Lk 9:37
least among you all is the one who is **g**." Lk 9:48
and how **g** is my distress until it is Lk 12:50
man once gave a **g** banquet and invited Lk 14:16
Now **g** crowds accompanied him, and Lk 14:25
if not, while the other is yet a **g** way off, Lk 14:32
us and you a **g** chasm has been fixed, Lk 16:26
There will be **g** earthquakes, and in Lk 21:11
be terrors and **g** signs from heaven. Lk 21:11
For there will be **g** distress upon the Lk 21:23
in a cloud with power and **g** glory. Lk 21:27
his sweat became like **g** drops of blood Lk 22:44
there followed him a **g** multitude of the Lk 23:27
and returned to Jerusalem with **g** joy, Lk 24:52
On the last day of the feast, the **g** day, Jn 7:37
comes, the **g** and magnificent day. Acts 2:20
And with **g** power the apostles were Acts 4:33
Jesus, and **g** grace was upon them all. Acts 4:33
And **g** fear came upon all who heard of Acts 5:5
And **g** fear came upon the whole Acts 5:11
and a **g** many of the priests became Acts 6:7
was doing **g** wonders and signs among Acts 6:8
all Egypt and Canaan, and **g** affliction, Acts 7:11
on that day a **g** persecution against the Acts 8:1
Stephen and made **g** lamentation over Acts 8:2
saying that he himself was somebody **g**. Acts 8:9
is the power of God that is called **G**." Acts 8:10
seeing signs and **g** miracles performed, Acts 8:13
something like a **g** sheet descending, Acts 10:11
something like a **g** sheet descending, Acts 11:5
and a **g** number who believed turned Acts 11:21
And a **g** many people were added to Acts 11:24
church and taught a **g** many people. Acts 11:26
there would be a **g** famine over all the Acts 11:28
made the people **g** during their stay Acts 13:17
a way that a **g** number of both Jews Acts 14:1
and brought **g** joy to all the brothers. Acts 15:3
suddenly there was a **g** earthquake, Acts 16:26
as did a **g** many of the devout Greeks Acts 17:4
and turned away a **g** many people, Acts 19:26
temple of the **g** goddess Artemis may Acts 19:27
out, "**G** is Artemis of the Ephesians!" Acts 19:28
"**G** is Artemis of the Ephesians!" Acts 19:34
is temple keeper of the **g** Artemis, Acts 19:35
And when there was a **g** hush, he Acts 21:40
about noon a **g** light from heaven Acts 22:6
Then a **g** clamor arose, and some of Acts 23:9
and Bernice came with **g** pomp, Acts 25:23
here testifying both to small and **g**, Acts 26:22
your **g** learning is driving you out of Acts 26:24
that I have **g** sorrow and unceasing Rom 9:2
in every way: by **g** endurance, 2 Cor 6:4
am acting with **g** boldness toward you; 2 Cor 7:4
toward you; I have **g** pride in you; 2 Cor 7:4
because of his **g** confidence in you. 2 Cor 8:22
to the working of his **g** might Eph 1:19
because of the **g** love with which he Eph 2:4
make known how **g** among the Col 1:27
you to know how **g** a struggle I have Col 2:1
more eagerly and with **g** desire to see 1 Thes 2:17
themselves and also **g** confidence in 1 Tm 3:13
G indeed, we confess, is the mystery of 1 Tm 3:16
Now there is **g** gain in godliness with 1 Tm 6:6
Now in a **g** house there are not only 2 Tm 2:20
the coppersmith did me **g** harm; 2 Tm 4:14
of the glory of our **g** God and Savior Jesus Ti 2:13
escape if we neglect such a **g** salvation? Heb 2:3
then we have a **g** high priest who has Heb 4:14
See how **g** this man was to whom Heb 7:4
since we have a **g** priest over the house Heb 10:21
confidence, which has a **g** reward. Heb 10:35
are surrounded by so **g** a cloud of Heb 12:1
Jesus, the **g** shepherd of the sheep, Heb 13:20
a small member, yet it boasts of **g** things. Jas 3:5
How **g** a forest is set ablaze by such a Jas 3:5
of a righteous person has **g** power as it is Jas 5:16
According to his **g** mercy, he has caused 1 Pt 1:3
to us his precious and very **g** promises, 2 Pt 1:4
until the judgment of the **g** day— Jude 1:6
the presence of his glory with **g** joy, Jude 1:24
with her I will throw into **g** tribulation, Rv 2:22
one another, and he was given a **g** sword. Rv 6:4
and behold, there was a **g** earthquake, Rv 6:12
the earth and the **g** ones and the generals Rv 6:15
for the **g** day of their wrath has come, Rv 6:17
a **g** multitude that no one could number, Rv 7:9
the ones coming out of the **g** tribulation. Rv 7:14
and something like a **g** mountain, Rv 8:8
trumpet, and a **g** star fell from heaven, Rv 8:10
rose smoke like the smoke of a **g** furnace, Rv 9:2
who are bound at the **g** river Euphrates." Rv 9:14
the street of the **g** city that symbolically Rv 11:8

and **g** fear fell on those who saw them. Rv 11:11
at that hour there was a **g** earthquake, Rv 11:13
have taken your **g** power and begun Rv 11:17
who fear your name, both small and **g**, Rv 11:18
And a **g** sign appeared in heaven: a Rv 12:1
behold, a **g** red dragon, with seven heads Rv 12:3
And the **g** dragon was thrown down, that Rv 12:9
devil has come down to you in **g** wrath, Rv 12:12
the two wings of the **g** eagle so that she Rv 12:14
power and his throne and **g** authority. Rv 13:2
It performs **g** signs, even making fire Rv 13:13
Also it causes all, both small and **g**, Rv 13:16
saying, "Fallen, fallen is Babylon the **g**, Rv 14:8
threw it into the **g** winepress of the Rv 14:19
another sign in heaven, **g** and amazing, Rv 15:1
saying, "**G** and amazing are your deeds, Rv 15:3
out his bowl on the **g** river Euphrates, Rv 16:12
them for battle on the **g** day of God the Rv 16:14
and a **g** earthquake such as there had Rv 16:18
on the earth, so **g** was that earthquake. Rv 16:18
The **g** city was split into three parts, Rv 16:19
and God remembered Babylon the **g**, Rv 16:19
And **g** hailstones, about one hundred Rv 16:21
the judgment of the **g** prostitute who is Rv 17:1
"Babylon the **g**, mother of prostitutes Rv 17:5
you saw is the **g** city that has dominion Rv 17:18
down from heaven, having **g** authority, Rv 18:1
voice, "Fallen, fallen is Babylon the **g**! Rv 18:2
Alas! You **g** city, you mighty city, Rv 18:10
for the **g** city that was clothed in fine Rv 18:16
"What city was like the **g** city?" Rv 18:18
for the **g** city where all who had ships at Rv 18:19
a stone like a **g** millstone and threw it Rv 18:21
"So will Babylon the **g** city be thrown Rv 18:21
your merchants were the **g** ones of the Rv 18:23
loud voice of a **g** multitude in heaven, Rv 19:1
has judged the **g** prostitute who Rv 19:2
you who fear him, small and **g**." Rv 19:5
seemed to be the voice of a **g** multitude, Rv 19:6
"Come, gather for the **g** supper of God, Rv 19:17
both free and slave, both small and **g**." Rv 19:18
key to the bottomless pit and a **g** chain. Rv 20:1
Then I saw a **g** white throne and him Rv 20:11
And I saw the dead, **g** and small, Rv 20:12
he carried me away in the Spirit to a **g**, Rv 21:10
It had a **g**, high wall, with twelve gates, Rv 21:12

GREATER (81)
two great lights—the **g** light to rule the Gn 1:16
"My punishment is **g** than I can bear. Gn 4:13
He is not **g** in this house than I am, nor Gn 39:9
the throne will I be **g** than you." Gn 41:40
his younger brother shall be **g** than he, Gn 48:19
I know that the LORD is **g** than all gods, Ex 18:11
of you a nation **g** and mightier than Nm 14:12
"The people are **g** and taller than we. Dt 1:28
before you nations **g** and mightier than Dt 4:38
your heart, 'These nations are **g** than I. Dt 7:17
to dispossess nations **g** and mightier than Dt 9:1
you a nation mightier and **g** than they.' Dt 9:14
will dispossess nations **g** and mightier Dt 11:23
cities, and because it was **g** than Ai, Jos 10:2
made this last kindness **g** than the first Ru 3:10
And David became **g** and greater, for 2 Sm 5:10
And David became greater and **g**, for 2 Sm 5:10
he hated her was **g** than the love with 2 Sm 13:15
sending me away is **g** than the other 2 Sm 13:16
make his throne **g** than the throne 1 Kgs 1:37
make his throne **g** than your throne.' 1 Kgs 1:47
And David became **g** and greater, for 1 Chr 11:9
And David became greater and **g**, for 1 Chr 11:9
be great, for our God is **g** than all gods. 2 Chr 2:5
And Jehoshaphat grew steadily **g**. He 2 Chr 17:12
will answer you, for God is **g** than man. Jb 33:12
carved images were **g** than those of Is 10:10
people has been **g** than the punishment Lam 4:6
But you will see still **g** abominations." Ezk 8:6
will see still **g** abominations that they Ezk 8:13
will see still **g** abominations than Ezk 8:15
and that seemed **g** than its companions. Dn 7:20
raise a multitude, **g** than the first. Dn 11:13
Or is their territory **g** than your territory, Am 6:2
of this house shall be **g** than the former, Hg 2:9
has arisen no one **g** than John the Mt 11:11
in the kingdom of heaven is **g** than he. Mt 11:11
something **g** than the temple is here. Mt 12:6
something **g** than Jonah is here. Mt 12:41
something **g** than Solomon is here. Mt 12:42
For which is **g**, the gold or the temple Mt 23:17
For which is **g**, the gift or the altar that Mt 23:19
other commandment **g** than these." Mk 12:31
will receive the **g** condemnation." Mk 12:40
born of women none is **g** than John. Lk 7:28
in the kingdom of God is **g** than he." Lk 7:28
something **g** than Solomon is here. Lk 11:31
something **g** than Jonah is here. Lk 11:32
They will receive the **g** condemnation." Lk 20:47
For who is the **g**, one who reclines at Lk 22:27
You will see **g** things than these." Jn 1:50
Are you **g** than our father Jacob? He gave Jn 4:12
And **g** works than these will he show Jn 5:20
that I have is **g** than that of John. Jn 5:36
Are you **g** than our father Abraham, Jn 8:53
who has given them to me, is **g** than all, Jn 10:29
you, a servant is not **g** than his master, Jn 13:16
nor is a messenger **g** than the one who Jn 13:16
and **g** works than these will he do, Jn 14:12
to the Father, for the Father is **g** than I. Jn 14:28
G love has no one than this, that Jn 15:13
you: 'A servant is not **g** than his master.' Jn 15:20
delivered me over to you has the **g** sin." Jn 19:11
lay on you no **g** burden than these Acts 15:28
to him at his lodging in **g** numbers. Acts 28:23
honorable we bestow the **g** honor, 1 Cor 12:23
parts are treated with **g** modesty, 1 Cor 12:23
giving **g** honor to the part that 1 Cor 12:24
one who prophesies is **g** than the one 1 Cor 14:5
And his affection for you is even **g**, as 2 Cor 7:15
like a madman—with far **g** labors, 2 Cor 11:23
he had no one **g** by whom to swear, Heb 6:13
swear by something **g** than themselves, Heb 6:16
then through the **g** and more perfect Heb 9:11
reproach of Christ **g** wealth than the Heb 11:26
teach will be judged with **g** strictness. Jas 3:1
angels, though **g** in might and power, 2 Pt 2:11
condemns us, God is **g** than our heart, 1 Jn 3:20
he who is in you is **g** than he who is in 1 Jn 4:4
of men, the testimony of God is **g**, 1 Jn 5:9
I have no **g** joy than to hear that my 3 Jn 1:4

GREATEST (20)
(Arba was the **g** man among the Jos 14:15
men and the **g** for a thousand. 1 Chr 12:14
that this man was the **g** of all the people of Jb 1:3
"For from the least to the **g** of them, Jer 6:13
the least to the **g** everyone is greedy for Jer 8:10
me, from the least of them to the **g**, Jer 31:34
and all the people from the least to the **g**, Jer 42:1
and all the people from the least to the **g**, Jer 42:8
From the least to the **g**, they shall die by Jer 44:12
from the **g** of them to the least of them. Jon 3:5
"Who is the **g** in the kingdom of Mt 18:1
like this child is the **g** in the kingdom of Mt 18:4
The **g** among you shall be your Mt 23:11
with one another about who was the **g**. Mk 9:34
them as to which of them was the **g**. Lk 9:46
of them was to be regarded as the **g**. Lk 22:24
let the **g** among you become as the Lk 22:26
to him, from the least to the **g**, Acts 8:10
these three; but the **g** of these is love. 1 Cor 13:13
me, from the least of them to the **g**. Heb 8:11

GREATLY (88)
prevailed and increased **g** on the earth, Gn 7:18
me and you, and may multiply you **g**." Gn 17:2
him fruitful and multiply him **g**. Gn 17:20
The LORD has **g** blessed my master, and Gn 24:35
the man increased **g** and had large Gn 30:43
because you longed **g** for your father's Gn 31:30
Then Jacob was **g** afraid and distressed. Gn 32:7
it, and were fruitful and multiplied **g**. Gn 47:27
of Israel were fruitful and increased **g**; Ex 1:7
marching after them, and they feared **g**. Ex 14:10
and the whole mountain trembled **g**. Ex 19:18
people of Israel, the people mourned **g**. Nm 14:39
with you, and that you may multiply **g**, Dt 6:3
—so we feared **g** for our lives because Jos 9:24
he feared **g**, because Gibeon was a great Jos 10:2
words, and his anger was **g** kindled. 1 Sm 11:6
and all the men of Israel rejoiced **g**. 1 Sm 11:15
and all the people **g** feared the LORD 1 Sm 12:18
And Saul loved him **g**, and he 1 Sm 16:21
they were dismayed and **g** afraid. 1 Sm 17:11
was afraid, and his heart trembled **g**. 1 Sm 28:5
And David was **g** distressed, for the 1 Sm 30:6
would not, for he feared **g**. 1 Sm 31:4
them, for the men were **g** ashamed. 2 Sm 10:5
David's anger was **g** kindled against 2 Sm 12:5
"I have sinned **g** in what I have done. 2 Sm 24:10
of Solomon, he rejoiced **g** and said, 1 Kgs 5:7
(Now Obadiah feared the LORD **g**, 1 Kgs 18:3
of Syria was **g** troubled because of 2 Kgs 6:11
and their fathers' houses increased **g**. 1 Chr 4:38
would not, for he feared **g**. 1 Chr 10:4
great is the LORD, and **g** to be praised, 1 Chr 16:25
them, for the men were **g** ashamed. 1 Chr 19:5
"I have sinned **g** in that I have done 1 Chr 21:8
LORD. David the king also rejoiced **g**. 1 Chr 29:9
and humbled himself **g** before the 2 Chr 33:12
for we have **g** transgressed in this Ezr 10:13
it displeased them **g** that someone had Neh 2:10
the wall, he was angry and **g** enraged, Neh 4:1
were afraid and fell **g** in their own Neh 6:16
My soul also is **g** troubled. But you, O Ps 6:3
shall be ashamed and **g** troubled; Ps 6:10
and in your salvation how **g** he exults! Ps 21:1
Great is the LORD and **g** to be praised in Ps 48:1
my fortress; I shall not be **g** shaken. Ps 62:2
the earth and water it; you **g** enrich it; Ps 65:9
a God **g** to be feared in the council of the Ps 89:7
For great is the LORD, and **g** to be praised; Ps 96:4
By his blessing they multiply **g**, and Ps 107:38
who **g** delights in his commandments! Ps 112:1
even when I spoke, "I am **g** afflicted"; Ps 116:10
"**G** have they afflicted me from my Ps 129:1
"**G** have they afflicted me from my Ps 129:2
Great is the LORD, and **g** to be praised, Ps 145:3
father of the righteous will **g** rejoice; Prv 23:24
the land, **g** distressed and hungry. Is 8:21
I will **g** rejoice in the LORD; my soul shall Is 61:10
her? Would not that land be **g** polluted? Jer 3:1
They will be **g** shamed, for they will not Jer 20:11
and my Sabbaths they **g** profaned. Ezk 20:13
Then King Belshazzar was **g** alarmed, Dn 5:9
me, Daniel, my thoughts **g** alarmed me, Dn 7:28
come to tell it to you, for you are **g** loved. Dn 9:23
he said to me, "O Daniel, man **g** loved, Dn 10:11
And he said, "O man **g** loved, fear not, Dn 10:19
Rejoice **g**, O daughter of Zion! Shout Zec 9:9
third day." And they were **g** distressed. Mt 17:23
had taken place, they were **g** distressed, Mt 18:31
heard this, they were **g** astonished, Mt 19:25
so that the governor was **g** amazed. Mt 27:14
he heard him, he was **g** perplexed, Mk 6:20
were **g** amazed and ran up to him and Mk 9:15
began to be **g** distressed and troubled. Mk 14:33
But she was **g** troubled at the saying, Lk 1:29
him, rejoices **g** at the bridegroom's voice. Jn 3:29
moved in his spirit and **g** troubled. Jn 11:33
g annoyed because they were teaching Acts 4:2
they were **g** perplexed about them, Acts 5:24
the disciples multiplied **g** in Jerusalem, Acts 6:7
Paul, having become **g** annoyed, Acts 16:18
he **g** helped those who through grace Acts 18:27
They also honored us **g**, and when we Acts 28:10
among you may be **g** enlarged, 2 Cor 10:15
rejoiced in the Lord **g** that now at Phil 4:10
g distressed by the sensual conduct of 2 Pt 2:7
I rejoiced **g** to find some of your children 2 Jn 1:4
For I rejoiced **g** when the brothers came 3 Jn 1:3
of Jesus. When I saw her, I marveled **g**. Rv 17:6

GREATNESS (34)
In the **g** of your majesty you overthrow Ex 15:7
them; because of the **g** of your arm, Ex 15:16
according to the **g** of your steadfast Nm 14:19
your servant your **g** and your mighty Dt 3:24
our God has shown us his glory and **g**, Dt 5:24
you have redeemed through your **g**, Dt 9:26
the discipline of the LORD your God, his **g**, Dt 11:2
name of the LORD; ascribe **g** to our God! Dt 32:3
you have brought about all this **g**, 2 Sm 7:21
own heart, you have done all this **g**, 1 Chr 17:19
is the **g** and the power and the glory 1 Chr 29:11
half the **g** of your wisdom was not told 2 Chr 9:6
according to the **g** of your steadfast Neh 13:22
and pomp of his **g** for many days, Est 1:4
he contend with me in the **g** of his power? Jb 23:6
and let not the **g** of the ransom turn you Jb 36:18
You will increase my **g** and comfort me Ps 71:21
to be praised, and his **g** is unsearchable. Ps 145:3
deeds, and I will declare your **g**. Ps 145:6
praise him according to his excellent **g**! Ps 150:2
them all by name, by the **g** of his might, Is 40:26
marching in the **g** of his strength? Is 63:1
it is for the **g** of your iniquity that your Jer 13:22
"Whom are you like in your **g**? Ezk 31:2
It was beautiful in its **g**, in the length of Ezk 31:7
in glory and in **g** among the trees of Ezk 31:18
I will show my **g** and my holiness and Ezk 38:23
Your **g** has grown and reaches to Dn 4:22
and still more **g** was added to me. Dn 4:36
father kingship and **g** and glory and Dn 5:18
And because of the **g** that he gave him, Dn 5:19
the dominion and the **g** of the kingdoms Dn 7:27
by the surpassing **g** of the revelations, 2 Cor 12:7
is the immeasurable **g** of his power Eph 1:19

GREECE (5)
And the goat is the king of **G**. And the Dn 8:21
out, behold, the prince of **G** will come. Dn 10:20
stir up all against the kingdom of **G**. Dn 11:2
sons, O Zion, against your sons, O **G**, Zec 9:13
much encouragement, he came to **G**. Acts 20:2

GREED (8)
delivered you to the **g** of your enemies, Ezk 16:27
His **g** is as wide as Sheol; like death he Hab 2:5
they are full of **g** and self-indulgence. Mt 23:25

inside you are full of **g** and wickedness. Lk 11:39
he is guilty of sexual immorality or **g**, 1 Cor 5:11
with a pretext for **g**—God is witness. 1 Thes 2:5
And in their **g** they will exploit you with 2 Pt 2:3
souls. They have hearts trained in **g**. 2 Pt 2:14

GREEDY (12)
and the one **g** for gain curses and Ps 10:3
of everyone who is **g** for unjust gain; Prv 1:19
Whoever is **g** for unjust gain troubles Prv 15:27
A **g** man stirs up strife, but the one Prv 28:25
of them, everyone is **g** for unjust gain; Jer 6:13
the greatest everyone is **g** for unjust gain; Jer 8:10
my people; they are **g** for their iniquity. Hos 4:8
of this world, or the **g** and swindlers, 1 Cor 5:10
nor thieves, nor the **g**, nor drunkards, 1 Cor 6:10
g to practice every kind of impurity. Eph 4:19
much wine, not **g** for dishonest gain. 1 Tm 3:8
or a drunkard or violent or **g** for gain, Ti 1:7

GREEK (13)
written in Aramaic, in Latin, and in **G**. Jn 19:20
was a believer, but his father was a **G**. Acts 16:1
they all knew that his father was a **G**. Acts 16:3
with not a few **G** women of high Acts 17:12
you?" And he said, "Do you know **G**? Acts 21:37
to the Jew first and also to the **G**. Rom 1:16
does evil, the Jew first and also the **G**, Rom 2:9
does good, the Jew first and also the **G**. Rom 2:10
is no distinction between Jew and **G**; Rom 10:12
to be circumcised, though he was a **G**. Gal 2:3
There is neither Jew nor **G**, there is Gal 3:28
Here there is not **G** and Jew, Col 3:11
and in **G** he is called Apollyon. Rv 9:11

GREEKS (17)
and Jerusalem to the **G** in order to remove Jl 3:6
Dispersion among the **G** and teach the Jn 7:35
among the Greeks and teach the **G**? Jn 7:35
up to worship at the feast were some **G**. Jn 12:20
number of both Jews and **G** believed. Acts 14:1
many of the devout **G** and not a few Acts 17:4
and tried to persuade Jews and **G**. Acts 18:4
the word of the Lord, both Jews and **G**. Acts 19:10
of Ephesus, both Jews and **G**. Acts 19:17
to Jews and to **G** of repentance toward Acts 20:21
he even brought **G** into the temple Acts 21:28
obligation both to **G** and to Rom 1:14
charged that all, both Jews and **G**, Rom 3:9
demand signs and **G** seek wisdom, 1 Cor 1:22
who are called, both Jews and **G**, 1 Cor 1:24
to Jews or to **G** or to the church 1 Cor 10:32
baptized into one body—Jews or **G**, 1 Cor 12:13

GREEN (33)
I have given every **g** plant for food." And Gn 1:30
And as I gave you the **g** plants, I give you Gn 9:3
hail had left. Not a **g** thing remained, Ex 10:15
and on the hills and under every **g** tree. Dt 12:2
high hill and under every **g** tree, 1 Kgs 14:23
on the hills and under every **g** tree. 2 Kgs 16:4
high hill and under every **g** tree, 2 Kgs 17:10
on the hills and under every **g** tree. 2 Chr 28:4
his time, and his branch will not be **g**. Jb 15:32
and he searches after every **g** thing. Jb 39:8
He makes me lie down in **g** pastures. He Ps 23:2
like the grass and wither like the **g** herb. Ps 37:2
spreading himself like a **g** laurel tree. Ps 37:35
But I am like a **g** olive tree in the house of Ps 52:8
the heat of thorns, whether **g** or ablaze, Ps 58:9
old age; they are ever full of sap and **g**, Ps 92:14
the righteous will flourish like a **g** leaf. Prv 11:28
beloved, truly delightful. Our couch is **g**; Sg 1:16
lust among the oaks, under every **g** tree, Is 57:5
hill and under every **g** tree you bowed Jer 2:20
on every high hill and under every **g** tree, Jer 3:6
among foreigners under every **g** tree, Jer 3:13
The LORD once called you 'a **g** olive tree, Jer 11:16
beside every **g** tree and on the high hills, Jer 17:2
when heat comes, for its leaves remain **g**, Jer 17:8
the mountaintops, under every **g** tree, Ezk 6:13
high the low tree, dry up the **g** tree, Ezk 17:24
it shall devour every **g** tree in you and Ezk 20:47
for the pastures of the wilderness are **g**; Jl 2:22
all to sit down in groups on the **g** grass. Mk 6:39
do these things when the wood is **g**, Lk 23:31
burned up, and all **g** grass was burned up. Rv 8:7
of the earth or any **g** plant or any tree, Rv 9:4

GREENERY (1)
the vegetation fails, the **g** is no more. Is 15:6

GREENISH (2)
if the disease is **g** or reddish in the Lv 13:49
of the house with **g** or reddish spots, Lv 14:37

GREET (44)
And they will **g** you and give you two 1 Sm 10:4
went out to meet him and **g** him. 1 Sm 13:10
go to Nabal and **g** him in my name. 1 Sm 25:5
And thus you shall **g** him: 'Peace be 1 Sm 25:6
out of the wilderness to **g** our master, 1 Sm 25:14
If you meet anyone, do not **g** him, and 2 Kgs 4:29
it rouses the shades to **g** you, all who were Is 14:9
And if you **g** only your brothers, what Mt 5:47
As you enter the house, **g** it. Mt 10:12
no sandals, and **g** no one on the road. Lk 10:4
G Prisca and Aquila, my fellow Rom 16:3
G also the church in their house. Rom 16:5
G my beloved Epaenetus, who was the Rom 16:5
G Mary, who has worked hard for you. Rom 16:6
G Andronicus and Junia, my Rom 16:7
G Ampliatus, my beloved in the Lord. Rom 16:8
G Urbanus, our fellow worker in Rom 16:9
G Apelles, who is approved in Christ. Rom 16:10
G those who belong to the family of Rom 16:10
G my kinsman Herodion. Greet those Rom 16:11
G those in the Lord who belong to the Rom 16:11
G those workers in the Lord, Rom 16:12
G the beloved Persis, who has worked Rom 16:12
G Rufus, chosen in the Lord; also his Rom 16:13
G Asyncritus, Phlegon, Hermes, Rom 16:14
G Philologus, Julia, Nereus and his Rom 16:15
G one another with a holy kiss. All Rom 16:16
All the churches of Christ **g** you. Rom 16:16
wrote this letter, **g** you in the Lord. Rom 16:22
and our brother Quartus, **g** you. Rom 16:23
G one another with a holy kiss. 1 Cor 16:20
G one another with a holy kiss. 2 Cor 13:12
All the saints **g** you. 2 Cor 13:13
G every saint in Christ Jesus. The Phil 4:21
The brothers who are with me **g** you. Phil 4:21
All the saints **g** you, especially those of Phil 4:22
G all the brothers with a holy kiss. 1 Thes 5:26
G Prisca and Aquila, and the 2 Tm 4:19
to you. **G** those who love us in the faith. Ti 3:15
G all your leaders and all the saints. Heb 13:24
G one another with the kiss of love. 1 Pt 5:14
The children of your elect sister **g** you. 2 Jn 1:13
Peace be to you. The friends **g** you. 3 Jn 1:15
you. **G** the friends, every one of them. 3 Jn 1:15

GREETED (9)
ranks and went and **g** his brothers. 1 Sm 17:22
came near to the people he **g** them. 1 Sm 30:21
And he **g** him and said to him, "Is 2 Kgs 10:15
amazed and ran up to him and **g** him. Mk 9:15
the house of Zechariah and **g** Elizabeth. Lk 1:40
he went up and **g** the church, Acts 18:22
and we **g** the brothers and stayed with Acts 21:7
arrived at Caesarea and **g** Festus. Acts 25:13
seen them and **g** them from afar, Heb 11:13

GREETING (10)
of the province Beyond the River, send **g**. Ezr 4:11
province Beyond the River, **g**. And now Ezr 4:17
to discern what sort of **g** this might be. Lk 1:29
when Elizabeth heard the **g** of Mary, Lk 1:41
the sound of your **g** came to my ears, Lk 1:44
After **g** them, he related one by one Acts 21:19
write this **g** with my own hand. 1 Cor 16:21
I, Paul, write this **g** with my own hand. Col 4:18
write this **g** with my own hand. 2 Thes 3:17
him into your house or give him any **g**, 2 Jn 1:10

GREETINGS (19)
and **g** in the marketplaces and being Mt 23:7
said, "**G**, Rabbi!" And he kissed him. Mt 26:49
"**G**!" And they came up and took hold of Mt 28:9
robes and like **g** in the marketplaces Mk 12:38
came to her and said, "**G**, O favored one, Lk 1:28
the synagogues and **g** in the Lk 11:43
and love **g** in the marketplaces and the Lk 20:46
in Antioch and Syria and Cilicia, **g**. Acts 15:23
his Excellency the governor Felix, **g**. Acts 23:26
The churches of Asia send you **g**. 1 Cor 16:19
send you hearty **g** in the Lord. 1 Cor 16:19
All the brothers send you **g**. Greet 1 Cor 16:20
Give my **g** to the brothers at Laodicea, Col 4:15
winter. Eubulus sends **g** to you, 2 Tm 4:21
All who are with me send **g** to you. Greet Ti 3:15
in Christ Jesus, sends **g** to you, Phlm 1:23
who come from Italy send you **g**. Heb 13:24
To the twelve tribes in the Dispersion: **G**. Jas 1:1
who is likewise chosen, sends you **g**, 1 Pt 5:13

GREETS (7)
do not greet him, and if anyone **g** you, 2 Kgs 4:29
Timothy, my fellow worker, **g** you; so Rom 16:21
me and to the whole church, **g** you. Rom 16:23
Aristarchus my fellow prisoner **g** you, Col 4:10
of you, a servant of Christ Jesus, **g** you, Col 4:12
Luke the beloved physician **g** you, as Col 4:14
for whoever **g** him takes part in his 2 Jn 1:11

GREW (55)
of the cities, and what **g** on the ground. Gn 19:25
And the child **g** and was weaned. And Gn 21:8
God was with the boy, and he **g** up. Gn 21:20
When the boys **g** up, Esau was a Gn 25:27
for his compassion **g** warm for his Gn 43:30
they multiplied and **g** exceedingly strong, Ex 1:7
the people multiplied and **g** very strong. Ex 1:20
When the child **g** up, she brought him Ex 2:10
eat; but when the sun **g** hot, it melted. Ex 16:21
But Moses' hands **g** weary, so they took Ex 17:12
of the trumpet **g** louder and louder, Ex 19:19
"But Jeshurun **g** fat, and kicked; you Dt 32:15
grew fat, and kicked; you **g** fat, Dt 32:15
Now when the people of Israel **g** strong, Jos 17:13
When Israel **g** strong, they put the Jgs 1:28
And when his wife's sons **g** up, they Jgs 11:2
And the young man **g**, and the LORD Jgs 13:24
young man Samuel **g** in the presence 1 Sm 2:21
And Samuel **g**, and the LORD was with 1 Sm 3:19
And David **g** stronger and stronger, 2 Sm 3:1
and it **g** up with him and with his 2 Sm 12:3
And the conspiracy **g** strong, and the 2 Sm 15:12
the Philistines. And David **g** weary. 2 Sm 21:15
while the heavens **g** black with 1 Kgs 18:45
So King Rehoboam **g** strong in 2 Chr 12:13
But Abijah **g** mighty. And he took 2 Chr 13:21
And Jehoshaphat **g** steadily greater. 2 Chr 17:12
But Jehoiada **g** old and full of days, 2 Chr 24:15
But when he was strong, he **g** proud, 2 Chr 26:16
for the man Mordecai **g** more and more Est 9:4
my youth the fatherless **g** up with me as Jb 31:18
to no avail, and my distress **g** worse. Ps 39:2
For he **g** up before him like a young Is 53:2
And you **g** up and became tall and Ezk 16:7
You **g** exceedingly beautiful and Ezk 16:13
its boughs **g** large and its branches Ezk 31:5
The tree **g** and became strong, and its Dn 4:11
you saw, which **g** and became strong, Dn 4:20
heaven till his hair **g** as long as eagles' Dn 4:33
which **g** exceedingly great toward the Dn 8:9
It **g** great, even to the host of heaven. Dn 8:10
us?" For the sea **g** more and more Jon 1:11
for the sea **g** more and more Jon 1:13
and the thorns **g** up and choked them. Mt 13:7
and the thorns **g** up and choked it, Mk 4:7
and was no better but rather **g** worse. Mk 5:26
And when it **g** late, his disciples came to Mk 6:35
And the child **g** and became strong in Lk 1:80
And the child **g** and became strong, Lk 2:40
And some fell on the rock, and as it **g** up, Lk 8:6
and the thorns **g** up with it and choked it. Lk 8:7
into good soil and **g** and yielded a Lk 8:8
his garden, and it **g** and became a tree, Lk 13:19
but he **g** strong in his faith as he gave Rom 4:20
had ships at sea **g** rich by her wealth! Rv 18:19

GRIDDLE (4)
offering is a grain offering baked on a **g**, Lv 2:5
It shall be made with oil on a **g**. You Lv 6:21
on a pan or a **g** shall belong to the priest Lv 7:9
And you, take an iron **g**, and place it as Ezk 4:3

GRIEF (16)
have no cause of **g** or pangs of 1 Sm 25:31
My eye wastes away because of **g**; it grows Ps 6:7
I am in distress; my eye is wasted from **g**; Ps 31:9
may ache, and the end of joy may be **g**. Prv 14:13
A foolish son is a **g** to his father and Prv 17:25
away in a day of **g** and incurable pain. Is 17:11
a man of sorrows, and acquainted with **g**; Is 53:3
LORD to crush him; he has put him to **g**; Is 53:10
My joy is gone; **g** is upon me; my heart is Jer 8:18
but, though he cause **g**, he will have Lam 3:32
my eyes cause me **g** at the fate of all Lam 3:51
with breaking heart and bitter **g**, groan Ezk 21:6
For you felt a godly **g**, so that you 2 Cor 7:9
For godly **g** produces a repentance 2 Cor 7:10
whereas worldly **g** produces death. 2 Cor 7:10
earnestness this godly **g** has produced 2 Cor 7:11

GRIEFS (1)
he has borne our **g** and carried our Is 53:4

GRIEVANCE (1)
one of you has a **g** against another, 1 Cor 6:1

GRIEVE (11)
to weep his eyes out to **g** his heart, 1 Sm 2:33
"How long will you **g** over Saul, 1 Sm 16:1
you, O Jerusalem, or who will **g** for you? Jer 15:5
mourning, or go to lament or **g** for them, Jer 16:5
not for him who is dead, nor **g** for him, Jer 22:10
G for him, all you who are around him, Jer 48:17
willingly afflict or **g** the children of Lam 3:33
Wasted is Nineveh; who will **g** for her? Na 3:7
For even if I made you **g** with my letter, 2 Cor 7:8
And do not **g** the Holy Spirit of God, by Eph 4:30
that you may not **g** as others do who 1 Thes 4:13

GRIEVED (21)
on the earth, and it **g** him to his heart. Gn 6:6
of his death, but Samuel **g** over Saul. 1 Sm 15:35
let Jonathan know this, lest he be **g**.' 1 Sm 20:3
of the month, for he was **g** for David, 1 Sm 20:34
And do not be **g**, for the joy of the LORD Neh 8:10
quiet, for this day is holy; do not be **g**." Neh 8:11
hard? Was not my soul **g** for the needy? Jb 30:25
about as though I **g** for my friend or Ps 35:14
in the wilderness and **g** him in the Ps 78:40
and all who work for pay will be **g**. Is 19:10
you like a wife deserted and **g** in spirit, Is 54:6
But they rebelled and **g** his Holy Spirit; Is 63:10
falsely, although I have not **g** him, Ezk 13:22
but are not **g** over the ruin of Joseph! Am 6:6
with anger, **g** at their hardness of heart, Mk 3:5
love me?" Peter was **g** because he said to Jn 21:17
if your brother is **g** by what you eat, Rom 14:15
regret it, for I see that that letter **g** you, 2 Cor 7:8
it is, I rejoice, not because you were **g**, 2 Cor 7:9
but because you were **g** into repenting. 2 Cor 7:9
you have been **g** by various trials, 1 Pt 1:6

GRIEVING (2)
that day, "The king is **g** for his son." 2 Sm 19:2
I have heard Ephraim **g**, 'You have Jer 31:18

GRIEVOUS (17)
with a very great and **g** lamentation, Gn 50:10
"This is a **g** mourning by the Gn 50:11
showed signs and wonders, great and **g**, Dt 6:22
on the legs with **g** boils of which you Dt 28:35
lasting, and sicknesses **g** and lasting. Dt 28:59
cursed me with a **g** curse on the day 1 Kgs 2:8
And see if there be any **g** way in me, Ps 139:24
is done under the sun was **g** to me, Eccl 2:17
There is a **g** evil that I have seen under Eccl 5:13
This also is a **g** evil: just as he came, so Eccl 5:16
enjoys them. This is vanity; it is a **g** evil. Eccl 6:2
me because of my hurt! My wound is **g**. Jer 10:19
with a great wound, with a very **g** blow. Jer 14:17
hurt is incurable, and your wound is **g**. Jer 30:12
that destroys with a **g** destruction. Mi 2:10
Therefore I strike you with a **g** blow, Mi 6:13
is no easing your hurt; your wound is **g**. Na 3:19

GRIEVOUSLY (3)
used to provoke her **g** to irritate her, 1 Sm 1:6
Jerusalem sinned **g**; therefore she Lam 1:8
of Judah and has **g** offended in taking Ezk 25:12

GRIND (4)
then let my wife **g** for another, and let Jb 31:10
Take the millstones and **g** flour, put off Is 47:2
He has made my teeth **g** on gravel, and Lam 3:16
men are compelled to **g** at the mill, Lam 5:13

GRINDERS (1)
and the **g** cease because they are few, Eccl 12:3

GRINDING (6)
it with fire and crushed it, **g** it very small, Dt 9:21
shut—when the sound of the **g** is low, Eccl 12:4
by **g** the face of the poor?" declares the Is 3:15
the **g** of the millstones and the light of Jer 25:10
Two women will be **g** at the mill; one Mt 24:41
There will be two women **g** together. Lk 17:35

GRINDS (1)
and he foams and **g** his teeth and Mk 9:18

GROAN (20)
From out of the city the dying **g**, and the Jb 24:12
poor are plundered, because the needy **g**, Ps 12:5
I **g** because of the tumult of my heart. Ps 38:8
and at the end of your life you **g**, when Prv 5:11
but when the wicked rule, the people **g**. Prv 29:2
all her land the wounded shall **g**. Jer 51:52
all her gates are desolate; her priests **g**; Lam 1:4
All her people **g** as they search for Lam 1:11
men who sigh and **g** over all the Ezk 9:4
g; with breaking heart and bitter grief, Ezk 21:6
and bitter grief, **g** before their eyes. Ezk 21:6
when they say to you, 'Why do you **g**?' Ezk 21:7
your iniquities and **g** to one another. Ezk 24:23
of your fall, when the wounded **g**, Ezk 26:15
and he will **g** before him like a man Ezk 30:24
How the beasts **g**! The herds of cattle are Jl 1:18
Writhe and **g**, O daughter of Zion, like a Mi 4:10
g inwardly as we wait eagerly for Rom 8:23
For in this tent we **g**, longing to put on 2 Cor 5:2
For while we are still in this tent, we **g**, 2 Cor 5:4

GROANED (1)
the people of Israel **g** because of their Ex 2:23

GROANING (14)
And God heard their **g**, and God Ex 2:24
I have heard the **g** of the people of Israel Ex 6:5
to pity by their **g** because of those who Jgs 2:18
my hand is heavy on account of my **g**. Jb 23:2
ear to my words, O LORD; consider my **g**. Ps 5:1
from saving me, from the words of my **g**? Ps 22:1
wasted away through my **g** all day long. Ps 32:3
Because of my loud **g** my bones cling to Ps 102:5
I am weary with my **g**, and I find no rest.' Jer 45:3
"They heard my **g**, yet there is no one Lam 1:21
with weeping and **g** because he no Mal 2:13
are in Egypt, and have heard their **g**, Acts 7:34
creation has been **g** together in the Rom 8:22
them do this with joy and not with **g**, Heb 13:17

GROANINGS (2)
and my **g** are poured out like water. Jb 3:24
intercedes for us with **g** too deep for Rom 8:26

GROANS (4)
Let the **g** of the prisoners come before Ps 79:11
to hear the **g** of the prisoners, to set free Ps 102:20
she herself **g** and turns her face away. Lam 1:8
my transgressions; for my **g** are many, Lam 1:22

GROPE (6)
and you shall **g** at noonday, as the Dt 28:29
at noonday, as the blind **g** in darkness, Dt 28:29
in the daytime and **g** at noonday as in Jb 5:14
They **g** in the dark without light, and he Jb 12:25
We **g** for the wall like the blind; we Is 59:10
blind; we **g** like those who have no eyes; Is 59:10

GROPING (1)
wore themselves out **g** for the door. Gn 19:11

GROUND (263)
that creeps on the **g** according to its Gn 1:25
and there was no man to work the **g**, Gn 2:5
was watering the whole face of the **g**— Gn 2:6
of dust from the **g** and breathed into his Gn 2:7
And out of the **g** the LORD God made to Gn 2:9
So out of the **g** the LORD God formed Gn 2:19
eat of it,' cursed is the **g** because of you; Gn 3:17
shall eat bread, till you return to the **g**, Gn 3:19
Eden to work the **g** from which he was Gn 3:23
of sheep, and Cain a worker of the **g**. Gn 4:2
the LORD an offering of the fruit of the **g**, Gn 4:3
blood is crying to me from the **g**. Gn 4:10
And now you are cursed from the **g**, Gn 4:11
When you work the **g**, it shall no longer Gn 4:12
have driven me today away from the **g**, Gn 4:14
"Out of the **g** that the LORD has cursed Gn 5:29
kinds, of every creeping thing of the **g**, Gn 6:20
I will blot out from the face of the **g**." Gn 7:4
and of everything that creeps on the **g**, Gn 7:8
thing that was on the face of the **g**, Gn 7:23
had subsided from the face of the **g**. Gn 8:8
and behold, the face of the **g** was dry. Gn 8:13
never again curse the **g** because of man, Gn 8:21
that creeps on the **g** and all the fish Gn 9:2
of the cities, and what grew on the **g**. Gn 19:25
bowing himself to the **g** seven times, Gn 33:3
to bow ourselves to the **g** before you?" Gn 37:10
wife he would waste the semen on the **g**, Gn 38:9
before him with their faces to the **g**. Gn 42:6
them and bowed down to him to the **g**. Gn 43:26
man quickly lowered his sack to the **g**, Gn 44:11
still there. They fell before him to the **g**. Gn 44:14
on which you are standing is holy **g**." Ex 3:5
"Throw it on the **g**." So he threw it on the Ex 4:3
it on the ground." So he threw it on the **g**, Ex 4:3
from the Nile and pour it on the dry **g**, Ex 4:9
the Nile will become blood on the dry **g**." Ex 4:9
flies, and also the **g** on which they stand. Ex 8:21
Israel may go through the sea on dry **g**. Ex 14:16
went into the midst of the sea on dry **g**, Ex 14:22
Israel walked on dry **g** through the sea, Ex 14:29
of Israel walked on dry **g** in the midst of Ex 15:19
flake-like thing, fine as frost on the **g**. Ex 16:14
the firstfruits of your **g** you shall bring Ex 23:19
it with fire and **g** it to powder and Ex 32:20
the firstfruits of your **g** you shall bring Ex 34:26
their feet, with which to hop on the **g**. Lv 11:21
swarming things that swarm on the **g**: Lv 11:29
that swarms on the **g** is detestable; Lv 11:41
swarming thing that swarms on the **g**, Lv 11:42
swarming thing that crawls on the **g**. Lv 11:44
every creature that swarms on the **g**, Lv 11:46
by anything with which the **g** crawls, Lv 20:25
and gathered it and **g** it in handmills or Nm 11:8
and about two cubits above the **g**. Nm 11:31
and the **g** opens its mouth and Nm 16:30
words, the **g** under them split apart. Nm 16:31
likeness of anything that creeps on the **g**, Dt 4:18
of your womb and the fruit of your **g**, Dt 7:13
scorpions and thirsty **g** where there was Dt 8:15
you shall pour it out on the **g** like water. Dt 15:23
a bird's nest in any tree or on the **g**, Dt 22:6
some of the first of all the fruit of the **g**, Dt 26:2
now I bring the first of the fruit of the **g**, Dt 26:10
people Israel and the **g** that you have Dt 26:15
and the fruit of your **g** and the fruit of Dt 28:4
livestock and in the fruit of your **g**, Dt 28:11
of your womb and the fruit of your **g**, Dt 28:18
up the fruit of your **g** and of all your Dt 28:33
all your trees and the fruit of your **g**. Dt 28:42
of your cattle and the fruit of your **g**, Dt 28:51
of her foot on the **g** because she is so Dt 28:56
of your cattle and in the fruit of your **g**. Dt 30:9
stood firmly on dry **g** in the midst of Jos 3:17
passing over on dry **g** until all the Jos 3:17
of the priests' feet were lifted up on dry **g**, Jos 4:18
'Israel passed over this Jordan on dry **g**.' Jos 4:22
and there clear **g** for yourselves in the Jos 17:15
from off this good **g** that the LORD your Jos 23:13
went down into the **g** while he was lying Jgs 4:21
the fleece alone, and it is dry on all the **g**, Jgs 6:37
only, and on all the **g** let there be dew." Jgs 6:39
only, and on all the **g** there was dew. Jgs 6:40
and they fell on their faces to the **g**. Jgs 13:20
And he **g** at the mill in the prison. Jgs 16:21
The men of Israel gave **g** to Benjamin, Jgs 20:36
she fell on her face, bowing to the **g**, Ru 2:10
and let none of his words fall to the **g**. 1 Sm 3:19
face downward on the **g** before the ark 1 Sm 5:3
face downward on the **g** before the ark 1 Sm 5:4
and some to plow his **g** and to reap his 1 Sm 8:12
behold, there was honey on the **g**. 1 Sm 14:25
and slaughtered them on the **g**. 1 Sm 14:32
not one hair of his head fall to the **g**, 1 Sm 14:45
and he fell on his face to the **g**. 1 Sm 17:49
his face to the **g** and bowed three 1 Sm 20:41
on her face and bowed to the **g**. 1 Sm 25:23
with her face to the **g** and said, 1 Sm 25:41
his spear stuck in the **g** at his head, 1 Sm 26:7
his face to the **g** and paid homage. 1 Sm 28:14
Saul fell at once full length on the **g**, 1 Sm 28:20
David, he fell to the **g** and paid homage. 2 Sm 1:2
me. Why should I strike you to the **g**? 2 Sm 2:22
a line, making them lie down on the **g**. 2 Sm 8:2
went in and lay all night on the **g**. 2 Sm 12:16
beside him, to raise him from the **g**, 2 Sm 12:17
her face to the **g** and paid homage and 2 Sm 14:4
hair of your son shall fall to the **g**." 2 Sm 14:11
we are like water spilled on the **g**, 2 Sm 14:14
his face to the **g** and paid homage 2 Sm 14:22
on his face to the **g** before the king, 2 Sm 14:33
upon him as the dew falls on the **g**, 2 Sm 17:12
did you not strike him there to the **g**? 2 Sm 18:11
entrails to the **g** without striking a 2 Sm 20:10
there was a plot of **g** full of lentils, 2 Sm 23:11
to the king with his face to the **g**. 2 Sm 24:20
before the king, with his face to the **g**. 1 Kgs 1:23
her face to the **g** and paid homage to 1 Kgs 1:31
in the clay **g** between Succoth and 1 Kgs 7:46
the two of them could go over on dry **g**. 2 Kgs 2:8
him and bowed to the **g** before him. 2 Kgs 2:15
and fell at his feet, bowing to the **g**. 2 Kgs 4:37
on the plot of **g** belonging to Naboth 2 Kgs 9:25
—I will repay you on this plot of **g**.' 2 Kgs 9:26
up and throw him on the plot of **g**, 2 Kgs 9:26
"Strike the **g** with them." And he 2 Kgs 13:18
There was a plot of **g** full of barley, 1 Chr 11:13
to David with his face to the **g**. 1 Chr 21:21
in the clay **g** between Succoth and 2 Chr 4:17
their faces to the **g** on the pavement 2 Chr 7:3
his head with his face to the **g**, 2 Chr 20:18
were dead bodies lying on the **g**; 2 Chr 20:24
the LORD with their faces to the **g**. Neh 8:6
firstfruits of our **g** and the firstfruits Neh 10:35
to the Levites the tithes from our **g**, Neh 10:37
his head and fell on the **g** and worshiped. Jb 1:20
with him on the **g** seven days and seven Jb 2:13
dust, nor does trouble sprout from the **g**, Jb 5:6
not spare; he pours out my gall on the **g**. Jb 16:13
A rope is hidden for him in the **g**, a trap Jb 18:10
they gnaw the dry **g** by night in waste Jb 30:3
and to make the **g** sprout with grass? Jb 38:27
earth and lets them be warmed on the **g**, Jb 39:14
fierceness and rage he swallows the **g**; Jb 39:24
trample my life to the **g** and lay my glory Ps 7:5
like silver refined in a furnace on the **g**, Ps 12:6
they set their eyes to cast us to the **g**. Ps 17:11
My foot stands on level **g**; in the great Ps 26:12
to the dust; our belly clings to the **g**. Ps 44:25
of your name, bringing it down to the **g**. Ps 74:7
You cleared the **g** for it; it took deep root Ps 80:9
at En-dor, who became dung for the **g**. Ps 83:10
Faithfulness springs up from the **g**, and Ps 85:11
to cease and cast his throne to the **g**. Ps 89:44
and you renew the face of the **g**. Ps 104:30
land and ate up the fruit of their **g**. Ps 105:35
a desert, springs of water into thirsty **g**, Ps 107:33
soul; he has crushed my life to the **g**; Ps 143:3
Let your good Spirit lead me on level **g**! Ps 143:10
humble; he casts the wicked to the **g**. Ps 147:6

The fallow **g** of the poor would yield Prv 13:23
the **g** was covered with nettles, and its Prv 24:31
princes walking on the **g** like slaves. Eccl 10:7
caves of the rocks and the holes of the **g**, Is 2:19
and mourn; empty, she shall sit on the **g**. Is 3:26
How you are cut down to the **g**, you who Is 14:12
of her gods he has shattered to the **g**." Is 21:9
bring down, lay low, and cast to the **g**, Is 25:12
He lays it low, lays it low to the **g**, casts it Is 26:5
he continually open and harrow his **g**? Is 28:24
shall come from the **g** like the voice of Is 29:4
for the seed with which you sow the **g**, Is 30:23
ground, and bread, the produce of the **g**, Is 30:23
that work the **g** will eat seasoned Is 30:24
a pool, and the thirsty **g** springs of water; Is 35:7
the uneven **g** shall become level, and the Is 40:4
into light, the rough places into level **g**. Is 42:16
the thirsty land, and streams on the dry **g**; Is 44:3
of Babylon; sit on the **g** without a throne, Is 47:1
their faces to the **g** they shall bow down Is 49:23
your back like the **g** and like the street Is 51:23
a young plant, and like a root out of dry **g**; Is 53:2
"Break up your fallow **g**, and sow not Jer 4:3
the trees of the field and the fruit of the **g**; Jer 7:20
shall be as dung on the surface of the **g**. Jer 8:2
Gather up your bundle from the **g**, O Jer 10:17
her people lament on the **g**, and the cry Jer 14:2
Because of the **g** that is dismayed, since Jer 14:4
shall be as dung on the surface of the **g**. Jer 16:4
shall be dung on the surface of the **g**. Jer 25:33
your glory, and sit on the parched **g**, Jer 48:18
of Babylon shall be leveled to the **g**, Jer 51:58
brought down to the **g** in dishonor the Lam 2:2
Her gates have sunk into the **g**; he has Lam 2:9
of Zion sit on the **g** in silence; Lam 2:10
have bowed their heads to the **g**. Lam 2:10
poured out to the **g** because of the Lam 2:11
whitewash, and bring it down to the **g**, Ezk 13:14
plucked up in fury, cast down to the **g**; Ezk 19:12
pour it out on the **g** to cover it with Ezk 24:7
your mighty pillars will fall to the **g**. Ezk 26:11
will sit on the **g** and tremble every Ezk 26:16
I cast you to the **g**; I exposed you before Ezk 28:17
And I will cast you on the **g**; on the Ezk 32:4
all creeping things that creep on the **g**, Ezk 38:20
and every wall shall tumble to the **g**. Ezk 38:20
set back from the **g** more than the Ezk 42:6
the base on the **g** to the lower ledge, Ezk 43:14
sought to find a **g** for complaint against Dn 6:4
they could find no **g** for complaint or any Dn 6:4
not find any **g** for complaint against Dn 6:5
lifted up from the **g** and made to stand Dn 7:4
the whole earth, without touching the **g**. Dn 8:5
him down to the **g** and trampled on him. Dn 8:7
threw down to the **g** and trampled on Dn 8:10
and it will throw truth to the **g**, Dn 8:12
into a deep sleep with my face to the **g**. Dn 8:18
face in deep sleep with my face to the **g**. Dn 10:9
my face toward the **g** and was mute. Dn 10:15
and the creeping things of the **g**. Hos 2:18
break up your fallow **g**, for it is the Hos 10:12
The fields are destroyed, the **g** mourns, Jl 1:10
Does a snare spring up from the **g**, when Am 3:5
altar shall be cut off and fall to the **g**. Am 3:14
I will destroy it from the surface of the **g**, Am 9:8
"Who will bring me down to the **g**?" Ob 1:3
wine, the oil, on what the **g** brings forth, Hg 1:11
its fruit, and the **g** shall give its produce, Zec 8:12
except on the **g** of sexual immorality, Mt 5:32
will fall to the **g** apart from your Mt 10:29
Other seeds fell on rocky **g**, where they Mt 13:5
As for what was sown on rocky **g**, this Mt 13:20
the crowd to sit down on the **g**, Mt 15:35
and dug in the **g** and hid his master's Mt 25:18
and I went and hid your talent in the **g**. Mt 25:25
Other seed fell on rocky **g**, where it did Mk 4:5
And these are the ones sown on rocky **g**: Mk 4:16
as if a man should scatter seed on the **g**. Mk 4:26
seed, which, when sown on the **g**, Mk 4:31
directed the crowd to sit down on the **g**. Mk 8:6
and he fell on the **g** and rolled about, Mk 9:20
he fell on the **g** and prayed that, Mk 14:35
a house on the **g** without a foundation. Lk 6:49
threw him to the **g** and convulsed him. Lk 9:42
it down. Why should it use up the **g**?' Lk 13:7
and tear you down to the **g**, you and Lk 19:44
drops of blood falling down to the **g**. Lk 22:44
and bowed their faces to the **g**, Lk 24:5
down and wrote with his finger on the **g**. Jn 8:6
more he bent down and wrote on the **g**. Jn 8:8
he spat on the **g** and made mud with the Jn 9:6
am he," they drew back and fell to the **g**. Jn 18:6
place where you are standing is holy **g**. Acts 7:33
enraged, and they **g** their teeth at him. Acts 7:54
And falling to the **g** he heard a voice Acts 9:4
Saul rose from the **g**, and although his Acts 9:8
And I fell to the **g** and heard a voice Acts 22:7
And when we had all fallen to the **g**, I Acts 26:14
deprive me of my **g** for boasting. 1 Cor 9:15
that gives me no **g** for boasting. 1 Cor 9:16
any question on the **g** of conscience. 1 Cor 10:25
any question on the **g** of conscience. 1 Cor 10:27
be disrespectful on the **g** that they are 1 Tm 6:2

GROUNDED (1)
—that you, being rooted and **g** in love, Eph 3:17

GROUP (4)
you will meet a **g** of prophets coming 1 Sm 10:5
behold, a **g** of prophets met him, 1 Sm 10:10
and became one **g** and took their 2 Sm 2:25
him to be in the **g** they went a day's Lk 2:44

GROUPINGS (2)
according to the **g** of the fathers' 2 Chr 35:5
according to the **g** of the fathers' 2 Chr 35:12

GROUPS (4)
Chaldeans formed three **g** and made a Jb 1:17
all to sit down in **g** on the green grass. Mk 6:39
So they sat down in **g**, by hundreds and Mk 6:40
them sit down in **g** of about fifty each." Lk 9:14

GROVES (1)
Like palm **g** that stretch afar, like Nm 24:6

GROW (52)
but when you **g** restless you shall Gn 27:40
and let them **g** into a multitude in the Gn 48:16
the Egyptians will **g** weary of drinking Ex 7:18
let the locks of hair of his head **g** long. Nm 6:5
lest the wild beasts **g** too numerous for Dt 7:22
of his head began to **g** again after it had Jgs 16:22
Samuel continued to **g** both in stature 1 Sm 2:26
eyesight had begun to **g** dim so that he 1 Sm 3:2
Why should damage **g** to the hurt of the Ezr 4:22
soon as it began to **g** dark at the gates Neh 13:19
"Can papyrus **g** where there is no marsh? Jb 8:11
Though its root **g** old in the earth, and its Jb 14:8
reach old age, and **g** mighty in power? Jb 21:7
let thorns **g** instead of wheat, and foul Jb 31:40
become strong; they **g** up in the open; Jb 39:4
My eyes **g** dim with waiting for my God. Ps 69:3
like the palm tree and **g** like a cedar in Ps 92:12
cause the grass to **g** for the livestock Ps 104:14
the earth; he makes grass **g** on the hills. Ps 147:8
dreams increase and words **g** many, Eccl 5:7
or hoed, and briers and thorns shall **g** up; Is 5:6
low, and the fat of his flesh will **g** lean. Is 17:4
though you make them **g** on the day Is 17:11
ashamed, no more shall his face **g** pale. Is 29:22
Thorns shall **g** over its strongholds, Is 34:13
He does not faint or **g** weary; his Is 40:28
He will not **g** faint or be discouraged till Is 42:4
oak and lets it **g** strong among the trees Is 44:14
for the spirit would **g** faint before me, Is 57:16
they take root; they **g** and produce fruit; Jer 12:2
of Israel, saying, 'The days **g** long, Ezk 12:22
the deep made it **g** tall, making its Ezk 31:4
the waters may **g** to towering height Ezk 31:14
their heads or let their locks **g** long; Ezk 44:20
there will **g** all kinds of trees for food. Ezk 47:12
Thorn and thistle shall **g** up on their Hos 10:8
peoples are in anguish; all faces **g** pale. Jl 2:6
did not labor, nor did you make it **g**, Jon 4:10
anguish is in all loins; all faces **g** pale! Na 2:10
not, O Zion; let not your hands **g** weak. Zep 3:16
the lilies of the field, how they **g**: Mt 6:28
Let both **g** together until the harvest, Mt 13:30
increased, the love of many will **g** cold. Mt 24:12
Consider the lilies, how they **g**: they Lk 12:27
with moneybags that do not **g** old, Lk 12:33
And let us not **g** weary of doing good, for Gal 6:9
we are to **g** up in every way into him Eph 4:15
makes the body **g** so that it builds itself Eph 4:16
do not **g** weary in doing good. 2 Thes 3:13
you may not **g** weary or fainthearted. Heb 12:3
that by it you may **g** up to salvation— 1 Pt 2:2
But **g** in the grace and knowledge of 2 Pt 3:18

GROWING (9)
plump and good, were **g** on one stalk. Gn 41:5
in my dream seven ears **g** on one stalk, Gn 41:22
and salt, nothing sown and nothing **g**, Dt 29:23
from which to water the forest of **g** trees. Eccl 2:6
the soil of my people **g** up in thorns and Is 32:13
g up and increasing and yielding Mk 4:8
it is bearing fruit and **g**—as it also does Col 1:6
because your faith is **g** abundantly, 2 Thes 1:3
is becoming obsolete and **g** old is ready Heb 8:13

GROWL (6)
But not a dog shall **g** against any of the Ex 11:7
about for food and **g** if they do not Ps 59:15
lions they roar; they **g** and seize their prey; Is 5:29
They will **g** over it on that day, like the Is 5:30
We all **g** like bears; we moan and moan Is 59:11
like lions; they shall **g** like lions' cubs. Jer 51:38

GROWLING (3)
A king's wrath is like the **g** of a lion, Prv 19:12
terror of a king is like the **g** of a lion; Prv 20:2
over it on that day, like the **g** of the sea. Is 5:30

GROWLS (1)
"As a lion or a young lion **g** over his prey, Is 31:4

GROWN (36)
For she saw that Shelah was **g** up, and Gn 38:14
One day, when Moses had **g** up, he went Ex 2:11
unchanged and black hair has **g** in it, Lv 13:37
children, and have **g** old in the land, Dt 4:25
they have eaten and are full and **g** fat, Dt 31:20
you therefore wait till they were **g**? Ru 1:13
your beards have **g** and then return." 2 Sm 10:5
young men who had **g** up with him 1 Kgs 12:8
young men who had **g** up with him 1 Kgs 12:10
When the child had **g**, he went out 2 Kgs 4:18
the housetops, blighted before it is **g**. 2 Kgs 19:26
your beards have **g** and then return." 1 Chr 19:5
young men who had **g** up with him 2 Chr 10:8
young men who had **g** up with him 2 Chr 10:10
My eye has **g** dim from vexation, and all Jb 17:7
in their youth be like plants full **g**, Ps 144:12
for lack of wine; all joy has **g** dark; Is 24:11
on the housetops, blighted before it is **g**. Is 37:27
they have **g** fat and sleek. They know no Jer 5:28
and not truth has **g** strong in the land; Jer 9:3
She who bore seven has **g** feeble; she has Jer 15:9
How the gold has **g** dim, how the pure Lam 4:1
for these things our eyes have **g** dim, Lam 5:17
Violence has **g** up into a rod of Ezk 7:11
were formed, and your hair had **g**; Ezk 16:7
O king, who have **g** and become strong. Dn 4:22
Your greatness has **g** and reaches to Dn 4:22
of Jacob? Has the LORD **g** impatient? Mi 2:7
For this people's heart has **g** dull, and Mt 13:15
but when it has **g** it is larger than all Mt 13:32
For this people's heart has **g** dull, and Acts 28:27
the appointed time has **g** very short. 1 Cor 7:29
By faith Moses, when he was **g** up, Heb 11:24
sin when it is fully **g** brings forth death. Jas 1:15
name's sake, and you have not **g** weary. Rv 2:3
of the earth have **g** rich from the power Rv 18:3

GROWS (19)
till Shelah my son **g** up"—for he feared Gn 38:11
eat every tree of yours that **g** in the field, Ex 10:5
shall not reap what **g** of itself in your Lv 25:5
sow nor reap what **g** of itself nor gather Lv 25:11
Or if he **g** rich he may redeem himself. Lv 25:49
to the hyssop that **g** out of the wall. 1 Kgs 4:33
this year eat what **g** of itself, and in 2 Kgs 19:29
has clean hands **g** stronger and stronger. Jb 17:9
eat, and let what **g** for me be rooted out. Jb 31:8
of grief; it **g** weak because of all my foes. Ps 6:7
my eye **g** dim through sorrow. Every day Ps 88:9
housetops, which withers before it **g** up, Ps 129:6
One gives freely, yet **g** all the richer; Prv 11:24
this year you shall eat what **g** of itself, Is 37:30
my compassion **g** warm and tender. Hos 11:8
and day, and the seed sprouts and **g**; Mk 4:27
it is sown it **g** up and becomes larger Mk 4:32
g into a holy temple in the Lord. Eph 2:21
g with a growth that is from God. Col 2:19

GROWTH (7)
it with showers, and blessing its **g**. Ps 65:10
gone and the new **g** appears and the Prv 27:25
when the latter **g** was just beginning Am 7:1
it was the latter **g** after the king's Am 7:1
Apollos watered, but God gave the **g**. 1 Cor 3:6
but only God who gives the **g**. 1 Cor 3:7
grows with a **g** that is from God. Col 2:19

GRUDGE (3)
vengeance or bear a **g** against the sons Lv 19:18
and in anger they bear a **g** against me. Ps 55:3
And Herodias had a **g** against him and Mk 6:19

GRUDGING (1)
heart shall not be **g** when you give to Dt 15:10

GRUDGINGLY (1)
and your eye look **g** on your poor Dt 15:9

GRUMBLE (10)
For what are we, that you **g** against us?" Ex 16:7
grumbling that you **g** against him— Ex 16:8
wicked congregation **g** against me? Nm 14:27
of Israel, which they **g** against me. Nm 14:27
all the congregation **g** against him by Nm 14:36
is Aaron that you **g** against him?" Nm 16:11
of Israel, which they **g** against you." Nm 17:5
them, "Do not **g** among yourselves. Jn 6:43

nor **g**, as some of them did and were 1 Cor 10:10
Do not **g** against one another, brothers, so Jas 5:9

GRUMBLED (11)
And the people **g** against Moses, saying, Ex 15:24
the people of Israel **g** against Moses and Ex 16:2
and the people **g** against Moses and said, Ex 17:3
the people of Israel **g** against Moses and Nm 14:2
and upward, who have **g** against me, Nm 14:29
people of Israel **g** against Moses and Nm 16:41
on receiving it they **g** at the master of Mt 20:11
and their scribes **g** at his disciples, Lk 5:30
And the Pharisees and the scribes **g**, Lk 15:2
And when they saw it, they all **g**, "He has Lk 19:7
So the Jews **g** about him, because he said, Jn 6:41

GRUMBLERS (1)
These are **g**, malcontents, following Jude 1:16

GRUMBLING (8)
he has heard your **g** against the LORD. Ex 16:7
LORD has heard your **g** that you grumble Ex 16:8
Your **g** is not against us but against the Ex 16:8
the LORD, for he has heard your **g**.'" Ex 16:9
"I have heard the **g** of the people of Ex 16:12
that his disciples were **g** about this, Jn 6:61
Do all things without **g** or questioning, Phil 2:14
hospitality to one another without **g**. 1 Pt 4:9

GRUMBLINGS (3)
I have heard the **g** of the people of Nm 14:27
to cease from me the **g** of the people of Nm 17:5
make an end of their **g** against me, Nm 17:10

GUARANTEE (3)
us his Spirit in our hearts as a **g**. 2 Cor 1:22
God, who has given us the Spirit as a **g**. 2 Cor 5:5
who is the **g** of our inheritance until we Eph 1:14

GUARANTEED (2)
on grace and be **g** to all his offspring Rom 4:16
of his purpose, he **g** it with an oath, Heb 6:17

GUARANTOR (1)
This makes Jesus the **g** of a better Heb 7:22

GUARD (134)
that turned every way to **g** the way to the Gn 3:24
officer of Pharaoh, the captain of the **g**. Gn 37:36
officer of Pharaoh, the captain of the **g**, Gn 39:1
in the house of the captain of the **g**, Gn 40:3
The captain of the **g** appointed Joseph to Gn 40:4
in the house of the captain of the **g**, Gn 41:10
us, a servant of the captain of the **g**. Gn 41:12
an angel before you to **g** you on the way Ex 23:20
Levites shall keep **g** over the tabernacle Nm 1:53
They shall keep **g** over him and over the Nm 3:7
They shall **g** all the furnishings of the Nm 3:8
and keep **g** over the people of Israel as Nm 3:8
sons, and they shall **g** their priesthood. Nm 3:10
And the **g** duty of the sons of Gershon Nm 3:25
8,600, keeping **g** over the sanctuary. Nm 3:28
And their **g** duty involved the ark, the Nm 3:31
of those who kept **g** over the sanctuary. Nm 3:32
And the appointed **g** duty of the sons of Nm 3:36
and their **g** duty is to be under the Nm 4:28
in the tent of meeting by keeping **g**, Nm 8:26
acting as the rear **g** of all the camps, Nm 10:25
They shall keep **g** over you and over Nm 18:3
join you and keep **g** over the tent of Nm 18:4
you shall keep **g** over the sanctuary Nm 18:5
with you shall **g** your priesthood for Nm 18:7
Levites who keep **g** over the Nm 31:30
Levites who kept **g** over the tabernacle Nm 31:47
and the rear **g** was walking after the ark, Jos 6:9
and the rear **g** was walking after the ark Jos 6:13
of the city and its rear **g** west of the city. Jos 8:13
of the cave and set men by it to **g** them, Jos 10:18
your enemies; attack their rear **g**. Jos 10:19
"He will **g** the feet of his faithful ones, 1 Sm 2:9
be on your **g** in the morning. 1 Sm 19:2
king said to the **g** who stood about 1 Sm 22:17
in a house under **g** and provided for 2 Sm 20:3
to the hands of the officers of the **g**, 1 Kgs 14:27
the **g** carried them and brought 1 Kgs 14:28
a man to me and said, '**G** this man; 1 Kgs 20:39
had been on **g** at Ramoth-gilead 2 Kgs 9:14
Jehu said to the **g** and to the officers, 2 Kgs 10:25
the **g** and the officers cast them out 2 Kgs 10:25
the Sabbath and **g** the king's house 2 Kgs 11:5
behind the guards) shall **g** the palace. 2 Kgs 11:6
on the Sabbath and **g** the house of the 2 Kgs 11:7
the noise of the **g** and of the people, 2 Kgs 11:13
who were with the captain of the **g**, 2 Kgs 25:10
captain of the **g** carried into exile. 2 Kgs 25:11
the captain of the **g** left some of the 2 Kgs 25:12
the captain of the **g** took away as 2 Kgs 25:15
the captain of the **g** took Seraiah the 2 Kgs 25:18
the captain of the **g** took them and 2 Kgs 25:20
to the hands of the officers of the **g**, 2 Chr 12:10
the **g** came and carried them and 2 Chr 12:11
set all the people as a **g** for the king, 2 Chr 23:10
G them and keep them until you weigh Ezr 8:29
house of the king at the court of the **g**. Neh 3:25
God and set a **g** as a protection against Neh 4:9
that they may be a **g** for us by night Neh 4:22
nor the men of the **g** who followed me, Neh 4:23
And while they are still standing **g**, let Neh 7:3
some at their **g** posts and some in front Neh 7:3
were gatekeepers standing **g** at the Neh 12:25
came to a halt at the Gate of the **G**. Neh 12:39
themselves and come and **g** the gates, Neh 13:22
a sea monster, that you set a **g** over me? Jb 7:12
you will **g** us from this generation Ps 12:7
Oh, **g** my soul, and deliver me! Let me Ps 25:20
I said, "I will **g** my ways, that I may not Ps 39:1
I will **g** my mouth with a muzzle, so long Ps 39:1
angels concerning you to **g** you in all Ps 91:11
G me, O LORD, from the hands of the Ps 140:4
Set a **g**, O LORD, over my mouth; keep Ps 141:3
over you, understanding will **g** you, Prv 2:11
keep you; love her, and she will **g** you. Prv 4:6
do not let go; **g** her, for she is your life. Prv 4:13
and your lips may **g** knowledge. Prv 5:2
G your steps when you go to the house Eccl 5:1
and the God of Israel will be your rear **g**. Is 52:12
the glory of the LORD shall be your rear **g**. Is 58:8
in the court of the **g** that was in the Jer 32:2
cousin came to me in the court of the **g**, Jer 32:8
who were sitting in the court of the **g**. Jer 32:12
he was still shut up in the court of the **g**: Jer 33:1
Jeremiah to the court of the **g**. Jer 37:21
remained in the court of the **g**. Jer 37:21
son, which was in the court of the **g**, Jer 38:6
remained in the court of the **g**. Jer 38:13
in the court of the **g** until the day that Jer 38:28
Then Nebuzaradan, the captain of the **g**, Jer 39:9
Nebuzaradan, the captain of the **g**, left Jer 39:10
Nebuzaradan, the captain of the **g**, Jer 39:11
So Nebuzaradan the captain of the **g**, Jer 39:13
took Jeremiah from the court of the **g**. Jer 39:14
he was shut up in the court of the **g**: Jer 39:15
the captain of the **g** had let him go Jer 40:1
The captain of the **g** took Jeremiah and Jer 40:2
the captain of the **g** gave him an Jer 40:5
Nebuzaradan, the captain of the **g**, Jer 41:10
the captain of the **g** had left with Jer 43:6
who were with the captain of the **g**, Jer 52:14
captain of the **g** carried away captive Jer 52:15
the captain of the **g** left some of the Jer 52:16
the captain of the **g** took away as gold, Jer 52:19
the captain of the **g** took Seraiah the Jer 52:24
the captain of the **g** took them and Jer 52:26
captain of the **g** carried away captive Jer 52:30
about you, and be a **g** for them. Ezk 38:7
to Arioch, the captain of the king's **g**, Dn 2:14
sea, and his rear **g** into the western sea; Jl 2:20
g the doors of your mouth from her who Mi 7:5
Then I will encamp at my house as a **g**, Zec 9:8
the lips of a priest should **g** knowledge, Mal 2:7
So **g** yourselves in your spirit, and let Mal 2:15
So **g** yourselves in your spirit, and do Mal 2:16
over to the judge, and the judge to the **g**, Mt 5:25
said to them, "You have a **g** of soldiers. Mt 27:65
by sealing the stone and setting a **g**. Mt 27:66
some of the **g** went into the city and Mt 28:11
"But be on your **g**. For they will deliver Mk 13:9
But be on **g**; I have told you all things Mk 13:23
Be on **g**, keep awake. For you do not Mk 13:33
him and lead him away under **g**." Mk 14:44
his angels concerning you, to **g** you,' Lk 4:10
He was kept under **g** and bound with Lk 8:29
be on your **g** against all covetousness, Lk 12:15
to four squads of soldiers to **g** him, Acts 12:4
had passed the first and the second **g**, Acts 12:10
the whole imperial **g** and to all Phil 1:13
will **g** your hearts and your minds in Phil 4:7
establish you and **g** you against the 2 Thes 3:3
g the deposit entrusted to you. 1 Tm 6:20
he is able to **g** until that Day what 2 Tm 1:12
g the good deposit entrusted to you. 2 Tm 1:14

GUARDED (10)
in vain have I **g** all that this fellow 1 Sm 25:21
the priests who **g** the threshold put 2 Kgs 12:9
king's eunuchs, who **g** the threshold, Est 2:21
the king's eunuchs, who **g** the threshold, Est 6:2
for a wife, and for a wife he **g** sheep. Hos 12:12
Egypt, and by a prophet he was **g**. Hos 12:13
I have **g** them, and not one of them has Jn 17:12
him to be **g** in Herod's praetorium. Acts 23:35
himself, with the soldier that **g** him. Acts 28:16
power are being **g** through faith for 1 Pt 1:5

GUARDIAN (4)
You were an anointed **g** cherub. I Ezk 28:14
God, and I destroyed you, O **g** cherub, Ezk 28:16
the law was our **g** until Christ came, Gal 3:24
has come, we are no longer under a **g**, Gal 3:25

GUARDIANS (3)
and to the **g** of the sons of Ahab, 2 Kgs 10:1
together with the elders and the **g**, 2 Kgs 10:5
but he is under **g** and managers until the Gal 4:2

GUARDING (5)
and his sons, **g** the sanctuary itself, Nm 3:38
pure? By **g** it according to your word. Ps 119:9
g the paths of justice and watching over Prv 2:8
before the door were **g** the prison. Acts 12:6
under King Aretas was **g** the city of 2 Cor 11:32

GUARDROOM (2)
and brought them back to the **g**. 1 Kgs 14:28
and brought them back to the **g**. 2 Chr 12:11

GUARDS (18)
captains of the Carites and of the **g**, 2 Kgs 11:4
the gate behind the **g**) shall guard the 2 Kgs 11:6
And the **g** stood, every man with his 2 Kgs 11:11
took the captains, the Carites, the **g**, 2 Kgs 11:19
the gate of the **g** to the king's house. 2 Kgs 11:19
that is, the house of the tent, as **g**. 1 Chr 9:23
Appoint **g** from among the inhabitants Neh 7:3
Whoever **g** his mouth preserves his life; Prv 13:3
Righteousness **g** him whose way is Prv 13:6
whoever **g** his way preserves his life. Prv 16:17
whoever **g** his soul will keep far from Prv 22:5
and he who **g** his master will be Prv 27:18
inside he sat with the **g** to see the end. Mt 26:58
fear of him the **g** trembled and became Mt 28:4
sitting with the **g** and warming Mk 14:54
"Prophesy!" And the **g** received him Mk 14:65
man, fully armed, **g** his own palace, Lk 11:21
locked and the **g** standing at the Acts 5:23

GUDGODAH (2)
From there they journeyed to **G**, and Dt 10:7
to Gudgodah, and from **G** to Jotbathah, Dt 10:7

GUEST (7)
no foreign **g** of the priest or hired Lv 22:10
to prepare for the **g** who had come to 2 Sm 12:4
For I am a sojourner with you, a **g**, like Ps 39:12
Teacher says, Where is my **g** room, Mk 14:14
has gone in to be the **g** of a man who is a Lk 19:7
says to you, Where is the **g** room, Lk 22:11
same time, prepare a **g** room for me, Phlm 1:22

GUESTS (16)
might eat with the **g**." So Saul ate with 1 Sm 9:24
from Jerusalem who were invited **g**, 2 Sm 15:11
Adonijah and all the **g** who were with 1 Kgs 1:41
Then all the **g** of Adonijah trembled 1 Kgs 1:49
The **g** in my house and my Jb 19:15
that her **g** are in the depths of Sheol. Prv 9:18
a sacrifice and consecrated his **g**. Zep 1:7
"Can the wedding **g** mourn as long as Mt 9:15
his oaths and his **g** he commanded it to Mt 14:9
So the wedding hall was filled with **g**. Mt 22:10
when the king came in to look at the **g**, Mt 22:11
"Can the wedding **g** fast while the Mk 2:19
danced, she pleased Herod and his **g**. Mk 6:22
of his oaths and his **g** he did not want to Mk 6:26
"Can you make wedding **g** fast while the Lk 5:34
So he invited them in to be his **g**. The Acts 10:23

GUIDANCE (7)
also consulted a medium, seeking **g**. 1 Chr 10:13
He did not seek **g** from the LORD. 1 Chr 10:14
They turn around and around by his **g**, Jb 37:12
and the one who understands obtain **g**, Prv 1:5
Where there is no **g**, a people falls, but Prv 11:14
by counsel; by wise **g** wage war. Prv 20:18
for by wise **g** you can wage your war, Prv 24:6

GUIDE (17)
or can you **g** the Bear with its children? Jb 38:32
your name's sake you lead me and **g** me; Ps 31:3
forever and ever. He will **g** us forever. Ps 48:14
with equity and **g** the nations upon Ps 67:4
You **g** me with your counsel, and Ps 73:24
who is righteous is a **g** to his neighbor, Prv 12:26
for those who **g** this people have been Is 9:16
that they have not known I will **g** them. Is 42:16
and by springs of water will **g** them. Is 49:10
There is none to **g** her among all the Is 51:18
And the LORD will **g** you continually and Is 58:11
to **g** our feet into the way of peace." Lk 1:79
comes, he will **g** you into all the truth, Jn 16:13
who became a **g** to those who arrested Acts 1:16
that you yourself are a **g** to the blind, Rom 2:19
obey us, we **g** their whole bodies as well. Jas 3:3
and he will **g** them to springs of living Rv 7:17

GUIDED (7)
you have **g** them by your strength to Ex 15:13

H

David hiding himself on the hill of **H**, 1 Sm 26:1
And Saul encamped on the hill of **H**, 1 Sm 26:3

HACHMONI (1)
the son of **H** attended the king's 1 Chr 27:32

HACHMONITE (1)
Jashobeam, a **H**, was chief of the 1 Chr 11:11

HACKED (1)
women." And Samuel **h** Agag to 1 Sm 15:33

HADAD (15)
H, Tema, Jetur, Naphish, and Gn 25:15
Husham died, and **H** the son of Bedad, Gn 36:35
H died, and Samlah of Masrekah Gn 36:36
against Solomon, **H** the Edomite. 1 Kgs 11:14
But **H** fled to Egypt, together with 1 Kgs 11:17
servants, **H** still being a little child. 1 Kgs 11:17
And **H** found great favor in the sight 1 Kgs 11:19
But when **H** heard in Egypt that 1 Kgs 11:21
army was dead, **H** said to Pharaoh, 1 Kgs 11:21
of Solomon, doing harm as **H** did. 1 Kgs 11:25
Mishma, Dumah, Massa, **H**, Tema, 1 Chr 1:30
died, and **H** the son of Bedad, 1 Chr 1:46
H died, and Samlah of Masrekah 1 Chr 1:47
died, and **H** reigned in his place, 1 Chr 1:50
And **H** died. The chiefs of Edom were: 1 Chr 1:51

HADAD-RIMMON (1)
as the mourning for **H** in the plain of Zec 12:11

HADADEZER (21)
David also defeated **H** the son of Rehob, 2 Sm 8:3
came to help **H** king of Zobah, 2 Sm 8:5
by the servants of **H** and brought them 2 Sm 8:7
Betah and from Berothai, cities of **H**, 2 Sm 8:8
had defeated the whole army of **H**, 2 Sm 8:9
had fought against **H** and defeated 2 Sm 8:10
for **H** had often been at war with Toi. 2 Sm 8:10
from the spoil of **H** the son of Rehob, 2 Sm 8:12
And **H** sent and brought out the 2 Sm 10:16
of the army of **H** at their head. 2 Sm 10:16
who were servants of **H** saw that they 2 Sm 10:19
from his master **H** king of Zobah. 1 Kgs 11:23
David also defeated **H** king of 1 Chr 18:3
came to help **H** king of Zobah, 1 Chr 18:5
the servants of **H** and brought them 1 Chr 18:7
Tibhath and from Cun, cities of **H**, 1 Chr 18:8
had defeated the whole army of **H**, 1 Chr 18:9
had fought against **H** and defeated 1 Chr 18:10
for **H** had often been at war with 1 Chr 18:10
of the army of **H** at their head. 1 Chr 19:16
the servants of **H** saw that they 1 Chr 19:19

HADAR (1)
died, and **H** reigned in his place, Gn 36:39

HADASHAH (1)
Zenan, **H**, Migdal-gad, Jos 15:37

HADASSAH (1)
He was bringing up **H**, that is Esther, the Est 2:7

HADES (9)
You will be brought down to **H**. Mt 11:23
You shall be brought down to **H**. Lk 10:15
and in **H**, being in torment, he lifted up Lk 16:23
you will not abandon my soul to **H**, Acts 2:27
that he was not abandoned to **H**, Acts 2:31
and I have the keys of Death and **H**. Rv 1:18
name was Death, and **H** followed him. Rv 6:8
Death and **H** gave up the dead who were Rv 20:13
Then Death and **H** were thrown into Rv 20:14

HADID (3)
The sons of Lod, **H**, and Ono, 725. Ezr 2:33
The sons of Lod, **H**, and Ono, 721. Neh 7:37
H, Zeboim, Neballat, Neh 11:34

HADLAI (1)
Shallum, and Amasa the son of **H**, 2 Chr 28:12

HADORAM (4)
H, Uzal, Diklah, Gn 10:27
H, Uzal, Diklah, 1 Chr 1:21
he sent his son **H** to King David, to 1 Chr 18:10
Then King Rehoboam sent **H**, who 2 Chr 10:18

HADRACH (1)
against the land of **H** and Damascus is Zec 9:1

HAELEPH (1)
Zela, **H**, Jebus (that is, Jerusalem), Jos 18:28

HAGAB (1)
the sons of **H**, the sons of Shamlai, the Ezr 2:46

HAGABA (1)
the sons of Lebana, the sons of **H**, the Neh 7:48

HAGABAH (1)
the sons of Lebanah, the sons of **H**, the Ezr 2:45

HAGAR (14)
Egyptian servant whose name was **H**. Gn 16:1
Abram's wife, took **H** the Egyptian, Gn 16:3
And he went in to **H**, and she conceived. Gn 16:4
And he said, "**H**, servant of Sarai, where Gn 16:8
And **H** bore Abram a son, and Abram Gn 16:15
the name of his son, whom **H** bore, Gn 16:15
years old when **H** bore Ishmael to Gn 16:16
Sarah saw the son of **H** the Egyptian, Gn 21:9
and a skin of water and gave it to **H**, Gn 21:14
of God called to **H** from heaven and Gn 21:17
her, "What troubles you, **H**? Fear not, Gn 21:17
Abraham's son, whom **H** the Egyptian, Gn 25:12
bearing children for slavery; she is **H**. Gal 4:24
Now **H** is Mount Sinai in Arabia; she Gal 4:25

HAGGAI (11)
H and Zechariah the son of Iddo, Ezr 5:1
the prophesying of **H** the prophet and Ezr 6:14
by the hand of **H** the prophet to Hg 1:1
LORD came by the hand of **H** the prophet, Hg 1:3
God, and the words of **H** the prophet, Hg 1:12
Then **H**, the messenger of the LORD, Hg 1:13
LORD came by the hand of **H** the prophet, Hg 2:1
word of the LORD came by **H** the prophet, Hg 2:10
Then **H** said, "If someone who is Hg 2:13
Then **H** answered and said, "So is it with Hg 2:14
a second time to **H** on the twenty-fourth Hg 2:20

HAGGARD (1)
are you so **h** morning after morning? 2 Sm 13:4

HAGGEDOLIM (1)
overseer was Zabdiel the son of **H**. Neh 11:14

HAGGI (2)
Ziphion, **H**, Shuni, Ezbon, Eri, Arodi, Gn 46:16
the clan of the Zephonites; of **H**, Nm 26:15

HAGGIAH (1)
Shimea his son, **H** his son, and 1 Chr 6:30

HAGGITES (1)
of Haggi, the clan of the **H**; Nm 26:15

HAGGITH (5)
and the fourth, Adonijah the son of **H**; 2 Sm 3:4
Adonijah the son of **H** exalted himself, 1 Kgs 1:5
the son of **H** has become king 1 Kgs 1:11
the son of **H** came to Bathsheba 1 Kgs 2:13
Adonijah, whose mother was **H**; 1 Chr 3:2

HAGRI (1)
of Nathan, Mibhar the son of **H**, 1 Chr 11:38

HAGRITE (1)
Over the flocks was Jaziz the **H**. 1 Chr 27:30

HAGRITES (4)
of Saul they waged war against the **H**, 1 Chr 5:10
They waged war against the **H**, Jetur, 1 Chr 5:19
the **H** and all who were with them 1 Chr 5:20
and the Ishmaelites, Moab and the **H**, Ps 83:6

HAHIROTH (1)
out from before **H** and passed through Nm 33:8

HAIL (33)
I will cause very heavy **h** to fall, Ex 9:18
will die when the **h** falls on them."'" Ex 9:19
so that there may be **h** in all the land of Ex 9:22
and the LORD sent thunder and **h**, Ex 9:23
And the LORD rained **h** upon the land of Ex 9:23
There was **h** and fire flashing Ex 9:24
continually in the midst of the **h**, Ex 9:24
in the midst of the hail, very heavy **h**, Ex 9:24
The **h** struck down everything that was Ex 9:25
And the **h** struck down every plant of the Ex 9:25
the people of Israel were, was there no **h**. Ex 9:26
been enough of God's thunder and **h**. Ex 9:28
will cease, and there will be no more **h**, Ex 9:29
LORD, and the thunder and the **h** ceased, Ex 9:33
the rain and the **h** and the thunder had Ex 9:34
shall eat what is left to you after the **h**, Ex 10:5
plant in the land, all that the **h** has left." Ex 10:12
the fruit of the trees that the **h** had left. Ex 10:15
have you seen the storehouses of the **h**, Jb 38:22
their vines with **h** and their sycamores Ps 78:47
their cattle to the **h** and their flocks to Ps 78:48
He gave them **h** for rain, and fiery Ps 105:32
fire and **h**, snow and mist, stormy wind Ps 148:8
like a storm of **h**, a destroying tempest, Is 28:2
and **h** will sweep away the refuge of lies, Is 28:17
And it will **h** when the forest falls down, Is 32:19
with blight and with mildew and with **h**, Hg 2:17
him, saying, "**H**, King of the Jews!" Mt 27:29
to salute him, "**H**, King of the Jews!" Mk 15:18
"**H**, King of the Jews!" and struck him Jn 19:3
his trumpet, and there followed **h** and fire, Rv 8:7
thunder, an earthquake, and heavy **h**. Rv 11:19
they cursed God for the plague of the **h**, Rv 16:21

HAILED (1)
of the garrison **h** Jonathan and his 1 Sm 14:12

HAILSTONES (8)
died because of the **h** than the sons of Jos 10:11
brightness before him **h** and coals of Ps 18:12
uttered his voice, **h** and coals of fire. Ps 18:13
fire, with a cloudburst and storm and **h**. Is 30:30
be a deluge of rain, and you, O great **h**, Ezk 13:11
and great **h** in wrath to make a full Ezk 13:13
are with him torrential rains and **h**, Ezk 38:22
And great **h**, about one hundred Rv 16:21

HAIR (82)
yarns and fine twined linen, goats' **h**, Ex 25:4
make curtains of goats' **h** for a tent over Ex 26:7
yarns and fine twined linen; goats' **h**, Ex 35:6
fine linen or goats' **h** or tanned rams' Ex 35:23
to use their skill spun the goats' **h**. Ex 35:26
made curtains of goats' **h** for a tent over Ex 36:14
"Do not let the **h** of your heads hang Lv 10:6
And if the **h** in the diseased area has Lv 13:3
and the **h** in it has not turned white, Lv 13:4
in the skin that has turned the **h** white, Lv 13:10
the skin and its **h** has turned white, Lv 13:20
it and there is no white **h** in it and it is Lv 13:21
and if the **h** in the spot has turned white Lv 13:25
and there is no white **h** in the spot and Lv 13:26
skin, and the **h** in it is yellow and thin, Lv 13:30
the skin and there is no black **h** in it, Lv 13:31
spread, and there is in it no yellow **h**, Lv 13:32
the priest need not seek for the yellow **h**; Lv 13:36
unchanged and black **h** has grown in Lv 13:37
"If a man's **h** falls out from his head, he Lv 13:40
And if a man's **h** falls out from his Lv 13:41
clothes and let the **h** of his head hang Lv 13:45
shave off all his **h** and bathe himself in Lv 14:8
shall shave off all his **h** from his head, Lv 14:9
He shall shave off all his **h**, and then he Lv 14:9
not round off the **h** on your temples or Lv 19:27
shall not let the **h** of his head hang Lv 21:10
LORD and unbind the **h** of the woman's Nm 5:18
shall let the locks of **h** of his head grow Nm 6:5
shall take the **h** from his consecrated Nm 6:18
has shaved the **h** of his consecration, Nm 6:19
article of skin, all work of goats' **h**, Nm 31:20
But the **h** of his head began to grow Jgs 16:22
could sling a stone at a **h** and not miss. Jgs 20:16
there shall not one **h** of his head fall 1 Sm 14:45
a pillow of goats' **h** at its head and 1 Sm 19:13
with the pillow of goats' **h** at its head. 1 Sm 19:16
not one **h** of your son shall fall to the 2 Sm 14:11
when he cut the **h** of his head (for 2 Sm 14:26
cut it), he weighed the **h** of his head, 2 Sm 14:26
him, "He wore a garment of **h**, 2 Kgs 1:8
my cloak and pulled **h** from my head Ezr 9:3
some of them and pulled out their **h**. Neh 13:25
past my face; the **h** of my flesh stood up. Jb 4:15
Gray **h** is a crown of glory; it is gained Prv 16:31
the splendor of old men is their gray **h**. Prv 20:29
Your **h** is like a flock of goats leaping Sg 4:1
overwhelm me—Your **h** is like a flock Sg 6:5
a rope; and instead of well-set **h**, baldness; Is 3:24
of Assyria—the head and the **h** of the feet, Is 7:20
"'Cut off your **h** and cast it away; raise a Jer 7:29
the desert who cut the corners of their **h**, Jer 9:26
and all who cut the corners of their **h**; Jer 25:23
those who cut the corners of their **h**, Jer 49:32
balances for weighing and divide the **h**. Ezk 5:1
were formed, and your **h** had grown; Ezk 16:7
and the **h** of their kings bristles with Ezk 27:35
and the **h** of their kings shall bristle Ezk 32:10
shall surely trim the **h** of their heads. Ezk 44:20
The **h** of their heads was not singed, Dn 3:27
dew of heaven till his **h** grew as long as Dn 4:33
and the **h** of his head like pure wool; Dn 7:9
yourselves bald and cut off your **h**, Mi 1:16
a garment of camel's **h** and a leather belt Mt 3:4
you cannot make one **h** white or black. Mt 5:36
was clothed with camel's **h** and wore a Mk 1:6
wiped them with the **h** of her head and Lk 7:38
her tears and wiped them with her **h**. Lk 7:44
But not a **h** of your head will perish. Lk 21:18
ointment and wiped his feet with her **h**, Jn 11:2
feet of Jesus and wiped his feet with her **h**. Jn 12:3
At Cenchreae he had cut his **h**, for he Acts 18:18
for not a **h** is to perish from the head Acts 27:34
head, then she should cut her **h** short. 1 Cor 11:6
to cut off her **h** or shave her head, 1 Cor 11:6
if a man wears long **h** it is a disgrace 1 Cor 11:14
but if a woman has long **h**, it is her 1 Cor 11:15
For her **h** is given to her for a 1 Cor 11:15
not with braided **h** and gold or pearls 1 Tm 2:9
be external—the braiding of **h**, 1 Pt 3:3
their **h** like women's hair, and their teeth Rv 9:8
their hair like women's **h**, and their teeth Rv 9:8

HAIRS (13)
bring down my gray **h** with sorrow to Gn 42:38

And **H** told his wife Zeresh and all his Est 6:13
and hurried to bring **H** to the feast that Est 6:14
So the king and **H** went in to feast with Est 7:1
This wicked **H**!" Then Haman was Est 7:6
wicked Haman!" Then **H** was terrified Est 7:6
but **H** stayed to beg for his life from Est 7:7
as **H** was falling on the couch where Est 7:8
the gallows that **H** has prepared for Est 7:9
that." So they hanged **H** on the gallows Est 7:10
gave to Queen Esther the house of **H**, Est 8:1
signet ring, which he had taken from **H**, Est 8:2
Esther set Mordecai over the house of **H**. Est 8:2
the evil plan of **H** the Agagite and the Est 8:3
the letters devised by **H** the Agagite, Est 8:5
I have given Esther the house of **H**, Est 8:7
the ten sons of **H** the son of Est 9:10
500 men and also the ten sons of **H**. Est 9:12
let the ten sons of **H** be hanged on the Est 9:13
Susa, and the ten sons of **H** were hanged. Est 9:14
For **H** the Agagite, the son of Est 9:24

HAMAN'S (2)
mouth of the king, they covered **H** face. Est 7:8
saved the king, is standing at **H** house, Est 7:9

HAMATH (23)
When Toi king of **H** heard that David 2 Sm 8:9
restored Damascus and **H** to Judah 2 Kgs 14:28
Cuthah, Avva, **H**, and Sepharvaim, 2 Kgs 17:24
Nergal, the men of **H** made Ashima, 2 Kgs 17:30
Where are the gods of **H** and Arpad? 2 Kgs 18:34
Where is the king of **H**, the king of 2 Kgs 19:13
in bonds at Riblah in the land of **H**, 2 Kgs 23:33
to death at Riblah in the land of **H**. 2 Kgs 25:21
Tou king of **H** heard that David 1 Chr 18:9
all the store cities that he built in **H**. 2 Chr 8:4
like Carchemish? Is not **H** like Arpad? Is 10:9
Cush, from Elam, from Shinar, from **H**, Is 11:11
Where are the gods of **H** and Arpad? Is 36:19
Where is the king of **H**, the king of Is 37:13
of Babylon, at Riblah, in the land of **H**; Jer 39:5
"**H** and Arpad are confounded, for they Jer 49:23
of Babylon at Riblah in the land of **H**, Jer 52:9
to death at Riblah in the land of **H**. Jer 52:27
the border between Damascus and **H**), Ezk 47:16
with the border of **H** to the north. Ezk 47:17
border of Damascus over against **H**), Ezk 48:1
and see, and from there go to **H** the great; Am 6:2
and on **H** also, which borders on it, Tyre Zec 9:2

HAMATH-ZOBAH (1)
And Solomon went to **H** and took it. 2 Chr 8:3

HAMATHITES (2)
the Arvadites, the Zemarites, and the **H**. Gn 10:18
Arvadites, the Zemarites, and the **H**. 1 Chr 1:16

HAMMATH (2)
cities are Ziddim, Zer, **H**, Rakkath, Jos 19:35
are the Kenites who came from **H**, 1 Chr 2:55

HAMMEDATHA (5)
Haman the Agagite, the son of **H**, Est 3:1
it to Haman the Agagite, the son of **H**, Est 3:10
by Haman the Agagite, the son of **H**, Est 8:5
the ten sons of Haman the son of **H**, the Est 9:10
For Haman the Agagite, the son of **H**, Est 9:24

HAMMER (7)
a tent peg, and took a **h** in her hand. Jgs 4:21
so that neither **h** nor axe nor any tool 1 Kgs 6:7
who smooths with the **h** him who strikes Is 41:7
they fasten it with **h** and nails so that it Jer 10:4
and like a **h** that breaks the rock in Jer 23:29
How the **h** of the whole earth is cut Jer 50:23
"You are my **h** and weapon of war: with Jer 51:20

HAMMERED (12)
of **h** work shall you make them, on the Ex 25:18
lampstand shall be made of **h** work: Ex 25:31
it a single piece of **h** work of pure gold. Ex 25:36
He made them of **h** work on the two ends Ex 37:7
gold. He made the lampstand of **h** work. Ex 37:17
a single piece of **h** work of pure gold. Ex 37:22
And they **h** out gold leaf, and he cut it Ex 39:3
of the lampstand, **h** work of gold. Nm 8:4
its base to its flowers, it was **h** work; Nm 8:4
Of **h** work you shall make them, and Nm 10:2
them be made into **h** plates as a Nm 16:38
and they were **h** out as a covering for Nm 16:39

HAMMERS (2)
they broke down with hatchets and **h**. Ps 74:6
He fashions it with **h** and works it with Is 44:12

HAMMOLECHETH (1)
And his sister **H** bore Ishhod, Abiezer 1 Chr 7:18

HAMMON (2)
Ebron, Rehob, **H**, Kanah, as far as Jos 19:28
H with its pasturelands, 1 Chr 6:76

HAMMOTH-DOR (1)
the manslayer, **H** with its pasturelands, Jos 21:32

HAMMUEL (1)
H his son, Zaccur his son, Shimei his 1 Chr 4:26

HAMON-GOG (2)
It will be called the Valley of **H**. Ezk 39:11
have buried it in the Valley of **H**. Ezk 39:15

HAMONAH (1)
(**H** is also the name of the city.) Thus Ezk 39:16

HAMOR (13)
And from the sons of **H**, Shechem's Gn 33:19
when Shechem the son of **H** the Hivite, Gn 34:2
So Shechem spoke to his father **H**, Gn 34:4
And **H** the father of Shechem went out Gn 34:6
But **H** spoke with them, saying, "The Gn 34:8
Shechem and his father **H** deceitfully, Gn 34:13
Their words pleased **H** and Hamor's Gn 34:18
So **H** and his son Shechem came to the Gn 34:20
his city listened to **H** and his son Gn 34:24
They killed **H** and his son Shechem Gn 34:26
from the sons of **H** the father of Jos 24:32
Serve the men of **H** the father of Jgs 9:28
silver from the sons of **H** in Shechem. Acts 7:16

HAMOR'S (1)
pleased Hamor and **H** son Shechem. Gn 34:18

HAMPERED (1)
you walk, your step will not be **h**, Prv 4:12

HAMSTRING (1)
You shall **h** their horses and burn their Jos 11:6

HAMSTRUNG (4)
and in their willfulness they **h** oxen. Gn 49:6
he **h** their horses and burned their Jos 11:9
And David **h** all the chariot horses but 2 Sm 8:4
And David **h** all the chariot horses, 1 Chr 18:4

HAMUL (3)
the sons of Perez were Hezron and **H**. Gn 46:12
the clan of the Hezronites; of **H**, Nm 26:21
The sons of Perez: Hezron and **H**. 1 Chr 2:5

HAMULITES (1)
of Hamul, the clan of the **H**. Nm 26:21

HAMUTAL (3)
mother's name was **H** the daughter 2 Kgs 23:31
mother's name was **H** the daughter 2 Kgs 24:18
mother's name was **H** the daughter of Jer 52:1

HANAMEL (4)
H the son of Shallum your uncle will Jer 32:7
Then **H** my cousin came to me in the Jer 32:8
the field at Anathoth from **H** my cousin, Jer 32:9
in the presence of **H** my cousin, Jer 32:12

HANAN (12)
Abdon, Zichri, **H**, 1 Chr 8:23
Ishmael, Sheariah, Obadiah, and **H**. 1 Chr 8:38
Ishmael, Sheariah, Obadiah, and **H**; 1 Chr 9:44
H the son of Maacah, and Joshaphat 1 Chr 11:43
the sons of Shamlai, the sons of **H**, Ezr 2:46
the sons of **H**, the sons of Giddel, the Neh 7:49
Kelita, Azariah, Jozabad, **H**, Pelaiah, Neh 8:7
Hodiah, Kelita, Pelaiah, **H**, Neh 10:10
Pelatiah, **H**, Anaiah, Neh 10:22
Ahiah, **H**, Anan, Neh 10:26
and as their assistant **H** the son of Neh 13:13
of the sons of **H** the son of Igdaliah, Jer 35:4

HANANEL (4)
of the Hundred, as far as the Tower of **H**. Neh 3:1
and the Tower of **H** and the Tower of Neh 12:39
from the tower of **H** to the Corner Gate. Jer 31:38
from the Tower of **H** to the king's Zec 14:10

HANANI (11)
to Jehu the son of **H** against Baasha, 1 Kgs 16:1
Jehu the son of **H** against Baasha and 1 Kgs 16:7
Jerimoth, Hananiah, **H**, Eliathah, 1 Chr 25:4
to the eighteenth, to **H**, his sons and 1 Chr 25:25
At that time **H** the seer came to Asa 2 Chr 16:7
Jehu the son of **H** the seer went out 2 Chr 19:2
the chronicles of Jehu the son of **H**, 2 Chr 20:34
Of the sons of Immer: **H** and Zebadiah. Ezr 10:20
that **H**, one of my brothers, came with Neh 1:2
I gave my brother **H** and Hananiah the Neh 7:2
Maai, Nethanel, Judah, and **H**, Neh 12:36

HANANIAH (29)
Meshullam and **H**, and Shelomith 1 Chr 3:19
The sons of **H**: Pelatiah and Jeshaiah, 1 Chr 3:21
H, Elam, Anthothijah, 1 Chr 8:24
Shebuel and Jerimoth, **H**, Hanani, 1 Chr 25:4
to the sixteenth, to **H**, his sons and 1 Chr 25:23
the officer, under the direction of **H**, 2 Chr 26:11
of Bebai were Jehohanan, **H**, Zabbai, Ezr 10:28
Next to him **H**, one of the perfumers, Neh 3:8
After him **H** the son of Shelemiah and Neh 3:30
brother Hanani and **H** the governor of Neh 7:2
Hoshea, **H**, Hasshub, Neh 10:23
of Seraiah, Meraiah; of Jeremiah, **H**; Neh 12:12
Micaiah, Elioenai, Zechariah, and **H**, Neh 12:41
of the fourth year, **H** the son of Azzur, Jer 28:1
Jeremiah spoke to **H** the prophet in Jer 28:5
Then the prophet **H** took the yoke-bars Jer 28:10
And **H** spoke in the presence of all the Jer 28:11
after the prophet **H** had broken the Jer 28:12
"Go, tell **H**, 'Thus says the LORD: You Jer 28:13
the prophet said to the prophet **H**, Jer 28:15
"Listen, **H**, the LORD has not sent you, Jer 28:15
the seventh month, the prophet **H** died. Jer 28:17
son of Shaphan, Zedekiah the son of **H**, Jer 36:12
Irijah the son of Shelemiah, son of **H**, Jer 37:13
Among these were Daniel, **H**, Mishael, Dn 1:6
Belteshazzar, **H** he called Shadrach, Dn 1:7
had assigned over Daniel, **H**, Mishael, Dn 1:11
none was found like Daniel, **H**, Mishael, Dn 1:19
house and made the matter known to **H**, Dn 2:17

HAND (1255)
lest he reach out his **h** and take also of Gn 3:22
your brother's blood from your **h**. Gn 4:11
So he put out his **h** and took her and Gn 8:9
of the sea. Into your **h** they are delivered. Gn 9:2
If you take the left **h**, then I will go to the Gn 13:9
go to the right, or if you take the right **h**, Gn 13:9
enemies into your **h**!" And Abram Gn 14:20
Sodom, "I have lifted my **h** to the LORD, Gn 14:22
his **h** against everyone and everyone's Gn 16:12
and everyone's **h** against him, Gn 16:12
wife and his two daughters by the **h**, Gn 19:16
the boy, and hold him fast with your **h**, Gn 21:18
ewe lambs you will take from my **h**, Gn 21:30
And he took in his **h** the fire and the Gn 22:6
reached out his **h** and took the Gn 22:10
"Do not lay your **h** on the boy or do Gn 22:12
he had, "Put your **h** under my thigh, Gn 24:2
the servant put his **h** under the thigh of Gn 24:9
her jar upon her **h** and gave him a Gn 24:18
I may turn to the right **h** or to the left." Gn 24:49
out with his **h** holding Esau's heel, Gn 25:26
prepared, into the **h** of her son Jacob. Gn 27:17
From my **h** you required it, whether Gn 31:39
deliver me from the **h** of my brother, Gn 32:11
of my brother, from the **h** of Esau, Gn 32:11
then accept my present from my **h**. Gn 33:10
but do not lay a **h** on him"—that he Gn 37:22
him out of their **h** to restore him to Gn 37:22
and let not our **h** be upon him, Gn 37:27
staff that is in your **h**." So he gave them Gn 38:18
back the pledge from the woman's **h**, Gn 38:20
when she was in labor, one put out a **h**, Gn 38:28
took and tied a scarlet thread on his **h**, Gn 38:28
But as he drew back his **h**, behold, his Gn 38:29
out with the scarlet thread on his **h**, Gn 38:30
his garment in her **h** and fled and got Gn 39:12
his garment in her **h** and had fled out Gn 39:13
Pharaoh's cup was in my **h**, and I took Gn 40:11
and placed the cup in Pharaoh's **h**." Gn 40:11
Pharaoh's cup in his **h** as formerly, Gn 40:13
and he placed the cup in Pharaoh's **h**. Gn 40:21
his signet ring from his **h** and put it on Gn 41:42
from his hand and put it on Joseph's **h**, Gn 41:42
no one shall lift up **h** or foot in all the Gn 41:44
From my **h** you shall require him. Gn 43:9
he also in whose **h** the cup has been Gn 44:16
the man in whose **h** the cup was found Gn 44:17
and Joseph's **h** shall close your eyes." Gn 46:4
put your **h** under my thigh and Gn 47:29
in his right **h** toward Israel's left Gn 48:13
in his right hand toward Israel's left **h**, Gn 48:13
in his left **h** toward Israel's right Gn 48:13
in his left hand toward Israel's right **h**, Gn 48:13
stretched out his right **h** and laid it on Gn 48:14
and his left **h** on the head of Manasseh, Gn 48:14
father laid his right **h** on the head of Gn 48:17
he took his father's **h** to move it from Gn 48:17
put your right **h** on his head." Gn 48:18
I took from the **h** of the Amorites with Gn 48:22
your **h** shall be on the neck of your Gn 49:8
us out of the **h** of the shepherds and Ex 2:19
them out of the **h** of the Egyptians and Ex 3:8
you go unless compelled by a mighty **h**. Ex 3:19
will stretch out my **h** and strike Egypt Ex 3:20
to him, "What is that in your **h**?" He said, Ex 4:2
"Put out your **h** and catch it by the tail"— Ex 4:4
tail"—so he put out his **h** and caught it, Ex 4:4
caught it, and it became a staff in his **h**— Ex 4:4
"Put your **h** inside your cloak." And he Ex 4:6
cloak." And he put his **h** inside his cloak, Ex 4:6
out, behold, his **h** was leprous like snow. Ex 4:6
"Put your **h** back inside your cloak." So Ex 4:7
So he put his **h** back inside his cloak, Ex 4:7

And take in your **h** this staff, with which Ex 4:17
And Moses took the staff of God in his **h**. Ex 4:20
have put a sword in their **h** to kill us." Ex 5:21
for with a strong **h** he will send them out, Ex 6:1
and with a strong **h** he will drive them out Ex 6:1
Then I will lay my **h** on Egypt and bring Ex 7:4
I stretch out my **h** against Egypt and Ex 7:5
and take in your **h** the staff that turned Ex 7:15
staff that is in my **h** I will strike the Ex 7:17
and stretch out your **h** over the waters of Ex 7:19
'Stretch out your **h** with your staff over Ex 8:5
Aaron stretched out his **h** over the waters Ex 8:6
Aaron stretched out his **h** with his staff Ex 8:17
the **h** of the LORD will fall with a very Ex 9:3
have put out my **h** and struck you and Ex 9:15
"Stretch out your **h** toward heaven, Ex 9:22
"Stretch out your **h** over the land of Ex 10:12
"Stretch out your **h** toward heaven, Ex 10:21
stretched out his **h** toward heaven, Ex 10:22
on your feet, and your staff in your **h**. Ex 12:11
for by a strong **h** the LORD brought you Ex 13:3
as a sign on your **h** and as a memorial Ex 13:9
For with a strong **h** the LORD has Ex 13:9
'By a strong **h** the LORD brought us out Ex 13:14
a mark on your **h** or frontlets between Ex 13:16
for by a strong **h** the LORD brought us Ex 13:16
and stretch out your **h** over the sea and Ex 14:16
Moses stretched out his **h** over the sea, Ex 14:21
them on their right **h** and on their left. Ex 14:22
Moses, "Stretch out your **h** over the sea, Ex 14:26
Moses stretched out his **h** over the sea, Ex 14:27
them on their right **h** and on their left. Ex 14:29
that day from the **h** of the Egyptians, Ex 14:30
Your right **h**, O LORD, glorious in power, Ex 15:6
O LORD, glorious in power, your right **h**, Ex 15:6
my sword; my **h** shall destroy them.' Ex 15:9
You stretched out your right **h**; the Ex 15:12
of Aaron, took a tambourine in her **h**, Ex 15:20
we had died by the **h** of the LORD in the Ex 16:3
and take in your **h** the staff with which Ex 17:5
of the hill with the staff of God in my **h**." Ex 17:9
Whenever Moses held up his **h**, Israel Ex 17:11
and whenever he lowered his **h**, Ex 17:11
"A **h** upon the throne of the LORD! Ex 17:16
them out of the **h** of the Egyptians. Ex 18:9
you out of the **h** of the Egyptians and Ex 18:10
and out of the **h** of Pharaoh and has Ex 18:10
from under the **h** of the Egyptians. Ex 18:10
No **h** shall touch him, but he shall be Ex 19:13
for him, but God let him fall into his **h**, Ex 21:13
a rod and the slave dies under his **h**, Ex 21:20
eye for eye, tooth for tooth, **h** for hand, Ex 21:24
eye for eye, tooth for tooth, hand for **h**, Ex 21:24
he has put his **h** to his neighbor's Ex 22:8
he has put his **h** to his neighbor's Ex 22:11
the inhabitants of the land into your **h**, Ex 23:31
he did not lay his **h** on the chief men of Ex 24:11
the gold from their **h** and fashioned it Ex 32:4
with great power and with a mighty **h**? Ex 32:11
two tablets of the testimony in his **h**, Ex 32:15
cover you with my **h** until I have Ex 33:22
Then I will take away my **h**, and you Ex 33:23
and took in his **h** two tablets of stone. Ex 34:4
the testimony in his **h** as he came down Ex 34:29
He shall lay his **h** on the head of the burnt Lv 1:4
And he shall lay his **h** on the head of his Lv 3:2
lay his **h** on the head of his offering, and Lv 3:8
and lay his **h** on its head and kill it in Lv 3:13
the LORD and lay his **h** on the head of the Lv 4:4
and shall lay his **h** on the head of the Lv 4:24
And he shall lay his **h** on the head of the Lv 4:29
and lay his **h** on the head of the sin Lv 4:33
the thumb of his right **h** and on the big Lv 8:23
the thumb of his right **h** and on the big Lv 14:14
pour it into the palm of his own left **h** Lv 14:15
is in his left **h** and sprinkle some oil Lv 14:16
that remains in his **h** the priest shall Lv 14:17
the thumb of his right **h** and on the big Lv 14:17
that is in the priest's **h** he shall put on Lv 14:18
the thumb of his right **h** and on the big Lv 14:25
of the oil into the palm of his own left **h**, Lv 14:26
is in his left **h** seven times before the Lv 14:27
the oil that is in his **h** on the lobe of the Lv 14:28
the thumb of his right **h** and on the big Lv 14:28
that is in the priest's **h** he shall put on Lv 14:29
the wilderness by the **h** of a man who Lv 16:21
has an injured foot or an injured **h**, Lv 21:19
shall remain in the **h** of the buyer until Lv 25:28
be delivered into the **h** of the enemy. Lv 26:25
And in his **h** the priest shall have the Nm 5:18
out of the woman's **h** and shall wave Nm 5:25
to Moses, "Is the LORD'S **h** shortened? Nm 11:23
who does anything with a high **h**, Nm 15:30
Moses lifted up his **h** and struck the Nm 20:11
turn aside to the right **h** or to the left Nm 20:17

will indeed give this people into my **h**, Nm 21:2
and taken all his land out of his **h**, Nm 21:26
him, for I have given him into your **h**, Nm 21:34
with the fees for divination in their **h**. Nm 22:7
the road, with a drawn sword in his **h**. Nm 22:23
I wish I had a sword in my **h**, for then Nm 22:29
way, with his drawn sword in his **h**. Nm 22:31
congregation and took a spear in his **h** Nm 25:7
is the Spirit, and lay your **h** on him. Nm 27:18
the trumpets for the alarm in his **h**. Nm 31:6
enmity struck him down with his **h**, Nm 35:21
manslayer from the **h** of the avenger Nm 35:25
to give us into the **h** of the Amorites, Dt 1:27
For indeed the **h** of the LORD was against Dt 2:15
given into your **h** Sihon the Amorite, Dt 2:24
that he might give him into your **h**, Dt 2:30
all his people and his land into your **h**. Dt 3:2
the LORD our God gave into our **h** Og also, Dt 3:3
at that time out of the **h** of the two kings of Dt 3:8
your greatness and your mighty **h**. Dt 3:24
by a mighty **h** and an outstretched arm, Dt 4:34
with a mighty **h** and an outstretched Dt 5:15
not turn aside to the right **h** or to the left. Dt 5:32
You shall bind them as a sign on your **h**, Dt 6:8
brought us out of Egypt with a mighty **h**. Dt 6:21
out with a mighty **h** and redeemed you Dt 7:8
from the **h** of Pharaoh king of Egypt. Dt 7:8
the signs, the wonders, the mighty **h**, Dt 7:19
And he will give their kings into your **h**, Dt 7:24
the might of my **h** have gotten me this Dt 8:17
brought out of Egypt with a mighty **h**. Dt 9:26
mountain with the two tablets in my **h**. Dt 10:3
his mighty **h** and his outstretched arm, Dt 11:2
shall bind them as a sign on your **h**, Dt 11:18
Your **h** shall be first against him to put Dt 13:9
and afterward the **h** of all the people. Dt 13:9
the devoted things shall stick to your **h**, Dt 13:17
up the money in your **h** and go to the Dt 14:25
is with your brother your **h** shall release. Dt 15:3
heart or shut your **h** against your poor Dt 15:7
you shall open your **h** to him and lend Dt 15:8
shall open wide your **h** to your brother, Dt 15:11
of a freewill offering from your **h**, Dt 16:10
The **h** of the witnesses shall be first Dt 17:7
and afterward the **h** of all the people. Dt 17:7
to you, either to the right **h** or to the left. Dt 17:11
either to the right **h** or to the left, Dt 17:20
and his **h** swings the axe to cut down a Dt 19:5
and **h** him over to the avenger of blood, Dt 19:12
eye for eye, tooth for tooth, **h** for hand, Dt 19:21
eye for eye, tooth for tooth, hand for **h**, Dt 19:21
the LORD your God gives it into your **h**, Dt 20:13
gives them into your **h** and you take Dt 21:10
you may pluck the ears with your **h**, Dt 23:25
and puts it in her **h** and sends her out of Dt 24:1
and puts it in her **h** and sends her out of Dt 24:3
her husband from the **h** of him who is Dt 25:11
and puts out her **h** and seizes him by Dt 25:11
then you shall cut off her **h**. Your eye Dt 25:12
the basket from your **h** and set it down Dt 26:4
with a mighty **h** and an outstretched Dt 26:8
you today, to the right **h** or to the left, Dt 28:14
prosperous in all the work of your **h**, Dt 30:9
they should say, "Our **h** is triumphant, Dt 32:27
for the day of their calamity is at **h**, and Dt 32:35
is none that can deliver out of my **h**. Dt 32:39
For I lift up my **h** to heaven and swear, Dt 32:40
flashing sword and my **h** takes hold on Dt 32:41
ones, with flaming fire at his right **h**. Dt 33:2
his people, all his holy ones were in his **h**; Dt 33:3
turn from it to the right **h** or to the left, Jos 1:7
But if a **h** is laid on anyone who is with Jos 2:19
earth may know that the **h** of the LORD is Jos 4:24
him with his drawn sword in his **h**. Jos 5:13
"See, I have given Jericho into your **h**, Jos 6:2
I have given into your **h** the king of Ai, Jos 8:1
the LORD your God will give it into your **h**. Jos 8:7
the javelin that is in your **h** toward Ai, Jos 8:18
it into your **h**." And Joshua stretched Jos 8:18
javelin that was in his **h** toward the city. Jos 8:18
as soon as he had stretched out his **h**, Jos 8:19
not draw back his **h** with which he Jos 8:26
provisions in your **h** for the journey Jos 9:11
And now, behold, we are in your **h**. Jos 9:25
them out of the **h** of the people of Jos 9:26
not relax your **h** from your servants. Jos 10:6
your God has given them into your **h**." Jos 10:19
it also and its king into the **h** of Israel. Jos 10:30
LORD gave Lachish into the **h** of Israel, Jos 10:32
the LORD gave them into the **h** of Israel, Jos 11:8
had commanded by the **h** of Moses for Jos 14:2
not give up the manslayer into his **h**, Jos 20:5
might not die by the **h** of the avenger of Jos 20:9
people of Israel from the **h** of the LORD." Jos 22:31
it neither to the right **h** nor to the left, Jos 23:6

with you, and I gave them into your **h**, Jos 24:8
you. So I delivered you out of his **h**. Jos 24:10
Jebusites. And I gave them into your **h**. Jos 24:11
behold, I have given the land into his **h**." Jgs 1:2
Canaanites and the Perizzites into their **h**, Jgs 1:4
but the **h** of the house of Joseph rested Jgs 1:35
them into the **h** of their surrounding Jgs 2:14
the **h** of the LORD was against them for Jgs 2:15
them out of the **h** of those who Jgs 2:16
saved them from the **h** of their enemies Jgs 2:18
did not give them into the **h** of Joshua. Jgs 2:23
their fathers by the **h** of Moses. Jgs 3:4
them into the **h** of Cushan-rishathaim Jgs 3:8
king of Mesopotamia into his **h**. Jgs 3:10
And his **h** prevailed over Jgs 3:10
And Ehud reached with his left **h**, took Jgs 3:21
the Moabites into your **h**." So they went Jgs 3:28
subdued that day under the **h** of Israel. Jgs 3:30
LORD sold them into the **h** of Jabin king of Jgs 4:2
troops, and I will give him into your **h**'?" Jgs 4:7
sell Sisera into the **h** of a woman." Then Jgs 4:9
the LORD has given Sisera into your **h**. Jgs 4:14
a tent peg, and took a hammer in her **h**. Jgs 4:21
And the **h** of the people of Israel pressed Jgs 4:24
She sent her **h** to the tent peg and her Jgs 5:26
peg and her right **h** to the workmen's Jgs 5:26
gave them into the **h** of Midian seven Jgs 6:1
And the **h** of Midian overpowered Israel, Jgs 6:2
delivered you from the **h** of the Egyptians Jgs 6:9
Egyptians and from the **h** of all who Jgs 6:9
us and given us into the **h** of Midian." Jgs 6:13
and save Israel from the **h** of Midian; Jgs 6:14
that was in his **h** and touched the meat Jgs 6:21
to God, "If you will save Israel by my **h**, Jgs 6:36
know that you will save Israel by my **h**, Jgs 6:37
for me to give the Midianites into their **h**, Jgs 7:2
me, saying, 'My own **h** has saved me.' Jgs 7:2
you and give the Midianites into your **h**, Jgs 7:7
the camp, for I have given it into your **h**. Jgs 7:9
has given into his **h** Midian and all the Jgs 7:14
given the host of Midian into your **h**." Jgs 7:15
Zebah and Zalmunna already in your **h**, Jgs 8:6
given Zebah and Zalmunna into my **h**, Jgs 8:7
and Zalmunna already in your **h**, Jgs 8:15
have saved us from the **h** of Midian." Jgs 8:22
delivered them from the **h** of all their Jgs 8:34
and delivered you from the **h** of Midian, Jgs 9:17
that this people were under my **h**! Jgs 9:29
may do to them as your **h** finds to do." Jgs 9:33
took an axe in his **h** and cut down a Jgs 9:48
sold them into the **h** of the Philistines Jgs 10:7
and into the **h** of the Ammonites, Jgs 10:7
to me, and I saved you out of their **h**. Jgs 10:12
and all his people into the **h** of Israel, Jgs 11:21
will give the Ammonites into my **h**, Jgs 11:30
and the LORD gave them into his **h**. Jgs 11:32
you, you did not save me from their **h**. Jgs 12:2
my life in my **h** and crossed over against Jgs 12:3
and the LORD gave them into my **h**. Jgs 12:3
gave them into the **h** of the Philistines Jgs 13:1
save Israel from the **h** of the Philistines." Jgs 13:5
and although he had nothing in his **h**, Jgs 14:6
a donkey, and put out his **h** and took it, Jgs 15:15
threw away the jawbone out of his **h**. Jgs 15:17
salvation by the **h** of your servant, Jgs 15:18
given Samson our enemy into our **h**." Jgs 16:23
god has given our enemy into our **h**, Jgs 16:24
the young man who held him by the **h**, Jgs 16:26
his right **h** on the one and his left hand Jgs 16:29
on the one and his left **h** on the other. Jgs 16:29
silver to the LORD from my **h** for my son, Jgs 17:3
put your **h** on your mouth and come Jgs 18:19
tomorrow I will give them into your **h**." Jgs 20:28
for your sake that the **h** of the LORD has Ru 1:13
you buy the field from the **h** of Naomi, Ru 4:5
have bought from the **h** of Naomi all that Ru 4:9
with a three-pronged fork in his **h**, 1 Sm 2:13
The **h** of the LORD was heavy against 1 Sm 5:6
for his **h** is hard against us and against 1 Sm 5:7
the **h** of the LORD was against the city, 1 Sm 5:9
The **h** of God was very heavy there. 1 Sm 5:11
to you why his **h** does not turn away 1 Sm 6:3
he will lighten his **h** from off you and 1 Sm 6:5
know that it is not his **h** that struck us; 1 Sm 6:9
you out of the **h** of the Philistines." 1 Sm 7:3
save us from the **h** of the Philistines." 1 Sm 7:8
And the **h** of the LORD was against the 1 Sm 7:13
territory from the **h** of the Philistines. 1 Sm 7:14
people from the **h** of the Philistines. 1 Sm 9:16
them from the **h** of their surrounding 1 Sm 10:1
which you shall accept from their **h**. 1 Sm 10:4
meet you, do what your **h** finds to do, 1 Sm 10:7
you from the **h** of the Egyptians 1 Sm 10:18
Egyptians and from the **h** of all the 1 Sm 10:18
of Israel by the **h** of messengers, 1 Sm 11:7

Or from whose **h** have I taken a bribe 1 Sm 12:3
taken anything from any man's **h**." 1 Sm 12:4
anything in my **h**." And they said, 1 Sm 12:5
And he sold them into the **h** of Sisera, 1 Sm 12:9
and into the **h** of the Philistines, 1 Sm 12:9
and into the **h** of the king of Moab. 1 Sm 12:9
us out of the **h** of our enemies, 1 Sm 12:10
you out of the **h** of your enemies on 1 Sm 12:11
then the **h** of the LORD will be against 1 Sm 12:15
nor spear found in the **h** of any of the 1 Sm 13:22
the LORD has given them into our **h**. 1 Sm 14:10
has given them into the **h** of Israel." 1 Sm 14:12
to the priest, "Withdraw your **h**." 1 Sm 14:19
but no one put his **h** to his mouth, 1 Sm 14:26
that was in his **h** and dipped it in 1 Sm 14:27
and put his **h** to his mouth, 1 Sm 14:27
give them into the **h** of Israel?" But 1 Sm 14:37
the tip of the staff that was in my **h**. 1 Sm 14:43
took the lyre and played it with his **h**. 1 Sm 16:23
me from the **h** of this Philistine." 1 Sm 17:37
his staff in his **h** and chose five 1 Sm 17:40
His sling was in his **h**, and he 1 Sm 17:40
the LORD will deliver you into my **h**, 1 Sm 17:46
and he will give you into our **h**." 1 Sm 17:47
And David put his **h** in his bag and 1 Sm 17:49
was no sword in the **h** of David. 1 Sm 17:50
the head of the Philistine in his **h**. 1 Sm 17:57
by day. Saul had his spear in his **h**. 1 Sm 18:10
"Let not my **h** be against him, 1 Sm 18:17
but let the **h** of the Philistines be 1 Sm 18:17
him and that the **h** of the Philistines 1 Sm 18:21
David fall by the **h** of the Philistines. 1 Sm 18:25
his life in his **h** and he struck down 1 Sm 19:5
in his house with his spear in his **h**. 1 Sm 19:9
yourself when the matter was in **h**, 1 Sm 20:19
Now then, what do you have on **h**? 1 Sm 21:3
"I have no common bread on **h**, 1 Sm 21:4
you not here a spear or a sword at **h**? 1 Sm 21:8
on the height with his spear in his **h**, 1 Sm 22:6
because their **h** also is with David, 1 Sm 22:17
not put out their **h** to strike the 1 Sm 22:17
I will give the Philistines into your **h**." 1 Sm 23:4
come down with an ephod in his **h**. 1 Sm 23:6
said, "God has given him into my **h**, 1 Sm 23:7
of Keilah surrender me into his **h**? 1 Sm 23:11
my men into the **h** of Saul?" And the 1 Sm 23:12
but God did not give him into his **h**. 1 Sm 23:14
and strengthened his **h** in God. 1 Sm 23:16
for the **h** of Saul my father shall not 1 Sm 23:17
to surrender him into the king's **h**." 1 Sm 23:20
I will give your enemy into your **h**, 1 Sm 24:4
to put out my **h** against him, 1 Sm 24:6
you today into my **h** in the cave. 1 Sm 24:10
not put out my **h** against my lord, 1 Sm 24:10
see the corner of your robe in my **h**. 1 Sm 24:11
but my **h** shall not be against you. 1 Sm 24:12
But my **h** shall not be against you. 1 Sm 24:13
cause and deliver me from your **h**." 1 Sm 24:15
Israel shall be established in your **h**. 1 Sm 24:20
you have at **h** to your servants 1 Sm 25:8
and from saving with your own **h**, 1 Sm 25:26
avenging myself with my own **h**! 1 Sm 25:33
received from her **h** what she had 1 Sm 25:35
insult I received at the **h** of Nabal, 1 Sm 25:39
your enemy into your **h** this day. 1 Sm 26:8
can put out his **h** against the LORD'S 1 Sm 26:9
put out my **h** against the LORD'S 1 Sm 26:11
the LORD gave you into my **h** today, 1 Sm 26:23
not put out my **h** against the LORD'S 1 Sm 26:23
I shall perish one day by the **h** of Saul. 1 Sm 27:1
Israel, and I shall escape out of his **h**." 1 Sm 27:1
kingdom out of your **h** and given it 1 Sm 28:17
with you into the **h** of the Philistines, 1 Sm 28:19
also into the **h** of the Philistines." 1 Sm 28:19
my life in my **h** and have listened to 1 Sm 28:21
and given into our **h** the band that 1 Sm 30:23
to put out your **h** to destroy the LORD'S 2 Sm 1:14
neither to the right **h** nor to the left 2 Sm 2:19
aside to your right **h** or to your left, 2 Sm 2:21
have not given you into the **h** of David. 2 Sm 3:8
my **h** shall be with you to bring over 2 Sm 3:12
'By the **h** of my servant David I will 2 Sm 3:18
Israel from the **h** of the Philistines, 2 Sm 3:18
and from the **h** of all their enemies.'" 2 Sm 3:18
his blood at your **h** and destroy you 2 Sm 4:11
give them into my **h**?" And the LORD 2 Sm 5:19
give the Philistines into your **h**." 2 Sm 5:19
Uzzah put out his **h** to the ark of God 2 Sm 6:6
out of the **h** of the Philistines. 2 Sm 8:1
to Joab and sent it by the **h** of Uriah. 2 Sm 11:14
I delivered you out of the **h** of Saul. 2 Sm 12:7
I may see it and eat it from her **h**.'" 2 Sm 13:5
my sight, that I may eat from her **h**." 2 Sm 13:6
eat from your **h**." And Tamar took 2 Sm 13:10
And she laid her **h** on her head and 2 Sm 13:19
his servant from the **h** of the man 2 Sm 14:16
"Is the **h** of Joab with you in all 2 Sm 14:19
turn to the right **h** or to the left 2 Sm 14:19
would put out his **h** and take hold of 2 Sm 15:5
were on his right **h** and on his left. 2 Sm 16:6
the kingdom into the **h** of your son 2 Sm 16:8
if I felt in my **h** the weight of a 2 Sm 18:12
reach out my **h** against the king's 2 Sm 18:12
On the other **h**, if I had dealt 2 Sm 18:13
javelins in his **h** and thrust them 2 Sm 18:14
him from the **h** of his enemies." 2 Sm 18:19
who raised their **h** against my lord 2 Sm 18:28
this day from the **h** of all who rose 2 Sm 18:31
delivered us from the **h** of our enemies 2 Sm 19:9
saved us from the **h** of the Philistines, 2 Sm 19:9
the beard with his right **h** to kiss him. 2 Sm 20:9
the sword that was in Joab's **h**. 2 Sm 20:10
lifted up his **h** against King David. 2 Sm 20:21
who had six fingers on each **h**, 2 Sm 21:20
they fell by the **h** of David and by 2 Sm 21:22
of David and by the **h** of his servants. 2 Sm 21:22
delivered him from the **h** of all his 2 Sm 22:1
his enemies, and from the **h** of Saul. 2 Sm 22:1
for they cannot be taken with the **h**; 2 Sm 23:6
the Philistines until his **h** was weary, 2 Sm 23:10
weary, and his **h** clung to the sword. 2 Sm 23:10
The Egyptian had a spear in his **h**, 2 Sm 23:21
of the Egyptian's **h** and killed him 2 Sm 23:21
Let us fall into the **h** of the LORD, for 2 Sm 24:14
let me not fall into the **h** of man." 2 Sm 24:14
stretched out his **h** toward Jerusalem 2 Sm 24:16
now stay your **h**." And the angel of 2 Sm 24:16
Please let your **h** be against me and 2 Sm 24:17
was established in the **h** of Solomon. 1 Kgs 2:46
who with his **h** has fulfilled what he 1 Kgs 8:15
and with your **h** have fulfilled it this 1 Kgs 8:24
your great name and your mighty **h**, 1 Kgs 8:42
I will tear it out of the **h** of your son. 1 Kgs 11:12
also lifted up his **h** against the king. 1 Kgs 11:26
he lifted up his **h** against the king. 1 Kgs 11:27
kingdom from the **h** of Solomon 1 Kgs 11:31
the whole kingdom out of his **h**, 1 Kgs 11:34
out of his son's **h** and will give it 1 Kgs 11:35
stretched out his **h** from the altar, 1 Kgs 13:4
altar, saying, "Seize him." And his **h**, 1 Kgs 13:4
that my **h** may be restored to me." 1 Kgs 13:6
and the king's **h** was restored to him 1 Kgs 13:6
me a morsel of bread in your **h**." 1 Kgs 17:11
give your servant into the **h** of Ahab, 1 Kgs 18:9
cloud like a man's **h** is rising from 1 Kgs 18:44
And the **h** of the LORD was on Elijah, 1 Kgs 18:46
I will give it into your **h** this day, 1 Kgs 20:13
all this great multitude into your **h**, 1 Kgs 20:28
let go out of your **h** the man whom I 1 Kgs 20:42
take it out of the **h** of the king of 1 Kgs 22:3
will give it into the **h** of the king." 1 Kgs 22:6
will give it into the **h** of the king." 1 Kgs 22:12
will give it into the **h** of the king." 1 Kgs 22:15
him on his right **h** and on his left; 1 Kgs 22:19
to give them into the **h** of Moab." 2 Kgs 3:10
to give them into the **h** of Moab." 2 Kgs 3:13
the **h** of the LORD came upon him. 2 Kgs 3:15
also give the Moabites into your **h**, 2 Kgs 3:18
and take my staff in your **h** and go. 2 Kgs 4:29
and wave his **h** over the place and 2 Kgs 5:11
accepting from his **h** what he 2 Kgs 5:20
took them from their **h** and put them 2 Kgs 5:24
So he reached out his **h** and took it. 2 Kgs 6:7
captain on whose **h** the king leaned 2 Kgs 7:2
the captain on whose **h** he leaned to 2 Kgs 7:17
and take this flask of oil in your **h**, 2 Kgs 9:1
give me your **h**." So he gave him his 2 Kgs 10:15
your hand." So he gave him his **h**. 2 Kgs 10:15
king, each with his weapons in his **h**. 2 Kgs 11:8
man with his weapons in his **h**, 2 Kgs 11:11
but **h** it over for the repair of the 2 Kgs 12:7
men into whose **h** they delivered the 2 Kgs 12:15
continually into the **h** of Hazael king 2 Kgs 13:3
Syria and into the **h** of Ben-hadad the 2 Kgs 13:3
escaped from the **h** of the Syrians, 2 Kgs 13:5
the royal power was firmly in his **h**, 2 Kgs 14:5
saved them by the **h** of Jeroboam the 2 Kgs 14:27
rescue me from the **h** of the king of 2 Kgs 16:7
of Syria and from the **h** of the king of 2 Kgs 16:7
from under the **h** of Pharaoh king 2 Kgs 17:7
gave them into the **h** of plunderers, 2 Kgs 17:20
you out of the **h** of all your 2 Kgs 17:39
which will pierce the **h** of any man 2 Kgs 18:21
be able to deliver you out of my **h**. 2 Kgs 18:29
not be given into the **h** of the king of 2 Kgs 18:30
his land out of the **h** of the king of 2 Kgs 18:33
they delivered Samaria out of my **h**? 2 Kgs 18:34
delivered their lands out of my **h**, 2 Kgs 18:35
deliver Jerusalem out of my **h**?'" 2 Kgs 18:35
not be given into the **h** of the king of 2 Kgs 19:10
letter from the **h** of the messengers 2 Kgs 19:14
our God, save us, please, from his **h**, 2 Kgs 19:19
this city out of the **h** of the king of 2 Kgs 20:6
them into the **h** of their enemies, 2 Kgs 21:14
be given into the **h** of the workmen 2 Kgs 22:5
money that is delivered into their **h**, 2 Kgs 22:7
delivered it into the **h** of the workmen 2 Kgs 22:9
and that your **h** might be with me, 1 Chr 4:10
the Hagrites, who fell into their **h**. 1 Chr 5:10
exile by the **h** of Nebuchadnezzar. 1 Chr 6:15
Asaph, who stood on his right **h**, 1 Chr 6:39
On the left **h** were their brothers, the 1 Chr 6:44
Egyptian had in his **h** a spear like a 1 Chr 11:23
of the Egyptian's **h** and killed him 1 Chr 11:23
with either the right or the left **h**; 1 Chr 12:2
Uzzah put out his **h** to take hold of 1 Chr 13:9
because he put out his **h** to the ark, 1 Chr 13:10
give them into my **h**?" And the LORD 1 Chr 14:10
and I will give them into your **h**." 1 Chr 14:10
through my enemies by my **h**, 1 Chr 14:11
villages out of the **h** of the Philistines. 1 Chr 18:1
six fingers on each **h** and six toes on 1 Chr 20:6
and they fell by the **h** of David and by 1 Chr 20:8
of David and by the **h** of his servants. 1 Chr 20:8
Let me fall into the **h** of the LORD, for 1 Chr 21:13
do not let me fall into the **h** of man." 1 Chr 21:13
now stay your **h**." And the angel of 1 Chr 21:15
and in his **h** a drawn sword 1 Chr 21:16
Please let your **h**, O LORD my God, be 1 Chr 21:17
inhabitants of the land into my **h**, 1 Chr 22:18
in writing from the **h** of the LORD, 1 Chr 28:19
In your **h** are power and might, and 1 Chr 29:12
and in your **h** it is to make great 1 Chr 29:12
name comes from your **h** and is all 1 Chr 29:16
who with his **h** has fulfilled what he 2 Chr 6:4
and with your **h** have fulfilled it this 2 Chr 6:15
and your mighty **h** and your 2 Chr 6:32
to him by the **h** of his servants ships 2 Chr 8:18
abandoned you to the **h** of Shishak.'" 2 Chr 12:5
on Jerusalem by the **h** of Shishak. 2 Chr 12:7
of the LORD in the **h** of the sons of 2 Chr 13:8
and God gave them into their **h**. 2 Chr 13:16
the LORD, he gave them into your **h**. 2 Chr 16:8
established the kingdom in his **h**. 2 Chr 17:5
will give it into the **h** of the king." 2 Chr 18:5
will give it into the **h** of the king." 2 Chr 18:11
they will be given into your **h**." 2 Chr 18:14
standing on his right **h** and on his 2 Chr 18:18
In your **h** are power and might, so 2 Chr 20:6
king, each with his weapons in his **h**. 2 Chr 23:7
every man with his weapon in his **h**, 2 Chr 23:10
delivered into their **h** a very great 2 Chr 24:24
their own people from your **h**?" 2 Chr 25:15
them into the **h** of their enemies, 2 Chr 25:20
a censer in his **h** to burn incense, 2 Chr 26:19
gave him into the **h** of the king of 2 Chr 28:5
also given into the **h** of the king of 2 Chr 28:5
Judah, he gave them into your **h**, 2 Chr 28:9
have escaped from the **h** of the kings 2 Chr 30:6
The **h** of God was also on Judah to 2 Chr 30:12
received from the **h** of the Levites. 2 Chr 30:16
deliver us from the **h** of the king of 2 Chr 32:11
to deliver their lands out of my **h**? 2 Chr 32:13
able to deliver his people from my **h**, 2 Chr 32:14
be able to deliver you from my **h**? 2 Chr 32:14
his people from my **h** or from the 2 Chr 32:15
hand or from the **h** of my fathers. 2 Chr 32:15
your God deliver you out of my **h**!'" 2 Chr 32:15
not deliver his people from my **h**." 2 Chr 32:17
from the **h** of Sennacherib 2 Chr 32:22
Assyria and from the **h** of all his 2 Chr 32:22
turn aside to the right **h** or to the left. 2 Chr 34:2
given it into the **h** of the overseers 2 Chr 34:17
or aged. He gave them all into his **h**. 2 Chr 36:17
them into the **h** of Nebuchadnezzar Ezr 5:12
who shall put out a **h** to alter this, Ezr 6:12
for the **h** of the LORD his God was on him. Ezr 7:6
for the good **h** of his God was on him. Ezr 7:9
Law of your God, which is in your **h**, Ezr 7:14
wisdom of your God that is in your **h**, Ezr 7:25
for the **h** of the LORD my God was on me, Ezr 7:28
And by the good **h** of our God on us, Ezr 8:18
"The **h** of our God is for good on all who Ezr 8:22
weighed out into their **h** 650 talents of Ezr 8:26
The **h** of our God was on us, and he Ezr 8:31
delivered us from the **h** of the enemy Ezr 8:31
in this faithlessness the **h** of the officials Ezr 9:2
have been given into the **h** of the kings of Ezr 9:7
your great power and by your strong **h**. Neh 1:10
for the good **h** of my God was upon me. Neh 2:8
I told them of the **h** of my God that had Neh 2:18
the work with one **h** and held his Neh 4:17
each kept his weapon at his right **h**. Neh 4:23
to me with an open letter in his **h**. Neh 6:5
Hilkiah, and Maaseiah on his right **h**, Neh 8:4

and Meshullam on his left **h**. Neh 8:4
and gave them into their **h**, Neh 9:24
gave them into the **h** of their enemies, Neh 9:27
them from the **h** of their enemies. Neh 9:27
them to the **h** of their enemies, Neh 9:28
gave them into the **h** of the peoples of Neh 9:30
his signet ring from his **h** and gave it to Est 3:10
the golden scepter that was in his **h**. Est 5:2
Jews, but they laid no **h** on the plunder. Est 9:10
But stretch out your **h** and touch all that Jb 1:11
"Behold, all that he has is in your **h**. Jb 1:12
not stretch out your **h**." So Satan went Jb 1:12
But stretch out your **h** and touch his bone Jb 2:5
said to Satan, "Behold, he is in your **h**; Jb 2:6
mouth and from the **h** of the mighty. Jb 5:15
he would let loose his **h** and cut me off! Jb 6:9
Or, 'Deliver me from the adversary's **h**'? Jb 6:23
'Redeem me from the **h** of the ruthless'? Jb 6:23
are not his days like the days of a hired **h**? Jb 7:1
and like a hired **h** who looks for his wages, Jb 7:2
them into the **h** of their transgression. Jb 8:4
man, nor take the **h** of evildoers. Jb 8:20
earth is given into the **h** of the wicked; Jb 9:24
us, who might lay his **h** on us both. Jb 9:33
and there is none to deliver out of your **h**? Jb 10:7
If iniquity is in your **h**, put it far away, Jb 11:14
secure, who bring their god in their **h**. Jb 12:6
does not know that the **h** of the LORD has Jb 12:9
In his **h** is the life of every living thing Jb 12:10
in my teeth and put my life in my **h**? Jb 13:14
withdraw your **h** far from me, and let Jb 13:21
alone, that he may enjoy, like a hired **h**, Jb 14:6
that a day of darkness is ready at his **h**; Jb 15:23
has stretched out his **h** against God and Jb 15:25
for the **h** of God has touched me! Jb 19:21
the **h** of everyone in misery will come Jb 20:22
and lay your **h** over your mouth. Jb 21:5
is not their prosperity in their **h**? Jb 21:16
my **h** is heavy on account of my Jb 23:2
on the left **h** when he is working, I do not Jb 23:9
he turns to the right **h**, but I do not see Jb 23:9
fair; his **h** pierced the fleeing serpent. Jb 26:13
will teach you concerning the **h** of God; Jb 27:11
"Man puts his **h** to the flinty rock and Jb 28:9
talking and laid their **h** on their mouth; Jb 29:9
me, and my bow ever new in my **h**.' Jb 29:20
On my right **h** the rabble rise; they Jb 30:12
the might of your **h** you persecute me. Jb 30:21
one in a heap of ruins stretch out his **h**, Jb 30:24
have raised my **h** against the fatherless, Jb 31:21
or because my **h** had found much, Jb 31:25
and my mouth has kissed my **h**, Jb 31:27
mighty are taken away by no human **h**. Jb 34:20
Or what does he receive from your **h**? Jb 35:7
He seals up the **h** of every man, that all Jb 37:7
I answer you? I lay my **h** on my mouth. Jb 40:4
you that your own right **h** can save you. Jb 40:14
Arise, O LORD; O God, lift up your **h**; Ps 10:12
because he is at my right **h**, I shall not be Ps 16:8
at your right **h** are pleasures Ps 16:11
from their adversaries at your right **h**. Ps 17:7
from men by your **h**, O LORD, from men Ps 17:14
rescued him from the **h** of all his Ps 18:T
all his enemies, and from the **h** of Saul. Ps 18:T
and your right **h** supported me, Ps 18:35
with the saving might of his right **h**. Ps 20:6
Your **h** will find out all your enemies; Ps 21:8
your right **h** will find out those who hate Ps 21:8
Into your **h** I commit my spirit; you have Ps 31:5
not delivered me into the **h** of the enemy; Ps 31:8
My times are in your **h**; rescue me from Ps 31:15
rescue me from the **h** of my enemies Ps 31:15
day and night your **h** was heavy upon Ps 32:4
nor the **h** of the wicked drive me away. Ps 36:11
headlong, for the LORD upholds his **h**. Ps 37:24
me, and your **h** has come down on me. Ps 38:2
I am spent by the hostility of your **h**. Ps 39:10
you with your own **h** drove out the Ps 44:2
them, but your right **h** and your arm, Ps 44:3
let your right **h** teach you awesome Ps 45:4
at your right **h** stands the queen in gold Ps 45:9
Your right **h** is filled with Ps 48:10
stretched out his **h** against his friends; Ps 55:20
salvation by your right **h** and answer us! Ps 60:5
clings to you; your right **h** upholds me. Ps 63:8
me, O my God, from the **h** of the wicked, Ps 71:4
with you; you hold my right **h**. Ps 73:23
Why do you hold back your **h**, your Ps 74:11
hold back your hand, your right **h**? Ps 74:11
For in the **h** of the LORD there is a cup Ps 75:8
in the night my **h** is stretched out Ps 77:2
years of the right **h** of the Most High." Ps 77:10
a flock by the **h** of Moses and Aaron. Ps 77:20
mountain which his right **h** had won. Ps 78:54
to captivity, his glory to the **h** of the foe. Ps 78:61
and guided them with his skillful **h**. Ps 78:72
the stock that your right **h** planted, and Ps 80:15
But let your **h** be on the man of your Ps 80:17
hand be on the man of your right **h**, Ps 80:17
and turn my **h** against their foes. Ps 81:14
deliver them from the **h** of the wicked." Ps 82:4
no more, for they are cut off from your **h**. Ps 88:5
strong is your **h**, high your right hand. Ps 89:13
strong is your hand, high your right **h**. Ps 89:13
so that my **h** shall be established with Ps 89:21
I will set his **h** on the sea and his right Ps 89:25
on the sea and his right **h** on the rivers. Ps 89:25
You have exalted the right **h** of his foes; Ps 89:42
your side, ten thousand at your right **h**, Ps 91:7
In his **h** are the depths of the earth; the Ps 95:4
of his pasture, and the sheep of his **h**. Ps 95:7
delivers them from the **h** of the wicked. Ps 97:10
His right **h** and his holy arm have Ps 98:1
when you open your **h**, they are filled Ps 104:28
saved them from the **h** of the foe and Ps 106:10
Therefore he raised his **h** and swore to Ps 106:26
he gave them into the **h** of the nations, Ps 106:41
by your right **h** and answer me! Ps 108:6
him; let an accuser stand at his right **h**. Ps 109:6
Let them know that this is your **h**; Ps 109:27
he stands at the right **h** of the needy, Ps 109:31
"Sit at my right **h**, until I make your Ps 110:1
The Lord is at your right **h**; he will Ps 110:5
"The right **h** of the LORD does Ps 118:15
the right **h** of the LORD exalts, the right Ps 118:16
the right **h** of the LORD does valiantly!" Ps 118:16
I hold my life in my **h** continually, Ps 119:109
Let your **h** be ready to help me, for I Ps 119:173
the LORD is your shade on your right **h**. Ps 121:5
of servants look to the **h** of their master, Ps 123:2
a maidservant to the **h** of her mistress, Ps 123:2
Like arrows in the **h** of a warrior are the Ps 127:4
does not fill his **h** nor the binder of Ps 129:7
with a strong **h** and an outstretched Ps 136:12
Jerusalem, let my right **h** forget its skill! Ps 137:5
stretch out your **h** against the wrath Ps 138:7
enemies, and your right **h** delivers me. Ps 138:7
and before, and lay your **h** upon me. Ps 139:5
even there your **h** shall lead me, and Ps 139:10
me, and your right **h** shall hold me. Ps 139:10
Stretch out your **h** from on high; rescue Ps 144:7
many waters, from the **h** of foreigners, Ps 144:7
lies and whose right **h** is a right hand Ps 144:8
right hand is a right **h** of falsehood. Ps 144:8
deliver me from the **h** of foreigners, Ps 144:11
lies and whose right **h** is a right hand Ps 144:11
right hand is a right **h** of falsehood. Ps 144:11
You open your **h**; you satisfy the desire Ps 145:16
have stretched out my **h** and no one has Prv 1:24
Long life is in her right **h**; in her left Prv 3:16
hand; in her left **h** are riches and honor. Prv 3:16
have come into the **h** of your neighbor: Prv 6:3
like a gazelle from the **h** of the hunter, Prv 6:5
like a bird from the **h** of the fowler. Prv 6:5
A slack **h** causes poverty, but the hand Prv 10:4
but the **h** of the diligent makes rich. Prv 10:4
work of a man's **h** comes back to him. Prv 12:14
The **h** of the diligent will rule, while Prv 12:24
have money in his **h** to buy wisdom Prv 17:16
The sluggard buries his **h** in the dish Prv 19:24
is a stream of water in the **h** of the LORD; Prv 21:1
sends a message by the **h** of a fool cuts Prv 26:6
that goes up into the **h** of a drunkard is Prv 26:9
The sluggard buries his **h** in the dish; Prv 26:15
wind or to grasp oil in one's right **h**. Prv 27:16
evil, put your **h** on your mouth. Prv 30:32
She opens her **h** to the poor and Prv 31:20
This also, I saw, is from the **h** of God, Eccl 2:24
of a son, but he has nothing in his **h**. Eccl 5:14
toil that he may carry away in his **h**. Eccl 5:15
and from that withhold not your **h**, Eccl 7:18
wise and their deeds are in the **h** of God. Eccl 9:1
Whatever your **h** finds to do, do it with Eccl 9:10
and at evening withhold not your **h**, Eccl 11:6
His left **h** is under my head, and his right Sg 2:6
my head, and his right **h** embraces me! Sg 2:6
My beloved put his **h** to the latch, and my Sg 5:4
are like jewels, the work of a master **h**. Sg 7:1
His left **h** is under my head, and his right Sg 8:3
my head, and his right **h** embraces me! Sg 8:3
I will turn my **h** against you and will Is 1:25
he stretched out his **h** against them and Is 5:25
away, and his **h** is stretched out still. Is 5:25
having in his **h** a burning coal that he had Is 6:6
thus to me with his strong **h** upon me, Is 8:11
away, and his **h** is stretched out still. Is 9:12
away, and his **h** is stretched out still. Is 9:17
away, and his **h** is stretched out still. Is 9:21
away, and his **h** is stretched out still. Is 10:4
As my **h** has reached to the kingdoms of Is 10:10
"By the strength of my **h** I have done it, Is 10:13
My **h** has found like a nest the wealth of Is 10:14
child shall put his **h** on the adder's den. Is 11:8
Lord will extend his **h** yet a second time Is 11:11
shall put out their **h** against Edom and Is 11:14
and will wave his **h** over the River with Is 11:15
wave the **h** for them to enter the gates of Is 13:2
its time is close at **h** and its days will not Is 13:22
and this is the **h** that is stretched out Is 14:26
His **h** is stretched out, and who will turn Is 14:27
the Egyptians into the **h** of a hard master, Is 19:4
with fear before the **h** that the LORD of Is 19:16
will commit your authority to his **h**. Is 22:21
He has stretched out his **h** over the sea; Is 23:11
For the **h** of the LORD will rest on this Is 25:10
O LORD, your **h** is lifted up, but they do Is 26:11
he casts down to the earth with his **h**. Is 28:2
it, he swallows it as soon as it is in his **h**. Is 28:4
When the LORD stretches out his **h**, the Is 31:3
his **h** has portioned it out to them with Is 34:17
which will pierce the **h** of any man who Is 36:6
not be given into the **h** of the king of Is 36:15
his land out of the **h** of the king of Is 36:18
they delivered Samaria out of my **h**? Is 36:19
have delivered their lands out of my **h**, Is 36:20
should deliver Jerusalem out of my **h**?'" Is 36:20
not be given into the **h** of the king of Is 37:10
the letter from the **h** of the messengers, Is 37:14
O LORD our God, save us from his **h**, Is 37:20
this city out of the **h** of the king of Is 38:6
received from the LORD'S **h** double for all Is 40:2
the hollow of his **h** and marked off the Is 40:12
uphold you with my righteous right **h**. Is 41:10
I, the LORD your God, hold your right **h**; Is 41:13
that the **h** of the LORD has done this, Is 41:20
I will take you by the **h** and keep you; Is 42:6
is none who can deliver from my **h**; Is 43:13
of Jacob, and another will write on his **h**, Is 44:5
or say, "Is there not a lie in my right **h**?" Is 44:20
to Cyrus, whose right **h** I have grasped, Is 45:1
my heritage; I gave them into your **h**; Is 47:6
My **h** laid the foundation of the earth, Is 48:13
and my right **h** spread out the heavens; Is 48:13
sword; in the shadow of his **h** he hid me; Is 49:2
I will lift up my **h** to the nations, Is 49:22
Is my **h** shortened, that it cannot redeem? Is 50:2
This you have from my **h**: you shall lie Is 50:11
and covered you in the shadow of my **h**, Is 51:16
have drunk from the **h** of the LORD the Is 51:17
to take her by the **h** among all the sons Is 51:18
have taken from your **h** the cup of Is 51:22
will put it into the **h** of your tormentors, Is 51:23
will of the LORD shall prosper in his **h**. Is 53:10
it, and keeps his **h** from doing any evil." Is 56:2
Behold, the LORD'S **h** is not shortened, that Is 59:1
be a crown of beauty in the **h** of the LORD, Is 62:3
and a royal diadem in the **h** of your God. Is 62:3
sworn by his right **h** and by his mighty Is 62:8
arm to go at the right **h** of Moses, Is 63:12
made us melt in the **h** of our iniquities. Is 64:7
our potter; we are all the work of your **h**. Is 64:8
All these things my **h** has made, and so Is 66:2
and the **h** of the LORD shall be known to Is 66:14
LORD put out his **h** and touched my Jer 1:9
grape-gatherer pass your **h** again over its Jer 6:9
stretch out my **h** against the inhabitants Jer 6:12
of the LORD, or you will die by our **h**"— Jer 11:21
have stretched out my **h** against you and Jer 15:6
sat alone, because your **h** was upon me, Jer 15:17
deliver you out of the **h** of the wicked, Jer 15:21
shall loosen your **h** from your heritage Jer 17:4
of clay was spoiled in the potter's **h**, Jer 18:4
Behold, like the clay in the potter's **h**, so Jer 18:6
in the potter's hand, so are you in my **h**, Jer 18:6
and by the **h** of those who seek their life. Jer 19:7
give all Judah into the **h** of the king of Jer 20:4
of Judah into the **h** of their enemies, Jer 20:5
life of the needy from the **h** of evildoers. Jer 20:13
you with outstretched **h** and strong arm, Jer 21:5
famine into the **h** of Nebuchadnezzar Jer 21:7
Babylon and into the **h** of their enemies, Jer 21:7
into the **h** of those who seek their lives. Jer 21:7
shall be given into the **h** of the king of Jer 21:10
and deliver from the **h** of the oppressor Jer 21:12
and deliver from the **h** of the oppressor Jer 22:3
were the signet ring on my right **h**, Jer 22:24
give you into the **h** of those who seek Jer 22:25
into the **h** of those of whom you are Jer 22:25
even into the **h** of Nebuchadnezzar Jer 22:25
and into the **h** of the Chaldeans. Jer 22:25
"Am I a God at **h**, declares the LORD, and Jer 23:23
"Take from my **h** this cup of the wine Jer 25:15
So I took the cup from the LORD'S **h**, and Jer 25:17
to accept the cup from your **h** to drink, Jer 25:28
But the **h** of Ahikam the son of Jer 26:24

king of Sidon by the **h** of the envoys who Jer 27:3
lands into the **h** of Nebuchadnezzar, Jer 27:6
LORD, until I have consumed it by his **h**. Jer 27:8
letter was sent by the **h** of Elasah the son Jer 29:3
them into the **h** of Nebuchadnezzar Jer 29:21
I took them by the **h** to bring them out Jer 31:32
giving this city into the **h** of the king of Jer 32:3
not escape out of the **h** of the Chaldeans, Jer 32:4
surely be given into the **h** of the king of Jer 32:4
with a strong **h** and outstretched arm, Jer 32:21
and into the **h** of Nebuchadnezzar king Jer 32:28
'It is given into the **h** of the king of Jer 32:36
it is given into the **h** of the Chaldeans.' Jer 32:43
giving this city into the **h** of the king of Jer 34:2
not escape from his **h** but shall surely be Jer 34:3
be captured and delivered into his **h**. Jer 34:3
give them into the **h** of their enemies Jer 34:20
enemies and into the **h** of those who Jer 34:20
will give into the **h** of their enemies and Jer 34:21
enemies and into the **h** of those who Jer 34:21
into the **h** of the army of the king of Jer 34:21
"Take in your **h** the scroll that you Jer 36:14
the scroll in his **h** and came to them. Jer 36:14
be delivered into the **h** of the king of Jer 37:17
surely be given into the **h** of the army of Jer 38:3
deliver you into the **h** of these men who Jer 38:16
be given into the **h** of the Chaldeans, Jer 38:18
and you shall not escape from their **h**." Jer 38:18
yourself shall not escape from their **h**, Jer 38:23
not be given into the **h** of the men of Jer 39:17
save you and to deliver you from his **h**. Jer 42:11
to deliver us into the **h** of the Chaldeans, Jer 43:3
of Egypt into the **h** of his enemies and Jer 44:30
enemies and into the **h** of those who Jer 44:30
Judah into the **h** of Nebuchadnezzar Jer 44:30
be delivered into the **h** of a people from Jer 46:24
deliver them into the **h** of those who Jer 46:26
into the **h** of Nebuchadnezzar king of Jer 46:26
The calamity of Moab is near at **h**, and Jer 48:16
was a golden cup in the LORD'S **h**, Jer 51:7
I will stretch out my **h** against you, and Jer 51:25
her people fell into the **h** of the foe, Lam 1:7
by his **h** they were fastened together; Lam 1:14
from them his right **h** in the face of Lam 2:3
an enemy, with his right **h** set like a foe; Lam 2:4
has delivered into the **h** of the enemy Lam 2:7
did not restrain his **h** from destroying; Lam 2:8
me he turns his **h** again and again the Lam 3:3
We have given the **h** to Egypt, and to Lam 5:6
there is none to deliver us from their **h**. Lam 5:8
and the **h** of the LORD was upon him Ezk 1:3
behold, a **h** was stretched out to me, Ezk 2:9
the **h** of the LORD being strong upon me. Ezk 3:14
but his blood I will require at your **h**. Ezk 3:18
but his blood I will require at your **h**. Ezk 3:20
And the **h** of the LORD was upon me Ezk 3:22
will stretch out my **h** against them and Ezk 6:14
the **h** of the Lord GOD fell upon me there. Ezk 8:1
put out the form of a **h** and took me by a Ezk 8:3
Each had his censer in his **h**, and the Ezk 8:11
with his destroying weapon in his **h**." Ezk 9:1
with his weapon for slaughter in his **h**, Ezk 9:2
stretched out his **h** from between the Ezk 10:7
form of a human **h** under their wings. Ezk 10:8
My **h** will be against the prophets who Ezk 13:9
and deliver my people out of your **h**, Ezk 13:21
shall be no more in your **h** as prey, Ezk 13:21
I will deliver my people out of your **h**. Ezk 13:23
will stretch out my **h** against him and Ezk 14:9
I stretch out my **h** against it and Ezk 14:13
I stretched out my **h** against you and Ezk 16:27
he gave his **h** and did all these things; Ezk 17:18
profit, withholds his **h** from injustice, Ezk 18:8
withholds his **h** from iniquity, takes Ezk 18:17
But I withheld my **h** and acted for the Ezk 20:22
with a mighty **h** and an outstretched Ezk 20:33
with a mighty **h** and an outstretched Ezk 20:34
that it may be grasped in the **h**. Ezk 21:11
to be given into the **h** of the slayer. Ezk 21:11
Into his right **h** comes the divination Ezk 21:22
you shall be taken in **h**. Ezk 21:24
I strike my **h** at the dishonest gain Ezk 22:13
I will give her cup into your **h**. Ezk 23:31
I have stretched out my **h** against you, Ezk 25:7
and will **h** you over as plunder to the Ezk 25:7
stretch out my **h** against Edom and Ezk 25:13
upon Edom by the **h** of my people Ezk 25:14
stretch out my **h** against the Ezk 25:16
uncircumcised by the **h** of foreigners; Ezk 28:10
when they grasped you with the **h**, you Ezk 29:7
by the **h** of Nebuchadnezzar king of Ezk 30:10
sell the land into the **h** of evildoers; Ezk 30:12
everything in it, by the **h** of foreigners; Ezk 30:12
I will make the sword fall from his **h**. Ezk 30:22
of Babylon and put my sword in his **h**, Ezk 30:24

put my sword into the **h** of the king of Ezk 30:25
will give it into the **h** of a mighty one Ezk 31:11
I will require at the watchman's **h**. Ezk 33:6
but his blood I will require at your **h**. Ezk 33:8
Now the **h** of the LORD had been upon Ezk 33:22
my sheep at their **h** and put a stop Ezk 34:10
deliver them from the **h** of those who Ezk 34:27
and I will stretch out my **h** against you, Ezk 35:3
The **h** of the LORD was upon me, and he Ezk 37:1
that they may become one in your **h**. Ezk 37:17
(that is in the **h** of Ephraim) and the Ezk 37:19
stick, that they may be one in my **h**. Ezk 37:19
write are in your **h** before their eyes, Ezk 37:20
to turn your **h** against the waste Ezk 38:12
I will strike your bow from your left **h**, Ezk 39:3
your arrows drop out of your right **h**. Ezk 39:3
and my **h** that I have laid on them. Ezk 39:21
them into the **h** of their adversaries, Ezk 39:23
day, the **h** of the LORD was upon me, Ezk 40:1
cord and a measuring reed in his **h**. Ezk 40:3
reed in the man's **h** was six long cubits, Ezk 40:5
with a measuring line in his **h**, Ezk 47:3
gave Jehoiakim king of Judah into his **h**, Dn 1:2
a stone was cut out by no human **h**, Dn 2:34
and into whose **h** he has given, wherever Dn 2:38
cut from a mountain by no human **h**, Dn 2:45
and he will deliver us out of your **h**, Dn 3:17
and none can stay his **h** or say to him, Dn 4:35
fingers of a human **h** appeared and wrote Dn 5:5
And the king saw the **h** as it wrote. Dn 5:5
but the God in whose **h** is your breath, Dn 5:23
"Then from his presence the **h** was sent, Dn 5:24
they shall be given into his **h** for a time, Dn 7:25
shall make deceit prosper under his **h**, Dn 8:25
shall be broken—but by no human **h**. Dn 8:25
out of the land of Egypt with a mighty **h**, Dn 9:15
a **h** touched me and set me trembling Dn 10:10
but it shall be given into his **h**. Dn 11:11
land, with destruction in his **h**. Dn 11:16
these shall be delivered out of his **h**: Dn 11:41
stretch out his **h** against the countries, Dn 11:42
he raised his right **h** and his left hand Dn 12:7
hand and his left **h** toward heaven and Dn 12:7
no one shall rescue her out of my **h**. Hos 2:10
he stretched out his **h** with mockers. Hos 7:5
How can I **h** you over, O Israel? Hos 11:8
your daughters into the **h** of the people of Jl 3:8
I will turn my **h** against Ekron, and the Am 1:8
and leaned his **h** against the wall, Am 5:19
a plumb line, with a plumb line in his **h**. Am 7:7
Sheol, from there shall my **h** take them; Am 9:2
do not **h** over his survivors in the day of Ob 1:14
not know their right **h** from their left, Jon 4:11
it, because it is in the power of their **h**. Mi 2:1
redeem you from the **h** of your enemies. Mi 4:10
Your **h** shall be lifted up over your Mi 5:9
and I will cut off sorceries from your **h**, Mi 5:12
has come; now their confusion is at **h**. Mi 7:4
in the LORD'S right **h** will come around Hab 2:16
like the light; rays flashed from his **h**; Hab 3:4
will stretch out my **h** against Judah and Zep 1:4
will stretch out his **h** against the north Zep 2:13
LORD came by the **h** of Haggai the prophet Hg 1:1
LORD came by the **h** of Haggai the Hg 1:3
LORD came by the **h** of Haggai the Hg 2:1
a man with a measuring line in his **h**! Zec 2:1
"Behold, I will shake my **h** over them, Zec 2:9
standing at his right **h** to accuse him. Zec 3:1
the plumb line in the **h** of Zerubbabel. Zec 4:10
each with staff in **h** because of great age. Zec 8:4
them to fall into the **h** of his neighbor, Zec 11:6
and each into the **h** of his king, Zec 11:6
and I will deliver none from their **h**." Zec 11:6
I will turn my **h** against the little ones. Zec 13:7
so that each will seize the **h** of another, Zec 14:13
and the **h** of the one will be raised Zec 14:13
be raised against the **h** of the other. Zec 14:13
With such a gift from your **h**, will he Mal 1:9
not accept an offering from your **h**. Mal 1:10
Shall I accept that from your **h**? Mal 1:13
or accepts it with favor from your **h**. Mal 2:13
for the kingdom of heaven is at **h**." Mt 3:2
His winnowing fork is in his **h**, and he Mt 3:12
for the kingdom of heaven is at **h**." Mt 4:17
lest your accuser **h** you over to the Mt 5:25
And if your right **h** causes you to sin, Mt 5:30
not let your left **h** know what your right Mt 6:3
hand know what your right **h** is doing, Mt 6:3
stretched out his **h** and touched him, Mt 8:3
He touched her **h**, and the fever left her, Mt 8:15
died, but come and lay your **h** on her, Mt 9:18
he went in and took her by the **h**, Mt 9:25
saying, 'The kingdom of heaven is at **h**.' Mt 10:7
a man was there with a withered **h**. Mt 12:10
"Stretch out your **h**." And the man Mt 12:13

stretching out his **h** toward his Mt 12:49
reached out his **h** and took hold Mt 14:31
And if your **h** or your foot causes you to Mt 18:8
one at your right **h** and one at your left, Mt 20:21
but to sit at my right **h** and at my left is Mt 20:23
'Bind him **h** and foot and cast him into Mt 22:13
Lord said to my Lord, Sit at my right **h**, Mt 22:44
'The Teacher says, My time is at **h**. Mt 26:18
who has dipped his **h** in the dish with Mt 26:23
See, the hour is at **h**, and the Son of Mt 26:45
us be going; see, my betrayer is at **h**." Mt 26:46
Jesus stretched out his **h** and drew his Mt 26:51
seated at the right **h** of Power and Mt 26:64
his head and put a reed in his right **h**. Mt 27:29
and the kingdom of God is at **h**; Mk 1:15
and took her by the **h** and lifted her up, Mk 1:31
he stretched out his **h** and touched him Mk 1:41
and a man was there with a withered **h**. Mk 3:1
he said to the man with the withered **h**, Mk 3:3
"Stretch out your **h**." He stretched it out, Mk 3:5
stretched it out, and his **h** was restored. Mk 3:5
Taking her by the **h** he said to her, Mk 5:41
they begged him to lay his **h** on him. Mk 7:32
the blind man by the **h** and led him out Mk 8:23
took him by the **h** and lifted him up, Mk 9:27
And if your **h** causes you to sin, cut it Mk 9:43
one at your right **h** and one at your Mk 10:37
but to sit at my right **h** or at my left is Mk 10:40
said to my Lord, Sit at my right **h**, Mk 12:36
us be going; see, my betrayer is at **h**." Mk 14:42
of Man seated at the right **h** of Power, Mk 14:62
and sat down at the right **h** of God. Mk 16:19
this child be?" For the **h** of the Lord was Lk 1:66
enemies and from the **h** of all who hate Lk 1:71
delivered from the **h** of our enemies, Lk 1:74
His winnowing fork is in his **h**, to clear Lk 3:17
stretched out his **h** and touched him, Lk 5:13
was there whose right **h** was withered. Lk 6:6
he said to the man with the withered **h**, Lk 6:8
him, "Stretch out your **h**." And he did so, Lk 6:10
And he did so, and his **h** was restored. Lk 6:10
But taking her by the **h** he called, Lk 8:54
"No one who puts his **h** to the plow and Lk 9:62
and the judge **h** you over to the officer, Lk 12:58
put it on him, and put a ring on his **h**, Lk 15:22
Lord said to my Lord, Sit at my right **h**, Lk 20:42
saying, 'I am he!' and, 'The time is at **h**!' Lk 21:8
the **h** of him who betrays me is with Lk 22:21
be seated at the right **h** of the power of Lk 22:69
The Passover of the Jews was at **h**, and Jn 2:13
Son and has given all things into his **h**. Jn 3:35
the Passover, the feast of the Jews, was at **h**. Jn 6:4
Now the Jews' Feast of Booths was at **h**. Jn 7:2
to arrest him, but no one laid a **h** on him, Jn 7:30
He who is a hired **h** and not a shepherd, Jn 10:12
he is a hired **h** and cares nothing for Jn 10:13
no one will snatch them out of my **h**. Jn 10:28
to snatch them out of the Father's **h**. Jn 10:29
Now the Passover of the Jews was at **h**, Jn 11:55
standing by struck Jesus with his **h**, Jn 18:22
since the tomb was close at **h**, Jn 19:42
the nails, and place my **h** into his side, Jn 20:25
and put out your **h**, and place it in my Jn 20:27
he is at my right **h** that I may not be Acts 2:25
therefore exalted at the right **h** of God, Acts 2:33
Lord said to my Lord, Sit at my right **h**, Acts 2:34
him by the right **h** and raised him up, Acts 3:7
to do whatever your **h** and your plan Acts 4:28
while you stretch out your **h** to heal, Acts 4:30
him at his right **h** as Leader and Acts 5:31
was giving them salvation by his **h**, Acts 7:25
and redeemer by the **h** of the angel Acts 7:35
Did not my **h** make all these things?' Acts 7:50
Jesus standing at the right **h** of God. Acts 7:55
of Man standing at the right **h** of God." Acts 7:56
led him by the **h** and brought him into Acts 9:8
he gave her his **h** and raised her up. Acts 9:41
And the **h** of the Lord was with them, Acts 11:21
the elders by the **h** of Barnabas and Acts 11:30
rescued me from the **h** of Herod and Acts 12:11
to them with his **h** to be silent, Acts 12:17
behold, the **h** of the Lord is upon you, Acts 13:11
seeking people to lead him by the **h**. Acts 13:11
up, and motioning with his **h** said: Acts 13:16
Alexander, motioning with his **h**, Acts 19:33
motioned with his **h** to the people. Acts 21:40
I was led by the **h** by those who were Acts 22:11
The tribune took him by the **h**, and Acts 23:19
Paul stretched out his **h** and made his Acts 26:1
of the heat and fastened on his **h**. Acts 28:3
saw the creature hanging from his **h**, Acts 28:4
I want to do right, evil lies close at **h**. Rom 7:21
raised—who is at the right **h** of God, Rom 8:34
The night is far gone; the day is at **h**. Rom 13:12
should say, "Because I am not a **h**, 1 Cor 12:15

The eye cannot say to the **h**, "I have 1 Cor 12:21
On the other **h**, the one who 1 Cor 14:3
write this greeting with my own **h**. 1 Cor 16:21
for the right **h** and for the 2 Cor 6:7
they gave the right **h** of fellowship to Gal 2:9
I am writing to you with my own **h**. Gal 6:11
him at his right **h** in the heavenly Eph 1:20
be known to everyone. The Lord is at **h**; Phil 4:5
Christ is, seated at the right **h** of God. Col 3:1
write this greeting with my own **h**. Col 4:18
write this greeting with my own **h**. 2 Thes 3:17
I, Paul, write this with my own **h**: I Phlm 1:19
sat down at the right **h** of the Majesty on Heb 1:3
"Sit at my right **h** until I make your Heb 1:13
On the one **h**, a former commandment Heb 7:18
but on the other **h**, a better hope is Heb 7:19
is seated at the right **h** of the throne of Heb 8:1
I took them by the **h** to bring them out Heb 8:9
sins, he sat down at the right **h** of God, Heb 10:12
is seated at the right **h** of the throne of Heb 12:2
hearts, for the coming of the Lord is at **h**. Jas 5:8
into heaven and is at the right **h** of God, 1 Pt 3:22
The end of all things is at **h**; therefore be 1 Pt 4:7
under the mighty **h** of God so that at the 1 Pt 5:6
In his right **h** he held seven stars, from Rv 1:16
But he laid his right **h** on me, saying, Rv 1:17
seven stars that you saw in my right **h**, Rv 1:20
who holds the seven stars in his right **h**, Rv 2:1
I saw in the right **h** of him who was seated Rv 5:1
scroll from the right **h** of him who was Rv 5:7
And its rider had a pair of scales in his **h**. Rv 6:5
rose before God from the **h** of the angel. Rv 8:4
He had a little scroll open in his **h**. And Rv 10:2
on the land raised his right **h** to heaven Rv 10:5
that is open in the **h** of the angel who is Rv 10:8
little scroll from the **h** of the angel and Rv 10:10
marked on the right **h** or the forehead, Rv 13:16
a mark on his forehead or on his **h**, Rv 14:9
on his head, and a sharp sickle in his **h**. Rv 14:14
holding in her **h** a golden cup full of Rv 17:4
of one mind and **h** over their power and Rv 17:13
holding in his **h** the key to the Rv 20:1

HANDBAGS (1)
robes, the mantles, the cloaks, and the **h**; Is 3:22

HANDBREADTH (7)
shall make a rim around it a **h** wide, Ex 25:25
And he made a rim around it a **h** wide, Ex 37:12
Its thickness was a **h**, and its brim 1 Kgs 7:26
Its thickness was a **h**. And its brim 2 Chr 4:5
each being a cubit and a **h** in length. Ezk 40:5
And hooks, a **h** long, were fastened all Ezk 40:43
(the cubit being a cubit and a **h**): Ezk 43:13

HANDBREADTHS (1)
Behold, you have made my days a few **h**, Ps 39:5

HANDED (10)
These he **h** over to his servants, every Gn 32:16
and Aaron's sons **h** him the blood, Lv 9:12
And they **h** the burnt offering to him, Lv 9:13
And Aaron's sons **h** him the blood, Lv 9:18
robes and the horse be **h** over to one of Est 6:9
lest I be **h** over to them and they deal Jer 38:19
All things have been **h** over to me by Mt 11:27
your tradition that you have **h** down. Mk 7:13
All things have been **h** over to me by Lk 10:22
whom I have **h** over to Satan that 1 Tm 1:20

HANDFUL (7)
shall take from it a **h** of the fine flour and Lv 2:2
the priest shall take a **h** of it as its Lv 5:12
shall take from it a **h** of the fine flour of Lv 6:15
the grain offering, took a **h** of it, Lv 9:17
priest shall take a **h** of the grain Nm 5:26
only a **h** of flour in a jar and a little 1 Kgs 17:12
Better is a **h** of quietness than two hands Eccl 4:6

HANDFULS (4)
and Aaron, "Take **h** of soot from the kiln, Ex 9:8
and two **h** of sweet incense beaten Lv 16:12
shall suffice for **h** for all the 1 Kgs 20:10
among my people for **h** of barley and Ezk 13:19

HANDING (2)
I am **h** you over to the people of the East Ezk 25:4
of one mind and **h** over their royal Rv 17:17

HANDIWORK (1)
God, and the sky above proclaims his **h**. Ps 19:1

HANDKERCHIEF (1)
mina, which I kept laid away in a **h**; Lk 19:20

HANDKERCHIEFS (1)
so that even **h** or aprons that had Acts 19:12

HANDLE (6)
head slips from the **h** and strikes his Dt 19:5
fit for war, able to **h** spear and shield. 2 Chr 25:5
Those who **h** the law did not know me; Jer 2:8
men of Cush and Put who **h** the shield, Jer 46:9
their ships come all who **h** the oar. Ezk 27:29
"Do not **h**, Do not taste, Do not touch" Col 2:21

HANDLED (3)
were pressed and their virgin bosoms **h**. Ezk 23:3
lain with her and **h** her virgin bosom Ezk 23:8
when the Egyptians **h** your bosom Ezk 23:21

HANDLES (4)
with liquid myrrh, on the **h** of the bolt. Sg 5:5
you making?' or 'Your work has no **h**'? Is 45:9
and the one who **h** the sickle in time of Jer 50:16
he who **h** the bow shall not stand, and Am 2:15

HANDLING (2)
shield, men of Lud, skilled in **h** the bow. Jer 46:9
ashamed, rightly **h** the word of truth. 2 Tm 2:15

HANDMAID (1)
your **h** is a servant to wash the feet of 1 Sm 25:41

HANDMILL (1)
of the slave girl who is behind the **h**, Ex 11:5

HANDMILLS (1)
it and ground it in **h** or beat it in Nm 11:8

HANDS (451)
and from the painful toil of our **h**." Gn 5:29
reached out their **h** and brought Lot Gn 19:10
the innocence of my **h** I have done this." Gn 20:5
she put on his **h** and on the smooth Gn 27:16
voice, but the **h** are the hands of Esau." Gn 27:22
voice, but the hands are the **h** of Esau." Gn 27:22
because his **h** were hairy like his Gn 27:23
were hairy like his brother Esau's **h**. Gn 27:23
the labor of my **h** and rebuked you last Gn 31:42
heard it, he rescued him out of their **h**, Gn 37:21
all that he did to succeed in his **h**. Gn 39:3
Put him in my **h**, and I will bring him Gn 42:37
crossing his **h** (for Manasseh was the Gn 48:14
made agile by the **h** of the Mighty One Gn 49:24
city, I will stretch out my **h** to the LORD. Ex 9:29
and stretched out his **h** to the LORD, Ex 9:33
O Lord, which your **h** have established. Ex 15:17
But Moses' **h** grew weary, so they took a Ex 17:12
it, while Aaron and Hur held up his **h**, Ex 17:12
So his **h** were steady until the going Ex 17:12
You shall not join **h** with a wicked man Ex 23:1
his sons shall lay their **h** on the head of Ex 29:10
his sons shall lay their **h** on the head of Ex 29:15
his sons shall lay their **h** on the head of Ex 29:19
thumbs of their right **h** and on the Ex 29:20
take them from their **h** and burn them Ex 29:25
sons shall wash their **h** and their feet. Ex 30:19
They shall wash their **h** and their feet, Ex 30:21
tablets out of his **h** and broke them at Ex 32:19
every skillful woman spun with her **h**, Ex 35:25
his sons washed their **h** and their feet. Ex 40:31
shall lay their **h** on the head Lv 4:15
His own **h** shall bring the LORD'S food Lv 7:30
and his sons laid their **h** on the head of Lv 8:14
and his sons laid their **h** on the head of Lv 8:18
and his sons laid their **h** on the head of Lv 8:22
thumbs of their right **h** and on the big Lv 8:24
put all these in the **h** of Aaron and in the Lv 8:27
of Aaron and in the **h** of his sons and Lv 8:27
them from their **h** and burned them Lv 8:28
Aaron lifted up his **h** toward the people Lv 9:22
having rinsed his **h** in water shall Lv 15:11
shall lay both his **h** on the head of Lv 16:21
who heard him lay their **h** on his head, Lv 24:14
and place in her **h** the grain offering of Nm 5:18
shall put them on the **h** of the Nazirite, Nm 6:19
of Israel shall lay their **h** on the Levites, Nm 8:10
Levites shall lay their **h** on the heads of Nm 8:12
Balaam, and he struck his **h** together. Nm 24:10
and he laid his **h** on him and Nm 27:23
And they took in their **h** some of the fruit Dt 1:25
has blessed you in all the work of your **h**. Dt 2:7
us. The LORD our God gave all into our **h**. Dt 2:36
of wood and stone, the work of human **h**, Dt 4:28
tablets of the covenant were in my two **h**. Dt 9:15
out of my two **h** and broke them before Dt 9:17
in all the work of your **h** that you do. Dt 14:29
produce and in all the work of your **h**, Dt 16:15
man shall wash their **h** over the heifer Dt 21:6
testify, 'Our **h** did not shed this blood, Dt 21:7
may bless you in all the work of your **h**. Dt 24:19
a thing made by the **h** of a craftsman, Dt 27:15
and to bless all the work of your **h**. Dt 28:12
to anger through the work of your **h**." Dt 31:29
With your **h** contend for him, and be a Dt 33:7
and accept the work of his **h**; Dt 33:11
for Moses had laid his **h** on him. Dt 34:9
LORD has given all the land into our **h**. Jos 2:24
all, to give us into the **h** of the Amorites, Jos 7:7
them, for I have given them into your **h**. Jos 10:8
had given all their enemies into their **h**. Jos 21:44
lapped, putting their **h** to their mouths, Jgs 7:6
So the people took provisions in their **h**, Jgs 7:8
and afterward your **h** shall be Jgs 7:11
put trumpets into the **h** of all of them Jgs 7:16
smashed the jars that were in their **h**. Jgs 7:19
They held in their left **h** the torches, and Jgs 7:20
and in their right **h** the trumpets to Jgs 7:20
has given into your **h** the princes of Jgs 8:3
"Are the **h** of Zebah and Zalmunna Jgs 8:6
'Are the **h** of Zebah and Zalmunna Jgs 8:15
who strengthened his **h** to kill his Jgs 9:24
offering and a grain offering at our **h**, Jgs 13:23
He scraped it out into his **h** and went on, Jgs 14:9
give you into the **h** of the Philistines." Jgs 15:12
bind you and give you into their **h**. Jgs 15:13
fire, and his bonds melted off his **h**. Jgs 15:14
fall into the **h** of the uncircumcised?" Jgs 15:18
her and brought the money in their **h**. Jgs 16:18
for God has given it into your **h**, Jgs 18:10
the house, with her **h** on the threshold. Jgs 19:27
Dagon and both his **h** were lying cut 1 Sm 5:4
climbed up on his **h** and feet, 1 Sm 14:13
Israel out of the **h** of those who 1 Sm 14:48
insane in their **h** and made marks 1 Sm 21:13
there is no wrong or treason in my **h**. 1 Sm 24:11
when the LORD put me into your **h**. 1 Sm 24:18
have I done? What evil is on my **h**? 1 Sm 26:18
deliver me into the **h** of my master, 1 Sm 30:15
Now therefore let your **h** be strong, and 2 Sm 2:7
Your **h** were not bound; your feet were 2 Sm 3:34
and cut off their **h** and feet and 2 Sm 4:12
and the **h** of all who are with you 2 Sm 16:21
them into the **h** of the Gibeonites, 2 Sm 21:9
cleanness of my **h** he rewarded me. 2 Sm 22:21
He trains my **h** for war, so that my 2 Sm 22:35
and spread out his **h** toward heaven, 1 Kgs 8:22
stretching out his **h** toward this 1 Kgs 8:38
had knelt with **h** outstretched toward 1 Kgs 8:54
them to the **h** of the officers 1 Kgs 14:27
gave them into the **h** of his servants. 1 Kgs 15:18
him to anger with the work of his **h**, 1 Kgs 16:7
servants and lay **h** on whatever 1 Kgs 20:6
who poured water on the **h** of Elijah." 2 Kgs 3:11
on his eyes, and his **h** on his hands. 2 Kgs 4:34
on his eyes, and his hands on his **h**. 2 Kgs 4:34
and the feet and the palms of her **h**. 2 Kgs 9:35
I give into your **h** to escape shall 2 Kgs 10:24
and they clapped their **h** and said, 2 Kgs 11:12
So they laid **h** on her; and she went 2 Kgs 11:16
out into the **h** of the workmen 2 Kgs 12:11
And Elisha laid his **h** on the king's 2 Kgs 13:16
laid his hands on the king's **h**. 2 Kgs 13:16
not gods, but the work of men's **h**, 2 Kgs 19:18
to anger with all the work of their **h**, 2 Kgs 22:17
with them were given into their **h**, 1 Chr 5:20
although there is no wrong in my **h**, 1 Chr 12:17
of Israel and spread out his **h**. 2 Chr 6:12
and spread out his **h** toward heaven, 2 Chr 6:13
stretching out his **h** toward this 2 Chr 6:29
them to the **h** of the officers 2 Chr 12:10
Do not let your **h** be weak, for your 2 Chr 15:7
So they laid **h** on her, and she went 2 Chr 23:15
repairing went forward in their **h**, 2 Chr 24:13
and they laid their **h** on them, 2 Chr 29:23
delivered their people from my **h**, 2 Chr 32:17
which are the work of men's **h**. 2 Chr 32:19
anger with all the works of their **h**, 2 Chr 34:25
goes on diligently and prospers in their **h**. Ezr 5:8
weighed into the **h** of Meremoth the Ezr 8:33
and spread out my **h** to the LORD my Ezr 9:5
they strengthened their **h** for the good Neh 2:18
"Their **h** will drop from the work, Neh 6:9
But now, O God, strengthen my **h**. Neh 6:9
"Amen, Amen," lifting up their **h**. Neh 8:6
I will lay **h** on you." From that time Neh 13:21
and sought to lay **h** on King Ahasuerus. Est 2:21
he disdained to lay **h** on Mordecai alone. Est 3:6
of silver into the **h** of those who have Est 3:9
had sought to lay **h** on King Ahasuerus. Est 6:2
because he intended to lay **h** on the Jews. Est 8:7
King Ahasuerus to lay **h** on those who Est 9:2
Susa, but they laid no **h** on the plunder. Est 9:15
them, but they laid no **h** on the plunder. Est 9:16
You have blessed the work of his **h**, and Jb 1:10
and you have strengthened the weak **h**. Jb 4:3
crafty, so that their **h** achieve no success. Jb 5:12
he binds up; he shatters, but his **h** heal. Jb 5:18
with snow and cleanse my **h** with lye, Jb 9:30
the work of your **h** and favor the designs Jb 10:3
Your **h** fashioned and made me, and now Jb 10:8
you will stretch out your **h** toward him. Jb 11:13
you would long for the work of your **h**. Jb 14:15
and casts me into the **h** of the wicked. Jb 16:11

although there is no violence in my **h**, Jb 16:17
he who has clean **h** grows stronger and Jb 17:9
and his **h** will give back his wealth. Jb 20:10
through the cleanness of your **h**." Jb 22:30
It claps its **h** at him and hisses at him Jb 27:23
could I gain from the strength of their **h**, Jb 30:2
eyes, and if any spot has stuck to my **h**, Jb 31:7
poor, for they are all the work of his **h**? Jb 34:19
he claps his **h** among us and multiplies Jb 34:37
He covers his **h** with the lightning and Jb 36:32
Lay your **h** on him; remember the battle Jb 41:8
I have done this, if there is wrong in my **h**, Ps 7:3
him dominion over the works of your **h**; Ps 8:6
are snared in the work of their own **h**. Ps 9:16
that you may take it into your **h**; Ps 10:14
the cleanness of my **h** he rewarded me. Ps 18:20
to the cleanness of my **h** in his sight. Ps 18:24
He trains my **h** for war, so that my Ps 18:34
me; they have pierced my **h** and feet— Ps 22:16
He who has clean **h** and a pure heart, Ps 24:4
I wash my **h** in innocence and go Ps 26:6
in whose **h** are evil devices, and whose Ps 26:10
and whose right **h** are full of bribes. Ps 26:10
I lift up my **h** toward your most holy Ps 28:2
to them according to the work of their **h**; Ps 28:4
works of the LORD or the work of his **h**, Ps 28:5
or spread out our **h** to a foreign god, Ps 44:20
Clap your **h**, all peoples! Shout to God Ps 47:1
your **h** deal out violence on earth. Ps 58:2
as I live; in your name I will lift up my **h**. Ps 63:4
shall hasten to stretch out her **h** to God. Ps 68:31
clean and washed my **h** in innocence. Ps 73:13
men of war were unable to use their **h**. Ps 76:5
your **h** were freed from the basket. Ps 81:6
you, O LORD; I spread out my **h** to you. Ps 88:9
establish the work of our **h** upon us; Ps 90:17
us; yes, establish the work of our **h**! Ps 90:17
On their **h** they will bear you up, lest Ps 91:12
at the works of your **h** I sing for joy. Ps 92:4
made it, and his **h** formed the dry land. Ps 95:5
Let the rivers clap their **h**; let the hills Ps 98:8
the heavens are the work of your **h**. Ps 102:25
The works of his **h** are faithful and just; Ps 111:7
silver and gold, the work of human **h**. Ps 115:4
They have **h**, but do not feel; feet, but do Ps 115:7
lift up my **h** toward your Ps 119:48
Your **h** have made and fashioned me; Ps 119:73
stretch out their **h** to do wrong. Ps 125:3
shall eat the fruit of the labor of your **h**; Ps 128:2
Lift up your **h** to the holy place and Ps 134:2
silver and gold, the work of human **h**. Ps 135:15
Do not forsake the work of your **h**. Ps 138:8
me, O LORD, from the **h** of the wicked; Ps 140:4
lifting up of my **h** as the evening Ps 141:2
have done; I ponder the work of your **h**. Ps 143:5
I stretch out my **h** to you; my soul Ps 143:6
my rock, who trains my **h** for war, Ps 144:1
throats and two-edged swords in their **h**, Ps 149:6
slumber, a little folding of the **h** to rest, Prv 6:10
tongue, and **h** that shed innocent blood, Prv 6:17
he who hates striking **h** in pledge is Prv 11:15
but folly with her own **h** tears it down. Prv 14:1
kills him, for his **h** refuse to labor. Prv 21:25
slumber, a little folding of the **h** to rest, Prv 24:33
the lizard you can take in your **h**, yet it Prv 30:28
and flax, and works with willing **h**. Prv 31:13
the fruit of her **h** she plants a vineyard. Prv 31:16
She puts her **h** to the distaff, and her Prv 31:19
the distaff, and her **h** hold the spindle. Prv 31:19
and reaches out her **h** to the needy. Prv 31:20
Give her of the fruit of her **h**, and let Prv 31:31
considered all that my **h** had done and Eccl 2:11
The fool folds his **h** and eats his own Eccl 4:5
of quietness than two **h** full of toil and Eccl 4:6
voice and destroy the work of your **h**? Eccl 5:6
and nets, and whose **h** are fetters. Eccl 7:26
beloved, and my **h** dripped with myrrh, Sg 5:5
When you spread out your **h**, I will hide Is 1:15
I will not listen; your **h** are full of blood. Is 1:15
and they strike **h** with the children of Is 2:6
they bow down to the work of their **h**, to Is 2:8
for what his **h** have dealt out shall be Is 3:11
deeds of the LORD, or see the work of his **h**. Is 5:12
my anger; the staff in their **h** is my fury! Is 10:5
Therefore all **h** will be feeble, and every Is 13:7
not look to the altars, the work of his **h**, Is 17:8
people, and Assyria the work of my **h**, Is 19:25
he will spread out his **h** in the midst of it Is 25:11
as a swimmer spreads his **h** out to swim, Is 25:11
pride together with the skill of his **h**. Is 25:11
he sees his children, the work of my **h**, Is 29:23
which your **h** have sinfully made for you. Is 31:7
gain of oppressions, who shakes his **h**, Is 33:15
Strengthen the weak **h**, and make firm Is 35:3
were no gods, but the work of men's **h**, Is 37:19
my children and the work of my **h**? Is 45:11
it was my **h** that stretched out the Is 45:12
engraved you on the palms of my **h**; Is 49:16
all the trees of the field shall clap their **h**. Is 55:12
For your **h** are defiled with blood and Is 59:3
and deeds of violence are in their **h**. Is 59:6
of my planting, the work of my **h**, Is 60:21
I spread out my **h** all the day to a Is 65:2
shall long enjoy the work of their **h**. Is 65:22
and worshiped the works of their own **h**. Jer 1:16
come away with your **h** on your head, Jer 2:37
gasping for breath, stretching out her **h**, Jer 4:31
heard the report of it; our **h** fall helpless; Jer 6:24
with an axe by the **h** of a craftsman. Jer 10:3
craftsman and of the **h** of the goldsmith; Jer 10:9
of my soul into the **h** of her enemies. Jer 12:7
that are in your **h** and with which you Jer 21:4
they strengthen the **h** of evildoers, so Jer 23:14
me to anger with the work of your **h**. Jer 25:6
the work of your **h** to your own harm. Jer 25:7
to their deeds and the work of their **h**." Jer 25:14
But as for me, behold, I am in your **h**. Jer 26:14
every man with his **h** on his stomach Jer 30:6
redeemed him from **h** too strong for Jer 31:11
is given into the **h** of the Chaldeans Jer 32:24
is given into the **h** of the Chaldeans.'" Jer 32:25
this city into the **h** of the Chaldeans Jer 32:28
me to anger by the work of their **h**, Jer 32:30
again pass under the **h** of the one who Jer 33:13
he is weakening the **h** of the soldiers who Jer 38:4
in this city, and the **h** of all the people, Jer 38:4
Zedekiah said, "Behold, he is in your **h**, Jer 38:5
you today from the chains on your **h**. Jer 40:4
"Take in your **h** large stones and hide Jer 43:9
me to anger with the works of your **h**, Jer 44:8
and have fulfilled it with your **h**, Jer 44:25
to their children, so feeble are their **h**, Jer 47:3
On all the **h** are gashes, and around the Jer 48:37
report of them, and his **h** fell helpless; Jer 50:43
has stretched out his **h** over all her Lam 1:10
gave me into the **h** of those whom I Lam 1:14
Zion stretches out her **h**, but there is Lam 1:17
pass along the way clap their **h** at you; Lam 2:15
Lift your **h** to him for the lives of your Lam 2:19
up our hearts and **h** to God in heaven: Lam 3:41
LORD, according to the work of their **h**. Lam 3:64
as earthen pots, the work of a potter's **h**! Lam 4:2
moment, and no **h** were wrung for her. Lam 4:6
The **h** of compassionate women have Lam 4:10
Princes are hung up by their **h**; no Lam 5:12
on their four sides they had human **h**. Ezk 1:8
"Clap your **h** and stamp your foot and Ezk 6:11
All **h** are feeble, and all knees turn to Ezk 7:17
give it into the **h** of foreigners for prey, Ezk 7:21
and the **h** of the people of the land are Ezk 7:27
Fill your **h** with burning coals from Ezk 10:2
and put it into the **h** of the man clothed Ezk 10:7
their wings the likeness of human **h**. Ezk 10:21
it, and give you into the **h** of foreigners, Ezk 11:9
I dug through the wall with my own **h**. Ezk 12:7
And I will give you into their **h**, and Ezk 16:39
heart will melt, and all **h** will be feeble; Ezk 21:7
Clap your **h** and let the sword come Ezk 21:14
I also will clap my **h**, and I will satisfy Ezk 21:17
deliver you into the **h** of brutish men, Ezk 21:31
endure, or can your **h** be strong, Ezk 22:14
I delivered her into the **h** of her lovers, Ezk 23:9
her lovers, into the **h** of the Assyrians, Ezk 23:9
deliver you into the **h** of those whom Ezk 23:28
into the **h** of those from whom you Ezk 23:28
adultery, and blood is on their **h**. Ezk 23:37
put bracelets on the **h** of the women, Ezk 23:42
adulteresses, and blood is on their **h**." Ezk 23:45
have clapped your **h** and stamped your Ezk 25:6
no god, in the **h** of those who slay you? Ezk 28:9
god who will deliver you out of my **h**?" Dn 3:15
set me trembling on my **h** and knees. Dn 10:10
in whose **h** are false balances, Hos 12:7
more, 'Our God,' to the work of our **h**. Hos 14:3
and from the violence that is in his **h**. Jon 3:8
down no more to the work of your **h**; Mi 5:13
Their **h** are on what is evil, to do it well; Mi 7:3
they shall lay their **h** on their mouths; Mi 7:16
news about you clap their **h** over you. Na 3:19
forth its voice; it lifted its **h** on high. Hab 3:10
not, O Zion; let not your **h** grow weak. Zep 3:16
LORD, and so with every work of their **h**. Hg 2:14
"The **h** of Zerubbabel have laid the Zec 4:9
of this house; his **h** shall also complete it. Zec 4:9
the LORD of hosts: "Let your **h** be strong, Zec 8:9
Fear not, but let your **h** be strong." Zec 8:13
and "'On their **h** they will bear you up, Mt 4:6
they do not wash their **h** when they eat." Mt 15:2
to eat with unwashed **h** does not defile Mt 15:20
of Man will certainly suffer at their **h**." Mt 17:12
about to be delivered into the **h** of men, Mt 17:22
or lame than with two **h** or two feet to be Mt 18:8
he might lay his **h** on them and pray. Mt 19:13
And he laid his **h** on them and went Mt 19:15
Man is betrayed into the **h** of sinners. Mt 26:45
came up and laid **h** on Jesus and seized Mt 26:50
and washed his **h** before the crowd, Mt 27:24
Come and lay your **h** on her, so that she Mk 5:23
are such mighty works done by his **h**? Mk 6:2
except that he laid his **h** on a few sick Mk 6:5
his disciples ate with **h** that were defiled, Mk 7:2
Jews do not eat unless they wash their **h**, Mk 7:3
of the elders, but eat with defiled **h**?" Mk 7:5
spit on his eyes and laid his **h** on him, Mk 8:23
Then Jesus laid his **h** on his eyes again; Mk 8:25
going to be delivered into the **h** of men, Mk 9:31
crippled than with two **h** to go to hell, Mk 9:43
blessed them, laying his **h** on them. Mk 10:16
Man is betrayed into the **h** of sinners. Mk 14:41
And they laid **h** on him and seized Mk 14:46
this temple that is made with **h**, Mk 14:58
will build another, not made with **h**.'" Mk 14:58
they will pick up serpents with their **h**; Mk 16:18
they will lay their **h** on the sick, and Mk 16:18
and "'On their **h** they will bear you up, Lk 4:11
and he laid his **h** on every one of them Lk 4:40
heads of grain, rubbing them in their **h**. Lk 6:1
about to be delivered into the **h** of men." Lk 9:44
And he laid his **h** on her, and Lk 13:13
priests sought to lay **h** on him at that Lk 20:19
they will lay their **h** on you and Lk 21:12
in the temple, you did not lay **h** on me. Lk 22:53
into your **h** I commit my spirit!" And Lk 23:46
be delivered into the **h** of sinful men and Lk 24:7
See my **h** and my feet, that it is I myself. Lk 24:39
this, he showed them his **h** and his feet. Lk 24:40
and lifting up his **h** he blessed them. Lk 24:50
to arrest him, but no one laid **h** on him. Jn 7:44
arrest him, but he escaped from their **h**. Jn 10:39
his **h** and feet bound with linen strips, Jn 11:44
Father had given all things into his **h**, Jn 13:3
feet only but also my **h** and my head!" Jn 13:9
of the Jews!" and struck him with their **h**. Jn 19:3
this, he showed them his **h** and his side. Jn 20:20
"Unless I see in his **h** the mark of the Jn 20:25
"Put your finger here, and see my **h**; Jn 20:27
you are old, you will stretch out your **h**, Jn 21:18
and killed by the **h** of lawless men. Acts 2:23
the people by the **h** of the apostles. Acts 5:12
they prayed and laid their **h** on them. Acts 6:6
were rejoicing in the works of their **h**. Acts 7:41
does not dwell in houses made by **h**, Acts 7:48
Then they laid their **h** on them and Acts 8:17
the laying on of the apostles' **h**, Acts 8:18
whom I lay my **h** may receive the Holy Acts 8:19
come in and lay his **h** on him so that Acts 9:12
And laying his **h** on him he said, Acts 9:17
the king laid violent **h** on some who Acts 12:1
quickly." And the chains fell off his **h**. Acts 12:7
praying they laid their **h** on them and Acts 13:3
and wonders to be done by their **h**. Acts 14:3
nor is he served by human **h**, as Acts 17:25
when Paul had laid his **h** on them, Acts 19:6
miracles by the **h** of Paul, Acts 19:11
that gods made with **h** are not gods. Acts 19:26
know that these **h** ministered to my Acts 20:34
bound his own feet and **h** and said, Acts 21:11
him into the **h** of the Gentiles.'" Acts 21:11
the whole crowd and laid **h** on him, Acts 21:27
tackle overboard with their own **h**. Acts 27:19
and putting his **h** on him healed him. Acts 28:8
Jerusalem into the **h** of the Romans. Acts 28:17
have held out my **h** to a disobedient Rom 10:21
we labor, working with our own **h**. 1 Cor 4:12
from God, a house not made with **h**, 2 Cor 5:1
I received at the **h** of the Jews the 2 Cor 11:24
in the wall and escaped his **h**. 2 Cor 11:33
which is made in the flesh by **h**— Eph 2:11
doing honest work with his own **h**, Eph 4:28
with a circumcision made without **h**, Col 2:11
affairs, and to work with your **h**, 1 Thes 4:11
lifting holy **h** without anger or 1 Tm 2:8
council of elders laid their **h** on you. 1 Tm 4:14
Do not be hasty in the laying on of **h**, 1 Tm 5:22
in you through the laying on of my **h**, 2 Tm 1:6
and the heavens are the work of your **h**; Heb 1:10
about washings, the laying on of **h**, Heb 6:2
more perfect tent (not made with **h**, Heb 9:11
not into holy places made with **h**, Heb 9:24
to fall into the **h** of the living God. Heb 10:31
lift your drooping **h** and strengthen Heb 12:12
Cleanse your **h**, you sinners, and purify Jas 4:8
upon and have touched with our **h**, 1 Jn 1:1
robes, with palm branches in their **h**, Rv 7:9
the works of their **h** nor give up Rv 9:20

my fathers destroyed, Gozan, **H**, Rezeph, Is 37:12
H, Canneh, Eden, traders of Sheba, Ezk 27:23
in Mesopotamia, before he lived in **H**, Acts 7:2
land of the Chaldeans and lived in **H**. Acts 7:4

HARARITE (5)
Shammah, the son of Agee the **H**. 2 Sm 23:11
Shammah the **H**, Ahiam the son of 2 Sm 23:33
Ahiam the son of Sharar the **H**, 2 Sm 23:33
Jonathan the son of Shagee the **H**, 1 Chr 11:34
Ahiam the son of Sachar the **H**, 1 Chr 11:35

HARASS (6)
"**H** the Midianites and strike them Nm 25:17
'Do not **h** Moab or contend with them in Dt 2:9
do not **h** them or contend with them, Dt 2:19
and those who **h** Judah shall be cut off; Is 11:13
Judah, and Judah shall not **h** Ephraim. Is 11:13
flesh, a messenger of Satan to **h** me, 2 Cor 12:7

HARASSED (3)
him, shot at him, and **h** him severely, Gn 49:23
for they have **h** you with their wiles, Nm 25:18
them, because they were **h** and helpless, Mt 9:36

HARBONA (2)
Biztha, **H**, Bigtha and Abagtha, Est 1:10
Then **H**, one of the eunuchs in Est 7:9

HARBOR (3)
for Tyre is laid waste, without house or **h**! Is 23:1
And because the **h** was not suitable Acts 27:12
could reach Phoenix, a **h** of Crete, Acts 27:12

HARBORS (1)
with his lips and **h** deceit in his heart; Prv 26:24

HARD (67)
Is anything too **h** for the LORD? At the Gn 18:14
Then they pressed **h** against the man Gn 19:9
If they are driven **h** for one day, all the Gn 33:13
went into labor, and she had **h** labor. Gn 35:16
made their lives bitter with **h** service, Ex 1:14
Any **h** case they brought to Moses, but Ex 18:26
And the case that is too **h** for you, you Dt 1:17
It shall not seem **h** to you when you let Dt 15:18
humiliated us and laid on us **h** labor. Dt 26:6
you today is not too **h** for you, Dt 30:11
he told her, because she pressed him **h**. Jgs 14:17
when she pressed him **h** with her words Jgs 16:16
out of all Israel, and the battle was **h**, Jgs 20:34
And they were pursued **h** to Gidom, Jgs 20:45
for his hand is **h** against us and 1 Sm 5:7
(for the people were **h** pressed), 1 Sm 13:6
they too followed **h** after them in the 1 Sm 14:22
of Israel had been **h** pressed that day, 1 Sm 14:24
There was **h** fighting against the 1 Sm 14:52
The battle pressed **h** against Saul, and 1 Sm 31:3
came to test him with **h** questions. 1 Kgs 10:1
therefore lighten the **h** service of your 1 Kgs 12:4
he said, "You have asked a **h** thing; 2 Kgs 2:10
The battle pressed **h** against Saul, 1 Chr 10:3
to test him with **h** questions, 2 Chr 9:1
therefore lighten the **h** service of your 2 Chr 10:4
"Has not man a **h** service on earth, and are Jb 7:1
Through want and **h** hunger they gnaw Jb 30:3
not I weep for him whose day was **h**? Jb 30:25
out the skies, **h** as a cast metal mirror? Jb 37:18
The waters become **h** like stone, and the Jb 38:30
His heart is **h** as a stone, hard as the Jb 41:24
as a stone, **h** as the lower millstone. Jb 41:24
You have made your people see **h** things; Ps 60:3
bowed their hearts down with **h** labor; Ps 107:12
I was pushed **h**, so that I was falling, Ps 118:13
and turmoil and the **h** service with which Is 14:3
the Egyptians into the hand of a **h** master, Is 19:4
the LORD with his **h** and great and strong Is 27:1
Crash follows **h** on crash; the whole Jer 4:20
arm! Nothing is too **h** for you. Jer 32:17
of all flesh. Is anything too **h** for me? Jer 32:27
because of affliction and **h** servitude; Lam 1:3
of foreign speech and a **h** language, Ezk 3:5
of foreign speech and a **h** language, Ezk 3:6
of Israel have a **h** forehead and a Ezk 3:7
I have made your face as **h** as their faces, Ezk 3:8
your forehead as **h** as their foreheads. Ezk 3:8
made his army labor **h** against Tyre. Ezk 29:18
the men rowed **h** to get back to dry land, Jon 1:13
"Your words have been **h** against me, Mal 3:13
and the way is **h** that leads to life, Mt 7:14
They tie up heavy burdens, **h** to bear, Mt 23:4
'Master, I knew you to be a **h** man, Mt 25:24
you load people with burdens **h** to bear, Lk 11:46
began to press him **h** and to provoke Lk 11:53
heard it, they said, "This is a **h** saying; Jn 6:60
you that by working **h** in this way we Acts 20:35
It is **h** for you to kick against the Acts 26:14
because of your **h** and impenitent heart Rom 2:5
Mary, who has worked **h** for you. Rom 16:6
Persis, who has worked **h** in the Lord. Rom 16:12
I am **h** pressed between the two. My Phil 1:23
that he has worked **h** for you and for Col 4:13
much to say, and it is **h** to explain, Heb 5:11
you endured a **h** struggle with Heb 10:32
in them that are **h** to understand, 2 Pt 3:16

HARD-FACED (1)
a **h** nation who shall not respect the old Dt 28:50

HARD-WORKING (1)
It is the **h** farmer who ought to have 2 Tm 2:6

HARDEN (12)
But I will **h** his heart, so that he will not Ex 4:21
But I will **h** Pharaoh's heart, and though I Ex 7:3
And I will **h** Pharaoh's heart, and he will Ex 14:4
And I will **h** the hearts of the Egyptians Ex 14:17
you shall not **h** your heart or shut your Dt 15:7
the LORD'S doing to **h** their hearts that Jos 11:20
Why should you **h** your hearts as the 1 Sm 6:6
do not **h** your hearts, as at Meribah, as Ps 95:8
wander from your ways and **h** our heart, Is 63:17
do not **h** your hearts as in the rebellion, Heb 3:8
do not **h** your hearts as in the Heb 3:15
hear his voice, do not **h** your hearts." Heb 4:7

HARDENED (26)
Still Pharaoh's heart was **h**, and he Ex 7:13
said to Moses, "Pharaoh's heart is **h**; Ex 7:14
So Pharaoh's heart remained **h**, and he Ex 7:22
he **h** his heart and would not listen to Ex 8:15
of God." But Pharaoh's heart was **h**, Ex 8:19
But Pharaoh **h** his heart this time also, Ex 8:32
But the heart of Pharaoh was **h**, and he Ex 9:7
But the LORD **h** the heart of Pharaoh, and Ex 9:12
he sinned yet again and **h** his heart, Ex 9:34
So the heart of Pharaoh was **h**, and he Ex 9:35
for I have **h** his heart and the heart of his Ex 10:1
But the LORD **h** Pharaoh's heart, and he Ex 10:20
But the LORD **h** Pharaoh's heart, and he Ex 10:27
and the LORD **h** Pharaoh's heart, Ex 11:10
And the LORD **h** the heart of Pharaoh Ex 14:8
the LORD your God **h** his spirit and made Dt 2:30
Egyptians and Pharaoh **h** their hearts? 1 Sm 6:6
his neck and **h** his heart against 2 Chr 36:13
—who has **h** himself against him, Jb 9:4
up and his spirit was **h** so that he dealt Dn 5:20
the loaves, but their hearts were **h**. Mk 6:52
or understand? Are your hearts **h**? Mk 8:17
has blinded their eyes and **h** their heart, Jn 12:40
elect obtained it, but the rest were **h**, Rom 11:7
But their minds were **h**. For to this 2 Cor 3:14
of you may be **h** by the deceitfulness of Heb 3:13

HARDENING (1)
a partial **h** has come upon Israel, Rom 11:25

HARDENS (3)
dirt; my skin **h**, then breaks out afresh. Jb 7:5
but whoever **h** his heart will fall into Prv 28:14
he wills, and he **h** whomever he wills. Rom 9:18

HARDER (5)
of Israel pressed **h** and harder against Jgs 4:24
pressed harder and **h** against Jabin the Jgs 4:24
They have made their faces **h** than rock; Jer 5:3
Like emery **h** than flint have I made Ezk 3:9
I worked **h** than any of them, 1 Cor 15:10

HARDEST (2)
And when her labor was at its **h**, the Gn 35:17
in the forefront of the **h** fighting, 2 Sm 11:15

HARDLY (1)
and shatters him, and will **h** leave him. Lk 9:39

HARDNESS (6)
shine, and the **h** of his face is changed. Eccl 8:1
"Because of your **h** of heart Moses Mt 19:8
with anger, grieved at their **h** of heart, Mk 3:5
"Because of your **h** of heart he wrote Mk 10:5
them for their unbelief and **h** of heart, Mk 16:14
that is in them, due to their **h** of heart. Eph 4:18

HARDSHIP (5)
me forget all my **h** and all my father's Gn 41:51
all the **h** that had come upon them in Ex 18:8
You know all the **h** that we have met: Nm 20:14
let not all the **h** seem little to you that Neh 9:32
in toil and **h**, through many a 2 Cor 11:27

HARDSHIPS (3)
in David's favor, all the **h** he endured, Ps 132:1
in afflictions, **h**, calamities, 2 Cor 6:4
weaknesses, insults, **h**, persecutions, 2 Cor 12:10

HARE (2)
And the **h**, because it chews the cud but Lv 11:6
the camel, the **h**, and the rock badger, Dt 14:7

HAREM (5)
young virgins to the **h** in Susa the Est 2:3
young women to the best place in the **h**. Est 2:9
of the court of the **h** to learn how Esther Est 2:11
with her from the **h** to the king's palace. Est 2:13
return to the second **h** in custody of Est 2:14

HAREPH (1)
and **H** the father of Beth-gader. 1 Chr 2:51

HARHAIAH (1)
Next to them Uzziel the son of **H**, Neh 3:8

HARHAS (1)
the son of Tikvah, son of **H**, 2 Kgs 22:14

HARHUR (2)
the sons of Hakupha, the sons of **H**, Ezr 2:51
the sons of Hakupha, the sons of **H**, Neh 7:53

HARIM (11)
the third to **H**, the fourth to Seorim, 1 Chr 24:8
The sons of **H**, 320. Ezr 2:32
The sons of **H**, 1,017. Ezr 2:39
Of the sons of **H**: Maaseiah, Elijah, Ezr 10:21
Of the sons of **H**: Eliezer, Isshijah, Ezr 10:31
the son of **H** and Hasshub the Neh 3:11
The sons of **H**, 320. Neh 7:35
The sons of **H**, 1,017. Neh 7:42
H, Meremoth, Obadiah, Neh 10:5
Malluch, **H**, Baanah. Neh 10:27
of **H**, Adna; of Meraioth, Helkai; Neh 12:15

HARIPH (2)
The sons of **H**, 112. Neh 7:24
H, Anathoth, Nebai, Neh 10:19

HARK (1)
"**H**! A cry from Horonaim, 'Desolation Jer 48:3

HARM (71)
that you will do us no **h**, just as we Gn 26:29
But God did not permit him to **h** me. Gn 31:7
It is in my power to do you **h**. But the Gn 31:29
this heap and this pillar to me, to do **h**. Gn 31:52
for he feared that **h** might happen to Gn 42:4
If **h** should happen to him on the Gn 42:38
also from me, and **h** happens to him, Gn 44:29
children come out, but there is no **h**, Ex 21:22
But if there is **h**, then you shall pay life Ex 21:23
not his enemy and did not seek his **h**, Nm 35:23
turn and do you **h** and consume you, Jos 24:20
hand of the LORD was against them for **h**, Jgs 2:15
to the Philistines, when I do them **h**." Jgs 15:3
it is he who has done us this great **h**, 1 Sm 6:9
then know that **h** is determined by 1 Sm 20:7
by my father that **h** should come to 1 Sm 20:9
it please my father to do you **h**, 1 Sm 20:13
that Saul was plotting **h** against him. 1 Sm 23:9
who say, 'Behold, David seeks your **h**'? 1 Sm 24:9
been with us, and we did them no **h**, 1 Sm 25:7
very good to us, and we suffered no **h**, 1 Sm 25:15
for **h** is determined against our 1 Sm 25:17
David, for I will no more do you **h**, 1 Sm 26:21
is dead? He may do himself some **h**." 2 Sm 12:18
LORD might bring **h** upon Absalom. 2 Sm 17:14
will do us more **h** than Absalom. 2 Sm 20:6
own heart all the **h** that you did to 1 Kgs 2:44
will bring back your **h** on your own 1 Kgs 2:44
of Solomon, doing **h** as Hadad did. 1 Kgs 11:25
I will bring **h** upon the house of 1 Kgs 14:10
eat." And there was no **h** in the pot. 2 Kgs 4:41
would keep me from **h** so that it 1 Chr 4:10
ones, do my prophets no **h**!" 1 Chr 16:22
of Ono." But they intended to do me **h**. Neh 6:2
for he saw that **h** was determined against Est 7:7
to lay hands on those who sought their **h**. Est 9:2
anointed ones, do my prophets no **h**!" Ps 105:15
no reason, when he has done you no **h**. Prv 3:30
for a stranger will surely suffer **h**, Prv 11:15
the companion of fools will suffer **h**. Prv 13:20
satisfied; he will not be visited by **h**. Prv 19:23
She does him good, and not **h**, all the Prv 31:12
do good, or do **h**, that we may be Is 41:23
do not go after other gods to your own **h**, Jer 7:6
against this city for **h** and not for good, Jer 21:10
of your hands. Then I will do you no **h**.' Jer 25:6
the work of your hands to your own **h**. Jer 25:7
to overthrow, destroy, and bring **h**, Jer 31:28
the welfare of this people, but their **h**." Jer 38:4
look after him well, and do him no **h**, Jer 39:12
against this city for **h** and not for good, Jer 39:16
I will set my face against you for **h**, Jer 44:11
will surely stand against you for **h**: Jer 44:29
before you, O king, I have done no **h**." Dn 6:22
and no kind of **h** was found on him, Dn 6:23
on high, to be safe from the reach of **h**! Hab 2:9
on the Sabbath to do good or to do **h**, Mk 3:4
came out of him, having done him no **h**. Lk 4:35
on the Sabbath to do good or to do **h**, Lk 6:9
with a loud voice, "Do not **h** yourself, Acts 16:28
and no one will attack you to **h** you, Acts 18:10

creature into the fire and suffered no **h**. Acts 28:5
the coppersmith did me great **h**; 2 Tm 4:14
God to their own **h** and holding him up Heb 6:6
Now who is there to **h** you if you are 1 Pt 3:13
denarius, and do not **h** the oil and wine!" Rv 6:6
had been given power to **h** earth and sea, Rv 7:2
"Do not **h** the earth or the sea or the trees, Rv 7:3
They were told not to **h** the grass of the Rv 9:4
And if anyone would **h** them, fire pours Rv 11:5
If anyone would **h** them, this is how he is Rv 11:5

HARMED (3)
them, and I have not **h** one of them." Nm 16:15
was not singed, their cloaks were not **h**, Dn 3:27
lions' mouths, and they have not **h** me, Dn 6:22

HARMFUL (5)
And I will remove **h** beasts from the Lv 26:6
The next day a **h** spirit from God 1 Sm 18:10
Then a **h** spirit from the LORD came 1 Sm 19:9
many senseless and **h** desires that 1 Tm 6:9
and **h** and painful sores came upon the Rv 16:2

HARMON (1)
be cast out into **H**," declares the LORD. Am 4:3

HARMONY (3)
Live in **h** with one another. Do not be Rom 12:16
you to live in such **h** with one another, Rom 15:5
binds everything together in perfect **h**. Col 3:14

HARNEPHER (1)
Zophah: Suah, **H**, Shual, Beri, Imrah. 1 Chr 7:36

HARNESS (2)
H the horses; mount, O horsemen! Take Jer 46:4
H the steeds to the chariots, inhabitants Mi 1:13

HAROD (4)
and encamped beside the spring of **H**. Jgs 7:1
Shammah of **H**, Elika of Harod, 2 Sm 23:25
Shammah of Harod, Elika of **H**, 2 Sm 23:25
Shammoth of **H**, Helez the Pelonite, 1 Chr 11:27

HAROEH (1)
other sons: **H**, half of the Menuhoth. 1 Chr 2:52

HAROSHETH-HAGOYIM (3)
of his army was Sisera, who lived in **H**. Jgs 4:2
with him, from **H** to the river Kishon. Jgs 4:13
pursued the chariots and the army to **H**, Jgs 4:16

HARP (18)
down from the high place with **h**, 1 Sm 10:5
melody to him with the **h** of ten strings! Ps 33:2
Awake, my glory! Awake, O **h** and lyre! I Ps 57:8
you with the **h** for your faithfulness, Ps 71:22
tambourine, the sweet lyre with the **h**. Ps 81:2
to the music of the lute and the **h**, to the Ps 92:3
Awake, O **h** and lyre! I will awake the Ps 108:2
upon a ten-stringed **h** I will play to you, Ps 144:9
sound; praise him with lute and **h**! Ps 150:3
They have lyre and **h**, tambourine and Is 5:12
"Take a **h**; go about the city, O forgotten Is 23:16
of the horn, pipe, lyre, trigon, **h**, bagpipe, Dn 3:5
of the horn, pipe, lyre, trigon, **h**, bagpipe, Dn 3:7
of the horn, pipe, lyre, trigon, **h**, bagpipe, Dn 3:10
of the horn, pipe, lyre, trigon, **h**, bagpipe, Dn 3:15
the sound of the **h** and like David invent Am 6:5
such as the flute or the **h**, 1 Cor 14:7
down before the Lamb, each holding a **h**, Rv 5:8

HARPISTS (2)
like the sound of **h** playing on their Rv 14:2
and the sound of **h** and musicians, of Rv 18:22

HARPOONS (1)
you fill his skin with **h** or his head with Jb 41:7

HARPS (18)
and lyres and **h** and tambourines and 2 Sm 6:5
also lyres and **h** for the singers. 1 Kgs 10:12
and lyres and **h** and tambourines 1 Chr 13:8
on **h** and lyres and cymbals, 1 Chr 15:16
were to play **h** according to 1 Chr 15:20
made loud music on **h** and lyres. 1 Chr 15:28
Jeiel, who were to play **h** and lyres; 1 Chr 16:5
who prophesied with lyres, with **h**, 1 Chr 25:1
h, and lyres for the service of the 1 Chr 25:6
linen, with cymbals, **h**, and lyres, 2 Chr 5:12
lyres also and **h** for the singers. 2 Chr 9:11
to Jerusalem with **h** and lyres and 2 Chr 20:28
the LORD with cymbals, **h**, and lyres, 2 Chr 29:25
singing, with cymbals, **h**, and lyres. Neh 12:27
down to Sheol, the sound of your **h**; Is 14:11
to the melody of your **h** I will not listen. Am 5:23
the sound of harpists playing on their **h**, Rv 14:2
the sea of glass with **h** of God in their Rv 15:2

HARROW (3)
ropes, or will he **h** the valleys after you? Jb 39:10
he continually open and **h** his ground? Is 28:24
must plow; Jacob must **h** for himself. Hos 10:11

HARSH (6)
of their broken spirit and **h** slavery. Ex 6:9
the man was **h** and badly behaved; 1 Sm 25:3
wrath, but a **h** word stirs up anger. Prv 15:1
I also will choose **h** treatment for them Is 66:4
your wives, and do not be **h** with them. Col 3:19
and of all the **h** things that ungodly Jude 1:15

HARSHA (2)
the sons of Mehida, the sons of **H**, Ezr 2:52
the sons of Mehida, the sons of **H**, Neh 7:54

HARSHLY (6)
you please." Then Sarai dealt **h** with her, Gn 16:6
how I have dealt **h** with the Egyptians Ex 10:2
And the Egyptians dealt **h** with us and Nm 20:15
Egyptians treated us **h** and humiliated Dt 26:6
And the king answered the people **h**, 1 Kgs 12:13
And the king answered them **h**; and 2 Chr 10:13

HARSHNESS (1)
and with force and **h** you have ruled Ezk 34:4

HARUM (1)
and the clans of Aharhel, the son of **H**. 1 Chr 4:8

HARUMAPH (1)
the son of **H** repaired opposite his Neh 3:10

HARUPHITE (1)
Shemariah, Shephatiah the **H**; 1 Chr 12:5

HARUZ (1)
the daughter of **H** of Jotbah. 2 Kgs 21:19

HARVEST (72)
the earth remains, seedtime and **h**, Gn 8:22
the days of wheat **h** Reuben went and Gn 30:14
there will be neither plowing nor **h**. Gn 45:6
the fullness of your **h** and from the Ex 22:29
You shall keep the Feast of **H**, of the Ex 23:16
In plowing time and in **h** you shall rest. Ex 34:21
of Weeks, the firstfruits of wheat **h**, Ex 34:22
"When you reap the **h** of your land, you Lv 19:9
you gather the gleanings after your **h**. Lv 19:9
the land that I give you and reap its **h**, Lv 23:10
of the firstfruits of your **h** to the priest, Lv 23:10
"And when you reap the **h** of your land, Lv 23:22
you gather the gleanings after your **h**. Lv 23:22
not reap what grows of itself in your **h**, Lv 25:5
shall last to the time of the grape **h**, Lv 26:5
and the grape **h** shall last to the time for Lv 26:5
"When you reap your **h** in your field Dt 24:19
which you **h** from your land that the Dt 26:2
all its banks throughout the time of **h**), Jos 3:15
better than the grape **h** of Abiezer? Jgs 8:2
After some days, at the time of wheat **h**, Jgs 15:1
Bethlehem at the beginning of barley **h**. Ru 1:22
men until they have finished all my **h**.'" Ru 2:21
reaping their wheat **h** in the valley. 1 Sm 6:13
to plow his ground and to reap his **h**, 1 Sm 8:12
Is it not wheat **h** today? I will call 1 Sm 12:17
were put to death in the first days of **h**, 2 Sm 21:9
harvest, at the beginning of barley **h**. 2 Sm 21:9
the beginning of **h** until rain fell 2 Sm 21:10
and came about **h** time to David 2 Sm 23:13
The hungry eat his **h**, and he takes it even Jb 5:5
in summer and gathers her food in **h**. Prv 6:8
but he who sleeps in **h** is a son who Prv 10:5
he will seek at **h** and have nothing. Prv 20:4
in the time of **h** is a faithful messenger Prv 25:13
Like snow in summer or rain in **h**, so Prv 26:1
they rejoice before you as with joy at the **h**, Is 9:3
summer fruit and your **h** the shout has Is 16:9
yet the **h** will flee away in a day of grief Is 17:11
like a cloud of dew in the heat of **h**." Is 18:4
For before the **h**, when the blossom is Is 18:5
was the grain of Shihor, the **h** of the Nile; Is 23:3
at the gleaning when the grape **h** is done. Is 24:13
for the grape **h** fails, the fruit harvest Is 32:10
harvest fails, the fruit **h** will not come. Is 32:10
holy to the LORD, the firstfruits of his **h**. Jer 2:3
They shall eat up your **h** and your food; Jer 5:17
for us the weeks appointed for the **h**.' Jer 5:24
"The **h** is past, the summer is ended, and Jer 8:20
one who handles the sickle in time of **h**; Jer 50:16
while and the time of her **h** will come." Jer 51:33
For you also, O Judah, a **h** is appointed, Hos 6:11
because the **h** of the field has perished. Jl 1:11
Put in the sickle, for the **h** is ripe. Go in, Jl 3:13
there were yet three months to the **h**; Am 4:7
said to his disciples, "The **h** is plentiful, Mt 9:37
to the Lord of the **h** to send out laborers Mt 9:38
harvest to send out laborers into his **h**." Mt 9:38
Let both grow together until the **h**, and Mt 13:30
and at **h** time I will tell the reapers, Mt 13:30
The **h** is the close of the age, and the Mt 13:39
in the sickle, because the **h** has come." Mk 4:29
And he said to them, "The **h** is plentiful, Lk 10:2
to the Lord of the **h** to send out laborers Lk 10:2
harvest to send out laborers into his **h**. Lk 10:2
are yet four months, then comes the **h**'? Jn 4:35
and see that the fields are white for **h**. Jn 4:35
I may reap some **h** among you as well Rom 1:13
and increase the **h** of your 2 Cor 9:10
And a **h** of righteousness is sown in Jas 3:18
for the **h** of the earth is fully ripe." Rv 14:15
and gathered the grape **h** of the earth Rv 14:19

HARVESTED (1)
You have sown much, and **h** little. You Hg 1:6

HARVESTERS (1)
the cries of the **h** have reached the ears Jas 5:4

HARVESTS (4)
And at the **h** you shall give a fifth to Gn 47:24
until the end of the barley and wheat **h**. Ru 2:23
standing grain and his arm **h** the ears, Is 17:5
be ashamed of their **h** because of the Jer 12:13

HASADIAH (1)
Berechiah, **H**, and Jushab-hesed, 1 Chr 3:20

HASHABIAH (16)
son of **H**, son of Amaziah, son of 1 Chr 6:45
Hasshub, son of Azrikam, son of **H**, 1 Chr 9:14
Jeshaiah, Shimei, **H**, and Mattithiah, 1 Chr 25:3
the twelfth to **H**, his sons and his 1 Chr 25:19
the Hebronites, **H** and his brothers, 1 Chr 26:30
for Levi, **H** the son of Kemuel; for 1 Chr 27:17
and **H** and Jeiel and Jozabad, 2 Chr 35:9
also **H**, and with him Jeshaiah of the Ezr 8:19
H, and ten of their kinsmen with them. Ezr 8:24
Mijamin, Eleazar, **H**, and Benaiah. Ezr 10:25
Next to him **H**, ruler of half the district Neh 3:17
Mica, Rehob, **H**, Neh 10:11
of Hasshub, son of Azrikam, son of **H**, Neh 11:15
was Uzzi the son of Bani, son of **H**, Neh 11:22
of Hilkiah, **H**; of Jedaiah, Nethanel. Neh 12:21
H, Sherebiah, and Jeshua the son of Neh 12:24

HASHABNAH (1)
Rehum, **H**, Maaseiah, Neh 10:25

HASHABNEIAH (2)
to him Hattush the son of **H** repaired. Neh 3:10
Jeshua, Kadmiel, Bani, **H**, Sherebiah, Neh 9:5

HASHBADDANAH (1)
Malchijah, Hashum, **H**, Zechariah, Neh 8:4

HASHEM (1)
H the Gizonite, Jonathan the son of 1 Chr 11:34

HASHMONAH (2)
out from Mithkah and camped at **H**. Nm 33:29
they set out from **H** and camped at Nm 33:30

HASHUBAH (1)
and **H**, Ohel, Berechiah, Hasadiah, 1 Chr 3:20

HASHUM (5)
The sons of **H**, 223. Ezr 2:19
Of the sons of **H**: Mattenai, Mattattah, Ezr 10:33
The sons of **H**, 328. Neh 7:22
Mishael, Malchijah, **H**, Hashbaddanah, Neh 8:4
Hodiah, **H**, Bezai, Neh 10:18

HASRAH (1)
the son of Tokhath, son of **H**, 2 Chr 34:22

HASSENAAH (1)
The sons of **H** built the Fish Gate. They Neh 3:3

HASSENUAH (2)
son of Hodaviah, son of **H**, 1 Chr 9:7
Judah the son of **H** was second over the Neh 11:9

HASSHUB (5)
Shemaiah the son of **H**, son of 1 Chr 9:14
son of Harim and **H** the son of Neh 3:11
Benjamin and **H** repaired opposite Neh 3:23
Hoshea, Hananiah, **H**, Neh 10:23
Shemaiah the son of **H**, son of Neh 11:15

HASSOPHERETH (1)
the sons of Sotai, the sons of **H**, the sons Ezr 2:55

HASTE (34)
in your hand. And you shall eat it in **h**. Ex 12:11
people to send them out of the land in **h**. Ex 12:33
the land of Egypt in **h**—that all the days Dt 16:3
Joshua. The people passed over in **h**. Jos 4:10
the king's business required **h**." 1 Sm 21:8
Then Abigail made **h** and took two 1 Sm 25:18
up and fled, and as she fled in her **h**, 2 Sm 4:4
Syrians had thrown away in their **h**. 2 Kgs 7:15
Then in **h** every man of them took 2 Kgs 9:13
they went in **h** to the Jews at Jerusalem Ezr 4:23
answer me, because of my **h** within me. Jb 20:2
Make **h** to help me, O Lord, my Ps 38:22
deliver me! O LORD, make **h** to help me! Ps 40:13
I am in distress; make **h** to answer me. Ps 69:17
Make **h**, O God, to deliver me! O LORD, Ps 70:1

deliver me! O LORD, make **h** to help me! Ps 70:1
me; O my God, make **h** to help me! Ps 71:12
to evil, and they make **h** to shed blood. Prv 1:16
plans, feet that make **h** to run to evil, Prv 6:18
and whoever makes **h** with his feet Prv 19:2
Make **h**, my beloved, and be like a Sg 8:14
'Whoever believes will not be in **h**.' Is 28:16
Your builders make **h**; your destroyers Is 49:17
For you shall not go out in **h**, and you Is 52:12
let them make **h** and raise a wailing over Jer 9:18
are beaten down and have fled in **h**; Jer 46:5
before the king in **h** and said thus to Dn 2:25
was astonished and rose up in **h**. Dn 3:24
king arose and went in **h** to the den of Dn 6:19
That is why I made **h** to flee to Tarshish; Jon 4:2
came in immediately with **h** to the king Mk 6:25
arose and went with **h** into the hill Lk 1:39
And they went with **h** and found Mary Lk 2:16
'Make **h** and get out of Jerusalem Acts 22:18

HASTEN (9)
Cush shall **h** to stretch out her hands to Ps 68:31
But I am poor and needy; **h** to me, O God! Ps 70:5
I **h** and do not delay to keep your Ps 119:60
O LORD, I call upon you; **h** to me! Give Ps 141:1
h, and plead urgently with your Prv 6:3
the stammerers will **h** to speak distinctly. Is 32:4
I am the LORD; in its time I will **h** it. Is 60:22
H and come, all you surrounding Jl 3:11
stumble as they go, they **h** to the wall; Na 2:5

HASTENED (1)
falsehood and my foot has **h** to deceit; Jb 31:5

HASTENING (3)
day of the LORD is near, near and **h** fast; Zep 1:14
Asia, for he was **h** to be at Jerusalem, Acts 20:16
waiting for and **h** the coming of the 2 Pt 3:12

HASTENS (5)
but whoever **h** to be rich will not go Prv 28:20
A stingy man **h** after wealth and does Prv 28:22
down, and **h** to the place where it rises. Eccl 1:5
at hand, and his affliction **h** swiftly. Jer 48:16
time; it **h** to the end—it will not lie. Hab 2:3

HASTILY (4)
Then Pharaoh **h** called Moses and Ex 10:16
Wealth gained **h** will dwindle, but Prv 13:11
An inheritance gained **h** in the Prv 20:21
do not **h** bring into court, for what will Prv 25:8

HASTY (8)
but he who has a **h** temper exalts folly. Prv 14:29
but everyone who is **h** comes only to Prv 21:5
you see a man who is **h** in his words? Prv 29:20
nor let your heart be **h** to utter a word Eccl 5:2
Be not **h** to go from his presence. Do not Eccl 8:3
The heart of the **h** will understand and Is 32:4
the Chaldeans, that bitter and **h** nation, Hab 1:6
Do not be **h** in the laying on of hands, 1 Tm 5:22

HASUPHA (2)
the sons of Ziha, the sons of **H**, the sons Ezr 2:43
the sons of Ziha, the sons of **H**, the sons Neh 7:46

HATCH (2)
They **h** adders' eggs; they weave the Is 59:5
that gathers a brood that she did not **h**, Jer 17:11

HATCHED (1)
and from one that is crushed a viper is **h**. Is 59:5

HATCHES (1)
nests and lays and **h** and gathers her Is 34:15

HATCHETS (1)
they broke down with **h** and hammers. Ps 74:6

HATE (94)
possess the gate of those who **h** them!" Gn 24:60
seeing that you **h** me and have sent me Gn 26:27
be that Joseph will **h** us and pay us Gn 50:15
who are trustworthy and **h** a bribe, Ex 18:21
the fourth generation of those who **h** me, Ex 20:5
"You shall not **h** your brother in your Lv 19:17
Those who **h** you shall rule over you, Lv 26:17
and let those who **h** you flee before Nm 10:35
and fourth generation of those who **h** me, Dt 5:9
and repays to their face those who **h** him, Dt 7:10
but he will lay them on all who **h** you. Dt 7:15
and will repay those who **h** me. Dt 32:41
repays those who **h** him and cleanses Dt 32:43
of his adversaries, of those who **h** him, Dt 33:11
and did not **h** him in the past. Jos 20:5
"Did you not **h** me and drive me out of Jgs 11:7
over him and said, "You only **h** me; Jgs 14:16
you love those who **h** you and hate 2 Sm 19:6
who hate you and **h** those who love 2 Sm 19:6
the son of Imlah, but I **h** him, 1 Kgs 22:8
honor, or the life of those who **h** you, 2 Chr 1:11
but I **h** him, for he never prophesies 2 Chr 18:7
and love those who **h** the LORD? 2 Chr 19:2
Those who **h** you will be clothed with Jb 8:22
stand before your eyes; you **h** all evildoers. Ps 5:5
See my affliction from those who **h** me, Ps 9:13
right hand will find out those who **h** you. Ps 21:8
and with what violent hatred they **h** me. Ps 25:19
I **h** the assembly of evildoers, and I will Ps 26:5
I **h** those who pay regard to worthless Ps 31:6
and those who **h** the righteous will be Ps 34:21
wink the eye who **h** me without cause. Ps 35:19
many are those who **h** me wrongfully. Ps 38:19
All who **h** me whisper together about Ps 41:7
and have put to shame those who **h** us. Ps 44:7
and those who **h** us have gotten spoil. Ps 44:10
For you **h** discipline, and you cast my Ps 50:17
and those who **h** him shall flee before Ps 68:1
head are those who **h** me without cause; Ps 69:4
Those who **h** the LORD would cringe Ps 81:15
those who **h** you have raised their heads. Ps 83:2
that those who **h** me may see and be put Ps 86:17
him and strike down those who **h** him. Ps 89:23
O you who love the LORD, **h** evil! He Ps 97:10
I **h** the work of those who fall away; it Ps 101:3
He turned their hearts to **h** his people, Ps 105:25
They encircle me with words of **h**, and Ps 109:3
look in triumph on those who **h** me. Ps 118:7
therefore I **h** every false way. Ps 119:104
I **h** the double-minded, but I love Ps 119:113
to be right; I **h** every false way. Ps 119:128
I **h** and abhor falsehood, but I love Ps 119:163
my dwelling among those who **h** peace. Ps 120:6
May all who **h** Zion be put to shame Ps 129:5
Do I not **h** those who hate you, O LORD? Ps 139:21
Do I not hate those who **h** you, O LORD? Ps 139:21
I **h** them with complete hatred; I count Ps 139:22
their scoffing and fools **h** knowledge? Prv 1:22
the way of evil and perverted speech I **h**. Prv 8:13
himself; all who **h** me love death." Prv 8:36
Do not reprove a scoffer, or he will **h** you; Prv 9:8
All a poor man's brothers **h** him; how Prv 19:7
lest he have his fill of you and **h** you. Prv 25:17
Bloodthirsty men **h** one who is Prv 29:10
a time to love, and a time to **h**; a time for Eccl 3:8
Whether it is love or **h**, man does not Eccl 9:1
Their love and their **h** and their envy Eccl 9:6
LORD love justice; I **h** robbery and wrong; Is 61:8
"Your brothers who **h** you and cast you Is 66:5
her voice against me; therefore I **h** her. Jer 12:8
do not do this abomination that I **h**!' Jer 44:4
into the hands of those whom you **h**, Ezk 23:28
because you did not **h** bloodshed, Ezk 35:6
be for those who **h** you and its Dn 4:19
is in Gilgal; there I began to **h** them. Hos 9:15
They **h** him who reproves in the gate, Am 5:10
H evil, and love good, and establish Am 5:15
"I **h**, I despise your feasts, and I take no Am 5:21
the pride of Jacob and **h** his strongholds, Am 6:8
you who **h** the good and love the evil, who Mi 3:2
no false oath, for all these things I **h**, Zec 8:17
love your neighbor and **h** your enemy.' Mt 5:43
for either he will **h** the one and love the Mt 6:24
betray one another and **h** one another. Mt 24:10
and from the hand of all who **h** us; Lk 1:71
are you when people **h** you and when Lk 6:22
enemies, do good to those who **h** you, Lk 6:27
me and does not **h** his own father and Lk 14:26
for either he will **h** the one and love the Lk 16:13
The world cannot **h** you, but it hates me Jn 7:7
what I want, but I do the very thing I **h**. Rom 7:15
you **h** the works of the Nicolaitans, Rv 2:6
works of the Nicolaitans, which I also **h**. Rv 2:6
they and the beast will **h** the prostitute. Rv 17:16

HATED (49)
Now Esau **h** Jacob because of the Gn 27:41
When the LORD saw that Leah was **h**, Gn 29:31
the LORD has heard that I am **h**, Gn 29:33
they **h** him and could not speak Gn 37:4
it to his brothers they **h** him even more. Gn 37:5
over us?" So they **h** him even more for Gn 37:8
'Because the LORD **h** us he has brought Dt 1:27
promised them, and because he **h** them, Dt 9:28
without having **h** him in Dt 19:4
since he had not **h** his neighbor in the Dt 19:6
"I really thought that you utterly **h** her, Jgs 15:2
who are **h** by David's soul." Therefore 2 Sm 5:8
Then Amnon **h** her with very great 2 Sm 13:15
with which he **h** her was greater 2 Sm 13:15
nor bad, for Absalom **h** Amnon, 2 Sm 13:22
strong enemy, from those who **h** me, 2 Sm 22:18
their backs to me, those who **h** me, 2 Sm 22:41
gained mastery over those who **h** them. Est 9:1
did as they pleased to those who **h** them. Est 9:5
and killed 75,000 of those who **h** them, Est 9:16
He has torn me in his wrath and **h** me; he Jb 16:9
rejoiced at the ruin of him who **h** me, Jb 31:29
enemy and from those who **h** me, Ps 18:17
to me, and those who **h** me I destroyed. Ps 18:40
his iniquity cannot be found out and **h**. Ps 36:2
loved righteousness and **h** wickedness. Ps 45:7
so that those who **h** them ruled over Ps 106:41
Because they **h** knowledge and did not Prv 1:29
and you say, "How I **h** discipline, and Prv 5:12
and a man of evil devices is **h**. Prv 14:17
So I **h** life, because what is done under Eccl 2:17
I **h** all my toil in which I toil under the Eccl 2:18
Whereas you have been forsaken and **h**, Is 60:15
those you loved and all those you **h**. Ezk 16:37
but Esau I have **h**. I have laid waste his Mal 1:3
and you will be **h** by all for my name's Mt 10:22
and you will be **h** by all nations for my Mt 24:9
And you will be **h** by all for my Mk 13:13
But his citizens **h** him and sent a Lk 19:14
You will be **h** by all for my name's Lk 21:17
know that it has **h** me before it hated Jn 15:18
that it has hated me before it **h** you. Jn 15:18
they have seen and **h** both me and my Jn 15:24
fulfilled: 'They **h** me without a cause.' Jn 15:25
and the world has **h** them because they Jn 17:14
written, "Jacob I loved, but Esau I **h**." Rom 9:13
For no one ever **h** his own flesh, but Eph 5:29
envy, **h** by others and hating one another. Ti 3:3
loved righteousness and **h** wickedness; Heb 1:9

HATERS (1)
slanderers, **h** of God, insolent, Rom 1:30

HATES (35)
donkey of one who **h** you lying down Ex 23:5
He will not be slack with one who **h** him. Dt 7:10
thing that the LORD **h** they have done for Dt 12:31
up a pillar, which the LORD your God **h**. Dt 16:22
"But if anyone **h** his neighbor and lies Dt 19:11
a wife and goes in to her and then **h** her Dt 22:13
to this man to marry, and he **h** her; Dt 22:16
and the latter man **h** her and writes her a Dt 24:3
Shall one who **h** justice govern? Will Jb 34:17
but his soul **h** the wicked and the one Ps 11:5
There are six things that the LORD **h**, Prv 6:16
but he who **h** striking hands in pledge Prv 11:15
but he who **h** reproof is stupid. Prv 12:1
The righteous **h** falsehood, but the Prv 13:5
Whoever spares the rod **h** his son, but Prv 13:24
the way; whoever **h** reproof will die. Prv 15:10
but he who **h** bribes will live. Prv 15:27
Whoever **h** disguises himself with his Prv 26:24
A lying tongue **h** its victims, and a Prv 26:28
but he who **h** unjust gain will prolong Prv 28:16
The partner of a thief **h** his own life; he Prv 29:24
and your appointed feasts my soul **h**; Is 1:14
"For the man who **h** and divorces, says Mal 2:16
who does wicked things **h** the light and Jn 3:20
but it **h** me because I testify about it that Jn 7:7
and whoever **h** his life in this world will Jn 12:25
"If the world **h** you, know that it has Jn 15:18
of the world, therefore the world **h** you. Jn 15:19
Whoever **h** me hates my Father also. Jn 15:23
Whoever hates me **h** my Father also. Jn 15:23
is in the light and **h** his brother is still in 1 Jn 2:9
But whoever **h** his brother is in the 1 Jn 2:11
brothers, that the world **h** you. 1 Jn 3:13
Everyone who **h** his brother is a 1 Jn 3:15
says, "I love God," and **h** his brother, 1 Jn 4:20

HATHACH (4)
Then Esther called for **H**, one of the Est 4:5
H went out to Mordecai in the open Est 4:6
And **H** went and told Esther what Est 4:9
Esther spoke to **H** and commanded him Est 4:10

HATHATH (1)
sons of Othniel: **H** and Meonothai. 1 Chr 4:13

HATING (2)
envy, hated by others and **h** one another. Ti 3:3
h even the garment stained by the Jude 1:23

HATIPHA (2)
the sons of Neziah, and the sons of **H**. Ezr 2:54
the sons of Neziah, the sons of **H**. Neh 7:56

HATITA (2)
the sons of Akkub, the sons of **H**, Ezr 2:42
the sons of Akkub, the sons of **H**, Neh 7:45

HATRED (16)
him out of **h** or hurled something Nm 35:20
Amnon hated her with very great **h**, 2 Sm 13:15
so that the **h** with which he hated 2 Sm 13:15
and with what violent **h** they hate me. Ps 25:19
Why do you look with **h**, O Ps 68:16
me evil for good, and **h** for my love. Ps 109:5
I hate them with complete **h**; I count Ps 139:22
The fear of the LORD is **h** of evil. Pride Prv 8:13
H stirs up strife, but love covers all Prv 10:12
one who conceals **h** has lying lips, Prv 10:18

love is than a fattened ox and **h** with it. Prv 15:17
though his **h** be covered with Prv 26:26
deal with you in **h** and take away all Ezk 23:29
because of your **h** against them. Ezk 35:11
of your great iniquity and great **h**. Hos 9:7
his ways, and **h** in the house of his God. Hos 9:8

HATS (1)
in their cloaks, their tunics, their **h**, Dn 3:21

HATTIL (2)
the sons of Shephatiah, the sons of **H**, Ezr 2:57
the sons of Shephatiah, the sons of **H**, Neh 7:59

HATTUSH (5)
H, Igal, Bariah, Neariah, and 1 Chr 3:22
Ithamar, Daniel. Of the sons of David, **H**. Ezr 8:2
And next to him **H** the son of Neh 3:10
H, Shebaniah, Malluch, Neh 10:4
Amariah, Malluch, **H**, Neh 12:2

HAUGHTILY (1)
your necks, and you shall not walk **h**, Mi 2:3

HAUGHTINESS (2)
And the **h** of man shall be humbled, and Is 2:17
his arrogance, and the **h** of his heart. Jer 48:29

HAUGHTY (19)
eyes are on the **h** to bring them 2 Sm 22:28
people, but the **h** eyes you bring down. Ps 18:27
horn on high, or speak with **h** neck.'" Ps 75:5
Whoever has a **h** look and an arrogant Ps 101:5
lowly, but the **h** he knows from afar. Ps 138:6
h eyes, a lying tongue, and hands that Prv 6:17
destruction, and a **h** spirit before a fall. Prv 16:18
Before destruction a man's heart is **h**, Prv 18:12
H eyes and a proud heart, the lamp of Prv 21:4
h man who acts with arrogant pride. Prv 21:24
The **h** looks of man shall be brought low, Is 2:11
daughters of Zion are **h** and walk with Is 3:16
low, and the eyes of the **h** are brought low. Is 5:15
They were **h** and did an abomination Ezk 16:50
shall no longer be **h** in my holy Zep 3:11
haters of God, insolent, **h**, boastful, Rom 1:30
Do not be **h**, but associate with the Rom 12:16
present age, charge them not to be **h**, 1 Tm 6:17
a mouth uttering **h** and blasphemous Rv 13:5

HAUL (2)
and they will **h** you up in my dragnet. Ezk 32:3
it, and now they were not able to **h** it in, Jn 21:6

HAULED (1)
Peter went aboard and **h** the net ashore, Jn 21:11

HAUNT (7)
It shall be the **h** of jackals, an abode for Is 34:13
springs of water; in the **h** of jackals, Is 35:7
Hazor shall become a **h** of jackals, an Jer 49:33
a heap of ruins, the **h** of jackals, Jer 51:37
for demons, a **h** for every unclean spirit, Rv 18:2
spirit, a **h** for every unclean bird, Rv 18:2
a **h** for every unclean and detestable Rv 18:2

HAURAN (2)
which is on the border of **H**. Ezk 47:16
shall run between **H** and Damascus; Ezk 47:18

HAVEN (2)
he shall become a **h** for ships, and his Gn 49:13
he brought them to their desired **h**. Ps 107:30

HAVENS (1)
we came to a place called Fair **H**, Acts 27:8

HAVILAH (7)
that flowed around the whole land of **H**, Gn 2:11
Seba, **H**, Sabtah, Raamah, and Sabteca. Gn 10:7
Ophir, **H**, and Jobab; all these were the Gn 10:29
They settled from **H** to Shur, which is Gn 25:18
the Amalekites from **H** as far as 1 Sm 15:7
Seba, **H**, Sabta, Raama, and Sabteca. 1 Chr 1:9
Ophir, **H**, and Jobab; all these were 1 Chr 1:23

HAVOC (1)
the man who made **h** in Jerusalem of Acts 9:21

HAVVOTH-JAIR (4)
their villages, and called them **H**. Nm 32:41
his own name, **H**, as it is to this day.) Dt 3:14
had thirty cities, called **H** to this day, Jgs 10:4
Geshur and Aram took from them **H**, 1 Chr 2:23

HAWK (4)
the sea gull, the **h** of any kind, Lv 11:16
the sea gull, the **h** of any kind; Dt 14:15
understanding that the **h** soars and Jb 39:26
But the **h** and the porcupine shall Is 34:11

HAWKS (1)
indeed, there the **h** are gathered, each Is 34:15

HAY (1)
precious stones, wood, **h**, straw— 1 Cor 3:12

HAZAEL (24)
you shall anoint **H** to be king over 1 Kgs 19:15
from the sword of **H** shall Jehu put 1 Kgs 19:17
the king said to **H**, "Take a present 2 Kgs 8:8
So **H** went to meet him, and took a 2 Kgs 8:9
And **H** said, "Why does my lord 2 Kgs 8:12
And **H** said, "What is your servant, 2 Kgs 8:13
And **H** became king in his place. 2 Kgs 8:15
to make war against **H** king of Syria 2 Kgs 8:28
he fought against **H** king of Syria. 2 Kgs 8:29
at Ramoth-gilead against **H** king of 2 Kgs 9:14
he fought with **H** king of Syria.) 2 Kgs 9:15
H defeated them throughout the 2 Kgs 10:32
At that time **H** king of Syria went up 2 Kgs 12:17
But when **H** set his face to go up 2 Kgs 12:17
and sent these to **H** king of Syria. 2 Kgs 12:18
Then **H** went away from Jerusalem. 2 Kgs 12:18
into the hand of **H** king of Syria and 2 Kgs 13:3
the hand of Ben-hadad the son of **H**. 2 Kgs 13:3
Now **H** king of Syria oppressed 2 Kgs 13:22
When **H** king of Syria died, 2 Kgs 13:24
the son of **H** the cities that 2 Kgs 13:25
to make war against **H** king of Syria 2 Chr 22:5
he fought against **H** king of Syria. 2 Chr 22:6
So I will send a fire upon the house of **H**, Am 1:4

HAZAIAH (1)
of Baruch, son of Col-hozeh, son of **H**, Neh 11:5

HAZAR-ADDAR (1)
Then it shall go on to **H**, and pass Nm 34:4

HAZAR-ENAN (4)
to Ziphron, and its limit shall be at **H**. Nm 34:9
eastern border from **H** to Shepham. Nm 34:10
boundary shall run from the sea to **H**, Ezk 47:17
as far as **H** (which is on the northern Ezk 48:1

HAZAR-GADDAH (1)
H, Heshmon, Beth-pelet, Jos 15:27

HAZAR-SHUAL (4)
H, Beersheba, Biziothiah, Jos 15:28
H, Balah, Ezem, Jos 19:3
They lived in Beersheba, Moladah, **H**, 1 Chr 4:28
in **H**, in Beersheba and its villages, Neh 11:27

HAZAR-SUSAH (1)
Ziklag, Beth-marcaboth, **H**, Jos 19:5

HAZAR-SUSIM (1)
Beth-marcaboth, **H**, Beth-biri, and 1 Chr 4:31

HAZARMAVETH (2)
fathered Almodad, Sheleph, **H**, Jerah, Gn 10:26
fathered Almodad, Sheleph, **H**, Jerah, 1 Chr 1:20

HAZAZON-TAMAR (2)
the Amorites who were dwelling in **H**. Gn 14:7
and, behold, they are in **H**" (that is, 2 Chr 20:2

HAZER-HATTICON (1)
Damascus and Hamath), as far as **H**, Ezk 47:16

HAZEROTH (6)
the people journeyed to **H**, Nm 11:35
to Hazeroth, and they remained at **H**. Nm 11:35
After that the people set out from **H**, Nm 12:16
Kibroth-hattaavah and camped at **H**. Nm 33:17
they set out from **H** and camped at Nm 33:18
and Tophel, Laban, **H**, and Dizahab. Dt 1:1

HAZIEL (1)
Shelomoth, **H**, and Haran, three. 1 Chr 23:9

HAZO (1)
Chesed, **H**, Pildash, Jidlaph, and Gn 22:22

HAZOR (18)
When Jabin, king of **H**, heard of this, he Jos 11:1
time and captured **H** and struck its Jos 11:10
for **H** formerly was the head of all those Jos 11:10
breathed. And he burned **H** with fire. Jos 11:11
did Israel burn, except **H** alone; Jos 11:13
king of Madon, one; the king of **H**, one; Jos 12:19
Kedesh, **H**, Ithnan, Jos 15:23
Kerioth-hezron (that is, **H**), Jos 15:25
Adamah, Ramah, **H**, Jos 19:36
Jabin king of Canaan, who reigned in **H**. Jgs 4:2
Jabin the king of **H** and the house of Jgs 4:17
Sisera, commander of the army of **H**, 1 Sm 12:9
of Jerusalem and **H** and Megiddo and 1 Kgs 9:15
Janoah, Kedesh, **H**, Gilead, 2 Kgs 15:29
H, Ramah, Gittaim, Neh 11:33
kingdoms of **H** that Nebuchadnezzar Jer 49:28
dwell in the depths, O inhabitants of **H**! Jer 49:30
H shall become a haunt of jackals, an Jer 49:33

HAZOR-HADATTAH (1)
H, Kerioth-hezron (that is, Hazor), Jos 15:25

HAZZELELPONI (1)
and the name of their sister was **H**, 1 Chr 4:3

HE-GOAT (1)
the strutting rooster, the **h**, and a king Prv 30:31

HE-GOATS (1)
earth—of rams, of lambs, and of **h**, Ezk 39:18

HEAD (370)
he shall bruise your **h**, and you shall Gn 3:15
man bowed his **h** and worshiped the Gn 24:26
Then I bowed my **h** and worshiped the Gn 24:48
he put it under his **h** and lay down in Gn 28:11
he had put under his **h** and set it up for Gn 28:18
will lift up your **h** and restore you to Gn 40:13
there were three cake baskets on my **h**, Gn 40:16
eating it out of the basket on my **h**." Gn 40:17
will lift up your **h**—from you! Gn 40:19
and lifted up the **h** of the chief Gn 40:20
chief cupbearer and the **h** of the chief Gn 40:20
bowed himself upon the **h** of his bed. Gn 47:31
hand and laid it on the **h** of Ephraim, Gn 48:14
his left hand on the **h** of Manasseh, Gn 48:14
his right hand on the **h** of Ephraim, Gn 48:17
it from Ephraim's **h** to Manasseh's Gn 48:17
from Ephraim's head to Manasseh's **h**. Gn 48:17
put your right hand on his **h**." Gn 48:18
May they be on the **h** of Joseph, and on Gn 49:26
its **h** with its legs and its inner parts. Ex 12:9
an opening for the **h** in the middle of Ex 28:32
set the turban on his **h** and put the holy Ex 29:6
oil and pour it on his **h** and anoint him. Ex 29:7
lay their hands on the **h** of the bull. Ex 29:10
lay their hands on the **h** of the ram, Ex 29:15
and put them with its pieces and its **h**, Ex 29:17
lay their hands on the **h** of the ram, Ex 29:19
quickly bowed his **h** toward the earth Ex 34:8
a beka a **h** (that is, half a shekel, by the Ex 38:26
his hand on the **h** of the burnt offering, Lv 1:4
the priests shall arrange the pieces, the **h**, Lv 1:8
cut it into pieces, with its **h** and its fat, Lv 1:12
altar and wring off its **h** and burn it on Lv 1:15
lay his hand on the **h** of his offering and Lv 3:2
lay his hand on the **h** of his offering, and Lv 3:8
lay his hand on its **h** and kill it in front Lv 3:13
lay his hand on the **h** of the bull and kill Lv 4:4
of the bull and all its flesh, with its **h**, Lv 4:11
their hands on the **h** of the bull before Lv 4:15
lay his hand on the **h** of the goat and kill Lv 4:24
lay his hand on the **h** of the sin offering Lv 4:29
lay his hand on the **h** of the sin offering Lv 4:33
He shall wring its **h** from its neck but Lv 5:8
And he set the turban on his **h**, and on the Lv 8:9
oil on Aaron's **h** and anointed him Lv 8:12
laid their hands on the **h** of the bull of Lv 8:14
laid their hands on the **h** of the ram. Lv 8:18
and Moses burned the **h** and the pieces Lv 8:20
laid their hands on the **h** of the ram. Lv 8:22
offering to him, piece by piece, and the **h**, Lv 9:13
of the diseased person from **h** to foot, Lv 13:12
has a disease on the **h** or the beard, Lv 13:29
a leprous disease of the **h** or the beard. Lv 13:30
"If a man's hair falls out from his **h**, he Lv 13:40
is on the bald **h** or the bald forehead Lv 13:42
out on his bald **h** or his bald forehead. Lv 13:42
reddish-white on his bald **h** or on his Lv 13:43
him unclean; his disease is on his **h**. Lv 13:44
and let the hair of his **h** hang loose, Lv 13:45
he shall shave off all his hair from his **h**, Lv 14:9
he shall put on the **h** of him who is to Lv 14:18
he shall put on the **h** of him who is to Lv 14:29
both his hands on the **h** of the live goat, Lv 16:21
shall put them on the **h** of the goat and Lv 16:21
up before the gray **h** and honor the face Lv 19:32
on whose **h** the anointing oil is poured Lv 21:10
let the hair of his **h** hang loose nor tear Lv 21:10
heard him lay their hands on his **h**, Lv 24:14
of names, every male, **h** by head. Nm 1:2
of names, every male, head by **h**. Nm 1:2
each man being the **h** of the house of his Nm 1:4
years old and upward, **h** by head, Nm 1:18
years old and upward, head by **h**, Nm 1:18
to the number of names, **h** by head, Nm 1:20
to the number of names, head by **h**, Nm 1:20
to the number of names, **h** by head, Nm 1:22
to the number of names, head by **h**, Nm 1:22
you shall take five shekels per **h**; you Nm 3:47
hair of the woman's **h** and place in her Nm 5:18
of separation, no razor shall touch his **h**. Nm 6:5
let the locks of hair of his **h** grow long. Nm 6:5
his separation to God is on his **h**. Nm 6:7
him and he defiles his consecrated **h**, Nm 6:9
then he shall shave his **h** on the day of Nm 6:9
he shall consecrate his **h** that same day Nm 6:11
shave his consecrated **h** at the entrance Nm 6:18
hair from his consecrated **h** and put it Nm 6:18
one staff for the **h** of each fathers' Nm 17:3
who was the tribal **h** of a father's Nm 25:15

for he shall go over at the **h** of this people, Dt 3:28
on your journey at the **h** of the people, Dt 10:11
and the **h** slips from the handle and Dt 19:5
shall be appointed at the **h** of the people. Dt 20:9
she shall shave her **h** and pare her Dt 21:12
will make you the **h** and not the tail, Dt 28:13
heavens over your **h** shall be bronze, Dt 28:23
sole of your foot to the crown of your **h**. Dt 28:35
He shall be the **h**, and you shall be the Dt 28:44
them, and Joshua will go over at your **h**, Dt 31:3
May these rest on the **h** of Joseph, on the Dt 33:16
street, his blood shall be on his own **h**, Jos 2:19
the house, his blood shall be on our **h**. Jos 2:19
Hazor formerly was the **h** of all those Jos 11:10
one of them the **h** of a family among Jos 22:14
she struck Sisera; she crushed his **h**; Jgs 5:26
Gaal went out at the **h** of the leaders of Jgs 9:39
on Abimelech's **h** and crushed Jgs 9:53
He shall be **h** over all the inhabitants Jgs 10:18
Ammonites and be our **h** over all the Jgs 11:8
gives them over to me, I will be your **h**." Jgs 11:9
the people made him **h** and leader over Jgs 11:11
No razor shall come upon his **h**, for the Jgs 13:5
seven locks of my **h** with the web and Jgs 16:13
seven locks of his **h** and wove them Jgs 16:14
"A razor has never come upon my **h**, Jgs 16:17
my mother's womb. If my **h** is shaved, Jgs 16:17
him shave off the seven locks of his **h**. Jgs 16:19
the hair of his **h** began to grow again Jgs 16:22
life, and no razor shall touch his **h**." 1 Sm 1:11
clothes torn and with dirt on his **h**. 1 Sm 4:12
and the **h** of Dagon and both his hands 1 Sm 5:4
them a place at the **h** of those who had 1 Sm 9:22
poured it on his **h** and kissed him and 1 Sm 10:1
one hair of his **h** fall to the ground, 1 Sm 14:45
are you not the **h** of the tribes of 1 Sm 15:17
He had a helmet of bronze on his **h**, 1 Sm 17:5
and his spear's **h** weighed six hundred 1 Sm 17:7
of bronze on his **h** and clothed him 1 Sm 17:38
strike you down and cut off your **h**. 1 Sm 17:46
killed him and cut off his **h** with it. 1 Sm 17:51
David took the **h** of the Philistine 1 Sm 17:54
Saul with the **h** of the Philistine 1 Sm 17:57
goats' hair at its **h** and covered it 1 Sm 19:13
with the pillow of goats' hair at its **h**. 1 Sm 19:16
Samuel standing as **h** over them, 1 Sm 19:20
on his own **h**." Then David sent 1 Sm 25:39
his spear stuck in the ground at his **h**, 1 Sm 26:7
spear that is at his **h** and the jar of 1 Sm 26:11
and the jar of water from Saul's **h**, 1 Sm 26:12
the jar of water that was at his **h**." 1 Sm 26:16
they cut off his **h** and stripped off his 1 Sm 31:9
with his clothes torn and dirt on his **h**. 2 Sm 1:2
that was on his **h** and the armlet that 2 Sm 1:10
to him, "Your blood be on your **h**, 2 Sm 1:16
his opponent by the **h** and thrust his 2 Sm 2:16
and said, "Am I a dog's **h** of Judah? 2 Sm 3:8
it fall upon the **h** of Joab and upon 2 Sm 3:29
They took his **h** and went by the way of 2 Sm 4:7
and brought the **h** of Ish-bosheth to 2 Sm 4:8
the king, "Here is the **h** of Ish-bosheth, 2 Sm 4:8
they took the **h** of Ish-bosheth and 2 Sm 4:12
of the army of Hadadezer at their **h**. 2 Sm 10:16
the crown of their king from his **h**. 2 Sm 12:30
stone, and it was placed on David's **h**. 2 Sm 12:30
put ashes on her **h** and tore the long 2 Sm 13:19
her hand on her **h** and went away, 2 Sm 13:19
the crown of his **h** there was no 2 Sm 14:25
cut the hair of his **h** (for at the end of 2 Sm 14:26
cut it), he weighed the hair of his **h**, 2 Sm 14:26
barefoot and with his **h** covered. 2 Sm 15:30
with his coat torn and dirt on his **h**. 2 Sm 15:32
Let me go over and take off his **h**." 2 Sm 16:9
and his **h** caught fast in the oak, 2 Sm 18:9
his **h** shall be thrown to you over the 2 Sm 20:21
they cut off the **h** of Sheba the son 2 Sm 20:22
you kept me as the **h** of the nations; 2 Sm 22:44
do not let his gray **h** go down to Sheol 1 Kgs 2:6
bring his gray **h** down with blood 1 Kgs 2:9
back his bloody deeds on his own **h**, 1 Kgs 2:32
come back on the **h** of Joab and on 1 Kgs 2:33
Joab and on the **h** of his descendants 1 Kgs 2:33
Your blood shall be on your own **h**." 1 Kgs 2:37
back your harm on your own **h**. 1 Kgs 2:44
bringing his conduct on his own **h**, 1 Kgs 8:32
the back of the throne was a calf's **h**, 1 Kgs 10:19
there was at his **h** a cake baked on 1 Kgs 19:6
and set Naboth at the **h** of the people. 1 Kgs 21:9
set Naboth at the **h** of the people. 1 Kgs 21:12
And he said to his father, "Oh, my **h**, 2 Kgs 4:19
my **h**!" The father said to his servant, 2 Kgs 4:19
a log, his axe **h** fell into the water, 2 Kgs 6:5
until a donkey's **h** was sold for eighty 2 Kgs 6:25
if the **h** of Elisha the son of Shaphat 2 Kgs 6:31
murderer has sent to take off my **h**? 2 Kgs 6:32
of oil and pour it on his **h** and say, 2 Kgs 9:3
the young man poured the oil on his **h**, 2 Kgs 9:6
and adorned her **h** and looked out 2 Kgs 9:30
she wags her **h** behind you—the 2 Kgs 19:21
him and took his **h** and his armor, 1 Chr 10:9
and fastened his **h** in the temple 1 Chr 10:10
of the army of Hadadezer at their **h**. 1 Chr 19:16
the crown of their king from his **h**. 1 Chr 20:2
stone. And it was placed on David's **h**. 1 Chr 20:2
the **h** of each father's house and his 1 Chr 24:31
and you are exalted as **h** above all. 1 Chr 29:11
bringing his conduct on his own **h**, 2 Chr 6:23
Behold, God is with us at our **h**, and 2 Chr 13:12
Jehoshaphat bowed his **h** with his 2 Chr 20:18
and Jehoshaphat at their **h**, 2 Chr 20:27
pulled hair from my **h** and beard and sat Ezr 9:3
royal crown on her **h** and made her Est 2:17
and on whose **h** a royal crown is set. Est 6:8
mourning and with his **h** covered. Est 6:12
the Jews should return on his own **h**, Est 9:25
his robe and shaved his **h** and fell on the Jb 1:20
the sole of his foot to the crown of his **h**. Jb 2:7
I am in the right, I cannot lift up my **h**, Jb 10:15
And were my **h** lifted up, you would Jb 10:16
against you and shake my **h** at you. Jb 16:4
glory and taken the crown from my **h**. Jb 19:9
heavens, and his **h** reach to the clouds, Jb 20:6
when his lamp shone upon my **h**, and by Jb 29:3
harpoons or his **h** with fishing spears? Jb 41:7
about me, my glory, and the lifter of my **h**. Ps 3:3
His mischief returns upon his own **h**, Ps 7:16
you made me the **h** of the nations; Ps 18:43
you set a crown of fine gold upon his **h**. Ps 21:3
of my enemies; you anoint my **h** with oil; Ps 23:5
And now my **h** shall be lifted up above Ps 27:6
I prayed with **h** bowed on my chest. Ps 35:13
For my iniquities have gone over my **h**; Ps 38:4
they are more than the hairs of my **h**; Ps 40:12
the hairs of my **h** are those who hate Ps 69:4
the way; therefore he will lift up his **h**. Ps 110:7
It is like the precious oil on the **h**, Ps 133:2
you have covered my **h** in the day of Ps 140:7
As for the **h** of those who surround me, Ps 140:9
let him rebuke me—it is oil for my **h**; Ps 141:5
is oil for my head; let my **h** not refuse it. Ps 141:5
garland for your **h** and pendants for Prv 1:9
at the **h** of the noisy streets she cries out; Prv 1:21
will place on your **h** a graceful garland; Prv 4:9
Blessings are on the **h** of the righteous, Prv 10:6
a blessing is on the **h** of him who sells Prv 11:26
you will heap burning coals on his **h**, Prv 25:22
The wise person has his eyes in his **h**, Eccl 2:14
white. Let not oil be lacking on your **h**. Eccl 9:8
His left hand is under my **h**, and his right Sg 2:6
my perfect one, for my **h** is wet with dew, Sg 5:2
His **h** is the finest gold; his locks are Sg 5:11
Your **h** crowns you like Carmel, and your Sg 7:5
His left hand is under my **h**, and his right Sg 8:3
you continue to rebel? The whole **h** is sick, Is 1:5
From the sole of the foot even to the **h**, Is 1:6
For the **h** of Syria is Damascus, and the Is 7:8
and the **h** of Damascus is Rezin. Is 7:8
"'And the **h** of Ephraim is Samaria, and Is 7:9
and the **h** of Samaria is the son of Is 7:9
king of Assyria—the **h** and the hair of the Is 7:20
So the LORD cut off from Israel **h** and tail, Is 9:14
the elder and honored man is the **h**, and Is 9:15
Moab wails. On every **h** is baldness; Is 15:2
will be nothing for Egypt that **h** or tail, Is 19:15
which is on the **h** of the rich valley of Is 28:1
which is on the **h** of the rich valley, Is 28:4
she wags her **h** behind you—the Is 37:22
they lie at the **h** of every street like an Is 51:20
Is it to bow down his **h** like a reed, and to Is 58:5
and a helmet of salvation on his **h**; Is 59:17
have shaved the crown of your **h**. Jer 2:16
come away with your hands on your **h**, Jer 2:37
Oh that my **h** were waters, and my eyes a Jer 9:1
crown has come down from your **h**." Jer 13:18
when they set as **h** over you those Jer 13:21
by it is horrified and shakes his **h**. Jer 18:16
it will burst upon the **h** of the wicked. Jer 23:19
it will burst upon the **h** of the wicked. Jer 30:23
you spoke of him you wagged your **h**? Jer 48:27
"For every **h** is shaved and every beard Jer 48:37
lifted up the **h** of Jehoiachin king of Jer 52:31
Her foes have become the **h**; her Lam 1:5
for hunger at the **h** of every street." Lam 2:19
water closed over my **h**; I said, 'I am Lam 3:54
lie scattered at the **h** of every street. Lam 4:1
The crown has fallen from our **h**; woe Lam 5:16
and pass it over your **h** and your beard. Ezk 5:1
a hand and took me by a lock of my **h**, Ezk 8:3
ears and a beautiful crown on your **h**. Ezk 16:12
At the **h** of every street you built your Ezk 16:25
chamber at the **h** of every street, Ezk 16:31
returned your deeds upon your **h**, Ezk 16:43
he broke. I will return it upon his **h**. Ezk 17:19
make it at the **h** of the way to a city. Ezk 21:19
of the way, at the **h** of the two ways, Ezk 21:21
Every **h** was made bald, and every Ezk 29:18
his blood shall be upon his own **h**. Ezk 33:4
would endanger my **h** with the king." Dn 1:10
and the visions of your **h** as you lay in Dn 2:28
The **h** of this image was of fine gold, its Dn 2:32
over them all—you are the **h** of gold. Dn 2:38
and the visions of my **h** alarmed me. Dn 4:5
The visions of my **h** as I lay in bed were Dn 4:10
in the visions of my **h** as I lay in bed, Dn 4:13
dream and visions of his **h** as he lay in Dn 7:1
and the hair of his **h** like pure wool; Dn 7:9
and the visions of my **h** alarmed me. Dn 7:15
about the ten horns that were on its **h**, Dn 7:20
they shall appoint for themselves one **h**. Hos 1:11
on your own **h** swiftly and speedily. Jl 3:4
I will return your payment on your own **h**. Jl 3:7
those who trample the **h** of the poor into Am 2:7
on every waist and baldness on every **h**; Am 8:10
your deeds shall return on your own **h**. Ob 1:15
me; weeds were wrapped about my **h** Jon 2:5
that it might be a shade over his **h**, Jon 4:6
sun beat down on the **h** of Jonah so that Jon 4:8
on before them, the LORD at their **h**. Mi 2:13
dashed in pieces at the **h** of every street; Na 3:10
You crushed the **h** of the house of the Hab 3:13
Judah, so that no one raised his **h**. Zec 1:21
a clean turban on his **h**." So they put a Zec 3:5
clean turban on his **h** and clothed him Zec 3:5
a crown, and set it on the **h** of Joshua, Zec 6:11
And do not take an oath by your **h**, for Mt 5:36
fast, anoint your **h** and wash your face, Mt 6:17
Son of Man has nowhere to lay his **h**." Mt 8:20
the hairs of your **h** are all numbered. Mt 10:30
"Give me the **h** of John the Baptist here Mt 14:8
and his **h** was brought on a platter and Mt 14:11
she poured it on his **h** as he reclined at Mt 26:7
they put it on his **h** and put a reed in Mt 27:29
took the reed and struck him on the **h**. Mt 27:30
And over his **h** they put the charge Mt 27:37
she said, "The **h** of John the Baptist." Mk 6:24
give me at once the **h** of John the Baptist Mk 6:25
with orders to bring John's **h**. Mk 6:27
and brought his **h** on a platter and gave Mk 6:28
struck him on the **h** and treated him Mk 12:4
broke the flask and poured it over his **h**. Mk 14:3
they were striking his **h** with a reed Mk 15:19
with the hair of her **h** and kissed his feet Lk 7:38
You did not anoint my **h** with oil, but Lk 7:46
Son of Man has nowhere to lay his **h**." Lk 9:58
the hairs of your **h** are all numbered. Lk 12:7
But not a hair of your **h** will perish. Lk 21:18
feet only but also my hands and my **h**!" Jn 13:9
and put it on his **h** and arrayed him in a Jn 19:2
and he bowed his **h** and gave up his Jn 19:30
face cloth, which had been on Jesus' **h**, Jn 20:7
had lain, one at the **h** and one at the feet. Jn 20:12
is to perish from the **h** of any of you." Acts 27:34
will heap burning coals on his **h**." Rom 12:20
to understand that the **h** of every man 1 Cor 11:3
Christ, the **h** of a wife is her husband, 1 Cor 11:3
husband, and the **h** of Christ is God. 1 Cor 11:3
with his **h** covered dishonors 1 Cor 11:4
his head covered dishonors his **h**, 1 Cor 11:4
with her **h** uncovered dishonors 1 Cor 11:5
uncovered dishonors her **h**—it is 1 Cor 11:5
it is the same as if her **h** were shaven. 1 Cor 11:5
For if a wife will not cover her **h**, then 1 Cor 11:6
wife to cut off her hair or shave her **h**, 1 Cor 11:6
or shave her head, let her cover her **h**. 1 Cor 11:6
For a man ought not to cover his **h**, 1 Cor 11:7
a symbol of authority on her **h**, 1 Cor 11:10
pray to God with her **h** uncovered? 1 Cor 11:13
of you," nor again the **h** to the feet, 1 Cor 12:21
and gave him as **h** over all things to Eph 1:22
up in every way into him who is the **h**, Eph 4:15
the husband is the **h** of the wife even Eph 5:23
even as Christ is the **h** of the church, Eph 5:23
And he is the **h** of the body, the church. Col 1:18
who is the **h** of all rule and authority. Col 2:10
and not holding fast to the **H**, from Col 2:19
in worship over the **h** of his staff. Heb 11:21
The hairs of his **h** were white like wool, Rv 1:14
in a cloud, with a rainbow over his **h**, Rv 10:1
feet, and on her **h** a crown of twelve stars. Rv 12:1
of man, with a golden crown on his **h**, Rv 14:14
of fire, and on his **h** are many diadems, Rv 19:12

HEADBANDS (1)
take away the finery of the anklets, the **h**, Is 3:18

HEADDRESS (2)
give them a beautiful **h** instead of ashes, Is 61:3
himself like a priest with a beautiful **h**, Is 61:10

HEADDRESSES (1)
the **h**, the armlets, the sashes, the perfume Is 3:20

HEADLONG (4)
pity; he flees from its power in **h** flight. Jb 27:22
though he fall, he shall not be cast **h**, Ps 37:24
like a horse plunging **h** into battle. Jer 8:6
and falling **h** he burst open in the Acts 1:18

HEADQUARTERS (6)
took Jesus into the governor's **h**, Mt 27:27
the palace (that is, the governor's **h**), Mk 15:16
house of Caiaphas to the governor's **h**. Jn 18:28
did not enter the governor's **h**, Jn 18:28
So Pilate entered his **h** again and called Jn 18:33
He entered his **h** again and said to Jesus, Jn 19:9

HEADS (166)
they bowed their **h** and prostrated Gn 43:28
they bowed their **h** and worshiped. Ex 4:31
These are the **h** of their fathers' houses: Ex 6:14
These are the **h** of the fathers' houses of Ex 6:25
people bowed their **h** and worshiped. Ex 12:27
Israel and made them **h** over the people, Ex 18:25
"Do not let the hair of your **h** hang loose, Lv 10:6
shall not make bald patches on their **h**, Lv 21:5
tribes, the **h** of the clans of Israel. Nm 1:16
chiefs of Israel, **h** of their fathers' houses, Nm 7:2
lay their hands on the **h** of the bulls, Nm 8:12
the chiefs, the **h** of the tribes of Israel, Nm 10:4
them men who were **h** of the people of Nm 13:3
Moses spoke to the **h** of the tribes of the Nm 30:1
the priest and the **h** of the fathers' Nm 31:26
Nun and to the **h** of the fathers' Nm 32:28
The **h** of the fathers' houses of the clan Nm 36:1
the **h** of the fathers' houses of the people Nm 36:1
men, and I will appoint them as your **h**.' Dt 1:13
So I took the **h** of your tribes, wise and Dt 1:15
men, and set them as **h** over you, Dt 1:15
came near to me, all the **h** of your tribes, Dt 5:23
the **h** of your tribes, your elders, and Dt 29:10
from the long-haired **h** of the enemy.' Dt 32:42
when the **h** of the people were gathered, Dt 33:5
and he came with the **h** of the people, Dt 33:21
of Israel. And they put dust on their **h**. Jos 7:6
of Nun and the **h** of the fathers' houses Jos 14:1
of Nun and the **h** of the fathers' houses Jos 19:51
Then the **h** of the fathers' houses of the Jos 21:1
Nun and to the **h** of the fathers' houses Jos 21:1
in answer to the **h** of the families of Jos 22:21
the **h** of the families of Israel who were Jos 22:30
summoned all Israel, its elders and **h**, Jos 23:2
and summoned the elders, the **h**, Jos 24:1
and they brought the **h** of Oreb and Jgs 7:25
Israel, and they raised their **h** no more. Jgs 8:28
the men of Shechem return on their **h**, Jgs 9:57
it not be with the **h** of the men here? 1 Sm 29:4
who were with him covered their **h**, 2 Sm 15:30
of Israel and all the **h** of the tribes, 1 Kgs 8:1
and ropes on our **h** and go out to 1 Kgs 20:31
put ropes on their **h** and went to the 1 Kgs 20:32
take the **h** of your master's sons and 2 Kgs 10:6
and put their **h** in baskets and sent 2 Kgs 10:7
have brought the **h** of the king's 2 Kgs 10:8
These were the **h** of their fathers' 1 Chr 5:24
men, **h** of their fathers' houses. 1 Chr 5:24
Shemuel, **h** of their fathers' houses, 1 Chr 7:2
and Iri, five, **h** of fathers' houses, 1 Chr 7:7
as **h** of their fathers' houses, 1 Chr 7:9
according to the **h** of their fathers' 1 Chr 7:11
men of Asher, **h** of fathers' houses, 1 Chr 7:40
of Ehud (they were **h** of fathers' houses 1 Chr 8:6
were his sons, **h** of fathers' houses. 1 Chr 8:10
Shema (they were **h** of fathers' 1 Chr 8:13
These were the **h** of fathers' houses, 1 Chr 8:28
All these were **h** of fathers' houses 1 Chr 9:9
kinsmen, **h** of their fathers' houses, 1 Chr 9:13
the **h** of fathers' houses of the Levites, 1 Chr 9:33
These were **h** of fathers' houses of the 1 Chr 9:34
"At peril to our **h** he will desert to 1 Chr 12:19
"You are the **h** of the fathers' houses 1 Chr 15:12
These were the **h** of the fathers' 1 Chr 23:9
the **h** of fathers' houses as they were 1 Chr 23:24
them under sixteen **h** of fathers' 1 Chr 24:4
of Abiathar and the **h** of the fathers' 1 Chr 24:6
and the **h** of fathers' houses of the 1 Chr 24:31
the **h** of the fathers' houses 1 Chr 26:21
the king and the **h** of the fathers' 1 Chr 26:26
men of ability, **h** of fathers' houses, 1 Chr 26:32
of Israel, the **h** of fathers' houses, 1 Chr 27:1
and bowed their **h** and paid homage 1 Chr 29:20
in all Israel, the **h** of fathers' houses. 2 Chr 1:2
of Israel and all the **h** of the tribes, 2 Chr 5:2
and priests and **h** of families of 2 Chr 19:8
and the **h** of fathers' houses of Israel, 2 Chr 23:2
number of the **h** of fathers' houses 2 Chr 26:12
Then rose up the **h** of the fathers' houses Ezr 1:5
Some of the **h** of families, when they Ezr 2:68
and Levites and **h** of fathers' houses, Ezr 3:12
Zerubbabel and the **h** of fathers' houses Ezr 4:2
and the rest of the **h** of fathers' houses in Ezr 4:3
These are the **h** of their fathers' houses, Ezr 8:1
the Levites and the **h** of fathers' houses Ezr 8:29
iniquities have risen higher than our **h**, Ezr 9:6
selected men, **h** of fathers' houses, Ezr 10:16
taunt on their own **h** and give them up Neh 4:4
Now some of the **h** of fathers' houses Neh 7:70
And some of the **h** of fathers' houses Neh 7:71
they bowed their **h** and worshiped the Neh 8:6
the second day the **h** of fathers' houses Neh 8:13
in sackcloth, and with earth on their **h**. Neh 9:1
and his brothers, **h** of fathers' houses, Neh 11:13
were priests, **h** of fathers' houses: Neh 12:12
were recorded as **h** of fathers' houses; Neh 12:22
their **h** of fathers' houses were written Neh 12:23
sprinkled dust on their **h** toward heaven. Jb 2:12
they are cut off like the **h** of grain. Jb 24:24
make mouths at me; they wag their **h**; Ps 22:7
Lift up your **h**, O gates! And be lifted up, Ps 24:7
Lift up your **h**, O gates! And lift them up, Ps 24:9
them; all who see them will wag their **h**. Ps 64:8
you let men ride over our **h**; we went Ps 66:12
But God will strike the **h** of his enemies, Ps 68:21
you broke the **h** of the sea monsters on Ps 74:13
You crushed the **h** of Leviathan; you Ps 74:14
those who hate you have raised their **h**. Ps 83:2
when they see me, they wag their **h**. Ps 109:25
with a scab the **h** of the daughters of Is 3:17
and covered your **h** (the seers). Is 29:10
everlasting joy shall be upon their **h**; Is 35:10
everlasting joy shall be upon their **h**; Is 51:11
and confounded and cover their **h**. Jer 14:3
farmers are ashamed; they cover their **h**. Jer 14:4
thrown dust on their **h** and put on Lam 2:10
have bowed their **h** to the ground. Lam 2:10
hiss and wag their **h** at the daughter of Lam 2:15
Over the **h** of the living creatures there Ezk 1:22
crystal, spread out above their **h**. Ezk 1:22
from above the expanse over their **h**. Ezk 1:25
the expanse over their **h** there was the Ezk 1:26
on all faces, and baldness on all their **h**. Ezk 7:18
I will bring their deeds upon their **h**." Ezk 9:10
that was over the **h** of the cherubim Ezk 10:1
bring their deeds upon their own **h**, Ezk 11:21
make veils for the **h** of persons of Ezk 13:18
have returned their way upon their **h**, Ezk 22:31
with flowing turbans on their **h**, Ezk 23:15
and beautiful crowns on their **h**. Ezk 23:42
shall be on your **h** and your shoes on Ezk 24:23
cast dust on their **h** and wallow in Ezk 27:30
whose swords were laid under their **h**, Ezk 32:27
shall have linen turbans on their **h**, Ezk 44:18
shall not shave their **h** or let their Ezk 44:20
shall surely trim the hair of their **h**. Ezk 44:20
The hair of their **h** was not singed, their Dn 3:27
And the beast had four **h**, and dominion Dn 7:6
The standing grain has no **h**; it shall Hos 8:7
shatter them on the **h** of all the people; Am 9:1
you **h** of Jacob and rulers of the house of Mi 3:1
you **h** of the house of Jacob and rulers of Mi 3:9
Its **h** give judgment for a bribe; its Mi 3:11
his own arrows the **h** of his warriors, Hab 3:14
they began to pluck **h** of grain and to Mt 12:1
passed by derided him, wagging their **h** Mt 27:39
his disciples began to pluck **h** of grain. Mk 2:23
him, wagging their **h** and saying, Mk 15:29
disciples plucked and ate some **h** of grain, Lk 6:1
place, straighten up and raise your **h**, Lk 21:28
them, "Your blood be on your own **h**! Acts 18:6
so that they may shave their **h**. Acts 21:24
garments, with golden crowns on their **h**. Rv 4:4
on their **h** were what looked like crowns Rv 9:7
and the **h** of the horses were like lions' Rv 9:17
the heads of the horses were like lions' **h**, Rv 9:17
for their tails are like serpents with **h**, Rv 9:19
red dragon, with seven **h** and ten horns, Rv 12:3
ten horns, and on his **h** seven diadems. Rv 12:3
of the sea, with ten horns and seven **h**, Rv 13:1
horns and blasphemous names on its **h**. Rv 13:1
One of its **h** seemed to have a mortal Rv 13:3
names, and it had seven **h** and ten horns. Rv 17:3
the beast with seven **h** and ten horns Rv 17:7
the seven **h** are seven mountains on Rv 17:9
threw dust on their **h** as they wept and Rv 18:19

HEADWAY (1)
saw that they were making **h** painfully, Mk 6:48

HEAL (41)
LORD, "O God, please **h** her—please." Nm 12:13
I kill and I make alive; I wound and I **h**; Dt 32:39
seen your tears. Behold, I will **h** you. 2 Kgs 20:5
be the sign that the LORD will **h** me, 2 Kgs 20:8
will forgive their sin and **h** their land. 2 Chr 7:14
he binds up; he shatters, but his hands **h**. Jb 5:18
h me, O LORD, for my bones are troubled. Ps 6:2
me; **h** me, for I have sinned against you!" Ps 41:4
a time to kill, and a time to **h**; a time to Eccl 3:3
to their pleas for mercy and **h** them. Is 19:22
I have seen his ways, but I will **h** him; I Is 57:18
near," says the LORD, "and I will **h** him. Is 57:19
I will **h** your faithlessness." "Behold, we Jer 3:22
H me, O LORD, and I shall be healed; Jer 17:14
to you, and your wounds I will **h**, Jer 30:17
and I will **h** them and reveal to them Jer 33:6
ruin is vast as the sea; who can **h** you? Lam 2:13
to **h** it by binding it with a bandage, Ezk 30:21
not able to cure you or **h** your wound. Hos 5:13
for he has torn us, that he may **h** us; Hos 6:1
When I would **h** Israel, the iniquity of Hos 7:1
I will **h** their apostasy; I will love them Hos 14:4
seek the young or **h** the maimed or Zec 11:16
he said to him, "I will come and **h** him." Mt 8:7
and to **h** every disease and every Mt 10:1
H the sick, raise the dead, cleanse lepers, Mt 10:8
"Is it lawful to **h** on the Sabbath?"—so Mt 12:10
heart and turn, and I would **h** them.' Mt 13:15
disciples, and they could not **h** him." Mt 17:16
see whether he would **h** him on the Mk 3:2
me this proverb, 'Physician, **h** yourself.' Lk 4:23
the power of the Lord was with him to **h**. Lk 5:17
see whether he would **h** on the Sabbath, Lk 6:7
asking him to come and **h** his servant. Lk 7:3
to proclaim the kingdom of God and to **h**. Lk 9:2
H the sick in it and say to them, 'The Lk 10:9
saying, "Is it lawful to **h** on the Sabbath, Lk 14:3
asked him to come down and **h** his son, Jn 4:47
heart, and turn, and I would **h** them." Jn 12:40
while you stretch out your hand to **h**, Acts 4:30
heart and turn, and I would **h** them.' Acts 28:27

HEALED (79)
prayed to God, and God **h** Abimelech, Gn 20:17
and also **h** his wife and female slaves Gn 20:17
time, and shall have him thoroughly **h**. Ex 21:19
in it, the itch is **h** and he is clean, Lv 13:37
of leprous disease is **h** in the leprous Lv 14:3
the house clean, for the disease is **h**. Lv 14:48
and itch, of which you cannot be **h**. Dt 28:27
boils of which you cannot be **h**, Dt 28:35
places in the camp until they were **h**. Jos 5:8
Then you will be **h**, and it will be 1 Sm 6:3
says the LORD, I have **h** this water; 2 Kgs 2:21
So the water has been **h** to this day, 2 Kgs 2:22
Joram returned to be **h** in Jezreel of 2 Kgs 8:29
had returned to be **h** in Jezreel of the 2 Kgs 9:15
he returned to be **h** in Jezreel of the 2 Chr 22:6
heard Hezekiah and **h** the people. 2 Chr 30:20
cried to you for help, and you have **h** me. Ps 30:2
He sent out his word and **h** them, and Ps 107:20
with their hearts, and turn and be **h**." Is 6:10
us peace, and with his stripes we are **h**. Is 53:5
They have **h** the wound of my people Jer 6:14
They have **h** the wound of my people Jer 8:11
my wound incurable, refusing to be **h**? Jer 15:18
Heal me, O LORD, and I shall be **h**; save Jer 17:14
for her pain; perhaps she may be **h**. Jer 51:8
We would have **h** Babylon, but she was Jer 51:9
have healed Babylon, but she was not **h**. Jer 51:9
strengthened, the sick you have not **h**, Ezk 34:4
but they did not know that I **h** them. Hos 11:3
and paralytics, and he **h** them. Mt 4:24
say the word, and my servant will be **h**. Mt 8:8
And the servant was **h** at that very Mt 8:13
with a word and **h** all who were sick. Mt 8:16
many followed him, and he **h** them all Mt 12:15
was brought to him, and he **h** him, Mt 12:22
compassion on them and **h** their sick. Mt 14:14
And her daughter was **h** instantly. Mt 15:28
put them at his feet, and he **h** them, Mt 15:30
of him, and the boy was **h** instantly. Mt 17:18
followed him, and he **h** them there. Mt 19:2
to him in the temple, and he **h** them. Mt 21:14
And he **h** many who were sick with Mk 1:34
for he had **h** many, so that all who had Mk 3:10
her body that she was **h** of her disease. Mk 5:29
go in peace, and be **h** of your disease." Mk 5:34
hands on a few sick people and **h** them. Mk 6:5
oil many who were sick and **h** them. Mk 6:13
hands on every one of them and **h** them. Lk 4:40
hear him and to be **h** of their infirmities. Lk 5:15
to hear him and to be **h** of their diseases. Lk 6:18
came out from him and **h** them all. Lk 6:19
But say the word, and let my servant be **h**. Lk 7:7

In that hour he **h** many people of Lk 7:21
women who had been **h** of evil spirits and Lk 8:2
the demon-possessed man had been **h**. Lk 8:36
she could not be **h** by anyone. Lk 8:43
and how she had been immediately **h**. Lk 8:47
the unclean spirit and **h** the boy, Lk 9:42
because Jesus had **h** on the Sabbath, Lk 13:14
Come on those days and be **h**, and not Lk 13:14
he took him and **h** him and sent him Lk 14:4
of them, when he saw that he was **h**, Lk 17:15
And he touched his ear and **h** him. Lk 22:51
he said to him, "Do you want to be **h**?" Jn 5:6
And at once the man was **h**, and he took Jn 5:9
the Jews said to the man who had been **h**, Jn 5:10
he answered them, "The man who **h** me, Jn 5:11
man who had been **h** did not know who Jn 5:13
the Jews that it was Jesus who had **h** him. Jn 5:15
by what means this man has been **h**, Acts 4:9
man who was **h** standing beside them, Acts 4:14
unclean spirits, and they were all **h**. Acts 5:16
who were paralyzed or lame were **h**. Acts 8:7
and putting his hands on him **h** him. Acts 28:8
not be put out of joint but rather be **h**. Heb 12:13
pray for one another, that you may be **h**. Jas 5:16
By his wounds you have been **h**. 1 Pt 2:24
wound, but its mortal wound was **h**, Rv 13:3
first beast, whose mortal wound was **h**. Rv 13:12

HEALER (2)
Egyptians, for I am the LORD, your **h**." Ex 15:26
he will speak out, saying: "I will not be a **h**; Is 3:7

HEALING (26)
It will be **h** to your flesh and refreshment Prv 3:8
who find them, and **h** to all their flesh. Prv 4:22
a moment he will be broken beyond **h**. Prv 6:15
but the tongue of the wise brings **h**. Prv 12:18
trouble, but a faithful envoy brings **h**. Prv 13:17
will suddenly be broken beyond **h**. Prv 29:1
LORD will strike Egypt, striking and **h**, Is 19:22
and your **h** shall spring up speedily; Is 58:8
came; for a time of **h**, but behold, terror. Jer 8:15
us down so that there is no **h** for us? Jer 14:19
for a time of **h**, but behold, terror. Jer 14:19
medicine for your wound, no **h** for you. Jer 30:13
Behold, I will bring to it health and **h**, Jer 33:6
many medicines; there is no **h** for you. Jer 46:11
will be for food, and their leaves for **h**." Ezk 47:12
shall rise with **h** in its wings. Mal 4:2
of the kingdom and **h** every disease and Mt 4:23
of the kingdom and **h** every disease and Mt 9:35
preaching the gospel and **h** everywhere. Lk 9:6
God and cured those who had need of **h**. Lk 9:11
this sign of **h** was performed was Acts 4:22
about doing good and **h** all who were Acts 10:38
to another gifts of **h** by the one Spirit, 1 Cor 12:9
then miracles, then gifts of **h**, 1 Cor 12:28
Do all possess gifts of **h**? Do all 1 Cor 12:30
of the tree were for the **h** of the nations. Rv 22:2

HEALS (5)
in the skin of one's body a boil and it **h**, Lv 13:18
your iniquity, who **h** all your diseases, Ps 103:3
He **h** the brokenhearted and binds up Ps 147:3
and **h** the wounds inflicted by his blow. Is 30:26
to him, "Aeneas, Jesus Christ **h** you; Acts 9:34

HEALTH (11)
to ask about his **h** and to bless him 2 Sm 8:10
to ask about his **h** and to bless him 1 Chr 18:10
there is no **h** in my bones because of my Ps 38:3
in his illness you restore him to full **h**. Ps 41:3
to the soul and **h** to the body. Prv 16:24
Oh restore me to **h** and make me live! Is 38:16
Why then has the **h** of the daughter of Jer 8:22
For I will restore **h** to you, and your Jer 30:17
Behold, I will bring to it **h** and healing, Jer 33:6
the man this perfect **h** in the presence Acts 3:16
with you and that you may be in good **h**, 3 Jn 1:2

HEALTHY (7)
or heal the maimed or nourish the **h**, Zec 11:16
So, if your eye is **h**, your whole body will Mt 6:22
So, every **h** tree bears good fruit, but the Mt 7:17
A **h** tree cannot bear bad fruit, nor can a Mt 7:18
and it was restored, **h** like the other. Mt 12:13
saw the mute speaking, the crippled **h**, Mt 15:31
When your eye is **h**, your whole body Lk 11:34

HEAP (43)
And they took stones and made a **h**, Gn 31:46
a heap, and they ate there by the **h**. Gn 31:46
"This **h** is a witness between you and Gn 31:48
said to Jacob, "See this **h** and the pillar, Gn 31:51
This **h** is a witness, and the pillar is a Gn 31:52
that I will not pass over this **h** to you, Gn 31:52
not pass over this **h** and this pillar to Gn 31:52
piled up; the floods stood up in a **h**; Ex 15:8
the camp to a clean place, to the ash **h**, Lv 4:12
On the ash **h** it shall be burned up. Lv 4:12
LORD your God. It shall be a **h** forever. Dt 13:16
"'And I will **h** disasters upon them; I Dt 32:23
down from above shall stand in one **h**." Jos 3:13
stood and rose up in a **h** very far away, Jos 3:16
over him a great **h** of stones that Jos 7:26
Ai and made it forever a **h** of ruins, Jos 8:28
city and raised over it a great **h** of stones, Jos 8:29
to lie down at the end of the **h** of grain. Ru 3:7
needy from the ash **h** to make them sit 1 Sm 2:8
hand, and remain beside the stone **h**. 1 Sm 20:19
from beside the stone **h** and fell on 1 Sm 20:41
over him a very great **h** of stones. 2 Sm 18:17
this house will become a **h** of ruins. 1 Kgs 9:8
His roots entwine the stone **h**; he looks Jb 8:17
Though he **h** up silver like dust, and Jb 27:16
does not one in a **h** of ruins stretch out Jb 30:24
He gathers the waters of the sea as a **h**; he Ps 33:7
it, and made the waters stand like a **h**. Ps 78:13
dust and lifts the needy from the ash **h**, Ps 113:7
for you will **h** burning coals on his Prv 25:22
Your belly is a **h** of wheat, encircled with Sg 7:2
and this **h** of ruins shall be under your Is 3:6
to be a city and will become a **h** of ruins. Is 17:1
For you have made the city a **h**, the Is 25:2
I will make Jerusalem a **h** of ruins, a lair Jer 9:11
Jerusalem shall become a **h** of ruins, Jer 26:18
and Babylon shall become a **h** of ruins, Jer 51:37
H on the logs, kindle the fire, boil the Ezk 24:10
will make Samaria a **h** in the open Mi 1:6
Jerusalem shall become a **h** of ruins, Mi 3:12
one came to a **h** of twenty measures, Hg 2:16
do not **h** up empty phrases as the Gentiles Mt 6:7
so doing you will **h** burning coals on Rom 12:20

HEAPED (2)
herself a rampart and **h** up silver like Zec 9:3
for her sins are **h** high as heaven, and Rv 18:5

HEAPING (1)
H oppression upon oppression, and deceit Jer 9:6

HEAPS (19)
And they gathered them together in **h**, Ex 8:14
the jawbone of a donkey, **h** upon heaps, Jgs 15:16
the jawbone of a donkey, heaps upon **h**, Jgs 15:16
"Lay them in two **h** at the entrance of 2 Kgs 10:8
turn fortified cities into **h** of ruins, 2 Kgs 19:25
LORD their God, and laid them in **h**. 2 Chr 31:6
month they began to pile up the **h**, 2 Chr 31:7
and the princes came and saw the **h**, 2 Chr 31:8
priests and the Levites about the **h**. 2 Chr 31:9
revive the stones out of the **h** of rubbish, Neh 4:2
and bringing in **h** of grain and Neh 13:15
which were ready to become **h** of ruins; Jb 15:28
man **h** up wealth and does not know Ps 39:6
fortified cities crash into **h** of ruins, Is 37:26
pile her up like **h** of grain, and devote Jer 50:26
brought up in purple embrace ash **h**. Lam 4:5
also are like stone **h** on the furrows of Hos 12:11
spear, hosts of slain, **h** of corpses, Na 3:3
"Woe to him who **h** up what is not his Hab 2:6

HEAR (468)
his wives: "Adah and Zillah, **h** my voice; Gn 4:23
"**H** us, my lord; you are a prince of God Gn 23:6
h me and entreat for me Ephron the son Gn 23:8
"No, my lord, **h** me: I give you the field, Gn 23:11
of the land, "But if you will, **h** me: Gn 23:13
"**H** this dream that I have dreamed: Gn 37:6
you that when you **h** a dream you can Gn 41:15
that the people may **h** when I speak with Ex 19:9
cry out to me, I will surely **h** their cry, Ex 22:23
And if he cries to me, I will **h**, for I am Ex 22:27
but the sound of singing that I **h**." Ex 32:18
that I may **h** what the LORD will Nm 9:8
And he said, "**H** my words: If there is a Nm 12:6
LORD, "Then the Egyptians will **h** of it, Nm 14:13
And Moses said to Korah, "**H** now, you Nm 16:8
the rock, and he said to them, "**H** now, Nm 20:10
and said, "Rise, Balak, and **h**; Nm 23:18
day that her husband comes to **h** of it, Nm 30:8
time, '**H** the cases between your brothers, Dt 1:16
You shall **h** the small and the great Dt 1:17
you shall bring to me, and I will **h** it.' Dt 1:17
who shall **h** the report of you and shall Dt 2:25
who, when they **h** all these statutes, Dt 4:6
to me, that I may let them **h** my words, Dt 4:10
of human hands, that neither see, nor **h**, Dt 4:28
Did any people ever **h** the voice of a god Dt 4:33
Out of heaven he let you **h** his voice, that Dt 4:36
all Israel and said to them, "**H**, O Israel, Dt 5:1
If we **h** the voice of the LORD our God any Dt 5:25
Go near and **h** all that the LORD our God Dt 5:27
speak to you, and we will **h** and do it.' Dt 5:27
H therefore, O Israel, and be careful to do Dt 6:3
"**H**, O Israel: The LORD our God, the LORD is Dt 6:4
"**H**, O Israel: you are to cross over the Dt 9:1
And all Israel shall **h** and fear and Dt 13:11
"If you **h** in one of your cities, which Dt 13:12
and it is told you and you **h** of it, then Dt 17:4
all the people shall **h** and fear and not Dt 17:13
'Let me not **h** again the voice of the Dt 18:16
And the rest shall **h** and fear, and shall Dt 19:20
and shall say to them, '**H**, O Israel, today Dt 20:3
from your midst, and all Israel shall **h**, Dt 21:21
said to all Israel, "Keep silence and **h**, Dt 27:9
to understand or eyes to see or ears to **h**. Dt 29:4
it to us, that we may **h** it and do it?' Dt 30:12
it to us, that we may **h** it and do it?' Dt 30:13
heart turns away, and you will not **h**, Dt 30:17
that they may **h** and learn to fear the Dt 31:12
may **h** and learn to fear the LORD your Dt 31:13
and let the earth **h** the words of my Dt 32:1
"**H**, O LORD, the voice of Judah, and bring Dt 33:7
when you **h** the sound of the trumpet, Jos 6:5
of the land will **h** of it and will Jos 7:9
"**H**, O kings; give ear, O princes; to the Jgs 5:3
to **h** the whistling for the flocks? Jgs 5:16
And you shall **h** what they say, and Jgs 7:11
"Put your riddle, that we may **h** it." Jgs 14:13
For I **h** of your evil dealings from all 1 Sm 2:23
good report that I **h** the people of the 1 Sm 2:24
the land, saying, "Let the Hebrews **h**." 1 Sm 13:3
and the lowing of the oxen that I **h**?" 1 Sm 15:14
who stood about him, "**H** now, 1 Sm 22:7
And Saul said, "**H** now, son of 1 Sm 22:12
I **h** that you have shearers. Now your 1 Sm 25:7
and **h** the words of your servant. 1 Sm 25:24
my lord the king **h** the words of his 1 Sm 26:19
And when you **h** the sound of 2 Sm 5:24
For the king will **h** and deliver his 2 Sm 14:16
man designated by the king to **h** you." 2 Sm 15:3
"As soon as you **h** the sound of the 2 Sm 15:10
So whatever you **h** from the king's 2 Sm 15:35
shall send to me everything you **h**." 2 Sm 15:36
and all Israel will **h** that you have 2 Sm 16:21
also, and let us **h** what he has to say." 2 Sm 17:5
all nations came to **h** the wisdom of 1 Kgs 4:34
your dwelling place, and when you **h**, 1 Kgs 8:30
then **h** in heaven and act and judge 1 Kgs 8:32
then **h** in heaven and forgive the sin 1 Kgs 8:34
then **h** in heaven and forgive the sin 1 Kgs 8:36
then **h** in heaven your dwelling place 1 Kgs 8:39
(for they shall **h** of your great name 1 Kgs 8:42
h in heaven your dwelling place and 1 Kgs 8:43
then **h** in heaven their prayer and 1 Kgs 8:45
then **h** in heaven your dwelling place 1 Kgs 8:49
stand before you and **h** your wisdom! 1 Kgs 10:8
of Solomon to **h** his wisdom, 1 Kgs 10:24
"Therefore **h** the word of the LORD: 1 Kgs 22:19
And he said, "**H**, all you peoples!" 1 Kgs 22:28
Elisha said, "**H** the word of the LORD: 2 Kgs 7:1
army of the Syrians **h** the sound of 2 Kgs 7:6
"**H** the word of the great king, the 2 Kgs 18:28
so that he shall **h** a rumor and return 2 Kgs 19:7
Incline your ear, O LORD, and **h**; 2 Kgs 19:16
and **h** the words of Sennacherib, 2 Kgs 19:16
to Hezekiah, "**H** the word of the LORD: 2 Kgs 20:16
And when you **h** the sound of 1 Chr 14:15
"**H** me, my brothers and my people. 1 Chr 28:2
your dwelling place, and when you **h**, 2 Chr 6:21
then **h** from heaven and act and 2 Chr 6:23
then **h** from heaven and forgive the 2 Chr 6:25
then **h** in heaven and forgive the sin 2 Chr 6:27
then **h** from heaven your dwelling 2 Chr 6:30
h from heaven your dwelling place 2 Chr 6:33
then **h** from heaven their prayer and 2 Chr 6:35
then **h** from heaven your dwelling 2 Chr 6:39
then I will **h** from heaven and will 2 Chr 7:14
stand before you and **h** your wisdom! 2 Chr 9:7
of Solomon to **h** his wisdom, 2 Chr 9:23
country of Ephraim and said, "**H** me, 2 Chr 13:4
to meet Asa and said to him, "**H** me, 2 Chr 15:2
"Therefore **h** the word of the LORD: 2 Chr 18:18
And he said, "**H**, all you peoples!" 2 Chr 18:27
affliction, and you will **h** and save.' 2 Chr 20:9
Jehoshaphat stood and said, "**H** me, 2 Chr 20:20
Now **h** me, and send back the 2 Chr 28:11
and said to them, "**H** me, Levites! 2 Chr 29:5
to **h** the prayer of your servant that I Neh 1:6
H, O our God, for we are despised. Turn Neh 4:4
the place where you **h** the sound of the Neh 4:20
And now the king will **h** of these reports. Neh 6:7
they **h** not the voice of the taskmaster. Jb 3:18
it is true. **H**, and know it for your good." Jb 5:27
H now my argument and listen to the Jb 13:6
h me, and what I have seen I will declare Jb 15:17
I **h** censure that insults me, and out of Jb 20:3
your prayer to him, and he will **h** you, Jb 22:27
how small a whisper do we **h** of him! Jb 26:14

Will God **h** his cry when distress comes Jb 27:9
Oh, that I had one to **h** me! (Here is my Jb 31:35
"But now, **h** my speech, O Job, and listen Jb 33:1
"**H** my words, you wise men, and give ear Jb 34:2
"Therefore, **h** me, you men of Jb 34:10
"If you have understanding, **h** this; Jb 34:16
Surely God does not **h** an empty cry, nor Jb 35:13
"**H** this, O Job; stop and consider the Jb 37:14
'**H**, and I will speak; I will question you, Jb 42:4
Be gracious to me and **h** my prayer! Ps 4:1
O LORD, in the morning you **h** my voice; Ps 5:3
O LORD, you **h** the desire of the afflicted; Ps 10:17
H a just cause, O LORD; attend to my cry! Ps 17:1
God; incline your ear to me; **h** my words. Ps 17:6
H, O LORD, when I cry aloud; be gracious Ps 27:7
H the voice of my pleas for mercy, when I Ps 28:2
H, O LORD, and be merciful to me! O Ps 30:10
For I **h** the whispering of many—terror Ps 31:13
the LORD; let the humble **h** and be glad. Ps 34:2
I do not **h**, like a mute man who does Ps 38:13
become like a man who does not **h**, Ps 38:14
"**H** my prayer, O LORD, and give ear to Ps 39:12
H, O daughter, and consider, and Ps 45:10
H this, all peoples! Give ear, all Ps 49:1
"**H**, O my people, and I will speak; O Ps 50:7
Let me **h** joy and gladness; let the bones Ps 51:8
O God, **h** my prayer; give ear to the words Ps 54:2
that it does not **h** the voice of charmers Ps 58:5
lips—for "Who," they think, "will **h** us?" Ps 59:7
H my cry, O God, listen to my prayer; Ps 61:1
H my voice, O God, in my complaint; Ps 64:1
Come and **h**, all you who fear God, and Ps 66:16
to God, aloud to God, and he will **h** me. Ps 77:1
of Egypt. I **h** a language I had not known: Ps 81:5
H, O my people, while I admonish you! O Ps 81:8
O LORD God of hosts, **h** my prayer; give Ps 84:8
Let me **h** what God the LORD will speak, Ps 85:8
He who planted the ear, does he not **h**? He Ps 94:9
of his hand. Today, if you **h** his voice, Ps 95:7
H my prayer, O LORD; let my cry come Ps 102:1
to **h** the groans of the prisoners, to set Ps 102:20
They have ears, but do not **h**; noses, but Ps 115:6
H my voice according to your Ps 119:149
O Lord, **h** my voice! Let your ears be Ps 130:2
they have ears, but do not **h**, nor is Ps 135:17
the cliff, then they shall **h** my words, Ps 141:6
H my prayer, O LORD; give ear to my Ps 143:1
Let me **h** in the morning of your Ps 143:8
Let the wise **h** and increase in learning, Prv 1:5
H, my son, your father's instruction, and Prv 1:8
H, O sons, a father's instruction, and be Prv 4:1
H, my son, and accept my words, that Prv 4:10
H, for I will speak noble things, and from Prv 8:6
H instruction and be wise, and do not Prv 8:33
Cease to **h** instruction, my son, and Prv 19:27
your ear, and **h** the words of the wise, Prv 22:17
H, my son, and be wise, and direct Prv 23:19
better for a man to **h** the rebuke of the Eccl 7:5
of the wise than to **h** the song of fools. Eccl 7:5
lest you **h** your servant cursing you. Eccl 7:21
let me see your face, let me **h** your voice, Sg 2:14
listening for your voice; let me **h** it. Sg 8:13
H, O heavens, and give ear, O earth; for the Is 1:2
H the word of the LORD, you rulers of Is 1:10
see with their eyes, and **h** with their ears, Is 6:10
And he said, "**H** then, O house of David! Is Is 7:13
see, or decide disputes by what his ears **h**, Is 11:3
look! When a trumpet is blown, **h**! Is 18:3
I am bowed down so that I cannot **h**; Is 21:3
ends of the earth we **h** songs of praise, Is 24:16
and this is repose"; yet they would not **h**. Is 28:12
Therefore **h** the word of the LORD, you Is 28:14
Give ear, and **h** my voice; give attention, Is 28:23
voice; give attention, and **h** my speech. Is 28:23
that day the deaf shall **h** the words of a Is 29:18
children unwilling to **h** the instruction of Is 30:9
let us **h** no more about the Holy One of Is 30:11
And your ears shall **h** a word behind Is 30:21
the ears of those who **h** will give attention. Is 32:3
you women who are at ease, **h** my voice; Is 32:9
H, you who are far off, what I have done; Is 33:13
Draw near, O nations, to **h**, and give Is 34:1
Let the earth **h**, and all that fills it; the Is 34:1
"**H** the words of the great king, the king Is 36:13
the LORD your God will **h** the words of the Is 37:4
so that he shall **h** a rumor and return to Is 37:7
Incline your ear, O LORD, and **h**; open Is 37:17
and **h** all the words of Sennacherib, Is 37:17
"**H** the word of the LORD of hosts: Is 39:5
Do you not know? Do you not **h**? Has it Is 40:21
H, you deaf, and look, you blind, that Is 42:18
his ears are open, but he does not **h**. Is 42:20
prove them right, and let them **h** and say, Is 43:9
"But now **h**, O Jacob my servant, Israel Is 44:1
Now therefore **h** this, you lover of Is 47:8
H this, O house of Jacob, who are called Is 48:1
Draw near to me, **h** this: from the Is 48:16
he awakens my ear to **h** as those who are Is 50:4
Therefore **h** this, you who are afflicted, Is 51:21
come to me; **h**, that your soul may live; Is 55:3
save, or his ear dull, that it cannot **h**; Is 59:1
his face from you so that he does not **h**. Is 59:2
while they are yet speaking I will **h**. Is 65:24
H the word of the LORD, you who tremble Is 66:5
H the word of the LORD, O house of Jacob, Jer 2:4
silent, for I **h** the sound of the trumpet, Jer 4:19
I see the standard and **h** the sound of the Jer 4:21
"**H** this, O foolish and senseless people, Jer 5:21
but see not, who have ears, but **h** not. Jer 5:21
and give warning, that they may **h**? Jer 6:10
Therefore **h**, O nations, and know, O Jer 6:18
H, O earth; behold, I am bringing Jer 6:19
this word, and say, **H** the word of the LORD, Jer 7:2
intercede with me, for I will not **h** you. Jer 7:16
H, O women, the word of the LORD, and Jer 9:20
H the word that the LORD speaks to you, Jer 10:1
"**H** the words of this covenant, and speak Jer 11:2
the man who does not **h** the words of this Jer 11:3
H the words of this covenant and do Jer 11:6
forefathers, who refused to **h** my words. Jer 11:10
evil people, who refuse to **h** my words, Jer 13:10
H and give ear; be not proud, for the Jer 13:15
Though they fast, I will not **h** their cry, Jer 14:12
'**H** the word of the LORD, you kings of Jer 17:20
they might not **h** and receive Jer 17:23
and there I will let you **h** my words." Jer 18:2
H me, O LORD, and listen to the voice of Jer 18:19
You shall say, '**H** the word of the LORD, O Jer 19:3
their neck, refusing to **h** my words." Jer 19:15
For I **h** many whispering. Terror is on Jer 20:10
let him **h** a cry in the morning and an Jer 20:16
of Judah say, '**H** the word of the LORD, Jer 21:11
and say, '**H** the word of the LORD, O King Jer 22:2
land, land, land, **h** the word of the LORD! Jer 22:29
of the LORD to see and to **h** his word, Jer 23:18
listened nor inclined your ears to **h**, Jer 25:4
Yet **h** now this word that I speak in your Jer 28:7
come and pray to me, and I will **h** you. Jer 29:12
H the word of the LORD, all you exiles Jer 29:20
"**H** the word of the LORD, O nations, and Jer 31:10
of the earth who shall **h** of all the good Jer 33:9
Yet **h** the word of the LORD, O Zedekiah Jer 34:4
house of Judah will **h** all the disaster that Jer 36:3
against them, but they would not **h**.'" Jer 36:31
Now **h**, please, O my lord the king: let Jer 37:20
If the officials **h** that I have spoken with Jer 38:25
shall not see war or **h** the sound of the Jer 42:14
then **h** the word of the LORD, O remnant Jer 42:15
all the women, "**H** the word of the LORD, Jer 44:24
Therefore **h** the word of the LORD, all Jer 44:26
Therefore **h** the plan that the LORD has Jer 49:20
Therefore **h** the plan that the LORD has Jer 50:45
I have rebelled against his word; but **h**, Lam 1:18
And whether they **h** or refuse to hear (for Ezk 2:5
they hear or refuse to **h** (for they are a Ezk 2:5
to them, whether they **h** or refuse to hear, Ezk 2:7
to them, whether they hear or refuse to **h**, Ezk 2:7
you, son of man, **h** what I say to you. Ezk 2:8
in your heart, and **h** with your ears. Ezk 3:10
GOD,' whether they **h** or refuse to hear." Ezk 3:11
GOD,' whether they hear or refuse to **h**." Ezk 3:11
Whenever you **h** a word from my Ezk 3:17
He who will **h**, let him hear; and he who Ezk 3:27
He who will hear, let him **h**; and he who Ezk 3:27
and he who will refuse to **h**, let him Ezk 3:27
of Israel, **h** the word of the Lord GOD! Ezk 6:3
with a loud voice, I will not **h** them." Ezk 8:18
to see, but see not, who have ears to **h**, Ezk 12:2
not, who have ears to hear, but **h** not, Ezk 12:2
own hearts: '**H** the word of the LORD!' Ezk 13:2
O prostitute, **h** the word of the LORD: Ezk 16:35
H now, O house of Israel: Is my way Ezk 18:25
of the Negeb, **H** the word of the LORD: Ezk 20:47
H the word of the Lord GOD: Ezk 25:3
Whenever you **h** a word from my Ezk 33:7
and **h** what the word is that comes Ezk 33:30
and they **h** what you say but they will Ezk 33:31
instrument, for they **h** what you say, Ezk 33:32
you shepherds, **h** the word of the LORD: Ezk 34:7
you shepherds, **h** the word of the LORD: Ezk 34:9
of Israel, **h** the word of the LORD. Ezk 36:1
of Israel, **h** the word of the Lord GOD: Ezk 36:4
not let you **h** anymore the reproach Ezk 36:15
O dry bones, **h** the word of the LORD. Ezk 37:4
with your eyes, and **h** with your ears, Ezk 40:4
and **h** with your ears all that I shall tell Ezk 44:5
that when you **h** the sound of the horn, Dn 3:5
are ready when you **h** the sound of the Dn 3:15
stone, which do not see or **h** or know, Dn 5:23
O my God, incline your ear and **h**. Open Dn 9:18
O Lord, **h**; O Lord, forgive. O Lord, pay Dn 9:19
H the word of the LORD, O children of Hos 4:1
H this, O priests! Pay attention, O house Hos 5:1
H this, you elders; give ear, all inhabitants Jl 1:2
H this word that the LORD has spoken Am 3:1
"**H**, and testify against the house of Am 3:13
"**H** this word, you cows of Bashan, who Am 4:1
H this word that I take up over you in Am 5:1
Now therefore **h** the word of the LORD. Am 7:16
H this, you who trample on the needy Am 8:4
H, you peoples, all of you; pay attention, O Mi 1:2
H, you heads of Jacob and rulers of the Mi 3:1
H this, you heads of the house of Jacob Mi 3:9
H what the LORD says: Arise, plead your Mi 6:1
mountains, and let the hills **h** your voice. Mi 6:1
H, you mountains, the indictment of the Mi 6:2
"**H** of the rod and of him who appointed Mi 6:9
God of my salvation; my God will **h** me. Mi 7:7
All who **h** the news about you clap their Na 3:19
shall I cry for help, and you will not **h**? Hab 1:2
I **h**, and my body trembles; my lips Hab 3:16
But they did not **h** or pay attention to me, Zec 1:4
H now, O Joshua the high priest, you and Zec 3:8
stopped their ears that they might not **h**. Zec 7:11
lest they should **h** the law and Zec 7:12
"As I called, and they would not **h**, so Zec 7:13
and I would not **h**," says the LORD of Zec 7:13
in the light, and what you **h** whispered, Mt 10:27
"Go and tell John what you **h** and see: Mt 11:4
walk, lepers are cleansed and the deaf **h**, Mt 11:5
He who has ears to **h**, let him hear. Mt 11:15
He who has ears to hear, let him **h**. Mt 11:15
nor will anyone **h** his voice in the Mt 12:19
of the earth to **h** the wisdom of Mt 12:42
He who has ears, let him **h**." Mt 13:9
do not see, and hearing they do not **h**, Mt 13:13
"'You will indeed **h** but never Mt 13:14
and with their ears they can barely **h**, Mt 13:15
with their eyes and **h** with their ears Mt 13:15
for they see, and your ears, for they **h**. Mt 13:16
did not see it, and to **h** what you hear, Mt 13:17
did not see it, and to hear what you **h**, Mt 13:17
to hear what you hear, and did not **h** it. Mt 13:17
"**H** then the parable of the sower: Mt 13:18
Father. He who has ears, let him **h**. Mt 13:43
and said to them, "**H** and understand: Mt 15:10
"Do you **h** what these are saying?" And Mt 21:16
"**H** another parable. There was a Mt 21:33
And you will **h** of wars and rumors of Mt 24:6
"Do you not **h** how many things they Mt 27:13
And he said, "He who has ears to **h**, let Mk 4:9
"He who has ears to hear, let him **h**." Mk 4:9
and may indeed **h** but not understand, Mk 4:12
when they **h**, Satan immediately comes Mk 4:15
the ones who, when they **h** the word, Mk 4:16
thorns. They are those who **h** the word, Mk 4:18
are the ones who **h** the word and accept Mk 4:20
If anyone has ears to **h**, let him hear." Mk 4:23
If anyone has ears to hear, let him **h**." Mk 4:23
to them, "Pay attention to what you **h**: Mk 4:24
word to them, as they were able to **h** it. Mk 4:33
to him again and said to them, "**H** me, Mk 7:14
even makes the deaf **h** and the mute Mk 7:37
not see, and having ears do you not **h**? Mk 8:18
"The most important is, '**H**, O Israel: Mk 12:29
And when you **h** of wars and rumors of Mk 13:7
was surprised to **h** that he should Mk 15:44
pressing in on him to **h** the word of God, Lk 5:1
great crowds gathered to **h** him and to Lk 5:15
who came to **h** him and to be healed of Lk 6:18
"But I say to you who **h**, Love your Lk 6:27
walk, lepers are cleansed, and the deaf **h**, Lk 7:22
he called out, "He who has ears to **h**, Lk 8:8
out, "He who has ears to hear, let him **h**." Lk 8:8
are those who, when they **h** the word, Lk 8:13
among the thorns, they are those who **h**, Lk 8:14
Take care then how you **h**, for to the one Lk 8:18
brothers are those who **h** the word of Lk 8:21
this about whom I **h** such things?" And Lk 9:9
did not see it, and to **h** what you hear, Lk 10:24
did not see it, and to hear what you **h**, Lk 10:24
hear what you hear, and did not **h** it." Lk 10:24
rather are those who **h** the word of God Lk 11:28
of the earth to **h** the wisdom of Lk 11:31
He who has ears to **h**, let him hear." Lk 14:35
He who has ears to hear, let him **h**." Lk 14:35
sinners were all drawing near to **h** him. Lk 15:1
to him, 'What is this that I **h** about you? Lk 16:2
and the Prophets; let them **h** them.' Lk 16:29
'If they do not **h** Moses and the Lk 16:31
"**H** what the unrighteous judge says. Lk 18:6
And when you **h** of wars and tumults, Lk 21:9
came to him in the temple to **h** him. Lk 21:38
where it wishes, and you **h** its sound, Jn 3:8
when the dead will **h** the voice of the Son Jn 5:25

the Son of God, and those who **h** will live. Jn 5:25
all who are in the tombs will **h** his voice Jn 5:28
As I **h**, I judge, and my judgment is just, Jn 5:30
because you cannot bear to **h** my word. Jn 8:43
why you do not **h** them is that you Jn 8:47
listen. Why do you want to **h** it again? Jn 9:27
gatekeeper opens. The sheep **h** his voice, Jn 10:3
My sheep **h** my voice, and I know them, Jn 10:27
I knew that you always **h** me, but I said Jn 11:42
the word that you **h** is not mine but Jn 14:24
And how is it that we **h**, each of us in Acts 2:8
and Arabians—we **h** them telling in Acts 2:11
"Men of Israel, **h** these words: Jesus of Acts 2:22
said: "Brothers and fathers, **h** me. Acts 7:2
his house and to **h** what you have to Acts 10:22
presence of God to **h** all that you have Acts 10:33
Saul and sought to **h** the word of God. Acts 13:7
whole city gathered to **h** the word of Acts 13:44
the Gentiles should **h** the word of Acts 15:7
"We will **h** you again about this." Acts 17:32
And you see and **h** that not only in Acts 19:26
They will certainly **h** that you have Acts 21:22
h the defense that I now make before Acts 22:1
Righteous One and to **h** a voice from Acts 22:14
you in your kindness to **h** us briefly. Acts 24:4
"I would like to **h** the man myself." Acts 25:22
said he, "you will **h** him." Acts 25:22
but also all who **h** me this day might Acts 26:29
But we desire to **h** from you what Acts 28:22
You will indeed **h** but never Acts 28:26
and with their ears they can barely **h**, Acts 28:27
with their eyes and **h** with their ears Acts 28:27
are they to **h** without someone Rom 10:14
not see and ears that would not **h**, Rom 11:8
I **h** that there are divisions among 1 Cor 11:18
that it may give grace to those who **h**. Eph 4:29
I may **h** of you that you are standing Phil 1:27
saw I had and now **h** that I still have. Phil 1:30
For we **h** that some among you 2 Thes 3:11
and all the Gentiles might **h** it. 2 Tm 4:17
because I **h** of your love and of the Phlm 1:5
Spirit says, "Today, if you **h** his voice, Heb 3:7
As it is said, "Today, if you **h** his voice, Heb 3:15
quoted, "Today, if you **h** his voice, Heb 4:7
let every person be quick to **h**, slow to Jas 1:19
greater joy than to **h** that my children 3 Jn 1:4
prophecy, and blessed are those who **h**, Rv 1:3
let him **h** what the Spirit says to the Rv 2:7
let him **h** what the Spirit says to the Rv 2:11
let him **h** what the Spirit says to the Rv 2:17
let him **h** what the Spirit says to the Rv 2:29
let him **h** what the Spirit says to the Rv 3:6
let him **h** what the Spirit says to the Rv 3:13
let him **h** what the Spirit says to the Rv 3:22
wood, which cannot see or **h** or walk, Rv 9:20
If anyone has an ear, let him **h**: Rv 13:9

HEARD (600)
And they **h** the sound of the LORD God Gn 3:8
said, "I **h** the sound of you in the garden, Gn 3:10
When Abram **h** that his kinsman had Gn 14:14
As for Ishmael, I have **h** you; behold, I Gn 17:20
And God **h** the voice of the boy, and the Gn 21:17
for God has **h** the voice of the boy Gn 21:17
me, and I have not **h** of it until today." Gn 21:26
and **h** the words of Rebekah his sister, Gn 24:30
Abraham's servant **h** their words, Gn 24:52
"I **h** your father speak to your brother Gn 27:6
As soon as Esau **h** the words of his Gn 27:34
As soon as Laban **h** the news about Gn 29:13
"Because the LORD has **h** that I am Gn 29:33
and has also **h** my voice and given me a Gn 30:6
Now Jacob **h** that the sons of Laban Gn 31:1
Now Jacob **h** that he had defiled his Gn 34:5
in from the field as soon as they **h** of it, Gn 34:7
father's concubine. And Israel **h** of it. Gn 35:22
have gone away, for I **h** them say, Gn 37:17
But when Reuben **h** it, he rescued him Gn 37:21
And as soon as he **h** that I lifted up my Gn 39:15
soon as his master **h** the words that his Gn 39:19
I have **h** it said of you that when you Gn 41:15
I have **h** that there is grain for sale in Gn 42:2
for they **h** that they should eat bread Gn 43:25
he wept aloud, so that the Egyptians **h** it, Gn 45:2
it, and the household of Pharaoh **h** it. Gn 45:2
the report was **h** in Pharaoh's house, Gn 45:16
When Pharaoh **h** of it, he sought to kill Ex 2:15
And God **h** their groaning, and God Ex 2:24
in Egypt and have **h** their cry because of Ex 3:7
and when they **h** that the LORD had Ex 4:31
I have **h** the groaning of the people of Ex 6:5
The peoples have **h**; they tremble; Ex 15:14
because he has **h** your grumbling Ex 16:7
the LORD has **h** your grumbling that Ex 16:8
the LORD, for he has **h** your grumbling.'" Ex 16:9
"I have **h** the grumbling of the people of Ex 16:12
h of all that God had done for Moses and Ex 18:1
other gods, nor let it be **h** on your lips. Ex 23:13
its sound shall be **h** when he goes into Ex 28:35
When Joshua **h** the noise of the people Ex 32:17
When the people **h** this disastrous word, Ex 33:4
And when Moses **h** that, he approved. Lv 10:20
and let all who **h** him lay their hands Lv 24:14
he **h** the voice speaking to him from Nm 7:89
misfortunes, and when the LORD **h** it, Nm 11:1
Moses **h** the people weeping Nm 11:10
through us also?" And the LORD **h** it. Nm 12:2
of this land. They have **h** that you, Nm 14:14
nations who have **h** your fame will Nm 14:15
I have **h** the grumblings of the people Nm 14:27
When Moses **h** it, he fell on his face, Nm 16:4
he **h** our voice and sent an angel and Nm 20:16
h that Israel was coming by the way of Nm 21:1
When Balak **h** that Balaam had Nm 22:36
and her husband **h** of it and said Nm 30:11
to her on the day that he **h** of them. Nm 30:14
null and void after he has **h** of them, Nm 30:15
h of the coming of the people of Israel. Nm 33:40
"And the LORD **h** your words and was Dt 1:34
You **h** the sound of words, but saw no Dt 4:12
this has ever happened or was ever **h** of. Dt 4:32
out of the midst of the fire, as you have **h**, Dt 4:33
and you **h** his words out of the midst of Dt 4:36
And as soon as you **h** the voice out of the Dt 5:23
and we have **h** his voice out of the midst Dt 5:24
that has **h** the voice of the living God Dt 5:26
"And the LORD **h** your words, when you Dt 5:28
to me, 'I have **h** the words of this people, Dt 5:28
know, and of whom you have **h** it said, Dt 9:2
and the LORD **h** our voice and saw our Dt 26:7
For we have **h** how the LORD dried up the Jos 2:10
And as soon as we **h** it, our hearts Jos 2:11
h that the LORD had dried up the waters of Jos 5:1
shall not shout or make your voice **h**, Jos 6:10
As soon as the people **h** the sound of the Jos 6:20
the Hivites, and the Jebusites, **h** of this, Jos 9:1
inhabitants of Gibeon **h** what Joshua had Jos 9:3
For we have **h** a report of him, and all Jos 9:9
they **h** that they were their neighbors Jos 9:16
h how Joshua had captured Ai and had Jos 10:1
When Jabin, king of Hazor, **h** of this, he Jos 11:1
for you **h** on that day how the Anakim Jos 14:12
And the people of Israel **h** it said, Jos 22:11
And when the people of Israel **h** of it, Jos 22:12
h the words that the people of Reuben Jos 22:30
for it has **h** all the words of the LORD Jos 24:27
As soon as Gideon **h** the telling of the Jgs 7:15
the ruler of the city **h** the words of Gaal Jgs 9:30
leaders of the Tower of Shechem **h** of it, Jgs 9:46
"Do not let your voice be **h** among us, Jgs 18:25
the people of Benjamin **h** that the people Jgs 20:3
for she had **h** in the fields of Moab that Ru 1:6
lips moved, and her voice was not **h**. 1 Sm 1:13
And when the Philistines **h** the noise of 1 Sm 4:6
When Eli **h** the sound of the outcry, 1 Sm 4:14
And when she **h** the news that the ark 1 Sm 4:19
when the Philistines **h** that the people 1 Sm 7:7
And when the people of Israel **h** of it, 1 Sm 7:7
And when Samuel had **h** all the words 1 Sm 8:21
upon Saul when he **h** these words, 1 Sm 11:6
at Geba, and the Philistines **h** of it. 1 Sm 13:3
And all Israel **h** it said that Saul had 1 Sm 13:4
country of Ephraim **h** that the 1 Sm 14:22
Jonathan had not **h** his father 1 Sm 14:27
Saul and all Israel **h** these words of 1 Sm 17:11
words as before. And David **h** him. 1 Sm 17:23
his eldest brother **h** when he spoke 1 Sm 17:28
the words that David spoke were **h**, 1 Sm 17:31
and all his father's house **h** it, 1 Sm 22:1
Now Saul **h** that David was 1 Sm 22:6
servant has surely **h** that Saul seeks 1 Sm 23:10
come down, as your servant has **h**? 1 Sm 23:11
And when Saul **h** that, he pursued 1 Sm 23:25
David **h** in the wilderness that Nabal 1 Sm 25:4
When David **h** that Nabal was dead, 1 Sm 25:39
of Jabesh-gilead **h** what the 1 Sm 31:11
Afterward, when David **h** of it, he said, 2 Sm 3:28
son, **h** that Abner had died at Hebron, 2 Sm 4:1
When the Philistines **h** that David 2 Sm 5:17
But David **h** of it and went down to the 2 Sm 5:17
to all that we have **h** with our ears. 2 Sm 7:22
Toi king of Hamath **h** that David had 2 Sm 8:9
And when David **h** of it, he sent Joab 2 Sm 10:7
the wife of Uriah **h** that Uriah her 2 Sm 11:26
When King David **h** of all these 2 Sm 13:21
And all the people **h** when the king 2 Sm 18:5
the people, for the people **h** that day, 2 Sm 19:2
From his temple he **h** my voice, and 2 Sm 22:7
as soon as they **h** of me, they obeyed 2 Sm 22:45
"Have you not **h** that Adonijah the 1 Kgs 1:11
who were with him **h** it as they 1 Kgs 1:41
And when Joab **h** the sound of the 1 Kgs 1:41
This is the noise that you have **h**. 1 Kgs 1:45
And all Israel **h** of the judgment that 1 Kgs 3:28
the earth, who had **h** of his wisdom. 1 Kgs 4:34
to Solomon when he **h** that they had 1 Kgs 5:1
As soon as Hiram **h** the words of 1 Kgs 5:7
"I have **h** the message that you have 1 Kgs 5:8
tool of iron was **h** in the house while 1 Kgs 6:7
"I have **h** your prayer and your plea, 1 Kgs 9:3
the queen of Sheba **h** of the fame of 1 Kgs 10:1
was true that I **h** in my own land 1 Kgs 10:6
prosperity surpass the report that I **h**. 1 Kgs 10:7
But when Hadad **h** in Egypt that 1 Kgs 11:21
the son of Nebat **h** of it (for he 1 Kgs 12:2
when all Israel **h** that Jeroboam had 1 Kgs 12:20
And when the king **h** the saying of 1 Kgs 13:4
him back from the way **h** of it, 1 Kgs 13:26
But when Ahijah **h** the sound of her 1 Kgs 14:6
And when Baasha **h** of it, he stopped 1 Kgs 15:21
troops who were encamped **h** it said, 1 Kgs 16:16
And when Elijah **h** it, he wrapped 1 Kgs 19:13
When Ben-hadad **h** this message as 1 Kgs 20:12
we have **h** that the kings of the 1 Kgs 20:31
soon as Jezebel **h** that Naboth had 1 Kgs 21:15
as soon as Ahab **h** that Naboth was 1 Kgs 21:16
And when Ahab **h** those words, he 1 Kgs 21:27
all the Moabites **h** that the kings 2 Kgs 3:21
the man of God **h** that the king of 2 Kgs 5:8
When the king **h** the words of the 2 Kgs 6:30
there was no one to be seen or **h** there, 2 Kgs 7:10
Jehu came to Jezreel, Jezebel **h** of it. 2 Kgs 9:30
When Athaliah **h** the noise of the 2 Kgs 11:13
As soon as King Hezekiah **h** it, he tore 2 Kgs 19:1
the LORD your God **h** all the words of 2 Kgs 19:4
words that the LORD your God has **h**; 2 Kgs 19:4
because of the words that you have **h**, 2 Kgs 19:6
for he **h** that the king had left 2 Kgs 19:8
the king **h** concerning Tirhakah 2 Kgs 19:9
you have **h** what the kings of 2 Kgs 19:11
king of Assyria I have **h**. 2 Kgs 19:20
"Have you not **h** that I determined it 2 Kgs 19:25
your father: I have **h** your prayer; 2 Kgs 20:5
for he **h** that Hezekiah had been 2 Kgs 20:12
When the king **h** the words of the 2 Kgs 22:11
the words that you have **h**, 2 Kgs 22:18
when you **h** how I spoke against this 2 Kgs 22:19
wept before me, I also have **h** you, 2 Kgs 22:19
and their men **h** that the king 2 Kgs 25:23
when all Jabesh-gilead **h** all that the 1 Chr 10:11
When the Philistines **h** that David 1 Chr 14:8
But David **h** of it and went out 1 Chr 14:8
to all that we have **h** with our ears. 1 Chr 17:20
king of Hamath **h** that David had 1 Chr 18:9
When David **h** of it, he sent Joab and 1 Chr 19:8
to make themselves **h** in unison in 2 Chr 5:13
"I have **h** your prayer and have 2 Chr 7:12
the queen of Sheba **h** of the fame of 2 Chr 9:1
was true that I **h** in my own land 2 Chr 9:5
me; you surpass the report that I **h**. 2 Chr 9:6
the son of Nebat **h** of it (for he 2 Chr 10:2
As soon as Asa **h** these words, the 2 Chr 15:8
And when Baasha **h** of it, he stopped 2 Chr 16:5
countries when they **h** that the LORD 2 Chr 20:29
When Athaliah **h** the noise of the 2 Chr 23:12
And the LORD **h** Hezekiah and 2 Chr 30:20
the people, and their voice was **h**, 2 Chr 30:27
by his entreaty and **h** his plea and 2 Chr 33:13
And when the king **h** the words of 2 Chr 34:19
the words that you have **h**, 2 Chr 34:26
God when you **h** his words against 2 Chr 34:27
wept before me, I also have **h** you, 2 Chr 34:27
shout, and the sound was **h** far away. Ezr 3:13
Judah and Benjamin **h** that the returned Ezr 4:1
As soon as I **h** this, I tore my garment Ezr 9:3
As soon as I **h** these words I sat down Neh 1:4
Tobiah, the Ammonite servant, **h** this, Neh 2:10
servant and Geshem the Arab **h** of it, Neh 2:19
Now when Sanballat **h** that we were Neh 4:1
and the Ashdodites **h** that the repairing Neh 4:7
When our enemies **h** that it was Neh 4:15
very angry when I **h** their outcry and Neh 5:6
the rest of our enemies **h** that I had built Neh 6:1
And when all our enemies **h** of it, all Neh 6:16
all who could understand what they **h**, Neh 8:2
people wept as they **h** the words of the Neh 8:9
fathers in Egypt and **h** their cry at the Neh 9:9
to you and you **h** them from heaven, Neh 9:27
and cried to you, you **h** from heaven, Neh 9:28
the joy of Jerusalem was **h** far away. Neh 12:43
As soon as the people **h** the law, they Neh 13:3
and Media who have **h** of the queen's Est 1:18
when Job's three friends **h** of all this evil Jb 2:11
eyes; there was silence, then I **h** a voice: Jb 4:16
all this, my ear has **h** and understood it. Jb 13:1
"I have **h** many such things; miserable Jb 16:2

'We have **h** a rumor of it with our ears.' Jb 28:22
When the ear **h**, it called me blessed, Jb 29:11
and I have **h** the sound of your words. Jb 33:8
him, and he **h** the cry of the afflicted— Jb 34:28
the lightnings when his voice is **h**. Jb 37:4
I had **h** of you by the hearing of the ear, Jb 42:5
for the LORD has **h** the sound of my Ps 6:8
The LORD has **h** my plea; the LORD accepts Ps 6:9
From his temple he **h** my voice, and my Ps 18:6
As soon as they **h** of me they obeyed me; Ps 18:44
nor are there words, whose voice is not **h**. Ps 19:3
hidden his face from him, but has **h**, Ps 22:24
for he has **h** the voice of my pleas for Ps 28:6
your sight." But you **h** the voice of my Ps 31:22
and the LORD **h** him and saved him out of Ps 34:6
LORD; he inclined to me and **h** my cry. Ps 40:1
O God, we have **h** with our ears, our Ps 44:1
As we have **h**, so have we seen in the city Ps 48:8
For you, O God, have **h** my vows; you Ps 61:5
God has spoken; twice have I **h** this: Ps 62:11
O peoples; let the sound of his praise be **h**, Ps 66:8
things that we have **h** and known, that Ps 78:3
Therefore, when the LORD **h**, he was full Ps 78:21
When God **h**, he was full of wrath, and Ps 78:59
my ears have **h** the doom of my evil Ps 92:11
their distress, when he **h** their cry. Ps 106:44
because he has **h** my voice and my Ps 116:1
Behold, we **h** of it in Ephrathah; we Ps 132:6
for they have **h** the words of your Ps 138:4
is despised and his words are not **h**. Eccl 9:16
words of the wise **h** in quiet are better Eccl 9:17
The end of the matter; all has been **h**. Eccl 12:13
voice of the turtledove is **h** in our land. Sg 2:12
And I **h** the voice of the Lord saying, Is 6:8
cry out; their voice is **h** as far as Jahaz; Is 15:4
We have **h** of the pride of Moab— Is 16:6
what I have **h** from the LORD of hosts, Is 21:10
for I have **h** a decree of destruction from Is 28:22
voice to be **h** and the descending Is 30:30
As soon as King Hezekiah **h** it, he tore his Is 37:1
the words that the LORD your God has **h**; Is 37:4
because of the words that you have **h**, Is 37:6
for he had **h** that the king had left Is 37:8
Now the king **h** concerning Tirhakah Is 37:9
to fight against you." And when he **h** it, Is 37:9
you have **h** what the kings of Assyria Is 37:11
"'Have you not **h** that I determined it Is 37:26
David your father: I have **h** your prayer; Is 38:5
for he **h** that he had been sick and had Is 39:1
Have you not known? Have you not **h**? Is 40:28
proclaimed, none who **h** your words. Is 41:26
lift up his voice, or make it **h** in the street; Is 42:2
"You have **h**; now see all this; and will Is 48:6
before today you have never **h** of them, Is 48:7
You have never **h**, you have never Is 48:8
which they have not **h** they understand. Is 52:15
Who has believed what they **h** from us? Is 53:1
will not make your voice to be **h** on high. Is 58:4
shall no more be **h** in your land, Is 60:18
of old no one has **h** or perceived by the Is 64:4
no more shall be **h** in it the sound of Is 65:19
Who has **h** such a thing? Who has seen Is 66:8
that have not **h** my fame or seen my Is 66:19
A voice on the bare heights is **h**, the Jer 3:21
For I **h** a cry as of a woman in labor, Jer 4:31
violence and destruction are **h** within her; Jer 6:7
We have **h** the report of it; our hands fall Jer 6:24
snorting of their horses is **h** from Dan; Jer 8:16
and the lowing of cattle is not **h**; Jer 9:10
For a sound of wailing is **h** from Zion: Jer 9:19
the nations, Who has **h** the like of this? Jer 18:13
May a cry be **h** from their houses, Jer 18:22
h Jeremiah prophesying these things. Jer 20:1
I have **h** what the prophets have said Jer 23:25
all the people **h** Jeremiah speaking these Jer 26:7
the officials of Judah **h** these things, Jer 26:10
as you have **h** with your own ears." Jer 26:11
and this city all the words you have **h**. Jer 26:12
and all the officials, **h** his words, Jer 26:21
But when Uriah **h** of it, he was afraid Jer 26:21
We have **h** a cry of panic, of terror, and Jer 30:5
"A voice is **h** in Ramah, lamentation Jer 31:15
I have **h** Ephraim grieving, 'You have Jer 31:18
or beast, there shall be **h** again Jer 33:10
h all the words of the LORD from the Jer 36:11
told them all the words that he had **h**, Jer 36:13
When they **h** all the words, they turned Jer 36:16
of his servants who **h** all these words Jer 36:24
were besieging Jerusalem **h** news about Jer 37:5
the son of Malchiah **h** the words that Jer 38:1
h that they had put Jeremiah into the Jer 38:7
country and their men **h** that the king of Jer 40:7
and in other lands **h** that the king of Jer 40:11
of the forces with him **h** of all the evil Jer 41:11
the prophet said to them, "I have **h** you. Jer 42:4
The nations have **h** of your shame, and Jer 46:12
Horonaim they have **h** the distressed cry Jer 48:5
We have **h** of the pride of Moab—he is Jer 48:29
battle cry to be **h** against Rabbah of the Jer 49:2
I have **h** a message from the LORD, and Jer 49:14
of their cry shall be **h** at the Red Sea. Jer 49:21
confounded, for they have **h** bad news; Jer 49:23
"The king of Babylon **h** the report of Jer 50:43
her cry shall be **h** among the nations." Jer 50:46
not fearful at the report **h** in the land, Jer 51:46
put to shame, for we have **h** reproach; Jer 51:51
"They **h** my groaning, yet there is no Lam 1:21
All my enemies have **h** of my trouble; Lam 1:21
you **h** my plea, 'Do not close your ear Lam 3:56
"You have **h** their taunts, O LORD, all Lam 3:61
I **h** the sound of their wings like the Ezk 1:24
face, and I **h** the voice of one speaking. Ezk 1:28
on my feet, and I **h** him speaking to me. Ezk 2:2
and I **h** behind me the voice of a great Ezk 3:12
of the cherubim was **h** as far as the Ezk 10:5
The nations **h** about him; he was Ezk 19:4
should no more be **h** on the mountains Ezk 19:9
of your lyres shall be **h** no more. Ezk 26:13
He **h** the sound of the trumpet and did Ezk 33:5
"I have **h** all the revilings that you Ezk 35:12
your words against me; I **h** it. Ezk 35:13
I **h** one speaking to me out of the Ezk 43:6
soon as all the peoples **h** the sound of the Dn 3:7
I have **h** of you that the spirit of the gods Dn 5:14
But I have **h** that you can give Dn 5:16
Then the king, when he **h** these words, Dn 6:14
Then I **h** a holy one speaking, and Dn 8:13
And I **h** a man's voice between the Dn 8:16
Then I **h** the sound of his words, and as I Dn 10:9
words, and as I **h** the sound of his words, Dn 10:9
your God, your words have been **h**, Dn 10:12
And I **h** the man clothed in linen, who Dn 12:7
I **h**, but I did not understand. Then I Dn 12:8
We have **h** a report from the LORD, and a Ob 1:1
of Sheol I cried, and you **h** my voice. Jon 2:2
of your messengers shall no longer be **h**. Na 2:13
O LORD, I have **h** the report of you, and Hab 3:2
"a cry will be **h** from the Fish Gate, Zep 1:10
"I have **h** the taunts of Moab and the Zep 2:8
for we have **h** that God is with you.'" Zec 8:23
The LORD paid attention and **h** them, Mal 3:16
When Herod the king **h** this, he was Mt 2:3
"A voice was **h** in Ramah, weeping and Mt 2:18
But when he **h** that Archelaus was Mt 2:22
Now when he **h** that John had been Mt 4:12
"You have **h** that it was said to those of Mt 5:21
"You have **h** that it was said, 'You shall Mt 5:27
"Again you have **h** that it was said to Mt 5:33
"You have **h** that it was said, 'An eye for Mt 5:38
"You have **h** that it was said, 'You shall Mt 5:43
that they will be **h** for their many words. Mt 6:7
When Jesus **h** this, he marveled and said Mt 8:10
But when he **h** it, he said, "Those who Mt 9:12
Now when John **h** in prison about the Mt 11:2
But when the Pharisees **h** it, they said, Mt 12:24
Herod the tetrarch **h** about the fame Mt 14:1
Now when Jesus **h** this, he withdrew Mt 14:13
But when the crowds **h** it, they followed Mt 14:13
offended when they **h** this saying?" Mt 15:12
When the disciples **h** this, they fell on Mt 17:6
When the young man **h** this he went Mt 19:22
When the disciples **h** this, they were Mt 19:25
And when the ten **h** it, they were Mt 20:24
and when they **h** that Jesus was passing Mt 20:30
and the Pharisees **h** his parables, Mt 21:45
When they **h** it, they marveled. And Mt 22:22
And when the crowd **h** it, they were Mt 22:33
But when the Pharisees **h** that he had Mt 22:34
need? You have now **h** his blasphemy. Mt 26:65
And when Jesus **h** it, he said to them, Mk 2:17
When the great crowd **h** all that he was Mk 3:8
And when his family **h** it, they went out Mk 3:21
She had **h** the reports about Jesus and Mk 5:27
and many who **h** him were astonished, Mk 6:2
King Herod **h** of it, for Jesus' name had Mk 6:14
But when Herod **h** of it, he said, "John, Mk 6:16
When he **h** him, he was greatly Mk 6:20
perplexed, and yet he **h** him gladly. Mk 6:20
When his disciples **h** of it, they came Mk 6:29
on their beds to wherever they **h** he was. Mk 6:55
by an unclean spirit **h** of him and Mk 7:25
And when the ten **h** it, they began to Mk 10:41
And when he **h** that it was Jesus of Mk 10:47
you again." And his disciples **h** it. Mk 11:14
priests and the scribes **h** it and were Mk 11:18
came up and **h** them disputing with Mk 12:28
And the great throng **h** him gladly. Mk 12:37
And when they **h** it, they were glad and Mk 14:11
"We **h** him say, 'I will destroy this Mk 14:58
You have **h** his blasphemy. What is Mk 14:64
But when they **h** that he was alive and Mk 16:11
Zechariah, for your prayer has been **h**, Lk 1:13
And when Elizabeth **h** the greeting of Lk 1:41
neighbors and relatives **h** that the Lord Lk 1:58
and all who **h** them laid them up in Lk 1:66
And all who **h** it wondered at what the Lk 2:18
praising God for all they had **h** and seen, Lk 2:20
And all who **h** him were amazed at his Lk 2:47
What we have **h** you did at Capernaum, Lk 4:23
When they **h** these things, all in the Lk 4:28
When the centurion **h** about Jesus, he Lk 7:3
When Jesus **h** these things, he marveled Lk 7:9
and tell John what you have seen and **h**: Lk 7:22
(When all the people **h** this, and the tax Lk 7:29
along the path are those who have **h**. Lk 8:12
Now Herod the tetrarch **h** about all that Lk 9:7
said in the dark shall be **h** in the light, Lk 12:3
at table with him **h** these things, Lk 14:15
to the house, he **h** music and dancing. Lk 15:25
lovers of money, **h** all these things, Lk 16:14
When Jesus **h** this, he said to him, Lk 18:22
But when he **h** these things, he became Lk 18:23
Those who **h** it said, "Then who can be Lk 18:26
As they **h** these things, he proceeded to Lk 19:11
vineyard to others." When they **h** this, Lk 20:16
We have **h** it ourselves from his own Lk 22:71
When Pilate **h** this, he asked whether Lk 23:6
to see him, because he had **h** about him, Lk 23:8
The two disciples **h** him say this, and Jn 1:37
of the two who **h** John speak and followed Jn 1:40
bears witness to what he has seen and **h**, Jn 3:32
that the Pharisees had **h** that Jesus was Jn 4:1
we believe, for we have **h** for ourselves, Jn 4:42
When this man **h** that Jesus had come Jn 4:47
His voice you have never **h**, his form you Jn 5:37
Everyone who has **h** and learned from Jn 6:45
When many of his disciples **h** it, they Jn 6:60
The Pharisees **h** the crowd muttering Jn 7:32
When they **h** these words, some of the Jn 7:40
But when they **h** it, they went away one by Jn 8:9
to the world what I have **h** from him." Jn 8:26
do what you have **h** from your father." Jn 8:38
has told you the truth that I **h** from God. Jn 8:40
began has it been **h** that anyone opened Jn 9:32
Jesus **h** that they had cast him out, and Jn 9:35
of the Pharisees near him **h** these things, Jn 9:40
But when Jesus **h** it he said, "This illness Jn 11:4
So, when he **h** that Lazarus was ill, he Jn 11:6
So when Martha **h** that Jesus was Jn 11:20
And when she **h** it, she rose quickly and Jn 11:29
I thank you that you have **h** me. Jn 11:41
come to the feast **h** that Jesus was Jn 12:12
him was that they **h** he had done this Jn 12:18
that stood there and **h** it said that it Jn 12:29
"We have **h** from the Law that the Jn 12:34
who has believed what he **h** from us, Jn 12:38
You **h** me say to you, 'I am going away, Jn 14:28
for all that I have **h** from my Father I Jn 15:15
Ask those who have **h** me what I said to Jn 18:21
When Pilate **h** this statement, he was Jn 19:8
So when Pilate **h** these words, he Jn 19:13
Lord!" When Simon Peter **h** that it was Jn 21:7
Father, which, he said, "you **h** from me; Acts 1:4
Now when they **h** this they were cut to Acts 2:37
of those who had **h** the word believed, Acts 4:4
but speak of what we have seen and **h**." Acts 4:20
And when they **h** it, they lifted their Acts 4:24
When Ananias **h** these words, he fell Acts 5:5
great fear came upon all who **h** of it. Acts 5:5
and upon all who **h** of these things. Acts 5:11
And when they **h** this, they entered the Acts 5:21
and the chief priests **h** these words, Acts 5:24
When they **h** this, they were enraged Acts 5:33
"We have **h** him speak blasphemous Acts 6:11
for we have **h** him say that this Jesus of Acts 6:14
But when Jacob **h** that there was grain Acts 7:12
in Egypt, and have **h** their groaning, Acts 7:34
Now when they **h** these things they Acts 7:54
by Philip when they **h** him and saw the Acts 8:6
apostles at Jerusalem **h** that Samaria Acts 8:14
ran to him and **h** him reading Isaiah Acts 8:30
to the ground he **h** a voice saying to Acts 9:4
I have **h** from many about this man, Acts 9:13
And all who **h** him were amazed and Acts 9:21
prayer has been **h** and your alms Acts 10:31
Holy Spirit fell on all who **h** the word. Acts 10:44
were throughout Judea **h** that the Acts 11:1
And I **h** a voice saying to me, 'Rise, Acts 11:7
When they **h** these things they fell Acts 11:18
And when the Gentiles **h** this, they Acts 13:48
apostles Barnabas and Paul **h** of it, Acts 14:14
Since we have **h** that some persons Acts 15:24
One who **h** us was a woman named Acts 16:14
afraid when they **h** that they were Acts 16:38
disturbed when they **h** these things. Acts 17:8

Now when they **h** of the resurrection Acts 17:32
when Priscilla and Aquila **h** him, Acts 18:26
we have not even **h** that there is a Holy Acts 19:2
the residents of Asia **h** the word of the Acts 19:10
When they **h** this they were enraged Acts 19:28
When we **h** this, we and the people Acts 21:12
And when they **h** it, they glorified Acts 21:20
And when they **h** that he was Acts 22:2
to the ground and **h** a voice saying to Acts 22:7
of what you have seen and **h**. Acts 22:15
When the centurion **h** this, he went Acts 22:26
of Paul's sister **h** of their ambush, Acts 23:16
sent for Paul and **h** him speak about Acts 24:24
I **h** a voice saying to me in the Acts 26:14
brothers there, when they **h** about us, Acts 28:15
in him of whom they have never **h**? Rom 10:14
has believed what he has **h** from us?" Rom 10:16
But I ask, have they not **h**? Indeed Rom 10:18
who have never **h** will understand." Rom 15:21
"What no eye has seen, nor ear **h**, 1 Cor 2:9
and he **h** things that cannot be told, 2 Cor 12:4
For you have **h** of my former life in Gal 1:13
you also, when you **h** the word of truth, Eph 1:13
because I have **h** of your faith in the Eph 1:15
that you have **h** of the stewardship Eph 3:2
that you have **h** about him and Eph 4:21
distressed because you **h** that he was Phil 2:26
learned and received and **h** and seen in Phil 4:9
since we **h** of your faith in Christ Jesus Col 1:4
Of this you have **h** before in the word of Col 1:5
since the day you **h** it and understood the Col 1:6
And so, from the day we **h**, we have not Col 1:9
from the hope of the gospel that you **h**, Col 1:23
word of God, which you **h** from us, 1 Thes 2:13
words that you have **h** from me, 2 Tm 1:13
and what you have **h** from me in the 2 Tm 2:2
closer attention to what we have **h**, Heb 2:1
and it was attested to us by those who **h**, Heb 2:3
who were those who **h** and yet rebelled? Heb 3:16
but the message they **h** did not benefit Heb 4:2
and he was **h** because of his reverence. Heb 5:7
You have **h** of the steadfastness of Job, Jas 5:11
we ourselves **h** this very voice borne 2 Pt 1:18
their lawless deeds that he saw and **h**); 2 Pt 2:8
from the beginning, which we have **h**, 1 Jn 1:1
we have seen and **h** we proclaim also to 1 Jn 1:3
the message we have **h** from him and 1 Jn 1:5
is the word that you have **h**. 1 Jn 2:7
and as you have **h** that antichrist is 1 Jn 2:18
Let what you **h** from the beginning 1 Jn 2:24
If what you **h** from the beginning 1 Jn 2:24
that you have **h** from the beginning, 1 Jn 3:11
which you **h** was coming and now is in 1 Jn 4:3
just as you have **h** from the beginning, 2 Jn 1:6
and I **h** behind me a loud voice like a Rv 1:10
then, what you received and **h**. Rv 3:3
which I had **h** speaking to me like a Rv 4:1
and I **h** around the throne and the living Rv 5:11
And I **h** every creature in heaven and on Rv 5:13
and I **h** one of the four living creatures Rv 6:1
seal, I **h** the second living creature say, Rv 6:3
third seal, I **h** the third living creature say, Rv 6:5
And I **h** what seemed to be a voice in the Rv 6:6
I **h** the voice of the fourth living creature Rv 6:7
And I **h** the number of the sealed, 144,000, Rv 7:4
and I **h** an eagle crying with a loud voice Rv 8:13
and I **h** a voice from the four horns of Rv 9:13
times ten thousand; I **h** their number. Rv 9:16
but I **h** a voice from heaven saying, Rv 10:4
voice that I had **h** from heaven spoke to Rv 10:8
Then they **h** a loud voice from heaven Rv 11:12
And I **h** a loud voice in heaven, saying, Rv 12:10
And I **h** a voice from heaven like the Rv 14:2
The voice I **h** was like the sound of Rv 14:2
And I **h** a voice from heaven saying, Rv 14:13
Then I **h** a loud voice from the temple Rv 16:1
And I **h** the angel in charge of the waters Rv 16:5
And I **h** the altar saying, "Yes, Lord God Rv 16:7
Then I **h** another voice from heaven Rv 18:4
trumpeters, will be **h** in you no more, Rv 18:22
of the mill will be **h** in you no more, Rv 18:22
and bride will be **h** in you no more, Rv 18:23
After this I **h** what seemed to be the loud Rv 19:1
Then I **h** what seemed to be the voice of a Rv 19:6
And I **h** a loud voice from the throne Rv 21:3
am the one who **h** and saw these things. Rv 22:8
things. And when I **h** and saw them, Rv 22:8

HEARER (2)
For if anyone is a **h** of the word and not Jas 1:23
being no **h** who forgets but a doer who Jas 1:25

HEARERS (5)
For it is not the **h** of the law who are Rom 2:13
will save both yourself and your **h**. 1 Tm 4:16
does no good, but only ruins the **h**. 2 Tm 2:14
whose words made the **h** beg that no Heb 12:19
But be doers of the word, and not **h** only, Jas 1:22

HEARING (68)
Abraham in the **h** of the Hittites, Gn 23:10
said to Ephron in the **h** of the people of Gn 23:13
he had named in the **h** of the Hittites, Gn 23:16
you may tell in the **h** of your son and of Ex 10:2
Speak now in the **h** of the people, that Ex 11:2
and read it in the **h** of the people. Ex 24:7
people complained in the **h** of the LORD Nm 11:1
for you have wept in the **h** of the LORD, Nm 11:18
you have said in my **h** I will do to you: Nm 14:28
and the rules that I speak in your **h** today, Dt 5:1
read this law before all Israel in their **h**. Dt 31:11
words of this song in the **h** of the people, Dt 32:44
and he kept **h** all that his sons were 1 Sm 2:22
for in our **h** the king commanded 2 Sm 18:12
of Judah within the **h** of the people 2 Kgs 18:26
And he read in their **h** all the words of 2 Kgs 23:2
of the LORD, and in the **h** of our God, 1 Chr 28:8
he read in their **h** all the words of 2 Chr 34:30
Book of Moses in the **h** of the people. Neh 13:1
I had heard of you by the **h** of the ear, but Jb 42:5
The **h** ear and the seeing eye, the LORD Prv 20:12
Do not speak in the **h** of a fool, for he Prv 23:9
one turns away his ear from **h** the law, Prv 28:9
with seeing, nor the ear filled with **h**. Eccl 1:8
The LORD of hosts has sworn in my **h**: Is 5:9
people: "'Keep on **h**, but do not understand; Is 6:9
stops his ears from **h** of bloodshed and Is 33:15
of Judah within the **h** of the people who Is 36:11
"Go and proclaim in the **h** of Jerusalem, Jer 2:2
that I speak in your **h** and in the hearing Jer 28:7
hearing and in the **h** of all the people. Jer 28:7
this letter in the **h** of Jeremiah the Jer 29:29
day of fasting in the **h** of all the people in Jer 36:6
read them also in the **h** of all the men of Jer 36:6
Then, in the **h** of all the people, Baruch Jer 36:10
read the scroll in the **h** of the people. Jer 36:13
that you read in the **h** of the people, Jer 36:14
And to the others he said in my **h**, "Pass Ezk 9:5
called in my **h** "the whirling wheels." Ezk 10:13
water, but of **h** the words of the LORD. Am 8:11
these days have been **h** these words from Zec 8:9
they do not see, and **h** they do not hear, Mt 13:13
And some of the bystanders, **h** it, said, Mt 27:47
And some of the bystanders **h** it said, Mk 15:35
Scripture has been fulfilled in your **h**." Lk 4:21
all his sayings in the **h** of the people, Lk 7:1
not see, and **h** they may not understand.' Lk 8:10
good soil, they are those who, **h** the word, Lk 8:15
But Jesus on **h** this answered him, "Do Lk 8:50
And **h** a crowd going by, he inquired Lk 18:36
And in the **h** of all the people he said to Lk 20:45
first giving him a **h** and learning what Jn 7:51
because each one was **h** them speak in Acts 2:6
that you yourselves are seeing and **h**. Acts 2:33
h the voice but seeing no one. Acts 9:7
the disciples, **h** that Peter was there, Acts 9:38
For they were **h** them speaking in Acts 10:46
except telling or **h** something new. Acts 17:21
of the Corinthians **h** Paul believed and Acts 18:8
On **h** this, they were baptized in the Acts 19:5
will give you a **h** when your accusers Acts 23:35
So faith comes from **h**, and hearing Rom 10:17
and **h** through the word of Christ. Rom 10:17
eye, where would be the sense of **h**? 1 Cor 12:17
They only were **h** it said, "He who used Gal 1:23
by works of the law or by **h** with faith? Gal 3:2
by works of the law, or by **h** with faith— Gal 3:5
since you have become dull of **h**. Heb 5:11

HEARS (57)
everyone who **h** will laugh over me." Gn 21:6
sins in that he **h** a public adjuration to Lv 5:1
oracle of him who **h** the words of God, Nm 24:4
oracle of him who **h** the words of God, Nm 24:16
and her father **h** of her vow and of her Nm 30:4
opposes her on the day that he **h** of it, Nm 30:5
and her husband **h** of it and says Nm 30:7
nothing to her on the day that he **h**, Nm 30:7
and void on the day that he **h** them, Nm 30:12
when he **h** the words of this sworn Dt 29:19
for your servant **h**.'" So Samuel went 1 Sm 3:9
said, "Speak, for your servant **h**." 1 Sm 3:10
ears of everyone who **h** it will tingle. 1 Sm 3:11
If Saul **h** it, he will kill me." And the 1 Sm 16:2
the first attack, whoever **h** it will say, 2 Sm 17:9
ears of everyone who **h** of it will 2 Kgs 21:12
and the wise man who **h** me will say: Jb 34:34
the city; he **h** not the shouts of the driver. Jb 39:7
for himself; the LORD **h** when I call to him. Ps 4:3
the LORD **h** and delivers them out of all Ps 34:17
and moan, and he **h** my voice. Ps 55:17
O you who **h** prayer, to you shall all flesh Ps 65:2
For the LORD **h** the needy and does not Ps 69:33
Zion **h** and is glad, and the daughters of Ps 97:8
he also **h** their cry and saves them. Ps 145:19
A wise son **h** his father's instruction, Prv 13:1
his wealth, but a poor man **h** no threat. Prv 13:8
but he **h** the prayer of the righteous. Prv 15:29
If one gives an answer before he **h**, it is Prv 18:13
the word of a man who **h** will endure. Prv 21:28
lest he who **h** you bring shame upon Prv 25:10
he **h** the curse, but discloses nothing. Prv 29:24
cry. As soon as he **h** it, he answers you. Is 30:19
ears of everyone who **h** of it will tingle. Jer 19:3
then if anyone who **h** the sound of the Ezk 33:4
that every man who **h** the sound of the Dn 3:10
"Everyone then who **h** these words of Mt 7:24
And everyone who **h** these words of Mt 7:26
When anyone **h** the word of the Mt 13:19
is the one who **h** the word and Mt 13:20
thorns, this is the one who **h** the word, Mt 13:22
is the one who **h** the word and Mt 13:23
comes to me and **h** my words and does Lk 6:47
But the one who **h** and does not do them Lk 6:49
"The one who **h** you hears me, and the Lk 10:16
"The one who hears you **h** me, and the Lk 10:16
the bridegroom, who stands and **h** him, Jn 3:29
whoever **h** my word and believes him Jn 5:24
Whoever is of God **h** the words of God. Jn 8:47
If anyone **h** my words and does not keep Jn 12:47
but whatever he **h** he will speak, Jn 16:13
me than he sees in me or **h** from me. 2 Cor 12:6
anything according to his will he **h** us. 1 Jn 5:14
if we know that he **h** us in whatever we 1 Jn 5:15
If anyone **h** my voice and opens the door, Rv 3:20
say, "Come." And let the one who **h** say, Rv 22:17
I warn everyone who **h** the words of the Rv 22:18

HEART (757)
the thoughts of his **h** was only evil Gn 6:5
on the earth, and it grieved him to his **h**. Gn 6:6
pleasing aroma, the LORD said in his **h**, Gn 8:21
the intention of man's **h** is evil from his Gn 8:21
the integrity of my **h** and the innocence Gn 20:5
have done this in the integrity of your **h**, Gn 20:6
I had finished speaking in my **h**, Gn 24:45
of Egypt." And his **h** became numb, Gn 45:26
he sees you, he will be glad in his **h**. Ex 4:14
But I will harden his **h**, so that he will Ex 4:21
But I will harden Pharaoh's **h**, and Ex 7:3
Still Pharaoh's **h** was hardened, and he Ex 7:13
said to Moses, "Pharaoh's **h** is hardened; Ex 7:14
arts. So Pharaoh's **h** remained hardened, Ex 7:22
house, and he did not take even this to **h**. Ex 7:23
he hardened his **h** and would not listen Ex 8:15
of God." But Pharaoh's **h** was hardened, Ex 8:19
Pharaoh hardened his **h** this time also, Ex 8:32
But the **h** of Pharaoh was hardened, and Ex 9:7
But the LORD hardened the **h** of Pharaoh, Ex 9:12
he sinned yet again and hardened his **h**, Ex 9:34
So the **h** of Pharaoh was hardened, and Ex 9:35
I have hardened his **h** and the heart of Ex 10:1
his heart and the **h** of his servants, Ex 10:1
But the LORD hardened Pharaoh's **h**, Ex 10:20
But the LORD hardened Pharaoh's **h**, Ex 10:27
and the LORD hardened Pharaoh's **h**, Ex 11:10
And I will harden Pharaoh's **h**, and he Ex 14:4
LORD hardened the **h** of Pharaoh king Ex 14:8
the deeps congealed in the **h** of the sea. Ex 15:8
You know the **h** of a sojourner, Ex 23:9
every man whose **h** moves him you Ex 25:2
in the breastpiece of judgment on his **h**, Ex 28:29
and they shall be on Aaron's **h**, Ex 28:30
of Israel on his **h** before the LORD Ex 28:30
Whoever is of a generous **h**, let him Ex 35:5
came, everyone whose **h** stirred him, Ex 35:21
of a willing **h** brought brooches and Ex 35:22
whose **h** moved them to bring Ex 35:29
everyone whose **h** stirred him up to Ex 36:2
shall not hate your brother in your **h**, Lv 19:17
consume the eyes and make the **h** ache. Lv 26:16
their uncircumcised **h** is humbled Lv 26:41
follow after your own **h** and your own Nm 15:39
will you discourage the **h** of the people Nm 32:7
they discouraged the **h** of the people of Nm 32:9
his spirit and made his **h** obstinate, Dt 2:30
lest they depart from your **h** all the days of Dt 4:9
burned with fire to the **h** of heaven, Dt 4:11
him with all your **h** and with all your Dt 4:29
therefore today, and lay it to your **h**, Dt 4:39
God with all your **h** and with all your Dt 6:5
I command you today shall be on your **h**. Dt 6:6
"If you say in your **h**, 'These nations are Dt 7:17
testing you to know what was in your **h**, Dt 8:2
Know then in your **h** that, as a man Dt 8:5
then your **h** be lifted up, and you forget Dt 8:14
Beware lest you say in your **h**, 'My power Dt 8:17
"Do not say in your **h**, after the LORD your Dt 9:4

the uprightness of your **h** are you going in Dt 9:5
God with all your **h** and with all your Dt 10:12
Yet the LORD set his **h** in love on your Dt 10:15
therefore the foreskin of your **h**, Dt 10:16
him with all your **h** and with all your Dt 11:13
Take care lest your **h** be deceived, and Dt 11:16
of mine in your **h** and in your soul, Dt 11:18
God with all your **h** and with all your Dt 13:3
shall not harden your **h** or shut your Dt 15:7
thought in your **h** and you say, Dt 15:9
and your **h** shall not be grudging when Dt 15:10
wives for himself, lest his **h** turn away, Dt 17:17
that his **h** may not be lifted up above Dt 17:20
And if you say in your **h**, 'How may we Dt 18:21
your enemies: let not your **h** faint. Dt 20:3
lest he make the **h** of his fellows melt like Dt 20:8
them with all your **h** and with all your Dt 26:16
God with joyfulness and gladness of **h**, Dt 28:47
there a trembling **h** and failing eyes Dt 28:65
of the dread that your **h** shall feel, Dt 28:67
not given you a **h** to understand or eyes Dt 29:4
clan or tribe whose **h** is turning away Dt 29:18
covenant, blesses himself in his **h**, Dt 29:19
I walk in the stubbornness of my **h**.' Dt 29:19
with all your **h** and with all your soul, Dt 30:2
will circumcise your **h** and the heart Dt 30:6
your heart and the **h** of your offspring, Dt 30:6
God with all your **h** and with all your Dt 30:6
God with all your **h** and with all your Dt 30:10
It is in your mouth and in your **h**, so Dt 30:14
But if your **h** turns away, and you will Dt 30:17
"Take to **h** all the words by which I am Dt 32:46
him word again as it was in my **h**. Jos 14:7
with me made the **h** of the people melt; Jos 14:8
him with all your **h** and with all your Jos 22:5
you, and incline your **h** to the LORD, Jos 24:23
My **h** goes out to the commanders of Jgs 5:9
Reuben there were great searchings of **h**. Jgs 5:15
Reuben there were great searchings of **h**. Jgs 5:16
love you,' when your **h** is not with me? Jgs 16:15
And he told her all his **h**, and said to Jgs 16:17
saw that he had told her all his **h**, Jgs 16:18
has told me all his **h**." Then the lords of Jgs 16:18
And the priest's **h** was glad. He took the Jgs 18:20
"Strengthen your **h** with a morsel of Jgs 19:5
the night, and let your **h** be merry." Jgs 19:6
"Strengthen your **h** and wait until the Jgs 19:8
Lodge here and let your **h** be merry, and Jgs 19:9
eaten and drunk, and his **h** was merry, Ru 3:7
do you not eat? And why is your **h** sad? 1 Sm 1:8
Hannah was speaking in her **h**; only 1 Sm 1:13
and said, "My **h** exults in the LORD; 1 Sm 2:1
to weep his eyes out to grieve his **h**, 1 Sm 2:33
to what is in my **h** and in my mind. 1 Sm 2:35
for his **h** trembled for the ark of God. 1 Sm 4:13
returning to the LORD with all your **h**, 1 Sm 7:3
you and direct your **h** to the LORD and 1 Sm 7:3
Samuel, God gave him another **h**. 1 Sm 10:9
but serve the LORD with all your **h**. 1 Sm 12:20
serve him faithfully with all your **h**. 1 Sm 12:24
sought out a man after his own **h**, 1 Sm 13:14
said to him, "Do all that is in your **h**. 1 Sm 14:7
Behold, I am with you **h** and soul." 1 Sm 14:7
but the LORD looks on the **h**." 1 Sm 16:7
presumption and the evil of your **h**, 1 Sm 17:28
"Let no man's **h** fail because of him. 1 Sm 17:32
took these words to **h** and was much 1 Sm 21:12
And afterward David's **h** struck him, 1 Sm 24:5
And Nabal's **h** was merry within 1 Sm 25:36
things, and his **h** died within him, 1 Sm 25:37
Then David said in his **h**, "Now I 1 Sm 27:1
afraid, and his **h** trembled greatly. 1 Sm 28:5
over all that your **h** desires." So David 2 Sm 3:21
LORD, and she despised him in her **h**. 2 Sm 6:16
to the king, "Go, do all that is in your **h**, 2 Sm 7:3
and according to your own **h**, 2 Sm 7:21
not take this to **h**." So Tamar lived, 2 Sm 13:20
"Mark when Amnon's **h** is merry 2 Sm 13:28
king so take it to **h** as to suppose that 2 Sm 13:33
knew that the king's **h** went out to 2 Sm 14:1
whose **h** is like the heart of a lion, 2 Sm 17:10
whose heart is like the **h** of a lion, 2 Sm 17:10
them into the **h** of Absalom while 2 Sm 18:14
And he swayed the **h** of all the men 2 Sm 19:14
Do not let the king take it to **h**. 2 Sm 19:19
Foreigners lost **h** and came 2 Sm 22:46
But David's **h** struck him after he 2 Sm 24:10
with all their **h** and with all 1 Kgs 2:4
know in your own **h** all the harm 1 Kgs 2:44
and in uprightness of **h** toward you. 1 Kgs 3:6
because her **h** yearned for her son, 1 Kgs 3:26
it was in the **h** of David my father 1 Kgs 8:17
it was in your **h** to build a house 1 Kgs 8:18
you did well that it was in your **h**. 1 Kgs 8:18
who walk before you with all their **h**, 1 Kgs 8:23
of his own **h** and stretching out 1 Kgs 8:38
render to each whose **h** you know, 1 Kgs 8:39
yet if they turn their **h** in the land to 1 Kgs 8:47
and with all their **h** in the land of 1 Kgs 8:48
Let your **h** therefore be wholly true to 1 Kgs 8:61
joyful and glad of **h** for all the 1 Kgs 8:66
My eyes and my **h** will be there for all 1 Kgs 9:3
with integrity of **h** and uprightness, 1 Kgs 9:4
turn away your **h** after their gods." 1 Kgs 11:2
And his wives turned away his **h**. 1 Kgs 11:3
turned away his **h** after other gods, 1 Kgs 11:4
and his **h** was not wholly true to the 1 Kgs 11:4
God, as was the **h** of David his father. 1 Kgs 11:4
because his **h** had turned away from 1 Kgs 11:9
And Jeroboam said in his **h**, "Now 1 Kgs 12:26
then the **h** of this people will turn 1 Kgs 12:27
that he had devised from his own **h**. 1 Kgs 12:33
and followed me with all his **h**, 1 Kgs 14:8
and his **h** was not wholly true to the 1 Kgs 15:3
his God, as the **h** of David his father. 1 Kgs 15:3
the **h** of Asa was wholly true to the 1 Kgs 15:14
eat bread and let your **h** be cheerful; 1 Kgs 21:7
"Did not my **h** go when the man 2 Kgs 5:26
so that the arrow pierced his **h**, 2 Kgs 9:24
"Is your **h** true to my heart as mine 2 Kgs 10:15
your heart true to my **h** as mine is to 2 Kgs 10:15
according to all that was in my **h**, 2 Kgs 10:30
LORD the God of Israel with all his **h**. 2 Kgs 10:31
that a man's **h** prompts him to 2 Kgs 12:4
Edom, and your **h** has lifted you up. 2 Kgs 14:10
in faithfulness and with a whole **h**, 2 Kgs 20:3
because your **h** was penitent, and 2 Kgs 22:19
statutes with all his **h** and all his 2 Kgs 23:3
LORD with all his **h** and with all his 2 Kgs 23:25
help me, my **h** will be joined to you; 1 Chr 12:17
and she despised him in her **h**. 1 Chr 15:29
to David, "Do all that is in your **h**, 1 Chr 17:2
LORD, and according to your own **h**, 1 Chr 17:19
I had it in my **h** to build a house to 1 Chr 22:7
set your mind and **h** to seek the 1 Chr 22:19
I had it in my **h** to build a house of 1 Chr 28:2
him with a whole **h** and with a 1 Chr 28:9
for with a whole **h** they had offered 1 Chr 29:9
you test the **h** and have pleasure 1 Chr 29:17
uprightness of my **h** I have freely 1 Chr 29:17
my son a whole **h** that he may keep 1 Chr 29:19
"Because this was in your **h**, 2 Chr 1:11
Now it was in the **h** of David my father 2 Chr 6:7
it was in your **h** to build a house 2 Chr 6:8
you did well that it was in your **h**. 2 Chr 6:8
who walk before you with all their **h**, 2 Chr 6:14
render to each whose **h** you know, 2 Chr 6:30
yet if they turn their **h** in the land to 2 Chr 6:37
and with all their **h** in the land of 2 Chr 6:38
joyful and glad of **h** for the prosperity 2 Chr 7:10
My eyes and my **h** will be there for all 2 Chr 7:16
he did not set his **h** to seek the LORD. 2 Chr 12:14
with all their **h** and with all their 2 Chr 15:12
with all their **h** and had sought 2 Chr 15:15
the **h** of Asa was wholly true all his 2 Chr 15:17
to those whose **h** is blameless toward 2 Chr 16:9
His **h** was courageous in the ways of 2 Chr 17:6
and have set your **h** to seek God." 2 Chr 19:3
faithfulness, and with your whole **h**: 2 Chr 19:9
LORD with all his **h**." And the house of 2 Chr 22:9
of the LORD, yet not with a whole **h**. 2 Chr 25:2
and your **h** has lifted you up in 2 Chr 25:19
it is in my **h** to make a covenant 2 Chr 29:10
of a willing **h** brought burnt 2 Chr 29:31
more upright in **h** than the priests 2 Chr 29:34
to give them one **h** to do what the 2 Chr 30:12
who sets his **h** to seek God, the LORD, 2 Chr 30:19
his God, he did with all his **h**, 2 Chr 31:21
done to him, for his **h** was proud. 2 Chr 32:25
himself for the pride of his **h**, 2 Chr 32:26
and to know all that was in his **h**. 2 Chr 32:31
because your **h** was tender and you 2 Chr 34:27
with all his **h** and all his soul, 2 Chr 34:31
and hardened his **h** against turning 2 Chr 36:13
and had turned the **h** of the king of Ezr 6:22
For Ezra had set his **h** to study the Law Ezr 7:10
a thing as this into the **h** of the king, Ezr 7:27
but sadness of the **h**." Then I was very Neh 2:2
had put into my **h** to do for Jerusalem. Neh 2:12
put it into my **h** to assemble the nobles Neh 7:5
You found his **h** faithful before you, Neh 9:8
when the **h** of the king was merry with Est 1:10
went out that day joyful and glad of **h**. Est 5:9
of him, and that you set your **h** on him, Jb 7:17
He is wise in **h** and mighty in strength— Jb 9:4
Yet these things you hid in your **h**; I Jb 10:13
"If you prepare your **h**, you will stretch Jb 11:13
Why does your **h** carry you away, and Jb 15:12
are broken off, the desires of my **h**. Jb 17:11
not another. My **h** faints within me! Jb 19:27
mouth, and lay up his words in your **h**. Jb 22:22
God has made my **h** faint; the Almighty Jb 23:16
my **h** does not reproach me for any of my Jb 27:6
I caused the widow's **h** to sing for joy. Jb 29:13
the way and my **h** has gone after my Jb 31:7
"If my **h** has been enticed toward a Jb 31:9
and my **h** has been secretly enticed, and Jb 31:27
words declare the uprightness of my **h**, Jb 33:3
If he should set his **h** to it and gather to Jb 34:14
"The godless in **h** cherish anger; they do Jb 36:13
"At this also my **h** trembles and leaps out Jb 37:1
His **h** is hard as a stone, hard as the Jb 41:24
more joy in my **h** than they have when Ps 4:7
is with God, who saves the upright in **h**. Ps 7:10
give thanks to the LORD with my whole **h**; Ps 9:1
He says in his **h**, "I shall not be moved; Ps 10:6
He says in his **h**, "God has forgotten, he Ps 10:11
wicked renounce God and say in his **h**, Ps 10:13
afflicted; you will strengthen their **h**; Ps 10:17
to shoot in the dark at the upright in **h**; Ps 11:2
flattering lips and a double **h** they speak. Ps 12:2
and have sorrow in my **h** all the day? Ps 13:2
my **h** shall rejoice in your salvation. Ps 13:5
The fool says in his **h**, "There is no God." Ps 14:1
what is right and speaks truth in his **h**; Ps 15:2
in the night also my **h** instructs me. Ps 16:7
Therefore my **h** is glad, and my whole Ps 16:9
You have tried my **h**, you have visited Ps 17:3
Foreigners lost **h** and came trembling Ps 18:45
of the LORD are right, rejoicing the **h**; Ps 19:8
the meditation of my **h** be acceptable in Ps 19:14
bones are out of joint; my **h** is like wax; Ps 22:14
He who has clean hands and a pure **h**, Ps 24:4
The troubles of my **h** are enlarged; Ps 25:17
and try me; test my **h** and my mind. Ps 26:2
encamp against me, my **h** shall not fear; Ps 27:3
said, "Seek my face." My **h** says to you, Ps 27:8
be strong, and let your **h** take courage; Ps 27:14
in him my **h** trusts, and I am helped; Ps 28:7
trusts, and I am helped; my **h** exults, Ps 28:7
Be strong, and let your **h** take courage, Ps 31:24
and shout for joy, all you upright in **h**! Ps 32:11
the plans of his **h** to all generations. Ps 33:11
For our **h** is glad in him, because we Ps 33:21
speaks to the wicked deep in his **h**; Ps 36:1
your righteousness to the upright of **h**! Ps 36:10
and he will give you the desires of your **h**. Ps 37:4
their sword shall enter their own **h**, and Ps 37:15
The law of his God is in his **h**; his steps Ps 37:31
I groan because of the tumult of my **h**. Ps 38:8
My **h** throbs; my strength fails me, and Ps 38:10
My **h** became hot within me. As I mused, Ps 39:3
O my God; your law is within my **h**." Ps 40:8
hidden your deliverance within my **h**; Ps 40:10
the hairs of my head; my **h** fails me. Ps 40:12
words, while his **h** gathers iniquity; Ps 41:6
Our **h** has not turned back, nor have Ps 44:18
this? For he knows the secrets of the **h**. Ps 44:21
My **h** overflows with a pleasing theme; I Ps 45:1
are sharp in the **h** of the king's enemies; Ps 45:5
be moved into the **h** of the sea, Ps 46:2
meditation of my **h** shall be Ps 49:3
you teach me wisdom in the secret **h**. Ps 51:6
Create in me a clean **h**, O God, and Ps 51:10
a broken and contrite **h**, O God, you Ps 51:17
The fool says in his **h**, "There is no God." Ps 53:1
My **h** is in anguish within me; the Ps 55:4
is in their dwelling place and in their **h**. Ps 55:15
smooth as butter, yet war was in his **h**; Ps 55:21
My **h** is steadfast, O God, my heart is Ps 57:7
is steadfast, O God, my **h** is steadfast! Ps 57:7
the earth I call to you when my **h** is faint. Ps 61:2
O people; pour out your **h** before him; Ps 62:8
riches increase, set not your **h** on them. Ps 62:10
For the inward mind and **h** of a man are Ps 64:6
in him! Let all the upright in **h** exult! Ps 64:10
If I had cherished iniquity in my **h**, the Ps 66:18
Reproaches have broken my **h**, so that I Ps 69:20
good to Israel, to those who are pure in **h**. Ps 73:1
have I kept my **h** clean and washed my Ps 73:13
embittered, when I was pricked in **h**, Ps 73:21
My flesh and my **h** may fail, but God is Ps 73:26
the strength of my **h** and my portion Ps 73:26
me meditate in my **h**." Then my spirit Ps 77:6
a generation whose **h** was not steadfast, Ps 78:8
tested God in their **h** by demanding the Ps 78:18
Their **h** was not steadfast toward him; Ps 78:37
With upright **h** he shepherded them Ps 78:72
my **h** and flesh sing for joy to the living Ps 84:2
in whose **h** are the highways to Zion. Ps 84:5
truth; unite my **h** to fear your name. Ps 86:11
you, O Lord my God, with my whole **h**, Ps 86:12
how I bear in my **h** the insults of all the Ps 89:50
our days that we may get a **h** of wisdom. Ps 90:12
and all the upright in **h** will follow it. Ps 94:15

When the cares of my **h** are many, Ps 94:19
are a people who go astray in their **h**, Ps 95:10
righteous, and joy for the upright in **h**. Ps 97:11
with integrity of **h** within my house; Ps 101:2
A perverse **h** shall be far from me; I will Ps 101:4
look and an arrogant **h** I will not Ps 101:5
My **h** is struck down like grass and has Ps 102:4
and wine to gladden the **h** of man, oil Ps 104:15
and bread to strengthen man's **h**. Ps 104:15
My **h** is steadfast, O God! I will sing and Ps 108:1
and my **h** is stricken within me. Ps 109:22
thanks to the LORD with my whole **h**, Ps 111:1
news; his **h** is firm, trusting in the LORD. Ps 112:7
His **h** is steady; he will not be afraid, Ps 112:8
who seek him with their whole **h**, Ps 119:2
I will praise you with an upright **h**, Ps 119:7
With my whole **h** I seek you; let me Ps 119:10
I have stored up your word in my **h**, Ps 119:11
when you enlarge my **h**! Ps 119:32
law and observe it with my whole **h**. Ps 119:34
Incline my **h** to your testimonies, and Ps 119:36
I entreat your favor with all my **h**; be Ps 119:58
but with my whole **h** I keep your Ps 119:69
their **h** is unfeeling like fat, but I Ps 119:70
May my **h** be blameless in your Ps 119:80
forever, for they are the joy of my **h**. Ps 119:111
I incline my **h** to perform your Ps 119:112
With my whole **h** I cry; answer me, O Ps 119:145
but my **h** stands in awe of your Ps 119:161
O LORD, my **h** is not lifted up; my eyes Ps 131:1
you thanks, O LORD, with my whole **h**; Ps 138:1
Search me, O God, and know my **h**! Ps 139:23
evil things in their **h** and stir up wars Ps 140:2
Do not let my **h** incline to any evil, to Ps 141:4
within me; my **h** within me is appalled. Ps 143:4
and inclining your **h** to understanding; Prv 2:2
for wisdom will come into your **h**, and Prv 2:10
but let your **h** keep my commandments, Prv 3:1
neck; write them on the tablet of your **h**. Prv 3:3
Trust in the LORD with all your **h**, and do Prv 3:5
to me, "Let your **h** hold fast my words; Prv 4:4
your sight; keep them within your **h**. Prv 4:21
Keep your **h** with all vigilance, for from Prv 4:23
discipline, and my **h** despised reproof! Prv 5:12
with perverted **h** devises evil, Prv 6:14
a **h** that devises wicked plans, feet that Prv 6:18
Bind them on your **h** always; tie them Prv 6:21
Do not desire her beauty in your **h**, and Prv 6:25
write them on the tablet of your **h**. Prv 7:3
him, dressed as a prostitute, wily of **h**. Prv 7:10
Let not your **h** turn aside to her ways; Prv 7:25
The wise of **h** will receive Prv 10:8
the **h** of the wicked is of little worth. Prv 10:20
Those of crooked **h** are an Prv 11:20
the fool will be servant to the wise of **h**. Prv 11:29
Deceit is in the **h** of those who devise Prv 12:20
but the **h** of fools proclaims folly. Prv 12:23
in a man's **h** weighs him down, Prv 12:25
Hope deferred makes the **h** sick, but a Prv 13:12
The **h** knows its own bitterness, and Prv 14:10
Even in laughter the **h** may ache, and Prv 14:13
The backslider in **h** will be filled with Prv 14:14
A tranquil **h** gives life to the flesh, but Prv 14:30
Wisdom rests in the **h** of a man of Prv 14:33
A glad **h** makes a cheerful face, but by Prv 15:13
but by sorrow of **h** the spirit is Prv 15:13
The **h** of him who has understanding Prv 15:14
but the cheerful of **h** has a continual Prv 15:15
The **h** of the righteous ponders how to Prv 15:28
The light of the eyes rejoices the **h**, and Prv 15:30
The plans of the **h** belong to man, but Prv 16:1
who is arrogant in **h** is an abomination Prv 16:5
The **h** of man plans his way, but the Prv 16:9
The wise of **h** is called discerning, and Prv 16:21
The **h** of the wise makes his speech Prv 16:23
A man of crooked **h** does not discover Prv 17:20
A joyful **h** is good medicine, but a Prv 17:22
destruction a man's **h** is haughty, Prv 18:12
An intelligent **h** acquires knowledge, Prv 18:15
to ruin, his **h** rages against the LORD. Prv 19:3
do not set your **h** on putting him to Prv 19:18
purpose in a man's **h** is like deep water, Prv 20:5
Who can say, "I have made my **h** pure; Prv 20:9
The king's **h** is a stream of water in the Prv 21:1
his own eyes, but the LORD weighs the **h**. Prv 21:2
Haughty eyes and a proud **h**, the lamp Prv 21:4
He who loves purity of **h**, and whose Prv 22:11
Folly is bound up in the **h** of a child, Prv 22:15
and apply your **h** to my knowledge, Prv 22:17
says to you, but his **h** is not with you. Prv 23:7
Apply your **h** to instruction and your Prv 23:12
My son, if your **h** is wise, my heart too Prv 23:15
heart is wise, my **h** too will be glad. Prv 23:15
Let not your **h** envy sinners, but Prv 23:17
be wise, and direct your **h** in the way. Prv 23:19
My son, give me your **h**, and let your Prv 23:26
and your **h** utter perverse things. Prv 23:33
not he who weighs the **h** perceive it? Prv 24:12
and let not your **h** be glad when he Prv 24:17
so the **h** of kings is unsearchable. Prv 25:3
songs to a heavy **h** is like one who Prv 25:20
vessel are fervent lips with an evil **h**. Prv 26:23
his lips and harbors deceit in his **h**; Prv 26:24
there are seven abominations in his **h**; Prv 26:25
Oil and perfume make the **h** glad, and Prv 27:9
Be wise, my son, and make my **h** glad, Prv 27:11
face, so the **h** of man reflects the man. Prv 27:19
whoever hardens his **h** will fall into Prv 28:14
you rest; he will give delight to your **h**. Prv 29:17
The **h** of her husband trusts in her, Prv 31:11
And I applied my **h** to seek and to Eccl 1:13
I said in my **h**, "I have acquired great Eccl 1:16
and my **h** has had great experience of Eccl 1:16
And I applied my **h** to know wisdom Eccl 1:17
I said in my **h**, "Come now, I will test Eccl 2:1
I searched with my **h** how to cheer my Eccl 2:3
with wine—my **h** still guiding me with Eccl 2:3
them. I kept my **h** from no pleasure, Eccl 2:10
for my **h** found pleasure in all my toil, Eccl 2:10
Then I said in my **h**, "What happens Eccl 2:15
And I said in my **h** that this also is Eccl 2:15
about and gave my **h** up to despair Eccl 2:20
toil and striving of **h** with which he Eccl 2:22
Even in the night his **h** does not rest. Eccl 2:23
Also, he has put eternity into man's **h**, Eccl 3:11
I said in my **h**, God will judge the Eccl 3:17
I said in my **h** with regard to the Eccl 3:18
nor let your **h** be hasty to utter a word Eccl 5:2
keeps him occupied with joy in his **h**. Eccl 5:20
mankind, and the living will lay it to **h**. Eccl 7:2
by sadness of face the **h** is made glad. Eccl 7:3
The **h** of the wise is in the house of Eccl 7:4
but the **h** of fools is in the house of Eccl 7:4
madness, and a bribe corrupts the **h**. Eccl 7:7
Do not take to **h** all the things that Eccl 7:21
Your **h** knows that many times you Eccl 7:22
I turned my **h** to know and to search Eccl 7:25
the woman whose **h** is snares and nets, Eccl 7:26
and the wise **h** will know the proper Eccl 8:5
while applying my **h** to all that Eccl 8:9
the **h** of the children of man is fully set Eccl 8:11
When I applied my **h** to know wisdom, Eccl 8:16
But all this I laid to **h**, examining it all, Eccl 9:1
and drink your wine with a merry **h**, Eccl 9:7
A wise man's **h** inclines him to the Eccl 10:2
to the right, but a fool's **h** to the left. Eccl 10:2
and let your **h** cheer you in the days of Eccl 11:9
in the ways of your **h** and the sight of Eccl 11:9
Remove vexation from your **h**, and Eccl 11:10
on the day of the gladness of his **h**. Sg 3:11
You have captivated my **h**, my sister, my Sg 4:9
you have captivated my **h** with one glance Sg 4:9
I slept, but my **h** was awake. A sound! My Sg 5:2
latch, and my **h** was thrilled within me. Sg 5:4
Set me as a seal upon your **h**, as a seal Sg 8:6
whole head is sick, and the whole **h** faint. Is 1:5
Make the **h** of this people dull, and their Is 6:10
league with Ephraim," the **h** of Ahaz and Is 7:2
heart of Ahaz and the **h** of his people shook Is 7:2
and do not let your **h** be faint because of Is 7:4
who say in pride and in arrogance of **h**: Is 9:9
not so intend, and his **h** does not so think; Is 10:7
but it is in his **h** to destroy, and to cut off Is 10:7
speech of the arrogant **h** of the king of Is 10:12
be feeble, and every human **h** will melt. Is 13:7
You said in your **h**, 'I will ascend to Is 14:13
My **h** cries out for Moab; her fugitives flee Is 15:5
and the **h** of the Egyptians will melt Is 19:1
My **h** staggers; horror has appalled me; Is 21:4
a holy feast is kept, and gladness of **h**, Is 30:29
The **h** of the hasty will understand and Is 32:4
folly, and his **h** is busy with iniquity, Is 32:6
Your **h** will muse on the terror: "Where Is 33:18
Say to those who have an anxious **h**, "Be Is 35:4
you in faithfulness and with a whole **h**, Is 38:3
him up, but he did not take it to **h**. Is 42:25
a deluded **h** has led him astray, and he Is 44:20
"Listen to me, you stubborn of **h**, you Is 46:12
lay these things to **h** or remember their Is 47:7
who sit securely, who say in your **h**, Is 47:8
led you astray, and you said in your **h**, Is 47:10
Then you will say in your **h**: 'Who has Is 49:21
the people in whose **h** is my law; Is 51:7
man perishes, and no one lays it to **h**; Is 57:1
did not remember me, did not lay it to **h**? Is 57:11
lowly, and to revive the **h** of the contrite. Is 57:15
on backsliding in the way of his own **h**. Is 57:17
and uttering from the **h** lying words. Is 59:13
your **h** shall thrill and exult, because the Is 60:5
For the day of vengeance was in my **h**, Is 63:4
from your ways and harden our **h**, Is 63:17
my servants shall sing for gladness of **h**, Is 65:14
cry out for pain of **h** and shall wail for Is 65:14
You shall see, and your **h** shall rejoice; Is 66:14
did not return to me with her whole **h**, Jer 3:10
I will give you shepherds after my own **h**, Jer 3:15
more stubbornly follow their own evil **h**. Jer 3:17
O Jerusalem, wash your **h** from evil, that Jer 4:14
it is bitter; it has reached your very **h**." Jer 4:18
I writhe in pain! Oh the walls of my **h**! Jer 4:19
My **h** is beating wildly; I cannot keep Jer 4:19
people has a stubborn and rebellious **h**; Jer 5:23
grief is upon me; my **h** is sick within me. Jer 8:18
daughter of my people is my **h** wounded; Jer 8:21
but in his **h** he plans an ambush for him. Jer 9:8
house of Israel is uncircumcised in **h**." Jer 9:26
walked in the stubbornness of his evil **h**. Jer 11:8
who tests the **h** and the mind, Jer 11:20
in their mouth and far from their **h**. Jer 12:2
you see me, and test my **h** toward you. Jer 12:3
made desolate, but no man lays it to **h**. Jer 12:11
follow their own **h** and have gone Jer 13:10
And if you say in your **h**, 'Why have Jer 13:22
yet my **h** would not turn toward this Jer 15:1
to me a joy and the delight of my **h**, Jer 15:16
it is engraved on the tablet of their **h**, Jer 17:1
whose **h** turns away from the LORD. Jer 17:5
The **h** is deceitful above all things, and Jer 17:9
the LORD search the **h** and test the mind, Jer 17:10
to the stubbornness of his evil **h**.' Jer 18:12
name," there is in my **h** as it were a Jer 20:9
righteous, who sees the **h** and the mind, Jer 20:12
you have eyes and **h** only for your Jer 22:17
the prophets: My **h** is broken within me; Jer 23:9
who stubbornly follows his own **h**, Jer 23:17
and accomplished the intents of his **h**. Jer 23:20
be lies in the **h** of the prophets who Jer 23:26
who prophesy the deceit of their own **h**, Jer 23:26
I will give them a **h** to know that I am Jer 24:7
shall return to me with their whole **h**. Jer 24:7
me. When you seek me with all your **h**, Jer 29:13
Therefore my **h** yearns for him; I will Jer 31:20
I will give them one **h** and one way, that Jer 32:39
with all my **h** and all my soul. Jer 32:41
and the haughtiness of his **h**. Jer 48:29
Therefore my **h** moans for Moab like a Jer 48:36
and my **h** moans like a flute for the Jer 48:36
The **h** of the warriors of Moab shall be Jer 48:41
in that day like the **h** of a woman in her Jer 48:41
deceived you, and the pride of your **h**, Jer 49:16
and the **h** of the warriors of Edom shall Jer 49:22
in that day like the **h** of a woman in her Jer 49:22
Let not your **h** faint, and be not fearful Jer 51:46
my **h** is wrung within me, because I Lam 1:20
groans are many, and my **h** is faint." Lam 1:22
Their **h** cried to the Lord. O wall of the Lam 2:18
Pour out your **h** like water before the Lam 2:19
You will give them dullness of **h**; your Lam 3:65
For this our **h** has become sick, for Lam 5:17
have a hard forehead and a stubborn **h**. Ezk 3:7
I shall speak to you receive in your **h**, Ezk 3:10
over their whoring **h** that has departed Ezk 6:9
And I will give them one **h**, and a new Ezk 11:19
I will remove the **h** of stone from their Ezk 11:19
their flesh and give them a **h** of flesh, Ezk 11:19
as for those whose **h** goes after their Ezk 11:21
his idols into his **h** and sets the Ezk 14:4
his idols into his **h** and putting the Ezk 14:7
"How lovesick is your **h**, declares the Ezk 16:30
make yourselves a new **h** and a new Ezk 18:31
for their **h** went after their idols. Ezk 20:16
with breaking **h** and bitter grief, groan Ezk 21:6
Every **h** will melt, and all hands will be Ezk 21:7
Your borders are in the **h** of the seas; Ezk 27:4
and heavily laden in the **h** of the seas. Ezk 27:25
has wrecked you in the **h** of the seas. Ezk 27:26
sink into the **h** of the seas on the day Ezk 27:27
the Lord GOD: "Because your **h** is proud, Ezk 28:2
the seat of the gods, in the **h** of the seas,' Ezk 28:2
though you make your **h** like the heart Ezk 28:2
make your heart like the **h** of a god— Ezk 28:2
and your **h** has become proud in your Ezk 28:5
you make your **h** like the heart Ezk 28:6
make your heart like the **h** of a god, Ezk 28:6
death of the slain in the **h** of the seas. Ezk 28:8
Your **h** was proud because of your Ezk 28:17
and its **h** was proud of its height, Ezk 31:10
they act; their **h** is set on their gain. Ezk 33:31
And I will give you a new **h**, and a new Ezk 36:26
I will remove the **h** of stone from your Ezk 36:26
your flesh and give you a **h** of flesh. Ezk 36:26
and set your **h** upon all that I shall Ezk 40:4
uncircumcised in **h** and flesh, Ezk 44:7
uncircumcised in **h** and flesh, Ezk 44:9
But when his **h** was lifted up and his Dn 5:20

Belshazzar, have not humbled your **h**, Dn 5:22
changed, but I kept the matter in my **h**." Dn 7:28
that you set your **h** to understand and Dn 10:12
is taken away, his **h** shall be exalted, Dn 11:12
his power and his **h** against the king of Dn 11:25
but his **h** shall be set against the holy Dn 11:28
They do not cry to me from the **h**, but Hos 7:14
Their **h** is false; now they must bear Hos 10:2
My **h** recoils within me; my Hos 11:8
were filled, and their **h** was lifted up; Hos 13:6
the LORD, "return to me with all your **h**, Jl 2:12
who is stout of **h** among the mighty Am 2:16
The pride of your **h** has deceived you, you Ob 1:3
in your lofty dwelling, who say in your **h**, Ob 1:3
me into the deep, into the **h** of the seas, Jon 2:3
that lived securely, that said in her **h**, Zep 2:15
Rejoice and exult with all your **h**, O Zep 3:14
devise evil against another in your **h**." Zec 7:10
will not take it to **h** to give honor to my Mal 2:2
them, because you do not lay it to **h**. Mal 2:2
"Blessed are the pure in **h**, for they shall Mt 5:8
committed adultery with her in his **h**. Mt 5:28
treasure is, there your **h** will be also. Mt 6:21
faith, he said to the paralytic, "Take **h**, Mt 9:2
turned, and seeing her he said, "Take **h**, Mt 9:22
me, for I am gentle and lowly in **h**, Mt 11:29
abundance of the **h** the mouth speaks. Mt 12:34
and three nights in the **h** of the earth. Mt 12:40
For this people's **h** has grown dull, and Mt 13:15
and understand with their **h** and turn, Mt 13:15
away what has been sown in his **h**. Mt 13:19
Jesus spoke to them, saying, "Take **h**; Mt 14:27
their lips, but their **h** is far from me; Mt 15:8
out of the mouth proceeds from the **h**, Mt 15:18
For out of the **h** come evil thoughts, Mt 15:19
not forgive your brother from your **h**." Mt 18:35
of your hardness of **h** Moses allowed you Mt 19:8
God with all your **h** and with all your Mt 22:37
anger, grieved at their hardness of **h**, Mk 3:5
he spoke to them and said, "Take **h**; Mk 6:50
with their lips, but their **h** is far from me; Mk 7:6
it enters not his **h** but his stomach, Mk 7:19
For from within, out of the **h** of man, Mk 7:21
of your hardness of **h** he wrote you this Mk 10:5
blind man, saying to him, "Take **h**. Mk 10:49
the sea,' and does not doubt in his **h**, Mk 11:23
God with all your **h** and with all your Mk 12:30
him with all the **h** and with all the Mk 12:33
for their unbelief and hardness of **h**, Mk 16:14
these things, pondering them in her **h**. Lk 2:19
treasured up all these things in her **h**. Lk 2:51
the good treasure of his **h** produces good, Lk 6:45
abundance of the **h** his mouth speaks. Lk 6:45
hold it fast in an honest and good **h**, Lk 8:15
God with all your **h** and with all your Lk 10:27
treasure is, there will your **h** be also. Lk 12:34
ought always to pray and not lose **h**. Lk 18:1
and slow of **h** to believe all that the Lk 24:25
'Out of his **h** will flow rivers of living Jn 7:38
blinded their eyes and hardened their **h**, Jn 12:40
their eyes, and understand with their **h**, Jn 12:40
already put it into the **h** of Judas Iscariot, Jn 13:2
things to you, sorrow has filled your **h**. Jn 16:6
But take **h**; I have overcome the world." Jn 16:33
therefore my **h** was glad, and my Acts 2:26
they heard this they were cut to the **h**, Acts 2:37
who believed were of one **h** and soul, Acts 4:32
why has Satan filled your **h** to lie to the Acts 5:3
you have contrived this deed in your **h**? Acts 5:4
it came into his **h** to visit his brothers, Acts 7:23
people, uncircumcised in **h** and ears, Acts 7:51
for your **h** is not right before God. Acts 8:21
the intent of your **h** may be forgiven Acts 8:22
the son of Jesse a man after my **h**, Acts 13:22
And God, who knows the **h**, bore Acts 15:8
Lord opened her **h** to pay attention Acts 16:14
doing, weeping and breaking my **h**? Acts 21:13
Yet now I urge you to take **h**, for there Acts 27:22
So take **h**, men, for I have faith in God Acts 27:25
For this people's **h** has grown dull, Acts 28:27
understand with their **h** and turn, Acts 28:27
hard and impenitent **h** you are storing Rom 2:5
and circumcision is a matter of the **h**, Rom 2:29
obedient from the **h** to the standard Rom 6:17
and unceasing anguish in my **h**. Rom 9:2
on faith says, "Do not say in your **h**, Rom 10:6
in your mouth and in your **h**" (that is, Rom 10:8
and believe in your **h** that God raised Rom 10:9
For with the **h** one believes and is Rom 10:10
ear heard, nor the **h** of man imagined, 1 Cor 2:9
and will disclose the purposes of the **h**. 1 Cor 4:5
is firmly established in his **h**, 1 Cor 7:37
and has determined this in his **h**, 1 Cor 7:37
the secrets of his **h** are disclosed, and 1 Cor 14:25
and anguish of **h** and with many 2 Cor 2:4
by the mercy of God, we do not lose **h**. 2 Cor 4:1
So we do not lose **h**. Though our 2 Cor 4:16
and not about what is in the **h**. 2 Cor 5:12
you, Corinthians; our **h** is wide open. 2 Cor 6:11
who put into the **h** of Titus the same 2 Cor 8:16
ask you not to lose **h** over what I am Eph 3:13
is in them, due to their hardness of **h**. Eph 4:18
melody to the Lord with all your **h**, Eph 5:19
fear and trembling, with a sincere **h**, Eph 6:5
Christ, doing the will of God from the **h**, Eph 6:6
you all, because I hold you in my **h**, Phil 1:7
people-pleasers, but with sincerity of **h**, Col 3:22
for a short time, in person not in **h**, 1 Thes 2:17
issues from a pure **h** and a good 1 Tm 1:5
who call on the Lord from a pure **h**. 2 Tm 2:22
him back to you, sending my very **h**. Phlm 1:12
in the Lord. Refresh my **h** in Christ. Phlm 1:20
said, 'They always go astray in their **h**; Heb 3:10
be in any of you an evil, unbelieving **h**, Heb 3:12
the thoughts and intentions of the **h**. Heb 4:12
near with a true **h** in full assurance of Heb 10:22
is good for the **h** to be strengthened by Heb 13:9
not bridle his tongue but deceives his **h**, Jas 1:26
one another earnestly from a pure **h**, 1 Pt 1:22
person of the **h** with the imperishable 1 Pt 3:4
sympathy, brotherly love, a tender **h**, 1 Pt 3:8
in need, yet closes his **h** against him, 1 Jn 3:17
truth and reassure our **h** before him; 1 Jn 3:19
for whenever our **h** condemns us, God 1 Jn 3:20
us, God is greater than our **h**, 1 Jn 3:20
Beloved, if our **h** does not condemn us, 1 Jn 3:21
that I am he who searches mind and **h**, Rv 2:23
and mourning, since in her **h** she says, Rv 18:7

HEART'S (5)
to all your **h** desire to come 1 Sm 23:20
he grant you your **h** desire and fulfill all Ps 20:4
have given him his **h** desire and have not Ps 21:2
"Aha, our **h** desire!" Let them not say, Ps 35:25
my **h** desire and prayer to God for Rom 10:1

HEARTH (5)
offering shall be on the **h** on the altar all Lv 6:9
with which to take fire from the **h**, Is 30:14
and the altar **h**, four cubits; and from Ezk 43:15
from the altar **h** projecting upward, Ezk 43:15
The altar **h** shall be square, twelve Ezk 43:16

HEARTHS (1)
with **h** made at the bottom of the rows Ezk 46:23

HEARTILY (1)
Whatever you do, work **h**, as for the Col 3:23

HEARTLESS (2)
foolish, faithless, **h**, ruthless. Rom 1:31
h, unappeasable, slanderous, without 2 Tm 3:3

HEARTS (146)
my sack!" At this their **h** failed them, Gn 42:28
I will harden the **h** of the Egyptians so Ex 14:17
All the women whose **h** stirred them to Ex 35:26
send faintness into their **h** in the lands Lv 26:36
Our brothers have made our **h** melt, Dt 1:28
And as soon as we heard it, our **h** melted, Jos 2:11
their **h** melted and there was no longer Jos 5:1
And the **h** of the people melted and Jos 7:5
to harden their **h** that they should Jos 11:20
and you know in your **h** and souls, Jos 23:14
and their **h** inclined to follow Abimelech, Jgs 9:3
And when their **h** were merry, they Jgs 16:25
As they were making their **h** merry, Jgs 19:22
you harden your **h** as the Egyptians 1 Sm 6:6
and Pharaoh hardened their **h**? 1 Sm 6:6
of valor whose **h** God had touched. 1 Sm 10:26
So Absalom stole the **h** of the men of 2 Sm 15:6
"The **h** of the men of Israel have 2 Sm 15:13
know the **h** of all the children of 1 Kgs 8:39
that he may incline our **h** to him, to 1 Kgs 8:58
that you have turned their **h** back." 1 Kgs 18:37
let the **h** of those who seek the LORD 1 Chr 16:10
LORD searches all **h** and understands 1 Chr 28:9
thoughts in the **h** of your people, 1 Chr 29:18
and direct their **h** toward you. 1 Chr 29:18
know the **h** of the children of 2 Chr 6:30
who had set their **h** to seek the LORD 2 Chr 11:16
not yet set their **h** upon the God of 2 Chr 20:33
cursed God in their **h**." Thus Job did Jb 1:5
have closed their **h** to understanding, Jb 17:4
ponder in your own **h** on your beds, and Ps 4:4
righteous—you who test the minds and **h**, Ps 7:9
They close their **h** to pity; with their Ps 17:10
the LORD! May your **h** live forever! Ps 22:26
their neighbors while evil is in their **h**. Ps 28:3
he who fashions the **h** of them all and Ps 33:15
Let them not say in their **h**, "Aha, our Ps 35:25
No, in your **h** you devise wrongs; your Ps 58:2
you who seek God, let your **h** revive. Ps 69:32
fatness; their **h** overflow with follies. Ps 73:7
So I gave them over to their stubborn **h**, Ps 81:12
do not harden your **h**, as at Meribah, as Ps 95:8
let the **h** of those who seek the LORD Ps 105:3
He turned their **h** to hate his people, to Ps 105:25
So he bowed their **h** down with hard Ps 107:12
and to those who are upright in their **h**! Ps 125:4
spread knowledge; not so the **h** of fools. Prv 15:7
how much more the **h** of the children Prv 15:11
furnace is for gold, and the LORD tests **h**. Prv 17:3
for their **h** devise violence, and their lips Prv 24:2
the **h** of the children of man are full of Eccl 9:3
madness is in their **h** while they live, Eccl 9:3
their ears, and understand with their **h**, Is 6:10
their lips, while their **h** are far from me, Is 29:13
eyes, so that they cannot see, and their **h**, Is 44:18
remove the foreskin of your **h**, O men of Jer 4:4
They do not say in their **h**, 'Let us fear Jer 5:24
and the stubbornness of their evil **h**, Jer 7:24
followed their own **h** and have gone Jer 9:14
them, and I will write it on their **h**. Jer 31:33
And I will put the fear of me in their **h**, Jer 32:40
Let us lift up our **h** and hands to God Lam 3:41
The joy of our **h** has ceased; our Lam 5:15
those who prophesy from their own **h**: Ezk 13:2
men have taken their idols into their **h**, Ezk 14:3
may lay hold of the **h** of the house of Ezk 14:5
that their **h** may melt, and many Ezk 21:15
"I will trouble the **h** of many peoples, Ezk 32:9
their **h** shall be bent on doing evil. Dn 11:27
For with **h** like an oven they approach Hos 7:6
and rend your **h** and not your garments." Jl 2:13
H melt and knees tremble; anguish is in Na 2:10
complacent, those who say in their **h**, Zep 1:12
They made their **h** diamond-hard lest Zec 7:12
evil in your **h** against one another, Zec 8:17
and their **h** shall be glad as with wine. Zec 10:7
be glad; their **h** shall rejoice in the LORD. Zec 10:7
And he will turn the **h** of fathers to their Mal 4:6
their children and the **h** of children to Mal 4:6
said, "Why do you think evil in your **h**? Mt 9:4
were sitting there, questioning in their **h**, Mk 2:6
do you question these things in your **h**? Mk 2:8
the loaves, but their **h** were hardened. Mk 6:52
or understand? Are your **h** hardened? Mk 8:17
to turn the **h** of the fathers to the Lk 1:17
the proud in the thoughts of their **h**; Lk 1:51
who heard them laid them up in their **h**, Lk 1:66
thoughts from many **h** may be Lk 2:35
questioning in their **h** concerning John, Lk 3:15
them, "Why do you question in your **h**? Lk 5:22
and takes away the word from their **h**, Lk 8:12
Jesus, knowing the reasoning of their **h**, Lk 9:47
before men, but God knows your **h**. Lk 16:15
yourselves lest your **h** be weighed down Lk 21:34
"Did not our **h** burn within us while he Lk 24:32
and why do doubts arise in your **h**? Lk 24:38
"Let not your **h** be troubled. Believe in Jn 14:1
Let not your **h** be troubled, neither let Jn 14:27
see you again and your **h** will rejoice, Jn 16:22
"You, Lord, who know the **h** of all, Acts 1:24
their food with glad and generous **h**, Acts 2:46
and in their **h** they turned to Egypt, Acts 7:39
satisfying your **h** with food and Acts 14:17
them, having cleansed their **h** by faith. Acts 15:9
and their foolish **h** were darkened. Rom 1:21
up in the lusts of their **h** to impurity, Rom 1:24
work of the law is written on their **h**, Rom 2:15
poured into our **h** through the Holy Rom 5:5
And he who searches **h** knows what is Rom 8:27
they deceive the **h** of the naive. Rom 16:18
us his Spirit in our **h** as a guarantee. 2 Cor 1:22
of recommendation, written on our **h**, 2 Cor 3:2
of stone but on tablets of human **h**. 2 Cor 3:3
Moses is read a veil lies over their **h**. 2 Cor 3:15
has shone in our **h** to give the light 2 Cor 4:6
as to children) widen your **h** also. 2 Cor 6:13
Make room in your **h** for us. We have 2 Cor 7:2
for I said before that you are in our **h**, 2 Cor 7:3
has sent the Spirit of his Son into our **h**, Gal 4:6
having the eyes of your **h** enlightened, Eph 1:18
may dwell in your **h** through faith— Eph 3:17
are, and that he may encourage your **h**. Eph 6:22
will guard your **h** and your minds in Phil 4:7
that their **h** may be encouraged, being Col 2:2
let the peace of Christ rule in your **h**, Col 3:15
with thankfulness in your **h** to God. Col 3:16
are and that he may encourage your **h**, Col 4:8
but to please God who tests our **h**. 1 Thes 2:4
may establish your **h** blameless in 1 Thes 3:13
comfort your **h** and establish them 2 Thes 2:17
the Lord direct your **h** to the love of 2 Thes 3:5
because the **h** of the saints have been Phlm 1:7
do not harden your **h** as in the rebellion, Heb 3:8
do not harden your **h** as in the Heb 3:15

hear his voice, do not harden your **h**.” Heb 4:7
their minds, and write them on their **h**, Heb 8:10
I will put my laws on their **h**, and Heb 10:16
with our **h** sprinkled clean from an Heb 10:22
jealousy and selfish ambition in your **h**, Jas 3:14
hands, you sinners, and purify your **h**, Jas 4:8
You have fattened your **h** in a day of Jas 5:5
Establish your **h**, for the coming of the Jas 5:8
but in your **h** regard Christ the Lord as 1 Pt 3:15
and the morning star rises in your **h**, 2 Pt 1:19
souls. They have **h** trained in greed. 2 Pt 2:14
has put it into their **h** to carry out his Rv 17:17

HEARTY (1)
send you **h** greetings in the Lord. 1 Cor 16:19

HEAT (32)
seedtime and harvest, cold and **h**, Gn 8:22
at the door of his tent in the **h** of the day. Gn 18:1
by day the **h** consumed me, and the Gn 31:40
with fever, inflammation and fiery **h**, Dt 28:22
What caused the **h** of this great anger?’ Dt 29:24
Ammonites until the **h** of the day. 1 Sm 11:11
and about the **h** of the day they came to 2 Sm 4:5
Drought and **h** snatch away the snow Jb 24:19
from me, and my bones burn with **h**. Jb 30:30
and there is nothing hidden from its **h**. Ps 19:6
was dried up as by the **h** of summer. Ps 32:4
than your pots can feel the **h** of thorns, Ps 58:9
be a booth for shade by day from the **h**, Is 4:6
my dwelling like clear **h** in sunshine, Is 18:4
like a cloud of dew in the **h** of harvest.” Is 18:4
from the storm and a shade from the **h**; Is 25:4
like **h** in a dry place. You subdue the Is 25:5
as **h** by the shade of a cloud, so the song Is 25:5
he poured on him the **h** of his anger and Is 42:25
wilderness, in her **h** sniffing the wind! Jer 2:24
stream, and does not fear when **h** comes, Jer 17:8
be cast out to the **h** by day and the frost Jer 36:30
an oven with the burning **h** of famine. Lam 5:10
went in bitterness in the **h** of my spirit, Ezk 3:14
princes became sick with the **h** of wine; Hos 7:5
Who can endure the **h** of his anger? Na 1:6
burden of the day and the scorching **h**.’ Mt 20:12
you say, ‘There will be scorching **h**,’ Lk 12:55
out because of the **h** and fastened on Acts 28:3
with its scorching **h** and withers the Jas 1:11
not strike them, nor any scorching **h**. Rv 7:16
They were scorched by the fierce **h**, and Rv 16:9

HEATED (3)
ordered the furnace **h** seven times more Dn 3:19
seven times more than it was usually **h**. Dn 3:19
they are like a **h** oven whose baker Hos 7:4

HEAVEN (491)
And God called the expanse **H**. And there Gn 1:8
in which is the breath of life under **h**. Gn 6:17
under the whole **h** were covered. Gn 7:19
Most High, Possessor of **h** and earth; Gn 14:19
Most High, Possessor of **h** and earth, Gn 14:22
him outside and said, “Look toward **h**, Gn 15:5
sulfur and fire from the LORD out of **h**. Gn 19:24
called to Hagar from **h** and said to her, Gn 21:17
the LORD called to him from **h** and said, Gn 22:11
to Abraham a second time from **h** Gn 22:15
as the stars of **h** and as the sand Gn 22:17
LORD, the God of **h** and God of the earth, Gn 24:3
The LORD, the God of **h**, who took me Gn 24:7
as the stars of **h** and will give to Gn 26:4
you of the dew of **h** and of the fatness of Gn 27:28
and away from the dew of **h** on high. Gn 27:39
the earth, and the top of it reached to **h**. Gn 28:12
house of God, and this is the gate of **h**.” Gn 28:17
bless you with blessings of **h** above, Gn 49:25
Moses, “Stretch out your hand toward **h**, Ex 9:22
Moses stretched out his staff toward **h**, Ex 9:23
“Stretch out your hand toward **h**, Ex 10:21
Moses stretched out his hand toward **h**, Ex 10:22
I am about to rain bread from **h** for you, Ex 16:4
the memory of Amalek from under **h**.” Ex 17:14
likeness of anything that is in **h** above, Ex 20:4
in six days the LORD made **h** and earth, Ex 20:11
that I have talked with you from **h**. Ex 20:22
stone, like the very **h** for clearness. Ex 24:10
in six days the LORD made **h** and earth, Ex 31:17
your offspring as the stars of **h**, Ex 32:13
are today as numerous as the stars of **h**. Dt 1:10
The cities are great and fortified up to **h**. Dt 1:28
the peoples who are under the whole **h**, Dt 2:25
what god is there in **h** or on earth who Dt 3:24
burned with fire to the heart of **h**, Dt 4:11
And beware lest you raise your eyes to **h**, Dt 4:19
the moon and the stars, all the host of **h**, Dt 4:19
to all the peoples under the whole **h**. Dt 4:19
I call **h** and earth to witness against you Dt 4:26
and ask from one end of **h** to the other, Dt 4:32
Out of **h** he let you hear his voice, that he Dt 4:36
the LORD is God in **h** above and on the Dt 4:39
likeness of anything that is in **h** above, Dt 5:8
make their name perish from under **h**. Dt 7:24
cities great and fortified up to **h**, Dt 9:1
and blot out their name from under **h**. Dt 9:14
LORD your God belong **h** and the heaven Dt 10:14
belong heaven and the **h** of heavens, Dt 10:14
you as numerous as the stars of **h**. Dt 10:22
which drinks water by the rain from **h**, Dt 11:11
sun or the moon or any of the host of **h**, Dt 17:3
the memory of Amalek from under **h**; Dt 25:19
from your holy habitation, from **h**, Dt 26:15
From **h** dust shall come down on you Dt 28:24
you were as numerous as the stars of **h**, Dt 28:62
will blot out his name from under **h**. Dt 29:20
outcasts are in the uttermost parts of **h**, Dt 30:4
It is not in **h**, that you should say, ‘Who Dt 30:12
‘Who will ascend to **h** for us and bring Dt 30:12
I call **h** and earth to witness against you Dt 30:19
their ears and call **h** and earth to Dt 31:28
For I lift up my hand to **h** and swear, As Dt 32:40
land, with the choicest gifts of **h** above, Dt 33:13
the smoke of the city went up to **h**, Jos 8:20
down large stones from **h** on them as Jos 10:11
in the midst of **h** and did not hurry Jos 10:13
From **h** the stars fought, from their Jgs 5:20
flame went up toward **h** from the altar, Jgs 13:20
of the city went up in smoke to **h**. Jgs 20:40
against them he will thunder in **h**. 1 Sm 2:10
and the cry of the city went up to **h**. 1 Sm 5:12
was suspended between **h** and earth, 2 Sm 18:9
The LORD thundered from **h**, and the 2 Sm 22:14
and spread out his hands toward **h**, 1 Kgs 8:22
you, in **h** above or on earth beneath, 1 Kgs 8:23
h and the highest heaven cannot 1 Kgs 8:27
and the highest **h** cannot contain 1 Kgs 8:27
And listen in **h** your dwelling place, 1 Kgs 8:30
then hear in **h** and act and judge 1 Kgs 8:32
then hear in **h** and forgive the sin of 1 Kgs 8:34
“When **h** is shut up and there is no 1 Kgs 8:35
then hear in **h** and forgive the sin of 1 Kgs 8:36
then hear in **h** your dwelling place 1 Kgs 8:39
hear in **h** your dwelling place and do 1 Kgs 8:43
then hear in **h** their prayer and their 1 Kgs 8:45
then hear in **h** your dwelling place 1 Kgs 8:49
with hands outstretched toward **h**. 1 Kgs 8:54
all the host of **h** standing beside him 1 Kgs 22:19
come down from **h** and consume you 2 Kgs 1:10
came down from **h** and consumed 2 Kgs 1:10
come down from **h** and consume you 2 Kgs 1:12
came down from **h** and consumed 2 Kgs 1:12
came down from **h** and consumed 2 Kgs 1:14
to take Elijah up to **h** by a whirlwind, 2 Kgs 2:1
Elijah went up by a whirlwind into **h**. 2 Kgs 2:11
himself should make windows in **h**, 2 Kgs 7:2
himself should make windows in **h**, 2 Kgs 7:19
out the name of Israel from under **h**, 2 Kgs 14:27
all the host of **h** and served Baal. 2 Kgs 17:16
earth; you have made **h** and earth. 2 Kgs 19:15
all the host of **h** and served them. 2 Kgs 21:3
for all the host of **h** in the two courts 2 Kgs 21:5
for Asherah, and for all the host of **h**. 2 Kgs 23:4
LORD standing between earth and **h**, 1 Chr 21:16
him with fire from **h** upon the altar 1 Chr 21:26
Israel as many as the stars of **h**. 1 Chr 27:23
is able to build him a house, since **h**, 2 Chr 2:6
a house, since heaven, even highest **h**, 2 Chr 2:6
God of Israel, who made **h** and earth, 2 Chr 2:12
and spread out his hands toward **h**, 2 Chr 6:13
is no God like you, in **h** or on earth, 2 Chr 6:14
h and the highest heaven cannot 2 Chr 6:18
and the highest **h** cannot contain 2 Chr 6:18
And listen from **h** your dwelling 2 Chr 6:21
then hear from **h** and act and judge 2 Chr 6:23
then hear from **h** and forgive the sin 2 Chr 6:25
“When **h** is shut up and there is no 2 Chr 6:26
then hear in **h** and forgive the sin of 2 Chr 6:27
then hear from **h** your dwelling place 2 Chr 6:30
hear from **h** your dwelling place and 2 Chr 6:33
then hear from **h** their prayer and 2 Chr 6:35
then hear from **h** your dwelling place 2 Chr 6:39
came down from **h** and consumed the 2 Chr 7:1
I will hear from **h** and will forgive 2 Chr 7:14
all the host of **h** standing on his 2 Chr 18:18
of our fathers, are you not God in **h**? 2 Chr 20:6
in a rage that has reached up to **h**. 2 Chr 28:9
came to his holy habitation in **h**. 2 Chr 30:27
because of this and cried to **h**. 2 Chr 32:20
all the host of **h** and served them. 2 Chr 33:3
for all the host of **h** in the two courts 2 Chr 33:5
of Persia, ‘The LORD, the God of **h**, 2 Chr 36:23
The LORD, the God of **h**, has given me all Ezr 1:2
the servants of the God of **h** and earth, Ezr 5:11
our fathers had angered the God of **h**, Ezr 5:12
sheep for burnt offerings to the God of **h**, Ezr 6:9
to the God of **h** and pray for the Ezr 6:10
the scribe of the Law of the God of **h**. Ezr 7:12
the scribe of the Law of the God of **h**, Ezr 7:21
Whatever is decreed by the God of **h**, let Ezr 7:23
in full for the house of the God of **h**, Ezr 7:23
fasting and praying before the God of **h**. Neh 1:4
And I said, “O LORD God of **h**, the great Neh 1:5
requesting?” So I prayed to the God of **h**. Neh 2:4
“The God of **h** will make us prosper, Neh 2:20
You have made **h**, the heaven of Neh 9:6
have made heaven, the **h** of heavens, Neh 9:6
of them; and the host of **h** worships you. Neh 9:6
with them from **h** and gave them Neh 9:13
them bread from **h** for their hunger Neh 9:15
their children as the stars of **h**, Neh 9:23
out to you and you heard them from **h**, Neh 9:27
and cried to you, you heard from **h**, Neh 9:28
fire of God fell from **h** and burned up the Jb 1:16
sprinkled dust on their heads toward **h**. Jb 2:12
It is higher than **h**—what can you do? Jb 11:8
Even now, behold, my witness is in **h**, Jb 16:19
not see, and he walks on the vault of **h**.’ Jb 22:14
with God; he makes peace in his high **h**. Jb 25:2
The pillars of **h** tremble and are Jb 26:11
Under the whole **h** he lets it go, and his Jb 37:3
who has given birth to the frost of **h**? Jb 38:29
Whatever is under the whole **h** is mine. Jb 41:11
his holy temple; the LORD’S throne is in **h**; Ps 11:4
LORD looks down from **h** on the children Ps 14:2
him from his holy **h** with the saving Ps 20:6
The LORD looks down from **h**; he sees all Ps 33:13
God looks down from **h** on the children Ps 53:2
He will send from **h** and save me; he will Ps 57:3
Let **h** and earth praise him, the seas and Ps 69:34
Whom have I in **h** but you? And there Ps 73:25
skies above and opened the doors of **h**, Ps 78:23
to eat and gave them the grain of **h**. Ps 78:24
Look down from **h**, and see; have regard Ps 80:14
from **h** the LORD looked at the earth, Ps 102:19
them bread from **h** in abundance. Ps 105:40
They mounted up to **h**; they went Ps 107:26
by the LORD, who made **h** and earth! Ps 115:15
from the LORD, who made **h** and earth. Ps 121:2
of the LORD, who made **h** and earth. Ps 124:8
from Zion, he who made **h** and earth! Ps 134:3
LORD pleases, he does, in **h** and on earth, Ps 135:6
Give thanks to the God of **h**, for his Ps 136:26
If I ascend to **h**, you are there! If I make Ps 139:8
who made **h** and earth, the sea, and all Ps 146:6
his majesty is above earth and **h**. Ps 148:13
wings, flying like an eagle toward **h**. Prv 23:5
has ascended to **h** and come down? Prv 30:4
by wisdom all that is done under **h**. Eccl 1:13
man to do under **h** during the few days Eccl 2:3
and a time for every matter under **h**: Eccl 3:1
for God is in **h** and you are on earth. Eccl 5:2
God; let it be deep as Sheol or high as **h**.” Is 7:11
“How you are fallen from **h**, O Day Star, Is 14:12
said in your heart, ‘I will ascend to **h**; Is 14:13
For the windows of **h** are opened, and the Is 24:18
day the LORD will punish the host of **h**, Is 24:21
will punish the host of heaven, in **h**, Is 24:21
All the host of **h** shall rot away, and the Is 34:4
of the earth; you have made **h** and earth. Is 37:16
snow come down from **h** and do not Is 55:10
Look down from **h** and see, from your Is 63:15
“**H** is my throne, and the earth is my Is 66:1
dough, to make cakes for the queen of **h**. Jer 7:18
sun and the moon and all the host of **h**, Jer 8:2
have been offered to all the host of **h**, Jer 19:13
the LORD. Do I not fill **h** and earth? Jer 23:24
As the host of **h** cannot be numbered Jer 33:22
night and the fixed order of **h** and earth, Jer 33:25
to the queen of **h** and pour out drink Jer 44:17
to the queen of **h** and pouring out drink Jer 44:18
to the queen of **h** and poured out drink Jer 44:19
to the queen of **h** and to pour out Jer 44:25
four winds from the four quarters of **h**. Jer 49:36
has reached up to **h** and has been lifted Jer 51:9
Babylon should mount up to **h**, Jer 51:53
has cast down from **h** to earth the Lam 2:1
up our hearts and hands to God in **h**: Lam 3:41
until the LORD from **h** looks down and Lam 3:50
up between earth and **h** and brought me Ezk 8:3
the bright lights of **h** will I make dark Ezk 32:8
the God of **h** concerning this mystery, Dn 2:18
night. Then Daniel blessed the God of **h**. Dn 2:19
is a God in **h** who reveals mysteries, Dn 2:28
whom the God of **h** has given the Dn 2:37
those kings the God of **h** will set up a Dn 2:44
became strong, and its top reached to **h**, Dn 4:11
watcher, a holy one, came down from **h**. Dn 4:13
field. Let him be wet with the dew of **h**. Dn 4:15
strong, so that its top reached to **h**, Dn 4:20

greatness has grown and reaches to **h**, Dn 4:22
one, coming down from **h** and saying, Dn 4:23
and let him be wet with the dew of **h**, Dn 4:23
and you shall be wet with the dew of **h**, Dn 4:25
the time that you know that **H** rules. Dn 4:26
king's mouth, there fell a voice from **h**, Dn 4:31
wet with the dew of **h** till his hair grew Dn 4:33
I, Nebuchadnezzar, lifted my eyes to **h**, Dn 4:34
among the host of **h** and among the Dn 4:35
and extol and honor the King of **h**, Dn 4:37
and his body was wet with the dew of **h**, Dn 5:21
lifted up yourself against the Lord of **h**. Dn 5:23
signs and wonders in **h** and on earth, Dn 6:27
the four winds of **h** were stirring up the Dn 7:2
with the clouds of **h** there came one like Dn 7:13
under the whole **h** shall be given Dn 7:27
horns toward the four winds of **h**. Dn 8:8
It grew great, even to the host of **h**. And Dn 8:10
For under the whole **h** there has not Dn 9:12
and divided toward the four winds of **h**, Dn 11:4
his left hand toward **h** and swore by Dn 12:7
if they climb up to **h**, from there I will Am 9:2
Hebrew, and I fear the LORD, the God of **h**, Jon 1:9
lifted up the basket between earth and **h**. Zec 5:9
are going out to the four winds of **h**, Zec 6:5
open the windows of **h** for you and Mal 3:10
"Repent, for the kingdom of **h** is at hand." Mt 3:2
and behold, a voice from **h** said, "This is Mt 3:17
for the kingdom of **h** is at hand." Mt 4:17
in spirit, for theirs is the kingdom of **h**. Mt 5:3
sake, for theirs is the kingdom of **h**. Mt 5:10
be glad, for your reward is great in **h**, Mt 5:12
give glory to your Father who is in **h**. Mt 5:16
I say to you, until **h** and earth pass away, Mt 5:18
will be called least in the kingdom of **h**, Mt 5:19
will be called great in the kingdom of **h**. Mt 5:19
you will never enter the kingdom of **h**. Mt 5:20
Do not take an oath at all, either by **h**, Mt 5:34
may be sons of your Father who is in **h**. Mt 5:45
no reward from your Father who is in **h**. Mt 6:1
"Our Father in **h**, hallowed be your Mt 6:9
your will be done, on earth as it is in **h**. Mt 6:10
but lay up for yourselves treasures in **h**, Mt 6:20
Father who is in **h** give good things to Mt 7:11
'Lord, Lord,' will enter the kingdom of **h**, Mt 7:21
does the will of my Father who is in **h**. Mt 7:21
Isaac, and Jacob in the kingdom of **h**, Mt 8:11
saying, 'The kingdom of **h** is at hand.' Mt 10:7
before my Father who is in **h**, Mt 10:32
will deny before my Father who is in **h**. Mt 10:33
in the kingdom of **h** is greater than he. Mt 11:11
the kingdom of **h** has suffered violence, Mt 11:12
Capernaum, will you be exalted to **h**? Mt 11:23
thank you, Father, Lord of **h** and earth, Mt 11:25
of my Father in **h** is my brother and Mt 12:50
know the secrets of the kingdom of **h**, Mt 13:11
"The kingdom of **h** may be compared Mt 13:24
"The kingdom of **h** is like a grain of Mt 13:31
"The kingdom of **h** is like leaven that a Mt 13:33
"The kingdom of **h** is like treasure Mt 13:44
the kingdom of **h** is like a merchant in Mt 13:45
the kingdom of **h** is like a net that was Mt 13:47
for the kingdom of **h** is like a master Mt 13:52
he looked up to **h** and said a blessing. Mt 14:19
asked him to show them a sign from **h**. Mt 16:1
this to you, but my Father who is in **h**. Mt 16:17
give you the keys of the kingdom of **h**, Mt 16:19
you bind on earth shall be bound in **h**, Mt 16:19
loose on earth shall be loosed in **h**." Mt 16:19
is the greatest in the kingdom of **h**?" Mt 18:1
you will never enter the kingdom of **h**. Mt 18:3
child is the greatest in the kingdom of **h**. Mt 18:4
tell you that in **h** their angels always Mt 18:10
see the face of my Father who is in **h**. Mt 18:10
my Father who is in **h** that one of these Mt 18:14
you bind on earth shall be bound in **h**, Mt 18:18
you loose on earth shall be loosed in **h**. Mt 18:18
be done for them by my Father in **h**. Mt 18:19
the kingdom of **h** may be compared Mt 18:23
for the sake of the kingdom of **h**. Mt 19:12
for to such belongs the kingdom of **h**." Mt 19:14
poor, and you will have treasure in **h**; Mt 19:21
a rich person enter the kingdom of **h**. Mt 19:23
"For the kingdom of **h** is like a master of Mt 20:1
From **h** or from man?" And they Mt 21:25
themselves, saying, "If we say, 'From **h**,' Mt 21:25
"The kingdom of **h** may be compared to Mt 22:2
in marriage, but are like angels in **h**. Mt 22:30
for you have one Father, who is in **h**. Mt 23:9
shut the kingdom of **h** in people's faces. Mt 23:13
whoever swears by **h** swears by the Mt 23:22
its light, and the stars will fall from **h**, Mt 24:29
Then will appear in **h** the sign of the Mt 24:30
on the clouds of **h** with power and great Mt 24:30
winds, from one end of **h** to the other. Mt 24:31

H and earth will pass away, but my Mt 24:35
no one knows, not even the angels of **h**, Mt 24:36
"Then the kingdom of **h** will be like ten Mt 25:1
Power and coming on the clouds of **h**." Mt 26:64
Lord descended from **h** and came and Mt 28:2
"All authority in **h** and on earth has Mt 28:18
And a voice came from **h**, "You are my Mk 1:11
he looked up to **h** and said a blessing Mk 6:41
And looking up to **h**, he sighed and said Mk 7:34
from him a sign from **h** to test him. Mk 8:11
poor, and you will have treasure in **h**; Mk 10:21
also who is in **h** may forgive you your Mk 11:25
baptism of John from **h** or from man? Mk 11:30
another, saying, "If we say, 'From **h**,' Mk 11:31
in marriage, but are like angels in **h**. Mk 12:25
and the stars will be falling from **h**, Mk 13:25
the ends of the earth to the ends of **h**. Mk 13:27
H and earth will pass away, but my Mk 13:31
one knows, not even the angels in **h**, Mk 13:32
and coming with the clouds of **h**." Mk 14:62
was taken up into **h** and sat down at Mk 16:19
the angels went away from them into **h**, Lk 2:15
and a voice came from **h**, "You are my Lk 3:22
joy, for behold, your reward is great in **h**; Lk 6:23
he looked up to **h** and said a blessing Lk 9:16
come down from **h** and consume Lk 9:54
Capernaum, will you be exalted to **h**? Lk 10:15
"I saw Satan fall like lightning from **h**. Lk 10:18
that your names are written in **h**." Lk 10:20
thank you, Father, Lord of **h** and earth, Lk 10:21
kept seeking from him a sign from **h**. Lk 11:16
be more joy in **h** over one sinner who Lk 15:7
I have sinned against **h** and before you. Lk 15:18
I have sinned against **h** and before you. Lk 15:21
But it is easier for **h** and earth to pass Lk 16:17
sulfur rained from **h** and destroyed Lk 17:29
off, would not even lift up his eyes to **h**, Lk 18:13
poor, and you will have treasure in **h**; Lk 18:22
Peace in **h** and glory in the highest!" Lk 19:38
baptism of John from **h** or from man?" Lk 20:4
one another, saying, "If we say, 'From **h**,' Lk 20:5
will be terrors and great signs from **h**. Lk 21:11
H and earth will pass away, but my Lk 21:33
there appeared to him an angel from **h**, Lk 22:43
from them and was carried up into **h**. Lk 24:51
saw the Spirit descend from **h** like a dove, Jn 1:32
truly, I say to you, you will see **h** opened, Jn 1:51
one has ascended into **h** except he who Jn 3:13
heaven except he who descended from **h**, Jn 3:13
one thing unless it is given him from **h**. Jn 3:27
way. He who comes from **h** is above all. Jn 3:31
'He gave them bread from **h** to eat.'" Jn 6:31
Moses who gave you the bread from **h**, Jn 6:32
Father gives you the true bread from **h**. Jn 6:32
who comes down from **h** and gives life to Jn 6:33
For I have come down from **h**, not to do Jn 6:38
"I am the bread that came down from **h**." Jn 6:41
he now say, 'I have come down from **h**'?" Jn 6:42
is the bread that comes down from **h**, Jn 6:50
the living bread that came down from **h**. Jn 6:51
is the bread that came down from **h**, Jn 6:58
your name." Then a voice came from **h**: Jn 12:28
these words, he lifted up his eyes to **h**, Jn 17:1
they were gazing into **h** as he went, Acts 1:10
why do you stand looking into **h**? Acts 1:11
who was taken up from you into **h**, Acts 1:11
same way as you saw him go into **h**." Acts 1:11
there came from **h** a sound like Acts 2:2
devout men from every nation under **h**. Acts 2:5
whom **h** must receive until the time Acts 3:21
other name under **h** given among men Acts 4:12
who made the **h** and the earth and the Acts 4:24
them over to worship the host of **h**, Acts 7:42
"'**H** is my throne, and the earth is my Acts 7:49
gazed into **h** and saw the glory of God, Acts 7:55
a light from **h** flashed around him. Acts 9:3
the thing was taken up at once to **h**. Acts 10:16
being let down from **h** by its four Acts 11:5
voice answered a second time from **h**, Acts 11:9
and all was drawn up again into **h**. Acts 11:10
who made the **h** and the earth and the Acts 14:15
you rains from **h** and fruitful Acts 14:17
in it, being Lord of **h** and earth, Acts 17:24
great light from **h** suddenly shone Acts 22:6
king, I saw on the way a light from **h**, Acts 26:13
is revealed from **h** against all Rom 1:18
'Who will ascend into **h**?'" (that is, Rom 10:6
be so-called gods in **h** or on earth— 1 Cor 8:5
of dust; the second man is from **h**. 1 Cor 15:47
of the dust, and as is the man of **h**, 1 Cor 15:48
so also are those who are of **h**. 1 Cor 15:48
also bear the image of the man of **h**. 1 Cor 15:49
up to the third **h**—whether in the 2 Cor 12:2
or an angel from **h** should preach to you Gal 1:8
him, things in **h** and things on earth. Eph 1:10

whom every family in **h** and on earth Eph 3:15
is both their Master and yours is in **h**, Eph 6:9
in **h** and on earth and under the earth, Phil 2:10
But our citizenship is in **h**, and from it Phil 3:20
because of the hope laid up for you in **h**. Col 1:5
things were created, in **h** and on earth, Col 1:16
all things, whether on earth or in **h**, Col 1:20
proclaimed in all creation under **h**, Col 1:23
that you also have a Master in **h**. Col 4:1
and to wait for his Son from **h**, 1 Thes 1:10
will descend from **h** with a cry 1 Thes 4:16
is revealed from **h** with his mighty 2 Thes 1:7
hand of the throne of the Majesty in **h**, Heb 8:1
of the true things, but into **h** itself, Heb 9:24
many as the stars of **h** and as many as Heb 11:12
of the firstborn who are enrolled in **h**, Heb 12:23
if we reject him who warns from **h**. Heb 12:25
either by **h** or by earth or by any other Jas 5:12
Then he prayed again, and **h** gave rain, Jas 5:18
and unfading, kept in **h** for you, 1 Pt 1:4
to you by the Holy Spirit sent from **h**, 1 Pt 1:12
who has gone into **h** and is at the right 1 Pt 3:22
heard this very voice borne from **h**, 2 Pt 1:18
comes down from my God out of **h**, Rv 3:12
and behold, a door standing open in **h**! Rv 4:1
the Spirit, and behold, a throne stood in **h**, Rv 4:2
And no one in **h** or on earth or under the Rv 5:3
heard every creature in **h** and on earth Rv 5:13
there was silence in **h** for about half an Rv 8:1
his trumpet, and a great star fell from **h**, Rv 8:10
and I saw a star fallen from **h** to earth, Rv 9:1
mighty angel coming down from **h**, Rv 10:1
write, but I heard a voice from **h** saying, Rv 10:4
on the land raised his right hand to **h** Rv 10:5
and ever, who created **h** and what is in it, Rv 10:6
I had heard from **h** spoke to me again, Rv 10:8
a loud voice from **h** saying to them, Rv 11:12
here!" And they went up to **h** in a cloud, Rv 11:12
terrified and gave glory to the God of **h**. Rv 11:13
and there were loud voices in **h**, Rv 11:15
Then God's temple in **h** was opened, Rv 11:19
And a great sign appeared in **h**: a woman Rv 12:1
And another sign appeared in **h**: behold, Rv 12:3
third of the stars of **h** and cast them to Rv 12:4
Now war arose in **h**, Michael and his Rv 12:7
was no longer any place for them in **h**. Rv 12:8
And I heard a loud voice in **h**, saying, Rv 12:10
dwelling, that is, those who dwell in **h**. Rv 13:6
fire come down from **h** to earth in front Rv 13:13
I heard a voice from **h** like the roar of Rv 14:2
and worship him who made **h** and earth, Rv 14:7
And I heard a voice from **h** saying, Rv 14:13
angel came out of the temple in **h**, Rv 14:17
Then I saw another sign in **h**, great and Rv 15:1
of the tent of witness in **h** was opened, Rv 15:5
cursed the God of **h** for their pain and Rv 16:11
pounds each, fell from **h** on people; Rv 16:21
saw another angel coming down from **h**, Rv 18:1
I heard another voice from **h** saying, Rv 18:4
for her sins are heaped high as **h**, and Rv 18:5
Rejoice over her, O **h**, and you saints Rv 18:20
the loud voice of a great multitude in **h**, Rv 19:1
Then I saw **h** opened, and behold, a Rv 19:11
And the armies of **h**, arrayed in fine Rv 19:14
I saw an angel coming down from **h**, Rv 20:1
came down from **h** and consumed them, Rv 20:9
Then I saw a new **h** and a new earth, for Rv 21:1
for the first **h** and the first earth had Rv 21:1
coming down out of **h** from God, Rv 21:2
coming down out of **h** from God, Rv 21:10

HEAVENLY (32)
little lower than the **h** beings and crowned Ps 8:5
Ascribe to the LORD, O **h** beings, ascribe Ps 29:1
have established the **h** lights and the Ps 74:16
Who among the **h** beings is like the Ps 89:6
be perfect, as your **h** Father is perfect. Mt 5:48
your **h** Father will also forgive you, Mt 6:14
barns, and yet your **h** Father feeds them. Mt 6:26
and your **h** Father knows that you need Mt 6:32
"Every plant that my **h** Father has not Mt 15:13
So also my **h** Father will do to every Mt 18:35
a multitude of the **h** host praising God Lk 2:13
much more will the **h** Father give the Lk 11:13
can you believe if I tell you **h** things? Jn 3:12
I was not disobedient to the **h** vision, Acts 26:19
There are **h** bodies and earthly 1 Cor 15:40
but the glory of the **h** is of one kind, 1 Cor 15:40
longing to put on our **h** dwelling, 2 Cor 5:2
every spiritual blessing in the **h** places, Eph 1:3
him at his right hand in the **h** places, Eph 1:20
with him in the **h** places in Christ Jesus, Eph 2:6
rulers and authorities in the **h** places. Eph 3:10
spiritual forces of evil in the **h** places. Eph 6:12
bring me safely into his **h** kingdom. 2 Tm 4:18
brothers, you who share in a **h** calling, Heb 3:1

enlightened, who have tasted the **h** gift, Heb 6:4
serve a copy and shadow of the **h** things. Heb 8:5
the copies of the **h** things to be purified Heb 9:23
but the **h** things themselves with better Heb 9:23
a better country, that is, a **h** one. Heb 11:16
city of the living God, the **h** Jerusalem, Heb 12:22
and the **h** bodies will be burned up and 2 Pt 3:10
and the **h** bodies will melt as they 2 Pt 3:12

HEAVENS (210)
God created the **h** and the earth. Gn 1:1
waters under the **h** be gathered together Gn 1:9
the expanse of the **h** to separate the day Gn 1:14
in the expanse of the **h** to give light upon Gn 1:15
in the expanse of the **h** to give light on Gn 1:17
the earth across the expanse of the **h**." Gn 1:20
the birds of the **h** and over the livestock Gn 1:26
the birds of the **h** and over every living Gn 1:28
every bird of the **h** and to everything Gn 1:30
Thus the **h** and the earth were finished, Gn 2:1
the generations of the **h** and the earth Gn 2:4
the LORD God made the earth and the **h**. Gn 2:4
every bird of the **h** and brought them to Gn 2:19
to the birds of the **h** and to every beast of Gn 2:20
and creeping things and birds of the **h**, Gn 6:7
and seven pairs of the birds of the **h** also, Gn 7:3
and the windows of the **h** were opened. Gn 7:11
and creeping things and birds of the **h**. Gn 7:23
and the windows of the **h** were closed, Gn 8:2
the rain from the **h** was restrained, Gn 8:2
of the earth and upon every bird of the **h**, Gn 9:2
a city and a tower with its top in the **h**, Gn 11:4
I will make your **h** like iron and your Lv 26:19
God belong heaven and the heaven of **h**, Dt 10:14
against you, and he will shut up the **h**, Dt 11:17
as long as the **h** are above the earth. Dt 11:21
open to you his good treasury, the **h**, Dt 28:12
And the **h** over your head shall be Dt 28:23
"Give ear, O **h**, and I will speak, and let Dt 32:1
"Rejoice with him, O **h**; bow down to Dt 32:43
who rides through the **h** to your help, Dt 33:26
and wine, whose **h** drop down dew. Dt 33:28
he is God in the **h** above and on the Jos 2:11
the earth trembled and the **h** dropped, Jgs 5:4
until rain fell upon them from the **h**. 2 Sm 21:10
foundations of the **h** trembled and 2 Sm 22:8
He bowed the **h** and came down; 2 Sm 22:10
country the birds of the **h** shall eat, 1 Kgs 14:11
the field the birds of the **h** shall eat." 1 Kgs 16:4
a little while the **h** grew black with 1 Kgs 18:45
country the birds of the **h** shall eat." 1 Kgs 21:24
and all the host of the **h**. 2 Kgs 23:5
are idols, but the LORD made the **h**. 1 Chr 16:26
Let the **h** be glad, and let the earth 1 Chr 16:31
all that is in the **h** and in the earth is 1 Chr 29:11
When I shut up the **h** so that there is 2 Chr 7:13
and our guilt has mounted up to the **h**. Ezr 9:6
You have made heaven, the heaven of **h**, Neh 9:6
alone stretched out the **h** and trampled the Jb 9:8
the birds of the **h**, and they will tell you; Jb 12:7
till the **h** are no more he will not awake Jb 14:12
ones, and the **h** are not pure in his sight; Jb 15:15
Though his height mount up to the **h**, Jb 20:6
The **h** will reveal his iniquity, and the Jb 20:27
"Is not God high in the **h**? See the Jb 22:12
By his wind the **h** were made fair; his Jb 26:13
earth and sees everything under the **h**. Jb 28:24
Look at the **h**, and see; and behold the Jb 35:5
makes us wiser than the birds of the **h**?' Jb 35:11
Do you know the ordinances of the **h**? Jb 38:33
Or who can tilt the waterskins of the **h**, Jb 38:37
He who sits in the **h** laughs; the Lord Ps 2:4
You have set your glory above the **h**. Ps 8:1
When I look at your **h**, the work of your Ps 8:3
the birds of the **h**, and the fish of the sea, Ps 8:8
He bowed the **h** and came down; thick Ps 18:9
The LORD also thundered in the **h**, and Ps 18:13
The **h** declare the glory of God, and the Ps 19:1
Its rising is from the end of the **h**, and its Ps 19:6
By the word of the LORD the **h** were made, Ps 33:6
steadfast love, O LORD, extends to the **h**, Ps 36:5
He calls to the **h** above and to the earth, Ps 50:4
The **h** declare his righteousness, for God Ps 50:6
Be exalted, O God, above the **h**! Let your Ps 57:5
For your steadfast love is great to the **h**, Ps 57:10
Be exalted, O God, above the **h**! Let your Ps 57:11
earth quaked, the **h** poured down rain, Ps 68:8
to him who rides in the **h**, the ancient Ps 68:33
who rides in the heavens, the ancient **h**; Ps 68:33
O God, reaches the high **h**. Ps 71:19
They set their mouths against the **h**, and Ps 73:9
From the **h** you uttered judgment; the Ps 76:8
caused the east wind to blow in the **h**, Ps 78:26
He built his sanctuary like the high **h**, Ps 78:69
servants to the birds of the **h** for food, Ps 79:2
in the **h** you will establish your Ps 89:2
Let the **h** praise your wonders, O LORD, Ps 89:5
The **h** are yours; the earth also is yours; Ps 89:11
and his throne as the days of the **h**. Ps 89:29
worthless idols, but the LORD made the **h**. Ps 96:5
Let the **h** be glad, and let the earth Ps 96:11
The **h** proclaim his righteousness, and Ps 97:6
and the **h** are the work of your hands. Ps 102:25
as high as the **h** are above the earth, Ps 103:11
has established his throne in the **h**, Ps 103:19
stretching out the **h** like a tent. Ps 104:2
Beside them the birds of the **h** dwell; Ps 104:12
your steadfast love is great above the **h**; Ps 108:4
Be exalted, O God, above the **h**! Let your Ps 108:5
all nations, and his glory above the **h**! Ps 113:4
looks far down on the **h** and the earth? Ps 113:6
Our God is in the **h**; he does all that he Ps 115:3
The **h** are the LORD'S heavens, but the Ps 115:16
The heavens are the LORD'S **h**, but the Ps 115:16
your word is firmly fixed in the **h**. Ps 119:89
eyes, O you who are enthroned in the **h**! Ps 123:1
him who by understanding made the **h**, Ps 136:5
Bow your **h**, O LORD, and come down! Ps 144:5
He covers the **h** with clouds; he prepares Ps 147:8
Praise the LORD from the **h**; praise him Ps 148:1
Praise him, you highest **h**, and you Ps 148:4
heavens, and you waters above the **h**! Ps 148:4
sanctuary; praise him in his mighty **h**! Ps 150:1
by understanding he established the **h**; Prv 3:19
When he established the **h**, I was there; Prv 8:27
As the **h** for height, and the earth for Prv 25:3
Hear, O **h**, and give ear, O earth; for the Is 1:2
from a distant land, from the end of the **h**, Is 13:5
stars of the **h** and their constellations Is 13:10
Therefore I will make the **h** tremble, and Is 13:13
For my sword has drunk its fill in the **h**; Is 34:5
hand and marked off the **h** with a span, Is 40:12
who stretches out the **h** like a curtain, Is 40:22
who created the **h** and stretched them out, Is 42:5
Sing, O **h**, for the LORD has done it; shout, Is 44:23
all things, who alone stretched out the **h**, Is 44:24
"Shower, O **h**, from above, and let the Is 45:8
it was my hands that stretched out the **h**, Is 45:12
the LORD, who created the **h** (he is God!), Is 45:18
and save you, those who divide the **h**, Is 47:13
and my right hand spread out the **h**; Is 48:13
Sing for joy, O **h**, and exult, O earth; Is 49:13
I clothe the **h** with blackness and make Is 50:3
Lift up your eyes to the **h**, and look at the Is 51:6
for the **h** vanish like smoke, the earth will Is 51:6
who stretched out the **h** and laid the Is 51:13
establishing the **h** and laying the Is 51:16
For as the **h** are higher than the earth, so Is 55:9
you would rend the **h** and come down, Is 64:1
behold, I create new **h** and a new earth, Is 65:17
"For as the new **h** and the new earth that Is 66:22
Be appalled, O **h**, at this; be shocked, be Jer 2:12
void; and to the **h**, and they had no light. Jer 4:23
shall mourn, and the **h** above be dark; Jer 4:28
Even the stork in the **h** knows her times, Jer 8:7
the signs of the **h** because the nations Jer 10:2
did not make the **h** and the earth shall Jer 10:11
from the earth and from under the **h**." Jer 10:11
his understanding stretched out the **h**. Jer 10:12
there is a tumult of waters in the **h**, Jer 10:13
bring rain? Or can the **h** give showers? Jer 14:22
"If the **h** above can be measured, and Jer 31:37
who has made the **h** and the earth by Jer 32:17
his understanding stretched out the **h**. Jer 51:15
there is a tumult of waters in the **h**, Jer 51:16
Then the **h** and the earth, and all that is Jer 51:48
and destroy them from under your **h**, Lam 3:66
were swifter than the eagles in the **h**; Lam 4:19
by the Chebar canal, the **h** were opened, Ezk 1:1
to the birds of the **h** I give you as food. Ezk 29:5
the birds of the **h** made their nests in Ezk 31:6
trunk dwell all the birds of the **h**, Ezk 31:13
all the birds of the **h** to settle on you, Ezk 32:4
I will cover the **h** and make their stars Ezk 32:7
and the birds of the **h** and the beasts of Ezk 38:20
beasts of the field, and the birds of the **h**, Dn 2:38
the birds of the **h** lived in its branches, Dn 4:12
branches the birds of the **h** lived— Dn 4:21
the beasts of the field, the birds of the **h**, Hos 2:18
declares the LORD, I will answer the **h**, Hos 2:21
beasts of the field and the birds of the **h**, Hos 4:3
bring them down like birds of the **h**; Hos 7:12
earth quakes before them; the **h** tremble. Jl 2:10
show wonders in the **h** and on the earth, Jl 2:30
Jerusalem, and the **h** and the earth quake. Jl 3:16
upper chambers in the **h** and founds his Am 9:6
merchants more than the stars of the **h**. Na 3:16
His splendor covered the **h**, and the Hab 3:3
away the birds of the **h** and the fish of the Zep 1:3
down on the roofs to the host of the **h**, Zep 1:5
Therefore the **h** above you have Hg 1:10
I will shake the **h** and the earth and the Hg 2:6
I am about to shake the **h** and the earth, Hg 2:21
you abroad as the four winds of the **h**, Zec 2:6
produce, and the **h** shall give their dew. Zec 8:12
stretched out the **h** and founded the Zec 12:1
and behold, the **h** were opened to him, Mt 3:16
and the powers of the **h** will be shaken. Mt 24:29
he saw the **h** opening and the Mk 1:10
the powers in the **h** will be shaken. Mk 13:25
and was praying, the **h** were opened, Lk 3:21
when the **h** were shut up three years and Lk 4:25
a treasure in the **h** that does not fail, Lk 12:33
For the powers of the **h** will be shaken. Lk 21:26
wonders in the **h** above and signs Acts 2:19
For David did not ascend into the **h**, Acts 2:34
he said, "Behold, I see the **h** opened, Acts 7:56
and saw the **h** opened and something Acts 10:11
not made with hands, eternal in the **h**. 2 Cor 5:1
who also ascended far above all the **h**, Eph 4:10
and the **h** are the work of your hands; Heb 1:10
priest who has passed through the **h**, Heb 4:14
from sinners, and exalted above the **h**. Heb 7:26
not only the earth but also the **h**." Heb 12:26
this fact, that the **h** existed long ago, 2 Pt 3:5
the same word the **h** and earth that now 2 Pt 3:7
and then the **h** will pass away with a 2 Pt 3:10
because of which the **h** will be set on 2 Pt 3:12
are waiting for new **h** and a new earth 2 Pt 3:13
O **h** and you who dwell in them! Rv 12:12

HEAVES (1)
the hills melt; the earth **h** before him, the Na 1:5

HEAVIER (3)
Let **h** work be laid on the men that they Ex 5:9
For then it would be **h** than the sand of the Jb 6:3
but a fool's provocation is **h** than both. Prv 27:3

HEAVILY (3)
chariot wheels so that they drove **h**. Ex 14:25
of the house of Joseph rested **h** on them, Jgs 1:35
you were filled and **h** laden in the Ezk 27:25

HEAVY (45)
them to afflict them with **h** burdens. Ex 1:11
tomorrow I will cause very **h** hail to fall, Ex 9:18
in the midst of the hail, very **h** hail, Ex 9:24
out, for the thing is too **h** for you. Ex 18:18
alone; the burden is too **h** for me. Nm 11:14
he died, for the man was old and **h**. 1 Sm 4:18
of the LORD was **h** against the people of 1 Sm 5:6
The hand of God was very **h** there. 1 Sm 5:11
when it was **h** on him, he cut it), he 2 Sm 14:26
"Your father made our yoke **h**. Now 1 Kgs 12:4
of your father and his **h** yoke on us, 1 Kgs 12:4
you, 'Your father made our yoke **h**, 1 Kgs 12:10
my father laid on you a **h** yoke, 1 Kgs 12:11
"My father made your yoke **h**, 1 Kgs 12:14
"Your father made our yoke **h**. Now 2 Chr 10:4
of your father and his **h** yoke on us, 2 Chr 10:4
you, 'Your father made our yoke **h**, 2 Chr 10:10
my father laid on you a **h** yoke, 2 Chr 10:11
"My father made your yoke **h**, 2 Chr 10:14
of this matter and because of the **h** rain. Ezr 10:9
are many, and it is a time of **h** rain; Ezr 10:13
were before me laid **h** burdens on the Neh 5:15
the service was too **h** on this people. Neh 5:18
my hand is **h** on account of my Jb 23:2
you; my pressure will not be **h** upon you. Jb 33:7
and night your hand was **h** upon me; Ps 32:4
like a **h** burden, they are too heavy for Ps 38:4
a heavy burden, they are too **h** for me. Ps 38:4
Your wrath lies **h** upon me, and you Ps 88:7
may our cattle be **h** with young, Ps 144:14
sings songs to a **h** heart is like one Prv 25:20
A stone is **h**, and sand is weighty, but a Prv 27:3
the sun, and it lies **h** on mankind: Eccl 6:1
although man's trouble lies **h** on him. Eccl 8:6
heart of this people dull, and their ears **h**, Is 6:10
its transgression lies **h** upon it, and it Is 24:20
aged you made your yoke exceedingly **h**. Is 47:6
escape; he has made my chains **h**; Lam 3:7
will make Jerusalem a **h** stone for all Zec 12:3
to me, all who labor and are **h** laden, Mt 11:28
They tie up **h** burdens, hard to bear, and Mt 23:4
them sleeping, for their eyes were **h**. Mt 26:43
sleeping, for their eyes were very **h**, Mk 14:40
who were with him were **h** with sleep, Lk 9:32
of thunder, an earthquake, and **h** hail. Rv 11:19

HEBER (11)
the sons of Beriah: **H** and Malchiel. Gn 46:17
Of the sons of Beriah: of **H**, the clan of Nm 26:45
Now **H** the Kenite had separated from Jgs 4:11
the tent of Jael, the wife of **H** the Kenite, Jgs 4:17
of Hazor and the house of **H** the Kenite. Jgs 4:17
But Jael the wife of **H** took a tent peg, and Jgs 4:21
women be Jael, the wife of **H** the Kenite, Jgs 5:24

father of Gedor, **H** the father of Soco, 1 Chr 4:18
H, and Malchiel, who fathered 1 Chr 7:31
H fathered Japhlet, Shomer, Hotham, 1 Chr 7:32
Zebadiah, Meshullam, Hizki, **H**, 1 Chr 8:17

HEBERITES (1)
of Beriah: of Heber, the clan of the **H**; Nm 26:45

HEBREW (21)
escaped came and told Abram the **H**, Gn 14:13
brought among us a **H** to laugh at us. Gn 39:14
the same story, saying, "The **H** servant, Gn 39:17
A young **H** was there with us, a servant Gn 41:12
the king of Egypt said to the **H** midwives, Ex 1:15
as midwife to the **H** women and see them Ex 1:16
"Because the **H** women are not like the Ex 1:19
a nurse from the **H** women to nurse the Ex 2:7
and he saw an Egyptian beating a **H**, Ex 2:11
When you buy a **H** slave, he shall serve Ex 21:2
brother, a **H** man or a Hebrew woman, Dt 15:12
brother, a Hebrew man or a **H** woman, Dt 15:12
everyone should set free his **H** slaves, Jer 34:9
set free the fellow **H** who has been sold Jer 34:14
And he said to them, "I am a **H**, and I fear Jon 1:9
he addressed them in the **H** language, Acts 21:40
addressing them in the **H** language, Acts 22:2
voice saying to me in the **H** language, Acts 26:14
of the tribe of Benjamin, a **H** of Hebrews; Phil 3:5
His name in **H** is Abaddon, and in Greek Rv 9:11
place that in **H** is called Armageddon. Rv 16:16

HEBREWS (21)
indeed stolen out of the land of the **H**, Gn 40:15
the Egyptians could not eat with the **H**, Gn 43:32
that is born to the **H** you shall cast into Ex 1:22
behold, two **H** were struggling together. Ex 2:13
say to him, 'The LORD, the God of the **H**, Ex 3:18
said, "The God of the **H** has met with us. Ex 5:3
say to him, 'The LORD, the God of the **H**, Ex 7:16
'Thus says the LORD, the God of the **H**, Ex 9:1
'Thus says the LORD, the God of the **H**, Ex 9:13
"Thus says the LORD, the God of the **H**, Ex 10:3
the camp of the **H** mean?" And when 1 Sm 4:6
become slaves to the **H** as they have 1 Sm 4:9
all the land, saying, "Let the **H** hear." 1 Sm 13:3
and some **H** crossed the fords of the 1 Sm 13:7
"Lest the **H** make themselves swords 1 Sm 13:19
H are coming out of the holes where 1 Sm 14:11
Now the **H** who had been with the 1 Sm 14:21
"What are these **H** doing here?" And 1 Sm 29:3
arose against the **H** because their Acts 6:1
Are they **H**? So am I. Are they 2 Cor 11:22
of the tribe of Benjamin, a Hebrew of **H**; Phil 3:5

HEBREWS' (1)
and said, "This is one of the **H** children." Ex 2:6

HEBRON (72)
by the oaks of Mamre, which are at **H**, Gn 13:18
(that is, **H**) in the land of Canaan, Gn 23:2
(that is, **H**) in the land of Canaan. Gn 23:19
H), where Abraham and Isaac had Gn 35:27
So he sent him from the Valley of **H**, Gn 37:14
Amram, Izhar, **H**, and Uzziel, the years Ex 6:18
clans: Amram, Izhar, **H**, and Uzziel. Nm 3:19
up into the Negeb and came to **H**. Nm 13:22
(**H** was built seven years before Zoan Nm 13:22
of Jerusalem sent to Hoham king of **H**, Jos 10:3
the king of Jerusalem, the king of **H**, Jos 10:5
the king of Jerusalem, the king of **H**, Jos 10:23
with him went up from Eglon to **H**. Jos 10:36
as he had done to **H** and to Libnah and Jos 10:39
Anakim from the hill country, from **H**, Jos 11:21
of Jerusalem, one; the king of **H**, one; Jos 12:10
and he gave **H** to Caleb the son of Jos 14:13
Therefore **H** became the inheritance of Jos 14:14
the name of **H** formerly was Jos 14:15
is, **H** (Arba was the father of Anak). Jos 15:13
Kiriath-arba (that is, **H**), and Zior: Jos 15:54
(that is, **H**) in the hill country of Judah. Jos 20:7
being the father of Anak), that is **H**, Jos 21:11
of Aaron the priest they gave **H**, Jos 21:13
who lived in **H** (now the name Jgs 1:10
the name of **H** was formerly Jgs 1:10
And **H** was given to Caleb, as Moses had Jgs 1:20
to the top of the hill that is in front of **H**. Jgs 16:3
in **H**, for all the places where David 1 Sm 30:31
shall I go up?" And he said, "To **H**." 2 Sm 2:1
and they lived in the towns of **H**. 2 Sm 2:3
David was king in **H** over the house of 2 Sm 2:11
and the day broke upon them at **H**. 2 Sm 2:32
And sons were born to David at **H**: his 2 Sm 3:2
wife. These were born to David in **H**. 2 Sm 3:5
to tell David at **H** all that Israel and 2 Sm 3:19
came with twenty men to David at **H**, 2 Sm 3:20
But Abner was not with David at **H**, 2 Sm 3:22
And when Abner returned to **H**, Joab 2 Sm 3:27
They buried Abner at **H**. And the 2 Sm 3:32
son, heard that Abner had died at **H**, 2 Sm 4:1
the head of Ish-bosheth to David at **H**. 2 Sm 4:8
and hanged them beside the pool at **H**. 2 Sm 4:12
buried it in the tomb of Abner at **H**. 2 Sm 4:12
of Israel came to David at **H** and said, 2 Sm 5:1
elders of Israel came to the king at **H**, 2 Sm 5:3
with them at **H** before the LORD, 2 Sm 5:3
At **H** he reigned over Judah seven years 2 Sm 5:5
Jerusalem, after he came from **H**, 2 Sm 5:13
which I have vowed to the LORD, in **H**. 2 Sm 15:7
in peace." So he arose and went to **H**. 2 Sm 15:9
then say, 'Absalom is king at **H**!'" 2 Sm 15:10
seven years in **H** and thirty-three 1 Kgs 2:11
Ziph. The son of Mareshah: **H**. 1 Chr 2:42
The sons of **H**: Korah, Tappuah, 1 Chr 2:43
of David who were born to him in **H**: 1 Chr 3:1
six were born to him in **H**, where he 1 Chr 3:4
Kohath: Amram, Izhar, **H**, and Uzziel. 1 Chr 6:2
Kohath: Amram, Izhar, **H** and Uzziel. 1 Chr 6:18
to them they gave **H** in the land of 1 Chr 6:55
H, Libnah with its pasturelands, 1 Chr 6:57
together to David at **H** and said, 1 Chr 11:1
elders of Israel came to the king at **H**, 1 Chr 11:3
with them at **H** before the LORD. 1 Chr 11:3
came to David in **H** to turn the 1 Chr 12:23
came to **H** with full intent to make 1 Chr 12:38
of the sons of **H**, Eliel the chief, with 1 Chr 15:9
Amram, Izhar, **H**, and Uzziel, four. 1 Chr 23:12
The sons of **H**: Jeriah the chief, 1 Chr 23:19
The sons of **H**: Jeriah the chief, 1 Chr 24:23
seven years in **H** and thirty-three 1 Chr 29:27
Zorah, Aijalon, and **H**, fortified 2 Chr 11:10

HEBRONITES (6)
and the clan of the **H** and the clan of Nm 3:27
clan of the Libnites, the clan of the **H**, Nm 26:58
the Amramites, the Izharites, the **H**, 1 Chr 26:23
Of the **H**, Hashabiah and his 1 Chr 26:30
Of the **H**, Jerijah was chief of the 1 Chr 26:31
chief of the **H** of whatever genealogy 1 Chr 26:31

HEDGE (5)
you not put a **h** around him and his Jb 1:10
way of a sluggard is like a **h** of thorns, Prv 15:19
I will remove its **h**, and it shall be Is 5:5
Therefore I will **h** up her way with Hos 2:6
brier, the most upright of them a thorn **h**. Mi 7:4

HEDGED (1)
way is hidden, whom God has **h** in? Jb 3:23

HEDGEHOG (2)
"And I will make it a possession of the **h**, Is 14:23
the owl and the **h** shall lodge in her Zep 2:14

HEDGES (2)
lament, and run to and fro among the **h**! Jer 49:3
the highways and **h** and compel people Lk 14:23

HEED (1)
that he stands take **h** lest he fall. 1 Cor 10:12

HEEDED (1)
out my hand and no one has **h**, Prv 1:24

HEEDS (3)
Whoever **h** instruction is on the path Prv 10:17
but whoever **h** reproof is honored. Prv 13:18
but whoever **h** reproof is prudent. Prv 15:5

HEEL (6)
your head, and you shall bruise his **h**." Gn 3:15
out with his hand holding Esau's **h**, Gn 25:26
A trap seizes him by the **h**; a snare lays Jb 18:9
ate my bread, has lifted his **h** against me. Ps 41:9
the womb he took his brother by the **h**, Hos 12:3
my bread has lifted his **h** against me.' Jn 13:18

HEELS (6)
that bites the horse's **h** so that his rider Gn 49:17
raid Gad, but he shall raid at their **h**. Gn 49:19
And 10,000 men went up at his **h**, and Jgs 4:10
into the valley they rushed at his **h**. Jgs 5:15
on every side, and chase him at his **h**. Jb 18:11
pestilence, and plague followed at his **h**. Hab 3:5

HEGAI (4)
in Susa the capital, under custody of **H**, Est 2:3
in Susa the citadel in custody of **H**, Est 2:8
the king's palace and put in custody of **H**, Est 2:8
nothing except what **H** the king's Est 2:15

HEGLAM (1)
is, **H**, who fathered Uzza and Ahihud. 1 Chr 8:7

HEIFER (16)
to him, "Bring me a **h** three years old, Gn 15:9
to bring you a red **h** without defect, Nm 19:2
And the **h** shall be burned in his sight. Nm 19:5
throw them into the fire burning the **h**. Nm 19:6
one who burns the **h** shall wash his Nm 19:8
the ashes of the **h** and deposit them Nm 19:9
the ashes of the **h** shall wash his Nm 19:10
man shall take a **h** that has never been Dt 21:3
city shall bring the **h** down to a valley Dt 21:4
their hands over the **h** whose neck was Dt 21:6
"If you had not plowed with my **h**, Jgs 14:18
said, "Take a **h** with you and say, 1 Sm 16:2
"A beautiful **h** is Egypt, but a biting fly Jer 46:20
you frolic like a **h** in the pasture, Jer 50:11
Like a stubborn **h**, Israel is stubborn; Hos 4:16
the ashes of a **h** sanctifies for the Heb 9:13

HEIFER'S (1)
and shall break the **h** neck there in the Dt 21:4

HEIGHT (58)
breadth 50 cubits, and its **h** 30 cubits. Gn 6:15
its breadth, and a cubit and a half its **h**. Ex 25:10
its breadth, and a cubit and a half its **h**. Ex 25:23
be square, and its **h** shall be three cubits. Ex 27:1
the breadth fifty, and the **h** five cubits, Ex 27:18
be square, and two cubits shall be its **h**. Ex 30:2
its breadth, and a cubit and a half its **h**. Ex 37:1
its breadth, and a cubit and a half its **h**. Ex 37:10
It was square, and two cubits was its **h**. Ex 37:25
It was square, and three cubits was its **h**. Ex 38:1
people that we saw in it are of great **h**. Nm 13:32
I will tell you." And he went to a bare **h**, Nm 23:3
appearance or on the **h** of his stature, 1 Sm 16:7
whose **h** was six cubits and a span. 1 Sm 17:4
tamarisk tree on the **h** with his spear 1 Sm 22:6
The **h** of one cherub was ten cubits, 1 Kgs 6:26
fifty cubits and its **h** thirty cubits, 1 Kgs 7:2
cubits was the **h** of one pillar, 1 Kgs 7:15
The **h** of the one capital was five 1 Kgs 7:16
and the **h** of the other capital was five 1 Kgs 7:16
and the **h** of a wheel was a cubit and 1 Kgs 7:32
The **h** of the one pillar was eighteen 2 Kgs 25:17
The **h** of the capital was three 2 Kgs 25:17
of the house, and its **h** was 120 cubits. 2 Chr 3:4
Ophel, and raised it to a very great **h**. 2 Chr 33:14
Its **h** shall be sixty cubits and its breadth Ezr 6:3
the wall was joined together to half its **h**, Neh 4:6
Though his **h** mount up to the heavens, Jb 20:6
that he looked down from his holy **h**; Ps 102:19
As the heavens for **h**, and the earth for Prv 25:3
the great in **h** will be hewn down, and Is 10:33
your shade like night at the **h** of noon; Is 16:3
a tomb on the **h** and carve a dwelling Is 22:16
he has humbled the inhabitants of the **h**, Is 26:5
cypresses, to come to its remotest **h**, Is 37:24
the mountain of the house a wooded **h**.' Jer 26:18
come and sing aloud on the **h** of Zion, Jer 31:12
of the rock, who hold the **h** of the hill. Jer 49:16
though she should fortify her strong **h**, Jer 51:53
the **h** of the one pillar was eighteen Jer 52:21
The **h** of the one capital was five cubits. Jer 52:22
On the mountain **h** of Israel will I Ezk 17:23
it was seen in its **h** with the mass of its Ezk 19:11
mountain, the mountain **h** of Israel, Ezk 20:40
and forest shade, and of towering **h**, Ezk 31:3
and its heart was proud of its **h**, Ezk 31:10
may grow to towering **h** or set their Ezk 31:14
water may reach up to them in **h**. Ezk 31:14
of the wall, one reed; and the **h**, one reed. Ezk 40:5
And this shall be the **h** of the altar: Ezk 43:13
whose **h** was sixty cubits and its breadth Dn 3:1
midst of the earth, and its **h** was great. Dn 4:10
whose **h** was like the height of the cedars Am 2:9
height was like the **h** of the cedars and Am 2:9
the mountain of the house a wooded **h**. Mi 3:12
nor **h** nor depth, nor anything else in Rom 8:39
breadth and length and **h** and depth, Eph 3:18
Its length and width and **h** are equal. Rv 21:16

HEIGHTS (28)
went up to the **h** of the hill country, Nm 14:40
to go up to the **h** of the hill country, Nm 14:44
and swallowed the **h** of the Arnon. Nm 21:28
death; Naphtali, too, on the **h** of the field. Jgs 5:18
of a deer and set me secure on the **h**. 2 Sm 22:34
voice and lifted your eyes to the **h**? 2 Kgs 19:22
gone up the **h** of the mountains, 2 Kgs 19:23
feet of a deer and set me secure on the **h**. Ps 18:33
the **h** of the mountains are his also. Ps 95:4
from the heavens; praise him in the **h**! Ps 148:1
On the **h** beside the way, at the Prv 8:2
I will ascend above the **h** of the clouds; I Is 14:14
places of the wooded **h** and the hilltops, Is 17:9
he will dwell on the **h**; his place of Is 33:16
your voice and lifted your eyes to the **h**? Is 37:23
I have gone up the **h** of the mountains, Is 37:24
I will open rivers on the bare **h**, and Is 41:18
ways; on all bare **h** shall be their pasture; Is 49:9
will make you ride on the **h** of the earth; Is 58:14
Lift up your eyes to the bare **h**, and see! Jer 3:2
A voice on the bare **h** is heard, the Jer 3:21
wind from the bare **h** in the desert Jer 4:11

raise a lamentation on the bare **h**, for the Jer 7:29
Upon all the bare **h** in the desert Jer 12:12
The wild donkeys stand on the bare **h**; Jer 14:6
and on the mountain **h** of Israel shall Ezk 34:14
'The ancient **h** have become our Ezk 36:2
and treads on the **h** of the earth— Am 4:13

HEINOUS (1)
For that would be a **h** crime; that would Jb 31:11

HEIR (16)
and the **h** of my house is Eliezer of Gn 15:2
of my household will be my **h**." Gn 15:3
to him: "This man shall not be your **h**; Gn 15:4
your very own son shall be your **h**." Gn 15:4
woman shall not be **h** with my son Gn 21:10
And so they would destroy the **h** also. 2 Sm 14:7
will in the end find him his **h**. Prv 29:21
LORD: "Has Israel no sons? Has he no **h**? Jer 49:1
they said to themselves, 'This is the **h**. Mt 21:38
said to one another, 'This is the **h**. Mk 12:7
they said to themselves, 'This is the **h**. Lk 20:14
that he would be **h** of the world did Rom 4:13
I mean that the **h**, as long as he is a child, Gal 4:1
son, and if a son, then an **h** through God. Gal 4:7
whom he appointed the **h** of all things, Heb 1:2
and became an **h** of the righteousness Heb 11:7

HEIRS (11)
of the law who are to be the **h**, Rom 4:14
then **h**—heirs of God and fellow heirs Rom 8:17
then heirs—**h** of God and fellow heirs Rom 8:17
heirs of God and fellow **h** with Christ, Rom 8:17
offspring, **h** according to promise. Gal 3:29
mystery is that the Gentiles are fellow **h**, Eph 3:6
we might become **h** according to the Ti 3:7
convincingly to the **h** of the promise Heb 6:17
Jacob, **h** with him of the same promise. Heb 11:9
to be rich in faith and **h** of the kingdom, Jas 2:5
since they are **h** with you of the grace of 1 Pt 3:7

HELAH (2)
Tekoa, had two wives, **H** and Naarah; 1 Chr 4:5
The sons of **H**: Zereth, Izhar, and 1 Chr 4:7

HELAM (2)
They came to **H**, with Shobach the 2 Sm 10:16
crossed the Jordan and came to **H**. 2 Sm 10:17

HELBAH (1)
or of Achzib or of **H** or of Aphik or of Jgs 1:31

HELBON (1)
kind; wine of **H** and wool of Sahar Ezk 27:18

HELD (63)
so Jacob **h** his peace until they came. Gn 34:5
Whenever Moses **h** up his hand, Israel Ex 17:11
while Aaron and Hur **h** up his hands, Ex 17:12
be glorified.'" And Aaron **h** his peace. Lv 10:3
but the LORD has **h** you back from Nm 24:11
But you who **h** fast to the LORD your God Dt 4:4
They **h** in their left hands the torches, Jgs 7:20
and trod them and **h** a festival; Jgs 9:27
the young man who **h** him by the Jgs 16:26
are wearing and hold it out." So she **h** it, Ru 3:15
and he is a man who is **h** in honor; 1 Sm 9:6
him no present. But he **h** his peace. 1 Sm 10:27
by them I shall be **h** in honor." 2 Sm 6:22
of a lily. It **h** two thousand baths. 1 Kgs 7:26
of bronze. Each basin **h** forty baths, 1 Kgs 7:38
So Solomon **h** the feast at that time, 1 Kgs 8:65
For he **h** fast to the LORD. He did not 2 Kgs 18:6
and he is to be **h** in awe above all 1 Chr 16:25
the flower of a lily. It **h** 3,000 baths. 2 Chr 4:5
At that time Solomon **h** the feast for 2 Chr 7:8
eighth day they **h** a solemn assembly, 2 Chr 7:9
So he **h** Judah and Benjamin. 2 Chr 11:12
on construction, and half **h** the spears, Neh 4:16
with one hand and **h** his weapon with Neh 4:17
and half of them **h** the spears from the Neh 4:21
his brother." And I **h** a great assembly Neh 5:7
and he **h** out to Esther the golden scepter Est 5:2
When the king **h** out the golden scepter Est 8:4
My foot has **h** fast to his steps; I have Jb 23:11
My steps have **h** fast to your paths; my Ps 17:5
I **h** my peace to no avail, and my distress Ps 39:2
your steadfast love, O LORD, **h** me up. Ps 94:18
pitied by all those who **h** them captive. Ps 106:46
and he is **h** fast in the cords of his sin. Prv 5:22
lest he curse you and you be **h** guilty. Prv 30:10
I found him whom my soul loves. I **h** him, Sg 3:4
purple; a king is **h** captive in the tresses. Sg 7:5
For a long time I have **h** my peace; I Is 42:14
Have I not **h** my peace, even for a long Is 57:11
your compassion are **h** back from me. Is 63:15
Your holy people **h** possession for a little Is 63:18
vomit, and he too shall be **h** in derision. Jer 48:26
took them captive have **h** them fast; Jer 50:33
those whom I **h** and raised my enemy Lam 2:22
shall be laughed at and **h** in derision, Ezk 23:32
because they **h** him to be a prophet. Mt 14:5
because they **h** him to be a prophet. Mt 21:46
out and immediately **h** counsel with the Mk 3:6
for they all **h** that John really was a Mk 11:32
the chief priests **h** a consultation with Mk 15:1
a hyssop branch and **h** it to his mouth. Jn 19:29
was not possible for him to be **h** by it. Acts 2:24
but the people **h** them in high esteem. Acts 5:13
a teacher of the law **h** in honor by all Acts 5:34
ordered him to be **h** until I could send Acts 25:21
world may be **h** accountable to God. Rom 3:19
having died to that which **h** us captive, Rom 7:6
day long I have **h** out my hands to Rom 10:21
you are strong. You are **h** in honor, 1 Cor 4:10
came, we were **h** captive under the law, Gal 3:23
joined and **h** together by every joint Eph 4:16
Let marriage be **h** in honor among all, Heb 13:4
In his right hand he **h** seven stars, from Rv 1:16

HELDAI (2)
month, was **H** the Netophathite, 1 Chr 27:15
"Take from the exiles **H**, Tobijah, and Zec 6:10

HELEB (1)
H the son of Baanah of Netophah, 2 Sm 23:29

HELECH (1)
Men of Arvad and **H** were on your Ezk 27:11

HELED (1)
H the son of Baanah of Netophah, 1 Chr 11:30

HELEK (2)
of Iezer, the clan of the Iezerites; of **H**, Nm 26:30
by their clans, Abiezer, **H**, Asriel, Jos 17:2

HELEKITES (1)
Iezerites; of Helek, the clan of the **H**; Nm 26:30

HELEM (2)
The sons of **H** his brother: Zophah, 1 Chr 7:35
temple of the LORD as a reminder to **H**, Zec 6:14

HELEPH (1)
And their boundary ran from **H**, from Jos 19:33

HELEZ (5)
H the Paltite, Ira the son of Ikkesh of 2 Sm 23:26
Azariah fathered **H**, and Helez 1 Chr 2:39
Helez, and **H** fathered Eleasah. 1 Chr 2:39
Shammoth of Harod, **H** the Pelonite, 1 Chr 11:27
seventh month, was **H** the Pelonite, 1 Chr 27:10

HELI (1)
was supposed) of Joseph, the son of **H**, Lk 3:23

HELIOPOLIS (1)
He shall break the obelisks of **H**, which Jer 43:13

HELKAI (1)
of Harim, Adna; of Meraioth, **H**; Neh 12:15

HELKATH (2)
Their territory included **H**, Hali, Beten, Jos 19:25
H with its pasturelands, and Rehob Jos 21:31

HELKATH-HAZZURIM (1)
Therefore that place was called **H**, 2 Sm 2:16

HELL (14)
'You fool!' will be liable to the **h** of fire. Mt 5:22
that your whole body be thrown into **h**. Mt 5:29
than that your whole body go into **h**. Mt 5:30
can destroy both soul and body in **h**. Mt 10:28
and the gates of **h** shall not prevail Mt 16:18
two eyes to be thrown into the **h** of fire. Mt 18:9
as much a child of **h** as yourselves. Mt 23:15
are you to escape being sentenced to **h**? Mt 23:33
crippled than with two hands to go to **h**, Mk 9:43
than with two feet to be thrown into **h**. Mk 9:45
than with two eyes to be thrown into **h**, Mk 9:47
has killed, has authority to cast into **h**. Lk 12:5
entire course of life, and set on fire by **h**. Jas 3:6
cast them into **h** and committed them 2 Pt 2:4

HELLENISTS (3)
a complaint by the **H** arose against the Acts 6:1
he spoke and disputed against the **H**. Acts 9:29
to Antioch spoke to the **H** also, Acts 11:20

HELMET (10)
He had a **h** of bronze on his head, and 1 Sm 17:5
He put a **h** of bronze on his head and 1 Sm 17:38
Manasseh is mine; Ephraim is my **h**; Ps 60:7
Ephraim is my **h**, Judah my scepter. Ps 108:8
and a **h** of salvation on his head; Is 59:17
every side with buckler, shield, and **h**; Ezk 23:24
They hung the shield and **h** in you; Ezk 27:10
them, all of them with shield and **h**; Ezk 38:5
and take the **h** of salvation, and the Eph 6:17
love, and for a **h** the hope of salvation. 1 Thes 5:8

HELMETS (2)
shields, spears, **h**, coats of mail, 2 Chr 26:14
Take your stations with your **h**, polish Jer 46:4

HELON (5)
from Zebulun, Eliab the son of **H**; Nm 1:9
of Zebulun being Eliab the son of **H**, Nm 2:7
On the third day Eliab the son of **H**, the Nm 7:24
was the offering of Eliab the son of **H**. Nm 7:29
of Zebulun was Eliab the son of **H**. Nm 10:16

HELP (155)
gotten a man with the **h** of the LORD." Gn 4:1
the God of your father who will **h** you, Gn 49:25
of their slavery and cried out for **h**. Ex 2:23
said, "The God of my father was my **h**, Ex 18:4
Aaron listed with the **h** of the chiefs of Nm 1:44
You shall **h** him to lift them up again. Dt 22:4
she did not cry for **h** though she was in Dt 22:24
young woman cried for **h** there was no Dt 22:27
and there shall be no one to **h** you. Dt 28:29
but there shall be no one to **h** you. Dt 28:31
Let them rise up and **h** you; let them be Dt 32:38
him, and be a **h** against his adversaries." Dt 33:7
rides through the heavens to your **h**, Dt 33:26
saved by the LORD, the shield of your **h**, Dt 33:29
before your brothers and shall **h** them, Jos 1:14
"Come up to me and **h** me, and let us Jos 10:4
up to us quickly and save us and **h** us, Jos 10:6
king of Gezer came up to **h** Lachish. Jos 10:33
people of Israel cried out to the LORD for **h**, Jgs 4:3
they did not come to the **h** of the LORD, Jgs 5:23
to the **h** of the LORD against the mighty. Jgs 5:23
people of Israel cried out for **h** to the LORD. Jgs 6:6
Damascus came to **h** Hadadezer king 2 Sm 8:5
strong for me, then you shall **h** me, 2 Sm 10:11
for you, then I will come and **h** you. 2 Sm 10:11
that you send us **h** from the city." 2 Sm 18:3
to prosper all my **h** and my desire? 2 Sm 23:5
cried out to him, saying, "**H**, my lord, 2 Kgs 6:26
he said, "If the LORD will not **h** you, 2 Kgs 6:27
will not help you, how shall I **h** you? 2 Kgs 6:27
free, and there was none to **h** Israel. 2 Kgs 14:26
that he might **h** him to confirm his 2 Kgs 15:19
come to me in friendship to **h** me, 1 Chr 12:17
(Yet he did not **h** them, for the 1 Chr 12:19
to day men came to David to **h** him, 1 Chr 12:22
to **h** David with singleness of 1 Chr 12:33
Damascus came to **h** Hadadezer king 1 Chr 18:5
strong for me, then you shall **h** me, 1 Chr 19:12
too strong for you, then I will **h** you. 1 Chr 19:12
of Israel to **h** Solomon his son, 1 Chr 22:17
With the **h** of Zadok of the sons of 1 Chr 24:3
"O LORD, there is none like you to **h**, 2 Chr 14:11
H us, O LORD our God, for we rely on 2 Chr 14:11
but sought **h** from physicians. 2 Chr 16:12
"Should you **h** the wicked and love 2 Chr 19:2
assembled to seek **h** from the LORD; 2 Chr 20:4
God has power to **h** or to cast down." 2 Chr 25:8
to **h** the king against the enemy. 2 Chr 26:13
sent to the king of Assyria for **h**. 2 Chr 28:16
of Assyria, but it did not **h** him. 2 Chr 28:21
them that they may **h** me." But they 2 Chr 28:23
to **h** us and to fight our battles." And 2 Chr 32:8
but it is not in our power to **h** it, Neh 5:5
accomplished with the **h** of our God. Neh 6:16
Have I any **h** in me, when resource is Jb 6:13
I call for **h**, but there is no justice. Jb 19:7
and the soul of the wounded cries for **h**; Jb 24:12
With whose **h** have you uttered words, Jb 26:4
I delivered the poor who cried for **h**, Jb 29:12
the fatherless who had none to **h** him. Jb 29:12
calamity; they need no one to **h** them. Jb 30:13
I cry to you for **h** and you do not answer Jb 30:20
his hand, and in his disaster cry for **h**? Jb 30:24
stand up in the assembly and cry for **h**. Jb 30:28
because I saw my **h** in the gate, Jb 31:21
they call for **h** because of the arm of the Jb 35:9
do not cry for **h** when he binds them. Jb 36:13
Will your cry for **h** avail to keep you Jb 36:19
when its young ones cry to God for **h**, Jb 38:41
upon the LORD; to my God I cried for **h**. Ps 18:6
They cried for **h**, but there was none to Ps 18:41
May he send you **h** from the sanctuary Ps 20:2
trouble is near, and there is none to **h**. Ps 22:11
O you my **h**, come quickly to my aid! Ps 22:19
in anger, O you who have been my **h**. Ps 27:9
pleas for mercy, when I cry to you for **h**, Ps 28:2
O LORD my God, I cried to you for **h**, and Ps 30:2
for mercy when I cried to you for **h**. Ps 31:22
for the LORD; he is our **h** and our shield. Ps 33:20
When the righteous cry for **h**, the LORD Ps 34:17
of shield and buckler and rise for my **h**! Ps 35:2
Make haste to **h** me, O Lord, my Ps 38:22
deliver me! O LORD, make haste to **h** me! Ps 40:13
for me. You are my **h** and my deliverer; Ps 40:17
Rise up; come to our **h**! Redeem us for Ps 44:26
and strength, a very present **h** in trouble. Ps 46:1

God will **h** her when morning dawns. Ps 46:5
Oh, grant us **h** against the foe, for vain Ps 60:11
for you have been my **h**, and in the Ps 63:7
deliver me! O LORD, make haste to **h** me! Ps 70:1
O God! You are my **h** and my deliverer; Ps 70:5
me; O my God, make haste to **h** me! Ps 71:12
talk of your righteous **h** all the day Ps 71:24
H us, O God of our salvation, for the Ps 79:9
"I have granted **h** to one who is mighty; Ps 89:19
If the LORD had not been my **h**, my soul Ps 94:17
your people; **h** me when you save them, Ps 106:4
labor; they fell down, with none to **h**. Ps 107:12
Oh grant us **h** against the foe, for vain Ps 108:12
H me, O LORD my God! Save me Ps 109:26
the LORD! He is their **h** and their shield. Ps 115:9
the LORD! He is their **h** and their shield. Ps 115:10
the LORD! He is their **h** and their shield. Ps 115:11
persecute me with falsehood; **h** me! Ps 119:86
I rise before dawn and cry for **h**; I Ps 119:147
Let your hand be ready to **h** me, for I Ps 119:173
praise you, and let your rules **h** me. Ps 119:175
the hills. From where does my **h** come? Ps 121:1
My **h** comes from the LORD, who made Ps 121:2
Our **h** is in the name of the LORD, who Ps 124:8
Blessed is he whose **h** is the God of Ps 146:5
fugitive until death; let no one **h** him. Prv 28:17
To whom will you flee for **h**, and where Is 10:3
to whom we fled for **h** to be delivered from Is 20:6
them, that brings neither **h** nor profit, Is 30:5
Egypt's **h** is worthless and empty; Is 30:7
go down to Egypt for **h** and rely on horses, Is 31:1
I will strengthen you, I will **h** you, I will Is 41:10
you from the womb and will **h** you: Is 44:2
I looked, but there was no one to **h**; I was Is 63:5
army that came to **h** you is about to Jer 37:7
of the foe, and there was none to **h** her, Lam 1:7
though I call and cry for **h**, he shuts out Lam 3:8
'Do not close your ear to my cry for **h**!' Lam 3:56
eyes failed, ever watching vainly for **h**; Lam 4:17
great company will not **h** him in war, Ezk 17:17
one of the chief princes, came to **h** me, Dn 10:13
stumble, they shall receive a little **h**. Dn 11:34
fortresses with the **h** of a foreign Dn 11:39
come to his end, with none to **h** him. Dn 11:45
"So you, by the **h** of your God, return, Hos 12:6
O LORD, how long shall I cry for **h**, and Hab 1:2
off shall come and **h** to build the temple Zec 6:15
knelt before him, saying, "Lord, **h** me." Mt 15:25
have compassion on us and **h** us." Mk 9:22
out and said, "I believe; **h** my unbelief!" Mk 9:24
in the other boat to come and **h** them. Lk 5:7
to serve alone? Tell her then to **h** me." Lk 10:40
moneybag he used to **h** himself to what Jn 12:6
"Come over to Macedonia and **h** us." Acts 16:9
this way we must **h** the weak and Acts 20:35
h! This is the man who is teaching Acts 21:28
I have had the **h** that comes from Acts 26:22
and **h** her in whatever she may need Rom 16:2
so that you may **h** me on my journey, 1 Cor 16:6
H him on his way in peace, that he 1 Cor 16:11
You also must **h** us by prayer, so that 2 Cor 1:11
your prayers and the **h** of the Spirit of Phil 1:19
also, true companion, **h** these women, Phil 4:3
you sent me **h** for my needs Phil 4:16
the fainthearted, **h** the weak, 1 Thes 5:14
works, so as to **h** cases of urgent need, Ti 3:14
he is able to **h** those who are being Heb 2:18
and find grace to **h** in time of need. Heb 4:16
the earth came to the **h** of the woman, Rv 12:16

HELPED (25)
he said, "Till now the LORD has **h** us." 1 Sm 7:12
they followed Adonijah and **h** him. 1 Kgs 1:7
and the thirty-two kings who **h** him. 1 Kgs 20:16
the mighty men who **h** him in war. 1 Chr 12:1
They **h** David against the band of 1 Chr 12:21
And because God **h** the Levites who 1 Chr 15:26
cried out, and the LORD **h** him; 2 Chr 18:31
they all **h** to destroy one another. 2 Chr 20:23
God **h** him against the Philistines 2 Chr 26:7
far, for he was marvelously **h**, 2 Chr 26:15
gods of the kings of Syria **h** them, 2 Chr 28:23
their brothers the Levites **h** them, 2 Chr 29:34
were outside the city; and they **h** him. 2 Chr 32:3
h the people to understand the Law, Neh 8:7
and the royal agents also **h** the Jews, Est 9:3
"How you have **h** him who has no power! Jb 26:2
in him my heart trusts, and I am **h**; Ps 28:7
LORD, have **h** me and comforted me. Ps 86:17
that I was falling, but the LORD **h** me. Ps 118:13
will stumble, and he who is **h** will fall, Is 31:3
you; in a day of salvation I have **h** you; Is 49:8
He has **h** his servant Israel, in Lk 1:54
he greatly **h** those who through grace Acts 18:27
and to be **h** on my journey there by Rom 15:24
day of salvation I have **h** you." Behold, 2 Cor 6:2

HELPER (15)
alone; I will make him a **h** fit for him." Gn 2:18
there was not found a **h** fit for him. Gn 2:20
you have been the **h** of the fatherless. Ps 10:14
be merciful to me! O LORD, be my **h**!" Ps 30:10
Behold, God is my **h**; the Lord is the Ps 54:4
calls, the poor and him who has no **h**. Ps 72:12
The LORD is on my side as my **h**; I shall Ps 118:7
out his hand, the **h** will stumble, Is 31:3
Tyre and Sidon every **h** that remains. Jer 47:4
for you are against me, against your **h**. Hos 13:9
Father, and he will give you another **H**, Jn 14:16
But the **H**, the Holy Spirit, whom the Jn 14:26
"But when the **H** comes, whom I will Jn 15:26
not go away, the **H** will not come to you. Jn 16:7
confidently say, "The Lord is my **h**; Heb 13:6

HELPERS (8)
peace to you, and peace to your **h**! 1 Chr 12:18
beneath him bowed the **h** of Rahab. Jb 9:13
evildoers and against the **h** of those who Is 31:2
around him, his **h** and all his troops, Ezk 12:14
fire to Egypt, and all her **h** are broken. Ezk 30:8
shall speak of them, with their **h**, Ezk 32:21
limit; Put and the Libyans were her **h**. Na 3:9
sent into Macedonia two of his **h**, Acts 19:22

HELPFUL (2)
for me," but not all things are **h**. 1 Cor 6:12
are lawful," but not all things are **h**. 1 Cor 10:23

HELPING (1)
gifts of healing, **h**, administrating, 1 Cor 12:28

HELPLESS (8)
them all day long, but you shall be **h**. Dt 28:32
His eyes stealthily watch for the **h**; Ps 10:8
The **h** are crushed, sink down, and fall Ps 10:10
hands; to you the **h** commits himself; Ps 10:14
youth up, I suffer your terrors; I am **h**. Ps 88:15
heard the report of it; our hands fall **h**; Jer 6:24
the report of them, and his hands fell **h**; Jer 50:43
them, because they were harassed and **h**, Mt 9:36

HELPS (11)
For your God **h** you." Then David 1 Chr 12:18
The LORD **h** them and delivers them; he Ps 37:40
but wisdom **h** one to succeed. Eccl 10:10
Everyone **h** his neighbor and says to his Is 41:6
you, "Fear not, I am the one who **h** you." Is 41:13
I am the one who **h** you, declares the Is 41:14
But the Lord GOD **h** me; therefore I have Is 50:7
Behold, the Lord GOD **h** me; who will Is 50:9
Likewise the Spirit **h** us in our Rom 8:26
For surely it is not angels that he **h**, but Heb 2:16
but he **h** the offspring of Abraham. Heb 2:16

HEM (8)
On its **h** you shall make pomegranates Ex 28:33
purple and scarlet yarns, around its **h**, Ex 28:33
pomegranate, around the **h** of the robe. Ex 28:34
On the **h** of the robe they made Ex 39:24
all around the **h** of the robe, Ex 39:25
a pomegranate around the **h** of the robe Ex 39:26
You **h** me in, behind and before, and Ps 139:5
and surround you and **h** you in on Lk 19:43

HEMAM (2)
The sons of Lotan were Hori and **H**; Gn 36:22
The sons of Lotan: Hori and **H**; and 1 Chr 1:39

HEMAN (17)
wiser than Ethan the Ezrahite, and **H**, 1 Kgs 4:31
Zimri, Ethan, **H**, Calcol, and Dara, five 1 Chr 2:6
H the singer the son of Joel, son of 1 Chr 6:33
So the Levites appointed **H** the son of 1 Chr 15:17
The singers, **H**, Asaph, and Ethan, 1 Chr 15:19
With them were **H** and Jeduthun 1 Chr 16:41
H and Jeduthun had trumpets and 1 Chr 16:42
service the sons of Asaph, and of **H**, 1 Chr 25:1
Of **H**, the sons of Heman: Bukkiah, 1 Chr 25:4
Of Heman, the sons of **H**: Bukkiah, 1 Chr 25:4
were the sons of **H** the king's seer, 1 Chr 25:5
God had given **H** fourteen sons and 1 Chr 25:5
and **H** were under the order of the 1 Chr 25:6
singers, Asaph, **H**, and Jeduthun, 2 Chr 5:12
and of the sons of **H**, Jehuel and 2 Chr 29:14
of David, and Asaph, and **H**, 2 Chr 35:15
Leannoth. A Maskil of **H** the Ezrahite. Ps 88:T

HEMDAN (2)
H, Eshban, Ithran, and Cheran. Gn 36:26
H, Eshban, Ithran, and Cheran. 1 Chr 1:41

HEN (3)
Jedaiah, and **H** the son of Zephaniah. Zec 6:14
together as a **h** gathers her brood Mt 23:37
together as a **h** gathers her brood Lk 13:34

HENA (3)
gods of Sepharvaim, **H**, and Ivvah? 2 Kgs 18:34
city of Sepharvaim, the king of **H**, 2 Kgs 19:13
of the city of Sepharvaim, the king of **H**, Is 37:13

HENADAD (4)
along with the sons of **H** and the Levites, Ezr 3:9
Bavvai the son of **H**, ruler of half the Neh 3:18
the son of **H** repaired another section, Neh 3:24
of Azaniah, Binnui of the sons of **H**, Neh 10:9

HENCEFORTH (3)
the house of Jeroboam today. And **h**, 1 Kgs 14:14
Also **h** I am he; there is none who can Is 43:13
H there is laid up for me the crown of 2 Tm 4:8

HENNA (2)
me a cluster of **h** blossoms in the Sg 1:14
with all choicest fruits, **h** with nard, Sg 4:13

HEPHER (9)
and of **H**, the clan of the Hepherites. Nm 26:32
Zelophehad the son of **H** had no sons, Nm 26:33
daughters of Zelophehad the son of **H**, Nm 27:1
of Tappuah, one; the king of **H**, one; Jos 12:17
Helek, Asriel, Shechem, **H**, and Shemida. Jos 17:2
Now Zelophehad the son of **H**, son of Jos 17:3
Socoh and all the land of **H**); 1 Kgs 4:10
bore him Ahuzzam, **H**, Temeni, 1 Chr 4:6
H the Mecherathite, Ahijah the 1 Chr 11:36

HEPHERITES (1)
and of Hepher, the clan of the **H**. Nm 26:32

HEPHZIBAH (1)
Jerusalem. His mother's name was **H**. 2 Kgs 21:1

HERALD (5)
a high mountain, O Zion, **h** of good news; Is 40:9
strength, O Jerusalem, **h** of good news; Is 40:9
and I give to Jerusalem a **h** of good news. Is 41:27
And the **h** proclaimed aloud, "You are Dn 3:4
preserved Noah, a **h** of righteousness, 2 Pt 2:5

HERB (3)
grass, and like showers upon the **h**. Dt 32:2
like the grass and wither like the green **h**. Ps 37:2
For you tithe mint and rue and every **h**, Lk 11:42

HERBS (5)
bread and bitter **h** they shall eat Ex 12:8
it with unleavened bread and bitter **h**. Nm 9:11
went out into the field to gather **h**, 2 Kgs 4:39
is a dinner of **h** where love is than Prv 15:17
of spices, mounds of sweet-smelling **h**. Sg 5:13

HERD (59)
Abraham ran to the **h** and took a calf, Gn 18:7
one bull of the **h** and two rams without Ex 29:1
of livestock from the **h** or from the flock. Lv 1:2
his offering is a burnt offering from the **h**, Lv 1:3
offering, if he offers an animal from the **h**, Lv 3:1
a bull from the **h** without blemish to the Lv 4:3
offer a bull from the **h** for a sin offering Lv 4:14
with a bull from the **h** for a sin offering Lv 16:3
freewill offering from the **h** or from the Lv 22:21
and one bull from the **h** and two rams. Lv 23:18
one bull from the **h**, one ram, one male Nm 7:15
one bull from the **h**, one ram, one male Nm 7:21
one bull from the **h**, one ram, one male Nm 7:27
one bull from the **h**, one ram, one male Nm 7:33
one bull from the **h**, one ram, one male Nm 7:39
one bull from the **h**, one ram, one male Nm 7:45
one bull from the **h**, one ram, one male Nm 7:51
one bull from the **h**, one ram, one male Nm 7:57
one bull from the **h**, one ram, one male Nm 7:63
one bull from the **h**, one ram, one male Nm 7:69
one bull from the **h**, one ram, one male Nm 7:75
one bull from the **h**, one ram, one male Nm 7:81
a bull from the **h** and its grain offering Nm 8:8
another bull from the **h** for a sin Nm 8:8
the LORD from the **h** or from the flock Nm 15:3
one bull from the **h** for a burnt Nm 15:24
two bulls from the **h**, one ram, seven Nm 28:11
two bulls from the **h**, one ram, and Nm 28:19
two bulls from the **h**, one ram, seven Nm 28:27
one bull from the **h**, one ram, seven Nm 29:2
one bull from the **h**, one ram, seven Nm 29:8
to the LORD, thirteen bulls from the **h**, Nm 29:13
second day twelve bulls from the **h**, Nm 29:17
the firstborn of your **h** and of your flock. Dt 12:6
the firstborn of your **h** or of your flock, Dt 12:17
may kill any of your **h** or your flock, Dt 12:21
and the firstborn of your **h** and flock, Dt 14:23
are born of your **h** and flock you shall Dt 15:19
do no work with the firstborn of your **h**, Dt 15:19
LORD your God, from the flock or the **h**, Dt 16:2
Curds from the **h**, and milk from the Dt 32:14
of his own flock or **h** to prepare for the 2 Sm 12:4
and sheep and cheese from the **h**, 2 Sm 17:29
the **h** of bulls with the calves of the Ps 68:30
over the young of the flock and the **h**; Jer 31:12
a bull from the **h** for a sin offering. Ezk 43:19

bull from the **h** without blemish and Ezk 43:23
a bull from the **h** and a ram from the Ezk 43:25
a bull from the **h** without blemish, Ezk 45:18
a bull from the **h** without blemish, Ezk 46:6
Let neither man nor beast, **h** nor flock, Jon 3:7
the fold and there be no **h** in the stalls, Hab 3:17
Now a **h** of many pigs was feeding at Mt 8:30
us out, send us away into the **h** of pigs." Mt 8:31
the whole **h** rushed down the steep bank Mt 8:32
Now a great **h** of pigs was feeding there Mk 5:11
out, and entered the pigs, and the **h**, Mk 5:13
Now a large **h** of pigs was feeding there Lk 8:32
and the **h** rushed down the steep bank Lk 8:33

HERDS (41)
Abram, also had flocks and **h** and tents, Gn 13:5
He has given him flocks and **h**, silver Gn 24:35
of flocks and **h** and many servants, Gn 26:14
him, and the flocks and **h** and camels, Gn 32:7
the nursing flocks and **h** are a care to Gn 33:13
They took their flocks and their **h**, Gn 34:28
children, and your flocks, your **h**, Gn 45:10
their flocks and their **h** and all that Gn 46:32
with their flocks and **h** and all that they Gn 47:1
for the horses, the flocks, the **h**, Gn 47:17
spent. The **h** of livestock are my lord's. Gn 47:18
and their **h** were left in the land of Gn 50:8
the horses, the donkeys, the camels, the **h**, Ex 9:3
daughters and with our flocks and **h**, Ex 10:9
flocks and your **h** remain behind." Ex 10:24
Take your flocks and your **h**, as you Ex 12:32
much livestock, both flocks and **h**. Ex 12:38
Let no flocks or **h** graze opposite that Ex 34:3
And every tithe of **h** and flocks, every Lv 27:32
Shall flocks and **h** be slaughtered for Nm 11:22
the increase of your **h** and the young of Dt 7:13
and when your **h** and flocks multiply Dt 8:13
the increase of your **h** and the young of Dt 28:4
the increase of your **h** and the young of Dt 28:18
the increase of your **h** or the young of Dt 28:51
also captured all the flocks and **h**, 1 Sm 30:20
man had very many flocks and **h**, 2 Sm 12:2
Over the **h** that pastured in Sharon 1 Chr 27:29
over the **h** in the valleys was 1 Chr 27:29
many cisterns, for he had large **h**, 2 Chr 26:10
and flocks and **h** in abundance, 2 Chr 32:29
the firstborn of our **h** and of our Neh 10:36
flocks, and give attention to your **h**, Prv 27:23
also great possessions of **h** and flocks, Eccl 2:7
Valley of Achor a place for **h** to lie down, Is 65:10
fathers labored, their flocks and their **h**, Jer 3:24
they shall eat up your flocks and your **h**; Jer 5:17
plunder, their **h** of livestock a spoil. Jer 49:32
With their flocks and **h** they shall go to Hos 5:6
The **h** of cattle are perplexed because Jl 1:18
H shall lie down in her midst, all kinds Zep 2:14

HERDSMAN (1)
but I was a **h** and a dresser of sycamore Am 7:14

HERDSMAN'S (1)
of all that pass under the **h** staff, Lv 27:32

HERDSMEN (10)
strife between the **h** of Abram's Gn 13:7
livestock and the **h** of Lot's livestock. Gn 13:7
and between your **h** and my herdsmen, Gn 13:8
and between your herdsmen and my **h**, Gn 13:8
the **h** of Gerar quarreled with Isaac's Gn 26:20
of Gerar quarreled with Isaac's **h**, Gn 26:20
the Edomite, the chief of Saul's **h**. 1 Sm 21:7
The **h** fled, and going into the city they Mt 8:33
The **h** fled and told it in the city and in Mk 5:14
When the **h** saw what had happened, Lk 8:34

HERE (289)
Now then, **h** is your wife; take her, and Gn 12:19
they shall come back **h** in the fourth Gn 15:16
"Truly **h** I have seen him who looks Gn 16:13
said to Lot, "Have you anyone else **h**? Gn 19:12
and your two daughters who are **h**, Gn 19:15
therefore swear to me **h** by God that Gn 21:23
"Abraham!" And he said, "**H** am I." Gn 22:1
young men, "Stay **h** with the donkey; Gn 22:5
"My father!" And he said, "**H** am I, Gn 22:7
Abraham!" And he said, "**H** am I." Gn 22:11
"My son"; and he answered, "**H** I am." Gn 27:1
said, "My father." And he said, "**H** I am. Gn 27:18
Then she said, "**H** is my servant Bilhah; Gn 30:3
the dream, 'Jacob,' and I said, '**H** I am!' Gn 31:11
Set it **h** before my kinsmen and your Gn 31:37
to them." And he said to him, "**H** I am." Gn 37:13
to one another, "**H** comes this dreamer. Gn 37:19
him into this pit **h** in the wilderness, Gn 37:22
said, "No cult prostitute has been **h**." Gn 38:21
said, 'No cult prostitute has been **h**.'" Gn 38:22
and **h** also I have done nothing that Gn 40:15
unless your youngest brother comes **h**. Gn 42:15
h it is in the mouth of my sack!" At Gn 42:28
with yourselves because you sold me **h**, Gn 45:5
So it was not you who sent me **h**, but Gn 45:8
Hurry and bring my father down **h**." Gn 45:13
"Jacob, Jacob." And he said, "**H** am I." Gn 46:2
Now **h** is seed for you, and you shall Gn 47:23
God has given me **h**." And he said, Gn 48:9
you shall carry up my bones from **h**." Gn 50:25
"Moses, Moses!" And he said, "**H** I am." Ex 3:4
Afterward he will let you go from **h**. Ex 11:1
carry up my bones with you from **h**." Ex 13:19
"Wait **h** for us until we return to you. Ex 24:14
go up from **h**, you and the people whom Ex 33:1
go with me, do not bring us up from **h**. Ex 33:15
of the hill country, saying, "**H** we are. Nm 14:40
this wilderness, that we should die **h**, Nm 20:4
And **h** we are in Kadesh, a city on the Nm 20:16
And he said to them, "Lodge **h** tonight, Nm 22:8
So you, too, please stay **h** tonight, that Nm 22:19
to Balak, "Build for me **h** seven altars, Nm 23:1
and prepare for me **h** seven bulls and Nm 23:1
"Stand **h** beside your burnt offering, Nm 23:15
"Build for me **h** seven altars and Nm 23:29
and prepare for me **h** seven bulls and Nm 23:29
brothers go to the war while you sit **h**? Nm 32:6
will build sheepfolds **h** for our Nm 32:16
with us, who are all of us **h** alive today. Dt 5:3
But you, stand **h** by me, and I will tell Dt 5:31
to me, 'Arise, go down quickly from **h**, Dt 9:12
to all that we are doing **h** today, Dt 12:8
which are not cities of the nations **h**. Dt 20:15
whoever is standing **h** with us today Dt 29:15
with whoever is not **h** with us today. Dt 29:15
of Israel have come **h** tonight to search Jos 2:2
"Come **h** and listen to the words of the Jos 3:9
"**H** is how you shall know that the living Jos 3:10
'Take twelve stones from **h** out of the Jos 4:3
H is our bread. It was still warm when Jos 9:12
and bring the description **h** to me. Jos 18:6
cast lots for you **h** before the LORD our Jos 18:6
will cast lots for you **h** before the LORD in Jos 18:8
man comes and asks you, 'Is anyone **h**?' Jgs 4:20
do not depart from **h** until I come to Jgs 6:18
your God on the top of the stronghold **h**, Jgs 6:26
you invited us **h** to impoverish us?" Jgs 14:15
"Samson has come **h**." And they Jgs 16:2
and said to him, "Who brought you **h**? Jgs 18:3
in this place? What is your business **h**?" Jgs 18:3
Lodge **h** and let your heart be merry, Jgs 19:9
h are my virgin daughter and his Jgs 19:24
of you, give your advice and counsel **h**." Jgs 20:7
"Come **h** and eat some bread and dip Ru 2:14
sit down **h**." And he turned aside and sat Ru 4:1
and said, "Sit down **h**." So they sat down. Ru 4:2
presence of those sitting **h** and in the Ru 4:4
who was standing **h** in your presence, 1 Sm 1:26
called Samuel, and he said, "**H** I am!" 1 Sm 3:4
and ran to Eli and said, "**H** I am, for 1 Sm 3:5
arose and went to Eli and said, "**H** I am, 1 Sm 3:6
arose and went to Eli and said, "**H** I am, 1 Sm 3:8
my son." And he said, "**H** I am." 1 Sm 3:16
covenant of the LORD **h** from Shiloh, 1 Sm 4:3
"**H**, I have with me a quarter of a shekel 1 Sm 9:8
water and said to them, "Is the seer **h**?" 1 Sm 9:11
"**H** is the man of whom I spoke to you! 1 Sm 9:17
passed on, stop **h** yourself for a while, 1 Sm 9:27
H I am; testify against me before the 1 Sm 12:3
"Bring the burnt offering **h** to me, 1 Sm 13:9
was dispersing **h** and there. 1 Sm 14:16
the ark of God **h**." For the ark of 1 Sm 14:18
roll a great stone to me **h**." 1 Sm 14:33
sheep and slaughter them **h** and eat, 1 Sm 14:34
said, "Let us draw near to God **h**." 1 Sm 14:36
And Saul said, "Come **h**, all you 1 Sm 14:38
was in my hand. **H** I am; I will die." 1 Sm 14:43
"Bring **h** to me Agag the king of the 1 Sm 15:32
"Are all your sons **h**?" And he said, 1 Sm 16:11
we will not sit down till he comes **h**." 1 Sm 16:11
"**H** is my elder daughter Merab. 1 Sm 18:17
five loaves of bread, or whatever is **h**." 1 Sm 21:3
"Then have you not **h** a spear or a 1 Sm 21:8
it is **h** wrapped in a cloth behind the 1 Sm 21:9
is none but that **h**." And David said, 1 Sm 21:9
Ahitub." And he answered, "**H** I am, 1 Sm 22:12
"Behold, we are afraid **h** in Judah; 1 Sm 23:3
the priest, "Bring the ephod **h**." 1 Sm 23:9
"**H** is the day of which the LORD said to 1 Sm 24:4
answered and said, "**H** is the spear, 1 Sm 26:22
these Hebrews doing **h**?" And Achish 1 Sm 29:3
it not be with the heads of the men **h**? 1 Sm 29:4
"**H** is a present for you from the spoil 1 Sm 30:26
called to me. And I answered, '**H** I am.' 2 Sm 1:7
I have brought them **h** to my lord." 2 Sm 1:10
the king, "**H** is the head of Ish-bosheth, 2 Sm 4:8
said to David, "You will not come in **h**, 2 Sm 5:6
—thinking, "David cannot come in **h**." 2 Sm 5:6
said to Uriah, "Remain **h** today also, 2 Sm 11:12
"Behold, I sent word to you, 'Come **h**, 2 Sm 14:32
no pleasure in you,' behold, **h** I am, 2 Sm 15:26
aside and stand **h**." So he turned 2 Sm 18:30
But **h** is your servant Chimham. 2 Sm 19:37
within three days, and be **h** yourself." 2 Sm 20:4
Tell Joab, 'Come **h**, that I may speak 2 Sm 20:16
H are the oxen for the burnt offering 2 Sm 24:22
"**H** is Nathan the prophet." And when 1 Kgs 1:23
I will die **h**." Then Benaiah brought 1 Kgs 2:30
"Depart from **h** and turn eastward 1 Kgs 17:3
tell your lord, 'Behold, Elijah is **h**.'" 1 Kgs 18:8
when they would say, 'He is not **h**,' 1 Kgs 18:10
tell your lord, "Behold, Elijah is **h**."' 1 Kgs 18:11
tell your lord, "Behold, Elijah is **h**"'; 1 Kgs 18:14
said to him, "What are you doing **h**, 1 Kgs 19:9
and said, "What are you doing **h**, 1 Kgs 19:13
your servant was busy **h** and there, 1 Kgs 20:40
"Is there not **h** another prophet of the 1 Kgs 22:7
Elijah said to Elisha, "Please stay **h**, 2 Kgs 2:2
said to him, "Elisha, please stay **h**, 2 Kgs 2:4
Elijah said to him, "Please stay **h**, 2 Kgs 2:6
"Is there no prophet of the LORD **h**, 2 Kgs 3:11
"Elisha the son of Shaphat is **h**, 2 Kgs 3:11
"Why are we sitting **h** until we die? 2 Kgs 7:3
die there. And if we sit **h**, we die also. 2 Kgs 7:4
those who are left **h** will fare like the 2 Kgs 7:13
said, "My lord, O king, **h** is the woman, 2 Kgs 8:5
and **h** is her son whom Elisha restored 2 Kgs 8:5
him, "The man of God has come **h**," 2 Kgs 8:7
no servant of the LORD **h** among you, 2 Kgs 10:23
will not come in **h**." Nevertheless, 1 Chr 11:5
"**H** shall be the house of the LORD God 1 Chr 22:1
the LORD God and **h** the altar of burnt 1 Chr 22:1
seen your people, who are present **h**, 1 Chr 29:17
"Is there not **h** another prophet of the 2 Chr 18:6
shall not bring the captives in **h**, 2 Chr 28:13
king of Assyria who brought us **h**." Ezr 4:2
had one to hear me! (**H** is my signature! Jb 31:35
and **h** shall your proud waves be Jb 38:11
they may go and say to you, '**H** we are'? Jb 38:35
H is the sea, great and wide, which Ps 104:25
h I will dwell, for I have desired it. Ps 132:14
let him turn in **h**!" To him who lacks Prv 9:4
let him turn in **h**!" And to him who Prv 9:16
"Come up **h**," than to be put lower in Prv 25:7
who will go for us?" Then I said, "**H** am I! Is 6:8
And behold, **h** come riders, horsemen in Is 21:9
What have you to do **h**, and whom have Is 22:16
you to do here, and whom have you **h**, Is 22:16
you have cut out **h** a tomb for yourself, Is 22:16
line upon line, line upon line, **h** a little, Is 28:10
line upon line, line upon line, **h** a little, Is 28:13
h they are!" and I give to Jerusalem a Is 41:27
what have I **h**," declares the LORD, Is 52:5
shall know that it is I who speak; **h** am I." Is 52:6
you shall cry, and he will say, '**H** I am.' Is 58:9
I said, "**H** am I, here am I," to a nation that Is 65:1
h am I," to a nation that was not called by Is 65:1
young camel running **h** and there, Jer 2:23
this place: "He shall return **h** no more, Jer 22:11
a great company, they shall return **h**. Jer 31:8
"Take three men with you from **h**, Jer 38:10
"Son of man, eat whatever you find **h**. Ezk 3:1
the house of Israel are committing **h**, Ezk 8:6
that they are committing **h**." Ezk 8:9
the abominations that they commit **h**, Ezk 8:17
for you were brought **h** in order that I Ezk 40:4
out, and come **h**!" Then Shadrach, Dn 3:26
"**H** is the end of the matter. As for me, Dn 7:28
access among those who are standing **h**. Zec 3:7
Have you come **h** to torment us before Mt 8:29
something greater than the temple is **h**. Mt 12:6
something greater than Jonah is **h**. Mt 12:41
something greater than Solomon is **h**. Mt 12:42
"**H** are my mother and my brothers! Mt 12:49
head of John the Baptist **h** on a platter." Mt 14:8
have only five loaves **h** and two fish." Mt 14:17
And he said, "Bring them **h** to me." Mt 14:18
there are some standing **h** who will not Mt 16:28
to Jesus, "Lord, it is good that we are **h**. Mt 17:4
If you wish, I will make three tents **h**, Mt 17:4
I to bear with you? Bring him **h** to me." Mt 17:17
this mountain, 'Move from **h** to there,' Mt 17:20
them, 'Why do you stand **h** idle all day?' Mt 20:6
did you get in **h** without a wedding Mt 22:12
will not be left **h** one stone upon another Mt 24:2
says to you, 'Look, **h** is the Christ!' Mt 24:23
there was a cry, '**H** is the bridegroom! Mt 25:6
h I have made five talents more.' Mt 25:20
h I have made two talents more.' Mt 25:22
the ground. **H** you have what is yours.' Mt 25:25
and he said to his disciples, "Sit **h**, Mt 26:36
sorrowful, even to death; remain **h**, Mt 26:38

He is not **h**, for he has risen, as he said. Mt 28:6
man with the withered hand, "Come **h**." Mk 3:3
"**H** are my mother and my brothers! Mk 3:34
are not his sisters **h** with us?" And they Mk 6:3
these people with bread **h** in this desolate Mk 8:4
there are some standing **h** who will not Mk 9:1
to Jesus, "Rabbi, it is good that we are **h**. Mk 9:5
and will send it back **h** immediately.'" Mk 11:3
will not be left **h** one stone upon Mk 13:2
says to you, 'Look, **h** is the Christ!' Mk 13:21
to his disciples, "Sit **h** while I pray." Mk 14:32
even to death. Remain **h** and watch." Mk 14:34
was crucified. He has risen; he is not **h**. Mk 16:6
Son of God, throw yourself down from **h**, Lk 4:9
do **h** in your hometown as well." Lk 4:23
"Come and stand **h**." And he rose and Lk 6:8
for we are **h** in a desolate place." Lk 9:12
there are some standing **h** who will not Lk 9:27
to Jesus, "Master, it is good that we are **h**. Lk 9:33
and bear with you? Bring your son **h**." Lk 9:41
something greater than Solomon is **h**. Lk 11:31
something greater than Jonah is **h**. Lk 11:32
and said to him, "Get away from **h**, Lk 13:31
bread, but I perish **h** with hunger! Lk 15:17
but now he is comforted **h**, and you are Lk 16:25
who would pass from **h** to you may not Lk 16:26
nor will they say, 'Look, **h** it is!' or Lk 17:21
'Look, **h**!' Do not go out or follow them. Lk 17:23
came, saying, 'Lord, **h** is your mina, Lk 19:20
bring them **h** and slaughter them Lk 19:27
has ever yet sat. Untie it and bring it **h**. Lk 19:30
will not be left **h** one stone upon another Lk 21:6
h are two swords." And he said to them, Lk 22:38
He is not **h**, but has risen. Remember Lk 24:6
to them, "Have you anything **h** to eat?" Lk 24:41
thirsty or have to come **h** to draw water." Jn 4:15
"Go, call your husband, and come **h**." Jn 4:16
But the hour is coming, and is now **h**, Jn 4:23
For **h** the saying holds true, 'One sows Jn 4:37
to you, an hour is coming, and is now **h**, Jn 5:25
"There is a boy **h** who has five barley Jn 6:9
to him, "Rabbi, when did you come **h**?" Jn 6:25
said to him, "Leave **h** and go to Judea, Jn 7:3
not yet come, but your time is always **h**. Jn 7:6
And **h** he is, speaking openly, and they Jn 7:26
love me, for I came from God and I am **h**. Jn 8:42
said to Jesus, "Lord, if you had been **h**, Jn 11:21
"The Teacher is **h** and is calling for Jn 11:28
saying to him, "Lord, if you had been **h**, Jn 11:32
I love the Father. Rise, let us go from **h**. Jn 14:31
he said to Thomas, "Put your finger **h**, Jn 20:27
yet **h** you have filled Jerusalem with Acts 5:28
and the eunuch said, "See, **h** is water! Acts 8:36
"Ananias." And he said, "**H** I am, Acts 9:10
And **h** he has authority from the chief Acts 9:14
has he not come **h** for this purpose, Acts 9:21
Now as Peter went **h** and there among Acts 9:32
therefore we are all **h** in the presence Acts 10:33
not harm yourself, for we are all **h**." Acts 16:28
world upside down have come **h** also, Acts 17:6
brought these men **h** who are neither Acts 19:37
they ought to be **h** before you and to Acts 24:19
So when they came together **h**, I made Acts 25:17
me, both in Jerusalem and **h**, Acts 25:24
And now I stand **h** on trial because of Acts 26:6
and so I stand **h** testifying both to Acts 26:22
the brothers coming **h** has reported Acts 28:21
H for the third time I am ready to 2 Cor 12:14
that I am put **h** for the defense of Phil 1:16
H there is not Greek and Jew, Col 3:11
you of everything that has taken place **h**. Col 4:9
For **h** we have no lasting city, but we Heb 13:14
"You sit **h** in a good place," while you say Jas 2:3
to me like a trumpet, said, "Come up **h**, Rv 4:1
"Come up **h**!" And they went up to Rv 11:12
H is a call for the endurance and faith Rv 13:10
H is a call for the endurance of the Rv 14:12

HEREAFTER (2)
Tell us what is to come **h**, that we may Is 41:23
every one of you his idols, now and **h**, Ezk 20:39

HEREBY (1)
"**H** you shall know that the LORD has Nm 16:28

HERES (2)
persisted in dwelling in Mount **H**, Jgs 1:35
from the battle by the ascent of **H**. Jgs 8:13

HERESH (1)
H, Galal and Mattaniah the son of 1 Chr 9:15

HERESIES (1)
who will secretly bring in destructive **h**, 2 Pt 2:1

HERETH (1)
departed and went into the forest of **H**. 1 Sm 22:5

HERITAGE (50)
GOD, destroy not your people and your **h**, Dt 9:26
For they are your people and your **h**, Dt 9:29
portion is his people, Jacob his allotted **h**. Dt 32:9
for the priesthood of the LORD is their **h**. Jos 18:7
anointed you to be prince over his **h**. 1 Sm 10:1
have no share in the **h** of the LORD, 1 Sm 26:19
my son together from the **h** of God.' 2 Sm 14:16
you swallow up the **h** of the LORD?" 2 Sm 20:19
that you may bless the **h** of the LORD?" 2 Sm 21:3
(for they are your people, and your **h**, 1 Kgs 8:51
the peoples of the earth to be your **h**, 1 Kgs 8:53
the remnant of my **h** and give them 2 Kgs 21:14
God, the **h** decreed for him by God." Jb 20:29
and the **h** that oppressors receive from Jb 27:13
God above and my **h** from the Almighty Jb 31:2
of me, and I will make the nations your **h**, Ps 2:8
Oh, save your people and bless your **h**! Ps 28:9
people whom he has chosen as his **h**! Ps 33:12
and their **h** will remain forever; Ps 37:18
He chose our **h** for us, the pride of Jacob Ps 47:4
have given me the **h** of those who fear Ps 61:5
have redeemed to be the tribe of your **h**! Ps 74:2
sword and vented his wrath on his **h**. Ps 78:62
your people, O LORD, and afflict your **h**. Ps 94:5
his people; he will not abandon his **h**; Ps 94:14
his people, and he abhorred his **h**; Ps 106:40
Your testimonies are my **h** forever, Ps 119:111
Behold, children are a **h** from the LORD, Ps 127:3
and gave their land as a **h**, a heritage Ps 135:12
as a heritage, a **h** to his people Israel. Ps 135:12
and gave their land as a **h**, for his Ps 136:21
a **h** to Israel his servant, for his Ps 136:22
angry with my people; I profaned my **h**; Is 47:6
This is the **h** of the servants of the LORD Is 54:17
feed you with the **h** of Jacob your father, Is 58:14
of your servants, the tribes of your **h**. Is 63:17
land and made my **h** an abomination. Jer 2:7
the land that I gave your fathers for a **h**. Jer 3:18
land, a **h** most beautiful of all nations. Jer 3:19
my house; I have abandoned my **h**; Jer 12:7
My **h** has become to me like a lion in the Jer 12:8
Is my **h** to me like a hyena's lair? Are the Jer 12:9
neighbors who touch the **h** that I have Jer 12:14
again each to his **h** and each to his Jer 12:15
your hand from your **h** that I gave to Jer 17:4
you exult, O plunderers of my **h**, Jer 50:11
O LORD, and make not your **h** a reproach, Jl 2:17
on behalf of my people and my **h** Israel, Jl 3:2
country and left his **h** to jackals of the Mal 1:3
The one who conquers will have this **h**, Rv 21:7

HERITAGES (1)
the land, to apportion the desolate **h**, Is 49:8

HERMAS (1)
H, and the brothers who are with Rom 16:14

HERMES (2)
H, because he was the chief speaker. Acts 14:12
Asyncritus, Phlegon, **H**, Patrobas, Rom 16:14

HERMOGENES (1)
among whom are Phygelus and **H**. 2 Tm 1:15

HERMON (14)
from the Valley of the Arnon to Mount **H** Dt 3:8
(the Sidonians call **H** Sirion, while the Dt 3:9
as far as Mount Sirion (that is, **H**), Dt 4:48
and the Hivites under **H** in the land of Jos 11:3
the Valley of Lebanon below Mount **H**. Jos 11:17
the Valley of the Arnon to Mount **H**, Jos 12:1
ruled over Mount **H** and Salecah and Jos 12:5
below Mount **H** to Lebo-hamath, Jos 13:5
and Maacathites, and all Mount **H**, Jos 13:11
to Baal-hermon, Senir, and Mount **H**. 1 Chr 5:23
you from the land of Jordan and of **H**, Ps 42:6
Tabor and **H** joyously praise your Ps 89:12
It is like the dew of **H**, which falls on the Ps 133:3
of Amana, from the peak of Senir and **H**, Sg 4:8

HEROD (40)
of Judea in the days of **H** the king, Mt 2:1
When **H** the king heard this, he was Mt 2:3
Then **H** summoned the wise men secretly Mt 2:7
warned in a dream not to return to **H**, Mt 2:12
for **H** is about to search for the child, Mt 2:13
and remained there until the death of **H**. Mt 2:15
Then **H**, when he saw that he had been Mt 2:16
But when **H** died, behold, an angel of the Mt 2:19
over Judea in place of his father **H**, Mt 2:22
At that time **H** the tetrarch heard about Mt 14:1
For **H** had seized John and bound him Mt 14:3
before the company and pleased **H**, Mt 14:6
King **H** heard of it, for Jesus' name had Mk 6:14
But when **H** heard of it, he said, "John, Mk 6:16
For it was **H** who had sent and seized Mk 6:17
For John had been saying to **H**, "It is not Mk 6:18
for **H** feared John, knowing that he was Mk 6:20
opportunity came when **H** on his Mk 6:21
danced, she pleased **H** and his guests. Mk 6:22
of the Pharisees and the leaven of **H**." Mk 8:15
In the days of **H**, king of Judea, there was a Lk 1:5
of Judea, and **H** being tetrarch of Galilee, Lk 3:1
But **H** the tetrarch, who had been Lk 3:19
for all the evil things that **H** had done, Lk 3:19
Now **H** the tetrarch heard about all that Lk 9:7
H said, "John I beheaded, but who is this Lk 9:9
from here, for **H** wants to kill you." Lk 13:31
jurisdiction, he sent him over to **H**, Lk 23:7
When **H** saw Jesus, he was very glad, for Lk 23:8
And **H** with his soldiers treated him Lk 23:11
And **H** and Pilate became friends with Lk 23:12
Neither did **H**, for he sent him back to Lk 23:15
anointed, both **H** and Pontius Pilate, Acts 4:27
About that time **H** the king laid Acts 12:1
Now when **H** was about to bring him Acts 12:6
from the hand of **H** and from all that Acts 12:11
And after **H** searched for him and did Acts 12:19
Now **H** was angry with the people of Acts 12:20
On an appointed day **H** put on his Acts 12:21
member of the court of **H** the tetrarch, Acts 13:1

HEROD'S (4)
But when **H** birthday came, the Mt 14:6
the wife of Chuza, **H** household manager, Lk 8:3
that he belonged to **H** jurisdiction, Lk 23:7
him to be guarded in **H** praetorium. Acts 23:35

HERODIANS (3)
their disciples to him, along with the **H**, Mt 22:16
held counsel with the **H** against him, Mk 3:6
of the Pharisees and some of the **H**, Mk 12:13

HERODIAS (5)
and put him in prison for the sake of **H**, Mt 14:3
the daughter of **H** danced before the Mt 14:6
bound him in prison for the sake of **H**, Mk 6:17
And **H** had a grudge against him and Mk 6:19
who had been reproved by him for **H**, Lk 3:19

HERODIAS'S (1)
For when **H** daughter came in and Mk 6:22

HERODION (1)
Greet my kinsman **H**. Greet those in Rom 16:11

HEROES (4)
He struck down two **h** of Moab. 1 Chr 11:22
Woe to those who are **h** at drinking wine, Is 5:22
Behold, their **h** cry in the streets; the Is 33:7
say, 'We are **h** and mighty men of war'? Jer 48:14

HERON (2)
the stork, the **h** of any kind, the hoopoe, Lv 11:19
the stork, the **h** of any kind; the hoopoe Dt 14:18

HESHBON (38)
in all the cities of the Amorites, in **H**, Nm 21:25
For **H** was the city of Sihon the king Nm 21:26
the ballad singers say, "Come to **H**, Nm 21:27
For fire came out from **H**, flame from Nm 21:28
them; **H**, as far as Dibon, perished; Nm 21:30
king of the Amorites, who lived at **H**." Nm 21:34
Dibon, Jazer, Nimrah, **H**, Elealeh, Nm 32:3
And the people of Reuben built **H**, Nm 32:37
the king of the Amorites, who lived in **H**, Dt 1:4
your hand Sihon the Amorite, king of **H**, Dt 2:24
of Kedemoth to Sihon the king of **H**, Dt 2:26
But Sihon the king of **H** would not let us Dt 2:30
the king of the Amorites, who lived at **H**.' Dt 3:2
as we did to Sihon the king of **H**, Dt 3:6
the king of the Amorites, who lived at **H**, Dt 4:46
Sihon the king of **H** and Og the king of Dt 29:7
the Jordan, to Sihon the king of **H**, Jos 9:10
Amorites who lived at **H** and ruled from Jos 12:2
to the boundary of Sihon king of **H**. Jos 12:5
king of the Amorites, who reigned in **H**, Jos 13:10
with **H**, and all its cities that are in the Jos 13:17
king of the Amorites, who reigned in **H**, Jos 13:21
and from **H** to Ramath-mizpeh and Jos 13:26
rest of the kingdom of Sihon king of **H**, Jos 13:27
H with its pasturelands, Jazer with its Jos 21:39
Sihon king of the Amorites, king of **H**, Jgs 11:19
While Israel lived in **H** and its villages, Jgs 11:26
H with its pasturelands, and Jazer 1 Chr 6:81
land of Sihon king of **H** and the land of Neh 9:22
Your eyes are pools in **H**, by the gate of Sg 7:4
H and Elealeh cry out; their voice is heard Is 15:4
For the fields of **H** languish, and the vine Is 16:8
you with my tears, O **H** and Elealeh; Is 16:9
In **H** they planned disaster against her: Jer 48:2
"From the outcry at **H** even to Elealeh, Jer 48:34
the shadow of **H** fugitives stop without Jer 48:45
strength, for fire came out from **H**, Jer 48:45
"Wail, O **H**, for Ai is laid waste! Cry out, Jer 49:3

HESHMON (1)
Hazar-gaddah, **H**, Beth-pelet, Jos 15:27

HESITATE (1)
they do not **h** to spit at the sight of me. Jb 30:10

HESITATION (1)
and accompany them without **h**, Acts 10:20

HETH (2)
fathered Sidon his firstborn and **H**, Gn 10:15
fathered Sidon his firstborn and **H**, 1 Chr 1:13

HETHLON (2)
Sea by way of **H** to Lebo-hamath, Ezk 47:15
beside the way of **H** to Lebo-hamath, Ezk 48:1

HEWED (3)
in my tomb that I **h** out for myself in Gn 50:5
in the midst of it, and **h** out a wine vat in it; Is 5:2
and **h** out cisterns for themselves, Jer 2:13

HEWN (8)
stone, you shall not build it of **h** stones, Ex 20:25
of all good things, cisterns already **h**, Neh 9:25
her house; she has **h** her seven pillars. Prv 9:1
the great in height will be **h** down, and Is 10:33
look to the rock from which you were **h**, Is 51:1
were four tables of **h** stone for the Ezk 40:42
Therefore I have **h** them by the prophets; Hos 6:5
him, you have built houses of **h** stone, Am 5:11

HEWS (1)
the axe boast over him who **h** with it, Is 10:15

HEZEKIAH (132)
and **H** his son reigned in his place. 2 Kgs 16:20
king of Israel, **H** the son of Ahaz, 2 Kgs 18:1
In the fourth year of King **H**, which 2 Kgs 18:9
In the sixth year of **H**, which was the 2 Kgs 18:10
In the fourteenth year of King **H**, 2 Kgs 18:13
And **H** king of Judah sent to the 2 Kgs 18:14
Assyria required of **H** king of Judah 2 Kgs 18:14
And **H** gave him all the silver that 2 Kgs 18:15
At that time **H** stripped the gold 2 Kgs 18:16
the doorposts that **H** king of Judah 2 Kgs 18:16
Lachish to King **H** at Jerusalem. 2 Kgs 18:17
Rabshakeh said to them, "Say to **H**, 2 Kgs 18:19
places and altars **H** has removed, 2 Kgs 18:22
'Do not let **H** deceive you, for he will 2 Kgs 18:29
Do not let **H** make you trust in the 2 Kgs 18:30
Do not listen to **H**, for thus says the 2 Kgs 18:31
do not listen to **H** when he misleads 2 Kgs 18:32
came to **H** with their clothes torn 2 Kgs 18:37
As soon as King **H** heard it, he tore 2 Kgs 19:1
They said to him, "Thus says **H**, This 2 Kgs 19:3
servants of King **H** came to Isaiah, 2 Kgs 19:5
So he sent messengers again to **H**, 2 Kgs 19:9
shall you speak to **H** king of Judah: 2 Kgs 19:10
H received the letter from the hand 2 Kgs 19:14
and **H** went up to the house of the 2 Kgs 19:14
And **H** prayed before the LORD and 2 Kgs 19:15
Isaiah the son of Amoz sent to **H**, 2 Kgs 19:20
In those days **H** became sick and was 2 Kgs 20:1
Then **H** turned his face to the wall 2 Kgs 20:2
in your sight." And **H** wept bitterly. 2 Kgs 20:3
and say to **H** the leader of my people, 2 Kgs 20:5
And **H** said to Isaiah, "What shall be 2 Kgs 20:8
And **H** answered, "It is an easy thing 2 Kgs 20:10
with letters and a present to **H**, 2 Kgs 20:12
for he heard that **H** had been sick. 2 Kgs 20:12
And **H** welcomed them, and he 2 Kgs 20:13
all his realm that **H** did not show 2 Kgs 20:13
Isaiah the prophet came to King **H**, 2 Kgs 20:14
did they come to you?" And **H** said, 2 Kgs 20:14
in your house?" And **H** answered, 2 Kgs 20:15
Then Isaiah said to **H**, "Hear the 2 Kgs 20:16
Then said **H** to Isaiah, "The word of 2 Kgs 20:19
of the deeds of **H** and all his might 2 Kgs 20:20
And **H** slept with his fathers, and 2 Kgs 20:21
the high places that **H** his father had 2 Kgs 21:3
Ahaz his son, **H** his son, Manasseh 1 Chr 3:13
by name, came in the days of **H**, 1 Chr 4:41
And **H** his son reigned in his place. 2 Chr 28:27
H began to reign when he was 2 Chr 29:1
they went in to **H** the king and said, 2 Chr 29:18
Then **H** the king rose early and 2 Chr 29:20
Then **H** commanded that the burnt 2 Chr 29:27
And **H** the king and the officials 2 Chr 29:30
Then **H** said, "You have now 2 Chr 29:31
And **H** and all the people rejoiced 2 Chr 29:36
H sent to all Israel and Judah, and 2 Chr 30:1
For **H** had prayed for them, saying, 2 Chr 30:18
the LORD heard **H** and healed the 2 Chr 30:20
And **H** spoke encouragingly to all 2 Chr 30:22
For **H** king of Judah gave the 2 Chr 30:24
And **H** appointed the divisions of the 2 Chr 31:2
When **H** and the princes came and 2 Chr 31:8
And **H** questioned the priests and the 2 Chr 31:9
Then **H** commanded them to 2 Chr 31:11
the appointment of **H** the king and 2 Chr 31:13
Thus **H** did throughout all Judah, 2 Chr 31:20
And when **H** saw that Sennacherib 2 Chr 32:2
from the words of **H** king of Judah. 2 Chr 32:8
to Jerusalem to **H** king of Judah 2 Chr 32:9
Is not **H** misleading you, that he 2 Chr 32:11
Has not this same **H** taken away his 2 Chr 32:12
do not let **H** deceive you or mislead 2 Chr 32:15
Lord GOD and against his servant **H**. 2 Chr 32:16
so the God of **H** will not deliver his 2 Chr 32:17
Then **H** the king and Isaiah the 2 Chr 32:20
the LORD saved **H** and the 2 Chr 32:22
precious things to **H** king of Judah, 2 Chr 32:23
In those days **H** became sick and 2 Chr 32:24
But **H** did not make return 2 Chr 32:25
But **H** humbled himself for the 2 Chr 32:26
come upon them in the days of **H**. 2 Chr 32:26
And **H** had very great riches and 2 Chr 32:27
This same **H** closed the upper outlet 2 Chr 32:30
And **H** prospered in all his works. 2 Chr 32:30
of the acts of **H** and his good deeds, 2 Chr 32:32
And **H** slept with his fathers, and 2 Chr 32:33
that his father **H** had broken down, 2 Chr 33:3
The sons of Ater, namely of **H**, 98. Ezr 2:16
The sons of Ater, namely of **H**, 98. Neh 7:21
Ater, **H**, Azzur, Neh 10:17
which the men of **H** king of Judah Prv 25:1
the days of Uzziah, Jotham, Ahaz, and **H**, Is 1:1
In the fourteenth year of King **H**, Is 36:1
from Lachish to King **H** at Jerusalem, Is 36:2
the Rabshakeh said to them, "Say to **H**, Is 36:4
high places and altars **H** has removed, Is 36:7
'Do not let **H** deceive you, for he will not Is 36:14
Do not let **H** make you trust in the LORD Is 36:15
Do not listen to **H**. For thus says the Is 36:16
Beware lest **H** mislead you by saying, Is 36:18
came to **H** with their clothes torn, Is 36:22
As soon as King **H** heard it, he tore his Is 37:1
They said to him, "Thus says **H**, 'This Is 37:3
the servants of King **H** came to Isaiah, Is 37:5
when he heard it, he sent messengers to **H**, Is 37:9
shall you speak to **H** king of Judah: Is 37:10
H received the letter from the hand of the Is 37:14
and **H** went up to the house of the LORD, Is 37:14
And **H** prayed to the LORD: Is 37:15
Then Isaiah the son of Amoz sent to **H**, Is 37:21
In those days **H** became sick and was at Is 38:1
Then **H** turned his face to the wall and Is 38:2
good in your sight." And **H** wept bitterly. Is 38:3
"Go and say to **H**, Thus says the LORD, the Is 38:5
A writing of **H** king of Judah, after he had Is 38:9
H also had said, "What is the sign that I Is 38:22
envoys with letters and a present to **H**, Is 39:1
And **H** welcomed them gladly. And he Is 39:2
in all his realm that **H** did not show them. Is 39:2
Then Isaiah the prophet came to King **H**, Is 39:3
where did they come to you?" **H** said, Is 39:3
they seen in your house?" **H** answered, Is 39:4
Then Isaiah said to **H**, "Hear the word of Is 39:5
Then said **H** to Isaiah, "The word of the Is 39:8
because of what Manasseh the son of **H**, Jer 15:4
in the days of **H** king of Judah, Jer 26:18
Did **H** king of Judah and all Judah put Jer 26:19
the days of Uzziah, Jotham, Ahaz, and **H**, Hos 1:1
in the days of Jotham, Ahaz, and **H**, Mi 1:1
of Gedaliah, son of Amariah, son of **H**, Zep 1:1
father of Ahaz, and Ahaz the father of **H**, Mt 1:9
and **H** the father of Manasseh, and Mt 1:10

HEZION (1)
the son of Tabrimmon, the son of **H**, 1 Kgs 15:18

HEZIR (2)
the seventeenth to **H**, the eighteenth 1 Chr 24:15
Magpiash, Meshullam, **H**, Neh 10:20

HEZRO (2)
H of Carmel, Paarai the Arbite, 2 Sm 23:35
H of Carmel, Naarai the son of 1 Chr 11:37

HEZRON (20)
Reuben: Hanoch, Pallu, **H**, and Carmi. Gn 46:9
the sons of Perez were **H** and Hamul. Gn 46:12
of Israel: Hanoch, Pallu, **H**, and Carmi; Ex 6:14
of **H**, the clan of the Hezronites; of Nm 26:6
And the sons of Perez were: of **H**, the Nm 26:21
up south of Kadesh-barnea, along by **H**, Jos 15:3
generations of Perez: Perez fathered **H**, Ru 4:18
H fathered Ram, Ram fathered Ru 4:19
The sons of Perez: **H** and Hamul. 1 Chr 2:5
The sons of **H** that were born to him: 1 Chr 2:9
the son of **H** fathered children by 1 Chr 2:18
Afterward **H** went in to the daughter 1 Chr 2:21
After the death of **H**, Caleb went in to 1 Chr 2:24
to Ephrathah, the wife of **H** his father, 1 Chr 2:24
sons of Jerahmeel, the firstborn of **H**: 1 Chr 2:25
Perez, **H**, Carmi, Hur, and Shobal. 1 Chr 4:1
Israel: Hanoch, Pallu, **H**, and Carmi. 1 Chr 5:3
by Tamar, and Perez the father of **H**, Mt 1:3
father of Hezron, and **H** the father of Ram, Mt 1:3
of Admin, the son of Arni, the son of **H**, Lk 3:33

HEZRONITES (2)
of Hezron, the clan of the **H**; of Carmi, Nm 26:6
were: of Hezron, the clan of the **H**; Nm 26:21

HID (43)
man and his wife **h** themselves from the Gn 3:8
because I was naked, and I **h** myself." Gn 3:10
Jacob **h** them under the terebinth tree Gn 35:4
was a fine child, she **h** him three months. Ex 2:2
down the Egyptian and **h** him in the Ex 2:12
the God of Jacob." And Moses **h** his face, Ex 3:6
up to the roof and **h** them with the stalks Jos 2:6
because she **h** the messengers whom we Jos 6:17
because she **h** the messengers whom Jos 6:25
five kings fled and **h** themselves in the Jos 10:16
of Jerubbaal was left, for he **h** himself. Jgs 9:5
him everything and **h** nothing from 1 Sm 3:18
the people **h** themselves in caves and 1 Sm 13:6
place where you **h** yourself when the 1 Sm 20:19
So David **h** himself in the field. And 1 Sm 20:24
hundred prophets and **h** them by 1 Kgs 18:4
how I **h** a hundred men of the LORD'S 1 Kgs 18:13
and clothing and went and **h** them. 2 Kgs 7:8
things from it and went and **h** them. 2 Kgs 7:8
Thus they **h** him from Athaliah, so 2 Kgs 11:2
who were with him **h** themselves. 1 Chr 21:20
of Ahaziah, **h** him from Athaliah, 2 Chr 22:11
Yet these things you **h** in your heart; I Jb 10:13
in the net that they **h** their own foot has Ps 9:15
mountain stand strong; you **h** your face; Ps 30:7
For without cause they **h** their net for Ps 35:7
And let the net that he **h** ensnare him; let Ps 35:8
sword; in the shadow of his hand he **h** me; Is 49:2
arrow; in his quiver he **h** me away. Is 49:2
I **h** not my face from disgrace and Is 50:6
for a moment I **h** my face from you, Is 54:8
I **h** my face and was angry, but he went Is 57:17
So I went and **h** it by the Euphrates, as Jer 13:5
the prophet, but the LORD **h** them. Jer 36:26
with me that I **h** my face from them Ezk 39:23
and **h** my face from them. Ezk 39:24
a woman took and **h** in three measures Mt 13:33
the ground and **h** his master's money. Mt 25:18
and I went and **h** your talent in the Mt 25:25
a woman took and **h** in three measures Lk 13:21
but Jesus **h** himself and went out of the Jn 8:59
he departed and **h** himself from them. Jn 12:36
h themselves in the caves and among Rv 6:15

HIDDAI (1)
Pirathon, **H** of the brooks of Gaash, 2 Sm 23:30

HIDDEN (86)
ground, and from your face I shall be **h**. Gn 4:14
and the thing is **h** from the eyes of Lv 4:13
and it is **h** from him and he has become Lv 5:2
becomes unclean, and it is **h** from him, Lv 5:3
that people swear, and it is **h** from him, Lv 5:4
and it is **h** from the eyes of her Nm 5:13
the seas and the **h** treasures of the Dt 33:19
had taken the two men and **h** them. Jos 2:4
they are **h** in the earth inside my tent, Jos 7:21
it was **h** in his tent with the silver Jos 7:22
found, **h** in the cave at Makkedah." Jos 10:17
the cave where they had **h** themselves, Jos 10:27
he has **h** himself among the 1 Sm 10:22
holes where they have **h** themselves." 1 Sm 14:11
of Israel who had **h** themselves in the 1 Sm 14:22
even now he has **h** himself in one of 2 Sm 17:9
there is nothing **h** from the king), 2 Sm 18:13
there was nothing **h** from the king 1 Kgs 10:3
and the LORD has **h** it from me and 2 Kgs 4:27
may eat him.' But she has **h** her son." 2 Kgs 6:29
six years, **h** in the house of the LORD, 2 Kgs 11:3
There was nothing **h** from Solomon 2 Chr 9:2
six years, **h** in the house of God, 2 Chr 22:12
Or why was I not as a **h** stillborn child, Jb 3:16
and dig for it more than for **h** treasures, Jb 3:21
is light given to a man whose way is **h**, Jb 3:23
You shall be **h** from the lash of the Jb 5:21
A rope is **h** for him in the ground, a trap Jb 18:10
and the thing that is **h** he brings out to Jb 28:11
It is **h** from the eyes of all living and Jb 28:21
"God has forgotten, he has **h** his face, Ps 10:11
and there is nothing **h** from its heat. Ps 19:6
Declare me innocent from **h** faults. Ps 19:12
and he has not **h** his face from him, Ps 22:24
take me out of the net they have **h** for me, Ps 31:4
you; my sighing is not **h** from you. Ps 38:9
I have not **h** your deliverance within Ps 40:10
wrongs I have done are not **h** from you. Ps 69:5
My frame was not **h** from you, when I Ps 139:15

The arrogant have **h** a trap for me, and Ps 140:5
where I walk they have **h** a trap for me. Ps 142:3
silver and search for it as for **h** treasures, Prv 2:4
Better is open rebuke than **h** love. Prv 27:5
of their discerning men shall be **h**." Is 29:14
O Israel, "My way is **h** from the LORD, Is 40:27
them trapped in holes and **h** in prisons; Is 42:22
h things that you have not known. Is 48:6
and your sins have **h** his face from you so Is 59:2
for you have **h** your face from us, and Is 64:7
are forgotten and are **h** from my eyes. Is 65:16
loincloth from the place where I had **h** it. Jer 13:7
They are not **h** from me, nor is their Jer 16:17
tell you great and **h** things that you have Jer 33:3
for I have **h** my face from this city Jer 33:5
and honey **h** in the fields." So he Jer 41:8
throne above these stones that I have **h**, Jer 43:10
than Daniel; no secret is **h** from you; Ezk 28:3
he reveals deep and **h** things; he knows Dn 2:22
Ephraim, and Israel is not **h** from me; Hos 5:3
sting? Compassion is **h** from my eyes. Hos 13:14
perhaps you may be **h** on the day of the Zep 2:3
world. A city set on a hill cannot be **h**. Mt 5:14
revealed, or **h** that will not be known. Mt 10:26
that you have **h** these things from the Mt 11:25
what has been **h** since the foundation Mt 13:35
of heaven is like treasure **h** in a field, Mt 13:44
For nothing is **h** except to be made Mk 4:22
anyone to know, yet he could not be **h**. Mk 7:24
and for five months she kept herself **h**, Lk 1:24
For nothing is **h** that will not be made Lk 8:17
the woman saw that she was not **h**, Lk 8:47
that you have **h** these things from the Lk 10:21
be revealed, or **h** that will not be known. Lk 12:2
This saying was **h** from them, and they Lk 18:34
But now they are **h** from your eyes. Lk 19:42
impart a secret and **h** wisdom of God, 1 Cor 2:7
light the things now **h** in darkness and 1 Cor 4:5
the plan of the mystery **h** for ages in God Eph 3:9
the mystery **h** for ages and generations Col 1:26
in whom are **h** all the treasures of Col 2:3
and your life is **h** with Christ in God. Col 3:3
those that are not cannot remain **h**. 1 Tm 5:25
And no creature is **h** from his sight, Heb 4:13
was **h** for three months by his Heb 11:23
your adorning be the **h** person of the 1 Pt 3:4
I will give some of the **h** manna, Rv 2:17

HIDE (69)

"Shall I **h** from Abraham what I am Gn 18:17
"We will not **h** from my lord that our Gn 47:18
When she could **h** him no longer, she Ex 2:3
who are left and **h** themselves from you Dt 7:20
will forsake them and **h** my face from Dt 31:17
And I will surely **h** my face in that day Dt 31:18
he said, 'I will **h** my face from them; Dt 32:20
and **h** there three days until the pursuers Jos 2:16
you have done; do not **h** it from me." Jos 7:19
in the winepress to **h** it from the Jgs 6:11
that he told you? Do not **h** it from me. 1 Sm 3:17
more also if you **h** anything from me 1 Sm 3:17
Stay in a secret place and **h** yourself. 1 Sm 19:2
should my father **h** this from me? 1 Sm 20:2
that I may **h** myself in the field till the 1 Sm 20:5
"Do not **h** from me anything I ask 2 Sm 14:18
turn eastward and **h** yourself by the 1 Kgs 17:3
an inner chamber to **h** yourself." 1 Kgs 22:25
of the camp to **h** themselves in the 2 Kgs 7:12
an inner chamber to **h** yourself." 2 Chr 18:24
womb, nor **h** trouble from my eyes. Jb 3:10
then I will not **h** myself from your face: Jb 13:20
Why do you **h** your face and count me Jb 13:24
Oh that you would **h** me in Sheol, that Jb 14:13
the poor of the earth all **h** themselves. Jb 24:4
where evildoers may **h** themselves. Jb 34:22
H them all in the dust together; bind Jb 40:13
Why do you **h** yourself in times of Ps 10:1
How long will you **h** your face from me? Ps 13:1
eye; **h** me in the shadow of your wings, Ps 17:8
For he will **h** me in his shelter in the day Ps 27:5
H not your face from me. Turn not your Ps 27:9
of your presence you **h** them from the Ps 31:20
Why do you **h** your face? Why do you Ps 44:24
H your face from my sins, and blot out Ps 51:9
and **h** not yourself from my plea for Ps 55:1
with me—then I could **h** from him. Ps 55:12
H me from the secret plots of the wicked, Ps 64:2
H not your face from your servant; for I Ps 69:17
We will not **h** them from their children, Ps 78:4
Why do you **h** your face from me? Ps 88:14
O LORD? Will you **h** yourself forever? Ps 89:46
Do not **h** your face from me in the day Ps 102:2
When you **h** your face, they are Ps 104:29
h not your commandments from me! Ps 119:19
H not your face from me, lest I be like Ps 143:7
the wicked rise, people **h** themselves. Prv 28:12
the wicked rise, people **h** themselves, Prv 28:28
your hands, I will **h** my eyes from you; Is 1:15
into the rock and **h** in the dust from Is 2:10
their sin like Sodom; they do not **h** it. Is 3:9
h yourselves for a little while until the Is 26:20
you who **h** deep from the LORD your Is 29:15
Teacher will not **h** himself anymore, Is 30:20
one from whom men **h** their faces he was Is 53:3
and not to **h** yourself from your own Is 58:7
go to the Euphrates and **h** it there in a Jer 13:4
that I commanded you to **h** there." Jer 13:6
Can a man **h** himself in secret places Jer 23:24
the officials said to Baruch, "Go and **h**, Jer 36:19
you a question; **h** nothing from me." Jer 38:14
h nothing from us and we will not put Jer 38:25
hands large stones and **h** them in the Jer 43:9
And I will not **h** my face anymore Ezk 39:29
them, and they fled to **h** themselves. Dn 10:7
If they **h** themselves on the top of Am 9:3
and if they **h** from my sight at the Am 9:3
he will **h** his face from them at that time, Mi 3:4
"Fall on us and **h** us from the face of Rv 6:16

HIDES (9)

of all the lurking places where he **h**, 1 Sm 23:23
with ice, and where the snow **h** itself. Jb 6:16
though he **h** it under his tongue, Jb 20:12
can condemn? When he **h** his face, Jb 34:29
is this that **h** counsel without Jb 42:3
The prudent sees danger and **h** himself, Prv 22:3
prudent sees danger and **h** himself, Prv 27:12
but he who **h** his eyes will get many a Prv 28:27
Truly, you are a God who **h** yourself, O Is 45:15

HIDING (14)

"Is not David **h** among us in the 1 Sm 23:19
"Is not David **h** himself on the hill of 1 Sm 26:1
he was captured while **h** in Samaria, 2 Chr 22:9
told, without **h** it from their fathers, Jb 15:18
as others do by **h** my iniquity in my Jb 31:33
in **h** places he murders the innocent. Ps 10:8
You are a **h** place for me; you preserve Ps 32:7
told Saul, "Is not David **h** among us?" Ps 54:T
You are my **h** place and my shield; I Ps 119:114
who is **h** his face from the house of Jacob, Is 8:17
Each will be like a **h** place from the wind, Is 32:2
I have uncovered his **h** places, and he is Jer 49:10
a bear lying in wait for me, a lion in **h**; Lam 3:10
also will be drunken; you will go into **h**; Na 3:11

HIEL (1)

In his days **H** of Bethel built Jericho. 1 Kgs 16:34

HIERAPOLIS (1)

you and for those in Laodicea and in **H**. Col 4:13

HIGGAION (1)

in the work of their own hands. **H**. Selah Ps 9:16

HIGH (358)

up the ark, and it rose **h** above the earth. Gn 7:17
that all the **h** mountains under the Gn 7:19
wine. (He was priest of God Most **H**.) Gn 14:18
"Blessed be Abram by God Most **H**, Gn 14:19
and blessed be God Most **H**, who has Gn 14:20
my hand to the LORD, God Most **H**, Gn 14:22
and away from the dew of heaven on **h**. Gn 27:39
He said, "Behold, it is still **h** day; it is not Gn 29:7
long and five cubits **h** in its breadth, Ex 38:18
I will destroy your **h** places and cut Lv 26:30
who does anything with a **h** hand, Nm 15:30
knows the knowledge of the Most **H**, Nm 24:16
and demolish all their **h** places. Nm 33:52
the death of the **h** priest who was Nm 35:25
refuge until the death of the **h** priest, Nm 35:28
the death of the **h** priest the manslayer Nm 35:28
land before the death of the **h** priest. Nm 35:32
Gilead, there was not a city too **h** for us. Dt 2:36
All these were cities fortified with **h** walls, Dt 3:5
on the **h** mountains and on the hills and Dt 12:2
fame and in honor **h** above all nations Dt 26:19
God will set you **h** above all the nations Dt 28:1
towns, until your **h** and fortified walls, Dt 28:52
When the Most **H** gave to the nations Dt 32:8
him ride on the **h** places of the land, Dt 32:13
The **H** God surrounds him all day long, Dt 33:12
death of him who is **h** priest at the time. Jos 20:6
have a sacrifice today on the **h** place. 1 Sm 9:12
before he goes up to the **h** place to eat. 1 Sm 9:13
them on his way up to the **h** place. 1 Sm 9:14
Go up before me to the **h** place, for 1 Sm 9:19
came down from the **h** place into the 1 Sm 9:25
down from the **h** place with harp, 1 Sm 10:5
prophesying, he came to the **h** place. 1 Sm 10:13
O Israel, is slain on your **h** places! 2 Sm 1:19
"Jonathan lies slain on your **h** places. 2 Sm 1:25
and the Most **H** uttered his voice. 2 Sm 22:14
"He sent from on **h**, he took me; he 2 Sm 22:17
of the man who was raised on **h**, 2 Sm 23:1
people were sacrificing at the **h** places, 1 Kgs 3:2
and made offerings at the **h** places. 1 Kgs 3:3
there, for that was the great **h** place. 1 Kgs 3:4
and these were his **h** officials: Azariah 1 Kgs 4:2
cubits wide, and thirty cubits **h**. 1 Kgs 6:2
the whole house, five cubits **h**, 1 Kgs 6:10
cubits wide, and twenty cubits **h**, 1 Kgs 6:20
of olivewood, each ten cubits **h**. 1 Kgs 6:23
from brim to brim, and five cubits **h**, 1 Kgs 7:23
four cubits wide, and three cubits **h**. 1 Kgs 7:27
was a round band half a cubit **h**; 1 Kgs 7:35
Solomon built a **h** place for 1 Kgs 11:7
made temples on **h** places and 1 Kgs 12:31
the priests of the **h** places that he 1 Kgs 12:32
the priests of the **h** places who make 1 Kgs 13:2
the houses of the **h** places that are in 1 Kgs 13:32
priests for the **h** places again from 1 Kgs 13:33
ordained to be priests of the **h** places. 1 Kgs 13:33
built for themselves **h** places and 1 Kgs 14:23
Asherim on every **h** hill and under 1 Kgs 14:23
But the **h** places were not taken 1 Kgs 15:14
Yet the **h** places were not taken 1 Kgs 22:43
and made offerings on the **h** places. 1 Kgs 22:43
man with his master and in **h** favor, 2 Kgs 5:1
the **h** places were not taken away; 2 Kgs 12:3
and make offerings on the **h** places. 2 Kgs 12:3
secretary and the **h** priest came up 2 Kgs 12:10
But the **h** places were not removed; 2 Kgs 14:4
and made offerings on the **h** places. 2 Kgs 14:4
the **h** places were not taken away. 2 Kgs 15:4
and made offerings on the **h** places. 2 Kgs 15:4
the **h** places were not removed. 2 Kgs 15:35
and made offerings on the **h** places. 2 Kgs 15:35
offerings on the **h** places and on 2 Kgs 16:4
built for themselves **h** places in all 2 Kgs 17:9
Asherim on every **h** hill and under 2 Kgs 17:10
made offerings on all the **h** places, 2 Kgs 17:11
the shrines of the **h** places that the 2 Kgs 17:29
of people as priests of the **h** places, 2 Kgs 17:32
them in the shrines of the **h** places. 2 Kgs 17:32
He removed the **h** places and broke 2 Kgs 18:4
it not he whose **h** places and altars 2 Kgs 18:22
he rebuilt the **h** places that Hezekiah 2 Kgs 21:3
"Go up to Hilkiah the **h** priest, that he 2 Kgs 22:4
And Hilkiah the **h** priest said to 2 Kgs 22:8
commanded Hilkiah the **h** priest and 2 Kgs 23:4
make offerings in the **h** places at the 2 Kgs 23:5
and defiled the **h** places where the 2 Kgs 23:8
he broke down the **h** places of the 2 Kgs 23:8
the priests of the **h** places did not 2 Kgs 23:9
king defiled the **h** places that were 2 Kgs 23:13
the **h** place erected by Jeroboam the 2 Kgs 23:15
that altar with the **h** place he pulled 2 Kgs 23:15
shrines also of the **h** places that were 2 Kgs 23:19
the priests of the **h** places who were 2 Kgs 23:20
of the LORD in the **h** place that was at 1 Chr 16:39
that time in the **h** place at Gibeon, 1 Chr 21:29
went to the **h** place that was at Gibeon, 2 Chr 1:3
came from the **h** place at Gibeon, 2 Chr 1:13
made two pillars thirty-five cubits **h**, 2 Chr 3:15
twenty cubits wide and ten cubits **h**. 2 Chr 4:1
from brim to brim, and five cubits **h**, 2 Chr 4:2
five cubits wide, and three cubits **h**, 2 Chr 6:13
own priests for the **h** places and for 2 Chr 11:15
altars and the **h** places and broke 2 Chr 14:3
cities of Judah the **h** places and the 2 Chr 14:5
But the **h** places were not taken out 2 Chr 15:17
he took the **h** places and the Asherim 2 Chr 17:6
The **h** places, however, were not 2 Chr 20:33
he made **h** places in the hill country 2 Chr 21:11
offerings on the **h** places and on 2 Chr 28:4
of Judah he made **h** places to make 2 Chr 28:25
and broke down the **h** places and the 2 Chr 31:1
taken away his **h** places and his 2 Chr 32:12
For he rebuilt the **h** places that his 2 Chr 33:3
people still sacrificed at the **h** places, 2 Chr 33:17
on which he built **h** places and set 2 Chr 33:19
Judah and Jerusalem of the **h** places, 2 Chr 34:3
came to Hilkiah the **h** priest and gave 2 Chr 34:9
Then Eliashib the **h** priest rose up with Neh 3:1
of the house of Eliashib the **h** priest. Neh 3:20
the son of Eliashib the **h** priest, Neh 13:28
to their husbands, **h** and low alike." Est 1:20
"Let a gallows fifty cubits **h** be made, Est 5:14
at Haman's house, fifty cubits **h**." Est 7:9
full account of the **h** honor of Mordecai, Est 10:2
he sets on **h** those who are lowly, and Jb 5:11
and he who testifies for me is on **h**. Jb 16:19
that he judges those who are on **h**? Jb 21:22
"Is not God **h** in the heavens? See the Jb 22:12
God; he makes peace in his **h** heaven. Jb 25:2
my heritage from the Almighty on **h**? Jb 31:2
mounts up and makes his nest on **h**? Jb 39:27
He sees everything that is **h**; he is king Jb 41:34

be gathered about you; over it return on **h**. Ps 7:7
to the name of the LORD, the Most **H**. Ps 7:17
I will sing praise to your name, O Most **H**. Ps 9:2
your judgments are on **h**, out of his Ps 10:5
and the Most **H** uttered his voice, Ps 18:13
He sent from on **h**, he took me; he drew Ps 18:16
love of the Most **H** he shall not be Ps 21:7
of his tent; he will lift me **h** upon a rock. Ps 27:5
a trifle, demanding no **h** price for them. Ps 44:12
God, the holy habitation of the Most **H**. Ps 46:4
For the LORD, the Most **H**, is to be feared, a Ps 47:2
both low and **h**, rich and poor together! Ps 49:2
and perform your vows to the Most **H**, Ps 50:14
I cry out to God Most **H**, to God who Ps 57:2
to thrust him down from his **h** position. Ps 62:4
a breath; those of **h** estate are a delusion; Ps 62:9
mouth, and **h** praise was on my tongue. Ps 66:17
You ascended on **h**, leading a host of Ps 68:18
let your salvation, O God, set me on **h**! Ps 69:29
O God, reaches the **h** heavens. Ps 71:19
Is there knowledge in the Most **H**?" Ps 73:11
do not lift up your horn on **h**, or speak Ps 75:5
years of the right hand of the Most **H**." Ps 77:10
against the Most **H** in the desert. Ps 78:17
rock, the Most **H** God their redeemer. Ps 78:35
rebelled against the Most **H** God and did Ps 78:56
him to anger with their **h** places; Ps 78:58
built his sanctuary like the **h** heavens, Ps 78:69
I said, "You are gods, sons of the Most **H**, Ps 82:6
LORD, are the Most **H** over all the earth. Ps 83:18
for the Most **H** himself will establish her. Ps 87:5
strong is your hand, **h** your right hand. Ps 89:13
the shelter of the Most **H** will abide in the Ps 91:1
LORD your dwelling place—the Most **H**, Ps 91:9
to sing praises to your name, O Most **H**; Ps 92:1
but you, O LORD, are on **h** forever. Ps 92:8
waves of the sea, the LORD on **h** is mighty! Ps 93:4
O LORD, are most **h** over all the earth; Ps 97:9
For as **h** as the heavens are above the Ps 103:11
The **h** mountains are for the wild Ps 104:18
spurned the counsel of the Most **H**. Ps 107:11
The LORD is **h** above all nations, and his Ps 113:4
the LORD our God, who is seated on **h**, Ps 113:5
lifted up; my eyes are not raised too **h**; Ps 131:1
For though the LORD is **h**, he regards the Ps 138:6
is too wonderful for me; it is **h**; Ps 139:6
Stretch out your hand from on **h**; Ps 144:7
Let the **h** praises of God be in their Ps 149:6
makes his door **h** seeks destruction. Prv 17:19
and like a **h** wall in his imagination. Prv 18:11
Wisdom is too **h** for a fool; in the gate Prv 24:7
are their eyes, how **h** their eyelids lift! Prv 30:13
a rock, the way of a ship on the **h** seas, Prv 30:19
for the **h** official is watched by a higher, Eccl 5:8
folly is set in many **h** places, and the Eccl 10:6
they are afraid also of what is **h**, and Eccl 12:5
against every **h** tower, and against every Is 2:15
Lord sitting upon a throne, **h** and lifted up; Is 6:1
let it be deep as Sheol or **h** as heaven." Is 7:11
stars of God I will set my throne on **h**; Is 14:13
I will make myself like the Most **H**.' Is 14:14
and to Dibon, to the **h** places to weep; Is 15:2
when he wearies himself on the **h** place, Is 16:12
And the **h** fortifications of his walls he Is 25:12
shall be to you like a breach in a **h** wall, Is 30:13
mountain and every **h** hill there will Is 30:25
the Spirit is poured upon us from on **h**, Is 32:15
The LORD is exalted, for he dwells on **h**; he Is 33:5
it not he whose **h** places and altars Is 36:7
Get you up to a **h** mountain, O Zion, Is 40:9
Lift up your eyes on **h** and see: who Is 40:26
act wisely; he shall be **h** and lifted up, Is 52:13
On a **h** and lofty mountain you have set Is 57:7
thus says the One who is **h** and lifted up, Is 57:15
"I dwell in the **h** and holy place, and also Is 57:15
not make your voice to be heard on **h**. Is 58:4
on every **h** hill and under every green Jer 2:20
went up on every **h** hill and under every Jer 3:6
they have built the **h** places of Topheth, Jer 7:31
beside every green tree and on the **h** hills, Jer 17:2
the price of your **h** places for sin Jer 17:3
throne set on **h** from the beginning Jer 17:12
and have built the **h** places of Baal to Jer 19:5
"'The LORD will roar from on **h**, and Jer 25:30
They built the **h** places of Baal in the Jer 32:35
sacrifice in the **h** place and makes Jer 48:35
you make your nest as **h** as the eagle's, Jer 49:16
and her **h** gates shall be burned with Jer 51:58
"From on **h** he sent fire; into my bones Lam 1:13
justice in the presence of the Most **H**, Lam 3:35
mouth of the Most **H** that good and Lam 3:38
you, and I will destroy your **h** places. Ezk 6:3
shall be waste and the **h** places ruined, Ezk 6:6
around their altars, on every **h** hill, Ezk 6:13
plant it on a **h** and lofty mountain. Ezk 17:22
I bring low the **h** tree, and make high Ezk 17:24
the high tree, and make **h** the low tree, Ezk 17:24
wherever they saw any **h** hill or any Ezk 20:28
What is the **h** place to which you go? Ezk 20:29
have brought you out into the **h** seas. Ezk 27:26
So it towered **h** above all the trees of the Ezk 31:5
Because it towered **h** and set its top Ezk 31:10
all the mountains and on every **h** hill. Ezk 34:6
and set me down on a very **h** mountain, Ezk 40:2
and a half broad, and one cubit **h**, Ezk 40:42
an altar of wood, three cubits **h**, two Ezk 41:22
bodies of their kings at their **h** places, Ezk 43:7
shall be one cubit **h** and one cubit Ezk 43:13
king gave Daniel **h** honors and many Dn 2:48
Abednego, servants of the Most **H** God, Dn 3:26
wonders that the Most **H** God has done Dn 4:2
that the Most **H** rules the kingdom Dn 4:17
It is a decree of the Most **H**, which has Dn 4:24
that the Most **H** rules the kingdom Dn 4:25
that the Most **H** rules the kingdom Dn 4:32
returned to me, and I blessed the Most **H**, Dn 4:34
the Most **H** God gave Nebuchadnezzar Dn 5:18
knew that the Most **H** God rules the Dn 5:21
saints of the Most **H** shall receive the Dn 7:18
was given for the saints of the Most **H**, Dn 7:22
shall speak words against the Most **H**, Dn 7:25
shall wear out the saints of the Most **H**, Dn 7:25
to the people of the saints of the Most **H**; Dn 7:27
It had two horns, and both horns were **h**, Dn 8:3
The **h** places of Aven, the sin of Israel, Hos 10:8
and though they call out to the Most **H**, Hos 11:7
the **h** places of Isaac shall be made Am 7:9
and tread upon the **h** places of the earth. Mi 1:3
And what is the **h** place of Judah? Mi 1:5
LORD, and bow myself before God on **h**? Mi 6:6
gain for his house, to set his nest on **h**, Hab 2:9
forth its voice; it lifted its hands on **h**. Hab 3:10
he makes me tread on my **h** places. Hab 3:19
Joshua the son of Jehozadak, the **h** priest: Hg 1:1
Joshua the son of Jehozadak, the **h** priest, Hg 1:12
Joshua the son of Jehozadak, the **h** priest, Hg 1:14
Joshua the son of Jehozadak, the **h** priest, Hg 2:2
O Joshua, son of Jehozadak, the **h** priest. Hg 2:4
me Joshua the **h** priest standing before Zec 3:1
Hear now, O Joshua the **h** priest, you and Zec 3:8
the son of Jehozadak, the **h** priest. Zec 6:11
him to a very **h** mountain and showed Mt 4:8
them up a **h** mountain by themselves. Mt 17:1
gathered in the palace of the **h** priest, Mt 26:3
the servant of the **h** priest and cut off Mt 26:51
Jesus led him to Caiaphas the **h** priest, Mt 26:57
as far as the courtyard of the **h** priest, Mt 26:58
And the **h** priest stood up and said, Mt 26:62
And the **h** priest said to him, "I adjure Mt 26:63
Then the **h** priest tore his robes and Mt 26:65
in the time of Abiathar the **h** priest, Mk 2:26
with me, Jesus, Son of the Most **H** God? Mk 5:7
them up a **h** mountain by themselves. Mk 9:2
the servant of the **h** priest and cut off Mk 14:47
And they led Jesus to the **h** priest. And Mk 14:53
right into the courtyard of the **h** priest. Mk 14:54
And the **h** priest stood up in the midst Mk 14:60
Again the **h** priest asked him, "Are Mk 14:61
And the **h** priest tore his garments and Mk 14:63
the servant girls of the **h** priest came, Mk 14:66
and will be called the Son of the Most **H**. Lk 1:32
of the Most **H** will overshadow you; Lk 1:35
will be called the prophet of the Most **H**; Lk 1:76
the sunrise shall visit us from on **h** Lk 1:78
during the **h** priesthood of Annas and Lk 3:2
mother-in-law was ill with a **h** fever, Lk 4:38
and you will be sons of the Most **H**, Lk 6:35
with me, Jesus, Son of the Most **H** God? Lk 8:28
the servant of the **h** priest and cut off Lk 22:50
bringing him into the **h** priest's house, Lk 22:54
you are clothed with power from on **h**." Lk 24:49
Caiaphas, who was **h** priest that year, Jn 11:49
but being **h** priest that year he Jn 11:51
it and struck the **h** priest's servant and Jn 18:10
of Caiaphas, who was **h** priest that year. Jn 18:13
that disciple was known to the **h** priest, Jn 18:15
with Jesus into the court of the **h** priest, Jn 18:15
disciple, who was known to the **h** priest, Jn 18:16
The **h** priest then questioned Jesus Jn 18:19
"Is that how you answer the **h** priest?" Jn 18:22
him bound to Caiaphas the **h** priest. Jn 18:24
One of the servants of the **h** priest, a Jn 18:26
(for that Sabbath was a **h** day), Jn 19:31
with Annas the **h** priest and Caiaphas Acts 4:6
but the people held them in **h** esteem. Acts 5:13
But the **h** priest rose up, and all who Acts 5:17
Now when the **h** priest came, and Acts 5:21
And the **h** priest questioned them, Acts 5:27
And the **h** priest said, "Are these things Acts 7:1
Yet the Most **H** does not dwell in Acts 7:48
disciples of the Lord, went to the **h** priest Acts 9:1
devout women of **h** standing and the Acts 13:50
men are servants of the Most **H** God, Acts 16:17
Greek women of **h** standing as well Acts 17:12
sons of a Jewish **h** priest named Sceva Acts 19:14
as the **h** priest and the whole council Acts 22:5
And the **h** priest Ananias commanded Acts 23:2
"Would you revile God's **h** priest?" Acts 23:4
brothers, that he was the **h** priest, Acts 23:5
five days the **h** priest Ananias came Acts 24:1
"When he ascended on **h** he led a host of Eph 4:8
kings and all who are in **h** positions, 1 Tm 2:2
at the right hand of the Majesty on **h**, Heb 1:3
a merciful and faithful **h** priest in the Heb 2:17
the apostle and **h** priest of our Heb 3:1
we have a great **h** priest who has passed Heb 4:14
we do not have a **h** priest who is unable Heb 4:15
For every **h** priest chosen from among Heb 5:1
not exalt himself to be made a **h** priest, Heb 5:5
designated by God a **h** priest after the Heb 5:10
having become a **h** priest forever after Heb 6:20
king of Salem, priest of the Most **H** God, Heb 7:1
that we should have such a **h** priest, Heb 7:26
He has no need, like those **h** priests, to Heb 7:27
men in their weakness as **h** priests, Heb 7:28
we have such a **h** priest, one who is Heb 8:1
For every **h** priest is appointed to offer Heb 8:3
into the second only the **h** priest goes, Heb 9:7
Christ appeared as a **h** priest of the Heb 9:11
as the **h** priest enters the holy places Heb 9:25
holy places by the **h** priest as a Heb 13:11
the winepress, as **h** as a horse's bridle, Rv 14:20
for her sins are heaped **h** as heaven, and Rv 18:5
in the Spirit to a great, **h** mountain, Rv 21:10
It had a great, **h** wall, with twelve gates, Rv 21:12

HIGH-PRIESTLY (1)
and all who were of the **h** family. Acts 4:6

HIGHER (15)
his king shall be **h** than Agag, and his Nm 24:7
you shall rise **h** and higher above Dt 28:43
you shall rise higher and **h** above you, Dt 28:43
iniquities have risen **h** than our heads, Ezr 9:6
It is **h** than heaven—what can you do? Jb 11:8
behold the clouds, which are **h** than you. Jb 35:5
Lead me to the rock that is **h** than I, Ps 61:2
for the high official is watched by a **h**, Eccl 5:8
and there are yet **h** ones over them. Eccl 5:8
For as the heavens are **h** than the earth, Is 55:9
so are my ways **h** than your ways and my Is 55:9
were high, but one was **h** than the other, Dn 8:3
the other, and the **h** one came up last. Dn 8:3
he may say to you, 'Friend, move up **h**.' Lk 14:10
But earnestly desire the **h** gifts. And I 1 Cor 12:31

HIGHEST (17)
heaven and the **h** heaven cannot 1 Kgs 8:27
a house, since heaven, even **h** heaven, 2 Chr 2:6
heaven and the **h** heaven cannot 2 Chr 6:18
See the **h** stars, how lofty they are! Jb 22:12
firstborn, the **h** of the kings of the earth. Ps 89:27
if I do not set Jerusalem above my **h** joy! Ps 137:6
Praise him, you **h** heavens, and you Ps 148:4
to call from the **h** places in the town, Prv 9:3
takes a seat on the **h** places of the town, Prv 9:14
be established as the **h** of the mountains, Is 2:2
or three berries in the top of the **h** bough, Is 17:6
the **h** people of the earth languish. Is 24:4
be established as the **h** of the mountains, Mi 4:1
name of the Lord! Hosanna in the **h**!" Mt 21:9
our father David! Hosanna in the **h**!" Mk 11:10
"Glory to God in the **h**, and on earth Lk 2:14
Peace in heaven and glory in the **h**!" Lk 19:38

HIGHLY (8)
so that his name was **h** esteemed. 1 Sm 18:30
his kingdom was **h** exalted for the 1 Chr 14:2
the earth belong to God; he is **h** exalted! Ps 47:9
Prize her **h**, and she will exalt you; she Prv 4:8
point of death, who was **h** valued by him. Lk 7:2
of himself more **h** than he ought Rom 12:3
Therefore God has **h** exalted him and Phil 2:9
esteem them very **h** in love because 1 Thes 5:13

HIGHWAY (20)
a well. We will go along the King's **H**. Nm 20:17
said to him, "We will go up by the **h**, Nm 20:19
go by the King's **H** until we have Nm 21:22
on the east of the **h** that goes up from Jgs 21:19
of Beth-shemesh along one **h**, 1 Sm 6:12
lay wallowing in his blood in the **h**. 2 Sm 20:12
Amasa out of the **h** into the field and 2 Sm 20:12
When he was taken out of the **h**, all 2 Sm 20:13
which is on the **h** to the Washer's 2 Kgs 18:17
but the path of the upright is a level **h**. Prv 15:19
The **h** of the upright turns aside from Prv 16:17
upper pool on the **h** to the Washer's Field. Is 7:3

there will be a **h** from Assyria for the Is 11:16
there will be a **h** from Egypt to Assyria, Is 19:23
And a **h** shall be there, and it shall be Is 35:8
upper pool on the **h** to the Washer's Field. Is 36:2
straight in the desert a **h** for our God. Is 40:3
for the people; build up, build up the **h**; Is 62:10
and to walk into side roads, not the **h**, Jer 18:15
consider well the **h**, the road by which Jer 31:21

HIGHWAYS (9)
in the days of Jael, the **h** were abandoned, Jgs 5:6
and kill some of the people in the **h**, Jgs 20:31
them away from the city to the **h**." Jgs 20:32
men of them were cut down in the **h**. Jgs 20:45
in you, in whose heart are the **h** to Zion. Ps 84:5
The **h** lie waste; the traveler ceases. Is 33:8
a road, and my **h** shall be raised up. Is 49:11
desolation and destruction are in their **h**. Is 59:7
'Go out to the **h** and hedges and compel Lk 14:23

HILEN (1)
H with its pasturelands, Debir with 1 Chr 6:58

HILKIAH (34)
out to them Eliakim the son of **H**, 2 Kgs 18:18
Then Eliakim the son of **H**, and 2 Kgs 18:26
Then Eliakim the son of **H**, who was 2 Kgs 18:37
"Go up to **H** the high priest, that he 2 Kgs 22:4
And **H** the high priest said to 2 Kgs 22:8
of the LORD." And **H** gave the book to 2 Kgs 22:8
"**H** the priest has given me a book." 2 Kgs 22:10
the king commanded **H** the priest, 2 Kgs 22:12
So **H** the priest, and Ahikam, and 2 Kgs 22:14
the king commanded **H** the high 2 Kgs 23:4
in the book that **H** the priest found 2 Kgs 23:24
Shallum fathered **H**, Hilkiah fathered 1 Chr 6:13
fathered Hilkiah, **H** fathered Azariah, 1 Chr 6:13
son of Amaziah, son of **H**, 1 Chr 6:45
and Azariah the son of **H**, son of 1 Chr 9:11
H the second, Tebaliah the third, 1 Chr 26:11
They came to **H** the high priest and 2 Chr 34:9
H the priest found the Book of the 2 Chr 34:14
Then **H** answered and said to 2 Chr 34:15
of the LORD." And **H** gave the book to 2 Chr 34:15
"**H** the priest has given me a book." 2 Chr 34:18
And the king commanded **H**, 2 Chr 34:20
So **H** and those whom the king had 2 Chr 34:22
H, Zechariah, and Jehiel, the chief 2 Chr 35:8
son of Seraiah, son of Azariah, son of **H**, Ezr 7:1
H, and Maaseiah on his right hand, Neh 8:4
Seraiah the son of **H**, son of Neh 11:11
Sallu, Amok, **H**, Jedaiah. These were Neh 12:7
of **H**, Hashabiah; of Jedaiah, Neh 12:21
call my servant Eliakim the son of **H**, Is 22:20
came out to him Eliakim the son of **H**, Is 36:3
Then Eliakim the son of **H**, who was Is 36:22
The words of Jeremiah, the son of **H**, one Jer 1:1
of Shaphan and Gemariah the son of **H**, Jer 29:3

HILL (151)
of Sephar to the **h** country of the east. Gn 10:30
he moved to the **h** country on the east Gn 12:8
the Horites in their **h** country of Seir as Gn 14:6
them, and the rest fled to the **h** country. Gn 14:10
face toward the **h** country of Gilead. Gn 31:21
after him into the **h** country of Gilead. Gn 31:23
had pitched his tent in the **h** country, Gn 31:25
tents in the **h** country of Gilead. Gn 31:25
a sacrifice in the **h** country and called Gn 31:54
and spent the night in the **h** country. Gn 31:54
So Esau settled in the **h** country of Seir. Gn 36:8
of the Edomites in the **h** country of Seir. Gn 36:9
on the top of the **h** with the staff of God Ex 17:9
and Hur went up to the top of the **h**. Ex 17:10
Negeb and go up into the **h** country, Nm 13:17
the Amorites dwell in the **h** country. Nm 13:29
up to the heights of the **h** country, Nm 14:40
go up to the heights of the **h** country, Nm 14:44
lived in that **h** country came down Nm 14:45
and go to the **h** country of the Amorites Dt 1:7
in the **h** country and in the lowland and Dt 1:7
the way to the **h** country of the Amorites, Dt 1:19
have come to the **h** country of the Dt 1:20
turned and went up into the **h** country, Dt 1:24
it easy to go up into the **h** country. Dt 1:41
went up into the **h** country. Dt 1:43
who lived in that **h** country came out Dt 1:44
Jabbok and the cities of the **h** country, Dt 2:37
and half the **h** country of Gilead with its Dt 3:12
that good **h** country and Lebanon.' Dt 3:25
the Jordan in the **h** country and in the Jos 9:1
who dwell in the **h** country are gathered Jos 10:6
the **h** country and the Negeb and the Jos 10:40
who were in the northern **h** country, Jos 11:2
and the Jebusites in the **h** country, Jos 11:3
the **h** country and all the Negeb and all Jos 11:16
the Arabah and the **h** country of Israel Jos 11:16
off the Anakim from the **h** country, Jos 11:21
and from all the **h** country of Judah, Jos 11:21
and from all the **h** country of Israel. Jos 11:21
in the **h** country, in the lowland, in the Jos 12:8
inhabitants of the **h** country from Jos 13:6
Zereth-shahar on the **h** of the valley, Jos 13:19
now give me this **h** country of which Jos 14:12
to the shoulder of the **h** north of Ekron, Jos 15:11
And in the **h** country, Shamir, Jattir, Jos 15:48
Jericho into the **h** country to Bethel. Jos 16:1
since the **h** country of Ephraim is too Jos 17:15
"The **h** country is not enough for us. Jos 17:16
but the **h** country shall be yours, for Jos 17:18
up through the **h** country westward, Jos 18:12
Timnath-serah in the **h** country of Jos 19:50
in Galilee in the **h** country of Naphtali, Jos 20:7
Shechem in the **h** country of Ephraim, Jos 20:7
is, Hebron) in the **h** country of Judah. Jos 20:7
is Hebron, in the **h** country of Judah, Jos 21:11
pasturelands in the **h** country of Jos 21:21
And I gave Esau the **h** country of Seir to Jos 24:4
which is in the **h** country of Ephraim, Jos 24:30
him in the **h** country of Ephraim. Jos 24:33
Canaanites who lived in the **h** country, Jgs 1:9
and he took possession of the **h** country, Jgs 1:19
people of Dan back into the **h** country, Jgs 1:34
in the **h** country of Ephraim, Jgs 2:9
trumpet in the **h** country of Ephraim. Jgs 3:27
down with him from the **h** country, Jgs 3:27
and Bethel in the **h** country of Ephraim, Jgs 4:5
was north of them, by the **h** of Moreh, Jgs 7:1
throughout all the **h** country of Jgs 7:24
at Shamir in the **h** country of Ephraim. Jgs 10:1
in the **h** country of the Amalekites. Jgs 12:15
them to the top of the **h** that is in front of Jgs 16:3
was a man of the **h** country of Ephraim, Jgs 17:1
he came to the **h** country of Ephraim to Jgs 17:8
they came to the **h** country of Ephraim, Jgs 18:2
there to the **h** country of Ephraim, Jgs 18:13
parts of the **h** country of Ephraim, Jgs 19:1
was from the **h** country of Ephraim, Jgs 19:16
parts of the **h** country of Ephraim, Jgs 19:18
of the **h** country of 1 Sm 1:1
it to the house of Abinadab on the **h**. 1 Sm 7:1
passed through the **h** country of 1 Sm 9:4
As they went up the **h** to the city, they 1 Sm 9:11
Michmash and the **h** country of 1 Sm 13:2
themselves in the **h** country of 1 Sm 14:22
in the **h** country of the Wilderness of 1 Sm 23:14
at Horesh, on the **h** of Hachilah, 1 Sm 23:19
hiding himself on the **h** of Hachilah, 1 Sm 26:1
Saul encamped on the **h** of Hachilah, 1 Sm 26:3
and stood far off on the top of the **h**, 1 Sm 26:13
down they came to the **h** of Ammah, 2 Sm 2:24
and took their stand on the top of a **h**. 2 Sm 2:25
of Abinadab, which was on the **h**. 2 Sm 6:3
a man of the **h** country of Ephraim, 2 Sm 20:21
Ben-hur, in the **h** country of Ephraim; 1 Kgs 4:8
80,000 stonecutters in the **h** country, 1 Kgs 5:15
Shechem in the **h** country of 1 Kgs 12:25
on every high **h** and under every 1 Kgs 14:23
He bought the **h** of Samaria from 1 Kgs 16:24
and he fortified the **h** and called the 1 Kgs 16:24
name of Shemer, the owner of the **h**. 1 Kgs 16:24
who was sitting on the top of a **h**, 2 Kgs 1:9
to me from the **h** country of Ephraim 2 Kgs 5:22
And when he came to the **h**, he took 2 Kgs 5:24
on every high **h** and under every 2 Kgs 17:10
pasturelands in the **h** country of 1 Chr 6:67
and 80,000 to quarry in the **h** country, 2 Chr 2:2
80,000 to quarry in the **h** country, 2 Chr 2:18
that is in the **h** country of Ephraim 2 Chr 13:4
taken in the **h** country of Ephraim, 2 Chr 15:8
Beersheba to the **h** country of 2 Chr 19:4
places in the **h** country of Judah 2 Chr 21:11
built cities in the **h** country of Judah, 2 Chr 27:4
I have set my King on Zion, my holy **h**." Ps 2:6
and he answered me from his holy **h**. Ps 3:4
tent? Who shall dwell on your holy **h**? Ps 15:1
Who shall ascend the **h** of the LORD? And Ps 24:3
me to your holy **h** and to your dwelling! Ps 43:3
of myrrh and the **h** of frankincense. Sg 4:6
beloved had a vineyard on a very fertile **h**. Is 5:1
the daughter of Zion, the **h** of Jerusalem. Is 10:32
On a bare **h** raise a signal; cry aloud to Is 13:2
top of a mountain, like a signal on a **h**. Is 30:17
mountain and every high **h** there will be Is 30:25
to fight on Mount Zion and on its **h**. Is 31:4
the **h** and the watchtower will become Is 32:14
and every mountain and **h** be made low; Is 40:4
on every high **h** and under every green Jer 2:20
up on every high **h** and under every green Jer 3:6
from every mountain and every **h**, Jer 16:16
the Shephelah, from the **h** country, Jer 17:26
will call in the **h** country of Ephraim: Jer 31:6
habitation of righteousness, O holy **h**!' Jer 31:23
go out farther, straight to the **h** Gareb, Jer 31:39
of Judah, in the cities of the **h** country, Jer 32:44
In the cities of the **h** country, in the Jer 33:13
the rock, who hold the height of the **h**. Jer 49:16
From mountain to **h** they have gone. Jer 50:6
around their altars, on every high **h**, Ezk 6:13
they saw any high **h** or any leafy tree, Ezk 20:28
all the mountains and on every high **h**. Ezk 34:6
the places all around my **h** a blessing, Ezk 34:26
from your city Jerusalem, your holy **h**, Dn 9:16
LORD my God for the holy **h** of my God, Dn 9:20
of the flock, **h** of the daughter of Zion, Mi 4:8
have laid waste his **h** country and left Mal 1:3
A city set on a **h** cannot be hidden. Mt 5:14
and went with haste into the **h** country, Lk 1:39
through all the **h** country of Judea, Lk 1:65
and every mountain and **h** shall be made Lk 3:5
to the brow of the **h** on which their town Lk 4:29

HILLEL (2)
the son of **H** the Pirathonite judged Jgs 12:13
the son of **H** the Pirathonite died Jgs 12:15

HILLS (64)
Escape to the **h**, lest you be swept Gn 19:17
But I cannot escape to the **h**, lest the Gn 19:19
and lived in the **h** with his two Gn 19:30
up to the bounties of the everlasting **h**. Gn 49:26
I see him, from the **h** I behold him; Nm 23:9
springs, flowing out in the valleys and **h**, Dt 8:7
and out of whose **h** you can dig copper. Dt 8:9
to possess is a land of **h** and valleys, Dt 11:11
mountains and on the **h** and under every Dt 12:2
and the abundance of the everlasting **h**, Dt 33:15
And she said to them, "Go into the **h**, or Jos 2:16
and went into the **h** and remained there Jos 2:22
came down from the **h** and passed over Jos 2:23
him, "Their gods are gods of the **h**, 1 Kgs 20:23
LORD is a god of the **h** but he is not a 1 Kgs 20:28
places and on the **h** and under every 2 Kgs 16:4
and vinedressers in the **h** and in the 2 Chr 26:10
and forts and towers on the wooded **h**. 2 Chr 27:4
places and on the **h** and under every 2 Chr 28:4
"Go out to the **h** and bring branches of Neh 8:15
Or were you brought forth before the **h**? Jb 15:7
is mine, the cattle on a thousand **h**. Ps 50:10
I know all the birds of the **h**, and all Ps 50:11
the **h** gird themselves with joy, Ps 65:12
bear prosperity for the people, and the **h**, Ps 72:3
their hands; let the **h** sing for joy together Ps 98:8
in the valleys; they flow between the **h**; Ps 104:10
skipped like rams, the **h** like lambs. Ps 114:4
that you skip like rams? O **h**, Ps 114:6
I lift up my eyes to the **h**. From where Ps 121:1
earth; he makes grass grow on the **h**. Ps 147:8
Mountains and all **h**, fruit trees and all Ps 148:9
had been shaped, before the **h**, Prv 8:25
over the mountains, bounding over the **h**. Sg 2:8
and shall be lifted up above the **h**; Is 2:2
mountains, and against all the uplifted **h**; Is 2:14
And as for all the **h** that used to be hoed Is 7:25
in scales and the **h** in a balance? Is 40:12
and you shall make the **h** like chaff; Is 41:15
I will lay waste mountains and **h**, and Is 42:15
may depart and the **h** be removed, Is 54:10
mountains and the **h** before you shall Is 55:12
the mountains and insulted me on the **h**, Is 65:7
Truly the **h** are a delusion, the orgies on Jer 3:23
quaking, and all the **h** moved to and fro. Jer 4:24
lewd whorings, on the **h** in the field. Jer 13:27
every green tree and on the high **h**, Jer 17:2
be satisfied on the **h** of Ephraim and in Jer 50:19
Lord GOD to the mountains and the **h**, Ezk 6:3
On your **h** and in your valleys and in Ezk 35:8
Lord GOD to the mountains and the **h**, Ezk 36:4
Israel, and say to the mountains and **h**, Ezk 36:6
and burn offerings on the **h**, Hos 4:13
the mountains, Cover us, and to the **h**, Hos 10:8
wine, and the **h** shall flow with milk, Jl 3:18
wine, and all the **h** shall flow with it. Am 9:13
and it shall be lifted up above the **h**; Mi 4:1
mountains, and let the **h** hear your voice. Mi 6:1
mountains quake before him; the **h** melt; Na 1:5
scattered; the everlasting **h** sank low. Hab 3:6
Quarter, a loud crash from the **h**. Zep 1:10
Go up to the **h** and bring wood and build Hg 1:8
for a drought on the land and the **h**, Hg 1:11
mountains, 'Fall on us,' and to the **h**, Lk 23:30

HILLSIDE (3)
along on the **h** opposite him and 2 Sm 16:13
herd of pigs was feeding there on the **h**, Mk 5:11
herd of pigs was feeding there on the **h**, Lk 8:32

HILLTOPS (1)
places of the wooded heights and the **h**, Is 17:9

HILT (1)
And the **h** also went in after the blade, Jgs 3:22

HIN (22)
with a fourth of a **h** of beaten oil, Ex 29:40
and a fourth of a **h** of wine for a drink Ex 29:40
of the sanctuary, and a **h** of olive oil. Ex 30:24
just weights, a just ephah, and a just **h**: Lv 19:36
with it shall be of wine, a fourth of a **h**. Lv 23:13
flour, mixed with a quarter of a **h** of oil; Nm 15:4
a quarter of a **h** of wine for the drink Nm 15:5
flour mixed with a third of a **h** of oil. Nm 15:6
you shall offer a third of a **h** of wine, Nm 15:7
of fine flour, mixed with half a **h** of oil. Nm 15:9
for the drink offering half a **h** of wine, Nm 15:10
with a quarter of a **h** of beaten oil. Nm 28:5
shall be a quarter of a **h** for each lamb. Nm 28:7
shall be half a **h** of wine for a Nm 28:14
for a bull, a third of a **h** for a ram, Nm 28:14
a ram, and a quarter of a **h** for a lamb. Nm 28:14
drink by measure, the sixth part of a **h**; Ezk 4:11
ram, and a **h** of oil to each ephah. Ezk 45:24
together with a **h** of oil to each ephah. Ezk 46:5
together with a **h** of oil to each ephah. Ezk 46:7
together with a **h** of oil to an ephah. Ezk 46:11
and one third of a **h** of oil to moisten Ezk 46:14

HINDER (6)
you his tomb to **h** you from burying Gn 23:6
'Let nothing **h** you from coming to Nm 22:16
for nothing can **h** the LORD from 1 Sm 14:6
come to me and do not **h** them, Mt 19:14
do not **h** them, for to such belongs the Mk 10:14
come to me, and do not **h** them, Lk 18:16

HINDERED (5)
and you **h** those who were entering." Lk 11:52
have so often been **h** from coming to Rom 15:22
Who **h** you from obeying the truth? Gal 5:7
again and again—but Satan **h** us. 1 Thes 2:18
life, so that your prayers may not be **h**. 1 Pt 3:7

HINDERING (2)
fear of God and **h** meditation before God. Jb 15:4
by **h** us from speaking to the 1 Thes 2:16

HINDRANCE (3)
behind me, Satan! You are a **h** to me. Mt 16:23
with all boldness and without **h**. Acts 28:31
a stumbling block or **h** in the way of Rom 14:13

HINGES (1)
As a door turns on its **h**, so does a Prv 26:14

HINNOM (13)
of the Son of **H** at the southern shoulder Jos 15:8
that lies over against the Valley of **H**, Jos 15:8
overlooks the Valley of the Son of **H**, Jos 18:16
And it then goes down the Valley of **H**, Jos 18:16
is in the Valley of the Son of **H**, 2 Kgs 23:10
of the Son of **H** and burned his sons 2 Chr 28:3
offering in the Valley of the Son of **H**, 2 Chr 33:6
from Beersheba to the valley of **H**. Neh 11:30
which is in the Valley of the Son of **H**, Jer 7:31
Topheth, or the Valley of the Son of **H**, Jer 7:32
Valley of the Son of **H** at the entry of the Jer 19:2
Topheth, or the Valley of the Son of **H**, Jer 19:6
of Baal in the Valley of the Son of **H**, Jer 32:35

HIP (8)
against Jacob, he touched his **h** socket, Gn 32:25
and Jacob's **h** was put out of joint as he Gn 32:25
Penuel, limping because of his **h**. Gn 32:31
of the thigh that is on the **h** socket, Gn 32:32
the socket of Jacob's **h** on the sinew of Gn 32:32
And he struck them **h** and thigh with a Jgs 15:8
your daughters shall be carried on the **h**. Is 60:4
nurse, you shall be carried upon her **h**, Is 66:12

HIPS (4)
shall reach from the **h** to the thighs; Ex 28:42
garments in the middle, at their **h**, 2 Sm 10:4
garments in the middle, at their **h**, 1 Chr 19:4
kings and binds a waistcloth on their **h**. Jb 12:18

HIRAH (2)
certain Adullamite, whose name was **H**. Gn 38:1
he and his friend **H** the Adullamite. Gn 38:12

HIRAM (31)
And **H** king of Tyre sent messengers 2 Sm 5:11
Now **H** king of Tyre sent his servants 1 Kgs 5:1
of his father, for **H** always loved David. 1 Kgs 5:1
And Solomon sent word to **H**, 1 Kgs 5:2
As soon as **H** heard the words of 1 Kgs 5:7
And **H** sent to Solomon, saying, "I have 1 Kgs 5:8
So **H** supplied Solomon with all the 1 Kgs 5:10
while Solomon gave **H** 20,000 cors of 1 Kgs 5:11
Solomon gave this to **H** year by year. 1 Kgs 5:11
was peace between **H** and Solomon, 1 Kgs 5:12
sent and brought **H** from Tyre. 1 Kgs 7:13
H also made the pots, the shovels, and 1 Kgs 7:40
So **H** finished all the work that he did 1 Kgs 7:40
which **H** made for King Solomon, 1 Kgs 7:45
and **H** king of Tyre had supplied 1 Kgs 9:11
Solomon gave to **H** twenty cities in 1 Kgs 9:11
But when **H** came from Tyre to see 1 Kgs 9:12
H had sent to the king 120 talents of 1 Kgs 9:14
And **H** sent with the fleet his servants, 1 Kgs 9:27
Moreover, the fleet of **H**, which 1 Kgs 10:11
of Tarshish at sea with the fleet of **H**. 1 Kgs 10:22
And **H** king of Tyre sent messengers 1 Chr 14:1
Solomon sent word to **H** the king of 2 Chr 2:3
Then **H** the king of Tyre answered in 2 Chr 2:11
H also said, "Blessed be the LORD God 2 Chr 2:12
H also made the pots, the shovels, and 2 Chr 4:11
So **H** finished the work that he did for 2 Chr 4:11
rebuilt the cities that **H** had given to 2 Chr 8:2
And **H** sent to him by the hand of his 2 Chr 8:18
the servants of **H** and the servants of 2 Chr 9:10
to Tarshish with the servants of **H**. 2 Chr 9:21

HIRAM'S (1)
builders and **H** builders and 1 Kgs 5:18

HIRE (4)
of silver to **h** chariots and horsemen 1 Chr 19:6
out silver in the scales, **h** a goldsmith, Is 46:6
Though they **h** allies among the Hos 8:10
in the morning to **h** laborers for his Mt 20:1

HIRED (41)
for I have **h** you with my son's Gn 30:16
No foreigner or **h** servant may eat of it. Ex 12:45
if it was **h**, it came for its hiring fee. Ex 22:15
The wages of a **h** servant shall not Lv 19:13
of the priest or **h** servant shall eat of Lv 22:10
slaves and for your **h** servant and the Lv 25:6
be with you as a **h** servant and as a Lv 25:40
shall be rated as the time of a **h** servant. Lv 25:50
treat him as a servant **h** year by year. Lv 25:53
the cost of a **h** servant he has served Dt 15:18
and because they **h** against you Balaam Dt 23:4
shall not oppress a **h** servant who is Dt 24:14
with which Abimelech **h** worthless and Jgs 9:4
he has **h** me, and I have become his Jgs 18:4
were full have **h** themselves out for 1 Sm 2:5
Ammonites sent and **h** the Syrians of 2 Sm 10:6
king of Israel has **h** against us the 2 Kgs 7:6
They **h** 32,000 chariots and the king 1 Chr 19:7
and they **h** masons and carpenters 2 Chr 24:12
He **h** also 100,000 mighty men of 2 Chr 25:6
Tobiah and Sanballat had **h** him. Neh 6:12
For this purpose he was **h**, that I Neh 6:13
but **h** Balaam against them to curse Neh 13:2
are not his days like the days of a **h** hand? Jb 7:1
and like a **h** hand who looks for his wages, Jb 7:2
alone, that he may enjoy, like a **h** hand, Jb 14:6
with a razor that is **h** beyond the River— Is 7:20
three years, like the years of a **h** worker, Is 16:14
according to the years of a **h** worker, Is 21:16
Even her **h** soldiers in her midst are Jer 46:21
wandering alone; Ephraim has **h** lovers. Hos 8:9
those who oppress the **h** worker in his Mal 3:5
said to him, 'Because no one has **h** us.' Mt 20:7
And when those **h** about the eleventh Mt 20:9
Now when those **h** first came, they Mt 20:10
boat with the **h** servants and followed Mk 1:20
So he went and **h** himself out to one of Lk 15:15
of my father's **h** servants have more Lk 15:17
Treat me as one of your **h** servants."' Lk 15:19
He who is a **h** hand and not a shepherd, Jn 10:12
because he is a **h** hand and cares Jn 10:13

HIRES (1)
everyone is one who **h** a passing fool Prv 26:10

HIRING (1)
if it was hired, it came for its **h** fee. Ex 22:15

HISS (7)
by it will be astonished and will **h**, 1 Kgs 9:8
be horrified and will **h** because of all its Jer 19:8
be horrified and will **h** because of all its Jer 49:17
and **h** because of all her wounds. Jer 50:13
they **h** and wag their heads at the Lam 2:15
your enemies rail against you; they **h**, Lam 2:16
among the peoples **h** at you; Ezk 27:36

HISSED (2)
land a horror, a thing to be **h** at forever. Jer 18:16
this city a horror, a thing to be **h** at. Jer 19:8

HISSES (2)
its hands at him and **h** at him from its Jb 27:23
who passes by her **h** and shakes his fist. Zep 2:15

HISSING (6)
of horror, of astonishment, and of **h**, 2 Chr 29:8
and make them a horror, a **h**, Jer 25:9
desolation and a waste, a **h** and a curse, Jer 25:18
of the earth, to be a curse, a terror, a **h**, Jer 29:18
the haunt of jackals, a horror and a **h**, Jer 51:37
a desolation, and your inhabitants a **h**; Mi 6:16

HISTORY (1)
not written in the **h** of Nathan the 2 Chr 9:29

HIT (3)
strive together and **h** a pregnant Ex 21:22
the one who **h** her shall surely be fined, Ex 21:22
and to fight and to **h** with a wicked fist. Is 58:4

HITTITE (25)
and Ephron the **H** answered Abraham Gn 23:10
field of Ephron the son of Zohar the **H**, Gn 25:9
daughter of Beeri the **H** to be his wife, Gn 26:34
Basemath the daughter of Elon the **H**, Gn 26:34
loathe my life because of the **H** women. Gn 27:46
marries one of the **H** women like these, Gn 27:46
Adah the daughter of Elon the **H**, Gn 36:2
that is in the field of Ephron the **H**, Gn 49:29
field from Ephron the **H** to possess as a Gn 49:30
field from Ephron the **H** to possess as a Gn 50:13
Then David said to Ahimelech the **H**, 1 Sm 26:6
of Eliam, the wife of Uriah the **H**?" 2 Sm 11:3
"Send me Uriah the **H**." And Joab sent 2 Sm 11:6
the people fell. Uriah the **H** also died. 2 Sm 11:17
servant Uriah the **H** is dead also.'" 2 Sm 11:21
servant Uriah the **H** is dead also." 2 Sm 11:24
down Uriah the **H** with the sword 2 Sm 12:9
wife of Uriah the **H** to be your wife.' 2 Sm 12:10
Uriah the **H**: thirty-seven in all. 2 Sm 23:39
Edomite, Sidonian, and **H** women, 1 Kgs 11:1
except in the matter of Uriah the **H**. 1 Kgs 15:5
Uriah the **H**, Zabad the son of 1 Chr 11:41
the land of the Canaanite, the **H**, Neh 9:8
was an Amorite and your mother a **H**. Ezk 16:3
Your mother was a **H** and your father Ezk 16:45

HITTITES (36)
the **H**, the Perizzites, the Rephaim, Gn 15:20
from before his dead and said to the **H**, Gn 23:3
The **H** answered Abraham, Gn 23:5
Abraham rose and bowed to the **H**, the Gn 23:7
Now Ephron was sitting among the **H**, Gn 23:10
Abraham in the hearing of the **H**, Gn 23:10
he had named in the hearing of the **H**, Gn 23:16
as a possession in the presence of the **H**, Gn 23:18
property for a burying place by the **H**. Gn 23:20
that Abraham purchased from the **H**. Gn 25:10
that is in it were bought from the **H**." Gn 49:32
to the place of the Canaanites, the **H**, Ex 3:8
to the land of the Canaanites, the **H**, Ex 3:17
into the land of the Canaanites, the **H**, Ex 13:5
Amorites and the **H** and the Perizzites Ex 23:23
Canaanites, and the **H** from before you. Ex 23:28
out the Canaanites, the Amorites, the **H**, Ex 33:2
the Amorites, the Canaanites, the **H**, Ex 34:11
dwell in the land of the Negeb. The **H**, Nm 13:29
away many nations before you, the **H**, Dt 7:1
destruction, the **H** and the Amorites, Dt 20:17
all the land of the **H** to the Great Sea Jos 1:4
from before you the Canaanites, the **H**, Jos 3:10
of the Great Sea toward Lebanon, the **H**, Jos 9:1
east and the west, the Amorites, the **H**, Jos 11:3
and in the Negeb, the land of the **H**, Jos 12:8
the Perizzites, the Canaanites, the **H**, Jos 24:11
to the land of the **H** and built a city and Jgs 1:26
Israel lived among the Canaanites, the **H**, Jgs 3:5
and to Kadesh in the land of the **H**; 2 Sm 24:6
who were left of the Amorites, the **H**, 1 Kgs 9:20
the kings of the **H** and the kings of 1 Kgs 10:29
us the kings of the **H** and the kings of 2 Kgs 7:6
all the kings of the **H** and the kings of 2 Chr 1:17
All the people who were left of the **H**, 2 Chr 8:7
from the Canaanites, the **H**, Ezr 9:1

HIVITE (2)
when Shechem the son of Hamor the **H**, Gn 34:2
of Anah the daughter of Zibeon the **H**, Gn 36:2

HIVITES (23)
the **H**, the Arkites, the Sinites, Gn 10:17
Hittites, the Amorites, the Perizzites, the **H**, Ex 3:8
the Amorites, the Perizzites, the **H**, Ex 3:17
the Hittites, the Amorites, the **H**, Ex 13:5
the Canaanites, the **H** and the Jebusites, Ex 23:23
before you, which shall drive out the **H**, Ex 23:28
the Hittites, the Perizzites, the **H**, Ex 33:2
the Hittites, the Perizzites, the **H**, Ex 34:11
the Canaanites, the Perizzites, the **H**, Dt 7:1
the Perizzites, the **H** and the Jebusites, Dt 20:17
you the Canaanites, the Hittites, the **H**, Jos 3:10
the Canaanites, the Perizzites, the **H**, Jos 9:1
But the men of Israel said to the **H**, Jos 9:7
and the **H** under Hermon in the land of Jos 11:3
with the people of Israel except the **H**, Jos 11:19
the Canaanites, the Perizzites, the **H**, Jos 12:8

the Hittites, the Girgashites, the **H**, Jos 24:11
the Sidonians and the **H** who lived on Jgs 3:3
the Amorites, the Perizzites, the **H**, Jgs 3:5
all the cities of the **H** and Canaanites; 2 Sm 24:7
the Hittites, the Perizzites, the **H**, 1 Kgs 9:20
the **H**, the Arkites, the Sinites, 1 Chr 1:15
the Amorites, the Perizzites, the **H**, 2 Chr 8:7

HIZKI (1)
Zebadiah, Meshullam, **H**, Heber, 1 Chr 8:17

HIZKIAH (1)
Elioenai, **H**, and Azrikam, three. 1 Chr 3:23

HOARDED (1)
It will not be stored or **h**, but her Is 23:18

HOARDS (1)
of darkness and the **h** in secret places, Is 45:3

HOARFROST (1)
like wool; he scatters **h** like ashes. Ps 147:16

HOBAB (2)
And Moses said to **H** the son of Reuel Nm 10:29
the descendants of **H** the father-in-law of Jgs 4:11

HOBAH (1)
defeated them and pursued them to **H**, Gn 14:15

HOBAIAH (1)
the sons of **H**, the sons of Hakkoz, the Neh 7:63

HOD (1)
Bezer, **H**, Shamma, Shilshah, Ithran, 1 Chr 7:37

HODAVIAH (4)
H, Eliashib, Pelaiah, Akkub, 1 Chr 3:24
Eliel, Azriel, Jeremiah, **H**, and Jahdiel, 1 Chr 5:24
Sallu the son of Meshullam, son of **H**, 1 Chr 9:7
of Jeshua and Kadmiel, of the sons of **H**, Ezr 2:40

HODESH (1)
He fathered sons by **H** his wife: Jobab, 1 Chr 8:9

HODEVAH (1)
namely of Kadmiel of the sons of **H**, Neh 7:43

HODIAH (6)
The sons of the wife of **H**, the sister of 1 Chr 4:19
Akkub, Shabbethai, **H**, Maaseiah, Neh 8:7
Hashabneiah, Sherebiah, **H**, Shebaniah, Neh 9:5
their brothers, Shebaniah, **H**, Kelita, Neh 10:10
H, Bani, Beninu. Neh 10:13
H, Hashum, Bezai, Neh 10:18

HOE (1)
all the hills that used to be hoed with a **h**, Is 7:25

HOED (2)
it shall not be pruned or **h**, and briers and Is 5:6
all the hills that used to be **h** with a hoe, Is 7:25

HOGLAH (4)
were Mahlah, Noah, **H**, Milcah, Nm 26:33
Mahlah, Noah, **H**, Milcah, and Tirzah. Nm 27:1
for Mahlah, Tirzah, **H**, Milcah, and Nm 36:11
Mahlah, Noah, **H**, Milcah, and Tirzah. Jos 17:3

HOHAM (1)
of Jerusalem sent to **H** king of Hebron, Jos 10:3

HOISTING (2)
After **h** it up, they used supports to Acts 27:17
Then **h** the foresail to the wind they Acts 27:40

HOLD (151)
and his mother and **h** fast to his wife, Gn 2:24
boy, and **h** him fast with your hand, Gn 21:18
that they may **h** a feast to me in the Ex 5:1
of Israel whom the Egyptians **h** as slaves, Ex 6:5
you refuse to let them go and still **h** them, Ex 9:2
herds, for we must **h** a feast to the LORD." Ex 10:9
first day you shall **h** a holy assembly, Ex 12:16
the LORD will not **h** him guiltless who Ex 20:7
I have set apart for you to **h** unclean. Lv 20:25
day. You shall **h** a holy convocation. Lv 23:21
day you shall **h** a holy convocation Lv 23:36
people of Israel shall **h** on to the Nm 36:7
the people of Israel shall **h** on to its own Nm 36:9
the LORD will not **h** him guiltless who Dt 5:11
So I took **h** of the two tablets and threw Dt 9:17
You shall serve him and **h** fast to him, Dt 10:20
you shall serve him and **h** fast to him. Dt 13:4
inheritance that you will **h** in the land Dt 19:14
his mother shall take **h** of him and Dt 21:19
and my hand takes **h** on judgment, Dt 32:41
honored, and go **h** sway over the trees?' Jgs 9:9
good fruit and go **h** sway over the trees?' Jgs 9:11
and men and go **h** sway over the trees?' Jgs 9:13
he arose and took **h** of the doors of Jgs 16:3
and taking **h** of his concubine he Jgs 19:29
So I took **h** of my concubine and cut her Jgs 20:6
you are wearing and **h** it out." So she Ru 3:15
Then David took **h** of his clothes and 2 Sm 1:11
hand to the ark of God and took **h** of it, 2 Sm 6:6
eat, he took **h** of her and said to her, 2 Sm 13:11
you? Now **h** your peace, my sister. 2 Sm 13:20
his hand and take **h** of him and kiss 2 Sm 15:5
"Let not my lord **h** me guilty or 2 Sm 19:19
and went and took **h** of the horns of 1 Kgs 1:50
he has laid **h** of the horns of the altar, 1 Kgs 1:51
Now therefore do not **h** him guiltless, 1 Kgs 2:9
the LORD and caught **h** of the horns of 1 Kgs 2:28
of Egypt and laid **h** on other gods and 1 Kgs 9:9
Then Ahijah laid **h** of the new 1 Kgs 11:30
Then he took **h** of his own clothes 2 Kgs 2:12
man of God, she caught **h** of his feet. 2 Kgs 4:27
shut the door and **h** the door fast 2 Kgs 6:32
him to confirm his **h** on the royal 2 Kgs 15:19
put out his hand to take **h** of the ark, 1 Chr 13:9
made could not **h** the burnt offering 2 Chr 7:7
of Egypt and laid **h** on other gods and 2 Chr 7:22
Stand firm, **h** your position, and see 2 Chr 20:17
give us a secure **h** within his holy place, Ezr 9:8
in Susa, and **h** a fast on my behalf, Est 4:16
h the fourteenth day of the month of Est 9:19
sons used to go and **h** a feast in the house Jb 1:4
to him, "Do you still **h** fast your integrity? Jb 2:9
but it does not stand; he lays **h** of it, Jb 8:15
for I know you will not **h** me innocent. Jb 9:28
him by the heel; a snare lays **h** of him. Jb 18:9
I **h** fast my righteousness and will not let Jb 27:6
days of affliction have taken **h** of me. Jb 30:16
that it might take **h** of the skirts of the Jb 38:13
portion and my cup; you **h** my lot. Ps 16:5
Take **h** of shield and buckler and rise for Ps 35:2
to my cry; **h** not your peace at my tears! Ps 39:12
Trembling took **h** of them there, Ps 48:6
them; you **h** all the nations in derision. Ps 59:8
They **h** fast to their evil purpose; they Ps 64:5
with you; you **h** my right hand. Ps 73:23
Why do you **h** back your hand, your Ps 74:11
You **h** my eyelids open; I am so troubled Ps 77:4
do not **h** your peace or be still, O God! Ps 83:1
For your servants **h** her stones dear Ps 102:14
me; the pangs of Sheol laid **h** on me; Ps 116:3
I **h** back my feet from every evil way, Ps 119:101
I **h** my life in my hand continually, Ps 119:109
H me up, that I may be safe and have Ps 119:117
me, and your right hand shall **h** me. Ps 139:10
h back your foot from their paths, Prv 1:15
is a tree of life to those who lay **h** of her; Prv 3:18
those who **h** her fast are called blessed. Prv 3:18
to me, "Let your heart **h** fast my words; Prv 4:4
Keep **h** of instruction; do not let go; Prv 4:13
and **h** it in pledge when he puts up Prv 20:16
righteous gives and does not **h** back. Prv 21:26
h back those who are stumbling to Prv 24:11
and **h** it in pledge when he puts up Prv 27:13
distaff, and her hands **h** the spindle. Prv 31:19
wisdom—and how to lay **h** on folly, Eccl 2:3
is good that you should take **h** of this, Eccl 7:18
climb the palm tree and lay **h** of its fruit. Sg 7:8
For a man will take **h** of his brother in the Is 3:6
seven women shall take **h** of one man in Is 4:1
strong man. He will seize firm **h** on you Is 22:17
Or let them lay **h** of my protection, let Is 27:5
shakes his hands, lest they **h** a bribe, Is 33:15
they cannot **h** the mast firm in its place Is 33:23
I, the LORD your God, **h** your right hand; Is 41:13
be stretched out; do not **h** back; Is 54:2
that please me and **h** fast my covenant, Is 56:4
"Cry aloud; do not **h** back; lift up your Is 58:1
who rouses himself to take **h** of you; Is 64:7
broken cisterns that can **h** no water. Jer 2:13
They lay **h** on bow and javelin; they are Jer 6:23
anguish has taken **h** of us, pain as of a Jer 6:24
They **h** fast to deceit; they refuse to return. Jer 8:5
I mourn, and dismay has taken **h** on me. Jer 8:21
Will not pangs take **h** of you like those Jer 13:21
to speak to them; do not **h** back a word. Jer 26:2
prophets and all the people laid **h** of him, Jer 26:8
of the rock, who **h** the height of the hill. Jer 49:16
and sorrows have taken **h** of her, Jer 49:24
They lay **h** of bow and spear; they are Jer 50:42
that I may lay **h** of the hearts of the Ezk 14:5
marriage, but they will not **h** together, Dn 2:43
God, return, **h** fast to love and justice, Hos 12:6
the mortar; take **h** of the brick mold! Na 3:14
every tongue shall take **h** of the robe of Zec 8:23
will not take **h** of it and lift it out? Mt 12:11
out his hand and took **h** of him, Mt 14:31
and his mother and **h** fast to his wife, Mt 19:5
for they all **h** that John was a prophet." Mt 21:26
they came up and took **h** of his feet and Mt 28:9
of God and **h** to the tradition Mk 7:8
father and mother and **h** fast to his wife, Mk 10:7
h it fast in an honest and good heart, Lk 8:15
do not **h** this sin against them." And Acts 7:60
And they took **h** of him and brought Acts 17:19
For we **h** that one is justified by faith Rom 3:28
what is evil; **h** fast to what is good. Rom 12:9
if you **h** fast to the word I preached to 1 Cor 15:2
father and mother and **h** fast to his Eph 5:31
you all, because I **h** you in my heart, Phil 1:7
Only let us **h** true to what we have Phil 3:16
and in him all things **h** together. Col 1:17
test everything; **h** fast what is good. 1 Thes 5:21
stand firm and **h** to the traditions 2 Thes 2:15
They must **h** the mystery of the faith 1 Tm 3:9
Take **h** of the eternal life to which 1 Tm 6:12
that they may take **h** of that which is 1 Tm 6:19
He must **h** firm to the trustworthy word as Ti 1:9
house if indeed we **h** fast our confidence Heb 3:6
if indeed we **h** our original confidence Heb 3:14
Son of God, let us **h** fast our confession. Heb 4:14
strong encouragement to **h** fast to the Heb 6:18
Let us **h** fast the confession of our Heb 10:23
no partiality as you **h** the faith in our Jas 2:1
Yet you **h** fast my name, and you did not Rv 2:13
have some there who **h** the teaching of Rv 2:14
you have some who **h** the teaching of the Rv 2:15
in Thyatira, who do not **h** this teaching, Rv 2:24
Only **h** fast what you have until I come. Rv 2:25
H fast what you have, so that no one Rv 3:11
of God and **h** to the testimony Rv 12:17
your brothers who **h** to the testimony Rv 19:10

HOLDERS (7)
lie, as **h** for the poles to carry the table. Ex 25:27
their rings of gold for **h** for the bars, Ex 26:29
and they shall be **h** for poles with which Ex 30:4
their rings of gold for **h** for the bars, Ex 36:34
as **h** for the poles to carry the table. Ex 37:14
as **h** for the poles with which to carry it. Ex 37:27
of the bronze grating as **h** for the poles. Ex 38:5

HOLDING (20)
came out with his hand **h** Esau's heel, Gn 25:26
spring or a cistern **h** water shall be Lv 11:36
in all his ways, and **h** fast to him, Dt 11:22
obeying his voice and **h** fast to him, Dt 30:20
behold, he was **h** a feast in his house, 1 Sm 25:36
wrath of the LORD; I am weary of **h** it in. Jer 6:11
my bones, and I am weary with **h** it in, Jer 20:9
hands, **h** to the tradition of the elders, Mk 7:3
the men who were **h** Jesus in custody Lk 22:63
that you are **h** with each other Lk 24:17
each **h** twenty or thirty gallons. Jn 2:6
h fast to the word of life, so that in the Phil 2:16
and not **h** fast to the Head, from whom Col 2:19
h faith and a good conscience. By 1 Tm 1:19
their own harm and **h** him up to Heb 6:6
which was a golden urn **h** the manna, Heb 9:4
fell down before the Lamb, each **h** a harp, Rv 5:8
earth, **h** back the four winds of the earth, Rv 7:1
h in her hand a golden cup full of Rv 17:4
h in his hand the key to the bottomless Rv 20:1

HOLDINGS (1)
lands and their **h** and came to 2 Chr 11:14

HOLDS (20)
for our clan **h** a sacrifice in the city, 1 Sm 20:29
is leprous or who **h** a spindle or who 2 Sm 3:29
to whom the king **h** out the golden Est 4:11
He still **h** fast his integrity, although you Jb 2:3
Yet the righteous **h** to his way, and he Jb 17:9
is loath to let it go and **h** it in his mouth, Jb 20:13
laughs; the Lord **h** them in derision. Ps 2:4
in the midst of the gods he **h** judgment: Ps 82:1
"Because he **h** fast to me in love, I will Ps 91:14
people curse him who **h** back grain, Prv 11:26
but a wise man quietly **h** it back. Prv 29:11
this, and the son of man who **h** it fast, Is 56:2
not profane it, and **h** fast my covenant— Is 56:6
Lord GOD of hosts **h** a sacrifice in the Jer 46:10
and him who **h** the scepter from Am 1:5
and him who **h** the scepter from Am 1:8
For here the saying **h** true, 'One sows and Jn 4:37
as it **h** promise for the present life and 1 Tm 4:8
but he **h** his priesthood permanently, Heb 7:24
words of him who **h** the seven stars in Rv 2:1

HOLE (5)
you shall dig a **h** with it and turn back Dt 23:13
a chest and bored a **h** in the lid of it 2 Kgs 12:9
and falls into the **h** that he has made. Ps 7:15
child shall play over the **h** of the cobra, Is 11:8
looked, behold, there was a **h** in the wall. Ezk 8:7

HOLES (8)
in caves and in **h** and in rocks and 1 Sm 13:6
coming out of the **h** where they have 1 Sm 14:11
dwell, in **h** of the earth and of the rocks. Jb 30:6
of the rocks and the **h** of the ground, Is 2:19
of them trapped in **h** and hidden in Is 42:22
does so to put them into a bag with **h**. Hg 1:6

And Jesus said to him, "Foxes have **h**, Mt 8:20
And Jesus said to him, "Foxes have **h**, Lk 9:58

HOLIDAY (3)
and joy among the Jews, a feast and a **h**. Est 8:17
a day for gladness and feasting, as a **h**, Est 9:19
gladness and from mourning into a **h**; Est 9:22

HOLINESS (33)
Who is like you, majestic in **h**, Ex 15:11
the LORD in the splendor of **h**; 1 Chr 16:29
worship the LORD in the splendor of **h**. Ps 29:2
God has spoken in his **h**: "With Ps 60:6
of your house, the **h** of your temple! Ps 65:4
Once for all I have sworn by my **h**; I Ps 89:35
h befits your house, O LORD, forevermore. Ps 93:5
Worship the LORD in the splendor of **h**; Ps 96:9
God has promised in his **h**: "With Ps 108:7
there, and it shall be called the Way of **H**; Is 35:8
I will manifest my **h** among you in Ezk 20:41
in her and manifest my **h** in her; Ezk 28:22
and manifest my **h** in them in the Ezk 28:25
I will vindicate the **h** of my great Ezk 36:23
you I vindicate my **h** before their eyes. Ezk 36:23
I vindicate my **h** before their eyes. Ezk 38:16
greatness and my **h** and make myself Ezk 38:23
have vindicated my **h** in the sight Ezk 39:27
lest they communicate **h** to the people Ezk 44:19
and so communicate **h** to the people." Ezk 46:20
The Lord GOD has sworn by his **h** that, Am 4:2
in **h** and righteousness before him all Lk 1:75
to the Spirit of **h** by his resurrection Rom 1:4
bringing **h** to completion in the fear of 2 Cor 7:1
of God in true righteousness and **h**. Eph 4:24
hearts blameless in **h** before our 1 Thes 3:13
control his own body in **h** and honor, 1 Thes 4:4
not called us for impurity, but in **h**. 1 Thes 4:7
they continue in faith and love and **h**, 1 Tm 2:15
for worship and an earthly place of **h**. Heb 9:1
for our good, that we may share his **h**. Heb 12:10
and for the **h** without which no one Heb 12:14
you to be in lives of **h** and godliness, 2 Pt 3:11

HOLLOW (7)
You shall make it **h**, with boards. As it Ex 27:8
it with them. He made it **h**, with boards. Ex 38:7
God split open the **h** place that is at Jgs 15:19
sling out as from the **h** of a sling. 1 Sm 25:29
It was **h**, and its thickness was four 1 Kgs 7:15
the waters in the **h** of his hand and Is 40:12
was four fingers, and it was **h**. Jer 52:21

HOLON (3)
Goshen, **H**, and Giloh: eleven cities Jos 15:51
H with its pasturelands, Debir with its Jos 21:15
has come upon the tableland, upon **H**, Jer 48:21

HOLY (665)
blessed the seventh day and made it **h**, Gn 2:3
on which you are standing is **h** ground." Ex 3:5
first day you shall hold a **h** assembly, Ex 12:16
and on the seventh day a **h** assembly. Ex 12:16
them by your strength to your **h** abode. Ex 15:13
of solemn rest, a **h** Sabbath to the LORD; Ex 16:23
me a kingdom of priests and a **h** nation. Ex 19:6
the Sabbath day, to keep it **h**. Ex 20:8
blessed the Sabbath day and made it **h**. Ex 20:11
separate for you the **H** Place from the Ex 26:33
for you the Holy Place from the Most **H**. Ex 26:33
of the testimony in the Most **H** Place. Ex 26:34
you shall make **h** garments for Aaron Ex 28:2
They shall make **h** garments for Aaron Ex 28:4
heart, when he goes into the **H** Place, Ex 28:29
he goes into the **H** Place before the Ex 28:35
engraving of a signet, 'H to the LORD.' Ex 28:36
any guilt from the **h** things that the Ex 28:38
of Israel consecrate as their **h** gifts. Ex 28:38
the altar to minister in the **H** Place, Ex 28:43
head and put the **h** crown on the turban. Ex 29:6
He and his garments shall be **h**, and his Ex 29:21
"The **h** garments of Aaron shall be for Ex 29:29
of meeting to minister in the **H** Place, Ex 29:30
and boil its flesh in a **h** place. Ex 29:31
not eat of them, because they are **h**. Ex 29:33
fire. It shall not be eaten, because it is **h**. Ex 29:34
it, and the altar shall be most **h**. Ex 29:37
touches the altar shall become **h**. Ex 29:37
generations. It is most **h** to the LORD." Ex 30:10
perfumer; it shall be a **h** anointing oil. Ex 30:25
them, that they may be most **h**. Ex 30:29
Whatever touches them will become **h**. Ex 30:29
shall be my **h** anointing oil Ex 30:31
It is **h**, and it shall be holy to you. Ex 30:32
It is holy, and it shall be **h** to you. Ex 30:32
seasoned with salt, pure and **h**. Ex 30:35
with you. It shall be most **h** for you. Ex 30:36
It shall be for you **h** to the LORD. Ex 30:37
the **h** garments for Aaron the priest and Ex 31:10
the fragrant incense for the **H** Place. Ex 31:11
the Sabbath, because it is **h** for you. Ex 31:14
a Sabbath of solemn rest, **h** to the LORD. Ex 31:15
a Sabbath of solemn rest, **h** to the LORD. Ex 35:2
for ministering in the **H** Place, Ex 35:19
the **h** garments for Aaron the priest, Ex 35:19
all its service, and for the **h** garments. Ex 35:21
He made the **h** anointing oil also, and Ex 37:29
for ministering in the **H** Place. Ex 39:1
They made the **h** garments for Aaron, Ex 39:1
the plate of the **h** crown of pure gold, Ex 39:30
engraving of a signet, "H to the LORD." Ex 39:30
for ministering in the **H** Place, Ex 39:41
the **h** garments for Aaron the priest, Ex 39:41
its furniture, so that it may become **h**. Ex 40:9
so that the altar may become most **h**. Ex 40:10
and put on Aaron the **h** garments. And Ex 40:13
it is a most **h** part of the LORD'S food Lv 2:3
it is a most **h** part of the LORD'S food Lv 2:10
in any of the **h** things of the LORD, Lv 5:15
done amiss in the **h** thing and shall add Lv 5:16
It shall be eaten unleavened in a **h** place. Lv 6:16
It is a thing most **h**, like the sin offering Lv 6:17
touches them shall become **h**." Lv 6:18
be killed before the LORD; it is most **h**. Lv 6:25
In a **h** place it shall be eaten, in the court Lv 6:26
Whatever touches its flesh shall be **h**, Lv 6:27
on which it was splashed in a **h** place. Lv 6:27
the priests may eat of it; it is most **h**. Lv 6:29
to make atonement in the **H** Place; Lv 6:30
is the law of the guilt offering. It is most **h**. Lv 7:1
may eat of it. It shall be eaten in a **h** place. Lv 7:6
shall be eaten in a holy place. It is most **h**. Lv 7:6
front, he set the golden plate, the **h** crown, Lv 8:9
distinguish between the **h** and the Lv 10:10
beside the altar, for it is most **h**. Lv 10:12
You shall eat it in a **h** place, because it Lv 10:13
it is a thing most **h** and has been given Lv 10:17
yourselves therefore, and be **h**, Lv 11:44
therefore, and be holy, for I am **h**. Lv 11:44
You shall therefore be **h**, for I am holy." Lv 11:45
You shall therefore be holy, for I am **h**." Lv 11:45
She shall not touch anything **h**, nor Lv 12:4
belongs to the priest; it is most **h**. Lv 14:13
any time into the **H** Place inside the veil, Lv 16:2
way Aaron shall come into the **H** Place: Lv 16:3
shall put on the **h** linen coat and shall Lv 16:4
linen turban; these are the **h** garments. Lv 16:4
shall make atonement for the **H** Place, Lv 16:16
atonement in the **H** Place until he Lv 16:17
of atoning for the **H** Place and the tent Lv 16:20
he went into the **H** Place and shall leave Lv 16:23
body in water in a **h** place and put on Lv 16:24
in to make atonement in the **H** Place, Lv 16:27
wearing the **h** linen garments. Lv 16:32
make atonement for the **h** sanctuary, Lv 16:33
of Israel and say to them, You shall be **h**, Lv 19:2
be holy, for I the LORD your God am **h**. Lv 19:2
he has profaned what is **h** to the LORD, Lv 19:8
in the fourth year all its fruit shall be **h**, Lv 19:24
unclean and to profane my **h** name. Lv 20:3
yourselves, therefore, and be **h**, Lv 20:7
You shall be **h** to me, for I the LORD am Lv 20:26
I the LORD am **h** and have separated you Lv 20:26
They shall be **h** to their God and not Lv 21:6
of their God; therefore they shall be **h**. Lv 21:6
husband, for the priest is **h** to his God. Lv 21:7
He shall be **h** to you, for I, the LORD, who Lv 21:8
for I, the LORD, who sanctify you, am **h**. Lv 21:8
both of the most **h** and of the holy Lv 21:22
of the most holy and of the **h** things, Lv 21:22
they abstain from the **h** things of the Lv 22:2
so that they do not profane my **h** name: Lv 22:2
approaches the **h** things that Lv 22:3
may eat of the **h** things until he is Lv 22:4
not eat of the **h** things unless he has Lv 22:6
and afterward he may eat of the **h** things, Lv 22:7
"A lay person shall not eat of a **h** thing; Lv 22:10
or hired servant shall eat of a **h** thing, Lv 22:10
eat of the contribution of the **h** things. Lv 22:12
eats of a **h** thing unintentionally, Lv 22:14
to it and give the **h** thing to the priest. Lv 22:14
shall not profane the **h** things of the Lv 22:15
and guilt, by eating their **h** things: Lv 22:16
And you shall not profane my **h** name, Lv 22:32
you shall proclaim as **h** convocations; Lv 23:2
of solemn rest, a **h** convocation. Lv 23:3
feasts of the LORD, the **h** convocations, Lv 23:4
first day you shall have a **h** convocation; Lv 23:7
On the seventh day is a **h** convocation; Lv 23:8
They shall be **h** to the LORD for the Lv 23:20
day. You shall hold a **h** convocation. Lv 23:21
blast of trumpets, a **h** convocation. Lv 23:24
be for you a time of **h** convocation, Lv 23:27
the first day shall be a **h** convocation; Lv 23:35
shall hold a **h** convocation and present Lv 23:36
proclaim as times of **h** convocation, Lv 23:37
sons, and they shall eat it in a **h** place, Lv 24:9
is for him a most **h** portion out of the Lv 24:9
For it is a jubilee. It shall be **h** to you. Lv 25:12
all of it that he gives to the LORD is **h**. Lv 27:9
both it and the substitute shall be **h**. Lv 27:10
his house as a **h** gift to the LORD, Lv 27:14
the jubilee, shall be a **h** gift to the LORD, Lv 27:21
on that day as a **h** gift to the LORD. Lv 27:23
devoted thing is most **h** to the LORD. Lv 27:28
the trees, is the LORD'S; it is **h** to the LORD. Lv 27:30
herdsman's staff, shall be **h** to the LORD. Lv 27:32
both it and the substitute shall be **h**; Lv 27:33
in the tent of meeting: the most **h** things. Nm 4:4
but they must not touch the **h** things, Nm 4:15
they come near to the most **h** things: Nm 4:19
in to look on the **h** things even for a Nm 4:20
all the **h** donations of the people of Israel, Nm 5:9
Each one shall keep his **h** donations: Nm 5:10
the priest shall take **h** water in an Nm 5:17
himself to the LORD, he shall be **h**. Nm 6:5
days of his separation he is **h** to the LORD. Nm 6:8
They are a **h** portion for the priest, Nm 6:20
the service of the **h** things that had to Nm 7:9
set out, carrying the **h** things, Nm 10:21
and be **h** to your God. Nm 15:40
For all in the congregation are **h**, every Nm 16:3
will show who is his, and who is **h**, Nm 16:5
the LORD chooses shall be the **h** one. Nm 16:7
far and wide, for they have become **h**. Nm 16:37
before the LORD, and they became **h**. Nm 16:38
shall be yours of the most **h** things, Nm 18:9
shall be most **h** to you and to your Nm 18:9
In a most **h** place shall you eat it. Nm 18:10
it. Every male may eat it; it is **h** to you. Nm 18:10
goat, you shall not redeem; they are **h**. Nm 18:17
All the **h** contributions that the Nm 18:19
shall not profane the **h** things of the Nm 18:32
to uphold me as **h** in the eyes of the Nm 20:12
through them he showed himself **h**. Nm 20:13
to uphold me as **h** at the waters before Nm 27:14
In the **H** Place you shall pour out a Nm 28:7
day there shall be a **h** convocation. Nm 28:18
day you shall have a **h** convocation. Nm 28:25
you shall have a **h** convocation. Nm 28:26
you shall have a **h** convocation. Nm 29:1
shall have a **h** convocation and afflict Nm 29:7
you shall have a **h** convocation. Nm 29:12
who was anointed with the **h** oil. Nm 35:25
"'Observe the Sabbath day, to keep it **h**, Dt 5:12
"For you are a people **h** to the LORD your Dt 7:6
But the **h** things that are due from you, Dt 12:26
For you are a people **h** to the LORD your Dt 14:2
For you are a people **h** to the LORD your Dt 14:21
you, therefore your camp must be **h**, Dt 23:14
Look down from your **h** habitation, Dt 26:15
you shall be a people **h** to the LORD your Dt 26:19
establish you as a people **h** to himself, Dt 28:9
did not treat me as **h** in the midst of the Dt 32:51
came from the ten thousands of **h** ones, Dt 33:2
people, all his **h** ones were in his hand; Dt 33:3
you are standing is **h**." And Joshua did Jos 5:15
of bronze and iron, are **h** to the LORD; Jos 6:19
able to serve the LORD, for he is a **h** God. Jos 24:19
"There is none **h** like the LORD; there is 1 Sm 2:2
to stand before the LORD, this **h** God? 1 Sm 6:20
but there is **h** bread—if the young 1 Sm 21:4
the young men are **h** even when it is 1 Sm 21:5
more today will their vessels be **h**?" 1 Sm 21:5
So the priest gave him the **h** bread, for 1 Sm 21:6
inner sanctuary, as the Most **H** Place. 1 Kgs 6:16
part of the house, the Most **H** Place, 1 Kgs 7:50
and all the **h** vessels that were in the 1 Kgs 8:4
of the house, in the Most **H** Place, 1 Kgs 8:6
were seen from the **H** Place before the 1 Kgs 8:8
the priests came out of the **H** Place, 1 Kgs 8:10
know that this is a **h** man of God who 2 Kgs 4:9
the money of the **h** things that is 2 Kgs 12:4
heights? Against the **H** One of Israel! 2 Kgs 19:22
for all the work of the Most **H** Place, 1 Chr 6:49
furniture and over all the **h** utensils, 1 Chr 9:29
Glory in his **h** name; let the hearts 1 Chr 16:10
may give thanks to your **h** name, 1 Chr 16:35
the LORD and the **h** vessels of God 1 Chr 22:19
apart to dedicate the most **h** things, 1 Chr 23:13
the cleansing of all that is **h**, 1 Chr 23:28
that I have provided for the **h** house, 1 Chr 29:3
house for your **h** name comes from 1 Chr 29:16
And he made the Most **H** Place. Its 2 Chr 3:8
In the Most **H** Place he made two 2 Chr 3:10
doors to the Most **H** Place and for the 2 Chr 4:22
and all the **h** vessels that were in the 2 Chr 5:5
of the house, in the Most **H** Place, 2 Chr 5:7
were seen from the **H** Place before the 2 Chr 5:9

came out of the **H** Place (for all the 2 Chr 5:11
the ark of the LORD has come are **h**." 2 Chr 8:11
the LORD and praise him in **h** attire, 2 Chr 20:21
They may enter, for they are **h**, but 2 Chr 23:6
carry out the filth from the **H** Place. 2 Chr 29:5
burnt offerings in the **H** Place to the 2 Chr 29:7
came to his **h** habitation in heaven. 2 Chr 30:27
the LORD and the most **h** offerings. 2 Chr 31:14
faithful in keeping themselves **h**. 2 Chr 31:18
all Israel and who were **h** to the LORD, 2 Chr 35:3
"Put the **h** ark in the house that 2 Chr 35:3
stand in the **H** Place according to 2 Chr 35:5
they boiled the **h** offerings in pots, 2 Chr 35:13
that he had made **h** in Jerusalem. 2 Chr 36:14
were not to partake of the most **h** food, Ezr 2:63
I said to them, "You are **h** to the LORD, Ezr 8:28
holy to the LORD, and the vessels are **h**, Ezr 8:28
so that the **h** race has mixed itself with Ezr 9:2
give us a secure hold within his **h** place, Ezr 9:8
partake of the most **h** food until a Neh 7:65
"This day is **h** to the LORD your God; Neh 8:9
ready, for this day is **h** to our Lord. Neh 8:10
saying, "Be quiet, for this day is **h**; Neh 8:11
to them your **h** Sabbath and Neh 9:14
them on the Sabbath or on a **h** day. Neh 10:31
the appointed feasts, the **h** things, Neh 10:33
of ten to live in Jerusalem the **h** city, Neh 11:1
All the Levites in the **h** city were 284. Neh 11:18
the gates, to keep the Sabbath day **h**. Neh 13:22
To which of the **h** ones will you turn? Jb 5:1
I have not denied the words of the **H** One. Jb 6:10
Behold, God puts no trust in his **h** ones, Jb 15:15
I have set my King on Zion, my **h** hill." Ps 2:6
LORD, and he answered me from his **h** hill. Ps 3:4
bow down toward your **h** temple in the Ps 5:7
The LORD is in his **h** temple; the LORD'S Ps 11:4
tent? Who shall dwell on your **h** hill? Ps 15:1
Sheol, or let your **h** one see corruption. Ps 16:10
answer him from his **h** heaven with the Ps 20:6
Yet you are **h**, enthroned on the praises Ps 22:3
And who shall stand in his **h** place? Ps 24:3
hands toward your most **h** sanctuary. Ps 28:2
saints, and give thanks to his **h** name. Ps 30:4
in him, because we trust in his **h** name. Ps 33:21
them bring me to your **h** hill and to your Ps 43:3
God, the **h** habitation of the Most High. Ps 46:4
the nations; God sits on his **h** throne. Ps 47:8
in the city of our God! His **h** mountain, Ps 48:1
and take not your **H** Spirit from me. Ps 51:11
of widows is God in his **h** habitation. Ps 68:5
to you with the lyre, O **H** One of Israel. Ps 71:22
Your way, O God, is **h**. What god is Ps 77:13
again and provoked the **H** One of Israel. Ps 78:41
And he brought them to his **h** land, to Ps 78:54
they have defiled your **h** temple; Ps 79:1
On the **h** mount stands the city he Ps 87:1
in the assembly of the **h** ones! Ps 89:5
to be feared in the council of the **h** ones, Ps 89:7
LORD, our king to the **H** One of Israel. Ps 89:18
with my **h** oil I have anointed him, Ps 89:20
and give thanks to his **h** name! Ps 97:12
right hand and his **h** arm have worked Ps 98:1
your great and awesome name! **H** is he! Ps 99:3
God; worship at his footstool! **H** is he! Ps 99:5
our God, and worship at his **h** mountain; Ps 99:9
mountain; for the LORD our God is **h**! Ps 99:9
he looked down from his **h** height; Ps 102:19
all that is within me, bless his **h** name! Ps 103:1
Glory in his **h** name; let the hearts of Ps 105:3
For he remembered his **h** promise, Ps 105:42
and Aaron, the **h** one of the LORD, Ps 106:16
give thanks to your **h** name and glory Ps 106:47
the day of your power, in **h** garments; Ps 110:3
forever. **H** and awesome is his name! Ps 111:9
your hands to the **h** place and bless the Ps 134:2
down toward your **h** temple and give Ps 138:2
all flesh bless his **h** name forever and Ps 145:21
the knowledge of the **H** One is insight. Prv 9:10
"It is **h**," and to reflect only after Prv 20:25
nor have I knowledge of the **H** One. Prv 30:3
and out of the **h** place and were praised Eccl 8:10
they have despised the **H** One of Israel, Is 1:4
and remains in Jerusalem will be called **h**, Is 4:3
and the **H** God shows himself holy in Is 5:16
God shows himself **h** in righteousness. Is 5:16
let the counsel of the **H** One of Israel draw Is 5:19
despised the word of the **H** One of Israel. Is 5:24
and said: "**H**, holy, holy is the LORD of hosts; Is 6:3
and said: "Holy, **h**, holy is the LORD of hosts; Is 6:3
and said: "Holy, holy, **h** is the LORD of hosts; Is 6:3
when it is felled." The **h** seed is its stump. Is 6:13
LORD of hosts, him you shall regard as **h**. Is 8:13
become a fire, and his **H** One a flame, Is 10:17
will lean on the LORD, the **H** One of Israel, Is 10:20
not hurt or destroy in all my **h** mountain; Is 11:9
great in your midst is the **H** One of Israel." Is 12:6
his eyes will look on the **H** One of Israel. Is 17:7
and her wages will be **h** to the LORD. Is 23:18
LORD on the **h** mountain at Jerusalem. Is 27:13
shall exult in the **H** One of Israel. Is 29:19
they will sanctify the **H** One of Jacob Is 29:23
hear no more about the **H** One of Israel." Is 30:11
Therefore thus says the **H** One of Israel, Is 30:12
said the Lord GOD, the **H** One of Israel, Is 30:15
as in the night when a **h** feast is kept, Is 30:29
do not look to the **H** One of Israel or Is 31:1
the heights? Against the **H** One of Israel! Is 37:23
I should be like him? says the **H** One. Is 40:25
your Redeemer is the **H** One of Israel. Is 41:14
in the **H** One of Israel you shall glory. Is 41:16
this, the **H** One of Israel has created it. Is 41:20
the LORD your God, the **H** One of Israel, Is 43:3
LORD, your Redeemer, the **H** One of Israel: Is 43:14
I am the LORD, your **H** One, the Creator Is 43:15
Thus says the LORD, the **H** One of Israel, Is 45:11
hosts is his name—is the **H** One of Israel. Is 47:4
For they call themselves after the **h** city, Is 48:2
LORD, your Redeemer, the **H** One of Israel: Is 48:17
the Redeemer of Israel and his **H** One, Is 49:7
LORD, who is faithful, the **H** One of Israel, Is 49:7
garments, O Jerusalem, the **h** city; Is 52:1
LORD has bared his **h** arm before the eyes Is 52:10
and the **H** One of Israel is your Redeemer, Is 54:5
LORD your God, and of the **H** One of Israel, Is 55:5
these I will bring to my **h** mountain, and Is 56:7
land and shall inherit my **h** mountain. Is 57:13
who inhabits eternity, whose name is **H**: Is 57:15
"I dwell in the high and **h** place, and also Is 57:15
from doing your pleasure on my **h** day, Is 58:13
a delight and the **h** day of the LORD Is 58:13
your God, and for the **H** One of Israel, Is 60:9
the LORD, the Zion of the **H** One of Israel. Is 60:14
And they shall be called The **H** People, Is 62:12
they rebelled and grieved his **H** Spirit; Is 63:10
put in the midst of them his **H** Spirit, Is 63:11
from your **h** and beautiful habitation. Is 63:15
Your **h** people held possession for a little Is 63:18
Your **h** cities have become a wilderness; Is 64:10
Our **h** and beautiful house, where our Is 64:11
for I am too **h** for you." These are a smoke Is 65:5
the LORD, who forget my **h** mountain, Is 65:11
destroy in all my **h** mountain," says the Is 65:25
to my **h** mountain Jerusalem, Is 66:20
Israel was **h** to the LORD, the firstfruits of Jer 2:3
any work, but keep the Sabbath day **h**, Jer 17:22
keep the Sabbath day **h** and do no work Jer 17:24
listen to me, to keep the Sabbath day **h**, Jer 17:27
of the LORD and because of his **h** words. Jer 23:9
and from his **h** habitation utter his Jer 25:30
habitation of righteousness, O **h** hill!' Jer 31:23
defied the LORD, the **H** One of Israel. Jer 50:29
is full of guilt against the **H** One of Israel. Jer 51:5
have come into the **h** places of the Jer 51:51
The **h** stones lie scattered at the head of Lam 4:1
and their **h** places shall be profaned. Ezk 7:24
keep my Sabbaths **h** that they may Ezk 20:20
but my **h** name you shall no more Ezk 20:39
"For on my **h** mountain, the Ezk 20:40
have despised my **h** things and Ezk 22:8
law and have profaned my **h** things. Ezk 22:26
distinction between the **h** and the Ezk 22:26
you were on the **h** mountain of God; Ezk 28:14
they came, they profaned my **h** name, Ezk 36:20
But I had concern for my **h** name, Ezk 36:21
to act, but for the sake of my **h** name, Ezk 36:22
"And my **h** name I will make known in Ezk 39:7
will not let my **h** name be profaned Ezk 39:7
that I am the LORD, the **H** One in Israel. Ezk 39:7
and I will be jealous for my **h** name. Ezk 39:25
said to me, "This is the Most **H** Place." Ezk 41:4
in front of the **H** Place was something Ezk 41:21
The nave and the **H** Place had each a Ezk 41:23
opposite the yard are the **h** chambers, Ezk 42:13
the LORD shall eat the most **h** offerings. Ezk 42:13
shall put the most **h** offerings—the Ezk 42:13
the guilt offering, for the place is **h**. Ezk 42:13
When the priests enter the **H** Place, Ezk 42:14
which they minister, for these are **h**. Ezk 42:14
separation between the **h** and the Ezk 42:20
Israel shall no more defile my **h** name, Ezk 43:7
They have defiled my **h** name by their Ezk 43:8
mountain all around shall be most **h**. Ezk 43:12
have not kept charge of my **h** things, Ezk 44:8
near any of my **h** things and the Ezk 44:13
things and the things that are most **h**, Ezk 44:13
and lay them in the **h** chambers. Ezk 44:19
difference between the **h** and the Ezk 44:23
and they shall keep my Sabbaths **h**. Ezk 44:24
the day that he goes into the **H** Place, Ezk 44:27
court, to minister in the **H** Place, Ezk 44:27
a portion of the land as a **h** district, Ezk 45:1
It shall be **h** throughout its whole Ezk 45:1
be the sanctuary, the Most **H** Place. Ezk 45:3
It shall be the **h** portion of the land. It Ezk 45:4
their houses and a **h** place for the Ezk 45:4
set apart as the **h** district you shall Ezk 45:6
both sides of the **h** district and the Ezk 45:7
alongside the **h** district and the Ezk 45:7
north row of the **h** chambers for the Ezk 46:19
be the allotments of the **h** portion: Ezk 48:10
portion from the **h** portion of the Ezk 48:12
portion of the land, a most **h** place, Ezk 48:12
of the land, for it is **h** to the LORD. Ezk 48:14
length alongside the **h** portion shall Ezk 48:18
and it shall be alongside the **h** portion. Ezk 48:18
the **h** portion together with the Ezk 48:20
both sides of the **h** portion and of the Ezk 48:21
25,000 cubits of the **h** portion to the Ezk 48:21
The **h** portion with the sanctuary of Ezk 48:21
is the spirit of the **h** gods—and I told Dn 4:8
that the spirit of the **h** gods is in you and Dn 4:9
in bed, and behold, a watcher, a **h** one, Dn 4:13
the decision by the word of the **h** ones, Dn 4:17
for the spirit of the **h** gods is in you." Dn 4:18
the king saw a watcher, a **h** one, Dn 4:23
in whom is the spirit of the **h** gods. Dn 5:11
Then I heard a **h** one speaking, and Dn 8:13
and another **h** one said to the one who Dn 8:13
from your city Jerusalem, your **h** hill, Dn 9:16
LORD my God for the **h** hill of my God, Dn 9:20
about your people and your **h** city, Dn 9:24
prophet, and to anoint a most **h** place. Dn 9:24
shall be set against the **h** covenant. Dn 11:28
take action against the **h** covenant. Dn 11:30
to those who forsake the **h** covenant. Dn 11:30
the sea and the glorious **h** mountain. Dn 11:45
of the power of the **h** people comes to an Dn 12:7
not a man, the **H** One in your midst, Hos 11:9
with God and is faithful to the **H** One. Hos 11:12
Zion; sound an alarm on my **h** mountain! Jl 2:1
God, who dwells in Zion, my **h** mountain. Jl 3:17
And Jerusalem shall be **h**, and strangers Jl 3:17
girl, so that my **h** name is profaned; Am 2:7
as you have drunk on my **h** mountain, Ob 1:16
be those who escape, and it shall be **h**, Ob 1:17
I shall again look upon your **h** temple.' Jon 2:4
prayer came to you, into your **h** temple. Jon 2:7
against you, the Lord from his **h** temple. Mi 1:2
O LORD my God, my **H** One? Hab 1:12
But the LORD is in his **h** temple; let all Hab 2:20
and the **H** One from Mount Paran. Hab 3:3
men; her priests profane what is **h**; Zep 3:4
longer be haughty in my **h** mountain. Zep 3:11
'If someone carries **h** meat in the fold of Hg 2:12
does it become **h**?'" The priests answered Hg 2:12
Judah as his portion in the **h** land, Zec 2:12
has roused himself from his **h** dwelling. Zec 2:13
of the LORD of hosts, the **h** mountain. Zec 8:3
will come, and all the **h** ones with him. Zec 14:5
"**H** to the LORD." And the pots in the Zec 14:20
and Judah shall be **h** to the LORD of Zec 14:21
found to be with child from the **H** Spirit. Mt 1:18
is conceived in her is from the **H** Spirit. Mt 1:20
baptize you with the **H** Spirit and with Mt 3:11
devil took him to the **h** city and set him Mt 4:5
"Do not give dogs what is **h**, and do not Mt 7:6
speaks against the **H** Spirit will not Mt 12:32
standing in the **h** place (let the reader Mt 24:15
they went into the **h** city and appeared Mt 27:53
and of the Son and of the **H** Spirit, Mt 28:19
he will baptize you with the **H** Spirit." Mk 1:8
know who you are—the **H** One of God." Mk 1:24
blasphemes against the **H** Spirit never Mk 3:29
that he was a righteous and **h** man, Mk 6:20
glory of his Father with the **h** angels." Mk 8:38
David himself, in the **H** Spirit, Mk 12:36
is not you who speak, but the **H** Spirit. Mk 13:11
and he will be filled with the **H** Spirit, Lk 1:15
her, "The **H** Spirit will come upon you, Lk 1:35
be born will be called **h**—the Son of Lk 1:35
Elizabeth was filled with the **H** Spirit, Lk 1:41
great things for me, and **h** is his name. Lk 1:49
filled with the **H** Spirit and prophesied, Lk 1:67
the mouth of his **h** prophets from of old, Lk 1:70
and to remember his **h** covenant, Lk 1:72
the womb shall be called **h** to the Lord") Lk 2:23
of Israel, and the **H** Spirit was upon him. Lk 2:25
to him by the **H** Spirit that he would Lk 2:26
baptize you with the **H** Spirit and with Lk 3:16
and the **H** Spirit descended on him in Lk 3:22
And Jesus, full of the **H** Spirit, returned Lk 4:1
I know who you are—the **H** One of God." Lk 4:34
glory of the Father and of the **h** angels. Lk 9:26
he rejoiced in the **H** Spirit and said, Lk 10:21
Father give the **H** Spirit to those Lk 11:13

blasphemes against the **H** Spirit will Lk 12:10
for the **H** Spirit will teach you in that Lk 12:12
this is he who baptizes with the **H** Spirit.' Jn 1:33
to know, that you are the **H** One of God." Jn 6:69
But the Helper, the **H** Spirit, whom the Jn 14:26
H Father, keep them in your name, Jn 17:11
and said to them, "Receive the **H** Spirit. Jn 20:22
commands through the **H** Spirit to the Acts 1:2
be baptized with the **H** Spirit not many Acts 1:5
power when the **H** Spirit has come Acts 1:8
which the **H** Spirit spoke beforehand Acts 1:16
all filled with the **H** Spirit and began to Acts 2:4
or let your **H** One see corruption. Acts 2:27
the Father the promise of the **H** Spirit, Acts 2:33
you will receive the gift of the **H** Spirit. Acts 2:38
you denied the **H** and Righteous One, Acts 3:14
the mouth of his **h** prophets long ago. Acts 3:21
Then Peter, filled with the **H** Spirit, said Acts 4:8
your servant, said by the **H** Spirit, Acts 4:25
together against your **h** servant Jesus, Acts 4:27
the name of your **h** servant Jesus." Acts 4:30
filled with the **H** Spirit and continued Acts 4:31
heart to lie to the **H** Spirit and to keep Acts 5:3
to these things, and so is the **H** Spirit, Acts 5:32
a man full of faith and of the **H** Spirit, Acts 6:5
words against this **h** place and the Acts 6:13
where you are standing is **h** ground. Acts 7:33
and ears, you always resist the **H** Spirit. Acts 7:51
But he, full of the **H** Spirit, gazed into Acts 7:55
that they might receive the **H** Spirit, Acts 8:15
on them and they received the **H** Spirit. Acts 8:17
my hands may receive the **H** Spirit." Acts 8:19
sight and be filled with the **H** Spirit." Acts 9:17
Lord and in the comfort of the **H** Spirit, Acts 9:31
was directed by a **h** angel to send for Acts 10:22
Nazareth with the **H** Spirit and with Acts 10:38
the **H** Spirit fell on all who heard the Acts 10:44
the gift of the **H** Spirit was poured out Acts 10:45
who have received the **H** Spirit just as Acts 10:47
the **H** Spirit fell on them just as on us Acts 11:15
will be baptized with the **H** Spirit.' Acts 11:16
man, full of the **H** Spirit and of faith. Acts 11:24
the Lord and fasting, the **H** Spirit said, Acts 13:2
So, being sent out by the **H** Spirit, they Acts 13:4
called Paul, filled with the **H** Spirit, Acts 13:9
will give you the **h** and sure blessings Acts 13:34
not let your **H** One see corruption.' Acts 13:35
filled with joy and with the **H** Spirit. Acts 13:52
by giving them the **H** Spirit just as he Acts 15:8
seemed good to the **H** Spirit and to us Acts 15:28
been forbidden by the **H** Spirit to speak Acts 16:6
"Did you receive the **H** Spirit when you Acts 19:2
not even heard that there is a **H** Spirit." Acts 19:2
on them, the **H** Spirit came on them, Acts 19:6
except that the **H** Spirit testifies to me Acts 20:23
in which the **H** Spirit has made you Acts 20:28
and said, "Thus says the **H** Spirit, Acts 21:11
temple and has defiled this **h** place." Acts 21:28
"The **H** Spirit was right in saying to Acts 28:25
his prophets in the **h** Scriptures, Rom 1:2
hearts through the **H** Spirit who has Rom 5:5
So the law is **h**, and the Rom 7:12
the commandment is **h** and righteous Rom 7:12
bears me witness in the **H** Spirit— Rom 9:1
If the dough offered as firstfruits is **h**, Rom 11:16
is the whole lump, and if the root is **h**, Rom 11:16
sacrifice, **h** and acceptable to God, Rom 12:1
and peace and joy in the **H** Spirit. Rom 14:17
the power of the **H** Spirit you may Rom 15:13
acceptable, sanctified by the **H** Spirit. Rom 15:16
Greet one another with a **h** kiss. All Rom 16:16
For God's temple is **h**, and you are 1 Cor 3:17
is a temple of the **H** Spirit within you, 1 Cor 6:19
husband is made **h** because of his 1 Cor 7:14
wife is made **h** because of her 1 Cor 7:14
be unclean, but as it is, they are **h**. 1 Cor 7:14
Lord, how to be **h** in body and spirit. 1 Cor 7:34
"Jesus is Lord" except in the **H** Spirit. 1 Cor 12:3
Greet one another with a **h** kiss. 1 Cor 16:20
patience, kindness, the **H** Spirit, 2 Cor 6:6
Greet one another with a **h** kiss. 2 Cor 13:12
the fellowship of the **H** Spirit be with 2 Cor 13:14
we should be **h** and blameless before Eph 1:4
were sealed with the promised **H** Spirit, Eph 1:13
grows into a **h** temple in the Lord. Eph 2:21
revealed to his **h** apostles and prophets Eph 3:5
And do not grieve the **H** Spirit of God, Eph 4:30
she might be **h** and without blemish. Eph 5:27
to present you **h** and blameless and Col 1:22
as God's chosen ones, **h** and beloved, Col 3:12
power and in the **H** Spirit and with 1 Thes 1:5
affliction, with the joy of the **H** Spirit, 1 Thes 1:6
how **h** and righteous and blameless 1 Thes 2:10
God, who gives his **H** Spirit to you. 1 Thes 4:8
Greet all the brothers with a **h** kiss. 1 Thes 5:26
lifting **h** hands without anger or 1 Tm 2:8
for it is made **h** by the word of God and 1 Tm 4:5
saved us and called us to a **h** calling, 2 Tm 1:9
By the **H** Spirit who dwells within us, 2 Tm 1:14
for honorable use, set apart as **h**, 2 Tm 2:21
upright, **h**, and disciplined. Ti 1:8
regeneration and renewal of the **H** Spirit, Ti 3:5
gifts of the **H** Spirit distributed Heb 2:4
Therefore, **h** brothers, you who share in Heb 3:1
Therefore, as the **H** Spirit says, "Today, if Heb 3:7
gift, and have shared in the **H** Spirit, Heb 6:4
have such a high priest, **h**, innocent, Heb 7:26
a minister in the **h** places, in the true Heb 8:2
of the Presence. It is called the **H** Place. Heb 9:2
second section called the Most **H** Place, Heb 9:3
By this the **H** Spirit indicates that the Heb 9:8
that the way into the **h** places is not yet Heb 9:8
he entered once for all into the **h** places, Heb 9:12
not into **h** places made with hands, Heb 9:24
priest enters the **h** places every year Heb 9:25
And the **H** Spirit also bears witness to Heb 10:15
confidence to enter the **h** places by the Heb 10:19
is brought into the **h** places by the Heb 13:11
to you by the **H** Spirit sent from 1 Pt 1:12
but as he who called you is **h**, you also 1 Pt 1:15
holy, you also be **h** in all your conduct, 1 Pt 1:15
since it is written, "You shall be **h**, for I 1 Pt 1:16
written, "You shall be holy, for I am **h**." 1 Pt 1:16
as a spiritual house, to be a **h** priesthood, 1 Pt 2:5
race, a royal priesthood, a **h** nation, 1 Pt 2:9
this is how the **h** women who hoped in 1 Pt 3:5
hearts regard Christ the Lord as **h**, 1 Pt 3:15
we were with him on the **h** mountain. 2 Pt 1:18
they were carried along by the **H** Spirit. 2 Pt 1:21
from the **h** commandment delivered 2 Pt 2:21
the predictions of the **h** prophets and the 2 Pt 3:2
you have been anointed by the **H** One, 1 Jn 2:20
came with ten thousands of his **h** ones, Jude 1:14
yourselves up in your most **h** faith; Jude 1:20
most holy faith; pray in the **H** Spirit; Jude 1:20
'The words of the **h** one, the true one, who Rv 3:7
night they never cease to say, "**H**, holy, Rv 4:8
they never cease to say, "Holy, **h**, holy, Rv 4:8
"Holy, holy, **h**, is the Lord God Almighty, Rv 4:8
voice, "O Sovereign Lord, **h** and true, Rv 6:10
they will trample the **h** city for forty-two Rv 11:2
the presence of the **h** angels and in the Rv 14:10
glorify your name? For you alone are **h**. Rv 15:4
of the waters say, "Just are you, O **H** One, Rv 16:5
Blessed and **h** is the one who shares in Rv 20:6
And I saw the **h** city, new Jerusalem, Rv 21:2
showed me the **h** city Jerusalem Rv 21:10
still do right, and the **h** still be holy." Rv 22:11
still do right, and the holy still be **h**." Rv 22:11
share in the tree of life and in the **h** city, Rv 22:19

HOMAGE (21)

with his face to the earth and paid **h**. 1 Sm 24:8
his face to the ground and paid **h**. 1 Sm 28:14
David, he fell to the ground and paid **h**. 2 Sm 1:2
to David and fell on his face and paid **h**. 2 Sm 9:6
And he paid **h** and said, "What is your 2 Sm 9:8
to the ground and paid **h** and said, 2 Sm 14:4
ground and paid **h** and blessed the 2 Sm 14:22
a man came near to pay **h** to him, 2 Sm 15:5
is now yours." And Ziba said, "I pay **h**; 2 Sm 16:4
went out and paid **h** to the king with 2 Sm 24:20
bowed and paid **h** to the king, 1 Kgs 1:16
the ground and paid **h** to the king 1 Kgs 1:31
he came and paid **h** to King Solomon, 1 Kgs 1:53
floor and paid **h** to David with 1 Chr 21:21
their heads and paid **h** to the LORD 1 Chr 29:20
Judah came and paid **h** to the king. 2 Chr 24:17
gate bowed down and paid **h** to Haman, Est 3:2
But Mordecai did not bow down or pay **h**. Est 3:2
did not bow down or pay **h** to him, Est 3:5
fell upon his face and paid **h** to Daniel, Dn 2:46
him and kneeling down in **h** to him. Mk 15:19

HOME (119)

I may go to my own **h** and country. Gn 30:25
Then Laban departed and returned **h**. Gn 31:55
by her until his master came **h**, Gn 39:16
When Joseph came **h**, they brought Gn 43:26
When they came **h** to their father Reuel, Ex 2:18
it that you have come **h** so soon today?" Ex 2:18
and is not brought **h** will die when the Ex 9:19
Moses' wife, after he had sent her **h**, Ex 18:2
up in the family or in another **h**. Lv 18:9
and you bring her **h** to your house, she Dt 21:12
he is, you shall bring it **h** to your house, Dt 22:2
He shall be free at **h** one year to be happy Dt 24:5
return to his own town and his own **h**, Jos 20:6
the half-tribe of Manasseh returned **h**, Jos 22:9
let him return **h** and hurry away from Jgs 7:3
let all the others go every man to his **h**." Jgs 7:7
was dead, everyone departed to his **h**. Jgs 9:55
"If you bring me **h** again to fight with Jgs 11:9
Jephthah came to his **h** at Mizpah. Jgs 11:34
of the young Levite, at the **h** of Micah, Jgs 18:15
gone a distance from the **h** of Micah, Jgs 18:22
him, he turned and went back to his **h**. Jgs 18:26
morning for your journey, and go **h**." Jgs 19:9
man rose up and went away to his **h**. Jgs 19:28
Then Elkanah went **h** to Ramah. And 1 Sm 2:11
So then they would return to their **h**. 1 Sm 2:20
and they fled, every man to his **h**. 1 Sm 4:10
to the cart, but take their calves **h**, 1 Sm 6:7
the cart and shut up their calves at **h**. 1 Sm 6:10
return to Ramah, for his **h** was there, 1 Sm 7:17
the people away, each one to his **h**. 1 Sm 10:25
Saul also went to his **h** at Gibeah, 1 Sm 10:26
The rest of the people he sent **h**, every 1 Sm 13:2
As they were coming **h**, when David 1 Sm 18:6
at Horesh, and Jonathan went **h**. 1 Sm 23:18
Then Saul went **h**, but David and his 1 Sm 24:22
Then David sent **h** to Tamar, saying, 2 Sm 13:7
not bring his banished one **h** again. 2 Sm 14:13
and also an exile from your **h**. 2 Sm 15:19
as a bride comes **h** to her husband. 2 Sm 17:3
donkey and went off **h** to his own 2 Sm 17:23
all Israel fled every one to his own **h**. 2 Sm 18:17
had fled every man to his own **h**. 2 Sm 19:8
my lord the king has come safely **h**." 2 Sm 19:30
him, and he returned to his own **h**. 2 Sm 19:39
from the city, every man to his **h**. 2 Sm 20:22
in Lebanon and two months at **h**. 1 Kgs 5:14
Every man return to his **h**, for this 1 Kgs 12:24
word of the LORD and went **h** again, 1 Kgs 12:24
to the man of God, "Come **h** with me, 1 Kgs 13:7
"Come **h** with me and eat bread." 1 Kgs 13:15
let each return to his **h** in peace.'" 1 Kgs 22:17
surrounded him, but his army fled **h**. 2 Kgs 8:21
with your glory, and stay at **h**, 2 Kgs 14:10
Israel, and every man fled to his **h**. 2 Kgs 14:12
departed and went **h** and lived at 2 Kgs 19:36
can I bring the ark of God **h** to me?" 1 Chr 13:12
not take the ark **h** into the city of 1 Chr 13:13
and David went **h** to bless his 1 Chr 16:43
Return every man to his **h**, for this 2 Chr 11:4
let each return to his **h** in peace.'" 2 Chr 18:16
to him from Ephraim to go **h** again. 2 Chr 25:10
Judah and returned **h** in fierce 2 Chr 25:10
in boastfulness. But now stay at **h**. 2 Chr 25:19
Israel, and every man fled to his **h**. 2 Chr 25:22
Mehetabel, who was confined to his **h**, Neh 6:10
Haman restrained himself and went **h**, Est 5:10
that you may discern the paths to its **h**? Jb 38:20
the arid plain for his **h** and the salt land Jb 39:6
On the rock he dwells and makes his **h**, Jb 39:28
God settles the solitary in a **h**; he leads Ps 68:6
flee!" The women at **h** divide the spoil— Ps 68:12
Even the sparrow finds a **h**, and the Ps 84:3
the stork has her **h** in the fir trees. Ps 104:17
He gives the barren woman a **h**, Ps 113:9
shall come **h** with shouts of joy, Ps 126:6
and wayward; her feet do not stay at **h**; Prv 7:11
For my husband is not at **h**; he has Prv 7:19
with him; at full moon he will come **h**." Prv 7:20
the righteous; do no violence to his **h**; Prv 24:15
its nest is a man who strays from his **h**. Prv 27:8
because man is going to his eternal **h**, Eccl 12:5
who did not let his prisoners go **h**?' Is 14:17
departed and returned **h** and lived at Is 37:37
of Shaphan, that he should take him **h**. Jer 39:14
people Israel, for they will soon come **h**. Ezk 36:8
And when you brought it **h**, I blew it Hg 1:9
I will bring them **h** from the land of Zec 10:10
"Lord, my servant is lying paralyzed at **h**, Mt 8:6
—"Rise, pick up your bed and go **h**." Mt 9:6
And he rose and went **h**. Mt 9:7
days, it was reported that he was at **h**. Mk 2:1
you, rise, pick up your bed, and go **h**." Mk 2:11
Then he went **h**, and the crowd Mk 3:20
"Go **h** to your friends and tell them how Mk 5:19
And she went **h** and found the child Mk 7:30
And he sent him to his **h**, saying, "Do Mk 8:26
when he leaves **h** and puts his servants Mk 13:34
of service was ended, he went to his **h**. Lk 1:23
three months and returned to her **h**. Lk 1:56
to you, rise, pick up your bed and go **h**." Lk 5:24
what he had been lying on and went **h**, Lk 5:25
"Return to your **h**, and declare how Lk 8:39
me first say farewell to those at my **h**." Lk 9:61
master to come **h** from the wedding Lk 12:36
And when he comes **h**, he calls together Lk 15:6
place, returned **h** beating their breasts. Lk 23:48
and he went **h** marveling at what had Lk 24:12
come to him and make our **h** with him. Jn 14:23
you will be scattered, each to his own **h**, Jn 16:32
hour the disciple took her to his own **h**. Jn 19:27

on board the ship, and they returned **h**. Acts 21:6
let him eat at **h**—so that when you 1 Cor 11:34
let them ask their husbands at **h**. 1 Cor 14:35
that if the tent, which is our earthly **h**, 2 Cor 5:1
that while we are at **h** in the body we 2 Cor 5:6
from the body and at **h** with the Lord. 2 Cor 5:8
So whether we are at **h** or away, we 2 Cor 5:9
to be self-controlled, pure, working at **h**, Ti 2:5

HOMEBORN (1)
"Is Israel a slave? Is he a **h** servant? Why Jer 2:14

HOMELAND (1)
it clear that they are seeking a **h**. Heb 11:14

HOMELESS (2)
hungry and bring the **h** poor into your Is 58:7
are poorly dressed and buffeted and **h**, 1 Cor 4:11

HOMER (9)
A **h** of barley seed shall be valued at Lv 27:16
and a **h** of seed shall yield but an ephah." Is 5:10
the bath containing one tenth of a **h**, Ezk 45:11
homer, and the ephah one tenth of a **h**; Ezk 45:11
the **h** shall be the standard measure. Ezk 45:11
of an ephah from each **h** of wheat, Ezk 45:13
of an ephah from each **h** of barley, Ezk 45:13
from each cor (the cor, like the **h**, Ezk 45:14
shekels of silver and a **h** and a lethech of Hos 3:2

HOMERS (1)
who gathered least gathered ten **h**. Nm 11:32

HOMES (15)
not return to our **h** until each of the Nm 32:18
them away to their **h** and blessed them, Jos 22:7
and went to their **h** joyful and glad of 1 Kgs 8:66
of Israel lived in their **h** as formerly. 2 Kgs 13:5
he sent the people away to their **h**, 2 Chr 7:10
daughters, your wives, and your **h**." Neh 4:14
posts and some in front of their own **h**." Neh 7:3
Their graves are their **h** forever, their Ps 49:11
yet they make their **h** in the cliffs; Prv 30:26
over to strangers, our **h** to foreigners. Lam 5:2
and I will return them to their **h**, Hos 11:11
if I send them away hungry to their **h**, Mk 8:3
we have left our **h** and followed you." Lk 18:28
Then the disciples went back to their **h**. Jn 20:10
and breaking bread in their **h**, Acts 2:46

HOMETOWN (7)
and coming to his **h** he taught them in Mt 13:54
honor except in his **h** and in his own Mt 13:57
went away from there and came to his **h**, Mk 6:1
except in his **h** and among his relatives Mk 6:4
Capernaum, do here in your **h** as well." Lk 4:23
to you, no prophet is acceptable in his **h**. Lk 4:24
a prophet has no honor in his own **h**.) Jn 4:44

HOMICIDE (1)
between one kind of **h** and another, Dt 17:8

HOMOSEXUALITY (2)
adulterers, nor men who practice **h**, 1 Cor 6:9
immoral, men who practice **h**, 1 Tm 1:10

HONEST (10)
are all sons of one man. We are **h** men. Gn 42:11
if you are **h** men, let one of your Gn 42:19
But we said to him, 'We are **h** men; we Gn 42:31
this I shall know that you are **h** men: Gn 42:33
know that you are not spies but **h** men, Gn 42:34
"As the LORD lives, you have been **h**, 1 Sm 29:6
speaks the truth gives **h** evidence, Prv 12:17
Whoever gives an **h** answer kisses the Prv 24:26
word, hold it fast in an **h** and good heart, Lk 8:15
doing **h** work with his own hands, Eph 4:28

HONESTLY (3)
out to the workmen, for they dealt **h**. 2 Kgs 12:15
into their hand, for they deal **h**." 2 Kgs 22:7
enters suit justly; no one goes to law **h**; Is 59:4

HONESTY (1)
So my **h** will answer for me later, when Gn 30:33

HONEY (58)
to the man, a little balm and a little **h**, Gn 43:11
land, a land flowing with milk and **h**, Ex 3:8
a land flowing with milk and **h**.'" Ex 3:17
you, a land flowing with milk and **h**, Ex 13:5
taste of it was like wafers made with **h**. Ex 16:31
Go up to a land flowing with milk and **h**; Ex 33:3
no leaven nor any **h** as a food offering Lv 2:11
a land flowing with milk and **h**.' Lv 20:24
It flows with milk and **h**, and this is Nm 13:27
us, a land that flows with milk and **h**. Nm 14:8
out of a land flowing with milk and **h**, Nm 16:13
into a land flowing with milk and **h**, Nm 16:14
you, in a land flowing with milk and **h**. Dt 6:3
pomegranates, a land of olive trees and **h**, Dt 8:8
a land flowing with milk and **h**. Dt 11:9
land, a land flowing with milk and **h**. Dt 26:9
a land flowing with milk and **h**.' Dt 26:15
you, a land flowing with milk and **h**, Dt 27:3
into the land flowing with milk and **h**, Dt 31:20
he suckled him with **h** out of the rock, Dt 32:13
to us, a land flowing with milk and **h**. Jos 5:6
of bees in the body of the lion, and **h**. Jgs 14:8
he had scraped the **h** from the carcass of Jgs 14:9
went down, "What is sweeter than **h**? Jgs 14:18
behold, there was **h** on the ground. 1 Sm 14:25
forest, behold, the **h** was dropping, 1 Sm 14:26
because I tasted a little of this **h**. 1 Sm 14:29
"I tasted a little **h** with the tip of the 1 Sm 14:43
h and curds and sheep and cheese 2 Sm 17:29
ten loaves, some cakes, and a jar of **h**, 1 Kgs 14:3
a land of olive trees and **h**, 2 Kgs 18:32
h, and of all the produce of the field. 2 Chr 31:5
the streams flowing with **h** and curds. Jb 20:17
sweeter also than **h** and drippings of the Ps 19:10
and with **h** from the rock I would Ps 81:16
taste, sweeter than **h** to my mouth! Ps 119:103
For the lips of a forbidden woman drip **h**, Prv 5:3
My son, eat **h**, for it is good, and the Prv 24:13
If you have found **h**, eat only enough Prv 25:16
It is not good to eat much **h**, nor is it Prv 25:27
One who is full loathes **h**, but to one Prv 27:7
bride; **h** and milk are under your tongue; Sg 4:11
my spice, I ate my honeycomb with my **h**, Sg 5:1
shall eat curds and **h** when he knows Is 7:15
is left in the land will eat curds and **h**. Is 7:22
them a land flowing with milk and **h**, Jer 11:5
them, a land flowing with milk and **h**. Jer 32:22
and **h** hidden in the fields." So he Jer 41:8
it, and it was in my mouth as sweet as **h**. Ezk 3:3
cloth. You ate fine flour and **h** and oil. Ezk 16:13
flour and oil and **h**—you set before Ezk 16:19
them, a land flowing with milk and **h**, Ezk 20:6
them, a land flowing with milk and **h**, Ezk 20:15
wheat of Minnith, meal, **h**, oil, Ezk 27:17
and his food was locusts and wild **h**. Mt 3:4
his waist and ate locusts and wild **h**. Mk 1:6
but in your mouth it will be sweet as **h**." Rv 10:9
It was sweet as **h** in my mouth, but Rv 10:10

HONEYCOMB (5)
dipped it in the **h** and put his hand 1 Sm 14:27
also than honey and drippings of the **h**. Ps 19:10
Gracious words are like a **h**, sweetness Prv 16:24
the drippings of the **h** are sweet to your Prv 24:13
with my spice, I ate my **h** with my honey, Sg 5:1

HONOR (140)
now my husband will **h** me, because I Gn 30:20
tell my father of all my **h** in Egypt, Gn 45:13
"**H** your father and your mother, that Ex 20:12
the gray head and **h** the face of an Lv 19:32
for I will surely do you great **h**, and Nm 22:17
come to me? Am I not able to **h** you?" Nm 22:37
I said, 'I will certainly **h** you,' but the Nm 24:11
the LORD has held you back from **h**." Nm 24:11
"'**H** your father and your mother, as the Dt 5:16
in fame and in **h** high above all nations Dt 26:19
your words come true, we may **h** you?" Jgs 13:17
sit with princes and inherit a seat of **h**. 1 Sm 2:8
and **h** your sons above me by 1 Sm 2:29
me, for those who **h** me I will honor, 1 Sm 2:30
me, for those who honor me I will **h**, 1 Sm 2:30
city, and he is a man who is held in **h**; 1 Sm 9:6
yet **h** me now before the elders of my 1 Sm 15:30
spoken, by them I shall be held in **h**." 2 Sm 6:22
have not asked, both riches and **h**, 1 Kgs 3:13
Both riches and **h** come from you, 1 Chr 29:12
good age, full of days, riches, and **h**. 1 Chr 29:28
h, or the life of those who hate you, 2 Chr 1:11
give you riches, possessions, and **h**, 2 Chr 1:12
they made a very great fire in his **h**. 2 Chr 16:14
and he had great riches and **h**. 2 Chr 17:5
Jehoshaphat had great riches and **h**, 2 Chr 18:1
His people made no fire in his **h**, like 2 Chr 21:19
will bring you no **h** from the LORD 2 Chr 26:18
had very great riches and **h**, 2 Chr 32:27
of Jerusalem did him **h** at his death. 2 Chr 32:33
all women will give **h** to their husbands, Est 1:20
"What **h** or distinction has been Est 6:3
the king delights to **h**?" And Haman said Est 6:6
the king delight to **h** more than me?" Est 6:6
the man whom the king delights to **h**, Est 6:7
the man whom the king delights to **h**, Est 6:9
to the man whom the king delights to **h**.'" Est 6:9
the man whom the king delights to **h**." Est 6:11
had light and gladness and joy and **h**. Est 8:16
full account of the high **h** of Mordecai, Est 10:2
His sons come to **h**, and he does not Jb 14:21
my **h** is pursued as by the wind, and my Jb 30:15
how long shall my **h** be turned into Ps 4:2
and crowned him with glory and **h**. Ps 8:5
of kings are among your ladies of **h**; Ps 45:9
shield; the LORD bestows favor and **h**. Ps 84:11
in trouble; I will rescue him and **h** him. Ps 91:15
endures forever; his horn is exalted in **h**. Ps 112:9
written! This is **h** for all his godly ones. Ps 149:9
H the LORD with your wealth and with Prv 3:9
hand; in her left hand are riches and **h**. Prv 3:16
The wise will inherit **h**, but fools get Prv 3:35
you; she will **h** you if you embrace her. Prv 4:8
lest you give your **h** to others and your Prv 5:9
Riches and **h** are with me, enduring Prv 8:18
A gracious woman gets **h**, and violent Prv 11:16
wisdom, and humility comes before **h**. Prv 15:33
but humility comes before **h**. Prv 18:12
It is an **h** for a man to keep aloof from Prv 20:3
will find life, righteousness, and **h**. Prv 21:21
fear of the LORD is riches and **h** and life. Prv 22:4
in harvest, so **h** is not fitting for a fool. Prv 26:1
in the sling is one who gives **h** to a fool. Prv 26:8
he who is lowly in spirit will obtain **h**. Prv 29:23
God gives wealth, possessions, and **h**, Eccl 6:2
a little folly outweighs wisdom and **h**. Eccl 10:1
shall be the pride and **h** of the survivors of Is 4:2
become a throne of **h** to his father's Is 22:23
on him the whole **h** of his father's house, Is 22:24
with their mouth and **h** me with their Is 29:13
The wild beasts will **h** me, the jackals Is 43:20
if you **h** it, not going your own ways, or Is 58:13
no **h** was shown to the priests, no favor Lam 4:16
from me gifts and rewards and great **h**. Dn 2:6
praise and extol and **h** the King of Dn 4:37
He shall **h** the god of fortresses instead Dn 11:38
not know he shall **h** with gold and Dn 11:38
acknowledge him he shall load with **h**. Dn 11:39
of the LORD and shall bear royal **h**, Zec 6:13
If then I am a father, where is my **h**? Mal 1:6
not take it to heart to give **h** to my name, Mal 2:2
prophet is not without **h** except in his Mt 13:57
'**H** your father and your mother,' Mt 15:4
he need not **h** his father.' So for the sake Mt 15:6
H your father and mother, and, You Mt 19:19
they love the place of **h** at feasts and the Mt 23:6
said to them, "A prophet is not without **h**, Mk 6:4
said, '**H** your father and your mother'; Mk 7:10
defraud, **H** your father and mother.'" Mk 10:19
and the places of **h** at feasts, Mk 12:39
noticed how they chose the places of **h**, Lk 14:7
feast, do not sit down in a place of **h**, Lk 14:8
witness, **H** your father and mother.'" Lk 18:20
and the places of **h** at feasts, Lk 20:46
a prophet has no **h** in his own Jn 4:44
that all may **h** the Son, just as they honor Jn 5:23
honor the Son, just as they **h** the Father. Jn 5:23
Whoever does not **h** the Son does not Jn 5:23
the Son does not **h** the Father who sent Jn 5:23
do not have a demon, but I **h** my Father, Jn 8:49
serves me, the Father will **h** him. Jn 12:26
of the law held in **h** by all the people, Acts 5:34
they did not **h** him as God or give Rom 1:21
seek for glory and **h** and immortality, Rom 2:7
but glory and **h** and peace for Rom 2:10
Outdo one another in showing **h**. Rom 12:10
is owed, **h** to whom honor is owed. Rom 13:7
is owed, honor to whom **h** is owed. Rom 13:7
the day, observes it in **h** of the Lord. Rom 14:6
The one who eats, eats in **h** of the Lord, Rom 14:6
abstains in **h** of the Lord and gives Rom 14:6
You are held in **h**, but we in 1 Cor 4:10
honorable we bestow the greater **h**, 1 Cor 12:23
giving greater **h** to the part that 1 Cor 12:24
through **h** and dishonor, through 2 Cor 6:8
"**H** your father and mother" (this is the Eph 6:2
the Lord with all joy, and **h** such men, Phil 2:29
his own body in holiness and **h**, 1 Thes 4:4
God, be **h** and glory forever and ever. 1 Tm 1:17
H widows who are truly widows. 1 Tm 5:3
be considered worthy of double **h**, 1 Tm 5:17
their own masters as worthy of all **h**, 1 Tm 6:1
To him be **h** and eternal dominion. 1 Tm 6:16
have crowned him with glory and **h**, Heb 2:7
crowned with glory and **h** because of the Heb 2:9
a house has more **h** than the house Heb 3:3
And no one takes this **h** for himself, but Heb 5:4
Let marriage be held in **h** among all, Heb 13:4
praise and glory and **h** at the revelation 1 Pt 1:7
So the **h** is for you who believe, but for 1 Pt 2:7
H everyone. Love the brotherhood. Fear 1 Pt 2:17
brotherhood. Fear God. **H** the emperor. 1 Pt 2:17
showing **h** to the woman as the weaker 1 Pt 3:7
For when he received **h** and glory from 2 Pt 1:17
creatures give glory and **h** and thanks to Rv 4:9
God, to receive glory and **h** and power, Rv 4:11
wisdom and might and **h** and glory and Rv 5:12
Lamb be blessing and **h** and glory and Rv 5:13
and thanksgiving and **h** and power and Rv 7:12

it the glory and the **h** of the nations. Rv 21:26

HONORABLE (13)
in number and more **h** than these. Nm 22:15
Jabez was more **h** than his brothers; 1 Chr 4:9
to the elder, and the despised to the **h**. Is 3:5
noble, nor the scoundrel said to be **h**. Is 32:5
a delight and the holy day of the LORD **h**; Is 58:13
thought to do what is **h** in the sight of Rom 12:17
that we think less **h** we bestow the 1 Cor 12:23
we aim at what is **h** not only in the 2 Cor 8:21
brothers, whatever is true, whatever is **h**, Phil 4:8
also of wood and clay, some for **h** use, 2 Tm 2:20
he will be a vessel for **h** use, 2 Tm 2:21
who blaspheme the **h** name by which Jas 2:7
your conduct among the Gentiles **h**, 1 Pt 2:12

HONORABLY (1)
desiring to act **h** in all things. Heb 13:18

HONORED (25)
he was the most **h** of all his father's Gn 34:19
by which gods and men are **h**, Jgs 9:9
bodyguard, and **h** in your house? 1 Sm 22:14
the king of Israel **h** himself today, 2 Sm 6:20
with which the king had **h** him, Est 5:11
but whoever heeds reproof is **h**. Prv 13:18
he who guards his master will be **h**. Prv 27:18
their **h** men go hungry, and their Is 5:13
the elder and **h** man is the head, and the Is 9:15
whose traders were the **h** of the earth? Is 23:8
glory, to dishonor all the **h** of the earth. Is 23:9
you are precious in my eyes, and **h**, Is 43:4
offerings, or **h** me with your sacrifices. Is 43:23
for I am **h** in the eyes of the LORD, Is 49:5
I will make them **h**, and they shall not Jer 30:19
all who **h** her despise her, for they have Lam 1:8
and praised and **h** him who lives Dn 4:34
whose are all your ways, you have not **h**. Dn 5:23
for her **h** men lots were cast, and all her Na 3:10
Then you will be **h** in the presence of Lk 14:10
They also **h** us greatly, and when we Acts 28:10
lump one vessel for **h** use and another Rom 9:21
if one member is **h**, all rejoice 1 Cor 12:26
as always Christ will be **h** in my body, Phil 1:20
the Lord may speed ahead and be **h**, 2 Thes 3:1

HONORING (3)
to you, that he is **h** your father? 2 Sm 10:3
David say to you for **h** your servant? 1 Chr 17:18
to you, that he is **h** your father? 1 Chr 19:3

HONORS (6)
but who **h** those who fear the LORD; Ps 15:4
he who is generous to the needy **h** him. Prv 14:31
gave Daniel high **h** and many great Dn 2:48
"A son **h** his father, and a servant his Mal 1:6
"'This people **h** me with their lips, but Mt 15:8
"'This people **h** me with their lips, Mk 7:6

HOOF (13)
not a **h** shall be left behind, for we must Ex 10:26
Whatever parts the **h** and is Lv 11:3
those that chew the cud or part the **h**, Lv 11:4
it chews the cud but does not part the **h**, Lv 11:4
it chews the cud but does not part the **h**, Lv 11:5
it chews the cud but does not part the **h**, Lv 11:6
it parts the **h** and is cloven-footed Lv 11:7
animal that parts the **h** but is not Lv 11:26
animal that parts the **h** and has the hoof Dt 14:6
the hoof and has the **h** cloven in two and Dt 14:6
cud or have the **h** cloven you shall not Dt 14:7
they chew the cud but do not part the **h**, Dt 14:7
because it parts the **h** but does not chew Dt 14:8

HOOFBEATS (1)
Why tarry the **h** of his chariots?' Jgs 5:28

HOOFS (8)
beat the horses' **h** with the galloping, Jgs 5:22
than an ox or a bull with horns and **h**. Ps 69:31
bows bent, their horses' **h** seem like flint, Is 5:28
of the stamping of the **h** of his stallions, Jer 47:3
With the **h** of his horses he will Ezk 26:11
nor shall the **h** of beasts trouble them. Ezk 32:13
iron, and I will make your **h** bronze; Mi 4:13
of the fat ones, tearing off even their **h**. Zec 11:16

HOOK (6)
I will put my **h** in your nose and my 2 Kgs 19:28
in his nose or pierce his jaw with a **h**? Jb 41:2
and lament, all who cast a **h** in the Nile; Is 19:8
I will put my **h** in your nose and my bit Is 37:29
He brings all of them up with a **h**; he Hab 1:15
the sea and cast a **h** and take the first Mt 17:27

HOOKS (26)
overlaid with gold, with **h** of gold, Ex 26:32
Their **h** shall be of gold, and you shall Ex 26:37
but the **h** of the pillars and their fillets Ex 27:10
but the **h** of the pillars and their fillets Ex 27:11
Their **h** shall be of silver, and their Ex 27:17
and its covering, its **h** and its frames, Ex 35:11
Their **h** were of gold, and he cast for Ex 36:36
and its five pillars with their **h**. He Ex 36:38
but the **h** of the pillars and their fillets Ex 38:10
but the **h** of the pillars and their fillets Ex 38:11
the **h** of the pillars and their fillets were Ex 38:12
but the **h** of the pillars and their fillets Ex 38:17
bases were of bronze, their **h** of silver, Ex 38:19
1,775 shekels he made **h** for the pillars Ex 38:28
Moses, the tent and all its utensils, its **h**, Ex 39:33
Manasseh with **h** and bound 2 Chr 33:11
and their spears into pruning **h**; Is 2:4
he cuts off the shoots with pruning **h**, Is 18:5
they brought him with **h** to the land of Ezk 19:4
With **h** they put him in a cage and Ezk 19:9
I will put **h** in your jaws, and make the Ezk 29:4
you about and put **h** into your jaws, Ezk 38:4
And **h**, a handbreadth long, were Ezk 40:43
swords, and your pruning **h** into spears; Jl 3:10
when they shall take you away with **h**, Am 4:2
and their spears into pruning **h**; Mi 4:3

HOOPOE (2)
the stork, the heron of any kind, the **h**, Lv 11:19
heron of any kind; the **h** and the bat. Dt 14:18

HOOT (1)
capitals; a voice shall **h** in the window; Zep 2:14

HOP (1)
feet, with which to **h** on the ground. Lv 11:21

HOPE (151)
If I should say I have **h**, even if I should Ru 1:12
even now there is **h** for Israel in spite Ezr 10:2
stars of its dawn be dark; let it **h** for light, Jb 3:9
and the integrity of your ways your **h**? Jb 4:6
So the poor have **h**, and injustice shuts Jb 5:16
request, and that God would fulfill my **h**, Jb 6:8
of Tema look, the travelers of Sheba **h**. Jb 6:19
shuttle and come to their end without **h**. Jb 7:6
God; the **h** of the godless shall perish. Jb 8:13
you will feel secure, because there is **h**; Jb 11:18
and their **h** is to breathe their last." Jb 11:20
Though he slay me, I will **h** in him; yet I Jb 13:15
"For there is **h** for a tree, if it be cut down, Jb 14:7
the earth; so you destroy the **h** of man. Jb 14:19
If I **h** for Sheol as my house, if I make Jb 17:13
where then is my **h**? Who will see my Jb 17:15
then is my hope? Who will see my **h**? Jb 17:15
and my **h** has he pulled up like a tree. Jb 19:10
For what is the **h** of the godless when God Jb 27:8
Behold, the **h** of a man is false; he is laid Jb 41:9
and the **h** of the poor shall not perish Ps 9:18
The war horse is a false **h** for salvation, Ps 33:17
on those who **h** in his steadfast love, Ps 33:18
O LORD, be upon us, even as we **h** in you. Ps 33:22
Lord, for what do I wait? My **h** is in you. Ps 39:7
H in God; for I shall again praise him, Ps 42:5
H in God; for I shall again praise him, Ps 42:11
H in God; for I shall again praise him, Ps 43:5
wait in silence, for my **h** is from him. Ps 62:5
the **h** of all the ends of the earth and of Ps 65:5
Let not those who **h** in you be put to Ps 69:6
For you, O Lord, are my **h**, my trust, O Ps 71:5
But I will **h** continually and will praise Ps 71:14
they should set their **h** in God and not Ps 78:7
my mouth, for my **h** is in your rules. Ps 119:43
in which you have made me **h**. Ps 119:49
for your salvation; I **h** in your word. Ps 119:81
and my shield; I **h** in your word. Ps 119:114
let me not be put to shame in my **h**! Ps 119:116
and cry for help; I **h** in your words. Ps 119:147
I **h** for your salvation, O LORD, and I Ps 119:166
my soul waits, and in his word I **h**; Ps 130:5
O Israel, **h** in the LORD! For with the Ps 130:7
h in the LORD from this time forth and Ps 131:3
of Jacob, whose **h** is in the LORD his God, Ps 146:5
in those who **h** in his steadfast love. Ps 147:11
The **h** of the righteous brings joy, but Prv 10:28
When the wicked dies, his **h** will perish, Prv 11:7
H deferred makes the heart sick, but a Prv 13:12
Discipline your son, for there is **h**; do Prv 19:18
a future, and your **h** will not be cut off. Prv 23:18
a future, and your **h** will not be cut off. Prv 24:14
There is more **h** for a fool than for Prv 26:12
There is more **h** for a fool than for Prv 29:20
who is joined with all the living has **h**, Eccl 9:4
the house of Jacob, and I will **h** in him. Is 8:17
because of Cush their **h** and of Egypt Is 20:5
to the pit do not **h** for your faithfulness. Is 38:18
judge the peoples; the coastlands **h** for me, Is 51:5
we **h** for light, and behold, darkness, and Is 59:9
doves; we **h** for justice, but there is none; Is 59:11
For the coastlands shall **h** for me, the Is 60:9
O you **h** of Israel, its savior in time of Jer 14:8
We set our **h** on you, for you do all Jer 14:22
O LORD, the **h** of Israel, all who forsake Jer 17:13
not for evil, to give you a future and a **h**. Jer 29:11
There is **h** for your future, declares the Jer 31:17
the LORD, the **h** of their fathers.' Jer 50:7
perished; so has my **h** from the LORD." Lam 3:18
I call to mind, and therefore I have **h**: Lam 3:21
my soul, "therefore I will **h** in him." Lam 3:24
in the dust—there may yet be **h**; Lam 3:29
she waited in vain, that her **h** was lost, Ezk 19:5
bones are dried up, and our **h** is lost; Ezk 37:11
make the Valley of Achor a door of **h**. Hos 2:15
idols forsake their **h** of steadfast love. Jon 2:8
to your stronghold, O prisoners of **h**; Zec 9:12
and in his name the Gentiles will **h**." Mt 12:21
Moses, on whom you have set your **h**. Jn 5:45
rejoiced; my flesh also will dwell in **h**. Acts 2:26
owners saw that their **h** of gain was Acts 16:19
in the **h** that they might feel their way Acts 17:27
respect to the **h** and the resurrection Acts 23:6
having a **h** in God, which these men Acts 24:15
trial because of my **h** in the promise Acts 26:6
to which our twelve tribes **h** to attain, Acts 26:7
And for this **h** I am accused by Jews, O Acts 26:7
all **h** of our being saved was at last Acts 27:20
it is because of the **h** of Israel that I Acts 28:20
In **h** he believed against hope, that he Rom 4:18
In hope he believed against **h**, that he Rom 4:18
and we rejoice in **h** of the glory of God. Rom 5:2
character, and character produces **h**, Rom 5:4
and **h** does not put us to shame, Rom 5:5
because of him who subjected it, in **h** Rom 8:20
For in this **h** we were saved. Now hope Rom 8:24
saved. Now **h** that is seen is not hope. Rom 8:24
saved. Now hope that is seen is not **h**. Rom 8:24
But if we **h** for what we do not see, we Rom 8:25
Rejoice in **h**, be patient in Rom 12:12
of the Scriptures we might have **h**. Rom 15:4
Gentiles; in him will the Gentiles **h**." Rom 15:12
May the God of **h** fill you with all joy Rom 15:13
the Holy Spirit you may abound in **h**. Rom 15:13
I **h** to see you in passing as I go to Rom 15:24
should plow in **h** and the thresher 1 Cor 9:10
the thresher thresh in **h** of sharing in 1 Cor 9:10
So now faith, **h**, and love abide, these 1 Cor 13:13
I **h** to spend some time with you, if the 1 Cor 16:7
Our **h** for you is unshaken, for we 2 Cor 1:7
we have set our **h** that he will deliver 2 Cor 1:10
acknowledge and I **h** you will fully 2 Cor 1:13
Since we have such a **h**, we are very 2 Cor 3:12
and I **h** it is known also to your 2 Cor 5:11
But our **h** is that as your faith 2 Cor 10:15
I **h** you will find out that we have not 2 Cor 13:6
eagerly wait for the **h** of righteousness. Gal 5:5
were the first to **h** in Christ might be Eph 1:12
know what is the **h** to which he has Eph 1:18
having no **h** and without God in the Eph 2:12
called to the one **h** that belongs to your Eph 4:4
my eager expectation and **h** that I will Phil 1:20
I **h** in the Lord Jesus to send Timothy Phil 2:19
I **h** therefore to send him just as soon Phil 2:23
because of the **h** laid up for you in Col 1:5
not shifting from the **h** of the gospel Col 1:23
which is Christ in you, the **h** of glory. Col 1:27
and steadfastness of **h** in our Lord 1 Thes 1:3
For what is our **h** or joy or crown of 1 Thes 2:19
grieve as others do who have no **h**. 1 Thes 4:13
and for a helmet the **h** of salvation. 1 Thes 5:8
comfort and good **h** through grace, 2 Thes 2:16
our Savior and of Christ Jesus our **h**, 1 Tm 1:1
I **h** to come to you soon, but I am 1 Tm 3:14
because we have our **h** set on the 1 Tm 4:10
has set her **h** on God and continues in 1 Tm 5:5
in **h** of eternal life, which God, who never Ti 1:2
waiting for our blessed **h**, the appearing Ti 2:13
heirs according to the **h** of eternal life. Ti 3:7
confidence and our boasting in our **h**. Heb 3:6
the full assurance of **h** until the end, Heb 6:11
to hold fast to the **h** set before us. Heb 6:18
a **h** that enters into the inner place Heb 6:19
the other hand, a better **h** is introduced, Heb 7:19
confession of our **h** without wavering, Heb 10:23
to a living **h** through the resurrection 1 Pt 1:3
set your **h** fully on the grace that will 1 Pt 1:13
so that your faith and **h** are in God. 1 Pt 1:21
you for a reason for the **h** that is in you; 1 Pt 3:15
Instead I **h** to come to you and talk face 2 Jn 1:12
I **h** to see you soon, and we will talk 3 Jn 1:14

HOPED (9)
enemies of the Jews **h** to gain the mastery Est 9:1
But when I **h** for good, evil came, and Jb 30:26
rejoice, because I have **h** in your word. Ps 119:74
to those in whom we **h** and to whom we Is 20:6
But we had **h** that he was the one to Lk 24:21
the same time he **h** that money would Acts 24:26

in this life only we have **h** in Christ, 1 Cor 15:19
faith is the assurance of things **h** for, Heb 11:1
the holy women who **h** in God used to 1 Pt 3:5

HOPELESS (2)
your way, but you did not say, "It is **h**"; Is 57:10
But you said, 'It is **h**, for I have loved Jer 2:25

HOPES (7)
in extortion; set no vain **h** on robbery; Ps 62:10
to you, filling you with vain **h**. Jer 23:16
also, because its **h** are confounded. Zec 9:5
not hope. For who **h** for what he sees? Rom 8:24
believes all things, **h** all things, 1 Cor 13:7
nor to set their **h** on the uncertainty 1 Tm 6:17
everyone who thus **h** in him purifies 1 Jn 3:3

HOPHNI (5)
the two sons of Eli, **H** and Phinehas, 1 Sm 1:3
upon your two sons, **H** and Phinehas, 1 Sm 2:34
the two sons of Eli, **H** and Phinehas, 1 Sm 4:4
the two sons of Eli, **H** and Phinehas, 1 Sm 4:11
Your two sons also, **H** and Phinehas, 1 Sm 4:17

HOPHRA (1)
I will give Pharaoh **H** king of Egypt Jer 44:30

HOPING (2)
and he was **h** to see some sign done by Lk 23:8
for I am **h** that through your prayers Phlm 1:22

HOPPER (1)
that the swarming locust has eaten, the **h**, Jl 2:25

HOPPING (2)
locust left, the **h** locust has eaten, Jl 1:4
locust has eaten, and what the **h** locust left, Jl 1:4

HOR (12)
congregation, came to Mount **H**. Nm 20:22
said to Moses and Aaron at Mount **H**, Nm 20:23
son and bring them up to Mount **H**. Nm 20:25
they went up Mount **H** in the sight of Nm 20:27
From Mount **H** they set out by the way Nm 21:4
Kadesh and camped at Mount **H**, Nm 33:37
went up Mount **H** at the command Nm 33:38
years old when he died on Mount **H**. Nm 33:39
set out from Mount **H** and camped at Nm 33:41
Sea you shall draw a line to Mount **H**. Nm 34:7
From Mount **H** you shall draw a line to Nm 34:8
died in Mount **H** and was gathered Dt 32:50

HOR-HAGGIDGAD (2)
from Bene-jaakan and camped at **H**. Nm 33:32
they set out from **H** and camped at Nm 33:33

HORAM (1)
Then **H** king of Gezer came up to help Jos 10:33

HORDE (6)
"This **h** will now lick up all that is Nm 22:4
came out with all their troops, a great **h**, Jos 11:4
against this great **h** that is coming 2 Chr 20:12
do not be dismayed at this great **h**, 2 Chr 20:15
they looked toward the **h**, 2 Chr 20:24
Assyria and all the **h** that is with 2 Chr 32:7

HORDES (5)
Gomer and all his **h**; Beth-togarmah Ezk 38:6
north with all his **h**—many peoples are Ezk 38:6
covering the land, you and all your **h**, Ezk 38:9
upon him and his **h** and the many Ezk 38:22
you and all your **h** and the peoples who Ezk 39:4

HOREB (17)
west side of the wilderness and came to **H**, Ex 3:1
stand before you there on the rock at **H**, Ex 17:6
their ornaments, from Mount **H** onward. Ex 33:6
eleven days' journey from **H** by the way of Dt 1:2
"The LORD our God said to us in **H**, 'You Dt 1:6
we set out from **H** and went through all Dt 1:19
you stood before the LORD your God at **H**, Dt 4:10
LORD spoke to you at **H** out of the midst of Dt 4:15
our God made a covenant with us in **H**. Dt 5:2
Even at **H** you provoked the LORD to wrath, Dt 9:8
the LORD your God at **H** on the day of the Dt 18:16
that he had made with them at **H**. Dt 29:1
of stone that Moses put there at **H**, 1 Kgs 8:9
food forty days and forty nights to **H**, 1 Kgs 19:8
two tablets that Moses put there at **H**, 2 Chr 5:10
made a calf in **H** and worshiped a Ps 106:19
I commanded him at **H** for all Israel. Mal 4:4

HOREM (1)
Yiron, Migdal-el, **H**, Beth-anath, and Jos 19:38

HORESH (4)
was in the Wilderness of Ziph at **H**. 1 Sm 23:15
son, rose and went to David at **H**, 1 Sm 23:16
David remained at **H**, and Jonathan 1 Sm 23:18
among us in the strongholds at **H**, 1 Sm 23:19

HORI (3)
The sons of Lotan were **H** and Hemam; Gn 36:22
tribe of Simeon, Shaphat the son of **H**; Nm 13:5
The sons of Lotan: **H** and Hemam; 1 Chr 1:39

HORITE (1)
These are the sons of Seir the **H**, the Gn 36:20

HORITES (6)
and the **H** in their hill country of Seir as Gn 14:6
these are the chiefs of the **H**, the sons of Gn 36:21
These are the chiefs of the **H**: the chiefs Gn 36:29
these are the chiefs of the **H**, chief by Gn 36:30
The **H** also lived in Seir formerly, but the Dt 2:12
when he destroyed the **H** before them and Dt 2:22

HORMAH (9)
them and pursued them, even to **H**. Nm 14:45
So the name of the place was called **H**. Nm 21:3
do and beat you down in Seir as far as **H**. Dt 1:44
the king of **H**, one; the king of Arad, Jos 12:14
Eltolad, Chesil, **H**, Jos 15:30
Eltolad, Bethul, **H**, Jos 19:4
So the name of the city was called **H**. Jgs 1:17
in **H**, in Bor-ashan, in Athach, 1 Sm 30:30
Bethuel, **H**, Ziklag, 1 Chr 4:30

HORN (37)
they make a long blast with the ram's **h**, Jos 6:5
king over Israel? Fill your **h** with oil, 1 Sm 16:1
Then Samuel took the **h** of oil and 1 Sm 16:13
shouting and with the sound of the **h**. 2 Sm 6:15
my shield, and the **h** of my salvation, 2 Sm 22:3
the priest took the **h** of oil from the 1 Kgs 1:39
with shouting, to the sound of the **h**, 1 Chr 15:28
my shield, and the **h** of my salvation, Ps 18:2
and to the wicked, 'Do not lift up your **h**; Ps 75:4
do not lift up your **h** on high, or speak Ps 75:5
strength; by your favor our **h** is exalted. Ps 89:17
and in my name shall his **h** be exalted. Ps 89:24
you have exalted my **h** like that of the Ps 92:10
the sound of the **h** make a joyful noise Ps 98:6
forever; his **h** is exalted in honor. Ps 112:9
I will make a **h** to sprout for David; Ps 132:17
He has raised up a **h** for his people, Ps 148:14
The **h** of Moab is cut off, and his arm is Jer 48:25
day I will cause a **h** to spring up for Ezk 29:21
that when you hear the sound of the **h**, Dn 3:5
all the peoples heard the sound of the **h**, Dn 3:7
every man who hears the sound of the **h**, Dn 3:10
ready when you hear the sound of the **h**, Dn 3:15
there came up among them another **h**, Dn 7:8
in this **h** were eyes like the eyes of a man, Dn 7:8
the great words that the **h** was speaking. Dn 7:11
and the other **h** that came up and before Dn 7:20
the **h** that had eyes and a mouth that Dn 7:20
this **h** made war with the saints and Dn 7:21
had a conspicuous **h** between his eyes. Dn 8:5
he was strong, the great **h** was broken, Dn 8:8
Out of one of them came a little **h**, which Dn 8:9
And the great **h** between his eyes is the Dn 8:21
As for the **h** that was broken, in place of Dn 8:22
Blow the **h** in Gibeah, the trumpet in Hos 5:8
of Zion, for I will make your **h** iron, Mi 4:13
and has raised up a **h** of salvation for us Lk 1:69

HORNET (1)
And I sent the **h** before you, which Jos 24:12

HORNETS (2)
And I will send **h** before you, which Ex 23:28
LORD your God will send **h** among them, Dt 7:20

HORNS (69)
a ram, caught in a thicket by his **h**. Gn 22:13
And you shall make **h** for it on its four Ex 27:2
its **h** shall be of one piece with it, and Ex 27:2
and put it on the **h** of the altar with Ex 29:12
height. Its **h** shall be of one piece with it. Ex 30:2
its top and around its sides and its **h**. Ex 30:3
make atonement on its **h** once a year. Ex 30:10
its height. Its **h** were of one piece with it. Ex 37:25
its top and around its sides and its **h**. Ex 37:26
He made **h** for it on its four corners. Its Ex 38:2
Its **h** were of one piece with it, and he Ex 38:2
of the blood on the **h** of the altar of Lv 4:7
of the blood on the **h** of the altar that is Lv 4:18
and put it on the **h** of the altar of burnt Lv 4:25
and put it on the **h** of the altar of burnt Lv 4:30
and put it on the **h** of the altar of burnt Lv 4:34
finger put it on the **h** of the altar around Lv 8:15
and put it on the **h** of the altar and poured Lv 9:9
and put it on the **h** of the altar all Lv 16:18
is for them like the **h** of the wild ox. Nm 23:22
and is for him like the **h** of the wild ox; Nm 24:8
and his **h** are the horns of a wild ox; Dt 33:17
and his horns are the **h** of a wild ox; Dt 33:17
seven trumpets of rams' **h** before the ark. Jos 6:4
seven trumpets of rams' **h** before the ark Jos 6:6
seven trumpets of rams' **h** before the LORD Jos 6:8
seven trumpets of rams' **h** before the ark Jos 6:13
and took hold of the **h** of the altar. 1 Kgs 1:50
he has laid hold of the **h** of the altar, 1 Kgs 1:51
and caught hold of the **h** of the altar. 1 Kgs 2:28
made for himself **h** of iron and 1 Kgs 22:11
and with trumpets and with **h**. 2 Chr 15:14
made for himself **h** of iron and 2 Chr 18:10
rescued me from the **h** of the wild oxen! Ps 22:21
than an ox or a bull with **h** and hoofs. Ps 69:31
All the **h** of the wicked I will cut off, but Ps 75:10
but the **h** of the righteous shall be lifted Ps 75:10
with cords, up to the **h** of the altar! Ps 118:27
their heart, and on the **h** of their altars, Jer 17:1
and thrust at all the weak with your **h**, Ezk 34:21
hearth projecting upward, four **h**. Ezk 43:15
put it on the four **h** of the altar and on Ezk 43:20
that were before it, and it had ten **h**. Dn 7:7
I considered the **h**, and behold, there Dn 7:8
three of the first **h** were plucked up by Dn 7:8
and about the ten **h** that were on its Dn 7:20
As for the ten **h**, out of this kingdom ten Dn 7:24
It had two **h**, and both horns were high, Dn 8:3
It had two horns, and both **h** were high, Dn 8:3
He came to the ram with the two **h**, Dn 8:6
and struck the ram and broke his two **h**. Dn 8:7
up four conspicuous **h** toward the four Dn 8:8
for the ram that you saw with the two **h**, Dn 8:20
and the **h** of the altar shall be cut off Am 3:14
my eyes and saw, and behold, four **h**! Zec 1:18
"These are the **h** that have scattered Zec 1:19
"These are the **h** that scattered Judah, Zec 1:21
to cast down the **h** of the nations who Zec 1:21
who lifted up their **h** against the land of Zec 1:21
slain, with seven **h** and with seven eyes, Rv 5:6
voice from the four **h** of the golden altar Rv 9:13
red dragon, with seven heads and ten **h**, Rv 12:3
of the sea, with ten **h** and seven heads, Rv 13:1
diadems on its **h** and blasphemous Rv 13:1
It had two **h** like a lamb and it spoke Rv 13:11
names, and it had seven heads and ten **h**. Rv 17:3
seven heads and ten **h** that carries her. Rv 17:7
And the ten **h** that you saw are ten Rv 17:12
And the ten **h** that you saw, they and Rv 17:16

HORONAIM (4)
on the road to **H** they raise a cry of Is 15:5
A cry from **H**, 'Desolation and great Jer 48:3
at the descent of **H** they have heard the Jer 48:5
from Zoar to **H** and Eglath-shelishiyah. Jer 48:34

HORONITE (3)
But when Sanballat the **H** and Tobiah, Neh 2:10
when Sanballat the **H** and Tobiah the Neh 2:19
was the son-in-law of Sanballat the **H**. Neh 13:28

HORRIBLE (4)
An appalling and **h** thing has happened Jer 5:30
virgin Israel has done a very **h** thing. Jer 18:13
of Jerusalem I have seen a **h** thing: Jer 23:14
the house of Israel I have seen a **h** thing; Hos 6:10

HORRIFIED (3)
passes by it is **h** and shakes his head. Jer 18:16
by it will be **h** and will hiss because Jer 19:8
by it will be **h** and will hiss because Jer 49:17

HORROR (29)
you shall be a **h** to all the kingdoms Dt 28:25
And you shall become a **h**, a proverb, Dt 28:37
and he has made them an object of **h**, 2 Chr 29:8
at his day, and **h** seizes them of the east. Jb 18:20
come upon me, and **h** overwhelms me. Ps 55:5
shun me; you have made me a **h** to them. Ps 88:8
My heart staggers; **h** has appalled me; the Is 21:4
I will make them a **h** to all the kingdoms Jer 15:4
making their land a **h**, a thing to be Jer 18:16
And I will make this city a **h**, a thing to Jer 19:8
I will make them a **h** to all the kingdoms Jer 24:9
them to destruction, and make them a **h**, Jer 25:9
will make them a **h** to all the kingdoms Jer 29:18
I will make you a **h** to all the kingdoms Jer 34:17
You shall become an execration, a **h**, a Jer 42:18
and they shall become an oath, a **h**, Jer 44:12
a derision and a **h** to all that are Jer 48:39
the LORD, that Bozrah shall become a **h**, Jer 49:13
The **h** you inspire has deceived you, Jer 49:16
"Edom shall become a **h**. Everyone Jer 49:17
has become a **h** among the nations! Jer 50:23
the haunt of jackals, a **h** and a hissing, Jer 51:37
has become a **h** among the nations! Jer 51:41
Her cities have become a **h**, a land of Jer 51:43
and a taunt, a warning and a **h**, Ezk 5:15
put on sackcloth, and **h** covers them. Ezk 7:18
A cup of **h** and desolation, the cup of Ezk 23:33
the hair of their kings bristles with **h**; Ezk 27:35
shall bristle with **h** because of you, Ezk 32:10

HORSE (40)
the **h** and his rider he has thrown into Ex 15:1

the **h** and his rider he has thrown into Ex 15:21
600 shekels of silver and a **h** for 150, 1 Kgs 10:29
Syria escaped on a **h** with horsemen. 1 Kgs 20:20
army that you have lost, **h** for horse, 1 Kgs 20:25
army that you have lost, horse for **h**, 1 Kgs 20:25
600 shekels of silver, and a **h** for 150. 2 Chr 1:17
the entrance of the **h** gate of the 2 Chr 23:15
Above the **H** Gate the priests repaired, Neh 3:28
worn, and the **h** that the king has ridden, Est 6:8
let the robes and the **h** be handed over to Est 6:9
lead him on the **h** through the square of Est 6:9
take the robes and the **h**, as you have Est 6:10
So Haman took the robes and the **h**, and Est 6:11
to flee, she laughs at the **h** and his rider. Jb 39:18
"Do you give the **h** his might? Do you Jb 39:19
Be not like a **h** or a mule, without Ps 32:9
The war **h** is a false hope for salvation, Ps 33:17
of Jacob, both rider and **h** lay stunned. Ps 76:6
delight is not in the strength of the **h**, Ps 147:10
The **h** is made ready for the day of Prv 21:31
A whip for the **h**, a bridle for the Prv 26:3
who brings forth chariot and **h**, army Is 43:17
Like a **h** in the desert, they did not Is 63:13
like a **h** plunging headlong into battle. Jer 8:6
the corner of the **H** Gate toward the east, Jer 31:40
I break in pieces the **h** and his rider; Jer 51:21
shall he who rides the **h** save his life; Am 2:15
galloping **h** and bounding chariot! Na 3:2
and behold, a man riding on a red **h**! Zec 1:8
and the war **h** from Jerusalem; Zec 9:10
LORD, I will strike every **h** with panic, Zec 12:4
when I strike every **h** of the peoples with Zec 12:4
And I looked, and behold, a white **h**! And Rv 6:2
And out came another **h**, bright red. Its Rv 6:4
And I looked, and behold, a black **h**! And Rv 6:5
And I looked, and behold, a pale **h**! And Rv 6:8
heaven opened, and behold, a white **h**! Rv 19:11
was sitting on the **h** and against his Rv 19:19
mouth of him who was sitting on the **h**, Rv 19:21

HORSE'S (2)
that bites the **h** heels so that his rider Gn 49:17
the winepress, as high as a **h** bridle, Rv 14:20

HORSEBACK (1)
So a man on **h** went to meet him and 2 Kgs 9:18

HORSEMAN (3)
"Take a **h** and send to meet them, 2 Kgs 9:17
Then he sent out a second **h**, who 2 Kgs 9:19
At the noise of **h** and archer every city Jer 4:29

HORSEMEN (56)
went up with him both chariots and **h**. Gn 50:9
and chariots and his **h** and his army, Ex 14:9
and all his host, his chariots, and his **h**. Ex 14:17
over Pharaoh, his chariots, and his **h**." Ex 14:18
horses, his chariots, and his **h**. Ex 14:23
upon their chariots, and upon their **h**." Ex 14:26
and covered the chariots and the **h**; Ex 14:28
his chariots and his **h** went into the sea, Ex 15:19
fathers with chariots and **h** to the Red Jos 24:6
and to be his **h** and to run before 1 Sm 8:11
and six thousand **h** and troops like 1 Sm 13:5
the chariots and the **h** were close upon 2 Sm 1:6
And David took from him 1,700 **h**, and 2 Sm 8:4
men of 700 chariots, and 40,000 **h**, 2 Sm 10:18
he prepared for himself chariots and **h**, 1 Kgs 1:5
horses for his chariots, and 12,000 **h**. 1 Kgs 4:26
his chariots, and the cities for his **h**, 1 Kgs 9:19
his chariot commanders and his **h**. 1 Kgs 9:22
gathered together chariots and **h**. 1 Kgs 10:26
He had 1,400 chariots and 12,000 **h**, 1 Kgs 10:26
of Syria escaped on a horse with **h**. 1 Kgs 20:20
of Israel and its **h**!" And he saw him 2 Kgs 2:12
So they took two **h**, and the king sent 2 Kgs 7:14
of more than fifty **h** and ten chariots 2 Kgs 13:7
The chariots of Israel and its **h**!" 2 Kgs 13:14
in Egypt for chariots and for **h**? 2 Kgs 18:24
7,000 **h**, and 20,000 foot soldiers. 1 Chr 18:4
chariots and **h** from Mesopotamia, 1 Chr 19:6
gathered together chariots and **h**. 2 Chr 1:14
He had 1,400 chariots and 12,000 **h**, 2 Chr 1:14
for his chariots and the cities for his **h**, 2 Chr 8:6
of his chariots, and his **h**. 2 Chr 8:9
for horses and chariots, and 12,000 **h**, 2 Chr 9:25
with 1,200 chariots and 60,000 **h**. 2 Chr 12:3
with very many chariots and **h**? 2 Chr 16:8
band of soldiers and **h** to protect us Ezr 8:22
sent with me officers of the army and **h**. Neh 2:9
When he sees riders, **h** in pairs, riders on Is 21:7
riders, **h** in pairs!" And he answered, Is 21:9
bore the quiver with chariots and **h**, Is 22:6
and the **h** took their stand at the gates. Is 22:7
are many and in **h** because they are very Is 31:1
you trust in Egypt for chariots and for **h**? Is 36:9
Harness the horses; mount, O **h**! Take Jer 46:4
young men, **h** riding on horses. Ezk 23:6
in full armor, **h** riding on horses, Ezk 23:12
and with **h** and a host of many soldiers. Ezk 26:7
the noise of the **h** and wagons and Ezk 26:10
out, and all your army, horses and **h**, Ezk 38:4
like a whirlwind, with chariots and **h**, Dn 11:40
sword or by war or by horses or by **h**." Hos 1:7
H charging, flashing sword and Na 3:3
wolves; their **h** press proudly on. Hab 1:8
Their **h** come from afar; they fly like an Hab 1:8
with seventy **h** and two hundred Acts 23:23
letting the **h** go on with him. Acts 23:32

HORSES (112)
gave them food in exchange for the **h**, Gn 47:17
your livestock that are in the field, the **h**, Ex 9:3
all Pharaoh's **h** and chariots and his Ex 14:9
the midst of the sea, all Pharaoh's **h**, Ex 14:23
For when the **h** of Pharaoh with his Ex 15:19
of Egypt, to their **h** and to their chariots, Dt 11:4
not acquire many **h** for himself or Dt 17:16
to Egypt in order to acquire many **h**, Dt 17:16
and see **h** and chariots and an army Dt 20:1
with very many **h** and chariots. Jos 11:4
shall hamstring their **h** and burn their Jos 11:6
he hamstrung their **h** and burned their Jos 11:9
all the chariot **h** but left enough 2 Sm 8:4
Absalom got himself a chariot and **h**, 2 Sm 15:1
had 40,000 stalls of **h** for his chariots, 1 Kgs 4:26
and straw for the **h** and swift steeds 1 Kgs 4:28
myrrh, spices, **h**, and mules, 1 Kgs 10:25
Solomon's import of **h** was from 1 Kgs 10:28
grass and save the **h** and mules alive, 1 Kgs 18:5
were with him, and **h** and chariots. 1 Kgs 20:1
out and struck the **h** and chariots, 1 Kgs 20:21
as your people, my **h** as your horses." 1 Kgs 22:4
as your people, my horses as your **h**." 1 Kgs 22:4
chariots of fire and **h** of fire separated 2 Kgs 2:11
as your people, my **h** as your horses." 2 Kgs 3:7
as your people, my horses as your **h**." 2 Kgs 3:7
came with his **h** and chariots and 2 Kgs 5:9
So he sent there **h** and chariots and a 2 Kgs 6:14
an army with **h** and chariots was all 2 Kgs 6:15
was full of **h** and chariots of 2 Kgs 6:17
hear the sound of chariots and of **h**, 2 Kgs 7:6
and abandoned their tents, their **h**, 2 Kgs 7:7
nothing but the **h** tied and the 2 Kgs 7:10
men take five of the remaining **h**, 2 Kgs 7:13
spattered on the wall and on the **h**, 2 Kgs 9:33
there are with you chariots and **h**, 2 Kgs 10:2
And they brought him on **h**; and he 2 Kgs 14:20
I will give you two thousand **h**, if 2 Kgs 18:23
And he removed the **h** that the kings 2 Kgs 23:11
David hamstrung all the chariot **h**, 1 Chr 18:4
Solomon's import of **h** was from 2 Chr 1:16
myrrh, spices, **h**, and mules, 2 Chr 9:24
had 4,000 stalls for **h** and chariots, 2 Chr 9:25
And **h** were imported for Solomon 2 Chr 9:28
And they brought him upon **h**, and 2 Chr 25:28
Their **h** were 736, their mules were 245, Ezr 2:66
Their **h** were 736, their mules 245, Neh 7:68
couriers riding on swift **h** that were used Est 8:10
mounted on their swift **h** that were used Est 8:14
Some trust in chariots and some in **h**, Ps 20:7
I have seen slaves on **h**, and princes Eccl 10:7
their land is filled with **h**, and there is no Is 2:7
drives his cart wheel over it with his **h**, Is 28:28
We will flee upon **h**"; therefore you shall Is 30:16
go down to Egypt for help and rely on **h**, Is 31:1
man, and not God, and their **h** are flesh, Is 31:3
I will give you two thousand **h**, if you are Is 36:8
on **h** and in chariots and in litters and Is 66:20
his **h** are swifter than eagles—woe to us, Jer 4:13
they ride on **h**, set in array as a man for Jer 6:23
"The snorting of their **h** is heard from Jer 8:16
you, how will you compete with **h**? Jer 12:5
of David, riding in chariots and on **h**, Jer 17:25
of David, riding in chariots and on **h**, Jer 22:4
Harness the **h**; mount, O horsemen! Jer 46:4
Advance, O **h**, and rage, O chariots! Let Jer 46:9
A sword against her **h** and against her Jer 50:37
they ride on **h**, arrayed as a man for Jer 50:42
her; bring up **h** like bristling locusts. Jer 51:27
they might give him **h** and a large Ezk 17:15
young men, horsemen riding on **h**. Ezk 23:6
in full armor, horsemen riding on **h**, Ezk 23:12
and whose issue was like that of **h**. Ezk 23:20
of renown, all of them riding on **h**. Ezk 23:23
king of kings, with **h** and chariots, Ezk 26:7
His **h** will be so many that their dust Ezk 26:10
the hoofs of his **h** he will trample all Ezk 26:11
Beth-togarmah they exchanged **h**, Ezk 27:14
they exchanged horses, war **h**, Ezk 27:14
and all your army, **h** and horsemen, Ezk 38:4
with you, all of them riding on **h**, Ezk 38:15
at my table with **h** and charioteers, Ezk 39:20
or by war or by **h** or by horsemen." Hos 1:7
shall not save us; we will not ride on **h**; Hos 14:3
appearance is like the appearance of **h**, Jl 2:4
of horses, and like war **h** they run. Jl 2:4
the sword, and carried away your **h**, Am 4:10
Do **h** run on rocks? Does one plow Am 6:12
will cut off your **h** from among you and Mi 5:10
Their **h** are swifter than leopards, more Hab 1:8
the sea, when you rode on your **h**, Hab 3:8
You trampled the sea with your **h**, the Hab 3:15
And the **h** and their riders shall go Hg 2:22
behind him were red, sorrel, and white **h**. Zec 1:8
The first chariot had red **h**, the second Zec 6:2
had red horses, the second black **h**, Zec 6:2
the third white **h**, and the fourth chariot Zec 6:3
the fourth chariot dappled **h**—all of Zec 6:3
chariot with the black **h** goes toward the Zec 6:6
When the strong **h** came out, they were Zec 6:7
they shall put to shame the riders on **h**. Zec 10:5
like this plague shall fall on the **h**, Zec 14:15
shall be inscribed on the bells of the **h**, Zec 14:20
into the mouths of **h** so that they obey Jas 3:3
the locusts were like **h** prepared for battle: Rv 9:7
many chariots with **h** rushing into battle. Rv 9:9
is how I saw the **h** in my vision and Rv 9:17
the heads of the **h** were like lions' heads, Rv 9:17
For the power of the **h** is in their mouths Rv 9:19
wheat, cattle and sheep, **h** and chariots, Rv 18:13
pure, were following him on white **h**. Rv 19:14
men, the flesh of **h** and their riders, Rv 19:18

HORSES' (3)
"Then loud beat the **h** hoofs with the Jgs 5:22
went through the **h** entrance to the 2 Kgs 11:16
bows bent, their **h** hoofs seem like flint, Is 5:28

HOSAH (5)
Then the boundary turns to **H**, and it Jos 19:29
and **H** were to be gatekeepers. 1 Chr 16:38
And **H**, of the sons of Merari, had 1 Chr 26:10
and brothers of **H** were thirteen. 1 Chr 26:11
For Shuppim and **H** it came out for 1 Chr 26:16

HOSANNA (6)
were shouting, "**H** to the Son of David! Mt 21:9
the name of the Lord! **H** in the highest!" Mt 21:9
"**H** to the Son of David!" they were Mt 21:15
"**H**! Blessed is he who comes in the Mk 11:9
of our father David! **H** in the highest!" Mk 11:10
"**H**! Blessed is he who comes in the Jn 12:13

HOSEA (4)
The word of the LORD that came to **H**, the Hos 1:1
When the LORD first spoke through **H**, Hos 1:2
spoke through Hosea, the LORD said to **H**, Hos 1:2
As indeed he says in **H**, "Those who Rom 9:25

HOSHAIAH (3)
And after them went **H** and half of the Neh 12:32
son of Kareah and Jezaniah the son of **H**, Jer 42:1
Azariah the son of **H** and Johanan the Jer 43:2

HOSHAMA (1)
Jekamiah, **H** and Nedabiah; 1 Chr 3:18

HOSHEA (12)
the tribe of Ephraim, **H** the son of Nun; Nm 13:8
And Moses called **H** the son of Nun Nm 13:16
Then **H** the son of Elah made a 2 Kgs 15:30
H the son of Elah began to reign in 2 Kgs 17:1
And **H** became his vassal and paid 2 Kgs 17:3
king of Assyria found treachery in **H**, 2 Kgs 17:4
In the ninth year of **H**, the king of 2 Kgs 17:6
In the third year of **H** son of Elah, 2 Kgs 18:1
was the seventh year of **H** son of Elah, 2 Kgs 18:9
the ninth year of **H** king of Israel, 2 Kgs 18:10
Ephraimites, **H** the son of Azaziah; 1 Chr 27:20
H, Hananiah, Hasshub, Neh 10:23

HOSPITABLE (2)
respectable, **h**, able to teach, 1 Tm 3:2
but **h**, a lover of good, self-controlled, Ti 1:8

HOSPITABLY (1)
us and entertained us **h** for three days. Acts 28:7

HOSPITALITY (4)
of the saints and seek to show **h**. Rom 12:13
brought up children, has shown **h**, 1 Tm 5:10
Do not neglect to show **h** to strangers, Heb 13:2
Show **h** to one another without 1 Pt 4:9

HOST (59)
earth were finished, and all the **h** of them. Gn 2:1
will get glory over Pharaoh and all his **h**, Ex 14:4
get glory over Pharaoh and all his **h**, Ex 14:17
was going before the **h** of Israel moved Ex 14:19
coming between the **h** of Egypt and the Ex 14:20
the host of Egypt and the **h** of Israel. Ex 14:20
of all the **h** of Pharaoh that had Ex 14:28
chariots and his **h** he cast into Ex 15:4

moon and the stars, all the **h** of heaven, Dt 4:19
or the moon or any of the **h** of heaven, Dt 17:3
LORD has given the **h** of Midian into Jgs 7:15
encampment as the **h** was going out 1 Sm 17:20
dead bodies of the **h** of the Philistines 1 Sm 17:46
Joab and all the **h** of the mighty men. 2 Sm 10:7
and all the **h** of heaven standing 1 Kgs 22:19
worshiped all the **h** of heaven and 2 Kgs 17:16
worshiped all the **h** of heaven and 2 Kgs 21:3
altars for all the **h** of heaven in the 2 Kgs 21:5
Asherah, and for all the **h** of heaven. 2 Kgs 23:4
and all the **h** of the heavens. 2 Kgs 23:5
and all the **h** of heaven standing on 2 Chr 18:18
worshiped all the **h** of heaven and 2 Chr 33:3
altars for all the **h** of heaven in the 2 Chr 33:5
the heaven of heavens, with all their **h**, Neh 9:6
them; and the **h** of heaven worships you. Neh 9:6
by the breath of his mouth all their **h**. Ps 33:6
who announce the news are a great **h**: Ps 68:11
leading a **h** of captives in your train Ps 68:18
Pharaoh and his **h** in the Red Ps 136:15
LORD of hosts is mustering a **h** for battle. Is 13:4
the LORD will punish the **h** of heaven, Is 24:21
nations, and furious against all their **h**; Is 34:2
All the **h** of heaven shall rot away, and Is 34:4
roll up like a scroll. All their **h** shall fall, Is 34:4
He who brings out their **h** by number, Is 40:26
heavens, and I commanded all their **h**. Is 45:12
sun and the moon and all the **h** of heaven, Jer 8:2
have been offered to all the **h** of heaven, Jer 19:13
As the **h** of heaven cannot be Jer 33:22
and wagons and a **h** of peoples. Ezk 23:24
"Bring up a vast **h** against them, and Ezk 23:46
And the **h** shall stone them and cut Ezk 23:47
horsemen and a **h** of many soldiers. Ezk 26:7
net over you with a **h** of many peoples, Ezk 32:3
of them clothed in full armor, a great **h**, Ezk 38:4
all of them riding on horses, a great **h**, Ezk 38:15
his will among the **h** of heaven and Dn 4:35
It grew great, even to the **h** of heaven. Dn 8:10
And some of the **h** and some of the stars Dn 8:10
even as great as the Prince of the **h**. Dn 8:11
And a **h** will be given over to it together Dn 8:12
of the sanctuary and **h** to be trampled Dn 8:13
The exiles of this **h** of the people of Israel Ob 1:20
down on the roofs to the **h** of the heavens, Zep 1:5
of the heavenly **h** praising God and Lk 2:13
so that when your **h** comes he may say Lk 14:10
them over to worship the **h** of heaven, Acts 7:42
who is **h** to me and to the whole Rom 16:23
ascended on high he led a **h** of captives, Eph 4:8

HOSTAGES (2)
of the king's house, also **h**, 2 Kgs 14:14
of the king's house, also **h**, 2 Chr 25:24

HOSTILE (2)
mind that is set on the flesh is **h** to God, Rom 8:7
who once were alienated and **h** in mind, Col 1:21

HOSTILITY (5)
me; I am spent by the **h** of your hand. Ps 39:10
jealousy, anger, **h**, slander, 2 Cor 12:20
down in his flesh the dividing wall of **h** Eph 2:14
the cross, thereby killing the **h**. Eph 2:16
from sinners such **h** against himself, Heb 12:3

HOSTS (296)
Israel from the land of Egypt by their **h**." Ex 6:26
lay my hand on Egypt and bring my **h**, Ex 7:4
day I brought your **h** out of the land Ex 12:17
all the **h** of the LORD went out from the Ex 12:41
out of the land of Egypt by their **h**. Ex 12:51
to sacrifice to the LORD of **h** at Shiloh, 1 Sm 1:3
vowed a vow and said, "O LORD of **h**, 1 Sm 1:11
the ark of the covenant of the LORD of **h**, 1 Sm 4:4
Thus says the LORD of **h**, 'I have noted 1 Sm 15:2
to you in the name of the LORD of **h**, 1 Sm 17:45
and greater, for the LORD, the God of **h**, 2 Sm 5:10
of the LORD of **h** who sits enthroned on 2 Sm 6:2
the people in the name of the LORD of **h** 2 Sm 6:18
David, 'Thus says the LORD of **h**, 2 Sm 7:8
'The LORD of **h** is God over Israel,' 2 Sm 7:26
For you, O LORD of **h**, the God of Israel, 2 Sm 7:27
Elijah said, "As the LORD of **h** lives, 1 Kgs 18:15
jealous for the LORD, the God of **h**. 1 Kgs 19:10
jealous for the LORD, the God of **h**. 1 Kgs 19:14
Elisha said, "As the LORD of **h** lives, 2 Kgs 3:14
for the LORD of **h** was with him. 1 Chr 11:9
David, 'Thus says the LORD of **h**, 1 Chr 17:7
forever, saying, 'The LORD of **h**, 1 Chr 17:24
The LORD of **h**, he is the King of glory! Ps 24:10
The LORD of **h** is with us; the God of Ps 46:7
The LORD of **h** is with us; the God of Ps 46:11
have we seen in the city of the LORD of **h**, Ps 48:8
You, LORD God of **h**, are God of Israel. Ps 59:5
to shame through me, O Lord GOD of **h**; Ps 69:6
O LORD God of **h**, how long will you be Ps 80:4
Restore us, O God of **h**; let your face Ps 80:7
Turn again, O God of **h**! Look down Ps 80:14
Restore us, O LORD God of **h**! let your Ps 80:19
is your dwelling place, O LORD of **h**! Ps 84:1
her young, at your altars, O LORD of **h**, Ps 84:3
O LORD God of **h**, hear my prayer; give Ps 84:8
O LORD of **h**, blessed is the one who Ps 84:12
O LORD God of **h**, who is mighty as you Ps 89:8
Bless the LORD, all his **h**, his ministers, Ps 103:21
all his angels; praise him, all his **h**! Ps 148:2
If the LORD of **h** had not left us a few Is 1:9
Therefore the Lord declares, the LORD of **h**, Is 1:24
For the LORD of **h** has a day against all Is 2:12
the Lord GOD of **h** is taking away from Is 3:1
of the poor?" declares the Lord GOD of **h**. Is 3:15
vineyard of the LORD of **h** is the house of Is 5:7
The LORD of **h** has sworn in my hearing: Is 5:9
But the LORD of **h** is exalted in justice, and Is 5:16
they have rejected the law of the LORD of **h**, Is 5:24
and said: "Holy, holy, holy is the LORD of **h**; Is 6:3
my eyes have seen the King, the LORD of **h**!" Is 6:5
But the LORD of **h**, him you shall regard as Is 8:13
and portents in Israel from the LORD of **h**, Is 8:18
The zeal of the LORD of **h** will do this. Is 9:7
struck them, nor inquire of the LORD of **h**. Is 9:13
of the LORD of **h** the land is scorched, Is 9:19
the Lord GOD of **h** will send wasting Is 10:16
For the Lord GOD of **h** will make a full Is 10:23
Therefore thus says the Lord GOD of **h**: Is 10:24
And the LORD of **h** will wield against Is 10:26
the Lord GOD of **h** will lop the boughs Is 10:33
The LORD of **h** is mustering a host for Is 13:4
wrath of the LORD of **h** in the day of his Is 13:13
up against them," declares the LORD of **h**, Is 14:22
of destruction," declares the LORD of **h**. Is 14:23
The LORD of **h** has sworn: "As I have Is 14:24
For the LORD of **h** has purposed, and who Is 14:27
children of Israel, declares the LORD of **h**. Is 17:3
to the LORD of **h** from a people tall Is 18:7
the place of the name of the LORD of **h**. Is 18:7
over them, declares the Lord GOD of **h**. Is 19:4
what the LORD of **h** has purposed against Is 19:12
that the LORD of **h** shakes over them. Is 19:16
that the LORD of **h** has purposed against Is 19:17
and swear allegiance to the LORD of **h**. Is 19:18
witness to the LORD of **h** in the land of Is 19:20
whom the LORD of **h** has blessed, saying, Is 19:25
what I have heard from the LORD of **h**, Is 21:10
For the Lord GOD of **h** has a day of tumult Is 22:5
the Lord GOD of **h** called for weeping and Is 22:12
The LORD of **h** has revealed himself in Is 22:14
until you die," says the Lord GOD of **h**. Is 22:14
Thus says the Lord GOD of **h**, "Come, go Is 22:15
In that day, declares the LORD of **h**, the Is 22:25
The LORD of **h** has purposed it, to defile the Is 23:9
for the LORD of **h** reigns on Mount Zion Is 24:23
mountain the LORD of **h** will make for all Is 25:6
that day the LORD of **h** will be a crown of Is 28:5
the Lord GOD of **h** against the whole Is 28:22
This also comes from the LORD of **h**; he Is 28:29
by the LORD of **h** with thunder and with Is 29:6
so the LORD of **h** will come down to fight Is 31:4
so the LORD of **h** will protect Jerusalem; Is 31:5
"O LORD of **h**, God of Israel, who is Is 37:16
The zeal of the LORD of **h** will do this. Is 37:32
Hezekiah, "Hear the word of the LORD of **h**: Is 39:5
of Israel and his Redeemer, the LORD of **h**: Is 44:6
for price or reward," says the LORD of **h**. Is 45:13
Redeemer—the LORD of **h** is his name— Is 47:4
God of Israel; the LORD of **h** is his name. Is 48:2
waves roar—the LORD of **h** is his name. Is 51:15
your husband, the LORD of **h** is his name; Is 54:5
is not in you, declares the Lord GOD of **h**. Jer 2:19
thus says the LORD, the God of **h**: Jer 5:14
For thus says the LORD of **h**: "Cut down Jer 6:6
Thus says the LORD of **h**: "They shall Jer 6:9
Thus says the LORD of **h**, the God of Israel: Jer 7:3
Thus says the LORD of **h**, the God of Jer 7:21
I have driven them, declares the LORD of **h**. Jer 8:3
Therefore thus says the LORD of **h**: Jer 9:7
Therefore thus says the LORD of **h**, the Jer 9:15
Thus says the LORD of **h**: "Consider, and Jer 9:17
inheritance; the LORD of **h** is his name. Jer 10:16
The LORD of **h**, who planted you, has Jer 11:17
But, O LORD of **h**, who judges Jer 11:20
therefore thus says the LORD of **h**: Jer 11:22
called by your name, O LORD, God of **h**. Jer 15:16
For thus says the LORD of **h**, the God of Jer 16:9
Thus says the LORD of **h**, the God of Jer 19:3
say to them, 'Thus says the LORD of **h**: Jer 19:11
"Thus says the LORD of **h**, the God of Jer 19:15
O LORD of **h**, who tests the righteous, Jer 20:12
the LORD of **h** concerning the prophets: Jer 23:15
Thus says the LORD of **h**: "Do not listen Jer 23:16
words of the living God, the LORD of **h**, Jer 23:36
"Therefore thus says the LORD of **h**: Jer 25:8
say to them, 'Thus says the LORD of **h**, Jer 25:27
say to them, 'Thus says the LORD of **h**: Jer 25:28
of the earth, declares the LORD of **h**.' Jer 25:29
"Thus says the LORD of **h**: Behold, Jer 25:32
'Thus says the LORD of **h**, "'Zion shall Jer 26:18
'Thus says the LORD of **h**, the God of Jer 27:4
let them intercede with the LORD of **h**, Jer 27:18
the LORD of **h** concerning the pillars, Jer 27:19
thus says the LORD of **h**, the God of Jer 27:21
"Thus says the LORD of **h**, the God of Jer 28:2
For thus says the LORD of **h**, the God of Jer 28:14
"Thus says the LORD of **h**, the God of Jer 29:4
For thus says the LORD of **h**, the God of Jer 29:8
'Thus says the LORD of **h**, behold, I am Jer 29:17
'Thus says the LORD of **h**, the God of Jer 29:21
"Thus says the LORD of **h**, the God of Jer 29:25
pass in that day, declares the LORD of **h**, Jer 30:8
Thus says the LORD of **h**, the God of Jer 31:23
waves roar—the LORD of **h** is his name: Jer 31:35
'Thus says the LORD of **h**, the God of Jer 32:14
For thus says the LORD of **h**, the God of Jer 32:15
God, whose name is the LORD of **h**, Jer 32:18
"'Give thanks to the LORD of **h**, for the Jer 33:11
"Thus says the LORD of **h**: In this place Jer 33:12
"Thus says the LORD of **h**, the God of Jer 35:13
thus says the LORD, the God of **h**, Jer 35:17
said, "Thus says the LORD of **h**, Jer 35:18
therefore thus says the LORD of **h**, the Jer 35:19
"Thus says the LORD, the God of **h**, Jer 38:17
the Ethiopian, 'Thus says the LORD of **h**, Jer 39:16
Thus says the LORD of **h**, the God of Jer 42:15
"For thus says the LORD of **h**, the God of Jer 42:18
say to them, 'Thus says the LORD of **h**, Jer 43:10
"Thus says the LORD of **h**, the God of Jer 44:2
And now thus says the LORD God of **h**, Jer 44:7
"Therefore thus says the LORD of **h**, the Jer 44:11
Thus says the LORD of **h**, the God of Jer 44:25
day is the day of the Lord GOD of **h**, Jer 46:10
the Lord GOD of **h** holds a sacrifice in Jer 46:10
the King, whose name is the LORD of **h**, Jer 46:18
The LORD of **h**, the God of Israel, said: Jer 46:25
Thus says the LORD of **h**, the God of Jer 48:1
the King, whose name is the LORD of **h**. Jer 48:15
upon you, declares the Lord GOD of **h**, Jer 49:5
Thus says the LORD of **h**: "Is wisdom no Jer 49:7
in that day, declares the LORD of **h**. Jer 49:26
Thus says the LORD of **h**: "Behold, I will Jer 49:35
Therefore, thus says the LORD of **h**, the Jer 50:18
for the Lord GOD of **h** has a work to do Jer 50:25
proud one, declares the Lord GOD of **h**, Jer 50:31
"Thus says the LORD of **h**: The people of Jer 50:33
is strong; the LORD of **h** is his name. Jer 50:34
forsaken by their God, the LORD of **h**, Jer 51:5
The LORD of **h** has sworn by himself: Jer 51:14
inheritance; the LORD of **h** is his name. Jer 51:19
For thus says the LORD of **h**, the God of Jer 51:33
the King, whose name is the LORD of **h**. Jer 51:57
"Thus says the LORD of **h**: The broad Jer 51:58
you and all your **h** that are assembled Ezk 38:7
you assembled your **h** to carry off Ezk 38:13
the LORD, the God of **h**, the LORD is his Hos 12:5
declares the Lord GOD, the God of **h**, Am 3:13
of the earth—the LORD, the God of **h**, Am 4:13
and so the LORD, the God of **h**, will be Am 5:14
it may be that the LORD, the God of **h**, Am 5:15
thus says the LORD, the God of **h**, Am 5:16
the LORD, whose name is the God of **h**. Am 5:27
himself, declares the LORD, the God of **h**: Am 6:8
Israel," declares the LORD, the God of **h**; Am 6:14
The Lord GOD of **h**, he who touches the Am 9:5
the mouth of the LORD of **h** has spoken. Mi 4:4
I am against you, declares the LORD of **h**, Na 2:13
sword and glittering spear, **h** of slain, Na 3:3
I am against you, declares the LORD of **h**, Na 3:5
from the LORD of **h** that peoples labor Hab 2:13
as I live," declares the LORD of **h**, Zep 2:9
against the people of the LORD of **h**. Zep 2:10
"Thus says the LORD of **h**: These people Hg 1:2
Now, therefore, thus says the LORD of **h**: Hg 1:5
"Thus says the LORD of **h**: Consider your Hg 1:7
it away. Why? declares the LORD of **h**. Hg 1:9
worked on the house of the LORD of **h**, Hg 1:14
for I am with you, declares the LORD of **h**, Hg 2:4
For thus says the LORD of **h**: Yet once Hg 2:6
this house with glory, says the LORD of **h**. Hg 2:7
the gold is mine, declares the LORD of **h**. Hg 2:8
than the former, says the LORD of **h**. Hg 2:9
I will give peace, declares the LORD of **h**.'" Hg 2:9
"Thus says the LORD of **h**: Ask the priests Hg 2:11
On that day, declares the LORD of **h**, I will Hg 2:23
chosen you, declares the LORD of **h**." Hg 2:23
say to them, Thus declares the LORD of **h**: Zec 1:3
Return to me, says the LORD of **h**, and I Zec 1:3

I will return to you, says the LORD of **h**. Zec 1:3
cried out, 'Thus says the LORD of **h**, Zec 1:4
As the LORD of **h** purposed to deal with us Zec 1:6
the angel of the LORD said, 'O LORD of **h**, Zec 1:12
to me, 'Cry out, Thus says the LORD of **h**: Zec 1:14
be built in it, declares the LORD of **h**, Zec 1:16
Cry out again, Thus says the LORD of **h**: Zec 1:17
For thus said the LORD of **h**, after his Zec 2:8
will know that the LORD of **h** has sent me. Zec 2:9
know that the LORD of **h** has sent me to Zec 2:11
"Thus says the LORD of **h**: If you will Zec 3:7
its inscription, declares the LORD of **h**, Zec 3:9
In that day, declares the LORD of **h**, every Zec 3:10
but by my Spirit, says the LORD of **h**. Zec 4:6
know that the LORD of **h** has sent me to Zec 4:9
I will send it out, declares the LORD of **h**, Zec 5:4
say to him, 'Thus says the LORD of **h**, Zec 6:12
know that the LORD of **h** has sent me to Zec 6:15
house of the LORD of **h** and the prophets, Zec 7:3
the word of the LORD of **h** came to me: Zec 7:4
"Thus says the LORD of **h**, Render true Zec 7:9
words that the LORD of **h** had sent by his Zec 7:12
great anger came from the LORD of **h**. Zec 7:12
I would not hear," says the LORD of **h**, Zec 7:13
And the word of the LORD of **h** came, Zec 8:1
"Thus says the LORD of **h**: I am jealous Zec 8:2
city, and the mountain of the LORD of **h**, Zec 8:3
Thus says the LORD of **h**: Old men and Zec 8:4
Thus says the LORD of **h**: If it is Zec 8:6
in my sight, declares the LORD of **h**? Zec 8:6
Thus says the LORD of **h**: behold, I will Zec 8:7
Thus says the LORD of **h**: "Let your hands Zec 8:9
of the house of the LORD of **h** was laid, Zec 8:9
the former days, declares the LORD of **h**. Zec 8:11
For thus says the LORD of **h**: "As I Zec 8:14
and I did not relent, says the LORD of **h**, Zec 8:14
the word of the LORD of **h** came to me, Zec 8:18
"Thus says the LORD of **h**: The fast of the Zec 8:19
"Thus says the LORD of **h**: Peoples shall Zec 8:20
of the LORD and to seek the LORD of **h**; Zec 8:21
seek the LORD of **h** in Jerusalem and to Zec 8:22
Thus says the LORD of **h**: In those days Zec 8:23
The LORD of **h** will protect them, and Zec 9:15
for the LORD of **h** cares for his flock, Zec 10:3
have strength through the LORD of **h**, Zec 12:5
on that day, declares the LORD of **h**, Zec 13:2
next to me," declares the LORD of **h**. Zec 13:7
to worship the King, the LORD of **h**, Zec 14:16
to worship the King, the LORD of **h**, Zec 14:17
Judah shall be holy to the LORD of **h**, Zec 14:21
the house of the LORD of **h** on that day. Zec 14:21
rebuild the ruins," the LORD of **h** says, Mal 1:4
says the LORD of **h** to you, O priests, who Mal 1:6
or show you favor? says the LORD of **h**. Mal 1:8
favor to any of you? says the LORD of **h**. Mal 1:9
no pleasure in you, says the LORD of **h**, Mal 1:10
among the nations, says the LORD of **h**. Mal 1:11
and you snort at it, says the LORD of **h**. Mal 1:13
I am a great King, says the LORD of **h**, Mal 1:14
honor to my name, says the LORD of **h**, Mal 2:2
with Levi may stand, says the LORD of **h**. Mal 2:4
for he is the messenger of the LORD of **h**. Mal 2:7
the covenant of Levi, says the LORD of **h**, Mal 2:8
brings an offering to the LORD of **h**! Mal 2:12
with violence, says the LORD of **h**. Mal 2:16
behold, he is coming, says the LORD of **h**. Mal 3:1
and do not fear me, says the LORD of **h**. Mal 3:5
I will return to you, says the LORD of **h**. Mal 3:7
put me to the test, says the LORD of **h**, Mal 3:10
shall not fail to bear, says the LORD of **h**. Mal 3:11
be a land of delight, says the LORD of **h**. Mal 3:12
as in mourning before the LORD of **h**? Mal 3:14
shall be mine, says the LORD of **h**, Mal 3:17
shall set them ablaze, says the LORD of **h**, Mal 4:1
on the day when I act, says the LORD of **h**. Mal 4:3
"If the Lord of **h** had not left us Rom 9:29
have reached the ears of the Lord of **h**. Jas 5:4

HOT (31)
Anah who found the **h** springs in the Gn 36:24
he went out from Pharaoh in **h** anger. Ex 11:8
eat; but when the sun grew **h**, it melted. Ex 16:21
wrath may burn **h** against them and Ex 32:10
your wrath burn **h** against your people, Ex 32:11
the dancing, Moses' anger burned **h**, Ex 32:19
"Let not the anger of my lord burn **h**. Ex 32:22
of the anger and **h** displeasure that the Dt 9:19
avenger of blood in **h** anger pursue the Dt 19:6
In **h** anger he went back to his father's Jgs 14:19
'Tomorrow, by the time the sun is **h**, 1 Sm 11:9
to be replaced by **h** bread on the day it 1 Sm 21:6
a cake baked on **h** stones and a jar 1 Kgs 19:6
Jerusalem be opened until the sun is **h**. Neh 7:3
when it is **h**, they vanish from their Jb 6:17
whose garments are **h** when the earth Jb 37:17
My heart became **h** within me. As I Ps 39:3
wrath; you turned from your **h** anger. Ps 85:3
H indignation seizes me because of the Ps 119:53
Or can one walk on **h** coals and his feet Prv 6:28
As charcoal to **h** embers and wood to Prv 26:21
"A **h** wind from the bare heights in the Jer 4:11
he poured out his **h** anger, and he Lam 4:11
Our skin is **h** as an oven with the Lam 5:10
upon the coals, that it may become **h**, Ezk 24:11
spoken in my **h** jealousy against the Ezk 36:5
All of them are **h** as an oven, and they Hos 7:7
"My anger is **h** against the shepherds, Zec 10:3
your works: you are neither cold nor **h**. Rv 3:15
Would that you were either cold or **h**! Rv 3:15
are lukewarm, and neither **h** nor cold, Rv 3:16

HOT-TEMPERED (1)
A **h** man stirs up strife, but he who is Prv 15:18

HOTHAM (2)
Shomer, **H**, and their sister Shua. 1 Chr 7:32
and Jeiel the sons of **H** the Aroerite, 1 Chr 11:44

HOTHIR (2)
Mallothi, **H**, Mahazioth. 1 Chr 25:4
to the twenty-first, to **H**, his sons and 1 Chr 25:28

HOTLY (3)
is my sin, that you have **h** pursued me? Gn 31:36
And the anger of the LORD blazed **h**, Nm 11:10
arrogance the wicked **h** pursue the poor; Ps 10:2

HOUR (98)
kept for you until the **h** appointed, 1 Sm 9:24
Egypt, 'Noisy one who lets the **h** go by.' Jer 46:17
anxious can add a single **h** to his span of Mt 6:27
are to say will be given to you in that **h**. Mt 10:19
out about the third **h** he saw others Mt 20:3
again about the sixth **h** and the ninth Mt 20:5
about the sixth hour and the ninth **h**, Mt 20:5
And about the eleventh **h** he went out Mt 20:6
those hired about the eleventh **h** came, Mt 20:9
saying, 'These last worked only one **h**, Mt 20:12
that day and **h** no one knows, Mt 24:36
is coming at an **h** you do not expect. Mt 24:44
him and at an **h** he does not know Mt 24:50
for you know neither the day nor the **h**. Mt 25:13
could you not watch with me one **h**? Mt 26:40
See, the **h** is at hand, and the Son of Mt 26:45
At that **h** Jesus said to the crowds, Mt 26:55
from the sixth **h** there was darkness Mt 27:45
over all the land until the ninth **h**. Mt 27:45
And about the ninth **h** Jesus cried out Mt 27:46
is a desolate place, and the **h** is now late. Mk 6:35
say whatever is given you in that **h**, Mk 13:11
"But concerning that day or that **h**, no Mk 13:32
possible, the **h** might pass from him. Mk 14:35
asleep? Could you not watch one **h**? Mk 14:37
rest? It is enough; the **h** has come. Mk 14:41
it was the third **h** when they crucified Mk 15:25
And when the sixth **h** had come, there Mk 15:33
over the whole land until the ninth **h**. Mk 15:33
And at the ninth **h** Jesus cried with a Mk 15:34
were praying outside at the **h** of incense. Lk 1:10
up at that very **h** she began to give Lk 2:38
In that **h** he healed many people of Lk 7:21
In that same **h** he rejoiced in the Holy Lk 10:21
you in that very **h** what you ought to Lk 12:12
can add a single **h** to his span of Lk 12:25
had known at what **h** the thief was Lk 12:39
is coming at an **h** you do not expect." Lk 12:40
him and at an **h** he does not know, Lk 12:46
At that very **h** some Pharisees came Lk 13:31
to lay hands on him at that very **h**, Lk 20:19
And when the **h** came, he reclined at Lk 22:14
But this is your **h**, and the power of Lk 22:53
of about an **h** still another insisted, Lk 22:59
It was now about the sixth **h**, and there Lk 23:44
over the whole land until the ninth **h**, Lk 23:44
they rose that same **h** and returned to Lk 24:33
that day, for it was about the tenth **h**. Jn 1:39
to do with me? My **h** has not yet come." Jn 2:4
beside the well. It was about the sixth **h**. Jn 4:6
the **h** is coming when neither on this Jn 4:21
But the **h** is coming, and is now here, Jn 4:23
So he asked them the **h** when he began to Jn 4:52
"Yesterday at the seventh **h** the fever left Jn 4:52
knew that was the **h** when Jesus had said Jn 4:53
truly, I say to you, an **h** is coming, Jn 5:25
for an **h** is coming when all who are in Jn 5:28
on him, because his **h** had not yet come. Jn 7:30
him, because his **h** had not yet come. Jn 8:20
"The **h** has come for the Son of Man to Jn 12:23
I say? 'Father, save me from this **h**'? Jn 12:27
for this purpose I have come to this **h**. Jn 12:27
Jesus knew that his **h** had come to depart Jn 13:1
the **h** is coming when whoever kills you Jn 16:2
that when their **h** comes you may Jn 16:4
she has sorrow because her **h** has come, Jn 16:21
The **h** is coming when I will no longer Jn 16:25
Behold, the **h** is coming, indeed it has Jn 16:32
and said, "Father, the **h** has come; Jn 17:1
of the Passover. It was about the sixth **h**. Jn 19:14
And from that **h** the disciple took Jn 19:27
since it is only the third **h** of the day. Acts 2:15
going up to the temple at the **h** of prayer, Acts 3:1
at the hour of prayer, the ninth **h**. Acts 3:1
About the ninth **h** of the day he saw Acts 10:3
the housetop about the sixth **h** to pray. Acts 10:9
said, "Four days ago, about this **h**, Acts 10:30
praying in my house at the ninth **h**, Acts 10:30
of her." And it came out that very **h**. Acts 16:18
took them the same **h** of the night Acts 16:33
And at that very **h** I received my sight Acts 22:13
Caesarea at the third **h** of the night. Acts 23:23
that the **h** has come for you to wake Rom 13:11
To the present **h** we hunger and 1 Cor 4:11
Why am I in danger every **h**? 1 Cor 15:30
Children, it is the last **h**, and as you 1 Jn 2:18
Therefore we know that it is the last **h**. 1 Jn 2:18
not know at what **h** I will come against Rv 3:3
will keep you from the **h** of trial that is Rv 3:10
was silence in heaven for about half an **h**. Rv 8:1
angels, who had been prepared for the **h**, Rv 9:15
And at that **h** there was a great Rv 11:13
because the **h** of his judgment has come, Rv 14:7
and reap, for the **h** to reap has come, Rv 14:15
to receive authority as kings for one **h**, Rv 17:12
For in a single **h** your judgment has Rv 18:10
For in a single **h** all this wealth has Rv 18:17
For in a single **h** she has been laid Rv 18:19

HOURS (3)
"Are there not twelve **h** in the day? Jn 11:9
interval of about three **h** his wife came Acts 5:7
for about two **h** they all cried out Acts 19:34

HOUSE (1785)
kindred and your father's **h** to the land Gn 12:1
woman was taken into Pharaoh's **h**. Gn 12:15
Pharaoh and his **h** with great plagues Gn 12:17
forth his trained men, born in his **h**, Gn 14:14
the heir of my **h** is Eliezer of Gn 15:2
born in your **h** or bought with Gn 17:12
who is born in your **h** and he who is Gn 17:13
those born in his **h** or bought with his Gn 17:23
male among the men of Abraham's **h**, Gn 17:23
And all the men of his **h**, those born in Gn 17:27
those born in the **h** and those bought Gn 17:27
aside to your servant's **h** and spend the Gn 19:2
turned aside to him and entered his **h**. Gn 19:3
to the last man, surrounded the **h**. Gn 19:4
brought Lot into the **h** with them and Gn 19:10
men who were at the entrance of the **h**, Gn 19:11
me to wander from my father's **h**, Gn 20:13
wombs of the **h** of Abimelech because Gn 20:18
me from my father's **h** and from the Gn 24:7
room in your father's **h** for us to spend Gn 24:23
the way to the **h** of my master's Gn 24:27
I have prepared the **h** and a place for Gn 24:31
came to the **h** and unharnessed the Gn 24:32
go to my father's **h** and to my clan Gn 24:38
from my clan and from my father's **h**. Gn 24:40
son, which were with her in the **h**, Gn 27:15
to Paddan-aram to the **h** of Bethuel your Gn 28:2
This is none other than the **h** of God, Gn 28:17
I come again to my father's **h** in peace, Gn 28:21
set up for a pillar, shall be God's **h**. Gn 28:22
kissed him and brought him to his **h**. Gn 29:13
inheritance left to us in our father's **h**? Gn 31:14
you longed greatly for your father's **h**, Gn 31:30
twenty years I have been in your **h**. Gn 31:41
and built himself a **h** and made booths Gn 33:17
the most honored of all his father's **h**. Gn 34:19
out of Shechem's **h** and went away. Gn 34:26
"Remain a widow in your father's **h**, Gn 38:11
went and remained in her father's **h**. Gn 38:11
he was in the **h** of his Egyptian master. Gn 39:2
him overseer of his **h** and put him in Gn 39:4
him overseer in his **h** and over all that Gn 39:5
blessed the Egyptian's **h** for Joseph's Gn 39:5
was on all that he had, in **h** and field. Gn 39:5
no concern about anything in the **h**, Gn 39:8
He is not greater in this **h** than I am, nor Gn 39:9
when he went into the **h** to do his work Gn 39:11
of the men of the **h** was there in the Gn 39:11
men of the house was there in the **h**, Gn 39:11
her hand and fled and got out of the **h**. Gn 39:12
in her hand and had fled out of the **h**, Gn 39:13
me and fled and got out of the **h**." Gn 39:15
beside me and fled out of the **h**." Gn 39:18
in custody in the **h** of the captain of Gn 40:3
with him in custody in his master's **h**, Gn 40:7
to Pharaoh, and so get me out of this **h**. Gn 40:14
in custody in the **h** of the captain of Gn 41:10

You shall be over my **h**, and all my Gn 41:40
all my hardship and all my father's **h**." Gn 41:51
them, he said to the steward of his **h**, Gn 43:16
of his house, "Bring the men into the **h**, Gn 43:16
and brought the men to Joseph's **h**. Gn 43:17
they were brought to Joseph's **h**, Gn 43:18
steward of Joseph's **h** and spoke with Gn 43:19
spoke with him at the door of the **h**, Gn 43:19
men into Joseph's **h** and given them Gn 43:24
they brought into the **h** to him the Gn 43:26
he commanded the steward of his **h**, Gn 44:1
steal silver or gold from your lord's **h**? Gn 44:8
and his brothers came to Joseph's **h**, Gn 44:14
and lord of all his **h** and ruler over all Gn 45:8
the report was heard in Pharaoh's **h**, Gn 45:16
the persons of the **h** of Jacob who came Gn 46:27
brought the money into Pharaoh's **h**. Gn 47:14
in Egypt, he and his father's **h**. Gn 50:22
Now a man from the **h** of Levi went and Ex 2:1
and any woman who lives in her **h**, Ex 3:22
Pharaoh turned and went into his **h**, and Ex 7:23
come up into your **h** and into your Ex 8:3
of flies into the **h** of Pharaoh and into Ex 8:24
of the door of his **h** until the morning. Ex 12:22
there was not a **h** where someone was Ex 12:30
It shall be eaten in one **h**; you shall not Ex 12:46
not take any of the flesh outside the **h**, Ex 12:46
out from Egypt, out of the **h** of slavery, Ex 13:3
us out of Egypt, from the **h** of slavery. Ex 13:14
Now the **h** of Israel called its name Ex 16:31
"Thus you shall say to the **h** of Jacob, Ex 19:3
the land of Egypt, out of the **h** of slavery. Ex 20:2
"You shall not covet your neighbor's **h**; Ex 20:17
safe, and it is stolen from the man's **h**, Ex 22:7
the owner of the **h** shall come near to Ex 22:8
shall bring into the **h** of the LORD your Ex 23:19
shall bring to the **h** of the LORD your Ex 34:26
sight of all the **h** of Israel throughout Ex 40:38
let your brothers, the whole **h** of Israel, Lv 10:6
of leprous disease in a **h** in the land of Lv 14:34
he who owns the **h** shall come and tell Lv 14:35
me to be some case of disease in my **h**.' Lv 14:35
that they empty the **h** before the priest Lv 14:36
all that is in the **h** be declared unclean. Lv 14:36
the priest shall go in to see the **h**. Lv 14:36
the walls of the **h** with greenish or Lv 14:37
shall go out of the **h** to the door of the Lv 14:38
to the door of the **h** and shut up the Lv 14:38
the house and shut up the **h** seven days. Lv 14:38
disease has spread in the walls of the **h**, Lv 14:39
the inside of the **h** scraped all around, Lv 14:41
take other plaster and plaster the **h**. Lv 14:42
the disease breaks out again in the **h**, Lv 14:43
and scraped the **h** and plastered it, Lv 14:43
And if the disease has spread in the **h**, it Lv 14:44
it is a persistent leprous disease in the **h**; Lv 14:44
And he shall break down the **h**, its Lv 14:45
and timber and all the plaster of the **h**, Lv 14:45
whoever enters the **h** while it is shut up Lv 14:46
whoever sleeps in the **h** shall wash his Lv 14:47
whoever eats in the **h** shall wash his Lv 14:47
not spread in the **h** after the house was Lv 14:48
in the house after the **h** was plastered, Lv 14:48
the priest shall pronounce the **h** clean, Lv 14:48
the cleansing of the **h** he shall take two Lv 14:49
water and sprinkle the **h** seven times. Lv 14:51
he shall cleanse the **h** with the blood of Lv 14:52
So he shall make atonement for the **h**, Lv 14:53
leprous disease in a garment or in a **h**, Lv 14:55
atonement for himself and for his **h**. Lv 16:6
atonement for himself and for his **h**. Lv 16:11
for himself and for his **h** and for all the Lv 16:17
If any one of the **h** of Israel kills an ox or Lv 17:3
say to them, Any one of the **h** of Israel, Lv 17:8
"If any one of the **h** of Israel or of the Lv 17:10
anyone born in his **h** may eat of his Lv 22:11
no child and returns to her father's **h**, Lv 22:13
When any one of the **h** of Israel or of Lv 22:18
man sells a dwelling **h** in a walled city, Lv 25:29
then the **h** in the walled city shall Lv 25:30
then the **h** that was sold in a city they Lv 25:33
a man dedicates his **h** as a holy gift Lv 27:14
if the donor wishes to redeem his **h**, Lv 27:15
being the head of the **h** of his fathers. Nm 1:4
men, each representing his fathers' **h**. Nm 1:44
in his clan, according to his fathers' **h**. Nm 2:34
of the fathers' **h** of the Gershonites. Nm 3:24
as chief of the fathers' **h** of the clans of Nm 3:30
the chief of the fathers' **h** of the clans of Nm 3:35
Moses. He is faithful in all my **h**. Nm 12:7
them staffs, one for each fathers' **h**, Nm 17:2
one staff for the head of each fathers' **h**. Nm 17:3
of Aaron for the **h** of Levi had sprouted Nm 17:8
sons and your father's **h** with you shall Nm 18:1
who is clean in your **h** may eat it. Nm 18:11

who is clean in your **h** may eat it. Nm 18:13
all the **h** of Israel wept for Aaron Nm 20:29
were to give me his **h** full of silver and Nm 22:18
should give me his **h** full of silver and Nm 24:13
chief of a father's **h** belonging to the Nm 25:14
tribal head of a father's **h** in Midian. Nm 25:15
within her father's **h** in her youth, Nm 30:3
in her husband's **h** or bound herself Nm 30:10
is in her youth within her father's **h**. Nm 30:16
of the land of Egypt, out of the **h** of slavery. Dt 5:6
you shall not desire your neighbor's **h**, Dt 5:21
shall talk of them when you sit in your **h**, Dt 6:7
the doorposts of your **h** and on your gates. Dt 6:9
the land of Egypt, out of the **h** of slavery. Dt 6:12
and redeemed you from the **h** of slavery, Dt 7:8
thing into your **h** and become devoted Dt 7:26
the land of Egypt, out of the **h** of slavery, Dt 8:14
of them when you are sitting in your **h**, Dt 11:19
the doorposts of your **h** and on your Dt 11:20
and redeemed you out of the **h** of slavery, Dt 13:5
the land of Egypt, out of the **h** of slavery. Dt 13:10
has built a new **h** and has not dedicated Dt 20:5
Let him go back to his **h**, lest he die in Dt 20:5
Let him go back to his **h**, lest he die in Dt 20:6
Let him go back to his **h**, lest he die in Dt 20:7
Let him go back to his **h**, lest he make Dt 20:8
and you bring her home to your **h**, she Dt 21:12
shall remain in your **h** and lament her Dt 21:13
he is, you shall bring it home to your **h**, Dt 22:2
"When you build a new **h**, you shall Dt 22:8
not bring the guilt of blood upon your **h**, Dt 22:8
woman to the door of her father's **h**, Dt 22:21
in Israel by whoring in her father's **h**. Dt 22:21
of a dog into the **h** of the LORD your God Dt 23:18
it in her hand and sends her out of his **h**, Dt 24:1
of his house, and she departs out of his **h**, Dt 24:1
it in her hand and sends her out of his **h**, Dt 24:3
not go into his **h** to collect his pledge. Dt 24:10
who does not build up his brother's **h**.' Dt 25:9
And the name of his **h** shall be called in Dt 25:10
'The **h** of him who had his sandal Dt 25:10
not have in your **h** two kinds of Dt 25:14
God has given to you and to your **h**, Dt 26:11
removed the sacred portion out of my **h**, Dt 26:13
You shall build a **h**, but you shall not Dt 28:30
and came into the **h** of a prostitute whose Jos 2:1
have come to you, who entered your **h**, Jos 2:3
also will deal kindly with my father's **h**, Jos 2:12
for her **h** was built into the city wall, Jos 2:15
shall gather into your **h** your father and Jos 2:18
out of the doors of your **h** into the street, Jos 2:19
laid on anyone who is with you in the **h**, Jos 2:19
all who are with her in her **h** shall live, Jos 6:17
"Go into the prostitute's **h** and bring out Jos 6:22
put into the treasury of the **h** of the LORD. Jos 6:24
drawers of water for the **h** of my God." Jos 9:23
Then Joshua said to the **h** of Joseph, to Jos 17:17
and the **h** of Joseph shall continue in Jos 18:5
had made to the **h** of Israel had failed; Jos 21:45
But as for me and my **h**, we will serve Jos 24:15
land of Egypt, out of the **h** of slavery, Jos 24:17
The **h** of Joseph also went up against Jgs 1:22
And the **h** of Joseph scouted out Bethel. Jgs 1:23
the hand of the **h** of Joseph rested heavily Jgs 1:35
of Hazor and the **h** of Heber the Kenite. Jgs 4:17
and brought you out of the **h** of bondage. Jgs 6:8
and I am the least in my father's **h**." Jgs 6:15
Gideon went into his **h** and prepared a Jgs 6:19
son of Joash went and lived in his own **h**. Jgs 8:29
silver out of the **h** of Baal-berith with Jgs 9:4
went to his father's **h** at Ophrah and Jgs 9:5
with Jerubbaal and his **h** and have done Jgs 9:16
up against my father's **h** this day and Jgs 9:18
with Jerubbaal and with his **h** this day, Jgs 9:19
and they went into the **h** of their god and Jgs 9:27
the stronghold of the **h** of El-berith. Jgs 9:46
Benjamin and against the **h** of Ephraim, Jgs 10:9
have an inheritance in our father's **h**, Jgs 11:2
me and drive me out of my father's **h**? Jgs 11:7
the doors of my **h** to meet me when Jgs 11:31
We will burn your **h** over you with fire." Jgs 12:1
burn you and your father's **h** with fire. Jgs 14:15
anger he went back to his father's **h**. Jgs 14:19
me feel the pillars on which the **h** rests, Jgs 16:26
Now the **h** was full of men and women. Jgs 16:27
middle pillars on which the **h** rested, Jgs 16:29
and the **h** fell upon the lords and upon Jgs 16:30
image. And it was in the **h** of Micah. Jgs 17:4
country of Ephraim to the **h** of Micah. Jgs 17:8
his priest, and was in the **h** of Micah. Jgs 17:12
country of Ephraim, to the **h** of Micah, Jgs 18:2
When they were by the **h** of Micah, they Jgs 18:3
Ephraim, and came to the **h** of Micah. Jgs 18:13
and came to the **h** of the young Levite, Jgs 18:15
these went into Micah's **h** and took the Jgs 18:18

for you to be priest to the **h** of one man, Jgs 18:19
houses near Micah's **h** were called out, Jgs 18:22
as long as the **h** of God was at Shiloh. Jgs 18:31
him to her father's **h** at Bethlehem in Jgs 19:2
she brought him into her father's **h**. Jgs 19:3
took them into his **h** to spend the night. Jgs 19:15
and I am going to the **h** of the Lord, Jgs 19:18
but no one has taken me into his **h**. Jgs 19:18
brought him into his **h** and gave the Jgs 19:21
worthless fellows, surrounded the **h**, Jgs 19:22
said to the old man, the master of the **h**, Jgs 19:22
out the man who came into your **h**, Jgs 19:22
And the man, the master of the **h**, went Jgs 19:23
since this man has come into my **h**, do Jgs 19:23
door of the man's **h** where her master Jgs 19:26
the doors of the **h** and went out to Jgs 19:27
concubine lying at the door of the **h**, Jgs 19:27
And when he entered his **h**, he took a Jgs 19:29
me and surrounded the **h** against me by Jgs 20:5
tent, and none of us will return to his **h**. Jgs 20:8
"Go, return each of you to her mother's **h**. Ru 1:8
of you in the **h** of her husband!" Then Ru 1:9
the woman, who is coming into your **h**, Ru 4:11
who together built up the **h** of Israel. Ru 4:11
and may your **h** be like the house of Ru 4:12
may your house be like the **h** of Perez, Ru 4:12
as she went up to the **h** of the LORD, 1 Sm 1:7
they went back to their **h** at Ramah. 1 Sm 1:19
Elkanah and all his **h** went up to offer 1 Sm 1:21
brought him to the **h** of the LORD at 1 Sm 1:24
reveal myself to the **h** of your father 1 Sm 2:27
in Egypt subject to the **h** of Pharaoh? 1 Sm 2:27
I gave to the **h** of your father all my 1 Sm 2:28
'I promised that your **h** and the house 1 Sm 2:30
your house and the **h** of your father 1 Sm 2:30
and the strength of your father's **h**, 1 Sm 2:31
will not be an old man in your **h**. 1 Sm 2:31
not be an old man in your **h** forever. 1 Sm 2:32
the descendants of your **h** shall die by 1 Sm 2:33
And I will build him a sure **h**, and he 1 Sm 2:35
is left in your **h** shall come to implore 1 Sm 2:36
that I have spoken concerning his **h**, 1 Sm 3:12
I am about to punish his **h** forever, 1 Sm 3:13
I swear to the **h** of Eli that the 1 Sm 3:14
the iniquity of Eli's **h** shall not be 1 Sm 3:14
opened the doors of the **h** of the LORD. 1 Sm 3:15
brought it into the **h** of Dagon and set 1 Sm 5:2
and all who enter the **h** of Dagon do not 1 Sm 5:5
brought it to the **h** of Abinadab on the 1 Sm 7:1
and all the **h** of Israel lamented after 1 Sm 7:2
And Samuel said to all the **h** of Israel, 1 Sm 7:3
"Tell me where is the **h** of the seer?" 1 Sm 9:18
for you and for all your father's **h**?" 1 Sm 9:20
went up to his **h** in Gibeah of Saul. 1 Sm 15:34
make his father's **h** free in Israel." 1 Sm 17:25
not let him return to his father's **h**. 1 Sm 18:2
raved within his **h** while David was 1 Sm 18:10
as he sat in his **h** with his spear in his 1 Sm 19:9
messengers to David's **h** to watch 1 Sm 19:11
steadfast love from my **h** forever, 1 Sm 20:15
a covenant with the **h** of David, 1 Sm 20:16
Shall this fellow come into my **h**?" 1 Sm 21:15
and all his father's **h** heard it, 1 Sm 22:1
son of Ahitub, and all his father's **h**, 1 Sm 22:11
bodyguard, and honored in your **h**? 1 Sm 22:14
servant or to all the **h** of my father, 1 Sm 22:15
you and all your father's **h**." 1 Sm 22:16
of all the persons of your father's **h**. 1 Sm 22:22
my name out of my father's **h**." 1 Sm 24:21
they buried him in his **h** at Ramah. 1 Sm 25:1
be to you, and peace be to your **h**, 1 Sm 25:6
our master and against all his **h**, 1 Sm 25:17
certainly make my lord a sure **h**, 1 Sm 25:28
to her, "Go up in peace to your **h**. 1 Sm 25:35
he was holding a feast in his **h**, 1 Sm 25:36
woman had a fattened calf in the **h**, 1 Sm 28:24
good news to the **h** of their idols and 1 Sm 31:9
of the LORD and for the **h** of Israel, 2 Sm 1:12
David king over the **h** of Judah. 2 Sm 2:4
and the **h** of Judah has anointed me 2 Sm 2:7
But the **h** of Judah followed David. 2 Sm 2:10
in Hebron over the **h** of Judah was 2 Sm 2:11
long war between the **h** of Saul and the 2 Sm 3:1
the house of Saul and the **h** of David. 2 Sm 3:1
while the **h** of Saul became weaker and 2 Sm 3:1
was war between the **h** of Saul and the 2 Sm 3:6
the house of Saul and the **h** of David, 2 Sm 3:6
himself strong in the **h** of Saul. 2 Sm 3:6
steadfast love to the **h** of Saul your 2 Sm 3:8
the kingdom from the **h** of Saul and 2 Sm 3:10
and the whole **h** of Benjamin thought 2 Sm 3:19
of Joab and upon all his father's **h**, 2 Sm 3:29
and may the **h** of Joab never be 2 Sm 3:29
they came to the **h** of Ish-bosheth as he 2 Sm 4:5
into the midst of the **h** as if to get wheat, 2 Sm 4:6

When they came into the **h**, as he lay 2 Sm 4:7
man in his own **h** on his bed, 2 Sm 4:11
the lame shall not come into the **h**." 2 Sm 5:8
and masons who built David a **h**. 2 Sm 5:11
brought it out of the **h** of Abinadab, 2 Sm 6:3
David and all the **h** of Israel were 2 Sm 6:5
it aside to the **h** of Obed-edom the 2 Sm 6:10
remained in the **h** of Obed-edom the 2 Sm 6:11
of God from the **h** of Obed-edom to the 2 Sm 6:12
David and all the **h** of Israel brought 2 Sm 6:15
all the people departed, each to his **h**. 2 Sm 6:19
above your father and above all his **h**, 2 Sm 6:21
king lived in his **h** and the LORD had 2 Sm 7:1
"See now, I dwell in a **h** of cedar, 2 Sm 7:2
Would you build me a **h** to dwell in? 2 Sm 7:5
have not lived in a **h** since the day I 2 Sm 7:6
have you not built me a **h** of cedar?"' 2 Sm 7:7
you that the LORD will make you a **h**. 2 Sm 7:11
He shall build a **h** for my name, and I 2 Sm 7:13
And your **h** and your kingdom shall 2 Sm 7:16
am I, O Lord GOD, and what is my **h**, 2 Sm 7:18
also of your servant's **h** for a great 2 Sm 7:19
your servant and concerning his **h**, 2 Sm 7:25
and the **h** of your servant David will 2 Sm 7:26
servant, saying, 'I will build you a **h**.' 2 Sm 7:27
you to bless the **h** of your servant, 2 Sm 7:29
blessing shall the **h** of your servant 2 Sm 7:29
there still anyone left of the **h** of Saul, 2 Sm 9:1
a servant of the **h** of Saul whose name 2 Sm 9:2
there not still someone of the **h** of Saul, 2 Sm 9:3
"He is in the **h** of Machir the son of 2 Sm 9:4
brought him from the **h** of Machir the 2 Sm 9:5
Saul and to all his **h** I have given to 2 Sm 9:9
in Ziba's **h** became Mephibosheth's 2 Sm 9:12
walking on the roof of the king's **h**, 2 Sm 11:2
Then she returned to her **h**. 2 Sm 11:4
"Go down to your **h** and wash your 2 Sm 11:8
And Uriah went out of the king's **h**, 2 Sm 11:8
door of the king's **h** with all the 2 Sm 11:9
his lord, and did not go down to his **h**. 2 Sm 11:9
go down to his **h**," David said to 2 Sm 11:10
did you not go down to your **h**?" 2 Sm 11:10
Shall I then go to my **h**, to eat and to 2 Sm 11:11
lord, but he did not go down to his **h**. 2 Sm 11:13
David sent and brought her to his **h**, 2 Sm 11:27
you your master's **h** and your 2 Sm 12:8
and gave you the **h** of Israel and of 2 Sm 12:8
shall never depart from your **h**, 2 Sm 12:10
evil against you out of your own **h**. 2 Sm 12:11
Then Nathan went to his **h**. And the 2 Sm 12:15
the elders of his **h** stood beside him, 2 Sm 12:17
he went into the **h** of the LORD and 2 Sm 12:20
He then went to his own **h**. 2 Sm 12:20
your brother Amnon's **h** and prepare 2 Sm 13:7
went to her brother Amnon's **h**, 2 Sm 13:8
woman, in her brother Absalom's **h**. 2 Sm 13:20
said to the woman, "Go to your **h**, 2 Sm 14:8
lord the king, and on my father's **h**; 2 Sm 14:9
"Let him dwell apart in his own **h**; 2 Sm 14:24
apart in his own **h** and did not come 2 Sm 14:24
to Absalom at his **h** and said to him, 2 Sm 14:31
left ten concubines to keep the **h**. 2 Sm 15:16
him. And they halted at the last **h**. 2 Sm 15:17
whatever you hear from the king's **h**, 2 Sm 15:35
'Today the **h** of Israel will give me 2 Sm 16:3
a man of the family of the **h** of Saul, 2 Sm 16:5
on you all the blood of the **h** of Saul, 2 Sm 16:8
whom he has left to keep the **h**, 2 Sm 16:21
and came to the **h** of a man at 2 Sm 17:18
came to the woman at the **h**, 2 Sm 17:20
He set his **h** in order and hanged 2 Sm 17:23
Joab came into the **h** to the king and 2 Sm 19:5
last to bring the king back to his **h**, 2 Sm 19:11
Ziba the servant of the **h** of Saul, 2 Sm 19:17
the first of all the **h** of Joseph to come 2 Sm 19:20
For all my father's **h** were but men 2 Sm 19:28
David came to his **h** at Jerusalem. 2 Sm 20:3
left to care for the **h** and put them in a 2 Sm 20:3
put them in a **h** under guard and 2 Sm 20:3
is bloodguilt on Saul and on his **h**, 2 Sm 21:1
or gold between us and Saul or his **h**; 2 Sm 21:4
For does not my **h** stand so with God? 2 Sm 23:5
me and against my father's **h**." 2 Sm 24:17
Solomon said to him, "Go to your **h**." 1 Kgs 1:53
my father, and who has made me a **h**, 1 Kgs 2:24
spoken concerning the **h** of Eli in 1 Kgs 2:27
and from my father's **h** the guilt for 1 Kgs 2:31
descendants and for his **h** and for his 1 Kgs 2:33
buried in his own **h** in the wilderness. 1 Kgs 2:34
"Build yourself a **h** in Jerusalem and 1 Kgs 2:36
building his own **h** and the house 1 Kgs 3:1
own house and the **h** of the LORD and 1 Kgs 3:1
because no **h** had yet been built for the 1 Kgs 3:2
this woman and I live in the same **h**, 1 Kgs 3:17
to a child while she was in the **h**. 1 Kgs 3:17
was no one else with us in the **h**; 1 Kgs 3:18
the house; only we two were in the **h**. 1 Kgs 3:18
could not build a **h** for the name of 1 Kgs 5:3
I intend to build a **h** for the name of 1 Kgs 5:5
place, shall build the **h** for my name.' 1 Kgs 5:5
foundation of the **h** with dressed 1 Kgs 5:17
timber and the stone to build the **h**. 1 Kgs 5:18
he began to build the **h** of the LORD. 1 Kgs 6:1
The **h** that King Solomon built for the 1 Kgs 6:2
the nave of the **h** was twenty cubits 1 Kgs 6:3
cubits long, equal to the width of the **h**, 1 Kgs 6:3
and ten cubits deep in front of the **h**. 1 Kgs 6:3
made for the **h** windows with recessed 1 Kgs 6:4
a structure against the wall of the **h**, 1 Kgs 6:5
running around the walls of the **h**, 1 Kgs 6:5
the outside of the **h** he made offsets on 1 Kgs 6:6
not be inserted into the walls of the **h**. 1 Kgs 6:6
When the **h** was built, it was with 1 Kgs 6:7
was heard in the **h** while it was being 1 Kgs 6:7
story was on the south side of the **h**, 1 Kgs 6:8
So he built the **h** and finished it, and 1 Kgs 6:9
the ceiling of the **h** of beams and 1 Kgs 6:9
the structure against the whole **h**, 1 Kgs 6:10
was joined to the **h** with timbers of 1 Kgs 6:10
"Concerning this **h** that you are 1 Kgs 6:12
Solomon built the **h** and finished it. 1 Kgs 6:14
the walls of the **h** on the inside with 1 Kgs 6:15
From the floor of the **h** to the walls of 1 Kgs 6:15
the floor of the **h** with boards of 1 Kgs 6:15
the rear of the **h** with boards of cedar 1 Kgs 6:16
The **h**, that is, the nave in front of the 1 Kgs 6:17
The cedar within the **h** was carved in 1 Kgs 6:18
in the innermost part of the **h**, 1 Kgs 6:19
the inside of the **h** with pure gold, 1 Kgs 6:21
he overlaid the whole **h** with gold, 1 Kgs 6:22
with gold, until all the **h** was finished. 1 Kgs 6:22
in the innermost part of the **h**. 1 Kgs 6:27
each other in the middle of the **h**. 1 Kgs 6:27
the walls of the **h** he carved engraved 1 Kgs 6:29
The floor of the **h** he overlaid with 1 Kgs 6:30
the foundation of the **h** of the LORD 1 Kgs 6:37
the **h** was finished in all its parts, 1 Kgs 6:38
was building his own **h** thirteen years, 1 Kgs 7:1
years, and he finished his entire **h**. 1 Kgs 7:1
He built the **H** of the Forest of 1 Kgs 7:2
His own **h** where he was to dwell, in the 1 Kgs 7:8
Solomon also made a **h** like this hall 1 Kgs 7:8
inner court of the **h** of the LORD and 1 Kgs 7:12
of the LORD and the vestibule of the **h**. 1 Kgs 7:12
stands, five on the south side of the **h**, 1 Kgs 7:39
and five on the north side of the **h**. 1 Kgs 7:39
sea at the southeast corner of the **h**. 1 Kgs 7:39
King Solomon on the **h** of the LORD: 1 Kgs 7:40
all these vessels in the **h** of the LORD, 1 Kgs 7:45
vessels that were in the **h** of the LORD: 1 Kgs 7:48
doors of the innermost part of the **h**, 1 Kgs 7:50
Solomon did on the **h** of the LORD was 1 Kgs 7:51
in the treasuries of the **h** of the LORD. 1 Kgs 7:51
place in the inner sanctuary of the **h**, 1 Kgs 8:6
Place, a cloud filled the **h** of the LORD, 1 Kgs 8:10
of the LORD filled the **h** of the LORD. 1 Kgs 8:11
I have indeed built you an exalted **h**, a 1 Kgs 8:13
tribes of Israel in which to build a **h**, 1 Kgs 8:16
my father to build a **h** for the name of 1 Kgs 8:17
your heart to build a **h** for my name, 1 Kgs 8:18
you shall not build the **h**, 1 Kgs 8:19
you shall build the **h** for my name.' 1 Kgs 8:19
and I have built the **h** for the name of 1 Kgs 8:20
how much less this **h** that I have 1 Kgs 8:27
be open night and day toward this **h**, 1 Kgs 8:29
his oath before your altar in this **h**, 1 Kgs 8:31
pray and plead with you in this **h**, 1 Kgs 8:33
out his hands toward this **h**, 1 Kgs 8:38
he comes and prays toward this **h**, 1 Kgs 8:42
may know that this **h** that I have 1 Kgs 8:43
have chosen and the **h** that I have 1 Kgs 8:44
and the **h** that I have built for your 1 Kgs 8:48
of Israel dedicated the **h** of the LORD. 1 Kgs 8:63
that was before the **h** of the LORD, 1 Kgs 8:64
had finished building the **h** of the LORD 1 Kgs 9:1
LORD and the king's **h** and all that 1 Kgs 9:1
have consecrated this **h** that you have 1 Kgs 9:3
and the **h** that I have consecrated for 1 Kgs 9:7
And this **h** will become a heap of 1 Kgs 9:8
done thus to this land and to this **h**?' 1 Kgs 9:8
the **h** of the LORD and the king's 1 Kgs 9:10
house of the LORD and the king's **h**, 1 Kgs 9:10
drafted to build the **h** of the LORD and 1 Kgs 9:15
LORD and his own **h** and the Millo 1 Kgs 9:15
David to her own **h** that Solomon had 1 Kgs 9:24
before the LORD. So he finished the **h**. 1 Kgs 9:25
of Solomon, the **h** that he had built, 1 Kgs 10:4
that he offered at the **h** of the LORD, 1 Kgs 10:5
wood supports for the **h** of the LORD 1 Kgs 10:12
of the LORD and for the king's **h**, 1 Kgs 10:12
put them in the **H** of the Forest of 1 Kgs 10:17
the vessels of the **H** of the Forest of 1 Kgs 10:21
He was of the royal **h** in Edom. 1 Kgs 11:14
who gave him a **h** and assigned him 1 Kgs 11:18
Tahpenes weaned in Pharaoh's **h**. 1 Kgs 11:20
was in Pharaoh's **h** among the sons 1 Kgs 11:20
the forced labor of the **h** of Joseph. 1 Kgs 11:28
you and will build you a sure **h**, 1 Kgs 11:38
Look now to your own **h**, David." So 1 Kgs 12:16
rebellion against the **h** of David to 1 Kgs 12:19
that followed the **h** of David but 1 Kgs 12:20
he assembled all the **h** of Judah and 1 Kgs 12:21
to fight against the **h** of Israel, 1 Kgs 12:21
and to all the **h** of Judah and 1 Kgs 12:23
will turn back to the **h** of David. 1 Kgs 12:26
a son shall be born to the **h** of David, 1 Kgs 13:2
the king, "If you give me half your **h**, 1 Kgs 13:8
with you into your **h** that he may 1 Kgs 13:18
ate bread in his **h** and drank water. 1 Kgs 13:19
became sin to the **h** of Jeroboam, 1 Kgs 13:34
Shiloh and came to the **h** of Ahijah. 1 Kgs 14:4
away from the **h** of David and 1 Kgs 14:8
harm upon the **h** of Jeroboam and 1 Kgs 14:10
and will burn up the **h** of Jeroboam, 1 Kgs 14:10
Arise therefore, go to your **h**. When 1 Kgs 14:12
God of Israel, in the **h** of Jeroboam. 1 Kgs 14:13
cut off the **h** of Jeroboam today. 1 Kgs 14:14
she came to the threshold of the **h**, 1 Kgs 14:17
the treasures of the **h** of the LORD and 1 Kgs 14:26
and the treasures of the king's **h**. 1 Kgs 14:26
who kept the door of the king's **h**. 1 Kgs 14:27
the king went into the **h** of the LORD, 1 Kgs 14:28
he brought into the **h** of the LORD the 1 Kgs 15:15
the treasures of the **h** of the LORD and 1 Kgs 15:18
of the king's **h** and gave them 1 Kgs 15:18
son of Ahijah, of the **h** of Issachar, 1 Kgs 15:27
king, he killed all the **h** of Jeroboam. 1 Kgs 15:29
He left to the **h** of Jeroboam not one 1 Kgs 15:29
utterly sweep away Baasha and his **h**, 1 Kgs 16:3
I will make your **h** like the house of 1 Kgs 16:3
your house like the **h** of Jeroboam the 1 Kgs 16:3
of Hanani against Baasha and his **h**, 1 Kgs 16:7
in being like the **h** of Jeroboam, 1 Kgs 16:7
himself drunk in the **h** of Arza, 1 Kgs 16:9
he struck down all the **h** of Baasha. 1 Kgs 16:11
Zimri destroyed all the **h** of Baasha, 1 Kgs 16:12
of the king's **h** and burned the 1 Kgs 16:18
burned the king's **h** over him with 1 Kgs 16:18
an altar for Baal in the **h** of Baal, 1 Kgs 16:32
of the woman, the mistress of the **h**, 1 Kgs 17:17
chamber into the **h** and delivered 1 Kgs 17:23
but you have, and your father's **h**, 1 Kgs 18:18
shall search your **h** and the houses 1 Kgs 20:6
the kings of the **h** of Israel are 1 Kgs 20:31
Israel went to his **h** vexed and sullen 1 Kgs 20:43
garden, because it is near my **h**, 1 Kgs 21:2
went into his **h** vexed and sullen 1 Kgs 21:4
I will make your **h** like the house of 1 Kgs 21:22
house like the **h** of Jeroboam the 1 Kgs 21:22
and like the **h** of Baasha the son of 1 Kgs 21:22
I will bring the disaster upon his **h**." 1 Kgs 21:29
and the ivory **h** that he built and all 1 Kgs 22:39
what have you in the **h**?" And she said, 2 Kgs 4:2
has nothing in the **h** except a jar of 2 Kgs 4:2
When Elisha came into the **h**, he saw 2 Kgs 4:32
walked once back and forth in the **h**, 2 Kgs 4:35
and stood at the door of Elisha's **h**. 2 Kgs 5:9
master goes into the **h** of Rimmon to 2 Kgs 5:18
I bow myself in the **h** of Rimmon, 2 Kgs 5:18
I bow myself in the **h** of Rimmon, 2 Kgs 5:18
their hand and put them in the **h**, 2 Kgs 5:24
Elisha was sitting in his **h**, and the 2 Kgs 6:32
to the king for her **h** and her land. 2 Kgs 8:3
to the king for her **h** and her land. 2 Kgs 8:5
of Israel, as the **h** of Ahab had done, 2 Kgs 8:18
in the way of the **h** of Ahab and did 2 Kgs 8:27
the LORD, as the **h** of Ahab had done, 2 Kgs 8:27
he was son-in-law to the **h** of Ahab. 2 Kgs 8:27
So he arose and went into the **h**. And 2 Kgs 9:6
shall strike down the **h** of Ahab your 2 Kgs 9:7
For the whole **h** of Ahab shall perish, 2 Kgs 9:8
And I will make the **h** of Ahab like the 2 Kgs 9:9
of Ahab like the **h** of Jeroboam the son 2 Kgs 9:9
and like the **h** of Baasha the son of 2 Kgs 9:9
throne and fight for your master's **h**." 2 Kgs 10:3
spoke concerning the **h** of Ahab, 2 Kgs 10:10
who remained of the **h** of Ahab in 2 Kgs 10:11
And they entered the **h** of Baal, and 2 Kgs 10:21
and the **h** of Baal was filled from one 2 Kgs 10:21
Jehu went into the **h** of Baal with 2 Kgs 10:23
into the inner room of the **h** of Baal, 2 Kgs 10:25
that was in the **h** of Baal and burned 2 Kgs 10:26
Baal, and demolished the **h** of Baal, 2 Kgs 10:27
done to the **h** of Ahab according 2 Kgs 10:30
six years, hidden in the **h** of the LORD, 2 Kgs 11:3

come to him in the **h** of the LORD. 2 Kgs 11:4
them under oath in the **h** of the LORD, 2 Kgs 11:4
the Sabbath and guard the king's **h** 2 Kgs 11:5
Sabbath and guard the **h** of the LORD 2 Kgs 11:7
which were in the **h** of the LORD. 2 Kgs 11:10
south side of the **h** to the north side 2 Kgs 11:11
the house to the north side of the **h**, 2 Kgs 11:11
the altar and the **h** on behalf of the 2 Kgs 11:11
she went into the **h** of the LORD to the 2 Kgs 11:13
be put to death in the **h** of the LORD." 2 Kgs 11:15
the horses' entrance to the king's **h**, 2 Kgs 11:16
land went to the **h** of Baal and tore 2 Kgs 11:18
watchmen over the **h** of the LORD. 2 Kgs 11:18
king down from the **h** of the LORD, 2 Kgs 11:19
the gate of the guards to the king's **h**. 2 Kgs 11:19
death with the sword at the king's **h**. 2 Kgs 11:20
that is brought into the **h** of the LORD, 2 Kgs 12:4
him to bring into the **h** of the LORD, 2 Kgs 12:4
them repair the **h** wherever any need 2 Kgs 12:5
priests had made no repairs on the **h**. 2 Kgs 12:6
"Why are you not repairing the **h**? 2 Kgs 12:7
hand it over for the repair of the **h**." 2 Kgs 12:7
and that they should not repair the **h**. 2 Kgs 12:8
side as one entered the **h** of the LORD. 2 Kgs 12:9
was brought into the **h** of the LORD. 2 Kgs 12:9
that was found in the **h** of the LORD. 2 Kgs 12:10
the oversight of the **h** of the LORD. 2 Kgs 12:11
who worked on the **h** of the LORD, 2 Kgs 12:11
making repairs on the **h** of the LORD, 2 Kgs 12:12
any outlay for the repairs of the **h**. 2 Kgs 12:12
not made for the **h** of the LORD 2 Kgs 12:13
was brought into the **h** of the LORD, 2 Kgs 12:13
who were repairing the **h** of the LORD 2 Kgs 12:14
not brought into the **h** of the LORD; 2 Kgs 12:16
the treasuries of the **h** of the LORD 2 Kgs 12:18
of the LORD and of the king's **h**, 2 Kgs 12:18
struck down Joash in the **h** of Millo, 2 Kgs 12:20
from the sins of the **h** of Jeroboam, 2 Kgs 13:6
were found in the **h** of the LORD and 2 Kgs 14:14
and in the treasuries of the king's **h**, 2 Kgs 14:14
his death, and he lived in a separate **h**. 2 Kgs 15:5
of the king's **h** with Argob and 2 Kgs 15:25
the upper gate of the **h** of the LORD. 2 Kgs 15:35
was found in the **h** of the LORD and 2 Kgs 16:8
treasures of the king's **h** and sent a 2 Kgs 16:8
he removed from the front of the **h**, 2 Kgs 16:14
his altar and the **h** of the LORD, 2 Kgs 16:14
been built inside the **h** and the outer 2 Kgs 16:18
to go around the **h** of the LORD, 2 Kgs 16:18
had torn Israel from the **h** of David, 2 Kgs 17:21
was found in the **h** of the LORD and 2 Kgs 18:15
and in the treasuries of the king's **h**. 2 Kgs 18:15
and went into the **h** of the LORD. 2 Kgs 19:1
went up to the **h** of the LORD and 2 Kgs 19:14
remnant of the **h** of Judah shall 2 Kgs 19:30
worshiping in the **h** of Nisroch his 2 Kgs 19:37
says the LORD, 'Set your **h** in order, 2 Kgs 20:1
you shall go up to the **h** of the LORD, 2 Kgs 20:5
shall go up to the **h** of the LORD on the 2 Kgs 20:8
he showed them all his treasure **h**, 2 Kgs 20:13
was nothing in his **h** or in all his 2 Kgs 20:13
seen in your **h**?" And Hezekiah 2 Kgs 20:15
"They have seen all that is in my **h**; 2 Kgs 20:15
coming, when all that is in your **h**, 2 Kgs 20:17
he built altars in the **h** of the LORD, 2 Kgs 21:4
in the two courts of the **h** of the LORD. 2 Kgs 21:5
he set in the **h** of which the LORD 2 Kgs 21:7
and to Solomon his son, "In this **h**, 2 Kgs 21:7
and the plumb line of the **h** of Ahab, 2 Kgs 21:13
was buried in the garden of his **h**, 2 Kgs 21:18
and put the king to death in his **h**. 2 Kgs 21:23
the secretary, to the **h** of the LORD, 2 Kgs 22:3
been brought into the **h** of the LORD, 2 Kgs 22:4
the oversight of the **h** of the LORD, 2 Kgs 22:5
who are at the **h** of the LORD, 2 Kgs 22:5
the house of the LORD, repairing the **h** 2 Kgs 22:5
and quarried stone to repair the **h**. 2 Kgs 22:6
of the Law in the **h** of the LORD." And 2 Kgs 22:8
was found in the **h** and have delivered 2 Kgs 22:9
the oversight of the **h** of the LORD." 2 Kgs 22:9
the king went up to the **h** of the LORD, 2 Kgs 23:2
had been found in the **h** of the LORD. 2 Kgs 23:2
the Asherah from the **h** of the LORD, 2 Kgs 23:6
who were in the **h** of the LORD, 2 Kgs 23:7
at the entrance to the **h** of the LORD, 2 Kgs 23:11
the two courts of the **h** of the LORD, 2 Kgs 23:12
the priest found in the **h** of the LORD. 2 Kgs 23:24
Jerusalem, and the **h** of which I said, 2 Kgs 23:27
the treasures of the **h** of the LORD and 2 Kgs 24:13
and the treasures of the king's **h**, 2 Kgs 24:13
And he burned the **h** of the LORD and 2 Kgs 25:9
LORD and the king's **h** and all the 2 Kgs 25:9
every great **h** he burned down. 2 Kgs 25:9
that were in the **h** of the LORD, 2 Kgs 25:13
sea that were in the **h** of the LORD, 2 Kgs 25:13
had made for the **h** of the LORD, 2 Kgs 25:16
the father of the **h** of Rechab. 1 Chr 2:55
the clans of the **h** of linen workers at 1 Chr 4:21
as priest in the **h** that Solomon built 1 Chr 6:10
of song in the **h** of the LORD after 1 Chr 6:31
until Solomon built the **h** of the LORD 1 Chr 6:32
of the tabernacle of the **h** of God. 1 Chr 6:48
because disaster had befallen his **h**. 1 Chr 7:23
the chief officer of the **h** of God; 1 Chr 9:11
work of the service of the **h** of God. 1 Chr 9:13
and his kinsmen of his fathers' **h**, 1 Chr 9:19
of the gates of the **h** of the LORD, 1 Chr 9:23
of the LORD, that is, the **h** of the tent, 1 Chr 9:23
and the treasures of the **h** of God. 1 Chr 9:26
And they lodged around the **h** of God, 1 Chr 9:27
three sons and all his **h** died together. 1 Chr 10:6
prince Jehoiada, of the **h** of Aaron, 1 Chr 12:27
from his own fathers' **h**. 1 Chr 12:28
their allegiance to the **h** of Saul. 1 Chr 12:29
a new cart, from the **h** of Abinadab, 1 Chr 13:7
it aside to the **h** of Obed-edom the 1 Chr 13:13
Obed-edom in his **h** three months. 1 Chr 13:14
and carpenters to build a **h** for him. 1 Chr 14:1
LORD from the **h** of Obed-edom with 1 Chr 15:25
all the people departed each to his **h**, 1 Chr 16:43
Now when David lived in his **h**, 1 Chr 17:1
"Behold, I dwell in a **h** of cedar, 1 Chr 17:1
who will build me a **h** to dwell in. 1 Chr 17:4
have not lived in a **h** since the day I 1 Chr 17:5
have you not built me a **h** of cedar?"' 1 Chr 17:6
you that the LORD will build you a **h**. 1 Chr 17:10
He shall build a **h** for me, and I will 1 Chr 17:12
confirm him in my **h** and in my 1 Chr 17:14
am I, O LORD God, and what is my **h**, 1 Chr 17:16
of your servant's **h** for a great 1 Chr 17:17
concerning his **h** be established 1 Chr 17:23
and the **h** of your servant David will 1 Chr 17:24
that you will build a **h** for him. 1 Chr 17:25
to bless the **h** of your servant, 1 Chr 17:27
me and against my father's **h**. 1 Chr 21:17
"Here shall be the **h** of the LORD God 1 Chr 22:1
stones for building the **h** of God. 1 Chr 22:2
and the **h** that is to be built for the 1 Chr 22:5
him to build a **h** for the LORD, 1 Chr 22:6
my heart to build a **h** to the name of 1 Chr 22:7
You shall not build a **h** to my name, 1 Chr 22:8
He shall build a **h** for my name. He 1 Chr 22:10
in building the **h** of the LORD 1 Chr 22:11
have provided for the **h** of the LORD 1 Chr 22:14
be brought into a **h** built for the 1 Chr 22:19
of the work in the **h** of the LORD, 1 Chr 23:4
counted as a single father's **h**. 1 Chr 23:11
for the service of the **h** of the LORD. 1 Chr 23:24
for the service of the **h** of the LORD, 1 Chr 23:28
work for the service of the **h** of God. 1 Chr 23:28
for the service of the **h** of the LORD. 1 Chr 23:32
one father's **h** being chosen for 1 Chr 24:6
to come into the **h** of the LORD 1 Chr 24:19
of each father's **h** and his younger 1 Chr 24:31
in the music in the **h** of the LORD with 1 Chr 25:6
lyres for the service of the **h** of God. 1 Chr 25:6
did, ministering in the **h** of the LORD. 1 Chr 26:12
the treasuries of the **h** of God and 1 Chr 26:20
of the treasuries of the **h** of the LORD. 1 Chr 26:22
maintenance of the **h** of the LORD. 1 Chr 26:27
my heart to build a **h** of rest for the 1 Chr 28:2
'You may not build a **h** for my name, 1 Chr 28:3
from all my father's **h** to be king over 1 Chr 28:4
and in the **h** of Judah my father's 1 Chr 28:4
in the house of Judah my father's **h**, 1 Chr 28:4
who shall build my **h** and my courts, 1 Chr 28:6
you to build a **h** for the sanctuary; 1 Chr 28:10
for the courts of the **h** of the LORD, 1 Chr 28:12
the treasuries of the **h** of God, 1 Chr 28:12
of the service in the **h** of the LORD; 1 Chr 28:13
for the service in the **h** of the LORD, 1 Chr 28:13
for the service of the **h** of the LORD is 1 Chr 28:20
for all the service of the **h** of God; 1 Chr 28:21
I have provided for the **h** of my God, 1 Chr 29:2
all that I have provided for the holy **h**, 1 Chr 29:3
of my devotion to the **h** of my God I 1 Chr 29:3
of my God I give it to the **h** of my God: 1 Chr 29:3
for overlaying the walls of the **h**, 1 Chr 29:4
the service of the **h** of God 5,000 1 Chr 29:7
to the treasury of the **h** of the LORD, 1 Chr 29:8
for building you a **h** for your holy 1 Chr 29:16
cedar to build himself a **h** to dwell in, 2 Chr 2:3
am about to build a **h** for the name of 2 Chr 2:4
The **h** that I am to build will be great, 2 Chr 2:5
But who is able to build him a **h**, since 2 Chr 2:6
Who am I to build a **h** for him, except 2 Chr 2:6
for the **h** I am to build will be great 2 Chr 2:9
began to build the **h** of the LORD in 2 Chr 3:1
for building the **h** of God: 2 Chr 3:3
the nave of the **h** was twenty cubits 2 Chr 3:4
long, equal to the width of the **h**, 2 Chr 3:4
He adorned the **h** with settings of 2 Chr 3:6
So he lined the **h** with gold—its 2 Chr 3:7
corresponding to the breadth of the **h**, 2 Chr 3:8
five cubits, touched the wall of the **h**, 2 Chr 3:11
five cubits, touched the wall of the **h**, 2 Chr 3:12
In front of the **h** he made two pillars 2 Chr 3:15
sea at the southeast corner of the **h**. 2 Chr 4:10
for King Solomon on the **h** of God: 2 Chr 4:11
King Solomon for the **h** of the LORD. 2 Chr 4:16
the vessels that were in the **h** of God: 2 Chr 4:19
Solomon did for the **h** of the LORD was 2 Chr 5:1
in the treasuries of the **h** of God. 2 Chr 5:1
place, in the inner sanctuary of the **h**, 2 Chr 5:7
steadfast love endures forever," the **h**, 2 Chr 5:13
forever," the house, the **h** of the LORD, 2 Chr 5:13
glory of the LORD filled the **h** of God. 2 Chr 5:14
But I have built you an exalted **h**, a 2 Chr 6:2
tribes of Israel in which to build a **h**, 2 Chr 6:5
my father to build a **h** for the name of 2 Chr 6:7
your heart to build a **h** for my name, 2 Chr 6:8
it is not you who shall build the **h**, 2 Chr 6:9
to you shall build the **h** for my name.' 2 Chr 6:9
and I have built the **h** for the name of 2 Chr 6:10
how much less this **h** that I have 2 Chr 6:18
be open day and night toward this **h**, 2 Chr 6:20
his oath before your altar in this **h**, 2 Chr 6:22
pray and plead with you in this **h**, 2 Chr 6:24
out his hands toward this **h**, 2 Chr 6:29
he comes and prays toward this **h**, 2 Chr 6:32
may know that this **h** that I have 2 Chr 6:33
have chosen and the **h** that I have 2 Chr 6:34
have chosen and the **h** that I have 2 Chr 6:38
could not enter the **h** of the LORD, 2 Chr 7:2
the glory of the LORD filled the LORD'S **h**. 2 Chr 7:2
all the people dedicated the **h** of God. 2 Chr 7:5
court that was before the **h** of the LORD, 2 Chr 7:7
Solomon finished the **h** of the LORD 2 Chr 7:11
house of the LORD and the king's **h**. 2 Chr 7:11
planned to do in the **h** of the LORD and 2 Chr 7:11
in his own **h** he successfully 2 Chr 7:11
place for myself as a **h** of sacrifice. 2 Chr 7:12
and consecrated this **h** that my name 2 Chr 7:16
and this **h** that I have consecrated for 2 Chr 7:20
And at this **h**, which was exalted, 2 Chr 7:21
done thus to this land and to this **h**?' 2 Chr 7:21
Solomon had built the **h** of the LORD 2 Chr 8:1
the house of the LORD and his own **h**, 2 Chr 8:1
of David to the **h** that he had built 2 Chr 8:11
not live in the **h** of David king of 2 Chr 8:11
the foundation of the **h** of the LORD 2 Chr 8:16
So the **h** of the LORD was completed. 2 Chr 8:16
of Solomon, the **h** that he had built, 2 Chr 9:3
that he offered at the **h** of the LORD, 2 Chr 9:4
wood supports for the **h** of the LORD 2 Chr 9:11
of the LORD and for the king's **h**, 2 Chr 9:11
put them in the **H** of the Forest of 2 Chr 9:16
all the vessels of the **H** of the Forest of 2 Chr 9:20
Look now to your own **h**, David." So 2 Chr 10:16
rebellion against the **h** of David to 2 Chr 10:19
he assembled the **h** of Judah and 2 Chr 11:1
the treasures of the **h** of the LORD and 2 Chr 12:9
and the treasures of the king's **h**. 2 Chr 12:9
who kept the door of the king's **h**. 2 Chr 12:10
the king went into the **h** of the LORD, 2 Chr 12:11
of the vestibule of the **h** of the LORD. 2 Chr 15:8
he brought into the **h** of God the 2 Chr 15:18
the treasures of the **h** of the LORD and 2 Chr 16:2
LORD and the king's **h** and sent them 2 Chr 16:2
in safety to his **h** in Jerusalem. 2 Chr 19:1
the governor of the **h** of Judah, 2 Chr 19:11
and Jerusalem, in the **h** of the LORD, 2 Chr 20:5
stand before this **h** and before you 2 Chr 20:9
your name is in this **h**—and cry out 2 Chr 20:9
and trumpets, to the **h** of the LORD. 2 Chr 20:28
of Israel, as the **h** of Ahab had done, 2 Chr 21:6
not willing to destroy the **h** of David, 2 Chr 21:7
as the **h** of Ahab led Israel into 2 Chr 21:13
your brothers, of your father's **h**, 2 Chr 21:13
found that belonged to the king's **h**, 2 Chr 21:17
walked in the ways of the **h** of Ahab, 2 Chr 22:3
the LORD, as the **h** of Ahab had done. 2 Chr 22:4
anointed to destroy the **h** of Ahab. 2 Chr 22:7
judgment on the **h** of Ahab, 2 Chr 22:8
his heart." And the **h** of Ahaziah had 2 Chr 22:9
the royal family of the **h** of Judah. 2 Chr 22:10
six years, hidden in the **h** of God, 2 Chr 22:12
with the king in the **h** of God. 2 Chr 23:3
be at the king's **h** and one third at 2 Chr 23:5
be in the courts of the **h** of the LORD. 2 Chr 23:5
no one enter the **h** of the LORD except 2 Chr 23:6
whoever enters the **h** shall be put 2 Chr 23:7
David's, which were in the **h** of God. 2 Chr 23:9
south side of the **h** to the north side 2 Chr 23:10
the house to the north side of the **h**, 2 Chr 23:10

house, around the altar and the **h**. 2 Chr 23:10
she went into the **h** of the LORD to the 2 Chr 23:12
her to death in the **h** of the LORD." 2 Chr 23:14
of the horse gate of the king's **h**, 2 Chr 23:15
people went to the **h** of Baal and tore 2 Chr 23:17
watchmen for the **h** of the LORD 2 Chr 23:18
to be in charge of the **h** of the LORD, 2 Chr 23:18
at the gates of the **h** of the LORD so 2 Chr 23:19
king down from the **h** of the LORD, 2 Chr 23:20
the upper gate to the king's **h**. 2 Chr 23:20
decided to restore the **h** of the LORD. 2 Chr 24:4
money to repair the **h** of your God 2 Chr 24:5
had broken into the **h** of God, 2 Chr 24:7
dedicated things of the **h** of the LORD 2 Chr 24:7
it outside the gate of the **h** of the LORD. 2 Chr 24:8
of the work of the **h** of the LORD, 2 Chr 24:12
to restore the **h** of the LORD, 2 Chr 24:12
bronze to repair the **h** of the LORD. 2 Chr 24:12
and they restored the **h** of God to its 2 Chr 24:13
made utensils for the **h** of the LORD, 2 Chr 24:14
burnt offerings in the **h** of the LORD 2 Chr 24:14
in Israel, and toward God and his **h**. 2 Chr 24:16
they abandoned the **h** of the LORD, 2 Chr 24:18
in the court of the **h** of the LORD. 2 Chr 24:21
the rebuilding of the **h** of God are 2 Chr 24:27
that were found in the **h** of God, 2 Chr 25:24
also the treasuries of the king's **h**, 2 Chr 25:24
of the priests in the **h** of the LORD, 2 Chr 26:19
being a leper lived in a separate **h**, 2 Chr 26:21
was excluded from the **h** of the LORD. 2 Chr 26:21
upper gate of the **h** of the LORD and 2 Chr 27:3
a portion from the **h** of the LORD and 2 Chr 28:21
the LORD and the **h** of the king and 2 Chr 28:21
the vessels of the **h** of God and cut 2 Chr 28:24
in pieces the vessels of the **h** of God, 2 Chr 28:24
up the doors of the **h** of the LORD, 2 Chr 28:24
the doors of the **h** of the LORD and 2 Chr 29:3
and consecrate the **h** of the LORD, 2 Chr 29:5
LORD, to cleanse the **h** of the LORD. 2 Chr 29:15
the inner part of the **h** of the LORD to 2 Chr 29:16
into the court of the **h** of the LORD. 2 Chr 29:16
they consecrated the **h** of the LORD, 2 Chr 29:17
have cleansed all the **h** of the LORD, 2 Chr 29:18
and went up to the **h** of the LORD. 2 Chr 29:20
the Levites in the **h** of the LORD with 2 Chr 29:25
offerings to the **h** of the LORD." 2 Chr 29:31
the service of the **h** of the LORD was 2 Chr 29:35
should come to the **h** of the LORD at 2 Chr 30:1
offerings into the **h** of the LORD. 2 Chr 30:15
priest, who was of the **h** of Zadok, 2 Chr 31:10
contributions into the **h** of the LORD, 2 Chr 31:10
chambers in the **h** of the LORD, 2 Chr 31:11
the chief officer of the **h** of God. 2 Chr 31:13
all who entered the **h** of the LORD as 2 Chr 31:16
in the service of the **h** of God and in 2 Chr 31:21
when he came into the **h** of his god, 2 Chr 32:21
he built altars in the **h** of the LORD, 2 Chr 33:4
in the two courts of the **h** of the LORD. 2 Chr 33:5
he had made he set in the **h** of God, 2 Chr 33:7
and to Solomon his son, "In this **h**, 2 Chr 33:7
and the idol from the **h** of the LORD, 2 Chr 33:15
the mountain of the **h** of the LORD 2 Chr 33:15
and they buried him in his **h**, 2 Chr 33:20
him and put him to death in his **h**. 2 Chr 33:24
he had cleansed the land and the **h**, 2 Chr 34:8
to repair the **h** of the LORD his God. 2 Chr 34:8
had been brought into the **h** of God, 2 Chr 34:9
were working in the **h** of the LORD. 2 Chr 34:10
were working in the **h** of the LORD 2 Chr 34:10
it for repairing and restoring the **h**. 2 Chr 34:10
been brought into the **h** of the LORD, 2 Chr 34:14
of the Law in the **h** of the LORD." And 2 Chr 34:15
was found in the **h** of the LORD and 2 Chr 34:17
king went up to the **h** of the LORD, 2 Chr 34:30
had been found in the **h** of the LORD. 2 Chr 34:30
in the service of the **h** of the LORD. 2 Chr 35:2
holy ark in the **h** that Solomon the 2 Chr 35:3
the chief officers of the **h** of God, 2 Chr 35:8
but against the **h** with which I am 2 Chr 35:21
of the vessels of the **h** of the LORD to 2 Chr 36:7
precious vessels of the **h** of the LORD, 2 Chr 36:10
And they polluted the **h** of the LORD 2 Chr 36:14
sword in the **h** of their sanctuary 2 Chr 36:17
And all the vessels of the **h** of God, 2 Chr 36:18
the treasures of the **h** of the LORD, 2 Chr 36:18
And they burned the **h** of God and 2 Chr 36:19
me to build him a **h** at Jerusalem, 2 Chr 36:23
me to build him a **h** at Jerusalem, Ezr 1:2
is in Judah, and rebuild the **h** of the LORD, Ezr 1:3
freewill offerings for the **h** of God that is Ezr 1:4
go up to rebuild the **h** of the LORD that is Ezr 1:5
out the vessels of the **h** of the LORD that Ezr 1:7
Jerusalem and placed in the **h** of his gods. Ezr 1:7
the sons of Jedaiah, of the **h** of Jeshua, Ezr 2:36
they came to the **h** of the LORD that Ezr 2:68
made freewill offerings for the **h** of God, Ezr 2:68
their coming to the **h** of God at Ezr 3:8
to supervise the work of the **h** of the LORD. Ezr 3:8
supervised the workmen in the **h** of God, Ezr 3:9
the foundation of the **h** of the LORD was Ezr 3:11
old men who had seen the first **h**, Ezr 3:12
saw the foundation of this **h** being laid, Ezr 3:12
to do with us in building a **h** to our God; Ezr 4:3
Then the work on the **h** of God that is in Ezr 4:24
and began to rebuild the **h** of God that is Ezr 5:2
a decree to build this **h** and to finish this Ezr 5:3
of Judah, to the **h** of the great God. Ezr 5:8
a decree to build this **h** and to finish this Ezr 5:9
we are rebuilding the **h** that was built Ezr 5:11
who destroyed this **h** and carried away Ezr 5:12
a decree that this **h** of God should be Ezr 5:13
gold and silver vessels of the **h** of God, Ezr 5:14
and let the **h** of God be rebuilt on its Ezr 5:15
the foundations of the **h** of God that is Ezr 5:16
the rebuilding of this **h** of God in Ezr 5:17
in the **h** of the archives where the Ezr 6:1
Concerning the **h** of God at Jerusalem, let Ezr 6:3
of God at Jerusalem, let the **h** be rebuilt, Ezr 6:3
the gold and silver vessels of the **h** of God, Ezr 6:5
You shall put them in the **h** of God. Ezr 6:5
Let the work on this **h** of God alone. Let Ezr 6:7
of the Jews rebuild this **h** of God on its Ezr 6:7
Jews for the rebuilding of this **h** of God. Ezr 6:8
a beam shall be pulled out of his **h**, Ezr 6:11
it, and his **h** shall be made a dunghill. Ezr 6:11
or to destroy this **h** of God that is in Ezr 6:12
and this **h** was finished on the third day Ezr 6:15
the dedication of this **h** of God with joy. Ezr 6:16
the dedication of this **h** of God 100 Ezr 6:17
aided them in the work of the **h** of God, Ezr 6:22
vowed willingly for the **h** of their God Ezr 7:16
on the altar of the **h** of your God that is Ezr 7:17
you for the service of the **h** of your God, Ezr 7:19
else is required for the **h** of your God, Ezr 7:20
done in full for the **h** of the God of Ezr 7:23
or other servants of this **h** of God. Ezr 7:24
to beautify the **h** of the LORD that is in Ezr 7:27
send us ministers for the **h** of our God. Ezr 8:17
the offering for the **h** of our God that the Ezr 8:25
the chambers of the **h** of the LORD." Ezr 8:29
them to Jerusalem, to the **h** of our God. Ezr 8:30
the fourth day, within the **h** of our God, Ezr 8:33
they aided the people and the **h** of God. Ezr 8:36
some reviving to set up the **h** of our God, Ezr 9:9
himself down before the **h** of God, Ezr 10:1
withdrew from before the **h** of God and Ezr 10:6
in the open square before the **h** of God, Ezr 10:9
Even I and my father's **h** have sinned. Neh 1:6
and for the **h** that I shall occupy." And Neh 2:8
of Harumaph repaired opposite his **h**. Neh 3:10
and as far as the **h** of the mighty men. Neh 3:16
to the door of the **h** of Eliashib the high Neh 3:20
the door of the **h** of Eliashib to the Neh 3:21
Eliashib to the end of the **h** of Eliashib. Neh 3:21
and Hasshub repaired opposite their **h**. Neh 3:23
of Ananiah repaired beside his own **h**. Neh 3:23
from the **h** of Azariah to the buttress Neh 3:24
projecting from the upper **h** of the king Neh 3:25
repaired, each one opposite his own **h**. Neh 3:28
of Immer repaired opposite his own **h**. Neh 3:29
as far as the **h** of the temple servants Neh 3:31
stood behind the whole **h** of Judah, Neh 4:16
every man from his **h** and from his Neh 5:13
I went into the **h** of Shemaiah the son Neh 6:10
"Let us meet together in the **h** of God, Neh 6:10
of Jedaiah, namely the **h** of Jeshua, Neh 7:39
and in the courts of the **h** of God, Neh 8:16
for the service of the **h** of our God: Neh 10:32
for all the work of the **h** of our God. Neh 10:33
to bring it into the **h** of our God, Neh 10:34
tree, year by year, to the **h** of the LORD; Neh 10:35
also to bring to the **h** of our God, to Neh 10:36
who minister in the **h** of our God, Neh 10:36
to the chambers of the **h** of our God; Neh 10:37
tithe of the tithes to the **h** of our God, Neh 10:38
We will not neglect the **h** of our God." Neh 10:39
son of Ahitub, ruler of the **h** of God, Neh 11:11
brothers who did the work of the **h**, Neh 11:12
over the outside work of the **h** of God; Neh 11:16
singers, over the work of the **h** of God. Neh 11:22
of the wall, above the **h** of David, Neh 12:37
gave thanks stood in the **h** of God, Neh 12:40
over the chambers of the **h** of our God, Neh 13:4
chamber in the courts of the **h** of God. Neh 13:7
back there the vessels of the **h** of God, Neh 13:9
"Why is the **h** of God forsaken?" And Neh 13:11
I have done for the **h** of my God and Neh 13:14
but you and your father's **h** will perish. Est 4:14
But Haman hurried to his **h**, mourning Est 6:12
in my own **h**?" As the word left the Est 7:8
saved the king, is standing at Haman's **h**, Est 7:9
gave to Queen Esther the **h** of Haman, Est 8:1
Esther set Mordecai over the **h** of Haman. Est 8:2
I have given Esther the **h** of Haman, Est 8:7
For Mordecai was great in the king's **h**, Est 9:4
and hold a feast in the **h** of each one on his Jb 1:4
around him and his **h** and all that he Jb 1:10
drinking wine in their oldest brother's **h**, Jb 1:13
drinking wine in their oldest brother's **h**, Jb 1:18
and struck the four corners of the **h**, Jb 1:19
he returns no more to his **h**, nor does his Jb 7:10
He leans against his **h**, but it does not Jb 8:15
stone heap; he looks upon a **h** of stones. Jb 8:17
If I hope for Sheol as my **h**, if I make my Jb 17:13
guests in my **h** and my maidservants Jb 19:15
he has seized a **h** that he did not build. Jb 20:19
The possessions of his **h** will be carried Jb 20:28
you say, 'Where is the **h** of the prince? Jb 21:28
He builds his **h** like a moth's, like a Jb 27:18
death and to the **h** appointed for all Jb 30:23
before, and ate bread with him in his **h**. Jb 42:11
of your steadfast love, will enter your **h**. Ps 5:7
I shall dwell in the **h** of the LORD forever. Ps 23:6
the habitation of your **h** and the place Ps 26:8
I may dwell in the **h** of the LORD all the Ps 27:4
They feast on the abundance of your **h**, Ps 36:8
in procession to the **h** of God with glad Ps 42:4
forget your people and your father's **h**, Ps 45:10
rich, when the glory of his **h** increases. Ps 49:16
a bull from your **h** or goats from your Ps 50:9
has come to the **h** of Ahimelech." Ps 52:T
am like a green olive tree in the **h** of God. Ps 52:8
within God's **h** we walked in the throng. Ps 55:14
sent men to watch his **h** in order to kill Ps 59:T
be satisfied with the goodness of your **h**, Ps 65:4
come into your **h** with burnt offerings; Ps 66:13
For zeal for your **h** has consumed me, Ps 69:9
Blessed are those who dwell in your **h**, Ps 84:4
a doorkeeper in the **h** of my God than Ps 84:10
They are planted in the **h** of the LORD; Ps 92:13
holiness befits your **h**, O LORD, Ps 93:5
love and faithfulness to the **h** of Israel. Ps 98:3
with integrity of heart within my **h**; Ps 101:2
practices deceit shall dwell in my **h**; Ps 101:7
made him lord of his **h** and ruler of all Ps 105:21
Wealth and riches are in his **h**, and his Ps 112:3
the **h** of Jacob from a people of strange Ps 114:1
O **h** of Aaron, trust in the LORD! He is Ps 115:10
bless us; he will bless the **h** of Israel; Ps 115:12
of Israel; he will bless the **h** of Aaron; Ps 115:12
in the courts of the **h** of the LORD, in Ps 116:19
Let the **h** of Aaron say, "His steadfast Ps 118:3
We bless you from the **h** of the LORD. Ps 118:26
my songs in the **h** of my sojourning. Ps 119:54
to me, "Let us go to the **h** of the LORD!" Ps 122:1
were set, the thrones of the **h** of David. Ps 122:5
For the sake of the **h** of the LORD our Ps 122:9
Unless the LORD builds the **h**, those who Ps 127:1
be like a fruitful vine within your **h**; Ps 128:3
"I will not enter my **h** or get into my Ps 132:3
who stand by night in the **h** of the LORD! Ps 134:1
who stand in the **h** of the LORD, in the Ps 135:2
LORD, in the courts of the **h** of our God! Ps 135:2
O **h** of Israel, bless the LORD! O house Ps 135:19
the LORD! O **h** of Aaron, bless the LORD! Ps 135:19
O **h** of Levi, bless the LORD! You who Ps 135:20
for her **h** sinks down to death, and her Prv 2:18
LORD'S curse is on the **h** of the wicked, Prv 3:33
her, and do not go near the door of her **h**, Prv 5:8
your labors go to the **h** of a foreigner, Prv 5:10
he will give all the goods of his **h**. Prv 6:31
at the window of my **h** I have looked out Prv 7:6
near her corner, taking the road to her **h** Prv 7:8
Her **h** is the way to Sheol, going down to Prv 7:27
Wisdom has built her **h**; she has hewn Prv 9:1
She sits at the door of her **h**; she takes a Prv 9:14
but the **h** of the righteous will stand. Prv 12:7
The wisest of women builds her **h**, but Prv 14:1
The **h** of the wicked will be destroyed, Prv 14:11
In the **h** of the righteous there is much Prv 15:6
LORD tears down the **h** of the proud but Prv 15:25
with quiet than a **h** full of feasting with Prv 17:1
good, evil will not depart from his **h**. Prv 17:13
H and wealth are inherited from Prv 19:14
housetop than in a **h** shared with a Prv 21:9
One observes the **h** of the wicked; Prv 21:12
By wisdom a **h** is built, and by Prv 24:3
the field, and after that build your **h**. Prv 24:27
foot be seldom in your neighbor's **h**, Prv 25:17
housetop than in a **h** shared with a Prv 25:24
not go to your brother's **h** in the day of Prv 27:10
and had slaves who were born in my **h**. Eccl 2:7
your steps when you go to the **h** of God. Eccl 5:1
to go to the **h** of mourning than to Eccl 7:2
than to go to the **h** of feasting, Eccl 7:2

of the wise is in the **h** of mourning, Eccl 7:4
the heart of fools is in the **h** of mirth. Eccl 7:4
and through indolence the **h** leaks. Eccl 10:18
day when the keepers of the **h** tremble, Eccl 12:3
the beams of our **h** are cedar; our rafters Sg 1:17
He brought me to the banqueting **h**, and Sg 2:4
I had brought him into my mother's **h**, Sg 3:4
and bring you into the **h** of my mother— Sg 8:2
offered for love all the wealth of his **h**, Sg 8:7
the mountain of the **h** of the LORD shall Is 2:2
of the LORD, to the **h** of the God of Jacob, Is 2:3
O **h** of Jacob, come, let us walk in the light Is 2:5
have rejected your people, the **h** of Jacob, Is 2:6
hold of his brother in the **h** of his father, Is 3:6
in my **h** there is neither bread nor cloak; Is 3:7
of the LORD of hosts is the **h** of Israel, Is 5:7
Woe to those who join **h** to house, who add Is 5:8
Woe to those who join house to **h**, who add Is 5:8
called, and the **h** was filled with smoke. Is 6:4
When the **h** of David was told, "Syria is in Is 7:2
And he said, "Hear then, O **h** of David! Is Is 7:13
and upon your father's **h** such days as Is 7:17
is hiding his face from the **h** of Jacob, Is 8:17
the survivors of the **h** of Jacob will no Is 10:20
will attach themselves to the **h** of Jacob. Is 14:1
and the **h** of Israel will possess them in Is 14:2
to the weapons of the **H** of the Forest, Is 22:8
chariots, you shame of your master's **h**. Is 22:18
of Jerusalem and to the **h** of Judah. Is 22:21
his shoulder the key of the **h** of David. Is 22:22
a throne of honor to his father's **h**. Is 22:23
him the whole honor of his father's **h**, Is 22:24
Tyre is laid waste, without **h** or harbor! Is 23:1
every **h** is shut up so that none can Is 24:10
Abraham, concerning the **h** of Jacob: Is 29:22
will arise against the **h** of the evildoers Is 31:2
sackcloth and went into the **h** of the LORD. Is 37:1
Hezekiah went up to the **h** of the LORD, Is 37:14
remnant of the **h** of Judah shall Is 37:31
was worshiping in the **h** of Nisroch his Is 37:38
"Thus says the LORD: Set your **h** in order, Is 38:1
the days of our lives, at the **h** of the LORD. Is 38:20
that I shall go up to the **h** of the LORD?" Is 38:22
And he showed them his treasure **h**, the Is 39:2
There was nothing in his **h** or in all his Is 39:2
they seen in your **h**?" Hezekiah answered, Is 39:4
"They have seen all that is in my **h**. Is 39:4
are coming, when all that is in your **h**, Is 39:6
with the beauty of a man, to dwell in a **h**. Is 44:13
"Listen to me, O **h** of Jacob, all the Is 46:3
of Jacob, all the remnant of the **h** of Israel, Is 46:3
Hear this, O **h** of Jacob, who are called by Is 48:1
I will give in my **h** and within my walls a Is 56:5
and make them joyful in my **h** of prayer; Is 56:7
for my **h** shall be called a house of prayer Is 56:7
house shall be called a **h** of prayer for all Is 56:7
transgression, to the **h** of Jacob their sins. Is 58:1
and bring the homeless poor into your **h**; Is 58:7
altar, and I will beautify my beautiful **h**. Is 60:7
great goodness to the **h** of Israel that he Is 63:7
Our holy and beautiful **h**, where our Is 64:11
what is the **h** that you would build for Is 66:1
in a clean vessel to the **h** of the LORD. Is 66:20
Hear the word of the LORD, O **h** of Jacob, Jer 2:4
Jacob, and all the clans of the **h** of Israel. Jer 2:4
so the **h** of Israel shall be shamed: Jer 2:26
In those days the **h** of Judah shall join Jer 3:18
house of Judah shall join the **h** of Israel, Jer 3:18
been treacherous to me, O **h** of Israel, Jer 3:20
For the **h** of Israel and the house of Jer 5:11
of Israel and the **h** of Judah have been Jer 5:11
you a nation from afar, O **h** of Israel, Jer 5:15
Declare this in the **h** of Jacob; proclaim Jer 5:20
"Stand in the gate of the LORD'S **h**, and Jer 7:2
then come and stand before me in this **h**, Jer 7:10
Has this **h**, which is called by my name, Jer 7:11
I will do to the **h** that is called by my Jer 7:14
detestable things in the **h** that is called Jer 7:30
and all the **h** of Israel is uncircumcised Jer 9:26
that the LORD speaks to you, O **h** of Israel. Jer 10:1
The **h** of Israel and the house of Judah Jer 11:10
of Israel and the **h** of Judah have Jer 11:10
What right has my beloved in my **h**, Jer 11:15
of the evil that the **h** of Israel and the Jer 11:17
of Israel and the **h** of Judah have done, Jer 11:17
your brothers and the **h** of your father, Jer 12:6
"I have forsaken my **h**; I have Jer 12:7
will pluck up the **h** of Judah from Jer 12:14
so I made the whole **h** of Israel and the Jer 13:11
Israel and the whole **h** of Judah cling to Jer 13:11
Do not enter the **h** of mourning, or go to Jer 16:5
shall not go into the **h** of feasting to sit Jer 16:8
thank offerings to the **h** of the LORD. Jer 17:26
"Arise, and go down to the potter's **h**, and Jer 18:2
So I went down to the potter's **h**, and Jer 18:3
"O **h** of Israel, can I not do with you as Jer 18:6
so are you in my hand, O **h** of Israel. Jer 18:6
the court of the LORD'S **h** and said to all Jer 19:14
was chief officer in the **h** of the LORD, Jer 20:1
Benjamin Gate of the **h** of the LORD. Jer 20:2
Pashhur, and all who dwell in your **h**, Jer 20:6
"And to the **h** of the king of Judah say, Jer 21:11
O **h** of David! Thus says the LORD: Jer 21:12
"Go down to the **h** of the king of Judah Jer 22:1
enter the gates of this **h** kings who sit on Jer 22:4
that this **h** shall become a desolation. Jer 22:5
the LORD concerning the **h** of the king of Jer 22:6
who builds his **h** by unrighteousness, Jer 22:13
myself a great **h** with spacious upper Jer 22:14
led the offspring of the **h** of Israel out of Jer 23:8
even in my **h** I have found their evil, Jer 23:11
Stand in the court of the LORD'S **h**, and Jer 26:2
come to worship in the **h** of the LORD all Jer 26:2
then I will make this **h** like Shiloh, and I Jer 26:6
these words in the **h** of the LORD. Jer 26:7
saying, 'This **h** shall be like Shiloh, Jer 26:9
around Jeremiah in the **h** of the LORD. Jer 26:9
up from the king's **h** to the house of Jer 26:10
king's house to the **h** of the LORD and Jer 26:10
of the New Gate of the **h** of the LORD. Jer 26:10
to prophesy against this **h** and this city Jer 26:12
the mountain of the **h** a wooded height.' Jer 26:18
vessels of the LORD'S **h** will now shortly Jer 27:16
vessels that are left in the **h** of the LORD, Jer 27:18
the LORD, in the **h** of the king of Judah, Jer 27:18
vessels that are left in the **h** of the LORD, Jer 27:21
the LORD, in the **h** of the king of Judah, Jer 27:21
Gibeon, spoke to me in the **h** of the LORD, Jer 28:1
this place all the vessels of the LORD'S **h**, Jer 28:3
who were standing in the **h** of the LORD, Jer 28:5
Babylon the vessels of the **h** of the LORD, Jer 28:6
to have charge in the **h** of the LORD over Jer 29:26
when I will sow the **h** of Israel and the Jer 31:27
of Israel and the **h** of Judah with the Jer 31:27
new covenant with the **h** of Israel and Jer 31:31
the house of Israel and the **h** of Judah, Jer 31:31
will make with the **h** of Israel after Jer 31:33
abominations in the **h** that is called Jer 32:34
thank offerings to the **h** of the LORD: Jer 33:11
I made to the **h** of Israel and the Jer 33:14
the house of Israel and the **h** of Judah. Jer 33:14
to sit on the throne of the **h** of Israel, Jer 33:17
land of Egypt, out of the **h** of bondage, Jer 34:13
before me in the **h** that is called by Jer 34:15
"Go to the **h** of the Rechabites and speak Jer 35:2
and bring them to the **h** of the LORD, Jer 35:2
sons and the whole **h** of the Rechabites. Jer 35:3
I brought them to the **h** of the LORD into Jer 35:4
You shall not build a **h**; you shall not Jer 35:7
But to the **h** of the Rechabites Jeremiah Jer 35:18
It may be that the **h** of Judah will hear Jer 36:3
banned from going to the **h** of the LORD, Jer 36:5
people in the LORD'S **h** you shall read the Jer 36:6
the words of the LORD in the LORD'S **h**. Jer 36:8
from the scroll, in the **h** of the LORD, Jer 36:10
entry of the New Gate of the LORD'S **h**. Jer 36:10
he went down to the king's **h**, into the Jer 36:12
the king was sitting in the winter **h**, Jer 36:22
him in the **h** of Jonathan the Jer 37:15
him secretly in his **h** and said, Jer 37:17
me back to the **h** of Jonathan the Jer 37:20
a eunuch who was in the king's **h**, Jer 38:7
went from the king's **h** and said to the Jer 38:8
with him and went to the **h** of the king, Jer 38:11
with fire, and you and your **h** shall live. Jer 38:17
the women left in the **h** of the king of Jer 38:22
me back to the **h** of Jonathan to die Jer 38:26
burned the king's **h** and the house Jer 39:8
the king's house and the **h** of the people, Jer 39:8
as the **h** of Israel was ashamed of Jer 48:13
Heshbon, flame from the **h** of Sihon; Jer 48:45
into the holy places of the LORD'S **h**.' Jer 51:51
And he burned the **h** of the LORD, and Jer 52:13
and the king's **h** and all the houses of Jer 52:13
every great **h** he burned down. Jer 52:13
of bronze that were in the **h** of the LORD, Jer 52:17
sea that were in the **h** of the LORD, Jer 52:17
the king had made for the **h** of the LORD, Jer 52:20
bereaves; in the **h** it is like death. Lam 1:20
raised a clamor in the **h** of the LORD as Lam 2:7
they are a rebellious **h**) they will know Ezk 2:5
at their looks, for they are a rebellious **h**. Ezk 2:6
refuse to hear, for they are a rebellious **h**. Ezk 2:7
Be not rebellious like that rebellious **h**; Ezk 2:8
scroll, and go, speak to the **h** of Israel." Ezk 3:1
go to the **h** of Israel and speak with my Ezk 3:4
a hard language, but to the **h** of Israel— Ezk 3:5
But the **h** of Israel will not be willing to Ezk 3:7
Because all the **h** of Israel have a hard Ezk 3:7
their looks, for they are a rebellious **h**." Ezk 3:9
you a watchman for the **h** of Israel. Ezk 3:17
to me, "Go, shut yourself within your **h**. Ezk 3:24
them, for they are a rebellious **h**. Ezk 3:26
him refuse, for they are a rebellious **h**. Ezk 3:27
it. This is a sign for the **h** of Israel. Ezk 4:3
the punishment of the **h** of Israel upon it. Ezk 4:4
bear the punishment of the **h** of Israel. Ezk 4:5
bear the punishment of the **h** of Judah. Ezk 4:6
fire will come out into all the **h** of Israel. Ezk 5:4
the evil abominations of the **h** of Israel, Ezk 6:11
fifth day of the month, as I sat in my **h**, Ezk 8:1
abominations that the **h** of Israel are Ezk 8:6
and all the idols of the **h** of Israel. Ezk 8:10
men of the elders of the **h** of Israel, Ezk 8:11
the elders of the **h** of Israel are doing Ezk 8:12
of the north gate of the **h** of the LORD, Ezk 8:14
into the inner court of the **h** of the LORD. Ezk 8:16
a thing for the **h** of Judah to commit Ezk 8:17
which it rested to the threshold of the **h**. Ezk 9:3
with the elders who were before the **h**. Ezk 9:6
Then he said to them, "Defile the **h**, and Ezk 9:7
"The guilt of the **h** of Israel and Judah is Ezk 9:9
standing on the south side of the **h**, Ezk 10:3
the cherub to the threshold of the **h**, Ezk 10:4
and the **h** was filled with the cloud, Ezk 10:4
went out from the threshold of the **h**, Ezk 10:18
of the east gate of the **h** of the LORD, Ezk 10:19
me to the east gate of the **h** of the LORD, Ezk 11:1
the LORD: So you think, O **h** of Israel. Ezk 11:5
your kinsmen, the whole **h** of Israel, Ezk 11:15
you dwell in the midst of a rebellious **h**, Ezk 12:2
but hear not, for they are a rebellious **h**. Ezk 12:2
though they are a rebellious **h**. Ezk 12:3
made you a sign for the **h** of Israel." Ezk 12:6
"Son of man, has not the **h** of Israel, the Ezk 12:9
not the house of Israel, the rebellious **h**, Ezk 12:9
Jerusalem and all the **h** of Israel who Ezk 12:10
divination within the **h** of Israel. Ezk 12:24
but in your days, O rebellious **h**, Ezk 12:25
behold, they of the **h** of Israel say, Ezk 12:27
or built up a wall for the **h** of Israel, Ezk 13:5
enrolled in the register of the **h** of Israel, Ezk 13:9
Any one of the **h** of Israel who takes his Ezk 14:4
lay hold of the hearts of the **h** of Israel, Ezk 14:5
"Therefore say to the **h** of Israel, Thus Ezk 14:6
For any one of the **h** of Israel, or of the Ezk 14:7
that the **h** of Israel may no more go Ezk 14:11
and speak a parable to the **h** of Israel; Ezk 17:2
"Say now to the rebellious **h**, Do you Ezk 17:12
up his eyes to the idols of the **h** of Israel, Ezk 18:6
his eyes to the idols of the **h** of Israel, Ezk 18:15
Hear now, O **h** of Israel: Is my way not Ezk 18:25
Yet the **h** of Israel says, 'The way of the Ezk 18:29
O **h** of Israel, are my ways not just? Ezk 18:29
I will judge you, O **h** of Israel, Ezk 18:30
spirit! Why will you die, O **h** of Israel? Ezk 18:31
swore to the offspring of the **h** of Jacob, Ezk 20:5
But the **h** of Israel rebelled against me Ezk 20:13
speak to the **h** of Israel and say to Ezk 20:27
"Therefore say to the **h** of Israel, Thus Ezk 20:30
I be inquired of by you, O **h** of Israel? Ezk 20:31
"As for you, O **h** of Israel, thus says the Ezk 20:39
the Lord GOD, there all the **h** of Israel, Ezk 20:40
to your corrupt deeds, O **h** of Israel, Ezk 20:44
the **h** of Israel has become dross to me; Ezk 22:18
behold, this is what they did in my **h**. Ezk 23:39
parable to the rebellious **h** and say to Ezk 24:3
'Say to the **h** of Israel, Thus says the Ezk 24:21
and over the **h** of Judah when they went Ezk 25:3
the **h** of Judah is like all the other Ezk 25:8
revengefully against the **h** of Judah Ezk 25:12
"And for the **h** of Israel there shall be Ezk 28:24
When I gather the **h** of Israel from the Ezk 28:25
been a staff of reed to the **h** of Israel; Ezk 29:6
again be the reliance of the **h** of Israel, Ezk 29:16
a horn to spring up for the **h** of Israel, Ezk 29:21
made a watchman for the **h** of Israel. Ezk 33:7
you, son of man, say to the **h** of Israel, Ezk 33:10
for why will you die, O **h** of Israel? Ezk 33:11
O **h** of Israel, I will judge each of you Ezk 33:20
them, and that they, the **h** of Israel, Ezk 34:30
over the inheritance of the **h** of Israel, Ezk 35:15
people on you, the whole **h** of Israel, Ezk 36:10
when the **h** of Israel lived in their own Ezk 36:17
which the **h** of Israel had profaned Ezk 36:21
"Therefore say to the **h** of Israel, Thus Ezk 36:22
It is not for your sake, O **h** of Israel, Ezk 36:22
for your ways, O **h** of Israel. Ezk 36:32
also I will let the **h** of Israel ask me to Ezk 36:37
these bones are the whole **h** of Israel. Ezk 37:11
and all the **h** of Israel associated Ezk 37:16
For seven months the **h** of Israel will Ezk 39:12
The **h** of Israel shall know that I am Ezk 39:22
shall know that the **h** of Israel went Ezk 39:23
have mercy on the whole **h** of Israel, Ezk 39:25

out my Spirit upon the **h** of Israel, Ezk 39:29
all that you see to the **h** of Israel." Ezk 40:4
And the **h** of Israel shall no more defile Ezk 43:7
describe to the **h** of Israel the temple, Ezk 43:10
And say to the rebellious **h**, to the Ezk 44:6
the rebellious house, to the **h** of Israel, Ezk 44:6
O **h** of Israel, enough of all your Ezk 44:6
block of iniquity to the **h** of Israel, Ezk 44:12
of the offspring of the **h** of Israel, Ezk 44:22
that a blessing may rest on your **h**. Ezk 44:30
It shall belong to the whole **h** of Israel. Ezk 45:6
they shall let the **h** of Israel have the Ezk 45:8
the appointed feasts of the **h** of Israel: Ezk 45:17
atonement on behalf of the **h** of Israel. Ezk 45:17
with some of the vessels of the **h** of God. Dn 1:2
to the land of Shinar, to the **h** of his god, Dn 1:2
Daniel went to his **h** and made the Dn 2:17
was at ease in my **h** and prospering in my Dn 4:4
of the temple, the **h** of God in Jerusalem, Dn 5:3
the vessels of his **h** have been brought Dn 5:23
he went to his **h** where he had windows Dn 6:10
while I will punish the **h** of Jehu for the Hos 1:4
an end to the kingdom of the **h** of Israel. Hos 1:4
no more have mercy on the **h** of Israel, Hos 1:6
But I will have mercy on the **h** of Judah, Hos 1:7
O priests! Pay attention, O **h** of Israel! Hos 5:1
house of Israel! Give ear, O **h** of the king! Hos 5:1
and like dry rot to the **h** of Judah. Hos 5:12
and like a young lion to the **h** of Judah. Hos 5:14
In the **h** of Israel I have seen a horrible Hos 6:10
like a vulture is over the **h** of the LORD, Hos 8:1
it shall not come to the **h** of the LORD. Hos 9:4
his ways, and hatred in the **h** of his God. Hos 9:8
deeds I will drive them out of my **h**. Hos 9:15
lies, and the **h** of Israel with deceit, Hos 11:12
offering are cut off from the **h** of the LORD. Jl 1:9
are withheld from the **h** of your God. Jl 1:13
of the land to the **h** of the LORD your God, Jl 1:14
joy and gladness from the **h** of our God? Jl 1:16
come forth from the **h** of the LORD and Jl 3:18
So I will send a fire upon the **h** of Hazael, Am 1:4
and in the **h** of their God they drink the Am 2:8
testify against the **h** of Jacob," declares Am 3:13
will strike the winter **h** along with the Am 3:15
winter house along with the summer **h**, Am 3:15
over you in lamentation, O **h** of Israel: Am 5:1
shall have ten left to the **h** of Israel." Am 5:3
For thus says the LORD to the **h** of Israel: Am 5:4
he break out like fire in the **h** of Joseph, Am 5:6
or went into the **h** and leaned his hand Am 5:19
years in the wilderness, O **h** of Israel? Am 5:25
nations, to whom the **h** of Israel comes! Am 6:1
And if ten men remain in one **h**, they Am 6:9
him up to bring the bones out of the **h**, Am 6:10
who is in the innermost parts of the **h**, Am 6:10
and the great **h** shall be struck down Am 6:11
fragments, and the little **h** into bits. Am 6:11
nation, O **h** of Israel," declares the LORD, Am 6:14
will rise against the **h** of Jeroboam with Am 7:9
you in the midst of the **h** of Israel. Am 7:10
do not preach against the **h** of Isaac.' Am 7:16
utterly destroy the **h** of Jacob," declares Am 9:8
and shake the **h** of Israel among all the Am 9:9
and the **h** of Jacob shall possess their Ob 1:17
The **h** of Jacob shall be a fire, and the Ob 1:18
be a fire, and the **h** of Joseph a flame, Ob 1:18
a flame, and the **h** of Esau stubble; Ob 1:18
shall be no survivor for the **h** of Esau, Ob 1:18
of Jacob and for the sins of the **h** of Israel. Mi 1:5
they oppress a man and his **h**, a man and Mi 2:2
Should this be said, O **h** of Jacob? Has the Mi 2:7
of Jacob and rulers of the **h** of Israel! Mi 3:1
you heads of the **h** of Jacob and rulers of Mi 3:9
of Jacob and rulers of the **h** of Israel, Mi 3:9
the mountain of the **h** a wooded height. Mi 3:12
the mountain of the **h** of the LORD shall Mi 4:1
of the LORD, to the **h** of the God of Jacob, Mi 4:2
and redeemed you from the **h** of slavery, Mi 6:4
of wickedness in the **h** of the wicked, Mi 6:10
and all the works of the **h** of Ahab; Mi 6:16
man's enemies are the men of his own **h**. Mi 7:6
from the **h** of your gods I will cut off the Na 1:14
to him who gets evil gain for his **h**, Hab 2:9
shame for your **h** by cutting off Hab 2:10
the head of the **h** of the wicked, Hab 3:13
fill their master's **h** with violence and Zep 1:9
of the remnant of the **h** of Judah, Zep 2:7
not yet come to rebuild the **h** of the LORD." Hg 1:2
paneled houses, while this **h** lies in ruins? Hg 1:4
the hills and bring wood and build the **h**, Hg 1:8
Because of my **h** that lies in ruins, while Hg 1:9
of you busies himself with his own **h**. Hg 1:9
came and worked on the **h** of the LORD of Hg 1:14
you who saw this **h** in its former glory? Hg 2:3
come in, and I will fill this **h** with glory, Hg 2:7
latter glory of this **h** shall be greater than Hg 2:9
my **h** shall be built in it, declares the Zec 1:16
you shall rule my **h** and have charge of Zec 3:7
have laid the foundation of this **h**; Zec 4:9
hosts, and it shall enter the **h** of the thief, Zec 5:4
and the **h** of him who swears falsely by Zec 5:4
it shall remain in his **h** and consume it, Zec 5:4
the land of Shinar, to build a **h** for it. Zec 5:11
and go the same day to the **h** of Josiah, Zec 6:10
to the priests of the **h** of the LORD of hosts Zec 7:3
the foundation of the **h** of the LORD of Zec 8:9
O **h** of Judah and house of Israel, Zec 8:13
O house of Judah and **h** of Israel, Zec 8:13
good to Jerusalem and to the **h** of Judah; Zec 8:15
shall be to the **h** of Judah seasons of Zec 8:19
Then I will encamp at my **h** as a guard, Zec 9:8
hosts cares for his flock, the **h** of Judah, Zec 10:3
"I will strengthen the **h** of Judah, and I Zec 10:6
of Judah, and I will save the **h** of Joseph. Zec 10:6
and threw them into the **h** of the LORD, Zec 11:13
for the sake of the **h** of Judah I will keep Zec 12:4
that the glory of the **h** of David and the Zec 12:7
and the **h** of David shall be like God, Zec 12:8
will pour out on the **h** of David and the Zec 12:10
the family of the **h** of David by itself, Zec 12:12
the family of the **h** of Nathan by itself, Zec 12:12
the family of the **h** of Levi by itself, Zec 12:13
fountain opened for the **h** of David and Zec 13:1
I received in the **h** of my friends.' Zec 13:6
And the pots in the **h** of the LORD shall Zec 14:20
be a trader in the **h** of the LORD of hosts Zec 14:21
that there may be food in my **h**. Mal 3:10
And going into the **h** they saw the child Mt 2:11
a stand, and it gives light to all in the **h**. Mt 5:15
a wise man who built his **h** on the rock. Mt 7:24
and the winds blew and beat on that **h**, Mt 7:25
man who built his **h** on the sand. Mt 7:26
the winds blew and beat against that **h**, Mt 7:27
And when Jesus entered Peter's **h**, he saw Mt 8:14
And as Jesus reclined at table in the **h**, Mt 9:10
came to the ruler's **h** and saw the flute Mt 9:23
When he entered the **h**, the blind men Mt 9:28
rather to the lost sheep of the **h** of Israel. Mt 10:6
As you enter the **h**, greet it. Mt 10:12
And if the **h** is worthy, let your peace Mt 10:13
feet when you leave that **h** or town. Mt 10:14
called the master of the **h** Beelzebul, Mt 10:25
how he entered the **h** of God and ate the Mt 12:4
and no city or **h** divided against itself Mt 12:25
enter a strong man's **h** and plunder his Mt 12:29
Then indeed he may plunder his **h**. Mt 12:29
will return to my **h** from which I Mt 12:44
when it comes, it finds the **h** empty, Mt 12:44
Jesus went out of the **h** and sat beside the Mt 13:1
of the master of the **h** came and said to Mt 13:27
he left the crowds and went into the **h**. Mt 13:36
of heaven is like a master of a **h**, Mt 13:52
only to the lost sheep of the **h** of Israel." Mt 15:24
"Yes." And when he came into the **h**, Mt 17:25
like a master of a **h** who went out early Mt 20:1
it they grumbled at the master of the **h**, Mt 20:11
'My **h** shall be called a house of prayer,' Mt 21:13
'My house shall be called a **h** of prayer,' Mt 21:13
a master of a **h** who planted a vineyard Mt 21:33
See, your **h** is left to you desolate. Mt 23:38
not go down to take what is in his **h**, Mt 24:17
the master of the **h** had known in what Mt 24:43
not have let his **h** be broken into. Mt 24:43
at Bethany in the **h** of Simon the leper, Mt 26:6
Passover at your **h** with my disciples.'" Mt 26:18
and entered the **h** of Simon and Mk 1:29
And as he reclined at table in his **h**, Mk 2:15
how he entered the **h** of God, in the time Mk 2:26
And if a **h** is divided against itself, that Mk 3:25
itself, that **h** will not be able to stand. Mk 3:25
enter a strong man's **h** and plunder his Mk 3:27
Then indeed he may plunder his **h**. Mk 3:27
came from the ruler's **h** some who said, Mk 5:35
They came to the **h** of the ruler of the Mk 5:38
said to them, "Whenever you enter a **h**, Mk 6:10
he had entered the **h** and left the people, Mk 7:17
And he entered a **h** and did not want Mk 7:24
And when he had entered the **h**, his Mk 9:28
when he was in the **h** he asked them, Mk 9:33
And in the **h** the disciples asked him Mk 10:10
one who has left **h** or brothers or Mk 10:29
'My **h** shall be called a house of prayer Mk 11:17
shall be called a **h** of prayer for all Mk 11:17
housetop not go down, nor enter his **h**, Mk 13:15
when the master of the **h** will come, Mk 13:35
at Bethany in the **h** of Simon the leper, Mk 14:3
he enters, say to the master of the **h**, Mk 14:14
name was Joseph, of the **h** of David. Lk 1:27
he will reign over the **h** of Jacob forever, Lk 1:33
and she entered the **h** of Zechariah and Lk 1:40
for us in the **h** of his servant David, Lk 1:69
he was of the **h** and lineage of David, Lk 2:4
know that I must be in my Father's **h**?" Lk 2:49
the synagogue and entered Simon's **h**. Lk 4:38
Levi made him a great feast in his **h**, Lk 5:29
how he entered the **h** of God and took and Lk 6:4
he is like a man building a **h**, who dug Lk 6:48
broke against that **h** and could not Lk 6:48
man who built a **h** on the ground Lk 6:49
it fell, and the ruin of that **h** was great." Lk 6:49
When he was not far from the **h**, the Lk 7:6
who had been sent returned to the **h**, Lk 7:10
went into the Pharisee's **h** and took his Lk 7:36
reclining at table in the Pharisee's **h**, Lk 7:37
I entered your **h**; you gave me no water Lk 7:44
not lived in a **h** but among the tombs. Lk 8:27
feet, he implored him to come to his **h**, Lk 8:41
from the ruler's **h** came and said, Lk 8:49
And when he came to the **h**, he allowed Lk 8:51
And whatever **h** you enter, stay there, and Lk 9:4
Whatever **h** you enter, first say, 'Peace Lk 10:5
you enter, first say, 'Peace be to this **h**!' Lk 10:5
And remain in the same **h**, eating and Lk 10:7
his wages. Do not go from **h** to house. Lk 10:7
his wages. Do not go from house to **h**. Lk 10:7
Martha welcomed him into her **h**. Lk 10:38
will return to my **h** from which I Lk 11:24
it finds the **h** swept and put in order. Lk 11:25
the master of the **h** had known at what Lk 12:39
not have left his **h** to be broken into. Lk 12:39
from now on in one **h** there will be five Lk 12:52
the master of the **h** has risen and shut Lk 13:25
Behold, your **h** is forsaken. And I tell Lk 13:35
he went to dine at the **h** of a ruler of the Lk 14:1
the master of the **h** became angry and Lk 14:21
to come in, that my **h** may be filled. Lk 14:23
and sweep the **h** and seek diligently Lk 15:8
and as he came and drew near to the **h**, Lk 15:25
father, to send him to my father's **h**— Lk 16:27
the housetop, with his goods in the **h**, Lk 17:31
this man went down to his **h** justified, Lk 18:14
one who has left **h** or wife or brothers Lk 18:29
down, for I must stay at your **h** today." Lk 19:5
"Today salvation has come to this **h**, Lk 19:9
'My **h** shall be a house of prayer,' Lk 19:46
'My house shall be a **h** of prayer,' Lk 19:46
Follow him into the **h** that he enters Lk 22:10
and tell the master of the **h**, 'The Lk 22:11
bringing him into the high priest's **h**, Lk 22:54
not make my Father's **h** a house of Jn 2:16
make my Father's house a **h** of trade." Jn 2:16
"Zeal for your **h** will consume me." Jn 2:17
[[They went each to his own **h**, Jn 7:53
slave does not remain in the **h** forever; Jn 8:35
but Mary remained seated in the **h**. Jn 11:20
the Jews who were with her in the **h**, Jn 11:31
The **h** was filled with the fragrance of the Jn 12:3
In my Father's **h** are many rooms. If it Jn 14:2
led Jesus from the **h** of Caiaphas to the Jn 18:28
it filled the entire **h** where they were Acts 2:2
Let all the **h** of Israel therefore know Acts 2:36
day, in the temple and from **h** to house, Acts 5:42
day, in the temple and from house to **h**, Acts 5:42
up for three months in his father's **h**, Acts 7:20
years in the wilderness, O **h** of Israel? Acts 7:42
it was Solomon who built a **h** for him. Acts 7:47
What kind of **h** will you build for me, Acts 7:49
the church, and entering **h** after house, Acts 8:3
the church, and entering house after **h**, Acts 8:3
and at the **h** of Judas look for a man of Acts 9:11
So Ananias departed and entered the **h**. Acts 9:17
a tanner, whose **h** is by the seaside." Acts 10:6
having made inquiry for Simon's **h**, Acts 10:17
you to come to his **h** and to hear what Acts 10:22
was praying in my **h** at the ninth Acts 10:30
He is lodging in the **h** of Simon, a Acts 10:32
men arrived at the **h** in which we Acts 11:11
me, and we entered the man's **h**. Acts 11:12
seen the angel stand in his **h** and say, Acts 11:13
realized this, he went to the **h** of Mary, Acts 12:12
come to my **h** and stay." And she Acts 16:15
to him and to all who were in his **h**. Acts 16:32
them up into his **h** and set food before Acts 16:34
an uproar, and attacked the **h** of Jason, Acts 17:5
and went to the **h** of a man named Acts 18:7
His **h** was next door to the synagogue. Acts 18:7
fled out of that **h** naked and wounded. Acts 19:16
you in public and from **h** to house, Acts 20:20
you in public and from house to **h**, Acts 20:20
and we entered the **h** of Philip the Acts 21:8
bringing us to the **h** of Mnason of Acts 21:16
Greet also the church in their **h**. Greet Rom 16:5
together with the church in their **h**, 1 Cor 16:19
from God, a **h** not made with hands, 2 Cor 5:1
to Nympha and the church in her **h**. Col 4:15

idlers, going about from **h** to house, 1 Tm 5:13
idlers, going about from house to **h**, 1 Tm 5:13
Now in a great **h** there are not only 2 Tm 2:20
as holy, useful to the master of the **h**, 2 Tm 2:21
soldier, and the church in your **h**: Phlm 1:2
as Moses also was faithful in all God's **h**. Heb 3:2
the builder of a **h** has more honor than Heb 3:3
house has more honor than the **h** itself. Heb 3:3
(For every **h** is built by someone, but Heb 3:4
was faithful in all God's **h** as a servant, Heb 3:5
Christ is faithful over God's **h** as a son. Heb 3:6
And we are his **h** if indeed we hold fast Heb 3:6
new covenant with the **h** of Israel and Heb 8:8
house of Israel and with the **h** of Judah, Heb 8:8
will make with the **h** of Israel after Heb 8:10
have a great priest over the **h** of God, Heb 10:21
are being built up as a spiritual **h**, 1 Pt 2:5
receive him into your **h** or give him 2 Jn 1:10

HOUSEHOLD (115)
"Go into the ark, you and all your **h**, Gn 7:1
and a member of my **h** will be my heir." Gn 15:3
his children and his **h** after him to Gn 18:19
said to his servant, the oldest of his **h**, Gn 24:2
told her mother's **h** about these things. Gn 24:28
shall I provide for my own **h** also?" Gn 30:30
and Rachel stole her father's **h** gods. Gn 31:19
Rachel had taken the **h** gods and put Gn 31:34
he searched but did not find the **h** gods. Gn 31:35
have you found of all your **h** goods? Gn 31:37
I shall be destroyed, both I and my **h**." Gn 34:30
So Jacob said to his **h** and to all who Gn 35:2
daughters, and all the members of his **h**, Gn 36:6
to the men of her **h** and said to them, Gn 39:14
heard it, and the **h** of Pharaoh heard it. Gn 45:2
to come, so that you and your **h**, Gn 45:11
to his brothers and to his father's **h**, Gn 46:31
him, 'My brothers and my father's **h**, Gn 46:31
and all his father's **h** with food, Gn 47:12
past, Joseph spoke to the **h** of Pharaoh, Gn 50:4
servants of Pharaoh, the elders of his **h**, Gn 50:7
as well as all the **h** of Joseph, his Gn 50:8
Joseph, his brothers, and his father's **h**. Gn 50:8
to Egypt with Jacob, each with his **h**: Ex 1:1
to their fathers' houses, a lamb for a **h**. Ex 12:3
And if the **h** is too small for a lamb, then Ex 12:4
Egypt and against Pharaoh and all his **h**, Dt 6:22
your God and rejoice, you and your **h**. Dt 14:26
you,' because he loves you and your **h**, Dt 15:16
You shall eat it, you and your **h**, before Dt 15:20
your brothers, and all your father's **h**. Jos 2:18
prostitute and her father's **h** and all who Jos 6:25
And the **h** that the LORD takes shall Jos 7:14
he brought near his **h** man by man, Jos 7:18
and he made an ephod and **h** gods, Jgs 17:5
these houses there are an ephod, **h** gods, Jgs 18:14
the carved image, the ephod, the **h** gods, Jgs 18:17
the carved image, the ephod, the **h** gods, Jgs 18:18
the ephod and the **h** gods and the Jgs 18:20
lose your life with the lives of your **h**." Jgs 18:25
he and his men, every man with his **h**, 1 Sm 27:3
were with him, everyone with his **h**, 2 Sm 2:3
LORD blessed Obed-edom and all his **h**. 2 Sm 6:11
has blessed the **h** of Obed-edom and 2 Sm 6:12
And David returned to bless his **h**. But 2 Sm 6:20
went out, and all his **h** after him. 2 Sm 15:16
donkeys are for the king's **h** to ride on, 2 Sm 16:2
bring over the king's **h** and to do his 2 Sm 19:18
the king and his **h** over the Jordan, 2 Sm 19:41
provided food for the king and his **h**. 1 Kgs 4:7
wishes by providing food for my **h**." 1 Kgs 5:9
20,000 cors of wheat as food for his **h**, 1 Kgs 5:11
Arza, who was over the **h** in Tirzah, 1 Kgs 16:9
and he and her **h** ate for many days. 1 Kgs 17:15
called Obadiah, who was over the **h**. 1 Kgs 18:3
come; let us go and tell the king's **h**." 2 Kgs 7:9
and it was told within the king's **h**. 2 Kgs 7:11
to life, "Arise, and depart with your **h**, 2 Kgs 8:1
She went with her **h** and sojourned in 2 Kgs 8:2
Jotham the king's son was over the **h**, 2 Kgs 15:5
son of Hilkiah, who was over the **h**, 2 Kgs 18:18
son of Hilkiah, who was over the **h**, 2 Kgs 18:37
he sent Eliakim, who was over the **h**, 2 Kgs 19:2
necromancers and the **h** gods and 2 Kgs 23:24
remained with the **h** of Obed-edom 1 Chr 13:14
LORD blessed the **h** of Obed-edom 1 Chr 13:14
and David went home to bless his **h**. 1 Chr 16:43
his son was over the king's **h**, 2 Chr 26:21
division of the Levites by fathers' **h**. 2 Chr 35:5
I threw all the **h** furniture of Tobiah Neh 13:8
in his own **h** and speak according Est 1:22
troubles his own **h** will inherit the Prv 11:29
for unjust gain troubles his own **h**, Prv 15:27
food of your **h** and maintenance for Prv 27:27
food for her **h** and portions for Prv 31:15
She is not afraid of snow for her **h**, for Prv 31:21
for all her **h** are clothed in scarlet. Prv 31:21
to the ways of her **h** and does not eat Prv 31:27
steward, to Shebna, who is over the **h**, Is 22:15
the son of Hilkiah, who was over the **h**, Is 36:3
the son of Hilkiah, who was over the **h**, Is 36:22
And he sent Eliakim, who was over the **h**, Is 37:2
LORD,' I will punish that man and his **h**. Jer 23:34
or pillar, without ephod or **h** gods. Hos 3:4
For the **h** gods utter nonsense, and the Zec 10:2
more will they malign those of his **h**. Mt 10:25
enemies will be those of his own **h**. Mt 10:36
in his hometown and in his own **h**." Mt 13:57
whom his master has set over his **h**, Mt 24:45
among his relatives and in his own **h**." Mk 6:4
the wife of Chuza, Herod's **h** manager, Lk 8:3
itself is laid waste, and a divided **h** falls. Lk 11:17
whom his master will set over his **h**, Lk 12:42
And he himself believed, and all his **h**. Jn 4:53
ruler over Egypt and over all his **h**. Acts 7:10
man who feared God with all his **h**, Acts 10:2
you will be saved, you and all your **h**.' Acts 11:14
she was baptized, and her **h** as well, Acts 16:15
you will be saved, you and your **h**." Acts 16:31
along with his entire **h** that he had Acts 16:34
in the Lord, together with his entire **h**. Acts 18:8
(I did baptize also the **h** of Stephanas. 1 Cor 1:16
know that the **h** of Stephanas were 1 Cor 16:15
to those who are of the **h** of faith. Gal 6:10
saints and members of the **h** of God, Eph 2:19
you, especially those of Caesar's **h**. Phil 4:22
He must manage his own **h** well, with 1 Tm 3:4
not know how to manage his own **h**, 1 Tm 3:5
one ought to behave in the **h** of God, 1 Tm 3:15
godliness to their own **h** and to make 1 Tm 5:4
and especially for members of his **h**, 1 Tm 5:8
grant mercy to the **h** of Onesiphorus, 2 Tm 1:16
Aquila, and the **h** of Onesiphorus. 2 Tm 4:19
an ark for the saving of his **h**. Heb 11:7
for judgment to begin at the **h** of God; 1 Pt 4:17

HOUSEHOLDS (12)
carry grain for the famine of your **h**, Gn 42:19
take grain for the famine of your **h**, Gn 42:33
and take your father and your **h**, and Gn 45:18
and as food for yourselves and your **h**, Gn 47:24
with their **h** and all the people who Nm 16:32
eat it in any place, you and your **h**, Nm 18:31
and swallowed them up, with their **h**, Dt 11:6
and you shall rejoice, you and your **h**, Dt 12:7
the LORD takes shall come near by **h**. Jos 7:14
their children and their own **h** well. 1 Tm 3:12
bear children, manage their **h**, 1 Tm 5:14
who creep into **h** and capture weak 2 Tm 3:6

HOUSES (215)
and their wives, all that was in the **h**, Gn 34:29
These are the heads of their fathers' **h**: Ex 6:14
heads of the fathers' **h** of the Levites by Ex 6:25
bed and into the **h** of your servants and Ex 8:3
off from you and your **h** and be left only Ex 8:9
from you and your **h** and your servants Ex 8:11
The frogs died out in the **h**, the Ex 8:13
and your people, and into your **h**. Ex 8:21
And the **h** of the Egyptians shall be filled Ex 8:21
of Pharaoh and into his servants' **h**. Ex 8:24
his slaves and his livestock into the **h**, Ex 9:20
they shall fill your **h** and the houses of Ex 10:6
your houses and the **h** of all your Ex 10:6
a lamb according to their fathers' **h**, Ex 12:3
and the lintel of the **h** in which they eat Ex 12:7
a sign for you, on the **h** where you are. Ex 12:13
you shall remove leaven out of your **h**, Ex 12:15
days no leaven is to be found in your **h**. Ex 12:19
destroyer to enter your **h** to strike you. Ex 12:23
for he passed over the **h** of the people of Ex 12:27
but spared our **h**.'" And the people Ex 12:27
But the **h** of the villages that have no Lv 25:31
at any time the **h** in the cities they Lv 25:32
For the **h** in the cities of the Levites are Lv 25:33
people of Israel, by clans, by fathers' **h**, Nm 1:2
themselves by clans, by fathers' **h**, Nm 1:18
by their clans, by their fathers' **h**, Nm 1:20
by their clans, by their fathers' **h**, Nm 1:22
by their clans, by their fathers' **h**, Nm 1:24
by their clans, by their fathers' **h**, Nm 1:26
by their clans, by their fathers' **h**, Nm 1:28
by their clans, by their fathers' **h**, Nm 1:30
by their clans, by their fathers' **h**, Nm 1:32
by their clans, by their fathers' **h**, Nm 1:34
by their clans, by their fathers' **h**, Nm 1:36
by their clans, by their fathers' **h**, Nm 1:38
by their clans, by their fathers' **h**, Nm 1:40
by their clans, by their fathers' **h**, Nm 1:42
the people of Israel, by their fathers' **h**, Nm 1:45
with the banners of their fathers' **h**. Nm 2:2
of Israel as listed by their fathers' **h**. Nm 2:32
sons of Levi, by fathers' **h** and by clans; Nm 3:15
clans of the Levites, by their fathers' **h**. Nm 3:20
Levi, by their clans and their fathers' **h**, Nm 4:2
by their fathers' **h** and by their clans. Nm 4:22
by their clans and their fathers' **h**. Nm 4:29
by their clans and their fathers' **h**, Nm 4:34
by their clans and their fathers' **h**, Nm 4:38
clans and their fathers' **h** were 2,630. Nm 4:40
by their clans and their fathers' **h**, Nm 4:42
by their clans and their fathers' **h**, Nm 4:46
chiefs of Israel, heads of their fathers' **h**, Nm 7:2
chiefs according to their fathers' **h**, Nm 17:2
chief, according to their fathers' **h**, Nm 17:6
old and upward, by their fathers' **h**, Nm 26:2
of the fathers' **h** of the congregation, Nm 31:26
heads of the fathers' **h** of the tribes of Nm 32:28
of Reuben by fathers' **h** and the tribe Nm 34:14
by their fathers' **h** have received their Nm 34:14
heads of the fathers' **h** of the clan of Nm 36:1
heads of the fathers' **h** of the people of Nm 36:1
and **h** full of all good things that you did Dt 6:11
and have built good **h** and live in them, Dt 8:12
and dwell in their cities and in their **h**, Dt 19:1
we took it from our **h** as our food for the Jos 9:12
the heads of the fathers' **h** of the tribes of Jos 14:1
heads of the fathers' **h** of the tribes of Jos 19:51
heads of the fathers' **h** of the Levites Jos 21:1
the heads of the fathers' **h** of the tribes of Jos 21:1
know that in these **h** there are an Jgs 18:14
who were in the **h** near Micah's house Jgs 18:22
leaders of the fathers' **h** of the people of 1 Kgs 8:1
which Solomon had built the two **h**, 1 Kgs 9:10
and against all the **h** of the high 1 Kgs 13:32
house and the **h** of your servants 1 Kgs 20:6
he broke down the **h** of the male cult 2 Kgs 23:7
house and all the **h** of Jerusalem; 2 Kgs 25:9
and their fathers' **h** increased greatly. 1 Chr 4:38
according to their fathers' **h**: 1 Chr 5:13
of Guni, was chief in their fathers' **h**, 1 Chr 5:15
were the heads of their fathers' **h**: 1 Chr 5:24
men, heads of their fathers' **h**. 1 Chr 5:24
and Shemuel, heads of their fathers' **h**, 1 Chr 7:2
according to their fathers' **h**, 1 Chr 7:4
and Iri, five, heads of fathers' **h**, 1 Chr 7:7
as heads of their fathers' **h**, 1 Chr 7:9
to the heads of their fathers' **h**, 1 Chr 7:11
men of Asher, heads of fathers' **h**, 1 Chr 7:40
heads of fathers' **h** of the inhabitants 1 Chr 8:6
were his sons, heads of fathers' **h**. 1 Chr 8:10
heads of fathers' **h** of the inhabitants 1 Chr 8:13
These were the heads of fathers' **h**, 1 Chr 8:28
heads of fathers' **h** according to their 1 Chr 9:9
houses according to their fathers' **h**. 1 Chr 9:9
kinsmen, heads of their fathers' **h**, 1 Chr 9:13
the heads of fathers' **h** of the Levites, 1 Chr 9:33
were heads of fathers' **h** of the Levites, 1 Chr 9:34
famous men in their fathers' **h**. 1 Chr 12:30
David built **h** for himself in the city 1 Chr 15:1
heads of the fathers' **h** of the Levites. 1 Chr 15:12
the heads of the fathers' **h** of Ladan. 1 Chr 23:9
the sons of Levi by their fathers' **h**, 1 Chr 23:24
the heads of fathers' **h** as they were 1 Chr 23:24
sixteen heads of fathers' **h** of the sons 1 Chr 24:4
heads of the fathers' **h** of the priests 1 Chr 24:6
Levites according to their fathers' **h**. 1 Chr 24:30
the heads of fathers' **h** of the priests 1 Chr 24:31
who were rulers in their fathers' **h**, 1 Chr 26:6
And they cast lots by fathers' **h**, 1 Chr 26:13
of the fathers' **h** belonging to Ladan 1 Chr 26:21
of the fathers' **h** and the officers 1 Chr 26:26
of whatever genealogy or fathers' **h**. 1 Chr 26:31
men of ability, heads of fathers' **h**, 1 Chr 26:32
of Israel, the heads of fathers' **h**, 1 Chr 27:1
vestibule of the temple, and of its **h**, 1 Chr 28:11
leaders of fathers' **h** made their 1 Chr 29:6
in all Israel, the heads of fathers' **h**. 2 Chr 1:2
leaders of the fathers' **h** of the people of 2 Chr 5:2
the muster of them by fathers' **h**: 2 Chr 17:14
and the heads of fathers' **h** of Israel, 2 Chr 23:2
by fathers' **h** under commanders 2 Chr 25:5
heads of fathers' **h** of mighty men 2 Chr 26:12
was according to their fathers' **h**; 2 Chr 31:17
to your fathers' **h** by your divisions, 2 Chr 35:4
of the fathers' **h** of your brothers 2 Chr 35:5
groupings of the fathers' **h** of the lay 2 Chr 35:12
heads of the fathers' **h** of Judah and Ezr 1:5
prove their fathers' **h** or their descent, Ezr 2:59
and Levites and heads of fathers' **h**, Ezr 3:12
the heads of fathers' **h** and said to them, Ezr 4:2
of the heads of fathers' **h** in Israel said to Ezr 4:3
These are the heads of their fathers' **h**, Ezr 8:1
the heads of fathers' **h** in Israel at Ezr 8:29
priest selected men, heads of fathers' **h**, Ezr 10:16
houses, according to their fathers' **h**, Ezr 10:16
and our **h** to get grain because of the Neh 5:3

their olive orchards, and their **h**, Neh 5:11
it were few, and no **h** had been rebuilt. Neh 7:4
prove their fathers' **h** nor their descent, Neh 7:61
the heads of fathers' **h** gave to the work. Neh 7:70
the heads of fathers' **h** gave into the Neh 7:71
the heads of fathers' **h** of all the people, Neh 8:13
and took possession of **h** full of all Neh 9:25
our God, according to our fathers' **h**, Neh 10:34
and his brothers, heads of fathers' **h**, Neh 11:13
were priests, heads of fathers' **h**: Neh 12:12
were recorded as heads of fathers' **h**; Neh 12:22
heads of fathers' **h** were written in Neh 12:23
had gold, who filled their **h** with silver. Jb 3:15
much more those who dwell in **h** of clay, Jb 4:19
cities, in **h** that none should inhabit, Jb 15:28
Their **h** are safe from fear, and no rod of Jb 21:9
what do they care for their **h** after them, Jb 21:21
Yet he filled their **h** with good things— Jb 22:18
In the dark they dig through **h**; by day Jb 24:16
goods, we shall fill our **h** with plunder; Prv 1:13
I built **h** and planted vineyards for Eccl 2:4
the spoil of the poor is in your **h**. Is 3:14
"Surely many **h** shall be desolate, large Is 5:9
shall be desolate, large and beautiful **h**, Is 5:9
inhabitant, and **h** without people, Is 6:11
a rock of stumbling to both **h** of Israel, Is 8:14
their **h** will be plundered and their wives Is 13:16
and their **h** will be full of howling Is 13:21
and you counted the **h** of Jerusalem, and Is 22:10
you broke down the **h** to fortify the wall. Is 22:10
for all the joyous **h** in the exultant city. Is 32:13
They shall build **h** and inhabit them; Is 65:21
adultery and trooped to the **h** of whores. Jer 5:7
full of birds, their **h** are full of deceit; Jer 5:27
Their **h** shall be turned over to others, Jer 6:12
burden out of your **h** on the Sabbath or Jer 17:22
May a cry be heard from their **h**, when Jer 18:22
The **h** of Jerusalem and the houses of Jer 19:13
of Jerusalem and the **h** of the kings of Jer 19:13
Judah—all the **h** on whose roofs Jer 19:13
Build **h** and live in them; plant gardens Jer 29:5
build **h** and live in them, and plant Jer 29:28
H and fields and vineyards shall again Jer 32:15
with the **h** on whose roofs offerings Jer 32:29
concerning the **h** of this city and the Jer 33:4
of this city and the **h** of the kings of Jer 33:4
and not to build **h** to dwell in. We have Jer 35:9
king's house and all the **h** of Jerusalem; Jer 52:13
nations to take possession of their **h**. Ezk 7:24
say, 'The time is not near to build **h**. Ezk 11:3
shall burn your **h** and execute Ezk 16:41
their daughters, and burn up their **h**. Ezk 23:47
walls and destroy your pleasant **h**. Ezk 26:12
they shall build **h** and plant Ezk 28:26
by the walls and at the doors of the **h**, Ezk 33:30
be a place for their **h** and a holy place Ezk 45:4
limb, and your **h** shall be laid in ruins. Dn 2:5
from limb, and their **h** laid in ruins, Dn 3:29
upon the walls, they climb up into the **h**, Jl 2:9
house, and the **h** of ivory shall perish, Am 3:15
and the great **h** shall come to an end," Am 3:15
him, you have built **h** of hewn stone, Am 5:11
the **h** of Achzib shall be a deceitful Mi 1:14
They covet fields and seize them, and **h**, Mi 2:2
you drive out from their delightful **h**; Mi 2:9
be plundered, and their **h** laid waste. Zep 1:13
Though they build **h**, they shall not Zep 1:13
and in the **h** of Ashkelon they shall lie Zep 2:7
you yourselves to dwell in your paneled **h**, Hg 1:4
be taken and the **h** plundered and the Zec 14:2
who wear soft clothing are in kings' **h**. Mt 11:8
everyone who has left **h** or brothers or Mt 19:29
h and brothers and sisters and Mk 10:30
who devour widows' **h** and for a Mk 12:40
people may receive me into their **h**.' Lk 16:4
who devour widows' **h** and for a Lk 20:47
owners of lands or **h** sold them and Acts 4:34
does not dwell in **h** made by hands, Acts 7:48
Do you not have **h** to eat and drink 1 Cor 11:22

HOUSETOP (7)
I am like a lonely sparrow on the **h**. Ps 102:7
in a corner of the **h** than in a house Prv 21:9
in a corner of the **h** than in a house Prv 25:24
one who is on the **h** not go down to take Mt 24:17
the one who is on the **h** not go down, Mk 13:15
On that day, let the one who is on the **h**, Lk 17:31
went up on the **h** about the sixth hour Acts 10:9

HOUSETOPS (8)
like tender grass, like grass on the **h**, 2 Kgs 19:26
Let them be like the grass on the **h**, Ps 129:6
on the **h** and in the squares everyone Is 15:3
that you have gone up, all of you, to the **h**, Is 22:1
and like tender grass, like grass on the **h**, Is 37:27
On all the **h** of Moab and in the squares Jer 48:38
you hear whispered, proclaim on the **h**. Mt 10:27
rooms shall be proclaimed on the **h**. Lk 12:3

HOVERING (2)
the Spirit of God was **h** over the face of the Gn 1:2
Like birds **h**, so the LORD of hosts will Is 31:5

HOW (585)
This is **h** you are to make it: the length Gn 6:15
h am I to know that I shall possess it?" Gn 15:8
And **h** have I sinned against you, that Gn 20:9
H then could you say, 'She is my Gn 26:9
"**H** is it that you have found it so Gn 27:20
and said, "**H** awesome is this place! Gn 28:17
"You yourself know **h** I have served Gn 30:29
and **h** your livestock has fared with Gn 30:29
H then can I do this great wickedness Gn 39:9
H then could we steal silver or gold from Gn 44:8
we speak? Or **h** can we clear ourselves? Gn 44:16
For **h** can I go back to my father if the Gn 44:34
"**H** many are the days of the years of Gn 47:8
for that is **h** many are required for Gn 50:3
"**H** is it that you have come home so Ex 2:18
H then shall Pharaoh listen to me, for I Ex 6:12
lips. **H** will Pharaoh listen to me?" Ex 6:30
and of your grandson **h** I have dealt Ex 10:2
'**H** long will you refuse to humble Ex 10:3
"**H** long shall this man be a snare to us? Ex 10:7
"**H** long will you refuse to keep my Ex 16:28
h the LORD had brought Israel out of Ex 18:1
way, and **h** the LORD had delivered them. Ex 18:8
and **h** I bore you on eagles' wings and Ex 19:4
For **h** shall it be known that I have Ex 33:16
and intelligence to know **h** to do any Ex 36:1
"**H** long will this people despise me? Nm 14:11
And **h** long will they not believe in Nm 14:11
"**H** long shall this wicked Nm 14:27
h our fathers went down to Egypt, and Nm 20:15
H can I curse whom God has not Nm 23:8
H can I denounce whom the LORD has Nm 23:8
H lovely are your tents, O Jacob, your Nm 24:5
H can I bear by myself the weight and Dt 1:12
where you have seen **h** the LORD your Dt 1:31
h on the day that you stood before the Dt 4:10
greater than I. **H** can I dispossess them?' Dt 7:17
and do not forget **h** you provoked the LORD Dt 9:7
h he made the water of the Red Sea flow Dt 11:4
and **h** the LORD has destroyed them to Dt 11:4
h the earth opened its mouth and Dt 11:6
'**H** did these nations serve their gods? Dt 12:30
'**H** may we know the word that the LORD Dt 18:21
h he attacked you on the way when you Dt 25:18
"You know **h** we lived in the land of Dt 29:16
and **h** we came through the midst of the Dt 29:16
For I know **h** rebellious and stubborn Dt 31:27
the LORD. **H** much more after my death! Dt 31:27
H could one have chased a thousand, Dt 32:30
For we have heard **h** the LORD dried up Jos 2:10
"Here is **h** you shall know that the living Jos 3:10
then **h** can we make a covenant with Jos 9:7
heard **h** Joshua had captured Ai and had Jos 10:1
and **h** the inhabitants of Gibeon had Jos 10:1
heard on that day **h** the Anakim were Jos 14:12
"**H** long will you put off going in to take Jos 18:3
to him, "Please, Lord, **h** can I save Israel? Jgs 6:15
lies, and **h** you might be bound, Jgs 16:6
Please tell me **h** you might be bound." Jgs 16:10
Tell me **h** you might be bound." And Jgs 16:13
And she said to him, "**H** can you say, 'I Jgs 16:15
to them, "This is **h** Micah dealt with me: Jgs 18:4
who were there, **h** they lived in security, Jgs 18:7
and **h** they were far from the Sidonians Jgs 18:7
H then do you ask me, 'What is the Jgs 18:24
said, "Tell us, **h** did this evil happen?" Jgs 20:3
and **h** you left your father and mother Ru 2:11
mother-in-law, she said, "**H** did you fare, Ru 3:16
until you learn **h** the matter turns out, Ru 3:18
"**H** long will you go on being drunk? 1 Sm 1:14
and **h** they lay with the women who 1 Sm 2:22
battle today." And he said, "**H** did it go, 1 Sm 4:16
the men of Ashdod saw **h** things were, 1 Sm 5:7
him previously saw **h** he prophesied 1 Sm 10:11
"**H** can this man save us?" And they 1 Sm 10:27
See **h** my eyes have become bright 1 Sm 14:29
H much better if the people had 1 Sm 14:30
and know and see **h** this sin has 1 Sm 14:38
"**H** long will you grieve over Saul, 1 Sm 16:1
And Samuel said, "**H** can I go? If Saul 1 Sm 16:2
H much more today will their vessels 1 Sm 21:5
h much more then if we go to Keilah 1 Sm 23:3
your eyes have seen **h** the LORD gave 1 Sm 24:10
declared this day **h** you have dealt 1 Sm 24:18
h he has cut off the mediums and the 1 Sm 28:9
For **h** could this fellow reconcile 1 Sm 29:4
And David said to him, "**H** did it go? 2 Sm 1:4
"**H** do you know that Saul and his son 2 Sm 1:5
"**H** is it you were not afraid to put out 2 Sm 1:14
places! **H** the mighty have fallen! 2 Sm 1:19
"**H** the mighty have fallen in the 2 Sm 1:25
"**H** the mighty have fallen, and the 2 Sm 1:27
H then could I lift up my face to your 2 Sm 2:22
H long will it be before you tell your 2 Sm 2:26
H much more, when wicked men 2 Sm 4:11
"**H** can the ark of the LORD come to 2 Sm 6:9
"**H** the king of Israel honored himself 2 Sm 6:20
David asked **h** Joab was doing and 2 Sm 11:7
Joab was doing and **h** the people were 2 Sm 11:7
people were doing and **h** the war was 2 Sm 11:7
H then can we say to him the child is 2 Sm 12:18
h much more now may this 2 Sm 16:11
guilty or remember **h** your servant 2 Sm 19:19
"**H** many years have I still to live, 2 Sm 19:34
And **h** shall I make atonement, that 2 Sm 21:3
h he dealt with the two commanders of 1 Kgs 2:5
I do not know **h** to go out or come in. 1 Kgs 3:7
among us who knows **h** to cut timber 1 Kgs 5:6
h much less this house that I have 1 Kgs 8:27
"**H** do you advise me to answer this 1 Kgs 12:6
h he warred and how he reigned, 1 Kgs 14:19
how he warred and **h** he reigned, 1 Kgs 14:19
And he said, "**H** have I sinned, that 1 Kgs 18:9
h I hid a hundred men of the LORD'S 1 Kgs 18:13
"**H** long will you go limping 1 Kgs 18:21
and **h** he had killed all the prophets 1 Kgs 19:1
and see **h** this man is seeking trouble, 1 Kgs 20:7
"Have you seen **h** Ahab has 1 Kgs 21:29
"**H** many times shall I make you 1 Kgs 22:16
"**H** did the Spirit of the LORD go from 1 Kgs 22:24
that he showed, and **h** he warred, 1 Kgs 22:45
"**H** can I set this before a hundred 2 Kgs 4:43
and see **h** he is seeking a quarrel with 2 Kgs 5:7
will not help you, **h** shall I help you? 2 Kgs 6:27
"Do you see **h** this murderer has sent 2 Kgs 6:32
telling the king **h** Elisha had restored 2 Kgs 8:5
h the LORD made this pronouncement 2 Kgs 9:25
before him. **H** then can we stand?" 2 Kgs 10:4
h the king of Syria oppressed them. 2 Kgs 13:4
and **h** he fought with Amaziah king 2 Kgs 14:15
he did, and his might, **h** he fought, 2 Kgs 14:28
and **h** he restored Damascus and 2 Kgs 14:28
and taught them **h** they should fear 2 Kgs 17:28
H then can you repulse a single 2 Kgs 18:24
please remember **h** I have walked 2 Kgs 20:3
all his might and **h** he made the 2 Kgs 20:20
when you heard **h** I spoke against 2 Kgs 22:19
"**H** can I bring the ark of God home 1 Chr 13:12
your servants know **h** to cut timber 2 Chr 2:8
h much less this house that I have 2 Chr 6:18
"**H** do you advise me to answer this 2 Chr 10:6
"**H** many times shall I make you 2 Chr 18:15
H much less will your God deliver 2 Chr 32:15
and **h** God was moved by his 2 Chr 33:19
and salt without prescribing **h** much. Ezr 7:22
beside him), "**H** long will you be gone, Neh 2:6
h Jerusalem lies in ruins with its gates Neh 2:17
the harem to learn **h** Esther was and Est 2:11
and **h** he had advanced him above the Est 5:11
it was found written **h** Mordecai had told Est 6:2
For **h** can I bear to see the calamity that Est 8:6
Or **h** can I bear to see the destruction of Est 8:6
h much more those who dwell in houses Jb 4:19
make me understand **h** I have gone Jb 6:24
H forceful are upright words! But what Jb 6:25
H long will you not look away from me, Jb 7:19
"**H** long will you say these things, and the Jb 8:2
But **h** can a man be in the right before Jb 9:2
H then can I answer him, choosing my Jb 9:14
H many are my iniquities and my sins? Jb 13:23
h much less one who is abominable Jb 15:16
and if I forbear, **h** much of it leaves me? Jb 16:6
"**H** long will you hunt for words? Jb 18:2
"**H** long will you torment me and break Jb 19:2
If you say, '**H** we will pursue him!' and, Jb 19:28
"**H** often is it that the lamp of the wicked Jb 21:17
H then will you comfort me with empty Jb 21:34
See the highest stars, **h** lofty they are! Jb 22:12
H then can man be in the right before Jb 25:4
H can he who is born of woman be pure? Jb 25:4
h much less man, who is a maggot, and Jb 25:6
"**H** you have helped him who has no Jb 26:2
H you have saved the arm that has no Jb 26:2
H you have counseled him who has no Jb 26:3
and **h** small a whisper do we hear of Jb 26:14
my eyes; **h** then could I gaze at a virgin? Jb 31:1
For I do not know **h** to flatter, else my Jb 32:22
I? **H** am I better off than if I had sinned?' Jb 35:3
H much less when you say that you do Jb 35:14
Do you know **h** God lays his command Jb 37:15
O LORD, **h** many are my foes! Many are Ps 3:1
h long shall my honor be turned into Ps 4:2
H long will you love vain words and seek Ps 4:2

troubled. But you, O LORD—**h** long? Ps 6:3
h majestic is your name in all the earth! Ps 8:1
h majestic is your name in all the earth! Ps 8:9
h can you say to my soul, "Flee like a Ps 11:1
H long, O LORD? Will you forget me Ps 13:1
H long will you hide your face from me? Ps 13:1
H long must I take counsel in my soul Ps 13:2
H long shall my enemy be exalted over Ps 13:2
in your salvation **h** greatly he exults! Ps 21:1
Consider **h** many are my foes, and with Ps 25:19
Oh, **h** abundant is your goodness, Ps 31:19
H long, O Lord, will you look on? Ps 35:17
H precious is your steadfast love, O God! Ps 36:7
of my days; let me know **h** fleeting I am! Ps 39:4
h I would go with the throng and lead Ps 42:4
h he has brought desolations on the Ps 46:8
H long will all of you attack a man to Ps 62:3
Say to God, "**H** awesome are your deeds! Ps 66:3
And they say, "**H** can God know? Is Ps 73:11
when I thought **h** to understand this, Ps 73:16
H they are destroyed in a moment, Ps 73:19
is none among us who knows **h** long. Ps 74:9
H long, O God, is the foe to scoff? Is the Ps 74:10
this, O LORD, **h** the enemy scoffs, Ps 74:18
remember **h** the foolish scoff at you all Ps 74:22
H often they rebelled against him in the Ps 78:40
H long, O LORD? Will you be angry Ps 79:5
h long will you be angry with your Ps 80:4
"**H** long will you judge unjustly and Ps 82:2
H lovely is your dwelling place, O LORD of Ps 84:1
H long, O LORD? Will you hide yourself Ps 89:46
H long will your wrath burn like fire? Ps 89:46
Remember **h** short my time is! For Ps 89:47
O Lord, **h** your servants are mocked, Ps 89:50
and **h** I bear in my heart the insults of Ps 89:50
Return, O LORD! **H** long? Have pity on Ps 90:13
H great are your works, O LORD! Your Ps 92:5
O LORD, **h** long shall the wicked, how Ps 94:3
wicked, **h** long shall the wicked exult? Ps 94:3
O LORD, **h** manifold are your works! In Ps 104:24
H can a young man keep his way pure? Ps 119:9
H long must your servant endure? Ps 119:84
Oh **h** I love your law! It is my Ps 119:97
H sweet are your words to my taste, Ps 119:103
Consider **h** I love your precepts! Give Ps 119:159
h he swore to the LORD and vowed to the Ps 132:2
h good and pleasant it is when brothers Ps 133:1
H shall we sing the LORD'S song in a Ps 137:4
the day of Jerusalem, **h** they said, Ps 137:7
H precious to me are your thoughts, O Ps 139:17
O God! **H** vast is the sum of them! Ps 139:17
"**H** long, O simple ones, will you love Prv 1:22
H long will scoffers delight in their Prv 1:22
and you say, "**H** I hated discipline, and Prv 5:12
H long will you lie there, O sluggard? Prv 6:9
h much more the wicked and the Prv 11:31
h much more the hearts of the Prv 15:11
and a word in season, **h** good it is! Prv 15:23
of the righteous ponders **h** to answer, Prv 15:28
H much better to get wisdom than Prv 16:16
h much more do his friends go far from Prv 19:7
h then can man understand his way? Prv 20:24
h much more when he brings it with Prv 21:27
There are those—**h** lofty are their eyes, Prv 30:13
are their eyes, **h** high their eyelids lift! Prv 30:13
searched with my heart **h** to cheer my Eccl 2:3
me with wisdom—and **h** to lay hold on Eccl 2:3
H the wise dies just like the fool! Eccl 2:16
but **h** can one keep warm alone? Eccl 4:11
who no longer knew **h** to take advice. Eccl 4:13
have who knows **h** to conduct himself Eccl 6:8
to be, for who can tell him **h** it will be? Eccl 8:7
h neither day nor night do one's eyes Eccl 8:16
h the righteous and the wise and their Eccl 9:1
H beautiful is your love, my sister, my Sg 4:10
H much better is your love than wine, Sg 4:10
put off my garment; **h** could I put it on? Sg 5:3
I had bathed my feet; **h** could I soil them? Sg 5:3
H beautiful are your feet in sandals, O Sg 7:1
H beautiful and pleasant you are, O loved Sg 7:6
H the faithful city has become a whore, Is 1:21
Then I said, "**H** long, O Lord?" And he Is 6:11
honey when he knows **h** to refuse the evil Is 7:15
before the boy knows **h** to refuse the evil Is 7:16
before the boy knows **h** to cry 'My father' Is 8:4
"**H** the oppressor has ceased, the insolent Is 14:4
"**H** you are fallen from heaven, O Day Is 14:12
H you are cut down to the ground, you Is 14:12
of the pride of Moab—**h** proud he is! Is 16:6
H can you say to Pharaoh, "I am a son Is 19:11
of Assyria! And we, **h** shall we escape?'" Is 20:6
H then can you repulse a single captain Is 36:9
remember **h** I have walked before you in Is 38:3
you will not know **h** to charm away; Is 47:11
it, for **h** should my name be profaned? Is 48:11
that I may know **h** to sustain with a word Is 50:4
H beautiful upon the mountains are the Is 52:7
Behold, I do not know **h** to speak, for I am Jer 1:6
h you followed me in the wilderness, Jer 2:2
H then have you turned degenerate and Jer 2:21
H can you say, 'I am not unclean, I have Jer 2:23
"**H** well you direct your course to seek Jer 2:33
H much you go about, changing your Jer 2:36
h she went up on every high hill and Jer 3:6
"'I said **H** I would set you among my Jer 3:19
H long shall your wicked thoughts lodge Jer 4:14
H long must I see the standard and hear Jer 4:21
evil! But **h** to do good they know not." Jer 4:22
"**H** can I pardon you? Your children have Jer 5:7
ashamed; they did not know **h** to blush. Jer 6:15
"**H** can you say, 'We are wise, and the law Jer 8:8
ashamed; they did not know **h** to blush. Jer 8:12
is heard from Zion: '**H** we are ruined! Jer 9:19
H long will the land mourn and the Jer 12:4
you, **h** will you compete with horses? Jer 12:5
H long will it be before you are made Jer 13:27
Remember **h** I stood before you to Jer 18:20
h you will be pitied when pangs come Jer 22:23
H long shall there be lies in the heart of Jer 23:26
H long will you waver, O faithless Jer 31:22
please, **h** did you write all these words? Jer 36:17
valley, **h** long will you gash yourselves? Jer 47:5
of the LORD! **H** long till you are quiet? Jer 47:6
H can it be quiet when the LORD has Jer 47:7
"**H** do you say, 'We are heroes and Jer 48:14
say, '**H** the mighty scepter is broken, Jer 48:17
H it is broken! How they wail! How Jer 48:39
How it is broken! **H** they wail! How Jer 48:39
H Moab has turned his back in shame! Jer 48:39
H is the famous city not forsaken, the Jer 49:25
H the hammer of the whole earth is cut Jer 50:23
H Babylon has become a horror Jer 50:23
"**H** Babylon is taken, the praise of the Jer 51:41
H Babylon has become a horror Jer 51:41
H lonely sits the city that was full of Lam 1:1
H like a widow has she become, she Lam 1:1
H the Lord in his anger has set the Lam 2:1
H the gold has grown dim, how the pure Lam 4:1
grown dim, **h** the pure gold is changed! Lam 4:1
h they are regarded as earthen pots, Lam 4:2
h I have been broken over their whoring Ezk 6:9
H much more when I send upon Ezk 14:21
h does the wood of the vine surpass any Ezk 15:2
H much less, when the fire has Ezk 15:5
"**H** lovesick is your heart, declares the Ezk 16:30
and say to you, "'**H** you have perished, Ezk 26:17
because of them. **H** then can we live?' Ezk 33:10
and show them **h** to distinguish Ezk 44:23
H great are his signs, how mighty his Dn 4:3
are his signs, **h** mighty his wonders! Dn 4:3
"For **h** long is the vision concerning the Dn 8:13
H can my lord's servant talk with my Dn 10:17
"**H** long shall it be till the end of these Dn 12:6
H long will they be incapable of Hos 8:5
H can I give you up, O Ephraim? How Hos 11:8
H can I hand you over, O Israel? Hos 11:8
Israel? **H** can I make you like Admah? Hos 11:8
H can I treat you like Zeboiim? Hos 11:8
H the beasts groan! The herds of cattle are Jl 1:18
"They do not know **h** to do right," Am 3:10
For I know **h** many are your Am 5:12
your transgressions and **h** great are Am 5:12
GOD, please forgive! **H** can Jacob stand? Am 7:2
GOD, please cease! **H** can Jacob stand? Am 7:5
came by night—**h** you have been Ob 1:5
H Esau has been pillaged, his treasures Ob 1:6
did, **h** they turned from their evil way, Jon 3:10
of my people; **h** he removes it from me! Mi 2:4
have I done to you? **H** have I wearied you? Mi 6:3
O LORD, **h** long shall I cry for help, and Hab 1:2
up what is not his own—for **h** long? Hab 2:6
h they have taunted my people and made Zep 2:8
in its former glory? **H** do you see it now? Hg 2:3
h did you fare? When one came to a Hg 2:16
h long will you have no mercy on Zec 1:12
For **h** great is his goodness, and how Zec 9:17
is his goodness, and **h** great his beauty! Zec 9:17
"**H** have you loved us?" "Is not Esau Mal 1:2
say, '**H** have we despised your name?' Mal 1:6
But you say, '**H** have we polluted you?' Mal 1:7
"**H** have we wearied him?" By saying, Mal 2:17
hosts. But you say, '**H** shall we return?' Mal 3:7
But you say, '**H** have we robbed you?' Mal 3:8
say, '**H** have we spoken against you?' Mal 3:13
its taste, **h** shall its saltiness be restored? Mt 5:13
you is darkness, **h** great is the darkness! Mt 6:23
the lilies of the field, **h** they grow: Mt 6:28
Or **h** can you say to your brother, 'Let me Mt 7:4
know **h** to give good gifts to your Mt 7:11
h much more will your Father who is in Mt 7:11
do not be anxious **h** you are to speak or Mt 10:19
h much more will they malign those of Mt 10:25
h he entered the house of God and ate the Mt 12:4
read in the Law **h** on the Sabbath the Mt 12:5
Of **h** much more value is a man than a Mt 12:12
against him, **h** to destroy him. Mt 12:14
H then will his kingdom stand? Mt 12:26
Or **h** can someone enter a strong man's Mt 12:29
H can you speak good, when you are Mt 12:34
your field? **H** then does it have weeds?' Mt 13:27
"**H** many loaves do you have?" They Mt 15:34
You know **h** to interpret the appearance Mt 16:3
and **h** many baskets you gathered? Mt 16:9
and **h** many baskets you gathered? Mt 16:10
H is it that you fail to understand that I Mt 16:11
generation, **h** long am I to be with you? Mt 17:17
you? **H** long am I to bear with you? Mt 17:17
h often will my brother sin against me, Mt 18:21
"**H** did the fig tree wither at once?" Mt 21:20
h did you get in here without a wedding Mt 22:12
went and plotted **h** to entangle him Mt 22:15
said to them, "**H** is it then that David, Mt 22:43
David calls him Lord, **h** is he his son?" Mt 22:45
h are you to escape being sentenced to Mt 23:33
H often would I have gathered your Mt 23:37
But **h** then should the Scriptures be Mt 26:54
"Do you not hear **h** many things they Mt 27:13
we remember **h** that impostor said, Mt 27:63
h he entered the house of God, in the Mk 2:26
Herodians against him, **h** to destroy him. Mk 3:6
parables, "**H** can Satan cast out Satan? Mk 3:23
H then will you understand all the Mk 4:13
seed sprouts and grows; he knows not **h**. Mk 4:27
friends and tell them **h** much the Lord Mk 5:19
you, and **h** he has had mercy on you." Mk 5:19
in the Decapolis **h** much Jesus had Mk 5:20
H are such mighty works done by his Mk 6:2
to them, "**H** many loaves do you have? Mk 6:38
"**H** can one feed these people with bread Mk 8:4
"**H** many loaves do you have?" They Mk 8:5
h many baskets full of broken pieces Mk 8:19
h many baskets full of broken pieces Mk 8:20
And **h** is it written of the Son of Man Mk 9:12
generation, **h** long am I to be with you? Mk 9:19
you? **H** long am I to bear with you? Mk 9:19
"**H** long has this been happening to Mk 9:21
h will you make it salty again? Mk 9:50
"**H** difficult it will be for those who Mk 10:23
h difficult it is to enter the kingdom of Mk 10:24
about the bush, **h** God spoke to him, Mk 12:26
"**H** can the scribes say that the Christ Mk 12:35
So **h** is he his son?" And the great Mk 12:37
the scribes were seeking **h** to arrest him Mk 14:1
And Peter remembered **h** Jesus had Mk 14:72
See **h** many charges they bring against Mk 15:4
said to the angel, "**H** shall I know this? Lk 1:18
Mary said to the angel, "**H** will this be, Lk 1:34
h he entered the house of God and took Lk 6:4
H can you say to your brother, 'Brother, Lk 6:42
Take care then **h** you hear, for to the one Lk 8:18
it told them **h** the demon-possessed man Lk 8:36
and declare **h** much God has done for Lk 8:39
the whole city **h** much Jesus had Lk 8:39
and **h** she had been immediately healed. Lk 8:47
h long am I to be with you and bear Lk 9:41
written in the Law? **H** do you read it?" Lk 10:26
know **h** to give good gifts to your Lk 11:13
h much more will the heavenly Father Lk 11:13
himself, **h** will his kingdom stand? Lk 11:18
be anxious about **h** you should defend Lk 12:11
Of **h** much more value are you than Lk 12:24
Consider the lilies, **h** they grow: they Lk 12:27
oven, **h** much more will he clothe you, Lk 12:28
and **h** great is my distress until it is Lk 12:50
You know **h** to interpret the Lk 12:56
do you not know **h** to interpret the Lk 12:56
H often would I have gathered your Lk 13:34
when he noticed **h** they chose the places Lk 14:7
taste, **h** shall its saltiness be restored? Lk 14:34
'**H** many of my father's hired servants Lk 15:17
first, '**H** much do you owe my master?' Lk 16:5
to another, 'And **h** much do you owe?' Lk 16:7
"**H** difficult it is for those who have Lk 18:24
"**H** can they say that the Christ is Lk 20:41
calls him Lord, so **h** is he his son?" Lk 20:44
h it was adorned with noble stones and Lk 21:5
to meditate beforehand **h** to answer, Lk 21:14
the scribes were seeking **h** to put him to Lk 22:2
priests and officers **h** he might betray Lk 22:4
of the Lord, **h** he had said to him, Lk 22:61
saw the tomb and **h** his body was laid. Lk 23:55
Remember **h** he told you, while he was Lk 24:6
and **h** our chief priests and rulers Lk 24:20
and **h** he was known to them in the Lk 24:35
"**H** do you know me?" Jesus answered Jn 1:48

“**H** can a man be born when he is old? Jn 3:4
said to him, “**H** can these things be?” Jn 3:9
h can you believe if I tell you heavenly Jn 3:12
woman said to him, “**H** is it that you, Jn 4:9
H can you believe, when you receive Jn 5:44
writings, **h** will you believe my words?” Jn 5:47
H does he now say, ‘I have come down Jn 6:42
“**H** can this man give us his flesh to eat?” Jn 6:52
“**H** is it that this man has learning, Jn 7:15
H is it that you say, ‘You will become Jn 8:33
to him, “Then **h** were your eyes opened?” Jn 9:10
again asked him **h** he had received Jn 9:15
“**H** can a man who is a sinner do such Jn 9:16
born blind? **H** then does he now see?” Jn 9:19
But **h** he now sees we do not know, nor do Jn 9:21
he do to you? **H** did he open your eyes?” Jn 9:26
“**H** long will you keep us in suspense? Jn 10:24
So the Jews said, “See **h** he loved him!” Jn 11:36
H can you say that the Son of Man Jn 12:34
you are going. **H** can we know the way?” Jn 14:5
H can you say, ‘Show us the Father’? Jn 14:9
h is it that you will manifest yourself to Jn 14:22
“Is that **h** you answer the high priest?” Jn 18:22
And **h** is it that we hear, each of us in Acts 2:8
“**H** is it that you have agreed together to Acts 5:9
And he said, “**H** can I, unless someone Acts 8:31
h much evil he has done to your saints Acts 9:13
I will show him **h** much he must Acts 9:16
and declared to them **h** on the road he Acts 9:27
and **h** at Damascus he had preached Acts 9:27
“You yourselves know **h** unlawful it Acts 10:28
h God anointed Jesus of Nazareth Acts 10:38
And he told us **h** he had seen the Acts 11:13
the word of the Lord, **h** he said, Acts 11:16
he described to them **h** the Lord had Acts 12:17
and **h** he had opened a door of faith to Acts 14:27
Simeon has related **h** God first visited Acts 15:14
word of the Lord, and see **h** they are.” Acts 15:36
“You yourselves know **h** I lived Acts 20:18
h I did not shrink from declaring to Acts 20:20
of the Lord Jesus, **h** he himself said, Acts 20:35
‘This is **h** the Jews at Jerusalem will Acts 21:11
h many thousands there are among Acts 21:20
Being at a loss **h** to investigate these Acts 25:20
For then **h** could God judge the world? Rom 3:6
H then was it counted to him? Was it Rom 4:10
H can we who died to sin still live in it? Rom 6:2
h will he not also with him graciously Rom 8:32
But **h** are they to call on him in Rom 10:14
And **h** are they to believe in him of Rom 10:14
And **h** are they to hear without Rom 10:14
And **h** are they to preach unless they Rom 10:15
“**H** beautiful are the feet of those who Rom 10:15
h he appeals to God against Israel? Rom 11:2
h much more will their full Rom 11:12
olive tree, **h** much more will these, Rom 11:24
H unsearchable are his judgments Rom 11:33
his judgments and **h** inscrutable his Rom 11:33
each one take care **h** he builds upon 1 Cor 3:10
This is **h** one should regard us, as 1 Cor 4:1
H much more, then, matters 1 Cor 6:3
h do you know whether you will save 1 Cor 7:16
h do you know whether you will save 1 Cor 7:16
of the Lord, **h** to please the Lord. 1 Cor 7:32
worldly things, **h** to please his wife, 1 Cor 7:33
Lord, **h** to be holy in body and spirit. 1 Cor 7:34
things, **h** to please her husband. 1 Cor 7:34
h will I benefit you unless I bring you 1 Cor 14:6
h will anyone know what is played? 1 Cor 14:7
h will anyone know what is said? 1 Cor 14:9
h can anyone in the position of an 1 Cor 14:16
h can some of you say that there is 1 Cor 15:12
will ask, “**H** are the dead raised? 1 Cor 15:35
h you received him with fear and 2 Cor 7:15
h I persecuted the church of God Gal 1:13
h can you force the Gentiles to live like Gal 2:14
h can you turn back again to the weak Gal 4:9
h the mystery was made known to me Eph 3:3
Look carefully then **h** you walk, not as Eph 5:15
you also may know **h** I am and what Eph 6:21
purpose, that you may know **h** we are, Eph 6:22
h I yearn for you all with the affection of Phil 1:8
h as a son with a father he has served Phil 2:22
as soon as I see **h** it will go with me, Phil 2:23
I know **h** to be brought low, and I Phil 4:12
brought low, and I know **h** to abound. Phil 4:12
to make known **h** great among the Col 1:27
I want you to know **h** great a struggle I Col 2:1
it clear, which is **h** I ought to speak. Col 4:4
that you may know **h** you ought to Col 4:6
that you may know **h** we are and that he Col 4:8
and **h** you turned to God from idols to 1 Thes 1:9
h holy and righteous and blameless 1 Thes 2:10
For you know **h**, like a father with 1 Thes 2:11
you received from us **h** you ought to 1 Thes 4:1
one of you know **h** to control his own 1 Thes 4:4
you yourselves know **h** you ought to 2 Thes 3:7
does not know **h** to manage his 1 Tm 3:5
h will he care for God’s church? 1 Tm 3:5
you may know **h** one ought to 1 Tm 3:15
and **h** from childhood you have been 2 Tm 3:15
to me, but **h** much more to you, Phlm 1:16
h shall we escape if we neglect such a Heb 2:3
See **h** great this man was to whom Heb 7:4
h much more will the blood of Christ, Heb 9:14
And let us consider **h** to stir up one Heb 10:24
H much worse punishment, do you Heb 10:29
H great a forest is set ablaze by such a Jas 3:5
See **h** the farmer waits for the precious Jas 5:7
h the Lord is compassionate and Jas 5:11
For this is **h** the holy women who hoped 1 Pt 3:5
then the Lord knows **h** to rescue the 2 Pt 2:9
him, **h** does God’s love abide in him? 1 Jn 3:17
and **h** you cannot bear with those who Rv 2:2
h long before you will judge and avenge Rv 6:10
And this is **h** I saw the horses in my Rv 9:17
them, this is **h** he is doomed to be killed. Rv 11:5

HOWEVER (22)
H, the people who dwell in the land are Nm 13:28
H, if they will not pass over with you Nm 32:30
“**H**, you may slaughter and eat meat Dt 12:15
H, they did not drive out the Jos 16:10
H, the kingdom has turned about 1 Kgs 2:15
h, because no house had yet been built 1 Kgs 3:2
H, I will not tear away all the 1 Kgs 11:13
H, they would not listen, but they 2 Kgs 17:40
H, the priests of the high places did 2 Kgs 23:9
high places, **h**, were not taken away; 2 Chr 20:33
H, some men of Asher, of Manasseh, 2 Chr 30:11
H, in the first year of Cyrus king of Ezr 5:13
H much man may toil in seeking, he Eccl 8:17
H, for father or mother, for son or Ezk 44:25
H, not to give offense to them, go to the Mt 17:27
h, shook off the creature into the fire Acts 28:5
h, are not in the flesh but in the Spirit, Rom 8:9
h, I am going to Jerusalem bringing Rom 15:25
H, not all possess this knowledge. But 1 Cor 8:7
astray to mute idols, **h** you were led. 1 Cor 12:2
H, let each one of you love his wife as Eph 5:33
You, **h**, have followed my teaching, 2 Tm 3:10

HOWL (1)
weep and **h** for the miseries that are Jas 5:1

HOWLING (4)
and in the **h** waste of the wilderness; Dt 32:10
h like dogs and prowling about the city. Ps 59:6
h like dogs and prowling about the city. Ps 59:14
their houses will be full of **h** creatures; Is 13:21

HUBS (1)
their spokes, and their **h** were all cast. 1 Kgs 7:33

HUDDLE (1)
bray; under the nettles they **h** together. Jb 30:7

HUGE (3)
was of costly stones, **h** stones, 1 Kgs 7:10
and the Libyans a **h** army with very 2 Chr 16:8
It is being built with **h** stones, and Ezr 5:8

HUKKOK (1)
Aznoth-tabor and goes from there to **H**, Jos 19:34

HUKOK (1)
H with its pasturelands, and Rehob 1 Chr 6:75

HUL (2)
of Aram: Uz, **H**, Gether, and Mash. Gn 10:23
Aram: Uz, **H**, Gether, and Meshech. 1 Chr 1:17

HULDAH (2)
Asaiah went to **H** the prophetess, 2 Kgs 22:14
had sent went to **H** the prophetess, 2 Chr 34:22

HUMAN (63)
or if he touches **h** uncleanness, of Lv 5:3
whether **h** uncleanness or an unclean Lv 7:21
“Whoever takes a **h** life shall surely be Lv 24:17
or touches a **h** bone or a grave, Nm 19:16
of wood and stone, the work of **h** hands, Dt 4:28
Are the trees in the field **h**, that they Dt 20:19
I will wipe them from **h** memory,” Dt 32:26
and **h** bones shall be burned on 1 Kgs 13:2
altars, and burned **h** bones on them. 2 Kgs 23:20
They are driven out from **h** company; Jb 30:5
mighty are taken away by no **h** hand. Jb 34:20
are silver and gold, the work of **h** hands. Ps 115:4
silver and gold, the work of **h** hands. Ps 135:15
will be feeble, and every **h** heart will melt. Is 13:7
to shame, and the craftsmen are only **h**. Is 44:11
was so marred, beyond **h** semblance, Is 52:14
their appearance: they had a **h** likeness, Ezk 1:5
on their four sides they had **h** hands. Ezk 1:8
of their faces, each had a **h** face. Ezk 1:10
was a likeness with a **h** appearance. Ezk 1:26
baking it in their sight on **h** dung.” Ezk 4:12
to you cow’s dung instead of **h** dung, Ezk 4:15
the form of a **h** hand under their wings. Ezk 10:8
and the second face was a **h** face, Ezk 10:14
their wings the likeness of **h** hands. Ezk 10:21
the prey; they have devoured **h** lives; Ezk 22:25
they exchanged **h** beings and vessels Ezk 27:13
are my sheep, **h** sheep of my pasture, Ezk 34:31
the land and anyone sees a **h** bone, Ezk 39:15
a **h** face toward the palm tree on the Ezk 41:19
a stone was cut out by no **h** hand, Dn 2:34
was cut from a mountain by no **h** hand, Dn 2:45
the fingers of a **h** hand appeared and Dn 5:5
he shall be broken—but by no **h** hand. Dn 8:25
“Those who offer **h** sacrifice kiss Hos 13:2
cut short, no **h** being would be saved. Mt 24:22
the days, no **h** being would be saved. Mk 13:20
for joy that a **h** being has been born Jn 16:21
nor is he served by **h** hands, as Acts 17:25
and distress for every **h** being who does Rom 2:9
wrath on us? (I speak in a **h** way.) Rom 3:5
of the law no **h** being will be justified Rom 3:20
I am speaking in **h** terms, because of Rom 6:19
it depends not on **h** will or exertion, Rom 9:16
so that no **h** being might boast in the 1 Cor 1:29
not taught by **h** wisdom but taught 1 Cor 2:13
flesh and behaving only in a **h** way? 1 Cor 3:3
Apollos,” are you not being merely **h**? 1 Cor 3:4
be judged by you or by any **h** court. 1 Cor 4:3
Do I say these things on **h** authority? 1 Cor 9:8
of stone but on tablets of **h** hearts. 2 Cor 3:3
To give a **h** example, brothers: even Gal 3:15
every wind of doctrine, by **h** cunning, Eph 4:14
And being found in **h** form, he Phil 2:8
empty deceit, according to **h** tradition, Col 2:8
—according to **h** precepts and Col 2:22
but no **h** being can tame the tongue. It is Jas 3:8
the Lord’s sake to every **h** institution, 1 Pt 2:13
flesh no longer for **h** passions but for the 1 Pt 4:2
donkey spoke with **h** voice and 2 Pt 2:16
of gold; their faces were like **h** faces, Rv 9:7
chariots, and slaves, that is, **h** souls. Rv 18:13
its wall, 144 cubits by **h** measurement, Rv 21:17

HUMANLY (1)
What do I gain if, **h** speaking, I 1 Cor 15:32

HUMANS (1)
the same, but there is one kind for **h**, 1 Cor 15:39

HUMBLE (40)
will you refuse to **h** yourself before me? Ex 10:3
in the wilderness, that he might **h** you, Dt 8:2
know, that he might **h** you and test you, Dt 8:16
him, that we may bind him to **h** him. Jgs 16:5
You save a **h** people, but your eyes 2 Sm 22:28
are called by my name **h** themselves, 2 Chr 7:14
And he did not **h** himself before the 2 Chr 33:23
He did not **h** himself before 2 Chr 36:12
that we might **h** ourselves before our Ezr 8:21
For you save a **h** people, but the Ps 18:27
He leads the **h** in what is right, and Ps 25:9
what is right, and teaches the **h** his way. Ps 25:9
in the LORD; let the **h** hear and be glad. Ps 34:2
God will give ear and **h** them, he who is Ps 55:19
When the **h** see it they will be glad; you Ps 69:32
judgment, to save all the **h** of the earth. Ps 76:9
outwit him; the wicked shall not **h** him. Ps 89:22
The LORD lifts up the **h**; he casts the Ps 147:6
people; he adorns the **h** with salvation. Ps 149:4
is scornful, but to the **h** he gives favor. Prv 3:34
disgrace, but with the **h** is wisdom. Prv 11:2
I choose, a day for a person to **h** himself? Is 58:5
he who is **h** and contrite in spirit and Is 66:2
let my **h** plea come before you and do Jer 37:20
‘I made a **h** plea to the king that he Jer 38:26
the kingdom might be **h** and not lift Ezk 17:14
those who walk in pride he is able to **h**. Dn 4:37
Seek the LORD, all you **h** of the land, who Zep 2:3
in your midst a people **h** and lowly. Zep 3:12
is he, **h** and mounted on a donkey, Zec 9:9
to you, **h**, and mounted on a donkey, Mt 21:5
has looked on the **h** estate of his servant. Lk 1:48
thrones and exalted those of **h** estate; Lk 1:52
—I who am **h** when face to face 2 Cor 10:1
again my God may **h** me before you, 2 Cor 12:21
the proud, but gives grace to the **h**.” Jas 4:6
H yourselves before the Lord, and he will Jas 4:10
love, a tender heart, and a **h** mind. 1 Pt 3:8
the proud but gives grace to the **h**.” 1 Pt 5:5
H yourselves, therefore, under the 1 Pt 5:6

HUMBLED (34)
uncircumcised heart is **h** and they Lv 26:41
And he **h** you and let you hunger and fed Dt 8:3
how Ahab has **h** himself before me? 1 Kgs 21:29

Because he has **h** himself before me, 1 Kgs 21:29
and you **h** yourself before the LORD, 2 Kgs 22:19
and the king **h** themselves and said, 2 Chr 12:6
the LORD saw that they **h** themselves, 2 Chr 12:7
Shemaiah: "They have **h** themselves. 2 Chr 12:7
And when he **h** himself the wrath of 2 Chr 12:12
For the LORD **h** Judah because of 2 Chr 28:19
and of Zebulun **h** themselves and 2 Chr 30:11
But Hezekiah **h** himself for the pride 2 Chr 32:26
his God and **h** himself greatly 2 Chr 33:12
and the images, before he **h** himself, 2 Chr 33:19
Manasseh his father had **h** himself, 2 Chr 33:23
tender and you **h** yourself before 2 Chr 34:27
and you have **h** yourself before me 2 Chr 34:27
For when they are **h** you say, 'It is Jb 22:29
God has loosed my cord and **h** me, Jb 30:11
When I wept and **h** my soul with Ps 69:10
So man is **h**, and each one is brought low Is 2:9
low, and the lofty pride of men shall be **h**, Is 2:11
And the haughtiness of man shall be **h**, Is 2:17
Man is **h**, and each one is brought low, Is 5:15
For he has **h** the inhabitants of the Is 26:5
Why have we **h** ourselves, and you take Is 58:3
They have not **h** themselves even to Jer 44:10
he raised up, and whom he would, he **h**. Dn 5:19
son, Belshazzar, have not **h** your heart, Dn 5:22
to understand and **h** yourself before Dn 10:12
Whoever exalts himself will be **h**, and Mt 23:12
everyone who exalts himself will be **h**, Lk 14:11
everyone who exalts himself will be **h**, Lk 18:14
he **h** himself by becoming obedient to Phil 2:8

HUMBLES (4)
Whoever **h** himself like this child is the Mt 18:4
and whoever **h** himself will be exalted. Mt 23:12
and he who **h** himself will be exalted." Lk 14:11
but the one who **h** himself will be Lk 18:14

HUMBLEST (1)
is not my clan the **h** of all the clans of 1 Sm 9:21

HUMBLING (1)
commit a sin in **h** myself so that you 2 Cor 11:7

HUMBLY (1)
kindness, and to walk **h** with your God? Mi 6:8

HUMILIATE (1)
of God and **h** those who have 1 Cor 11:22

HUMILIATED (4)
he seized her and lay with her and **h** her. Gn 34:2
her as a slave, since you have **h** her. Dt 21:14
treated us harshly and **h** us and laid on Dt 26:6
we would be **h**—to say nothing of you 2 Cor 9:4

HUMILIATION (3)
shelter in the shadow of Egypt to your **h**. Is 30:3
In his **h** justice was denied him. Who Acts 8:33
and the rich in his **h**, because like a Jas 1:10

HUMILITY (9)
in wisdom, and **h** comes before honor. Prv 15:33
is haughty, but **h** comes before honor. Prv 18:12
The reward for **h** and fear of the LORD is Prv 22:4
commands; seek righteousness; seek **h**; Zep 2:3
the Lord with all **h** and with tears and Acts 20:19
with all **h** and gentleness, with patience, Eph 4:2
but in **h** count others more significant Phil 2:3
compassion, kindness, **h**, meekness, Col 3:12
all of you, with **h** toward one another, 1 Pt 5:5

HUMPS (1)
and their treasures on the **h** of camels, Is 30:6

HUMTAH (1)
H, Kiriath-arba (that is, Hebron), and Jos 15:54

HUNCHBACK (1)
or a **h** or a dwarf or a man with a defect Lv 21:20

HUNDRED (128)
Noah was six **h** years old when the flood Gn 7:6
In the six **h** and first year, in the first Gn 8:13
they will be afflicted for four **h** years. Gn 15:13
be born to a man who is a **h** years old? Gn 17:17
Abraham was a **h** years old when his Gn 21:5
of land worth four **h** shekels of silver, Gn 23:15
of the Hittites, four **h** shekels of silver, Gn 23:16
and there are four **h** men with him." Gn 32:6
two **h** female goats and twenty male Gn 32:14
goats, two **h** ewes and twenty rams, Gn 32:14
was coming, and four **h** men with him. Gn 33:1
he bought for a **h** pieces of money the Gn 33:19
he gave three **h** shekels of silver Gn 45:22
about six **h** thousand men on foot, Ex 12:37
and took six **h** chosen chariots and all Ex 14:7
fine twined linen a **h** cubits long for one Ex 27:9
shall be hangings a **h** cubits long, Ex 27:11
length of the court shall be a **h** cubits, Ex 27:18
were of fine twined linen, a **h** cubits; Ex 38:9
side there were hangings of a **h** cubits, Ex 38:11
were recorded was a **h** talents and 1,775 Ex 38:25
The **h** talents of silver were for casting Ex 38:27
a **h** bases for the hundred talents, a Ex 38:27
a hundred bases for the **h** talents, a Ex 38:27
Five of you shall chase a **h**, and a Lv 26:8
and a **h** of you shall chase ten thousand, Lv 26:8
I am number six **h** thousand on foot, Nm 11:21
went out to battle, one out of five **h**, Nm 31:28
shall fine him a **h** shekels of silver and Dt 22:19
of Shechem for a **h** pieces of money. Jos 24:32
So Gideon and the **h** men who were with Jgs 7:19
ten men of a **h** throughout all the Jgs 20:10
tribes of Israel, and a **h** of a thousand, Jgs 20:10
people of Israel were three **h** thousand, 1 Sm 11:8
present with him, about six **h** men. 1 Sm 13:15
were with him were about six **h** men, 1 Sm 14:2
Telaim, two **h** thousand men on foot, 1 Sm 15:4
head weighed six **h** shekels of iron. 1 Sm 17:7
bride-price except a **h** foreskins of 1 Sm 18:25
and killed two **h** of the Philistines. 1 Sm 18:27
were with him about four **h** men. 1 Sm 22:2
and his men, who were about six **h**, 1 Sm 23:13
And about four **h** men went up after 1 Sm 25:13
while two **h** remained with the 1 Sm 25:13
haste and took two **h** loaves and two 1 Sm 25:18
grain and a **h** clusters of raisins 1 Sm 25:18
of raisins and two **h** cakes of figs, 1 Sm 25:18
he and the six **h** men who were with 1 Sm 27:2
and the six **h** men who were with him, 1 Sm 30:9
David pursued, he and four **h** men. 1 Sm 30:10
Two **h** stayed behind, who were too 1 Sm 30:10
escaped, except four **h** young men, 1 Sm 30:17
came to the two **h** men who had 1 Sm 30:21
bridal price of a **h** foreskins of the 2 Sm 3:14
horses but left enough for a **h** chariots. 2 Sm 8:4
two **h** shekels by the king's weight. 2 Sm 14:26
Absalom went two **h** men from 2 Sm 15:11
and all the six **h** Gittites who had 2 Sm 15:18
bearing two **h** loaves of bread, 2 Sm 16:1
of bread, a **h** bunches of raisins, 2 Sm 16:1
of raisins, a **h** of summer fruits, 2 Sm 16:1
spear weighed three **h** shekels of 2 Sm 21:16
spear against eight **h** whom he killed 2 Sm 23:8
spear against three **h** men and killed 2 Sm 23:18
add to the people a **h** times as many as 2 Sm 24:3
twenty pasture-fed cattle, a **h** sheep, 1 Kgs 4:23
In the four **h** and eightieth year after 1 Kgs 6:1
Its length was a **h** cubits and its 1 Kgs 7:2
There were two **h** pomegranates in 1 Kgs 7:20
and the four **h** pomegranates for the 1 Kgs 7:42
Obadiah took a **h** prophets and hid 1 Kgs 18:4
how I hid a **h** men of the LORD'S 1 Kgs 18:13
prophets together, about four **h** men, 1 Kgs 22:6
set this before a **h** men?" So he 2 Kgs 4:43
wall of Jerusalem for four **h** cubits, 2 Kgs 14:13
of Judah three **h** talents of silver 2 Kgs 18:14
a tribute of a **h** talents of silver and 2 Kgs 23:33
of them, five **h** men of the Simeonites, 1 Chr 4:42
a match for a **h** men and the 1 Chr 12:14
to his people a **h** times as many as 1 Chr 21:3
he made a **h** pomegranates and put 2 Chr 3:16
north. And he made a **h** basins of gold. 2 Chr 4:8
the prophets together, four **h** men, 2 Chr 18:5
we do about the **h** talents that I have 2 Chr 25:9
a tribute of a **h** talents of silver and 2 Chr 36:3
it as far as the Tower of the **H**, Neh 3:1
of Hananel and the Tower of the **H**, Neh 12:39
understanding than a **h** blows into a Prv 17:10
a man fathers a **h** children and lives Eccl 6:3
sinner does evil a **h** times and prolongs Eccl 8:12
and the keepers of the fruit two **h**. Sg 8:12
struck down a **h** and eighty-five Is 37:36
the young man shall die a **h** years old, Is 65:20
and the sinner a **h** years old shall be Is 65:20
pomegranates were a **h** upon the Jer 52:23
a **h** cubits on the east side and on the Ezk 40:19
from gate to gate, a **h** cubits. Ezk 40:23
to gate toward the south, a **h** cubits. Ezk 40:27
a **h** cubits long and a hundred cubits Ezk 40:47
cubits long and a **h** cubits broad, Ezk 40:47
measured the temple, a **h** cubits long; Ezk 41:13
with its walls, a **h** cubits long; Ezk 41:13
of the temple and the yard, a **h** cubits. Ezk 41:14
its galleries on either side, a **h** cubits. Ezk 41:15
whose door faced north was a **h** cubits, Ezk 42:2
ten cubits wide and a **h** cubits long, Ezk 42:4
opposite the nave were a **h** cubits long. Ezk 42:8
one sheep from every flock of two **h**, Ezk 45:15
went out a thousand shall have a **h** left, Am 5:3
which went out a **h** shall have ten left Am 5:3
If a man has a **h** sheep and one of them Mt 18:12
servants who owed him a **h** denarii, Mt 18:28
go and buy two **h** denarii worth of Mk 6:37
for more than three **h** denarii and given Mk 14:5
One owed five **h** denarii, and the other Lk 7:41
"What man of you, having a **h** sheep, if Lk 15:4
He said, 'A **h** measures of oil.' He said to Lk 16:6
owe?' He said, 'A **h** measures of wheat.' Lk 16:7
"Two **h** denarii would not buy enough Jn 6:7
not sold for three **h** denarii and given to Jn 12:5
from the land, but about a **h** yards off. Jn 21:8
and a number of men, about four **h**, Acts 5:36
them and afflict them four **h** years. Acts 7:6
and said, "Get ready two **h** soldiers, Acts 23:23
horsemen and two **h** spearmen to go Acts 23:23
(since he was about a **h** years old), Rom 4:19
to more than five **h** brothers at one 1 Cor 15:6
hailstones, about one **h** pounds each, Rv 16:21

HUNDREDFOLD (8)
land and reaped in the same year a **h**. Gn 26:12
good soil and produced grain, some a **h**, Mt 13:8
bears fruit and yields, in one case a **h**, Mt 13:23
will receive a **h** and will inherit eternal Mt 19:29
thirtyfold and sixtyfold and a **h**." Mk 4:8
fruit, thirtyfold and sixtyfold and a **h**." Mk 4:20
will not receive a **h** now in this time, Mk 10:30
grew and yielded a **h**." As he said these Lk 8:8

HUNDREDS (20)
the people as chiefs of thousands, of **h**, Ex 18:21
the people, chiefs of thousands, of **h**, Ex 18:25
thousands and the commanders of **h**, Nm 31:14
thousands and the commanders of **h**, Nm 31:48
thousands and the commanders of **h**, Nm 31:52
commanders of thousands and of **h**, Nm 31:54
of thousands, commanders of **h**, Dt 1:15
of thousands and commanders of **h**, 1 Sm 22:7
passing on by **h** and by thousands, 1 Sm 29:2
of thousands and commanders of **h**. 2 Sm 18:1
marched out by **h** and by thousands. 2 Sm 18:4
commanders of thousands and of **h**, 1 Chr 13:1
thousands and the **h** and the 1 Chr 26:26
the commanders of thousands and **h**, 1 Chr 27:1
of thousands, the commanders of **h**, 1 Chr 28:1
commanders of thousands and of **h**, 1 Chr 29:6
commanders of thousands and of **h**, 2 Chr 1:2
covenant with the commanders of **h**, 2 Chr 23:1
of thousands and of **h** for all Judah 2 Chr 25:5
sat down in groups, by **h** and by fifties. Mk 6:40

HUNDREDTH (1)
In the six **h** year of Noah's life, in the Gn 7:11

HUNG (7)
And they **h** on the trees until evening. Jos 10:26
On the willows there we **h** up our lyres. Ps 137:2
Princes are **h** up by their hands; no Lam 5:12
They **h** the shield and helmet in you; Ezk 27:10
They **h** their shields on your walls all Ezk 27:11
great millstone were **h** around his neck Mk 9:42
if a millstone were **h** around his neck Lk 17:2

HUNGER (26)
to kill this whole assembly with **h**." Ex 16:3
you and let you **h** and fed you with Dt 8:3
will send against you, in **h** and thirst, Dt 28:48
they shall be wasted with **h**, and Dt 32:24
who were hungry have ceased to **h**. 1 Sm 2:5
heaven for their **h** and brought water Neh 9:15
Through want and hard **h** they gnaw the Jb 30:3
The young lions suffer want and **h**; but Ps 34:10
sleep, and an idle person will suffer **h**. Prv 19:15
and awakes with his **h** not satisfied, Is 29:8
they shall not **h** or thirst, neither Is 49:10
the cistern, and he will die there of **h**, Jer 38:9
who faint for **h** at the head of every Lam 2:19
of the sword than the victims of **h**, Lam 4:9
They cannot satisfy their **h** or fill their Ezk 7:19
more be consumed with **h** in the land, Ezk 34:29
for their bread shall be for their **h** only; Hos 9:4
and there shall be **h** within you; Mi 6:14
"Blessed are those who **h** and thirst for Mt 5:6
enough bread, but I perish here with **h**! Lk 15:17
whoever comes to me shall not **h**, and Jn 6:35
To the present hour we **h** and thirst, 1 Cor 4:11
riots, labors, sleepless nights, **h**; 2 Cor 6:5
a sleepless night, in **h** and thirst, 2 Cor 11:27
the secret of facing plenty and **h**, Phil 4:12
They shall **h** no more, neither thirst Rv 7:16

HUNGRY (49)
but those who were **h** have ceased to 1 Sm 2:5
"The people are **h** and weary and 2 Sm 17:29
done to us. They know that we are **h**. 2 Kgs 7:12
The **h** eat his harvest, and he takes it even Jb 5:5
and you have withheld bread from the **h**. Jb 22:7
clothing; **h**, they carry the sheaves; Jb 24:10
"If I were **h**, I would not tell you, for the Ps 50:12
h and thirsty, their soul fainted within Ps 107:5
and the **h** soul he fills with good things. Ps 107:9
And there he lets the **h** dwell, and they Ps 107:36
the oppressed, who gives food to the **h**. Ps 146:7

to satisfy his appetite when he is **h**, Prv 6:30
LORD does not let the righteous go **h**, Prv 10:3
If your enemy is **h**, give him bread to Prv 25:21
to one who is **h** everything bitter is Prv 27:7
their honored men go **h**, and their Is 5:13
the land, greatly distressed and **h**. Is 8:21
And when they are **h**, they will be enraged Is 8:21
slice meat on the right, but are still **h**, Is 9:20
As when a **h** man dreams he is eating and Is 29:8
to leave the craving of the **h** unsatisfied, Is 32:6
He becomes **h**, and his strength fails; he Is 44:12
your bread with the **h** and bring the Is 58:7
yourself out for the **h** and satisfy the Is 58:10
servants shall eat, but you shall be **h**; Is 65:13
sound of the trumpet or be **h** for bread, Jer 42:14
his bread to the **h** and covers the naked Ezk 18:7
his bread to the **h** and covers the Ezk 18:16
forty days and forty nights, he was **h**. Mt 4:2
His disciples were **h**, and they began to Mt 12:1
not read what David did when he was **h**, Mt 12:3
I am unwilling to send them away **h**, Mt 15:32
was returning to the city, he became **h**. Mt 21:18
For I was **h** and you gave me food, I was Mt 25:35
when did we see you **h** and feed you, Mt 25:37
For I was **h** and you gave me no food, I Mt 25:42
when did we see you **h** or thirsty or a Mt 25:44
did, when he was in need and was **h**, Mk 2:25
if I send them away **h** to their homes, Mk 8:3
they came from Bethany, he was **h**. Mk 11:12
he has filled the **h** with good things, and Lk 1:53
And when they were ended, he was **h**. Lk 4:2
not read what David did when he was **h**, Lk 6:3
"Blessed are you who are **h** now, for you Lk 6:21
you who are full now, for you shall be **h**. Lk 6:25
And he became **h** and wanted Acts 10:10
To the contrary, "if your enemy is **h**, Rom 12:20
One goes **h**, another gets drunk. 1 Cor 11:21
if anyone is **h**, let him eat at home— 1 Cor 11:34

HUNT (12)
go out to the field and **h** game for me, Gn 27:3
went to the field to **h** for game and bring Gn 27:5
you, though you **h** my life to take it. 1 Sm 24:11
you would **h** me like a lion and again Jb 10:16
"How long will you **h** for words? Jb 18:2
"Can you **h** the prey for the lion, or Jb 38:39
let evil **h** down the violent man Ps 140:11
and they shall **h** them from every Jer 16:16
of every stature, in the **h** for souls! Ezk 13:18
Will you **h** down souls belonging to Ezk 13:18
bands with which you **h** the souls like Ezk 13:20
I will let the souls whom you **h** go free, Ezk 13:20

HUNTED (4)
was it then that **h** game and brought it Gn 27:33
And like a **h** gazelle, or like sheep with Is 13:14
"Israel is a **h** sheep driven away by Jer 50:17
"I have been **h** like a bird by those Lam 3:52

HUNTER (4)
He was a mighty **h** before the LORD. Gn 10:9
Nimrod a mighty **h** before the LORD." Gn 10:9
boys grew up, Esau was a skillful **h**, Gn 25:27
like a gazelle from the hand of the **h**, Prv 6:5

HUNTERS (1)
And afterward I will send for many **h**, Jer 16:16

HUNTING (2)
Esau his brother came in from his **h**. Gn 27:30
who takes in **h** any beast or bird that Lv 17:13

HUNTS (3)
flea like one who **h** a partridge in the 1 Sm 26:20
a married woman **h** down a precious Prv 6:26
for blood, and each **h** the other with a net. Mi 7:2

HUPHAM (1)
the clan of the Shuphamites; of **H**, Nm 26:39

HUPHAMITES (1)
of Hupham, the clan of the **H**. Nm 26:39

HUPPAH (1)
the thirteenth to **H**, the fourteenth to 1 Chr 24:13

HUPPIM (3)
Ehi, Rosh, Muppim, **H**, and Ard. Gn 46:21
And Shuppim and **H** were the sons of 1 Chr 7:12
took a wife for **H** and for Shuppim. 1 Chr 7:15

HUR (15)
and **H** went up to the top of the hill. Ex 17:10
while Aaron and **H** held up his hands, Ex 17:12
And behold, Aaron and **H** are with you. Ex 24:14
by name Bezalel the son of Uri, son of **H**, Ex 31:2
name Bezalel the son of Uri, son of **H**, Ex 35:30
Bezalel the son of Uri, son of **H**, of the Ex 38:22
slain, Evi, Rekem, Zur, **H**, and Reba, Nm 31:8
and Rekem and Zur and **H** and Reba, Jos 13:21
married Ephrath, who bore him **H**. 1 Chr 2:19
H fathered Uri, and Uri fathered 1 Chr 2:20
The sons of **H** the firstborn of 1 Chr 2:50
Perez, Hezron, Carmi, **H**, and Shobal. 1 Chr 4:1
These were the sons of **H**, the firstborn 1 Chr 4:4
that Bezalel the son of Uri, son of **H**, 2 Chr 1:5
Next to them Rephaiah the son of **H**, Neh 3:9

HURAI (1)
H of the brooks of Gaash, Abiel the 1 Chr 11:32

HURAM (1)
Gera, Shephuphan, and **H**. 1 Chr 8:5

HURAM-ABI (2)
man, who has understanding, **H**, 2 Chr 2:13
equipment for these **H** made of 2 Chr 4:16

HURI (1)
were the sons of Abihail the son of **H**, 1 Chr 5:14

HURL (4)
the LORD will **h** you away violently, Is 22:17
Therefore I will **h** you out of this land Jer 16:13
I will **h** you and the mother who bore Jer 22:26
"Pick me up and **h** me into the sea; Jon 1:12

HURLED (8)
out of hatred or **h** something at him, Nm 35:20
or **h** anything on him without lying Nm 35:22
And Saul **h** the spear, for he thought, 1 Sm 18:11
But Saul **h** his spear at him to strike 1 Sm 20:33
he and his children **h** and cast into a Jer 22:28
But the LORD **h** a great wind upon the sea, Jon 1:4
And they **h** the cargo that was in the ship Jon 1:5
picked up Jonah and **h** him into the sea, Jon 1:15

HURLS (2)
It **h** at him without pity; he flees from its Jb 27:22
He **h** down his crystals of ice like Ps 147:17

HURRICANE (1)
tempest and terrify them with your **h**! Ps 83:15

HURRIED (16)
Then Joseph **h** out, for his compassion Gn 43:30
the servants of Pharaoh **h** his slaves and Ex 9:20
h and went out early to the appointed Jos 8:14
it. And they **h** to set the city on fire. Jos 8:19
men in ambush **h** and rushed against Jgs 20:37
Then the man **h** and came and 1 Sm 4:14
she **h** and got down from the donkey 1 Sm 25:23
unless you had **h** and come to meet 1 Sm 25:34
And Abigail **h** and rose and 1 Sm 25:42
h to come down with the men of 2 Sm 19:16
And King Rehoboam **h** to mount 1 Kgs 12:18
Then he **h** to take the bandage away 1 Kgs 20:41
quickly, and he himself **h** to go out, 2 Chr 26:20
But Haman **h** to his house, mourning Est 6:12
eunuchs arrived and **h** to bring Haman Est 6:14
So he **h** and came down and received Lk 19:6

HURRIEDLY (2)
The couriers went out **h** by order of the Est 3:15
used in the king's service, rode out **h**, Est 8:14

HURRY (12)
H and go up to my father and say to Gn 45:9
H and bring my father down here." Gn 45:13
of heaven and did not **h** to set for about Jos 10:13
return home and **h** away from Mount Jgs 7:3
seen me do, **h** and do as I have done." Jgs 9:48
H. He has come just now to the city, 1 Sm 9:12
called after the boy, "**H**! Be quick! 1 Sm 20:38
came to Saul, saying, "**H** and come, 1 Sm 23:27
And God has commanded me to **h**. 2 Chr 35:21
"**H**; take the robes and the horse, Est 6:10
I would **h** to find a shelter from the Ps 55:8
to him, "Zacchaeus, **h** and come down, Lk 19:5

HURRYING (1)
And David was **h** to get away from 1 Sm 23:26

HURT (25)
damage grow to the **h** of the king?" Ezr 4:22
swears to his own **h** and does not change; Ps 15:4
those who seek my **h** speak of ruin and Ps 38:12
brought to dishonor who desire my **h**! Ps 40:14
brought to dishonor who desire my **h**! Ps 70:2
may they be covered who seek my **h**. Ps 71:13
disappointed who sought to do me **h**. Ps 71:24
His feet were **h** with fetters; his neck Ps 105:18
me," you will say, "but I was not **h**; Prv 23:35
were kept by their owner to his **h**, Eccl 5:13
man had power over man to his **h**. Eccl 8:9
He who quarries stones is **h** by them, Eccl 10:9
They shall not **h** or destroy in all my holy Is 11:9
They shall not **h** or destroy in all my Is 65:25
Woe is me because of my **h**! My wound Jer 10:19
Your **h** is incurable, and your wound Jer 30:12
Why do you cry out over your **h**? Your Jer 30:15
or a thorn to **h** them among all their Ezk 28:24
the midst of the fire, and they are not **h**; Dn 3:25
There is no easing your **h**; your wound Na 3:19
All who lift it will surely **h** themselves. Zec 12:3
any deadly poison, it will not **h** them; Mk 16:18
of the enemy, and nothing shall **h** you. Lk 10:19
conquers will not be **h** by the second Rv 2:11
and their power to **h** people for five Rv 9:10

HURTFUL (1)
city, **h** to kings and provinces, Ezr 4:15

HURTING (1)
who has restrained me from **h** you, 1 Sm 25:34

HURTS (1)
himself, but a cruel man **h** himself. Prv 11:17

HUSBAND (115)
gave some to her **h** who was with her, Gn 3:6
Your desire shall be for your **h**, and he Gn 3:16
and gave her to Abram her **h** as a wife. Gn 16:3
affliction; for now my **h** will love me." Gn 29:32
"Now this time my **h** will be attached Gn 29:34
that you have taken away my **h**? Gn 30:15
my servant to my **h**." So she called his Gn 30:18
now my **h** will honor me, because I Gn 30:20
as the woman's **h** shall impose on him, Ex 21:22
is near to him because she has had no **h**; Lv 21:3
unclean as a **h** among his people Lv 21:4
marry a woman divorced from her **h**, Lv 21:7
and it is hidden from the eyes of her **h**, Nm 5:13
man other than your **h** has lain with Nm 5:20
and has broken faith with her **h**, Nm 5:27
If she marries a **h**, while under her Nm 30:6
and her **h** hears of it and says nothing Nm 30:7
on the day that her **h** comes to hear of Nm 30:8
and her **h** heard of it and said nothing Nm 30:11
But if her **h** makes them null and Nm 30:12
Her **h** has made them void, and the Nm 30:12
to afflict herself, her **h** may establish, Nm 30:13
establish, or her **h** may make void. Nm 30:13
But if her **h** says nothing to her from Nm 30:14
that you may go in to her and be her **h**, Dt 21:13
then her former **h**, who sent her away, Dt 24:4
near to rescue her **h** from the hand of Dt 25:11
will begrudge to the **h** she embraces, Dt 28:56
Then the woman came and told her **h**, Jgs 13:6
But Manoah her **h** was not with her. Jgs 13:9
the woman ran quickly and told her **h**, Jgs 13:10
"Entice your **h** to tell us what the riddle Jgs 14:15
Then her **h** arose and went after her, to Jgs 19:3
the **h** of the woman who was murdered, Jgs 20:4
But Elimelech, the **h** of Naomi, died, and Ru 1:3
was left without her two sons and her **h**. Ru 1:5
the house of her **h**!" Then she kissed Ru 1:9
go your way, for I am too old to have a **h**. Ru 1:12
I should have a **h** this night and should Ru 1:12
the death of your **h** has been fully told Ru 2:11
And Elkanah, her **h**, said to her, 1 Sm 1:8
did not go up, for she said to her **h**, 1 Sm 1:22
Elkanah her **h** said to her, "Do what 1 Sm 1:23
went up with her **h** to offer the yearly 1 Sm 2:19
her father-in-law and her **h** were dead, 1 Sm 4:19
of her father-in-law and her **h**. 1 Sm 4:21
But she did not tell her **h** Nabal. 1 Sm 25:19
took her from her **h** Paltiel the son of 2 Sm 3:15
But her **h** went with her, weeping after 2 Sm 3:16
heard that Uriah her **h** was dead, 2 Sm 11:26
was dead, she lamented over her **h**. 2 Sm 11:26
"Alas, I am a widow; my **h** is dead. 2 Sm 14:5
and leave to my **h** neither name nor 2 Sm 14:7
you as a bride comes home to her **h**. 2 Sm 17:3
to Elisha, "Your servant my **h** is dead, 2 Kgs 4:1
And she said to her **h**, "Behold now, I 2 Kgs 4:9
she has no son, and her **h** is old." 2 Kgs 4:14
Then she called to her **h** and said, 2 Kgs 4:22
well with you? Is all well with your **h**? 2 Kgs 4:26
For my **h** is not at home; he has gone Prv 7:19
An excellent wife is the crown of her **h**, Prv 12:4
an unloved woman when she gets a **h**, Prv 30:23
The heart of her **h** trusts in her, and he Prv 31:11
Her **h** is known in the gates when he Prv 31:23
rise up and call her blessed; her **h** also, Prv 31:28
For your Maker is your **h**, the LORD of Is 54:5
as a treacherous wife leaves her **h**, Jer 3:20
both **h** and wife shall be taken, the Jer 6:11
that they broke, though I was their **h**, Jer 31:32
receives strangers instead of her **h**! Ezk 16:32
who loathed her **h** and her children; Ezk 16:45
and I am not her **h**—that she put away Hos 2:2
say, 'I will go and return to my first **h**, Hos 2:7
the LORD, you will call me 'My **H**,' Hos 2:16
Jacob the father of Joseph the **h** of Mary, Mt 1:16
And her **h** Joseph, being a just man and Mt 1:19
she divorces her **h** and marries Mk 10:12
lived with her **h** seven years from Lk 2:36
divorced from her **h** commits adultery. Lk 16:18
Jesus said to her, "Go, call your **h**, and Jn 4:16

him, "I have no **h**." Jesus said to her, Jn 4:17
"You are right in saying, 'I have no **h**'; Jn 4:17
and the one you now have is not your **h**. Jn 4:18
who have buried your **h** are at the door, Acts 5:9
her out and buried her beside her **h**. Acts 5:10
is bound by law to her **h** while he lives, Rom 7:2
but if her **h** dies she is released from the Rom 7:2
with another man while her **h** is alive. Rom 7:3
But if her **h** dies, she is free from that Rom 7:3
own wife and each woman her own **h**. 1 Cor 7:2
The **h** should give to his wife her 1 Cor 7:3
rights, and likewise the wife to her **h**. 1 Cor 7:3
over her own body, but the **h** does. 1 Cor 7:4
Likewise the **h** does not have authority 1 Cor 7:4
wife should not separate from her **h** 1 Cor 7:10
or else be reconciled to her **h**), 1 Cor 7:11
and the **h** should not divorce his wife. 1 Cor 7:11
any woman has a **h** who is an 1 Cor 7:13
For the unbelieving **h** is made holy 1 Cor 7:14
wife is made holy because of her **h**. 1 Cor 7:14
know whether you will save your **h**? 1 Cor 7:16
H, how do you know whether you 1 Cor 7:16
worldly things, how to please her **h**. 1 Cor 7:34
wife is bound to her **h** as long as he 1 Cor 7:39
But if her **h** dies, she is free to be 1 Cor 7:39
is Christ, the head of a wife is her **h**, 1 Cor 11:3
for you, for I betrothed you to one **h**, 2 Cor 11:2
than those of the one who has a **h**." Gal 4:27
For the **h** is the head of the wife even as Eph 5:23
let the wife see that she respects her **h**. Eph 5:33
be above reproach, the **h** of one wife, 1 Tm 3:2
Let deacons each be the **h** of one wife, 1 Tm 3:12
of age, having been the wife of one **h**, 1 Tm 5:9
is above reproach, the **h** of one wife, Ti 1:6
prepared as a bride adorned for her **h**. Rv 21:2

HUSBAND'S (9)
while you were under your **h** authority, Nm 5:19
you are under your **h** authority, Nm 5:20
a wife, though under her **h** authority, Nm 5:29
she vowed in her **h** house or bound Nm 30:10
Her **h** brother shall go in to her and take Dt 25:5
perform the duty of a **h** brother to her. Dt 25:5
'My **h** brother refuses to perpetuate his Dt 25:7
perform the duty of a **h** brother to me.' Dt 25:7
Now Naomi had a relative of her **h**, a Ru 2:1

HUSBANDS (18)
womb that they may become your **h**? Ru 1:11
them to look at their **h** with contempt, Est 1:17
all women will give honor to their **h**, Est 1:20
who loathed their **h** and their Ezk 16:45
who crush the needy, who say to your **h**, Am 4:1
for you have had five **h**, and the one you Jn 4:18
learn, let them ask their **h** at home. 1 Cor 14:35
Wives, submit to your own **h**, as to the Eph 5:22
should submit in everything to their **h**. Eph 5:24
H, love your wives, as Christ loved the Eph 5:25
In the same way **h** should love their Eph 5:28
Wives, submit to your **h**, as is fitting in Col 3:18
H, love your wives, and do not be harsh Col 3:19
women to love their **h** and children, Ti 2:4
kind, and submissive to their own **h**, Ti 2:5
wives, be subject to your own **h**, 1 Pt 3:1
themselves, by submitting to their **h**, 1 Pt 3:5
h, live with your wives in an 1 Pt 3:7

HUSBANDS' (1)
was it without our **h** approval that we Jer 44:19

HUSH (1)
And when there was a great **h**, he Acts 21:40

HUSHAH (1)
fathered Gedor, and Ezer fathered **H**. 1 Chr 4:4

HUSHAI (14)
H the Archite came to meet him 2 Sm 15:32
So **H**, David's friend, came into the 2 Sm 15:37
And when **H** the Archite, David's 2 Sm 16:16
to Absalom, **H** said to Absalom, 2 Sm 16:16
And Absalom said to **H**, "Is this your 2 Sm 16:17
And **H** said to Absalom, "No, for 2 Sm 16:18
said, "Call **H** the Archite also, 2 Sm 17:5
And when **H** came to Absalom, 2 Sm 17:6
Then **H** said to Absalom, "This time 2 Sm 17:7
H said, "You know that your father 2 Sm 17:8
"The counsel of **H** the Archite is 2 Sm 17:14
Then **H** said to Zadok and Abiathar 2 Sm 17:15
Baana the son of **H**, in Asher and 1 Kgs 4:16
and **H** the Archite was the king's 1 Chr 27:33

HUSHAM (4)
and **H** of the land of the Temanites Gn 36:34
H died, and Hadad the son of Bedad, Gn 36:35
and **H** of the land of the Temanites 1 Chr 1:45
H died, and Hadad the son of Bedad, 1 Chr 1:46

HUSHATHITE (5)
Then Sibbecai the **H** struck down 2 Sm 21:18
of Anathoth, Mebunnai the **H**, 2 Sm 23:27
Sibbecai the **H**, Ilai the Ahohite, 1 Chr 11:29
Then Sibbecai the **H** struck down 1 Chr 20:4
eighth month, was Sibbecai the **H**, 1 Chr 27:11

HUSHED (2)
the voice of the nobles was **h**, and their Jb 29:10
still, and the waves of the sea were **h**. Ps 107:29

HUSHIM (4)
The sons of Dan: **H**. Gn 46:23
were the sons of Ir, **H** the son of Aher. 1 Chr 7:12
he had sent away **H** and Baara his 1 Chr 8:8
He also fathered sons by **H**: Abitub 1 Chr 8:11

HUT (1)
like a drunken man; it sways like a **h**; Is 24:20

HYENA'S (1)
Is my heritage to me like a **h** lair? Are Jer 12:9

HYENAS (3)
H will cry in its towers, and jackals in Is 13:22
And wild animals shall meet with **h**; the Is 34:14
beasts shall dwell with **h** in Babylon, Jer 50:39

HYMENAEUS (2)
among whom are **H** and Alexander, 1 Tm 1:20
Among them are **H** and Philetus, 2 Tm 2:17

HYMN (3)
And when they had sung a **h**, they went Mt 26:30
And when they had sung a **h**, they Mk 14:26
come together, each one has a **h**, 1 Cor 14:26

HYMNS (3)
were praying and singing **h** to God, Acts 16:25
in psalms and **h** and spiritual songs, Eph 5:19
singing psalms and **h** and spiritual Col 3:16

HYPOCRISY (5)
you are full of **h** and lawlessness. Mt 23:28
But, knowing their **h**, he said to them, Mk 12:15
the leaven of the Pharisees, which is **h**. Lk 12:1
Barnabas was led astray by their **h**. Gal 2:13
and all deceit and **h** and envy and all 1 Pt 2:1

HYPOCRITE (2)
You **h**, first take the log out of your own Mt 7:5
the log that is in your own eye? You **h**, Lk 6:42

HYPOCRITES (16)
of falsehood, nor do I consort with **h**. Ps 26:4
as the **h** do in the synagogues and in the Mt 6:2
you pray, you must not be like the **h**. Mt 6:5
you fast, do not look gloomy like the **h**, Mt 6:16
You **h**! Well did Isaiah prophesy of you, Mt 15:7
said, "Why put me to the test, you **h**? Mt 22:18
h! For you shut the kingdom of heaven Mt 23:13
h! For you travel across sea and land to Mt 23:15
h! For you tithe mint and dill and Mt 23:23
h! For you clean the outside of the cup Mt 23:25
h! For you are like whitewashed Mt 23:27
h! For you build the tombs of the Mt 23:29
him in pieces and put him with the **h**. Mt 24:51
"Well did Isaiah prophesy of you **h**, Mk 7:6
You **h**! You know how to interpret the Lk 12:56
Then the Lord answered him, "You **h**! Lk 13:15

HYPOCRITICALLY (1)
rest of the Jews acted **h** along with him, Gal 2:13

HYSSOP (12)
Take a bunch of **h** and dip it in the Ex 12:22
and cedarwood and scarlet yarn and **h**. Lv 14:4
and the scarlet yarn and the **h**, Lv 14:6
with cedarwood and scarlet yarn and **h**, Lv 14:49
the cedarwood and the **h** and the scarlet Lv 14:51
the cedarwood and **h** and scarlet yarn. Lv 14:52
take cedarwood and **h** and scarlet yarn, Nm 19:6
clean person shall take **h** and dip it in Nm 19:18
in Lebanon to the **h** that grows out of 1 Kgs 4:33
Purge me with **h**, and I shall be clean; Ps 51:7
the sour wine on a **h** branch and held it Jn 19:29
with water and scarlet wool and **h**, Heb 9:19

I

I (3) [Part of God's Name]
to Moses, "**I** AM WHO I AM." And he said, Ex 3:14
to Moses, "I AM WHO **I** AM." And he said, Ex 3:14
of Israel, '**I** AM has sent me to you.'" Ex 3:14

IBEX (1)
gazelle, the roebuck, the wild goat, the **i**, Dt 14:5

IBHAR (3)
I, Elishua, Nepheg, Japhia, 2 Sm 5:15
then **I**, Elishama, Eliphelet, 1 Chr 3:6
I, Elishua, Elpelet, 1 Chr 14:5

IBLEAM (4)
and its villages, and **I** and its villages, Jos 17:11
or the inhabitants of **I** and its villages, Jgs 1:27
at the ascent of Gur, which is by **I**. 2 Kgs 9:27
struck him down at **I** and put him 2 Kgs 15:10

IBNEIAH (1)
I the son of Jeroham, Elah the son of 1 Chr 9:8

IBNIJAH (1)
of Shephatiah, son of Reuel, son of **I**; 1 Chr 9:8

IBRI (1)
Beno, Shoham, Zaccur and **I**. 1 Chr 24:27

IBSAM (1)
Jeriel, Jahmai, **I**, and Shemuel, 1 Chr 7:2

IBZAN (2)
After him **I** of Bethlehem judged Israel. Jgs 12:8
Then **I** died and was buried at Jgs 12:10

ICE (4)
which are dark with **i**, and where the Jb 6:16
By the breath of God **i** is given, and the Jb 37:10
From whose womb did the **i** come forth, Jb 38:29
down his crystals of **i** like crumbs; Ps 147:17

ICHABOD (1)
And she named the child **I**, saying, 1 Sm 4:21

ICHABOD'S (1)
Ahijah the son of Ahitub, **I** brother, 1 Sm 14:3

ICONIUM (6)
their feet against them and went to **I**. Acts 13:51
Now at **I** they entered together into the Acts 14:1
But Jews came from Antioch and **I**, Acts 14:19
to Lystra and to **I** and to Antioch, Acts 14:21
of by the brothers at Lystra and **I**. Acts 16:2
that happened to me at Antioch, at **I**, 2 Tm 3:11

IDALAH (1)
I, and Bethlehem—twelve cities with Jos 19:15

IDBASH (1)
the sons of Etam: Jezreel, Ishma, and **I**; 1 Chr 4:3

IDDO (14)
Ahinadab the son of **I**, in Mahanaim; 1 Kgs 4:14
Joah his son, **I** his son, Zerah his son, 1 Chr 6:21
in Gilead, **I** the son of Zechariah; 1 Chr 27:21
in the visions of **I** the seer concerning 2 Chr 9:29
the prophet and of **I** the seer? 2 Chr 12:15
written in the story of the prophet **I**. 2 Chr 13:22
Haggai and Zechariah the son of **I**, Ezr 5:1
the prophet and Zechariah the son of **I**. Ezr 6:14
and sent them to **I**, the leading man at Ezr 8:17
what to say to **I** and his brothers and Ezr 8:17
I, Ginnethoi, Abijah, Neh 12:4
of **I**, Zechariah; of Ginnethon, Neh 12:16
Zechariah, the son of Berechiah, son of **I**, Zec 1:1
Zechariah, the son of Berechiah, son of **I**, Zec 1:7

IDEA (1)
king to the feast." This **i** pleased Haman, Est 5:14

IDENTIFIED (2)
And he **i** it and said, "It is my son's Gn 37:33
Then Judah **i** them and said, "She is Gn 38:26

IDENTIFY (2)
please **i** whether it is your son's robe or Gn 37:32
And she said, "Please **i** whose these are, Gn 38:25

IDLE (12)
shall by no means reduce it, for they are **i**. Ex 5:8
But he said, "You are **i**, you are idle; that Ex 5:17
But he said, "You are idle, you are **i**; that Ex 5:17
and an **i** person will suffer hunger. Prv 19:15
in his **i** boasting he is not right. Is 16:6
who sing **i** songs to the sound of the harp Am 6:5
saw others standing **i** in the Mt 20:3
them, 'Why do you stand here **i** all day?' Mt 20:6
these words seemed to them an **i** tale, Lk 24:11
urge you, brothers, admonish the **i**, 1 Thes 5:14
because we were not **i** when we were 2 Thes 3:7
condemnation from long ago is not **i**, 2 Pt 2:3

IDLENESS (3)
and does not eat the bread of **i**. Prv 31:27
who is walking in **i** and not in accord 2 Thes 3:6
that some among you walk in **i**, 2 Thes 3:11

IDLERS (2)
Besides that, they learn to be **i**, going 1 Tm 5:13
from house to house, and not only **i**, 1 Tm 5:13

IDLY (3)
seeking your own pleasure, or talking **i**; Is 58:13
and why do you **i** look at wrong? Hab 1:3
why do you **i** look at traitors and are Hab 1:13

IDOL (15)
carved image of the **i** that he had 2 Chr 33:7
gods and the **i** from the house 2 Chr 33:15
An **i**! A craftsman casts it, and a Is 40:19

to set up an **i** that will not move. Is 40:20
a god or casts an **i** that is profitable for Is 44:10
he makes it an **i** and falls down before it. Is 44:15
the rest of it he makes into a god, his **i**, Is 44:17
you, lest you should say, 'My **i** did them, Is 48:5
frankincense, like one who blesses an **i**. Is 66:3
and Israel shall be ashamed of his **i**. Hos 10:6
"What profit is an **i** when its maker Hab 2:18
a sacrifice to the **i** and were rejoicing Acts 7:41
we know that "an **i** has no real 1 Cor 8:4
idols, eat food as really offered to an **i**, 1 Cor 8:7
anything, or that an **i** is anything? 1 Cor 10:19

IDOL'S (1)
have knowledge eating in an **i** temple, 1 Cor 8:10

IDOLATER (2)
sexual immorality or greed, or is an **i**, 1 Cor 5:11
or who is covetous (that is, an **i**), Eph 5:5

IDOLATERS (5)
or the greedy and swindlers, or **i**, 1 Cor 5:10
neither the sexually immoral, nor **i**, 1 Cor 6:9
Do not be **i** as some of them were; as it 1 Cor 10:7
immoral, sorcerers, **i**, and all liars, Rv 21:8
sexually immoral and murderers and **i**, Rv 22:15

IDOLATROUS (2)
and so do its **i** priests—those who Hos 10:5
the name of the **i** priests along with the Zep 1:4

IDOLATRY (6)
and presumption is as iniquity and **i**. 1 Sm 15:23
bear the penalty for your sinful **i**, Ezk 23:49
Therefore, my beloved, flee from **i**. 1 Cor 10:14
i, sorcery, enmity, strife, jealousy, fits of Gal 5:20
evil desire, and covetousness, which is **i**. Col 3:5
orgies, drinking parties, and lawless **i**. 1 Pt 4:3

IDOLS (121)
Do not turn to **i** or make for yourselves Lv 19:4
"You shall not make **i** for yourselves or Lv 26:1
bodies upon the dead bodies of your **i**, Lv 26:30
things, their **i** of wood and stone, Dt 29:17
have provoked me to anger with their **i**. Dt 32:21
turned back at the **i** near Gilgal and Jgs 3:19
he passed beyond the **i** and escaped to Jgs 3:26
the house of their **i** and to the people. 1 Sm 31:9
And the Philistines left their **i** there, 2 Sm 5:21
removed all the **i** that his fathers 1 Kgs 15:12
God of Israel to anger with their **i**. 1 Kgs 16:13
the God of Israel, to anger by their **i**. 1 Kgs 16:26
very abominably in going after **i**, 1 Kgs 21:26
and they served **i**, of which the LORD 2 Kgs 17:12
went after false **i** and became false, 2 Kgs 17:15
made Judah also to sin with his **i**, 2 Kgs 21:11
and served the **i** that his father 2 Kgs 21:21
household gods and the **i** and all the 2 Kgs 23:24
good news to their **i** and to the people. 1 Chr 10:9
For all the gods of the peoples are **i**, 1 Chr 16:26
and for the goat **i** and for the calves 2 Chr 11:15
put away the detestable **i** from all the 2 Chr 15:8
and served the Asherim and the **i**. 2 Chr 24:18
hate those who pay regard to worthless **i**, Ps 31:6
they moved him to jealousy with their **i**. Ps 78:58
all the gods of the peoples are worthless **i**, Ps 96:5
who make their boast in worthless **i**; Ps 97:7
They served their **i**, which became a Ps 106:36
they sacrificed to the **i** of Canaan, Ps 106:38
Their **i** are silver and gold, the work of Ps 115:4
The **i** of the nations are silver and Ps 135:15
Their land is filled with **i**; they bow down Is 2:8
And the **i** shall utterly pass away. Is 2:18
will cast away their **i** of silver and their Is 2:20
their idols of silver and their **i** of gold, Is 2:20
has reached to the kingdoms of the **i**, Is 10:10
do to Jerusalem and her **i** as I have done Is 10:11
and the **i** of Egypt will tremble at his Is 19:1
will inquire of the **i** and the sorcerers, Is 19:3
defile your carved **i** overlaid with silver Is 30:22
shall cast away his **i** of silver and his Is 31:7
away his idols of silver and his **i** of gold, Is 31:7
give to no other, nor my praise to carved **i**. Is 42:8
put to shame, who trust in carved **i**, Is 42:17
All who fashion **i** are nothing, and the Is 44:9
the makers of **i** go in confusion together. Is 45:16
who carry about their wooden **i**, Is 45:20
stoops; their **i** are on beasts and livestock; Is 46:1
out, let your collection of **i** deliver you! Is 57:13
carved images and with their foreign **i**?" Jer 8:19
Their **i** are like scarecrows in a Jer 10:5
foolish; the instruction of **i** is but wood! Jer 10:8
goldsmith is put to shame by his **i**, Jer 10:14
with the carcasses of their detestable **i**, Jer 16:18
are put to shame, her **i** are dismayed.' Jer 50:2
land of images, and they are mad over **i**. Jer 50:38
goldsmith is put to shame by his **i**, Jer 51:17
I will cast down your slain before your **i**. Ezk 6:4
of the people of Israel before their **i**, Ezk 6:5
and ruined, your **i** broken and destroyed, Ezk 6:6
their eyes that go whoring after their **i**. Ezk 6:9
lie among their **i** around their altars, Ezk 6:13
offered pleasing aroma to all their **i**. Ezk 6:13
and all the **i** of the house of Israel. Ezk 8:10
have taken their **i** into their hearts, Ezk 14:3
Israel who takes his **i** into his heart and Ezk 14:4
as he comes with the multitude of his **i**, Ezk 14:4
all estranged from me through their **i**. Ezk 14:5
Repent and turn away from your **i**, and Ezk 14:6
taking his **i** into his heart and putting Ezk 14:7
and with all your abominable **i**, Ezk 16:36
up his eyes to the **i** of the house of Israel, Ezk 18:6
the pledge, lifts up his eyes to the **i**, Ezk 18:12
up his eyes to the **i** of the house of Ezk 18:15
not defile yourselves with the **i** of Egypt; Ezk 20:7
on, nor did they forsake the **i** of Egypt. Ezk 20:8
for their heart went after their **i**. Ezk 20:16
nor defile yourselves with their **i**. Ezk 20:18
their eyes were set on their fathers' **i**. Ezk 20:24
yourselves with all your **i** to this day. Ezk 20:31
Go serve every one of you his **i**, now Ezk 20:39
profane with your gifts and your **i**. Ezk 20:39
come, and that makes **i** to defile herself! Ezk 22:3
and defiled by the **i** that you have made, Ezk 22:4
herself with all the **i** of everyone after Ezk 23:7
and defiled yourself with their **i**. Ezk 23:30
With their **i** they have committed Ezk 23:37
their children in sacrifice to their **i**, Ezk 23:39
"I will destroy the **i** and put an end to Ezk 30:13
up your eyes to your **i** and shed blood; Ezk 33:25
for the **i** with which they had defiled it. Ezk 36:18
and from all your **i** I will cleanse you. Ezk 36:25
anymore with their **i** and their Ezk 37:23
from me after their **i** when Israel went Ezk 44:10
to them before their **i** and became a Ezk 44:12
Ephraim is joined to **i**; leave him alone. Hos 4:17
and gold they made **i** for their own Hos 8:4
to the Baals and burning offerings to **i**. Hos 11:2
images, **i** skillfully made of their silver, Hos 13:2
O Ephraim, what have I to do with **i**? It Hos 14:8
pay regard to vain **i** forsake their hope of Jon 2:8
with fire, and all her **i** I will lay waste, Mi 1:7
creation when he makes speechless **i**! Hab 2:18
cut off the names of the **i** from the land, Zec 13:2
abstain from the things polluted by **i**, Acts 15:20
from what has been sacrificed to **i**, Acts 15:29
as he saw that the city was full of **i**. Acts 17:16
from what has been sacrificed to **i**, Acts 21:25
You who abhor **i**, do you rob temples? Rom 2:22
Now concerning food offered to **i**: we 1 Cor 8:1
as to the eating of food offered to **i**, 1 Cor 8:4
through former association with **i**, 1 Cor 8:7
is weak, to eat food offered to **i**? 1 Cor 8:10
That food offered to **i** is anything, or 1 Cor 10:19
pagans you were led astray to mute **i**, 1 Cor 12:2
has the temple of God with **i**? 2 Cor 6:16
turned to God from **i** to serve the 1 Thes 1:9
Little children, keep yourselves from **i**. 1 Jn 5:21
food sacrificed to **i** and practice sexual Rv 2:14
and to eat food sacrificed to **i**. Rv 2:20
up worshiping demons and **i** of gold and Rv 9:20

IDUMEA (1)
and Jerusalem and **I** and from beyond Mk 3:8

IEZER (1)
These are the sons of Gilead: of **I**, the Nm 26:30

IEZERITES (1)
of Gilead: of Iezer, the clan of the **I**; Nm 26:30

IGAL (3)
the tribe of Issachar, **I** the son of Joseph; Nm 13:7
I the son of Nathan of Zobah, Bani 2 Sm 23:36
Hattush, **I**, Bariah, Neariah, and 1 Chr 3:22

IGDALIAH (1)
of the sons of Hanan the son of **I**, Jer 35:4

IGNORANCE (6)
who has sinned through error or **i**; Ezk 45:20
brothers, I know that you acted in **i**, Acts 3:17
The times of **i** God overlooked, but Acts 17:30
of God because of the **i** that is in them, Eph 4:18
to the passions of your former **i**, 1 Pt 1:14
put to silence the **i** of foolish people. 1 Pt 2:15

IGNORANT (8)
I was brutish and **i**; I was like a beast Ps 73:22
being **i** of the righteousness that Rom 10:3
For we do not want you to be **i**, 2 Cor 1:8
Satan; for we are not **i** of his designs. 2 Cor 2:11
to do with foolish, **i** controversies; 2 Tm 2:23
can deal gently with the **i** and wayward, Heb 5:2
about matters of which they are **i**, 2 Pt 2:12
which the **i** and unstable twist to their 2 Pt 3:16

IGNORANTLY (1)
because I had acted **i** in unbelief, 1 Tm 1:13

IGNORE (3)
ox or his sheep going astray and **i** them. Dt 22:1
he loses and you find; you may not **i** it. Dt 22:3
ox fallen down by the way and **i** them. Dt 22:4

IGNORED (2)
disowned his brothers and **i** his children. Dt 33:9
because you have **i** all my counsel and Prv 1:25

IGNORES (3)
at once, but the prudent **i** an insult. Prv 12:16
come to him who **i** instruction, Prv 13:18
Whoever **i** instruction despises Prv 15:32

IIM (1)
Baalah, **I**, Ezem, Jos 15:29

IJON (3)
the cities of Israel and conquered **I**, 1 Kgs 15:20
of Assyria came and captured **I**, 2 Kgs 15:29
cities of Israel, and they conquered **I**, 2 Chr 16:4

IKKESH (3)
the Paltite, Ira the son of **I** of Tekoa, 2 Sm 23:26
Ira the son of **I** of Tekoa, Abiezer of 1 Chr 11:28
was Ira, the son of **I** the Tekoite; 1 Chr 27:9

ILAI (1)
the Hushathite, **I** the Ahohite, 1 Chr 11:29

ILL (23)
your father is **i**." So he took with him Gn 48:1
have you dealt **i** with your servant? Nm 11:11
that he made himself **i** because of his 2 Sm 13:2
down on your bed and pretend to be **i**. 2 Sm 13:5
lay down and pretended to be **i**. 2 Sm 13:6
the mistress of the house, became **i**. 1 Kgs 17:17
and it went **i** with Moses on their Ps 106:32
No **i** befalls the righteous, but the Prv 12:21
you, and your **i** repute have no end. Prv 25:10
It shall be **i** with him, for what his hands Is 3:11
LORD will not do good, nor will he do **i**.' Zep 1:12
Simon's mother-in-law lay **i** with a Mk 1:30
Simon's mother-in-law was **i** with a Lk 4:38
there was an official whose son was **i**. Jn 4:46
Now a certain man was **i**, Lazarus of Jn 11:1
her hair, whose brother Lazarus was **i**. Jn 11:2
saying, "Lord, he whom you love is **i**." Jn 11:3
So, when he heard that Lazarus was **i**, he Jn 11:6
In those days she became **i** and died, Acts 9:37
is why many of you are weak and **i**, 1 Cor 11:30
because you heard that he was **i**. Phil 2:26
Indeed he was **i**, near to death. But God Phil 2:27
and I left Trophimus, who was **i**, 2 Tm 4:20

ILLEGITIMATE (1)
then you are **i** children and not sons. Heb 12:8

ILLNESS (4)
And his **i** was so severe that there 1 Kgs 17:17
fallen sick with the **i** of which he 2 Kgs 13:14
in his **i** you restore him to full health. Ps 41:3
it he said, "This **i** does not lead to death. Jn 11:4

ILLNESSES (1)
"He took our **i** and bore our diseases." Mt 8:17

ILLUSIONS (1)
speak to us smooth things, prophesy **i**, Is 30:10

ILLYRICUM (1)
the way around to **I** I have fulfilled Rom 15:19

IMAGE (79)
God said, "Let us make man in our **i**, Gn 1:26
So God created man in his own **i**, in the Gn 1:27
image, in the **i** of God he created him; Gn 1:27
a son in his own likeness, after his **i**, Gn 5:3
be shed, for God made man in his own **i**. Gn 9:6
shall not make for yourself a carved **i**, Ex 20:4
idols for yourselves or erect an **i** or pillar, Lv 26:1
by making a carved **i** for yourselves, Dt 4:16
he made with you, and make a carved **i**, Dt 4:23
by making a carved **i** in the form of Dt 4:25
shall not make for yourself a carved **i**, Dt 5:8
they have made themselves a metal **i**.' Dt 9:12
who makes a carved or cast metal **i**, Dt 27:15
to make a carved **i** and a metal image. Jgs 17:3
to make a carved image and a metal **i**. Jgs 17:3
it into a carved **i** and a metal image. Jgs 17:4
it into a carved image and a metal **i**. Jgs 17:4
an ephod, household gods, a carved **i**, Jgs 18:14
gods, a carved image, and a metal **i**? Jgs 18:14
up and entered and took the carved **i**, Jgs 18:17
the household gods, and the metal **i**, Jgs 18:17
Micah's house and took the carved **i**, Jgs 18:18
the household gods, and the metal **i**, Jgs 18:18
gods and the carved **i** and went along Jgs 18:20
Dan set up the carved **i** for themselves, Jgs 18:30
set up Micah's carved **i** that he made, Jgs 18:31

Michal took an **i** and laid it on the 1 Sm 19:13
came in, behold, the **i** was in the bed, 1 Sm 19:16
made an abominable **i** for Asherah. 1 Kgs 15:13
Asa cut down her **i** and burned it at 1 Kgs 15:13
And the carved **i** of Asherah that he 2 Kgs 21:7
had made a detestable **i** for Asherah. 2 Chr 15:16
Asa cut down her **i**, crushed it, and 2 Chr 15:16
And the carved **i** of the idol that he 2 Chr 33:7
calf in Horeb and worshiped a metal **i**. Ps 106:19
glory of God for the **i** of an ox that eats Ps 106:20
my carved **i** and my metal image Is 48:5
and my metal **i** commanded them.' Is 48:5
for her bearing her **i** and poured out Jer 44:19
where was the seat of the **i** of jealousy, Ezk 8:3
in the entrance, was this **i** of jealousy. Ezk 8:5
"You saw, O king, and behold, a great **i**. Dn 2:31
king, and behold, a great image. This **i**, Dn 2:31
The head of this **i** was of fine gold, its Dn 2:32
and it struck the **i** on its feet of iron and Dn 2:34
stone that struck the **i** became a great Dn 2:35
King Nebuchadnezzar made an **i** of gold, Dn 3:1
dedication of the **i** that King Dn 3:2
dedication of the **i** that King Dn 3:3
stood before the **i** that Nebuchadnezzar Dn 3:3
worship the golden **i** that King Dn 3:5
worshiped the golden **i** that King Dn 3:7
fall down and worship the golden **i**. Dn 3:10
or worship the golden **i** that you have set Dn 3:12
or worship the golden **i** that I have set Dn 3:14
down and worship the **i** that I have Dn 3:15
or worship the golden **i** that you have set Dn 3:18
cut off the carved **i** and the metal image. Na 1:14
cut off the carved image and the metal **i**. Na 1:14
its maker has shaped it, a metal **i**, Hab 2:18
an **i** formed by the art and Acts 17:29
to be conformed to the **i** of his Son, Rom 8:29
since he is the **i** and glory of God, 1 Cor 11:7
as we have borne the **i** of the man of 1 Cor 15:49
we shall also bear the **i** of the man of 1 Cor 15:49
into the same **i** from one degree 2 Cor 3:18
the glory of Christ, who is the **i** of God. 2 Cor 4:4
He is the **i** of the invisible God, the Col 1:15
in knowledge after the **i** of its creator. Col 3:10
them to make an **i** for the beast that Rv 13:14
to give breath to the **i** of the beast, Rv 13:15
so that the **i** of the beast might even Rv 13:15
would not worship the **i** of the beast to Rv 13:15
the beast and its **i** and receives a mark Rv 14:9
these worshipers of the beast and its **i**, Rv 14:11
the beast and its **i** and the number of Rv 15:2
mark of the beast and worshiped its **i**. Rv 16:2
the beast and those who worshiped its **i**. Rv 19:20
the beast or its **i** and had not received Rv 20:4

IMAGES (44)
all their metal **i** and demolish all Nm 33:52
Asherim and burn their carved **i** with fire. Dt 7:5
The carved **i** of their gods you shall burn Dt 7:25
chop down the carved **i** of their gods and Dt 12:3
So you must make **i** of your tumors 1 Sm 6:5
of your tumors and **i** of your mice that 1 Sm 6:5
golden mice and the **i** of their tumors. 1 Sm 6:11
for yourself other gods and metal **i**, 1 Kgs 14:9
his altars and his **i** they broke in 2 Kgs 11:18
for themselves metal **i** of two calves; 2 Kgs 17:16
LORD and also served their carved **i**. 2 Kgs 17:41
his altars and his **i** they broke in 2 Chr 23:17
He even made metal **i** for the Baals, 2 Chr 28:2
and set up the Asherim and the **i**, 2 Chr 33:19
to all the **i** that Manasseh his 2 Chr 33:22
and the carved and the metal **i**. 2 Chr 34:3
and the carved and the metal **i**, 2 Chr 34:4
Asherim and the **i** into powder and 2 Chr 34:7
All worshipers of **i** are put to shame, who Ps 97:7
whose carved **i** were greater than those Is 10:10
as I have done to Samaria and her **i**?" Is 10:11
and all the carved **i** of her gods he has Is 21:9
with silver and your gold-plated metal **i**. Is 30:22
nothing; their metal **i** are empty wind. Is 41:29
trust in carved idols, who say to metal **i**, Is 42:17
anger with their carved **i** and with their Jer 8:19
to shame by his idols, for his **i** are false, Jer 10:14
Her **i** are put to shame, her idols are Jer 50:2
For it is a land of **i**, and they are mad Jer 50:38
to shame by his idols, for his **i** are false, Jer 51:17
when I will punish the **i** of Babylon; Jer 51:47
I will execute judgment upon her **i**, Jer 51:52
made their abominable **i** and their Ezk 7:20
you, and made for yourself **i** of men, Ezk 16:17
the **i** of the Chaldeans portrayed in Ezk 23:14
and put an end to the **i** in Memphis; Ezk 30:13
with their metal **i** and their precious Dn 11:8
more, and make for themselves metal **i**, Hos 13:2
your star-god—your **i** that you made Am 5:26
All her carved **i** shall be beaten to pieces, Mi 1:7
cut off your carved **i** and your pillars Mi 5:13
out your Asherah **i** from among you Mi 5:14
the **i** that you made to worship; Acts 7:43
immortal God for **i** resembling mortal Rom 1:23

IMAGINATION (2)
city, and like a high wall in his **i**. Prv 18:11
formed by the art and **i** of man. Acts 17:29

IMAGINE (1)
about me; they **i** the worst for me. Ps 41:7

IMAGINED (1)
nor ear heard, nor the heart of man **i**, 1 Cor 2:9

IMAGINES (1)
If anyone **i** that he knows something, 1 Cor 8:2

IMAGINING (1)
i that godliness is a means of gain. 1 Tm 6:5

IMITATE (5)
know how you ought to **i** us, 2 Thes 3:7
give you in ourselves an example to **i**. 2 Thes 3:9
of their way of life, and **i** their faith. Heb 13:7
Beloved, do not **i** evil but imitate good. 3 Jn 1:11
Beloved, do not imitate evil but **i** good. 3 Jn 1:11

IMITATING (1)
Brothers, join in **i** me, and keep your Phil 3:17

IMITATORS (6)
I urge you, then, be **i** of me. 1 Cor 4:16
Be **i** of me, as I am of Christ. 1 Cor 11:1
Therefore be **i** of God, as beloved Eph 5:1
And you became **i** of us and of the 1 Thes 1:6
became **i** of the churches of God in 1 Thes 2:14
but **i** of those who through faith and Heb 6:12

IMLAH (4)
of the LORD, Micaiah the son of **I**, 1 Kgs 22:8
"Bring quickly Micaiah the son of **I**." 1 Kgs 22:9
of the LORD, Micaiah the son of **I**; 2 Chr 18:7
"Bring quickly Micaiah the son of **I**." 2 Chr 18:8

IMMANUEL (3)
and bear a son, and shall call his name **I**. Is 7:14
will fill the breadth of your land, O **I**." Is 8:8
shall call his name **I**" (which means, Mt 1:23

IMMEASURABLE (2)
and what is the **i** greatness of his power Eph 1:19
he might show the **i** riches of his grace Eph 2:7

IMMEDIATELY (83)
Now go up, for you will meet him **i**." 1 Sm 9:13
down and worship shall **i** be cast into a Dn 3:6
you shall **i** be cast into a burning fiery Dn 3:15
I the word was fulfilled against Dn 4:33
I the fingers of a human hand appeared Dn 5:5
baptized, **i** he went up from the water, Mt 3:16
I they left their nets and followed him. Mt 4:20
I they left the boat and their father and Mt 4:22
be clean." And **i** his leprosy was cleansed. Mt 8:3
have much soil, and **i** they sprang up, Mt 13:5
hears the word and **i** receives it with Mt 13:20
on account of the word, **i** he falls away. Mt 13:21
I he made the disciples get into the boat Mt 14:22
But **i** Jesus spoke to them, saying, Mt 14:27
Jesus **i** reached out his hand and took Mt 14:31
and **i** they recovered their sight and Mt 20:34
of you, and **i** you will find a donkey tied, Mt 21:2
"**I** after the tribulation of those days the Mt 24:29
the man." And **i** the rooster crowed. Mt 26:74
i he saw the heavens opening and the Mk 1:10
The Spirit **i** drove him out into the Mk 1:12
And **i** they left their nets and followed Mk 1:18
And **i** he called them, and they left their Mk 1:20
and **i** on the Sabbath he entered the Mk 1:21
And **i** there was in their synagogue a Mk 1:23
And **i** he left the synagogue and entered Mk 1:29
a fever, and **i** they told him about her. Mk 1:30
And **i** the leprosy left him, and he was Mk 1:42
And **i** Jesus, perceiving in his spirit that Mk 2:8
And he rose and **i** picked up his bed and Mk 2:12
went out and **i** held counsel with Mk 3:6
not have much soil, and **i** it sprang up, Mk 4:5
Satan **i** comes and takes away the word Mk 4:15
they hear the word, **i** receive it with joy. Mk 4:16
on account of the word, **i** they fall away. Mk 4:17
i there met him out of the tombs a man Mk 5:2
And **i** the flow of blood dried up, and Mk 5:29
i turned about in the crowd and said, Mk 5:30
And **i** the girl got up and began Mk 5:42
and they were **i** overcome with Mk 5:42
And she came in **i** with haste to the Mk 6:25
And **i** the king sent an executioner with Mk 6:27
I he made his disciples get into the boat Mk 6:45
But **i** he spoke to them and said, "Take Mk 6:50
of the boat, the people **i** recognized him Mk 6:54
But **i** a woman whose little daughter Mk 7:25
And **i** he got into the boat with his Mk 8:10
And **i** all the crowd, when they saw Mk 9:15
spirit saw him, **i** it convulsed the boy, Mk 9:20
I the father of the child cried out and Mk 9:24
made you well." And **i** he recovered his Mk 10:52
and **i** as you enter it you will find a colt Mk 11:2
need of it and will send it back here **i**.'" Mk 11:3
And **i**, while he was still speaking, Mk 14:43
And **i** the rooster crowed a second Mk 14:72
And **i** his mouth was opened and his Lk 1:64
and **i** she rose and began to serve them. Lk 4:39
be clean." And **i** the leprosy left him. Lk 5:13
And **i** he rose up before them and picked Lk 5:25
the stream broke against it, **i** it fell, Lk 6:49
and **i** her discharge of blood ceased. Lk 8:44
him, and how she had been **i** healed. Lk 8:47
on her, and **i** she was made straight, Lk 13:13
a Sabbath day, will not **i** pull him out?" Lk 14:5
And **i** he recovered his sight and Lk 18:43
the kingdom of God was to appear **i**. Lk 19:11
what you are talking about." And **i**, Lk 22:60
and **i** the boat was at the land to which Jn 6:21
the morsel of bread, he **i** went out. Jn 13:30
and **i** his feet and ankles were made Acts 3:7
I she fell down at his feet and breathed Acts 5:10
And **i** something like scales fell from Acts 9:18
And **i** he proclaimed Jesus in the Acts 9:20
and make your bed." And **i** he rose. Acts 9:34
one street, and **i** the angel left him. Acts 12:10
I an angel of the Lord struck him Acts 12:23
sun for a time." **I** mist and darkness Acts 13:11
i we sought to go on into Macedonia, Acts 16:10
And **i** all the doors were opened, and Acts 16:26
The brothers **i** sent Paul and Silas Acts 17:10
Then the brothers **i** sent Paul off on Acts 17:14
examine him withdrew from him **i**, Acts 22:29
I did not **i** consult with anyone; Gal 1:16

IMMER (10)
son of Meshillemith, son of **I**; 1 Chr 9:12
fifteenth to Bilgah, the sixteenth to **I**, 1 Chr 24:14
The sons of **I**, 1,052. Ezr 2:37
Tel-harsha, Cherub, Addan, and **I**, Ezr 2:59
Of the sons of **I**: Hanani and Zebadiah. Ezr 10:20
Zadok the son of **I** repaired opposite his Neh 3:29
The sons of **I**, 1,052. Neh 7:40
Tel-harsha, Cherub, Addon, and **I**, Neh 7:61
Ahzai, son of Meshillemoth, son of **I**, Neh 11:13
Now Pashhur the priest, the son of **I**, Jer 20:1

IMMORAL (11)
your daughter-in-law has been **i**. Gn 38:24
to associate with sexually **i** people— 1 Cor 5:9
meaning the sexually **i** of this world, 1 Cor 5:10
neither the sexually **i**, nor idolaters, 1 Cor 6:9
but the sexually **i** person sins against 1 Cor 6:18
everyone who is sexually **i** or impure, Eph 5:5
the sexually **i**, men who practice 1 Tm 1:10
no one is sexually **i** or unholy like Heb 12:16
judge the sexually **i** and adulterous. Heb 13:4
as for murderers, the sexually **i**, Rv 21:8
and the sexually **i** and murderers and Rv 22:15

IMMORALITY (34)
she is pregnant by **i**." And Judah said, Gn 38:24
wife, except on the ground of sexual **i**, Mt 5:32
thoughts, murder, adultery, sexual **i**, Mt 15:19
divorces his wife, except for sexual **i**, Mt 19:9
of man, come evil thoughts, sexual **i**, Mk 7:21
to him, "We were not born of sexual **i**. Jn 8:41
polluted by idols, and from sexual **i**, Acts 15:20
been strangled, and from sexual **i**. Acts 15:29
been strangled, and from sexual **i**." Acts 21:25
not in sexual **i** and sensuality, Rom 13:13
that there is sexual **i** among you, 1 Cor 5:1
if he is guilty of sexual **i** or greed, 1 Cor 5:11
The body is not meant for sexual **i**, 1 Cor 6:13
Flee from sexual **i**. Every other sin a 1 Cor 6:18
because of the temptation to sexual **i**, 1 Cor 7:2
not indulge in sexual **i** as some of 1 Cor 10:8
repented of the impurity, sexual **i**, 2 Cor 12:21
works of the flesh are evident: sexual **i**, Gal 5:19
But sexual **i** and all impurity or Eph 5:3
therefore what is earthly in you: sexual **i**, Col 3:5
that you abstain from sexual **i**; 1 Thes 4:3
indulged in sexual **i** and pursued Jude 1:7
sacrificed to idols and practice sexual **i**. Rv 2:14
servants to practice sexual **i** and to eat Rv 2:20
but she refuses to repent of her sexual **i**. Rv 2:21
sorceries or their sexual **i** or their thefts. Rv 9:21
the wine of the passion of her sexual **i**." Rv 14:8
of the earth have committed sexual **i**, Rv 17:2
wine of whose sexual **i** the dwellers on Rv 17:2
and the impurities of her sexual **i**. Rv 17:4
the wine of the passion of her sexual **i**, Rv 18:3
of the earth have committed **i** with her, Rv 18:3
who committed sexual **i** and lived in Rv 18:9
who corrupted the earth with her **i**, Rv 19:2

IMMORTAL (2)
the glory of the **i** God for images Rom 1:23
To the King of ages, **i**, invisible, the 1 Tm 1:17

IMMORTALITY (5)
seek for glory and honor and **i**, Rom 2:7
and this mortal body must put on **i**. 1 Cor 15:53
and the mortal puts on **i**, 1 Cor 15:54
who alone has **i**, who dwells in 1 Tm 6:16
brought life and **i** to light through 2 Tm 1:10

IMMOVABLE (4)
stick together, firmly cast on him and **i**. Jb 41:23
an untroubled habitation, an **i** tent, Is 33:20
The bow stuck and remained **i**, and Acts 27:41
i, always abounding in the work of 1 Cor 15:58

IMNA (1)
Zophah, **I**, Shelesh, and Amal. 1 Chr 7:35

IMNAH (4)
I, Ishvah, Ishvi, Beriah, with Serah Gn 46:17
of Asher according to their clans: of **I**, Nm 26:44
I, Ishvah, Ishvi, Beriah, and their 1 Chr 7:30
And Kore the son of **I** the Levite, 2 Chr 31:14

IMNITES (1)
their clans: of Imnah, the clan of the **I**; Nm 26:44

IMPAIR (1)
it for myself, lest I **i** my own inheritance. Ru 4:6

IMPAIRED (1)
or toll, and the royal revenue will be **i**. Ezr 4:13

IMPALED (1)
out of his house, and he shall be **i** on it, Ezr 6:11

IMPART (4)
that I may **i** to you some spiritual gift Rom 1:11
Yet among the mature we do **i** wisdom, 1 Cor 2:6
But we **i** a secret and hidden wisdom of 1 Cor 2:7
And we **i** this in words not taught by 1 Cor 2:13

IMPARTIAL (1)
of mercy and good fruits, **i** and sincere. Jas 3:17

IMPARTIALLY (1)
Father who judges **i** according to each 1 Pt 1:17

IMPARTS (1)
it **i** understanding to the simple. Ps 119:130

IMPATIENT (8)
And the people became **i** on the way. Nm 21:4
and he became **i** over the misery of Jgs 10:16
ventures a word with you, will you be **i**? Jb 4:2
But now it has come to you, and you are **i**; Jb 4:5
against man? Why should I not be **i**? Jb 21:4
O house of Jacob? Has the LORD grown **i**? Mi 2:7
out, they were **i** to go and patrol the earth. Zec 6:7
But I became **i** with them, and they also Zec 11:8

IMPEDIMENT (1)
a man who was deaf and had a speech **i**, Mk 7:32

IMPENETRABLE (1)
forest, declares the LORD, though it is **i**, Jer 46:23

IMPENITENT (1)
of your hard and **i** heart you are storing Rom 2:5

IMPERIAL (1)
throughout the whole **i** guard and to Phil 1:13

IMPERISHABLE (9)
a perishable wreath, but we an **i**. 1 Cor 9:25
is perishable; what is raised is **i**. 1 Cor 15:42
nor does the perishable inherit the **i**. 1 Cor 15:50
sound, and the dead will be raised **i**, 1 Cor 15:52
perishable body must put on the **i**, 1 Cor 15:53
When the perishable puts on the **i**, 1 Cor 15:54
to an inheritance that is **i**, undefiled, and 1 Pt 1:4
again, not of perishable seed but of **i**, 1 Pt 1:23
of the heart with the **i** beauty of a gentle 1 Pt 3:4

IMPLANTED (1)
and receive with meekness the **i** word, Jas 1:21

IMPLEMENTS (1)
and to make his **i** of war and the 1 Sm 8:12

IMPLIES (1)
Now an intermediary **i** more than one, Gal 3:20

IMPLORE (2)
house shall come to **i** him for a piece 1 Sm 2:36
We **i** you on behalf of Christ, be 2 Cor 5:20

IMPLORED (6)
But Moses **i** the LORD his God and said, Ex 32:11
So we fasted and **i** our God for this, and Ezr 8:23
and **i** him that they might only touch Mt 14:36
and **i** him earnestly, saying, "My little Mk 5:23
in the marketplaces and **i** him that they Mk 6:56
Jesus' feet, he **i** him to come to his house, Lk 8:41

IMPLORING (2)
So the servant fell on his knees, **i** him, Mt 18:26
And a leper came to him, **i** him, and Mk 1:40

IMPLY (2)
What do I **i** then? That food offered 1 Cor 10:19
I **i** that what pagans sacrifice they 1 Cor 10:20

IMPORT (2)
And Solomon's **i** of horses was from 1 Kgs 10:28
And Solomon's **i** of horses was from 2 Chr 1:16

IMPORTANCE (1)
to you as of first **i** what I also received: 1 Cor 15:3

IMPORTANT (2)
commandment is the most **i** of all?" Mk 12:28
Jesus answered, "The most **i** is, 'Hear, Mk 12:29

IMPORTED (3)
A chariot could be **i** from Egypt for 1 Kgs 10:29
They **i** a chariot from Egypt for 600 2 Chr 1:17
And horses were **i** for Solomon from 2 Chr 9:28

IMPOSE (5)
they made in the past you shall **i** on them, Ex 5:8
the woman's husband shall **i** on him, Ex 21:22
Whatever you **i** on me I will bear." 2 Kgs 18:14
that it shall not be lawful to **i** tribute, Ezr 7:24
To **i** a fine on a righteous man is not Prv 17:26

IMPOSED (5)
If a ransom is **i** on him, then he shall Ex 21:30
of his life whatever is **i** on him. Ex 21:30
King Ahasuerus **i** tax on the land and Est 10:1
and her inhabitants **i** their terror on Ezk 26:17
for the body **i** until the time Heb 9:10

IMPOSING (1)
an altar by the Jordan, an altar of **i** size. Jos 22:10

IMPOSSIBLE (11)
propose to do will now be **i** for them. Gn 11:6
and it seemed **i** to Amnon to do 2 Sm 13:2
move, and nothing will be **i** for you." Mt 17:20
at them and said, "With man this is **i**, Mt 19:26
at them and said, "With man it is **i**, Mk 10:27
For nothing will be **i** with God." Lk 1:37
"What is **i** with men is possible with Lk 18:27
For it is **i** to restore again to repentance Heb 6:4
things, in which it is **i** for God to lie, Heb 6:18
For it is **i** for the blood of bulls and Heb 10:4
And without faith it is **i** to please him, Heb 11:6

IMPOSTOR (1)
said, "Sir, we remember how that **i** said, Mt 27:63

IMPOSTORS (2)
We are treated as **i**, and yet are true; 2 Cor 6:8
while evil people and **i** will go on 2 Tm 3:13

IMPOVERISH (1)
fire. Have you invited us here to **i** us?" Jgs 14:15

IMPOVERISHED (1)
He who is too **i** for an offering chooses Is 40:20

IMPRINT (1)
of God and the exact **i** of his nature, Heb 1:3

IMPRISONED (6)
For Zedekiah king of Judah had **i** him, Jer 32:3
they beat him and **i** him in the house Jer 37:15
ready not only to be **i** but even to die Acts 21:13
after another I **i** and beat those Acts 22:19
But the Scripture **i** everything under Gal 3:22
i until the coming faith would be Gal 3:23

IMPRISONMENT (11)
or for confiscation of his goods or for **i**." Ezr 7:26
every city that **i** and afflictions await Acts 20:23
with nothing deserving death or **i**. Acts 23:29
doing nothing to deserve death or **i**." Acts 26:31
both in my **i** and in the defense and Phil 1:7
to all the rest that my **i** is for Christ. Phil 1:13
become confident in the Lord by my **i**, Phil 1:14
but thinking to afflict me in my **i**. Phil 1:17
whose father I became in my **i**. Phlm 1:10
behalf during my **i** for the gospel, Phlm 1:13
and flogging, and even chains and **i**. Heb 11:36

IMPRISONMENTS (2)
beatings, **i**, riots, labors, sleepless 2 Cor 6:5
—with far greater labors, far more **i**, 2 Cor 11:23

IMPRISONS (1)
passes through and **i** and summons the Jb 11:10

IMPROVED (2)
as his country **i**, he improved his Hos 10:1
his country improved, he **i** his pillars. Hos 10:1

IMPUDENCE (1)
yet because of his **i** he will rise and give Lk 11:8

IMPUDENT (1)
descendants also are **i** and stubborn: Ezk 2:4

IMPURE (2)
is a land **i** with the impurity of the Ezr 9:11
everyone who is sexually immoral or **i**, Eph 5:5

IMPURITIES (1)
of abominations and the **i** of her sexual Rv 17:4

IMPURITY (29)
be in her menstrual **i** for seven days, Lv 15:19
during her menstrual **i** shall be Lv 15:20
and her menstrual **i** comes upon him, Lv 15:24
days, not at the time of her menstrual **i**, Lv 15:25
a discharge beyond the time of her **i**, Lv 15:25
As in the days of her **i**, she shall be Lv 15:25
shall be to her as the bed of her **i**. Lv 15:26
in the uncleanness of her menstrual **i**. Lv 15:26
her who is unwell with her menstrual **i**, Lv 15:33
If a man takes his brother's wife, it is **i**. Lv 20:21
for the water for **i** for the congregation Nm 19:9
the water for **i** was not thrown Nm 19:13
Because the water for **i** has not been Nm 19:20
the water for **i** shall wash his Nm 19:21
the water for **i** shall be unclean Nm 19:21
also be purified with the water for **i**. Nm 31:23
land impure with the **i** of the peoples of Ezr 9:11
a woman in her time of menstrual **i**, Ezk 18:6
who are unclean in their menstrual **i**. Ezk 22:10
of a woman in her menstrual **i**. Ezk 36:17
them up in the lusts of their hearts to **i**, Rom 1:24
as slaves to **i** and to lawlessness Rom 6:19
and have not repented of the **i**, 2 Cor 12:21
sexual immorality, **i**, sensuality, Gal 5:19
greedy to practice every kind of **i**. Eph 4:19
immorality and all **i** or covetousness Eph 5:3
sexual immorality, **i**, passion, evil desire, Col 3:5
spring from error or **i** or any attempt 1 Thes 2:3
For God has not called us for **i**, but in 1 Thes 4:7

IMPUTE (1)
Let not the king **i** anything to his 1 Sm 22:15

IMPUTED (1)
LORD, bloodguilt shall be **i** to that man. Lv 17:4

IMRAH (1)
Suah, Harnepher, Shual, Beri, **I**. 1 Chr 7:36

IMRI (2)
of Ammihud, son of Omri, son of **I**, 1 Chr 9:4
next to them Zaccur the son of **I** built. Neh 3:2

INASMUCH (4)
i as the king does not bring his 2 Sm 14:13
i as you do not keep my ways but show Mal 2:9
I as many have undertaken to compile a Lk 1:1
I then as I am an apostle to the Rom 11:13

INAUGURATED (1)
the first covenant was **i** without blood. Heb 9:18

INCAPABLE (1)
How long will they be **i** of innocence? Hos 8:5

INCENSE (94)
the anointing oil and for the fragrant **i**, Ex 25:6
shall make its plates and dishes for **i**, Ex 25:29
shall make an altar on which to burn **i**; Ex 30:1
And Aaron shall burn fragrant **i** on it. Ex 30:7
a regular **i** offering before the LORD Ex 30:8
You shall not offer unauthorized **i** on it, Ex 30:9
and its utensils, and the altar of **i**, Ex 30:27
and make an **i** blended as by the Ex 30:35
And the **i** that you shall make Ex 30:37
with all its utensils, and the altar of **i**, Ex 31:8
oil and the fragrant **i** for the Holy Place. Ex 31:11
the anointing oil and for the fragrant **i**, Ex 35:8
and the altar of **i**, with its poles, and the Ex 35:15
the anointing oil and the fragrant **i**, Ex 35:15
the anointing oil, and for the fragrant **i**. Ex 35:28
on the table, its plates and dishes for **i**, Ex 37:16
He made the altar of **i** of acacia wood. Ex 37:25
oil also, and the pure fragrant **i**, Ex 37:29
the anointing oil and the fragrant **i**, Ex 39:38
the golden altar for **i** before the ark of Ex 40:5
and burned fragrant **i** on it, as the LORD Ex 40:27
the altar of fragrant **i** before the LORD that Lv 4:7
fire in it and laid **i** on it and offered Lv 10:1
two handfuls of sweet **i** beaten small, Lv 16:12
and put the **i** on the fire before the LORD, Lv 16:13
the cloud of the **i** may cover the mercy Lv 16:13
and cut down your **i** altars and cast Lv 26:30
and put on it the plates, the dishes for **i**, Nm 4:7
of the oil for the light, the fragrant **i**, Nm 4:16
one golden dish of 10 shekels, full of **i**; Nm 7:14
one golden dish of 10 shekels, full of **i**; Nm 7:20
one golden dish of 10 shekels, full of **i**; Nm 7:26
one golden dish of 10 shekels, full of **i**; Nm 7:32
one golden dish of 10 shekels, full of **i**; Nm 7:38
one golden dish of 10 shekels, full of **i**; Nm 7:44
one golden dish of 10 shekels, full of **i**; Nm 7:50
one golden dish of 10 shekels, full of **i**; Nm 7:56
one golden dish of 10 shekels, full of **i**; Nm 7:62
one golden dish of 10 shekels, full of **i**; Nm 7:68

one golden dish of 10 shekels, full of **i**; Nm 7:74
one golden dish of 10 shekels, full of **i**; Nm 7:80
the twelve golden dishes, full of **i**, Nm 7:86
in them and put **i** on them before the Nm 16:7
of you take his censer and put **i** on it, Nm 16:17
in them and laid **i** on them and stood Nm 16:18
consumed the 250 men offering the **i**. Nm 16:35
draw near to burn **i** before the LORD, Nm 16:40
off the altar and lay **i** on it and carry it Nm 16:46
he put on the **i** and made atonement Nm 16:47
they shall put **i** before you and whole Dt 33:10
priest, to go up to my altar, to burn **i**, 1 Sm 2:28
the cups, snuffers, basins, dishes for **i**, 1 Kgs 7:50
those also who burned **i** to Baal, to 2 Kgs 23:5
and the dishes for **i** and all the 2 Kgs 25:14
and on the altar of **i** for all the work 1 Chr 6:49
the fine flour, the wine, the oil, the **i**, 1 Chr 9:29
for the altar of **i** made of refined 1 Chr 28:18
for the burning of **i** of sweet spices 2 Chr 2:4
the snuffers, basins, dishes for **i**, and 2 Chr 4:22
burnt offerings and **i** of sweet spices, 2 Chr 13:11
the high places and the **i** altars. 2 Chr 14:5
and dishes for **i** and vessels of gold 2 Chr 24:14
of the LORD to burn **i** on the altar of 2 Chr 26:16
to burn incense on the altar of **i**. 2 Chr 26:16
you, Uzziah, to burn **i** to the LORD, 2 Chr 26:18
who are consecrated to burn **i**. 2 Chr 26:18
had a censer in his hand to burn **i**, 2 Chr 26:19
house of the LORD, by the altar of **i**. 2 Chr 26:19
have not burned **i** or offered burnt 2 Chr 29:7
altars for burning **i** they took away 2 Chr 30:14
he cut down the **i** altars that stood 2 Chr 34:4
down all the **i** altars throughout all 2 Chr 34:7
my prayer be counted as **i** before you, Ps 141:2
vain offerings; **i** is an abomination to me. Is 1:13
either the Asherim or the altars of **i**. Is 17:8
no Asherim or **i** altars will remain Is 27:9
grain offerings and **i** to present at Jer 41:5
and the dishes for **i** and all the vessels Jer 52:18
and the dishes for **i** and the bowls for Jer 52:19
and your **i** altars shall be broken, Ezk 6:4
and destroyed, your **i** altars cut down, Ezk 6:6
and the smoke of the cloud of **i** went up. Ezk 8:11
and set my oil and my **i** before them. Ezk 16:18
you had placed my **i** and my oil. Ezk 23:41
that an offering and **i** be offered up to Dn 2:46
and in every place **i** will be offered to Mal 1:11
to enter the temple of the Lord and burn **i**. Lk 1:9
were praying outside at the hour of **i**. Lk 1:10
on the right side of the altar of **i**. Lk 1:11
the golden altar of **i** and the ark of Heb 9:4
holding a harp, and golden bowls full of **i**, Rv 5:8
and he was given much **i** to offer with the Rv 8:3
and the smoke of the **i**, with the prayers of Rv 8:4
cinnamon, spice, **i**, myrrh, Rv 18:13

INCENSED (2)
all who are **i** against you shall be put to Is 41:11
be ashamed all who were **i** against him. Is 45:24

INCIDENT (1)
against the LORD in the **i** of Peor, Nm 31:16

INCITED (5)
Israel, and he **i** David against them, 2 Sm 24:1
like Ahab, whom Jezebel his wife **i**. 1 Kgs 21:25
against Israel and **i** David to number 1 Chr 21:1
although you **i** me against him to destroy Jb 2:3
But the Jews **i** the devout women of Acts 13:50

INCLINE (30)
you, and **i** your heart to the LORD, Jos 24:23
that he may **i** our hearts to him, to 1 Kgs 8:58
I your ear, O LORD, and hear; open 2 Kgs 19:16
their heart; you will **i** your ear Ps 10:17
will answer me, O God; **i** your ear to me; Ps 17:6
I your ear to me; rescue me speedily! Be a Ps 31:2
daughter, and consider, and **i** your ear: Ps 45:10
I will **i** my ear to a proverb; I will solve Ps 49:4
rescue me; **i** your ear to me, and save me! Ps 71:2
i your ears to the words of my mouth! Ps 78:1
I your ear, O LORD, and answer me, for I Ps 86:1
come before you; **i** your ear to my cry! Ps 88:2
I your ear to me; answer me speedily in Ps 102:2
I my heart to your testimonies, and Ps 119:36
I **i** my heart to perform your statutes Ps 119:112
Do not let my heart **i** to any evil, to busy Ps 141:4
to my words; **i** your ear to my sayings. Prv 4:20
wisdom; **i** your ear to my understanding, Prv 5:1
voice of my teachers or **i** my ear to my Prv 5:13
I your ear, and hear the words of the Prv 22:17
I your ear, O LORD, and hear; open your Is 37:17
I your ear, and come to me; hear, that Is 55:3
But they did not obey or **i** their ear, but Jer 7:24
they did not listen to me or **i** their ear, Jer 7:26
Yet they did not obey or **i** their ear, but Jer 11:8
Yet they did not listen or **i** their ear, but Jer 17:23
did not listen to me or **i** their ears to me. Jer 34:14
But you did not **i** your ear or listen to Jer 35:15
But they did not listen or **i** their ear, to Jer 44:5
O my God, **i** your ear and hear. Open Dn 9:18

INCLINED (7)
eyes, which you are **i** to whore after. Nm 15:39
I know what they are **i** to do even today, Dt 31:21
and their hearts **i** to follow Abimelech, Jgs 9:3
the LORD; he **i** to me and heard my cry. Ps 40:1
Because he **i** his ear to me, therefore I Ps 116:2
have neither listened nor **i** your ears to Jer 25:4
If anyone is **i** to be contentious, we 1 Cor 11:16

INCLINES (1)
A wise man's heart **i** him to the right, Eccl 10:2

INCLINING (1)
attentive to wisdom and **i** your heart to Prv 2:2

INCLUDE (1)
But he did not **i** Levi and Benjamin 1 Chr 21:6

INCLUDED (4)
Their territory **i** Jezreel, Chesulloth, Jos 19:18
Their territory **i** Helkath, Hali, Beten, Jos 19:25
the territory of its inheritance **i** Zorah, Jos 19:41
attack them, children and women **i**, Est 8:11

INCLUDING (4)
descendants, not **i** Jacob's sons' wives, Gn 46:26
Dan to Beersheba, **i** the land of Gilead, Jgs 20:1
i Ahijah the son of Ahitub, Ichabod's 1 Sm 14:3
i you who are called to belong to Jesus Rom 1:6

INCLUSION (1)
much more will their full **i** mean! Rom 11:12

INCOME (2)
but trouble befalls the **i** of the wicked. Prv 15:6
nor he who loves wealth with his **i**; Eccl 5:10

INCOMPETENT (1)
by you, are you **i** to try trivial cases? 1 Cor 6:2

INCORRUPTIBLE (1)
love our Lord Jesus Christ with love **i**. Eph 6:24

INCREASE (42)
may eat of its fruit, to **i** its yield for you: Lv 19:25
years are many, you shall **i** the price, Lv 25:16
season, and the land shall yield its **i**, Lv 26:4
vain, for your land shall not yield its **i**, Lv 26:20
to **i** still more the fierce anger of the Nm 32:14
the **i** of your herds and the young of your Dt 7:13
the **i** of your herds and the young of your Dt 28:4
the **i** of your herds and the young of Dt 28:18
the **i** of your herds or the young of your Dt 28:51
of Sheol, devours the earth and its **i**, Dt 32:22
I would say to Abimelech, '**I** your army, Jgs 9:29
against me and **i** your vexation toward Jb 10:17
and it would burn to the root all my **i**. Jb 31:12
if riches **i**, set not your heart on them. Ps 62:10
The earth has yielded its **i**; God, our God, Ps 67:6
You will **i** my greatness and comfort Ps 71:21
wicked; always at ease, they **i** in riches. Ps 73:12
is good, and our land will yield its **i**. Ps 85:12
May the LORD give you **i**, you and your Ps 115:14
Let the wise hear and **i** in learning, and Prv 1:5
righteous man, and he will **i** in learning. Prv 9:9
whoever gathers little by little will **i** it. Prv 13:11
oppresses the poor to **i** his own wealth, Prv 22:16
but when they perish, the righteous **i**. Prv 28:28
When the righteous **i**, the people Prv 29:2
When the wicked **i**, transgression Prv 29:16
For when dreams **i** and words grow Eccl 5:7
When goods **i**, they increase who eat Eccl 5:11
goods increase, they **i** who eat them, Eccl 5:11
Of the **i** of his government and of peace Is 9:7
fruit, and the earth shall yield its **i**, Ezk 34:27
the tree and the **i** of the field abundant, Ezk 36:30
for them: to **i** their people like a flock. Ezk 36:37
run to and fro, and knowledge shall **i**." Dn 12:4
apostles said to the Lord, "**I** our faith!" Lk 17:5
He must **i**, but I must decrease." Jn 3:30
And the word of God continued to **i**, and Acts 6:7
Lord continued to **i** and prevail Acts 19:20
Now the law came in to **i** the trespass, Rom 5:20
more people it may **i** thanksgiving, 2 Cor 4:15
seed for sowing and **i** the harvest of 2 Cor 9:10
the Lord make you **i** and abound in 1 Thes 3:12

INCREASED (27)
The waters **i** and bore up the ark, and it Gn 7:17
waters prevailed and **i** greatly on the Gn 7:18
before I came, and it has **i** abundantly, Gn 30:30
Thus the man **i** greatly and had large Gn 30:43
people of Israel were fruitful and **i** greatly; Ex 1:7
until you have **i** and possess the land. Ex 23:30
of the Philistines **i** more and more. 1 Sm 14:19
and their fathers' houses **i** greatly. 1 Chr 4:38
women, and so **i** the guilt of Israel. Ezr 10:10
and his possessions have **i** in the land. Jb 1:10
answered me; my strength of soul you **i**. Ps 138:3
multiplied the nation; you have **i** its joy; Is 9:3
But you have **i** the nation, O LORD, you Is 26:15
nation, O LORD, you have **i** the nation; Is 26:15
you have multiplied and **i** in the land, Jer 3:16
Yet she **i** her whoring, remembering Ezk 23:19
in your trade you have **i** your wealth, Ezk 28:5
The more they **i**, the more they sinned Hos 4:7
The more his fruit **i**, the more altars he Hos 10:1
You **i** your merchants more than the Na 3:16
And because lawlessness will be **i**, the Mt 24:12
And Jesus **i** in wisdom and in stature Lk 2:52
the people **i** and multiplied in Egypt Acts 7:17
But Saul **i** all the more in strength, and Acts 9:22
But the word of God **i** and multiplied. Acts 12:24
the faith, and they **i** in numbers daily. Acts 16:5
increase the trespass, but where sin **i**, Rom 5:20

INCREASES (9)
rich, when the glory of his house **i**. Ps 49:16
sweetness of speech **i** persuasiveness. Prv 16:21
like a robber and **i** the traitors among Prv 23:28
the wicked increase, transgression **i**, Prv 29:16
and he who **i** knowledge increases Eccl 1:18
he who increases knowledge **i** sorrow. Eccl 1:18
to him who has no might he **i** strength. Is 40:29
But our hope is that as your faith **i**, 2 Cor 10:15
but I seek the fruit that **i** to your credit. Phil 4:17

INCREASING (7)
and the people with Absalom kept **i**. 2 Sm 15:12
growing up and **i** and yielding thirtyfold Mk 4:8
When the crowds were **i**, he began to Lk 11:29
when the disciples were **i** in number, Acts 6:1
every good work and **i** in the knowledge Col 1:10
every one of you for one another is **i**. 2 Thes 1:3
For if these qualities are yours and are **i**, 2 Pt 1:8

INCREDIBLE (1)
Why is it thought **i** by any of you that Acts 26:8

INCUR (5)
neighbor, lest you **i** sin because of him. Lv 19:17
that they may not **i** guilt before the 2 Chr 19:10
shall do, and you will not **i** guilt. 2 Chr 19:10
and those who resist will **i** judgment. Rom 13:2
and so **i** condemnation for having 1 Tm 5:12

INCURABLE (7)
him in his bowels with an **i** disease. 2 Chr 21:18
my wound is **i**, though I am without Jb 34:6
will flee away in a day of grief and **i** pain. Is 17:11
is my pain unceasing, my wound **i**, Jer 15:18
Your hurt is **i**, and your wound is Jer 30:12
cry out over your hurt? Your pain is **i**. Jer 30:15
For her wound is **i**, and it has come to Mi 1:9

INCURRED (5)
he has indeed **i** guilt before the LORD." Lv 5:19
but this Amon **i** guilt more and 2 Chr 33:23
All who ate of it **i** guilt; disaster came Jer 2:3
but he **i** guilt through Baal and died. Hos 13:1
sail from Crete and **i** this injury and Acts 27:21

INCURS (1)
he who reproves a wicked man **i** injury. Prv 9:7

INDEBTED (1)
ourselves forgive everyone who is **i** to us. Lk 11:4

INDECENCY (1)
eyes because he has found some **i** in her, Dt 24:1

INDECENT (1)
may not see anything **i** among you and Dt 23:14

INDEED (104)
laugh and say, 'Shall I **i** bear a child, Gn 18:13
"Will you **i** sweep away the righteous Gn 18:23
Besides, she is **i** my sister, the daughter Gn 20:12
us, and he has **i** devoured our money. Gn 31:15
said to him, "Are you **i** to reign over us? Gn 37:8
Or are you **i** to rule over us?" So they Gn 37:8
and your brothers **i** come to bow Gn 37:10
For I was **i** stolen out of the land of the Gn 40:15
like me can **i** practice divination?" Gn 44:15
if you will **i** obey my voice and keep my Ex 19:5
he has **i** incurred guilt before the LORD." Lv 5:19
"Has the LORD **i** spoken only through Nm 12:2
"If you will **i** give this people into my Nm 21:2
For **i** the hand of the LORD was against Dt 2:15
if you will **i** obey my commandments Dt 11:13
you may **i** set a king over you whom Dt 17:15
not listen to Balaam. **I**, he blessed you. Jos 24:10
princesses answer, **i**, she answers herself, Jgs 5:29
if you will **i** look on the affliction of 1 Sm 1:11
I the LORD visited Hannah, and she 1 Sm 2:21
'Did I **i** reveal myself to the house of 1 Sm 2:27
'If the LORD will **i** bring me back to 2 Sm 15:8
I have **i** built you an exalted house, a 1 Kgs 8:13

“But will God i dwell on the earth? 1 Kgs 8:27
You have i struck down Edom, and 2 Kgs 14:10
“But will God i dwell with man on 2 Chr 6:18
“I, the light of the wicked is put out, and Jb 18:5
If i you magnify yourselves against me Jb 19:5
places; i, I have a beautiful inheritance. Ps 16:6
I, none who wait for you shall be put to Ps 25:3
Do you i decree what is right, you gods? Ps 58:1
they were afraid; i, the deep trembled. Ps 77:16
i, for the king it is made ready, its pyre Is 30:33
i, there the night bird settles and finds Is 34:14
i, there the hawks are gathered, each one Is 34:15
I will repay; I will i repay into their bosom Is 65:6
‘Do we not i know that every jar will be Jer 13:12
For if you will i obey this word, then Jer 22:4
Should I i let myself be consulted by Ezk 14:3
you are i wiser than Daniel; no secret is Ezk 28:3
I, he shall turn his insolence back Dn 11:18
Is it not i so, O people of Israel?” Am 2:11
I, the vine, the fig tree, the pomegranate, Hg 2:19
I, I have already cursed them, because Mal 2:2
Then i he may plunder his house. Mt 12:29
I, in their case the prophecy of Isaiah is Mt 13:14
“‘You will i hear but never understand, Mt 13:14
and you will i see but never perceive. Mt 13:14
He i bears fruit and yields, in one case a Mt 13:23
i, he said nothing to them without a Mt 13:34
into temptation. The spirit i is willing, Mt 26:41
man. Then i he may plunder his house. Mk 3:27
so that “they may i see but not perceive, Mk 4:12
and may i hear but not understand, Mk 4:12
into temptation. The spirit i is willing, Mk 14:38
And we i justly, for we are receiving the Lk 23:41
saying, “The Lord has risen i, and has Lk 24:34
and said of him, “Behold, an Israelite i, Jn 1:47
we know that this is i the Savior of the Jn 4:42
“This is i the Prophet who is to come into Jn 6:14
if the Son sets you free, you will be free i. Jn 8:36
I, the hour is coming when whoever kills Jn 16:2
the hour is coming, i it has come, Jn 16:32
have said, “‘For we are i his offspring.’ Acts 17:28
You will i hear but never understand, Acts 28:26
and you will i see but never perceive. Acts 28:26
For circumcision i is of value if you Rom 2:25
for sin i was in the world before the Rom 5:13
not submit to God’s law; i, it cannot. Rom 8:7
of God, who i is interceding for us. Rom 8:34
As i he says in Hosea, “Those who Rom 9:25
I they have, for “Their voice has gone Rom 10:18
Everything is i clean, but it is wrong Rom 14:20
to do it, and i they owe it to them. Rom 15:27
on earth—as i there are many “gods” 1 Cor 8:5
I, we felt that we had received the 2 Cor 1:9
I, in this case, what once had glory 2 Cor 3:10
if i by putting it on we may not be 2 Cor 5:3
i, in every way we have made this 2 Cor 11:6
—unless i you fail to meet the test! 2 Cor 13:5
many things in vain—if i it was in vain? Gal 3:4
then righteousness would i be by the Gal 3:21
Some i preach Christ from envy and Phil 1:15
I he was ill, near to death. But God had Phil 2:27
I, I count everything as loss because of Phil 3:8
You were i concerned for me, but you Phil 4:10
as i in the whole world it is bearing fruit Col 1:6
if i you continue in the faith, stable and Col 1:23
These have i an appearance of wisdom Col 2:23
to which i you were called in one body. Col 3:15
for that i is what you are doing to all 1 Thes 4:10
since i God considers it just to repay 2 Thes 1:6
Great i, we confess, is the mystery of 1 Tm 3:16
I, all who desire to live a godly life in 2 Tm 3:12
but now he is i useful to you and to Phlm 1:11
we are his house if i we hold fast our Heb 3:6
if i we hold our original confidence Heb 3:14
For it was i fitting that we should have Heb 7:26
I, under the law almost everything is Heb 9:22
I, so terrifying was the sight that Heb 12:21
if i you have tasted that the Lord is good. 1 Pt 2:3
and i our fellowship is with the Father 1 Jn 1:3
truth, as i you are walking in the truth. 3 Jn 1:3
now on.” “Blessed i,” says the Spirit, Rv 14:13

INDEPENDENT (1)
Lord woman is not i of man nor 1 Cor 11:11

INDESTRUCTIBLE (1)
descent, but by the power of an i life. Heb 7:16

INDIA (2)
who reigned from I to Ethiopia over Est 1:1
of the provinces from I to Ethiopia, Est 8:9

INDICATE (1)
not to i the charges against him.” Acts 25:27

INDICATES (2)
By this the Holy Spirit i that the way into Heb 9:8
“Yet once more,” i the removal of Heb 12:27

INDICATING (1)
Christ in them was i when he predicted 1 Pt 1:11

INDICTMENT (5)
that I had the i written by my Jb 31:35
the LORD has an i against the nations; Jer 25:31
The LORD has an i against Judah and Hos 12:2
Hear, you mountains, the i of the LORD, Mi 6:2
for the LORD has an i against his people, Mi 6:2

INDIGNANT (9)
of it, and the men were i and very angry, Gn 34:7
be angry forever, will he be i to the end?’ Jer 3:5
heard it, they were i at the two brothers. Mt 20:24
to the Son of David!” they were i, Mt 21:15
when the disciples saw it, they were i, Mt 26:8
Jesus saw it, he was i and said to them, Mk 10:14
they began to be i at James and John. Mk 10:41
i because Jesus had healed on the Lk 13:14
Who is made to fall, and I am not i? 2 Cor 11:29

INDIGNANTLY (1)
were some who said to themselves i, Mk 14:4

INDIGNATION (23)
judge, and a God who feels i every day. Ps 7:11
soundness in my flesh because of your i; Ps 38:3
Pour out your i upon them, and let Ps 69:24
burning anger, wrath, i, and distress, Ps 78:49
and put away your i toward us! Ps 85:4
because of your i and anger; for you Ps 102:10
Hot i seizes me because of the wicked, Ps 119:53
the LORD and the weapons of his i, Is 13:5
he shall show his i against his enemies. Is 66:14
and the nations cannot endure his i. Jer 10:10
upon me, for you had filled me with i. Jer 15:17
my anger and my wrath and in great i. Jer 32:37
and in his fierce i has spurned king and Lam 2:6
And I will pour out my i upon you; I Ezk 21:31
or rained upon in the day of i. Ezk 22:24
I have poured out my i upon them. Ezk 22:31
what shall be at the latter end of the i, Dn 8:19
shall prosper till the i is accomplished; Dn 11:36
I will bear the i of the LORD because I have Mi 7:9
Who can stand before his i? Who can Na 1:6
the rivers, or your i against the sea, Hab 3:8
kingdoms, to pour out upon them my i, Zep 3:8
eagerness to clear yourselves, what i, 2 Cor 7:11

INDISPENSABLE (1)
body that seem to be weaker are i, 1 Cor 12:22

INDISTINCT (1)
And if the bugle gives an i sound, 1 Cor 14:8

INDIVIDUALLY (3)
Christ, and i members one of another. Rom 12:5
apportions to each one i as he wills. 1 Cor 12:11
body of Christ and i members of it. 1 Cor 12:27

INDIVIDUALS (1)
the names of the i from twenty years 1 Chr 23:24

INDOLENCE (1)
in, and through i the house leaks. Eccl 10:18

INDOORS (1)
the sword shall bereave, and i terror, Dt 32:25

INDUCED (1)
and i him to go up against 2 Chr 18:2

INDULGE (2)
We must not i in sexual immorality 1 Cor 10:8
and especially those who i in the lust of 2 Pt 2:10

INDULGED (1)
which likewise i in sexual immorality Jude 1:7

INDULGENCE (1)
of no value in stopping the i of the flesh. Col 2:23

INDUSTRIOUS (1)
the young man was i he gave him 1 Kgs 11:28

INEFFECTIVE (1)
keep you from being i or unfruitful in 2 Pt 1:8

INEXPERIENCED (2)
“Solomon my son is young and i, 1 Chr 22:5
God has chosen, is young and i, 1 Chr 29:1

INEXPRESSIBLE (2)
Thanks be to God for his i gift! 2 Cor 9:15
with joy that is i and filled with glory, 1 Pt 1:8

INFANT (5)
both man and woman, child and i, 1 Sm 15:3
both man and woman, child and i, 1 Sm 22:19
there be in it an i who lives but a few Is 65:20
from you man and woman, i and child, Jer 44:7
tongue of the nursing i sticks to the Lam 4:4

INFANTS (18)
child, as i who never see the light? Jb 3:16
Out of the mouth of babes and i, you have Ps 8:2
they leave their abundance to their i. Ps 17:14
their princes, and i shall rule over them. Is 3:4
My people—i are their oppressors, and Is 3:12
Their i will be dashed in pieces before Is 13:16
because i and babies faint in the Lam 2:11
elders; gather the children, even nursing i. Jl 2:16
her i were dashed in pieces at the head of Na 3:10
of the mouth of i and nursing babies Mt 21:16
those who are nursing i in those days! Mt 24:19
those who are nursing i in those days! Mk 13:17
they were bringing even i to him that Lk 18:15
those who are nursing i in those days! Lk 21:23
and forced our fathers to expose their i, Acts 7:19
but as people of the flesh, as i in Christ. 1 Cor 3:1
Be i in evil, but in your thinking be 1 Cor 14:20
Like newborn i, long for the pure 1 Pt 2:2

INFERIOR (6)
as well as you; I am not i to you. Jb 12:3
you know, I also know; I am not i to you. Jb 13:2
Another kingdom i to you shall arise Dn 2:39
in the least i to these super-apostles. 2 Cor 11:5
not at all i to these super-apostles, 2 Cor 12:11
beyond dispute that the i is blessed by Heb 7:7

INFIRMITIES (2)
to hear him and to be healed of their i. Lk 5:15
who had been healed of evil spirits and i: Lk 8:2

INFLAMED (1)
While they are i I will prepare them a Jer 51:39

INFLAMES (1)
tarry late into the evening as wine i them! Is 5:11

INFLAMMATION (1)
disease and with fever, i and fiery heat, Dt 28:22

INFLICT (2)
Egypt, which you knew, will he i on you, Dt 7:15
God is unrighteous to i wrath on us? Rom 3:5

INFLICTED (4)
And Asa i cruelties upon some of 2 Chr 16:10
and heals the wounds i by his blow. Is 30:26
which the LORD i on the day of his Lam 1:12
when they had i many blows upon Acts 16:23

INFLICTING (1)
i vengeance on those who do not 2 Thes 1:8

INFLUENCE (3)
to the area of i God assigned to us, 2 Cor 10:13
our area of i among you may be 2 Cor 10:15
already done in another’s area of i. 2 Cor 10:16

INFLUENTIAL (3)
those who seemed i) the gospel that Gal 2:2
who seemed to be i (what they were Gal 2:6
I say, who seemed i added nothing to me. Gal 2:6

INFORM (2)
until word comes from you to i me.” 2 Sm 15:28
therefore we send and i the king, Ezr 4:14

INFORMATION (2)
and come back to me with sure i. 1 Sm 23:23
also asked them their names, for your i, Ezr 5:10

INFORMED (2)
one that you have i me of these Acts 23:22
it, for the sake of the one who i you, 1 Cor 10:28

INFORMS (1)
He who i against his friends to get a share Jb 17:5

INGATHERING (2)
shall keep the Feast of I at the end of the Ex 23:16
and the Feast of I at the year’s end. Ex 34:22

INHABIT (8)
you come into the land you are to i, Nm 15:2
cities, in houses that none should i, Jb 15:28
seeking food far from the ruins they i! Ps 109:10
For the upright will i the land, and Prv 2:21
They shall build houses and i them; Is 65:21
They shall not build and another i; they Is 65:22
rebuild the ruined cities and i them; Am 9:14
build houses, they shall not i them; Zep 1:13

INHABITANT (26)
large and beautiful houses, without i. Is 5:9
“Until cities lie waste without i, and Is 6:11
Shout, and sing for joy, O i of Zion, for Is 12:6
the snare are upon you, O i of the earth! Is 24:17
And no i will say, “I am sick”; the people Is 33:24
a waste; his cities are in ruins, without i. Jer 2:15
waste; your cities will be ruins without i. Jer 4:7
cities of Judah a desolation, without i.” Jer 9:11
I am against you, O i of the valley, Jer 21:13
O i of Lebanon, nested among the Jer 22:23
without i’?” And all the people gathered Jer 26:9
are desolate, without man or i or beast, Jer 33:10
cities of Judah a desolation without i.” Jer 34:22
and a waste and a curse, without i, Jer 44:22
shall become a waste, a ruin, without i. Jer 46:19

out, and every **i** of the land shall wail. Jer 47:2
become a desolation, with no **i** in them. Jer 48:9
on the parched ground, O **i** of Dibon! Jer 48:18
by the way and watch, O **i** of Aroer! Jer 48:19
and snare are before you, O **i** of Moab! Jer 48:43
land of Babylon a desolation, without **i**. Jer 51:29
be upon Babylon," let the **i** of Zion say. Jer 51:35
a horror and a hissing, without **i**. Jer 51:37
doom has come to you, O **i** of the land. Ezk 7:7
and I will destroy you until no **i** is left. Zep 2:5
desolate, without a man, without an **i**. Zep 3:6

INHABITANTS (214)

all the valley, and all the **i** of the cities, Gn 19:25
making me stink to the **i** of the land, Gn 34:30
sons of Seir the Horite, the **i** of the land: Gn 36:20
When the **i** of the land, the Canaanites, Gn 50:11
pangs have seized the **i** of Philistia. Ex 15:14
all the **i** of Canaan have melted away. Ex 15:15
for I will give the **i** of the land into your Ex 23:31
a covenant with the **i** of the land to Ex 34:12
make a covenant with the **i** of the land, Ex 34:15
iniquity, and the land vomited out its **i**. Lv 18:25
liberty throughout the land to all its **i**. Lv 25:10
spy it out, is a land that devours its **i**, Nm 13:32
and they will tell the **i** of this land. Nm 14:14
cities because of the **i** of the land. Nm 32:17
drive out all the **i** of the land from Nm 33:52
do not drive out the **i** of the land from Nm 33:55
and have drawn away the **i** of their city, Dt 13:13
you shall surely put the **i** of that city to Dt 13:15
and that all the **i** of the land melt away Jos 2:9
all the **i** of the land melt away because of Jos 2:24
Canaanites and all the **i** of the land will Jos 7:9
had finished killing all the **i** of Ai in the Jos 8:24
had devoted all the **i** of Ai to destruction. Jos 8:26
But when the **i** of Gibeon heard what Jos 9:3
elders and all the **i** of our country said Jos 9:11
and to destroy all the **i** of the land from Jos 9:24
and how the **i** of Gibeon had made peace Jos 10:1
except the Hivites, the **i** of Gibeon. Jos 11:19
all the **i** of the hill country from Jos 13:6
up from there against the **i** of Debir. Jos 15:15
But the Jebusites, the **i** of Jerusalem, the Jos 15:63
along southward to the **i** of En-tappuah. Jos 17:7
and the **i** of Dor and its villages, Jos 17:11
and the **i** of En-dor and its villages, Jos 17:11
and the **i** of Taanach and its villages, Jos 17:11
and the **i** of Megiddo and its villages; Jos 17:11
there they went against the **i** of Debir. Jgs 1:11
not drive out the **i** of the plain because Jgs 1:19
not drive out the **i** of Beth-shean and its Jgs 1:27
villages, or the **i** of Dor and its villages, Jgs 1:27
or the **i** of Ibleam and its villages, Jgs 1:27
or the **i** of Megiddo and its villages, Jgs 1:27
did not drive out the **i** of Kitron, Jgs 1:30
of Kitron, or the **i** of Nahalol, Jgs 1:30
Asher did not drive out the **i** of Acco, or Jgs 1:31
or the **i** of Sidon or of Ahlab or of Jgs 1:31
among the Canaanites, the **i** of the land, Jgs 1:32
did not drive out the **i** of Beth-shemesh, Jgs 1:33
of Beth-shemesh, or the **i** of Beth-anath, Jgs 1:33
among the Canaanites, the **i** of the land. Jgs 1:33
the **i** of Beth-shemesh and of Beth-anath Jgs 1:33
make no covenant with the **i** of this land; Jgs 2:2
angel of the LORD, curse its **i** thoroughly, Jgs 5:23
shall be head over all the **i** of Gilead." Jgs 10:18
and be our head over all the **i** of Gilead." Jgs 11:8
drew the sword, besides the **i** of Gibeah, Jgs 20:15
not one of the **i** of Jabesh-gilead was Jgs 21:9
and strike the **i** of Jabesh-gilead with Jgs 21:10
found among the **i** of Jabesh-gilead 400 Jgs 21:12
messengers to the **i** of Kiriath-jearim, 1 Sm 6:21
blow. So David saved the **i** of Keilah. 1 Sm 23:5
for these were the **i** of the land from of 1 Sm 27:8
But when the **i** of Jabesh-gilead 1 Sm 31:11
against the Jebusites, the **i** of the land, 2 Sm 5:6
while their **i**, shorn of strength, are 2 Kgs 19:26
upon this place and upon its **i**, 2 Kgs 22:16
against this place and against its **i**, 2 Kgs 22:19
Judah and all the **i** of Jerusalem and 2 Kgs 23:2
the potters who were **i** of Netaim and 1 Chr 4:23
for the former **i** there belonged to 1 Chr 4:40
of fathers' houses of the **i** of Geba, 1 Chr 8:6
of fathers' houses of the **i** of Aijalon, 1 Chr 8:13
who caused the **i** of Gath to flee); 1 Chr 8:13
the Jebusites were, the **i** of the land. 1 Chr 11:4
The **i** of Jebus said to David, "You 1 Chr 11:5
he has delivered the **i** of the land 1 Chr 22:18
afflicted all the **i** of the lands. 2 Chr 15:5
drive out the **i** of this land before 2 Chr 20:7
all Judah and **i** of Jerusalem and 2 Chr 20:15
all Judah and the **i** of Jerusalem fell 2 Chr 20:18
"Hear me, Judah and **i** of Jerusalem! 2 Chr 20:20
rose against the **i** of Mount Seir, 2 Chr 20:23
had made an end of the **i** of Seir, 2 Chr 20:23
Judah and led the **i** of Jerusalem into 2 Chr 21:11
Judah and the **i** of Jerusalem into 2 Chr 21:13
And the **i** of Jerusalem made Ahaziah 2 Chr 22:1
Hezekiah and the **i** of Jerusalem 2 Chr 32:22
both he and the **i** of Jerusalem, 2 Chr 32:26
all Judah and the **i** of Jerusalem did 2 Chr 32:33
Judah and the **i** of Jerusalem astray, 2 Chr 33:9
and from the **i** of Jerusalem. 2 Chr 34:9
upon this place and upon its **i**, 2 Chr 34:24
words against this place and its **i**, 2 Chr 34:27
place and its **i**.'" And they brought 2 Chr 34:28
of Judah and the **i** of Jerusalem and 2 Chr 34:30
And the **i** of Jerusalem did 2 Chr 34:32
were present, and the **i** of Jerusalem. 2 Chr 35:18
an accusation against the **i** of Judah and Ezr 4:6
Hanun and the **i** of Zanoah repaired Neh 3:13
guards from among the **i** of Jerusalem, Neh 7:3
subdued before them the **i** of the land, Neh 9:24
tremble under the waters and their **i**. Jb 26:5
let all the **i** of the world stand in awe of Ps 33:8
he looks out on all the **i** of the earth, Ps 33:14
all peoples! Give ear, all **i** of the world, Ps 49:1
When the earth totters, and all its **i**, it is I Ps 75:3
and Amalek, Philistia with the **i** of Tyre; Ps 83:7
salty waste, because of the evil of its **i**. Ps 107:34
now, O **i** of Jerusalem and men of Judah, Is 5:3
a trap and a snare to the **i** of Jerusalem. Is 8:14
will know, Ephraim and the **i** of Samaria, Is 9:9
is in flight; the **i** of Gebim flee for safety. Is 10:31
All you **i** of the world, you who dwell on Is 18:3
And the **i** of this coastland will say in that Is 20:6
with bread, O **i** of the land of Tema. Is 21:14
be a father to the **i** of Jerusalem and to Is 22:21
Be still, O **i** of the coast; the merchants of Is 23:2
over to Tarshish; wail, O **i** of the coast! Is 23:6
he will twist its surface and scatter its **i**. Is 24:1
The earth lies defiled under its **i**; for they Is 24:5
the earth, and its **i** suffer for their guilt; Is 24:6
therefore the **i** of the earth are scorched, Is 24:6
For he has humbled the **i** of the height, Is 26:5
the **i** of the world learn righteousness. Is 26:9
and the **i** of the world have not fallen. Is 26:18
his place to punish the **i** of the earth for Is 26:21
while their **i**, shorn of strength, are Is 37:27
man no more among the **i** of the world. Is 38:11
the earth, and its **i** are like grasshoppers; Is 40:22
all that fills it, the coastlands and their **i**. Is 42:10
now you will be too narrow for your **i**, Is 49:19
be let loose upon all the **i** of the land. Jer 1:14
hearts, O men of Judah and **i** of Jerusalem; Jer 4:4
my hand against the **i** of the land," Jer 6:12
the bones of the **i** of Jerusalem shall be Jer 8:1
I am slinging out the **i** of the land at Jer 10:18
the men of Judah and the **i** of Jerusalem. Jer 11:2
the men of Judah and the **i** of Jerusalem. Jer 11:9
of Judah and the **i** of Jerusalem will go Jer 11:12
with drunkenness all the **i** of this land: Jer 13:13
the prophets, and all the **i** of Jerusalem. Jer 13:13
all Judah, and all the **i** of Jerusalem, Jer 17:20
men of Judah and the **i** of Jerusalem. Jer 17:25
men of Judah and the **i** of Jerusalem: Jer 18:11
O kings of Judah and **i** of Jerusalem. Jer 19:3
this place, declares the LORD, and to its **i**, Jer 19:12
And I will strike down the **i** of this city, Jer 21:6
Sodom to me, and its **i** like Gomorrah." Jer 23:14
of Judah and all the **i** of Jerusalem: Jer 25:2
bring them against this land and its **i**, Jer 25:9
a sword against all the **i** of the earth, Jer 25:29
grapes, against all the **i** of the earth. Jer 25:30
yourselves and upon this city and its **i**, Jer 26:15
men of Judah and the **i** of Jerusalem. Jer 32:32
people of Judah and the **i** of Jerusalem, Jer 35:13
Judah and all the **i** of Jerusalem all the Jer 35:17
them and upon the **i** of Jerusalem and Jer 36:31
were poured out on the **i** of Jerusalem, Jer 42:18
the earth, I will destroy cities and their **i**.' Jer 46:8
baggage for exile, O **i** of Egypt! Jer 46:19
and dwell in the rock, O **i** of Moab! Jer 48:28
back, dwell in the depths, O **i** of Dedan! Jer 49:8
he has formed against the **i** of Teman: Jer 49:20
away, dwell in the depths, O **i** of Hazor! Jer 49:30
Merathaim, and against the **i** of Pekod. Jer 50:21
earth, but unrest to the **i** of Babylon. Jer 50:34
the LORD, and against the **i** of Babylon, Jer 50:35
Babylon, against the **i** of Leb-kamai, Jer 51:1
he spoke concerning the **i** of Babylon. Jer 51:12
Babylon and all the **i** of Chaldea before Jer 51:24
blood be upon the **i** of Chaldea," let Jer 51:35
believe, nor any of the **i** of the world, Lam 4:12
those of whom the **i** of Jerusalem have Ezk 11:15
GOD concerning the **i** of Jerusalem in Ezk 12:19
so have I given up the **i** of Jerusalem. Ezk 15:6
she and her **i** imposed their terror on Ezk 26:17
imposed their terror on all her **i**! Ezk 26:17
The **i** of Sidon and Arvad were your Ezk 27:8
All the **i** of the coastlands are appalled Ezk 27:35
Then all the **i** of Egypt shall know that Ezk 29:6
the **i** of these waste places in the land Ezk 33:24
all the **i** of the earth are accounted as Dn 4:35
of heaven and among the **i** of the earth; Dn 4:35
to the men of Judah, to the **i** of Jerusalem, Dn 9:7
has a controversy with the **i** of the land. Hos 4:1
The **i** of Samaria tremble for the calf of Hos 10:5
this, you elders; give ear, all **i** of the land! Jl 1:2
the elders and all the **i** of the land to the Jl 1:14
Let all the **i** of the land tremble, for the day Jl 2:1
and cut off the **i** from the Valley of Aven, Am 1:5
I will cut off the **i** from Ashdod, and him Am 1:8
Pass on your way, **i** of Shaphir, in Mi 1:11
shame; the **i** of Zaanan do not come out; Mi 1:11
For the **i** of Maroth wait anxiously for Mi 1:12
the steeds to the chariots, **i** of Lachish; Mi 1:13
a conqueror to you, **i** of Mareshah; Mi 1:15
your **i** speak lies, and their tongue is Mi 6:12
you a desolation, and your **i** a hissing; Mi 6:16
the earth will be desolate because of its **i**, Mi 7:13
Judah and against all the **i** of Jerusalem; Zep 1:4
Wail, O **i** of the Mortar! For all the Zep 1:11
end he will make of all the **i** of the earth. Zep 1:18
Woe to you **i** of the seacoast, you nation Zep 2:5
yet come, even the **i** of many cities. Zec 8:20
The **i** of one city shall go to another, Zec 8:21
no longer have pity on the **i** of this land, Zec 11:6
'The **i** of Jerusalem have strength Zec 12:5
the glory of the **i** of Jerusalem may not Zec 12:7
the LORD will protect the **i** of Jerusalem, Zec 12:8
of David and the **i** of Jerusalem a spirit Zec 12:10
house of David and the **i** of Jerusalem, Zec 13:1
known to all the **i** of Jerusalem, Acts 1:19
is evident to all the **i** of Jerusalem, Acts 4:16
the earth and its **i** worship the first Rv 13:12

INHABITED (27)

the Canaanites who **i** Zephath and Jgs 1:17
of the Amorites, who **i** that country. Jgs 11:21
rejoicing in his **i** world and delighting Prv 8:31
It will never be **i** or lived in for all Is 13:20
who says of Jerusalem, 'She shall be **i**,' Is 44:26
not create it empty, he formed it to be **i**!): Is 45:18
And this city shall be **i** forever. Jer 17:25
Afterward Egypt shall be **i** as in the Jer 46:26
LORD she shall not be **i** but shall be an Jer 50:13
have people, nor be **i** for all generations. Jer 50:39
And the **i** cities shall be laid waste, Ezk 12:20
you who were **i** from the seas, Ezk 26:17
laid waste, like the cities that are not **i**, Ezk 26:19
to the pit, so that you will not be **i**; Ezk 26:20
and in all the **i** places of the country. Ezk 34:13
and your cities shall not be **i**. Ezk 35:9
The cities shall be **i** and the waste Ezk 36:10
cause you to be **i** as in your former Ezk 36:11
iniquities, I will cause the cities to be **i**, Ezk 36:33
ruined cities are now fortified and **i**.' Ezk 36:35
the waste places that are now **i**, Ezk 38:12
But Judah shall be **i** forever, and Jl 3:20
'Jerusalem shall be **i** as villages without Zec 2:4
when Jerusalem was **i** and prosperous, Zec 7:7
and the South and the lowland were **i**?" Zec 7:7
Jerusalem shall again be **i** in its place, Zec 12:6
And it shall be **i**, for there shall never Zec 14:11

INHABITS (2)

up their voice, the villages that Kedar **i**; Is 42:11
who is high and lifted up, who **i** eternity, Is 57:15

INHERIT (45)

offspring, and they shall **i** it forever.'" Ex 32:13
have said to you, 'You shall **i** their land, Lv 20:24
sons after you to **i** as a possession Lv 25:46
the tribes of their fathers they shall **i**. Nm 26:55
For we will not **i** with them on the Nm 32:19
You shall **i** the land by lot according Nm 33:54
the tribes of your fathers you shall **i**. Nm 33:54
is the land that you shall **i** by lot, Nm 34:13
him, for he shall cause Israel to **i** it. Dt 1:38
the LORD your God is giving you to **i**, Dt 12:10
you may live and **i** the land that the Dt 16:20
shall cause this people to **i** the land that I Jos 1:6
of the people of Israel gave them to **i**. Jos 14:1
sit with princes and **i** a seat of honor. 1 Sm 2:8
which you have given us to **i**. 2 Chr 20:11
me and make me **i** the iniquities of my Jb 13:26
and his offspring shall **i** the land. Ps 25:13
who wait for the LORD shall **i** the land. Ps 37:9
But the meek shall **i** the land and Ps 37:11
blessed by the LORD shall **i** the land, Ps 37:22
The righteous shall **i** the land and dwell Ps 37:29
way, and he will exalt you to **i** the land; Ps 37:34
the offspring of his servants shall **i** it, Ps 69:36
the earth; for you shall **i** all the nations! Ps 82:8
The wise will **i** honor, but fools get Prv 3:35
his own household will **i** the wind, Prv 11:29

The simple **i** folly, but the prudent are Prv 14:18
the land and shall **i** my holy mountain. Is 57:13
that I have given my people Israel to **i**: Jer 12:14
And the LORD will **i** Judah as his portion Zec 2:12
are the meek, for they shall **i** the earth. Mt 5:5
a hundredfold and will **i** eternal life. Mt 19:29
i the kingdom prepared for you from Mt 25:34
what must I do to **i** eternal life?" Mk 10:17
what shall I do to **i** eternal life?" Lk 10:25
what must I do to **i** eternal life?" Lk 18:18
unrighteous will not **i** the kingdom of 1 Cor 6:9
nor swindlers will **i** the kingdom of 1 Cor 6:10
and blood cannot **i** the kingdom of 1 Cor 15:50
the perishable **i** the imperishable. 1 Cor 15:50
slave woman shall not **i** with the son of Gal 4:30
such things will not **i** the kingdom of Gal 5:21
the sake of those who are to **i** salvation? Heb 1:14
faith and patience **i** the promises. Heb 6:12
when he desired to **i** the blessing, Heb 12:17

INHERITANCE (208)

"Is there any portion or **i** left to us in Gn 31:14
by the name of their brothers in their **i**. Gn 48:6
and our sin, and take us for your **i**." Ex 34:9
nor given us **i** of fields and vineyards. Nm 16:14
"You shall have no **i** in their land, Nm 18:20
portion and your **i** among the people Nm 18:20
given every tithe in Israel for an **i**, Nm 18:21
people of Israel they shall have no **i**. Nm 18:23
I have given to the Levites for an **i**. Nm 18:24
they shall have no **i** among the people Nm 18:24
I have given you from them for your **i**, Nm 18:26
shall be divided for **i** according to the Nm 26:53
a large tribe you shall give a large **i**, Nm 26:54
a small tribe you shall give a small **i**; Nm 26:54
shall be given its **i** in proportion to its Nm 26:54
Their **i** shall be divided according to Nm 26:56
because there was no **i** given to them Nm 26:62
possession of an **i** among their father's Nm 27:7
and transfer the **i** of their father Nm 27:7
you shall transfer his **i** to his daughter. Nm 27:8
you shall give his **i** to his brothers. Nm 27:9
you shall give his **i** to his father's Nm 27:10
you shall give his **i** to the nearest Nm 27:11
of the people of Israel has gained his **i**. Nm 32:18
because our **i** has come to us on this Nm 32:19
possession of our **i** shall remain with Nm 32:32
a large tribe you shall give a large **i**, Nm 33:54
a small tribe you shall give a small **i**. Nm 33:54
is the land that shall fall to you for an **i**, Nm 34:2
fathers' houses have received their **i**, Nm 34:14
have received their **i** beyond the Nm 34:15
who shall divide the land to you for **i**: Nm 34:17
every tribe to divide the land for **i**. Nm 34:18
to divide the **i** for the people Nm 34:29
Levites some of the **i** of their possession Nm 35:2
in proportion to the **i** that it inherits, Nm 35:8
to give the land for **i** by lot to the people Nm 36:2
LORD to give the **i** of Zelophehad our Nm 36:2
then their **i** will be taken from the Nm 36:3
be taken from the **i** of our fathers and Nm 36:3
and added to the **i** of the tribe into Nm 36:3
will be taken away from the lot of our **i**. Nm 36:3
then their **i** will be added to the Nm 36:4
will be added to the **i** of the tribe into Nm 36:4
and their **i** will be taken from the Nm 36:4
will be taken from the **i** of the tribe of Nm 36:4
The **i** of the people of Israel shall not be Nm 36:7
shall hold on to the **i** of the tribe of his Nm 36:7
who possesses an **i** in any tribe Nm 36:8
Israel may possess the **i** of his fathers. Nm 36:8
So no **i** shall be transferred from one Nm 36:9
of Israel shall hold on to its own **i**.'" Nm 36:9
and their **i** remained in the tribe of Nm 36:12
out of Egypt, to be a people of his own **i**, Dt 4:20
the LORD your God is giving you for an **i**. Dt 4:21
you in, to give you their land for an **i**, Dt 4:38
has no portion or **i** with his brothers. Dt 10:9
The LORD is his **i**, as the LORD your God Dt 10:9
the rest and to the **i** that the LORD your Dt 12:9
since he has no portion or **i** with you. Dt 12:12
for he has no portion or **i** with you. Dt 14:27
he has no portion or **i** with you, Dt 14:29
God is giving you for an **i** to possess— Dt 15:4
shall have no portion or **i** with Israel. Dt 18:1
eat the LORD'S food offerings as their **i**. Dt 18:1
shall have no **i** among their brothers; Dt 18:2
the LORD is their **i**, as he promised them. Dt 18:2
LORD your God is giving you for an **i**, Dt 19:10
in the **i** that you will hold in the land Dt 19:14
LORD your God is giving you for an **i**, Dt 20:16
his possessions as an **i** to his sons, Dt 21:16
LORD your God is giving you for an **i**. Dt 21:23
the LORD your God is giving you for an **i**. Dt 24:4
God is giving you for an **i** to possess, Dt 25:19
giving you for an **i** and have taken Dt 26:1
and gave it for an **i** to the Reubenites, Dt 29:8
the Most High gave to the nations their **i**, Dt 32:8
gave it for an **i** to Israel according to Jos 11:23
Only allot the land to Israel for an **i**, as I Jos 13:6
divide this land for an **i** to the nine tribes Jos 13:7
and the Gadites received their **i**, Jos 13:8
the tribe of Levi alone Moses gave no **i**. Jos 13:14
fire to the LORD God of Israel are their **i**, Jos 13:14
And Moses gave an **i** to the tribe of the Jos 13:15
This was the **i** of the people of Reuben, Jos 13:23
Moses gave an **i** also to the tribe of Gad, Jos 13:24
This is the **i** of the people of Gad Jos 13:28
And Moses gave an **i** to the half-tribe of Jos 13:29
But to the tribe of Levi Moses gave no **i**; Jos 13:33
the LORD God of Israel is their **i**, just as Jos 13:33
Their **i** was by lot, just as the LORD had Jos 14:2
For Moses had given an **i** to the two and Jos 14:3
to the Levites he gave no **i** among them. Jos 14:3
trodden shall be an **i** for you and your Jos 14:9
to Caleb the son of Jephunneh for an **i**. Jos 14:13
Hebron became the **i** of Caleb the Jos 14:14
This is the **i** of the tribe of the people of Jos 15:20
Manasseh and Ephraim, received their **i**. Jos 16:4
the boundary of their **i** on the east was Jos 16:5
Such is the **i** of the tribe of the people of Jos 16:8
Ephraim within the **i** of the Manassites, Jos 16:9
to give us an **i** along with our brothers." Jos 17:4
he gave them an **i** among the brothers of Jos 17:4
Manasseh received an **i** along with his Jos 17:6
me but one lot and one portion as an **i**, Jos 17:14
Israel seven tribes whose **i** had not yet Jos 18:2
have received their **i** beyond the Jordan Jos 18:7
This is the **i** of the people of Benjamin, Jos 18:20
This is the **i** of the people of Benjamin Jos 18:28
and their **i** was in the midst of the Jos 19:1
in the midst of the **i** of the people of Jos 19:1
And they had for their **i** Beersheba, Jos 19:2
This was the **i** of the tribe of the people of Jos 19:8
The **i** of the people of Simeon formed Jos 19:9
of Simeon obtained an **i** in the midst of Jos 19:9
an inheritance in the midst of their **i**. Jos 19:9
the territory of their **i** reached as far as Jos 19:10
This is the **i** of the people of Zebulun, Jos 19:16
This is the **i** of the tribe of the people of Jos 19:23
This is the **i** of the tribe of the people of Jos 19:31
This is the **i** of the tribe of the people of Jos 19:39
the territory of its **i** included Zorah, Jos 19:41
This is the **i** of the tribe of the people of Jos 19:48
of Israel gave an **i** among them to Jos 19:49
cities and pasturelands out of their **i**. Jos 21:3
to you as an **i** for your tribes those Jos 23:4
the people away, every man to his **i**. Jos 24:28
him in his own **i** at Timnath-serah, Jos 24:30
It became an **i** of the descendants of Jos 24:32
went each to his **i** to take possession of Jgs 2:6
the boundaries of his **i** in Timnath-heres, Jgs 2:9
shall not have an **i** in our father's house, Jgs 11:2
was seeking for itself an **i** to dwell in, Jgs 18:1
for until then no **i** among the tribes of Jgs 18:1
all the country of the **i** of Israel, Jgs 20:6
"There must be an **i** for the survivors Jgs 21:17
and returned to their **i** and rebuilt the Jgs 21:23
went out from there every man to his **i**. Jgs 21:24
perpetuate the name of the dead in his **i**." Ru 4:5
it for myself, lest I impair my own **i**. Ru 4:6
perpetuate the name of the dead in his **i**, Ru 4:10
and we have no **i** in the son of Jesse; 2 Sm 20:1
you have given to your people as an **i**. 1 Kgs 8:36
We have no **i** in the son of Jesse. 1 Kgs 12:16
I should give you the **i** of my fathers." 1 Kgs 21:3
not give you the **i** of my fathers." And 1 Kgs 21:4
of Canaan, as your portion for an **i**." 1 Chr 16:18
leave it for an **i** to your children after 1 Chr 28:8
you have given to your people as an **i**. 2 Chr 6:27
We have no **i** in the son of Jesse. 2 Chr 10:16
leave it for an **i** to your children forever.' Ezr 9:12
the towns of Judah, every one in his **i**. Neh 11:20
gave them an **i** among their brothers. Jb 42:15
places; indeed, I have a beautiful **i**. Ps 16:6
you restored your **i** as it languished; Ps 68:9
shepherd Jacob his people, Israel his **i**. Ps 78:71
God, the nations have come into your **i**; Ps 79:1
of Canaan as your portion for an **i**." Ps 105:11
nation, that I may glory with your **i**. Ps 106:5
in giving them the **i** of the nations. Ps 111:6
granting an **i** to those who love me, and Prv 8:21
good man leaves an **i** to his children's Prv 13:22
and will share the **i** as one of the Prv 17:2
An **i** gained hastily in the beginning Prv 20:21
but the blameless will have a goodly **i**. Prv 28:10
Wisdom is good with an **i**, an Eccl 7:11
the work of my hands, and Israel my **i**." Is 19:25
all things, and Israel is the tribe of his **i**; Jer 10:16
have filled my **i** with their Jer 16:18
all things, and Israel is the tribe of his **i**; Jer 51:19
Our **i** has been turned over to strangers, Lam 5:2
you rejoiced over the **i** of the house of Ezk 35:15
possess you, and you shall be their **i**, Ezk 36:12
"This shall be their **i**: I am their Ezk 44:28
shall be their inheritance: I am their **i**: Ezk 44:28
"When you allot the land as an **i**, you Ezk 45:1
makes a gift to any of his sons as his **i**, Ezk 46:16
to his sons. It is their property by **i**. Ezk 46:16
a gift out of his **i** to one of his servants, Ezk 46:17
surely it is his **i**—it shall belong to his Ezk 46:17
not take any of the **i** of the people, Ezk 46:18
give his sons their **i** out of his own Ezk 46:18
divide the land for **i** among the twelve Ezk 47:13
This land shall fall to you as your **i**. Ezk 47:14
allot it as an **i** for yourselves and for Ezk 47:22
shall be allotted an **i** among the tribes Ezk 47:22
there you shall assign him his **i**, Ezk 47:23
shall allot as an **i** among the tribes of Ezk 48:29
a man and his house, a man and his **i**. Mi 2:2
with your staff, the flock of your **i**, Mi 7:14
transgression for the remnant of his **i**? Mi 7:18
Come, let us kill him and have his **i**.' Mt 21:38
let us kill him, and the **i** will be ours.' Mk 12:7
tell my brother to divide the **i** with me." Lk 12:13
us kill him, so that the **i** may be ours.' Lk 20:14
Yet he gave him no **i** in it, not even a Acts 7:5
he gave them their land as an **i**. Acts 13:19
to give you the **i** among all those who Acts 20:32
For if the **i** comes by the law, it no Gal 3:18
In him we have obtained an **i**, having Eph 1:11
the guarantee of our **i** until we acquire Eph 1:14
the riches of his glorious **i** in the saints, Eph 1:18
has no **i** in the kingdom of Christ and Eph 5:5
you to share in the **i** of the saints in Col 1:12
you will receive the **i** as your reward. Col 3:24
may receive the promised eternal **i**, Heb 9:15
to a place that he was to receive as an **i**. Heb 11:8
to an **i** that is imperishable, undefiled, 1 Pt 1:4

INHERITANCES (5)

These are the **i** that Moses distributed Jos 13:32
These are the **i** that the people of Israel Jos 14:1
a description of it with a view to their **i**, Jos 18:4
the several territories of the land as **i**, Jos 19:49
These are the **i** that Eleazar the priest Jos 19:51

INHERITED (5)

whether man or beast, or of his **i** field, Lv 27:28
House and wealth are **i** from fathers, Prv 19:14
"Our fathers have **i** nothing but lies, Jer 16:19
the name he has **i** is more excellent than Heb 1:4
the futile ways **i** from your forefathers, 1 Pt 1:18

INHERITS (1)

proportion to the inheritance that it **i**, Nm 35:8

INIQUITIES (49)

confess over it all the **i** of the people of Lv 16:21
goat shall bear all their **i** on itself to a Lv 16:22
also because of the **i** of their fathers Lv 26:39
for our **i** have risen higher than our Ezr 9:6
And for our **i** we, our kings, and our Ezr 9:7
us less than our **i** deserved and have Ezr 9:13
their sins and the **i** of their fathers. Neh 9:2
How many are my **i** and my sins? Make Jb 13:23
and make me inherit the **i** of my youth. Jb 13:26
evil abundant? There is no end to your **i**. Jb 22:5
For my **i** have gone over my head; like a Ps 38:4
my **i** have overtaken me, and I cannot Ps 40:12
face from my sins, and blot out all my **i**. Ps 51:9
When **i** prevail against me, you atone for Ps 65:3
not remember against us our former **i**; Ps 79:8
You have set our **i** before you, our secret Ps 90:8
sins, nor repay us according to our **i**. Ps 103:10
because of their **i** suffered affliction; Ps 107:17
If you, O LORD, should mark **i**, O Lord, Ps 130:3
And he will redeem Israel from all his **i**. Ps 130:8
The **i** of the wicked ensnare him, and Prv 5:22
sins; you have wearied me with your **i**. Is 43:24
Behold, for your **i** you were sold, and for Is 50:1
transgressions; he was crushed for our **i**; Is 53:5
righteous, and he shall bear their **i**. Is 53:11
but your **i** have made a separation Is 59:2
are with us, and we know our **i**: Is 59:12
We all fade like a leaf, and our **i**, like the Is 64:6
have made us melt in the hand of our **i**. Is 64:7
both your **i** and your fathers' iniquities Is 65:7
iniquities and your fathers' **i** together, Is 65:7
Your **i** have turned these away, and your Jer 5:25
turned back to the **i** of their forefathers, Jer 11:10
"Though our **i** testify against us, act, O Jer 14:7
of her prophets and the **i** of her priests, Lam 4:13
and are no more; and we bear their **i**. Lam 5:7
rot away in your **i** and groan to one Ezk 24:23
By the multitude of your **i**, in the Ezk 28:18
and whose **i** are upon their bones; Ezk 32:27
yourselves for your **i** and your Ezk 36:31

day that I cleanse you from all your **i**, Ezk 36:33
that they may be ashamed of their **i**; Ezk 43:10
and your **i** by showing mercy to the Dn 4:27
turning from our **i** and gaining insight Dn 9:13
for our sins, and for the **i** of our fathers, Dn 9:16
therefore I will punish you for all your **i**. Am 3:2
on us; he will tread our **i** under foot. Mi 7:19
For I will be merciful toward their **i**, Heb 8:12
heaven, and God has remembered her **i**. Rv 18:5

INIQUITOUS (1)
Woe to those who decree **i** decrees, and Is 10:1

INIQUITY (164)
for the **i** of the Amorites is not yet Gn 15:16
visiting the **i** of the fathers on the Ex 20:5
forgiving **i** and transgression and sin, Ex 34:7
visiting the **i** of the fathers on the Ex 34:7
people, and pardon our **i** and our sin, Ex 34:9
yet does not speak, he shall bear his **i**; Lv 5:1
then realizes his guilt, he shall bear his **i**. Lv 5:17
and he who eats of it shall bear his **i**. Lv 7:18
you may bear the **i** of the congregation, Lv 10:17
or bathe his flesh, he shall bear his **i**." Lv 17:16
unclean, so that I punished its **i**, Lv 18:25
and everyone who eats it shall bear his **i**, Lv 19:8
nakedness, and he shall bear his **i**. Lv 20:17
one's relative; they shall bear their **i**. Lv 20:19
and so cause them to bear **i** and guilt, Lv 22:16
your enemies' lands because of their **i**, Lv 26:39
if they confess their **i** and the iniquity Lv 26:40
their iniquity and the **i** of their fathers Lv 26:40
and they make amends for their **i**, Lv 26:41
and they shall make amends for their **i**, Lv 26:43
bringing **i** to remembrance. Nm 5:15
The man shall be free from **i**, but the Nm 5:31
but the woman shall bear her **i**." Nm 5:31
love, forgiving **i** and transgression, Nm 14:18
visiting the **i** of the fathers on the Nm 14:18
Please pardon the **i** of this people, Nm 14:19
day, you shall bear your **i** forty years, Nm 14:34
utterly cut off; his **i** shall be on him." Nm 15:31
you shall bear **i** connected with the Nm 18:1
you shall bear **i** connected with your Nm 18:1
of meeting, and they shall bear their **i**. Nm 18:23
of them, then he shall bear her **i**." Nm 30:15
visiting the **i** of the fathers on the children Dt 5:9
A God of faithfulness and without **i**, just Dt 32:4
And he did not perish alone for his **i**.'" Jos 22:20
house forever, for the **i** that he knew, 1 Sm 3:13
of Eli that the **i** of Eli's house shall 1 Sm 3:14
and presumption is as **i** and idolatry. 1 Sm 15:23
When he commits **i**, I will discipline 2 Sm 7:14
take away the **i** of your servant, 2 Sm 24:10
take away the **i** of your servant, 1 Chr 21:8
those who plow **i** and sow trouble reap the Jb 4:8
my transgression and take away my **i**? Jb 7:21
that you seek out my **i** and search for my Jb 10:6
watch me and do not acquit me of my **i**. Jb 10:14
when he sees **i**, will he not consider it? Jb 11:11
If **i** is in your hand, put it far away, and Jb 11:14
a bag, and you would cover over my **i**. Jb 14:17
For your **i** teaches your mouth, and you Jb 15:5
The heavens will reveal his **i**, and the Jb 20:27
'God stores up their **i** for their children.' Jb 21:19
and disaster for the workers of **i**? Jb 31:3
that would be an **i** to be punished by the Jb 31:11
also would be an **i** to be punished by Jb 31:28
others do by hiding my **i** in my bosom, Jb 31:33
I am clean, and there is no **i** in me. Jb 33:9
see; if I have done **i**, I will do it no more'? Jb 34:32
and commands that they return from **i**. Jb 36:10
do not turn to **i**, for this you have Jb 36:21
under his tongue are mischief and **i**. Ps 10:7
my strength fails because of my **i**, and Ps 31:10
man against whom the LORD counts no **i**, Ps 32:2
my sin to you, and I did not cover my **i**; Ps 32:5
LORD," and you forgave the **i** of my sin. Ps 32:5
own eyes that his **i** cannot be found out Ps 36:2
I confess my **i**; I am sorry for my sin. Ps 38:18
empty words, while his heart gathers **i**; Ps 41:6
when the **i** of those who cheat me Ps 49:5
Wash me thoroughly from my **i**, and Ps 51:2
Behold, I was brought forth in **i**, and in Ps 51:5
They are corrupt, doing abominable **i**; Ps 53:1
its walls, and **i** and trouble are within it; Ps 55:10
If I had cherished **i** in my heart, the Ps 66:18
atoned for their **i** and did not destroy Ps 78:38
You forgave the **i** of your people; you Ps 85:2
with the rod and their **i** with stripes, Ps 89:32
back on them their **i** and wipe them out Ps 94:23
who forgives all your **i**, who heals all Ps 103:3
have sinned; we have committed **i**; Ps 106:6
and were brought low through their **i**. Ps 106:43
May the **i** of his fathers be Ps 109:14
and let no **i** get dominion over me. Ps 119:133
in company with men who work **i**, Ps 141:4
love and faithfulness **i** is atoned for, Prv 16:6
the mouth of the wicked devours **i**. Prv 19:28
Ah, sinful nation, a people laden with **i**, Is 1:4
I cannot endure **i** and solemn assembly. Is 1:13
to those who draw **i** with cords of Is 5:18
for its evil, and the wicked for their **i**; Is 13:11
"Surely this **i** will not be atoned for you Is 22:14
the inhabitants of the earth for their **i**, Is 26:21
therefore this **i** shall be to you like a Is 30:13
against the helpers of those who work **i**. Is 31:2
speaks folly, and his heart is busy with **i**, Is 32:6
who dwell there will be forgiven their **i**. Is 33:24
warfare is ended, that her **i** is pardoned, Is 40:2
the LORD has laid on him the **i** of us all. Is 53:6
Because of the **i** of his unjust gain I was Is 57:17
defiled with blood and your fingers with **i**; Is 59:3
conceive mischief and give birth to **i**. Is 59:4
Their works are works of **i**, and deeds of Is 59:6
blood; their thoughts are thoughts of **i**; Is 59:7
O LORD, and remember not **i** forever. Is 64:9
lies; they weary themselves committing **i**. Jer 9:5
the greatness of your **i** that your skirts Jer 13:22
will remember their **i** and punish their Jer 14:10
O LORD, and the **i** of our fathers, Jer 14:20
great evil against us? What is our **i**? Jer 16:10
nor is their **i** concealed from my eyes. Jer 16:17
I will doubly repay their **i** and their sin, Jer 16:18
Forgive not their **i**, nor blot out their Jer 18:23
the land of the Chaldeans, for their **i**, Jer 25:12
For I will forgive their **i**, and I will Jer 31:34
that I may forgive their **i** and their sin." Jer 36:3
offspring and his servants for their **i**. Jer 36:31
the LORD, **i** shall be sought in Israel, Jer 50:20
have not exposed your **i** to restore your Lam 2:14
The punishment of your **i**, O daughter Lam 4:22
but your **i**, O daughter of Edom, he Lam 4:22
that wicked person shall die for his **i**, Ezk 3:18
his wicked way, he shall die for his **i**, Ezk 3:19
and because of his **i**, none can Ezk 7:13
of them moaning, each one over his **i**. Ezk 7:16
it was the stumbling block of their **i**. Ezk 7:19
the men who devise **i** and who give Ezk 11:2
block of their **i** before their faces. Ezk 14:3
block of his **i** before his face, Ezk 14:4
block of his **i** before his face, Ezk 14:7
withholds his hand from **i**, takes no Ezk 18:17
he shall not die for his father's **i**; Ezk 18:17
people, behold, he shall die for his **i**. Ezk 18:18
the son suffer for the **i** of the father?' Ezk 18:19
shall not suffer for the **i** of the father, Ezk 18:20
the father suffer for the **i** of the son. Ezk 18:20
transgressions, lest **i** be your ruin. Ezk 18:30
of the house of Israel, recalling their **i**, Ezk 29:16
that person is taken away in his **i**, Ezk 33:6
that wicked person shall die in his **i**, Ezk 33:8
his way, that person shall die in his **i**, Ezk 33:9
of Israel went into captivity for their **i**, Ezk 39:23
a stumbling block of **i** to the house of Ezk 44:12
to put an end to sin, and to atone for **i**, Dn 9:24
of my people; they are greedy for their **i**. Hos 4:8
heal Israel, the **i** of Ephraim is revealed, Hos 7:1
will remember their **i** and punish their Hos 8:13
because of your great **i** and great hatred. Hos 9:7
days of Gibeah: he will remember their **i**; Hos 9:9
they are bound up for their double **i**. Hos 10:10
You have plowed **i**; you have reaped Hos 10:13
labors they cannot find in me **i** or sin." Hos 12:8
If there is **i** in Gilead, they shall surely Hos 12:11
The **i** of Ephraim is bound up; his sin Hos 13:12
you have stumbled because of your **i**. Hos 14:1
the LORD; say to him, "Take away all **i**; Hos 14:2
Zion with blood and Jerusalem with **i**. Mi 3:10
pardoning **i** and passing over Mi 7:18
Why do you make me see **i**, and why do Hab 1:3
with blood and founds a city on **i**! Hab 2:12
I have taken your **i** away from you, Zec 3:4
and I will remove the **i** of this land in a Zec 3:9
he said, "This is their **i** in all the land." Zec 5:6
and he turned many from **i**. Mal 2:6
gall of bitterness and in the bond of **i**." Acts 8:23
the name of the Lord depart from **i**." 2 Tm 2:19

INJUNCTION (7)
establish an ordinance and enforce an **i**, Dn 6:7
establish the **i** and sign the document, Dn 6:8
King Darius signed the document and **i**. Dn 6:9
said before the king, concerning the **i**, Dn 6:12
Did you not sign an **i**, that anyone who Dn 6:12
to you, O king, or the **i** you have signed, Dn 6:13
and Persians that no **i** or ordinance that Dn 6:15

INJURE (1)
All day long they **i** my cause; all their Ps 56:5

INJURED (6)
safe, and it dies or is **i** or is driven away, Ex 22:10
of his neighbor, and it is **i** or dies, Ex 22:14
a man who has an **i** foot or an injured Lv 21:19
who has an injured foot or an **i** hand, Lv 21:19
healed, the **i** you have not bound up, Ezk 34:4
the strayed, and I will bind up the **i**, Ezk 34:16

INJURES (2)
If anyone **i** his neighbor, as he has done Lv 24:19
but he who fails to find me **i** himself; all Prv 8:36

INJURY (4)
whatever **i** he has given a person shall Lv 24:20
he who reproves a wicked man incurs **i**. Prv 9:7
voyage will be with **i** and much loss, Acts 27:10
Crete and incurred this **i** and loss. Acts 27:21

INJUSTICE (28)
"You shall do no **i** in court. You shall Lv 19:15
for there is no **i** with the LORD our 2 Chr 19:7
poor have hope, and **i** shuts her mouth. Jb 5:16
Please turn; let no **i** be done. Turn now; Jb 6:29
Is there any **i** on my tongue? Cannot my Jb 6:30
away, and let not **i** dwell in your tents. Jb 11:14
corrupt, a man who drinks **i** like water! Jb 15:16
up; if you remove **i** far from your tents, Jb 22:23
They search out **i**, saying, "We have Ps 64:6
with you, those who frame **i** by statute? Ps 94:20
food, but it is swept away through **i**. Prv 13:23
than great revenues with **i**. Prv 16:8
Whoever sows **i** will reap calamity, and Prv 22:8
and his upper rooms by **i**, Jer 22:13
from his righteousness and commits **i**, Ezk 3:20
land is full of blood, and the city full of **i**. Ezk 9:9
any profit, withholds his hand from **i**, Ezk 18:8
righteousness and does **i** and does the Ezk 18:24
from his righteousness and does **i**, Ezk 18:26
for the **i** that he has done he shall die. Ezk 18:26
trusts in his righteousness and does **i**, Ezk 33:13
but in his **i** that he has done he shall Ezk 33:13
in the statutes of life, not doing **i**, Ezk 33:15
from his righteousness and does **i**, Ezk 33:18
plowed iniquity; you have reaped **i**; Hos 10:13
within her is righteous; he does no **i**; Zep 3:5
they shall do no **i** and speak no lies, Zep 3:13
we say then? Is there **i** on God's part? Rom 9:14

INK (4)
while I wrote them with **i** on the scroll." Jer 36:18
written not with **i** but with the Spirit of 2 Cor 3:3
you, I would rather not use paper and **i**. 2 Jn 1:12
I would rather not write with pen and **i**. 3 Jn 1:13

INLAID (2)
its interior was **i** with love by the Sg 3:10
from the coasts of Cyprus, **i** with ivory. Ezk 27:6

INLAND (1)
passed through the **i** country and Acts 19:1

INMOST (3)
in their mouth; their **i** self is destruction; Ps 5:9
My **i** being will exult when your lips Prv 23:16
for Moab, and my **i** self for Kir-hareseth. Is 16:11

INN (2)
there was no place for them in the **i**. Lk 2:7
brought him to an **i** and took care of Lk 10:34

INNER (68)
its head with its legs and its **i** parts. Ex 12:9
not brought into the **i** part of the Lv 10:18
men lying in ambush in an **i** chamber. Jgs 16:9
in ambush were in an **i** chamber. Jgs 16:12
both the nave and the **i** sanctuary. 1 Kgs 6:5
built this within as an **i** sanctuary, 1 Kgs 6:16
the nave in front of the **i** sanctuary, 1 Kgs 6:17
The **i** sanctuary he prepared in the 1 Kgs 6:19
The **i** sanctuary was twenty cubits 1 Kgs 6:20
across, in front of the **i** sanctuary, 1 Kgs 6:21
belonged to the **i** sanctuary he 1 Kgs 6:22
In the **i** sanctuary he made two 1 Kgs 6:23
flowers, in the **i** and outer rooms. 1 Kgs 6:29
with gold in the **i** and outer rooms. 1 Kgs 6:30
entrance to the **i** sanctuary he made 1 Kgs 6:31
He built the **i** court with three 1 Kgs 6:36
so had the **i** court of the house of the 1 Kgs 7:12
on the north, before the **i** sanctuary; 1 Kgs 7:49
its place in the **i** sanctuary of the 1 Kgs 8:6
the Holy Place before the **i** sanctuary; 1 Kgs 8:8
fled and entered an **i** chamber in the 1 Kgs 20:30
you go into an **i** chamber to hide 1 Kgs 22:25
fellows, and lead him to an **i** chamber. 2 Kgs 9:2
and went into the **i** room of the 2 Kgs 10:25
its upper rooms, and its **i** chambers, 1 Chr 28:11
gold to burn before the **i** sanctuary, 2 Chr 4:20
for the **i** doors to the Most Holy Place 2 Chr 4:22
place, in the **i** sanctuary of the house, 2 Chr 5:7
the Holy Place before the **i** sanctuary, 2 Chr 5:9
you go into an **i** chamber to hide 2 Chr 18:24
priests went into the **i** part of the 2 Chr 29:16

king inside the **i** court without being Est 4:11
and stood in the **i** court of the king's Est 5:1
go down into the **i** parts of the body. Prv 18:8
go down into the **i** parts of the body. Prv 26:22
Therefore my **i** parts moan like a lyre Is 16:11
The stirring of your **i** parts and your Is 63:15
the gateway of the **i** court that faces Ezk 8:3
brought me into the **i** court of the Ezk 8:16
went in, and a cloud filled the **i** court. Ezk 10:3
by the vestibule of the gate at the **i** end, Ezk 40:7
the vestibule of the gate was at the **i** end. Ezk 40:9
the front of the **i** vestibule of the gate Ezk 40:15
the distance from the **i** front of the Ezk 40:19
gate to the outer front of the **i** court, Ezk 40:19
as on the east, was a gate to the **i** court. Ezk 40:23
was a gate on the south of the **i** court. Ezk 40:27
brought me to the **i** court through the Ezk 40:28
brought me to the **i** court on the east Ezk 40:32
the outside of the **i** gateway there were Ezk 40:44
were two chambers in the **i** court, Ezk 40:44
he went into the **i** room and measured Ezk 41:3
above the door, even to the **i** room, Ezk 41:17
cubits that belonged to the **i** court, Ezk 42:3
me up and brought me into the **i** court; Ezk 43:5
they enter the gates of the **i** court, Ezk 44:17
minister at the gates of the **i** court, Ezk 44:17
drink wine when he enters the **i** court. Ezk 44:21
into the Holy Place, into the **i** court, Ezk 44:27
and the posts of the gate of the **i** court. Ezk 45:19
The gate of the **i** court that faces east Ezk 46:1
had gone down into the **i** part of the ship Jon 1:5
If they say, 'Look, he is in the **i** rooms,' Mt 24:26
them into the **i** prison and fastened Acts 16:24
in the law of God, in my **i** being, Rom 7:22
our **i** nature is being renewed day by 2 Cor 4:16
through his Spirit in your **i** being, Eph 3:16
that enters into the **i** place behind the Heb 6:19

INNERMOST (7)
were sitting in the **i** parts of the cave. 1 Sm 24:3
he prepared in the **i** part of the house, 1 Kgs 6:19
the cherubim in the **i** part of the 1 Kgs 6:27
for the doors of the **i** part of the house, 1 Kgs 7:50
of the LORD, searching all his **i** parts. Prv 20:27
evil; strokes make clean the **i** parts. Prv 20:30
him who is in the **i** parts of the house, Am 6:10

INNKEEPER (1)
out two denarii and gave them to the **i**, Lk 10:35

INNOCENCE (6)
of my heart and the **i** of my hands I have Gn 20:5
It is a sign of your **i** in the eyes of all Gn 20:16
went in their **i** and knew nothing. 2 Sm 15:11
wash my hands in **i** and go around your Ps 26:6
heart clean and washed my hands in **i**. Ps 73:13
How long will they be incapable of **i**? Hos 8:5

INNOCENT (50)
he said, "Lord, will you kill an **i** people? Gn 20:4
servant, and the rest of you shall be **i**." Gn 44:10
and do not kill the **i** and righteous, Ex 23:7
lest **i** blood be shed in your land that Dt 19:10
purge the guilt of **i** blood from Israel, Dt 19:13
not set the guilt of **i** blood in the midst of Dt 21:8
purge the guilt of **i** blood from your Dt 21:9
acquitting the **i** and condemning the Dt 25:1
who takes a bribe to shed **i** blood.' Dt 27:25
"This time I shall be **i** in regard to the Jgs 15:3
will you sin against **i** blood by killing 1 Sm 19:5
and said to all the people, "You are **i**. 2 Kgs 10:9
Manasseh shed very much **i** blood, 2 Kgs 21:16
and also for the **i** blood that he had 2 Kgs 24:4
For he filled Jerusalem with **i** blood, 2 Kgs 24:4
"Remember: who that was **i** ever perished? Jb 4:7
death, he mocks at the calamity of the **i**. Jb 9:23
for I know you will not hold me **i**. Jb 9:28
and the **i** stirs himself up against the Jb 17:8
it and are glad; the **i** one mocks at them, Jb 22:19
He delivers even the one who is not **i**, Jb 22:30
wear it, and the **i** will divide the silver. Jb 27:17
in hiding places he murders the **i**. Ps 10:8
and does not take a bribe against the **i**. Ps 15:5
errors? Declare me **i** from hidden faults. Ps 19:12
blameless, and **i** of great transgression. Ps 19:13
righteous and condemn the **i** to death. Ps 94:21
they poured out **i** blood, the blood of Ps 106:38
let us ambush the **i** without reason; Prv 1:11
tongue, and hands that shed **i** blood, Prv 6:17
for a bribe, and deprive the **i** of his right! Is 5:23
to evil, and they are swift to shed **i** blood; Is 59:7
you say, 'I am **i**; surely his anger has Jer 2:35
or the widow, or shed **i** blood in this place, Jer 7:6
the widow, nor shed **i** blood in this place. Jer 22:3
dishonest gain, for shedding **i** blood, Jer 22:17
you will bring **i** blood upon yourselves Jer 26:15
because they have shed **i** blood in their Jl 3:19
man's life, and lay not on us **i** blood, Jon 1:14
so be wise as serpents and **i** as doves. Mt 10:16
from the blood of **i** Abel to the blood of Mt 23:35
sinned by betraying **i** blood." They said, Mt 27:4
saying, "I am **i** of this man's blood; Mt 27:24
saying, "Certainly this man was **i**!" Lk 23:47
blood be on your own heads! I am **i**. Acts 18:6
this day that I am **i** of the blood of all Acts 20:26
to what is good and **i** as to what is Rom 16:19
have proved yourselves **i** in the 2 Cor 7:11
that you may be blameless and **i**, Phil 2:15
such a high priest, holy, **i**, unstained, Heb 7:26

INNOCENTS (1)
have filled this place with the blood of **i**, Jer 19:4

INNUMERABLE (4)
him, and those who go before him are **i**. Jb 21:33
wide, which teems with creatures **i**, Ps 104:25
as many as the **i** grains of sand by Heb 11:12
and to **i** angels in festal gathering, Heb 12:22

INQUIRE (50)
to me?" So she went to **i** of the LORD. Gn 25:22
the people come to me to **i** of God; Ex 18:15
who shall **i** for him by the judgment Nm 27:21
and that you do not **i** about their gods, Dt 12:30
then you shall **i** and make search and Dt 13:14
you hear of it, then you shall **i** diligently, Dt 17:4
The judges shall **i** diligently, and if the Dt 19:18
And they said to him, "**I** of God, please, Jgs 18:5
in Israel, when a man went to **i** of God, 1 Sm 9:9
king said, "**I** whose son the boy is." 1 Sm 17:56
may go to her and **i** of her." And his 1 Sm 28:7
is coming to **i** of you concerning 1 Kgs 14:5
"**I** first for the word of the LORD." 1 Kgs 22:5
of the LORD of whom we may **i**?" 1 Kgs 22:7
man by whom we may **i** of the LORD, 1 Kgs 22:8
telling them, "Go, **i** of Baal-zebub, 2 Kgs 1:2
that you are going to **i** of Baal-zebub, 2 Kgs 1:3
you are sending to **i** of Baal-zebub, 2 Kgs 1:6
sent messengers to **i** of Baal-zebub, 2 Kgs 1:16
is no God in Israel to **i** of his word? 2 Kgs 1:16
whom we may **i** of the LORD?" 2 Kgs 3:11
of God, and **i** of the LORD through him, 2 Kgs 8:8
bronze altar shall be for me to **i** by." 2 Kgs 16:15
"Go, **i** of the LORD for me, and for the 2 Kgs 22:13
Judah, who sent you to **i** of the LORD, 2 Kgs 22:18
could not go before it to **i** of God, 1 Chr 21:30
"**I** first for the word of the LORD." 2 Chr 18:4
of the LORD of whom we may **i**?" 2 Chr 18:6
man by whom we may **i** of the LORD, 2 Chr 18:7
sent to him to **i** about the sign that 2 Chr 32:31
i of the LORD for me and for those 2 Chr 34:21
Judah, who sent you to **i** of the LORD, 2 Chr 34:26
"For **i**, please, of bygone ages, and consider Jb 8:8
beauty of the LORD and to **i** in his temple. Ps 27:4
"**I** of the mediums and the necromancers Is 8:19
should not a people **i** of their God? Is 8:19
Should they **i** of the dead on behalf of the Is 8:19
struck them, nor **i** of the LORD of hosts. Is 9:13
the peoples—of him shall the nations **i**, Is 11:10
and they will **i** of the idols and the Is 19:3
If you will **i**, inquire; come back again." Is 21:12
If you will inquire, **i**; come back again." Is 21:12
are stupid and do not **i** of the LORD; Jer 10:21
"**I** of the LORD for us, for Jer 21:2
of Judah who sent you to me to **i** of me, Jer 37:7
the elders of Israel came to **i** of the LORD, Ezk 20:1
Lord GOD, Is it to **i** of me that you come? Ezk 20:3
My people **i** of a piece of wood, and their Hos 4:12
who do not seek the LORD or **i** of him." Zep 1:6
were going to **i** somewhat more Acts 23:20

INQUIRED (31)
And he **i** about their welfare and said, Gn 43:27
Now Moses diligently **i** about the goat Lv 10:16
of Joshua, the people of Israel **i** of the LORD, Jgs 1:1
And after they had searched and **i**, Jgs 6:29
and went up to Bethel and **i** of God, Jgs 20:18
And they **i** of the LORD, "Shall we again Jgs 20:23
the people of Israel **i** of the LORD (for Jgs 20:27
So they **i** again of the LORD, "Is there a 1 Sm 10:22
And Saul **i** of God, "Shall I go down 1 Sm 14:37
and he **i** of the LORD for him and gave 1 Sm 22:10
a sword and have **i** of God for him, 1 Sm 22:13
time that I have **i** of God for him? 1 Sm 22:15
Therefore David **i** of the LORD, "Shall I 1 Sm 23:2
Then David **i** of the LORD again. And 1 Sm 23:4
And when Saul **i** of the LORD, the LORD 1 Sm 28:6
And David **i** of the LORD, "Shall I 1 Sm 30:8
After this David **i** of the LORD, "Shall I 2 Sm 2:1
And David **i** of the LORD, "Shall I go up 2 Sm 5:19
And when David **i** of the LORD, he said, 2 Sm 5:23
David sent and **i** about the woman. 2 Sm 11:3
And David **i** of God, "Shall I go up 1 Chr 14:10
And when David again **i** of God, 1 Chr 14:14
the Lord GOD, I will not be **i** of by you. Ezk 20:3
And shall I be **i** of by you, O house of Ezk 20:31
the Lord GOD, I will not be **i** of by you. Ezk 20:31
about which the king **i** of them, Dn 1:20
he **i** of them where the Christ was to be Mt 2:4
a crowd going by, he **i** what this meant. Lk 18:36
they had set them in the midst, they **i**, Acts 4:7
He **i** who he was and what he had Acts 21:33
to be yours searched and **i** carefully, 1 Pt 1:10

INQUIRER (1)
the punishment of the **i** shall be alike Ezk 14:10

INQUIRIES (1)
counselors to make **i** about Judah and Ezr 7:14

INQUIRING (2)
i what he wanted him to be called. Lk 1:62
i what person or time the Spirit of 1 Pt 1:11

INQUIRY (2)
When he makes **i**, what shall I answer Jb 31:14
having made **i** for Simon's house, Acts 10:17

INSANE (2)
and pretended to be **i** in their hands 1 Sm 21:13
of them said, "He has a demon, and is **i**; Jn 10:20

INSATIABLE (1)
have eyes full of adultery, **i** for sin. 2 Pt 2:14

INSCRIBE (1)
before them on a tablet and **i** it in a book, Is 30:8

INSCRIBED (7)
written! Oh that they were **i** in a book! Jb 19:23
He has **i** a circle on the face of the Jb 26:10
hand was sent, and this writing was **i**. Dn 5:24
And this is the writing that was **i**: MENE, Dn 5:25
will tell you what is **i** in the book of Dn 10:21
that day there shall be **i** on the bells of Zec 14:20
tribes of the sons of Israel were **i**— Rv 21:12

INSCRIPTION (10)
crown of pure gold, and wrote on it an **i**, Ex 39:30
stone with seven eyes, I will engrave its **i**, Zec 3:9
them, "Whose likeness and **i** is this?" Mt 22:20
"Whose likeness and **i** is this?" They Mk 12:16
And the **i** of the charge against him Mk 15:26
Whose likeness and **i** does it have?" Lk 20:24
There was also an **i** over him, "This is Lk 23:38
Pilate also wrote an **i** and put it on the Jn 19:19
Many of the Jews read this **i**, for the Jn 19:20
I found also an altar with this **i**, Acts 17:23

INSCRUTABLE (1)
his judgments and how **i** his ways! Rom 11:33

INSECTS (4)
"All winged **i** that go on all fours are Lv 11:20
Yet among the winged **i** that go on all Lv 11:21
But all other winged **i** that have four Lv 11:23
And all winged **i** are unclean for you; Dt 14:19

INSERTED (1)
beams should not be **i** into the walls of 1 Kgs 6:6

INSIDE (42)
ark, and cover it **i** and out with pitch. Gn 6:14
"Put your hand **i** your cloak." And he put Ex 4:6
cloak." And he put his hand **i** his cloak, Ex 4:6
"Put your hand back **i** your cloak." So he Ex 4:7
So he put his hand back **i** his cloak, Ex 4:7
gold, **i** and outside shall you overlay it, Ex 25:11
on its **i** edge next to the ephod. Ex 28:26
overlaid it with pure gold **i** and outside, Ex 37:2
on its **i** edge next to the ephod. Ex 39:19
he shall have the **i** of the house scraped Lv 14:41
at any time into the Holy Place **i** the veil, Lv 16:2
small, and he shall bring it **i** the veil Lv 16:12
and bring its blood **i** the veil and do Lv 16:15
camp. He shall not come **i** the camp, Dt 23:10
the sun sets, he may come **i** the camp. Dt 23:11
Jericho was shut up **i** and outside because Jos 6:1
they are hidden in the earth **i** my tent, Jos 7:21
and empty jars, with torches **i** the jars. Jgs 7:16
i the tent that David had pitched for it. 2 Sm 6:17
the house on the **i** with boards of 1 Kgs 6:15
he covered them on the **i** with wood, 1 Kgs 6:15
Solomon overlaid the **i** of the house 1 Kgs 6:21
that had been built **i** the house and 2 Kgs 16:18
of God and set it **i** the tent that David 1 Chr 16:1
He overlaid it on the **i** with pure gold. 2 Chr 3:4
goes to the king **i** the inner court Est 4:11
on his royal throne **i** the throne room Est 5:1
the vestibule of the gateway, on the **i**, Ezk 40:8
vestibule had windows all around **i**, Ezk 40:16
The **i** of the nave and the vestibules of Ezk 41:15
all the walls all around, **i** and outside, Ezk 41:17
On the **i**, around each of the four Ezk 46:23
but **i** they are full of greed and Mt 23:25
First clean the **i** of the cup and the Mt 23:26

and going **i** he sat with the guards to Mt 26:58
led him away **i** the palace (that Mk 15:16
but **i** you are full of greed and Lk 11:39
who made the outside make the **i** also? Lk 11:40
and let those who are **i** the city depart, Lk 21:21
days later, his disciples were **i** again, Jn 20:26
we opened them we found no one **i**." Acts 5:23
Is it not those **i** the church whom you 1 Cor 5:12

INSIGHT (15)
and Elnathan, who were men of **i**, Ezr 8:16
knowledge; his words are without **i**.' Jb 34:35
instruction, to understand words of **i**, Prv 1:2
if you call out for **i** and raise your voice Prv 2:3
and be attentive, that you may gain **i**, Prv 4:1
Get wisdom; get **i**; do not forget, and do Prv 4:5
Get wisdom, and whatever you get, get **i**. Prv 4:7
sister," and call **i** your intimate friend, Prv 7:4
counsel and sound wisdom; I have **i**; Prv 8:14
ways, and live, and walk in the way of **i**." Prv 9:6
and the knowledge of the Holy One is **i**. Prv 9:10
iniquities and gaining **i** by your truth. Dn 9:13
out to give you **i** and understanding. Dn 9:22
he lavished upon us, in all wisdom and **i** Eph 1:8
you can perceive my **i** into the mystery Eph 3:4

INSINCERITY (1)
through the **i** of liars whose 1 Tm 4:2

INSIST (2)
It does not **i** on its own way; it is not 1 Cor 13:5
and I want you to **i** on these things, Ti 3:8

INSISTED (1)
of about an hour still another **i**, Lk 22:59

INSISTING (2)
mind." But she kept **i** that it was so, Acts 12:15
i on asceticism and worship of angels, Col 2:18

INSOFAR (1)
But rejoice **i** as you share Christ's 1 Pt 4:13

INSOLENCE (6)
By **i** comes nothing but strife, but Prv 13:10
of his arrogance, his pride, and his **i**; Is 16:6
I know his **i**, declares the LORD; his Jer 48:30
a commander shall put an end to his **i**. Dn 11:18
he shall turn his **i** back upon him. Dn 11:18
sword because of the **i** of their tongue. Hos 7:16

INSOLENT (13)
O God, **i** men have risen up against me; Ps 86:14
You rebuke the **i**, accursed ones, who Ps 119:21
The **i** utterly deride me, but I do not Ps 119:51
The **i** smear me with lies, but with my Ps 119:69
Let the **i** be put to shame, because they Ps 119:78
The **i** have dug pitfalls for me; they do Ps 119:85
of good; let not the **i** oppress me. Ps 119:122
the youth will be **i** to the elder, and the Is 3:5
oppressor has ceased, the **i** fury ceased! Is 14:4
You will see no more the **i** people, the Is 33:19
Kareah and all the **i** men said to Jer 43:2
slanderers, haters of God, **i**, haughty, Rom 1:30
persecutor, and **i** opponent. 1 Tm 1:13

INSOLENTLY (3)
they have struck me **i** on the cheek; Jb 16:10
which speak **i** against the righteous in Ps 31:18
an adversary who deals **i** with me— Ps 55:12

INSPECT (1)
and you shall **i** your fold and miss Jb 5:24

INSPECTED (2)
and I **i** the walls of Jerusalem that were Neh 2:13
the night by the valley and **i** the wall, Neh 2:15

INSPIRE (2)
to succeed; perhaps you may **i** terror. Is 47:12
The horror you **i** has deceived you, and Jer 49:16

INSPIRED (1)
And he has **i** him to teach, both him Ex 35:34

INSTANT (2)
like passing chaff. And in an **i**, suddenly, Is 29:5
breaking comes suddenly, in an **i**; Is 30:13

INSTANTLY (3)
made you well." And **i** the woman was Mt 9:22
desire." And her daughter was healed **i**. Mt 15:28
out of him, and the boy was healed **i**. Mt 17:18

INSTEAD (59)
for me another offspring **i** of Abel, Gn 4:25
it up as a burnt offering **i** of his son. Gn 22:13
let your servant remain **i** of the boy as Gn 44:33
the people of Israel **i** of every firstborn Nm 3:12
I am the LORD—**i** of all the firstborn Nm 3:41
cattle of the Levites **i** of all the firstborn Nm 3:41
"Take the Levites **i** of all the firstborn Nm 3:45
the cattle of the Levites **i** of their cattle. Nm 3:45
I of all who open the womb, the Nm 8:16
have taken the Levites **i** of all the Nm 8:18
i the LORD your God turned the curse into Dt 23:5
beautiful than she? Please take her **i**." Jgs 15:2
set Amasa over the army **i** of Joab. 2 Sm 17:25
Would I had died **i** of you, O 2 Sm 18:33
and made him king **i** of his father 2 Kgs 14:21
the cities of Samaria **i** of the people 2 Kgs 17:24
and made him king **i** of his father 2 Chr 26:1
and afflicted him **i** of strengthening 2 Chr 28:20
the king be queen **i** of Vashti." This Est 2:4
head and made her queen **i** of Vashti. Est 2:17
For my sighing comes **i** of my bread, and Jb 3:24
let thorns grow **i** of wheat, and foul Jb 31:40
and foul weeds **i** of barley." The words Jb 31:40
Take my instruction **i** of silver, and Prv 8:10
trouble, and the wicked walks into it **i**. Prv 11:8
I of perfume there will be rottenness; and Is 3:24
will be rottenness; and **i** of a belt, a rope; Is 3:24
a rope; and **i** of well-set hair, baldness; Is 3:24
and **i** of a rich robe, a skirt of sackcloth; Is 3:24
of sackcloth; and branding **i** of beauty. Is 3:24
I of the thorn shall come up the cypress; Is 55:13
i of the brier shall come up the myrtle; Is 55:13
I of bronze I will bring gold, and instead Is 60:17
gold, and **i** of iron I will bring silver; Is 60:17
i of wood, bronze, instead of stones, iron. Is 60:17
instead of wood, bronze, **i** of stones, iron. Is 60:17
them a beautiful headdress **i** of ashes, Is 61:3
ashes, the oil of gladness **i** of mourning, Is 61:3
the garment of praise **i** of a faint spirit; Is 61:3
I of your shame there shall be a double Is 61:7
i of dishonor they shall rejoice in their Is 61:7
who reigned **i** of Josiah his father, Jer 22:11
has made you priest **i** of Jehoiada the Jer 29:26
reigned **i** of Coniah the son of Jer 37:1
to you cow's dung **i** of human dung, Ezk 4:15
who receives strangers **i** of her Ezk 16:32
i of being the desolation that it was in Ezk 36:34
and **i** of it there came up four Dn 8:8
honor the god of fortresses **i** of these. Dn 11:38
will have your fill of shame **i** of glory. Hab 2:16
have him release for them Barabbas **i**. Mk 15:11
a fish, will **i** of a fish give him a serpent; Lk 11:11
I, seek his kingdom, and these things Lk 12:31
before the unrighteous **i** of the saints? 1 Cor 6:1
of place, but **i** let there be thanksgiving. Eph 5:4
works of darkness, but **i** expose them. Eph 5:11
good things to come **i** of the true form Heb 10:1
I you ought to say, "If the Lord wills, we Jas 4:15
I I hope to come to you and talk face to 2 Jn 1:12

INSTIGATED (1)
Then they secretly **i** men who said, Acts 6:11

INSTINCT (1)
like irrational animals, creatures of **i**, 2 Pt 2:12

INSTINCTIVELY (1)
unreasoning animals, understand **i**. Jude 1:10

INSTITUTED (2)
And he **i** a feast for the people of 1 Kgs 12:33
those that exist have been **i** by God. Rom 13:1

INSTITUTION (1)
for the Lord's sake to every human **i**, 1 Pt 2:13

INSTRUCT (7)
and I will **i** you in the good and the 1 Sm 12:23
your good Spirit to **i** them and did not Neh 9:20
Him will he **i** in the way that he should Ps 25:12
I will **i** you and teach you in the way you Ps 32:8
knowledge and able to **i** one another. Rom 15:14
the Lord so as to **i** him?" But we have 1 Cor 2:16
with my mind in order to **i** others, 1 Cor 14:19

INSTRUCTED (16)
He **i** the first, "When Esau my brother Gn 32:17
He likewise **i** the second and the third Gn 32:19
she rose to glean, Boaz **i** his young men, Ru 2:15
And he **i** the messenger, "When you 2 Sm 11:19
because Jehoiada the priest **i** him. 2 Kgs 12:2
who **i** him in the fear of God, 2 Chr 26:5
Behold, you have **i** many, and you have Jb 4:3
when a wise man is **i**, he gains Prv 21:11
For he is rightly **i**; his God teaches him. Is 28:26
away, I relented, and after I was **i**, Jer 31:19
answered them as the king had **i** him. Jer 38:27
And Moses was **i** in all the wisdom of Acts 7:22
He had been **i** in the way of the Lord. Acts 18:25
because you are **i** from the law; Rom 2:18
work with your hands, as we **i** you, 1 Thes 4:11
about to erect the tent, he was **i** by God, Heb 8:5

INSTRUCTING (3)
i them, "Thus you shall say to my lord Gn 32:4
These twelve Jesus sent out, **i** them, "Go Mt 10:5
Jesus had finished **i** his twelve disciples, Mt 11:1

INSTRUCTION (42)
which I have written for their **i**." Ex 24:12
to come, and this is **i** for mankind, 2 Sm 7:19
all the king's provinces with **i** to destroy, Est 3:13
Receive **i** from his mouth, and lay up Jb 22:22
their ears to **i** and commands that Jb 36:10
A Miktam of David; for **i**; when he strove Ps 60:T
To know wisdom and **i**, to understand Prv 1:2
to receive **i** in wise dealing, in Prv 1:3
of knowledge; fools despise wisdom and **i**. Prv 1:7
Hear, my son, your father's **i**, and forsake Prv 1:8
Hear, O sons, a father's **i**, and be Prv 4:1
Keep hold of **i**; do not let go; guard her, Prv 4:13
Take my **i** instead of silver, and Prv 8:10
Hear **i** and be wise, and do not neglect it. Prv 8:33
Give **i** to a wise man, and he will be still Prv 9:9
Whoever heeds **i** is on the path to life, Prv 10:17
A wise son hears his father's **i**, but a Prv 13:1
disgrace come to him who ignores **i**, Prv 13:18
A fool despises his father's **i**, but Prv 15:5
Whoever ignores **i** despises himself, Prv 15:32
The fear of the LORD is **i** in wisdom, Prv 15:33
who has it, but the **i** of fools is folly. Prv 16:22
Listen to advice and accept **i**, that you Prv 19:20
Cease to hear **i**, my son, and you will Prv 19:27
Apply your heart to **i** and your ear to Prv 23:12
it; buy wisdom, **i**, and understanding. Prv 23:23
considered it; I looked and received **i**. Prv 24:32
and those who murmur will accept **i**." Is 29:24
unwilling to hear the **i** of the LORD; Is 30:9
and foolish; the **i** of idols is but wood! Jer 10:8
that they might not hear and receive **i**. Jer 17:23
they have not listened to receive **i**. Jer 32:33
Will you not receive **i** and listen to my Jer 35:13
True **i** was in his mouth, and no wrong Mal 2:6
people should seek **i** from his mouth, Mal 2:7
have caused many to stumble by your **i**. Mal 2:8
my ways but show partiality in your **i**." Mal 2:9
in former days was written for our **i**, Rom 15:4
but they were written down for our **i**, 1 Cor 10:11
up in the discipline and **i** of the Lord. Eph 6:4
be able to give **i** in sound doctrine and Ti 1:9
and of **i** about washings, the laying on Heb 6:2

INSTRUCTIONS (6)
According to the **i** that they give you, Dt 17:11
minds, although we gave them no **i**, Acts 15:24
So the soldiers, according to their **i**, Acts 23:31
But in the following **i** I do not 1 Cor 11:17
whom you have received **i**—if he comes Col 4:10
For you know what **i** we gave you 1 Thes 4:2

INSTRUCTOR (2)
called instructors, for you have one **i**, Mt 23:10
an **i** of the foolish, a teacher of Rom 2:20

INSTRUCTORS (2)
my teachers or incline my ear to my **i**. Prv 5:13
Neither be called **i**, for you have one Mt 23:10

INSTRUCTS (2)
counsel; in the night also my heart **i** me. Ps 16:7
LORD; therefore he **i** sinners in the way. Ps 25:8

INSTRUMENT (2)
beautiful voice and plays well on an **i**, Ezk 33:32
for he is a chosen **i** of mine to carry Acts 9:15

INSTRUMENTS (27)
was the forger of all **i** of bronze and iron. Gn 4:22
with songs of joy, and with musical **i**. 1 Sm 18:6
should play loudly on musical **i**, 1 Chr 15:16
for the music and **i** for sacred song. 1 Chr 16:42
the LORD with the **i** that I have made 1 Chr 23:5
and cymbals and other musical **i**, 2 Chr 5:13
with the **i** for music to the LORD that 2 Chr 7:6
with their musical **i** leading in the 2 Chr 23:13
Levites stood with the **i** of David, 2 Chr 29:26
accompanied by the **i** of David king 2 Chr 29:27
who were skillful with **i** of music, 2 Chr 34:12
with the musical **i** of David the man Neh 12:36
To the choirmaster: with stringed **i**. A Ps 4:T
To the choirmaster: with stringed **i**; Ps 6:T
ivory palaces stringed **i** make you glad; Ps 45:8
To the choirmaster: with stringed **i**. A Ps 54:T
To the choirmaster: with stringed **i**. A Ps 55:T
To the choirmaster: with stringed **i**. Of Ps 61:T
To the choirmaster: with stringed **i**. A Ps 67:T
To the choirmaster: with stringed **i**. A Ps 76:T
my music on stringed **i** all the days of Is 38:20
on which the **i** were to be laid with Ezk 40:42
David invent for themselves **i** of music, Am 6:5
To the choirmaster: with stringed **i**. Hab 3:19
to sin as **i** for unrighteousness, Rom 6:13
to God as **i** for righteousness. Rom 6:13
If even lifeless **i**, such as the flute or 1 Cor 14:7

INSUBORDINATE (1)
For there are many who are **i**, empty Ti 1:10

INSUBORDINATION (1)
not open to the charge of debauchery or **i**. Ti 1:6

INSULT (3)
who has avenged the **i** I received at 1 Sm 25:39
at once, but the prudent ignores an **i**. Prv 12:16
in saying these things you **i** us also." Lk 11:45

INSULTED (2)
on the mountains and **i** me on the hills, Is 65:7
If you are **i** for the name of Christ, you 1 Pt 4:14

INSULTS (7)
I hear censure that **i** me, and out of my Jb 20:3
bear in my heart the **i** of all the many Ps 89:50
oppresses a poor man **i** his Maker, Prv 14:31
Whoever mocks the poor **i** his Maker; Prv 17:5
strikes, and let him be filled with **i**. Lam 3:30
whoever **i** his brother will be liable to Mt 5:22
with weaknesses, **i**, hardships, 2 Cor 12:10

INSURRECTION (3)
who had committed murder in the **i**, Mk 15:7
into prison for an **i** started in the city Lk 23:19
thrown into prison for **i** and murder, Lk 23:25

INTEGRITY (25)
In the **i** of my heart and the innocence Gn 20:5
you have done this in the **i** of your heart, Gn 20:6
in good faith and **i** when you made Jgs 9:16
in good faith and **i** with Jerubbaal and Jgs 9:19
with **i** of heart and uprightness, 1 Kgs 9:4
He still holds fast his **i**, although you Jb 2:3
said to him, "Do you still hold fast your **i**? Jb 2:9
and the **i** of your ways your hope? Jb 4:6
till I die I will not put away my **i** from me. Jb 27:5
a just balance, and let God know my **i**!) Jb 31:6
and according to the **i** that is in me. Ps 7:8
May **i** and uprightness preserve me, for Ps 25:21
me, O LORD, for I have walked in my **i**, Ps 26:1
But as for me, I shall walk in my **i**; Ps 26:11
you have upheld me because of my **i**, Ps 41:12
I will walk with **i** of heart within my Ps 101:2
he is a shield to those who walk in **i**, Prv 2:7
land, and those with **i** will remain in it, Prv 2:21
Whoever walks in **i** walks securely, but Prv 10:9
The **i** of the upright guides them, but Prv 11:3
who walks in his **i** than one who is Prv 19:1
who walks in his **i**—blessed are his Prv 20:7
who walks in his **i** than a rich man Prv 28:6
Whoever walks in **i** will be delivered, Prv 28:18
good works, and in your teaching show **i**, Ti 2:7

INTELLIGENCE (5)
with the Spirit of God, with ability and **i**, Ex 31:3
with the Spirit of God, with skill, with **i**, Ex 35:31
LORD has put skill and **i** to know how to Ex 36:1
but he who listens to reproof gains **i**. Prv 15:32
proconsul, Sergius Paulus, a man of **i**, Acts 13:7

INTELLIGENT (3)
when he closes his lips, he is deemed **i**. Prv 17:28
An **i** heart acquires knowledge, and Prv 18:15
bread to the wise, nor riches to the **i**, Eccl 9:11

INTELLIGIBLE (1)
tongue you utter speech that is not **i**, 1 Cor 14:9

INTEND (11)
And so I **i** to build a house for the 1 Kgs 5:5
And now you **i** to subjugate the 2 Chr 28:10
says it, that you and the Jews **i** to rebel; Neh 6:6
But he does not so **i**, and his heart does Is 10:7
of the disaster that I **i** to do to them Jer 26:3
hear all the disaster that I **i** to do to them, Jer 36:3
"Where does this man **i** to go that we will Jn 7:35
Does he **i** to go to the Dispersion among Jn 7:35
and you **i** to bring this man's blood Acts 5:28
for I **i** to pass through Macedonia, 1 Cor 16:5
Therefore I **i** always to remind you of 2 Pt 1:12

INTENDED (9)
by not telling him that he **i** to flee. Gn 31:20
brothers, for he **i** to make him king. 2 Chr 11:22
had come and **i** to fight against 2 Chr 32:2
plain of Ono." But they **i** to do me harm. Neh 6:2
because he **i** to lay hands on the Jews. Est 8:7
relent of the disaster that I **i** to do to it. Jer 18:8
relent of the good that I had **i** to do to it. Jer 18:10
and that he himself **i** to go there Acts 25:4
that I have often **i** to come to you (but Rom 1:13

INTENDING (5)
near Bethlehem, **i** to go to Egypt Jer 41:17
i after the Passover to bring him out to Acts 12:4
with them, **i** to depart on the next day, Acts 20:7
for Assos, **i** to take Paul aboard there, Acts 20:13
had arranged, **i** himself to go by land. Acts 20:13

INTENSELY (1)
and his clothes became radiant, **i** white, Mk 9:3

INTENT (10)
say, 'With evil **i** did he bring them out, Ex 32:12
any person without **i** may flee there. Nm 35:11
any person without **i** may flee there. Nm 35:15
any person without **i** or unknowingly Jos 20:3
killed a person without **i** could flee there, Jos 20:9
to Hebron with full **i** to make David 1 Chr 12:38
speak against you with malicious **i**; Ps 139:20
more when he brings it with evil **i**. Prv 21:27
woman with lustful **i** has already Mt 5:28
the **i** of your heart may be forgiven Acts 8:22

INTENTION (2)
and that every **i** of the thoughts of his Gn 6:5
for the **i** of man's heart is evil from his Gn 8:21

INTENTIONS (2)
and accomplished the **i** of his mind. Jer 30:24
the thoughts and **i** of the heart. Heb 4:12

INTENTLY (4)
with the Holy Spirit, looked **i** at him Acts 13:9
looking **i** at him and seeing that he Acts 14:9
And looking **i** at the council, Paul Acts 23:1
a man who looks **i** at his natural face Jas 1:23

INTENTS (1)
and accomplished the **i** of his heart. Jer 23:20

INTERCEDE (4)
who can **i** for him?" But they would 1 Sm 2:25
and wondered that there was no one to **i**; Is 59:16
or prayer for them, and do not **i** with me, Jer 7:16
then let them **i** with the LORD of hosts, Jer 27:18

INTERCEDES (2)
but the Spirit himself **i** for us with Rom 8:26
because the Spirit **i** for the saints Rom 8:27

INTERCEDING (1)
hand of God, who indeed is **i** for us. Rom 8:34

INTERCESSION (2)
and makes **i** for the transgressors. Is 53:12
he always lives to make **i** for them. Heb 7:25

INTERCESSIONS (1)
i, and thanksgivings be made for all 1 Tm 2:1

INTEREST (20)
and you shall not exact **i** from him. Ex 22:25
Take no **i** from him or profit, but fear Lv 25:36
shall not lend him your money at **i**, Lv 25:37
"You shall not charge **i** on loans to Dt 23:19
on loans to your brother, **i** on money, Dt 23:19
brother, interest on money, **i** on food, Dt 23:19
i on anything that is lent for interest. Dt 23:19
interest on anything that is lent for **i**. Dt 23:19
You may charge a foreigner **i**, but you Dt 23:20
but you may not charge your brother **i**, Dt 23:20
I said to them, "You are exacting **i**, each Neh 5:7
Let us abandon this exacting of **i**. Neh 5:10
put out his money at **i** and does not take Ps 15:5
his wealth by **i** and profit gathers Prv 28:8
does not lend at **i** or take any profit, Ezk 18:8
lends at **i**, and takes profit; shall he Ezk 18:13
from iniquity, takes no **i** or profit, Ezk 18:17
you take **i** and profit and make gain of Ezk 22:12
have received what was my own with **i**. Mt 25:27
I might have collected it with **i**?' Lk 19:23

INTERESTS (4)
and his **i** are divided. And the 1 Cor 7:34
each of you look not only to his own **i**, Phil 2:4
own interests, but also to the **i** of others. Phil 2:4
They all seek their own **i**, not those of Phil 2:21

INTERIOR (2)
its **i** was inlaid with love by the Sg 3:10
finished measuring the **i** of the temple Ezk 42:15

INTERMARRY (2)
You shall not **i** with them, giving your Dt 7:3
commandments again and **i** with the Ezr 9:14

INTERMEDIARY (2)
put in place through angels by an **i**. Gal 3:19
Now an **i** implies more than one, but Gal 3:20

INTERPRET (14)
is no one to **i** them." And Joseph said Gn 40:8
was none who could **i** them to Pharaoh. Gn 41:8
dream, and there is no one who can **i** it. Gn 41:15
when you hear a dream you can **i** it." Gn 41:15
You shall not **i** omens or tell fortunes. Lv 19:26
and understanding to **i** dreams, Dn 5:12
You know how to **i** the appearance of Mt 16:3
but you cannot **i** the signs of the times. Mt 16:3
You know how to **i** the appearance of Lk 12:56
not know how to **i** the present time? Lk 12:56
Do all speak with tongues? Do all **i**? 1 Cor 12:30
should pray for the power to **i**. 1 Cor 14:13
and each in turn, and let someone **i**. 1 Cor 14:27
But if there is no one to **i**, let each of 1 Cor 14:28

INTERPRETATION (41)
dream, and each dream with its own **i**. Gn 40:5
Then Joseph said to him, "This is its **i**: Gn 40:12
baker saw that the **i** was favorable, Gn 40:16
Joseph answered and said, "This is its **i**: Gn 40:18
I, each having a dream with its own **i**. Gn 41:11
giving an **i** to each man according to Gn 41:12
heard the telling of the dream and its **i**, Jgs 7:15
wise? And who knows the **i** of a thing? Eccl 8:1
the dream, and we will show the **i**." Dn 2:4
make known to me the dream and its **i**, Dn 2:5
But if you show the dream and its **i**, you Dn 2:6
Therefore show me the dream and its **i**." Dn 2:6
the dream, and we will show its **i**." Dn 2:7
I shall know that you can show me its **i**." Dn 2:9
that he might show the **i** to the king. Dn 2:16
the king, and I will show the king the **i**." Dn 2:24
who will make known to the king the **i**." Dn 2:25
me the dream that I have seen and its **i**?" Dn 2:26
in order that the **i** may be made known Dn 2:30
dream. Now we will tell the king its **i**. Dn 2:36
The dream is certain, and its **i** sure." Dn 2:45
make known to me the **i** of the dream. Dn 4:6
they could not make known to me its **i**. Dn 4:7
of my dream that I saw and their **i**. Dn 4:9
And you, O Belteshazzar, tell me the **i**, Dn 4:18
are not able to make known to me the **i**, Dn 4:18
dream or the **i** alarm you." Belteshazzar Dn 4:19
who hate you and its **i** for your enemies! Dn 4:19
this is the **i**, O king: It is a decree of the Dn 4:24
reads this writing, and shows me its **i**, Dn 5:7
writing or make known to the king the **i**. Dn 5:8
Daniel be called, and he will show the **i**." Dn 5:12
writing and make known to me its **i**, Dn 5:15
they could not show the **i** of the matter. Dn 5:15
the writing and make known to me its **i**, Dn 5:16
the king and make known to him the **i**. Dn 5:17
This is the **i** of the matter: MENE, God Dn 5:26
made known to me the **i** of the things. Dn 7:16
tongues, to another the **i** of tongues. 1 Cor 12:10
a revelation, a tongue, or an **i**. 1 Cor 14:26
Scripture comes from someone's own **i**. 2 Pt 1:20

INTERPRETATIONS (2)
said to them, "Do not **i** belong to God? Gn 40:8
that you can give **i** and solve problems. Dn 5:16

INTERPRETED (5)
chief baker, as Joseph had **i** to them. Gn 40:22
we told him, he **i** our dreams to us, Gn 41:12
And as he **i** to us, so it came about. I Gn 41:13
he **i** to them in all the Scriptures the Lk 24:27
Now this may be **i** allegorically: these Gal 4:24

INTERPRETER (1)
them, for there was an **i** between them. Gn 42:23

INTERPRETING (1)
i spiritual truths to those who are 1 Cor 2:13

INTERPRETS (2)
divination or tells fortunes or **i** omens, Dt 18:10
speaks in tongues, unless someone **i**, 1 Cor 14:5

INTERVAL (2)
And after an **i** of about an hour still Lk 22:59
After an **i** of about three hours his wife Acts 5:7

INTERVENED (2)
Then Phinehas stood up and **i**, and the Ps 106:30
for you have **i** on behalf of your Ezk 16:52

INTERWOVEN (1)
in her chamber, with robes **i** with gold. Ps 45:13

INTIMATE (2)
All my **i** friends abhor me, and those Jb 19:19
my sister," and call insight your **i** friend, Prv 7:4

INTIMIDATED (1)
You shall not be **i** by anyone, for the Dt 1:17

INTOXICATED (2)
with delight; be **i** always in her love. Prv 5:19
Why should you be **i**, my son, with a Prv 5:20

INTRICATELY (1)
i woven in the depths of the earth. Ps 139:15

INTRIGUE (1)
like an oven they approach their **i**; Hos 7:6

INTRODUCED (2)
in the customs that Israel had **i**. 2 Kgs 17:19
on the other hand, a better hope is **i**, Heb 7:19

INVADE (3)
of Moabites used to **i** the land in the 2 Kgs 13:20
not let Israel **i** when they came 2 Chr 20:10
trouble to come upon people who **i** us. Hab 3:16

INVADED (4)
the king of Assyria **i** all the land and 2 Kgs 17:5
against Judah and **i** it and carried 2 Chr 21:17

Edomites had again **i** and defeated 2 Chr 28:17
Assyria came and **i** Judah and 2 Chr 32:1

INVALID (1)
who had been an **i** for thirty-eight years. Jn 5:5

INVALIDS (1)
In these lay a multitude of **i**—blind, lame, Jn 5:3

INVENT (1)
and like David **i** for themselves Am 6:5

INVENTED (1)
he made engines, **i** by skillful men, 2 Chr 26:15

INVENTING (1)
for you are **i** them out of your own Neh 6:8

INVENTORS (1)
insolent, haughty, boastful, **i** of evil, Rom 1:30

INVEST (1)
You shall **i** him with some of your Nm 27:20

INVESTED (1)
you ought to have **i** my money with the Mt 25:27

INVESTIGATE (1)
at a loss how to **i** these questions, Acts 25:20

INVESTIGATED (1)
When the affair was **i** and found to be Est 2:23

INVESTIGATION (1)
the mighty without **i** and sets others Jb 34:24

INVISIBLE (5)
For his **i** attributes, namely, his Rom 1:20
He is the image of the **i** God, the Col 1:15
in heaven and on earth, visible and **i**, Col 1:16
of ages, immortal, **i**, the only God, 1 Tm 1:17
for he endured as seeing him who is **i**. Heb 11:27

INVITE (8)
And **i** Jesse to the sacrifice, and I will 1 Sm 16:3
but he did not **i** Nathan the prophet 1 Kgs 1:10
they would send and **i** their three sisters to Jb 1:4
one of you will **i** his neighbor to come Zec 3:10
the main roads and **i** to the wedding Mt 22:9
do not **i** your friends or your brothers Lk 14:12
lest they also **i** you in return and you Lk 14:12
But when you give a feast, **i** the poor, Lk 14:13

INVITED (34)
sacrifice to their gods and you are **i**, Ex 34:15
These **i** the people to the sacrifices of Nm 25:2
And he sent and **i** Balaam the son of Jos 24:9
Have you **i** us here to impoverish us?" Jgs 14:15
afterward those who are **i** will eat. 1 Sm 9:13
at the head of those who had been **i**, 1 Sm 9:22
and his sons and **i** them to the 1 Sm 16:5
And David **i** him, and he ate in his 2 Sm 11:13
and Absalom **i** all the king's sons. 2 Sm 13:23
from Jerusalem who were **i** guests, 2 Sm 15:11
En-rogel, and he **i** all his brothers, 1 Kgs 1:9
and has **i** all the sons of the king, 1 Kgs 1:19
Solomon your servant he has not **i**. 1 Kgs 1:19
and has **i** all the king's sons, 1 Kgs 1:25
your servant Solomon he has not **i**. 1 Kgs 1:26
tomorrow also I am **i** by her together Est 5:12
call those who were **i** to the wedding Mt 22:3
servants, saying, 'Tell those who are **i**, Mt 22:4
is ready, but those **i** were not worthy. Mt 22:8
the Pharisee who had **i** him saw this, Lk 7:39
he told a parable to those who were **i**, Lk 14:7
"When you are **i** by someone to a Lk 14:8
distinguished than you be **i** by him, Lk 14:8
and he who **i** you both will come and Lk 14:9
But when you are **i**, go and sit in the Lk 14:10
He said also to the man who had **i** him, Lk 14:12
once gave a great banquet and **i** many. Lk 14:16
servant to say to those who had been **i**, Lk 14:17
those men who were **i** shall taste my Lk 14:24
Jesus also was **i** to the wedding with his Jn 2:2
guides me?" And he **i** Philip to come Acts 8:31
So he **i** them in to be his guests. The Acts 10:23
brothers and were **i** to stay with Acts 28:14
are those who are **i** to the marriage Rv 19:9

INVITES (2)
into a fight, and his mouth **i** a beating. Prv 18:6
of the unbelievers **i** you to dinner 1 Cor 10:27

INVOKE (5)
"Please let the king **i** the LORD your 2 Sm 14:11
before the ark of the LORD, to **i**, 1 Chr 16:4
Then he began to **i** a curse on himself Mt 26:74
But he began to **i** a curse on himself Mk 14:71
exorcists undertook to **i** the name of Acts 19:13

INVOKED (3)
and blessings **i** for him all the day! Ps 72:15
shall no more be **i** by the mouth of Jer 44:26
By faith Isaac **i** future blessings on Heb 11:20

INVOLVED (5)
in the tent of meeting **i** the tabernacle, Nm 3:25
And their guard duty **i** the ark, the Nm 3:31
of the sons of Merari **i** the frames of the Nm 3:36
whole population was **i** in the Nm 15:26
For where a will is **i**, the death of the Heb 9:16

INVOLVING (1)
vow to the LORD **i** the valuation of Lv 27:2

INWARD (9)
the city all around from the Millo **i**. 2 Sm 5:9
them, and all their rear parts were **i**. 1 Kgs 7:25
on them, and all their rear parts were **i**. 2 Chr 4:4
My **i** parts are in turmoil and never still; Jb 30:27
put wisdom in the **i** parts or given Jb 38:36
you delight in truth in the **i** being, Ps 51:6
search." For the **i** mind and heart Ps 64:6
For you formed my **i** parts; you Ps 139:13
before the chambers was a passage **i**, Ezk 42:4

INWARDLY (6)
bless with their mouths, but **i** they curse. Ps 62:4
for he is like one who is **i** calculating. Prv 23:7
sheep's clothing but **i** are ravenous Mt 7:15
Now while Peter was **i** perplexed as to Acts 10:17
But a Jew is one **i**, and circumcision is Rom 2:29
groan **i** as we wait eagerly for adoption Rom 8:23

INWARDS (1)
narrowing **i** toward the side rooms Ezk 40:16

IOTA (1)
heaven and earth pass away, not an **i**, Mt 5:18

IPHDEIAH (1)
I, and Penuel were the sons of 1 Chr 8:25

IPHTAH (1)
I, Ashnah, Nezib, Jos 15:43

IPHTAHEL (2)
and it ends at the Valley of **I**; Jos 19:14
the Valley of **I** northward to Beth-emek Jos 19:27

IR (1)
and Huppim were the sons of **I**, 1 Chr 7:12

IR-NAHASH (1)
and Tehinnah, the father of **I**. 1 Chr 4:12

IR-SHEMESH (1)
inheritance included Zorah, Eshtaol, **I**, Jos 19:41

IRA (6)
and **I** the Jairite was also David's 2 Sm 20:26
Paltite, **I** the son of Ikkesh of Tekoa, 2 Sm 23:26
I the Ithrite, Gareb the Ithrite, 2 Sm 23:38
I the son of Ikkesh of Tekoa, 1 Chr 11:28
I the Ithrite, Gareb the Ithrite, 1 Chr 11:40
Sixth, for the sixth month, was **I**, the 1 Chr 27:9

IRAD (2)
To Enoch was born **I**, and Irad fathered Gn 4:18
was born Irad, and **I** fathered Mehujael, Gn 4:18

IRAM (2)
Magdiel, and **I**; these are the chiefs of Gn 36:43
Magdiel, and **I**; these are the chiefs of 1 Chr 1:54

IRI (1)
Ezbon, Uzzi, Uzziel, Jerimoth, and **I**, 1 Chr 7:7

IRIJAH (2)
a sentry there named **I** the son of Jer 37:13
the Chaldeans." But **I** would not listen Jer 37:14

IRON (97)
of all instruments of bronze and **i**. Gn 4:22
your heavens like **i** and your earth Lv 26:19
the gold, the silver, the bronze, the **i**, Nm 31:22
he struck him down with an **i** object, Nm 35:16
Rephaim. Behold, his bed was a bed of **i**. Dt 3:11
and brought you out of the **i** furnace, Dt 4:20
lack nothing, a land whose stones are **i**, Dt 8:9
stones. You shall wield no **i** tool on them; Dt 27:5
and the earth under you shall be **i**. Dt 28:23
will put a yoke of **i** on your neck until Dt 28:48
Your bars shall be **i** and bronze, and as Dt 33:25
gold, and every vessel of bronze and **i**, Jos 6:19
gold, and the vessels of bronze and of **i**, Jos 6:24
man has wielded an **i** tool." And they Jos 8:31
dwell in the plain have chariots of **i**, Jos 17:16
though they have chariots of **i**, Jos 17:18
livestock, with silver, gold, bronze, and **i**, Jos 22:8
the plain because they had chariots of **i**. Jgs 1:19
had 900 chariots of **i** and he oppressed the Jgs 4:3
out all his chariots, 900 chariots of **i**, Jgs 4:13
head weighed six hundred shekels of **i**. 1 Sm 17:7
labor with saws and **i** picks and iron 2 Sm 12:31
and iron picks and **i** axes and made 2 Sm 12:31
arms himself with **i** and the shaft 2 Sm 23:7
axe nor any tool of **i** was heard in the 1 Kgs 6:7
from the midst of the **i** furnace). 1 Kgs 8:51
for himself horns of **i** and said, 1 Kgs 22:11
threw it in there and made the **i** float. 2 Kgs 6:6
labor with saws and **i** picks and axes. 1 Chr 20:3
great quantities of **i** for nails for 1 Chr 22:3
and bronze and **i** beyond weighing, 1 Chr 22:14
gold, silver, bronze, and **i**. Arise and 1 Chr 22:16
of bronze, the **i** for the things of iron, 1 Chr 29:2
of bronze, the iron for the things of **i**, 1 Chr 29:2
of bronze and 100,000 talents of **i**. 1 Chr 29:7
to work in gold, silver, bronze, and **i**, 2 Chr 2:7
work in gold, silver, bronze, **i**, stone, 2 Chr 2:14
for himself horns of **i** and said, 2 Chr 18:10
and also workers in **i** and bronze to 2 Chr 24:12
Oh that with an **i** pen and lead they were Jb 19:24
He will flee from an **i** weapon; a bronze Jb 20:24
I is taken out of the earth, and copper is Jb 28:2
tubes of bronze, his limbs like bars of **i**. Jb 40:18
He counts **i** as straw, and bronze as Jb 41:27
them with a rod of **i** and dash them in Ps 2:9
his neck was put in a collar of **i**; Ps 105:18
of bronze and cuts in two the bars of **i**. Ps 107:16
chains and their nobles with fetters of **i**, Ps 149:8
I sharpens iron, and one man Prv 27:17
Iron sharpens **i**, and one man Prv 27:17
If the **i** is blunt, and one does not Eccl 10:10
of bronze and cut through the bars of **i**, Is 45:2
your neck is an **i** sinew and your Is 48:4
gold, and instead of **i** I will bring silver; Is 60:17
of wood, bronze, instead of stones, **i**. Is 60:17
you this day a fortified city, an **i** pillar, Jer 1:18
with slanders; they are bronze and **i**; Jer 6:28
of the land of Egypt, from the **i** furnace, Jer 11:4
Can one break **i**, iron from the north, Jer 15:12
Can one break iron, **i** from the north, Jer 15:12
sin of Judah is written with a pen of **i**; Jer 17:1
you have made in their place bars of **i**. Jer 28:13
all these nations an **i** yoke to serve Jer 28:14
And you, take an **i** griddle, and place it Ezk 4:3
and place it as an **i** wall between you and Ezk 4:3
bronze and tin and **i** and lead in the Ezk 22:18
silver and bronze and **i** and lead and Ezk 22:20
silver, **i**, tin, and lead they exchanged Ezk 27:12
exchanged for your wares; wrought **i**, Ezk 27:19
its legs of **i**, its feet partly of iron and Dn 2:33
iron, its feet partly of **i** and partly of clay. Dn 2:33
struck the image on its feet of **i** and clay, Dn 2:34
Then the **i**, the clay, the bronze, the Dn 2:35
shall be a fourth kingdom, strong as **i**, Dn 2:40
because **i** breaks to pieces and shatters Dn 2:40
all things. And like **i** that crushes, Dn 2:40
partly of potter's clay and partly of **i**, Dn 2:41
some of the firmness of **i** shall be in it, Dn 2:41
just as you saw **i** mixed with the soft Dn 2:41
of the feet were partly **i** and partly clay, Dn 2:42
As you saw the **i** mixed with soft clay, so Dn 2:43
just as **i** does not mix with clay. Dn 2:43
hand, and that it broke in pieces the **i**, Dn 2:45
bound with a band of **i** and bronze, Dn 4:15
bound with a band of **i** and bronze, Dn 4:23
gods of gold and silver, bronze, **i**, wood, Dn 5:4
of silver and gold, of bronze, **i**, wood, Dn 5:23
It had great **i** teeth; it devoured and broke Dn 7:7
with its teeth of **i** and claws of bronze, Dn 7:19
Gilead with threshing sledges of **i**. Am 1:3
of Zion, for I will make your horn **i**, Mi 4:13
they came to the **i** gate leading into Acts 12:10
and he will rule them with a rod of **i**, as Rv 2:27
had breastplates like breastplates of **i**, Rv 9:9
is to rule all the nations with a rod of **i**, Rv 12:5
of costly wood, bronze, **i** and marble, Rv 18:12
and he will rule them with a rod of **i**. Rv 19:15

IRONS (2)
death, prisoners in affliction and in **i**, Ps 107:10
to put him in the stocks and neck **i**. Jer 29:26

IRONSMITH (1)
The **i** takes a cutting tool and works it Is 44:12

IRPEEL (1)
Rekem, **I**, Taralah, Jos 18:27

IRRATIONAL (1)
But these, like **i** animals, creatures of 2 Pt 2:12

IRRESOLUTE (1)
was young and **i** and could not 2 Chr 13:7

IRREVERENT (3)
Have nothing to do with **i**, silly myths. 1 Tm 4:7
Avoid the **i** babble and 1 Tm 6:20
But avoid **i** babble, for it will lead 2 Tm 2:16

IRREVOCABLE (1)
the gifts and the calling of God are **i**. Rom 11:29

IRRIGATED (1)
where you sowed your seed and **i** it, Dt 11:10

IRRITABLE (1)
on its own way; it is not **i** or resentful; 1 Cor 13:5

IRRITATE (1)
used to provoke her grievously to **i** her, 1 Sm 1:6

IRU (1)
son of Jephunneh: **I**, Elah, and Naam; 1 Chr 4:15

ISAAC (129)
a son, and you shall call his name **I**. Gn 17:19
I will establish my covenant with **I**, Gn 17:21
born to him, whom Sarah bore him, **I**. Gn 21:3
circumcised his son **I** when he was Gn 21:4
old when his son **I** was born to him. Gn 21:5
great feast on the day that **I** was weaned. Gn 21:8
shall not be heir with my son **I**." Gn 21:10
for through **I** shall your offspring be Gn 21:12
said, "Take your son, your only son **I**, Gn 22:2
his young men with him, and his son **I**. Gn 22:3
burnt offering and laid it on **I** his son. Gn 22:6
And **I** said to his father Abraham, "My Gn 22:7
in order and bound **I** his son and laid Gn 22:9
kindred, and take a wife for my son **I**." Gn 24:4
you have appointed for your servant **I**. Gn 24:14
Now **I** had returned from Gn 24:62
And **I** went out to meditate in the field Gn 24:63
lifted up her eyes, and when she saw **I**, Gn 24:64
And the servant told **I** all the things Gn 24:66
Then **I** brought her into the tent of Gn 24:67
So **I** was comforted after his mother's Gn 24:67
Abraham gave all he had to **I**. Gn 25:5
living he sent them away from his son **I**, Gn 25:6
I and Ishmael his sons buried him in Gn 25:9
of Abraham, God blessed **I** his son. Gn 25:11
his son. And **I** settled at Beer-lahai-roi. Gn 25:11
These are the generations of **I**, Gn 25:19
Abraham's son: Abraham fathered **I**, Gn 25:19
and **I** was forty years old when he took Gn 25:20
And **I** prayed to the LORD for his wife, Gn 25:21
I was sixty years old when she bore Gn 25:26
I loved Esau because he ate of his Gn 25:28
And **I** went to Gerar to Abimelech king Gn 26:1
So **I** settled in Gerar. Gn 26:6
window and saw **I** laughing with Gn 26:8
So Abimelech called **I** and said, "Behold, Gn 26:9
say, 'She is my sister'?" **I** said to him, Gn 26:9
And **I** sowed in that land and reaped in Gn 26:12
And Abimelech said to **I**, "Go away Gn 26:16
So **I** departed from there and encamped Gn 26:17
And **I** dug again the wells of water that Gn 26:18
I said to them, "Why have you come to Gn 26:27
And **I** sent them on their way, and they Gn 26:31
they made life bitter for **I** and Rebekah. Gn 26:35
When **I** was old and his eyes were dim Gn 27:1
was listening when **I** spoke to his Gn 27:5
But **I** said to his son, "How is it that you Gn 27:20
Then **I** said to Jacob, "Please come Gn 27:21
So Jacob went near to **I** his father, who Gn 27:22
Then his father **I** said to him, "Come Gn 27:26
And **I** smelled the smell of his Gn 27:27
As soon as **I** had finished blessing Gn 27:30
out from the presence of **I** his father, Gn 27:30
His father **I** said to him, "Who are Gn 27:32
Then **I** trembled very violently and Gn 27:33
I answered and said to Esau, "Behold, I Gn 27:37
Then **I** his father answered and said to Gn 27:39
Then Rebekah said to **I**, "I loathe my Gn 27:46
Then **I** called Jacob and blessed him Gn 28:1
Thus **I** sent Jacob away. And he went to Gn 28:5
Now Esau saw that **I** had blessed Jacob Gn 28:6
women did not please **I** his father, Gn 28:8
Abraham your father and the God of **I**. Gn 28:13
go to the land of Canaan to his father **I**. Gn 31:18
the God of Abraham and the Fear of **I**, Gn 31:42
Jacob swore by the Fear of his father **I**, Gn 31:53
father Abraham and God of my father **I**, Gn 32:9
I gave to Abraham and **I** I will give to Gn 35:12
Jacob came to his father **I** at Mamre, Gn 35:27
where Abraham and **I** had sojourned. Gn 35:27
Now the days of **I** were 180 years. Gn 35:28
And **I** breathed his last, and he died Gn 35:29
sacrifices to the God of his father **I**. Gn 46:1
my fathers Abraham and **I** walked, Gn 48:15
name of my fathers Abraham and **I**; Gn 48:16
There they buried **I** and Rebekah his Gn 49:31
land that he swore to Abraham, to **I**, Gn 50:24
his covenant with Abraham, with **I**, Ex 2:24
father, the God of Abraham, the God of **I**, Ex 3:6
the God of Abraham, the God of **I**, Ex 3:15
your fathers, the God of Abraham, of **I**, Ex 3:16
fathers, the God of Abraham, the God of **I**, Ex 4:5
I appeared to Abraham, to **I**, and to Jacob, Ex 6:3
land that I swore to give to Abraham, to **I**, Ex 6:8
Remember Abraham, **I**, and Israel, Ex 32:13
which I swore to Abraham, **I**, and Jacob, Ex 33:1
my covenant with **I** and my covenant Lv 26:42
that I swore to give to Abraham, to **I**, Nm 32:11
swore to your fathers, to Abraham, to **I**, Dt 1:8
swore to your fathers, to Abraham, to **I**, Dt 6:10
swore to your fathers, to Abraham, to **I**, Dt 9:5
your servants, Abraham, **I**, and Jacob. Dt 9:27
swore to your fathers, to Abraham, to **I**, Dt 29:13
swore to your fathers, to Abraham, to **I**, Dt 30:20
land of which I swore to Abraham, to **I**, Dt 34:4
made his offspring many. I gave him **I**. Jos 24:3
And to **I** I gave Jacob and Esau. And I Jos 24:4
LORD, God of Abraham, **I**, and Israel, 1 Kgs 18:36
with Abraham, **I**, and Jacob, 2 Kgs 13:23
The sons of Abraham: **I** and Ishmael. 1 Chr 1:28
Abraham fathered **I**. The sons of 1 Chr 1:34
Isaac. The sons of **I**: Esau and Israel. 1 Chr 1:34
Abraham, his sworn promise to **I**, 1 Chr 16:16
the God of Abraham, **I**, and Israel, 1 Chr 29:18
the God of Abraham, **I**, and Israel, 2 Chr 30:6
with Abraham, his sworn promise to **I**, Ps 105:9
the offspring of Abraham, **I**, and Jacob. Jer 33:26
the high places of **I** shall be made Am 7:9
do not preach against the house of **I**.' Am 7:16
Abraham was the father of **I**, and Isaac Mt 1:2
father of Isaac, and **I** the father of Jacob, Mt 1:2
I, and Jacob in the kingdom of heaven, Mt 8:11
the God of Abraham, and the God of **I**, Mt 22:32
the God of Abraham, and the God of **I**, Mk 12:26
the son of Jacob, the son of **I**, the son of Lk 3:34
you see Abraham and **I** and Jacob and Lk 13:28
and the God of **I** and the God of Lk 20:37
The God of Abraham, the God of **I**, and Acts 3:13
so Abraham became the father of **I**, Acts 7:8
day, and **I** became the father of Jacob, Acts 7:8
of Abraham and of **I** and of Jacob.' Acts 7:32
but "Through **I** shall your offspring be Rom 9:7
children by one man, our forefather **I**, Rom 9:10
Now you, brothers, like **I**, are children Gal 4:28
land, living in tents with **I** and Jacob, Heb 11:9
when he was tested, offered up **I**, Heb 11:17
"Through **I** shall your offspring be Heb 11:18
By faith **I** invoked future blessings on Heb 11:20
he offered up his son **I** on the altar? Jas 2:21

ISAAC'S (4)
But when **I** servants dug in the valley Gn 26:19
of Gerar quarreled with **I** herdsmen, Gn 26:20
there. And there **I** servants dug a well. Gn 26:25
That same day **I** servants came and Gn 26:32

ISAIAH (54)
to the prophet **I** the son of Amoz. 2 Kgs 19:2
servants of King Hezekiah came to **I**, 2 Kgs 19:5
I said to them, "Say to your master, 2 Kgs 19:6
Then **I** the son of Amoz sent to 2 Kgs 19:20
And **I** the prophet the son of Amoz 2 Kgs 20:1
And before **I** had gone out of the 2 Kgs 20:4
And **I** said, "Bring a cake of figs. And 2 Kgs 20:7
And Hezekiah said to **I**, "What shall 2 Kgs 20:8
And **I** said, "This shall be the sign to 2 Kgs 20:9
And **I** the prophet called to the LORD, 2 Kgs 20:11
Then **I** the prophet came to King 2 Kgs 20:14
Then **I** said to Hezekiah, "Hear the 2 Kgs 20:16
Then said Hezekiah to **I**, "The word 2 Kgs 20:19
I the prophet the son of Amoz wrote. 2 Chr 26:22
Hezekiah the king and **I** the prophet, 2 Chr 32:20
in the vision of **I** the prophet the son 2 Chr 32:32
The vision of **I** the son of Amoz, which he Is 1:1
The word that **I** the son of Amoz saw Is 2:1
And the LORD said to **I**, "Go out to meet Is 7:3
concerning Babylon which **I** the son of Is 13:1
time the LORD spoke by **I** the son of Amoz, Is 20:2
"As my servant **I** has walked naked and Is 20:3
to the prophet **I** the son of Amoz. Is 37:2
the servants of King Hezekiah came to **I**, Is 37:5
I said to them, "Say to your master, 'Thus Is 37:6
Then **I** the son of Amoz sent to Is 37:21
And **I** the prophet the son of Amoz came Is 38:1
Then the word of the LORD came to **I**: Is 38:4
Now **I** had said, "Let them take a cake of Is 38:21
Then **I** the prophet came to King Is 39:3
Then **I** said to Hezekiah, "Hear the word Is 39:5
Then said Hezekiah to **I**, "The word of the Is 39:8
spoken of by the prophet **I** when he said, Mt 3:3
by the prophet **I** might be fulfilled: Mt 4:14
fulfill what was spoken by the prophet **I**: Mt 8:17
what was spoken by the prophet **I**: Mt 12:17
case the prophecy of **I** is fulfilled that Mt 13:14
Well did **I** prophesy of you, when he Mt 15:7
As it is written in **I** the prophet, "Behold, I Mk 1:2
"Well did **I** prophesy of you hypocrites, Mk 7:6
in the book of the words of **I** the prophet, Lk 3:4
scroll of the prophet **I** was given to him. Lk 4:17
way of the Lord,' as the prophet **I** said." Jn 1:23
by the prophet **I** might be fulfilled: Jn 12:38
they could not believe. For again **I** said, Jn 12:39
I said these things because he saw his Jn 12:41
and he was reading the prophet **I**. Acts 8:28
heard him reading **I** the prophet and Acts 8:30
to your fathers through **I** the prophet: Acts 28:25
And **I** cries out concerning Israel: Rom 9:27
And as **I** predicted, "If the Lord of hosts Rom 9:29
not all obeyed the gospel. For **I** says, Rom 10:16
Then **I** is so bold as to say, "I have Rom 10:20
And again **I** says, "The root of Jesse Rom 15:12

ISCAH (1)
of Haran the father of Milcah and **I**. Gn 11:29

ISCARIOT (11)
Simon the Cananaean, and Judas **I**, who Mt 10:4
of the twelve, whose name was Judas **I**, Mt 26:14
and Judas **I**, who betrayed him. Mk 3:19
Then Judas **I**, who was one of the Mk 14:10
and Judas the son of James, and Judas **I**, Lk 6:16
Then Satan entered into Judas called **I**, Lk 22:3
He spoke of Judas the son of Simon **I**, for Jn 6:71
But Judas **I**, one of his disciples (he who Jn 12:4
already put it into the heart of Judas **I**, Jn 13:2
he gave it to Judas, the son of Simon **I**. Jn 13:26
Judas (not **I**) said to him, "Lord, how is Jn 14:22

ISH-BOSHETH (14)
took **I** the son of Saul and brought him 2 Sm 2:8
I, Saul's son, was forty years old when 2 Sm 2:10
and the servants of **I** the son of Saul, 2 Sm 2:12
twelve for Benjamin and **I** the son of 2 Sm 2:15
And **I** said to Abner, "Why have you 2 Sm 3:7
very angry over the words of **I** and said, 2 Sm 3:8
And **I** could not answer Abner 2 Sm 3:11
Then David sent messengers to **I**, 2 Sm 3:14
And **I** sent and took her from her 2 Sm 3:15
When **I**, Saul's son, heard that Abner 2 Sm 4:1
came to the house of **I** as he was taking 2 Sm 4:5
brought the head of **I** to David at 2 Sm 4:8
said to the king, "Here is the head of **I**, 2 Sm 4:8
they took the head of **I** and buried it in 2 Sm 4:12

ISHBAH (1)
and bore Miriam, Shammai, and **I**, 1 Chr 4:17

ISHBAK (2)
Jokshan, Medan, Midian, **I**, and Shuah. Gn 25:2
Medan, Midian, **I**, and Shuah. 1 Chr 1:32

ISHBI-BENOB (1)
And **I**, one of the descendants of the 2 Sm 21:16

ISHHOD (1)
And his sister Hammolecheth bore **I**, 1 Chr 7:18

ISHI (5)
The son of Appaim: **I**. The son of Ishi: 1 Chr 2:31
Appaim: Ishi. The son of **I**: Sheshan. 1 Chr 2:31
The sons of **I**: Zoheth and 1 Chr 4:20
Rephaiah, and Uzziel, the sons of **I**. 1 Chr 4:42
Epher, **I**, Eliel, Azriel, Jeremiah, 1 Chr 5:24

ISHMA (1)
the sons of Etam: Jezreel, **I**, and Idbash; 1 Chr 4:3

ISHMAEL (47)
You shall call his name **I**, because the Gn 16:11
name of his son, whom Hagar bore, **I**. Gn 16:15
years old when Hagar bore **I** to Abram. Gn 16:16
God, "Oh that **I** might live before you!" Gn 17:18
As for **I**, I have heard you; behold, I Gn 17:20
Then Abraham took **I** his son and all Gn 17:23
And **I** his son was thirteen years old Gn 17:25
and his son **I** were circumcised. Gn 17:26
Isaac and **I** his sons buried him in the Gn 25:9
These are the generations of **I**, Gn 25:12
These are the names of the sons of **I**, Gn 25:13
their birth: Nebaioth, the firstborn of **I**; Gn 25:13
are the sons of **I** and these are their Gn 25:16
(These are the years of the life of **I**: 137 Gn 25:17
Esau went to **I** and took as his wife, Gn 28:9
he had, Mahalath the daughter of **I**, Gn 28:9
namely, **I** the son of Nethaniah, 2 Kgs 25:23
month, **I** the son of Nethaniah, 2 Kgs 25:25
The sons of Abraham: Isaac and **I**. 1 Chr 1:28
the firstborn of **I**, Nebaioth, and 1 Chr 1:29
and Kedemah. These are the sons of **I**. 1 Chr 1:31
Azrikam, Bocheru, **I**, Sheariah, 1 Chr 8:38
Azrikam, Bocheru, **I**, Sheariah, 1 Chr 9:44
and Zebadiah the son of **I**, the 2 Chr 19:11
of Jeroham, **I** the son of Jehohanan, 2 Chr 23:1
Elioenai, Maaseiah, **I**, Nethanel, Ezr 10:22
Gedaliah at Mizpah—**I** the son of Jer 40:8
the Ammonites has sent **I** the son of Jer 40:14
go and strike down **I** the son of Jer 40:15
thing, for you are speaking falsely of **I**." Jer 40:16
seventh month, **I** the son of Nethaniah, Jer 41:1
I the son of Nethaniah and the ten men Jer 41:2
I also struck down all the Judeans who Jer 41:3
And **I** the son of Nethaniah came out Jer 41:6
I the son of Nethaniah and the men with Jer 41:7
were ten men among them who said to **I**, Jer 41:8
the cistern into which **I** had thrown all Jer 41:9
I the son of Nethaniah filled it with the Jer 41:9

Then **I** took captive all the rest of the Jer 41:10
I the son of Nethaniah took them Jer 41:10
all the evil that **I** the son of Nethaniah Jer 41:11
went to fight against **I** the son of Jer 41:12
people who were with **I** saw Johanan the Jer 41:13
all the people whom **I** had carried away Jer 41:14
But **I** the son of Nethaniah escaped Jer 41:15
he had recovered from **I** the son of Jer 41:16
because **I** the son of Nethaniah had Jer 41:18

ISHMAEL'S (1)
and Basemath, **I** daughter, the sister of Gn 36:3

ISHMAELITE (3)
the son of a man named Ithra the **I**, 2 Sm 17:25
the father of Amasa was Jether the **I**. 1 Chr 2:17
Over the camels was Obil the **I**; and 1 Chr 27:30

ISHMAELITES (6)
a caravan of **I** coming from Gilead, Gn 37:25
Come, let us sell him to the **I**, and let Gn 37:27
sold him to the **I** for twenty shekels of Gn 37:28
him from the **I** who had brought Gn 39:1
golden earrings, because they were **I**.) Jgs 8:24
the tents of Edom and the **I**, Moab and Ps 83:6

ISHMAIAH (2)
I of Gibeon, a mighty man among 1 Chr 12:4
for Zebulun, **I** the son of Obadiah; 1 Chr 27:19

ISHMERAI (1)
I, Izliah, and Jobab were the sons of 1 Chr 8:18

ISHPAH (1)
I, and Joha were sons of Beriah. 1 Chr 8:16

ISHPAN (1)
I, Eber, Eliel, 1 Chr 8:22

ISHVAH (2)
Imnah, **I**, Ishvi, Beriah, with Serah Gn 46:17
Imnah, **I**, Ishvi, Beriah, and their 1 Chr 7:30

ISHVI (4)
Imnah, Ishvah, **I**, Beriah, with Serah Gn 46:17
of Imnah, the clan of the Imnites; of **I**, Nm 26:44
were Jonathan, **I**, and Malchi-shua. 1 Sm 14:49
Imnah, Ishvah, **I**, Beriah, and their 1 Chr 7:30

ISHVITES (1)
the Imnites; of Ishvi, the clan of the **I**; Nm 26:44

ISLAND (10)
gone through the whole **i** as far as Acts 13:6
the lee of a small **i** called Cauda, Acts 27:16
But we must run aground on some **i**." Acts 27:26
learned that the **i** was called Malta. Acts 28:1
belonging to the chief man of the **i**, Acts 28:7
the people on the **i** who had diseases Acts 28:9
in a ship that had wintered in the **i**, Acts 28:11
was on the **i** called Patmos on account of Rv 1:9
every mountain and **i** was removed from Rv 6:14
And every **i** fled away, and no Rv 16:20

ISLANDS (1)
I will turn the rivers into **i**, and dry up Is 42:15

ISMACHIAH (1)
Jerimoth, Jozabad, Eliel, **I**, Mahath, 2 Chr 31:13

ISOLATES (1)
Whoever **i** himself seeks his own desire; Prv 18:1

ISRAEL (2566)
shall no longer be called Jacob, but **I**, Gn 32:28
this day the people of **I** do not eat the Gn 32:32
an outrageous thing in **I** by lying with Gn 34:7
but **I** shall be your name." So he called Gn 35:10
your name." So he called his name **I**. Gn 35:10
I journeyed on and pitched his tent Gn 35:21
While **I** lived in that land, Reuben Gn 35:22
father's concubine. And **I** heard of it. Gn 35:22
Now **I** loved Joseph more than any other Gn 37:3
And **I** said to Joseph, "Are not your Gn 37:13
Thus the sons of **I** came to buy among Gn 42:5
I said, "Why did you treat me so badly Gn 43:6
And Judah said to **I** his father, "Send the Gn 43:8
Then their father **I** said to them, "If it Gn 43:11
The sons of **I** did so: and Joseph gave Gn 45:21
And **I** said, "It is enough; Joseph my Gn 45:28
So **I** took his journey with all that he Gn 46:1
And God spoke to **I** in visions of the Gn 46:2
The sons of **I** carried Jacob their father, Gn 46:5
are the names of the descendants of **I**, Gn 46:8
went up to meet **I** his father in Goshen. Gn 46:29
I said to Joseph, "Now let me die, since I Gn 46:30
Thus **I** settled in the land of Egypt, in Gn 47:27
the time drew near that **I** must die, Gn 47:29
Then **I** bowed himself upon the head of Gn 47:31
to you." Then **I** summoned his strength Gn 48:2
When **I** saw Joseph's sons, he said, Gn 48:8
Now the eyes of **I** were dim with age, so Gn 48:10
And **I** said to Joseph, "I never expected Gn 48:11
And **I** stretched out his right hand and Gn 48:14
"By you **I** will pronounce blessings, Gn 48:20
Then **I** said to Joseph, "Behold, I am Gn 48:21
O sons of Jacob, listen to **I** your father. Gn 49:2
them in Jacob and scatter them in **I**. Gn 49:7
judge his people as one of the tribes of **I**. Gn 49:16
there is the Shepherd, the Stone of **I**), Gn 49:24
All these are the twelve tribes of **I**. This Gn 49:28
father. So the physicians embalmed **I**. Gn 50:2
Then Joseph made the sons of **I** swear, Gn 50:25
names of the sons of **I** who came to Egypt Ex 1:1
But the people of **I** were fruitful and Ex 1:7
the people of **I** are too many and too Ex 1:9
Egyptians were in dread of the people of **I**. Ex 1:12
made the people of **I** work as slaves Ex 1:13
and the people of **I** groaned because of Ex 2:23
God saw the people of **I**—and God knew. Ex 2:25
the cry of the people of **I** has come to me, Ex 3:9
may bring my people, the children of **I**, Ex 3:10
bring the children of **I** out of Egypt?" Ex 3:11
I come to the people of **I** and say to them, Ex 3:13
And he said, "Say this to the people of **I**, Ex 3:14
said to Moses, "Say this to the people of **I**, Ex 3:15
gather the elders of **I** together and say to Ex 3:16
you and the elders of **I** shall go to the Ex 3:18
says the LORD, **I** is my firstborn son, Ex 4:22
together all the elders of the people of **I**. Ex 4:29
visited the people of **I** and that he had Ex 4:31
"Thus says the LORD, the God of **I**, Ex 5:1
that I should obey his voice and let **I** go? Ex 5:2
the LORD, and moreover, I will not let **I** go." Ex 5:2
And the foremen of the people of **I**, whom Ex 5:14
of the people of **I** came and cried to Ex 5:15
of the people of **I** saw that they were Ex 5:19
of the people of **I** whom the Egyptians Ex 6:5
Say therefore to the people of **I**, 'I am the Ex 6:6
Moses spoke thus to the people of **I**, but Ex 6:9
to let the people of **I** go out of his land." Ex 6:11
the people of **I** have not listened to me. Ex 6:12
about the people of **I** and about Pharaoh Ex 6:13
to bring the people of **I** out of the land of Ex 6:13
the sons of Reuben, the firstborn of **I**: Ex 6:14
out the people of **I** from the land of Ex 6:26
bringing out the people of **I** from Egypt, Ex 6:27
to let the people of **I** go out of his land. Ex 7:2
my hosts, my people the children of **I**, Ex 7:4
out the people of **I** from among them." Ex 7:5
the livestock of **I** and the livestock Ex 9:4
that belongs to the people of **I** shall die.""" Ex 9:4
one of the livestock of the people of **I** died. Ex 9:6
not one of the livestock of **I** was dead. Ex 9:7
of Goshen, where the people of **I** were, Ex 9:26
and he did not let the people of **I** go, Ex 9:35
and he did not let the people of **I** go. Ex 10:20
all the people of **I** had light where they Ex 10:23
shall growl against any of the people of **I**, Ex 11:7
a distinction between Egypt and **I**. Ex 11:7
not let the people of **I** go out of his land. Ex 11:10
all the congregation of **I** that on the Ex 12:3
of the congregation of **I** shall kill their Ex 12:6
day, that person shall be cut off from **I**. Ex 12:15
be cut off from the congregation of **I**, Ex 12:19
all the elders of **I** and said to them, Ex 12:21
the houses of the people of **I** in Egypt, Ex 12:27
Then the people of **I** went and did so; as Ex 12:28
my people, both you and the people of **I**; Ex 12:31
The people of **I** had also done as Moses Ex 12:35
the people of **I** journeyed from Rameses Ex 12:37
that the people of **I** lived in Egypt was Ex 12:40
the people of **I** throughout their Ex 12:42
All the congregation of **I** shall keep it. Ex 12:47
All the people of **I** did just as the LORD Ex 12:50
brought the people of **I** out of the land Ex 12:51
to open the womb among the people of **I**, Ex 13:2
And the people of **I** went up out of the Ex 13:18
had made the sons of **I** solemnly swear, Ex 13:19
"Tell the people of **I** to turn back and Ex 14:2
For Pharaoh will say of the people of **I**, Ex 14:3
that we have let **I** go from serving us?" Ex 14:5
pursued the people of **I** while the people Ex 14:8
while the people of **I** were going out Ex 14:8
near, the people of **I** lifted up their eyes, Ex 14:10
And the people of **I** cried out to the LORD. Ex 14:10
to me? Tell the people of **I** to go forward. Ex 14:15
that the people of **I** may go through the Ex 14:16
before the host of **I** moved and went Ex 14:19
the host of Egypt and the host of **I**. Ex 14:20
And the people of **I** went into the midst Ex 14:22
said, "Let us flee from before **I**, Ex 14:25
But the people of **I** walked on dry Ex 14:29
Thus the LORD saved **I** that day from the Ex 14:30
and **I** saw the Egyptians dead on the Ex 14:30
I saw the great power that the LORD used Ex 14:31
and the people of **I** sang this song to Ex 15:1
but the people of **I** walked on dry Ex 15:19
Then Moses made **I** set out from the Ex 15:22
of the people of **I** came to the wilderness Ex 16:1
the people of **I** grumbled against Moses Ex 16:2
and the people of **I** said to them, "Would Ex 16:3
and Aaron said to all the people of **I**, Ex 16:6
the whole congregation of the people of **I**, Ex 16:9
whole congregation of the people of **I**, Ex 16:10
heard the grumbling of the people of **I**. Ex 16:12
When the people of **I** saw it, they said to Ex 16:15
And the people of **I** did so. They Ex 16:17
Now the house of **I** called its name Ex 16:31
The people of **I** ate the manna forty Ex 16:35
of the people of **I** moved on from the Ex 17:1
taking with you some of the elders of **I**, Ex 17:5
did so, in the sight of the elders of **I**. Ex 17:6
of the quarreling of the people of **I**, Ex 17:7
came and fought with **I** at Rephidim. Ex 17:8
Moses held up his hand, **I** prevailed, Ex 17:11
had done for Moses and for **I** his people, Ex 18:1
how the LORD had brought **I** out of Egypt. Ex 18:1
all the good that the LORD had done to **I**, Ex 18:9
with all the elders of **I** to eat bread with Ex 18:12
men out of all **I** and made them heads Ex 18:25
after the people of **I** had gone out of Ex 19:1
There **I** encamped before the mountain, Ex 19:2
house of Jacob, and tell the people of **I**: Ex 19:3
that you shall speak to the people of **I**." Ex 19:6
"Thus you shall say to the people of **I**: Ex 20:22
and Abihu, and seventy of the elders of **I**, Ex 24:1
according to the twelve tribes of **I**. Ex 24:4
And he sent young men of the people of **I**, Ex 24:5
and seventy of the elders of **I** went up, Ex 24:9
and they saw the God of **I**. There was Ex 24:10
hand on the chief men of the people of **I**; Ex 24:11
mountain in the sight of the people of **I**. Ex 24:17
"Speak to the people of **I**, that they take Ex 25:2
in commandment for the people of **I**. Ex 25:22
the people of **I** that they bring Ex 27:20
their generations by the people of **I**. Ex 27:21
with him, from among the people of **I**, Ex 28:1
on them the names of the sons of **I**, Ex 28:9
stones with the names of the sons of **I**. Ex 28:11
of remembrance for the sons of **I**. Ex 28:12
according to the names of the sons of **I**. Ex 28:21
of the sons of **I** in the breastpiece of Ex 28:29
of the people of **I** on his heart before Ex 28:30
that the people of **I** consecrate as their Ex 28:38
as a perpetual due from the people of **I**, Ex 29:28
from the people of **I** from their peace Ex 29:28
There I will meet with the people of **I**, Ex 29:43
among the people of **I** and will be their Ex 29:45
you take the census of the people of **I**, Ex 30:12
from the people of **I** and shall give it Ex 30:16
the people of **I** to remembrance before Ex 30:16
And you shall say to the people of **I**, Ex 30:31
are to speak to the people of **I** and say, Ex 31:13
Therefore the people of **I** shall keep the Ex 31:16
me and the people of **I** that in six days Ex 31:17
And they said, "These are your gods, O **I**, Ex 32:4
to it and said, 'These are your gods, O **I**, Ex 32:8
Remember Abraham, Isaac, and **I**, Ex 32:13
water and made the people of **I** drink it. Ex 32:20
to them, "Thus says the LORD God of **I**, Ex 32:27
had said to Moses, "Say to the people of **I**, Ex 33:5
the people of **I** stripped themselves of Ex 33:6
before the LORD God, the God of **I**. Ex 34:23
made a covenant with you and with **I**." Ex 34:27
Aaron and all the people of **I** saw Moses, Ex 34:30
Afterward all the people of **I** came near, Ex 34:32
told the people of **I** what he was Ex 34:34
the people of **I** would see the face of Ex 34:35
of the people of **I** and said to them, Ex 35:1
to all the congregation of the people of **I**, Ex 35:4
of the people of **I** departed from the Ex 35:20
All the men and women, the people of **I**, Ex 35:29
Then Moses said to the people of **I**, "See, Ex 35:30
that the people of **I** had brought for Ex 36:3
according to the names of the sons of **I**. Ex 39:6
stones of remembrance for the sons of **I**. Ex 39:7
according to the names of the sons of **I**. Ex 39:14
and the people of **I** did according to all Ex 39:32
so the people of **I** had done all the work. Ex 39:42
tabernacle, the people of **I** would set out. Ex 40:36
all the house of **I** throughout all their Ex 40:38
"Speak to the people of **I** and say to them, Lv 1:2
"Speak to the people of **I**, saying, If anyone Lv 4:2
congregation of **I** sins unintentionally Lv 4:13
"Speak to the people of **I**, saying, You Lv 7:23
"Speak to the people of **I**, saying, Lv 7:29
I have taken from the people of **I**, Lv 7:34
as a perpetual due from the people of **I**. Lv 7:34
this to be given them by the people of **I**, Lv 7:36
commanded the people of **I** to bring their Lv 7:38
Aaron and his sons and the elders of **I**, Lv 9:1
And say to the people of **I**, 'Take a male Lv 9:3
let your brothers, the whole house of **I**, Lv 10:6

teach the people of **I** all the statutes that Lv 10:11
of the peace offerings of the people of **I**. Lv 10:14
"Speak to the people of **I**, saying, These Lv 11:2
"Speak to the people of **I**, saying, 'If a Lv 12:2
"Speak to the people of **I** and say to them, Lv 15:2
keep the people of **I** separate from their Lv 15:31
of the people of **I** two male goats for Lv 16:5
of the people of **I** and because of their Lv 16:16
his house and for all the assembly of **I**. Lv 16:17
the uncleannesses of the people of **I**. Lv 16:19
it all the iniquities of the people of **I**, Lv 16:21
made for the people of **I** once in the year Lv 16:34
and to all the people of **I** and say to them, Lv 17:2
any one of the house of **I** kills an ox or a Lv 17:3
that the people of **I** may bring their Lv 17:5
say to them, Any one of the house of **I**, Lv 17:8
one of the house of **I** or of the strangers Lv 17:10
Therefore I have said to the people of **I**, Lv 17:12
"Any one also of the people of **I**, or of the Lv 17:13
Therefore I have said to the people of **I**, Lv 17:14
"Speak to the people of **I** and say to them, Lv 18:2
of the people of **I** and say to them, Lv 19:2
"Say to the people of **I**, Any one of the Lv 20:2
one of the people of **I** or of the strangers Lv 20:2
who sojourn in **I** who gives any Lv 20:2
and to his sons and to all the people of **I**. Lv 21:24
from the holy things of the people of **I**, Lv 22:2
that the people of **I** dedicate to the LORD, Lv 22:3
the holy things of the people of **I**, Lv 22:15
and all the people of **I** and say to them, Lv 22:18
of the house of **I** or of the sojourners Lv 22:18
of the sojourners in **I** presents a burnt Lv 22:18
be sanctified among the people of **I**. Lv 22:32
"Speak to the people of **I** and say to them, Lv 23:2
to the people of **I** and say to them, Lv 23:10
"Speak to the people of **I**, saying, In the Lv 23:24
"Speak to the people of **I**, saying, On the Lv 23:34
made the people of **I** dwell in booths Lv 23:43
to the people of **I** the appointed feasts of Lv 23:44
"Command the people of **I** to bring you Lv 24:2
from the people of **I** as a covenant Lv 24:8
went out among the people of **I**. Lv 24:10
son and a man of **I** fought in the camp, Lv 24:10
And speak to the people of **I**, saying, Lv 24:15
So Moses spoke to the people of **I**, and Lv 24:23
Thus the people of **I** did as the LORD Lv 24:23
"Speak to the people of **I** and say to them, Lv 25:2
their possession among the people of **I**. Lv 25:33
brothers the people of **I** you shall not Lv 25:46
is to me that the people of **I** are servants. Lv 25:55
and the people of **I** through Moses on Lv 26:46
"Speak to the people of **I** and say to them, Lv 27:2
for the people of **I** on Mount Sinai. Lv 27:34
of all the congregation of the people of **I**, Nm 1:2
all in **I** who are able to go to war, Nm 1:3
tribes, the heads of the clans of **I**. Nm 1:16
listed with the help of the chiefs of **I**, Nm 1:44
So all those listed of the people of **I**, by Nm 1:45
every man able to go to war in **I**— Nm 1:45
a census of them among the people of **I**. Nm 1:49
The people of **I** shall pitch their tents Nm 1:52
on the congregation of the people of **I**. Nm 1:53
Thus did the people of **I**; they did Nm 1:54
"The people of **I** shall camp each by his Nm 2:2
are the people of **I** as listed by their Nm 2:32
were not listed among the people of **I**, Nm 2:33
Thus did the people of **I**. According to Nm 2:34
over the people of **I** as they minister at Nm 3:8
given to him from among the people of **I**. Nm 3:9
among the people of **I** instead of every Nm 3:12
opens the womb among the people of **I**. Nm 3:12
for my own all the firstborn in **I**, Nm 3:13
itself, to protect the people of **I**. Nm 3:38
all the firstborn males of the people of **I**, Nm 3:40
all the firstborn among the people of **I**, Nm 3:41
among the cattle of the people of **I**." Nm 3:41
all the firstborn among the people of **I**, Nm 3:42
all the firstborn among the people of **I**, Nm 3:45
273 of the firstborn of the people of **I**, Nm 3:46
of the people of **I** he took the money, Nm 3:50
and Aaron and the chiefs of **I** listed, Nm 4:46
"Command the people of **I** that they put Nm 5:2
And the people of **I** did so, and put them Nm 5:4
LORD said to Moses, so the people of **I** did. Nm 5:4
"Speak to the people of **I**, When a man or Nm 5:6
all the holy donations of the people of **I**, Nm 5:9
"Speak to the people of **I**, If any man's Nm 5:12
"Speak to the people of **I** and say to them, Nm 6:2
Thus you shall bless the people of **I**: Nm 6:23
they put my name upon the people of **I**, Nm 6:27
the chiefs of **I**, heads of their fathers' Nm 7:2
it was anointed, from the chiefs of **I**: Nm 7:84
among the people of **I** and cleanse them. Nm 8:6
the whole congregation of the people of **I**. Nm 8:9
the people of **I** shall lay their hands on Nm 8:10
as a wave offering from the people of **I**, Nm 8:11
the Levites from among the people of **I**, Nm 8:14
given to me from among the people of **I**. Nm 8:16
the firstborn of all the people of **I**, Nm 8:16
among the people of **I** are mine, Nm 8:17
all the firstborn among the people of **I**. Nm 8:18
his sons from among the people of **I**, Nm 8:19
service for the people of **I** at the tent of Nm 8:19
to make atonement for the people of **I**, Nm 8:19
among the people of **I** when the people Nm 8:19
when the people of **I** come near the Nm 8:19
of the people of **I** to the Levites. Nm 8:20
the Levites, the people of **I** did to them. Nm 8:20
"Let the people of **I** keep the Passover at Nm 9:2
told the people of **I** that they should keep Nm 9:4
Moses, so the people of **I** did. Nm 9:5
appointed time among the people of **I**?" Nm 9:7
"Speak to the people of **I**, saying, If any Nm 9:10
the tent, after that the people of **I** set out, Nm 9:17
down, there the people of **I** camped. Nm 9:17
of the LORD the people of **I** set out, Nm 9:18
the people of **I** kept the charge of the Nm 9:19
the people of **I** remained in camp and Nm 9:22
the chiefs, the heads of the tribes of **I**, Nm 10:4
and the people of **I** set out by stages Nm 10:12
of the people of **I** by their companies, Nm 10:28
for the LORD has promised good to **I**." Nm 10:29
to the ten thousand thousands of **I**." Nm 10:36
And the people of **I** also wept again and Nm 11:4
for me seventy men of the elders of **I**, Nm 11:16
and the elders of **I** returned to the Nm 11:30
which I am giving to the people of **I**. Nm 13:2
men who were heads of the people of **I**. Nm 13:3
that the people of **I** cut down from Nm 13:24
of the people of **I** in the wilderness of Nm 13:26
to the people of **I** a bad report of Nm 13:32
the people of **I** grumbled against Moses Nm 14:2
of the congregation of the people of **I**. Nm 14:5
all the congregation of the people of **I**, Nm 14:7
tent of meeting to all the people of **I**. Nm 14:10
the grumblings of the people of **I**, Nm 14:27
told these words to all the people of **I**, Nm 14:39
to the people of **I** and say to them, Nm 15:2
to the people of **I** and say to them, Nm 15:18
all the congregation of the people of **I**, Nm 15:25
of the people of **I** shall be forgiven, Nm 15:26
among the people of **I** and for the Nm 15:29
While the people of **I** were in the Nm 15:32
"Speak to the people of **I**, and tell them Nm 15:38
Moses, with a number of the people of **I**, Nm 16:2
that the God of **I** has separated you Nm 16:9
you from the congregation of **I**, Nm 16:9
and the elders of **I** followed him. Nm 16:25
And all **I** who were around them fled Nm 16:34
they shall be a sign to the people of **I**." Nm 16:38
to be a reminder to the people of **I**, so Nm 16:40
the people of **I** grumbled against Nm 16:41
"Speak to the people of **I**, and get from Nm 17:2
me the grumblings of the people of **I**, Nm 17:5
Moses spoke to the people of **I**. And all Nm 17:6
before the LORD to all the people of **I**. Nm 17:9
And the people of **I** said to Moses, Nm 17:12
never again be wrath on the people of **I**. Nm 18:5
the Levites from among the people of **I**. Nm 18:6
consecrated things of the people of **I**. Nm 18:8
all the wave offerings of the people of **I**. Nm 18:11
devoted thing in **I** shall be yours. Nm 18:14
that the people of **I** present to the LORD Nm 18:19
inheritance among the people of **I**. Nm 18:20
every tithe in **I** for an inheritance, Nm 18:21
that the people of **I** do not come near Nm 18:22
among the people of **I** they shall have Nm 18:23
For the tithe of the people of **I**, which Nm 18:24
no inheritance among the people of **I**." Nm 18:24
from the people of **I** the tithe that I Nm 18:26
you receive from the people of **I**. Nm 18:28
the holy things of the people of **I**, Nm 18:32
Tell the people of **I** to bring you a red Nm 19:2
for the congregation of the people of **I**; Nm 19:9
a perpetual statute for the people of **I**, Nm 19:10
that person shall be cut off from **I**; Nm 19:13
And the people of **I**, the whole Nm 20:1
as holy in the eyes of the people of **I**, Nm 20:12
the people of **I** quarreled with the Nm 20:13
of Edom: "Thus says your brother **I**: Nm 20:14
And the people of **I** said to him, "We Nm 20:19
refused to give **I** passage through his Nm 20:21
territory, so **I** turned away from him. Nm 20:21
from Kadesh, and the people of **I**, Nm 20:22
that I have given to the people of **I**, Nm 20:24
all the house of **I** wept for Aaron thirty Nm 20:29
heard that **I** was coming by the way of Nm 21:1
way of Atharim, he fought against **I**, Nm 21:1
And **I** vowed a vow to the LORD and said, Nm 21:2
obeyed the voice of **I** and gave over the Nm 21:3
people, so that many people of **I** died. Nm 21:6
And the people of **I** set out and camped Nm 21:10
Then **I** sang this song: "Spring up, O Nm 21:17
Then **I** sent messengers to Sihon king Nm 21:21
would not allow **I** to pass through Nm 21:23
went out against **I** to the wilderness Nm 21:23
came to Jahaz and fought against **I**. Nm 21:23
And **I** defeated him with the edge of Nm 21:24
And **I** took all these cities, and Israel Nm 21:25
and **I** settled in all the cities of the Nm 21:25
Thus **I** lived in the land of the Nm 21:31
Then the people of **I** set out and camped Nm 22:1
of Zippor saw all that **I** had done to the Nm 22:2
overcome with fear of the people of **I**. Nm 22:3
Jacob for me, and come, denounce **I**!' Nm 23:7
Jacob or number the fourth part of **I**? Nm 23:10
in Jacob, nor has he seen trouble in **I**. Nm 23:21
against Jacob, no divination against **I**; Nm 23:23
now it shall be said of Jacob and **I**, Nm 23:23
saw that it pleased the LORD to bless **I**, Nm 24:1
his eyes and saw **I** camping tribe by Nm 24:2
tents, O Jacob, your encampments, O **I**! Nm 24:5
Jacob, and a scepter shall rise out of **I**; Nm 24:17
be dispossessed. **I** is doing valiantly. Nm 24:18
While **I** lived in Shittim, the people Nm 25:1
So **I** yoked himself to Baal of Peor. And Nm 25:3
anger of the LORD was kindled against **I**. Nm 25:3
of the LORD may turn away from **I**." Nm 25:4
And Moses said to the judges of **I**, Nm 25:5
of the people of **I** came and brought a Nm 25:6
whole congregation of the people of **I**, Nm 25:6
after the man of **I** into the chamber Nm 25:8
the man of **I** and the woman through Nm 25:8
plague on the people of **I** was stopped. Nm 25:8
back my wrath from the people of **I**, Nm 25:11
the people of **I** in my jealousy. Nm 25:11
made atonement for the people of **I**.'" Nm 25:13
The name of the slain man of **I**, who Nm 25:14
all the congregation of the people of **I**, Nm 26:2
all in **I** who are able to go to war." Nm 26:2
The people of **I** who came out of the Nm 26:4
Reuben, the firstborn of **I**; the sons of Nm 26:5
This was the list of the people of **I**, Nm 26:51
were not listed among the people of **I**, Nm 26:62
given to them among the people of **I**. Nm 26:62
listed the people of **I** in the plains of Nm 26:63
listed the people of **I** in the wilderness Nm 26:64
And you shall speak to the people of **I**, Nm 27:8
be for the people of **I** a statute and rule, Nm 27:11
that I have given to the people of **I**. Nm 27:12
of the people of **I** may obey. Nm 27:20
he and all the people of **I** with him, Nm 27:21
"Command the people of **I** and say to Nm 28:2
told the people of **I** everything just as Nm 29:40
the heads of the tribes of the people of **I**, Nm 30:1
the people of **I** on the Midianites. Nm 31:2
from each of the tribes of **I** to the war." Nm 31:4
were provided, out of the thousands of **I**, Nm 31:5
And the people of **I** took captive the Nm 31:9
to the congregation of the people of **I**, Nm 31:12
the people of **I** to act treacherously Nm 31:16
for the people of **I** before the LORD. Nm 31:54
down before the congregation of **I**, Nm 32:4
of the people of **I** from going over into Nm 32:7
of the people of **I** from going into the Nm 32:9
LORD'S anger was kindled against **I**, Nm 32:13
the fierce anger of the LORD against **I**! Nm 32:14
ready to go before the people of **I**, Nm 32:17
of the people of **I** has gained his Nm 32:18
free of obligation to the LORD and to **I**, Nm 32:22
houses of the tribes of the people of **I**. Nm 32:28
These are the stages of the people of **I**, Nm 33:1
the people of **I** went out triumphantly Nm 33:3
So the people of **I** set out from Rameses Nm 33:5
after the people of **I** had come out of Nm 33:38
heard of the coming of the people of **I**. Nm 33:40
to the people of **I** and say to them, Nm 33:51
"Command the people of **I**, and say to Nm 34:2
Moses commanded the people of **I**, Nm 34:13
for the people of **I** in the land of Nm 34:29
"Command the people of **I** to give to the Nm 35:2
from the possession of the people of **I**, Nm 35:8
to the people of **I** and say to them, Nm 35:10
shall be for refuge for the people of **I**, Nm 35:15
dwell in the midst of the people of **I**." Nm 35:34
of the fathers' houses of the people of **I**. Nm 36:1
for inheritance by lot to the people of **I**, Nm 36:2
of the other tribes of the people of **I**, Nm 36:3
the jubilee of the people of **I** comes, Nm 36:4
the people of **I** according to the Nm 36:5
of the people of **I** shall not be Nm 36:7
one of the people of **I** shall hold on to Nm 36:7
tribe of the people of **I** shall be wife to Nm 36:8
of the people of **I** may possess the Nm 36:8
tribes of the people of **I** shall hold on to Nm 36:9

Moses to the people of **I** in the plains of Nm 36:13
Moses spoke to all **I** beyond the Jordan in Dt 1:1
to the people of **I** according to all that Dt 1:3
him, for he shall cause **I** to inherit it. Dt 1:38
as **I** did to the land of their possession, Dt 2:12
before your brothers, the people of **I**. Dt 3:18
"And now, O **I**, listen to the statutes and Dt 4:1
law that Moses set before the people of **I**. Dt 4:44
to the people of **I** when they came out Dt 4:45
and the people of **I** defeated when they Dt 4:46
And Moses summoned all **I** and said to Dt 5:1
all Israel and said to them, "Hear, O **I**, Dt 5:1
Hear therefore, O **I**, and be careful to do Dt 6:3
"Hear, O **I**: The LORD our God, the LORD is Dt 6:4
"Hear, O **I**: you are to cross over the Jordan Dt 9:1
(The people of **I** journeyed from Beeroth Dt 10:6
I, what does the LORD your God require Dt 10:12
that followed them, in the midst of all **I**. Dt 11:6
And all **I** shall hear and fear and never Dt 13:11
an abomination has been done in **I**, Dt 17:4
die. So you shall purge the evil from **I**. Dt 17:12
his kingdom, he and his children, in **I**. Dt 17:20
have no portion or inheritance with **I**. Dt 18:1
from any of your towns out of all **I**, Dt 18:6
the guilt of innocent blood from **I**, Dt 19:13
and shall say to them, 'Hear, O **I**, today Dt 20:3
atonement, O LORD, for your people **I**, Dt 21:8
blood in the midst of your people **I**, Dt 21:8
from your midst, and all **I** shall hear, Dt 21:21
brought a bad name upon a virgin of **I**. Dt 22:19
an outrageous thing in **I** by whoring in Dt 22:21
So you shall purge the evil from **I**. Dt 22:22
of the daughters of **I** shall be a cult Dt 23:17
none of the sons of **I** shall be a cult Dt 23:17
one of his brothers, of the people of **I**, Dt 24:7
his name may not be blotted out of **I**. Dt 25:6
to perpetuate his brother's name in **I**; Dt 25:7
name of his house shall be called in **I**, Dt 25:10
and bless your people **I** and the ground Dt 26:15
the elders of **I** commanded the people, Dt 27:1
and the Levitical priests said to all **I**, Dt 27:9
to all Israel, "Keep silence and hear, O **I**: Dt 27:9
to all the men of **I** in a loud voice: Dt 27:14
make with the people of **I** in the land of Dt 29:1
And Moses summoned all **I** and said to Dt 29:2
and your officers, all the men of **I**, Dt 29:10
out from all the tribes of **I** for calamity, Dt 29:21
continued to speak these words to all **I**. Dt 31:1
and said to him in the sight of all **I**, Dt 31:7
of the LORD, and to all the elders of **I**. Dt 31:9
when all **I** comes to appear before the Dt 31:11
this law before all **I** in their hearing. Dt 31:11
this song and teach it to the people of **I**. Dt 31:19
a witness for me against the people of **I**. Dt 31:19
same day and taught it to the people of **I**. Dt 31:22
bring the people of **I** into the land that Dt 31:23
in the ears of all the assembly of **I**: Dt 31:30
speaking all these words to all **I**, Dt 32:45
giving to the people of **I** for a possession. Dt 32:49
midst of the people of **I** at the waters of Dt 32:51
as holy in the midst of the people of **I**. Dt 32:51
land that I am giving to the people of **I**." Dt 32:52
blessed the people of **I** before his death. Dt 33:1
were gathered, all the tribes of **I** together. Dt 33:5
teach Jacob your rules and **I** your law; Dt 33:10
with **I** he executed the justice of the Dt 33:21
of the LORD, and his judgments for **I**." Dt 33:21
So **I** lived in safety, Jacob lived alone, in Dt 33:28
Happy are you, O **I**! Who is like you, a Dt 33:29
And the people of **I** wept for Moses in the Dt 34:8
So the people of **I** obeyed him and did as Dt 34:9
arisen a prophet since in **I** like Moses, Dt 34:10
terror that Moses did in the sight of all **I**. Dt 34:12
that I am giving to them, to the people of **I**. Jos 1:2
men of **I** have come here tonight to Jos 2:2
to the Jordan, he and all the people of **I**, Jos 3:1
will begin to exalt you in the sight of all **I**, Jos 3:7
And Joshua said to the people of **I**, "Come Jos 3:9
take twelve men from the tribes of **I**, Jos 3:12
and all **I** was passing over on dry ground Jos 3:17
called the twelve men from the people of **I**, Jos 4:4
the number of the tribes of the people of **I**, Jos 4:5
be to the people of **I** a memorial forever." Jos 4:7
And the people of **I** did just as Joshua Jos 4:8
the number of the tribes of the people of **I**, Jos 4:8
passed over armed before the people of **I**, Jos 4:12
LORD exalted Joshua in the sight of all **I**, Jos 4:14
And he said to the people of **I**, "When Jos 4:21
'**I** passed over this Jordan on dry ground.' Jos 4:22
for the people of **I** until they had crossed Jos 5:1
spirit in them because of the people of **I**. Jos 5:1
circumcise the sons of **I** a second time." Jos 5:2
the sons of **I** at Gibeath-haaraloth. Jos 5:3
For the people of **I** walked forty years in Jos 5:6
While the people of **I** were encamped at Jos 5:10
was no longer manna for the people of **I**, Jos 5:12
and outside because of the people of **I**. Jos 6:1
make the camp of **I** a thing for Jos 6:18
and put them outside the camp of **I**. Jos 6:23
And she has lived in **I** to this day, Jos 6:25
But the people of **I** broke faith in regard to Jos 7:1
of the LORD burned against the people of **I**. Jos 7:1
until the evening, he and the elders of **I**. Jos 7:6
when **I** has turned their backs before Jos 7:8
I has sinned; they have transgressed my Jos 7:11
the people of **I** cannot stand before Jos 7:12
for thus says the LORD, God of **I**, "There Jos 7:13
are devoted things in your midst, O **I**. Jos 7:13
he has done an outrageous thing in **I**.'" Jos 7:15
morning and brought **I** near tribe by Jos 7:16
to the LORD God of **I** and give praise to Jos 7:19
I have sinned against the LORD God of **I**, Jos 7:20
them to Joshua and to all the people of **I**. Jos 7:23
And Joshua and all **I** with him took Jos 7:24
you today." And all **I** stoned him with Jos 7:25
and went up, he and the elders of **I**, Jos 8:10
toward the Arabah to meet **I** in battle. Jos 8:14
And Joshua and all **I** pretended to be Jos 8:15
in Ai or Bethel who did not go out after **I**. Jos 8:17
They left the city open and pursued **I**. Jos 8:17
when Joshua and all **I** saw that the Jos 8:21
them, so they were in the midst of **I**, Jos 8:22
And **I** struck them down, until there was Jos 8:22
When **I** had finished killing all the Jos 8:24
all **I** returned to Ai and struck it down Jos 8:24
spoil of that city **I** took as their plunder, Jos 8:27
built an altar to the LORD, the God of **I**, Jos 8:30
the LORD had commanded the people of **I**, Jos 8:31
there, in the presence of the people of **I**, Jos 8:32
And all **I**, sojourner as well as native Jos 8:33
at the first, to bless the people of **I**. Jos 8:33
did not read before all the assembly of **I**, Jos 8:35
as one to fight against Joshua and **I**. Jos 9:2
and said to him and to the men of **I**, Jos 9:6
But the men of **I** said to the Hivites, Jos 9:7
And the people of **I** set out and reached Jos 9:17
But the people of **I** did not attack them, Jos 9:18
sworn to them by the LORD, the God of **I**. Jos 9:18
sworn to them by the LORD, the God of **I**, Jos 9:19
them out of the hand of the people of **I**, Jos 9:26
had made peace with **I** and were among Jos 10:1
with Joshua and with the people of **I**." Jos 10:4
LORD threw them into a panic before **I**, Jos 10:10
And as they fled before **I**, while they Jos 10:11
than the sons of **I** killed with the sword. Jos 10:11
gave the Amorites over to the sons of **I**, Jos 10:12
of Israel, and he said in the sight of **I**, Jos 10:12
of a man, for the LORD fought for **I**. Jos 10:14
So Joshua returned, and all **I** with him, Jos 10:15
and the sons of **I** had finished striking Jos 10:20
tongue against any of the people of **I**. Jos 10:21
all the men of **I** and said to the Jos 10:24
Then Joshua and all **I** with him passed Jos 10:29
it also and its king into the hand of **I**. Jos 10:30
Then Joshua and all **I** with him passed Jos 10:31
LORD gave Lachish into the hand of **I**, Jos 10:32
Then Joshua and all **I** with him passed Jos 10:34
Then Joshua and all **I** with him went Jos 10:36
Then Joshua and all **I** with him turned Jos 10:38
just as the LORD God of **I** commanded. Jos 10:40
the LORD God of **I** fought for Israel. Jos 10:42
the LORD God of Israel fought for **I**. Jos 10:42
Joshua returned, and all **I** with him, Jos 10:43
at the waters of Merom to fight with **I**. Jos 11:5
I will give over all of them, slain, to **I**. Jos 11:6
the LORD gave them into the hand of **I**, Jos 11:8
cities that stood on mounds did **I** burn, Jos 11:13
the people of **I** took for their plunder. Jos 11:14
the hill country of **I** and its lowland Jos 11:16
with the people of **I** except the Hivites, Jos 11:19
they should come against **I** in battle, Jos 11:20
and from all the hill country of **I**. Jos 11:21
left in the land of the people of **I**. Jos 11:22
an inheritance to **I** according to their Jos 11:23
whom the people of **I** defeated and took Jos 12:1
LORD, and the people of **I** defeated them. Jos 12:6
and the people of **I** defeated on the west Jos 12:7
to the tribes of **I** as a possession Jos 12:7
them out from before the people of **I**. Jos 13:6
allot the land to **I** for an inheritance, Jos 13:6
Yet the people of **I** did not drive out the Jos 13:13
dwell in the midst of **I** to this day. Jos 13:13
the LORD God of **I** are their inheritance, Jos 13:14
by the people of **I** among the rest of Jos 13:22
the LORD God of **I** is their inheritance, Jos 13:33
that the people of **I** received in the land Jos 14:1
of the people of **I** gave them to inherit. Jos 14:1
The people of **I** did as the LORD Jos 14:5
while **I** walked in the wilderness. Jos 14:10
wholly followed the LORD, the God of **I**. Jos 14:14
Now when the people of **I** grew strong, Jos 17:13
of the people of **I** assembled at Shiloh Jos 18:1
among the people of **I** seven tribes whose Jos 18:2
So Joshua said to the people of **I**, "How Jos 18:3
apportioned the land to the people of **I**, Jos 18:10
the people of **I** gave an inheritance Jos 19:49
of the people of **I** distributed by lot at Jos 19:51
"Say to the people of **I**, 'Appoint the cities Jos 20:2
for all the people of **I** and for the stranger Jos 20:9
houses of the tribes of the people of **I**. Jos 21:1
LORD the people of **I** gave to the Levites Jos 21:3
pasturelands the people of **I** gave by lot Jos 21:8
of the people of **I** were in all forty-eight Jos 21:41
the LORD gave to **I** all the land that Jos 21:43
had made to the house of **I** had failed; Jos 21:45
parting from the people of **I** at Shiloh, Jos 22:9
And the people of **I** heard it said, Jos 22:11
the side that belongs to the people of **I**." Jos 22:11
And when the people of **I** heard of it, the Jos 22:12
of the people of **I** gathered at Shiloh to Jos 22:12
Then the people of **I** sent to the people of Jos 22:13
from each of the tribal families of **I**, Jos 22:14
head of a family among the clans of **I**. Jos 22:14
against the God of **I** in turning away Jos 22:16
angry with the whole congregation of **I**. Jos 22:18
fell upon all the congregation of **I**? Jos 22:20
answer to the heads of the families of **I**, Jos 22:21
LORD! He knows; and let **I** itself know! Jos 22:22
you to do with the LORD, the God of **I**? Jos 22:24
of the families of **I** who were with him, Jos 22:30
delivered the people of **I** from the hand Jos 22:31
to the land of Canaan, to the people of **I**, Jos 22:32
was good in the eyes of the people of **I**. Jos 22:33
And the people of **I** blessed God and Jos 22:33
had given rest to **I** from all their Jos 23:1
Joshua summoned all **I**, its elders and Jos 23:2
all the tribes of **I** to Shechem and Jos 24:1
heads, the judges, and the officers of **I**. Jos 24:1
people, "Thus says the LORD, the God of **I**, Jos 24:2
of Moab, arose and fought against **I**. Jos 24:9
your heart to the LORD, the God of **I**." Jos 24:23
I served the LORD all the days of Joshua, Jos 24:31
all the work that the LORD did for **I**. Jos 24:31
which the people of **I** brought up from Jos 24:32
the people of **I** inquired of the LORD, Jgs 1:1
When **I** grew strong, they put the Jgs 1:28
spoke these words to all the people of **I**, Jgs 2:4
the people of **I** went each to his Jgs 2:6
great work that the LORD had done for **I**. Jgs 2:7
LORD or the work that he had done for **I**. Jgs 2:10
And the people of **I** did what was evil in Jgs 2:11
anger of the LORD was kindled against **I**, Jgs 2:14
anger of the LORD was kindled against **I**, Jgs 2:20
in order to test **I** by them, whether they Jgs 2:22
that the LORD left, to test **I** by them, Jgs 3:1
all in **I** who had not experienced all the Jgs 3:1
of the people of **I** might know war, Jgs 3:2
They were for the testing of **I**, to know Jgs 3:4
to know whether **I** would obey the Jgs 3:4
So the people of **I** lived among the Jgs 3:5
And the people of **I** did what was evil in Jgs 3:7
anger of the LORD was kindled against **I**, Jgs 3:8
the people of **I** served Cushan-rishathaim Jgs 3:8
But when the people of **I** cried out to the Jgs 3:9
raised up a deliverer for the people of **I**, Jgs 3:9
the LORD was upon him, and he judged **I**. Jgs 3:10
And the people of **I** again did what was Jgs 3:12
Eglon the king of Moab against **I**, Jgs 3:12
the Amalekites, and went and defeated **I**. Jgs 3:13
And the people of **I** served Eglon the king Jgs 3:14
Then the people of **I** cried out to the Jgs 3:15
The people of **I** sent tribute by him to Jgs 3:15
Then the people of **I** went down with Jgs 3:27
subdued that day under the hand of **I**. Jgs 3:30
with an oxgoad, and he also saved **I**. Jgs 3:31
And the people of **I** again did what was Jgs 4:1
Then the people of **I** cried out to the LORD Jgs 4:3
the people of **I** cruelly for twenty Jgs 4:3
of Lappidoth, was judging **I** at that time. Jgs 4:4
and the people of **I** came up to her for Jgs 4:5
to him, "Has not the LORD, the God of **I**, Jgs 4:6
king of Canaan before the people of **I**. Jgs 4:23
of the people of **I** pressed harder and Jgs 4:24
"That the leaders took the lead in **I**, that Jgs 5:2
make melody to the LORD, the God of **I**. Jgs 5:3
even Sinai before the LORD, the God of **I**. Jgs 5:5
The villagers ceased in **I**; they ceased to be Jgs 5:7
I arose; I, Deborah, arose as a mother in **I**. Jgs 5:7
to be seen among forty thousand in **I**? Jgs 5:8
the commanders of **I** who offered Jgs 5:9
righteous triumphs of his villagers in **I**. Jgs 5:11
The people of **I** did what was evil in the Jgs 6:1
And the hand of Midian overpowered **I**, Jgs 6:2
the people of **I** made for themselves Jgs 6:2
leave no sustenance in **I** and no sheep or Jgs 6:4

And **I** was brought very low because of Jgs 6:6
And the people of **I** cried out for help to Jgs 6:6
When the people of **I** cried out to the LORD Jgs 6:7
the LORD sent a prophet to the people of **I**. Jgs 6:8
to them, "Thus says the LORD, the God of **I**: Jgs 6:8
of yours and save **I** from the hand of Jgs 6:14
to him, "Please, Lord, how can I save **I**? Jgs 6:15
to God, "If you will save **I** by my hand, Jgs 6:36
know that you will save **I** by my hand, Jgs 6:37
into their hand, lest **I** boast over me, Jgs 7:2
sent all the rest of **I** every man to his tent, Jgs 7:8
of Gideon the son of Joash, a man of **I**; Jgs 7:14
he returned to the camp of **I** and said, Jgs 7:15
And the men of **I** were called out from Jgs 7:23
Then the men of **I** said to Gideon, "Rule Jgs 8:22
And all **I** whored after it there, and it Jgs 8:27
was subdued before the people of **I**, Jgs 8:28
the people of **I** turned again and whored Jgs 8:33
And the people of **I** did not remember the Jgs 8:34
for all the good that he had done to **I**. Jgs 8:35
Abimelech ruled over **I** three years. Jgs 9:22
when the men of **I** saw that Abimelech Jgs 9:55
there arose to save **I** Tola the son of Jgs 10:1
And he judged **I** twenty-three years. Jgs 10:2
Gileadite, who judged **I** twenty-two years. Jgs 10:3
The people of **I** again did what was evil Jgs 10:6
anger of the LORD was kindled against **I**, Jgs 10:7
and oppressed the people of **I** that year. Jgs 10:8
all the people of **I** who were beyond the Jgs 10:8
so that **I** was severely distressed. Jgs 10:9
And the people of **I** cried out to the Jgs 10:10
And the LORD said to the people of **I**, Jgs 10:11
And the people of **I** said to the LORD, Jgs 10:15
became impatient over the misery of **I**. Jgs 10:16
And the people of **I** came together, and Jgs 10:17
the Ammonites made war against **I**. Jgs 11:4
the Ammonites made war against **I**, Jgs 11:5
"Because **I** on coming up from Egypt Jgs 11:13
I did not take away the land of Moab or Jgs 11:15
I went through the wilderness to the Jgs 11:16
I then sent messengers to the king of Jgs 11:17
not consent. So **I** remained at Kadesh. Jgs 11:17
I then sent messengers to Sihon king of Jgs 11:19
king of Heshbon, and **I** said to him, Jgs 11:19
Sihon did not trust **I** to pass through Jgs 11:20
encamped at Jahaz and fought with **I**. Jgs 11:20
And the LORD, the God of **I**, gave Sihon Jgs 11:21
and all his people into the hand of **I**, Jgs 11:21
So **I** took possession of all the land of Jgs 11:21
So then the LORD, the God of **I**, Jgs 11:23
the Amorites from before his people **I**; Jgs 11:23
Did he ever contend against **I**, or did he Jgs 11:25
While **I** lived in Heshbon and its Jgs 11:26
between the people of **I** and the people of Jgs 11:27
were subdued before the people of **I**. Jgs 11:33
a man, and it became a custom in **I** Jgs 11:39
that the daughters of **I** went year by Jgs 11:40
Jephthah judged **I** six years. Then Jgs 12:7
After him Ibzan of Bethlehem judged **I**. Jgs 12:8
for his sons. And he judged **I** seven years. Jgs 12:9
him Elon the Zebulunite judged **I**, Jgs 12:11
judged Israel, and he judged **I** ten years. Jgs 12:11
son of Hillel the Pirathonite judged **I**. Jgs 12:13
donkeys, and he judged **I** eight years. Jgs 12:14
And the people of **I** again did what was Jgs 13:1
he shall begin to save **I** from the hand of Jgs 13:5
At that time the Philistines ruled over **I**. Jgs 14:4
And he judged **I** in the days of the Jgs 15:20
father. He had judged **I** twenty years. Jgs 16:31
In those days there was no king in **I**. Jgs 17:6
In those days there was no king in **I**. And Jgs 18:1
among the tribes of **I** had fallen to them. Jgs 18:1
or to be priest to a tribe and clan in **I**?" Jgs 18:19
Dan their ancestor, who was born to **I**; Jgs 18:29
those days, when there was no king in **I**, Jgs 19:1
who do not belong to the people of **I**, Jgs 19:12
her throughout all the territory of **I**. Jgs 19:29
day that the people of **I** came up out of Jgs 19:30
Then all the people of **I** came out, from Jgs 20:1
of all the people, of all the tribes of **I**, Jgs 20:2
heard that the people of **I** had gone up to Jgs 20:3
And the people of **I** said, "Tell us, how Jgs 20:3
all the country of the inheritance of **I**, Jgs 20:6
abomination and outrage in **I**. Jgs 20:6
Behold, you people of **I**, all of you, give Jgs 20:7
hundred throughout all the tribes of **I**, Jgs 20:10
outrage that they have committed in **I**." Jgs 20:10
all the men of **I** gathered against the Jgs 20:11
And the tribes of **I** sent men through Jgs 20:12
purge evil from **I**." But the Jgs 20:13
voice of their brothers, the people of **I**. Jgs 20:13
go out to battle against the people of **I**. Jgs 20:14
And the men of **I**, apart from Jgs 20:17
The people of **I** arose and went up to Jgs 20:18
Then the people of **I** rose in the Jgs 20:19

And the men of **I** went out to fight Jgs 20:20
and the men of **I** drew up the battle line Jgs 20:20
But the people, the men of **I**, took Jgs 20:22
And the people of **I** went up and wept Jgs 20:23
So the people of **I** came near against the Jgs 20:24
destroyed 18,000 men of the people of **I**. Jgs 20:25
Then all the people of **I**, the whole Jgs 20:26
And the people of **I** inquired of the LORD Jgs 20:27
So **I** set men in ambush around Jgs 20:29
And the people of **I** went up against the Jgs 20:30
open country, about thirty men of **I**. Jgs 20:31
as at the first." But the people of **I** said, Jgs 20:32
And all the men of **I** rose up out of their Jgs 20:33
and the men of **I** who were in ambush Jgs 20:33
Gibeah 10,000 chosen men out of all **I**, Jgs 20:34
the LORD defeated Benjamin before **I**, Jgs 20:35
the people of **I** destroyed 25,100 men Jgs 20:35
The men of **I** gave ground to Benjamin, Jgs 20:36
between the men of **I** and the men in Jgs 20:38
the men of **I** should turn in battle. Now Jgs 20:39
to strike and kill about thirty men of **I**. Jgs 20:39
Then the men of **I** turned, and the men Jgs 20:41
before the men of **I** in the direction of Jgs 20:42
And the men of **I** turned back against Jgs 20:48
Now the men of **I** had sworn at Mizpah, Jgs 21:1
And they said, "O LORD, the God of **I**, why Jgs 21:3
of Israel, why has this happened in **I**, Jgs 21:3
there should be one tribe lacking in **I**?" Jgs 21:3
And the people of **I** said, "Which of all Jgs 21:5
of all the tribes of **I** did not come up in Jgs 21:5
And the people of **I** had compassion for Jgs 21:6
said, "One tribe is cut off from **I** this day. Jgs 21:6
there of the tribes of **I** that did not come Jgs 21:8
had made a breach in the tribes of **I**. Jgs 21:15
that a tribe not be blotted out from **I**. Jgs 21:17
For the people of **I** had sworn, Jgs 21:18
And the people of **I** departed from there Jgs 21:24
In those days there was no king in **I**. Jgs 21:25
be given you by the LORD, the God of **I**, Ru 2:12
former times in **I** concerning redeeming Ru 4:7
and this was the manner of attesting in **I**. Ru 4:7
who together built up the house of **I**. Ru 4:11
and may his name be renowned in **I**! Ru 4:14
and the God of **I** grant your petition 1 Sm 1:17
all that his sons were doing to all **I**, 1 Sm 2:22
out of all the tribes of **I** to be my priest, 1 Sm 2:28
offerings by fire from the people of **I**. 1 Sm 2:28
parts of every offering of my people **I**?' 1 Sm 2:29
the LORD the God of **I** declares: 1 Sm 2:30
prosperity that shall be bestowed on **I**, 1 Sm 2:32
to do a thing in **I** at which the two ears 1 Sm 3:11
And all **I** from Dan to Beersheba 1 Sm 3:20
And the word of Samuel came to all **I**. 1 Sm 4:1
Now **I** went out to battle against the 1 Sm 4:1
Philistines drew up in line against **I**, 1 Sm 4:2
I was defeated by the Philistines, 1 Sm 4:2
came to the camp, the elders of **I** said, 1 Sm 4:3
the camp, all **I** gave a mighty shout, 1 Sm 4:5
Philistines fought, and **I** was defeated, 1 Sm 4:10
for there fell of **I** thirty thousand foot 1 Sm 4:10
said, "**I** has fled before the Philistines, 1 Sm 4:17
heavy. He had judged **I** forty years. 1 Sm 4:18
has departed from **I**!" because the ark 1 Sm 4:21
said, "The glory has departed from **I**, 1 Sm 4:22
of the God of **I** must not remain with 1 Sm 5:7
ark of the God of **I**?" They answered, 1 Sm 5:8
of the God of **I** be brought around to 1 Sm 5:8
brought the ark of the God of **I** there. 1 Sm 5:8
ark of the God of **I** to kill us and our 1 Sm 5:10
"Send away the ark of the God of **I**, 1 Sm 5:11
you send away the ark of the God of **I**, 1 Sm 6:3
the land, and give glory to the God of **I**. 1 Sm 6:5
all the house of **I** lamented after the 1 Sm 7:2
And Samuel said to all the house of **I**, 1 Sm 7:3
So the people of **I** put away the Baals 1 Sm 7:4
Samuel said, "Gather all **I** at Mizpah, 1 Sm 7:5
judged the people of **I** at Mizpah. 1 Sm 7:6
that the people of **I** had gathered at 1 Sm 7:7
of the Philistines went up against **I**. 1 Sm 7:7
And when the people of **I** heard of it, 1 Sm 7:7
And the people of **I** said to Samuel, "Do 1 Sm 7:8
And Samuel cried out to the LORD for **I**, 1 Sm 7:9
the Philistines drew near to attack **I**. 1 Sm 7:10
and they were routed before **I**. 1 Sm 7:10
And the men of **I** went out from 1 Sm 7:11
did not again enter the territory of **I**. 1 Sm 7:13
had taken from **I** were restored to 1 Sm 7:14
taken from Israel were restored to **I**, 1 Sm 7:14
and **I** delivered their territory from the 1 Sm 7:14
peace also between **I** and the 1 Sm 7:14
Samuel judged **I** all the days of his life. 1 Sm 7:15
And he judged **I** in all these places. 1 Sm 7:16
was there, and there also he judged **I**. 1 Sm 7:17
old, he made his sons judges over **I**. 1 Sm 8:1
all the elders of **I** gathered together and 1 Sm 8:4

Samuel then said to the men of **I**, 1 Sm 8:22
the people of **I** more handsome than 1 Sm 9:2
(Formerly in **I**, when a man went to 1 Sm 9:9
him to be prince over my people **I**. 1 Sm 9:16
for whom is all that is desirable in **I**? 1 Sm 9:20
from the least of the tribes of **I**? 1 Sm 9:21
you to be prince over his people **I**? 1 Sm 10:1
And he said to the people of **I**, "Thus 1 Sm 10:18
"Thus says the LORD, the God of **I**, 1 Sm 10:18
of Israel, 'I brought up **I** out of Egypt, 1 Sm 10:18
brought all the tribes of **I** near, 1 Sm 10:20
eyes, and thus bring disgrace on all **I**." 1 Sm 11:2
through all the territory of **I**. 1 Sm 11:3
all the territory of **I** by the hand of 1 Sm 11:7
the people of **I** were three hundred 1 Sm 11:8
the LORD has worked salvation in **I**." 1 Sm 11:13
and all the men of **I** rejoiced greatly. 1 Sm 11:15
And Samuel said to all **I**, "Behold, I 1 Sm 12:1
and he reigned … and two years over **I**. 1 Sm 13:1
Saul chose three thousand men of **I**. 1 Sm 13:2
And all **I** heard it said that Saul had 1 Sm 13:4
and also that **I** had become a stench 1 Sm 13:4
Philistines mustered to fight with **I**, 1 Sm 13:5
When the men of **I** saw that they were 1 Sm 13:6
your kingdom over **I** forever. 1 Sm 13:13
found throughout all the land of **I**, 1 Sm 13:19
has given them into the hand of **I**." 1 Sm 14:12
went at that time with the people of **I**. 1 Sm 14:18
all the men of **I** who had hidden 1 Sm 14:22
So the LORD saved **I** that day. And the 1 Sm 14:23
And the men of **I** had been hard 1 Sm 14:24
into the hand of **I**?" But he did not 1 Sm 14:37
For as the LORD lives who saves **I**, 1 Sm 14:39
Then he said to all **I**, "You shall be 1 Sm 14:40
Saul said, "O LORD God of **I**, 1 Sm 14:41
Jonathan my son, O LORD, God of **I**, 1 Sm 14:41
But if this guilt is in your people **I**, 1 Sm 14:41
has worked this great salvation in **I**? 1 Sm 14:45
Saul had taken the kingship over **I**, 1 Sm 14:47
Amalekites and delivered **I** out of the 1 Sm 14:48
to anoint you king over his people **I**; 1 Sm 15:1
Amalek did to **I** in opposing them 1 Sm 15:2
all the people of **I** when they came up 1 Sm 15:6
you not the head of the tribes of **I**? 1 Sm 15:17
The LORD anointed you king over **I**. 1 Sm 15:17
rejected you from being king over **I**." 1 Sm 15:26
torn the kingdom of **I** from you this 1 Sm 15:28
And also the Glory of **I** will not lie or 1 Sm 15:29
the elders of my people and before **I**, 1 Sm 15:30
that he had made Saul king over **I**. 1 Sm 15:35
rejected him from being king over **I**? 1 Sm 16:1
Saul and the men of **I** were gathered, 1 Sm 17:2
and **I** stood on the mountain on the 1 Sm 17:3
He stood and shouted to the ranks of **I**, 1 Sm 17:8
said, "I defy the ranks of **I** this day. 1 Sm 17:10
Saul and all **I** heard these words 1 Sm 17:11
all the men of **I** were in the valley 1 Sm 17:19
And **I** and the Philistines drew up for 1 Sm 17:21
All the men of **I**, when they saw the 1 Sm 17:24
And the men of **I** said, "Have you 1 Sm 17:25
up? Surely he has come up to defy **I**. 1 Sm 17:25
make his father's house free in **I**." 1 Sm 17:25
and takes away the reproach from **I**? 1 Sm 17:26
of hosts, the God of the armies of **I**, 1 Sm 17:45
may know that there is a God in **I**, 1 Sm 17:46
And the men of **I** and Judah rose 1 Sm 17:52
And the people of **I** came back from 1 Sm 17:53
women came out of all the cities of **I**, 1 Sm 18:6
But all **I** and Judah loved David, for 1 Sm 18:16
my relatives, my father's clan in **I**, 1 Sm 18:18
LORD worked a great salvation for all **I**. 1 Sm 19:5
to David, "The LORD, the God of **I**, 1 Sm 20:12
said David, "O LORD, the God of **I**, 1 Sm 23:10
O LORD, the God of **I**, please tell your 1 Sm 23:11
You shall be king over **I**, and I shall 1 Sm 23:17
men out of all **I** and went to seek 1 Sm 24:2
whom has the king of **I** come out? 1 Sm 24:14
the kingdom of **I** shall be established 1 Sm 24:20
And all **I** assembled and mourned for 1 Sm 25:1
and has appointed you prince over **I**, 1 Sm 25:30
"Blessed be the LORD, the God of **I**, 1 Sm 25:32
surely as the LORD the God of **I** lives, 1 Sm 25:34
chosen men of **I** to seek David 1 Sm 26:2
not a man? Who is like you in **I**? 1 Sm 26:15
for the king of **I** has come out to seek 1 Sm 26:20
me any longer within the borders of **I**, 1 Sm 27:1
an utter stench to his people **I**; 1 Sm 27:12
their forces for war, to fight against **I**. 1 Sm 28:1
and all **I** had mourned for him and 1 Sm 28:3
And Saul gathered all **I**, and they 1 Sm 28:4
the LORD will give **I** also with you 1 Sm 28:19
give the army of **I** also into the hand 1 Sm 28:19
David, the servant of Saul, king of **I**, 1 Sm 29:3
and a rule for **I** from that day 1 Sm 30:25
Now the Philistines fought against **I**, 1 Sm 31:1

and the men of **I** fled before the 1 Sm 31:1
when the men of **I** who were on the 1 Sm 31:7
saw that the men of **I** had fled and that 1 Sm 31:7
"I have escaped from the camp of **I**." 2 Sm 1:3
of the LORD and for the house of **I**, 2 Sm 1:12
"Your glory, O **I**, is slain on your high 2 Sm 1:19
"You daughters of **I**, weep over Saul, 2 Sm 1:24
and Ephraim and Benjamin and all **I**. 2 Sm 2:9
old when he began to reign over **I**, 2 Sm 2:10
and the men of **I** were beaten before 2 Sm 2:17
men stopped and pursued **I** no more, 2 Sm 2:28
throne of David over **I** and over Judah, 2 Sm 3:10
be with you to bring over all **I** to you." 2 Sm 3:12
Abner conferred with the elders of **I**, 2 Sm 3:17
will save my people **I** from the hand of 2 Sm 3:18
at Hebron all that **I** and the whole 2 Sm 3:19
go and will gather all **I** to my lord the 2 Sm 3:21
people and all **I** understood that day 2 Sm 3:37
a great man has fallen this day in **I**? 2 Sm 3:38
courage failed, and all **I** was dismayed. 2 Sm 4:1
all the tribes of **I** came to David at 2 Sm 5:1
was you who led out and brought in **I**. 2 Sm 5:2
'You shall be shepherd of my people **I**, 2 Sm 5:2
Israel, and you shall be prince over **I**.'" 2 Sm 5:2
So all the elders of **I** came to the king at 2 Sm 5:3
and they anointed David king over **I**. 2 Sm 5:3
reigned over all **I** and Judah 2 Sm 5:5
LORD had established him king over **I**, 2 Sm 5:12
kingdom for the sake of his people **I**. 2 Sm 5:12
David had been anointed king over **I**, 2 Sm 5:17
again gathered all the chosen men of **I**, 2 Sm 6:1
all the house of **I** were making merry 2 Sm 6:5
all the house of **I** brought up the ark 2 Sm 6:15
the people, the whole multitude of **I**, 2 Sm 6:19
the king of **I** honored himself today, 2 Sm 6:20
house, to appoint me as prince over **I**, 2 Sm 6:21
up the people of **I** from Egypt to this 2 Sm 7:6
I have moved with all the people of **I**, 2 Sm 7:7
a word with any of the judges of **I**, 2 Sm 7:7
I commanded to shepherd my people **I**, 2 Sm 7:7
you should be prince over my people **I**. 2 Sm 7:8
place for my people **I** and will plant 2 Sm 7:10
I appointed judges over my people **I**. 2 Sm 7:11
And who is like your people **I**, the one 2 Sm 7:23
for yourself your people **I** to be your 2 Sm 7:24
'The LORD of hosts is God over **I**,' 2 Sm 7:26
For you, O LORD of hosts, the God of **I**, 2 Sm 7:27
So David reigned over all **I**. And David 2 Sm 8:15
the best men of **I** and arrayed them 2 Sm 10:9
saw that they had been defeated by **I**, 2 Sm 10:15
he gathered all **I** together and crossed 2 Sm 10:17
And the Syrians fled before **I**, and 2 Sm 10:18
saw that they had been defeated by **I**, 2 Sm 10:19
made peace with **I** and became 2 Sm 10:19
and his servants with him, and all **I**. 2 Sm 11:1
"The ark and **I** and Judah dwell in 2 Sm 11:11
Thus says the LORD, the God of **I**, 'I 2 Sm 12:7
of Israel, 'I anointed you king over **I**, 2 Sm 12:7
gave you the house of **I** and of Judah. 2 Sm 12:8
this thing before all **I** and before the 2 Sm 12:12
me, for such a thing is not done in **I**; 2 Sm 13:12
be as one of the outrageous fools in **I**. 2 Sm 13:13
Now in all **I** there was no one so 2 Sm 14:25
is of such and such a tribe in **I**," 2 Sm 15:2
did to all of **I** who came to the 2 Sm 15:6
stole the hearts of the men of **I**. 2 Sm 15:6
throughout all the tribes of **I**, 2 Sm 15:10
of the men of **I** have gone after 2 Sm 15:13
'Today the house of **I** will give me 2 Sm 16:3
and all the people, the men of **I**, 2 Sm 16:15
and all the men of **I** have chosen, 2 Sm 16:18
and all **I** will hear that you have 2 Sm 16:21
concubines in the sight of all **I**. 2 Sm 16:22
eyes of Absalom and all the elders of **I**. 2 Sm 17:4
for all **I** knows that your father is a 2 Sm 17:10
counsel is that all **I** be gathered to 2 Sm 17:11
then all **I** will bring ropes to that 2 Sm 17:13
Absalom and all the men of **I** said, 2 Sm 17:14
counsel Absalom and the elders of **I**, 2 Sm 17:15
the Jordan with all the men of **I**. 2 Sm 17:24
And **I** and Absalom encamped in the 2 Sm 17:26
army went out into the field against **I**, 2 Sm 18:6
And the men of **I** were defeated there 2 Sm 18:7
troops came back from pursuing **I**, 2 Sm 18:16
And all **I** fled every one to his own 2 Sm 18:17
Now **I** had fled every man to his own 2 Sm 19:8
arguing throughout all the tribes of **I**, 2 Sm 19:9
the word of all **I** has come to the 2 Sm 19:11
anyone be put to death in **I** this day? 2 Sm 19:22
that I am this day king over **I**?" 2 Sm 19:22
of Judah, and also half the people of **I**, 2 Sm 19:40
all the men of **I** came to the king 2 Sm 19:41
men of Judah answered the men of **I**, 2 Sm 19:42
And the men of **I** answered the men 2 Sm 19:43
than the words of the men of **I**. 2 Sm 19:43

of Jesse; every man to his tents, O **I**!" 2 Sm 20:1
all the men of **I** withdrew from David 2 Sm 20:2
all the tribes of **I** to Abel of 2 Sm 20:14
who are peaceable and faithful in **I**. 2 Sm 20:19
to destroy a city that is a mother in **I**. 2 Sm 20:19
was in command of all the army of **I**; 2 Sm 20:23
of the people of **I** but of the remnant 2 Sm 21:2
Although the people of **I** had sworn to 2 Sm 21:2
his zeal for the people of **I** and Judah. 2 Sm 21:2
any man to death in **I**." And he said, 2 Sm 21:4
have no place in all the territory of **I**, 2 Sm 21:5
again between the Philistines and **I**, 2 Sm 21:15
lest you quench the lamp of **I**." 2 Sm 21:17
And when he taunted **I**, Jonathan the 2 Sm 21:21
God of Jacob, the sweet psalmist of **I**: 2 Sm 23:1
The God of **I** has spoken; the Rock of 2 Sm 23:3
spoken; the Rock of **I** has said to me: 2 Sm 23:3
for battle, and the men of **I** withdrew. 2 Sm 23:9
of the LORD was kindled against **I**, 2 Sm 24:1
saying, "Go, number **I** and Judah." 2 Sm 24:1
him, "Go through all the tribes of **I**, 2 Sm 24:2
of the king to number the people of **I**. 2 Sm 24:4
in **I** there were 800,000 valiant men 2 Sm 24:9
a pestilence on **I** from the morning 2 Sm 24:15
and the plague was averted from **I**. 2 Sm 24:25
throughout all the territory of **I**, 1 Kgs 1:3
the king, the eyes of all **I** are on you, 1 Kgs 1:20
swore to you by the LORD, the God of **I**, 1 Kgs 1:30
prophet there anoint him king over **I**. 1 Kgs 1:34
to be ruler over **I** and over Judah." 1 Kgs 1:35
said, 'Blessed be the LORD, the God of **I**, 1 Kgs 1:48
not lack a man on the throne of **I**.' 1 Kgs 2:4
the two commanders of the armies of **I**, 1 Kgs 2:5
David reigned over **I** was forty years. 1 Kgs 2:11
and that all **I** fully expected me to 1 Kgs 2:15
of Ner, commander of the army of **I**, 1 Kgs 2:32
And all **I** heard of the judgment that 1 Kgs 3:28
King Solomon was king over all **I**, 1 Kgs 4:1
Solomon had twelve officers over all **I**, 1 Kgs 4:7
Judah and **I** were as many as the sand 1 Kgs 4:20
And Judah and **I** lived in safety, from 1 Kgs 4:25
drafted forced labor out of all **I**, 1 Kgs 5:13
after the people of **I** came out of the 1 Kgs 6:1
fourth year of Solomon's reign over **I**, 1 Kgs 6:1
among the children of **I** and will not 1 Kgs 6:13
and will not forsake my people **I**." 1 Kgs 6:13
assembled the elders of **I** and all the 1 Kgs 8:1
of the fathers' houses of the people of **I**, 1 Kgs 8:1
all the men of **I** assembled to King 1 Kgs 8:2
And all the elders of **I** came, and the 1 Kgs 8:3
Solomon and all the congregation of **I**, 1 Kgs 8:5
made a covenant with the people of **I**, 1 Kgs 8:9
and blessed all the assembly of **I**, 1 Kgs 8:14
while all the assembly of **I** stood. 1 Kgs 8:14
"Blessed be the LORD, the God of **I**, 1 Kgs 8:15
I brought my people **I** out of Egypt, 1 Kgs 8:16
of all the tribes of **I** in which to build 1 Kgs 8:16
I chose David to be over my people **I**.' 1 Kgs 8:16
for the name of the LORD, the God of **I**. 1 Kgs 8:17
my father, and sit on the throne of **I**, 1 Kgs 8:20
for the name of the LORD, the God of **I**. 1 Kgs 8:20
all the assembly of **I** and spread out 1 Kgs 8:22
and said, "O LORD, God of **I**, there is no 1 Kgs 8:23
Now therefore, O LORD, God of **I**, keep 1 Kgs 8:25
to sit before me on the throne of **I**, 1 Kgs 8:25
Now therefore, O God of **I**, let your 1 Kgs 8:26
of your servant and of your people **I**, 1 Kgs 8:30
"When your people **I** are defeated 1 Kgs 8:33
sin of your people **I** and bring them 1 Kgs 8:34
the sin of your servants, your people **I**, 1 Kgs 8:36
by any man or by all your people **I**, 1 Kgs 8:38
foreigner, who is not of your people **I**, 1 Kgs 8:41
and fear you, as do your people **I**, 1 Kgs 8:43
and to the plea of your people **I**, 1 Kgs 8:52
all the assembly of **I** with a loud 1 Kgs 8:55
who has given rest to his people **I**, 1 Kgs 8:56
servant and the cause of his people **I**, 1 Kgs 8:59
Then the king, and all **I** with him, 1 Kgs 8:62
all the people of **I** dedicated the house 1 Kgs 8:63
feast at that time, and all **I** with him, 1 Kgs 8:65
David his servant and to **I** his people. 1 Kgs 8:66
your royal throne over **I** forever, 1 Kgs 9:5
not lack a man on the throne of **I**.' 1 Kgs 9:5
then I will cut off **I** from the land that I 1 Kgs 9:7
and **I** will become a proverb and a 1 Kgs 9:7
who were not of the people of **I**— 1 Kgs 9:20
whom the people of **I** were unable to 1 Kgs 9:21
of the people of **I** Solomon made no 1 Kgs 9:22
in you and set you on the throne of **I**! 1 Kgs 10:9
Because the LORD loved **I** forever, he 1 Kgs 10:9
the LORD had said to the people of **I**, 1 Kgs 11:2
away from the LORD, the God of **I**, 1 Kgs 11:9
Joab and all **I** remained there six 1 Kgs 11:16
was an adversary of **I** all the days of 1 Kgs 11:25
And he loathed **I** and reigned over 1 Kgs 11:25

for thus says the LORD, the God of **I**, 1 Kgs 11:31
chosen out of all the tribes of **I**), 1 Kgs 11:32
desires, and you shall be king over **I**. 1 Kgs 11:37
for David, and I will give **I** to you. 1 Kgs 11:38
Jerusalem over all **I** was forty years. 1 Kgs 11:42
for all **I** had come to Shechem to 1 Kgs 12:1
all the assembly of **I** came and said to 1 Kgs 12:3
And when all **I** saw that the king did 1 Kgs 12:16
in the son of Jesse. To your tents, O **I**! 1 Kgs 12:16
David." So **I** went to their tents. 1 Kgs 12:16
over the people of **I** who lived in the 1 Kgs 12:17
and all **I** stoned him to death with 1 Kgs 12:18
So **I** has been in rebellion against 1 Kgs 12:19
And when all **I** heard that Jeroboam 1 Kgs 12:20
and made him king over all **I**. 1 Kgs 12:20
to fight against the house of **I**, 1 Kgs 12:21
against your relatives the people of **I**. 1 Kgs 12:24
Behold your gods, O **I**, who brought 1 Kgs 12:28
for the people of **I** and went up to 1 Kgs 12:33
'Thus says the LORD, the God of **I**: 1 Kgs 14:7
and made you leader over my people **I** 1 Kgs 14:7
every male, both bond and free in **I**, 1 Kgs 14:10
And all **I** shall mourn for him and 1 Kgs 14:13
pleasing to the LORD, the God of **I**, 1 Kgs 14:13
himself a king over **I** who shall cut 1 Kgs 14:14
the LORD will strike **I** as a reed is 1 Kgs 14:15
and root up **I** out of this good land 1 Kgs 14:15
And he will give **I** up because of the 1 Kgs 14:16
which he sinned and made **I** to sin." 1 Kgs 14:16
And all **I** buried him and mourned 1 Kgs 14:18
of the Chronicles of the Kings of **I**. 1 Kgs 14:19
had chosen out of all the tribes of **I**, 1 Kgs 14:21
LORD drove out before the people of **I**. 1 Kgs 14:24
twentieth year of Jeroboam king of **I**, 1 Kgs 15:9
and Baasha king of **I** all their days. 1 Kgs 15:16
Baasha king of **I** went up against 1 Kgs 15:17
covenant with Baasha king of **I**, 1 Kgs 15:19
the cities of **I** and conquered Ijon, 1 Kgs 15:20
began to reign over **I** in the second 1 Kgs 15:25
and he reigned over **I** two years. 1 Kgs 15:25
in his sin which he made **I** to sin. 1 Kgs 15:26
for Nadab and all **I** were laying siege 1 Kgs 15:27
he sinned and that he made **I** to sin, 1 Kgs 15:30
he provoked the LORD, the God of **I**. 1 Kgs 15:30
of the Chronicles of the Kings of **I**? 1 Kgs 15:31
and Baasha king of **I** all their days. 1 Kgs 15:32
began to reign over all **I** at Tirzah, 1 Kgs 15:33
in his sin which he made **I** to sin. 1 Kgs 15:34
made you leader over my people **I**, 1 Kgs 16:2
and have made my people **I** to sin, 1 Kgs 16:2
of the Chronicles of the Kings of **I**? 1 Kgs 16:5
began to reign over **I** in Tirzah, 1 Kgs 16:8
and which they made **I** to sin, 1 Kgs 16:13
the LORD God of **I** to anger with their 1 Kgs 16:13
of the Chronicles of the Kings of **I**? 1 Kgs 16:14
king." Therefore all **I** made Omri, 1 Kgs 16:16
king over **I** that day in the camp. 1 Kgs 16:16
from Gibbethon, and all **I** with him, 1 Kgs 16:17
he committed, making **I** to sin. 1 Kgs 16:19
of the Chronicles of the Kings of **I**? 1 Kgs 16:20
the people of **I** were divided into 1 Kgs 16:21
of Judah, Omri began to reign over **I**, 1 Kgs 16:23
and in the sins that he made **I** to sin, 1 Kgs 16:26
sin, provoking the LORD, the God of **I**, 1 Kgs 16:26
of the Chronicles of the Kings of **I**? 1 Kgs 16:27
son of Omri began to reign over **I**, 1 Kgs 16:29
Omri reigned over **I** in Samaria 1 Kgs 16:29
to provoke the LORD, the God of **I**, 1 Kgs 16:33
all the kings of **I** who were before 1 Kgs 16:33
Ahab, "As the LORD the God of **I** lives, 1 Kgs 17:1
For thus says the LORD the God of **I**, 1 Kgs 17:14
to him, "Is it you, you troubler of **I**?" 1 Kgs 18:17
he answered, "I have not troubled **I**, 1 Kgs 18:18
send and gather all **I** to me at Mount 1 Kgs 18:19
all the people of **I** and gathered the 1 Kgs 18:20
saying, "**I** shall be your name," 1 Kgs 18:31
LORD, God of Abraham, Isaac, and **I**, 1 Kgs 18:36
this day that you are God in **I**, 1 Kgs 18:36
the people of **I** have forsaken your 1 Kgs 19:10
the people of **I** have forsaken your 1 Kgs 19:14
you shall anoint to be king over **I**, 1 Kgs 19:16
Yet I will leave seven thousand in **I**, 1 Kgs 19:18
to Ahab king of **I** and said to him, 1 Kgs 20:2
And the king of **I** answered, "As you 1 Kgs 20:4
Then the king of **I** called all the elders 1 Kgs 20:7
And the king of **I** answered, "Tell 1 Kgs 20:11
near to Ahab king of **I** and said, 1 Kgs 20:13
them he mustered all the people of **I**, 1 Kgs 20:15
Syrians fled, and **I** pursued them, 1 Kgs 20:20
And the king of **I** went out and 1 Kgs 20:21
near to the king of **I** and said to him, 1 Kgs 20:22
went up to Aphek to fight against **I**. 1 Kgs 20:26
the people of **I** were mustered and 1 Kgs 20:27
The people of **I** encamped before 1 Kgs 20:27
came near and said to the king of **I**, 1 Kgs 20:28

And the people of **I** struck down of 1 Kgs 20:29
of the house of **I** are merciful kings. 1 Kgs 20:31
our heads and go out to the king of **I**. 1 Kgs 20:31
and went to the king of **I** and said, 1 Kgs 20:32
was gone." The king of **I** said to him, 1 Kgs 20:40
and the king of **I** recognized him as 1 Kgs 20:41
And the king of **I** went to his house 1 Kgs 20:43
said to him, "Do you now govern **I**? 1 Kgs 21:7
go down to meet Ahab king of **I**, 1 Kgs 21:18
Ahab every male, bond or free, in **I**. 1 Kgs 21:21
and because you have made **I** to sin. 1 Kgs 21:22
LORD cast out before the people of **I**.) 1 Kgs 21:26
years Syria and **I** continued without 1 Kgs 22:1
of Judah came down to the king of **I**. 1 Kgs 22:2
And the king of **I** said to his servants, 1 Kgs 22:3
And Jehoshaphat said to the king of **I**, 1 Kgs 22:4
And Jehoshaphat said to the king of **I**, 1 Kgs 22:5
the king of **I** gathered the prophets 1 Kgs 22:6
And the king of **I** said to Jehoshaphat, 1 Kgs 22:8
the king of **I** summoned an officer 1 Kgs 22:9
the king of **I** and Jehoshaphat the 1 Kgs 22:10
"I saw all **I** scattered on the 1 Kgs 22:17
the king of **I** said to Jehoshaphat, 1 Kgs 22:18
And the king of **I** said, "Seize 1 Kgs 22:26
So the king of **I** and Jehoshaphat the 1 Kgs 22:29
the king of **I** said to Jehoshaphat, 1 Kgs 22:30
the king of **I** disguised himself and 1 Kgs 22:30
great, but only with the king of **I**." 1 Kgs 22:31
surely the king of **I**." So they turned 1 Kgs 22:32
saw that it was not the king of **I**, 1 Kgs 22:33
the king of **I** between the scale 1 Kgs 22:34
of the Chronicles of the Kings of **I**? 1 Kgs 22:39
in the fourth year of Ahab king of **I**. 1 Kgs 22:41
also made peace with the king of **I**. 1 Kgs 22:44
began to reign over **I** in Samaria in 1 Kgs 22:51
and he reigned two years over **I**. 1 Kgs 22:51
the son of Nebat, who made **I** to sin. 1 Kgs 22:52
and provoked the LORD, the God of **I**, 1 Kgs 22:53
of Ahab, Moab rebelled against **I**. 2 Kgs 1:1
there is no God in **I** that you are going 2 Kgs 1:3
is no God in **I** that you are sending 2 Kgs 1:6
there is no God in **I** to inquire of his 2 Kgs 1:16
of the Chronicles of the Kings of **I**? 2 Kgs 1:18
The chariots of **I** and its horsemen!" 2 Kgs 2:12
Ahab became king over **I** in Samaria, 2 Kgs 3:1
son of Nebat, which he made **I** to sin; 2 Kgs 3:3
to the king of **I** 100,000 lambs and the 2 Kgs 3:4
of Moab rebelled against the king of **I**. 2 Kgs 3:5
at that time and mustered all **I**. 2 Kgs 3:6
So the king of **I** went with the king of 2 Kgs 3:9
Then the king of **I** said, "Alas! The 2 Kgs 3:10
So the king of **I** and Jehoshaphat and 2 Kgs 3:12
And Elisha said to the king of **I**, 2 Kgs 3:13
But the king of **I** said to him, 2 Kgs 3:13
But when they came to the camp of **I**, 2 Kgs 3:24
And there came great wrath against **I**. 2 Kgs 3:27
off a little girl from the land of **I**, 2 Kgs 5:2
so spoke the girl from the land of **I**." 2 Kgs 5:4
a letter to the king of **I**." So he went, 2 Kgs 5:5
he brought the letter to the king of **I**, 2 Kgs 5:6
And when the king of **I** read the letter, 2 Kgs 5:7
that the king of **I** had torn his clothes, 2 Kgs 5:8
may know that there is a prophet in **I**." 2 Kgs 5:8
better than all the waters of **I**? 2 Kgs 5:12
is no God in all the earth but in **I**; 2 Kgs 5:15
king of Syria was warring against **I**, 2 Kgs 6:8
man of God sent word to the king of **I**, 2 Kgs 6:9
And the king of **I** sent to the place 2 Kgs 6:10
me who of us is for the king of **I**?" 2 Kgs 6:11
but Elisha, the prophet who is in **I**, 2 Kgs 6:12
tells the king of **I** the words that you 2 Kgs 6:12
As soon as the king of **I** saw them, he 2 Kgs 6:21
again on raids into the land of **I**. 2 Kgs 6:23
as the king of **I** was passing by on 2 Kgs 6:26
the king of **I** has hired against us the 2 Kgs 7:6
whole multitude of **I** who have 2 Kgs 7:13
evil that you will do to the people of **I**. 2 Kgs 8:12
of Joram the son of Ahab, king of **I**, 2 Kgs 8:16
he walked in the way of the kings of **I**, 2 Kgs 8:18
of Joram the son of Ahab, king of **I**, 2 Kgs 8:25
a granddaughter of Omri king of **I**. 2 Kgs 8:26
says the LORD, I anoint you king over **I**.' 2 Kgs 9:3
him, "Thus says the LORD the God of **I**, 2 Kgs 9:6
king over the people of the LORD, over **I**. 2 Kgs 9:6
Ahab every male, bond or free, in **I**. 2 Kgs 9:8
the LORD, I anoint you king over **I**.'" 2 Kgs 9:12
(Now Joram with all **I** had been on 2 Kgs 9:14
Joram king of **I** and Ahaziah king 2 Kgs 9:21
And Jehu sent throughout all **I**, and 2 Kgs 10:21
Thus Jehu wiped out Baal from **I**. 2 Kgs 10:28
which he made **I** to sin—that is, 2 Kgs 10:29
shall sit on the throne of **I**." 2 Kgs 10:30
LORD the God of **I** with all his heart. 2 Kgs 10:31
of Jeroboam, which he made **I** to sin. 2 Kgs 10:31
the LORD began to cut off parts of **I**. 2 Kgs 10:32
them throughout the territory of **I**: 2 Kgs 10:32
of the Chronicles of the Kings of **I**? 2 Kgs 10:34
Jehu reigned over **I** in Samaria was 2 Kgs 10:36
began to reign over **I** in Samaria, 2 Kgs 13:1
son of Nebat, which he made **I** to sin; 2 Kgs 13:2
of the LORD was kindled against **I**, 2 Kgs 13:3
to him, for he saw the oppression of **I**, 2 Kgs 13:4
(Therefore the LORD gave **I** a savior, so 2 Kgs 13:5
and the people of **I** lived in their 2 Kgs 13:5
of Jeroboam, which he made **I** to sin, 2 Kgs 13:6
of the Chronicles of the Kings of **I**? 2 Kgs 13:8
began to reign over **I** in Samaria, 2 Kgs 13:10
of Nebat, which he made **I** to sin, 2 Kgs 13:11
of the Chronicles of the Kings of **I**? 2 Kgs 13:12
in Samaria with the kings of **I**. 2 Kgs 13:13
Joash king of **I** went down to him 2 Kgs 13:14
The chariots of **I** and its horsemen!" 2 Kgs 13:14
Then he said to the king of **I**, "Draw 2 Kgs 13:16
And he said to the king of **I**, "Strike 2 Kgs 13:18
king of Syria oppressed **I** all the days 2 Kgs 13:22
him and recovered the cities of **I**. 2 Kgs 13:25
of Joash the son of Joahaz, king of **I**, 2 Kgs 14:1
son of Jehoahaz, son of Jehu, king of **I**, 2 Kgs 14:8
And Jehoash king of **I** sent word to 2 Kgs 14:9
So Jehoash king of **I** went up, and he 2 Kgs 14:11
And Judah was defeated by **I**, and 2 Kgs 14:12
Jehoash king of **I** captured Amaziah 2 Kgs 14:13
of the Chronicles of the Kings of **I**? 2 Kgs 14:15
in Samaria with the kings of **I**, 2 Kgs 14:16
of Jehoash son of Jehoahaz, king of **I**. 2 Kgs 14:17
Jeroboam the son of Joash, king of **I**, 2 Kgs 14:23
of Nebat, which he made **I** to sin. 2 Kgs 14:24
the border of **I** from Lebo-hamath 2 Kgs 14:25
to the word of the LORD, the God of **I**, 2 Kgs 14:25
the affliction of **I** was very bitter, 2 Kgs 14:26
or free, and there was none to help **I**. 2 Kgs 14:26
the name of **I** from under heaven, 2 Kgs 14:27
and Hamath to Judah in **I**, 2 Kgs 14:28
of the Chronicles of the Kings of **I**? 2 Kgs 14:28
slept with his fathers, the kings of **I**, 2 Kgs 14:29
year of Jeroboam king of **I**, 2 Kgs 15:1
Jeroboam reigned over **I** in Samaria 2 Kgs 15:8
son of Nebat, which he made **I** to sin. 2 Kgs 15:9
of the Chronicles of the Kings of **I**. 2 Kgs 15:11
on the throne of **I** to the fourth 2 Kgs 15:12
of the Chronicles of the Kings of **I**. 2 Kgs 15:15
the son of Gadi began to reign over **I**, 2 Kgs 15:17
of Nebat, which he made **I** to sin. 2 Kgs 15:18
exacted the money from **I**, 2 Kgs 15:20
of the Chronicles of the Kings of **I**? 2 Kgs 15:21
began to reign over **I** in Samaria, 2 Kgs 15:23
of Nebat, which he made **I** to sin. 2 Kgs 15:24
of the Chronicles of the Kings of **I**. 2 Kgs 15:26
began to reign over **I** in Samaria, 2 Kgs 15:27
of Nebat, which he made **I** to sin. 2 Kgs 15:28
In the days of Pekah king of **I**, 2 Kgs 15:29
of the Chronicles of the Kings of **I**. 2 Kgs 15:31
the son of Remaliah, king of **I**, 2 Kgs 15:32
he walked in the way of the kings of **I**. 2 Kgs 16:3
LORD drove out before the people of **I**. 2 Kgs 16:3
Pekah the son of Remaliah, king of **I**, 2 Kgs 16:5
and from the hand of the king of **I**, 2 Kgs 16:7
began to reign in Samaria over **I**, 2 Kgs 17:1
as the kings of **I** who were before him. 2 Kgs 17:2
the people of **I** had sinned against 2 Kgs 17:7
LORD drove out before the people of **I**, 2 Kgs 17:8
that the kings of **I** had practiced. 2 Kgs 17:8
the people of **I** did secretly against 2 Kgs 17:9
Yet the LORD warned **I** and Judah by 2 Kgs 17:13
very angry with **I** and removed them 2 Kgs 17:18
the customs that **I** had introduced. 2 Kgs 17:19
the descendants of **I** and afflicted 2 Kgs 17:20
When he had torn **I** from the house 2 Kgs 17:21
Jeroboam drove **I** from following 2 Kgs 17:21
The people of **I** walked in all the sins 2 Kgs 17:22
until the LORD removed **I** out of his 2 Kgs 17:23
So **I** was exiled from their own land 2 Kgs 17:23
of Samaria instead of the people of **I**. 2 Kgs 17:24
of Jacob, whom he named **I**. 2 Kgs 17:34
year of Hoshea son of Elah, king of **I**, 2 Kgs 18:1
the people of **I** had made offerings 2 Kgs 18:4
He trusted in the LORD the God of **I**, so 2 Kgs 18:5
year of Hoshea son of Elah, king of **I**, 2 Kgs 18:9
the ninth year of Hoshea king of **I**, 2 Kgs 18:10
"O LORD the God of **I**, who is 2 Kgs 19:15
"Thus says the LORD, the God of **I**: 2 Kgs 19:20
heights? Against the Holy One of **I**! 2 Kgs 19:22
LORD drove out before the people of **I**. 2 Kgs 21:2
Asherah, as Ahab king of **I** had done, 2 Kgs 21:3
I have chosen out of all the tribes of **I**, 2 Kgs 21:7
cause the feet of **I** to wander anymore 2 Kgs 21:8
LORD destroyed before the people of **I**. 2 Kgs 21:9
thus says the LORD, the God of **I**: 2 Kgs 21:12
"Thus says the LORD, the God of **I**: 2 Kgs 22:15
Thus says the LORD, the God of **I**: 2 Kgs 22:18
Solomon the king of **I** had built for 2 Kgs 23:13
the son of Nebat, who made **I** to sin, 2 Kgs 23:15
which kings of **I** had made, 2 Kgs 23:19
the days of the judges who judged **I**, 2 Kgs 23:22
days of the kings of **I** or of the kings 2 Kgs 23:22
out of my sight, as I have removed **I**, 2 Kgs 23:27
which Solomon king of **I** had made, 2 Kgs 24:13
Isaac. The sons of Isaac: Esau and **I**. 1 Chr 1:34
any king reigned over the people of **I**: 1 Chr 1:43
These are the sons of **I**: Reuben, 1 Chr 2:1
Achan, the troubler of **I**, who broke 1 Chr 2:7
Jabez called upon the God of **I**, 1 Chr 4:10
Reuben the firstborn of **I** (for he was 1 Chr 5:1
given to the sons of Joseph the son of **I**, 1 Chr 5:1
the sons of Reuben, the firstborn of **I**: 1 Chr 5:3
and in the days of Jeroboam king of **I**. 1 Chr 5:17
So the God of **I** stirred up the spirit of 1 Chr 5:26
son of Kohath, son of Levi, son of **I**; 1 Chr 6:38
Place, and to make atonement for **I**, 1 Chr 6:49
So the people of **I** gave the Levites the 1 Chr 6:64
lived the sons of Joseph the son of **I**. 1 Chr 7:29
So all **I** was recorded in genealogies, 1 Chr 9:1
written in the Book of the Kings of **I**. 1 Chr 9:1
their possessions in their cities were **I**, 1 Chr 9:2
Now the Philistines fought against **I**, 1 Chr 10:1
and the men of **I** fled before the 1 Chr 10:1
when all the men of **I** who were in the 1 Chr 10:7
Then all **I** gathered together to David 1 Chr 11:1
you who led out and brought in **I**. 1 Chr 11:2
shall be shepherd of my people **I**, 1 Chr 11:2
shall be prince over my people **I**.'" 1 Chr 11:2
So all the elders of **I** came to the king 1 Chr 11:3
And they anointed David king over **I**, 1 Chr 11:3
David and all **I** went to Jerusalem, 1 Chr 11:4
in his kingdom, together with all **I**, 1 Chr 11:10
the word of the LORD concerning **I**. 1 Chr 11:10
times, to know what **I** ought to do, 1 Chr 12:32
intent to make David king over all **I**. 1 Chr 12:38
all the rest of **I** were of a single mind 1 Chr 12:38
and sheep, for there was joy in **I**. 1 Chr 12:40
David said to all the assembly of **I**, 1 Chr 13:2
who remain in all the lands of **I**, 1 Chr 13:2
David assembled all **I** from the Nile 1 Chr 13:5
And David and all **I** went up to 1 Chr 13:6
David and all **I** were rejoicing before 1 Chr 13:8
had established him as king over **I**, 1 Chr 14:2
exalted for the sake of his people **I**. 1 Chr 14:2
had been anointed king over all **I**, 1 Chr 14:8
David assembled all **I** at Jerusalem to 1 Chr 15:3
up the ark of the LORD, the God of **I**, 1 Chr 15:12
up the ark of the LORD, the God of **I**. 1 Chr 15:14
the elders of **I** and the commanders 1 Chr 15:25
So all **I** brought up the ark of the 1 Chr 15:28
and distributed to all **I**, both men and 1 Chr 16:3
and to praise the LORD, the God of **I**. 1 Chr 16:4
O offspring of **I** his servant, sons of 1 Chr 16:13
as an everlasting covenant to **I**, 1 Chr 16:17
Blessed be the LORD, the God of **I**, 1 Chr 16:36
of the LORD that he commanded **I**. 1 Chr 16:40
the day I brought up **I** to this day, 1 Chr 17:5
places where I have moved with all **I**, 1 Chr 17:6
a word with any of the judges of **I**, 1 Chr 17:6
sheep, to be prince over my people **I**, 1 Chr 17:7
place for my people **I** and will plant 1 Chr 17:9
I appointed judges over my people **I**. 1 Chr 17:10
And who is like your people **I**, the 1 Chr 17:21
you made your people **I** to be your 1 Chr 17:22
'The LORD of hosts, the God of **I**, 1 Chr 17:24
So David reigned over all **I**, and he 1 Chr 18:14
the best men of **I** and arrayed them 1 Chr 19:10
saw that they had been defeated by **I**, 1 Chr 19:16
he gathered all **I** together and 1 Chr 19:17
And the Syrians fled before **I**, and 1 Chr 19:18
saw that they had been defeated by **I**, 1 Chr 19:19
And when he taunted **I**, Jonathan the 1 Chr 20:7
Satan stood against **I** and incited 1 Chr 21:1
Israel and incited David to number **I**. 1 Chr 21:1
of the army, "Go, number **I**, 1 Chr 21:2
should it be a cause of guilt for **I**?" 1 Chr 21:3
went throughout all **I** and came 1 Chr 21:4
In all **I** there were 1,100,000 men who 1 Chr 21:5
with this thing, and he struck **I**. 1 Chr 21:7
throughout all the territory of **I**.' 1 Chr 21:12
So the LORD sent a pestilence on **I**, 1 Chr 21:14
on Israel, and 70,000 men of **I** fell. 1 Chr 21:14
here the altar of burnt offering for **I**." 1 Chr 22:1
aliens who were in the land of **I**, 1 Chr 22:2
a house for the LORD, the God of **I**. 1 Chr 22:6
give peace and quiet to **I** in his days. 1 Chr 22:9
his royal throne in **I** forever.' 1 Chr 22:10
you charge over **I** you may keep 1 Chr 22:12
the LORD commanded Moses for **I**. 1 Chr 22:13
all the leaders of **I** to help Solomon 1 Chr 22:17
made Solomon his son king over **I**. 1 Chr 23:1
all the leaders of **I** and the priests and 1 Chr 23:2

David said, "The LORD, the God of **I**, 1 Chr 23:25
LORD God of **I** had commanded him. 1 Chr 24:19
appointed to external duties for **I**, 1 Chr 26:29
the oversight of **I** westward of the 1 Chr 26:30
This is the number of the people of **I**, 1 Chr 27:1
Over the tribes of **I**, for the 1 Chr 27:16
were the leaders of the tribes of **I**. 1 Chr 27:22
had promised to make **I** as many as 1 Chr 27:23
Yet wrath came upon **I** for this, and 1 Chr 27:24
at Jerusalem all the officials of **I**, 1 Chr 28:1
the LORD God of **I** chose me from all 1 Chr 28:4
house to be king over **I** forever. 1 Chr 28:4
in me to make me king over all **I**. 1 Chr 28:4
of the kingdom of the LORD over **I**. 1 Chr 28:5
Now therefore in the sight of all **I**, the 1 Chr 28:8
you, O LORD, the God of **I** our father, 1 Chr 29:10
the God of Abraham, Isaac, and **I**, 1 Chr 29:18
sacrifices in abundance for all **I**. 1 Chr 29:21
he prospered, and all **I** obeyed him. 1 Chr 29:23
the sight of all **I** and bestowed on 1 Chr 29:25
been on any king before him in **I**. 1 Chr 29:25
the son of Jesse reigned over all **I**. 1 Chr 29:26
he reigned over **I** was forty years. 1 Chr 29:27
upon him and upon **I** and upon all 1 Chr 29:30
Solomon spoke to all **I**, to the 2 Chr 1:2
judges, and to all the leaders in all **I**, 2 Chr 1:2
to Jerusalem. And he reigned over **I**. 2 Chr 1:13
LORD our God, as ordained forever for **I**. 2 Chr 2:4
said, "Blessed be the LORD God of **I**, 2 Chr 2:12
aliens who were in the land of **I**, 2 Chr 2:17
assembled the elders of **I** and all the 2 Chr 5:2
of the fathers' houses of the people of **I**, 2 Chr 5:2
all the men of **I** assembled before the 2 Chr 5:3
And all the elders of **I** came, and the 2 Chr 5:4
Solomon and all the congregation of **I**, 2 Chr 5:6
made a covenant with the people of **I**, 2 Chr 5:10
and blessed all the assembly of **I**, 2 Chr 6:3
while all the assembly of **I** stood. 2 Chr 6:3
said, "Blessed be the LORD, the God of **I**, 2 Chr 6:4
of all the tribes of **I** in which to build a 2 Chr 6:5
no man as prince over my people **I**; 2 Chr 6:5
chosen David to be over my people **I**.' 2 Chr 6:6
for the name of the LORD, the God of **I**. 2 Chr 6:7
my father and sit on the throne of **I**, 2 Chr 6:10
for the name of the LORD, the God of **I**. 2 Chr 6:10
that he made with the people of **I**." 2 Chr 6:11
all the assembly of **I** and spread out 2 Chr 6:12
the presence of all the assembly of **I**, 2 Chr 6:13
and said, "O LORD, God of **I**, there is no 2 Chr 6:14
Now therefore, O LORD, God of **I**, keep 2 Chr 6:16
to sit before me on the throne of **I**, 2 Chr 6:16
Now therefore, O LORD, God of **I**, let 2 Chr 6:17
of your servant and of your people **I**, 2 Chr 6:21
"If your people **I** are defeated before 2 Chr 6:24
sin of your people **I** and bring them 2 Chr 6:25
sin of your servants, your people **I**, 2 Chr 6:27
by any man or by all your people **I**, 2 Chr 6:29
foreigner, who is not of your people **I**, 2 Chr 6:32
and fear you, as do your people **I**, 2 Chr 6:33
all the people of **I** saw the fire come 2 Chr 7:3
sounded trumpets, and all **I** stood. 2 Chr 7:6
feast for seven days, and all **I** with him, 2 Chr 7:8
and to Solomon and to **I** his people. 2 Chr 7:10
'You shall not lack a man to rule **I**.' 2 Chr 7:18
and settled the people of **I** in them. 2 Chr 8:2
and the Jebusites, who were not of **I**, 2 Chr 8:7
whom the people of **I** had not destroyed 2 Chr 8:8
of the people of **I** Solomon made no 2 Chr 8:9
live in the house of David king of **I**, 2 Chr 8:11
your God loved **I** and would establish 2 Chr 9:8
in Jerusalem over all **I** forty years. 2 Chr 9:30
for all **I** had come to Shechem to 2 Chr 10:1
Jeroboam and all **I** came and said 2 Chr 10:3
And when all **I** saw that the king did 2 Chr 10:16
Jesse. Each of you to your tents, O **I**! 2 Chr 10:16
David." So all **I** went to their tents. 2 Chr 10:16
over the people of **I** who lived in the 2 Chr 10:17
and the people of **I** stoned him to 2 Chr 10:18
So **I** has been in rebellion against 2 Chr 10:19
chosen warriors, to fight against **I**, 2 Chr 11:1
and to all **I** in Judah and Benjamin, 2 Chr 11:3
were in all **I** presented themselves to 2 Chr 11:13
the LORD God of **I** came after them 2 Chr 11:16
all the tribes of **I** to Jerusalem to 2 Chr 11:16
law of the LORD, and all **I** with him. 2 Chr 12:1
Then the princes of **I** and the king 2 Chr 12:6
of all the tribes of **I** to put his name 2 Chr 12:13
said, "Hear me, O Jeroboam and all **I**! 2 Chr 13:4
the LORD God of **I** gave the kingship 2 Chr 13:5
the kingship over **I** forever to David 2 Chr 13:5
O sons of **I**, do not fight against the 2 Chr 13:12
Jeroboam and all **I** before Abijah 2 Chr 13:15
The men of **I** fled before Judah, and 2 Chr 13:16
fell slain of **I** 500,000 chosen men. 2 Chr 13:17
Thus the men of **I** were subdued at 2 Chr 13:18

For a long time **I** was without the 2 Chr 15:3
they turned to the LORD, the God of **I**, 2 Chr 15:4
deserted to him from **I** when they saw 2 Chr 15:9
not seek the LORD, the God of **I**, 2 Chr 15:13
high places were not taken out of **I**. 2 Chr 15:17
Baasha king of **I** went up against 2 Chr 16:1
your covenant with Baasha king of **I**, 2 Chr 16:3
of his armies against the cities of **I**, 2 Chr 16:4
Book of the Kings of Judah and **I**. 2 Chr 16:11
and strengthened himself against **I**. 2 Chr 17:1
not according to the practices of **I**. 2 Chr 17:4
Ahab king of **I** said to Jehoshaphat 2 Chr 18:3
And Jehoshaphat said to the king of **I**, 2 Chr 18:4
the king of **I** gathered the prophets 2 Chr 18:5
And the king of **I** said to Jehoshaphat, 2 Chr 18:7
the king of **I** summoned an officer 2 Chr 18:8
the king of **I** and Jehoshaphat the 2 Chr 18:9
"I saw all **I** scattered on the 2 Chr 18:16
the king of **I** said to Jehoshaphat, 2 Chr 18:17
'Who will entice Ahab the king of **I**, 2 Chr 18:19
And the king of **I** said, "Seize 2 Chr 18:25
So the king of **I** and Jehoshaphat the 2 Chr 18:28
the king of **I** said to Jehoshaphat, 2 Chr 18:29
And the king of **I** disguised himself, 2 Chr 18:29
great, but only with the king of **I**." 2 Chr 18:30
"It is the king of **I**." So they turned to 2 Chr 18:31
saw that it was not the king of **I**, 2 Chr 18:32
the king of **I** between the scale 2 Chr 18:33
and the king of **I** was propped up in 2 Chr 18:34
and priests and heads of families of **I**, 2 Chr 19:8
of this land before your people **I**, 2 Chr 20:7
would not let **I** invade when they 2 Chr 20:10
up to praise the LORD, the God of **I**, 2 Chr 20:19
had fought against the enemies of **I**. 2 Chr 20:29
in the Book of the Kings of **I**. 2 Chr 20:34
joined with Ahaziah king of **I**, 2 Chr 20:35
and also some of the princes of **I**. 2 Chr 21:4
he walked in the way of the kings of **I**, 2 Chr 21:6
of the kings of **I** and have enticed 2 Chr 21:13
house of Ahab led **I** into whoredom, 2 Chr 21:13
of Ahab king of **I** to make war 2 Chr 22:5
and the heads of fathers' houses of **I**, 2 Chr 23:2
and gather from all **I** money to repair 2 Chr 24:5
and the congregation of **I** for the tent 2 Chr 24:6
of God laid on **I** in the wilderness. 2 Chr 24:9
because he had done good in **I**, 2 Chr 24:16
men of valor from **I** for 100 talents of 2 Chr 25:6
do not let the army of **I** go with you, 2 Chr 25:7
go with you, for the LORD is not with **I**, 2 Chr 25:7
to the army of **I**?" The man of God 2 Chr 25:9
of Jehoahaz, son of Jehu, king of **I**, 2 Chr 25:17
Joash the king of **I** sent word to 2 Chr 25:18
So Joash king of **I** went up, and he 2 Chr 25:21
And Judah was defeated by **I**, and 2 Chr 25:22
Joash king of **I** captured Amaziah 2 Chr 25:23
Joash the son of Jehoahaz, king of **I**. 2 Chr 25:25
Book of the Kings of Judah and **I**? 2 Chr 25:26
the Book of the Kings of **I** and Judah. 2 Chr 27:7
walked in the ways of the kings of **I**. 2 Chr 28:2
LORD drove out before the people of **I**. 2 Chr 28:3
given into the hand of the king of **I**, 2 Chr 28:5
The men of **I** took captive 200,000 of 2 Chr 28:8
and there is fierce wrath against **I**." 2 Chr 28:13
Judah because of Ahaz king of **I**, 2 Chr 28:19
were the ruin of him and of all **I**. 2 Chr 28:23
Book of the Kings of Judah and **I**. 2 Chr 28:26
him into the tombs of the kings of **I**. 2 Chr 28:27
in the Holy Place to the God of **I**. 2 Chr 29:7
covenant with the LORD, the God of **I**, 2 Chr 29:10
altar, to make atonement for all **I**. 2 Chr 29:24
sin offering should be made for all **I**. 2 Chr 29:24
the instruments of David king of **I**. 2 Chr 29:27
Hezekiah sent to all **I** and Judah, and 2 Chr 30:1
the Passover to the LORD, the God of **I**. 2 Chr 30:1
a proclamation throughout all **I**, 2 Chr 30:5
the Passover to the LORD, the God of **I**, 2 Chr 30:5
went throughout all **I** and Judah with 2 Chr 30:6
commanded, saying, "O people of **I**, 2 Chr 30:6
the God of Abraham, Isaac, and **I**, 2 Chr 30:6
And the people of **I** who were present 2 Chr 30:21
whole assembly that came out of **I**, 2 Chr 30:25
who came out of the land of **I**, 2 Chr 30:25
of David king of **I** there had been 2 Chr 30:26
all **I** who were present went out to the 2 Chr 31:1
all the people of **I** returned to their 2 Chr 31:1
the people of **I** gave in abundance the 2 Chr 31:5
And the people of **I** and Judah who 2 Chr 31:6
they blessed the LORD and his people **I**. 2 Chr 31:8
the God of **I** and to speak against 2 Chr 32:17
Book of the Kings of Judah and **I**. 2 Chr 32:32
LORD drove out before the people of **I**. 2 Chr 33:2
I have chosen out of all the tribes of **I**, 2 Chr 33:7
remove the foot of **I** from the land 2 Chr 33:8
LORD destroyed before the people of **I**. 2 Chr 33:9
Judah to serve the LORD, the God of **I**. 2 Chr 33:16

in the name of the LORD, the God of **I**, 2 Chr 33:18
in the Chronicles of the Kings of **I**. 2 Chr 33:18
altars throughout all the land of **I**. 2 Chr 34:7
all the remnant of **I** and from all 2 Chr 34:9
those who are left in **I** and in Judah, 2 Chr 34:21
"Thus says the LORD, the God of **I**: 2 Chr 34:23
Thus says the LORD, the God of **I**: 2 Chr 34:26
to the people of **I** and made all who 2 Chr 34:33
who were present in **I** serve the LORD 2 Chr 34:33
who taught all **I** and who were 2 Chr 35:3
Solomon the son of David, king of **I**, 2 Chr 35:3
the LORD your God and his people **I**. 2 Chr 35:3
of David king of **I** and the document 2 Chr 35:4
And the people of **I** who were present 2 Chr 35:17
had been kept in **I** since the days of 2 Chr 35:18
of the kings of **I** had kept such a 2 Chr 35:18
all Judah and **I** who were present, 2 Chr 35:18
They made these a rule in **I**; behold, 2 Chr 35:25
Book of the Kings of **I** and Judah. 2 Chr 35:27
the Book of the Kings of **I** and Judah. 2 Chr 36:8
turning to the LORD, the God of **I**. 2 Chr 36:13
the God of **I**—he is the God who is in Ezr 1:3
The number of the men of the people of **I**: Ezr 2:2
descent, whether they belonged to **I**: Ezr 2:59
and all the rest of **I** in their towns. Ezr 2:70
and the children of **I** were in the towns, Ezr 3:1
and they built the altar of the God of **I**, Ezr 3:2
to the directions of David king of **I**. Ezr 3:10
endures forever toward **I**." And all the Ezr 3:11
a temple to the LORD, the God of **I**, Ezr 4:1
heads of fathers' houses in **I** said to them, Ezr 4:3
alone will build to the LORD, the God of **I**, Ezr 4:3
name of the God of **I** who was over them. Ezr 5:1
a great king of **I** built and finished. Ezr 5:11
decree of the God of **I** and by decree of Ezr 6:14
And the people of **I**, the priests and the Ezr 6:16
as a sin offering for all **I** 12 male goats, Ezr 6:17
to the number of the tribes of **I**. Ezr 6:17
by the people of **I** who had returned Ezr 6:21
land to worship the LORD, the God of **I**. Ezr 6:21
work of the house of God, the God of **I**. Ezr 6:22
that the LORD the God of **I** had given, Ezr 7:6
the king, some of the people of **I**, Ezr 7:7
and to teach his statutes and rules in **I**. Ezr 7:10
of the LORD and his statutes for **I**: Ezr 7:11
of the people of **I** or their priests or Ezr 7:13
have freely offered to the God of **I**, Ezr 7:15
gathered leading men from **I** to go up Ezr 7:28
sons of Mahli the son of Levi, son of **I**, Ezr 8:18
his lords and all **I** there present had Ezr 8:25
of fathers' houses in **I** at Jerusalem, Ezr 8:29
offered burnt offerings to the God of **I**, Ezr 8:35
to the God of Israel, twelve bulls for all **I**, Ezr 8:35
"The people of **I** and the priests and the Ezr 9:1
who trembled at the words of the God of **I**, Ezr 9:4
O LORD the God of **I**, you are just, for we Ezr 9:15
and children, gathered to him out of **I**, Ezr 10:1
now there is hope for **I** in spite of this. Ezr 10:2
and Levites and all **I** take oath that they Ezr 10:5
women, and so increased the guilt of **I**. Ezr 10:10
And of **I**: of the sons of Parosh: Ezr 10:25
night for the people of **I** your servants, Neh 1:6
confessing the sins of the people of **I**, Neh 1:6
to seek the welfare of the people of **I**. Neh 2:10
number of the men of the people of **I**: Neh 7:7
descent, whether they belonged to **I**: Neh 7:61
people, the temple servants, and all **I**, Neh 7:73
the people of **I** were in their towns. Neh 7:73
Moses that the LORD had commanded **I**. Neh 8:1
that the people of **I** should dwell in Neh 8:14
that day the people of **I** had not done so. Neh 8:17
the people of **I** were assembled with Neh 9:1
sin offerings to make atonement for **I**, Neh 10:33
For the people of **I** and the sons of Levi Neh 10:39
I, the priests, the Levites, the temple Neh 11:3
And the rest of **I**, and of the priests and Neh 11:20
And all **I** in the days of Zerubbabel Neh 12:47
meet the people of **I** with bread and Neh 13:2
they separated from **I** all those of Neh 13:3
more wrath on **I** by profaning the Neh 13:18
not Solomon king of **I** sin on account Neh 13:26
and God made him king over all **I**. Neh 13:26
that salvation for **I** would come out of Ps 14:7
his people, let Jacob rejoice, let **I** be glad. Ps 14:7
are holy, enthroned on the praises of **I**. Ps 22:3
in awe of him, all you offspring of **I**! Ps 22:23
Redeem **I**, O God, out of all his troubles. Ps 25:22
Blessed be the LORD, the God of **I**, from Ps 41:13
"Hear, O my people, and I will speak; O **I**, Ps 50:7
that salvation for **I** would come out of Ps 53:6
his people, Let Jacob rejoice, let **I** be glad. Ps 53:6
You, LORD God of hosts, are God of **I**. Ps 59:5
the One of Sinai, before God, the God of **I**. Ps 68:8
power to God, whose majesty is over **I**, Ps 68:34
the God of **I**—he is the one who gives Ps 68:35

to dishonor through me, O God of **I**. Ps 69:6
to you with the lyre, O Holy One of **I**. Ps 71:22
Blessed be the LORD, the God of **I**, who Ps 72:18
Truly God is good to **I**, to those who are Ps 73:1
God is known; his name is great in **I**. Ps 76:1
in Jacob and appointed a law in **I**, Ps 78:5
against Jacob; his anger rose against **I**, Ps 78:21
them and laid low the young men of **I**. Ps 78:31
again and provoked the Holy One of **I**. Ps 78:41
and settled the tribes of **I** in their tents. Ps 78:55
full of wrath, and he utterly rejected **I**. Ps 78:59
Jacob his people, **I** his inheritance. Ps 78:71
Give ear, O Shepherd of **I**, you who lead Ps 80:1
For it is a statute for **I**, a rule of the God of Ps 81:4
O my people, while I admonish you! O **I**, Ps 81:8
to my voice; **I** would not submit to me. Ps 81:11
to me, that **I** would walk in my ways! Ps 81:13
let the name of **I** be remembered no Ps 83:4
the LORD, our king to the Holy One of **I**. Ps 89:18
love and faithfulness to the house of **I**. Ps 98:3
ways to Moses, his acts to the people of **I**. Ps 103:7
statute, to **I** as an everlasting covenant, Ps 105:10
Then **I** came to Egypt; Jacob Ps 105:23
Then he brought out **I** with silver and Ps 105:37
Blessed be the LORD, the God of **I**, from Ps 106:48
When **I** went out from Egypt, the house Ps 114:1
became his sanctuary, **I** his dominion. Ps 114:2
O **I**, trust in the LORD! He is their help Ps 115:9
bless us; he will bless the house of **I**; Ps 115:12
Let **I** say, "His steadfast love endures Ps 118:2
he who keeps **I** will neither slumber nor Ps 121:4
tribes of the LORD, as was decreed for **I**, Ps 122:4
who was on our side—let **I** now say— Ps 124:1
away with evildoers! Peace be upon **I**! Ps 125:5
children's children! Peace be upon **I**! Ps 128:6
me from my youth"—let **I** now say— Ps 129:1
O **I**, hope in the LORD! For with the LORD Ps 130:7
And he will redeem **I** from all his Ps 130:8
O **I**, hope in the LORD from this time Ps 131:3
for himself, **I** as his own possession. Ps 135:4
as a heritage, a heritage to his people **I**. Ps 135:12
O house of **I**, bless the LORD! O house of Ps 135:19
and brought **I** out from among them, Ps 136:11
and made **I** pass through the midst of Ps 136:14
a heritage to **I** his servant, for his Ps 136:22
Jerusalem; he gathers the outcasts of **I**. Ps 147:2
to Jacob, his statutes and rules to **I**. Ps 147:19
for the people of **I** who are near to him. Ps 148:14
Let **I** be glad in his Maker; let the Ps 149:2
of Solomon, son of David, king of **I**: Prv 1:1
have been king over **I** in Jerusalem. Eccl 1:12
mighty men, some of the mighty men of **I**, Sg 3:7
its master's crib, but **I** does not know, Is 1:3
LORD, they have despised the Holy One of **I**, Is 1:4
the LORD of hosts, the Mighty One of **I**: Is 1:24
be the pride and honor of the survivors of **I**. Is 4:2
of the LORD of hosts is the house of **I**, Is 5:7
counsel of the Holy One of **I** draw near, Is 5:19
despised the word of the Holy One of **I**. Is 5:24
Remaliah the king of **I** came up to Is 7:1
a rock of stumbling to both houses of **I**, Is 8:14
signs and portents in **I** from the LORD of Is 8:18
a word against Jacob, and it will fall on **I**; Is 9:8
on the west devour **I** with open mouth. Is 9:12
So the LORD cut off from **I** head and tail, Is 9:14
The light of **I** will become a fire, and his Is 10:17
day the remnant of **I** and the survivors Is 10:20
will lean on the LORD, the Holy One of **I**, Is 10:20
For though your people **I** be as the sand Is 10:22
and will assemble the banished of **I**, Is 11:12
as there was for **I** when they came up Is 11:16
great in your midst is the Holy One of **I**." Is 12:6
on Jacob and will again choose **I**, Is 14:1
and the house of **I** will possess them in the Is 14:2
will be like the glory of the children of **I**, Is 17:3
of a fruit tree, declares the LORD God of **I**. Is 17:6
his eyes will look on the Holy One of **I**. Is 17:7
they deserted because of the children of **I**, Is 17:9
In that day **I** will be the third with Egypt Is 19:24
of my hands, and **I** my inheritance." Is 19:25
from the LORD of hosts, the God of **I**, Is 21:10
will be few, for the LORD, the God of **I**, Is 21:17
to the name of the LORD, the God of **I**. Is 24:15
I shall blossom and put forth shoots and Is 27:6
will be gleaned one by one, O people of **I**. Is 27:12
shall exult in the Holy One of **I**. Is 29:19
and will stand in awe of the God of **I**. Is 29:23
hear no more about the Holy One of **I**." Is 30:11
Therefore thus says the Holy One of **I**, Is 30:12
said the Lord GOD, the Holy One of **I**, Is 30:15
mountain of the LORD, to the Rock of **I**. Is 30:29
to the Holy One of **I** or consult the LORD! Is 31:1
have deeply revolted, O children of **I**. Is 31:6
"O LORD of hosts, God of **I**, who is Is 37:16
"Thus says the LORD, the God of **I**: Is 37:21
the heights? Against the Holy One of **I**! Is 37:23
do you say, O Jacob, and speak, O **I**, Is 40:27
But you, **I**, my servant, Jacob, whom I Is 41:8
Fear not, you worm Jacob, you men of **I**! Is 41:14
LORD; your Redeemer is the Holy One of **I**. Is 41:14
in the Holy One of **I** you shall glory. Is 41:16
I the God of **I** will not forsake them. Is 41:17
this, the Holy One of **I** has created it. Is 41:20
to the looter, and **I** to the plunderers? Is 42:24
you, O Jacob, he who formed you, O **I**: Is 43:1
I am the LORD your God, the Holy One of **I**, Is 43:3
LORD, your Redeemer, the Holy One of **I**: Is 43:14
the LORD, your Holy One, the Creator of **I**, Is 43:15
but you have been weary of me, O **I**! Is 43:22
to utter destruction and **I** to reviling. Is 43:28
Jacob my servant, **I** whom I have chosen! Is 44:1
and name himself by the name of **I**." Is 44:5
the LORD, the King of **I** and his Redeemer, Is 44:6
Remember these things, O Jacob, and **I**, Is 44:21
you are my servant; O **I**, you will not be Is 44:21
Jacob, and will be glorified in **I**. Is 44:23
know that it is I, the LORD, the God of **I**, Is 45:3
of my servant Jacob, and **I** my chosen, Is 45:4
Thus says the LORD, the Holy One of **I**, Is 45:11
are a God who hides yourself, O God of **I**, Is 45:15
But **I** is saved by the LORD with Is 45:17
all the offspring of **I** shall be justified Is 45:25
of Jacob, all the remnant of the house of **I**, Is 46:3
put salvation in Zion, for **I** my glory." Is 46:13
of hosts is his name—is the Holy One of **I**. Is 47:4
of Jacob, who are called by the name of **I**, Is 48:1
name of the LORD and confess the God of **I**, Is 48:1
city, and stay themselves on the God of **I**; Is 48:2
"Listen to me, O Jacob, and **I**, whom I Is 48:12
LORD, your Redeemer, the Holy One of **I**: Is 48:17
servant, **I**, in whom I will be glorified." Is 49:3
and that **I** might be gathered to him— Is 49:5
and to bring back the preserved of **I**; Is 49:6
LORD, the Redeemer of **I** and his Holy One, Is 49:7
LORD, who is faithful, the Holy One of **I**, Is 49:7
and the God of **I** will be your rear guard. Is 52:12
and the Holy One of **I** is your Redeemer, Is 54:5
LORD your God, and of the Holy One of **I**, Is 55:5
Lord GOD, who gathers the outcasts of **I**, Is 56:8
LORD your God, and for the Holy One of **I**, Is 60:9
of the LORD, the Zion of the Holy One of **I**. Is 60:14
to the house of **I** that he has granted Is 63:7
know us, and **I** does not acknowledge us; Is 63:16
I was holy to the LORD, the firstfruits of his Jer 2:3
Jacob, and all the clans of the house of **I**. Jer 2:4
"Is **I** a slave? Is he a homeborn servant? Jer 2:14
so the house of **I** shall be shamed: Jer 2:26
Have I been a wilderness to **I**, or a land of Jer 2:31
I, how she went up on every high hill and Jer 3:6
I, I had sent her away with a decree of Jer 3:8
"Faithless **I** has shown herself more Jer 3:11
the north, and say, "'Return, faithless **I**, Jer 3:12
house of Judah shall join the house of **I**, Jer 3:18
been treacherous to me, O house of **I**, Jer 3:20
in the LORD our God is the salvation of **I**. Jer 3:23
"If you return, O **I**, declares the LORD, to Jer 4:1
For the house of **I** and the house of Judah Jer 5:11
you a nation from afar, O house of **I**, Jer 5:15
thoroughly as a vine the remnant of **I**; Jer 6:9
Thus says the LORD of hosts, the God of **I**: Jer 7:3
to it because of the evil of my people **I**. Jer 7:12
Thus says the LORD of hosts, the God of **I**: Jer 7:21
thus says the LORD of hosts, the God of **I**: Jer 9:15
all the house of **I** is uncircumcised in Jer 9:26
that the LORD speaks to you, O house of **I**. Jer 10:1
and **I** is the tribe of his inheritance; Jer 10:16
to them, Thus says the LORD, the God of **I**: Jer 11:3
The house of **I** and the house of Judah Jer 11:10
evil that the house of **I** and the house of Jer 11:17
that I have given my people **I** to inherit: Jer 12:14
the whole house of **I** and the whole Jer 13:11
'Thus says the LORD, the God of **I**, Jer 13:12
O you hope of **I**, its savior in time of Jer 14:8
thus says the LORD of hosts, the God of **I**: Jer 16:9
up the people of **I** out of the land Jer 16:14
up the people of **I** out of the north Jer 16:15
O LORD, the hope of **I**, all who forsake Jer 17:13
"O house of **I**, can I not do with you as Jer 18:6
so are you in my hand, O house of **I**. Jer 18:6
The virgin **I** has done a very horrible Jer 18:13
Thus says the LORD of hosts, the God of **I**: Jer 19:3
says the LORD of hosts, the God of **I**, Jer 19:15
'Thus says the LORD, the God of **I**: Jer 21:4
thus says the LORD, the God of **I**, Jer 23:2
will be saved, and **I** will dwell securely. Jer 23:6
brought up the people of **I** out of the land Jer 23:7
of the house of **I** out of the north Jer 23:8
by Baal and led my people **I** astray. Jer 23:13
"Thus says the LORD, the God of **I**: Like Jer 24:5
Thus the LORD, the God of **I**, said to me: Jer 25:15
says the LORD of hosts, the God of **I**: Jer 25:27
'Thus says the LORD of hosts, the God of **I**: Jer 27:4
thus says the LORD of hosts, the God of **I**, Jer 27:21
says the LORD of hosts, the God of **I**: Jer 28:2
thus says the LORD of hosts, the God of **I**: Jer 28:14
says the LORD of hosts, the God of **I**, Jer 29:4
thus says the LORD of hosts, the God of **I**: Jer 29:8
says the LORD of hosts, the God of **I**, Jer 29:21
have done an outrageous thing in **I**, Jer 29:23
says the LORD of hosts, the God of **I**: Jer 29:25
"Thus says the LORD, the God of **I**: Write Jer 30:2
the fortunes of my people, **I** and Judah, Jer 30:3
the LORD spoke concerning **I** and Judah: Jer 30:4
declares the LORD, nor be dismayed, O **I**; Jer 30:10
I will be the God of all the clans of **I**, Jer 31:1
in the wilderness; when **I** sought for rest, Jer 31:2
you, and you shall be built, O virgin **I**! Jer 31:4
LORD, save your people, the remnant of **I**.' Jer 31:7
shall not stumble, for I am a father to **I**, Jer 31:9
say, 'He who scattered **I** will gather him, Jer 31:10
Return, O virgin **I**, return to these your Jer 31:21
says the LORD of hosts, the God of **I**: Jer 31:23
will sow the house of **I** and the house of Jer 31:27
with the house of **I** and the house of Jer 31:31
with the house of **I** after those days, Jer 31:33
shall the offspring of **I** cease from being Jer 31:36
off all the offspring of **I** for all that they Jer 31:37
says the LORD of hosts, the God of **I**: Jer 32:14
thus says the LORD of hosts, the God of **I**: Jer 32:15
to this day in **I** and among all Jer 32:20
You brought your people **I** out of the Jer 32:21
For the children of **I** and the children of Jer 32:30
The children of **I** have done nothing Jer 32:30
of the children of **I** and the children of Jer 32:32
thus says the LORD, the God of **I**, Jer 32:36
For thus says the LORD, the God of **I**, Jer 33:4
fortunes of Judah and the fortunes of **I**, Jer 33:7
made to the house of **I** and the house of Jer 33:14
to sit on the throne of the house of **I**, Jer 33:17
"Thus says the LORD, the God of **I**: Go and Jer 34:2
"Thus says the LORD, the God of **I**: I Jer 34:13
says the LORD of hosts, the God of **I**: Jer 35:13
the LORD, the God of hosts, the God of **I**: Jer 35:17
says the LORD of hosts, the God of **I**: Jer 35:18
thus says the LORD of hosts, the God of **I**: Jer 35:19
spoken to you against **I** and Judah and Jer 36:2
"Thus says the LORD, God of **I**: Thus Jer 37:7
the LORD, the God of hosts, the God of **I**: Jer 38:17
says the LORD of hosts, the God of **I**: Jer 39:16
for defense against Baasha king of **I**; Jer 41:9
them, "Thus says the LORD, the God of **I**, Jer 42:9
says the LORD of hosts, the God of **I**: Jer 42:15
thus says the LORD of hosts, the God of **I**: Jer 42:18
says the LORD of hosts, the God of **I**: Jer 43:10
says the LORD of hosts, the God of **I**: Jer 44:2
says the LORD God of hosts, the God of **I**: Jer 44:7
thus says the LORD of hosts, the God of **I**: Jer 44:11
says the LORD of hosts, the God of **I**: Jer 44:25
"Thus says the LORD, the God of **I**, to you, Jer 45:2
The LORD of hosts, the God of **I**, said: Jer 46:25
Jacob my servant, nor be dismayed, O **I**, Jer 46:27
Thus says the LORD of hosts, the God of **I**: Jer 48:1
as the house of **I** was ashamed of Bethel, Jer 48:13
Was not **I** a derision to you? Was he Jer 48:27
Thus says the LORD: "Has **I** no sons? Jer 49:1
then **I** shall dispossess those who Jer 49:2
the people of **I** and the people of Judah Jer 50:4
"**I** is a hunted sheep driven away by Jer 50:17
thus says the LORD of hosts, the God of **I**: Jer 50:18
I will restore **I** to his pasture, and he Jer 50:19
the LORD, iniquity shall be sought in **I**, Jer 50:20
defied the LORD, the Holy One of **I**. Jer 50:29
The people of **I** are oppressed, and the Jer 50:33
For **I** and Judah have not been forsaken Jer 51:5
is full of guilt against the Holy One of **I**. Jer 51:5
and **I** is the tribe of his inheritance; Jer 51:19
thus says the LORD of hosts, the God of **I**: Jer 51:33
Babylon must fall for the slain of **I**, just Jer 51:49
from heaven to earth the splendor of **I**; Lam 2:1
down in fierce anger all the might of **I**; Lam 2:3
like an enemy; he has swallowed up **I**; Lam 2:5
"Son of man, I send you to the people of **I**, Ezk 2:3
scroll, and go, speak to the house of **I**." Ezk 3:1
go to the house of **I** and speak with my Ezk 3:4
a hard language, but to the house of **I**— Ezk 3:5
But the house of **I** will not be willing to Ezk 3:7
all the house of **I** have a hard forehead Ezk 3:7
you a watchman for the house of **I**. Ezk 3:17
it. This is a sign for the house of **I**. Ezk 4:3
the punishment of the house of **I** upon it. Ezk 4:4
bear the punishment of the house of **I**. Ezk 4:5
shall the people of **I** eat their bread Ezk 4:13
fire will come out into all the house of **I**. Ezk 5:4
set your face toward the mountains of **I**, Ezk 6:2
and say, You mountains of **I**, hear the Ezk 6:3

bodies of the people of **I** before their idols,	Ezk 6:5
the evil abominations of the house of **I**,	Ezk 6:11
thus says the Lord GOD to the land of **I**:	Ezk 7:2
the glory of the God of **I** was there,	Ezk 8:4
that the house of **I** are committing here,	Ezk 8:6
and all the idols of the house of **I**.	Ezk 8:10
men of the elders of the house of **I**,	Ezk 8:11
elders of the house of **I** are doing in the	Ezk 8:12
glory of the God of **I** had gone up from	Ezk 9:3
all the remnant of **I** in the outpouring of	Ezk 9:8
of the house of **I** and Judah is	Ezk 9:9
glory of the God of **I** was over them.	Ezk 10:19
the God of **I** by the Chebar	Ezk 10:20
the LORD: So you think, O house of **I**.	Ezk 11:5
I will judge you at the border of **I**, and	Ezk 11:10
of it. I will judge you at the border of **I**,	Ezk 11:11
make a full end of the remnant of **I**?"	Ezk 11:13
your kinsmen, the whole house of **I**,	Ezk 11:15
and I will give you the land of **I**.'	Ezk 11:17
glory of the God of **I** was over them.	Ezk 11:22
made you a sign for the house of **I**."	Ezk 12:6
"Son of man, has not the house of **I**, the	Ezk 12:9
and all the house of **I** who are in it.'	Ezk 12:10
of Jerusalem in the land of **I**:	Ezk 12:19
that you have about the land of **I**,	Ezk 12:22
shall no more use it as a proverb in **I**.'	Ezk 12:23
divination within the house of **I**.	Ezk 12:24
behold, they of the house of **I** say,	Ezk 12:27
prophesy against the prophets of **I**,	Ezk 13:2
been like jackals among ruins, O **I**.	Ezk 13:4
or built up a wall for the house of **I**,	Ezk 13:5
enrolled in the register of the house of **I**,	Ezk 13:9
Israel, nor shall they enter the land of **I**.	Ezk 13:9
the prophets of **I** who prophesied	Ezk 13:16
certain of the elders of **I** came to me and	Ezk 14:1
one of the house of **I** who takes his idols	Ezk 14:4
lay hold of the hearts of the house of **I**,	Ezk 14:5
"Therefore say to the house of **I**, Thus	Ezk 14:6
For any one of the house of **I**, or of the	Ezk 14:7
or of the strangers who sojourn in **I**,	Ezk 14:7
him from the midst of my people **I**.	Ezk 14:9
that the house of **I** may no more go	Ezk 14:11
and speak a parable to the house of **I**;	Ezk 17:2
the mountain height of **I** will I plant it,	Ezk 17:23
this proverb concerning the land of **I**,	Ezk 18:2
shall no more be used by you in **I**.	Ezk 18:3
up his eyes to the idols of the house of **I**,	Ezk 18:6
his eyes to the idols of the house of **I**,	Ezk 18:15
Hear now, O house of **I**: Is my way not	Ezk 18:25
Yet the house of **I** says, 'The way of the	Ezk 18:29
O house of **I**, are my ways not just?	Ezk 18:29
I will judge you, O house of **I**,	Ezk 18:30
spirit! Why will you die, O house of **I**?	Ezk 18:31
up a lamentation for the princes of **I**,	Ezk 19:1
more be heard on the mountains of **I**.	Ezk 19:9
of the elders of **I** came to inquire of	Ezk 20:1
"Son of man, speak to the elders of **I**,	Ezk 20:3
On the day when I chose **I**, I swore to the	Ezk 20:5
But the house of **I** rebelled against me	Ezk 20:13
to the house of **I** and say to them,	Ezk 20:27
"Therefore say to the house of **I**, Thus	Ezk 20:30
I be inquired of by you, O house of **I**?	Ezk 20:31
but they shall not enter the land of **I**.	Ezk 20:38
"As for you, O house of **I**, thus says the	Ezk 20:39
mountain, the mountain height of **I**,	Ezk 20:40
the Lord GOD, there all the house of **I**,	Ezk 20:40
when I bring you into the land of **I**,	Ezk 20:42
to your corrupt deeds, O house of **I**,	Ezk 20:44
Prophesy against the land of **I**	Ezk 21:2
and say to the land of **I**, Thus says the	Ezk 21:3
people. It is against all the princes of **I**.	Ezk 21:12
you, O profane wicked one, prince of **I**,	Ezk 21:25
"Behold, the princes of **I** in you, every	Ezk 22:6
the house of **I** has become dross to me;	Ezk 22:18
'Say to the house of **I**, Thus says the	Ezk 24:21
and over the land of **I** when it was made	Ezk 25:3
within your soul against the land of **I**,	Ezk 25:6
Edom by the hand of my people **I**,	Ezk 25:14
and the land of **I** traded with you;	Ezk 27:17
for the house of **I** there shall be no	Ezk 28:24
gather the house of **I** from the peoples	Ezk 28:25
been a staff of reed to the house of **I**;	Ezk 29:6
again be the reliance of the house of **I**,	Ezk 29:16
a horn to spring up for the house of **I**,	Ezk 29:21
made a watchman for the house of **I**.	Ezk 33:7
you, son of man, say to the house of **I**,	Ezk 33:10
for why will you die, O house of **I**?	Ezk 33:11
O house of **I**, I will judge each of you	Ezk 33:20
places in the land of **I** keep saying,	Ezk 33:24
and the mountains of **I** shall be so	Ezk 33:28
prophesy against the shepherds of **I**;	Ezk 34:2
shepherds of **I** who have been feeding	Ezk 34:2
I will feed them on the mountains of **I**,	Ezk 34:13
mountain heights of **I** shall be their	Ezk 34:14
they shall feed on the mountains of **I**.	Ezk 34:14
them, and that they, the house of **I**,	Ezk 34:30
gave over the people of **I** to the power of	Ezk 35:5
uttered against the mountains of **I**,	Ezk 35:12
over the inheritance of the house of **I**,	Ezk 35:15
of man, prophesy to the mountains of **I**,	Ezk 36:1
of Israel, and say, O mountains of **I**,	Ezk 36:1
therefore, O mountains of **I**, hear the	Ezk 36:4
prophesy concerning the land of **I**,	Ezk 36:6
"But you, O mountains of **I**, shall shoot	Ezk 36:8
and yield your fruit to my people **I**,	Ezk 36:8
people on you, the whole house of **I**,	Ezk 36:10
people walk on you, even my people **I**.	Ezk 36:12
when the house of **I** lived in their own	Ezk 36:17
the house of **I** had profaned among	Ezk 36:21
"Therefore say to the house of **I**, Thus	Ezk 36:22
It is not for your sake, O house of **I**,	Ezk 36:22
for your ways, O house of **I**.	Ezk 36:32
I will let the house of **I** ask me to do for	Ezk 36:37
these bones are the whole house of **I**.	Ezk 37:11
And I will bring you into the land of **I**.	Ezk 37:12
the people of **I** associated with him';	Ezk 37:16
all the house of **I** associated with him.'	Ezk 37:16
the tribes of **I** associated with him.	Ezk 37:19
take the people of **I** from the nations	Ezk 37:21
in the land, on the mountains of **I**.	Ezk 37:22
that I am the LORD who sanctifies **I**,	Ezk 37:28
many peoples upon the mountains of **I**,	Ezk 38:8
when my people **I** are dwelling	Ezk 38:14
You will come up against my people **I**,	Ezk 38:16
days by my servants the prophets of **I**,	Ezk 38:17
Gog shall come against the land of **I**,	Ezk 38:18
be a great earthquake in the land of **I**.	Ezk 38:19
lead you against the mountains of **I**.	Ezk 39:2
You shall fall on the mountains of **I**,	Ezk 39:4
known in the midst of my people **I**,	Ezk 39:7
that I am the LORD, the Holy One in **I**.	Ezk 39:7
dwell in the cities of **I** will go out and	Ezk 39:9
will give to Gog a place for burial in **I**,	Ezk 39:11
months the house of **I** will be burying	Ezk 39:12
sacrificial feast on the mountains of **I**,	Ezk 39:17
The house of **I** shall know that I am	Ezk 39:22
that the house of **I** went into captivity	Ezk 39:23
have mercy on the whole house of **I**,	Ezk 39:25
out my Spirit upon the house of **I**,	Ezk 39:29
of God he brought me to the land of **I**,	Ezk 40:2
all that you see to the house of **I**."	Ezk 40:4
of the God of **I** was coming from the	Ezk 43:2
in the midst of the people of **I** forever.	Ezk 43:7
And the house of **I** shall no more defile	Ezk 43:7
describe to the house of **I** the temple,	Ezk 43:10
enter by it, for the LORD, the God of **I**,	Ezk 44:2
the rebellious house, to the house of **I**,	Ezk 44:6
O house of **I**, enough of all your	Ezk 44:6
who are among the people of **I**,	Ezk 44:9
after their idols when **I** went astray,	Ezk 44:10
block of iniquity to the house of **I**,	Ezk 44:12
when the people of **I** went astray from	Ezk 44:15
of the offspring of the house of **I**,	Ezk 44:22
you shall give them no possession in **I**;	Ezk 44:28
every devoted thing in **I** shall be theirs.	Ezk 44:29
It shall belong to the whole house of **I**.	Ezk 45:6
of the land. It is to be his property in **I**.	Ezk 45:8
let the house of **I** have the land	Ezk 45:8
the Lord GOD: Enough, O princes of **I**!	Ezk 45:9
watering places of **I** for grain offering,	Ezk 45:15
to give this offering to the prince in **I**.	Ezk 45:16
the appointed feasts of the house of **I**:	Ezk 45:17
atonement on behalf of the house of **I**.	Ezk 45:17
among the twelve tribes of **I**.	Ezk 47:13
between Gilead and the land of **I**;	Ezk 47:18
you according to the tribes of **I**.	Ezk 47:21
be to you as native-born children of **I**.	Ezk 47:22
an inheritance among the tribes of **I**.	Ezk 47:22
when the people of **I** went astray,	Ezk 48:11
of the city, from all the tribes of **I**,	Ezk 48:19
an inheritance among the tribes of **I**,	Ezk 48:29
city being named after the tribes of **I**.	Ezk 48:31
eunuch, to bring some of the people of **I**,	Dn 1:3
the inhabitants of Jerusalem, and to all **I**,	Dn 9:7
All **I** has transgressed your law and	Dn 9:11
my sin and the sin of my people **I**,	Dn 9:20
of Jeroboam the son of Joash, king of **I**.	Hos 1:1
an end to the kingdom of the house of **I**.	Hos 1:4
will break the bow of **I** in the Valley of	Hos 1:5
no more have mercy on the house of **I**,	Hos 1:6
of the children of **I** shall be like the	Hos 1:10
and the children of **I** shall be gathered	Hos 1:11
even as the LORD loves the children of **I**,	Hos 3:1
For the children of **I** shall dwell many	Hos 3:4
the children of **I** shall return and	Hos 3:5
the word of the LORD, O children of **I**,	Hos 4:1
Though you play the whore, O **I**, let not	Hos 4:15
Like a stubborn heifer, **I** is stubborn;	Hos 4:16
O priests! Pay attention, O house of **I**!	Hos 5:1
Ephraim, and **I** is not hidden from me;	Hos 5:3
you have played the whore; **I** is defiled.	Hos 5:3
The pride of **I** testifies to his face; Israel	Hos 5:5
I and Ephraim shall stumble in his	Hos 5:5
among the tribes of **I** I make known	Hos 5:9
In the house of **I** I have seen a horrible	Hos 6:10
whoredom is there; **I** is defiled.	Hos 6:10
When I would heal **I**, the iniquity of	Hos 7:1
The pride of **I** testifies to his face; yet	Hos 7:10
me they cry, My God, we—**I**—know you.	Hos 8:2
I has spurned the good; the enemy shall	Hos 8:3
For it is from **I**; a craftsman made it; it is	Hos 8:6
I is swallowed up; already they are	Hos 8:8
For **I** has forgotten his Maker and built	Hos 8:14
Rejoice not, O **I**! Exult not like the	Hos 9:1
recompense have come; **I** shall know it.	Hos 9:7
Like grapes in the wilderness, I found **I**.	Hos 9:10
I is a luxuriant vine that yields its fruit.	Hos 10:1
and **I** shall be ashamed of his idol.	Hos 10:6
The high places of Aven, the sin of **I**,	Hos 10:8
days of Gibeah, you have sinned, O **I**;	Hos 10:9
dawn the king of **I** shall be utterly cut	Hos 10:15
When **I** was a child, I loved him, and	Hos 11:1
How can I hand you over, O **I**?	Hos 11:8
lies, and the house of **I** with deceit,	Hos 11:12
there **I** served for a wife, and for a wife	Hos 12:12
the LORD brought **I** up from Egypt,	Hos 12:13
he was exalted in **I**, but he incurred	Hos 13:1
He destroys you, O **I**, for you are against	Hos 13:9
Return, O **I**, to the LORD your God, for	Hos 14:1
I will be like the dew to **I**; he shall	Hos 14:5
shall know that I am in the midst of **I**,	Jl 2:27
on behalf of my people and my heritage **I**,	Jl 3:2
his people, a stronghold to the people of **I**.	Jl 3:16
which he saw concerning **I** in the days	Am 1:1
of Jeroboam the son of Joash, king of **I**,	Am 1:1
"For three transgressions of **I**, and for	Am 2:6
so, O people of **I**?" declares the LORD.	Am 2:11
has spoken against you, O people of **I**,	Am 3:1
shall the people of **I** who dwell in	Am 3:12
day I punish **I** for his transgressions,	Am 3:14
do, O people of **I**!" declares the Lord GOD.	Am 4:5
"Therefore thus I will do to you, O **I**;	Am 4:12
to you, prepare to meet your God, O **I**!"	Am 4:12
up over you in lamentation, O house of **I**:	Am 5:1
"Fallen, no more to rise, is the virgin **I**;	Am 5:2
shall have ten left to the house of **I**."	Am 5:3
For thus says the LORD to the house of **I**:	Am 5:4
years in the wilderness, O house of **I**?	Am 5:25
nations, to whom the house of **I** comes!	Am 6:1
nation, O house of **I**," declares the LORD,	Am 6:14
a plumb line in the midst of my people **I**;	Am 7:8
and the sanctuaries of **I** shall be laid	Am 7:9
of Bethel sent to Jeroboam king of **I**,	Am 7:10
you in the midst of the house of **I**.	Am 7:10
and **I** must go into exile away from his	Am 7:11
to me, 'Go, prophesy to my people **I**.'	Am 7:15
"You say, 'Do not prophesy against **I**,	Am 7:16
and **I** shall surely go into exile away	Am 7:17
"The end has come upon my people **I**;	Am 8:2
to me, O people of **I**?" declares the LORD.	Am 9:7
"Did I not bring up **I** from the land of	Am 9:7
shake the house of **I** among all the	Am 9:9
I will restore the fortunes of my people **I**,	Am 9:14
of the people of **I** shall possess the land	Ob 1:20
of Jacob and for the sins of the house of **I**.	Mi 1:5
you were found the transgressions of **I**.	Mi 1:13
be a deceitful thing to the kings of **I**.	Mi 1:14
the glory of **I** shall come to Adullam.	Mi 1:15
O Jacob; I will gather the remnant of **I**;	Mi 2:12
of Jacob and rulers of the house of **I**!	Mi 3:1
to Jacob his transgression and to **I** his sin.	Mi 3:8
of Jacob and rulers of the house of **I**,	Mi 3:9
rod they strike the judge of **I** on the cheek.	Mi 5:1
forth for me one who is to be ruler in **I**,	Mi 5:2
his brothers shall return to the people of **I**.	Mi 5:3
his people, and he will contend with **I**.	Mi 6:2
the majesty of Jacob as the majesty of **I**,	Na 2:2
declares the LORD of hosts, the God of **I**,	Zep 2:9
those who are left in **I**; they shall do no	Zep 3:13
aloud, O daughter of Zion; shout, O **I**!	Zep 3:14
The King of **I**, the LORD, is in your	Zep 3:15
have scattered Judah, **I**, and Jerusalem."	Zec 1:19
O house of Judah and house of **I**,	Zec 8:13
eye on mankind and on all the tribes of **I**,	Zec 9:1
the brotherhood between Judah and **I**.	Zec 11:14
of the word of the LORD concerning **I**:	Zec 12:1
of the word of the LORD to **I** by Malachi.	Mal 1:1
is the LORD beyond the border of **I**!"	Mal 1:5
been committed in **I** and in Jerusalem.	Mal 2:11
divorces, says the LORD, the God of **I**,	Mal 2:16
I commanded him at Horeb for all **I**.	Mal 4:4
a ruler who will shepherd my people **I**.'"	Mt 2:6
and his mother and go to the land of **I**,	Mt 2:20
and his mother and went to the land of **I**.	Mt 2:21
with no one in **I** have I found such faith.	Mt 8:10

His body is polished **i**, bedecked with Sg 5:14
Your neck is like an **i** tower. Your eyes are Sg 7:4
from the coasts of Cyprus, inlaid with **i**. Ezk 27:6
you in payment **i** tusks and ebony. Ezk 27:15
house, and the houses of **i** shall perish, Am 3:15
lie on beds of **i** and stretch themselves Am 6:4
scented wood, all kinds of articles of **i**, Rv 18:12

IVVAH (3)
gods of Sepharvaim, Hena, and **I**? 2 Kgs 18:34
the king of Hena, or the king of **I**?'" 2 Kgs 19:13
the king of Hena, or the king of **I**?'" Is 37:13

IYE-ABARIM (2)
set out from Oboth and camped at **I**, Nm 21:11
set out from Oboth and camped at **I**, Nm 33:44

IYIM (1)
they set out from **I** and camped at Nm 33:45

IZHAR (10)
Amram, **I**, Hebron, and Uzziel, the years Ex 6:18
The sons of **I**: Korah, Nepheg, and Ex 6:21
clans: Amram, **I**, Hebron, and Uzziel. Nm 3:19
Now Korah the son of **I**, son of Kohath, Nm 16:1
sons of Helah: Zereth, **I**, and Ethnan. 1 Chr 4:7
Amram, **I**, Hebron, and Uzziel. 1 Chr 6:2
Amram, **I**, Hebron and Uzziel. 1 Chr 6:18
son of **I**, son of Kohath, son of Levi, 1 Chr 6:38
Amram, **I**, Hebron, and Uzziel, four. 1 Chr 23:12
The sons of **I**: Shelomith the chief. 1 Chr 23:18

IZHARITES (4)
and the clan of the **I** and the clan of the Nm 3:27
Of the **I**, Shelomoth; of the sons of 1 Chr 24:22
Of the Amramites, the **I**, the 1 Chr 26:23
Of the **I**, Chenaniah and his sons 1 Chr 26:29

IZLIAH (1)
I, and Jobab were the sons of Elpaal. 1 Chr 8:18

IZRAHIAH (2)
of Uzzi: **I**. And the sons of Izrahiah: 1 Chr 7:3
And the sons of **I**: Michael, Obadiah, 1 Chr 7:3

IZRAHITE (1)
the fifth month, was Shamhuth the **I**; 1 Chr 27:8

IZRI (1)
the fourth to **I**, his sons and his 1 Chr 25:11

IZZIAH (1)
Ramiah, **I**, Malchijah, Mijamin, Ezr 10:25

J

JAAKOBAH (1)
Elioenai, **J**, Jeshohaiah, Asaiah, Adiel, 1 Chr 4:36

JAALA (1)
the sons of **J**, the sons of Darkon, the Neh 7:58

JAALAH (1)
the sons of **J**, the sons of Darkon, the Ezr 2:56

JAAR (1)
Ephrathah; we found it in the fields of **J**. Ps 132:6

JAARE-OREGIM (1)
at Gob, and Elhanan the son of **J**, 2 Sm 21:19

JAARESHIAH (1)
J, Elijah, and Zichri were the sons of 1 Chr 8:27

JAASIEL (2)
Eliel, and Obed, and **J** the Mezobaite. 1 Chr 11:47
for Benjamin, **J** the son of Abner; 1 Chr 27:21

JAASU (1)
Mattaniah, Mattenai, **J**. Ezr 10:37

JAAZANIAH (4)
and **J** the son of the Maacathite. 2 Kgs 25:23
So I took **J** the son of Jeremiah, son of Jer 35:3
with **J** the son of Shaphan standing Ezk 8:11
I saw among them **J** the son of Azzur, Ezk 11:1

JAAZIAH (2)
and Mushi. The sons of **J**: Beno. 1 Chr 24:26
The sons of Merari: of **J**, Beno, 1 Chr 24:27

JAAZIEL (1)
order, Zechariah, **J**, Shemiramoth, 1 Chr 15:18

JABAL (1)
Adah bore **J**; he was the father of those Gn 4:20

JABBOK (7)
children, and crossed the ford of the **J**. Gn 32:22
of his land from the Arnon to the **J**, Nm 21:24
the banks of the river **J** and the cities of Dt 2:37
as a border, as far over as the river **J**, Dt 3:16
middle of the valley as far as the river **J**, Jos 12:2
the Arnon to the **J** and to the Jordan; Jgs 11:13
the Arnon to the **J** and from the Jgs 11:22

JABESH (12)
and all the men of **J** said to Nahash, 1 Sm 11:1
The elders of **J** said to him, "Give us 1 Sm 11:3
they told him the news of the men of **J**. 1 Sm 11:5
came and told the men of **J**, 1 Sm 11:9
Therefore the men of **J** said, 1 Sm 11:10
and they came to **J** and burned them 1 Sm 31:12
tamarisk tree in **J** and fasted seven 1 Sm 31:13
the son of **J** conspired against him 2 Kgs 15:10
Shallum the son of **J** began to reign 2 Kgs 15:13
Shallum the son of **J** in Samaria and 2 Kgs 15:14
of his sons, and brought them to **J**. 1 Chr 10:12
under the oak in **J** and fasted seven 1 Chr 10:12

JABESH-GILEAD (12)
no one had come to the camp from **J**, Jgs 21:8
not one of the inhabitants of **J** was there. Jgs 21:9
strike the inhabitants of **J** with the edge Jgs 21:10
the inhabitants of **J** 400 young virgins Jgs 21:12
they had saved alive of the women of **J**, Jgs 21:14
the Ammonite went up and besieged **J**, 1 Sm 11:1
"Thus shall you say to the men of **J**: 1 Sm 11:9
the inhabitants of **J** heard what the 1 Sm 31:11
"It was the men of **J** who buried Saul," 2 Sm 2:4
to the men of **J** and said to them, 2 Sm 2:5
his son Jonathan from the men of **J**, 2 Sm 21:12
But when all **J** heard all that the 1 Chr 10:11

JABEZ (4)
also of the scribes who lived at **J**: 1 Chr 2:55
J was more honorable than his 1 Chr 4:9
and his mother called his name **J**, 1 Chr 4:9
J called upon the God of Israel, 1 Chr 4:10

JABIN (7)
When **J**, king of Hazor, heard of this, he Jos 11:1
them into the hand of **J** king of Canaan, Jgs 4:2
there was peace between **J** the king of Jgs 4:17
that day God subdued **J** the king of Jgs 4:23
harder and harder against **J** the king of Jgs 4:24
until they destroyed **J** king of Canaan. Jgs 4:24
as to Sisera and **J** at the river Kishon, Ps 83:9

JABIN'S (1)
draw out Sisera, the general of **J** army, Jgs 4:7

JABNEEL (2)
to Mount Baalah and goes out to **J**. Jos 15:11
Zaanannim, and Adami-nekeb, and **J**, Jos 19:33

JABNEH (1)
Gath and the wall of **J** and the wall of 2 Chr 26:6

JACAN (1)
Sheba, Jorai, **J**, Zia and Eber, 1 Chr 5:13

JACHIN (8)
Jemuel, Jamin, Ohad, **J**, Zohar, and Gn 46:10
Jemuel, Jamin, Ohad, **J**, Zohar, and Ex 6:15
Jamin, the clan of the Jaminites; of **J**, Nm 26:12
on the south and called its name **J**, 1 Kgs 7:21
Of the priests: Jedaiah, Jehoiarib, **J**, 1 Chr 9:10
the twenty-first to **J**, the 1 Chr 24:17
that on the south he called **J**, and that 2 Chr 3:17
priests: Jedaiah the son of Joiarib, **J**, Neh 11:10

JACHINITES (1)
Jaminites; of Jachin, the clan of the **J**; Nm 26:12

JACINTH (3)
and the third row a **j**, an agate, and an Ex 28:19
and the third row, a **j**, an agate, and an Ex 39:12
the tenth chrysoprase, the eleventh **j**, Rv 21:20

JACKALS (17)
I am a brother of **j** and a companion of Jb 30:29
us in the place of **j** and covered us with Ps 44:19
the sword; they shall be a portion for **j**. Ps 63:10
its towers, and **j** in the pleasant palaces; Is 13:22
It shall be the haunt of **j**, an abode for Is 34:13
in the haunt of **j**, where they lie down, the Is 35:7
will honor me, the **j** and the ostriches, Is 43:20
Jerusalem a heap of ruins, a lair of **j**, Jer 9:11
cities of Judah a desolation, a lair of **j**. Jer 10:22
the bare heights; they pant for air like **j**; Jer 14:6
Hazor shall become a haunt of **j**, an Jer 49:33
become a heap of ruins, the haunt of **j**, Jer 51:37
Even **j** offer the breast; they nurse their Lam 4:3
which lies desolate; **j** prowl over it. Lam 5:18
prophets have been like **j** among ruins, Ezk 13:4
I will make lamentation like the **j**, and Mi 1:8
and left his heritage to **j** of the desert." Mal 1:3

JACOB (371)
Esau's heel, so his name was called **J**. Gn 25:26
of the field, while **J** was a quiet man, Gn 25:27
ate of his game, but Rebekah loved **J**. Gn 25:28
Once when **J** was cooking stew, Esau Gn 25:29
And Esau said to **J**, "Let me eat some of Gn 25:30
J said, "Sell me your birthright now." Gn 25:31
J said, "Swear to me now." So he swore Gn 25:33
to him and sold his birthright to **J**. Gn 25:33
Then **J** gave Esau bread and lentil stew, Gn 25:34
Rebekah said to her son **J**, "I heard your Gn 27:6
But **J** said to Rebekah his mother, Gn 27:11
and put them on **J** her younger son. Gn 27:15
prepared, into the hand of her son **J**. Gn 27:17
J said to his father, "I am Esau your Gn 27:19
Then Isaac said to **J**, "Please come Gn 27:21
So **J** went near to Isaac his father, who Gn 27:22
soon as Isaac had finished blessing **J**, Gn 27:30
when **J** had scarcely gone out from the Gn 27:30
Esau said, "Is he not rightly named **J**? Gn 27:36
Now Esau hated **J** because of the Gn 27:41
then I will kill my brother **J**." Gn 27:41
she sent and called **J** her younger son Gn 27:42
If **J** marries one of the Hittite women Gn 27:46
Then Isaac called **J** and blessed him and Gn 28:1
Thus Isaac sent **J** away. And he went to Gn 28:5
that Isaac had blessed **J** and sent him Gn 28:6
and that **J** had obeyed his father and his Gn 28:7
J left Beersheba and went toward Gn 28:10
Then **J** awoke from his sleep and said, Gn 28:16
early in the morning **J** took the stone Gn 28:18
Then **J** made a vow, saying, "If God will Gn 28:20
Then **J** went on his journey and came to Gn 29:1
J said to them, "My brothers, where do Gn 29:4
Now as soon as **J** saw Rachel the Gn 29:10
J came near and rolled the stone from Gn 29:10
Then **J** kissed Rachel and wept aloud. Gn 29:11
And **J** told Rachel that he was her Gn 29:12
soon as Laban heard the news about **J**, Gn 29:13
his house. **J** told Laban all these things, Gn 29:13
Then Laban said to **J**, "Because you are Gn 29:15
J loved Rachel. And he said, "I will Gn 29:18
So **J** served seven years for Rachel, and Gn 29:20
Then **J** said to Laban, "Give me my Gn 29:21
daughter Leah and brought her to **J**, Gn 29:23
And **J** said to Laban, "What is this you Gn 29:25
J did so, and completed her week. Then Gn 29:28
So **J** went in to Rachel also, and he Gn 29:30
Rachel saw that she bore **J** no children, Gn 30:1
She said to **J**, "Give me children, or I Gn 30:1
Bilhah as a wife, and **J** went in to her. Gn 30:4
And Bilhah conceived and bore **J** a son. Gn 30:5
again and bore **J** a second son. Gn 30:7
Zilpah and gave her to **J** as a wife. Gn 30:9
Leah's servant Zilpah bore **J** a son. Gn 30:10
servant Zilpah bore **J** a second son. Gn 30:12
When **J** came from the field in the Gn 30:16
she conceived and bore **J** a fifth son. Gn 30:17
again, and she bore **J** a sixth son. Gn 30:19
had borne Joseph, **J** said to Laban, Gn 30:25
J said to him, "You yourself know how Gn 30:29
He said, "What shall I give you?" **J** said, Gn 30:31
days' journey between himself and **J**, Gn 30:36
and **J** pastured the rest of Laban's Gn 30:36
Then **J** took fresh sticks of poplar and Gn 30:37
And **J** separated the lambs and set the Gn 30:40
J would lay the sticks in the troughs Gn 30:41
Now **J** heard that the sons of Laban were Gn 31:1
"**J** has taken all that was our father's, Gn 31:1
And **J** saw that Laban did not regard Gn 31:2
Then the LORD said to **J**, "Return to the Gn 31:3
So **J** sent and called Rachel and Leah Gn 31:4
said to me in the dream, '**J**,' and I said, Gn 31:11
So **J** arose and set his sons and his Gn 31:17
And **J** tricked Laban the Aramean, by Gn 31:20
Laban on the third day that **J** had fled, Gn 31:22
"Be careful not to say anything to **J**, Gn 31:24
And Laban overtook **J**. Now Jacob had Gn 31:25
Now **J** had pitched his tent in the hill Gn 31:25
And Laban said to **J**, "What have you Gn 31:26
'Be careful not to say anything to **J**,' Gn 31:29
J answered and said to Laban, Gn 31:31
and take it." Now **J** did not know that Gn 31:32
Then **J** became angry and berated Gn 31:36
J said to Laban, "What is my offense? Gn 31:36
Then Laban answered and said to **J**, Gn 31:43
So **J** took a stone and set it up as a Gn 31:45
And **J** said to his kinsmen, "Gather Gn 31:46
Jegar-sahadutha, but **J** called it Galeed. Gn 31:47
Then Laban said to **J**, "See this heap Gn 31:51
judge between us." So **J** swore by the Gn 31:53
and **J** offered a sacrifice in the hill Gn 31:54
J went on his way, and the angels of God Gn 32:1
And when **J** saw them he said, "This is Gn 32:2
And **J** sent messengers before him to Gn 32:3
Thus says your servant **J**, 'I have Gn 32:4
And the messengers returned to **J**, Gn 32:6
Then **J** was greatly afraid and distressed. Gn 32:7
And **J** said, "O God of my father Gn 32:9
say, 'They belong to your servant **J**. Gn 32:18
your servant **J** is behind us.'" For he Gn 32:20
And **J** was left alone. And a man Gn 32:24
saw that he did not prevail against **J**, Gn 32:25
go, for the day has broken." But **J** said, Gn 32:26

"What is your name?" And he said, "**J**." Gn 32:27
name shall no longer be called **J**, Gn 32:28
Then **J** asked him, "Please tell me your Gn 32:29
So **J** called the name of the place Peniel, Gn 32:30
And **J** lifted up his eyes and looked, and Gn 33:1
said, "Who are these with you?" **J** said, Gn 33:5
this company that I met?" **J** answered, Gn 33:8
J said, "No, please, if I have found favor Gn 33:10
But **J** said to him, "My lord knows that Gn 33:13
But **J** journeyed to Succoth, and built Gn 33:17
And **J** came safely to the city of Gn 33:18
of Leah, whom she had borne to **J**, Gn 34:1
was drawn to Dinah the daughter of **J**. Gn 34:3
Now **J** heard that he had defiled his Gn 34:5
field, so **J** held his peace until they came. Gn 34:5
Shechem went out to **J** to speak with Gn 34:6
The sons of **J** had come in from the field Gn 34:7
The sons of **J** answered Shechem and Gn 34:13
they were sore, two of the sons of **J**, Gn 34:25
The sons of **J** came upon the slain and Gn 34:27
Then **J** said to Simeon and Levi, "You Gn 34:30
God said to **J**, "Arise, go up to Bethel and Gn 35:1
So **J** said to his household and to all who Gn 35:2
So they gave to **J** all the foreign gods that Gn 35:4
J hid them under the terebinth tree that Gn 35:4
so that they did not pursue the sons of **J**. Gn 35:5
And **J** came to Luz (that is, Bethel), Gn 35:6
God appeared to **J** again, when he came Gn 35:9
And God said to him, "Your name is **J**; Gn 35:10
no longer shall your name be called **J**, Gn 35:10
And **J** set up a pillar in the place where Gn 35:14
So **J** called the name of the place where Gn 35:15
and **J** set up a pillar over her tomb. It is Gn 35:20
of it. Now the sons of **J** were twelve. Gn 35:22
were the sons of **J** who were born to Gn 35:26
And **J** came to his father Isaac at Gn 35:27
And his sons Esau and **J** buried him. Gn 35:29
into a land away from his brother **J**. Gn 36:6
J lived in the land of his father's Gn 37:1
These are the generations of **J**. Joseph, Gn 37:2
Then **J** tore his garments and put Gn 37:34
When **J** learned that there was grain for Gn 42:1
But **J** did not send Benjamin, Joseph's Gn 42:4
When they came to **J** their father in the Gn 42:29
And **J** their father said to them, "You Gn 42:36
to the land of Canaan to their father **J**. Gn 45:25
him, the spirit of their father **J** revived. Gn 45:27
night and said, "**J**, Jacob." And he said, Gn 46:2
night and said, "Jacob, **J**." And he said, Gn 46:2
Then **J** set out from Beersheba. The sons Gn 46:5
The sons of Israel carried **J** their father, Gn 46:5
Egypt, **J** and all his offspring with him, Gn 46:6
who came into Egypt, **J** and his sons. Gn 46:8
whom she bore to **J** in Paddan-aram, Gn 46:15
these she bore to **J**—sixteen persons. Gn 46:18
who were born to **J**—fourteen persons Gn 46:22
these she bore to **J**—seven persons in Gn 46:25
persons belonging to **J** who came into Gn 46:26
of the house of **J** who came into Egypt Gn 46:27
Then Joseph brought in **J** his father and Gn 47:7
before Pharaoh, and **J** blessed Pharaoh. Gn 47:7
And Pharaoh said to **J**, "How many are Gn 47:8
And **J** said to Pharaoh, "The days of the Gn 47:9
And **J** blessed Pharaoh and went out Gn 47:10
And **J** lived in the land of Egypt Gn 47:28
So the days of **J**, the years of his life, Gn 47:28
And it was told to **J**, "Your son Joseph Gn 48:2
And **J** said to Joseph, "God Almighty Gn 48:3
Then **J** called his sons and said, "Gather Gn 49:1
"Assemble and listen, O sons of **J**, listen Gn 49:2
will divide them in **J** and scatter them in Gn 49:7
the Mighty One of **J** (from there is the Gn 49:24
When **J** finished commanding his Gn 49:33
swore to Abraham, to Isaac, and to **J**." Gn 50:24
sons of Israel who came to Egypt with **J**, Ex 1:1
the descendants of **J** were seventy persons; Ex 1:5
with Abraham, with Isaac, and with **J**. Ex 2:24
and the God of **J**." And Moses hid his face, Ex 3:6
the God of Isaac, and the God of **J**, Ex 3:15
the God of Abraham, of Isaac, and of **J**, Ex 3:16
the God of Isaac, and the God of **J**, Ex 4:5
I appeared to Abraham, to Isaac, and to **J**, Ex 6:3
to give to Abraham, to Isaac, and to **J**. Ex 6:8
"Thus you shall say to the house of **J**, Ex 19:3
which I swore to Abraham, Isaac, and **J**, Ex 33:1
I will remember my covenant with **J**, Lv 26:42
'Come, curse **J** for me, and come, Nm 23:7
count the dust of **J** or number the Nm 23:10
He has not beheld misfortune in **J**, nor Nm 23:21
there is no enchantment against **J**, Nm 23:23
now it shall be said of **J** and Israel, Nm 23:23
How lovely are your tents, O **J**, your Nm 24:5
a star shall come out of **J**, and a Nm 24:17
And one from **J** shall exercise Nm 24:19
to give to Abraham, to Isaac, and to **J**, Nm 32:11
fathers, to Abraham, to Isaac, and to **J**, Dt 1:8
fathers, to Abraham, to Isaac, and to **J**, Dt 6:10
fathers, to Abraham, to Isaac, and to **J**. Dt 9:5
your servants, Abraham, Isaac, and **J**. Dt 9:27
fathers, to Abraham, to Isaac, and to **J**. Dt 29:13
fathers, to Abraham, to Isaac, and to **J**, Dt 30:20
is his people, **J** his allotted heritage. Dt 32:9
law, as a possession for the assembly of **J**. Dt 33:4
They shall teach **J** your rules and Israel Dt 33:10
So Israel lived in safety, **J** lived alone, in Dt 33:28
I swore to Abraham, to Isaac, and to **J**, Dt 34:4
And to Isaac I gave **J** and Esau. And I Jos 24:4
but **J** and his children went down to Jos 24:4
piece of land that **J** bought from the Jos 24:32
When **J** went into Egypt, and the 1 Sm 12:8
on high, the anointed of the God of **J**, 2 Sm 23:1
number of the tribes of the sons of **J**, 1 Kgs 18:31
with Abraham, Isaac, and **J**, 2 Kgs 13:23
LORD commanded the children of **J**, 2 Kgs 17:34
of Israel his servant, sons of **J**, 1 Chr 16:13
which he confirmed as a statute to **J**, 1 Chr 16:17
the fortunes of his people, let **J** rejoice, Ps 14:7
the name of the God of **J** protect you! Ps 20:1
All you offspring of **J**, glorify him, and Ps 22:23
him, who seek the face of the God of **J**. Ps 24:6
my King, O God; ordain salvation for **J**! Ps 44:4
is with us; the God of **J** is our fortress. Ps 46:7
is with us; the God of **J** is our fortress. Ps 46:11
for us, the pride of **J** whom he loves. Ps 47:4
the fortunes of his people, Let **J** rejoice, Ps 53:6
that God rules over **J** to the ends of Ps 59:13
forever; I will sing praises to the God of **J**. Ps 75:9
At your rebuke, O God of **J**, both rider Ps 76:6
people, the children of **J** and Joseph. Ps 77:15
a testimony in **J** and appointed a Ps 78:5
of wrath; a fire was kindled against **J**; Ps 78:21
brought him to shepherd **J** his people, Ps 78:71
For they have devoured **J** and laid waste Ps 79:7
strength; shout for joy to the God of **J**! Ps 81:1
a statute for Israel, a rule of the God of **J**. Ps 81:4
hear my prayer; give ear, O God of **J**! Ps 84:8
your land; you restored the fortunes of **J**. Ps 85:1
more than all the dwelling places of **J**. Ps 87:2
not see; the God of **J** does not perceive." Ps 94:7
executed justice and righteousness in **J**. Ps 99:4
of Abraham, his servant, children of **J**, Ps 105:6
which he confirmed to **J** as a statute, to Ps 105:10
Egypt; **J** sojourned in the land of Ham. Ps 105:23
the house of **J** from a people of strange Ps 114:1
the Lord, at the presence of the God of **J**, Ps 114:7
LORD and vowed to the Mighty One of **J**, Ps 132:2
dwelling place for the Mighty One of **J**." Ps 132:5
For the LORD has chosen **J** for himself, Ps 135:4
Blessed is he whose help is the God of **J**, Ps 146:5
He declares his word to **J**, his statutes Ps 147:19
of the LORD, to the house of the God of **J**, Is 2:3
O house of **J**, come, let us walk in the light Is 2:5
have rejected your people, the house of **J**, Is 2:6
who is hiding his face from the house of **J**, Is 8:17
The Lord has sent a word against **J**, and it Is 9:8
of the house of **J** will no more lean Is 10:20
A remnant will return, the remnant of **J**, Is 10:21
will have compassion on **J** and will again Is 14:1
will attach themselves to the house of **J**. Is 14:1
day the glory of **J** will be brought low, Is 17:4
In days to come **J** shall take root, Israel Is 27:6
by this the guilt of **J** will be atoned for, Is 27:9
Abraham, concerning the house of **J**: Is 29:22
"**J** shall no more be ashamed, no more Is 29:22
the Holy One of **J** and will stand in Is 29:23
Why do you say, O **J**, and speak, O Israel, Is 40:27
Israel, my servant, **J**, whom I have chosen, Is 41:8
Fear not, you worm **J**, you men of Israel! Is 41:14
bring your proofs, says the King of **J**. Is 41:21
Who gave up **J** to the looter, and Israel to Is 42:24
says the LORD, he who created you, O **J**, Is 43:1
"Yet you did not call upon me, O **J**; but Is 43:22
and deliver **J** to utter destruction and Is 43:28
"But now hear, O **J** my servant, Israel Is 44:1
Fear not, O **J** my servant, Jeshurun whom Is 44:2
LORD'S,' another will call on the name of **J**, Is 44:5
Remember these things, O **J**, and Israel, Is 44:21
For the LORD has redeemed **J**, and will be Is 44:23
For the sake of my servant **J**, and Israel Is 45:4
I did not say to the offspring of **J**, 'Seek Is 45:19
"Listen to me, O house of **J**, all the Is 46:3
Hear this, O house of **J**, who are called by Is 48:1
"Listen to me, O **J**, and Israel, whom I Is 48:12
"The LORD has redeemed his servant **J**!" Is 48:20
to be his servant, to bring **J** back to him; Is 49:5
raise up the tribes of **J** and to bring back Is 49:6
your Redeemer, the Mighty One of **J**." Is 49:26
transgression, to the house of **J** their sins. Is 58:1
you with the heritage of **J** your father, Is 58:14
to those in **J** who turn from Is 59:20
and your Redeemer, the Mighty One of **J**. Is 60:16
I will bring forth offspring from **J**, and Is 65:9
Hear the word of the LORD, O house of **J**, Jer 2:4
Declare this in the house of **J**; proclaim it Jer 5:20
like these is he who is the portion of **J**, Jer 10:16
on your name, for they have devoured **J**; Jer 10:25
is none like it; it is a time of distress for **J**; Jer 30:7
"Then fear not, O **J** my servant, declares Jer 30:10
J shall return and have quiet and ease, Jer 30:10
of the tents of **J** and have compassion Jer 30:18
"Sing aloud with gladness for **J**, and raise Jer 31:7
LORD has ransomed **J** and has redeemed Jer 31:11
reject the offspring of **J** and David my Jer 33:26
the offspring of Abraham, Isaac, and **J**. Jer 33:26
"But fear not, O **J** my servant, nor be Jer 46:27
J shall return and have quiet and ease, Jer 46:27
Fear not, O **J** my servant, declares the Jer 46:28
like these is he who is the portion of **J**, Jer 51:19
has commanded against **J** that his Lam 1:17
without mercy all the habitations of **J**; Lam 2:2
he has burned like a flaming fire in **J**, Lam 2:3
I swore to the offspring of the house of **J**, Ezk 20:5
own land that I gave to my servant **J**. Ezk 28:25
in the land that I gave to my servant **J**, Ezk 37:25
the fortunes of **J** and have mercy Ezk 39:25
must plow; **J** must harrow for himself. Hos 10:11
and will punish **J** according to his Hos 12:2
J fled to the land of Aram; there Israel Hos 12:12
the house of **J**," declares the Lord Am 3:13
abhor the pride of **J** and hate his Am 6:8
GOD, please forgive! How can **J** stand? Am 7:2
Lord GOD, please cease! How can **J** stand? Am 7:5
The LORD has sworn by the pride of **J**: Am 8:7
destroy the house of **J**," declares the LORD. Am 9:8
of the violence done to your brother **J**, Ob 1:10
and the house of **J** shall possess their Ob 1:17
The house of **J** shall be a fire, and the Ob 1:18
for the transgression of **J** and for the sins Mi 1:5
of Israel. What is the transgression of **J**? Mi 1:5
Should this be said, O house of **J**? Has the Mi 2:7
I will surely assemble all of you, O **J**; I Mi 2:12
you heads of **J** and rulers of the house of Mi 3:1
to declare to **J** his transgression and to Mi 3:8
heads of the house of **J** and rulers of the Mi 3:9
of the LORD, to the house of the God of **J**, Mi 4:2
Then the remnant of **J** shall be in the Mi 5:7
And the remnant of **J** shall be among the Mi 5:8
show faithfulness to **J** and steadfast love Mi 7:20
restoring the majesty of **J** as the majesty Na 2:2
declares the LORD. "Yet I have loved **J** Mal 1:2
May the LORD cut off from the tents of **J**, Mal 2:12
therefore you, O children of **J**, are not Mal 3:6
father of Isaac, and Isaac the father of **J**, Mt 1:2
and **J** the father of Judah and his brothers, Mt 1:2
of Matthan, and Matthan the father of **J**, Mt 1:15
and **J** the father of Joseph the husband of Mt 1:16
Isaac, and **J** in the kingdom of heaven, Mt 8:11
and the God of Isaac, and the God of **J**'? Mt 22:32
and the God of Isaac, and the God of **J**'? Mk 12:26
he will reign over the house of **J** forever, Lk 1:33
the son of **J**, the son of Isaac, the son of Lk 3:34
Abraham and Isaac and **J** and all the Lk 13:28
and the God of Isaac and the God of **J**. Lk 20:37
near the field that **J** had given to his son Jn 4:5
Are you greater than our father **J**? He Jn 4:12
the God of Isaac, and the God of **J**, Acts 3:13
day, and Isaac became the father of **J**, Acts 7:8
of Jacob, and **J** of the twelve patriarchs. Acts 7:8
But when **J** heard that there was grain Acts 7:12
sent and summoned **J** his father and Acts 7:14
And **J** went down into Egypt, and he Acts 7:15
God of Abraham and of Isaac and of **J**.' Acts 7:32
to find a dwelling place for the God of **J**. Acts 7:46
As it is written, "**J** I loved, but Esau I Rom 9:13
he will banish ungodliness from **J**"; Rom 11:26
land, living in tents with Isaac and **J**, Heb 11:9
future blessings on **J** and Esau. Heb 11:20
By faith **J**, when dying, blessed each of Heb 11:21

JACOB'S (15)
felt him and said, "The voice is **J** voice, Gn 27:22
of Rebekah, **J** and Esau's mother. Gn 28:5
J anger was kindled against Rachel, and Gn 30:2
would be Laban's, and the stronger **J**. Gn 30:42
So Laban went into **J** tent and into Gn 31:33
and **J** hip was put out of joint as he Gn 32:25
touched the socket of **J** hip on the Gn 32:32
thing in Israel by lying with **J** daughter, Gn 34:7
because he delighted in **J** daughter. Gn 34:19
The sons of Leah: Reuben (**J** firstborn), Gn 35:23
Jacob and his sons. Reuben, **J** firstborn, Gn 46:8
The sons of Rachel, **J** wife: Joseph and Gn 46:19
not including **J** sons' wives, Gn 46:26
us?" "Is not Esau **J** brother?" declares the Mal 1:2
J well was there; so Jesus, wearied as he was Jn 4:6

JADA (2)
The sons of Onam: Shammai and **J**. 1 Chr 2:28
The sons of **J**, Shammai's brother: 1 Chr 2:32

JADDAI (1)
Jeiel, Mattithiah, Zabad, Zebina, **J**, Joel, Ezr 10:43

JADDUA (3)
Meshezabel, Zadok, **J**, Neh 10:21
and Jonathan the father of **J**. Neh 12:11
of Eliashib, Joiada, Johanan, and **J**, Neh 12:22

JADON (1)
the Gibeonite and **J** the Meronothite, Neh 3:7

JAEL (6)
Sisera fled away on foot to the tent of **J**, Jgs 4:17
And **J** came out to meet Sisera and said Jgs 4:18
But **J** the wife of Heber took a tent peg, Jgs 4:21
J went out to meet him and said to him, Jgs 4:22
of Shamgar, son of Anath, in the days of **J**, Jgs 5:6
"Most blessed of women be **J**, the wife of Jgs 5:24

JAGUR (1)
of Edom, were Kabzeel, Eder, **J**, Jos 15:21

JAHATH (8)
Reaiah the son of Shobal fathered **J**, 1 Chr 4:2
and **J** fathered Ahumai and Lahad. 1 Chr 4:2
Libni his son, **J** his son, Zimmah his 1 Chr 6:20
son of **J**, son of Gershom, son of Levi. 1 Chr 6:43
J, Zina, and Jeush and Beriah. 1 Chr 23:10
J was the chief, and Zizah the 1 Chr 23:11
of the sons of Shelomoth, **J**. 1 Chr 24:22
them were set **J** and Obadiah the 2 Chr 34:12

JAHAZ (7)
and came to **J** and fought against Nm 21:23
us, he and all his people, to battle at **J**. Dt 2:32
and **J**, and Kedemoth, and Mephaath, Jos 13:18
pasturelands, **J** with its pasturelands, Jos 21:36
and encamped at **J** and fought with Jgs 11:20
cry out; their voice is heard as far as **J**; Is 15:4
Elealeh, as far as **J** they utter their voice, Jer 48:34

JAHAZIEL (6)
Jeremiah, **J**, Johanan, Jozabad of 1 Chr 12:4
and Benaiah and **J** the priests were to 1 Chr 16:6
Amariah the second, **J** the third, 1 Chr 23:19
Amariah the second, **J** the third, 1 Chr 24:23
the LORD came upon **J** the son of 2 Chr 20:14
the sons of Zattu, Shecaniah the son of **J**, Ezr 8:5

JAHDAI (1)
The sons of **J**: Regem, Jotham, 1 Chr 2:47

JAHDIEL (1)
Azriel, Jeremiah, Hodaviah, and **J**, 1 Chr 5:24

JAHDO (1)
of Michael, son of Jeshishai, son of **J**, 1 Chr 5:14

JAHLEEL (2)
sons of Zebulun: Sered, Elon, and **J**. Gn 46:14
of Elon, the clan of the Elonites; of **J**, Nm 26:26

JAHLEELITES (1)
Elonites; of Jahleel, the clan of the **J**. Nm 26:26

JAHMAI (1)
Uzzi, Rephaiah, Jeriel, **J**, Ibsam, and 1 Chr 7:2

JAHZAH (2)
pasturelands, **J** with its pasturelands, 1 Chr 6:78
upon the tableland, upon Holon, and **J**, Jer 48:21

JAHZEEL (2)
of Naphtali: **J**, Guni, Jezer, and Shillem. Gn 46:24
according to their clans: of **J**, Nm 26:48

JAHZEELITES (1)
their clans: of Jahzeel, the clan of the **J**; Nm 26:48

JAHZEIAH (1)
son of Asahel and **J** the son of Tikvah Ezr 10:15

JAHZERAH (1)
and Maasai the son of Adiel, son of **J**, 1 Chr 9:12

JAHZIEL (1)
J, Guni, Jezer and Shallum, the 1 Chr 7:13

JAILER (4)
ordering the **j** to keep them safely. Acts 16:23
When the **j** woke and saw that the Acts 16:27
And the **j** called for lights and rushed Acts 16:29
And the **j** reported these words to Acts 16:36

JAILERS (1)
anger his master delivered him to the **j**, Mt 18:34

JAIR (9)
And **J** the son of Manasseh went and Nm 32:41
J the Manassite took all the region of Dt 3:14
king of Bashan, and all the towns of **J**, Jos 13:30
After him arose **J** the Gileadite, who Jgs 10:3
And **J** died and was buried in Kamon. Jgs 10:5
had the villages of **J** the son of 1 Kgs 4:13
And Segub fathered **J**, who had 1 Chr 2:22
the son of **J** struck down Lahmi 1 Chr 20:5
whose name was Mordecai, the son of **J**, Est 2:5

JAIRITE (1)
and Ira the **J** was also David's priest. 2 Sm 20:26

JAIRUS (2)
the rulers of the synagogue, **J** by name, Mk 5:22
And there came a man named **J**, who Lk 8:41

JAKEH (1)
The words of Agur son of **J**. The oracle. Prv 30:1

JAKIM (2)
J, Zichri, Zabdi, 1 Chr 8:19
eleventh to Eliashib, the twelfth to **J**, 1 Chr 24:12

JALAM (4)
Oholibamah bore Jeush, **J**, and Korah. Gn 36:5
she bore to Esau Jeush, **J**, and Korah. Gn 36:14
wife: the chiefs Jeush, **J**, and Korah; Gn 36:18
Eliphaz, Reuel, Jeush, **J**, and Korah. 1 Chr 1:35

JALON (1)
of Ezrah: Jether, Mered, Epher, and **J**. 1 Chr 4:17

JAMBRES (1)
Just as Jannes and **J** opposed Moses, so 2 Tm 3:8

JAMBS (18)
eight cubits; and its **j**, two cubits; Ezk 40:9
and the **j** on either side were of the Ezk 40:10
the side rooms and toward their **j**, Ezk 40:16
inside, and on the **j** were palm trees. Ezk 40:16
and its **j** and its vestibule were of the Ezk 40:21
he measured its **j** and its vestibule; Ezk 40:24
them, and it had palm trees on its **j**, Ezk 40:26
Its side rooms, its **j**, and its vestibule Ezk 40:29
court, and palm trees were on its **j**, Ezk 40:31
Its side rooms, its **j**, and its vestibule Ezk 40:33
court, and it had palm trees on its **j**, Ezk 40:34
Its side rooms, its **j**, and its vestibule Ezk 40:36
court, and it had palm trees on its **j**, Ezk 40:37
and measured the **j** of the vestibule, Ezk 40:48
And there were pillars beside the **j**, one Ezk 40:49
me to the nave and measured the **j**. Ezk 41:1
side six cubits was the breadth of the **j**. Ezk 41:1
and measured the **j** of the entrance, Ezk 41:3

JAMES (42)
J the son of Zebedee and John his Mt 4:21
J the son of Zebedee, and John his Mt 10:2
J the son of Alphaeus, and Thaddaeus; Mt 10:3
are not his brothers **J** and Joseph and Mt 13:55
six days Jesus took with him Peter and **J**, Mt 17:1
Mary the mother of **J** and Joseph and Mt 27:56
he saw **J** the son of Zebedee and John his Mk 1:19
of Simon and Andrew, with **J** and John. Mk 1:29
J the son of Zebedee and John the Mk 3:17
John the brother of **J** (to whom he gave Mk 3:17
and Thomas, and **J** the son of Alphaeus, Mk 3:18
him except Peter and **J** and John the Mk 5:37
and James and John the brother of **J**. Mk 5:37
Mary and brother of **J** and Joses and Mk 6:3
took with him Peter and **J** and John, Mk 9:2
And **J** and John, the sons of Zebedee, Mk 10:35
began to be indignant at **J** and John. Mk 10:41
Peter and **J** and John and Andrew asked Mk 13:3
he took with him Peter and **J** and John, Mk 14:33
Mary the mother of **J** the younger and Mk 15:40
the mother of **J** and Salome bought Mk 16:1
and so also were **J** and John, sons of Lk 5:10
and Andrew his brother, and **J** and John, Lk 6:14
and Thomas, and **J** the son of Alphaeus, Lk 6:15
and Judas the son of **J**, and Judas Lk 6:16
with him, except Peter and John and **J**, Lk 8:51
Peter and John and **J** and went up on Lk 9:28
And when his disciples **J** and John saw Lk 9:54
Mary the mother of **J** and the other Lk 24:10
Peter and John and **J** and Andrew, Acts 1:13
J the son of Alphaeus and Simon the Acts 1:13
the Zealot and Judas the son of **J**. Acts 1:13
He killed **J** the brother of John with the Acts 12:2
"Tell these things to **J** and to the Acts 12:17
After they finished speaking, **J** replied, Acts 15:13
day Paul went in with us to **J**, Acts 21:18
Then he appeared to **J**, then to all the 1 Cor 15:7
other apostles except **J** the Lord's Gal 1:19
and when **J** and Cephas and John, who Gal 2:9
For before certain men came from **J**, he Gal 2:12
J, a servant of God and of the Lord Jesus Jas 1:1
servant of Jesus Christ and brother of **J**, Jude 1:1

JAMIN (6)
Jemuel, **J**, Ohad, Jachin, Zohar, and Gn 46:10
Jemuel, **J**, Ohad, Jachin, Zohar, and Ex 6:15
the clan of the Nemuelites; of **J**, Nm 26:12
of Jerahmeel: Maaz, **J**, and Eker. 1 Chr 2:27
Nemuel, **J**, Jarib, Zerah, Shaul; 1 Chr 4:24
Also Jeshua, Bani, Sherebiah, **J**, Akkub, Neh 8:7

JAMINITES (1)
Nemuelites; of Jamin, the clan of the **J**; Nm 26:12

JAMLECH (1)
J, Joshah the son of Amaziah, 1 Chr 4:34

JANAI (1)
the second, **J**, and Shaphat in Bashan. 1 Chr 5:12

JANIM (1)
J, Beth-tappuah, Aphekah, Jos 15:53

JANNAI (1)
of Levi, the son of Melchi, the son of **J**, Lk 3:24

JANNES (1)
Just as **J** and Jambres opposed Moses, 2 Tm 3:8

JANOAH (3)
passes along beyond it on the east to **J**, Jos 16:6
it goes down from **J** to Ataroth and to Jos 16:7
Ijon, Abel-beth-maacah, **J**, Kedesh, 2 Kgs 15:29

JAPHETH (11)
old, Noah fathered Shem, Ham, and **J**. Gn 5:32
Noah had three sons, Shem, Ham, and **J**. Gn 6:10
and his sons, Shem and Ham and **J**, Gn 7:13
from the ark were Shem, Ham, and **J**. Gn 9:18
Then Shem and **J** took a garment, laid it Gn 9:23
May God enlarge **J**, and let him dwell in Gn 9:27
of the sons of Noah, Shem, Ham, and **J**. Gn 10:1
The sons of **J**: Gomer, Magog, Madai, Gn 10:2
children of Eber, the elder brother of **J**, Gn 10:21
Noah, Shem, Ham, and **J**. 1 Chr 1:4
The sons of **J**: Gomer, Magog, Madai, 1 Chr 1:5

JAPHIA (5)
king of Jarmuth, to **J** king of Lachish, Jos 10:3
there it goes to Daberath, then up to **J**. Jos 19:12
Ibhar, Elishua, Nepheg, **J**, 2 Sm 5:15
Nogah, Nepheg, **J**, 1 Chr 3:7
Nogah, Nepheg, **J**, 1 Chr 14:6

JAPHLET (3)
Heber fathered **J**, Shomer, Hotham, 1 Chr 7:32
The sons of **J**: Pasach, Bimhal, and 1 Chr 7:33
and Ashvath. These are the sons of **J**. 1 Chr 7:33

JAPHLETITES (1)
down westward to the territory of the **J**, Jos 16:3

JAR (26)
'Please let down your **j** that I may Gn 24:14
out with her water **j** on her shoulder. Gn 24:15
the spring and filled her **j** and came up. Gn 24:16
me a little water to drink from your **j**." Gn 24:17
quickly let down her **j** upon her hand Gn 24:18
quickly emptied her **j** into the trough Gn 24:20
me a little water from your **j** to drink," Gn 24:43
out with her water **j** on her shoulder, Gn 24:45
let down her **j** from her shoulder Gn 24:46
And Moses said to Aaron, "Take a **j**, Ex 16:33
that is at his head and the **j** of water, 1 Sm 26:11
the spear and the **j** of water from 1 Sm 26:12
spear is and the **j** of water that was 1 Sm 26:16
loaves, some cakes, and a **j** of honey, 1 Kgs 14:3
handful of flour in a **j** and a little oil 1 Kgs 17:12
'The **j** of flour shall not be spent, 1 Kgs 17:14
The **j** of flour was not spent, neither 1 Kgs 17:16
baked on hot stones and a **j** of water. 1 Kgs 19:6
nothing in the house except a **j** of oil." 2 Kgs 4:2
"Every **j** shall be filled with wine."' And Jer 13:12
indeed know that every **j** will be filled Jer 13:12
a man carrying a **j** of water will meet Mk 14:13
lamp covers it with a **j** or puts it under a Lk 8:16
a man carrying a **j** of water will meet Lk 22:10
woman left her water **j** and went away Jn 4:28
A **j** full of sour wine stood there, so they Jn 19:29

JARAH (2)
And Ahaz fathered **J**, and Jarah 1 Chr 9:42
Jarah, and **J** fathered Alemeth, 1 Chr 9:42

JARED (7)
had lived 65 years, he fathered **J**. Gn 5:15
lived after he fathered **J** 830 years and Gn 5:16
When **J** had lived 162 years he fathered Gn 5:18
J lived after he fathered Enoch 800 years Gn 5:19
Thus all the days of **J** were 962 years, Gn 5:20
Kenan, Mahalalel, **J**; 1 Chr 1:2
the son of Enoch, the son of **J**, Lk 3:37

JARHA (2)
an Egyptian slave whose name was **J**. 1 Chr 2:34
daughter in marriage to **J** his slave, 1 Chr 2:35

JARIB (3)
Nemuel, Jamin, **J**, Zerah, Shaul; 1 Chr 4:24
Ariel, Shemaiah, Elnathan, **J**, Elnathan, Ezr 8:16
Maaseiah, Eliezer, **J**, and Gedaliah, Ezr 10:18

JARMUTH (7)
king of Hebron, to Piram king of **J**, Jos 10:3
the king of Hebron, the king of **J**, Jos 10:5

JEDIDAH (1)
mother's name was J the daughter of 2 Kgs 22:1

JEDIDIAH (1)
So he called his name J, because of 2 Sm 12:25

JEDUTHUN (17)
of Shemaiah, son of Galal, son of J, 1 Chr 9:16
while Obed-edom, the son of J, 1 Chr 16:38
them were Heman and J and the rest 1 Chr 16:41
Heman and J had trumpets and 1 Chr 16:42
The sons of J were appointed to the 1 Chr 16:42
of Asaph, and of Heman, and of J, 1 Chr 25:1
Of J, the sons of Jeduthun: Gedaliah, 1 Chr 25:3
Of Jeduthun, the sons of J: Gedaliah, 1 Chr 25:3
under the direction of their father J, 1 Chr 25:3
J, and Heman were under the order of 1 Chr 25:6
singers, Asaph, Heman, and J, 2 Chr 5:12
and of the sons of J, Shemaiah and 2 Chr 29:14
and Heman, and J the king's seer; 2 Chr 35:15
of Shammua, son of Galal, son of J. Neh 11:17
To the choirmaster: to J. A Psalm of Ps 39:T
To the choirmaster: according to J. A Ps 62:T
To the choirmaster: according to J. A Ps 77:T

JEERED (3)
came out of the city and j at him, 2 Kgs 2:23
it, they j at us and despised us and said, Neh 2:19
and greatly enraged, and he j at the Jews. Neh 4:1

JEGAR-SAHADUTHA (1)
Laban called it J, but Jacob called it Gn 31:47

JEHALLELEL (2)
The sons of J: Ziph, Ziphah, Tiria, 1 Chr 4:16
of Abdi, and Azariah the son of J; 2 Chr 29:12

JEHDEIAH (2)
Shubael; of the sons of Shubael, J. 1 Chr 24:20
the donkeys was J the Meronothite. 1 Chr 27:30

JEHEZKEL (1)
to Pethahiah, the twentieth to J, 1 Chr 24:16

JEHIAH (1)
Obed-edom and J were to be 1 Chr 15:24

JEHIEL (13)
Jaaziel, Shemiramoth, J, Unni, 1 Chr 15:18
Aziel, Shemiramoth, J, Unni, 1 Chr 15:20
Jeiel, Shemiramoth, J, Mattithiah, 1 Chr 16:5
J the chief, and Zetham, and Joel, 1 Chr 23:8
He and J the son of Hachmoni 1 Chr 27:32
LORD, in the care of J the Gershonite. 1 Chr 29:8
Azariah, J, Zechariah, Azariah, 2 Chr 21:2
while J, Azaziah, Nahath, Asahel, 2 Chr 31:13
Hilkiah, Zechariah, and J, the chief 2 Chr 35:8
Of the sons of Joab, Obadiah the son of J, Ezr 8:9
And Shecaniah the son of J, of the sons Ezr 10:2
Elijah, Shemaiah, J, and Uzziah. Ezr 10:21
Mattaniah, Zechariah, J, Abdi, Ezr 10:26

JEHIELI (2)
to Ladan the Gershonite: J. 1 Chr 26:21
The sons of J, Zetham, and Joel his 1 Chr 26:22

JEHIZKIAH (1)
Meshillemoth, J the son of Shallum, 2 Chr 28:12

JEHOADDAH (2)
Ahaz fathered J, and Jehoaddah 1 Chr 8:36
Jehoaddah, and J fathered Alemeth, 1 Chr 8:36

JEHOADDAN (1)
mother's name was J of Jerusalem. 2 Chr 25:1

JEHOADDIN (1)
mother's name was J of Jerusalem. 2 Kgs 14:2

JEHOAHAZ (21)
And J his son reigned in his place. 2 Kgs 10:35
J the son of Jehu began to reign over 2 Kgs 13:1
Then J sought the favor of the LORD, 2 Kgs 13:4
was not left to J an army of more 2 Kgs 13:7
rest of the acts of J and all that he did, 2 Kgs 13:8
So J slept with his fathers, and they 2 Kgs 13:9
Jehoash the son of J began to reign 2 Kgs 13:10
oppressed Israel all the days of J. 2 Kgs 13:22
Jehoash the son of J took again from 2 Kgs 13:25
he had taken from J his father in 2 Kgs 13:25
messengers to Jehoash the son of J, 2 Kgs 14:8
after the death of Jehoash son of J, 2 Kgs 14:17
of the land took J the son of Josiah, 2 Kgs 23:30
J was twenty-three years old when he 2 Kgs 23:31
But he took J away, and he came to 2 Kgs 23:34
that no son was left to him except J, 2 Chr 21:17
and sent to Joash the son of J, 2 Chr 25:17
after the death of Joash the son of J, 2 Chr 25:25
of the land took J the son of Josiah 2 Chr 36:1
J was twenty-three years old when he 2 Chr 36:2
But Neco took J his brother and 2 Chr 36:4

JEHOASH (17)
J was seven years old when he began 2 Kgs 11:21
seventh year of Jehu, J began to reign, 2 Kgs 12:1
And J did what was right in the eyes 2 Kgs 12:2
J said to the priests, "All the money of 2 Kgs 12:4
by the twenty-third year of King J, 2 Kgs 12:6
Therefore King J summoned 2 Kgs 12:7
J king of Judah took all the sacred 2 Kgs 12:18
J the son of Jehoahaz began to reign 2 Kgs 13:10
Then J the son of Jehoahaz took 2 Kgs 13:25
sent messengers to J the son of 2 Kgs 14:8
And J king of Israel sent word to 2 Kgs 14:9
So J king of Israel went up, and he 2 Kgs 14:11
And J king of Israel captured 2 Kgs 14:13
Amaziah king of Judah, the son of J, 2 Kgs 14:13
the rest of the acts of J that he did, 2 Kgs 14:15
And J slept with his fathers and was 2 Kgs 14:16
after the death of J son of Jehoahaz, 2 Kgs 14:17

JEHOHANAN (8)
Elam the fifth, J the sixth, Eliehoenai 1 Chr 26:3
and next to him J the commander, 2 Chr 17:15
son of Jeroham, Ishmael the son of J, 2 Chr 23:1
to the chamber of J the son of Eliashib, Ezr 10:6
Of the sons of Bebai were J, Hananiah, Ezr 10:28
and his son J had taken the daughter of Neh 6:18
of Ezra, Meshullam; of Amariah, J; Neh 12:13
Eleazar, Uzzi, J, Malchijah, Neh 12:42

JEHOIACHIN (13)
and J his son reigned in his place. 2 Kgs 24:6
J was eighteen years old when he 2 Kgs 24:8
and J the king of Judah gave himself 2 Kgs 24:12
And he carried away J to Babylon. 2 Kgs 24:15
year of the exile of J king of Judah, 2 Kgs 25:27
graciously freed J king of Judah 2 Kgs 25:27
So J put off his prison garments. 2 Kgs 25:29
And J his son reigned in his place. 2 Chr 36:8
J was eight years old when he became 2 Chr 36:9
year of the exile of J king of Judah, Jer 52:31
lifted up the head of J king of Judah and Jer 52:31
So J put off his prison garments. And Jer 52:33
was the fifth year of the exile of King J), Ezk 1:2

JEHOIACHIN'S (1)
Babylon made Mattaniah, J uncle, 2 Kgs 24:17

JEHOIADA (53)
Benaiah the son of J was over the 2 Sm 8:18
the son of J was in command 2 Sm 20:23
Benaiah the son of J was a valiant 2 Sm 23:20
things did Benaiah the son of J, 2 Sm 23:22
Benaiah the son of J and Nathan the 1 Kgs 1:8
the priest, and Benaiah the son of J, 1 Kgs 1:26
Benaiah the son of J." So they came 1 Kgs 1:32
the son of J answered the king, 1 Kgs 1:36
the prophet, and Benaiah the son of J, 1 Kgs 1:38
the prophet, and Benaiah the son of J, 1 Kgs 1:44
Solomon sent Benaiah the son of J, 1 Kgs 2:25
Solomon sent Benaiah the son of J, 1 Kgs 2:29
Benaiah the son of J went up and 1 Kgs 2:34
Benaiah the son of J over the army in 1 Kgs 2:35
commanded Benaiah the son of J, 1 Kgs 2:46
Benaiah the son of J was in command 1 Kgs 4:4
the seventh year J sent and brought 2 Kgs 11:4
to all that J the priest commanded, 2 Kgs 11:9
the Sabbath, and came to J the priest. 2 Kgs 11:9
Then J the priest commanded the 2 Kgs 11:15
And J made a covenant between the 2 Kgs 11:17
because J the priest instructed him. 2 Kgs 12:2
King Jehoash summoned J the priest 2 Kgs 12:7
Then J the priest took a chest and 2 Kgs 12:9
Benaiah the son of J was a valiant 1 Chr 11:22
Benaiah the son of J and won a 1 Chr 11:24
The prince J, of the house of Aaron, 1 Chr 12:27
Benaiah the son of J was over the 1 Chr 18:17
Benaiah, the son of J the chief priest; 1 Chr 27:5
was succeeded by J the son of 1 Chr 27:34
Jehoram and wife of J the priest, 2 Chr 22:11
the seventh year J took courage and 2 Chr 23:1
And J said to them, "Behold, the 2 Chr 23:3
to all that J the priest commanded, 2 Chr 23:8
for J the priest did not dismiss the 2 Chr 23:8
And J the priest gave to the captains 2 Chr 23:9
and J and his sons anointed him, 2 Chr 23:11
Then J the priest brought out the 2 Chr 23:14
And J made a covenant between 2 Chr 23:16
And J posted watchmen for the 2 Chr 23:18
of the LORD all the days of J the priest. 2 Chr 24:2
J got for him two wives, and he had 2 Chr 24:3
the king summoned J the chief and 2 Chr 24:6
And the king and J gave it to those 2 Chr 24:12
of the money before the king and J, 2 Chr 24:14
the LORD regularly all the days of J. 2 Chr 24:14
But J grew old and full of days, and 2 Chr 24:15
after the death of J the princes of 2 Chr 24:17
Zechariah the son of J the priest, 2 Chr 24:20
not remember the kindness that J, 2 Chr 24:22
of the blood of the son of J the priest, 2 Chr 24:25
And one of the sons of J, the son of Neh 13:28
made you priest instead of J the priest, Jer 29:26

JEHOIAKIM (36)
father, and changed his name to J. 2 Kgs 23:34
And J gave the silver and the gold to 2 Kgs 23:35
J was twenty-five years old when he 2 Kgs 23:36
and J became his servant three years. 2 Kgs 24:1
rest of the deeds of J and all that he 2 Kgs 24:5
So J slept with his fathers, and 2 Kgs 24:6
according to all that J had done. 2 Kgs 24:19
Johanan the firstborn, the second J, 1 Chr 3:15
The descendants of J: Jeconiah his 1 Chr 3:16
and changed his name to J. 2 Chr 36:4
J was twenty-five years old when he 2 Chr 36:5
Now the rest of the acts of J, and the 2 Chr 36:8
also in the days of J the son of Josiah, Jer 1:3
says the LORD concerning J the son of Jer 22:18
the LORD, though Coniah the son of J, Jer 22:24
from Jerusalem Jeconiah the son of J, Jer 24:1
in the fourth year of J the son of Josiah, Jer 25:1
of the reign of J the son of Josiah, Jer 26:1
And when King J, with all his warriors Jer 26:21
Then King J sent to Egypt certain men, Jer 26:22
from Egypt and brought him to King J, Jer 26:23
to Babylon Jeconiah the son of J, Jer 27:20
back to this place Jeconiah the son of J, Jer 28:4
the LORD in the days of J the son of Josiah, Jer 35:1
In the fourth year of J the son of Josiah, Jer 36:1
In the fifth year of J the son of Josiah, Jer 36:9
which J the king of Judah has burned. Jer 36:28
And concerning J king of Judah you Jer 36:29
the LORD concerning J king of Judah: Jer 36:30
of the scroll that J king of Judah had Jer 36:32
reigned instead of Coniah the son of J. Jer 37:1
in the fourth year of J the son of Josiah, Jer 45:1
in the fourth year of J the son of Josiah, Jer 46:2
LORD, according to all that J had done. Jer 52:2
third year of the reign of J king of Judah, Dn 1:1
And the Lord gave J king of Judah into Dn 1:2

JEHOIARIB (2)
Of the priests: Jedaiah, J, Jachin, 1 Chr 9:10
The first lot fell to J, the second to 1 Chr 24:7

JEHONADAB (3)
he met J the son of Rechab coming 2 Kgs 10:15
mine is to yours?" And J answered, 2 Kgs 10:15
house of Baal with J the son of 2 Kgs 10:23

JEHONATHAN (2)
Asahel, Shemiramoth, J, Adonijah, 2 Chr 17:8
of Bilgah, Shammua; of Shemaiah, J; Neh 12:18

JEHORAM (22)
and J his son reigned in his place. 1 Kgs 22:50
J became king in his place in the 2 Kgs 1:17
the second year of J the son of 2 Kgs 1:17
J the son of Ahab became king over 2 Kgs 3:1
So King J marched out of Samaria at 2 Kgs 3:6
way shall we march?" J answered, 2 Kgs 3:8
of Judah, J the son of Jehoshaphat, 2 Kgs 8:16
king of Israel, Ahaziah the son of J, 2 Kgs 8:25
Ahaziah the son of J king of Judah 2 Kgs 8:29
that Jehoshaphat and J and Ahaziah 2 Kgs 12:18
Levites, the priests Elishama and J. 2 Chr 17:8
and J his son reigned in his place. 2 Chr 21:1
Judah, but he gave the kingdom to J, 2 Chr 21:3
When J had ascended the throne of 2 Chr 21:4
J was thirty-two years old when he 2 Chr 21:5
Then J passed over with his 2 Chr 21:9
stirred up against J the anger of 2 Chr 21:16
Ahaziah the son of J king of Judah 2 Chr 22:1
counsel and went with J the son of 2 Chr 22:5
Ahaziah the son of J king of Judah 2 Chr 22:6
he went out with J to meet Jehu the 2 Chr 22:7
the daughter of King J and wife of 2 Chr 22:11

JEHOSHABEATH (2)
But J, the daughter of the king, took 2 Chr 22:11
and his nurse in a bedroom. Thus J, 2 Chr 22:11

JEHOSHAPHAT (86)
and J the son of Ahilud was recorder, 2 Sm 8:16
and J the son of Ahilud was the 2 Sm 20:24
J the son of Ahilud was recorder; 1 Kgs 4:3
J the son of Paruah, in Issachar; 1 Kgs 4:17
and J his son reigned in his place. 1 Kgs 15:24
in the third year J the king of Judah 1 Kgs 22:2
And he said to J, "Will you go with 1 Kgs 22:4
at Ramoth-gilead?" And J said to the 1 Kgs 22:4
And J said to the king of Israel, 1 Kgs 22:5
But J said, "Is there not here another 1 Kgs 22:7
And the king of Israel said to J, 1 Kgs 22:8
concerning me, but evil." And J said, 1 Kgs 22:8
king of Israel and J the king of 1 Kgs 22:10
And the king of Israel said to J, "Did 1 Kgs 22:18
king of Israel and J the king of 1 Kgs 22:29
And the king of Israel said to J, "I 1 Kgs 22:30

the captains of the chariots saw **J**, 1 Kgs 22:32
to fight against him. And **J** cried out. 1 Kgs 22:32
J the son of Asa began to reign over 1 Kgs 22:41
J was thirty-five years old when he 1 Kgs 22:42
J also made peace with the king of 1 Kgs 22:44
Now the rest of the acts of **J**, and his 1 Kgs 22:45
J made ships of Tarshish to go to 1 Kgs 22:48
Ahaziah the son of Ahab said to **J**, 1 Kgs 22:49
in the ships," but **J** was not willing. 1 Kgs 22:49
And **J** slept with his fathers and was 1 Kgs 22:50
seventeenth year of **J** king of Judah, 1 Kgs 22:51
second year of Jehoram the son of **J**, 2 Kgs 1:17
the eighteenth year of **J** king of Judah, 2 Kgs 3:1
went and sent word to **J** king of Judah, 2 Kgs 3:7
And **J** said, "Is there no prophet of the 2 Kgs 3:11
And **J** said, "The word of the LORD is 2 Kgs 3:12
king of Israel and **J** and the king of 2 Kgs 3:12
I have regard for **J** the king of Judah, 2 Kgs 3:14
of Israel, when **J** was king of Judah, 2 Kgs 8:16
king of Judah, Jehoram the son of **J**, 2 Kgs 8:16
arrive, look there for Jehu the son of **J**, 2 Kgs 9:2
Jehu the son of **J** the son of Nimshi 2 Kgs 9:14
sacred gifts that **J** and Jehoram and 2 Kgs 12:18
Abijah his son, Asa his son, **J** his son, 1 Chr 3:10
and **J** the son of Ahilud was 1 Chr 18:15
J his son reigned in his place and 2 Chr 17:1
The LORD was with **J**, because he 2 Chr 17:3
And all Judah brought tribute to **J**, 2 Chr 17:5
and they made no war against **J**. 2 Chr 17:10
Philistines brought **J** presents and 2 Chr 17:11
And **J** grew steadily greater. He built 2 Chr 17:12
Now **J** had great riches and honor, 2 Chr 18:1
king of Israel said to **J** king of Judah, 2 Chr 18:3
And **J** said to the king of Israel, 2 Chr 18:4
But **J** said, "Is there not here another 2 Chr 18:6
And the king of Israel said to **J**, 2 Chr 18:7
me, but always evil." And **J** said, 2 Chr 18:7
king of Israel and **J** the king of Judah 2 Chr 18:9
And the king of Israel said to **J**, "Did 2 Chr 18:17
king of Israel and **J** the king of 2 Chr 18:28
And the king of Israel said to **J**, "I 2 Chr 18:29
as the captains of the chariots saw **J**, 2 Chr 18:31
And **J** cried out, and the LORD helped 2 Chr 18:31
J the king of Judah returned in safety 2 Chr 19:1
out to meet him and said to King **J**, 2 Chr 19:2
J lived at Jerusalem. And he went out 2 Chr 19:4
in Jerusalem **J** appointed certain 2 Chr 19:8
Meunites, came against **J** for battle. 2 Chr 20:1
Some men came and told **J**, "A great 2 Chr 20:2
Then **J** was afraid and set his face to 2 Chr 20:3
And **J** stood in the assembly of Judah 2 Chr 20:5
of Jerusalem and King **J**: 2 Chr 20:15
Then **J** bowed his head with his face 2 Chr 20:18
they went out, **J** stood and said, 2 Chr 20:20
When **J** and his people came to take 2 Chr 20:25
and Jerusalem, and **J** at their head, 2 Chr 20:27
So the realm of **J** was quiet, for his 2 Chr 20:30
Thus **J** reigned over Judah. He was 2 Chr 20:31
Now the rest of the acts of **J**, from 2 Chr 20:34
After this **J** king of Judah joined 2 Chr 20:35
of Mareshah prophesied against **J**, 2 Chr 20:37
J slept with his fathers and was 2 Chr 21:1
He had brothers, the sons of **J**: 2 Chr 21:2
these were the sons of **J** king of Judah. 2 Chr 21:2
walked in the ways of **J** your father, 2 Chr 21:12
for they said, "He is the grandson of **J**, 2 Chr 22:9
and bring them down to the Valley of **J**. Jl 3:2
up and come up to the Valley of **J**; Jl 3:12
and Asaph the father of **J**, and Mt 1:8
of Jehoshaphat, and **J** the father of Joram, Mt 1:8

JEHOSHEBA (1)
But **J**, the daughter of King Joram, 2 Kgs 11:2

JEHOZABAD (4)
son of Shimeath and **J** the son of 2 Kgs 12:21
Shemaiah the firstborn, **J** the second, 1 Chr 26:4
next to him **J** with 180,000 armed 2 Chr 17:18
and **J** the son of Shimrith the 2 Chr 24:26

JEHOZADAK (8)
fathered Seraiah, Seraiah fathered **J**; 1 Chr 6:14
and **J** went into exile when the LORD 1 Chr 6:15
of Judah, and to Joshua the son of **J**, Hg 1:1
son of Shealtiel, and Joshua the son of **J**, Hg 1:12
and the spirit of Joshua the son of **J**, Hg 1:14
of Judah, and to Joshua the son of **J**, Hg 2:2
Be strong, O Joshua, son of **J**, the high Hg 2:4
set it on the head of Joshua, the son of **J**, Zec 6:11

JEHU (61)
the LORD came to **J** the son of Hanani 1 Kgs 16:1
came by the prophet **J** the son of 1 Kgs 16:7
against Baasha by **J** the prophet, 1 Kgs 16:12
And **J** the son of Nimshi you shall 1 Kgs 19:16
sword of Hazael shall **J** put to death, 1 Kgs 19:17
from the sword of **J** shall Elisha put 1 Kgs 19:17
look there for **J** the son of Jehoshaphat, 2 Kgs 9:2
for you, O commander." And **J** said, 2 Kgs 9:5
When **J** came out to the servants of 2 Kgs 9:11
trumpet and proclaimed, "**J** is king." 2 Kgs 9:13
Thus **J** the son of Jehoshaphat the son 2 Kgs 9:14
with Hazael king of Syria.) So **J** said, 2 Kgs 9:15
Then **J** mounted his chariot and went 2 Kgs 9:16
saw the company of **J** as he came and 2 Kgs 9:17
the king, 'Is it peace?'" And **J** said, 2 Kgs 9:18
said, 'Is it peace?'" And **J** answered, 2 Kgs 9:19
like the driving of **J** the son of 2 Kgs 9:20
in his chariot, and went to meet **J**, 2 Kgs 9:21
And when Joram saw **J**, he said, "Is it 2 Kgs 9:22
he said, "Is it peace, **J**?" He answered, 2 Kgs 9:22
And **J** drew his bow with his full 2 Kgs 9:24
J said to Bidkar his aide, "Take him 2 Kgs 9:25
And **J** pursued him and said, "Shoot 2 Kgs 9:27
When **J** came to Jezreel, Jezebel heard 2 Kgs 9:30
And as **J** entered the gate, she said, "Is 2 Kgs 9:31
So **J** wrote letters and sent them to 2 Kgs 10:1
the elders and the guardians, sent to **J**, 2 Kgs 10:5
So **J** struck down all who remained 2 Kgs 10:11
J met the relatives of Ahaziah king 2 Kgs 10:13
Jehonadab answered, "It is." **J** said, 2 Kgs 10:15
And **J** took him up with him into 2 Kgs 10:15
Then **J** assembled all the people and 2 Kgs 10:18
a little, but **J** will serve him much. 2 Kgs 10:18
shall not live." But **J** did it with 2 Kgs 10:19
And **J** ordered, "Sanctify a solemn 2 Kgs 10:20
And **J** sent throughout all Israel, and 2 Kgs 10:21
Then **J** went into the house of Baal 2 Kgs 10:23
Now **J** had stationed eighty men 2 Kgs 10:24
J said to the guard and to the 2 Kgs 10:25
Thus **J** wiped out Baal from Israel. 2 Kgs 10:28
But **J** did not turn aside from the 2 Kgs 10:29
And the LORD said to **J**, "Because you 2 Kgs 10:30
But **J** was not careful to walk in the 2 Kgs 10:31
rest of the acts of **J** and all that he 2 Kgs 10:34
So **J** slept with his fathers, and they 2 Kgs 10:35
The time that **J** reigned over Israel in 2 Kgs 10:36
In the seventh year of **J**, Jehoash 2 Kgs 12:1
Jehoahaz the son of **J** began to reign 2 Kgs 13:1
Jehoash the son of Jehoahaz, son of **J**, 2 Kgs 14:8
promise of the LORD that he gave to **J**, 2 Kgs 15:12
Obed fathered **J**, and Jehu fathered 1 Chr 2:38
fathered Jehu, and **J** fathered Azariah. 1 Chr 2:38
Joel, **J** the son of Joshibiah, son of 1 Chr 4:35
of Azmaveth; Beracah, **J** of Anathoth, 1 Chr 12:3
But **J** the son of Hanani the seer went 2 Chr 19:2
in the chronicles of **J** the son of 2 Chr 20:34
with Jehoram to meet **J** the son of 2 Chr 22:7
And when **J** was executing judgment 2 Chr 22:8
he was brought to **J** and put to death. 2 Chr 22:9
Joash the son of Jehoahaz, son of **J**, 2 Chr 25:17
punish the house of **J** for the blood of Hos 1:4

JEHUBBAH (1)
his brother: Rohgah, **J**, and Aram. 1 Chr 7:34

JEHUCAL (1)
King Zedekiah sent **J** the son of Jer 37:3

JEHUD (1)
J, Bene-berak, Gath-rimmon, Jos 19:45

JEHUDI (4)
all the officials sent **J** the son of Jer 36:14
Then the king sent **J** to get the scroll, Jer 36:21
And **J** read it to the king and all the Jer 36:21
As **J** read three or four columns, the Jer 36:23

JEHUEL (1)
of the sons of Heman, **J** and Shimei; 2 Chr 29:14

JEIEL (12)
recorded: the chief, **J**, and Zechariah, 1 Chr 5:7
J the father of Gibeon lived in 1 Chr 8:29
J, and the name of his wife was 1 Chr 9:35
Shama and **J** the sons of Hotham 1 Chr 11:44
the gatekeepers Obed-edom and **J**. 1 Chr 15:18
J, and Azaziah were to lead with 1 Chr 15:21
were Zechariah, **J**, Shemiramoth, 1 Chr 16:5
Eliab, Benaiah, Obed-edom, and **J**, 1 Chr 16:5
Zechariah, son of Benaiah, son of **J**, 2 Chr 20:14
muster made by **J** the secretary and 2 Chr 26:11
and Hashabiah and **J** and Jozabad, 2 Chr 35:9
J, Mattithiah, Zabad, Zebina, Jaddai, Ezr 10:43

JEKABZEEL (1)
its villages, and in **J** and its villages, Neh 11:25

JEKAMEAM (2)
Jahaziel the third, and **J** the fourth. 1 Chr 23:19
Jahaziel the third, **J** the fourth. 1 Chr 24:23

JEKAMIAH (3)
Shallum fathered **J**, and Jekamiah 1 Chr 2:41
Jekamiah, and **J** fathered Elishama. 1 Chr 2:41
J, Hoshama and Nedabiah; 1 Chr 3:18

JEKUTHIEL (1)
of Soco, and **J** the father of Zanoah. 1 Chr 4:18

JEMIMAH (1)
called the name of the first daughter **J**, Jb 42:14

JEMUEL (2)
J, Jamin, Ohad, Jachin, Zohar, and Gn 46:10
J, Jamin, Ohad, Jachin, Zohar, and Ex 6:15

JEPHTHAH (30)
Now **J** the Gileadite was a mighty Jgs 11:1
of a prostitute. Gilead was the father of **J**. Jgs 11:1
up, they drove **J** out and said to him, Jgs 11:2
Then **J** fled from his brothers and lived Jgs 11:3
fellows collected around **J** and went out Jgs 11:3
Gilead went to bring **J** from the land of Jgs 11:5
And they said to **J**, "Come and be our Jgs 11:6
But **J** said to the elders of Gilead, "Did Jgs 11:7
And the elders of Gilead said to **J**, "That Jgs 11:8
J said to the elders of Gilead, "If you Jgs 11:9
And the elders of Gilead said to **J**, "The Jgs 11:10
So **J** went with the elders of Gilead, and Jgs 11:11
And **J** spoke all his words before the Jgs 11:11
Then **J** sent messengers to the king of Jgs 11:12
answered the messengers of **J**, Jgs 11:13
J again sent messengers to the king of Jgs 11:14
and said to him, "Thus says **J**: Israel did Jgs 11:15
listen to the words of **J** that he sent to Jgs 11:28
Then the Spirit of the LORD was upon **J**, Jgs 11:29
And **J** made a vow to the LORD and said, Jgs 11:30
So **J** crossed over to the Ammonites to Jgs 11:32
Then **J** came to his home at Mizpah. Jgs 11:34
the daughter of **J** the Gileadite four Jgs 11:40
and they crossed to Zaphon and said to **J**, Jgs 12:1
And **J** said to them, "I and my people had Jgs 12:2
Then **J** gathered all the men of Gilead Jgs 12:4
J judged Israel six years. Then Jephthah Jgs 12:7
Then **J** the Gileadite died and was buried Jgs 12:7
and Barak and **J** and Samuel and 1 Sm 12:11
J, of David and Samuel and the Heb 11:32

JEPHUNNEH (16)
the tribe of Judah, Caleb the son of **J**; Nm 13:6
the son of Nun and Caleb the son of **J**, Nm 14:6
Caleb the son of **J** and Joshua the son Nm 14:30
and Caleb the son of **J** remained alive. Nm 14:38
Caleb the son of **J** and Joshua the son Nm 26:65
Caleb the son of **J** the Kenizzite and Nm 32:12
the tribe of Judah, Caleb the son of **J**. Nm 34:19
except Caleb the son of **J**. He shall see it, Dt 1:36
Caleb the son of **J** the Kenizzite said to Jos 14:6
to Caleb the son of **J** for an inheritance. Jos 14:13
Caleb the son of **J** the Kenizzite to this Jos 14:14
Caleb the son of **J** a portion among the Jos 15:13
to Caleb the son of **J** as his possession. Jos 21:12
The sons of Caleb the son of **J**: Iru, 1 Chr 4:15
they gave to Caleb the son of **J**. 1 Chr 6:56
The sons of Jether: **J**, Pispa, and Ara. 1 Chr 7:38

JERAH (2)
Almodad, Sheleph, Hazarmaveth, **J**, Gn 10:26
Almodad, Sheleph, Hazarmaveth, **J**, 1 Chr 1:20

JERAHMEEL (8)
born to him: **J**, Ram, and Chelubai. 1 Chr 2:9
The sons of **J**, the firstborn of Hezron: 1 Chr 2:25
J also had another wife, whose name 1 Chr 2:26
The sons of Ram, the firstborn of **J**: 1 Chr 2:27
Zaza. These were the descendants of **J**. 1 Chr 2:33
The sons of Caleb the brother of **J**: 1 Chr 2:42
Of Kish, the sons of Kish: **J**. 1 Chr 24:29
the king commanded **J** the king's son Jer 36:26

JERAHMEELITES (2)
or, "Against the Negeb of the **J**," or, 1 Sm 27:10
in Racal, in the cities of the **J**, in the 1 Sm 30:29

JERED (1)
his Judahite wife bore **J** the father of 1 Chr 4:18

JEREMAI (1)
Zabad, Eliphelet, **J**, Manasseh, Ezr 10:33

JEREMIAH (148)
the daughter of **J** of Libnah. 2 Kgs 23:31
the daughter of **J** of Libnah. 2 Kgs 24:18
Epher, Ishi, Eliel, Azriel, **J**, Hodaviah, 1 Chr 5:24
J, Jahaziel, Johanan, Jozabad of 1 Chr 12:4
Mishmannah fourth, **J** fifth, 1 Chr 12:10
J tenth, Machbannai eleventh. 1 Chr 12:13
J also uttered a lament for Josiah; 2 Chr 35:25
himself before **J** the prophet, 2 Chr 36:12
word of the LORD by the mouth of **J**, 2 Chr 36:21
by the mouth of **J** might be fulfilled, 2 Chr 36:22
LORD by the mouth of **J** might be fulfilled, Ezr 1:1
Seraiah, Azariah, **J**, Neh 10:2
Shealtiel, and Jeshua: Seraiah, **J**, Ezra, Neh 12:1
of Seraiah, Meraiah; of **J**, Hananiah; Neh 12:12
Judah, Benjamin, Shemaiah, and **J**, Neh 12:34
The words of **J**, the son of Hilkiah, one of Jer 1:1

saying, "J, what do you see?" And I said, Jer 1:11
The word that came to J from the LORD: Jer 7:1
The word that came to J from the LORD: Jer 11:1
that came to J concerning the drought: Jer 14:1
The word that came to J from the LORD: Jer 18:1
said, "Come, let us make plots against J, Jer 18:18
Then J came from Topheth, where the Jer 19:14
LORD, heard J prophesying these things. Jer 20:1
Then Pashhur beat J the prophet, and Jer 20:2
when Pashhur released J from the Jer 20:3
Jeremiah from the stocks, J said to him, Jer 20:3
is the word that came to J from the LORD, Jer 21:1
Then J said to them: Jer 21:3
said to me, "What do you see, J?" I said, Jer 24:3
word that came to J concerning all the Jer 25:1
which J the prophet spoke to all the Jer 25:2
which J prophesied against all the Jer 25:13
the people heard J speaking these words Jer 26:7
And when J had finished speaking all Jer 26:8
people gathered around J in the house Jer 26:9
Then J spoke to all the officials and all Jer 26:12
this land in words like those of J. Jer 26:20
of Shaphan was with J so that he was Jer 26:24
this word came to J from the LORD. Jer 27:1
Then the prophet J spoke to Hananiah Jer 28:5
and the prophet J said, "Amen! May the Jer 28:6
from the neck of J the prophet and Jer 28:10
two years." But J the prophet went Jer 28:11
from off the neck of J the prophet, Jer 28:12
prophet, the word of the LORD came to J: Jer 28:12
And J the prophet said to the prophet Jer 28:15
of the letter that J the prophet sent from Jer 29:1
you not rebuked J of Anathoth who Jer 29:27
letter in the hearing of J the prophet. Jer 29:29
Then the word of the LORD came to J: Jer 29:30
The word that came to J from the LORD: Jer 30:1
word that came to J from the LORD in Jer 32:1
and J the prophet was shut up in the Jer 32:2
J said, "The word of the LORD came to me: Jer 32:6
The word of the LORD came to J: Jer 32:26
word of the LORD came to J a second time, Jer 33:1
The word of the LORD came to J: Jer 33:19
The word of the LORD came to J: Jer 33:23
The word that came to J from the LORD, Jer 34:1
Then J the prophet spoke all these words Jer 34:6
The word that came to J from the LORD, Jer 34:8
of the LORD came to J from the LORD: Jer 34:12
word that came to J from the LORD in Jer 35:1
So I took Jaazaniah the son of J, son of Jer 35:3
Then the word of the LORD came to J: Jer 35:12
to the house of the Rechabites J said, Jer 35:18
this word came to J from the LORD: Jer 36:1
Then J called Baruch the son of Neriah, Jer 36:4
scroll at the dictation of J all the words of Jer 36:4
And J ordered Baruch, saying, "I am Jer 36:5
Neriah did all that J the prophet ordered Jer 36:8
read the words of J from the scroll, Jer 36:10
said to Baruch, "Go and hide, you and J, Jer 36:19
Baruch the secretary and J the prophet, Jer 36:26
the word of the LORD came to J: Jer 36:27
Then J took another scroll and gave it Jer 36:32
it at the dictation of J all the words of Jer 36:32
that he spoke through J the prophet. Jer 37:2
the son of Maaseiah, to J the prophet, Jer 37:3
Now J was still going in and out among Jer 37:4
word of the LORD came to J the prophet: Jer 37:6
J set out from Jerusalem to go to the Jer 37:12
son of Hananiah, seized J the prophet, Jer 37:13
And J said, "It is a lie; I am not deserting Jer 37:14
and seized J and brought him to the Jer 37:14
And the officials were enraged at J, and Jer 37:15
When J had come to the dungeon cells Jer 37:16
there any word from the LORD?" J said, Jer 37:17
J also said to King Zedekiah, "What Jer 37:18
and they committed J to the court of the Jer 37:21
So J remained in the court of the guard. Jer 37:21
heard the words that J was saying to all Jer 38:1
So they took J and cast him into the Jer 38:6
of the guard, letting J down by ropes. Jer 38:6
but only mud, and J sank in the mud. Jer 38:6
that they had put J into the cistern— Jer 38:7
that they did to J the prophet by casting Jer 38:9
and lift J the prophet out of the cistern Jer 38:10
which he let down to J in the cistern by Jer 38:11
Ebed-melech the Ethiopian said to J, Jer 38:12
your armpits and the ropes." J did so. Jer 38:12
Then they drew J up with ropes and Jer 38:13
And J remained in the court of the Jer 38:13
Zedekiah sent for J the prophet and Jer 38:14
The king said to J, "I will ask you a Jer 38:14
J said to Zedekiah, "If I tell you, will you Jer 38:15
Then King Zedekiah swore secretly to J, Jer 38:16
Then J said to Zedekiah, "Thus says the Jer 38:17
King Zedekiah said to J, "I am afraid of Jer 38:19
J said, "You shall not be given to them. Jer 38:20
Then Zedekiah said to J, "Let no one Jer 38:24
the officials came to J and asked him, Jer 38:27
And J remained in the court of the Jer 38:28
command concerning J through Jer 39:11
sent and took J from the court of the Jer 39:14
of the LORD came to J while he was shut Jer 39:15
word that came to J from the LORD after Jer 40:1
of the guard took J and said to him, Jer 40:2
Then J went to Gedaliah the son of Jer 40:6
and said to J the prophet, "Let our plea Jer 42:2
J the prophet said to them, "I have heard Jer 42:4
Then they said to J, "May the LORD be a Jer 42:5
ten days the word of the LORD came to J. Jer 42:7
When J finished speaking to all the Jer 43:1
and all the insolent men said to J, Jer 43:2
also J the prophet and Baruch the son of Jer 43:6
of the LORD came to J in Tahpanhes: Jer 43:8
word that came to J concerning all the Jer 44:1
in the land of Egypt, answered J: Jer 44:15
Then J said to all the people, men and Jer 44:20
J said to all the people and all the Jer 44:24
The word that J the prophet spoke to Jer 45:1
words in a book at the dictation of J, Jer 45:1
that came to J the prophet concerning Jer 46:1
the LORD spoke to J the prophet about Jer 46:13
that came to J the prophet concerning Jer 47:1
that came to J the prophet concerning Jer 49:34
land of the Chaldeans, by J the prophet: Jer 50:1
The word that J the prophet Jer 51:59
J wrote in a book all the disaster that Jer 51:60
And J said to Seraiah: "When you come Jer 51:61
exhausted.'" Thus far are the words of J. Jer 51:64
Hamutal the daughter of J of Libnah. Jer 52:1
to the word of the LORD to J the prophet, Dn 9:2
what was spoken by the prophet J: Mt 2:17
and others J or one of the prophets." Mt 16:14
what had been spoken by the prophet J, Mt 27:9

JEREMIAH'S (1)
words that Baruch wrote at J dictation, Jer 36:27

JEREMOTH (8)
Eliezer, Elioenai, Omri, J, Abijah, 1 Chr 7:8
and Ahio, Shashak, and J. 1 Chr 8:14
of Mushi: Mahli, Eder, and J, three. 1 Chr 23:23
to the fifteenth, to J, his sons and his 1 Chr 25:22
for Naphtali, J the son of Azriel; 1 Chr 27:19
Zechariah, Jehiel, Abdi, J, and Elijah. Ezr 10:26
Eliashib, Mattaniah, J, Zabad, Ezr 10:27
Malluch, Adaiah, Jashub, Sheal, and J. Ezr 10:29

JERIAH (2)
J the chief, Amariah the second, 1 Chr 23:19
J the chief, Amariah the second, 1 Chr 24:23

JERIBAI (1)
Eliel the Mahavite, and J, and 1 Chr 11:46

JERICHO (64)
plains of Moab beyond the Jordan at J. Nm 22:1
the plains of Moab by the Jordan at J, Nm 26:3
the plains of Moab by the Jordan at J. Nm 26:63
the plains of Moab by the Jordan at J. Nm 31:12
the plains of Moab by the Jordan at J; Nm 33:48
the plains of Moab by the Jordan at J, Nm 33:50
beyond the Jordan east of J, Nm 34:15
the plains of Moab by the Jordan at J, Nm 35:1
the plains of Moab by the Jordan at J. Nm 36:13
which is in the land of Moab, opposite J, Dt 32:49
to the top of Pisgah, which is opposite J. Dt 34:1
is, the Valley of J the city of palm trees, Dt 34:3
especially J." And they went and came Jos 2:1
And it was told to the king of J, "Behold, Jos 2:2
Then the king of J sent to Rahab, saying, Jos 2:3
off. And the people passed over opposite J. Jos 3:16
the LORD for battle, to the plains of J. Jos 4:13
at Gilgal on the east border of J. Jos 4:19
month in the evening on the plains of J. Jos 5:10
When Joshua was by J, he lifted up his Jos 5:13
Now J was shut up inside and outside Jos 6:1
"See, I have given J into your hand, Jos 6:2
whom Joshua sent to spy out J. Jos 6:25
who rises up and rebuilds this city, J. Jos 6:26
Joshua sent men from J to Ai, which is Jos 7:2
and its king as you did to J and its king. Jos 8:2
what Joshua had done to J and to Ai, Jos 9:3
its king as he had done to J and its king, Jos 10:1
just as he had done to the king of J. Jos 10:28
its king as he had done to the king of J. Jos 10:30
the king of J, one; the king of Ai, which Jos 12:9
of Moab, beyond the Jordan east of J. Jos 13:32
of Joseph went from the Jordan by J, Jos 16:1
Jordan by Jericho, east of the waters of J, Jos 16:1
going up from J into the hill country to Jos 16:1
to Ataroth and to Naarah, and touches J, Jos 16:7
goes up to the shoulder north of J, Jos 18:12
according to their clans were J, Jos 18:21
And beyond the Jordan east of J, they Jos 20:8
you went over the Jordan and came to J, Jos 24:11
and the leaders of J fought against you, Jos 24:11
"Remain at J until your beards have 2 Sm 10:5
In his days Hiel of Bethel built J. He 1 Kgs 16:34
the LORD has sent me to J." But he said, 2 Kgs 2:4
I will not leave you." So they came to J. 2 Kgs 2:4
prophets who were at J drew near to 2 Kgs 2:5
who were at J saw him opposite 2 Kgs 2:15
to him while he was staying at J, 2 Kgs 2:18
and overtook him in the plains of J, 2 Kgs 25:5
and beyond the Jordan at J, on the 1 Chr 6:78
"Remain at J until your beards have 1 Chr 19:5
brought them to their kinsfolk at J, 2 Chr 28:15
The sons of J, 345. Ezr 2:34
And next to him the men of J built. And Neh 3:2
The sons of J, 345. Neh 7:36
and overtook Zedekiah in the plains of J. Jer 39:5
and overtook Zedekiah in the plains of J. Jer 52:8
And as they went out of J, a great crowd Mt 20:29
And they came to J. And as he was Mk 10:46
as he was leaving J with his disciples Mk 10:46
was going down from Jerusalem to J, Lk 10:30
As he drew near to J, a blind man was Lk 18:35
He entered J and was passing through. Lk 19:1
faith the walls of J fell down after they Heb 11:30

JERIEL (1)
Uzzi, Rephaiah, J, Jahmai, Ibsam, and 1 Chr 7:2

JERIJAH (1)
J was chief of the Hebronites of 1 Chr 26:31

JERIMOTH (6)
Ezbon, Uzzi, Uzziel, J, and Iri, five, 1 Chr 7:7
Eluzai, J, Bealiah, Shemariah, 1 Chr 12:5
sons of Mushi: Mahli, Eder, and J. 1 Chr 24:30
Mattaniah, Uzziel, Shebuel and J, 1 Chr 25:4
the daughter of J the son of 2 Chr 11:18
Azaziah, Nahath, Asahel, J, Jozabad, 2 Chr 31:13

JERIOTH (1)
by his wife Azubah, and by J; 1 Chr 2:18

JEROBOAM (102)
J the son of Nebat, an Ephraimite of 1 Kgs 11:26
The man J was very able, and when 1 Kgs 11:28
time, when J went out of Jerusalem, 1 Kgs 11:29
And he said to J, "Take for yourself 1 Kgs 11:31
Solomon sought therefore to kill J. 1 Kgs 11:40
But J arose and fled into Egypt, to 1 Kgs 11:40
And as soon as J the son of Nebat 1 Kgs 12:2
then J returned from Egypt. 1 Kgs 12:2
and J and all the assembly of Israel 1 Kgs 12:3
So J and all the people came to 1 Kgs 12:12
Ahijah the Shilonite to J the son of 1 Kgs 12:15
all Israel heard that J had returned, 1 Kgs 12:20
Then J built Shechem in the hill 1 Kgs 12:25
And J said in his heart, "Now the 1 Kgs 12:26
And J appointed a feast on the 1 Kgs 12:32
J was standing by the altar to make 1 Kgs 13:1
J stretched out his hand from the 1 Kgs 13:4
After this thing J did not turn from 1 Kgs 13:33
thing became sin to the house of J, 1 Kgs 13:34
that time Abijah the son of J fell sick. 1 Kgs 14:1
And J said to his wife, "Arise, and 1 Kgs 14:2
be known that you are the wife of J, 1 Kgs 14:2
the wife of J is coming to inquire of 1 Kgs 14:5
the door, he said, "Come in, wife of J. 1 Kgs 14:6
Go, tell J, 'Thus says the LORD, the God 1 Kgs 14:7
upon the house of J and will cut off 1 Kgs 14:10
and will cut off from J every male, 1 Kgs 14:10
and will burn up the house of J, 1 Kgs 14:10
Anyone belonging to J who dies in 1 Kgs 14:11
for he only of J shall come to the 1 Kgs 14:13
the God of Israel, in the house of J. 1 Kgs 14:13
shall cut off the house of J today. 1 Kgs 14:14
Israel up because of the sins of J, 1 Kgs 14:16
Now the rest of the acts of J, how he 1 Kgs 14:19
the time that J reigned was 1 Kgs 14:20
Rehoboam and J continually. 1 Kgs 14:30
eighteenth year of King J the son of 1 Kgs 15:1
between Rehoboam and J all the days 1 Kgs 15:6
there was war between Abijam and J. 1 Kgs 15:7
the twentieth year of J king of Israel, 1 Kgs 15:9
Nadab the son of J began to reign 1 Kgs 15:25
was king, he killed all the house of J. 1 Kgs 15:29
to the house of J not one that 1 Kgs 15:29
for the sins of J that he sinned and 1 Kgs 15:30
walked in the way of J and in his sin 1 Kgs 15:34
in the way of J and have made my 1 Kgs 16:2
like the house of J the son of Nebat. 1 Kgs 16:3
hands, in being like the house of J, 1 Kgs 16:7
of the LORD, walking in the way of J, 1 Kgs 16:19
in all the way of J the son of Nebat, 1 Kgs 16:26
in the sins of J the son of Nebat, 1 Kgs 16:31
like the house of J the son of Nebat, 1 Kgs 21:22
and in the way of J the son of Nebat, 1 Kgs 22:52
clung to the sin of J the son of Nebat, 2 Kgs 3:3

like the house of **J** the son of Nebat, 2 Kgs 9:9
from the sins of **J** the son of Nebat, 2 Kgs 10:29
He did not turn from the sins of **J**, 2 Kgs 10:31
followed the sins of **J** the son of Nebat, 2 Kgs 13:2
depart from the sins of the house of **J**, 2 Kgs 13:6
all the sins of **J** the son of Nebat, 2 Kgs 13:11
his fathers, and **J** sat on his throne. 2 Kgs 13:13
and **J** his son reigned in his place. 2 Kgs 14:16
king of Judah, **J** the son of Joash, 2 Kgs 14:23
all the sins of **J** the son of Nebat, 2 Kgs 14:24
by the hand of **J** the son of Joash. 2 Kgs 14:27
rest of the acts of **J** and all that he 2 Kgs 14:28
And **J** slept with his fathers, the 2 Kgs 14:29
twenty-seventh year of **J** king of 2 Kgs 15:1
the son of **J** reigned over Israel 2 Kgs 15:8
from the sins of **J** the son of Nebat, 2 Kgs 15:9
all the sins of **J** the son of Nebat, 2 Kgs 15:18
from the sins of **J** the son of Nebat, 2 Kgs 15:24
from the sins of **J** the son of Nebat, 2 Kgs 15:28
they made **J** the son of Nebat king. 2 Kgs 17:21
And **J** drove Israel from following 2 Kgs 17:21
walked in all the sins that **J** did. 2 Kgs 17:22
high place erected by **J** the son of 2 Kgs 23:15
and in the days of **J** king of Israel. 1 Chr 5:17
Iddo the seer concerning **J** the son of 2 Chr 9:29
And as soon as **J** the son of Nebat 2 Chr 10:2
then **J** returned from Egypt. 2 Chr 10:2
And **J** and all Israel came and said to 2 Chr 10:3
So **J** and all the people came to 2 Chr 10:12
Ahijah the Shilonite to **J** the son of 2 Chr 10:15
and returned and did not go against **J**. 2 Chr 11:4
because **J** and his sons cast them 2 Chr 11:14
wars between Rehoboam and **J**. 2 Chr 12:15
In the eighteenth year of King **J**, 2 Chr 13:1
there was war between Abijah and **J**. 2 Chr 13:2
And **J** drew up his line of battle 2 Chr 13:3
and said, "Hear me, O **J** and all Israel! 2 Chr 13:4
Yet **J** the son of Nebat, a servant of 2 Chr 13:6
the golden calves that **J** made you for 2 Chr 13:8
J had sent an ambush around to 2 Chr 13:13
God defeated **J** and all Israel before 2 Chr 13:15
And Abijah pursued **J** and took 2 Chr 13:19
J did not recover his power in the 2 Chr 13:20
and in the days of **J** the son of Joash, Hos 1:1
and in the days of **J** the son of Joash, Am 1:1
against the house of **J** with the sword." Am 7:9
priest of Bethel sent to **J** king of Israel, Am 7:10
has said, "**J** shall die by the sword, Am 7:11

JEROBOAM'S (2)
J wife did so. She arose and went to 1 Kgs 14:4
Then **J** wife arose and departed and 1 Kgs 14:17

JEROHAM (10)
whose name was Elkanah the son of **J**, 1 Sm 1:1
Eliab his son, **J** his son, Elkanah his 1 Chr 6:27
son of Elkanah, son of **J**, son of Eliel, 1 Chr 6:34
Elijah, and Zichri were the sons of **J**. 1 Chr 8:27
Ibneiah the son of **J**, Elah the son of 1 Chr 9:8
and Adaiah the son of **J**, son of 1 Chr 9:12
and Zebadiah, the sons of **J** of Gedor. 1 Chr 12:7
for Dan, Azarel the son of **J**. These 1 Chr 27:22
of hundreds, Azariah the son of **J**, 2 Chr 23:1
and Adaiah the son of **J**, son of Neh 11:12

JERUBBAAL (14)
on that day Gideon was called **J**, Jgs 6:32
Then **J** (that is, Gideon) and all the people Jgs 7:1
J the son of Joash went and lived in his Jgs 8:29
steadfast love to the family of **J** (that is, Jgs 8:35
Abimelech the son of **J** went to Shechem Jgs 9:1
all seventy of the sons of **J** rule over you, Jgs 9:2
and killed his brothers the sons of **J**, Jgs 9:5
But Jotham the youngest son of **J** was left, Jgs 9:5
have dealt well with **J** and his house and Jgs 9:16
faith and integrity with **J** and with his Jgs 9:19
to the seventy sons of **J** might come, Jgs 9:24
Is he not the son of **J**, and is not Zebul Jgs 9:28
came the curse of Jotham the son of **J**. Jgs 9:57
And the LORD sent **J** and Barak and 1 Sm 12:11

JERUBBESHETH (1)
Who killed Abimelech the son of **J**? 2 Sm 11:21

JERUEL (1)
the valley, east of the wilderness of **J**. 2 Chr 20:16

JERUSALEM (809)
As soon as Adoni-zedek, king of **J**, heard Jos 10:1
So Adoni-zedek king of **J** sent to Hoham Jos 10:3
five kings of the Amorites, the king of **J**, Jos 10:5
out to him from the cave, the king of **J**, Jos 10:23
the king of **J**, one; the king of Hebron, Jos 12:10
J). And the boundary goes up to the top Jos 15:8
But the Jebusites, the inhabitants of **J**, Jos 15:63
with the people of Judah at **J** to this day. Jos 15:63
J), Gibeah and Kiriath-jearim— Jos 18:28
repaid me." And they brought him to **J**, Jgs 1:7
of Judah fought against **J** and captured it Jgs 1:8
not drive out the Jebusites who lived in **J**, Jgs 1:21
the people of Benjamin in **J** to this day. Jgs 1:21
J). He had with him a couple of saddled Jgs 19:10
of the Philistine and brought it to **J**, 1 Sm 17:54
and at **J** he reigned over all Israel and 2 Sm 5:5
his men went to **J** against the Jebusites, 2 Sm 5:6
more concubines and wives from **J**, 2 Sm 5:13
of those who were born to him in **J**: 2 Sm 5:14
of Hadadezer and brought them to **J**. 2 Sm 8:7
So Mephibosheth lived in **J**, for he ate 2 Sm 9:13
the Ammonites and came to **J**. 2 Sm 10:14
Rabbah. But David remained at **J**. 2 Sm 11:1
So Uriah remained in **J** that day and 2 Sm 11:12
and all the people returned to **J**. 2 Sm 12:31
Geshur and brought Absalom to **J**. 2 Sm 14:23
So Absalom lived two full years in **J**, 2 Sm 14:28
LORD will indeed bring me back to **J**, 2 Sm 15:8
hundred men from **J** who were 2 Sm 15:11
his servants who were with him at **J**, 2 Sm 15:14
carried the ark of God back to **J**, 2 Sm 15:29
city, just as Absalom was entering **J**. 2 Sm 15:37
to the king, "Behold, he remains in **J**, 2 Sm 16:3
people, the men of Israel, came to **J**, 2 Sm 16:15
not find them, they returned to **J**. 2 Sm 17:20
on the day my lord the king left **J**. 2 Sm 19:19
when he came to **J** to meet the king, 2 Sm 19:25
I will provide for you with me in **J**." 2 Sm 19:33
I should go up with the king to **J**? 2 Sm 19:34
king steadfastly from the Jordan to **J**. 2 Sm 20:2
And David came to his house at **J**. 2 Sm 20:3
They went out from **J** to pursue Sheba 2 Sm 20:7
And Joab returned to **J** to the king. 2 Sm 20:22
they came to **J** at the end of nine 2 Sm 24:8
out his hand toward **J** to destroy it, 2 Sm 24:16
in Hebron and thirty-three years in **J**. 1 Kgs 2:11
yourself a house in **J** and dwell there, 1 Kgs 2:36
do." So Shimei lived in **J** many days. 1 Kgs 2:38
Shimei had gone from **J** to Gath and 1 Kgs 2:41
of the LORD and the wall around **J**. 1 Kgs 3:1
Then he came to **J** and stood before 1 Kgs 3:15
of Israel, before King Solomon in **J**, 1 Kgs 8:1
and the wall of **J** and Hazor and 1 Kgs 9:15
Solomon desired to build in **J**, 1 Kgs 9:19
She came to **J** with a very great 1 Kgs 10:2
chariot cities and with the king in **J**. 1 Kgs 10:26
silver as common in **J** as stone, 1 Kgs 10:27
on the mountain east of **J**. 1 Kgs 11:7
for the sake of **J** that I have chosen." 1 Kgs 11:13
time, when Jeroboam went out of **J**, 1 Kgs 11:29
servant David and for the sake of **J**, 1 Kgs 11:32
always have a lamp before me in **J**, 1 Kgs 11:36
Solomon reigned in **J** over all Israel 1 Kgs 11:42
to mount his chariot to flee to **J**. 1 Kgs 12:18
When Rehoboam came to **J**, he 1 Kgs 12:21
in the temple of the LORD at **J**, 1 Kgs 12:27
"You have gone up to **J** long enough. 1 Kgs 12:28
and he reigned seventeen years in **J**, 1 Kgs 14:21
king of Egypt came up against **J**. 1 Kgs 14:25
He reigned for three years in **J**. His 1 Kgs 15:2
LORD his God gave him a lamp in **J**, 1 Kgs 15:4
his son after him, and establishing **J**, 1 Kgs 15:4
and he reigned forty-one years in **J**. 1 Kgs 15:10
and he reigned twenty-five years in **J**. 1 Kgs 22:42
king, and he reigned eight years in **J**. 2 Kgs 8:17
to reign, and he reigned one year in **J**. 2 Kgs 8:26
servants carried him in a chariot to **J**, 2 Kgs 9:28
reign, and he reigned forty years in **J**. 2 Kgs 12:1
Hazael set his face to go up against **J**, 2 Kgs 12:17
Then Hazael went away from **J**. 2 Kgs 12:18
and he reigned twenty-nine years in **J**. 2 Kgs 14:2
mother's name was Jehoaddin of **J**. 2 Kgs 14:2
and came to **J** and broke down the 2 Kgs 14:13
down the wall of **J** for four hundred 2 Kgs 14:13
made a conspiracy against him in **J**, 2 Kgs 14:19
he was buried in **J** with his fathers 2 Kgs 14:20
and he reigned fifty-two years in **J**. 2 Kgs 15:2
His mother's name was Jecoliah of **J**. 2 Kgs 15:2
and he reigned sixteen years in **J**. 2 Kgs 15:33
and he reigned sixteen years in **J**. 2 Kgs 16:2
of Israel, came up to wage war on **J**, 2 Kgs 16:5
and he reigned twenty-nine years in **J**. 2 Kgs 18:2
from Lachish to King Hezekiah at **J**. 2 Kgs 18:17
And they went up and came to **J**. 2 Kgs 18:17
removed, saying to Judah and to **J**, 2 Kgs 18:22
shall worship before this altar in **J**"? 2 Kgs 18:22
the LORD should deliver **J** out of my 2 Kgs 18:35
you by promising that **J** will not be 2 Kgs 19:10
head behind you—the daughter of **J**. 2 Kgs 19:21
For out of **J** shall go a remnant, and 2 Kgs 19:31
and he reigned fifty-five years in **J**. 2 Kgs 21:1
had said, "In **J** will I put my name." 2 Kgs 21:4
his son, "In this house, and in **J**, 2 Kgs 21:7
am bringing upon **J** and Judah such 2 Kgs 21:12
will stretch over **J** the measuring 2 Kgs 21:13
and I will wipe **J** as one wipes a dish, 2 Kgs 21:13
till he had filled **J** from one end to 2 Kgs 21:16
reign, and he reigned two years in **J**. 2 Kgs 21:19
and he reigned thirty-one years in **J**. 2 Kgs 22:1
(now she lived in **J** in the Second 2 Kgs 22:14
elders of Judah and **J** were gathered to 2 Kgs 23:1
all the inhabitants of **J** and the priests 2 Kgs 23:2
He burned them outside **J** in the fields 2 Kgs 23:4
at the cities of Judah and around **J**; 2 Kgs 23:5
from the house of the LORD, outside **J**, 2 Kgs 23:6
come up to the altar of the LORD in **J**, 2 Kgs 23:9
the high places that were east of **J**, 2 Kgs 23:13
on them. Then he returned to **J**. 2 Kgs 23:20
Passover was kept to the LORD in **J**. 2 Kgs 23:23
seen in the land of Judah and in **J**, 2 Kgs 23:24
J, and the house of which I said, 2 Kgs 23:27
brought him to **J** and buried him 2 Kgs 23:30
and he reigned three months in **J**. 2 Kgs 23:31
that he might not reign in **J**, 2 Kgs 23:33
and he reigned eleven years in **J**. 2 Kgs 23:36
For he filled **J** with innocent blood, 2 Kgs 24:4
and he reigned three months in **J**. 2 Kgs 24:8
the daughter of Elnathan of **J**. 2 Kgs 24:8
king of Babylon came up to **J**, 2 Kgs 24:10
He carried away all **J** and all the 2 Kgs 24:14
into captivity from **J** to Babylon. 2 Kgs 24:15
and he reigned eleven years in **J**. 2 Kgs 24:18
to the point in **J** and Judah that he 2 Kgs 24:20
all his army against **J** and laid siege 2 Kgs 25:1
of the king of Babylon, came to **J**. 2 Kgs 25:8
king's house and all the houses of **J**; 2 Kgs 25:9
broke down the walls around **J**. 2 Kgs 25:10
And he reigned thirty-three years in **J**. 1 Chr 3:4
These were born to him in **J**: Shimea, 1 Chr 3:5
in the house that Solomon built in **J**). 1 Chr 6:10
LORD sent Judah and **J** into exile by 1 Chr 6:15
built the house of the LORD in **J**, 1 Chr 6:32
chief men. These lived in **J**. 1 Chr 8:28
also lived opposite their kinsmen in **J**, 1 Chr 8:32
Ephraim, and Manasseh lived in **J**: 1 Chr 9:3
generations, leaders. These lived in **J**. 1 Chr 9:34
also lived opposite their kinsmen in **J**, 1 Chr 9:38
And David and all Israel went to **J**, 1 Chr 11:4
And David took more wives in **J**, and 1 Chr 14:3
of the children born to him in **J**: 1 Chr 14:4
assembled all Israel at **J** to bring up 1 Chr 15:3
of Hadadezer and brought them to **J**. 1 Chr 18:7
the city. Then Joab came to **J**. 1 Chr 19:15
Rabbah. But David remained at **J**. 1 Chr 20:1
David and all the people returned to **J**. 1 Chr 20:3
all Israel and came back to **J**. 1 Chr 21:4
God sent the angel to **J** to destroy it, 1 Chr 21:15
a drawn sword stretched out over **J**. 1 Chr 21:16
his people, and he dwells in **J** forever. 1 Chr 23:25
David assembled at **J** all the officials 1 Chr 28:1
Hebron and thirty-three years in **J**. 1 Chr 29:27
it, for he had pitched a tent for it in **J**.) 2 Chr 1:4
from before the tent of meeting, to **J**. 2 Chr 1:13
chariot cities and with the king in **J**. 2 Chr 1:14
and gold as common in **J** as stone, 2 Chr 1:15
who are with me in Judah and **J**, 2 Chr 2:7
so that you may take it up to **J**." 2 Chr 2:16
of the LORD in **J** on Mount Moriah, 2 Chr 3:1
houses of the people of Israel, in **J**, 2 Chr 5:2
but I have chosen **J** that my name 2 Chr 6:6
Solomon desired to build in **J**, 2 Chr 8:6
she came to **J** to test him with hard 2 Chr 9:1
chariot cities and with the king in **J**. 2 Chr 9:25
made silver as common in **J** as stone, 2 Chr 9:27
Solomon reigned in **J** over all Israel 2 Chr 9:30
mounted his chariot to flee to **J**. 2 Chr 10:18
When Rehoboam came to **J**, he 2 Chr 11:1
Rehoboam lived in **J**, and he built 2 Chr 11:5
holdings and came to Judah and **J**, 2 Chr 11:14
tribes of Israel to **J** to sacrifice to the 2 Chr 11:16
king of Egypt came up against **J** 2 Chr 12:2
cities of Judah and came as far as **J**. 2 Chr 12:4
had gathered at **J** because of Shishak, 2 Chr 12:5
not be poured out on **J** by the hand of 2 Chr 12:7
king of Egypt came up against **J**. 2 Chr 12:9
grew strong in **J** and reigned. 2 Chr 12:13
and he reigned seventeen years in **J**, 2 Chr 12:13
He reigned for three years in **J**. His 2 Chr 13:2
and camels. Then they returned to **J**. 2 Chr 14:15
They were gathered at **J** in the third 2 Chr 15:10
soldiers, mighty men of valor, in **J**. 2 Chr 17:13
returned in safety to his house in **J**. 2 Chr 19:1
Jehoshaphat lived at **J**. And he went 2 Chr 19:4
in **J** Jehoshaphat appointed certain 2 Chr 19:8
cases. They had their seat at **J**. 2 Chr 19:8
stood in the assembly of Judah and **J**, 2 Chr 20:5
and inhabitants of **J** and King 2 Chr 20:15
LORD on your behalf, O Judah and **J**.' 2 Chr 20:17
the inhabitants of **J** fell down before 2 Chr 20:18
me, Judah and inhabitants of **J**! 2 Chr 20:20

returned, every man of Judah and **J**, 2 Chr 20:27
at their head, returning to **J** with joy, 2 Chr 20:27
They came to **J** with harps and lyres 2 Chr 20:28
he reigned twenty-five years in **J**. 2 Chr 20:31
king, and he reigned eight years in **J**. 2 Chr 21:5
the inhabitants of **J** into whoredom 2 Chr 21:11
the inhabitants of **J** into whoredom, 2 Chr 21:13
and he reigned eight years in **J**. 2 Chr 21:20
the inhabitants of **J** made Ahaziah 2 Chr 22:1
to reign, and he reigned one year in **J**. 2 Chr 22:2
houses of Israel, and they came to **J**. 2 Chr 23:2
reign, and he reigned forty years in **J**. 2 Chr 24:1
in from Judah and **J** the tax levied by 2 Chr 24:6
throughout Judah and **J** to bring in 2 Chr 24:9
upon Judah and **J** for this guilt 2 Chr 24:18
to Judah and **J** and destroyed all 2 Chr 24:23
and he reigned twenty-nine years in **J**. 2 Chr 25:1
mother's name was Jehoaddan of **J**. 2 Chr 25:1
brought him to **J** and broke down 2 Chr 25:23
down the wall of **J** for 400 cubits, 2 Chr 25:23
made a conspiracy against him in **J**, 2 Chr 25:27
and he reigned fifty-two years in **J**. 2 Chr 26:3
His mother's name was Jecoliah of **J**. 2 Chr 26:3
Uzziah built towers in **J** at the Corner 2 Chr 26:9
In **J** he made engines, invented by 2 Chr 26:15
and he reigned sixteen years in **J**. 2 Chr 27:1
and he reigned sixteen years in **J**. 2 Chr 27:8
and he reigned sixteen years in **J**. 2 Chr 28:1
subjugate the people of Judah and **J**, 2 Chr 28:10
himself altars in every corner of **J**. 2 Chr 28:24
and they buried him in the city, in **J**, 2 Chr 28:27
and he reigned twenty-nine years in **J**. 2 Chr 29:1
of the LORD came on Judah and **J**, 2 Chr 29:8
of the LORD at **J** to keep the Passover 2 Chr 30:1
the assembly in **J** had taken counsel 2 Chr 30:2
nor had the people assembled in **J**— 2 Chr 30:3
to the LORD, the God of Israel, at **J**, 2 Chr 30:5
humbled themselves and came to **J**. 2 Chr 30:11
people came together in **J** to keep the 2 Chr 30:13
removed the altars that were in **J**, 2 Chr 30:14
who were present at **J** kept the Feast 2 Chr 30:21
So there was great joy in **J**, for since 2 Chr 30:26
had been nothing like this in **J**. 2 Chr 30:26
people who lived in **J** to give the 2 Chr 31:4
come and intended to fight against **J**, 2 Chr 32:2
his servants to **J** to Hezekiah king 2 Chr 32:9
all the people of Judah who were in **J**, 2 Chr 32:9
that you endure the siege in **J**? 2 Chr 32:10
altars and commanded Judah and **J**, 2 Chr 32:12
to the people of **J** who were on the 2 Chr 32:18
spoke of the God of **J** as they spoke of 2 Chr 32:19
the inhabitants of **J** from the hand 2 Chr 32:22
to the LORD to **J** and precious things 2 Chr 32:23
came upon him and Judah and **J**. 2 Chr 32:25
both he and the inhabitants of **J**, 2 Chr 32:26
the inhabitants of **J** did him honor 2 Chr 32:33
and he reigned fifty-five years in **J**. 2 Chr 33:1
said, "In **J** shall my name be forever." 2 Chr 33:4
his son, "In this house, and in **J**, 2 Chr 33:7
Judah and the inhabitants of **J** astray, 2 Chr 33:9
him again to **J** into his kingdom. 2 Chr 33:13
of the house of the LORD and in **J**, 2 Chr 33:15
reign, and he reigned two years in **J**. 2 Chr 33:21
and he reigned thirty-one years in **J**. 2 Chr 34:1
to purge Judah and **J** of the high 2 Chr 34:3
their altars and cleansed Judah and **J**. 2 Chr 34:5
land of Israel. Then he returned to **J**. 2 Chr 34:7
and from the inhabitants of **J**. 2 Chr 34:9
(now she lived in **J** in the Second 2 Chr 34:22
together all the elders of Judah and **J**. 2 Chr 34:29
the inhabitants of **J** and the priests 2 Chr 34:30
were present in **J** and in Benjamin 2 Chr 34:32
the inhabitants of **J** did according to 2 Chr 34:32
kept a Passover to the LORD in **J**. 2 Chr 35:1
present, and the inhabitants of **J**. 2 Chr 35:18
chariot and brought him to **J**. 2 Chr 35:24
All Judah and **J** mourned for Josiah. 2 Chr 35:24
him king in his father's place in **J**. 2 Chr 36:1
and he reigned three months in **J**. 2 Chr 36:2
Egypt deposed him in **J** and laid on 2 Chr 36:3
his brother king over Judah and **J**, 2 Chr 36:4
and he reigned eleven years in **J**. 2 Chr 36:5
three months and ten days in **J**. 2 Chr 36:9
Zedekiah king over Judah and **J**. 2 Chr 36:10
and he reigned eleven years in **J**. 2 Chr 36:11
the LORD that he had made holy in **J**. 2 Chr 36:14
down the wall of **J** and burned all its 2 Chr 36:19
me to build him a house at **J**, 2 Chr 36:23
charged me to build him a house at **J**, Ezr 1:2
God be with him, and let him go up to **J**, Ezr 1:3
God of Israel—he is the God who is in **J**. Ezr 1:3
for the house of God that is in **J**." Ezr 1:4
rebuild the house of the LORD that is in **J**. Ezr 1:5
had carried away from **J** and placed in Ezr 1:7
were brought up from Babylonia to **J**. Ezr 1:11

They returned to **J** and Judah, each to his Ezr 2:1
to the house of the LORD that is in **J**, Ezr 2:68
the people gathered as one man to **J**. Ezr 3:1
their coming to the house of God at **J**, Ezr 3:8
all who had come to **J** from the captivity. Ezr 3:8
against the inhabitants of Judah and **J**. Ezr 4:6
wrote a letter against **J** to Artaxerxes the Ezr 4:8
came up from you to us have gone to **J**. Ezr 4:12
And mighty kings have been over **J**, Ezr 4:20
haste to the Jews at **J** and by force and Ezr 4:23
on the house of God that is in **J** stopped, Ezr 4:24
to the Jews who were in Judah and **J**, Ezr 5:1
to rebuild the house of God that is in **J**, Ezr 5:2
temple that was in **J** and brought into Ezr 5:14
and put them in the temple that is in **J**, Ezr 5:15
of the house of God that is in **J**, Ezr 5:16
the rebuilding of this house of God in **J**. Ezr 5:17
Concerning the house of God at **J**, let the Ezr 6:3
temple that is in **J** and brought to Ezr 6:5
brought back to the temple that is in **J**, Ezr 6:5
as the priests at **J** require—let that be Ezr 6:9
to destroy this house of God that is in **J**. Ezr 6:12
divisions, for the service of God at **J**, Ezr 6:18
And there went up also to **J**, in the Ezr 7:7
And he came to **J** in the fifth month, Ezr 7:8
first day of the fifth month he came to **J**, Ezr 7:9
my kingdom, who freely offers to go to **J**, Ezr 7:13
about Judah and **J** according to the Ezr 7:14
the God of Israel, whose dwelling is in **J**, Ezr 7:15
for the house of their God that is in **J**. Ezr 7:16
of the house of your God that is in **J**. Ezr 7:17
you shall deliver before the God of **J**. Ezr 7:19
the house of the LORD that is in **J**, Ezr 7:27
the heads of fathers' houses in Israel at **J**, Ezr 8:29
gold and the vessels, to bring them to **J**, Ezr 8:30
twelfth day of the first month, to go to **J**. Ezr 8:31
We came to **J**, and there we remained Ezr 8:32
and to give us protection in Judea and **J**. Ezr 9:9
made throughout Judah and **J** to all the Ezr 10:7
exiles that they should assemble at **J**, Ezr 10:7
Benjamin assembled at **J** within the Ezr 10:9
survived the exile, and concerning **J**. Neh 1:2
shame. The wall of **J** is broken down, Neh 1:3
So I went to **J** and was there three days. Neh 2:11
God had put into my heart to do for **J**. Neh 2:12
the walls of **J** that were broken Neh 2:13
how **J** lies in ruins with its gates Neh 2:17
Come, let us build the wall of **J**, that we Neh 2:17
have no portion or right or claim in **J**." Neh 2:20
and they restored **J** as far as the Broad Neh 3:8
son of Hur, ruler of half the district of **J**, Neh 3:9
Hallohesh, ruler of half the district of **J**, Neh 3:12
of the walls of **J** was going forward and Neh 4:7
come and fight against **J** and to cause Neh 4:8
and his servant pass the night within **J**, Neh 4:22
to proclaim concerning you in **J**, Neh 6:7
the governor of the castle charge over **J**, Neh 7:2
"Let not the gates of **J** be opened until the Neh 7:3
from among the inhabitants of **J**, Neh 7:3
They returned to **J** and Judah, each to Neh 7:6
publish it in all their towns and in **J**, Neh 8:15
Now the leaders of the people lived in **J**. Neh 11:1
one out of ten to live in **J** the holy city, Neh 11:1
men who willingly offered to live in **J**. Neh 11:2
chiefs of the province who lived in **J**; Neh 11:3
And in **J** lived certain of the sons of Neh 11:4
Perez who lived in **J** were 468 valiant Neh 11:6
of the Levites in **J** was Uzzi the son Neh 11:22
of the wall of **J** they sought the Levites Neh 12:27
to bring them to **J** to celebrate the Neh 12:27
the district surrounding **J** and from Neh 12:28
built for themselves villages around **J**. Neh 12:29
And the joy of **J** was heard far away. Neh 12:43
this was taking place, I was not in **J**, Neh 13:6
and came to **J**, and I then discovered Neh 13:7
they brought into **J** on the Sabbath Neh 13:15
to the people of Judah, in **J** itself! Neh 13:16
at the gates of **J** before the Sabbath, Neh 13:19
wares lodged outside **J** once or twice. Neh 13:20
carried away from **J** among the captives Est 2:6
good pleasure; build up the walls of **J**; Ps 51:18
of your temple at **J** kings shall bear gifts Ps 68:29
holy temple; they have laid **J** in ruins. Ps 79:1
out their blood like water all around **J**, Ps 79:3
name of the LORD, and in **J** his praise, Ps 102:21
house of the LORD, in your midst, O **J**. Ps 116:19
been standing within your gates, O **J**! Ps 122:2
J—built as a city that is bound firmly Ps 122:3
Pray for the peace of **J**! "May they be Ps 122:6
As the mountains surround **J**, so the Ps 125:2
you see the prosperity of **J** all the days of Ps 128:5
LORD from Zion, he who dwells in **J**! Ps 135:21
If I forget you, O **J**, let my right hand Ps 137:5
if I do not set **J** above my highest joy! Ps 137:6
LORD, against the Edomites the day of **J**, Ps 137:7

The LORD builds up **J**; he gathers the Ps 147:2
Praise the LORD, O **J**! Praise your God, Ps 147:12
the Preacher, the son of David, king in **J**. Eccl 1:1
have been king over Israel in **J**. Eccl 1:12
all who were over **J** before me, Eccl 1:16
than any who had been before me in **J**. Eccl 2:7
surpassed all who were before me in **J**. Eccl 2:9
am very dark, but lovely, O daughters of **J**, Sg 1:5
I adjure you, O daughters of **J**, by the Sg 2:7
I adjure you, O daughters of **J**, by the Sg 3:5
inlaid with love by the daughters of **J**. Sg 3:10
I adjure you, O daughters of **J**, if you find Sg 5:8
and this is my friend, O daughters of **J**. Sg 5:16
beautiful as Tirzah, my love, lovely as **J**, Sg 6:4
I adjure you, O daughters of **J**, that you not Sg 8:4
saw concerning Judah and **J** in the days of Is 1:1
son of Amoz saw concerning Judah and **J**. Is 2:1
go the law, and the word of the LORD from **J**. Is 2:3
is taking away from **J** and from Judah Is 3:1
For **J** has stumbled, and Judah has fallen, Is 3:8
Zion and remains in **J** will be called holy, Is 4:3
who has been recorded for life in **J**, Is 4:3
cleansed the bloodstains of **J** from its midst Is 4:4
now, O inhabitants of **J** and men of Judah, Is 5:3
and the nobility of **J** and her multitude Is 5:14
of Israel came up to **J** to wage war against Is 7:1
a trap and a snare to the inhabitants of **J**. Is 8:14
greater than those of **J** and Samaria, Is 10:10
shall I not do to **J** and her idols as I have Is 10:11
all his work on Mount Zion and on **J**, Is 10:12
of the daughter of Zion, the hill of **J**. Is 10:32
and you counted the houses of **J**, and Is 22:10
to the inhabitants of **J** and to the house Is 22:21
of hosts reigns on Mount Zion and in **J**, Is 24:23
the LORD on the holy mountain at **J**. Is 27:13
you scoffers, who rule this people in **J**! Is 28:14
For a people shall dwell in Zion, in **J**; you Is 30:19
so the LORD of hosts will protect **J**; Is 31:5
fire is in Zion, and whose furnace is in **J**. Is 31:9
Your eyes will see **J**, an untroubled Is 33:20
from Lachish to King Hezekiah at **J**, Is 36:2
has removed, saying to Judah and to **J**, Is 36:7
the LORD should deliver **J** out of my Is 36:20
you by promising that **J** will not be Is 37:10
her head behind you—the daughter of **J**. Is 37:22
For out of **J** shall go a remnant, and out Is 37:32
Speak tenderly to **J**, and cry to her that her Is 40:2
lift up your voice with strength, O **J**, Is 40:9
are!" and I give to **J** a herald of good Is 41:27
counsel of his messengers, who says of **J**, Is 44:26
saying of **J**, 'She shall be built,' and of Is 44:28
yourself, wake yourself, stand up, O **J**, Is 51:17
put on your beautiful garments, O **J**, the Is 52:1
from the dust and arise; be seated, O **J**; Is 52:2
into singing, you waste places of **J**, Is 52:9
comforted his people; he has redeemed **J**. Is 52:9
On your walls, O **J**, I have set watchmen; Is 62:6
rest until he establishes **J** and makes it a Is 62:7
has become a wilderness, **J** a desolation. Is 64:10
for behold, I create **J** to be a joy, and her Is 65:18
I will rejoice in **J** and be glad in my Is 65:19
"Rejoice with **J**, and be glad for her, all Is 66:10
you; you shall be comforted in **J**. Is 66:13
on dromedaries, to my holy mountain **J**, Is 66:20
until the captivity of **J** in the fifth month. Jer 1:3
throne at the entrance of the gates of **J**, Jer 1:15
"Go and proclaim in the hearing of **J**, Jer 2:2
At that time **J** shall be called the throne Jer 3:17
to it, to the presence of the LORD in **J**, Jer 3:17
says the LORD to the men of Judah and **J**: Jer 4:3
O men of Judah and inhabitants of **J**; Jer 4:4
Declare in Judah, and proclaim in **J**, and Jer 4:5
have utterly deceived this people and **J**, Jer 4:10
time it will be said to this people and to **J**, Jer 4:11
O **J**, wash your heart from evil, that you Jer 4:14
announce to **J**, "Besiegers come from a Jer 4:16
Run to and fro through the streets of **J**, Jer 5:1
O people of Benjamin, from the midst of **J**! Jer 6:1
her trees; cast up a siege mound against **J**. Jer 6:6
Be warned, O **J**, lest I turn from you in Jer 6:8
the cities of Judah and in the streets of **J**? Jer 7:17
and in the streets of **J** the voice of mirth Jer 7:34
of the inhabitants of **J** shall be brought Jer 8:1
I will make **J** a heap of ruins, a lair of Jer 9:11
men of Judah and the inhabitants of **J**. Jer 11:2
the cities of Judah and in the streets of **J**: Jer 11:6
men of Judah and the inhabitants of **J**. Jer 11:9
and the inhabitants of **J** will go and cry Jer 11:12
as the streets of **J** are the altars you Jer 11:13
the pride of Judah and the great pride of **J**. Jer 13:9
prophets, and all the inhabitants of **J**. Jer 13:13
on the hills in the field. Woe to you, O **J**! Jer 13:27
on the ground, and the cry of **J** goes up. Jer 14:2
shall be cast out in the streets of **J**, Jer 14:16
son of Hezekiah, king of Judah, did in **J**. Jer 15:4

"Who will have pity on you, O **J**, or who Jer 15:5
they go out, and in all the gates of **J**, Jer 17:19
all Judah, and all the inhabitants of **J**, Jer 17:20
day or bring it in by the gates of **J**. Jer 17:21
men of Judah and the inhabitants of **J**. Jer 17:25
cities of Judah and the places around **J**, Jer 17:26
by the gates of **J** on the Sabbath day, Jer 17:27
devour the palaces of **J** and shall not be Jer 17:27
men of Judah and the inhabitants of **J**: Jer 18:11
O kings of Judah and inhabitants of **J**. Jer 19:3
I will make void the plans of Judah and **J**, Jer 19:7
The houses of **J** and the houses of the Jer 19:13
and dumped beyond the gates of **J**." Jer 22:19
But in the prophets of **J** I have seen a Jer 23:14
the prophets of **J** ungodliness has gone Jer 23:15
taken into exile from **J** Jeconiah the son Jer 24:1
the remnant of **J** who remain in this Jer 24:8
of Judah and all the inhabitants of **J**: Jer 25:2
J and the cities of Judah, its kings and Jer 25:18
J shall become a heap of ruins, and the Jer 26:18
who have come to **J** to Zedekiah king of Jer 27:3
Judah, and in **J** may not go to Babylon. Jer 27:18
into exile from **J** to Babylon Jeconiah Jer 27:20
and all the nobles of Judah and **J**— Jer 27:20
the house of the king of Judah, and in **J**: Jer 27:21
the prophet sent from **J** to the surviving Jer 29:1
had taken into exile from **J** to Babylon. Jer 29:1
the eunuchs, the officials of Judah and **J**, Jer 29:2
the metal workers had departed from **J**. Jer 29:2
I have sent into exile from **J** to Babylon: Jer 29:4
whom I sent away from **J** to Babylon: Jer 29:20
name to all the people who are in **J**, Jer 29:25
of the king of Babylon was besieging **J**, Jer 32:2
men of Judah and the inhabitants of **J**. Jer 32:32
land of Benjamin, in the places about **J**, Jer 32:44
and the streets of **J** that are desolate, Jer 33:10
land of Benjamin, the places about **J**, Jer 33:13
will be saved and **J** will dwell securely. Jer 33:16
peoples were fighting against **J** and all of Jer 34:1
words to Zedekiah king of Judah, in **J**, Jer 34:6
was fighting against **J** and against all Jer 34:7
all the people in **J** to make a Jer 34:8
the officials of Judah, the officials of **J**, Jer 34:19
and let us go to **J** for fear of the army of Jer 35:11
of the Syrians.' So we are living in **J**." Jer 35:11
of Judah and the inhabitants of **J**, Jer 35:13
all the inhabitants of **J** all the disaster Jer 35:17
all the people in **J** and all the people who Jer 36:9
cities of Judah to **J** proclaimed a fast Jer 36:9
upon the inhabitants of **J** and upon the Jer 36:31
who were besieging **J** heard news about Jer 37:5
news about them, they withdrew from **J**. Jer 37:5
had withdrawn from **J** at the approach Jer 37:11
Jeremiah set out from **J** to go to the land Jer 37:12
guard until the day that **J** was taken. Jer 38:28
his army came against **J** and besieged it. Jer 39:1
the people, and broke down the walls of **J**. Jer 39:8
all the captives of **J** and Judah who were Jer 40:1
were poured out on the inhabitants of **J**, Jer 42:18
that I brought upon **J** and upon all the Jer 44:2
the cities of Judah and in the streets of **J**, Jer 44:6
the land of Judah and in the streets of **J**? Jer 44:9
the land of Egypt, as I have punished **J**, Jer 44:13
the cities of Judah and in the streets of **J**. Jer 44:17
the cities of Judah and in the streets of **J**, Jer 44:21
the inhabitants of Chaldea," let **J** say. Jer 51:35
away, and let **J** come into your mind: Jer 51:50
king; and he reigned eleven years in **J**. Jer 52:1
came to the point in **J** and Judah that he Jer 52:3
came with all his army against **J**, Jer 52:4
served the king of Babylon, entered **J**. Jer 52:12
the king's house and all the houses of **J**; Jer 52:13
broke down all the walls around **J**. Jer 52:14
away captive from **J** 832 persons; Jer 52:29
J remembers in the days of her Lam 1:7
J sinned grievously; therefore she Lam 1:8
J has become a filthy thing among Lam 1:17
young women of **J** have bowed their Lam 2:10
to what compare you, O daughter of **J**? Lam 2:13
wag their heads at the daughter of **J**; Lam 2:15
foe or enemy could enter the gates of **J**. Lam 4:12
you, and engrave on it a city, even **J**. Ezk 4:1
shall set your face toward the siege of **J**, Ezk 4:7
I will break the supply of bread in **J**. Ezk 4:16
"Thus says the Lord GOD: This is **J**. I Ezk 5:5
and brought me in visions of God to **J**, Ezk 8:3
him, "Pass through the city, through **J**, Ezk 9:4
in the outpouring of your wrath on **J**?" Ezk 9:8
whom the inhabitants of **J** have said, Ezk 11:15
concerns the prince in **J** and all the Ezk 12:10
the inhabitants of **J** in the land Ezk 12:19
who prophesied concerning **J** and saw Ezk 13:16
when I send upon **J** my four disastrous Ezk 14:21
disaster that I have brought upon **J**, Ezk 14:22
so have I given up the inhabitants of **J**. Ezk 15:6
make known to **J** her abominations, Ezk 16:2
and say, Thus says the Lord GOD to **J**: Ezk 16:3
behold, the king of Babylon came to **J**, Ezk 17:12
your face toward **J** and preach against Ezk 21:2
and to Judah, into **J** the fortified. Ezk 21:20
right hand comes the divination for **J**, Ezk 21:22
I will gather you into the midst of **J**. Ezk 22:19
Oholah is Samaria, and Oholibah is **J**. Ezk 23:4
has laid siege to **J** this very day. Ezk 24:2
man, because Tyre said concerning **J**, Ezk 26:2
a fugitive from **J** came to me and said, Ezk 33:21
the flock at **J** during her appointed Ezk 36:38
of Babylon came to **J** and besieged it. Dn 1:1
taken out of the temple in **J** be brought, Dn 5:2
out of the temple, the house of God in **J**, Dn 5:3
in his upper chamber open toward **J**. Dn 6:10
pass before the end of the desolations of **J**, Dn 9:2
the men of Judah, to the inhabitants of **J**, Dn 9:7
like what has been done against **J**. Dn 9:12
your wrath turn away from your city **J**, Dn 9:16
J and your people have become a Dn 9:16
to restore and build **J** to the coming of Dn 9:25
Mount Zion and in **J** there shall be those Jl 2:32
when I restore the fortunes of Judah and **J**, Jl 3:1
the people of Judah and **J** to the Greeks in Jl 3:6
from Zion, and utters his voice from **J**, Jl 3:16
And **J** shall be holy, and strangers shall Jl 3:17
inhabited forever, and **J** to all generations. Jl 3:20
from Zion and utters his voice from **J**; Am 1:2
and it shall devour the strongholds of **J**." Am 2:5
entered his gates and cast lots for **J**, Ob 1:11
and the exiles of **J** who are in Sepharad Ob 1:20
which he saw concerning Samaria and **J**. Mi 1:1
is the high place of Judah? Is it not **J**? Mi 1:5
has reached to the gate of my people, to **J**. Mi 1:9
down from the LORD to the gate of **J**. Mi 1:12
Zion with blood and **J** with iniquity. Mi 3:10
J shall become a heap of ruins, and the Mi 3:12
the law, and the word of the LORD from **J**. Mi 4:2
come, kingship for the daughter of **J**. Mi 4:8
and against all the inhabitants of **J**; Zep 1:4
At that time I will search **J** with lamps, Zep 1:12
with all your heart, O daughter of **J**! Zep 3:14
On that day it shall be said to **J**: "Fear Zep 3:16
you have no mercy on **J** and the cities of Zec 1:12
exceedingly jealous for **J** and for Zion. Zec 1:14
LORD, I have returned to **J** with mercy; Zec 1:16
line shall be stretched out over **J**. Zec 1:16
comfort Zion and again choose **J**.'" Zec 1:17
that have scattered Judah, Israel, and **J**." Zec 1:19
And he said to me, "To measure **J**, Zec 2:2
'**J** shall be inhabited as villages without Zec 2:4
the holy land, and will again choose **J**." Zec 2:12
The LORD who has chosen **J** rebuke you! Zec 3:2
when **J** was inhabited and prosperous, Zec 7:7
to Zion and will dwell in the midst of **J**, Zec 8:3
and **J** shall be called the faithful city, Zec 8:3
women shall again sit in the streets of **J**, Zec 8:4
will bring them to dwell in the midst of **J**. Zec 8:8
days to bring good to **J** and to the house Zec 8:15
the LORD of hosts in **J** and to entreat the Zec 8:22
of Zion! Shout aloud, O daughter of **J**! Zec 9:9
Ephraim and the war horse from **J**; Zec 9:10
am about to make **J** a cup of staggering Zec 12:2
The siege of **J** will also be against Judah. Zec 12:2
that day I will make **J** a heavy stone for Zec 12:3
'The inhabitants of **J** have strength Zec 12:5
while **J** shall again be inhabited in its Zec 12:6
again be inhabited in its place, in **J**. Zec 12:6
of the inhabitants of **J** may not surpass Zec 12:7
LORD will protect the inhabitants of **J**, Zec 12:8
all the nations that come against **J**. Zec 12:9
and the inhabitants of **J** a spirit of Zec 12:10
day the mourning in **J** will be as great Zec 12:11
house of David and the inhabitants of **J**, Zec 13:1
gather all the nations against **J** to battle, Zec 14:2
of Olives that lies before **J** on the east, Zec 14:4
day living waters shall flow out from **J**, Zec 14:8
from Geba to Rimmon south of **J**. Zec 14:10
But **J** shall remain aloft on its site Zec 14:10
destruction. **J** shall dwell in security. Zec 14:11
all the peoples that wage war against **J**: Zec 14:12
Even Judah will fight against **J**. And Zec 14:14
that have come against **J** shall go up Zec 14:16
do not go up to **J** to worship the King, Zec 14:17
And every pot in **J** and Judah shall be Zec 14:21
has been committed in Israel and in **J**. Mal 2:11
offering of Judah and **J** will be pleasing Mal 3:4
behold, wise men from the east came to **J**, Mt 2:1
this, he was troubled, and all **J** with him; Mt 2:3
Then **J** and all Judea and all the region Mt 3:5
and the Decapolis, and from **J** and Judea, Mt 4:25
the earth, for it is his footstool, or by **J**, Mt 5:35
scribes came to Jesus from **J** and said, Mt 15:1
he must go to **J** and suffer many things Mt 16:21
And as Jesus was going up to **J**, he took Mt 20:17
"See, we are going up to **J**. And the Son Mt 20:18
they drew near to **J** and came to Mt 21:1
And when he entered **J**, the whole city Mt 21:10
"O **J**, Jerusalem, the city that kills the Mt 23:37
J, the city that kills the prophets and Mt 23:37
of Judea and all **J** were going out to Mk 1:5
and **J** and Idumea and from beyond the Mk 3:8
who came down from **J** were saying, Mk 3:22
of the scribes who had come from **J**, Mk 7:1
they were on the road, going up to **J**, Mk 10:32
saying, "See, we are going up to **J**, and Mk 10:33
Now when they drew near to **J**, to Mk 11:1
And he entered **J** and went into the Mk 11:11
And they came to **J**. And he entered the Mk 11:15
And they came again to **J**. And as he Mk 11:27
women who came up with him to **J**. Mk 15:41
brought him up to **J** to present him to Lk 2:22
Now there was a man in **J**, whose name Lk 2:25
were waiting for the redemption of **J**. Lk 2:38
his parents went to **J** every year at the Lk 2:41
the boy Jesus stayed behind in **J**. Lk 2:43
they did not find him, they returned to **J**, Lk 2:45
And he took him to **J** and set him on the Lk 4:9
village of Galilee and Judea and from **J**. Lk 5:17
from all Judea and **J** and the seacoast of Lk 6:17
which he was about to accomplish at **J**. Lk 9:31
to be taken up, he set his face to go to **J**. Lk 9:51
him, because his face was set toward **J**. Lk 9:53
man was going down from **J** to Jericho, Lk 10:30
than all the others who lived in **J**? Lk 13:4
teaching and journeying toward **J**. Lk 13:22
a prophet should perish away from **J**.' Lk 13:33
O **J**, Jerusalem, the city that kills the Lk 13:34
J, the city that kills the prophets and Lk 13:34
On the way to **J** he was passing along Lk 17:11
said to them, "See, we are going up to **J**, Lk 18:31
tell a parable, because he was near to **J**, Lk 19:11
things, he went on ahead, going up to **J**. Lk 19:28
when you see **J** surrounded by armies, Lk 21:20
and **J** will be trampled underfoot by the Lk 21:24
Herod, who was himself in **J** at that time. Lk 23:7
to them Jesus said, "Daughters of **J**, Lk 23:28
Emmaus, about seven miles from **J**, Lk 24:13
the only visitor to **J** who does not know Lk 24:18
rose that same hour and returned to **J**. Lk 24:33
name to all nations, beginning from **J**. Lk 24:47
him and returned to **J** with great joy, Lk 24:52
priests and Levites from **J** to ask him, Jn 1:19
Jews was at hand, and Jesus went up to **J**. Jn 2:13
when he was in **J** at the Passover Feast, Jn 2:23
but you say that in **J** is the place where Jn 4:20
this mountain nor in **J** will you worship Jn 4:21
seen all that he had done in **J** at the feast. Jn 4:45
a feast of the Jews, and Jesus went up to **J**. Jn 5:1
Now there is in **J** by the Sheep Gate a pool, Jn 5:2
Some of the people of **J** therefore said, "Is Jn 7:25
the Feast of Dedication took place at **J**. Jn 10:22
Bethany was near **J**, about two miles off, Jn 11:18
the country to **J** before the Passover Jn 11:55
feast heard that Jesus was coming to **J**. Jn 12:12
he ordered them not to depart from **J**, Acts 1:4
be my witnesses in **J** and in all Judea Acts 1:8
they returned to **J** from the mount Acts 1:12
mount called Olivet, which is near **J**, Acts 1:12
known to all the inhabitants of **J**, Acts 1:19
Now there were dwelling in **J** Jews, Acts 2:5
"Men of Judea and all who dwell in **J**, Acts 2:14
elders and scribes gathered together in **J**, Acts 4:5
is evident to all the inhabitants of **J**, Acts 4:16
also gathered from the towns around **J**, Acts 5:16
you have filled **J** with your teaching, Acts 5:28
of the disciples multiplied greatly in **J**, Acts 6:7
persecution against the church in **J**, Acts 8:1
the apostles at **J** heard that Samaria Acts 8:14
the word of the Lord, they returned to **J**, Acts 8:25
that goes down from **J** to Gaza." This is Acts 8:26
treasure. He had come to **J** to worship Acts 8:27
he might bring them bound to **J**. Acts 9:2
evil he has done to your saints at **J**. Acts 9:13
who made havoc in **J** of those who Acts 9:21
And when he had come to **J**, he Acts 9:26
he went in and out among them at **J**, Acts 9:28
in the country of the Jews and in **J**. Acts 10:39
So when Peter went up to **J**, the Acts 11:2
came to the ears of the church in **J**, Acts 11:22
came down from **J** to Antioch. Acts 11:27
Saul returned from **J** when they had Acts 12:25
And John left them and returned to **J**, Acts 13:13
those who live in **J** and their rulers, Acts 13:27
come up with him from Galilee to **J**, Acts 13:31
to go up to **J** to the apostles and Acts 15:2
When they came to **J**, they were Acts 15:4
the apostles and elders who were in **J**. Acts 16:4
Macedonia and Achaia and go to **J**, Acts 19:21

Asia, for he was hastening to be at **J**, Acts 20:16
And now, behold, I am going to **J**, Acts 20:22
they were telling Paul not to go on to **J**. Acts 21:4
is how the Jews at **J** will bind the man Acts 21:11
there urged him not to go up to **J**. Acts 21:12
but even to die in **J** for the name of the Acts 21:13
days we got ready and went up to **J**. Acts 21:15
When we had come to **J**, the brothers Acts 21:17
the cohort that all **J** was in confusion. Acts 21:31
them in bonds to **J** to be punished. Acts 22:5
I had returned to **J** and was praying in Acts 22:17
'Make haste and get out of **J** quickly, Acts 22:18
testified to the facts about me in **J**, Acts 23:11
days since I went up to worship in **J**, Acts 24:11
he went up to **J** from Caesarea. Acts 25:1
he summon him to **J**—because they Acts 25:3
come down from **J** stood around him, Acts 25:7
wish to go up to **J** and there be tried on Acts 25:9
and when I was at **J**, the chief priests Acts 25:15
he wanted to go to **J** and be tried there Acts 25:20
petitioned me, both in **J** and here, Acts 25:24
among my own nation and in **J**, Acts 26:4
And I did so in **J**. I not only locked up Acts 26:10
then in **J** and throughout all the Acts 26:20
as a prisoner from **J** into the hands of Acts 28:17
God—so that from **J** and all the way Rom 15:19
I am going to **J** bringing aid to the Rom 15:25
for the poor among the saints at **J**. Rom 15:26
my service for **J** may be acceptable Rom 15:31
by letter to carry your gift to **J**. 1 Cor 16:3
did I go up to **J** to those who were Gal 1:17
years I went up to **J** to visit Cephas and Gal 1:18
years I went up again to **J** with Barnabas, Gal 2:1
she corresponds to the present **J**, for she Gal 4:25
But the **J** above is free, and she is our Gal 4:26
city of the living God, the heavenly **J**, Heb 12:22
name of the city of my God, the new **J**, Rv 3:12
And I saw the holy city, new **J**, coming Rv 21:2
me the holy city **J** coming down out of Rv 21:10

JERUSALEM'S (1)
silent, and for **J** sake I will not be quiet, Is 62:1

JERUSHA (1)
mother's name was **J** the daughter of 2 Kgs 15:33

JERUSHAH (1)
mother's name was **J** the daughter of 2 Chr 27:1

JESHAIAH (7)
Pelatiah and **J**, his son Rephaiah, his 1 Chr 3:21
Gedaliah, Zeri, **J**, Shimei, Hashabiah, 1 Chr 25:3
the eighth to **J**, his sons and his 1 Chr 25:15
his son Rehabiah, and his son **J**, 1 Chr 26:25
the sons of Elam, **J** the son of Athaliah, Ezr 8:7
and with him **J** of the sons of Merari, Ezr 8:19
son of Maaseiah, son of Ithiel, son of **J**, Neh 11:7

JESHANAH (1)
its villages and **J** with its villages 2 Chr 13:19

JESHARELAH (1)
the seventh to **J**, his sons and his 1 Chr 25:14

JESHEBEAB (1)
to Huppah, the fourteenth to **J**, 1 Chr 24:13

JESHER (1)
were her sons: **J**, Shobab, and Ardon. 1 Chr 2:18

JESHIMON (4)
hill of Hachilah, which is south of **J**? 1 Sm 23:19
in the Arabah to the south of **J**. 1 Sm 23:24
Hachilah, which is on the east of **J**?" 1 Sm 26:1
is beside the road on the east of **J**. 1 Sm 26:3

JESHISHAI (1)
of Gilead, son of Michael, son of **J**, 1 Chr 5:14

JESHOHAIAH (1)
Elioenai, Jaakobah, **J**, Asaiah, Adiel, 1 Chr 4:36

JESHUA (30)
the ninth to **J**, the tenth to 1 Chr 24:11
Eden, Miniamin, **J**, Shemaiah, 2 Chr 31:15
came with Zerubbabel, **J**, Nehemiah, Ezr 2:2
namely the sons of **J** and Joab, Ezr 2:6
the sons of Jedaiah, of the house of **J**, Ezr 2:36
the sons of **J** and Kadmiel, of the sons of Ezr 2:40
Then arose **J** the son of Jozadak, with his Ezr 3:2
son of Shealtiel and **J** the son of Jozadak Ezr 3:8
And **J** with his sons and his brothers, and Ezr 3:9
J, and the rest of the heads of fathers' Ezr 4:3
son of Shealtiel and **J** the son of Jozadak Ezr 5:2
Jozabad the son of **J** and Noadiah the Ezr 8:33
some of the sons of **J** the son of Jozadak Ezr 10:18
Next to him Ezer the son of **J**, ruler of Neh 3:19
came with Zerubbabel, **J**, Nehemiah, Neh 7:7
namely the sons of **J** and Joab, Neh 7:11
sons of Jedaiah, namely the house of **J**, Neh 7:39
the sons of **J**, namely of Kadmiel of the Neh 7:43
Also **J**, Bani, Sherebiah, Jamin, Akkub, Neh 8:7
for from the days of **J** the son of Nun to Neh 8:17
On the stairs of the Levites stood **J**, Bani, Neh 9:4
Then the Levites, **J**, Kadmiel, Bani, Neh 9:5
J the son of Azaniah, Binnui of the Neh 10:9
and in **J** and in Moladah and Neh 11:26
Zerubbabel the son of Shealtiel, and **J**: Neh 12:1
and of their brothers in the days of **J**. Neh 12:7
J, Binnui, Kadmiel, Sherebiah, Judah, Neh 12:8
And **J** was the father of Joiakim, Neh 12:10
Sherebiah, and **J** the son of Kadmiel, Neh 12:24
of Joiakim the son of **J** son of Jozadak, Neh 12:26

JESHURUN (4)
"But **J** grew fat, and kicked; you grew Dt 32:15
Thus the LORD became king in **J**, when Dt 33:5
"There is none like God, O **J**, who rides Dt 33:26
Jacob my servant, **J** whom I have chosen. Is 44:2

JESIMIEL (1)
Jeshohaiah, Asaiah, Adiel, **J**, Benaiah, 1 Chr 4:36

JESSE (47)
He was the father of **J**, the father of Ru 4:17
Obed fathered **J**, and Jesse fathered Ru 4:22
fathered Jesse, and **J** fathered David. Ru 4:22
I will send you to **J** the Bethlehemite, 1 Sm 16:1
And invite **J** to the sacrifice, and I will 1 Sm 16:3
And he consecrated **J** and his sons 1 Sm 16:5
Then **J** called Abinadab and made 1 Sm 16:8
Then **J** made Shammah pass by. And 1 Sm 16:9
And **J** made seven of his sons pass 1 Sm 16:10
And Samuel said to **J**, "The LORD has 1 Sm 16:10
Then Samuel said to **J**, "Are all your 1 Sm 16:11
the sheep." And Samuel said to **J**, 1 Sm 16:11
have seen a son of **J** the Bethlehemite, 1 Sm 16:18
Saul sent messengers to **J** and said, 1 Sm 16:19
And **J** took a donkey laden with 1 Sm 16:20
And Saul sent to **J**, saying, "Let David 1 Sm 16:22
of Bethlehem in Judah, named **J**, 1 Sm 17:12
oldest sons of **J** had followed Saul 1 Sm 17:13
And **J** said to David his son, "Take 1 Sm 17:17
and went, as **J** had commanded him. 1 Sm 17:20
of your servant **J** the Bethlehemite." 1 Sm 17:58
has not the son of **J** come to the meal, 1 Sm 20:27
chosen the son of **J** to your own 1 Sm 20:30
long as the son of **J** lives on the earth, 1 Sm 20:31
will the son of **J** give every one of you 1 Sm 22:7
makes a covenant with the son of **J**. 1 Sm 22:8
"I saw the son of **J** coming to Nob, 1 Sm 22:9
against me, you and the son of **J**, 1 Sm 22:13
"Who is David? Who is the son of **J**? 1 Sm 25:10
we have no inheritance in the son of **J**; 2 Sm 20:1
The oracle of David, the son of **J**, the 2 Sm 23:1
have no inheritance in the son of **J**. 1 Kgs 12:16
Boaz fathered Obed, Obed fathered **J**. 1 Chr 2:12
J fathered Eliab his firstborn, 1 Chr 2:13
kingdom over to David the son of **J**. 1 Chr 10:14
O David, and with you, O son of **J**! 1 Chr 12:18
David the son of **J** reigned over all 1 Chr 29:26
have no inheritance in the son of **J**. 2 Chr 10:16
the daughter of Eliab the son of **J**, 2 Chr 11:18
The prayers of David, the son of **J**, are Ps 72:20
come forth a shoot from the stump of **J**, Is 11:1
In that day the root of **J**, who shall stand Is 11:10
of Obed by Ruth, and Obed the father of **J**, Mt 1:5
and **J** the father of David the king. And Mt 1:6
the son of **J**, the son of Obed, the son of Lk 3:32
in David the son of **J** a man after my Acts 13:22
Isaiah says, "The root of **J** will come, Rom 15:12

JESTING (1)
he seemed to his sons-in-law to be **j**. Gn 19:14

JESUS (958)
The book of the genealogy of **J** Christ, the Mt 1:1
husband of Mary, of whom **J** was born, Mt 1:16
Now the birth of **J** Christ took place in Mt 1:18
a son, and you shall call his name **J**, Mt 1:21
birth to a son. And he called his name **J**. Mt 1:25
Now after **J** was born in Bethlehem of Mt 2:1
Then **J** came from Galilee to the Jordan Mt 3:13
But **J** answered him, "Let it be so now, Mt 3:15
And when **J** was baptized, immediately Mt 3:16
Then **J** was led up by the Spirit into the Mt 4:1
J said to him, "Again it is written, 'You Mt 4:7
Then **J** said to him, "Be gone, Satan! For Mt 4:10
From that time **J** began to preach, Mt 4:17
And when **J** finished these sayings, the Mt 7:28
And **J** stretched out his hand and touched Mt 8:3
And **J** said to him, "See that you say Mt 8:4
When **J** heard this, he marveled and said Mt 8:10
And to the centurion **J** said, "Go; let it be Mt 8:13
And when **J** entered Peter's house, he saw Mt 8:14
Now when **J** saw a great crowd around Mt 8:18
And **J** said to him, "Foxes have holes, Mt 8:20
And **J** said to him, "Follow me, and leave Mt 8:22
behold, all the city came out to meet **J**, Mt 8:34
And when **J** saw their faith, he said to the Mt 9:2
But **J**, knowing their thoughts, said, Mt 9:4
As **J** passed on from there, he saw a man Mt 9:9
And as **J** reclined at table in the house, Mt 9:10
were reclining with **J** and his disciples. Mt 9:10
And **J** said to them, "Can the wedding Mt 9:15
And **J** rose and followed him, with his Mt 9:19
J turned, and seeing her he said, "Take Mt 9:22
And when **J** came to the ruler's house Mt 9:23
And as **J** passed on from there, two blind Mt 9:27
men came to him, and **J** said to them, Mt 9:28
And **J** sternly warned them, "See that no Mt 9:30
And **J** went throughout all the cities and Mt 9:35
These twelve **J** sent out, instructing Mt 10:5
When **J** had finished instructing his Mt 11:1
And **J** answered them, "Go and tell John Mt 11:4
J began to speak to the crowds Mt 11:7
At that time **J** declared, "I thank you, Mt 11:25
At that time **J** went through the Mt 12:1
J, aware of this, withdrew from there. Mt 12:15
That same day **J** went out of the house Mt 13:1
All these things **J** said to the crowds in Mt 13:34
And when **J** had finished these Mt 13:53
But **J** said to them, "A prophet is not Mt 13:57
the tetrarch heard about the fame of **J**, Mt 14:1
and buried it, and they went and told **J**. Mt 14:12
Now when **J** heard this, he withdrew Mt 14:13
But **J** said, "They need not go away; you Mt 14:16
But immediately **J** spoke to them, Mt 14:27
and walked on the water and came to **J**. Mt 14:29
J immediately reached out his hand Mt 14:31
scribes came to **J** from Jerusalem and Mt 15:1
And **J** went away from there and Mt 15:21
Then **J** answered her, "O woman, great Mt 15:28
J went on from there and walked beside Mt 15:29
Then **J** called his disciples to him and Mt 15:32
And **J** said to them, "How many loaves Mt 15:34
J said to them, "Watch and beware of Mt 16:6
But **J**, aware of this, said, "O you of little Mt 16:8
Now when **J** came into the district of Mt 16:13
And **J** answered him, "Blessed are you, Mt 16:17
From that time **J** began to show his Mt 16:21
Then **J** told his disciples, "If anyone Mt 16:24
And after six days **J** took with him Peter Mt 17:1
And Peter said to **J**, "Lord, it is good that Mt 17:4
But **J** came and touched them, saying, Mt 17:7
up their eyes, they saw no one but **J** only. Mt 17:8
the mountain, **J** commanded them, Mt 17:9
And **J** answered, "O faithless and Mt 17:17
And **J** rebuked him, and the demon Mt 17:18
disciples came to **J** privately and said, Mt 17:19
gathering in Galilee, **J** said to them, Mt 17:22
into the house, **J** spoke to him first, Mt 17:25
he said, "From others," **J** said to him, Mt 17:26
At that time the disciples came to **J**, Mt 18:1
J said to him, "I do not say to you seven Mt 18:22
Now when **J** had finished these sayings, Mt 19:1
but **J** said, "Let the little children come Mt 19:14
said to him, "Which ones?" And **J** said, Mt 19:18
J said to him, "If you would be perfect, Mt 19:21
And **J** said to his disciples, "Truly, I say Mt 19:23
But **J** looked at them and said, "With Mt 19:26
J said to them, "Truly, I say to you, in Mt 19:28
And as **J** was going up to Jerusalem, he Mt 20:17
J answered, "You do not know what Mt 20:22
But **J** called them to him and said, Mt 20:25
when they heard that **J** was passing by, Mt 20:30
And stopping, **J** called them and said, Mt 20:32
And **J** in pity touched their eyes, and Mt 20:34
of Olives, then **J** sent two disciples, Mt 21:1
went and did as **J** had directed them. Mt 21:6
the crowds said, "This is the prophet **J**, Mt 21:11
And **J** entered the temple and drove out Mt 21:12
these are saying?" And **J** said to them, Mt 21:16
And **J** answered them, "Truly, I say to Mt 21:21
J answered them, "I also will ask you Mt 21:24
So they answered **J**, "We do not know." Mt 21:27
They said, "The first." **J** said to them, Mt 21:31
J said to them, "Have you never read in Mt 21:42
And again **J** spoke to them in parables, Mt 22:1
But **J**, aware of their malice, said, "Why Mt 22:18
And **J** said to them, "Whose likeness Mt 22:20
But **J** answered them, "You are wrong, Mt 22:29
together, **J** asked them a question, Mt 22:41
Then **J** said to the crowds and to his Mt 23:1
J left the temple and was going away, Mt 24:1
And **J** answered them, "See that no one Mt 24:4
When **J** had finished all these sayings, Mt 26:1
in order to arrest **J** by stealth and kill Mt 26:4
Now when **J** was at Bethany in the house Mt 26:6
But **J**, aware of this, said to them, "Why Mt 26:10
Bread the disciples came to **J**, Mt 26:17
the disciples did as **J** had directed them, Mt 26:19
Now as they were eating, **J** took bread, Mt 26:26
Then **J** said to them, "You will all fall Mt 26:31
J said to him, "Truly, I tell you, this Mt 26:34

Then **J** went with them to a place called Mt 26:36
And he came up to **J** at once and said, Mt 26:49
J said to him, "Friend, do what you Mt 26:50
up and laid hands on **J** and seized him. Mt 26:50
those who were with **J** stretched out his Mt 26:51
Then **J** said to him, "Put your sword Mt 26:52
At that hour **J** said to the crowds, "Have Mt 26:55
those who had seized **J** led him to Mt 26:57
false testimony against **J** that they Mt 26:59
But **J** remained silent. And the high Mt 26:63
J said to him, "You have said so. But I Mt 26:64
"You also were with **J** the Galilean." Mt 26:69
"This man was with **J** of Nazareth." Mt 26:71
And Peter remembered the saying of **J**, Mt 26:75
people took counsel against **J** to put him Mt 27:1
his betrayer, saw that **J** was condemned, Mt 27:3
Now **J** stood before the governor, and Mt 27:11
"Are you the King of the Jews?" **J** said, Mt 27:11
Barabbas, or **J** who is called Christ?" Mt 27:17
to ask for Barabbas and destroy **J**. Mt 27:20
shall I do with **J** who is called Christ?" Mt 27:22
Barabbas, and having scourged **J**, Mt 27:26
the governor took **J** into the governor's Mt 27:27
against him, which read, "This is **J**, Mt 27:37
about the ninth hour **J** cried out with a Mt 27:46
And **J** cried out again with a loud voice Mt 27:50
were with him, keeping watch over **J**, Mt 27:54
who had followed **J** from Galilee, Mt 27:55
Joseph, who also was a disciple of **J**. Mt 27:57
to Pilate and asked for the body of **J**. Mt 27:58
know that you seek **J** who was crucified. Mt 28:5
And behold, **J** met them and said, Mt 28:9
Then **J** said to them, "Do not be afraid; Mt 28:10
mountain to which **J** had directed Mt 28:16
And **J** came and said to them, "All Mt 28:18
The beginning of the gospel of **J** Christ, Mk 1:1
In those days **J** came from Nazareth of Mk 1:9
John was arrested, **J** came into Galilee, Mk 1:14
And **J** said to them, "Follow me, and I Mk 1:17
have you to do with us, **J** of Nazareth? Mk 1:24
But **J** rebuked him, saying, "Be silent, Mk 1:25
And **J** sternly charged him and sent Mk 1:43
so that **J** could no longer openly enter a Mk 1:45
And when **J** saw their faith, he said to the Mk 2:5
And immediately **J**, perceiving in his Mk 2:8
were reclining with **J** and his disciples, Mk 2:15
And when **J** heard it, he said to them, Mk 2:17
And **J** said to them, "Can the wedding Mk 2:19
And they watched **J**, to see whether he Mk 3:2
J withdrew with his disciples to the sea, Mk 3:7
And when **J** had stepped out of the boat, Mk 5:2
And when he saw **J** from afar, he ran and Mk 5:6
do with me, **J**, Son of the Most High God? Mk 5:7
And **J** asked him, "What is your name?" Mk 5:9
And they came to **J** and saw the Mk 5:15
they began to beg **J** to depart from their Mk 5:17
the Decapolis how much **J** had done for Mk 5:20
And when **J** had crossed again in the Mk 5:21
heard the reports about **J** and came up Mk 5:27
And **J**, perceiving in himself that power Mk 5:30
said, **J** said to the ruler of the synagogue, Mk 5:36
the synagogue, and **J** saw a commotion, Mk 5:38
And **J** said to them, "A prophet is not Mk 6:4
The apostles returned to **J** and told him Mk 6:30
And **J** charged them to tell no one. But Mk 7:36
And **J**, aware of this, said to them, "Why Mk 8:17
Then **J** laid his hands on his eyes again; Mk 8:25
And **J** went on with his disciples to the Mk 8:27
And after six days **J** took with him Peter Mk 9:2
with Moses, and they were talking with **J**. Mk 9:4
And Peter said to **J**, "Rabbi, it is good that Mk 9:5
longer saw anyone with them but **J** only. Mk 9:8
And **J** asked his father, "How long has Mk 9:21
And **J** said to him, "If you can! All Mk 9:23
And when **J** saw that a crowd came Mk 9:25
But **J** took him by the hand and lifted Mk 9:27
But **J** said, "Do not stop him, for no one Mk 9:39
And **J** said to them, "Because of your Mk 10:5
But when **J** saw it, he was indignant Mk 10:14
And **J** said to him, "Why do you call Mk 10:18
And **J**, looking at him, loved him, and Mk 10:21
And **J** looked around and said to his Mk 10:23
But **J** said to them again, "Children, Mk 10:24
J looked at them and said, "With man Mk 10:27
J said, "Truly, I say to you, there is no Mk 10:29
and **J** was walking ahead of them. Mk 10:32
J said to them, "You do not know what Mk 10:38
"We are able." And **J** said to them, Mk 10:39
And **J** called them to him and said to Mk 10:42
he heard that it was **J** of Nazareth, Mk 10:47
to cry out and say, "**J**, Son of David, Mk 10:47
And **J** stopped and said, "Call him." Mk 10:49
his cloak, he sprang up and came to **J**. Mk 10:50
And **J** said to him, "What do you want Mk 10:51
And **J** said to him, "Go your way; your Mk 10:52

of Olives, **J** sent two of his disciples Mk 11:1
And they told them what **J** had said, and Mk 11:6
brought the colt to **J** and threw their Mk 11:7
And **J** answered them, "Have faith in Mk 11:22
J said to them, "I will ask you one Mk 11:29
So they answered **J**, "We do not know." Mk 11:33
"We do not know." And **J** said to them, Mk 11:33
J said to them, "Render to Caesar the Mk 12:17
J said to them, "Is this not the reason Mk 12:24
J answered, "The most important is, Mk 12:29
And when **J** saw that he answered Mk 12:34
And as **J** taught in the temple, he said, Mk 12:35
And **J** said to him, "Do you see these Mk 13:2
And **J** began to say to them, "See that no Mk 13:5
But **J** said, "Leave her alone. Why do Mk 14:6
reclining at table and eating, **J** said, Mk 14:18
And **J** said to them, "You will all fall Mk 14:27
And **J** said to him, "Truly, I tell you, Mk 14:30
And **J** said to them, "Have you come Mk 14:48
And they led **J** to the high priest. And Mk 14:53
seeking testimony against **J** to put him Mk 14:55
stood up in the midst and asked **J**, Mk 14:60
And **J** said, "I am, and you will see the Mk 14:62
"You also were with the Nazarene, **J**." Mk 14:67
Peter remembered how **J** had said to Mk 14:72
And they bound **J** and led him away Mk 15:1
But **J** made no further answer, so that Mk 15:5
Barabbas, and having scourged **J**, Mk 15:15
at the ninth hour **J** cried with a loud Mk 15:34
And **J** uttered a loud cry and breathed Mk 15:37
to Pilate and asked for the body of **J**. Mk 15:43
not be alarmed. You seek **J** of Nazareth, Mk 16:6
So then the Lord **J**, after he had spoken Mk 16:19
a son, and you shall call his name **J**. Lk 1:31
he was circumcised, he was called **J**, Lk 2:21
when the parents brought in the child **J**, Lk 2:27
the boy **J** stayed behind in Jerusalem. Lk 2:43
And **J** increased in wisdom and in Lk 2:52
and when **J** also had been baptized and Lk 3:21
J, when he began his ministry, was Lk 3:23
And **J**, full of the Holy Spirit, returned Lk 4:1
And **J** answered him, "It is written, 'Man Lk 4:4
And **J** answered him, "It is written, "'You Lk 4:8
And **J** answered him, "It is said, 'You Lk 4:12
And **J** returned in the power of the Spirit Lk 4:14
have you to do with us, **J** of Nazareth? Lk 4:34
But **J** rebuked him, saying, "Be silent Lk 4:35
And **J** said to Simon, "Do not be afraid; Lk 5:10
And when he saw **J**, he fell on his face Lk 5:12
And **J** stretched out his hand and Lk 5:13
to bring him in and lay him before **J**, Lk 5:18
through the tiles into the midst before **J**. Lk 5:19
When **J** perceived their thoughts, he Lk 5:22
And **J** answered them, "Those who are Lk 5:31
And **J** said to them, "Can you make Lk 5:34
And **J** answered them, "Have you not read Lk 6:3
And **J** said to them, "I ask you, is it lawful Lk 6:9
one another what they might do to **J**. Lk 6:11
When the centurion heard about **J**, he Lk 7:3
And when they came to **J**, they pleaded Lk 7:4
And **J** went with them. When he was not Lk 7:6
When **J** heard these things, he marveled Lk 7:9
to speak, and **J** gave him to his mother. Lk 7:15
J began to speak to the crowds Lk 7:24
And **J** answering said to him, "Simon, I Lk 7:40
When **J** had stepped out on land, there Lk 8:27
When he saw **J**, he cried out and fell Lk 8:28
do with me, **J**, Son of the Most High God? Lk 8:28
J then asked him, "What is your name?" Lk 8:30
and they came to **J** and found the man Lk 8:35
demons had gone, sitting at the feet of **J**, Lk 8:35
might be with him, but **J** sent him away, Lk 8:38
whole city how much **J** had done for Lk 8:39
Now when **J** returned, the crowd Lk 8:40
of age, and she was dying. As **J** went, Lk 8:42
And **J** said, "Who was it that touched Lk 8:45
But **J** said, "Someone touched me, for I Lk 8:46
But **J** on hearing this answered him, "Do Lk 8:50
were parting from him, Peter said to **J**, Lk 9:33
the voice had spoken, **J** was found alone. Lk 9:36
J answered, "O faithless and twisted Lk 9:41
But **J** rebuked the unclean spirit and Lk 9:42
he was doing, **J** said to his disciples, Lk 9:43
But **J**, knowing the reasoning of their Lk 9:47
But **J** said to him, "Do not stop him, for Lk 9:50
And **J** said to him, "Foxes have holes, Lk 9:58
And **J** said to him, "Leave the dead to Lk 9:60
J said to him, "No one who puts his Lk 9:62
he, desiring to justify himself, said to **J**, Lk 10:29
J replied, "A man was going down from Lk 10:30
showed him mercy." And **J** said to him, Lk 10:37
went on their way, **J** entered a village. Lk 10:38
Now **J** was praying in a certain place, Lk 11:1
While **J** was speaking, a Pharisee asked Lk 11:37
When **J** saw her, he called her over and Lk 13:12

indignant because **J** had healed on the Lk 13:14
And **J** responded to the lawyers and Lk 14:3
lifted up their voices, saying, "**J**, Master, Lk 17:13
Then **J** answered, "Were not ten Lk 17:17
But **J** called them to him, saying, "Let Lk 18:16
And **J** said to him, "Why do you call Lk 18:19
When **J** heard this, he said to him, Lk 18:22
J, looking at him with sadness, said, Lk 18:24
told him, "**J** of Nazareth is passing by." Lk 18:37
And he cried out, "**J**, Son of David, have Lk 18:38
And **J** stopped and commanded him to Lk 18:40
And **J** said to him, "Recover your sight; Lk 18:42
And he was seeking to see who **J** was, but Lk 19:3
And when **J** came to the place, he looked Lk 19:5
And **J** said to him, "Today salvation has Lk 19:9
And they brought it to **J**, and throwing Lk 19:35
their cloaks on the colt, they set **J** on it. Lk 19:35
as **J** was teaching the people in the Lk 20:1
And **J** said to them, "Neither will I tell Lk 20:8
And **J** said to them, "The sons of this Lk 20:34
J looked up and saw the rich putting Lk 21:1
So **J** sent Peter and John, saying, "Go and Lk 22:8
J said, "I tell you, Peter, the rooster will Lk 22:34
them. He drew near to **J** to kiss him, Lk 22:47
but **J** said to him, "Judas, would you Lk 22:48
But **J** said, "No more of this!" And he Lk 22:51
Then **J** said to the chief priests and Lk 22:52
who were holding **J** in custody were Lk 22:63
When Herod saw **J**, he was very glad, for Lk 23:8
them once more, desiring to release **J**, Lk 23:20
but he delivered **J** over to their will. Lk 23:25
on him the cross, to carry it behind **J**. Lk 23:26
But turning to them **J** said, "Daughters Lk 23:28
And **J** said, "Father, forgive them, for Lk 23:34
"**J**, remember me when you come into Lk 23:42
Then **J**, calling out with a loud voice, Lk 23:46
to Pilate and asked for the body of **J**. Lk 23:52
they did not find the body of the Lord **J**. Lk 24:3
J himself drew near and went with Lk 24:15
to him, "Concerning **J** of Nazareth, Lk 24:19
things, **J** himself stood among them, Lk 24:36
grace and truth came through **J** Christ. Jn 1:17
next day he saw **J** coming toward him, Jn 1:29
and he looked at **J** as he walked by and Jn 1:36
heard him say this, and they followed **J**. Jn 1:37
J turned and saw them following and Jn 1:38
John speak and followed **J** was Andrew, Jn 1:40
He brought him to **J**. Jesus looked at him Jn 1:42
J looked at him and said, "So you are Jn 1:42
The next day **J** decided to go to Galilee. He Jn 1:43
also the prophets wrote, **J** of Nazareth, Jn 1:45
J saw Nathanael coming toward him Jn 1:47
"How do you know me?" **J** answered him, Jn 1:48
J answered him, "Because I said to you, 'I Jn 1:50
in Galilee, and the mother of **J** was there. Jn 2:1
J also was invited to the wedding with his Jn 2:2
wine ran out, the mother of **J** said to him, Jn 2:3
And **J** said to her, "Woman, what does this Jn 2:4
J said to the servants, "Fill the jars with Jn 2:7
first of his signs, **J** did at Cana in Galilee, Jn 2:11
was at hand, and **J** went up to Jerusalem. Jn 2:13
J answered them, "Destroy this temple, Jn 2:19
Scripture and the word that **J** had spoken. Jn 2:22
But **J** on his part did not entrust himself Jn 2:24
This man came to **J** by night and said to Jn 3:2
J answered him, "Truly, truly, I say to you, Jn 3:3
J answered, "Truly, truly, I say to you, Jn 3:5
J answered him, "Are you the teacher of Jn 3:10
After this **J** and his disciples went into the Jn 3:22
Now when **J** learned that the Pharisees Jn 4:1
had heard that **J** was making and Jn 4:1
(although **J** himself did not baptize, but Jn 4:2
Jacob's well was there; so **J**, wearied as he Jn 4:6
water. **J** said to her, "Give me a drink." Jn 4:7
J answered her, "If you knew the gift of Jn 4:10
J said to her, "Everyone who drinks of Jn 4:13
J said to her, "Go, call your husband, and Jn 4:16
him, "I have no husband." **J** said to her, Jn 4:17
J said to her, "Woman, believe me, the Jn 4:21
J said to her, "I who speak to you am he." Jn 4:26
J said to them, "My food is to do the will Jn 4:34
(For **J** himself had testified that a prophet Jn 4:44
this man heard that **J** had come from Jn 4:47
So **J** said to him, "Unless you see signs Jn 4:48
J said to him, "Go; your son will live." Jn 4:50
believed the word that **J** spoke to him and Jn 4:50
was the hour when **J** had said to him, Jn 4:53
the second sign that **J** did when he had Jn 4:54
of the Jews, and **J** went up to Jerusalem. Jn 5:1
When **J** saw him lying there and knew Jn 5:6
J said to him, "Get up, take up your bed, Jn 5:8
know who it was, for **J** had withdrawn, Jn 5:13
Afterward **J** found him in the temple and Jn 5:14
Jews that it was **J** who had healed him. Jn 5:15
this was why the Jews were persecuting **J**, Jn 5:16

But **J** answered them, "My Father is Jn 5:17
So **J** said to them, "Truly, truly, I say to Jn 5:19
After this **J** went away to the other side of Jn 6:1
J went up on the mountain, and there he Jn 6:3
was coming toward him, **J** said to Philip, Jn 6:5
J said, "Have the people sit down." Now Jn 6:10
J then took the loaves, and when he had Jn 6:11
J withdrew again to the mountain by Jn 6:15
dark, and **J** had not yet come to them. Jn 6:17
they saw **J** walking on the sea and Jn 6:19
and that **J** had not entered the boat with Jn 6:22
when the crowd saw that **J** was not there, Jn 6:24
boats and went to Capernaum, seeking **J**. Jn 6:24
J answered them, "Truly, truly, I say to Jn 6:26
J answered them, "This is the work of Jn 6:29
J then said to them, "Truly, truly, I say to Jn 6:32
J said to them, "I am the bread of life; Jn 6:35
They said, "Is not this **J**, the son of Joseph, Jn 6:42
J answered them, "Do not grumble Jn 6:43
So **J** said to them, "Truly, truly, I say to Jn 6:53
J said these things in the synagogue, as Jn 6:59
But **J**, knowing in himself that his Jn 6:61
do not believe." (For **J** knew from the Jn 6:64
So **J** said to the Twelve, "Do you want to Jn 6:67
J answered them, "Did I not choose you, Jn 6:70
After this **J** went about in Galilee. He Jn 7:1
J said to them, "My time has not yet come, Jn 7:6
the middle of the feast **J** went up into the Jn 7:14
So **J** answered them, "My teaching is not Jn 7:16
J answered them, "I did one deed, and you Jn 7:21
So **J** proclaimed, as he taught in the Jn 7:28
J then said, "I will be with you a little Jn 7:33
the great day, **J** stood up and cried out, Jn 7:37
given, because **J** was not yet glorified. Jn 7:39
but **J** went to the Mount of Olives. Jn 8:1
J bent down and wrote with his finger on Jn 8:6
and **J** was left alone with the woman Jn 8:9
J stood up and said to her, "Woman, Jn 8:10
She said, "No one, Lord." And **J** said, Jn 8:11
Again **J** spoke to them, saying, "I am the Jn 8:12
J answered, "Even if I do bear witness Jn 8:14
"Where is your Father?" **J** answered, Jn 8:19
to him, "Who are you?" **J** said to them, Jn 8:25
So **J** said to them, "When you have lifted Jn 8:28
So **J** said to the Jews who had believed in Jn 8:31
J answered them, "Truly, truly, I say to Jn 8:34
"Abraham is our father." **J** said to them, Jn 8:39
J said to them, "If God were your Father, Jn 8:42
J answered, "I do not have a demon, but I Jn 8:49
J answered, "If I glorify myself, my glory Jn 8:54
J said to them, "Truly, truly, I say to you, Jn 8:58
but **J** hid himself and went out of the Jn 8:59
J answered, "It was not that this man Jn 9:3
"The man called **J** made mud and Jn 9:11
a Sabbath day when **J** made the mud and Jn 9:14
if anyone should confess **J** to be Christ, Jn 9:22
J heard that they had cast him out, and Jn 9:35
J said to him, "You have seen him, and it Jn 9:37
J said, "For judgment I came into this Jn 9:39
J said to them, "If you were blind, you Jn 9:41
This figure of speech **J** used with them, Jn 10:6
So **J** again said to them, "Truly, truly, I Jn 10:7
and **J** was walking in the temple, in the Jn 10:23
J answered them, "I told you, and you do Jn 10:25
J answered them, "I have shown you Jn 10:32
J answered them, "Is it not written in Jn 10:34
But when **J** heard it he said, "This illness Jn 11:4
Now **J** loved Martha and her sister and Jn 11:5
J answered, "Are there not twelve hours Jn 11:9
Now **J** had spoken of his death, but they Jn 11:13
Then **J** told them plainly, "Lazarus has Jn 11:14
Now when **J** came, he found that Jn 11:17
when Martha heard that **J** was coming, Jn 11:20
Martha said to **J**, "Lord, if you had been Jn 11:21
J said to her, "Your brother will rise Jn 11:23
J said to her, "I am the resurrection and Jn 11:25
Now **J** had not yet come into the village, Jn 11:30
Mary came to where **J** was and saw him, Jn 11:32
When **J** saw her weeping, and the Jews Jn 11:33
J wept. Jn 11:35
Then **J**, deeply moved again, came to the Jn 11:38
J said, "Take away the stone." Martha, Jn 11:39
J said to her, "Did I not tell you that if Jn 11:40
And **J** lifted up his eyes and said, Jn 11:41
J said to them, "Unbind him, and let Jn 11:44
and told them what **J** had done. Jn 11:46
year he prophesied that **J** would die for Jn 11:51
J therefore no longer walked openly Jn 11:54
They were looking for **J** and saying to Jn 11:56
Passover, **J** therefore came to Bethany, Jn 12:1
was, whom **J** had raised from the dead. Jn 12:1
anointed the feet of **J** and wiped his feet Jn 12:3
J said, "Leave her alone, so that she may Jn 12:7
crowd of the Jews learned that **J** was there, Jn 12:9
Jews were going away and believing in **J**. Jn 12:11

the feast heard that **J** was coming to Jn 12:12
And **J** found a young donkey and sat on Jn 12:14
things at first, but when **J** was glorified, Jn 12:16
and asked him, "Sir, we wish to see **J**." Jn 12:21
Andrew and Philip went and told **J**. Jn 12:22
And **J** answered them, "The hour has Jn 12:23
J answered, "This voice has come for Jn 12:30
So **J** said to them, "The light is among Jn 12:35
sons of light." When **J** had said these Jn 12:36
And **J** cried out and said, "Whoever Jn 12:44
when **J** knew that his hour had come to Jn 13:1
J, knowing that the Father had given all Jn 13:3
J answered him, "What I am doing you Jn 13:7
never wash my feet." **J** answered him, Jn 13:8
J said to him, "The one who has bathed Jn 13:10
these things, **J** was troubled in his spirit, Jn 13:21
One of his disciples, whom **J** loved, was Jn 13:23
loved, was reclining at table close to **J**, Jn 13:23
to him to ask **J** of whom he was Jn 13:24
So that disciple, leaning back against **J**, Jn 13:25
J answered, "It is he to whom I will give Jn 13:26
J said to him, "What you are going to Jn 13:27
had the moneybag, **J** was telling him, Jn 13:29
When he had gone out, **J** said, "Now is Jn 13:31
where are you going?" **J** answered him, Jn 13:36
J answered, "Will you lay down your Jn 13:38
J said to him, "I am the way, and the Jn 14:6
J said to him, "Have I been with you so Jn 14:9
J answered him, "If anyone loves me, he Jn 14:23
J knew that they wanted to ask him, so Jn 16:19
J answered them, "Do you now believe? Jn 16:31
When **J** had spoken these words, he lifted Jn 17:1
God, and **J** Christ whom you have sent. Jn 17:3
When **J** had spoken these words, he went Jn 18:1
for **J** often met there with his disciples. Jn 18:2
Then **J**, knowing all that would happen Jn 18:4
him, "**J** of Nazareth." Jesus said to them, Jn 18:5
him, "Jesus of Nazareth." **J** said to them, Jn 18:5
When **J** said to them, "I am he," they Jn 18:6
you seek?" And they said, "**J** of Nazareth." Jn 18:7
J answered, "I told you that I am he. So, if Jn 18:8
So **J** said to Peter, "Put your sword into Jn 18:11
of the Jews arrested **J** and bound him. Jn 18:12
Simon Peter followed **J**, and so did Jn 18:15
he entered with **J** into the court of the Jn 18:15
priest then questioned **J** about his Jn 18:19
J answered him, "I have spoken openly Jn 18:20
standing by struck **J** with his hand, Jn 18:22
J answered him, "If what I said is wrong, Jn 18:23
Then they led **J** from the house of Jn 18:28
fulfill the word that **J** had spoken to Jn 18:32
again and called **J** and said to Jn 18:33
J answered, "Do you say this of your Jn 18:34
J answered, "My kingdom is not of this Jn 18:36
to him, "So you are a king?" **J** answered, Jn 18:37
Then Pilate took **J** and flogged him. Jn 19:1
So **J** came out, wearing the crown of Jn 19:5
his headquarters again and said to **J**, Jn 19:9
are you from?" But **J** gave him no Jn 19:9
J answered him, "You would have no Jn 19:11
he brought **J** out and sat down on the Jn 19:13
to them to be crucified. So they took **J**, Jn 19:16
one on either side, and **J** between them. Jn 19:18
It read, "**J** of Nazareth, the King of the Jn 19:19
for the place where **J** was crucified was Jn 19:20
When the soldiers had crucified **J**, they Jn 19:23
by the cross of **J** were his mother and Jn 19:25
When **J** saw his mother and the disciple Jn 19:26
J, knowing that all was now finished, Jn 19:28
When **J** had received the sour wine, he Jn 19:30
when they came to **J** and saw that he Jn 19:33
of Arimathea, who was a disciple of **J**, Jn 19:38
that he might take away the body of **J**, Jn 19:38
also, who earlier had come to **J** by night, Jn 19:39
they took the body of **J** and bound it in Jn 19:40
was close at hand, they laid **J** there. Jn 19:42
the other disciple, the one whom **J** loved, Jn 20:2
sitting where the body of **J** had lain, Jn 20:12
she turned around and saw **J** standing, Jn 20:14
but she did not know that it was **J**. Jn 20:14
J said to her, "Woman, why are you Jn 20:15
J said to her, "Mary." She turned and Jn 20:16
J said to her, "Do not cling to me, for I Jn 20:17
J came and stood among them and said Jn 20:19
J said to them again, "Peace be with Jn 20:21
Twin, was not with them when **J** came. Jn 20:24
J came and stood among them and said, Jn 20:26
J said to him, "Have you believed Jn 20:29
Now **J** did many other signs in the Jn 20:30
that you may believe that **J** is the Christ, Jn 20:31
After this **J** revealed himself again to the Jn 21:1
as day was breaking, **J** stood on the shore; Jn 21:4
the disciples did not know that it was **J**. Jn 21:4
J said to them, "Children, do you have Jn 21:5
That disciple whom **J** loved therefore said Jn 21:7

J said to them, "Bring some of the fish Jn 21:10
J said to them, "Come and have Jn 21:12
J came and took the bread and gave it to Jn 21:13
the third time that **J** was revealed to the Jn 21:14
breakfast, **J** said to Simon Peter, Jn 21:15
you know that I love you." **J** said to him, Jn 21:17
the disciple whom **J** loved following Jn 21:20
When Peter saw him, he said to **J**, "Lord, Jn 21:21
J said to him, "If it is my will that he Jn 21:22
yet **J** did not say to him that he was not Jn 21:23
are also many other things that **J** did. Jn 21:25
dealt with all that **J** began to do and Acts 1:1
you stand looking into heaven? This **J**, Acts 1:11
the women and Mary the mother of **J**, Acts 1:14
became a guide to those who arrested **J**. Acts 1:16
time that the Lord **J** went in and out Acts 1:21
J of Nazareth, a man attested to you by Acts 2:22
this **J**, delivered up according to the Acts 2:23
This **J** God raised up, and of that we all Acts 2:32
Christ, this **J** whom you crucified." Acts 2:36
in the name of **J** Christ for the Acts 2:38
In the name of **J** Christ of Nazareth, rise Acts 3:6
of our fathers, glorified his servant **J**, Acts 3:13
faith that is through **J** has given the Acts 3:16
send the Christ appointed for you, **J**, Acts 3:20
and proclaiming in **J** the resurrection Acts 4:2
by the name of **J** Christ of Nazareth, Acts 4:10
This **J** is the stone that was rejected by Acts 4:11
recognized that they had been with **J**. Acts 4:13
speak or teach at all in the name of **J**. Acts 4:18
together against your holy servant **J**, Acts 4:27
the name of your holy servant **J**." Acts 4:30
to the resurrection of the Lord **J**, Acts 4:33
The God of our fathers raised **J**, whom Acts 5:30
them not to speak in the name of **J**, Acts 5:40
teaching and preaching **J** as the Acts 5:42
him say that this **J** of Nazareth will Acts 6:14
and **J** standing at the right hand of Acts 7:55
stoning Stephen, he called out, "Lord **J**, Acts 7:59
of God and the name of **J** Christ, Acts 8:12
baptized in the name of the Lord **J**. Acts 8:16
he told him the good news about **J**. Acts 8:35
are you, Lord?" And he said, "I am **J**, Acts 9:5
the Lord **J** who appeared to you on the Acts 9:17
immediately he proclaimed **J** in the Acts 9:20
by proving that **J** was the Christ. Acts 9:22
had preached boldly in the name of **J**. Acts 9:27
to him, "Aeneas, **J** Christ heals you; Acts 9:34
news of peace through **J** Christ (he is Acts 10:36
how God anointed **J** of Nazareth with Acts 10:38
to be baptized in the name of **J** Christ. Acts 10:48
when we believed in the Lord **J** Christ, Acts 11:17
Hellenists also, preaching the Lord **J**. Acts 11:20
to Israel a Savior, **J**, as he promised. Acts 13:23
to us their children by raising **J**, Acts 13:33
saved through the grace of the Lord **J**, Acts 15:11
lives for the sake of our Lord **J** Christ. Acts 15:26
but the Spirit of **J** did not allow them. Acts 16:7
in the name of **J** Christ to come out Acts 16:18
And they said, "Believe in the Lord **J**, Acts 16:31
rise from the dead, and saying, "This **J**, Acts 17:3
saying that there is another king, **J**." Acts 17:7
he was preaching **J** and the Acts 17:18
to the Jews that the Christ was **J**. Acts 18:5
accurately the things concerning **J**, Acts 18:25
the Scriptures that the Christ was **J**. Acts 18:28
who was to come after him, that is, **J**." Acts 19:4
baptized in the name of the Lord **J**. Acts 19:5
name of the Lord **J** over those who Acts 19:13
spirits, saying, "I adjure you by the **J**, Acts 19:13
evil spirit answered them, "**J** I know, Acts 19:15
the name of the Lord **J** was extolled. Acts 19:17
God and of faith in our Lord **J** Christ. Acts 20:21
that I received from the Lord **J**, Acts 20:24
remember the words of the Lord **J**, Acts 20:35
Jerusalem for the name of the Lord **J**." Acts 21:13
And he said to me, 'I am **J** of Nazareth, Acts 22:8
him speak about faith in Christ **J**. Acts 24:24
own religion and about a certain **J**, Acts 25:19
in opposing the name of **J** of Nazareth. Acts 26:9
'I am **J** whom you are persecuting. Acts 26:15
convince them about **J** both from the Acts 28:23
about the Lord **J** Christ with all Acts 28:31
Paul, a servant of Christ **J**, called to be Rom 1:1
from the dead, **J** Christ our Lord, Rom 1:4
you who are called to belong to **J** Christ, Rom 1:6
God our Father and the Lord **J** Christ. Rom 1:7
thank my God through **J** Christ for all Rom 1:8
judges the secrets of men by Christ **J**. Rom 2:16
God through faith in **J** Christ for all Rom 3:22
the redemption that is in Christ **J**, Rom 3:24
justifier of the one who has faith in **J**. Rom 3:26
who raised from the dead **J** our Lord, Rom 4:24
with God through our Lord **J** Christ. Rom 5:1
in God through our Lord **J** Christ, Rom 5:11

of that one man J Christ abounded for Rom 5:15
in life through the one man J Christ. Rom 5:17
eternal life through J Christ our Lord. Rom 5:21
baptized into Christ J were baptized into Rom 6:3
dead to sin and alive to God in Christ J. Rom 6:11
God is eternal life in Christ J our Lord. Rom 6:23
be to God through J Christ our Lord! Rom 7:25
for those who are in Christ J. Rom 8:1
set you free in Christ J from the law of Rom 8:2
of him who raised J from the dead Rom 8:11
he who raised Christ J from the dead Rom 8:11
Christ J is the one who died—more Rom 8:34
the love of God in Christ J our Lord. Rom 8:39
with your mouth that J is Lord and Rom 10:9
But put on the Lord J Christ, and Rom 13:14
in the Lord J that nothing is Rom 14:14
one another, in accord with Christ J, Rom 15:5
God and Father of our Lord J Christ. Rom 15:6
a minister of Christ J to the Gentiles Rom 15:16
In Christ J, then, I have reason to be Rom 15:17
by our Lord J Christ and by the love Rom 15:30
Aquila, my fellow workers in Christ J, Rom 16:3
grace of our Lord J Christ be with Rom 16:20
gospel and the preaching of J Christ, Rom 16:25
glory forevermore through J Christ! Rom 16:27
will of God to be an apostle of Christ J, 1 Cor 1:1
Corinth, to those sanctified in Christ J, 1 Cor 1:2
upon the name of our Lord J Christ, 1 Cor 1:2
God our Father and the Lord J Christ. 1 Cor 1:3
of God that was given you in Christ J, 1 Cor 1:4
for the revealing of our Lord J Christ, 1 Cor 1:7
in the day of our Lord J Christ. 1 Cor 1:8
of his Son, J Christ our Lord. 1 Cor 1:9
by the name of our Lord J Christ, 1 Cor 1:10
is the source of your life in Christ J, 1 Cor 1:30
among you except J Christ and him 1 Cor 2:2
that which is laid, which is J Christ. 1 Cor 3:11
father in Christ J through the gospel. 1 Cor 4:15
the name of the Lord J and my spirit is 1 Cor 5:4
is present, with the power of our Lord J, 1 Cor 5:4
name of the Lord J Christ and by the 1 Cor 6:11
whom we exist, and one Lord, J Christ, 1 Cor 8:6
an apostle? Have I not seen J our Lord? 1 Cor 9:1
that the Lord J on the night when he 1 Cor 11:23
of God ever says "J is accursed!" and 1 Cor 12:3
no one can say "J is Lord" except in 1 Cor 12:3
which I have in Christ J our Lord, 1 Cor 15:31
victory through our Lord J Christ. 1 Cor 15:57
The grace of the Lord J be with you. 1 Cor 16:23
My love be with you all in Christ J. 1 Cor 16:24
an apostle of Christ J by the will of 2 Cor 1:1
God our Father and the Lord J Christ. 2 Cor 1:2
God and Father of our Lord J Christ, 2 Cor 1:3
the day of our Lord J you will boast of 2 Cor 1:14
For the Son of God, J Christ, whom 2 Cor 1:19
is not ourselves, but J Christ as Lord, 2 Cor 4:5
the glory of God in the face of J Christ. 2 Cor 4:6
carrying in the body the death of J, 2 Cor 4:10
that the life of J may also be 2 Cor 4:10
that the life of J also may be 2 Cor 4:11
who raised the Lord J will raise us 2 Cor 4:14
raise us also with J and bring us with 2 Cor 4:14
know the grace of our Lord J Christ, 2 Cor 8:9
and proclaims another J than the one 2 Cor 11:4
The God and Father of the Lord J, he 2 Cor 11:31
yourselves, that J Christ is in you? 2 Cor 13:5
grace of the Lord J Christ and the 2 Cor 13:14
but through J Christ and God the Father, Gal 1:1
God our Father and the Lord J Christ, Gal 1:3
it through a revelation of J Christ. Gal 1:12
out our freedom that we have in Christ J, Gal 2:4
of the law but through faith in J Christ, Gal 2:16
so we also have believed in Christ J, Gal 2:16
your eyes that J Christ was publicly Gal 3:1
so that in Christ J the blessing of Gal 3:14
promise by faith in J Christ might be Gal 3:22
for in Christ J you are all sons of God, Gal 3:26
female, for you are all one in Christ J. Gal 3:28
me as an angel of God, as Christ J. Gal 4:14
For in Christ J neither circumcision nor Gal 5:6
belong to Christ J have crucified the Gal 5:24
except in the cross of our Lord J Christ, Gal 6:14
for I bear on my body the marks of J. Gal 6:17
grace of our Lord J Christ be with your Gal 6:18
an apostle of Christ J by the will of God, Eph 1:1
in Ephesus, and are faithful in Christ J: Eph 1:1
God our Father and the Lord J Christ. Eph 1:2
the God and Father of our Lord J Christ, Eph 1:3
us for adoption through J Christ, Eph 1:5
faith in the Lord J and your love toward Eph 1:15
that the God of our Lord J Christ, the Eph 1:17
him in the heavenly places in Christ J, Eph 2:6
grace in kindness toward us in Christ J. Eph 2:7
created in Christ J for good works, Eph 2:10
But now in Christ J you who once were Eph 2:13
Christ J himself being the cornerstone, Eph 2:20
a prisoner for Christ J on behalf of you Eph 3:1
promise in Christ J through the gospel. Eph 3:6
he has realized in Christ J our Lord, Eph 3:11
and in Christ J throughout all Eph 3:21
were taught in him, as the truth is in J, Eph 4:21
in the name of our Lord J Christ, Eph 5:20
God the Father and the Lord J Christ. Eph 6:23
who love our Lord J Christ with love Eph 6:24
Paul and Timothy, servants of Christ J, Phil 1:1
the saints in Christ J who are at Phil 1:1
God our Father and the Lord J Christ. Phil 1:2
it to completion at the day of J Christ. Phil 1:6
for you all with the affection of Christ J. Phil 1:8
that comes through J Christ, Phil 1:11
of the Spirit of J Christ this will turn Phil 1:19
have ample cause to glory in Christ J, Phil 1:26
yourselves, which is yours in Christ J, Phil 2:5
at the name of J every knee should Phil 2:10
tongue confess that J Christ is Lord, Phil 2:11
I hope in the Lord J to send Timothy to Phil 2:19
own interests, not those of J Christ. Phil 2:21
and glory in Christ J and put no Phil 3:3
worth of knowing Christ J my Lord. Phil 3:8
because Christ J has made me his own. Phil 3:12
of the upward call of God in Christ J. Phil 3:14
it we await a Savior, the Lord J Christ, Phil 3:20
your hearts and your minds in Christ J. Phil 4:7
to his riches in glory in Christ J. Phil 4:19
Greet every saint in Christ J. The Phil 4:21
grace of the Lord J Christ be with your Phil 4:23
an apostle of Christ J by the will of God, Col 1:1
God, the Father of our Lord J Christ, Col 1:3
of your faith in Christ J and of the love Col 1:4
as you received Christ J the Lord, Col 2:6
do everything in the name of the Lord J, Col 3:17
and J who is called Justus. These are the Col 4:11
who is one of you, a servant of Christ J, Col 4:12
God the Father and the Lord J Christ: 1 Thes 1:1
of hope in our Lord J Christ. 1 Thes 1:3
J who delivers us from the wrath to 1 Thes 1:10
of God in Christ J that are in Judea. 1 Thes 2:14
both the Lord J and the prophets, 1 Thes 2:15
before our Lord J at his coming? 1 Thes 2:19
and Father himself, and our Lord J, 1 Thes 3:11
coming of our Lord J with all his 1 Thes 3:13
we ask and urge you in the Lord J, 1 Thes 4:1
we gave you through the Lord J. 1 Thes 4:2
since we believe that J died and rose 1 Thes 4:14
and rose again, even so, through J, 1 Thes 4:14
salvation through our Lord J Christ, 1 Thes 5:9
is the will of God in Christ J for you. 1 Thes 5:18
at the coming of our Lord J Christ. 1 Thes 5:23
grace of our Lord J Christ be with 1 Thes 5:28
God our Father and the Lord J Christ: 2 Thes 1:1
God our Father and the Lord J Christ. 2 Thes 1:2
when the Lord J is revealed from 2 Thes 1:7
do not obey the gospel of our Lord J. 2 Thes 1:8
name of our Lord J may be glorified 2 Thes 1:12
of our God and the Lord J Christ. 2 Thes 1:12
coming of our Lord J Christ and our 2 Thes 2:1
whom the Lord J will kill with the 2 Thes 2:8
the glory of our Lord J Christ. 2 Thes 2:14
Now may our Lord J Christ himself, 2 Thes 2:16
in the name of our Lord J Christ, 2 Thes 3:6
encourage in the Lord J Christ to do 2 Thes 3:12
grace of our Lord J Christ be with 2 Thes 3:18
an apostle of Christ J by command of 1 Tm 1:1
our Savior and of Christ J our hope, 1 Tm 1:1
God the Father and Christ J our Lord. 1 Tm 1:2
given me strength, Christ J our Lord, 1 Tm 1:12
the faith and love that are in Christ J. 1 Tm 1:14
that Christ J came into the world to 1 Tm 1:15
J Christ might display his perfect 1 Tm 1:16
God and men, the man Christ J, 1 Tm 2:5
in the faith that is in Christ J. 1 Tm 3:13
you will be a good servant of Christ J, 1 Tm 4:6
of God and of Christ J and of the elect 1 Tm 5:21
words of our Lord J Christ and the 1 Tm 6:3
gives life to all things, and of Christ J, 1 Tm 6:13
the appearing of our Lord J Christ, 1 Tm 6:14
an apostle of Christ J by the will of God 2 Tm 1:1
promise of the life that is in Christ J, 2 Tm 1:1
God the Father and Christ J our Lord. 2 Tm 1:2
gave us in Christ J before the ages 2 Tm 1:9
the appearing of our Savior Christ J, 2 Tm 1:10
the faith and love that are in Christ J. 2 Tm 1:13
by the grace that is in Christ J, 2 Tm 2:1
suffering as a good soldier of Christ J. 2 Tm 2:3
Remember J Christ, risen from the 2 Tm 2:8
that is in Christ J with eternal glory. 2 Tm 2:10
life in Christ J will be persecuted, 2 Tm 3:12
salvation through faith in Christ J. 2 Tm 3:15
in the presence of God and of Christ J, 2 Tm 4:1
a servant of God and an apostle of J Christ, Ti 1:1
God the Father and Christ J our Savior. Ti 1:4
of our great God and Savior J Christ, Ti 2:13
on us richly through J Christ our Savior, Ti 3:6
Paul, a prisoner for Christ J, and Phlm 1:1
God our Father and the Lord J Christ. Phlm 1:3
have toward the Lord J and all the Phlm 1:5
and now a prisoner also for Christ J— Phlm 1:9
my fellow prisoner in Christ J, Phlm 1:23
grace of the Lord J Christ be with Phlm 1:25
made lower than the angels, namely J, Heb 2:9
share in a heavenly calling, consider J, Heb 3:1
For J has been counted worthy of more Heb 3:3
through the heavens, J, the Son of God, Heb 4:14
J offered up prayers and supplications, Heb 5:7
where J has gone as a forerunner on Heb 6:20
This makes J the guarantor of a better Heb 7:22
of the body of J Christ once for all. Heb 10:10
enter the holy places by the blood of J, Heb 10:19
looking to J, the founder and perfecter Heb 12:2
and to J, the mediator of a new Heb 12:24
J Christ is the same yesterday and Heb 13:8
So J also suffered outside the gate in Heb 13:12
again from the dead our Lord J, Heb 13:20
in his sight, through J Christ, Heb 13:21
a servant of God and of the Lord J Christ, Jas 1:1
as you hold the faith in our Lord J Christ, Jas 2:1
Peter, an apostle of J Christ, To those 1 Pt 1:1
for obedience to J Christ and for 1 Pt 1:2
the God and Father of our Lord J Christ! 1 Pt 1:3
the resurrection of J Christ from the 1 Pt 1:3
and honor at the revelation of J Christ. 1 Pt 1:7
to you at the revelation of J Christ. 1 Pt 1:13
acceptable to God through J Christ. 1 Pt 2:5
through the resurrection of J Christ, 1 Pt 3:21
God may be glorified through J Christ. 1 Pt 4:11
Peter, a servant and apostle of J Christ, 2 Pt 1:1
of our God and Savior J Christ: 2 Pt 1:1
the knowledge of God and of J our Lord. 2 Pt 1:2
in the knowledge of our Lord J Christ. 2 Pt 1:8
of our Lord and Savior J Christ. 2 Pt 1:11
as our Lord J Christ made clear to me. 2 Pt 1:14
power and coming of our Lord J Christ, 2 Pt 1:16
of our Lord and Savior J Christ, 2 Pt 2:20
of our Lord and Savior J Christ. 2 Pt 3:18
the Father and with his Son J Christ. 1 Jn 1:3
and the blood of J his Son cleanses us 1 Jn 1:7
with the Father, J Christ the righteous. 1 Jn 2:1
but he who denies that J is the Christ? 1 Jn 2:22
name of his Son J Christ and love one 1 Jn 3:23
that confesses that J Christ has come 1 Jn 4:2
that does not confess J is not from God. 1 Jn 4:3
Whoever confesses that J is the Son of 1 Jn 4:15
who believes that J is the Christ 1 Jn 5:1
the one who believes that J is the Son of 1 Jn 5:5
came by water and blood—J Christ; 1 Jn 5:6
in him who is true, in his Son J Christ. 1 Jn 5:20
Father and from J Christ the Father's 2 Jn 1:3
confess the coming of J Christ in the 2 Jn 1:7
a servant of J Christ and brother of Jude 1:1
in God the Father and kept for J Christ: Jude 1:1
deny our only Master and Lord, J Christ. Jude 1:4
although you once fully knew it, that J, Jude 1:5
of the apostles of our Lord J Christ. Jude 1:17
mercy of our Lord J Christ that leads to Jude 1:21
our Savior, through J Christ our Lord, Jude 1:25
The revelation of J Christ, which God Rv 1:1
of God and to the testimony of J Christ, Rv 1:2
and from J Christ the faithful witness, the Rv 1:5
and the patient endurance that are in J, Rv 1:9
of the word of God and the testimony of J. Rv 1:9
of God and hold to the testimony of J. Rv 12:17
of God and their faith in J. Rv 14:12
the saints, the blood of the martyrs of J. Rv 17:6
brothers who hold to the testimony of J. Rv 19:10
For the testimony of J is the spirit of Rv 19:10
for the testimony of J and for the word Rv 20:4
J, have sent my angel to testify to you Rv 22:16
coming soon." Amen. Come, Lord J! Rv 22:20
The grace of the Lord J be with all. Rv 22:21

JESUS' (7)

of it, for J name had become known. Mk 6:14
Peter saw it, he fell down at J knees, Lk 5:8
And falling at J feet, he implored him to Lk 8:41
and he fell on his face at J feet, giving Lk 17:16
the face cloth, which had been on J head, Jn 20:7
ourselves as your servants for J sake. 2 Cor 4:5
being given over to death for J sake, 2 Cor 4:11

JETHER (8)

So he said to J his firstborn, "Rise and Jgs 8:20
the son of Ner, and Amasa the son of J, 1 Kgs 2:5
of Israel, and Amasa the son of J, 1 Kgs 2:32
father of Amasa was J the Ishmaelite. 1 Chr 2:17
Shammai's brother: J and Jonathan; 1 Chr 2:32
and Jonathan; and J died childless. 1 Chr 2:32

of Ezrah: **J**, Mered, Epher, and Jalon. 1 Chr 4:17
The sons of **J**: Jephunneh, Pispa, and 1 Chr 7:38

JETHETH (2)
names: the chiefs Timna, Alvah, **J**, Gn 36:40
Edom were: chiefs Timna, Alvah, **J**, 1 Chr 1:51

JETHRO (10)
of his father-in-law, **J**, the priest of Midian, Ex 3:1
went back to **J** his father-in-law and Ex 4:18
they are still alive." And **J** said to Moses, Ex 4:18
J, the priest of Midian, Moses' Ex 18:1
Now **J**, Moses' father-in-law, had taken Ex 18:2
J, Moses' father-in-law, came with his Ex 18:5
word to Moses, "I, your father-in-law **J**, Ex 18:6
And **J** rejoiced for all the good that the Ex 18:9
J said, "Blessed be the LORD, who has Ex 18:10
And **J**, Moses' father-in-law, brought a Ex 18:12

JETTISON (1)
they began the next day to **j** the cargo. Acts 27:18

JETUR (3)
Hadad, Tema, **J**, Naphish, and Gn 25:15
J, Naphish, and Kedemah. These are 1 Chr 1:31
war against the Hagrites, **J**, Naphish, 1 Chr 5:19

JEUEL (3)
of Zerah: **J** and their kinsmen, 690. 1 Chr 9:6
the sons of Elizaphan, Shimri and **J**; 2 Chr 29:13
being Eliphelet, **J**, and Shemaiah, Ezr 8:13

JEUSH (9)
and Oholibamah bore **J**, Jalam, and Gn 36:5
she bore to Esau **J**, Jalam, and Korah. Gn 36:14
wife: the chiefs **J**, Jalam, and Korah; Gn 36:18
Eliphaz, Reuel, **J**, Jalam, and Korah. 1 Chr 1:35
J, Benjamin, Ehud, Chenaanah, 1 Chr 7:10
Ulam his firstborn, **J** the second, and 1 Chr 8:39
Jahath, Zina, and **J** and Beriah. 1 Chr 23:10
but **J** and Beriah did not have many 1 Chr 23:11
she bore him sons, **J**, Shemariah, 2 Chr 11:19

JEUZ (1)
J, Sachia, and Mirmah. These were 1 Chr 8:10

JEW (32)
Now there was a **J** in Susa the citadel Est 2:5
for he had told them that he was a **J**. Est 3:4
I see Mordecai the **J** sitting at the king's Est 5:13
do so to Mordecai the **J** who sits at the Est 6:10
to Queen Esther and to Mordecai the **J**, Est 8:7
and Mordecai the **J** gave full written Est 9:29
as Mordecai the **J** and Queen Esther Est 9:31
For Mordecai the **J** was second in rank Est 10:3
female, so that no one should enslave a **J**, Jer 34:9
tongue shall take hold of the robe of a **J**, Zec 8:23
John's disciples and a **J** over purification. Jn 3:25
said to him, "How is it that you, a **J**, Jn 4:9
Pilate answered, "Am I a **J**? Your own Jn 18:35
it is for a **J** to associate with or Acts 10:28
And he found a **J** named Aquila, a Acts 18:2
Now a **J** named Apollos, a native of Acts 18:24
when they recognized that he was a **J**, Acts 19:34
Paul replied, "I am a **J**, from Tarsus Acts 21:39
"I am a **J**, born in Tarsus in Cilicia, Acts 22:3
to the **J** first and also to the Greek. Rom 1:16
does evil, the **J** first and also the Greek, Rom 2:9
good, the **J** first and also the Greek. Rom 2:10
if you call yourself a **J** and rely on the Rom 2:17
For no one is a **J** who is merely one Rom 2:28
But a **J** is one inwardly, and Rom 2:29
Then what advantage has the **J**? Or Rom 3:1
no distinction between **J** and Greek; Rom 10:12
To the Jews I became as a **J**, in order 1 Cor 9:20
before them all, "If you, though a **J**, Gal 2:14
a Jew, live like a Gentile and not like a **J**, Gal 2:14
There is neither **J** nor Greek, there is Gal 3:28
Here there is not Greek and **J**, Col 3:11

JEWEL (4)
the lips of knowledge are a precious **j**. Prv 20:15
of your eyes, with one **j** of your necklace. Sg 4:9
of God, its radiance like a most rare **j**, Rv 21:11
city were adorned with every kind of **j**. Rv 21:19

JEWELER (1)
As a **j** engraves signets, so shall you Ex 28:11

JEWELRY (5)
the servant brought out **j** of silver and Gn 24:53
lives in her house, for silver and gold **j**, Ex 3:22
of her neighbor, for silver and gold **j**." Ex 11:2
for silver and gold **j** and for clothing. Ex 12:35
and adorned herself with her ring and **j**, Hos 2:13

JEWELS (15)
can it be exchanged for **j** of fine gold. Jb 28:17
She is more precious than **j**, and Prv 3:15
for wisdom is better than **j**, and all that Prv 8:11
find? She is far more precious than **j**. Prv 31:10
ornaments, your neck with strings of **j**. Sg 1:10
His arms are rods of gold, set with **j**. His Sg 5:14
Your rounded thighs are like **j**, the work Sg 7:1
and as a bride adorns herself with her **j**. Is 61:10
also took your beautiful **j** of my gold Ezk 16:17
take your beautiful **j** and leave you Ezk 16:39
and take away your beautiful **j**. Ezk 23:26
for like the **j** of a crown they shall shine Zec 9:16
and adorned with gold and **j** and pearls, Rv 17:4
cargo of gold, silver, **j**, pearls, fine linen, Rv 18:12
and scarlet, adorned with gold, with **j**, Rv 18:16

JEWISH (17)
of their wives against their **J** brothers. Neh 5:1
bought back our **J** brothers who have Neh 5:8
you have begun to fall, is of the **J** people, Est 6:13
Joseph, from the **J** town of Arimathea. Lk 23:50
jars there for the **J** rites of purification, Jn 2:6
So because of the **J** day of Preparation, Jn 19:42
well spoken of by the whole **J** nation, Acts 10:22
all that the **J** people were expecting." Acts 12:11
a **J** false prophet named Bar-Jesus. Acts 13:6
together into the **J** synagogue and Acts 14:1
the son of a **J** woman who was a Acts 16:1
they went into the **J** synagogue. Acts 17:10
of the itinerant **J** exorcists undertook Acts 19:13
Seven sons of a **J** high priest named Acts 19:14
with his wife Drusilla, who was **J**, Acts 24:24
whom the whole **J** people petitioned Acts 25:24
devoting themselves to **J** myths and the Ti 1:14

JEWS (225)
along with the **J** and the Chaldeans 2 Kgs 25:25
to the king that the **J** who came up from Ezr 4:12
in haste to the **J** at Jerusalem and by Ezr 4:23
prophesied to the **J** who were in Judah Ezr 5:1
eye of their God was on the elders of the **J**, Ezr 5:5
Let the governor of the **J** and the elders of Ezr 6:7
the elders of the **J** rebuild this house of Ezr 6:7
these elders of the **J** for the rebuilding of Ezr 6:8
the elders of the **J** built and prospered Ezr 6:14
them concerning the **J** who escaped, Neh 1:2
I was doing, and I had not yet told the **J**, Neh 2:16
greatly enraged, and he jeered at the **J**. Neh 4:1
"What are these feeble **J** doing? Neh 4:2
At that time the **J** who lived near them Neh 4:12
at my table 150 men, **J** and officials, Neh 5:17
says it, that you and the **J** intend to rebel; Neh 6:6
also I saw the **J** who had married Neh 13:23
Haman sought to destroy all the **J**, Est 3:6
son of Hammedatha, the enemy of the **J**. Est 3:10
to destroy, to kill, and to annihilate all **J**, Est 3:13
there was great mourning among the **J**, Est 4:3
treasuries for the destruction of the **J**. Est 4:7
escape any more than all the other **J**. Est 4:13
will rise for the **J** from another place, Est 4:14
"Go, gather all the **J** to be found in Susa, Est 4:16
the house of Haman, the enemy of the **J**. Est 8:1
the plot that he had devised against the **J**. Est 8:3
he wrote to destroy the **J** who are in all the Est 8:5
because he intended to lay hands on the **J**. Est 8:7
write as you please with regard to the **J**, Est 8:8
Mordecai commanded concerning the **J**, Est 8:9
and also to the **J** in their script and their Est 8:9
the king allowed the **J** who were in every Est 8:11
and the **J** were to be ready on that day to Est 8:13
The **J** had light and gladness and joy Est 8:16
there was gladness and joy among the **J**, Est 8:17
of the country declared themselves **J**, Est 8:17
Jews, for fear of the **J** had fallen on them. Est 8:17
the enemies of the **J** hoped to gain the Est 9:1
the **J** gained mastery over those who Est 9:1
The **J** gathered in their cities throughout Est 9:2
and the royal agents also helped the **J**, Est 9:3
The **J** struck all their enemies with the Est 9:5
the citadel itself the **J** killed and destroyed Est 9:6
son of Hammedatha, the enemy of the **J**, Est 9:10
Susa the citadel the **J** have killed and Est 9:12
let the **J** who are in Susa be allowed Est 9:13
The **J** who were in Susa gathered also on Est 9:15
Now the rest of the **J** who were in the Est 9:16
But the **J** who were in Susa gathered on Est 9:18
Therefore the **J** of the villages, who live Est 9:19
sent letters to all the **J** who were in all the Est 9:20
days on which the **J** got relief from their Est 9:22
So the **J** accepted what they had started Est 9:23
of Hammedatha, the enemy of all the **J**, Est 9:24
had plotted against the **J** to destroy them, Est 9:24
devised against the **J** should return on Est 9:25
the **J** firmly obligated themselves and Est 9:27
never fall into disuse among the **J**, Est 9:28
Letters were sent to all the **J**, to the 127 Est 9:30
was great among the **J** and popular with Est 10:3
forward and maliciously accused the **J**. Dn 3:8
There are certain **J** whom you have Dn 3:12
is he who has been born king of the **J**? Mt 2:2
"Are you the King of the **J**?" Jesus said, Mt 27:11
him, saying, "Hail, King of the **J**!" Mt 27:29
read, "This is Jesus, the King of the **J**." Mt 27:37
been spread among the **J** to this day. Mt 28:15
Pharisees and all the **J** do not eat unless Mk 7:3
the King of the **J**?" And he answered Mk 15:2
me to release for you the King of the **J**?" Mk 15:9
the man you call the King of the **J**?" Mk 15:12
to salute him, "Hail, King of the **J**!" Mk 15:18
against him read, "The King of the **J**." Mk 15:26
about Jesus, he sent to him elders of the **J**, Lk 7:3
the King of the **J**?" And he answered Lk 23:3
and saying, "If you are the King of the **J**, Lk 23:37
over him, "This is the King of the **J**." Lk 23:38
when the **J** sent priests and Levites from Jn 1:19
The Passover of the **J** was at hand, and Jn 2:13
So the **J** said to him, "What sign do you Jn 2:18
The **J** then said, "It has taken forty-six Jn 2:20
named Nicodemus, a ruler of the **J**. Jn 3:1
of Samaria?" (For **J** have no dealings Jn 4:9
what we know, for salvation is from the **J**. Jn 4:22
After this there was a feast of the **J**, and Jn 5:1
So the **J** said to the man who had been Jn 5:10
went away and told the **J** that it was Jesus Jn 5:15
this was why the **J** were persecuting Jesus, Jn 5:16
This was why the **J** were seeking all the Jn 5:18
Now the Passover, the feast of the **J**, was at Jn 6:4
So the **J** grumbled about him, because he Jn 6:41
The **J** then disputed among themselves, Jn 6:52
because the **J** were seeking to kill him. Jn 7:1
The **J** were looking for him at the feast, Jn 7:11
Yet for fear of the **J** no one spoke openly Jn 7:13
The **J** therefore marveled, saying, "How is Jn 7:15
The **J** said to one another, "Where does Jn 7:35
So the **J** said, "Will he kill himself, since Jn 8:22
So Jesus said to the **J** who had believed in Jn 8:31
The **J** answered him, "Are we not right in Jn 8:48
The **J** said to him, "Now we know that Jn 8:52
So the **J** said to him, "You are not yet fifty Jn 8:57
The **J** did not believe that he had been Jn 9:18
these things because they feared the **J**, Jn 9:22
for the **J** had already agreed that if Jn 9:22
a division among the **J** because of these Jn 10:19
So the **J** gathered around him and said Jn 10:24
The **J** picked up stones again to stone Jn 10:31
The **J** answered him, "It is not for a good Jn 10:33
the **J** were just now seeking to stone you, Jn 11:8
and many of the **J** had come to Martha Jn 11:19
When the **J** who were with her in the Jn 11:31
and the **J** who had come with her also Jn 11:33
So the **J** said, "See how he loved him!" Jn 11:36
Many of the **J** therefore, who had come Jn 11:45
no longer walked openly among the **J**, Jn 11:54
Now the Passover of the **J** was at hand, Jn 11:55
large crowd of the **J** learned that Jesus Jn 12:9
him many of the **J** were going away and Jn 12:11
will seek me, and just as I said to the **J**, Jn 13:33
the officers of the **J** arrested Jesus and Jn 18:12
who had advised the **J** that it would be Jn 18:14
in the temple, where all **J** come together. Jn 18:20
by your own law." The **J** said to him, Jn 18:31
said to him, "Are you the King of the **J**?" Jn 18:33
I might not be delivered over to the **J**. Jn 18:36
back outside to the **J** and told them, Jn 18:38
me to release to you the King of the **J**?" Jn 18:39
King of the **J**!" and struck him with their Jn 19:3
The **J** answered him, "We have a law, Jn 19:7
to release him, but the **J** cried out, Jn 19:12
He said to the **J**, "Behold your King!" Jn 19:14
"Jesus of Nazareth, the King of the **J**." Jn 19:19
Many of the **J** read this inscription, for Jn 19:20
So the chief priests of the **J** said to Pilate, Jn 19:21
Pilate, "Do not write, 'The King of the **J**,' Jn 19:21
'This man said, I am King of the **J**.'" Jn 19:21
the **J** asked Pilate that their legs might Jn 19:31
of Jesus, but secretly for fear of the **J**, Jn 19:38
spices, as is the burial custom of the **J**. Jn 19:40
where the disciples were for fear of the **J**, Jn 20:19
Now there were dwelling in Jerusalem **J**, Acts 2:5
both **J** and proselytes, Cretans and Acts 2:11
and confounded the **J** who lived in Acts 9:22
had passed, the **J** plotted to kill him, Acts 9:23
the country of the **J** and in Jerusalem. Acts 10:39
speaking the word to no one except **J**. Acts 11:19
and when he saw that it pleased the **J**, Acts 12:3
word of God in the synagogues of the **J**. Acts 13:5
many **J** and devout converts to Acts 13:43
But when the **J** saw the crowds, they Acts 13:45
But the **J** incited the devout women of Acts 13:50
number of both **J** and Greeks believed. Acts 14:1
But the unbelieving **J** stirred up the Acts 14:2
some sided with the **J** and some with Acts 14:4
was made by both Gentiles and **J**, Acts 14:5
But **J** came from Antioch and Acts 14:19
him because of the **J** who were in those Acts 16:3
they said, "These men are **J**, Acts 16:20

where there was a synagogue of the J. Acts 17:1
But the J were jealous, and taking Acts 17:5
Now these J were more noble than Acts 17:11
But when the J from Thessalonica Acts 17:13
synagogue with the J and the devout Acts 17:17
commanded all the J to leave Rome. Acts 18:2
and tried to persuade J and Greeks. Acts 18:4
testifying to the J that the Christ was Acts 18:5
the J made a united attack on Paul Acts 18:12
open his mouth, Gallio said to the J, Acts 18:14
of wrongdoing or vicious crime, O J, Acts 18:14
synagogue and reasoned with the J. Acts 18:19
he powerfully refuted the J in public, Acts 18:28
word of the Lord, both J and Greeks. Acts 19:10
of Ephesus, both J and Greeks. Acts 19:17
whom the J had put forward. Acts 19:33
against him by the J as he was about Acts 20:3
to me through the plots of the J; Acts 20:19
testifying both to J and to Greeks of Acts 20:21
'This is how the J at Jerusalem will Acts 21:11
there are among the J of those who Acts 21:20
you teach all the J who are among the Acts 21:21
almost completed, the J from Asia, Acts 21:27
spoken of by all the J who lived there, Acts 22:12
why he was being accused by the J, Acts 22:30
the J made a plot and bound Acts 23:12
"The J have agreed to ask you to Acts 23:20
was seized by the J and was about to Acts 23:27
among all the J throughout the world Acts 24:5
The J also joined in the charge, Acts 24:9
or tumult. But some J from Asia— Acts 24:18
And desiring to do the J a favor, Felix Acts 24:27
principal men of the J laid out their Acts 25:2
the J who had come down from Acts 25:7
"Neither against the law of the J, Acts 25:8
But Festus, wishing to do the J a favor, Acts 25:9
To the J I have done no wrong, as you Acts 25:10
the elders of the J laid out their case Acts 25:15
against all the accusations of the J, Acts 26:2
the customs and controversies of the J. Acts 26:3
in Jerusalem, is known by all the J. Acts 26:4
And for this hope I am accused by J, O Acts 26:7
For this reason the J seized me in the Acts 26:21
together the local leaders of the J, Acts 28:17
But because the J objected, I was Acts 28:19
the J were entrusted with the oracles of Rom 3:2
What then? Are we J any better off? No, Rom 3:9
charged that all, both J and Greeks, Rom 3:9
Or is God the God of J only? Is he not Rom 3:29
not from the J only but also from the Rom 9:24
to make my fellow J jealous, Rom 11:14
For J demand signs and Greeks seek 1 Cor 1:22
a stumbling block to J and folly to 1 Cor 1:23
who are called, both J and Greeks, 1 Cor 1:24
To the J I became as a Jew, in order to 1 Cor 9:20
I became as a Jew, in order to win J. 1 Cor 9:20
Give no offense to J or to Greeks or to 1 Cor 10:32
baptized into one body—J or Greeks, 1 Cor 12:13
the hands of the J the forty lashes 2 Cor 11:24
rest of the J acted hypocritically along Gal 2:13
you force the Gentiles to live like J?" Gal 2:14
We ourselves are J by birth and not Gal 2:15
countrymen as they did from the J, 1 Thes 2:14
those who say that they are J and are not, Rv 2:9
Satan who say that they are J and are not, Rv 3:9

JEWS' (1)
Now the J Feast of Booths was at hand. Jn 7:2

JEZANIAH (2)
J the son of the Maacathite, Jer 40:8
son of Kareah and J the son of Hoshaiah, Jer 42:1

JEZEBEL (22)
took for his wife J the daughter of 1 Kgs 16:31
and when J cut off the prophets of the 1 Kgs 18:4
what I did when J killed the prophets 1 Kgs 18:13
Ahab told J all that Elijah had done, 1 Kgs 19:1
Then J sent a messenger to Elijah, 1 Kgs 19:2
But J his wife came to him and said to 1 Kgs 21:5
And J his wife said to him, "Do you 1 Kgs 21:7
city, did as J had sent word to them. 1 Kgs 21:11
Then they sent to J, saying, "Naboth 1 Kgs 21:14
As soon as J heard that Naboth had 1 Kgs 21:15
stoned and was dead, J said to Ahab, 1 Kgs 21:15
And of J the LORD also said, 'The 1 Kgs 21:23
'The dogs shall eat J within the walls 1 Kgs 21:23
like Ahab, whom J his wife incited. 1 Kgs 21:25
that I may avenge on J the blood of my 2 Kgs 9:7
the dogs shall eat J in the territory of 2 Kgs 9:10
of your mother J are so many?" 2 Kgs 9:22
Jehu came to Jezreel, J heard of it. 2 Kgs 9:30
Jezreel the dogs shall eat the flesh of J, 2 Kgs 9:36
and the corpse of J shall be as dung 2 Kgs 9:37
so that no one can say, This is J.'" 2 Kgs 9:37
you, that you tolerate that woman J, Rv 2:20

JEZEBEL'S (1)
of Asherah, who eat at J table." 1 Kgs 18:19

JEZER (3)
Naphtali: Jahzeel, Guni, J, and Shillem. Gn 46:24
of J, the clan of the Jezerites; of Nm 26:49
Jahziel, Guni, J and Shallum, the 1 Chr 7:13

JEZERITES (1)
of Jezer, the clan of the J; of Shillem, Nm 26:49

JEZIEL (1)
also J and Pelet, the sons of 1 Chr 12:3

JEZRAHIAH (1)
the singers sang with J as their leader. Neh 12:42

JEZREEL (39)
J, Jokdeam, Zanoah, Jos 15:56
its villages and those in the Valley of J." Jos 17:16
Their territory included J, Chesulloth, Jos 19:18
Jordan and encamped in the Valley of J. Jgs 6:33
David also took Ahinoam of J, and 1 Sm 25:43
with his two wives, Ahinoam of J, 1 Sm 27:3
encamped by the spring that is in J. 1 Sm 29:1
But the Philistines went up to J. 1 Sm 29:11
Ahinoam of J and Abigail the widow 1 Sm 30:5
Ahinoam of J and Abigail the widow of 2 Sm 2:2
the Ashurites and J and Ephraim and 2 Sm 2:9
firstborn was Amnon, of Ahinoam of J; 2 Sm 3:2
about Saul and Jonathan came from J, 2 Sm 4:4
that is beside Zarethan below J, 1 Kgs 4:12
rain. And Ahab rode and went to J. 1 Kgs 18:45
ran before Ahab to the entrance of J. 1 Kgs 18:46
the Jezreelite had a vineyard in J, 1 Kgs 21:1
eat Jezebel within the walls of J.' 1 Kgs 21:23
to be healed in J of the wounds that 2 Kgs 8:29
to see Joram the son of Ahab in J, 2 Kgs 8:29
shall eat Jezebel in the territory of J, 2 Kgs 9:10
to be healed in J of the wounds that 2 Kgs 9:15
of the city to go and tell the news in J." 2 Kgs 9:15
mounted his chariot and went to J, 2 Kgs 9:16
was standing on the tower in J, 2 Kgs 9:17
When Jehu came to J, Jezebel heard of 2 Kgs 9:30
'In the territory of J the dogs shall eat 2 Kgs 9:36
face of the field in the territory of J, 2 Kgs 9:37
come to me at J tomorrow at this 2 Kgs 10:6
in baskets and sent them to him at J. 2 Kgs 10:7
remained of the house of Ahab in J, 2 Kgs 10:11
the sons of Etam: J, Ishma, and Idbash; 1 Chr 4:3
to be healed in J of the wounds that 2 Chr 22:6
to see Joram the son of Ahab in J, 2 Chr 22:6
the LORD said to him, "Call his name J, Hos 1:4
the house of Jehu for the blood of J, Hos 1:4
the bow of Israel in the Valley of J." Hos 1:5
the land, for great shall be the day of J. Hos 1:11
and the oil, and they shall answer J, Hos 2:22

JEZREELITE (9)
Now Naboth the J had a vineyard in 1 Kgs 21:1
of what Naboth the J had said to him, 1 Kgs 21:4
spoke to Naboth the J and said to 1 Kgs 21:6
you the vineyard of Naboth the J." 1 Kgs 21:7
of the vineyard of Naboth the J, 1 Kgs 21:15
to the vineyard of Naboth the J, 1 Kgs 21:16
him at the property of Naboth the J. 2 Kgs 9:21
of ground belonging to Naboth the J. 2 Kgs 9:25
firstborn, Amnon, by Ahinoam the J; 1 Chr 3:1

JIDLAPH (1)
Chesed, Hazo, Pildash, J, and Bethuel." Gn 22:22

JOAB (141)
And J the son of Zeruiah and the 2 Sm 2:13
And Abner said to J, "Let the young 2 Sm 2:14
and compete before us." And J said, 2 Sm 2:14
sons of Zeruiah were there, J, Abishai, 2 Sm 2:18
I lift up my face to your brother J?" 2 Sm 2:22
But J and Abishai pursued Abner. 2 Sm 2:24
Then Abner called to J, "Shall the 2 Sm 2:26
And J said, "As God lives, if you had 2 Sm 2:27
So J blew the trumpet, and all the men 2 Sm 2:28
J returned from the pursuit of Abner. 2 Sm 2:30
And J and his men marched all night, 2 Sm 2:32
of David arrived with J from a raid, 2 Sm 3:22
When J and all the army that was 2 Sm 3:23
that was with him came, it was told J, 2 Sm 3:23
Then J went to the king and said, 2 Sm 3:24
When J came out from David's 2 Sm 3:26
J took him aside into the midst of the 2 Sm 3:27
upon the head of J and upon all his 2 Sm 3:29
may the house of J never be without 2 Sm 3:29
So J and Abishai his brother killed 2 Sm 3:30
Then David said to J and to all the 2 Sm 3:31
J the son of Zeruiah was over the 2 Sm 8:16
he sent J and all the host of the mighty 2 Sm 10:7
When J saw that the battle was set 2 Sm 10:9
So J and the people who were with 2 Sm 10:13
Then J returned from fighting 2 Sm 10:14
kings go out to battle, David sent J, 2 Sm 11:1
So David sent word to J, "Send me 2 Sm 11:6
Uriah the Hittite." And J sent Uriah to 2 Sm 11:6
David asked how J was doing and how 2 Sm 11:7
and my lord J and the servants of my 2 Sm 11:11
David wrote a letter to J and sent it by 2 Sm 11:14
And as J was besieging the city, he 2 Sm 11:16
the city came out and fought with J, 2 Sm 11:17
Then J sent and told David all the 2 Sm 11:18
told David all that J had sent him to 2 Sm 11:22
messenger, "Thus shall you say to J, 2 Sm 11:25
Now J fought against Rabbah of the 2 Sm 12:26
And J sent messengers to David and 2 Sm 12:27
Now J the son of Zeruiah knew that 2 Sm 14:1
And J sent to Tekoa and brought 2 Sm 14:2
thus to him." So J put the words in 2 Sm 14:3
"Is the hand of J with you in all 2 Sm 14:19
was your servant J who commanded 2 Sm 14:19
of things your servant J did this. 2 Sm 14:20
Then the king said to J, "Behold now, 2 Sm 14:21
And J fell on his face to the ground 2 Sm 14:22
and blessed the king. And J said, 2 Sm 14:22
So J arose and went to Geshur and 2 Sm 14:23
Then Absalom sent for J, to send 2 Sm 14:29
king, but J would not come to him. 2 Sm 14:29
a second time, but J would not come. 2 Sm 14:29
Then J arose and went to Absalom at 2 Sm 14:31
Absalom answered J, "Behold, I sent 2 Sm 14:32
Then J went to the king and told 2 Sm 14:33
set Amasa over the army instead of J. 2 Sm 17:25
one third under the command of J, 2 Sm 18:2
the king ordered J and Abishai and 2 Sm 18:5
And a certain man saw it and told J, 2 Sm 18:10
J said to the man who told him, 2 Sm 18:11
But the man said to J, "Even if I felt 2 Sm 18:12
J said, "I will not waste time like this 2 Sm 18:14
Then J blew the trumpet, and the 2 Sm 18:16
Israel, for J restrained them. 2 Sm 18:16
And J said to him, "You are not to 2 Sm 18:20
Then J said to the Cushite, "Go, tell 2 Sm 18:21
seen." The Cushite bowed before J, 2 Sm 18:21
the son of Zadok said again to J, 2 Sm 18:22
run after the Cushite." And J said, 2 Sm 18:22
"When J sent the king's servant, 2 Sm 18:29
It was told J, "Behold, the king is 2 Sm 19:1
Then J came into the house to the 2 Sm 19:5
my army from now on in place of J.'" 2 Sm 19:13
Now J was wearing a soldier's 2 Sm 20:8
And J said to Amasa, "Is it well with 2 Sm 20:9
my brother?" And J took Amasa by 2 Sm 20:9
So J struck him with it in the 2 Sm 20:10
Then J and Abishai his brother 2 Sm 20:10
Amasa and said, "Whoever favors J, 2 Sm 20:11
is for David, let him follow J." 2 Sm 20:11
went on after J to pursue Sheba 2 Sm 20:13
who were with J came and besieged 2 Sm 20:15
Listen! Tell J, 'Come here, that I may 2 Sm 20:16
said, "Are you J?" He answered, 2 Sm 20:17
J answered, "Far be it from me, far be 2 Sm 20:20
the city." And the woman said to J, 2 Sm 20:21
son of Bichri and threw it out to J. 2 Sm 20:22
And J returned to Jerusalem to the 2 Sm 20:22
Now J was in command of all the 2 Sm 20:23
Now Abishai, the brother of J, the 2 Sm 23:18
Asahel the brother of J was one of the 2 Sm 23:24
the armor-bearer of J the son of 2 Sm 23:37
So the king said to J, the commander 2 Sm 24:2
But J said to the king, "May the LORD 2 Sm 24:3
word prevailed against J and the 2 Sm 24:4
So J and the commanders of the army 2 Sm 24:4
And J gave the sum of the numbering 2 Sm 24:9
He conferred with J the son of Zeruiah 1 Kgs 1:7
and J the commander of the army, 1 Kgs 1:19
And when J heard the sound of the 1 Kgs 1:41
you also know what J the son of 1 Kgs 2:5
Abiathar the priest and J the son of 1 Kgs 2:22
the news came to J—for Joab had 1 Kgs 2:28
Joab—for J had supported Adonijah 1 Kgs 2:28
not supported Absalom—J fled to the 1 Kgs 2:28
"J has fled to the tent of the LORD, 1 Kgs 2:29
word again, saying, "Thus said J, 1 Kgs 2:30
the blood that J shed without cause. 1 Kgs 2:31
back on the head of J and on the head 1 Kgs 2:33
Jehoiada over the army in place of J, 1 Kgs 2:35
and J the commander of the army 1 Kgs 11:15
(for J and all Israel remained there 1 Kgs 11:16
fathers and that J the commander of 1 Kgs 11:21
Abishai, J, and Asahel, three. 1 Chr 2:16
and Seraiah fathered J, the father of 1 Chr 4:14
and commander." And J the son of 1 Chr 11:6
and J repaired the rest of the city. 1 Chr 11:8
Now Abishai, the brother of J, was 1 Chr 11:20
men were Asahel the brother of J, 1 Chr 11:26
the armor-bearer of J the son of 1 Chr 11:39
And J the son of Zeruiah was over 1 Chr 18:15
he sent J and all the army of the 1 Chr 19:8

When J saw that the battle was set 1 Chr 19:10
So J and the people who were with 1 Chr 19:14
the city. Then J came to Jerusalem. 1 Chr 19:15
J led out the army and ravaged the 1 Chr 20:1
And J struck down Rabbah and 1 Chr 20:1
David said to J and the commanders 1 Chr 21:2
But J said, "May the LORD add to his 1 Chr 21:3
the king's word prevailed against J. 1 Chr 21:4
So J departed and went throughout 1 Chr 21:4
And J gave the sum of the 1 Chr 21:5
king's command was abhorrent to J. 1 Chr 21:6
son of Ner and J the son of Zeruiah 1 Chr 26:28
Asahel the brother of J was fourth, 1 Chr 27:7
J the son of Zeruiah began to count, 1 Chr 27:24
J was commander of the king's 1 Chr 27:34
namely the sons of Jeshua and J, Ezr 2:6
Of the sons of J, Obadiah the son of Jehiel, Ezr 8:9
namely the sons of Jeshua and J, Neh 7:11
and when J on his return struck down Ps 60:T

JOAB'S (9)
and to J brother Abishai the son of 1 Sm 26:6
servants, "See, J field is next to mine, 2 Sm 14:30
Nahash, sister of Zeruiah, J mother. 2 Sm 17:25
Abishai the son of Zeruiah, J brother, 2 Sm 18:2
ten young men, J armor-bearers, 2 Sm 18:15
went out after him J men and the 2 Sm 20:7
observe the sword that was in J hand. 2 Sm 20:10
And one of J young men took his 2 Sm 20:11
fled before Abishai, J brother, 1 Chr 19:15

JOAH (11)
the secretary, and J the son of Asaph, 2 Kgs 18:18
son of Hilkiah, and Shebnah, and J, 2 Kgs 18:26
the secretary, and J the son of Asaph, 2 Kgs 18:37
J his son, Iddo his son, Zerah his son, 1 Chr 6:21
Jehozabad the second, J the third, 1 Chr 26:4
Gershonites, J the son of Zimmah, 2 Chr 29:12
of Zimmah, and Eden the son of J; 2 Chr 29:12
of the city, and J the son of Joahaz, 2 Chr 34:8
the secretary, and J the son of Asaph, Is 36:3
Shebna, and J said to the Rabshakeh, Is 36:11
the secretary, and J the son of Asaph, Is 36:22

JOAHAZ (2)
the second year of Joash the son of J, 2 Kgs 14:1
of the city, and Joah the son of J, 2 Chr 34:8

JOANAN (1)
the son of J, the son of Rhesa, the son of Lk 3:27

JOANNA (2)
and J, the wife of Chuza, Herod's Lk 8:3
Mary Magdalene and J and Mary the Lk 24:10

JOASH (50)
which belonged to J the Abiezrite, Jgs 6:11
"Gideon the son of J has done this Jgs 6:29
Then the men of the town said to J, Jgs 6:30
But J said to all who stood against him, Jgs 6:31
than the sword of Gideon the son of J, Jgs 7:14
Gideon the son of J returned from the Jgs 8:13
Jerubbaal the son of J went and lived in Jgs 8:29
And Gideon the son of J died in a good Jgs 8:32
was buried in the tomb of J his father, Jgs 8:32
of the city and to J the king's son, 1 Kgs 22:26
took J the son of Ahaziah and stole 2 Kgs 11:2
rest of the acts of J and all that he 2 Kgs 12:19
and struck down J in the house 2 Kgs 12:20
the twenty-third year of J the son of 2 Kgs 13:1
and J his son reigned in his place. 2 Kgs 13:9
thirty-seventh year of J king of 2 Kgs 13:10
rest of the acts of J and all that he 2 Kgs 13:12
So J slept with his fathers, and 2 Kgs 13:13
And J was buried in Samaria with 2 Kgs 13:13
J king of Israel went down to him 2 Kgs 13:14
Three times J defeated him and 2 Kgs 13:25
the second year of J the son of Joahaz, 2 Kgs 14:1
king of Israel, Amaziah the son of J, 2 Kgs 14:1
in all things as J his father had done. 2 Kgs 14:3
Amaziah the son of J, king of Judah, 2 Kgs 14:17
year of Amaziah the son of J, 2 Kgs 14:23
king of Judah, Jeroboam the son of J, 2 Kgs 14:23
the hand of Jeroboam the son of J. 2 Kgs 14:27
his son, Ahaziah his son, J his son, 1 Chr 3:11
Jokim, and the men of Cozeba, and J, 1 Chr 4:22
Zemirah, J, Eliezer, Elioenai, Omri, 1 Chr 7:8
The chief was Ahiezer, then J, both 1 Chr 12:3
and over the stores of oil was J. 1 Chr 27:28
of the city and to J the king's son, 2 Chr 18:25
took J the son of Ahaziah and stole 2 Chr 22:11
J was seven years old when he began 2 Chr 24:1
And J did what was right in the eyes 2 Chr 24:2
After this J decided to restore the 2 Chr 24:4
Thus J the king did not remember 2 Chr 24:22
of the Syrians came up against J. 2 Chr 24:23
Thus they executed judgment on J. 2 Chr 24:24
counsel and sent to J the son of 2 Chr 25:17
And J the king of Israel sent word to 2 Chr 25:18
So J king of Israel went up, and he 2 Chr 25:21
And J king of Israel captured 2 Chr 25:23
Amaziah king of Judah, the son of J, 2 Chr 25:23
Amaziah the son of J, king of Judah, 2 Chr 25:25
after the death of J the son of 2 Chr 25:25
and in the days of Jeroboam the son of J, Hos 1:1
and in the days of Jeroboam the son of J, Am 1:1

JOB (56)
man in the land of Uz whose name was J, Jb 1:1
course, J would send and consecrate them, Jb 1:5
to the number of them all. For J said, Jb 1:5
in their hearts." Thus J did continually. Jb 1:5
Satan, "Have you considered my servant J, Jb 1:8
and said, "Does J fear God for no reason? Jb 1:9
and there came a messenger to J and said, Jb 1:14
Then J arose and tore his robe and Jb 1:20
In all this J did not sin or charge God Jb 1:22
Satan, "Have you considered my servant J, Jb 2:3
LORD and struck J with loathsome sores Jb 2:7
receive evil?" In all this J did not sin with Jb 2:10
After this J opened his mouth and cursed Jb 3:1
And J said: Jb 3:2
Then J answered and said: Jb 6:1
Then J answered and said: Jb 9:1
Then J answered and said: Jb 12:1
Then J answered and said: Jb 16:1
Then J answered and said: Jb 19:1
Then J answered and said: Jb 21:1
Then J answered and said: Jb 23:1
Then J answered and said: Jb 26:1
And J again took up his discourse, and Jb 27:1
And J again took up his discourse, and Jb 29:1
of barley." The words of J are ended. Jb 31:40
So these three men ceased to answer J, Jb 32:1
with anger at J because he justified Jb 32:2
although they had declared J to be in the Jb 32:3
waited to speak to J because they were Jb 32:4
you who refuted J or who answered Jb 32:12
"But now, hear my speech, O J, and listen Jb 33:1
Pay attention, O J, listen to me; be silent, Jb 33:31
For J has said, 'I am in the right, and God Jb 34:5
What man is like J, who drinks up Jb 34:7
'J speaks without knowledge; his words Jb 34:35
Would that J were tried to the end, Jb 34:36
J opens his mouth in empty talk; he Jb 35:16
"Hear this, O J; stop and consider the Jb 37:14
Then the LORD answered J out of the Jb 38:1
And the LORD said to J: Jb 40:1
Then J answered the LORD and said: Jb 40:3
Then the LORD answered J out of the Jb 40:6
Then J answered the LORD and said: Jb 42:1
the LORD had spoken these words to J, Jb 42:7
of me what is right, as my servant J has. Jb 42:7
and go to my servant J and offer up a Jb 42:8
And my servant J shall pray for you, for I Jb 42:8
of me what is right, as my servant J has." Jb 42:8
And the LORD restored the fortunes of J, Jb 42:10
And the LORD gave J twice as much as Jb 42:10
the latter days of J more than his Jb 42:12
And after this J lived 140 years, and saw Jb 42:16
And J died, an old man, and full of days. Jb 42:17
these three men, Noah, Daniel, and J, Ezk 14:14
even if Noah, Daniel, and J were in it, Ezk 14:20
You have heard of the steadfastness of J, Jas 5:11

JOB'S (4)
Now when J three friends heard of all this Jb 2:11
with anger also at J three friends because Jb 32:3
told them, and the LORD accepted J prayer. Jb 42:9
no women so beautiful as J daughters. Jb 42:15

JOBAB (9)
Ophir, Havilah, and J; all these were the Gn 10:29
and J the son of Zerah of Bozrah Gn 36:33
J died, and Husham of the land of the Gn 36:34
heard of this, he sent to J king of Madon, Jos 11:1
Ophir, Havilah, and J; all these were 1 Chr 1:23
and J the son of Zerah of Bozrah 1 Chr 1:44
J died, and Husham of the land of the 1 Chr 1:45
his wife: J, Zibia, Mesha, Malcam, 1 Chr 8:9
Izliah, and J were the sons of Elpaal. 1 Chr 8:18

JOCHEBED (2)
took as his wife J his father's sister, Ex 6:20
of Amram's wife was J the daughter of Nm 26:59

JODA (1)
of Semein, the son of Josech, the son of J, Lk 3:26

JOED (1)
Sallu the son of Meshullam, son of J, Neh 11:7

JOEL (21)
The name of his firstborn son was J, 1 Sm 8:2
J, Jehu the son of Joshibiah, son of 1 Chr 4:35
The sons of J: Shemaiah his son, Gog 1 Chr 5:4
the son of Azaz, son of Shema, son of J, 1 Chr 5:8
J the chief, Shapham the second, 1 Chr 5:12
J his firstborn, the second Abijah. 1 Chr 6:28
Heman the singer the son of J, son of 1 Chr 6:33
son of Elkanah, son of J, son of 1 Chr 6:36
Michael, Obadiah, J, and Isshiah, all 1 Chr 7:3
J the brother of Nathan, Mibhar the 1 Chr 11:38
of the sons of Gershom, J the chief, 1 Chr 15:7
Levites Uriel, Asaiah, J, Shemaiah, 1 Chr 15:11
appointed Heman the son of J; 1 Chr 15:17
Jehiel the chief, and Zetham, and J, 1 Chr 23:8
of Jehieli, Zetham, and J his brother, 1 Chr 26:22
of Manasseh, J the son of Pedaiah; 1 Chr 27:20
of Amasai, and J the son of Azariah, 2 Chr 29:12
Zabad, Zebina, Jaddai, J, and Benaiah. Ezr 10:43
J the son of Zichri was their overseer; Neh 11:9
The word of the LORD that came to J, the Jl 1:1
was uttered through the prophet J: Acts 2:16

JOELAH (1)
And J and Zebadiah, the sons of 1 Chr 12:7

JOEZER (1)
Isshiah, Azarel, J, and Jashobeam, 1 Chr 12:6

JOGBEHAH (2)
Atroth-shophan, Jazer, J, Nm 32:35
east of Nobah and J and attacked the Jgs 8:11

JOGLI (1)
of Dan a chief, Bukki the son of J. Nm 34:22

JOHA (2)
Ishpah, and J were sons of Beriah. 1 Chr 8:16
the son of Shimri, and J his brother, 1 Chr 11:45

JOHANAN (26)
Nethaniah, and J the son of Kareah, 2 Kgs 25:23
J the firstborn, the second Jehoiakim, 1 Chr 3:15
Eliashib, Pelaiah, Akkub, J, Delaiah, 1 Chr 3:24
fathered Azariah, Azariah fathered J, 1 Chr 6:9
and J fathered Azariah (it was he who 1 Chr 6:10
Jahaziel, J, Jozabad of Gederah, 1 Chr 12:4
J eighth, Elzabad ninth, 1 Chr 12:12
of Ephraim, Azariah the son of J, 2 Chr 28:12
sons of Azgad, J the son of Hakkatan, Ezr 8:12
days of Eliashib, Joiada, J, and Jaddua, Neh 12:22
until the days of J the son of Eliashib. Neh 12:23
son of Nethaniah, J the son of Kareah, Jer 40:8
Now J the son of Kareah and all the Jer 40:13
Then J the son of Kareah spoke secretly Jer 40:15
of Ahikam said to J the son of Kareah, Jer 40:16
But when J the son of Kareah and all Jer 41:11
were with Ishmael saw J the son of Jer 41:13
back, and went to J the son of Kareah. Jer 41:14
Nethaniah escaped from J with eight Jer 41:15
Then J the son of Kareah and all the Jer 41:16
whom J brought back from Gibeon. Jer 41:16
and J the son of Kareah and Jezaniah the Jer 42:1
Then he summoned J the son of Kareah Jer 42:8
son of Hoshaiah and J the son of Kareah Jer 43:2
So J the son of Kareah and all the Jer 43:4
But J the son of Kareah and all the Jer 43:5

JOHN (130)
In those days J the Baptist came Mt 3:1
Now J wore a garment of camel's hair Mt 3:4
came from Galilee to the Jordan to J, Mt 3:13
J would have prevented him, saying, "I Mt 3:14
when he heard that J had been arrested, Mt 4:12
the son of Zebedee and J his brother, Mt 4:21
Then the disciples of J came to him, Mt 9:14
the son of Zebedee, and J his brother; Mt 10:2
Now when J heard in prison about the Mt 11:2
"Go and tell J what you hear and see: Mt 11:4
to speak to the crowds concerning J: Mt 11:7
arisen no one greater than J the Baptist. Mt 11:11
From the days of J the Baptist until Mt 11:12
and the Law prophesied until J, Mt 11:13
For J came neither eating nor Mt 11:18
to his servants, "This is J the Baptist. Mt 14:2
For Herod had seized J and bound him Mt 14:3
because J had been saying to him, "It is Mt 14:4
me the head of J the Baptist here on Mt 14:8
He sent and had J beheaded in the Mt 14:10
And they said, "Some say J the Baptist, Mt 16:14
him Peter and James, and J his brother, Mt 17:1
was speaking to them of J the Baptist. Mt 17:13
The baptism of J, from where did it Mt 21:25
for they all hold that J was a prophet." Mt 21:26
For J came to you in the way of Mt 21:32
J appeared, baptizing in the wilderness Mk 1:4
Now J was clothed with camel's hair and Mk 1:6
and was baptized by J in the Jordan. Mk 1:9
Now after J was arrested, Jesus came Mk 1:14
the son of Zebedee and J his brother, Mk 1:19
Simon and Andrew, with James and J. Mk 1:29
son of Zebedee and J the brother of Mk 3:17
Peter and James and J the brother of Mk 5:37
"J the Baptist has been raised from the Mk 6:14

heard of it, he said, "**J**, whom I beheaded, Mk 6:16
had sent and seized **J** and bound him in Mk 6:17
For **J** had been saying to Herod, "It is Mk 6:18
for Herod feared **J**, knowing that he was Mk 6:20
she said, "The head of **J** the Baptist." Mk 6:24
at once the head of **J** the Baptist on a Mk 6:25
And they told him, "**J** the Baptist; and Mk 8:28
took with him Peter and James and **J**, Mk 9:2
J said to him, "Teacher, we saw Mk 9:38
And James and **J**, the sons of Zebedee, Mk 10:35
began to be indignant at James and **J**. Mk 10:41
Was the baptism of **J** from heaven or Mk 11:30
they all held that **J** really was a Mk 11:32
and James and **J** and Andrew asked Mk 13:3
took with him Peter and James and **J**, Mk 14:33
you a son, and you shall call his name **J**. Lk 1:13
answered, "No; he shall be called **J**." Lk 1:60
"His name is **J**." And they all wondered. Lk 1:63
of God came to **J** the son of Zechariah Lk 3:2
in their hearts concerning **J**, Lk 3:15
J answered them all, saying, "I baptize Lk 3:16
to them all, that he locked up **J** in prison. Lk 3:20
and so also were James and **J**, sons of Lk 5:10
"The disciples of **J** fast often and offer Lk 5:33
Andrew his brother, and James and **J**, Lk 6:14
The disciples of **J** reported all these Lk 7:18
reported all these things to him. And **J**, Lk 7:18
said, "**J** the Baptist has sent us to you, Lk 7:20
"Go and tell **J** what you have seen and Lk 7:22
to speak to the crowds concerning **J**: Lk 7:24
born of women none is greater than **J**. Lk 7:28
been baptized with the baptism of **J**, Lk 7:29
For **J** the Baptist has come eating no Lk 7:33
with him, except Peter and **J** and James, Lk 8:51
said by some that **J** had been raised from Lk 9:7
Herod said, "**J** I beheaded, but who is this Lk 9:9
And they answered, "**J** the Baptist. But Lk 9:19
with him Peter and **J** and James and Lk 9:28
J answered, "Master, we saw someone Lk 9:49
when his disciples James and **J** saw it, Lk 9:54
us to pray, as **J** taught his disciples." Lk 11:1
Law and the Prophets were until **J**; Lk 16:16
Was the baptism of **J** from heaven or Lk 20:4
they are convinced that **J** was a prophet." Lk 20:6
So Jesus sent Peter and **J**, saying, "Go and Lk 22:8
a man sent from God, whose name was **J**. Jn 1:6
(**J** bore witness about him, and cried out, Jn 1:15
And this is the testimony of **J**, when the Jn 1:19
J answered them, "I baptize with water, Jn 1:26
across the Jordan, where **J** was baptizing. Jn 1:28
And **J** bore witness: "I saw the Spirit Jn 1:32
The next day again **J** was standing with Jn 1:35
the two who heard **J** speak and followed Jn 1:40
and said, "So you are Simon the son of **J**? Jn 1:42
J also was baptizing at Aenon near Jn 3:23
(for **J** had not yet been put in prison). Jn 3:24
And they came to **J** and said to him, Jn 3:26
J answered, "A person cannot receive Jn 3:27
and baptizing more disciples than **J** Jn 4:1
You sent to **J**, and he has borne witness to Jn 5:33
that I have is greater than that of **J**. Jn 5:36
to the place where **J** had been baptizing Jn 10:40
And they said, "**J** did no sign, but Jn 10:41
but everything that **J** said about this Jn 10:41
said to Simon Peter, "Simon, son of **J**, Jn 21:15
to him a second time, "Simon, son of **J**, Jn 21:16
to him the third time, "Simon, son of **J**, Jn 21:17
for **J** baptized with water, but you will Acts 1:5
Peter and **J** and James and Andrew, Acts 1:13
from the baptism of **J** until the day Acts 1:22
Now Peter and **J** were going up to the Acts 3:1
Seeing Peter and **J** about to go into the Acts 3:3
Peter directed his gaze at him, as did **J**, Acts 3:4
While he clung to Peter and **J**, all the Acts 3:11
and Caiaphas and **J** and Alexander, Acts 4:6
they saw the boldness of Peter and **J**, Acts 4:13
But Peter and **J** answered them, Acts 4:19
of God, they sent to them Peter and **J**, Acts 8:14
after the baptism that **J** proclaimed: Acts 10:37
how he said, '**J** baptized with water, Acts 11:16
James the brother of **J** with the sword, Acts 12:2
the mother of **J** whose other name Acts 12:12
their service, bringing with them **J**, Acts 12:25
the Jews. And they had **J** to assist them. Acts 13:5
And **J** left them and returned to Acts 13:13
J had proclaimed a baptism of Acts 13:24
And as **J** was finishing his course, he Acts 13:25
to take with them **J** called Mark. Acts 15:37
he knew only the baptism of **J**. Acts 18:25
"**J** baptized with the baptism of Acts 19:4
and when James and Cephas and **J**, who Gal 2:9
by sending his angel to his servant **J**, Rv 1:1
J to the seven churches that are in Asia: Rv 1:4
J, your brother and partner in the Rv 1:9
J, am the one who heard and saw these Rv 22:8

JOHN'S (6)

Now **J** disciples and the Pharisees were Mk 2:18
"Why do **J** disciples and the disciples of Mk 2:18
executioner with orders to bring **J** head. Mk 6:27
When **J** messengers had gone, Jesus Lk 7:24
arose between some of **J** disciples and a Jn 3:25
baptized?" They said, "Into **J** baptism." Acts 19:3

JOIADA (4)

J the son of Paseah and Meshullam the Neh 3:6
of Eliashib, Eliashib the father of **J**, Neh 12:10
J the father of Jonathan, and Jonathan Neh 12:11
In the days of Eliashib, **J**, Johanan, Neh 12:22

JOIAKIM (4)

And Jeshua was the father of **J**, Neh 12:10
of Joiakim, **J** the father of Eliashib, Neh 12:10
And in the days of **J** were priests, Neh 12:12
were in the days of **J** the son of Jeshua Neh 12:26

JOIARIB (5)

leading men, and for **J** and Elnathan, Ezr 8:16
son of Hazaiah, son of Adaiah, son of **J**, Neh 11:5
priests: Jedaiah the son of **J**, Jachin, Neh 11:10
Shemaiah, **J**, Jedaiah, Neh 12:6
of **J**, Mattenai; of Jedaiah, Uzzi; Neh 12:19

JOIN (23)

they **j** our enemies and fight against us Ex 1:10
You shall not **j** hands with a wicked Ex 23:1
that they may **j** you and minister to Nm 18:2
They shall **j** you and keep guard over Nm 18:4
were called out to **j** Saul at Gilgal. 1 Sm 13:4
And my servants will **j** your servants, 1 Kgs 5:6
j with their brothers, their nobles, Neh 10:29
I could **j** words together against you and Jb 16:4
and do not **j** with those who do Prv 24:21
Woe to those who **j** house to house, who Is 5:8
and sojourners will **j** them and will Is 14:1
the foreigners who **j** themselves to the Is 56:6
house of Judah shall **j** the house of Israel, Jer 3:18
let us **j** ourselves to the LORD in an Jer 50:5
And **j** them one to another into one Ezk 37:17
And I will **j** with it the stick of Judah, Ezk 37:19
And many shall **j** themselves to them Dn 11:34
many nations shall **j** themselves to the Zec 2:11
None of the rest dared **j** them, but the Acts 5:13
to Philip, "Go over and **j** this chariot." Acts 8:29
he attempted to **j** the disciples. Acts 9:26
Brothers, **j** in imitating me, and keep Phil 3:17
when you do not **j** them in the same 1 Pt 4:4

JOINED (36)

And all these **j** forces in the Valley of Gn 14:3
and they **j** battle in the Valley of Siddim Gn 14:8
O my glory, be not **j** to their company. Gn 49:6
be separate beneath, but **j** at the top, Ex 26:24
its two edges, so that it may be **j** together. Ex 28:7
were separate beneath but **j** at the top, Ex 36:29
shoulder pieces, **j** to it at its two edges. Ex 39:4
And all these kings **j** their forces and Jos 11:5
and it was **j** to the house with timbers 1 Kgs 6:10
on the seventh day the battle was **j**. 1 Kgs 20:29
And all the people **j** in the covenant. 2 Kgs 23:3
to help me, my heart will be **j** to you; 1 Chr 12:17
was **j** to the wing of the first cherub. 2 Chr 3:12
king of Judah **j** with Ahaziah king 2 Chr 20:35
He **j** him in building ships to go to 2 Chr 20:36
"Because you have **j** with Ahaziah, 2 Chr 20:37
everyone who had **j** them and separated Ezr 6:21
And all the wall was **j** together to half its Neh 4:6
and their offspring and all who **j** them, Est 9:27
They are **j** one to another; they clasp Jb 41:17
Asshur also has **j** them; they are the Ps 83:8
But he who is **j** with all the living has Eccl 9:4
You will not be **j** with them in burial, Is 14:20
the foreigner who has **j** himself to the Is 56:3
Ephraim is **j** to idols; leave him alone. Hos 4:17
What therefore God has **j** together, let Mt 19:6
What therefore God has **j** together, let Mk 10:9
of men, about four hundred, **j** him. Acts 5:36
The crowd **j** in attacking them, and Acts 16:22
were persuaded and **j** Paul and Silas, Acts 17:4
But some men **j** him and believed, Acts 17:34
The Jews also **j** in the charge, Acts 24:9
that he who is **j** to a prostitute 1 Cor 6:16
But he who is **j** to the Lord becomes 1 Cor 6:17
the whole structure, being **j** together, Eph 2:21
j and held together by every joint with Eph 4:16

JOINT (4)

hip was put out of **j** as he wrestled with Gn 32:25
like water, and all my bones are out of **j**; Ps 22:14
held together by every **j** with which it is Eph 4:16
be put out of **j** but rather be healed. Heb 12:13

JOINTED (1)

eat those that have **j** legs above their Lv 11:21

JOINTS (2)

together through its **j** and ligaments, Col 2:19
of soul and of spirit, of **j** and of marrow, Heb 4:12

JOKDEAM (1)

Jezreel, **J**, Zanoah, Jos 15:56

JOKE (1)

Doing wrong is like a **j** to a fool, but Prv 10:23

JOKIM (1)

and **J**, and the men of Cozeba, and 1 Chr 4:22

JOKING (2)

his neighbor and says, "I am only **j**!" Prv 26:19
filthiness nor foolish talk nor crude **j**, Eph 5:4

JOKMEAM (2)

as far as the other side of **J**; 1 Kgs 4:12
J with its pasturelands, Beth-horon 1 Chr 6:68

JOKNEAM (3)

one; the king of **J** in Carmel, one; Jos 12:22
then the brook that is east of **J**. Jos 19:11
of Zebulun, **J** with its pasturelands, Jos 21:34

JOKSHAN (4)

She bore him Zimran, **J**, Medan, Gn 25:2
J fathered Sheba and Dedan. The sons of Gn 25:3
she bore Zimran, **J**, Medan, Midian, 1 Chr 1:32
The sons of **J**: Sheba and Dedan. 1 Chr 1:32

JOKTAN (6)

divided, and his brother's name was **J**. Gn 10:25
J fathered Almodad, Sheleph, Gn 10:26
and Jobab; all these were the sons of **J**. Gn 10:29
and his brother's name was **J**. 1 Chr 1:19
J fathered Almodad, Sheleph, 1 Chr 1:20
and Jobab; all these were the sons of **J**. 1 Chr 1:23

JOKTHEEL (2)

Dilean, Mizpeh, **J**, Jos 15:38
took Sela by storm, and called it **J**, 2 Kgs 14:7

JONADAB (12)

had a friend, whose name was **J**, 2 Sm 13:3
brother. And **J** was a very crafty man. 2 Sm 13:3
J said to him, "Lie down on your bed 2 Sm 13:5
But **J** the son of Shimeah, David's 2 Sm 13:32
And **J** said to the king, "Behold, the 2 Sm 13:35
drink no wine, for **J** the son of Rechab, Jer 35:6
obeyed the voice of **J** the son of Rechab, Jer 35:8
done all that **J** our father commanded Jer 35:10
The command that **J** the son of Rechab Jer 35:14
The sons of **J** the son of Rechab have Jer 35:16
the command of **J** your father and Jer 35:18
J the son of Rechab shall never lack a Jer 35:19

JONAH (28)

spoke by his servant **J** the son of 2 Kgs 14:25
of the LORD came to **J** the son of Amittai, Jon 1:1
But **J** rose to flee to Tarshish from the Jon 1:3
But **J** had gone down into the inner part Jon 1:5
us." So they cast lots, and the lot fell on **J**. Jon 1:7
So they picked up **J** and hurled him into Jon 1:15
appointed a great fish to swallow up **J**. Jon 1:17
And **J** was in the belly of the fish three Jon 1:17
Then **J** prayed to the LORD his God from Jon 2:1
and it vomited **J** out upon the dry land. Jon 2:10
of the LORD came to **J** the second time, Jon 3:1
So **J** arose and went to Nineveh, Jon 3:3
J began to go into the city, going a day's Jon 3:4
But it displeased **J** exceedingly, and he Jon 4:1
J went out of the city and sat to the east of Jon 4:5
a plant and made it come up over **J**, Jon 4:6
So **J** was exceedingly glad because of the Jon 4:6
down on the head of **J** so that he was Jon 4:8
But God said to **J**, "Do you do well to be Jon 4:9
to it except the sign of the prophet **J**. Mt 12:39
For just as **J** was three days and three Mt 12:40
for they repented at the preaching of **J**, Mt 12:41
something greater than **J** is here. Mt 12:41
it except the sign of **J**." So he left them Mt 16:4
will be given to it except the sign of **J**. Lk 11:29
For as **J** became a sign to the people of Lk 11:30
for they repented at the preaching of **J**, Lk 11:32
something greater than **J** is here. Lk 11:32

JONAM (1)

of Judah, the son of Joseph, the son of **J**, Lk 3:30

JONATHAN (120)

themselves, and **J** the son of Gershom, Jgs 18:30
a thousand were with **J** in Gibeah of 1 Sm 13:2
J defeated the garrison of the 1 Sm 13:3
And Saul and **J** his son and the 1 Sm 13:16
of any of the people with Saul and **J**, 1 Sm 13:22
but Saul and **J** his son had them. 1 Sm 13:22
One day **J** the son of Saul said to the 1 Sm 14:1
people did not know that **J** had gone. 1 Sm 14:3
by which **J** sought to go over to the 1 Sm 14:4
J said to the young man who carried 1 Sm 14:6

Then **J** said, "Behold, we will cross 1 Sm 14:8
the garrison hailed **J** and his 1 Sm 14:12
you a thing." And **J** said to his 1 Sm 14:12
Then **J** climbed up on his hands and 1 Sm 14:13
And they fell before **J**, and his 1 Sm 14:13
which **J** and his armor-bearer made, 1 Sm 14:14
J and his armor-bearer were not 1 Sm 14:17
Israelites who were with Saul and **J**. 1 Sm 14:21
But **J** had not heard his father charge 1 Sm 14:27
Then **J** said, "My father has troubled 1 Sm 14:29
saves Israel, though it be in **J** my son, 1 Sm 14:39
and I and **J** my son will be on the 1 Sm 14:40
If this guilt is in me or in **J** my son, O 1 Sm 14:41
give Thummim." And **J** and Saul 1 Sm 14:41
and my son **J**." And Jonathan was 1 Sm 14:42
my son Jonathan." And **J** was taken. 1 Sm 14:42
Then Saul said to **J**, "Tell me what 1 Sm 14:43
you have done." And **J** told him, 1 Sm 14:43
more also; you shall surely die, **J**." 1 Sm 14:44
the people said to Saul, "Shall **J** die, 1 Sm 14:45
this day." So the people ransomed **J**, 1 Sm 14:45
Now the sons of Saul were **J**, Ishvi, 1 Sm 14:49
the soul of **J** was knit to the soul of 1 Sm 18:1
and **J** loved him as his own soul. 1 Sm 18:1
Then **J** made a covenant with David, 1 Sm 18:3
And **J** stripped himself of the robe that 1 Sm 18:4
And Saul spoke to **J** his son and to all 1 Sm 19:1
that they should kill David. But **J**, 1 Sm 19:1
And **J** told David, "Saul my father 1 Sm 19:2
And **J** spoke well of David to Saul his 1 Sm 19:4
And Saul listened to the voice of **J**. 1 Sm 19:6
And **J** called David, and Jonathan 1 Sm 19:7
and **J** reported to him all these things. 1 Sm 19:7
And **J** brought David to Saul, and he 1 Sm 19:7
in Ramah and came and said before **J**, 1 Sm 20:1
and he thinks, 'Do not let **J** know this, 1 Sm 20:3
Then **J** said to David, "Whatever you 1 Sm 20:4
David said to **J**, "Behold, tomorrow is 1 Sm 20:5
And **J** said, "Far be it from you! If I 1 Sm 20:9
Then David said to **J**, "Who will tell 1 Sm 20:10
And **J** said to David, "Come, let us go 1 Sm 20:11
And **J** said to David, "The LORD, the 1 Sm 20:12
the LORD do so to **J** and more also if I 1 Sm 20:13
And **J** made a covenant with the 1 Sm 20:16
And **J** made David swear again by 1 Sm 20:17
Then **J** said to him, "Tomorrow is 1 Sm 20:18
J sat opposite, and Abner sat by 1 Sm 20:25
And Saul said to **J** his son, "Why has 1 Sm 20:27
J answered Saul, "David earnestly 1 Sm 20:28
Saul's anger was kindled against **J**, 1 Sm 20:30
Then **J** answered Saul his father, 1 Sm 20:32
So **J** knew that his father was 1 Sm 20:33
And **J** rose from the table in fierce 1 Sm 20:34
In the morning **J** went out into the 1 Sm 20:35
the place of the arrow that **J** had shot, 1 Sm 20:37
shot, **J** called after the boy and said, 1 Sm 20:37
And **J** called after the boy, "Hurry! Be 1 Sm 20:38
Only **J** and David knew the matter. 1 Sm 20:39
And **J** gave his weapons to his boy 1 Sm 20:40
Then **J** said to David, "Go in peace, 1 Sm 20:42
departed, and **J** went into the city. 1 Sm 20:42
And **J**, Saul's son, rose and went to 1 Sm 23:16
at Horesh, and **J** went home. 1 Sm 23:18
struck down **J** and Abinadab 1 Sm 31:2
and Saul and his son **J** are also dead." 2 Sm 1:4
know that Saul and his son **J** are dead?" 2 Sm 1:5
for Saul and for **J** his son and for 2 Sm 1:12
lamentation over Saul and **J** his son, 2 Sm 1:17
mighty, the bow of **J** turned not back, 2 Sm 1:22
"Saul and **J**, beloved and lovely! In life 2 Sm 1:23
"**J** lies slain on your high places. 2 Sm 1:25
I am distressed for you, my brother **J**; 2 Sm 1:26
J, the son of Saul, had a son who was 2 Sm 4:4
about Saul and **J** came from Jezreel, 2 Sm 4:4
to the king, "There is still a son of **J**; 2 Sm 9:3
And Mephibosheth the son of **J**, son of 2 Sm 9:6
kindness for the sake of your father **J**, 2 Sm 9:7
your son, and **J** the son of Abiathar. 2 Sm 15:27
there, Ahimaaz, Zadok's son, and **J**, 2 Sm 15:36
Now **J** and Ahimaaz were waiting at 2 Sm 17:17
are Ahimaaz and **J**?" And the 2 Sm 17:20
Mephibosheth, the son of Saul's son **J**, 2 Sm 21:7
between David and **J** the son of Saul. 2 Sm 21:7
bones of his son **J** from the men of 2 Sm 21:12
of Saul and the bones of his son **J**; 2 Sm 21:13
of Saul and his son **J** in the land of 2 Sm 21:14
he taunted Israel, **J** the son of Shimei, 2 Sm 21:21
the Shaalbonite, the sons of Jashen, **J**, 2 Sm 23:32
J the son of Abiathar the priest came. 1 Kgs 1:42
J answered Adonijah, "No, for our 1 Kgs 1:43
Shammai's brother: Jether and **J**; 1 Chr 2:32
The sons of **J**: Peleth and Zaza. These 1 Chr 2:33
father of Kish, Kish of Saul, Saul of **J**, 1 Chr 8:33
and the son of **J** was Merib-baal; and 1 Chr 8:34
Kish fathered Saul, Saul fathered **J**, 1 Chr 9:39
And the son of **J** was Merib-baal, and 1 Chr 9:40
struck down **J** and Abinadab 1 Chr 10:2
J the son of Shagee the Hararite, 1 Chr 11:34
he taunted Israel, **J** the son of Shimea, 1 Chr 20:7
the towers, was **J** the son of Uzziah; 1 Chr 27:25
J, David's uncle, was a counselor, 1 Chr 27:32
Of the sons of Adin, Ebed the son of **J**, and Ezr 8:6
Only **J** the son of Asahel and Jahzeiah Ezr 10:15
Joiada the father of **J**, and Jonathan Neh 12:11
Jonathan, and **J** the father of Jaddua. Neh 12:11
of Malluchi, **J**; of Shebaniah, Joseph; Neh 12:14
Zechariah the son of **J**, son of Neh 12:35
him in the house of **J** the secretary, Jer 37:15
me back to the house of **J** the secretary, Jer 37:20
me back to the house of **J** to die there.'" Jer 38:26

JONATHAN'S (2)
Do not stay!" So **J** boy gathered up 1 Sm 20:38
I may show him kindness for **J** sake?" 2 Sm 9:1

JOPPA (14)
with the territory over against **J**. Jos 19:46
and bring it to you in rafts by sea to **J**, 2 Chr 2:16
cedar trees from Lebanon to the sea, to **J**, Ezr 3:7
He went down to **J** and found a ship going Jon 1:3
Now there was in **J** a disciple named Acts 9:36
Since Lydda was near **J**, the disciples, Acts 9:38
it became known throughout all **J**, Acts 9:42
And he stayed in **J** for many days with Acts 9:43
now send men to **J** and bring one Acts 10:5
everything to them, he sent them to **J**. Acts 10:8
brothers from **J** accompanied him. Acts 10:23
Send therefore to **J** and ask for Simon Acts 10:32
"I was in the city of **J** praying, and in a Acts 11:5
'Send to **J** and bring Simon who is Acts 11:13

JORAH (1)
The sons of **J**, 112. Ezr 2:18

JORAI (1)
Michael, Meshullam, Sheba, **J**, Jacan, 1 Chr 5:13

JORAM (31)
Toi sent his son **J** to King David, to 2 Sm 8:10
And **J** brought with him articles of 2 Sm 8:10
In the fifth year of **J** the son of Ahab, 2 Kgs 8:16
Then **J** passed over to Zair with all his 2 Kgs 8:21
Now the rest of the acts of **J**, and all 2 Kgs 8:23
So **J** slept with his fathers and was 2 Kgs 8:24
the twelfth year of **J** the son of Ahab, 2 Kgs 8:25
He went with **J** the son of Ahab to 2 Kgs 8:28
and the Syrians wounded **J**. 2 Kgs 8:28
And King **J** returned to be healed in 2 Kgs 8:29
went down to see **J** the son of Ahab 2 Kgs 8:29
son of Nimshi conspired against **J**. 2 Kgs 9:14
(Now **J** with all Israel had been on 2 Kgs 9:14
but King **J** had returned to be healed 2 Kgs 9:15
and went to Jezreel, for **J** lay there. 2 Kgs 9:16
of Judah had come down to visit **J**. 2 Kgs 9:16
said, "I see a company." And **J** said, 2 Kgs 9:17
J said, "Make ready." And they made 2 Kgs 9:21
Then **J** king of Israel and Ahaziah 2 Kgs 9:21
And when **J** saw Jehu, he said, "Is it 2 Kgs 9:22
Then **J** reined about and fled, saying 2 Kgs 9:23
and shot **J** between the shoulders, 2 Kgs 9:24
the eleventh year of **J** the son of Ahab, 2 Kgs 9:29
Jehosheba, the daughter of King **J**, 2 Kgs 11:2
J his son, Ahaziah his son, Joash his 1 Chr 3:11
and his son Jeshaiah, and his son **J**, 1 Chr 26:25
And the Syrians wounded **J**, 2 Chr 22:5
went down to see **J** the son of Ahab 2 Chr 22:6
about through his going to visit **J**. 2 Chr 22:7
and Jehoshaphat the father of **J**, Mt 1:8
of Joram, and **J** the father of Uzziah, Mt 1:8

JORDAN (199)
and saw that the **J** Valley was well Gn 13:10
Lot chose for himself all the **J** Valley, Gn 13:11
for with only my staff I crossed this **J**, Gn 32:10
floor of Atad, which is beyond the **J**, Gn 50:10
Abel-mizraim; it is beyond the **J**. Gn 50:11
dwell by the sea, and along the **J**." Nm 13:29
plains of Moab beyond the **J** at Jericho. Nm 22:1
the plains of Moab by the **J** at Jericho, Nm 26:3
the plains of Moab by the **J** at Jericho. Nm 26:63
the plains of Moab by the **J** at Jericho. Nm 31:12
possession. Do not take us across the **J**." Nm 32:5
on the other side of the **J** and beyond, Nm 32:19
to us on this side of the **J** to the east." Nm 32:19
will pass over the **J** before the LORD, Nm 32:21
with you over the **J** and the land shall Nm 32:29
shall remain with us beyond the **J**." Nm 32:32
the plains of Moab by the **J** at Jericho; Nm 33:48
camped by the **J** from Beth-jeshimoth Nm 33:49
the plains of Moab by the **J** at Jericho, Nm 33:50
you pass over the **J** into the land of Nm 33:51
And the border shall go down to the **J**, Nm 34:12
inheritance beyond the **J** east of Nm 34:15
the plains of Moab by the **J** at Jericho, Nm 35:1
When you cross the **J** into the land of Nm 35:10
shall give three cities beyond the **J**, Nm 35:14
the plains of Moab by the **J** at Jericho. Nm 36:13
to all Israel beyond the **J** in the wilderness, Dt 1:1
Beyond the **J**, in the land of Moab, Moses Dt 1:5
until I go over the **J** into the land that the Dt 2:29
of the Amorites who were beyond the **J**, Dt 3:8
the Arabah also, with the **J** as the border, Dt 3:17
LORD your God gives them beyond the **J**. Dt 3:20
over and see the good land beyond the **J**, Dt 3:25
your eyes, for you shall not go over this **J**. Dt 3:27
he swore that I should not cross the **J**, Dt 4:21
die in this land; I must not go over the **J**. Dt 4:22
that you are going over the **J** to possess. Dt 4:26
apart three cities in the east beyond the **J**, Dt 4:41
beyond the **J** in the valley opposite Dt 4:46
who lived to the east beyond the **J**; Dt 4:47
on the east side of the **J** as far as the Sea of Dt 4:49
you are to cross over the **J** today, to go in to Dt 9:1
Are they not beyond the **J**, west of the Dt 11:30
are to cross over the **J** to go in to take Dt 11:31
when you go over the **J** and live in the Dt 12:10
day you cross over the **J** to the land that Dt 27:2
And when you have crossed over the **J**, Dt 27:4
"When you have crossed over the **J**, Dt 27:12
are going over the **J** to enter and possess. Dt 30:18
said to me, 'You shall not go over this **J**.' Dt 31:2
that you are going over the **J** to possess." Dt 31:13
that you are going over the **J** to possess." Dt 32:47
Now therefore arise, go over this **J**, you Jos 1:2
you are to pass over this **J** to go in to take Jos 1:11
land that Moses gave you beyond the **J**, Jos 1:14
you beyond the **J** toward the sunrise." Jos 1:15
on the way to the **J** as far as the fords. Jos 2:7
of the Amorites who were beyond the **J**, Jos 2:10
And they came to the **J**, he and all the Jos 3:1
come to the brink of the waters of the **J**, Jos 3:8
the Jordan, you shall stand still in the **J**.'" Jos 3:8
is passing over before you into the **J**. Jos 3:11
the earth, shall rest in the waters of the **J**, Jos 3:13
the waters of the **J** shall be cut off from Jos 3:13
to pass over the **J** with the priests bearing Jos 3:14
bearing the ark had come as far as the **J**, Jos 3:15
the water (now the **J** overflows all its Jos 3:15
on dry ground in the midst of the **J**, Jos 3:17
all the nation finished passing over the **J**. Jos 3:17
the nation had finished passing over the **J**, Jos 4:1
stones from here out of the midst of the **J**, Jos 4:3
the LORD your God into the midst of the **J**, Jos 4:5
that the waters of the **J** were cut off before Jos 4:7
When it passed over the **J**, the waters of Jos 4:7
the Jordan, the waters of the **J** were cut off. Jos 4:7
up twelve stones out of the midst of the **J**, Jos 4:8
set up twelve stones in the midst of the **J**, Jos 4:9
the midst of the **J** until everything was Jos 4:10
of the testimony to come up out of the **J**." Jos 4:16
the priests, "Come up out of the **J**." Jos 4:17
LORD came up from the midst of the **J**, Jos 4:18
the waters of the **J** returned to their place Jos 4:18
came up out of the **J** on the tenth day of Jos 4:19
stones, which they took out of the **J**, Jos 4:20
'Israel passed over this **J** on dry ground.' Jos 4:22
up the waters of the **J** for you until you Jos 4:23
who were beyond the **J** to the west, Jos 5:1
up the waters of the **J** for the people of Jos 5:1
you brought this people over the **J** at all, Jos 7:7
had been content to dwell beyond the **J**! Jos 7:7
who were beyond the **J** in the hill country Jos 9:1
of the Amorites who were beyond the **J**, Jos 9:10
land beyond the **J** toward the sunrise, Jos 12:1
of Israel defeated on the west side of the **J**, Jos 12:7
Moses gave them, beyond the **J** eastward, Jos 13:8
of Reuben was the **J** as a boundary. Jos 13:23
Heshbon, having the **J** as a boundary, Jos 13:27
of Chinnereth, eastward beyond the **J**. Jos 13:27
of Moab, beyond the **J** east of Jericho. Jos 13:32
the two and one-half tribes beyond the **J**, Jos 14:3
is the Salt Sea, to the mouth of the **J**. Jos 15:5
the bay of the sea at the mouth of the **J**. Jos 15:5
of Joseph went from the **J** by Jericho, Jos 16:1
and touches Jericho, ending at the **J**. Jos 16:7
which is on the other side of the **J**, Jos 17:5
their inheritance beyond the **J** eastward, Jos 18:7
side their boundary began at the **J**. Jos 18:12
of the Salt Sea, at the south end of the **J**: Jos 18:19
The **J** forms its boundary on the Jos 18:20
boundary ends at the **J**—sixteen cities Jos 19:22
as far as Lakkum, and it ended at the **J**. Jos 19:33
the west and Judah on the east at the **J**. Jos 19:34
And beyond the **J** east of Jericho, they Jos 20:8
LORD gave you on the other side of the **J**. Jos 22:4
their brothers in the land west of the **J**. Jos 22:7
to the region of the **J** that is in the land Jos 22:10
Manasseh built there an altar by the **J**, Jos 22:10

of Canaan, in the region about the **J**, Jos 22:11
has made the **J** a boundary between Jos 22:25
from the **J** to the Great Sea in the west. Jos 23:4
who lived on the other side of the **J**. Jos 24:8
you went over the **J** and came to Jos 24:11
the fords of the **J** against the Moabites Jgs 3:28
Gilead stayed beyond the **J**; and Dan, Jgs 5:17
and they crossed the **J** and encamped in Jgs 6:33
and also the **J**." So all the men of Jgs 7:24
as far as Beth-barah, and also the **J**. Jgs 7:24
of Oreb and Zeeb to Gideon across the **J**. Jgs 7:25
Gideon came to the **J** and crossed over, Jgs 8:4
who were beyond the **J** in the land of Jgs 10:8
Ammonites crossed the **J** to fight also Jgs 10:9
the Arnon to the Jabbok and to the **J**; Jgs 11:13
and from the wilderness to the **J**. Jgs 11:22
fords of the **J** against the Ephraimites. Jgs 12:5
and slaughtered him at the fords of the **J**. Jgs 12:6
crossed the fords of the **J** to the land of 1 Sm 13:7
and those beyond the **J** saw that the 1 Sm 31:7
They crossed the **J**, and marching the 2 Sm 2:29
and crossed the **J** and came to 2 Sm 10:17
were with him, arrived weary at the **J**. 2 Sm 16:14
with him, and they crossed the **J**. 2 Sm 17:22
was left who had not crossed the **J**. 2 Sm 17:22
Absalom crossed the **J** with all the 2 Sm 17:24
So the king came back to the **J**, and 2 Sm 19:15
king and to bring the king over the **J**. 2 Sm 19:15
rushed down to the **J** before the king, 2 Sm 19:17
king, as he was about to cross the **J**, 2 Sm 19:18
and he went on with the king to the **J**, 2 Sm 19:31
the Jordan, to escort him over the **J**. 2 Sm 19:31
a little way over the **J** with the king. 2 Sm 19:36
Then all the people went over the **J**, 2 Sm 19:39
king and his household over the **J**, 2 Sm 19:41
steadfastly from the **J** to Jerusalem. 2 Sm 20:2
They crossed the **J** and began from 2 Sm 24:5
he came down to meet me at the **J**, 1 Kgs 2:8
the plain of the **J** the king cast them, 1 Kgs 7:46
brook Cherith, which is east of the **J**. 1 Kgs 17:3
the brook Cherith that is east of the **J**. 1 Kgs 17:5
LORD has sent me to the **J**." But he said, 2 Kgs 2:6
as they both were standing by the **J**. 2 Kgs 2:7
back and stood on the bank of the **J**. 2 Kgs 2:13
"Go and wash in the **J** seven times, 2 Kgs 5:10
dipped himself seven times in the **J**, 2 Kgs 5:14
Let us go to the **J** and each of us get 2 Kgs 6:2
And when they came to the **J**, they cut 2 Kgs 6:4
So they went after them as far as the **J**, 2 Kgs 7:15
from the **J** eastward, all the land of 2 Kgs 10:33
and beyond the **J** at Jericho, on the 1 Chr 6:78
at Jericho, on the east side of the **J**, 1 Chr 6:78
men who crossed the **J** in the first 1 Chr 12:15
of Manasseh from beyond the **J**, 1 Chr 12:37
and crossed the **J** and came to 1 Chr 19:17
Israel westward of the **J** for all the 1 Chr 26:30
the plain of the **J** the king cast them, 2 Chr 4:17
is confident though **J** rushes against his Jb 40:23
you from the land of **J** and of Hermon, Ps 42:6
The sea looked and fled; **J** turned back. Ps 114:3
What ails you, O sea, that you flee? O **J**, Ps 114:5
the way of the sea, the land beyond the **J**, Is 9:1
what will you do in the thicket of the **J**? Jer 12:5
the jungle of the **J** against a perennial Jer 49:19
the thicket of the **J** against a perennial Jer 50:44
along the **J** between Gilead and the Ezk 47:18
lions, for the thicket of the **J** is ruined! Zec 11:3
the region about the **J** were going out to Mt 3:5
they were baptized by him in the river **J**, Mt 3:6
Jesus came from Galilee to the **J** to John, Mt 3:13
the way of the sea, beyond the **J**, Mt 4:15
and Judea, and from beyond the **J**. Mt 4:25
entered the region of Judea beyond the **J**. Mt 19:1
were being baptized by him in the river **J**, Mk 1:5
Galilee and was baptized by John in the **J**. Mk 1:9
and from beyond the **J** and from around Mk 3:8
to the region of Judea and beyond the **J**, Mk 10:1
he went into all the region around the **J**, Lk 3:3
returned from the **J** and was led by the Lk 4:1
things took place in Bethany across the **J**, Jn 1:28
he who was with you across the **J**, Jn 3:26
away again across the **J** to the place Jn 10:40

JORIM (1)
of Joshua, the son of Eliezer, the son of **J**, Lk 3:29

JORKEAM (1)
fathered Raham, the father of **J**; 1 Chr 2:44

JOSECH (1)
the son of Semein, the son of **J**, Lk 3:26

JOSEPH (229)
And she called his name **J**, saying, Gn 30:24
As soon as Rachel had borne **J**, Jacob Gn 30:25
children, and Rachel and **J** last of all. Gn 33:2
And last **J** and Rachel drew near, and Gn 33:7
The sons of Rachel: **J** and Benjamin. Gn 35:24
J, being seventeen years old, was Gn 37:2
And **J** brought a bad report of them to Gn 37:2
Now Israel loved **J** more than any other Gn 37:3
Now **J** had a dream, and when he told it Gn 37:5
And Israel said to **J**, "Are not your Gn 37:13
go to Dothan.'" So **J** went after his Gn 37:17
So when **J** came to his brothers, they Gn 37:23
And they drew **J** up and lifted him out Gn 37:28
shekels of silver. They took **J** to Egypt. Gn 37:28
the pit and saw that **J** was not in the pit, Gn 37:29
him. **J** is without doubt torn to pieces." Gn 37:33
Now **J** had been brought down to Egypt, Gn 39:1
The LORD was with **J**, and he became a Gn 39:2
So **J** found favor in his sight and Gn 39:4
Now **J** was handsome in form and Gn 39:6
master's wife cast her eyes on **J** and said, Gn 39:7
And as she spoke to **J** day after day, he Gn 39:10
the LORD was with **J** and showed him Gn 39:21
of the prison put **J** in charge of all Gn 39:22
in the prison where **J** was confined. Gn 40:3
of the guard appointed **J** to be with them, Gn 40:4
When **J** came to them in the morning, Gn 40:6
to interpret them." And **J** said to them, Gn 40:8
told his dream to **J** and said to him, Gn 40:9
Then **J** said to him, "This is its Gn 40:12
was favorable, he said to **J**, Gn 40:16
And **J** answered and said, "This is its Gn 40:18
baker, as **J** had interpreted to them. Gn 40:22
chief cupbearer did not remember **J**, Gn 40:23
Then Pharaoh sent and called **J**, and Gn 41:14
And Pharaoh said to **J**, "I have had a Gn 41:15
J answered Pharaoh, "It is not in me; Gn 41:16
Then Pharaoh said to **J**, "Behold, in my Gn 41:17
Then **J** said to Pharaoh, "The dreams Gn 41:25
Then Pharaoh said to **J**, "Since God Gn 41:39
And Pharaoh said to **J**, "See, I have set Gn 41:41
Moreover, Pharaoh said to **J**, "I am Gn 41:44
So **J** went out over the land of Egypt. Gn 41:45
J was thirty years old when he entered Gn 41:46
And **J** went out from the presence of Gn 41:46
And **J** stored up grain in great Gn 41:49
famine came, two sons were born to **J**. Gn 41:50
J called the name of the firstborn Gn 41:51
of famine began to come, as **J** had said. Gn 41:54
said to all the Egyptians, "Go to **J**. Gn 41:55
J opened all the storehouses and sold to Gn 41:56
earth came to Egypt to **J** to buy grain, Gn 41:57
Now **J** was governor over the land. He Gn 42:6
J saw his brothers and recognized them, Gn 42:7
And **J** recognized his brothers, but they Gn 42:8
And **J** remembered the dreams that he Gn 42:9
But **J** said to them, "It is as I said to you. Gn 42:14
On the third day **J** said to them, "Do Gn 42:18
did not know that **J** understood them, Gn 42:23
And **J** gave orders to fill their bags with Gn 42:25
J is no more, and Simeon is no more, Gn 42:36
went down to Egypt and stood before **J**. Gn 43:15
When **J** saw Benjamin with them, he Gn 43:16
The man did as **J** told him and Gn 43:17
When **J** came home, they brought into Gn 43:26
Then **J** hurried out, for his compassion Gn 43:30
for the grain." And he did as **J** told him. Gn 44:2
Now **J** said to his steward, "Up, follow Gn 44:4
J said to them, "What deed is this that Gn 44:15
Then **J** could not control himself before Gn 45:1
with him when **J** made himself known Gn 45:1
And **J** said to his brothers, "I am Joseph! Gn 45:3
And Joseph said to his brothers, "I am **J**! Gn 45:3
So **J** said to his brothers, "Come near to Gn 45:4
brother, **J**, whom you sold into Egypt. Gn 45:4
and say to him, 'Thus says your son **J**, Gn 45:9
And Pharaoh said to **J**, "Say to your Gn 45:17
And you, **J**, are commanded to say, 'Do Gn 45:19
and **J** gave them wagons, according to Gn 45:21
And they told him, "**J** is still alive, and Gn 45:26
when they told him all the words of **J**, Gn 45:27
saw the wagons that **J** had sent to carry Gn 45:27
"It is enough; **J** my son is still alive. Gn 45:28
Rachel, Jacob's wife: **J** and Benjamin. Gn 46:19
And to **J** in the land of Egypt were born Gn 46:20
And the sons of **J**, who were born to Gn 46:27
ahead of him to **J** to show the way Gn 46:28
Then **J** prepared his chariot and went Gn 46:29
Israel said to **J**, "Now let me die, since I Gn 46:30
J said to his brothers and to his father's Gn 46:31
So **J** went in and told Pharaoh, "My Gn 47:1
Then Pharaoh said to **J**, "Your father Gn 47:5
Then **J** brought in Jacob his father and Gn 47:7
Then **J** settled his father and his Gn 47:11
And **J** provided his father, his brothers, Gn 47:12
And **J** gathered up all the money that Gn 47:14
And **J** brought the money into Gn 47:14
all the Egyptians came to **J** and said, Gn 47:15
And **J** answered, "Give your livestock, Gn 47:16
So they brought their livestock to **J**, Gn 47:17
and **J** gave them food in exchange for Gn 47:17
So **J** bought all the land of Egypt for Gn 47:20
Then **J** said to the people, "Behold, I Gn 47:23
So **J** made it a statute concerning the Gn 47:26
die, he called his son **J** and said to him, Gn 47:29
After this, **J** was told, "Behold, your Gn 48:1
"Your son **J** has come to you." Then Gn 48:2
And Jacob said to **J**, "God Almighty Gn 48:3
J said to his father, "They are my sons, Gn 48:9
So **J** brought them near him, and he Gn 48:10
And Israel said to **J**, "I never expected to Gn 48:11
Then **J** removed them from his knees, Gn 48:12
And **J** took them both, Ephraim in his Gn 48:13
And he blessed **J** and said, "The God Gn 48:15
When **J** saw that his father laid his Gn 48:17
And **J** said to his father, "Not this way, Gn 48:18
Then Israel said to **J**, "Behold, I am Gn 48:21
"**J** is a fruitful bough, a fruitful bough Gn 49:22
May they be on the head of **J**, and on Gn 49:26
Then **J** fell on his father's face and wept Gn 50:1
And **J** commanded his servants the Gn 50:2
J spoke to the household of Pharaoh, Gn 50:4
So **J** went up to bury his father. With Gn 50:7
as well as all the household of **J**, his Gn 50:8
J returned to Egypt with his brothers Gn 50:14
"It may be that **J** will hate us and pay Gn 50:15
So they sent a message to **J**, saying, Gn 50:16
'Say to **J**, Please forgive the Gn 50:17
God of your father." **J** wept when they Gn 50:17
But **J** said to them, "Do not fear, for am Gn 50:19
So **J** remained in Egypt, he and his Gn 50:22
his father's house. **J** lived 110 years. Gn 50:22
And **J** saw Ephraim's children of the Gn 50:23
And **J** said to his brothers, "I am about Gn 50:24
Then **J** made the sons of Israel swear, Gn 50:25
So **J** died, being 110 years old. They Gn 50:26
seventy persons; **J** was already in Egypt. Ex 1:5
Then **J** died, and all his brothers and all Ex 1:6
new king over Egypt, who did not know **J**. Ex 1:8
Moses took the bones of **J** with him, for Ex 13:19
for **J** had made the sons of Israel Ex 13:19
from the sons of **J**, from Ephraim, Nm 1:10
Of the people of **J**, namely, of the people Nm 1:32
the tribe of Issachar, Igal the son of **J**; Nm 13:7
from the tribe of **J** (that is, from the Nm 13:11
The sons of **J** according to their clans: Nm 26:28
are the sons of **J** according to their Nm 26:37
the clans of Manasseh the son of **J**. Nm 27:1
half-tribe of Manasseh the son of **J**, Nm 32:33
Of the people of **J**: of the tribe of the Nm 34:23
from the clans of the people of **J**, Nm 36:1
"The tribe of the people of **J** is right. Nm 36:5
of the people of Manasseh the son of **J**, Nm 36:12
Levi, Judah, Issachar, **J**, and Benjamin. Dt 27:12
And of **J** he said, "Blessed by the LORD be Dt 33:13
May these rest on the head of **J**, on the Dt 33:16
For the people of **J** were two tribes, Jos 14:4
of the people of **J** went from the Jordan Jos 16:1
The people of **J**, Manasseh and Ephraim, Jos 16:4
Manasseh, for he was the firstborn of **J**. Jos 17:1
descendants of Manasseh the son of **J**, Jos 17:2
Then the people of **J** spoke to Joshua, Jos 17:14
The people of **J** said, "The hill country Jos 17:16
Then Joshua said to the house of **J**, to Jos 17:17
and the house of **J** shall continue in Jos 18:5
the people of Judah and the people of **J**. Jos 18:11
As for the bones of **J**, which the people Jos 24:32
an inheritance of the descendants of **J**. Jos 24:32
The house of **J** also went up against Jgs 1:22
And the house of **J** scouted out Bethel. Jgs 1:23
of the house of **J** rested heavily on them, Jgs 1:35
of all the house of **J** to come down to 2 Sm 19:20
all the forced labor of the house of **J**. 1 Kgs 11:28
Dan, **J**, Benjamin, Naphtali, Gad, and 1 Chr 2:2
given to the sons of **J** the son of Israel, 1 Chr 5:1
him, yet the birthright belonged to **J**), 1 Chr 5:2
lived the sons of **J** the son of Israel. 1 Chr 7:29
Zaccur, **J**, Nethaniah, and 1 Chr 25:2
The first lot fell for Asaph to **J**; the 1 Chr 25:9
Shallum, Amariah, and **J**. Ezr 10:42
Malluchi, Jonathan; of Shebaniah, **J**; Neh 12:14
your people, the children of Jacob and **J**. Ps 77:15
He rejected the tent of **J**; he did not Ps 78:67
of Israel, you who lead **J** like a flock! Ps 80:1
made it a decree in **J** when he went out Ps 81:5
of them, **J**, who was sold as a slave. Ps 105:17
'For **J** (the stick of Ephraim) and all Ezk 37:16
to take the stick of **J** (that is in the Ezk 37:19
of Israel. **J** shall have two portions. Ezk 47:13
4,500 cubits, three gates, the gate of **J**, Ezk 48:32
he break out like fire in the house of **J**, Am 5:6
will be gracious to the remnant of **J**. Am 5:15
but are not grieved over the ruin of **J**! Am 6:6
be a fire, and the house of **J** a flame, Ob 1:18

of Judah, and I will save the house of **J**. Zec 10:6
Jacob the father of **J** the husband of Mt 1:16
mother Mary had been betrothed to **J**, Mt 1:18
And her husband **J**, being a just man Mt 1:19
him in a dream, saying, "**J**, son of David, Mt 1:20
When **J** woke from sleep, he did as the Mt 1:24
of the Lord appeared to **J** in a dream and Mt 2:13
Lord appeared in a dream to **J** in Egypt, Mt 2:19
brothers James and **J** and Simon and Mt 13:55
mother of James and **J** and the mother Mt 27:56
a rich man from Arimathea, named **J**, Mt 27:57
And **J** took the body and wrapped it in a Mt 27:59
J of Arimathea, a respected member of Mk 15:43
he was dead, he granted the corpse to **J**. Mk 15:45
And **J** bought a linen shroud, and Mk 15:46
betrothed to a man whose name was **J**, Lk 1:27
And **J** also went up from Galilee, from the Lk 2:4
went with haste and found Mary and **J**, Lk 2:16
age, being the son (as was supposed) of **J**, Lk 3:23
of Melchi, the son of Jannai, the son of **J**, Lk 3:24
of Simeon, the son of Judah, the son of **J**, Lk 3:30
Now there was a man named **J**, from Lk 23:50
wrote, Jesus of Nazareth, the son of **J**." Jn 1:45
the field that Jacob had given to his son **J** Jn 4:5
They said, "Is not this Jesus, the son of **J**, Jn 6:42
After these things **J** of Arimathea, who Jn 19:38
put forward two, **J** called Barsabbas, Acts 1:23
Thus **J**, who was also called by the Acts 4:36
"And the patriarchs, jealous of **J**, sold Acts 7:9
the second visit **J** made himself known Acts 7:13
And **J** sent and summoned Jacob his Acts 7:14
another king who did not know **J**. Acts 7:18
dying, blessed each of the sons of **J**, Heb 11:21
By faith **J**, at the end of his life, made Heb 11:22
of Zebulun, 12,000 from the tribe of **J**, Rv 7:8

JOSEPH'S (24)
Then they took **J** robe and slaughtered Gn 37:31
blessed the Egyptian's house for **J** sake; Gn 39:5
So he left all that he had in **J** charge, and Gn 39:6
And **J** master took him and put him Gn 39:20
to anything that was in **J** charge, Gn 39:23
from his hand and put it on **J** hand, Gn 41:42
Pharaoh called **J** name Gn 41:45
So ten of **J** brothers went down to buy Gn 42:3
Jacob did not send Benjamin, **J** brother, Gn 42:4
And **J** brothers came and bowed Gn 42:6
him and brought the men to **J** house. Gn 43:17
because they were brought to **J** house, Gn 43:18
to the steward of **J** house and spoke Gn 43:19
the men into **J** house and given Gn 43:24
the present for **J** coming at noon, Gn 43:25
were taken to them from **J** table, Gn 43:34
and his brothers came to **J** house, Gn 44:14
"**J** brothers have come," it pleased Gn 45:16
again, and **J** hand shall close your eyes." Gn 46:4
When Israel saw **J** sons, he said, "Who Gn 48:8
When **J** brothers saw that their father Gn 50:15
of Manasseh were counted as **J** own. Gn 50:23
And they said, "Is not this **J** son?" Lk 4:22
and **J** family became known to Acts 7:13

JOSES (3)
brother of James and **J** and Judas and Mk 6:3
mother of James the younger and of **J**, Mk 15:40
Mary the mother of **J** saw where he Mk 15:47

JOSHAH (1)
Jamlech, **J** the son of Amaziah, 1 Chr 4:34

JOSHAPHAT (2)
son of Maacah, and **J** the Mithnite, 1 Chr 11:43
Shebaniah, **J**, Nethanel, Amasai, 1 Chr 15:24

JOSHAVIAH (1)
the Mahavite, and Jeribai, and **J**, 1 Chr 11:46

JOSHBEKASHAH (2)
and Romamti-ezer, **J**, Mallothi, 1 Chr 25:4
to the seventeenth, to **J**, his sons and 1 Chr 25:24

JOSHEB-BASSHEBETH (1)
whom David had: **J** a Tahchemonite; 2 Sm 23:8

JOSHIBIAH (1)
Joel, Jehu the son of **J**, son of Seraiah, 1 Chr 4:35

JOSHUA (222)
So Moses said to **J**, "Choose for us men, Ex 17:9
So **J** did as Moses told him, and fought Ex 17:10
And **J** overwhelmed Amalek and his Ex 17:13
in a book and recite it in the ears of **J**, Ex 17:14
So Moses rose with his assistant **J**, and Ex 24:13
When **J** heard the noise of the people as Ex 32:17
camp, his assistant **J** the son of Nun, Ex 33:11
And **J** the son of Nun, the assistant of Nm 11:28
Moses called Hoshea the son of Nun **J**. Nm 13:16
And **J** the son of Nun and Caleb the Nm 14:6
son of Jephunneh and **J** the son of Nm 14:30
only **J** the son of Nun and Caleb the Nm 14:38
son of Jephunneh and **J** the son of Nm 26:65
said to Moses, "Take **J** the son of Nun, Nm 27:18
He took **J** and made him stand before Nm 27:22
the Kenizzite and **J** the son of Nm 32:12
the priest and to **J** the son of Nun Nm 32:28
Eleazar the priest and **J** the son of Nm 34:17
J the son of Nun, who stands before you, Dt 1:38
And I commanded **J** at that time, 'Your Dt 3:21
But charge **J**, and encourage and Dt 3:28
them, and **J** will go over at your head, Dt 31:3
Then Moses summoned **J** and said to Dt 31:7
Call **J** and present yourselves in the tent Dt 31:14
And Moses and **J** went and presented Dt 31:14
the LORD commissioned **J** the son of Dt 31:23
of the people, he and **J** the son of Nun. Dt 32:44
And **J** the son of Nun was full of the Dt 34:9
LORD, the LORD said to **J** the son of Nun, Jos 1:1
And **J** commanded the officers of the Jos 1:10
and the half-tribe of Manasseh **J** said, Jos 1:12
And they answered **J**, "All that you have Jos 1:16
And **J** the son of Nun sent two men Jos 2:1
over and came to **J** the son of Nun, Jos 2:23
And they said to **J**, "Truly the LORD has Jos 2:24
Then **J** rose early in the morning and Jos 3:1
Then **J** said to the people, "Consecrate Jos 3:5
And **J** said to the priests, "Take up the ark Jos 3:6
The LORD said to **J**, "Today I will begin to Jos 3:7
And **J** said to the people of Israel, "Come Jos 3:9
And **J** said, "Here is how you shall know Jos 3:10
passing over the Jordan, the LORD said to **J**, Jos 4:1
Then **J** called the twelve men from the Jos 4:4
And **J** said to them, "Pass on before the Jos 4:5
Israel did just as **J** commanded and took Jos 4:8
the people of Israel, just as the LORD told **J**. Jos 4:8
And **J** set up twelve stones in the midst of Jos 4:9
that the LORD commanded **J** to tell the Jos 4:10
to all that Moses had commanded **J**. Jos 4:10
that day the LORD exalted **J** in the sight of Jos 4:14
And the LORD said to **J**, Jos 4:15
So **J** commanded the priests, "Come up Jos 4:17
took out of the Jordan, **J** set up at Gilgal. Jos 4:20
At that time the LORD said to **J**, "Make flint Jos 5:2
So **J** made flint knives and circumcised Jos 5:3
is the reason why **J** circumcised them: Jos 5:4
up in their place, that **J** circumcised. Jos 5:7
And the LORD said to **J**, "Today I have Jos 5:9
When **J** was by Jericho, he lifted up his Jos 5:13
And **J** went to him and said to him, "Are Jos 5:13
Now I have come." And **J** fell on his face Jos 5:14
commander of the LORD'S army said to **J**, Jos 5:15
you are standing is holy." And **J** did so. Jos 5:15
And the LORD said to **J**, "See, I have given Jos 6:2
So **J** the son of Nun called the priests and Jos 6:6
And just as **J** had commanded the people, Jos 6:8
But **J** commanded the people, "You shall Jos 6:10
Then **J** rose early in the morning, and Jos 6:12
blown the trumpets, **J** said to the people, Jos 6:16
men who had spied out the land, **J** said, Jos 6:22
all who belonged to her, **J** saved alive. Jos 6:25
hid the messengers whom **J** sent to spy Jos 6:25
J laid an oath on them at that time, Jos 6:26
So the LORD was with **J**, and his fame was Jos 6:27
J sent men from Jericho to Ai, which is Jos 7:2
And they returned to **J** and said to him, Jos 7:3
Then **J** tore his clothes and fell to the Jos 7:6
And **J** said, "Alas, O Lord GOD, why have Jos 7:7
The LORD said to **J**, "Get up! Why have Jos 7:10
So **J** rose early in the morning and Jos 7:16
Then **J** said to Achan, "My son, give Jos 7:19
And Achan answered **J**, "Truly I have Jos 7:20
So **J** sent messengers, and they ran to the Jos 7:22
tent and brought them to **J** and to all the Jos 7:23
And **J** and all Israel with him took Jos 7:24
And **J** said, "Why did you bring trouble Jos 7:25
And the LORD said to **J**, "Do not fear and do Jos 8:1
So **J** and all the fighting men arose to go Jos 8:3
And **J** chose 30,000 mighty men of valor Jos 8:3
So **J** sent them out. And they went to the Jos 8:9
but **J** spent that night among the people. Jos 8:9
J arose early in the morning and Jos 8:10
city. But **J** spent that night in the valley. Jos 8:13
And **J** and all Israel pretended to be Jos 8:15
and as they pursued **J** they were drawn Jos 8:16
Then the LORD said to **J**, "Stretch out the Jos 8:18
into your hand." And **J** stretched out the Jos 8:18
And when **J** and all Israel saw that the Jos 8:21
took alive, and brought him near to **J**. Jos 8:23
But **J** did not draw back his hand with Jos 8:26
word of the LORD that he commanded **J**. Jos 8:27
So **J** burned Ai and made it forever a Jos 8:28
And at sunset **J** commanded, and they Jos 8:29
At that time **J** built an altar to the LORD, Jos 8:30
Moses commanded that **J** did not read Jos 8:35
as one to fight against **J** and Israel. Jos 9:2
of Gibeon heard what **J** had done to Jos 9:3
And they went to **J** in the camp at Gilgal Jos 9:6
They said to **J**, "We are your servants." Jos 9:8
are your servants." And **J** said to them, Jos 9:8
And **J** made peace with them and made a Jos 9:15
J summoned them, and he said to them, Jos 9:22
They answered **J**, "Because it was told to Jos 9:24
But **J** made them that day cutters of Jos 9:27
heard how **J** had captured Ai and had Jos 10:1
has made peace with **J** and with the Jos 10:4
men of Gibeon sent to **J** at the camp in Jos 10:6
So **J** went up from Gilgal, he and all the Jos 10:7
And the LORD said to **J**, "Do not fear Jos 10:8
So **J** came upon them suddenly, having Jos 10:9
At that time **J** spoke to the LORD in the Jos 10:12
So **J** returned, and all Israel with him, Jos 10:15
And it was told to **J**, "The five kings Jos 10:17
And **J** said, "Roll large stones against Jos 10:18
When **J** and the sons of Israel had Jos 10:20
people returned safe to **J** in the camp at Jos 10:21
Then **J** said, "Open the mouth of the Jos 10:22
when they brought those kings out to **J**, Jos 10:24
J summoned all the men of Israel and Jos 10:24
And **J** said to them, "Do not be afraid or Jos 10:25
And afterward **J** struck them and put Jos 10:26
going down of the sun, **J** commanded, Jos 10:27
J captured it on that day and struck it, Jos 10:28
Then **J** and all Israel with him passed Jos 10:29
Then **J** and all Israel with him passed Jos 10:31
And **J** struck him and his people, until Jos 10:33
Then **J** and all Israel with him passed Jos 10:34
Then **J** and all Israel with him went up Jos 10:36
Then **J** and all Israel with him turned Jos 10:38
So **J** struck the whole land, the hill Jos 10:40
And **J** struck them from Jos 10:41
And **J** captured all these kings and Jos 10:42
Then **J** returned, and all Israel with Jos 10:43
And the LORD said to **J**, "Do not be afraid Jos 11:6
So **J** and all his warriors came suddenly Jos 11:7
And **J** did to them just as the LORD said to Jos 11:9
And **J** turned back at that time and Jos 11:10
kings, and all their kings, **J** captured, Jos 11:12
except Hazor alone; that **J** burned. Jos 11:13
his servant, so Moses commanded **J**, Jos 11:15
commanded Joshua, and so **J** did. Jos 11:15
So **J** took all that land, the hill country Jos 11:16
J made war a long time with all those Jos 11:18
And **J** came at that time and cut off the Jos 11:21
J devoted them to destruction with their Jos 11:21
So **J** took the whole land, according to Jos 11:23
And **J** gave it for an inheritance to Jos 11:23
of the land whom **J** and the people of Jos 12:7
rises toward Seir (and **J** gave their land Jos 12:7
Now **J** was old and advanced in years, Jos 13:1
Eleazar the priest and **J** the son of Nun Jos 14:1
the people of Judah came to **J** at Gilgal. Jos 14:6
Then **J** blessed him, and he gave Jos 14:13
to the commandment of the LORD to **J**, Jos 15:13
Eleazar the priest and **J** the son of Nun Jos 17:4
Then the people of Joseph spoke to **J**, Jos 17:14
And **J** said to them, "If you are a Jos 17:15
Then **J** said to the house of Joseph, to Jos 17:17
So **J** said to the people of Israel, "How Jos 18:3
and **J** charged those who went to write Jos 18:8
Then they came to **J** to the camp at Jos 18:9
and **J** cast lots for them in Shiloh Jos 18:10
And there **J** apportioned the land to the Jos 18:10
inheritance among them to **J** the son of Jos 19:49
Eleazar the priest and **J** the son of Nun Jos 19:51
Then the LORD said to **J**, Jos 20:1
Eleazar the priest and to **J** the son of Nun Jos 21:1
At that time **J** summoned the Reubenites Jos 22:1
So **J** blessed them and sent them away, Jos 22:6
to the other half **J** had given a possession Jos 22:7
And when **J** sent them away to their Jos 22:7
and **J** was old and well advanced in Jos 23:1
J summoned all Israel, its elders and Jos 23:2
J gathered all the tribes of Israel to Jos 24:1
And **J** said to all the people, "Thus says Jos 24:2
But **J** said to the people, "You are not Jos 24:19
And the people said to **J**, "No, but we Jos 24:21
Then **J** said to the people, "You are Jos 24:22
And the people said to **J**, "The LORD our Jos 24:24
So **J** made a covenant with the people Jos 24:25
And **J** wrote these words in the Book of Jos 24:26
And **J** said to all the people, "Behold, Jos 24:27
So **J** sent the people away, every man to Jos 24:28
After these things **J** the son of Nun, the Jos 24:29
Israel served the LORD all the days of **J**, Jos 24:31
elders who outlived **J** and had known Jos 24:31
After the death of **J**, the people of Israel Jgs 1:1
When **J** dismissed the people, the people of Jgs 2:6
the people served the LORD all the days of **J**, Jgs 2:7
all the days of the elders who outlived **J**, Jgs 2:7
And **J** the son of Nun, the servant of the Jgs 2:8
of the nations that **J** left when he died, Jgs 2:21

he did not give them into the hand of **J**. Jgs 2:23
into the field of **J** of Beth-shemesh and 1 Sm 6:14
day in the field of **J** of Beth-shemesh. 1 Sm 6:18
which he spoke by **J** the son of Nun. 1 Kgs 16:34
of the gate of **J** the governor of the 2 Kgs 23:8
Nun his son, **J** his son. 1 Chr 7:27
of Judah, and to **J** the son of Jehozadak, Hg 1:1
of Shealtiel, and **J** the son of Jehozadak, Hg 1:12
and the spirit of **J** the son of Jehozadak, Hg 1:14
of Judah, and to **J** the son of Jehozadak, Hg 2:2
Be strong, O **J**, son of Jehozadak, the high Hg 2:4
Then he showed me **J** the high priest Zec 3:1
Now **J** was standing before the angel, Zec 3:3
the angel of the LORD solemnly assured **J**, Zec 3:6
Hear now, O **J** the high priest, you and Zec 3:8
on the stone that I have set before **J**, Zec 3:9
a crown, and set it on the head of **J**, Zec 6:11
the son of **J**, the son of Eliezer, the son of Lk 3:29
it in with **J** when they dispossessed Acts 7:45
For if **J** had given them rest, God would Heb 4:8

JOSIAH (55)
to the house of David, **J** by name, 1 Kgs 13:2
of the land made **J** his son king in 2 Kgs 21:24
and **J** his son reigned in his place. 2 Kgs 21:26
J was eight years old when he began 2 Kgs 22:1
In the eighteenth year of King **J**, the 2 Kgs 22:3
And as **J** turned, he saw the tombs 2 Kgs 23:16
And **J** removed all the shrines also of 2 Kgs 23:19
year of King **J** this Passover was 2 Kgs 23:23
J put away the mediums and the 2 Kgs 23:24
rest of the acts of **J** and all that he 2 Kgs 23:28
King **J** went to meet him, and 2 Kgs 23:29
the land took Jehoahaz the son of **J**, 2 Kgs 23:30
Eliakim the son of **J** king in the 2 Kgs 23:34
king in the place of **J** his father, 2 Kgs 23:34
Amon his son, **J** his son. 1 Chr 3:14
The sons of **J**: Johanan the firstborn, 1 Chr 3:15
of the land made **J** his son king in 2 Chr 33:25
J was eight years old when he began 2 Chr 34:1
And **J** took away all the 2 Chr 34:33
J kept a Passover to the LORD in 2 Chr 35:1
Then **J** contributed to the lay people, 2 Chr 35:7
to the command of King **J**. 2 Chr 35:16
such a Passover as was kept by **J**, 2 Chr 35:18
of the reign of **J** this Passover was 2 Chr 35:19
when **J** had prepared the temple, 2 Chr 35:20
on the Euphrates and **J** went out to 2 Chr 35:20
J did not turn away from him, 2 Chr 35:22
And the archers shot King **J**. And 2 Chr 35:23
Judah and Jerusalem mourned for **J**. 2 Chr 35:24
Jeremiah also uttered a lament for **J**; 2 Chr 35:25
have spoken of **J** in their laments 2 Chr 35:25
Now the rest of the acts of **J**, and his 2 Chr 35:26
Jehoahaz the son of **J** and made him 2 Chr 36:1
came in the days of **J** the son of Amon, Jer 1:2
also in the days of Jehoiakim the son of **J**, Jer 1:3
the eleventh year of Zedekiah, the son of **J**, Jer 1:3
The LORD said to me in the days of King **J**: Jer 3:6
LORD concerning Shallum the son of **J**, Jer 22:11
who reigned instead of **J** his father, Jer 22:11
concerning Jehoiakim the son of **J**, Jer 22:18
the fourth year of Jehoiakim the son of **J**, Jer 25:1
the thirteenth year of **J** the son of Amon, Jer 25:3
of the reign of Jehoiakim the son of **J**, Jer 26:1
of the reign of Zedekiah the son of **J**, Jer 27:1
in the days of Jehoiakim the son of **J**, Jer 35:1
the fourth year of Jehoiakim the son of **J**, Jer 36:1
to you, from the days of **J** until today. Jer 36:2
In the fifth year of Jehoiakim the son of **J**, Jer 36:9
Zedekiah the son of **J**, whom Jer 37:1
the fourth year of Jehoiakim the son of **J**, Jer 45:1
the fourth year of Jehoiakim the son of **J**, Jer 46:2
in the days of **J** the son of Amon, Zep 1:1
and go the same day to the house of **J**, Zec 6:10
father of Amos, and Amos the father of **J**, Mt 1:10
and **J** the father of Jechoniah and his Mt 1:11

JOSIPHIAH (1)
the sons of Bani, Shelomith the son of **J**, Ezr 8:10

JOSTLE (1)
They do not **j** one another; each marches Jl 2:8

JOTBAH (1)
the daughter of Haruz of **J**. 2 Kgs 21:19

JOTBATHAH (3)
from Hor-haggidgad and camped at **J**. Nm 33:33
they set out from **J** and camped at Nm 33:34
to Gudgodah, and from Gudgodah to **J**, Dt 10:7

JOTHAM (26)
But **J** the youngest son of Jerubbaal was Jgs 9:5
When it was told to **J**, he went and stood Jgs 9:7
And **J** ran away and fled and went to Jgs 9:21
came the curse of **J** the son of Jerubbaal. Jgs 9:57
And **J** the king's son was over the 2 Kgs 15:5
and **J** his son reigned in his place. 2 Kgs 15:7
the twentieth year of **J** the son of 2 Kgs 15:30
king of Israel, **J** the son of Uzziah, 2 Kgs 15:32
rest of the acts of **J** and all that he 2 Kgs 15:36
J slept with his fathers and was 2 Kgs 15:38
son of Remaliah, Ahaz the son of **J**, 2 Kgs 16:1
Regem, **J**, Geshan, Pelet, Ephah, and 1 Chr 2:47
his son, Azariah his son, **J** his son, 1 Chr 3:12
in the days of **J** king of Judah, 1 Chr 5:17
And **J** his son was over the king's 2 Chr 26:21
is a leper." And **J** his son reigned in 2 Chr 26:23
J was twenty-five years old when he 2 Chr 27:1
So **J** became mighty, because he 2 Chr 27:6
Now the rest of the acts of **J**, and all 2 Chr 27:7
And **J** slept with his fathers, and they 2 Chr 27:9
Jerusalem in the days of Uzziah, **J**, Ahaz, Is 1:1
In the days of Ahaz the son of **J**, son of Is 7:1
of Beeri, in the days of Uzziah, **J**, Ahaz, Hos 1:1
to Micah of Moresheth in the days of **J**, Mi 1:1
and Uzziah the father of **J**, and Jotham the Mt 1:9
father of Jotham, and **J** the father of Ahaz, Mt 1:9

JOURNEY (56)
the LORD had prospered his **j** or not. Gn 24:21
Jacob went on his **j** and came to the Gn 29:1
of three days' **j** between himself and Gn 30:36
Then Esau said, "Let us **j** on our way, Gn 33:12
and to give them provisions for the **j**. Gn 42:25
happen to him on the **j** that you are to Gn 42:38
and gave them provisions for the **j**. Gn 45:21
and provision for his father on the **j**. Gn 45:23
So Israel took his **j** with all that he had Gn 46:1
us go a three days' **j** into the wilderness, Ex 3:18
go a three days' **j** into the wilderness that Ex 5:3
must go three days' **j** into the wilderness Ex 8:27
touching a dead body, or is on a long **j**, Nm 9:10
and is not on a **j** fails to keep the Nm 9:13
the mount of the LORD three days' **j**. Nm 10:33
LORD went before them three days' **j**, Nm 10:33
about a day's **j** on this side and a day's Nm 11:31
side and a day's **j** on the other side, Nm 11:31
went a three days' **j** in the wilderness of Nm 33:8
It is eleven days' **j** from Horeb by the way Dt 1:2
Turn and take your **j**, and go to the hill Dt 1:7
and **j** into the wilderness in the direction Dt 1:40
set out on your **j** and go over the Valley Dt 2:24
go on your **j** at the head of the people, Dt 10:11
a **j** that I promised that you should Dt 28:68
in your hand for the **j** and go to meet Jos 9:11
as our food for the **j** on the day we set Jos 9:12
ours are worn out from the very long **j**." Jos 9:13
may know whether the **j** on which we Jgs 18:5
The **j** on which you go is under the eye Jgs 18:6
arise early in the morning for your **j**, Jgs 19:9
are holy even when it is an ordinary **j**. 1 Sm 21:5
Uriah, "Have you not come from a **j**? 2 Sm 11:10
is relieving himself, or he is on a **j**, 1 Kgs 18:27
went a day's **j** into the wilderness 1 Kgs 19:4
and eat, for the **j** is too great for you." 1 Kgs 19:7
to seek from him a safe **j** for ourselves, Ezr 8:21
is not at home; he has gone on a long **j**; Prv 7:19
great city, three days' **j** in breadth. Jon 3:3
began to go into the city, going a day's **j**. Jon 3:4
no bag for your **j**, nor two tunics nor Mt 10:10
"For it will be like a man going on a **j**, Mt 25:14
to take nothing for their **j** except a staff— Mk 6:8
And as he was setting out on his **j**, a Mk 10:17
It is like a man going on a **j**, when he Mk 13:34
to be in the group they went a day's **j**, Lk 2:44
he said to them, "Take nothing for your **j**, Lk 9:3
for a friend of mine has arrived on a **j**, Lk 11:6
he had and took a **j** into a far country, Lk 15:13
so Jesus, wearied as he was from his **j**, was Jn 4:6
Jerusalem, a Sabbath day's **j** away. Acts 1:12
were on their **j** and approaching the Acts 10:9
ended, we departed and went on our **j**, Acts 21:5
to be helped on my **j** there by you, Rom 15:24
so that you may help me on my **j**, 1 Cor 16:6
send them on their **j** in a manner 3 Jn 1:6

JOURNEYED (22)
And Abram **j** on, still going toward the Gn 12:9
And he **j** on from the Negeb as far as Gn 13:3
all the Jordan Valley, and Lot **j** east. Gn 13:11
From there Abraham **j** toward the Gn 20:1
But Jacob **j** to Succoth, and built Gn 33:17
And as they **j**, a terror from God fell Gn 35:5
Then they **j** from Bethel. When they Gn 35:16
Israel **j** on and pitched his tent beyond Gn 35:21
the people of Israel **j** from Rameses to Ex 12:37
the people **j** to Hazeroth, Nm 11:35
And they **j** from Kadesh, and the Nm 20:22
"Then we turned and **j** into the wilderness Dt 2:1
people of Israel **j** from Beeroth Dt 10:6
From there they **j** to Gudgodah, and Dt 10:7
"Then they **j** through the wilderness Jgs 11:18
And as he **j**, he came to the hill country Jgs 17:8
They **j** to the entrance of Gedor, to the 1 Chr 4:39
You **j** to the king with oil and multiplied Is 57:9
But a Samaritan, as he **j**, came to where Lk 10:33
and I **j** toward Damascus to take those Acts 22:5
this connection I **j** to Damascus with Acts 26:12
around me and those who **j** with me. Acts 26:13

JOURNEYING (1)
teaching and **j** toward Jerusalem. Lk 13:22

JOURNEYS (3)
Throughout all their **j**, whenever the Ex 40:36
house of Israel throughout all their **j**. Ex 40:38
on frequent **j**, in danger from rivers, 2 Cor 11:26

JOY (179)
saw him, he came with **j** to meet him. Jgs 19:3
with tambourines, with songs of **j**, 1 Sm 18:6
on pipes, and rejoicing with great **j**, 1 Kgs 1:40
and sheep, for there was **j** in Israel. 1 Chr 12:40
and cymbals, to raise sounds of **j**. 1 Chr 15:16
him; strength and **j** are in his place. 1 Chr 16:27
the forest sing for **j** before the LORD, 1 Chr 16:33
head, returning to Jerusalem with **j**, 2 Chr 20:27
So there was great **j** in Jerusalem, for 2 Chr 30:26
laid, though many shouted aloud for **j**, Ezr 3:12
dedication of this house of God with **j**. Ezr 6:16
of Unleavened Bread seven days with **j**, Ezr 6:22
for the **j** of the LORD is your strength." Neh 8:10
had made them rejoice with great **j**; Neh 12:43
And the **j** of Jerusalem was heard far Neh 12:43
had light and gladness and **j** and honor. Est 8:16
was gladness and **j** among the Jews, Est 8:17
Behold, this is the **j** of his way, and out of Jb 8:19
and the **j** of the godless but for a Jb 20:5
I caused the widow's heart to sing for **j**. Jb 29:13
he sees his face with a shout of **j**, and he Jb 33:26
and all the sons of God shouted for **j**? Jb 38:7
You have put more **j** in my heart than Ps 4:7
let them ever sing for **j**, and spread your Ps 5:11
in your presence there is fullness of **j**; Ps 16:11
like a strong man, runs its course with **j**. Ps 19:5
May we shout for **j** over your salvation, Ps 20:5
him glad with the **j** of your presence. Ps 21:6
in his tent sacrifices with shouts of **j**; Ps 27:6
the night, but **j** comes with the morning. Ps 30:5
rejoice, O righteous, and shout for **j**, Ps 32:11
Shout for **j** in the LORD, O you righteous! Ps 33:1
righteousness shout for **j** and be glad Ps 35:27
the altar of God, to God my exceeding **j**, Ps 43:4
With **j** and gladness they are led along Ps 45:15
Shout to God with loud songs of **j**! Ps 47:1
in elevation, is the **j** of all the earth, Ps 48:2
Let me hear **j** and gladness; let the bones Ps 51:8
Restore to me the **j** of your salvation, Ps 51:12
the shadow of your wings I will sing for **j**. Ps 63:7
morning and the evening to shout for **j**. Ps 65:8
the hills gird themselves with **j**, Ps 65:12
they shout and sing together for **j**. Ps 65:13
Shout for **j** to God, all the earth; Ps 66:1
Let the nations be glad and sing for **j**, for Ps 67:4
before God; they shall be jubilant with **j**! Ps 68:3
My lips will shout for **j**, when I sing Ps 71:23
strength; shout for **j** to the God of Jacob! Ps 81:1
and flesh sing for **j** to the living God. Ps 84:2
at the works of your hands I sing for **j**. Ps 92:4
shall all the trees of the forest sing for **j** Ps 96:12
righteous, and **j** for the upright in heart. Ps 97:11
hands; let the hills sing for **j** together Ps 98:8
So he brought his people out with **j**, Ps 105:43
and tell of his deeds in songs of **j**! Ps 107:22
forever, for they are the **j** of my heart. Ps 119:111
and our tongue with shouts of **j**; Ps 126:2
sow in tears shall reap with shouts of **j**! Ps 126:5
shall come home with shouts of **j**, Ps 126:6
and let your saints shout for **j**. Ps 132:9
and her saints will shout for **j**. Ps 132:16
not set Jerusalem above my highest **j**! Ps 137:6
glory; let them sing for **j** on their beds. Ps 149:5
The hope of the righteous brings **j**, but Prv 10:28
evil, but those who plan peace have **j**. Prv 12:20
bitterness, and no stranger shares its **j**. Prv 14:10
ache, and the end of **j** may be grief. Prv 14:13
Folly is a **j** to him who lacks sense, Prv 15:21
To make an apt answer is a **j** to a man, Prv 15:23
and the father of a fool has no **j**. Prv 17:21
it is a **j** to the righteous but terror to Prv 21:15
given wisdom and knowledge and **j**, Eccl 2:26
keeps him occupied with **j** in his heart. Eccl 5:20
And I commend **j**, for man has no Eccl 8:15
Go, eat your bread in **j**, and drink your Eccl 9:7
the nation; you have increased its **j**; Is 9:3
rejoice before you as with **j** at the harvest, Is 9:3
With **j** you will draw water from the wells Is 12:3
Shout, and sing for **j**, O inhabitant of Is 12:6
And **j** and gladness are taken away from Is 16:10

and behold, **j** and gladness, killing oxen Is 22:13
for lack of wine; all **j** has grown dark; Is 24:11
They lift up their voices, they sing for **j**; Is 24:14
dwell in the dust, awake and sing for **j**! Is 26:19
meek shall obtain fresh **j** in the LORD, Is 29:19
become dens forever, a **j** of wild donkeys, Is 32:14
and rejoice with **j** and singing. Is 35:2
deer, and the tongue of the mute sing for **j**. Is 35:6
everlasting **j** shall be upon their heads; Is 35:10
they shall obtain gladness and **j**, and Is 35:10
let the habitants of Sela sing for **j**, let Is 42:11
Chaldea, declare this with a shout of **j**, Is 48:20
Sing for **j**, O heavens, and exult, O earth; Is 49:13
j and gladness will be found in her, Is 51:3
everlasting **j** shall be upon their heads; Is 51:11
they shall obtain gladness and **j**, and Is 51:11
lift up their voice; together they sing for **j**; Is 52:8
you shall go out in **j** and be led forth in Is 55:12
you majestic forever, a **j** from age to age. Is 60:15
portion; they shall have everlasting **j**. Is 61:7
for behold, I create Jerusalem to be a **j**, Is 65:18
LORD be glorified, that we may see your **j**'; Is 66:5
rejoice with her in **j**, all you who mourn Is 66:10
My **j** is gone; grief is upon me; my heart Jer 8:18
became to me a **j** and the delight of Jer 15:16
I will turn their mourning into **j**; I will Jer 31:13
And this city shall be to me a name of **j**, Jer 33:9
Gladness and **j** have been taken away Jer 48:33
no one treads them with shouts of **j**; Jer 48:33
of joy; the shouting is not the shout of **j**. Jer 48:33
city not forsaken, the city of my **j**? Jer 49:25
in them, shall sing for **j** over Babylon, Jer 51:48
of beauty, the **j** of all the earth?" Lam 2:15
The **j** of our hearts has ceased; our Lam 5:15
their stronghold, their **j** and glory, Ezk 24:25
with wholehearted **j** and utter Ezk 36:5
j and gladness from the house of our God? Jl 1:16
I will take **j** in the God of my salvation. Hab 3:18
of Judah seasons of **j** and gladness and Zec 8:19
they rejoiced exceedingly with great **j**. Mt 2:10
and immediately receives it with **j**, Mt 13:20
Then in his **j** he goes and sells all that Mt 13:44
much. Enter into the **j** of your master.' Mt 25:21
much. Enter into the **j** of your master.' Mt 25:23
from the tomb with fear and great **j**, Mt 28:8
the word, immediately receive it with **j**. Mk 4:16
And you will have **j** and gladness, and Lk 1:14
ears, the baby in my womb leaped for **j**. Lk 1:44
good news of a great **j** that will be for all Lk 2:10
Rejoice in that day, and leap for **j**, for Lk 6:23
they hear the word, receive it with **j**. Lk 8:13
The seventy-two returned with **j**, Lk 10:17
there will be more **j** in heaven over one Lk 15:7
there is **j** before the angels of God over Lk 15:10
still disbelieved for **j** and were Lk 24:41
and returned to Jerusalem with great **j**, Lk 24:52
Therefore this **j** of mine is now complete. Jn 3:29
spoken to you, that my **j** may be in you, Jn 15:11
be in you, and that your **j** may be full. Jn 15:11
but your sorrow will turn into **j**. Jn 16:20
for **j** that a human being has been born Jn 16:21
and no one will take your **j** from you. Jn 16:22
you will receive, that your **j** may be full. Jn 16:24
may have my **j** fulfilled in themselves. Jn 17:13
So there was much **j** in that city. Acts 8:8
in her **j** she did not open the gate but Acts 12:14
were filled with **j** and with the Acts 13:52
and brought great **j** to all the brothers. Acts 15:3
and peace and **j** in the Holy Rom 14:17
fill you with all **j** and peace in Rom 15:13
come to you with **j** and be refreshed Rom 15:32
but we work with you for your **j**, 2 Cor 1:24
that my **j** would be the joy of you all. 2 Cor 2:3
that my joy would be the **j** of you all. 2 Cor 2:3
our affliction, I am overflowing with **j**. 2 Cor 7:4
we rejoiced still more at the **j** of Titus, 2 Cor 7:13
their abundance of **j** and their extreme 2 Cor 8:2
But the fruit of the Spirit is love, **j**, peace, Gal 5:22
for you all making my prayer with **j**, Phil 1:4
all, for your progress and **j** in the faith, Phil 1:25
complete my **j** by being of the same Phil 2:2
So receive him in the Lord with all **j**, Phil 2:29
I love and long for, my **j** and crown, Phil 4:1
for all endurance and patience with **j**, Col 1:11
affliction, with the **j** of the Holy Spirit, 1 Thes 1:6
is our hope or **j** or crown of boasting 1 Thes 2:19
For you are our glory and **j**. 1 Thes 2:20
for all the **j** that we feel for your sake 1 Thes 3:9
to see you, that I may be filled with **j**. 2 Tm 1:4
have derived much **j** and comfort Phlm 1:7
who for the **j** that was set before him Heb 12:2
them do this with **j** and not with Heb 13:17
Count it all **j**, my brothers, when you Jas 1:2
turned to mourning and your **j** to gloom. Jas 4:9
and rejoice with **j** that is inexpressible 1 Pt 1:8
things so that our **j** may be complete. 1 Jn 1:4
to face, so that our **j** may be complete. 2 Jn 1:12
I have no greater **j** than to hear that my 3 Jn 1:4
the presence of his glory with great **j**, Jude 1:24

JOYFUL (19)

hands, so that you will be altogether **j**. Dt 16:15
went to their homes **j** and glad of 1 Kgs 8:66
j and glad of heart for the prosperity 2 Chr 7:10
the sound of the **j** shout from the sound Ezr 3:13
LORD had made them **j** and had turned Ezr 6:22
went out that day **j** and glad of heart. Est 5:9
that night be barren; let no **j** cry enter it. Jb 3:7
my mouth will praise you with **j** lips, Ps 63:5
let us make a **j** noise to the rock of our Ps 95:1
let us make a **j** noise to him with songs Ps 95:2
Make a **j** noise to the LORD, all the earth; Ps 98:4
the horn make a **j** noise before the King, Ps 98:6
Make a **j** noise to the LORD, all the earth! Ps 100:1
A **j** heart is good medicine, but a Prv 17:22
for them than to be **j** and to do good as Eccl 3:12
In the day of prosperity be **j**, and in the Eccl 7:14
the sun but to eat and drink and be **j**, Eccl 8:15
and make them **j** in my house of prayer; Is 56:7
and not of **j** shouting on the mountains. Ezk 7:7

JOYFULLY (4)

Then go **j** with the king to the feast." Est 5:14
meet him who **j** works righteousness, Is 64:5
and came down and received him **j**. Lk 19:6
and you **j** accepted the plundering of Heb 10:34

JOYFULNESS (1)

LORD your God with **j** and gladness of Dt 28:47

JOYOUS (3)

break forth into **j** song and sing praises! Ps 98:4
making her the **j** mother of children. Ps 113:9
for all the **j** houses in the exultant city. Is 32:13

JOYOUSLY (2)

here, offering freely and **j** to you. 1 Chr 29:17
Tabor and Hermon **j** praise your name. Ps 89:12

JOZABAD (10)

Jahaziel, Johanan, **J** of Gederah, 1 Chr 12:4
Adnah, **J**, Jediael, Michael, Jozabad, 1 Chr 12:20
Jozabad, Jediael, Michael, **J**, Elihu, 1 Chr 12:20
Nahath, Asahel, Jerimoth, **J**, Eliel, 2 Chr 31:13
and Hashabiah and Jeiel and **J**, 2 Chr 35:9
J the son of Jeshua and Noadiah the son Ezr 8:33
Ishmael, Nethanel, **J**, and Elasah. Ezr 10:22
J, Shimei, Kelaiah (that is, Kelita), Ezr 10:23
Maaseiah, Kelita, Azariah, **J**, Hanan, Neh 8:7
and Shabbethai and **J**, of the chiefs of Neh 11:16

JOZACAR (1)

It was **J** the son of Shimeath and 2 Kgs 12:21

JOZADAK (5)

Then arose Jeshua the son of **J**, with his Ezr 3:2
Jeshua the son of **J** made a beginning, Ezr 3:8
Jeshua the son of **J** arose and began to Ezr 5:2
of Jeshua the son of **J** and his brothers. Ezr 10:18
of Joiakim the son of Jeshua son of **J**, Neh 12:26

JUBAL (1)

His brother's name was **J**; he was the Gn 4:21

JUBILANT (2)

exult before God; they shall be **j** with joy! Ps 68:3
is stilled, the noise of the **j** has ceased, Is 24:8

JUBILEE (21)

It shall be a **j** for you, when each of you Lv 25:10
That fiftieth year shall be a **j** for you; in Lv 25:11
For it is a **j**. It shall be holy to you. You Lv 25:12
"In this year of **j** each of you shall Lv 25:13
to the number of years after the **j**, Lv 25:15
the hand of the buyer until the year of **j**. Lv 25:28
In the **j** it shall be released, and he shall Lv 25:28
it shall not be released in the **j**. Lv 25:30
and they shall be released in the **j**. Lv 25:31
they possess shall be released in the **j**. Lv 25:33
serve with you until the year of the **j**. Lv 25:40
sold himself to him until the year of **j**, Lv 25:50
but a few years until the year of **j**, Lv 25:52
him shall be released in the year of **j**. Lv 25:54
he dedicates his field from the year of **j**, Lv 27:17
but if he dedicates his field after the **j**, Lv 27:18
the years that remain until the year of **j**, Lv 27:18
But the field, when it is released in the **j**, Lv 27:21
of the valuation for it up to the year of **j**, Lv 27:23
In the year of **j** the field shall return to Lv 27:24
And when the **j** of the people of Israel Nm 36:4

JUCAL (1)

son of Pashhur, **J** the son of Shelemiah, Jer 38:1

JUDAH (845)

LORD." Therefore she called his name **J**. Gn 29:35
firstborn), Simeon, Levi, **J**, Issachar, Gn 35:23
Then **J** said to his brothers, "What Gn 37:26
at that time that **J** went down from his Gn 38:1
There **J** saw the daughter of a certain Gn 38:2
J was in Chezib when she bore him. Gn 38:5
And **J** took a wife for Er his firstborn, Gn 38:6
Then **J** said to Onan, "Go in to your Gn 38:8
Then **J** said to Tamar his Gn 38:11
In the course of time the wife of **J**, Gn 38:12
When **J** was comforted, he went up to Gn 38:12
When **J** saw her, he thought she was a Gn 38:15
When **J** sent the young goat by his Gn 38:20
So he returned to **J** and said, "I have not Gn 38:22
And **J** replied, "Let her keep the things Gn 38:23
About three months later **J** was told, Gn 38:24
pregnant by immorality." And **J** said, Gn 38:24
Then **J** identified them and said, "She is Gn 38:26
But **J** said to him, "The man solemnly Gn 43:3
And **J** said to Israel his father, "Send the Gn 43:8
When **J** and his brothers came to Gn 44:14
And **J** said, "What shall we say to my Gn 44:16
Then **J** went up to him and said, "O my Gn 44:18
The sons of **J**: Er, Onan, Shelah, Perez, Gn 46:12
He had sent **J** ahead of him to Joseph to Gn 46:28
"**J**, your brothers shall praise you; your Gn 49:8
J is a lion's cub; from the prey, my son, Gn 49:9
The scepter shall not depart from **J**, nor Gn 49:10
Reuben, Simeon, Levi, and **J**, Ex 1:2
son of Uri, son of Hur, of the tribe of **J**, Ex 31:2
son of Uri, son of Hur, of the tribe of **J**; Ex 35:30
son of Uri, son of Hur, of the tribe of **J**, Ex 38:22
from **J**, Nahshon the son of Nm 1:7
Of the people of **J**, their generations, by Nm 1:26
those listed of the tribe of **J** were 74,600. Nm 1:27
of the camp of **J** by their companies, Nm 2:3
of the people of **J** being Nahshon the son Nm 2:3
All those listed of the camp of **J**, by their Nm 2:9
the son of Amminadab, of the tribe of **J**. Nm 7:12
camp of the people of **J** set out first by Nm 10:14
from the tribe of **J**, Caleb the son of Nm 13:6
The sons of **J** were Er and Onan; and Nm 26:19
And the sons of **J** according to their Nm 26:20
are the clans of **J** as they were listed, Nm 26:22
Of the tribe of **J**, Caleb the son of Nm 34:19
Simeon, Levi, **J**, Issachar, Joseph, and Dt 27:12
And this he said of **J**: "Hear, O LORD, the Dt 33:7
"Hear, O LORD, the voice of **J**, and bring Dt 33:7
all the land of **J** as far as the western sea, Dt 34:2
of Zabdi, son of Zerah, of the tribe of **J**, Jos 7:1
by tribe, and the tribe of **J** was taken. Jos 7:16
And he brought near the clans of **J**, and Jos 7:17
of Zabdi, son of Zerah, of the tribe of **J**, Jos 7:18
and from all the hill country of **J**, Jos 11:21
Then the people of **J** came to Joshua at Jos 14:6
of the people of **J** according to their clans Jos 15:1
the people of **J** according to their Jos 15:12
a portion among the people of **J**, Jos 15:13
of the people of **J** according to their Jos 15:20
of the people of **J** in the extreme south, Jos 15:21
the people of **J** could not drive out, Jos 15:63
with the people of **J** at Jerusalem to this Jos 15:63
J shall continue in his territory on the Jos 18:5
between the people of **J** and the people of Jos 18:11
a city belonging to the people of **J**. Jos 18:14
of the inheritance of the people of **J**. Jos 19:1
part of the territory of the people of **J**. Jos 19:9
of the people of **J** was too large for Jos 19:9
Asher on the west and **J** on the east at Jos 19:34
(that is, Hebron) in the hill country of **J**. Jos 20:7
priest received by lot from the tribes of **J**, Jos 21:4
tribe of the people of **J** and the tribe of the Jos 21:9
that is Hebron, in the hill country of **J**, Jos 21:11
The LORD said, "**J** shall go up; behold, I Jgs 1:2
And **J** said to Simeon his brother, "Come Jgs 1:3
Then **J** went up and the LORD gave the Jgs 1:4
the men of **J** fought against Jerusalem Jgs 1:8
afterward the men of **J** went down to fight Jgs 1:9
And **J** went against the Canaanites who Jgs 1:10
up with the people of **J** from the city of Jgs 1:16
the city of palms into the wilderness of **J**, Jgs 1:16
And **J** went with Simeon his brother, Jgs 1:17
J also captured Gaza with its territory, Jgs 1:18
And the LORD was with **J**, and he took Jgs 1:19
fight also against **J** and against Jgs 10:9
up and encamped in **J** and made a raid Jgs 15:9
And the men of **J** said, "Why have you Jgs 15:10
Then 3,000 men of **J** went down to the Jgs 15:11
was a young man of Bethlehem in **J**, Jgs 17:7
of Bethlehem in Judah, of the family of **J**, Jgs 17:7
town of Bethlehem in **J** to sojourn where Jgs 17:8
to him, "I am a Levite of Bethlehem in **J**, Jgs 17:9
and encamped at Kiriath-jearim in **J**. Jgs 18:12
a concubine from Bethlehem in **J**. Jgs 19:1
to her father's house at Bethlehem in **J**, Jgs 19:2
from Bethlehem in **J** to the remote Jgs 19:18
I went to Bethlehem in **J**, and I am Jgs 19:18

And the LORD said, "**J** shall go up first." Jgs 20:18
man of Bethlehem in **J** went to sojourn in Ru 1:1
were Ephrathites from Bethlehem in **J**. Ru 1:2
went on the way to return to the land of **J**. Ru 1:7
house of Perez, whom Tamar bore to **J**, Ru 4:12
and the men of **J** thirty thousand. 1 Sm 11:8
on foot, and ten thousand men of **J**. 1 Sm 15:4
gathered at Socoh, which belongs to **J**, 1 Sm 17:1
of an Ephrathite of Bethlehem in **J**, 1 Sm 17:12
men of Israel and **J** rose with a shout 1 Sm 17:52
But all Israel and **J** loved David, for 1 Sm 18:16
into the land of **J**." So David departed 1 Sm 22:5
him, "Behold, we are afraid here in **J**; 1 Sm 23:3
out among all the thousands of **J**." 1 Sm 23:23
belonged to the kings of **J** to this day. 1 Sm 27:6
say, "Against the Negeb of **J**," or, 1 Sm 27:10
which belongs to **J** and against the 1 Sm 30:14
Philistines and from the land of **J**. 1 Sm 30:16
the spoil to his friends, the elders of **J**, 1 Sm 30:26
it should be taught to the people of **J**; 2 Sm 1:18
of the cities of **J**?" And the LORD said 2 Sm 2:1
And the men of **J** came, and there they 2 Sm 2:4
David king over the house of **J**. 2 Sm 2:4
and the house of **J** has anointed me 2 Sm 2:7
But the house of **J** followed David. 2 Sm 2:10
over the house of **J** was seven years 2 Sm 2:11
and said, "Am I a dog's head of **J**? 2 Sm 3:8
throne of David over Israel and over **J**, 2 Sm 3:10
he reigned over **J** seven years and 2 Sm 5:5
over all Israel and **J** thirty-three years. 2 Sm 5:5
ark and Israel and **J** dwell in booths, 2 Sm 11:11
gave you the house of Israel and of **J**. 2 Sm 12:8
the priests, "Say to the elders of **J**, 2 Sm 19:11
heart of all the men of **J** as one man, 2 Sm 19:14
and **J** came to Gilgal to meet the king 2 Sm 19:15
with the men of **J** to meet King 2 Sm 19:16
All the people of **J**, and also half the 2 Sm 19:40
the men of **J** stolen you away 2 Sm 19:41
All the men of **J** answered the men of 2 Sm 19:42
men of Israel answered the men of **J**, 2 Sm 19:43
of the men of **J** were fiercer than the 2 Sm 19:43
But the men of **J** followed their king 2 Sm 20:2
"Call the men of **J** together to me 2 Sm 20:4
So Amasa went to summon **J**, but he 2 Sm 20:5
his zeal for the people of Israel and **J**. 2 Sm 21:2
saying, "Go, number Israel and **J**." 2 Sm 24:1
out to the Negeb of **J** at Beersheba. 2 Sm 24:7
sword, and the men of **J** were 500,000. 2 Sm 24:9
sons, and all the royal officials of **J**, 1 Kgs 1:9
to be ruler over Israel and over **J**." 1 Kgs 1:35
Jether, commander of the army of **J**. 1 Kgs 2:32
J and Israel were as many as the sand 1 Kgs 4:20
And **J** and Israel lived in safety, from 1 Kgs 4:25
in the wilderness, in the land of **J**, 1 Kgs 9:18
of Israel who lived in the cities of **J**. 1 Kgs 12:17
of David but the tribe of **J** only. 1 Kgs 12:20
all the house of **J** and the tribe of 1 Kgs 12:21
the son of Solomon, king of **J**, 1 Kgs 12:23
to all the house of **J** and Benjamin, 1 Kgs 12:23
to their lord, to Rehoboam king of **J**, 1 Kgs 12:27
and return to Rehoboam king of **J**." 1 Kgs 12:27
month like the feast that was in **J**, 1 Kgs 12:32
of God came out of **J** by the word of 1 Kgs 13:1
of God who came from **J** had gone. 1 Kgs 13:12
God who came from **J**?" And he said, 1 Kgs 13:14
to the man of God who came from **J**, 1 Kgs 13:21
the son of Solomon reigned in **J**. 1 Kgs 14:21
And **J** did what was evil in the sight 1 Kgs 14:22
of the Chronicles of the Kings of **J**? 1 Kgs 14:29
Nebat, Abijam began to reign over **J**. 1 Kgs 15:1
of the Chronicles of the Kings of **J**? 1 Kgs 15:7
of Israel, Asa began to reign over **J**, 1 Kgs 15:9
went up against **J** and built Ramah, 1 Kgs 15:17
to go out or come in to Asa king of **J**. 1 Kgs 15:17
Asa made a proclamation to all **J**, 1 Kgs 15:22
of the Chronicles of the Kings of **J**? 1 Kgs 15:23
in the second year of Asa king of **J**, 1 Kgs 15:25
of Asa king of **J** and reigned in his 1 Kgs 15:28
In the third year of Asa king of **J**, 1 Kgs 15:33
the twenty-sixth year of Asa king of **J**, 1 Kgs 16:8
twenty-seventh year of Asa king of **J**, 1 Kgs 16:10
twenty-seventh year of Asa king of **J**, 1 Kgs 16:15
the thirty-first year of Asa king of **J**, 1 Kgs 16:23
thirty-eighth year of Asa king of **J**, 1 Kgs 16:29
to Beersheba, which belongs to **J**, 1 Kgs 19:3
the king of **J** came down to 1 Kgs 22:2
the king of **J** were sitting on 1 Kgs 22:10
Jehoshaphat the king of **J** went up to 1 Kgs 22:29
began to reign over **J** in the fourth 1 Kgs 22:41
of the Chronicles of the Kings of **J**? 1 Kgs 22:45
year of Jehoshaphat king of **J**, 1 Kgs 22:51
the son of Jehoshaphat, king of **J**, 2 Kgs 1:17
year of Jehoshaphat king of **J**, 2 Kgs 3:1
and sent word to Jehoshaphat king of **J**, 2 Kgs 3:7
went with the king of **J** and the king of 2 Kgs 3:9
regard for Jehoshaphat the king of **J**, 2 Kgs 3:14
when Jehoshaphat was king of **J**, 2 Kgs 8:16
the son of Jehoshaphat, king of **J**, 2 Kgs 8:16
the LORD was not willing to destroy **J**, 2 Kgs 8:19
revolted from the rule of **J** and set up a 2 Kgs 8:20
revolted from the rule of **J** to this day. 2 Kgs 8:22
of the Chronicles of the Kings of **J**? 2 Kgs 8:23
the son of Jehoram, king of **J**, 2 Kgs 8:25
of Jehoram king of **J** went down to see 2 Kgs 8:29
Ahaziah king of **J** had come down 2 Kgs 9:16
Israel and Ahaziah king of **J** set out, 2 Kgs 9:21
When Ahaziah the king of **J** saw this, 2 Kgs 9:27
Ahab, Ahaziah began to reign over **J**. 2 Kgs 9:29
the relatives of Ahaziah king of **J**, 2 Kgs 10:13
Jehoash king of **J** took all the sacred 2 Kgs 12:18
Ahaziah his fathers, the kings of **J**, 2 Kgs 12:18
of the Chronicles of the Kings of **J**? 2 Kgs 12:19
of Joash the son of Ahaziah, king of **J**, 2 Kgs 13:1
year of Joash king of **J**, 2 Kgs 13:10
fought against Amaziah king of **J**, 2 Kgs 13:12
Amaziah the son of Joash, king of **J**, 2 Kgs 14:1
Israel sent word to Amaziah king of **J**, 2 Kgs 14:9
that you fall, you and **J** with you?" 2 Kgs 14:10
Amaziah king of **J** faced one 2 Kgs 14:11
Beth-shemesh, which belongs to **J**. 2 Kgs 14:11
And **J** was defeated by Israel, and 2 Kgs 14:12
Israel captured Amaziah king of **J**, 2 Kgs 14:13
he fought with Amaziah king of **J**, 2 Kgs 14:15
Amaziah the son of Joash, king of **J**, 2 Kgs 14:17
of the Chronicles of the Kings of **J**? 2 Kgs 14:18
And all the people of **J** took Azariah, 2 Kgs 14:21
He built Elath and restored it to **J**, 2 Kgs 14:22
Amaziah the son of Joash, king of **J**, 2 Kgs 14:23
and Hamath to **J** in Israel, 2 Kgs 14:28
the son of Amaziah, king of **J**, 2 Kgs 15:1
of the Chronicles of the Kings of **J**? 2 Kgs 15:6
year of Azariah king of **J**, 2 Kgs 15:8
year of Uzziah king of **J**, 2 Kgs 15:13
year of Azariah king of **J**, 2 Kgs 15:17
the fiftieth year of Azariah king of **J**, 2 Kgs 15:23
year of Azariah king of **J**, 2 Kgs 15:27
Jotham the son of Uzziah, king of **J**, 2 Kgs 15:32
of the Chronicles of the Kings of **J**? 2 Kgs 15:36
the son of Remaliah against **J**. 2 Kgs 15:37
Ahaz the son of Jotham, king of **J**, 2 Kgs 16:1
and drove the men of **J** from Elath, 2 Kgs 16:6
of the Chronicles of the Kings of **J**? 2 Kgs 16:19
In the twelfth year of Ahaz king of **J**, 2 Kgs 17:1
warned Israel and **J** by every prophet 2 Kgs 17:13
None was left but the tribe of **J** only. 2 Kgs 17:18
J also did not keep the 2 Kgs 17:19
Hezekiah the son of Ahaz, king of **J**, 2 Kgs 18:1
among all the kings of **J** after him, 2 Kgs 18:5
fortified cities of **J** and took them. 2 Kgs 18:13
And Hezekiah king of **J** sent to the 2 Kgs 18:14
Hezekiah king of **J** three hundred 2 Kgs 18:14
Hezekiah king of **J** had overlaid and 2 Kgs 18:16
saying to **J** and to Jerusalem, 2 Kgs 18:22
the language of **J** within the hearing 2 Kgs 18:26
in a loud voice in the language of **J**: 2 Kgs 18:28
you speak to Hezekiah king of **J**: 2 Kgs 19:10
of the house of **J** shall again take 2 Kgs 19:30
of the Chronicles of the Kings of **J**? 2 Kgs 20:20
Manasseh king of **J** has committed 2 Kgs 21:11
and has made **J** also to sin with his 2 Kgs 21:11
upon Jerusalem and **J** such disaster 2 Kgs 21:12
the sin that he made **J** to sin so that 2 Kgs 21:16
of the Chronicles of the Kings of **J**? 2 Kgs 21:17
of the Chronicles of the Kings of **J**? 2 Kgs 21:25
me, and for the people, and for all **J**, 2 Kgs 22:13
the book that the king of **J** has read. 2 Kgs 22:16
But to the king of **J**, who sent you to 2 Kgs 22:18
all the elders of **J** and Jerusalem were 2 Kgs 23:1
all the men of **J** and all the 2 Kgs 23:2
whom the kings of **J** had ordained to 2 Kgs 23:5
the cities of **J** and around Jerusalem; 2 Kgs 23:5
all the priests out of the cities of **J**, 2 Kgs 23:8
that the kings of **J** had dedicated to 2 Kgs 23:11
which the kings of **J** had made, 2 Kgs 23:12
who came from **J** and predicted 2 Kgs 23:17
kings of Israel or of the kings of **J**. 2 Kgs 23:22
in the land of **J** and in Jerusalem, 2 Kgs 23:24
his anger was kindled against **J**, 2 Kgs 23:26
"I will remove **J** also out of my sight, 2 Kgs 23:27
of the Chronicles of the Kings of **J**? 2 Kgs 23:28
and sent them against **J** to destroy it, 2 Kgs 24:2
this came upon **J** at the command 2 Kgs 24:3
of the Chronicles of the Kings of **J**? 2 Kgs 24:5
the king of **J** gave himself up 2 Kgs 24:12
point in Jerusalem and **J** that he cast 2 Kgs 24:20
So **J** was taken into exile out of its 2 Kgs 25:21
who remained in the land of **J**, 2 Kgs 25:22
of the exile of Jehoiachin king of **J**, 2 Kgs 25:27
Jehoiachin king of **J** from prison. 2 Kgs 25:27
Reuben, Simeon, Levi, **J**, Issachar, 1 Chr 2:1
The sons of **J**: Er, Onan and Shelah; 1 Chr 2:3
Perez and Zerah. **J** had five sons in all. 1 Chr 2:4
Nahshon, prince of the sons of **J**. 1 Chr 2:10
The sons of **J**: Perez, Hezron, Carmi, 1 Chr 4:1
The sons of Shelah the son of **J**: Er the 1 Chr 4:21
their clan multiply like the men of **J**. 1 Chr 4:27
in the days of Hezekiah, king of **J**, 1 Chr 4:41
though **J** became strong among his 1 Chr 5:2
in the days of Jotham king of **J**, 1 Chr 5:17
the LORD sent **J** and Jerusalem into 1 Chr 6:15
in the land of **J** and its surrounding 1 Chr 6:55
They gave by lot out of the tribes of **J**, 1 Chr 6:65
And **J** was taken into exile in Babylon 1 Chr 9:1
And some of the people of **J**, Benjamin, 1 Chr 9:3
from the sons of Perez the son of **J**. 1 Chr 9:4
men of Benjamin and **J** came to the 1 Chr 12:16
The men of **J** bearing shield and 1 Chr 12:24
is, to Kiriath-jearim that belongs to **J**, 1 Chr 13:6
and in **J** 470,000 who drew the sword. 1 Chr 21:5
for **J**, Elihu, one of David's brothers; 1 Chr 27:18
For he chose **J** as leader, and in the 1 Chr 28:4
in the house of **J** my father's house, 1 Chr 28:4
who are with me in **J** and Jerusalem, 2 Chr 2:7
like of them before in the land of **J**. 2 Chr 9:11
of Israel who lived in the cities of **J**. 2 Chr 10:17
the house of **J** and Benjamin, 2 Chr 11:1
the son of Solomon, king of **J**, 2 Chr 11:3
and to all Israel in **J** and Benjamin, 2 Chr 11:3
and he built cities for defense in **J**. 2 Chr 11:5
cities that are in **J** and in Benjamin. 2 Chr 11:10
strong. So he held **J** and Benjamin. 2 Chr 11:12
and came to **J** and Jerusalem, 2 Chr 11:14
strengthened the kingdom of **J**, 2 Chr 11:17
all the districts of **J** and Benjamin, 2 Chr 11:23
the fortified cities of **J** and came as far 2 Chr 12:4
to Rehoboam and to the princes of **J**, 2 Chr 12:5
Moreover, conditions were good in **J**. 2 Chr 12:12
Abijah began to reign over **J**. 2 Chr 13:1
Thus his troops were in front of **J**, 2 Chr 13:13
And when **J** looked, behold, the 2 Chr 13:14
Then the men of **J** raised the battle 2 Chr 13:15
And when the men of **J** shouted, God 2 Chr 13:15
and all Israel before Abijah and **J**. 2 Chr 13:15
The men of Israel fled before **J**, and 2 Chr 13:16
time, and the men of **J** prevailed, 2 Chr 13:18
and commanded **J** to seek the LORD, 2 Chr 14:4
all the cities of **J** the high places and 2 Chr 14:5
He built fortified cities in **J**, for the 2 Chr 14:6
And he said to **J**, "Let us build these 2 Chr 14:7
Asa had an army of 300,000 from **J**, 2 Chr 14:8
Ethiopians before Asa and before **J**, 2 Chr 14:12
The men of **J** carried away very 2 Chr 14:13
me, Asa, and all **J** and Benjamin: 2 Chr 15:2
all the land of **J** and Benjamin and 2 Chr 15:8
And he gathered all **J** and Benjamin, 2 Chr 15:9
And all **J** rejoiced over the oath, for 2 Chr 15:15
went up against **J** and built Ramah, 2 Chr 16:1
to go out or come in to Asa king of **J**. 2 Chr 16:1
Then King Asa took all **J**, and they 2 Chr 16:6
to Asa king of **J** and said to him, 2 Chr 16:7
the Book of the Kings of **J** and Israel. 2 Chr 16:11
fortified cities of **J** and set garrisons 2 Chr 17:2
and set garrisons in the land of **J**, 2 Chr 17:2
And all **J** brought tribute to 2 Chr 17:5
high places and the Asherim out of **J**. 2 Chr 17:6
Micaiah, to teach in the cities of **J**; 2 Chr 17:7
And they taught in **J**, having the 2 Chr 17:9
all the cities of **J** and taught among 2 Chr 17:9
of the lands that were around **J**, 2 Chr 17:10
He built in **J** fortresses and store 2 Chr 17:12
had large supplies in the cities of **J**. 2 Chr 17:13
of them by fathers' houses: Of **J**, 2 Chr 17:14
the fortified cities throughout all **J**. 2 Chr 17:19
of Israel said to Jehoshaphat king of **J**, 2 Chr 18:3
the king of **J** were sitting on 2 Chr 18:9
Jehoshaphat the king of **J** went up to 2 Chr 18:28
the king of **J** returned in safety 2 Chr 19:1
the land in all the fortified cities of **J**, 2 Chr 19:5
the governor of the house of **J**, 2 Chr 19:11
proclaimed a fast throughout all **J**. 2 Chr 20:3
And **J** assembled to seek help from 2 Chr 20:4
all the cities of **J** they came to seek 2 Chr 20:4
in the assembly of **J** and Jerusalem, 2 Chr 20:5
Meanwhile all **J** stood before the 2 Chr 20:13
all **J** and inhabitants of Jerusalem 2 Chr 20:15
on your behalf, O **J** and Jerusalem.' 2 Chr 20:17
and all **J** and the inhabitants of 2 Chr 20:18
me, **J** and inhabitants of Jerusalem! 2 Chr 20:20
Seir, who had come against **J**, 2 Chr 20:22
When **J** came to the watchtower of 2 Chr 20:24
every man of **J** and Jerusalem, 2 Chr 20:27
Thus Jehoshaphat reigned over **J**. He 2 Chr 20:31
Jehoshaphat king of **J** joined with 2 Chr 20:35
the sons of Jehoshaphat king of **J**. 2 Chr 21:2
together with fortified cities in **J**, 2 Chr 21:3

 JUDAH

from the rule of **J** and set up a 2 Chr 21:8
from the rule of **J** to this day. 2 Chr 21:10
the hill country of **J** and led the 2 Chr 21:11
whoredom and made **J** go astray. 2 Chr 21:11
or in the ways of Asa king of **J**, 2 Chr 21:12
and have enticed **J** and the 2 Chr 21:13
came up against **J** and invaded it 2 Chr 21:17
the son of Jehoram king of **J** reigned. 2 Chr 22:1
of Jehoram king of **J** went down to see 2 Chr 22:6
he met the princes of **J** and the sons of 2 Chr 22:8
all the royal family of the house of **J**. 2 Chr 22:10
went about through **J** and gathered 2 Chr 23:2
the Levites from all the cities of **J**, 2 Chr 23:2
The Levites and all **J** did according to 2 Chr 23:8
to the cities of **J** and gather from all 2 Chr 24:5
to bring in from **J** and Jerusalem the 2 Chr 24:6
made throughout **J** and Jerusalem 2 Chr 24:9
the princes of **J** came and paid 2 Chr 24:17
wrath came upon **J** and Jerusalem 2 Chr 24:18
They came to **J** and Jerusalem and 2 Chr 24:23
because **J** had forsaken the LORD, 2 Chr 24:24
assembled the men of **J** and set them 2 Chr 25:5
of hundreds for all **J** and Benjamin. 2 Chr 25:5
very angry with **J** and returned 2 Chr 25:10
The men of **J** captured another 2 Chr 25:12
him to battle, raided the cities of **J**, 2 Chr 25:13
Amaziah king of **J** took counsel and 2 Chr 25:17
sent word to Amaziah king of **J**, 2 Chr 25:18
that you fall, you and **J** with you?" 2 Chr 25:19
Amaziah king of **J** faced one 2 Chr 25:21
Beth-shemesh, which belongs to **J**. 2 Chr 25:21
And **J** was defeated by Israel, and 2 Chr 25:22
Israel captured Amaziah king of **J**, 2 Chr 25:23
Amaziah the son of Joash, king of **J**, 2 Chr 25:25
Book of the Kings of **J** and Israel? 2 Chr 25:26
And all the people of **J** took Uzziah, 2 Chr 26:1
He built Eloth and restored it to **J**, 2 Chr 26:2
he built cities in the hill country of **J**, 2 Chr 27:4
the Book of the Kings of Israel and **J**. 2 Chr 27:7
killed 120,000 from **J** in one day, 2 Chr 28:6
God of your fathers, was angry with **J**, 2 Chr 28:9
the people of **J** and Jerusalem, 2 Chr 28:10
invaded and defeated **J** and carried 2 Chr 28:17
in the Shephelah and the Negeb of **J**, 2 Chr 28:18
the LORD humbled **J** because of 2 Chr 28:19
for he had made **J** act sinfully and 2 Chr 28:19
In every city of **J** he made high 2 Chr 28:25
the Book of the Kings of **J** and Israel. 2 Chr 28:26
of the LORD came on **J** and Jerusalem, 2 Chr 29:8
and for the sanctuary and for **J**. 2 Chr 29:21
Hezekiah sent to all Israel and **J**, and 2 Chr 30:1
all Israel and **J** with letters from 2 Chr 30:6
God was also on **J** to give them one 2 Chr 30:12
Hezekiah king of **J** gave the 2 Chr 30:24
The whole assembly of **J**, and the 2 Chr 30:25
and the sojourners who lived in **J**, 2 Chr 30:25
to the cities of **J** and broke in pieces 2 Chr 31:1
throughout all **J** and Benjamin, 2 Chr 31:1
people of Israel and **J** who lived in the 2 Chr 31:6
in the cities of **J** also brought in the 2 Chr 31:6
Thus Hezekiah did throughout all **J**, 2 Chr 31:20
came and invaded **J** and encamped 2 Chr 32:1
from the words of Hezekiah king of **J**. 2 Chr 32:8
to Hezekiah king of **J** and to all the 2 Chr 32:9
all the people of **J** who were in 2 Chr 32:9
and commanded **J** and Jerusalem, 2 Chr 32:12
in the language of **J** to the people of 2 Chr 32:18
things to Hezekiah king of **J**, 2 Chr 32:23
upon him and **J** and Jerusalem. 2 Chr 32:25
the Book of the Kings of **J** and Israel. 2 Chr 32:32
and all **J** and the inhabitants of 2 Chr 32:33
Manasseh led **J** and the inhabitants 2 Chr 33:9
army in all the fortified cities in **J**. 2 Chr 33:14
and he commanded **J** to serve the 2 Chr 33:16
he began to purge **J** and Jerusalem of 2 Chr 34:3
altars and cleansed **J** and Jerusalem. 2 Chr 34:5
and from all **J** and Benjamin and 2 Chr 34:9
that the kings of **J** had let go to 2 Chr 34:11
those who are left in Israel and in **J**, 2 Chr 34:21
that was read before the king of **J**. 2 Chr 34:24
But to the king of **J**, who sent you to 2 Chr 34:26
all the elders of **J** and Jerusalem. 2 Chr 34:29
all the men of **J** and the inhabitants 2 Chr 34:30
and all **J** and Israel who were 2 Chr 35:18
we to do with each other, king of **J**? 2 Chr 35:21
All **J** and Jerusalem mourned for 2 Chr 35:24
the Book of the Kings of Israel and **J**. 2 Chr 35:27
brother king over **J** and Jerusalem, 2 Chr 36:4
the Book of the Kings of Israel and **J**. 2 Chr 36:8
Zedekiah king over **J** and Jerusalem. 2 Chr 36:10
a house at Jerusalem, which is in **J**. 2 Chr 36:23
him a house at Jerusalem, which is in **J**. Ezr 1:2
let him go up to Jerusalem, which is in **J**, Ezr 1:3
of the fathers' houses of **J** and Benjamin, Ezr 1:5
them out to Sheshbazzar the prince of **J**. Ezr 1:8

They returned to Jerusalem and **J**, each to Ezr 2:1
and Kadmiel and his sons, the sons of **J**, Ezr 3:9
the adversaries of **J** and Benjamin heard Ezr 4:1
the people of **J** and made them Ezr 4:4
the inhabitants of **J** and Jerusalem. Ezr 4:6
to the Jews who were in **J** and Jerusalem, Ezr 5:1
the king that we went to the province of **J**, Ezr 5:8
make inquiries about **J** and Jerusalem Ezr 7:14
was made throughout **J** and Jerusalem Ezr 10:7
the men of **J** and Benjamin assembled Ezr 10:9
is, Kelita), Pethahiah, **J**, and Eliezer. Ezr 10:23
brothers, came with certain men from **J**. Neh 1:2
in your sight, that you send me to **J**, Neh 2:5
let me pass through until I come to **J**, Neh 2:7
In **J** it was said, "The strength of those Neh 4:10
stood behind the whole house of **J**, Neh 4:16
to be their governor in the land of **J**, Neh 5:14
you in Jerusalem, 'There is a king in **J**.' Neh 6:7
days the nobles of **J** sent many letters to Neh 6:17
For many in **J** were bound by oath to Neh 6:18
They returned to Jerusalem and **J**, each Neh 7:6
in the towns of **J** everyone lived on his Neh 11:3
certain of the sons of **J** and of the sons Neh 11:4
Of the sons of **J**: Athaiah the son of Neh 11:4
and **J** the son of Hassenuah was second Neh 11:9
the Levites, were in all the towns of **J**, Neh 11:20
of the sons of Zerah the son of **J**, Neh 11:24
of the people of **J** lived in Kiriath-arba Neh 11:25
of the Levites in **J** were assigned to Neh 11:36
Kadmiel, Sherebiah, **J**, and Mattaniah, Neh 12:8
brought the leaders of **J** up onto the Neh 12:31
Hoshaiah and half of the leaders of **J**, Neh 12:32
J, Benjamin, Shemaiah, and Neh 12:34
Maai, Nethanel, **J**, and Hanani, Neh 12:36
for **J** rejoiced over the priests and the Neh 12:44
Then all **J** brought the tithe of the Neh 13:12
I saw in **J** people treading winepresses Neh 13:15
on the Sabbath to the people of **J**, Neh 13:16
confronted the nobles of **J** and said to Neh 13:17
could not speak the language of **J**, Neh 13:24
carried away with Jeconiah king of **J**, Est 2:6
Let the daughters of **J** rejoice because of Ps 48:11
Ephraim is my helmet; **J** is my scepter. Ps 60:7
when he was in the wilderness of **J**. Ps 63:T
the lead, the princes of **J** in their throng, Ps 68:27
save Zion and build up the cities of **J**, Ps 69:35
In **J** God is known; his name is great in Ps 76:1
but he chose the tribe of **J**, Mount Zion, Ps 78:68
is glad, and the daughters of **J** rejoice, Ps 97:8
Ephraim is my helmet, **J** my scepter. Ps 108:8
J became his sanctuary, Israel his Ps 114:2
the men of Hezekiah king of **J** copied. Prv 25:1
he saw concerning **J** and Jerusalem in Is 1:1
Jotham, Ahaz, and Hezekiah, kings of **J**. Is 1:1
of Amoz saw concerning **J** and Jerusalem. Is 2:1
Jerusalem and from **J** support and supply, Is 3:1
Jerusalem has stumbled, and **J** has fallen, Is 3:8
O inhabitants of Jerusalem and men of **J**, Is 5:3
and the men of **J** are his pleasant planting; Is 5:7
the son of Jotham, son of Uzziah, king of **J**, Is 7:1
"Let us go up against **J** and terrify it, and let Is 7:6
that Ephraim departed from **J**—the king Is 7:17
and it will sweep on into **J**, it will overflow Is 8:8
Manasseh; together they are against **J**. Is 9:21
gather the dispersed of **J** from the four Is 11:12
and those who harass **J** shall be cut off; Is 11:13
Ephraim shall not be jealous of **J**, and Is 11:13
Judah, and **J** shall not harass Ephraim. Is 11:13
And the land of **J** will become a terror to Is 19:17
He has taken away the covering of **J**. In Is 22:8
of Jerusalem and to the house of **J**. Is 22:21
day this song will be sung in the land of **J**: Is 26:1
all the fortified cities of **J** and took them. Is 36:1
removed, saying to **J** and to Jerusalem, Is 36:7
in the language of **J** within the hearing Is 36:11
out in a loud voice in the language of **J**: Is 36:13
shall you speak to Hezekiah king of **J**: Is 37:10
of the house of **J** shall again take root Is 37:31
A writing of Hezekiah king of **J**, after he Is 38:9
say to the cities of **J**, "Behold your God!" Is 40:9
shall be inhabited,' and of the cities of **J**, Is 44:26
Israel, and who came from the waters of **J**, Is 48:1
and from **J** possessors of my mountains; Is 65:9
days of Josiah the son of Amon, king of **J**, Jer 1:2
of Jehoiakim the son of Josiah, king of **J**, Jer 1:3
of Zedekiah, the son of Josiah, king of **J**, Jer 1:3
all around and against all the cities of **J**. Jer 1:15
the whole land, against the kings of **J**, Jer 1:18
as many as your cities are your gods, O **J**. Jer 2:28
return, and her treacherous sister **J** saw it. Jer 3:7
Yet her treacherous sister **J** did not fear, Jer 3:8
her treacherous sister **J** did not return Jer 3:10
more righteous than treacherous **J**. Jer 3:11
days the house of **J** shall join the house Jer 3:18
the LORD to the men of **J** and Jerusalem: Jer 4:3

O men of **J** and inhabitants of Jerusalem; Jer 4:4
Declare in **J**, and proclaim in Jerusalem, Jer 4:5
land; they shout against the cities of **J**. Jer 4:16
and the house of **J** have been utterly Jer 5:11
in the house of Jacob; proclaim it in **J**: Jer 5:20
all you men of **J** who enter these gates to Jer 7:2
doing in the cities of **J** and in the streets Jer 7:17
"For the sons of **J** have done evil in my Jer 7:30
silence in the cities of **J** and in the streets Jer 7:34
the LORD, the bones of the kings of **J**, Jer 8:1
I will make the cities of **J** a desolation, Jer 9:11
Egypt, **J**, Edom, the sons of Ammon, Jer 9:26
to make the cities of **J** a desolation, Jer 10:22
to the men of **J** and the inhabitants of Jer 11:2
words in the cities of **J** and in the streets Jer 11:6
among the men of **J** and the inhabitants Jer 11:9
and the house of **J** have broken my Jer 11:10
Then the cities of **J** and the inhabitants Jer 11:12
become as many as your cities, O **J**, Jer 11:13
of Israel and the house of **J** have done, Jer 11:17
up the house of **J** from among them. Jer 12:14
I spoil the pride of **J** and the great pride of Jer 13:9
and the whole house of **J** cling to me, Jer 13:11
all **J** is taken into exile, wholly taken Jer 13:19
"**J** mourns and her gates languish; her Jer 14:2
Have you utterly rejected **J**? Does your Jer 14:19
Manasseh the son of Hezekiah, king of **J**, Jer 15:4
"The sin of **J** is written with a pen of iron; Jer 17:1
which the kings of **J** enter and by Jer 17:19
the word of the LORD, you kings of **J**, Jer 17:20
the LORD, you kings of Judah, and all **J**, Jer 17:20
the men of **J** and the inhabitants of Jer 17:25
from the cities of **J** and the places Jer 17:26
to the men of **J** and the inhabitants of Jer 18:11
O kings of **J** and inhabitants of Jer 19:3
fathers nor the kings of **J** have known; Jer 19:4
make void the plans of **J** and Jerusalem, Jer 19:7
houses of the kings of **J**—all the houses Jer 19:13
And I will give all **J** into the hand of the Jer 20:4
of the kings of **J** into the hand of Jer 20:5
give Zedekiah king of **J** and his servants Jer 21:7
"And to the house of the king of **J** say, Jer 21:11
of the king of **J** and speak there this Jer 22:1
'Hear the word of the LORD, O King of **J**, Jer 22:2
concerning the house of the king of **J**: Jer 22:6
Shallum the son of Josiah, king of **J**, Jer 22:11
Jehoiakim the son of Josiah, king of **J**: Jer 22:18
Coniah the son of Jehoiakim, king of **J**, Jer 22:24
throne of David and ruling again in **J**." Jer 22:30
In his days **J** will be saved, and Israel will Jer 23:6
Jeconiah the son of Jehoiakim, king of **J**, Jer 24:1
of Judah, together with the officials of **J**, Jer 24:1
so I will regard as good the exiles from **J**, Jer 24:5
so will I treat Zedekiah the king of **J**, Jer 24:8
Jeremiah concerning all the people of **J**, Jer 25:1
king of **J** (that was the first year of Jer 25:1
all the people of **J** and all the inhabitants Jer 25:2
year of Josiah the son of Amon, king of **J**, Jer 25:3
Jerusalem and the cities of **J**, its kings Jer 25:18
of Jehoiakim the son of Josiah, king of **J**, Jer 26:1
to all the cities of **J** that come to worship Jer 26:2
the officials of **J** heard these things, Jer 26:10
in the days of Hezekiah king of **J**, Jer 26:18
of Judah, and said to all the people of **J**: Jer 26:18
Did Hezekiah king of **J** and all Judah Jer 26:19
of Judah and all **J** put him to death? Jer 26:19
of Zedekiah the son of Josiah, king of **J**, Jer 27:1
come to Jerusalem to Zedekiah king of **J**. Jer 27:3
To Zedekiah king of **J** I spoke in like Jer 27:12
of the LORD, in the house of the king of **J**, Jer 27:18
the son of Jehoiakim, king of **J**, Jer 27:20
and all the nobles of **J** and Jerusalem— Jer 27:20
of the LORD, in the house of the king of **J**, Jer 27:21
of the reign of Zedekiah king of **J**, Jer 28:1
Jeconiah the son of Jehoiakim, king of **J**, Jer 28:4
all the exiles from **J** who went to Jer 28:4
eunuchs, the officials of **J** and Jerusalem, Jer 29:2
Zedekiah king of **J** sent to Babylon Jer 29:3
used by all the exiles from **J** in Babylon: Jer 29:22
the fortunes of my people, Israel and **J**, Jer 30:3
the LORD spoke concerning Israel and **J**: Jer 30:4
words in the land of **J** and in its cities, Jer 31:23
And **J** and all its cities shall dwell there Jer 31:24
Israel and the house of **J** with the seed of Jer 31:27
the house of Israel and the house of **J**, Jer 31:31
in the tenth year of Zedekiah king of **J**, Jer 32:1
that was in the palace of the king of **J**. Jer 32:2
Zedekiah king of **J** had imprisoned him, Jer 32:3
Zedekiah king of **J** shall not escape out Jer 32:4
and the children of **J** have done nothing Jer 32:30
and the children of **J** that they did to Jer 32:32
the men of **J** and the inhabitants of Jer 32:32
do this abomination, to cause **J** to sin. Jer 32:35
about Jerusalem, and in the cities of **J**, Jer 32:44
of the kings of **J** that were torn down Jer 33:4

restore the fortunes of J and the fortunes — Jer 33:7
in the cities of J and the streets of — Jer 33:10
about Jerusalem, and in the cities of J, — Jer 33:13
to the house of Israel and the house of J. — Jer 33:14
In those days J will be saved and — Jer 33:16
to Zedekiah king of J and say to him, — Jer 34:2
word of the LORD, O Zedekiah king of J! — Jer 34:4
all these words to Zedekiah king of J, — Jer 34:6
against all the cities of J that were left, — Jer 34:7
only fortified cities of J that remained. — Jer 34:7
the officials of J, the officials of — Jer 34:19
Zedekiah king of J and his officials — Jer 34:21
the cities of J a desolation without — Jer 34:22
of Jehoiakim the son of Josiah, king of J: — Jer 35:1
to the people of J and the inhabitants of — Jer 35:13
I am bringing upon J and all the — Jer 35:17
of Jehoiakim the son of Josiah, king of J, — Jer 36:1
you against Israel and J and all the — Jer 36:2
be that the house of J will hear all the — Jer 36:3
of all the men of J who come out of their — Jer 36:6
of Jehoiakim the son of Josiah, king of J, — Jer 36:9
the cities of J to Jerusalem proclaimed — Jer 36:9
Jehoiakim the king of J has burned. — Jer 36:28
Jehoiakim king of J you shall say, — Jer 36:29
LORD concerning Jehoiakim king of J: — Jer 36:30
upon the people of J all the disaster that — Jer 36:31
that Jehoiakim king of J had burned in — Jer 36:32
of Babylon made king in the land of J, — Jer 37:1
say to the king of J who sent you to me — Jer 37:7
house of the king of J were being led out — Jer 38:22
In the ninth year of Zedekiah king of J, — Jer 39:1
When Zedekiah king of J and all the — Jer 39:4
Babylon slaughtered all the nobles of J. — Jer 39:6
left in the land of J some of the poor — Jer 39:10
of Jerusalem and J who were being — Jer 40:1
appointed governor of the cities of J, — Jer 40:5
left a remnant in J and had appointed — Jer 40:11
been driven and came to the land of J, — Jer 40:12
and the remnant of J would perish?" — Jer 40:15
the word of the LORD, O remnant of J. — Jer 42:15
LORD has said to you, O remnant of J, — Jer 42:19
of the LORD, to remain in the land of J. — Jer 43:4
all the remnant of J who had returned to — Jer 43:5
live in the land of J from all the nations — Jer 43:5
Tahpanhes, in the sight of the men of J, — Jer 43:9
Jerusalem and upon all the cities of J. — Jer 44:2
kindled in the cities of J and in the streets — Jer 44:6
infant and child, from the midst of J, — Jer 44:7
of your fathers, the evil of the kings of J, — Jer 44:9
in the land of J and in the streets — Jer 44:9
against you for harm, to cut off all J. — Jer 44:11
take the remnant of J who have set their — Jer 44:12
of the remnant of J who have come to — Jer 44:14
or survive or return to the land of J, — Jer 44:14
in the cities of J and in the streets of — Jer 44:17
in the cities of J and in the streets — Jer 44:21
all you of J who are in the land of Egypt. — Jer 44:24
all you of J who dwell in the land of — Jer 44:26
mouth of any man of J in all the land of — Jer 44:26
All the men of J who are in the land of — Jer 44:27
from the land of Egypt to the land of J, — Jer 44:28
and all the remnant of J, who came to — Jer 44:28
gave Zedekiah king of J into the hand — Jer 44:30
of Jehoiakim the son of Josiah, king of J: — Jer 45:1
of Jehoiakim the son of Josiah, king of J: — Jer 46:2
of the reign of Zedekiah king of J. — Jer 49:34
and the people of J shall come together, — Jer 50:4
And sin in J, and none shall be found, — Jer 50:20
and the people of J with them. — Jer 50:33
For Israel and J have not been forsaken — Jer 51:5
with Zedekiah king of J to Babylon, — Jer 51:59
point in Jerusalem and J that he cast — Jer 52:3
all the officials of J at Riblah. — Jer 52:10
So J was taken into exile out of its land. — Jer 52:27
year of the exile of Jehoiachin king of J, — Jer 52:31
Jehoiachin king of J and brought him — Jer 52:31
J has gone into exile because of — Lam 1:3
in a winepress the virgin daughter of J. — Lam 1:15
the strongholds of the daughter of J; — Lam 2:2
the daughter of J mourning and — Lam 2:5
Zion, young women in the towns of J. — Lam 5:11
bear the punishment of the house of J. — Ezk 4:6
with the elders of J sitting before me, — Ezk 8:1
for the house of J to commit the — Ezk 8:17
house of Israel and J is exceedingly great. — Ezk 9:9
to Rabbah of the Ammonites and to J, — Ezk 21:20
over the house of J when they went into — Ezk 25:3
the house of J is like all the other — Ezk 25:8
the house of J and has grievously — Ezk 25:12
J and the land of Israel traded with — Ezk 27:17
take a stick and write on it, 'For J, — Ezk 37:16
And I will join with it the stick of J, — Ezk 37:19
the east side to the west, J, one portion. — Ezk 48:7
"Adjoining the territory of J, from the — Ezk 48:8
the territory of J and the territory — Ezk 48:22
gates, the gate of Reuben, the gate of J, — Ezk 48:31
year of the reign of Jehoiakim king of J, — Dn 1:1
gave Jehoiakim king of J into his hand, — Dn 1:2
Mishael, and Azariah of the tribe of J. — Dn 1:6
among the exiles from J a man who will — Dn 2:25
are that Daniel, one of the exiles of J, — Dn 5:13
the king my father brought from J. — Dn 5:13
"Daniel, who is one of the exiles from J, — Dn 6:13
shame, as at this day, to the men of J, — Dn 9:7
Jotham, Ahaz, and Hezekiah, kings of J, — Hos 1:1
But I will have mercy on the house of J, — Hos 1:7
And the children of J and the children — Hos 1:11
whore, O Israel, let not J become guilty. — Hos 4:15
his guilt; J also shall stumble with them. — Hos 5:5
The princes of J have become like those — Hos 5:10
and like dry rot to the house of J. — Hos 5:12
saw his sickness, and J his wound, — Hos 5:13
and like a young lion to the house of J. — Hos 5:14
Ephraim? What shall I do with you, O J? — Hos 6:4
For you also, O J, a harvest is appointed, — Hos 6:11
and J has multiplied fortified cities; — Hos 8:14
put Ephraim to the yoke; J must plow; — Hos 10:11
but J still walks with God and is — Hos 11:12
an indictment against J and will — Hos 12:2
I restore the fortunes of J and Jerusalem, — Jl 3:1
sold the people of J and Jerusalem to the — Jl 3:6
daughters into the hand of the people of J, — Jl 3:8
all the streambeds of J shall flow with — Jl 3:18
for the violence done to the people of J, — Jl 3:19
But J shall be inhabited forever, and — Jl 3:20
days of Uzziah king of J and in the days — Am 1:1
"For three transgressions of J, and for — Am 2:4
So I will send a fire upon J, and it shall — Am 2:5
"O seer, go, flee away to the land of J, — Am 7:12
rejoice over the people of J in the day of — Ob 1:12
of Jotham, Ahaz, and Hezekiah, kings of J, — Mi 1:1
Samaria? And what is the high place of J? — Mi 1:5
wound is incurable, and it has come to J; — Mi 1:9
are too little to be among the clans of J, — Mi 5:2
Keep your feasts, O J; fulfill your vows, — Na 1:15
days of Josiah the son of Amon, king of J. — Zep 1:1
out my hand against J and against all — Zep 1:4
of the remnant of the house of J, — Zep 2:7
the son of Shealtiel, governor of J, — Hg 1:1
the son of Shealtiel, governor of J, — Hg 1:14
the son of Shealtiel, governor of J, — Hg 2:2
"Speak to Zerubbabel, governor of J, — Hg 2:21
mercy on Jerusalem and the cities of J, — Zec 1:12
are the horns that have scattered J, — Zec 1:19
"These are the horns that scattered J, — Zec 1:21
horns against the land of J to scatter it." — Zec 1:21
the LORD will inherit J as his portion in — Zec 2:12
O house of J and house of Israel, — Zec 8:13
good to Jerusalem and to the house of J; — Zec 8:15
be to the house of J seasons of joy and — Zec 8:19
it shall be like a clan in J, and Ekron — Zec 9:7
For I have bent J as my bow; I have — Zec 9:13
hosts cares for his flock, the house of J, — Zec 10:3
"I will strengthen the house of J, and I — Zec 10:6
the brotherhood between J and Israel. — Zec 11:14
siege of Jerusalem will also be against J. — Zec 12:2
sake of the house of J I will keep my eyes — Zec 12:4
Then the clans of J shall say to — Zec 12:5
make the clans of J like a blazing pot — Zec 12:6
will give salvation to the tents of J first, — Zec 12:7
of Jerusalem may not surpass that of J. — Zec 12:7
in the days of Uzziah king of J. — Zec 14:5
Even J will fight against Jerusalem. — Zec 14:14
pot in Jerusalem and J shall be holy to — Zec 14:21
J has been faithless, and abomination — Mal 2:11
For J has profaned the sanctuary of the — Mal 2:11
Then the offering of J and Jerusalem will — Mal 3:4
and Jacob the father of J and his brothers, — Mt 1:2
and J the father of Perez and Zerah by — Mt 1:3
"'And you, O Bethlehem, in the land of J, — Mt 2:6
by no means least among the rulers of J; — Mt 2:6
into the hill country, to a town in J, — Lk 1:39
the son of Simeon, the son of J, the son of — Lk 3:30
of Hezron, the son of Perez, the son of J, — Lk 3:33
that our Lord was descended from J, — Heb 7:14
house of Israel and with the house of J, — Heb 8:8
behold, the Lion of the tribe of J, the Root — Rv 5:5
12,000 from the tribe of J were sealed, — Rv 7:5

JUDAH'S (2)

But Er, J firstborn, was wicked in the — Gn 38:7
Now Er, J firstborn, was evil in the — 1 Chr 2:3

JUDAHITE (1)

And his J wife bore Jered the father of — 1 Chr 4:18

JUDAISM (3)

devout converts to J followed Paul — Acts 13:43
you have heard of my former life in J, — Gal 1:13
I was advancing in J beyond many of — Gal 1:14

JUDAS (32)

Simon the Cananaean, and J Iscariot, — Mt 10:4
James and Joseph and Simon and J? — Mt 13:55
the twelve, whose name was J Iscariot, — Mt 26:14
J, who would betray him, answered, "Is — Mt 26:25
While he was still speaking, J came, — Mt 26:47
Then when J, his betrayer, saw that — Mt 27:3
and J Iscariot, who betrayed him. — Mk 3:19
of James and Joses and J and Simon? — Mk 6:3
Then J Iscariot, who was one of the — Mk 14:10
while he was still speaking, J came, — Mk 14:43
and J the son of James, and Judas — Lk 6:16
Judas the son of James, and J Iscariot, — Lk 6:16
Then Satan entered into J called Iscariot, — Lk 22:3
came a crowd, and the man called J, — Lk 22:47
"J, would you betray the Son of Man — Lk 22:48
He spoke of J the son of Simon Iscariot, — Jn 6:71
But J Iscariot, one of his disciples (he — Jn 12:4
already put it into the heart of J Iscariot, — Jn 13:2
he had dipped the morsel, he gave it to J, — Jn 13:26
that, because J had the moneybag, — Jn 13:29
J (not Iscariot) said to him, "Lord, how — Jn 14:22
Now J, who betrayed him, also knew the — Jn 18:2
So J, having procured a band of soldiers — Jn 18:3
Jesus said to them, "I am he." J, — Jn 18:5
Simon the Zealot and J the son of — Acts 1:13
by the mouth of David concerning J, — Acts 1:16
apostleship from which J turned aside — Acts 1:25
After him J the Galilean rose up in the — Acts 5:37
and at the house of J look for a man of — Acts 9:11
They sent J called Barsabbas, — Acts 15:22
We have therefore sent J and Silas, — Acts 15:27
And J and Silas, who were themselves — Acts 15:32

JUDE (1)

J, a servant of Jesus Christ and brother — Jude 1:1

JUDEA (46)

to give us protection in J and Jerusalem. — Ezr 9:9
was born in Bethlehem of J in the days of — Mt 2:1
They told him, "In Bethlehem of J, for so — Mt 2:5
was reigning over J in place of — Mt 2:22
came preaching in the wilderness of J, — Mt 3:1
Then Jerusalem and all J and all the — Mt 3:5
the Decapolis, and from Jerusalem and J, — Mt 4:25
the region of J beyond the Jordan. — Mt 19:1
those who are in J flee to the — Mt 24:16
all the country of J and all Jerusalem — Mk 1:5
great crowd followed, from Galilee and J — Mk 3:7
to the region of J and beyond the Jordan, — Mk 10:1
those who are in J flee to the — Mk 13:14
In the days of Herod, king of J, there was a — Lk 1:5
about through all the hill country of J, — Lk 1:65
Galilee, from the town of Nazareth, to J, — Lk 2:4
Pontius Pilate being governor of J, — Lk 3:1
he was preaching in the synagogues of J. — Lk 4:44
of Galilee and J and from Jerusalem. — Lk 5:17
of people from all J and Jerusalem and — Lk 6:17
through the whole of J and all the — Lk 7:17
those who are in J flee to the — Lk 21:21
up the people, teaching throughout all J, — Lk 23:5
he left J and departed again for Galilee. — Jn 4:3
that Jesus had come from J to Galilee, — Jn 4:47
did when he had come from J to Galilee. — Jn 4:54
He would not go about in J, because the — Jn 7:1
said to him, "Leave here and go to J, — Jn 7:3
to the disciples, "Let us go to J again." — Jn 11:7
in Jerusalem and in all J and Samaria, — Acts 1:8
of Mesopotamia, J and Cappadocia, — Acts 2:9
"Men of J and all who dwell in — Acts 2:14
the regions of J and Samaria, — Acts 8:1
church throughout all J and Galilee — Acts 9:31
what happened throughout all J, — Acts 10:37
who were throughout J heard that the — Acts 11:1
send relief to the brothers living in J. — Acts 11:29
he went down from J to Caesarea and — Acts 12:19
came down from J and were teaching — Acts 15:1
named Agabus came down from J. — Acts 21:10
and throughout all the region of J, — Acts 26:20
received no letters from J about you, — Acts 28:21
delivered from the unbelievers in J, — Rom 15:31
have you send me on my way to J. — 2 Cor 1:16
to the churches of J that are in Christ. — Gal 1:22
of God in Christ Jesus that are in J. — 1 Thes 2:14

JUDEAN (1)

his disciples went into the J countryside, — Jn 3:22

JUDEANS (9)

presence of all the J who were sitting in — Jer 32:12
am afraid of the J who have deserted to — Jer 38:19
when all the J who were in Moab and — Jer 40:11
then all the J returned from all the — Jer 40:12
so that all the J who are gathered about — Jer 40:15
struck down all the J who were with — Jer 41:3
concerning all the J who lived in — Jer 44:1
captive: in the seventh year, 3,023 J; — Jer 52:28

away captive of the **J** 745 persons; Jer 52:30

JUDGE (144)

May the LORD **j** between you and me!" Gn 16:5
Shall not the **J** of all the earth do what Gn 18:25
to sojourn, and he has become the **j**! Gn 19:9
j between us." So Jacob swore by the Gn 31:53
"Dan shall **j** his people as one of the Gn 49:16
made you a prince and a **j** over us? Ex 2:14
to them, "The LORD look on you and **j**, Ex 5:21
The next day Moses sat to **j** the people, Ex 18:13
And let them **j** the people at all times. Ex 18:22
shall you **j** your neighbor. Lv 19:15
the congregation shall **j** between the Nm 35:24
and **j** righteously between a man and his Dt 1:16
and they shall **j** the people with Dt 16:18
priests and to the **j** who is in office Dt 17:9
there before the LORD your God, or the **j**, Dt 17:12
the **j** shall cause him to lie down and be Dt 25:2
judges for them, the LORD was with the **j**, Jgs 2:18
of their enemies all the days of the **j**. Jgs 2:18
But whenever the **j** died, they turned Jgs 2:19
The LORD, the **J**, decide this day between Jgs 11:27
The LORD will **j** the ends of the earth; 1 Sm 2:10
for us a king to **j** us like all the 1 Sm 8:5
us a king to **j** us." And Samuel prayed 1 Sm 8:6
and that our king may **j** us and go out 1 Sm 8:20
May the LORD **j** between me and you, 1 Sm 24:12
LORD therefore be **j** and give sentence 1 Sm 24:15
say, "Oh that I were **j** in the land! 2 Sm 15:4
heaven and act and **j** your servants, 1 Kgs 8:32
the LORD, for he comes to **j** the earth. 1 Chr 16:33
heaven and act and **j** your servants, 2 Chr 6:23
for you **j** not for man but for the 2 Chr 19:6
and judges who may **j** all the people in Ezr 7:25
Can he **j** through the deep darkness? Jb 22:13
and I would be acquitted forever by my **j**. Jb 23:7
j me, O LORD, according to my Ps 7:8
God is a righteous **j**, and a God who feels Ps 7:11
and to the earth, that he may **j** his people: Ps 50:4
his righteousness, for God himself is **j**! Ps 50:6
Do you **j** the children of man uprightly? Ps 58:1
for you **j** the peoples with equity and Ps 67:4
May he **j** your people with righteousness, Ps 72:2
set time that I appoint I will **j** with equity. Ps 75:2
"How long will you **j** unjustly and show Ps 82:2
Arise, O God, **j** the earth; for you shall Ps 82:8
Rise up, O **j** of the earth; repay to the Ps 94:2
he will **j** the peoples with equity." Ps 96:10
he comes, for he comes to **j** the earth. Ps 96:13
He will **j** the world in righteousness, Ps 96:13
the LORD, for he comes to **j** the earth. Ps 98:9
He will **j** the world with righteousness, Ps 98:9
When will you **j** those who persecute Ps 119:84
Open your mouth, **j** righteously, defend Prv 31:9
God will **j** the righteous and the Eccl 3:17
He shall **j** between the nations, and shall Is 2:4
man and the soldier, the **j** and the prophet, Is 3:2
place to contend; he stands to **j** peoples. Is 3:13
of Judah, **j** between me and my vineyard. Is 5:3
He shall not **j** by what his eyes see, or Is 11:3
with righteousness he shall **j** the poor, Is 11:4
For the LORD is our **j**; the LORD is our Is 33:22
gone out, and my arms will **j** the peoples; Is 51:5
they **j** not with justice the cause of the Jer 5:28
wrong done to me, O LORD; **j** my cause. Lam 3:59
I will **j** you according to your ways, and I Ezk 7:3
you, and **j** you according to your ways, Ezk 7:8
to their judgments I will **j** them, Ezk 7:27
I will **j** you at the border of Israel, and Ezk 11:10
of it. I will **j** you at the border of Israel, Ezk 11:11
And I will **j** you as women who Ezk 16:38
"Therefore I will **j** you, O house of Ezk 18:30
Will you **j** them, son of man, will you Ezk 20:4
them, son of man, will you **j** them? Ezk 20:4
in the land of your origin, I will **j** you. Ezk 21:30
"And you, son of man, will you **j**, will Ezk 22:2
you judge, will you **j** the bloody city? Ezk 22:2
and they shall **j** you according to their Ezk 23:24
will you **j** Oholah and Oholibah? Ezk 23:36
I will **j** each of you according to his Ezk 33:20
Behold, I **j** between sheep and sheep, Ezk 34:17
I myself will **j** between the fat sheep Ezk 34:20
And I will **j** between sheep and sheep. Ezk 34:22
known among them, when I **j** you. Ezk 35:11
and they shall **j** it according to my Ezk 44:24
I will sit to **j** all the surrounding nations. Jl 3:12
He shall **j** between many peoples, and Mi 4:3
a rod they strike the **j** of Israel on the Mi 5:1
well; the prince and the **j** ask for a bribe, Mi 7:3
lest your accuser hand you over to the **j**, Mt 5:25
over to the judge, and the **j** to the guard, Mt 5:25
"**J** not, that you be not judged. Mt 7:1
"**J** not, and you will not be judged; Lk 6:37
who made me a **j** or arbitrator over Lk 12:14
why do you not **j** for yourselves what is Lk 12:57
on the way, lest he drag you to the **j**, Lk 12:58
and the **j** hand you over to the officer, Lk 12:58
city there was a **j** who neither feared God Lk 18:2
said, "Hear what the unrighteous **j** says. Lk 18:6
As I hear, I **j**, and my judgment is just, Jn 5:30
Do not **j** by appearances, but judge with Jn 7:24
appearances, but **j** with right judgment." Jn 7:24
"Does our law **j** a man without first Jn 7:51
You **j** according to the flesh; I judge no Jn 8:15
judge according to the flesh; I **j** no one. Jn 8:15
Yet even if I do **j**, my judgment is true, for Jn 8:16
is true, for it is not I alone who **j**, Jn 8:16
much to say about you and much to **j**, Jn 8:26
there is One who seeks it, and he is the **j**. Jn 8:50
and does not keep them, I do not **j** him; Jn 12:47
I did not come to **j** the world but to save Jn 12:47
and does not receive my words has a **j**; Jn 12:48
that I have spoken will **j** him on the last Jn 12:48
him yourselves and **j** him by your Jn 18:31
to you rather than to God, you must **j**, Acts 4:19
'But I will **j** the nation that they serve,' Acts 7:7
made you a ruler and a **j** over us? Acts 7:27
'Who made you a ruler and a **j**?' Acts 7:35
by God to be **j** of the living and Acts 10:42
it aside and **j** yourselves unworthy of Acts 13:46
on which he will **j** the world in Acts 17:31
I refuse to be a **j** of these things." Acts 18:15
Are you sitting to **j** me according to Acts 23:3
you have been a **j** over this nation, Acts 24:10
condemn yourself, because you, the **j**, Rom 2:1
O man—you who **j** those who do such Rom 2:3
For then how could God **j** the world? Rom 3:6
court. In fact, I do not even **j** myself. 1 Cor 4:3
inside the church whom you are to **j**? 1 Cor 5:12
know that the saints will **j** the world? 1 Cor 6:2
you not know that we are to **j** angels? 1 Cor 6:3
people; **j** for yourselves what I say. 1 Cor 10:15
J for yourselves: is it proper for a wife 1 Cor 11:13
who is to **j** the living and the dead, 2 Tm 4:1
which the Lord, the righteous **j**, 2 Tm 4:8
again, "The Lord will **j** his people." Heb 10:30
in heaven, and to God, the **j** of all, Heb 12:23
for God will **j** the sexually immoral Heb 13:4
But if you **j** the law, you are not a doer of Jas 4:11
law, you are not a doer of the law but a **j**. Jas 4:11
There is only one lawgiver and **j**, he who Jas 4:12
But who are you to **j** your neighbor? Jas 4:12
behold, the **J** is standing at the door. Jas 5:9
him who is ready to **j** the living and the 1 Pt 4:5
long before you will **j** and avenge our Rv 6:10
whom the authority to **j** was committed. Rv 20:4

JUDGED (50)

Then Rachel said, "God has **j** me, and Gn 30:6
And they **j** the people at all times. Any Ex 18:26
the LORD was upon him, and he **j** Israel. Jgs 3:10
And he **j** Israel twenty-three years. Then Jgs 10:2
Gileadite, who **j** Israel twenty-two years. Jgs 10:3
Jephthah **j** Israel six years. Then Jgs 12:7
After him Ibzan of Bethlehem **j** Israel. Jgs 12:8
for his sons. And he **j** Israel seven years. Jgs 12:9
After him Elon the Zebulunite **j** Israel, Jgs 12:11
judged Israel, and he **j** Israel ten years. Jgs 12:11
the son of Hillel the Pirathonite **j** Israel. Jgs 12:13
donkeys, and he **j** Israel eight years. Jgs 12:14
And he **j** Israel in the days of the Jgs 15:20
his father. He had **j** Israel twenty years. Jgs 16:31
and heavy. He had **j** Israel forty years. 1 Sm 4:18
the LORD." And Samuel **j** the people of 1 Sm 7:6
Samuel **j** Israel all the days of his life. 1 Sm 7:15
And he **j** Israel in all these places. 1 Sm 7:16
was there, and there also he **j** Israel. 1 Sm 7:17
the days of the judges who **j** Israel, 2 Kgs 23:22
and a man full of talk be **j** right? Jb 11:2
prevail; let the nations be **j** before you! Ps 9:19
He **j** the cause of the poor and needy; Jer 22:16
commit adultery and shed blood are **j**, Ezk 16:38
ways and your deeds you will be **j**, Ezk 24:14
their ways and their deeds I **j** them. Ezk 36:19
"Judge not, that you be not **j**. Mt 7:1
judgment you pronounce you will be **j**, Mt 7:2
"Judge not, and you will not be **j**; Lk 6:37
he said to him, "You have **j** rightly." Lk 7:43
because the ruler of this world is **j**. Jn 16:11
"If you have **j** me to be faithful to the Acts 16:15
under the law will be **j** by the law. Rom 2:12
words, and prevail when you are **j**." Rom 3:4
but is himself to be **j** by no one. 1 Cor 2:15
thing that I should be **j** by you or by 1 Cor 4:3
And if the world is to be **j** by you, are 1 Cor 6:2
But if we **j** ourselves truly, we would 1 Cor 11:31
ourselves truly, we would not be **j**. 1 Cor 11:31
But when we are **j** by the Lord, we 1 Cor 11:32
our Lord, because he **j** me faithful, 1 Tm 1:12
those who are to be **j** under the law of Jas 2:12
teach will be **j** with greater strictness. Jas 3:1
brothers, so that you may not be **j**; Jas 5:9
that though **j** in the flesh the way people 1 Pt 4:6
came, and the time for the dead to be **j**, Rv 11:18
mighty is the Lord God who has **j** her." Rv 18:8
for he has **j** the great prostitute who Rv 19:2
And the dead were **j** by what was Rv 20:12
dead who were in them, and they were **j**, Rv 20:13

JUDGES (62)

and he shall pay as the **j** determine. Ex 21:22
And Moses said to the **j** of Israel, "Each Nm 25:5
And I charged your **j** at that time, 'Hear Dt 1:16
"You shall appoint **j** and officers in all Dt 16:18
the priests and the **j** who are in office Dt 19:17
The **j** shall inquire diligently, and if the Dt 19:18
your elders and your **j** shall come out, Dt 21:2
into court and the **j** decide between them, Dt 25:1
with their elders and officers and their **j**, Jos 8:33
its elders and heads, its **j** and officers, Jos 23:2
summoned the elders, the heads, the **j**, Jos 24:1
Then the LORD raised up **j**, who saved Jgs 2:16
Yet they did not listen to their **j**, for they Jgs 2:17
Whenever the LORD raised up **j** for them, Jgs 2:18
In the days when the **j** ruled there was a Ru 1:1
old, he made his sons **j** over Israel. 1 Sm 8:1
Abijah; they were **j** in Beersheba. 1 Sm 8:2
speak a word with any of the **j** of Israel, 2 Sm 7:7
time that I appointed **j** over my people 2 Sm 7:11
the days of the **j** who judged Israel, 2 Kgs 23:22
a word with any of the **j** of Israel, 1 Chr 17:6
that I appointed **j** over my people 1 Chr 17:10
the LORD, 6,000 shall be officers and **j**, 1 Chr 23:4
duties for Israel, as officers and **j**. 1 Chr 26:29
of thousands and of hundreds, to the **j**, 2 Chr 1:2
He appointed **j** in the land in all the 2 Chr 19:5
and said to the **j**, "Consider what you 2 Chr 19:6
and the rest of their associates, the **j**, Ezr 4:9
appoint magistrates and **j** who may Ezr 7:25
with them the elders and **j** of every city, Ezr 10:14
he covers the faces of its **j**—if it is not he, Jb 9:24
away stripped, and **j** he makes fools. Jb 12:17
seeing that he **j** those who are on high? Jb 21:22
be an iniquity to be punished by the **j**; Jb 31:11
be an iniquity to be punished by the **j**, Jb 31:28
For by these he **j** peoples; he gives food Jb 36:31
The LORD **j** the peoples; judge me, O LORD, Ps 7:8
and he **j** the world with righteousness; he Ps 9:8
he **j** the peoples with uprightness. Ps 9:8
surely there is a God who **j** on earth." Ps 58:11
When their **j** are thrown over the cliff, Ps 141:6
If a king faithfully **j** the poor, his Prv 29:14
And I will restore your **j** as at the first, and Is 1:26
of David one who **j** and seeks justice and Is 16:5
But, O LORD of hosts, who **j** righteously, Jer 11:20
In a dispute, they shall act as **j**, and Ezk 44:24
her **j** are evening wolves that leave Zep 3:3
out? Therefore they will be your **j**. Mt 12:27
out? Therefore they will be your **j**. Lk 11:19
The Father **j** no one, but has given all Jn 5:22
that he gave them **j** until Samuel the Acts 13:20
excuse, O man, every one of you who **j**. Rom 2:1
God **j** the secrets of men by Christ Rom 2:16
The spiritual person **j** all things, but 1 Cor 2:15
acquitted. It is the Lord who **j** me. 1 Cor 4:4
God **j** those outside. "Purge the evil 1 Cor 5:13
yourselves and become **j** with evil Jas 2:4
against a brother or **j** his brother, Jas 4:11
speaks evil against the law and **j** the law. Jas 4:11
as Father who **j** impartially according 1 Pt 1:17
entrusting himself to him who **j** justly. 1 Pt 2:23
in righteousness he **j** and makes war. Rv 19:11

JUDGING (5)

of Lappidoth, was **j** Israel at that time. Jgs 4:4
of the wise. Partiality in **j** is not good. Prv 24:23
thrones, **j** the twelve tribes of Israel. Mt 19:28
and sit on thrones **j** the twelve tribes of Lk 22:30
what have I to do with **j** outsiders? 1 Cor 5:12

JUDGMENT (170)

But I will bring **j** on the nation that Gn 15:14
outstretched arm and with great acts of **j**. Ex 6:6
out of the land of Egypt by great acts of **j**. Ex 7:4
"You shall make a breastpiece of **j**, in Ex 28:15
in the breastpiece of **j** on his heart, Ex 28:29
in the breastpiece of **j** you shall put the Ex 28:30
Aaron shall bear the **j** of the people of Ex 28:30
"You shall do no wrong in **j**, in Lv 19:35
for him by the **j** of the Urim before Nm 27:21
stands before the congregation for **j**. Nm 35:12
You shall not be partial in **j**. You shall Dt 1:17
intimidated by anyone, for the **j** is God's. Dt 1:17
shall judge the people with righteous **j**. Dt 16:18
sword and my hand takes hold on **j**, Dt 32:41
has stood before the congregation for **j**, Jos 20:6
the people of Israel came up to her for **j**. Jgs 4:5
a dispute to come before the king for **j**, 2 Sm 15:2

of Israel who came to the king for **j**. 2 Sm 15:6
Israel heard of the **j** that the king had 1 Kgs 3:28
Throne where he was to pronounce **j**, 1 Kgs 7:7
judgment, even the Hall of **J**. 1 Kgs 7:7
said to him, "So shall your **j** be; 1 Kgs 20:40
the LORD. He is with you in giving **j**. 2 Chr 19:6
to give **j** for the LORD and to decide 2 Chr 19:8
upon us, the sword, **j**, or pestilence, 2 Chr 20:9
God, will you not execute **j** on them? 2 Chr 20:12
Jehu was executing **j** on the house 2 Chr 22:8
Thus they executed **j** on Joash. 2 Chr 24:24
king, let **j** be strictly executed on him, Ezr 7:26
toward all who were versed in law and **j**, Est 1:13
such a one and bring me into **j** with you? Jb 14:3
sword, that you may know there is a **j**." Jb 19:29
reproves you and enters into **j** with you? Jb 22:4
are not times of **j** kept by the Almighty, Jb 24:1
that he should go before God in **j**. Jb 34:23
"But you are full of the **j** on the wicked; Jb 36:17
on the wicked; **j** and justice seize you. Jb 36:17
the wicked will not stand in the **j**, Ps 1:5
awake for me; you have appointed a **j**. Ps 7:6
have sat on the throne, giving righteous **j**. Ps 9:4
made himself known; he has executed **j**; Ps 9:16
in your words and blameless in your **j**. Ps 51:4
but it is God who executes **j**, putting Ps 75:7
From the heavens you uttered **j**; the earth Ps 76:8
when God arose to establish **j**, to save all Ps 76:9
in the midst of the gods he holds **j**: Ps 82:1
He will execute **j** among the nations, Ps 110:6
Teach me good **j** and knowledge, for I Ps 119:66
There thrones for **j** were set, the thrones Ps 122:5
Enter not into **j** with your servant, for Ps 143:2
to execute on them the **j** written! This is Ps 149:9
of a king; his mouth does not sin in **j**. Prv 16:10
he breaks out against all sound **j**. Prv 18:1
on the throne of **j** winnows all evil with Prv 20:8
these things God will bring you into **j**. Eccl 11:9
For God will bring every deed into **j**, Eccl 12:14
LORD will enter into **j** with the elders and Is 3:14
its midst by a spirit of **j** and by a spirit of Is 4:4
and a spirit of justice to him who sits in **j**, Is 28:6
reel in vision, they stumble in giving **j**. Is 28:7
behold, it descends for **j** upon Edom, Is 34:5
speak; let us together draw near for **j**. Is 41:1
By oppression and **j** he was taken away; Is 53:8
every tongue that rises against you in **j**. Is 54:17
and did not forsake the **j** of their God; Is 58:2
For by fire will the LORD enter into **j**, and Is 66:16
Behold, I will bring you to **j** for saying, 'I Jer 2:35
Now it is I who speak in **j** upon them." Jer 4:12
he is entering into **j** with all flesh, and Jer 25:31
"**J** has come upon the tableland, upon Jer 48:21
the LORD." Thus far is the **j** on Moab. Jer 48:47
for her **j** has reached up to heaven and Jer 51:9
when I will execute **j** upon her images, Jer 51:52
Jerusalem my four disastrous acts of **j**, Ezk 14:21
and enter into **j** with him there Ezk 17:20
there I will enter into **j** with you face to Ezk 20:35
As I entered into **j** with your fathers in Ezk 20:36
of Egypt, so I will enter into **j** with you, Ezk 20:36
he comes, the one to whom **j** belongs, Ezk 21:27
when **j** had been executed on her. Ezk 23:10
and I will commit the **j** to them, and Ezk 23:24
men shall pass **j** on them with Ezk 23:45
bloodshed I will enter into **j** with him, Ezk 38:22
nations shall see my **j** that I have Ezk 39:21
the court sat in **j**, and the books were Dn 7:10
and **j** was given for the saints of the Dn 7:22
But the court shall sit in **j**, and his Dn 7:26
For the **j** is for you; for you have been a Hos 5:1
Ephraim is oppressed, crushed in **j**, Hos 5:11
mouth, and my **j** goes forth as the light. Hos 6:5
so **j** springs up like poisonous weeds in Hos 10:4
And I will enter into **j** with them there, on Jl 3:2
the Lord GOD was calling for a **j** by fire, Am 7:4
Its heads give **j** for a bribe; its priests Mi 3:11
he pleads my cause and executes **j** for me. Mi 7:9
O LORD, you have ordained them as a **j**, Hab 1:12
"Then I will draw near to you for **j**. I will Mal 3:5
and whoever murders will be liable to **j**.' Mt 5:21
angry with his brother will be liable to **j**; Mt 5:22
For with the **j** you pronounce you will be Mt 7:2
bearable on the day of **j** for the land of Mt 10:15
on the day of **j** for Tyre and Sidon Mt 11:22
tolerable on the day of **j** for the land of Mt 11:24
on the day of **j** people will give account Mt 12:36
rise up at the **j** with this generation and Mt 12:41
rise up at the **j** with this generation and Mt 12:42
What is your **j**?" They answered, "He Mt 26:66
while he was sitting on the **j** seat, Mt 27:19
more bearable in the **j** for Tyre and Lk 10:14
will rise up at the **j** with the men of this Lk 11:31
rise up at the **j** with this generation and Lk 11:32
And this is the **j**: the light has come into Jn 3:19
no one, but has given all **j** to the Son, Jn 5:22
He does not come into **j**, but has passed Jn 5:24
he has given him authority to execute **j**, Jn 5:27
have done evil to the resurrection of **j**. Jn 5:29
As I hear, I judge, and my **j** is just, Jn 5:30
by appearances, but judge with right **j**." Jn 7:24
Yet even if I do judge, my **j** is true, for it is Jn 8:16
Jesus said, "For **j** I came into this world, Jn 9:39
Now is the **j** of this world; now will the Jn 12:31
concerning sin and righteousness and **j**: Jn 16:8
concerning **j**, because the ruler of this Jn 16:11
and sat down on the **j** seat at a place Jn 19:13
Therefore my **j** is that we should not Acts 15:19
a letter with our **j** that they should Acts 21:25
and self-control and the coming **j**, Acts 24:25
For in passing **j** on another you Rom 2:1
We know that the **j** of God rightly falls Rom 2:2
—that you will escape the **j** of God? Rom 2:3
when God's righteous **j** will be revealed. Rom 2:5
For the **j** following one trespass Rom 5:16
to think, but to think with sober **j**, Rom 12:3
and those who resist will incur **j**. Rom 13:2
one who abstains pass **j** on the one Rom 14:3
are you to pass **j** on the servant of Rom 14:4
Why do you pass **j** on your brother? Rom 14:10
will all stand before the **j** seat of God; Rom 14:10
let us not pass **j** on one another any Rom 14:13
no reason to pass **j** on himself for Rom 14:22
in the same mind and the same **j**. 1 Cor 1:10
do not pronounce **j** before the time, 1 Cor 4:5
I have already pronounced **j** on the one 1 Cor 5:3
but I give my **j** as one who by the 1 Cor 7:25
Yet in my **j** she is happier if she 1 Cor 7:40
body eats and drinks **j** on himself. 1 Cor 11:29
come together it will not be for **j**. 1 Cor 11:34
all appear before the **j** seat of Christ, 2 Cor 5:10
And in this matter I give my **j**: this 2 Cor 8:10
let no one pass **j** on you in questions Col 2:16
is evidence of the righteous **j** of God, 2 Thes 1:5
conspicuous, going before them to **j**, 1 Tm 5:24
resurrection of the dead, and eternal **j**. Heb 6:2
man to die once, and after that comes **j**, Heb 9:27
but a fearful expectation of **j**, and a Heb 10:27
For **j** is without mercy to one who has Jas 2:13
no mercy. Mercy triumphs over **j**. Jas 2:13
For it is time for **j** to begin at the 1 Pt 4:17
gloomy darkness to be kept until the **j**; 2 Pt 2:4
under punishment until the day of **j**, 2 Pt 2:9
a blasphemous **j** against them 2 Pt 2:11
until the day of **j** and destruction of the 2 Pt 3:7
may have confidence for the day of **j**, 1 Jn 4:17
gloomy darkness until the **j** of the great Jude 1:6
presume to pronounce a blasphemous **j**, Jude 1:9
to execute **j** on all and to convict all the Jude 1:15
because the hour of his **j** has come, Rv 14:7
will show you the **j** of the great prostitute Rv 17:1
For in a single hour your **j** has come." Rv 18:10
for God has given **j** for you against Rv 18:20

JUDGMENTS (36)
on all the gods of Egypt I will execute **j**: Ex 12:12
On their gods also the LORD executed **j**. Nm 33:4
justice of the LORD, and his **j** for Israel." Dt 33:21
his miracles and the **j** he uttered, 1 Chr 16:12
our God, his **j** are in all the earth. 1 Chr 16:14
times; your **j** are on high, out of his sight; Ps 10:5
of God; your **j** are like the great deep; Ps 36:6
of Judah rejoice because of your **j**! Ps 48:11
of Judah rejoice, because of your **j**, Ps 97:8
done, his miracles, and the **j** he uttered, Ps 105:5
LORD our God; his **j** are in all the earth. Ps 105:7
fear of you, and I am afraid of your **j**. Ps 119:120
In the path of your **j**, O LORD, we wait for Is 26:8
For when your **j** are in the earth, the Is 26:9
of their God; they ask of me righteous **j**; Is 58:2
And I will declare my **j** against them, for Jer 1:16
And I will execute **j** in your midst in the Ezk 5:8
And I will execute **j** on you, and any of Ezk 5:10
when I execute **j** on you in anger and Ezk 5:15
and according to their **j** I will judge Ezk 7:27
of foreigners, and execute **j** upon you. Ezk 11:9
houses and execute **j** upon you in Ezk 16:41
shall judge you according to their **j**. Ezk 23:24
and I will execute **j** upon Moab. Then Ezk 25:11
LORD when I execute **j** in her and Ezk 28:22
when I execute **j** upon all their Ezk 28:26
to Zoan and will execute **j** on Thebes. Ezk 30:14
Thus I will execute **j** on Egypt. Then Ezk 30:19
they shall judge it according to my **j**. Ezk 44:24
LORD has taken away the **j** against you; Zep 3:15
says the LORD of hosts, Render true **j**, Zec 7:9
render in your gates **j** that are true and Zec 8:16
unsearchable are his **j** and how Rom 11:33
is and who was, for you brought these **j**. Rv 16:5
the Almighty, true and just are your **j**!" Rv 16:7
for his **j** are true and just; for he has Rv 19:2

JUDICIOUS (1)
makes his speech **j** and adds Prv 16:23

JUDITH (1)
he took **J** the daughter of Beeri the Gn 26:34

JUG (3)
of flour in a jar and a little oil in a **j**. 1 Kgs 17:12
and the **j** of oil shall not be empty, 1 Kgs 17:14
neither did the **j** of oil become 1 Kgs 17:16

JUICE (3)
and shall not drink any **j** of grapes or eat Nm 6:3
or is there any taste in the **j** of the mallow? Jb 6:6
wine to drink, the **j** of my pomegranate. Sg 8:2

JULIA (1)
Philologus, **J**, Nereus and his sister, Rom 16:15

JULIUS (2)
of the Augustan Cohort named **J**. Acts 27:1
And **J** treated Paul kindly and gave Acts 27:3

JUMP (1)
could swim to **j** overboard first and Acts 27:43

JUNGLE (1)
coming up from the **j** of the Jordan Jer 49:19

JUNIA (1)
Greet Andronicus and **J**, my kinsmen Rom 16:7

JUNIPER (1)
You will be like a **j** in the desert! Jer 48:6

JURISDICTION (2)
to the authority and **j** of the governor. Lk 20:20
he learned that he belonged to Herod's **j**, Lk 23:7

JUSHAB-HESED (1)
Ohel, Berechiah, Hasadiah, and **J**, 1 Chr 3:20

JUST (206)
the Judge of all the earth do what is **j**?" Gn 18:25
j as we have not touched you and have Gn 26:29
they did **j** as the LORD commanded them. Ex 7:6
to Pharaoh and did **j** as the LORD Ex 7:10
j as the LORD had spoken through Moses. Ex 9:35
people of Israel did **j** as the LORD Ex 12:50
(**j** as these are taken from the ox of the Lv 4:10
The guilt offering is **j** like the sin offering; Lv 7:7
You shall have **j** balances, just weights, Lv 19:36
You shall have just balances, **j** weights, Lv 19:36
just balances, just weights, a **j** ephah, Lv 19:36
just weights, a just ephah, and a **j** hin: Lv 19:36
You shall not eat **j** one day, or two Nm 11:19
j as you have forgiven this people, Nm 14:19
surely **j** now I would have killed you Nm 22:33
of Israel everything **j** as the LORD Nm 29:40
j as he did for you in Egypt before your Dt 1:30
j as the LORD our God commanded us.' Dt 1:41
J as the gazelle or the deer is eaten, so Dt 12:22
j as you desired of the LORD your God at Dt 18:16
and without iniquity, **j** and upright is he. Dt 32:4
given to you, **j** as I promised to Moses. Jos 1:3
J as I was with Moses, so I will be with Jos 1:5
J as we obeyed Moses in all things, so we Jos 1:17
of Israel did **j** as Joshua commanded Jos 4:8
people of Israel, **j** as the LORD told Joshua. Jos 4:8
stood in awe of him **j** as they had stood Jos 4:14
And **j** as Joshua had commanded the Jos 6:8
they come out against us **j** as before, Jos 8:5
say, 'They are fleeing from us, **j** as before.' Jos 8:6
j as Moses the servant of the LORD had Jos 8:31
j as Moses the servant of the LORD had Jos 8:33
j as the leaders had said of them. Jos 9:21
the king of Makkedah **j** as he had done Jos 10:28
J as he had done to Hebron and to Jos 10:39
j as the LORD God of Israel commanded. Jos 10:40
Joshua did to them **j** as the LORD said Jos 11:9
j as Moses the servant of the LORD had Jos 11:12
J as the LORD had commanded Moses Jos 11:15
j as the LORD commanded Moses. Jos 11:20
their inheritance, **j** as he said to them. Jos 13:33
j as the LORD had commanded by the Jos 14:2
the LORD has kept me alive, **j** as he said, Jos 14:10
shall drive them out **j** as the LORD said." Jos 14:12
rest on every side **j** as he had sworn Jos 21:44
j as the LORD your God promised you. Jos 23:5
to the LORD your God **j** as you have done Jos 23:8
fights for you, **j** as he promised you. Jos 23:10
But **j** as all the good things that the Jos 23:15
against me; let me speak **j** once more. Jgs 6:39
Please let me test **j** once more with the Jgs 6:39
watch, when they had **j** set the watch. Jgs 7:19
floor and did **j** as her mother-in-law Ru 3:6
"He is; behold, he is **j** ahead of you. 1 Sm 9:12
He has come **j** now to the city, 1 Sm 9:12
J then the servants of David arrived 2 Sm 3:22
j as Absalom was entering 2 Sm 15:37
'There have **j** now come to me from 2 Kgs 5:22
j as their brothers the sons of 1 Chr 24:31

had duties, **j** as their brothers did, 1 Chr 26:12
O LORD the God of Israel, you are **j**, for Ezr 9:15
Esther obeyed Mordecai **j** as when she Est 2:20
Now Haman had **j** entered the outer Est 6:4
he answered me, a **j** and blameless man, Jb 12:4
(Let me be weighed in a **j** balance, and let Jb 31:6
"Do you think this to be **j**? Do you say, 'It Jb 35:2
For you have maintained my **j** cause; you Ps 9:4
Hear a **j** cause, O LORD; attend to my cry! Ps 17:1
In **j** a little while, the wicked will be no Ps 37:10
works of his hands are faithful and **j**; Ps 111:7
I have done what is **j** and right; do not Ps 119:121
kings reign, and rulers decree what is **j**; Prv 8:15
to the LORD, but a **j** weight is his delight. Prv 11:1
The thoughts of the righteous are **j**; the Prv 12:5
A **j** balance and scales are the LORD'S; Prv 16:11
because they refuse to do what is **j**. Prv 21:7
How the wise dies **j** like the fool! Eccl 2:16
j as he came, so shall he go, and what Eccl 5:16
will know the proper time and the **j** way. Eccl 8:5
j as the Israelites bring their grain Is 66:20
Have you not **j** now called to me, 'My Jer 3:4
I will discipline you in **j** measure, and I Jer 30:11
J as I have brought all this great Jer 32:42
I will discipline you in **j** measure, and I Jer 46:28
j as for Babylon have fallen the slain of Jer 51:49
righteous and does what is **j** and right— Ezk 18:5
the son has done what is **j** and right, Ezk 18:19
statutes and does what is **j** and right, Ezk 18:21
you say, 'The way of the Lord is not **j**.' Ezk 18:25
O house of Israel: Is my way not **j**? Ezk 18:25
just? Is it not your ways that are not **j**? Ezk 18:25
and does what is **j** and right, Ezk 18:27
says, 'The way of the Lord is not **j**.' Ezk 18:29
O house of Israel, are my ways not **j**? Ezk 18:29
just? Is it not your ways that are not **j**? Ezk 18:29
his sin and does what is **j** and right, Ezk 33:14
He has done what is **j** and right; he Ezk 33:16
say, 'The way of the Lord is not **j**,' Ezk 33:17
when it is their own way that is not **j**. Ezk 33:17
and does what is **j** and right, Ezk 33:19
you say, 'The way of the Lord is not **j**.' Ezk 33:20
vision I saw was **j** like the vision that Ezk 43:3
and **j** like the vision that I had seen by Ezk 43:3
"You shall have **j** balances, a just Ezk 45:10
shall have just balances, a **j** ephah, Ezk 45:10
balances, a just ephah, and a **j** bath. Ezk 45:10
j as you saw iron mixed with the soft Dn 2:41
j as iron does not mix with clay. Dn 2:43
j as you saw that a stone was cut from a Dn 2:45
his works are right and his ways are **j**; Dn 4:37
for in **j** a little while I will punish the Hos 1:4
latter growth was **j** beginning to sprout, Am 7:1
of the land, who do his **j** commands; Zep 2:3
being a **j** man and unwilling to put her Mt 1:19
sends rain on the **j** and on the unjust. Mt 5:45
him, saying, "My daughter has **j** died, Mt 9:18
For **j** as Jonah was three days and three Mt 12:40
J as the weeds are gathered and burned Mt 13:40
him with them in the boat, **j** as he was. Mk 4:36
the city and found it **j** as he had told Mk 14:16
you will see him, **j** as he told you." Mk 16:7
j as those who from the beginning were Lk 1:2
the disobedient to the wisdom of the **j**, Lk 1:17
tax collectors too, they declared God **j**, Lk 7:29
be repaid at the resurrection of the **j**." Lk 14:14
J so, I tell you, there will be more joy in Lk 15:7
J so, I tell you, there is joy before the Lk 15:10
J as it was in the days of Noah, so will it Lk 17:26
j as it was in the days of Lot—they were Lk 17:28
went away and found it **j** as he had told Lk 19:32
they went and found it **j** as he had told Lk 22:13
tomb and found it **j** as the women had Lk 24:24
J then his disciples came back. They Jn 4:27
the Son, **j** as they honor the Father. Jn 5:23
As I hear, I judge, and my judgment is **j**, Jn 5:30
"**J** what I have been telling you from the Jn 8:25
but speak **j** as the Father taught me. Jn 8:28
j as the Father knows me and I know Jn 10:15
the Jews were **j** now seeking to stone you, Jn 11:8
donkey and sat on it, **j** as it is written, Jn 12:14
that you also should do **j** as I have done Jn 13:15
will seek me, and **j** as I said to the Jews, Jn 13:33
j as I have loved you, you also are to love Jn 13:34
j as I have kept my Father's Jn 15:10
of the world, **j** as I am not of the world. Jn 17:14
of the world, **j** as I am not of the world. Jn 17:16
that they may all be one, **j** as you, Jn 17:21
J as day was breaking, Jesus stood on the Jn 21:4
of the fish that you have **j** caught." Jn 21:10
j as he who spoke to Moses directed Acts 7:44
received the Holy Spirit **j** as we have?" Acts 10:47
Holy Spirit fell on them **j** as on us at Acts 11:15
them the Holy Spirit **j** as he did to Acts 15:8
grace of the Lord Jesus, **j** as they will." Acts 15:11
of the prophets agree, **j** as it is written, Acts 15:15
of both the **j** and the unjust. Acts 24:15
with saying. Their condemnation is **j**. Rom 3:8
that he might be **j** and the justifier of Rom 3:26
j as David also speaks of the blessing of Rom 4:6
j as sin came into the world through Rom 5:12
j as Christ was raised from the dead by Rom 6:4
For **j** as you once presented your Rom 6:19
J as you were at one time disobedient Rom 11:30
j as I try to please everyone in 1 Cor 10:33
For **j** as the body is one and has 1 Cor 12:12
J as we have borne the image of the 1 Cor 15:49
not want to see you now **j** in passing. 1 Cor 16:7
j as you did partially acknowledge us, 2 Cor 1:14
But **j** as everything we said to you was 2 Cor 7:14
him remind himself that **j** as he is 2 Cor 10:7
j as Peter had been entrusted with the Gal 2:7
j as Abraham "believed God, and it was Gal 3:6
But **j** as at that time he who was born Gal 4:29
and one Spirit—**j** as you were called Eph 4:4
it, **j** as Christ does the church, Eph 5:29
therefore to send him **j** as soon as I Phil 2:23
whatever is honorable, whatever is **j**, Phil 4:8
j as you learned it from Epaphras our Col 1:7
in the faith, **j** as you were taught, Col 2:7
but **j** as we have been approved by 1 Thes 2:4
affliction, **j** as it has come to pass, 1 Thes 3:4
has come to pass, and **j** as you know. 1 Thes 3:4
and to please God, **j** as you are doing, 1 Thes 4:1
one another up, **j** as you are doing. 1 Thes 5:11
God considers it **j** to repay with 2 Thes 1:6
laid down for the **j** but for the lawless 1 Tm 1:9
J as Jannes and Jambres opposed 2 Tm 3:8
or disobedience received a **j** retribution, Heb 2:2
j as Moses also was faithful in all God's Heb 3:2
For good news came to us **j** as to them, Heb 4:2
sacrifice for his own sins **j** as he does for Heb 5:3
when called by God, **j** as Aaron was. Heb 5:4
And **j** as it is appointed for man to die Heb 9:27
j as there will be false teachers among 2 Pt 2:1
j as our beloved brother Paul also 2 Pt 3:15
he is faithful and **j** to forgive us our sins 1 Jn 1:9
j as it has taught you—abide in him. 1 Jn 2:27
another, **j** as he has commanded us. 1 Jn 3:23
j as we were commanded by the Father. 2 Jn 1:4
j as you have heard from the beginning, 2 Jn 1:6
j as Sodom and Gomorrah and the Jude 1:7
j as he announced to his servants the Rv 10:7
J and true are your ways, O King of the Rv 15:3
in charge of the waters say, "**J** are you, Rv 16:5
true and **j** are your judgments!" Rv 16:7
for his judgments are true and **j**; for he Rv 19:2

JUSTICE (135)

the LORD by doing righteousness and **j**, Gn 18:19
siding with the many, so as to pervert **j**, Ex 23:2
shall not pervert the **j** due to your poor Ex 23:6
He executes **j** for the fatherless and the Dt 10:18
You shall not pervert **j**. You shall not Dt 16:19
J, and only justice, you shall follow, Dt 16:20
Justice, and only **j**, you shall follow, Dt 16:20
shall not pervert the **j** due to the Dt 24:17
anyone who perverts the **j** due to the Dt 27:19
his work is perfect, for all his ways are **j**. Dt 32:4
with Israel he executed the **j** of the LORD, Dt 33:21
gain. They took bribes and perverted **j**. 1 Sm 8:3
And David administered **j** and equity 2 Sm 8:15
come to me, and I would give him **j**." 2 Sm 15:4
the wisdom of God was in him to do **j**. 1 Kgs 3:28
may execute **j** and righteousness." 1 Kgs 10:9
and he administered **j** and equity to 1 Chr 18:14
you may execute **j** and righteousness." 2 Chr 9:8
Does God pervert **j**? Or does the Almighty Jb 8:3
If it is a matter of **j**, who can summon Jb 9:19
answered; I call for help, but there is no **j**. Jb 19:7
me; my **j** was like a robe and a turban. Jb 29:14
and the Almighty will not pervert **j**. Jb 34:12
Shall one who hates **j** govern? Will you Jb 34:17
the wicked; judgment and **j** seize you. Jb 36:17
j and abundant righteousness he will Jb 37:23
forever; he has established his throne for **j**, Ps 9:7
to do **j** to the fatherless and the Ps 10:18
He loves righteousness and **j**; the earth is Ps 33:5
as the light, and your **j** as the noonday. Ps 37:6
For the LORD loves **j**; he will not forsake Ps 37:28
utters wisdom, and his tongue speaks **j**. Ps 37:30
Give the king your **j**, O God, and your Ps 72:1
righteousness, and your poor with **j**! Ps 72:2
Give **j** to the weak and the fatherless; Ps 82:3
Righteousness and **j** are the foundation Ps 89:14
for **j** will return to the righteous, and all Ps 94:15
righteousness and **j** are the foundation of Ps 97:2
The King in his might loves **j**. You have Ps 99:4
you have executed **j** and righteousness in Ps 99:4
I will sing of steadfast love and **j**; to you, Ps 101:1
works righteousness and **j** for all who Ps 103:6
Blessed are they who observe **j**, who do Ps 106:3
lends; who conducts his affairs with **j**. Ps 112:5
LORD, according to your **j** give me life. Ps 119:149
and will execute **j** for the needy. Ps 140:12
who executes **j** for the oppressed, who Ps 146:7
dealing, in righteousness, **j**, and equity; Prv 1:3
the paths of **j** and watching over Prv 2:8
righteousness and **j** and equity, Prv 2:9
way of righteousness, in the paths of **j**, Prv 8:20
bribe in secret to pervert the ways of **j**. Prv 17:23
wicked or to deprive the righteous of **j**. Prv 18:5
A worthless witness mocks at **j**, and Prv 19:28
do righteousness and **j** is more Prv 21:3
When **j** is done, it is a joy to the Prv 21:15
Evil men do not understand **j**, but those Prv 28:5
By **j** a king builds up the land, but he Prv 29:4
it is from the LORD that a man gets **j**. Prv 29:26
under the sun that in the place of **j**, Eccl 3:16
and the violation of **j** and righteousness, Eccl 5:8
learn to do good; seek **j**, correct Is 1:17
bring **j** to the fatherless, plead the widow's Is 1:17
become a whore, she who was full of **j**! Is 1:21
They do not bring **j** to the fatherless, and Is 1:23
Zion shall be redeemed by **j**, and those in Is 1:27
and he looked for **j**, but behold, bloodshed; Is 5:7
But the LORD of hosts is exalted in **j**, and Is 5:16
to uphold it with **j** and with righteousness Is 9:7
turn aside the needy from **j** and to rob the Is 10:2
"Give counsel; grant **j**; make your shade Is 16:3
one who judges and seeks **j** and is swift to Is 16:5
and a spirit of **j** to him who sits in Is 28:6
And I will make **j** the line, and Is 28:17
For the LORD is a God of **j**; blessed are all Is 30:18
righteousness, and princes will rule in **j**. Is 32:1
Then **j** will dwell in the wilderness, and Is 32:16
he will fill Zion with **j** and righteousness, Is 33:5
Who taught him the path of **j**, and Is 40:14
him; he will bring forth **j** to the nations. Is 42:1
quench; he will faithfully bring forth **j**. Is 42:3
till he has established **j** in the earth; Is 42:4
and I will set my **j** for a light to the Is 51:4
Thus says the LORD: "Keep **j**, and do Is 56:1
not know, and there is no **j** in their paths; Is 59:8
Therefore **j** is far from us, and Is 59:9
doves; we hope for **j**, but there is none; Is 59:11
J is turned back, and righteousness Is 59:14
and it displeased him that there was no **j**. Is 59:15
For I the LORD love **j**; I hate robbery and Is 61:8
swear, 'As the LORD lives,' in truth, in **j**, Jer 4:2
a man, one who does **j** and seeks truth, Jer 5:1
the way of the LORD, the **j** of their God. Jer 5:4
the **j** of their God." But they all alike had Jer 5:5
they judge not with **j** the cause of the Jer 5:28
if you truly execute **j** one with another, Jer 7:5
love, **j**, and righteousness in the earth. Jer 9:24
Correct me, O LORD, but in **j**; not in Jer 10:24
so is he who gets riches but not by **j**; Jer 17:11
"'Execute **j** in the morning, and deliver Jer 21:12
Do **j** and righteousness, and deliver from Jer 22:3
and drink and do **j** and righteousness? Jer 22:15
and shall execute **j** and righteousness in Jer 23:5
he shall execute **j** and righteousness in Jer 33:15
to deny a man **j** in the presence of the Lam 3:35
executes true **j** between man and man, Ezk 18:8
extorted from the sojourner without **j**. Ezk 22:29
I will destroy. I will feed them in **j**. Ezk 34:16
and execute **j** and righteousness. Ezk 45:9
you to me in righteousness and in **j**, Hos 2:19
your God, return, hold fast to love and **j**, Hos 12:6
O you who turn **j** to wormwood and cast Am 5:7
love good, and establish **j** in the gate; Am 5:15
But let **j** roll down like waters, and Am 5:24
But you have turned **j** into poison and Am 6:12
house of Israel! Is it not for you to know **j**? Mi 3:1
Spirit of the LORD, and with **j** and might, Mi 3:8
who detest **j** and make crooked all that is Mi 3:9
does the LORD require of you but to do **j**, Mi 6:8
law is paralyzed, and **j** never goes forth. Hab 1:4
the righteous; so **j** goes forth perverted. Hab 1:4
their **j** and dignity go forth from Hab 1:7
every morning he shows forth his **j**; Zep 3:5
Or by asking, "Where is the God of **j**?" Mal 2:17
and he will proclaim **j** to the Gentiles. Mt 12:18
quench, until he brings **j** to victory; Mt 12:20
the law: **j** and mercy and faithfulness. Mt 23:23
herb, and neglect **j** and the love of God. Lk 11:42
'Give me **j** against my adversary.' Lk 18:3
keeps bothering me, I will give her **j**, Lk 18:5
And will not God give **j** to his elect, who Lk 18:7
I tell you, he will give **j** to them speedily. Lk 18:8
In his humiliation **j** was denied him. Acts 8:33
the sea, **J** has not allowed him to live." Acts 28:4
faith conquered kingdoms, enforced **j**, Heb 11:33

JUSTICES (2)

the counselors, the treasurers, the **j**, Dn 3:2

the counselors, the treasurers, the **j**, Dn 3:3

JUSTIFICATION (4)
for our trespasses and raised for our **j**. Rom 4:25
following many trespasses brought **j**. Rom 5:16
of righteousness leads to **j** and life for Rom 5:18
of God, for if **j** were through the law, Gal 2:21

JUSTIFIED (30)
at Job because he **j** himself rather than Jb 32:2
so that you may be **j** in your words and Ps 51:4
of Israel shall be **j** and shall glory." Is 45:25
sinners!' Yet wisdom is **j** by her deeds." Mt 11:19
for by your words you will be **j**, and by Mt 12:37
Yet wisdom is **j** by all her children." Lk 7:35
this man went down to his house **j**, Lk 18:14
but the doers of the law who will be **j**. Rom 2:13
"That you may be **j** in your words, Rom 3:4
no human being will be **j** in his sight, Rom 3:20
and are **j** by his grace as a gift, Rom 3:24
hold that one is **j** by faith apart from Rom 3:28
For if Abraham was **j** by works, he has Rom 4:2
since we have been **j** by faith, Rom 5:1
we have now been **j** by his blood, Rom 5:9
and those whom he called he also **j**, Rom 8:30
and those whom he **j** he also glorified. Rom 8:30
with the heart one believes and is **j**, Rom 10:10
you were **j** in the name of the Lord 1 Cor 6:11
that a person is not **j** by works of the Gal 2:16
in order to be **j** by faith in Christ and Gal 2:16
by works of the law no one will be **j**. Gal 2:16
But if, in our endeavor to be **j** in Christ, Gal 2:17
that no one is **j** before God by the Gal 3:11
in order that we might be **j** by faith. Gal 3:24
Christ, you who would be **j** by the law; Gal 5:4
so that being **j** by his grace we might Ti 3:7
Abraham our father **j** by works when Jas 2:21
see that a person is **j** by works and not Jas 2:24
Rahab the prostitute **j** by works when Jas 2:25

JUSTIFIER (1)
might be just and the **j** of the one who Rom 3:26

JUSTIFIES (3)
He who **j** the wicked and he who Prv 17:15
work but trusts him who **j** the ungodly, Rom 4:5
against God's elect? It is God who **j**. Rom 8:33

JUSTIFY (6)
answer me; speak, for I desire to **j** you. Jb 33:32
But he, desiring to **j** himself, said to Lk 10:29
are those who **j** yourselves before men, Lk 16:15
we can give to **j** this commotion." Acts 19:40
He will **j** the circumcised by faith and Rom 3:30
that God would **j** the Gentiles by Gal 3:8

JUSTLY (6)
When one rules **j** over men, ruling in 2 Sm 23:3
rule, and nobles, all who govern **j**. Prv 8:16
No one enters suit **j**; no one goes to law Is 59:4
And we indeed **j**, for we are receiving Lk 23:41
Masters, treat your slaves **j** and fairly, Col 4:1
himself to him who judges **j**. 1 Pt 2:23

JUSTUS (3)
Barsabbas, who was also called **J**, Acts 1:23
to the house of a man named Titius **J**, Acts 18:7
and Jesus who is called **J**. These are the Col 4:11

JUTTAH (2)
Maon, Carmel, Ziph, **J**, Jos 15:55
pasturelands, **J** with its pasturelands, Jos 21:16

K

KAB (1)
fourth part of a **k** of dove's dung for 2 Kgs 6:25

KABZEEL (3)
toward the boundary of Edom, were **K**, Jos 15:21
of Jehoiada was a valiant man of **K**, 2 Sm 23:20
of Jehoiada was a valiant man of **K**, 1 Chr 11:22

KADESH (16)
(that is, **K**) and defeated all the country Gn 14:7
it lies between **K** and Bered. Gn 16:14
Negeb and lived between **K** and Shur; Gn 20:1
Israel in the wilderness of Paran, at **K**. Nm 13:26
first month, and the people stayed in **K**. Nm 20:1
sent messengers from **K** to the king Nm 20:14
And here we are in **K**, a city on the Nm 20:16
And they journeyed from **K**, and the Nm 20:22
of Meribah of **K** in the wilderness Nm 27:14
in the wilderness of Zin (that is, **K**). Nm 33:36
they set out from **K** and camped at Nm 33:37
So you remained at **K** many days, the Dt 1:46
to the Red Sea and came to **K**. Jgs 11:16
not consent. So Israel remained at **K**. Jgs 11:17
and to **K** in the land of the Hittites; 2 Sm 24:6
the LORD shakes the wilderness of **K**. Ps 29:8

KADESH-BARNEA (10)
I sent them from **K** to see the land. Nm 32:8
to Zin, and its limit shall be south of **K**. Nm 34:4
Horeb by the way of Mount Seir to **K**. Dt 1:2
God commanded us. And we came to **K**. Dt 1:19
time from our leaving **K** until we crossed Dt 2:14
And when the LORD sent you from **K**, Dt 9:23
Joshua struck them from **K** as far as Jos 10:41
man of God in **K** concerning you and Jos 14:6
the LORD sent me from **K** to spy out the Jos 14:7
along to Zin, and goes up south of **K**, Jos 15:3

KADMIEL (8)
the sons of Jeshua and **K**, of the sons of Ezr 2:40
and his brothers, and **K** and his sons, Ezr 3:9
namely of **K** of the sons of Hodevah, Neh 7:43
stood Jeshua, Bani, **K**, Shebaniah, Neh 9:4
Then the Levites, Jeshua, **K**, Bani, Neh 9:5
Binnui of the sons of Henadad, **K**; Neh 10:9
Jeshua, Binnui, **K**, Sherebiah, Judah, Neh 12:8
Sherebiah, and Jeshua the son of **K**, Neh 12:24

KADMONITES (1)
of the Kenites, the Kenizzites, the **K**, Gn 15:19

KAIN (2)
K shall be burned when Asshur takes Nm 24:22
K, Gibeah, and Timnah: ten cities with Jos 15:57

KALLAI (1)
of Sallai, **K**; of Amok, Eber; Neh 12:20

KAMON (1)
And Jair died and was buried in **K**. Jgs 10:5

KANAH (3)
westward to the brook **K** and ends at the Jos 16:8
the boundary went down to the brook **K**. Jos 17:9
Hammon, **K**, as far as Sidon the Great. Jos 19:28

KAREAH (14)
and Johanan the son of **K**, 2 Kgs 25:23
son of Nethaniah, Johanan the son of **K**, Jer 40:8
Johanan the son of **K** and all the leaders Jer 40:13
Johanan the son of **K** spoke secretly to Jer 40:15
Ahikam said to Johanan the son of **K**, Jer 40:16
Johanan the son of **K** and all the leaders Jer 41:11
Johanan the son of **K** and all the leaders Jer 41:13
and went to Johanan the son of **K**. Jer 41:14
Johanan the son of **K** and all the leaders Jer 41:16
Johanan the son of **K** and Jezaniah the Jer 42:1
Johanan the son of **K** and all the Jer 42:8
Johanan the son of **K** and all the insolent Jer 43:2
Johanan the son of **K** and all the Jer 43:4
Johanan the son of **K** and all the Jer 43:5

KARKA (1)
Hezron, up to Addar, turns about to **K**, Jos 15:3

KARKOR (1)
Zalmunna were in **K** with their army, Jgs 8:10

KARNAIM (1)
strength captured **K** for ourselves?" Am 6:13

KARTAH (1)
pasturelands, **K** with its pasturelands, Jos 21:34

KARTAN (1)
and **K** with its pasturelands—three Jos 21:32

KATTATH (1)
and **K**, Nahalal, Shimron, Idalah, and Jos 19:15

KEDAR (12)
the firstborn of Ishmael; and **K**, Gn 25:13
of Ishmael, Nebaioth, and **K**, 1 Chr 1:29
that I dwell among the tents of **K**! Ps 120:5
daughters of Jerusalem, like the tents of **K**, Sg 1:5
all the glory of **K** will come to an end. Is 21:16
mighty men of the sons of **K** will be few, Is 21:17
their voice, the villages that **K** inhabits; Is 42:11
All the flocks of **K** shall be gathered to Is 60:7
see, or send to **K** and examine with care; Jer 2:10
Concerning **K** and the kingdoms of Jer 49:28
the LORD: "Rise up, advance against **K**! Jer 49:28
all the princes of **K** were your favored Ezk 27:21

KEDEMAH (2)
Hadad, Tema, Jetur, Naphish, and **K**. Gn 25:15
Jetur, Naphish, and **K**. These are the 1 Chr 1:31

KEDEMOTH (4)
from the wilderness of **K** to Sihon the Dt 2:26
and Jahaz, and **K**, and Mephaath, Jos 13:18
K with its pasturelands, and Mephaath Jos 21:37
K with its pasturelands, and 1 Chr 6:79

KEDESH (11)
the king of **K**, one; the king of Jokneam Jos 12:22
K, Hazor, Ithnan, Jos 15:23
K, Edrei, En-hazor, Jos 19:37
So they set apart **K** in Galilee in the hill Jos 20:7
K in Galilee with its pasturelands, Jos 21:32
Deborah arose and went with Barak to **K**. Jgs 4:9
called out Zebulun and Naphtali to **K**. Jgs 4:10
the oak in Zaanannim, which is near **K**. Jgs 4:11
Janoah, **K**, Hazor, 2 Kgs 15:29
K with its pasturelands, Daberath 1 Chr 6:72
K in Galilee with its pasturelands, 1 Chr 6:76

KEDESH-NAPHTALI (1)
son of Abinoam from **K** and said to him, Jgs 4:6

KEEP (379)
in the garden of Eden to work it and **k** it. Gn 2:15
into the ark to **k** them alive with you. Gn 6:19
shall come in to you to **k** them alive. Gn 6:20
to **k** their offspring alive on the face of all Gn 7:3
"As for you, you shall **k** my covenant, Gn 17:9
is my covenant, which you shall **k**, Gn 17:10
household after him to **k** the way of the Gn 18:19
with you and will **k** you wherever you Gn 28:15
be with me and will **k** me in this way Gn 28:20
I will again pasture your flock and **k** it: Gn 30:31
brother; **k** what you have for yourself." Gn 33:9
"Let her **k** the things as her own, Gn 38:23
for food in the cities, and let them **k** it. Gn 41:35
and to **k** alive for you many survivors. Gn 45:7
and you shall **k** it until the fourteenth Ex 12:6
and you shall **k** it as a feast to the LORD; Ex 12:14
statute forever, you shall **k** it as a feast. Ex 12:14
has promised, you shall **k** this service. Ex 12:25
All the congregation of Israel shall **k** it. Ex 12:47
with you and would **k** the Passover to Ex 12:48
Then he may come near and **k** it; he Ex 12:48
you shall **k** this service in this month. Ex 13:5
You shall therefore **k** this statute at its Ex 13:10
his commandments and **k** all his Ex 15:26
you refuse to **k** my commandments Ex 16:28
obey my voice and **k** my covenant, Ex 19:5
who love me and **k** my commandments. Ex 20:6
the Sabbath day, to **k** it holy. Ex 20:8
his neighbor money or goods to **k** safe, Ex 22:7
an ox or a sheep or any beast to **k** safe, Ex 22:10
K far from a false charge, and do not kill Ex 23:7
in the year you shall **k** a feast to me. Ex 23:14
You shall **k** the Feast of Unleavened Ex 23:15
You shall **k** the Feast of Harvest, of the Ex 23:16
You shall **k** the Feast of Ingathering at Ex 23:16
'Above all you shall **k** my Sabbaths, Ex 31:13
You shall **k** the Sabbath, because it is Ex 31:14
the people of Israel shall **k** the Sabbath, Ex 31:16
"You shall **k** the Feast of Unleavened Ex 34:18
"Thus you shall **k** the people of Israel Lv 15:31
follow my rules and **k** my statutes and Lv 18:4
You shall therefore **k** my statutes and Lv 18:5
But you shall **k** my statutes and my Lv 18:26
So **k** my charge never to practice any of Lv 18:30
his father, and you shall **k** my Sabbaths: Lv 19:3
"You shall **k** my statutes. You shall not Lv 19:19
You shall **k** my Sabbaths and Lv 19:30
K my statutes and do them; I am the Lv 20:8
"You shall therefore **k** all my statutes Lv 20:22
They shall therefore **k** my charge, lest Lv 22:9
"So you shall **k** my commandments Lv 22:31
to evening shall you **k** your Sabbath." Lv 23:32
the land shall **k** a Sabbath to the LORD. Lv 25:2
do my statutes and **k** my rules and Lv 25:18
You shall **k** my Sabbaths and reverence Lv 26:2
And the Levites shall **k** guard over the Nm 1:53
They shall **k** guard over him and over Nm 3:7
and **k** guard over the people of Israel as Nm 3:8
Each one shall **k** his holy donations: Nm 5:10
The LORD bless you and **k** you; Nm 6:24
the people of Israel **k** the Passover at its Nm 9:2
you shall **k** it at its appointed time; Nm 9:3
statutes and all its rules you shall **k** it." Nm 9:3
of Israel that they should **k** the Passover. Nm 9:4
that they could not **k** the Passover on Nm 9:6
he shall still **k** the Passover to the LORD. Nm 9:10
day at twilight they shall **k** it. Nm 9:11
statute for the Passover they shall **k** it. Nm 9:12
not on a journey fails to **k** the Passover, Nm 9:13
you and would **k** the Passover to Nm 9:14
They shall **k** guard over you and over Nm 18:3
shall join you and **k** guard over the Nm 18:4
And you shall **k** guard over the Nm 18:5
and you shall **k** a feast to the LORD Nm 29:12
lying with him **k** alive for yourselves. Nm 31:18
to the Levites who **k** guard over the Nm 31:30
that you may **k** the commandments of Dt 4:2
K them and do them, for that will be your Dt 4:6
take care, and **k** your soul diligently, Dt 4:9
Therefore you shall **k** his statutes and Dt 4:40
who love me and **k** my commandments. Dt 5:10
"'Observe the Sabbath day, to **k** it holy, Dt 5:12
commanded you to **k** the Sabbath day. Dt 5:15

fear me and to **k** all my commandments, Dt 5:29
shall diligently **k** the commandments Dt 6:17
who love him and **k** his commandments, Dt 7:9
listen to these rules and **k** and do them, Dt 7:12
LORD your God will **k** with you the Dt 7:12
whether you would **k** his commandments Dt 8:2
So you shall **k** the commandments of the Dt 8:6
and to **k** the commandments and Dt 10:13
love the LORD your God and **k** his charge, Dt 11:1
"You shall therefore **k** the whole Dt 11:8
fear him and **k** his commandments and Dt 13:4
month of Abib and **k** the Passover to the Dt 16:1
Then you shall **k** the Feast of Weeks to Dt 16:10
"You shall **k** the Feast of Booths seven Dt 16:13
seven days you shall **k** the feast to the Dt 16:15
are careful to **k** all this commandment, Dt 19:9
then you shall **k** yourself from every evil Dt 23:9
and **k** his statutes and his Dt 26:17
you are to **k** all his commandments, Dt 26:18
"**K** the whole commandment that I Dt 27:1
said to all Israel, "**K** silence and hear, Dt 27:9
if you **k** the commandments of the LORD Dt 28:9
to **k** his commandments and his Dt 28:45
Therefore **k** the words of this covenant Dt 29:9
the LORD and **k** all his commandments Dt 30:8
to **k** his commandments and his Dt 30:10
k yourselves from the things devoted to Jos 6:18
have been careful to **k** the charge of the Jos 22:3
ways and to **k** his commandments and Jos 22:5
be very strong to **k** and to do all that is Jos 23:6
And they said to him, "**K** quiet; put Jgs 18:19
this one, but **k** close to my young women. Ru 2:8
'You shall **k** close by my young men Ru 2:21
"Your servant used to **k** sheep for his 1 Sm 17:34
To this day I **k** showing steadfast love 2 Sm 3:8
left ten concubines to **k** the house. 2 Sm 15:16
whom he has left to **k** the house, 2 Sm 16:21
have no son to **k** my name in 2 Sm 18:18
and **k** the charge of the LORD your God, 1 Kgs 2:3
my rules and **k** all my 1 Kgs 6:12
k for your servant David my father 1 Kgs 8:25
ways and to **k** his commandments, 1 Kgs 8:58
and do not **k** my commandments and 1 Kgs 9:6
But he did not **k** what the LORD 1 Kgs 11:10
and we **k** quiet and do not take it out 1 Kgs 22:3
And he said, "Yes, I know it; **k** quiet." 2 Kgs 2:3
he answered, "Yes, I know it; **k** quiet." 2 Kgs 2:5
ways and **k** my commandments 2 Kgs 17:13
also did not **k** the commandments 2 Kgs 17:19
LORD and to **k** his commandments 2 Kgs 23:3
"**K** the Passover to the LORD your 2 Kgs 23:21
and that you would **k** me from harm 1 Chr 4:10
that he did not **k** the command of 1 Chr 10:13
over Israel you may **k** the law of the 1 Chr 22:12
Thus they were to **k** charge of the 1 Chr 23:32
k forever such purposes and 1 Chr 29:18
he may **k** your commandments, 1 Chr 29:19
k for your servant David my father 2 Chr 6:16
For we **k** the charge of the LORD our 2 Chr 13:11
and to **k** the law and the 2 Chr 14:4
all the people shall **k** the charge of 2 Chr 23:6
at Jerusalem to **k** the Passover to 2 Chr 30:1
taken counsel to **k** the Passover in 2 Chr 30:2
for they could not **k** it at that time 2 Chr 30:3
should come and **k** the Passover to 2 Chr 30:5
in Jerusalem to **k** the Feast of 2 Chr 30:13
agreed together to **k** the feast for 2 Chr 30:23
LORD and to **k** his commandments 2 Chr 34:31
to **k** the Passover and to offer burnt 2 Chr 35:16
in the province Beyond the River, **k** away. Ezr 6:6
Guard them and **k** them until you Ezr 8:29
love him and **k** his commandments, Neh 1:5
to me and **k** my commandments and Neh 1:9
get grain, that we may eat and **k** alive." Neh 5:2
his labor who does not **k** this promise. Neh 5:13
the gates, to **k** the Sabbath day holy. Neh 13:22
people, and they do not **k** the king's laws, Est 3:8
For if you **k** silent at this time, relief and Est 4:14
obliging them to **k** the fourteenth day of Est 9:21
without fail they would **k** these two days Est 9:27
impatient? Yet who can **k** from speaking? Jb 4:2
Oh that you would **k** silent, and it would Jb 13:5
K listening to my words, and let my Jb 13:17
you would not **k** watch over my sin; Jb 14:16
"**K** listening to my words, and let this be Jb 21:2
Will you **k** to the old way that wicked Jb 22:15
They abhor me; they **k** aloof from me; Jb 30:10
He does not **k** the wicked alive, but gives Jb 36:6
cry for help avail to **k** you from distress, Jb 36:19
K listening to the thunder of his voice Jb 37:2
"I will not **k** silence concerning his Jb 41:12
You, O LORD, will **k** them; you will guard Ps 12:7
K me as the apple of your eye; hide me in Ps 17:8
K back your servant also from Ps 19:13
the one who could not **k** himself alive. Ps 22:29
for those who **k** his covenant and his Ps 25:10
soul from death and **k** them alive in Ps 33:19
K your tongue from evil and your lips Ps 34:13
Wait for the LORD and **k** his way, and he Ps 37:34
Our God comes; he does not **k** silence; Ps 50:3
and you **k** company with adulterers. Ps 50:18
whose eyes **k** watch on the nations— Ps 66:7
it is I who **k** steady its pillars. Ps 75:3
of God, but **k** his commandments; Ps 78:7
They did not **k** God's covenant, but Ps 78:10
High God and did not **k** his testimonies, Ps 78:56
O God, do not **k** silence; do not hold your Ps 83:1
steadfast love I will **k** for him forever, Ps 89:28
and do not **k** my commandments, Ps 89:31
chide, nor will he **k** his anger forever. Ps 103:9
to those who **k** his covenant and Ps 103:18
that they might **k** his statutes and Ps 105:45
Blessed are those who **k** his testimonies, Ps 119:2
I will **k** your statutes; do not utterly Ps 119:8
How can a young man **k** his way pure? Ps 119:9
that I may live and **k** your word. Ps 119:17
your statutes; and I will **k** it to the end. Ps 119:33
that I may **k** your law and observe it Ps 119:34
I will **k** your law continually, forever Ps 119:44
in the night, O LORD, and **k** your law. Ps 119:55
my portion; I promise to **k** your words. Ps 119:57
not delay to **k** your commandments. Ps 119:60
fear you, of those who **k** your precepts. Ps 119:63
I went astray, but now I **k** your word. Ps 119:67
with my whole heart I **k** your precepts; Ps 119:69
that I may **k** the testimonies of your Ps 119:88
than the aged, for I **k** your precepts. Ps 119:100
evil way, in order to **k** your word. Ps 119:101
it, to **k** your righteous rules. Ps 119:106
that I may **k** the commandments of Ps 119:115
K steady my steps according to your Ps 119:133
that I may **k** your precepts. Ps 119:134
because people do not **k** your law. Ps 119:136
me, O LORD! I will **k** your statutes. Ps 119:145
they do not **k** your commands. Ps 119:158
I **k** your precepts and testimonies, for Ps 119:168
The LORD will **k** you from all evil; he Ps 121:7
you from all evil; he will **k** your life. Ps 121:7
The LORD will **k** your going out and Ps 121:8
If your sons **k** my covenant and my Ps 132:12
k watch over the door of my lips! Ps 141:3
K me from the trap that they have laid Ps 141:9
way of the good and **k** to the paths of the Prv 2:20
let your heart **k** my commandments, Prv 3:1
sight of these—**k** sound wisdom and Prv 3:21
confidence and will **k** your foot from Prv 3:26
words; **k** my commandments, and live. Prv 4:4
Do not forsake her, and she will **k** you; Prv 4:6
K hold of instruction; do not let go; Prv 4:13
your sight; **k** them within your heart. Prv 4:21
K your heart with all vigilance, for Prv 4:23
that you may **k** discretion, and your lips Prv 5:2
K your way far from her, and do not go Prv 5:8
son, **k** your father's commandment, Prv 6:20
k my words and treasure up my Prv 7:1
k my commandments and live; keep my Prv 7:2
k my teaching as the apple of your eye; Prv 7:2
to **k** you from the forbidden woman, Prv 7:5
to me: blessed are those who **k** my ways. Prv 8:32
honor for a man to **k** aloof from strife, Prv 20:3
guards his soul will **k** far from them. Prv 22:5
of the LORD **k** watch over knowledge, Prv 22:12
be pleasant if you **k** them within you, Prv 22:18
but those who **k** the law strive against Prv 28:4
my eyes desired I did not **k** from them. Eccl 2:10
a time to **k**, and a time to cast away; Eccl 3:6
a time to **k** silence, and a time to speak; Eccl 3:7
Again, if two lie together, they **k** warm, Eccl 4:11
but how can one **k** warm alone? Eccl 4:11
K the king's command, because of Eccl 8:2
Fear God and **k** his commandments, Eccl 12:13
"'**K** on hearing, but do not understand; Is 6:9
k on seeing, but do not perceive.' Is 6:9
that day a man will **k** alive a young cow Is 7:21
and the writers who **k** writing oppression, Is 10:1
You **k** him in perfect peace whose mind Is 26:3
anyone punish it, I **k** it night and day; Is 27:3
firm in its place or **k** the sail spread out. Is 33:23
I will take you by the hand and **k** you; Is 42:6
and **k** on praying to a god that cannot Is 45:20
I will **k** you and give you as a covenant to Is 49:8
"**K** justice, and do righteousness, for soon Is 56:1
"To the eunuchs who **k** my Sabbaths, Is 56:4
For Zion's sake I will not **k** silent, and for Is 62:1
Will you **k** silent, and afflict us so Is 64:12
who say, "**K** to yourself, do not come near Is 65:5
me: "I will not **k** silent, but I will repay; Is 65:6
K your feet from going unshod and your Jer 2:25
I cannot **k** silent, for I hear the sound of Jer 4:19
and crane **k** the time of their coming, Jer 8:7
you **k** going backward, so I have Jer 15:6
any work, but **k** the Sabbath day holy, Jer 17:22
but **k** the Sabbath day holy and do no Jer 17:24
listen to me, to **k** the Sabbath day holy, Jer 17:27
and will **k** him as a shepherd keeps his Jer 31:10
"**K** your voice from weeping, and your Jer 31:16
covenant and did not **k** the terms of the Jer 34:18
you. I will **k** nothing back from you." Jer 42:4
fatherless children; I will **k** them alive; Jer 49:11
he will **k** you in exile no longer; Lam 4:22
in my statutes and **k** my rules and Ezk 11:20
to my people and **k** your own souls Ezk 13:18
and **k** his covenant that it might Ezk 17:14
of your fathers, nor **k** their rules, Ezk 20:18
and **k** my Sabbaths holy that they Ezk 20:20
places in the land of Israel **k** saying, Ezk 33:24
"Be ready and **k** ready, you and all your Ezk 38:7
have set others to **k** my charge for you Ezk 44:8
will appoint them to **k** charge of the Ezk 44:14
to me, and they shall **k** my charge. Ezk 44:16
They shall **k** my laws and my statutes Ezk 44:24
and they shall **k** my Sabbaths holy. Ezk 44:24
who love him and **k** his commandments, Dn 9:4
which shall **k** coming and overflow Dn 11:10
who is prudent will **k** silent in such a Am 5:13
K your feasts, O Judah; fulfill your vows, Na 1:15
Is he then to **k** on emptying his net and Hab 1:17
let all the earth **k** silence before him." Hab 2:20
will walk in my ways and **k** my charge, Zec 3:7
k them." And they weighed out as my Zec 11:12
house of Judah I will **k** my eyes open, Zec 12:4
of hosts, and to **k** the Feast of Booths. Zec 14:16
do not go up to **k** the Feast of Booths. Zec 14:18
do not go up to **k** the Feast of Booths. Zec 14:19
as you do not **k** my ways but show Mal 2:9
enter life, **k** the commandments." Mt 19:17
I will **k** the Passover at your house with Mt 26:18
will satisfy him and **k** you out of Mt 28:14
Be on guard, **k** awake. For you do not Mk 13:33
who hear the word of God and **k** it!" Lk 11:28
for action and **k** your lamps burning, Lk 12:35
it, but whoever loses his life will **k** it. Lk 17:33
you, but I do know him and I **k** his word. Jn 8:55
for he does not **k** the Sabbath." But Jn 9:16
"How long will you **k** us in suspense? Jn 10:24
so that she may **k** it for the day of my Jn 12:7
life in this world will **k** it for eternal life. Jn 12:25
hears my words and does not **k** them, Jn 12:47
me, you will **k** my commandments. Jn 14:15
"If anyone loves me, he will **k** my word, Jn 14:23
does not love me does not **k** my words. Jn 14:24
If you **k** my commandments, you will Jn 15:10
kept my word, they will also **k** yours. Jn 15:20
things to you to **k** you from falling away. Jn 16:1
Holy Father, **k** them in your name, Jn 17:11
but that you **k** them from the evil one. Jn 17:15
Holy Spirit and to **k** back for yourself Acts 5:3
k away from these men and let them Acts 5:38
as delivered by angels and did not **k** it." Acts 7:53
to order them to **k** the law of Moses." Acts 15:5
If you **k** yourselves from these, you Acts 15:29
ordering the jailer to **k** them safely. Acts 16:23
evil I do not want is what I **k** on doing. Rom 7:19
have, **k** between yourself and God. Rom 14:22
in his heart, to **k** her as his betrothed, 1 Cor 7:37
my body and **k** it under control, 1 Cor 9:27
let each of them **k** silent in church 1 Cor 14:28
the women should **k** silent in the 1 Cor 14:34
to **k** them from seeing the light of the 2 Cor 4:4
So to **k** me from being too elated by 2 Cor 12:7
me, to **k** me from being too elated. 2 Cor 12:7
that he is obligated to **k** the whole law. Gal 5:3
to **k** you from doing the things you Gal 5:17
K watch on yourself, lest you too be Gal 6:1
do not themselves **k** the law, Gal 6:13
To that end **k** alert with all Eph 6:18
and **k** your eyes on those who walk Phil 3:17
do, but let us **k** awake and be sober. 1 Thes 5:6
that you **k** away from any brother 2 Thes 3:6
K a close watch on yourself and on 1 Tm 4:16
I charge you to **k** these rules without 1 Tm 5:21
in the sins of others; **k** yourself pure. 1 Tm 5:22
to **k** the commandment unstained 1 Tm 6:14
have been glad to **k** him with me, Phlm 1:13
K your life free from love of money, Heb 13:5
and to **k** oneself unstained from the Jas 1:27
K your conduct among the Gentiles 1 Pt 2:12
let him **k** his tongue from evil and his 1 Pt 3:10
all, **k** loving one another earnestly, 1 Pt 4:8
they **k** you from being ineffective or 2 Pt 1:8
and to **k** the unrighteous under 2 Pt 2:9
know him, if we **k** his commandments. 1 Jn 2:3
but does not **k** his commandments is 1 Jn 2:4
and he cannot **k** on sinning because he 1 Jn 3:9
because we **k** his commandments and 1 Jn 3:22

of God, that we **k** his commandments. 1 Jn 5:3
born of God does not **k** on sinning, 1 Jn 5:18
Little children, **k** yourselves from idols. 1 Jn 5:21
k yourselves in the love of God, waiting Jude 1:21
who is able to **k** you from stumbling Jude 1:24
who hear, and who **k** what is written in it, Rv 1:3
you received and heard. **K** it, and repent. Rv 3:3
I will **k** you from the hour of trial that is Rv 3:10
on those who **k** the commandments of Rv 12:17
those who **k** the commandments of Rv 14:12
and with those who **k** the words of this Rv 22:9

KEEPER (17)
Now Abel was a **k** of sheep, and Cain a Gn 4:2
"I do not know; am I my brother's **k**?" Gn 4:9
favor in the sight of the **k** of the prison. Gn 39:21
And the **k** of the prison put Joseph in Gn 39:22
The **k** of the prison paid no attention to Gn 39:23
the sheep with a **k** and took the 1 Sm 17:20
in charge of the **k** of the baggage and 1 Sm 17:22
k of the wardrobe (now she lived in 2 Kgs 22:14
Imnah the Levite, **k** of the east gate, 2 Chr 31:14
k of the wardrobe (now she lived in 2 Chr 34:22
letter to Asaph, the **k** of the king's forest, Neh 2:8
of Shecaniah, the **k** of the East Gate, Neh 3:29
The LORD is your **k**; the LORD is your Ps 121:5
with me; they made me **k** of the vineyards, Sg 1:6
I, the LORD, am its **k**; every moment I Is 27:3
the son of Shallum, **k** of the threshold. Jer 35:4
the Ephesians is temple **k** of the great Acts 19:35

KEEPERS (13)
for they have been **k** of livestock, Gn 46:32
servants have been **k** of livestock from Gn 46:34
which the **k** of the threshold have 2 Kgs 22:4
order and the **k** of the threshold 2 Kgs 23:4
and the three **k** of the threshold, 2 Kgs 25:18
service, **k** of the thresholds of the tent, 1 Chr 9:19
camp of the LORD, **k** of the entrance. 1 Chr 9:19
the Levites, the **k** of the threshold, 2 Chr 34:9
the day when the **k** of the house Eccl 12:3
Baal-hamon; he let out the vineyard to **k**; Sg 8:11
and the **k** of the fruit two hundred. Sg 8:12
Like **k** of a field are they against her all Jer 4:17
priest, and the three **k** of the threshold; Jer 52:24

KEEPING (40)
Now Moses was **k** the flock of his Ex 3:1
k steadfast love for thousands, forgiving Ex 34:7
were 8,600, **k** guard over the sanctuary. Nm 3:28
in the tent of meeting by **k** guard, Nm 8:26
by **k** all his statutes and his Dt 6:2
LORD loves you and is **k** the oath that he Dt 7:8
God by not **k** his commandments and Dt 8:11
k all his commandments that I am Dt 13:18
the LORD his God by **k** all the words of Dt 17:19
k his commandments and his statutes, Dt 27:10
and by **k** his commandments and his Dt 30:16
he is **k** the sheep." And Samuel said 1 Sm 16:11
while we were with them **k** the sheep. 1 Sm 25:16
walking in his ways and **k** his statutes, 1 Kgs 2:3
k my statutes and my commandments, 1 Kgs 3:14
k covenant and showing steadfast 1 Kgs 8:23
statutes and **k** his commandments, 1 Kgs 8:61
you, and **k** my statutes and my rules, 1 Kgs 9:4
in my sight and **k** my statutes and 1 Kgs 11:33
in my eyes by **k** my statutes and my 1 Kgs 11:38
strong in **k** my commandments 1 Chr 28:7
k covenant and showing steadfast 2 Chr 6:14
commanded you and **k** my statutes 2 Chr 7:17
were faithful in **k** themselves holy. 2 Chr 31:18
warned; in **k** them there is great reward. Ps 19:11
songs of praise, a multitude **k** festival. Ps 42:4
may be steadfast in **k** your statutes! Ps 119:5
place, **k** watch on the evil and the good. Prv 15:3
should not die and **k** alive souls who Ezk 13:19
is the profit of our **k** his charge or of Mal 3:14
Bear fruit in **k** with repentance. Mt 3:8
who were with him, **k** watch over Jesus, Mt 27:54
field, **k** watch over their flock by night. Lk 2:8
Bear fruits in **k** with repentance. And do Lk 3:8
a servant plowing or **k** sheep say to him Lk 17:7
performing deeds in **k** with their Acts 26:20
but **k** the commandments of God. 1 Cor 7:19
with all dignity **k** his children 1 Tm 3:4
for they are **k** watch over your souls, Heb 13:17
who stays awake, **k** his garments on, Rv 16:15

KEEPS (51)
faithful God who **k** covenant and Dt 7:9
awesome God who **k** covenant and Neh 1:5
who **k** covenant and steadfast love, Neh 9:32
he **k** back his soul from the pit, his life Jb 33:18
He **k** all his bones; not one of them is Ps 34:20
the LORD protects him and **k** him alive; Ps 41:2
wonderful; therefore my soul **k** them. Ps 119:129
My soul **k** your testimonies; I love Ps 119:167
moved; he who **k** you will not slumber. Ps 121:3
he who **k** Israel will neither slumber Ps 121:4
all that is in them, who **k** faith forever; Ps 146:6
of the blameless **k** his way straight, Prv 11:5
trustworthy in spirit **k** a thing Prv 11:13
Even a fool who **k** silent is considered Prv 17:28
he who **k** understanding will discover Prv 19:8
Whoever **k** the commandment keeps Prv 19:16
keeps the commandment **k** his life; Prv 19:16
Whoever **k** his mouth and his tongue Prv 21:23
and his tongue **k** himself out of Prv 21:23
Does not he who **k** watch over your Prv 24:12
The one who **k** the law is a son with Prv 28:7
but blessed is he who **k** the law. Prv 29:18
life because God **k** him occupied with Eccl 5:20
Whoever **k** a command will know no Eccl 8:5
righteous nation that **k** faith may enter Is 26:2
who holds it fast, who **k** the Sabbath, Is 56:2
it, and **k** his hand from doing any evil." Is 56:2
everyone who **k** the Sabbath and does not Is 56:6
and **k** for us the weeks appointed for the Jer 5:24
As a well **k** its water fresh, so she keeps Jer 6:7
its water fresh, so she **k** fresh her evil; Jer 6:7
keep him as a shepherd **k** his flock.' Jer 31:10
cursed is he who **k** back his sword Jer 48:10
and **k** my rules by acting faithfully— Ezk 18:9
has committed and **k** all my statutes Ezk 18:21
who **k** covenant and steadfast love with Dn 9:4
on his adversaries and **k** wrath for his Na 1:2
yet because this widow **k** bothering me, Lk 18:5
you the law? Yet none of you **k** the law. Jn 7:19
truly, I say to you, if anyone **k** my word, Jn 8:51
yet you say, 'If anyone **k** my word, Jn 8:52
has my commandments and **k** them, Jn 14:21
who is uncircumcised **k** the precepts Rom 2:26
uncircumcised but **k** the law Rom 2:27
For whoever **k** the whole law but fails in Jas 2:10
but whoever **k** his word, in him truly 1 Jn 2:5
No one who abides in him **k** on sinning; 1 Jn 3:6
no one who **k** on sinning has either seen 1 Jn 3:6
Whoever **k** his commandments abides 1 Jn 3:24
conquers and who **k** my works until Rv 2:26
Blessed is the one who **k** the words of the Rv 22:7

KEHELATHAH (2)
set out from Rissah and camped at **K**. Nm 33:22
they set out from **K** and camped at Nm 33:23

KEILAH (18)
K, Achzib, and Mareshah: nine cities Jos 15:44
are fighting against **K** and are 1 Sm 23:1
attack the Philistines and save **K**." 1 Sm 23:2
if we go to **K** against the armies of 1 Sm 23:3
answered him, "Arise, go down to **K**, 1 Sm 23:4
his men went to **K** and fought with 1 Sm 23:5
So David saved the inhabitants of **K**. 1 Sm 23:5
of Ahimelech had fled to David to **K**, 1 Sm 23:6
told Saul that David had come to **K**. 1 Sm 23:7
all the people to war, to go down to **K**, 1 Sm 23:8
heard that Saul seeks to come to **K**, 1 Sm 23:10
Will the men of **K** surrender me into 1 Sm 23:11
the men of **K** surrender me and 1 Sm 23:12
hundred, arose and departed from **K**, 1 Sm 23:13
told that David had escaped from **K**, 1 Sm 23:13
were the fathers of **K** the Garmite and 1 Chr 4:19
ruler of half the district of **K**, Neh 3:17
Henadad, ruler of half the district of **K**. Neh 3:18

KELAIAH (1)
Jozabad, Shimei, **K** (that is, Kelita), Ezr 10:23

KELITA (3)
Kelaiah (that is, **K**), Pethahiah, Ezr 10:23
Hodiah, Maaseiah, **K**, Azariah, Neh 8:7
Shebaniah, Hodiah, **K**, Pelaiah, Neh 10:10

KEMUEL (3)
Buz his brother, **K** the father of Aram, Gn 22:21
a chief, **K** the son of Shiphtan. Nm 34:24
for Levi, Hashabiah the son of **K**; for 1 Chr 27:17

KENAN (6)
Enosh had lived 90 years, he fathered **K**. Gn 5:9
lived after he fathered **K** 815 years and Gn 5:10
When **K** had lived 70 years, he fathered Gn 5:12
K lived after he fathered Mahalalel 840 Gn 5:13
Thus all the days of **K** were 910 years, Gn 5:14
K, Mahalalel, Jared; 1 Chr 1:2

KENATH (2)
went and captured **K** and its villages, Nm 32:42
Havvoth-jair, **K**, and its villages, 1 Chr 2:23

KENAZ (11)
Teman, Omar, Zepho, Gatam, and **K**. Gn 36:11
the chiefs Teman, Omar, Zepho, **K**, Gn 36:15
K, Teman, Mibzar, Gn 36:42
And Othniel the son of **K**, the brother Jos 15:17
And Othniel the son of **K**, Caleb's Jgs 1:13
who saved them, Othniel the son of **K**, Jgs 3:9
years. Then Othniel the son of **K** died. Jgs 3:11
Zepho, Gatam, **K**, and of Timna, 1 Chr 1:36
K, Teman, Mibzar, 1 Chr 1:53
The sons of **K**: Othniel and Seraiah; 1 Chr 4:13
and Naam; and the son of Elah: **K**. 1 Chr 4:15

KENITE (6)
And he looked on the **K**, and took up Nm 24:21
And the descendants of the **K**, Moses' Jgs 1:16
Now Heber the **K** had separated from the Jgs 4:11
to the tent of Jael, the wife of Heber the **K**, Jgs 4:17
of Hazor and the house of Heber the **K**. Jgs 4:17
women be Jael, the wife of Heber the **K**, Jgs 5:24

KENITES (7)
the land of the **K**, the Kenizzites, the Gn 15:19
the Kenite had separated from the **K**, Jgs 4:11
Then Saul said to the **K**, "Go, depart; 1 Sm 15:6
Egypt." So the **K** departed from among 1 Sm 15:6
or, "Against the Negeb of the **K**." 1 Sm 27:10
Jerahmeelites, in the cities of the **K**, 1 Sm 30:29
These are the **K** who came from 1 Chr 2:55

KENIZZITE (3)
of Jephunneh the **K** and Joshua the Nm 32:12
the son of Jephunneh the **K** said to him, Jos 14:6
the son of Jephunneh the **K** to this day, Jos 14:14

KENIZZITES (1)
the land of the Kenites, the **K**, the Gn 15:19

KEPT (176)
it was I who **k** you from sinning against Gn 20:6
obeyed my voice and **k** my charge, Gn 26:5
but his father **k** the saying in mind. Gn 37:11
nor has he **k** back anything from me Gn 39:9
that many people should be **k** alive, Gn 50:20
is a night of watching **k** to the LORD by Ex 12:42
over lay aside to be **k** till the morning.'" Ex 16:23
of it be **k** throughout your generations, Ex 16:32
LORD to be **k** throughout your Ex 16:33
placed it before the testimony to be **k**. Ex 16:34
has been warned but has not **k** it in, Ex 21:29
the past, and its owner has not **k** it in, Ex 21:36
They still **k** bringing him freewill Ex 36:3
fire of the altar shall be **k** burning on it. Lv 6:9
fire on the altar shall be **k** burning on it; Lv 6:12
Fire shall be **k** burning on the altar Lv 6:13
that a light may be **k** burning regularly. Lv 24:2
You shall eat old store long **k**, and you Lv 26:10
oversight of those who **k** guard over the Nm 3:32
And they **k** the Passover in the first Nm 9:5
Why are we **k** from bringing the LORD'S Nm 9:7
the people of Israel **k** the charge of the Nm 9:19
They **k** the charge of the LORD, at the Nm 9:23
to be **k** as a sign for the rebels, Nm 17:10
And they shall be **k** for the water for Nm 19:9
to the Levites who **k** guard over the Nm 31:47
him, he **k** him as the apple of his eye. Dt 32:10
your word and **k** your covenant. Dt 33:9
they **k** the Passover on the fourteenth Jos 5:10
now, behold, the LORD has **k** me alive, Jos 14:10
"You have **k** all that Moses the servant Jos 22:2
and travelers **k** to the byways. Jgs 5:6
They **k** quiet all night, saying, "Let us Jgs 16:2
So she **k** close to the young women of Ru 2:23
and he **k** hearing all that his sons 1 Sm 2:22
"See, what was **k** is set before you. 1 Sm 9:24
because it was **k** for you until the 1 Sm 9:24
You have not **k** the command of the 1 Sm 13:13
you have not **k** what the LORD 1 Sm 13:14
young men have **k** themselves from 1 Sm 21:4
women have been **k** from us as 1 Sm 21:5
who have **k** me this day from 1 Sm 25:33
and has **k** back his servant from 1 Sm 25:39
then have you not **k** watch over your 1 Sm 26:15
you have not **k** watch over your 1 Sm 26:16
young man who **k** the watch lifted 2 Sm 13:34
people with Absalom **k** increasing. 2 Sm 15:12
For I have **k** the ways of the LORD and 2 Sm 22:22
him, and I **k** myself from guilt. 2 Sm 22:24
you **k** me as the head of the nations; 2 Sm 22:44
then have you not **k** your oath to the 1 Kgs 2:43
And you have **k** for him this great and 1 Kgs 3:6
who have **k** with your servant David 1 Kgs 8:24
you have not **k** my covenant and 1 Kgs 11:11
who **k** my commandments and my 1 Kgs 11:34
and have not **k** the command that 1 Kgs 13:21
who **k** my commandments and 1 Kgs 14:8
who **k** the door of the king's house. 1 Kgs 14:27
but **k** the commandments that the 2 Kgs 18:6
Passover had been **k** since the days 2 Kgs 23:22
this Passover was **k** to the LORD 2 Kgs 23:23
and they **k** a genealogical record. 1 Chr 4:33
to that point **k** their allegiance to 1 Chr 12:29
who have **k** with your servant David 2 Chr 6:15
for they had **k** the dedication of the 2 Chr 7:9
who **k** the door of the king's house. 2 Chr 12:10

for they had not **k** it as often as 2 Chr 30:5
present at Jerusalem **k** the Feast of 2 Chr 30:21
So they **k** it for another seven days 2 Chr 30:23
our fathers have not **k** the word of 2 Chr 34:21
Josiah **k** a Passover to the LORD in 2 Chr 35:1
who were present **k** the Passover at 2 Chr 35:17
like it had been **k** in Israel since the 2 Chr 35:18
of Israel had **k** such a Passover 2 Chr 35:18
such a Passover as was **k** by Josiah, 2 Chr 35:18
reign of Josiah this Passover was **k**. 2 Chr 35:19
But they **k** mocking the messengers 2 Chr 36:16
that it lay desolate it **k** Sabbath, 2 Chr 36:21
And they **k** the Feast of Booths, as it is Ezr 3:4
the returned exiles **k** the Passover. Ezr 6:19
And they **k** the Feast of Unleavened Ezr 6:22
and have not **k** the commandments, Neh 1:7
each **k** his weapon at his right hand. Neh 4:23
They **k** the feast seven days, and on the Neh 8:18
And you have **k** your promise, for you Neh 9:8
our fathers have not **k** your law or paid Neh 9:34
brothers, who **k** watch at the gates, Neh 11:19
be remembered and **k** throughout every Est 9:28
to the grave, watch is **k** over his tomb. Jb 21:32
I have **k** his way and have not turned Jb 23:11
times of judgment **k** by the Almighty, Jb 24:1
me and waited and **k** silence for my Jb 29:21
families terrified me, so that I **k** silence, Jb 31:34
For I have **k** the ways of the LORD, and Ps 18:21
him, and I **k** myself from my guilt. Ps 18:23
For when I **k** silent, my bones wasted Ps 32:3
You have **k** count of my tossings; put Ps 56:8
who has **k** our soul among the living Ps 66:9
All in vain have I **k** my heart clean and Ps 73:13
they **k** his testimonies and the statute Ps 99:7
your precepts to be **k** diligently. Ps 119:4
for I have **k** your testimonies. Ps 119:22
to me, that I have **k** your precepts. Ps 119:56
I **k** my heart from no pleasure, for my Eccl 2:10
riches were **k** by their owner to his Eccl 5:13
but my own vineyard I have not **k**! Sg 1:6
as in the night when a holy feast is **k**, Is 30:29
I have **k** still and restrained myself; Is 42:14
and your sins have **k** good from you. Jer 5:25
forsaken me and have not **k** my law, Jer 16:11
his sons, to drink no wine, has been **k**, Jer 35:14
of Rechab have **k** the command that Jer 35:16
your father and **k** all his precepts Jer 35:18
And you have not **k** charge of my holy Ezk 44:8
who **k** the charge of my sanctuary Ezk 44:15
the sons of Zadok, who **k** my charge, Ezk 48:11
killed, and whom he would, he **k** alive; Dn 5:19
but I **k** the matter in my heart." Dn 7:28
the LORD has **k** ready the calamity Dn 9:14
they **k** sacrificing to the Baals and Hos 11:2
is bound up; his sin is **k** in store. Hos 13:12
perpetually, and he **k** his wrath forever. Am 1:11
of the LORD, and have not **k** his statutes, Am 2:4
For you have **k** the statutes of Omri, and Mi 6:16
from my statutes and have not **k** them. Mal 3:7
man said to him, "All these I have **k**. Mt 19:20
they sat down and **k** watch over him Mt 27:36
and holy man, and he **k** him safe. Mk 6:20
So they **k** the matter to themselves, Mk 9:10
But they **k** silent, for on the way they Mk 9:34
all these I have **k** from my youth." Mk 10:20
And he **k** making signs to them and Lk 1:22
for five months she **k** herself hidden, Lk 1:24
and would have **k** him from leaving Lk 4:42
He was **k** under guard and bound with Lk 8:29
And they **k** silent and told no one in Lk 9:36
k seeking from him a sign from Lk 11:16
in that city who **k** coming to him and Lk 18:3
"All these I have **k** from my youth." Lk 18:21
which I **k** laid away in a handkerchief; Lk 19:20
blindfolded him and **k** asking him, Lk 22:64
but they **k** shouting, "Crucify, crucify Lk 23:21
their eyes were **k** from recognizing Lk 24:16
But you have **k** the good wine until now." Jn 2:10
said, "No, but he is like him." He **k** saying, Jn 9:9
blind man also have **k** this man from Jn 11:37
as I have **k** my Father's Jn 15:10
also persecute you. If they **k** my word, Jn 15:20
them to me, and they have **k** your word. Jn 17:6
I was with them, I **k** them in your name, Jn 17:12
the servant girl who **k** watch at the Jn 18:16
wife's knowledge he **k** back for himself Acts 5:2
so that they would not be **k** alive. Acts 7:19
So Peter was **k** in prison, but earnest Acts 12:5
mind." But she **k** insisting that it Acts 12:15
that it was so, and they **k** saying, Acts 12:15
And this she **k** doing for many days. Acts 16:18
that he should be **k** in custody but Acts 24:23
that Paul was being **k** at Caesarea and Acts 25:4
had appealed to be **k** in custody for Acts 25:21
k them from carrying out their plan. Acts 27:43
"I have **k** for myself seven thousand Rom 11:4
the mystery that was **k** secret for long Rom 16:25
we **k** telling you beforehand that we 1 Thes 3:4
soul and body be **k** blameless at the 1 Thes 5:23
finished the race, I have **k** the faith. 2 Tm 4:7
By faith he **k** the Passover and Heb 11:28
your fields, which you **k** back by fraud, Jas 5:4
and unfading, **k** in heaven for you, 1 Pt 1:4
darkness to be **k** until the judgment; 2 Pt 2:4
being **k** until the day of judgment and 2 Pt 3:7
in God the Father and **k** for Jesus Christ: Jude 1:1
he has **k** in eternal chains under Jude 1:6
and yet you have **k** my word and have not Rv 3:8
Because you have **k** my word about Rv 3:10
of the day might be **k** from shining, Rv 8:12

KEREN-HAPPUCH (1)
Keziah, and the name of the third **K**. Jb 42:14

KERIOTH (2)
and **K**, and Bozrah, and all the cities of Jer 48:24
and it shall devour the strongholds of **K**, Am 2:2

KERIOTH-HEZRON (1)
Hazor-hadattah, **K** (that is, Hazor), Jos 15:25

KERNEL (1)
the body that is to be, but a bare **k**, 1 Cor 15:37

KEROS (2)
the sons of **K**, the sons of Siaha, the sons Ezr 2:44
the sons of **K**, the sons of Sia, the sons Neh 7:47

KETTLE (1)
it into the pan or **k** or cauldron or pot. 1 Sm 2:14

KETURAH (4)
took another wife, whose name was **K**. Gn 25:1
Eldaah. All these were the children of **K**. Gn 25:4
The sons of **K**, Abraham's 1 Chr 1:32
All these were the descendants of **K**. 1 Chr 1:33

KEY (6)
they took the **k** and opened them, Jgs 3:25
on his shoulder the **k** of the house of Is 22:22
have taken away the **k** of knowledge. Lk 11:52
one, the true one, who has the **k** of David, Rv 3:7
and he was given the **k** to the shaft of the Rv 9:1
in his hand the **k** to the bottomless pit Rv 20:1

KEYS (2)
I will give you the **k** of the kingdom of Mt 16:19
and I have the **k** of Death and Hades. Rv 1:18

KEZIAH (1)
and the name of the second **K**, Jb 42:14

KIBROTH-HATTAAVAH (5)
the name of that place was called **K**, Nm 11:34
From **K** the people journeyed to Nm 11:35
wilderness of Sinai and camped at **K**. Nm 33:16
they set out from **K** and camped at Nm 33:17
at Massah and at **K** you provoked the Dt 9:22

KIBZAIM (1)
K with its pasturelands, Beth-horon Jos 21:22

KICK (1)
hard for you to **k** against the goads.' Acts 26:14

KICKED (1)
"But Jeshurun grew fat, and **k**; you grew Dt 32:15

KIDNEYS (19)
and the two **k** with the fat that is on Ex 29:13
the liver and the two **k** with the fat that Ex 29:22
and the two **k** with the fat that is on them Lv 3:4
the liver that he shall remove with the **k**. Lv 3:4
and the two **k** with the fat that is on Lv 3:10
the liver that he shall remove with the **k**. Lv 3:10
and the two **k** with the fat that is on Lv 3:15
the liver that he shall remove with the **k**. Lv 3:15
and the two **k** with the fat that is on them Lv 4:9
the liver that he shall remove with the **k** Lv 4:9
the two **k** with the fat that is on them at Lv 7:4
the liver that he shall remove with the **k**. Lv 7:4
of the liver and the two **k** with their fat, Lv 8:16
the liver and the two **k** with their fat and Lv 8:25
But the fat and the **k** and the long lobe of Lv 9:10
the entrails and the **k** and the long lobe Lv 9:19
He slashes open my **k** and does not Jb 16:13
and goats, with the fat of the **k** of rams. Is 34:6
He drove into my **k** the arrows of his Lam 3:13

KIDRON (12)
and the king crossed the brook **K**, 2 Sm 15:23
you go out and cross the brook **K**, 1 Kgs 2:37
image and burned it at the brook **K**. 1 Kgs 15:13
the fields of the **K** and carried their 2 Kgs 23:4
outside Jerusalem, to the brook **K**, 2 Kgs 23:6
it at the brook **K** and beat it to 2 Kgs 23:6
the dust of them into the brook **K**. 2 Kgs 23:12
it, and burned it at the brook **K**. 2 Chr 15:16
it and carried it out to the brook **K**. 2 Chr 29:16
away and threw into the **K** valley. 2 Chr 30:14
and all the fields as far as the brook **K**, Jer 31:40
with his disciples across the **K** Valley, Jn 18:1

KILL (176)
earth, and whoever finds me will **k** me." Gn 4:14
Then they will **k** me, but they will let Gn 12:12
"Lord, will you **k** an innocent people? Gn 20:4
and they will **k** me because of my wife. Gn 20:11
of the place should **k** me because of Gn 26:7
then I will **k** my brother Jacob." Gn 27:41
about you by planning to **k** you. Gn 27:42
they conspired against him to **k** him. Gn 37:18
let us **k** him and throw him into one of Gn 37:20
is it if we **k** our brother and conceal Gn 37:26
"**K** my two sons if I do not bring him Gn 42:37
birthstool, if it is a son, you shall **k** him, Ex 1:16
Do you mean to **k** me as you killed the Ex 2:14
heard of it, he sought to **k** Moses. Ex 2:15
go, behold, I will **k** your firstborn son.'" Ex 4:23
have put a sword in their hand to **k** us." Ex 5:21
of Israel shall **k** their lambs at Ex 12:6
to your clans, and **k** the Passover lamb. Ex 12:21
this wilderness to **k** this whole assembly Ex 16:3
to **k** us and our children and our Ex 17:3
attacks another to **k** him by cunning, Ex 21:14
burn, and I will **k** you with the sword, Ex 22:24
and do not **k** the innocent and righteous, Ex 23:7
Then you shall **k** the bull before the Ex 29:11
and you shall **k** the ram and shall take Ex 29:16
and you shall **k** the ram and take part Ex 29:20
to **k** them in the mountains and to Ex 32:12
and each of you **k** his brother and his Ex 32:27
Then he shall **k** the bull before the LORD, Lv 1:5
and he shall **k** it on the north side of the Lv 1:11
of his offering and **k** it at the entrance Lv 3:2
and **k** it in front of the tent of meeting; Lv 3:8
hand on its head and **k** it in front of the Lv 3:13
head of the bull and **k** the bull before the Lv 4:4
head of the goat and **k** it in the place Lv 4:24
the place where they **k** the burnt offering Lv 4:24
the sin offering and **k** the sin offering in Lv 4:29
of the sin offering and **k** it for a sin Lv 4:33
place where they **k** the burnt offering. Lv 4:33
the place where they **k** the burnt offering Lv 7:2
offering they shall **k** the guilt offering, Lv 7:2
shall command them to **k** one of the Lv 14:5
And he shall **k** the lamb in the place Lv 14:13
the place where they **k** the sin offering Lv 14:13
afterward he shall **k** the burnt offering. Lv 14:19
And he shall **k** the lamb of the guilt Lv 14:25
and shall **k** one of the birds in an Lv 14:50
He shall **k** the bull as a sin offering for Lv 16:11
"Then he shall **k** the goat of the sin Lv 16:15
to death, and you shall **k** the animal. Lv 20:15
you shall **k** the woman and the animal; Lv 20:16
But you shall not **k** an ox or a sheep Lv 22:28
will treat me like this, **k** me at once, Nm 11:15
Now if you **k** this people as one man, Nm 14:15
and honey, to **k** us in the wilderness, Nm 16:13
in my hand, for then I would **k** you." Nm 22:29
"Each of you **k** those of his men who Nm 25:5
k every male among the little ones, Nm 31:17
and **k** every woman who has known Nm 31:17
then you may **k** any of your herd or Dt 12:21
But you shall **k** him. Your hand shall be Dt 13:9
no god besides me; I **k** and I make alive; Dt 32:39
people of Israel, and they did not **k** them. Jos 9:26
saved them alive, I would not **k** you." Jgs 8:19
"Rise and **k** them!" But the young man Jgs 8:20
his hands to **k** his brothers. Jgs 9:24
to him, "Draw your sword and **k** me, Jgs 9:54
to him, "If the LORD had meant to **k** us, Jgs 13:23
We will surely not **k** you." So they Jgs 15:13
of the morning; then we will **k** him." Jgs 16:2
They meant to **k** me, and they violated Jgs 20:5
began to strike and **k** some of the Jgs 20:31
begun to strike and **k** about thirty men Jgs 20:39
God of Israel to **k** us and our people." 1 Sm 5:10
that it may not **k** us and our people." 1 Sm 5:11
them, but **k** both man and woman, 1 Sm 15:3
it, he will **k** me." And the LORD said, 1 Sm 16:2
If he is able to fight with me and **k** me, 1 Sm 17:9
if I prevail against him and **k** him, 1 Sm 17:9
servants, that they should **k** David. 1 Sm 19:1
David, "Saul my father seeks to **k** you. 1 Sm 19:2
that he might **k** him in the morning. 1 Sm 19:11
to me in the bed, that I may **k** him." 1 Sm 19:15
'Let me go. Why should I **k** you?'" 1 Sm 19:17
if there is guilt in me, **k** me yourself, 1 Sm 20:8
"Turn and **k** the priests of the LORD, 1 Sm 22:17
And some told me to **k** you, but I 1 Sm 24:10
of your robe and did not **k** you, 1 Sm 24:11
that you did not **k** me when the LORD 1 Sm 24:18
that you will not **k** me or deliver me 1 Sm 30:15
said to me 'Stand beside me and **k** me, 2 Sm 1:9

to you, 'Strike Amnon,' then **k** him. 2 Sm 13:28
that the avenger of blood **k** no more, 2 Sm 14:11
a new sword, thought to **k** David. 2 Sm 21:16
sought therefore to **k** Jeroboam. 1 Kgs 11:40
and they will **k** me and return to 1 Kgs 12:27
into the hand of Ahab, to **k** me? 1 Kgs 18:9
he cannot find you, he will **k** me, 1 Kgs 18:12
Elijah is here"'; and he will **k** me." 1 Kgs 18:14
"Am I God, to **k** and to make alive, 2 Kgs 5:7
live, and if they **k** us we shall but die." 2 Kgs 7:4
and you will **k** their young men with 2 Kgs 8:12
among them and **k** them and stop Neh 4:11
temple, for they are coming to **k** you. Neh 6:10
They are coming to **k** you by night." Neh 6:10
with instruction to destroy, to **k**, Est 3:13
and defend their lives, to destroy, to **k**, Est 8:11
cobras; the tongue of a viper will **k** him. Jb 20:16
light, that he may **k** the poor and needy, Jb 24:14
to watch his house in order to **k** him. Ps 59:T
K them not, lest my people forget; make Ps 59:11
They **k** the widow and the sojourner, and Ps 94:6
a time to **k**, and a time to heal; a time to Eccl 3:3
breath of his lips he shall **k** the wicked. Is 11:4
but I will **k** your root with famine, and Is 14:30
the sword to **k**, the dogs to tear, and the Jer 15:3
O LORD, know all their plotting to **k** me. Jer 18:23
because he did not **k** me in the womb; Jer 20:17
that they may **k** us or take us into exile Jer 43:3
K, and devote them to destruction, Jer 50:21
K all her bulls; let them go down to the Jer 50:27
K old men outright, young men and Ezk 9:6
They shall **k** their sons and their Ezk 23:47
He will **k** with the sword your Ezk 26:8
He will **k** your people with the sword, Ezk 26:11
in the presence of those who **k** you, Ezk 28:9
Daniel and his companions, to **k** them. Dn 2:13
who had gone out to **k** the wise men of Dn 2:14
a parched land, and **k** her with thirst. Hos 2:3
and will **k** all its princes with him," says Am 2:3
are left of them I will **k** with the sword; Am 9:1
the sword, and it shall **k** them; Am 9:4
not fear those who **k** the body but Mt 10:28
kill the body but cannot **k** the soul. Mt 10:28
and they will **k** him, and he will be Mt 17:23
let us **k** him and have his inheritance.' Mt 21:38
some of whom you will **k** and crucify, Mt 23:34
to arrest Jesus by stealth and **k** him. Mt 26:4
to save life or to **k**?" But they were silent. Mk 3:4
the hands of men, and they will **k** him. Mk 9:31
spit on him, and flog him and **k** him. Mk 10:34
Come, let us **k** him, and the inheritance Mk 12:7
how to arrest him by stealth and **k** him, Mk 14:1
of whom they will **k** and persecute,' Lk 11:49
do not fear those who **k** the body, Lk 12:4
from here, for Herod wants to **k** you." Lk 13:31
And bring the fattened calf and **k** it, Lk 15:23
after flogging him, they will **k** him, Lk 18:33
Let us **k** him, so that the inheritance Lk 20:14
Jews were seeking all the more to **k** him, Jn 5:18
because the Jews were seeking to **k** him. Jn 7:1
the law. Why do you seek to **k** me?" Jn 7:19
a demon! Who is seeking to **k** you?" Jn 7:20
not this the man whom they seek to **k**? Jn 7:25
So the Jews said, "Will he **k** himself, Jn 8:22
yet you seek to **k** me because my word Jn 8:37
but now you seek to **k** me, a man who Jn 8:40
comes only to steal and **k** and destroy. Jn 10:10
were enraged and wanted to **k** them. Acts 5:33
Do you want to **k** me as you killed the Acts 7:28
had passed, the Jews plotted to **k** him, Acts 9:23
gates day and night in order to **k** him, Acts 9:24
But they were seeking to **k** him. Acts 9:29
voice to him: "Rise, Peter; **k** and eat." Acts 10:13
saying to me, 'Rise, Peter; **k** and eat.' Acts 11:7
sword and was about to **k** himself, Acts 16:27
And as they were seeking to **k** him, Acts 21:31
we are ready to **k** him before he Acts 23:15
planning an ambush to **k** him on the Acts 25:3
me in the temple and tried to **k** me. Acts 26:21
soldiers' plan was to **k** the prisoners, Acts 27:42
the Lord Jesus will **k** with the breath 2 Thes 2:8
to **k** with sword and with famine and with Rv 6:8
them for five months, but not to **k** them, Rv 9:5
were released to **k** a third of mankind. Rv 9:15
on them and conquer them and **k** them, Rv 11:7

KILLED (193)
up against his brother Abel and **k** him. Gn 4:8
I have **k** a man for wounding me, Gn 4:23
instead of Abel, for Cain **k** him." Gn 4:25
while it felt secure and **k** all the males. Gn 34:25
They **k** Hamor and his son Shechem Gn 34:26
For in their anger they **k** men, and in Gn 49:6
kill me as you **k** the Egyptian?" Then Ex 2:14
the LORD **k** all the firstborn in the land Ex 13:15
and the bull shall be **k** before the LORD. Lv 4:15
the burnt offering is **k** shall the sin Lv 6:25
the sin offering be **k** before the LORD; Lv 6:25
And he **k** it, and Moses took the blood, Lv 8:15
And he **k** it, and Moses threw the blood Lv 8:19
And he **k** it, and Moses took some of its Lv 8:23
near to the altar and **k** the calf of the sin Lv 9:8
Then he **k** the burnt offering, and Lv 9:12
was for the people and **k** it and offered it Lv 9:15
Then he **k** the ox and the ram, the Lv 9:18
the bird that was **k** over the fresh water. Lv 14:6
of the bird that was **k** and in the fresh Lv 14:51
them that he has **k** them in the Nm 14:16
"You have **k** the people of the LORD." Nm 16:41
someone who was **k** with a sword Nm 19:16
now I would have **k** you and let her Nm 22:33
who was **k** with the Midianite Nm 25:14
woman who was **k** was Cozbi the Nm 25:15
who was **k** on the day of the plague on Nm 25:18
commanded Moses, and **k** every male. Nm 31:7
They **k** the kings of Midian with the Nm 31:8
And they also **k** Balaam the son of Beor Nm 31:8
Whoever of you has **k** any person and Nm 31:19
country, and it is not known who **k** him, Dt 21:1
the men of Ai **k** about thirty-six of their Jos 7:5
the sons of Israel **k** with the sword. Jos 10:11
was **k** with the sword by the people of Jos 13:22
that anyone who **k** a person without Jos 20:9
And they **k** at that time about 10,000 of Jgs 3:29
who **k** 600 of the Philistines with an Jgs 3:31
They **k** Oreb at the rock of Oreb, and Jgs 7:25
and Zeeb they **k** at the winepress of Zeeb. Jgs 7:25
the tower of Penuel and **k** the men of the Jgs 8:17
the men whom you **k** at Tabor?" They Jgs 8:18
Gideon arose and **k** Zebah and Jgs 8:21
house at Ophrah and **k** his brothers the Jgs 9:5
house this day and have **k** his sons, Jgs 9:18
Abimelech their brother, who **k** them, Jgs 9:24
So he rose against them and **k** them. Jgs 9:43
all who were in the field and **k** them. Jgs 9:44
captured the city and **k** the people who Jgs 9:45
'A woman **k** him.'" And his young man Jgs 9:54
of our country, who has **k** many of us." Jgs 16:24
the dead whom he **k** at his death were Jgs 16:30
those whom he had **k** during his life. Jgs 16:30
who **k** about four thousand men on 1 Sm 4:2
and his armor-bearer **k** them after 1 Sm 14:13
k about twenty men within as it 1 Sm 14:14
beard and struck him and **k** him. 1 Sm 17:35
and struck the Philistine and **k** him. 1 Sm 17:50
of its sheath and **k** him and cut off 1 Sm 17:51
and **k** two hundred of the Philistines. 1 Sm 18:27
tonight, tomorrow you will be **k**." 1 Sm 19:11
and he **k** on that day eighty-five 1 Sm 22:18
David that Saul had **k** the priests of 1 Sm 22:21
meat that I have **k** for my shearers 1 Sm 25:11
in the house, and she quickly **k** it, 1 Sm 28:24
They **k** no one, but carried them off 1 Sm 30:2
So I stood beside him and **k** him, 2 Sm 1:10
saying, 'I have **k** the LORD'S anointed.'" 2 Sm 1:16
and Abishai his brother **k** Abner, 2 Sm 3:30
I seized him and **k** him at Ziklag, 2 Sm 4:10
wicked men have **k** a righteous man 2 Sm 4:11
and they **k** them and cut off their 2 Sm 4:12
and David **k** of the Syrians the men 2 Sm 10:18
Who **k** Abimelech the son of 2 Sm 11:21
your wife and have **k** him with the 2 Sm 12:9
that they have **k** all the young 2 Sm 13:32
and one struck the other and **k** him. 2 Sm 14:6
for the life of his brother whom he **k**.' 2 Sm 14:7
and struck him and **k** him. 2 Sm 18:15
day the Philistines **k** Saul on Gilboa. 2 Sm 21:12
attacked the Philistine and **k** him. 2 Sm 21:17
eight hundred whom he **k** at one time. 2 Sm 23:8
hundred men and **k** them and won 2 Sm 23:18
Egyptian's hand and **k** him with his 2 Sm 23:21
Amasa the son of Jether, whom he **k**, 1 Kgs 2:5
he attacked and **k** with the sword two 1 Kgs 2:32
and had **k** the Canaanites who lived 1 Kgs 9:16
met him on the road and **k** him. 1 Kgs 13:24
which has torn him and **k** him, 1 Kgs 13:26
So Baasha **k** him in the third year of 1 Kgs 15:28
he **k** all the house of Jeroboam. 1 Kgs 15:29
in and struck him down and **k** him, 1 Kgs 16:10
and he has **k** the king." Therefore 1 Kgs 16:16
I did when Jezebel **k** the prophets of 1 Kgs 18:13
and how he had **k** all the prophets 1 Kgs 19:1
and **k** your prophets with the sword, 1 Kgs 19:10
and **k** your prophets with the sword, 1 Kgs 19:14
"Have you **k** and also taken 1 Kgs 21:19
against my master and **k** him, 2 Kgs 10:9
and they **k** Mattan the priest of Baal 2 Kgs 11:18
people captive to Kir, and he **k** Rezin. 2 Kgs 16:9
them, which **k** some of them. 2 Kgs 17:25
and Pharaoh Neco **k** him at 2 Kgs 23:29
of Gath who were born in the land **k**, 1 Chr 7:21
against 300 whom he **k** at one time. 1 Chr 11:11
defended it and **k** the Philistines. 1 Chr 11:14
300 men and **k** them and won 1 Chr 11:20
Egyptian's hand and **k** him with his 1 Chr 11:23
k 18,000 Edomites in the Valley of 1 Chr 18:12
and David **k** of the Syrians the men 1 Chr 19:18
And Ahab **k** an abundance of sheep 2 Chr 18:2
he **k** all his brothers with the sword, 2 Chr 21:4
and also you have **k** your brothers, 2 Chr 21:13
to the camp had **k** all the older sons. 2 Chr 22:1
attended Ahaziah, and he **k** them. 2 Chr 22:8
and they **k** Mattan the priest of Baal 2 Chr 23:17
had shown him, but **k** his son. 2 Chr 24:22
the priest, and **k** him on his bed. 2 Chr 24:25
he **k** his servants who had struck 2 Chr 25:3
son of Remaliah **k** 120,000 from 2 Chr 28:6
k Maaseiah the king's son and 2 Chr 28:7
but you have **k** them in a rage that 2 Chr 28:9
who **k** their young men with the 2 Chr 36:17
their back and **k** your prophets, Neh 9:26
I and my people, to be destroyed, to be **k**, Est 7:4
citadel itself the Jews **k** and destroyed 500 Est 9:6
and also **k** Parshandatha and Dalphon Est 9:7
the number of those **k** in Susa the Est 9:11
the Jews have **k** and destroyed 500 Est 9:12
of Adar and they **k** 300 men in Susa, Est 9:15
their enemies and **k** 75,000 of those Est 9:16
for your sake we are **k** all the day long; Ps 44:22
and he **k** the strongest of them and laid Ps 78:31
When he **k** them, they sought him; Ps 78:34
many nations and **k** mighty kings, Ps 135:10
and **k** mighty kings, for his steadfast Ps 136:18
For the simple are **k** by their turning Prv 1:32
outside! I shall be **k** in the streets!" Prv 22:13
of Shaphan, with the sword, and **k** him, Jer 41:2
and he has **k** all who were delightful in Lam 2:4
and prophet be **k** in the sanctuary Lam 2:20
you have **k** them in the day of your Lam 2:21
as for her, they **k** her with the sword; Ezk 23:10
the mainland shall be **k** by the sword. Ezk 26:6
with those who are **k** by the sword; Ezk 32:29
and the wise men were about to be **k**; Dn 2:13
flame of the fire **k** those men who took Dn 3:22
Whom he would, he **k**, and whom he Dn 5:19
Belshazzar the Chaldean king was **k**. Dn 5:30
And as I looked, the beast was **k**, and its Dn 7:11
I **k** your young men with the sword, Am 4:10
and he sent and **k** all the male children Mt 2:16
and chief priests and scribes, and be **k**, Mt 16:21
his servants and beat one, **k** another, Mt 21:35
him out of the vineyard and **k** him. Mt 21:39
treated them shamefully, and **k** them. Mt 22:6
chief priests and the scribes and be **k**, Mk 8:31
And when he is **k**, after three days he Mk 9:31
And he sent another, and him they **k**. Mk 12:5
some they beat, and some they **k**. Mk 12:5
they took him and **k** him and threw Mk 12:8
and chief priests and scribes, and be **k**, Lk 9:22
of the prophets whom your fathers **k**. Lk 11:47
deeds of your fathers, for they **k** them, Lk 11:48
fear him who, after he has **k**, has Lk 12:5
the tower in Siloam fell and **k** them: Lk 13:4
and your father has **k** the fattened calf, Lk 15:27
you **k** the fattened calf for him!' Lk 15:30
him out of the vineyard and **k** him. Lk 20:15
you crucified and **k** by the hands of Acts 2:23
and you **k** the Author of life, whom Acts 3:15
whom you **k** by hanging him on a Acts 5:30
He was **k**, and all who followed him Acts 5:36
me as you **k** the Egyptian yesterday?' Acts 7:28
And they **k** those who announced Acts 7:52
He **k** James the brother of John with Acts 12:2
the garments of those who **k** him.' Acts 22:20
to eat nor drink till they had **k** Paul. Acts 23:12
to taste no food till we have **k** Paul. Acts 23:14
to eat nor drink till they have **k** him. Acts 23:21
was about to be **k** by them when I Acts 23:27
deceived me and through it **k** me. Rom 7:11
sake we are being **k** all the day long; Rom 8:36
"Lord, they have **k** your prophets, they Rom 11:3
we live; as punished, and yet not **k**; 2 Cor 6:9
who **k** both the Lord Jesus and the 1 Thes 2:15
in two, they were **k** with the sword. Heb 11:37
faithful witness, who was **k** among you, Rv 2:13
who were to be **k** as they themselves had Rv 6:11
three plagues a third of mankind was **k**, Rv 9:18
who were not **k** by these plagues, Rv 9:20
them, this is how he is doomed to be **k**. Rv 11:5
thousand people were **k** in the Rv 11:13

KILLING (11)
Israel had finished **k** all the inhabitants Jos 8:24
his father in **k** his seventy brothers. Jgs 9:56
innocent blood by **k** David without 1 Sm 19:5
band, after the **k** by David. 1 Kgs 11:24
whom I sojourn, by **k** her son?" 1 Kgs 17:20

them, and behold, they are **k** them, 2 Kgs 17:26
with the sword, **k** and destroying them, Est 9:5
k oxen and slaughtering sheep, Is 22:13
anger and pursued us, **k** without pity; Lam 3:43
net and mercilessly **k** nations forever? Hab 1:17
the cross, thereby **k** the hostility. Eph 2:16

KILLS (24)
If anyone **k** Cain, vengeance shall be Gn 4:15
kept it in, and it **k** a man or a woman, Ex 21:29
steals an ox or a sheep, and **k** it or sells it, Ex 22:1
of the house of Israel **k** an ox or a lamb Lv 17:3
in the camp, or **k** it outside the camp, Lv 17:3
Whoever **k** an animal shall make it Lv 24:21
and whoever **k** a person shall be put to Lv 24:21
the manslayer who **k** any person Nm 35:11
that anyone who **k** any person Nm 35:15
the avenger of blood **k** the manslayer, Nm 35:27
"If anyone **k** a person, the murderer Nm 35:30
anyone who **k** his neighbor Dt 4:42
If anyone **k** his neighbor Dt 19:4
The LORD **k** and brings to life; he 1 Sm 2:6
the man who **k** him with great 1 Sm 17:25
the man who **k** this Philistine and 1 Sm 17:26
it be done to the man who **k** him." 1 Sm 17:27
Surely vexation **k** the fool, and jealousy Jb 5:2
The desire of the sluggard **k** him, for Prv 21:25
slaughters an ox is like one who **k** a man; Is 66:3
the city that **k** the prophets and stones Mt 23:37
the city that **k** the prophets and stones Lk 13:34
coming when whoever **k** you will think Jn 16:2
For the letter **k**, but the Spirit gives life. 2 Cor 3:6

KILN (3)
Aaron, "Take handfuls of soot from the **k**, Ex 9:8
took soot from the **k** and stood before Ex 9:10
of it went up like the smoke of a **k**, Ex 19:18

KILNS (1)
and made them toil at the brick **k**. 2 Sm 12:31

KIN (2)
has no next of **k** to whom restitution Nm 5:8
plague, and my nearest **k** stand far off. Ps 38:11

KINAH (1)
K, Dimonah, Adadah, Jos 15:22

KIND (73)
is their seed, each according to its **k**, Gn 1:11
is their seed, each according to its **k**. Gn 1:12
every winged bird according to its **k**. Gn 1:21
creeps on the ground according to its **k**. Gn 1:25
thing of the ground, according to its **k**, Gn 6:20
they and every beast, according to its **k**, Gn 7:14
creeps on the earth, according to its **k**, Gn 7:14
kind, and every bird, according to its **k**, Gn 7:14
for a cloak, or for any **k** of lost thing, Ex 22:9
the kite, the falcon of any **k**, Lv 11:14
every raven of any **k**, Lv 11:15
the sea gull, the hawk of any **k**, Lv 11:16
the stork, the heron of any **k**, the Lv 11:19
the locust of any **k**, the bald locust of Lv 11:22
of any kind, the bald locust of any **k**, Lv 11:22
locust of any kind, the cricket of any **k**, Lv 11:22
any kind, and the grasshopper of any **k**. Lv 11:22
rat, the mouse, the great lizard of any **k**, Lv 11:29
let your cattle breed with a different **k**. Lv 19:19
land and plant any **k** of tree for food, Lv 19:23
the kite, the falcon of any **k**; Dt 14:13
every raven of any **k**; Dt 14:14
the sea gull, the hawk of any **k**; Dt 14:15
the stork, the heron of any **k**; the Dt 14:18
decision between one **k** of homicide and Dt 17:8
another, one **k** of legal right and another, Dt 17:8
another, or one **k** of assault and another, Dt 17:8
anyone who lies with any **k** of animal.' Dt 27:21
"What **k** of cities are these that you 1 Kgs 9:13
"What **k** of man was he who came to 2 Kgs 1:7
who has skill for any **k** of service; 1 Chr 28:21
who did work in every **k** of service, 2 Chr 34:13
they loathed any **k** of food, and they Ps 107:18
all his words and **k** in all his works.] Ps 145:13
in all his ways and **k** in all his works. Ps 145:17
A man who is **k** benefits himself, but Prv 11:17
And under it will dwell every **k** of bird; Ezk 17:23
of your great wealth of every **k**; Ezk 27:12
of your great wealth of every **k**; Ezk 27:18
harp, bagpipe, and every **k** of music, Dn 3:5
harp, bagpipe, and every **k** of music, Dn 3:7
harp, bagpipe, and every **k** of music, Dn 3:10
harp, bagpipe, and every **k** of music, Dn 3:15
and no **k** of harm was found on him, Dn 6:23
or stew or wine or oil or any **k** of food, Hg 2:12
the sea and gathered fish of every **k**. Mt 13:47
"This **k** cannot be driven out by Mk 9:29
for he is **k** to the ungrateful and the evil. Lk 6:35
this to show by what **k** of death he was Jn 12:33
to show by what **k** of death he was Jn 18:32
said to show by what **k** of death he was Jn 21:19
What **k** of house will you build for Acts 7:49
you have been **k** enough to come. Acts 10:33
It is excluded. By what **k** of law? Rom 3:27
and of a **k** that is not tolerated even 1 Cor 5:1
God, one of one **k** and one of another. 1 Cor 7:7
Love is patient and **k**; love does not 1 Cor 13:4
With what **k** of body do they 1 Cor 15:35
and to each **k** of seed its own body. 1 Cor 15:38
but there is one **k** for humans, 1 Cor 15:39
the glory of the heavenly is of one **k**, 1 Cor 15:40
greedy to practice every **k** of impurity. Eph 4:19
Be **k** to one another, tenderhearted, Eph 4:32
Yet it was **k** of you to share my trouble. Phil 4:14
You know what **k** of men we proved 1 Thes 1:5
concerning us the **k** of reception we 1 Thes 1:9
be quarrelsome but **k** to everyone, 2 Tm 2:24
k, and submissive to their own husbands, Ti 2:5
that we should be a **k** of firstfruits of his Jas 1:18
For every **k** of beast and bird, of reptile Jas 3:7
See what **k** of love the Father has given 1 Jn 3:1
to strike the earth with every **k** of plague, Rv 11:6
city were adorned with every **k** of jewel. Rv 21:19

KINDLE (12)
You shall **k** no fire in all your dwelling Ex 35:3
Behold, all you who **k** a fire, who equip Is 50:11
children gather wood, the fathers **k** fire, Jer 7:18
day, then I will **k** a fire in its gates, Jer 17:27
I will **k** a fire in her forest, and it shall Jer 21:14
I shall **k** a fire in the temples of the gods Jer 43:12
And I will **k** a fire in the wall of Jer 49:27
him up, and I will **k** a fire in his cities, Jer 50:32
Lord GOD, Behold, I will **k** a fire in you, Ezk 20:47
Heap on the logs, **k** the fire, boil the Ezk 24:10
So I will **k** a fire in the wall of Rabbah, Am 1:14
that you might not **k** fire on my altar Mal 1:10

KINDLED (52)
Jacob's anger was **k** against Rachel, and Gn 30:2
servant treated me," his anger was **k**. Gn 39:19
of the LORD was **k** against Moses and he Ex 4:14
bewail the burning that the LORD has **k**. Lv 10:6
the LORD heard it, his anger was **k**, Nm 11:1
of the LORD was **k** against the people, Nm 11:33
anger of the LORD was **k** against them, Nm 12:9
God's anger was **k** because he went, Nm 22:22
And Balaam's anger was **k**, and he Nm 22:27
Balak's anger was **k** against Balaam, Nm 24:10
anger of the LORD was **k** against Israel. Nm 25:3
the LORD'S anger was **k** on that day, Nm 32:10
the LORD'S anger was **k** against Israel, Nm 32:13
of the LORD your God be **k** against you, Dt 6:15
anger of the LORD would be **k** against you, Dt 7:4
anger of the LORD will be **k** against you, Dt 11:17
of the LORD was **k** against this land, Dt 29:27
my anger will be **k** against them in that Dt 31:17
For a fire is **k** by my anger, and it Dt 32:22
anger of the LORD will be **k** against you, Jos 23:16
anger of the LORD was **k** against Israel, Jgs 2:14
anger of the LORD was **k** against Israel, Jgs 2:20
the anger of the LORD was **k** against Israel, Jgs 3:8
of Gaal the son of Ebed, his anger was **k**. Jgs 9:30
anger of the LORD was **k** against Israel, Jgs 10:7
words, and his anger was greatly **k**. 1 Sm 11:6
Eliab's anger was **k** against David, 1 Sm 17:28
Saul's anger was **k** against Jonathan, 1 Sm 20:30
anger of the LORD was **k** against Uzzah, 2 Sm 6:7
anger was greatly **k** against the man, 2 Sm 12:5
anger of the LORD was **k** against Israel, 2 Sm 24:1
of the LORD was **k** against Israel, 2 Kgs 13:3
of the LORD that is **k** against us, 2 Kgs 22:13
wrath will be **k** against this place, 2 Kgs 22:17
his anger was **k** against Judah, 2 Kgs 23:26
of the LORD was **k** against Uzzah, 1 Chr 13:10
He has **k** his wrath against me and Jb 19:11
in the way, for his wrath is quickly **k**. Ps 2:12
full of wrath; a fire was **k** against Jacob; Ps 78:21
of the LORD was **k** against his people, Ps 106:40
when their anger was **k** against us; Ps 124:3
of the LORD was **k** against his people, Is 5:25
and under his glory a burning will be **k**, Is 10:16
fire, and by the torches that you have **k**! Is 50:11
anger a fire is **k** that shall burn Jer 15:14
anger a fire is **k** that shall burn forever." Jer 17:4
were poured out and **k** in the cities of Jer 44:6
and he **k** a fire in Zion that consumed Lam 4:11
flesh shall see that I the LORD have **k** it; Ezk 20:48
earth, and would that it were already **k**! Lk 12:49
And when they had **k** a fire in the Lk 22:55
for they **k** a fire and welcomed us all, Acts 28:2

KINDLES (5)
His breath **k** coals, and a flame comes Jb 41:21
it **k** the thickets of the forest, and they roll Is 9:18
of the LORD, like a stream of sulfur, **k** it. Is 30:33
himself; he **k** a fire and bakes bread. Is 44:15
as when fire **k** brushwood and the fire Is 64:2

KINDLING (1)
so is a quarrelsome man for **k** strife. Prv 26:21

KINDLY (18)
but as I have dealt **k** with you, Gn 21:23
and promise to deal **k** and truly with Gn 47:29
comforted them and spoke **k** to them. Gn 50:21
the LORD that, as I have dealt **k** with you, Jos 2:12
you also will deal **k** with my father's Jos 2:12
land we will deal **k** and faithfully with Jos 2:14
the city, and we will deal **k** with you." Jgs 1:24
to speak **k** to her and bring her back. Jgs 19:3
May the LORD deal **k** with you, as you Ru 1:8
me and spoken **k** to your servant, Ru 2:13
Therefore deal **k** with your servant, 1 Sm 20:8
go out and speak **k** to your servants, 2 Sm 19:7
And he spoke **k** to him and gave 2 Kgs 25:28
"I will deal **k** with Hanun the son of 1 Chr 19:2
for his father dealt **k** with me." So 1 Chr 19:2
And he spoke **k** to him, and gave him a Jer 52:32
Julius treated Paul **k** and gave him Acts 27:3
always remember us **k** and long to 1 Thes 3:6

KINDNESS (31)
have shown me great **k** in saving my Gn 19:19
to her, 'This is the **k** you must do me: Gn 20:13
please do me the **k** to mention me to Gn 40:14
whose **k** has not forsaken the living or Ru 2:20
have made this last **k** greater than the Ru 3:10
For you showed **k** to all the people of 1 Sm 15:6
may show him **k** for Jonathan's sake?" 2 Sm 9:1
that I may show the **k** of God to him?" 2 Sm 9:3
for I will show you **k** for the sake of 2 Sm 9:7
not remember the **k** that Jehoiada, 2 Chr 24:22
"He who withholds **k** from a friend Jb 6:14
Let there be none to extend **k** to him, Ps 109:12
For he did not remember to show **k**, Ps 109:16
a righteous man strike me—it is a **k**; Ps 141:5
pursues righteousness and **k** will find Prv 21:21
and the teaching of **k** is on her tongue. Prv 31:26
I led them with cords of **k**, with the Hos 11:4
of you but to do justice, and to love **k**, Mi 6:8
show **k** and mercy to one another, Zec 7:9
I beg you in your **k** to hear us briefly. Acts 24:4
native people showed us unusual **k**, Acts 28:2
the riches of his **k** and forbearance and Rom 2:4
not knowing that God's **k** is meant to Rom 2:4
Note then the **k** and the severity of Rom 11:22
who have fallen, but God's **k** to you, Rom 11:22
you, provided you continue in his **k**. Rom 11:22
knowledge, patience, **k**, the Holy Spirit, 2 Cor 6:6
is love, joy, peace, patience, **k**, goodness, Gal 5:22
of his grace in **k** toward us in Christ Eph 2:7
and beloved, compassion, **k**, humility, Col 3:12
the goodness and loving **k** of God our Ti 3:4

KINDRED (14)
of his father Terah in the land of his **k**, Gn 11:28
country and your **k** and your father's Gn 12:1
but will go to my country and to my **k**, Gn 24:4
house and from the land of my **k**, Gn 24:7
to the land of your fathers and to your **k**, Gn 31:3
land and return to the land of your **k**.'" Gn 31:13
'Return to your country and to your **k**, Gn 32:9
us carefully about ourselves and our **k**, Gn 43:7
depart to my own land and to my **k**." Nm 10:30
had not made known her people or **k**, Est 2:10
not made known her **k** or her people, Est 2:20
I bear to see the destruction of my **k**?" Est 8:6
land and from your **k** and go into the Acts 7:3
Jacob his father and all his **k**, Acts 7:14

KINDS (47)
yielding seed according to their own **k**, Gn 1:12
the waters swarm, according to their **k**, Gn 1:21
according to their **k**—livestock and Gn 1:24
earth according to their **k**." And it was Gn 1:24
according to their **k** and the livestock Gn 1:25
and the livestock according to their **k**, Gn 1:25
Of the birds according to their **k**, and of Gn 6:20
and of the animals according to their **k**, Gn 6:20
all the livestock according to their **k**, Gn 7:14
brick, and in all **k** of work in the field. Ex 1:14
not sow your field with two **k** of seed, Lv 19:19
of cloth made of two **k** of material. Lv 19:19
not sow your vineyard with two **k** of seed, Dt 22:9
not have in your bag two **k** of weights, Dt 25:13
have in your house two **k** of measures, Dt 25:14
with him, all **k** of goods of Damascus, 2 Kgs 8:9
and all **k** of craftsmen without 1 Chr 22:15
filled with various **k** of spices 2 Chr 16:14
and for all **k** of costly vessels; 2 Chr 32:27
and stalls for all **k** of cattle, and 2 Chr 32:28
every ten days all **k** of wine in Neh 5:18
wine, grapes, figs, and all **k** of loads, Neh 13:15

in fish and all **k** of goods and sold Neh 13:16
and sellers of all **k** of wares lodged Neh 13:20
in golden vessels, vessels of different **k**, Est 1:7
be full, providing all **k** of produce; Ps 144:13
and planted in them all **k** of fruit trees. Eccl 2:5
appoint over them four **k** of destroyers, Jer 15:3
wares the best of all **k** of spices and all Ezk 27:22
mighty men and all **k** of warriors,' Ezk 39:20
the first of all the firstfruits of all **k**, Ezk 44:30
every offering of all **k** from all your Ezk 44:30
Its fish will be of very many **k**, like the Ezk 47:10
there will grow all **k** of trees for food. Ezk 47:12
lie down in her midst, all **k** of beasts; Zep 2:14
you and utter all **k** of evil against you Mt 5:11
In it were all **k** of animals and reptiles Acts 10:12
produced in me all **k** of covetousness. Rom 7:8
to another various **k** of tongues, 1 Cor 12:10
and various **k** of tongues. 1 Cor 12:28
of money is a root of all **k** of evils. 1 Tm 6:10
when you meet trials of various **k**, Jas 1:2
that the same **k** of suffering are 1 Pt 5:9
silk, scarlet cloth, all **k** of scented wood, Rv 18:12
scented wood, all **k** of articles of ivory, Rv 18:12
of ivory, all **k** of articles of costly wood, Rv 18:12
the tree of life with its twelve **k** of fruit, Rv 22:2

KING (2316)
In the days of Amraphel **k** of Shinar, Gn 14:1
king of Shinar, Arioch **k** of Ellasar, Gn 14:1
of Ellasar, Chedorlaomer **k** of Elam, Gn 14:1
king of Elam, and Tidal **k** of Goiim, Gn 14:1
kings made war with Bera **k** of Sodom, Gn 14:2
king of Sodom, Birsha **k** of Gomorrah, Gn 14:2
king of Gomorrah, Shinab **k** of Admah, Gn 14:2
of Admah, Shemeber **k** of Zeboiim, Gn 14:2
of Zeboiim, and the **k** of Bela (that is, Gn 14:2
Then the **k** of Sodom, the king of Gn 14:8
the king of Sodom, the **k** of Gomorrah, Gn 14:8
the king of Gomorrah, the **k** of Admah, Gn 14:8
the king of Admah, the **k** of Zeboiim, Gn 14:8
of Zeboiim, and the **k** of Bela (that is, Gn 14:8
with Chedorlaomer **k** of Elam, Tidal Gn 14:9
king of Elam, Tidal **k** of Goiim, Gn 14:9
king of Goiim, Amraphel **k** of Shinar, Gn 14:9
king of Shinar, and Arioch **k** of Ellasar, Gn 14:9
the **k** of Sodom went out to meet him at Gn 14:17
And Melchizedek **k** of Salem brought Gn 14:18
And the **k** of Sodom said to Abram, Gn 14:21
But Abram said to the **k** of Sodom, "I Gn 14:22
sister." And Abimelech **k** of Gerar sent Gn 20:2
Gerar to Abimelech **k** of the Philistines. Gn 26:1
Abimelech **k** of the Philistines looked Gn 26:8
before any **k** reigned over the Israelites. Gn 36:31
the cupbearer of the **k** of Egypt and his Gn 40:1
offense against their lord the **k** of Egypt. Gn 40:1
and the baker of the **k** of Egypt, Gn 40:5
the service of Pharaoh **k** of Egypt. Gn 41:46
Now there arose a new **k** over Egypt, who Ex 1:8
Then the **k** of Egypt said to the Hebrew Ex 1:15
not do as the **k** of Egypt commanded Ex 1:17
So the **k** of Egypt called the midwives Ex 1:18
those many days the **k** of Egypt died, Ex 2:23
Israel shall go to the **k** of Egypt and say Ex 3:18
But I know that the **k** of Egypt will not Ex 3:19
But the **k** of Egypt said to them, "Moses Ex 5:4
tell Pharaoh **k** of Egypt to let the people Ex 6:11
of Israel and about Pharaoh **k** of Egypt: Ex 6:13
who spoke to Pharaoh **k** of Egypt about Ex 6:27
tell Pharaoh **k** of Egypt all that I say to Ex 6:29
When the **k** of Egypt was told that the Ex 14:5
the heart of Pharaoh **k** of Egypt, Ex 14:8
from Kadesh to the **k** of Edom: Nm 20:14
When the Canaanite, the **k** of Arad, Nm 21:1
messengers to Sihon **k** of the Nm 21:21
city of Sihon the **k** of the Amorites, Nm 21:26
against the former **k** of Moab and Nm 21:26
daughters captives, to an Amorite **k**, Nm 21:29
And Og the **k** of Bashan came out Nm 21:33
as you did to Sihon **k** of the Amorites, Nm 21:34
who was **k** of Moab at that time, Nm 22:4
"Balak the son of Zippor, **k** of Moab, Nm 22:10
the **k** of Moab from the eastern Nm 23:7
and the shout of a **k** is among them. Nm 23:21
his **k** shall be higher than Agag, and Nm 24:7
kingdom of Sihon **k** of the Amorites Nm 32:33
and the kingdom of Og **k** of Bashan, Nm 32:33
And the Canaanite, the **k** of Arad, Nm 33:40
had defeated Sihon the **k** of the Amorites, Dt 1:4
lived in Heshbon, and Og the **k** of Bashan, Dt 1:4
hand Sihon the Amorite, **k** of Heshbon, Dt 2:24
of Kedemoth to Sihon the **k** of Heshbon, Dt 2:26
But Sihon the **k** of Heshbon would not Dt 2:30
And Og the **k** of Bashan came out against Dt 3:1
as you did to Sihon the **k** of the Amorites, Dt 3:2
into our hand Og also, the **k** of Bashan, Dt 3:3
as we did to Sihon the **k** of Heshbon, Dt 3:6
(For only Og the **k** of Bashan was left of Dt 3:11
the land of Sihon the **k** of the Amorites, Dt 4:46
land and the land of Og, the **k** of Bashan, Dt 4:47
from the hand of Pharaoh **k** of Egypt. Dt 7:8
Egypt to Pharaoh the **k** of Egypt and to Dt 11:3
in it and then say, 'I will set a **k** over me, Dt 17:14
may indeed set a **k** over you whom the Dt 17:15
brothers you shall set as **k** over you. Dt 17:15
bring you and your **k** whom you set Dt 28:36
Sihon the **k** of Heshbon and Og the king Dt 29:7
Heshbon and Og the **k** of Bashan came Dt 29:7
Thus the LORD became **k** in Jeshurun, Dt 33:5
And it was told to the **k** of Jericho, Jos 2:2
Then the **k** of Jericho sent to Rahab, Jos 2:3
hand, with its **k** and mighty men of valor. Jos 6:2
I have given into your hand the **k** of Ai, Jos 8:1
do to Ai and its **k** as you did to Jericho Jos 8:2
its king as you did to Jericho and its **k**. Jos 8:2
And as soon as the **k** of Ai saw this, he Jos 8:14
But the **k** of Ai they took alive, and Jos 8:23
And he hanged the **k** of Ai on a tree until Jos 8:29
the Jordan, to Sihon the **k** of Heshbon, Jos 9:10
king of Heshbon, and to Og **k** of Bashan, Jos 9:10
As soon as Adoni-zedek, **k** of Jerusalem, Jos 10:1
doing to Ai and its **k** as he had done to Jos 10:1
king as he had done to Jericho and its **k**, Jos 10:1
So Adoni-zedek **k** of Jerusalem sent to Jos 10:3
Jerusalem sent to Hoham **k** of Hebron, Jos 10:3
king of Hebron, to Piram **k** of Jarmuth, Jos 10:3
king of Jarmuth, to Japhia **k** of Lachish, Jos 10:3
of Lachish, and to Debir **k** of Eglon, Jos 10:3
of the Amorites, the **k** of Jerusalem, Jos 10:5
the king of Jerusalem, the **k** of Hebron, Jos 10:5
the king of Hebron, the **k** of Jarmuth, Jos 10:5
the king of Jarmuth, the **k** of Lachish, Jos 10:5
the king of Lachish, and the **k** of Eglon, Jos 10:5
him from the cave, the **k** of Jerusalem, Jos 10:23
the king of Jerusalem, the **k** of Hebron, Jos 10:23
the king of Hebron, the **k** of Jarmuth, Jos 10:23
the king of Jarmuth, the **k** of Lachish, Jos 10:23
king of Lachish, and the **k** of Eglon. Jos 10:23
it on that day and struck it, and its **k**, Jos 10:28
he did to the **k** of Makkedah just as Jos 10:28
just as he had done to the **k** of Jericho. Jos 10:28
gave it also and its **k** into the hand of Jos 10:30
And he did to its **k** as he had done to the Jos 10:30
king as he had done to the **k** of Jericho. Jos 10:30
Then Horam **k** of Gezer came up to Jos 10:33
of the sword, and its **k** and its towns, Jos 10:37
captured it with its **k** and all its towns. Jos 10:39
to Hebron and to Libnah and its **k**, Jos 10:39
its king, so he did to Debir and to its **k**. Jos 10:39
When Jabin, **k** of Hazor, heard of this, Jos 11:1
of this, he sent to Jobab **k** of Madon, Jos 11:1
king of Madon, and to the **k** of Shimron, Jos 11:1
of Shimron, and to the **k** of Achshaph, Jos 11:1
Hazor and struck its **k** with the sword, Jos 11:10
Sihon **k** of the Amorites who lived at Jos 12:2
and Og **k** of Bashan, one of the remnant Jos 12:4
to the boundary of Sihon **k** of Heshbon. Jos 12:5
the **k** of Jericho, one; the king of Ai, Jos 12:9
the **k** of Ai, which is beside Bethel, one; Jos 12:9
the **k** of Jerusalem, one; the king of Jos 12:10
of Jerusalem, one; the **k** of Hebron, one; Jos 12:10
the **k** of Jarmuth, one; the king of Jos 12:11
of Jarmuth, one; the **k** of Lachish, one; Jos 12:11
the **k** of Eglon, one; the king of Gezer, Jos 12:12
king of Eglon, one; the **k** of Gezer, one; Jos 12:12
the **k** of Debir, one; the king of Geder, Jos 12:13
king of Debir, one; the **k** of Geder, one; Jos 12:13
the **k** of Hormah, one; the king of Arad, Jos 12:14
of Hormah, one; the **k** of Arad, one; Jos 12:14
the **k** of Libnah, one; the king of Jos 12:15
of Libnah, one; the **k** of Adullam, one; Jos 12:15
the **k** of Makkedah, one; the king of Jos 12:16
of Makkedah, one; the **k** of Bethel, one; Jos 12:16
the **k** of Tappuah, one; the king of Jos 12:17
of Tappuah, one; the **k** of Hepher, one; Jos 12:17
the **k** of Aphek, one; the king of Jos 12:18
of Aphek, one; the **k** of Lasharon, one; Jos 12:18
the **k** of Madon, one; the king of Hazor, Jos 12:19
of Madon, one; the **k** of Hazor, one; Jos 12:19
the **k** of Shimron-meron, one; the king Jos 12:20
one; the **k** of Achshaph, one; Jos 12:20
the **k** of Taanach, one; the king of Jos 12:21
of Taanach, one; the **k** of Megiddo, one; Jos 12:21
the **k** of Kedesh, one; the king of Jos 12:22
one; the **k** of Jokneam in Carmel, one; Jos 12:22
the **k** of Dor in Naphath-dor, one; the Jos 12:23
one; the **k** of Goiim in Galilee, one; Jos 12:23
the **k** of Tirzah, one: in all, thirty-one Jos 12:24
all the cities of Sihon **k** of the Amorites, Jos 13:10
kingdom of Sihon **k** of the Amorites, Jos 13:21
of the kingdom of Sihon **k** of Heshbon, Jos 13:27
the whole kingdom of Og **k** of Bashan, Jos 13:30
Balak the son of Zippor, **k** of Moab, Jos 24:9
of Cushan-rishathaim **k** of Jgs 3:8
gave Cushan-rishathaim **k** of Jgs 3:10
strengthened Eglon the **k** of Moab Jgs 3:12
served Eglon the **k** of Moab eighteen Jgs 3:14
tribute by him to Eglon the **k** of Moab. Jgs 3:15
the tribute to Eglon **k** of Moab. Jgs 3:17
for you, O **k**." And he commanded, Jgs 3:19
them into the hand of Jabin **k** of Canaan, Jgs 4:2
peace between Jabin the **k** of Hazor and Jgs 4:17
subdued Jabin the **k** of Canaan before Jgs 4:23
harder against Jabin the **k** of Canaan, Jgs 4:24
until they destroyed Jabin **k** of Canaan. Jgs 4:24
one of them resembled the son of a **k**." Jgs 8:18
and they went and made Abimelech **k**, Jgs 9:6
once went out to anoint a **k** over them, Jgs 9:8
faith you are anointing me **k** over you, Jgs 9:15
integrity when you made Abimelech **k**, Jgs 9:16
servant, **k** over the leaders of Shechem, Jgs 9:18
messengers to the **k** of the Ammonites Jgs 11:12
And the **k** of the Ammonites answered Jgs 11:13
messengers to the **k** of the Ammonites Jgs 11:14
then sent messengers to the **k** of Edom, Jgs 11:17
but the **k** of Edom would not listen. Jgs 11:17
And they sent also to the **k** of Moab, Jgs 11:17
messengers to Sihon **k** of the Amorites, Jgs 11:19
king of the Amorites, **k** of Heshbon, Jgs 11:19
Balak the son of Zippor, **k** of Moab? Jgs 11:25
But the **k** of the Ammonites did not Jgs 11:28
In those days there was no **k** in Israel. Jgs 17:6
In those days there was no **k** in Israel. Jgs 18:1
days, when there was no **k** in Israel, Jgs 19:1
In those days there was no **k** in Israel. Jgs 21:25
give strength to his **k** and exalt the 1 Sm 2:10
Now appoint for us a **k** to judge us like 1 Sm 8:5
"Give us a **k** to judge us." And Samuel 1 Sm 8:6
rejected me from being **k** over them. 1 Sm 8:7
the ways of the **k** who shall reign over 1 Sm 8:9
who were asking for a **k** from him. 1 Sm 8:10
the ways of the **k** who will reign over 1 Sm 8:11
you will cry out because of your **k**, 1 Sm 8:18
"No! But there shall be a **k** over us, 1 Sm 8:19
and that our **k** may judge us and go 1 Sm 8:20
make them a **k**." Samuel then said 1 Sm 8:22
have said to him, 'Set a **k** over us.' 1 Sm 10:19
the people shouted, "Long live the **k**!" 1 Sm 10:24
they made Saul **k** before the LORD 1 Sm 11:15
to me and have made a **k** over you. 1 Sm 12:1
now, behold, the **k** walks before you, 1 Sm 12:2
and into the hand of the **k** of Moab. 1 Sm 12:9
that Nahash the **k** of the Ammonites 1 Sm 12:12
me, 'No, but a **k** shall reign over us,' 1 Sm 12:12
when the LORD your God was your **k**. 1 Sm 12:12
now behold the **k** whom you have 1 Sm 12:13
behold, the LORD has set a **k** over you. 1 Sm 12:13
both you and the **k** who reigns over 1 Sm 12:14
LORD will be against you and your **k**. 1 Sm 12:15
LORD, in asking for yourselves a **k**." 1 Sm 12:17
this evil, to ask for ourselves a **k**." 1 Sm 12:19
swept away, both you and your **k**." 1 Sm 12:25
me to anoint you **k** over his people 1 Sm 15:1
he took Agag the **k** of the Amalekites 1 Sm 15:8
"I regret that I have made Saul **k**, for 1 Sm 15:11
The LORD anointed you **k** over Israel. 1 Sm 15:17
have brought Agag the **k** of Amalek, 1 Sm 15:20
has also rejected you from being **k**." 1 Sm 15:23
you from being **k** over Israel." 1 Sm 15:26
to me Agag the **k** of the Amalekites." 1 Sm 15:32
that he had made Saul **k** over Israel. 1 Sm 15:35
rejected him from being **k** over Israel? 1 Sm 16:1
for myself a **k** among his sons." 1 Sm 16:1
And the **k** will enrich the man who 1 Sm 17:25
Abner said, "As your soul lives, O **k**, 1 Sm 17:55
And the **k** said, "Inquire whose son 1 Sm 17:56
singing and dancing, to meet **K** Saul, 1 Sm 18:6
that I should be son-in-law to the **k**?" 1 Sm 18:18
say, 'Behold, the **k** has delight in you, 1 Sm 18:22
'The **k** desires no bride-price except a 1 Sm 18:25
were given in full number to the **k**, 1 Sm 18:27
"Let not the **k** sin against his servant 1 Sm 19:4
not fail to sit at table with the **k**. 1 Sm 20:5
came, the **k** sat down to eat food. 1 Sm 20:24
The **k** sat on his seat, as at other 1 Sm 20:25
"The **k** has charged me with a matter 1 Sm 21:2
and went to Achish the **k** of Gath. 1 Sm 21:10
"Is not this David the **k** of the land? 1 Sm 21:11
afraid of Achish the **k** of Gath. 1 Sm 21:12
And he said to the **k** of Moab, "Please 1 Sm 22:3
And he left them with the **k** of Moab, 1 Sm 22:4
Then the **k** sent to summon 1 Sm 22:11
Nob, and all of them came to the **k**. 1 Sm 22:11
Then Ahimelech answered the **k**, 1 Sm 22:14
Let not the **k** impute anything to his 1 Sm 22:15
And the **k** said, "You shall surely die, 1 Sm 22:16
And the **k** said to the guard who 1 Sm 22:17

the servants of the **k** would not put 1 Sm 22:17
Then the **k** said to Doeg, "You turn 1 Sm 22:18
You shall be **k** over Israel, and I 1 Sm 23:17
Now come down, O **k**, according to 1 Sm 23:20
"My lord the **k**!" And when Saul 1 Sm 24:8
After whom has the **k** of Israel come 1 Sm 24:14
I know that you shall surely be **k**, 1 Sm 24:20
in his house, like the feast of a **k**. 1 Sm 25:36
"Who are you who calls to the **k**?" 1 Sm 26:14
not kept watch over your lord the **k**? 1 Sm 26:15
came in to destroy the **k** your lord. 1 Sm 26:15
said, "It is my voice, my lord, O **k**." 1 Sm 26:17
let my lord the **k** hear the words of 1 Sm 26:19
for the **k** of Israel has come out to 1 Sm 26:20
and said, "Here is the spear, O **k**! 1 Sm 26:22
Achish the son of Maoch, **k** of Gath. 1 Sm 27:2
The **k** said to her, "Do not be afraid. 1 Sm 28:13
David, the servant of Saul, **k** of Israel, 1 Sm 29:3
against the enemies of my lord the **k**?" 1 Sm 29:8
they anointed David **k** over the house 2 Sm 2:4
Judah has anointed me **k** over them." 2 Sm 2:7
and he made him **k** over Gilead and the 2 Sm 2:9
time that David was **k** in Hebron over 2 Sm 2:11
the daughter of Talmai **k** of Geshur; 2 Sm 3:3
been seeking David as **k** over you. 2 Sm 3:17
will gather all Israel to my lord the **k**, 2 Sm 3:21
"Abner the son of Ner came to the **k**, 2 Sm 3:23
Then Joab went to the **k** and said, 2 Sm 3:24
before Abner." And **K** David followed 2 Sm 3:31
And the **k** lifted up his voice and wept 2 Sm 3:32
And the **k** lamented for Abner, 2 Sm 3:33
as everything that the **k** did pleased all 2 Sm 3:36
And the **k** said to his servants, "Do 2 Sm 3:38
I was gentle today, though anointed **k**. 2 Sm 3:39
And they said to the **k**, "Here is the head 2 Sm 4:8
avenged my lord the **k** this day on Saul 2 Sm 4:8
In times past, when Saul was **k** over us, 2 Sm 5:2
elders of Israel came to the **k** at Hebron, 2 Sm 5:3
and **K** David made a covenant with 2 Sm 5:3
and they anointed David **k** over Israel. 2 Sm 5:3
And the **k** and his men went to 2 Sm 5:6
And Hiram **k** of Tyre sent messengers 2 Sm 5:11
had established him **k** over Israel, 2 Sm 5:12
had been anointed **k** over Israel, 2 Sm 5:17
And it was told **K** David, "The LORD 2 Sm 6:12
window and saw **K** David leaping and 2 Sm 6:16
"How the **k** of Israel honored himself 2 Sm 6:20
Now when the **k** lived in his house and 2 Sm 7:1
the **k** said to Nathan the prophet, "See 2 Sm 7:2
And Nathan said to the **k**, "Go, do all 2 Sm 7:3
Then **K** David went in and sat before 2 Sm 7:18
the son of Rehob, **k** of Zobah, 2 Sm 8:3
came to help Hadadezer **k** of Zobah, 2 Sm 8:5
K David took very much bronze. 2 Sm 8:8
When Toi **k** of Hamath heard that 2 Sm 8:9
Toi sent his son Joram to **K** David, to 2 Sm 8:10
These also **K** David dedicated to the 2 Sm 8:11
the son of Rehob, **k** of Zobah. 2 Sm 8:12
And the **k** said to him, "Are you Ziba?" 2 Sm 9:2
And the **k** said, "Is there not still 2 Sm 9:3
of God to him?" Ziba said to the **k**, 2 Sm 9:3
The **k** said to him, "Where is he?" And 2 Sm 9:4
"Where is he?" And Ziba said to the **k**, 2 Sm 9:4
Then **K** David sent and brought him 2 Sm 9:5
Then the **k** called Ziba, Saul's servant, 2 Sm 9:9
Then Ziba said to the **k**, "According 2 Sm 9:11
my lord the **k** commands his servant, 2 Sm 9:11
After this the **k** of the Ammonites 2 Sm 10:1
And the **k** said, "Remain at Jericho 2 Sm 10:5
and the **k** of Maacah with 1,000 men, 2 Sm 10:6
followed him a present from the **k**. 2 Sm 11:8
the news about the fighting to the **k**, 2 Sm 11:19
of Israel, 'I anointed you **k** over Israel, 2 Sm 12:7
the crown of their **k** from his head. 2 Sm 12:30
And he said to him, "O son of the **k**, 2 Sm 13:4
And when the **k** came to see him, 2 Sm 13:6
came to see him, Amnon said to the **k**, 2 Sm 13:6
Now therefore, please speak to the **k**, 2 Sm 13:13
the virgin daughters of the **k** dressed. 2 Sm 13:18
When **K** David heard of all these 2 Sm 13:21
Absalom came to the **k** and said, 2 Sm 13:24
Please let the **k** and his servants go 2 Sm 13:24
But the **k** said to Absalom, "No, my 2 Sm 13:25
go with us." And the **k** said to him, 2 Sm 13:26
Then the **k** arose and tore his 2 Sm 13:31
let not my lord the **k** so take it to 2 Sm 13:33
And Jonadab said to the **k**, "Behold, 2 Sm 13:35
And the **k** also and all his servants 2 Sm 13:36
the son of Ammihud, **k** of Geshur. 2 Sm 13:37
the spirit of the **k** longed to go out 2 Sm 13:39
Go to the **k** and speak thus to him." So 2 Sm 14:3
the woman of Tekoa came to the **k**, 2 Sm 14:4
paid homage and said, "Save me, O **k**." 2 Sm 14:4
And the **k** said to her, "What is your 2 Sm 14:5
Then the **k** said to the woman, "Go to 2 Sm 14:8
the woman of Tekoa said to the **k**, 2 Sm 14:9
"On me be the guilt, my lord the **k**, 2 Sm 14:9
let the **k** and his throne be guiltless." 2 Sm 14:9
The **k** said, "If anyone says anything 2 Sm 14:10
"Please let the **k** invoke the LORD 2 Sm 14:11
a word to my lord the **k**." He said, 2 Sm 14:12
this decision the **k** convicts himself, 2 Sm 14:13
inasmuch as the **k** does not bring 2 Sm 14:13
to my lord the **k** because the people 2 Sm 14:15
thought, 'I will speak to the **k**; 2 Sm 14:15
may be that the **k** will perform the 2 Sm 14:15
For the **k** will hear and deliver his 2 Sm 14:16
word of my lord the **k** will set me at 2 Sm 14:17
for my lord the **k** is like the angel of 2 Sm 14:17
Then the **k** answered the woman, 2 Sm 14:18
said, "Let my lord the **k** speak." 2 Sm 14:18
The **k** said, "Is the hand of Joab with 2 Sm 14:19
"As surely as you live, my lord the **k**, 2 Sm 14:19
that my lord the **k** has said. 2 Sm 14:19
Then the **k** said to Joab, "Behold 2 Sm 14:21
and paid homage and blessed the **k**. 2 Sm 14:22
favor in your sight, my lord the **k**, 2 Sm 14:22
in that the **k** has granted the request 2 Sm 14:22
And the **k** said, "Let him dwell apart 2 Sm 14:24
sent for Joab, to send him to the **k**, 2 Sm 14:29
here, that I may send you to the **k**, 2 Sm 14:32
let me go into the presence of the **k**, 2 Sm 14:32
Joab went to the **k** and told him, 2 Sm 14:33
he came to the **k** and bowed himself 2 Sm 14:33
his face to the ground before the **k**, 2 Sm 14:33
the king, and the **k** kissed Absalom. 2 Sm 14:33
to come before the **k** for judgment, 2 Sm 15:2
man designated by the **k** to hear you." 2 Sm 15:3
who came to the **k** for judgment. 2 Sm 15:6
of four years Absalom said to the **k**, 2 Sm 15:7
The **k** said to him, "Go in peace." So 2 Sm 15:9
then say, 'Absalom is **k** at Hebron!'" 2 Sm 15:10
And the king's servants said to the **k**, 2 Sm 15:15
do whatever my lord the **k** decides." 2 Sm 15:15
So the **k** went out, and all his 2 Sm 15:16
And the **k** left ten concubines to 2 Sm 15:16
And the **k** went out, and all the 2 Sm 15:17
from Gath, passed on before the **k**. 2 Sm 15:18
Then the **k** said to Ittai the Gittite, 2 Sm 15:19
Go back and stay with the **k**, for you 2 Sm 15:19
But Ittai answered the **k**, "As the 2 Sm 15:21
LORD lives, and as my lord the **k** lives, 2 Sm 15:21
wherever my lord the **k** shall be, 2 Sm 15:21
and the **k** crossed the brook Kidron, 2 Sm 15:23
Then the **k** said to Zadok, "Carry the 2 Sm 15:25
The **k** also said to Zadok the priest, 2 Sm 15:27
'I will be your servant, O **k**; 2 Sm 15:34
And the **k** said to Ziba, "Why have 2 Sm 16:2
And the **k** said, "And where is your 2 Sm 16:3
your master's son?" Ziba said to the **k**, 2 Sm 16:3
Then the **k** said to Ziba, "Behold, all 2 Sm 16:4
favor in your sight, my lord the **k**." 2 Sm 16:4
When **K** David came to Bahurim, 2 Sm 16:5
and at all the servants of **K** David, 2 Sm 16:6
the son of Zeruiah said to the **k**, 2 Sm 16:9
this dead dog curse my lord the **k**? 2 Sm 16:9
But the **k** said, "What have I to do 2 Sm 16:10
And the **k**, and all the people who 2 Sm 16:14
said to Absalom, "Long live the **k**! 2 Sm 16:16
live the king! Long live the **k**!" 2 Sm 16:16
will flee. I will strike down only the **k**, 2 Sm 17:2
lest the **k** and all the people who are 2 Sm 17:16
and they were to go and tell **K** David, 2 Sm 17:17
the well, and went and told **K** David. 2 Sm 17:21
And the **k** said to the men, "I myself 2 Sm 18:2
The **k** said to them, "Whatever seems 2 Sm 18:4
I will do." So the **k** stood at the side of 2 Sm 18:4
And the **k** ordered Joab and Abishai 2 Sm 18:5
heard when the **k** gave orders to 2 Sm 18:5
our hearing the **k** commanded you 2 Sm 18:12
there is nothing hidden from the **k**), 2 Sm 18:13
carry news to the **k** that the LORD has 2 Sm 18:19
tell the **k** what you have seen." The 2 Sm 18:21
watchman called out and told the **k**. 2 Sm 18:25
And the **k** said, "If he is alone, there 2 Sm 18:25
man running alone!" The **k** said, 2 Sm 18:26
the son of Zadok." And the **k** said, 2 Sm 18:27
Then Ahimaaz cried out to the **k**, 2 Sm 18:28
he bowed before the **k** with his face 2 Sm 18:28
their hand against my lord the **k**." 2 Sm 18:28
And the **k** said, "Is it well with the 2 Sm 18:29
And the **k** said, "Turn aside and 2 Sm 18:30
said, "Good news for my lord the **k**! 2 Sm 18:31
The **k** said to the Cushite, "Is it well 2 Sm 18:32
of my lord the **k** and all who rise 2 Sm 18:32
And the **k** was deeply moved and 2 Sm 18:33
the **k** is weeping and mourning for 2 Sm 19:1
day, "The **k** is grieving for his son." 2 Sm 19:2
The **k** covered his face, and the king 2 Sm 19:4
face, and the **k** cried with a loud voice, 2 Sm 19:4
came into the house to the **k** and said, 2 Sm 19:5
Then the **k** arose and took his seat in 2 Sm 19:8
the **k** is sitting in the gate." And all the 2 Sm 19:8
And all the people came before the **k**. 2 Sm 19:8
"The **k** delivered us from the hand of 2 Sm 19:9
about bringing the **k** back?" 2 Sm 19:10
And **K** David sent this message to 2 Sm 19:11
last to bring the **k** back to his house, 2 Sm 19:11
word of all Israel has come to the **k**? 2 Sm 19:11
you be the last to bring back the **k**?' 2 Sm 19:12
man, so that they sent word to the **k**, 2 Sm 19:14
So the **k** came back to the Jordan, 2 Sm 19:15
Gilgal to meet the **k** and to bring the 2 Sm 19:15
and to bring the **k** over the Jordan. 2 Sm 19:15
the men of Judah to meet **K** David. 2 Sm 19:16
down to the Jordan before the **k**, 2 Sm 19:17
son of Gera fell down before the **k**, 2 Sm 19:18
and said to the **k**, "Let not my lord 2 Sm 19:19
the day my lord the **k** left Jerusalem. 2 Sm 19:19
Do not let the **k** take it to heart. 2 Sm 19:19
come down to meet my lord the **k**." 2 Sm 19:20
that I am this day **k** over Israel?" 2 Sm 19:22
And the **k** said to Shimei, "You shall 2 Sm 19:23
not die." And the **k** gave him his 2 Sm 19:23
son of Saul came down to meet the **k**. 2 Sm 19:24
from the day the **k** departed until the 2 Sm 19:24
he came to Jerusalem to meet the **k**, 2 Sm 19:25
to meet the king, the **k** said to him, 2 Sm 19:25
He answered, "My lord, O **k**, my 2 Sm 19:26
I may ride on it and go with the **k**.' 2 Sm 19:26
your servant to my lord the **k**. 2 Sm 19:27
But my lord the **k** is like the angel of 2 Sm 19:27
to death before my lord the **k**, 2 Sm 19:28
right have I, then, to cry to the **k**?" 2 Sm 19:28
And the **k** said to him, "Why speak 2 Sm 19:29
And Mephibosheth said to the **k**, 2 Sm 19:30
since my lord the **k** has come safely 2 Sm 19:30
he went on with the **k** to the Jordan, 2 Sm 19:31
had provided the **k** with food while 2 Sm 19:32
And the **k** said to Barzillai, "Come 2 Sm 19:33
But Barzillai said to the **k**, "How 2 Sm 19:34
go up with the **k** to Jerusalem? 2 Sm 19:34
an added burden to my lord the **k**? 2 Sm 19:35
little way over the Jordan with the **k**. 2 Sm 19:36
Why should the **k** repay me with 2 Sm 19:36
Let him go over with my lord the **k**, 2 Sm 19:37
And the **k** answered, "Chimham 2 Sm 19:38
over the Jordan, and the **k** went over. 2 Sm 19:39
And the **k** kissed Barzillai and 2 Sm 19:39
The **k** went on to Gilgal, and 2 Sm 19:40
of Israel, brought the **k** on his way. 2 Sm 19:40
of Israel came to the **k** and said to the 2 Sm 19:41
came to the king and said to the **k**, 2 Sm 19:41
and brought the **k** and his 2 Sm 19:41
"Because the **k** is our close relative. 2 Sm 19:42
Judah, "We have ten shares in the **k**, 2 Sm 19:43
bringing back our **k**?" But the 2 Sm 19:43
followed their **k** steadfastly from 2 Sm 20:2
And the **k** took the ten concubines 2 Sm 20:3
Then the **k** said to Amasa, "Call the 2 Sm 20:4
lifted up his hand against **K** David. 2 Sm 20:21
Joab returned to Jerusalem to the **k**. 2 Sm 20:22
So the **k** called the Gibeonites and 2 Sm 21:2
They said to the **k**, "The man who 2 Sm 21:5
chosen of the LORD." And the **k** said, 2 Sm 21:6
But the **k** spared Mephibosheth, the 2 Sm 21:7
The **k** took the two sons of Rizpah the 2 Sm 21:8
they did all that the **k** commanded. 2 Sm 21:14
Great salvation he brings to his **k**, 2 Sm 22:51
So the **k** said to Joab, the commander 2 Sm 24:2
But Joab said to the **k**, "May the LORD 2 Sm 24:3
the eyes of my lord the **k** still see it, 2 Sm 24:3
does my lord the **k** delight in this 2 Sm 24:3
the presence of the **k** to number the 2 Sm 24:4
the numbering of the people to the **k**: 2 Sm 24:9
he saw the **k** and his servants 2 Sm 24:20
paid homage to the **k** with his face to 2 Sm 24:20
has my lord the **k** come to his 2 Sm 24:21
"Let my lord the **k** take and offer up 2 Sm 24:22
All this, O **k**, Araunah gives to the 2 Sm 24:23
gives to the **k**." And Araunah said 2 Sm 24:23
king." And Araunah said to the **k**, 2 Sm 24:23
But the **k** said to Araunah, "No, but I 2 Sm 24:24
Now **K** David was old and advanced in 1 Kgs 1:1
woman be sought for my lord the **k**, 1 Kgs 1:2
let her wait on the **k** and be in his 1 Kgs 1:2
that my lord the **k** may be warm." 1 Kgs 1:2
and brought her to the **k**. 1 Kgs 1:3
of service to the **k** and attended to him, 1 Kgs 1:4
to him, but the **k** knew her not. 1 Kgs 1:4
"I will be **k**." And he prepared for 1 Kgs 1:5
Haggith has become **k** and David our 1 Kgs 1:11
Go in at once to **K** David, and say to 1 Kgs 1:13
to him, 'Did you not, my lord the **k**, 1 Kgs 1:13
throne"? Why then is Adonijah **k**?' 1 Kgs 1:13

you are still speaking with the **k**,	1 Kgs 1:14
went to the **k** in his chamber	1 Kgs 1:15
his chamber (now the **k** was very old,	1 Kgs 1:15
Shunammite was attending to the **k**).	1 Kgs 1:15
bowed and paid homage to the **k**,	1 Kgs 1:16
homage to the king, and the **k** said,	1 Kgs 1:16
And now, behold, Adonijah is **k**,	1 Kgs 1:18
is king, although you, my lord the **k**,	1 Kgs 1:18
and has invited all the sons of the **k**,	1 Kgs 1:19
And now, my lord the **k**, the eyes of	1 Kgs 1:20
the throne of my lord the **k** after him.	1 Kgs 1:20
when my lord the **k** sleeps with his	1 Kgs 1:21
she was still speaking with the **k**,	1 Kgs 1:22
And they told the **k**, "Here is Nathan	1 Kgs 1:23
And when he came in before the **k**,	1 Kgs 1:23
the king, he bowed before the **k**,	1 Kgs 1:23
And Nathan said, "My lord the **k**,	1 Kgs 1:24
and saying, 'Long live **K** Adonijah!'	1 Kgs 1:25
by my lord the **k** and you have not	1 Kgs 1:27
throne of my lord the **k** after him?"	1 Kgs 1:27
Then **K** David answered, "Call	1 Kgs 1:28
presence and stood before the **k**.	1 Kgs 1:28
And the **k** swore, saying, "As the LORD	1 Kgs 1:29
and paid homage to the **k** and said,	1 Kgs 1:31
"May my lord **K** David live forever!"	1 Kgs 1:31
K David said, "Call to me Zadok the	1 Kgs 1:32
Jehoiada." So they came before the **k**.	1 Kgs 1:32
And the **k** said to them, "Take with	1 Kgs 1:33
there anoint him **k** over Israel.	1 Kgs 1:34
and say, 'Long live **K** Solomon!'	1 Kgs 1:34
throne, for he shall be **k** in my place.	1 Kgs 1:35
the son of Jehoiada answered the **k**,	1 Kgs 1:36
the LORD, the God of my lord the **k**,	1 Kgs 1:36
the LORD has been with my lord the **k**,	1 Kgs 1:37
than the throne of my lord **K** David."	1 Kgs 1:37
Solomon ride on **K** David's mule and	1 Kgs 1:38
people said, "Long live **K** Solomon!"	1 Kgs 1:39
for our lord **K** David has made	1 Kgs 1:43
King David has made Solomon **k**,	1 Kgs 1:43
and the **k** has sent with him Zadok	1 Kgs 1:44
have anointed him **k** at Gihon,	1 Kgs 1:45
to congratulate our lord **K** David,	1 Kgs 1:47
And the **k** bowed himself on the bed.	1 Kgs 1:47
And the **k** also said, 'Blessed be the	1 Kgs 1:48
"Behold, Adonijah fears **K** Solomon,	1 Kgs 1:51
'Let **K** Solomon swear to me first that	1 Kgs 1:51
So **K** Solomon sent, and they brought	1 Kgs 1:53
and paid homage to **K** Solomon,	1 Kgs 1:53
"Please ask **K** Solomon—he will not	1 Kgs 2:17
well; I will speak for you to the **k**."	1 Kgs 2:18
Bathsheba went to **K** Solomon to	1 Kgs 2:19
And the **k** rose to meet her and bowed	1 Kgs 2:19
not refuse me." And the **k** said to her,	1 Kgs 2:20
K Solomon answered his mother,	1 Kgs 2:22
Then **K** Solomon swore by the LORD,	1 Kgs 2:23
So **K** Solomon sent Benaiah the son	1 Kgs 2:25
And to Abiathar the priest the **k** said,	1 Kgs 2:26
And when it was told **K** Solomon,	1 Kgs 2:29
and said to him, "The **k** commands,	1 Kgs 2:30
Benaiah brought the **k** word again,	1 Kgs 2:30
The **k** replied to him, "Do as he has	1 Kgs 2:31
The **k** put Benaiah the son of	1 Kgs 2:35
and the **k** put Zadok the priest in the	1 Kgs 2:35
Then the **k** sent and summoned	1 Kgs 2:36
And Shimei said to the **k**, "What you	1 Kgs 2:38
as my lord the **k** has said, so will your	1 Kgs 2:38
to Achish, son of Maacah, **k** of Gath.	1 Kgs 2:39
the **k** sent and summoned Shimei	1 Kgs 2:42
The **k** also said to Shimei, "You	1 Kgs 2:44
But **K** Solomon shall be blessed, and	1 Kgs 2:45
Then the **k** commanded Benaiah the	1 Kgs 2:46
alliance with Pharaoh **k** of Egypt.	1 Kgs 3:1
And the **k** went to Gibeon to sacrifice	1 Kgs 3:4
have made your servant **k** in place of	1 Kgs 3:7
so that no other **k** shall compare with	1 Kgs 3:13
came to the **k** and stood before	1 Kgs 3:16
mine." Thus they spoke before the **k**.	1 Kgs 3:22
Then the **k** said, "The one says, 'This	1 Kgs 3:23
And the **k** said, "Bring me a sword."	1 Kgs 3:24
So a sword was brought before the **k**.	1 Kgs 3:24
And the **k** said, "Divide the living	1 Kgs 3:25
whose son was alive said to the **k**,	1 Kgs 3:26
Then the **k** answered and said, "Give	1 Kgs 3:27
the judgment that the **k** had rendered,	1 Kgs 3:28
and they stood in awe of the **k**,	1 Kgs 3:28
K Solomon was king over all Israel,	1 Kgs 4:1
King Solomon was **k** over all Israel,	1 Kgs 4:1
food for the **k** and his household.	1 Kgs 4:7
country of Sihon **k** of the Amorites	1 Kgs 4:19
the Amorites and of Og **k** of Bashan.	1 Kgs 4:19
supplied provisions for **K** Solomon,	1 Kgs 4:27
all who came to **K** Solomon's table,	1 Kgs 4:27
Now Hiram **k** of Tyre sent his servants	1 Kgs 5:1
they had anointed him **k** in place of	1 Kgs 5:1
K Solomon drafted forced labor out	1 Kgs 5:13
The house that **K** Solomon built for	1 Kgs 6:2
And **K** Solomon sent and brought	1 Kgs 7:13
He came to **K** Solomon and did all his	1 Kgs 7:14
that he did for **K** Solomon on the	1 Kgs 7:40
which Hiram made for **K** Solomon,	1 Kgs 7:45
plain of the Jordan the **k** cast them,	1 Kgs 7:46
all the work that **K** Solomon did on	1 Kgs 7:51
Israel, before **K** Solomon in Jerusalem,	1 Kgs 8:1
Israel assembled to **K** Solomon at the	1 Kgs 8:2
And **K** Solomon and all the	1 Kgs 8:5
Then the **k** turned around and	1 Kgs 8:14
Then the **k**, and all Israel with him,	1 Kgs 8:62
So the **k** and all the people of Israel	1 Kgs 8:63
same day the **k** consecrated the	1 Kgs 8:64
and they blessed the **k** and went to	1 Kgs 8:66
and Hiram **k** of Tyre had supplied	1 Kgs 9:11
K Solomon gave to Hiram twenty	1 Kgs 9:11
had sent to the **k** 120 talents of gold.	1 Kgs 9:14
forced labor that **K** Solomon drafted	1 Kgs 9:15
(Pharaoh **k** of Egypt had gone up and	1 Kgs 9:16
K Solomon built a fleet of ships at	1 Kgs 9:26
and they brought it to **K** Solomon.	1 Kgs 9:28
hidden from the **k** that he could	1 Kgs 10:3
And she said to the **k**, "The report was	1 Kgs 10:6
Israel forever, he has made you **k**,	1 Kgs 10:9
Then she gave the **k** 120 talents of	1 Kgs 10:10
queen of Sheba gave to **K** Solomon.	1 Kgs 10:10
And the **k** made of the almug wood	1 Kgs 10:12
And **K** Solomon gave to the queen of	1 Kgs 10:13
her by the bounty of **K** Solomon.	1 Kgs 10:13
K Solomon made 200 large shields	1 Kgs 10:16
And the **k** put them in the House of	1 Kgs 10:17
The **k** also made a great ivory	1 Kgs 10:18
All **K** Solomon's drinking vessels	1 Kgs 10:21
For the **k** had a fleet of ships of	1 Kgs 10:22
Thus **K** Solomon excelled all the	1 Kgs 10:23
cities and with the **k** in Jerusalem.	1 Kgs 10:26
And the **k** made silver as common	1 Kgs 10:27
Now **K** Solomon loved many foreign	1 Kgs 11:1
to Egypt, to Pharaoh **k** of Egypt,	1 Kgs 11:18
his master Hadadezer **k** of Zobah.	1 Kgs 11:23
and made him **k** in Damascus.	1 Kgs 11:24
also lifted up his hand against the **k**.	1 Kgs 11:26
he lifted up his hand against the **k**.	1 Kgs 11:27
and you shall be **k** over Israel.	1 Kgs 11:37
into Egypt, to Shishak **k** of Egypt,	1 Kgs 11:40
come to Shechem to make him **k**.	1 Kgs 12:1
where he had fled from **K** Solomon),	1 Kgs 12:2
Then **K** Rehoboam took counsel	1 Kgs 12:6
the third day, as the **k** said,	1 Kgs 12:12
And the **k** answered the people	1 Kgs 12:13
So the **k** did not listen to the people,	1 Kgs 12:15
Israel saw that the **k** did not listen to	1 Kgs 12:16
to them, the people answered the **k**,	1 Kgs 12:16
Then **K** Rehoboam sent Adoram,	1 Kgs 12:18
And **K** Rehoboam hurried to mount	1 Kgs 12:18
and made him **k** over all Israel.	1 Kgs 12:20
the son of Solomon, **k** of Judah,	1 Kgs 12:23
their lord, to Rehoboam **k** of Judah,	1 Kgs 12:27
return to Rehoboam **k** of Judah."	1 Kgs 12:27
So the **k** took counsel and made two	1 Kgs 12:28
And when the **k** heard the saying of	1 Kgs 13:4
And the **k** said to the man of God,	1 Kgs 13:6
And the **k** said to the man of God,	1 Kgs 13:7
And the man of God said to the **k**, "If	1 Kgs 13:8
words that he had spoken to the **k**.	1 Kgs 13:11
me that I should be **k** over this people.	1 Kgs 14:2
up for himself a **k** over Israel who	1 Kgs 14:14
In the fifth year of **K** Rehoboam,	1 Kgs 14:25
Shishak **k** of Egypt came up against	1 Kgs 14:25
and **K** Rehoboam made in their	1 Kgs 14:27
as often as the **k** went into the house	1 Kgs 14:28
eighteenth year of **K** Jeroboam the	1 Kgs 15:1
year of Jeroboam **k** of Israel,	1 Kgs 15:9
Asa and Baasha **k** of Israel all	1 Kgs 15:16
Baasha **k** of Israel went up against	1 Kgs 15:17
go out or come in to Asa **k** of Judah.	1 Kgs 15:17
And **K** Asa sent them to Ben-hadad	1 Kgs 15:18
the son of Hezion, **k** of Syria,	1 Kgs 15:18
covenant with Baasha **k** of Israel,	1 Kgs 15:19
Ben-hadad listened to **K** Asa and	1 Kgs 15:20
Then **K** Asa made a proclamation	1 Kgs 15:22
and with them **K** Asa built Geba of	1 Kgs 15:22
in the second year of Asa **k** of Judah,	1 Kgs 15:25
third year of Asa **k** of Judah and	1 Kgs 15:28
And as soon as he was **k**, he killed	1 Kgs 15:29
Asa and Baasha **k** of Israel all	1 Kgs 15:32
In the third year of Asa **k** of Judah,	1 Kgs 15:33
twenty-sixth year of Asa **k** of Judah,	1 Kgs 16:8
year of Asa **k** of Judah,	1 Kgs 16:10
year of Asa **k** of Judah,	1 Kgs 16:15
has killed the **k**." Therefore all Israel	1 Kgs 16:16
k over Israel that day in the camp.	1 Kgs 16:16
the son of Ginath, to make him **k**,	1 Kgs 16:21
So Tibni died, and Omri became **k**.	1 Kgs 16:22
thirty-first year of Asa **k** of Judah,	1 Kgs 16:23
thirty-eighth year of Asa **k** of Judah,	1 Kgs 16:29
daughter of Ethbaal **k** of the	1 Kgs 16:31
anoint Hazael to be **k** over Syria.	1 Kgs 19:15
you shall anoint to be **k** over Israel,	1 Kgs 19:16
Ben-hadad the **k** of Syria gathered all	1 Kgs 20:1
the city to Ahab **k** of Israel and said	1 Kgs 20:2
And the **k** of Israel answered, "As you	1 Kgs 20:4
answered, "As you say, my lord, O **k**,	1 Kgs 20:4
Then the **k** of Israel called all the	1 Kgs 20:7
of Ben-hadad, "Tell my lord the **k**,	1 Kgs 20:9
And the **k** of Israel answered, "Tell	1 Kgs 20:11
came near to Ahab **k** of Israel and	1 Kgs 20:13
but Ben-hadad **k** of Syria escaped on	1 Kgs 20:20
And the **k** of Israel went out and	1 Kgs 20:21
came near to the **k** of Israel and said	1 Kgs 20:22
in the spring the **k** of Syria will	1 Kgs 20:22
the servants of the **k** of Syria said to	1 Kgs 20:23
came near and said to the **k** of Israel,	1 Kgs 20:28
heads and go out to the **k** of Israel.	1 Kgs 20:31
and went to the **k** of Israel and said,	1 Kgs 20:32
and waited for the **k** by the way,	1 Kgs 20:38
And as the **k** passed, he cried to the	1 Kgs 20:39
passed, he cried to the **k** and said,	1 Kgs 20:39
he was gone." The **k** of Israel said to	1 Kgs 20:40
and the **k** of Israel recognized him	1 Kgs 20:41
And the **k** of Israel went to his house	1 Kgs 20:43
the palace of Ahab **k** of Samaria.	1 Kgs 21:1
'You have cursed God and the **k**.'	1 Kgs 21:10
cursed God and the **k**." So they took	1 Kgs 21:13
go down to meet Ahab **k** of Israel,	1 Kgs 21:18
year Jehoshaphat the **k** of Judah	1 Kgs 22:2
of Judah came down to the **k** of Israel.	1 Kgs 22:2
And the **k** of Israel said to his	1 Kgs 22:3
it out of the hand of the **k** of Syria?"	1 Kgs 22:3
Jehoshaphat said to the **k** of Israel,	1 Kgs 22:4
Jehoshaphat said to the **k** of Israel,	1 Kgs 22:5
Then the **k** of Israel gathered the	1 Kgs 22:6
will give it into the hand of the **k**."	1 Kgs 22:6
And the **k** of Israel said to	1 Kgs 22:8
said, "Let not the **k** say so."	1 Kgs 22:8
Then the **k** of Israel summoned an	1 Kgs 22:9
Now the **k** of Israel and Jehoshaphat	1 Kgs 22:10
and Jehoshaphat the **k** of Judah were	1 Kgs 22:10
will give it into the hand of the **k**."	1 Kgs 22:12
one accord are favorable to the **k**.	1 Kgs 22:13
And when he had come to the **k**, the	1 Kgs 22:15
come to the king, the **k** said to him,	1 Kgs 22:15
will give it into the hand of the **k**."	1 Kgs 22:15
But the **k** said to him, "How many	1 Kgs 22:16
And the **k** of Israel said to	1 Kgs 22:18
And the **k** of Israel said, "Seize	1 Kgs 22:26
and say, 'Thus says the **k**, "Put this	1 Kgs 22:27
So the **k** of Israel and Jehoshaphat	1 Kgs 22:29
and Jehoshaphat the **k** of Judah	1 Kgs 22:29
And the **k** of Israel said to	1 Kgs 22:30
robes." And the **k** of Israel disguised	1 Kgs 22:30
Now the **k** of Syria had commanded	1 Kgs 22:31
great, but only with the **k** of Israel."	1 Kgs 22:31
"It is surely the **k** of Israel." So they	1 Kgs 22:32
saw that it was not the **k** of Israel,	1 Kgs 22:33
and struck the **k** of Israel between	1 Kgs 22:34
and the **k** was propped up in his	1 Kgs 22:35
So the **k** died, and was brought to	1 Kgs 22:37
And they buried the **k** in Samaria.	1 Kgs 22:37
the fourth year of Ahab **k** of Israel.	1 Kgs 22:41
also made peace with the **k** of Israel.	1 Kgs 22:44
There was no **k** in Edom; a deputy	1 Kgs 22:47
no king in Edom; a deputy was **k**.	1 Kgs 22:47
year of Jehoshaphat **k** of Judah,	1 Kgs 22:51
the messengers of the **k** of Samaria,	2 Kgs 1:3
The messengers returned to the **k**, and	2 Kgs 1:5
to us, 'Go back to the **k** who sent you,	2 Kgs 1:6
Then the **k** sent to him a captain of	2 Kgs 1:9
said to him, "O man of God, the **k** says,	2 Kgs 1:9
Again the **k** sent to him another	2 Kgs 1:11
Again the **k** sent the captain of a	2 Kgs 1:13
and went down with him to the **k**	2 Kgs 1:15
Jehoram became **k** in his place in the	2 Kgs 1:17
the son of Jehoshaphat, **k** of Judah,	2 Kgs 1:17
year of Jehoshaphat **k** of Judah,	2 Kgs 3:1
son of Ahab became **k** over Israel in	2 Kgs 3:1
Now Mesha **k** of Moab was a sheep	2 Kgs 3:4
to deliver to the **k** of Israel 100,000	2 Kgs 3:4
the **k** of Moab rebelled against the	2 Kgs 3:5
Moab rebelled against the **k** of Israel.	2 Kgs 3:5
So **K** Jehoram marched out of Samaria	2 Kgs 3:6
sent word to Jehoshaphat **k** of Judah,	2 Kgs 3:7
"The **k** of Moab has rebelled against	2 Kgs 3:7
So the **k** of Israel went with the king of	2 Kgs 3:9
Israel went with the **k** of Judah and the	2 Kgs 3:9
the king of Judah and the **k** of Edom.	2 Kgs 3:9
Then the **k** of Israel said, "Alas! The	2 Kgs 3:10
Then one of the **k** of Israel's servants	2 Kgs 3:11
with him." So the **k** of Israel and	2 Kgs 3:12

Jehoshaphat and the **k** of Edom went	2 Kgs 3:12
And Elisha said to the **k** of Israel,	2 Kgs 3:13
your mother." But the **k** of Israel said	2 Kgs 3:13
for Jehoshaphat the **k** of Judah,	2 Kgs 3:14
When the **k** of Moab saw that the	2 Kgs 3:26
through, opposite the **k** of Edom,	2 Kgs 3:26
your behalf to the **k** or to the	2 Kgs 4:13
of the army of the **k** of Syria,	2 Kgs 5:1
And the **k** of Syria said, "Go now, and I	2 Kgs 5:5
send a letter to the **k** of Israel." So he	2 Kgs 5:5
he brought the letter to the **k** of Israel,	2 Kgs 5:6
And when the **k** of Israel read the letter,	2 Kgs 5:7
God heard that the **k** of Israel had torn	2 Kgs 5:8
had torn his clothes, he sent to the **k**,	2 Kgs 5:8
Once when the **k** of Syria was warring	2 Kgs 6:8
man of God sent word to the **k** of Israel,	2 Kgs 6:9
And the **k** of Israel sent to the place	2 Kgs 6:10
the mind of the **k** of Syria was greatly	2 Kgs 6:11
me who of us is for the **k** of Israel?"	2 Kgs 6:11
servants said, "None, my lord, O **k**;	2 Kgs 6:12
tells the **k** of Israel the words that you	2 Kgs 6:12
As soon as the **k** of Israel saw them,	2 Kgs 6:21
Afterward Ben-hadad **k** of Syria	2 Kgs 6:24
Now as the **k** of Israel was passing by	2 Kgs 6:26
to him, saying, "Help, my lord, O **k**!"	2 Kgs 6:26
And the **k** asked her, "What is your	2 Kgs 6:28
When the **k** heard the words of the	2 Kgs 6:30
Now the **k** had dispatched a man	2 Kgs 6:32
on whose hand the **k** leaned said to the	2 Kgs 7:2
the **k** of Israel has hired against us the	2 Kgs 7:6
And the **k** rose in the night and said	2 Kgs 7:12
and the **k** sent them after the army of	2 Kgs 7:14
messengers returned and told the **k**.	2 Kgs 7:15
Now the **k** had appointed the captain	2 Kgs 7:17
had said when the **k** came down to	2 Kgs 7:17
the man of God had said to the **k**,	2 Kgs 7:18
to appeal to the **k** for her house and	2 Kgs 8:3
Now the **k** was talking with Gehazi the	2 Kgs 8:4
he was telling the **k** how Elisha had	2 Kgs 8:5
life appealed to the **k** for her house and	2 Kgs 8:5
And Gehazi said, "My lord, O **k**, here is	2 Kgs 8:5
And when the **k** asked the woman, she	2 Kgs 8:6
So the **k** appointed an official for her,	2 Kgs 8:6
Ben-hadad the **k** of Syria was sick.	2 Kgs 8:7
the **k** said to Hazael, "Take a present	2 Kgs 8:8
"Your son Ben-hadad **k** of Syria has	2 Kgs 8:9
me that you are to be **k** over Syria."	2 Kgs 8:13
And Hazael became **k** in his place.	2 Kgs 8:15
of Joram the son of Ahab, **k** of Israel,	2 Kgs 8:16
when Jehoshaphat was **k** of Judah,	2 Kgs 8:16
the son of Jehoshaphat, **k** of Judah,	2 Kgs 8:16
years old when he became **k**,	2 Kgs 8:17
of Judah and set up a **k** of their own.	2 Kgs 8:20
of Joram the son of Ahab, **k** of Israel,	2 Kgs 8:25
the son of Jehoram, **k** of Judah,	2 Kgs 8:25
a granddaughter of Omri **k** of Israel.	2 Kgs 8:26
war against Hazael **k** of Syria at	2 Kgs 8:28
And **K** Joram returned to be healed in	2 Kgs 8:29
he fought against Hazael **k** of Syria.	2 Kgs 8:29
the son of Jehoram **k** of Judah went	2 Kgs 8:29
the LORD, I anoint you **k** over Israel.'	2 Kgs 9:3
I anoint you **k** over the people of the	2 Kgs 9:6
the LORD, I anoint you **k** over Israel.'"	2 Kgs 9:12
trumpet and proclaimed, "Jehu is **k**."	2 Kgs 9:13
against Hazael **k** of Syria,	2 Kgs 9:14
but **K** Joram had returned to be	2 Kgs 9:15
he fought with Hazael **k** of Syria.)	2 Kgs 9:15
And Ahaziah **k** of Judah had come	2 Kgs 9:16
meet him and said, "Thus says the **k**,	2 Kgs 9:18
them and said, "Thus the **k** has said,	2 Kgs 9:19
Then Joram **k** of Israel and Ahaziah	2 Kgs 9:21
of Israel and Ahaziah **k** of Judah set	2 Kgs 9:21
When Ahaziah the **k** of Judah saw	2 Kgs 9:27
tell us. We will not make anyone **k**.	2 Kgs 10:5
the relatives of Ahaziah **k** of Judah,	2 Kgs 10:13
Jehosheba, the daughter of **K** Joram,	2 Kgs 11:2
house of the LORD on behalf of the **k**,	2 Kgs 11:7
shall surround the **k**, each with his	2 Kgs 11:8
Be with the **k** when he goes out and	2 Kgs 11:8
and shields that had been **K** David's,	2 Kgs 11:10
and the house on behalf of the **k**.	2 Kgs 11:11
proclaimed him **k** and anointed	2 Kgs 11:12
hands and said, "Long live the **k**!"	2 Kgs 11:12
there was the **k** standing by the	2 Kgs 11:14
and the trumpeters beside the **k**,	2 Kgs 11:14
the LORD and the **k** and people,	2 Kgs 11:17
also between the **k** and the people.	2 Kgs 11:17
they brought the **k** down from the	2 Kgs 11:19
by the twenty-third year of **K** Jehoash,	2 Kgs 12:6
Therefore **K** Jehoash summoned	2 Kgs 12:7
At that time Hazael **k** of Syria went	2 Kgs 12:17
Jehoash **k** of Judah took all the	2 Kgs 12:18
and sent these to Hazael **k** of Syria.	2 Kgs 12:18
Joash the son of Ahaziah, **k** of Judah,	2 Kgs 13:1
the hand of Hazael **k** of Syria and into	2 Kgs 13:3
how the **k** of Syria oppressed them.	2 Kgs 13:4
for the **k** of Syria had destroyed them	2 Kgs 13:7
year of Joash **k** of Judah,	2 Kgs 13:10
fought against Amaziah **k** of Judah,	2 Kgs 13:12
Joash **k** of Israel went down to him	2 Kgs 13:14
Then he said to the **k** of Israel,	2 Kgs 13:16
And he said to the **k** of Israel, "Strike	2 Kgs 13:18
Now Hazael **k** of Syria oppressed	2 Kgs 13:22
When Hazael **k** of Syria died,	2 Kgs 13:24
his son became **k** in his place.	2 Kgs 13:24
of Joash the son of Joahaz, **k** of Israel,	2 Kgs 14:1
Amaziah the son of Joash, **k** of Judah,	2 Kgs 14:1
had struck down the **k** his father.	2 Kgs 14:5
of Jehoahaz, son of Jehu, **k** of Israel,	2 Kgs 14:8
And Jehoash **k** of Israel sent word to	2 Kgs 14:9
sent word to Amaziah **k** of Judah,	2 Kgs 14:9
So Jehoash **k** of Israel went up, and	2 Kgs 14:11
he and Amaziah **k** of Judah faced	2 Kgs 14:11
And Jehoash **k** of Israel captured	2 Kgs 14:13
Israel captured Amaziah **k** of Judah,	2 Kgs 14:13
he fought with Amaziah **k** of Judah,	2 Kgs 14:15
the son of Joash, **k** of Judah,	2 Kgs 14:17
Jehoash son of Jehoahaz, **k** of Israel.	2 Kgs 14:17
and made him **k** instead of his	2 Kgs 14:21
after the **k** slept with his fathers.	2 Kgs 14:22
the son of Joash, **k** of Judah,	2 Kgs 14:23
the son of Joash, **k** of Israel,	2 Kgs 14:23
year of Jeroboam **k** of Israel,	2 Kgs 15:1
the son of Amaziah, **k** of Judah,	2 Kgs 15:1
And the LORD touched the **k**, so that	2 Kgs 15:5
year of Azariah **k** of Judah,	2 Kgs 15:8
year of Uzziah **k** of Judah,	2 Kgs 15:13
year of Azariah **k** of Judah,	2 Kgs 15:17
Pul the **k** of Assyria came against	2 Kgs 15:19
man, to give to the **k** of Assyria.	2 Kgs 15:20
So the **k** of Assyria turned back and	2 Kgs 15:20
fiftieth year of Azariah **k** of Judah,	2 Kgs 15:23
year of Azariah **k** of Judah,	2 Kgs 15:27
In the days of Pekah **k** of Israel,	2 Kgs 15:29
Tiglath-pileser **k** of Assyria came	2 Kgs 15:29
the son of Remaliah, **k** of Israel,	2 Kgs 15:32
the son of Uzziah, **k** of Judah,	2 Kgs 15:32
to send Rezin the **k** of Syria and	2 Kgs 15:37
Ahaz the son of Jotham, **k** of Judah,	2 Kgs 16:1
Then Rezin **k** of Syria and Pekah the	2 Kgs 16:5
the son of Remaliah, **k** of Israel,	2 Kgs 16:5
time Rezin the **k** of Syria recovered	2 Kgs 16:6
to Tiglath-pileser **k** of Assyria,	2 Kgs 16:7
the hand of the **k** of Syria and from	2 Kgs 16:7
and from the hand of the **k** of Israel,	2 Kgs 16:7
and sent a present to the **k** of Assyria.	2 Kgs 16:8
And the **k** of Assyria listened to him.	2 Kgs 16:9
The **k** of Assyria marched up against	2 Kgs 16:9
When **K** Ahaz went to Damascus to	2 Kgs 16:10
to meet Tiglath-pileser **k** of Assyria,	2 Kgs 16:10
And **K** Ahaz sent to Uriah the priest	2 Kgs 16:10
with all that **K** Ahaz had sent	2 Kgs 16:11
before **K** Ahaz arrived from	2 Kgs 16:11
And when the **k** came from	2 Kgs 16:12
Damascus, the **k** viewed the altar.	2 Kgs 16:12
Then the **k** drew near to the altar	2 Kgs 16:12
And **K** Ahaz commanded Uriah the	2 Kgs 16:15
did all this, as **K** Ahaz commanded.	2 Kgs 16:16
And **K** Ahaz cut off the frames of the	2 Kgs 16:17
outer entrance for the **k** he caused to	2 Kgs 16:18
LORD, because of the **k** of Assyria.	2 Kgs 16:18
In the twelfth year of Ahaz **k** of Judah,	2 Kgs 17:1
came up Shalmaneser **k** of Assyria.	2 Kgs 17:3
But the **k** of Assyria found treachery	2 Kgs 17:4
had sent messengers to So, **k** of Egypt,	2 Kgs 17:4
offered no tribute to the **k** of Assyria,	2 Kgs 17:4
Therefore the **k** of Assyria shut him	2 Kgs 17:4
Then the **k** of Assyria invaded all the	2 Kgs 17:5
the **k** of Assyria captured Samaria,	2 Kgs 17:6
the hand of Pharaoh **k** of Egypt,	2 Kgs 17:7
made Jeroboam the son of Nebat **k**.	2 Kgs 17:21
And the **k** of Assyria brought people	2 Kgs 17:24
So the **k** of Assyria was told, "The	2 Kgs 17:26
Then the **k** of Assyria commanded,	2 Kgs 17:27
of Hoshea son of Elah, **k** of Israel,	2 Kgs 18:1
Hezekiah the son of Ahaz, **k** of Judah,	2 Kgs 18:1
rebelled against the **k** of Assyria and	2 Kgs 18:7
In the fourth year of **K** Hezekiah,	2 Kgs 18:9
of Hoshea son of Elah, **k** of Israel,	2 Kgs 18:9
Shalmaneser **k** of Assyria came up	2 Kgs 18:9
the ninth year of Hoshea **k** of Israel,	2 Kgs 18:10
The **k** of Assyria carried the	2 Kgs 18:11
the fourteenth year of **K** Hezekiah,	2 Kgs 18:13
Sennacherib **k** of Assyria came up	2 Kgs 18:13
And Hezekiah **k** of Judah sent to the	2 Kgs 18:14
Judah sent to the **k** of Assyria at	2 Kgs 18:14
bear." And the **k** of Assyria required	2 Kgs 18:14
required of Hezekiah **k** of Judah	2 Kgs 18:14
doorposts that Hezekiah **k** of Judah	2 Kgs 18:16
and gave it to the **k** of Assyria.	2 Kgs 18:16
And the **k** of Assyria sent the	2 Kgs 18:17
from Lachish to **K** Hezekiah at	2 Kgs 18:17
And when they called for the **k**,	2 Kgs 18:18
to Hezekiah, 'Thus says the great **k**,	2 Kgs 18:19
says the great king, the **k** of Assyria:	2 Kgs 18:19
Such is Pharaoh **k** of Egypt to all	2 Kgs 18:21
with my master the **k** of Assyria:	2 Kgs 18:23
"Hear the word of the great **k**, the	2 Kgs 18:28
of the great king, the **k** of Assyria!	2 Kgs 18:28
Thus says the **k**: 'Do not let	2 Kgs 18:29
into the hand of the **k** of Assyria.'	2 Kgs 18:30
for thus says the **k** of Assyria:	2 Kgs 18:31
out of the hand of the **k** of Assyria?	2 Kgs 18:33
As soon as **K** Hezekiah heard it, he	2 Kgs 19:1
his master the **k** of Assyria has	2 Kgs 19:4
the servants of **K** Hezekiah came to	2 Kgs 19:5
the servants of the **k** of Assyria have	2 Kgs 19:6
and found the **k** of Assyria fighting	2 Kgs 19:8
he heard that the **k** had left Lachish.	2 Kgs 19:8
Now the **k** heard concerning	2 Kgs 19:9
concerning Tirhakah **k** of Cush,	2 Kgs 19:9
you speak to Hezekiah **k** of Judah:	2 Kgs 19:10
into the hand of the **k** of Assyria.	2 Kgs 19:10
Where is the **k** of Hamath, the king	2 Kgs 19:13
the king of Hamath, the **k** of Arpad,	2 Kgs 19:13
the **k** of the city of Sepharvaim,	2 Kgs 19:13
city of Sepharvaim, the **k** of Hena,	2 Kgs 19:13
the king of Hena, or the **k** of Ivvah?'"	2 Kgs 19:13
me about Sennacherib **k** of Assyria	2 Kgs 19:20
LORD concerning the **k** of Assyria:	2 Kgs 19:32
Then Sennacherib **k** of Assyria	2 Kgs 19:36
out of the hand of the **k** of Assyria,	2 Kgs 20:6
the son of Baladan, **k** of Babylon,	2 Kgs 20:12
the prophet came to **K** Hezekiah,	2 Kgs 20:14
in the palace of the **k** of Babylon."	2 Kgs 20:18
as Ahab **k** of Israel had done,	2 Kgs 21:3
"Because Manasseh **k** of Judah has	2 Kgs 21:11
him and put the **k** to death in his	2 Kgs 21:23
had conspired against **K** Amon,	2 Kgs 21:24
made Josiah his son **k** in his place.	2 Kgs 21:24
In the eighteenth year of **K** Josiah, the	2 Kgs 22:3
the **k** sent Shaphan the son of	2 Kgs 22:3
Shaphan the secretary came to the **k**,	2 Kgs 22:9
to the king, and reported to the **k**,	2 Kgs 22:9
Shaphan the secretary told the **k**,	2 Kgs 22:10
And Shaphan read it before the **k**.	2 Kgs 22:10
When the **k** heard the words of the	2 Kgs 22:11
And the **k** commanded Hilkiah the	2 Kgs 22:12
the book that the **k** of Judah has	2 Kgs 22:16
But to the **k** of Judah, who sent you	2 Kgs 22:18
they brought back word to the **k**.	2 Kgs 22:20
Then the **k** sent, and all the elders of	2 Kgs 23:1
And the **k** went up to the house of the	2 Kgs 23:2
And the **k** stood by the pillar and	2 Kgs 23:3
And the **k** commanded Hilkiah the	2 Kgs 23:4
And the **k** defiled the high places	2 Kgs 23:13
which Solomon the **k** of Israel had	2 Kgs 23:13
And the **k** commanded all the	2 Kgs 23:21
eighteenth year of **K** Josiah this	2 Kgs 23:23
Before him there was no **k** like him,	2 Kgs 23:25
days Pharaoh Neco **k** of Egypt went	2 Kgs 23:29
went up to the **k** of Assyria to the	2 Kgs 23:29
K Josiah went to meet him, and	2 Kgs 23:29
and made him **k** in his father's	2 Kgs 23:30
the son of Josiah **k** in the place of	2 Kgs 23:34
Nebuchadnezzar **k** of Babylon came	2 Kgs 24:1
And the **k** of Egypt did not come	2 Kgs 24:7
for the **k** of Babylon had taken all	2 Kgs 24:7
that belonged to the **k** of Egypt from	2 Kgs 24:7
eighteen years old when he became **k**,	2 Kgs 24:8
of Nebuchadnezzar **k** of Babylon	2 Kgs 24:10
And Nebuchadnezzar **k** of Babylon	2 Kgs 24:11
and Jehoiachin the **k** of Judah gave	2 Kgs 24:12
gave himself up to the **k** of Babylon,	2 Kgs 24:12
The **k** of Babylon took him prisoner	2 Kgs 24:12
which Solomon **k** of Israel had	2 Kgs 24:13
And the **k** of Babylon brought	2 Kgs 24:16
And the **k** of Babylon made	2 Kgs 24:17
Jehoiachin's uncle, **k** in his place,	2 Kgs 24:17
years old when he became **k**,	2 Kgs 24:18
rebelled against the **k** of Babylon.	2 Kgs 24:20
Nebuchadnezzar **k** of Babylon came	2 Kgs 25:1
till the eleventh year of **K** Zedekiah.	2 Kgs 25:2
pursued the **k** and overtook	2 Kgs 25:5
they captured the **k** and brought him	2 Kgs 25:6
him up to the **k** of Babylon at Riblah,	2 Kgs 25:6
year of **K** Nebuchadnezzar,	2 Kgs 25:8
k of Babylon—Nebuzaradan,	2 Kgs 25:8
a servant of the **k** of Babylon,	2 Kgs 25:8
had deserted to the **k** of Babylon,	2 Kgs 25:11
brought them to the **k** of Babylon at	2 Kgs 25:20
And the **k** of Babylon struck them	2 Kgs 25:21
whom Nebuchadnezzar **k** of	2 Kgs 25:22
heard that the **k** of Babylon had	2 Kgs 25:23
the land and serve the **k** of Babylon,	2 Kgs 25:24

of the exile of Jehoiachin **k** of Judah, 2 Kgs 25:27
Evil-merodach **k** of Babylon, 2 Kgs 25:27
freed Jehoiachin **k** of Judah 2 Kgs 25:27
allowance was given him by the **k**, 2 Kgs 25:30
Edom before any **k** reigned over the 1 Chr 1:43
the daughter of Talmai, **k** of Geshur; 1 Chr 3:2
in the days of Hezekiah, **k** of Judah, 1 Chr 4:41
whom Tiglath-pileser **k** of Assyria 1 Chr 5:6
in the days of Jotham **k** of Judah, 1 Chr 5:17
in the days of Jeroboam **k** of Israel. 1 Chr 5:17
up the spirit of Pul **k** of Assyria, 1 Chr 5:26
spirit of Tiglath-pileser **k** of Assyria, 1 Chr 5:26
In times past, even when Saul was **k**, 1 Chr 11:2
of Israel came to the **k** at Hebron, 1 Chr 11:3
they anointed David **k** over Israel, 1 Chr 11:3
with all Israel, to make him **k**, 1 Chr 11:10
named to come and make David **k**. 1 Chr 12:31
to make David **k** over all Israel. 1 Chr 12:38
of a single mind to make David **k**. 1 Chr 12:38
And Hiram **k** of Tyre sent 1 Chr 14:1
had established him as **k** over Israel, 1 Chr 14:2
had been anointed **k** over all Israel, 1 Chr 14:8
window and saw **K** David dancing 1 Chr 15:29
Then **K** David went in and sat 1 Chr 17:16
defeated Hadadezer **k** of 1 Chr 18:3
came to help Hadadezer **k** of Zobah, 1 Chr 18:5
When Tou **k** of Hamath heard that 1 Chr 18:9
army of Hadadezer, **k** of Zobah, 1 Chr 18:9
sent his son Hadoram to **K** David, 1 Chr 18:10
These also **K** David dedicated to the 1 Chr 18:11
chief officials in the service of the **k**. 1 Chr 18:17
this Nahash the **k** of the Ammonites 1 Chr 19:1
And the **k** said, "Remain at Jericho 1 Chr 19:5
chariots and the **k** of Maacah with 1 Chr 19:7
the crown of their **k** from his head. 1 Chr 20:2
Are they not, my lord the **k**, all of 1 Chr 21:3
let my lord the **k** do what seems 1 Chr 21:23
But **K** David said to Ornan, "No, but 1 Chr 21:24
made Solomon his son **k** over Israel. 1 Chr 23:1
the presence of the **k** and the princes 1 Chr 24:6
Aaron, in the presence of **K** David, 1 Chr 24:31
under the direction of the **k**. 1 Chr 25:2
Heman were under the order of the **k**. 1 Chr 25:6
gifts that David the **k** and the heads 1 Chr 26:26
the LORD and for the service of the **k**. 1 Chr 26:30
K David appointed him and his 1 Chr 26:32
to God and for the affairs of the **k**. 1 Chr 26:32
who served the **k** in all matters 1 Chr 27:1
in the chronicles of **K** David. 1 Chr 27:24
were stewards of **K** David's property. 1 Chr 27:31
of the divisions that served the **k**, 1 Chr 28:1
and livestock of the **k** and his sons, 1 Chr 28:1
Then **K** David rose to his feet and 1 Chr 28:2
house to be **k** over Israel forever. 1 Chr 28:4
in me to make me **k** over all Israel. 1 Chr 28:4
And David the **k** said to all the 1 Chr 29:1
David the **k** also rejoiced greatly. 1 Chr 29:9
homage to the LORD and to the **k**. 1 Chr 29:20
the son of David **k** the second time, 1 Chr 29:22
of the LORD as **k** in place of David 1 Chr 29:23
and also all the sons of **K** David, 1 Chr 29:24
their allegiance to **K** Solomon. 1 Chr 29:24
not been on any **k** before him in 1 Chr 29:25
Now the acts of **K** David, from first 1 Chr 29:29
and have made me **k** in his place. 2 Chr 1:8
you have made me **k** over a people as 2 Chr 1:9
people over whom I have made you **k**, 2 Chr 1:11
cities and with the **k** in Jerusalem. 2 Chr 1:14
And the **k** made silver and gold as 2 Chr 1:15
sent word to Hiram the **k** of Tyre: 2 Chr 2:3
Then Hiram the **k** of Tyre answered 2 Chr 2:11
he has made you **k** over them." 2 Chr 2:11
who has given **K** David a wise son, 2 Chr 2:12
that he did for **K** Solomon on the 2 Chr 4:11
burnished bronze for **K** Solomon for 2 Chr 4:16
plain of the Jordan the **k** cast them, 2 Chr 4:17
assembled before the **k** at the feast 2 Chr 5:3
And **K** Solomon and all the 2 Chr 5:6
Then the **k** turned around and blessed 2 Chr 6:3
Then the **k** and all the people offered 2 Chr 7:4
K Solomon offered as a sacrifice 2 Chr 7:5
So the **k** and all the people dedicated 2 Chr 7:5
to the LORD that **K** David had made for 2 Chr 7:6
were the chief officers of **K** Solomon, 2 Chr 8:10
live in the house of David **k** of Israel, 2 Chr 8:11
from what the **k** had commanded the 2 Chr 8:15
of gold and brought it to **K** Solomon. 2 Chr 8:18
And she said to the **k**, "The report was 2 Chr 9:5
on his throne as **k** for the LORD your 2 Chr 9:8
forever, he has made you **k** over them, 2 Chr 9:8
Then she gave the **k** 120 talents of 2 Chr 9:9
the queen of Sheba gave to **K** Solomon. 2 Chr 9:9
And the **k** made from the algum 2 Chr 9:11
And **K** Solomon gave to the queen of 2 Chr 9:12
what she had brought to the **k**. 2 Chr 9:12
K Solomon made 200 large shields of 2 Chr 9:15
and the **k** put them in the House of 2 Chr 9:16
The **k** also made a great ivory throne 2 Chr 9:17
All **K** Solomon's drinking vessels 2 Chr 9:20
Thus **K** Solomon excelled all the 2 Chr 9:22
cities and with the **k** in Jerusalem. 2 Chr 9:25
And the **k** made silver as common in 2 Chr 9:27
come to Shechem to make him **k**. 2 Chr 10:1
where he had fled from **K** Solomon), 2 Chr 10:2
Then **K** Rehoboam took counsel 2 Chr 10:6
the third day, as the **k** said, 2 Chr 10:12
And the **k** answered them harshly; 2 Chr 10:13
K Rehoboam spoke to them 2 Chr 10:14
So the **k** did not listen to the people, 2 Chr 10:15
Israel saw that the **k** did not listen to 2 Chr 10:16
to them, the people answered the **k**, 2 Chr 10:16
Then **K** Rehoboam sent Hadoram, 2 Chr 10:18
And **K** Rehoboam quickly mounted 2 Chr 10:18
the son of Solomon, **k** of Judah, 2 Chr 11:3
for he intended to make him **k**. 2 Chr 11:22
In the fifth year of **K** Rehoboam, 2 Chr 12:2
Shishak **k** of Egypt came up against 2 Chr 12:2
Israel and the **k** humbled themselves 2 Chr 12:6
So Shishak **k** of Egypt came up 2 Chr 12:9
and **K** Rehoboam made in their 2 Chr 12:10
as often as the **k** went into the house 2 Chr 12:11
So **K** Rehoboam grew strong in 2 Chr 12:13
In the eighteenth year of **K** Jeroboam, 2 Chr 13:1
K Asa removed from being queen 2 Chr 15:16
Baasha **k** of Israel went up against 2 Chr 16:1
go out or come in to Asa **k** of Judah. 2 Chr 16:1
sent them to Ben-hadad **k** of Syria, 2 Chr 16:2
covenant with Baasha **k** of Israel, 2 Chr 16:3
Ben-hadad listened to **K** Asa and sent 2 Chr 16:4
Then **K** Asa took all Judah, and they 2 Chr 16:6
seer came to Asa **k** of Judah and said 2 Chr 16:7
"Because you relied on the **k** of Syria, 2 Chr 16:7
the army of the **k** of Syria has 2 Chr 16:7
These were in the service of the **k**, 2 Chr 17:19
those whom the **k** had placed in 2 Chr 17:19
Ahab **k** of Israel said to Jehoshaphat 2 Chr 18:3
Israel said to Jehoshaphat **k** of Judah, 2 Chr 18:3
Jehoshaphat said to the **k** of Israel, 2 Chr 18:4
Then the **k** of Israel gathered the 2 Chr 18:5
will give it into the hand of the **k**." 2 Chr 18:5
And the **k** of Israel said to 2 Chr 18:7
said, "Let not the **k** say so." 2 Chr 18:7
Then the **k** of Israel summoned an 2 Chr 18:8
Now the **k** of Israel and Jehoshaphat 2 Chr 18:9
and Jehoshaphat the **k** of Judah were 2 Chr 18:9
will give it into the hand of the **k**." 2 Chr 18:11
one accord are favorable to the **k**. 2 Chr 18:12
And when he had come to the **k**, the 2 Chr 18:14
come to the king, the **k** said to him, 2 Chr 18:14
But the **k** said to him, "How many 2 Chr 18:15
And the **k** of Israel said to 2 Chr 18:17
will entice Ahab the **k** of Israel, 2 Chr 18:19
And the **k** of Israel said, "Seize 2 Chr 18:25
and say, 'Thus says the **k**, Put this 2 Chr 18:26
So the **k** of Israel and Jehoshaphat 2 Chr 18:28
and Jehoshaphat the **k** of Judah 2 Chr 18:28
And the **k** of Israel said to 2 Chr 18:29
robes." And the **k** of Israel disguised 2 Chr 18:29
Now the **k** of Syria had commanded 2 Chr 18:30
great, but only with the **k** of Israel." 2 Chr 18:30
"It is the **k** of Israel." So they turned 2 Chr 18:31
saw that it was not the **k** of Israel, 2 Chr 18:32
and struck the **k** of Israel between 2 Chr 18:33
and the **k** of Israel was propped up 2 Chr 18:34
Jehoshaphat the **k** of Judah returned 2 Chr 19:1
meet him and said to **K** Jehoshaphat, 2 Chr 19:2
of Jerusalem and **K** Jehoshaphat: 2 Chr 20:15
After this Jehoshaphat **k** of Judah 2 Chr 20:35
joined with Ahaziah **k** of Israel, 2 Chr 20:35
the sons of Jehoshaphat **k** of Judah. 2 Chr 21:2
years old when he became **k**, 2 Chr 21:5
of Judah and set up a **k** of their own. 2 Chr 21:8
or in the ways of Asa **k** of Judah, 2 Chr 21:12
his youngest son **k** in his place, 2 Chr 22:1
son of Jehoram **k** of Judah reigned. 2 Chr 22:1
the son of Ahab **k** of Israel to make 2 Chr 22:5
war against Hazael **k** of Syria at 2 Chr 22:5
he fought against Hazael **k** of Syria. 2 Chr 22:6
the son of Jehoram **k** of Judah went 2 Chr 22:6
Jehoshabeath, the daughter of the **k**, 2 Chr 22:11
the daughter of **K** Jehoram and wife 2 Chr 22:11
a covenant with the **k** in the house of 2 Chr 23:3
The Levites shall surround the **k**, 2 Chr 23:7
Be with the **k** when he comes in and 2 Chr 23:7
shields that had been **K** David's, 2 Chr 23:9
all the people as a guard for the **k**, 2 Chr 23:10
And they proclaimed him **k**, and 2 Chr 23:11
and they said, "Long live the **k**." 2 Chr 23:11
people running and praising the **k**, 2 Chr 23:12
there was the **k** standing by his 2 Chr 23:13
and the trumpeters beside the **k**, 2 Chr 23:13
people and the **k** that they should 2 Chr 23:16
they brought the **k** down from the 2 Chr 23:20
And they set the **k** on the royal 2 Chr 23:20
So the **k** summoned Jehoiada the 2 Chr 24:6
So the **k** commanded, and they made 2 Chr 24:8
And the **k** and Jehoiada gave it to 2 Chr 24:12
money before the **k** and Jehoiada, 2 Chr 24:14
came and paid homage to the **k**. 2 Chr 24:17
king. Then the **k** listened to them. 2 Chr 24:17
command of the **k** they stoned him 2 Chr 24:21
Thus Joash the **k** did not remember 2 Chr 24:22
all their spoil to the **k** of Damascus. 2 Chr 24:23
had struck down the **k** his father. 2 Chr 25:3
of God came to him and said, "O **k**, 2 Chr 25:7
he was speaking, the **k** said to him, 2 Chr 25:16
Then Amaziah **k** of Judah took 2 Chr 25:17
of Jehoahaz, son of Jehu, **k** of Israel, 2 Chr 25:17
And Joash the **k** of Israel sent word 2 Chr 25:18
sent word to Amaziah **k** of Judah, 2 Chr 25:18
So Joash **k** of Israel went up, and he 2 Chr 25:21
he and Amaziah **k** of Judah faced 2 Chr 25:21
And Joash **k** of Israel captured 2 Chr 25:23
Israel captured Amaziah **k** of Judah, 2 Chr 25:23
the son of Joash, **k** of Judah, 2 Chr 25:25
the son of Jehoahaz, **k** of Israel. 2 Chr 25:25
and made him **k** instead of his father 2 Chr 26:1
after the **k** slept with his fathers. 2 Chr 26:2
to help the **k** against the enemy. 2 Chr 26:13
and they withstood **K** Uzziah and 2 Chr 26:18
And **K** Uzziah was a leper to the day 2 Chr 26:21
fought with the **k** of the Ammonites 2 Chr 27:5
him into the hand of the **k** of Syria, 2 Chr 28:5
given into the hand of the **k** of Israel, 2 Chr 28:5
the next in authority to the **k**. 2 Chr 28:7
At that time **K** Ahaz sent to the king 2 Chr 28:16
Ahaz sent to the **k** of Assyria for 2 Chr 28:16
Judah because of Ahaz **k** of Israel, 2 Chr 28:19
So Tiglath-pileser **k** of Assyria 2 Chr 28:20
the house of the **k** and of the 2 Chr 28:21
and gave tribute to the **k** of Assyria, 2 Chr 28:21
to the LORD—this same **K** Ahaz. 2 Chr 28:22
went in as the **k** had commanded, 2 Chr 29:15
went in to Hezekiah the **k** and said, 2 Chr 29:18
the utensils that **K** Ahaz discarded 2 Chr 29:19
Then Hezekiah the **k** rose early and 2 Chr 29:20
brought to the **k** and the assembly, 2 Chr 29:23
For the **k** commanded that the 2 Chr 29:24
the instruments of David **k** of Israel. 2 Chr 29:27
the **k** and all who were present with 2 Chr 29:29
And Hezekiah the **k** and the 2 Chr 29:30
For the **k** and his princes and all the 2 Chr 30:2
seemed right to the **k** and all the 2 Chr 30:4
letters from the **k** and his princes, 2 Chr 30:6
princes, as the **k** had commanded, 2 Chr 30:6
to do what the **k** and the princes 2 Chr 30:12
For Hezekiah **k** of Judah gave the 2 Chr 30:24
the son of David **k** of Israel there 2 Chr 30:26
contribution of the **k** from his own 2 Chr 31:3
of Hezekiah the **k** and Azariah the 2 Chr 31:13
Sennacherib **k** of Assyria came and 2 Chr 32:1
dismayed before the **k** of Assyria and 2 Chr 32:7
the words of Hezekiah **k** of Judah. 2 Chr 32:8
After this, Sennacherib, **k** of Assyria, 2 Chr 32:9
Jerusalem to Hezekiah **k** of Judah 2 Chr 32:9
says Sennacherib **k** of Assyria, 2 Chr 32:10
from the hand of the **k** of Assyria"? 2 Chr 32:11
Then Hezekiah the **k** and Isaiah the 2 Chr 32:20
in the camp of the **k** of Assyria. 2 Chr 32:21
hand of Sennacherib **k** of Assyria 2 Chr 32:22
things to Hezekiah **k** of Judah, 2 Chr 32:23
of the army of the **k** of Assyria, 2 Chr 33:11
had conspired against **K** Amon. 2 Chr 33:25
made Josiah his son **k** in his place. 2 Chr 33:25
Shaphan brought the book to the **k**, 2 Chr 34:16
king, and further reported to the **k**, 2 Chr 34:16
Shaphan the secretary told the **k**, 2 Chr 34:18
Shaphan read from it before the **k**. 2 Chr 34:18
And when the **k** heard the words of 2 Chr 34:19
And the **k** commanded Hilkiah, 2 Chr 34:20
those whom the **k** had sent went 2 Chr 34:22
that was read before the **k** of Judah. 2 Chr 34:24
But to the **k** of Judah, who sent you 2 Chr 34:26
they brought back word to the **k**. 2 Chr 34:28
Then the **k** sent and gathered 2 Chr 34:29
And the **k** went up to the house of 2 Chr 34:30
And the **k** stood in his place and 2 Chr 34:31
Solomon the son of David, **k** of Israel, 2 Chr 35:3
the writing of David **k** of Israel and 2 Chr 35:4
to the command of **K** Josiah. 2 Chr 35:16
Neco **k** of Egypt went up to fight at 2 Chr 35:20
to do with each other, **k** of Judah? 2 Chr 35:21
And the archers shot **K** Josiah. And 2 Chr 35:23
And the **k** said to his servants, 2 Chr 35:23
and made him **k** in his father's 2 Chr 36:1

Then the **k** of Egypt deposed him in 2 Chr 36:3
And the **k** of Egypt made Eliakim his 2 Chr 36:4
Eliakim his brother **k** over Judah 2 Chr 36:4
up Nebuchadnezzar **k** of Babylon 2 Chr 36:6
eight years old when he became **k**, 2 Chr 36:9
of the year **K** Nebuchadnezzar sent 2 Chr 36:10
his brother Zedekiah **k** over Judah 2 Chr 36:10
against **K** Nebuchadnezzar, 2 Chr 36:13
against them the **k** of the 2 Chr 36:17
the treasures of the **k** and of his 2 Chr 36:18
in the first year of Cyrus **k** of Persia, 2 Chr 36:22
up the spirit of Cyrus **k** of Persia, 2 Chr 36:22
"Thus says Cyrus **k** of Persia, 'The 2 Chr 36:23
In the first year of Cyrus **k** of Persia, that Ezr 1:1
stirred up the spirit of Cyrus **k** of Persia, Ezr 1:1
"Thus says Cyrus **k** of Persia: The LORD, Ezr 1:2
Cyrus the **k** also brought out the vessels Ezr 1:7
Cyrus **k** of Persia brought these out in Ezr 1:8
Nebuchadnezzar the **k** of Babylon Ezr 2:1
that they had from Cyrus **k** of Persia. Ezr 3:7
to the directions of David **k** of Israel. Ezr 3:10
the days of Esarhaddon **k** of Assyria who Ezr 4:2
as **K** Cyrus the king of Persia has Ezr 4:3
as King Cyrus the **k** of Persia has Ezr 4:3
purpose, all the days of Cyrus **k** of Persia, Ezr 4:5
even until the reign of Darius **k** of Persia. Ezr 4:5
wrote to Artaxerxes **k** of Persia. Ezr 4:7
Jerusalem to Artaxerxes the **k** as follows: Ezr 4:8
"To Artaxerxes the **k**: Your servants, the Ezr 4:11
be it known to the **k** that the Jews who Ezr 4:12
be it known to the **k** that if this city is Ezr 4:13
therefore we send and inform the **k**, Ezr 4:14
make known to the **k** that if this city Ezr 4:16
The **k** sent an answer: "To Rehum the Ezr 4:17
damage grow to the hurt of the **k**?" Ezr 4:22
the copy of **K** Artaxerxes' letter was Ezr 4:23
year of the reign of Darius **k** of Persia. Ezr 4:24
Beyond the River sent to Darius the **k**. Ezr 5:6
as follows: "To Darius the **k**, all peace. Ezr 5:7
Be it known to the **k** that we went to the Ezr 5:8
which a great **k** of Israel built and Ezr 5:11
hand of Nebuchadnezzar **k** of Babylon, Ezr 5:12
in the first year of Cyrus **k** of Babylon, Ezr 5:13
Cyrus the **k** made a decree that this Ezr 5:13
these Cyrus the **k** took out of the temple Ezr 5:14
Therefore, if it seems good to the **k**, let Ezr 5:17
issued by Cyrus the **k** for the rebuilding Ezr 5:17
And let the **k** send us his pleasure in Ezr 5:17
Then Darius the **k** made a decree, and Ezr 6:1
In the first year of Cyrus the **k**, Cyrus the Ezr 6:3
the king, Cyrus the **k** issued a decree: Ezr 6:3
pray for the life of the **k** and his sons. Ezr 6:10
there overthrow any **k** or people who Ezr 6:12
to the word sent by Darius the **k**, Ezr 6:13
what Darius the **k** had ordered. Ezr 6:13
and Darius and Artaxerxes **k** of Persia; Ezr 6:14
sixth year of the reign of Darius the **k**. Ezr 6:15
the heart of the **k** of Assyria to them, Ezr 6:22
in the reign of Artaxerxes **k** of Persia, Ezr 7:1
and the **k** granted him all that he asked, Ezr 7:6
in the seventh year of Artaxerxes the **k**, Ezr 7:7
which was in the seventh year of the **k**. Ezr 7:8
of the letter that **K** Artaxerxes gave to Ezr 7:11
"Artaxerxes, **k** of kings, to Ezra the Ezr 7:12
are sent by the **k** and his seven Ezr 7:14
and gold that the **k** and his counselors Ezr 7:15
"And I, Artaxerxes the **k**, make a decree Ezr 7:21
against the realm of the **k** and his sons. Ezr 7:23
the law of your God and the law of the **k**, Ezr 7:26
a thing as this into the heart of the **k**, Ezr 7:27
love before the **k** and his counselors, Ezr 7:28
in the reign of Artaxerxes the **k**: Ezr 8:1
was ashamed to ask the **k** for a band of Ezr 8:22
on our way, since we had told the **k**, Ezr 8:22
our God that the **k** and his counselors Ezr 8:25
man." Now I was cupbearer to the **k**. Neh 1:11
in the twentieth year of **K** Artaxerxes, Neh 2:1
I took up the wine and gave it to the **k**. Neh 2:1
And the **k** said to me, "Why is your face Neh 2:2
I said to the **k**, "Let the king live forever! Neh 2:3
I said to the king, "Let the **k** live forever! Neh 2:3
Then the **k** said to me, "What are you Neh 2:4
And I said to the **k**, "If it pleases the king, Neh 2:5
And I said to the king, "If it pleases the **k**, Neh 2:5
And the **k** said to me (the queen sitting Neh 2:6
So it pleased the **k** to send me when Neh 2:6
And I said to the **k**, "If it pleases the king, Neh 2:7
And I said to the king, "If it pleases the **k**, Neh 2:7
occupy." And the **k** granted me what Neh 2:8
Now the **k** had sent with me officers of Neh 2:9
the words that the **k** had spoken to me. Neh 2:18
Are you rebelling against the **k**?" Neh 2:19
the upper house of the **k** at the court of Neh 3:25
thirty-second year of Artaxerxes the **k**, Neh 5:14
reports you wish to become their **k**. Neh 6:6

in Jerusalem, 'There is a **k** in Judah.' Neh 6:7
And now the **k** will hear of these reports. Neh 6:7
Nebuchadnezzar the **k** of Babylon Neh 7:6
the land of Sihon **k** of Heshbon and the Neh 9:22
and the land of Og **k** of Bashan. Neh 9:22
from the **k** concerning them, Neh 11:23
year of Artaxerxes **k** of Babylon I Neh 13:6
king of Babylon I went to the **k**. Neh 13:6
after some time I asked leave of the **k** Neh 13:6
Did not Solomon **k** of Israel sin on Neh 13:26
nations there was no **k** like him, Neh 13:26
and God made him **k** over all Israel. Neh 13:26
in those days when **K** Ahasuerus sat on Est 1:2
the **k** gave for all the people present in Est 1:5
according to the bounty of the **k**. Est 1:7
compulsion." For the **k** had given orders Est 1:8
the palace that belonged to **K** Ahasuerus. Est 1:9
the heart of the **k** was merry with wine, Est 1:10
served in the presence of **K** Ahasuerus, Est 1:10
Vashti before the **k** with her royal Est 1:11
At this the **k** became enraged, and his Est 1:12
Then the **k** said to the wise men who Est 1:13
the command of **K** Ahasuerus delivered Est 1:15
in the presence of the **k** and the officials, Est 1:16
only against the **k** has Queen Vashti Est 1:16
are in all the provinces of **K** Ahasuerus. Est 1:16
'**K** Ahasuerus commanded Queen Est 1:17
If it please the **k**, let a royal order go out Est 1:19
again to come before **K** Ahasuerus. Est 1:19
And let the **k** give her royal position to Est 1:19
made by the **k** is proclaimed Est 1:20
advice pleased the **k** and the princes, Est 1:21
and the **k** did as Memucan proposed. Est 1:21
the anger of **K** Ahasuerus had abated, Est 2:1
young virgins be sought out for the **k**. Est 2:2
And let the **k** appoint officers in all the Est 2:3
who pleases the **k** be queen instead Est 2:4
instead of Vashti." This pleased the **k**, Est 2:4
carried away with Jeconiah **k** of Judah, Est 2:6
whom Nebuchadnezzar **k** of Babylon Est 2:6
young woman to go in to **K** Ahasuerus, Est 2:12
woman went in to the **k** in this way, Est 2:13
She would not go in to the **k** again, Est 2:14
unless the **k** delighted in her and she Est 2:14
as his own daughter, to go in to the **k**, Est 2:15
was taken to **K** Ahasuerus into his Est 2:16
the **k** loved Esther more than all the Est 2:17
Then the **k** gave a great feast for all his Est 2:18
sought to lay hands on **K** Ahasuerus. Est 2:21
and Esther told the **k** in the name of Est 2:22
the chronicles in the presence of the **k**. Est 2:23
After these things **K** Ahasuerus promoted Est 3:1
for the **k** had so commanded concerning Est 3:2
in the twelfth year of **K** Ahasuerus, Est 3:7
Then Haman said to **K** Ahasuerus, Est 3:8
If it please the **k**, let it be decreed that they Est 3:9
So the **k** took his signet ring from his Est 3:10
And the **k** said to Haman, "The money Est 3:11
in the name of **K** Ahasuerus and sealed Est 3:12
went out hurriedly by order of the **k**, Est 3:15
And the **k** and Haman sat down to Est 3:15
her to go to the **k** to beg his favor and Est 4:8
woman goes to the **k** inside the inner Est 4:11
one to whom the **k** holds out the golden Est 4:11
to come in to the **k** these thirty days." Est 4:11
Then I will go to the **k**, though it is Est 4:16
while the **k** was sitting on his royal Est 5:1
And when the **k** saw Queen Esther Est 5:2
And the **k** said to her, "What is it, Queen Est 5:3
And Esther said, "If it please the **k**, let the Est 5:4
let the **k** and Haman come today to a Est 5:4
to a feast that I have prepared for the **k**." Est 5:4
Then the **k** said, "Bring Haman quickly, Est 5:5
has asked." So the **k** and Haman came to Est 5:5
wine after the feast, the **k** said to Esther, Est 5:6
If I have found favor in the sight of the **k**, Est 5:8
and if it please the **k** to grant my wish Est 5:8
let the **k** and Haman come to the feast Est 5:8
and tomorrow I will do as the **k** has said." Est 5:8
with which the **k** had honored him, Est 5:11
the officials and the servants of the **k**. Est 5:11
but me come with the **k** to the feast she Est 5:12
I am invited by her together with the **k**. Est 5:12
the morning tell the **k** to have Mordecai Est 5:14
go joyfully with the **k** to the feast." This Est 5:14
On that night the **k** could not sleep. And Est 6:1
and they were read before the **k**. Est 6:1
had sought to lay hands on **K** Ahasuerus. Est 6:2
And the **k** said, "What honor or Est 6:3
And the **k** said, "Who is in the court?" Est 6:4
to speak to the **k** about having Mordecai Est 6:4
standing in the court." And the **k** said, Est 6:5
Haman came in, and the **k** said to him, Est 6:6
the man whom the **k** delights to honor?" Est 6:6
"Whom would the **k** delight to honor Est 6:6

And Haman said to the **k**, "For the man Est 6:7
the man whom the **k** delights to honor, Est 6:7
robes be brought, which the **k** has worn, Est 6:8
worn, and the horse that the **k** has ridden, Est 6:8
the man whom the **k** delights to honor, Est 6:9
the man whom the **k** delights to honor.'" Est 6:9
Then the **k** said to Haman, "Hurry; take Est 6:10
the man whom the **k** delights to honor." Est 6:11
So the **k** and Haman went in to feast with Est 7:1
after the feast, the **k** again said to Esther, Est 7:2
"If I have found favor in your sight, O **k**, Est 7:3
your sight, O king, and if it please the **k**, Est 7:3
to be compared with the loss to the **k**." Est 7:4
Then **K** Ahasuerus said to Queen Esther, Est 7:5
was terrified before the **k** and the queen. Est 7:6
And the **k** arose in his wrath from the Est 7:7
was determined against him by the **k**. Est 7:7
And the **k** returned from the palace Est 7:8
And the **k** said, "Will he even assault the Est 7:8
As the word left the mouth of the **k**, Est 7:8
of the eunuchs in attendance on the **k**, Est 7:9
for Mordecai, whose word saved the **k**, Est 7:9
And the **k** said, "Hang him on that." So Est 7:10
Then the wrath of the **k** abated. Est 7:10
On that day **K** Ahasuerus gave to Queen Est 8:1
And Mordecai came before the **k**, for Est 8:1
And the **k** took off his signet ring, which Est 8:2
Then Esther spoke again to the **k**. She fell Est 8:3
When the **k** held out the golden scepter to Est 8:4
Esther rose and stood before the **k**. And Est 8:5
And she said, "If it please the **k**, and if I Est 8:5
and if the thing seems right before the **k**, Est 8:5
Jews who are in all the provinces of the **k**. Est 8:5
Then **K** Ahasuerus said to Queen Esther Est 8:7
regard to the Jews, in the name of the **k**, Est 8:8
in the name of the **k** and sealed with the Est 8:8
in the name of **K** Ahasuerus and sealed Est 8:10
saying that the **k** allowed the Jews who Est 8:11
all the provinces of **K** Ahasuerus, Est 8:12
the presence of the **k** in royal robes of Est 8:15
all the provinces of **K** Ahasuerus to lay Est 9:2
in Susa the citadel was reported to the **k**. Est 9:11
And the **k** said to Queen Esther, "In Susa Est 9:12
And Esther said, "If it please the **k**, let the Est 9:13
So the **k** commanded this to be done. A Est 9:14
in all the provinces of **K** Ahasuerus, Est 9:20
But when it came before the **k**, he gave Est 9:25
K Ahasuerus imposed tax on the land Est 10:1
to which the **k** advanced him, Est 10:2
Jew was second in rank to **K** Ahasuerus, Est 10:3
against him, like a **k** ready for battle. Jb 15:24
and is brought to the **k** of terrors. Jb 18:14
and I lived like a **k** among his troops, Jb 29:25
who says to a **k**, 'Worthless one,' and to Jb 34:18
high; he is **k** over all the sons of pride." Jb 41:34
"As for me, I have set my **K** on Zion, my Ps 2:6
to the sound of my cry, my **K** and my God, Ps 5:2
The LORD is **k** forever and ever; the Ps 10:16
Great salvation he brings to his **k**, and Ps 18:50
O LORD, save the **k**! May he answer us Ps 20:9
O LORD, in your strength the **k** rejoices, Ps 21:1
For the **k** trusts in the LORD, and through Ps 21:7
doors, that the **K** of glory may come in. Ps 24:7
Who is this **K** of glory? The LORD, strong Ps 24:8
doors, that the **K** of glory may come in. Ps 24:9
Who is this **K** of glory? The LORD of Ps 24:10
The LORD of hosts, he is the **K** of glory! Ps 24:10
the LORD sits enthroned as **k** forever. Ps 29:10
The **k** is not saved by his great army; a Ps 33:16
You are my **K**, O God; ordain salvation Ps 44:4
theme; I address my verses to the **k**; Ps 45:1
and the **k** will desire your beauty. Since Ps 45:11
many-colored robes she is led to the **k**, Ps 45:14
along as they enter the palace of the **k**. Ps 45:15
is to be feared, a great **k** over all the earth. Ps 47:2
Sing praises to our **K**, sing praises! Ps 47:6
For God is the **K** of all the earth; sing Ps 47:7
in the far north, the city of the great **K**. Ps 48:2
Prolong the life of the **k**; may his years Ps 61:6
But the **k** shall rejoice in God; all who Ps 63:11
O God, the procession of my God, my **K**, Ps 68:24
Give the **k** your justice, O God, and your Ps 72:1
Yet God my **K** is from of old, working Ps 74:12
O LORD of hosts, my **K** and my God. Ps 84:3
the LORD, our **k** to the Holy One of Israel. Ps 89:18
a great God, and a great **K** above all gods. Ps 95:3
horn make a joyful noise before the **K**, Ps 98:6
The **K** in his might loves justice. You Ps 99:4
The **k** sent and released him; the ruler Ps 105:20
Sihon, **k** of the Amorites, and Og, king Ps 135:11
of the Amorites, and Og, **k** of Bashan, Ps 135:11
Sihon, **k** of the Amorites, for his Ps 136:19
and Og, **k** of Bashan, for his steadfast Ps 136:20
I will extol you, my God and **K**, and Ps 145:1
the children of Zion rejoice in their **K**! Ps 149:2

of Solomon, son of David, **k** of Israel: Prv 1:1
multitude of people is the glory of a **k**, Prv 14:28
An oracle is on the lips of a **k**; his Prv 16:10
Righteous lips are the delight of a **k**, Prv 16:13
The terror of a **k** is like the growling of Prv 20:2
A **k** who sits on the throne of judgment Prv 20:8
A wise **k** winnows the wicked and Prv 20:26
love and faithfulness preserve the **k**, Prv 20:28
gracious, will have the **k** as his friend. Prv 22:11
My son, fear the LORD and the **k**, and Prv 24:21
the men of Hezekiah **k** of Judah copied. Prv 25:1
the wicked from the presence of the **k**, Prv 25:5
By justice a **k** builds up the land, but he Prv 29:4
If a **k** faithfully judges the poor, his Prv 29:14
a slave when he becomes **k**, and a fool Prv 30:22
the locusts have no **k**, yet all of them Prv 30:27
and a **k** whose army is with him. Prv 30:31
The words of **K** Lemuel. An oracle that Prv 31:1
the son of David, **k** in Jerusalem. Eccl 1:1
the Preacher have been **k** over Israel in Eccl 1:12
the man do who comes after the **k**? Eccl 2:12
an old and foolish **k** who no longer Eccl 4:13
way: a **k** committed to cultivated fields. Eccl 5:9
For the word of the **k** is supreme, and Eccl 8:4
and a great **k** came against it and Eccl 9:14
you, O land, when your **k** is a child, Eccl 10:16
when your **k** is the son of the Eccl 10:17
in your thought, do not curse the **k**, Eccl 10:20
The **k** has brought me into his chambers. Sg 1:4
While the **k** was on his couch, my nard Sg 1:12
K Solomon made himself a carriage from Sg 3:9
of Zion, and look upon **K** Solomon, Sg 3:11
purple; a **k** is held captive in the tresses. Sg 7:5
In the year that **K** Uzziah died I saw the Is 6:1
for my eyes have seen the **K**, the LORD of Is 6:5
son of Jotham, son of Uzziah, **k** of Judah, Is 7:1
Rezin the **k** of Syria and Pekah the son of Is 7:1
son of Remaliah the **k** of Israel came up Is 7:1
the son of Tabeel as **k** in the midst of it," Is 7:6
departed from Judah—the **k** of Assyria." Is 7:17
the River—with the **k** of Assyria—the Is 7:20
be carried away before the **k** of Assyria." Is 8:4
many, the **k** of Assyria and all his glory. Is 8:7
contemptuously against their **k** and their Is 8:21
arrogant heart of the **k** of Assyria and Is 10:12
up this taunt against the **k** of Babylon: Is 14:4
In the year that **K** Ahaz died came this Is 14:28
master, and a fierce **k** will rule over them, Is 19:4
who was sent by Sargon the **k** of Assyria, Is 20:1
so shall the **k** of Assyria lead away the Is 20:4
help to be delivered from the **k** of Assyria! Is 20:6
for seventy years, like the days of one **k**. Is 23:15
indeed, for the **k** it is made ready, its pyre Is 30:33
Behold, a **k** will reign in righteousness, Is 32:1
eyes will behold the **k** in his beauty; Is 33:17
LORD is our lawgiver; the LORD is our **k**; Is 33:22
In the fourteenth year of **K** Hezekiah, Is 36:1
Sennacherib **k** of Assyria came up Is 36:1
And the **k** of Assyria sent the Rabshakeh Is 36:2
from Lachish to **K** Hezekiah at Is 36:2
"Say to Hezekiah, 'Thus says the great **k**, Is 36:4
says the great king, the **k** of Assyria: Is 36:4
Such is Pharaoh **k** of Egypt to all who Is 36:6
a wager with my master the **k** of Assyria: Is 36:8
"Hear the words of the great **k**, the king Is 36:13
words of the great king, the **k** of Assyria! Is 36:13
Thus says the **k**: 'Do not let Hezekiah Is 36:14
given into the hand of the **k** of Assyria." Is 36:15
For thus says the **k** of Assyria: Make Is 36:16
land out of the hand of the **k** of Assyria? Is 36:18
As soon as **K** Hezekiah heard it, he tore Is 37:1
whom his master the **k** of Assyria has Is 37:4
the servants of **K** Hezekiah came to Is 37:5
young men of the **k** of Assyria have Is 37:6
and found the **k** of Assyria fighting Is 37:8
he had heard that the **k** had left Lachish. Is 37:8
Now the **k** heard concerning Tirhakah Is 37:9
heard concerning Tirhakah **k** of Cush, Is 37:9
shall you speak to Hezekiah **k** of Judah: Is 37:10
given into the hand of the **k** of Assyria. Is 37:10
Where is the **k** of Hamath, the king of Is 37:13
is the king of Hamath, the **k** of Arpad, Is 37:13
Arpad, the **k** of the city of Sepharvaim, Is 37:13
of the city of Sepharvaim, the **k** of Hena, Is 37:13
the king of Hena, or the **k** of Ivvah?'" Is 37:13
concerning Sennacherib **k** of Assyria, Is 37:21
the LORD concerning the **k** of Assyria: Is 37:33
Then Sennacherib **k** of Assyria departed Is 37:37
city out of the hand of the **k** of Assyria, Is 38:6
A writing of Hezekiah **k** of Judah, after he Is 38:9
the son of Baladan, **k** of Babylon, Is 39:1
Isaiah the prophet came to **K** Hezekiah, Is 39:3
in the palace of the **k** of Babylon." Is 39:7
bring your proofs, says the **K** of Jacob. Is 41:21
Holy One, the Creator of Israel, your **K**." Is 43:15
the LORD, the **K** of Israel and his Redeemer, Is 44:6
You journeyed to the **k** with oil and Is 57:9
of Josiah the son of Amon, **k** of Judah, Jer 1:2
of Jehoiakim the son of Josiah, **k** of Judah, Jer 1:3
of Zedekiah, the son of Josiah, **k** of Judah, Jer 1:3
LORD said to me in the days of **K** Josiah: Jer 3:6
courage shall fail both **k** and officials. Jer 4:9
Is her **K** not in her?" "Why have they Jer 8:19
would not fear you, O **K** of the nations? Jer 10:7
is the living God and the everlasting **K**. Jer 10:10
Say to the **k** and the queen mother: Jer 13:18
the son of Hezekiah, **k** of Judah, Jer 15:4
Judah into the hand of the **k** of Babylon. Jer 20:4
when **K** Zedekiah sent to him Pashhur Jer 21:1
for Nebuchadnezzar **k** of Babylon is Jer 21:2
fighting against the **k** of Babylon and Jer 21:4
I will give Zedekiah **k** of Judah and his Jer 21:7
hand of Nebuchadnezzar **k** of Babylon Jer 21:7
given into the hand of the **k** of Babylon, Jer 21:10
"And to the house of the **k** of Judah say, Jer 21:11
to the house of the **k** of Judah and speak Jer 22:1
'Hear the word of the LORD, O **K** of Judah, Jer 22:2
concerning the house of the **k** of Judah: Jer 22:6
Shallum the son of Josiah, **k** of Judah, Jer 22:11
think you are a **k** because you compete Jer 22:15
Jehoiakim the son of Josiah, **k** of Judah: Jer 22:18
the son of Jehoiakim, **k** of Judah, Jer 22:24
hand of Nebuchadnezzar **k** of Babylon Jer 22:25
and he shall reign as **k** and deal wisely, Jer 23:5
After Nebuchadnezzar **k** of Babylon had Jer 24:1
the son of Jehoiakim, **k** of Judah, Jer 24:1
so will I treat Zedekiah the **k** of Judah, Jer 24:8
k of Judah (that was the first year of Jer 25:1
year of Nebuchadnezzar **k** of Babylon), Jer 25:1
of Josiah the son of Amon, **k** of Judah, Jer 25:3
for Nebuchadnezzar the **k** of Babylon, Jer 25:9
shall serve the **k** of Babylon seventy Jer 25:11
I will punish the **k** of Babylon and that Jer 25:12
Pharaoh **k** of Egypt, his servants, his Jer 25:19
And after them the **k** of Babylon shall Jer 25:26
Jehoiakim the son of Josiah, **k** of Judah, Jer 26:1
in the days of Hezekiah **k** of Judah, Jer 26:18
Did Hezekiah **k** of Judah and all Judah Jer 26:19
And when **K** Jehoiakim, with all his Jer 26:21
words, the **k** sought to put him to death. Jer 26:21
Then **K** Jehoiakim sent to Egypt Jer 26:22
and brought him to **K** Jehoiakim, Jer 26:23
of Zedekiah the son of Josiah, **k** of Judah, Jer 27:1
Send word to the **k** of Edom, the king of Jer 27:3
word to the king of Edom, the **k** of Moab, Jer 27:3
of Moab, the **k** of the sons of Ammon, Jer 27:3
of the sons of Ammon, the **k** of Tyre, Jer 27:3
and the **k** of Sidon by the hand of the Jer 27:3
to Jerusalem to Zedekiah **k** of Judah. Jer 27:3
of Nebuchadnezzar, the **k** of Babylon, Jer 27:6
this Nebuchadnezzar **k** of Babylon, Jer 27:8
neck under the yoke of the **k** of Babylon, Jer 27:8
'You shall not serve the **k** of Babylon.' Jer 27:9
the yoke of the **k** of Babylon and serve Jer 27:11
To Zedekiah **k** of Judah I spoke in like Jer 27:12
under the yoke of the **k** of Babylon, Jer 27:12
that will not serve the **k** of Babylon? Jer 27:13
'You shall not serve the **k** of Babylon,' Jer 27:14
them; serve the **k** of Babylon and live. Jer 27:17
the LORD, in the house of the **k** of Judah, Jer 27:18
which Nebuchadnezzar **k** of Babylon Jer 27:20
the son of Jehoiakim, **k** of Judah, Jer 27:20
the LORD, in the house of the **k** of Judah, Jer 27:21
of the reign of Zedekiah **k** of Judah, Jer 28:1
broken the yoke of the **k** of Babylon. Jer 28:2
which Nebuchadnezzar **k** of Babylon Jer 28:3
the son of Jehoiakim, **k** of Judah, Jer 28:4
will break the yoke of the **k** of Babylon." Jer 28:4
yoke of Nebuchadnezzar **k** of Babylon Jer 28:11
to serve Nebuchadnezzar **k** of Babylon, Jer 28:14
This was after **K** Jeconiah and the queen Jer 29:2
whom Zedekiah **k** of Judah sent to Jer 29:3
to Nebuchadnezzar **k** of Babylon. Jer 29:3
the LORD concerning the **k** who sits on Jer 29:16
hand of Nebuchadnezzar **k** of Babylon, Jer 29:21
whom the **k** of Babylon roasted in the Jer 29:22
the LORD their God and David their **k**, Jer 30:9
in the tenth year of Zedekiah **k** of Judah, Jer 32:1
the army of the **k** of Babylon was Jer 32:2
that was in the palace of the **k** of Judah. Jer 32:2
For Zedekiah **k** of Judah had imprisoned Jer 32:3
city into the hand of the **k** of Babylon, Jer 32:3
Zedekiah **k** of Judah shall not escape out Jer 32:4
given into the hand of the **k** of Babylon, Jer 32:4
hand of Nebuchadnezzar **k** of Babylon, Jer 32:28
the hand of the **k** of Babylon by sword, Jer 32:36
when Nebuchadnezzar **k** of Babylon Jer 34:1
and speak to Zedekiah **k** of Judah and Jer 34:2
city into the hand of the **k** of Babylon, Jer 34:2
You shall see the **k** of Babylon eye to eye Jer 34:3
word of the LORD, O Zedekiah **k** of Judah! Jer 34:4
all these words to Zedekiah **k** of Judah, Jer 34:6
the army of the **k** of Babylon was Jer 34:7
after **K** Zedekiah had made a covenant Jer 34:8
And Zedekiah **k** of Judah and his Jer 34:21
the army of the **k** of Babylon which Jer 34:21
Jehoiakim the son of Josiah, **k** of Judah: Jer 35:1
when Nebuchadnezzar **k** of Babylon Jer 35:11
Jehoiakim the son of Josiah, **k** of Judah, Jer 36:1
Jehoiakim the son of Josiah, **k** of Judah, Jer 36:9
must report all these words to the **k**." Jer 36:16
So they went into the court to the **k**, Jer 36:20
and they reported all the words to the **k**. Jer 36:20
Then the **k** sent Jehudi to get the scroll, Jer 36:21
read it to the **k** and all the officials Jer 36:21
all the officials who stood beside the **k**. Jer 36:21
and the **k** was sitting in the winter Jer 36:22
the **k** would cut them off with a knife Jer 36:23
Yet neither the **k** nor any of his Jer 36:24
and Gemariah urged the **k** not to burn Jer 36:25
And the **k** commanded Jerahmeel the Jer 36:26
Now after the **k** had burned the scroll Jer 36:27
which Jehoiakim the **k** of Judah has Jer 36:28
And concerning Jehoiakim **k** of Judah Jer 36:29
in it that the **k** of Babylon will Jer 36:29
LORD concerning Jehoiakim **k** of Judah: Jer 36:30
scroll that Jehoiakim **k** of Judah had Jer 36:32
whom Nebuchadnezzar **k** of Babylon Jer 37:1
king of Babylon made **k** in the land of Jer 37:1
K Zedekiah sent Jehucal the son of Jer 37:3
shall you say to the **k** of Judah who sent Jer 37:7
K Zedekiah sent for him and received Jer 37:17
The **k** questioned him secretly in his Jer 37:17
into the hand of the **k** of Babylon." Jer 37:17
Jeremiah also said to **K** Zedekiah, Jer 37:18
'The **k** of Babylon will not come Jer 37:19
Now hear, please, O my lord the **k**: let Jer 37:20
So **K** Zedekiah gave orders, and they Jer 37:21
of the army of the **k** of Babylon and be Jer 38:3
Then the officials said to the **k**, "Let this Jer 38:4
K Zedekiah said, "Behold, he is in your Jer 38:5
for the **k** can do nothing against you." Jer 38:5
into the cistern—the **k** was sitting in the Jer 38:7
from the king's house and said to the **k**, Jer 38:8
"My lord the **k**, these men have done evil Jer 38:9
Then the **k** commanded Ebed-melech Jer 38:10
him and went to the house of the **k**, Jer 38:11
K Zedekiah sent for Jeremiah the Jer 38:14
The **k** said to Jeremiah, "I will ask you Jer 38:14
Then **K** Zedekiah swore secretly to Jer 38:16
to the officials of the **k** of Babylon, Jer 38:17
to the officials of the **k** of Babylon, Jer 38:18
K Zedekiah said to Jeremiah, "I am Jer 38:19
the house of the **k** of Judah were being Jer 38:22
the officials of the **k** of Babylon and Jer 38:22
but shall be seized by the **k** of Babylon, Jer 38:23
you said to the **k** and what the king Jer 38:25
to the king and what the **k** said to you; Jer 38:25
humble plea to the **k** that he would not Jer 38:26
them as the **k** had instructed him. Jer 38:27
In the ninth year of Zedekiah **k** of Judah, Jer 39:1
Nebuchadnezzar **k** of Babylon and all Jer 39:1
the officials of the **k** of Babylon came Jer 39:3
rest of the officers of the **k** of Babylon. Jer 39:3
When Zedekiah **k** of Judah and all the Jer 39:4
up to Nebuchadnezzar **k** of Babylon, Jer 39:5
The **k** of Babylon slaughtered the sons Jer 39:6
and the **k** of Babylon slaughtered all the Jer 39:6
Nebuchadnezzar **k** of Babylon gave Jer 39:11
all the chief officers of the **k** of Babylon Jer 39:13
whom the **k** of Babylon appointed Jer 40:5
men heard that the **k** of Babylon had Jer 40:7
in the land and serve the **k** of Babylon, Jer 40:9
lands heard that the **k** of Babylon had Jer 40:11
that Baalis the **k** of the Ammonites Jer 40:14
family, one of the chief officers of the **k**, Jer 41:1
whom the **k** of Babylon had appointed Jer 41:2
the large cistern that **K** Asa had made Jer 41:9
for defense against Baasha **k** of Israel; Jer 41:9
whom the **k** of Babylon had made Jer 41:18
Do not fear the **k** of Babylon, of whom Jer 42:11
Nebuchadnezzar the **k** of Babylon, Jer 43:10
give Pharaoh Hophra **k** of Egypt into Jer 44:30
as I gave Zedekiah **k** of Judah into the Jer 44:30
hand of Nebuchadnezzar **k** of Babylon, Jer 44:30
Jehoiakim the son of Josiah, **k** of Judah: Jer 45:1
the army of Pharaoh Neco, **k** of Egypt, Jer 46:2
which Nebuchadnezzar **k** of Babylon Jer 46:2
Jehoiakim the son of Josiah, **k** of Judah: Jer 46:2
of Nebuchadnezzar **k** of Babylon Jer 46:13
Call the name of Pharaoh, **k** of Egypt, Jer 46:17
"As I live, declares the **K**, whose name is Jer 46:18
hand of Nebuchadnezzar **k** of Babylon Jer 46:26
gone down to slaughter, declares the **K**, Jer 48:15
that Nebuchadnezzar **k** of Babylon Jer 49:28

For Nebuchadnezzar **k** of Babylon has	Jer 49:30
of the reign of Zedekiah **k** of Judah.	Jer 49:34
Elam and destroy their **k** and officials,	Jer 49:38
First the **k** of Assyria devoured him,	Jer 50:17
at last Nebuchadnezzar **k** of Babylon	Jer 50:17
punishment on the **k** of Babylon and	Jer 50:18
his land, as I punished the **k** of Assyria.	Jer 50:18
"The **k** of Babylon heard the report of	Jer 50:43
to tell the **k** of Babylon that his city is	Jer 51:31
"Nebuchadnezzar the **k** of Babylon has	Jer 51:34
sleep and not wake, declares the **K**,	Jer 51:57
he went with Zedekiah **k** of Judah to	Jer 51:59
twenty-one years old when he became **k**;	Jer 52:1
rebelled against the **k** of Babylon.	Jer 52:3
Nebuchadnezzar **k** of Babylon came	Jer 52:4
till the eleventh year of **K** Zedekiah.	Jer 52:5
Chaldeans pursued the **k** and overtook	Jer 52:8
they captured the **k** and brought him	Jer 52:9
him up to the **k** of Babylon at Riblah	Jer 52:9
The **k** of Babylon slaughtered the sons	Jer 52:10
and the **k** of Babylon took him to	Jer 52:11
nineteenth year of **K** Nebuchadnezzar,	Jer 52:12
k of Babylon—Nebuzaradan the	Jer 52:12
who served the **k** of Babylon,	Jer 52:12
who had deserted to the **k** of Babylon,	Jer 52:15
which Solomon the **k** had made for the	Jer 52:20
brought them to the **k** of Babylon at	Jer 52:26
And the **k** of Babylon struck them	Jer 52:27
of the exile of Jehoiachin **k** of Judah,	Jer 52:31
month, Evil-merodach **k** of Babylon,	Jer 52:31
Babylon, in the year that he became **k**,	Jer 52:31
the head of Jehoiachin **k** of Judah and	Jer 52:31
given him by the **k** according to his	Jer 52:34
indignation has spurned **k** and priest.	Lam 2:6
her **k** and princes are among the	Lam 2:9
fifth year of the exile of **K** Jehoiachin),	Ezk 1:2
The **k** mourns, the prince is wrapped in	Ezk 7:27
the **k** of Babylon came to Jerusalem,	Ezk 17:12
and took her **k** and her princes and	Ezk 17:12
place where the **k** dwells who made	Ezk 17:16
the king dwells who made him **k**,	Ezk 17:16
and brought him to the **k** of Babylon;	Ezk 19:9
wrath poured out I will be **k** over you.	Ezk 20:33
the sword of the **k** of Babylon to come.	Ezk 21:19
For the **k** of Babylon stands at the	Ezk 21:21
The **k** of Babylon has laid siege to	Ezk 24:2
north Nebuchadnezzar **k** of Babylon,	Ezk 26:7
king of Babylon, **k** of kings,	Ezk 26:7
raise a lamentation over the **k** of Tyre,	Ezk 28:12
your face against Pharaoh **k** of Egypt,	Ezk 29:2
I am against you, Pharaoh **k** of Egypt,	Ezk 29:3
Nebuchadnezzar **k** of Babylon made	Ezk 29:18
to Nebuchadnezzar **k** of Babylon;	Ezk 29:19
of Nebuchadnezzar **k** of Babylon.	Ezk 30:10
the arm of Pharaoh **k** of Egypt,	Ezk 30:21
I am against Pharaoh **k** of Egypt and	Ezk 30:22
the arms of the **k** of Babylon and put	Ezk 30:24
the arms of the **k** of Babylon,	Ezk 30:25
the hand of the **k** of Babylon and he	Ezk 30:25
say to Pharaoh **k** of Egypt and to his	Ezk 31:2
lamentation over Pharaoh **k** of Egypt	Ezk 32:2
The sword of the **k** of Babylon shall	Ezk 32:11
And one **k** shall be king over them all,	Ezk 37:22
And one king shall be **k** over them all,	Ezk 37:22
servant David shall be **k** over them,	Ezk 37:24
year of the reign of Jehoiakim **k** of Judah,	Dn 1:1
Nebuchadnezzar **k** of Babylon came to	Dn 1:1
the Lord gave Jehoiakim **k** of Judah into	Dn 1:2
Then the **k** commanded Ashpenaz, his	Dn 1:3
The **k** assigned them a daily portion of	Dn 1:5
a daily portion of the food that the **k** ate,	Dn 1:5
that time they were to stand before the **k**.	Dn 1:5
said to Daniel, "I fear my lord the **k**,	Dn 1:10
would endanger my head with the **k**."	Dn 1:10
when the **k** had commanded that they	Dn 1:18
And the **k** spoke with them, and among	Dn 1:19
Therefore they stood before the **k**.	Dn 1:19
about which the **k** inquired of them,	Dn 1:20
was there until the first year of **K** Cyrus.	Dn 1:21
Then the **k** commanded that the	Dn 2:2
be summoned to tell the **k** his dreams.	Dn 2:2
So they came in and stood before the **k**.	Dn 2:2
And the **k** said to them, "I had a dream,	Dn 2:3
the Chaldeans said to the **k** in Aramaic,	Dn 2:4
said to the king in Aramaic, "O **k**,	Dn 2:4
The **k** answered and said to the	Dn 2:5
"Let the **k** tell his servants the dream,	Dn 2:7
The **k** answered and said, "I know with	Dn 2:8
The Chaldeans answered the **k** and said,	Dn 2:10
no great and powerful **k** has asked such	Dn 2:10
The thing that the **k** asks is difficult,	Dn 2:11
one can show it to the **k** except the gods,	Dn 2:11
Because of this the **k** was angry and	Dn 2:12
the decree of the **k** so urgent?" Then	Dn 2:15
in and requested the **k** to appoint him a	Dn 2:16
might show the interpretation to the **k**.	Dn 2:16
whom the **k** had appointed to destroy	Dn 2:24
bring me in before the **k**, and I will	Dn 2:24
and I will show the **k** the interpretation."	Dn 2:24
in Daniel before the **k** in haste and said	Dn 2:25
known to the **k** the interpretation."	Dn 2:25
The **k** said to Daniel, whose name was	Dn 2:26
Daniel answered the **k** and said, "No	Dn 2:27
can show to the **k** the mystery that the	Dn 2:27
king the mystery that the **k** has asked,	Dn 2:27
known to **K** Nebuchadnezzar what	Dn 2:28
To you, O **k**, as you lay in bed came	Dn 2:29
may be made known to the **k**,	Dn 2:30
"You saw, O **k**, and behold, a great	Dn 2:31
Now we will tell the **k** its interpretation.	Dn 2:36
You, O **k**, the king of kings, to whom	Dn 2:37
You, O king, the **k** of kings, to whom	Dn 2:37
made known to the **k** what shall be after	Dn 2:45
Then **K** Nebuchadnezzar fell upon his	Dn 2:46
The **k** answered and said to Daniel,	Dn 2:47
Then the **k** gave Daniel high honors	Dn 2:48
Daniel made a request of the **k**, and he	Dn 2:49
K Nebuchadnezzar made an image of	Dn 3:1
Then **K** Nebuchadnezzar sent to gather	Dn 3:2
the image that **K** Nebuchadnezzar had	Dn 3:2
the image that **K** Nebuchadnezzar had	Dn 3:3
image that **K** Nebuchadnezzar has	Dn 3:5
image that **K** Nebuchadnezzar had	Dn 3:7
They declared to **K** Nebuchadnezzar, "O	Dn 3:9
declared to King Nebuchadnezzar, "O **k**,	Dn 3:9
You, O **k**, have made a decree, that every	Dn 3:10
These men, O **k**, pay no attention to you;	Dn 3:12
So they brought these men before the **k**.	Dn 3:13
Abednego answered and said to the **k**,	Dn 3:16
he will deliver us out of your hand, O **k**.	Dn 3:17
But if not, be it known to you, O **k**, that	Dn 3:18
Then **K** Nebuchadnezzar was	Dn 3:24
fire?" They answered and said to the **k**,	Dn 3:24
and said to the king, "True, O **k**."	Dn 3:24
Then the **k** promoted Shadrach,	Dn 3:30
K Nebuchadnezzar to all peoples,	Dn 4:1
This dream I, **K** Nebuchadnezzar, saw.	Dn 4:18
The **k** answered and said, "Belteshazzar,	Dn 4:19
it is you, O **k**, who have grown and	Dn 4:22
And because the **k** saw a watcher, a	Dn 4:23
this is the interpretation, O **k**: It is a	Dn 4:24
which has come upon my lord the **k**,	Dn 4:24
Therefore, O **k**, let my counsel be	Dn 4:27
All this came upon **K** Nebuchadnezzar.	Dn 4:28
and the **k** answered and said, "Is not this	Dn 4:30
from heaven, "O **K** Nebuchadnezzar,	Dn 4:31
and extol and honor the **K** of heaven,	Dn 4:37
K Belshazzar made a great feast for a	Dn 5:1
be brought, that the **k** and his lords,	Dn 5:2
in Jerusalem, and the **k** and his lords,	Dn 5:3
And the **k** saw the hand as it wrote.	Dn 5:5
The **k** called loudly to bring in the	Dn 5:7
The **k** declared to the wise men of	Dn 5:7
make known to the **k** the interpretation.	Dn 5:8
Then **K** Belshazzar was greatly alarmed,	Dn 5:9
of the words of the **k** and his lords,	Dn 5:10
hall, and the queen declared, "O **k**,	Dn 5:10
found in him, and **K** Nebuchadnezzar,	Dn 5:11
—your father the **k**—made him chief	Dn 5:11
whom the **k** named Belteshazzar.	Dn 5:12
Daniel was brought in before the **k**.	Dn 5:13
The **k** answered and said to Daniel,	Dn 5:13
whom the **k** my father brought from	Dn 5:13
Daniel answered and said before the **k**,	Dn 5:17
the writing to the **k** and make known to	Dn 5:17
O **k**, the Most High God gave	Dn 5:18
Belshazzar the Chaldean **k** was killed.	Dn 5:30
so that the **k** might suffer no loss.	Dn 6:2
And the **k** planned to set him over the	Dn 6:3
by agreement to the **k** and said to him,	Dn 6:6
to the king and said to him, "O **K** Darius,	Dn 6:6
are agreed that the **k** should establish an	Dn 6:7
or man for thirty days, except to you, O **k**,	Dn 6:7
Now, O **k**, establish the injunction and	Dn 6:8
Therefore **K** Darius signed the document	Dn 6:9
they came near and said before the **k**,	Dn 6:12
king, concerning the injunction, "O **k**!	Dn 6:12
within thirty days except to you, O **k**,	Dn 6:12
den of lions?" The **k** answered and said,	Dn 6:12
they answered and said before the **k**,	Dn 6:13
Judah, pays no attention to you, O **k**,	Dn 6:13
Then the **k**, when he heard these words,	Dn 6:14
by agreement to the **k** and said to the	Dn 6:15
agreement to the king and said to the **k**,	Dn 6:15
king and said to the king, "Know, O **k**,	Dn 6:15
ordinance that the **k** establishes can be	Dn 6:15
Then the **k** commanded, and Daniel	Dn 6:16
The **k** declared to Daniel, "May your	Dn 6:16
and the **k** sealed it with his own signet	Dn 6:17
Then the **k** went to his palace and spent	Dn 6:18
the **k** arose and went in haste to the den	Dn 6:19
The **k** declared to Daniel, "O Daniel,	Dn 6:20
Then Daniel said to the **k**, "O king, live	Dn 6:21
Then Daniel said to the king, "O **k**, live	Dn 6:21
and also before you, O **k**, I have done no	Dn 6:22
Then the **k** was exceedingly glad, and	Dn 6:23
And the **k** commanded, and those men	Dn 6:24
Then **K** Darius wrote to all the peoples,	Dn 6:25
the first year of Belshazzar **k** of Babylon,	Dn 7:1
of the reign of **K** Belshazzar a vision	Dn 8:1
And the goat is the **k** of Greece. And the	Dn 8:21
great horn between his eyes is the first **k**.	Dn 8:21
reached their limit, a **k** of bold face,	Dn 8:23
who was made **k** over the realm of the	Dn 9:1
third year of Cyrus **k** of Persia a word	Dn 10:1
Then a mighty **k** shall arise, who shall	Dn 11:3
"Then the **k** of the south shall be strong,	Dn 11:5
the daughter of the **k** of the south shall	Dn 11:6
south shall come to the **k** of the north to	Dn 11:6
enter the fortress of the **k** of the north,	Dn 11:7
from attacking the **k** of the north.	Dn 11:8
into the realm of the **k** of the south but	Dn 11:9
Then the **k** of the south, moved with	Dn 11:11
out and fight with the **k** of the north.	Dn 11:11
For the **k** of the north shall again raise	Dn 11:13
shall rise against the **k** of the south,	Dn 11:14
Then the **k** of the north shall come	Dn 11:15
his heart against the **k** of the south	Dn 11:25
And the **k** of the south shall wage war	Dn 11:25
"And the **k** shall do as he wills. He	Dn 11:36
the **k** of the south shall attack him,	Dn 11:40
but the **k** of the north shall rush upon	Dn 11:40
of Jeroboam the son of Joash, **k** of Israel.	Hos 1:1
dwell many days without **k** or prince,	Hos 3:4
the LORD their God, and David their **k**,	Hos 3:5
of Israel! Give ear, O house of the **k**!	Hos 5:1
went to Assyria, and sent to the great **k**.	Hos 5:13
By their evil they make the **k** glad, and	Hos 7:3
On the day of our **k**, the princes became	Hos 7:5
And the **k** and princes shall soon	Hos 8:10
"We have no **k**, for we do not fear the	Hos 10:3
and a **k**—what could he do for us?"	Hos 10:3
to Assyria as tribute to the great **k**.	Hos 10:6
Samaria's **k** shall perish like a twig on	Hos 10:7
At dawn the **k** of Israel shall be utterly	Hos 10:15
of Egypt, but Assyria shall be their **k**,	Hos 11:5
Where now is your **k**, to save you in	Hos 13:10
you said, "Give me a **k** and princes"?	Hos 13:10
I gave you a **k** in my anger, and I took	Hos 13:11
in the days of Uzziah **k** of Judah and in	Am 1:1
of Jeroboam the son of Joash, **k** of Israel,	Am 1:1
and their **k** shall go into exile, he and	Am 1:15
to lime the bones of the **k** of Edom.	Am 2:1
You shall take up Sikkuth your **k**, and	Am 5:26
of Bethel sent to Jeroboam **k** of Israel,	Am 7:10
The word reached the **k** of Nineveh, and	Jon 3:6
"By the decree of the **k** and his nobles:	Jon 3:7
Their **k** passes on before them, the LORD	Mi 2:13
do you cry aloud? Is there no **k** in you?	Mi 4:9
remember what Balak **k** of Moab devised,	Mi 6:5
shepherds are asleep, O **k** of Assyria;	Na 3:18
of Josiah the son of Amon, **k** of Judah.	Zep 1:1
The **K** of Israel, the LORD, is in your	Zep 3:15
In the second year of Darius the **k**, in the	Hg 1:1
in the second year of Darius the **k**.	Hg 1:15
In the fourth year of **K** Darius, the word	Zec 7:1
The **k** shall perish from Gaza; Ashkelon	Zec 9:5
behold, your **k** is coming to you;	Zec 9:9
and each into the hand of his **k**,	Zec 11:6
in the days of Uzziah **k** of Judah.	Zec 14:5
the LORD will be **k** over all the earth.	Zec 14:9
go up year after year to worship the **K**,	Zec 14:16
go up to Jerusalem to worship the **K**,	Zec 14:17
For I am a great **K**, says the LORD of	Mal 1:14
and Jesse the father of David the **k**. And	Mt 1:6
of Judea in the days of Herod the **k**,	Mt 2:1
is he who has been born **k** of the Jews?	Mt 2:2
When Herod the **k** heard this, he was	Mt 2:3
After listening to the **k**, they went on their	Mt 2:9
Jerusalem, for it is the city of the great **K**.	Mt 5:35
And the **k** was sorry, but because of his	Mt 14:9
be compared to a **k** who wished to settle	Mt 18:23
Zion, 'Behold, your **k** is coming to you,	Mt 21:5
be compared to a **k** who gave a wedding	Mt 22:2
The **k** was angry, and he sent his troops	Mt 22:7
"But when the **k** came in to look at the	Mt 22:11
Then the **k** said to the attendants, 'Bind	Mt 22:13
Then the **K** will say to those on his	Mt 25:34
And the **K** will answer them, 'Truly, I	Mt 25:40
"Are you the **K** of the Jews?" Jesus said,	Mt 27:11
him, saying, "Hail, **K** of the Jews!"	Mt 27:29
read, "This is Jesus, the **K** of the Jews."	Mt 27:37
He is the **K** of Israel; let him come down	Mt 27:42
K Herod heard of it, for Jesus' name had	Mk 6:14
And the **k** said to the girl, "Ask me for	Mk 6:22

with haste to the **k** and asked, Mk 6:25
And the **k** was exceedingly sorry, but Mk 6:26
And immediately the **k** sent an Mk 6:27
"Are you the **K** of the Jews?" And he Mk 15:2
me to release for you the **K** of the Jews?" Mk 15:9
the man you call the **K** of the Jews?" Mk 15:12
to salute him, "Hail, **K** of the Jews!" Mk 15:18
against him read, "The **K** of the Jews." Mk 15:26
Let the Christ, the **K** of Israel, come Mk 15:32
In the days of Herod, **k** of Judea, there was Lk 1:5
Or what **k**, going out to encounter Lk 14:31
out to encounter another **k** in war, Lk 14:31
"Blessed is the **K** who comes in the Lk 19:38
saying that he himself is Christ, a **k**." Lk 23:2
"Are you the **K** of the Jews?" And he Lk 23:3
saying, "If you are the **K** of the Jews, Lk 23:37
over him, "This is the **K** of the Jews." Lk 23:38
the Son of God! You are the **K** of Israel!" Jn 1:49
and take him by force to make him **k**, Jn 6:15
name of the Lord, even the **K** of Israel!" Jn 12:13
behold, your **k** is coming, sitting on a Jn 12:15
said to him, "Are you the **K** of the Jews?" Jn 18:33
him, "So you are a **k**?" Jesus answered, Jn 18:37
Jesus answered, "You say that I am a **k**. Jn 18:37
me to release to you the **K** of the Jews?" Jn 18:39
K of the Jews!" and struck him with their Jn 19:3
makes himself a **k** opposes Caesar." Jn 19:12
He said to the Jews, "Behold your **K**!" Jn 19:14
I crucify your **K**?" The chief priests Jn 19:15
answered, "We have no **k** but Caesar." Jn 19:15
"Jesus of Nazareth, the **K** of the Jews." Jn 19:19
Pilate, "Do not write, 'The **K** of the Jews,' Jn 19:21
'This man said, I am **K** of the Jews.'" Jn 19:21
wisdom before Pharaoh, **k** of Egypt, Acts 7:10
over Egypt another **k** who did not Acts 7:18
time Herod the **k** laid violent hands Acts 12:1
Then they asked for a **k**, and God Acts 13:21
him, he raised up David to be their **k**, Acts 13:22
Caesar, saying that there is another **k**, Acts 17:7
Agrippa the **k** and Bernice arrived at Acts 25:13
Festus laid Paul's case before the **k**, Acts 25:14
"**K** Agrippa and all who are present Acts 25:24
and especially before you, **K** Agrippa, Acts 25:26
that it is before you, **K** Agrippa, Acts 26:2
this hope I am accused by Jews, O **k**! Acts 26:7
At midday, O **k**, I saw on the way a Acts 26:13
"Therefore, O **K** Agrippa, I was not Acts 26:19
For the **k** knows about these things, Acts 26:26
K Agrippa, do you believe the Acts 26:27
Then the **k** rose, and the governor Acts 26:30
the governor under **K** Aretas was 2 Cor 11:32
To the **K** of ages, immortal, invisible, 1 Tm 1:17
the **K** of kings and Lord of lords, 1 Tm 6:15
For this Melchizedek, **k** of Salem, priest Heb 7:1
of his name, **k** of righteousness, Heb 7:2
and then he is also **k** of Salem, Heb 7:2
is also king of Salem, that is, **k** of peace. Heb 7:2
not being afraid of the anger of the **k**, Heb 11:27
They have as **k** over them the angel of Rv 9:11
true are your ways, O **K** of the nations! Rv 15:3
for he is Lord of lords and **K** of kings, Rv 17:14
written, **K** of kings and Lord of lords. Rv 19:16

KING'S (254)
of Shaveh (that is, the **K** Valley). Gn 14:17
place where the **k** prisoners were Gn 39:20
well. We will go along the **K** Highway. Nm 20:17
will go by the **K** Highway until we Nm 21:22
then become the **k** son-in-law.'" 1 Sm 18:22
thing to become the **k** son-in-law, 1 Sm 18:23
avenged of the **k** enemies.'" Now 1 Sm 18:25
David well to be the **k** son-in-law. 1 Sm 18:26
he might become the **k** son-in-law. 1 Sm 18:27
he has not come to the **k** table." 1 Sm 20:29
because the **k** business required 1 Sm 21:8
as David, who is the **k** son-in-law, 1 Sm 22:14
to surrender him into the **k** hand." 1 Sm 23:20
now see where the **k** spear is and the 1 Sm 26:16
it had not been the **k** will to put to 2 Sm 3:37
at David's table, like one of the **k** sons. 2 Sm 9:11
for he ate always at the **k** table. 2 Sm 9:13
walking on the roof of the **k** house, 2 Sm 11:2
And Uriah went out of the **k** house, 2 Sm 11:8
at the door of the **k** house with all the 2 Sm 11:9
then, if the **k** anger rises, and if he 2 Sm 11:20
wall. Some of the **k** servants are dead, 2 Sm 11:24
and Absalom invited all the **k** sons. 2 Sm 13:23
Amnon and all the **k** sons go with 2 Sm 13:27
Then all the **k** sons arose, and each 2 Sm 13:29
has struck down all the **k** sons, 2 Sm 13:30
killed all the young men the **k** sons, 2 Sm 13:32
suppose that all the **k** sons are dead, 2 Sm 13:33
king, "Behold, the **k** sons have come; 2 Sm 13:35
the **k** sons came and lifted up their 2 Sm 13:36
knew that the **k** heart went out 2 Sm 14:1
did not come into the **k** presence. 2 Sm 14:24
hundred shekels by the **k** weight. 2 Sm 14:26
without coming into the **k** presence. 2 Sm 14:28
And the **k** servants said to the king, 2 Sm 15:15
whatever you hear from the **k** house, 2 Sm 15:35
are for the **k** household to ride 2 Sm 16:2
out my hand against the **k** son, 2 Sm 18:12
the pillar that is in the **K** Valley, 2 Sm 18:18
no news, because the **k** son is dead." 2 Sm 18:20
"When Joab sent the **k** servant, 2 Sm 18:29
to bring over the **k** household and to 2 Sm 19:18
Have we eaten at all at the **k** expense? 2 Sm 19:42
But the **k** word prevailed against Joab 2 Sm 24:4
he invited all his brothers, the **k** sons, 1 Kgs 1:9
and has invited all the **k** sons, 1 Kgs 1:25
came into the **k** presence and stood 1 Kgs 1:28
And they had him ride on the **k** mule. 1 Kgs 1:44
the **k** servants came to congratulate 1 Kgs 1:47
had a seat brought for the **k** mother, 1 Kgs 2:19
son of Nathan was priest and **k** friend; 1 Kgs 4:5
At the **k** command they quarried out 1 Kgs 5:17
the LORD and the **k** house and all that 1 Kgs 9:1
house of the LORD and the **k** house, 1 Kgs 9:10
of the LORD and for the **k** house, 1 Kgs 10:12
and the **k** traders received them 1 Kgs 10:28
so through the **k** traders they were 1 Kgs 10:29
and the **k** hand was restored to him 1 Kgs 13:6
and the treasures of the **k** house. 1 Kgs 14:26
who kept the door of the **k** house. 1 Kgs 14:27
treasures of the **k** house and gave 1 Kgs 15:18
citadel of the **k** house and burned 1 Kgs 16:18
and burned the **k** house over him 1 Kgs 16:18
of the city and to Joash the **k** son, 1 Kgs 22:26
"O man of God, this is the **k** order, 2 Kgs 1:11
let us go and tell the **k** household." 2 Kgs 7:9
it was told within the **k** household. 2 Kgs 7:11
bury her, for she is a **k** daughter." 2 Kgs 9:34
at this time." Now the **k** sons, 2 Kgs 10:6
they took the **k** sons and slaughtered 2 Kgs 10:7
the heads of the **k** sons," he said, 2 Kgs 10:8
from among the **k** sons who were 2 Kgs 11:2
LORD, and he showed them the **k** son. 2 Kgs 11:4
the Sabbath and guard the **k** house 2 Kgs 11:5
he brought out the **k** son and put 2 Kgs 11:12
the horses' entrance to the **k** house, 2 Kgs 11:16
the gate of the guards to the **k** house. 2 Kgs 11:19
death with the sword at the **k** house. 2 Kgs 11:20
the **k** secretary and the high priest 2 Kgs 12:10
of the LORD and of the **k** house, 2 Kgs 12:18
laid his hands on the **k** hands. 2 Kgs 13:16
and in the treasuries of the **k** house, 2 Kgs 14:14
And Jotham the **k** son was over the 2 Kgs 15:5
citadel of the **k** house with Argob 2 Kgs 15:25
the treasures of the **k** house and sent 2 Kgs 16:8
offering and the **k** burnt offering 2 Kgs 16:15
and in the treasuries of the **k** house. 2 Kgs 18:15
not a word, for the **k** command was, 2 Kgs 18:36
secretary, and Asaiah the **k** servant, 2 Kgs 22:12
and the treasures of the **k** house, 2 Kgs 24:13
to Babylon. The **k** mother, 2 Kgs 24:15
The king's mother, the **k** wives, his 2 Kgs 24:15
the two walls, by the **k** garden, 2 Kgs 25:4
the LORD and the **k** house and all the 2 Kgs 25:9
five men of the **k** council who were 2 Kgs 25:19
life he dined regularly at the **k** table, 2 Kgs 25:29
They lived there in the **k** service. 1 Chr 4:23
they were in the **k** gate on the east 1 Chr 9:18
But the **k** word prevailed against 1 Chr 21:4
for the **k** command was abhorrent to 1 Chr 21:6
were the sons of Heman the **k** seer, 1 Chr 25:5
Over the **k** treasuries was Azmaveth 1 Chr 27:25
of Hachmoni attended the **k** sons. 1 Chr 27:32
Ahithophel was the **k** counselor, 1 Chr 27:33
Hushai the Archite was the **k** friend. 1 Chr 27:33
was commander of the **k** army. 1 Chr 27:34
and the officers over the **k** work. 1 Chr 29:6
and the **k** traders would buy them 2 Chr 1:16
house of the LORD and the **k** house. 2 Chr 7:11
of the LORD and for the **k** house, 2 Chr 9:11
For the **k** ships went to Tarshish 2 Chr 9:21
LORD and the treasures of the **k** house. 2 Chr 12:9
who kept the door of the **k** house. 2 Chr 12:10
the LORD and the **k** house and sent 2 Chr 16:2
of the city and to Joash the **k** son, 2 Chr 18:25
house of Judah, in all the **k** matters, 2 Chr 19:11
found that belonged to the **k** house, 2 Chr 21:17
from among the **k** sons who were 2 Chr 22:11
said to them, "Behold, the **k** son! 2 Chr 23:3
shall be at the **k** house and one third 2 Chr 23:5
they brought out the **k** son and put 2 Chr 23:11
of the horse gate of the **k** house, 2 Chr 23:15
the upper gate to the **k** house. 2 Chr 23:20
was brought to the **k** officers by the 2 Chr 24:11
the **k** secretary and the officer of the 2 Chr 24:11
also the treasures of the **k** house, 2 Chr 25:24
one of the **k** commanders. 2 Chr 26:11
his son was over the **k** household, 2 Chr 26:21
killed Maaseiah the **k** son and 2 Chr 28:7
and of Gad the **k** seer and of Nathan 2 Chr 29:25
secretary, and Asaiah the **k** servant, 2 Chr 34:20
these were from the **k** possessions. 2 Chr 35:7
according to the **k** command. 2 Chr 35:10
Heman, and Jeduthun the **k** seer; 2 Chr 35:15
fitting for us to witness the **k** dishonor, Ezr 4:14
you may provide it out of the **k** treasury. Ezr 7:20
and before all the **k** mighty officers. Ezr 7:28
also delivered the **k** commissions to the Ezr 8:36
commissions to the **k** satraps and to Ezr 8:36
letter to Asaph, the keeper of the **k** forest, Neh 2:8
the River and gave them the **k** letters. Neh 2:9
to the Fountain Gate and to the **K** Pool, Neh 2:14
of the Pool of Shelah of the **k** garden, Neh 3:15
borrowed money for the **k** tax on our Neh 5:4
was at the **k** side in all matters Neh 11:24
in the court of the garden of the **k** palace. Est 1:5
to come at the **k** command delivered by Est 1:12
(for this was the **k** procedure toward all Est 1:13
of Persia and Media, who saw the **k** face, Est 1:14
will say the same to all the **k** officials, Est 1:18
Then the **k** young men who attended Est 2:2
under custody of Hegai, the **k** eunuch, Est 2:3
So when the **k** order and his edict were Est 2:8
was taken into the **k** palace and put in Est 2:8
chosen young women from the **k** palace, Est 2:9
with her from the harem to the **k** palace. Est 2:13
in custody of Shaashgaz, the **k** eunuch, Est 2:14
except what Hegai the **k** eunuch, Est 2:15
time, Mordecai was sitting at the **k** gate. Est 2:19
as Mordecai was sitting at the **k** gate, Est 2:21
and Teresh, two of the **k** eunuchs, Est 2:21
And all the **k** servants who were at the Est 3:2
who were at the **k** gate bowed down and Est 3:2
Then the **k** servants who were at the Est 3:3
who were at the **k** gate said to Mordecai, Est 3:3
do you transgress the **k** command?" Est 3:3
people, and they do not keep the **k** laws, Est 3:8
it is not to the **k** profit to tolerate them. Est 3:8
those who have charge of the **k** business, Est 3:9
they may put it into the **k** treasuries." Est 3:9
Then the **k** scribes were summoned on Est 3:12
was written to the **k** satraps and to the Est 3:12
and sealed with the **k** signet ring. Est 3:12
to all the **k** provinces with instruction Est 3:13
He went up to the entrance of the **k** gate, Est 4:2
allowed to enter the **k** gate clothed in Est 4:2
wherever the **k** command and his decree Est 4:3
called for Hathach, one of the **k** eunuchs, Est 4:5
square of the city in front of the **k** gate, Est 4:6
to pay into the **k** treasuries for the Est 4:7
"All the **k** servants and the people of the Est 4:11
the people of the **k** provinces know that Est 4:11
yourself that in the **k** palace you will Est 4:13
stood in the inner court of the **k** palace, Est 5:1
king's palace, in front of the **k** quarters, Est 5:1
when Haman saw Mordecai in the **k** gate, Est 5:9
Mordecai the Jew sitting at the **k** gate." Est 5:13
and Teresh, two of the **k** eunuchs, Est 6:2
for this?" The **k** young men who Est 6:3
the outer court of the **k** palace to speak to Est 6:4
And the **k** young men told him, "Haman Est 6:5
over to one of the **k** most noble officials. Est 6:9
Mordecai the Jew who sits at the **k** gate. Est 6:10
Then Mordecai returned to the **k** gate. Est 6:12
the **k** eunuchs arrived and hurried to Est 6:14
of the king, and seal it with the **k** ring, Est 8:8
and sealed with the **k** ring cannot be Est 8:8
The **k** scribes were summoned at that Est 8:9
and sealed it with the **k** signet ring. Est 8:10
horses that were used in the **k** service, Est 8:10
horses that were used in the **k** service, Est 8:14
hurriedly, urged by the **k** command. Est 8:14
wherever the **k** command and his edict Est 8:17
when the **k** command and edict were Est 9:1
For Mordecai was great in the **k** house, Est 9:4
they done in the rest of the **k** provinces! Est 9:12
were in the **k** provinces also gathered Est 9:16
are sharp in the heart of the **k** enemies; Ps 45:5
who deals wisely has the **k** favor, Prv 14:35
A **k** wrath is a messenger of death, and Prv 16:14
In the light of a **k** face there is life, and Prv 16:15
A **k** wrath is like the growling of a Prv 19:12
The **k** heart is a stream of water in the Prv 21:1
forward in the **k** presence or stand Prv 25:6
youth who was to stand in the **k** place. Eccl 4:15
Keep the **k** command, because of God's Eccl 8:2
not a word, for the **k** command was, Is 36:21
came up from the **k** house to the house Jer 26:10
he went down to the **k** house, into the Jer 36:12
commanded Jerahmeel the **k** son and Jer 36:26
into the cistern of Malchiah, the **k** son, Jer 38:6
a eunuch who was in the **k** house, Jer 38:7

went from the **k** house and said Jer 38:8
by way of the **k** garden through the gate Jer 39:4
Chaldeans burned the **k** house and the Jer 39:8
the **k** daughters and all the people who Jer 41:10
between the two walls, by the **k** garden, Jer 52:7
and the **k** house and all the houses of Jer 52:13
of war, and seven men of the **k** council, Jer 52:25
his life he dined regularly at the **k** table, Jer 52:33
and competent to stand in the **k** palace, Dn 1:4
would not defile himself with the **k** food, Dn 1:8
youths who eat the **k** food be observed Dn 1:13
than all the youths who ate the **k** food. Dn 1:15
on earth who can meet the **k** demand, Dn 2:10
to Arioch, the captain of the **k** guard, Dn 2:14
He declared to Arioch, the **k** captain, Dn 2:15
have made known to us the **k** matter." Dn 2:23
But Daniel remained at the **k** court. Dn 2:49
Because the **k** order was urgent and the Dn 3:22
and the **k** counselors gathered together Dn 3:27
in him, and set aside the **k** command, Dn 3:28
the words were still in the **k** mouth, Dn 4:31
on the plaster of the wall of the **k** palace, Dn 5:5
Then the **k** color changed, and his Dn 5:6
Then all the **k** wise men came in, but Dn 5:8
I rose and went about the **k** business, Dn 8:27
the latter growth after the **k** mowings. Am 7:1
at Bethel, for it is the **k** sanctuary, Am 7:13
the officials and the **k** sons and all who Zep 1:8
of Hananel to the **k** winepresses. Zec 14:10
Blastus, the **k** chamberlain, Acts 12:20
depended on the **k** country for food. Acts 12:20
and they were not afraid of the **k** edict. Heb 11:23

KINGDOM (320)

The beginning of his **k** was Babel, Gn 10:10
brought on me and my **k** a great sin? Gn 20:9
shall be to me a **k** of priests and a holy Ex 19:6
than Agag, and his **k** shall be exalted. Nm 24:7
the **k** of Sihon king of the Amorites Nm 32:33
the Amorites and the **k** of Og king of Nm 32:33
region of Argob, the **k** of Og in Bashan. Dt 3:4
and Edrei, cities of the **k** of Og in Bashan. Dt 3:10
of Gilead, and all Bashan, the **k** of Og, Dt 3:13
when he sits on the throne of his **k**, Dt 17:18
so that he may continue long in his **k**, Dt 17:20
all the **k** of Og in Bashan, who reigned Jos 13:12
and all the **k** of Sihon king of the Jos 13:21
the rest of the **k** of Sihon king of Jos 13:27
the whole **k** of Og king of Bashan, Jos 13:30
the cities of the **k** of Og in Bashan. Jos 13:31
But about the matter of the **k**, 1 Sm 10:16
go to Gilgal and there renew the **k**." 1 Sm 11:14
have established your **k** over Israel 1 Sm 13:13
But now your **k** shall not continue. 1 Sm 13:14
LORD has torn the **k** of Israel from 1 Sm 15:28
what more can he have but the **k**?" 1 Sm 18:8
you nor your **k** shall be established. 1 Sm 20:31
and that the **k** of Israel shall be 1 Sm 24:20
LORD has torn the **k** out of your hand 1 Sm 28:17
to transfer the **k** from the house of 2 Sm 3:10
"I and my **k** are forever guiltless 2 Sm 3:28
he had exalted his **k** for the sake of 2 Sm 5:12
your body, and I will establish his **k**. 2 Sm 7:12
establish the throne of his **k** forever. 2 Sm 7:13
your house and your **k** shall be made 2 Sm 7:16
will give me back the **k** of my father.'" 2 Sm 16:3
LORD has given the **k** into the hand of 2 Sm 16:8
and his **k** was firmly established. 1 Kgs 2:12
said, "You know that the **k** was mine, 1 Kgs 2:15
the **k** has turned about and become 1 Kgs 2:15
Ask for him the **k** also, for he is my 1 Kgs 2:22
So the **k** was established in the hand 1 Kgs 2:46
like of it was never made in any **k**. 1 Kgs 10:20
will surely tear the **k** from you and 1 Kgs 11:11
I will not tear away all the **k**, 1 Kgs 11:13
about to tear the **k** from the hand of 1 Kgs 11:31
not take the whole **k** out of his hand, 1 Kgs 11:34
But I will take the **k** out of his son's 1 Kgs 11:35
to restore the **k** to Rehoboam the son 1 Kgs 12:21
"Now the **k** will turn back to the 1 Kgs 12:26
and tore the **k** away from the house of 1 Kgs 14:8
is no nation or **k** where my lord has 1 Kgs 18:10
take an oath of the **k** or nation, 1 Kgs 18:10
and turned the **k** over to David 1 Chr 10:14
gave him strong support in his **k**, 1 Chr 11:10
Hebron to turn the **k** of Saul over to 1 Chr 12:23
and that his **k** was highly exalted for 1 Chr 14:2
from one **k** to another people, 1 Chr 16:20
own sons, and I will establish his **k**. 1 Chr 17:11
in my house and in my **k** forever, 1 Chr 17:14
the throne of the **k** of the LORD over 1 Chr 28:5
I will establish his **k** forever if he 1 Chr 28:7
Yours is the **k**, O LORD, and you are 1 Chr 29:11
of David established himself in his **k**, 2 Chr 1:1
like it was ever made for any **k**. 2 Chr 9:19
Israel, to restore the **k** to Rehoboam. 2 Chr 11:1
They strengthened the **k** of Judah, 2 Chr 11:17
think to withstand the **k** of the LORD 2 Chr 13:8
altars. And the **k** had rest under him. 2 Chr 14:5
LORD established the **k** in his hand. 2 Chr 17:5
Judah, but he gave the **k** to Jehoram, 2 Chr 21:3
had no one able to rule the **k**. 2 Chr 22:9
sin offering for the **k** and for the 2 Chr 29:21
of any nation or **k** has been able to 2 Chr 32:15
him again to Jerusalem into his **k**. 2 Chr 33:13
the establishment of the **k** of Persia, 2 Chr 36:20
throughout all his **k** and also put 2 Chr 36:22
throughout all his **k** and also put Ezr 1:1
Israel or their priests or Levites in my **k**, Ezr 7:13
Even in their own **k**, enjoying your Neh 9:35
the king's face, and sat first in the **k**): Est 1:14
is proclaimed throughout all his **k**, Est 1:20
all the provinces of his **k** to gather all the Est 2:3
throughout the whole **k** of Ahasuerus. Est 3:6
the peoples in all the provinces of your **k**. Est 3:8
have not come to the **k** for such a time Est 4:14
be given you, even to the half of my **k**." Est 5:3
Even to the half of my **k**, it shall be Est 5:6
Even to the half of my **k**, it shall be Est 7:2
the 127 provinces of the **k** of Ahasuerus, Est 9:30
The scepter of your **k** is a scepter of Ps 45:6
the heavens, and his **k** rules over all. Ps 103:19
nation, from one **k** to another people, Ps 105:13
of the glory of your **k** and tell of your Ps 145:11
and the glorious splendor of your **k**. Ps 145:12
Your **k** is an everlasting kingdom, Ps 145:13
Your kingdom is an everlasting **k**, Ps 145:13
though in his own **k** he had been born Eccl 4:14
end, on the throne of David and over his **k**, Is 9:7
Ephraim, and the **k** from Damascus; Is 17:3
city against city, **k** against kingdom; Is 19:2
city against city, kingdom against **k**; Is 19:2
—there is no one there to call it a **k**, Is 34:12
For the nation and **k** that will not serve Is 60:12
I declare concerning a nation or a **k**, Jer 18:7
a nation or a **k** that I will build Jer 18:9
if any nation or **k** will not serve this Jer 27:8
ground in dishonor the **k** and its rulers. Lam 2:2
that the **k** might be humble and not Ezk 17:14
and there they shall be a lowly **k**. Ezk 29:14
and enchanters that were in all his **k**. Dn 1:20
the God of heaven has given the **k**, Dn 2:37
Another **k** inferior to you shall arise Dn 2:39
after you, and yet a third **k** of bronze, Dn 2:39
And there shall be a fourth **k**, strong as Dn 2:40
and partly of iron, it shall be a divided **k**, Dn 2:41
so the **k** shall be partly strong and Dn 2:42
will set up a **k** that shall never be Dn 2:44
nor shall the **k** be left to another people. Dn 2:44
His **k** is an everlasting kingdom, and his Dn 4:3
His kingdom is an everlasting **k**, and his Dn 4:3
Most High rules the **k** of men and gives Dn 4:17
the wise men of my **k** are not able to Dn 4:18
Most High rules the **k** of men and gives Dn 4:25
your **k** shall be confirmed for you from Dn 4:26
is spoken: The **k** has departed from you, Dn 4:31
Most High rules the **k** of men and gives Dn 4:32
and his **k** endures from generation to Dn 4:34
to me, and for the glory of my **k**, Dn 4:36
me, and I was established in my **k**, Dn 4:36
and shall be the third ruler in the **k**." Dn 5:7
is a man in your **k** in whom is the spirit Dn 5:11
and shall be the third ruler in the **k**." Dn 5:16
High God rules the **k** of mankind and Dn 5:21
the days of your **k** and brought it to Dn 5:26
your **k** is divided and given to the Medes Dn 5:28
he should be the third ruler in the **k**. Dn 5:29
And Darius the Mede received the **k**, Dn 5:31
Darius to set over the **k** 120 satraps, Dn 6:1
satraps, to be throughout the whole **k**; Dn 6:1
king planned to set him over the whole **k**. Dn 6:3
against Daniel with regard to the **k**, Dn 6:4
All the presidents of the **k**, the prefects Dn 6:7
his **k** shall never be destroyed, and his Dn 6:26
was given dominion and glory and a **k**, Dn 7:14
and his **k** one that shall not be Dn 7:14
High shall receive the **k** and possess the Dn 7:18
the kingdom and possess the **k** forever, Dn 7:18
came when the saints possessed the **k**. Dn 7:22
beast, there shall be a fourth **k** on earth, Dn 7:23
horns, out of this **k** ten kings shall arise, Dn 7:24
And the **k** and the dominion and the Dn 7:27
their **k** shall be an everlasting kingdom, Dn 7:27
their kingdom shall be an everlasting **k**, Dn 7:27
And at the latter end of their **k**, when the Dn 8:23
The prince of the **k** of Persia withstood Dn 10:13
shall stir up all against the **k** of Greece. Dn 11:2
his **k** shall be broken and divided Dn 11:4
for his **k** shall be plucked up and go to Dn 11:4
come with the strength of his whole **k**, Dn 11:17
daughter of women to destroy the **k**, Dn 11:17
exactor of tribute for the glory of the **k**. Dn 11:20
warning and obtain the **k** by flatteries. Dn 11:21
put an end to the **k** of the house of Israel. Hos 1:4
sanctuary, and it is a temple of the **k**." Am 7:13
of the Lord GOD are upon the sinful **k**, Am 9:8
Esau, and the **k** shall be the LORD'S. Ob 1:21
"Repent, for the **k** of heaven is at hand." Mt 3:2
"Repent, for the **k** of heaven is at hand." Mt 4:17
the gospel of the **k** and healing every Mt 4:23
poor in spirit, for theirs is the **k** of heaven. Mt 5:3
sake, for theirs is the **k** of heaven. Mt 5:10
will be called least in the **k** of heaven, Mt 5:19
will be called great in the **k** of heaven. Mt 5:19
you will never enter the **k** of heaven. Mt 5:20
Your **k** come, your will be done, on Mt 6:10
But seek first the **k** of God and his Mt 6:33
'Lord, Lord,' will enter the **k** of heaven, Mt 7:21
Isaac, and Jacob in the **k** of heaven, Mt 8:11
the sons of the **k** will be thrown into Mt 8:12
the gospel of the **k** and healing every Mt 9:35
go, saying, 'The **k** of heaven is at hand.' Mt 10:7
is least in the **k** of heaven is greater Mt 11:11
Baptist until now the **k** of heaven has Mt 11:12
"Every **k** divided against itself is laid Mt 12:25
himself. How then will his **k** stand? Mt 12:26
then the **k** of God has come upon you. Mt 12:28
to know the secrets of the **k** of heaven, Mt 13:11
the word of the **k** and does not Mt 13:19
"The **k** of heaven may be compared to Mt 13:24
"The **k** of heaven is like a grain of Mt 13:31
"The **k** of heaven is like leaven that a Mt 13:33
the good seed is the children of the **k**. Mt 13:38
will gather out of his **k** all causes of sin Mt 13:41
like the sun in the **k** of their Father. Mt 13:43
"The **k** of heaven is like treasure Mt 13:44
the **k** of heaven is like a merchant in Mt 13:45
the **k** of heaven is like a net that was Mt 13:47
been trained for the **k** of heaven is like Mt 13:52
give you the keys of the **k** of heaven, Mt 16:19
see the Son of Man coming in his **k**." Mt 16:28
"Who is the greatest in the **k** of heaven?" Mt 18:1
you will never enter the **k** of heaven. Mt 18:3
child is the greatest in the **k** of heaven. Mt 18:4
"Therefore the **k** of heaven may be Mt 18:23
for the sake of the **k** of heaven. Mt 19:12
for to such belongs the **k** of heaven." Mt 19:14
will a rich person enter the **k** of heaven. Mt 19:23
for a rich person to enter the **k** of God." Mt 19:24
"For the **k** of heaven is like a master of a Mt 20:1
hand and one at your left, in your **k**." Mt 20:21
prostitutes go into the **k** of God before Mt 21:31
the **k** of God will be taken away from Mt 21:43
"The **k** of heaven may be compared to a Mt 22:2
For you shut the **k** of heaven in Mt 23:13
against nation, and **k** against kingdom, Mt 24:7
against nation, and kingdom against **k**, Mt 24:7
this gospel of the **k** will be proclaimed Mt 24:14
"Then the **k** of heaven will be like ten Mt 25:1
inherit the **k** prepared for you from the Mt 25:34
it new with you in my Father's **k**." Mt 26:29
is fulfilled, and the **k** of God is at hand; Mk 1:15
If a **k** is divided against itself, that Mk 3:24
against itself, that **k** cannot stand. Mk 3:24
been given the secret of the **k** of God, Mk 4:11
"The **k** of God is as if a man should Mk 4:26
what can we compare the **k** of God, Mk 4:30
me, I will give you, up to half of my **k**." Mk 6:23
death until they see the **k** of God after it Mk 9:1
for you to enter the **k** of God with one Mk 9:47
them, for to such belongs the **k** of God. Mk 10:14
does not receive the **k** of God like a Mk 10:15
have wealth to enter the **k** of God!" Mk 10:23
how difficult it is to enter the **k** of God! Mk 10:24
for a rich person to enter the **k** of God." Mk 10:25
Blessed is the coming **k** of our father Mk 11:10
not far from the **k** of God." And after Mk 12:34
against nation, and **k** against kingdom. Mk 13:8
against nation, and kingdom against **k**. Mk 13:8
when I drink it new in the **k** of God." Mk 14:25
also himself looking for the **k** of God, Mk 15:43
and of his **k** there will be no end." Lk 1:33
the good news of the **k** of God to the Lk 4:43
who are poor, for yours is the **k** of God. Lk 6:20
who is least in the **k** of God is greater Lk 7:28
bringing the good news of the **k** of God. Lk 8:1
given to know the secrets of the **k** of God, Lk 8:10
them out to proclaim the **k** of God and to Lk 9:2
spoke to them of the **k** of God and cured Lk 9:11
taste death until they see the **k** of God." Lk 9:27
for you, go and proclaim the **k** of God." Lk 9:60
and looks back is fit for the **k** of God." Lk 9:62
'The **k** of God has come near to you.' Lk 10:9
this, that the **k** of God has come near.' Lk 10:11
hallowed be your name. Your **k** come. Lk 11:2
"Every **k** divided against itself is laid Lk 11:17

against himself, how will his **k** stand? Lk 11:18
then the **k** of God has come upon you. Lk 11:20
Instead, seek his **k**, and these things Lk 12:31
good pleasure to give you the **k**. Lk 12:32
therefore, "What is the **k** of God like? Lk 13:18
"To what shall I compare the **k** of God? Lk 13:20
all the prophets in the **k** of God but you Lk 13:28
and recline at table in the **k** of God. Lk 13:29
who will eat bread in the **k** of God!" Lk 14:15
good news of the **k** of God is preached, Lk 16:16
the Pharisees when the **k** of God would Lk 17:20
"The **k** of God is not coming with signs Lk 17:20
the **k** of God is in the midst of you." Lk 17:21
them, for to such belongs the **k** of God. Lk 18:16
does not receive the **k** of God like a Lk 18:17
who have wealth to enter the **k** of God! Lk 18:24
for a rich person to enter the **k** of God." Lk 18:25
or children, for the sake of the **k** of God, Lk 18:29
they supposed that the **k** of God was to Lk 19:11
receive for himself a **k** and then return. Lk 19:12
he returned, having received the **k**, Lk 19:15
nation, and **k** against kingdom. Lk 21:10
nation, and kingdom against **k**. Lk 21:10
you know that the **k** of God is near. Lk 21:31
it until it is fulfilled in the **k** of God." Lk 22:16
of the vine until the **k** of God comes." Lk 22:18
you, as my Father assigned to me, a **k**, Lk 22:29
at my table in my **k** and sit on thrones Lk 22:30
me when you come into your **k**." Lk 23:42
and he was looking for the **k** of God. Lk 23:51
is born again he cannot see the **k** of God." Jn 3:3
the Spirit, he cannot enter the **k** of God. Jn 3:5
answered, "My **k** is not of this world. Jn 18:36
If my **k** were of this world, my servants Jn 18:36
Jews. But my **k** is not from the world." Jn 18:36
days and speaking about the **k** of God. Acts 1:3
you at this time restore the **k** to Israel?" Acts 1:6
good news about the **k** of God and the Acts 8:12
we must enter the **k** of God. Acts 14:22
persuading them about the **k** of God. Acts 19:8
about proclaiming the **k** will see my Acts 20:25
testifying to the **k** of God and trying Acts 28:23
proclaiming the **k** of God and Acts 28:31
For the **k** of God is not a matter of Rom 14:17
For the **k** of God does not consist in 1 Cor 4:20
will not inherit the **k** of God? 1 Cor 6:9
swindlers will inherit the **k** of God. 1 Cor 6:10
when he delivers the **k** to God the 1 Cor 15:24
blood cannot inherit the **k** of God, 1 Cor 15:50
things will not inherit the **k** of God. Gal 5:21
no inheritance in the **k** of Christ and Eph 5:5
transferred us to the **k** of his beloved Col 1:13
my fellow workers for the **k** of God, Col 4:11
calls you into his own **k** and glory. 1 Thes 2:12
be considered worthy of the **k** of God, 2 Thes 1:5
dead, and by his appearing and his **k**: 2 Tm 4:1
bring me safely into his heavenly **k**. 2 Tm 4:18
of uprightness is the scepter of your **k**. Heb 1:8
for receiving a **k** that cannot be Heb 12:28
to be rich in faith and heirs of the **k**, Jas 2:5
entrance into the eternal **k** of our Lord 2 Pt 1:11
and made us a **k**, priests to his God and Rv 1:6
the tribulation and the **k** and the patient Rv 1:9
have made them a **k** and priests to our Rv 5:10
"The **k** of the world has become the Rv 11:15
world has become the **k** of our Lord Rv 11:15
and the power and the **k** of our God and Rv 12:10
and its **k** was plunged into darkness. Rv 16:10

KINGDOMS (56)
LORD do to all the **k** into which you are Dt 3:21
be a horror to all the **k** of the earth. Dt 28:25
formerly was the head of all those **k**. Jos 11:10
of all the **k** that were oppressing 1 Sm 10:18
over all the **k** from the Euphrates 1 Kgs 4:21
you alone, of all the **k** of the earth; 2 Kgs 19:15
that all the **k** of the earth may know 2 Kgs 19:19
and upon all the **k** of the countries. 1 Chr 29:30
the service of the **k** of the countries." 2 Chr 12:8
fell upon all the **k** of the lands that 2 Chr 17:10
You rule over all the **k** of the nations. 2 Chr 20:6
came on all the **k** of the countries 2 Chr 20:29
has given me all the **k** of the earth, 2 Chr 36:23
has given me all the **k** of the earth, Ezr 1:2
"And you gave them **k** and peoples and Neh 9:22
The nations rage, the **k** totter; he utters Ps 46:6
O **k** of the earth, sing to God; sing Ps 68:32
and on the **k** that do not call upon your Ps 79:6
when peoples gather together, and **k**, to Ps 102:22
of Bashan, and all the **k** of Canaan, Ps 135:11
hand has reached to the **k** of the idols, Is 10:10
The sound of an uproar of **k**, of nations Is 13:4
And Babylon, the glory of **k**, the Is 13:19
made the earth tremble, who shook **k**, Is 14:16
hand over the sea; he has shaken the **k**; Is 23:11
herself with all the **k** of the world on Is 23:17
God, you alone, of all the **k** of the earth; Is 37:16
that all the **k** of the earth may know that Is 37:20
shall no more be called the mistress of **k**. Is 47:5
set you this day over nations and over **k**, Jer 1:10
all the tribes of the **k** of the north, Jer 1:15
and in all their **k** there is none like Jer 10:7
a horror to all the **k** of the earth because Jer 15:4
them a horror to all the **k** of the earth, Jer 24:9
and all the **k** of the world that are on Jer 25:26
against many countries and great **k**. Jer 28:8
them a horror to all the **k** of the earth, Jer 29:18
his army and all the **k** of the earth under Jer 34:1
you a horror to all the **k** of the earth. Jer 34:17
Kedar and the **k** of Hazor that Jer 49:28
nations in pieces; with you I destroy **k**; Jer 51:20
summon against her the **k**, Ararat, Jer 51:27
It shall be the most lowly of the **k**, and Ezk 29:15
and no longer divided into two **k**. Ezk 37:22
in pieces all these **k** and bring them to Dn 2:44
which shall be different from all the **k**, Dn 7:23
the greatness of the **k** under the whole Dn 7:27
arose, four **k** shall arise from his nation, Dn 8:22
Philistines. Are you better than these **k**? Am 6:2
at your nakedness and **k** at your shame. Na 3:5
is to gather nations, to assemble **k**, Zep 3:8
and to overthrow the throne of **k**. I am Hg 2:22
the strength of the **k** of the nations, Hg 2:22
showed him all the **k** of the world and Mt 4:8
and showed him all the **k** of the world in Lk 4:5
who through faith conquered **k**, Heb 11:33

KINGLY (1)
was brought down from his **k** throne, Dn 5:20

KINGS (323)
these **k** made war with Bera king of Gn 14:2
Chedorlaomer and the **k** who were with Gn 14:5
king of Ellasar, four **k** against five. Gn 14:9
and as the **k** of Sodom and Gomorrah Gn 14:10
Chedorlaomer and the **k** who were Gn 14:17
nations, and **k** shall come from you. Gn 17:6
k of peoples shall come from her." Gn 17:16
and **k** shall come from your own body. Gn 35:11
These are the **k** who reigned in the Gn 36:31
They killed the **k** of Midian with the Nm 31:8
Hur, and Reba, the five **k** of Midian. Nm 31:8
the hand of the two **k** of the Amorites who Dt 3:8
LORD your God has done to these two **k**. Dt 3:21
of Bashan, the two **k** of the Amorites, Dt 4:47
And he will give their **k** into your hand, Dt 7:24
to Sihon and Og, the **k** of the Amorites, Dt 31:4
you did to the two **k** of the Amorites who Jos 2:10
As soon as all the **k** of the Amorites who Jos 5:1
and all the **k** of the Canaanites who were Jos 5:1
As soon as all the **k** who were beyond the Jos 9:1
he did to the two **k** of the Amorites who Jos 9:10
Then the five **k** of the Amorites, the king Jos 10:5
for all the **k** of the Amorites who dwell Jos 10:6
These five **k** fled and hid themselves in Jos 10:16
to Joshua, "The five **k** have been found, Jos 10:17
and bring those five **k** out to me from Jos 10:22
and brought those five **k** out to him Jos 10:23
they brought those **k** out to Joshua, Jos 10:24
the necks of these **k**." Then they came Jos 10:24
lowland and the slopes, and all their **k**. Jos 10:40
captured all these **k** and their land Jos 10:42
and to the **k** who were in the northern Jos 11:2
And all these **k** joined their forces and Jos 11:5
And all the cities of those **k**, and all Jos 11:12
the cities of those kings, and all their **k**, Jos 11:12
captured all their **k** and struck them Jos 11:17
made war a long time with all those **k**. Jos 11:18
Now these are the **k** of the land whom Jos 12:1
And these are the **k** of the land whom Jos 12:7
king of Tirzah, one: in all, thirty-one **k**. Jos 12:24
before you, the two **k** of the Amorites; Jos 24:12
"Seventy **k** with their thumbs and their Jgs 1:7
"Hear, O **k**; give ear, O princes; to the LORD Jgs 5:3
"The **k** came, they fought; then fought Jgs 5:19
then fought the **k** of Canaan, at Jgs 5:19
Zebah and Zalmunna, the **k** of Midian." Jgs 8:5
them and captured the two **k** of Midian, Jgs 8:12
garments worn by the **k** of Midian, Jgs 8:26
Edom, against the **k** of Zobah, 1 Sm 14:47
has belonged to the **k** of Judah to this 1 Sm 27:6
when all the **k** who were servants 2 Sm 10:19
year, the time when **k** go out to battle, 2 Sm 11:1
over all the **k** west of the Euphrates. 1 Kgs 4:24
and from all the **k** of the earth, 1 Kgs 4:34
and from all the **k** of the west and 1 Kgs 10:15
excelled all the **k** of the earth 1 Kgs 10:23
exported to all the **k** of the Hittites 1 Kgs 10:29
of the Hittites and the **k** of Syria. 1 Kgs 10:29
of the Chronicles of the **K** of Israel. 1 Kgs 14:19
of the Chronicles of the **K** of Judah? 1 Kgs 14:29
of the Chronicles of the **K** of Judah? 1 Kgs 15:7
of the Chronicles of the **K** of Judah? 1 Kgs 15:23
of the Chronicles of the **K** of Israel? 1 Kgs 15:31
of the Chronicles of the **K** of Israel? 1 Kgs 16:5
of the Chronicles of the **K** of Israel? 1 Kgs 16:14
of the Chronicles of the **K** of Israel? 1 Kgs 16:20
of the Chronicles of the **K** of Israel? 1 Kgs 16:27
anger than all the **k** of Israel who 1 Kgs 16:33
Thirty-two **k** were with him, and 1 Kgs 20:1
drinking with the **k** in the booths, 1 Kgs 20:12
and the thirty-two **k** who helped 1 Kgs 20:16
remove the **k**, each from his post, 1 Kgs 20:24
have heard that the **k** of the house of 1 Kgs 20:31
of the house of Israel are merciful **k**. 1 Kgs 20:31
of the Chronicles of the **K** of Israel? 1 Kgs 22:39
of the Chronicles of the **K** of Judah? 1 Kgs 22:45
of the Chronicles of the **K** of Israel? 2 Kgs 1:18
has called these three **k** to give them 2 Kgs 3:10
has called these three **k** to give them 2 Kgs 3:13
heard that the **k** had come up 2 Kgs 3:21
the **k** have surely fought together and 2 Kgs 3:23
hired against us the **k** of the Hittites 2 Kgs 7:6
the Hittites and the **k** of Egypt to come 2 Kgs 7:6
walked in the way of the **k** of Israel, 2 Kgs 8:18
of the Chronicles of the **K** of Judah? 2 Kgs 8:23
the two **k** could not stand before him. 2 Kgs 10:4
of the Chronicles of the **K** of Israel? 2 Kgs 10:34
took his seat on the throne of the **k**. 2 Kgs 11:19
Ahaziah his fathers, the **k** of Judah, 2 Kgs 12:18
of the Chronicles of the **K** of Judah? 2 Kgs 12:19
of the Chronicles of the **K** of Israel? 2 Kgs 13:8
of the Chronicles of the **K** of Israel? 2 Kgs 13:12
in Samaria with the **k** of Israel. 2 Kgs 13:13
of the Chronicles of the **K** of Israel? 2 Kgs 14:15
in Samaria with the **k** of Israel, 2 Kgs 14:16
of the Chronicles of the **K** of Judah? 2 Kgs 14:18
of the Chronicles of the **K** of Israel? 2 Kgs 14:28
slept with his fathers, the **k** of Israel, 2 Kgs 14:29
of the Chronicles of the **K** of Judah? 2 Kgs 15:6
of the Chronicles of the **K** of Israel. 2 Kgs 15:11
of the Chronicles of the **K** of Israel. 2 Kgs 15:15
of the Chronicles of the **K** of Israel? 2 Kgs 15:21
of the Chronicles of the **K** of Israel. 2 Kgs 15:26
of the Chronicles of the **K** of Israel. 2 Kgs 15:31
of the Chronicles of the **K** of Judah? 2 Kgs 15:36
walked in the way of the **k** of Israel. 2 Kgs 16:3
of the Chronicles of the **K** of Judah? 2 Kgs 16:19
yet not as the **k** of Israel who were 2 Kgs 17:2
the customs that the **k** of Israel had 2 Kgs 17:8
him among all the **k** of Judah after 2 Kgs 18:5
heard what the **k** of Assyria have 2 Kgs 19:11
the **k** of Assyria have laid waste the 2 Kgs 19:17
of the Chronicles of the **K** of Judah? 2 Kgs 20:20
of the Chronicles of the **K** of Judah? 2 Kgs 21:17
of the Chronicles of the **K** of Judah? 2 Kgs 21:25
the priests whom the **k** of Judah had 2 Kgs 23:5
the horses that the **k** of Judah had 2 Kgs 23:11
which the **k** of Judah had made, 2 Kgs 23:12
which **k** of Israel had made, 2 Kgs 23:19
all the days of the **k** of Israel or of the 2 Kgs 23:22
kings of Israel or of the **k** of Judah. 2 Kgs 23:22
of the Chronicles of the **K** of Judah? 2 Kgs 23:28
of the Chronicles of the **K** of Judah? 2 Kgs 24:5
the seats of the **k** who were with him 2 Kgs 25:28
These are the **k** who reigned in the 1 Chr 1:43
written in the Book of the **K** of Israel. 1 Chr 9:1
he rebuked **k** on their account, 1 Chr 16:21
and the **k** who had come were by 1 Chr 19:9
year, the time when **k** go out to battle, 1 Chr 20:1
as none of the **k** had who were before 2 Chr 1:12
exported to all the **k** of the Hittites 2 Chr 1:17
of the Hittites and the **k** of Syria. 2 Chr 1:17
And all the **k** of Arabia and the 2 Chr 9:14
excelled all the **k** of the earth 2 Chr 9:22
And all the **k** of the earth sought the 2 Chr 9:23
over all the **k** from the Euphrates 2 Chr 9:26
the Book of the **K** of Judah and 2 Chr 16:11
in the Book of the **K** of Israel. 2 Chr 20:34
walked in the way of the **k** of Israel, 2 Chr 21:6
the way of the **k** of Israel and have 2 Chr 21:13
David, but not in the tombs of the **k**. 2 Chr 21:20
in the city of David among the **k**, 2 Chr 24:16
not bury him in the tombs of the **k**. 2 Chr 24:25
in the Story of the Book of the **K**. 2 Chr 24:27
the Book of the **K** of Judah and 2 Chr 25:26
burial field that belonged to the **k**, 2 Chr 26:23
the Book of the **K** of Israel and Judah. 2 Chr 27:7
walked in the ways of the **k** of Israel. 2 Chr 28:2
the gods of the **k** of Syria helped 2 Chr 28:23
the Book of the **K** of Judah and 2 Chr 28:26
into the tombs of the **k** of Israel. 2 Chr 28:27
from the hand of the **k** of Assyria. 2 Chr 30:6
"Why should the **k** of Assyria come 2 Chr 32:4
the Book of the **K** of Judah and 2 Chr 32:32
in the Chronicles of the **K** of Israel. 2 Chr 33:18
buildings that the **k** of Judah had 2 Chr 34:11

None of the **k** of Israel had kept 2 Chr 35:18
the Book of the **K** of Israel and 2 Chr 35:27
the Book of the **K** of Israel and Judah. 2 Chr 36:8
city, hurtful to **k** and provinces, Ezr 4:15
this city from of old has risen against **k**, Ezr 4:19
And mighty **k** have been over Ezr 4:20
"Artaxerxes, king of **k**, to Ezra the priest, Ezr 7:12
And for our iniquities we, our **k**, and our Ezr 9:7
given into the hand of the **k** of the lands, Ezr 9:7
his steadfast love before the **k** of Persia, Ezr 9:9
with their **k** and the peoples of the land, Neh 9:24
that has come upon us, upon our **k**, Neh 9:32
the time of the **k** of Assyria until this Neh 9:32
Our **k**, our princes, our priests, and our Neh 9:34
yield goes to the **k** whom you have set Neh 9:37
the Chronicles of the **k** of Media and Est 10:2
with **k** and counselors of the earth who Jb 3:14
looses the bonds of **k** and binds a Jb 12:18
but with **k** on the throne he sets them Jb 36:7
The **k** of the earth set themselves, and the Ps 2:2
Now therefore, O **k**, be wise; be warned, O Ps 2:10
daughters of **k** are among your ladies of Ps 45:9
For behold, the **k** assembled; they came Ps 48:4
"The **k** of the armies—they flee, they Ps 68:12
When the Almighty scatters **k** there, let Ps 68:14
temple at Jerusalem **k** shall bear gifts Ps 68:29
May the **k** of Tarshish and of the Ps 72:10
may the **k** of Sheba and Seba bring Ps 72:10
May all **k** fall down before him, all Ps 72:11
who is to be feared by the **k** of the earth. Ps 76:12
the highest of the **k** of the earth. Ps 89:27
and all the **k** of the earth will fear your Ps 102:15
them; he rebuked **k** on their account, Ps 105:14
frogs, even in the chambers of their **k**. Ps 105:30
he will shatter **k** on the day of his Ps 110:5
your testimonies before **k** and shall Ps 119:46
many nations and killed mighty **k**, Ps 135:10
to him who struck down great **k**, for Ps 136:17
and killed mighty **k**, for his steadfast Ps 136:18
All the **k** of the earth shall give you Ps 138:4
who gives victory to **k**, who rescues Ps 144:10
K of the earth and all peoples, princes Ps 148:11
to bind their **k** with chains and their Ps 149:8
By me **k** reign, and rulers decree what is Prv 8:15
It is an abomination to **k** to do evil, for Prv 16:12
He will stand before **k**; he will not Prv 22:29
but the glory of **k** is to search things Prv 25:2
depth, so the heart of **k** is unsearchable. Prv 25:3
your ways to those who destroy **k**. Prv 31:3
It is not for **k**, O Lemuel, it is not for Prv 31:4
O Lemuel, it is not for **k** to drink wine, Prv 31:4
and the treasure of **k** and provinces. Eccl 2:8
Jotham, Ahaz, and Hezekiah, **k** of Judah. Is 1:1
the land whose two **k** you dread will be Is 7:16
he says: "Are not my commanders all **k**? Is 10:8
thrones all who were **k** of the nations. Is 14:9
All the **k** of the nations lie in glory, each Is 14:18
a son of the wise, a son of ancient **k**"? Is 19:11
in heaven, and the **k** of the earth, Is 24:21
have heard what the **k** of Assyria have Is 37:11
the **k** of Assyria have laid waste all the Is 37:18
him, so that he tramples **k** underfoot; Is 41:2
before him and to loose the belts of **k**, Is 45:1
servant of rulers: "**K** shall see and arise; Is 49:7
K shall be your foster fathers, and their Is 49:23
k shall shut their mouths because of Is 52:15
and **k** to the brightness of your rising. Is 60:3
walls, and their **k** shall minister to you; Is 60:10
nations, with their **k** led in procession. Is 60:11
you shall nurse at the breast of **k**; Is 60:16
righteousness, and all the **k** your glory, Is 62:2
the whole land, against the **k** of Judah, Jer 1:18
they, their **k**, their officials, their priests, Jer 2:26
the LORD, the bones of the **k** of Judah, Jer 8:1
the **k** who sit on David's throne, the Jer 13:13
by which the **k** of Judah enter and by Jer 17:19
the word of the LORD, you **k** of Judah, Jer 17:20
gates of this city **k** and princes who sit Jer 17:25
O **k** of Judah and inhabitants of Jer 19:3
their fathers nor the **k** of Judah have Jer 19:4
and the houses of the **k** of Judah—all Jer 19:13
the treasures of the **k** of Judah into the Jer 20:5
the gates of this house **k** who sit on the Jer 22:4
nations and great **k** shall make slaves Jer 25:14
the cities of Judah, its **k** and officials, Jer 25:18
all the **k** of the land of Uz and all the Jer 25:20
of Uz and all the **k** of the land of the Jer 25:20
all the **k** of Tyre, all the kings of Sidon, Jer 25:22
all the kings of Tyre, all the **k** of Sidon, Jer 25:22
and the **k** of the coastland across the Jer 25:22
all the **k** of Arabia and all the kings of Jer 25:24
Arabia and all the **k** of the mixed tribes Jer 25:24
all the **k** of Zimri, all the kings of Elam, Jer 25:25
all the kings of Zimri, all the **k** of Elam, Jer 25:25
kings of Elam, and all the **k** of Media; Jer 25:25
all the **k** of the north, far and near, one Jer 25:26
nations and great **k** shall make him Jer 27:7
to anger—their **k** and their officials, Jer 32:32
the houses of the **k** of Judah that were Jer 33:4
the former **k** who were before you, Jer 34:5
of your fathers, the evil of the **k** of Judah, Jer 44:9
and our fathers, our **k** and our officials, Jer 44:17
your fathers, your **k** and your officials, Jer 44:21
and Egypt and her gods and her **k**, Jer 46:25
nation and many **k** are stirring from Jer 50:41
up the spirit of the **k** of the Medes, Jer 51:11
for war against her, the **k** of the Medes, Jer 51:28
the seats of the **k** who were with him Jer 52:32
The **k** of the earth did not believe, nor Lam 4:12
king of Babylon, king of **k**, Ezk 26:7
you enriched the **k** of the earth. Ezk 27:33
the hair of their **k** bristles with horror; Ezk 27:35
I exposed you before **k**, to feast their Ezk 28:17
the hair of their **k** shall bristle with Ezk 32:10
is there, her **k** and all her princes, Ezk 32:29
holy name, neither they, nor their **k**, Ezk 43:7
dead bodies of their **k** at their high Ezk 43:7
the dead bodies of their **k** far from me, Ezk 43:9
seasons; he removes **k** and sets up kings; Dn 2:21
seasons; he removes kings and sets up **k**; Dn 2:21
You, O king, the king of **k**, to whom the Dn 2:37
in the days of those **k** the God of heaven Dn 2:44
your God is God of gods and Lord of **k**, Dn 2:47
great beasts are four **k** who shall arise Dn 7:17
out of this kingdom ten **k** shall arise, Dn 7:24
former ones, and shall put down three **k**. Dn 7:24
these are the **k** of Media and Persia. Dn 8:20
who spoke in your name to our **k**, Dn 9:6
us, O Lord, belongs open shame, to our **k**, Dn 9:8
for I was left there with the **k** of Persia, Dn 10:13
three more **k** shall arise in Persia, Dn 11:2
And as for the two **k**, their hearts shall Dn 11:27
Jotham, Ahaz, and Hezekiah, **k** of Judah, Hos 1:1
their rulers. All their **k** have fallen, Hos 7:7
They made **k**, but not through me. They Hos 8:4
Jotham, Ahaz, and Hezekiah, **k** of Judah, Mi 1:1
be a deceitful thing to the **k** of Israel. Mi 1:14
At **k** they scoff, and at rulers they Hab 1:10
before governors and **k** for my sake, Mt 10:18
From whom do **k** of the earth take toll Mt 17:25
before governors and **k** for my sake, Mk 13:9
that many prophets and **k** desired to see Lk 10:24
be brought before **k** and governors for Lk 21:12
"The **k** of the Gentiles exercise lordship Lk 22:25
The **k** of the earth set themselves, and Acts 4:26
the Gentiles and **k** and the children Acts 9:15
rich! Without us you have become **k**! 1 Cor 4:8
for **k** and all who are in high positions, 1 Tm 2:2
the King of **k** and Lord of lords, 1 Tm 6:15
the slaughter of the **k** and blessed him, Heb 7:1
of the dead, and the ruler of **k** on earth. Rv 1:5
Then the **k** of the earth and the great Rv 6:15
and nations and languages and **k**." Rv 10:11
prepare the way for the **k** from the east. Rv 16:12
go abroad to the **k** of the whole world, Rv 16:14
with whom the **k** of the earth have Rv 17:2
they are also seven **k**, five of whom Rv 17:10
that you saw are ten **k** who have not yet Rv 17:12
to receive authority as **k** for one hour, Rv 17:12
for he is Lord of lords and King of **k**, Rv 17:14
has dominion over the **k** of the earth." Rv 17:18
and the **k** of the earth have committed Rv 18:3
And the **k** of the earth, who committed Rv 18:9
written, King of **k** and Lord of lords. Rv 19:16
to eat the flesh of **k**, the flesh of Rv 19:18
the beast and the **k** of the earth with Rv 19:19
and the **k** of the earth will bring their Rv 21:24

KINGS' (3)
in your hands, yet it is in **k** palaces. Prv 30:28
who wear soft clothing are in **k** houses. Mt 11:8
and live in luxury are in **k** courts. Lk 7:25

KINGSHIP (6)
people the rights and duties of the **k**, 1 Sm 10:25
Saul had taken the **k** over Israel, 1 Sm 14:47
of Israel gave the **k** over Israel forever 2 Chr 13:5
For **k** belongs to the LORD, and he rules Ps 22:28
your father **k** and greatness Dn 5:18
come, **k** for the daughter of Jerusalem. Mi 4:8

KINSFOLK (1)
brought them to their **k** at Jericho, 2 Chr 28:15

KINSMAN (8)
heard that his **k** had been taken Gn 14:14
also brought back his **k** Lot with his Gn 14:16
daughter of my master's **k** for his son. Gn 24:48
told Rachel that he was her father's **k**, Gn 29:12
said to Jacob, "Because you are my **k**, Gn 29:15
to the nearest **k** of his clan, Nm 27:11
set me among the chariots of my **k**, Sg 6:12
Greet my **k** Herodion. Greet those in Rom 16:11

KINSMEN (43)
and my herdsmen, for we are **k**. Gn 13:8
he shall dwell over against all his **k**." Gn 16:12
the way to the house of my master's **k**." Gn 24:27
He settled over against all his **k**. Gn 25:18
he took his **k** with him and pursued Gn 31:23
and Laban with his **k** pitched tents in Gn 31:25
the presence of our **k** point out what I Gn 31:32
it here before my **k** and your kinsmen, Gn 31:37
it here before my kinsmen and your **k**, Gn 31:37
And Jacob said to his **k**, "Gather Gn 31:46
country and called his **k** to eat bread. Gn 31:54
following you, Benjamin, with your **k**; Jgs 5:14
And his **k** by their clans, when the 1 Chr 5:7
And their **k** according to their 1 Chr 5:13
Their **k** belonging to all the clans of 1 Chr 7:5
lived opposite their **k** in Jerusalem, 1 Chr 8:32
kinsmen in Jerusalem, with their **k**. 1 Chr 8:32
sons of Zerah: Jeuel and their **k**, 690. 1 Chr 9:6
and their **k** according to their 1 Chr 9:9
besides their **k**, heads of their fathers' 1 Chr 9:13
and their **k** (Shallum was the chief); 1 Chr 9:17
and his **k** of his fathers' house, 1 Chr 9:19
And their **k** who were in their 1 Chr 9:25
some of their **k** of the Kohathites 1 Chr 9:32
lived opposite their **k** in Jerusalem, 1 Chr 9:38
kinsmen in Jerusalem, with their **k**. 1 Chr 9:38
they were Benjaminites, Saul's **k**. 1 Chr 12:2
Of the Benjaminites, the **k** of Saul, 1 Chr 12:29
and all their **k** under their 1 Chr 12:32
no sons, but only daughters; their **k**, 1 Chr 23:22
and Jeduthun, their sons and **k**, 2 Chr 5:12
the son of Shealtiel with his **k**, Ezr 3:2
together with the rest of their **k**, Ezr 3:8
namely Sherebiah with his sons and **k**, Ezr 8:18
of Merari, with his **k** and their sons, Ezr 8:19
and ten of their **k** with them. Ezr 8:24
out of my sight, as I cast out all your **k**, Jer 7:15
your **k** who did not go out with you Jer 29:16
me and to my **k** be upon Babylon," let Jer 51:35
brothers, even your brothers, your **k**, Ezk 11:15
brothers, my **k** according to the flesh. Rom 9:3
Junia, my **k** and my fellow prisoners. Rom 16:7
and Jason and Sosipater, my **k**. Rom 16:21

KIR (5)
it, carrying its people captive to **K**, 2 Kgs 16:9
because **K** of Moab is laid waste in a Is 15:1
horsemen, and **K** uncovered the shield. Is 22:6
shall go into exile to **K**," says the LORD. Am 1:5
from Caphtor and the Syrians from **K**? Am 9:7

KIR-HARESETH (5)
trees, till only its stones were left in **K**, 2 Kgs 3:25
utterly stricken, for the raisin cakes of **K**. Is 16:7
lyre for Moab, and my inmost self for **K**. Is 16:11
for all Moab; for the men of **K** I mourn. Jer 48:31
moans like a flute for the men of **K**. Jer 48:36

KIRIATH-ARBA (9)
And Sarah died at **K** (that is, Hebron) in Gn 23:2
father Isaac at Mamre, or **K** (that is, Gn 35:27
the name of Hebron formerly was **K**. Jos 14:15
among the people of Judah, **K**, that is, Jos 15:13
Humtah, **K** (that is, Hebron), and Zior: Jos 15:54
hill country of Ephraim, and **K** (that is, Jos 20:7
They gave them **K** (Arba being the Jos 21:11
the name of Hebron was formerly **K**), Jgs 1:10
of Judah lived in **K** and its villages, Neh 11:25

KIRIATH-ARIM (1)
The sons of **K**, Chephirah, and Beeroth, Ezr 2:25

KIRIATH-BAAL (2)
K (that is, Kiriath-jearim), and Jos 15:60
Beth-horon, and it ends at **K** (that is, Jos 18:14

KIRIATH-HUZOTH (1)
went with Balak, and they came to **K**. Nm 22:39

KIRIATH-JEARIM (19)
Gibeon, Chephirah, Beeroth, and **K**. Jos 9:17
bends around to Baalah (that is, **K**). Jos 15:9
Kiriath-baal (that is, **K**), and Rabbah: Jos 15:60
K), a city belonging to the people of Jos 18:14
side begins at the outskirts of **K**. Jos 18:15
Gibeah and **K**—fourteen cities with Jos 18:28
went up and encamped at **K** in Judah. Jgs 18:12
to this day; behold, it is west of **K**. Jgs 18:12
messengers to the inhabitants of **K**, 1 Sm 6:21
And the men of **K** came and took up 1 Sm 7:1
the day that the ark was lodged at **K**, 1 Sm 7:2
of Ephrathah: Shobal the father of **K**, 1 Chr 2:50
the father of **K** had other sons: 1 Chr 2:52
And the clans of **K**: the Ithrites, the 1 Chr 2:53
to bring the ark of God from **K**. 1 Chr 13:5
that is, to **K** that belongs to Judah, 1 Chr 13:6
the ark of God from **K** to the place that 2 Chr 1:4

The men of **K**, Chephirah, and — Neh 7:29
Uriah the son of Shemaiah from **K**. — Jer 26:20

KIRIATH-SANNAH (1)
Dannah, **K** (that is, Debir), — Jos 15:49

KIRIATH-SEPHER (4)
the name of Debir formerly was **K**. — Jos 15:15
"Whoever strikes **K** and captures it, — Jos 15:16
The name of Debir was formerly **K**. — Jgs 1:11
said, "He who attacks **K** and captures it, — Jgs 1:12

KIRIATHAIM (6)
of Reuben built Heshbon, Elealeh, **K**, — Nm 32:37
and **K**, and Sibmah, and Zereth-shahar — Jos 13:19
and **K** with its pasturelands. — 1 Chr 6:76
K is put to shame, it is taken; the fortress — Jer 48:1
and **K**, and Beth-gamul, and — Jer 48:23
Beth-jeshimoth, Baal-meon, and **K**. — Ezk 25:9

KISH (22)
man of Benjamin whose name was **K**, — 1 Sm 9:1
Now the donkeys of **K**, Saul's father, — 1 Sm 9:3
So **K** said to Saul his son, "Take one of — 1 Sm 9:3
"What has come over the son of **K**? — 1 Sm 10:11
Saul the son of **K** was taken by lot. — 1 Sm 10:21
K was the father of Saul, and Ner the — 1 Sm 14:51
in Zela, in the tomb of **K** his father. — 2 Sm 21:14
Abdon, then Zur, **K**, Baal, Nadab, — 1 Chr 8:30
Ner was the father of **K**, Kish of Saul, — 1 Chr 8:33
Ner was the father of Kish, **K** of Saul, — 1 Chr 8:33
son Abdon, then Zur, **K**, Baal, — 1 Chr 9:36
Ner fathered **K**, Kish fathered Saul, — 1 Chr 9:39
Ner fathered Kish, **K** fathered Saul, — 1 Chr 9:39
freely because of Saul the son of **K**. — 1 Chr 12:1
The sons of Mahli: Eleazar and **K**. — 1 Chr 23:21
their kinsmen, the sons of **K**, — 1 Chr 23:22
Of **K**, the sons of Kish: Jerahmeel. — 1 Chr 24:29
Of Kish, the sons of **K**: Jerahmeel. — 1 Chr 24:29
Saul the son of **K** and Abner the son — 1 Chr 26:28
sons of Merari, **K** the son of Abdi, — 2 Chr 29:12
the son of Jair, son of Shimei, son of **K**, — Est 2:5
and God gave them Saul the son of **K**, — Acts 13:21

KISHI (1)
Ethan the son of **K**, son of Abdi, son — 1 Chr 6:44

KISHION (2)
Rabbith, **K**, Ebez, — Jos 19:20
of Issachar, **K** with its pasturelands, — Jos 21:28

KISHON (6)
you by the river **K** with his chariots and — Jgs 4:7
from Harosheth-hagoyim to the river **K**. — Jgs 4:13
The torrent **K** swept them away, the — Jgs 5:21
away, the ancient torrent, the torrent **K**. — Jgs 5:21
to the brook **K** and slaughtered — 1 Kgs 18:40
as to Sisera and Jabin at the river **K**, — Ps 83:9

KISS (21)
said to him, "Come near and **k** me, — Gn 27:26
not permit me to **k** my sons and my — Gn 31:28
and take hold of him and **k** him. — 2 Sm 15:5
beard with his right hand to **k** him. — 2 Sm 20:9
"Let me **k** my father and my — 1 Kgs 19:20
K the Son, lest he be angry, and you — Ps 2:12
righteousness and peace **k** each other. — Ps 85:10
Let him **k** me with the kisses of his — Sg 1:2
If I found you outside, I would **k** you, and — Sg 8:1
who offer human sacrifice **k** calves!" — Hos 13:2
saying, "The one I will **k** is the man; — Mt 26:48
saying, "The one I will **k** is the man. — Mk 14:44
You gave me no **k**, but from the time I — Lk 7:45
came in she has not ceased to **k** my feet. — Lk 7:45
them. He drew near to Jesus to **k** him, — Lk 22:47
you betray the Son of Man with a **k**?" — Lk 22:48
Greet one another with a holy **k**. All — Rom 16:16
Greet one another with a holy **k**. — 1 Cor 16:20
Greet one another with a holy **k**. — 2 Cor 13:12
Greet all the brothers with a holy **k**. — 1 Thes 5:26
Greet one another with the **k** of love. — 1 Pt 5:14

KISSED (23)
So he came near and **k** him. And Isaac — Gn 27:27
Then Jacob **k** Rachel and wept aloud. — Gn 29:11
embraced him and **k** him and — Gn 29:13
Laban arose and **k** his grandchildren — Gn 31:55
him and fell on his neck and **k** him, — Gn 33:4
And he **k** all his brothers and wept — Gn 45:15
and he **k** them and embraced them. — Gn 48:10
face and wept over him and **k** him. — Gn 50:1
him at the mountain of God and **k** him. — Ex 4:27
and bowed down and **k** him. — Ex 18:7
house of her husband!" Then she **k** them, — Ru 1:9
again. And Orpah **k** her mother-in-law, — Ru 1:14
it on his head and **k** him and said, — 1 Sm 10:1
And they **k** one another and wept — 1 Sm 20:41
the king, and the king **k** Absalom. — 2 Sm 14:33
And the king **k** Barzillai and blessed — 2 Sm 19:39
every mouth that has not **k** him." — 1 Kgs 19:18
enticed, and my mouth has **k** my hand, — Jb 31:27
"Greetings, Rabbi!" And he **k** him. — Mt 26:49
once and said, "Rabbi!" And he **k** him. — Mk 14:45
of her head and **k** his feet and anointed — Lk 7:38
and ran and embraced him and **k** him. — Lk 15:20
all; they embraced Paul and **k** him, — Acts 20:37

KISSES (4)
She seizes him and **k** him, and with — Prv 7:13
gives an honest answer **k** the lips. — Prv 24:26
a friend; profuse are the **k** of an enemy. — Prv 27:6
Let him kiss me with the **k** of his mouth! — Sg 1:2

KITCHENS (1)
"These are the **k** where those who — Ezk 46:24

KITE (2)
the **k**, the falcon of any kind, — Lv 11:14
the **k**, the falcon of any kind; — Dt 14:13

KITRON (1)
did not drive out the inhabitants of **K**, — Jgs 1:30

KITTIM (4)
Elishah, Tarshish, **K**, and Dodanim. — Gn 10:4
shall come from **K** and shall afflict — Nm 24:24
Elishah, Tarshish, **K**, and Rodanim. — 1 Chr 1:7
For ships of **K** shall come against him, — Dn 11:30

KIYYUN (1)
and **K** your star-god—your images that — Am 5:26

KNAPSACK (3)
Carry no moneybag, no **k**, no sandals, — Lk 10:4
out with no moneybag or **k** or sandals, — Lk 22:35
a moneybag take it, and likewise a **k**. — Lk 22:36

KNEAD (2)
of fine flour! **K** it, and make cakes." — Gn 18:6
kindle fire, and the women **k** dough, — Jer 7:18

KNEADED (2)
she took flour and **k** it and baked — 1 Sm 28:24
she took dough and **k** it and made — 2 Sm 13:8

KNEADING (5)
and into your ovens and your **k** bowls. — Ex 8:3
their **k** bowls being bound up in their — Ex 12:34
shall be your basket and your **k** bowl. — Dt 28:5
shall be your basket and your **k** bowl. — Dt 28:17
from the **k** of the dough until it is — Hos 7:4

KNEE (5)
"Bow the **k**!" Thus he set him over all — Gn 41:43
'To me every **k** shall bow, every tongue — Is 45:23
who have not bowed the **k** to Baal." — Rom 11:4
the Lord, every **k** shall bow to me, — Rom 14:11
the name of Jesus every **k** should bow, — Phil 2:10

KNEE-DEEP (1)
led me through the water, and it was **k**. — Ezk 47:4

KNEEL (2)
he made the camels **k** down outside the — Gn 24:11
let us **k** before the LORD, our Maker! — Ps 95:6

KNEELING (6)
came up to him and, **k** before him, — Mt 17:14
and **k** before him she asked him for — Mt 20:20
And **k** before him, they mocked him, — Mt 27:29
him, imploring him, and **k** said to him, — Mk 1:40
on him and **k** down in homage — Mk 15:19
And **k** down on the beach, we prayed — Acts 21:5

KNEELS (1)
every one who **k** down to drink." — Jgs 7:5

KNEES (24)
Then Joseph removed them from his **k**, — Gn 48:12
will strike you on the **k** and on the legs — Dt 28:35
She made him sleep on her **k**. And she — Jgs 16:19
earth and put his face between his **k**. — 1 Kgs 18:42
all the **k** that have not bowed to — 1 Kgs 19:18
and fell on his **k** before Elijah and — 2 Kgs 1:13
he knelt on his **k** in the presence of — 2 Chr 6:13
and fell upon my **k** and spread out my — Ezr 9:5
Why did the **k** receive me? Or why the — Jb 3:12
and you have made firm the feeble **k**. — Jb 4:4
My **k** are weak through fasting; my — Ps 109:24
weak hands, and make firm the feeble **k**. — Is 35:3
upon her hip, and bounced upon her **k**. — Is 66:12
are feeble, and all **k** turn to water. — Ezk 7:17
faint, and all **k** will be weak as water. — Ezk 21:7
gave way, and his **k** knocked together. — Dn 5:6
He got down on his **k** three times a day — Dn 6:10
set me trembling on my hands and **k**. — Dn 10:10
Hearts melt and **k** tremble; anguish is — Na 2:10
So the servant fell on his **k**, imploring — Mt 18:26
Peter saw it, he fell down at Jesus' **k**, — Lk 5:8
And falling to his **k** he cried out with a — Acts 7:60
reason I bow my **k** before the Father, — Eph 3:14
hands and strengthen your weak **k**, — Heb 12:12

KNELT (10)
rest of the people **k** down to drink water. — Jgs 7:6
where he had **k** with hands — 1 Kgs 8:54
Then he **k** on his knees in the — 2 Chr 6:13
a leper came to him and **k** before him, — Mt 8:2
a ruler came in and **k** before him, — Mt 9:18
But she came and **k** before him, — Mt 15:25
man ran up and **k** before him and — Mk 10:17
stone's throw, and **k** down and prayed, — Lk 22:41
all outside, and **k** down and prayed; — Acts 9:40
he **k** down and prayed with them all. — Acts 20:36

KNEW (90)
opened, and they **k** that they were naked. — Gn 3:7
Now Adam **k** Eve his wife, and she — Gn 4:1
Cain **k** his wife, and she conceived and — Gn 4:17
And Adam **k** his wife again, and she — Gn 4:25
So Noah **k** that the waters had subsided — Gn 8:11
from his wine and **k** what his youngest — Gn 9:24
But Onan **k** that the offspring would not — Gn 38:9
God saw the people of Israel—and God **k**. — Ex 2:25
of the evil diseases of Egypt, which you **k**, — Dt 7:15
the LORD from the day that I **k** you. — Dt 9:24
Moses, whom the LORD **k** face to face, — Dt 34:10
Then Manoah **k** that he was the angel — Jgs 13:21
And they **k** her and abused her all — Jgs 19:25
And Elkanah **k** Hannah his wife, and — 1 Sm 1:19
forever, for the iniquity that he **k**, — 1 Sm 3:13
Dan to Beersheba **k** that Samuel was — 1 Sm 3:20
when all who **k** him previously saw — 1 Sm 10:11
when Saul saw and **k** that the LORD — 1 Sm 18:28
If I **k** that it was determined by my — 1 Sm 20:9
So Jonathan **k** that his father was — 1 Sm 20:33
But the boy **k** nothing. Only — 1 Sm 20:39
Jonathan and David **k** the matter. — 1 Sm 20:39
and they **k** that he fled and did not — 1 Sm 22:17
said to Abiathar, "I **k** on that day, — 1 Sm 22:22
David **k** that Saul was plotting harm — 1 Sm 23:9
No man saw it or **k** it, nor did any — 1 Sm 26:12
a robe." And Saul **k** that it was — 1 Sm 28:14
And David **k** that the LORD had — 2 Sm 5:12
place where he **k** there were valiant — 2 Sm 11:16
the son of Zeruiah **k** that the king's — 2 Sm 14:1
in their innocence and **k** nothing. — 2 Sm 15:11
to him, but the king **k** her not. — 1 Kgs 1:4
And David **k** that the LORD had — 1 Chr 14:2
Then Manasseh **k** that the LORD was — 2 Chr 33:13
for you **k** that they acted arrogantly — Neh 9:10
the wise men who **k** the times (for this — Est 1:13
and those who **k** me are wholly — Jb 19:13
"Because he **k** no contentment in his — Jb 20:20
Oh, that I **k** where I might find him, that — Jb 23:3
king who no longer **k** how to take — Eccl 4:13
lest you should say, 'Behold, I **k** them.' — Is 48:7
For I **k** that you would surely deal — Is 48:8
"Before I formed you in the womb I **k** you, — Jer 1:5
The LORD made it known to me and I **k**; — Jer 11:18
Then I **k** that this was the word of the — Jer 32:8
of Gedaliah, before anyone **k** of it, — Jer 41:4
and serve other gods that they **k** not, — Jer 44:3
all the men who **k** that their wives had — Jer 44:15
and I **k** that they were cherubim. — Ezk 10:20
until he **k** that the Most High God rules — Dn 5:21
your heart, though you **k** all this, — Dn 5:22
When Daniel **k** that the document had — Dn 6:10
me. They set up princes, but I **k** it not. — Hos 8:4
It was I who **k** you in the wilderness, in — Hos 13:5
done!" For the men **k** that he was — Jon 1:10
for I **k** that you are a gracious God and — Jon 4:2
me, **k** that it was the word of the LORD. — Zec 11:11
but **k** her not until she had given birth — Mt 1:25
will I declare to them, 'I never **k** you; — Mt 7:23
'Master, I **k** you to be a hard man, — Mt 25:24
You **k** that I reap where I have not — Mt 25:26
For he **k** that it was out of envy that — Mt 27:18
demons to speak, because they **k** him. — Mk 1:34
because they **k** that he was the Christ. — Lk 4:41
But he **k** their thoughts, and he said to the — Lk 6:8
that servant who **k** his master's will — Lk 12:47
You **k** that I was a severe man, taking — Lk 19:22
the servants who had drawn the water **k**), — Jn 2:9
himself to them, because he **k** all people — Jn 2:24
man, for he himself **k** what was in man. — Jn 2:25
answered her, "If you **k** the gift of God, — Jn 4:10
The father **k** that was the hour when — Jn 4:53
him lying there and **k** that he had already — Jn 5:6
him, for he himself **k** what he would do. — Jn 6:6
believe." (For Jesus **k** from the beginning — Jn 6:64
If you **k** me, you would know my Father — Jn 8:19
I **k** that you always hear me, but I said — Jn 11:42
orders that if anyone **k** where he was, — Jn 11:57
when Jesus **k** that his hour had come to — Jn 13:1
For he **k** who was to betray him; that — Jn 13:11
no one at the table **k** why he said this to — Jn 13:28
Jesus **k** that they wanted to ask him, so — Jn 16:19
who betrayed him, also **k** the place, — Jn 18:2
"Who are you?" They **k** it was the Lord. — Jn 21:12
for they all **k** that his father was a — Acts 16:3

though he **k** only the baptism of — Acts 18:25
For although they **k** God, they did not — Rom 1:21
he made him to be sin who **k** no sin, — 2 Cor 5:21
since you **k** that you yourselves had a — Heb 10:34
you, although you once fully **k** it, — Jude 1:5

KNIFE (5)
he took in his hand the fire and the **k**. — Gn 22:6
hand and took the **k** to slaughter his — Gn 22:10
when he entered his house, he took a **k**, — Jgs 19:29
and put a **k** to your throat if you are — Prv 23:2
them off with a **k** and throw them into — Jer 36:23

KNIT (5)
soul of Jonathan was **k** to the soul of — 1 Sm 18:1
and **k** me together with bones and — Jb 10:11
the sinews of his thighs are **k** together. — Jb 40:17
be encouraged, being **k** together in love, — Col 2:2
nourished and **k** together through its — Col 2:19

KNITTED (1)
you **k** me together in my mother's — Ps 139:13

KNIVES (3)
"Make flint **k** and circumcise the sons of — Jos 5:2
Joshua made flint **k** and circumcised the — Jos 5:3
teeth are swords, whose fangs are **k**, — Prv 30:14

KNOCK (4)
will find; **k**, and it will be opened to you. — Mt 7:7
will find; **k**, and it will be opened to you. — Lk 11:9
to stand outside and to **k** at the door, — Lk 13:25
Behold, I stand at the door and **k**. If — Rv 3:20

KNOCKED (2)
limbs gave way, and his knees **k** together. — Dn 5:6
And when he **k** at the door of the — Acts 12:13

KNOCKING (2)
was awake. A sound! My beloved is **k**. — Sg 5:2
But Peter continued **k**, and when they — Acts 12:16

KNOCKS (4)
If he **k** out the tooth of his slave, male — Ex 21:27
and to the one who **k** it will be opened. — Mt 7:8
and to the one who **k** it will be opened. — Lk 11:10
to him at once when he comes and **k**. — Lk 12:36

KNOW (958)
Abel your brother?" He said, "I do not **k**; — Gn 4:9
"I **k** that you are a woman beautiful in — Gn 12:11
how am I to **k** that I shall possess it?" — Gn 15:8
"**K** for certain that your offspring will — Gn 15:13
has come to me. And if not, I will **k**." — Gn 18:21
them out to us, that we may **k** them." — Gn 19:5
He did not **k** when she lay down or — Gn 19:33
and he did not **k** when she lay down or — Gn 19:35
I **k** that you have done this in the — Gn 20:6
return her, **k** that you shall surely die, — Gn 20:7
"I do not **k** who has done this thing; — Gn 21:26
to him, for now I **k** that you fear God, — Gn 22:12
By this I shall **k** that you have shown — Gn 24:14
I am old; I do not **k** the day of my death. — Gn 27:2
to **k** whether you are really my son — Gn 27:21
LORD is in this place, and I did not **k** it." — Gn 28:16
"Do you **k** Laban the son of Nahor?" — Gn 29:5
son of Nahor?" They said, "We **k** him." — Gn 29:5
for you **k** the service that I have given — Gn 30:26
"You yourself **k** how I have served you, — Gn 30:29
You **k** that I have served your father — Gn 31:6
Now Jacob did not **k** that Rachel had — Gn 31:32
you," for he did not **k** that she was his — Gn 38:16
Shelah." And he did not **k** her again. — Gn 38:26
They did not **k** that Joseph understood — Gn 42:23
'By this I shall **k** that you are honest — Gn 42:33
Then I shall **k** that you are not spies — Gn 42:34
we in any way **k** that he would say, — Gn 43:7
We do not **k** who put our money in — Gn 43:22
Do you not **k** that a man like me can — Gn 44:15
'You **k** that my wife bore me two sons. — Gn 44:27
seen your face and **k** that you are still — Gn 46:30
and if you **k** any able men among them, — Gn 47:6
But his father refused and said, "I **k**, — Gn 48:19
refused and said, "I know, my son, I **k**. — Gn 48:19
king over Egypt, who did not **k** Joseph. — Ex 1:8
at a distance to **k** what would be done — Ex 2:4
of their taskmasters. I **k** their sufferings, — Ex 3:7
But I **k** that the king of Egypt will not let — Ex 3:19
the Levite? I **k** that he can speak well. — Ex 4:14
I do not **k** the LORD, and moreover, I will — Ex 5:2
and you shall **k** that I am the LORD your — Ex 6:7
The Egyptians shall **k** that I am the LORD, — Ex 7:5
"By this you shall **k** that I am the LORD: — Ex 7:17
so that you may **k** that there is no one — Ex 8:10
that you may **k** that I am the LORD in the — Ex 8:22
so that you may **k** that there is none like — Ex 9:14
so that you may **k** that the earth is the — Ex 9:29
I **k** that you do not yet fear the LORD — Ex 9:30
that you may **k** that I am the LORD." — Ex 10:2
and we do not **k** with what we must — Ex 10:26
that you may **k** that the LORD makes a — Ex 11:7
and the Egyptians shall **k** that I am the — Ex 14:4
And the Egyptians shall **k** that I am the — Ex 14:18
"At evening you shall **k** that it was the — Ex 16:6
Then you shall **k** that I am the LORD — Ex 16:12
is it?" For they did not **k** what it was. — Ex 16:15
Now I **k** that the LORD is greater than all — Ex 18:11
and I make them **k** the statutes of God — Ex 18:16
and make them **k** the way in which — Ex 18:20
You **k** the heart of a sojourner, for you — Ex 23:9
And they shall **k** that I am the LORD — Ex 29:46
generations, that you may **k** that I, — Ex 31:13
we do not **k** what has become of him." — Ex 32:1
You **k** the people, that they are set on — Ex 32:22
we do not **k** what has become of him.' — Ex 32:23
that I may **k** what to do with you.'" — Ex 33:5
have not let me **k** whom you will send — Ex 33:12
Yet you have said, 'I **k** you by name, — Ex 33:12
that I may **k** you in order to find favor — Ex 33:13
in my sight, and I **k** you by name." — Ex 33:17
Moses did not **k** that the skin of his face — Ex 34:29
skill and intelligence to **k** how to do any — Ex 36:1
he has seen or come to **k** the matter, — Lv 5:1
hidden from him, when he comes to **k** it, — Lv 5:3
hidden from him, when he comes to **k** it, — Lv 5:4
not to be done, though he did not **k** it, — Lv 5:17
your generations may **k** that I made — Lv 23:43
for you **k** where we should camp in — Nm 10:31
whom you **k** to be the elders of the — Nm 11:16
and they shall **k** the land that you — Nm 14:31
and you shall **k** my displeasure.' — Nm 14:34
"Hereby you shall **k** that the LORD has — Nm 16:28
then you shall **k** that these men have — Nm 16:30
You **k** all the hardship that we have — Nm 20:14
for I **k** that he whom you bless is — Nm 22:6
that I may **k** what more the LORD will — Nm 22:19
for I did not **k** that you stood in the — Nm 22:34
I will let you **k** what this people will do — Nm 24:14
and your livestock (I **k** that you have — Dt 3:19
that you might **k** that the LORD is God; — Dt 4:35
k therefore today, and lay it to your — Dt 4:39
K therefore that the LORD your God is God, — Dt 7:9
testing you to **k** what was in your heart, — Dt 8:2
fed you with manna, which you did not **k**, — Dt 8:3
you did not know, nor did your fathers **k**, — Dt 8:3
he might make you **k** that man does not — Dt 8:3
K then in your heart that, as a man — Dt 8:5
with manna that your fathers did not **k**, — Dt 8:16
tall, the sons of the Anakim, whom you **k**, — Dt 9:2
K therefore today that he who goes over — Dt 9:3
"**K**, therefore, that the LORD your God is — Dt 9:6
to **k** whether you love the LORD your God — Dt 13:3
'How may we **k** the word that the LORD — Dt 18:21
the trees that you **k** are not trees for — Dt 20:20
live near you and you do not **k** who he is, — Dt 22:2
that you may **k** that I am the LORD your — Dt 29:6
"You **k** how we lived in the land of — Dt 29:16
For I **k** what they are inclined to do — Dt 31:21
For I **k** how rebellious and stubborn — Dt 31:27
For I **k** that after my death you will — Dt 31:29
me, but I did not **k** where they were from. — Jos 2:4
went out. I do not **k** where the men went. — Jos 2:5
"I **k** that the LORD has given you the land, — Jos 2:9
order that you may **k** the way you shall — Jos 3:4
sight of all Israel, that they may **k** that, — Jos 3:7
is how you shall **k** that the living God — Jos 3:10
then you shall let your children **k**, — Jos 4:22
of the earth may **k** that the hand of — Jos 4:24
But he did not **k** that there was an — Jos 8:14
"You **k** what the LORD said to Moses the — Jos 14:6
LORD! He knows; and let Israel itself **k**! — Jos 22:22
"Today we **k** that the LORD is in our — Jos 22:31
k for certain that the LORD your God — Jos 23:13
and you **k** in your hearts and souls, — Jos 23:14
after them who did not **k** the LORD or the — Jgs 2:10
of the people of Israel might **k** war, — Jgs 3:2
to **k** whether Israel would obey the — Jgs 3:4
then I shall **k** that you will save Israel by — Jgs 6:37
(For Manoah did not **k** that he was the — Jgs 13:16
and mother did not **k** that it was from — Jgs 14:4
"Do you not **k** that the Philistines are — Jgs 15:11
free." But he did not **k** that the LORD had — Jgs 16:20
"Now I **k** that the LORD will prosper me, — Jgs 17:13
that we may **k** whether the journey on — Jgs 18:5
"Do you **k** that in these houses there — Jgs 18:14
into your house, that we may **k** him." — Jgs 19:22
Benjaminites did not **k** that disaster — Jgs 20:34
to a people that you did not **k** before. — Ru 2:11
all my fellow townsmen **k** that you are a — Ru 3:11
But if you will not, tell me, that I may **k**, — Ru 4:4
men. They did not **k** the LORD. — 1 Sm 2:12
Now Samuel did not yet **k** the LORD, — 1 Sm 3:7
then we shall **k** that it is not his hand — 1 Sm 6:9
And you shall **k** and see that your — 1 Sm 12:17
the people did not **k** that Jonathan had — 1 Sm 14:3
and **k** and see how this sin has — 1 Sm 14:38
I **k** your presumption and the evil of — 1 Sm 17:28
all the earth may **k** that there is a — 1 Sm 17:46
this assembly may **k** that the LORD — 1 Sm 17:47
your soul lives, O king, I do not **k**." — 1 Sm 17:55
he thinks, 'Do not let Jonathan **k** this, — 1 Sm 20:3
then **k** that harm is determined by — 1 Sm 20:7
do I not **k** that you have chosen the — 1 Sm 20:30
'Let no one **k** anything of the matter — 1 Sm 21:2
you, till I **k** what God will do for me." — 1 Sm 22:3
K and see the place where his foot is, — 1 Sm 23:22
you may **k** and see that there is no — 1 Sm 24:11
I **k** that you shall surely be king, — 1 Sm 24:20
who come from I do not **k** where?" — 1 Sm 25:11
Now therefore **k** this and consider — 1 Sm 25:17
you shall **k** what your servant can — 1 Sm 28:2
"Surely you **k** what Saul has done, — 1 Sm 28:9
"I **k** that you are as blameless in my — 1 Sm 29:9
"How do you **k** that Saul and his son — 2 Sm 1:5
Do you not **k** that the end will be — 2 Sm 2:26
You **k** that Abner the son of Ner — 2 Sm 3:25
deceive you and to **k** your going out — 2 Sm 3:25
in, and to **k** all that you are doing." — 2 Sm 3:25
of Sirah. But David did not **k** about it. — 2 Sm 3:26
"Do you not **k** that a prince and a — 2 Sm 3:38
say to you? For you **k** your servant, — 2 Sm 7:20
greatness, to make your servant **k** it. — 2 Sm 7:21
Did you not **k** that they would shoot — 2 Sm 11:20
angel of God to **k** all things that are — 2 Sm 14:20
with us, since I go I **k** not where? — 2 Sm 15:20
"You **k** that your father and his men — 2 Sm 17:8
but I do not **k** what it was." — 2 Sm 18:29
for today I **k** that if Absalom were — 2 Sm 19:6
For do I not **k** that I am this day king — 2 Sm 19:22
that I may **k** the number of the — 2 Sm 24:2
and David our lord does not **k** it? — 1 Kgs 1:11
you, my lord the king, do not **k** it. — 1 Kgs 1:18
you also **k** what Joab the son of — 1 Kgs 2:5
You will **k** what you ought to do to — 1 Kgs 2:9
"You **k** that the kingdom was mine, — 1 Kgs 2:15
k for certain that you shall die. — 1 Kgs 2:37
'**K** for certain that on the day you go — 1 Kgs 2:42
"You **k** in your own heart all the — 1 Kgs 2:44
I do not **k** how to go out or come in. — 1 Kgs 3:7
"You **k** that David my father could not — 1 Kgs 5:3
for you **k** that there is no one among — 1 Kgs 5:6
render to each whose heart you **k**, — 1 Kgs 8:39
k the hearts of all the children of — 1 Kgs 8:39
of the earth may **k** your name and — 1 Kgs 8:43
and that they may **k** that this house — 1 Kgs 8:43
of the earth may **k** that the LORD is — 1 Kgs 8:60
"Now I **k** that you are a man of God, — 1 Kgs 17:24
LORD will carry you I **k** not where. — 1 Kgs 18:12
me, that this people may **k** that you, — 1 Kgs 18:37
and you shall **k** that I am the LORD." — 1 Kgs 20:13
and you shall **k** that I am the LORD.'" — 1 Kgs 20:28
"Do you **k** that Ramoth-gilead — 1 Kgs 22:3
"Do you **k** that today the LORD will take — 2 Kgs 2:3
over you?" And he said, "Yes, I **k** it; — 2 Kgs 2:3
"Do you **k** that today the LORD will take — 2 Kgs 2:5
you?" And he answered, "Yes, I **k** it; — 2 Kgs 2:5
and you **k** that your servant feared the — 2 Kgs 4:1
I **k** that this is a holy man of God who — 2 Kgs 4:9
k that I have sent to you Naaman my — 2 Kgs 5:6
that he may **k** that there is a prophet in — 2 Kgs 5:8
I **k** that there is no God in all the — 2 Kgs 5:15
to us. They **k** that we are hungry. — 2 Kgs 7:12
"Because I **k** the evil that you will do — 2 Kgs 8:12
them, "You **k** the fellow and his talk." — 2 Kgs 9:11
K then that there shall fall to the — 2 Kgs 10:10
of Samaria do not **k** the law of the — 2 Kgs 17:26
because they do not **k** the law of the — 2 Kgs 17:26
of the earth may **k** that you, — 2 Kgs 19:19
"But I **k** your sitting down and your — 2 Kgs 19:27
times, to **k** what Israel ought to do, — 1 Chr 12:32
servant? For you **k** your servant. — 1 Chr 17:18
a report, that I may **k** their number." — 1 Chr 21:2
k the God of your father and serve — 1 Chr 28:9
I **k**, my God, that you test the heart — 1 Chr 29:17
for I **k** that your servants know how to — 2 Chr 2:8
know that your servants **k** how to cut — 2 Chr 2:8
render to each whose heart you **k**, — 2 Chr 6:30
k the hearts of the children of — 2 Chr 6:30
of the earth may **k** your name and — 2 Chr 6:33
and that they may **k** that this house — 2 Chr 6:33
that they may **k** my service and the — 2 Chr 12:8
Ought you not to **k** that the LORD God — 2 Chr 13:5
against us. We do not **k** what to do, — 2 Chr 20:12
"I **k** that God has determined to — 2 Chr 25:16
Do you not **k** what I and my fathers — 2 Chr 32:13
to test him and to **k** all that was in — 2 Chr 32:31
all such as **k** the laws of your God. — Ezr 7:25
And those who do not **k** them, you shall — Ezr 7:25
the officials did not **k** where I had gone — Neh 2:16
"They will not **k** or see till we come — Neh 4:11

of the king's provinces **k** that if any Est 4:11
You shall **k** that your tent is at peace, Jb 5:24
You shall **k** also that your offspring Jb 5:25
it is true. Hear, and **k** it for your good." Jb 5:27
nor does his place **k** him anymore. Jb 7:10
For we are but of yesterday and **k** nothing, Jb 8:9
"Truly I **k** that it is so: But how can a man Jb 9:2
removes mountains, and they **k** it not, Jb 9:5
for I **k** you will not hold me innocent. Jb 9:28
let me **k** why you contend against me. Jb 10:2
although you **k** that I am not guilty, and Jb 10:7
heart; I **k** that this was your purpose. Jb 10:13
K then that God exacts of you less than Jb 11:6
do? Deeper than Sheol—what can you **k**? Jb 11:8
Who does not **k** such things as these? Jb 12:3
all these does not **k** that the hand of Jb 12:9
What you **k**, I also know; I am not Jb 13:2
What you know, I also **k**; I am not Jb 13:2
my case; I **k** that I shall be in the right. Jb 13:18
Make me **k** my transgression and my Jb 13:23
come to honor, and he does not **k** it; Jb 14:21
What do you **k** that we do not know? Jb 15:9
What do you know that we do not **k**? Jb 15:9
k then that God has put me in the wrong Jb 19:6
For I **k** that my Redeemer lives, and at Jb 19:25
that you may **k** there is a judgment." Jb 19:29
Do you not **k** this from of old, since man Jb 20:4
pay it out to them, that they may **k** it. Jb 21:19
I **k** your thoughts and your schemes to Jb 21:27
But you say, 'What does God **k**? Can he Jb 22:13
I would **k** what he would answer me and Jb 23:5
why do those who **k** him never see his Jb 24:1
themselves up; they do not **k** the light. Jb 24:16
Man does not **k** its worth, and it is not Jb 28:13
out the cause of him whom I did not **k**. Jb 29:16
For I **k** that you will bring me to death Jb 30:23
balance, and let God **k** my integrity!) Jb 31:6
For I do not **k** how to flatter, else my Jb 32:22
and what my lips **k** they speak sincerely. Jb 33:3
wise men, and give ear to me, you who **k**; Jb 34:2
let us **k** among ourselves what is good. Jb 34:4
and not I; therefore declare what you **k**. Jb 34:33
Behold, God is great, and we **k** him not; Jb 36:26
that all men whom he made may **k** it. Jb 37:7
Do you **k** how God lays his command Jb 37:15
Do you **k** the balancings of the clouds, Jb 37:16
its measurements—surely you **k**! Jb 38:5
and caused the dawn to **k** its place, Jb 38:12
of the earth? Declare, if you **k** all this. Jb 38:18
You **k**, for you were born then, and the Jb 38:21
Do you **k** the ordinances of the Jb 38:33
"Do you **k** when the mountain goats give Jb 39:1
and do you **k** the time when they give Jb 39:2
"I **k** that you can do all things, and that Jb 42:2
too wonderful for me, which I did not **k**. Jb 42:3
But **k** that the LORD has set apart the godly Ps 4:3
And those who **k** your name put their Ps 9:10
Let the nations **k** that they are but men! Ps 9:20
Now I **k** that the LORD saves his anointed; Ps 20:6
Make me to **k** your ways, O LORD; teach Ps 25:4
come upon him when he does not **k** it! Ps 35:8
they ask me of things that I do not **k**. Ps 35:11
whom I did not **k** tore at me without Ps 35:15
your steadfast love to those who **k** you, Ps 36:10
make me **k** my end and what is the Ps 39:4
of my days; let me **k** how fleeting I am! Ps 39:4
wealth and does not **k** who will gather! Ps 39:6
I have not restrained my lips, as you **k**, Ps 40:9
By this I **k** that you delight in me: my Ps 41:11
"Be still, and **k** that I am God. I will be Ps 46:10
I **k** all the birds of the hills, and all that Ps 50:11
For I **k** my transgressions, and my sin is Ps 51:3
when I call. This I **k**, that God is for me. Ps 56:9
that they may **k** that God rules over Ps 59:13
O God, you **k** my folly; the wrongs I have Ps 69:5
You **k** my reproach, and my shame Ps 69:19
And they say, "How can God **k**? Is there Ps 73:11
that the next generation might **k** them, Ps 78:6
anger on the nations that do not **k** you, Ps 79:6
that they may **k** that you alone, whose Ps 83:18
Among those who **k** me I mention Ps 87:4
are the people who **k** the festal shout, Ps 89:15
The stupid man cannot **k**; the fool Ps 92:6
K that the LORD, he is God! It is he who Ps 100:3
be far from me; I will **k** nothing of evil. Ps 101:4
Let them **k** that this is your hand; you, Ps 109:27
I **k**, O LORD, that your rules are Ps 119:75
me, that they may **k** your testimonies. Ps 119:79
that I may **k** your testimonies! Ps 119:125
For I **k** that the LORD is great, and that Ps 135:5
You **k** when I sit down and when I rise Ps 139:2
behold, O LORD, you **k** it altogether. Ps 139:4
Search me, O God, and **k** my heart! Ps 139:23
my heart! Try me and **k** my thoughts! Ps 139:23
I **k** that the LORD will maintain the Ps 140:12
spirit faints within me, you **k** my way! Ps 142:3
Make me **k** the way I should go, for to Ps 143:8
other nation; they do not **k** his rules. Ps 147:20
To **k** wisdom and instruction, to Prv 1:2
they do not **k** over what they stumble. Prv 4:19
her ways wander, and she does not **k** it. Prv 5:6
he does not **k** that it will cost him his Prv 7:23
But he does not **k** that the dead are Prv 9:18
of the righteous **k** what is acceptable, Prv 10:32
to make you **k** what is right and true, Prv 22:21
we did not **k** this," does not he who Prv 24:12
who keeps watch over your soul **k** it, Prv 24:12
K that wisdom is such to your soul; if Prv 24:14
for you do not **k** what a day may bring. Prv 27:1
K well the condition of your flocks, Prv 27:23
wealth and does not **k** that poverty will Prv 28:22
what is his son's name? Surely you **k**! Prv 30:4
applied my heart to **k** wisdom and to Eccl 1:17
wisdom and to **k** madness and folly. Eccl 1:17
for they do not **k** that they are doing Eccl 5:1
turned my heart to **k** and to search out Eccl 7:25
and to **k** the wickedness of folly and Eccl 7:25
keeps a command will **k** no evil thing, Eccl 8:5
the wise heart will **k** the proper time and Eccl 8:5
For he does not **k** what is to be, for who Eccl 8:7
yet I **k** that it will be well with those Eccl 8:12
When I applied my heart to **k** wisdom, Eccl 8:16
Even though a wise man claims to **k**, Eccl 8:17
it is love or hate, man does not **k**; Eccl 9:1
For the living **k** that they will die, but Eccl 9:5
they will die, but the dead **k** nothing, Eccl 9:5
For man does not **k** his time. Like fish Eccl 9:12
for he does not **k** the way to the city. Eccl 10:15
for you **k** not what disaster may Eccl 11:2
As you do not **k** the way the spirit Eccl 11:5
so you do not **k** the work of God who Eccl 11:5
for you do not **k** which will prosper, Eccl 11:6
But **k** that for all these things God will Eccl 11:9
If you do not **k**, O most beautiful among Sg 1:8
its master's crib, but Israel does not **k**, Is 1:3
near, and let it come, that we may **k** it!" Is 5:19
and all the people will **k**, Ephraim and the Is 9:9
you that they might **k** what the LORD of Is 19:12
and the Egyptians will **k** the LORD in that Is 19:21
heart of the hasty will understand and **k**, Is 32:4
of the earth may **k** that you alone are Is 37:20
"'I **k** your sitting down and your going Is 37:28
Do you not **k**? Do you not hear? Has it Is 40:21
that they may see and **k**, may consider Is 41:20
them, that we may **k** their outcome; Is 41:22
that we may **k** that you are gods; Is 41:23
it from the beginning, that we might **k**, Is 41:26
the blind in a way that they do not **k**, Is 42:16
that you may **k** and believe me and Is 43:10
me? There is no Rock; I **k** not any." Is 44:8
Their witnesses neither see nor **k**, that Is 44:9
They **k** not, nor do they discern, for he Is 44:18
secret places, that you may **k** that it is I, Is 45:3
I name you, though you do not **k** me. Is 45:4
God; I equip you, though you do not **k** me, Is 45:5
that people may **k**, from the rising of the Is 45:6
sit as a widow or **k** the loss of children": Is 47:8
which you will not **k** how to charm Is 47:11
you suddenly, of which you **k** nothing. Is 47:11
Because I **k** that you are obstinate, and Is 48:4
Then you will **k** that I am the LORD; Is 49:23
Then all flesh shall **k** that I am the LORD Is 49:26
that I may **k** how to sustain with a word Is 50:4
and I **k** that I shall not be put to shame. Is 50:7
"Listen to me, you who **k** righteousness, Is 51:7
Therefore my people shall **k** my name. Is 52:6
in that day they shall **k** that it is I who Is 52:6
you shall call a nation that you do not **k**, Is 55:5
a nation that did not **k** you shall run to Is 55:5
seek me daily and delight to **k** my ways, Is 58:2
The way of peace they do not **k**, and there Is 59:8
are with us, and we **k** our iniquities: Is 59:12
and you shall **k** that I, the LORD, am your Is 60:16
Father, though Abraham does not **k** us, Is 63:16
"For I **k** their works and their thoughts, Is 66:18
Behold, I do not **k** how to speak, for I am Jer 1:6
Those who handle the law did not **k** me; Jer 2:8
K and see that it is evil and bitter for you Jer 2:19
k what you have done—a restless young Jer 2:23
my people are foolish; they **k** me not; Jer 4:22
evil! But how to do good they **k** not." Jer 4:22
for they do not **k** the way of the LORD, the Jer 5:4
to them, for they **k** the way of the LORD, Jer 5:5
a nation whose language you do not **k**, Jer 5:15
They **k** no bounds in deeds of evil; they Jer 5:28
ashamed; they did not **k** how to blush. Jer 6:15
Therefore hear, O nations, and **k**, O Jer 6:18
that you may **k** and test their ways. Jer 6:27
but my people **k** not the rules of the LORD. Jer 8:7
ashamed; they did not **k** how to blush. Jer 8:12
from evil to evil, and they do not **k** me, Jer 9:3
deceit upon deceit, they refuse to **k** me, Jer 9:6
I **k**, O LORD, that the way of man is not Jer 10:23
wrath on the nations that **k** you not, Jer 10:25
I did not **k** it was against me they Jer 11:19
But you, O LORD, **k** me; you see me, and Jer 12:3
'Do we not indeed **k** that every jar will Jer 13:12
enemies in a land that you do not **k**, Jer 15:14
O LORD, you **k**; remember me and visit Jer 15:15
k that for your sake I bear reproach. Jer 15:15
"Therefore, behold, I will make them **k**, Jer 16:21
I will make them **k** my power and my Jer 16:21
and they shall **k** that my name is the Jer 16:21
enemies in a land that you do not **k**, Jer 17:4
You **k** what came out of my lips; it was Jer 17:16
O LORD, **k** all their plotting to kill me. Jer 18:23
then it was well. Is not this to **k** me? Jer 22:16
and cast into a land that they do not **k**? Jer 22:28
give them a heart to **k** that I am the LORD, Jer 24:7
Only **k** for certain that if you put me to Jer 26:15
For I **k** the plans I have for you, Jer 29:11
each his brother, saying, '**K** the LORD,' Jer 31:34
'Know the LORD,' for they shall all **k** me, Jer 31:34
and let no one **k** where you are." Jer 36:19
Jeremiah, "Let no one **k** of these words, Jer 38:24
"Do you **k** that Baalis the king of the Jer 40:14
son of Nethaniah, and no one will **k** it. Jer 40:15
K for a certainty that I have warned Jer 42:19
Now therefore **k** for a certainty that Jer 42:22
to live, shall **k** whose word will stand, Jer 44:28
order that you may **k** that my words Jer 44:29
around him, and all who **k** his name; Jer 48:17
I **k** his insolence, declares the LORD; his Jer 48:30
taken, O Babylon, and you did not **k** it; Jer 50:24
house) they will **k** that a prophet Ezk 2:5
And they shall **k** that I am the LORD— Ezk 5:13
and you shall **k** that I am the LORD. Ezk 6:7
And they shall **k** that I am the LORD. I Ezk 6:10
And you shall **k** that I am the LORD, Ezk 6:13
Then they will **k** that I am the LORD." Ezk 6:14
Then you will **k** that I am the LORD. Ezk 7:4
Then you will **k** that I am the LORD, who Ezk 7:9
and they shall **k** that I am the LORD." Ezk 7:27
For I **k** the things that come into your Ezk 11:5
and you shall **k** that I am the LORD. Ezk 11:10
and you shall **k** that I am the LORD. Ezk 11:12
And they shall **k** that I am the LORD, Ezk 12:15
go, and may **k** that I am the LORD." Ezk 12:16
and you shall **k** that I am the LORD." Ezk 12:20
And you shall **k** that I am the Lord Ezk 13:9
it, and you shall **k** that I am the LORD. Ezk 13:14
and you shall **k** that I am the LORD. Ezk 13:21
And you shall **k** that I am the LORD." Ezk 13:23
and you shall **k** that I am the LORD. Ezk 14:8
and you shall **k** that I have not done Ezk 14:23
and you will **k** that I am the LORD, Ezk 15:7
and you shall **k** that I am the LORD, Ezk 16:62
Do you not **k** what these things mean? Ezk 17:12
and you shall **k** that I am the LORD. Ezk 17:21
trees of the field shall **k** that I am the Ezk 17:24
Let them **k** the abominations of their Ezk 20:4
that they might **k** that I am the LORD Ezk 20:12
that you may **k** that I am the LORD Ezk 20:20
did it that they might **k** that I am the Ezk 20:26
Then you will **k** that I am the LORD. Ezk 20:38
And you shall **k** that I am the LORD, Ezk 20:42
And you shall **k** that I am the LORD, Ezk 20:44
And all flesh shall **k** that I am the LORD. Ezk 21:5
and you shall **k** that I am the LORD." Ezk 22:16
it, and you shall **k** that I am the LORD; Ezk 22:22
and you shall **k** that I am the Lord Ezk 23:49
then you will **k** that I am the Lord Ezk 24:24
and they will **k** that I am the LORD." Ezk 24:27
Then you will **k** that I am the LORD. Ezk 25:5
Then you will **k** that I am the LORD. Ezk 25:7
Then they will **k** that I am the LORD. Ezk 25:11
and they shall **k** my vengeance, Ezk 25:14
Then they will **k** that I am the LORD, Ezk 25:17
Then they will **k** that I am the LORD. Ezk 26:6
All who **k** you among the peoples are Ezk 28:19
And they shall **k** that I am the LORD Ezk 28:22
Then they will **k** that I am the LORD. Ezk 28:23
Then they will **k** that I am the Lord Ezk 28:24
Then they will **k** that I am the LORD Ezk 28:26
inhabitants of Egypt shall **k** that I am Ezk 29:6
Then they will **k** that I am the LORD. Ezk 29:9
Then they will **k** that I am the Lord Ezk 29:16
Then they will **k** that I am the LORD." Ezk 29:21
Then they will **k** that I am the LORD, Ezk 30:8
Then they will **k** that I am the LORD." Ezk 30:19
Then they shall **k** that I am the LORD. Ezk 30:25
Then they will **k** that I am the LORD." Ezk 30:26
it, then they will **k** that I am the LORD. Ezk 32:15
Then they will **k** that I am the LORD, Ezk 33:29
—then they will **k** that a prophet has Ezk 33:33

And they shall **k** that I am the LORD,	Ezk 34:27
And they shall **k** that I am the LORD	Ezk 34:30
and you shall **k** that I am the LORD.	Ezk 35:4
Then you will **k** that I am the LORD.	Ezk 35:9
And you shall **k** that I am the LORD. "I	Ezk 35:12
it. Then they will **k** that I am the LORD.	Ezk 35:15
Then you will **k** that I am the LORD.	Ezk 36:11
And the nations will **k** that I am the	Ezk 36:23
all around you shall **k** that I am the	Ezk 36:36
Then they will **k** that I am the LORD."	Ezk 36:38
And I answered, "O Lord GOD, you **k**."	Ezk 37:3
and you shall **k** that I am the LORD."	Ezk 37:6
And you shall **k** that I am the LORD,	Ezk 37:13
Then you shall **k** that I am the LORD; I	Ezk 37:14
Then the nations will **k** that I am the	Ezk 37:28
dwelling securely, will you not **k** it?	Ezk 38:14
my land, that the nations may **k** me,	Ezk 38:16
Then they will **k** that I am the LORD.	Ezk 38:23
and they shall **k** that I am the LORD.	Ezk 39:6
And the nations shall **k** that I am the	Ezk 39:7
house of Israel shall **k** that I am the	Ezk 39:22
And the nations shall **k** that the house	Ezk 39:23
Then they shall **k** that I am the LORD	Ezk 39:28
and my spirit is troubled to **k** the dream."	Dn 2:3
"I **k** with certainty that you are trying to	Dn 2:8
and I shall **k** that you can show me its	Dn 2:9
and that you may **k** the thoughts of	Dn 2:30
because I **k** that the spirit of the holy gods	Dn 4:9
that the living may **k** that the Most	Dn 4:17
till you **k** that the Most High rules the	Dn 4:25
the time that you **k** that Heaven rules.	Dn 4:26
until you **k** that the Most High rules the	Dn 4:32
and stone, which do not see or hear or **k**,	Dn 5:23
king and said to the king, "**K**, O king,	Dn 6:15
"Then I desired to **k** the truth about the	Dn 7:19
K therefore and understand that from	Dn 9:25
"Do you **k** why I have come to you?	Dn 10:20
but the people who **k** their God shall	Dn 11:32
his fathers did not **k** he shall honor	Dn 11:38
And she did not **k** that it was I who gave	Hos 2:8
faithfulness. And you shall **k** the LORD.	Hos 2:20
I **k** Ephraim, and Israel is not hidden	Hos 5:3
is within them, and they **k** not the LORD.	Hos 5:4
Let us **k**; let us press on to know the	Hos 6:3
us know; let us press on to **k** the LORD;	Hos 6:3
they cry, My God, we—Israel—**k** you.	Hos 8:2
recompense have come; Israel shall **k** it.	Hos 9:7
but they did not **k** that I healed them.	Hos 11:3
you **k** no God but me, and besides me	Hos 13:4
whoever is discerning, let him **k** them;	Hos 14:9
You shall **k** that I am in the midst of	Jl 2:27
"So you shall **k** that I am the LORD your	Jl 3:17
"They do not **k** how to do right,"	Am 3:10
For I **k** how many are your	Am 5:12
that we may **k** on whose account this	Jon 1:7
for I **k** it is because of me that this great	Jon 1:12
persons who do not **k** their right hand	Jon 4:11
of Israel! Is it not for you to **k** justice?	Mi 3:1
But they do not **k** the thoughts of the	Mi 4:12
that you may **k** the saving acts of the	Mi 6:5
Then you will **k** that the LORD of hosts	Zec 2:9
and you shall **k** that the LORD of hosts	Zec 2:11
me, "Do you not **k** what these are?" I said,	Zec 4:5
Then you will **k** that the LORD of hosts	Zec 4:9
"Do you not **k** what these are?" I said,	Zec 4:13
And you shall **k** that the LORD of hosts	Zec 6:15
So shall you **k** that I have sent this	Mal 2:4
let your left hand **k** what your right hand	Mt 6:3
k how to give good gifts to your	Mt 7:11
But that you may **k** that the Son of Man	Mt 9:6
it has been given to **k** the secrets of the	Mt 13:11
"Do you **k** that the Pharisees were	Mt 15:12
You **k** how to interpret the appearance	Mt 16:3
"You do not **k** what you are asking.	Mt 20:22
"You **k** that the rulers of the Gentiles	Mt 20:25
"We do not **k**." And he said to them,	Mt 21:27
we **k** that you are true and teach the	Mt 22:16
because you **k** neither the Scriptures	Mt 22:29
its leaves, you **k** that summer is near.	Mt 24:32
all these things, you **k** that he is near,	Mt 24:33
for you do not **k** on what day your Lord	Mt 24:42
But **k** this, that if the master of the	Mt 24:43
him and at an hour he does not **k**	Mt 24:50
'Truly, I say to you, I do not **k** you.'	Mt 25:12
for you **k** neither the day nor the hour.	Mt 25:13
"You **k** that after two days the Passover	Mt 26:2
all, saying, "I do not **k** what you mean."	Mt 26:70
it with an oath: "I do not **k** the man."	Mt 26:72
"I do not **k** the man." And immediately	Mt 26:74
for I **k** that you seek Jesus who was	Mt 28:5
I **k** who you are—the Holy One of God."	Mk 1:24
But that you may **k** that the Son of Man	Mk 2:10
them that no one should **k** this,	Mk 5:43
a house and did not want anyone to **k**,	Mk 7:24
For he did not **k** what to say, for they	Mk 9:6
And he did not want anyone to **k**,	Mk 9:30
You **k** the commandments: 'Do not	Mk 10:19
"You do not **k** what you are asking.	Mk 10:38
"You **k** that those who are considered	Mk 10:42
"We do not **k**." And Jesus said to them,	Mk 11:33
we **k** that you are true and do not care	Mk 12:14
because you **k** neither the Scriptures	Mk 12:24
its leaves, you **k** that summer is near.	Mk 13:28
taking place, you **k** that he is near,	Mk 13:29
For you do not **k** when the time will	Mk 13:33
—for you do not **k** when the master of	Mk 13:35
and they did not **k** what to answer	Mk 14:40
"I neither **k** nor understand what you	Mk 14:68
"I do not **k** this man of whom you	Mk 14:71
said to the angel, "How shall I **k** this?	Lk 1:18
in Jerusalem. His parents did not **k** it,	Lk 2:43
Did you not **k** that I must be in my	Lk 2:49
I **k** who you are—the Holy One of God."	Lk 4:34
But that you may **k** that the Son of Man	Lk 5:24
it has been given to **k** the secrets of the	Lk 8:10
off against you. Nevertheless **k** this,	Lk 10:11
k how to give good gifts to your	Lk 11:13
But **k** this, that if the master of the	Lk 12:39
him and at an hour he does not **k**,	Lk 12:46
But the one who did not **k**, and did	Lk 12:48
You **k** how to interpret the appearance	Lk 12:56
why do you not **k** how to interpret the	Lk 12:56
you, 'I do not **k** where you come from.'	Lk 13:25
you, I do not **k** where you come from.	Lk 13:27
You **k** the commandments: 'Do not	Lk 18:20
that he might **k** what they had gained	Lk 19:15
because you did not **k** the time of your	Lk 19:44
that they did not **k** where it came from.	Lk 20:7
we **k** that you speak and teach rightly,	Lk 20:21
then **k** that its desolation has come	Lk 21:20
for yourselves and **k** that the summer	Lk 21:30
you **k** that the kingdom of God is near.	Lk 21:31
you deny three times that you **k** me."	Lk 22:34
it, saying, "Woman, I do not **k** him."	Lk 22:57
I do not **k** what you are talking about."	Lk 22:60
for they **k** not what they do." And they	Lk 23:34
who does not **k** the things that	Lk 24:18
him, yet the world did not **k** him.	Jn 1:10
but among you stands one you do not **k**,	Jn 1:26
I myself did not **k** him, but for this	Jn 1:31
I myself did not **k** him, but he who sent	Jn 1:33
"How do you **k** me?" Jesus answered him,	Jn 1:48
and did not **k** where it came from (though	Jn 2:9
we **k** that you are a teacher come from	Jn 3:2
but you do not **k** where it comes from or	Jn 3:8
truly, I say to you, we speak of what we **k**,	Jn 3:11
You worship what you do not **k**; we	Jn 4:22
we worship what we **k**, for salvation is	Jn 4:22
"I **k** that Messiah is coming (he who is	Jn 4:25
have food to eat that you do not **k** about."	Jn 4:32
and we **k** that this is indeed the Savior of	Jn 4:42
had been healed did not **k** who it was,	Jn 5:13
and I **k** that the testimony that he bears	Jn 5:32
But I **k** that you do not have the love of	Jn 5:42
of Joseph, whose father and mother we **k**?	Jn 6:42
we have believed, and have come to **k**,	Jn 6:69
he will **k** whether the teaching is from	Jn 7:17
that the authorities really **k** that this is	Jn 7:26
But we **k** where this man comes from,	Jn 7:27
no one will **k** where he comes from."	Jn 7:27
as he taught in the temple, "You **k** me,	Jn 7:28
know me, and you **k** where I come from?	Jn 7:28
sent me is true, and him you do not **k**.	Jn 7:28
I **k** him, for I come from him, and he sent	Jn 7:29
crowd that does not **k** the law is	Jn 7:49
for I **k** where I came from and where I am	Jn 8:14
but you do not **k** where I come from or	Jn 8:14
"You **k** neither me nor my Father.	Jn 8:19
knew me, you would **k** my Father also."	Jn 8:19
Son of Man, then you will **k** that I am he,	Jn 8:28
and you will **k** the truth, and the truth	Jn 8:32
I **k** that you are offspring of Abraham;	Jn 8:37
him, "Now we **k** that you have a demon!	Jn 8:52
But you have not known him. I **k** him. If	Jn 8:55
If I were to say that I do not **k** him, I	Jn 8:55
you, but I do **k** him and I keep his word.	Jn 8:55
him, "Where is he?" He said, "I do not **k**."	Jn 9:12
"We **k** that this is our son and that he	Jn 9:20
But how he now sees we do not **k**, nor do	Jn 9:21
know, nor do we **k** who opened his eyes.	Jn 9:21
to God. We **k** that this man is a sinner."	Jn 9:24
"Whether he is a sinner I do not **k**.	Jn 9:25
One thing I do **k**, that though I was blind,	Jn 9:25
We **k** that God has spoken to Moses, but	Jn 9:29
man, we do not **k** where he comes from."	Jn 9:29
You do not **k** where he comes from, and	Jn 9:30
We **k** that God does not listen to sinners,	Jn 9:31
the sheep follow him, for they **k** his voice.	Jn 10:4
for they do not **k** the voice of strangers."	Jn 10:5
I **k** my own and my own know me,	Jn 10:14
I know my own and my own **k** me,	Jn 10:14
the Father knows me and I **k** the Father;	Jn 10:15
My sheep hear my voice, and I **k** them,	Jn 10:27
that you may **k** and understand that the	Jn 10:38
But even now I **k** that whatever you ask	Jn 11:22
"I **k** that he will rise again in the	Jn 11:24
said to them, "You **k** nothing at all.	Jn 11:49
where he was, he should let them **k**,	Jn 11:57
the darkness does not **k** where he is	Jn 12:35
And I **k** that his commandment is	Jn 12:50
If you **k** these things, blessed are you if	Jn 13:17
of all of you; I **k** whom I have chosen.	Jn 13:18
By this all people will **k** that you are my	Jn 13:35
And you **k** the way to where I am going."	Jn 14:4
"Lord, we do not **k** where you are going.	Jn 14:5
you are going. How can we **k** the way?"	Jn 14:5
now on you do **k** him and have seen	Jn 14:7
you so long, and you still do not **k** me,	Jn 14:9
sees him nor knows him. You **k** him,	Jn 14:17
In that day you will **k** that I am in my	Jn 14:20
so that the world may **k** that I love the	Jn 14:31
the servant does not **k** what his master	Jn 15:15
k that it has hated me before it hated	Jn 15:18
because they do not **k** him who sent me.	Jn 15:21
We do not **k** what he is talking about."	Jn 16:18
Now we **k** that you know all things and	Jn 16:30
we know that you **k** all things and do	Jn 16:30
life, that they **k** you the only true God,	Jn 17:3
Now they **k** that everything that you	Jn 17:7
them and have come to **k** in truth that I	Jn 17:8
that the world may **k** that you sent me	Jn 17:23
even though the world does not **k** you,	Jn 17:25
the world does not know you, I **k** you,	Jn 17:25
you, and these **k** that you have sent me.	Jn 17:25
what I said to them; they **k** what I said."	Jn 18:21
to you that you may **k** that I find no guilt	Jn 19:4
Do you not **k** that I have authority to	Jn 19:10
and we do not **k** where they have laid	Jn 20:2
and I do not **k** where they have laid	Jn 20:13
but she did not **k** that it was Jesus.	Jn 20:14
the disciples did not **k** that it was Jesus.	Jn 21:4
you **k** that I love you." He said to him,	Jn 21:15
you **k** that I love you." He said to him,	Jn 21:16
he said to him, "Lord, you **k** everything;	Jn 21:17
you **k** that I love you." Jesus said to him,	Jn 21:17
and we **k** that his testimony is true.	Jn 21:24
is not for you to **k** times or seasons that	Acts 1:7
"You, Lord, who **k** the hearts of all,	Acts 1:24
in your midst, as you yourselves **k**—	Acts 2:22
of Israel therefore **k** for certain that	Acts 2:36
this man strong whom you see and **k**,	Acts 3:16
I **k** that you acted in ignorance,	Acts 3:17
another king who did not **k** Joseph.	Acts 7:18
we do not **k** what has become of him.'	Acts 7:40
"You yourselves **k** how unlawful it is	Acts 10:28
you yourselves **k** what happened	Acts 10:37
He did not **k** that what was being done	Acts 12:9
you **k** that in the early days God made	Acts 15:7
"May we **k** what this new teaching is	Acts 17:19
We wish to **k** therefore what these	Acts 17:20
evil spirit answered them, "Jesus I **k**,	Acts 19:15
you **k** that from this business we	Acts 19:25
of them did not **k** why they had come	Acts 19:32
is there who does not **k** that the city of	Acts 19:35
"You yourselves **k** how I lived among	Acts 20:18
I **k** that none of you among whom I	Acts 20:25
I **k** that after my departure fierce	Acts 20:29
You yourselves **k** that these hands	Acts 20:34
Thus all will **k** that there is nothing	Acts 21:24
you?" And he said, "Do you **k** Greek?	Acts 21:37
fathers appointed you to **k** his will,	Acts 22:14
they themselves **k** that in one	Acts 22:19
desiring to **k** the real reason why he	Acts 22:30
And Paul said, "I did not **k**, brothers,	Acts 23:5
And desiring to **k** the charge for	Acts 23:28
wrong, as you yourselves **k** very well.	Acts 25:10
the prophets? I **k** that you believe."	Acts 26:27
to this sect we **k** that everywhere it is	Acts 28:22
I want you to **k**, brothers, that I have	Rom 1:13
Though they **k** God's decree that those	Rom 1:32
We **k** that the judgment of God rightly	Rom 2:2
and **k** his will and approve what is	Rom 2:18
Now we **k** that whatever the law says it	Rom 3:19
Do you not **k** that all of us who have	Rom 6:3
We **k** that our old self was crucified	Rom 6:6
We **k** that Christ being raised from the	Rom 6:9
Do you not **k** that if you present	Rom 6:16
Or do you not **k**, brothers—for I am	Rom 7:1
speaking to those who **k** the law—that	Rom 7:1
For we **k** that the law is spiritual, but I	Rom 7:14
For I **k** that nothing good dwells in	Rom 7:18
For we **k** that the whole creation has	Rom 8:22
For we do not **k** what to pray for as we	Rom 8:26
And we **k** that for those who love God	Rom 8:28
Do you not **k** what the Scripture says	Rom 11:2

Besides this you **k** the time, that the Rom 13:11
I **k** and am persuaded in the Lord Rom 14:14
I **k** that when I come to you I will Rom 15:29
I do not **k** whether I baptized anyone 1 Cor 1:16
world did not **k** God through wisdom, 1 Cor 1:21
For I decided to **k** nothing among you 1 Cor 2:2
Do you not **k** that you are God's 1 Cor 3:16
Do you not **k** that a little leaven 1 Cor 5:6
Or do you not **k** that the saints will 1 Cor 6:2
Do you not **k** that we are to judge 1 Cor 6:3
Do you not **k** that the unrighteous will 1 Cor 6:9
Do you not **k** that your bodies are 1 Cor 6:15
Or do you not **k** that he who is joined 1 Cor 6:16
Or do you not **k** that your body is a 1 Cor 6:19
how do you **k** whether you will save 1 Cor 7:16
how do you **k** whether you will save 1 Cor 7:16
we **k** that "all of us possess 1 Cor 8:1
he does not yet **k** as he ought to know. 1 Cor 8:2
he does not yet know as he ought to **k**. 1 Cor 8:2
we **k** that "an idol has no real 1 Cor 8:4
Do you not **k** that those who are 1 Cor 9:13
Do you not **k** that in a race all the 1 Cor 9:24
I want you to **k**, brothers, that our 1 Cor 10:1
You **k** that when you were pagans 1 Cor 12:2
For we **k** in part and we prophesy in 1 Cor 13:9
then face to face. Now I **k** in part; 1 Cor 13:12
then I shall **k** fully, even as I have 1 Cor 13:12
how will anyone **k** what is played? 1 Cor 14:7
how will anyone **k** what is said? 1 Cor 14:9
but if I do not **k** the meaning of the 1 Cor 14:11
when he does not **k** what you are 1 Cor 14:16
brothers—you **k** that the household 1 Cor 16:15
for we **k** that as you share in our 2 Cor 1:7
but to let you **k** the abundant love that 2 Cor 2:4
might test you and **k** whether you are 2 Cor 2:9
For we **k** that if the tent, which is our 2 Cor 5:1
We **k** that while we are at home in the 2 Cor 5:6
We want you to **k**, brothers, about the 2 Cor 8:1
For you **k** the grace of our Lord Jesus 2 Cor 8:9
for I **k** your readiness, of which I boast 2 Cor 9:2
I **k** a man in Christ who fourteen 2 Cor 12:2
the body or out of the body I do not **k**, 2 Cor 12:2
And I **k** that this man was caught up 2 Cor 12:3
the body or out of the body I do not **k**, 2 Cor 12:3
For I would have you **k**, brothers, that Gal 1:11
yet we **k** that a person is not justified by Gal 2:16
K then that it is those of faith who are the Gal 3:7
Formerly, when you did not **k** God, you Gal 4:8
But now that you have come to **k** God, or Gal 4:9
You **k** it was because of a bodily Gal 4:13
that you may **k** what is the hope to Eph 1:18
and to **k** the love of Christ that Eph 3:19
So that you also may **k** how I am and Eph 6:21
purpose, that you may **k** how we are, Eph 6:22
I want you to **k**, brothers, that what Phil 1:12
for I **k** that through your prayers and Phil 1:19
I **k** that I will remain and continue Phil 1:25
But you **k** Timothy's proven worth, Phil 2:22
that I may **k** him and the power of his Phil 3:10
I **k** how to be brought low, and I know Phil 4:12
brought low, and I **k** how to abound. Phil 4:12
you Philippians yourselves **k** that in Phil 4:15
For I want you to **k** how great a struggle I Col 2:1
so that you may **k** how you ought to Col 4:6
that you may **k** how we are and that he Col 4:8
For we **k**, brothers loved by God, that 1 Thes 1:4
You **k** what kind of men we proved to 1 Thes 1:5
For you yourselves **k**, brothers, that 1 Thes 2:1
treated at Philippi, as you **k**, 1 Thes 2:2
came with words of flattery, as you **k**, 1 Thes 2:5
For you **k** how, like a father with his 1 Thes 2:11
For you yourselves **k** that we are 1 Thes 3:3
it has come to pass, and just as you **k**. 1 Thes 3:4
For you **k** what instructions we gave 1 Thes 4:2
each one of you **k** how to control his 1 Thes 4:4
like the Gentiles who do not **k** God; 1 Thes 4:5
those who do not **k** God and on those 2 Thes 1:8
And you **k** what is restraining him 2 Thes 2:6
For you yourselves **k** how you ought 2 Thes 3:7
Now we **k** that the law is good, if one 1 Tm 1:8
if someone does not **k** how to manage 1 Tm 3:5
you may **k** how one ought to behave 1 Tm 3:15
by those who believe and **k** the truth. 1 Tm 4:3
for I **k** whom I have believed, 2 Tm 1:12
—and you well **k** all the service he 2 Tm 1:18
you **k** that they breed quarrels. 2 Tm 2:23
They profess to **k** God, but they deny Ti 1:16
one his brother, saying, '**K** the Lord,' Heb 8:11
'Know the Lord,' for they shall all **k** me, Heb 8:11
For we **k** him who said, "Vengeance is Heb 10:30
For you **k** that afterward, when he Heb 12:17
You should **k** that our brother Heb 13:23
for you **k** that the testing of your faith Jas 1:3
K this, my beloved brothers: let every Jas 1:19
for you **k** that we who teach will be Jas 3:1
Do you not **k** that friendship with the Jas 4:4
yet you do not **k** what tomorrow will Jas 4:14
let him **k** that whoever brings back a Jas 5:20
though you **k** them and are established 2 Pt 1:12
since I **k** that the putting off of my 2 Pt 1:14
And by this we **k** that we have come to 1 Jn 2:3
we know that we have come to **k** him, 1 Jn 2:3
Whoever says "I **k** him" but does not 1 Jn 2:4
and does not **k** where he is going, 1 Jn 2:11
because you **k** him who is from the 1 Jn 2:13
children, because you **k** the Father. 1 Jn 2:13
because you **k** him who is from the 1 Jn 2:14
Therefore we **k** that it is the last hour. 1 Jn 2:18
not because you do not **k** the truth, 1 Jn 2:21
know the truth, but because you **k** it, 1 Jn 2:21
If you **k** that he is righteous, you may 1 Jn 2:29
why the world does not **k** us is that it did 1 Jn 3:1
not know us is that it did not **k** him. 1 Jn 3:1
but we **k** that when he appears we shall 1 Jn 3:2
You **k** that he appeared to take away 1 Jn 3:5
We **k** that we have passed out of death 1 Jn 3:14
and you **k** that no murderer has 1 Jn 3:15
By this we **k** love, that he laid down his 1 Jn 3:16
By this we shall **k** that we are of the 1 Jn 3:19
And by this we **k** that he abides in us, 1 Jn 3:24
By this you **k** the Spirit of God: every 1 Jn 4:2
By this we **k** the Spirit of truth and the 1 Jn 4:6
who does not love does not **k** God, 1 Jn 4:8
By this we **k** that we abide in him and 1 Jn 4:13
So we have come to **k** and to believe the 1 Jn 4:16
By this we **k** that we love the children of 1 Jn 5:2
God that you may **k** that you have 1 Jn 5:13
And if we **k** that he hears us in 1 Jn 5:15
we **k** that we have the requests that we 1 Jn 5:15
We **k** that everyone who has been born 1 Jn 5:18
We **k** that we are from God, and the 1 Jn 5:19
And we **k** that the Son of God has come 1 Jn 5:20
so that we may **k** him who is true; 1 Jn 5:20
not only I, but also all who **k** the truth, 2 Jn 1:1
and you **k** that our testimony is true. 3 Jn 1:12
"'I **k** your works, your toil and your Rv 2:2
I **k** you are enduring patiently and Rv 2:3
"'I **k** your tribulation and your poverty Rv 2:9
"'I **k** where you dwell, where Satan's Rv 2:13
"'I **k** your works, your love and faith and Rv 2:19
And all the churches will **k** that I am he Rv 2:23
God and the seven stars. "'I **k** your works. Rv 3:1
and you will not **k** at what hour I will Rv 3:3
"'I **k** your works. Behold, I have set before Rv 3:8
I **k** that you have but little power, and yet Rv 3:8
"'I **k** your works: you are neither cold Rv 3:15
to him, "Sir, you **k**." And he said to me, Rv 7:14

KNOWING (45)
you will be like God, **k** good and evil." Gn 3:5
like one of us in **k** good and evil. Gn 3:22
each **k** the affliction of his own heart 1 Kgs 8:38
the pot of stew, not **k** what they were. 2 Kgs 4:39
each **k** his own affliction and his 2 Chr 6:29
Thus, **k** their works, he overturns them Jb 34:25
But Jesus, **k** their thoughts, said, "Why do Mt 9:4
K their thoughts, he said to them, Mt 12:25
woman, **k** what had happened to her, Mk 5:33
k that he was a righteous and holy Mk 6:20
But, **k** their hypocrisy, he said to them, Mk 12:15
laughed at him, **k** that she was dead. Lk 8:53
and one for Elijah"—not **k** what he said. Lk 9:33
Jesus, **k** the reasoning of their hearts, Lk 9:47
But he, **k** their thoughts, said to them, Lk 11:17
people walk over them without **k** it." Lk 11:44
k in himself that his disciples were Jn 6:61
k that the Father had given all things Jn 13:3
Jesus, **k** all that would happen to him, Jn 18:4
this, Jesus, **k** that all was now finished, Jn 19:28
and **k** that God had sworn with an Acts 2:30
wife came in, not **k** what had happened. Acts 5:7
not **k** what will happen to me there, Acts 20:22
"**K** that for many years you have Acts 24:10
not **k** that God's kindness is meant to Rom 2:4
k that suffering produces endurance, Rom 5:3
k that in the Lord your labor is not 1 Cor 15:58
k that he who raised the Lord Jesus 2 Cor 4:14
Therefore, **k** the fear of the Lord, we 2 Cor 5:11
k that whatever good anyone does, this Eph 6:8
k that he who is both their Master and Eph 6:9
k that I am put here for the defense of Phil 1:16
surpassing worth of **k** Christ Jesus my Phil 3:8
k that from the Lord you will receive Col 3:24
k that you also have a Master in heaven. Col 4:1
believed, **k** from whom you learned it 2 Tm 3:14
k that such a person is warped and Ti 3:11
k that you will do even more than I Phlm 1:21
he went out, not **k** where he was going. Heb 11:8
k that you were ransomed from the 1 Pt 1:18
k that the same kinds of suffering are 1 Pt 5:9
k this first of all, that no prophecy of 2 Pt 1:20
of righteousness than after **k** it to turn 2 Pt 2:21
k this first of all, that scoffers will come 2 Pt 3:3
therefore, beloved, **k** this beforehand, 2 Pt 3:17

KNOWLEDGE (161)
and the tree of the **k** of good and evil. Gn 2:9
of the tree of the **k** of good and evil you Gn 2:17
with **k** and all craftsmanship, Ex 31:3
with skill, with intelligence, with **k**, Ex 35:31
unintentionally without the **k** of the Nm 15:24
and knows the **k** of the Most High, Nm 24:16
who today have no **k** of good or evil, Dt 1:39
for the LORD is a God of **k**, and by him 1 Sm 2:3
without the **k** of my father David, 1 Kgs 2:32
me now wisdom and **k** to go out and 2 Chr 1:10
asked wisdom and **k** for yourself that 2 Chr 1:11
wisdom and **k** are granted to you. I 2 Chr 1:12
all who have **k** and understanding, Neh 10:28
And this came to the **k** of Mordecai, and Est 2:22
a wise man answer with windy **k**, Jb 15:2
us! We do not desire the **k** of your ways. Jb 21:14
Will any teach God **k**, seeing that he Jb 21:22
and plentifully declared sound **k**! Jb 26:3
'Job speaks without **k**; his words are Jb 34:35
talk; he multiplies words without **k**." Jb 35:16
I will get my **k** from afar and ascribe Jb 36:3
false; one who is perfect in **k** is with you. Jb 36:4
perish by the sword and die without **k**. Jb 36:12
works of him who is perfect in **k**, Jb 37:16
darkens counsel by words without **k**? Jb 38:2
is this that hides counsel without **k**?' Jb 42:3
Have they no **k**, all the evildoers who eat Ps 14:4
out speech, and night to night reveals **k**. Ps 19:2
Have those who work evil no **k**, who eat Ps 53:4
the day, for their number is past my **k**. Ps 71:15
know? Is there **k** in the Most High?" Ps 73:11
They have neither **k** nor understanding, Ps 82:5
not rebuke? He who teaches man **k**— Ps 94:10
Teach me good judgment and **k**, for I Ps 119:66
Such **k** is too wonderful for me; it is Ps 139:6
simple, **k** and discretion to the youth— Prv 1:4
fear of the LORD is the beginning of **k**; Prv 1:7
in their scoffing and fools hate **k**? Prv 1:22
Because they hated **k** and did not Prv 1:29
the fear of the LORD and find the **k** of God. Prv 2:5
his mouth come **k** and understanding; Prv 2:6
and **k** will be pleasant to your soul; Prv 2:10
by his **k** the deeps broke open, and the Prv 3:20
discretion, and your lips may guard **k**. Prv 5:2
and right to those who find **k**. Prv 8:9
of silver, and **k** rather than choice gold, Prv 8:10
prudence, and I find **k** and discretion. Prv 8:12
and the **k** of the Holy One is insight. Prv 9:10
The wise lay up **k**, but the mouth of a Prv 10:14
but by **k** the righteous are delivered. Prv 11:9
Whoever loves discipline loves **k**, but Prv 12:1
A prudent man conceals **k**, but the Prv 12:23
In everything the prudent acts with **k**, Prv 13:16
but **k** is easy for a man of Prv 14:6
for there you do not meet words of **k**. Prv 14:7
but the prudent are crowned with **k**. Prv 14:18
The tongue of the wise commends **k**, Prv 15:2
The lips of the wise spread **k**; not so the Prv 15:7
him who has understanding seeks **k**, Prv 15:14
Whoever restrains his words has **k**, Prv 17:27
An intelligent heart acquires **k**, and Prv 18:15
and the ear of the wise seeks **k**. Prv 18:15
Desire without **k** is not good, and Prv 19:2
of understanding, and he will gain **k**. Prv 19:25
and you will stray from the words of **k**. Prv 19:27
but the lips of **k** are a precious jewel. Prv 20:15
a wise man is instructed, he gains **k**. Prv 21:11
eyes of the LORD keep watch over **k**, Prv 22:12
the wise, and apply your heart to my **k**, Prv 22:17
you thirty sayings of counsel and **k**, Prv 22:20
instruction and your ear to words of **k**. Prv 23:12
by **k** the rooms are filled with all Prv 24:4
and a man of **k** enhances his might, Prv 24:5
with a man of understanding and **k**, Prv 28:2
man does not understand such **k**. Prv 29:7
wisdom, nor have I **k** of the Holy One. Prv 30:3
great experience of wisdom and **k**." Eccl 1:16
he who increases **k** increases sorrow. Eccl 1:18
with wisdom and **k** and skill must Eccl 2:21
God has given wisdom and **k** and joy, Eccl 2:26
and the advantage of **k** is that wisdom Eccl 7:12
work or thought or **k** or wisdom in Eccl 9:10
intelligent, nor favor to those with **k**, Eccl 9:11
the Preacher also taught the people **k**, Eccl 12:9
my people go into exile for lack of **k**; Is 5:13
the Spirit of **k** and the fear of the LORD. Is 11:2
shall be full of the **k** of the LORD as the Is 11:9
"To whom will he teach **k**, and to whom Is 28:9
abundance of salvation, wisdom, and **k**; Is 33:6
the path of justice, and taught him **k**, Is 40:14
nor is there **k** or discernment to say, Is 44:19

men back and makes their **k** foolish, Is 44:25
They have no **k** who carry about their Is 45:20
your wisdom and your **k** led you astray, Is 47:10
by his **k** shall the righteous one, my Is 53:11
are blind; they are all without **k**; Is 56:10
ourselves, and you take no **k** of it?' Is 58:3
will feed you with **k** and understanding. Jer 3:15
Every man is stupid and without **k**; Jer 10:14
trade through the land and have no **k**.'" Jer 14:18
Every man is stupid and without **k**; Jer 51:17
skillful in all wisdom, endowed with **k**, Dn 1:4
to the wise and **k** to those who have Dn 2:21
k, and understanding to interpret Dn 5:12
run to and fro, and **k** shall increase." Dn 12:4
love, and no **k** of God in the land; Hos 4:1
My people are destroyed for lack of **k**; Hos 4:6
because you have rejected **k**, I reject you Hos 4:6
the **k** of God rather than burnt offerings. Hos 6:6
will be filled with the **k** of the glory of Hab 2:14
For the lips of a priest should guard **k**, Mal 2:7
to give **k** of salvation to his people in the Lk 1:77
For you have taken away the key of **k**. Lk 11:52
and with his wife's **k** he kept back for Acts 5:2
a rather accurate **k** of the Way, Acts 24:22
law the embodiment of **k** and truth— Rom 2:20
since through the law comes **k** of sin. Rom 3:20
a zeal for God, but not according to **k**. Rom 10:2
the riches and wisdom and **k** of God! Rom 11:33
filled with all **k** and able to instruct Rom 15:14
in him in all speech and all **k**— 1 Cor 1:5
of us possess **k**." This "knowledge" 1 Cor 8:1
possess knowledge." This "**k**" puffs up, 1 Cor 8:1
However, not all possess this **k**. But 1 Cor 8:7
sees you who have **k** eating in an 1 Cor 8:10
And so by your **k** this weak person is 1 Cor 8:11
the utterance of **k** according to the 1 Cor 12:8
understand all mysteries and all **k**, 1 Cor 13:2
will cease; as for **k**, it will pass away. 1 Cor 13:8
some revelation or **k** or prophecy or 1 Cor 14:6
sinning. For some have no **k** of God. 1 Cor 15:34
fragrance of the **k** of him everywhere. 2 Cor 2:14
give the light of the **k** of the glory of 2 Cor 4:6
by purity, **k**, patience, kindness, the 2 Cor 6:6
everything—in faith, in speech, in **k**, 2 Cor 8:7
opinion raised against the **k** of God, 2 Cor 10:5
in speaking, I am not so in **k**; 2 Cor 11:6
and of revelation in the **k** of him, Eph 1:17
the love of Christ that surpasses **k**, Eph 3:19
the faith and of the **k** of the Son of God, Eph 4:13
and more, with **k** and all discernment, Phil 1:9
may be filled with the **k** of his will in all Col 1:9
work and increasing in the **k** of God. Col 1:10
understanding and the **k** of God's Col 2:2
hidden all the treasures of wisdom and **k**. Col 2:3
is being renewed in **k** after the image of Col 3:10
saved and to come to the **k** of the truth. 1 Tm 2:4
of what is falsely called "**k**," 1 Tm 6:20
repentance leading to a **k** of the truth, 2 Tm 2:25
never able to arrive at a **k** of the truth. 2 Tm 3:7
faith of God's elect and their **k** of the truth, Ti 1:1
effective for the full **k** of every good Phlm 1:6
after receiving the **k** of the truth, Heb 10:26
multiplied to you in the **k** of God and of 2 Pt 1:2
through the **k** of him who called us to 2 Pt 1:3
your faith with virtue, and virtue with **k**, 2 Pt 1:5
and **k** with self-control, and self-control 2 Pt 1:6
or unfruitful in the **k** of our Lord Jesus 2 Pt 1:8
the world through the **k** of our Lord 2 Pt 2:20
in the grace and **k** of our Lord and 2 Pt 3:18
by the Holy One, and you all have **k**. 1 Jn 2:20

KNOWN (221)

two daughters who have not **k** any man. Gn 19:8
a maiden whom no man had **k**. Gn 24:16
no one would have **k** that they had Gn 41:21
Joseph made himself **k** to his brothers. Gn 45:1
and thought, "Surely the thing is **k**." Ex 2:14
the LORD I did not make myself **k** to them. Ex 6:3
Or if it is **k** that the ox has been Ex 21:36
For how shall it be **k** that I have found Ex 33:16
which they have committed becomes **k**, Lv 4:14
he has committed is made **k** to him, Lv 4:23
he has committed is made **k** to him, Lv 4:28
I the LORD make myself **k** to him in a Nm 12:6
woman who has **k** man by lying Nm 31:17
girls who have not **k** man by lying Nm 31:18
women who had not **k** man by lying Nm 31:35
Make them **k** to your children and your Dt 4:9
your children who have not **k** or seen it), Dt 11:2
go after other gods that you have not **k**. Dt 11:28
after other gods,' which you have not **k**, Dt 13:2
neither you nor your fathers have **k**, Dt 13:6
serve other gods,' which you have not **k**, Dt 13:13
country, and it is not **k** who killed him, Dt 21:1
that you have not **k** shall eat up the Dt 28:33
neither you nor your fathers have **k**. Dt 28:36
neither you nor your fathers have **k**. Dt 28:64
whom they had not **k** and whom he Dt 29:26
that their children, who have not **k** it, Dt 31:13
were no gods, to gods they had never **k**, Dt 32:17
outlived Joshua and had **k** all the work Jos 24:31
war to those who had not **k** it before. Jgs 3:2
She had never **k** a man, and it became Jgs 11:39
So the secret of his strength was not **k**. Jgs 16:9
virgins who had not **k** a man by lying Jgs 21:12
do not make yourself **k** to the man until Ru 3:3
"Let it not be **k** that the woman came to Ru 3:14
and it will be **k** to you why his hand 1 Sm 6:3
that I may make **k** to you the word of 1 Sm 9:27
for your servant has **k** nothing of all 1 Sm 22:15
grain on it, and nothing was **k** of it. 2 Sm 17:19
people whom I had not **k** served me. 2 Sm 22:44
that it not be **k** that you are the wife 1 Kgs 14:2
let it be **k** this day that you are God 1 Kgs 18:36
make **k** his deeds among the peoples! 1 Chr 16:8
in making **k** all these great things. 1 Chr 17:19
be it **k** to the king that the Jews who Ezr 4:12
Now be it **k** to the king that if this city Ezr 4:13
We make **k** to the king that if this city Ezr 4:16
Be it **k** to the king that we went to the Ezr 5:8
heard that it was **k** to us and that Neh 4:15
and you made **k** to them your holy Neh 9:14
behavior will be made **k** to all women, Est 1:17
Esther had not made **k** her people or Est 2:10
had commanded her not to make it **k**. Est 2:10
Esther had not made **k** her kindred or Est 2:20
as they had made **k** to him the people of Est 3:6
question you, and you make it **k** to me. Jb 38:3
question you, and you make it **k** to me. Jb 40:7
question you, and you make it **k** to me.' Jb 42:4
sisters and all who had **k** him before, Jb 42:11
The LORD has made himself **k**; he has Ps 9:16
You make **k** to me the path of life; in Ps 16:11
people whom I had not **k** served me. Ps 18:43
and he makes **k** to them his covenant. Ps 25:14
you have **k** the distress of my soul, Ps 31:7
God has made himself **k** as a fortress. Ps 48:3
that your way may be **k** on earth, your Ps 67:2
my dishonor; my foes are all **k** to you. Ps 69:19
In Judah God is **k**; his name is great in Ps 76:1
you have made **k** your might among Ps 77:14
things that we have heard and **k**, that Ps 78:3
your servants be **k** among the nations Ps 79:10
of Egypt. I hear a language I had not **k**: Ps 81:5
Are your wonders **k** in the darkness, or Ps 88:12
mouth I will make **k** your faithfulness to Ps 89:1
heart, and they have not **k** my ways." Ps 95:10
The LORD has made **k** his salvation; he Ps 98:2
He made **k** his ways to Moses, his acts Ps 103:7
make **k** his deeds among the peoples! Ps 105:1
he might make **k** his mighty power. Ps 106:8
Long have I **k** from your testimonies Ps 119:152
LORD, you have searched me and **k** me! Ps 139:1
to make **k** to the children of man your Ps 145:12
to you; I will make my words **k** to you. Prv 1:23
The vexation of a fool is **k** at once, but Prv 12:16
but it makes itself **k** even in the midst Prv 14:33
a child makes himself **k** by his acts, Prv 20:11
I have made them **k** to you today, Prv 22:19
Her husband is **k** in the gates when he Prv 31:23
it has not seen the sun or **k** anything, Eccl 6:5
been named, and it is **k** what man is, Eccl 6:10
make **k** his deeds among the peoples, Is 12:4
let this be made **k** in all the earth. Is 12:5
will make himself **k** to the Egyptians, Is 19:21
the father makes **k** to the children your Is 38:19
Have you not **k**? Have you not heard? Is 40:28
that they have not **k** I will guide them. Is 42:16
the new moons make **k** what shall come Is 47:13
hidden things that you have not **k**. Is 48:6
You have never heard, you have never **k**, Is 48:8
offspring shall be **k** among the nations, Is 61:9
to make your name **k** to your adversaries, Is 64:2
of the LORD shall be **k** to his servants, Is 66:14
go after other gods that you have not **k**, Jer 7:9
neither they nor their fathers have **k**, Jer 9:16
The LORD made it **k** to me and I knew; Jer 11:18
neither you nor your fathers have **k**, Jer 16:13
fathers nor the kings of Judah have **k**; Jer 19:4
then it will be **k** that the LORD has truly Jer 28:9
and hidden things that you have not **k**. Jer 33:3
make **k** to Jerusalem her Ezk 16:2
making myself **k** to them in the land of Ezk 20:5
sight I made myself **k** to them in Ezk 20:9
my statutes and made **k** to them my Ezk 20:11
into the countries that you have not **k**. Ezk 32:9
I will make myself **k** among them, Ezk 35:11
the Lord GOD; let that be **k** to you. Ezk 36:32
and make myself **k** in the eyes Ezk 38:23
holy name I will make **k** in the midst of Ezk 39:7
make **k** to them the design of the Ezk 43:11
and make **k** to them as well all its Ezk 43:11
if you do not make **k** to me the dream Dn 2:5
if you do not make the dream **k** to me, Dn 2:9
Arioch made the matter **k** to Daniel. Dn 2:15
and made the matter **k** to Hananiah, Dn 2:17
and have now made **k** to me what we Dn 2:23
for you have made **k** to us the king's Dn 2:23
a man who will make **k** to the king the Dn 2:25
you able to make **k** to me the dream Dn 2:26
he has made **k** to King Nebuchadnezzar Dn 2:28
reveals mysteries made **k** to you what Dn 2:29
may be made **k** to the king, Dn 2:30
great God has made **k** to the king what Dn 2:45
But if not, be it **k** to you, O king, that we Dn 3:18
that they might make **k** to me the Dn 4:6
they could not make **k** to me its Dn 4:7
not able to make **k** to me the Dn 4:18
the writing or make **k** to the king the Dn 5:8
this writing and make **k** to me its Dn 5:15
the writing and make **k** to me its Dn 5:16
the king and make **k** to him the Dn 5:17
told me and made **k** to me the Dn 7:16
I will make **k** to you what shall be at the Dn 8:19
the tribes of Israel I make **k** what is sure. Hos 5:9
"You only have I **k** of all the families of Am 3:2
it; in the midst of the years make it **k**; Hab 3:2
all the nations that they had not **k**. Zec 7:14
be a unique day, which is **k** to the LORD, Zec 14:7
revealed, or hidden that will not be **k**. Mt 10:26
And if you had **k** what this means, 'I Mt 12:7
and ordered them not to make him **k**. Mt 12:16
its fruit bad, for the tree is **k** by its fruit. Mt 12:33
of the house had **k** in what part of Mt 24:43
ordered them not to make him **k**. Mk 3:12
of it, for Jesus' name had become **k**. Mk 6:14
which the Lord has made **k** to us." Lk 2:15
they made **k** the saying that had been Lk 2:17
for each tree is **k** by its own fruit. For Lk 6:44
he would have **k** who and what sort of Lk 7:39
that will not be **k** and come to light. Lk 8:17
be revealed, or hidden that will not be **k**. Lk 12:2
of the house had **k** at what hour the Lk 12:39
had **k** on this day the things that make Lk 19:42
and how he was **k** to them in the Lk 24:35
at the Father's side, he has made him **k**. Jn 1:18
works in secret if he seeks to be **k** openly. Jn 7:4
But you have not **k** him. I know him. If I Jn 8:55
If you had **k** me, you would have known Jn 14:7
me, you would have **k** my Father also. Jn 14:7
from my Father I have made **k** to you. Jn 15:15
because they have not **k** the Father, Jn 16:3
I made **k** to them your name, and I will Jn 17:26
name, and I will continue to make it **k**, Jn 17:26
Since that disciple was **k** to the high Jn 18:15
disciple, who was **k** to the high priest, Jn 18:16
And it became **k** to all the inhabitants Acts 1:19
dwell in Jerusalem, let this be **k** to you, Acts 2:14
You have made **k** to me the paths of Acts 2:28
let it be **k** to all of you and to all the Acts 4:10
Joseph made himself **k** to his brothers, Acts 7:13
Joseph's family became **k** to Pharaoh. Acts 7:13
but their plot became **k** to Saul. They Acts 9:24
And it became **k** throughout all Joppa, Acts 9:42
centurion of what was **k** as the Italian Acts 10:1
Let it be **k** to you therefore, brothers, Acts 13:38
k from of old.' Acts 15:18
And this became **k** to all the residents Acts 19:17
and in Jerusalem, is **k** by all the Jews. Acts 26:4
They have **k** for a long time, if they are Acts 26:5
Therefore let it be **k** to you that this Acts 28:28
For what can be **k** about God is plain Rom 1:19
and the way of peace they have not **k**." Rom 3:17
been for the law, I would not have **k** sin. Rom 7:7
I would not have **k** what it is to covet if Rom 7:7
his wrath and to make **k** his power, Rom 9:22
in order to make **k** the riches of his Rom 9:23
"For who has **k** the mind of the Lord, Rom 11:34
They are well **k** to the apostles, Rom 16:7
For your obedience is **k** to all, so that Rom 16:19
has been made **k** to all nations, Rom 16:26
if anyone loves God, he is **k** by God. 1 Cor 8:3
fully, even as I have been fully **k**. 1 Cor 13:12
on our hearts, to be **k** and read by all. 2 Cor 3:2
But what we are is **k** to God, and I 2 Cor 5:11
I hope it is **k** also to your conscience. 2 Cor 5:11
as unknown, and yet well **k**; as dying, 2 Cor 6:9
to know God, or rather to be **k** by God, Gal 4:9
making **k** to us the mystery of his will, Eph 1:9
the mystery was made **k** to me by Eph 3:3
which was not made **k** to the sons of Eph 3:5
might now be made **k** to the rulers and Eph 3:10
it has become **k** throughout the whole Phil 1:13
your reasonableness be **k** to everyone. Phil 4:5
let your requests be made **k** to God. Phil 4:6
and has made **k** to us your love in the Col 1:8

you, to make the word of God fully **k**, Col 1:25
God chose to make **k** how great among Col 1:27
their heart; they have not **k** my ways.' Heb 3:10
myths when we made **k** to you the 2 Pt 1:16
them never to have **k** the way of 2 Pt 2:21
sinning has either seen him or **k** him. 1 Jn 3:6
He made it **k** by sending his angel to his Rv 1:1

KNOWS (92)
For God **k** that when you eat of it your Gn 3:5
"My lord **k** that the children are frail, Gn 33:13
and **k** the knowledge of the Most Nm 24:16
He **k** your going through this great Dt 2:7
but no one **k** the place of his burial to Dt 34:6
The Mighty One, God, the LORD! He **k**; Jos 22:22
"Your father **k** well that I have found 1 Sm 20:3
to you. Saul my father also **k** this." 1 Sm 23:17
'Who **k** whether the LORD will be 2 Sm 12:22
"Today your servant **k** that I have 2 Sm 14:22
for all Israel **k** that your father is a 2 Sm 17:10
For your servant **k** that I have 2 Sm 19:20
one among us who **k** how to cut 1 Kgs 5:6
And who **k** whether you have not come Est 4:14
For he **k** worthless men; when he sees Jb 11:11
He **k** that a day of darkness is ready at Jb 15:23
is the place of him who **k** not God." Jb 18:21
But he **k** the way that I take; when he Jb 23:10
"That path no bird of prey **k**, and the Jb 28:7
the way to it, and he **k** its place. Jb 28:23
for the LORD **k** the way of the righteous, Ps 1:6
The LORD **k** the days of the blameless, Ps 37:18
this? For he **k** the secrets of the heart. Ps 44:21
there is none among us who **k** how long. Ps 74:9
protect him, because he **k** my name. Ps 91:14
the LORD—**k** the thoughts of man, that Ps 94:11
For he **k** our frame; he remembers Ps 103:14
it is gone, and its place **k** it no more. Ps 103:16
seasons; the sun **k** its time for setting. Ps 104:19
lowly, but the haughty he **k** from afar. Ps 138:6
are your works; my soul **k** it very well. Ps 139:14
is loud; she is seductive and **k** nothing. Prv 9:13
The heart **k** its own bitterness, and no Prv 14:10
and who **k** the ruin that will come Prv 24:22
A righteous man **k** the rights of the Prv 29:7
and who **k** whether he will be wise or a Eccl 2:19
Who **k** whether the spirit of man goes Eccl 3:21
poor man have who **k** how to conduct Eccl 6:8
For who **k** what is good for man while Eccl 6:12
Your heart **k** that many times you Eccl 7:22
And who **k** the interpretation of a Eccl 8:1
though no man **k** what is to be, Eccl 10:14
The ox **k** its owner, and the donkey its Is 1:3
and honey when he **k** how to refuse the Is 7:15
For before the boy **k** how to refuse the evil Is 7:16
for before the boy **k** how to cry 'My father' Is 8:4
and who say, "Who sees us? Who **k** us?" Is 29:15
no one who treads on them **k** peace. Is 59:8
Even the stork in the heavens **k** her times, Jer 8:7
in this, that he understands and **k** me, Jer 9:24
I am the one who **k**, and I am witness, Jer 29:23
he **k** what is in the darkness, and the Dn 2:22
devour his strength, and he **k** it not; Hos 7:9
are sprinkled upon him, and he **k** it not. Hos 7:9
Who **k** whether he will not turn and Jl 2:14
Who **k**? God may turn and relent and Jon 3:9
he **k** those who take refuge in him. Na 1:7
they fly away; no one **k** where they are. Na 3:17
does not fail; but the unjust **k** no shame. Zep 3:5
for your Father **k** what you need before Mt 6:8
your heavenly Father **k** that you need Mt 6:32
them, "See that no one **k** about it." Mt 9:30
and no one **k** the Son except the Father, Mt 11:27
and no one **k** the Father except the Son Mt 11:27
that day and hour no one **k**, Mt 24:36
seed sprouts and grows; he **k** not how. Mk 4:27
that day or that hour, no one **k**, Mk 13:32
and no one **k** who the Son is except the Lk 10:22
and your Father **k** that you need them. Lk 12:30
before men, but God **k** your hearts. Lk 16:15
just as the Father **k** me and I know the Jn 10:15
because it neither sees him nor **k** him. Jn 14:17
and he **k** that he is telling the truth — Jn 19:35
And God, who **k** the heart, bore Acts 15:8
For the king **k** about these things, Acts 26:26
he who searches hearts **k** what is the Rom 8:27
For who **k** a person's thoughts except 1 Cor 2:11
"The Lord **k** the thoughts of the wise, 1 Cor 3:20
anyone imagines that he **k** something, 1 Cor 8:2
I do not love you? God **k** I do! 2 Cor 11:11
forever, **k** that I am not lying. 2 Cor 11:31
out of the body I do not know, God **k**. 2 Cor 12:2
of the body I do not know, God **k** — 2 Cor 12:3
"The Lord **k** those who are his," and, 2 Tm 2:19
So whoever **k** the right thing to do and Jas 4:17
then the Lord **k** how to rescue the godly 2 Pt 2:9
than our heart, and he **k** everything. 1 Jn 3:20
Whoever **k** God listens to us; whoever is 1 Jn 4:6
loves has been born of God and **k** God. 1 Jn 4:7
stone that no one **k** except the one who Rv 2:17
because he **k** that his time is short!" Rv 12:12
written that no one **k** but himself. Rv 19:12

KOA (1)
Chaldeans, Pekod and Shoa and **K**, Ezk 23:23

KOHATH (26)
sons of Levi: Gershon, **K**, and Merari. Gn 46:11
Gershon, **K**, and Merari, the years of the Ex 6:16
The sons of **K**: Amram, Izhar, Hebron, Ex 6:18
the years of the life of **K** being 133 years. Ex 6:18
names: Gershon and **K** and Merari. Nm 3:17
And the sons of **K** by their clans: Nm 3:19
To **K** belonged the clan of the Nm 3:27
clans of the sons of **K** were to camp on Nm 3:29
of the sons of **K** from among the sons Nm 4:2
service of the sons of **K** in the tent of Nm 4:4
that the sons of **K** shall come to carry Nm 4:15
meeting that the sons of **K** are to carry. Nm 4:15
But to the sons of **K** he gave none, Nm 7:9
Now Korah the son of Izhar, son of **K**, Nm 16:1
the clan of the Gershonites; of **K**, Nm 26:57
And **K** was the father of Amram. Nm 26:58
sons of Levi: Gershon, **K**, and Merari. 1 Chr 6:1
The sons of **K**: Amram, Izhar, Hebron, 1 Chr 6:2
of Levi: Gershom, **K**, and Merari. 1 Chr 6:16
The sons of **K**: Amram, Izhar, 1 Chr 6:18
The sons of **K**: Amminadab his son, 1 Chr 6:22
son of Izhar, son of **K**, son of Levi, son 1 Chr 6:38
of the sons of **K** had cities of their 1 Chr 6:66
of the sons of **K**, Uriel the chief, with 1 Chr 15:5
sons of Levi: Gershon, **K**, and Merari. 1 Chr 23:6
The sons of **K**: Amram, Izhar, 1 Chr 23:12

KOHATHITE (1)
belonging to the **K** clans of the Jos 21:20

KOHATHITES (20)
Uzzielites; these are the clans of the **K**. Nm 3:27
the fathers' house of the clans of the **K**. Nm 3:30
the clans of the **K** be destroyed from Nm 4:18
congregation listed the sons of the **K**, Nm 4:34
This was the list of the clans of the **K**, Nm 4:37
Then the **K** set out, carrying the holy Nm 10:21
of Kohath, the clan of the **K**; Nm 26:57
The lot came out for the clans of the **K**. Jos 21:4
the rest of the **K** received by lot from Jos 21:5
the clans of the **K** who belonged to the Jos 21:10
the rest of the **K** belonging to the Jos 21:20
of the rest of the **K** were ten in all with Jos 21:26
Of the sons of the **K**: Heman the 1 Chr 6:33
to the sons of Aaron of the clans of **K**, 1 Chr 6:54
To the rest of the **K** were given by lot 1 Chr 6:61
for the rest of the clans of the **K**. 1 Chr 6:70
their kinsmen of the **K** had charge of 1 Chr 9:32
Levites, of the **K** and the Korahites, 2 Chr 20:19
son of Azariah, of the sons of the **K**; 2 Chr 29:12
Meshullam, of the sons of the **K**, 2 Chr 34:12

KOLAIAH (2)
son of Joed, son of Pedaiah, son of **K**, Neh 11:7
Ahab the son of **K** and Zedekiah the Jer 29:21

KORAH (37)
Oholibamah bore Jeush, Jalam, and **K**. Gn 36:5
she bore to Esau Jeush, Jalam, and **K**. Gn 36:14
K, Gatam, and Amalek; these are the Gn 36:16
wife: the chiefs Jeush, Jalam, and **K**; Gn 36:18
sons of Izhar: **K**, Nepheg, and Zichri. Ex 6:21
The sons of **K**: Assir, Elkanah, and Ex 6:24
Now **K** the son of Izhar, son of Kohath, Nm 16:1
and he said to **K** and all his company, Nm 16:5
take censers, **K** and all his company; Nm 16:6
And Moses said to **K**, "Hear now, you Nm 16:8
And Moses said to **K**, "Be present, you Nm 16:16
Then **K** assembled all the Nm 16:19
Get away from the dwelling of **K**, Nm 16:24
they got away from the dwelling of **K**, Nm 16:27
people who belonged to **K** and all their Nm 16:32
he become like **K** and his company Nm 16:40
those who died in the affair of **K**. Nm 16:49
Moses and Aaron in the company of **K**, Nm 26:9
swallowed them up together with **K**, Nm 26:10
But the sons of **K** did not die. Nm 26:11
against the LORD in the company of **K**, Nm 27:3
Eliphaz, Reuel, Jeush, Jalam, and **K**. 1 Chr 1:35
K, Tappuah, Rekem and Shema. 1 Chr 2:43
Amminadab his son, **K** his son, 1 Chr 6:22
of Assir, son of Ebiasaph, son of **K**, 1 Chr 6:37
of Kore, son of Ebiasaph, son of **K**, 1 Chr 9:19
choirmaster. A Maskil of the Sons of **K**. Ps 42:T
choirmaster. A Maskil of the Sons of **K**. Ps 44:T
A Maskil of the Sons of **K**; a love song. Ps 45:T
To the choirmaster. Of the Sons of **K**. Ps 46:T
choirmaster. A Psalm of the Sons of **K**. Ps 47:T
A Song. A Psalm of the Sons of **K**. Ps 48:T
choirmaster. A Psalm of the Sons of **K**. Ps 49:T
to The Gittith. A Psalm of the Sons of **K**. Ps 84:T
choirmaster. A Psalm of the Sons of **K**. Ps 85:T
A Psalm of the Sons of **K**. A Song. Ps 87:T
A Song. A Psalm of the Sons of **K**. To the Ps 88:T

KORAH'S (1)
error and perished in **K** rebellion. Jude 1:11

KORAHITE (1)
the firstborn of Shallum the **K**, 1 Chr 9:31

KORAHITES (7)
Abiasaph; these are the clans of the **K**. Ex 6:24
of the Mushites, the clan of the **K**. Nm 26:58
kinsmen of his fathers' house, the **K**, 1 Chr 9:19
Azarel, Joezer, and Jashobeam, the **K**; 1 Chr 12:6
of the **K**, Meshelemiah the son of 1 Chr 26:1
gatekeepers among the **K** and the 1 Chr 26:19
Levites, of the Kohathites and the **K**, 2 Chr 20:19

KORE (3)
Shallum the son of **K**, son of 1 Chr 9:19
Korahites, Meshelemiah the son of **K**, 1 Chr 26:1
And **K** the son of Imnah the Levite, 2 Chr 31:14

KOZ (1)
K fathered Anub, Zobebah, and the 1 Chr 4:8

KUE (4)
of horses was from Egypt and **K**, 1 Kgs 10:28
received them from **K** at a price. 1 Kgs 10:28
of horses was from Egypt and **K**, 2 Chr 1:16
would buy them from **K** for a price. 2 Chr 1:16

KUSHAIAH (1)
their brothers, Ethan the son of **K**; 1 Chr 15:17

L

LAADAH (1)
of Lecah, **L** the father of Mareshah, 1 Chr 4:21

LABAN (55)
had a brother whose name was **L**. Gn 24:29
L ran out toward the man, to the Gn 24:29
Then **L** and Bethuel answered and Gn 24:50
the sister of **L** the Aramean. Gn 25:20
Arise, flee to **L** my brother in Haran Gn 27:43
the daughters of **L** your mother's Gn 28:2
And he went to Paddan-aram, to **L**, the Gn 28:5
"Do you know **L** the son of Nahor?" Gn 29:5
the daughter of **L** his mother's brother, Gn 29:10
the sheep of **L** his mother's brother, Gn 29:10
the flock of **L** his mother's brother. Gn 29:10
As soon as **L** heard the news about Gn 29:13
his house. Jacob told **L** all these things, Gn 29:13
and **L** said to him, "Surely you are my Gn 29:14
Then **L** said to Jacob, "Because you are Gn 29:15
Now **L** had two daughters. The name Gn 29:16
L said, "It is better that I give her to you Gn 29:19
Then Jacob said to **L**, "Give me my Gn 29:21
So **L** gathered together all the people of Gn 29:22
(**L** gave his female servant Zilpah to Gn 29:24
And Jacob said to **L**, "What is this you Gn 29:25
L said, "It is not so done in our Gn 29:26
Then **L** gave him his daughter Rachel Gn 29:28
(**L** gave his female servant Bilhah to Gn 29:29
and served **L** for another seven years. Gn 29:30
had borne Joseph, Jacob said to **L**, Gn 30:25
But **L** said to him, "If I have found Gn 30:27
L said, "Good! Let it be as you have Gn 30:34
But that day **L** removed the male goats Gn 30:35
and all the black in the flock of **L**. Gn 30:40
heard that the sons of **L** were saying, Gn 31:1
And Jacob saw that **L** did not regard Gn 31:2
I have seen all that **L** is doing to you. Gn 31:12
L had gone to shear his sheep, and Gn 31:19
And Jacob tricked **L** the Aramean, by Gn 31:20
When it was told **L** on the third day Gn 31:22
But God came to **L** the Aramean in a Gn 31:24
And **L** overtook Jacob. Now Jacob had Gn 31:25
and **L** with his kinsmen pitched tents Gn 31:25
And **L** said to Jacob, "What have you Gn 31:26
Jacob answered and said to **L**, "Because Gn 31:31
So **L** went into Jacob's tent and into Gn 31:33
L felt all about the tent, but did not Gn 31:34
Jacob became angry and berated **L**. Gn 31:36
Jacob said to **L**, "What is my offense? Gn 31:36
Then **L** answered and said to Jacob, Gn 31:43
L called it Jegar-sahadutha, but Jacob Gn 31:47
L said, "This heap is a witness between Gn 31:48
Then **L** said to Jacob, "See this heap Gn 31:51
in the morning **L** arose and kissed Gn 31:55
Then **L** departed and returned home. Gn 31:55
have sojourned with **L** and stayed until Gn 32:4

whom **L** gave to Leah his daughter; Gn 46:18
whom **L** gave to Rachel his daughter, Gn 46:25
between Paran and Tophel, **L**, Hazeroth, Dt 1:1

LABAN'S (3)
and Jacob pastured the rest of **L** flock. Gn 30:36
and did not put them with **L** flock. Gn 30:40
So the feebler would be **L**, and the Gn 30:42

LABOR (92)
my affliction and the **l** of my hands Gn 31:42
from Ephrath, Rachel went into **l**, Gn 35:16
went into labor, and she had hard **l**. Gn 35:16
And when her **l** was at its hardest, the Gn 35:17
When the time of her **l** came, there Gn 38:27
And when she was in **l**, one put out a Gn 38:28
bear, and became a servant at forced **l**. Gn 49:15
the men that they may **l** at it and pay no Ex 5:9
Six days you shall **l**, and do all your Ex 20:9
of Harvest, of the firstfruits of your **l**, Ex 23:16
in from the field the fruit of your **l**. Ex 23:16
Six days you shall **l** and do all your Dt 5:13
in it shall do forced **l** for you and shall Dt 20:11
and humiliated us and laid on us hard **l**. Dt 26:6
day but have been made to do forced **l**. Jos 16:10
they put the Canaanites to forced **l**, Jos 17:13
they put the Canaanites to forced **l**, Jgs 1:28
them, but became subject to forced **l**. Jgs 1:30
became subject to forced **l** for them. Jgs 1:33
and they became subject to forced **l**. Jgs 1:35
and set them to **l** with saws and iron 2 Sm 12:31
was in charge of the forced **l**; 2 Sm 20:24
of Abda was in charge of the forced **l**. 1 Kgs 4:6
Solomon drafted forced **l** out of all 1 Kgs 5:13
of the forced **l** that King Solomon 1 Kgs 9:15
over all the forced **l** of the house of 1 Kgs 11:28
was taskmaster over the forced **l**, 1 Kgs 12:18
and set them to **l** with saws and iron 1 Chr 20:3
—these Solomon drafted as forced **l**, 2 Chr 8:8
was taskmaster over the forced **l**, 2 Chr 10:18
for us by night and may **l** by day." Neh 4:22
house and from his **l** who does not Neh 5:13
the tithes in all our towns where we **l**. Neh 10:37
be condemned; why then do I **l** in vain? Jb 9:29
great, and will you leave to him your **l**? Jb 39:11
though her **l** be in vain, yet she has no Jb 39:16
them there, anguish as of a woman in **l**. Ps 48:6
and the fruit of their **l** to the locust. Ps 78:46
his work and to his **l** until the evening. Ps 104:23
bowed their hearts down with hard **l**; Ps 107:12
the house, those who build it **l** in vain. Ps 127:1
shall eat the fruit of the **l** of your hands; Ps 128:2
the slothful will be put to forced **l**. Prv 12:24
kills him, for his hands refuse to **l**. Prv 21:25
There your mother was in **l** with you; Sg 8:5
with you; there she who bore you was in **l**. Sg 8:5
they will be in anguish like a woman in **l**. Is 13:8
seized me, like the pangs of a woman in **l**; Is 21:3
do not **l** to comfort me concerning the Is 22:4
his young men shall be put to forced **l**. Is 31:8
now I will cry out like a woman in **l**; Is 42:14
to a woman, 'With what are you in **l**?'" Is 45:10
cry aloud, you who have not been in **l**! Is 54:1
and your **l** for that which does not Is 55:2
They shall not **l** in vain or bear children Is 65:23
"Before she was in **l** she gave birth; before Is 66:7
as Zion was in **l** she brought forth her Is 66:8
For I heard a cry as of a woman in **l**, Jer 4:31
hold of us, pain as of a woman in **l**. Jer 6:24
hold of you like those of a woman in **l**? Jer 13:21
upon you, pain as of a woman in **l**!" Jer 22:23
on his stomach like a woman in **l**? Jer 30:6
the pregnant woman and she who is in **l**, Jer 31:8
taken hold of her, as of a woman in **l**. Jer 49:24
seized him, pain as of a woman in **l**. Jer 50:43
with fire. The peoples **l** for nothing, Jer 51:58
the fruit of your **l** and leave you naked Ezk 23:29
made his army **l** hard against Tyre. Ezk 29:18
to pay for the **l** that he had performed Ezk 29:18
pity the plant, for which you did not **l**, Jon 4:10
that pain seized you like a woman in **l**? Mi 4:9
O daughter of Zion, like a woman in **l**, Mi 4:10
time when she who is in **l** has given birth; Mi 5:3
of hosts that peoples **l** merely for fire, Hab 2:13
to me, all who **l** and are heavy laden, Mt 11:28
you to reap that for which you did not **l**. Jn 4:38
and you have entered into their **l**." Jn 4:38
Do not **l** for the food that perishes, but for Jn 6:27
receive his wages according to his **l**. 1 Cor 3:8
and we **l**, working with our own 1 Cor 4:12
that in the Lord your **l** is not in vain. 1 Cor 15:58
and cry aloud, you who are not in **l**! Gal 4:27
no longer steal, but rather let him **l**, Eph 4:28
the flesh, that means fruitful **l** for me. Phil 1:22
that I did not run in vain or **l** in vain. Phil 2:16
work of faith and **l** of love and 1 Thes 1:3
remember, brothers, our **l** and toil: 1 Thes 2:9
tempted you and our **l** would be in 1 Thes 3:5
upon them as **l** pains come upon 1 Thes 5:3
respect those who **l** among you and 1 Thes 5:12
but with toil and **l** we worked night 2 Thes 3:8
especially those who **l** in preaching 1 Tm 5:17

LABORED (15)
which you had not **l** and cities that you Jos 24:13
who were engaged in the work **l**, 2 Chr 24:13
a way that each **l** on the work with Neh 4:17
So we **l** at the work, and half of them Neh 4:21
saying: "I have neither **l** nor given birth, Is 23:4
with which you have **l** from your youth; Is 47:12
to you are those with whom you have **l**, Is 47:15
But I said, "I have **l** in vain; I have spent Is 49:4
drink your wine for which you have **l**; Is 62:8
has devoured all for which our fathers **l**, Jer 3:24
Egypt as his payment for which he **l**, Ezk 29:20
And he **l** till the sun went down to Dn 6:14
Others have **l**, and you have entered into Jn 4:38
afraid I may have **l** over you in vain. Gal 4:11
who have **l** side by side with me in the Phil 4:3

LABORER (5)
Sweet is the sleep of a **l**, whether he eats Eccl 5:12
nor a staff, for the **l** deserves his food. Mt 10:10
they provide, for the **l** deserves his wages. Lk 10:7
and to every fellow worker and **l**. 1 Cor 16:16
and, "The **l** deserves his wages." 1 Tm 5:18

LABORERS (8)
harvest is plentiful, but the **l** are few; Mt 9:37
harvest to send out **l** into his harvest." Mt 9:38
in the morning to hire **l** for his vineyard. Mt 20:1
After agreeing with the **l** for a denarius a Mt 20:2
'Call the **l** and pay them their wages, Mt 20:8
harvest is plentiful, but the **l** are few. Lk 10:2
the harvest to send out **l** into his harvest. Lk 10:2
the wages of the **l** who mowed your fields, Jas 5:4

LABORS (9)
fruit of your ground and of all your **l**, Dt 28:33
and your **l** go to the house of a Prv 5:10
over all the toil of my **l** under the sun, Eccl 2:20
in all my **l** they cannot find in me Hos 12:8
on man and beast, and on all their **l**." Hg 1:11
riots, **l**, sleepless nights, 2 Cor 6:5
boast beyond limit in the **l** of others. 2 Cor 10:15
like a madman—with far greater **l**, 2 Cor 11:23
Spirit, "that they may rest from their **l**, Rv 14:13

LACE (2)
the rings of the ephod with a **l** of blue, Ex 28:28
the rings of the ephod with a **l** of blue, Ex 39:21

LACHISH (24)
king of Jarmuth, to Japhia king of **L**, Jos 10:3
the king of Jarmuth, the king of **L**, Jos 10:5
the king of Jarmuth, the king of **L**, Jos 10:23
on from Libnah to **L** and laid siege to Jos 10:31
And the LORD gave **L** into the hand of Jos 10:32
king of Gezer came up to help **L**. Jos 10:33
with him passed on from **L** to Eglon. Jos 10:34
that day, as he had done to **L**. Jos 10:35
of Jarmuth, one; the king of **L**, one; Jos 12:11
L, Bozkath, Eglon, Jos 15:39
him in Jerusalem, and he fled to **L**. 2 Kgs 14:19
sent after him to **L** and put him to 2 Kgs 14:19
sent to the king of Assyria at **L**, 2 Kgs 18:14
great army from **L** to King Hezekiah 2 Kgs 18:17
for he heard that the king had left **L**. 2 Kgs 19:8
Adoraim, **L**, Azekah, 2 Chr 11:9
him in Jerusalem, and he fled to **L**. 2 Chr 25:27
sent after him to **L** and put him to 2 Chr 25:27
who was besieging **L** with all his 2 Chr 32:9
and their villages, **L** and its fields, Neh 11:30
the Rabshakeh from **L** to King Hezekiah Is 36:2
for he had heard that the king had left **L**. Is 37:8
of Judah that were left, **L** and Azekah, Jer 34:7
steeds to the chariots, inhabitants of **L**; Mi 1:13

LACK (40)
the whole city for **l** of five?" And he Gn 18:28
and whoever gathered little had no **l**. Ex 16:18
scarcity, in which you will **l** nothing, Dt 8:9
where there is no **l** of anything that is Jgs 18:10
servants. There is no **l** of anything." Jgs 19:19
Do I **l** madmen, that you have 1 Sm 21:15
you shall not **l** a man on the throne of 1 Kgs 2:4
'You shall not **l** a man to sit before 1 Kgs 8:25
'You shall not **l** a man on the throne of 1 Kgs 9:5
'You shall not **l** a man to sit before 2 Chr 6:16
'You shall not **l** a man to rule Israel.' 2 Chr 7:18
The strong lion perishes for **l** of prey, and Jb 4:11
and cling to the rock for **l** of shelter. Jb 24:8
seen anyone perish for **l** of clothing, Jb 31:19
for help, and wander about for **l** of food? Jb 38:41
saints, for those who fear him have no **l**! Ps 34:9
who seek the LORD **l** no good thing. Ps 34:10
He dies for **l** of discipline, and because Prv 5:23
feed many, but fools die for **l** of sense. Prv 10:21
than to play the great man and **l** bread. Prv 12:9
For **l** of wood the fire goes out, and Prv 26:20
in her, and he will have no **l** of gain. Prv 31:11
my people go into exile for **l** of knowledge; Is 5:13
is an outcry in the streets for **l** of wine; Is 24:11
their fish stink for **l** of water and die of Is 50:2
David shall never **l** a man to sit on the Jer 33:17
Levitical priests shall never **l** a man in Jer 33:18
of Rechab shall never **l** a man to stand Jer 35:19
pierced by **l** of the fruits of the field. Lam 4:9
do this that they may **l** bread and water, Ezk 4:17
people are destroyed for **l** of knowledge; Hos 4:6
cities, and **l** of bread in all your places, Am 4:6
they are afflicted for **l** of a shepherd. Zec 10:2
these I have kept. What do I still **l**?" Mt 19:20
and said to him, "You **l** one thing: Mk 10:21
he said to him, "One thing you still **l**. Lk 18:22
did you **l** anything?" They said, Lk 22:35
you because of your **l** of self-control. 1 Cor 7:5
and whoever gathered little had no **l**." 2 Cor 8:15
on their way; see that they **l** nothing. Ti 3:13

LACKED (5)
has been with you. You have **l** nothing."' Dt 2:7
"What have you **l** with me that you 1 Kgs 11:22
in the wilderness, and they **l** nothing. Neh 9:21
we have **l** everything and have been Jer 44:18
greater honor to the part that **l** it, 1 Cor 12:24

LACKING (19)
Suppose five of the fifty righteous are **l**. Gn 18:28
thirst, in nakedness, and **l** everything. Dt 28:48
because **l** everything she will eat them Dt 28:57
l nothing that is in the earth and Jgs 18:7
there should be one tribe **l** in Israel?" Jgs 21:3
in his month. They let nothing be **l**. 1 Kgs 4:27
among the youths, a young man **l** sense, Prv 7:7
words are many, transgression is not **l**, Prv 10:19
by the vineyard of a man **l** sense, Prv 24:30
and what is **l** cannot be counted. Eccl 1:15
white. Let not oil be **l** on your head. Eccl 9:8
to the pit, neither shall his bread be **l**. Is 51:14
Truth is **l**, and he who departs from evil Is 59:15
that you are not **l** in any spiritual gift, 1 Cor 1:7
to complete what was **l** in your service Phil 2:30
up what is **l** in Christ's afflictions Col 1:24
and supply what is **l** in your faith? 1 Thes 3:10
be perfect and complete, **l** in nothing. Jas 1:4
is poorly clothed and **l** in daily food, Jas 2:15

LACKS (15)
falls by the sword or who **l** bread!" 2 Sm 3:29
He who commits adultery **l** sense; he Prv 6:32
in here!" To him who **l** sense she says, Prv 9:4
here!" And to him who **l** sense she says, Prv 9:16
rod is for the back of him who **l** sense. Prv 10:13
belittles his neighbor **l** sense, Prv 11:12
who follows worthless pursuits **l** sense. Prv 12:11
Folly is a joy to him who **l** sense, but a Prv 15:21
One who **l** sense gives a pledge and Prv 17:18
A ruler who **l** understanding is a cruel Prv 28:16
so that he **l** nothing of all that he Eccl 6:2
the fool walks on the road, he **l** sense, Eccl 10:3
is a rounded bowl that never **l** mixed wine. Sg 7:2
If any of you **l** wisdom, let him ask God, Jas 1:5
For whoever **l** these qualities is so 2 Pt 1:9

LADAN (7)
L his son, Ammihud his son, 1 Chr 7:26
sons of Gershon were **L** and Shimei. 1 Chr 23:7
The sons of **L**: Jehiel the chief, and 1 Chr 23:8
the heads of the fathers' houses of **L**. 1 Chr 23:9
The sons of **L**, the sons of the 1 Chr 26:21
of the Gershonites belonging to **L**, 1 Chr 26:21
belonging to **L** the Gershonite: 1 Chr 26:21

LADDER (1)
there was a **l** set up on the earth, Gn 28:12

LADEN (4)
Jesse took a donkey **l** with bread and 1 Sm 16:20
Ah, sinful nation, a people **l** with iniquity, Is 1:4
were filled and heavily **l** in the heart of Ezk 27:25
to me, all who labor and are heavy **l**, Mt 11:28

LADIES (1)
of kings are among your **l** of honor; Ps 45:9

LADY (2)
The elder to the elect **l** and her children, 2 Jn 1:1
dear **l**—not as though I were writing you 2 Jn 1:5

LAEL (1)
the son of **L** as chief of the fathers' Nm 3:24

LAGGING (1)
your tail, those who were **l** behind you, Dt 25:18

LAHAD (1)
and Jahath fathered Ahumai and **L**. 1 Chr 4:2

LAHMAM (1)
Cabbon, **L**, Chitlish, Jos 15:40

LAHMI (1)
of Jair struck down **L** the brother of 1 Chr 20:5

LAID (243)
a garment, **l** it on both their shoulders, Gn 9:23
and **l** each half over against the other. Gn 15:10
the burnt offering and **l** it on Isaac his Gn 22:6
the altar there and **l** the wood in order Gn 22:9
Isaac his son and **l** him on the altar, Gn 22:9
Then she **l** up his garment by her until Gn 39:16
out his right hand and **l** it on the head Gn 48:14
saw that his father **l** his right hand on Gn 48:17
Let heavier work be **l** on the men that Ex 5:9
So they **l** it aside till the morning, as Ex 16:24
He **l** its bases, and set up its frames, and Ex 40:18
Aaron and his sons **l** their hands on the Lv 8:14
Aaron and his sons **l** their hands on the Lv 8:18
Aaron and his sons **l** their hands on the Lv 8:22
put fire in it and **l** incense on it and Lv 10:1
fire in them and **l** incense on them Nm 16:18
and we **l** waste as far as Nophah; Nm 21:30
and he **l** his hands on him and Nm 27:23
and humiliated us and **l** on us hard Dt 26:6
"'Is not this **l** up in store with me, sealed Dt 32:34
for Moses had **l** his hands on him. Dt 34:9
of flax that she had **l** in order on the roof. Jos 2:6
But if a hand is **l** on anyone who is with Jos 2:19
where they lodged and **l** them down there. Jos 4:8
Joshua **l** an oath on them at that time, Jos 6:26
And they **l** them down before the LORD. Jos 7:23
Libnah to Lachish and **l** siege to it and Jos 10:31
And they **l** siege to it and fought Jos 10:34
counted—so that they **l** waste the land as Jgs 6:5
here, with stones **l** in due order. Jgs 6:26
and their blood be **l** on Abimelech their Jgs 9:24
and took it up and **l** it on his shoulder. Jgs 9:48
took the child and **l** him on her lap Ru 4:16
them in a book and **l** it up before the 1 Sm 10:25
so Saul had **l** an oath on the people, 1 Sm 14:24
took an image and **l** it on the bed 1 Sm 19:13
cakes of figs, and **l** them on donkeys. 1 Sm 25:18
And she **l** her hand on her head and 2 Sm 13:19
foundations of the world were **l** bare, 2 Sm 22:16
he has **l** hold of the horns of the altar, 1 Kgs 1:51
servant slept, and **l** him at her breast, 1 Kgs 3:20
and **l** her dead son at my breast. 1 Kgs 3:20
of the house of the LORD was **l**, 1 Kgs 6:37
land of Egypt and **l** hold on other gods 1 Kgs 9:9
Then Ahijah **l** hold of the new 1 Kgs 11:30
whereas my father **l** on you a heavy 1 Kgs 12:11
man of God and **l** it on the donkey 1 Kgs 13:29
And he **l** the body in his own grave. 1 Kgs 13:30
He **l** its foundation at the cost of 1 Kgs 16:34
he lodged, and **l** him on his own bed. 1 Kgs 17:19
bull in pieces and **l** it on the wood. 1 Kgs 18:33
she went up and **l** him on the bed 2 Kgs 4:21
went on ahead and **l** the staff on the 2 Kgs 4:31
and **l** them on two of his servants. 2 Kgs 5:23
So they **l** hands on her; and she went 2 Kgs 11:16
And Elisha **l** his hands on the king's 2 Kgs 13:16
of Assyria have **l** waste the nations 2 Kgs 19:17
and **l** on the land a tribute of a 2 Kgs 23:33
against Jerusalem and **l** siege to it. 2 Kgs 25:1
land of Egypt and **l** hold on other 2 Chr 7:22
of the LORD was **l** until it was finished. 2 Chr 8:16
whereas my father **l** on you a heavy 2 Chr 10:11
They **l** him on a bier that had been 2 Chr 16:14
So they **l** hands on her, and she went 2 Chr 23:15
the servant of God **l** on Israel in the 2 Chr 24:9
and they **l** their hands on them, 2 Chr 29:23
LORD their God, and **l** them in heaps. 2 Chr 31:6
him in Jerusalem and **l** on the land a 2 Chr 36:3
of the temple of the LORD was not yet **l**. Ezr 3:6
when the builders **l** the foundation of Ezr 3:10
of the house of the LORD was **l**. Ezr 3:11
the foundation of this house being **l**, Ezr 3:12
old. That was why this city was **l** waste. Ezr 4:15
huge stones, and timber is **l** in the walls. Ezr 5:8
came and **l** the foundations Ezr 5:16
They **l** its beams and set its doors, its Neh 3:3
They **l** its beams and set its doors, its Neh 3:6
were before me **l** heavy burdens on Neh 5:15
Jews, but they **l** no hand on the plunder. Est 9:10
but they **l** no hands on the plunder. Est 9:15
but they **l** no hands on the plunder. Est 9:16
and all my calamity **l** in the balances! Jb 6:2
But a man dies and is **l** low; man Jb 14:10
the years that are **l** up for the ruthless. Jb 15:20
my skin and have **l** my strength in the Jb 16:15
Utter darkness is **l** up for his treasures; Jb 20:26
from talking and **l** their hand on Jb 29:9
and who **l** on him the whole world? Jb 34:13
were you when I **l** the foundation of the Jb 38:4
its bases sunk, or who **l** its cornerstone, Jb 38:6
false; he is **l** low even at the sight of him. Jb 41:9
of the world were **l** bare at your rebuke, Ps 18:15
you **l** a crushing burden on our backs; Ps 66:11
strongest of them and **l** low the young Ps 78:31
temple; they have **l** Jerusalem in ruins. Ps 79:1
devoured Jacob and **l** waste his Ps 79:7
you have **l** his strongholds in ruins. Ps 89:40
Of old you **l** the foundation of the Ps 102:25
me; the pangs of Sheol **l** hold on me; Ps 116:3
The wicked have **l** a snare for me, Ps 119:110
trap that they have **l** for me and from Ps 141:9
for many a victim has she **l** low, and all Prv 7:26
the sinner's wealth is **l** up for the Prv 13:22
But all this I **l** to heart, examining it all, Eccl 9:1
as well as old, which I have **l** up for you, Sg 7:13
of Lebanon, saying, 'Since you were **l** low, Is 14:8
maggots are **l** as a bed beneath you, and Is 14:11
the ground, you who **l** the nations low! Is 14:12
Because Ar of Moab is **l** waste in a night, Is 15:1
because Kir of Moab is **l** waste in a night, Is 15:1
and what they have **l** up they carry away Is 15:7
O ships of Tarshish, for Tyre is **l** waste, Is 23:1
Tarshish, for your stronghold is **l** waste. Is 23:14
am the one who has **l** as a foundation in Is 28:16
down, and the city will be utterly **l** low. Is 32:19
kings of Assyria have **l** waste all the Is 37:18
the temple, 'Your foundation shall be **l**.'" Is 44:28
My hand **l** the foundation of the earth, Is 48:13
destroyers and those who **l** you waste go Is 49:17
out the heavens and **l** the foundations of Is 51:13
and the LORD has **l** on him the iniquity of Is 53:6
those nations shall be utterly **l** waste. Is 60:12
hard on crash; the whole land is **l** waste. Jer 4:20
Suddenly my tents are **l** waste, my Jer 4:20
all its cities were **l** in ruins before the Jer 4:26
because they are **l** waste so that no one Jer 9:10
the land ruined and **l** waste like a Jer 9:12
him, and have **l** waste his habitation. Jer 10:25
a pit to take me and **l** snares for my feet. Jer 18:22
prophets and all the people **l** hold of him, Jer 26:8
of Israel: "Woe to Nebo, for it is **l** waste! Jer 48:1
beside the Arnon, that Moab is **l** waste. Jer 48:20
"Wail, O Heshbon, for Ai is **l** waste! Cry Jer 49:3
army against Jerusalem, and **l** siege to it. Jer 52:4
he has **l** in ruins its strongholds, and he Lam 2:5
He has **l** waste his booth like a garden, Lam 2:6
a garden, **l** in ruins his meeting place; Lam 2:6
sit alone in silence when it is **l** on him; Lam 3:28
slain whom you have **l** in the midst of Ezk 11:7
the inhabited cities shall be **l** waste, Ezk 12:20
so that its foundation will be **l** bare. Ezk 13:14
He **l** waste their cities, and the land was Ezk 19:7
of Babylon has **l** siege to Jerusalem Ezk 24:2
be replenished, now that she is **l** waste,' Ezk 26:2
When I make you a city **l** waste, like Ezk 26:19
years among cities that are **l** waste. Ezk 29:12
be in the midst of cities that are **l** waste. Ezk 30:7
Go down and be **l** to rest with the Ezk 32:19
whose swords were **l** under their Ezk 32:27
all their might are **l** with those who Ezk 32:29
and he shall be **l** to rest among the Ezk 32:32
of Israel, saying, 'They are **l** desolate; Ezk 35:12
and my hand that I have **l** on them. Ezk 39:21
were to be **l** with which the Ezk 40:42
the flesh of the offering was to be **l**. Ezk 40:43
limb, and your houses shall be **l** in ruins. Dn 2:5
from limb, and their houses **l** in ruins. Dn 3:29
stone was brought and **l** on the mouth Dn 6:17
It has **l** waste my vine and splintered my fig Jl 1:7
the sanctuaries of Israel shall be **l** waste, Am 7:9
O daughter of troops; siege is **l** against us; Mi 5:1
be plundered, and their houses **l** waste. Zep 1:13
for her cedar work will be **l** bare. Zep 2:14
I have **l** waste their streets so that no one Zep 3:6
foundation of the LORD'S temple was **l**, Hg 2:18
of Zerubbabel have **l** the foundation of Zec 4:9
of the house of the LORD of hosts was **l**, Zec 8:9
The pride of Assyria shall be **l** low, Zec 10:11
I have **l** waste his hill country and left Mal 1:3
Even now the axe is **l** to the root of the Mt 3:10
divided against itself is **l** waste, Mt 12:25
And he **l** his hands on them and went Mt 19:15
they came up and **l** hands on Jesus and Mt 26:50
and **l** it in his own new tomb, which he Mt 27:60
except that he **l** his hands on a few sick Mk 6:5
and took his body and **l** it in a tomb. Mk 6:29
they **l** the sick in the marketplaces and Mk 6:56
spit on his eyes and **l** his hands on him, Mk 8:23
Then Jesus **l** his hands on his eyes Mk 8:25
And they **l** hands on him and seized Mk 14:46
the linen shroud and **l** him in a tomb Mk 15:46
the mother of Joses saw where he was **l**. Mk 15:47
not here. See the place where they **l** him. Mk 16:6
all who heard them **l** them up in their Lk 1:66
in swaddling cloths and **l** him in a Lk 2:7
Even now the axe is **l** to the root of the Lk 3:9
and he **l** his hands on every one of them Lk 4:40
who dug deep and **l** the foundation on Lk 6:48
divided against itself is **l** waste, Lk 11:17
you have ample goods **l** up for many Lk 12:19
And he **l** his hands on her, and Lk 13:13
when he has **l** a foundation and is not Lk 14:29
at his gate was **l** a poor man named Lk 16:20
which I kept **l** away in a handkerchief; Lk 19:20
the country, and **l** on him the cross, Lk 23:26
in a linen shroud and **l** him in a tomb Lk 23:53
stone, where no one had ever yet been **l**. Lk 23:53
saw the tomb and how his body was **l**. Lk 23:55
arrest him, but no one **l** a hand on him, Jn 7:30
to arrest him, but no one **l** hands on him. Jn 7:44
"Where have you **l** him?" They said to Jn 11:34
He **l** aside his outer garments, and taking Jn 13:4
tomb in which no one had yet been **l**. Jn 19:41
was close at hand, they **l** Jesus there. Jn 19:42
we do not know where they have **l** him." Jn 20:2
I do not know where they have **l** him." Jn 20:13
away, tell me where you have **l** him, Jn 20:15
fire in place, with fish **l** out on it, Jn 21:9
whom they **l** daily at the gate of the Acts 3:2
and **l** it at the apostles' feet, and it was Acts 4:35
brought the money and **l** it at the Acts 4:37
a part of it and **l** it at the apostles' feet. Acts 5:2
into the streets and **l** them on cots and Acts 5:15
and they prayed and **l** their hands on Acts 6:6
back to Shechem and **l** in the tomb Acts 7:16
And the witnesses **l** down their Acts 7:58
Then they **l** their hands on them and Acts 8:17
her, they **l** her in an upper room. Acts 9:37
time Herod the king **l** violent hands on Acts 12:1
and praying they **l** their hands on Acts 13:3
from the tree and **l** him in a tomb. Acts 13:29
fell asleep and was **l** with his fathers Acts 13:36
And when Paul had **l** his hands on Acts 19:6
the whole crowd and **l** hands on him, Acts 21:27
They **l** before the governor their case Acts 24:1
believing everything **l** down by the Acts 24:14
men of the Jews **l** out their case against Acts 25:2
Festus **l** Paul's case before the king, Acts 25:14
elders of the Jews **l** out their case Acts 25:15
concerning the charge **l** against him. Acts 25:16
master builder I **l** a foundation, 1 Cor 3:10
other than that which is **l**, 1 Cor 3:11
boasting. For necessity is **l** upon me. 1 Cor 9:16
because of the hope **l** up for you in Col 1:5
that the law is not **l** down for the just 1 Tm 1:9
the council of elders **l** their hands on 1 Tm 4:14
Henceforth there is **l** up for me the 2 Tm 4:8
l the foundation of the earth in the Heb 1:10
You have **l** up treasure in the last days. Jas 5:3
love, that he **l** down his life for us, 1 Jn 3:16
But he **l** his right hand on me, saying, Rv 1:17
this wealth has been **l** waste." And all Rv 18:17
in a single hour she has been **l** waste. Rv 18:19

LAIN (9)
might easily have **l** with your wife, Gn 26:10
oath, saying, 'If no man has **l** with you, Nm 5:19
than your husband has **l** with you, Nm 5:20
every woman that has **l** with a male Jgs 21:11
then I would have **l** down and been quiet; Jb 3:13
and I have **l** in wait at my neighbor's Jb 31:9
her youth men had **l** with her and Ezk 23:8
of the ship and had **l** down and was fast Jon 1:5
sitting where the body of Jesus had **l**, Jn 20:12

LAIR (5)
Jerusalem a heap of ruins, a **l** of jackals, Jer 9:11
of Judah a desolation, a **l** of jackals. Jer 10:22
Is my heritage to me like a hyena's **l**? Are Jer 12:9
Like a lion he has left his **l**, for their Jer 25:38
she has become, a **l** for wild beasts! Zep 2:15

LAIRS (1)
Then the beasts go into their **l**, and Jb 37:8

LAISH (6)
departed and came to **L** and saw the Jgs 18:7
out the country of **L** said to their Jgs 18:14
belonged to him, and they came to **L**, Jgs 18:27
the name of the city was **L** at the first. Jgs 18:29
David's wife, to Palti the son of **L**, 1 Sm 25:44
from her husband Paltiel the son of **L**. 2 Sm 3:15

LAISHAH (1)
daughter of Gallim! Give attention, O **L**! Is 10:30

LAKE (13)
of the LORD, possess the **l** and the south." Dt 33:23
waters fail from a **l** and a river wastes Jb 14:11
he was standing by the **l** of Gennesaret, Lk 5:1

and he saw two boats by the **l**, but the Lk 5:2
to the other side of the **l**." So they set out, Lk 8:22
And a windstorm came down on the **l**, Lk 8:23
steep bank into the **l** and were drowned. Lk 8:33
thrown alive into the **l** of fire that Rv 19:20
was thrown into the **l** of fire and sulfur Rv 20:10
and Hades were thrown into the **l** of fire. Rv 20:14
This is the second death, the **l** of fire. Rv 20:14
of life, he was thrown into the **l** of fire. Rv 20:15
will be in the **l** that burns with fire Rv 21:8

LAKKUM (1)
Adami-nekeb, and Jabneel, as far as **L**, Jos 19:33

LAMB (112)
but where is the **l** for a burnt offering?" Gn 22:7
provide for himself the **l** for a burnt Gn 22:8
and spotted sheep and every black **l**, Gn 30:32
white on it, and every **l** that was black, Gn 30:35
man shall take a **l** according to their Ex 12:3
their fathers' houses, a **l** for a household. Ex 12:3
And if the household is too small for a **l**, Ex 12:4
eat you shall make your count for the **l**. Ex 12:4
Your **l** shall be without blemish, a male Ex 12:5
to your clans, and kill the Passover **l**. Ex 12:21
of a donkey you shall redeem with a **l**, Ex 13:13
One **l** you shall offer in the morning, Ex 29:39
and the other **l** you shall offer at Ex 29:39
And with the first **l** a tenth seah of fine Ex 29:40
The other **l** you shall offer at twilight, Ex 29:41
of a donkey you shall redeem with a **l**, Ex 34:20
If he offers a **l** for his offering, then he Lv 3:7
"If he brings a **l** as his offering for a sin Lv 4:32
as the fat of the **l** is removed from the Lv 4:35
a female from the flock, a **l** or a goat, Lv 5:6
"But if he cannot afford a **l**, then he shall Lv 5:7
goat for a sin offering, and a calf and a **l**, Lv 9:3
of the tent of meeting a **l** a year old for a Lv 12:6
And if she cannot afford a **l**, then she Lv 12:8
and one ewe **l** a year old without Lv 14:10
he shall kill the **l** in the place where Lv 14:13
shall take one male **l** for a guilt offering Lv 14:21
priest shall take the **l** of the guilt Lv 14:24
he shall kill the **l** of the guilt offering. Lv 14:25
Israel kills an ox or a **l** or a goat in the Lv 17:3
present a bull or a **l** that has a part too Lv 22:23
shall offer a male **l** a year old without Lv 23:12
and bring a male **l** a year old for Nm 6:12
one male **l** a year old without blemish Nm 6:14
and one ewe **l** a year old without Nm 6:14
herd, one ram, one male **l** a year old, Nm 7:15
herd, one ram, one male **l** a year old, Nm 7:21
herd, one ram, one male **l** a year old, Nm 7:27
herd, one ram, one male **l** a year old, Nm 7:33
herd, one ram, one male **l** a year old, Nm 7:39
herd, one ram, one male **l** a year old, Nm 7:45
herd, one ram, one male **l** a year old, Nm 7:51
herd, one ram, one male **l** a year old, Nm 7:57
herd, one ram, one male **l** a year old, Nm 7:63
herd, one ram, one male **l** a year old, Nm 7:69
herd, one ram, one male **l** a year old, Nm 7:75
herd, one ram, one male **l** a year old, Nm 7:81
of wine for the drink offering for each **l**. Nm 15:5
or ram, or for each **l** or young goat. Nm 15:11
The one **l** you shall offer in the Nm 28:4
and the other **l** you shall offer at Nm 28:4
shall be a quarter of a hin for each **l**. Nm 28:7
The other **l** you shall offer at twilight. Nm 28:8
with oil as a grain offering for every **l**; Nm 28:13
a ram, and a quarter of a hin for a **l**. Nm 28:14
Samuel took a nursing **l** and offered it 1 Sm 7:9
a bear, and took a **l** from the flock, 1 Sm 17:34
man had nothing but one little ewe **l**, 2 Sm 12:3
took the poor man's **l** and prepared it 2 Sm 12:4
and he shall restore the **l** fourfold, 2 Sm 12:6
slaughtered the Passover **l** on the 2 Chr 30:15
the Passover **l** for everyone 2 Chr 30:17
slaughtered the Passover **l** on the 2 Chr 35:1
And slaughter the Passover **l**, and 2 Chr 35:6
And they slaughtered the Passover **l**, 2 Chr 35:11
roasted the Passover **l** with fire 2 Chr 35:13
slaughtered the Passover **l** for all the Ezr 6:20
The wolf shall dwell with the **l**, and the Is 11:6
Send the **l** to the ruler of the land, from Is 16:1
like a **l** that is led to the slaughter, and Is 53:7
The wolf and the **l** shall graze together; Is 65:25
he who sacrifices a **l**, like one who breaks Is 66:3
I was like a gentle **l** led to the slaughter. Jer 11:19
"You shall provide a **l** a year old Ezk 46:13
Thus the **l** and the meal offering and Ezk 46:15
feed them like a **l** in a broad pasture? Hos 4:16
when they sacrificed the Passover **l**, Mk 14:12
on which the Passover **l** had to be Lk 22:7
him, and said, "Behold, the **L** of God, Jn 1:29
by and said, "Behold, the **L** of God!" Jn 1:36
slaughter and like a **l** before its shearer Acts 8:32
For Christ, our Passover **l**, has been 1 Cor 5:7
like that of a **l** without blemish or spot. 1 Pt 1:19
and among the elders I saw a **L** standing, Rv 5:6
twenty-four elders fell down before the **L**, Rv 5:8
voice, "Worthy is the **L** who was slain, Rv 5:12
throne and to the **L** be blessing and Rv 5:13
I watched when the **L** opened one of the Rv 6:1
the throne, and from the wrath of the **L**, Rv 6:16
before the throne and before the **L**, Rv 7:9
who sits on the throne, and to the **L**!" Rv 7:10
made them white in the blood of the **L**. Rv 7:14
For the **L** in the midst of the throne will Rv 7:17
When the **L** opened the seventh seal, there Rv 8:1
by the blood of the **L** and by the word of Rv 12:11
in the book of life of the **L** that was slain. Rv 13:8
had two horns like a **l** and it spoke like Rv 13:11
and behold, on Mount Zion stood the **L**, Rv 14:1
these who follow the **L** wherever he goes. Rv 14:4
mankind as firstfruits for God and the **L**, Rv 14:4
angels and in the presence of the **L**. Rv 14:10
the servant of God, and the song of the **L**, Rv 15:3
They will make war on the **L**, and the Rv 17:14
Lamb, and the **L** will conquer them, Rv 17:14
for the marriage of the **L** has come, Rv 19:7
marriage supper of the **L**." And he said to Rv 19:9
show you the Bride, the wife of the **L**." Rv 21:9
names of the twelve apostles of the **L**. Rv 21:14
is the Lord God the Almighty and the **L**. Rv 21:22
God gives it light, and its lamp is the **L**. Rv 21:23
from the throne of God and of the **L** Rv 22:1
throne of God and of the **L** will be in it, Rv 22:3

LAMB'S (1)
who are written in the **L** book of life. Rv 21:27

LAMBS (85)
Abraham set seven ewe **l** of the flock Gn 21:28
of these seven ewe **l** that you have set Gn 21:29
"These seven ewe **l** you will take from Gn 21:30
the goats and black among the **l**, Gn 30:33
And Jacob separated the **l** and set the Gn 30:40
of Israel shall kill their **l** at twilight. Ex 12:6
"Go and select **l** for yourselves Ex 12:21
two **l** a year old day by day regularly. Ex 29:38
shall take two male **l** without blemish, Lv 14:10
take one of the male **l** and offer it for a Lv 14:12
with the bread seven **l** a year old Lv 23:18
and two male **l** a year old as a sacrifice Lv 23:19
offering before the LORD, with the two **l**. Lv 23:20
male goats, and five male **l** a year old. Nm 7:17
male goats, and five male **l** a year old. Nm 7:23
male goats, and five male **l** a year old. Nm 7:29
male goats, and five male **l** a year old. Nm 7:35
male goats, and five male **l** a year old. Nm 7:41
male goats, and five male **l** a year old. Nm 7:47
male goats, and five male **l** a year old. Nm 7:53
male goats, and five male **l** a year old. Nm 7:59
male goats, and five male **l** a year old. Nm 7:65
male goats, and five male **l** a year old. Nm 7:71
male goats, and five male **l** a year old. Nm 7:77
male goats, and five male **l** a year old. Nm 7:83
twelve rams, twelve male **l** a year old, Nm 7:87
goats sixty, the male **l** a year old sixty. Nm 7:88
two male **l** a year old without blemish, Nm 28:3
two male **l** a year old without blemish, Nm 28:9
seven male **l** a year old without Nm 28:11
one ram, and seven male **l** a year old; Nm 28:19
shall you offer for each of the seven **l**; Nm 28:21
herd, one ram, seven male **l** a year old; Nm 28:27
a tenth for each of the seven **l**; Nm 28:29
seven male **l** a year old without Nm 29:2
and one tenth for each of the seven **l**; Nm 29:4
herd, one ram, seven male **l** a year old: Nm 29:8
a tenth for each of the seven **l**: Nm 29:10
two rams, fourteen male **l** a year old; Nm 29:13
and a tenth for each of the fourteen **l**; Nm 29:15
fourteen male **l** a year old without Nm 29:17
the bulls, for the rams, and for the **l**, Nm 29:18
fourteen male **l** a year old without Nm 29:20
the bulls, for the rams, and for the **l**, Nm 29:21
fourteen male **l** a year old without Nm 29:23
the bulls, for the rams, and for the **l**, Nm 29:24
fourteen male **l** a year old without Nm 29:26
the bulls, for the rams, and for the **l**, Nm 29:27
fourteen male **l** a year old without Nm 29:29
the bulls, for the rams, and for the **l**, Nm 29:30
fourteen male **l** a year old without Nm 29:32
the bulls, for the rams, and for the **l**, Nm 29:33
seven male **l** a year old without Nm 29:36
for the bull, for the ram, and for the **l**, Nm 29:37
and milk from the flock, with fat of **l**, Dt 32:14
and of the fattened calves and the **l**, 1 Sm 15:9
king of Israel 100,000 **l** and the wool of 2 Kgs 3:4
1,000 bulls, 1,000 rams, and 1,000 **l**, 1 Chr 29:21
seven bulls, seven rams, seven **l**, 2 Chr 29:21
they slaughtered the **l** and their 2 Chr 29:22
was 70 bulls, 100 rams, and 200 **l**; 2 Chr 29:32
l and young goats from the flock to 2 Chr 35:7
offerings 2,600 Passover **l** and 300 2 Chr 35:8
Passover offerings 5,000 **l** and young 2 Chr 35:9
house of God 100 bulls, 200 rams, 400 **l**, Ezr 6:17
all diligence buy bulls, rams, and **l**, Ezr 7:17
Israel, ninety-six rams, seventy-seven **l**, Ezr 8:35
skipped like rams, the hills like **l**. Ps 114:4
that you skip like rams? O hills, like **l**? Ps 114:6
the **l** will provide your clothing, and Prv 27:26
do not delight in the blood of bulls, or of **l**, Is 1:11
Then shall the **l** graze as in their pasture, Is 5:17
with fat, with the blood of **l** and goats, Is 34:6
he will gather the **l** in his arms; Is 40:11
them down like **l** to the slaughter, Jer 51:40
Kedar were your favored dealers in **l**, Ezk 27:21
the princes of the earth—of rams, of **l**, Ezk 39:18
day shall be six **l** without blemish and Ezk 46:4
grain offering with the **l** shall be as Ezk 46:5
without blemish, and six **l** and a ram, Ezk 46:6
and with the **l** as much as he is able, Ezk 46:7
and with the **l** as much as one is able Ezk 46:11
and eat **l** from the flock and calves from Am 6:4
am sending you out as **l** in the midst of Lk 10:3
I love you." He said to him, "Feed my **l**." Jn 21:15

LAME (31)
shall draw near, a man blind or **l**, Lv 21:18
if it is **l** or blind or has any serious Dt 15:21
fled in her haste, he fell and became **l**. 2 Sm 4:4
the blind and the **l** will ward you off" 2 Sm 5:6
shaft to attack 'the **l** and the blind,' 2 Sm 5:8
"The blind and the **l** shall not come 2 Sm 5:8
table. Now he was **l** in both his feet. 2 Sm 9:13
with the king.' For your servant is **l**. 2 Sm 19:26
I was eyes to the blind and feet to the **l**. Jb 29:15
Like a **l** man's legs, which hang useless, Prv 26:7
be divided; even the **l** will take the prey. Is 33:23
then shall the **l** man leap like a deer, and Is 35:6
earth, among them the blind and the **l**, Jer 31:8
I will assemble the **l** and gather those who Mi 4:6
and the **l** I will make the remnant, and Mi 4:7
I will save the **l** and gather the outcast, Zep 3:19
when you offer those that are **l** or sick, Mal 1:8
been taken by violence or is **l** or sick, Mal 1:13
blind receive their sight and the **l** walk, Mt 11:5
came to him, bringing with them the **l**, Mt 15:30
the crippled healthy, the **l** walking, Mt 15:31
enter life crippled or **l** than with two Mt 18:8
And the blind and the **l** came to him in Mt 21:14
for you to enter life **l** than with two feet Mk 9:45
the blind receive their sight, the **l** walk, Lk 7:22
feast, invite the poor, the crippled, the **l**, Lk 14:13
the poor and crippled and blind and **l**.' Lk 14:21
of invalids—blind, **l**, and paralyzed. Jn 5:3
And a man **l** from birth was being Acts 3:2
who were paralyzed or **l** were healed. Acts 8:7
so that what is **l** may not be put out of Heb 12:13

LAMECH (11)
and Methushael fathered **L**. Gn 4:18
And **L** took two wives. The name of the Gn 4:19
L said to his wives: "Adah and Zillah, Gn 4:23
you wives of **L**, listen to what I say: Gn 4:23
had lived 187 years, he fathered **L**. Gn 5:25
lived after he fathered **L** 782 years and Gn 5:26
When **L** had lived 182 years, he fathered Gn 5:28
L lived after he fathered Noah 595 years Gn 5:30
Thus all the days of **L** were 777 years, Gn 5:31
Enoch, Methuselah, **L**; 1 Chr 1:3
of Shem, the son of Noah, the son of **L**, Lk 3:36

LAMECH'S (1)
sevenfold, then **L** is seventy-sevenfold." Gn 4:24

LAMENT (20)
in your house and **l** her father and her Dt 21:13
year by year to **l** the daughter of Jgs 11:40
Jeremiah also uttered a **l** for Josiah; 2 Chr 35:25
And her gates shall **l** and mourn; empty, Is 3:26
The fishermen will mourn and **l**, all who Is 19:8
For this put on sackcloth, **l**, and wail, for Jer 4:8
teach to your daughters a **l**, and each to Jer 9:20
her people **l** on the ground, and the cry of Jer 14:2
mourning, or go to **l** or grieve for them, Jer 16:5
and no one shall **l** for them or cut Jer 16:6
"They shall not **l** for him, saying, 'Ah, Jer 22:18
They shall not **l** for him, saying, 'Ah, Jer 22:18
shall burn spices for you and **l** for you, Jer 34:5
l, and run to and fro among the hedges! Jer 49:3
he caused rampart and wall to **l**; Lam 2:8
a lamentation for you and **l** over you: Ezk 27:32
L like a virgin wearing sackcloth for the Jl 1:8
Put on sackcloth and **l**, O priests; wail, O Jl 1:13
For this I will **l** and wail; I will go stripped Mi 1:8
truly, I say to you, you will weep and **l**, Jn 16:20

LAMENTATION (27)
there with a very great and grievous **l**, Gn 50:10
lamented with this **l** over Saul and 2 Sm 1:17
the sword, and their widows made no **l**. Ps 78:64
Ariel, and there shall be moaning and **l**, Is 29:2
as for an only son, most bitter **l**, Jer 6:26
raise a **l** on the bare heights, for the LORD Jer 7:29
and a **l** for the pastures of the wilderness, Jer 9:10
heard in Ramah, **l** and bitter weeping. Jer 31:15
in the squares there is nothing but **l**, Jer 48:38
the daughter of Judah mourning and **l**. Lam 2:5
on it words of **l** and mourning and woe. Ezk 2:10
you, take up a **l** for the princes of Israel, Ezk 19:1
This is a **l** and has become a Ezk 19:14
is a lamentation and has become a **l**. Ezk 19:14
they will raise a **l** over you and say Ezk 26:17
you, son of man, raise a **l** over Tyre, Ezk 27:2
wailing they raise a **l** for you and Ezk 27:32
of man, raise a **l** over the king of Tyre, Ezk 28:12
raise a **l** over Pharaoh king of Egypt Ezk 32:2
This is a **l** that shall be chanted; the Ezk 32:16
this word that I take up over you in **l**, Am 5:1
to wailing those who are skilled in **l**, Am 5:16
mourning and all your songs into **l**; Am 8:10
and naked; I will make **l** like the jackals, Mi 1:8
the **l** of Beth-ezel shall take away from Mi 1:11
heard in Ramah, weeping and loud **l**, Mt 2:18
Stephen and made great **l** over him. Acts 8:2

LAMENTED (7)
they **l** there with a very great and Gn 50:10
all the house of Israel **l** after the LORD. 1 Sm 7:2
And David **l** with this lamentation 2 Sm 1:17
And the king **l** for Abner, saying, 2 Sm 3:33
was dead, she **l** over her husband. 2 Sm 11:26
They shall not be **l**, nor shall they be Jer 16:4
They shall not be **l**, or gathered, or Jer 25:33

LAMENTING (4)
the Jews, with fasting and weeping and **l**, Est 4:3
with regard to their fasts and their **l**. Est 9:31
she is carried off, her slave girls **l**, Na 2:7
who were mourning and **l** for him. Lk 23:27

LAMENTS (3)
of Josiah in their **l** to this day. 2 Chr 35:25
behold, they are written in the **L**. 2 Chr 35:25
as one who **l** his mother, I bowed down Ps 35:14

LAMP (37)
that a **l** may regularly be set up to Ex 27:20
you pure oil from beaten olives for the **l**, Lv 24:2
The **l** of God had not yet gone out, and 1 Sm 3:3
lest you quench the **l** of Israel." 2 Sm 21:17
For you are my **l**, O LORD, and my 2 Sm 22:29
may always have a **l** before me in 1 Kgs 11:36
his God gave him a **l** in Jerusalem, 1 Kgs 15:4
for him a bed, a table, a chair, and a **l**, 2 Kgs 4:10
he promised to give a **l** to him and to 2 Kgs 8:19
promised to give a **l** to him and to 2 Chr 21:7
his tent, and his **l** above him is put out. Jb 18:6
often is it that the **l** of the wicked is put Jb 21:17
when his **l** shone upon my head, and by Jb 29:3
For it is you who light my **l**; the LORD Ps 18:28
Your word is a **l** to my feet and a light Ps 119:105
I have prepared a **l** for my anointed. Ps 132:17
commandment is a **l** and the teaching Prv 6:23
but the **l** of the wicked will be put out. Prv 13:9
his **l** will be put out in utter darkness. Prv 20:20
The spirit of man is the **l** of the LORD, Prv 20:27
and a proud heart, the **l** of the wicked, Prv 21:4
the **l** of the wicked will be put out. Prv 24:20
Her **l** does not go out at night. Prv 31:18
of the millstones and the light of the **l**. Jer 25:10
Nor do people light a **l** and put it under a Mt 5:15
"The eye is the **l** of the body. So, if your Mt 6:22
"Is a **l** brought in to be put under a Mk 4:21
"No one after lighting a **l** covers it with a Lk 8:16
"No one after lighting a **l** puts it in a Lk 11:33
Your eye is the **l** of your body. When Lk 11:34
as when a **l** with its rays gives you Lk 11:36
does not light a **l** and sweep the house Lk 15:8
He was a burning and shining **l**, and you Jn 5:35
pay attention as to a **l** shining in a dark 2 Pt 1:19
and the light of a **l** will shine in you no Rv 18:23
God gives it light, and its **l** is the Lamb. Rv 21:23
They will need no light of **l** or sun, for Rv 22:5

LAMPS (34)
oil for the **l**, spices for the anointing oil Ex 25:6
You shall make seven **l** for it. And the Ex 25:37
And the **l** shall be set up so as to give Ex 25:37
when he dresses the **l** he shall burn it, Ex 30:7
and when Aaron sets up the **l** at twilight, Ex 30:8
for the light, with its utensils and its **l**, Ex 35:14
he made its seven **l** and its tongs and Ex 37:23
of pure gold and its **l** with the lamps set Ex 39:37
and its lamps with the **l** set and all its Ex 39:37
bring in the lampstand and set up its **l**. Ex 40:4
and set up the **l** before the LORD, as the Ex 40:25
He shall arrange the **l** on the lampstand Lv 24:4
the lampstand for the light, with its **l**, Nm 4:9
and say to him, When you set up the **l**, Nm 8:2
the seven **l** shall give light in front of the Nm 8:2
he set up its **l** in front of the lampstand, Nm 8:3
the flowers, the **l**, and the tongs, of 1 Kgs 7:49
the golden lampstands and their **l**, 1 Chr 28:15
of gold for each lampstand and its **l**, 1 Chr 28:15
of silver for a lampstand and its **l**, 1 Chr 28:15
lampstands and their **l** of pure gold 2 Chr 4:20
the flowers, the **l**, and the tongs, of 2 Chr 4:21
lampstand that its **l** may burn every 2 Chr 13:11
and put out the **l** and have not 2 Chr 29:7
that time I will search Jerusalem with **l**, Zep 1:12
a bowl on the top of it, and seven **l** on it, Zec 4:2
lips on each of the **l** that are on the top Zec 4:2
virgins who took their **l** and went to Mt 25:1
For when the foolish took their **l**, they Mt 25:3
the wise took flasks of oil with their **l**. Mt 25:4
those virgins rose and trimmed their **l**. Mt 25:7
some of your oil, for our **l** are going out.' Mt 25:8
for action and keep your **l** burning, Lk 12:35
There were many **l** in the upper room Acts 20:8

LAMPSTAND (36)
"You shall make a **l** of pure gold. The Ex 25:31
The **l** shall be made of hammered Ex 25:31
three branches of the **l** out of one side of Ex 25:32
three branches of the **l** out of the other Ex 25:32
for the six branches going out of the **l**. Ex 25:33
And on the **l** itself there shall be four Ex 25:34
the six branches going out from the **l**. Ex 25:35
and the **l** on the south side of the Ex 26:35
its utensils, and the **l** and its utensils, Ex 30:27
and the pure **l** with all its utensils, Ex 31:8
the **l** also for the light, with its utensils Ex 35:14
He also made the **l** of pure gold. He Ex 37:17
gold. He made the **l** of hammered work. Ex 37:17
three branches of the **l** out of one side of Ex 37:18
three branches of the **l** out of the other Ex 37:18
for the six branches going out of the **l**. Ex 37:19
And on the **l** itself were four cups made Ex 37:20
the **l** of pure gold and its lamps with the Ex 39:37
you shall bring in the **l** and set up its Ex 40:4
He put the **l** in the tent of meeting, Ex 40:24
the lamps on the **l** of pure gold before Lv 24:4
duty involved the ark, the table, the **l**, Nm 3:31
of blue and cover the **l** for the light, Nm 4:9
lamps shall give light in front of the **l**." Nm 8:2
he set up its lamps in front of the **l**, as the Nm 8:3
And this was the workmanship of the **l**, Nm 8:4
LORD had shown Moses, so he made the **l**. Nm 8:4
of gold for each **l** and its lamps, 1 Chr 28:15
weight of silver for a **l** and its lamps, 1 Chr 28:15
to the use of each **l** in the service, 1 Chr 28:15
care for the golden **l** that its lamps 2 Chr 13:11
wall of the king's palace, opposite the **l**. Dn 5:5
I said, "I see, and behold, a **l** all of gold, Zec 4:2
trees on the right and the left of the **l**?" Zec 4:11
in which were the **l** and the table and the Heb 9:2
to you and remove your **l** from its place, Rv 2:5

LAMPSTANDS (11)
the **l** of pure gold, five on the south 1 Kgs 7:49
of the golden **l** and their lamps, 1 Chr 28:15
he made ten golden **l** as prescribed, 2 Chr 4:7
the **l** and their lamps of pure gold to 2 Chr 4:20
and the pots and the **l** and the dishes for Jer 52:19
me, and on turning I saw seven golden **l**, Rv 1:12
and in the midst of the **l** one like a son of Rv 1:13
in my right hand, and the seven golden **l**, Rv 1:20
and the seven **l** are the seven churches. Rv 1:20
who walks among the seven golden **l**. Rv 2:1
trees and the two **l** that stand before the Rv 11:4

LANCES (1)
their custom with swords and **l**, 1 Kgs 18:28

LAND (1811)
and let the dry **l** appear." And it was so. Gn 1:9
God called the dry **l** Earth, and the Gn 1:10
field was yet in the **l** and no small plant of Gn 2:5
God had not caused it to rain on the **l**, Gn 2:5
going up from the **l** and was watering the Gn 2:6
flowed around the whole **l** of Havilah, Gn 2:11
And the gold of that **l** is good; bdellium Gn 2:12
that flowed around the whole **l** of Cush. Gn 2:13
of the LORD and settled in the **l** of Nod, Gn 4:16
the face of the **l** and daughters were born Gn 6:1
I have created from the face of the **l**, Gn 6:7
on the dry **l** in whose nostrils Gn 7:22
Accad, and Calneh, in the **l** of Shinar. Gn 10:10
From that **l** he went into Assyria and Gn 10:11
a plain in the **l** of Shinar and settled Gn 11:2
his father Terah in the **l** of his kindred, Gn 11:28
Chaldeans to go into the **l** of Canaan, Gn 11:31
father's house to the **l** that I will show Gn 12:1
and they set out to go to the **l** of Canaan. Gn 12:5
When they came to the **l** of Canaan, Gn 12:5
Abram passed through the **l** to the place Gn 12:6
that time the Canaanites were in the **l**. Gn 12:6
I will give this **l**." So he built there Gn 12:7
Now there was a famine in the **l**. So Gn 12:10
there, for the famine was severe in the **l**. Gn 12:10
so that the **l** could not support both of Gn 13:6
and the Perizzites were dwelling in the **l**. Gn 13:7
Is not the whole **l** before you? Separate Gn 13:9
garden of the LORD, like the **l** of Egypt, Gn 13:10
Abram settled in the **l** of Canaan, Gn 13:12
for all the **l** that you see I will give to Gn 13:15
the length and the breadth of the **l**, Gn 13:17
Chaldeans to give you this **l** to possess." Gn 15:7
be sojourners in a **l** that is not theirs Gn 15:13
saying, "To your offspring I give this **l**, Gn 15:18
the **l** of the Kenites, the Kenizzites, the Gn 15:19
had lived ten years in the **l** of Canaan, Gn 16:3
after you the **l** of your sojournings, Gn 17:8
of your sojournings, all the **l** of Canaan, Gn 17:8
and toward all the **l** of the valley, Gn 19:28
the smoke of the **l** went up like the Gn 19:28
said, "Behold, my **l** is before you; Gn 20:15
took a wife for him from the **l** of Egypt. Gn 21:21
me and with the **l** where you have Gn 21:23
and returned to the **l** of the Philistines. Gn 21:32
many days in the **l** of the Philistines. Gn 21:34
you love, and go to the **l** of Moriah, Gn 22:2
(that is, Hebron) in the **l** of Canaan, Gn 23:2
bowed to the Hittites, the people of the **l**. Gn 23:7
bowed down before the people of the **l**. Gn 23:12
in the hearing of the people of the **l**, Gn 23:13
a piece of **l** worth four hundred shekels Gn 23:15
(that is, Hebron) in the **l** of Canaan. Gn 23:19
may not be willing to follow me to this **l**. Gn 24:5
son back to the **l** from which you Gn 24:5
house and from the **l** of my kindred, Gn 24:7
me, 'To your offspring I will give this **l**,' Gn 24:7
of the Canaanites, in whose **l** I dwell, Gn 24:37
Now there was a famine in the **l**, besides Gn 26:1
dwell in the **l** of which I shall tell you. Gn 26:2
Sojourn in this **l**, and I will be with you Gn 26:3
Isaac sowed in that **l** and reaped in the Gn 26:12
for us, and we shall be fruitful in the **l**." Gn 26:22
like these, one of the women of the **l**, Gn 27:46
possession of the **l** of your sojournings Gn 28:4
The **l** on which you lie I will give to Gn 28:13
go, and will bring you back to this **l**. Gn 28:15
and came to the **l** of the people of Gn 29:1
"Return to the **l** of your fathers and to Gn 31:3
go out from this **l** and return to the Gn 31:13
and return to the **l** of your kindred.'" Gn 31:13
to go to the **l** of Canaan to his father Gn 31:18
him to Esau his brother in the **l** of Seir, Gn 32:3
Shechem, which is in the **l** of Canaan, Gn 33:18
money the piece of **l** on which he had Gn 33:19
went out to see the women of the **l**. Gn 34:1
of Hamor the Hivite, the prince of the **l**, Gn 34:2
with us, and the **l** shall be open to you. Gn 34:10
let them dwell in the **l** and trade in it, Gn 34:21
behold, the **l** is large enough for them. Gn 34:21
me stink to the inhabitants of the **l**, Gn 34:30
is, Bethel), which is in the **l** of Canaan, Gn 35:6
The **l** that I gave to Abraham and Gn 35:12
I will give the **l** to your offspring after Gn 35:12
While Israel lived in that **l**, Reuben Gn 35:22
were born to him in the **l** of Canaan. Gn 36:5
that he had acquired in the **l** of Canaan. Gn 36:6
He went into a **l** away from his brother Gn 36:6
The **l** of their sojournings could not Gn 36:7
the chiefs of Eliphaz in the **l** of Edom; Gn 36:16
are the chiefs of Reuel in the **l** of Edom; Gn 36:17
Seir the Horite, the inhabitants of the **l**: Gn 36:20
the sons of Seir in the **l** of Edom. Gn 36:21
Horites, chief by chief in the **l** of Seir. Gn 36:30
the kings who reigned in the **l** of Edom, Gn 36:31
and Husham of the **l** of the Temanites Gn 36:34
places in the **l** of their possession. Gn 36:43
Jacob lived in the **l** of his father's Gn 37:1
father's sojournings, in the **l** of Canaan. Gn 37:1
stolen out of the **l** of the Hebrews, Gn 40:15
as I had never seen in all the **l** of Egypt. Gn 41:19
plenty throughout all the **l** of Egypt, Gn 41:29
will be forgotten in the **l** of Egypt. Gn 41:30
Egypt. The famine will consume the **l**, Gn 41:30
be unknown in the **l** by reason of the Gn 41:31
man, and set him over the **l** of Egypt. Gn 41:33
overseers over the **l** and take one-fifth Gn 41:34
the produce of the **l** of Egypt during the Gn 41:34
a reserve for the **l** against the seven Gn 41:36
that are to occur in the **l** of Egypt, Gn 41:36
so that the **l** may not perish through Gn 41:36

I have set you over all the **l** of Egypt." Gn 41:41
Thus he set him over all the **l** of Egypt. Gn 41:43
up hand or foot in all the **l** of Egypt." Gn 41:44
So Joseph went out over the **l** of Egypt. Gn 41:45
and went through all the **l** of Egypt. Gn 41:46
years, which occurred in the **l** of Egypt, Gn 41:48
me fruitful in the **l** of my affliction." Gn 41:52
that occurred in the **l** of Egypt came to Gn 41:53
but in all the **l** of Egypt there was Gn 41:54
When all the **l** of Egypt was famished, Gn 41:55
the famine had spread over all the **l**, Gn 41:56
the famine was severe in the **l** of Egypt. Gn 41:56
for the famine was in the **l** of Canaan. Gn 42:5
Now Joseph was governor over the **l**. He Gn 42:6
the one who sold to all the people of the **l**. Gn 42:6
They said, "From the **l** of Canaan, to Gn 42:7
have come to see the nakedness of the **l**." Gn 42:9
the nakedness of the **l** that you have Gn 42:12
the sons of one man in the **l** of Canaan, Gn 42:13
to Jacob their father in the **l** of Canaan, Gn 42:29
"The man, the lord of the **l**, spoke Gn 42:30
to us and took us to be spies of the **l**. Gn 42:30
day with our father in the **l** of Canaan.' Gn 42:32
Then the man, the lord of the **l**, said to Gn 42:33
to you, and you shall trade in the **l**.'" Gn 42:34
Now the famine was severe in the **l**. Gn 43:1
the choice fruits of the **l** in your bags, Gn 43:11
back to you from the **l** of Canaan. Gn 44:8
famine has been in the **l** these two years, Gn 45:6
house and ruler over all the **l** of Egypt. Gn 45:8
You shall dwell in the **l** of Goshen, and Gn 45:10
beasts and go back to the **l** of Canaan, Gn 45:17
I will give you the best of the **l** of Egypt, Gn 45:18
Egypt, and you shall eat the fat of the **l**.' Gn 45:18
take wagons from the **l** of Egypt for Gn 45:19
the best of all the **l** of Egypt is yours.'" Gn 45:20
and came to the **l** of Canaan to their Gn 45:25
is ruler over all the **l** of Egypt." And his Gn 45:26
they had gained in the **l** of Canaan, Gn 46:6
Er and Onan died in the **l** of Canaan); Gn 46:12
to Joseph in the **l** of Egypt were born Gn 46:20
and they came into the **l** of Goshen. Gn 46:28
who were in the **l** of Canaan, Gn 46:31
that you may dwell in the **l** of Goshen, Gn 46:34
have come from the **l** of Canaan. Gn 47:1
They are now in the **l** of Goshen." Gn 47:1
"We have come to sojourn in the **l**, Gn 47:4
the famine is severe in the **l** of Canaan. Gn 47:4
your servants dwell in the **l** of Goshen." Gn 47:4
The **l** of Egypt is before you. Settle your Gn 47:6
and your brothers in the best of the **l**. Gn 47:6
Let them settle in the **l** of Goshen, and if Gn 47:6
them a possession in the **l** of Egypt, Gn 47:11
in the land of Egypt, in the best of the **l**, Gn 47:11
the best of the land, in the **l** of Rameses, Gn 47:11
Now there was no food in all the **l**, for Gn 47:13
so that the **l** of Egypt and the land of Gn 47:13
Egypt and the **l** of Canaan languished Gn 47:13
that was found in the **l** of Egypt and in Gn 47:14
land of Egypt and in the **l** of Canaan, Gn 47:14
was all spent in the **l** of Egypt and in Gn 47:15
land of Egypt and in the **l** of Canaan, Gn 47:15
of my lord but our bodies and our **l**. Gn 47:18
die before your eyes, both we and our **l**? Gn 47:19
Buy us and our **l** for food, and we with Gn 47:19
and we with our **l** will be servants to Gn 47:19
die, and that the **l** may not be desolate." Gn 47:19
Joseph bought all the **l** of Egypt for Gn 47:20
on them. The **l** became Pharaoh's. Gn 47:20
Only the **l** of the priests he did not buy, Gn 47:22
them; therefore they did not sell their **l**. Gn 47:22
bought you and your **l** for Pharaoh. Gn 47:23
is seed for you, and you shall sow the **l**. Gn 47:23
it a statute concerning the **l** of Egypt, Gn 47:26
the **l** of the priests alone did not Gn 47:26
Thus Israel settled in the **l** of Egypt, in Gn 47:27
in the land of Egypt, in the **l** of Goshen. Gn 47:27
Jacob lived in the **l** of Egypt seventeen Gn 47:28
at Luz in the **l** of Canaan and blessed Gn 48:3
and will give this **l** to your offspring Gn 48:4
born to you in the **l** of Egypt before I Gn 48:5
Rachel died in the **l** of Canaan on the Gn 48:7
you again to the **l** of your fathers. Gn 48:21
was good, and that the **l** was pleasant, Gn 49:15
the east of Mamre, in the **l** of Canaan, Gn 49:30
hewed out for myself in the **l** of Canaan, Gn 50:5
and all the elders of the **l** of Egypt, Gn 50:7
their herds were left in the **l** of Goshen. Gn 50:8
When the inhabitants of the **l**, the Gn 50:11
carried him to the **l** of Canaan and Gn 50:13
you up out of this **l** to the land that he Gn 50:24
of this land to the **l** that he swore to Gn 50:24
strong, so that the **l** was filled with them. Ex 1:7
fight against us and escape from the **l**." Ex 1:10
Pharaoh and stayed in the **l** of Midian. Ex 2:15
"I have been a sojourner in a foreign **l**." Ex 2:22
them up out of that **l** to a good and broad Ex 3:8
up out of that land to a good and broad **l**, Ex 3:8
land, a **l** flowing with milk and honey, Ex 3:8
of Egypt to the **l** of the Canaanites, Ex 3:17
a **l** flowing with milk and honey."' Ex 3:17
donkey, and went back to the **l** of Egypt. Ex 4:20
"Behold, the people of the **l** are now many, Ex 5:5
scattered throughout all the **l** of Egypt to Ex 5:12
hand he will drive them out of his **l**." Ex 6:1
with them to give them the **l** of Canaan, Ex 6:4
the **l** in which they lived as sojourners. Ex 6:4
will bring you into the **l** that I swore to Ex 6:8
to let the people of Israel go out of his **l**." Ex 6:11
the people of Israel out of the **l** of Egypt. Ex 6:13
of Israel from the **l** of Egypt by their Ex 6:26
the LORD spoke to Moses in the **l** of Egypt, Ex 6:28
to let the people of Israel go out of his **l**. Ex 7:2
my signs and wonders in the **l** of Egypt, Ex 7:3
out of the **l** of Egypt by great acts of Ex 7:4
be blood throughout all the **l** of Egypt, Ex 7:19
was blood throughout all the **l** of Egypt. Ex 7:21
make frogs come up on the **l** of Egypt!'" Ex 8:5
frogs came up and covered the **l** of Egypt. Ex 8:6
and made frogs come up on the **l** of Egypt. Ex 8:7
them together in heaps, and the **l** stank. Ex 8:14
may become gnats in all the **l** of Egypt.'" Ex 8:16
earth became gnats in all the **l** of Egypt. Ex 8:17
that day I will set apart the **l** of Goshen, Ex 8:22
Throughout all the **l** of Egypt the land Ex 8:24
the land of Egypt the **l** was ruined by the Ex 8:24
"Go, sacrifice to your God within the **l**." Ex 8:25
the LORD will do this thing in the **l**." Ex 9:5
become fine dust over all the **l** of Egypt, Ex 9:9
and beast throughout all the **l** of Egypt." Ex 9:9
there may be hail in all the **l** of Egypt, Ex 9:22
every plant of the field, in the **l** of Egypt." Ex 9:22
the LORD rained hail upon the **l** of Egypt. Ex 9:23
never been in all the **l** of Egypt since it Ex 9:24
that was in the field in all the **l** of Egypt, Ex 9:25
Only in the **l** of Goshen, where the people Ex 9:26
and they shall cover the face of the **l**, so Ex 10:5
of the land, so that no one can see the **l**. Ex 10:5
your hand over the **l** of Egypt for the Ex 10:12
may come upon the **l** of Egypt and eat Ex 10:12
of Egypt and eat every plant in the **l**, Ex 10:12
out his staff over the **l** of Egypt, Ex 10:13
an east wind upon the **l** all that day and Ex 10:13
up over all the **l** of Egypt and settled Ex 10:14
They covered the face of the whole **l**, so Ex 10:15
whole land, so that the **l** was darkened, Ex 10:15
all the plants in the **l** and all the fruit of Ex 10:15
of the field, through all the **l** of Egypt. Ex 10:15
may be darkness over the **l** of Egypt, Ex 10:21
darkness in all the **l** of Egypt three days. Ex 10:22
Moses was very great in the **l** of Egypt, Ex 11:3
every firstborn in the **l** of Egypt shall die, Ex 11:5
a great cry throughout all the **l** of Egypt, Ex 11:6
may be multiplied in the **l** of Egypt." Ex 11:9
not let the people of Israel go out of his **l**. Ex 11:10
to Moses and Aaron in the **l** of Egypt, Ex 12:1
will pass through the **l** of Egypt that Ex 12:12
strike all the firstborn in the **l** of Egypt, Ex 12:12
destroy you, when I strike the **l** of Egypt. Ex 12:13
your hosts out of the **l** of Egypt. Ex 12:17
he is a sojourner or a native of the **l**. Ex 12:19
you come to the **l** that the LORD will Ex 12:25
down all the firstborn in the **l** of Egypt, Ex 12:29
people to send them out of the **l** in haste. Ex 12:33
of the LORD went out from the **l** of Egypt. Ex 12:41
to bring them out of the **l** of Egypt; Ex 12:42
keep it; he shall be as a native of the **l**. Ex 12:48
of Israel out of the **l** of Egypt by their Ex 12:51
brings you into the **l** of the Canaanites, Ex 13:5
you, a **l** flowing with milk and honey, Ex 13:5
brings you into the **l** of the Canaanites, Ex 13:11
killed all the firstborn in the **l** of Egypt, Ex 13:15
them by way of the **l** of the Philistines, Ex 13:17
up out of the **l** of Egypt equipped for Ex 13:18
of Israel, 'They are wandering in the **l**; Ex 14:3
wind all night and made the sea dry **l**, Ex 14:21
they had departed from the **l** of Egypt. Ex 16:1
by the hand of the LORD in the **l** of Egypt, Ex 16:3
who brought you out of the **l** of Egypt, Ex 16:6
I brought you out of the **l** of Egypt.'" Ex 16:32
years, till they came to a habitable **l**. Ex 16:35
came to the border of the **l** of Canaan. Ex 16:35
"I have been a sojourner in a foreign **l**"), Ex 18:3
of Israel had gone out of the **l** of Egypt, Ex 19:1
who brought you out of the **l** of Egypt, Ex 20:2
may be long in the **l** that the LORD your Ex 20:12
you were sojourners in the **l** of Egypt. Ex 22:21
for you were sojourners in the **l** of Egypt. Ex 23:9
you shall sow your **l** and gather in its Ex 23:10
shall miscarry or be barren in your **l**; Ex 23:26
lest the **l** become desolate and the wild Ex 23:29
you have increased and possess the **l**. Ex 23:30
the inhabitants of the **l** into your hand, Ex 23:31
They shall not dwell in your **l**, lest they Ex 23:33
them out of the **l** of Egypt that I Ex 29:46
who brought us up out of the **l** of Egypt, Ex 32:1
brought you up out of the **l** of Egypt!" Ex 32:4
you brought up out of the **l** of Egypt, Ex 32:7
brought you up out of the **l** of Egypt!'" Ex 32:8
brought out of the **l** of Egypt with great Ex 32:11
and all this **l** that I have promised I will Ex 32:13
who brought us up out of the **l** of Egypt, Ex 32:23
have brought up out of the **l** of Egypt, Ex 33:1
to the **l** of which I swore to Abraham, Ex 33:1
Go up to a **l** flowing with milk and Ex 33:3
the inhabitants of the **l** to which you Ex 34:12
covenant with the inhabitants of the **l**, Ex 34:15
no one shall covet your **l**, when you go Ex 34:24
you up out of the **l** of Egypt to be your Lv 11:45
"When you come into the **l** of Canaan, Lv 14:34
in a house in the **l** of your possession, Lv 14:34
shall not do as they do in the **l** of Egypt, Lv 18:3
not do as they do in the **l** of Canaan, Lv 18:3
and the **l** became unclean, so that I Lv 18:25
and the **l** vomited out its inhabitants. Lv 18:25
(for the people of the **l**, who were before Lv 18:27
so that the **l** became unclean), Lv 18:27
lest the **l** vomit you out when you make Lv 18:28
"When you reap the harvest of your **l**, Lv 19:9
you come into the **l** and plant any kind Lv 19:23
lest the **l** fall into prostitution and the Lv 19:29
prostitution and the **l** become full of Lv 19:29
a stranger sojourns with you in your **l**, Lv 19:33
for you were strangers in the **l** of Egypt: Lv 19:34
who brought you out of the **l** of Egypt. Lv 19:36
The people of the **l** shall stone him with Lv 20:2
if the people of the **l** do at all close their Lv 20:4
that the **l** where I am bringing you to Lv 20:22
said to you, 'You shall inherit their **l**, Lv 20:24
a **l** flowing with milk and honey.' Lv 20:24
LORD; you shall not do it within your **l**, Lv 22:24
brought you out of the **l** of Egypt to be Lv 22:33
you come into the **l** that I give you Lv 23:10
when you reap the harvest of your **l**, Lv 23:22
have gathered in the produce of the **l**, Lv 23:39
I brought them out of the **l** of Egypt: Lv 23:43
you come into the **l** that I give you, Lv 25:2
the **l** shall keep a Sabbath to the LORD. Lv 25:2
be a Sabbath of solemn rest for the **l**, Lv 25:4
It shall be a year of solemn rest for the **l**. Lv 25:5
The Sabbath of the **l** shall provide food Lv 25:6
for the wild animals that are in your **l**: Lv 25:7
the trumpet throughout all your **l**. Lv 25:9
liberty throughout the **l** to all its Lv 25:10
then you will dwell in the **l** securely. Lv 25:18
The **l** will yield its fruit, and you will Lv 25:19
"The **l** shall not be sold in perpetuity, Lv 25:23
be sold in perpetuity, for the **l** is mine. Lv 25:23
you shall allow a redemption of the **l**. Lv 25:24
be classified with the fields of the **l**. Lv 25:31
brought you out of the **l** of Egypt to give Lv 25:38
of Egypt to give you the **l** of Canaan, Lv 25:38
whom I brought out of the **l** of Egypt; Lv 25:42
you, who have been born in your **l**, Lv 25:45
whom I brought out of the **l** of Egypt: Lv 25:55
a figured stone in your **l** to bow down to Lv 26:1
season, and the **l** shall yield its increase, Lv 26:4
to the full and dwell in your **l** securely. Lv 26:5
I will give peace in the **l**, and you shall lie Lv 26:6
I will remove harmful beasts from the **l**, Lv 26:6
the sword shall not go through your **l**. Lv 26:6
who brought you out of the **l** of Egypt, Lv 26:13
for your **l** shall not yield its increase, Lv 26:20
the trees of the **l** shall not yield their Lv 26:20
And I myself will devastate the **l**, so that Lv 26:32
you, and your **l** shall be a desolation, Lv 26:33
"Then the **l** shall enjoy its Sabbaths as Lv 26:34
while you are in your enemies' **l**; Lv 26:34
your enemies' land; then the **l** shall rest, Lv 26:34
and the **l** of your enemies shall eat you Lv 26:38
them into the **l** of their enemies Lv 26:41
Abraham, and I will remember the **l**. Lv 26:42
But the **l** shall be abandoned by them Lv 26:43
when they are in the **l** of their enemies, Lv 26:44
I brought out of the **l** of Egypt in the Lv 26:45
LORD part of the **l** that is his possession, Lv 27:16
to whom the **l** belongs as a possession. Lv 27:24
"Every tithe of the **l**, whether of the seed Lv 27:30
of the seed of the **l** or of the fruit of Lv 27:30
after they had come out of the **l** of Egypt, Nm 1:1
down all the firstborn in the **l** of Egypt, Nm 3:13
the firstborn in the **l** of Egypt I Nm 8:17
after they had come out of the **l** of Egypt, Nm 9:1
to war in your **l** against the adversary Nm 10:9
depart to my own **l** and to my Nm 10:30

to the **l** that you swore to give their Nm 11:12
"Send men to spy out the **l** of Canaan, Nm 13:2
whom Moses sent to spy out the **l**. Nm 13:16
to spy out the **l** of Canaan and said Nm 13:17
and see what the **l** is, and whether the Nm 13:18
and whether the **l** that they dwell in is Nm 13:19
and whether the **l** is rich or poor, and Nm 13:20
of the fruit of the **l**." Now the time was Nm 13:20
spied out the **l** from the wilderness Nm 13:21
they returned from spying out the **l**. Nm 13:25
and showed them the fruit of the **l**. Nm 13:26
"We came to the **l** to which you sent Nm 13:27
people who dwell in the **l** are strong, Nm 13:28
dwell in the **l** of the Negeb. Nm 13:29
bad report of the **l** that they had spied Nm 13:32
that they had spied out, saying, "The **l**, Nm 13:32
out, is a **l** that devours its inhabitants, Nm 13:32
that we had died in the **l** of Egypt! Nm 14:2
is the LORD bringing us into this **l**, Nm 14:3
among those who had spied out the **l**, Nm 14:6
of the people of Israel, "The **l**, Nm 14:7
to spy it out, is an exceedingly good **l**. Nm 14:7
will bring us into this **l** and give it to Nm 14:8
us, a **l** that flows with milk and honey. Nm 14:8
And do not fear the people of the **l**, for Nm 14:9
they will tell the inhabitants of this **l**. Nm 14:14
this people into the **l** that he swore to Nm 14:16
shall see the **l** that I swore to give to Nm 14:23
will bring into the **l** into which he Nm 14:24
shall come into the **l** where I swore Nm 14:30
they shall know the **l** that you have Nm 14:31
the days in which you spied out the **l**, Nm 14:34
whom Moses sent to spy out the **l**, Nm 14:36
bringing up a bad report about the **l**— Nm 14:36
a bad report of the **l**—died by plague Nm 14:37
those men who went to spy out the **l**, Nm 14:38
you come into the **l** you are to inhabit, Nm 15:2
you come into the **l** to which I bring Nm 15:18
and when you eat of the bread of the **l**, Nm 15:19
brought you out of the **l** of Egypt to be Nm 15:41
us up out of a **l** flowing with milk and Nm 16:13
brought us into a **l** flowing with milk Nm 16:14
first ripe fruits of all that is in their **l**, Nm 18:13
shall have no inheritance in their **l**, Nm 18:20
this assembly into the **l** that I have Nm 20:12
Please let us pass through your **l**. We Nm 20:17
Hor, on the border of the **l** of Edom, Nm 20:23
shall not enter the **l** that I have given Nm 20:24
the Red Sea, to go around the **l** of Edom. Nm 21:4
"Let me pass through your **l**. We will Nm 21:22
possession of his **l** from the Arnon Nm 21:24
and taken all his **l** out of his hand, Nm 21:26
Israel lived in the **l** of the Amorites. Nm 21:31
hand, and all his people, and his **l**. Nm 21:34
survivor left. And they possessed his **l**. Nm 21:35
near the River in the **l** of the people of Nm 22:5
defeat them and drive them from the **l**, Nm 22:6
princes of Balak, "Go to your own **l**, Nm 22:13
who came out of the **l** of Egypt were: Nm 26:4
Er and Onan died in the **l** of Canaan. Nm 26:19
"Among these the **l** shall be divided Nm 26:53
But the **l** shall be divided by lot. Nm 26:55
Abarim and see the **l** that I have given Nm 27:12
And they saw the **l** of Jazer and the land Nm 32:1
saw the land of Jazer and the **l** of Gilead, Nm 32:1
the **l** that the LORD struck down before Nm 32:4
of Israel, is a **l** for livestock, Nm 32:4
let this **l** be given to your servants for a Nm 32:5
going over into the **l** that the LORD has Nm 32:7
them from Kadesh-barnea to see the **l**. Nm 32:8
to the Valley of Eshcol and saw the **l**, Nm 32:9
from going into the **l** that the LORD had Nm 32:9
shall see the **l** that I swore to give to Nm 32:11
because of the inhabitants of the **l**. Nm 32:17
and the **l** is subdued before the LORD; Nm 32:22
and this **l** shall be your possession Nm 32:22
the Jordan and the **l** shall be subdued Nm 32:29
shall give them the **l** of Gilead for a Nm 32:29
among you in the **l** of Canaan." Nm 32:30
before the LORD into the **l** of Canaan, Nm 32:32
the **l** and its cities with their Nm 32:33
cities of the **l** throughout the country. Nm 32:33
they went out of the **l** of Egypt by their Nm 33:1
Hor, on the edge of the **l** of Edom. Nm 33:37
Israel had come out of the **l** of Egypt, Nm 33:38
lived in the Negeb in the **l** of Canaan, Nm 33:40
over the Jordan into the **l** of Canaan, Nm 33:51
inhabitants of the **l** from before you Nm 33:52
take possession of the **l** and settle in it, Nm 33:53
for I have given the **l** to you to possess Nm 33:53
shall inherit the **l** by lot according Nm 33:54
inhabitants of the **l** from before you, Nm 33:55
trouble you in the **l** where you dwell. Nm 33:55
When you enter the **l** of Canaan (this Nm 34:2
of Canaan (this is the **l** that shall fall to Nm 34:2
the **l** of Canaan as defined by its Nm 34:2
This shall be your **l** as defined by its Nm 34:12
"This is the **l** that you shall inherit by Nm 34:13
who shall divide the **l** to you for Nm 34:17
tribe to divide the **l** for inheritance. Nm 34:18
people of Israel in the **l** of Canaan." Nm 34:29
cross the Jordan into the **l** of Canaan, Nm 35:10
and three cities in the **l** of Canaan, Nm 35:14
may return to the **l** of his possession. Nm 35:28
to dwell in the **l** before the death of Nm 35:32
shall not pollute the **l** in which you Nm 35:33
you live, for blood pollutes the **l**, Nm 35:33
be made for the **l** for the blood that Nm 35:33
shall not defile the **l** in which you live, Nm 35:34
lord to give the **l** for inheritance by lot Nm 36:2
Beyond the Jordan, in the **l** of Moab, Dt 1:5
by the seacoast, the **l** of the Canaanites, Dt 1:7
See, I have set the **l** before you. Go in and Dt 1:8
take possession of the **l** that the LORD Dt 1:8
LORD your God has set the **l** before you. Dt 1:21
they may explore the **l** for us and bring Dt 1:22
of the fruit of the **l** and brought it down Dt 1:25
'It is a good **l** that the LORD our God is Dt 1:25
he has brought us out of the **l** of Egypt, Dt 1:27
shall see the good **l** that I swore to Dt 1:35
children I will give the **l** on which he has Dt 1:36
them, for I will not give you any of their **l**, Dt 2:5
not give you any of their **l** for a possession, Dt 2:9
as Israel did to the **l** of their possession, Dt 2:12
give you any of the **l** of the people of Dt 2:19
(It is also counted as a **l** of Rephaim. Dt 2:20
the Amorite, king of Heshbon, and his **l**. Dt 2:24
'Let me pass through your **l**. I will go Dt 2:27
the Jordan into the **l** that the LORD our Dt 2:29
to give Sihon and his **l** over to you. Dt 2:31
possession, that you may occupy his **l**.' Dt 2:31
Only to the **l** of the sons of Ammon you Dt 2:37
all his people and his **l** into your hand. Dt 3:2
So we took the **l** at that time out of the Dt 3:8
we took possession of this **l** at that time, Dt 3:12
of Bashan is called the **l** of Rephaim. Dt 3:13
your God has given you this **l** to possess. Dt 3:18
they also occupy the **l** that the LORD your Dt 3:20
and see the good **l** beyond the Jordan, Dt 3:25
in possession of the **l** that you shall see.' Dt 3:28
and take possession of the **l** that the LORD, Dt 4:1
do them in the **l** that you are entering Dt 4:5
do them in the **l** that you are going Dt 4:14
not enter the good **l** that the LORD your Dt 4:21
For I must die in this **l**; I must not go Dt 4:22
over and take possession of that good **l**. Dt 4:22
children, and have grown old in the **l**, Dt 4:25
utterly perish from the **l** that you are Dt 4:26
in, to give you their **l** for an inheritance, Dt 4:38
your days in the **l** that the LORD your Dt 4:40
in the **l** of Sihon the king of the Dt 4:46
took possession of his **l** and the land of Dt 4:47
possession of his land and the **l** of Og, Dt 4:47
who brought you out of the **l** of Egypt, Dt 5:6
that you were a slave in the **l** of Egypt, Dt 5:15
well with you in the **l** that the LORD your Dt 5:16
may do them in the **l** that I am giving Dt 5:31
live long in the **l** that you shall possess. Dt 5:33
may do them in the **l** to which you are Dt 6:1
you, in a **l** flowing with milk and honey. Dt 6:3
brings you into the **l** that he swore to Dt 6:10
who brought you out of the **l** of Egypt, Dt 6:12
possession of the good **l** that the LORD Dt 6:18
in and give us the **l** that he swore to give Dt 6:23
brings you into the **l** that you are entering Dt 7:1
in the **l** that he swore to your fathers to Dt 7:13
go in and possess the **l** that the LORD swore Dt 8:1
your God is bringing you into a good **l**, Dt 8:7
into a good land, a **l** of brooks of water, Dt 8:7
a **l** of wheat and barley, of vines and fig Dt 8:8
pomegranates, a **l** of olive trees and honey, Dt 8:8
a **l** in which you will eat bread without Dt 8:9
lack nothing, a **l** whose stones are iron, Dt 8:9
your God for the good **l** he has given you. Dt 8:10
who brought you out of the **l** of Egypt, Dt 8:14
LORD has brought me in to possess this **l**,' Dt 9:4
heart are you going in to possess their **l**, Dt 9:5
giving you this good **l** to possess because Dt 9:6
you came out of the **l** of Egypt until you Dt 9:7
take possession of the **l** that I have given Dt 9:23
lest the **l** from which you brought us Dt 9:28
bring them into the **l** that he promised Dt 9:28
to Jotbathah, a **l** with brooks of water. Dt 10:7
so that they may go in and possess the **l**, Dt 10:11
you were sojourners in the **l** of Egypt. Dt 10:19
the king of Egypt and to all his **l**, Dt 11:3
take possession of the **l** that you are Dt 11:8
may live long in the **l** that the LORD swore Dt 11:9
a **l** flowing with milk and honey. Dt 11:9
For the **l** that you are entering to take Dt 11:10
possession of it is not like the **l** of Egypt, Dt 11:10
But the **l** that you are going over to Dt 11:11
over to possess is a **l** of hills and valleys, Dt 11:11
a **l** that the LORD your God cares for. Dt 11:12
give the rain for your **l** in its season, Dt 11:14
be no rain, and the **l** will yield no fruit, Dt 11:17
quickly off the good **l** that the LORD is Dt 11:17
be multiplied in the **l** that the LORD Dt 11:21
of you on all the **l** that you shall tread, Dt 11:25
brings you into the **l** that you are Dt 11:29
in the **l** of the Canaanites who live in Dt 11:30
take possession of the **l** that the LORD Dt 11:31
be careful to do in the **l** that the LORD, Dt 12:1
and live in the **l** that the LORD your Dt 12:10
the Levite as long as you live in your **l**. Dt 12:19
dispossess them and dwell in their **l**, Dt 12:29
you out of the **l** of Egypt and redeemed Dt 13:5
who brought you out of the **l** of Egypt, Dt 13:10
will bless you in the **l** that the LORD your Dt 15:4
your towns within your **l** that the LORD Dt 15:7
there will never cease to be poor in the **l**. Dt 15:11
to the needy and to the poor, in your **l**.' Dt 15:11
that you were a slave in the **l** of Egypt, Dt 15:15
you came out of the **l** of Egypt in haste— Dt 16:3
day when you came out of the **l** of Egypt. Dt 16:3
live and inherit the **l** that the LORD your Dt 16:20
you come to the **l** that the LORD your Dt 17:14
you come into the **l** that the LORD your Dt 18:9
off the nations whose **l** the LORD your Dt 19:1
for yourselves in the **l** that the LORD your Dt 19:2
parts the area of the **l** that the LORD your Dt 19:3
gives you all the **l** that he promised to Dt 19:8
be shed in your **l** that the LORD your Dt 19:10
you will hold in the **l** that the LORD your Dt 19:14
who brought you up out of the **l** of Egypt. Dt 20:1
"If in the **l** that the LORD your God is Dt 21:1
shall not defile your **l** that the LORD Dt 21:23
because you were a sojourner in his **l**. Dt 23:7
you undertake in the **l** that you are Dt 23:20
bring sin upon the **l** that the LORD your Dt 24:4
who are in your **l** within your towns. Dt 24:14
that you were a slave in the **l** of Egypt; Dt 24:22
may be long in the **l** that the LORD your Dt 25:15
in the **l** that the LORD your God is giving Dt 25:19
you come into the **l** that the LORD your Dt 26:1
you harvest from your **l** that the LORD Dt 26:2
have come into the **l** that the LORD swore Dt 26:3
us into this place and gave us this **l**, Dt 26:9
land, a **l** flowing with milk and honey. Dt 26:9
a **l** flowing with milk and honey.' Dt 26:15
the Jordan to the **l** that the LORD your Dt 27:2
over to enter the **l** that the LORD your Dt 27:3
you, a **l** flowing with milk and honey, Dt 27:3
will bless you in the **l** that the LORD your Dt 28:8
within the **l** that the LORD swore to your Dt 28:11
give the rain to your **l** in its season and Dt 28:12
consumed you off the **l** that you are Dt 28:21
will make the rain of your **l** powder. Dt 28:24
come down throughout all your **l**. Dt 28:52
in all your towns throughout all your **l**, Dt 28:52
be plucked off the **l** that you are Dt 28:63
with the people of Israel in the **l** of Moab, Dt 29:1
did before your eyes in the **l** of Egypt, Dt 29:2
and to all his servants and to all his **l**, Dt 29:2
We took their **l** and gave it for an Dt 29:8
know how we lived in the **l** of Egypt, Dt 29:16
the foreigner who comes from a far **l**, Dt 29:22
afflictions of that **l** and the sicknesses Dt 29:22
the whole **l** burned out with brimstone Dt 29:23
'Why has the LORD done thus to this **l**? Dt 29:24
he brought them out of the **l** of Egypt, Dt 29:25
of the LORD was kindled against this **l**, Dt 29:27
them from their **l** in anger and Dt 29:28
wrath, and cast them into another **l**, Dt 29:28
bring you into the **l** that your fathers Dt 30:5
bless you in the **l** that you are entering Dt 30:16
not live long in the **l** that you are going Dt 30:18
may dwell in the **l** that the LORD swore Dt 30:20
the kings of the Amorites, and to their **l**, Dt 31:4
this people into the **l** that the LORD has Dt 31:7
as you live in the **l** that you are going Dt 31:13
among them in the **l** that they are Dt 31:16
them into the **l** flowing with milk Dt 31:20
brought them into the **l** that I swore to Dt 31:21
people of Israel into the **l** that I swore to Dt 31:23
"He found him in a desert **l**, and in the Dt 32:10
him ride on the high places of the **l**, Dt 32:13
hate him and cleanses his people's **l**." Dt 32:43
live long in the **l** that you are going Dt 32:47
Mount Nebo, which is in the **l** of Moab, Dt 32:49
Jericho, and view the **l** of Canaan, Dt 32:49
For you shall see the **l** before you, but Dt 32:52
into the **l** that I am giving to the people Dt 32:52
he said, "Blessed by the LORD be his **l**, Dt 33:13
He chose the best of the **l** for himself, for Dt 33:21

lived alone, in a **l** of grain and wine, Dt 33:28
And the LORD showed him all the **l**, Dt 34:1
the **l** of Ephraim and Manasseh, Dt 34:2
all the **l** of Judah as far as the western sea, Dt 34:2
"This is the **l** of which I swore to Dt 34:4
of the LORD died there in the **l** of Moab, Dt 34:5
the valley in the **l** of Moab opposite Dt 34:6
the LORD sent him to do in the **l** of Egypt, Dt 34:11
and to all his servants and to all his **l**, Dt 34:11
people, into the **l** that I am giving to them, Jos 1:2
all the **l** of the Hittites to the Great Sea Jos 1:4
this people to inherit the **l** that I swore to Jos 1:6
take possession of the **l** that the LORD Jos 1:11
a place of rest and will give you this **l**.' Jos 1:13
shall remain in the **l** that Moses gave Jos 1:14
take possession of the **l** that the LORD Jos 1:15
shall return to the **l** of your possession Jos 1:15
the **l** that Moses the servant of the LORD Jos 1:15
Shittim as spies, saying, "Go, view the **l**, Jos 2:1
come here tonight to search out the **l**." Jos 2:2
they have come to search out all the **l**." Jos 2:3
"I know that the LORD has given you the **l**, Jos 2:9
the inhabitants of the **l** melt away before Jos 2:9
LORD gives us the **l** we will deal kindly Jos 2:14
Behold, when we come into the **l**, you Jos 2:18
LORD has given all the **l** into our hands. Jos 2:24
inhabitants of the **l** melt away because Jos 2:24
not let them see the **l** that the LORD had Jos 5:6
to us, a **l** flowing with milk and honey. Jos 5:6
very day, they ate of the produce of the **l**, Jos 5:11
day after they ate of the produce of the **l**. Jos 5:12
of the fruit of the **l** of Canaan that year. Jos 5:12
to the two men who had spied out the **l**, Jos 6:22
Joshua, and his fame was in all the **l**. Jos 6:27
up and spy out the **l**." And the men went Jos 7:2
all the inhabitants of the **l** will hear of it Jos 7:9
of Ai, and his people, his city, and his **l**. Jos 8:1
to give you all the **l** and to destroy all the Jos 9:24
the inhabitants of the **l** from before you Jos 9:24
So Joshua struck the whole **l**, the hill Jos 10:40
all these kings and their **l** at one time, Jos 10:42
under Hermon in the **l** of Mizpah. Jos 11:3
So Joshua took all that **l**, the hill Jos 11:16
Negeb and all the **l** of Goshen and the Jos 11:16
the Anakim left in the **l** of the people of Jos 11:22
So Joshua took the whole **l**, according Jos 11:23
And the **l** had rest from war. Jos 11:23
are the kings of the **l** whom the people of Jos 12:1
possession of their **l** beyond the Jordan Jos 12:1
the LORD gave their **l** for a possession to Jos 12:6
the kings of the **l** whom Joshua and the Jos 12:7
(and Joshua gave their **l** to the tribes of Jos 12:7
and in the Negeb, the **l** of the Hittites, Jos 12:8
remains yet very much **l** to possess. Jos 13:1
This is the **l** that yet remains: all the Jos 13:2
in the south, all the **l** of the Canaanites, Jos 13:4
and the **l** of the Gebalites, and all Jos 13:5
Only allot the **l** to Israel for an Jos 13:6
therefore divide this **l** for an inheritance Jos 13:7
the princes of Sihon, who lived in the **l**. Jos 13:21
and half the **l** of the Ammonites, Jos 13:25
of Israel received in the **l** of Canaan, Jos 14:1
portion was given to the Levites in the **l**, Jos 14:4
commanded Moses; they allotted the **l**. Jos 14:5
me from Kadesh-barnea to spy out the **l**, Jos 14:7
'Surely the **l** on which your foot has Jos 14:9
Anakim.) And the **l** had rest from war. Jos 14:15
you have given me the **l** of the Negeb, Jos 15:19
besides the **l** of Gilead and Bashan, Jos 17:5
The **l** of Gilead was allotted to the rest of Jos 17:6
The **l** of Tappuah belonged to Jos 17:8
the **l** to the south being Ephraim's and Jos 17:10
persisted in dwelling in that **l**. Jos 17:12
for yourselves in the **l** of the Perizzites Jos 17:15
there. The **l** lay subdued before them. Jos 18:1
off going in to take possession of the **l**, Jos 18:3
may set out and go up and down the **l**. Jos 18:4
shall describe the **l** in seven divisions Jos 18:6
went to write the description of the **l**, Jos 18:8
and down in the **l** and write a Jos 18:8
up and down in the **l** and wrote in a Jos 18:9
Joshua apportioned the **l** to the people Jos 18:10
territories of the **l** as inheritances, Jos 19:49
meeting. So they finished dividing the **l**. Jos 19:51
to them at Shiloh in the **l** of Canaan, Jos 21:2
gave to Israel all the **l** that he swore to Jos 21:43
your tents in the **l** where your possession Jos 22:4
their brothers in the **l** west of the Jordan. Jos 22:7
at Shiloh, which is in the **l** of Canaan, Jos 22:9
land of Canaan, to go to the **l** of Gilead, Jos 22:9
their own **l** of which they had possessed Jos 22:9
of the Jordan that is in the **l** of Canaan, Jos 22:10
altar at the frontier of the **l** of Canaan, Jos 22:11
of Manasseh, in the **l** of Gilead, Jos 22:13
of Manasseh, in the **l** of Gilead, Jos 22:15

if the **l** of your possession is unclean, Jos 22:19
over into the LORD'S **l** where the LORD'S Jos 22:19
people of Gad in the **l** of Gilead to the Jos 22:32
in the land of Gilead to the **l** of Canaan, Jos 22:32
them to destroy the **l** where the people Jos 22:33
And you shall possess their **l**, just as the Jos 23:5
from off this good **l** that the LORD your Jos 23:15
from off the good **l** that he has given Jos 23:16
and led him through all the **l** of Canaan, Jos 24:3
I brought you to the **l** of the Amorites, Jos 24:8
hand, and you took possession of their **l**, Jos 24:8
I gave you a **l** on which you had not Jos 24:13
of the Amorites in whose **l** you dwell. Jos 24:15
and our fathers up from the **l** of Egypt, Jos 24:17
peoples, the Amorites who lived in the **l**. Jos 24:18
in the piece of **l** that Jacob bought from Jos 24:32
behold, I have given the **l** into his hand." Jgs 1:2
you have set me in the **l** of the Negeb, Jgs 1:15
the man went to the **l** of the Hittites and Jgs 1:26
persisted in dwelling in that **l**. Jgs 1:27
the Canaanites, the inhabitants of the **l**, Jgs 1:32
the Canaanites, the inhabitants of the **l**. Jgs 1:33
and brought you into the **l** that I swore to Jgs 2:1
covenant with the inhabitants of this **l**; Jgs 2:2
his inheritance to take possession of the **l**. Jgs 2:6
had brought them out of the **l** of Egypt. Jgs 2:12
So the **l** had rest forty years. Then Jgs 3:11
Israel. And the **l** had rest for eighty years. Jgs 3:30
his might." And the **l** had rest for forty Jgs 5:31
them and devour the produce of the **l**, Jgs 6:4
that they laid waste the **l** as they came in. Jgs 6:5
them out before you and gave you their **l**. Jgs 6:9
of the Amorites in whose **l** you dwell.' Jgs 6:10
And the **l** had rest forty years in the days Jgs 8:28
coming down from the center of the **l**, Jgs 9:37
to this day, which are in the **l** of Gilead. Jgs 10:4
the Jordan in the **l** of the Amorites, Jgs 10:8
his brothers and lived in the **l** of Tob, Jgs 11:3
to bring Jephthah from the **l** of Tob. Jgs 11:5
come to me to fight against my **l**?" Jgs 11:12
coming up from Egypt took away my **l**, Jgs 11:13
did not take away the **l** of Moab or the Jgs 11:15
of Moab or the **l** of the Ammonites, Jgs 11:15
'Please let us pass through your **l**,' Jgs 11:17
and went around the **l** of Edom and the Jgs 11:18
of Edom and the **l** of Moab and arrived Jgs 11:18
east side of the **l** of Moab and camped Jgs 11:18
us pass through your **l** to our country,' Jgs 11:19
possession of all the **l** of the Amorites, Jgs 11:21
buried at Aijalon in the **l** of Zebulun. Jgs 12:12
buried at Pirathon in the **l** of Ephraim, Jgs 12:15
Eshtaol, to spy out the **l** and to explore it. Jgs 18:2
"Go and explore the **l**." And they came to Jgs 18:2
up against them, for we have seen the **l**, Jgs 18:9
slow to go, to enter in and possess the **l**. Jgs 18:9
The **l** is spacious, for God has given it Jgs 18:10
to scout out the **l** went up and entered Jgs 18:17
until the day of the captivity of the **l**. Jgs 18:30
came up out of the **l** of Egypt until this Jgs 19:30
to Beersheba, including the **l** of Gilead, Jgs 20:1
at Shiloh, which is in the **l** of Canaan. Jgs 21:12
of Shiloh, and go to the **l** of Benjamin. Jgs 21:21
judges ruled there was a famine in the **l**, Ru 1:1
on the way to return to the **l** of Judah. Ru 1:7
mother and your native **l** and came to a Ru 2:11
selling the parcel of **l** that belonged to our Ru 4:3
images of your mice that ravage the **l**, 1 Sm 6:5
from off you and your gods and your **l**. 1 Sm 6:5
If it goes up on the way to its own **l**, to 1 Sm 6:9
and passed through the **l** of Shalishah, 1 Sm 9:4
they passed through the **l** of Shaalim, 1 Sm 9:4
they passed through the **l** of Benjamin, 1 Sm 9:4
When they came to the **l** of Zuph, Saul 1 Sm 9:5
to you a man from the **l** of Benjamin, 1 Sm 9:16
your fathers up out of the **l** of Egypt. 1 Sm 12:6
blew the trumpet throughout all the **l**, 1 Sm 13:3
the Jordan to the **l** of Gad and Gilead. 1 Sm 13:7
toward Ophrah, to the **l** of Shual; 1 Sm 13:17
found throughout all the **l** of Israel, 1 Sm 13:19
half a furrow's length in an acre of **l**. 1 Sm 14:14
said, "My father has troubled the **l**. 1 Sm 14:29
"Is not this David the king of the **l**? 1 Sm 21:11
and go into the **l** of Judah." So David 1 Sm 22:5
And if he is in the **l**, I will search him 1 Sm 23:23
have made a raid against the **l**." 1 Sm 23:27
escape to the **l** of the Philistines. 1 Sm 27:1
the inhabitants of the **l** from of old, 1 Sm 27:8
of old, as far as Shur, to the **l** of Egypt. 1 Sm 27:8
would strike the **l** and would leave 1 Sm 27:9
and the necromancers out of the **l**. 1 Sm 28:3
and the necromancers from the **l**. 1 Sm 28:9
to return to the **l** of the Philistines. 1 Sm 29:11
were spread abroad over all the **l**, 1 Sm 30:16
taken from the **l** of the Philistines 1 Sm 30:16
Philistines and from the **l** of Judah. 1 Sm 30:16

messengers throughout the **l** of the 1 Sm 31:9
saying, "To whom does the **l** belong? 2 Sm 3:12
the Jebusites, the inhabitants of the **l**, 2 Sm 5:6
to you all the **l** of Saul your father, 2 Sm 9:7
servants shall till the **l** for him and 2 Sm 9:10
came into the **l** of the Ammonites. 2 Sm 10:2
say, "Oh that I were judge in the **l**! 2 Sm 15:4
And all the **l** wept aloud as all the 2 Sm 15:23
encamped in the **l** of Gilead. 2 Sm 17:26
he has fled out of the **l** from Absalom. 2 Sm 19:9
you and Ziba shall divide the **l**." 2 Sm 19:29
son Jonathan in the **l** of Benjamin in 2 Sm 21:14
God responded to the plea for the **l**. 2 Sm 21:14
and to Kadesh in the **l** of the Hittites; 2 Sm 24:6
when they had gone through all the **l**, 2 Sm 24:8
of famine come to you in your **l**? 2 Sm 24:13
be three days' pestilence in your **l**? 2 Sm 24:13
LORD responded to the plea for the **l**, 2 Sm 24:25
Socoh and all the **l** of Hepher); 1 Kgs 4:10
the son of Uri, in the **l** of Gilead, 1 Kgs 4:19
was one governor who was over the **l**. 1 Kgs 4:19
Euphrates to the **l** of the Philistines 1 Kgs 4:21
of Israel came out of the **l** of Egypt, 1 Kgs 6:1
when they came out of the **l** of Egypt. 1 Kgs 8:9
brought them out of the **l** of Egypt." 1 Kgs 8:21
them again to the **l** that you gave to 1 Kgs 8:34
walk, and grant rain upon your **l**, 1 Kgs 8:36
"If there is famine in the **l**, if there is 1 Kgs 8:37
besieges them in the **l** at their gates, 1 Kgs 8:37
that they live in the **l** that you gave to 1 Kgs 8:40
away captive to the **l** of the enemy, 1 Kgs 8:46
their heart in the **l** to which they have 1 Kgs 8:47
with you in the **l** of their captors, 1 Kgs 8:47
their heart in the **l** of their enemies, 1 Kgs 8:48
and pray to you toward their **l**, 1 Kgs 8:48
off Israel from the **l** that I have given 1 Kgs 9:7
done thus to this **l** and to this house?' 1 Kgs 9:8
fathers out of the **l** of Egypt and laid 1 Kgs 9:9
Hiram twenty cities in the **l** of Galilee. 1 Kgs 9:11
they are called the **l** of Cabul to this 1 Kgs 9:13
in the wilderness, in the **l** of Judah, 1 Kgs 9:18
and in all the **l** of his dominion. 1 Kgs 9:19
who were left after them in the **l**, 1 Kgs 9:21
shore of the Red Sea, in the **l** of Edom. 1 Kgs 9:26
heard in my own **l** of your words and 1 Kgs 10:6
back to her own **l** with her servants. 1 Kgs 10:13
west and from the governors of the **l**. 1 Kgs 10:15
allowance of food and gave him **l**. 1 Kgs 11:18
you up out of the **l** of Egypt." 1 Kgs 12:28
out of this good **l** that he gave to 1 Kgs 14:15
also male cult prostitutes in the **l**. 1 Kgs 14:24
out of the **l** and removed all 1 Kgs 15:12
with all the **l** of Naphtali. 1 Kgs 15:20
up, because there was no rain in the **l**. 1 Kgs 17:7
"Go through the **l** to all the springs of 1 Kgs 18:5
So they divided the **l** between them to 1 Kgs 18:6
called all the elders of the **l** and said, 1 Kgs 20:7
And from the **l** he exterminated the 1 Kgs 22:46
water is bad, and the **l** is unfruitful." 2 Kgs 2:19
every good piece of **l** with stones." 2 Kgs 3:19
every good piece of **l** every man threw 2 Kgs 3:25
from him and returned to their own **l**. 2 Kgs 3:27
when there was a famine in the **l**. 2 Kgs 4:38
off a little girl from the **l** of Israel, 2 Kgs 5:2
so spoke the girl from the **l** of Israel." 2 Kgs 5:4
again on raids into the **l** of Israel. 2 Kgs 6:23
will come upon the **l** for seven years." 2 Kgs 8:1
sojourned in the **l** of the Philistines 2 Kgs 8:2
returned from the **l** of the Philistines, 2 Kgs 8:3
to the king for her house and her **l**. 2 Kgs 8:3
to the king for her house and her **l**. 2 Kgs 8:5
the day that she left the **l** until now." 2 Kgs 8:6
Jordan eastward, all the **l** of Gilead, 2 Kgs 10:33
while Athaliah reigned over the **l**. 2 Kgs 11:3
people of the **l** rejoicing and blowing 2 Kgs 11:14
the people of the **l** went to the house 2 Kgs 11:18
guards, and all the people of the **l**, 2 Kgs 11:19
So all the people of the **l** rejoiced, and 2 Kgs 11:20
used to invade the **l** in the spring of 2 Kgs 13:20
governing the people of the **l**. 2 Kgs 15:5
king of Assyria came against the **l**, 2 Kgs 15:19
back and did not stay there in the **l**. 2 Kgs 15:20
and Galilee, all the **l** of Naphtali, 2 Kgs 15:29
offering of all the people of the **l**, 2 Kgs 16:15
Assyria invaded all the **l** and came to 2 Kgs 17:5
up out of the **l** of Egypt from under 2 Kgs 17:7
from their own **l** to Assyria until 2 Kgs 17:23
not know the law of the god of the **l**. 2 Kgs 17:26
not know the law of the god of the **l**." 2 Kgs 17:26
them the law of the god of the **l**." 2 Kgs 17:27
you out of the **l** of Egypt with great 2 Kgs 17:36
LORD said to me, Go up against this **l**, 2 Kgs 18:25
you away to a **l** like your own land, 2 Kgs 18:32
you away to a land like your own **l**, 2 Kgs 18:32
own land, a **l** of grain and wine, 2 Kgs 18:32

and wine, a **l** of bread and vineyards, 2 Kgs 18:32
a **l** of olive trees and honey, 2 Kgs 18:32
nations ever delivered his **l** out of the 2 Kgs 18:33
hear a rumor and return to his own **l**, 2 Kgs 19:7
him fall by the sword in his own **l**.'" 2 Kgs 19:7
and escaped into the **l** of Ararat. 2 Kgs 19:37
anymore out of the **l** that I gave to 2 Kgs 21:8
the people of the **l** struck down all 2 Kgs 21:24
the people of the **l** made Josiah his 2 Kgs 21:24
were seen in the **l** of Judah and in 2 Kgs 23:24
the people of the **l** took Jehoahaz the 2 Kgs 23:30
bonds at Riblah in the **l** of Hamath, 2 Kgs 23:33
and laid on the **l** a tribute of a 2 Kgs 23:33
but he taxed the **l** to give the money 2 Kgs 23:35
and the gold of the people of the **l**, 2 Kgs 23:35
Egypt did not come again out of his **l**, 2 Kgs 24:7
except the poorest people of the **l**. 2 Kgs 24:14
chief men of the **l** he took into 2 Kgs 24:15
was no food for the people of the **l**. 2 Kgs 25:3
the poorest of the **l** to be vinedressers 2 Kgs 25:12
who mustered the people of the **l**, 2 Kgs 25:19
the people of the **l** who were found in 2 Kgs 25:19
death at Riblah in the **l** of Hamath. 2 Kgs 25:21
was taken into exile out of its **l**. 2 Kgs 25:21
who remained in the **l** of Judah, 2 Kgs 25:22
Live in the **l** and serve the king of 2 Kgs 25:24
who reigned in the **l** of Edom before 1 Chr 1:43
Husham of the **l** of the Temanites 1 Chr 1:45
twenty-three cities in the **l** of Gilead. 1 Chr 2:22
pasture, and the **l** was very broad, 1 Chr 4:40
had multiplied in the **l** of Gilead. 1 Chr 5:9
against them in the **l** of Bashan as far 1 Chr 5:11
half-tribe of Manasseh lived in the **l**. 1 Chr 5:23
after the gods of the peoples of the **l**, 1 Chr 5:25
gave Hebron in the **l** of Judah and its 1 Chr 6:55
of Gath who were born in the **l** killed, 1 Chr 7:21
messengers throughout the **l** of the 1 Chr 10:9
were, the inhabitants of the **l**. 1 Chr 11:4
"To you I will give the **l** of Canaan, 1 Chr 16:18
came to the **l** of the Ammonites 1 Chr 19:2
to overthrow and to spy out the **l**?" 1 Chr 19:3
of the LORD, pestilence on the **l**, 1 Chr 21:12
aliens who were in the **l** of Israel, 1 Chr 22:2
inhabitants of the **l** into my hand, 1 Chr 22:18
and the **l** is subdued before the LORD 1 Chr 22:18
may possess this good **l** and leave it 1 Chr 28:8
aliens who were in the **l** of Israel, 2 Chr 2:17
my people out of the **l** of Egypt, 2 Chr 6:5
them again to the **l** that you gave to 2 Chr 6:25
walk, and grant rain upon your **l**, 2 Chr 6:27
"If there is famine in the **l**, if there is 2 Chr 6:28
besiege them in the **l** at their gates, 2 Chr 6:28
that they live in the **l** that you gave to 2 Chr 6:31
away captive to a **l** far or near, 2 Chr 6:36
their heart in the **l** to which they 2 Chr 6:37
with you in the **l** of their captivity, 2 Chr 6:37
their heart in the **l** of their captivity 2 Chr 6:38
captive, and pray toward their **l**, 2 Chr 6:38
command the locust to devour the **l**, 2 Chr 7:13
will forgive their sin and heal their **l**. 2 Chr 7:14
you up from my **l** that I have given 2 Chr 7:20
done thus to this **l** and to this house?' 2 Chr 7:21
them out of the **l** of Egypt and laid 2 Chr 7:22
and in all the **l** of his dominion. 2 Chr 8:6
who were left after them in the **l**, 2 Chr 8:8
the shore of the sea, in the **l** of Edom. 2 Chr 8:17
I heard in my own **l** of your words and 2 Chr 9:5
like of them before in the **l** of Judah. 2 Chr 9:11
back to her own **l** with her servants. 2 Chr 9:12
governors of the **l** brought gold and 2 Chr 9:14
Euphrates to the **l** of the Philistines 2 Chr 9:26
In his days the **l** had rest for ten years. 2 Chr 14:1
cities in Judah, for the **l** had rest. 2 Chr 14:6
The **l** is still ours, because we have 2 Chr 14:7
idols from all the **l** of Judah and 2 Chr 15:8
and set garrisons in the **l** of Judah, 2 Chr 17:2
destroyed the Asherahs out of the **l**, 2 Chr 19:3
appointed judges in the **l** in all the 2 Chr 19:5
inhabitants of this **l** before your 2 Chr 20:7
when they came from the **l** of Egypt, 2 Chr 20:10
while Athaliah reigned over the **l**. 2 Chr 22:12
people of the **l** rejoicing and 2 Chr 23:13
the people, and all the people of the **l**, 2 Chr 23:20
So all the people of the **l** rejoiced, 2 Chr 23:21
governing the people of the **l**. 2 Chr 26:21
their captors and return to this **l**. 2 Chr 30:9
who came out of the **l** of Israel, 2 Chr 30:25
fields of common **l** belonging to 2 Chr 31:19
the brook that flowed through the **l**, 2 Chr 32:4
with shame of face to his own **l**. 2 Chr 32:21
the sign that had been done in the **l**, 2 Chr 32:31
of Israel from the **l** that I appointed 2 Chr 33:8
the people of the **l** struck down all 2 Chr 33:25
the people of the **l** made Josiah his 2 Chr 33:25
altars throughout all the **l** of Israel. 2 Chr 34:7
he had cleansed the **l** and the house, 2 Chr 34:8
The people of the **l** took Jehoahaz the 2 Chr 36:1
and laid on the **l** a tribute of a 2 Chr 36:3
until the **l** had enjoyed its Sabbaths. 2 Chr 36:21
the people of the **l** discouraged the people Ezr 4:4
the peoples of the **l** to worship the LORD, Ezr 6:21
saying, 'The **l** that you are entering, Ezr 9:11
is a **l** impure with the impurity of the Ezr 9:11
eat the good of the **l** and leave it for an Ezr 9:12
foreign women from the peoples of the **l**, Ezr 10:2
the peoples of the **l** and from the Ezr 10:11
be plundered in a **l** where they are Neh 4:4
to be their governor in the **l** of Judah, Neh 5:14
on this wall, and we acquired no **l**, Neh 5:16
to his offspring the **l** of the Canaanite, Neh 9:8
his servants and all the people of his **l**, Neh 9:10
through the midst of the sea on dry **l**, Neh 9:11
in to possess the **l** that you had sworn Neh 9:15
took possession of the **l** of Sihon king Neh 9:22
of Heshbon and the **l** of Og king of Neh 9:22
brought them into the **l** that you had Neh 9:23
went in and possessed the **l**, Neh 9:24
before them the inhabitants of the **l**, Neh 9:24
their kings and the peoples of the **l**, Neh 9:24
captured fortified cities and a rich **l**, Neh 9:25
the large and rich **l** that you set before Neh 9:35
in the **l** that you gave to our fathers to Neh 9:36
the peoples of the **l** or take their Neh 10:30
if the peoples of the **l** bring in goods or Neh 10:31
imposed tax on the **l** and on the Est 10:1
was a man in the **l** of Uz whose name was Jb 1:1
his possessions have increased in the **l**. Jb 1:10
return—to the **l** of darkness and deep Jb 10:21
the **l** of gloom like thick darkness, like Jb 10:22
sends them out, they overwhelm the **l**. Jb 12:15
to whom alone the **l** was given, and no Jb 15:19
The man with power possessed the **l**, and Jb 22:8
waters; their portion is cursed in the **l**; Jb 24:18
and it is not found in the **l** of the living. Jb 28:13
they have been whipped out of the **l**. Jb 30:8
"If my **l** has cried out against me and its Jb 31:38
for correction or for his **l** or for love, Jb 37:13
to bring rain on a **l** where no man is, on Jb 38:26
to satisfy the waste and desolate **l**, and to Jb 38:27
home and the salt **l** for his dwelling Jb 39:6
And in all the **l** there were no women so Jb 42:15
and ever; the nations perish from his **l**. Ps 10:16
As for the saints in the **l**, they are the Ps 16:3
and his offspring shall inherit the **l**. Ps 25:13
of the LORD in the **l** of the living! Ps 27:13
are quiet in the **l** they devise words of Ps 35:20
dwell in the **l** and befriend faithfulness. Ps 37:3
who wait for the LORD shall inherit the **l**. Ps 37:9
shall inherit the **l** and delight Ps 37:11
blessed by the LORD shall inherit the **l**, Ps 37:22
shall inherit the **l** and dwell upon Ps 37:29
and he will exalt you to inherit the **l**; Ps 37:34
him alive; he is called blessed in the **l**; Ps 41:2
remember you from the **l** of Jordan and Ps 42:6
by their own sword did they win the **l**, Ps 44:3
will uproot you from the **l** of the living. Ps 52:5
You have made the **l** to quake; you have Ps 60:2
in a dry and weary **l** where there is no Ps 63:1
He turned the sea into dry **l**; they passed Ps 66:6
but the rebellious dwell in a parched **l**. Ps 68:6
there be abundance of grain in the **l**; Ps 72:16
all the meeting places of God in the **l**. Ps 74:8
the dark places of the **l** are full of the Ps 74:20
he performed wonders in the **l** of Egypt, Ps 78:12
And he brought them to his holy **l**, to Ps 78:54
for it; it took deep root and filled the **l**. Ps 80:9
when he went out over the **l** of Egypt. Ps 81:5
brought you up out of the **l** of Egypt. Ps 81:10
LORD, you were favorable to your **l**; you Ps 85:1
fear him, that glory may dwell in our **l**. Ps 85:9
is good, and our **l** will yield its increase. Ps 85:12
righteousness in the **l** of forgetfulness? Ps 88:12
soon have lived in the **l** of silence. Ps 94:17
made it, and his hands formed the dry **l**. Ps 95:5
look with favor on the faithful in the **l**, Ps 101:6
I will destroy all the wicked in the **l**, Ps 101:8
you I will give the **l** of Canaan as your Ps 105:11
a famine on the **l** and broke all supply Ps 105:16
Jacob sojourned in the **l** of Ham. Ps 105:23
them and miracles in the **l** of Ham. Ps 105:27
He sent darkness, and made the **l** dark; Ps 105:28
Their **l** swarmed with frogs, even in Ps 105:30
fiery lightning bolts through their **l**. Ps 105:32
the vegetation in their **l** and ate up the Ps 105:35
down all the firstborn in their **l**, Ps 105:36
wondrous works in the **l** of Ham, and Ps 106:22
Then they despised the pleasant **l**, Ps 106:24
and the **l** was polluted with blood. Ps 106:38
a fruitful **l** into a salty waste, because Ps 107:34
a parched **l** into springs of water. Ps 107:35
His offspring will be mighty in the **l**; the Ps 112:2
before the LORD in the **l** of the living. Ps 116:9
not rest on the **l** allotted to the Ps 125:3
and gave their **l** as a heritage, a Ps 135:12
and gave their **l** as a heritage, for his Ps 136:21
we sing the LORD'S song in a foreign **l**? Ps 137:4
the slanderer be established in the **l**; Ps 140:11
my portion in the **l** of the living." Ps 142:5
my soul thirsts for you like a parched **l**. Ps 143:6
For the upright will inhabit the **l**, and Prv 2:21
the wicked will be cut off from the **l**, Prv 2:22
but the wicked will not dwell in the **l**. Prv 10:30
Whoever works his **l** will have plenty Prv 12:11
live in a desert **l** than with a Prv 21:19
When a **l** transgresses, it has many Prv 28:2
Whoever works his **l** will have plenty Prv 28:19
By justice a king builds up the **l**, but he Prv 29:4
womb, the **l** never satisfied with water, Prv 30:16
when he sits among the elders of the **l**. Prv 31:23
But this is gain for a **l** in every way: a Eccl 5:9
Woe to you, O **l**, when your king is a Eccl 10:16
Happy are you, O **l**, when your king is Eccl 10:17
voice of the turtledove is heard in our **l**. Sg 2:12
very presence foreigners devour your **l**; Is 1:7
obedient, you shall eat the good of the **l**; Is 1:19
Their **l** is filled with silver and gold, and Is 2:7
their **l** is filled with horses, and there is no Is 2:7
Their **l** is filled with idols; they bow down Is 2:8
and the fruit of the **l** shall be the pride and Is 4:2
made to dwell alone in the midst of the **l**. Is 5:8
And if one looks to the **l**, behold, darkness Is 5:30
people, and the **l** is a desolate waste, Is 6:11
places are many in the midst of the **l**. Is 6:12
the **l** whose two kings you dread will be Is 7:16
and for the bee that is in the **l** of Assyria. Is 7:18
who is left in the **l** will eat curds and Is 7:22
for all the **l** will be briers and thorns. Is 7:24
wings will fill the breadth of your **l**, Is 8:8
They will pass through the **l**, greatly Is 8:21
into contempt the **l** of Zebulun and Is 9:1
the land of Zebulun and the **l** of Naphtali, Is 9:1
the way of the sea, the **l** beyond the Jordan, Is 9:1
those who dwelt in a **l** of deep darkness, on Is 9:2
of the LORD of hosts the **l** is scorched, Is 9:19
and of his fruitful **l** the LORD will destroy, Is 10:18
when they came up from the **l** of Egypt. Is 11:16
They come from a distant **l**, from the end Is 13:5
of his indignation, to destroy the whole **l**. Is 13:5
to make the **l** a desolation and to destroy Is 13:9
people, and each will flee to his own **l**. Is 13:14
Israel, and will set them in their own **l**, Is 14:1
them in the LORD'S **l** as male and female Is 14:2
because you have destroyed your **l**, Is 14:20
that I will break the Assyrian in my **l**, Is 14:25
For a cry has gone around the **l** of Moab; Is 15:8
who escape, for the remnant of the **l**. Is 15:9
Send the lamb to the ruler of the **l**, from Is 16:1
underfoot has vanished from the **l**, Is 16:4
l of whirring wings that is beyond the Is 18:1
and conquering, whose **l** the rivers divide. Is 18:2
and conquering, whose **l** the rivers divide, Is 18:7
are the pillars of the **l** will be crushed, Is 19:10
And the **l** of Judah will become a terror Is 19:17
be five cities in the **l** of Egypt that speak Is 19:18
to the LORD in the midst of the **l** of Egypt, Is 19:19
to the LORD of hosts in the **l** of Egypt. Is 19:20
from the wilderness, from a terrible **l**. Is 21:1
bread, O inhabitants of the **l** of Tema. Is 21:14
and throw you like a ball into a wide **l**. Is 22:18
From the **l** of Cyprus it is revealed to Is 23:1
Cross over your **l** like the Nile, O Is 23:10
Behold the **l** of the Chaldeans! This is Is 23:13
this song will be sung in the **l** of Judah: Is 26:1
in the **l** of uprightness he deals corruptly Is 26:10
have enlarged all the borders of the **l**. Is 26:15
were lost in the **l** of Assyria and those Is 27:13
driven out to the **l** of Egypt will come Is 27:13
Lord GOD of hosts against the whole **l**. Is 28:22
Through a **l** of trouble and anguish, Is 30:6
like the shade of a great rock in a weary **l**. Is 32:2
The **l** mourns and languishes; Lebanon Is 33:9
they will see a **l** that stretches afar. Is 33:17
a great slaughter in the **l** of Edom. Is 34:6
Their **l** shall drink its fill of blood, and Is 34:7
sulfur; her **l** shall become burning pitch. Is 34:9
wilderness and the dry **l** shall be glad; Is 35:1
have come up against this **l** to destroy it? Is 36:10
me, Go up against this **l** and destroy it.'" Is 36:10
take you away to a **l** like your own land, Is 36:17
take you away to a land like your own **l**, Is 36:17
your own land, a **l** of grain and wine, Is 36:17
and wine, a **l** of bread and vineyards. Is 36:17
the nations delivered his **l** out of the Is 36:18
hear a rumor and return to his own **l**, Is 37:7
him fall by the sword in his own **l**.'" Is 37:7

after they escaped into the **l** of Ararat, Is 37:38
the LORD, the LORD in the **l** of the living; Is 38:11
of water, and the dry **l** springs of water. Is 41:18
For I will pour water on the thirsty **l**, and Is 44:3
not speak in secret, in a **l** of darkness; Is 45:19
a covenant to the people, to establish the **l**, Is 49:8
the west, and these from the **l** of Syene." Is 49:12
and your devastated **l**—surely now Is 49:19
he was cut off out of the **l** of the living, Is 53:8
me shall possess the **l** and shall inherit Is 57:13
shall no more be heard in your **l**, Is 60:18
they shall possess the **l** forever, the Is 60:21
therefore in their **l** they shall possess a Is 61:7
and your **l** shall no more be termed Is 62:4
My Delight Is in Her, and your **l** Married; Is 62:4
in you, and your **l** shall be married. Is 62:4
himself in the **l** shall bless himself Is 65:16
takes an oath in the **l** shall swear by the Is 65:16
things? Shall a **l** be born in one day? Is 66:8
were in Anathoth in the **l** of Benjamin, Jer 1:1
let loose upon all the inhabitants of the **l**. Jer 1:14
and bronze walls, against the whole **l**, Jer 1:18
its priests, and the people of the **l**. Jer 1:18
me in the wilderness, in a **l** not sown. Jer 2:2
who brought us up from the **l** of Egypt, Jer 2:6
in the wilderness, in a **l** of deserts and pits, Jer 2:6
pits, in a **l** of drought and deep darkness, Jer 2:6
darkness, in a **l** that none passes through, Jer 2:6
you into a plentiful **l** to enjoy its fruits Jer 2:7
you defiled my **l** and made my heritage an Jer 2:7
They have made his **l** a waste; his cities Jer 2:15
to Israel, or a **l** of thick darkness? Jer 2:31
her? Would not that **l** be greatly polluted? Jer 3:1
You have polluted the **l** with your vile Jer 3:2
her whoredom lightly, she polluted the **l**, Jer 3:9
have multiplied and increased in the **l**, Jer 3:16
shall come from the **l** of the north to Jer 3:18
of the north to the **l** that I gave your Jer 3:18
my sons, and give you a pleasant **l**, Jer 3:19
and say, "Blow the trumpet through the **l**; Jer 4:5
out from his place to make your **l** a waste; Jer 4:7
"Besiegers come from a distant **l**; Jer 4:16
hard on crash; the whole **l** is laid waste. Jer 4:20
and behold, the fruitful **l** was a desert, Jer 4:26
LORD, "The whole **l** shall be a desolation; Jer 4:27
me and served foreign gods in your **l**, Jer 5:19
serve foreigners in a **l** that is not yours.'" Jer 5:19
horrible thing has happened in the **l**: Jer 5:30
you a desolation, an uninhabited **l**." Jer 6:8
inhabitants of the **l**," declares the LORD. Jer 6:12
Sheba, or sweet cane from a distant **l**? Jer 6:20
in the **l** that I gave of old to your fathers Jer 7:7
that I brought them out of the **l** of Egypt, Jer 7:22
fathers came out of the **l** of Egypt to this Jer 7:25
the bride, for the **l** shall become a waste. Jer 7:34
of their stallions the whole **l** quakes. Jer 8:16
come and devour the **l** and all that fills Jer 8:16
from the length and breadth of the **l**: Jer 8:19
and not truth has grown strong in the **l**; Jer 9:3
Why is the **l** ruined and laid waste like a Jer 9:12
shamed, because we have left the **l**, Jer 9:19
out the inhabitants of the **l** at this time, Jer 10:18
I brought them out of the **l** of Egypt, Jer 11:4
to give them a **l** flowing with milk and Jer 11:5
I brought them up out of the **l** of Egypt, Jer 11:7
us cut him off from the **l** of the living, Jer 11:19
How long will the **l** mourn and the grass Jer 12:4
And if in a safe **l** you are so trusting, Jer 12:5
The whole **l** is made desolate, but no Jer 12:11
from one end of the **l** to the other; Jer 12:12
I will pluck them up from their **l**, Jer 12:14
each to his heritage and each to his **l**. Jer 12:15
all the inhabitants of this **l**: Jer 13:13
dismayed, since there is no rain on the **l**, Jer 14:4
should you be like a stranger in the **l**, Jer 14:8
and famine shall not come upon this **l**': Jer 14:15
their trade through the **l** and have no Jer 14:18
a winnowing fork in the gates of the **l**; Jer 15:7
of strife and contention to the whole **l**! Jer 15:10
your enemies in a **l** that you do not Jer 15:14
the fathers who fathered them in this **l**: Jer 16:3
Both great and small shall die in this **l**. Jer 16:6
hurl you out of this **l** into a land that Jer 16:13
of this land into a **l** that neither you nor Jer 16:13
the people of Israel out of the **l** of Egypt,' Jer 16:14
them back to their own **l** that I gave to Jer 16:15
have polluted my **l** with the carcasses Jer 16:18
serve your enemies in a **l** that you do not Jer 17:4
the wilderness, in an uninhabited salt **l**. Jer 17:6
Jerusalem, from the **l** of Benjamin, Jer 17:26
making their **l** a horror, a thing to be Jer 18:16
shall return no more to see his native **l**. Jer 22:10
die, and he shall never see this **l** again." Jer 22:12
But to the **l** to which they will long to Jer 22:27
hurled and cast into a **l** that they do not Jer 22:28

O **l**, land, land, hear the word of the Jer 22:29
O land, **l**, land, hear the word of the Jer 22:29
land, land, **l**, hear the word of the LORD! Jer 22:29
justice and righteousness in the **l**. Jer 23:5
the people of Israel out of the **l** of Egypt,' Jer 23:7
Then they shall dwell in their own **l**." Jer 23:8
For the **l** is full of adulterers; because of Jer 23:10
because of the curse the **l** mourns, and Jer 23:10
ungodliness has gone out into all the **l**." Jer 23:15
from this place to the **l** of the Chaldeans. Jer 24:5
and I will bring them back to this **l**. Jer 24:6
of Jerusalem who remain in this **l**, Jer 24:8
and those who dwell in the **l** of Egypt. Jer 24:8
utterly destroyed from the **l** that I gave Jer 24:10
and dwell upon the **l** that the LORD has Jer 25:5
them against this **l** and its inhabitants, Jer 25:9
This whole **l** shall become a ruin and a Jer 25:11
and that nation, the **l** of the Chaldeans, Jer 25:12
making the **l** an everlasting waste. Jer 25:12
will bring upon that **l** all the words that Jer 25:13
all the kings of the **l** of Uz and all the Jer 25:20
the kings of the **l** of the Philistines Jer 25:20
for their **l** has become a waste because Jer 25:38
of the elders of the **l** arose and spoke to Jer 26:17
city and against this **l** in words like Jer 26:20
until the time of his own **l** comes. Jer 27:7
you will be removed far from your **l**, Jer 27:10
and serve him, I will leave on its own **l**, Jer 27:11
bring them back to the **l** that I gave to Jer 30:3
offspring from the **l** of their captivity. Jer 30:10
come back from the **l** of the enemy. Jer 31:16
use these words in the **l** of Judah and in Jer 31:23
to bring them out of the **l** of Egypt, Jer 31:32
that is at Anathoth in the **l** of Benjamin, Jer 32:8
shall again be bought in this **l**.' Jer 32:15
signs and wonders in the **l** of Egypt, Jer 32:20
Israel out of the **l** of Egypt with signs Jer 32:21
And you gave them this **l**, which you Jer 32:22
them, a **l** flowing with milk and honey. Jer 32:22
will plant them in this **l** in faithfulness, Jer 32:41
be bought in this **l** of which you are Jer 32:43
and witnessed, in the **l** of Benjamin, Jer 32:44
restore the fortunes of the **l** as at first, Jer 33:11
of the Negeb, in the **l** of Benjamin, Jer 33:13
justice and righteousness in the **l**. Jer 33:15
I brought them out of the **l** of Egypt, Jer 34:13
the people of the **l** who passed between Jer 34:19
many days in the **l** where you sojourn.' Jer 35:7
king of Babylon came up against the **l**, Jer 35:11
you shall dwell in the **l** that I gave to Jer 35:15
will certainly come and destroy this **l**, Jer 36:29
of Babylon made king in the **l** of Judah, Jer 37:1
the people of the **l** listened to the words Jer 37:2
is about to return to Egypt, to its own **l**. Jer 37:7
to go to the **l** of Benjamin to receive Jer 37:12
come against you and against this **l**'? Jer 37:19
Babylon, at Riblah, in the **l** of Hamath; Jer 39:5
left in the **l** of Judah some of the poor Jer 39:10
See, the whole **l** is before you; go Jer 40:4
among the people who were left in the **l**. Jer 40:6
governor in the **l** and had committed Jer 40:7
of the poorest of the **l** who had not been Jer 40:7
Dwell in the **l** and serve the king of Jer 40:9
been driven and came to the **l** of Judah, Jer 40:12
had appointed governor in the **l**. Jer 41:2
Babylon had made governor over the **l**. Jer 41:18
If you will remain in this **l**, then I will Jer 42:10
you and let you remain in your own **l**. Jer 42:12
you say, 'We will not remain in this **l**,' Jer 42:13
saying, 'No, we will go to the **l** of Egypt, Jer 42:14
overtake you there in the **l** of Egypt, Jer 42:16
of the LORD, to remain in the **l** of Judah. Jer 43:4
returned to live in the **l** of Judah from all Jer 43:5
And they came into the **l** of Egypt, for Jer 43:7
He shall come and strike the **l** of Egypt, Jer 43:11
And he shall clean the **l** of Egypt as a Jer 43:12
of Heliopolis, which is in the **l** of Egypt, Jer 43:13
the Judeans who lived in the **l** of Egypt, Jer 44:1
at Memphis, and in the **l** of Pathros, Jer 44:1
to other gods in the **l** of Egypt where you Jer 44:8
they committed in the **l** of Judah and in Jer 44:9
faces to come to the **l** of Egypt to live, Jer 44:12
In the **l** of Egypt they shall fall; by the Jer 44:12
those who dwell in the **l** of Egypt, Jer 44:13
to live in the **l** of Egypt shall escape Jer 44:14
or survive or return to the **l** of Judah, Jer 44:14
who lived in Pathros in the **l** of Egypt, Jer 44:15
your officials, and the people of the **l**, Jer 44:21
Therefore your **l** has become a Jer 44:22
you of Judah who are in the **l** of Egypt. Jer 44:24
of Judah who dwell in the **l** of Egypt: Jer 44:26
any man of Judah in all the **l** of Egypt, Jer 44:26
Judah who are in the **l** of Egypt shall be Jer 44:27
shall return from the **l** of Egypt to the Jer 44:28
from the land of Egypt to the **l** of Judah, Jer 44:28

who came to the **l** of Egypt to live, Jer 44:28
I am plucking up—that is, the whole **l**. Jer 45:4
king of Babylon to strike the **l** of Egypt: Jer 46:13
our own people and to the **l** of our birth, Jer 46:16
offspring from the **l** of their captivity. Jer 46:27
they shall overflow the **l** and all that fills Jer 47:2
and every inhabitant of the **l** shall wail. Jer 47:2
and all the cities of the **l** of Moab, Jer 48:24
taken away from the fruitful **l** of Moab; Jer 48:33
concerning the **l** of the Chaldeans, Jer 50:1
her, which shall make her **l** a desolation, Jer 50:3
and go out of the **l** of the Chaldeans, Jer 50:8
last of the nations, a wilderness, a dry **l**, Jer 50:12
and every one shall flee to his own **l**. Jer 50:16
on the king of Babylon and his **l**, Jer 50:18
"Go up against the **l** of Merathaim, and Jer 50:21
The noise of battle is in the **l**, and great Jer 50:22
a work to do in the **l** of the Chaldeans. Jer 50:25
flee and escape from the **l** of Babylon, Jer 50:28
For it is a **l** of images, and they are mad Jer 50:38
formed against the **l** of the Chaldeans: Jer 50:45
winnow her, and they shall empty her **l**, Jer 51:2
fall down slain in the **l** of the Chaldeans, Jer 51:4
but the **l** of the Chaldeans is full of guilt Jer 51:5
and every **l** under their dominion. Jer 51:28
The **l** trembles and writhes in pain, for Jer 51:29
to make the **l** of Babylon a desolation, Jer 51:29
a horror, a **l** of drought and a desert, Jer 51:43
and a desert, a **l** in which no one dwells, Jer 51:43
not fearful at the report heard in the **l**, Jer 51:46
in another year, and violence is in the **l**, Jer 51:46
her whole **l** shall be put to shame, and Jer 51:47
through all her **l** the wounded shall Jer 51:52
destruction from the **l** of the Jer 51:54
there was no food for the people of the **l**. Jer 52:6
of Babylon at Riblah in the **l** of Hamath, Jer 52:9
the poorest of the **l** to be vinedressers Jer 52:16
army who mustered the people of the **l**; Jer 52:25
and sixty men of the people of the **l**, who Jer 52:25
to death at Riblah in the **l** of Hamath. Jer 52:27
Judah was taken into exile out of its **l**. Jer 52:27
of Edom, you who dwell in the **l** of Uz; Lam 4:21
in the **l** of the Chaldeans by the Chebar Ezk 1:3
and make the **l** desolate and waste, Ezk 6:14
thus says the Lord GOD to the **l** of Israel: Ezk 7:2
has come upon the four corners of the **l**. Ezk 7:2
has come to you, O inhabitant of the **l**. Ezk 7:7
For the **l** is full of bloody crimes and Ezk 7:23
the people of the **l** are paralyzed by Ezk 7:27
not see us, the LORD has forsaken the **l**.'" Ezk 8:12
they should fill the **l** with violence and Ezk 8:17
The **l** is full of blood, and the city full of Ezk 9:9
they say, 'The LORD has forsaken the **l**, Ezk 9:9
to us this **l** is given for a possession.' Ezk 11:15
and I will give you the **l** of Israel.' Ezk 11:17
your face that you may not see the **l**, Ezk 12:6
that he may not see the **l** with his eyes. Ezk 12:12
to Babylon, the **l** of the Chaldeans, Ezk 12:13
And say to the people of the **l**, Thus Ezk 12:19
of Jerusalem in the **l** of Israel: Ezk 12:19
In this way her **l** will be stripped of all Ezk 12:19
and the **l** shall become a desolation; Ezk 12:20
that you have about the **l** of Israel, Ezk 12:22
nor shall they enter the **l** of Israel. Ezk 13:9
when a **l** sins against me by acting Ezk 14:13
wild beasts to pass through the **l**, Ezk 14:15
delivered, but the **l** would be desolate. Ezk 14:16
if I bring a sword upon that **l** and say, Ezk 14:17
say, Let a sword pass through the **l**, Ezk 14:17
a pestilence into that **l** and pour out Ezk 14:19
And I will make the **l** desolate, because Ezk 15:8
birth are of the **l** of the Canaanites; Ezk 16:3
also with the trading **l** of Chaldea, Ezk 16:29
and carried it to a **l** of trade and set it Ezk 17:4
of the seed of the **l** and planted it in Ezk 17:5
chief men of the **l** he had taken away), Ezk 17:13
this proverb concerning the **l** of Israel, Ezk 18:2
him with hooks to the **l** of Egypt. Ezk 19:4
and the **l** was appalled and all who were Ezk 19:7
the wilderness, in a dry and thirsty **l**. Ezk 19:13
myself known to them in the **l** of Egypt; Ezk 20:5
bring them out of the **l** of Egypt into a Ezk 20:6
of Egypt into a **l** that I had searched Ezk 20:6
them, a **l** flowing with milk and honey, Ezk 20:6
them in the midst of the **l** of Egypt. Ezk 20:8
in bringing them out of the **l** of Egypt. Ezk 20:9
them out of the **l** of Egypt and brought Ezk 20:10
bring them into the **l** that I had given Ezk 20:15
a **l** flowing with milk and honey, Ezk 20:15
brought them into the **l** that I swore to Ezk 20:28
in the wilderness of the **l** of Egypt, Ezk 20:36
them out of the **l** where they sojourn, Ezk 20:38
but they shall not enter the **l** of Israel. Ezk 20:38
all of them, shall serve me in the **l**. Ezk 20:40
when I bring you into the **l** of Israel, Ezk 20:42

against the forest l in the Negeb. Ezk 20:46
Prophesy against the l of Israel Ezk 21:2
and say to the l of Israel, Thus says the Ezk 21:3
of them shall come from the same l. Ezk 21:19
were created, in the l of your origin, Ezk 21:30
blood shall be in the midst of the l. Ezk 21:32
You are a l that is not cleansed or Ezk 22:24
people of the l have practiced extortion Ezk 22:29
in the breach before me for the l, Ezk 22:30
whose native l was Chaldea. Ezk 23:15
she played the whore in the l of Egypt Ezk 23:19
your whoring begun in the l of Egypt, Ezk 23:27
will I put an end to lewdness in the l, Ezk 23:48
and over the l of Israel when it was Ezk 25:3
within your soul against the l of Israel, Ezk 25:6
I will set beauty in the l of the living. Ezk 26:20
Judah and the l of Israel traded with Ezk 27:17
all the pilots of the sea stand on the l Ezk 27:29
shall dwell in their own l that I gave to Ezk 28:25
and the l of Egypt shall be a desolation Ezk 29:9
and I will make the l of Egypt an utter Ezk 29:10
I will make the l of Egypt a desolation Ezk 29:12
bring them back to the l of Pathros, Ezk 29:14
land of Pathros, the l of their origin, Ezk 29:14
I will give the l of Egypt to Ezk 29:19
I have given him the l of Egypt as his Ezk 29:20
and the people of the l that is in league, Ezk 30:5
shall be brought in to destroy the l, Ezk 30:11
Egypt and fill the l with the slain. Ezk 30:11
Nile and will sell the l into the hand of Ezk 30:12
desolation upon the l and everything Ezk 30:12
longer be a prince from the l of Egypt; Ezk 30:13
so I will put fear in the l of Egypt. Ezk 30:13
stretches it out against the l of Egypt. Ezk 30:25
been broken in all the ravines of the l, Ezk 31:12
I will drench the l even to the Ezk 32:6
over you, and put darkness on your l, Ezk 32:8
When I make the l of Egypt desolate, Ezk 32:15
and when the l is desolate of all that Ezk 32:15
who spread terror in the l of the living. Ezk 32:23
their terror in the l of the living; Ezk 32:24
them was spread in the l of the living, Ezk 32:25
their terror in the l of the living. Ezk 32:26
mighty men was in the l of the living. Ezk 32:27
I spread terror in the l of the living; Ezk 32:32
to them, If I bring the sword upon a l, Ezk 33:2
and the people of the l take a man from Ezk 33:2
sword coming upon the l and blows the Ezk 33:3
waste places in the l of Israel keep Ezk 33:24
one man, yet he got possession of the l; Ezk 33:24
the l is surely given us to possess.' Ezk 33:24
blood; shall you then possess the l? Ezk 33:25
wife; shall you then possess the l? Ezk 33:26
I will make the l a desolation and a Ezk 33:28
I have made the l a desolation and a Ezk 33:29
and will bring them into their own l. Ezk 34:13
of Israel shall be their grazing l. Ezk 34:14
they shall lie down in good grazing l, Ezk 34:14
and banish wild beasts from the l, Ezk 34:25
and they shall be secure in their l. Ezk 34:27
shall the beasts of the l devour them. Ezk 34:28
be consumed with hunger in the l, Ezk 34:29
who gave my l to themselves as a Ezk 36:5
prophesy concerning the l of Israel, Ezk 36:6
the house of Israel lived in their own l, Ezk 36:17
the blood that they had shed in the l, Ezk 36:18
and yet they had to go out of his l.' Ezk 36:20
and bring you into your own l. Ezk 36:24
You shall dwell in the l that I gave to Ezk 36:28
And the l that was desolate shall be Ezk 36:34
'This l that was desolate has become Ezk 36:35
I will bring you into the l of Israel. Ezk 37:12
and I will place you in your own l. Ezk 37:14
and bring them to their own l. Ezk 37:21
I will make them one nation in the l, Ezk 37:22
They shall dwell in the l that I gave to Ezk 37:25
set them in their l and multiply them, Ezk 37:26
your face toward Gog, of the l of Magog, Ezk 38:2
will go against the l that is restored Ezk 38:8
the l whose people were gathered from Ezk 38:8
You will be like a cloud covering the l, Ezk 38:9
up against the l of unwalled villages. Ezk 38:11
Israel, like a cloud covering the l. Ezk 38:16
days I will bring you against my l, Ezk 38:16
Gog shall come against the l of Israel, Ezk 38:18
be a great earthquake in the l of Israel. Ezk 38:19
them, in order to cleanse the l. Ezk 39:12
All the people of the l will bury them, Ezk 39:13
travel through the l regularly and Ezk 39:14
remaining on the face of the l, Ezk 39:14
travel through the l and anyone sees Ezk 39:15
city.) Thus shall they cleanse the l. Ezk 39:16
dwell securely in their l with none to Ezk 39:26
then assembled them into their own l. Ezk 39:28
of God he brought me to the l of Israel, Ezk 40:2

you allot the l as an inheritance, Ezk 45:1
LORD a portion of the l as a holy district, Ezk 45:1
It shall be the holy portion of the l. It Ezk 45:4
prince shall belong the l on both sides Ezk 45:7
of the l. It is to be his property in Israel. Ezk 45:8
of Israel have the l according to their Ezk 45:8
the people of the l shall be obliged to Ezk 45:16
all the people of the l a young bull for Ezk 45:22
The people of the l shall bow down at Ezk 46:3
the people of the l come before the LORD Ezk 46:9
shall divide the l for inheritance Ezk 47:13
This l shall fall to you as your Ezk 47:14
"This shall be the boundary of the l: Ezk 47:15
between Gilead and the l of Israel; Ezk 47:18
shall divide this l among you Ezk 47:21
portion from the holy portion of the l, Ezk 48:12
alienate this choice portion of the l, Ezk 48:14
And the city shall have open l: on the Ezk 48:17
This is the l that you shall allot as an Ezk 48:29
And he brought them to the l of Shinar, Dn 1:2
toward the east, and toward the glorious l. Dn 8:9
our fathers, and to all the people of the l. Dn 9:6
your people out of the l of Egypt with a Dn 9:15
the south but shall return to his own l. Dn 11:9
And he shall stand in the glorious l, Dn 11:16
back toward the fortresses of his own l, Dn 11:19
shall return to his l with great wealth, Dn 11:28
work his will and return to his own l. Dn 11:28
many and shall divide the l for a price. Dn 11:39
He shall come into the glorious l. And Dn 11:41
and the l of Egypt shall not escape. Dn 11:42
for the l commits great whoredom by Hos 1:2
And they shall go up from the l, for Hos 1:11
and make her like a parched l, Hos 2:3
when she came out of the l of Egypt. Hos 2:15
the bow, the sword, and war from the l, Hos 2:18
and I will sow her for myself in the l. Hos 2:23
with the inhabitants of the l. Hos 4:1
love, and no knowledge of God in the l; Hos 4:1
Therefore the l mourns, and all who Hos 4:3
shall be their derision in the l of Egypt. Hos 7:16
shall not remain in the l of the LORD, Hos 9:3
They shall not return to the l of Egypt, Hos 11:5
and like doves from the l of Assyria, Hos 11:11
the LORD your God from the l of Egypt; Hos 12:9
Jacob fled to the l of Aram; there Israel Hos 12:12
the LORD your God from the l of Egypt; Hos 13:4
in the wilderness, in the l of drought; Hos 13:5
you elders; give ear, all inhabitants of the l! Jl 1:2
For a nation has come up against my l, Jl 1:6
all the inhabitants of the l to the house of Jl 1:14
Let all the inhabitants of the l tremble, for Jl 2:1
The l is like the garden of Eden before Jl 2:3
became jealous for his l and had pity on Jl 2:18
drive him into a parched and desolate l, Jl 2:20
"Fear not, O l; be glad and rejoice, for the Jl 2:21
the nations and have divided up my l, Jl 3:2
they have shed innocent blood in their l. Jl 3:19
you up out of the l of Egypt and led you Am 2:10
to possess the l of the Amorite. Am 2:10
that I brought up out of the l of Egypt: Am 3:1
and to the strongholds in the l of Egypt, Am 3:9
shall surround the l and bring down Am 3:11
forsaken on her l, with none to raise her Am 5:2
had finished eating the grass of the l, Am 7:2
the great deep and was eating up the l. Am 7:4
The l is not able to bear all his words. Am 7:10
must go into exile away from his l.'" Am 7:11
"O seer, go, flee away to the l of Judah, Am 7:12
and your l shall be divided up with a Am 7:17
you yourself shall die in an unclean l, Am 7:17
surely go into exile away from its l.'" Am 7:17
and bring the poor of the l to an end, Am 8:4
Shall not the l tremble on this account, Am 8:8
send a famine on the l—not a famine of Am 8:11
I not bring up Israel from the l of Egypt, Am 9:7
I will plant them on their l, and they Am 9:15
uprooted out of the l that I have given Am 9:15
shall possess the l of the Philistines; Ob 1:19
they shall possess the l of Ephraim and Ob 1:19
land of Ephraim and the l of Samaria, Ob 1:19
shall possess the l of the Canaanites Ob 1:20
heaven, who made the sea and the dry l." Jon 1:9
the men rowed hard to get back to dry l, Jon 1:13
went down to the l whose bars closed Jon 2:6
and it vomited Jonah out upon the dry l. Jon 2:10
Assyrian comes into our l and treads in Mi 5:5
they shall shepherd the l of Assyria with Mi 5:6
and the l of Nimrod at its entrances; Mi 5:6
he comes into our l and treads within our Mi 5:6
the cities of your l and throw down all Mi 5:11
you up from the l of Egypt and redeemed Mi 6:4
in a forest in the midst of a garden l; Mi 7:14
when you came out of the l of Egypt, Mi 7:15
The gates of your l are wide open to your Na 3:13

the curtains of the l of Midian did Hab 3:7
Seek the LORD, all you humble of the l, Zep 2:3
you, O Canaan, l of the Philistines; Zep 2:5
a l possessed by nettles and salt pits, Zep 2:9
for a drought on the l and the hills, Hg 1:11
Be strong, all you people of the l, declares Hg 2:4
and the earth and the sea and the dry l. Hg 2:6
their horns against the l of Judah to Zec 1:21
Up! Flee from the l of the north, declares Zec 2:6
Judah as his portion in the holy l, Zec 2:12
the iniquity of this l in a single day. Zec 3:9
that goes out over the face of the whole l. Zec 5:3
said, "This is their iniquity in all the l." Zec 5:6
He said to me, "To the l of Shinar, to Zec 5:11
to all the people of the l and the priests, Zec 7:5
Thus the l they left was desolate, so that Zec 7:14
and the pleasant l was made desolate." Zec 7:14
LORD is against the l of Hadrach and Zec 9:1
of a crown they shall shine on his l. Zec 9:16
bring them home from the l of Egypt, Zec 10:10
bring them to the l of Gilead and to Zec 10:10
have pity on the inhabitants of this l, Zec 11:6
of his king, and they shall crush the l, Zec 11:6
raising up in the l a shepherd who Zec 11:16
The l shall mourn, each family by Zec 12:12
cut off the names of the idols from the l, Zec 13:2
will remove from the l the prophets and Zec 13:2
In the whole l, declares the LORD, two Zec 13:8
The whole l shall be turned into a Zec 14:10
blessed, for you will be a l of delight, Mal 3:12
I come and strike the l with a decree of Mal 4:6
"'And you, O Bethlehem, in the l of Judah, Mt 2:6
and his mother and go to the l of Israel, Mt 2:20
his mother and went to the l of Israel. Mt 2:21
"The l of Zebulun and the land of Mt 4:15
land of Zebulun and the l of Naphtali, Mt 4:15
of judgment for the l of Sodom and Mt 10:15
of judgment for the l of Sodom than for Mt 11:24
by this time was a long way from the l, Mt 14:24
over, they came to l at Gennesaret. Mt 14:34
travel across sea and l to make a single Mt 23:15
darkness over all the l until the ninth Mt 27:45
whole crowd was beside the sea on the l. Mk 4:1
on the sea, and he was alone on the l. Mk 6:47
they came to l at Gennesaret and Mk 6:53
over the whole l until the ninth Mk 15:33
and a great famine came over all the l, Lk 4:25
but only to Zarephath, in the l of Sidon, Lk 4:26
he asked him to put out a little from the l. Lk 5:3
when they had brought their boats to l, Lk 5:11
When Jesus had stepped out on l, there Lk 8:27
"The l of a rich man produced Lk 12:16
over the whole l until the ninth Lk 23:44
the boat was at the l to which they were Jn 6:21
of fish, for they were not far from the l, Jn 21:8
When they got out on l, they saw a Jn 21:9
for yourself part of the proceeds of the l? Acts 5:3
whether you sold the l for so much." Acts 5:8
'Go out from your l and from your Acts 7:3
and go into the l that I will show Acts 7:3
went out from the l of the Chaldeans Acts 7:4
from there into this l in which you are Acts 7:4
be sojourners in a l belonging to others, Acts 7:6
and became an exile in the l of Midian, Acts 7:29
who led us out from the l of Egypt, Acts 7:40
during their stay in the l of Egypt, Acts 13:17
seven nations in the l of Canaan, Acts 13:19
gave them their l as an inheritance. Acts 13:19
intending himself to go by l. Acts 20:13
northeaster, struck down from the l. Acts 27:14
suspected that they were nearing l. Acts 27:27
was day, they did not recognize the l, Acts 27:39
overboard first and make for the l, Acts 27:43
was that all were brought safely to l. Acts 27:44
you and that you may live long in the l." Eph 6:3
For l that has drunk the rain that often Heb 6:7
hand to bring them out of the l of Egypt. Heb 8:9
faith he went to live in the l of promise, Heb 11:9
in the land of promise, as in a foreign l, Heb 11:9
thinking of that l from which they Heb 11:15
crossed the Red Sea as if on dry l, Heb 11:29
who saved a people out of the l of Egypt, Jude 1:5
foot on the sea, and his left foot on the l, Rv 10:2
the sea and on the l raised his right hand Rv 10:5
who is standing on the sea and on the l." Rv 10:8

LANDED (2)
When he had l at Caesarea, he went Acts 18:22
the left we sailed to Syria and l at Tyre, Acts 21:3

LANDINGS (1)
at the coast of the sea, staying by his l. Jgs 5:17

LANDMARK (5)
"You shall not move your neighbor's l, Dt 19:14
be anyone who moves his neighbor's l.' Dt 27:17
move the ancient l that your fathers Prv 22:28

not move an ancient **l** or enter the Prv 23:10
have become like those who move the **l**; Hos 5:10

LANDMARKS (1)
Some move **l**; they seize flocks and Jb 24:2

LANDS (53)
the coastland peoples spread in their **l**, Gn 10:5
by their clans, their languages, their **l**, Gn 10:20
by their clans, their languages, their **l**, Gn 10:31
to your offspring I will give all these **l**, Gn 26:3
will give to your offspring all these **l**. Gn 26:4
There was famine in all **l**, but in all the Gn 41:54
their hearts in the **l** of their enemies. Lv 26:36
in your enemies' **l** because of their Lv 26:39
the gods of the **l** have delivered their 2 Kgs 18:35
have delivered their **l** out of my 2 Kgs 18:35
kings of Assyria have done to all **l**, 2 Kgs 19:11
laid waste the nations and their **l** 2 Kgs 19:17
who remain in all the **l** of Israel, 1 Chr 13:2
the fame of David went out into all **l**, 1 Chr 14:17
of fame and glory throughout all **l**. 1 Chr 22:5
Solomon from Egypt and from all **l**. 2 Chr 9:28
left their common **l** and their 2 Chr 11:14
yourselves like the peoples of other **l**? 2 Chr 13:9
afflicted all the inhabitants of the **l**. 2 Chr 15:5
kingdoms of the **l** that were around 2 Chr 17:10
in the hills and in the fertile **l**, 2 Chr 26:10
done to all the peoples of other **l**? 2 Chr 32:13
of the nations of those **l** at all able to 2 Chr 32:13
able to deliver their **l** out of my 2 Chr 32:13
the nations of the **l** who have not 2 Chr 32:17
on them because of the peoples of the **l**, Ezr 3:3
peoples of the **l** with their abominations, Ezr 9:1
has mixed itself with the peoples of the **l**. Ezr 9:2
given into the hand of the kings of the **l**, Ezr 9:7
with the impurity of the peoples of the **l**, Ezr 9:11
into the hand of the peoples of the **l**. Neh 9:30
from the peoples of the **l** to the Law of Neh 10:28
though they called **l** by their own Ps 49:11
And he gave them the **l** of the nations, Ps 105:44
nations, scattering them among the **l**. Ps 106:27
and gathered in from the **l**, from the Ps 107:3
the gods of these **l** have delivered their Is 36:20
lands have delivered their **l** out of my Is 36:20
the kings of Assyria have done to all **l**, Is 37:11
laid waste all the nations and their **l**, Is 37:18
I have given all these **l** into the hand of Jer 27:6
Edom and in other **l** heard that the Jer 40:11
and honey, the most glorious of all **l**. Ezk 20:6
and honey, the most glorious of all **l**, Ezk 20:15
gathered them from their enemies' **l**, Ezk 39:27
in all the **l** to which you have driven Dn 9:7
each in its place, all the **l** of the nations. Zep 2:11
or father or mother or children or **l**, Mt 19:29
or mother or father or children or **l**, Mk 10:29
and mothers and children and **l**, Mk 10:30
as were owners of **l** or houses sold Acts 4:34
of that place were **l** belonging to the Acts 28:7
preach the gospel in **l** beyond you, 2 Cor 10:16

LANES (1)
quickly to the streets and **l** of the city, Lk 14:21

LANGUAGE (37)
in their lands, each with his own **l**, Gn 10:5
whole earth had one **l** and the same Gn 11:1
are one people, and they have all one **l**, Gn 11:6
let us go down and there confuse their **l**, Gn 11:7
the LORD confused the **l** of all the earth. Gn 11:9
a nation whose **l** you do not Dt 28:49
to us in the **l** of Judah within the 2 Kgs 18:26
out in a loud voice in the **l** of Judah: 2 Kgs 18:28
a loud voice in the **l** of Judah to the 2 Chr 32:18
their children spoke the **l** of Ashdod, Neh 13:24
they could not speak the **l** of Judah, Neh 13:24
of Judah, but the **l** of each people. Neh 13:24
script and to every people in its own **l**, Est 1:22
speak according to the **l** of his people. Est 1:22
own script and every people in its own **l**. Est 3:12
own script and to each people in its own **l**, Est 8:9
also to the Jews in their script and their **l**. Est 8:9
land of Egypt. I hear a **l** I had not known: Ps 81:5
of Jacob from a people of strange **l**, Ps 114:1
Egypt that speak the **l** of Canaan and Is 19:18
speak to us in the **l** of Judah within the Is 36:11
out in a loud voice in the **l** of Judah: Is 36:13
a nation whose **l** you do not know, Jer 5:15
to a people of foreign speech and a hard **l**, Ezk 3:5
peoples of foreign speech and a hard **l**, Ezk 3:6
the literature and **l** of the Chaldeans. Dn 1:4
or **l** that speaks anything against the Dn 3:29
was called in their own **l** Akeldama, Acts 1:19
was hearing them speak in his own **l**. Acts 2:6
we hear, each of us in his own native **l**? Acts 2:8
he addressed them in the Hebrew **l**, Acts 21:40
was addressing them in the Hebrew **l**, Acts 22:2
a voice saying to me in the Hebrew **l**, Acts 26:14
I do not know the meaning of the **l**, 1 Cor 14:11
from every tribe and **l** and people and Rv 5:9
every tribe and people and **l** and nation, Rv 13:7
every nation and tribe and **l** and people. Rv 14:6

LANGUAGES (13)
the sons of Ham, by their clans, their **l**, Gn 10:20
sons of Shem, by their clans, their **l**, Gn 10:31
commanded, O peoples, nations, and **l**, Dn 3:4
and **l** fell down and worshiped the golden Dn 3:7
to all peoples, nations, and **l**, Dn 4:1
and **l** trembled and feared before him. Dn 5:19
nations, and **l** that dwell in all the earth: Dn 6:25
peoples, nations, and **l** should serve him; Dn 7:14
doubtless many different **l** in the 1 Cor 14:10
nation, from all tribes and peoples and **l**, Rv 7:9
peoples and nations and **l** and kings." Rv 10:11
peoples and tribes and **l** and nations will Rv 11:9
and multitudes and nations and **l**. Rv 17:15

LANGUISH (6)
For the fields of Heshbon **l**, and the vine Is 16:8
and they will **l** who spread nets on the Is 19:8
withers; the highest people of the earth **l**. Is 24:4
"Judah mourns and her gates **l**; her Jer 14:2
garden, and they shall **l** no more. Jer 31:12
land mourns, and all who dwell in it **l**, Hos 4:3

LANGUISHED (3)
the land of Canaan **l** by reason of the Gn 47:13
you restored your inheritance as it **l**; Ps 68:9
and wall to lament; they **l** together. Lam 2:8

LANGUISHES (5)
and withers; the world **l** and withers; Is 24:4
The wine mourns, the vine **l**, all the Is 24:7
The land mourns and **l**; Lebanon is Is 33:9
is destroyed, the wine dries up, the oil **l**. Jl 1:10
The vine dries up; the fig tree **l**. Jl 1:12

LANGUISHING (3)
heart and failing eyes and a **l** soul. Dt 28:65
Be gracious to me, O LORD, for I am **l**; heal Ps 6:2
soul, and every **l** soul I will replenish." Jer 31:25

LANTERNS (1)
went there with **l** and torches and Jn 18:3

LAODICEA (6)
you and for those at **L** and for all who Col 2:1
and for those in **L** and in Hierapolis. Col 4:13
Give my greetings to the brothers at **L**, Col 4:15
see that you also read the letter from **L**. Col 4:16
to Sardis and to Philadelphia and to **L**." Rv 1:11
to the angel of the church in **L** write: Rv 3:14

LAODICEANS (1)
have it also read in the church of the **L**; Col 4:16

LAP (6)
laid him on her **l** and became his nurse. Ru 4:16
the child sat on her **l** till noon, 2 Kgs 4:20
gathered from it his **l** full of wild 2 Kgs 4:39
sevenfold into the **l** of our neighbors Ps 79:12
The lot is cast into the **l**, but its every Prv 16:33
running over, will be put into your **l**. Lk 6:38

LAPPED (2)
And the number of those who **l**, putting Jgs 7:6
"With the 300 men who **l** I will save you Jgs 7:7

LAPPIDOTH (1)
Now Deborah, a prophetess, the wife of **L**, Jgs 4:4

LAPS (2)
"Every one who **l** the water with his Jgs 7:5
laps the water with his tongue, as a dog **l**, Jgs 7:5

LARGE (56)
The stone on the well's mouth was **l**, Gn 29:2
increased greatly and had **l** flocks, Gn 30:43
behold, the land is **l** enough for them. Gn 34:21
and the cities are fortified and very **l**. Nm 13:28
against them with a **l** army and with Nm 20:20
To a **l** tribe you shall give a large Nm 26:54
tribe you shall give a **l** inheritance, Nm 26:54
To a **l** tribe you shall give a large Nm 33:54
tribe you shall give a **l** inheritance, Nm 33:54
two kinds of weights, a **l** and a small. Dt 25:13
two kinds of measures, a **l** and a small. Dt 25:14
you shall set up **l** stones and plaster them Dt 27:2
LORD threw down **l** stones from heaven Jos 10:11
"Roll **l** stones against the mouth of the Jos 10:18
and they set **l** stones against the mouth Jos 10:27
of the people of Judah was too **l** for them, Jos 19:9
And he took a **l** stone and set it up there Jos 24:26
Solomon made 200 **l** shields of 1 Kgs 10:16
said to his servant, "Set on the **l** pot, 2 Kgs 4:38
David took a **l** amount of bronze. 1 Chr 18:8
Solomon made 200 **l** shields of 2 Chr 9:15
armed with **l** shields and spears, 2 Chr 14:8
and he had **l** supplies in the cities of 2 Chr 17:13
the spears and the **l** and small shields 2 Chr 23:9
many cisterns, for he had **l** herds, 2 Chr 26:10
so that we have this **l** amount left." 2 Chr 31:10
The city was wide and **l**, but the people Neh 7:4
and in the **l** and rich land that you set Neh 9:35
for Tobiah a **l** chamber where they Neh 13:5
shall be desolate, **l** and beautiful houses, Is 5:9
"Take a **l** tablet and write on it in common Is 8:1
your livestock will graze in **l** pastures, Is 30:23
Gedaliah was the **l** cistern that King Jer 41:9
"Take in your hands **l** stones and hide Jer 43:9
might give him horses and a **l** army. Ezk 17:15
your sister's cup that is deep and **l**; Ezk 23:32
its boughs grew **l** and its branches long Ezk 31:5
And **l** crowds followed him, and he Mt 19:2
have been sold for a **l** sum and given to Mt 26:9
And a very **l** crowd gathered about him, Mk 4:1
garden plants and puts out **l** branches, Mk 4:32
box. Many rich people put in **l** sums. Mk 12:41
show you a **l** upper room furnished Mk 14:15
had been rolled back—it was very **l**. Mk 16:4
this, they enclosed a **l** number of fish, Lk 5:6
and there was a **l** company of tax Lk 5:29
Now a **l** herd of pigs was feeding there on Lk 8:32
show you a **l** upper room furnished; Lk 22:12
And a **l** crowd was following him, because Jn 6:2
and seeing that a **l** crowd was coming Jn 6:5
When the **l** crowd of the Jews learned Jn 12:9
The next day the **l** crowd that had come Jn 12:12
and hauled the net ashore, full of **l** fish, Jn 21:11
citizenship for a **l** sum." Paul said, Acts 22:28
See with what **l** letters I am writing to Gal 6:11
though they are so **l** and are driven by Jas 3:4

LARGER (8)
to lot between the **l** and the smaller." Nm 26:56
from the **l** tribes you shall take many, Nm 35:8
chariots and an army **l** than your own, Dt 20:1
from the smaller ledge to the **l** ledge, Ezk 43:14
it has grown it is **l** than all the garden Mt 13:32
grows up and becomes **l** than all the Mk 4:32
whom he cancelled the **l** debt." And he Lk 7:43
tear down my barns and build **l** ones, Lk 12:18

LASEA (1)
Havens, near which was the city of **L**. Acts 27:8

LASH (1)
shall be hidden from the **l** of the tongue, Jb 5:21

LASHA (1)
Admah, and Zeboiim, as far as **L**. Gn 10:19

LASHARON (1)
king of Aphek, one; the king of **L**, one; Jos 12:18

LASHES (1)
hands of the Jews the forty **l** less one. 2 Cor 11:24

LAST (106)
"This at **l** is bone of my bones and flesh Gn 2:23
and old, all the people to the **l** man, Gn 19:4
"Behold, I lay **l** night with my father. Gn 19:34
Abraham breathed his **l** and died in a Gn 25:8
He breathed his **l** and died, and was Gn 25:17
God of your father spoke to me **l** night, Gn 31:29
of my hands and rebuked you **l** night." Gn 31:42
children, and Rachel and Joseph **l** of all. Gn 33:2
And **l** Joseph and Rachel drew near, and Gn 33:7
And Isaac breathed his **l**, and he died Gn 35:29
and breathed his **l** and was gathered Gn 49:33
Your threshing shall **l** to the time of the Lv 26:5
the grape harvest shall **l** to the time for Lv 26:5
They shall set out **l**, standard by Nm 2:31
until the **l** of your dead bodies lies in Nm 14:33
and to the **l** of the children whom he Dt 28:54
of them to the very **l** had fallen by the Jos 8:24
have made this **l** kindness greater than Ru 3:10
him. And they halted at the **l** house. 2 Sm 15:17
should you be the **l** to bring the king 2 Sm 19:11
should you be the **l** to bring back 2 Sm 19:12
Now these are the **l** words of David: 2 Sm 23:1
For by the **l** words of David the sons 1 Chr 23:27
acts of King David, from first to **l**, 1 Chr 29:29
of the acts of Solomon, from first to **l**, 2 Chr 9:29
acts of Rehoboam, from first to **l**, 2 Chr 12:15
The acts of Asa, from first to **l**, are 2 Chr 16:11
acts of Jehoshaphat, from first to **l**, 2 Chr 20:34
the deeds of Amaziah, from first to **l**, 2 Chr 25:26
of the acts of Uzziah, from first to **l**, 2 Chr 26:22
acts and all his ways, from first to **l**, 2 Chr 28:26
and his acts, first and **l**, behold, they 2 Chr 35:27
by day, from the first day to the **l** day, Neh 8:18
and their hope is to breathe their **l**." Jb 11:20
man breathes his **l**, and where is he? Jb 14:10
and at the **l** he will stand upon the earth. Jb 19:25
and made its owners breathe their **l**, Jb 31:39
the singers in front, the musicians **l**, Ps 68:25

him, and their fate would **l** forever. Ps 81:15
for riches do not **l** forever; and does a Prv 27:24
I, the LORD, the first, and with the **l**; I am Is 41:4
of hosts: "I am the first and I am the **l**; Is 44:6
I am he; I am the first, and I am the **l**. Is 48:12
vessel, that they may **l** for a long time. Jer 32:14
Behold, she shall be the **l** of the nations, Jer 50:12
and now at **l** Nebuchadnezzar king of Jer 50:17
At **l** Daniel came in before me—he who Dn 4:8
the other, and the higher one came up **l**. Dn 8:3
hooks, even the **l** of you with fishhooks. Am 4:2
get out until you have paid the **l** penny. Mt 5:26
and the **l** state of that person is worse Mt 12:45
But many who are first will be **l**, and Mt 19:30
who are first will be last, and the **l** first. Mt 19:30
them their wages, beginning with the **l**, Mt 20:8
saying, 'These **l** worked only one hour, Mt 20:12
choose to give to this **l** worker as I give Mt 20:14
So the **l** will be first, and the first last." Mt 20:16
So the last will be first, and the first **l**." Mt 20:16
came forward. At **l** two came forward Mt 26:60
and the **l** fraud will be worse than the Mt 27:64
he must be **l** of all and servant of all." Mk 9:35
But many who are first will be **l**, and Mk 10:31
are first will be last, and the **l** first." Mk 10:31
offspring. **L** of all the woman also died. Mk 12:22
uttered a loud cry and breathed his **l**. Mk 15:37
saw that in this way he breathed his **l**, Mk 15:39
And the **l** state of that person is worse Lk 11:26
until you have paid the very **l** penny." Lk 12:59
behold, some are **l** who will be first, Lk 13:30
first, and some are first who will be **l**." Lk 13:30
And having said this he breathed his **l**. Lk 23:46
has given me, but raise it up on the **l** day. Jn 6:39
life, and I will raise him up on the **l** day." Jn 6:40
him. And I will raise him up on the **l** day. Jn 6:44
life, and I will raise him up on the **l** day. Jn 6:54
On the **l** day of the feast, the great day, Jn 7:37
again in the resurrection on the **l** day." Jn 11:24
spoken will judge him on the **l** day. Jn 12:48
"'And in the **l** days it shall be, God Acts 2:17
words, he fell down and breathed his **l**. Acts 5:5
fell down at his feet and breathed her **l**. Acts 5:10
eaten by worms and breathed his **l**. Acts 12:23
our being saved was at **l** abandoned. Acts 27:20
I may now at **l** succeed in coming to Rom 1:10
has exhibited us apostles as **l** of all, 1 Cor 4:9
L of all, as to one untimely born, he 1 Cor 15:8
The **l** enemy to be destroyed is death. 1 Cor 15:26
the **l** Adam became a life-giving 1 Cor 15:45
twinkling of an eye, at the **l** trumpet. 1 Cor 15:52
Achaia has been ready since **l** year. 2 Cor 9:2
wrath has come upon them at **l**! 1 Thes 2:16
that in the **l** days there will come times 2 Tm 3:1
but in these **l** days he has spoken to us Heb 1:2
You have laid up treasure in the **l** days. Jas 5:3
ready to be revealed in the **l** time. 1 Pt 1:5
made manifest in the **l** times for your 1 Pt 1:20
the **l** state has become worse for them 2 Pt 2:20
will come in the **l** days with scoffing, 2 Pt 3:3
Children, it is the **l** hour, and as you 1 Jn 2:18
Therefore we know that it is the **l** hour. 1 Jn 2:18
"In the **l** time there will be scoffers, Jude 1:18
saying, "Fear not, I am the first and the **l**, Rv 1:17
'The words of the first and the **l**, who died Rv 2:8
with seven plagues, which are the **l**, Rv 15:1
full of the seven **l** plagues and spoke to Rv 21:9
and the Omega, the first and the **l**, Rv 22:13

LASTED (1)

him the seven days that their feast **l**, Jgs 14:17

LASTING (4)

afflictions, afflictions severe and **l**, Dt 28:59
lasting, and sicknesses grievous and **l**. Dt 28:59
a feast **l** for seven days in the court of the Est 1:5
For here we have no **l** city, but we seek Heb 13:14

LATCH (1)

My beloved put his hand to the **l**, and my Sg 5:4

LATE (9)

down, for they are **l** in coming up.) Ex 9:32
It happened, **l** one afternoon, when 2 Sm 11:2
that you rise up early and go **l** to rest, Ps 127:2
who tarry **l** into the evening as wine Is 5:11
And when it grew **l**, his disciples came Mk 6:35
a desolate place, and the hour is now **l**. Mk 6:35
at everything, as it was already **l**, Mk 11:11
until it receives the early and the **l** rains. Jas 5:7
fruitless trees in **l** autumn, twice dead, Jude 1:12

LATELY (1)

But **l** my people have risen up as an Mi 2:8

LATER (17)

So my honesty will answer for me **l**, Gn 30:33
About three months **l** Judah was told, Gn 38:24
its season, the early rain and the **l** rain, Dt 11:14
And about ten days **l** the LORD struck 1 Sm 25:38
sons of Adonikam, those who came **l**, Ezr 8:13
be any remembrance of **l** things yet to Eccl 1:11
Yet those who come **l** will not rejoice Eccl 4:16
to them, "Sleep and take your rest **l** on. Mt 26:45
Not many days **l**, the younger son Lk 15:13
And a little **l** someone else saw him and Lk 22:58
Eight days **l**, his disciples were inside Jn 20:26
expressly says that in **l** times some will 1 Tm 4:1
but the sins of others appear **l**. 1 Tm 5:24
to the things that were to be spoken **l**, Heb 3:5
not have spoken of another day **l** on. Heb 4:8
of the oath, which came **l** than the law, Heb 7:28
but **l** it yields the peaceful fruit of Heb 12:11

LATIN (1)

and it was written in Aramaic, in **L**, Jn 19:20

LATRINE (1)

of Baal, and made it a **l** to this day. 2 Kgs 10:27

LATTER (30)

the first sign, they may believe the **l** sign. Ex 4:8
will do to your people in the **l** days." Nm 24:14
things come upon you in the **l** days, Dt 4:30
and the **l** man hates her and writes her a Dt 24:3
her out of his house, or if the **l** man dies, Dt 24:3
this; they would discern their **l** end! Dt 32:29
was small, your **l** days will be very great. Jb 8:7
the LORD blessed the **l** days of Job more Jb 42:12
to pass in the **l** days that the mountain Is 2:2
but in the **l** time he has made glorious the Is 9:1
they said, "He will not see our **l** end." Jer 12:4
In the **l** days you will understand it Jer 23:20
In the **l** days you will understand this. Jer 30:24
the fortunes of Moab in the **l** days, Jer 48:47
"But in the **l** days I will restore the Jer 49:39
In the **l** years you will go against the Ezk 38:8
In the **l** days I will bring you against Ezk 38:16
what will be in the **l** days. Dn 2:28
shall be at the **l** end of the indignation, Dn 8:19
And at the **l** end of their kingdom, when Dn 8:23
to happen to your people in the **l** days. Dn 10:14
Then the **l** shall come into the realm of Dn 11:9
LORD and to his goodness in the **l** days. Hos 3:5
abundant rain, the early and the **l** rain, Jl 2:23
locusts when the **l** growth was just Am 7:1
it was the **l** growth after the king's Am 7:1
to pass in the **l** days that the mountain Mi 4:1
The **l** glory of this house shall be greater Hg 2:9
The **l** do it out of love, knowing that I Phil 1:16
and that your **l** works exceed the first. Rv 2:19

LATTICE (6)

mother of Sisera wailed through the **l**: Jgs 5:28
a **l** for the one capital and a lattice for 1 Kgs 7:17
one capital and a **l** for the other 1 Kgs 7:17
Ahaziah fell through the **l** in his upper 2 Kgs 1:2
house I have looked out through my **l**, Prv 7:6
the windows, looking through the **l**. Sg 2:9

LATTICES (1)

There were **l** of checker work with 1 Kgs 7:17

LATTICEWORK (6)

rows around the one **l** to cover the 1 Kgs 7:18
projection which was beside the **l**. 1 Kgs 7:20
two rows of pomegranates for each **l**, 1 Kgs 7:42
A **l** and pomegranates, all of bronze, 2 Kgs 25:17
pillar had the same, with the **l**. 2 Kgs 25:17
two rows of pomegranates for each **l**, 2 Chr 4:13

LATTICEWORKS (4)

and the two **l** to cover the two bowls 1 Kgs 7:41
hundred pomegranates for the two **l**, 1 Kgs 7:42
and the two **l** to cover the two bowls 2 Chr 4:12
the 400 pomegranates for the two **l**, 2 Chr 4:13

LAUGH (17)

Abraham, "Why did Sarah **l** and say, Gn 18:13
saying, "I did not **l**," for she was afraid. Gn 18:15
was afraid. He said, "No, but you did **l**." Gn 18:15
me; everyone who hears will **l** over me." Gn 21:6
brought among us a Hebrew to **l** at us. Gn 39:14
among us, came in to me to **l** at me. Gn 39:17
At destruction and famine you shall **l**, Jb 5:22
"But now they **l** at me, men who are Jb 30:1
shall see and fear, and shall **l** at him, Ps 52:6
But you, O LORD, **l** at them; you hold all Ps 59:8
and our enemies **l** among themselves. Ps 80:6
I also will **l** at your calamity; I will Prv 1:26
a time to weep, and a time to **l**; a time to Eccl 3:4
At kings they scoff, and at rulers they **l**. Hab 1:10
They **l** at every fortress, for they pile up Hab 1:10
are you who weep now, for you shall **l**. Lk 6:21
"Woe to you who **l** now, for you shall Lk 6:25

LAUGHED (8)

on his face and **l** and said to himself, Gn 17:17
So Sarah **l** to herself, saying, "After I Gn 18:12
things as her own, or we shall be **l** at. Gn 38:23
but they **l** them to scorn and 2 Chr 30:10
you shall be **l** at and held in derision, Ezk 23:32
dead but sleeping." And they **l** at him. Mt 9:24
And they **l** at him. But he put them all Mk 5:40
And they **l** at him, knowing that she was Lk 8:53

LAUGHING (2)

whom she had borne to Abraham, **l**. Gn 21:9
and saw Isaac **l** with Rebekah his Gn 26:8

LAUGHINGSTOCK (5)

I am a **l** to my friends; I, who called to Jb 12:4
me, a just and blameless man, am a **l**. Jb 12:4
the nations, a **l** among the peoples. Ps 44:14
I have become a **l** all the day; everyone Jer 20:7
I have become the **l** of all peoples, the Lam 3:14

LAUGHS (7)

to flee, she **l** at the horse and his rider. Jb 39:18
He **l** at fear and is not dismayed; he does Jb 39:22
as stubble; he **l** at the rattle of javelins. Jb 41:29
He who sits in the heavens **l**; the Lord Ps 2:4
but the Lord **l** at the wicked, for he sees Ps 37:13
with a fool, the fool only rages and **l**, Prv 29:9
clothing, and she **l** at the time to come. Prv 31:25

LAUGHTER (9)

And Sarah said, "God has made **l** for me; Gn 21:6
He will yet fill your mouth with **l**, and Jb 8:21
Then our mouth was filled with **l**, and Ps 126:2
Even in **l** the heart may ache, and the Prv 14:13
I said of **l**, "It is mad," and of pleasure, Eccl 2:2
Sorrow is better than **l**, for by sadness of Eccl 7:3
under a pot, so is the **l** of the fools; Eccl 7:6
Bread is made for **l**, and wine Eccl 10:19
Let your **l** be turned to mourning and Jas 4:9

LAUREL (1)

spreading himself like a green **l** tree. Ps 37:35

LAVISH (1)

Those who **l** gold from the purse, and Is 46:6

LAVISHED (4)

the royal wine was **l** according to the Est 1:7
your renown and **l** your whorings on Ezk 16:15
the oil, and who **l** on her silver and gold, Hos 2:8
which he **l** upon us, in all wisdom and Eph 1:8

LAW (415)

There shall be one **l** for the native and Ex 12:49
that the **l** of the LORD may be in your Ex 13:9
whether they will walk in my **l** or not. Ex 16:4
with the **l** and the commandment, Ex 24:12
saying, This is the **l** of the burnt offering. Lv 6:9
"And this is the **l** of the grain offering. Lv 6:14
saying, This is the **l** of the sin offering. Lv 6:25
"This is the **l** of the guilt offering. It is Lv 7:1
the sin offering; there is one **l** for them. Lv 7:7
"And this is the **l** of the sacrifice of peace Lv 7:11
This is the **l** of the burnt offering, of the Lv 7:37
This is the **l** about beast and bird and Lv 11:46
This is the **l** for her who bears a child, Lv 12:7
This is the **l** for a case of leprous disease Lv 13:59
"This shall be the **l** of the leprous person Lv 14:2
This is the **l** for him in whom is a case Lv 14:32
This is the **l** for any case of leprous Lv 14:54
clean. This is the **l** for leprous disease. Lv 14:57
And this is the **l** of his uncleanness for a Lv 15:3
This is the **l** for him who has a Lv 15:32
"This is the **l** in cases of jealousy, when Nm 5:29
priest shall carry out for her all this **l**. Nm 5:30
"And this is the **l** for the Nazirite, when Nm 6:13
"This is the **l** of the Nazirite. But if he Nm 6:21
do in addition to the **l** of the Nazirite." Nm 6:21
One **l** and one rule shall be for you Nm 15:16
You shall have one **l** for him who Nm 15:29
is the statute of the **l** that the LORD has Nm 19:2
"This is the **l** when someone dies in a Nm 19:14
is the statute of the **l** that the LORD has Nm 31:21
Moab, Moses undertook to explain this **l**, Dt 1:5
so righteous as all this **l** that I set before Dt 4:8
This is the **l** that Moses set before the Dt 4:44
for himself in a book a copy of this **l**, Dt 17:18
all the words of this **l** and these statutes, Dt 17:19
write on them all the words of this **l**, Dt 27:3
all the words of this **l** very plainly." Dt 27:8
the words of this **l** by doing them.' Dt 27:26
all the words of this **l** that are written in Dt 28:58
that is not recorded in the book of this **l**, Dt 28:61
covenant written in this Book of the **L**. Dt 29:21
that we may do all the words of this **l**. Dt 29:29
that are written in this Book of the **L**, Dt 30:10
Then Moses wrote this **l** and gave it to Dt 31:9
you shall read this **l** before all Israel in Dt 31:11
be careful to do all the words of this **l**, Dt 31:12
writing the words of this **l** in a book to Dt 31:24
"Take this Book of the **L** and put it by Dt 31:26

be careful to do all the words of this **l**. Dt 32:46
when Moses commanded us a **l**, as a Dt 33:4
Jacob your rules and Israel your **l**; Dt 33:10
according to all the **l** that Moses my Jos 1:7
This Book of the **L** shall not depart from Jos 1:8
is written in the Book of the **L** of Moses, Jos 8:31
on the stones a copy of the **l** of Moses, Jos 8:32
afterward he read all the words of the **l**, Jos 8:34
to all that is written in the Book of the **L**. Jos 8:34
commandment and the **l** that Moses the Jos 22:5
is written in the Book of the **L** of Moses, Jos 23:6
these words in the Book of the **L** of God. Jos 24:26
as it is written in the **L** of Moses, 1 Kgs 2:3
to walk in the **l** of the LORD the 2 Kgs 10:31
written in the Book of the **L** of Moses, 2 Kgs 14:6
with all the **L** that I commanded 2 Kgs 17:13
do not know the **l** of the god of 2 Kgs 17:26
they do not know the **l** of the god of 2 Kgs 17:26
and teach them the **l** of the god of 2 Kgs 17:27
rules or the **l** or the commandment 2 Kgs 17:34
rules and the **l** and the 2 Kgs 17:37
to all the **L** that my servant 2 Kgs 21:8
the Book of the **L** in the house of 2 Kgs 22:8
heard the words of the Book of the **L**, 2 Kgs 22:11
the words of the **l** that were written 2 Kgs 23:24
according to all the **L** of Moses, 2 Kgs 23:25
is written in the **L** of the LORD that 1 Chr 16:40
you may keep the **l** of the LORD your 1 Chr 22:12
to walk in my **l** as you have walked 2 Chr 6:16
he abandoned the **l** of the LORD, 2 Chr 12:1
to keep the **l** and the commandment. 2 Chr 14:4
a teaching priest and without **l**, 2 Chr 15:3
the Book of the **L** of the LORD with 2 Chr 17:9
bloodshed, **l** or commandment, 2 Chr 19:10
as it is written in the **L** of Moses, 2 Chr 23:18
according to what is written in the **L**, 2 Chr 25:4
according to the **L** of Moses the 2 Chr 30:16
as it is written in the **L** of the LORD. 2 Chr 31:3
give themselves to the **L** of the LORD. 2 Chr 31:4
accordance with the **l** and the 2 Chr 31:21
I have commanded them, all the **l**, 2 Chr 33:8
the Book of the **L** of the LORD given 2 Chr 34:14
the Book of the **L** in the house of 2 Chr 34:15
the king heard the words of the **L**, 2 Chr 34:19
what is written in the **L** of the LORD, 2 Chr 35:26
it is written in the **L** of Moses the man of Ezr 3:2
a scribe skilled in the **L** of Moses that the Ezr 7:6
set his heart to study the **L** of the LORD, Ezr 7:10
the scribe of the **L** of the God of heaven. Ezr 7:12
according to the **L** of your God, Ezr 7:14
the scribe of the **L** of the God of heaven, Ezr 7:21
will not obey the **l** of your God and Ezr 7:26
law of your God and the **l** of the king, Ezr 7:26
and let it be done according to the **L**. Ezr 10:3
the Book of the **L** of Moses that the Neh 8:1
priest brought the **L** before the Neh 8:2
were attentive to the Book of the **L**. Neh 8:3
helped the people to understand the **L**, Neh 8:7
read from the book, from the **L** of God, Neh 8:8
wept as they heard the words of the **L**. Neh 8:9
in order to study the words of the **L**. Neh 8:13
it written in the **L** that the LORD had Neh 8:14
he read from the Book of the **L** of God. Neh 8:18
from the Book of the **L** of the LORD their Neh 9:3
and statutes and a **l** by Moses your Neh 9:14
you and cast your **l** behind their back Neh 9:26
in order to turn them back to your **l**. Neh 9:29
have not kept your **l** or paid attention Neh 9:34
peoples of the lands to the **L** of God, Neh 10:28
to walk in God's **L** that was given by Neh 10:29
LORD our God, as it is written in the **L**. Neh 10:34
of our cattle, as it is written in the **L**, Neh 10:36
required by the **L** for the priests Neh 12:44
As soon as the people heard the **l**, they Neh 13:3
all who were versed in **l** and judgment, Est 1:13
"According to the **l**, what is to be done to Est 1:15
there is but one **l**—to be put to death, Est 4:11
go to the king, though it is against the **l**, Est 4:16
but his delight is in the **l** of the LORD, and Ps 1:2
and on his **l** he meditates day and night. Ps 1:2
The **l** of the LORD is perfect, reviving the Ps 19:7
The **l** of his God is in his heart; his steps Ps 37:31
O my God; your **l** is within my heart." Ps 40:8
in Jacob and appointed a **l** in Israel, Ps 78:5
but refused to walk according to his **l**. Ps 78:10
his children forsake my **l** and do not Ps 89:30
and whom you teach out of your **l**, Ps 94:12
who walk in the **l** of the LORD! Ps 119:1
behold wondrous things out of your **l**. Ps 119:18
me and graciously teach me your **l**! Ps 119:29
I may keep your **l** and observe it with Ps 119:34
I will keep your **l** continually, forever Ps 119:44
but I do not turn away from your **l**. Ps 119:51
of the wicked, who forsake your **l**. Ps 119:53
in the night, O LORD, and keep your **l**. Ps 119:55
ensnare me, I do not forget your **l**. Ps 119:61
like fat, but I delight in your **l**. Ps 119:70
The **l** of your mouth is better to me Ps 119:72
I may live; for your **l** is my delight. Ps 119:77
they do not live according to your **l**. Ps 119:85
If your **l** had not been my delight, I Ps 119:92
Oh how I love your **l**! It is my Ps 119:97
but I do not forget your **l**. Ps 119:109
the double-minded, but I love your **l**. Ps 119:113
to act, for your **l** has been broken. Ps 119:126
because people do not keep your **l**. Ps 119:136
righteous forever, and your **l** is true. Ps 119:142
evil purpose; they are far from your **l**. Ps 119:150
deliver me, for I do not forget your **l**. Ps 119:153
abhor falsehood, but I love your **l**. Ps 119:163
peace have those who love your **l**; Ps 119:165
O LORD, and your **l** is my delight. Ps 119:174
who forsake the **l** praise the wicked, Prv 28:4
who keep the **l** strive against them. Prv 28:4
The one who keeps the **l** is a son with Prv 28:7
turns away his ear from hearing the **l**, Prv 28:9
but blessed is he who keeps the **l**. Prv 29:18
in his paths." For out of Zion shall go the **l**, Is 2:3
for they have rejected the **l** of the LORD of Is 5:24
earth; and the coastlands wait for his **l**. Is 42:4
to magnify his **l** and make it glorious. Is 42:21
walk, and whose **l** they would not obey? Is 42:24
for a **l** will go out from me, and I will set Is 51:4
the people in whose heart is my **l**; Is 51:7
suit justly; no one goes to **l** honestly; Is 59:4
Those who handle the **l** did not know me; Jer 2:8
and as for my **l**, they have rejected it. Jer 6:19
are wise, and the **l** of the LORD is with us'? Jer 8:8
they have forsaken my **l** that I set before Jer 9:13
forsaken me and have not kept my **l**, Jer 16:11
for the **l** shall not perish from the priest, Jer 18:18
to walk in my **l** that I have set before Jer 26:4
I will put my **l** within them, and I will Jer 31:33
not obey your voice or walk in your **l**. Jer 32:23
nor walked in my **l** and my statutes Jer 44:10
LORD or walk in his **l** and in his statutes Jer 44:23
the **l** is no more, and her prophets find Lam 2:9
while the **l** perishes from the priest and Ezk 7:26
violence to my **l** and have profaned Ezk 22:26
This is the **l** of the temple: the whole Ezk 43:12
holy. Behold, this is the **l** of the temple. Ezk 43:12
it in connection with the **l** of his God." Dn 6:5
according to the **l** of the Medes and the Dn 6:8
according to the **l** of the Medes and Dn 6:12
that it is a **l** of the Medes and Persians Dn 6:15
think to change the times and the **l**; Dn 7:25
has transgressed your **l** and turned Dn 9:11
are written in the **L** of Moses the servant Dn 9:11
As it is written in the **L** of Moses, all this Dn 9:13
you have forgotten the **l** of your God, Hos 4:6
my covenant and rebelled against my **l**. Hos 8:1
they have rejected the **l** of the LORD, Am 2:4
For out of Zion shall go forth the **l**, Mi 4:2
So the **l** is paralyzed, and justice never Hab 1:4
what is holy; they do violence to the **l**. Zep 3:4
LORD of hosts: Ask the priests about the **l**: Hg 2:11
they should hear the **l** and the words Zec 7:12
"Remember the **l** of my servant Moses, Mal 4:4
come to abolish the **L** or the Prophets; Mt 5:17
will pass from the **L** until all is Mt 5:18
them, for this is the **L** and the Prophets. Mt 7:12
Prophets and the **L** prophesied until Mt 11:13
not read in the **L** how on the Sabbath Mt 12:5
is the great commandment in the **L**?" Mt 22:36
depend all the **L** and the Prophets." Mt 22:40
neglected the weightier matters of the **l**: Mt 23:23
according to the **L** of Moses, Lk 2:22
(as it is written in the **L** of the Lord, Lk 2:23
to what is said in the **L** of the Lord, Lk 2:24
him according to the custom of the **L**, Lk 2:27
according to the **L** of the Lord, Lk 2:39
and teachers of the **l** were sitting there, Lk 5:17
said to him, "What is written in the **L**? Lk 10:26
"The **L** and the Prophets were until Lk 16:16
for one dot of the **L** to become void. Lk 16:17
about me in the **L** of Moses and the Lk 24:44
For the **l** was given through Moses; grace Jn 1:17
whom Moses in the **L** and also the Jn 1:45
Has not Moses given you the **l**? Yet none Jn 7:19
you the law? Yet none of you keeps the **l**. Jn 7:19
so that the **l** of Moses may not be broken, Jn 7:23
that does not know the **l** is accursed." Jn 7:49
"Does our **l** judge a man without first Jn 7:51
Now in the **L** Moses commanded us to Jn 8:5
In your **L** it is written that the testimony Jn 8:17
them, "Is it not written in your **L**, Jn 10:34
have heard from the **L** that the Christ Jn 12:34
is written in their **L** must be fulfilled: Jn 15:25
him by your own **l**." The Jews said to Jn 18:31
The Jews answered him, "We have a **l**, Jn 19:7
and according to that **l** he ought to die Jn 19:7
a teacher of the **l** held in honor by all Acts 5:34
words against this holy place and the **l**, Acts 6:13
you who received the **l** as delivered by Acts 7:53
reading from the **L** and the Prophets, Acts 13:15
could not be freed by the **l** of Moses. Acts 13:39
to order them to keep the **l** of Moses." Acts 15:5
to worship God contrary to the **l**." Acts 18:13
words and names and your own **l**, Acts 18:15
They are all zealous for the **l**, Acts 21:20
also live in observance of the **l**. Acts 21:24
the people and the **l** and this place. Acts 21:28
strict manner of the **l** of our fathers, Acts 22:3
a devout man according to the **l**, Acts 22:12
sitting to judge me according to the **l**, Acts 23:3
yet contrary to the **l** you order me to Acts 23:3
accused about questions of their **l**, Acts 23:29
laid down by the **L** and written in the Acts 24:14
"Neither against the **l** of the Jews, Acts 25:8
Jesus both from the **L** of Moses and Acts 28:23
sinned without the **l** will also perish Rom 2:12
the law will also perish without the **l**, Rom 2:12
have sinned under the **l** will be judged Rom 2:12
under the law will be judged by the **l**. Rom 2:12
the hearers of the **l** who are righteous Rom 2:13
the doers of the **l** who will be justified. Rom 2:13
when Gentiles, who do not have the **l**, Rom 2:14
law, by nature do what the **l** requires, Rom 2:14
law requires, they are a **l** to themselves, Rom 2:14
even though they do not have the **l**. Rom 2:14
the work of the **l** is written on their Rom 2:15
Jew and rely on the **l** and boast in God Rom 2:17
because you are instructed from the **l**; Rom 2:18
having in the **l** the embodiment of Rom 2:20
who boast in the **l** dishonor God by Rom 2:23
law dishonor God by breaking the **l**. Rom 2:23
indeed is of value if you obey the **l**, Rom 2:25
obey the law, but if you break the **l**, Rom 2:25
keeps the precepts of the **l**, Rom 2:26
but keeps the **l** will condemn you Rom 2:27
and circumcision but break the **l**. Rom 2:27
that whatever the **l** says it speaks Rom 3:19
it speaks to those who are under the **l**, Rom 3:19
by works of the **l** no human being will Rom 3:20
since through the **l** comes knowledge Rom 3:20
has been manifested apart from the **l**, Rom 3:21
although the **L** and the Prophets bear Rom 3:21
It is excluded. By what kind of **l**? Rom 3:27
By what kind of law? By a **l** of works? Rom 3:27
law of works? No, but by the **l** of faith. Rom 3:27
by faith apart from works of the **l**. Rom 3:28
we then overthrow the **l** by this faith? Rom 3:31
On the contrary, we uphold the **l**. Rom 3:31
come through the **l** but through the Rom 4:13
is the adherents of the **l** who are to be Rom 4:14
For the **l** brings wrath, but where Rom 4:15
where there is no **l** there is no Rom 4:15
to the adherent of the **l** but also to the Rom 4:16
in the world before the **l** was given, Rom 5:13
sin is not counted where there is no **l**. Rom 5:13
Now the **l** came in to increase the Rom 5:20
you are not under **l** but under grace. Rom 6:14
we are not under **l** but under grace? Rom 6:15
to those who know the **l**—that the law Rom 7:1
the law—that the **l** is binding on a Rom 7:1
woman is bound by **l** to her husband Rom 7:2
she is released from the **l** of marriage. Rom 7:2
her husband dies, she is free from that **l**, Rom 7:3
have died to the **l** through the body of Rom 7:4
our sinful passions, aroused by the **l**, Rom 7:5
But now we are released from the **l**, Rom 7:6
then shall we say? That the **l** is sin? Rom 7:7
Yet if it had not been for the **l**, I would Rom 7:7
what it is to covet if the **l** had not said, Rom 7:7
Apart from the **l**, sin lies dead. Rom 7:8
I was once alive apart from the **l**, but Rom 7:9
So the **l** is holy, and the Rom 7:12
For we know that the **l** is spiritual, but Rom 7:14
what I do not want, I agree with the **l**, Rom 7:16
I find it to be a **l** that when I want to do Rom 7:21
For I delight in the **l** of God, in my Rom 7:22
my members another **l** waging war Rom 7:23
waging war against the **l** of my mind Rom 7:23
me captive to the **l** of sin that dwells Rom 7:23
I myself serve the **l** of God with my Rom 7:25
but with my flesh I serve the **l** of sin. Rom 7:25
For the **l** of the Spirit of life has set you Rom 8:2
Christ Jesus from the **l** of sin and death. Rom 8:2
For God has done what the **l**, weakened Rom 8:3
requirement of the **l** might be fulfilled Rom 8:4
to God, for it does not submit to God's **l**; Rom 8:7
glory, the covenants, the giving of the **l**, Rom 9:4
Israel who pursued a **l** that would lead Rom 9:31
did not succeed in reaching that **l**. Rom 9:31
the end of the **l** for righteousness to Rom 10:4

righteousness that is based on the **l**, Rom 10:5
who loves another has fulfilled the **l**. Rom 13:8
therefore love is the fulfilling of the **l**. Rom 13:10
he dare go to **l** before the unrighteous 1 Cor 6:1
but brother goes to **l** against brother, 1 Cor 6:6
Does not the **L** say the same? 1 Cor 9:8
For it is written in the **L** of Moses, 1 Cor 9:9
To those under the **l** I became as one 1 Cor 9:20
as one under the **l** (though not being 1 Cor 9:20
myself under the **l**) that I might 1 Cor 9:20
that I might win those under the **l**. 1 Cor 9:20
To those outside the **l** I became as one 1 Cor 9:21
as one outside the **l** (not being outside 1 Cor 9:21
(not being outside the **l** of God but 1 Cor 9:21
God but under the **l** of Christ) that I 1 Cor 9:21
that I might win those outside the **l**. 1 Cor 9:21
In the **L** it is written, "By people of 1 Cor 14:21
be in submission, as the **L** also says. 1 Cor 14:34
is sin, and the power of sin is the **l**. 1 Cor 15:56
by works of the **l** but through faith in Gal 2:16
in Christ and not by works of the **l**, Gal 2:16
because by works of the **l** no one will be Gal 2:16
For through the **l** I died to the law, so Gal 2:19
For through the law I died to the **l**, so Gal 2:19
for if justification were through the **l**, Gal 2:21
by works of the **l** or by hearing with Gal 3:2
among you do so by works of the **l**, Gal 3:5
rely on works of the **l** are under a curse; Gal 3:10
all things written in the Book of the **L**, Gal 3:10
no one is justified before God by the **l**, Gal 3:11
But the **l** is not of faith, rather "The one Gal 3:12
the curse of the **l** by becoming a curse Gal 3:13
This is what I mean: the **l**, which came Gal 3:17
For if the inheritance comes by the **l**, it Gal 3:18
Why then the **l**? It was added because of Gal 3:19
Is the **l** then contrary to the promises of Gal 3:21
For if a **l** had been given that could give Gal 3:21
righteousness would indeed be by the **l**. Gal 3:21
came, we were held captive under the **l**, Gal 3:23
the **l** was our guardian until Christ Gal 3:24
Son, born of woman, born under the **l**, Gal 4:4
to redeem those who were under the **l**, so Gal 4:5
me, you who desire to be under the **l**, Gal 4:21
under the law, do you not listen to the **l**? Gal 4:21
that he is obligated to keep the whole **l**. Gal 5:3
you who would be justified by the **l**; Gal 5:4
For the whole **l** is fulfilled in one word: Gal 5:14
led by the Spirit, you are not under the **l**. Gal 5:18
against such things there is no **l**. Gal 5:23
burdens, and so fulfill the **l** of Christ. Gal 6:2
do not themselves keep the **l**, Gal 6:13
by abolishing the **l** of commandments Eph 2:15
of Hebrews; as to the **l**, a Pharisee; Phil 3:5
to righteousness, under the **l** blameless. Phil 3:6
of my own that comes from the **l**, Phil 3:9
desiring to be teachers of the **l**, without 1 Tm 1:7
Now we know that the **l** is good, if one 1 Tm 1:8
that the **l** is not laid down for the just 1 Tm 1:9
dissensions, and quarrels about the **l**, Ti 3:9
a commandment in the **l** to take tithes Heb 7:5
(for under it the people received the **l**), Heb 7:11
is necessarily a change in the **l** as well. Heb 7:12
(for the **l** made nothing perfect); but on Heb 7:19
For the **l** appoints men in their Heb 7:28
the oath, which came later than the **l**, Heb 7:28
priests who offer gifts according to the **l**. Heb 8:4
commandment of the **l** had been Heb 9:19
under the **l** almost everything is Heb 9:22
For since the **l** has but a shadow of the Heb 10:1
(these are offered according to the **l**), Heb 10:8
has set aside the **l** of Moses dies Heb 10:28
But the one who looks into the perfect **l**, Jas 1:25
looks into the perfect law, the **l** of liberty, Jas 1:25
really fulfill the royal **l** according to the Jas 2:8
are convicted by the **l** as transgressors. Jas 2:9
whoever keeps the whole **l** but fails in Jas 2:10
you have become a transgressor of the **l**. Jas 2:11
are to be judged under the **l** of liberty. Jas 2:12
speaks evil against the **l** and judges the Jas 4:11
evil against the law and judges the **l**. Jas 4:11
But if you judge the **l**, you are not a doer Jas 4:11
you are not a doer of the **l** but a judge. Jas 4:11

LAW-BREAKERS (1)
his kingdom all causes of sin and all **l**, Mt 13:41

LAWFUL (28)
that it shall not be **l** to impose tribute, Ezr 7:24
are doing what is not **l** to do on the Mt 12:2
which it was not **l** for him to eat nor for Mt 12:4
"Is it **l** to heal on the Sabbath?"—so Mt 12:10
So it is **l** to do good on the Sabbath." Mt 12:12
to him, "It is not **l** for you to have her." Mt 14:4
"Is it **l** to divorce one's wife for any Mt 19:3
Is it **l** to pay taxes to Caesar, or not?" Mt 22:17
"It is not **l** to put them into the treasury, Mt 27:6
doing what is not **l** on the Sabbath?" Mk 2:24
which it is not **l** for any but the priests Mk 2:26
"Is it **l** on the Sabbath to do good or to do Mk 3:4
"It is not **l** for you to have your Mk 6:18
"Is it **l** for a man to divorce his wife?" Mk 10:2
Is it **l** to pay taxes to Caesar, or not? Mk 12:14
you doing what is not **l** to do on the Lk 6:2
which is not **l** for any but the priests to Lk 6:4
is it **l** on the Sabbath to do good or to do Lk 6:9
saying, "Is it **l** to heal on the Sabbath, Lk 14:3
Is it **l** for us to give tribute to Caesar, or Lk 20:22
and it is not **l** for you to take up your Jn 5:10
"It is not **l** for us to put anyone to death." Jn 18:31
customs that are not **l** for us as Acts 16:21
"Is it **l** for you to flog a man who is a Acts 22:25
"All things are **l** for me," but not all 1 Cor 6:12
"All things are **l** for me," but I will 1 Cor 6:12
"All things are **l**," but not all things 1 Cor 10:23
"All things are **l**," but not all things 1 Cor 10:23

LAWFULLY (1)
that the law is good, if one uses it **l**, 1 Tm 1:8

LAWGIVER (2)
the LORD is our judge; the LORD is our **l**; Is 33:22
There is only one **l** and judge, he who is Jas 4:12

LAWLESS (9)
and killed by the hands of **l** men. Acts 2:23
are those whose **l** deeds are forgiven, Rom 4:7
And then the **l** one will be revealed, 2 Thes 2:8
The coming of the **l** one is by the 2 Thes 2:9
the just but for the **l** and disobedient, 1 Tm 1:9
their sins and their **l** deeds no more." Heb 10:17
orgies, drinking parties, and **l** idolatry. 1 Pt 4:3
righteous soul over their **l** deeds that he 2 Pt 2:8
with the error of **l** people and lose your 2 Pt 3:17

LAWLESSNESS (11)
you; depart from me, you workers of **l**.' Mt 7:23
within you are full of hypocrisy and **l**. Mt 23:28
And because **l** will be increased, the Mt 24:12
to impurity and to **l** leading to more Rom 6:19
and to lawlessness leading to more **l**, Rom 6:19
partnership has righteousness with **l**? 2 Cor 6:14
first, and the man of **l** is revealed, 2 Thes 2:3
For the mystery of **l** is already at 2 Thes 2:7
to redeem us from all **l** and to purify for Ti 2:14
a practice of sinning also practices **l**; 1 Jn 3:4
also practices lawlessness; sin is **l**. 1 Jn 3:4

LAWS (20)
my statutes, and my **l**." Gn 26:5
to keep my commandments and my **l**? Ex 16:28
know the statutes of God and his **l**." Ex 18:16
warn them about the statutes and the **l**, Ex 18:20
statutes and rules and **l** that the LORD Lv 26:46
all such as know the **l** of your God. Ezr 7:25
and gave them right rules and true **l**, Neh 9:13
be written among the **l** of the Persians Est 1:19
Their **l** are different from those of every Est 3:8
people, and they do not keep the king's **l**, Est 3:8
keep his statutes and observe his **l**. Ps 105:45
for they have transgressed the **l**, violated Is 24:5
and its whole design and all its **l**, Ezk 43:11
may observe all its **l** and all its Ezk 43:11
of the temple of the LORD and all its **l**. Ezk 44:5
They shall keep my **l** and my statutes Ezk 44:24
of the LORD our God by walking in his **l**, Dn 9:10
write for him my **l** by the ten Hos 8:12
I will put my **l** into their minds, and Heb 8:10
I will put my **l** on their hearts, and Heb 10:16

LAWSUIT (4)
do evil, nor shall you bear witness in a **l**, Ex 23:2
you be partial to a poor man in his **l**. Ex 23:3
the justice due to your poor in his **l**. Ex 23:6
to subvert a man in his **l**, the Lord Lam 3:36

LAWSUITS (1)
To have **l** at all with one another is 1 Cor 6:7

LAWYER (3)
And one of them, a **l**, asked him a Mt 22:35
a **l** stood up to put him to the test, Lk 10:25
to speed Zenas the **l** and Apollos on their Ti 3:13

LAWYERS (5)
Pharisees and the **l** rejected the purpose Lk 7:30
One of the **l** answered him, "Teacher, Lk 11:45
And he said, "Woe to you **l** also! For Lk 11:46
Woe to you **l**! For you have taken away Lk 11:52
Jesus responded to the **l** and Pharisees, Lk 14:3

LAY (217)
became drunk and **l** uncovered in his Gn 9:21
But before they **l** down, the men of the Gn 19:4
firstborn went in and **l** with her father. Gn 19:33
not know when she **l** down or when Gn 19:33
"Behold, I **l** last night with my father. Gn 19:34
And the younger arose and **l** with him, Gn 19:35
not know when she **l** down or when Gn 19:35
"Do not **l** your hand on the boy or do Gn 22:12
under his head and **l** down in that Gn 28:11
son's mandrakes." So he **l** with her that Gn 30:16
Jacob would **l** the sticks in the troughs Gn 30:41
of the flock he would not **l** them there. Gn 30:42
he seized her and **l** with her and Gn 34:2
Reuben went and **l** with Bilhah his Gn 35:22
but do not **l** a hand on him"—that he Gn 37:22
Then I will **l** my hand on Egypt and bring Ex 7:4
in the morning dew **l** around the camp. Ex 16:13
all that is left over **l** aside to be kept till Ex 16:23
And he did not **l** his hand on the chief Ex 24:11
and his sons shall **l** their hands on the Ex 29:10
and his sons shall **l** their hands on the Ex 29:15
and his sons shall **l** their hands on the Ex 29:19
He shall **l** his hand on the head of the Lv 1:4
put oil on it and **l** frankincense on it; Lv 2:15
And he shall **l** his hand on the head of his Lv 3:2
l his hand on the head of his offering, and Lv 3:8
and **l** his hand on its head and kill it in Lv 3:13
before the LORD and **l** his hand on the Lv 4:4
the congregation shall **l** their hands on Lv 4:15
and shall **l** his hand on the head of the Lv 4:24
And he shall **l** his hand on the head of Lv 4:29
and **l** his hand on the head of the sin Lv 4:33
And Aaron shall **l** both his hands on Lv 16:21
"A **l** person shall not eat of a holy thing; Lv 22:10
food; yet no **l** person shall eat of it. Lv 22:13
all who heard him **l** their hands on his Lv 24:14
And I will **l** your cities waste and will Lv 26:31
people of Israel shall **l** their hands on Nm 8:10
Then the Levites shall **l** their hands on Nm 8:12
that you **l** the burden of all this people Nm 11:11
off the altar and **l** incense on it and Nm 16:46
of the LORD, she **l** down under Balaam. Nm 22:27
he **l** down like a lion and like a lioness; Nm 24:9
is the Spirit, and **l** your hand on him. Nm 27:18
therefore today, and **l** it to your heart, Dt 4:39
but he will **l** them on all who hate you. Dt 7:15
Then I **l** prostrate before the LORD as Dt 9:18
"So I **l** prostrate before the LORD for these Dt 9:25
"You shall therefore **l** up these words of Dt 11:18
The LORD your God will **l** the fear of you Dt 11:25
in the same year and **l** it up within your Dt 14:28
die, the man who **l** with the woman, Dt 22:22
only the man who **l** with her shall die. Dt 22:25
then the man who **l** with her shall give Dt 22:29
Before the men **l** down, she came up to Jos 2:8
over with you and **l** them down in the Jos 4:3
of his firstborn shall he **l** its foundation, Jos 6:26
L an ambush against the city, behind it." Jos 8:2
of ambush and **l** between Bethel and Jos 8:9
there. The land **l** subdued before them. Jos 18:1
and there **l** their lord dead on the floor. Jgs 3:25
in to her tent, and there **l** Sisera dead, Jgs 4:22
her feet he sank, he fell, he **l** still; Jgs 5:27
people of the East **l** along the valley like Jgs 7:12
it upside down, so that the tent **l** flat." Jgs 7:13
But Samson **l** till midnight, and at Jgs 16:3
softly and uncovered his feet and **l** down. Ru 3:7
over, and behold, a woman **l** at his feet! Ru 3:8
So she **l** at his feet until the morning, Ru 3:14
and how they **l** with the women who 1 Sm 2:22
lie down again." So he went and **l** down. 1 Sm 3:5
So Samuel went and **l** down in his 1 Sm 3:9
Samuel **l** until morning; then he 1 Sm 3:15
on the roof, and he **l** down to sleep. 1 Sm 9:25
the city of Amalek and **l** in wait in the 1 Sm 15:5
before Samuel and **l** naked all that 1 Sm 19:24
And David saw the place where Saul **l**, 1 Sm 26:5
And there **l** Saul sleeping within the 1 Sm 26:7
Abner and the army **l** around him. 1 Sm 26:7
as he **l** on his bed in his bedroom, 2 Sm 4:7
she came to him, and he **l** with her. 2 Sm 11:4
and went in and **l** all night on the 2 Sm 12:16
and went in to her and **l** with her, 2 Sm 12:24
So Amnon **l** down and pretended to be 2 Sm 13:6
she, he violated her and **l** with her. 2 Sm 13:14
tore his garments and **l** on the earth. 2 Sm 13:31
And Amasa **l** wallowing in his blood 2 Sm 20:12
in the night, because she **l** on him. 1 Kgs 3:19
stones in order to **l** the foundation of 1 Kgs 5:17
buried; **l** my bones beside his bones. 1 Kgs 13:31
cut it in pieces and **l** it on the wood, 1 Kgs 18:23
the other bull and **l** it on the wood 1 Kgs 18:23
And he **l** down and slept under a 1 Kgs 19:5
he ate and drank and **l** down again. 1 Kgs 19:6
your servants and **l** hands on 1 Kgs 20:6
my fathers." And he **l** down on his 1 Kgs 21:4
and fasted and **l** in sackcloth and 1 Kgs 21:27
upper chamber in Samaria, and **l** sick; 2 Kgs 1:2
And **l** my staff on the face of the 2 Kgs 4:29
Then he went up and **l** on the child, 2 Kgs 4:34
and went to Jezreel, for Joram **l** there. 2 Kgs 9:16

"**L** them in two heaps at the entrance 2 Kgs 10:8
And let them take and **l** it on the boil, 2 Kgs 20:7
for on them **l** the duty of watching, 1 Chr 9:27
houses of your brothers the **l** people, 2 Chr 35:5
Josiah contributed to the **l** people, 2 Chr 35:7
of the fathers' houses of the **l** people, 2 Chr 35:12
them quickly to all the **l** people. 2 Chr 35:13
the days that it **l** desolate it kept 2 Chr 36:21
I will **l** hands on you." From that time Neh 13:21
angry and sought to **l** hands on King Est 2:21
But he disdained to **l** hands on Mordecai Est 3:6
and many of them **l** in sackcloth and Est 4:3
who had sought to **l** hands on King Est 6:2
because he intended to **l** hands on the Est 8:7
of King Ahasuerus to **l** hands on those Est 9:2
us, who might **l** his hand on us both. Jb 9:33
"**L** down a pledge for me with yourself; Jb 17:3
and **l** your hand over your mouth. Jb 21:5
and **l** up his words in your heart. Jb 22:22
if you **l** gold in the dust, and gold of Jb 22:24
I would **l** my case before him and fill my Jb 23:4
I answer you? I **l** my hand on my mouth. Jb 40:4
L your hands on him; remember the Jb 41:8
I **l** down and slept; I woke again, for the Ps 3:5
life to the ground and **l** my glory in the Ps 7:5
my jaws; you **l** me in the dust of death. Ps 22:15
Those who seek my life **l** their snares; Ps 38:12
I rebuke you and **l** the charge before Ps 50:21
of Jacob, both rider and horse **l** stunned. Ps 76:6
They **l** crafty plans against your people; Ps 83:3
for herself, where she may **l** her young, Ps 84:3
of Jerusalem, how they said, "**L** it bare, Ps 137:7
how they said, "Lay it bare, **l** it bare, Ps 137:7
and before, and **l** your hand upon me. Ps 139:5
is a tree of life to those who **l** hold of her; Prv 3:18
The wise **l** up knowledge, but the Prv 10:14
wisdom—and how to **l** hold on folly, Eccl 2:3
and the living will **l** it to heart. Eccl 7:2
for calmness will **l** great offenses to Eccl 10:4
climb the palm tree and **l** hold of its fruit. Sg 7:8
and the LORD will **l** bare their secret parts. Is 3:17
and **l** low the pompous pride of the Is 13:11
Go up, O Elam; **l** siege, O Media; all the Is 21:2
but the LORD will **l** low his pompous Is 25:11
of his walls he will bring down, **l** low, Is 25:12
Or let them **l** hold of my protection, let Is 27:5
and **l** a snare for him who reproves in Is 29:21
I will **l** waste mountains and hills, and Is 42:15
so that you did not **l** these things to heart Is 47:7
and **l** your foundations with sapphires. Is 54:11
not remember me, did not **l** it to heart? Is 57:11
I will **l** before this people stumbling Jer 6:21
They **l** hold on bow and javelin; they are Jer 6:23
They **l** hold of bow and spear; they are Jer 50:42
The LORD determined to **l** in ruins the Lam 2:8
they **l** in wait for us in the wilderness. Lam 4:19
and I **l** a stumbling block before him, Ezk 3:20
of man, take a brick and **l** it before you, Ezk 4:1
And I will **l** the dead bodies of the people Ezk 6:5
that I may **l** hold of the hearts of the Ezk 14:5
therefore I will **l** open the flank of Moab Ezk 25:9
And I will **l** my vengeance upon Edom Ezk 25:14
when I **l** my vengeance upon them." Ezk 25:17
I will **l** your cities waste, and you shall Ezk 35:4
it abundant and **l** no famine upon Ezk 36:29
And I will **l** sinews upon you, and will Ezk 37:6
been ministering and **l** them in the Ezk 44:19
of your head as you **l** in bed are these: Dn 2:28
as you **l** in bed came thoughts of what Dn 2:29
As I **l** in bed the fancies and the visions of Dn 4:5
of my head as I **l** in bed were these: Dn 4:10
in the visions of my head as I **l** in bed, Dn 4:13
and visions of his head as he **l** in his bed. Dn 7:1
was overcome and **l** sick for some days. Dn 8:27
And I will **l** waste her vines and her fig Hos 2:12
they **l** themselves down beside every Am 2:8
life, and **l** not on us innocent blood, Jon 1:14
with fire, and all her idols I will **l** waste, Mi 1:7
they shall **l** their hands on their mouths; Mi 7:16
them, because you do not **l** it to heart. Mal 2:2
"Do not **l** up for yourselves treasures on Mt 6:19
but **l** up for yourselves treasures in Mt 6:20
Son of Man has nowhere to **l** his head." Mt 8:20
died, but come and **l** your hand on her, Mt 9:18
him that he might **l** his hands on them Mt 19:13
bear, and **l** them on people's shoulders, Mt 23:4
he said. Come, see the place where he **l**. Mt 28:6
Now Simon's mother-in-law **l** ill with a Mk 1:30
down the bed on which the paralytic **l**. Mk 2:4
Come and **l** your hands on her, so that Mk 5:23
they begged him to **l** his hand on him. Mk 7:32
they will **l** their hands on the sick, and Mk 16:18
to bring him in and **l** him before Jesus, Lk 5:18
Son of Man has nowhere to **l** his head." Lk 9:58
chief priests sought to **l** hands on him Lk 20:19
all this they will **l** their hands on you Lk 21:12
the temple, you did not **l** hands on me. Lk 22:53
In these **l** a multitude of invalids—blind, Jn 5:3
and I **l** down my life for the sheep. Jn 10:15
because I **l** down my life that I may take Jn 10:17
me, but I **l** it down of my own accord. Jn 10:18
I have authority to **l** it down, and I have Jn 10:18
It was a cave, and a stone **l** against it. Jn 11:38
you now? I will **l** down my life for you." Jn 13:37
"Will you **l** down your life for me? Jn 13:38
anyone on whom I **l** my hands may Acts 8:19
Ananias come in and **l** his hands on Acts 9:12
Spirit and to us to **l** on you no greater Acts 15:28
days, and no small tempest **l** on us, Acts 27:20
the father of Publius **l** sick with fever Acts 28:8
For no one can **l** a foundation other 1 Cor 3:11
why do you **l** them before those who 1 Cor 6:4
not to **l** any restraint upon you, 1 Cor 7:35
let us also **l** aside every weight, Heb 12:1
and we ought to **l** down our lives for the 1 Jn 3:16
I say, I do not **l** on you any other burden. Rv 2:24

LAYER (1)
layers of great stones and one **l** of timber. Ezr 6:4

LAYERS (1)
with three **l** of great stones and one layer Ezr 6:4

LAYING (19)
I am **l** a fleece of wool on the threshing Jgs 6:37
Why then are you **l** a trap for my life 1 Sm 28:9
all Israel were **l** siege to Gibbethon. 1 Kgs 15:27
they talk of **l** snares secretly, thinking, Ps 64:5
the heavens and **l** the foundations of Is 51:16
For the LORD is **l** waste their pasture, Jer 25:36
For the LORD is **l** Babylon waste and Jer 51:55
outer court without **l** there the Ezk 42:14
wicked, **l** him bare from thigh to neck. Hab 3:13
blessed them, **l** his hands on them. Mk 10:16
was given through the **l** on of the Acts 8:18
And **l** his hands on him he said, Acts 9:17
under pretense of **l** out anchors from Acts 27:30
I am **l** in Zion a stone of stumbling, Rom 9:33
Do not be hasty in the **l** on of hands, 1 Tm 5:22
in you through the **l** on of my hands, 2 Tm 1:6
not **l** again a foundation of repentance Heb 6:1
about washings, the **l** on of hands, Heb 6:2
"Behold, I am **l** in Zion a stone, a 1 Pt 2:6

LAYMAN (1)
If a priest's daughter marries a **l**, she Lv 22:12

LAYS (15)
he **l** hold of it, but it does not endure. Jb 8:15
him by the heel; a snare **l** hold of him. Jb 18:9
know how God **l** his command upon Jb 37:15
He **l** the beams of his chambers on the Ps 104:3
The fear of man **l** a snare, but whoever Prv 29:25
He **l** it low, lays it low to the ground, casts Is 26:5
He lays it low, **l** it low to the ground, casts Is 26:5
staff that the LORD **l** on them will be Is 30:32
the owl nests and **l** and hatches and Is 34:15
man perishes, and no one **l** it to heart; Is 57:1
made desolate, but no man **l** it to heart. Jer 12:11
is the one who **l** up treasure for himself Lk 12:21
he has found it, he **l** it on his shoulders, Lk 15:5
The good shepherd **l** down his life for Jn 10:11
that someone **l** down his life for his Jn 15:13

LAZARUS (17)
his gate was laid a poor man named **L**, Lk 16:20
saw Abraham far off and **L** at his side. Lk 16:23
and send **L** to dip the end of his finger Lk 16:24
and **L** in like manner bad things; Lk 16:25
Now a certain man was ill, **L** of Bethany, Jn 11:1
with her hair, whose brother **L** was ill. Jn 11:2
Jesus loved Martha and her sister and **L**. Jn 11:5
So, when he heard that **L** was ill, he Jn 11:6
to them, "Our friend **L** has fallen asleep, Jn 11:11
Jesus told them plainly, "**L** has died, Jn 11:14
he found that **L** had already been in the Jn 11:17
out with a loud voice, "**L**, come out." Jn 11:43
therefore came to Bethany, where **L** was, Jn 12:1
and **L** was one of those reclining with Jn 12:2
only on account of him but also to see **L**, Jn 12:9
made plans to put **L** to death as well, Jn 12:10
him when he called **L** out of the tomb Jn 12:17

LAZY (1)
are always liars, evil beasts, **l** gluttons." Ti 1:12

LEAD (75)
of his servant, and I will **l** on slowly, Gn 33:14
God did not **l** them by way of the land Ex 13:17
pillar of cloud to **l** them along the way, Ex 13:21
they sank like **l** in the mighty waters. Ex 15:10
l the people to the place about which I Ex 32:34
who shall **l** them out and bring them Nm 27:17
the bronze, the iron, the tin, and the **l**, Nm 31:22
peoples where the LORD will **l** you away. Dt 28:37
This will **l** to the sweeping away of Dt 29:19
you are going will not **l** to your glory, Jgs 4:9
"That the leaders took the **l** in Israel, that Jgs 5:2
Arise, Barak, **l** away your captives, O Jgs 5:12
that each man may **l** away his wife 1 Sm 30:22
and **l** him to an inner chamber. 2 Kgs 9:2
Azaziah were to **l** with lyres 1 Chr 15:21
The pillar of cloud to **l** them in the way Neh 9:19
and let them **l** him on the horse through Est 6:9
an iron pen and **l** they were engraved in Jb 19:24
Can you **l** forth the Mazzaroth in their Jb 38:32
L me, O LORD, in your righteousness Ps 5:8
L me in your truth and teach me, for you Ps 25:5
and **l** me on a level path because of my Ps 27:11
your name's sake you **l** me and guide Ps 31:3
with the throng and **l** them in procession Ps 42:4
your light and your truth; let them **l** me; Ps 43:3
fortified city? Who will **l** me to Edom? Ps 60:9
L me to the rock that is higher than I, Ps 61:2
is Benjamin, the least of them, in the **l**, Ps 68:27
of Israel, you who **l** Joseph like a flock! Ps 80:1
fortified city? Who will **l** me to Edom? Ps 108:10
L me in the path of your Ps 119:35
the LORD will **l** away with evildoers! Ps 125:5
even there your hand shall **l** me, and Ps 139:10
in me, and **l** me in the way everlasting! Ps 139:24
Let your good Spirit **l** me on level Ps 143:10
When you walk, they will **l** you; when Prv 6:22
of the diligent **l** surely to abundance, Prv 21:5
Let not your mouth **l** you into sin, and Eccl 5:6
I would **l** you and bring you into the Sg 8:2
together; and a little child shall **l** them. Is 11:6
and he will **l** people across in sandals. Is 11:15
the king of Assyria **l** away the Egyptian Is 20:4
and gently **l** those that are with young. Is 40:11
And I will **l** the blind in a way that they Is 42:16
for he who has pity on them will **l** them, Is 49:10
I will **l** him and restore comfort to him Is 57:18
fiercely; the **l** is consumed by the fire; Jer 6:29
who tell them and **l** my people astray Jer 23:32
with pleas for mercy I will **l** them back, Jer 31:9
and tin and iron and **l** in the furnace; Ezk 22:18
bronze and iron and **l** and tin into a Ezk 22:20
and **l** they exchanged for your wares. Ezk 27:12
and **l** you against the mountains of Ezk 39:2
but Ephraim must **l** his children out to Hos 9:13
the prophets who **l** my people astray, Mi 3:5
And **l** us not into temptation, but deliver Mt 6:13
And if the blind **l** the blind, both will Mt 15:14
the Christ,' and they will **l** many astray. Mt 24:5
prophets will arise and **l** many astray. Mt 24:11
signs and wonders, so as to **l** astray, Mt 24:24
'I am he!' and they will **l** many astray. Mk 13:6
perform signs and wonders, to **l** astray, Mk 13:22
Seize him and **l** him away under Mk 14:44
"Can a blind man **l** a blind man? Lk 6:39
to us. And **l** us not into temptation." Lk 11:4
from the manger and **l** it away to water Lk 13:15
he said, "This illness does not **l** to death. Jn 11:4
about seeking people to **l** him by the Acts 13:11
is meant to **l** you to repentance? Rom 2:4
a law that would **l** to righteousness did Rom 9:31
Only let each person **l** the life that the 1 Cor 7:17
that we may **l** a peaceful and quiet life, 1 Tm 2:2
for it will **l** people into more and more 2 Tm 2:16
who commit sins that do not **l** to death. 1 Jn 5:16
but there is sin that does not **l** to death. 1 Jn 5:17

LEADEN (2)
And behold, the **l** cover was lifted, and Zec 5:7
and thrust down the **l** weight on its Zec 5:8

LEADER (23)
"When a **l** sins, doing unintentionally Lv 4:22
"Let us choose a **l** and go back to Nm 14:4
from the hill country, and he was their **l**. Jgs 3:27
said to Jephthah, "Come and be our **l**, Jgs 11:6
people made him head and **l** over them. Jgs 11:11
him and became **l** of a marauding 1 Kgs 11:24
people and made you **l** over my people 1 Kgs 14:7
dust and made you **l** over my people 1 Kgs 16:2
say to Hezekiah the **l** of my people, 2 Kgs 20:5
the Reubenite, a **l** of the Reubenites, 1 Chr 11:42
the thirty and a **l** over the thirty; 1 Chr 12:4
and of hundreds, with every **l**. 1 Chr 13:1
l of the Levites in music, 1 Chr 15:22
and Chenaniah the **l** of the music 1 Chr 15:27
For he chose Judah as **l**, and in the 1 Chr 28:4
neck and appointed a **l** to return to Neh 9:17
of Asaph, who was the **l** of the praise, Neh 11:17
singers sang with Jezrahiah as their **l**. Neh 12:42
you shall be our **l**, and this heap of ruins Is 3:6
you shall not make me **l** of the people." Is 3:7
a **l** and commander for the peoples. Is 55:4
youngest, and the **l** as one who serves. Lk 22:26
him at his right hand as **L** and Savior, Acts 5:31

LEADERS (62)
trembling seizes the **l** of Moab; Ex 15:15
And when all the **l** of the congregation Ex 16:22
Aaron and all the **l** of the congregation Ex 34:31
And the **l** brought onyx stones and Ex 35:27
and the **l** of the congregation swore to Jos 9:15
because the **l** of the congregation had Jos 9:18
congregation murmured against the **l**. Jos 9:18
But all the **l** said to all the congregation, Jos 9:19
And the **l** said to them, "Let them live." Jos 9:21
just as the **l** had said of them. Jos 9:21
Moses defeated with the **l** of Midian, Jos 13:21
the son of Nun and the **l** and said, Jos 17:4
and the **l** of Jericho fought against you, Jos 24:11
"That the **l** took the lead in Israel, that the Jgs 5:2
"Say in the ears of all the **l** of Shechem, Jgs 9:2
behalf in the ears of all the **l** of Shechem, Jgs 9:3
And all the **l** of Shechem came together, Jgs 9:6
to them, "Listen to me, you **l** of Shechem, Jgs 9:7
servant, king over the **l** of Shechem, Jgs 9:18
and devour the **l** of Shechem and Jgs 9:20
come out from the **l** of Shechem and Jgs 9:20
Abimelech and the **l** of Shechem, Jgs 9:23
and the **l** of Shechem dealt Jgs 9:23
And the **l** of Shechem put men in Jgs 9:25
and the **l** of Shechem put confidence in Jgs 9:26
the head of the **l** of Shechem and fought Jgs 9:39
When all the **l** of the Tower of Shechem Jgs 9:46
was told that all the **l** of the Tower of Jgs 9:47
and women and all the **l** of the city fled Jgs 9:51
And the people, the **l** of Gilead, said one Jgs 10:18
And the **l** of Gibeah rose against me and Jgs 20:5
"Come here, all you **l** of the people, 1 Sm 14:38
the **l** of the fathers' houses of the people 1 Kgs 8:1
the elders and the **l** who lived with 1 Kgs 21:8
the elders and the **l** who lived in his 1 Kgs 21:11
Seir, having as their **l** Pelatiah, 1 Chr 4:42
according to their generations, **l**. These 1 Chr 9:34
also commanded all the **l** of Israel to 1 Chr 22:17
assembled all the **l** of Israel and 1 Chr 23:2
These were the **l** of the tribes of 1 Chr 27:22
Then the **l** of fathers' houses made 1 Chr 29:6
as did also the **l** of the tribes, 1 Chr 29:6
All the **l** and the mighty men, and 1 Chr 29:24
the judges, and to all the **l** in all Israel, 2 Chr 1:2
the **l** of the fathers' houses of the people 2 Chr 5:2
might write down the names of their **l**. Ezr 5:10
And the **l** stood behind the whole Neh 4:16
Now the **l** of the people lived in Neh 11:1
Then I brought the **l** of Judah up onto Neh 12:31
Hoshaiah and half of the **l** of Judah, Neh 12:32
to greet you, all who were **l** of the earth; Is 14:9
All your **l** have fled together; without the Is 22:3
of Kareah and all the **l** of the forces in Jer 40:13
Kareah and all the **l** of the forces with Jer 41:11
Kareah and all the **l** of the forces with Jer 41:13
Kareah and all the **l** of the forces with Jer 41:16
Tarshish and all its **l** will say to you, Ezk 38:13
the shepherds, and I will punish the **l**; Zec 10:3
called together the local **l** of the Jews, Acts 28:17
Remember your **l**, those who spoke to Heb 13:7
Obey your **l** and submit to them, for Heb 13:17
Greet all your **l** and all the saints. Heb 13:24

LEADERSHIP (1)
companies under the **l** of Moses and Nm 33:1

LEADING (23)
their musical instruments **l** in the 2 Chr 23:13
and I gathered **l** men from Israel to go Ezr 7:28
Zechariah, and Meshullam, **l** men, Ezr 8:16
to Iddo, the **l** man at the place Casiphia, Ezr 8:17
Then I set apart twelve of the **l** priests: Ezr 8:24
arose and made the **l** priests and Levites Ezr 10:5
l a host of captives in your train and Ps 68:18
guide this people have been **l** them astray, Is 9:16
And there were seven steps **l** up to it, Ezk 40:26
commanders and the **l** men of Galilee. Mk 6:21
Judas, one of the twelve, was **l** them. Lk 22:47
others said, "No, he is **l** the people astray." Jn 7:12
came to the iron gate **l** into the city. Acts 12:10
high standing and the **l** men of the Acts 13:50
and Silas, **l** men among the brothers, Acts 15:22
which is a **l** city of the district of Acts 16:12
Greeks and not a few of the **l** women. Acts 17:4
through righteousness **l** to eternal Rom 5:21
and to lawlessness **l** to more Rom 6:19
to righteousness **l** to sanctification. Rom 6:19
grant them repentance **l** to a 2 Tm 2:25
l you to fall away from the living God. Heb 3:12
committing a sin not **l** to death, 1 Jn 5:16

LEADS (30)
He **l** counselors away stripped, and Jb 12:17
He **l** priests away stripped and Jb 12:19
he enlarges nations, and **l** them away. Jb 12:23
pastures. He **l** me beside still waters. Ps 23:2
He **l** me in paths of righteousness for his Ps 23:3
He **l** the humble in what is right, and Ps 25:9
he **l** out the prisoners to prosperity, but Ps 68:6
The wage of the righteous **l** to life, the Prv 10:16
he who rejects reproof **l** others astray. Prv 10:17
the way of the wicked **l** them astray. Prv 12:26
The path of life **l** upward for the Prv 15:24
entices his neighbor and **l** him in a Prv 16:29
The fear of the LORD **l** to life, and Prv 19:23
jaws of the peoples a bridle that **l** astray. Is 30:28
who **l** you in the way you should go. Is 48:17
and the way is easy that **l** to destruction, Mt 7:13
narrow and the way is hard that **l** to life, Mt 7:14
them, "See that no one **l** you astray. Mt 24:4
to them, "See that no one **l** you astray. Mk 13:5
his own sheep by name and **l** them out. Jn 10:3
has granted repentance that **l** to life." Acts 11:18
act of righteousness **l** to justification Rom 5:18
obey, either of sin, which **l** to death, Rom 6:16
obedience, which **l** to righteousness? Rom 6:16
the fruit you get **l** to sanctification and Rom 6:22
in generosity; the one who **l**, with zeal; Rom 12:8
in Christ always **l** us in triumphal 2 Cor 2:14
a repentance that **l** to salvation 2 Cor 7:10
There is sin that **l** to death; I do not say 1 Jn 5:16
Lord Jesus Christ that **l** to eternal life. Jude 1:21

LEAF (10)
her mouth was a freshly plucked olive **l**. Gn 8:11
And they hammered out gold **l**, and he Ex 39:3
sound of a driven **l** shall put them to Lv 26:36
you frighten a driven **l** and pursue dry Jb 13:25
in its season, and its **l** does not wither. Ps 1:3
righteous will flourish like a green **l**. Prv 11:28
you shall be like an oak whose **l** withers, Is 1:30
We all fade like a **l**, and our iniquities, Is 64:6
seeing in the distance a fig tree in **l**, Mk 11:13
As soon as they come out in **l**, you see Lk 21:30

LEAFY (5)
trees and boughs of **l** trees and willows Lv 23:40
palm, and other **l** trees to make booths, Neh 8:15
every green tree, and under every **l** oak, Ezk 6:13
they saw any high hill or any **l** tree, Ezk 20:28
and others spread **l** branches that they Mk 11:8

LEAGUE (3)
For you shall be in **l** with the stones of Jb 5:23
"Syria is in **l** with Ephraim," the heart of Is 7:2
and the people of the land that is in **l**, Ezk 30:5

LEAH (28)
The name of the older was **L**, and the Gn 29:16
took his daughter **L** and brought her Gn 29:23
Zilpah to his daughter **L** to be her Gn 29:24
And in the morning, behold, it was **L**! Gn 29:25
also, and he loved Rachel more than **L**, Gn 29:30
When the LORD saw that **L** was hated, Gn 29:31
And **L** conceived and bore a son, and Gn 29:32
When **L** saw that she had ceased Gn 30:9
And **L** said, "Good fortune has come!" Gn 30:11
And **L** said, "Happy am I! For women Gn 30:13
and brought them to his mother **L**. Gn 30:14
Then Rachel said to **L**, "Please give me Gn 30:14
L went out to meet him and said, Gn 30:16
And God listened to **L**, and she Gn 30:17
L said, "God has given me my wages Gn 30:18
And **L** conceived again, and she bore Gn 30:19
Then **L** said, "God has endowed me Gn 30:20
and called Rachel and **L** into the field Gn 31:4
Then Rachel and **L** answered and said Gn 31:14
the children among **L** and Rachel and Gn 33:1
in front, then **L** with her children, Gn 33:2
L likewise and her children drew near Gn 33:7
Now Dinah the daughter of **L**, whom Gn 34:1
The sons of **L**: Reuben (Jacob's Gn 35:23
These are the sons of **L**, whom she bore Gn 46:15
whom Laban gave to **L** his daughter; Gn 46:18
his wife, and there I buried **L**— Gn 49:31
into your house, like Rachel and **L**, Ru 4:11

LEAH'S (6)
L eyes were weak, but Rachel was Gn 29:17
Then **L** servant Zilpah bore Jacob a Gn 30:10
L servant Zilpah bore Jacob a second Gn 30:12
Jacob's tent and into **L** tent and into Gn 31:33
he went out of **L** tent and entered Gn 31:33
The sons of Zilpah, **L** servant: Gad and Gn 35:26

LEAKS (1)
and through indolence the house **l**. Eccl 10:18

LEAN (8)
The seven **l** and ugly cows that came Gn 41:27
house rests, that I may **l** against them." Jgs 16:26
and do not **l** on your own understanding. Prv 3:5
Jacob will no more **l** on him who struck Is 10:20
who struck them, but will **l** on the LORD, Is 10:20
low, and the fat of his flesh will grow **l**. Is 17:4
between the fat sheep and the **l** sheep. Ezk 34:20
yet they **l** on the LORD and say, "Is not the Mi 3:11

LEANED (6)
and he **l** his weight against them, Jgs 16:29
whose hand the king **l** said to the man 2 Kgs 7:2
on whose hand he **l** to have charge of 2 Kgs 7:17
Upon you I have **l** from before my birth; Ps 71:6
and when they **l** on you, you broke and Ezk 29:7
into the house and **l** his hand against Am 5:19

LEANING (5)
and there was Saul **l** on his spear, 2 Sm 1:6
to worship there, **l** on my arm, 2 Kgs 5:18
attack a man to batter him, like a **l** wall, Ps 62:3
up from the wilderness, **l** on her beloved? Sg 8:5
So that disciple, **l** back against Jesus, Jn 13:25

LEANNESS (1)
me, and my **l** has risen up against me; Jb 16:8

LEANNOTH (1)
choirmaster: according to Mahalath **L**. Ps 88:T

LEANS (4)
of Ar, and **l** to the border of Moab." Nm 21:15
the hand of any man who **l** on it. 2 Kgs 18:21
He **l** against his house, but it does not Jb 8:15
pierce the hand of any man who **l** on it. Is 36:6

LEAP (9)
and by my God I can **l** over a wall. 2 Sm 22:30
Do you make him **l** like the locust? His Jb 39:20
flaming torches; sparks of fire **l** forth. Jb 41:19
and by my God I can **l** over a wall. Ps 18:29
gathers; as locusts **l**, it is leapt upon. Is 33:4
then shall the lame man **l** like a deer, and Is 35:6
they **l** on the tops of the mountains, Jl 2:5
They **l** upon the city, they run upon the Jl 2:9
Rejoice in that day, and **l** for joy, for Lk 6:23

LEAPED (3)
of Mary, the baby **l** in her womb. Lk 1:41
my ears, the baby in my womb **l** for joy. Lk 1:44
in whom was the evil spirit **l** on them, Acts 19:16

LEAPING (7)
saw King David **l** and dancing before 2 Sm 6:16
Behold, he comes, **l** over the mountains, Sg 2:8
like a flock of goats **l** down the slopes of Sg 4:1
like a flock of goats **l** down the slopes of Sg 6:5
You shall go out **l** like calves from the Mal 4:2
And **l** up he stood and began to walk, Acts 3:8
them, walking and **l** and praising God. Acts 3:8

LEAPS (3)
is a lion's cub that **l** from Bashan." Dt 33:22
my heart trembles and **l** out of its place. Jb 37:1
punish everyone who **l** over the Zep 1:9

LEAPT (1)
gathers; as locusts leap, it is **l** upon. Is 33:4

LEARN (43)
her in silence to **l** whether the LORD had Gn 24:21
so that they may **l** to fear me all the days Dt 4:10
and you shall **l** them and be careful to do Dt 5:1
that you may **l** to fear the LORD your Dt 14:23
that he may **l** to fear the LORD his God Dt 17:19
you shall not **l** to follow the abominable Dt 18:9
they may hear and **l** to fear the LORD Dt 31:12
may hear and **l** to fear the LORD your Dt 31:13
until you **l** how the matter turns out, Ru 3:18
And if I **l** anything I will tell you." 1 Sm 19:3
of the records and **l** that this city is Ezr 4:15
of the harem to **l** how Esther was and Est 2:11
to go to Mordecai to **l** what this was and Est 4:5
heart, when I **l** your righteous rules. Ps 119:7
afflicted, that I might **l** your statutes. Ps 119:71
that I may **l** your commandments. Ps 119:73
O simple ones, **l** prudence; O fools, learn Prv 8:5
ones, learn prudence; O fools, **l** sense. Prv 8:5
scoffer, and the simple will **l** prudence; Prv 19:25
lest you **l** his ways and entangle Prv 22:25
l to do good; seek justice, correct Is 1:17
nation, neither shall they **l** war anymore. Is 2:4
inhabitants of the world **l** righteousness. Is 26:9
the wicked, he does not **l** righteousness; Is 26:10
"**L** not the way of the nations, nor be Jer 10:2
if they will diligently **l** the ways of my Jer 12:16
nation, neither shall they **l** war anymore; Mi 4:3
Go and **l** what this means, 'I desire Mt 9:13
my yoke upon you, and **l** from me, Mt 11:29
"From the fig tree **l** its lesson: as soon Mt 24:32
"From the fig tree **l** its lesson: as soon Mk 13:28
as he could not **l** the facts because of Acts 21:34
that you may **l** by us not to go beyond 1 Cor 4:6
so that all may **l** and all be 1 Cor 14:31
If there is anything they desire to **l**, 1 Cor 14:35
no longer, I sent to **l** about your faith, 1 Thes 3:5
that they may **l** not to blaspheme. 1 Tm 1:20

Let a woman **l** quietly with all 1 Tm 2:11
let them first **l** to show godliness to 1 Tm 5:4
Besides that, they **l** to be idlers, going 1 Tm 5:13
And let our people **l** to devote themselves Ti 3:14
your feet and they will **l** that I have loved Rv 3:9
No one could **l** that song except the Rv 14:3

LEARNED (32)
I have **l** by divination that the LORD has Gn 30:27
When Jacob **l** that there was grain for Gn 42:1
mean?" And when they **l** that the ark of 1 Sm 4:6
sent out spies and **l** that Saul had 1 Sm 26:4
a man **l** in matters of the Ezr 7:11
When Mordecai **l** all that had been done, Est 4:1
with the nations and **l** to do as they Ps 106:35
I have not **l** wisdom, nor have I Prv 30:3
a young lion, and he **l** to catch prey; Ezk 19:3
a young lion, and he **l** to catch prey; Ezk 19:6
And when he **l** from the centurion Mk 15:45
when she **l** that he was reclining at table Lk 7:37
When the crowds **l** it, they followed him, Lk 9:11
And when he **l** that he belonged to Lk 23:7
Now when Jesus **l** that the Pharisees had Jn 4:1
who has heard and **l** from the Father Jn 6:45
crowd of the Jews **l** that Jesus was there, Jn 12:9
And when the brothers **l** this, they Acts 9:30
they **l** of it and fled to Lystra and Acts 14:6
Jews from Thessalonica **l** that the Acts 17:13
having **l** that he was a Roman citizen. Acts 23:27
And when he **l** that he was from Acts 23:34
we then **l** that the island was called Acts 28:1
But that is not the way you **l** Christ!— Eph 4:20
What you have **l** and received and Phil 4:9
for I have **l** in whatever situation I am Phil 4:11
I have **l** the secret of facing plenty and Phil 4:12
just as you **l** it from Epaphras our Col 1:7
in what you have **l** and have firmly 2 Tm 3:14
knowing from whom you **l** it 2 Tm 3:14
he **l** obedience through what he suffered. Heb 5:8
who have not **l** what some call the deep Rv 2:24

LEARNING (8)
Let the wise hear and increase in **l**, and Prv 1:5
righteous man, and he will increase in **l**. Prv 9:9
with knowledge, understanding **l**, Dn 1:4
God gave them **l** and skill in all Dn 1:17
saying, "How is it that this man has **l**, Jn 7:15
him a hearing and **l** what he does?" Jn 7:51
your great **l** is driving you out of your Acts 26:24
always **l** and never able to arrive at a 2 Tm 3:7

LEASED (2)
it and built a tower and **l** it to tenants, Mt 21:33
and **l** it to tenants and went into Mk 12:1

LEASH (1)
or will you put him on a **l** for your girls? Jb 41:5

LEAST (33)
remain with us a while, at **l** ten days; Gn 24:55
am not worthy of the **l** of all the deeds Gn 32:10
your work will not be reduced in the **l**.'" Ex 5:11
Those who gathered **l** gathered ten Nm 11:32
and I am the **l** in my father's house." Jgs 6:15
from the **l** of the tribes of Israel? 1 Sm 9:21
captain among the **l** of my master's 2 Kgs 18:24
the **l** was a match for a hundred 1 Chr 12:14
There is Benjamin, the **l** of them, in the Ps 68:27
captain among the **l** of my master's Is 36:9
The **l** one shall become a clan, and the Is 60:22
"For from the **l** to the greatest of them, Jer 6:13
because from the **l** to the greatest Jer 8:10
me, from the **l** of them to the greatest, Jer 31:34
all the people from the **l** to the greatest, Jer 42:1
all the people from the **l** to the greatest, Jer 42:8
From the **l** to the greatest, they shall die Jer 44:12
from the greatest of them to the **l** of them. Jon 3:5
are by no means **l** among the rulers of Mt 2:6
one of the **l** of these commandments Mt 5:19
same will be called **l** in the kingdom of Mt 5:19
Yet the one who is **l** in the kingdom of Mt 11:11
it to one of the **l** of these my brothers, Mt 25:40
you did not do it to one of the **l** of these, Mt 25:45
Yet the one who is **l** in the kingdom of Lk 7:28
For he who is **l** among you all is the one Lk 9:48
Peter came by at **l** his shadow might Acts 5:15
to him, from the **l** to the greatest, Acts 8:10
I am not an apostle, at **l** I am to you, 1 Cor 9:2
For I am the **l** of the apostles, 1 Cor 15:9
am not in the **l** inferior to these 2 Cor 11:5
though I am the very **l** of all the saints, Eph 3:8
me, from the **l** of them to the greatest. Heb 8:11

LEATHER (4)
with a belt of **l** about his waist." And 2 Kgs 1:8
cloth and shod you with fine **l**. Ezk 16:10
camel's hair and a **l** belt around his Mt 3:4
hair and wore a **l** belt around his waist Mk 1:6

LEAVE (136)
Therefore a man shall **l** his father and Gn 2:24
For I will not **l** you until I have done Gn 28:15
"Let me **l** with you some of the people Gn 33:15
l one of your brothers with me, and Gn 42:33
my lord, 'The boy cannot **l** his father, Gn 44:22
his father, for if he should **l** his father, Gn 44:22
'**L** us alone that we may serve the Ex 14:12
"Let no one **l** any of it over till the Ex 16:19
and what they **l** the beasts of the field Ex 23:11
He shall not **l** any of it until the Lv 7:15
the Holy Place and shall **l** them there. Lv 16:23
You shall **l** them for the poor and for Lv 19:10
you shall **l** none of it until morning: Lv 22:30
You shall **l** them for the poor and for Lv 23:22
They shall **l** none of it until the Nm 9:12
And he said, "Please do not **l** us, for Nm 10:31
He will not **l** you or destroy you or forget Dt 4:31
to make you **l** the way in which the LORD Dt 13:5
it also shall not **l** you grain, wine, or oil, Dt 28:51
you. He will not **l** you or forsake you." Dt 31:6
you; he will not **l** you or forsake you. Dt 31:8
with you. I will not **l** you or forsake you. Jos 1:5
and they did not **l** any who breathed. Jos 11:14
and **l** no sustenance in Israel and no Jgs 6:4
said to them, 'Shall I **l** my abundance, Jgs 9:9
'Shall I **l** my sweetness and my good Jgs 9:11
'Shall I **l** my wine that cheers God and Jgs 9:13
l me alone two months, that I may go Jgs 11:37
is shaved, then my strength will **l** me, Jgs 16:17
"Do not urge me to **l** you or to return Ru 1:16
go to glean in another field or **l** this one, Ru 2:8
the bundles for her and **l** it for her to Ru 2:16
he turned his back to **l** Samuel, 1 Sm 10:9
let us not **l** a man of them." And they 1 Sm 14:36
'David earnestly asked **l** of me to run 1 Sm 20:6
"David earnestly asked **l** of me to go 1 Sm 20:28
if by morning I **l** so much as one 1 Sm 25:22
the land and would **l** neither man nor 1 Sm 27:9
And David would **l** neither man nor 1 Sm 27:11
that is left and **l** to my husband 2 Sm 14:7
L him alone, and let him curse, for 2 Sm 16:11
fathers. May he not **l** us or forsake us, 1 Kgs 8:57
He did not **l** him a single male of his 1 Kgs 16:11
Yet I will **l** seven thousand in Israel, 1 Kgs 19:18
I will not **l** you." So they went down to 2 Kgs 2:2
I will not **l** you." So they came to 2 Kgs 2:4
I will not **l** you." So the two of them 2 Kgs 2:6
the man of God said, "**L** her alone, 2 Kgs 4:27
I will not **l** you." So he arose and 2 Kgs 4:30
this good land and **l** it for an 1 Chr 28:8
He will not **l** you or forsake you, 1 Chr 28:20
to **l** us a remnant and to give us a secure Ezr 9:8
of the land and **l** it for an inheritance Ezr 9:12
the work stop while I **l** it and come down Neh 6:3
after some time I asked **l** of the king Neh 13:6
L out nothing that you have Est 6:10
L me alone, for my days are a breath. Jb 7:16
me, nor **l** me alone till I swallow my spit? Jb 7:19
Then cease, and **l** me alone, that I may Jb 10:20
look away from him and **l** him alone, Jb 14:6
great, and will you **l** to him your labor? Jb 39:11
and they **l** their abundance to their Ps 17:14
alike must perish and **l** their wealth to Ps 49:10
right; do not **l** me to my oppressors. Ps 119:121
you I seek refuge; **l** me not defenseless! Ps 141:8
L your simple ways, and live, and walk Prv 9:6
L the presence of a fool, for there you do Prv 14:7
seeing that I must **l** it to the man who Eccl 2:18
and skill must **l** everything to be Eccl 2:21
rises against you, do not **l** your place, Eccl 10:4
help, and where will you **l** your wealth? Is 10:3
l the way, turn aside from the path, let us Is 30:11
to **l** the craving of the hungry unsatisfied, Is 32:6
You shall **l** your name to my chosen for Is 65:15
that I might **l** my people and go away Jer 9:2
we are called by your name; do not **l** us." Jer 14:9
in the midst of his days they will **l** him, Jer 17:11
the snow of Lebanon **l** the crags of Jer 18:14
and serve him, I will **l** on its own land, Jer 27:11
I will by no means **l** you unpunished. Jer 30:11
I will by no means **l** you unpunished." Jer 46:28
"**L** the cities, and dwell in the rock, O Jer 48:28
came to you, would they not **l** gleanings? Jer 49:9
L your fatherless children; I will keep Jer 49:11
pardon those whom I **l** as a remnant. Jer 50:20
"Yet I will **l** some of you alive. When you Ezk 6:8
beautiful jewels and **l** you naked and Ezk 16:39
of your labor and **l** you naked and Ezk 23:29
I will **l** none of them remaining Ezk 39:28
But **l** the stump of its roots in the earth, Dn 4:15
but **l** the stump of its roots in the earth, Dn 4:23
it was commanded to **l** the stump of the Dn 4:26
Ephraim is joined to idols; **l** him alone. Hos 4:17
so his Lord will **l** his bloodguilt on Hos 12:14
and relent, and **l** a blessing behind him, Jl 2:14
Let the bridegroom **l** his room, and the Jl 2:16
came to you, would they not **l** gleanings? Ob 1:5
are evening wolves that **l** nothing till the Zep 3:3
But I will **l** in your midst a people Zep 3:12
so that it will **l** them neither root nor Mal 4:1
l your gift there before the altar and go. Mt 5:24
and **l** the dead to bury their own dead." Mt 8:22
him, they begged him to **l** their region. Mt 8:34
your feet when you **l** that house or Mt 10:14
does he not **l** the ninety-nine on the Mt 18:12
'Therefore a man shall **l** his father and Mt 19:5
they will not listen to you, when you **l**, Mk 6:11
And after he had taken **l** of them, he Mk 6:46
You **l** the commandment of God and Mk 7:8
'Therefore a man shall **l** his father and Mk 10:7
But Jesus said, "**L** her alone. Why do Mk 14:6
when you **l** that town shake off the dust Lk 9:5
and shatters him, and will hardly **l** him. Lk 9:39
him, "**L** the dead to bury their own dead. Lk 9:60
does not **l** the ninety-nine in the open Lk 15:4
And they will not **l** one stone upon Lk 19:44
said to him, "**L** here and go to Judea, Jn 7:3
Jesus said, "**L** her alone, so that she may Jn 12:7
"I will not **l** you as orphans; I will come Jn 14:18
Peace I **l** with you; my peace I give to Jn 14:27
to his own home, and will **l** me alone. Jn 16:32
commanded them to **l** the council, Acts 4:15
he did not **l** himself without witness, Acts 14:17
them out and asked them to **l** the city. Acts 16:39
commanded all the Jews to **l** Rome. Acts 18:2
longer and then took **l** of the brothers Acts 18:18
But on taking **l** of them he said, "I Acts 18:21
Paul kindly and gave him **l** to go to his Acts 27:3
but **l** it to the wrath of God, Rom 12:19
I will **l** for Spain by way of you. Rom 15:28
So I took **l** of them and went on to 2 Cor 2:13
Lord about this, that it should **l** me. 2 Cor 12:8
"Therefore a man shall **l** his father and Eph 5:31
Therefore let us **l** the elementary Heb 6:1
"I will never **l** you nor forsake you." Heb 13:5
l that out, for it is given over to the Rv 11:2

LEAVEN (21)
day you shall remove **l** out of your Ex 12:15
For seven days no **l** is to be found in Ex 12:19
and no **l** shall be seen with you in all Ex 13:7
bring to the LORD shall be made with **l**, Lv 2:11
for you shall burn no **l** nor any honey as Lv 2:11
It shall not be baked with **l**. I have given Lv 6:17
flour, and they shall be baked with **l**, Lv 23:17
No **l** shall be seen with you in all your Dt 16:4
of heaven is like **l** that a woman took Mt 13:33
and beware of the **l** of the Pharisees and Mt 16:6
Beware of the **l** of the Pharisees and Mt 16:11
not tell them to beware of the **l** of bread, Mt 16:12
beware of the **l** of the Pharisees and the Mk 8:15
of the Pharisees and the **l** of Herod." Mk 8:15
first, "Beware of the **l** of the Pharisees, Lk 12:1
It is like **l** that a woman took and hid Lk 13:21
know that a little **l** leavens the whole 1 Cor 5:6
Cleanse out the old **l** that you may be a 1 Cor 5:7
celebrate the festival, not with the old **l**, 1 Cor 5:8
the old leaven, the **l** of malice and evil, 1 Cor 5:8
A little **l** leavens the whole lump. Gal 5:9

LEAVENED (15)
houses, for if anyone eats what is **l**, Ex 12:15
If anyone eats what is **l**, that person will Ex 12:19
You shall eat nothing **l**; in all your Ex 12:20
people took their dough before it was **l**, Ex 12:34
brought out of Egypt, for it was not **l**, Ex 12:39
this place. No **l** bread shall be eaten. Ex 13:3
no **l** bread shall be seen with you, and no Ex 13:7
blood of my sacrifice with anything **l**, Ex 23:18
blood of my sacrifice with anything **l**, Ex 34:25
bring his offering with loaves of **l** bread. Lv 7:13
You shall eat no **l** bread with it. Seven Dt 16:3
the kneading of the dough until it is **l**. Hos 7:4
of thanksgiving of that which is **l**, Am 4:5
three measures of flour, till it was all **l**." Mt 13:33
measures of flour, until it was all **l**." Lk 13:21

LEAVENS (2)
that a little leaven **l** the whole lump? 1 Cor 5:6
A little leaven **l** the whole lump. Gal 5:9

LEAVES (32)
And they sewed fig **l** together and made Gn 3:7
The two **l** of the one door were 1 Kgs 6:34
and the two **l** of the other door were 1 Kgs 6:34
and if I forbear, how much of it **l** me? Jb 16:6
they pick saltwort and the **l** of bushes, Jb 30:4
For she **l** her eggs to the earth and lets Jb 39:14
Behind him he **l** a shining wake; one Jb 41:32
A good man **l** an inheritance to his Prv 13:22
the poor is a beating rain that **l** no food. Prv 28:3

and Bashan and Carmel shake off their **l**. Is 33:9
their host shall fall, as **l** fall from the vine, Is 34:4
the vine, like **l** falling from the fig tree. Is 34:4
as a treacherous wife **l** her husband, Jer 3:20
on the fig tree; even the **l** are withered, Jer 8:13
when heat comes, for its **l** remain green, Jer 17:8
so that all its fresh sprouting **l** wither? Ezk 17:9
The double doors had two **l** apiece, Ezk 41:24
apiece, two swinging **l** for each door. Ezk 41:24
Their **l** will not wither, nor their fruit Ezk 47:12
be for food, and their **l** for healing." Ezk 47:12
Its **l** were beautiful and its fruit Dn 4:12
strip off its **l** and scatter its fruit. Dn 4:14
whose **l** were beautiful and its fruit Dn 4:21
to it and found nothing on it but only **l**. Mt 21:19
becomes tender and puts out its **l**, Mt 24:32
he came to it, he found nothing but **l**, Mk 11:13
if a man's brother dies and **l** a wife, Mk 12:19
dies and leaves a wife, but **l** no child, Mk 12:19
becomes tender and puts out its **l**, Mk 13:28
when he **l** home and puts his servants Mk 13:34
the wolf coming and **l** the sheep and Jn 10:12
The **l** of the tree were for the healing of Rv 22:2

LEAVING (18)
you shall refrain from **l** him with it; Ex 23:5
time from our **l** Kadesh-barnea until we Dt 2:14
their donkeys, **l** the camp as it was, 2 Kgs 7:7
from him, **l** him severely wounded, 2 Chr 24:25
out like a bridegroom **l** his chamber, Ps 19:5
the midst of Judah, **l** you no remnant? Jer 44:7
And **l** Nazareth he went and lived in Mt 4:13
And **l** them, he went out of the city to Mt 21:17
So, **l** them again, he went away and Mt 26:44
And **l** the crowd, they took him with Mk 4:36
And as he was **l** Jericho with his Mk 10:46
took her, and died, **l** no offspring. Mk 12:21
and would have kept him from **l** them, Lk 4:42
And **l** everything, he rose and followed Lk 5:28
beat him and departed, **l** him half dead. Lk 10:30
and now I am **l** the world and going to Jn 16:28
l it on the left we sailed to Syria and Acts 21:3
also suffered for you, **l** you an example, 1 Pt 2:21

LEB-KAMAI (1)
Babylon, against the inhabitants of **L**, Jer 51:1

LEBANA (1)
the sons of **L**, the sons of Hagaba, the Neh 7:48

LEBANAH (1)
the sons of **L**, the sons of Hagabah, the Ezr 2:45

LEBANON (71)
the land of the Canaanites, and **L**, Dt 1:7
the Jordan, that good hill country and **L**.' Dt 3:25
the wilderness to the **L** and from the Dt 11:24
the wilderness and this **L** as far as the Jos 1:4
along the coast of the Great Sea toward **L**, Jos 9:1
the Valley of **L** below Mount Hermon. Jos 11:17
in the Valley of **L** to Mount Halak, Jos 12:7
and the land of the Gebalites, and all **L**, Jos 13:5
country from **L** to Misrephoth-maim, Jos 13:6
and the Hivites who lived on Mount **L**, Jgs 3:3
the bramble and devour the cedars of **L**.' Jgs 9:15
cedar that is in **L** to the hyssop that 1 Kgs 4:33
command that cedars of **L** be cut for 1 Kgs 5:6
shall bring it down to the sea from **L**, 1 Kgs 5:9
And he sent them to **L**, 10,000 a 1 Kgs 5:14
be a month in **L** and two months at 1 Kgs 5:14
He built the House of the Forest of **L**. 1 Kgs 7:2
desired to build in Jerusalem, in **L**, 1 Kgs 9:19
them in the House of the Forest of **L**. 1 Kgs 10:17
of the Forest of **L** were of pure gold. 1 Kgs 10:21
"A thistle on **L** sent to a cedar on 2 Kgs 14:9
on Lebanon sent to a cedar on **L**, 2 Kgs 14:9
a wild beast of **L** passed by and 2 Kgs 14:9
mountains, to the far recesses of **L**; 2 Kgs 19:23
cypress, and algum timber from **L**, 2 Chr 2:8
servants know how to cut timber in **L**. 2 Chr 2:8
timber you need from **L** and bring it 2 Chr 2:16
desired to build in Jerusalem, in **L**, 2 Chr 8:6
them in the House of the Forest of **L**. 2 Chr 9:16
of the Forest of **L** were of pure gold. 2 Chr 9:20
"A thistle on **L** sent to a cedar on 2 Chr 25:18
on Lebanon sent to a cedar on **L**, 2 Chr 25:18
a wild beast of **L** passed by and 2 Chr 25:18
to bring cedar trees from **L** to the sea, Ezr 3:7
cedars; the LORD breaks the cedars of **L**. Ps 29:5
He makes **L** to skip like a calf, and Sirion Ps 29:6
may it wave; may its fruit be like **L**; Ps 72:16
palm tree and grow like a cedar in **L**. Ps 92:12
the cedars of **L** that he planted. Ps 104:16
himself a carriage from the wood of **L**. Sg 3:9
Come with me from **L**, my bride; come Sg 4:8
my bride; come with me from **L**. Sg 4:8
your garments is like the fragrance of **L**. Sg 4:11
water, and flowing streams from **L**. Sg 4:15
His appearance is like **L**, choice as the Sg 5:15
Your nose is like a tower of **L**, which Sg 7:4
against all the cedars of **L**, lofty and lifted Is 2:13
axe, and **L** will fall by the Majestic One. Is 10:34
cypresses rejoice at you, the cedars of **L**, Is 14:8
very little while until **L** shall be turned Is 29:17
L is confounded and withers away; Is 33:9
The glory of **L** shall be given to it, the Is 35:2
of the mountains, to the far recesses of **L**, Is 37:24
L would not suffice for fuel, nor are its Is 40:16
The glory of **L** shall come to you, the Is 60:13
Does the snow of **L** leave the crags of Jer 18:14
like Gilead to me, like the summit of **L**, Jer 22:6
"Go up to **L**, and cry out, and lift up Jer 22:20
O inhabitant of **L**, nested among the Jer 22:23
came to **L** and took the top of the cedar. Ezk 17:3
took a cedar from **L** to make a mast Ezk 27:5
Behold, Assyria was a cedar in **L**, with Ezk 31:3
I clothed **L** in gloom for it, and all the Ezk 31:15
trees of Eden, the choice and best of **L**, Ezk 31:16
lily; he shall take root like the trees of **L**; Hos 14:5
like the olive, and his fragrance like **L**. Hos 14:6
their fame shall be like the wine of **L**. Hos 14:7
Carmel wither; the bloom of **L** withers. Na 1:4
violence done to **L** will overwhelm you, Hab 2:17
them to the land of Gilead and to **L**, Zec 10:10
Open your doors, O **L**, that the fire may Zec 11:1

LEBAOTH (1)
L, Shilhim, Ain, and Rimmon: in all, Jos 15:32

LEBO-HAMATH (12)
the wilderness of Zin to Rehob, near **L**. Nm 13:21
Mount Hor you shall draw a line to **L**, Nm 34:8
Baal-gad below Mount Hermon to **L**, Jos 13:5
from Mount Baal-hermon as far as **L**. Jgs 3:3
from **L** to the Brook of Egypt, 1 Kgs 8:65
border of Israel from **L** as far as the 2 Kgs 14:25
all Israel from the Nile of Egypt to **L**, 1 Chr 13:5
from **L** to the Brook of Egypt. 2 Chr 7:8
the Great Sea by way of Hethlon to **L**, Ezk 47:15
be the boundary to a point opposite **L**. Ezk 47:20
extreme, beside the way of Hethlon to **L**, Ezk 48:1
shall oppress you from **L** to the Brook Am 6:14

LEBONAH (1)
Bethel to Shechem, and south of **L**." Jgs 21:19

LECAH (1)
Er the father of **L**, Laadah the father 1 Chr 4:21

LED (109)
captive, he **l** forth his trained men, Gn 14:14
the LORD has **l** me in the way to the Gn 24:27
who had **l** me by the right way to take Gn 24:48
and he **l** his flock to the west side of the Ex 3:1
But God **l** the people around by the way Ex 13:18
"You have **l** in your steadfast love the Ex 15:13
LORD your God has **l** you these forty years Dt 8:2
who **l** you through the great and Dt 8:15
I have **l** you forty years in the wilderness. Dt 29:5
beyond the River and **l** him through all Jos 24:3
I **l** you up from Egypt and brought you Jgs 6:8
it was you who **l** out and brought in 2 Sm 5:2
you seek." And he **l** them to Samaria. 2 Kgs 6:19
and Manasseh **l** them astray to do 2 Kgs 21:9
it was you who **l** out and brought in 1 Chr 11:2
Joab **l** out the army and ravaged the 1 Chr 20:1
of Judah and **l** the inhabitants of 2 Chr 21:11
house of Ahab **l** Israel into 2 Chr 21:13
took courage and **l** out his people 2 Chr 25:11
Manasseh **l** Judah and the 2 Chr 33:9
a pillar of cloud you **l** them in the day, Neh 9:12
dressed Mordecai and **l** him through the Est 6:11
many-colored robes she is **l** to the king, Ps 45:14
and gladness they are **l** along as they Ps 45:15
You **l** your people like a flock by the Ps 77:20
In the daytime he **l** them with a cloud, Ps 78:14
by his power he **l** out the south wind; Ps 78:26
Then he **l** out his people like sheep and Ps 78:52
He **l** them in safety, so that they were Ps 78:53
and he **l** them through the deep as Ps 106:9
He **l** them by a straight way till they Ps 107:7
to him who **l** his people through the Ps 136:16
I have **l** you in the paths of uprightness. Prv 4:11
because of his great folly he is **l** astray. Prv 5:23
and whoever is **l** astray by it is not wise. Prv 20:1
end of all the people, all of whom he **l**. Eccl 4:16
a deluded heart has **l** him astray, and he Is 44:20
and your knowledge **l** you astray, Is 47:10
not thirst when he **l** them through the Is 48:21
like a lamb that is **l** to the slaughter, and Is 53:7
go out in joy and be **l** forth in peace; Is 55:12
nations, with their kings **l** in procession. Is 60:11
who **l** them through the depths? Like a Is 63:13
gave them rest. So you **l** your people, Is 63:14
land of Egypt, who **l** us in the wilderness, Jer 2:6
your God, when he **l** you in the way? Jer 2:17
like a gentle lamb **l** to the slaughter. Jer 11:19
who brought up and **l** the offspring of Jer 23:8
by Baal and **l** my people Israel Jer 23:13
of Judah were being **l** out to the officials Jer 38:22
your sons shall be **l** out to the Jer 38:23
camels shall be **l** away from them, Jer 49:29
Their shepherds have **l** them astray, Jer 50:6
So I **l** them out of the land of Egypt Ezk 20:10
And he **l** me around among them, and Ezk 37:2
And he **l** me toward the south, and Ezk 40:24
Then he **l** me out into the outer court, Ezk 42:1
he **l** me out by the gate that faced east, Ezk 42:15
Then he **l** me to the gate, the gate facing Ezk 43:1
the outer court and **l** me around to the Ezk 46:21
the north gate and **l** me around on the Ezk 47:2
and then **l** me through the water, Ezk 47:3
thousand, and **l** me through the water, Ezk 47:4
thousand, and **l** me through the water, Ezk 47:4
seen this?" Then he **l** me back to the Ezk 47:6
a spirit of whoredom has **l** them astray, Hos 4:12
I **l** them with cords of kindness, with Hos 11:4
but their lies have **l** them astray, Am 2:4
land of Egypt and **l** you forty years in Am 2:10
Then Jesus was **l** up by the Spirit into the Mt 4:1
and **l** them up a high mountain by Mt 17:1
who had seized Jesus **l** him to Caiaphas Mt 26:57
they bound him and **l** him away and Mt 27:2
clothes on him and **l** him away to Mt 27:31
man by the hand and **l** him out of the Mk 8:23
and **l** them up a high mountain by Mk 9:2
And they **l** Jesus to the high priest. And Mk 14:53
they bound Jesus and **l** him away and Mk 15:1
And the soldiers **l** him away inside the Mk 15:16
And they **l** him out to crucify him. Mk 15:20
from the Jordan and was **l** by the Spirit in Lk 4:1
he said, "See that you are not **l** astray. Lk 21:8
the sword and be **l** captive among all Lk 21:24
Then they seized him and **l** him away, Lk 22:54
And they **l** him away to their council, Lk 22:66
And as they **l** him away, they seized one Lk 23:26
were **l** away to be put to death with Lk 23:32
Then he **l** them out as far as Bethany, Lk 24:50
First they **l** him to Annas, for he was the Jn 18:13
Then they **l** Jesus from the house of Jn 18:28
This man **l** them out, performing Acts 7:36
for this Moses who **l** us out from the Acts 7:40
a sheep he was **l** to the slaughter and Acts 8:32
So they **l** him by the hand and brought Acts 9:8
with uplifted arm he **l** them out of it. Acts 13:17
up a revolt and **l** the four thousand Acts 21:38
I was **l** by the hand by those who were Acts 22:11
as one trespass **l** to condemnation for Rom 5:18
For all who are **l** by the Spirit of God Rom 8:14
pagans you were **l** astray to mute 1 Cor 12:2
to mute idols, however you were **l**. 1 Cor 12:2
your thoughts will be **l** astray from a 2 Cor 11:3
even Barnabas was **l** astray by their Gal 2:13
But if you are **l** by the Spirit, you are not Gal 5:18
ascended on high he **l** a host of captives, Eph 4:8
with sins and **l** astray by various 2 Tm 3:6
were once foolish, disobedient, **l** astray, Ti 3:3
not all those who left Egypt **l** by Moses? Heb 3:16
Do not be **l** away by diverse and Heb 13:9

LEDGE (8)
shall set it under the **l** of the altar so that Ex 27:5
grating, a network of bronze, under its **l**, Ex 38:4
the base on the ground to the lower **l**, Ezk 43:14
and from the smaller **l** to the larger Ezk 43:14
from the smaller ledge to the larger **l**, Ezk 43:14
The **l** also shall be square, fourteen Ezk 43:17
four corners of the **l** and upon the rim Ezk 43:20
the four corners of the **l** of the altar, Ezk 45:19

LEE (3)
there we sailed under the **l** of Cyprus, Acts 27:4
we sailed under the **l** of Crete off Acts 27:7
Running under the **l** of a small island Acts 27:16

LEECH (1)
The **l** has two daughters; "Give" and Prv 30:15

LEEKS (1)
the cucumbers, the melons, the **l**, Nm 11:5

LEFT (368)
Only Noah was **l**, and those who were Gn 7:23
earth, and they **l** off building the city. Gn 11:8
If you take the **l** hand, then I will go to Gn 13:9
the right hand, then I will go to the **l**." Gn 13:9
may turn to the right hand or to the **l**." Gn 24:49
Jacob **l** Beersheba and went toward Gn 28:10
any portion or inheritance **l** to us in Gn 31:14
it, then the camp that is **l** will escape." Gn 32:8
And Jacob was **l** alone. And a man Gn 32:24
So he **l** all that he had in Joseph's Gn 39:6
with me." But he **l** his garment in her Gn 39:12
saw that he had **l** his garment in her Gn 39:13

he **l** his garment beside me and fled	Gn 39:15
he **l** his garment beside me and fled out	Gn 39:18
is dead, and he is the only one **l**.	Gn 42:38
and he alone is **l** of his mother's	Gn 44:20
One **l** me, and I said, Surely he has	Gn 44:28
There is nothing **l** in the sight of my	Gn 47:18
his right hand toward Israel's **l** hand,	Gn 48:13
Manasseh in his **l** hand toward Israel's	Gn 48:13
and his **l** hand on the head of	Gn 48:14
and their herds were **l** in the land of	Gn 50:8
where is he? Why have you **l** the man?	Ex 2:20
your houses and be **l** only in the Nile."	Ex 8:9
people. They shall be **l** only in the Nile."	Ex 8:11
the word of the LORD **l** his slaves and his	Ex 9:21
they shall eat what is **l** to you after the	Ex 10:5
in the land, all that the hail has **l**."	Ex 10:12
the fruit of the trees that the hail had **l**.	Ex 10:15
a single locust was **l** in all the country	Ex 10:19
not a hoof shall be **l** behind, for we	Ex 10:26
them on their right hand and on their **l**.	Ex 14:22
them on their right hand and on their **l**.	Ex 14:29
gathered much had nothing **l** over,	Ex 16:18
Some **l** part of it till the morning, and it	Ex 16:20
and all that is **l** over lay aside to be kept	Ex 16:23
grain offering that is **l** of the LORD'S food	Lv 10:12
pour it into the palm of his own **l** hand	Lv 14:15
that is in his **l** hand and sprinkle some	Lv 14:16
the oil into the palm of his own **l** hand,	Lv 14:26
that is in his **l** hand seven times before	Lv 14:27
and anything **l** over until the third day	Lv 19:6
If there are still many years **l**, he shall	Lv 25:51
And as for those of you who are **l**, I will	Lv 26:36
those of you who are **l** shall rot away in	Lv 26:39
hand or to the **l** until we have passed	Nm 20:17
his people, until he had no survivor **l**.	Nm 21:35
to turn either to the right or to the **l**.	Nm 22:26
he rose and **l** the congregation and	Nm 25:7
wilderness." Not one of them was **l**,	Nm 26:65
aside neither to the right nor to the **l**.	Dt 2:27
women, and children. We **l** no survivors.	Dt 2:34
him down until he had no survivor **l**.	Dt 3:3
king of Bashan was **l** of the remnant of	Dt 3:11
and you will be **l** few in number among	Dt 4:27
turn aside to the right hand or to the **l**.	Dt 5:32
those who are **l** and hide themselves	Dt 7:20
you, either to the right hand or to the **l**.	Dt 17:11
either to the right hand or to the **l**,	Dt 17:20
you today, to the right hand or to the **l**,	Dt 28:14
the last of the children whom he has **l**,	Dt 28:54
is eating, because he has nothing else **l**,	Dt 28:55
heaven, you shall be **l** few in number,	Dt 28:62
turn from it to the right hand or to the **l**,	Jos 1:7
there was no spirit **l** in any man because	Jos 2:11
Not a man was **l** in Ai or Bethel who did	Jos 8:17
They **l** the city open and pursued Israel.	Jos 8:17
until there was **l** none that survived or	Jos 8:22
every person in it; he **l** none remaining.	Jos 10:28
person in it; he **l** none remaining in it.	Jos 10:30
his people, until he **l** none remaining.	Jos 10:33
He **l** none remaining, as he had done to	Jos 10:37
every person in it; he **l** none remaining.	Jos 10:39
He **l** none remaining, but devoted to	Jos 10:40
struck them until he **l** none remaining.	Jos 11:8
there was none **l** that breathed.	Jos 11:11
He **l** nothing undone of all that the	Jos 11:15
none of the Anakim **l** in the land of	Jos 11:22
Edrei (he alone was **l** of the remnant of	Jos 13:12
it neither to the right hand nor to the **l**,	Jos 23:6
the nations that Joshua **l** when he died,	Jgs 2:21
So the LORD **l** those nations, not driving	Jgs 2:23
Now these are the nations that the LORD **l**,	Jgs 3:1
And Ehud reached with his **l** hand, took	Jgs 3:21
the edge of the sword; not a man was **l**.	Jgs 4:16
They held in their **l** hands the torches,	Jgs 7:20
all who were **l** of all the army of the	Jgs 8:10
the youngest son of Jerubbaal was **l**,	Jgs 9:5
to torment him, and his strength **l** him.	Jgs 16:19
did not know that the LORD had **l** him.	Jgs 16:20
on the one and his **l** hand on the other.	Jgs 16:29
priest, and go away, and what have I **l**?	Jgs 18:24
shall we do for wives for those who are **l**,	Jgs 21:7
we do for wives for those who are **l**,	Jgs 21:16
died, and she was **l** with her two sons.	Ru 1:3
that the woman was **l** without her two	Ru 1:5
and how you **l** your father and mother	Ru 2:11
was satisfied, and she had some **l** over.	Ru 2:14
what food she had **l** over after being	Ru 2:18
who has not **l** you this day without a	Ru 4:14
And everyone who is **l** in your house	1 Sm 2:36
Only the trunk of Dagon was **l** to him.	1 Sm 5:4
turned neither to the right nor to the **l**,	1 Sm 6:12
that no two of them were **l** together.	1 Sm 11:11
in the morning and **l** the sheep with	1 Sm 17:20
And David **l** the things in charge of	1 Sm 17:22
whom have you **l** those few sheep	1 Sm 17:28
And he **l** them with the king of Moab,	1 Sm 22:4
Saul rose up and **l** the cave and went	1 Sm 24:7
there had not been **l** to Nabal so	1 Sm 25:34
where those who were **l** behind stayed.	1 Sm 30:9
and my master **l** me behind because	1 Sm 30:13
and who had been **l** at the brook	1 Sm 30:21
nor to the **l** from following Abner.	2 Sm 2:19
aside to your right hand or to your **l**,	2 Sm 2:21
And the Philistines **l** their idols there,	2 Sm 5:21
the chariot horses but **l** enough for a	2 Sm 8:4
"Is there still anyone **l** of the house of	2 Sm 9:1
sons, and not one of them is **l**."	2 Sm 13:30
my coal that is **l** and leave to my	2 Sm 14:7
hand or to the **l** from anything that	2 Sm 14:19
And the king **l** ten concubines to	2 Sm 15:16
were on his right hand and on his **l**.	2 Sm 16:6
whom he has **l** to keep the house,	2 Sm 16:21
the men with him not one will be **l**.	2 Sm 17:12
daybreak not one was **l** who had not	2 Sm 17:22
the day my lord the king **l** Jerusalem.	2 Sm 19:19
concubines whom he had **l** to care for	2 Sm 20:3
And Solomon **l** all the vessels	1 Kgs 7:47
the people who were **l** of the Amorites,	1 Kgs 9:20
descendants who were **l** after them in	1 Kgs 9:21
the gold that were **l** in the treasures	1 Kgs 15:18
He **l** to the house of Jeroboam not	1 Kgs 15:29
that there was no breath **l** in him.	1 Kgs 17:17
I only, am **l** a prophet of the LORD,	1 Kgs 18:22
to Judah, and **l** his servant there.	1 Kgs 19:3
the sword, and I, even I only, am **l**,	1 Kgs 19:10
the sword, and I, even I only, am **l**,	1 Kgs 19:14
And he **l** the oxen and ran after	1 Kgs 19:20
fell upon 27,000 men who were **l**.	1 Kgs 20:30
him on his right hand and on his **l**;	1 Kgs 22:19
only its stones were **l** in Kir-hareseth,	2 Kgs 3:25
'They shall eat and have some **l**.'"	2 Kgs 4:43
And they ate and had some **l**,	2 Kgs 4:44
that those who are **l** here will fare like	2 Kgs 7:13
the day that she **l** the land until now."	2 Kgs 8:6
until he **l** him none remaining.	2 Kgs 10:11
was not a man **l** who did not come.	2 Kgs 10:21
For there was not **l** to Jehoahaz an	2 Kgs 13:7
was very bitter, for there was none **l**,	2 Kgs 14:26
None was **l** but the tribe of Judah	2 Kgs 17:18
your prayer for the remnant that is **l**."	2 Kgs 19:4
he heard that the king had **l** Lachish.	2 Kgs 19:8
Nothing shall be **l**, says the LORD.	2 Kgs 20:17
not turn aside to the right or to the **l**.	2 Kgs 22:2
which were on one's **l** at the gate of	2 Kgs 23:8
the people who were **l** in the city and	2 Kgs 25:11
captain of the guard **l** some of the	2 Kgs 25:12
king of Babylon had **l**,	2 Kgs 25:22
On the **l** hand were their brothers, the	1 Chr 6:44
with either the right or the **l** hand;	1 Chr 12:2
And they **l** their gods there, and	1 Chr 14:12
So David **l** Asaph and his brothers	1 Chr 16:37
And he **l** Zadok the priest and his	1 Chr 16:39
horses, but **l** enough for 100 chariots.	1 Chr 18:4
the people who were **l** of the Hittites,	2 Chr 8:7
descendants who were **l** after them in	2 Chr 8:8
For the Levites **l** their common	2 Chr 11:14
on his right hand and on his **l**.	2 Chr 18:18
that no son was **l** to him except	2 Chr 21:17
So the armed men **l** the captives and	2 Chr 28:14
and had enough and have plenty **l**,	2 Chr 31:10
that we have this large amount **l**."	2 Chr 31:10
in the land, God **l** him to himself,	2 Chr 32:31
aside to the right hand or to the **l**.	2 Chr 34:2
for those who are **l** in Israel and in	2 Chr 34:21
for we are **l** a remnant that has escaped,	Ezr 9:15
there was no breach **l** in it (although up	Neh 6:1
and Meshullam on his **l** hand.	Neh 8:4
house?" As the word **l** the mouth of the	Est 7:8
There was nothing **l** after he had eaten;	Jb 20:21
what is **l** in his tent will be consumed.	Jb 20:26
There is nothing **l** of your answers but	Jb 21:34
and what they **l** the fire has consumed.'	Jb 22:20
on the **l** hand when he is working, I do	Jb 23:9
adversaries; not one of them was **l**.	Ps 106:11
in her **l** hand are riches and honor.	Prv 3:16
Do not swerve to the right or to the **l**;	Prv 4:27
a city broken into and **l** without walls.	Prv 25:28
but a child **l** to himself brings shame	Prv 29:15
to the right, but a fool's heart to the **l**.	Eccl 10:2
His **l** hand is under my head, and his right	Sg 2:6
His **l** hand is under my head, and his right	Sg 8:3
the daughter of Zion is **l** like a booth in a	Is 1:8
LORD of hosts had not **l** us a few survivors,	Is 1:9
And he who is **l** in Zion and remains in	Is 4:3
for everyone who is **l** in the land will eat	Is 7:22
are still hungry, and they devour on the **l**,	Is 9:20
Gleanings will be **l** in it, as when an olive	Is 17:6
shall all of them be **l** to the birds of prey	Is 18:6
the earth are scorched, and few men are **l**.	Is 24:6
Desolation is **l** in the city; the gates are	Is 24:12
are full of filthy vomit, with no space **l**.	Is 28:8
till you are **l** like a flagstaff on the top of	Is 30:17
to the right or when you turn to the **l**.	Is 30:21
up your prayer for the remnant that is **l**.'"	Is 37:4
he had heard that the king had **l** Lachish.	Is 37:8
Nothing shall be **l**, says the LORD.	Is 39:6
Behold, I was **l** alone; from where have	Is 49:21
spread abroad to the right and to the **l**,	Is 54:3
shamed, because we have **l** the land,	Jer 9:19
and none of them shall be **l**. For I will	Jer 11:23
Like a lion he has **l** his lair, for their	Jer 25:38
that the vessels that are **l** in the house of	Jer 27:18
rest of the vessels that are **l** in this city,	Jer 27:19
the vessels that are **l** in the house of	Jer 27:21
against all the cities of Judah that were **l**,	Jer 34:7
of the soldiers who are **l** in this city,	Jer 38:4
for there is no bread **l** in the city."	Jer 38:9
all the women **l** in the house of the king	Jer 38:22
rest of the people who were **l** in the city,	Jer 39:9
l in the land of Judah some of the poor	Jer 39:10
among the people who were **l** in the land.	Jer 40:6
king of Babylon had **l** a remnant in	Jer 40:11
and all the people who were **l** at Mizpah,	Jer 41:10
—because we are **l** with but a few,	Jer 42:2
of the guard had **l** with Gedaliah the son	Jer 43:6
But since we **l** off making offerings to	Jer 44:18
to destruction; let nothing be **l** of her.	Jer 50:26
of the people who were **l** in the city and	Jer 52:15
captain of the guard **l** some of the	Jer 52:16
turned me back; he has **l** me stunned,	Lam 1:13
The old men have **l** the city gate, the	Lam 5:14
four had the face of an ox on the **l** side,	Ezk 1:10
"Then lie on your **l** side, and place the	Ezk 4:4
and he who is **l** and is preserved shall	Ezk 6:12
they were striking, and I was **l** alone,	Ezk 9:8
behold, some survivors will be **l** in it,	Ezk 14:22
set yourself to the **l**, wherever your	Ezk 21:16
daughters whom you **l** behind shall	Ezk 24:21
of nations, have cut it down and **l** it.	Ezk 31:12
gone away from its shadow and **l** it.	Ezk 31:12
the nations that are **l** all around you	Ezk 36:36
will strike your bow from your **l** hand,	Ezk 39:3
become fresh; they are to be **l** for salt.	Ezk 47:11
spirit was troubled, and his sleep **l** him.	Dn 2:1
the kingdom be **l** to another people.	Dn 2:44
and stamped what was **l** with its feet.	Dn 7:7
and stamped what was **l** with its feet,	Dn 7:19
So I was **l** alone and saw this great	Dn 10:8
vision, and no strength was **l** in me.	Dn 10:8
for I was **l** there with the kings of	Dn 10:13
in me, and no breath is **l** in me."	Dn 10:17
hand and his **l** hand toward heaven	Dn 12:7
and they have **l** their God to play the	Hos 4:12
I will bereave them till none is **l**.	Hos 9:12
What the cutting locust **l**, the swarming	Jl 1:4
What the swarming locust **l**, the hopping	Jl 1:4
has eaten, and what the hopping locust **l**,	Jl 1:4
out a thousand shall have a hundred **l**,	Am 5:3
hundred shall have ten **l** to the house of	Am 5:3
and those who are **l** of them I will kill	Am 9:1
not know their right hand from their **l**,	Jon 4:11
will destroy you until no inhabitant is **l**.	Zep 2:5
those who are **l** in Israel; they shall do	Zep 3:13
'Who is **l** among you who saw this house	Hg 2:3
right of the bowl and the other on its **l**."	Zec 4:3
the right and the **l** of the lampstand?"	Zec 4:11
Thus the land they **l** was desolate, so	Zec 7:14
let those who are **l** devour the flesh of	Zec 11:9
right and to the **l** all the surrounding	Zec 12:6
and all the families that are **l**, each by	Zec 12:14
perish, and one third shall be **l** alive.	Zec 13:8
his hill country and **l** his heritage to	Mal 1:3
Then the devil **l** him, and behold, angels	Mt 4:11
Immediately they **l** their nets and	Mt 4:20
Immediately they **l** the boat and their	Mt 4:22
do not let your **l** hand know what your	Mt 6:3
He touched her hand, and the fever **l** her,	Mt 8:15
Then he **l** the crowds and went into the	Mt 13:36
baskets full of the broken pieces **l** over.	Mt 14:20
baskets full of the broken pieces **l** over.	Mt 15:37
of Jonah." So he **l** them and departed.	Mt 16:4
we have **l** everything and followed you.	Mt 19:27
everyone who has **l** houses or brothers	Mt 19:29
at your right hand and one at your **l**,	Mt 20:21
right hand and at my **l** is not mine to	Mt 20:23
And they **l** him and went away.	Mt 22:22
and having no children **l** his wife to his	Mt 22:25
See, your house is **l** to you desolate.	Mt 23:38
Jesus **l** the temple and was going away,	Mt 24:1
there will not be **l** here one stone upon	Mt 24:2
in the field; one will be taken and one **l**.	Mt 24:40
at the mill; one will be taken and one **l**.	Mt 24:41
on his right, but the goats on the **l**.	Mt 25:33
"Then he will say to those on his **l**,	Mt 25:41
Then all the disciples **l** him and fled.	Mt 26:56

him, one on the right and one on the **l**. Mt 27:38
And immediately they **l** their nets and Mk 1:18
and they **l** their father Zebedee in the Mk 1:20
And immediately he **l** the synagogue Mk 1:29
and lifted her up, and the fever **l** her, Mk 1:31
And immediately the leprosy **l** him, and Mk 1:42
had entered the house and **l** the people, Mk 7:17
way; the demon has **l** your daughter." Mk 7:29
they took up the broken pieces **l** over, Mk 8:8
And he **l** them, got into the boat again, Mk 8:13
And he **l** there and went to the region of Mk 10:1
we have **l** everything and followed Mk 10:28
no one who has **l** house or brothers or Mk 10:29
at your right hand and one at your **l**, Mk 10:37
right hand or at my **l** is not mine to Mk 10:40
them. So they **l** him and went away. Mk 12:12
a wife, and when he died **l** no offspring. Mk 12:20
And the seven **l** no offspring. Last of Mk 12:22
There will not be **l** here one stone upon Mk 13:2
And they all **l** him and fled. Mk 14:50
but he **l** the linen cloth and ran away Mk 14:52
one on his right and one on his **l**. Mk 15:27
And he arose and **l** the synagogue and Lk 4:38
her and rebuked the fever, and it **l** her, Lk 4:39
they **l** everything and followed him. Lk 5:11
And immediately the leprosy **l** him. Lk 5:13
And what was **l** over was picked up, Lk 9:17
that my sister has **l** me to serve alone? Lk 10:40
he would not have **l** his house to be Lk 12:39
bed. One will be taken and the other **l**. Lk 17:34
One will be taken and the other **l**." Lk 17:35
we have **l** our homes and followed Lk 18:28
is no one who has **l** house or wife or Lk 18:29
likewise all seven **l** no children and Lk 20:31
there will not be **l** here one stone upon Lk 21:6
one on his right and one on his **l**. Lk 23:33
he **l** Judea and departed again for Galilee. Jn 4:3
So the woman **l** her water jar and went Jn 4:28
at the seventh hour the fever **l** him." Jn 4:52
barley loaves, **l** by those who had eaten. Jn 6:13
and Jesus was **l** alone with the woman Jn 8:9
He has not **l** me alone, for I always do the Jn 8:29
Then they **l** the presence of the Acts 5:41
and immediately the angel **l** him. Acts 12:10
And John **l** them and returned to Acts 13:13
After this Paul **l** Athens and went to Acts 18:1
And he **l** there and went to the house of Acts 18:7
came to Ephesus, and he **l** them there, Acts 18:19
and their diseases **l** them and the evil Acts 19:12
leaving it on the **l** we sailed to Syria Acts 21:3
Jews a favor, Felix **l** Paul in prison. Acts 24:27
"There is a man **l** prisoner by Felix, Acts 25:14
off the anchors and **l** them in the sea, Acts 27:40
Lord of hosts had not **l** us offspring, Rom 9:29
your altars, and I alone am **l**, Rom 11:3
for the right hand and for the **l**; 2 Cor 6:7
gathered much had nothing **l** over, 2 Cor 8:15
of the gospel, when I **l** Macedonia, Phil 4:15
were willing to be **l** behind at Athens 1 Thes 3:1
who are **l** until the coming of the 1 Thes 4:15
Then we who are alive, who are **l**, 1 Thes 4:17
She who is truly a widow, **l** all alone, 1 Tm 5:5
the cloak that I **l** with Carpus at 2 Tm 4:13
at Corinth, and I **l** Trophimus, 2 Tm 4:20
This is why I **l** you in Crete, so that you Ti 1:5
to him, he **l** nothing outside his control. Heb 2:8
not all those who **l** Egypt led by Moses? Heb 3:16
By faith he **l** Egypt, not being afraid of Heb 11:27
If you are **l** without discipline, in Heb 12:8
of authority, but **l** their proper dwelling, Jude 1:6
foot on the sea, and his **l** foot on the land, Rv 10:2

LEFT-HANDED (2)
son of Gera, the Benjaminite, a **l** man. Jgs 3:15
these were 700 chosen men who were **l**; Jgs 20:16

LEFTOVER (1)
his disciples, "Gather up the **l** fragments, Jn 6:12

LEG (1)
cook took up the **l** and what was on 1 Sm 9:24

LEGAL (3)
another, one kind of **l** right and another, Dt 17:8
stood against us with its **l** demands. Col 2:14
basis of a **l** requirement concerning Heb 7:16

LEGION (3)
your name?" He replied, "My name is **L**, Mk 5:9
man, the one who had had the **l**, Mk 5:15
"**L**," for many demons had entered him. Lk 8:30

LEGIONS (1)
send me more than twelve **l** of angels? Mt 26:53

LEGS (25)
its head with its **l** and its inner parts. Ex 12:9
rings to the four corners at its four **l**. Ex 25:26
pieces, and wash its entrails and its **l**, Ex 29:17
rings to the four corners at its four **l**. Ex 37:13
its entrails and its **l** he shall wash with Lv 1:9
the entrails and the **l** he shall wash with Lv 1:13
bull and all its flesh, with its head, its **l**, Lv 4:11
washed the entrails and the **l** with water, Lv 8:21
the entrails and the **l** and burned them Lv 9:14
that have jointed **l** above their feet, Lv 11:21
knees and on the **l** with grievous boils Dt 28:35
And he had bronze armor on his **l**, 1 Sm 17:6
nor his pleasure in the **l** of a man, Ps 147:10
Like a lame man's **l**, which hang Prv 26:7
His **l** are alabaster columns, set on bases Sg 5:15
veil, strip off your robe, uncover your **l**, Is 47:2
Their **l** were straight, and the soles of Ezk 1:7
its **l** of iron, its feet partly of iron and Dn 2:33
his arms and **l** like the gleam of Dn 10:6
from the mouth of the lion two **l**, Am 3:12
my bones; my **l** tremble beneath me. Hab 3:16
Pilate that their **l** might be broken Jn 19:31
came and broke the **l** of the first, Jn 19:32
already dead, they did not break his **l**. Jn 19:33
like the sun, and his **l** like pillars of fire. Rv 10:1

LEHABIM (2)
Ludim, Anamim, **L**, Naphtuhim, Gn 10:13
Ludim, Anamim, **L**, Naphtuhim, 1 Chr 1:11

LEHEM (1)
and returned to **L** (now the records 1 Chr 4:22

LEHI (5)
in Judah and made a raid on **L**. Jgs 15:9
When he came to **L**, the Philistines Jgs 15:14
split open the hollow place that is at **L**, Jgs 15:19
called En-hakkore; it is at **L** to this day. Jgs 15:19
Philistines gathered together at **L**, 2 Sm 23:11

LEISURE (1)
and going, and they had no **l** even to eat. Mk 6:31

LEMA (2)
"Eli, Eli, **l** sabachthani?" that is, Mt 27:46
Eloi, **l** sabachthani?" which means, Mk 15:34

LEMUEL (2)
The words of King **L**. An oracle that his Prv 31:1
It is not for kings, O **L**, it is not for kings Prv 31:4

LEND (12)
"If you **l** money to any of my people Ex 22:25
You shall not **l** him your money at Lv 25:37
you, and you shall **l** to many nations, Dt 15:6
hand to him and **l** him sufficient for his Dt 15:8
And you shall **l** to many nations, Dt 28:12
He shall **l** to you, and you shall not lend Dt 28:44
lend to you, and you shall not **l** to him. Dt 28:44
does not **l** at interest or take any profit, Ezk 18:8
And if you **l** to those from whom you Lk 6:34
is that to you? Even sinners **l** to sinners, Lk 6:34
love your enemies, and do good, and **l**, Lk 6:35
say to him, 'Friend, **l** me three loaves, Lk 11:5

LENDER (2)
and the borrower is the slave of the **l**. Prv 22:7
seller; as with the **l**, so with the borrower; Is 24:2

LENDING (2)
and my servants are **l** them money and Neh 5:10
He is ever **l** generously, and his children Ps 37:26

LENDS (3)
the man who deals generously and **l**; Ps 112:5
is generous to the poor **l** to the LORD, Prv 19:17
l at interest, and takes profit; shall he Ezk 18:13

LENGTH (74)
the **l** of the ark 300 cubits, its breadth 50 Gn 6:15
walk through the **l** and the breadth of Gn 13:17
Two cubits and a half shall be its **l**, a Ex 25:10
Two cubits and a half shall be its **l**, and Ex 25:17
Two cubits shall be its **l**, a cubit its Ex 25:23
The **l** of each curtain shall be Ex 26:2
The **l** of each curtain shall be thirty Ex 26:8
that remains in the **l** of the curtains, Ex 26:13
Ten cubits shall be the **l** of a frame, Ex 26:16
And likewise for its **l** on the north side Ex 27:11
The **l** of the court shall be a hundred Ex 27:18
a span its **l** and a span its breadth. Ex 28:16
A cubit shall be its **l**, and a cubit its Ex 30:2
The **l** of each curtain was twenty-eight Ex 36:9
The **l** of each curtain was thirty cubits, Ex 36:15
Ten cubits was the **l** of a frame, and a Ex 36:21
Two cubits and a half was its **l**, a cubit Ex 37:1
Two cubits and a half was its **l**, and a Ex 37:6
Two cubits was its **l**, a cubit its Ex 37:10
Its **l** was a cubit, and its breadth was a Ex 37:25
Five cubits was its **l**, and five cubits its Ex 38:1
a span its **l** and a span its breadth when Ex 39:9
in measures of **l** or weight or quantity. Lv 19:35
Nine cubits was its **l**, and four cubits its Dt 3:11
to him, for he is your life and **l** of days, Dt 30:20
you and it, about 2,000 cubits in **l**. Jos 3:4
a sword with two edges, a cubit in **l**, Jgs 3:16
it were half a furrow's **l** in an acre of 1 Sm 14:14
Saul fell at once full **l** on the ground, 1 Sm 28:20
Five cubits was the **l** of one wing of 1 Kgs 6:24
and five cubits the **l** of the other wing 1 Kgs 6:24
Its **l** was a hundred cubits and its 1 Kgs 7:2
its **l** was fifty cubits, and its breadth 1 Kgs 7:6
for building the house of God: the **l**, 2 Chr 3:3
he made the Most Holy Place. Its **l**, 2 Chr 3:8
aged, and understanding in **l** of days. Jb 12:12
gave it to him, **l** of days forever and ever. Ps 21:4
for **l** of days and years of life and peace Prv 3:2
You were wearied with the **l** of your way, Is 57:10
my people from the **l** and breadth of the Jer 8:19
in its greatness, in the **l** of its branches; Ezk 31:7
and the **l** of the measuring reed in the Ezk 40:5
being a cubit and a handbreadth in **l**. Ezk 40:5
and the **l** of the gateway, thirteen Ezk 40:11
corresponding to the **l** of the gates. Ezk 40:18
he measured its **l** and its breadth. Ezk 40:20
Its **l** was fifty cubits, and its breadth Ezk 40:21
Its **l** was fifty cubits, and its breadth Ezk 40:25
Its **l** was fifty cubits, and its breadth Ezk 40:29
Its **l** was fifty cubits, and its breadth Ezk 40:33
Its **l** was fifty cubits, and its breadth Ezk 40:36
The **l** of the vestibule was twenty Ezk 40:49
And he measured the **l** of the nave, forty Ezk 41:2
And he measured the **l** of the room, Ezk 41:4
all around, and its **l** ninety cubits. Ezk 41:12
he measured the **l** of the building Ezk 41:15
The **l** of the building whose door faced Ezk 42:2
the north, of the same **l** and breadth, Ezk 42:11
corresponding in **l** to one of the tribal Ezk 45:7
and in **l** equal to one of the tribal Ezk 48:8
for the LORD shall be 25,000 cubits in **l**, Ezk 48:9
and 25,000 in **l** on the southern side, Ezk 48:10
25,000 cubits in **l** and 10,000 in Ezk 48:13
The whole **l** shall be 25,000 cubits Ezk 48:13
cubits in breadth and 25,000 in **l**, Ezk 48:15
remainder of the **l** alongside the holy Ezk 48:18
to see what is its width and what is its **l**." Zec 2:2
Its **l** is twenty cubits, and its width ten Zec 5:2
So he questioned him at some **l**, but he Lk 23:9
no inheritance in it, not even a foot's **l**, Acts 7:5
is the breadth and **l** and height and Eph 3:18
greatly that now at **l** you have revived Phil 4:10
foursquare; its **l** the same as its width. Rv 21:16
Its **l** and width and height are equal. Rv 21:16

LENGTHEN (4)
walked, then I will **l** your days." 1 Kgs 3:14
thing for the shadow to **l** ten steps. 2 Kgs 20:10
l your cords and strengthen your stakes. Is 54:2
day declines, for the shadows of evening **l**! Jer 6:4

LENGTHENING (1)
may perhaps be a **l** of your prosperity." Dn 4:27

LENT (5)
release what he has **l** to his neighbor. Dt 15:2
on anything that is **l** for interest. Dt 23:19
Therefore I have **l** him to the LORD. As 1 Sm 1:28
he is **l** to the LORD." And he worshiped 1 Sm 1:28
I have not **l**, nor have I borrowed, yet all Jer 15:10

LENTIL (1)
Jacob gave Esau bread and **l** stew, Gn 25:34

LENTILS (3)
flour, parched grain, beans and **l**, 2 Sm 17:28
there was a plot of ground full of **l**, 2 Sm 23:11
you, take wheat and barley, beans and **l**, Ezk 4:9

LEOPARD (6)
and the **l** shall lie down with the young Is 11:6
A **l** is watching their cities; everyone who Jer 5:6
change his skin or the **l** his spots? Jer 13:23
I looked, and behold, another, like a **l**, Dn 7:6
a lion; like a **l** I will lurk beside the way. Hos 13:7
And the beast that I saw was like a **l**; its Rv 13:2

LEOPARDS (2)
the dens of lions, from the mountains of **l**. Sg 4:8
Their horses are swifter than **l**, more Hab 1:8

LEPER (11)
a mighty man of valor, but he was a **l**. 2 Kgs 5:1
hand over the place and cure the **l**. 2 Kgs 5:11
So he went out from his presence a **l**, 2 Kgs 5:27
so that he was a **l** to the day of his 2 Kgs 15:5
King Uzziah was a **l** to the day of 2 Chr 26:21
and being a **l** lived in a separate 2 Chr 26:21
"He is a **l**." And Jotham his son 2 Chr 26:23
a **l** came to him and knelt before him, Mt 8:2
at Bethany in the house of Simon the **l**, Mt 26:6
And a **l** came to him, imploring him, Mk 1:40
at Bethany in the house of Simon the **l**, Mk 14:3

LEPERS (7)
four men who were l at the entrance to 2 Kgs 7:3
And when these l came to the edge of 2 Kgs 7:8
Heal the sick, raise the dead, cleanse l, Mt 10:8
walk, l are cleansed and the deaf hear, Mt 11:5
And there were many l in Israel in the Lk 4:27
their sight, the lame walk, l are cleansed, Lk 7:22
entered a village, he was met by ten l, Lk 17:12

LEPROSY (9)
Samaria! He would cure him of his l." 2 Kgs 5:3
that you may cure him of his l." 2 Kgs 5:6
word to me to cure a man of his l? 2 Kgs 5:7
Therefore the l of Naaman shall 2 Kgs 5:27
l broke out on his forehead in the 2 Chr 26:19
And immediately his l was cleansed. Mt 8:3
And immediately the l left him, and he Mk 1:42
of the cities, there came a man full of l. Lk 5:12
clean." And immediately the l left him. Lk 5:13

LEPROUS (41)
it out, behold, his hand was l like snow. Ex 4:6
turns into a case of l disease on the skin Lv 13:2
skin of his body, it is a case of l disease. Lv 13:3
pronounce him unclean; it is a l disease. Lv 13:8
a man is afflicted with a l disease, Lv 13:9
it is a chronic l disease in the skin of Lv 13:11
And if the l disease breaks out in the Lv 13:12
so that the l disease covers all the skin Lv 13:12
and if the l disease has covered all his Lv 13:13
Raw flesh is unclean, for it is a l disease. Lv 13:15
It is a case of l disease that has broken Lv 13:20
than the skin, then it is a l disease. Lv 13:25
him unclean; it is a case of l disease. Lv 13:25
him unclean; it is a case of l disease. Lv 13:27
itch, a l disease of the head or the beard. Lv 13:30
it is a l disease breaking out on his bald Lv 13:42
like the appearance of l disease in the Lv 13:43
he is a l man, he is unclean. The priest Lv 13:44
"The l person who has the disease shall Lv 13:45
there is a case of l disease in a garment, Lv 13:47
made of skin, it is a case of l disease, Lv 13:49
skin, the disease is a persistent l disease; Lv 13:51
is diseased, for it is a persistent l disease. Lv 13:52
law for a case of l disease in a garment Lv 13:59
be the law of the l person for the day of Lv 14:2
if the case of l disease is healed in the Lv 14:3
leprous disease is healed in the l person, Lv 14:3
who is to be cleansed of the l disease. Lv 14:7
for him in whom is a case of l disease, Lv 14:32
I put a case of l disease in a house in Lv 14:34
it is a persistent l disease in the house; Lv 14:44
This is the law for any case of l disease: Lv 14:54
for l disease in a garment or in a house, Lv 14:55
it is clean. This is the law for l disease. Lv 14:57
Aaron who has a l disease or a discharge Lv 22:4
camp everyone who is l or has a Nm 5:2
over the tent, behold, Miriam was l, Nm 12:10
toward Miriam, and behold, she was l. Nm 12:10
"Take care, in a case of l disease, to be Dt 24:8
a discharge or who is l or who holds a 2 Sm 3:29
behold, he was l in his forehead! 2 Chr 26:20

LESHEM (2)
of Dan went up and fought against L, Jos 19:47
of it and settled in it, calling L, Jos 19:47

LESS (25)
so. They gathered, some more, some l. Ex 16:17
give more, and the poor shall not give l, Ex 30:15
of the LORD my God to do l or more. Nm 22:18
how much l this house that I have 1 Kgs 8:27
how much l this house that I have 2 Chr 6:18
How much l will your God deliver 2 Chr 32:15
have punished us l than our iniquities Ezr 9:13
God exacts of you l than your guilt Jb 11:6
how much l one who is abominable Jb 15:16
how much l man, who is a maggot, and Jb 25:6
How much l when you say that you do Jb 35:14
a fool; still l is false speech to a prince. Prv 17:7
much l for a slave to rule over princes. Prv 19:10
by him as l than nothing and Is 40:17
and your work is l than nothing; Is 41:24
How much l, when the fire has Ezk 15:5
would not make it any l a part of the 1 Cor 12:15
would not make it any l a part of the 1 Cor 12:16
that we think l honorable we bestow 1 Cor 12:23
of the Jews the forty lashes l one. 2 Cor 11:24
in what were you l favored than the 2 Cor 12:13
If I love you more, am I to be loved l? 2 Cor 12:15
again, and that I may be l anxious. Phil 2:28
if she is not l than sixty years of 1 Tm 5:9
much l will we escape if we reject him Heb 12:25

LESSER (1)
rule the day and the l light to rule the Gn 1:16

LESSON (4)
them taught the men of Succoth a l. Jgs 8:16
"From the fig tree learn its l: as soon as Mt 24:32
"From the fig tree learn its l: as soon as Mk 13:28
together, each one has a hymn, a l, 1 Cor 14:26

LEST (195)
neither shall you touch it, l you die.'" Gn 3:3
l he reach out his hand and take also of Gn 3:22
l any who found him should attack Gn 4:15
l we be dispersed over the face of the Gn 11:4
that is yours, l you should say, Gn 14:23
l you be swept away in the punishment Gn 19:15
to the hills, l you be swept away." Gn 19:17
l the disaster overtake me and I die. Gn 19:19
"l the men of the place should kill me Gn 26:7
I thought, 'L I die because of her.'" Gn 26:9
shrewdly with them, l they multiply, Ex 1:10
l he fall upon us with pestilence or with Ex 5:3
"L the people change their minds when Ex 13:17
l they break through to the LORD to Ex 19:21
l the LORD break out against them." Ex 19:22
the LORD, l he break out against them." Ex 19:24
but do not let God speak to us, l we die." Ex 20:19
l the land become desolate and the wild Ex 23:29
land, l they make you sin against me; Ex 23:33
the Holy Place, l they bear guilt and die. Ex 28:43
among you, l I consume you on the way, Ex 33:3
l you make a covenant with the Ex 34:12
go, l it become a snare in your midst. Ex 34:12
l you make a covenant with the Ex 34:15
and do not tear your clothes, l you die, Lv 10:6
entrance of the tent of meeting, l you die, Lv 10:7
you go into the tent of meeting, l you die. Lv 10:9
l all that is in the house be declared Lv 14:36
l they die in their uncleanness by Lv 15:31
l the land vomit you out when you Lv 18:28
l you incur sin because of him. Lv 19:17
l the land fall into prostitution and the Lv 19:29
l he profane the sanctuary of his God, Lv 21:12
l they bear sin for it and die thereby Lv 22:9
not touch the holy things, l they die. Nm 4:15
things even for a moment, l they die." Nm 4:20
l you be struck down before your Nm 14:42
l you be swept away with all their Nm 16:26
they said, "L the earth swallow us up!" Nm 16:34
l he become like Korah and his Nm 16:40
grumblings against me, l they die." Nm 17:10
of the sanctuary or to the altar l they, Nm 18:3
of meeting, l they bear sin and die. Nm 18:22
of the people of Israel, l you die.'" Nm 18:32
l I come out with the sword against Nm 20:18
l you be defeated before your enemies.' Dt 1:42
l you forget the things that your eyes have Dt 4:9
and l they depart from your heart all the Dt 4:9
beware l you act corruptly by making a Dt 4:16
And beware l you raise your eyes to Dt 4:19
l you forget the covenant of the LORD Dt 4:23
then take care l you forget the LORD, who Dt 6:12
l the anger of the LORD your God be Dt 6:15
l the wild beasts grow too numerous for Dt 7:22
it for yourselves, l you be ensnared by it, Dt 7:25
"Take care l you forget the LORD your Dt 8:11
l, when you have eaten and are full and Dt 8:12
Beware l you say in your heart, 'My Dt 8:17
l the land from which you brought us Dt 9:28
Take care l your heart be deceived, and Dt 11:16
Take care l there be an unworthy Dt 15:9
wives for himself, l his heart turn away, Dt 17:17
or see this great fire any more, l I die.' Dt 18:16
l the avenger of blood in hot anger Dt 19:6
l innocent blood be shed in your land Dt 19:10
l he die in the battle and another man Dt 20:5
l he die in the battle and another man Dt 20:6
l he die in the battle and another man Dt 20:7
l he make the heart of his fellows melt Dt 20:8
of seed, l the whole yield be forfeited, Dt 22:9
on it), l he cry against you to the LORD, Dt 24:15
l, if one should go on to beat him with Dt 25:3
Beware l there be among you a man or Dt 29:18
Beware l there be among you a root Dt 29:18
l their adversaries should Dt 32:27
misunderstand, l they should say, Dt 32:27
l when you have devoted them you take Jos 6:18
let them live, l wrath be upon us, Jos 9:20
you, l you deal falsely with your God." Jos 24:27
into their hand, l Israel boast over me, Jgs 7:2
your sword and kill me, l they say of me, Jgs 9:54
l we burn you and your father's house Jgs 14:15
us, l angry fellows fall upon you, Jgs 18:25
l in another field you be assaulted." Ru 2:22
myself, l I impair my own inheritance. Ru 4:6
l you become slaves to the Hebrews as 1 Sm 4:9
l my father cease to care about the 1 Sm 9:5
"L the Hebrews make themselves 1 Sm 13:19
Amalekites, l I destroy you with them. 1 Sm 15:6
Jonathan know this, l he be grieved.' 1 Sm 20:3
"L they should tell about us and say, 1 Sm 27:11
l in the battle he become an adversary 1 Sm 29:4
l these uncircumcised come and 1 Sm 31:4
l the daughters of the Philistines 2 Sm 1:20
l the daughters of the uncircumcised 2 Sm 1:20
l I take the city and it be called by 2 Sm 12:28
l we be burdensome to you." He 2 Sm 13:25
l he overtake us quickly and bring 2 Sm 15:14
l the king and all the people who are 2 Sm 17:16
l he get himself to fortified cities and 2 Sm 20:6
l you quench the lamp of Israel." 2 Sm 21:17
and go down, l the rain stop you.'" 1 Kgs 18:44
l these uncircumcised come and 1 Chr 10:4
who is with me, l he destroy you." 2 Chr 35:21
l his wrath be against the realm of the Ezr 7:23
Beware l you say, 'We have found Jb 32:13
Beware l wrath entice you into scoffing, Jb 36:18
Kiss the Son, l he be angry, and you Ps 2:12
l like a lion they tear my soul apart, Ps 7:2
up my eyes, l I sleep the sleep of death, Ps 13:3
l my enemy say, "I have prevailed over Ps 13:4
prevailed over him," l my foes rejoice Ps 13:4
be not deaf to me, l, if you be silent to me, Ps 28:1
you who forget God, l I tear you apart, Ps 50:22
Kill them not, l my people forget; make Ps 59:11
l you strike your foot against a stone. Ps 91:12
l the righteous stretch out their hands Ps 125:3
l I be like those who go down to the pit. Ps 143:7
l you give your honor to others and your Prv 5:9
l strangers take their fill of your Prv 5:10
Love not sleep, l you come to poverty; Prv 20:13
l you learn his ways and entangle Prv 22:25
l the LORD see it and be displeased, and Prv 24:18
l he who hears you bring shame upon Prv 25:10
l you have your fill of it and vomit it. Prv 25:16
l he have his fill of you and hate you. Prv 25:17
to his folly, l you be like him yourself. Prv 26:4
to his folly, l he be wise in his own eyes. Prv 26:5
l he rebuke you and you be found a Prv 30:6
l I be full and deny you and say, "Who Prv 30:9
"Who is the LORD?" or l I be poor and Prv 30:9
l he curse you and you be held guilty. Prv 30:10
l they drink and forget what has been Prv 31:5
l you hear your servant cursing you. Eccl 7:21
l they see with their eyes, and hear with Is 6:10
fathers, l they rise and possess the earth, Is 14:21
L anyone punish it, I keep it night and Is 27:3
not scoff, l your bonds be made strong; Is 28:22
shakes his hands, l they hold a bribe, Is 33:15
Beware l Hezekiah mislead you by Is 36:18
them to you, l you should say, Is 48:5
never heard of them, l you should say, Is 48:7
by them, l I dismay you before them. Jer 1:17
l my wrath go forth like fire, and burn Jer 4:4
O Jerusalem, l I turn from you in disgust, Jer 6:8
you in disgust, l I make you a desolation, Jer 6:8
your anger, l you bring me to nothing. Jer 10:24
robbed, l my wrath go forth like fire, Jer 21:12
of Jonathan the secretary, l I die there." Jer 37:20
l I be handed over to them and they deal Jer 38:19
l iniquity be your ruin. Ezk 18:30
l they communicate holiness to the Ezk 44:19
l I strip her naked and make her as in Hos 2:3
l he break out like fire in the house of Am 5:6
hearts diamond-hard l they should Zec 7:12
l I come and strike the land with a Mal 4:6
l you strike your foot against a stone.'" Mt 4:6
l your accuser hand you over to the Mt 5:25
l they trample them underfoot and turn Mt 7:6
l they should see with their eyes and Mt 13:15
l in gathering the weeds you root up the Mt 13:29
away hungry, l they faint on the way." Mt 15:32
l there be an uproar among the people." Mt 26:5
l his disciples go and steal him away Mt 27:64
because of the crowd, l they crush him, Mk 3:9
l they should turn and be forgiven." Mk 4:12
l he come suddenly and find you Mk 13:36
l there be an uproar from the people." Mk 14:2
l you strike your foot against a stone.'" Lk 4:11
Therefore be careful l the light in you Lk 11:35
on the way, l he drag you to the judge, Lk 12:58
l someone more distinguished than you Lk 14:8
l they also invite you in return and you Lk 14:12
l they also come into this place of Lk 16:28
"But watch yourselves l your hearts be Lk 21:34
to the light, l his deeds should be exposed. Jn 3:20
have the light, l darkness overtake you. Jn 12:35
their heart, l they see with their eyes, Jn 12:40
l what is said in the Prophets should Acts 13:40
l any should swim away and escape. Acts 27:42
l they should see with their eyes and Acts 28:27
L you be wise in your own conceits, I Rom 11:25
l I build on someone else's Rom 15:20
l the cross of Christ be emptied of its 1 Cor 1:17

meat, **l** I make my brother stumble. 1 Cor 8:13
l after preaching to others I myself 1 Cor 9:27
that he stands take heed **l** he fall. 1 Cor 10:12
watch on yourself, **l** you too be tempted. Gal 6:1
l I should have sorrow upon sorrow. Phil 2:27
children, **l** they become discouraged. Col 3:21
we have heard, **l** we drift away from it. Heb 2:1
l there be in any of you an evil, Heb 3:12
let us fear **l** any of you should seem to Heb 4:1
my people, **l** you take part in her sins, Rv 18:4
in her sins, **l** you share in her plagues; Rv 18:4

LET (1492)
"**L** there be light," and there was light. Gn 1:3
"**L** there be an expanse in the midst of the Gn 1:6
and **l** it separate the waters from the Gn 1:6
"**L** the waters under the heavens be Gn 1:9
and **l** the dry land appear." And it was so. Gn 1:9
God said, "**L** the earth sprout vegetation, Gn 1:11
"**L** there be lights in the expanse of the Gn 1:14
And **l** them be for signs and for seasons, Gn 1:14
and **l** them be lights in the expanse of Gn 1:15
"**L** the waters swarm with swarms of Gn 1:20
and **l** birds fly above the earth across Gn 1:20
seas, and **l** birds multiply on the earth." Gn 1:22
"**L** the earth bring forth living creatures Gn 1:24
said, "**L** us make man in our image, Gn 1:26
And **l** them have dominion over the fish Gn 1:26
of Shem; and **l** Canaan be his servant. Gn 9:26
and **l** him dwell in the tents of Shem, Gn 9:27
of Shem, and **l** Canaan be his servant." Gn 9:27
one another, "Come, **l** us make bricks, Gn 11:3
l us build ourselves a city and a tower Gn 11:4
and **l** us make a name for ourselves, Gn 11:4
l us go down and there confuse their Gn 11:7
will kill me, but they will **l** you live. Gn 12:12
"**L** there be no strife between you and Gn 13:8
L Aner, Eshcol, and Mamre take their Gn 14:24
L a little water be brought, and wash Gn 18:4
he said, "Oh **l** not the Lord be angry, Gn 18:30
he said, "Oh **l** not the Lord be angry, Gn 18:32
L me bring them out to you, and do to Gn 19:8
L me escape there—is it not a little Gn 19:20
l us make our father drink wine, Gn 19:32
L us make him drink wine tonight Gn 19:34
me. Therefore I did not **l** you touch her. Gn 20:6
"**L** me not look on the death of the Gn 21:16
For the full price **l** him give it to me in Gn 23:9
L the young woman to whom I shall Gn 24:14
'Please **l** down your jar that I may Gn 24:14
water your camels'—**l** her be the one Gn 24:14
lord." And she quickly **l** down her jar Gn 24:18
L the virgin who comes out to draw Gn 24:43
for your camels also," **l** her be the Gn 24:44
water. I said to her, 'Please **l** me drink.' Gn 24:45
She quickly **l** down her jar from her Gn 24:46
and **l** her be the wife of your master's Gn 24:51
"**L** the young woman remain with us a Gn 24:55
"**L** us call the young woman and ask Gn 24:57
Jacob, "**L** me eat some of that red stew, Gn 25:30
l there be a sworn pact between us, Gn 26:28
us, and **l** us make a covenant with you, Gn 26:28
said to him, "**L** your curse be on me, Gn 27:13
L peoples serve you, and nations bow Gn 27:29
"**L** my father arise and eat of his son's Gn 27:31
l me pass through all your flock today, Gn 30:32
said, "Good! **L** it be as you have said." Gn 30:34
"**L** not my lord be angry that I cannot Gn 31:35
Come now, **l** us make a covenant, you Gn 31:44
And **l** it be a witness between you and Gn 31:44
Then he said, "**L** me go, for the day has Gn 32:26
"I will not **l** you go unless you bless Gn 32:26
Esau said, "**L** us journey on our way, Gn 33:12
L my lord pass on ahead of his servant, Gn 33:14
"**L** me leave with you some of the Gn 33:15
L me find favor in the sight of my Gn 33:15
brothers, "**L** me find favor in your eyes, Gn 34:11
l them dwell in the land and trade in it, Gn 34:21
L us take their daughters as wives, and Gn 34:21
and **l** us give them our daughters. Gn 34:21
Only **l** us agree with them, and they Gn 34:23
Then **l** us arise and go up to Bethel, so Gn 35:3
'**L** us go to Dothan.'" So Joseph went Gn 37:17
l us kill him and throw him into one Gn 37:20
hands, saying, "**L** us not take his life." Gn 37:21
Come, **l** us sell him to the Ishmaelites, Gn 37:27
and **l** not our hand be upon him, Gn 37:27
l me come in to you," for he did not Gn 38:16
"**L** her keep the things as her own, Gn 38:23
"Bring her out, and **l** her be burned." Gn 38:24
Now therefore **l** Pharaoh select a Gn 41:33
L Pharaoh proceed to appoint Gn 41:34
And **l** them gather all the food of these Gn 41:35
for food in the cities, and **l** them keep it. Gn 41:35
of you, and **l** him bring your brother, Gn 42:16
l one of your brothers remain confined Gn 42:19
and **l** the rest go and carry grain for the Gn 42:19
you, then **l** me bear the blame forever. Gn 43:9
He said, "**L** it be as you say: he who is Gn 44:10
please **l** your servant speak a word in Gn 44:18
and **l** not your anger burn against Gn 44:18
please **l** your servant remain instead of Gn 44:33
and **l** the boy go back with his Gn 44:33
Israel said to Joseph, "Now **l** me die, Gn 46:30
please **l** your servants dwell in the land Gn 47:4
L them settle in the land of Goshen, and Gn 47:6
but **l** me lie with my fathers. Carry me Gn 47:30
God has **l** me see your offspring also." Gn 48:11
and in them **l** my name be carried on, Gn 48:16
and **l** them grow into a multitude in Gn 48:16
L my soul come not into their council; Gn 49:6
"Naphtali is a doe **l** loose that bears Gn 49:21
l me please go up and bury my father. Gn 50:5
Come, **l** us deal shrewdly with them, lest Ex 1:10
them, but **l** the male children live. Ex 1:17
done this, and **l** the male children live?" Ex 1:18
but you shall **l** every daughter live." Ex 1:22
please **l** us go a three days' journey into Ex 3:18
of Egypt will not **l** you go unless Ex 3:19
I will do in it; after that he will **l** you go. Ex 3:20
"Please **l** me go back to my brothers in Ex 4:18
heart, so that he will not **l** the people go. Ex 4:21
"**L** my son go that he may serve me." If Ex 4:23
may serve me." If you refuse to **l** him go, Ex 4:23
So he **l** him alone. It was then that she Ex 4:26
LORD, the God of Israel, '**L** my people go, Ex 5:1
I should obey his voice and **l** Israel go? Ex 5:2
LORD, and moreover, I will not **l** Israel go." Ex 5:2
Please **l** us go a three days' journey into Ex 5:3
l them go and gather straw for Ex 5:7
'**L** us go and offer sacrifice to our God.' Ex 5:8
L heavier work be laid on the men that Ex 5:9
say, '**L** us go and sacrifice to the LORD.' Ex 5:17
king of Egypt to **l** the people of Israel Ex 6:11
shall tell Pharaoh to **l** the people of Israel Ex 7:2
is hardened; he refuses to **l** the people go. Ex 7:14
sent me to you, saying, "**L** my people go, Ex 7:16
'Thus says the LORD, "**L** my people go, Ex 8:1
But if you refuse to **l** them go, behold, I Ex 8:2
and I will **l** the people go to sacrifice to the Ex 8:8
'Thus says the LORD, "**L** my people go, Ex 8:20
Or else, if you will not **l** my people go, Ex 8:21
"I will **l** you go to sacrifice to the LORD Ex 8:28
Only **l** not Pharaoh cheat again by not Ex 8:29
this time also, and did not **l** the people go. Ex 8:32
the God of the Hebrews, "**L** my people go, Ex 9:1
For if you refuse to **l** them go and still Ex 9:2
hardened, and he did not **l** the people go. Ex 9:7
and **l** Moses throw them in the air in the Ex 9:8
the God of the Hebrews, "**L** my people go, Ex 9:13
my people and will not **l** them go. Ex 9:17
of God's thunder and hail. I will **l** you go, Ex 9:28
and he did not **l** the people of Israel go, Ex 9:35
L my people go, that they may serve me. Ex 10:3
For if you refuse to **l** my people go, Ex 10:4
L the men go, that they may serve the Ex 10:7
if ever I **l** you and your little ones go! Ex 10:10
and he did not **l** the people of Israel go. Ex 10:20
only **l** your flocks and your herds Ex 10:24
"You must also **l** us have sacrifices and Ex 10:25
heart, and he would not **l** them go. Ex 10:27
Afterward he will **l** you go from here. Ex 11:1
and he did not **l** the people of Israel go Ex 11:10
And you shall **l** none of it remain until Ex 12:10
so that they **l** them have what they Ex 12:36
LORD, **l** all his males be circumcised. Ex 12:48
Pharaoh stubbornly refused to **l** us go, Ex 13:15
When Pharaoh **l** the people go, God did Ex 13:17
that we have **l** Israel go from serving Ex 14:5
said, "**L** us flee from before Israel, Ex 14:25
"**L** no one leave any of it over till the Ex 16:19
l no one go out of his place on the Ex 16:29
'**L** an omer of it be kept throughout Ex 16:32
And **l** them judge the people at all Ex 18:22
Then Moses **l** his father-in-law depart, Ex 18:27
and **l** them wash their garments Ex 19:10
Also **l** the priests who come near to the Ex 19:22
But do not **l** the priests and the people Ex 19:24
but do not **l** God speak to us, lest we Ex 20:19
himself, then he shall **l** her be redeemed. Ex 21:8
him, but God **l** him fall into his hand, Ex 21:13
he shall **l** the slave go free because of Ex 21:26
he shall **l** the slave go free because of Ex 21:27
by beasts, **l** him bring it as evidence. Ex 22:13
seventh year you shall **l** it rest and lie Ex 23:11
gods, nor **l** it be heard on your lips. Ex 23:13
or **l** the fat of my feast remain until the Ex 23:18
has a dispute, **l** him go to them." Ex 24:14
And **l** them make me a sanctuary, that I Ex 25:8
Now therefore **l** me alone, that my Ex 32:10
"**L** not the anger of my lord burn hot. Ex 32:22
them, '**L** any who have gold take it off.' Ex 32:24
(for Aaron had **l** them break loose, Ex 32:25
but you have not **l** me know whom you Ex 33:12
and **l** no one be seen throughout all the Ex 34:3
L no flocks or herds graze opposite that Ex 34:3
please **l** the Lord go in the midst of us, Ex 34:9
or **l** the sacrifice of the Feast of the Ex 34:25
l him bring the LORD'S contribution: Ex 35:5
"**L** every skillful craftsman among you Ex 35:10
"**L** no man or woman do anything more Ex 36:6
You shall not **l** the salt of the covenant Lv 2:13
"Do not **l** the hair of your heads hang Lv 10:6
but **l** your brothers, the whole house of Lv 10:6
wear torn clothes and **l** the hair of his Lv 13:45
him clean and shall **l** the living bird go Lv 14:7
And he shall **l** the live bird go out of the Lv 14:53
and he shall **l** the goat go free in the Lv 16:22
You shall not **l** your cattle breed with a Lv 19:19
shall not **l** the hair of his head hang Lv 21:10
and **l** all who heard him lay their Lv 24:14
and **l** all the congregation stone him. Lv 24:14
l him calculate the years since he sold Lv 25:27
And I will **l** loose the wild beasts Lv 26:22
"**L** not the tribe of the clans of the Nm 4:18
then' (**l** the priest make the woman Nm 5:21
He shall **l** the locks of hair of his head Nm 6:5
and **l** them go with a razor over all their Nm 8:7
Then **l** them take a bull from the herd Nm 8:8
"**L** the people of Israel keep the Passover Nm 9:2
LORD, and **l** your enemies be scattered, Nm 10:35
and **l** those who hate you flee before Nm 10:35
and **l** them take their stand there with Nm 11:16
from the sea and **l** them fall beside the Nm 11:31
L her not be as one dead, whose flesh Nm 12:12
L her be shut outside the camp seven Nm 12:14
"**L** us go up at once and occupy it, Nm 13:30
"**L** us choose a leader and go back to Nm 14:4
please **l** the power of the Lord be great Nm 14:17
And **l** every one of you take his censer Nm 16:17
l them be made into hammered plates Nm 16:38
Please **l** us pass through your land. Nm 20:17
L me only pass through on foot, Nm 20:19
"**L** Aaron be gathered to his people, for Nm 20:24
"**L** me pass through your land. We Nm 21:22
say, "Come to Heshbon, **l** it be built; Nm 21:27
l the city of Sihon be established. Nm 21:27
LORD has refused to **l** me go with you." Nm 22:13
'**L** nothing hinder you from coming Nm 22:16
would have killed you and **l** her live." Nm 22:33
L me die the death of the upright, and Nm 23:10
the upright, and **l** my end be like his!" Nm 23:10
I will **l** you know what this people will Nm 24:14
"**L** the LORD, the God of the spirits of Nm 27:16
them, "Have you **l** all the women live? Nm 31:15
l this land be given to your servants for Nm 32:5
of them whom you **l** remain shall be Nm 33:55
'**L** them marry whom they think best, Nm 36:6
me and said, '**L** us send men before us, Dt 1:22
'**L** me pass through your land. I will go Dt 2:27
drink. Only **l** me pass through on foot, Dt 2:28
of Heshbon would not **l** us pass by him, Dt 2:30
Please **l** me go over and see the good land Dt 3:25
to me, that I may **l** them hear my words, Dt 4:10
Out of heaven he **l** you hear his voice, Dt 4:36
And on earth he **l** you see his great fire, Dt 4:36
he humbled you and **l** you hunger and fed Dt 8:3
L me alone, that I may destroy them and Dt 9:14
and if he says, '**L** us go after other gods,' Dt 13:2
have not known, 'and **l** us serve them,' Dt 13:2
saying, '**L** us go and serve other gods,' Dt 13:6
saying, '**L** us go and serve other gods,' Dt 13:13
seventh year you shall **l** him go free Dt 15:12
And when you **l** him go free from you, Dt 15:13
you shall not **l** him go empty-handed. Dt 15:13
to you when you **l** him go free from Dt 15:18
'**L** me not hear again the voice of the Dt 18:16
your enemies: **l** not your heart faint. Dt 20:3
L him go back to his house, lest he die in Dt 20:5
L him go back to his house, lest he die in Dt 20:6
L him go back to his house, lest he die in Dt 20:7
L him go back to his house, lest he make Dt 20:8
her, you shall **l** her go where she wants. Dt 21:14
You shall **l** the mother go, but the young Dt 22:7
and **l** the earth hear the words of my Dt 32:1
L them rise up and help you; let them Dt 32:38
help you; **l** them be your protection! Dt 32:38
"**L** Reuben live, and not die, but let his Dt 33:6
live, and not die, but **l** his men be few." Dt 33:6
l him be the favorite of his brothers, Dt 33:24
brothers, and **l** him dip his foot in oil. Dt 33:24
I have **l** you see it with your eyes, but you Dt 34:4
Then she **l** them down by a rope Jos 2:15
window through which you **l** us down, Jos 2:18
then you shall **l** your children know, Jos 4:22
that he would not **l** them see the land Jos 5:6

of the covenant and **l** seven priests bear Jos 6:6
around the city and **l** the armed men pass Jos 6:7
but **l** about two or three thousand men go Jos 7:3
a covenant with them, to **l** them live, Jos 9:15
l them live, lest wrath be upon us, Jos 9:20
"**L** them live." So they became cutters of Jos 9:21
me and help me, and **l** us strike Gibeon. Jos 10:4
Do not **l** them enter their cities, for the Jos 10:19
He knows; and **l** Israel itself know! Jos 22:22
we said, '**L** us now build an altar, Jos 22:26
but they **l** the man and all his family go. Jgs 1:25
If he is a god, **l** him contend for himself, Jgs 6:31
"**L** Baal contend against him," because Jgs 6:32
"**L** not your anger burn against me; Jgs 6:39
against me; **l** me speak just once more. Jgs 6:39
Please **l** me test just once more with the Jgs 6:39
Please **l** it be dry on the fleece only, and Jgs 6:39
and on all the ground **l** there be dew." Jgs 6:39
l him return home and hurry away from Jgs 7:3
and **l** all the others go every man to his Jgs 7:7
to them, "**L** me make a request of you: Jgs 8:24
l fire come out of the bramble and Jgs 9:15
and **l** him also rejoice in you. Jgs 9:19
l fire come out from Abimelech and Jgs 9:20
and **l** fire come out from the leaders of Jgs 9:20
l them save you in the time of your Jgs 10:14
'Please **l** us pass through your land,' Jgs 11:17
'Please **l** us pass through your land to Jgs 11:19
her father, "**L** this thing be done for me: Jgs 11:37
"**L** me go over," the men of Gilead said to Jgs 12:5
please **l** the man of God whom you sent Jgs 13:8
I said to the woman **l** her be careful. Jgs 13:13
neither **l** her drink wine or strong Jgs 13:14
that I commanded her **l** her observe." Jgs 13:14
"Please **l** us detain you and prepare a Jgs 13:15
to them, "**L** me now put a riddle to you. Jgs 14:12
he **l** the foxes go into the standing grain Jgs 15:5
"**L** us wait till the light of the morning; Jgs 16:2
"**L** me feel the pillars on which the Jgs 16:26
"**L** me die with the Philistines." Then Jgs 16:30
said, "Arise, and **l** us go up against them, Jgs 18:9
"Do not **l** your voice be heard among Jgs 18:25
the night, and **l** your heart be merry." Jgs 19:6
Lodge here and **l** your heart be merry, Jgs 19:9
l us turn aside to this city of the Jgs 19:11
"Come and **l** us draw near to one of Jgs 19:13
concubine. **L** me bring them out now. Jgs 19:24
the dawn began to break, they **l** her go. Jgs 19:25
l us be going." But there was no Jgs 19:28
"**L** us flee and draw them away from Jgs 20:32
"**L** me go to the field and glean among the Ru 2:2
'Please **l** me glean and gather among the Ru 2:7
L your eyes be on the field that they are Ru 2:9
"**L** her glean even among the sheaves, Ru 2:15
if he will redeem you, good; **l** him do it. Ru 3:13
"**L** it not be known that the woman Ru 3:14
"**L** your servant find favor in your 1 Sm 1:18
l not arrogance come from your 1 Sm 2:3
said to him, "**L** them burn the fat first, 1 Sm 2:16
L him do what seems good to him." 1 Sm 3:18
was with him and **l** none of his words 1 Sm 3:19
L us bring the ark of the covenant of 1 Sm 4:3
"**L** the ark of the God of Israel be 1 Sm 5:8
Israel, and **l** it return to its own place, 1 Sm 5:11
Then send it off and **l** it go its way 1 Sm 6:8
was with him, "Come, **l** us go back, 1 Sm 9:5
says comes true. So now **l** us go there. 1 Sm 9:6
l us go to the seer," for today's "prophet" 1 Sm 9:9
l us go." So they went to the city where 1 Sm 9:10
in the morning I will **l** you go and will 1 Sm 9:19
l us go to Gilgal and there renew the 1 Sm 11:14
land, saying, "**L** the Hebrews hear." 1 Sm 13:3
l us go over to the Philistine garrison 1 Sm 14:1
l us go over to the garrison of these 1 Sm 14:6
'**L** every man bring his ox or his 1 Sm 14:34
"**L** us go down after the Philistines 1 Sm 14:36
l us not leave a man of them." And 1 Sm 14:36
said, "**L** us draw near to God here." 1 Sm 14:36
L our lord now command your 1 Sm 16:16
"**L** David remain in my service, 1 Sm 16:22
and **l** him come down to me. 1 Sm 17:8
"**L** no man's heart fail because of 1 Sm 17:32
day and would not **l** him return to his 1 Sm 18:2
"**L** not my hand be against him, 1 Sm 18:17
but **l** the hand of the Philistines be 1 Sm 18:17
Saul thought, "**L** me give her to him, 1 Sm 18:21
"**L** not the king sin against his 1 Sm 19:4
So Michal **l** David down through the 1 Sm 19:12
me thus and **l** my enemy go, 1 Sm 19:17
Saul, "He said to me, '**L** me go. 1 Sm 19:17
thinks, 'Do not **l** Jonathan know this, 1 Sm 20:3
But **l** me go, that I may hide myself in 1 Sm 20:5
l us go out into the field." So they 1 Sm 20:11
He said, '**L** me go, for our clan holds 1 Sm 20:29
l me get away and see my brothers.' 1 Sm 20:29

'**L** no one know anything of the 1 Sm 21:2
of the gate and **l** his spittle run down 1 Sm 21:13
"Please **l** my father and my mother 1 Sm 22:3
L not the king impute anything to 1 Sm 22:15
enemy, will he **l** him go away safe? 1 Sm 24:19
Therefore **l** my young men find favor 1 Sm 25:8
Please **l** your servant speak in your 1 Sm 25:24
L not my lord regard this worthless 1 Sm 25:25
now then **l** your enemies and those 1 Sm 25:26
And now **l** this present that your 1 Sm 25:27
Now please **l** me pin him to the earth 1 Sm 26:8
and the jar of water, and **l** us go." 1 Sm 26:11
Now therefore **l** my lord the king 1 Sm 26:19
l not my blood fall to the earth away 1 Sm 26:20
L one of the young men come over 1 Sm 26:22
l a place be given me in one of the 1 Sm 27:5
L me set a morsel of bread before 1 Sm 28:22
l there be no dew or rain upon you, 2 Sm 1:21
Now therefore **l** your hands be strong, 2 Sm 2:7
"**L** the young men arise and compete 2 Sm 2:14
us." And Joab said, "**L** them arise." 2 Sm 2:14
came to the king, and he has **l** him go, 2 Sm 3:23
l him get up the water shaft to attack 2 Sm 5:8
and **l** us be courageous for our 2 Sm 10:12
'Do not **l** this matter trouble you, 2 Sm 11:25
'**L** my sister Tamar come and give me 2 Sm 13:5
"Please **l** my sister Tamar come and 2 Sm 13:6
Please **l** the king and his servants go 2 Sm 13:24
"No, my son, **l** us not all go, 2 Sm 13:25
please **l** my brother Amnon go with 2 Sm 13:26
him until he **l** Amnon and all 2 Sm 13:27
"**L** not my lord suppose that they 2 Sm 13:32
Now therefore **l** not my lord the king 2 Sm 13:33
l the king and his throne be guiltless." 2 Sm 14:9
"Please **l** the king invoke the LORD 2 Sm 14:11
"Please **l** your servant speak a word 2 Sm 14:12
said, "**L** my lord the king speak." 2 Sm 14:18
"**L** him dwell apart in his own house; 2 Sm 14:24
still." Now therefore **l** me go into 2 Sm 14:32
guilt in me, **l** him put me to death.'" 2 Sm 14:32
king, "Please **l** me go and pay my vow, 2 Sm 15:7
at Jerusalem, "Arise, and **l** us flee, 2 Sm 15:14
bring me back and **l** me see both it 2 Sm 15:25
l him do to me what seems good to 2 Sm 15:26
l me ever find favor in your sight, my 2 Sm 16:4
L me go over and take off his head." 2 Sm 16:9
Leave him alone, and **l** him curse, 2 Sm 16:11
"**L** me choose twelve thousand men, 2 Sm 17:1
and **l** us hear what he has to say." 2 Sm 17:5
"**L** me run and carry news to the 2 Sm 18:19
l me also run after the Cushite." And 2 Sm 18:22
"**L** not my lord hold me guilty or 2 Sm 19:19
Do not **l** the king take it to heart. 2 Sm 19:19
to the king, "Oh, **l** him take it all, 2 Sm 19:30
Please **l** your servant return, that I 2 Sm 19:37
L him go over with my lord the king, 2 Sm 19:37
is for David, **l** him follow Joab." 2 Sm 20:11
'**L** them but ask counsel at Abel,' 2 Sm 20:18
l seven of his sons be given to us, so 2 Sm 21:6
L us fall into the hand of the LORD, 2 Sm 24:14
but **l** me not fall into the hand of 2 Sm 24:14
Please **l** your hand be against me 2 Sm 24:17
"**L** my lord the king take and offer 2 Sm 24:22
"**L** a young woman be sought for my 1 Kgs 1:2
and **l** her wait on the king and be in 1 Kgs 1:2
L her lie in your arms, that my lord 1 Kgs 1:2
therefore come, **l** me give you advice, 1 Kgs 1:12
And **l** Zadok the priest and Nathan 1 Kgs 1:34
'**L** King Solomon swear to me first 1 Kgs 1:51
but do not **l** his gray head go down to 1 Kgs 2:6
and **l** them be among those who eat at 1 Kgs 2:7
"**L** Abishag the Shunammite be 1 Kgs 2:21
month. They **l** nothing be lacking. 1 Kgs 4:27
of Israel, **l** your word be confirmed, 1 Kgs 8:26
L your eyes be open to the plea of 1 Kgs 8:52
L these words of mine, with which I 1 Kgs 8:59
L your heart therefore be wholly true 1 Kgs 8:61
said to Pharaoh, "**L** me depart, 1 Kgs 11:21
he said to him, "Only **l** me depart." 1 Kgs 11:22
"**L** there be a covenant between me 1 Kgs 15:19
l this child's life come into him 1 Kgs 17:21
L two bulls be given to us, and let 1 Kgs 18:23
and **l** them choose one bull for 1 Kgs 18:23
l it be known this day that you are 1 Kgs 18:36
l not one of them escape." And they 1 Kgs 18:40
"**L** me kiss my father and my 1 Kgs 19:20
'**L** not him who straps on his armor 1 Kgs 20:11
But **l** us fight against them in the 1 Kgs 20:23
L us put sackcloth around our 1 Kgs 20:31
says, 'Please, **l** me live.'" And he said, 1 Kgs 20:32
"I will **l** you go on these terms." So 1 Kgs 20:34
a covenant with him and **l** him go. 1 Kgs 20:34
'Because you have **l** go out of your 1 Kgs 20:42
and eat bread and **l** your heart be 1 Kgs 21:7
and **l** them bring a charge against 1 Kgs 21:10

said, "**L** not the king say so." 1 Kgs 22:8
L your word be like the word of one 1 Kgs 22:13
l each return to his home in peace.'" 1 Kgs 22:17
"**L** my servants go with your 1 Kgs 22:49
l fire come down from heaven and 2 Kgs 1:10
l fire come down from heaven and 2 Kgs 1:12
him, "O man of God, please **l** my life, 2 Kgs 1:13
but now **l** my life be precious in your 2 Kgs 1:14
"Please **l** there be a double portion of 2 Kgs 2:9
Please **l** them go and seek your 2 Kgs 2:16
L us make a small room on the roof 2 Kgs 4:10
L him come now to me, that he may 2 Kgs 5:8
please **l** there be given to your servant 2 Kgs 5:17
L us go to the Jordan and each of us get 2 Kgs 6:2
and **l** us make a place for us to dwell 2 Kgs 6:2
If we say, '**L** us enter the city,' the 2 Kgs 7:4
l us go over to the camp of the Syrians. 2 Kgs 7:4
l us go and tell the king's household." 2 Kgs 7:9
"**L** some men take five of the 2 Kgs 7:13
already perished. **L** us send and see." 2 Kgs 7:13
then **l** no one slip out of the city to go 2 Kgs 9:15
and send to meet them, and **l** him say, 2 Kgs 9:17
L none be missing, for I have a great 2 Kgs 10:19
l not a man escape." So when they 2 Kgs 10:25
"**L** her not be put to death in the 2 Kgs 11:15
l the priests take, each from his 2 Kgs 12:5
and **l** them repair the house wherever 2 Kgs 12:5
l us look one another in the face." 2 Kgs 14:8
and **l** him go and dwell there and 2 Kgs 17:27
'Do not **l** Hezekiah deceive you, for 2 Kgs 18:29
Do not **l** Hezekiah make you trust in 2 Kgs 18:30
'Do not **l** your God in whom you 2 Kgs 19:10
And **l** them take and lay it on the 2 Kgs 20:7
Rather **l** the shadow go back ten 2 Kgs 20:10
And **l** it be given into the hand of the 2 Kgs 22:5
and **l** them give it to the workmen 2 Kgs 22:5
and **l** them use it for buying timber 2 Kgs 22:6
And he said, "**L** him be; let no man 2 Kgs 23:18
l no man move his bones." So they 2 Kgs 23:18
bones." So they **l** his bones alone, 2 Kgs 23:18
l us send abroad to our brothers who 1 Chr 13:2
Then **l** us bring again the ark of our 1 Chr 13:3
l the hearts of those who seek the 1 Chr 16:10
L the heavens be glad, and let the 1 Chr 16:31
be glad, and **l** the earth rejoice, 1 Chr 16:31
and **l** them say among the nations, 1 Chr 16:31
L the sea roar, and all that fills it; let 1 Chr 16:32
l the field exult, and everything in it! 1 Chr 16:32
l the word that you have spoken 1 Chr 17:23
and **l** us use our strength for our 1 Chr 19:13
L me fall into the hand of the LORD, 1 Chr 21:13
but do not **l** me fall into the hand of 1 Chr 21:13
Please **l** your hand, O LORD my God, 1 Chr 21:17
But do not **l** the plague be on your 1 Chr 21:17
and **l** my lord the king do what 1 Chr 21:23
l your word to David my father be now 2 Chr 1:9
spoken, **l** him send to his servants. 2 Chr 2:15
of Israel, **l** your word be confirmed, 2 Chr 6:17
l your eyes be open and your ears 2 Chr 6:40
L your priests, O LORD God, be 2 Chr 6:41
and **l** your saints rejoice in your 2 Chr 6:41
"**L** us build these cities and surround 2 Chr 14:7
God; **l** not man prevail against you." 2 Chr 14:11
Do not **l** your hands be weak, for 2 Chr 15:7
building Ramah and **l** his work 2 Chr 16:5
said, "**L** not the king say so." 2 Chr 18:7
L your word be like the word of one 2 Chr 18:12
l each return to his home in peace.'" 2 Chr 18:16
l the fear of the LORD be upon you. 2 Chr 19:7
you would not **l** Israel invade when 2 Chr 20:10
L him reign, as the LORD spoke 2 Chr 23:3
L no one enter the house of the LORD 2 Chr 23:6
do not **l** the army of Israel go with 2 Chr 25:7
l us look one another in the face." 2 Chr 25:17
do not **l** Hezekiah deceive you or 2 Chr 32:15
the kings of Judah had **l** go to ruin. 2 Chr 34:11
his God be with him. **L** him go up.'" 2 Chr 36:23
with him, and **l** him go up to Jerusalem, Ezr 1:3
And **l** each survivor, in whatever place Ezr 1:4
and said to them, "**L** us build with you, Ezr 4:2
and **l** the house of God be rebuilt on its Ezr 5:15
l search be made in the royal archives Ezr 5:17
And **l** the king send us his pleasure in Ezr 5:17
God at Jerusalem, **l** the house be rebuilt, Ezr 6:3
offered, and **l** its foundations be retained. Ezr 6:3
L the cost be paid from the royal Ezr 6:4
And also **l** the gold and silver vessels of Ezr 6:5
L the work on this house of God alone. Ezr 6:7
L the governor of the Jews and the elders Ezr 6:7
at Jerusalem require—**l** that be given to Ezr 6:9
a decree; **l** it be done with all diligence." Ezr 6:12
of you, **l** it be done with all diligence, Ezr 7:21
l it be done in full for the house of the Ezr 7:23
l judgment be strictly executed on him, Ezr 7:26
Therefore **l** us make a covenant with Ezr 10:3

and **l** it be done according to the Law. Ezr 10:3
L our officials stand for the whole Ezr 10:14
L all in our cities who have taken Ezr 10:14
l your ear be attentive and your eyes Neh 1:6
l your ear be attentive to the prayer of Neh 1:11
said to the king, "**L** the king live forever! Neh 2:3
l letters be given me to the governors of Neh 2:7
that they may **l** me pass through until I Neh 2:7
Come, **l** us build the wall of Jerusalem, Neh 2:17
"**L** us rise up and build." So they Neh 2:18
and **l** not their sin be blotted out from Neh 4:5
"**L** every man and his servant pass the Neh 4:22
So **l** us get grain, that we may eat and Neh 5:2
L us abandon this exacting of interest. Neh 5:10
"Come and **l** us meet together at Neh 6:2
So now come and **l** us take counsel Neh 6:7
"**L** us meet together in the house of Neh 6:10
L us close the doors of the temple, for Neh 6:10
"**L** not the gates of Jerusalem be opened Neh 7:3
guard, **l** them shut and bar the doors. Neh 7:3
l not all the hardship seem little to you Neh 9:32
king, **l** a royal order go out from him, Est 1:19
and **l** it be written among the laws of the Est 1:19
And **l** the king give her royal position to Est 1:19
"**L** beautiful young virgins be sought out Est 2:2
And **l** the king appoint officers in all the Est 2:3
women. **L** their cosmetics be given them. Est 2:3
And **l** the young woman who pleases the Est 2:4
l it be decreed that they be destroyed, Est 3:9
l the king and Haman come today to a Est 5:4
l the king and Haman come to the feast Est 5:8
"Even Queen Esther **l** no one but me Est 5:12
"**L** a gallows fifty cubits high be made, Est 5:14
And the king said, "**L** him come in." Est 6:5
l royal robes be brought, which the king Est 6:8
And **l** the robes and the horse be handed Est 6:9
L them dress the man whom the king Est 6:9
and **l** them lead him on the horse Est 6:9
l my life be granted me for my wish, Est 7:3
l an order be written to revoke the letters Est 8:5
l the Jews who are in Susa be allowed Est 9:13
And **l** the ten sons of Haman be hanged Est 9:13
"**L** the day perish on which I was born, Jb 3:3
L that day be darkness! May God above Jb 3:4
L gloom and deep darkness claim it. Let Jb 3:5
L clouds dwell upon it; let the blackness of Jb 3:5
it; **l** the blackness of the day terrify it. Jb 3:5
That night—**l** thick darkness seize it! Let Jb 3:6
L it not rejoice among the days of the year; Jb 3:6
l it not come into the number of the Jb 3:6
Behold, **l** that night be barren; let no Jb 3:7
night be barren; **l** no joyful cry enter it. Jb 3:7
L those curse it who curse the day, who Jb 3:8
L the stars of its dawn be dark; let it hope Jb 3:9
l it hope for light, but have none, nor see Jb 3:9
that he would **l** loose his hand and cut me Jb 6:9
Please turn; **l** no injustice be done. Turn Jb 6:29
he will not **l** me get my breath, but fills Jb 9:18
L him take his rod away from me, and let Jb 9:34
me, and **l** not dread of him terrify me. Jb 9:34
l me know why you contend against me. Jb 10:2
and **l** not injustice dwell in your tents. Jb 11:14
"**L** me have silence, and I will speak, Jb 13:13
will speak, and **l** come on me what may. Jb 13:13
and **l** my declaration be in your ears. Jb 13:17
me, and **l** not dread of you terrify me. Jb 13:21
or **l** me speak, and you reply to me. Jb 13:22
L him not trust in emptiness, deceiving Jb 15:31
and **l** my cry find no resting place. Jb 16:18
therefore you will not **l** them triumph. Jb 17:4
though he is loath to **l** it go and holds it Jb 20:13
he will not **l** anything in which he Jb 20:20
to my words, and **l** this be your comfort. Jb 21:2
L him pay it out to them, that they may Jb 21:19
L their own eyes see their destruction, Jb 21:20
and **l** them drink of the wrath of the Jb 21:20
fast my righteousness and will not **l** it go; Jb 27:6
"**L** my enemy be as the wicked, and let Jb 27:7
and **l** him who rises up against me be as Jb 27:7
(**L** me be weighed in a just balance, and Jb 31:6
balance, and **l** God know my integrity!) Jb 31:6
then **l** me sow, and another eat, and let Jb 31:8
and **l** what grows for me be rooted out. Jb 31:8
then **l** my wife grind for another, and let Jb 31:10
another, and **l** others bow down on her. Jb 31:10
then **l** my shoulder blade fall from my Jb 31:22
and **l** my arm be broken from its Jb 31:22
(I have not **l** my mouth sin by asking Jb 31:30
signature! **L** the Almighty answer me!) Jb 31:35
l thorns grow instead of wheat, and foul Jb 31:40
I said, '**L** days speak, and many years Jb 32:7
to me; **l** me also declare my opinion.' Jb 32:10
l his flesh become fresh with youth; let Jb 33:25
l him return to the days of his youthful Jb 33:25
L us choose what is right; let us know Jb 34:4
l us know among ourselves what is good. Jb 34:4
and **l** not the greatness of the ransom Jb 36:18
"Who has **l** the wild donkey go free? Jb 39:5
who argues with God, **l** him answer it." Jb 40:2
l him who made him bring near his Jb 40:19
"**L** us burst their bonds apart and cast Ps 2:3
O God; **l** them fall by their own counsels; Ps 5:10
But **l** all who take refuge in you rejoice; Ps 5:11
l them ever sing for joy, and spread your Ps 5:11
l the enemy pursue my soul and overtake Ps 7:5
and **l** him trample my life to the ground Ps 7:5
L the assembly of the peoples be gathered Ps 7:7
l the evil of the wicked come to an end, Ps 7:9
L not man prevail; let the nations be Ps 9:19
l the nations be judged before you! Ps 9:19
L the nations know that they are but Ps 9:20
l them be caught in the schemes that Ps 10:2
L him rain coals on the wicked; fire and Ps 11:6
the fortunes of his people, **l** Jacob rejoice, Ps 14:7
people, let Jacob rejoice, **l** Israel be glad. Ps 14:7
Sheol, or **l** your holy one see corruption. Ps 16:10
From your presence **l** my vindication Ps 17:2
come! **L** your eyes behold the right! Ps 17:2
l them not have dominion over me! Ps 19:13
L the words of my mouth and the Ps 19:14
"He trusts in the LORD; **l** him deliver him; Ps 22:8
l him rescue him, for he delights in Ps 22:8
in you I trust; **l** me not be put to shame; Ps 25:2
shame; **l** not my enemies exult over me. Ps 25:2
L me not be put to shame, for I take Ps 25:20
strong, and **l** your heart take courage; Ps 27:14
up and have not **l** my foes rejoice over Ps 30:1
I take refuge; **l** me never be put to shame; Ps 31:1
O LORD, **l** me not be put to shame, for I Ps 31:17
upon you; **l** the wicked be put to shame; Ps 31:17
to shame; **l** them go silently to Sheol. Ps 31:17
L the lying lips be mute, which speak Ps 31:18
strong, and **l** your heart take courage, Ps 31:24
Therefore **l** everyone who is godly offer Ps 32:6
L all the earth fear the LORD; let all the Ps 33:8
l all the inhabitants of the world stand in Ps 33:8
L your steadfast love, O LORD, be upon Ps 33:22
the LORD; **l** the humble hear and be glad. Ps 34:2
me, and **l** us exalt his name together! Ps 34:3
L them be put to shame and dishonor Ps 35:4
L them be turned back and disappointed Ps 35:4
L them be like chaff before the wind, Ps 35:5
L their way be dark and slippery, with Ps 35:6
L destruction come upon him when he Ps 35:8
And **l** the net that he hid ensnare him; let Ps 35:8
l him fall into it—to his destruction! Ps 35:8
L not those rejoice over me who are Ps 35:19
and **l** not those wink the eye who hate Ps 35:19
and **l** them not rejoice over me! Ps 35:24
L them not say in their hearts, "Aha, Ps 35:25
our heart's desire!" **L** them not say, Ps 35:25
L them be put to shame and Ps 35:26
L them be clothed with shame and Ps 35:26
L those who delight in my Ps 35:27
L not the foot of arrogance come upon Ps 36:11
to his power or **l** him be condemned Ps 37:33
I said, "Only **l** them not rejoice over me, Ps 38:16
of my days; **l** me know how fleeting I am! Ps 39:4
L those be put to shame and Ps 40:14
l those be turned back and brought to Ps 40:14
L those be appalled because of their Ps 40:15
light and your truth; **l** them lead me; Ps 43:3
l them bring me to your holy hill and to Ps 43:3
l your right hand teach you awesome Ps 45:4
L Mount Zion be glad! Let the Ps 48:11
L the daughters of Judah rejoice Ps 48:11
L me hear joy and gladness; let the bones Ps 51:8
l the bones that you have broken rejoice. Ps 51:8
fortunes of his people, **L** Jacob rejoice, Ps 53:6
people, Let Jacob rejoice, **l** Israel be glad. Ps 53:6
L death steal over them; let them go Ps 55:15
them; **l** them go down to Sheol alive; Ps 55:15
L your glory be over all the earth! Ps 57:5
L your glory be over all the earth! Ps 57:11
L them vanish like water that runs Ps 58:7
he aims his arrows, **l** them be blunted. Ps 58:7
L them be like the snail that dissolves Ps 58:8
God will **l** me look in triumph on my Ps 59:10
lips, **l** them be trapped in their pride. Ps 59:12
L me dwell in your tent forever! Let me Ps 61:4
L me take refuge under the shelter of Ps 61:4
L the righteous one rejoice in the LORD Ps 64:10
in him! **L** all the upright in heart exult! Ps 64:10
on the nations—**l** not the rebellious exalt Ps 66:7
l the sound of his praise be heard, Ps 66:8
the living and has not **l** our feet slip. Ps 66:9
you **l** men ride over our heads; we went Ps 66:12
L the peoples praise you, O God; let all the Ps 67:3
you, O God; **l** all the peoples praise you! Ps 67:3
L the nations be glad and sing for joy, for Ps 67:4
L the peoples praise you, O God; let all the Ps 67:5
you, O God; **l** all the peoples praise you! Ps 67:5
us; **l** all the ends of the earth fear him! Ps 67:7
kings there, **l** snow fall on Zalmon. Ps 68:14
L not those who hope in you be put to Ps 69:6
l not those who seek you be brought to Ps 69:6
l me be delivered from my enemies and Ps 69:14
L not the flood sweep over me, or the Ps 69:15
L their own table before them become a Ps 69:22
they are at peace, **l** it become a trap. Ps 69:22
L their eyes be darkened, so that they Ps 69:23
and **l** your burning anger overtake Ps 69:24
desolation; **l** no one dwell in their tents. Ps 69:25
L them be blotted out of the book of the Ps 69:28
l them not be enrolled among the Ps 69:28
l your salvation, O God, set me on high! Ps 69:29
you who seek God, **l** your hearts revive. Ps 69:32
L heaven and earth praise him, the seas Ps 69:34
L them be put to shame and confusion Ps 70:2
L them be turned back and brought to Ps 70:2
L them turn back because of their Ps 70:3
I take refuge; **l** me never be put to shame! Ps 71:1
L the mountains bear prosperity for the Ps 72:3
L not the downtrodden turn back in Ps 74:21
l the poor and needy praise your name. Ps 74:21
l all around him bring gifts to him who Ps 76:11
"**L** me remember my song in the night; Ps 77:6
l me meditate in my heart." Then my Ps 77:6
divided the sea and **l** them pass through Ps 78:13
he **l** them fall in the midst of their Ps 78:28
He **l** loose on them his burning anger, Ps 78:49
l your compassion come speedily to meet Ps 79:8
"Where is their God?" **L** the avenging of Ps 79:10
L the groans of the prisoners come Ps 79:11
l your face shine, that we may be saved! Ps 80:3
l your face shine, that we may be saved! Ps 80:7
But **l** your hand be on the man of your Ps 80:17
l your face shine, that we may be saved! Ps 80:19
"Come, **l** us wipe them out as a nation; Ps 83:4
l the name of Israel be remembered no Ps 83:4
"**L** us take possession for ourselves of Ps 83:12
L them be put to shame and dismayed Ps 83:17
forever; **l** them perish in disgrace, Ps 83:17
L me hear what God the LORD will speak, Ps 85:8
saints; but **l** them not turn back to folly. Ps 85:8
L my prayer come before you; incline Ps 88:2
L the heavens praise your wonders, O Ps 89:5
L your work be shown to your servants, Ps 90:16
L the favor of the Lord our God be upon Ps 90:17
Oh come, **l** us sing to the LORD; let us Ps 95:1
l us make a joyful noise to the rock of Ps 95:1
L us come into his presence with Ps 95:2
l us make a joyful noise to him with Ps 95:2
Oh come, **l** us worship and bow down; let Ps 95:6
l us kneel before the LORD, our Maker! Ps 95:6
L the heavens be glad, and let the earth Ps 96:11
heavens be glad, and **l** the earth rejoice; Ps 96:11
rejoice; **l** the sea roar, and all that fills it; Ps 96:11
l the field exult, and everything in it! Ps 96:12
The LORD reigns, **l** the earth rejoice; let Ps 97:1
rejoice; **l** the many coastlands be glad! Ps 97:1
L the sea roar, and all that fills it; the Ps 98:7
L the rivers clap their hands; let the hills Ps 98:8
hands; **l** the hills sing for joy together Ps 98:8
The LORD reigns; **l** the peoples tremble! Ps 99:1
upon the cherubim; **l** the earth quake! Ps 99:1
L them praise your great and awesome Ps 99:3
prayer, O LORD; **l** my cry come to you! Ps 102:1
L this be recorded for a generation to Ps 102:18
L sinners be consumed from the Ps 104:35
earth, and **l** the wicked be no more! Ps 104:35
l the hearts of those who seek the LORD Ps 105:3
And **l** all the people say, "Amen!" Ps 106:48
L the redeemed of the LORD say so, Ps 107:2
L them thank the LORD for his steadfast Ps 107:8
L them thank the LORD for his Ps 107:15
L them thank the LORD for his Ps 107:21
And **l** them offer sacrifices of Ps 107:22
L them thank the LORD for his Ps 107:31
L them extol him in the congregation Ps 107:32
he does not **l** their livestock diminish. Ps 107:38
is wise, **l** him attend to these things; Ps 107:43
l them consider the steadfast love of Ps 107:43
L your glory be over all the earth! Ps 108:5
l an accuser stand at his right hand. Ps 109:6
he is tried, **l** him come forth guilty; Ps 109:7
guilty; **l** his prayer be counted as sin! Ps 109:7
L there be none to extend kindness to Ps 109:12
and **l** not the sin of his mother be Ps 109:14
L them be before the LORD Ps 109:15
to curse; **l** curses come upon him! Ps 109:17
L them know that this is your hand; Ps 109:27
L them curse, but you will bless! They Ps 109:28
L Israel say, "His steadfast love endures Ps 118:2
L the house of Aaron say, "His steadfast Ps 118:3

L those who fear the LORD say, "His Ps 118:4
has made; **l** us rejoice and be glad in it. Ps 118:24
l me not wander from your Ps 119:10
O LORD; **l** me not be put to shame! Ps 119:31
L your steadfast love come to me, O Ps 119:41
L your steadfast love comfort me Ps 119:76
L your mercy come to me, that I may Ps 119:77
L the insolent be put to shame, Ps 119:78
L those who fear you turn to me, that Ps 119:79
and **l** me not be put to shame in my Ps 119:116
of good; **l** not the insolent oppress me. Ps 119:122
and **l** no iniquity get dominion over Ps 119:133
L my cry come before you, O LORD; Ps 119:169
L my plea come before you; deliver Ps 119:170
L your hand be ready to help me, for I Ps 119:173
L my soul live and praise you, and let Ps 119:175
praise you, and **l** your rules help me. Ps 119:175
He will not **l** your foot be moved; he Ps 121:3
me, "**L** us go to the house of the LORD!" Ps 122:1
was on our side—**l** Israel now say— Ps 124:1
me from my youth"—**l** Israel now say— Ps 129:1
L them be like the grass on the Ps 129:6
L your ears be attentive to the voice of Ps 130:2
"**L** us go to his dwelling place; let us Ps 132:7
place; **l** us worship at his footstool!" Ps 132:7
L your priests be clothed with Ps 132:9
and **l** your saints shout for joy. Ps 132:9
l my right hand forget its skill! Ps 137:5
L my tongue stick to the roof of my Ps 137:6
l the mischief of their lips overwhelm Ps 140:9
L burning coals fall upon them! Let Ps 140:10
L them be cast into fire, into miry pits, Ps 140:10
L not the slanderer be established in Ps 140:11
l evil hunt down the violent man Ps 140:11
L my prayer be counted as incense Ps 141:2
Do not **l** my heart incline to any evil, to Ps 141:4
and **l** me not eat of their delicacies! Ps 141:4
L a righteous man strike me—it is a Ps 141:5
l him rebuke me—it is oil for my head; Ps 141:5
oil for my head; **l** my head not refuse it. Ps 141:5
L the wicked fall into their own nets, Ps 141:10
L me hear in the morning of your Ps 143:8
L your good Spirit lead me on level Ps 143:10
and **l** all flesh bless his holy name Ps 145:21
L them praise the name of the LORD! For Ps 148:5
L them praise the name of the LORD, Ps 148:13
L Israel be glad in his Maker; let the Ps 149:2
l the children of Zion rejoice in their Ps 149:2
L them praise his name with dancing, Ps 149:3
L the godly exult in glory; let them sing Ps 149:5
glory; **l** them sing for joy on their beds. Ps 149:5
L the high praises of God be in their Ps 149:6
L everything that has breath praise the Ps 150:6
L the wise hear and increase in learning, Prv 1:5
with us, **l** us lie in wait for blood; Prv 1:11
l us ambush the innocent without Prv 1:11
like Sheol **l** us swallow them alive, and Prv 1:12
but **l** your heart keep my Prv 3:1
L not steadfast love and faithfulness Prv 3:3
to me, "**L** your heart hold fast my words; Prv 4:4
Keep hold of instruction; do not **l** go; Prv 4:13
L them not escape from your sight; Prv 4:21
L your eyes look directly forward, and Prv 4:25
L them be for yourself alone, and not Prv 5:17
L your fountain be blessed, and rejoice Prv 5:18
L her breasts fill you at all times with Prv 5:19
and do not **l** her capture you with her Prv 6:25
l us take our fill of love till morning; Prv 7:18
l us delight ourselves with love. Prv 7:18
L not your heart turn aside to her ways; Prv 7:25
l him turn in here!" To him who lacks Prv 9:4
l him turn in here!" And to him who Prv 9:16
The LORD does not **l** the righteous go Prv 10:3
L a man meet a she-bear robbed of her Prv 17:12
L not your heart envy sinners, but Prv 23:17
L your father and mother be glad; let Prv 23:25
be glad; **l** her who bore you rejoice. Prv 23:25
and **l** your eyes observe my ways. Prv 23:26
and **l** not your heart be glad when he Prv 24:17
L your foot be seldom in your Prv 25:17
L another praise you, and not your own Prv 27:2
fugitive until death; **l** no one help him. Prv 28:17
l them drink and forget their poverty Prv 31:7
and **l** her works praise her in the gates. Prv 31:31
nor **l** your heart be hasty to utter a word Eccl 5:2
on earth. Therefore **l** your words be few. Eccl 5:2
L not your mouth lead you into sin, and Eccl 5:6
of the rich will not **l** him sleep. Eccl 5:12
L your garments be always white. Let Eccl 9:8
L not oil be lacking on your head. Eccl 9:8
many years, **l** him rejoice in them all; Eccl 11:8
but **l** him remember that the days of Eccl 11:8
and **l** your heart cheer you in the days Eccl 11:9
L him kiss me with the kisses of his Sg 1:2
Draw me after you; **l** us run. The king has Sg 1:4
crannies of the cliff, **l** me see your face, Sg 2:14
me see your face, **l** me hear your voice, Sg 2:14
and would not **l** him go until I had Sg 3:4
Blow upon my garden, **l** its spices flow. Sg 4:16
L my beloved come to his garden, and Sg 4:16
l us go out into the fields and lodge in the Sg 7:11
l us go out early to the vineyards and see Sg 7:12
he **l** out the vineyard to keepers; Sg 8:11
listening for your voice; **l** me hear it. Sg 8:13
"Come now, **l** us reason together, says the Is 1:18
l us go up to the mountain of the LORD, Is 2:3
come, **l** us walk in the light of the LORD. Is 2:5
clothes, only **l** us be called by your name; Is 4:1
L me sing for my beloved my love song Is 5:1
"**L** him be quick, let him speed his work Is 5:19
l him speed his work that we may see it; Is 5:19
l the counsel of the Holy One of Israel Is 5:19
One of Israel draw near, and **l** it come, Is 5:19
and do not **l** your heart be faint because of Is 7:4
"**L** us go up against Judah and terrify it, Is 7:6
terrify it, and **l** us conquer it for ourselves, Is 7:6
l it be deep as Sheol or high as heaven." Is 7:11
place where cattle are **l** loose and where Is 7:25
L him be your fear, and let him be your Is 8:13
be your fear, and **l** him be your dread. Is 8:13
l this be made known in all the earth. Is 12:5
who did not **l** his prisoners go home?' Is 14:17
l the outcasts of Moab sojourn among Is 16:4
Therefore **l** Moab wail for Moab, let Is 16:7
let Moab wail for Moab, **l** everyone wail. Is 16:7
L them tell you that they might know Is 19:12
watchman; **l** him announce what he sees. Is 21:6
riders on camels, **l** him listen diligently, Is 21:7
away from me; **l** me weep bitter tears; Is 22:4
"**L** us eat and drink, for tomorrow we Is 22:13
l us be glad and rejoice in his salvation." Is 25:9
L them see your zeal for your people, and Is 26:11
L the fire for your adversaries consume Is 26:11
Or **l** them lay hold of my protection, let Is 27:5
protection, **l** them make peace with me, Is 27:5
with me, **l** them make peace with me." Is 27:5
year to year; **l** the feasts run their round. Is 29:1
l us hear no more about the Holy One of Is 30:11
who **l** the feet of the ox and the donkey Is 32:20
L the earth hear, and all that fills it; the Is 34:1
'Do not **l** Hezekiah deceive you, for he Is 36:14
Do not **l** Hezekiah make you trust in the Is 36:15
'Do not **l** your God in whom you trust Is 37:10
"**L** them take a cake of figs and apply it Is 38:21
l the peoples renew their strength; Is 41:1
l them approach, then let them speak; Is 41:1
let them approach, then **l** them speak; Is 41:1
l us together draw near for judgment. Is 41:1
L them bring them, and tell us what is Is 41:22
L the desert and its cities lift up their Is 42:11
l the habitants of Sela sing for joy, let Is 42:11
l them shout from the top of the Is 42:11
L them give glory to the LORD, and Is 42:12
L them bring their witnesses to prove Is 43:9
them right, and **l** them hear and say, Is 43:9
in remembrance; **l** us argue together; Is 43:26
Who is like me? **L** him proclaim it. Let Is 44:7
L him declare and set it before me, since I Is 44:7
L them declare what is to come, and what Is 44:7
L them all assemble, let them stand Is 44:11
them all assemble, **l** them stand forth. Is 44:11
and **l** the clouds rain down righteousness; Is 45:8
l the earth open, that salvation and Is 45:8
l the earth cause them both to sprout; Is 45:8
your case; **l** them take counsel together! Is 45:21
l them stand forth and save you, those Is 47:13
contend with me? **L** us stand up together. Is 50:8
is my adversary? **L** him come near to me. Is 50:8
L him who walks in darkness and has Is 50:10
and **l** the curtains of your habitations be Is 54:2
l the wicked forsake his way, and the Is 55:7
l him return to the LORD, that he may Is 55:7
L not the foreigner who has joined Is 56:3
and **l** not the eunuch say, "Behold, I am a Is 56:3
"Come," they say, "**l** me get wine; let us Is 56:12
l us fill ourselves with strong drink; Is 56:12
l your collection of idols deliver you! Is 57:13
of the yoke, to **l** the oppressed go free, Is 58:6
sake have said, '**L** the LORD be glorified, Is 66:5
north disaster shall be **l** loose upon all Jer 1:14
L them arise, if they can save you, in Jer 2:28
L us lie down in our shame, and let our Jer 3:25
our shame, and **l** our dishonor cover us. Jer 3:25
and **l** us go into the fortified cities!' Jer 4:5
their hearts, '**L** us fear the LORD our God, Jer 5:24
against her; arise, and **l** us attack at noon! Jer 6:4
and **l** us attack by night and destroy her Jer 6:5
deeds, and I will **l** you dwell in this place. Jer 7:3
then I will **l** you dwell in this place, in the Jer 7:7
l us go into the fortified cities and perish Jer 8:14
L everyone beware of his neighbor, and Jer 9:4
l them make haste and raise a wailing Jer 9:18
and **l** your ear receive the word of his Jer 9:20
"**L** not the wise man boast in his Jer 9:23
l not the mighty man boast in his Jer 9:23
l not the rich man boast in his riches, Jer 9:23
but **l** him who boasts boast in this, that Jer 9:24
"**L** us destroy the tree with its fruit, Jer 11:19
l us cut him off from the land of the Jer 11:19
l me see your vengeance upon them, Jer 11:20
'**L** my eyes run down with tears night Jer 14:17
night and day, and **l** them not cease, Jer 14:17
them out of my sight, and **l** them go! Jer 15:1
is the word of the LORD? **L** it come!" Jer 17:15
L those be put to shame who persecute Jer 17:18
me, but **l** me not be put to shame; Jer 17:18
l them be dismayed, but let me not be Jer 17:18
be dismayed, but **l** me not be dismayed; Jer 17:18
and there I will **l** you hear my words." Jer 18:2
l us make plots against Jeremiah, Jer 18:18
Come, **l** us strike him with the tongue, Jer 18:18
and **l** us not pay attention to any of his Jer 18:18
l their wives become childless and Jer 18:21
L them be overthrown before you; deal Jer 18:23
L us denounce him!" say all my close Jer 20:10
l me see your vengeance upon them, Jer 20:12
my mother bore me, **l** it not be blessed! Jer 20:14
L that man be like the cities that the Jer 20:16
l him hear a cry in the morning and an Jer 20:16
L the prophet who has a dream tell the Jer 23:28
but **l** him who has my word speak my Jer 23:28
then **l** them intercede with the LORD of Jer 27:18
Do not **l** your prophets and your diviners Jer 29:8
'Arise, and **l** us go up to Zion, to the LORD Jer 31:6
and **l** us go to Jerusalem for fear of the Jer 35:11
and **l** no one know where you are." Jer 36:19
l my humble plea come before you and Jer 37:20
to the king, "**L** this man be put to death, Jer 38:4
which he **l** down to Jeremiah in the Jer 38:11
"**L** no one know of these words, Jer 38:24
of the guard had **l** him go from Ramah, Jer 40:1
of food and a present, and **l** him go. Jer 40:5
"Please **l** me go and strike down Jer 40:15
"**L** our plea for mercy come before you, Jer 42:2
mercy on you and **l** you remain in Jer 42:12
L the warriors go out: men of Cush and Jer 46:9
and **l** us go back to our own people and Jer 46:16
l us cut her off from being a nation!' Jer 48:2
alive; and **l** your widows trust in me." Jer 49:11
l us join ourselves to the LORD in an Jer 50:5
to destruction; **l** nothing be left of her. Jer 50:26
bulls; **l** them go down to the slaughter. Jer 50:27
Encamp around her; **l** no one escape. Jer 50:29
held them fast; they refuse to **l** them go. Jer 50:33
L not the archer bend his bow, and let Jer 51:3
and **l** him not stand up in his armor. Jer 51:3
of Babylon; **l** every one save his life! Jer 51:6
her, and **l** us go each to his own country, Jer 51:9
l us declare in Zion the work of the Jer 51:10
be upon Babylon," **l** the inhabitant of Jer 51:35
of Chaldea," **l** Jerusalem say. Jer 51:35
L every one save his life from the fierce Jer 51:45
L not your heart faint, and be not Jer 51:46
and **l** Jerusalem come into your mind: Jer 51:50
announced; now **l** them be as I am. Lam 1:21
"**L** all their evildoing come before you, Lam 1:22
l tears stream down like a torrent day Lam 2:18
L him sit alone in silence when it is Lam 3:28
l him put his mouth in the dust— Lam 3:29
l him give his cheek to the one who Lam 3:30
and **l** him be filled with insults. Lam 3:30
L us test and examine our ways, and Lam 3:40
L us lift up our hearts and hands to Lam 3:41
they stood still, they **l** down their wings. Ezk 1:24
they stood still, they **l** down their wings. Ezk 1:25
He who will hear, **l** him hear; and he Ezk 3:27
he who will refuse to hear, **l** him refuse, Ezk 3:27
toward it, and **l** it be in a state of siege, Ezk 4:3
L not the buyer rejoice, nor the seller Ezk 7:12
But I will **l** a few of them escape from Ezk 12:16
and I will **l** the souls whom you hunt Ezk 13:20
Should I indeed **l** myself be consulted Ezk 14:3
say, **L** a sword pass through the land, Ezk 14:17
L them know the abominations of Ezk 20:4
the thought, '**L** us be like the nations, Ezk 20:32
your hands and **l** the sword come Ezk 21:14
spices, and **l** the bones be burned up. Ezk 24:10
I will **l** people walk on you, even my Ezk 36:12
And I will not **l** you hear anymore the Ezk 36:15
the Lord GOD; **l** that be known to you. Ezk 36:32
This also I will **l** the house of Israel Ezk 36:37
and I will not **l** my holy name be Ezk 39:7
Now **l** them put away their whoring Ezk 43:9
shave their heads or **l** their locks grow Ezk 44:20
but they shall **l** the house of Israel have Ezk 45:8

l us be given vegetables to eat and water Dn 1:12
Then **l** our appearance and the Dn 1:13
"**L** the king tell his servants the dream, Dn 2:7
L the beasts flee from under it and the Dn 4:14
L him be wet with the dew of heaven. Dn 4:15
L his portion be with the beasts in the Dn 4:15
L his mind be changed from a man's, Dn 4:16
and **l** a beast's mind be given to him; Dn 4:16
and **l** seven periods of time pass over Dn 4:16
l not the dream or the interpretation Dn 4:19
and **l** him be wet with the dew of heaven, Dn 4:23
and **l** his portion be with the beasts of Dn 4:23
king, **l** my counsel be acceptable to you: Dn 4:27
L not your thoughts alarm you or your Dn 5:10
Now **l** Daniel be called, and he will Dn 5:12
the king, "**L** your gifts be for yourself, Dn 5:17
l your anger and your wrath turn away Dn 9:16
and said, "**L** my lord speak, Dn 10:19
Yet **l** no one contend, and let none Hos 4:4
let no one contend, and **l** none accuse, Hos 4:4
O Israel, **l** not Judah become guilty. Hos 4:15
"Come, **l** us return to the LORD; for he has Hos 6:1
L us know; let us press on to know the Hos 6:3
us know; **l** us press on to know the LORD; Hos 6:3
is wise, **l** him understand these things; Hos 14:9
is discerning, **l** him know them; Hos 14:9
of it, and **l** your children tell their children, Jl 1:3
L all the inhabitants of the land tremble, Jl 2:1
L the bridegroom leave his room, and the Jl 2:16
the vestibule and the altar **l** the priests, Jl 2:17
L all the men of war draw near; let them Jl 3:9
the men of war draw near; **l** them come up. Jl 3:9
spears; **l** the weak say, "I am a warrior." Jl 3:10
L the nations stir themselves up and Jl 3:12
But **l** justice roll down like waters, and Am 5:24
"Rise up! **L** us rise against her for battle!" Ob 1:1
said to one another, "Come, **l** us cast lots, Jon 1:7
LORD, **l** us not perish for this man's life, Jon 1:14
L neither man nor beast, herd nor flock, Jon 3:7
anything. **L** them not feed or drink water, Jon 3:7
but **l** man and beast be covered with Jon 3:8
and **l** them call out mightily to God. Jon 3:8
L everyone turn from his evil way and Jon 3:8
and **l** the Lord GOD be a witness against Mi 1:2
l us go up to the mountain of the LORD, Mi 4:2
against you, saying, "**L** her be defiled, Mi 4:11
defiled, and **l** our eyes gaze upon Zion." Mi 4:11
and **l** the hills hear your voice. Mi 6:1
l them graze in Bashan and Gilead as in Mi 7:14
l all the earth keep silence before him." Hab 2:20
O Zion; **l** not your hands grow weak. Zep 3:16
"**L** them put a clean turban on his head." Zec 3:5
and **l** none of you devise evil against Zec 7:10
"**L** your hands be strong, you who in Zec 8:9
Fear not, but **l** your hands be strong." Zec 8:13
'**L** us go at once to entreat the favor of Zec 8:21
robe of a Jew, saying, '**L** us go with you, Zec 8:23
be your shepherd. What is to die, **l** it die. Zec 11:9
is to be destroyed, **l** it be destroyed. Zec 11:9
And **l** those who are left devour the flesh Zec 11:9
L his arm be wholly withered, his Zec 11:17
and **l** none of you be faithless to the Mal 2:15
But Jesus answered him, "**L** it be so now, Mt 3:15
way, **l** your light shine before others, Mt 5:16
l him give her a certificate of divorce.' Mt 5:31
L what you say be simply 'Yes' or 'No'; Mt 5:37
tunic, **l** him have your cloak as well. Mt 5:40
do not **l** your left hand know what your Mt 6:3
'**L** me take the speck out of your eye,' Mt 7:4
l it be done for you as you have Mt 8:13
"Lord, **l** me first go and bury my father." Mt 8:21
is worthy, **l** your peace come upon it, Mt 10:13
not worthy, **l** your peace return to you. Mt 10:13
He who has ears to hear, **l** him hear. Mt 11:15
He who has ears, **l** him hear." Mt 13:9
L both grow together until the harvest, Mt 13:30
Father. He who has ears, **l** him hear. Mt 13:43
L them alone; they are blind guides. Mt 15:14
l him deny himself and take up his Mt 16:24
l him be to you as a Gentile and a tax Mt 18:17
has joined together, **l** not man separate." Mt 19:6
L the one who is able to receive this Mt 19:12
"**L** the little children come to me and Mt 19:14
to him, "Lord, **l** our eyes be opened." Mt 20:33
l us kill him and have his inheritance.' Mt 21:38
miserable death and **l** out the vineyard Mt 21:41
the holy place (**l** the reader Mt 24:15
then **l** those who are in Judea flee to the Mt 24:16
L the one who is on the housetop not go Mt 24:17
and **l** the one who is in the field not Mt 24:18
and would not have **l** his house be Mt 24:43
it be possible, **l** this cup pass from me; Mt 26:39
Rise, **l** us be going; see, my betrayer is Mt 26:46
They all said, "**L** him be crucified!" Mt 27:22
all the more, "**L** him be crucified!" Mt 27:23
l him come down now from the cross, Mt 27:42
l God deliver him now, if he desires Mt 27:43
l us see whether Elijah will come to Mt 27:49
to them, "**L** us go on to the next towns, Mk 1:38
they **l** down the bed on which the Mk 2:4
"He who has ears to hear, **l** him hear." Mk 4:9
If anyone has ears to hear, **l** him hear." Mk 4:23
them, "**L** us go across to the other side." Mk 4:35
"Send us to the pigs; **l** us enter them." Mk 5:12
said to her, "**L** the children be fed first, Mk 7:27
l him deny himself and take up his Mk 8:34
L us make three tents, one for you and Mk 9:5
joined together, **l** not man separate." Mk 10:9
to them, "**L** the children come to me; Mk 10:14
him, "Rabbi, **l** me recover my sight." Mk 10:51
what Jesus had said, and they **l** them go. Mk 11:6
Come, **l** us kill him, and the Mk 12:7
me a denarius and **l** me look at it." Mk 12:15
not to be (**l** the reader understand), Mk 13:14
then **l** those who are in Judea flee to the Mk 13:14
L the one who is on the housetop not Mk 13:15
and **l** the one who is in the field not Mk 13:16
Rise, **l** us be going; see, my betrayer is Mk 14:42
me. But **l** the Scriptures be fulfilled." Mk 14:49
L the Christ, the King of Israel, come Mk 15:32
l us see whether Elijah will come to Mk 15:36
l it be to me according to your word." Lk 1:38
"**L** us go over to Bethlehem and see this Lk 2:15
out into the deep and **l** down your nets for Lk 5:4
But at your word I will **l** down the nets." Lk 5:5
up on the roof and **l** him down with his Lk 5:19
l me take out the speck that is in your Lk 6:42
say the word, and **l** my servant be healed. Lk 7:7
"He who has ears to hear, **l** him hear." Lk 8:8
"**L** us go across to the other side of the Lk 8:22
they begged him to **l** them enter these. Lk 8:32
l him deny himself and take up his Lk 9:23
L us make three tents, one for you and Lk 9:33
"**L** these words sink into your ears: The Lk 9:44
"Lord, **l** me first go and bury my father." Lk 9:59
but **l** me first say farewell to those at my Lk 9:61
him, 'Sir, **l** it alone this year also, Lk 13:8
He who has ears to hear, **l** him hear." Lk 14:35
and kill it, and **l** us eat and celebrate. Lk 15:23
and the Prophets; **l** them hear them.' Lk 16:29
day, **l** the one who is on the housetop, Lk 17:31
and likewise **l** the one who is in the Lk 17:31
saying, "**L** the children come to me, Lk 18:16
He said, "Lord, **l** me recover my sight." Lk 18:41
planted a vineyard and **l** it out to tenants Lk 20:9
L us kill him, so that the inheritance Lk 20:14
Then **l** those who are in Judea flee to Lk 21:21
and **l** those who are inside the city Lk 21:21
and **l** not those who are out in the Lk 21:21
l the greatest among you become as the Lk 22:26
"But now **l** the one who has a Lk 22:36
And **l** the one who has no sword sell his Lk 22:36
l him save himself, if he is the Christ of Lk 23:35
thirsts, **l** him come to me and drink. Jn 7:37
"**L** him who is without sin among you be Jn 8:7
to the disciples, "**L** us go to Judea again." Jn 11:7
you may believe. But **l** us go to him." Jn 11:15
said to his fellow disciples, "**L** us also go, Jn 11:16
to them, "Unbind him, and **l** him go." Jn 11:44
If we **l** him go on like this, everyone will Jn 11:48
where he was, he should **l** them know, Jn 11:57
"**L** not your hearts be troubled. Believe in Jn 14:1
L not your hearts be troubled, neither Jn 14:27
be troubled, neither **l** them be afraid. Jn 14:27
I love the Father. Rise, **l** us go from here. Jn 14:31
he. So, if you seek me, **l** these men go." Jn 18:8
said to one another, "**L** us not tear it, Jn 19:24
and **l** there be no one to dwell in it'; Acts 1:20
in it'; and "'**L** another take his office.' Acts 1:20
in Jerusalem, **l** this be known to you, Acts 2:14
or **l** your Holy One see corruption. Acts 2:27
L all the house of Israel therefore know Acts 2:36
l it be known to all of you and to all Acts 4:10
l us warn them to speak no more to Acts 4:17
threatened them, they **l** them go, Acts 4:21
from these men and **l** them alone, Acts 5:38
in the name of Jesus, and **l** them go. Acts 5:40
him by night and **l** him down through Acts 9:25
being **l** down by its four corners Acts 10:11
being **l** down from heaven by its four Acts 11:5
"'You will not **l** your Holy One see Acts 13:35
L it be known to you therefore, Acts 13:38
"**L** us return and visit the brothers in Acts 15:36
the police, saying, "**L** those men go." Acts 16:35
magistrates have sent to **l** you go. Acts 16:36
L them come themselves and take us Acts 16:37
from Jason and the rest, they **l** them go. Acts 17:9
crowd, the disciples would not **l** him. Acts 19:30
L them bring charges against one Acts 19:38
said, "**L** the will of the Lord be done." Acts 21:14
Or else **l** these men themselves say Acts 24:20
"**l** the men of authority among you go Acts 25:5
l them bring charges against him." Acts 25:5
they **l** down four anchors from the Acts 27:29
the ropes of the ship's boat and **l** it go. Acts 27:32
Therefore **l** it be known to you that Acts 28:28
L God be true though every one were a Rom 3:4
L not sin therefore reign in your Rom 6:12
"**L** their table become a snare and a Rom 11:9
l their eyes be darkened so that they Rom 11:10
to the grace given to us, **l** us use them: Rom 12:6
L love be genuine. Abhor what is evil; Rom 12:9
L every person be subject to the Rom 13:1
So then **l** us cast off the works of Rom 13:12
L us walk properly as in the daytime, Rom 13:13
L not the one who eats despise the one Rom 14:3
and **l** not the one who abstains pass Rom 14:3
Therefore **l** us not pass judgment on Rom 14:13
So do not **l** what you regard as good Rom 14:16
So then **l** us pursue what makes for Rom 14:19
L each of us please his neighbor for Rom 15:2
and **l** all the peoples extol him." Rom 15:11
as it is written, "**L** the one who boasts, 1 Cor 1:31
L each one take care how he builds 1 Cor 3:10
L no one deceive himself. If anyone 1 Cor 3:18
l him become a fool that he may 1 Cor 3:18
So **l** no one boast in men. For all 1 Cor 3:21
L him who has done this be removed 1 Cor 5:2
L us therefore celebrate the festival, 1 Cor 5:8
partner separates, **l** it be so. 1 Cor 7:15
Only **l** each person lead the life that 1 Cor 7:17
L him not seek to remove the marks 1 Cor 7:18
L him not seek circumcision. 1 Cor 7:18
called, there **l** him remain with God. 1 Cor 7:24
l those who have wives live as though 1 Cor 7:29
it has to be, **l** him do as he wishes: 1 Cor 7:36
he wishes: **l** them marry—it is no sin. 1 Cor 7:36
Therefore **l** anyone who thinks that 1 Cor 10:12
and he will not **l** you be tempted 1 Cor 10:13
L no one seek his own good, but the 1 Cor 10:24
shave her head, **l** her cover her head. 1 Cor 11:6
L a person examine himself, then, 1 Cor 11:28
l him eat at home—so that when 1 Cor 11:34
L all things be done for building up. 1 Cor 14:26
l there be only two or at most three, 1 Cor 14:27
in turn, and **l** someone interpret. 1 Cor 14:27
l each of them keep silent in church 1 Cor 14:28
L two or three prophets speak, and 1 Cor 14:29
and **l** the others weigh what is said. 1 Cor 14:29
sitting there, **l** the first be silent. 1 Cor 14:30
l them ask their husbands at home. 1 Cor 14:35
are not raised, "**L** us eat and drink, 1 Cor 15:32
So **l** no one despise him. Help him 1 Cor 16:11
L all that you do be done in love. 1 Cor 16:14
love for the Lord, **l** him be accursed. 1 Cor 16:22
you pain but to **l** you know the 2 Cor 2:4
"**L** light shine out of darkness," has 2 Cor 4:6
l us cleanse ourselves from every 2 Cor 7:1
l him remind himself that just as he 2 Cor 10:7
L such a person understand that 2 Cor 10:11
"**L** the one who boasts, boast in the 2 Cor 10:17
I repeat, **l** no one think me foolish. 2 Cor 11:16
but I was **l** down in a basket 2 Cor 11:33
we preached to you, **l** him be accursed. Gal 1:8
the one you received, **l** him be accursed. Gal 1:9
L me ask you only this: Did you receive Gal 3:2
the Spirit, **l** us also walk by the Spirit. Gal 5:25
L us not become conceited, provoking Gal 5:26
But **l** each one test his own work, and Gal 6:4
And **l** us not grow weary of doing good, Gal 6:9
opportunity, **l** us do good to everyone, Gal 6:10
From now on **l** no one cause me Gal 6:17
l each one of you speak the truth with Eph 4:25
do not **l** the sun go down on your Eph 4:26
L the thief no longer steal, but rather Eph 4:28
no longer steal, but rather **l** him labor, Eph 4:28
L no corrupting talk come out of your Eph 4:29
L all bitterness and wrath and anger Eph 4:31
L there be no filthiness nor foolish talk Eph 5:4
but instead **l** there be thanksgiving. Eph 5:4
L no one deceive you with empty words, Eph 5:6
l each one of you love his wife as Eph 5:33
and **l** the wife see that she respects her Eph 5:33
Only **l** your manner of life be worthy Phil 1:27
L each of you look not only to his own Phil 2:4
L those of us who are mature think Phil 3:15
Only **l** us hold true to what we have Phil 3:16
L your reasonableness be known to Phil 4:5
with thanksgiving **l** your requests Phil 4:6
Therefore **l** no one pass judgment on Col 2:16
L no one disqualify you, insisting on Col 2:18
And **l** the peace of Christ rule in your Col 3:15
L the word of Christ dwell in you Col 3:16
L your speech always be gracious, Col 4:6
So then **l** us not sleep, as others do, 1 Thes 5:6

do, but **l** us keep awake and be sober. 1 Thes 5:6
we belong to the day, **l** us be sober, 1 Thes 5:8
L no one deceive you in any way. For 2 Thes 2:3
is not willing to work, **l** him not eat. 2 Thes 3:10
L a woman learn quietly with all 1 Tm 2:11
And **l** them also be tested first; then 1 Tm 3:10
then **l** them serve as deacons if they 1 Tm 3:10
L deacons each be the husband of 1 Tm 3:12
L no one despise you for your youth, 1 Tm 4:12
l them first learn to show godliness to 1 Tm 5:4
L a widow be enrolled if she is not less 1 Tm 5:9
who are widows, **l** her care for them. 1 Tm 5:16
L the church not be burdened, so 1 Tm 5:16
L the elders who rule well be 1 Tm 5:17
L all who are under a yoke as slaves 1 Tm 6:1
"**L** everyone who names the name of 2 Tm 2:19
all authority. **L** no one disregard you. Ti 2:15
And **l** our people learn to devote Ti 3:14
says, "**L** all God's angels worship him." Heb 1:6
l us fear lest any of you should seem to Heb 4:1
L us therefore strive to enter that rest, Heb 4:11
of God, **l** us hold fast our confession. Heb 4:14
L us then with confidence draw near to Heb 4:16
Therefore **l** us leave the elementary Heb 6:1
l us draw near with a true heart in full Heb 10:22
L us hold fast the confession of our Heb 10:23
And **l** us consider how to stir up one Heb 10:24
l us also lay aside every weight, Heb 12:1
and **l** us run with endurance the race Heb 12:1
Therefore **l** us be grateful for Heb 12:28
and thus **l** us offer to God acceptable Heb 12:28
L brotherly love continue. Heb 13:1
L marriage be held in honor among Heb 13:4
and **l** the marriage bed be undefiled, Heb 13:4
Therefore **l** us go to him outside the Heb 13:13
Through him then **l** us continually Heb 13:15
L them do this with joy and not with Heb 13:17
And **l** steadfastness have its full effect, Jas 1:4
any of you lacks wisdom, **l** him ask God, Jas 1:5
But **l** him ask in faith, with no doubting, Jas 1:6
L the lowly brother boast in his Jas 1:9
L no one say when he is tempted, "I am Jas 1:13
l every person be quick to hear, slow to Jas 1:19
By his good conduct **l** him show his Jas 3:13
L your laughter be turned to mourning Jas 4:9
but **l** your "yes" be yes and your "no" be Jas 5:12
among you suffering? **L** him pray. Jas 5:13
Is anyone cheerful? **L** him sing praise. Jas 5:13
L him call for the elders of the church, Jas 5:14
the church, and **l** them pray over him, Jas 5:14
l him know that whoever brings back a Jas 5:20
Do not **l** your adorning be external—the 1 Pt 3:3
but **l** your adorning be the hidden 1 Pt 3:4
l him keep his tongue from evil and his 1 Pt 3:10
l him turn away from evil and do good; 1 Pt 3:11
do good; **l** him seek peace and pursue it. 1 Pt 3:11
But **l** none of you suffer as a murderer 1 Pt 4:15
as a Christian, **l** him not be ashamed, 1 Pt 4:16
but **l** him glorify God in that name. 1 Pt 4:16
Therefore **l** those who suffer according 1 Pt 4:19
L what you heard from the beginning 1 Jn 2:24
Little children, **l** no one deceive you. 1 Jn 3:7
l us not love in word or talk but in deed 1 Jn 3:18
Beloved, **l** us love one another, for love is 1 Jn 4:7
l him hear what the Spirit says to the Rv 2:7
l him hear what the Spirit says to the Rv 2:11
l him hear what the Spirit says to the Rv 2:17
l him hear what the Spirit says to the Rv 2:29
l him hear what the Spirit says to the Rv 3:6
l him hear what the Spirit says to the Rv 3:13
l him hear what the Spirit says to the Rv 3:22
bodies and refuse to **l** them be placed in Rv 11:9
If anyone has an ear, **l** him hear: Rv 13:9
l the one who has understanding Rv 13:18
L us rejoice and exult and give him the Rv 19:7
L the evildoer still do evil, and the filthy Rv 22:11
"Come." And **l** the one who hears say, Rv 22:17
"Come." And **l** the one who is thirsty Rv 22:17
l the one who desires take the water of Rv 22:17

LETHECH (1)
of silver and a homer and a **l** of barley. Hos 3:2

LETS (8)
let you go from here. When he **l** you go, Ex 11:1
or **l** his beast loose and it feeds in Ex 22:5
And he who **l** the goat go to Azazel shall Lv 16:26
Under the whole heaven he **l** it go, and Jb 37:3
to the earth and **l** them be warmed on Jb 39:14
And there he **l** the hungry dwell, and Ps 107:36
or an oak and **l** it grow strong among Is 44:14
Egypt, 'Noisy one who **l** the hour go by.' Jer 46:17

LETTER (53)
morning David wrote a **l** to Joab and 2 Sm 11:14
In the **l** he wrote, "Set Uriah in the 2 Sm 11:15
and I will send a **l** to the king of Israel." 2 Kgs 5:5
And he brought the **l** to the king of 2 Kgs 5:6
which read, "When this **l** reaches you, 2 Kgs 5:6
And when the king of Israel read the **l**, 2 Kgs 5:7
then, as soon as this **l** comes to you, 2 Kgs 10:2
Then he wrote to them a second **l**, 2 Kgs 10:6
And as soon as the **l** came to them, 2 Kgs 10:7
Hezekiah received the **l** from the 2 Kgs 19:14
of Tyre answered in a **l** that he sent to 2 Chr 2:11
And a **l** came to him from Elijah 2 Chr 21:12
The **l** was written in Aramaic and Ezr 4:7
the scribe wrote a **l** against Jerusalem to Ezr 4:8
(This is a copy of the **l** that they sent.) Ezr 4:11
the **l** that you sent to us has been Ezr 4:18
of King Artaxerxes' **l** was read before Ezr 4:23
answer be returned by **l** concerning it. Ezr 5:5
a copy of the **l** that Tattenai the governor Ezr 5:6
a copy of the **l** that King Artaxerxes Ezr 7:11
and a **l** to Asaph, the keeper of the king's Neh 2:8
to me with an open **l** in his hand. Neh 6:5
because of all that was written in this **l**, Est 9:26
confirming this second **l** about Purim. Est 9:29
Hezekiah received the **l** from the hand of Is 37:14
the words of the **l** that Jeremiah the Jer 29:1
The **l** was sent by the hand of Elasah the Jer 29:3
the priest read this **l** in the hearing of Jer 29:29
with the following **l**: "The brothers, Acts 15:23
together, they delivered the **l**. Acts 15:30
we have sent a **l** with our judgment Acts 21:25
And he wrote a **l** to this effect: Acts 23:25
and delivered the **l** to the governor, Acts 23:33
On reading the **l**, he asked what Acts 23:34
of the heart, by the Spirit, not by the **l**. Rom 2:29
I Tertius, who wrote this **l**, greet you Rom 16:22
to you in my **l** not to associate with 1 Cor 5:9
whom you accredit by **l** to carry your 1 Cor 16:3
are our **l** of recommendation, 2 Cor 3:2
that you are a **l** from Christ delivered 2 Cor 3:3
covenant, not of the **l** but of the Spirit. 2 Cor 3:6
For the **l** kills, but the Spirit gives life. 2 Cor 3:6
even if I made you grieve with my **l**, 2 Cor 7:8
it, for I see that that **l** grieved you, 2 Cor 7:8
that what we say by **l** when absent, 2 Cor 10:11
And when this **l** has been read among Col 4:16
that you also read the **l** from Laodicea. Col 4:16
the Lord to have this **l** read to all the 1 Thes 5:27
word, or a **l** seeming to be from us, 2 Thes 2:2
by our spoken word or by our **l**. 2 Thes 2:15
does not obey what we say in this **l**, 2 Thes 3:14
of genuineness in every **l** of mine; 2 Thes 3:17
is now the second **l** that I am writing 2 Pt 3:1

LETTERS (31)
So she wrote **l** in Ahab's name and 1 Kgs 21:8
and she sent the **l** to the elders and the 1 Kgs 21:8
And she wrote in the **l**, "Proclaim a 1 Kgs 21:9
was written in the **l** that she had sent 1 Kgs 21:11
So Jehu wrote **l** and sent them to 2 Kgs 10:1
sent envoys with **l** and a present to 2 Kgs 20:12
and wrote **l** also to Ephraim and 2 Chr 30:1
Israel and Judah with **l** from the king 2 Chr 30:6
And he wrote **l** to cast contempt on 2 Chr 32:17
let **l** be given me to the governors of the Neh 2:7
the River and gave them the king's **l**. Neh 2:9
nobles of Judah sent many **l** to Tobiah, Neh 6:17
Tobiah, and Tobiah's **l** came to them. Neh 6:17
And Tobiah sent **l** to make me afraid. Neh 6:19
He sent **l** to all the royal provinces, to Est 1:22
L were sent by couriers to all the king's Est 3:13
written to revoke the **l** devised by Haman Est 8:5
Then he sent the **l** by mounted couriers Est 8:10
these things and sent **l** to all the Jews Est 9:20
L were sent to all the Jews, to the 127 Est 9:30
sent envoys with **l** and a present to Is 39:1
You have sent **l** in your name to all the Jer 29:25
and asked him for **l** to the synagogues Acts 9:2
From them I received **l** to the brothers, Acts 22:5
have received no **l** from Judea about Acts 28:21
some do, **l** of recommendation to you, 2 Cor 3:1
ministry of death, carved in **l** on stone, 2 Cor 3:7
to be frightening you with my **l**. 2 Cor 10:9
say, "His **l** are weighty and strong, 2 Cor 10:10
See with what large **l** I am writing to Gal 6:11
he does in all his **l** when he speaks in 2 Pt 3:16

LETTING (6)
cheat again by not **l** the people go to Ex 8:29
not **l** them go with him to battle, 2 Chr 25:13
beginning of strife is like **l** out water, Prv 17:14
of the guard, **l** Jeremiah down by ropes. Jer 38:6
now you are **l** your servant depart in Lk 2:29
l the horsemen go on with him. Acts 23:32

LETUSHIM (1)
were Asshurim, **L**, and Leummim. Gn 25:3

LEUKODERMA (1)
it is **l** that has broken out in the skin; Lv 13:39

LEUMMIM (1)
were Asshurim, Letushim, and **L**. Gn 25:3

LEVEL (12)
My foot stands on **l** ground; in the great Ps 26:12
and lead me on a **l** path because of my Ps 27:11
your good Spirit lead me on **l** ground! Ps 143:10
the path of the upright is a **l** highway. Prv 15:19
The path of the righteous is **l**; you make Is 26:7
level; you make **l** the way of the righteous. Is 26:7
the uneven ground shall become **l**, and Is 40:4
light, the rough places into **l** ground. Is 42:16
will go before you and **l** the exalted places, Is 45:2
and I will make all his ways **l**; Is 45:13
the rough places shall become **l** ways, Lk 3:5
down with them and stood on a **l** place, Lk 6:17

LEVELED (2)
When he has **l** its surface, does he not Is 28:25
of Babylon shall be **l** to the ground, Jer 51:58

LEVI (70)
Therefore his name was called **L**. Gn 29:34
two of the sons of Jacob, Simeon and **L**, Gn 34:25
Then Jacob said to Simeon and **L**, Gn 34:30
(Jacob's firstborn), Simeon, **L**, Judah, Gn 35:23
The sons of **L**: Gershon, Kohath, and Gn 46:11
"Simeon and **L** are brothers; weapons of Gn 49:5
Reuben, Simeon, **L**, and Judah, Ex 1:2
from the house of **L** went and took as Ex 2:1
of the sons of **L** according to their Ex 6:16
the years of the life of **L** being 137 years. Ex 6:16
all the sons of **L** gathered around him. Ex 32:26
And the sons of **L** did according to the Ex 32:28
"Only the tribe of **L** you shall not list, Nm 1:49
"Bring the tribe of **L** near, and set them Nm 3:6
"List the sons of **L**, by fathers' houses Nm 3:15
these were the sons of **L** by their names: Nm 3:17
of Kohath from among the sons of **L**, Nm 4:2
son of Izhar, son of Kohath, son of **L**, Nm 16:1
one. You have gone too far, sons of **L**!" Nm 16:7
to Korah, "Hear now, you sons of **L**: Nm 16:8
your brothers the sons of **L** with you? Nm 16:10
write Aaron's name on the staff of **L**. Nm 17:3
for the house of **L** had sprouted and put Nm 17:8
bring your brothers also, the tribe of **L**, Nm 18:2
These are the clans of **L**: the clan of Nm 26:58
wife was Jochebed the daughter of **L**, Nm 26:59
of Levi, who was born to **L** in Egypt. Nm 26:59
set apart the tribe of **L** to carry the ark of Dt 10:8
Therefore **L** has no portion or Dt 10:9
"The Levitical priests, all the tribe of **L**, Dt 18:1
Then the priests, the sons of **L**, shall Dt 21:5
Simeon, **L**, Judah, Issachar, Joseph, and Dt 27:12
and gave it to the priests, the sons of **L**, Dt 31:9
And of **L** he said, "Give to Levi your Dt 33:8
Levi he said, "Give to **L** your Thummim, Dt 33:8
To the tribe of **L** alone Moses gave no Jos 13:14
to the tribe of **L** Moses gave no Jos 13:33
who belonged to the people of **L**; Jos 21:10
Reuben, Simeon, **L**, Judah, Issachar, 1 Chr 2:1
The sons of **L**: Gershon, Kohath, and 1 Chr 6:1
The sons of **L**: Gershom, Kohath, and 1 Chr 6:16
son of Izhar, son of Kohath, son of **L**, 1 Chr 6:38
of Jahath, son of Gershom, son of **L**. 1 Chr 6:43
son of Mushi, son of Merari, son of **L**. 1 Chr 6:47
did not include **L** and Benjamin in 1 Chr 21:6
corresponding to the sons of **L**: 1 Chr 23:6
were named among the tribe of **L**. 1 Chr 23:14
were the sons of **L** by their fathers' 1 Chr 23:24
the sons of **L** were numbered from 1 Chr 23:27
And of the rest of the sons of **L**: of 1 Chr 24:20
for **L**, Hashabiah the son of Kemuel; 1 Chr 27:17
I found there none of the sons of **L**. Ezr 8:15
of the sons of Mahli the son of **L**, Ezr 8:18
and the sons of **L** shall bring the Neh 10:39
As for the sons of **L**, their heads of Neh 12:23
O house of **L**, bless the LORD! You who Ps 135:20
among the sons of **L** may come near Ezk 40:46
the gate of Judah, and the gate of **L**, Ezk 48:31
the family of the house of **L** by itself, Zec 12:13
that my covenant with **L** may stand, Mal 2:4
You have corrupted the covenant of **L**, Mal 2:8
purify the sons of **L** and refine them like Mal 3:3
he saw **L** the son of Alphaeus sitting at Mk 2:14
the son of Matthat, the son of **L**, the son Lk 3:24
of Jorim, the son of Matthat, the son of **L**, Lk 3:29
out and saw a tax collector named **L**, Lk 5:27
And **L** made him a great feast in his Lk 5:29
those descendants of **L** who receive the Heb 7:5
One might even say that **L** himself, who Heb 7:9
of Simeon, 12,000 from the tribe of **L**, Rv 7:7

LEVIATHAN (6)
curse the day, who are ready to rouse up **L**. Jb 3:8
"Can you draw out **L** with a fishhook or Jb 41:1
You crushed the heads of **L**; you gave Ps 74:14

There go the ships, and **L**, which you Ps 104:26
sword will punish **L** the fleeing serpent, Is 27:1
the fleeing serpent, **L** the twisting serpent, Is 27:1

LEVIED (1)
and Jerusalem the tax **l** by Moses, 2 Chr 24:6

LEVITE (30)
went and took as his wife a **L** woman. Ex 2:1
"Is there not Aaron, your brother, the **L**? Ex 4:14
and the **L** that is within your towns, Dt 12:12
and the **L** who is within your towns. Dt 12:18
you do not neglect the **L** as long as you Dt 12:19
shall not neglect the **L** who is within Dt 14:27
And the **L**, because he has no portion or Dt 14:29
the **L** who is within your towns, Dt 16:11
servant and your female servant, the **L**, Dt 16:14
"And if a **L** comes from any of your Dt 18:6
you and to your house, you, and the **L**, Dt 26:11
is the year of tithing, giving it to the **L**, Dt 26:12
and moreover, I have given it to the **L**, Dt 26:13
of the family of Judah, who was a **L**, Jgs 17:7
to him, "I am a **L** of Bethlehem in Judah, Jgs 17:9
and your living." And the **L** went in. Jgs 17:10
And the **L** was content to dwell with the Jgs 17:11
And Micah ordained the **L**, and the Jgs 17:12
me, because I have a **L** as priest." Jgs 17:13
they recognized the voice of the young **L**. Jgs 18:3
and came to the house of the young **L**, Jgs 18:15
a certain **L** was sojourning in the Jgs 19:1
And the **L**, the husband of the woman Jgs 20:4
Shemaiah, the son of Nethanel, a **L**, 1 Chr 24:6
Mattaniah, a **L** of the sons of Asaph, 2 Chr 20:14
of them was Conaniah the **L**, 2 Chr 31:12
And Kore the son of Imnah the **L**, 2 Chr 31:14
and Shabbethai the **L** supported them. Ezr 10:15
So likewise a **L**, when he came to the Lk 10:32
means son of encouragement), a **L**, Acts 4:36

LEVITES (251)
the clans of the **L** according to their Ex 6:19
fathers' houses of the **L** by their clans. Ex 6:25
responsibility of the **L** under the Ex 38:21
As for the cities of the **L**, the Levites Lv 25:32
the **L** may redeem at any time the Lv 25:32
And if one of the **L** exercises his right of Lv 25:33
the cities of the **L** are their possession Lv 25:33
But the **L** were not listed along with Nm 1:47
But appoint the **L** over the tabernacle Nm 1:50
is to set out, the **L** shall take it down, Nm 1:51
is to be pitched, the **L** shall set it up. Nm 1:51
But the **L** shall camp around the Nm 1:53
And the **L** shall keep guard over the Nm 1:53
with the camp of the **L** in the midst of Nm 2:17
But the **L** were not listed among the Nm 2:33
you shall give the **L** to Aaron and his Nm 3:9
I have taken the **L** from among the Nm 3:12
people of Israel. The **L** shall be mine, Nm 3:12
These are the clans of the **L**, by their Nm 3:20
was to be chief over the chiefs of the **L**, Nm 3:32
All those listed among the **L**, whom Nm 3:39
And you shall take the **L** for me—I am Nm 3:41
and the cattle of the **L** instead of all the Nm 3:41
"Take the **L** instead of all the firstborn Nm 3:45
the cattle of the **L** instead of their cattle. Nm 3:45
The **L** shall be mine: I am the LORD. Nm 3:45
and above the number of the male **L**, Nm 3:46
and above those redeemed by the **L**. Nm 3:49
be destroyed from among the **L**, Nm 4:18
All those who were listed of the **L**, Nm 4:46
tent of meeting, and give them to the **L**, Nm 7:5
and the oxen and gave them to the **L**. Nm 7:6
"Take the **L** from among the people of Nm 8:6
you shall bring the **L** before the tent of Nm 8:9
When you bring the **L** before the LORD, Nm 8:10
of Israel shall lay their hands on the **L**, Nm 8:10
Aaron shall offer the **L** before the LORD Nm 8:11
Then the **L** shall lay their hands on the Nm 8:12
the LORD to make atonement for the **L**. Nm 8:12
you shall set the **L** before Aaron and Nm 8:13
shall separate the **L** from among the Nm 8:14
of Israel, and the **L** shall be mine. Nm 8:14
And after that the **L** shall go in to serve Nm 8:15
and I have taken the **L** instead of all the Nm 8:18
And I have given the **L** as a gift to Nm 8:19
of the people of Israel to the **L**. Nm 8:20
commanded Moses concerning the **L**, Nm 8:20
And the **L** purified themselves from sin Nm 8:21
And after that the **L** went in to do their Nm 8:22
commanded Moses concerning the **L**, Nm 8:22
"This applies to the **L**: from twenty-five Nm 8:24
you do to the **L** in assigning their Nm 8:26
your brothers the **L** from among the Nm 18:6
"To the **L** I have given every tithe in Nm 18:21
But the **L** shall do the service of the Nm 18:23
have given to the **L** for an inheritance. Nm 18:24
you shall speak and say to the **L**, Nm 18:26
be counted to the **L** as produce of the Nm 18:30
the list of the **L** according to their Nm 26:57
give them to the **L** who keep guard Nm 31:30
gave them to the **L** who kept guard Nm 31:47
to give to the **L** some of the inheritance Nm 35:2
give to the **L** pasturelands around the Nm 35:2
the cities, which you shall give to the **L**, Nm 35:4
that you give to the **L** shall be the six Nm 35:6
you give to the **L** shall be forty-eight, Nm 35:7
inherits, shall give of its cities to the **L**." Nm 35:8
like all his fellow **L** who stand to Dt 18:7
And the **L** shall declare to all the men of Dt 27:14
Moses commanded the **L** who carried Dt 31:25
but to the **L** he gave no inheritance Jos 14:3
portion was given to the **L** in the land, Jos 14:4
The **L** have no portion among you, for Jos 18:7
fathers' houses of the **L** came to Eleazar Jos 21:1
Israel gave to the **L** the following cities Jos 21:3
So those **L** who were descendants of Jos 21:4
the people of Israel gave by lot to the **L**, Jos 21:8
to the Kohathite clans of the **L**, Jos 21:20
Gershonites, one of the clans of the **L**, Jos 21:27
And to the rest of the **L**, the Merarite Jos 21:34
is, the remainder of the clans of the **L**, Jos 21:40
The cities of the **L** in the midst of the Jos 21:41
And the **L** took down the ark of the 1 Sm 6:15
Zadok came also with all the **L**, 2 Sm 15:24
the priests and the **L** brought them up. 1 Kgs 8:4
all the people, who were not of the **L**. 1 Kgs 12:31
the clans of the **L** according to their 1 Chr 6:19
their brothers the **L** were appointed 1 Chr 6:48
of Israel gave the **L** the cities with 1 Chr 6:64
cities were Israel, the priests, the **L**, 1 Chr 9:2
Of the **L**: Shemaiah the son of 1 Chr 9:14
the gatekeepers of the camps of the **L**. 1 Chr 9:18
four chief gatekeepers, who were **L**, 1 Chr 9:26
and Mattithiah, one of the **L**, the 1 Chr 9:31
the heads of fathers' houses of the **L**, 1 Chr 9:33
were heads of fathers' houses of the **L**, 1 Chr 9:34
Of the **L** 4,600. 1 Chr 12:26
to the priests and **L** in the cities that 1 Chr 13:2
no one but the **L** may carry the ark 1 Chr 15:2
together the sons of Aaron and the **L**: 1 Chr 15:4
and Abiathar, and the **L** Uriel, 1 Chr 15:11
heads of the fathers' houses of the **L**. 1 Chr 15:12
and the **L** consecrated themselves 1 Chr 15:14
And the **L** carried the ark of God on 1 Chr 15:15
the chiefs of the **L** to appoint their 1 Chr 15:16
So the **L** appointed Heman the son 1 Chr 15:17
leader of the **L** in music, 1 Chr 15:22
God helped the **L** who were carrying 1 Chr 15:26
were all the **L** who were carrying 1 Chr 15:27
some of the **L** as ministers before 1 Chr 16:4
of Israel and the priests and the **L**. 1 Chr 23:2
The **L**, thirty years old and upward, 1 Chr 23:3
And so the **L** no longer need to carry 1 Chr 23:26
houses of the priests and of the **L**, 1 Chr 24:6
the sons of the **L** according to their 1 Chr 24:30
houses of the priests and of the **L**. 1 Chr 24:31
And of the **L**, Ahijah had charge of 1 Chr 26:20
divisions of the priests and of the **L**, 1 Chr 28:13
the priests and the **L** for all the 1 Chr 28:21
Israel came, and the **L** took up the ark. 2 Chr 5:4
priests stood at their posts; the **L** also, 2 Chr 7:6
and the **L** for their offices of praise 2 Chr 8:14
the priests and **L** concerning any 2 Chr 8:15
the priests and the **L** who were in all 2 Chr 11:13
For the **L** left their common lands 2 Chr 11:14
LORD, the sons of Aaron, and the **L**, 2 Chr 13:9
of Aaron, and **L** for their service. 2 Chr 13:10
and with them the **L**, Shemaiah, 2 Chr 17:8
and with these **L**, the priests 2 Chr 17:8
appointed certain **L** and priests 2 Chr 19:8
and the **L** will serve you as officers. 2 Chr 19:11
And the **L**, of the Kohathites and the 2 Chr 20:19
Judah and gathered the **L** from all the 2 Chr 23:2
of you priests and **L** who come off 2 Chr 23:4
except the priests and ministering **L**. 2 Chr 23:6
The **L** shall surround the king, each 2 Chr 23:7
The **L** and all Judah did according to 2 Chr 23:8
priests and the **L** whom David had 2 Chr 23:18
the priests and the **L** and said to 2 Chr 24:5
act quickly." But the **L** did not act 2 Chr 24:5
you not required the **L** to bring in 2 Chr 24:6
to the king's officers by the **L**, 2 Chr 24:11
priests and the **L** and assembled 2 Chr 29:4
me, **L**! Now consecrate yourselves, 2 Chr 29:5
Then the **L** arose, Mahath the son of 2 Chr 29:12
And the **L** took it and carried it out 2 Chr 29:16
And he stationed the **L** in the house 2 Chr 29:25
The **L** stood with the instruments of 2 Chr 29:26
officials commanded the **L** to sing 2 Chr 29:30
their brothers the **L** helped them, 2 Chr 29:34
—for the **L** were more upright 2 Chr 29:34
the priests and the **L** were ashamed, 2 Chr 30:15
received from the hand of the **L**. 2 Chr 30:16
Therefore the **L** had to slaughter the 2 Chr 30:17
and the **L** and the priests praised the 2 Chr 30:21
to all the **L** who showed good 2 Chr 30:22
of Judah, and the priests and the **L**, 2 Chr 30:25
priests and the **L** arose and blessed 2 Chr 30:27
divisions of the priests and of the **L**, 2 Chr 31:2
to his service, the priests and the **L**, 2 Chr 31:2
portion due to the priests and the **L**, 2 Chr 31:4
the priests and the **L** about the heaps. 2 Chr 31:9
that of the **L** from twenty years old 2 Chr 31:17
everyone among the **L** who was 2 Chr 31:19
into the house of God, which the **L**, 2 Chr 34:9
were set Jahath and Obadiah the **L**, 2 Chr 34:12
to have oversight. The **L**, 2 Chr 34:12
and some of the **L** were scribes and 2 Chr 34:13
Jerusalem and the priests and the **L**, 2 Chr 34:30
he said to the **L** who taught all Israel 2 Chr 35:3
division of the **L** by fathers' 2 Chr 35:5
the people, to the priests, and to the **L**. 2 Chr 35:8
Jeiel and Jozabad, the chiefs of the **L**, 2 Chr 35:9
gave to the **L** for the Passover 2 Chr 35:9
and the **L** in their divisions 2 Chr 35:10
them while the **L** flayed the 2 Chr 35:11
so the **L** prepared for themselves and 2 Chr 35:14
their brothers the **L** prepared for 2 Chr 35:15
by Josiah, and the priests and the **L**, 2 Chr 35:18
and Benjamin, and the priests and the **L**, Ezr 1:5
The **L**: the sons of Jeshua and Kadmiel, Ezr 2:40
Now the priests, the **L**, some of the Ezr 2:70
the priests and the **L** and all who had Ezr 3:8
They appointed the **L**, from twenty years Ezr 3:8
with the sons of Henadad and the **L**, Ezr 3:9
came forward with trumpets, and the **L**, Ezr 3:10
of the priests and **L** and heads of fathers' Ezr 3:12
the people of Israel, the priests and the **L**, Ezr 6:16
divisions and the **L** in their divisions, Ezr 6:18
priests and the **L** had purified Ezr 6:20
of Israel, and some of the priests and **L**, Ezr 7:7
or their priests or **L** in my kingdom, Ezr 7:13
or toll on anyone of the priests, the **L**, Ezr 7:24
officials had set apart to attend the **L**. Ezr 8:20
chief priests and the **L** and the heads of Ezr 8:29
the priests and the **L** took over the Ezr 8:30
of Phinehas, and with them were the **L**, Ezr 8:33
the priests and the **L** have not separated Ezr 9:1
the leading priests and **L** and all Israel Ezr 10:5
Of the **L**: Jozabad, Shimei, Kelaiah Ezr 10:23
After him the **L** repaired: Rehum the Neh 3:17
singers, and the **L** had been appointed, Neh 7:1
The **L**: the sons of Jeshua, namely of Neh 7:43
So the priests, the **L**, the gatekeepers, Neh 7:73
Azariah, Jozabad, Hanan, Pelaiah, the **L**, Neh 8:7
and the **L** who taught the people said to Neh 8:9
So the **L** calmed all the people, saying, Neh 8:11
the people, with the priests and the **L**, Neh 8:13
On the stairs of the **L** stood Jeshua, Bani, Neh 9:4
Then the **L**, Jeshua, Kadmiel, Bani, Neh 9:5
are the names of our princes, our **L**, Neh 9:38
And the **L**: Jeshua the son of Azaniah, Neh 10:9
rest of the people, the priests, the **L**, Neh 10:28
We, the priests, the **L**, and the people, Neh 10:34
to bring to the **L** the tithes from our Neh 10:37
for it is the **L** who collect the tithes in Neh 10:37
shall be with the **L** when the Levites Neh 10:38
Levites when the **L** receive the tithes. Neh 10:38
And the **L** shall bring up the tithe of Neh 10:38
Israel, the priests, the **L**, the temple Neh 11:3
And of the **L**: Shemaiah the son of Neh 11:15
and Jozabad, of the chiefs of the **L**, Neh 11:16
All the **L** in the holy city were 284. Neh 11:18
of Israel, and of the priests and the **L**, Neh 11:20
overseer of the **L** in Jerusalem was Neh 11:22
divisions of the **L** in Judah were Neh 11:36
the priests and the **L** who came up with Neh 12:1
And the **L**: Jeshua, Binnui, Kadmiel, Neh 12:8
the **L** were recorded as heads of Neh 12:22
And the chiefs of the **L**: Hashabiah, Neh 12:24
they sought the **L** in all their Neh 12:27
priests and the **L** purified themselves, Neh 12:30
priests and for the **L** according to the Neh 12:44
the priests and the **L** who ministered. Neh 12:44
set apart that which was for the **L**; Neh 12:47
and the **L** set apart that which was for Neh 12:47
were given by commandment to the **L**, Neh 13:5
the portions of the **L** had not been Neh 13:10
to them, so that the **L** and the singers, Neh 13:10
the scribe, and Pedaiah of the **L**, Neh 13:13
I commanded the **L** that they should Neh 13:22
covenant of the priesthood and the **L**. Neh 13:29
the duties of the priests and **L**, Neh 13:30
also I will take for priests and for **L**, Is 66:21
But the **L** who went far from me, Ezk 44:10
shall be for the **L** who minister at the Ezk 45:5
of Israel went astray, as the **L** did. Ezk 48:11

place, adjoining the territory of the **L**. Ezk 48:12
the **L** shall have an allotment 25,000 Ezk 48:13
the property of the **L** and the property Ezk 48:22
Jews sent priests and **L** from Jerusalem to Jn 1:19

LEVITICAL (16)
you shall come to the **L** priests and to the Dt 17:9
of this law, approved by the **L** priests. Dt 17:18
"The **L** priests, all the tribe of Levi, shall Dt 18:1
to all that the **L** priests shall direct you. Dt 24:8
Then Moses and the **L** priests said to all Dt 27:9
your God being carried by the **L** priests, Jos 3:3
the ark before the **L** priests who carried Jos 8:33
tent; the **L** priests brought them up. 2 Chr 5:5
and all the **L** singers, Asaph, Heman, 2 Chr 5:12
the direction of the **L** priests and the 2 Chr 23:18
and the **L** priests shall never lack a Jer 33:18
covenant with the **L** priests my Jer 33:21
and the **L** priests who minister to me." Jer 33:22
shall give to the **L** priests of the family Ezk 43:19
"But the **L** priests, the sons of Zadok, Ezk 44:15
through the **L** priesthood (for Heb 7:11

LEVY (1)
And **l** for the LORD a tribute from the Nm 31:28

LEWD (3)
and neighings, your **l** whorings, Jer 13:27
who were ashamed of your **l** behavior. Ezk 16:27
to Oholah and to Oholibah, **l** women! Ezk 23:44

LEWDLY (1)
another **l** defiles his daughter-in-law; Ezk 22:11

LEWDNESS (12)
you not committed **l** in addition to Ezk 16:43
penalty of your **l** and your Ezk 16:58
they commit **l** in your midst. Ezk 22:9
you longed for the **l** of your youth, Ezk 23:21
an end to your **l** and your whoring Ezk 23:27
uncovered. Your **l** and your whoring Ezk 23:29
consequences of your **l** and whoring." Ezk 23:35
Thus will I put an end to **l** in the land, Ezk 23:48
and not commit **l** as you have Ezk 23:48
they shall return your **l** upon you, Ezk 23:49
On account of your unclean **l**, Ezk 24:13
Now I will uncover her **l** in the sight of Hos 2:10

LIABLE (6)
but the owner of the ox shall not be **l**. Ex 21:28
the army or be **l** for any other public Dt 24:5
whoever murders will be **l** to judgment.' Mt 5:21
with his brother will be **l** to judgment; Mt 5:22
his brother will be **l** to the council; Mt 5:22
'You fool!' will be **l** to the hell of fire. Mt 5:22

LIAR (13)
will prove me a **l** and show that there Jb 24:25
in spite of my right I am counted a **l**; my Jb 34:6
and a **l** gives ear to a mischievous Prv 17:4
love, and a poor man is better than a **l**. Prv 19:22
lest he rebuke you and you be found a **l**. Prv 30:6
for he is a **l** and the father of lies. Jn 8:44
do not know him, I would be a **l** like you, Jn 8:55
God be true though every one were a **l**, Rom 3:4
we have not sinned, we make him a **l**, 1 Jn 1:10
does not keep his commandments is a **l**, 1 Jn 2:4
Who is the **l** but he who denies that 1 Jn 2:22
God," and hates his brother, he is a **l**; 1 Jn 4:20
does not believe God has made him a **l**, 1 Jn 5:10

LIARS (7)
for the mouths of **l** will be stopped. Ps 63:11
in my alarm, "All mankind are **l**." Ps 116:11
frustrates the signs of **l** and makes fools Is 44:25
enslavers, **l**, perjurers, 1 Tm 1:10
the insincerity of **l** whose consciences 1 Tm 4:2
of their own, said, "Cretans are always **l**, Ti 1:12
immoral, sorcerers, idolaters, and all **l**, Rv 21:8

LIBERALLY (1)
You shall furnish him **l** out of your Dt 15:14

LIBERTY (14)
and proclaim **l** throughout the land to Lv 25:10
to proclaim **l** to the captives, Is 61:1
to make a proclamation of **l** to them, Jer 34:8
was right in my eyes by proclaiming **l**, Jer 34:15
have not obeyed me by proclaiming **l**, Jer 34:17
behold, I proclaim to you **l** to the sword, Jer 34:17
servants, it shall be his to the year of **l**. Ezk 46:17
sent me to proclaim **l** to the captives and Lk 4:18
blind, to set at **l** those who are oppressed, Lk 4:18
be kept in custody but have some **l**, Acts 24:23
me, they wished to set me at **l**, Acts 28:18
why should my **l** be determined by 1 Cor 10:29
looks into the perfect law, the law of **l**, Jas 1:25
who are to be judged under the law of **l**. Jas 2:12

LIBNAH (18)
from Rimmon-perez and camped at **L**. Nm 33:20
they set out from **L** and camped at Nm 33:21
from Makkedah to **L** and fought Jos 10:29
to Libnah and fought against **L**. Jos 10:29
him passed on from **L** to Lachish and Jos 10:31
every person in it, as he had done to **L**. Jos 10:32
done to Hebron and to **L** and its king, Jos 10:39
the king of **L**, one; the king of Adullam, Jos 12:15
L, Ether, Ashan, Jos 15:42
pasturelands, **L** with its pasturelands, Jos 21:13
Then **L** revolted at the same time. 2 Kgs 8:22
king of Assyria fighting against **L**, 2 Kgs 19:8
the daughter of Jeremiah of **L**. 2 Kgs 23:31
the daughter of Jeremiah of **L**. 2 Kgs 24:18
Hebron, **L** with its pasturelands, 1 Chr 6:57
At that time **L** also revolted from his 2 Chr 21:10
the king of Assyria fighting against **L**, Is 37:8
Hamutal the daughter of Jeremiah of **L**. Jer 52:1

LIBNI (5)
Gershon: **L** and Shimei, by their clans. Ex 6:17
Gershon by their clans: **L** and Shimei. Nm 3:18
the sons of Gershom: **L** and Shimei. 1 Chr 6:17
L his son, Jahath his son, Zimmah 1 Chr 6:20
Mahli, **L** his son, Shimei his son, 1 Chr 6:29

LIBNITES (2)
the clan of the **L** and the clan of Nm 3:21
the clan of the **L**, the clan of the Nm 26:58

LIBYA (2)
Put, and Lud, and all Arabia, and **L**, Ezk 30:5
and the parts of **L** belonging to Cyrene, Acts 2:10

LIBYANS (4)
who came with him from Egypt—**L**, 2 Chr 12:3
Ethiopians and the **L** a huge army 2 Chr 16:8
and the **L** and the Cushites shall follow Dn 11:43
limit; Put and the **L** were her helpers. Na 3:9

LICK (5)
"This horde will now **l** up all that is Nm 22:4
Naboth shall dogs **l** your own 1 Kgs 21:19
before him and his enemies **l** the dust! Ps 72:9
down to you, and **l** the dust of your feet. Is 49:23
they shall **l** the dust like a serpent, like Mi 7:17

LICKED (4)
and **l** up the water that was in the 1 Kgs 18:38
the place where dogs **l** up the blood 1 Kgs 21:19
and the dogs **l** up his blood, 1 Kgs 22:38
even the dogs came and **l** his sores. Lk 16:21

LICKS (1)
as the ox **l** up the grass of the field." So Nm 22:4

LID (1)
bored a hole in the **l** of it and set it 2 Kgs 12:9

LIE (143)
drink wine, and we will **l** with him, Gn 19:32
Then you go in and **l** with him, that we Gn 19:34
The land on which you **l** I will give to Gn 28:13
"Then he may **l** with you tonight in Gn 30:15
eyes on Joseph and said, "**L** with me." Gn 39:7
to her, to **l** beside her or to be with her. Gn 39:10
"**L** with me." But he left his garment in Gn 39:12
He came in to me to **l** with me, and I Gn 39:14
but let me **l** with my fathers. Carry me Gn 47:30
But if he did not **l** in wait for him, but Ex 21:13
year you shall let it rest and **l** fallow, Ex 23:11
Close to the frame the rings shall **l**, as Ex 25:27
so that it may **l** on the skillfully woven Ex 28:28
so that it should **l** on the skillfully Ex 39:21
And you shall not **l** sexually with your Lv 18:20
You shall not **l** with a male as with a Lv 18:22
And you shall not **l** with any animal Lv 18:23
give herself to an animal to **l** with it: Lv 18:23
falsely; you shall not **l** to one another. Lv 19:11
peace in the land, and you shall **l** down, Lv 26:6
God is not man, that he should **l**, or a Nm 23:19
it does not **l** down until it has Nm 23:24
walk by the way, and when you **l** down, Dt 6:7
by the way, and when you **l** down, Dt 11:19
shall cause him to **l** down and be beaten Dt 25:2
you are about to **l** down with your Dt 31:16
you shall **l** in ambush against the city, Jos 8:4
"Go and **l** in ambush in the vineyards Jgs 21:20
Then go and uncover his feet and **l** down, Ru 3:4
he went to **l** down at the end of the heap of Ru 3:7
redeem you. **L** down until the morning." Ru 3:13
l down again." So he went and lay 1 Sm 3:5
"I did not call, my son; **l** down again." 1 Sm 3:6
Eli said to Samuel, "Go, **l** down, 1 Sm 3:9
of Israel will not **l** or have regret, 1 Sm 15:29
up my servant against me, to **l** in wait, 1 Sm 22:8
he has risen against me, to **l** in wait, 1 Sm 22:13
are fulfilled and you **l** down with your 2 Sm 7:12
making them **l** down on the ground. 2 Sm 8:2
and to drink and to **l** with my wife? 2 Sm 11:11
he went out to **l** on his couch with 2 Sm 11:13
drink from his cup and **l** in his arms, 2 Sm 12:3
and he shall **l** with your wives in the 2 Sm 12:11
"**L** down on your bed and pretend to 2 Sm 13:5
and said to her, "Come, **l** with me, 2 Sm 13:11
Let her **l** in your arms, that my lord 1 Kgs 1:2
man of God; do not **l** to your servant." 2 Kgs 4:16
to look at me, for I will not **l** to your face. Jb 6:28
When I **l** down I say, 'When shall I arise?' Jb 7:4
For now I shall **l** in the earth; you will Jb 7:21
You will **l** down, and none will make Jb 11:19
but it will **l** down with him in the dust. Jb 20:11
They **l** down alike in the dust, and the Jb 21:26
They **l** all night naked, without clothing, Jb 24:7
crouch in their dens or **l** in wait in their Jb 38:40
In peace I will both **l** down and sleep; for Ps 4:8
He makes me **l** down in green pastures. Ps 23:2
There the evildoers **l** fallen; they are Ps 36:12
proud, to those who go astray after a **l**! Ps 40:4
I **l** down amid fiery beasts—the children Ps 57:4
For behold, they **l** in wait for my life; Ps 59:3
though you men **l** among the Ps 68:13
the dead, like the slain that **l** in the grave, Ps 88:5
by my holiness; I will not **l** to David. Ps 89:35
I **l** awake; I am like a lonely sparrow on Ps 102:7
they steal away and **l** down in their Ps 104:22
The wicked **l** in wait to destroy me, Ps 119:95
with us, let us **l** in wait for blood; Prv 1:11
but these men **l** in wait for their own Prv 1:18
If you **l** down, you will not be afraid; Prv 3:24
when you **l** down, your sleep will be Prv 3:24
How long will you **l** there, O sluggard? Prv 6:9
when you **l** down, they will watch over Prv 6:22
words of the wicked **l** in wait for blood, Prv 12:6
A faithful witness does not **l**, but a false Prv 14:5
Sheol and Abaddon **l** open before the Prv 15:11
L not in wait as a wicked man against Prv 24:15
Again, if two **l** together, they keep Eccl 4:11
place where the tree falls, there it will **l**. Eccl 11:3
flock, where you make it **l** down at noon; Sg 1:7
"Until cities **l** waste without inhabitant, Is 6:11
and the leopard shall **l** down with the Is 11:6
graze; their young shall **l** down together; Is 11:7
will make their flocks **l** down there. Is 13:20
But wild animals will **l** down there, and Is 13:21
All the kings of the nations **l** in glory, Is 14:18
graze, and the needy **l** down in safety; Is 14:30
they will be for flocks, which will **l** down, Is 17:2
The highways **l** waste; the traveler ceases. Is 33:8
generation to generation it shall **l** waste; Is 34:10
the haunt of jackals, where they **l** down, Is 35:7
horse, army and warrior; they **l** down, Is 43:17
say, "Is there not a **l** in my right hand?" Is 44:20
my hand: you shall **l** down in torment. Is 50:11
they **l** at the head of every street like an Is 51:20
of Achor a place for herds to **l** down, Is 65:10
Let us **l** down in our shame, and let our Jer 3:25
pen of the scribes has made it into a **l**. Jer 8:8
For it is a **l** that they are prophesying to Jer 27:10
for it is a **l** that they are prophesying to Jer 27:14
for it is a **l** that they are prophesying to Jer 27:16
you have made this people trust in a **l**. Jer 28:15
for it is a **l** that they are prophesying to Jer 29:9
who are prophesying a **l** to you in my Jer 29:21
him, and has made you trust in a **l**, Jer 29:31
And Jeremiah said, "It is a **l**; I am not Jer 37:14
said to Jeremiah, "You are telling a **l**. Jer 43:2
dust of the streets **l** the young and the Lam 2:21
The holy stones **l** scattered at the head Lam 4:1
"Then **l** on your left side, and place the Ezk 4:4
the number of the days that you **l** on it, Ezk 4:4
these, you shall **l** down a second time, Ezk 4:6
number of days that you **l** on your side, Ezk 4:9
when their slain **l** among their idols Ezk 6:13
You shall **l** among the Ezk 31:18
'They have come down, they **l** still, the Ezk 32:21
And they do not **l** with the mighty, the Ezk 32:27
be broken and **l** among the Ezk 32:28
they **l** with the uncircumcised, with Ezk 32:29
they **l** uncircumcised with those who Ezk 32:30
There they shall **l** down in good Ezk 34:14
and I myself will make them **l** down, Ezk 34:15
the prince shall **l** between the territory Ezk 48:22
and I will make you **l** down in safety. Hos 2:18
As robbers **l** in wait for a man, so the Hos 6:9
"Woe to those who **l** on beds of ivory and Am 6:4
they all **l** in wait for blood, and each Mi 7:2
time; it hastens to the end—it will not **l**. Hab 2:3
Ashkelon they shall **l** down at evening. Zep 2:7
Herds shall **l** down in her midst, all Zep 2:14
For they shall graze and **l** down, and Zep 3:13
filled your heart to **l** to the Holy Spirit Acts 5:3
about God for a **l** and worshiped and Rom 1:25
if through my **l** God's truth abounds Rom 3:7
writing to you, before God, I do not **l**!) Gal 1:20
Do not **l** to one another, seeing that you Col 3:9

in which it is impossible for God to **l**, Heb 6:18
we **l** and do not practice the truth. 1 Jn 1:6
it, and because no **l** is of the truth. 1 Jn 2:21
everything—and is true and is no **l**, 1 Jn 2:27
they are Jews and are not, but **l**—behold, Rv 3:9
their dead bodies will **l** in the street of Rv 11:8
and in their mouth no **l** was found, for Rv 14:5

LIED (6)
has found something lost and **l** about it, Lv 6:3
they have stolen and **l** and put them Jos 7:11
and drink water.'" But he **l** to him. 1 Kgs 13:18
they **l** to him with their tongues. Ps 78:36
did you dread and fear, so that you **l**, Is 57:11
You have not **l** to men but to God." Acts 5:4

LIES (125)
it **l** between Kadesh and Bered. Gn 16:14
engaged to be married and **l** with her, Ex 22:16
"Whoever **l** with an animal shall be Ex 22:19
with the discharge **l** shall be unclean, Lv 15:4
If a man **l** with a woman and has an Lv 15:18
on which she **l** during her menstrual Lv 15:20
And if any man **l** with her and her Lv 15:24
bed on which he **l** shall be unclean. Lv 15:24
Every bed on which she **l**, all the days Lv 15:26
for the man who **l** with a woman who Lv 15:33
"If a man **l** sexually with a woman who Lv 19:20
If a man **l** with his father's wife, he has Lv 20:11
If a man **l** with his daughter-in-law, Lv 20:12
If a man **l** with a male as with a Lv 20:13
If a man **l** with an animal, he shall Lv 20:15
approaches any animal and **l** with it, Lv 20:16
If a man **l** with a woman during her Lv 20:18
If a man **l** with his uncle's wife, he has Lv 20:20
its Sabbaths as long as it **l** desolate, Lv 26:34
As long as it **l** desolate it shall have rest, Lv 26:35
Sabbaths while it **l** desolate without Lv 26:43
if a man **l** with her sexually, and it is Nm 5:13
your dead bodies **l** in the wilderness. Nm 14:33
hates his neighbor and **l** in wait for Dt 19:11
meets her in the city and **l** with her, Dt 22:23
and the man seizes her and **l** with her, Dt 22:25
betrothed, and seizes her and **l** with her, Dt 22:28
be anyone who **l** with his father's Dt 27:20
be anyone who **l** with any kind Dt 27:21
be anyone who **l** with his sister, Dt 27:22
be anyone who **l** with his Dt 27:23
of the mountain that **l** over against the Jos 15:8
on the mountain that **l** south of Lower Jos 18:13
from the mountain that **l** to the south, Jos 18:14
in the land where your possession **l**, Jos 22:4
Judah, which **l** in the Negeb near Arad, Jgs 1:16
him, and see where his great strength **l**, Jgs 16:5
tell me where your great strength **l**, Jgs 16:6
you have mocked me and told me **l**. Jgs 16:10
you have mocked me and told me **l**. Jgs 16:13
told me where your great strength **l**." Jgs 16:15
But when he **l** down, observe the place Ru 3:4
he lies down, observe the place where he **l**. Ru 3:4
"Jonathan **l** slain on your high places. 2 Sm 1:25
which **l** before Giah on the way to the 2 Sm 2:24
place of my fathers' graves, **l** in ruins, Neh 2:3
how Jerusalem **l** in ruins with its gates Neh 2:17
As for you, you whitewash with **l**; Jb 13:4
so a man **l** down and rises not again; till Jb 14:12
Under the lotus plants he **l**, in the Jb 40:21
will you love vain words and seek after **l**? Ps 4:2
You destroy those who speak **l**; the LORD Ps 5:6
with mischief and gives birth to **l**. Ps 7:14
Everyone utters **l** to his neighbor; with Ps 12:2
he will not rise again from where he **l**." Ps 41:8
they go astray from birth, speaking **l**. Ps 58:3
For the cursing and **l** that they utter, Ps 59:12
destroy me, those who attack me with **l**. Ps 69:4
Your wrath **l** heavy upon me, and you Ps 88:7
one who utters **l** shall continue before Ps 101:7
The insolent smear me with **l**, but Ps 119:69
whose mouths speak **l** and whose right Ps 144:8
whose mouths speak **l** and whose Ps 144:11
a false witness who breathes out **l**, and Prv 6:19
and at every corner she **l** in wait. Prv 7:12
lie, but a false witness breathes out **l**. Prv 14:5
but one who breathes out **l** is deceitful. Prv 14:25
he who breathes out **l** will not escape. Prv 19:5
and he who breathes out **l** will perish. Prv 19:9
She **l** in wait like a robber and Prv 23:28
be like one who **l** down in the midst Prv 23:34
sea, like one who **l** on the top of a mast. Prv 23:34
the sun, and it **l** heavy on mankind: Eccl 6:1
although man's trouble **l** heavy on Eccl 8:6
of myrrh that **l** between my breasts. Sg 1:13
Your country **l** desolate; your cities are Is 1:7
and the prophet who teaches **l** is the tail; Is 9:15
The earth **l** defiled under its inhabitants; Is 24:5
its transgression **l** heavy upon it, and it Is 24:20
there it **l** down and strips its branches. Is 27:10
to us, for we have made **l** our refuge, Is 28:15
and hail will sweep away the refuge of **l**, Is 28:17
with iniquity; your lips have spoken **l**; Is 59:3
they rely on empty pleas, they speak **l**, Is 59:4
they have taught their tongue to speak **l**; Jer 9:5
you have forgotten me and trusted in **l**. Jer 13:25
prophets are prophesying **l** in my Jer 14:14
fathers have inherited nothing but **l**, Jer 16:19
they commit adultery and walk in **l**; Jer 23:14
have said who prophesy **l** in my name, Jer 23:25
How long shall there be **l** in the heart of Jer 23:26
heart of the prophets who prophesy **l**, Jer 23:26
astray by their **l** and their recklessness, Jer 23:32
for Mount Zion which **l** desolate; Lam 5:18
lying to my people, who listen to **l**. Ezk 13:19
while they divine **l** for you—to place Ezk 21:29
false visions and divining **l** for them, Ezk 22:28
the great dragon that **l** in the midst of Ezk 29:3
Sibraim (which **l** on the border Ezk 47:16
They shall speak **l** at the same table, Dn 11:27
them, but they speak **l** against me. Hos 7:13
injustice; you have eaten the fruit of **l**. Hos 10:13
Ephraim has surrounded me with **l**, Hos 11:12
statutes, but their **l** have led them astray, Am 2:4
should go about and utter wind and **l**, Mi 2:11
your inhabitants speak **l**, and their Mi 6:12
mouth from her who **l** in your arms; Mi 7:5
all full of **l** and plunder—no end to the Na 3:1
shaped it, a metal image, a teacher of **l**? Hab 2:18
shall do no injustice and speak no **l**, Zep 3:13
houses, while this house **l** in ruins? Hg 1:4
Because of my house that **l** in ruins, Hg 1:9
utter nonsense, and the diviners see **l**; Zec 10:2
for you speak **l** in the name of the LORD.' Zec 13:3
of Olives that **l** before Jerusalem on Zec 14:4
When he **l**, he speaks out of his own Jn 8:44
for he is a liar and the father of **l**. Jn 8:44
Apart from the law, sin **l** dead. Rom 7:8
I want to do right, evil **l** close at hand. Rom 7:21
Moses is read a veil **l** over their hearts. 2 Cor 3:15
forgetting what **l** behind and straining Phil 3:13
and straining forward to what **l** ahead, Phil 3:13
of eternal life, which God, who never **l**, Ti 1:2
and the whole world **l** in the power of 1 Jn 5:19
The city **l** foursquare; its length the Rv 21:16

LIEUTENANT'S (1)
from Zebulun those who bear the **l** staff; Jgs 5:14

LIFE (563)
everything that has the breath of **l**, Gn 1:30
breathed into his nostrils the breath of **l**, Gn 2:7
The tree of **l** was in the midst of the Gn 2:9
dust you shall eat all the days of your **l**. Gn 3:14
you shall eat of it all the days of your **l**; Gn 3:17
and take also of the tree of **l** and eat, Gn 3:22
way to guard the way to the tree of **l**. Gn 3:24
which is the breath of **l** under heaven. Gn 6:17
In the six hundredth year of Noah's **l**, in Gn 7:11
flesh in which there was the breath of **l**. Gn 7:15
whose nostrils was the breath of **l** died. Gn 7:22
But you shall not eat flesh with its **l**, that Gn 9:4
will require a reckoning for the **l** of man. Gn 9:5
and that my **l** may be spared for your Gn 12:13
them out, one said, "Escape for your **l** Gn 19:17
me great kindness in saving my **l**. Gn 19:19
a little one?—and my **l** will be saved!" Gn 19:20
these were the years of the **l** of Sarah. Gn 23:1
are the days of the years of Abraham's **l**, Gn 25:7
(These are the years of the **l** of Ishmael: Gn 25:17
and they made **l** bitter for Isaac and Gn 26:35
"I loathe my **l** because of the Hittite Gn 27:46
land, what good will my **l** be to me?" Gn 27:46
face, and yet my **l** has been delivered." Gn 32:30
hands, saying, "Let us not take his **l**." Gn 37:21
you shall be tested: by the **l** of Pharaoh, Gn 42:15
Or else, by the **l** of Pharaoh, surely you Gn 42:16
as his **l** is bound up in the boy's life, Gn 44:30
as his life is bound up in the boy's **l**, Gn 44:30
the blame before my father all my **l**.' Gn 44:32
for God sent me before you to preserve **l**. Gn 45:5
are the days of the years of your **l**?" Gn 47:8
have been the days of the years of my **l**, Gn 47:9
of the years of the **l** of my fathers in the Gn 47:9
So the days of Jacob, the years of his **l**, Gn 47:28
my shepherd all my **l** long to this day, Gn 48:15
men who were seeking your **l** are dead." Ex 4:19
the years of the **l** of Levi being 137 years. Ex 6:16
the years of the **l** of Kohath being 133 Ex 6:18
the years of the **l** of Amram being 137 Ex 6:20
is harm, then you shall pay **l** for life, Ex 21:23
is harm, then you shall pay life for **l**, Ex 21:23
redemption of his **l** whatever is imposed Ex 21:30
a ransom for his **l** to the LORD when Ex 30:12
For the **l** of the flesh is in the blood, and Lv 17:11
blood that makes atonement by the **l**. Lv 17:11
For the **l** of every creature is its blood: Lv 17:14
creature is its blood: its blood is its **l**. Lv 17:14
for the **l** of every creature is its blood. Lv 17:14
stand up against the **l** of your neighbor: Lv 19:16
takes a human **l** shall surely be Lv 24:17
takes an animal's **l** shall make it Lv 24:18
life shall make it good, **l** for life. Lv 24:18
life shall make it good, life for **l**. Lv 24:18
have ridden all your **l** long to this Nm 22:30
no ransom for the **l** of a murderer, Nm 35:31
from your heart all the days of your **l**. Dt 4:9
flee to one of these cities and save his **l**: Dt 4:42
I command you, all the days of your **l**, Dt 6:2
not eat the blood, for the blood is the **l**, Dt 12:23
you shall not eat the **l** with the flesh. Dt 12:23
the days of your **l** you may remember Dt 16:3
he shall read in it all the days of his **l**, Dt 17:19
who by fleeing there may save his **l**. Dt 19:4
It shall be **l** for life, eye for eye, tooth for Dt 19:21
It shall be life for **l**, eye for eye, tooth for Dt 19:21
for that would be taking a **l** in pledge. Dt 24:6
Your **l** shall hang in doubt before you. Dt 28:66
dread and have no assurance of your **l**. Dt 28:66
I have set before you today **l** and good, Dt 30:15
that I have set before you **l** and death, Dt 30:19
Therefore choose **l**, that you and your Dt 30:19
him, for he is your **l** and length of days, Dt 30:20
no empty word for you, but your very **l**, Dt 32:47
to stand before you all the days of your **l**. Jos 1:5
to her, "Our **l** for yours even to death! Jos 2:14
in awe of Moses, all the days of his **l**. Jos 4:14
you and risked his **l** and delivered you Jgs 9:17
I took my **l** in my hand and crossed over Jgs 12:3
what is to be the child's manner of **l**, Jgs 13:12
those whom he had killed during his **l**. Jgs 16:30
and you lose your **l** with the lives of Jgs 18:25
to you a restorer of **l** and a nourisher of Ru 4:15
him to the LORD all the days of his **l**, 1 Sm 1:11
The LORD kills and brings to **l**; he 1 Sm 2:6
judged Israel all the days of his **l**. 1 Sm 7:15
For he took his **l** in his hand and he 1 Sm 19:5
do not escape with your **l** tonight, 1 Sm 19:11
your father, that he seeks my **l**?" 1 Sm 20:1
for he who seeks my **l** seeks your life. 1 Sm 22:23
for he who seeks my life seeks your **l**. 1 Sm 22:23
that Saul had come out to seek his **l**. 1 Sm 23:15
you, though you hunt my **l** to take it. 1 Sm 24:11
up to pursue you and to seek your **l**, 1 Sm 25:29
the **l** of my lord shall be bound in 1 Sm 25:29
because my **l** was precious in your 1 Sm 26:21
as your **l** was precious this day in 1 Sm 26:24
so may my **l** be precious in the sight 1 Sm 26:24
I will make you my bodyguard for **l**." 1 Sm 28:2
a trap for my **l** to bring about my 1 Sm 28:9
I have taken my **l** in my hand and 1 Sm 28:21
seized me, and yet my **l** still lingers.' 2 Sm 1:9
In **l** and in death they were not 2 Sm 1:23
Saul, your enemy, who sought your **l**. 2 Sm 4:8
who has redeemed my **l** out of every 2 Sm 4:9
to death for the **l** of his brother whom 2 Sm 14:7
But God will not take away **l**, and he 2 Sm 14:14
shall be, whether for death or for **l**, 2 Sm 15:21
"Behold, my own son seeks my **l**; 2 Sm 16:11
You seek the **l** of only one man, and 2 Sm 17:3
against his **l** (and there 2 Sm 18:13
this day saved your **l** and the lives of 2 Sm 19:5
may save your own **l** and the life of 1 Kgs 1:12
own life and the **l** of your son 1 Kgs 1:12
word does not cost Adonijah his **l**! 1 Kgs 2:23
asked for yourself long **l** or riches or 1 Kgs 3:11
life or riches or the **l** of your enemies, 1 Kgs 3:11
served Solomon all the days of his **l**. 1 Kgs 4:21
make him ruler all the days of his **l**, 1 Kgs 11:34
commanded him all the days of his **l**, 1 Kgs 15:5
and Jeroboam all the days of his **l**. 1 Kgs 15:6
let this child's **l** come into him 1 Kgs 17:21
And the **l** of the child came into him 1 Kgs 17:22
I do not make your **l** as the life of one 1 Kgs 19:2
make your life as the **l** of one of them 1 Kgs 19:2
and ran for his **l** and came to 1 Kgs 19:3
now, O LORD, take away my **l**, for I am 1 Kgs 19:4
I only, am left, and they seek my **l**, 1 Kgs 19:10
I only, am left, and they seek my **l**, 1 Kgs 19:14
Israel. Perhaps he will spare your **l**." 1 Kgs 20:31
missing, your **l** shall be for his life, 1 Kgs 20:39
missing, your life shall be for his **l**, 1 Kgs 20:39
therefore your **l** shall be for his life, 1 Kgs 20:42
therefore your life shall be for his **l**, 1 Kgs 20:42
him, "O man of God, please let my **l**, 2 Kgs 1:13
and the **l** of these fifty servants of 2 Kgs 1:13
but now let my **l** be precious in your 2 Kgs 1:14
but there was no sound or sign of **l**. 2 Kgs 4:31
woman whose son he had restored to **l**, 2 Kgs 8:1
how Elisha had restored the dead to **l**, 2 Kgs 8:5

he had restored to **l** appealed to the 2 Kgs 8:5
is her son whom Elisha restored to **l**." 2 Kgs 8:5
hands to escape shall forfeit his **l**." 2 Kgs 10:24
and I will add fifteen years to your **l**. I 2 Kgs 20:6
every day of his **l** he dined regularly 2 Kgs 25:29
honor, or the **l** of those who hate you, 2 Chr 1:11
you, and have not even asked long **l**, 2 Chr 1:11
and pray for the **l** of the king and Ezr 6:10
king, let my **l** be granted me for my wish, Est 7:3
stayed to beg for his **l** from Queen Esther, Est 7:7
All that a man has he will give for his **l**. Jb 2:4
he is in your hand; only spare his **l**." Jb 2:6
is in misery, and **l** to the bitter in soul, Jb 3:20
"Remember that my **l** is a breath; my eye Jb 7:7
I loathe my **l**; I would not live forever. Jb 7:16
I regard not myself; I loathe my **l**. Jb 9:21
"I loathe my **l**; I will give free utterance to Jb 10:1
have granted me **l** and steadfast love, Jb 10:12
And your **l** will be brighter than the Jb 11:17
In his hand is the **l** of every living thing Jb 12:10
in my teeth and put my **l** in my hand? Jb 13:14
Yet God prolongs the **l** of the mighty by Jb 24:22
they rise up when they despair of **l**. Jb 24:22
cuts him off, when God takes away his **l**? Jb 27:8
sin by asking for his **l** with a curse), Jb 31:30
the breath of the Almighty gives me **l**. Jb 33:4
pit, his **l** from perishing by the sword. Jb 33:18
so that his **l** loathes bread, and his Jb 33:20
pit, and his **l** to those who bring death. Jb 33:22
pit, and my **l** shall look upon the light.' Jb 33:28
he may be lighted with the light of **l**. Jb 33:30
and their **l** ends among the cult Jb 36:14
Turn, O LORD, deliver my **l**; save me for the Ps 6:4
let him trample my **l** to the ground and Ps 7:5
You make known to me the path of **l**; in Ps 16:11
of the world whose portion is in this **l**. Ps 17:14
He asked **l** of you; you gave it to him, Ps 21:4
my precious **l** from the power of the Ps 22:20
shall follow me all the days of my **l**, Ps 23:6
sinners, nor my **l** with bloodthirsty men, Ps 26:9
The LORD is the stronghold of my **l**; of Ps 27:1
the house of the LORD all the days of my **l**, Ps 27:4
you restored me to **l** from among those Ps 30:3
For my **l** is spent with sorrow, and my Ps 31:10
against me, as they plot to take my **l**. Ps 31:13
is there who desires **l** and loves many Ps 34:12
The LORD redeems the **l** of his servants; Ps 34:22
and dishonor who seek after my **l**! Ps 35:4
without cause they dug a pit for my **l**. Ps 35:7
my precious **l** from the lions! Ps 35:17
For with you is the fountain of **l**; in your Ps 36:9
Those who seek my **l** lay their snares; Ps 38:12
who seek to snatch away my **l**; Ps 40:14
is with me, a prayer to the God of my **l**. Ps 42:8
another, or give to God the price of his **l**, Ps 49:7
the ransom of their **l** is costly and can Ps 49:8
against me; ruthless men seek my **l**; Ps 54:3
helper; the Lord is the upholder of my **l**. Ps 54:4
my steps, as they have waited for my **l**. Ps 56:6
I may walk before God in the light of **l**. Ps 56:13
For behold, they lie in wait for my **l**; Ps 59:3
Prolong the **l** of the king; may his years Ps 61:6
your steadfast love is better than **l**, Ps 63:3
seek to destroy my **l** shall go down into Ps 63:9
preserve my **l** from dread of the enemy. Ps 64:1
to shame and confusion who seek my **l**! Ps 70:2
who watch for my **l** consult together Ps 71:10
and violence he redeems their **l**, Ps 72:14
do not forget the **l** of your poor forever. Ps 74:19
give us **l**, and we will call upon your Ps 80:18
Preserve my **l**, for I am godly; save your Ps 86:2
a band of ruthless men seek my **l**, and Ps 86:14
troubles, and my **l** draws near to Sheol. Ps 88:3
The years of our **l** are seventy, or even Ps 90:10
With long **l** I will satisfy him and show Ps 91:16
together against the **l** of the righteous Ps 94:21
who redeems your **l** from the pit, who Ps 103:4
of those who speak evil against my **l**! Ps 109:20
give me **l** according to your word! Ps 119:25
things; and give me **l** in your ways. Ps 119:37
in your righteousness give me **l**! Ps 119:40
that your promise gives me **l**. Ps 119:50
In your steadfast love give me **l**, that I Ps 119:88
for by them you have given me **l**. Ps 119:93
give me **l**, O LORD, according to your Ps 119:107
I hold my **l** in my hand continually, Ps 119:109
according to your justice give me **l**. Ps 119:149
give me **l** according to your promise! Ps 119:154
give me **l** according to your rules. Ps 119:156
Give me **l** according to your steadfast Ps 119:159
you from all evil; he will keep your **l**. Ps 121:7
of Jerusalem all the days of your **l**! Ps 128:5
the blessing, **l** forevermore. Ps 133:3
the midst of trouble, you preserve my **l**; Ps 138:7
he has crushed my **l** to the ground; Ps 143:3

name's sake, O LORD, preserve my **l**! Ps 143:11
it takes away the **l** of its possessors. Prv 1:19
back, nor do they regain the paths of **l**. Prv 2:19
of days and years of **l** and peace they will Prv 3:2
Long **l** is in her right hand; in her left Prv 3:16
She is a tree of **l** to those who lay hold of Prv 3:18
and they will be **l** for your soul and Prv 3:22
that the years of your **l** may be many. Prv 4:10
do not let go; guard her, for she is your **l**. Prv 4:13
For they are **l** to those who find them, Prv 4:22
for from it flow the springs of **l**. Prv 4:23
she does not ponder the path of **l**; her Prv 5:6
and at the end of your **l** you groan, Prv 5:11
reproofs of discipline are the way of **l**, Prv 6:23
woman hunts down a precious **l**. Prv 6:26
not know that it will cost him his **l**. Prv 7:23
finds me finds **l** and obtains favor Prv 8:35
and years will be added to your **l**. Prv 9:11
of the righteous is a fountain of **l**, Prv 10:11
The wage of the righteous leads to **l**, Prv 10:16
heeds instruction is on the path to **l**, Prv 10:17
The fear of the LORD prolongs **l**, but the Prv 10:27
The fruit of the righteous is a tree of **l**, Prv 11:30
has regard for the **l** of his beast, Prv 12:10
In the path of righteousness is **l**, and in Prv 12:28
guards his mouth preserves his **l**; Prv 13:3
The ransom of a man's **l** is his wealth, Prv 13:8
sick, but a desire fulfilled is a tree of **l**. Prv 13:12
teaching of the wise is a fountain of **l**, Prv 13:14
The fear of the LORD is a fountain of **l**, Prv 14:27
A tranquil heart gives **l** to the flesh, Prv 14:30
A gentle tongue is a tree of **l**, but Prv 15:4
The path of **l** leads upward for the Prv 15:24
In the light of a king's face there is **l**, Prv 16:15
guards his way preserves his **l**. Prv 16:17
sense is a fountain of **l** to him who has Prv 16:22
of glory; it is gained in a righteous **l**. Prv 16:31
Death and **l** are in the power of the Prv 18:21
keeps the commandment keeps his **l**; Prv 19:16
The fear of the LORD leads to **l**, and Prv 19:23
provokes him to anger forfeits his **l**. Prv 20:2
righteousness and kindness will find **l**, Prv 21:21
of the LORD is riches and honor and **l**. Prv 22:4
cause and rob of **l** those who rob Prv 22:23
Listen to your father who gave you **l**, Prv 23:22
and seek the **l** of the upright. Prv 29:10
The partner of a thief hates his own **l**; Prv 29:24
and not harm, all the days of her **l**. Prv 31:12
heaven during the few days of their **l**. Eccl 2:3
So I hated **l**, because what is done Eccl 2:17
the few days of his **l** that God has given Eccl 5:18
the days of his **l** because God keeps Eccl 5:20
while he lives the few days of his vain **l**, Eccl 6:12
wisdom preserves the **l** of him who Eccl 7:12
In my vain **l** I have seen everything. Eccl 7:15
who prolongs his **l** in his evildoing. Eccl 7:15
a hundred times and prolongs his **l**, Eccl 8:12
the days of his **l** that God has given Eccl 8:15
Enjoy **l** with the wife whom you love, all Eccl 9:9
the days of your vain **l** that he has given Eccl 9:9
that is your portion in **l** and in your toil Eccl 9:9
for laughter, and wine gladdens **l**, Eccl 10:19
youth and the dawn of **l** are vanity. Eccl 11:10
who has been recorded for **l** in Jerusalem, Is 4:3
Behold, I will add fifteen years to your **l**. Is 38:5
tent; like a weaver I have rolled up my **l**; Is 38:12
live, and in all these is the **l** of my spirit. Is 38:16
you have delivered my **l** from the pit of Is 38:17
for you, peoples in exchange for your **l**. Is 43:4
you found new **l** for your strength, Is 57:10
me, and the breath of **l** that I made. Is 57:16
the sword has reached their very **l**." Jer 4:10
Your lovers despise you; they seek your **l**. Jer 4:30
shall be preferred to **l** by all the remnant Jer 8:3
the men of Anathoth, who seek your **l**, Jer 11:21
evil? Yet they have dug a pit for my **l**. Jer 18:20
by the hand of those who seek their **l**. Jer 19:7
and those who seek their **l** afflict them.' Jer 19:9
he has delivered the **l** of the needy from Jer 20:13
before you the way of **l** and the way of Jer 21:8
live and shall have his **l** as a prize of war. Jer 21:9
into the hand of those who seek your **l**, Jer 22:25
their **l** shall be like a watered garden, Jer 31:12
He shall have his **l** as a prize of war, and Jer 38:2
the hand of these men who seek your **l**." Jer 38:16
of Babylon, then your **l** shall be spared, Jer 38:17
with you, and your **l** shall be spared. Jer 38:20
but you shall have your **l** as a prize of Jer 39:18
to take your **l**?" But Gedaliah the Jer 40:14
Why should he take your **l**, so that all Jer 40:15
into the hand of those who seek his **l**, Jer 44:30
who was his enemy and sought his **l**." Jer 44:30
I will give you your **l** as a prize of war Jer 45:5
into the hand of those who seek their **l**, Jer 46:26
and before those who seek their **l**. Jer 49:37

of Babylon; let every one save his **l**! Jer 51:6
has come; the thread of your **l** is cut. Jer 51:13
every one save his **l** from the fierce Jer 51:45
every day of his **l** he dined regularly at Jer 52:33
as their **l** is poured out on their Lam 2:12
O Lord; you have redeemed my **l**. Lam 3:58
his wicked way, in order to save his **l**, Ezk 3:18
his iniquity, none can maintain his **l**. Ezk 7:13
turn from his evil way to save his **l**, Ezk 13:22
is just and right, he shall save his **l**. Ezk 18:27
rules by which they could not have **l**, Ezk 20:25
every moment, every one for his own **l**, Ezk 32:10
warning, he would have saved his **l**. Ezk 33:5
robbery, and walks in the statutes of **l**, Ezk 33:15
earth shall awake, some to everlasting **l**, Dn 12:2
nor shall the mighty save his **l**; Am 2:14
shall he who rides the horse save his **l**; Am 2:15
LORD, let us not perish for this man's **l**, Jon 1:14
waters closed in over me to take my **l**; Jon 2:5
yet you brought up my **l** from the pit, O Jon 2:6
When my **l** was fainting away, I Jon 2:7
now, O LORD, please take my **l** from me, Jon 4:3
peoples; you have forfeited your **l**. Hab 2:10
with him was one of **l** and peace, Mal 2:5
those who sought the child's **l** are dead." Mt 2:20
tell you, do not be anxious about your **l**, Mt 6:25
Is not **l** more than food, and the body Mt 6:25
can add a single hour to his span of **l**? Mt 6:27
and the way is hard that leads to **l**, Mt 7:14
Whoever finds his **l** will lose it, and Mt 10:39
and whoever loses his **l** for my sake Mt 10:39
whoever would save his **l** will lose it, Mt 16:25
but whoever loses his **l** for my sake will Mt 16:25
the whole world and forfeits his **l**? Mt 16:26
shall a man give in return for his **l**? Mt 16:26
for you to enter **l** crippled or lame than Mt 18:8
for you to enter **l** with one eye than Mt 18:9
good deed must I do to have eternal **l**?" Mt 19:16
If you would enter **l**, keep the Mt 19:17
hundredfold and will inherit eternal **l**. Mt 19:29
and to give his **l** as a ransom for Mt 20:28
but the righteous into eternal **l**." Mt 25:46
to save **l** or to kill?" But they were silent. Mk 3:4
whoever would save his **l** will lose it, Mk 8:35
but whoever loses his **l** for my sake and Mk 8:35
gain the whole world and forfeit his **l**? Mk 8:36
what can a man give in return for his **l**? Mk 8:37
for you to enter **l** crippled than with two Mk 9:43
for you to enter **l** lame than with two Mk 9:45
what must I do to inherit eternal **l**?" Mk 10:17
and in the age to come eternal **l**. Mk 10:30
and to give his **l** as a ransom for Mk 10:45
or to do harm, to save **l** or to destroy it?" Lk 6:9
the cares and riches and pleasures of **l**, Lk 8:14
For whoever would save his **l** will lose it, Lk 9:24
but whoever loses his **l** for my sake will Lk 9:24
what shall I do to inherit eternal **l**?" Lk 10:25
for one's **l** does not consist in the Lk 12:15
you, do not be anxious about your **l**, Lk 12:22
For **l** is more than food, and the body Lk 12:23
can add a single hour to his span of **l**? Lk 12:25
and sisters, yes, and even his own **l**, Lk 14:26
seeks to preserve his **l** will lose it, Lk 17:33
it, but whoever loses his **l** will keep it. Lk 17:33
what must I do to inherit eternal **l**?" Lk 18:18
time, and in the age to come eternal **l**." Lk 18:30
and drunkenness and cares of this **l**, Lk 21:34
In him was **l**, and the life was the light of Jn 1:4
was life, and the **l** was the light of men. Jn 1:4
believes in him may have eternal **l**. Jn 3:15
him should not perish but have eternal **l**. Jn 3:16
believes in the Son has eternal **l**; Jn 3:36
does not obey the Son shall not see **l**, Jn 3:36
a spring of water welling up to eternal **l**." Jn 4:14
wages and gathering fruit for eternal **l**, Jn 4:36
Father raises the dead and gives them **l**, Jn 5:21
so also the Son gives **l** to whom he will. Jn 5:21
believes him who sent me has eternal **l**. Jn 5:24
judgment, but has passed from death to **l**. Jn 5:24
For as the Father has **l** in himself, so he Jn 5:26
granted the Son also to have **l** in himself. Jn 5:26
have done good to the resurrection of **l**, Jn 5:29
think that in them you have eternal **l**; Jn 5:39
to come to me that you may have **l**. Jn 5:40
but for the food that endures to eternal **l**, Jn 6:27
from heaven and gives **l** to the world." Jn 6:33
Jesus said to them, "I am the bread of **l**; Jn 6:35
believes in him should have eternal **l**, Jn 6:40
say to you, whoever believes has eternal **l**. Jn 6:47
I am the bread of **l**. Jn 6:48
that I will give for the **l** of the world is my Jn 6:51
drink his blood, you have no **l** in you. Jn 6:53
flesh and drinks my blood has eternal **l**, Jn 6:54
It is the Spirit who gives **l**; the flesh is of Jn 6:63
that I have spoken to you are spirit and **l**. Jn 6:63

we go? You have the words of eternal **l**, Jn 6:68
in darkness, but will have the light of **l**." Jn 8:12
that they may have **l** and have it Jn 10:10
shepherd lays down his **l** for the sheep. Jn 10:11
and I lay down my **l** for the sheep. Jn 10:15
because I lay down my **l** that I may take Jn 10:17
I give them eternal **l**, and they will never Jn 10:28
to her, "I am the resurrection and the **l**. Jn 11:25
Whoever loves his **l** loses it, and Jn 12:25
and whoever hates his **l** in this world Jn 12:25
in this world will keep it for eternal **l**. Jn 12:25
that his commandment is eternal **l**. Jn 12:50
you now? I will lay down my **l** for you." Jn 13:37
"Will you lay down your **l** for me? Jn 13:38
"I am the way, and the truth, and the **l**. Jn 14:6
someone lays down his **l** for his friends. Jn 15:13
to give eternal **l** to all whom you have Jn 17:2
And this is eternal **l**, that they know you Jn 17:3
believing you may have **l** in his name. Jn 20:31
have made known to me the paths of **l**; Acts 2:28
and you killed the Author of **l**, whom Acts 3:15
to the people all the words of this **L**." Acts 5:20
For his **l** is taken away from the Acts 8:33
granted repentance that leads to **l**." Acts 11:18
yourselves unworthy of eternal **l**, Acts 13:46
were appointed to eternal **l** believed. Acts 13:48
to all mankind **l** and breath and Acts 17:25
not be alarmed, for his **l** is in him." Acts 20:10
do not account my **l** of any value nor Acts 20:24
I have lived my **l** before God in all good Acts 23:1
"My manner of **l** from my youth, spent Acts 26:4
there will be no loss of **l** among you, Acts 27:22
and immortality, he will give eternal **l**; Rom 2:7
who gives **l** to the dead and calls into Rom 4:17
reconciled, shall we be saved by his **l**. Rom 5:10
righteousness reign in **l** through the Rom 5:17
leads to justification and **l** for all men. Rom 5:18
leading to eternal **l** through Jesus Rom 5:21
we too might walk in newness of **l**. Rom 6:4
all, but the **l** he lives he lives to God. Rom 6:10
have been brought from death to **l**, Rom 6:13
to sanctification and its end, eternal **l**. Rom 6:22
of God is eternal **l** in Christ Jesus our Rom 6:23
code but in the new **l** of the Spirit. Rom 7:6
that promised **l** proved to Rom 7:10
law of the Spirit of **l** has set you free in Rom 8:2
set the mind on the Spirit is **l** and peace. Rom 8:6
the Spirit is **l** because of righteousness. Rom 8:10
dead will also give **l** to your mortal Rom 8:11
For I am sure that neither death nor **l**, Rom 8:38
I alone am left, and they seek my **l**." Rom 11:3
acceptance mean but **l** from the Rom 11:15
who risked their necks for my **l**, to Rom 16:4
is the source of your **l** in Christ Jesus, 1 Cor 1:30
or the world or **l** or death or the 1 Cor 3:22
then, matters pertaining to this **l**! 1 Cor 6:3
each person lead the **l** that the Lord 1 Cor 7:17
If in this **l** only we have hoped in 1 Cor 15:19
sow does not come to **l** unless it dies. 1 Cor 15:36
strength that we despaired of **l** itself. 2 Cor 1:8
to the other a fragrance from **l** to life. 2 Cor 2:16
to the other a fragrance from life to **l**. 2 Cor 2:16
the letter kills, but the Spirit gives **l**. 2 Cor 3:6
so that the **l** of Jesus may also be 2 Cor 4:10
so that the **l** of Jesus also may be 2 Cor 4:11
So death is at work in us, but **l** in you. 2 Cor 4:12
is mortal may be swallowed up by **l**. 2 Cor 5:4
have heard of my former **l** in Judaism, Gal 1:13
And the **l** I now live in the flesh I live by Gal 2:20
a law had been given that could give **l**, Gal 3:21
Spirit will from the Spirit reap eternal **l**. Gal 6:8
alienated from the **l** of God because of Eph 4:18
your former manner of **l** and is corrupt Eph 4:22
in my body, whether by **l** or by death. Phil 1:20
let your manner of **l** be worthy of the Phil 1:27
holding fast to the word of **l**, so that in Phil 2:16
risking his **l** to complete what was Phil 2:30
whose names are in the book of **l**. Phil 4:3
and your **l** is hidden with Christ in God. Col 3:3
When Christ who is your **l** appears, then Col 3:4
were to believe in him for eternal **l**. 1 Tm 1:16
we may lead a peaceful and quiet **l**, 1 Tm 2:2
promise for the present **l** and also for 1 Tm 4:8
present life and also for the **l** to come. 1 Tm 4:8
hold of the eternal **l** to which you 1 Tm 6:12
of God, who gives **l** to all things, 1 Tm 6:13
take hold of that which is truly **l**. 1 Tm 6:19
to the promise of the **l** that is in Christ 2 Tm 1:1
death and brought **l** and immortality 2 Tm 1:10
teaching, my conduct, my aim in **l**, 2 Tm 3:10
to live a godly **l** in Christ Jesus will 2 Tm 3:12
in hope of eternal **l**, which God, who never Ti 1:2
heirs according to the hope of eternal **l**. Ti 3:7
neither beginning of days nor end of **l**, Heb 7:3
but by the power of an indestructible **l**. Heb 7:16
By faith Joseph, at the end of his **l**, Heb 11:22
that they might rise again to a better **l**. Heb 11:35
Keep your **l** free from love of money, Heb 13:5
Consider the outcome of their way of **l**, Heb 13:7
the test he will receive the crown of **l**, Jas 1:12
body, setting on fire the entire course of **l**, Jas 3:6
tomorrow will bring. What is your **l**? Jas 4:14
they are heirs with you of the grace of **l**, 1 Pt 3:7
"Whoever desires to love **l** and see good 1 Pt 3:10
all things that pertain to **l** and godliness, 2 Pt 1:3
our hands, concerning the word of **l**— 1 Jn 1:1
the **l** was made manifest, and we have 1 Jn 1:2
to it and proclaim to you the eternal **l**, 1 Jn 1:2
promise that he made to us—eternal **l**. 1 Jn 2:25
that we have passed out of death into **l**, 1 Jn 3:14
murderer has eternal **l** abiding in him. 1 Jn 3:15
love, that he laid down his **l** for us, 1 Jn 3:16
testimony, that God gave us eternal **l**, 1 Jn 5:11
us eternal life, and this **l** is in his Son. 1 Jn 5:11
Whoever has the Son has **l**; whoever 1 Jn 5:12
not have the Son of God does not have **l**. 1 Jn 5:12
you may know that you have eternal **l**. 1 Jn 5:13
and God will give him **l**—to those who 1 Jn 5:16
Christ. He is the true God and eternal **l**. 1 Jn 5:20
Lord Jesus Christ that leads to eternal **l**. Jude 1:21
conquers I will grant to eat of the tree of **l**, Rv 2:7
first and the last, who died and came to **l**. Rv 2:8
death, and I will give you the crown of **l**. Rv 2:10
never blot his name out of the book of **l**. Rv 3:5
days a breath of **l** from God entered Rv 11:11
world in the book of **l** of the Lamb that Rv 13:8
in the book of **l** from the foundation of Rv 17:8
They came to **l** and reigned with Christ Rv 20:4
did not come to **l** until the thousand Rv 20:5
was opened, which is the book of **l**. Rv 20:12
was not found written in the book of **l**, Rv 20:15
spring of the water of **l** without payment. Rv 21:6
are written in the Lamb's book of **l**. Rv 21:27
showed me the river of the water of **l**, Rv 22:1
the tree of **l** with its twelve kinds of fruit, Rv 22:2
right to the tree of **l** and that they may Rv 22:14
desires take the water of **l** without price. Rv 22:17
share in the tree of **l** and in the holy Rv 22:19

LIFE'S (1)
soul is not satisfied with **l** good things, Eccl 6:3

LIFE-GIVING (2)
ear that listens to **l** reproof will dwell Prv 15:31
the last Adam became a **l** spirit. 1 Cor 15:45

LIFEBLOOD (5)
And for your **l** I will require a reckoning: Gn 9:5
Shall I drink the **l** of these men? 1 Chr 11:19
their **l** spattered on my garments, and Is 63:3
and I poured out their **l** on the earth." Is 63:6
skirts is found the **l** of the guiltless poor; Jer 2:34

LIFELESS (1)
If even **l** instruments, such as the 1 Cor 14:7

LIFELONG (1)
fear of death were subject to **l** slavery. Heb 2:15

LIFETIME (5)
as priests in the **l** of Aaron their father. Nm 3:4
Absalom in his **l** had taken and 2 Sm 18:18
but for a moment, and his favor is for a **l**. Ps 30:5
and my **l** is as nothing before you. Ps 39:5
that you in your **l** received your good Lk 16:25

LIFT (95)
"**L** up your eyes and look from the Gn 13:14
L up the boy, and hold him fast with Gn 21:18
And he said, '**L** up your eyes and see, all Gn 31:12
three days Pharaoh will **l** up your head Gn 40:13
three days Pharaoh will **l** up your head Gn 40:19
consent no one shall **l** up hand or foot Gn 41:44
L up your staff, and stretch out your Ex 14:16
the LORD **l** up his countenance upon Nm 6:26
top of Pisgah and **l** up your eyes Dt 3:27
You shall help him to **l** them up again. Dt 22:4
For I **l** up my hand to heaven and Dt 32:40
How then could I **l** up my face to your 2 Sm 2:22
therefore **l** up your prayer for the 2 Kgs 19:4
ashamed and blush to **l** my face to you, Ezr 9:6
I am in the right, I cannot **l** up my head, Jb 10:15
Surely then you will **l** up your face Jb 11:15
in the Almighty and **l** up your face to Jb 22:26
You **l** me up on the wind; you make me Jb 30:22
"Can you **l** up your voice to the clouds, Jb 38:34
L up the light of your face upon us, O Ps 4:6
l yourself up against the fury of my Ps 7:6
O you who **l** me up from the gates of Ps 9:13
Arise, O LORD; O God, **l** up your hand; Ps 10:12
who does not **l** up his soul to what is false Ps 24:4
L up your heads, O gates! And be lifted Ps 24:7
L up your heads, O gates! And lift them Ps 24:9
And **l** them up, O ancient doors, that the Ps 24:9
To you, O LORD, I **l** up my soul. Ps 25:1
of his tent; he will **l** me high upon a rock. Ps 27:5
when I **l** up my hands toward your most Ps 28:2
I live; in your name I will **l** up my hands. Ps 63:4
l up a song to him who rides through the Ps 68:4
to the wicked, 'Do not **l** up your horn; Ps 75:4
do not **l** up your horn on high, or speak Ps 75:5
for to you, O Lord, do I **l** up my soul. Ps 86:4
their voice; the floods **l** up their roaring. Ps 93:3
the way; therefore he will **l** up his head. Ps 110:7
I will **l** up the cup of salvation and call Ps 116:13
I will **l** up my hands toward your Ps 119:48
I **l** up my eyes to the hills. From where Ps 121:1
To you I **l** up my eyes, O you who are Ps 123:1
L up your hands to the holy place and Ps 134:2
I should go, for to you I **l** up my soul. Ps 143:8
are their eyes, how high their eyelids **l**! Prv 30:13
For if they fall, one will **l** up his fellow. Eccl 4:10
falls and has not another to **l** him up! Eccl 4:10
nation shall not **l** up sword against nation, Is 2:4
as if a staff should **l** him who is not Is 10:15
with the rod and **l** up their staff against Is 10:24
the sea, and he will **l** it as he did in Egypt. Is 10:26
They **l** up their voices, they sing for joy; Is 24:14
noise peoples flee; when you **l** yourself up, Is 33:3
says the LORD, "now I will **l** myself up; Is 33:10
therefore **l** up your prayer for the Is 37:4
l up your voice with strength, O Is 40:9
herald of good news; **l** it up, fear not; Is 40:9
L up your eyes on high and see: who Is 40:26
He will not cry aloud or **l** up his voice, or Is 42:2
the desert and its cities **l** up their voice, Is 42:11
They **l** it to their shoulders, they carry it, Is 46:7
L up your eyes around and see; they all Is 49:18
I will **l** up my hand to the nations, Is 49:22
L up your eyes to the heavens, and look at Is 51:6
of your watchmen—they **l** up their voice; Is 52:8
hold back; **l** up your voice like a trumpet; Is 58:1
L up your eyes all around, and see; they Is 60:4
it of stones; **l** up a signal over the peoples. Is 62:10
L up your eyes to the bare heights, and Jer 3:2
people, or **l** up a cry or prayer for them, Jer 7:16
or **l** up a cry or prayer on their behalf, Jer 11:14
"**L** up your eyes and see those who Jer 13:20
I myself will **l** up your skirts over your Jer 13:26
cry out, and **l** up your voice in Bashan; Jer 22:20
I will surely **l** you up and cast you away Jer 23:39
and **l** Jeremiah the prophet out of the Jer 38:10
L your hands to him for the lives of Lam 2:19
Let us **l** up our hearts and hands to Lam 3:41
l up your eyes now toward the north." So Ezk 8:5
sight you shall **l** the baggage upon Ezk 12:6
among them shall **l** his baggage upon Ezk 12:12
might be humble and not **l** itself up, Ezk 17:14
upon the mountains or **l** up his eyes to Ezk 18:6
upon the mountains or **l** up his eyes to Ezk 18:15
to **l** up the voice with shouting, Ezk 21:22
so that you shall not **l** up your eyes to Ezk 23:27
with the blood and **l** up your eyes to Ezk 33:25
own people shall **l** themselves up in Dn 11:14
nation shall not **l** up sword against Mi 4:3
and will **l** up your skirts over your face; Na 3:5
"**L** your eyes and see what this is that is Zec 5:5
All who **l** it will surely hurt themselves. Zec 12:3
will not take hold of it and **l** it out? Mt 12:11
would not even **l** up his eyes to heaven, Lk 18:13
Look, I tell you, **l** up your eyes, and see Jn 4:35
Therefore **l** your drooping hands and Heb 12:12

LIFTED (123)
And Lot **l** up his eyes and saw that the Gn 13:10
Sodom, "I have **l** my hand to the LORD, Gn 14:22
He **l** up his eyes and looked, and behold, Gn 18:2
him, she **l** up her voice and wept. Gn 21:16
the third day Abraham **l** up his eyes and Gn 22:4
And Abraham **l** up his eyes and Gn 22:13
And he **l** up his eyes and saw, and Gn 24:63
And Rebekah **l** up her eyes, and when Gn 24:64
my father." And Esau **l** up his voice Gn 27:38
season of the flock I **l** up my eyes and Gn 31:10
And Jacob **l** up his eyes and looked, and Gn 33:1
And when Esau **l** up his eyes and saw Gn 33:5
drew Joseph up and **l** him out of the Gn 37:28
as he heard that I **l** up my voice and Gn 39:15
But as soon as I **l** up my voice and Gn 39:18
for all his servants and **l** up the head of Gn 40:20
And he **l** up his eyes and saw his Gn 43:29
sight of his servants he **l** up the staff and Ex 7:20
which **l** the locusts and drove them Ex 10:19
near, the people of Israel **l** up their eyes, Ex 14:10
Then Aaron **l** up his hands toward the Lv 9:22
whenever the cloud **l** from over the Nm 9:17
And when the cloud **l** in the morning, Nm 9:21
a night, when the cloud **l** they set out. Nm 9:21
not set out, but when it **l** they set out. Nm 9:22
the cloud **l** from over the tabernacle Nm 10:11

And Moses **l** up his hand and struck Nm 20:11
And Balaam **l** up his eyes and saw Nm 24:2
then your heart be **l** up, and you forget Dt 8:14
heart may not be **l** up above his Dt 17:20
the priests' feet were **l** up on dry ground, Jos 4:18
by Jericho, he **l** up his eyes and looked, Jos 5:13
the people **l** up their voices and wept. Jgs 2:4
And he **l** up his eyes and saw the Jgs 19:17
and they **l** up their voices and wept Jgs 21:2
them, and they **l** up their voices and wept. Ru 1:9
Then they **l** up their voices and wept Ru 1:14
And when they **l** up their eyes and saw 1 Sm 6:13
son David?" And Saul **l** up his voice 1 Sm 24:16
And the king **l** up his voice and wept 2 Sm 3:32
who kept the watch **l** up his eyes and 2 Sm 13:34
sons came and **l** up their voice 2 Sm 13:36
and when he **l** up his eyes and 2 Sm 18:24
has **l** up his hand against King 2 Sm 20:21
also **l** up his hand against the king. 1 Kgs 11:26
the reason why he **l** up his hand 1 Kgs 11:27
And when he had **l** him and brought 2 Kgs 4:20
And he **l** up his face to the window 2 Kgs 9:32
Edom, and your heart has **l** you up. 2 Kgs 14:10
raised your voice and **l** your eyes to 2 Kgs 19:22
And David **l** his eyes and saw the 1 Chr 21:16
and your heart has **l** you up in 2 Chr 25:19
and those who mourn are **l** to safety. Jb 5:11
And were my head **l** up, you would hunt Jb 10:16
And be **l** up, O ancient doors, that the Ps 24:7
my head shall be **l** up above my enemies Ps 27:6
ate my bread, has **l** his heel against me. Ps 41:9
the horns of the righteous shall be **l** up. Ps 75:10
The floods have **l** up, O LORD, the floods Ps 93:3
O LORD, the floods have **l** up their voice; Ps 93:3
wind, which **l** up the waves of the sea. Ps 107:25
O LORD, my heart is not **l** up; my eyes Ps 131:1
and shall be **l** up above the hills; Is 2:2
against all that is **l** up—and it shall be Is 2:12
all the cedars of Lebanon, lofty and **l** up; Is 2:13
Lord sitting upon a throne, high and **l** up; Is 6:1
O LORD, your hand is **l** up, but they do Is 26:11
raised your voice and **l** your eyes to the Is 37:23
Every valley shall be **l** up, and every Is 40:4
he shall be high and **l** up, and shall be Is 52:13
thus says the One who is high and **l** up, Is 57:15
he **l** them up and carried them all the Is 63:9
forest; she has **l** up her voice against me; Jer 12:8
that your skirts are **l** up and you suffer Jer 13:22
up with ropes and **l** him out of the Jer 38:13
to heaven and has been **l** up even to the Jer 51:9
l up the head of Jehoiachin king of Jer 52:31
Then the Spirit **l** me up, and I heard Ezk 3:12
The Spirit **l** me up and took me away, Ezk 3:14
and the Spirit **l** me up between earth and Ezk 8:3
the north." So I **l** up my eyes toward Ezk 8:5
when the cherubim **l** up their wings Ezk 10:16
And the cherubim **l** up their wings Ezk 10:19
The Spirit **l** me up and brought me to Ezk 11:1
Then the cherubim **l** up their wings, Ezk 11:22
And the Spirit **l** me up and brought Ezk 11:24
the Spirit **l** me up and brought me into Ezk 43:5
I, Nebuchadnezzar, **l** my eyes to heaven, Dn 4:34
when his heart was **l** up and his spirit Dn 5:20
but you have **l** up yourself against the Dn 5:23
and it was **l** up from the ground and Dn 7:4
I **l** up my eyes and looked, and behold, a Dn 10:5
were filled, and their heart was **l** up; Hos 13:6
and it shall be **l** up above the hills; Mi 4:1
Your hand shall be **l** up over your Mi 5:9
forth its voice; it **l** its hands on high. Hab 3:10
And I **l** my eyes and saw, and behold, Zec 1:18
of the nations who **l** up their horns Zec 1:21
And I **l** my eyes and saw, and behold, a Zec 2:1
Again I **l** my eyes and saw, and behold, a Zec 5:1
And behold, the leaden cover was **l**, and Zec 5:7
Then I **l** my eyes and saw, and behold, Zec 5:9
and they **l** up the basket between earth Zec 5:9
Again I **l** my eyes and saw, and behold, Zec 6:1
And when they **l** up their eyes, they saw Mt 17:8
and took her by the hand and **l** her up, Mk 1:31
took him by the hand and **l** him up, Mk 9:27
And he **l** up his eyes on his disciples, and Lk 6:20
he **l** up his eyes and saw Abraham far Lk 16:23
and **l** up their voices, saying, "Jesus, Lk 17:13
And as Moses **l** up the serpent in the Jn 3:14
so must the Son of Man be **l** up, Jn 3:14
"When you have **l** up the Son of Man, Jn 8:28
And Jesus **l** up his eyes and said, Jn 11:41
And I, when I am **l** up from the earth, Jn 12:32
say that the Son of Man must be **l** up? Jn 12:34
ate my bread has **l** his heel against me.' Jn 13:18
these words, he **l** up his eyes to heaven, Jn 17:1
as they were looking on, he was **l** up, Acts 1:9
l up his voice and addressed them, Acts 2:14
they **l** their voices together to God and Acts 4:24
But Peter **l** him up, saying, "Stand up; Acts 10:26
Paul had done, they **l** up their voices, Acts 14:11

LIFTER (1)
about me, my glory, and the **l** of my head. Ps 3:3

LIFTING (7)
"Amen, Amen," **l** up their hands. Neh 8:6
and not from the wilderness comes **l** up, Ps 75:6
putting down one and **l** up another. Ps 75:7
and the **l** up of my hands as the evening Ps 141:2
and **l** up his hands he blessed them. Lk 24:50
L up his eyes, then, and seeing that a large Jn 6:5
l holy hands without anger or 1 Tm 2:8

LIFTS (8)
it rises up and as a lion it **l** itself; Nm 23:24
he **l** the needy from the ash heap to 1 Sm 2:8
The east wind **l** him up and he is gone; Jb 27:21
from the dust and **l** the needy from the Ps 113:7
The LORD **l** up those who are bowed Ps 146:8
The LORD **l** up the humble; he casts the Ps 147:6
As if a rod should wield him who **l** it, or Is 10:15
the pledge, **l** up his eyes to the idols, Ezk 18:12

LIGAMENTS (1)
knit together through its joints and **l**, Col 2:19

LIGHT (244)
said, "Let there be **l**," and there was light. Gn 1:3
said, "Let there be light," and there was **l**. Gn 1:3
And God saw that the **l** was good. And Gn 1:4
God separated the **l** from the darkness. Gn 1:4
God called the **l** Day, and the darkness he Gn 1:5
the heavens to give **l** upon the earth." Gn 1:15
great lights—the greater **l** to rule the day Gn 1:16
the day and the lesser **l** to rule the night Gn 1:16
of the heavens to give **l** on the earth, Gn 1:17
and to separate the **l** from the darkness. Gn 1:18
As soon as the morning was **l**, the men Gn 44:3
people of Israel had **l** where they lived. Ex 10:23
night in a pillar of fire to give them **l**, Ex 13:21
up so as to give **l** on the space in front Ex 25:37
to you pure beaten olive oil for the **l**, Ex 27:20
oil for the **l**, spices for the anointing oil Ex 35:8
the lampstand also for the **l**, with its Ex 35:14
and its lamps, and the oil for the **l**; Ex 35:14
and spices and oil for the **l**, and for the Ex 35:28
and all its utensils, and the oil for the **l**; Ex 39:37
that a **l** may be kept burning regularly. Lv 24:2
blue and cover the lampstand for the **l**, Nm 4:9
shall have charge of the oil for the **l**, Nm 4:16
seven lamps shall give **l** in front of the Nm 8:2
"Let us wait till the **l** of the morning; Jgs 16:2
where her master was, until it was **l**. Jgs 19:26
plunder them until the morning **l**; 1 Sm 14:36
nothing at all until the morning **l**. 1 Sm 25:36
and depart as soon as you have **l**." 1 Sm 29:10
and we shall **l** upon him as the dew 2 Sm 17:12
he dawns on them like the morning **l**, 2 Sm 23:4
if it had been a **l** thing for him to 1 Kgs 16:31
This is a **l** thing in the sight of the 2 Kgs 3:18
are silent and wait until the morning **l**, 2 Kgs 7:9
fire in the night to **l** for them the way Neh 9:12
of fire by night to **l** for them the way by Neh 9:19
The Jews had **l** and gladness and joy and Est 8:16
God above not seek it, nor **l** shine upon it. Jb 3:4
let it hope for **l**, but have none, nor see the Jb 3:9
child, as infants who never see the **l**? Jb 3:16
"Why is **l** given to him who is in misery, Jb 3:20
Why is **l** given to a man whose way is Jb 3:23
any order, where **l** is as thick darkness." Jb 10:22
darkness and brings deep darkness to **l**. Jb 12:22
They grope in the dark without **l**, and Jb 12:25
They make night into day; 'The **l**,' they Jb 17:12
"Indeed, the **l** of the wicked is put out, and Jb 18:5
The **l** is dark in his tent, and his lamp Jb 18:6
He is thrust from **l** into darkness, and Jb 18:18
for you, and **l** will shine on your ways. Jb 22:28
"There are those who rebel against the **l**, Jb 24:13
The murderer rises before it is **l**, that he Jb 24:14
themselves up; they do not know the **l**. Jb 24:16
armies? Upon whom does his **l** not arise? Jb 25:3
the boundary between **l** and darkness. Jb 26:10
thing that is hidden he brings out to **l**. Jb 28:11
and by his **l** I walked through darkness, Jb 29:3
and the **l** of my face they did not cast Jb 29:24
good, evil came, and when I waited for **l**, Jb 30:26
pit, and my life shall look upon the **l**.' Jb 33:28
that he may be lighted with the **l** of life. Jb 33:30
no one looks on the **l** when it is bright Jb 37:21
From the wicked their **l** is withheld, and Jb 38:15
"Where is the way to the dwelling of **l**, Jb 38:19
to the place where the **l** is distributed, Jb 38:24
His sneezings flash forth **l**, and his eyes Jb 41:18
Lift up the **l** of your face upon us, O LORD!" Ps 4:6
l up my eyes, lest I sleep the sleep of death, Ps 13:3
For it is you who **l** my lamp; the LORD Ps 18:28
The LORD is my **l** and my salvation; Ps 27:1
fountain of life; in your **l** do we see light. Ps 36:9
fountain of life; in your light do we see **l**. Ps 36:9
bring forth your righteousness as the **l**, Ps 37:6
and the **l** of my eyes—it also has gone Ps 38:10
Send out your **l** and your truth; let them Ps 43:3
and your arm, and the **l** of your face, Ps 44:3
his fathers, who will never again see **l**. Ps 49:19
I may walk before God in the **l** of life. Ps 56:13
a cloud, and all the night with a fiery **l**. Ps 78:14
who walk, O LORD, in the **l** of your face, Ps 89:15
our secret sins in the **l** of your presence. Ps 90:8
His lightnings **l** up the world; the earth Ps 97:4
L is sown for the righteous, and joy for Ps 97:11
covering yourself with **l** as with a Ps 104:2
a covering, and fire to give **l** by night. Ps 105:39
L dawns in the darkness for the Ps 112:4
he has made his **l** to shine upon us. Ps 118:27
a lamp to my feet and a **l** to my path. Ps 119:105
The unfolding of your words gives **l**; Ps 119:130
me, and the **l** about me be night," Ps 139:11
the day, for darkness is as **l** with you. Ps 139:12
of the righteous is like the **l** of dawn, Prv 4:18
is a lamp and the teaching a **l**, Prv 6:23
The **l** of the righteous rejoices, but the Prv 13:9
The **l** of the eyes rejoices the heart, and Prv 15:30
In the **l** of a king's face there is life, and Prv 16:15
When your eyes **l** on it, it is gone, for Prv 23:5
the LORD gives **l** to the eyes of both. Prv 29:13
is more gain in **l** than in darkness. Eccl 2:13
L is sweet, and it is pleasant for the eyes Eccl 11:7
the sun and the **l** and the moon and Eccl 12:2
come, let us walk in the **l** of the LORD. Is 2:5
who put darkness for **l** and light for Is 5:20
put darkness for light and **l** for darkness, Is 5:20
and the **l** is darkened by its clouds. Is 5:30
walked in darkness have seen a great **l**; Is 9:2
of deep darkness, on them has **l** shined. Is 9:2
The **l** of Israel will become a fire, and his Is 10:17
their constellations will not give their **l**; Is 13:10
rising, and the moon will not shed its **l**. Is 13:10
For your dew is a dew of **l**, and the earth Is 26:19
the **l** of the moon will be as the light of Is 30:26
of the moon will be as the **l** of the sun, Is 30:26
and the **l** of the sun will be sevenfold, Is 30:26
will be sevenfold, as the **l** of seven days, Is 30:26
for the people, a **l** for the nations, Is 42:6
turn the darkness before them into **l**, Is 42:16
I form **l** and create darkness, I make Is 45:7
"It is too **l** a thing that you should be my Is 49:6
I will make you as a **l** for the nations, that Is 49:6
darkness and has no **l** trust in the name Is 50:10
torches! Walk by the **l** of your fire, Is 50:11
I will set my justice for a **l** to the peoples. Is 51:4
Then shall your **l** break forth like the Is 58:8
then shall your **l** rise in the darkness Is 58:10
we hope for **l**, and behold, darkness, and Is 59:9
Arise, shine, for your **l** has come, and the Is 60:1
And nations shall come to your **l**, and Is 60:3
The sun shall be no more your **l** by day, Is 60:19
for brightness shall the moon give you **l**; Is 60:19
but the LORD will be your everlasting **l**, Is 60:19
for the LORD will be your everlasting **l**, Is 60:20
and to the heavens, and they had no **l**. Jer 4:23
and while you look for **l** he turns it into Jer 13:16
of the millstones and the **l** of the lamp. Jer 25:10
who gives the sun for **l** by day and the Jer 31:35
of the moon and the stars for **l** by night, Jer 31:35
me into darkness without any **l**; Lam 3:2
Is it too **l** a thing for the house of Judah Ezk 8:17
cloud, and the moon shall not give its **l**. Ezk 32:7
the darkness, and the **l** dwells with him. Dn 2:22
l and understanding and wisdom like Dn 5:11
and that **l** and understanding and Dn 5:14
and my judgment goes forth as the **l**. Hos 6:5
of the LORD? It is darkness, and not **l**, Am 5:18
the day of the LORD darkness, and not **l**, Am 5:20
sit in darkness, the LORD will be a **l** to me. Mi 7:8
He will bring me out to the **l**; I shall look Mi 7:9
His brightness was like the **l**; rays Hab 3:4
in their place at the **l** of your arrows as Hab 3:11
On that day there shall be no **l**, cold, or Zec 14:6
but at evening time there shall be **l**. Zec 14:7
dwelling in darkness have seen a great **l**, Mt 4:16
of death, on them a **l** has dawned." Mt 4:16
"You are the **l** of the world. A city set on Mt 5:14
Nor do people **l** a lamp and put it under Mt 5:15
a stand, and it gives **l** to all in the house. Mt 5:15
same way, let your **l** shine before others, Mt 5:16
your whole body will be full of **l**, Mt 6:22
If then the **l** in you is darkness, how Mt 6:23
What I tell you in the dark, say in the **l**, Mt 10:27
my yoke is easy, and my burden is **l**." Mt 11:30
sun, and his clothes became white as **l**. Mt 17:2
and the moon will not give its **l**, Mt 24:29

is anything secret except to come to **l**. Mk 4:22
and the moon will not give its **l**, Mk 13:24
to give **l** to those who sit in darkness and Lk 1:79
a **l** for revelation to the Gentiles, and for Lk 2:32
so that those who enter may see the **l**. Lk 8:16
that will not be known and come to **l**. Lk 8:17
so that those who enter may see the **l**. Lk 11:33
is healthy, your whole body is full of **l**, Lk 11:34
be careful lest the **l** in you be darkness. Lk 11:35
If then your whole body is full of **l**, Lk 11:36
when a lamp with its rays gives you **l**." Lk 11:36
said in the dark shall be heard in the **l**, Lk 12:3
a beating, will receive a **l** beating. Lk 12:48
does not **l** a lamp and sweep the house Lk 15:8
their own generation than the sons of **l**. Lk 16:8
as he sat in the **l** and looking closely at Lk 22:56
while the sun's **l** failed. And the curtain Lk 23:45
him was life, and the life was the **l** of men. Jn 1:4
The **l** shines in the darkness, and the Jn 1:5
as a witness, to bear witness about the **l**, Jn 1:7
He was not the **l**, but came to bear witness Jn 1:8
but came to bear witness about the **l**. Jn 1:8
The true **l**, which enlightens everyone, Jn 1:9
the **l** has come into the world, and people Jn 3:19
rather than the **l** because their deeds Jn 3:19
wicked things hates the **l** and does not Jn 3:20
hates the light and does not come to the **l**, Jn 3:20
whoever does what is true comes to the **l**, Jn 3:21
were willing to rejoice for a while in his **l**. Jn 5:35
to them, saying, "I am the **l** of the world. Jn 8:12
in darkness, but will have the **l** of life." Jn 8:12
I am in the world, I am the **l** of the world." Jn 9:5
because he sees the **l** of this world. Jn 11:9
stumbles, because the **l** is not in him." Jn 11:10
"The **l** is among you for a little while Jn 12:35
Walk while you have the **l**, lest Jn 12:35
While you have the **l**, believe in the Jn 12:36
you have the light, believe in the **l**, Jn 12:36
may become sons of **l**." When Jesus had Jn 12:36
I have come into the world as **l**, so that Jn 12:46
and suddenly a **l** from heaven flashed Acts 9:3
next to him, and a **l** shone in the cell. Acts 12:7
"'I have made you a **l** for the Gentiles, Acts 13:47
noon a great **l** from heaven suddenly Acts 22:6
with me saw the **l** but did not Acts 22:9
see because of the brightness of that **l**, Acts 22:11
I saw on the way a **l** from heaven, Acts 26:13
turn from darkness to **l** and from the Acts 26:18
he would proclaim **l** both to our Acts 26:23
blind, a **l** to those who are in darkness, Rom 2:19
darkness and put on the armor of **l**. Rom 13:12
who will bring to **l** the things now 1 Cor 4:5
them from seeing the **l** of the gospel of 2 Cor 4:4
"Let **l** shine out of darkness," has 2 Cor 4:6
hearts to give the **l** of the knowledge of 2 Cor 4:6
what fellowship has **l** with darkness? 2 Cor 6:14
disguises himself as an angel of **l**. 2 Cor 11:14
and to bring to **l** for everyone what is the Eph 3:9
darkness, but now you are **l** in the Lord. Eph 5:8
light in the Lord. Walk as children of **l** Eph 5:8
(for the fruit of **l** is found in all that is Eph 5:9
But when anything is exposed by the **l**, Eph 5:13
for anything that becomes visible is **l**. Eph 5:14
in the inheritance of the saints in **l**. Col 1:12
For you are all children of **l**, children 1 Thes 5:5
who dwells in unapproachable **l**, 1 Tm 6:16
and immortality to **l** through the 2 Tm 1:10
out of darkness into his marvelous **l**. 1 Pt 2:9
him and proclaim to you, that God is **l**, 1 Jn 1:5
But if we walk in the **l**, as he is in the 1 Jn 1:7
if we walk in the light, as he is in the **l**, 1 Jn 1:7
away and the true **l** is already shining. 1 Jn 2:8
says he is in the **l** and hates his brother 1 Jn 2:9
loves his brother abides in the **l**, 1 Jn 2:10
that a third of their **l** might be darkened, Rv 8:12
and the **l** of a lamp will shine in you no Rv 18:23
on it, for the glory of God gives it **l**, Rv 21:23
By its **l** will the nations walk, and the Rv 21:24
They will need no **l** of lamp or sun, Rv 22:5
or sun, for the Lord God will be their **l**, Rv 22:5

LIGHTED (2)
that he may be **l** with the light of life. Jb 33:30
your lightnings **l** up the world; Ps 77:18

LIGHTEN (8)
Perhaps he will **l** his hand from off you 1 Sm 6:5
Now therefore **l** the hard service of 1 Kgs 12:4
'**L** the yoke that your father put on 1 Kgs 12:9
our yoke heavy, but you **l** it for us,' 1 Kgs 12:10
Now therefore **l** the hard service of 2 Chr 10:4
'**L** the yoke that your father put on 2 Chr 10:9
our yoke heavy, but you **l** it for us'; 2 Chr 10:10
in the ship into the sea to **l** it for them. Jon 1:5

LIGHTENED (1)
had eaten enough, they **l** the ship, Acts 27:38

LIGHTENS (2)
O LORD, and my God **l** my darkness. 2 Sm 22:29
lamp; the LORD my God **l** my darkness. Ps 18:28

LIGHTER (1)
go up; they are together **l** than a breath. Ps 62:9

LIGHTING (2)
"No one after **l** a lamp covers it with a Lk 8:16
"No one after **l** a lamp puts it in a cellar Lk 11:33

LIGHTLY (5)
who despise me shall be **l** esteemed. 1 Sm 2:30
Because she took her whoredom **l**, she Jer 3:9
have healed the wound of my people **l**, Jer 6:14
have healed the wound of my people **l**, Jer 8:11
do not regard **l** the discipline of the Heb 12:5

LIGHTNING (28)
and the flashes of **l** and the sound of Ex 20:18
scattered them; **l**, and routed them. 2 Sm 22:15
rain and a way for the **l** of the thunder, Jb 28:26
he scatters his **l** about him and covers Jb 36:30
his hands with the **l** and commands it Jb 36:32
it go, and his **l** to the corners of the earth. Jb 37:3
with moisture; the clouds scatter his **l**. Jb 37:11
them and causes the **l** of his cloud to Jb 37:15
and fiery **l** bolts through their land. Ps 105:32
Flash forth the **l** and scatter them; send Ps 144:6
He makes **l** for the rain, and he brings Jer 10:13
He makes **l** for the rain, and he brings Jer 51:16
bright, and out of the fire went forth **l**. Ezk 1:13
fro, like the appearance of a flash of **l**. Ezk 1:14
for slaughter, polished to flash like **l**! Ezk 21:10
Ah, it is made like **l**; it is taken up for Ezk 21:15
to consume and to flash like **l**— Ezk 21:28
beryl, his face like the appearance of **l**, Dn 10:6
they gleam like torches; they dart like **l**. Na 2:4
them, and his arrow will go forth like **l**; Zec 9:14
For as the **l** comes from the east and Mt 24:27
His appearance was like **l**, and his Mt 28:3
"I saw Satan fall like **l** from heaven. Lk 10:18
For as the **l** flashes and lights up the Lk 17:24
From the throne came flashes of **l**, and Rv 4:5
peals of thunder, rumblings, flashes of **l**, Rv 8:5
There were flashes of **l**, rumblings, Rv 11:19
And there were flashes of **l**, rumblings, Rv 16:18

LIGHTNINGS (7)
there were thunders and **l** and a thick Ex 19:16
does not restrain the **l** when his voice is Jb 37:4
Can you send forth **l**, that they may go Jb 38:35
he flashed forth **l** and routed them. Ps 18:14
whirlwind; your **l** lighted up the world; Ps 77:18
His **l** light up the world; the earth sees Ps 97:4
who makes **l** for the rain and brings Ps 135:7

LIGHTS (10)
"Let there be **l** in the expanse of the Gn 1:14
and let them be **l** in the expanse of the Gn 1:15
made the two great **l**—the greater light Gn 1:16
established the heavenly **l** and the sun. Ps 74:16
to him who made the great **l**, for his Ps 136:7
All the bright **l** of heaven will I make Ezk 32:8
the lightning flashes and **l** up the sky Lk 17:24
the jailer called for **l** and rushed in, Acts 16:29
whom you shine as **l** in the world, Phil 2:15
from the Father of **l** with whom there is Jas 1:17

LIKEN (3)
To whom then will you **l** God, or what Is 40:18
"To whom will you **l** me and make me Is 46:5
What can I **l** to you, that I may Lam 2:13

LIKENESS (36)
us make man in our image, after our **l**. Gn 1:26
man, he made him in the **l** of God. Gn 5:1
130 years, he fathered a son in his own **l**, Gn 5:3
or any **l** of anything that is in heaven Ex 20:4
of any figure, the **l** of male or female, Dt 4:16
the **l** of any animal that is on the earth, Dt 4:17
the **l** of any winged bird that flies in the Dt 4:17
the **l** of anything that creeps on the Dt 4:18
the **l** of any fish that is in the water under Dt 4:18
or any **l** of anything that is in heaven Dt 5:8
I awake, I shall be satisfied with your **l**. Ps 17:15
liken God, or what **l** compare with him? Is 40:18
of it came the **l** of four living creatures. Ezk 1:5
their appearance: they had a human **l**, Ezk 1:5
As for the **l** of their faces, each had a Ezk 1:10
As for the **l** of the living creatures, their Ezk 1:13
And the four had the same **l**, their Ezk 1:16
creatures there was the **l** of an expanse, Ezk 1:22
their heads there was the **l** of a throne, Ezk 1:26
and seated above the **l** of a throne was a Ezk 1:26
a throne was a **l** with a human Ezk 1:26
the appearance of the **l** of the glory of Ezk 1:28
appearance, the four had the same **l**, Ezk 10:10
their wings the **l** of human hands. Ezk 10:21
And as for the **l** of their faces, they Ezk 10:22
a **l** of Babylonians whose native land Ezk 23:15
one in the **l** of the children of man Dn 10:16
"Whose **l** and inscription is this?" Mt 22:20
"Whose **l** and inscription is this?" Mk 12:16
Whose **l** and inscription does it have?" Lk 20:24
come down to us in the **l** of men!" Acts 14:11
his own Son in the **l** of sinful flesh and Rom 8:3
created after the **l** of God in true Eph 4:24
of a servant, being born in the **l** of men. Phil 2:7
priest arises in the **l** of Melchizedek, Heb 7:15
curse people who are made in the **l** of God. Jas 3:9

LIKES (1)
Diotrephes, who **l** to put himself first, 3 Jn 1:9

LIKEWISE (57)
He **l** instructed the second and the Gn 32:19
Leah **l** and her children drew near and Gn 33:7
eat. You shall do **l** with your vineyard, Ex 23:11
L you shall make loops on the edge of Ex 26:4
And **l** for its length on the north side Ex 27:11
L he made them on the edge of the Ex 36:11
And I **l** will go with you into the territory Jgs 1:3
L, every one who kneels down to drink." Jgs 7:5
he said to them, "Look at me, and do **l**. Jgs 7:17
L, when all the men of Israel who 1 Sm 14:22
they **l** fled before Abishai and 2 Sm 10:14
L he made pomegranates in two rows 1 Kgs 7:18
"**L**, when a foreigner, who is not of 1 Kgs 8:41
Their children did **l**, and their 2 Kgs 17:41
L, all the rest of Israel were of a 1 Chr 12:38
fled, they **l** fled before Abishai, 1 Chr 19:15
praising the LORD, and **l** at evening, 1 Chr 23:30
L through them these were exported 2 Chr 1:17
"**L**, when a foreigner, who is not of 2 Chr 6:32
He **l** provided cities for himself, and 2 Chr 32:29
and the people **l** were exceedingly 2 Chr 36:14
have **l** cast lots for the wood offering, Neh 10:34
'Fall on the earth,' **l** to the downpour, Jb 37:6
L, when all the Judeans who were in Jer 40:11
has done; he sees, and does not do **l**: Ezk 18:14
and **l** the vestibule had windows all Ezk 40:16
leaving no offspring. And the third **l**. Mk 12:21
none, and whoever has food is to do **l**." Lk 3:11
So **l** a Levite, when he came to the place Lk 10:32
Jesus said to him, "You go, and do **l**." Lk 10:37
unless you repent, you will all **l** perish. Lk 13:3
unless you repent, you will all **l** perish." Lk 13:5
L, just as it was in the days of Lot— Lk 17:28
and **l** let the one who is in the field not Lk 17:31
and **l** all seven left no children and Lk 20:31
And **l** the cup after they had eaten, Lk 22:20
a moneybag take it, and **l** a knapsack. Lk 22:36
the Father does, that the Son does **l**. Jn 5:19
and the men **l** gave up natural Rom 1:27
L, my brothers, you also have died to Rom 7:4
L the Spirit helps us in our weakness. Rom 8:26
rights, and **l** the wife to her husband. 1 Cor 7:3
L the husband does not have authority 1 Cor 7:4
L he who was free when called is a 1 Cor 7:22
L you also should be glad and rejoice Phil 2:18
l also that women should adorn 1 Tm 2:9
Deacons **l** must be dignified, not 1 Tm 3:8
Their wives **l** must be dignified, not 1 Tm 3:11
Older women **l** are to be reverent in Ti 2:3
L, urge the younger men to be Ti 2:6
he himself **l** partook of the same Heb 2:14
L, wives, be subject to your own 1 Pt 3:1
L, husbands, live with your wives in an 1 Pt 3:7
L, you who are younger, be subject to 1 Pt 5:5
She who is at Babylon, who is **l** chosen, 1 Pt 5:13
which **l** indulged in sexual immorality Jude 1:7
from shining, and **l** a third of the night. Rv 8:12

LIKHI (1)
were Ahian, Shechem, **L**, and Aniam. 1 Chr 7:19

LILIES (11)
To the choirmaster: according to **L**. A Ps 45:T
To the choirmaster: according to **L**. Of Ps 69:T
To the choirmaster: according to **L**. A Ps 80:T
and I am his; he grazes among the **l**. Sg 2:16
twins of a gazelle, that graze among the **l**. Sg 4:5
His lips are **l**, dripping liquid myrrh. Sg 5:13
to graze in the gardens and to gather **l**. Sg 6:2
beloved is mine; he grazes among the **l**. Sg 6:3
belly is a heap of wheat, encircled with **l**. Sg 7:2
Consider the **l** of the field, how they Mt 6:28
Consider the **l**, how they grow: they Lk 12:27

LILY (5)
brim of a cup, like the flower of a **l**. 1 Kgs 7:26
the brim of a cup, like the flower of a **l**. 2 Chr 4:5
I am a rose of Sharon, a **l** of the valleys. Sg 2:1
As a **l** among brambles, so is my love Sg 2:2
to Israel; he shall blossom like the **l**; Hos 14:5

LILY-WORK (2)
of the pillars in the vestibule were of **l**, 1 Kgs 7:19
And on the tops of the pillars was **l**. 1 Kgs 7:22

LIMB (7)
has a mutilated face or a **l** too long, Lv 21:18
concubine he divided her, **l** by limb, Jgs 19:29
concubine he divided her, limb by **l**, Jgs 19:29
you shall be torn **l** from limb, Dn 2:5
you shall be torn limb from **l**, Dn 2:5
Abednego shall be torn **l** from limb, Dn 3:29
Abednego shall be torn limb from **l**, Dn 3:29

LIMBS (4)
the firstborn of death consumes his **l**. Jb 18:13
tubes of bronze, his **l** like bars of iron. Jb 40:18
"I will not keep silence concerning his **l**, Jb 41:12
his **l** gave way, and his knees knocked Dn 5:6

LIME (2)
And the peoples will be as if burned to **l**, Is 33:12
because he burned to **l** the bones of the Am 2:1

LIMIT (14)
and its **l** shall be south of Nm 34:4
of Egypt, and its **l** shall be at the sea. Nm 34:5
and the **l** of the border shall be at Nm 34:8
and its **l** shall be at Hazar-enan. Nm 34:9
and its **l** shall be at the Salt Sea. Nm 34:12
Can you find out the **l** of the Almighty? Jb 11:7
paths; you set a **l** for the soles of my feet. Jb 13:27
of God? And do you **l** wisdom to yourself? Jb 15:8
out to the farthest **l** the ore in gloom Jb 28:3
I have seen a **l** to all perfection, but Ps 119:96
when he assigned to the sea its **l**, so that Prv 8:29
the transgressors have reached their **l**, Dn 8:23
strength; Egypt too, and that without **l**; Na 3:9
do not boast beyond **l** in the labors 2 Cor 10:15

LIMITATIONS (1)
terms, because of your natural **l**. Rom 6:19

LIMITED (1)
perhaps by agreement for a **l** time, 1 Cor 7:5

LIMITS (6)
And you shall set **l** for the people all Ex 19:12
'Set **l** around the mountain and Ex 19:23
the pasturelands of Sharon to their **l**. 1 Chr 5:16
you have appointed his **l** that he cannot Jb 14:5
and prescribed **l** for it and set bars and Jb 38:10
But we will not boast beyond **l**, but 2 Cor 10:13

LIMPED (1)
And they **l** around the altar that 1 Kgs 18:26

LIMPING (2)
he passed Penuel, **l** because of his hip. Gn 32:31
will you go **l** between two different 1 Kgs 18:21

LINE (46)
Sea you shall draw a **l** to Mount Hor. Nm 34:7
you shall draw a **l** to Lebo-hamath, Nm 34:8
"You shall draw a **l** for your eastern Nm 34:10
drew up the battle **l** against them at Jgs 20:20
again formed the battle **l** in the same Jgs 20:22
Philistines drew up in **l** against Israel, 1 Sm 4:2
ran from the battle **l** and came to 1 Sm 4:12
and drew up in **l** of battle against the 1 Sm 17:2
the host was going out to the battle **l**, 1 Sm 17:20
toward the battle **l** to meet the 1 Sm 17:48
Moab and he measured them with a **l**, 2 Sm 8:2
put to death, and one full **l** to be spared. 2 Sm 8:2
and a **l** of twelve cubits measured its 1 Kgs 7:15
and a **l** of thirty cubits measured its 1 Kgs 7:23
the measuring **l** of Samaria, 2 Kgs 21:13
and the plumb **l** of the house of 2 Kgs 21:13
and a **l** of thirty cubits measured its 2 Chr 4:2
drew up his **l** of battle against 2 Chr 13:3
know! Or who stretched the **l** upon it? Jb 38:5
Their measuring **l** goes out through all Ps 19:4
precept upon precept, **l** upon line, Is 28:10
precept upon precept, line upon **l**, Is 28:10
upon precept, line upon line, **l** upon line, Is 28:10
upon precept, line upon line, line upon **l**, Is 28:10
precept upon precept, **l** upon line, Is 28:13
precept upon precept, line upon **l**, Is 28:13
upon precept, line upon line, **l** upon line, Is 28:13
upon precept, line upon line, line upon **l**, Is 28:13
And I will make justice the **l**, and Is 28:17
the line, and righteousness the plumb **l**; Is 28:17
He shall stretch the **l** of confusion over Is 34:11
over it, and the plumb **l** of emptiness. Is 34:11
has portioned it out to them with the **l**; Is 34:17
The carpenter stretches a **l**; he marks it Is 44:13
And the measuring **l** shall go out Jer 31:39
Zion; he stretched out the measuring **l**; Lam 2:8
with a measuring **l** in his hand, Ezk 47:3
beside a wall built with a plumb **l**, Am 7:7
plumb line, with a plumb **l** in his hand. Am 7:7
I said, "A plumb **l**." Then the Lord said, Am 7:8
I am setting a plumb **l** in the midst of Am 7:8
shall be divided up with a measuring **l**; Am 7:17
have none to cast the **l** by lot in the Mi 2:5
and the measuring **l** shall be stretched Zec 1:16
a man with a measuring **l** in his hand! Zec 2:1
and shall see the plumb **l** in the hand of Zec 4:10

LINEAGE (1)
he was of the house and **l** of David, Lk 2:4

LINED (3)
He **l** the walls of the house on the 1 Kgs 6:15
The nave he **l** with cypress and 2 Chr 3:5
So he **l** the house with gold—its 2 Chr 3:7

LINEN (104)
in garments of fine **l** and put a gold Gn 41:42
and scarlet yarns and fine twined **l**, Ex 25:4
curtains of fine twined **l** and blue and Ex 26:1
and scarlet yarns and fine twined **l**. Ex 26:31
and scarlet yarns and fine twined **l**, Ex 26:36
of fine twined **l** a hundred cubits Ex 27:9
and scarlet yarns and fine twined **l**, Ex 27:16
hangings of fine twined **l** and bases of Ex 27:18
and scarlet yarns, and fine twined **l**. Ex 28:5
and scarlet yarns, and of fine twined **l**, Ex 28:6
and scarlet yarns, and fine twined **l**. Ex 28:8
and fine twined **l** shall you make it. Ex 28:15
the coat in checker work of fine **l**, Ex 28:39
and you shall make a turban of fine **l**, Ex 28:39
make for them **l** undergarments to Ex 28:42
and scarlet yarns and fine twined **l**; Ex 35:6
scarlet yarns or fine **l** or goats' hair or Ex 35:23
and scarlet yarns and fine twined **l**. Ex 35:25
and scarlet yarns and fine twined **l**, Ex 35:35
made of fine twined **l** and blue and Ex 36:8
and scarlet yarns and fine twined **l**; Ex 36:35
and scarlet yarns and fine twined **l**, Ex 36:37
of the court were of fine twined **l**, Ex 38:9
around the court were of fine twined **l**. Ex 38:16
and scarlet yarns and fine twined **l**. Ex 38:18
and scarlet yarns and fine twined **l**. Ex 38:23
and scarlet yarns, and fine twined **l**. Ex 39:2
scarlet yarns, and into the fine twined **l**, Ex 39:3
and scarlet yarns, and fine twined **l**, Ex 39:5
and scarlet yarns, and fine twined **l**. Ex 39:8
and scarlet yarns and fine twined **l**. Ex 39:24
also made the coats, woven of fine **l**, Ex 39:27
and the turban of fine **l**, and the caps of Ex 39:28
of fine linen, and the caps of fine **l**, Ex 39:28
and the **l** undergarments of fine twined Ex 39:28
linen undergarments of fine twined **l**, Ex 39:28
the sash of fine twined **l** and of blue and Ex 39:29
shall put on his **l** garment and put his Lv 6:10
and put his **l** undergarment on his Lv 6:10
whether a woolen or a **l** garment, Lv 13:47
in warp or woof of **l** or wool, or in a Lv 13:48
the warp or the woof, the wool or the **l**, Lv 13:52
disease in a garment of wool or **l**, Lv 13:59
put on the holy **l** coat and shall have Lv 16:4
shall have the **l** undergarment on his Lv 16:4
he shall tie the **l** sash around his waist, Lv 16:4
around his waist, and wear the **l** turban; Lv 16:4
shall take off the **l** garments that he put Lv 16:23
wearing the holy **l** garments. Lv 16:32
wear cloth of wool and **l** mixed together. Dt 22:11
give you thirty **l** garments and thirty Jgs 14:12
give me thirty **l** garments and thirty Jgs 14:13
the LORD, a boy clothed with a **l** ephod. 1 Sm 2:18
persons who wore the **l** ephod. 1 Sm 22:18
And David was wearing a **l** ephod. 2 Sm 6:14
the house of **l** workers at 1 Chr 4:21
was clothed with a robe of fine **l**, 1 Chr 15:27
singers. And David wore a **l** ephod. 1 Chr 15:27
blue, and crimson fabrics and fine **l**, 2 Chr 2:14
and crimson fabrics and fine **l**, 2 Chr 3:14
sons and kinsmen, arrayed in fine **l**, 2 Chr 5:12
with cords of fine **l** and purple to silver Est 1:6
crown and a robe of fine **l** and purple, Est 8:15
colored linens from Egyptian **l**; Prv 7:16
her clothing is fine **l** and purple. Prv 31:22
She makes **l** garments and sells them; Prv 31:24
the mirrors, the **l** garments, the turbans, Is 3:23
"Go and buy a **l** loincloth and put it Jer 13:1
and with them was a man clothed in **l**, Ezk 9:2
And he called to the man clothed in **l**, Ezk 9:3
And behold, the man clothed in **l**, with Ezk 9:11
And he said to the man clothed in **l**, Ezk 10:2
he commanded the man clothed in **l**, Ezk 10:6
into the hands of the man clothed in **l**, Ezk 10:7
wrapped you in fine **l** and covered you Ezk 16:10
clothing was of fine **l** and silk and Ezk 16:13
Of fine embroidered **l** from Egypt was Ezk 27:7
purple, embroidered work, fine **l**, Ezk 27:16
with a **l** cord and a measuring reed in Ezk 40:3
court, they shall wear **l** garments. Ezk 44:17
They shall have **l** turbans on their Ezk 44:18
and **l** undergarments around their Ezk 44:18
looked, and behold, a man clothed in **l**, Dn 10:5
someone said to the man clothed in **l**, Dn 12:6
And I heard the man clothed in **l**, who Dn 12:7
and wrapped it in a clean **l** shroud Mt 27:59
with nothing but a **l** cloth about his Mk 14:51
but he left the **l** cloth and ran away Mk 14:52
And Joseph bought a **l** shroud, and Mk 15:46
wrapped him in the **l** shroud and laid Mk 15:46
in purple and fine **l** and who feasted Lk 16:19
wrapped it in a **l** shroud and laid him Lk 23:53
in, he saw the **l** cloths by themselves; Lk 24:12
his hands and feet bound with **l** strips, Jn 11:44
and bound it in **l** cloths with the spices, Jn 19:40
to look in, he saw the **l** cloths lying there, Jn 20:5
the tomb. He saw the **l** cloths lying there, Jn 20:6
not lying with the **l** cloths but folded up Jn 20:7
seven plagues, clothed in pure, bright **l**, Rv 15:6
of gold, silver, jewels, pearls, fine **l**, Rv 18:12
the great city that was clothed in fine **l**, Rv 18:16
granted her to clothe herself with fine **l**, Rv 19:8
—for the fine **l** is the righteous deeds Rv 19:8
the armies of heaven, arrayed in fine **l**, Rv 19:14

LINENS (1)
colored **l** from Egyptian linen; Prv 7:16

LINES (3)
Two **l** he measured to be put to death, 2 Sm 8:2
they drew up their **l** of battle in the 2 Chr 14:10
The **l** have fallen for me in pleasant Ps 16:6

LINGER (1)
Then open the door and flee; do not **l**." 2 Kgs 9:3

LINGERED (1)
But he **l**. So the men seized him and his Gn 19:16

LINGERS (1)
has seized me, and yet my life still **l**.' 2 Sm 1:9

LINTEL (4)
two doorposts and the **l** of the houses in Ex 12:7
and touch the **l** and the two doorposts Ex 12:22
sees the blood on the **l** and on the two Ex 12:23
the **l** and the doorposts were 1 Kgs 6:31

LINUS (1)
as do Pudens and **L** and Claudia and 2 Tm 4:21

LION (91)
he crouched as a **l** and as a lioness; Gn 49:9
it rises up and as a **l** it lifts itself; Nm 23:24
he lay down like a **l** and like a lioness; Nm 24:9
Gad crouches like a **l**; he tears off arm Dt 33:20
a young **l** came toward him roaring. Jgs 14:5
he tore the **l** in pieces as one tears a Jgs 14:6
he turned aside to see the carcass of the **l**, Jgs 14:8
was a swarm of bees in the body of the **l**, Jgs 14:8
the honey from the carcass of the **l**. Jgs 14:9
is stronger than a **l**?" And he said to Jgs 14:18
And when there came a **l**, or a bear, 1 Sm 17:34
the paw of the **l** and from the paw 1 Sm 17:37
whose heart is like the heart of a **l**, 2 Sm 17:10
down and struck down a **l** in a pit on 2 Sm 23:20
as he went away a **l** met him on the 1 Kgs 13:24
it; the **l** also stood beside the body. 1 Kgs 13:24
the road and the **l** standing by the 1 Kgs 13:25
the LORD has given him to the **l**, 1 Kgs 13:26
donkey and the **l** standing beside the 1 Kgs 13:28
The **l** had not eaten the body or torn 1 Kgs 13:28
a **l** shall strike you down." And as 1 Kgs 20:36
a **l** met him and struck him down. 1 Kgs 20:36
and struck down a **l** in a pit on 1 Chr 11:22
The roar of the **l**, the voice of the fierce Jb 4:10
roar of the lion, the voice of the fierce **l**, Jb 4:10
The strong **l** perishes for lack of prey, Jb 4:11
hunt me like a **l** and again work Jb 10:16
not trodden it; the **l** has not passed over it. Jb 28:8
"Can you hunt the prey for the **l**, or Jb 38:39
lest like a **l** they tear my soul apart, Ps 7:2
lurks in ambush like a **l** in his thicket; Ps 10:9
He is like a **l** eager to tear, as a young Ps 17:12
tear, as a young **l** lurking in ambush. Ps 17:12
at me, like a ravening and roaring **l**. Ps 22:13
Save me from the mouth of the **l**! You Ps 22:21
You will tread on the **l** and the adder; Ps 91:13
the young **l** and the serpent you will Ps 91:13
king's wrath is like the growling of a **l**, Prv 19:12
of a king is like the growling of a **l**; Prv 20:2
sluggard says, "There is a **l** outside! Prv 22:13
says, "There is a **l** in the road! Prv 26:13
in the road! There is a **l** in the streets!" Prv 26:13
but the righteous are bold as a **l**. Prv 28:1
Like a roaring **l** or a charging bear is Prv 28:15
the **l**, which is mightiest among beasts Prv 30:30
for a living dog is better than a dead **l**. Eccl 9:4
Their roaring is like a **l**, like young lions Is 5:29
and the calf and the **l** and the fattened calf Is 11:6
and the **l** shall eat straw like the ox. Is 11:7

more, a **l** for those of Moab who escape, Is 15:9
from where come the lioness and the **l**, Is 30:6
"As a **l** or a young lion growls over his Is 31:4
a lion or a young **l** growls over his prey, Is 31:4
No **l** shall be there, nor shall any Is 35:9
like a **l** he breaks all my bones; Is 38:13
the **l** shall eat straw like the ox, and dust Is 65:25
your prophets like a ravening **l**. Jer 2:30
A **l** has gone up from his thicket, a Jer 4:7
Therefore a **l** from the forest shall strike Jer 5:6
has become to me like a **l** in the forest; Jer 12:8
Like a **l** he has left his lair, for their Jer 25:38
like a **l** coming up from the jungle of Jer 49:19
like a **l** coming up from the thicket of Jer 50:44
bear lying in wait for me, a **l** in hiding; Lam 3:10
four had the face of a **l** on the right side, Ezk 1:10
face, and the third the face of a **l**, Ezk 10:14
he became a young **l**, and he learned to Ezk 19:3
of her cubs and made him a young **l**. Ezk 19:5
he became a young **l**, and he learned to Ezk 19:6
is like a roaring **l** tearing the prey; Ezk 22:25
consider yourself a **l** of the nations, Ezk 32:2
face of a young **l** toward the palm tree Ezk 41:19
first was like a **l** and had eagles' wings. Dn 7:4
For I will be like a **l** to Ephraim, and Hos 5:14
and like a young **l** to the house of Hos 5:14
go after the LORD; he will roar like a **l**; Hos 11:10
So I am to them like a **l**; like a leopard I Hos 13:7
and there I will devour them like a **l**, Hos 13:8
Does a **l** roar in the forest, when he has Am 3:4
Does a young **l** cry out from his den, if Am 3:4
The **l** has roared; who will not fear? The Am 3:8
from the mouth of the **l** two legs, Am 3:12
as if a man fled from a **l**, and a bear met Am 5:19
like a **l** among the beasts of the forest, Mi 5:8
like a young **l** among the flocks of sheep, Mi 5:8
lions, where the **l** and lioness went, Na 2:11
The **l** tore enough for his cubs and Na 2:12
the devil prowls around like a roaring **l**, 1 Pt 5:8
the first living creature like a **l**, the second Rv 4:7
behold, the **L** of the tribe of Judah, the Rv 5:5
out with a loud voice, like a **l** roaring. Rv 10:3

LION'S (4)
Judah is a **l** cub; from the prey, my son, Gn 49:9
"Dan is a **l** cub that leaps from Dt 33:22
it. So I was rescued from the **l** mouth. 2 Tm 4:17
bear's, and its mouth was like a **l** mouth. Rv 13:2

LIONESS (8)
down; he crouched as a lion and as a **l**; Gn 49:9
As a **l** it rises up and as a lion it lifts Nm 23:24
he lay down like a lion and like a **l**; Nm 24:9
prey, and the cubs of the **l** are scattered. Jb 4:11
from where come the **l** and the lion, Is 30:6
and say: What was your mother? A **l**! Ezk 19:2
are lions' teeth, and it has the fangs of a **l**. Jl 1:6
young lions, where the lion and **l** went, Na 2:11

LIONESSES (1)
for his cubs and strangled prey for his **l**; Na 2:12

LIONS (40)
has struck down both **l** and bears, 1 Sm 17:36
than eagles; they were stronger than **l**. 2 Sm 1:23
that were set in the frames were **l**, 1 Kgs 7:29
both above and below the **l** and oxen, 1 Kgs 7:29
carved cherubim, **l**, and palm trees, 1 Kgs 7:36
armrests and two **l** standing beside 1 Kgs 10:19
while twelve **l** stood there, one on 1 Kgs 10:20
the LORD sent **l** among them, 2 Kgs 17:25
he has sent **l** among them, 2 Kgs 17:26
like the faces of **l** and who were swift 1 Chr 12:8
rests and two **l** standing beside the 2 Chr 9:18
while twelve **l** stood there, one on 2 Chr 9:19
lion, the teeth of the young **l** are broken. Jb 4:10
or satisfy the appetite of the young **l**, Jb 38:39
The young **l** suffer want and hunger; Ps 34:10
destruction, my precious life from the **l**! Ps 35:17
My soul is in the midst of **l**; I lie down Ps 57:4
tear out the fangs of the young **l**, O LORD! Ps 58:6
The young **l** roar for their prey, Ps 104:21
of Senir and Hermon, from the dens of **l**, Sg 4:8
is like a lion, like young **l** they roar; Is 5:29
The **l** have roared against him; they Jer 2:15
is a hunted sheep driven away by **l**. Jer 50:17
"They shall roar together like **l**; they Jer 51:38
Among **l** she crouched; in the midst of Ezk 19:2
the midst of young **l** she reared her Ezk 19:2
He prowled among the **l**; he became a Ezk 19:6
O king, shall be cast into the den of **l**. Dn 6:7
into the den of **l**?" The king answered Dn 6:12
was brought and cast into the den of **l**. Dn 6:16
arose and went in haste to the den of **l**. Dn 6:19
been able to deliver you from the **l**?" Dn 6:20
and cast into the den of **l**—they, Dn 6:24
the **l** overpowered them and broke all Dn 6:24
saved Daniel from the power of the **l**." Dn 6:27
den, the feeding place of the young **l**, Na 2:11
the sword shall devour your young **l**. Na 2:13
Her officials within her are roaring **l**; her Zep 3:3
The sound of the roar of the **l**, for the Zec 11:3
promises, stopped the mouths of **l**, Heb 11:33

LIONS' (6)
like lions; they shall growl like **l** cubs. Jer 51:38
sent his angel and shut the **l** mouths, Dn 6:22
its teeth are **l** teeth, and it has the fangs of Jl 1:6
Where is the **l** den, the feeding place of Na 2:11
women's hair, and their teeth like **l** teeth; Rv 9:8
the heads of the horses were like **l** heads, Rv 9:17

LIP (1)
he shall cover his upper **l** and cry out, Lv 13:45

LIPS (114)
to me, for I am of uncircumcised **l**?" Ex 6:12
LORD, "Behold, I am of uncircumcised **l**. Ex 6:30
other gods, nor let it be heard on your **l**. Ex 23:13
if anyone utters with his **l** a rash oath to Lv 5:4
utterance of her **l** by which she Nm 30:6
utterance of her **l** by which she Nm 30:8
out of her **l** concerning her vows Nm 30:12
be careful to do what has passed your **l**, Dt 23:23
only her **l** moved, and her voice was 1 Sm 1:13
evil?" In all this Job did not sin with his **l**. Jb 2:10
with laughter, and your **l** with shouting. Jb 8:21
God would speak and open his **l** to you, Jb 11:5
and listen to the pleadings of my **l**. Jb 13:6
and not I; your own **l** testify against you. Jb 15:6
the solace of my **l** would assuage your Jb 16:5
from the commandment of his **l**; Jb 23:12
my **l** will not speak falsehood, and my Jb 27:4
find relief; I must open my **l** and answer. Jb 32:20
and what my **l** know they speak Jb 33:3
with flattering **l** and a double heart they Ps 12:2
May the LORD cut off all flattering **l**, the Ps 12:3
tongue we will prevail, our **l** are with us; Ps 12:4
pour out or take their names on my **l**. Ps 16:4
ear to my prayer from **l** free of deceit! Ps 17:1
by the word of your **l** I have avoided the Ps 17:4
have not withheld the request of his **l**. Ps 21:2
Let the lying **l** be mute, which speak Ps 31:18
evil and your **l** from speaking deceit. Ps 34:13
behold, I have not restrained my **l**, as you Ps 40:9
sons of men; grace is poured upon your **l**; Ps 45:2
statutes or take my covenant on your **l**? Ps 50:16
O Lord, open my **l**, and my mouth will Ps 51:15
with swords in their **l**—for "Who," they Ps 59:7
sin of their mouths, the words of their **l**, Ps 59:12
is better than life, my **l** will praise you. Ps 63:3
my mouth will praise you with joyful **l**, Ps 63:5
that which my **l** uttered and my mouth Ps 66:14
My **l** will shout for joy, when I sing Ps 71:23
the word that went forth from my **l**. Ps 89:34
bitter, and he spoke rashly with his **l**. Ps 106:33
With my **l** I declare all the rules of Ps 119:13
My **l** will pour forth praise, for you Ps 119:171
Deliver me, O LORD, from lying **l**, from a Ps 120:2
and under their **l** is the venom of asps. Ps 140:3
the mischief of their **l** overwhelm them! Ps 140:9
keep watch over the door of my **l**! Ps 141:3
and your **l** may guard knowledge. Prv 5:2
For the **l** of a forbidden woman drip Prv 5:3
and from my **l** will come what is right, Prv 8:6
wickedness is an abomination to my **l**. Prv 8:7
On the **l** of him who has Prv 10:13
one who conceals hatred has lying **l**, Prv 10:18
but whoever restrains his **l** is prudent. Prv 10:19
The **l** of the righteous feed many, but Prv 10:21
The **l** of the righteous know what is Prv 10:32
ensnared by the transgression of his **l**, Prv 12:13
Truthful **l** endure forever, but a lying Prv 12:19
Lying **l** are an abomination to the Prv 12:22
he who opens wide his **l** comes to ruin. Prv 13:3
but the **l** of the wise will preserve them. Prv 14:3
The **l** of the wise spread knowledge; not Prv 15:7
An oracle is on the **l** of a king; his Prv 16:10
Righteous **l** are the delight of a king, Prv 16:13
and adds persuasiveness to his **l**. Prv 16:23
he who purses his **l** brings evil to pass. Prv 16:30
An evildoer listens to wicked **l**, and a Prv 17:4
when he closes his **l**, he is deemed Prv 17:28
A fool's **l** walk into a fight, and his Prv 18:6
ruin, and his **l** are a snare to his soul. Prv 18:7
he is satisfied by the yield of his **l**. Prv 18:20
but the **l** of knowledge are a precious Prv 20:15
you, if all of them are ready on your **l**. Prv 22:18
will exult when your **l** speak what is Prv 23:16
violence, and their **l** talk of trouble. Prv 24:2
gives an honest answer kisses the **l**. Prv 24:26
cause, and do not deceive with your **l**. Prv 24:28
earthen vessel are fervent **l** with an evil Prv 26:23
himself with his **l** and harbors deceit Prv 26:24
mouth; a stranger, and not your own **l**. Prv 27:2
but the **l** of a fool consume him. Eccl 10:12
Your **l** are like a scarlet thread, and your Sg 4:3
Your **l** drip nectar, my bride; honey and Sg 4:11
His **l** are lilies, dripping liquid myrrh. Sg 5:13
for my beloved, gliding over **l** and teeth. Sg 7:9
for I am a man of unclean **l**, and I dwell in Is 6:5
I dwell in the midst of a people of unclean **l**; Is 6:5
and said: "Behold, this has touched your **l**; Is 6:7
with the breath of his **l** he shall kill the Is 11:4
by people of strange **l** and with a foreign Is 28:11
their mouth and honor me with their **l**, Is 29:13
his **l** are full of fury, and his tongue is Is 30:27
creating the fruit of the **l**. Peace, peace, to Is 57:19
with iniquity; your **l** have spoken lies; Is 59:3
has perished; it is cut off from their **l**. Jer 7:28
You know what came out of my **l**; it Jer 17:16
The **l** and thoughts of my assailants Lam 3:62
do not cover your **l**, nor eat the bread Ezk 24:17
you shall not cover your **l**, nor eat the Ezk 24:22
and I will open your **l** among them. Ezk 29:21
of the children of man touched my **l**. Dn 10:16
Set the trumpet to your **l**! One like a Hos 8:1
we will pay with bulls the vows of our **l**. Hos 14:2
they shall all cover their **l**, for there is no Mi 3:7
trembles; my **l** quiver at the sound; Hab 3:16
with seven **l** on each of the lamps that Zec 4:2
and no wrong was found on his **l**. Mal 2:6
For the **l** of a priest should guard Mal 2:7
"This people honors me with their **l**, but Mt 15:8
"This people honors me with their **l**, Mk 7:6
heard it ourselves from his own **l**." Lk 22:71
"The venom of asps is under their **l**." Rom 3:13
and by the **l** of foreigners will 1 Cor 14:21
the fruit of **l** that acknowledge his Heb 13:15
evil and his **l** from speaking deceit; 1 Pt 3:10

LIQUID (3)
of **l** myrrh 500 shekels, and of Ex 30:23
with myrrh, my fingers with **l** myrrh, Sg 5:5
His lips are lilies, dripping **l** myrrh. Sg 5:13

LIST (16)
go to war, you and Aaron shall **l** them, Nm 1:3
"Only the tribe of Levi you shall not **l**, Nm 1:49
"**L** the sons of Levi, by fathers' houses Nm 3:15
a month old and upward you shall **l**." Nm 3:15
"**L** all the firstborn males of the people Nm 3:40
up to fifty years old, you shall **l** them, Nm 4:23
you shall **l** them by their clans and Nm 4:29
up to fifty years old, you shall **l** them, Nm 4:30
And you shall **l** by name the objects Nm 4:32
This was the **l** of the clans of the Nm 4:37
This was the **l** of the clans of the sons Nm 4:41
This was the **l** of the clans of the sons Nm 4:45
This was the **l** of the people of Israel, Nm 26:51
its inheritance in proportion to its **l**. Nm 26:54
This was the **l** of the Levites Nm 26:57
The **l** of those who did the work and 1 Chr 25:1

LISTED (78)
for everyone who was **l** in the records, Ex 38:26
So he **l** them in the wilderness of Sinai. Nm 1:19
those **l** of the tribe of Reuben were Nm 1:21
houses, those of them who were **l**, Nm 1:22
those **l** of the tribe of Simeon were Nm 1:23
those **l** of the tribe of Gad were 45,650. Nm 1:25
those **l** of the tribe of Judah were 74,600. Nm 1:27
those **l** of the tribe of Issachar were Nm 1:29
those **l** of the tribe of Zebulun were Nm 1:31
those **l** of the tribe of Ephraim were Nm 1:33
those **l** of the tribe of Manasseh were Nm 1:35
those **l** of the tribe of Benjamin were Nm 1:37
those **l** of the tribe of Dan were 62,700. Nm 1:39
those **l** of the tribe of Asher were 41,500. Nm 1:41
those **l** of the tribe of Naphtali were Nm 1:43
These are those who were **l**, whom Nm 1:44
whom Moses and Aaron **l** with the help Nm 1:44
So all those **l** of the people of Israel, by Nm 1:45
all those **l** were 603,550. Nm 1:46
the Levites were not **l** along with them Nm 1:47
his company as **l** being 74,600. Nm 2:4
his company as **l** being 54,400. Nm 2:6
his company as **l** being 57,400. Nm 2:8
All those **l** of the camp of Judah, by their Nm 2:9
his company as **l** being 46,500. Nm 2:11
his company as **l** being 59,300. Nm 2:13
his company as **l** being 45,650. Nm 2:15
All those **l** of the camp of Reuben, by Nm 2:16
his company as **l** being 40,500. Nm 2:19
his company as **l** being 32,200. Nm 2:21
his company as **l** being 35,400. Nm 2:23
All those **l** of the camp of Ephraim, by Nm 2:24
his company as **l** being 62,700. Nm 2:26
his company as **l** being 41,500. Nm 2:28
his company as **l** being 53,400. Nm 2:30
All those **l** of the camp of Dan were Nm 2:31

people of Israel as **l** by their fathers' Nm 2:32
All those **l** in the camps by their Nm 2:32
the Levites were not **l** among the people Nm 2:33
So Moses **l** them according to the word Nm 3:16
All those **l** among the Levites, whom Nm 3:39
Moses and Aaron **l** at the Nm 3:39
So Moses **l** all the firstborn among the Nm 3:42
old and upward as **l** were 22,273. Nm 3:43
chiefs of the congregation **l** the sons of Nm 4:34
and those **l** by clans were 2,750. Nm 4:36
Moses and Aaron **l** according to the Nm 4:37
Those **l** of the sons of Gershon, by their Nm 4:38
those **l** by their clans and their fathers' Nm 4:40
Moses and Aaron **l** according to the Nm 4:41
Those **l** of the clans of the sons of Nm 4:42
those **l** by clans were 3,200. Nm 4:44
Moses and Aaron **l** according to the Nm 4:45
All those who were **l** of the Levites, Nm 4:46
and Aaron and the chiefs of Israel **l**, Nm 4:46
those **l** were 8,580. Nm 4:48
of the LORD through Moses they were **l**, Nm 4:49
Thus they were **l** by him, as the LORD Nm 4:49
tribes, who were over those who were **l**, Nm 7:2
l in the census from twenty years old Nm 14:29
the Reubenites, and those **l** were 43,730. Nm 26:7
clans of the sons of Gad as they were **l**, Nm 26:18
are the clans of Judah as they were **l**, Nm 26:22
the clans of Issachar as they were **l**, Nm 26:25
of the Zebulunites as they were **l**, Nm 26:27
of Manasseh, and those **l** were 52,700. Nm 26:34
of the sons of Ephraim as they were **l**, Nm 26:37
to their clans, and those **l** were 45,600. Nm 26:41
of the Shuhamites, as they were **l**, Nm 26:43
of the sons of Asher as they were **l**, Nm 26:47
to their clans, and those **l** were 45,400. Nm 26:50
And those **l** were 23,000, every male Nm 26:62
For they were not **l** among the people Nm 26:62
These were those **l** by Moses and Nm 26:63
who **l** the people of Israel in the plains Nm 26:63
not one of those **l** by Moses and Aaron Nm 26:64
who had **l** the people of Israel in the Nm 26:64
as they were **l** according to the 1 Chr 23:24

LISTEN (195)

you wives of Lamech, **l** to what I say: Gn 4:23
"My lord, **l** to me: a piece of land worth Gn 23:15
But if you will not **l** to us and be Gn 34:17
day after day, he would not **l** to her, Gn 39:10
when he begged us and we did not **l**. Gn 42:21
sin against the boy? But you did not **l**. Gn 42:22
"Assemble and **l**, O sons of Jacob, listen Gn 49:2
O sons of Jacob, **l** to Israel your father. Gn 49:2
And they will **l** to your voice, and you Ex 3:18
they will not believe me or **l** to my voice, Ex 4:1
you," God said, "or **l** to the first sign, Ex 4:8
even these two signs or **l** to your voice, Ex 4:9
of Israel, but they did not **l** to Moses, Ex 6:9
How then shall Pharaoh **l** to me, for I am Ex 6:12
lips. How will Pharaoh **l** to me?" Ex 6:30
Pharaoh will not **l** to you. Then I will lay Ex 7:4
hardened, and he would not **l** to them, Ex 7:13
hardened, and he would not **l** to them, Ex 7:22
his heart and would not **l** to them, Ex 8:15
hardened, and he would not **l** to them, Ex 8:19
of Pharaoh, and he did not **l** to them, Ex 9:12
said to Moses, "Pharaoh will not **l** to you, Ex 11:9
"If you will diligently **l** to the voice of Ex 15:26
But they did not **l** to Moses. Some left Ex 16:20
Moses, "You speak to us, and we will **l**; Ex 20:19
"But if you will not **l** to me and will not Lv 26:14
if in spite of this you will not **l** to me, Lv 26:18
contrary to me and will not **l** to me, Lv 26:21
if in spite of this you will not **l** to me, Lv 26:27
So I spoke to you, and you would not **l**; Dt 1:43
but the LORD did not **l** to your voice or Dt 1:45
because of you and would not **l** to me. Dt 3:26
l to the statutes and the rules that I am Dt 4:1
"And because you **l** to these rules and Dt 7:12
you shall not **l** to the words of that Dt 13:3
you shall not yield to him or **l** to him, Dt 13:8
l to fortune-tellers and to diviners. Dt 18:14
brothers—it is to him you shall **l**— Dt 18:15
And whoever will not **l** to my words Dt 18:19
they discipline him, will not **l** to them, Dt 21:18
LORD your God would not **l** to Balaam; Dt 23:5
"Come here and **l** to the words of the LORD Jos 3:9
but I would not **l** to Balaam. Indeed, he Jos 24:10
Yet they did not **l** to their judges, for they Jgs 2:17
cried aloud and said to them, "**L** to me, Jgs 9:7
of Shechem, that God may **l** to you. Jgs 9:7
but the king of Edom would not **l**. Jgs 11:17
the Ammonites did not **l** to the words of Jgs 11:28
But the men would not **l** to him. So the Jgs 19:25
Benjaminites would not **l** to the voice Jgs 20:13
Boaz said to Ruth, "Now, **l**, my daughter, Ru 2:8
But they would not **l** to the voice of 1 Sm 2:25
now therefore **l** to the words of the 1 Sm 15:1
and to **l** than the fat of rams. 1 Sm 15:22
"Why do you **l** to the words of men 1 Sm 24:9
Who would **l** to you in this matter? 1 Sm 30:24
spoke to him, and he did not **l** to us. 2 Sm 12:18
But he would not **l** to her, and being 2 Sm 13:14
did to me." But he would not **l** to her. 2 Sm 13:16
Can I still **l** to the voice of singing 2 Sm 19:35
called from the city, "**L**! Listen! 2 Sm 20:16
L! Tell Joab, 'Come here, that I may 2 Sm 20:16
"**L** to the words of your servant." And 2 Sm 20:17
that you may **l** to the prayer that your 1 Kgs 8:29
And **l** to the plea of your servant and 1 Kgs 8:30
And **l** in heaven your dwelling place, 1 Kgs 8:30
And if you will **l** to all that I 1 Kgs 11:38
So the king did not **l** to the people, 1 Kgs 12:15
saw that the king did not **l** to them, 1 Kgs 12:16
said to him, "Do not **l** or consent." 1 Kgs 20:8
But Amaziah would not **l**. So 2 Kgs 14:11
But they would not **l**, but were 2 Kgs 17:14
However, they would not **l**, but they 2 Kgs 17:40
Do not **l** to Hezekiah, for thus says 2 Kgs 18:31
And do not **l** to Hezekiah when he 2 Kgs 18:32
But they did not **l**, and Manasseh led 2 Kgs 21:9
that you may **l** to the prayer that 2 Chr 6:20
And **l** to the pleas of your servant and 2 Chr 6:21
And **l** from heaven your dwelling 2 Chr 6:21
So the king did not **l** to the people, 2 Chr 10:15
saw that the king did not **l** to them, 2 Chr 10:16
"**L**, all Judah and inhabitants of 2 Chr 20:15
But Amaziah would not **l**, for it was 2 Chr 25:20
He did not **l** to the words of Neco 2 Chr 35:22
Shall we then **l** to you and do all this Neh 13:27
day after day and he would not **l** to them, Est 3:4
now my argument and **l** to the pleadings Jb 13:6
Therefore I say, '**L** to me; let me also Jb 32:10
my speech, O Job, and **l** to all my words. Jb 33:1
Pay attention, O Job, **l** to me; be silent, Jb 33:31
If not, **l** to me; be silent, and I will teach Jb 33:33
understanding, hear this; **l** to what I say. Jb 34:16
If they **l** and serve him, they complete Jb 36:11
But if they do not **l**, they perish by the Jb 36:12
Come, O children, **l** to me; I will teach Ps 34:11
Hear my cry, O God, **l** to my prayer; Ps 61:1
you! O Israel, if you would but **l** to me! Ps 81:8
"But my people did not **l** to my voice; Ps 81:11
Oh, that my people would **l** to me, that Ps 81:13
LORD, to my prayer; **l** to my plea for grace. Ps 86:6
I have called and you refused to **l**, Prv 1:24
And now, O sons, **l** to me, and do not Prv 5:7
I did not **l** to the voice of my teachers or Prv 5:13
And now, O sons, **l** to me, and be Prv 7:24
"And now, O sons, **l** to me: blessed are Prv 8:32
but a scoffer does not **l** to rebuke. Prv 13:1
L to advice and accept instruction, Prv 19:20
L to your father who gave you life, and Prv 23:22
To draw near to **l** is better than to offer Eccl 5:1
you make many prayers, I will not **l**; Is 1:15
and he will **l** to their pleas for mercy and Is 19:22
riders on camels, let him **l** diligently, Is 21:7
Do not **l** to Hezekiah. For thus says the Is 36:16
L to me in silence, O coastlands; let the Is 41:1
will attend and **l** for the time to come? Is 42:23
"**L** to me, O house of Jacob, all the Is 46:3
"**L** to me, you stubborn of heart, you Is 46:12
"**L** to me, O Jacob, and Israel, whom I Is 48:12
"Assemble, all of you, and **l**! who among Is 48:14
L to me, O coastlands, and give attention, Is 49:1
"**L** to me, you who pursue righteousness, Is 51:1
"**L** to me, you who know righteousness, Is 51:7
L diligently to me, and eat what is good, Is 55:2
when I spoke, you did not **l**, but you did Is 65:12
one answered, when I spoke they did not **l**; Is 66:4
ears are uncircumcised, they cannot **l**; Jer 6:10
I spoke to you persistently you did not **l**, Jer 7:13
Yet they did not **l** to me or incline their Jer 7:26
words to them, but they will not **l** to you. Jer 7:27
the iron furnace, saying, **L** to my voice, Jer 11:4
they cry to me, I will not **l** to them. Jer 11:11
for I will not **l** when they call to me in Jer 11:14
But if any nation will not **l**, then I will Jer 12:17
and a glory, but they would not **l**. Jer 13:11
But if you will not **l**, my soul will weep Jer 13:17
stubborn, evil will, refusing to **l** to me. Jer 16:12
Yet they did not **l** or incline their ear, Jer 17:23
"'But if you **l** to me, declares the LORD, Jer 17:24
But if you do not **l** to me, to keep the Jer 17:27
and **l** to the voice of my adversaries. Jer 18:19
prosperity, but you said, 'I will not **l**.' Jer 22:21
"Do not **l** to the words of the prophets Jer 23:16
It may be they will **l**, and every one turn Jer 26:3
If you will not **l** to me, to walk in my law Jer 26:4
and to **l** to the words of my servants the Jer 26:5
So do not **l** to your prophets, your Jer 27:9
Do not **l** to the words of the prophets Jer 27:14
Do not **l** to the words of your prophets Jer 27:16
Do not **l** to them; serve the king of Jer 27:17
the prophet Hananiah, "**L**, Hananiah, Jer 28:15
and do not **l** to the dreams that they Jer 29:8
the prophets, but you would not **l**, Jer 29:19
your fathers did not **l** to me or incline Jer 34:14
receive instruction and **l** to my words? Jer 35:13
you did not incline your ear or **l** to me. Jer 35:15
burn the scroll, he would not **l** to them. Jer 36:25
But Irijah would not **l** to him, Jer 37:14
give you counsel, you will not **l** to me." Jer 38:15
But they did not **l** or incline their ear, to Jer 44:5
name of the LORD, we will not **l** to you. Jer 44:16
if I sent you to such, they would **l** to you. Ezk 3:6
of Israel will not be willing to **l** to you, Ezk 3:7
to you, for they are not willing to **l** to me. Ezk 3:7
your lying to my people, who **l** to lies. Ezk 13:19
me and were not willing to **l** to me. Ezk 20:8
and hereafter, if you will not **l** to me; Ezk 20:39
l to the prayer of your servant and to his Dn 9:17
to the melody of your harps I will not **l**. Am 5:23
If you will not **l**, if you will not take it to Mal 2:2
will not receive you or **l** to your words, Mt 10:14
with whom I am well pleased; **l** to him." Mt 17:5
But if he does not **l**, take one or two Mt 18:16
If he refuses to **l** to them, tell it to the Mt 18:17
if he refuses to **l** even to the church, Mt 18:17
"**L**! A sower went out to sow. Mk 4:3
receive you and they will not **l** to you, Mk 6:11
"This is my beloved Son; **l** to him." Mk 9:7
is my Son, my Chosen One; **l** to him!" Lk 9:35
"This is a hard saying; who can **l** to it?" Jn 6:60
told you already, and you would not **l**. Jn 9:27
We know that God does not **l** to sinners, Jn 9:31
robbers, but the sheep did not **l** to them. Jn 10:8
them also, and they will **l** to my voice. Jn 10:16
a demon, and is insane; why **l** to him?" Jn 10:20
You shall **l** to him in whatever he tells Acts 3:22
soul who does not **l** to that prophet Acts 3:23
the sight of God to **l** to you rather than Acts 4:19
of Israel and you who fear God, **l**. Acts 13:16
James replied, "Brothers, **l** to me. Acts 15:13
I beg you to **l** to me patiently. Acts 26:3
been sent to the Gentiles; they will **l**." Acts 28:28
and even then they will not **l** to me, 1 Cor 14:21
under the law, do you not **l** to the law? Gal 4:21
L, my beloved brothers, has not God Jas 2:5
whoever is not from God does not **l** to us. 1 Jn 4:6

LISTENED (53)

"Because you have **l** to the voice of your Gn 3:17
by her." And Abram **l** to the voice of Gn 16:2
the LORD has **l** to your affliction. Gn 16:11
Abraham **l** to Ephron, and Abraham Gn 23:16
And God **l** to Leah, and she conceived Gn 30:17
and God **l** to her and opened her womb. Gn 30:22
the gate of his city **l** to Hamor and his Gn 34:24
own flesh." And his brothers **l** to him. Gn 37:27
the people of Israel have not **l** to me. Ex 6:12
So Moses **l** to the voice of his Ex 18:24
you. But the LORD **l** to me that time also. Dt 9:19
and the LORD **l** to me that time also. Dt 10:10
And God **l** to the voice of Manoah, and Jgs 13:9
And Saul **l** to the voice of Jonathan. 1 Sm 19:6
my hand and have **l** to what you 1 Sm 28:21
urged him, and he **l** to their words. 1 Sm 28:23
is from me.'" So they **l** to the word of 1 Kgs 12:24
And Ben-hadad **l** to King Asa and 1 Kgs 15:20
And the LORD **l** to the voice of Elijah. 1 Kgs 17:22
than they." And he **l** to their voice 1 Kgs 20:25
of the LORD, and the LORD **l** to him, 2 Kgs 13:4
And the king of Assyria **l** to him. The 2 Kgs 16:9
They neither **l** nor obeyed. 2 Kgs 18:12
is from me.'" So they **l** to the word of 2 Chr 11:4
And Ben-hadad **l** to King Asa and 2 Chr 16:4
to the king. Then the king **l** to them. 2 Chr 24:17
this and have not **l** to my counsel." 2 Chr 25:16
God for this, and he **l** to our entreaty. Ezr 8:23
Have you **l** in the council of God? And do Jb 15:8
"Men **l** to me and waited and kept Jb 29:21
for your words, I **l** for your wise sayings, Jb 32:11
in my heart, the Lord would not have **l**. Ps 66:18
But truly God has **l**; he has attended to Ps 66:19
I have paid attention and **l**, but they have Jer 8:6
has paid attention to his word and **l**? Jer 23:18
persistently to you, but you have not **l**. Jer 25:3
You have neither **l** nor inclined your Jer 25:4
Yet you have not **l** to me, declares the Jer 25:7
to you urgently, though you have not **l**, Jer 26:5
they have not **l** to receive instruction. Jer 32:33
persistently, but you have not **l** to me. Jer 35:14
spoken to them and they have not **l**, Jer 35:17
the people of the land **l** to the words of the Jer 37:2
So he **l** to them in this matter, and tested Dn 1:14
We have not **l** to your servants the Dn 9:6
them because they have not **l** to him; Hos 9:17

at the Lord's feet and **l** to his teaching. Lk 10:39
He **l** to Paul speaking. And Paul, Acts 14:9
and they **l** to Barnabas and Paul as Acts 15:12
Up to this word they **l** to him. Then Acts 22:22
you should have **l** to me and not have Acts 27:21
he says, "In a favorable time I **l** to you, 2 Cor 6:2
not united by faith with those who **l**. Heb 4:2

LISTENING (16)
a son." And Sarah was **l** at the tent door Gn 18:10
Now Rebekah was **l** when Isaac spoke to Gn 27:5
servant." And he answered, "I am **l**." 2 Sm 20:17
l to the cry and to the prayer that 1 Kgs 8:28
l to the cry and to the prayer that 2 Chr 6:19
not believe that he was **l** to my voice. Jb 9:16
Keep **l** to my words, and let my Jb 13:17
"Keep **l** to my words, and let this be your Jb 21:2
Keep **l** to the thunder of his voice and the Jb 37:2
of gold is a wise reprover to a **l** ear. Prv 25:12
with companions **l** for your voice; Sg 8:13
does evil in my sight, not **l** to my voice, Jer 18:10
After **l** to the king, they went on their way. Mt 2:9
l to them and asking them questions. Lk 2:46
God, and the prisoners were **l** to them, Acts 16:25
will turn away from **l** to the truth and 2 Tm 4:4

LISTENS (13)
but whoever **l** to me will dwell secure Prv 1:33
Blessed is the one who **l** to me, watching Prv 8:34
own eyes, but a wise man **l** to advice. Prv 12:15
The ear that **l** to life-giving reproof Prv 15:31
but he who **l** to reproof gains Prv 15:32
An evildoer **l** to wicked lips, and a liar Prv 17:4
If a ruler **l** to falsehood, all his officials Prv 29:12
She **l** to no voice; she accepts no Zep 3:2
you and him alone. If he **l** to you, Mt 18:15
of God and does his will, God **l** to him. Jn 9:31
who is of the truth **l** to my voice." Jn 18:37
from the world, and the world **l** to them. 1 Jn 4:5
Whoever knows God **l** to us; whoever is 1 Jn 4:6

LISTING (2)
Their **l** according to the number of all Nm 3:22
Their **l** according to the number of all Nm 3:34

LIT (1)
And it **l** up the night without one Ex 14:20

LITERATURE (2)
to teach them the **l** and language of the Dn 1:4
learning and skill in all **l** and wisdom, Dn 1:17

LITTER (1)
Behold, it is the **l** of Solomon! Around it Sg 3:7

LITTERED (1)
all the way was **l** with garments and 2 Kgs 7:15

LITTERS (1)
in chariots and in **l** and on mules and Is 66:20

LITTLE (211)
Let a **l** water be brought, and wash your Gn 18:4
near enough to flee to, and it is a **l** one. Gn 19:20
Let me escape there—is it not a **l** one? Gn 19:20
"Please give me a **l** water to drink from Gn 24:17
"Please give me a **l** water from your jar Gn 24:43
For you had **l** before I came, and it has Gn 30:30
wealth, all their **l** ones and their wives, Gn 34:29
to them, "Go again, buy us a **l** food." Gn 43:2
die, both we and you and also our **l** ones. Gn 43:8
to the man, a **l** balm and a little honey, Gn 43:11
to the man, a little balm and a **l** honey, Gn 43:11
father said, 'Go again, buy us a **l** food,' Gn 44:25
of Egypt for your **l** ones and for your Gn 45:19
carried Jacob their father, their **l** ones, Gn 46:5
and as food for your **l** ones." Gn 47:24
for you and your **l** ones." Thus he Gn 50:21
you, if ever I let you and your **l** ones go! Ex 10:10
LORD; your **l** ones also may go with you; Ex 10:24
and whoever gathered **l** had no lack. Ex 16:18
L by little I will drive them out from Ex 23:30
Little by **l** I will drive them out from Ex 23:30
the **l** owl, the cormorant, the Lv 11:17
Our wives and our **l** ones will become a Nm 14:3
But your **l** ones, who you said would Nm 14:31
wives, their sons, and their **l** ones. Nm 16:27
the women of Midian and their **l** ones, Nm 31:9
kill every male among the **l** ones, Nm 31:17
our livestock, and cities for our **l** ones, Nm 32:16
And our **l** ones shall live in the Nm 32:17
Build cities for your **l** ones and folds Nm 32:24
Our **l** ones, our wives, our livestock, Nm 32:26
And as for your **l** ones, who you said Dt 1:39
Only your wives, your **l** ones, and your Dt 3:19
away these nations before you **l** by little. Dt 7:22
away these nations before you little by **l**. Dt 7:22
the **l** owl and the short-eared owl, the Dt 14:16
but the women and the **l** ones, the Dt 20:14
seed into the field and shall gather in **l**, Dt 28:38
your **l** ones, your wives, and the Dt 29:11
the people, men, women, and **l** ones, Dt 31:12
Your wives, your **l** ones, and your Jos 1:14
of Israel, and the women, and the **l** ones, Jos 8:35
to her, "Please give me a **l** water to drink, Jgs 4:19
putting the **l** ones and the livestock and Jgs 18:21
sword; also the women and the **l** ones. Jgs 21:10
to make for him a **l** robe and take it to 1 Sm 2:19
because I tasted a **l** of this honey. 1 Sm 14:29
"I tasted a **l** honey with the tip of the 1 Sm 14:43
"Though you are **l** in your own eyes, 1 Sm 15:17
seem to you a **l** thing to become the 1 Sm 18:23
with David, and with him a **l** boy. 1 Sm 20:35
nothing of all this, much or **l**." 1 Sm 22:15
man had nothing but one **l** ewe lamb, 2 Sm 12:3
And if this were too **l**, I would add to 2 Sm 12:8
men and all the **l** ones who were with 2 Sm 15:22
had passed a **l** beyond the summit, 2 Sm 16:1
servant will go a **l** way over the 2 Sm 19:36
my father, although I am but a **l** child. 1 Kgs 3:7
servants, Hadad still being a **l** child. 1 Kgs 11:17
'My **l** finger is thicker than my 1 Kgs 12:10
said, "Bring me a **l** water in a vessel, 1 Kgs 17:10
of flour in a jar and a **l** oil in a jug. 1 Kgs 17:12
But first make me a **l** cake of it and 1 Kgs 17:13
a **l** cloud like a man's hand is rising 1 Kgs 18:44
And in a **l** while the heavens grew 1 Kgs 18:45
them like two **l** flocks of goats, 1 Kgs 20:27
had carried off a **l** girl from the land 2 Kgs 5:2
was restored like the flesh of a **l** child, 2 Kgs 5:14
dash in pieces their **l** ones and rip 2 Kgs 8:12
said to them, "Ahab served Baal a **l**, 2 Kgs 10:18
few in number, and of **l** account, 1 Chr 16:19
'My **l** finger is thicker than my 2 Chr 10:10
before the LORD, with their **l** ones, 2 Chr 20:13
enrolled with all their **l** children, 2 Chr 31:18
and grant us a **l** reviving in our slavery. Ezr 9:8
all the hardship seem **l** to you that has Neh 9:32
leave me alone, that I may find a **l** cheer Jb 10:20
They send out their **l** boys like a flock, Jb 21:11
They are exalted a **l** while, and then are Jb 24:24
"Bear with me a **l**, and I will show you, Jb 36:2
have made him a **l** lower than the Ps 8:5
In just a **l** while, the wicked will be no Ps 37:10
Better is the **l** that the righteous has Ps 37:16
they were few in number, of **l** account, Ps 105:12
he who takes your **l** ones and dashes Ps 137:9
A **l** sleep, a little slumber, a little folding Prv 6:10
A little sleep, a **l** slumber, a little folding Prv 6:10
slumber, a **l** folding of the hands to rest, Prv 6:10
the heart of the wicked is of **l** worth. Prv 10:20
but whoever gathers **l** by little will Prv 13:11
gathers little by **l** will increase it. Prv 13:11
Better is a **l** with the fear of the LORD Prv 15:16
Better is a **l** with righteousness than Prv 16:8
A **l** sleep, a little slumber, a little Prv 24:33
A little sleep, a **l** slumber, a little Prv 24:33
a **l** folding of the hands to rest, Prv 24:33
a laborer, whether he eats **l** or much, Eccl 5:12
There was a **l** city with few men in it, Eccl 9:14
so a **l** folly outweighs wisdom and Eccl 10:1
for us, the **l** foxes that spoil the vineyards, Sg 2:15
We have a **l** sister, and she has no breasts. Sg 8:8
Is it too **l** for you to weary men, that you Is 7:13
For in a very **l** while my fury will come Is 10:25
together; and a **l** child shall lead them. Is 11:6
hide yourselves for a **l** while until the Is 26:20
line upon line, line upon line, here a **l**, Is 28:10
line upon line, here a little, there a **l**." Is 28:10
line upon line, line upon line, here a **l**, Is 28:13
line, line upon line, here a little, there a **l**, Is 28:13
not yet a very **l** while until Lebanon Is 29:17
In **l** more than a year you will shudder, Is 32:10
holy people held possession for a **l** while; Is 63:18
is destroyed; her **l** ones have made a cry. Jer 48:4
Even the **l** ones of the flock shall be Jer 49:20
Surely the **l** ones of their flock shall be Jer 50:45
yet a **l** while and the time of her harvest Jer 51:33
and maidens, **l** children and women, Ezk 9:6
within a very **l** time you were more Ezk 16:47
up among them another horn, a **l** one, Dn 7:8
Out of one of them came a **l** horn, which Dn 8:9
stumble, they shall receive a **l** help. Dn 11:34
for in just a **l** while I will punish the Hos 1:4
their **l** ones shall be dashed in pieces, Hos 13:16
fragments, and the **l** house into bits. Am 6:11
who are too **l** to be among the clans of Mi 5:2
You have sown much, and harvested **l**. Hg 1:6
looked for much, and behold, it came to **l**. Hg 1:9
Yet once more, in a **l** while, I will shake Hg 2:6
for while I was angry but a **l**, they Zec 1:15
I will turn my hand against the **l** ones. Zec 13:7
much more clothe you, O you of **l** faith? Mt 6:30
O you of **l** faith?" Then he rose and Mt 8:26
gives one of these **l** ones even a cup Mt 10:42
and revealed them to **l** children; Mt 11:25
of him, saying to him, "O you of **l** faith, Mt 14:31
aware of this, said, "O you of **l** faith, Mt 16:8
said to them, "Because of your **l** faith. Mt 17:20
causes one of these **l** ones who believe in Mt 18:6
you do not despise one of these **l** ones. Mt 18:10
that one of these **l** ones should perish. Mt 18:14
"Let the **l** children come to me and do Mt 19:14
You have been faithful over a **l**; I will Mt 25:21
You have been faithful over a **l**; I will Mt 25:23
And going a **l** farther he fell on his face Mt 26:39
After a **l** while the bystanders came up Mt 26:73
And going on a **l** farther, he saw James Mk 1:19
"My **l** daughter is at the point of death. Mk 5:23
"Talitha cumi," which means, "**L** girl, Mk 5:41
a woman whose **l** daughter was Mk 7:25
causes one of these **l** ones who believe Mk 9:42
And going a **l** farther, he fell on the Mk 14:35
And after a **l** while the bystanders Mk 14:70
he asked him to put out a **l** from the land. Lk 5:3
But he who is forgiven **l**, loves little." Lk 7:47
But he who is forgiven little, loves **l**." Lk 7:47
and revealed them to **l** children; Lk 10:21
will he clothe you, O you of **l** faith! Lk 12:28
"Fear not, **l** flock, for it is your Father's Lk 12:32
is faithful in a very **l** is also faithful in Lk 16:10
dishonest in a very **l** is also dishonest Lk 16:10
should cause one of these **l** ones to sin. Lk 17:2
you have been faithful in a very **l**, Lk 19:17
And a **l** later someone else saw him and Lk 22:58
enough bread for each of them to get a **l**." Jn 6:7
then said, "I will be with you a **l** longer, Jn 7:33
light is among you for a **l** while longer. Jn 12:35
L children, yet a little while I am with Jn 13:33
children, yet a **l** while I am with you. Jn 13:33
Yet a **l** while and the world will see me Jn 14:19
"A **l** while, and you will see me no Jn 16:16
and again a **l** while, and you will see Jn 16:16
is this that he says to us, 'A **l** while, Jn 16:17
you will not see me, and again a **l** while, Jn 16:17
"What does he mean by 'a **l** while'? Jn 16:18
'A **l** while and you will not see me, Jn 16:19
and again a **l** while and you will see Jn 16:19
to put the men outside for a **l** while. Acts 5:34
there was no **l** disturbance among Acts 12:18
And they remained no **l** time with the Acts 14:28
arose no **l** disturbance concerning Acts 19:23
brought no **l** business to the Acts 19:24
alive, and were not a **l** comforted. Acts 20:12
A **l** farther on they took a sounding Acts 27:28
not know that a **l** leaven leavens the 1 Cor 5:6
and whoever gathered **l** had no lack." 2 Cor 8:15
even if I boast a **l** too much of our 2 Cor 10:8
bear with me in a **l** foolishness. 2 Cor 11:1
as a fool, so that I too may boast a **l**. 2 Cor 11:16
my **l** children, for whom I am again in Gal 4:19
A **l** leaven leavens the whole lump. Gal 5:9
but use a **l** wine for the sake of your 1 Tm 5:23
made him for a **l** while lower than the Heb 2:7
him who for a **l** while was made lower Heb 2:9
For, "Yet a **l** while, and the coming Heb 10:37
that appears for a **l** time and then Jas 4:14
you rejoice, though now for a **l** while, 1 Pt 1:6
And after you have suffered a **l** while, 1 Pt 5:10
My **l** children, I am writing these things 1 Jn 2:1
I am writing to you, **l** children, because 1 Jn 2:12
And now, **l** children, abide in him, so 1 Jn 2:28
L children, let no one deceive you. 1 Jn 3:7
L children, let us not love in word or 1 Jn 3:18
L children, you are from God and have 1 Jn 4:4
L children, keep yourselves from idols. 1 Jn 5:21
I know that you have but **l** power, and yet Rv 3:8
a white robe and told to rest a **l** longer, Rv 6:11
He had a **l** scroll open in his hand. And Rv 10:2
and told him to give me the **l** scroll. Rv 10:9
And I took the **l** scroll from the hand of Rv 10:10
come he must remain only a **l** while. Rv 17:10
that he must be released for a **l** while. Rv 20:3

LIVE (339)
of the tree of life and eat, and **l** forever—" Gn 3:22
they will kill me, but they will let you **l**. Gn 12:12
"Oh that Ishmael might **l** before you!" Gn 17:18
for he was afraid to **l** in Zoar. Gn 19:30
he will pray for you, and you shall **l**. Gn 20:7
By your sword you shall **l**, and you Gn 27:40
whom you find your gods shall not **l**. Gn 31:32
for us there, that we may **l** and not die." Gn 42:2
said to them, "Do this and you will **l**, Gn 42:18
arise and go, that we may **l** and not die, Gn 43:8
give us seed that we may **l** and not die, Gn 47:19
him, but if it is a daughter, she shall **l**." Ex 1:16
them, but let the male children **l**. Ex 1:17
done this, and let the male children **l**?" Ex 1:18
Nile, but you shall let every daughter **l**." Ex 1:22
whether beast or man, he shall not **l**.' Ex 19:13

they shall sell the l ox and share its Ex 21:35
"You shall not permit a sorceress to l. Ex 22:18
face, for man shall not see me and l." Ex 33:20
disease. He is unclean. He shall l alone. Lv 13:46
to be cleansed two l clean birds and Lv 14:4
He shall take the l bird with the Lv 14:6
and dip them and the l bird in the blood Lv 14:6
camp, but l outside his tent seven days. Lv 14:8
the scarlet yarn, along with the l bird, Lv 14:51
water and with the l bird and with the Lv 14:52
And he shall let the l bird go out of the Lv 14:53
and the altar, he shall present the l goat. Lv 16:20
his hands on the head of the l goat, Lv 16:21
if a person does them, he shall l by them: Lv 18:5
am bringing you to l may not vomit Lv 20:22
a sojourner, and he shall l with you. Lv 25:35
that your brother may l beside you. Lv 25:36
that they may l and not die when they Nm 4:19
But truly, as I l, and as all the earth Nm 14:21
Say to them, 'As I l, declares the LORD, Nm 14:28
who is bitten, when he sees it, shall l." Nm 21:8
would look at the bronze serpent and l. Nm 21:9
I would have killed you and let her l." Nm 22:33
who shall l when God does this? Nm 24:23
them, "Have you let all the women l? Nm 31:15
our little ones shall l in the fortified Nm 32:17
and he shall l in it until the death of Nm 35:25
not pollute the land in which you l, Nm 35:33
not defile the land in which you l, Nm 35:34
brothers, the people of Esau, who l in Seir; Dt 2:4
brothers, the people of Esau, who l in Seir, Dt 2:8
did for the people of Esau, who l in Seir, Dt 2:22
the sons of Esau who l in Seir and the Dt 2:29
Seir and the Moabites who l in Ar did for Dt 2:29
you, and do them, that you may l, Dt 4:1
me all the days that they l on the earth, Dt 4:10
to possess. You will not l long in it, Dt 4:26
of the fire, as you have heard, and still l? Dt 4:33
God speak with man and man still l. Dt 5:24
has commanded you, that you may l, Dt 5:33
and that you may l long in the land that Dt 5:33
to do, that you may l and multiply, Dt 8:1
know that man does not l by bread alone, Dt 8:3
have built good houses and l in them, Dt 8:12
and that you may l long in the land that Dt 11:9
of the Canaanites who l in the Arabah, Dt 11:30
you. And when you possess it and l in it, Dt 11:31
all the days that you l on the earth. Dt 12:1
go over the Jordan and l in the land that Dt 12:10
enemies around, so that you l in safety, Dt 12:10
the Levite as long as you l in your land. Dt 12:19
that you may l and inherit the land that Dt 16:20
—he may flee to one of these cities and l, Dt 19:5
And if he does not l near you and you do Dt 22:2
well with you, and that you may l long. Dt 22:7
have taken possession of it and l in it, Dt 26:1
and with all your soul, that you may l. Dt 30:6
his rules, then you shall l and multiply, Dt 30:16
You shall not l long in the land that Dt 30:18
life, that you and your offspring may l, Dt 30:19
as long as you l in the land that you are Dt 31:13
witness (for it will l unforgotten in the Dt 31:21
to heaven and swear, As I l forever, Dt 32:40
this word you shall l long in the land Dt 32:47
"Let Reuben l, and not die, but let his Dt 33:6
all who are with her in her house shall l, Jos 6:17
to the Hivites, "Perhaps you l among us; Jos 9:7
a covenant with them, to let them l, Jos 9:15
let them l, lest wrath be upon us, Jos 9:20
"Let them l." So they became cutters of Jos 9:21
As you l, my lord, I am the woman 1 Sm 1:26
people shouted, "Long l the king!" 1 Sm 10:24
not be found in you so long as you l. 1 Sm 25:28
that he could not l after he had fallen. 2 Sm 1:10
As you l, and as your soul lives, I will 2 Sm 11:11
to me, that the child may l?' 2 Sm 12:22
and said, "As surely as you l, 2 Sm 14:19
said to Absalom, "Long l the king! 2 Sm 16:16
live the king! Long l the king!" 2 Sm 16:16
"How many years have I still to l, 2 Sm 19:34
and saying, 'Long l King Adonijah!' 1 Kgs 1:25
"May my lord King David l forever!" 1 Kgs 1:31
and say, 'Long l King Solomon!' 1 Kgs 1:34
people said, "Long l King Solomon!" 1 Kgs 1:39
this woman and I l in the same 1 Kgs 3:17
the days that they l in the land that 1 Kgs 8:40
says, 'Please, let me l.'" And he said, 1 Kgs 20:32
live.'" And he said, "Does he still l? 1 Kgs 20:32
the LORD lives, and as you yourself l, 2 Kgs 2:2
the LORD lives, and as you yourself l, 2 Kgs 2:4
the LORD lives, and as you yourself l, 2 Kgs 2:6
you and your sons can l on the rest." 2 Kgs 4:7
the LORD lives and as you yourself l, 2 Kgs 4:30
If they spare our lives we shall l, and if 2 Kgs 7:4
is missing shall not l." But Jehu did 2 Kgs 10:19

hands and said, "Long l the king!" 2 Kgs 11:12
trees and honey, that you may l, 2 Kgs 18:32
L in the land and serve the king of 2 Kgs 25:24
the days that they l in the land that 2 Chr 6:31
"My wife shall not l in the house of 2 Chr 8:11
your brothers who l in their cities, 2 Chr 19:10
and they said, "Long l the king." 2 Chr 23:11
of their associates who l in Samaria and Ezr 4:17
I said to the king, "Let the king l forever! Neh 2:3
as I could go into the temple and l? Neh 6:11
a person does them, he shall l by them, Neh 9:29
one out of ten to l in Jerusalem the holy Neh 11:1
who willingly offered to l in Jerusalem. Neh 11:2
out the golden scepter so that he may l. Est 4:11
of the villages, who l in the rural towns, Est 9:19
I loathe my life; I would not l forever. Jb 7:16
If a man dies, shall he l again? All the Jb 14:14
and no survivor where he used to l. Jb 18:19
Why do the wicked l, reach old age, and Jb 21:7
the LORD! May your hearts l forever! Ps 22:26
that he should l on forever and never see Ps 49:9
and treachery shall not l out half their Ps 55:23
So I will bless you as long as I l; in your Ps 63:4
Long may he l; may gold of Sheba be Ps 72:15
What man can l and never see death? Ps 89:48
I will sing to the LORD as long as I l; I Ps 104:33
dwell, and they establish a city to l in; Ps 107:36
I will call on him as long as I l. Ps 116:2
I shall not die, but I shall l, and Ps 118:17
that I may l and keep your word. Ps 119:17
your mercy come to me, that I may l; Ps 119:77
they do not l according to your law. Ps 119:85
to your promise, that I may l, Ps 119:116
give me understanding that I may l. Ps 119:144
Let my soul l and praise you, and let Ps 119:175
I will praise the LORD as long as I l; I will Ps 146:2
words; keep my commandments, and l. Prv 4:4
keep my commandments and l; keep my Prv 7:2
Leave your simple ways, and l, and walk Prv 9:6
is steadfast in righteousness will l, Prv 11:19
but he who hates bribes will l. Prv 15:27
It is not fitting for a fool to l in luxury, Prv 19:10
It is better to l in a corner of the Prv 21:9
It is better to l in a desert land than Prv 21:19
It is better to l in a corner of the Prv 25:24
joyful and to do good as long as they l; Eccl 3:12
though he should l a thousand years Eccl 6:6
madness is in their hearts while they l, Eccl 9:3
They are dead, they will not l; they are Is 26:14
Your dead shall l; their bodies shall rise. Is 26:19
O Lord, by these things men l, and in all Is 38:16
Oh restore me to health and make me l! Is 38:16
As I l, declares the LORD, you shall put Is 49:18
come to me; hear, that your soul may l; Is 55:3
are besieging you shall l and shall have Jer 21:9
"As I l, declares the LORD, though Jer 22:24
and serve him and his people and l. Jer 27:12
them; serve the king of Babylon and l. Jer 27:17
Build houses and l in them; plant Jer 29:5
build houses and l in them, and plant Jer 29:28
but you shall l in tents all your days, Jer 35:7
that you may l many days in the land Jer 35:7
he who goes out to the Chaldeans shall l. Jer 38:2
shall have his life as a prize of war, and l. Jer 38:2
fire, and you and your house shall l. Jer 38:17
faces to enter Egypt and go to l there, Jer 42:15
to go to Egypt to l there shall die by the Jer 42:17
in the place where you desire to go to l." Jer 42:22
you to say, 'Do not go to Egypt to l there,' Jer 43:2
who had returned to l in the land of Jer 43:5
land of Egypt where you have come to l, Jer 44:8
faces to come to the land of Egypt to l, Jer 44:12
Judah who have come to l in the land of Jer 44:14
who came to the land of Egypt to l, Jer 44:28
"As I l, declares the King, whose name Jer 46:18
you who l in the clefts of the rock, Jer 49:16
shadow we shall l among the nations." Lam 4:20
and he does not sin, he shall surely l, Ezk 3:21
Therefore, as I l, declares the Lord GOD, Ezk 5:11
return to what he has sold, while they l. Ezk 7:13
keeping alive souls who should not l, Ezk 13:19
even if these three men were in it, as I l, Ezk 14:16
these three men were in it, as I l, Ezk 14:18
Noah, Daniel, and Job were in it, as I l, Ezk 14:20
blood, 'L!' I said to you in your blood, Ezk 16:6
'Live!' I said to you in your blood, 'L!' Ezk 16:6
As I l, declares the Lord GOD, your Ezk 16:48
"As I l, declares the Lord GOD, surely Ezk 17:16
As I l, surely it is my oath that he Ezk 17:19
As I l, declares the Lord GOD, this Ezk 18:3
he shall surely l, declares the Lord GOD. Ezk 18:9
and takes profit; shall he then l? Ezk 18:13
shall he then live? He shall not l. Ezk 18:13
his father's iniquity; he shall surely l. Ezk 18:17
all my statutes, he shall surely l. Ezk 18:19

is just and right, he shall surely l; Ezk 18:21
that he has done he shall l. Ezk 18:22
he should turn from his way and l? Ezk 18:23
the wicked person does, shall he l? Ezk 18:24
he had committed, he shall surely l; Ezk 18:28
declares the Lord GOD; so turn, and l." Ezk 18:32
As I l, declares the Lord GOD, I will not Ezk 20:3
if a person does them, he shall l. Ezk 20:11
if a person does them, he shall l; Ezk 20:13
if a person does them, he shall l; Ezk 20:21
As I l, declares the Lord GOD, I will not Ezk 20:31
"As I l, declares the Lord GOD, surely Ezk 20:33
because of them. How then can we l?' Ezk 33:10
Say to them, As I l, declares the Lord Ezk 33:11
the wicked turn from his way and l; Ezk 33:11
not be able to l by his righteousness Ezk 33:12
to the righteous that he shall surely l, Ezk 33:13
not doing injustice, he shall surely l; Ezk 33:15
is just and right; he shall surely l. Ezk 33:16
is just and right, he shall l by them. Ezk 33:19
As I l, surely those who are in the Ezk 33:27
As I l, declares the Lord GOD, surely Ezk 34:8
therefore, as I l, declares the Lord GOD, I Ezk 35:6
therefore, as I l, declares the Lord GOD, Ezk 35:11
can these bones l?" And I answered, Ezk 37:3
breath to enter you, and you shall l. Ezk 37:5
and put breath in you, and you shall l, Ezk 37:6
breathe on these slain, that they may l." Ezk 37:9
my Spirit within you, and you shall l, Ezk 37:14
as their possession for cities to l in. Ezk 45:5
living creature that swarms will l, Ezk 47:9
so everything will l where the river Ezk 47:9
the king in Aramaic, "O king, l forever! Dn 2:4
Nebuchadnezzar, "O king, l forever! Dn 3:9
the queen declared, "O king, l forever! Dn 5:10
said to him, "O King Darius, l forever! Dn 6:6
said to the king, "O king, l forever! Dn 6:21
raise us up, that we may l before him. Hos 6:2
to the house of Israel: "Seek me and l; Am 5:4
Seek the LORD and l, lest he break out Am 5:6
Seek good, and not evil, that you may l; Am 5:14
you, you who l in the clefts of the rock, Ob 1:3
me, for it is better for me to die than to l." Jon 4:3
said, "It is better for me to die than to l." Jon 4:8
but the righteous shall l by his faith. Hab 2:4
as I l," declares the LORD of hosts, Zep 2:9
they? And the prophets, do they l forever? Zec 1:5
their children they shall l and return. Zec 10:9
him will say to him, 'You shall not l, Zec 13:3
written, "'Man shall not l by bread alone, Mt 4:4
lay your hand on her, and she will l." Mt 9:18
so that she may be made well and l." Mk 5:23
she had, all she had to l on." Mk 12:44
written, 'Man shall not l by bread alone.'" Lk 4:4
in splendid clothing and l in luxury are Lk 7:25
correctly; do this, and you will l." Lk 10:28
dead, but of the living, for all l to him." Lk 20:38
of her poverty put in all she had to l on." Lk 21:4
your son will l." The man believed the Jn 4:50
"Your son will l." And he himself Jn 4:53
the Son of God, and those who hear will l. Jn 5:25
eats of this bread, he will l forever. Jn 6:51
sent me, and I l because of the Father, Jn 6:57
feeds on me, he also will l because of me. Jn 6:57
feeds on this bread will l forever." Jn 6:58
in me, though he die, yet shall he l, Jn 11:25
see me. Because I l, you also will live. Jn 14:19
see me. Because I live, you also will l. Jn 14:19
For those who l in Jerusalem and Acts 13:27
does not l in temples made by man, Acts 17:24
nation of mankind to l on all the face Acts 17:26
for "'In him we l and move and have Acts 17:28
you yourself also l in observance of Acts 21:24
For he should not be allowed to l." Acts 22:22
that he ought not to l any longer. Acts 25:24
sea, Justice has not allowed him to l." Acts 28:4
"The righteous shall l by faith." Rom 1:17
How can we who died to sin still l in it? Rom 6:2
we believe that we will also l with him. Rom 6:8
For those who l according to the flesh Rom 8:5
but those who l according to the Spirit Rom 8:5
to the flesh, to l according to the flesh. Rom 8:12
For if you l according to the flesh you Rom 8:13
death the deeds of the body, you will l. Rom 8:13
the commandments shall l by them. Rom 10:5
L in harmony with one another. Do Rom 12:16
depends on you, l peaceably with all. Rom 12:18
If we l, we live to the Lord, and if we die, Rom 14:8
If we live, we l to the Lord, and if we die, Rom 14:8
then, whether we l or whether we die, Rom 14:8
for it is written, "As I l, says the Lord, Rom 14:11
grant you to l in such harmony Rom 15:5
and she consents to l with him, 1 Cor 7:12
and he consents to l with her, 1 Cor 7:13
who have wives l as though they 1 Cor 7:29

For we who **l** are always being given 2 Cor 4:11
that those who **l** might no longer live 2 Cor 5:15
might no longer **l** for themselves but 2 Cor 5:15
well known; as dying, and behold, we **l**; 2 Cor 6:9
hearts, to die together and to **l** together. 2 Cor 7:3
with you we will **l** with him by the 2 Cor 13:4
agree with one another, **l** in peace; 2 Cor 13:11
a Jew, **l** like a Gentile and not like a Jew, Gal 2:14
you force the Gentiles to **l** like Jews?" Gal 2:14
I died to the law, so that I might **l** to God. Gal 2:19
It is no longer I who **l**, but Christ who Gal 2:20
And the life I now **l** in the flesh I live by Gal 2:20
live in the flesh I **l** by faith in the Son Gal 2:20
law, for "The righteous shall **l** by faith." Gal 3:11
one who does them shall **l** by them." Gal 3:12
If we **l** by the Spirit, let us also walk by Gal 5:25
and that you may **l** long in the land." Eph 6:3
For to me to **l** is Christ, and to die is Phil 1:21
If I am to **l** in the flesh, that means Phil 1:22
For now we **l**, if you are standing fast 1 Thes 3:8
how you ought to **l** and to please God, 1 Thes 4:1
and to aspire to **l** quietly, and to 1 Thes 4:11
that you may **l** properly before 1 Thes 4:12
or asleep we might **l** with him. 1 Thes 5:10
with him, we will also **l** with him; 2 Tm 2:11
all who desire to **l** a godly life in 2 Tm 3:12
worldly passions, and to **l** self-controlled, Ti 2:12
but my righteous one shall **l** by faith, Heb 10:38
By faith he went to **l** in the land of Heb 11:9
be subject to the Father of spirits and **l**? Heb 12:9
Lord wills, we will **l** and do this or that." Jas 4:15
L as people who are free, not using your 1 Pt 2:16
might die to sin and **l** to righteousness. 1 Pt 2:24
l with your wives in an understanding 1 Pt 3:7
so as to **l** for the rest of the time in the 1 Pt 4:2
they might **l** in the spirit the way God 1 Pt 4:6
escaping from those who **l** in error. 2 Pt 2:18
world, so that we might **l** through him. 1 Jn 4:9

LIVED (252)
When Adam had **l** 130 years, he fathered Gn 5:3
all the days that Adam **l** were 930 years, Gn 5:5
When Seth had **l** 105 years, he fathered Gn 5:6
Seth **l** after he fathered Enosh 807 years Gn 5:7
When Enosh had **l** 90 years, he fathered Gn 5:9
Enosh **l** after he fathered Kenan 815 Gn 5:10
When Kenan had **l** 70 years, he fathered Gn 5:12
Kenan **l** after he fathered Mahalalel 840 Gn 5:13
When Mahalalel had **l** 65 years, he Gn 5:15
Mahalalel **l** after he fathered Jared 830 Gn 5:16
When Jared had **l** 162 years he fathered Gn 5:18
Jared **l** after he fathered Enoch 800 years Gn 5:19
When Enoch had **l** 65 years, he fathered Gn 5:21
When Methuselah had **l** 187 years, he Gn 5:25
Methuselah **l** after he fathered Lamech Gn 5:26
When Lamech had **l** 182 years, he Gn 5:28
Lamech **l** after he fathered Noah 595 Gn 5:30
After the flood Noah **l** 350 years. Gn 9:28
in which they **l** extended from Mesha Gn 10:30
And Shem **l** after he fathered Gn 11:11
When Arpachshad had **l** 35 years, he Gn 11:12
And Arpachshad **l** after he fathered Gn 11:13
When Shelah had **l** 30 years, he Gn 11:14
And Shelah **l** after he fathered Eber 403 Gn 11:15
When Eber had **l** 34 years, he fathered Gn 11:16
And Eber **l** after he fathered Peleg 430 Gn 11:17
When Peleg had **l** 30 years, he fathered Gn 11:18
And Peleg **l** after he fathered Reu 209 Gn 11:19
When Reu had **l** 32 years, he fathered Gn 11:20
And Reu **l** after he fathered Serug 207 Gn 11:21
When Serug had **l** 30 years, he fathered Gn 11:22
And Serug **l** after he fathered Nahor Gn 11:23
When Nahor had **l** 29 years, he Gn 11:24
And Nahor **l** after he fathered Terah Gn 11:25
When Terah had **l** 70 years, he Gn 11:26
after Abram had **l** ten years in the land Gn 16:3
overthrew the cities in which Lot had **l**. Gn 19:29
up out of Zoar and **l** in the hills with Gn 19:30
So he **l** in a cave with his two Gn 19:30
of the Negeb and **l** between Kadesh and Gn 20:1
He **l** in the wilderness and became an Gn 21:20
He **l** in the wilderness of Paran, and his Gn 21:21
And Abraham **l** at Beersheba. Gn 22:19
Sarah **l** 127 years; these were the years of Gn 23:1
While Israel **l** in that land, Reuben Gn 35:22
Jacob **l** in the land of his father's Gn 37:1
from Pharaoh and **l** on the allowance Gn 47:22
And Jacob **l** in the land of Egypt Gn 47:28
his father's house. Joseph **l** 110 years. Gn 50:22
the land in which they **l** as sojourners. Ex 6:4
people of Israel had light where they **l**. Ex 10:23
the people of Israel **l** in Egypt was 430 Ex 12:40
they do in the land of Egypt, where you **l**, Lv 18:3
and the Canaanites who **l** in that hill Nm 14:45
Egypt, and we **l** in Egypt a long time. Nm 20:15
the king of Arad, who **l** in the Negeb, Nm 21:1
Thus Israel **l** in the land of the Nm 21:31
of the Amorites, who **l** at Heshbon." Nm 21:34
While Israel **l** in Shittim, the people Nm 25:1
their cities in the places where they **l**, Nm 31:10
who **l** in the Negeb in the land of Nm 33:40
king of the Amorites, who **l** in Heshbon, Dt 1:4
Bashan, who **l** in Ashtaroth and in Edrei. Dt 1:4
Then the Amorites who **l** in that hill Dt 1:44
(The Emim formerly **l** there, a people Dt 2:10
The Horites also **l** in Seir formerly, but Dt 2:12
Rephaim formerly **l** there—but the Dt 2:20
Avvim, who **l** in villages as far as Gaza, Dt 2:23
king of the Amorites, who **l** at Heshbon.' Dt 3:2
king of the Amorites, who **l** at Heshbon, Dt 4:46
who **l** to the east beyond the Jordan; Dt 4:47
midst of fire as we have, and has still **l**? Dt 5:26
"You know how we **l** in the land of Dt 29:16
So Israel **l** in safety, Jacob lived alone, in Dt 33:28
So Israel lived in safety, Jacob **l** alone, in Dt 33:28
the city wall, so that she **l** in the wall. Jos 2:15
And she has **l** in Israel to this day, Jos 6:25
and the sojourners who **l** among them. Jos 8:35
Og king of Bashan, who **l** in Ashtaroth. Jos 9:10
neighbors and that they **l** among them. Jos 9:16
of the Amorites who **l** at Heshbon and Jos 12:2
who **l** at Ashtaroth and at Edrei Jos 12:4
the princes of Sihon, who **l** in the land. Jos 13:21
out the Canaanites who **l** in Gezer, Jos 16:10
so the Canaanites have **l** in the midst of Jos 16:10
your fathers **l** beyond the Euphrates, Jos 24:2
And you **l** in the wilderness a long time. Jos 24:7
who **l** on the other side of the Jordan. Jos 24:8
peoples, the Amorites who **l** in the land. Jos 24:18
against the Canaanites who **l** in the hill Jgs 1:9
the Canaanites who **l** in Hebron (now Jgs 1:10
out the Jebusites who **l** in Jerusalem, Jgs 1:21
so the Jebusites have **l** with the people of Jgs 1:21
drive out the Canaanites who **l** in Gezer, Jgs 1:29
so the Canaanites **l** in Gezer among Jgs 1:29
so the Canaanites **l** among them, Jgs 1:30
so the Asherites **l** among the Jgs 1:32
so they **l** among the Canaanites, Jgs 1:33
and the Hivites who **l** on Mount Lebanon, Jgs 3:3
people of Israel **l** among the Canaanites, Jgs 3:5
was Sisera, who **l** in Harosheth-hagoyim. Jgs 4:2
of Joash went and **l** in his own house. Jgs 8:29
and fled and went to Beer and **l** there, Jgs 9:21
And Abimelech **l** at Arumah, and Zebul Jgs 9:41
and he **l** at Shamir in the hill country of Jgs 10:1
from his brothers and **l** in the land of Jgs 11:3
While Israel **l** in Heshbon and its Jgs 11:26
who were there, how they **l** in security, Jgs 18:7
Then they rebuilt the city and **l** in it. Jgs 18:28
and rebuilt the towns and **l** in them. Jgs 21:23
other Ruth. They **l** there about ten years, Ru 1:4
And she **l** with her mother-in-law. Ru 2:23
on every side, and you **l** in safety. 1 Sm 12:11
he and Samuel went and **l** at Naioth. 1 Sm 19:18
to the rock and **l** in the wilderness of 1 Sm 23:25
from there and **l** in the strongholds 1 Sm 23:29
And David **l** with Achish at Gath, he 1 Sm 27:3
the days that David **l** in the country of 1 Sm 27:7
all the while he **l** in the country of 1 Sm 27:11
the Philistines came and **l** in them. 1 Sm 31:7
and they **l** in the towns of Hebron. 2 Sm 2:3
And David **l** in the stronghold and 2 Sm 5:9
Now when the king **l** in his house and 2 Sm 7:1
I have not **l** in a house since the day I 2 Sm 7:6
And all who **l** in Ziba's house became 2 Sm 9:12
So Mephibosheth **l** in Jerusalem, for 2 Sm 9:13
not take this to heart." So Tamar **l**, 2 Sm 13:20
presence." So Absalom **l** apart in his 2 Sm 14:24
So Absalom **l** two full years in 2 Sm 14:28
a vow while I **l** at Geshur in Aram, 2 Sm 15:8
do." So Shimei **l** in Jerusalem many 1 Kgs 2:38
And Judah and Israel **l** in safety, from 1 Kgs 4:25
the Canaanites who **l** in the city, 1 Kgs 9:16
to Damascus and **l** there and made 1 Kgs 11:24
people of Israel who **l** in the cities of 1 Kgs 12:17
hill country of Ephraim and **l** there. 1 Kgs 12:25
Now an old prophet **l** in Bethel. And 1 Kgs 13:11
it in the city where the old prophet **l**. 1 Kgs 13:25
king of Syria, who **l** in Damascus, 1 Kgs 15:18
building Ramah, and he **l** in Tirzah. 1 Kgs 15:21
He went and **l** by the brook Cherith 1 Kgs 17:5
and the leaders who **l** with Naboth in 1 Kgs 21:8
and the leaders who **l** in his city, 1 Kgs 21:11
to Shunem, where a wealthy woman **l**, 2 Kgs 4:8
the people of Israel **l** in their homes as 2 Kgs 13:5
l fifteen years after the death of 2 Kgs 14:17
death, and he **l** in a separate house. 2 Kgs 15:5
of Samaria and **l** in its cities. 2 Kgs 17:24
Samaria came and **l** in Bethel and 2 Kgs 17:28
nation in the cities in which they **l**. 2 Kgs 17:29
and went home and **l** at Nineveh. 2 Kgs 19:36
wardrobe (now she **l** in Jerusalem in 2 Kgs 22:14
to his daily needs, as long as he **l**. 2 Kgs 25:30
also of the scribes who **l** at Jabez: 1 Chr 2:55
They **l** there in the king's service. 1 Chr 4:23
They **l** in Beersheba, Moladah, 1 Chr 4:28
and they have **l** there to this day. 1 Chr 4:43
of Shema, son of Joel, who **l** in Aroer, 1 Chr 5:8
He also **l** to the east as far as the 1 Chr 5:9
And they **l** in their tents throughout 1 Chr 5:10
The sons of Gad **l** over against them 1 Chr 5:11
and they **l** in Gilead, in Bashan and 1 Chr 5:16
And they **l** in their place until the 1 Chr 5:22
half-tribe of Manasseh **l** in the land. 1 Chr 5:23
In these **l** the sons of Joseph the son of 1 Chr 7:29
chief men. These **l** in Jerusalem. 1 Chr 8:28
Jeiel the father of Gibeon **l** in Gibeon, 1 Chr 8:29
Now these also **l** opposite their 1 Chr 8:32
and Manasseh **l** in Jerusalem: 1 Chr 9:3
who **l** in the villages of the 1 Chr 9:16
leaders. These **l** in Jerusalem. 1 Chr 9:34
In Gibeon **l** the father of Gibeon, Jeiel, 1 Chr 9:35
and these also **l** opposite their 1 Chr 9:38
the Philistines came and **l** in them. 1 Chr 10:7
And David **l** in the stronghold; 1 Chr 11:7
Now when David **l** in his house, 1 Chr 17:1
For I have not **l** in a house since the 1 Chr 17:5
people of Israel who **l** in the cities of 2 Chr 10:17
Rehoboam **l** in Jerusalem, and he 2 Chr 11:5
to him from all places where they **l**. 2 Chr 11:13
king of Syria, who **l** in Damascus, 2 Chr 16:2
Jehoshaphat **l** at Jerusalem. And he 2 Chr 19:4
And they have **l** in it and have built 2 Chr 20:8
l fifteen years after the death of 2 Chr 25:25
the Arabians who **l** in Gurbaal and 2 Chr 26:7
and being a leper **l** in a separate 2 Chr 26:21
and the sojourners who **l** in Judah, 2 Chr 30:25
the people who **l** in Jerusalem to 2 Chr 31:4
Israel and Judah who **l** in the cities of 2 Chr 31:6
wardrobe (now she **l** in Jerusalem 2 Chr 34:22
and the temple servants **l** in their towns, Ezr 2:70
time the Jews who **l** near them came Neh 4:12
servants, and all Israel, **l** in their towns. Neh 7:73
made booths and **l** in the booths, Neh 8:17
the leaders of the people **l** in Jerusalem. Neh 11:1
of the province who **l** in Jerusalem; Neh 11:3
of Judah everyone **l** on his property Neh 11:3
And in Jerusalem **l** certain of the sons Neh 11:4
sons of Perez who **l** in Jerusalem were Neh 11:6
But the temple servants **l** on Ophel; Neh 11:21
people of Judah **l** in Kiriath-arba and Neh 11:25
of Benjamin also **l** from Geba Neh 11:31
Tyrians also, who **l** in the city, Neh 13:16
and has **l** in desolate cities, in houses Jb 15:28
is the tent in which the wicked **l**?' Jb 21:28
the land, and the favored man **l** in it. Jb 22:8
and I **l** like a king among his troops, Jb 29:25
And after this Job **l** 140 years, and saw Jb 42:16
soul would soon have **l** in the land of Ps 94:17
never be inhabited or **l** in for all Is 13:20
and returned home and **l** at Nineveh. Is 37:37
but we have **l** in tents and have obeyed Jer 35:10
him home. So he **l** among the people. Jer 39:14
and **l** with him among the people who Jer 40:6
all the Judeans who **l** in the land of Jer 44:1
all the people who **l** in Pathros in the Jer 44:15
the day of his death as long as he **l**. Jer 52:34
who **l** with her daughters to the north Ezk 16:46
sister, who **l** to the south of you, Ezk 16:46
of the nations among whom they **l**, Ezk 20:9
under its shadow **l** all great nations. Ezk 31:6
who **l** under its shadow among the Ezk 31:17
the house of Israel **l** in their own land, Ezk 36:17
and they **l** and stood on their feet, Ezk 37:10
servant Jacob, where your fathers **l**. Ezk 37:25
birds of the heavens **l** in its branches, Dn 4:12
branches the birds of the heavens **l**— Dn 4:21
This is the exultant city that **l** securely, Zep 2:15
And he went and **l** in a city called Mt 2:23
he went and **l** in Capernaum by Mt 4:13
'If we had **l** in the days of our fathers, Mt 23:30
He **l** among the tombs. And no one could Mk 5:3
having **l** with her husband seven years Lk 2:36
and he had not **l** in a house but among Lk 8:27
than all the others who **l** in Jerusalem? Lk 13:4
in Mesopotamia, before he **l** in Haran, Acts 7:2
land of the Chaldeans and **l** in Haran. Acts 7:4
the Jews who **l** in Damascus by Acts 9:22
down also to the saints who **l** at Lydda. Acts 9:32
the foreigners who **l** there would Acts 17:21
know how I **l** among you the Acts 20:18
spoken of by all the Jews who **l** there, Acts 22:12
I have **l** my life before God in all good Acts 23:1
of our religion I have **l** as a Pharisee. Acts 26:5
He **l** there two whole years at his own Acts 28:30
For to this end Christ died and **l** again, Rom 14:9

whom we all once **l** in the passions of Eph 2:3
You have **l** on the earth in luxury and in Jas 5:5
that righteous man **l** among them day 2 Pt 2:8
was wounded by the sword and yet **l**. Rv 13:14
As she glorified herself and **l** in luxury, Rv 18:7
sexual immorality and **l** in luxury with Rv 18:9

LIVER (13)
the entrails, and the long lobe of the **l**, Ex 29:13
long lobe of the **l** and the two kidneys Ex 29:22
the long lobe of the **l** that he shall remove Lv 3:4
long lobe of the **l** that he shall remove Lv 3:10
long lobe of the **l** that he shall remove Lv 3:15
the long lobe of the **l** that he shall remove Lv 4:9
the long lobe of the **l** that he shall remove Lv 7:4
the long lobe of the **l** and the two kidneys Lv 8:16
the long lobe of the **l** and the two kidneys Lv 8:25
long lobe of the **l** from the sin offering Lv 9:10
the kidneys and the long lobe of the **l**— Lv 9:19
till an arrow pierces its **l**; as a bird Prv 7:23
the teraphim; he looks at the **l**. Ezk 21:21

LIVES (134)
Every moving thing that **l** shall be food Gn 9:3
And they said, "You have saved our **l**; Gn 47:25
and made their **l** bitter with hard service, Ex 1:14
and any woman who **l** in her house, Ex 3:22
offering to make atonement for your **l**. Ex 30:15
so as to make atonement for your **l**." Ex 30:16
and the sojourner who **l** with you, Lv 25:6
who have sinned at the cost of their **l**, Nm 16:38
but man **l** by every word that comes from Dt 8:3
where he **l**—and he may come when he Dt 18:6
city at the gate of the place where he **l**, Dt 21:19
to them, and deliver our **l** from death." Jos 2:13
feared greatly for our **l** because of you Jos 9:24
a people who risked their **l** to the death; Jgs 5:18
As the LORD **l**, if you had saved them Jgs 8:19
your life with the **l** of your household." Jgs 18:25
to redeem you, then, as the LORD **l**, Ru 3:13
As long as he **l**, he is lent to the LORD." 1 Sm 1:28
For as the LORD **l** who saves Israel, 1 Sm 14:39
As the LORD **l**, there shall not one 1 Sm 14:45
And Abner said, "As your soul **l**, 1 Sm 17:55
Saul swore, "As the LORD **l**, he shall 1 Sm 19:6
as the LORD **l** and as your soul lives, 1 Sm 20:3
as the LORD lives and as your soul **l**, 1 Sm 20:3
you are to come, for, as the LORD **l**, 1 Sm 20:21
long as the son of Jesse **l** on the earth, 1 Sm 20:31
Now then, my lord, as the LORD **l**, and 1 Sm 25:26
as the LORD lives, and as your soul **l**, 1 Sm 25:26
And the **l** of your enemies he shall 1 Sm 25:29
surely as the LORD the God of Israel **l**, 1 Sm 25:34
And David said, "As the LORD **l**, the 1 Sm 26:10
As the LORD **l**, you deserve to die, 1 Sm 26:16
to her by the LORD, "As the LORD **l**, 1 Sm 28:10
David and said to him, "As the LORD **l**, 1 Sm 29:6
And Joab said, "As God **l**, if you had 2 Sm 2:27
Rimmon the Beerothite, "As the LORD **l**, 2 Sm 4:9
As you live, and as your soul **l**, I will 2 Sm 11:11
and he said to Nathan, "As the LORD **l**, 2 Sm 12:5
destroyed." He said, "As the LORD **l**, 2 Sm 14:11
answered the king, "As the LORD **l**, 2 Sm 15:21
LORD lives, and as my lord the king **l**, 2 Sm 15:21
your life and the **l** of your sons and 2 Sm 19:5
daughters and the **l** of your wives 2 Sm 19:5
"The LORD **l**, and blessed be my rock, 2 Sm 22:47
risk of their **l**?" Therefore he would 2 Sm 23:17
the king swore, saying, "As the LORD **l**, 1 Kgs 1:29
Now therefore as the LORD **l**, who has 1 Kgs 2:24
Ahab, "As the LORD the God of Israel **l**, 1 Kgs 17:1
she said, "As the LORD your God **l**, 1 Kgs 17:12
And Elijah said, "See, your son **l**." 1 Kgs 17:23
As the LORD your God **l**, there is no 1 Kgs 18:10
Elijah said, "As the LORD of hosts **l**, 1 Kgs 18:15
But Micaiah said, "As the LORD **l**, 1 Kgs 22:14
Bethel." But Elisha said, "As the LORD **l**, 2 Kgs 2:2
to Jericho." But he said, "As the LORD **l**, 2 Kgs 2:4
the Jordan." But he said, "As the LORD **l**, 2 Kgs 2:6
Elisha said, "As the LORD of hosts **l**, 2 Kgs 3:14
"As the LORD **l** and as you yourself 2 Kgs 4:30
But he said, "As the LORD **l**, before 2 Kgs 5:16
As the LORD **l**, I will run after him and 2 Kgs 5:20
If they spare our **l** we shall live, and if 2 Kgs 7:4
the camp as it was, and fled for their **l**. 2 Kgs 7:7
the risk of their **l** they brought it." 1 Chr 11:19
But Micaiah said, "As the LORD **l**, 2 Chr 18:13
in every city to gather and defend their **l**, Est 8:11
provinces also gathered to defend their **l**, Est 9:16
For I know that my Redeemer **l**, and at Jb 19:25
"As God **l**, who has taken away my right, Jb 27:2
in a valley away from where anyone **l**; Jb 28:4
The LORD **l**, and blessed be my rock, Ps 18:46
For though, while he **l**, he counts Ps 49:18
the needy, and saves the **l** of the needy. Ps 72:13
but gave their **l** over to the plague. Ps 78:50
hate evil! He preserves the **l** of his saints; Ps 97:10
they set an ambush for their own **l**. Prv 1:18
A truthful witness saves **l**, but one Prv 14:25
a hundred children and **l** many years, Eccl 6:3
good for man while he **l** the few days of Eccl 6:12
So if a person **l** many years, let him Eccl 11:8
instruments all the days of our **l**, Is 38:20
be in it an infant who **l** but a few days, Is 65:20
and if you swear, 'As the LORD **l**,' in truth, Jer 4:2
say, "As the LORD **l**," yet they swear falsely. Jer 5:2
to swear by my name, 'As the LORD **l**,' Jer 12:16
'As the LORD **l** who brought up the Jer 16:14
but 'As the LORD **l** who brought up the Jer 16:15
Take care for the sake of your **l**, and do Jer 17:21
into the hand of those who seek their **l**. Jer 21:7
'As the LORD **l** who brought up the people Jer 23:7
but 'As the LORD **l** who brought up and Jer 23:8
into the hand of those who seek their **l**. Jer 34:20
into the hand of those who seek their **l**, Jer 34:21
secretly to Jeremiah, "As the LORD **l**, Jer 38:16
have gone astray at the cost of your **l**. Jer 42:20
of Egypt, saying, 'As the Lord GOD **l**.' Jer 44:26
to him for the **l** of your children, Lam 2:19
We get our bread at the peril of our **l**, Lam 5:9
but their own **l** by their righteousness, Ezk 14:14
but their own **l** by their righteousness. Ezk 14:20
and siege walls built to cut off many **l**. Ezk 17:17
the prey; they have devoured human **l**; Ezk 22:25
destroying **l** to get dishonest gain. Ezk 22:27
praised and honored him who **l** forever, Dn 4:34
but their **l** were prolonged for a season Dn 7:12
swore by him who **l** forever that it Dn 12:7
and swear not, "As the LORD **l**." Hos 4:15
of Samaria, and say, 'As your god **l**, Am 8:14
Dan,' and, 'As the Way of Beersheba **l**,' Am 8:14
for by them he **l** in luxury, and his Hab 1:16
your endurance you will gain your **l**. Lk 21:19
and everyone who **l** and believes in me Jn 11:26
who have risked their **l** for the sake of Acts 15:26
cargo and the ship, but also of our **l**." Acts 27:10
for all, but the life he **l** he lives to God. Rom 6:10
for all, but the life he lives he **l** to God. Rom 6:10
on a person only as long as he **l**? Rom 7:1
by law to her husband while he **l**, Rom 7:2
an adulteress if she **l** with another man Rom 7:3
For none of us **l** to himself, and none Rom 14:7
bound to her husband as long as he **l**. 1 Cor 7:39
weakness, but **l** by the power of God. 2 Cor 13:4
I who live, but Christ who **l** in me. Gal 2:20
self-indulgent is dead even while she **l**. 1 Tm 5:6
upright, and godly **l** in the present age, Ti 2:12
for everyone who **l** on milk is unskilled Heb 5:13
by one of whom it is testified that he **l**. Heb 7:8
since he always **l** to make intercession Heb 7:25
you to be in **l** of holiness and godliness, 2 Pt 3:11
to lay down our **l** for the brothers. 1 Jn 3:16
on the throne, who **l** forever and ever, Rv 4:9
and worship him who **l** forever and ever. Rv 4:10
swore by him who **l** forever and ever, Rv 10:6
they loved not their **l** even unto death. Rv 12:11
the wrath of God who **l** forever and ever, Rv 15:7

LIVESTOCK (98)
to their kinds—**l** and creeping things Gn 1:24
their kinds and the **l** according to their Gn 1:25
heavens and over the **l** and over all the Gn 1:26
man gave names to all **l** and to the birds Gn 2:20
are you above all **l** and above all beasts Gn 3:14
of those who dwell in tents and have **l**. Gn 4:20
and all the **l** according to their kinds, Gn 7:14
that moved on the earth, birds, **l**, beasts, Gn 7:21
beasts and all the **l** that were with him Gn 8:1
creature that is with you, the birds, the **l**, Gn 9:10
Now Abram was very rich in **l**, in silver, Gn 13:2
herdsmen of Abram's **l** and the Gn 13:7
livestock and the herdsmen of Lot's **l**. Gn 13:7
not time for the **l** to be gathered together. Gn 29:7
you, and how your **l** has fared with me. Gn 30:29
has taken away the **l** of your father and Gn 31:9
He drove away all his **l**, all his property Gn 31:18
the **l** in his possession that he had Gn 31:18
at the pace of the **l** that are ahead of me Gn 33:14
a house and made booths for his **l**. Gn 33:17
But his sons were with his **l** in the field, Gn 34:5
Will not their **l**, their property and all Gn 34:23
all the members of his household, his **l**, Gn 36:6
not support them because of their **l**. Gn 36:7
They also took their **l** and their goods, Gn 46:6
for they have been keepers of **l**, Gn 46:32
have been keepers of **l** from our youth Gn 46:34
them, put them in charge of my **l**." Gn 47:6
And Joseph answered, "Give your **l**, and Gn 47:16
give you food in exchange for your **l**, Gn 47:16
So they brought their **l** to Joseph, and Gn 47:17
in exchange for all their **l** that year. Gn 47:17
all spent. The herds of **l** are my lord's. Gn 47:18
severe plague upon your **l** that are in the Ex 9:3
a distinction between the **l** of Israel and Ex 9:4
the livestock of Israel and the **l** of Egypt, Ex 9:4
All the **l** of the Egyptians died, but not one Ex 9:6
but not one of the **l** of the people of Israel Ex 9:6
behold, not one of the **l** of Israel was dead. Ex 9:7
get your **l** and all that you have in the Ex 9:19
his slaves and his **l** into the houses, Ex 9:20
LORD left his slaves and his **l** in the field. Ex 9:21
Our **l** also must go with us; not a hoof Ex 10:26
dungeon, and all the firstborn of the **l**. Ex 12:29
went up with them, and very much **l**, Ex 12:38
and our children and our **l** with thirst?" Ex 17:3
or your female servant, or your **l**, Ex 20:10
the womb are mine, all your male **l**, Ex 34:19
bring your offering of **l** from the herd or Lv 1:2
or a carcass of unclean **l** or a carcass of Lv 5:2
and destroy your **l** and make you Lv 26:22
the congregation drank, and their **l**. Nm 20:11
if we drink of your water, I and my **l**, Nm 20:19
of Gad had a very great number of **l**. Nm 32:1
and behold, the place was a place for **l**. Nm 32:1
congregation of Israel, is a land for **l**, Nm 32:4
livestock, and your servants have **l**." Nm 32:4
will build sheepfolds here for our **l**, Nm 32:16
Our little ones, our wives, our **l**, and Nm 32:26
cattle and for their **l** and for all their Nm 35:3
Only the **l** we took as spoil for ourselves, Dt 2:35
But all the **l** and the spoil of the cities we Dt 3:7
and your **l** (I know that you have much Dt 3:19
that you have much **l**) shall remain in Dt 3:19
your ox or your donkey or any of your **l**, Dt 5:14
barren among you or among your **l**. Dt 7:14
will give grass in your fields for your **l**, Dt 11:15
but the women and the little ones, the **l**, Dt 20:14
in the fruit of your **l** and in the fruit of Dt 28:11
and your **l** shall remain in the land that Jos 1:14
Only its spoil and its **l** you shall take as Jos 8:2
Only the **l** and the spoil of that city Israel Jos 8:27
all the spoil of these cities and the **l**, Jos 11:14
pasturelands for their **l** and their Jos 14:4
along with their pasturelands for our **l**." Jos 21:2
much wealth and with very much **l**, Jos 22:8
come up with their **l** and their tents; Jgs 6:5
the little ones and the **l** and the goods in Jgs 18:21
brought away their **l** and struck them 1 Sm 23:5
the people drove the **l** before him, 1 Sm 30:20
so that you shall drink, you, your **l**, 2 Kgs 3:17
because their **l** had multiplied in the 1 Chr 5:9
They carried off their **l**: 50,000 of 1 Chr 5:21
they came down to raid their **l**. 1 Chr 7:21
all the property and **l** of the king and 1 Chr 28:1
of those who had **l** and carried away 2 Chr 14:15
bodies and over our **l** as they please, Neh 9:37
to grow for the **l** and plants for man Ps 104:14
and he does not let their **l** diminish. Ps 107:38
Beasts and all **l**, creeping things and Ps 148:10
In that day your **l** will graze in large Is 30:23
stoops; their idols are on beasts and **l**; Is 46:1
Like **l** that go down into the valley, the Is 63:14
become plunder, their herds of **l** a spoil. Jer 49:32
who have acquired **l** and goods, Ezk 38:12
and gold, to take away **l** and goods, Ezk 38:13
of the multitude of people and **l** in it. Zec 2:4
from it himself, as did his sons and his **l**." Jn 4:12

LIVING (184)
swarm with swarms of **l** creatures, Gn 1:20
creatures and every **l** creature that Gn 1:21
earth bring forth **l** creatures according Gn 1:24
and over every **l** thing that moves Gn 1:28
of life, and the man became a **l** creature. Gn 2:7
the man called every **l** creature, Gn 2:19
Eve, because she was the mother of all **l**. Gn 3:20
And of every **l** thing of all flesh, you Gn 6:19
and every **l** thing that I have made I will Gn 7:4
He blotted out every **l** thing that was on Gn 7:23
out with you every **l** thing that is with Gn 8:17
again strike down every **l** creature as I Gn 8:21
and with every **l** creature that is with Gn 9:10
and you and every **l** creature that is with Gn 9:12
and you and every **l** creature of all flesh. Gn 9:15
between God and every **l** creature of all Gn 9:16
who was **l** by the oaks of Mamre the Gn 14:13
while he was still **l** he sent them away Gn 25:6
These are the **l** things that you may eat Lv 11:2
waters and of the **l** creatures that are in Lv 11:10
bird and every **l** creature that moves Lv 11:46
and between the **l** creature that may Lv 11:47
be eaten and the **l** creature that may Lv 11:47
clean and shall let the **l** bird go into the Lv 14:7
or anyone is **l** permanently among Nm 15:14
he stood between the dead and the **l**, Nm 16:48
the voice of the **l** God speaking out of Dt 5:26
and every **l** thing that followed them, Dt 11:6
shall know that the **l** God is among you Jos 3:10

of clothes and your l." And the Levite Jgs 17:10
has not forsaken the l or the dead!" Ru 2:20
should defy the armies of the l God?" 1 Sm 17:26
has defied the armies of the l God." 1 Sm 17:36
in the bundle of the l in the care of 1 Sm 25:29
of their death, l as if in widowhood. 2 Sm 20:3
woman said, "No, the l child is mine, 1 Kgs 3:22
and the l child is mine." Thus they 1 Kgs 3:22
son is dead, and my son is the l one.'" 1 Kgs 3:23
king said, "Divide the l child in two, 1 Kgs 3:25
son, "Oh, my lord, give her the l child, 1 Kgs 3:26
"Give the l child to the first woman, 1 Kgs 3:27
of Assyria has sent to mock the l God, 2 Kgs 19:4
he has sent to mock the l God. 2 Kgs 19:16
the temple servants l on Ophel repaired Neh 3:26
is the life of every l thing and the breath Jb 12:10
and it is not found in the land of the l. Jb 28:13
the eyes of all l and concealed from the Jb 28:21
and to the house appointed for all l. Jb 30:23
goodness of the LORD in the land of the l! Ps 27:13
My soul thirsts for God, for the l God. Ps 42:2
he will uproot you from the land of the l. Ps 52:5
kept our soul among the l and has not let Ps 66:9
them be blotted out of the book of the l; Ps 69:28
heart and flesh sing for joy to the l God. Ps 84:2
l things both small and great. Ps 104:25
walk before the LORD in the land of the l. Ps 116:9
refuge, my portion in the land of the l." Ps 142:5
for no one l is righteous before you. Ps 143:2
you satisfy the desire of every l thing. Ps 145:16
more fortunate than the l who are still Eccl 4:2
I saw all the l who move about under Eccl 4:15
how to conduct himself before the l? Eccl 6:8
mankind, and the l will lay it to heart. Eccl 7:2
he who is joined with all the l has hope, Eccl 9:4
for a l dog is better than a dead lion. Eccl 9:4
For the l know that they will die, but the Eccl 9:5
a garden fountain, a well of l water, and Sg 4:15
they inquire of the dead on behalf of the l? Is 8:19
of Assyria has sent to mock the l God, Is 37:4
which he has sent to mock the l God. Is 37:17
see the LORD, the LORD in the land of the l; Is 38:11
The l, the living, he thanks you, as I do Is 38:19
The living, the l, he thanks you, as I do Is 38:19
that he was cut off out of the land of the l, Is 53:8
forsaken me, the fountain of l waters, Jer 2:13
he is the l God and the everlasting King. Jer 10:10
let us cut him off from the land of the l, Jer 11:19
the LORD, the fountain of l water. Jer 17:13
and you pervert the words of the l God, Jer 23:36
not have anyone l among this people, Jer 29:32
the Syrians.' So we are l in Jerusalem." Jer 35:11
Why should a l man complain, a Lam 3:39
it came the likeness of four l creatures. Ezk 1:5
As for the likeness of the l creatures, Ezk 1:13
to and fro among the l creatures. Ezk 1:13
And the l creatures darted to and fro, Ezk 1:14
Now as I looked at the l creatures, I saw Ezk 1:15
on the earth beside the l creatures, Ezk 1:15
And when the l creatures went, the Ezk 1:19
and when the l creatures rose from the Ezk 1:19
the spirit of the l creatures was in the Ezk 1:20
the spirit of the l creatures was in the Ezk 1:21
the heads of the l creatures there was Ezk 1:22
the wings of the l creatures as they Ezk 3:13
These were the l creatures that I saw Ezk 10:15
the spirit of the l creatures was in Ezk 10:17
These were the l creatures that I saw Ezk 10:20
I will set beauty in the land of the l. Ezk 26:20
who spread terror in the land of the l. Ezk 32:23
spread their terror in the land of the l; Ezk 32:24
of them was spread in the land of the l, Ezk 32:25
spread their terror in the land of the l. Ezk 32:26
mighty men was in the land of the l. Ezk 32:27
For I spread terror in the land of the l; Ezk 32:32
every l creature that swarms will live, Ezk 47:9
wisdom that I have more than all the l, Dn 2:30
to the end that the l may know that the Dn 4:17
Daniel, "O Daniel, servant of the l God, Dn 6:20
the God of Daniel, for he is the l God, Dn 6:26
be said to them, "Children of the l God." Hos 1:10
On that day l waters shall flow out from Zec 14:8
are the Christ, the Son of the l God." Mt 16:16
He is not God of the dead, but of the l." Mt 22:32
said to him, "I adjure you by the l God, Mt 26:63
He is not God of the dead, but of the l. Mk 12:27
she had spent all her l on physicians, Lk 8:43
squandered his property in reckless l. Lk 15:13
he is not God of the dead, but of the l, Lk 20:38
"Why do you seek the l among the dead? Lk 24:5
and he would have given you l water." Jn 4:10
is deep. Where do you get that l water? Jn 4:11
I am the l bread that came down from Jn 6:51
As the l Father sent me, and I live Jn 6:57
of his heart will flow rivers of l water.'" Jn 7:38
into this land in which you are now l. Acts 7:4
He received l oracles to give to us. Acts 7:38
God to be judge of the l and the dead. Acts 10:42
send relief to the brothers l in Judea. Acts 11:29
from these vain things to a l God, Acts 14:15
For while we were l in the flesh, our Rom 7:5
they will be called 'sons of the l God.'" Rom 9:26
to present your bodies as a l sacrifice, Rom 12:1
be Lord both of the dead and of the l. Rom 14:9
right to refrain from working for a l? 1 Cor 9:6
gospel should get their l by the gospel. 1 Cor 9:14
first man Adam became a l being"; 1 Cor 15:45
ink but with the Spirit of the l God, 2 Cor 3:3
For we are the temple of the l God; as 2 Cor 6:16
once walked, when you were l in them. Col 3:7
from idols to serve the l and true God, 1 Thes 1:9
work quietly and to earn their own l. 2 Thes 3:12
which is the church of the l God, 1 Tm 3:15
we have our hope set on the l God, 1 Tm 4:10
who is to judge the l and the dead, 2 Tm 4:1
leading you to fall away from the l God. Heb 3:12
For the word of God is l and active, Heb 4:12
from dead works to serve the l God. Heb 9:14
by the new and l way that he opened Heb 10:20
to fall into the hands of the l God. Heb 10:31
land, l in tents with Isaac and Jacob, Heb 11:9
Zion and to the city of the l God, Heb 12:22
born again to a l hope through the 1 Pt 1:3
through the l and abiding word of God; 1 Pt 1:23
a l stone rejected by men but in the sight 1 Pt 2:4
you yourselves like l stones are being 1 Pt 2:5
for evil, but l as servants of God. 1 Pt 2:16
the Gentiles want to do, l in sensuality, 1 Pt 4:3
who is ready to judge the l and the dead. 1 Pt 4:5
and the l one. I died, and behold I am Rv 1:18
side of the throne, are four l creatures, Rv 4:6
the first l creature like a lion, the second Rv 4:7
a lion, the second l creature like an ox, Rv 4:7
the third l creature with the face of a man, Rv 4:7
and the fourth l creature like an eagle in Rv 4:7
And the four l creatures, each of them Rv 4:8
And whenever the l creatures give glory Rv 4:9
and the four l creatures and among Rv 5:6
the four l creatures and the twenty-four Rv 5:8
the throne and the l creatures and the Rv 5:11
And the four l creatures said, "Amen!" Rv 5:14
one of the four l creatures say with a Rv 6:1
seal, I heard the second l creature say, Rv 6:3
third seal, I heard the third l creature say, Rv 6:5
a voice in the midst of the four l creatures, Rv 6:6
the voice of the fourth l creature say, Rv 6:7
of the sun, with the seal of the l God, Rv 7:2
the elders and the four l creatures, Rv 7:11
he will guide them to springs of l water, Rv 7:17
A third of the l creatures in the sea died, Rv 8:9
before the four l creatures and before Rv 14:3
one of the four l creatures gave to the Rv 15:7
and every l thing died that was in the sea. Rv 16:3
rich from the power of her luxurious l." Rv 18:3
elders and the four l creatures fell down Rv 19:4

LIZARD (5)
rat, the mouse, the great l of any kind, Lv 11:29
the gecko, the monitor l, the lizard, the Lv 11:30
the gecko, the monitor lizard, the l, the Lv 11:30
monitor lizard, the lizard, the sand l, Lv 11:30
the l you can take in your hands, yet it Prv 30:28

LO-DEBAR (4)
of Machir the son of Ammiel, at L." 2 Sm 9:4
of Machir the son of Ammiel, at L. 2 Sm 9:5
Machir the son of Ammiel from L, 2 Sm 17:27
you who rejoice in L, who say, "Have Am 6:13

LOAD (7)
l your beasts and go back to the land Gn 45:17
to your servant two mules' l of earth, 2 Kgs 5:17
that no l might be brought in on the Neh 13:19
and the l that was on it will be cut off, Is 22:25
him he shall l with honor. Dn 11:39
For you l people with burdens hard to Lk 11:46
For each will have to bear his own l. Gal 6:5

LOADED (5)
Then they l their donkeys with their Gn 42:26
clothes, and every man l his donkey, Gn 44:13
ten donkeys l with the good things of Gn 45:23
and ten female donkeys l with grain, Gn 45:23
who carried burdens were l in such a Neh 4:17

LOADING (1)
of grain and l them on donkeys, Neh 13:15

LOADS (5)
of goods of Damascus, forty camel l. 2 Kgs 8:9
wine, grapes, figs, and all kinds of l, Neh 13:15
He l the thick cloud with moisture; the Jb 37:11
mill, and boys stagger under l of wood. Lam 5:13
long?—and l himself with pledges!" Hab 2:6

LOAF (12)
and one l of bread and one cake of Ex 29:23
it he shall offer one l from each offering, Lv 7:14
he took one unleavened l and one loaf of Lv 8:26
unleavened loaf and one l of bread with Lv 8:26
two tenths of an ephah shall be in each l. Lv 24:5
and one unleavened l out of the basket Nm 6:19
shall present a l as a contribution; Nm 15:20
piece of silver or a l of bread and shall 1 Sm 2:36
men and women, to each a l of bread, 1 Chr 16:3
price of a prostitute is only a l of bread, Prv 6:26
And a l of bread was given him daily Jer 37:21
they had only one l with them in the Mk 8:14

LOAN (2)
you make your neighbor a l of any sort, Dt 24:10
whom you make the l shall bring the Dt 24:11

LOANS (1)
not charge interest on l to your brother, Dt 23:19

LOATH (1)
though he is l to let it go and holds it in Jb 20:13

LOATHE (9)
"I l my life because of the Hittite Gn 27:46
no water, and we l this worthless food." Nm 21:5
I l my life; I would not live forever. Leave Jb 7:16
blameless; I regard not myself; I l my life. Jb 9:21
"I l my life; I will give free utterance to Jb 10:1
And do I not l those who rise up Ps 139:21
rejected Judah? Does your soul l Zion? Jer 14:19
and you shall l yourselves for all the Ezk 20:43
and you will l yourselves for your Ezk 36:31

LOATHED (6)
And he l Israel and reigned over 1 Kgs 11:25
For forty years I l that generation and Ps 95:10
they l any kind of food, and they drew Ps 107:18
away from your grave, like a l branch, Is 14:19
who l her husband and her children; Ezk 16:45
who l their husbands and their Ezk 16:45

LOATHES (2)
so that his life l bread, and his appetite Jb 33:20
One who is full l honey, but to one who Prv 27:7

LOATHSOME (5)
at your nostrils and becomes l to you, Nm 11:20
and struck Job with l sores from the sole Jb 2:7
them; they are as food that is l to me. Jb 6:7
And they will be l in their own sight for Ezk 6:9
form of creeping things and l beasts, Ezk 8:10

LOAVES (40)
it shall be unleavened l of fine flour Lv 2:4
sacrifice unleavened l mixed with Lv 7:12
and l of fine flour well mixed with oil. Lv 7:12
his offering with l of leavened bread. Lv 7:13
your dwelling places two l of bread to Lv 23:17
take fine flour and bake twelve l from it; Lv 24:5
bread, l of fine flour mixed with oil, Nm 6:15
"Please give l of bread to the people who Jgs 8:5
another carrying three l of bread, 1 Sm 10:3
greet you and give you two l of bread, 1 Sm 10:4
of this parched grain, and these ten l, 1 Sm 17:17
Give me five l of bread, or whatever is 1 Sm 21:3
took two hundred l and two skins 1 Sm 25:18
bearing two hundred l of bread, 2 Sm 16:1
Take with you ten l, some cakes, and 1 Kgs 14:3
twenty l of barley and fresh ears of 2 Kgs 4:42
these stones to become l of bread." Mt 4:3
"We have only five l here and two fish." Mt 14:17
and taking the five l and the two fish, Mt 14:19
Then he broke the l and gave them to Mt 14:19
"How many l do you have?" They said, Mt 15:34
he took the seven l and the fish, and Mt 15:36
not remember the five l for the five Mt 16:9
Or the seven l for the four thousand, Mt 16:10
to them, "How many l do you have? Mk 6:38
And taking the five l and the two fish he Mk 6:41
blessing and broke the l and gave them Mk 6:41
those who ate the l were five thousand Mk 6:44
for they did not understand about the l, Mk 6:52
"How many l do you have?" They said, Mk 8:5
And he took the seven l, and having Mk 8:6
I broke the five l for the five thousand, Mk 8:19
have no more than five l and two fish— Lk 9:13
And taking the five l and the two fish, he Lk 9:16
Then he broke the l and gave them to Lk 9:16
and say to him, 'Friend, lend me three l, Lk 11:5
here who has five barley l and two fish, Jn 6:9
Jesus then took the l, and when he had Jn 6:11
with fragments from the five barley l, Jn 6:13
but because you ate your fill of the l. Jn 6:26

LOBE (16)
the entrails, and the long l of the liver, Ex 29:13
and the long l of the liver and the two Ex 29:22

and the long **l** of the liver that he shall Lv 3:4
the loins and the long **l** of the liver that Lv 3:10
the loins and the long **l** of the liver that Lv 3:15
the loins and the long **l** of the liver that he Lv 4:9
and the long **l** of the liver that he shall Lv 7:4
entrails and the long **l** of the liver and Lv 8:16
and put it on the **l** of Aaron's right ear Lv 8:23
entrails and the long **l** of the liver and Lv 8:25
kidneys and the long **l** of the liver from Lv 9:10
the kidneys and the long **l** of the liver— Lv 9:19
shall put it on the **l** of the right ear of Lv 14:14
priest shall put on the **l** of the right ear Lv 14:17
and put it on the **l** of the right ear of Lv 14:25
is in his hand on the **l** of the right ear of Lv 14:28

LOBES (1)
of the blood on the **l** of their right ears Lv 8:24

LOCAL (1)
he called together the **l** leaders of the Acts 28:17

LOCK (1)
of a hand and took me by a **l** of my head, Ezk 8:3

LOCKED (9)
roof chamber behind him and **l** them. Jgs 3:23
the doors of the roof chamber were **l**, Jgs 3:24
A garden **l** is my sister, my bride, a Sg 4:12
locked is my sister, my bride, a spring **l**, Sg 4:12
to them all, that he **l** up John in prison. Lk 3:20
the doors being **l** where the disciples Jn 20:19
Although the doors were **l**, Jesus came Jn 20:26
the prison securely **l** and the guards Acts 5:23
I not only **l** up many of the saints in Acts 26:10

LOCKS (8)
He shall let the **l** of hair of his head grow Nm 6:5
you weave the seven **l** of my head with Jgs 16:13
Delilah took the seven **l** of his head and Jgs 16:14
him shave off the seven **l** of his head. Jgs 16:19
dew, my **l** with the drops of the night." Sg 5:2
gold; his **l** are wavy, black as a raven. Sg 5:11
and your flowing **l** are like purple; Sg 7:5
their heads or let their **l** grow long; Ezk 44:20

LOCUST (22)
Not a single **l** was left in all the country Ex 10:19
the **l** of any kind, the bald locust of any Lv 11:22
of any kind, the bald **l** of any kind, Lv 11:22
in little, for the **l** shall consume it. Dt 28:38
or blight or mildew or **l** or caterpillar, 1 Kgs 8:37
blight or mildew or **l** or caterpillar, 2 Chr 6:28
or command the **l** to devour the land, 2 Chr 7:13
Do you make him leap like the **l**? His Jb 39:20
crops to the destroying **l** and the fruit of Ps 78:46
and the fruit of their labor to the **l**. Ps 78:46
at evening; I am shaken off like a **l**. Ps 109:23
What the cutting **l** left, the swarming Jl 1:4
locust left, the swarming **l** has eaten. Jl 1:4
What the swarming **l** left, the hopping Jl 1:4
locust left, the hopping **l** has eaten, Jl 1:4
has eaten, and what the hopping **l** left, Jl 1:4
locust left, the destroying **l** has eaten. Jl 1:4
the years that the swarming **l** has eaten, Jl 2:25
trees and your olive trees the **l** devoured; Am 4:9
cut you off. It will devour you like the **l**. Na 3:15
Multiply yourselves like the **l**; multiply Na 3:15
The **l** spreads its wings and flies away. Na 3:16

LOCUSTS (21)
I will bring **l** into your country, Ex 10:4
hand over the land of Egypt for the **l**, Ex 10:12
the east wind had brought the **l**. Ex 10:13
The **l** came up over all the land of Ex 10:14
a dense swarm of **l** as had never been Ex 10:14
which lifted the **l** and drove them into Ex 10:19
they would come like **l** in number—both Jgs 6:5
lay along the valley like **l** in abundance, Jgs 7:12
He spoke, and the **l** came, young Ps 105:34
came, young **l** without number, Ps 105:34
the **l** have no king, yet all of them Prv 30:27
as the caterpillar gathers; as **l** leap, Is 33:4
they are more numerous than **l**; Jer 46:23
I will fill you with men, as many as **l**, Jer 51:14
her; bring up horses like bristling **l**. Jer 51:27
he was forming **l** when the latter growth Am 7:1
scribes like clouds of **l** settling on the Na 3:17
waist, and his food was **l** and wild honey. Mt 3:4
his waist and ate **l** and wild honey. Mk 1:6
from the smoke came **l** on the earth, Rv 9:3
In appearance the **l** were like horses Rv 9:7

LOD (4)
who built Ono and **L** with its towns, 1 Chr 8:12
The sons of **L**, Hadid, and Ono, 725. Ezr 2:33
The sons of **L**, Hadid, and Ono, 721. Neh 7:37
L, and Ono, the valley of craftsmen. Neh 11:35

LODGE (14)
And he said to them, "**L** here tonight, Nm 22:8
down in the place where you **l** tonight.'" Jos 4:3
L here and let your heart be merry, and Jgs 19:9
go I will go, and where you **l** I will lodge. Ru 1:16
go I will go, and where you lodge I will **l**. Ru 1:16
"Why do you **l** outside the wall? Neh 13:21
far away; I would **l** in the wilderness; Ps 55:7
go out into the fields and **l** in the villages; Sg 7:11
in a vineyard, like a **l** in a cucumber field, Is 1:8
the pass; at Geba they **l** for the night; Is 10:29
In the thickets in Arabia you will **l**, O Is 21:13
your wicked thoughts **l** within you? Jer 4:14
and the hedgehog shall **l** in her capitals; Zep 2:14
disciple, with whom we should **l**. Acts 21:16

LODGED (13)
whose name was Rahab and **l** there. Jos 2:1
Israel, and **l** there before they passed over. Jos 3:1
the place where they **l** and laid them Jos 4:8
to the house of Micah, and **l** there. Jgs 18:2
that the ark was **l** at Kiriath-jearim, 1 Sm 7:2
into the upper chamber where he **l**, 1 Kgs 17:19
There he came to a cave and **l** in it. 1 Kgs 19:9
And they **l** around the house of God, 1 Chr 9:27
kinds of wares **l** outside Jerusalem Neh 13:20
(the sojourner has not **l** in the street; I Jb 31:32
Righteousness **l** in her, but now Is 1:21
out of the city to Bethany and **l** there. Mt 21:17
he went out and **l** on the mount called Lk 21:37

LODGES (1)
angry, for anger **l** in the bosom of fools. Eccl 7:9

LODGING (10)
to give his donkey fodder at the **l** place, Gn 42:27
we came to the **l** place we opened our Gn 43:21
At a **l** place on the way the LORD met him Ex 4:24
I entered its farthest **l** place, its most 2 Kgs 19:23
that I had in the desert a travelers' **l** place, Jer 9:2
countryside to find **l** and get provisions, Lk 9:12
He is **l** with one Simon, a tanner, Acts 10:6
who was called Peter was **l** there. Acts 10:18
He is **l** in the house of Simon, a Acts 10:32
to him at his **l** in greater numbers. Acts 28:23

LOFTILY (1)
with malice; **l** they threaten oppression. Ps 73:8

LOFTINESS (1)
of Moab—he is very proud—of his **l**, Jer 48:29

LOFTY (22)
See the highest stars, how **l** they are! Jb 22:12
From your **l** abode you water the Ps 104:13
There are those—how **l** are their eyes, Prv 30:13
and the **l** pride of men shall be humbled, Is 2:11
has a day against all that is proud and **l**, Is 2:12
all the cedars of Lebanon, **l** and lifted up; Is 2:13
against all the **l** mountains, and against Is 2:14
and the **l** pride of men shall be brought Is 2:17
down, and the **l** will be brought low. Is 10:33
the inhabitants of the height, the **l** city. Is 26:5
And on every **l** mountain and every Is 30:25
On a high and **l** mountain you have set Is 57:7
and made yourself a **l** place in every Ezk 16:24
street you built your **l** place and made Ezk 16:25
and making your **l** place in every Ezk 16:31
and break down your **l** places. Ezk 16:39
take a sprig from the **l** top of the cedar Ezk 17:22
plant it on a high and **l** mountain. Ezk 17:22
the clefts of the rock, in your **l** dwelling, Ob 1:3
cities and against the **l** battlements. Zep 1:16
of God with **l** speech or wisdom. 1 Cor 2:1
arguments and every **l** opinion raised 2 Cor 10:5

LOG (14)
the LORD, and the LORD showed him a **l**, Ex 15:25
flour mixed with oil, and one **l** of oil. Lv 14:10
a guilt offering, along with the **l** of oil, Lv 14:12
shall take some of the **l** of oil and pour Lv 14:15
oil for a grain offering, and a **l** of oil; Lv 14:21
of the guilt offering and the **l** of oil, Lv 14:24
the Jordan and each of us get there a **l**, 2 Kgs 6:2
But as one was felling a **l**, his axe head 2 Kgs 6:5
but do not notice the **l** that is in your own Mt 7:3
eye,' when there is the **l** in your own eye? Mt 7:4
first take the **l** out of your own eye, Mt 7:5
but do not notice the **l** that is in your Lk 6:41
yourself do not see the **l** that is in your Lk 6:42
first take the **l** out of your own eye, Lk 6:42

LOGS (3)
and he who splits **l** is endangered by Eccl 10:9
one of the flock; pile the **l** under it; Ezk 24:5
Heap on the **l**, kindle the fire, boil the Ezk 24:10

LOINCLOTH (8)
"Go and buy a linen **l** and put it around Jer 13:1
So I bought a **l** according to the word of Jer 13:2
"Take the **l** that you have bought, which Jer 13:4
take from there the **l** that I commanded Jer 13:6
and I took the **l** from the place where I Jer 13:7
And behold, the **l** was spoiled; it was Jer 13:7
and worship them, shall be like this **l**, Jer 13:10
For as the **l** clings to the waist of a man, Jer 13:11

LOINCLOTHS (1)
fig leaves together and made themselves **l**. Gn 3:7

LOINS (14)
sackcloth on his **l** and mourned for Gn 37:34
with the fat that is on them at the **l**, Lv 3:4
is on them at the **l** and the long lobe of Lv 3:10
is on them at the **l** and the long lobe of Lv 3:15
is on them at the **l** and the long lobe of Lv 4:9
with the fat that is on them at the **l**, Lv 7:4
crush the **l** of his adversaries, of those Dt 33:11
Behold, his strength in his **l**, and his Jb 40:16
and make their **l** tremble continually. Ps 69:23
waist, and faithfulness the belt of his **l**. Is 11:5
Therefore my **l** are filled with anguish; Is 21:3
broke and made all their **l** to shake. Ezk 29:7
and knees tremble; anguish is in all **l**; Na 2:10
was still in the **l** of his ancestor when Heb 7:10

LOIS (1)
in your grandmother **L** and your 2 Tm 1:5

LONELY (3)
gracious to me, for I am **l** and afflicted. Ps 25:16
I am like a **l** sparrow on the housetop. Ps 102:7
How **l** sits the city that was full of Lam 1:1

LONG (308)
When he had been there a **l** time, Gn 26:8
my shepherd all my life **l** to this day, Gn 48:15
'How **l** will you refuse to humble Ex 10:3
"How **l** shall this man be a snare to us? Ex 10:7
"How **l** will you refuse to keep my Ex 16:28
When the trumpet sounds a **l** blast, Ex 19:13
that your days may be **l** in the land that Ex 20:12
wood, five cubits **l** and five cubits broad. Ex 27:1
linen a hundred cubits **l** for one side. Ex 27:9
shall be hangings a hundred cubits **l**, Ex 27:11
there shall be a screen twenty cubits **l**, Ex 27:16
the entrails, and the **l** lobe of the liver, Ex 29:13
and the **l** lobe of the liver and the two Ex 29:22
It was twenty cubits **l** and five cubits Ex 38:18
and the **l** lobe of the liver that he shall Lv 3:4
at the loins and the **l** lobe of the liver that Lv 3:10
at the loins and the **l** lobe of the liver that Lv 3:15
at the loins and the **l** lobe of the liver that Lv 4:9
and the **l** lobe of the liver that he shall Lv 7:4
on the entrails and the **l** lobe of the liver Lv 8:16
on the entrails and the **l** lobe of the liver Lv 8:25
the kidneys and the **l** lobe of the liver Lv 9:10
the kidneys and the **l** lobe of the liver Lv 9:19
shall remain unclean as **l** as he has the Lv 13:46
has a mutilated face or a limb too **l**, Lv 21:18
that has a part too **l** or too short for a Lv 22:23
You shall eat old store **l** kept, and you Lv 26:10
enjoy its Sabbaths as **l** as it lies Lv 26:34
As **l** as it lies desolate it shall have rest, Lv 26:35
let the locks of hair of his head grow **l**. Nm 6:5
a dead body, or is on a **l** journey, Nm 9:10
As **l** as the cloud rested over the Nm 9:18
together, you shall blow a **l** blast, Nm 10:7
"How **l** will this people despise me? Nm 14:11
And how **l** will they not believe in me, Nm 14:11
"How **l** shall this wicked Nm 14:27
Egypt, and we lived in Egypt a **l** time. Nm 20:15
have ridden all your life **l** to this day? Nm 22:30
'You have stayed **l** enough at this Dt 1:6
around this mountain country **l** enough. Dt 2:3
You will not live **l** in it, but will be Dt 4:26
you, that your days may be **l**, Dt 5:16
and that you may live **l** in the land that Dt 5:33
of your life, and that your days may be **l**. Dt 6:2
and that you may live **l** in the land that Dt 11:9
as **l** as the heavens are above the earth. Dt 11:21
not neglect the Levite as **l** as you live in Dt 12:19
And if the way is too **l** for you, so that Dt 14:24
that he may continue **l** in his kingdom, Dt 17:20
and overtake him, because the way is **l**, Dt 19:6
"When you besiege a city for a **l** time, Dt 20:19
go well with you, and that you may live **l**. Dt 22:7
that your days may be **l** in the land that Dt 25:15
and fail with longing for them all day **l**, Dt 28:32
You shall not live **l** in the land that you Dt 30:18
as **l** as you live in the land that you are Dt 31:13
word you shall live **l** in the land that Dt 32:47
The High God surrounds him all day **l**, Dt 33:12
when they make a **l** blast with the ram's Jos 6:5
are worn out from the very **l** journey." Jos 9:13
Joshua made war a **l** time with all those Jos 11:18
"How **l** will you put off going in to take Jos 18:3
A **l** time afterward, when the LORD had Jos 23:1
says the LORD, the God of Israel, '**L** ago, Jos 24:2
And you lived in the wilderness a **l** time. Jos 24:7

'Why is his chariot so **l** in coming? Jgs 5:28
as **l** as the house of God was at Shiloh. Jgs 18:31
"How **l** will you go on being drunk? 1 Sm 1:14
As **l** as he lives, he is lent to the LORD." 1 Sm 1:28
at Kiriath-jearim, a **l** time passed, 1 Sm 7:2
the people shouted, "**L** live the king!" 1 Sm 10:24
"How **l** will you grieve over Saul, 1 Sm 16:1
For as **l** as the son of Jesse lives on 1 Sm 20:31
the fields, as **l** as we went with them. 1 Sm 25:15
not be found in you so **l** as you live. 1 Sm 25:28
How **l** will it be before you tell your 2 Sm 2:26
There was a **l** war between the house of 2 Sm 3:1
was wearing a **l** robe with sleeves, 2 Sm 13:18
head and tore the **l** robe that she 2 Sm 13:19
said to Absalom, "**L** live the king! 2 Sm 16:16
"Long live the king! **L** live the king!" 2 Sm 16:16
and saying, '**L** live King Adonijah!' 1 Kgs 1:25
and say, '**L** live King Solomon!' 1 Kgs 1:34
people said, "**L** live King Solomon!" 1 Kgs 1:39
not asked for yourself **l** life or riches 1 Kgs 3:11
built for the LORD was sixty cubits **l**, 1 Kgs 6:2
nave of the house was twenty cubits **l**, 1 Kgs 6:3
inner sanctuary, was forty cubits **l**. 1 Kgs 6:17
inner sanctuary was twenty cubits **l**, 1 Kgs 6:20
Each stand was four cubits **l**, four 1 Kgs 7:27
And the poles were so **l** that the ends of 1 Kgs 8:8
have gone up to Jerusalem **l** enough. 1 Kgs 12:28
"How **l** will you go limping between 1 Kgs 18:21
so **l** as the whorings and the sorceries 2 Kgs 9:22
hands and said, "**L** live the king!" 2 Kgs 11:12
not heard that I determined it **l** ago? 2 Kgs 19:25
to his daily needs, as **l** as he lived. 2 Kgs 25:30
you, and have not even asked **l** life, 2 Chr 1:11
nave of the house was twenty cubits **l**, 2 Chr 3:4
twenty cubits **l** and twenty cubits wide 2 Chr 4:1
And the poles were so **l** that the ends of 2 Chr 5:9
made a bronze platform five cubits **l**, 2 Chr 6:13
For a **l** time Israel was without the 2 Chr 15:3
and they said, "**L** live the king." 2 Chr 23:11
God, and as **l** as he sought the LORD, 2 Chr 26:5
beside him), "How **l** will you be gone, Neh 2:6
For **l** ago in the days of David and Neh 12:46
so **l** as I see Mordecai the Jew sitting at Est 5:13
who **l** for death, but it comes not, and dig Jb 3:21
But the night is **l**, and I am full of tossing Jb 7:4
How **l** will you not look away from me, Jb 7:19
"How **l** will you say these things, and the Jb 8:2
you would **l** for the work of your hands. Jb 14:15
"How **l** will you hunt for words? Jb 18:2
"How **l** will you torment me and break Jb 19:2
as **l** as my breath is in me, and the spirit Jb 27:3
Do not **l** for the night, when peoples Jb 36:20
how **l** shall my honor be turned into Ps 4:2
How **l** will you love vain words and seek Ps 4:2
greatly troubled. But you, O LORD—how **l**? Ps 6:3
How **l**, O LORD? Will you forget me Ps 13:1
How **l** will you hide your face from me? Ps 13:1
How **l** must I take counsel in my soul Ps 13:2
How **l** shall my enemy be exalted over Ps 13:2
my salvation; for you I wait all the day **l**. Ps 25:5
away through my groaning all day **l**. Ps 32:3
How **l**, O Lord, will you look on? Rescue Ps 35:17
and of your praise all the day **l**. Ps 35:28
of ruin and meditate treachery all day **l**. Ps 38:12
so **l** as the wicked are in my presence." Ps 39:1
All day **l** my disgrace is before me, and Ps 44:15
for your sake we are killed all the day **l**; Ps 44:22
me; all day **l** an attacker oppresses me; Ps 56:1
my enemies trample on me all day **l**, for Ps 56:2
All day **l** they injure my cause; all their Ps 56:5
How **l** will all of you attack a man to Ps 62:3
So I will bless you as **l** as I live; in your Ps 63:4
talk of your righteous help all the day **l**, Ps 71:24
the sun endures, and as **l** as the moon, Ps 72:5
L may he live; may gold of Sheba be Ps 72:15
his fame continue as **l** as the sun! Ps 72:17
For all the day **l** I have been stricken Ps 73:14
is none among us who knows how **l**. Ps 74:9
How **l**, O God, is the foe to scoff? Is the Ps 74:10
I consider the days of old, the years **l** ago. Ps 77:5
How **l**, O LORD? Will you be angry Ps 79:5
how **l** will you be angry with your Ps 80:4
"How **l** will you judge unjustly and show Ps 82:2
They surround me like a flood all day **l**; Ps 88:17
his throne as **l** as the sun before me. Ps 89:36
How **l**, O LORD? Will you hide yourself Ps 89:46
How **l** will your wrath burn like fire? Ps 89:46
Return, O LORD! How **l**? Have pity on Ps 90:13
With **l** life I will satisfy him and show Ps 91:16
O LORD, how **l** shall the wicked, how long Ps 94:3
the wicked, how **l** shall the wicked exult? Ps 94:3
I will sing to the LORD as **l** as I live; I Ps 104:33
therefore I will call on him as **l** as I live. Ps 116:2
Behold, I **l** for your precepts; in your Ps 119:40
My eyes **l** for your promise; I ask, Ps 119:82
How **l** must your servant endure? Ps 119:84
My eyes **l** for your salvation and for Ps 119:123
because I **l** for your commandments. Ps 119:131
L have I known from your Ps 119:152
I **l** for your salvation, O LORD, and Ps 119:174
Too **l** have I had my dwelling among Ps 120:6
my back; they made **l** their furrows." Ps 129:3
me sit in darkness like those **l** dead. Ps 143:3
I will praise the LORD as **l** as I live; I will Ps 146:2
"How **l**, O simple ones, will you love Prv 1:22
How **l** will scoffers delight in their Prv 1:22
L life is in her right hand; in her left Prv 3:16
How **l** will you lie there, O sluggard? Prv 6:9
not at home; he has gone on a **l** journey; Prv 7:19
All day **l** he craves and craves, but the Prv 21:26
Those who tarry **l** over wine; those Prv 23:30
knowledge, its stability will **l** continue. Prv 28:2
to come all will have been **l** forgotten. Eccl 2:16
joyful and to do good as **l** as they live; Eccl 3:12
Then I said, "How **l**, O Lord?" And he said: Is 6:11
did it, or see him who planned it **l** ago. Is 22:11
For a burning place has **l** been prepared; Is 30:33
you not heard that I determined it **l** ago? Is 37:26
For a **l** time I have held my peace; I have Is 42:14
counsel together! Who told this **l** ago? Is 45:21
They are created now, not **l** ago; before Is 48:7
as in days of old, the generations of **l** ago. Is 51:9
I not held my peace, even for a **l** time, Is 57:11
in our sins we have been a **l** time, and Is 64:5
and my chosen shall **l** enjoy the work of Is 65:22
"For **l** ago I broke your yoke and burst Jer 2:20
How **l** shall your wicked thoughts lodge Jer 4:14
How **l** must I see the standard and hear Jer 4:21
How **l** will the land mourn and the grass Jer 12:4
How **l** will it be before you are made Jer 13:27
for me a reproach and derision all day **l**. Jer 20:8
the land to which they will **l** to return, Jer 22:27
How **l** shall there be lies in the heart of Jer 23:26
Babylon, saying, "Your exile will be **l**; Jer 29:28
How **l** will you waver, O faithless Jer 31:22
vessel, that they may last for a **l** time. Jer 32:14
valley, how **l** will you gash yourselves? Jer 47:5
of the LORD! How **l** till you are quiet? Jer 47:6
the day of his death as **l** as he lived. Jer 52:34
has left me stunned, faint all the day **l**. Lam 1:13
his word, which he commanded **l** ago; Lam 2:17
hand again and again the whole day **l**. Lam 3:3
dwell in darkness like the dead of **l** ago. Lam 3:6
the object of their taunts all day **l**. Lam 3:14
assailants are against me all the day **l**. Lam 3:62
So **l** shall you bear the punishment of Ezk 4:5
of Israel, saying, 'The days grow **l**, Ezk 12:22
eagle with great wings and **l** pinions, Ezk 17:3
and its branches **l** from abundant Ezk 31:5
reed in the man's hand was six **l** cubits, Ezk 40:5
rooms, one reed **l** and one reed broad; Ezk 40:7
twenty-five cubits **l** and five cubits Ezk 40:30
burnt offering, a cubit and a half **l**, Ezk 40:42
And hooks, a handbreadth **l**, were Ezk 40:43
a hundred cubits **l** and a hundred Ezk 40:47
measured a full reed of six **l** cubits. Ezk 41:8
the temple, a hundred cubits **l**; Ezk 41:13
with its walls, a hundred cubits **l**; Ezk 41:13
wood, three cubits high, two cubits **l**, Ezk 41:22
ten cubits wide and a hundred cubits **l**, Ezk 42:4
opposite the chambers, fifty cubits **l**. Ezk 42:7
on the outer court were fifty cubits **l**, Ezk 42:8
the nave were a hundred cubits **l**. Ezk 42:8
it, 500 cubits **l** and 500 cubits broad, Ezk 42:20
twelve cubits **l** by twelve broad. Ezk 43:16
fourteen cubits **l** by fourteen broad, Ezk 43:17
their heads or let their locks grow **l**; Ezk 44:20
25,000 cubits **l** and 20,000 cubits Ezk 45:1
section 25,000 cubits **l** and 10,000 Ezk 45:3
25,000 cubits **l** and 10,000 cubits Ezk 45:5
5,000 cubits broad and 25,000 cubits **l**. Ezk 45:6
courts, forty cubits **l** and thirty broad; Ezk 46:22
till his hair grew as **l** as eagles' feathers, Dn 4:33
"For how **l** is the vision concerning the Dn 8:13
"How **l** shall it be till the end of these Dn 12:6
How **l** will they be incapable of Hos 8:5
and pursues the east wind all day **l**; Hos 12:1
O LORD, how **l** shall I cry for help, and Hab 1:2
up what is not his own—for how **l**? Hab 2:6
how **l** will you have no mercy on Zec 1:12
guests mourn as **l** as the bridegroom Mt 9:15
would have repented **l** ago in sackcloth Mt 11:21
by this time was a **l** way from the land, Mt 14:24
generation, how **l** am I to be with you? Mt 17:17
with you? How **l** am I to bear with you? Mt 17:17
phylacteries broad and their fringes **l**, Mt 23:5
Now after a **l** time the master of those Mt 25:19
As **l** as they have the bridegroom with Mk 2:19
generation, how **l** am I to be with you? Mk 9:19
with you? How **l** am I to bear with you? Mk 9:19
"How **l** has this been happening to Mk 9:21
to walk around in **l** robes and like Mk 12:38
and for a pretense make **l** prayers. Mk 12:40
For a **l** time he had worn no clothes, and Lk 8:27
how **l** am I to be with you and bear with Lk 9:41
Sidon, they would have repented **l** ago, Lk 10:13
But while he was still a **l** way off, his Lk 15:20
and night? Will he delay **l** over them? Lk 18:7
went into another country for a **l** while. Lk 20:9
who like to walk around in **l** robes, Lk 20:46
and for a pretense make **l** prayers. Lk 20:47
very glad, for he had **l** desired to see him, Lk 23:8
that he had already been there a **l** time, Jn 5:6
As **l** as I am in the world, I am the light of Jn 9:5
"How **l** will you keep us in suspense? Jn 10:24
said to him, "Have I been with you so **l**, Jn 14:9
the mouth of his holy prophets **l** ago. Acts 3:21
him because for a **l** time he had Acts 8:11
So they remained for a **l** time, speaking Acts 14:3
he conversed with them a **l** while, Acts 20:11
They have known for a **l** time, if they Acts 26:5
And Paul said, "Whether short or **l**, I Acts 26:29
had been without food for a **l** time, Acts 27:21
they had waited a **l** time and saw no Acts 28:6
For I **l** to see you, that I may impart to Rom 1:11
on a person only as **l** as he lives? Rom 7:1
sake we are being killed all the day **l**; Rom 8:36
"All day **l** I have held out my hands Rom 10:21
that was kept secret for **l** ages Rom 16:25
bound to her husband as **l** as he lives. 1 Cor 7:39
that if a man wears **l** hair it is a 1 Cor 11:14
but if a woman has **l** hair, it is her 1 Cor 11:15
while they **l** for you and pray for you, 2 Cor 9:14
I mean that the heir, as **l** as he is a child, Gal 4:1
you and that you may live **l** in the land." Eph 6:3
my brothers, whom I love and **l** for, Phil 4:1
remember us kindly and **l** to see us, 1 Thes 3:6
and long to see us, as we **l** to see you— 1 Thes 3:6
I remember your tears, I **l** to see you, 2 Tm 1:4
L ago, at many times and in many ways, Heb 1:1
as **l** as it is called "today," that none of Heb 3:13
saying through David so **l** afterward, Heb 4:7
is not yet opened as **l** as the first section Heb 9:8
is not in force as **l** as the one who made Heb 9:17
things into which angels **l** to look. 1 Pt 1:12
infants, **l** for the pure spiritual milk, 1 Pt 2:2
think it right, as **l** as I am in this body, 2 Pt 1:13
Their condemnation from **l** ago is not 2 Pt 2:3
this fact, that the heavens existed **l** ago, 2 Pt 3:5
in unnoticed who **l** ago were designated Jude 1:4
clothed with a **l** robe and with a golden Rv 1:13
how **l** before you will judge and avenge Rv 6:10
and will not find it. They will **l** to die, Rv 9:6

LONG-HAIRED (1)

captives, from the **l** heads of the enemy.' Dt 32:42

LONGED (8)

away because you **l** greatly for your Gn 31:30
the spirit of the king **l** to go out to 2 Sm 13:39
the twilight I **l** for has been turned for me Is 21:4
Ah, this is the day we **l** for; now we Lam 2:16
Thus you **l** for the lewdness of your Ezk 23:21
and righteous people **l** to see what Mt 13:17
and since I have **l** for many years to Rom 15:23
for which your soul **l** has gone from Rv 18:14

LONGER (121)

it shall no **l** yield to you its strength. Gn 4:12
No **l** shall your name be called Abram, Gn 17:5
"Your name shall no **l** be called Jacob, Gn 32:28
no **l** shall your name be called Jacob, Gn 35:10
When she could hide him no **l**, she took Ex 2:3
"You shall no **l** give the people straw to Ex 5:7
I will let you go, and you shall stay no **l**." Ex 9:28
and the rain no **l** poured upon the earth. Ex 9:33
it was two days, or a month, or a **l** time, Nm 9:22
of your heart, and be no **l** stubborn. Dt 10:16
But if you no **l** delight in her, you shall Dt 21:14
I am no **l** able to go out and come in. Dt 31:2
they are no **l** his children because they Dt 32:5
and there was no **l** any spirit in them Jos 5:1
And there was no **l** manna for the people Jos 5:12
your God will no **l** drive out these Jos 23:13
they could no **l** withstand their enemies. Jgs 2:14
I will no **l** drive out before them any of Jgs 2:21
way and ate, and her face was no **l** sad. 1 Sm 1:18
seeking me any **l** within the borders 1 Sm 27:1
had fled to Gath, he no **l** sought him. 1 Sm 27:4
"You shall no **l** go out with us to 2 Sm 21:17
should I wait for the LORD any **l**?" 2 Kgs 6:33
so the Levites no **l** need to carry the 1 Chr 23:26
that we may no **l** suffer derision." Neh 2:17
Its measure is **l** than the earth and Jb 11:9
they are no **l** remembered, so Jb 24:20
there is no **l** any prophet, and there is Ps 74:9
foolish king who no **l** knew how to Eccl 4:13

to pieces so that it will no **l** be a people.) Is 7:8
the LORD, when it shall no **l** be said, Jer 16:14
the LORD, when they shall no **l** say, Jer 23:7
In those days they shall no **l** say: "'The Jer 31:29
And no **l** shall each one teach his Jer 31:34
so that they are no **l** a nation in their Jer 33:24
The LORD could no **l** bear your evil Jer 44:22
shall be destroyed and be no **l** a people, Jer 48:42
The nations shall no **l** flow to him; the Jer 51:44
"They shall stay with us no **l**." Lam 4:15
he will keep you in exile no **l**; Lam 4:22
It will no **l** be delayed, but in your Ezk 12:25
of my words will be delayed any **l**, Ezk 12:28
and you shall speak and be no **l** mute. Ezk 24:27
there shall no **l** be a prince from the Ezk 30:13
was opened, and I was no **l** mute. Ezk 33:22
No **l** shall the shepherds feed Ezk 34:10
my flock; they shall no **l** be a prey. Ezk 34:22
and no **l** suffer the reproach of the Ezk 34:29
and you shall no **l** bereave them of Ezk 36:12
you shall no **l** devour people and Ezk 36:14
people and no **l** bereave your nation Ezk 36:14
and you shall no **l** bear the disgrace of Ezk 36:15
the peoples and no **l** cause your nation Ezk 36:15
all, and they shall be no **l** two nations, Ezk 37:22
and no **l** divided into two kingdoms. Ezk 37:22
and no **l** will you call me 'My Baal.' Hos 2:16
Can I forget any **l** the treasures of Mi 6:10
of your messengers shall no **l** be heard. Na 2:13
and you shall no **l** be haughty in my Zep 3:11
so that you will no **l** suffer reproach. Zep 3:18
For I will no **l** have pity on the Zec 11:6
And there shall no **l** be a trader in the Zec 14:21
because he no **l** regards the offering Mal 2:13
It is no **l** good for anything except to be Mt 5:13
So they are no **l** two but one flesh. What Mt 19:6
that Jesus could no **l** openly enter a Mk 1:45
then you no **l** permit him to do Mk 7:12
they no **l** saw anyone with them but Mk 9:8
flesh.' So they are no **l** two but one flesh. Mk 10:8
I am no **l** worthy to be called your son. Lk 15:19
I am no **l** worthy to be called your son.' Lk 15:21
for you can no **l** be manager.' Lk 16:2
For they no **l** dared to ask him any Lk 20:40
"It is no **l** because of what you said that Jn 4:42
turned back and no **l** walked with him. Jn 6:66
then said, "I will be with you a little **l**, Jn 7:33
he stayed two days **l** in the place where he Jn 11:6
Jesus therefore no **l** walked openly Jn 11:54
light is among you for a little while **l**. Jn 12:35
I will no **l** talk much with you, for the Jn 14:30
No **l** do I call you servants, for the Jn 15:15
to the Father, and you will see me no **l**; Jn 16:10
"A little while, and you will see me no **l**; Jn 16:16
baby, she no **l** remembers the anguish, Jn 16:21
coming when I will no **l** speak to you in Jn 16:25
And I am no **l** in the world, but they are Jn 17:11
stayed many days **l** and then took Acts 18:18
they asked him to stay for a **l** period, Acts 18:20
into a deep sleep as Paul talked still **l**. Acts 20:9
that he ought not to live any **l**. Acts 25:24
so that we would no **l** be enslaved to sin. Rom 6:6
death no **l** has dominion over him. Rom 6:9
So now it is no **l** I who do it, but sin Rom 7:17
I do not want, it is no **l** I who do it, Rom 7:20
grace, it is no **l** on the basis of works; Rom 11:6
otherwise grace would no **l** be grace. Rom 11:6
pass judgment on one another any **l**, Rom 14:13
you eat, you are no **l** walking in love. Rom 14:15
since I no **l** have any room for work Rom 15:23
live might no **l** live for themselves 2 Cor 5:15
to the flesh, we regard him thus no **l**. 2 Cor 5:16
with Christ. It is no **l** I who live, Gal 2:20
by the law, it no **l** comes by promise; Gal 3:18
has come, we are no **l** under a guardian, Gal 3:25
So you are no **l** a slave, but a son, and if a Gal 4:7
then you are no **l** strangers and aliens, Eph 2:19
so that we may no **l** be children, tossed Eph 4:14
that you must no **l** walk as the Gentiles Eph 4:17
Let the thief no **l** steal, but rather let Eph 4:28
Therefore when we could bear it no **l**, 1 Thes 3:1
this reason, when I could bear it no **l**, 1 Thes 3:5
(No **l** drink only water, but use a 1 Tm 5:23
no **l** as a slave but more than a slave, Phlm 1:16
would no **l** have any consciousness of Heb 10:2
these, there is no **l** any offering for sin. Heb 10:18
there no **l** remains a sacrifice for sins, Heb 10:26
in the flesh no **l** for human passions but 1 Pt 4:2
a white robe and told to rest a little **l**, Rv 6:11
and there was no **l** any place for them Rv 12:8
he might not deceive the nations any **l**, Rv 20:3
No **l** will there be anything accursed, Rv 22:3

LONGING (10)
look on and fail with **l** for them all day Dt 28:32
O Lord, all my **l** is before you; my Ps 38:9
For he satisfies the **l** soul, and the Ps 107:9
soul is consumed with **l** for your rules Ps 119:20
And he was **l** to be fed with the pods Lk 15:16
waits with eager **l** for the revealing Rom 8:19
l to put on our heavenly dwelling, 2 Cor 5:2
by you, as he told us of your **l**, 2 Cor 7:7
what indignation, what fear, what **l**, 2 Cor 7:11
for he has been **l** for you all and has Phil 2:26

LONGINGLY (2)
And David said **l**, "Oh, that someone 2 Sm 23:15
And David said **l**, "Oh that someone 1 Chr 11:17

LONGS (5)
of my son Shechem **l** for your daughter. Gn 34:8
Like a slave who **l** for the shadow, and like Jb 7:2
place him in the safety for which he **l**." Ps 12:5
My soul **l**, yes, faints for the courts of the Ps 84:2
My soul **l** for your salvation; I hope in Ps 119:81

LOOK (207)
up your eyes and **l** from the place Gn 13:14
him outside and said, "**L** toward heaven, Gn 15:5
Do not **l** back or stop anywhere in the Gn 19:17
"Let me not **l** on the death of the child." Gn 21:16
when you come to **l** into my wages Gn 30:33
sons, "Why do you **l** at one another?" Gn 42:1
hid his face, for he was afraid to **l** at God. Ex 3:6
to them, "The LORD **l** on you and judge, Ex 5:21
L, you have some evil purpose in mind. Ex 10:10
l for able men from all the people, Ex 18:21
to the LORD to **l** and many of them Ex 19:21
And the priest shall **l**, and if the eruption Lv 13:8
and the priest shall **l**. And if there is a Lv 13:10
then the priest shall **l**, and if the leprous Lv 13:13
And the priest shall **l**, and if it appears Lv 13:20
the priest shall **l**, and if the spots on the Lv 13:39
go out of the camp, and the priest shall **l**. Lv 14:3
come again on the seventh day, and **l**. Lv 14:39
then the priest shall go and **l**. And if the Lv 14:44
shall not go in to **l** on the holy things Nm 4:20
nothing at all but this manna to **l** at." Nm 11:6
tassel for you to **l** at and remember all Nm 15:39
he would **l** at the bronze serpent and Nm 21:9
not go, as at other times, to **l** for omens, Nm 24:1
and eastward, and **l** at it with your eyes, Dt 3:27
and your eye **l** grudgingly on your poor Dt 15:9
L down from your holy habitation, Dt 26:15
while your eyes **l** on and fail with Dt 28:32
And he said to them, "**L** at me, and do Jgs 7:17
"**L**, people are coming down from the Jgs 9:36
"**L**, people are coming down from the Jgs 9:37
if you will indeed **l** on the affliction of 1 Sm 1:11
in distress you will **l** with envious eye 1 Sm 2:32
and arise, go and **l** for the donkeys." 1 Sm 9:3
"**L**, Hebrews are coming out of the 1 Sm 14:11
"Do not **l** on his appearance or on the 1 Sm 16:7
'**L**, the arrows are on this side of you, 1 Sm 20:21
'**L**, the arrows are beyond you,' 1 Sm 20:22
that the LORD will **l** on the wrong 2 Sm 16:12
L now to your own house, David." 1 Kgs 12:16
l toward the sea." And he went up 1 Kgs 18:43
I would neither **l** at you nor see you. 2 Kgs 3:14
servant, "**L**, there is the Shunammite. 2 Kgs 4:25
L, when the messenger comes, shut 2 Kgs 6:32
l there for Jehu the son of Jehoshaphat, 2 Kgs 9:2
let us **l** one another in the face." 2 Kgs 14:8
L now to your own house, David." 2 Chr 10:16
let us **l** one another in the face." 2 Chr 25:17
her beauty, for she was lovely to **l** at. Est 1:11
causing them to **l** at their husbands Est 1:17
a beautiful figure and was lovely to **l** at, Est 2:7
The caravans of Tema **l**, the travelers of Jb 6:19
"But now, be pleased to **l** at me, for I will Jb 6:28
How long will you not **l** away from me, Jb 7:19
with disgrace and **l** on my affliction. Jb 10:15
you will **l** around and take your rest in Jb 11:18
l away from him and leave him alone, Jb 14:6
He will not **l** upon the rivers, the Jb 20:17
L at me and be appalled, and lay your Jb 21:5
me; I stand, and you only **l** at me. Jb 30:20
pit, and my life shall **l** upon the light.' Jb 33:28
L at the heavens, and see; and behold the Jb 35:5
and **l** on everyone who is proud and Jb 40:11
L on everyone who is proud and bring Jb 40:12
When I **l** at your heavens, the work of Ps 8:3
believe that I shall **l** upon the goodness Ps 27:13
Those who **l** to him are radiant, and Ps 34:5
How long, O Lord, will you **l** on? Rescue Ps 35:17
though you **l** carefully at his place, he Ps 37:10
you will **l** on when the wicked are cut Ps 37:34
L away from me, that I may smile Ps 39:13
God will let me **l** in triumph on my Ps 59:10
Why do you **l** with hatred, O Ps 68:16
L down from heaven, and see; have Ps 80:14
O God; **l** on the face of your anointed! Ps 84:9
You will only **l** with your eyes and see Ps 91:8
has a haughty **l** and an arrogant Ps 101:5
I will **l** with favor on the faithful in the Ps 101:6
These all **l** to you, to give them their Ps 104:27
that I may **l** upon the prosperity of your Ps 106:5
I shall **l** in triumph on those who hate Ps 118:7
L on my affliction and deliver me, for Ps 119:153
I **l** at the faithless with disgust, Ps 119:158
as the eyes of servants **l** to the hand of Ps 123:2
so our eyes **l** to the LORD our God, Ps 123:2
L to the right and see: there is none who Ps 142:4
The eyes of all **l** to you, and you give Ps 145:15
Let your eyes **l** directly forward, and Prv 4:25
Do not **l** at wine when it is red, when it Prv 23:31
the righteous will **l** upon their Prv 29:16
and those who **l** through the windows Eccl 12:3
of Zion, and **l** upon King Solomon, Sg 3:11
to the nut orchard to **l** at the blossoms of Sg 6:11
return, return, that we may **l** upon you. Sg 6:13
Why should you **l** upon the Sg 6:13
For the **l** on their faces bears witness Is 3:9
And they will **l** to the earth, but behold, Is 8:22
of Assyria and the boastful **l** in his eyes. Is 10:12
They will **l** aghast at one another; their Is 13:8
In that day man will **l** to his Maker, and Is 17:7
and his eyes will **l** on the Holy One of Is 17:7
He will not **l** to the altars, the work of his Is 17:8
and he will not **l** on what his own fingers Is 17:8
mountains, **l**! When a trumpet is blown, Is 18:3
"I will quietly **l** from my dwelling like Is 18:4
Therefore I said: "**L** away from me; let me Is 22:4
But you did not **l** to him who did it, or Is 22:11
but do not **l** to the Holy One of Israel or Is 31:1
I shall **l** on man no more among the Is 38:11
But when I **l** there is no one; among Is 41:28
Hear, you deaf, and **l**, you blind, that you Is 42:18
l to the rock from which you were hewn, Is 51:1
L to Abraham your father and to Sarah Is 51:2
to the heavens, and **l** at the earth beneath; Is 51:6
form or majesty that we should **l** at him, Is 53:2
L down from heaven and see, from your Is 63:15
did awesome things that we did not **l** for, Is 64:3
Behold, please **l**, we are all your people. Is 64:9
But this is the one to whom I will **l**: he Is 66:2
shall go out and **l** on the dead bodies Is 66:24
L at your way in the valley; know what Jer 2:23
I will not **l** on you in anger, for I am Jer 3:12
the streets of Jerusalem, **l** and take note! Jer 5:1
O LORD, do not your eyes **l** for truth? You Jer 5:3
"Stand by the roads, and **l**, and ask for Jer 6:16
and while you **l** for light he turns it into Jer 13:16
sword of their enemies while you **l** on. Jer 20:4
"Take him, **l** after him well, and do Jer 39:12
come, and I will **l** after you well, Jer 40:4
they **l** not back—terror on every side! Jer 46:5
the fathers **l** not back to their children, Jer 47:3
"**L**, O LORD, and see, for I am despised." Lam 1:11
L and see if there is any sorrow like Lam 1:12
"**L**, O LORD, for I am in distress; my Lam 1:20
L, O LORD, and see! With whom have Lam 2:20
has befallen us; **l**, and see our disgrace! Lam 5:1
water, and **l** at one another in dismay, Ezk 4:17
to me, "Son of man, **l** with your eyes, Ezk 40:4
idols? It is I who answer and **l** after you. Hos 14:8
animals, I will not **l** upon them. Am 5:22
Yet I shall again **l** upon your holy Jon 2:4
But as for me, I will **l** to the LORD; I will Mi 7:7
to the light; I shall **l** upon his vindication. Mi 7:9
your God?" My eyes will **l** upon her; Mi 7:10
I will make nations **l** at your nakedness Na 3:5
And all who **l** at you will shrink from Na 3:7
and why do you idly **l** at wrong? Hab 1:3
"**L** among the nations, and see; wonder Hab 1:5
than to see evil and cannot **l** at wrong, Hab 1:13
why do you idly **l** at traitors and are Hab 1:13
and **l** out to see what he will say to me, Hab 2:1
for mercy, so that, when they **l** on me, Zec 12:10
fast, do not **l** gloomy like the hypocrites, Mt 6:16
L at the birds of the air: they neither sow Mt 6:26
is to come, or shall we **l** for another?" Mt 11:3
and drinking, and they say, '**L** at him! Mt 11:19
"**L**, your disciples are doing what is not Mt 12:2
the king came in to **l** at the guests, Mt 22:11
says to you, '**L**, here is the Christ!' Mt 24:23
say to you, '**L**, he is in the wilderness,' Mt 24:26
If they say, '**L**, he is in the inner rooms,' Mt 24:26
"**L**, why are they doing what is not Mk 2:24
said, "I see men, but they **l** like trees, Mk 8:24
l! The fig tree that you cursed has Mk 11:21
Bring me a denarius and let me **l** at it." Mk 12:15
of his disciples said to him, "**L**, Teacher, Mk 13:1
says to you, '**L**, here is the Christ!' Mk 13:21
to you, 'Look, here is the Christ!' or '**L**, Mk 13:21
is to come, or shall we **l** for another?" Lk 7:19
is to come, or shall we **l** for another?'" Lk 7:20
and drinking, and you say, '**L** at him! Lk 7:34

out, "Teacher, I beg you to **l** at my son, Lk 9:38
'**L**, for three years now I have come Lk 13:7
'**L**, these many years I have served you, Lk 15:29
nor will they say, '**L**, here it is!' or Lk 17:21
And they will say to you, '**L**, there!' or Lk 17:23
they will say to you, 'Look, there!' or '**L**, Lk 17:23
"**L** at the fig tree, and all the trees. Lk 21:29
And they said, "**L**, Lord, here are two Lk 22:38
L, nothing deserving death has been Lk 23:15
the Jordan, to whom you bore witness—**l**, Jn 3:26
L, I tell you, lift up your eyes, and see that Jn 4:35
L, the world has gone after him." Jn 12:19
"They will **l** on him whom they have Jn 19:37
And stooping to **l** in, he saw the linen Jn 20:5
she wept she stooped to **l** into the tomb. Jn 20:11
at him, as did John, and said, "**L** at us." Acts 3:4
l upon their threats and grant to your Acts 4:29
"**L**! The men whom you put in prison Acts 5:25
at the sight, and as he drew near to **l**, Acts 7:31
Moses trembled and did not dare to **l**. Acts 7:32
at the house of Judas **l** for a man of Acts 9:11
went to Tarsus to **l** for Saul, Acts 11:25
"**L**, you scoffers, be astounded and Acts 13:41
as we **l** not to the things that are seen 2 Cor 4:18
L at what is before your eyes. If 2 Cor 10:7
L: I, Paul, say to you that if you accept Gal 5:2
L carefully then how you walk, not as Eph 5:15
Let each of you **l** not only to his own Phil 2:4
L out for the dogs, look out for the Phil 3:2
out for the dogs, **l** out for the evildoers, Phil 3:2
l out for those who mutilate the flesh. Phil 3:2
have been no occasion to **l** for a second. Heb 8:7
L at the ships also: though they are so Jas 3:4
things into which angels long to **l**. 1 Pt 1:12
was able to open the scroll or to **l** into it, Rv 5:3
worthy to open the scroll or to **l** into it. Rv 5:4

LOOKED (133)
removed the covering of the ark and **l**, Gn 8:13
she **l** with contempt on her mistress. Gn 16:4
conceived, she **l** on me with contempt. Gn 16:5
He lifted up his eyes and **l**, and behold, Gn 18:2
there, and they **l** down toward Sodom. Gn 18:16
But Lot's wife, behind him, **l** back, and Gn 19:26
And he **l** down toward Sodom and Gn 19:28
all the land of the valley, and he **l** and, Gn 19:28
And Abraham lifted up his eyes and **l**, Gn 22:13
king of the Philistines **l** out of a window Gn 26:8
As he **l**, he saw a well in the field, and Gn 29:2
the LORD has **l** upon my affliction; Gn 29:32
And Jacob lifted up his eyes and **l**, and Gn 33:1
And the men **l** at one another in Gn 43:33
out to his people and **l** on their burdens, Ex 2:11
He **l** this way and that, and seeing no Ex 2:12
of fire out of the midst of a bush. He **l**, Ex 3:2
fire and of cloud **l** down on the Ex 14:24
of Israel, they **l** toward the wilderness, Ex 16:10
And they **l**, and each man took his Nm 17:9
Then he **l** on Amalek and took up his Nm 24:20
And he **l** on the Kenite, and took up Nm 24:21
And I **l**, and behold, you had sinned Dt 9:16
by Jericho, he lifted up his eyes and **l**, Jos 5:13
So when the men of Ai **l** back, behold, Jos 8:20
And he **l** and saw the people coming out Jgs 9:43
who **l** on while Samson entertained. Jgs 16:27
the Benjaminites **l** behind them, Jgs 20:40
because they **l** upon the ark of the 1 Sm 6:19
of Saul in Gibeah of Benjamin **l**, 1 Sm 14:16
they came, he **l** on Eliab and thought, 1 Sm 16:6
when the Philistine **l** and saw David, 1 Sm 17:42
king!" And when Saul **l** behind him, 1 Sm 24:8
And when he **l** behind him, he saw me, 2 Sm 1:7
Then Abner **l** behind him and said, 2 Sm 2:20
the daughter of Saul **l** out of the 2 Sm 6:16
the watch lifted up his eyes and **l**, 2 Sm 13:34
and when he lifted up his eyes and **l**, 2 Sm 18:24
They **l**, but there was none to save; 2 Sm 22:42
And when Araunah **l** down, he saw 2 Sm 24:20
But when I **l** at him closely in the 1 Kgs 3:21
sea." And he went up and **l** and said, 1 Kgs 18:43
And he **l**, and behold, there was at his 1 Kgs 19:6
by on the wall—and the people **l**, 2 Kgs 6:30
adorned her head and **l** out of the 2 Kgs 9:30
Two or three eunuchs **l** out at him. 2 Kgs 9:32
And when she **l**, there was the king 2 Kgs 11:14
the daughter of Saul **l** out of the 1 Chr 15:29
Ornan **l** and saw David and went 1 Chr 21:21
And when Judah **l**, behold, the 2 Chr 13:14
wilderness, they **l** toward the horde, 2 Chr 20:24
And when she **l**, there was the king 2 Chr 23:13
priest and all the priests **l** at him, 2 Chr 26:20
And I **l** and arose and said to the nobles Neh 4:14
if I have **l** at the sun when it shone, or Jb 31:26
All mankind has **l** on it; man beholds it Jb 36:25
and my eye has **l** in triumph on my Ps 54:7
So I have **l** upon you in the sanctuary, Ps 63:2
I **l** for pity, but there was none, and for Ps 69:20
that he **l** down from his holy height; Ps 102:19
from heaven the LORD **l** at the earth, Ps 102:19
Nevertheless, he **l** upon their distress, Ps 106:44
The sea **l** and fled; Jordan turned back. Ps 114:3
my house I have **l** out through my Prv 7:6
it; I **l** and received instruction. Prv 24:32
I am dark, because the sun has **l** upon me. Sg 1:6
and he **l** for it to yield grapes, but it yielded Is 5:2
When I **l** for it to yield grapes, why did it Is 5:4
his pleasant planting; and he **l** for justice, Is 5:7
In that day you **l** to the weapons of the Is 22:8
loved their bed, you have **l** on nakedness. Is 57:8
I **l**, but there was no one to help; I was Is 63:5
I **l** on the earth, and behold, it was Jer 4:23
I **l** on the mountains, and behold, they Jer 4:24
I **l**, and behold, there was no man, and Jer 4:25
I **l**, and behold, the fruitful land was a Jer 4:26
We **l** for peace, but no good came; for a Jer 8:15
We **l** for peace, but no good came; for a Jer 14:19
At this I awoke and **l**, and my sleep was Jer 31:26
As I **l**, behold, a stormy wind came out of Ezk 1:4
Now as I **l** at the living creatures, I saw Ezk 1:15
And when I **l**, behold, a hand was Ezk 2:9
Then I **l**, and behold, a form that had the Ezk 8:2
to the entrance of the court, and when I **l**, Ezk 8:7
Then I **l**, and behold, on the expanse Ezk 10:1
And I **l**, and behold, there were four Ezk 10:9
And I **l**, and behold, there were sinews Ezk 37:8
gate to the front of the temple, and I **l**, Ezk 44:4
As you **l**, a stone was cut out by no Dn 2:34
Then as I **l** its wings were plucked off, Dn 7:4
After this I **l**, and behold, another, like a Dn 7:6
As I **l**, thrones were placed, and the Dn 7:9
I **l** then because of the sound of the great Dn 7:11
And as I **l**, the beast was killed, and its Dn 7:11
As I **l**, this horn made war with the Dn 7:21
I lifted up my eyes and **l**, and behold, a Dn 10:5
Then I, Daniel, **l**, and behold, two others Dn 12:5
the earth; he **l** and shook the nations; Hab 3:6
You **l** for much, and behold, it came to Hg 1:9
he **l** up to heaven and said a blessing. Mt 14:19
But Jesus **l** at them and said, "With Mt 19:26
And he **l** around at them with anger, Mk 3:5
And he **l** around to see who had done it. Mk 5:32
and the two fish he **l** up to heaven and Mk 6:41
And he **l** up and said, "I see men, but Mk 8:24
And Jesus **l** around and said to his Mk 10:23
Jesus **l** at them and said, "With man it Mk 10:27
when he had **l** around at everything, Mk 11:11
himself, she **l** at him and said, Mk 14:67
done for me in the days when he **l** on me, Lk 1:25
for he has **l** on the humble estate of his Lk 1:48
he **l** up to heaven and said a blessing Lk 9:16
to the place, he **l** up and said to him, Lk 19:5
But he **l** directly at them and said, Lk 20:17
Jesus **l** up and saw the rich putting their Lk 21:1
And the Lord turned and **l** at Peter. And Lk 22:61
and he **l** at Jesus as he walked by and Jn 1:36
Jesus **l** at him and said, "So you are Jn 1:42
The disciples **l** at one another, Jn 13:22
with the Holy Spirit, **l** intently at him Acts 13:9
which we **l** upon and have touched with 1 Jn 1:1
After this I **l**, and behold, a door standing Rv 4:1
Then I **l**, and I heard around the throne Rv 5:11
And I **l**, and behold, a white horse! And its Rv 6:2
third living creature say, "Come!" And I **l**, Rv 6:5
And I **l**, and behold, a pale horse! And its Rv 6:8
When he opened the sixth seal, I **l**, and Rv 6:12
After this I **l**, and behold, a great Rv 7:9
Then I **l**, and I heard an eagle crying Rv 8:13
their heads were what **l** like crowns of Rv 9:7
Then I **l**, and behold, on Mount Zion Rv 14:1
Then I **l**, and behold, a white cloud, and Rv 14:14
After this I **l**, and the sanctuary of the Rv 15:5

LOOKING (34)
And **l** up they saw a caravan of Gn 37:25
my eyes from **l** at worthless things; Ps 119:37
the windows, **l** through the lattice. Sg 2:9
and shuts his eyes from **l** on evil, Is 33:15
a dove. My eyes are weary with **l** upward. Is 38:14
women there, **l** on from a distance, Mt 27:55
and said to him, "Everyone is **l** for you." Mk 1:37
And **l** about at those who sat around Mk 3:34
And **l** up to heaven, he sighed and said Mk 7:34
And suddenly, **l** around, they no longer Mk 9:8
And Jesus, **l** at him, loved him, and Mk 10:21
There were also women **l** on from a Mk 15:40
was also himself **l** for the kingdom Mk 15:43
And **l** up, they saw that the stone had Mk 16:4
said to them, "Why were you **l** for me? Lk 2:49
And after **l** around at them all he said to Lk 6:10
Jesus, **l** at him with sadness, said, "How Lk 18:24
he sat in the light and **l** closely at him, Lk 22:56
and he was **l** for the kingdom of God. Lk 23:51
stooping and **l** in, he saw the linen Lk 24:12
you walk?" And they stood still, **l** sad. Lk 24:17
The Jews were **l** for him at the feast, and Jn 7:11
They were **l** for Jesus and saying to one Jn 11:56
had said these things, as they were **l** on, Acts 1:9
why do you stand **l** into heaven? Acts 1:11
him, "Behold, three men are **l** for you. Acts 10:19
and said, "I am the one you are **l** for. Acts 10:21
L at it closely, I observed animals and Acts 11:6
l intently at him and seeing that he Acts 14:9
And **l** intently at the council, Paul Acts 23:1
For he was **l** forward to the city that Heb 11:10
of Egypt, for he was **l** to the reward. Heb 11:26
l to Jesus, the founder and perfecter of Heb 12:2
you without fear, **l** after themselves; Jude 1:12

LOOKS (34)
here I have seen him who **l** after me." Gn 16:13
"But if the priest comes and **l**, and if the Lv 14:48
top of Pisgah that **l** down on the Nm 21:20
toward the border that **l** down on the 1 Sm 13:18
man **l** on the outward appearance, 1 Sm 16:7
but the LORD **l** on the heart." 1 Sm 16:7
and like a hired hand who **l** for his wages, Jb 7:2
stone heap; he **l** upon a house of stones. Jb 8:17
For he **l** to the ends of the earth and sees Jb 28:24
"And now no one **l** on the light when it Jb 37:21
The LORD **l** down from heaven on the Ps 14:2
The LORD **l** down from heaven; he sees Ps 33:13
he sits enthroned he **l** out on all the Ps 33:14
God **l** down from heaven on the children Ps 53:2
and righteousness **l** down from the sky. Ps 85:11
who **l** on the earth and it trembles, Ps 104:32
until he **l** in triumph on his Ps 112:8
who **l** far down on the heavens and the Ps 113:6
and a backbiting tongue, angry **l**. Prv 25:23
She **l** well to the ways of her household Prv 31:27
"Who is this who **l** down like the dawn, Sg 6:10
of Lebanon, which **l** toward Damascus. Sg 7:4
The haughty **l** of man shall be brought Is 2:11
of the sea. And if one **l** to the land, Is 5:30
the LORD from heaven **l** down and sees; Lam 3:50
of their words, nor be dismayed at their **l**, Ezk 2:6
them not, nor be dismayed at their **l**, Ezk 3:9
consults the teraphim; he **l** at the liver. Ezk 21:21
you that everyone who **l** at a woman Mt 5:28
hand to the plow and **l** back is fit for the Lk 9:62
that everyone who **l** on the Son and Jn 6:40
like a man who **l** intently at his natural Jas 1:23
For he **l** at himself and goes away and at Jas 1:24
But the one who **l** into the perfect law, Jas 1:25

LOOM (2)
his sleep and pulled away the pin, the **l**, Jgs 16:14
up my life; he cuts me off from the **l**; Is 38:12

LOOMS (1)
for disaster **l** out of the north, Jer 6:1

LOOPS (14)
And you shall make **l** of blue on the edge Ex 26:4
Likewise you shall make **l** on the edge of Ex 26:4
Fifty **l** you shall make on the one Ex 26:5
and fifty **l** you shall make on the edge of Ex 26:5
set; the **l** shall be opposite one another. Ex 26:5
You shall make fifty **l** on the edge of the Ex 26:10
and fifty **l** on the edge of the curtain Ex 26:10
of bronze, and put the clasps into the **l**, Ex 26:11
He made **l** of blue on the edge of the Ex 36:11
He made fifty **l** on the one curtain, and Ex 36:12
and he made fifty **l** on the edge of the Ex 36:12
set. The **l** were opposite one another. Ex 36:12
And he made fifty **l** on the edge of the Ex 36:17
and fifty **l** on the edge of the other Ex 36:17

LOOSE (25)
is a doe let **l** that bears beautiful fawns. Gn 49:21
or lets his beast **l** and it feeds in another Ex 22:5
shall not come **l** from the ephod. Ex 28:28
the people had broken **l** (for Aaron had Ex 32:25
loose (for Aaron had let them break **l**, Ex 32:25
should not come **l** from the ephod, Ex 39:21
"Do not let the hair of your heads hang **l**, Lv 10:6
and let the hair of his head hang **l**, Lv 13:45
of his head hang **l** nor tear his clothes. Lv 21:10
And I will let **l** the wild beasts against Lv 26:22
that he would let **l** his hand and cut me Jb 6:9
of the Pleiades or **l** the cords of Orion? Jb 38:31
He let **l** on them his burning anger, Ps 78:49
like one set **l** among the dead, like the Ps 88:5
slumbers or sleeps, not a waistband is **l**, Is 5:27
where cattle are let **l** and where sheep Is 7:25
and **l** the sackcloth from your waist and Is 20:2
Your cords hang **l**; they cannot hold the Is 33:23
before him and to **l** the belts of kings, Is 45:1
l the bonds from your neck, O captive Is 52:2
of the adulterer and the **l** woman. Is 57:3
to **l** the bonds of wickedness, to undo the Is 58:6

disaster shall be let **l** upon all the Jer 1:14
and whatever you **l** on earth shall be Mt 16:19
and whatever you **l** on earth shall be Mt 18:18

LOOSED (8)
Because God has **l** my cord and Jb 30:11
Who has **l** the bonds of the swift donkey, Jb 39:5
you have **l** my sackcloth and clothed Ps 30:11
maidservant. You have **l** my bonds. Ps 116:16
loose on earth shall be **l** in heaven." Mt 16:19
you loose on earth shall be **l** in heaven. Mt 18:18
his mouth was opened and his tongue **l**, Lk 1:64
be **l** from this bond on the Sabbath Lk 13:16

LOOSEN (1)
You shall **l** your hand from your Jer 17:4

LOOSENING (1)
at the same time **l** the ropes that tied Acts 27:40

LOOSENS (1)
contempt on princes and **l** the belt of Jb 12:21

LOOSES (1)
He **l** the bonds of kings and binds a Jb 12:18

LOOSING (1)
raised him up, **l** the pangs of death, Acts 2:24

LOOT (3)
This is the portion of those who **l** us, and Is 17:14
your riches and **l** your merchandise. Ezk 26:12
do not **l** his wealth in the day of his Ob 1:13

LOOTED (1)
But this is a people plundered and **l**; they Is 42:22

LOOTER (1)
Who gave up Jacob to the **l**, and Israel to Is 42:24

LOP (2)
GOD of hosts will **l** the boughs with Is 10:33
down the tree and **l** off its branches, Dn 4:14

LOPS (1)
the spreading branches he **l** off and clears Is 18:5

LORD (7776)
in the day that the **L** God made the earth Gn 2:4
sprung up—for the **L** God had not caused Gn 2:5
then the **L** God formed the man of dust Gn 2:7
And the **L** God planted a garden in Eden, Gn 2:8
of the ground the **L** God made to spring Gn 2:9
The **L** God took the man and put him in Gn 2:15
And the **L** God commanded the man, Gn 2:16
Then the **L** God said, "It is not good that Gn 2:18
of the ground the **L** God formed every Gn 2:19
So the **L** God caused a deep sleep to fall Gn 2:21
the rib that the **L** God had taken from Gn 2:22
of the field that the **L** God had made. Gn 3:1
the sound of the **L** God walking in the Gn 3:8
the presence of the **L** God among the trees Gn 3:8
But the **L** God called to the man and said Gn 3:9
Then the **L** God said to the woman, Gn 3:13
The **L** God said to the serpent, "Because Gn 3:14
And the **L** God made for Adam and for Gn 3:21
Then the **L** God said, "Behold, the man Gn 3:22
therefore the **L** God sent him out from Gn 3:23
have gotten a man with the help of the **L**." Gn 4:1
Cain brought to the **L** an offering of the Gn 4:3
And the **L** had regard for Abel and his Gn 4:4
The **L** said to Cain, "Why are you angry, Gn 4:6
Then the **L** said to Cain, "Where is Abel Gn 4:9
And the **L** said, "What have you done? Gn 4:10
Cain said to the **L**, "My punishment is Gn 4:13
Then the **L** said to him, "Not so! If Gn 4:15
him sevenfold." And the **L** put a mark Gn 4:15
the presence of the **L** and settled in the Gn 4:16
began to call upon the name of the **L**. Gn 4:26
the ground that the **L** has cursed this Gn 5:29
Then the **L** said, "My Spirit shall not Gn 6:3
The **L** saw that the wickedness of man Gn 6:5
And the **L** was sorry that he had made Gn 6:6
So the **L** said, "I will blot out man whom I Gn 6:7
But Noah found favor in the eyes of the **L**. Gn 6:8
Then the **L** said to Noah, "Go into the Gn 7:1
did all that the **L** had commanded him. Gn 7:5
him. And the **L** shut him in. Gn 7:16
built an altar to the **L** and took some of Gn 8:20
And when the **L** smelled the pleasing Gn 8:21
pleasing aroma, the **L** said in his heart, Gn 8:21
He also said, "Blessed be the **L**, the God Gn 9:26
He was a mighty hunter before the **L**. Gn 10:9
Nimrod a mighty hunter before the **L**." Gn 10:9
And the **L** came down to see the city and Gn 11:5
And the **L** said, "Behold, they are one Gn 11:6
So the **L** dispersed them from there over Gn 11:8
because there the **L** confused the Gn 11:9
from there the **L** dispersed them over Gn 11:9
Now the **L** said to Abram, "Go from Gn 12:1
So Abram went, as the **L** had told him, Gn 12:4
Then the **L** appeared to Abram and said, Gn 12:7
land." So he built there an altar to the **L**, Gn 12:7
an altar to the **L** and called upon the Gn 12:8
LORD and called upon the name of the **L**. Gn 12:8
But the **L** afflicted Pharaoh and his Gn 12:17
Abram called upon the name of the **L**. Gn 13:4
everywhere like the garden of the **L**, Gn 13:10
was before the **L** destroyed Sodom and Gn 13:10
wicked, great sinners against the **L**. Gn 13:13
The **L** said to Abram, after Lot had Gn 13:14
and there he built an altar to the **L**. Gn 13:18
Sodom, "I have lifted my hand to the **L**, Gn 14:22
the word of the **L** came to Abram in Gn 15:1
But Abram said, "O **L** GOD, what will Gn 15:2
behold, the word of the **L** came to him: Gn 15:4
And he believed the **L**, and he counted it Gn 15:6
"I am the **L** who brought you out from Gn 15:7
But he said, "O **L** GOD, how am I to know Gn 15:8
Then the **L** said to Abram, "Know for Gn 15:13
On that day the **L** made a covenant Gn 15:18
the **L** has prevented me from bearing Gn 16:2
May the **L** judge between you and me!" Gn 16:5
The angel of the **L** found her by a spring Gn 16:7
The angel of the **L** said to her, "Return to Gn 16:9
The angel of the **L** also said to her, "I Gn 16:10
And the angel of the **L** said to her, Gn 16:11
because the **L** has listened to your Gn 16:11
the name of the **L** who spoke to her, Gn 16:13
years old the **L** appeared to Abram Gn 17:1
And the **L** appeared to him by the oaks Gn 18:1
and said, "O **L**, if I have found favor in Gn 18:3
The **L** said, "I will surely return to you Gn 18:10
"After I am worn out, and my **l** is old, Gn 18:12
The **L** said to Abraham, "Why did Gn 18:13
Is anything too hard for the **L**? At the Gn 18:14
The **L** said, "Shall I hide from Gn 18:17
way of the **L** by doing righteousness Gn 18:19
so that the **L** may bring to Abraham Gn 18:19
Then the **L** said, "Because the outcry Gn 18:20
but Abraham still stood before the **L**. Gn 18:22
And the **L** said, "If I find at Sodom fifty Gn 18:26
I have undertaken to speak to the **L**, Gn 18:27
he said, "Oh let not the **L** be angry, Gn 18:30
I have undertaken to speak to the **L**. Gn 18:31
he said, "Oh let not the **L** be angry, Gn 18:32
And the **L** went his way, when he had Gn 18:33
people has become great before the **L**, Gn 19:13
and the **L** has sent us to destroy it." Gn 19:13
for the **L** is about to destroy the city." Gn 19:14
the hand, the **L** being merciful to him, Gn 19:16
Then the **L** rained on Sodom and Gn 19:24
and fire from the **L** out of heaven. Gn 19:24
place where he had stood before the **L**. Gn 19:27
"**L**, will you kill an innocent people? Gn 20:4
For the **L** had closed all the wombs of Gn 20:18
The **L** visited Sarah as he had said, and Gn 21:1
and the **L** did to Sarah as he had Gn 21:1
and called there on the name of the **L**, Gn 21:33
the angel of the **L** called to him from Gn 22:11
of that place, "The **L** will provide"; Gn 22:14
the mount of the **L** it shall be Gn 22:14
the angel of the **L** called to Abraham a Gn 22:15
myself I have sworn, declares the **L**, Gn 22:16
"Hear us, my **l**; you are a prince of God Gn 23:6
"No, my **l**, hear me: I give you the field, Gn 23:11
"My **l**, listen to me: a piece of land Gn 23:15
And the **L** had blessed Abraham in all Gn 24:1
that I may make you swear by the **L**, the Gn 24:3
The **L**, the God of heaven, who took me Gn 24:7
And he said, "O **L**, God of my master Gn 24:12
my **l**." And she quickly let down her Gn 24:18
learn whether the **L** had prospered his Gn 24:21
bowed his head and worshiped the **L** Gn 24:26
and said, "Blessed be the **L**, the God of Gn 24:27
the **L** has led me in the way to the Gn 24:27
He said, "Come in, O blessed of the **L**. Gn 24:31
The **L** has greatly blessed my master, Gn 24:35
But he said to me, 'The **L**, before whom Gn 24:40
came today to the spring and said, 'O **L**, Gn 24:42
woman whom the **L** has appointed for Gn 24:44
and worshiped the **L** and blessed the Gn 24:48
worshiped the LORD and blessed the **L**, Gn 24:48
said, "The thing has come from the **L**; Gn 24:50
master's son, as the **L** has spoken." Gn 24:51
himself to the earth before the **L**. Gn 24:52
me, since the **L** has prospered my way. Gn 24:56
And Isaac prayed to the **L** for his wife, Gn 25:21
And the **L** granted his prayer, and Gn 25:21
to me?" So she went to inquire of the **L**. Gn 25:22
And the **L** said to her, "Two nations are Gn 25:23
And the **L** appeared to him and said, "Do Gn 26:2
year a hundredfold. The **L** blessed him, Gn 26:12
"For now the **L** has made room for us, Gn 26:22
And the **L** appeared to him the same Gn 26:24
the name of the **L** and pitched his tent Gn 26:25
see plainly that the **L** has been with Gn 26:28
You are now the blessed of the **L**." Gn 26:29
it and bless you before the **L** before I die.' Gn 27:7
"Because the **L** your God granted me Gn 27:20
smell of a field that the **L** has blessed! Gn 27:27
Be **l** over your brothers, and may your Gn 27:29
"Behold, I have made him **l** over you, Gn 27:37
behold, the **L** stood above it and said, Gn 28:13
stood above it and said, "I am the **L**, Gn 28:13
and said, "Surely the **L** is in this place, Gn 28:16
in peace, then the **L** shall be my God, Gn 28:21
When the **L** saw that Leah was hated, Gn 29:31
"Because the **L** has looked upon my Gn 29:32
"Because the **L** has heard that I am Gn 29:33
will praise the **L**." Therefore she called Gn 29:35
"May the **L** add to me another son!" Gn 30:24
divination that the **L** has blessed me Gn 30:27
and the **L** has blessed you wherever I Gn 30:30
Then the **L** said to Jacob, "Return to the Gn 31:3
"Let not my **l** be angry that I cannot Gn 31:35
"The **L** watch between you and me, Gn 31:49
them, "Thus you shall say to my **l** Esau: Gn 32:4
I have sent to tell my **l**, in order that I Gn 32:5
of my father Isaac, O **L** who said to me, Gn 32:9
They are a present sent to my **l** Esau. Gn 32:18
"To find favor in the sight of my **l**." Gn 33:8
"My **l** knows that the children are frail, Gn 33:13
Let my **l** pass on ahead of his servant, Gn 33:14
children, until I come to my **l** in Seir." Gn 33:14
Let me find favor in the sight of my **l**." Gn 33:15
was wicked in the sight of the **L**, Gn 38:7
of the LORD, and the **L** put him to death. Gn 38:7
he did was wicked in the sight of the **L**, Gn 38:10
The **L** was with Joseph, and he became a Gn 39:2
master saw that the **L** was with him and Gn 39:3
him and that the **L** caused all that he Gn 39:3
that he had the **L** blessed the Egyptian's Gn 39:5
the blessing of the **L** was on all that he Gn 39:5
But the **L** was with Joseph and showed Gn 39:21
charge, because the **L** was with him. Gn 39:23
whatever he did, the **L** made it succeed. Gn 39:23
an offense against their **l** the king of Gn 40:1
They said to him, "No, my **l**, your Gn 42:10
"The man, the **l** of the land, spoke Gn 42:30
Then the man, the **l** of the land, said to Gn 42:33
and said, "Oh, my **l**, we came down the Gn 43:20
Is it not from this that my **l** drinks, and Gn 44:5
"Why does my **l** speak such words as Gn 44:7
said, "What shall we say to my **l**? Gn 44:16
went up to him and said, "O my **l**, Gn 44:18
My **l** asked his servants, saying, 'Have Gn 44:19
And we said to my **l**, 'We have a father, Gn 44:20
We said to my **l**, 'The boy cannot leave Gn 44:22
father, we told him the words of my **l**. Gn 44:24
instead of the boy as a servant to my **l**, Gn 44:33
and **l** of all his house and ruler over all Gn 45:8
Joseph, God has made me **l** of all Egypt. Gn 45:9
not hide from my **l** that our money is Gn 47:18
in the sight of my **l** but our bodies and Gn 47:18
may it please my **l**, we will be servants Gn 47:25
I wait for your salvation, O **L**. Gn 49:18
And the angel of the **L** appeared to him in Ex 3:2
When the **L** saw that he turned aside to Ex 3:4
Then the **L** said, "I have surely seen the Ex 3:7
"Say this to the people of Israel, 'The **L**, Ex 3:15
Israel together and say to them, 'The **L**, Ex 3:16
the king of Egypt and say to him, 'The **L**, Ex 3:18
that we may sacrifice to the **L** our God.' Ex 3:18
will say, 'The **L** did not appear to you.'" Ex 4:1
The **L** said to him, "What is that in your Ex 4:2
But the **L** said to Moses, "Put out your Ex 4:4
"that they may believe that the **L**, the God Ex 4:5
Again, the **L** said to him, "Put your hand Ex 4:6
But Moses said to the **L**, "Oh, my Lord, I Ex 4:10
But Moses said to the LORD, "Oh, my **L**, I Ex 4:10
Then the **L** said to him, "Who has made Ex 4:11
deaf, or seeing, or blind? Is it not I, the **L**? Ex 4:11
But he said, "Oh, my **L**, please send Ex 4:13
the anger of the **L** was kindled against Ex 4:14
And the **L** said to Moses in Midian, "Go Ex 4:19
And the **L** said to Moses, "When you go Ex 4:21
shall say to Pharaoh, 'Thus says the **L**, Ex 4:22
on the way the **L** met him and sought Ex 4:24
The **L** said to Aaron, "Go into the Ex 4:27
all the words of the **L** with which he had Ex 4:28
the words that the **L** had spoken to Ex 4:30
they heard that the **L** had visited the Ex 4:31
and said to Pharaoh, "Thus says the **L**, Ex 5:1
But Pharaoh said, "Who is the **L**, that I Ex 5:2
I do not know the **L**, and moreover, I will Ex 5:2
that we may sacrifice to the **L** our God, Ex 5:3
you say, 'Let us go and sacrifice to the **L**.' Ex 5:17
to them, "The **L** look on you and judge, Ex 5:21
Then Moses turned to the **L** and said, "O Ex 5:22
Moses turned to the LORD and said, "O **L**, Ex 5:22
But the **L** said to Moses, "Now you shall Ex 6:1

to Moses and said to him, "I am the **L**. Ex 6:2
but by my name the **L** I did not make Ex 6:3
to the people of Israel, 'I am the **L**, Ex 6:6
you shall know that I am the **L** your God, Ex 6:7
give it to you for a possession. I am the **L**.'" Ex 6:8
So the **L** said to Moses, Ex 6:10
But Moses said to the **L**, "Behold, the Ex 6:12
But the **L** spoke to Moses and Aaron and Ex 6:13
Aaron and Moses to whom the **L** said: Ex 6:26
On the day when the **L** spoke to Moses in Ex 6:28
the **L** said to Moses, "I am the LORD; tell Ex 6:29
the LORD said to Moses, "I am the **L**; tell Ex 6:29
But Moses said to the **L**, "Behold, I am of Ex 6:30
And the **L** said to Moses, "See, I have made Ex 7:1
Egyptians shall know that I am the **L**, Ex 7:5
they did just as the **L** commanded them. Ex 7:6
Then the **L** said to Moses and Aaron, Ex 7:8
and did just as the **L** commanded. Ex 7:10
not listen to them, as the **L** had said. Ex 7:13
Then the **L** said to Moses, "Pharaoh's Ex 7:14
And you shall say to him, 'The **L**, the Ex 7:16
Thus says the **L**, "By this you shall Ex 7:17
"By this you shall know that I am the **L**: Ex 7:17
And the **L** said to Moses, "Say to Aaron, Ex 7:19
and Aaron did as the **L** commanded. Ex 7:20
not listen to them, as the **L** had said. Ex 7:22
days passed after the **L** had struck the Ex 7:25
Then the **L** said to Moses, "Go in to Ex 8:1
and say to him, 'Thus says the **L**, Ex 8:1
And the **L** said to Moses, "Say to Aaron, Ex 8:5
"Plead with the **L** to take away the frogs Ex 8:8
will let the people go to sacrifice to the **L**." Ex 8:8
that there is no one like the **L** our God. Ex 8:10
and Moses cried to the **L** about the frogs, Ex 8:12
And the **L** did according to the word of Ex 8:13
not listen to them, as the **L** had said. Ex 8:15
Then the **L** said to Moses, "Say to Aaron, Ex 8:16
not listen to them, as the **L** had said. Ex 8:19
Then the **L** said to Moses, "Rise up early Ex 8:20
water, and say to him, 'Thus says the **L**, Ex 8:20
know that I am the **L** in the midst of the Ex 8:22
And the **L** did so. There came great Ex 8:24
we shall sacrifice to the **L** our God are an Ex 8:26
and sacrifice to the **L** our God as he Ex 8:27
go to sacrifice to the **L** your God in the Ex 8:28
I will plead with the **L** that the swarms of Ex 8:29
letting the people go to sacrifice to the **L**." Ex 8:29
out from Pharaoh and prayed to the **L**. Ex 8:30
And the **L** did as Moses asked, and Ex 8:31
Then the **L** said to Moses, "Go in to Ex 9:1
and say to him, 'Thus says the **L**, Ex 9:1
the hand of the **L** will fall with a very Ex 9:3
But the **L** will make a distinction between Ex 9:4
And the **L** set a time, saying, "Tomorrow Ex 9:5
"Tomorrow the **L** will do this thing in the Ex 9:5
And the next day the **L** did this thing. All Ex 9:6
And the **L** said to Moses and Aaron, Ex 9:8
But the **L** hardened the heart of Pharaoh, Ex 9:12
to them, as the **L** had spoken to Moses. Ex 9:12
Then the **L** said to Moses, "Rise up early Ex 9:13
and say to him, 'Thus says the **L**, Ex 9:13
the word of the **L** among the servants of Ex 9:20
to the word of the **L** left his slaves and his Ex 9:21
Then the **L** said to Moses, "Stretch out Ex 9:22
heaven, and the **L** sent thunder and hail, Ex 9:23
And the **L** rained hail upon the land of Ex 9:23
the **L** is in the right, and I and my people Ex 9:27
Plead with the **L**, for there has been Ex 9:28
city, I will stretch out my hands to the **L**. Ex 9:29
know that you do not yet fear the **L** God." Ex 9:30
and stretched out his hands to the **L**, Ex 9:33
just as the **L** had spoken through Moses. Ex 9:35
Then the **L** said to Moses, "Go in to Ex 10:1
that you may know that I am the **L**." Ex 10:2
and said to him, "Thus says the **L**, Ex 10:3
go, that they may serve the **L** their God. Ex 10:7
said to them, "Go, serve the **L** your God. Ex 10:8
herds, for we must hold a feast to the **L**." Ex 10:9
he said to them, "The **L** be with you, Ex 10:10
the men among you, and serve the **L**, Ex 10:11
Then the **L** said to Moses, "Stretch out Ex 10:12
and the **L** brought an east wind upon Ex 10:13
"I have sinned against the **L** your God, Ex 10:16
and plead with the **L** your God only to Ex 10:17
from Pharaoh and pleaded with the **L**. Ex 10:18
And the **L** turned the wind into a very Ex 10:19
But the **L** hardened Pharaoh's heart, Ex 10:20
Then the **L** said to Moses, "Stretch out Ex 10:21
called Moses and said, "Go, serve the **L**; Ex 10:24
that we may sacrifice to the **L** our God. Ex 10:25
take of them to serve the **L** our God, Ex 10:26
we must serve the **L** until we arrive Ex 10:26
But the **L** hardened Pharaoh's heart, Ex 10:27
The **L** said to Moses, "Yet one plague Ex 11:1
And the **L** gave the people favor in the Ex 11:3

So Moses said, "Thus says the **L**: About Ex 11:4
know that the **L** makes a distinction Ex 11:7
Then the **L** said to Moses, "Pharaoh will Ex 11:9
and the **L** hardened Pharaoh's heart, Ex 11:10
The **L** said to Moses and Aaron in the Ex 12:1
I will execute judgments: I am the **L**. Ex 12:12
and you shall keep it as a feast to the **L**; Ex 12:14
For the **L** will pass through to strike the Ex 12:23
the **L** will pass over the door and will Ex 12:23
to the land that the **L** will give you, Ex 12:25
as the **L** had commanded Moses and Ex 12:28
At midnight the **L** struck down all the Ex 12:29
and go, serve the **L**, as you have said. Ex 12:31
And the **L** had given the people favor in Ex 12:36
all the hosts of the **L** went out from the Ex 12:41
It was a night of watching by the **L**, to Ex 12:42
watching kept to the **L** by all the people Ex 12:42
And the **L** said to Moses and Aaron, Ex 12:43
and would keep the Passover to the **L**, Ex 12:48
just as the **L** commanded Moses and Ex 12:50
that very day the **L** brought the people Ex 12:51
The **L** said to Moses, Ex 13:1
a strong hand the **L** brought you out Ex 13:3
And when the **L** brings you into the land Ex 13:5
day there shall be a feast to the **L**. Ex 13:6
is because of what the **L** did for me when Ex 13:8
that the law of the **L** may be in your Ex 13:9
a strong hand the **L** has brought you out Ex 13:9
"When the **L** brings you into the land Ex 13:11
set apart to the **L** all that first opens Ex 13:12
a strong hand the **L** brought us out of Ex 13:14
the **L** killed all the firstborn in the land Ex 13:15
I sacrifice to the **L** all the males that Ex 13:15
a strong hand the **L** brought us out of Ex 13:16
And the **L** went before them by day in a Ex 13:21
Then the **L** said to Moses, Ex 14:1
know that I am the **L**." And they did so. Ex 14:4
And the **L** hardened the heart of Ex 14:8
the people of Israel cried out to the **L**. Ex 14:10
firm, and see the salvation of the **L**, Ex 14:13
The **L** will fight for you, and you have Ex 14:14
The **L** said to Moses, "Why do you cry Ex 14:15
Egyptians shall know that I am the **L**, Ex 14:18
and the **L** drove the sea back by a Ex 14:21
the morning watch the **L** in the pillar Ex 14:24
for the **L** fights for them against the Ex 14:25
Then the **L** said to Moses, "Stretch out Ex 14:26
the **L** threw the Egyptians into the Ex 14:27
Thus the **L** saved Israel that day from Ex 14:30
great power that the **L** used against the Ex 14:31
Egyptians, so the people feared the **L**, Ex 14:31
they believed in the **L** and in his Ex 14:31
people of Israel sang this song to the **L**, Ex 15:1
to the LORD, saying, "I will sing to the **L**, Ex 15:1
The **L** is my strength and my song, and Ex 15:2
The **L** is a man of war; the LORD is his Ex 15:3
LORD is a man of war; the **L** is his name. Ex 15:3
Your right hand, O **L**, glorious in power, Ex 15:6
glorious in power, your right hand, O **L**, Ex 15:6
"Who is like you, O **L**, among the gods? Ex 15:11
are still as a stone, till your people, O **L**, Ex 15:16
on your own mountain, the place, O **L**, Ex 15:17
for your abode, the sanctuary, O **L**, Ex 15:17
The **L** will reign forever and ever." Ex 15:18
the **L** brought back the waters of the Ex 15:19
"Sing to the **L**, for he has triumphed Ex 15:21
And he cried to the **L**, and the LORD Ex 15:25
the LORD, and the **L** showed him a log, Ex 15:25
There the **L** made for them a statute Ex 15:25
listen to the voice of the **L** your God, Ex 15:26
I put on the Egyptians, for I am the **L**, Ex 15:26
by the hand of the **L** in the land of Egypt, Ex 16:3
Then the **L** said to Moses, "Behold, I am Ex 16:4
that it was the **L** who brought you out Ex 16:6
morning you shall see the glory of the **L**, Ex 16:7
heard your grumbling against the **L**. Ex 16:7
"When the **L** gives you in the evening Ex 16:8
because the **L** has heard your Ex 16:8
is not against us but against the **L**." Ex 16:8
people of Israel, 'Come near before the **L**, Ex 16:9
the glory of the **L** appeared in the cloud. Ex 16:10
And the **L** said to Moses, Ex 16:11
shall know that I am the **L** your God.'" Ex 16:12
is the bread that the **L** has given you to Ex 16:15
This is what the **L** has commanded: Ex 16:16
"This is what the **L** has commanded: Ex 16:23
of solemn rest, a holy Sabbath to the **L**; Ex 16:23
it today, for today is a Sabbath to the **L**; Ex 16:25
And the **L** said to Moses, "How long will Ex 16:28
The **L** has given you the Sabbath; Ex 16:29
"This is what the **L** has commanded: Ex 16:32
place it before the **L** to be kept Ex 16:33
As the **L** commanded Moses, so Aaron Ex 16:34
to the commandment of the **L**, Ex 17:1
with me? Why do you test the **L**?" Ex 17:2

So Moses cried to the **L**, "What shall I do Ex 17:4
And the **L** said to Moses, "Pass on before Ex 17:5
and because they tested the **L** by saying, Ex 17:7
by saying, "Is the **L** among us or not?" Ex 17:7
Then the **L** said to Moses, "Write this Ex 17:14
the name of it, The **L** is my banner, Ex 17:15
"A hand upon the throne of the **L**! Ex 17:16
The **L** will have war with Amalek from Ex 17:16
how the **L** had brought Israel out of Ex 18:1
father-in-law all that the **L** had done to Ex 18:8
way, and how the **L** had delivered them. Ex 18:8
all the good that the **L** had done to Israel, Ex 18:9
Jethro said, "Blessed be the **L**, who has Ex 18:10
I know that the **L** is greater than all Ex 18:11
The **L** called to him out of the Ex 19:3
words that the **L** had commanded him. Ex 19:7
"All that the **L** has spoken we will do." Ex 19:8
reported the words of the people to the **L**. Ex 19:8
And the **L** said to Moses, "Behold, I am Ex 19:9
told the words of the people to the **L**, Ex 19:9
the **L** said to Moses, "Go to the people Ex 19:10
the third day the **L** will come down on Ex 19:11
smoke because the **L** had descended on Ex 19:18
The **L** came down on Mount Sinai, to Ex 19:20
And the **L** called Moses to the top of the Ex 19:20
And the **L** said to Moses, "Go down and Ex 19:21
break through to the **L** to look and Ex 19:21
near to the **L** consecrate themselves, Ex 19:22
lest the **L** break out against them." Ex 19:22
And Moses said to the **L**, "The people Ex 19:23
And the **L** said to him, "Go down, and Ex 19:24
break through to come up to the **L**, Ex 19:24
"I am the **L** your God, who brought you Ex 20:2
for I the **L** your God am a jealous God, Ex 20:5
take the name of the **L** your God in vain, Ex 20:7
for the **L** will not hold him guiltless who Ex 20:7
day is a Sabbath to the **L** your God. Ex 20:10
in six days the **L** made heaven and Ex 20:11
Therefore the **L** blessed the Sabbath Ex 20:11
the land that the **L** your God is giving Ex 20:12
And the **L** said to Moses, "Thus you Ex 20:22
an oath by the **L** shall be between them Ex 22:11
to any god, other than the **L** alone, Ex 22:20
all your males appear before the **L** GOD. Ex 23:17
bring into the house of the **L** your God. Ex 23:19
You shall serve the **L** your God, and he Ex 23:25
he said to Moses, "Come up to the **L**, Ex 24:1
Moses alone shall come near to the **L**, Ex 24:2
all the words of the **L** and all the rules. Ex 24:3
the words that the **L** has spoken we will Ex 24:3
Moses wrote down all the words of the **L**. Ex 24:4
peace offerings of oxen to the **L**. Ex 24:5
"All that the **L** has spoken we will do, Ex 24:7
the covenant that the **L** has made with Ex 24:8
The **L** said to Moses, "Come up to me Ex 24:12
The glory of the **L** dwelt on Mount Ex 24:16
the glory of the **L** was like a devouring Ex 24:17
The **L** said to Moses, Ex 25:1
from evening to morning before the **L**. Ex 27:21
their names before the **L** on his two Ex 28:12
to regular remembrance before the **L**. Ex 28:29
heart, when he goes in before the **L**. Ex 28:30
on his heart before the **L** regularly. Ex 28:30
he goes into the Holy Place before the **L**, Ex 28:35
engraving of a signet, 'Holy to the **L**.' Ex 28:36
that they may be accepted before the **L**. Ex 28:38
the bull before the **L** at the entrance of Ex 29:11
the altar. It is a burnt offering to the **L**. Ex 29:18
pleasing aroma, a food offering to the **L**. Ex 29:18
unleavened bread that is before the **L**. Ex 29:23
them for a wave offering before the **L**. Ex 29:24
as a pleasing aroma before the **L**. Ex 29:25
the LORD. It is a food offering to the **L**. Ex 29:25
wave it for a wave offering before the **L**, Ex 29:26
offerings, their contribution to the **L**. Ex 29:28
pleasing aroma, a food offering to the **L**. Ex 29:41
of the tent of meeting before the **L**, Ex 29:42
shall know that I am the **L** their God, Ex 29:46
among them. I am the **L** their God. Ex 29:46
offering before the **L** throughout your Ex 30:8
generations. It is most holy to the **L**." Ex 30:10
The **L** said to Moses, Ex 30:11
his life to the **L** when you number Ex 30:12
half a shekel as an offering to the **L**. Ex 30:13
of Israel to remembrance before the **L**, Ex 30:16
The **L** said to Moses, Ex 30:17
to burn a food offering to the **L**, Ex 30:20
The **L** said to Moses, Ex 30:22
The **L** said to Moses, "Take sweet Ex 30:34
It shall be for you holy to the **L**. Ex 30:37
The **L** said to Moses, Ex 31:1
And the **L** said to Moses, Ex 31:12
that you may know that I, the **L**, Ex 31:13
a Sabbath of solemn rest, holy to the **L**. Ex 31:15
in six days the **L** made heaven and Ex 31:17

"Tomorrow shall be a feast to the **L**." Ex 32:5
And the **L** said to Moses, "Go down, for Ex 32:7
And the **L** said to Moses, "I have seen this Ex 32:9
But Moses implored the **L** his God and Ex 32:11
the LORD his God and said, "O **L**, Ex 32:11
And the **L** relented from the disaster Ex 32:14
"Let not the anger of my **l** burn hot. Ex 32:22
to them, "Thus says the **L** God of Israel, Ex 32:27
been ordained for the service of the **L**, Ex 32:29
And now I will go up to the **L**; perhaps I Ex 32:30
So Moses returned to the **L** and said, Ex 32:31
But the **L** said to Moses, "Whoever has Ex 32:33
Then the **L** sent a plague on the people, Ex 32:35
The **L** said to Moses, "Depart; go up from Ex 33:1
For the **L** had said to Moses, "Say to the Ex 33:5
everyone who sought the **L** would go out Ex 33:7
tent, and the **L** would speak with Moses. Ex 33:9
Thus the **L** used to speak to Moses face Ex 33:11
Moses said to the **L**, "See, you say to me, Ex 33:12
And the **L** said to Moses, "This very Ex 33:17
proclaim before you my name 'The **L**.' Ex 33:19
And the **L** said, "Behold, there is a place Ex 33:21
The **L** said to Moses, "Cut for yourself Ex 34:1
Sinai, as the **L** had commanded him, Ex 34:4
The **L** descended in the cloud and stood Ex 34:5
there, and proclaimed the name of the **L**. Ex 34:5
The **L** passed before him and Ex 34:6
before him and proclaimed, "The **L**, Ex 34:6
him and proclaimed, "The LORD, the **L**, Ex 34:6
I have found favor in your sight, O **L**, Ex 34:9
please let the **L** go in the midst of us, Ex 34:9
you are shall see the work of the **L**, Ex 34:10
shall worship no other god, for the **L**, Ex 34:14
all your males appear before the **L** God, Ex 34:23
to appear before the **L** your God three Ex 34:24
bring to the house of the **L** your God. Ex 34:26
And the **L** said to Moses, "Write these Ex 34:27
was there with the **L** forty days and Ex 34:28
them all that the **L** had spoken with Ex 34:32
went in before the **L** to speak with him, Ex 34:34
things that the **L** has commanded you Ex 35:1
a Sabbath of solemn rest, holy to the **L**. Ex 35:2
is the thing that the **L** has commanded. Ex 35:4
among you a contribution to the **L**. Ex 35:5
make all that the **L** has commanded: Ex 35:10
dedicating an offering of gold to the **L**. Ex 35:22
work that the **L** had commanded by Ex 35:29
brought it as a freewill offering to the **L**. Ex 35:29
the **L** has called by name Bezalel the Ex 35:30
craftsman in whom the **L** has put skill Ex 36:1
with all that the **L** has commanded." Ex 36:1
in whose mind the **L** had put skill, Ex 36:2
the work that the **L** has commanded us Ex 36:5
made all that the **L** commanded Moses; Ex 38:22
Aaron, as the **L** had commanded Moses. Ex 39:1
linen, as the **L** had commanded Moses. Ex 39:5
Israel, as the **L** had commanded Moses. Ex 39:7
ephod, as the **L** had commanded Moses. Ex 39:21
as the **L** had commanded Moses. Ex 39:26
as the **L** had commanded Moses. Ex 39:29
engraving of a signet, "Holy to the **L**." Ex 39:30
above, as the **L** had commanded Moses. Ex 39:31
all that the **L** had commanded Moses; Ex 39:32
all that the **L** had commanded Moses, Ex 39:42
had done it; as the **L** had commanded, Ex 39:43
The **L** spoke to Moses, saying, Ex 40:1
to all that the **L** commanded him, Ex 40:16
it, as the **L** had commanded Moses. Ex 40:19
as the **L** had commanded Moses. Ex 40:21
arranged the bread on it before the **L**, Ex 40:23
LORD, as the **L** had commanded Moses. Ex 40:23
and set up the lamps before the **L**, as the Ex 40:25
LORD, as the **L** had commanded Moses. Ex 40:25
on it, as the **L** had commanded Moses. Ex 40:27
as the **L** had commanded Moses. Ex 40:29
washed, as the **L** commanded Moses. Ex 40:32
the glory of the **L** filled the tabernacle. Ex 40:34
the glory of the **L** filled the tabernacle. Ex 40:35
the cloud of the **L** was on the Ex 40:38
The **L** called Moses and spoke to him Lv 1:1
any one of you brings an offering to the **L**, Lv 1:2
that he may be accepted before the **L**. Lv 1:3
Then he shall kill the bull before the **L**, Lv 1:5
offering with a pleasing aroma to the **L**. Lv 1:9
the north side of the altar before the **L**, Lv 1:11
offering with a pleasing aroma to the **L**. Lv 1:13
his offering to the **L** is a burnt offering Lv 1:14
offering with a pleasing aroma to the **L**. Lv 1:17
a grain offering as an offering to the **L**, Lv 2:1
offering with a pleasing aroma to the **L**. Lv 2:2
that is made of these things to the **L**, Lv 2:8
offering with a pleasing aroma to the **L**. Lv 2:9
you bring to the **L** shall be made with Lv 2:11
nor any honey as a food offering to the **L**. Lv 2:11
firstfruits you may bring them to the **L**, Lv 2:12

a grain offering of firstfruits to the **L**, Lv 2:14
it is a food offering to the **L**. Lv 2:16
offer it without blemish before the **L**. Lv 3:1
peace offering, as a food offering to the **L**, Lv 3:3
offering with a pleasing aroma to the **L**. Lv 3:5
peace offering to the **L** is an animal from Lv 3:6
offering, then he shall offer it before the **L**, Lv 3:7
offer as a food offering to the **L** its fat; Lv 3:9
it on the altar as a food offering to the **L**. Lv 3:11
a goat, then he shall offer it before the **L** Lv 3:12
his offering for a food offering to the **L**, Lv 3:14
And the **L** spoke to Moses, saying, Lv 4:1
without blemish to the **L** for a sin Lv 4:3
of meeting before the **L** and lay his hand Lv 4:4
of the bull and kill the bull before the **L**. Lv 4:4
seven times before the **L** in front of the Lv 4:6
fragrant incense before the **L** that is in the Lv 4:7
on the head of the bull before the **L**, Lv 4:15
and the bull shall be killed before the **L**. Lv 4:15
it seven times before the **L** in front of the Lv 4:17
that is in the tent of meeting before the **L**, Lv 4:18
commandments of the **L** his God ought Lv 4:22
they kill the burnt offering before the **L**; Lv 4:24
the altar for a pleasing aroma to the **L**. Lv 4:31
shall bring to the **L** as his compensation Lv 5:6
shall bring to the **L** as his compensation Lv 5:7
The **L** spoke to Moses, saying, Lv 5:14
in any of the holy things of the **L**, Lv 5:15
bring to the **L** as his compensation, Lv 5:15
has indeed incurred guilt before the **L**." Lv 5:19
The **L** spoke to Moses, saying, Lv 6:1
of faith against the **L** by deceiving his Lv 6:2
his compensation to the **L** a ram without Lv 6:6
make atonement for him before the **L**, Lv 6:7
The **L** spoke to Moses, saying, Lv 6:8
shall offer it before the **L** in front of the Lv 6:14
on the altar, a pleasing aroma to the **L**. Lv 6:15
The **L** spoke to Moses, saying, Lv 6:19
sons shall offer to the **L** on the day when Lv 6:20
and offer it for a pleasing aroma to the **L**. Lv 6:21
shall offer it to the **L** as decreed forever. Lv 6:22
The **L** spoke to Moses, saying, Lv 6:24
the sin offering be killed before the **L**; Lv 6:25
on the altar as a food offering to the **L**; Lv 7:5
offerings that one may offer to the **L**. Lv 7:11
loaf from each offering, as a gift to the **L**. Lv 7:14
The **L** spoke to Moses, saying, Lv 7:22
may be made to the **L** shall be cut off Lv 7:25
The **L** spoke to Moses, saying, Lv 7:28
peace offerings to the **L** shall bring his Lv 7:29
his offering to the **L** from the sacrifice of Lv 7:29
be waved as a wave offering before the **L**. Lv 7:30
were presented to serve as priests of the **L**. Lv 7:35
The **L** commanded this to be given them Lv 7:36
which the **L** commanded Moses on Lv 7:38
of Israel to bring their offerings to the **L**, Lv 7:38
The **L** spoke to Moses, saying, Lv 8:1
And Moses did as the **L** commanded him, Lv 8:4
the thing that the **L** has commanded to be Lv 8:5
holy crown, as the **L** commanded Moses. Lv 8:9
on them, as the **L** commanded Moses. Lv 8:13
the camp, as the **L** commanded Moses. Lv 8:17
pleasing aroma, a food offering for the **L**, Lv 8:21
the LORD, as the **L** commanded Moses. Lv 8:21
that was before the **L** he took one Lv 8:26
them as a wave offering before the **L**. Lv 8:27
pleasing aroma, a food offering to the **L**. Lv 8:28
waved it for a wave offering before the **L**. Lv 8:29
ordination, as the **L** commanded Moses. Lv 8:29
the **L** has commanded to be done to Lv 8:34
performing what the **L** has charged, Lv 8:35
things that the **L** commanded by Moses. Lv 8:36
blemish, and offer them before the **L**. Lv 9:2
peace offerings, to sacrifice before the **L**, Lv 9:4
oil, for today the **L** will appear to you.'" Lv 9:4
drew near and stood before the **L**. Lv 9:5
the thing that the **L** commanded you to Lv 9:6
that the glory of the **L** may appear to you." Lv 9:6
for them, as the **L** has commanded." Lv 9:7
on the altar, as the **L** commanded Moses. Lv 9:10
waved for a wave offering before the **L**, Lv 9:21
and the glory of the **L** appeared to all the Lv 9:23
out from before the **L** and consumed the Lv 9:24
offered unauthorized fire before the **L**, Lv 10:1
from before the **L** and consumed them, Lv 10:2
them, and they died before the **L**. Lv 10:2
to Aaron, "This is what the **L** has said, Lv 10:3
the burning that the **L** has kindled. Lv 10:6
anointing oil of the **L** is upon you." And Lv 10:7
And the **L** spoke to Aaron, saying, Lv 10:8
the statutes that the **L** has spoken to Lv 10:11
to wave for a wave offering before the **L**, Lv 10:15
due forever, as the **L** has commanded." Lv 10:15
make atonement for them before the **L**? Lv 10:17
and their burnt offering before the **L**, Lv 10:19

today, would the **L** have approved?" Lv 10:19
And the **L** spoke to Moses and Aaron, Lv 11:1
For I am the **L** your God. Consecrate Lv 11:44
For I am the **L** who brought you up out Lv 11:45
The **L** spoke to Moses, saying, Lv 12:1
offer it before the **L** and make atonement Lv 12:7
The **L** spoke to Moses and Aaron, Lv 13:1
The **L** spoke to Moses, saying, Lv 14:1
cleansed and these things before the **L**, Lv 14:11
them for a wave offering before the **L**. Lv 14:12
with his finger seven times before the **L**. Lv 14:16
make atonement for him before the **L**. Lv 14:18
of the tent of meeting, before the **L**. Lv 14:23
them for a wave offering before the **L**. Lv 14:24
his left hand seven times before the **L**. Lv 14:27
make atonement for him before the **L**. Lv 14:29
atonement before the **L** for him who Lv 14:31
The **L** spoke to Moses and Aaron, Lv 14:33
The **L** spoke to Moses and Aaron, Lv 15:1
and come before the **L** to the entrance Lv 15:14
for him before the **L** for his discharge. Lv 15:15
for her before the **L** for her unclean Lv 15:30
The **L** spoke to Moses after the death of Lv 16:1
they drew near before the **L** and died, Lv 16:1
and the **L** said to Moses, "Tell Aaron Lv 16:2
set them before the **L** at the entrance of Lv 16:7
one lot for the **L** and the other lot for Lv 16:8
which the lot fell for the **L** and use it as a Lv 16:9
alive before the **L** to make atonement Lv 16:10
coals of fire from the altar before the **L**, Lv 16:12
put the incense on the fire before the **L**, Lv 16:13
is before the **L** and make atonement Lv 16:18
be clean before the **L** from all your Lv 16:30
Moses did as the **L** commanded him. Lv 16:34
And the **L** spoke to Moses, saying, Lv 17:1
is the thing that the **L** has commanded. Lv 17:2
as a gift to the **L** in front of the Lv 17:4
LORD in front of the tabernacle of the **L**, Lv 17:4
field, that they may bring them to the **L**, Lv 17:5
as sacrifices of peace offerings to the **L**. Lv 17:5
on the altar of the **L** at the entrance of Lv 17:6
the fat for a pleasing aroma to the **L**. Lv 17:6
of the tent of meeting to offer it to the **L**, Lv 17:9
And the **L** spoke to Moses, saying, Lv 18:1
and say to them, I am the **L** your God. Lv 18:2
and walk in them. I am the **L** your God. Lv 18:4
them, he shall live by them: I am the **L**. Lv 18:5
to uncover nakedness. I am the **L**. Lv 18:6
the name of your God: I am the **L**. Lv 18:21
by them: I am the **L** your God." Lv 18:30
And the **L** spoke to Moses, saying, Lv 19:1
be holy, for I the **L** your God am holy. Lv 19:2
keep my Sabbaths: I am the **L** your God. Lv 19:3
gods of cast metal: I am the **L** your God. Lv 19:4
a sacrifice of peace offerings to the **L**, Lv 19:5
he has profaned what is holy to the **L**, Lv 19:8
for the sojourner: I am the **L** your God. Lv 19:10
the name of your God: I am the **L**. Lv 19:12
but you shall fear your God: I am the **L**. Lv 19:14
the life of your neighbor: I am the **L**. Lv 19:16
your neighbor as yourself: I am the **L**. Lv 19:18
shall bring his compensation to the **L**, Lv 19:21
guilt offering before the **L** for his sin Lv 19:22
be holy, an offering of praise to the **L**. Lv 19:24
its yield for you: I am the **L** your God. Lv 19:25
dead or tattoo yourselves: I am the **L**. Lv 19:28
reverence my sanctuary: I am the **L**. Lv 19:30
unclean by them: I am the **L** your God. Lv 19:31
and you shall fear your God: I am the **L**. Lv 19:32
the land of Egypt: I am the **L** your God. Lv 19:34
I am the **L** your God, who brought you Lv 19:36
all my rules, and do them: I am the **L**." Lv 19:37
The **L** spoke to Moses, saying, Lv 20:1
and be holy, for I am the **L** your God. Lv 20:7
do them; I am the **L** who sanctifies you. Lv 20:8
I am the **L** your God, who have Lv 20:24
for I the **L** am holy and have separated Lv 20:26
And the **L** said to Moses, "Speak to the Lv 21:1
He shall be holy to you, for I, the **L**, who Lv 21:8
oil of his God is on him: I am the **L**. Lv 21:12
for I am the **L** who sanctifies him." Lv 21:15
And the **L** spoke to Moses, saying, Lv 21:16
for I am the **L** who sanctifies them." Lv 21:23
And the **L** spoke to Moses, saying, Lv 22:1
not profane my holy name: I am the **L**. Lv 22:2
that the people of Israel dedicate to the **L**, Lv 22:3
be cut off from my presence: I am the **L**. Lv 22:3
make himself unclean by it: I am the **L**.' Lv 22:8
it: I am the **L** who sanctifies them. Lv 22:9
Israel, which they contribute to the **L**, Lv 22:15
for I am the **L** who sanctifies them." Lv 22:16
And the **L** spoke to Moses, saying, Lv 22:17
offerings that they offer to the **L**, Lv 22:18
peace offerings to the **L** to fulfill a vow Lv 22:21
shall not offer to the **L** or give them to Lv 22:22

or give them to the **L** as a food offering Lv 22:22
torn or cut you shall not offer to the **L**; Lv 22:24
And the **L** spoke to Moses, saying, Lv 22:26
acceptable as a food offering to the **L**. Lv 22:27
a sacrifice of thanksgiving to the **L**, Lv 22:29
none of it until morning: I am the **L**. Lv 22:30
and do them: I am the **L**. Lv 22:31
of Israel. I am the **L** who sanctifies you, Lv 22:32
of Egypt to be your God: I am the **L**." Lv 22:33
The **L** spoke to Moses, saying, Lv 23:1
appointed feasts of the **L** that you shall Lv 23:2
is a Sabbath to the **L** in all your dwelling Lv 23:3
"These are the appointed feasts of the **L**, Lv 23:4
is the Feast of Unleavened bread to the **L**; Lv 23:6
a food offering to the **L** for seven days. Lv 23:8
And the **L** spoke to Moses, saying, Lv 23:9
he shall wave the sheaf before the **L**, Lv 23:11
blemish as a burnt offering to the **L**. Lv 23:12
food offering to the **L** with a pleasing Lv 23:13
a grain offering of new grain to the **L**. Lv 23:16
with leaven, as firstfruits to the **L**. Lv 23:17
They shall be a burnt offering to the **L**, Lv 23:18
offering with a pleasing aroma to the **L**. Lv 23:18
as a wave offering before the **L**, Lv 23:20
shall be holy to the **L** for the priest. Lv 23:20
for the sojourner: I am the **L** your God." Lv 23:22
And the **L** spoke to Moses, saying, Lv 23:23
shall present a food offering to the **L**." Lv 23:25
And the **L** spoke to Moses, saying, Lv 23:26
and present a food offering to the **L**. Lv 23:27
for you before the **L** your God. Lv 23:28
And the **L** spoke to Moses, saying, Lv 23:33
days is the Feast of Booths to the **L**. Lv 23:34
shall present food offerings to the **L**. Lv 23:36
and present a food offering to the **L**. Lv 23:36
"These are the appointed feasts of the **L**, Lv 23:37
for presenting to the **L** food offerings, Lv 23:37
offerings, which you give to the **L**. Lv 23:38
celebrate the feast of the **L** seven days. Lv 23:39
rejoice before the **L** your God seven Lv 23:40
it as a feast to the **L** for seven days in the Lv 23:41
the land of Egypt: I am the **L** your God." Lv 23:43
of Israel the appointed feasts of the **L**. Lv 23:44
The **L** spoke to Moses, saying, Lv 24:1
to morning before the **L** regularly. Lv 24:3
of pure gold before the **L** regularly. Lv 24:4
on the table of pure gold before the **L**. Lv 24:6
portion as a food offering to the **L**. Lv 24:7
shall arrange it before the **L** regularly; Lv 24:8
till the will of the **L** should be clear to Lv 24:12
Then the **L** spoke to Moses, saying, Lv 24:13
the name of the **L** shall surely be put Lv 24:16
for the native, for I am the **L** your God." Lv 24:22
Israel did as the **L** commanded Moses. Lv 24:23
The **L** spoke to Moses on Mount Sinai, Lv 25:1
the land shall keep a Sabbath to the **L**. Lv 25:2
rest for the land, a Sabbath to the **L**. Lv 25:4
fear your God, for I am the **L** your God. Lv 25:17
I am the **L** your God, who brought you Lv 25:38
the land of Egypt: I am the **L** your God. Lv 25:55
bow down to it, for I am the **L** your God. Lv 26:1
and reverence my sanctuary: I am the **L**. Lv 26:2
I am the **L** your God, who brought you Lv 26:13
with them, for I am the **L** their God. Lv 26:44
that I might be their God: I am the **L**." Lv 26:45
and laws that the **L** made between him Lv 26:46
The **L** spoke to Moses, saying, Lv 27:1
vow to the **L** involving the valuation Lv 27:2
may be offered as an offering to the **L**, Lv 27:9
all of it that he gives to the **L** is holy. Lv 27:9
not be offered as an offering to the **L**, Lv 27:11
his house as a holy gift to the **L**, Lv 27:14
man dedicates to the **L** part of the land Lv 27:16
the jubilee, shall be a holy gift to the **L**, Lv 27:21
If he dedicates to the **L** a field that he Lv 27:22
on that day as a holy gift to the **L**. Lv 27:23
which as a firstborn belongs to the **L**, Lv 27:26
thing that a man devotes to the **L**, Lv 27:28
devoted thing is most holy to the **L**. Lv 27:28
the trees, is the LORD'S; it is holy to the **L**. Lv 27:30
herdsman's staff, shall be holy to the **L**. Lv 27:32
that the **L** commanded Moses Lv 27:34
The **L** spoke to Moses in the wilderness Nm 1:1
as the **L** commanded Moses. So he Nm 1:19
For the **L** spoke to Moses, saying, Nm 1:48
to all that the **L** commanded Moses. Nm 1:54
The **L** spoke to Moses and Aaron, Nm 2:1
of Israel, as the **L** commanded Moses. Nm 2:33
to all that the **L** commanded Moses, Nm 2:34
the time when the **L** spoke with Moses Nm 3:1
died before the **L** when they offered Nm 3:4
fire before the **L** in the wilderness Nm 3:4
And the **L** spoke to Moses, saying, Nm 3:5
And the **L** spoke to Moses, saying, Nm 3:11
beast. They shall be mine: I am the **L**." Nm 3:13
And the **L** spoke to Moses in the Nm 3:14
them according to the word of the **L**, Nm 3:16
listed at the commandment of the **L**, Nm 3:39
And the **L** said to Moses, "List all the Nm 3:40
for me—I am the **L**—instead of all the Nm 3:41
of Israel, as the **L** commanded him. Nm 3:42
And the **L** spoke to Moses, saying, Nm 3:44
The Levites shall be mine: I am the **L**. Nm 3:45
sons, according to the word of the **L**, Nm 3:51
the LORD, as the **L** commanded Moses. Nm 3:51
The **L** spoke to Moses and Aaron, Nm 4:1
The **L** spoke to Moses and Aaron, Nm 4:17
The **L** spoke to Moses, saying, Nm 4:21
the commandment of the **L** by Moses. Nm 4:37
to the commandment of the **L**. Nm 4:41
the commandment of the **L** by Moses. Nm 4:45
of the **L** through Moses Nm 4:49
by him, as the **L** commanded Moses. Nm 4:49
The **L** spoke to Moses, saying, Nm 5:1
as the **L** said to Moses, so the people of Nm 5:4
And the **L** spoke to Moses, saying, Nm 5:5
commit by breaking faith with the **L**, Nm 5:6
for wrong shall go to the **L** for the priest, Nm 5:8
And the **L** spoke to Moses, saying, Nm 5:11
bring her near and set her before the **L**. Nm 5:16
woman before the **L** and unbind the Nm 5:18
to the woman) 'the **L** make you a curse Nm 5:21
when the **L** makes your thigh fall away Nm 5:21
grain offering before the **L** and bring it Nm 5:25
he shall set the woman before the **L**, Nm 5:30
And the **L** spoke to Moses, saying, Nm 6:1
of a Nazirite, to separate himself to the **L**, Nm 6:2
for which he separates himself to the **L**, Nm 6:5
separates himself to the **L** he shall not go Nm 6:6
days of his separation he is holy to the **L**. Nm 6:8
separate himself to the **L** for the days of Nm 6:12
and he shall bring his gift to the **L**, one Nm 6:14
bring them before the **L** and offer his Nm 6:16
as a sacrifice of peace offering to the **L**, Nm 6:17
them for a wave offering before the **L**. Nm 6:20
an offering to the **L** above his Nazirite Nm 6:21
The **L** spoke to Moses, saying, Nm 6:22
The **L** bless you and keep you; Nm 6:24
the **L** make his face to shine upon you Nm 6:25
the **L** lift up his countenance upon you Nm 6:26
and brought their offerings before the **L**, Nm 7:3
Then the **L** said to Moses, Nm 7:4
And the **L** said to Moses, "They shall Nm 7:11
the tent of meeting to speak with the **L**, Nm 7:89
Now the **L** spoke to Moses, saying, Nm 8:1
lampstand, as the **L** commanded Moses. Nm 8:3
the pattern that the **L** had shown Moses, Nm 8:4
And the **L** spoke to Moses, saying, Nm 8:5
you bring the Levites before the **L**, Nm 8:10
the Levites before the **L** as a wave Nm 8:11
that they may do the service of the **L**. Nm 8:11
offering to the **L** to make atonement Nm 8:12
offer them as a wave offering to the **L**. Nm 8:13
all that the **L** commanded Moses Nm 8:20
them as a wave offering before the **L**, Nm 8:21
as the **L** had commanded Moses Nm 8:22
And the **L** spoke to Moses, saying, Nm 8:23
And the **L** spoke to Moses in the Nm 9:1
to all that the **L** commanded Moses, Nm 9:5
hear what the **L** will command Nm 9:8
The **L** spoke to Moses, saying, Nm 9:9
he shall still keep the Passover to the **L**. Nm 9:10
and would keep the Passover to the **L**, Nm 9:14
the command of the **L** the people of Nm 9:18
at the command of the **L** they camped. Nm 9:18
kept the charge of the **L** and did not set Nm 9:19
command of the **L** they remained in Nm 9:20
to the command of the **L** they set out. Nm 9:20
At the command of the **L** they camped, Nm 9:23
at the command of the **L** they set out. Nm 9:23
They kept the charge of the **L**, at the Nm 9:23
at the command of the **L** by Moses. Nm 9:23
The **L** spoke to Moses, saying, Nm 10:1
be remembered before the **L** your God, Nm 10:9
your God: I am the **L** your God." Nm 10:10
at the command of the **L** by Moses. Nm 10:13
out for the place of which the **L** said, Nm 10:29
for the **L** has promised good to Israel." Nm 10:29
us, whatever good the **L** will do to us, Nm 10:32
mount of the **L** three days' journey. Nm 10:33
covenant of the **L** went before them Nm 10:33
the cloud of the **L** was over them by Nm 10:34
ark set out, Moses said, "Arise, O **L**, Nm 10:35
when it rested, he said, "Return, O **L**, Nm 10:36
hearing of the **L** about their Nm 11:1
misfortunes, and when the **L** heard it, Nm 11:1
the fire of the **L** burned among them Nm 11:1
to Moses, and Moses prayed to the **L**, Nm 11:2
the fire of the **L** burned among them. Nm 11:3
And the anger of the **L** blazed hotly, Nm 11:10
Moses said to the **L**, "Why have you Nm 11:11
Then the **L** said to Moses, "Gather for Nm 11:16
you have wept in the hearing of the **L**, Nm 11:18
Egypt." Therefore the **L** will give you Nm 11:18
you have rejected the **L** who is among Nm 11:20
And the **L** said to Moses, "Is the LORD'S Nm 11:23
and told the people the words of the **L**. Nm 11:24
Then the **L** came down in the cloud Nm 11:25
from his youth, said, "My **l** Moses, Nm 11:28
that the **L** would put his Spirit on Nm 11:29
Then a wind from the **L** sprang up, Nm 11:31
the anger of the **L** was kindled against Nm 11:33
and the **L** struck down the people with Nm 11:33
"Has the **L** indeed spoken only through Nm 12:2
through us also?" And the **L** heard it. Nm 12:2
And suddenly the **L** said to Moses and Nm 12:4
And the **L** came down in a pillar of Nm 12:5
I the **L** make myself known to him in a Nm 12:6
and he beholds the form of the **L**. Nm 12:8
the anger of the **L** was kindled against Nm 12:9
And Aaron said to Moses, "Oh, my **l**, Nm 12:11
And Moses cried to the **L**, "O God, Nm 12:13
But the **L** said to Moses, "If her father Nm 12:14
The **L** spoke to Moses, saying, Nm 13:1
according to the command of the **L**, Nm 13:3
Why is the **L** bringing us into this Nm 14:3
If the **L** delights in us, he will bring us Nm 14:8
Only do not rebel against the **L**. And do Nm 14:9
from them, and the **L** is with us; Nm 14:9
the glory of the **L** appeared at the tent Nm 14:10
And the **L** said to Moses, "How long Nm 14:11
But Moses said to the **L**, "Then the Nm 14:13
They have heard that you, O **L**, are in Nm 14:14
For you, O **L**, are seen face to face, and Nm 14:14
'It is because the **L** was not able to Nm 14:16
let the power of the **L** be great as you Nm 14:17
'The **L** is slow to anger and Nm 14:18
Then the **L** said, "I have pardoned, Nm 14:20
shall be filled with the glory of the **L**, Nm 14:21
And the **L** spoke to Moses and to Nm 14:26
Say to them, 'As I live, declares the **L**, Nm 14:28
I, the **L**, have spoken. Surely this will I Nm 14:35
the land—died by plague before the **L**. Nm 14:37
to the place that the **L** has promised, Nm 14:40
transgressing the command of the **L**, Nm 14:41
not go up, for the **L** is not among you, Nm 14:42
turned back from following the **L**, Nm 14:43
the LORD, the **L** will not be with you." Nm 14:43
covenant of the **L** nor Moses departed Nm 14:44
The **L** spoke to Moses, saying, Nm 15:1
and you offer to the **L** from the herd or Nm 15:3
to make a pleasing aroma to the **L**, Nm 15:3
shall offer to the **L** a grain offering of Nm 15:4
hin of wine, a pleasing aroma to the **L**. Nm 15:7
a vow or for peace offerings to the **L**, Nm 15:8
offering, a pleasing aroma to the **L**. Nm 15:10
with a pleasing aroma to the **L**. Nm 15:13
with a pleasing aroma to the **L**, Nm 15:14
sojourner shall be alike before the **L**. Nm 15:15
The **L** spoke to Moses, saying, Nm 15:17
shall present a contribution to the **L**. Nm 15:19
shall give to the **L** as a contribution Nm 15:21
that the **L** has spoken Nm 15:22
all that the **L** has commanded you by Nm 15:23
day that the **L** gave commandment, Nm 15:23
offering, a pleasing aroma to the **L**, Nm 15:24
their offering, a food offering to the **L**, Nm 15:25
offering before the **L** for their mistake. Nm 15:25
atonement before the **L** for the person Nm 15:28
is native or a sojourner, reviles the **L**, Nm 15:30
the word of the **L** and has broken his Nm 15:31
And the **L** said to Moses, "The man Nm 15:35
stones, as the **L** commanded Moses. Nm 15:36
The **L** said to Moses, Nm 15:37
all the commandments of the **L**, Nm 15:39
I am the **L** your God, who brought Nm 15:41
to be your God: I am the **L** your God." Nm 15:41
one of them, and the **L** is among them. Nm 16:3
above the assembly of the **L**?" Nm 16:3
"In the morning the **L** will show who is Nm 16:5
on them before the **L** tomorrow, Nm 16:7
the man whom the **L** chooses shall be Nm 16:7
the tabernacle of the **L** and to stand Nm 16:9
it is against the **L** that you and all Nm 16:11
was very angry and said to the **L**, Nm 16:15
and all your company, before the **L**, Nm 16:16
of you bring before the **L** his censer, Nm 16:17
the glory of the **L** appeared to all the Nm 16:19
And the **L** spoke to Moses and to Nm 16:20
And the **L** spoke to Moses, saying, Nm 16:23
shall know that the **L** has sent me to Nm 16:28
mankind, then the **L** has not sent me. Nm 16:29
But if the **L** creates something new, Nm 16:30
that these men have despised the **L**." Nm 16:30
out from the **L** and consumed the Nm 16:35

Then the **L** spoke to Moses, saying, Nm 16:36
for they offered them before the **L**, Nm 16:38
near to burn incense before the **L**, Nm 16:40
company—as the **L** said to him Nm 16:40
"You have killed the people of the **L**." Nm 16:41
it, and the glory of the **L** appeared. Nm 16:42
and the **L** spoke to Moses, saying, Nm 16:44
for wrath has gone out from the **L**; Nm 16:46
The **L** spoke to Moses, saying, Nm 17:1
the staffs before the **L** in the tent of Nm 17:7
staffs from before the **L** to all the people Nm 17:9
And the **L** said to Moses, "Put back Nm 17:10
did Moses; as the **L** commanded him, Nm 17:11
comes near to the tabernacle of the **L**, Nm 17:13
So the **L** said to Aaron, "You and your Nm 18:1
They are a gift to you, given to the **L**, to Nm 18:6
Then the **L** spoke to Aaron, "Behold, I Nm 18:8
firstfruits of what they give to the **L**, Nm 18:12
their land, which they bring to the **L**, Nm 18:13
or beast, which they offer to the **L**, Nm 18:15
with a pleasing aroma to the **L**. Nm 18:17
of Israel present to the **L** I give to you, Nm 18:19
salt forever before the **L** for you and Nm 18:19
And the **L** said to Aaron, "You shall Nm 18:20
present as a contribution to the **L**, Nm 18:24
And the **L** spoke to Moses, saying, Nm 18:25
a contribution from it to the **L**, Nm 18:26
a contribution to the **L** from all your Nm 18:28
every contribution due to the **L**; Nm 18:29
Now the **L** spoke to Moses and to Nm 19:1
of the law that the **L** has commanded: Nm 19:2
defiles the tabernacle of the **L**, Nm 19:13
he has defiled the sanctuary of the **L**. Nm 19:20
our brothers perished before the **L**! Nm 20:3
assembly of the **L** into this wilderness, Nm 20:4
the glory of the **L** appeared to them, Nm 20:6
and the **L** spoke to Moses, saying, Nm 20:7
Moses took the staff from before the **L**, Nm 20:9
And the **L** said to Moses and Aaron, Nm 20:12
people of Israel quarreled with the **L**, Nm 20:13
And when we cried to the **L**, he heard Nm 20:16
And the **L** said to Moses and Aaron at Nm 20:23
Moses did as the **L** commanded. And Nm 20:27
Israel vowed a vow to the **L** and said, Nm 21:2
And the **L** obeyed the voice of Israel Nm 21:3
Then the **L** sent fiery serpents among Nm 21:6
spoken against the **L** and against you. Nm 21:7
Pray to the **L**, that he take away the Nm 21:7
And the **L** said to Moses, "Make a fiery Nm 21:8
said in the Book of the Wars of the **L**, Nm 21:14
the well of which the **L** said to Moses, Nm 21:16
But the **L** said to Moses, "Do not fear Nm 21:34
as the **L** speaks to me." So the princes of Nm 22:8
for the **L** has refused to let me go with Nm 22:13
the command of the **L** my God to do Nm 22:18
know what more the **L** will say to Nm 22:19
the angel of the **L** took his stand in Nm 22:22
the angel of the **L** standing in the Nm 22:23
the angel of the **L** stood in a narrow Nm 22:24
the donkey saw the angel of the **L**, Nm 22:25
the angel of the **L** went ahead and Nm 22:26
the donkey saw the angel of the **L**, Nm 22:27
Then the **L** opened the mouth of the Nm 22:28
Then the **L** opened the eyes of Balaam, Nm 22:31
the angel of the **L** standing in the way, Nm 22:31
And the angel of the **L** said to him, Nm 22:32
Balaam said to the angel of the **L**, Nm 22:34
And the angel of the **L** said to Balaam, Nm 22:35
Perhaps the **L** will come to meet me, Nm 23:3
And the **L** put a word in Balaam's Nm 23:5
denounce whom the **L** has not Nm 23:8
to speak what the **L** puts in my Nm 23:12
while I meet the **L** over there." Nm 23:15
And the **L** met Balaam and put a word Nm 23:16
to him, "What has the **L** spoken?" Nm 23:17
The **L** their God is with them, and the Nm 23:21
"Did I not tell you, 'All that the **L** says, Nm 23:26
saw that it pleased the **L** to bless Israel, Nm 24:1
river, like aloes that the **L** has planted, Nm 24:6
but the **L** has held you back from Nm 24:11
be able to go beyond the word of the **L**, Nm 24:13
What the **L** speaks, that will I speak'? Nm 24:13
the anger of the **L** was kindled against Nm 25:3
And the **L** said to Moses, "Take all the Nm 25:4
and hang them in the sun before the **L**, Nm 25:4
fierce anger of the **L** may turn away Nm 25:4
And the **L** said to Moses, Nm 25:10
And the **L** spoke to Moses, saying, Nm 25:16
the **L** said to Moses and to Eleazar the Nm 26:1
upward," as the **L** commanded Moses. Nm 26:4
when they contended against the **L** Nm 26:9
The **L** spoke to Moses, saying, Nm 26:52
offered unauthorized fire before the **L**. Nm 26:61
For the **L** had said of them, "They Nm 26:65
together against the **L** in the company Nm 27:3

Moses brought their case before the **L**. Nm 27:5
And the **L** said to Moses, Nm 27:6
rule, as the **L** commanded Moses.'" Nm 27:11
The **L** said to Moses, "Go up into this Nm 27:12
Moses spoke to the **L**, saying, Nm 27:15
"Let the **L**, the God of the spirits of all Nm 27:16
the congregation of the **L** may not be Nm 27:17
So the **L** said to Moses, "Take Joshua Nm 27:18
judgment of the Urim before the **L**. Nm 27:21
Moses did as the **L** commanded him. Nm 27:22
him as the **L** directed through Moses. Nm 27:23
The **L** spoke to Moses, saying, Nm 28:1
offering that you shall offer to the **L**: Nm 28:3
aroma, a food offering to the **L**. Nm 28:6
drink offering of strong drink to the **L**. Nm 28:7
with a pleasing aroma to the **L**. Nm 28:8
shall offer a burnt offering to the **L**: Nm 28:11
aroma, a food offering to the **L**. Nm 28:13
male goat for a sin offering to the **L**; Nm 28:15
offering, a burnt offering to the **L**: Nm 28:19
with a pleasing aroma to the **L**. Nm 28:24
of new grain to the **L** at your Feast of Nm 28:26
with a pleasing aroma to the **L**: Nm 28:27
offering, for a pleasing aroma to the **L**: Nm 29:2
aroma, a food offering to the **L**. Nm 29:6
shall offer a burnt offering to the **L**, Nm 29:8
shall keep a feast to the **L** seven days. Nm 29:12
with a pleasing aroma to the **L**, Nm 29:13
with a pleasing aroma to the **L**: Nm 29:36
shall offer to the **L** at your appointed Nm 29:39
just as the **L** had commanded Moses. Nm 29:40
"This is what the **L** has commanded. Nm 30:1
If a man vows a vow to the **L**, or swears Nm 30:2
a vow to the **L** and binds herself by Nm 30:3
And the **L** will forgive her, because her Nm 30:5
herself. And the **L** will forgive her. Nm 30:8
them void, and the **L** will forgive her. Nm 30:12
statutes that the **L** commanded Moses Nm 30:16
The **L** spoke to Moses, saying, Nm 31:1
Midian, as the **L** commanded Moses, Nm 31:7
treacherously against the **L** in the Nm 31:16
among the congregation of the **L**. Nm 31:16
law that the **L** has commanded Nm 31:21
The **L** said to Moses, Nm 31:25
And levy for the **L** a tribute from the Nm 31:28
the priest as a contribution to the **L**. Nm 31:29
guard over the tabernacle of the **L**." Nm 31:30
priest did as the **L** commanded Moses. Nm 31:31
which was the contribution for the **L**, Nm 31:41
priest, as the **L** commanded Moses. Nm 31:41
guard over the tabernacle of the **L**, Nm 31:47
the LORD, as the **L** commanded Moses. Nm 31:47
atonement for ourselves before the **L**." Nm 31:50
that they presented to the **L**, Nm 31:52
for the people of Israel before the **L**. Nm 31:54
the land that the **L** struck down before Nm 32:4
the land that the **L** has given them? Nm 32:7
the land that the **L** had given them. Nm 32:9
for they have wholly followed the **L**.' Nm 32:12
evil in the sight of the **L** was gone. Nm 32:13
the fierce anger of the **L** against Israel! Nm 32:14
up arms to go before the **L** for the war, Nm 32:20
will pass over the Jordan before the **L**, Nm 32:21
and the land is subdued before the **L**; Nm 32:22
of obligation to the **L** and to Israel, Nm 32:22
shall be your possession before the **L**. Nm 32:22
you have sinned against the **L**, Nm 32:23
servants will do as my **l** commands. Nm 32:25
armed for war, before the **L** to battle, Nm 32:27
the LORD to battle, as my **l** orders." Nm 32:27
who is armed to battle before the **L**, Nm 32:29
"What the **L** has said to your Nm 32:31
over armed before the **L** into the land Nm 32:32
stage by stage, by command of the **L**, Nm 33:2
whom the **L** had struck down among Nm 33:4
gods also the **L** executed judgments. Nm 33:4
the command of the **L** and died there, Nm 33:38
And the **L** spoke to Moses in the Nm 33:50
The **L** spoke to Moses, saying, Nm 34:1
which the **L** has commanded to give Nm 34:13
The **L** spoke to Moses, saying, Nm 34:16
men whom the **L** commanded to Nm 34:29
The **L** spoke to Moses in the plains of Nm 35:1
And the **L** spoke to Moses, saying, Nm 35:9
for I the **L** dwell in the midst of the Nm 35:34
"The **L** commanded my lord to give the Nm 36:2
"The LORD commanded my **l** to give the Nm 36:2
and my **l** was commanded by the LORD Nm 36:2
was commanded by the **L** to give the Nm 36:2
of Israel according to the word of the **L**, Nm 36:5
is what the **L** commands concerning Nm 36:6
did as the **L** commanded Moses, Nm 36:10
rules that the **L** commanded through Nm 36:13
to all that the **L** had given him in Dt 1:3
"The **L** our God said to us in Horeb, 'You Dt 1:6

the land that the **L** swore to your fathers, Dt 1:8
The **L** your God has multiplied you, and Dt 1:10
May the **L**, the God of your fathers, make Dt 1:11
as the **L** our God commanded us. Dt 1:19
which the **L** our God is giving us. Dt 1:20
the **L** your God has set the land before Dt 1:21
Go up, take possession, as the **L**, the God Dt 1:21
a good land that the **L** our God is giving Dt 1:25
against the command of the **L** your God. Dt 1:26
'Because the **L** hated us he has brought Dt 1:27
The **L** your God who goes before you will Dt 1:30
have seen how the **L** your God carried Dt 1:31
word you did not believe the **L** your God, Dt 1:32
"And the **L** heard your words and was Dt 1:34
because he has wholly followed the **L**!' Dt 1:36
Even with me the **L** was angry on your Dt 1:37
me, 'We have sinned against the **L**. Dt 1:41
just as the **L** our God commanded us.' Dt 1:41
And the **L** said to me, 'Say to them, Do Dt 1:42
command of the **L** and presumptuously Dt 1:43
And you returned and wept before the **L**, Dt 1:45
but the **L** did not listen to your voice or Dt 1:45
direction of the Red Sea, as the **L** told me. Dt 2:1
Then the **L** said to me, Dt 2:2
For the **L** your God has blessed you in all Dt 2:7
These forty years the **L** your God has been Dt 2:7
And the **L** said to me, 'Do not harass Dt 2:9
possession, which the **L** gave to them.) Dt 2:12
the camp, as the **L** had sworn to them. Dt 2:14
the hand of the **L** was against them, Dt 2:15
the **L** said to me, Dt 2:17
but the **L** destroyed them before the Dt 2:21
into the land that the **L** our God is giving Dt 2:29
for the **L** your God hardened his spirit Dt 2:30
And the **L** said to me, 'Behold, I have Dt 2:31
And the **L** our God gave him over to us, Dt 2:33
The **L** our God gave all into our hands. Dt 2:36
whatever the **L** our God had forbidden Dt 2:37
But the **L** said to me, 'Do not fear him, for I Dt 3:2
So the **L** our God gave into our hand Og Dt 3:3
'The **L** your God has given you this land Dt 3:18
until the **L** gives rest to your brothers, as Dt 3:20
the land that the **L** your God gives them Dt 3:20
seen all that the **L** your God has done Dt 3:21
So will the **L** do to all the kingdoms into Dt 3:21
for it is the **L** your God who fights for Dt 3:22
"And I pleaded with the **L** at that time, Dt 3:23
'O **L** GOD, you have only begun to show Dt 3:24
But the **L** was angry with me because of Dt 3:26
And the **L** said to me, 'Enough from you; Dt 3:26
and take possession of the land that the **L**, Dt 4:1
commandments of the **L** your God that Dt 4:2
eyes have seen what the **L** did at Baal-peor, Dt 4:3
for the **L** your God destroyed from among Dt 4:3
who held fast to the **L** your God are all Dt 4:4
rules, as the **L** my God commanded me, Dt 4:5
a god so near to it as the **L** our God is to us, Dt 4:7
you stood before the **L** your God at Dt 4:10
LORD your God at Horeb, the **L** said to me, Dt 4:10
Then the **L** spoke to you out of the midst Dt 4:12
And the **L** commanded me at that time Dt 4:14
on the day that the **L** spoke to you at Dt 4:15
things that the **L** your God has allotted to Dt 4:19
But the **L** has taken you and brought Dt 4:20
the **L** was angry with me because of you, Dt 4:21
good land that the **L** your God is giving Dt 4:21
forget the covenant of the **L** your God, Dt 4:23
of anything that the **L** your God has Dt 4:23
For the **L** your God is a consuming fire, Dt 4:24
is evil in the sight of the **L** your God, Dt 4:25
And the **L** will scatter you among the Dt 4:27
the nations where the **L** will drive you. Dt 4:27
you will seek the **L** your God and you Dt 4:29
will return to the **L** your God and obey Dt 4:30
For the **L** your God is a merciful God. He Dt 4:31
all of which the **L** your God did for you Dt 4:34
that you might know that the **L** is God; Dt 4:35
that the **L** is God in heaven above and on Dt 4:39
in the land that the **L** your God is giving Dt 4:40
The **L** our God made a covenant with us Dt 5:2
our fathers did the **L** make this covenant, Dt 5:3
The **L** spoke with you face to face at the Dt 5:4
I stood between the **L** and you at that Dt 5:5
time, to declare to you the word of the **L**. Dt 5:5
"'I am the **L** your God, who brought you Dt 5:6
for I the **L** your God am a jealous God, Dt 5:9
take the name of the **L** your God in vain, Dt 5:11
for the **L** will not hold him guiltless who Dt 5:11
as the **L** your God commanded you. Dt 5:12
day is a Sabbath to the **L** your God. Dt 5:14
and the **L** your God brought you out Dt 5:15
Therefore the **L** your God commanded Dt 5:15
as the **L** your God commanded you, Dt 5:16
in the land that the **L** your God is giving Dt 5:16
"These words the **L** spoke to all your Dt 5:22

the **L** our God has shown us his glory Dt 5:24
the voice of the **L** our God any more, Dt 5:25
and hear all that the **L** our God will say Dt 5:27
to us all that the **L** our God will speak to Dt 5:27
"And the **L** heard your words, when you Dt 5:28
And the **L** said to me, 'I have heard the Dt 5:28
to do as the **L** your God has commanded Dt 5:32
the way that the **L** your God has Dt 5:33
the rules that the **L** your God commanded Dt 6:1
that you may fear the **L** your God, you Dt 6:2
that you may multiply greatly, as the **L**, Dt 6:3
O Israel: The **L** our God, the LORD is one. Dt 6:4
O Israel: The LORD our God, the **L** is one. Dt 6:4
You shall love the **L** your God with all Dt 6:5
"And when the **L** your God brings you Dt 6:10
then take care lest you forget the **L**, who Dt 6:12
It is the **L** your God you shall fear. Him Dt 6:13
for the **L** your God in your midst is a Dt 6:15
the anger of the **L** your God be kindled Dt 6:15
"You shall not put the **L** your God to the Dt 6:16
the commandments of the **L** your God, Dt 6:17
is right and good in the sight of the **L**, Dt 6:18
the good land that the **L** swore to give to Dt 6:18
from before you, as the **L** has promised. Dt 6:19
the rules that the **L** our God has Dt 6:20
And the **L** brought us out of Egypt with a Dt 6:21
And the **L** showed signs and wonders, Dt 6:22
And the **L** commanded us to do all these Dt 6:24
all these statutes, to fear the **L** our God, Dt 6:24
commandment before the **L** our God, Dt 6:25
"When the **L** your God brings you into Dt 7:1
and when the **L** your God gives them over Dt 7:2
the anger of the **L** would be kindled Dt 7:4
you are a people holy to the **L** your God. Dt 7:6
The **L** your God has chosen you to be a Dt 7:6
any other people that the **L** set his love on Dt 7:7
but it is because the **L** loves you and is Dt 7:8
that the **L** has brought you out with a Dt 7:8
Know therefore that the **L** your God is Dt 7:9
the **L** your God will keep with you the Dt 7:12
And the **L** will take away from you all Dt 7:15
the peoples that the **L** your God will give Dt 7:16
shall remember what the **L** your God did Dt 7:18
by which the **L** your God brought you Dt 7:19
So will the **L** your God do to all the Dt 7:19
the **L** your God will send hornets among Dt 7:20
for the **L** your God is in your midst, Dt 7:21
The **L** your God will clear away these Dt 7:22
But the **L** your God will give them over to Dt 7:23
it is an abomination to the **L** your God. Dt 7:25
possess the land that the **L** swore to give to Dt 8:1
the whole way that the **L** your God has led Dt 8:2
word that comes from the mouth of the **L**. Dt 8:3
his son, the **L** your God disciplines you. Dt 8:5
the commandments of the **L** your God by Dt 8:6
For the **L** your God is bringing you into a Dt 8:7
you shall bless the **L** your God for the Dt 8:10
lest you forget the **L** your God by not Dt 8:11
lifted up, and you forget the **L** your God, Dt 8:14
You shall remember the **L** your God, for Dt 8:18
And if you forget the **L** your God and go Dt 8:19
the nations that the **L** makes to perish Dt 8:20
not obey the voice of the **L** your God. Dt 8:20
as a consuming fire is the **L** your God. Dt 9:3
perish quickly, as the **L** has promised you. Dt 9:3
after the **L** your God has thrust them out Dt 9:4
righteousness that the **L** has brought me Dt 9:4
these nations that the **L** is driving them Dt 9:4
of these nations the **L** your God is driving Dt 9:5
the word that the **L** swore to your fathers, Dt 9:5
that the **L** your God is not giving you this Dt 9:6
how you provoked the **L** your God to Dt 9:7
you have been rebellious against the **L**. Dt 9:7
at Horeb you provoked the **L** to wrath, Dt 9:8
and the **L** was so angry with you that he Dt 9:8
of the covenant that the **L** made with you, Dt 9:9
And the **L** gave me the two tablets of Dt 9:10
the words that the **L** had spoken with Dt 9:10
and forty nights the **L** gave me the two Dt 9:11
Then the **L** said to me, 'Arise, go down Dt 9:12
"Furthermore, the **L** said to me, 'I have Dt 9:13
you had sinned against the **L** your God. Dt 9:16
the way that the **L** had commanded you. Dt 9:16
I lay prostrate before the **L** as before, Dt 9:18
in the sight of the **L** to provoke him to Dt 9:18
displeasure that the **L** bore against you, Dt 9:19
But the **L** listened to me that time also. Dt 9:19
And the **L** was so angry with Aaron that Dt 9:20
you provoked the **L** to wrath. Dt 9:22
And when the **L** sent you from Dt 9:23
commandment of the **L** your God and Dt 9:23
rebellious against the **L** from the day Dt 9:24
lay prostrate before the **L** for these forty Dt 9:25
because the **L** had said he would destroy Dt 9:25
And I prayed to the **L**, 'O Lord GOD, Dt 9:26
And I prayed to the LORD, 'O **L** GOD, Dt 9:26
"Because the **L** was not able to bring Dt 9:28
"At that time the **L** said to me, 'Cut for Dt 10:1
Commandments that the **L** had spoken Dt 10:4
assembly. And the **L** gave them to me. Dt 10:4
there they are, as the **L** commanded me." Dt 10:5
At that time the **L** set apart the tribe of Dt 10:8
the covenant of the **L** to stand before the Dt 10:8
to stand before the **L** to minister to him Dt 10:8
The **L** is his inheritance, as the LORD Dt 10:9
as the **L** your God said to him.) Dt 10:9
and the **L** listened to me that time also. Dt 10:10
The **L** was unwilling to destroy you. Dt 10:10
And the **L** said to me, 'Arise, go on your Dt 10:11
what does the **L** your God require of Dt 10:12
of you, but to fear the **L** your God, Dt 10:12
to serve the **L** your God with all your Dt 10:12
commandments and statutes of the **L**, Dt 10:13
to the **L** your God belong heaven and Dt 10:14
Yet the **L** set his heart in love on your Dt 10:15
For the **L** your God is God of gods and Dt 10:17
your God is God of gods and **L** of lords, Dt 10:17
You shall fear the **L** your God. You Dt 10:20
and now the **L** your God has made you Dt 10:22
shall therefore love the **L** your God and Dt 11:1
consider the discipline of the **L** your God, Dt 11:2
and how the **L** has destroyed them to this Dt 11:4
all the great work of the **L** that he did. Dt 11:7
the land that the **L** swore to your fathers Dt 11:9
a land that the **L** your God cares for. Dt 11:12
The eyes of the **L** your God are always Dt 11:12
you today, to love the **L** your God, Dt 11:13
the anger of the **L** will be kindled Dt 11:17
the good land that the **L** is giving you. Dt 11:17
the land that the **L** swore to your fathers Dt 11:21
you to do, loving the **L** your God, Dt 11:22
then the **L** will drive out all these Dt 11:23
The **L** your God will lay the fear of you Dt 11:25
the commandments of the **L** your God, Dt 11:27
the commandments of the **L** your God, Dt 11:28
And when the **L** your God brings you Dt 11:29
of the land that the **L** your God is giving Dt 11:31
be careful to do in the land that the **L**, Dt 12:1
shall not worship the **L** your God in that Dt 12:4
the place that the **L** your God will choose Dt 12:5
there you shall eat before the **L** your God, Dt 12:7
in which the **L** your God has blessed Dt 12:7
the inheritance that the **L** your God is Dt 12:9
the land that the **L** your God is giving Dt 12:10
the place that the **L** your God will Dt 12:11
vow offerings that you vow to the **L**. Dt 12:11
you shall rejoice before the **L** your God, Dt 12:12
the place that the **L** will choose in one Dt 12:14
to the blessing of the **L** your God that he Dt 12:15
eat them before the **L** your God in the Dt 12:18
the place that the **L** your God will Dt 12:18
shall rejoice before the **L** your God in Dt 12:18
"When the **L** your God enlarges your Dt 12:20
the place that the **L** your God will Dt 12:21
your flock, which the **L** has given you, Dt 12:21
do what is right in the sight of the **L**. Dt 12:25
go to the place that the **L** will choose, Dt 12:26
blood, on the altar of the **L** your God. Dt 12:27
out on the altar of the **L** your God, Dt 12:27
and right in the sight of the **L** your God. Dt 12:28
"When the **L** your God cuts off before Dt 12:29
shall not worship the **L** your God in Dt 12:31
thing that the **L** hates they have Dt 12:31
For the **L** your God is testing you, to Dt 13:3
whether you love the **L** your God with all Dt 13:3
shall walk after the **L** your God and fear Dt 13:4
taught rebellion against the **L** your God, Dt 13:5
in which the **L** your God commanded Dt 13:5
to draw you away from the **L** your God, Dt 13:10
which the **L** your God is giving you to Dt 13:12
whole burnt offering to the **L** your God. Dt 13:16
that the **L** may turn from the fierceness Dt 13:17
if you obey the voice of the **L** your God, Dt 13:18
is right in the sight of the **L** your God. Dt 13:18
"You are the sons of the **L** your God. You Dt 14:1
you are a people holy to the **L** your God, Dt 14:2
and the **L** has chosen you to be a people Dt 14:2
you are a people holy to the **L** your God. Dt 14:21
And before the **L** your God, in the place Dt 14:23
learn to fear the **L** your God always. Dt 14:23
tithe, when the **L** your God blesses you, Dt 14:24
you, which the **L** your God chooses, Dt 14:24
to the place that the **L** your God chooses Dt 14:25
eat there before the **L** your God and Dt 14:26
that the **L** your God may bless you in Dt 14:29
for the **L** will bless you in the land that Dt 15:4
in the land that the **L** your God is giving Dt 15:4
strictly obey the voice of the **L** your God, Dt 15:5
For the **L** your God will bless you, as he Dt 15:6
your land that the **L** your God is giving Dt 15:7
nothing, and he cry to the **L** against you, Dt 15:9
because for this the **L** your God will Dt 15:10
As the **L** your God has blessed you, you Dt 15:14
and the **L** your God redeemed you; Dt 15:15
So the **L** your God will bless you in all Dt 15:18
you shall dedicate to the **L** your God. Dt 15:19
before the **L** your God year by year at Dt 15:20
year at the place that the **L** will choose. Dt 15:20
shall not sacrifice it to the **L** your God. Dt 15:21
and keep the Passover to the **L** your God, Dt 16:1
month of Abib the **L** your God brought Dt 16:1
the Passover sacrifice to the **L** your God, Dt 16:2
herd, at the place that the **L** will choose, Dt 16:2
your towns that the **L** your God is giving Dt 16:5
the place that the **L** your God will Dt 16:6
the place that the **L** your God will Dt 16:7
be a solemn assembly to the **L** your God. Dt 16:8
of Weeks to the **L** your God with the Dt 16:10
shall give as the **L** your God blesses Dt 16:10
you shall rejoice before the **L** your God, Dt 16:11
the place that the **L** your God will Dt 16:11
keep the feast to the **L** your God at the Dt 16:15
God at the place that the **L** will choose, Dt 16:15
because the **L** your God will bless you Dt 16:15
shall appear before the **L** your God at Dt 16:16
not appear before the **L** empty-handed. Dt 16:16
to the blessing of the **L** your God that he Dt 16:17
your towns that the **L** your God is Dt 16:18
the land that the **L** your God is giving Dt 16:20
the altar of the **L** your God that you Dt 16:21
up a pillar, which the **L** your God hates. Dt 16:22
not sacrifice to the **L** your God an ox Dt 17:1
is an abomination to the **L** your God. Dt 17:1
your towns that the **L** your God is giving Dt 17:2
is evil in the sight of the **L** your God, Dt 17:2
the place that the **L** your God will Dt 17:8
from that place that the **L** will choose. Dt 17:10
to minister there before the **L** your God, Dt 17:12
to the land that the **L** your God is giving Dt 17:14
over you whom the **L** your God will Dt 17:15
horses, since the **L** has said to you, Dt 17:16
learn to fear the **L** his God by keeping Dt 17:19
the **L** is their inheritance, as he promised Dt 18:2
For the **L** your God has chosen him out Dt 18:5
stand and minister in the name of the **L**, Dt 18:5
—to the place that the **L** will choose, Dt 18:6
ministers in the name of the **L** his God, Dt 18:7
who stand to minister there before the **L**, Dt 18:7
the land that the **L** your God is giving Dt 18:9
these things is an abomination to the **L**. Dt 18:12
these abominations the **L** your God is Dt 18:12
be blameless before the **L** your God, Dt 18:13
the **L** your God has not allowed you to Dt 18:14
"The **L** your God will raise up for you a Dt 18:15
you desired of the **L** your God at Horeb Dt 18:16
again the voice of the **L** my God or see Dt 18:16
And the **L** said to me, 'They are right in Dt 18:17
the word that the **L** has not spoken?' Dt 18:21
a prophet speaks in the name of the **L**, Dt 18:22
that is a word that the **L** has not spoken; Dt 18:22
"When the **L** your God cuts off the Dt 19:1
nations whose land the **L** your God is Dt 19:1
in the land that the **L** your God is giving Dt 19:2
of the land that the **L** your God gives you Dt 19:3
And if the **L** your God enlarges your Dt 19:8
by loving the **L** your God and by Dt 19:9
your land that the **L** your God is giving Dt 19:10
the land that the **L** your God is giving Dt 19:14
to the dispute shall appear before the **L**, Dt 19:17
of them, for the **L** your God is with you, Dt 20:1
for the **L** your God is he who goes with Dt 20:4
And when the **L** your God gives it into Dt 20:13
which the **L** your God has given you. Dt 20:14
these peoples that the **L** your God is Dt 20:16
as the **L** your God has commanded, Dt 20:17
and so you sin against the **L** your God. Dt 20:18
in the land that the **L** your God is giving Dt 21:1
for the **L** your God has chosen them to Dt 21:5
to him and to bless in the name of the **L**, Dt 21:5
Accept atonement, O **L**, for your people Dt 21:8
you do what is right in the sight of the **L**. Dt 21:9
and the **L** your God gives them into Dt 21:10
your land that the **L** your God is giving Dt 21:23
is an abomination to the **L** your God. Dt 22:5
cut off shall enter the assembly of the **L**. Dt 23:1
union may enter the assembly of the **L**. Dt 23:2
may enter the assembly of the **L**. Dt 23:2
may enter the assembly of the **L**. Dt 23:3
may enter the assembly of the **L** forever, Dt 23:3
But the **L** your God would not listen to Dt 23:5
instead the **L** your God turned the curse Dt 23:5
you, because the **L** your God loved you. Dt 23:5
may enter the assembly of the **L**. Dt 23:8
Because the **L** your God walks in the Dt 23:14
the house of the **L** your God in payment Dt 23:18

are an abomination to the **L** your God. Dt 23:18
that the **L** your God may bless you in Dt 23:20
"If you make a vow to the **L** your God, Dt 23:21
for the **L** your God will surely require it Dt 23:21
vowed to the **L** your God what Dt 23:23
for that is an abomination before the **L**. Dt 24:4
the land that the **L** your God is giving Dt 24:4
Remember what the **L** your God did to Dt 24:9
for you before the **L** your God. Dt 24:13
on it), lest he cry against you to the **L**, Dt 24:15
in Egypt and the **L** your God redeemed Dt 24:18
that the **L** your God may bless you in Dt 24:19
the land that the **L** your God is giving Dt 25:15
are an abomination to the **L** your God. Dt 25:16
Therefore when the **L** your God has Dt 25:19
the land that the **L** your God is giving Dt 25:19
the land that the **L** your God is giving Dt 26:1
your land that the **L** your God is giving Dt 26:2
the place that the **L** your God will Dt 26:2
'I declare today to the **L** your God that I Dt 26:3
the land that the **L** swore to our fathers Dt 26:3
down before the altar of the **L** your God. Dt 26:4
make response before the **L** your God, Dt 26:5
Then we cried to the **L**, the God of our Dt 26:7
and the **L** heard our voice and saw our Dt 26:7
And the **L** brought us out of Egypt with a Dt 26:8
the fruit of the ground, which you, O **L**, Dt 26:10
it down before the **L** your God and Dt 26:10
God and worship before the **L** your God. Dt 26:10
the good that the **L** your God has given Dt 26:11
you shall say before the **L** your God, Dt 26:13
I have obeyed the voice of the **L** my God. Dt 26:14
"This day the **L** your God commands Dt 26:16
declared today that the **L** is your God, Dt 26:17
And the **L** has declared today that you Dt 26:18
shall be a people holy to the **L** your God, Dt 26:19
to the land that the **L** your God is giving Dt 27:2
the land that the **L** your God is giving Dt 27:3
flowing with milk and honey, as the **L**, Dt 27:3
shall build an altar to the **L** your God, Dt 27:5
build an altar to the **L** your God of uncut Dt 27:6
burnt offerings on it to the **L** your God, Dt 27:6
you shall rejoice before the **L** your God. Dt 27:7
become the people of the **L** your God. Dt 27:9
obey the voice of the **L** your God, Dt 27:10
metal image, an abomination to the **L**, Dt 27:15
obey the voice of the **L** your God, Dt 28:1
the **L** your God will set you high above Dt 28:1
if you obey the voice of the **L** your God. Dt 28:2
"The **L** will cause your enemies who rise Dt 28:7
The **L** will command the blessing on Dt 28:8
in the land that the **L** your God is giving Dt 28:8
The **L** will establish you as a people holy Dt 28:9
commandments of the **L** your God and Dt 28:9
you are called by the name of the **L**, Dt 28:10
And the **L** will make you abound in Dt 28:11
the land that the **L** swore to your fathers Dt 28:11
The **L** will open to you his good Dt 28:12
And the **L** will make you the head and Dt 28:13
the commandments of the **L** your God, Dt 28:13
obey the voice of the **L** your God or be Dt 28:15
"The **L** will send on you curses, Dt 28:20
The **L** will make the pestilence stick to Dt 28:21
The **L** will strike you with wasting Dt 28:22
The **L** will make the rain of your land Dt 28:24
"The **L** will cause you to be defeated Dt 28:25
The **L** will strike you with the boils of Dt 28:27
The **L** will strike you with madness and Dt 28:28
The **L** will strike you on the knees and Dt 28:35
"The **L** will bring you and your king Dt 28:36
the peoples where the **L** will lead you Dt 28:37
not obey the voice of the **L** your God, Dt 28:45
did not serve the **L** your God with Dt 28:47
enemies whom the **L** will send against Dt 28:48
The **L** will bring a nation against you Dt 28:49
which the **L** your God has given you. Dt 28:52
whom the **L** your God has given you, Dt 28:53
and awesome name, the **L** your God, Dt 28:58
then the **L** will bring on you and your Dt 28:59
of this law, the **L** will bring upon you, Dt 28:61
not obey the voice of the **L** your God. Dt 28:62
And as the **L** took delight in doing you Dt 28:63
so the **L** will take delight in bringing Dt 28:63
"And the **L** will scatter you among all Dt 28:64
but the **L** will give you there a Dt 28:65
And the **L** will bring you back in ships Dt 28:68
covenant that the **L** commanded Moses Dt 29:1
seen all that the **L** did before your eyes Dt 29:2
But to this day the **L** has not given you a Dt 29:4
you may know that I am the **L** your God. Dt 29:6
today all of you before the **L** your God: Dt 29:10
the sworn covenant of the **L** your God, Dt 29:12
which the **L** your God is making with Dt 29:12
here with us today before the **L** our God, Dt 29:15
away today from the **L** our God to go Dt 29:18

The **L** will not be willing to forgive Dt 29:20
the anger of the **L** and his jealousy will Dt 29:20
and the **L** will blot out his name from Dt 29:20
And the **L** will single him out from all Dt 29:21
with which the **L** has made it Dt 29:22
which the **L** overthrew in his anger and Dt 29:23
'Why has the **L** done thus to this land? Dt 29:24
they abandoned the covenant of the **L**, Dt 29:25
the anger of the **L** was kindled against Dt 29:27
and the **L** uprooted them from their Dt 29:28
secret things belong to the **L** our God, Dt 29:29
the nations where the **L** your God has Dt 30:1
and return to the **L** your God, you and Dt 30:2
then the **L** your God will restore your Dt 30:3
the peoples where the **L** your God has Dt 30:3
from there the **L** your God will gather Dt 30:4
And the **L** your God will bring you into Dt 30:5
And the **L** your God will circumcise Dt 30:6
that you will love the **L** your God with all Dt 30:6
And the **L** your God will put all these Dt 30:7
obey the voice of the **L** and keep all his Dt 30:8
The **L** your God will make you Dt 30:9
For the **L** will again take delight in Dt 30:9
you obey the voice of the **L** your God, Dt 30:10
you turn to the **L** your God with all Dt 30:10
commandments of the **L** your God that Dt 30:16
you today, by loving the **L** your God, Dt 30:16
and the **L** your God will bless you in the Dt 30:16
loving the **L** your God, obeying his Dt 30:20
the land that the **L** swore to your Dt 30:20
The **L** has said to me, 'You shall not go Dt 31:2
The **L** your God himself will go over Dt 31:3
over at your head, as the **L** has spoken. Dt 31:3
And the **L** will do to them as he did to Dt 31:4
And the **L** will give them over to you, and Dt 31:5
for it is the **L** your God who goes with Dt 31:6
the land that the **L** has sworn to their Dt 31:7
It is the **L** who goes before you. He will be Dt 31:8
carried the ark of the covenant of the **L**, Dt 31:9
to appear before the **L** your God at the Dt 31:11
hear and learn to fear the **L** your God, Dt 31:12
hear and learn to fear the **L** your God, Dt 31:13
And the **L** said to Moses, "Behold, the Dt 31:14
And the **L** appeared in the tent in a Dt 31:15
And the **L** said to Moses, "Behold, you Dt 31:16
And the **L** commissioned Joshua the Dt 31:23
carried the ark of the covenant of the **L**, Dt 31:25
ark of the covenant of the **L** your God, Dt 31:26
you have been rebellious against the **L**. Dt 31:27
will do what is evil in the sight of the **L**, Dt 31:29
For I will proclaim the name of the **L**; Dt 32:3
Do you thus repay the **L**, you foolish and Dt 32:6
the **L** alone guided him, no foreign god Dt 32:12
"The **L** saw it and spurned them, Dt 32:19
it was not the **L** who did all this."' Dt 32:27
them, and the **L** had given them up? Dt 32:30
For the **L** will vindicate his people and Dt 32:36
That very day the **L** spoke to Moses, Dt 32:48
"The **L** came from Sinai and dawned Dt 33:2
Thus the **L** became king in Jeshurun, Dt 33:5
"Hear, O **L**, the voice of Judah, and bring Dt 33:7
Bless, O **L**, his substance, and accept Dt 33:11
"The beloved of the **L** dwells in safety. Dt 33:12
he said, "Blessed by the **L** be his land, Dt 33:13
Israel he executed the justice of the **L**, Dt 33:21
favor, and full of the blessing of the **L**, Dt 33:23
is like you, a people saved by the **L**, Dt 33:29
And the **L** showed him all the land, Dt 34:1
And the **L** said to him, "This is the land Dt 34:4
the servant of the **L** died there in the Dt 34:5
of Moab, according to the word of the **L**, Dt 34:5
and did as the **L** had commanded Moses. Dt 34:9
Moses, whom the **L** knew face to face, Dt 34:10
the wonders that the **L** sent him to do Dt 34:11
the death of Moses the servant of the **L**, Jos 1:1
LORD, the **L** said to Joshua the son of Nun, Jos 1:1
for the **L** your God is with you wherever Jos 1:9
of the land that the **L** your God is giving Jos 1:11
the servant of the **L** commanded you, Jos 1:13
'The **L** your God is providing you a Jos 1:13
until the **L** gives rest to your brothers as Jos 1:15
of the land that the **L** your God is giving Jos 1:15
the servant of the **L** gave you beyond the Jos 1:15
Only may the **L** your God be with you, Jos 1:17
"I know that the **L** has given you the land, Jos 2:9
have heard how the **L** dried up the water Jos 2:10
man because of you, for the **L** your God, Jos 2:11
then, please swear to me by the **L** that, Jos 2:12
then when the **L** gives us the land we Jos 2:14
"Truly the **L** has given all the land into Jos 2:24
the covenant of the **L** your God being Jos 3:3
for tomorrow the **L** will do wonders Jos 3:5
The **L** said to Joshua, "Today I will begin Jos 3:7
and listen to the words of the **L** your God." Jos 3:9
of the covenant of the **L** of all the earth is Jos 3:11

of the priests bearing the ark of the **L**, Jos 3:13
the ark of the LORD, the **L** of all the earth, Jos 3:13
the covenant of the **L** stood firmly on Jos 3:17
over the Jordan, the **L** said to Joshua, Jos 4:1
before the ark of the **L** your God into the Jos 4:5
off before the ark of the covenant of the **L**. Jos 4:7
people of Israel, just as the **L** told Joshua. Jos 4:8
finished that the **L** commanded Joshua Jos 4:10
the ark of the **L** and the priests passed Jos 4:11
war passed over before the **L** for battle, Jos 4:13
On that day the **L** exalted Joshua in the Jos 4:14
And the **L** said to Joshua, Jos 4:15
the covenant of the **L** came up from the Jos 4:18
For the **L** your God dried up the waters Jos 4:23
as the **L** your God did to the Red Sea, Jos 4:23
know that the hand of the **L** is mighty, Jos 4:24
you may fear the **L** your God forever." Jos 4:24
heard that the **L** had dried up the waters Jos 5:1
At that time the **L** said to Joshua, "Make Jos 5:2
they did not obey the voice of the **L**; Jos 5:6
the **L** swore to them that he would not let Jos 5:6
see the land that the **L** had sworn to their Jos 5:6
And the **L** said to Joshua, "Today I have Jos 5:9
am the commander of the army of the **L**. Jos 5:14
"What does my **l** say to his servant?" Jos 5:14
And the **L** said to Joshua, "See, I have Jos 6:2
of rams' horns before the ark of the **L**." Jos 6:6
men pass on before the ark of the **L**." Jos 6:7
of rams' horns before the **L** went forward, Jos 6:8
of the covenant of the **L** following them. Jos 6:8
caused the ark of the **L** to circle the city, Jos 6:11
and the priests took up the ark of the **L**. Jos 6:12
horns before the ark of the **L** walked on, Jos 6:13
guard was walking after the ark of the **L**, Jos 6:13
"Shout, for the **L** has given you the city. Jos 6:16
shall be devoted to the **L** for destruction. Jos 6:17
of bronze and iron, are holy to the **L**; Jos 6:19
they shall go into the treasury of the **L**." Jos 6:19
into the treasury of the house of the **L**. Jos 6:24
"Cursed before the **L** be the man who Jos 6:26
So the **L** was with Joshua, and his fame Jos 6:27
the anger of the **L** burned against the Jos 7:1
before the ark of the **L** until the evening, Jos 7:6
And Joshua said, "Alas, O **L** GOD, why Jos 7:7
O **L**, what can I say, when Israel has Jos 7:8
The **L** said to Joshua, "Get up! Why Jos 7:10
for thus says the **L**, God of Israel, "There Jos 7:13
the tribe that the **L** takes by lot shall Jos 7:14
the clan that the **L** takes shall come Jos 7:14
household that the **L** takes shall come Jos 7:14
has transgressed the covenant of the **L**, Jos 7:15
give glory to the **L** God of Israel and give Jos 7:19
I have sinned against the **L** God of Israel, Jos 7:20
And they laid them down before the **L**. Jos 7:23
The **L** brings trouble on you today." Jos 7:25
Then the **L** turned from his burning Jos 7:26
And the **L** said to Joshua, "Do not fear and Jos 8:1
for the **L** your God will give it into your Jos 8:7
shall do according to the word of the **L**. Jos 8:8
Then the **L** said to Joshua, "Stretch out Jos 8:18
the word of the **L** that he commanded Jos 8:27
that time Joshua built an altar to the **L**, Jos 8:30
the servant of the **L** had commanded the Jos 8:31
offerings to the **L** and sacrificed peace Jos 8:31
carried the ark of the covenant of the **L**, Jos 8:33
the servant of the **L** had commanded at Jos 8:33
because of the name of the **L** your God. Jos 9:9
but did not ask counsel from the **L**. Jos 9:14
had sworn to them by the **L**, Jos 9:18
"We have sworn to them by the **L**, Jos 9:19
a certainty that the **L** your God had Jos 9:24
congregation and for the altar of the **L**, Jos 9:27
And the **L** said to Joshua, "Do not fear Jos 10:8
And the **L** threw them into a panic Jos 10:10
the **L** threw down large stones from Jos 10:11
Joshua spoke to the **L** in the day when Jos 10:12
the day when the **L** gave the Amorites Jos 10:12
when the **L** obeyed the voice of a man, Jos 10:14
of a man, for the **L** fought for Israel. Jos 10:14
for the **L** your God has given them into Jos 10:19
For thus the **L** will do to all your Jos 10:25
And the **L** gave it also and its king into Jos 10:30
And the **L** gave Lachish into the hand Jos 10:32
just as the **L** God of Israel commanded. Jos 10:40
because the **L** God of Israel fought for Jos 10:42
And the **L** said to Joshua, "Do not be Jos 11:6
And the **L** gave them into the hand of Jos 11:8
did to them just as the **L** said to him: Jos 11:9
the servant of the **L** had commanded. Jos 11:12
Just as the **L** had commanded Moses Jos 11:15
all that the **L** had commanded Moses. Jos 11:15
just as the **L** commanded Moses. Jos 11:20
to all that the **L** had spoken to Moses. Jos 11:23
Moses, the servant of the **L**, and the Jos 12:6
the servant of the **L** gave their land for Jos 12:6

in years, and the **L** said to him, Jos 13:1
as Moses the servant of the **L** gave them: Jos 13:8
by fire to the **L** God of Israel are Jos 13:14
the **L** God of Israel is their inheritance, Jos 13:33
just as the **L** had commanded by the Jos 14:2
of Israel did as the **L** commanded Moses; Jos 14:5
"You know what the **L** said to Moses the Jos 14:6
the servant of the **L** sent me from Jos 14:7
melt; yet I wholly followed the **L** my God. Jos 14:8
you have wholly followed the **L** my God.' Jos 14:9
now, behold, the **L** has kept me alive, Jos 14:10
the time that the **L** spoke this word to Jos 14:10
country of which the **L** spoke on that Jos 14:12
It may be that the **L** will be with me, Jos 14:12
shall drive them out just as the **L** said." Jos 14:12
day, because he wholly followed the **L**, Jos 14:14
the commandment of the **L** to Joshua, Jos 15:13
"The **L** commanded Moses to give us an Jos 17:4
to the mouth of the **L** he gave them an Jos 17:4
since all along the **L** has blessed me?" Jos 17:14
take possession of the land, which the **L**, Jos 18:3
lots for you here before the **L** our God. Jos 18:6
the priesthood of the **L** is their heritage. Jos 18:7
Moses the servant of the **L** gave them." Jos 18:7
lots for you here before the **L** in Shiloh." Jos 18:8
lots for them in Shiloh before the **L**. Jos 18:10
By command of the **L** they gave him Jos 19:50
by lot at Shiloh before the **L**, Jos 19:51
Then the **L** said to Joshua, Jos 20:1
"The **L** commanded through Moses that Jos 21:2
by command of the **L** the people of Israel Jos 21:3
as the **L** had commanded through Jos 21:8
Thus the **L** gave to Israel all the land Jos 21:43
And the **L** gave them rest on every side Jos 21:44
for the **L** had given all their enemies Jos 21:44
good promises that the **L** had made to Jos 21:45
servant of the **L** commanded you and Jos 22:2
to keep the charge of the **L** your God. Jos 22:3
And now the **L** your God has given rest Jos 22:4
the servant of the **L** gave you on the Jos 22:4
the servant of the **L** commanded you, Jos 22:5
commanded you, to love the **L** your God, Jos 22:5
by command of the **L** through Moses. Jos 22:9
says the whole congregation of the **L**, Jos 22:16
from following the **L** by building Jos 22:16
this day in rebellion against the **L**? Jos 22:16
plague upon the congregation of the **L**, Jos 22:17
away this day from following the **L**? Jos 22:18
rebel against the **L** today then Jos 22:18
not rebel against the **L** or make us as Jos 22:19
other than the altar of the **L** our God. Jos 22:19
"The Mighty One, God, the **L**! The Jos 22:22
the LORD! The Mighty One, God, the **L**! Jos 22:22
or in breach of faith against the **L**, Jos 22:22
to turn away from following the **L**. Jos 22:23
it, may the **L** himself take vengeance. Jos 22:23
'What have you to do with the **L**, Jos 22:24
For the **L** has made the Jordan a Jos 22:25
of Gad. You have no portion in the **L**.' Jos 22:25
our children cease to worship the **L**. Jos 22:25
the service of the **L** in his presence with Jos 22:27
come, "You have no portion in the **L**."' Jos 22:27
'Behold, the copy of the altar of the **L**, Jos 22:28
rebel against the **L** and turn away Jos 22:29
from following the **L** by building an Jos 22:29
the altar of the **L** our God that stands Jos 22:29
we know that the **L** is in our midst, Jos 22:31
this breach of faith against the **L**. Jos 22:31
people of Israel from the hand of the **L**." Jos 22:31
a witness between us that the **L** is God." Jos 22:34
when the **L** had given rest to Israel from Jos 23:1
seen all that the **L** your God has done Jos 23:3
for it is the **L** your God who has fought Jos 23:3
The **L** your God will push them back Jos 23:5
just as the **L** your God promised you. Jos 23:5
you shall cling to the **L** your God just as Jos 23:8
For the **L** has driven out before you Jos 23:9
since it is the **L** your God who fights for Jos 23:10
therefore, to love the **L** your God. Jos 23:11
for certain that the **L** your God will no Jos 23:13
good ground that the **L** your God has Jos 23:13
things that the **L** your God promised Jos 23:14
things that the **L** your God promised Jos 23:15
so the **L** will bring upon you all the evil Jos 23:15
good land that the **L** your God has Jos 23:15
the covenant of the **L** your God, Jos 23:16
the anger of the **L** will be kindled Jos 23:16
said to all the people, "Thus says the **L**, Jos 24:2
And when they cried to the **L**, he put Jos 24:7
therefore fear the **L** and serve him Jos 24:14
the River and in Egypt, and serve the **L**. Jos 24:14
if it is evil in your eyes to serve the **L**, Jos 24:15
me and my house, we will serve the **L**." Jos 24:15
we should forsake the **L** to serve other Jos 24:16
for it is the **L** our God who brought us Jos 24:17
And the **L** drove out before us all the Jos 24:18
Therefore we also will serve the **L**, for Jos 24:18
people, "You are not able to serve the **L**, Jos 24:19
If you forsake the **L** and serve foreign Jos 24:20
to Joshua, "No, but we will serve the **L**." Jos 24:21
yourselves that you have chosen the **L**, Jos 24:22
you, and incline your heart to the **L**, Jos 24:23
Joshua, "The **L** our God we will serve, Jos 24:24
that was by the sanctuary of the **L**. Jos 24:26
all the words of the **L** that he spoke to Jos 24:27
the son of Nun, the servant of the **L**, Jos 24:29
Israel served the **L** all the days of Jos 24:31
all the work that the **L** did for Israel. Jos 24:31
the people of Israel inquired of the **L**, Jgs 1:1
The **L** said, "Judah shall go up; behold, I Jgs 1:2
went up and the **L** gave the Canaanites Jgs 1:4
And the **L** was with Judah, and he took Jgs 1:19
against Bethel, and the **L** was with them. Jgs 1:22
the angel of the **L** went up from Gilgal Jgs 2:1
as the angel of the **L** spoke these words to Jgs 2:4
And they sacrificed there to the **L**. Jgs 2:5
And the people served the **L** all the days of Jgs 2:7
great work that the **L** had done for Israel. Jgs 2:7
the son of Nun, the servant of the **L**, Jgs 2:8
who did not know the **L** or the work that Jgs 2:10
in the sight of the **L** and served the Baals. Jgs 2:11
And they abandoned the **L**, the God of Jgs 2:12
them. And they provoked the **L** to anger. Jgs 2:12
They abandoned the **L** and served the Jgs 2:13
the anger of the **L** was kindled against Jgs 2:14
the hand of the **L** was against them for Jgs 2:15
them for harm, as the **L** had warned, Jgs 2:15
warned, and as the **L** had sworn to them. Jgs 2:15
Then the **L** raised up judges, who saved Jgs 2:16
obeyed the commandments of the **L**, Jgs 2:17
Whenever the **L** raised up judges for Jgs 2:18
for them, the **L** was with the judge, Jgs 2:18
For the **L** was moved to pity by their Jgs 2:18
the anger of the **L** was kindled against Jgs 2:20
in the way of the **L** as their fathers did, Jgs 2:22
So the **L** left those nations, not driving Jgs 2:23
Now these are the nations that the **L** left, Jgs 3:1
would obey the commandments of the **L**, Jgs 3:4
did what was evil in the sight of the **L**. Jgs 3:7
They forgot the **L** their God and served Jgs 3:7
the anger of the **L** was kindled against Jgs 3:8
the people of Israel cried out to the **L**, Jgs 3:9
the **L** raised up a deliverer for the people of Jgs 3:9
The Spirit of the **L** was upon him, and Jgs 3:10
and the **L** gave Cushan-rishathaim Jgs 3:10
did what was evil in the sight of the **L**, Jgs 3:12
and the **L** strengthened Eglon the king Jgs 3:12
done what was evil in the sight of the **L**. Jgs 3:12
the people of Israel cried out to the **L**, Jgs 3:15
and the **L** raised up for them a deliverer, Jgs 3:15
and there lay their **l** dead on the floor. Jgs 3:25
for the **L** has given your enemies the Jgs 3:28
evil in the sight of the **L** after Ehud died. Jgs 4:1
And the **L** sold them into the hand of Jgs 4:2
people of Israel cried out to the **L** for help, Jgs 4:3
and said to him, "Has not the **L**, Jgs 4:6
for the **L** will sell Sisera into the hand of a Jgs 4:9
day in which the **L** has given Sisera into Jgs 4:14
Does not the **L** go out before you?" So Jgs 4:14
And the **L** routed Sisera and all his Jgs 4:15
and said to him, "Turn aside, my **l**; Jgs 4:18
offered themselves willingly, bless the **L**! Jgs 5:2
give ear, O princes; to the **L** I will sing; Jgs 5:3
I will make melody to the **L**, the God of Jgs 5:3
"**L**, when you went out from Seir, when Jgs 5:4
The mountains quaked before the **L**, even Jgs 5:5
before the LORD, even Sinai before the **L**, Jgs 5:5
willingly among the people. Bless the **L**. Jgs 5:9
repeat the righteous triumphs of the **L**, Jgs 5:11
to the gates marched the people of the **L**. Jgs 5:11
the people of the **L** marched down for me Jgs 5:13
"Curse Meroz, says the angel of the **L**, Jgs 5:23
they did not come to the help of the **L**, Jgs 5:23
to the help of the **L** against the mighty. Jgs 5:23
"So may all your enemies perish, O **L**! Jgs 5:31
did what was evil in the sight of the **L**, Jgs 6:1
and the **L** gave them into the hand of Jgs 6:1
people of Israel cried out for help to the **L**. Jgs 6:6
Israel cried out to the **L** on account of the Jgs 6:7
the **L** sent a prophet to the people of Israel. Jgs 6:8
And he said to them, "Thus says the **L**, Jgs 6:8
And I said to you, 'I am the **L** your God; Jgs 6:10
the angel of the **L** came and sat under Jgs 6:11
the angel of the **L** appeared to him and Jgs 6:12
him and said to him, "The **L** is with you, Jgs 6:12
to him, "Please, sir, if the **L** is with us, Jgs 6:13
'Did not the **L** bring us up from Egypt?' Jgs 6:13
But now the **L** has forsaken us and Jgs 6:13
And the **L** turned to him and said, "Go Jgs 6:14
to him, "Please, **L**, how can I save Israel? Jgs 6:15
And the **L** said to him, "But I will be Jgs 6:16
the angel of the **L** reached out the tip Jgs 6:21
the angel of the **L** vanished from his Jgs 6:21
perceived that he was the angel of the **L**. Jgs 6:22
LORD. And Gideon said, "Alas, O **L** GOD! Jgs 6:22
have seen the angel of the **L** face to face." Jgs 6:22
But the **L** said to him, "Peace be to you. Jgs 6:23
built an altar there to the **L** and called it, Jgs 6:24
to the LORD and called it, The **L** is Peace. Jgs 6:24
That night the **L** said to him, "Take Jgs 6:25
build an altar to the **L** your God on the Jgs 6:26
servants and did as the **L** had told him. Jgs 6:27
But the Spirit of the **L** clothed Gideon, Jgs 6:34
The **L** said to Gideon, "The people with Jgs 7:2
And the **L** said to Gideon, "The people are Jgs 7:4
And the **L** said to Gideon, "Every one who Jgs 7:5
And the **L** said to Gideon, "With the 300 Jgs 7:7
That same night the **L** said to him, Jgs 7:9
for the **L** has given the host of Midian Jgs 7:15
and shout, 'For the **L** and for Gideon.'" Jgs 7:18
out, "A sword for the **L** and for Gideon!" Jgs 7:20
the **L** set every man's sword against his Jgs 7:22
when the **L** has given Zebah and Jgs 8:7
As the **L** lives, if you had saved them Jgs 8:19
rule over you; the **L** will rule over you." Jgs 8:23
Israel did not remember the **L** their God, Jgs 8:34
in the sight of the **L** and served the Baals Jgs 10:6
And they forsook the **L** and did not serve Jgs 10:6
the anger of the **L** was kindled against Jgs 10:7
the people of Israel cried out to the **L**, Jgs 10:10
And the **L** said to the people of Israel, Jgs 10:11
And the people of Israel said to the **L**, Jgs 10:15
from among them and served the **L**, Jgs 10:16
and the **L** gives them over to me, Jgs 11:9
"The **L** will be witness between us, Jgs 11:10
all his words before the **L** at Mizpah. Jgs 11:11
And the **L**, the God of Israel, gave Sihon Jgs 11:21
So then the **L**, the God of Israel, Jgs 11:23
And all that the **L** our God has Jgs 11:24
wrong by making war on me. The **L**, Jgs 11:27
the Spirit of the **L** was upon Jephthah, Jgs 11:29
Jephthah made a vow to the **L** and said, Jgs 11:30
and the **L** gave them into his hand. Jgs 11:32
For I have opened my mouth to the **L**, Jgs 11:35
you have opened your mouth to the **L**; Jgs 11:36
now that the **L** has avenged you on Jgs 11:36
and the **L** gave them into my hand. Jgs 12:3
did what was evil in the sight of the **L**, Jgs 13:1
so the **L** gave them into the hand of the Jgs 13:1
the angel of the **L** appeared to the Jgs 13:3
Then Manoah prayed to the **L** and said, Jgs 13:8
prayed to the LORD and said, "O **L**, Jgs 13:8
And the angel of the **L** said to Manoah, Jgs 13:13
Manoah said to the angel of the **L**, Jgs 13:15
And the angel of the **L** said to Manoah, Jgs 13:16
offer it to the **L**." (For Manoah did not Jgs 13:16
know that he was the angel of the **L**.) Jgs 13:16
And Manoah said to the angel of the **L**, Jgs 13:17
And the angel of the **L** said to him, Jgs 13:18
and offered it on the rock to the **L**, Jgs 13:19
the angel of the **L** went up in the flame Jgs 13:20
The angel of the **L** appeared no more to Jgs 13:21
knew that he was the angel of the **L**. Jgs 13:21
to him, "If the **L** had meant to kill us, Jgs 13:23
man grew, and the **L** blessed him. Jgs 13:24
the Spirit of the **L** began to stir him Jgs 13:25
did not know that it was from the **L**, Jgs 14:4
the Spirit of the **L** rushed upon him, Jgs 14:6
the Spirit of the **L** rushed upon him, Jgs 14:19
the Spirit of the **L** rushed upon him, Jgs 15:14
and he called upon the **L** and said, Jgs 15:18
did not know that the **L** had left him. Jgs 16:20
Then Samson called to the **L** and said, Jgs 16:28
called to the LORD and said, "O **L** GOD, Jgs 16:28
said, "Blessed be my son by the **L**." Jgs 17:2
the silver to the **L** from my hand for Jgs 17:3
I know that the **L** will prosper me, Jgs 17:13
which you go is under the eye of the **L**." Jgs 18:6
and I am going to the house of the **L**, Jgs 19:18
as one man to the **L** at Mizpah. Jgs 20:1
people of Benjamin?" And the **L** said, Jgs 20:18
and wept before the **L** until the evening. Jgs 20:23
And they inquired of the **L**, "Shall we Jgs 20:23
people of Benjamin?" And the **L** said, Jgs 20:23
sat there before the **L** and fasted that Jgs 20:26
and peace offerings before the **L**. Jgs 20:26
Israel inquired of the **L** (for the ark of Jgs 20:27
or shall we cease?" And the **L** said, Jgs 20:28
And the **L** defeated Benjamin before Jgs 20:35
And they said, "O **L**, the God of Israel, Jgs 21:3
the assembly to the **L**?" For they had Jgs 21:5
who did not come up to the **L** to Mizpah, Jgs 21:5
we have sworn by the **L** that we will not Jgs 21:7
come up to the **L** to Mizpah?" And Jgs 21:8
Benjamin because the **L** had made a Jgs 21:15

is the yearly feast of the **L** at Shiloh, Jgs 21:19
of Moab that the **L** had visited his people Ru 1:6
May the **L** deal kindly with you, as you Ru 1:8
The **L** grant that you may find rest, each Ru 1:9
the hand of the **L** has gone out against Ru 1:13
May the **L** do so to me and more also if Ru 1:17
and the **L** has brought me back empty. Ru 1:21
when the **L** has testified against me and Ru 1:21
"The **L** be with you!" And they answered, Ru 2:4
And they answered, "The **L** bless you." Ru 2:4
The **L** repay you for what you have Ru 2:12
and a full reward be given you by the **L**, Ru 2:12
"I have found favor in your eyes, my **l**, Ru 2:13
"May he be blessed by the **L**, Ru 2:20
he said, "May you be blessed by the **L**, Ru 3:10
to redeem you, then, as the **L** lives, Ru 3:13
May the **L** make the woman, who is Ru 4:11
the offspring that the **L** will give you by Ru 4:12
in to her, and the **L** gave her conception, Ru 4:13
women said to Naomi, "Blessed be the **L**, Ru 4:14
to sacrifice to the **L** of hosts at Shiloh, 1 Sm 1:3
and Phinehas, were priests of the **L**. 1 Sm 1:3
though the **L** had closed her womb. 1 Sm 1:5
because the **L** had closed her womb. 1 Sm 1:6
as she went up to the house of the **L**, 1 Sm 1:7
the doorpost of the temple of the **L**. 1 Sm 1:9
and prayed to the **L** and wept bitterly. 1 Sm 1:10
vowed a vow and said, "O **L** of hosts, 1 Sm 1:11
will give him to the **L** all the days of 1 Sm 1:11
she continued praying before the **L**, 1 Sm 1:12
But Hannah answered, "No, my **l**, I 1 Sm 1:15
pouring out my soul before the **L**. 1 Sm 1:15
morning and worshiped before the **L**; 1 Sm 1:19
his wife, and the **L** remembered her. 1 Sm 1:19
"I have asked for him from the **L**." 1 Sm 1:20
to offer to the **L** the yearly sacrifice 1 Sm 1:21
the presence of the **L** and dwell there 1 Sm 1:22
may the **L** establish his word." So the 1 Sm 1:23
him to the house of the **L** at Shiloh. 1 Sm 1:24
And she said, "Oh, my **l**! As you live, 1 Sm 1:26
As you live, my **l**, I am the woman 1 Sm 1:26
in your presence, praying to the **L**. 1 Sm 1:26
and the **L** has granted me my petition 1 Sm 1:27
Therefore I have lent him to the **L**. As 1 Sm 1:28
is lent to the **L**." And he worshiped the 1 Sm 1:28
LORD." And he worshiped the **L** there. 1 Sm 1:28
and said, "My heart exults in the **L**; 1 Sm 2:1
LORD; my strength is exalted in the **L**. 1 Sm 2:1
"There is none holy like the **L**; there is 1 Sm 2:2
for the **L** is a God of knowledge, and by 1 Sm 2:3
The **L** kills and brings to life; he brings 1 Sm 2:6
The **L** makes poor and makes rich; he 1 Sm 2:7
adversaries of the **L** shall be broken 1 Sm 2:10
The **L** will judge the ends of the earth; 1 Sm 2:10
ministered to the **L** in the presence 1 Sm 2:11
men. They did not know the **L**. 1 Sm 2:12
was very great in the sight of the **L**, 1 Sm 2:17
the offering of the **L** with contempt. 1 Sm 2:17
Samuel was ministering before the **L**, 1 Sm 2:18
"May the **L** give you children by this 1 Sm 2:20
she asked of the **L**." So then they 1 Sm 2:20
Indeed the **L** visited Hannah, and she 1 Sm 2:21
Samuel grew in the presence of the **L**. 1 Sm 2:21
the people of the **L** spreading abroad. 1 Sm 2:24
but if someone sins against the **L**, 1 Sm 2:25
was the will of the **L** to put them to 1 Sm 2:25
in favor with the **L** and also with 1 Sm 2:26
and said to him, "Thus the **L** has said, 1 Sm 2:27
Therefore the **L** the God of Israel 1 Sm 2:30
me forever,' but now the **L** declares: 1 Sm 2:30
was ministering to the **L** under Eli. 1 Sm 3:1
And the word of the **L** was rare in those 1 Sm 3:1
was lying down in the temple of the **L**, 1 Sm 3:3
Then the **L** called Samuel, and he said, 1 Sm 3:4
And the **L** called again, "Samuel!" and 1 Sm 3:6
Now Samuel did not yet know the **L**, 1 Sm 3:7
and the word of the **L** had not yet been 1 Sm 3:7
And the **L** called Samuel again the 1 Sm 3:8
Eli perceived that the **L** was calling the 1 Sm 3:8
L, for your servant hears.'" So Samuel 1 Sm 3:9
And the **L** came and stood, calling as 1 Sm 3:10
Then the **L** said to Samuel, "Behold, I 1 Sm 3:11
opened the doors of the house of the **L**. 1 Sm 3:15
from him. And he said, "It is the **L**. 1 Sm 3:18
and the **L** was with him and let none 1 Sm 3:19
was established as a prophet of the **L**. 1 Sm 3:20
And the **L** appeared again at Shiloh, 1 Sm 3:21
for the **L** revealed himself to Samuel 1 Sm 3:21
Samuel at Shiloh by the word of the **L**. 1 Sm 3:21
"Why has the **L** defeated us today 1 Sm 4:3
the covenant of the **L** here from Shiloh, 1 Sm 4:3
ark of the covenant of the **L** of hosts, 1 Sm 4:4
the covenant of the **L** came into the 1 Sm 4:5
that the ark of the **L** had come to the 1 Sm 4:6
on the ground before the ark of the **L**. 1 Sm 5:3
on the ground before the ark of the **L**, 1 Sm 5:4
The hand of the **L** was heavy against 1 Sm 5:6
the hand of the **L** was against the city, 1 Sm 5:9
The ark of the **L** was in the country of 1 Sm 6:1
shall we do with the ark of the **L**? 1 Sm 6:2
take the ark of the **L** and place it on the 1 Sm 6:8
put the ark of the **L** on the cart and 1 Sm 6:11
the cows as a burnt offering to the **L**. 1 Sm 6:14
down the ark of the **L** and the box that 1 Sm 6:15
sacrifices on that day to the **L**. 1 Sm 6:15
returned as a guilt offering to the **L**: 1 Sm 6:17
down the ark of the **L** is a witness to 1 Sm 6:18
they looked upon the ark of the **L**. 1 Sm 6:19
mourned because the **L** had struck 1 Sm 6:19
"Who is able to stand before the **L**, 1 Sm 6:20
have returned the ark of the **L**. 1 Sm 6:21
up the ark of the **L** and brought it to 1 Sm 7:1
to have charge of the ark of the **L**. 1 Sm 7:1
the house of Israel lamented after the **L**. 1 Sm 7:2
are returning to the **L** with all your 1 Sm 7:3
your heart to the **L** and serve him only, 1 Sm 7:3
Ashtaroth, and they served the **L** only. 1 Sm 7:4
and I will pray to the **L** for you." 1 Sm 7:5
it out before the **L** and fasted on that 1 Sm 7:6
sinned against the **L**." And Samuel 1 Sm 7:6
cease to cry out to the **L** our God for us, 1 Sm 7:8
it as a whole burnt offering to the **L**. 1 Sm 7:9
Samuel cried out to the **L** for Israel, 1 Sm 7:9
for Israel, and the **L** answered him. 1 Sm 7:9
But the **L** thundered with a mighty 1 Sm 7:10
said, "Till now the **L** has helped us." 1 Sm 7:12
the hand of the **L** was against the 1 Sm 7:13
And he built there an altar to the **L**. 1 Sm 7:17
judge us." And Samuel prayed to the **L**. 1 Sm 8:6
And the **L** said to Samuel, "Obey the 1 Sm 8:7
the words of the **L** to the people who 1 Sm 8:10
but the **L** will not answer you in that 1 Sm 8:18
he repeated them in the ears of the **L**. 1 Sm 8:21
And the **L** said to Samuel, "Obey their 1 Sm 8:22
came, the **L** had revealed to Samuel: 1 Sm 9:15
Samuel saw Saul, the **L** told him, 1 Sm 9:17
"Has not the **L** anointed you to be 1 Sm 10:1
the people of the **L** and you will save 1 Sm 10:1
to you that the **L** has anointed you to 1 Sm 10:1
the Spirit of the **L** will rush upon you, 1 Sm 10:6
people together to the **L** at Mizpah. 1 Sm 10:17
the people of Israel, "Thus says the **L**, 1 Sm 10:18
yourselves before the **L** by your 1 Sm 10:19
So they inquired again of the **L**, "Is 1 Sm 10:22
a man still to come?" and the **L** said, 1 Sm 10:22
see him whom the **L** has chosen? 1 Sm 10:24
in a book and laid it up before the **L**. 1 Sm 10:25
the dread of the **L** fell upon the people, 1 Sm 11:7
for today the **L** has worked salvation 1 Sm 11:13
Saul king before the **L** in Gilgal. 1 Sm 11:15
peace offerings before the **L**, 1 Sm 11:15
against me before the **L** and before his 1 Sm 12:3
them, "The **L** is witness against you, 1 Sm 12:5
said to the people, "The **L** is witness, 1 Sm 12:6
you before the **L** concerning all the 1 Sm 12:7
deeds of the **L** that he performed 1 Sm 12:7
cried out to the **L** and the LORD sent 1 Sm 12:8
the LORD and the **L** sent Moses and 1 Sm 12:8
But they forgot the **L** their God. And 1 Sm 12:9
And they cried out to the **L** and said, 1 Sm 12:10
have forsaken the **L** and have served 1 Sm 12:10
And the **L** sent Jerubbaal and Barak 1 Sm 12:11
when the **L** your God was your king. 1 Sm 12:12
behold, the **L** has set a king over you. 1 Sm 12:13
you will fear the **L** and serve him 1 Sm 12:14
against the commandment of the **L**, 1 Sm 12:14
over you will follow the **L** your God, 1 Sm 12:14
you will not obey the voice of the **L**, 1 Sm 12:15
against the commandment of the **L**, 1 Sm 12:15
the hand of the **L** will be against you 1 Sm 12:15
great thing that the **L** will do before 1 Sm 12:16
I will call upon the **L**, that he may 1 Sm 12:17
you have done in the sight of the **L**, 1 Sm 12:17
So Samuel called upon the **L**, and the 1 Sm 12:18
and the **L** sent thunder and rain that 1 Sm 12:18
greatly feared the **L** and Samuel. 1 Sm 12:18
for your servants to the **L** your God, 1 Sm 12:19
not turn aside from following the **L**, 1 Sm 12:20
but serve the **L** with all your heart. 1 Sm 12:20
For the **L** will not forsake his people, 1 Sm 12:22
it has pleased the **L** to make you a 1 Sm 12:22
sin against the **L** by ceasing to 1 Sm 12:23
Only fear the **L** and serve him 1 Sm 12:24
I have not sought the favor of the **L**.' 1 Sm 13:12
the command of the **L** your God, 1 Sm 13:13
For then the **L** would have 1 Sm 13:13
The **L** has sought out a man after 1 Sm 13:14
and the **L** has commanded him to be 1 Sm 13:14
kept what the **L** commanded you." 1 Sm 13:14
son of Eli, the priest of the **L** in Shiloh, 1 Sm 14:3
It may be that the **L** will work for us, 1 Sm 14:6
can hinder the **L** from saving by 1 Sm 14:6
for the **L** has given them into our 1 Sm 14:10
for the **L** has given them into the 1 Sm 14:12
So the **L** saved Israel that day. And 1 Sm 14:23
sinning against the **L** by eating with 1 Sm 14:33
not sin against the **L** by eating with 1 Sm 14:34
And Saul built an altar to the **L**; it 1 Sm 14:35
the first altar that he built to the **L**. 1 Sm 14:35
For as the **L** lives who saves Israel, 1 Sm 14:39
Saul said, "O **L** God of Israel, 1 Sm 14:41
is in me or in Jonathan my son, O **L**, 1 Sm 14:41
As the **L** lives, there shall not one 1 Sm 14:45
"The **L** sent me to anoint you king 1 Sm 15:1
therefore listen to the words of the **L**. 1 Sm 15:1
Thus says the **L** of hosts, 'I have noted 1 Sm 15:2
The word of the **L** came to Samuel: 1 Sm 15:10
angry, and he cried to the **L** all night. 1 Sm 15:11
said to him, "Blessed be you to the **L**. 1 Sm 15:13
the commandment of the **L**." 1 Sm 15:13
oxen to sacrifice to the **L** your God, 1 Sm 15:15
tell you what the **L** said to me this 1 Sm 15:16
The **L** anointed you king over Israel. 1 Sm 15:17
And the **L** sent you on a mission and 1 Sm 15:18
did you not obey the voice of the **L**? 1 Sm 15:19
what was evil in the sight of the **L**?" 1 Sm 15:19
"I have obeyed the voice of the **L**. 1 Sm 15:20
the mission on which the **L** sent me. 1 Sm 15:20
to sacrifice to the **L** your God in 1 Sm 15:21
"Has the **L** as great delight in burnt 1 Sm 15:22
as in obeying the voice of the **L**? 1 Sm 15:22
you have rejected the word of the **L**, 1 Sm 15:23
commandment of the **L** and your 1 Sm 15:24
with me that I may worship the **L**." 1 Sm 15:25
you have rejected the word of the **L**, 1 Sm 15:26
and the **L** has rejected you from 1 Sm 15:26
"The **L** has torn the kingdom of 1 Sm 15:28
I may bow before the **L** your God." 1 Sm 15:30
Saul, and Saul bowed before the **L**. 1 Sm 15:31
Agag to pieces before the **L** in Gilgal. 1 Sm 15:33
And the **L** regretted that he had made 1 Sm 15:35
The **L** said to Samuel, "How long will 1 Sm 16:1
it, he will kill me." And the **L** said, 1 Sm 16:2
say, 'I have come to sacrifice to the **L**.' 1 Sm 16:2
did what the **L** commanded and came 1 Sm 16:4
I have come to sacrifice to the **L**. 1 Sm 16:5
But the **L** said to Samuel, "Do not look 1 Sm 16:7
For the **L** sees not as man sees: man 1 Sm 16:7
but the **L** looks on the heart." 1 Sm 16:7
"Neither has the **L** chosen this one." 1 Sm 16:8
"Neither has the **L** chosen this one." 1 Sm 16:9
Jesse, "The **L** has not chosen these." 1 Sm 16:10
And the **L** said, "Arise, anoint him, 1 Sm 16:12
the Spirit of the **L** rushed upon David 1 Sm 16:13
Spirit of the **L** departed from Saul, 1 Sm 16:14
evil spirit from the **L** tormented him. 1 Sm 16:14
Let our **l** now command your 1 Sm 16:16
presence, and the **L** is with him." 1 Sm 16:18
"The **L** who delivered me from the 1 Sm 17:37
David, "Go, and the **L** be with you!" 1 Sm 17:37
to you in the name of the **L** of hosts, 1 Sm 17:45
This day the **L** will deliver you into 1 Sm 17:46
may know that the **L** saves not with 1 Sm 17:47
of David because the **L** was with him 1 Sm 18:12
for the **L** was with him. 1 Sm 18:14
and knew that the **L** was with David, 1 Sm 18:28
and the **L** worked a great salvation for 1 Sm 19:5
Saul swore, "As the **L** lives, he shall 1 Sm 19:6
spirit from the **L** came upon Saul, 1 Sm 19:9
as the **L** lives and as your soul lives, 1 Sm 20:3
into a covenant of the **L** with you. 1 Sm 20:8
And Jonathan said to David, "The **L**, 1 Sm 20:12
the **L** do so to Jonathan and more 1 Sm 20:13
May the **L** be with you, as he has 1 Sm 20:13
show me the steadfast love of the **L**, 1 Sm 20:14
when the **L** cuts off every one of the 1 Sm 20:15
"May the **L** take vengeance on 1 Sm 20:16
you are to come, for, as the **L** lives, 1 Sm 20:21
then go, for the **L** has sent you away. 1 Sm 20:22
the **L** is between you and me 1 Sm 20:23
both of us in the name of the **L**, 1 Sm 20:42
'The **L** shall be between me and you, 1 Sm 20:42
which is removed from before the **L**, 1 Sm 21:6
there that day, detained before the **L**. 1 Sm 21:7
he inquired of the **L** for him and 1 Sm 22:10
And he answered, "Here I am, my **l**." 1 Sm 22:12
"Turn and kill the priests of the **L**, 1 Sm 22:17
hand to strike the priests of the **L**. 1 Sm 22:17
Saul had killed the priests of the **L**. 1 Sm 22:21
Therefore David inquired of the **L**, 1 Sm 23:2
Philistines?" And the **L** said to David, 1 Sm 23:2
Then David inquired of the **L** again. 1 Sm 23:4
LORD again. And the **L** answered him, 1 Sm 23:4
Then said David, "O **L**, the God of 1 Sm 23:10
as your servant has heard? O **L**, 1 Sm 23:11

tell your servant." And the **L** said, 1 Sm 23:11
the hand of Saul?" And the **L** said, 1 Sm 23:12
them made a covenant before the **L**. 1 Sm 23:18
said, "May you be blessed by the **L**, 1 Sm 23:21
is the day of which the **L** said to you, 1 Sm 24:4
"The **L** forbid that I should do this 1 Sm 24:6
that I should do this thing to my **l**, 1 Sm 24:6
"My **l** the king!" And when Saul 1 Sm 24:8
have seen how the **L** gave you today 1 Sm 24:10
not put out my hand against my **l**, 1 Sm 24:10
May the **L** judge between me and 1 Sm 24:12
may the **L** avenge me against you, 1 Sm 24:12
May the **L** therefore be judge and 1 Sm 24:15
kill me when the **L** put me into your 1 Sm 24:18
So may the **L** reward you with good 1 Sm 24:19
me therefore by the **L** that you will 1 Sm 24:21
his feet and said, "On me alone, my **l**, 1 Sm 25:24
Let not my **l** regard this worthless 1 Sm 25:25
did not see the young men of my **l**, 1 Sm 25:25
Now then, my **l**, as the LORD lives, 1 Sm 25:26
Now then, my lord, as the **L** lives, 1 Sm 25:26
because the **L** has restrained you 1 Sm 25:26
seek to do evil to my **l** be as Nabal. 1 Sm 25:26
has brought to my **l** be given to the 1 Sm 25:27
to the young men who follow my **l**. 1 Sm 25:27
For the **L** will certainly make my 1 Sm 25:28
certainly make my **l** a sure house, 1 Sm 25:28
because my **l** is fighting the battles 1 Sm 25:28
lord is fighting the battles of the **L**, 1 Sm 25:28
the life of my **l** shall be bound in the 1 Sm 25:29
living in the care of the **L** your God. 1 Sm 25:29
And when the **L** has done to my lord 1 Sm 25:30
has done to my **l** according to all the 1 Sm 25:30
my **l** shall have no cause of grief or 1 Sm 25:31
or for my **l** taking vengeance 1 Sm 25:31
And when the **L** has dealt well with 1 Sm 25:31
the LORD has dealt well with my **l**, 1 Sm 25:31
said to Abigail, "Blessed be the **L**, 1 Sm 25:32
as surely as the **L** the God of Israel 1 Sm 25:34
ten days later the **L** struck Nabal, 1 Sm 25:38
"Blessed be the **L** who has avenged 1 Sm 25:39
The **L** has returned the evil of Nabal 1 Sm 25:39
wash the feet of the servants of my **l**." 1 Sm 25:41
And David said, "As the **L** lives, the 1 Sm 26:10
the LORD lives, the **L** will strike him, 1 Sm 26:10
The **L** forbid that I should put out 1 Sm 26:11
sleep from the **L** had fallen upon 1 Sm 26:12
not kept watch over your **l** the king? 1 Sm 26:15
came in to destroy the king your **l**. 1 Sm 26:15
As the **L** lives, you deserve to die, 1 Sm 26:16
you have not kept watch over your **l**, 1 Sm 26:16
And David said, "It is my voice, my **l**, 1 Sm 26:17
"Why does my **l** pursue after his 1 Sm 26:18
Now therefore let my **l** the king hear 1 Sm 26:19
If it is the **L** who has stirred you up 1 Sm 26:19
may they be cursed before the **L**, 1 Sm 26:19
no share in the heritage of the **L**, 1 Sm 26:19
away from the presence of the **L**, 1 Sm 26:20
The **L** rewards every man for his 1 Sm 26:23
for the **L** gave you into my hand 1 Sm 26:23
life be precious in the sight of the **L**, 1 Sm 26:24
And when Saul inquired of the **L**, the 1 Sm 28:6
of the LORD, the **L** did not answer him, 1 Sm 28:6
But Saul swore to her by the **L**, "As 1 Sm 28:10
to her by the LORD, "As the **L** lives, 1 Sm 28:10
since the **L** has turned from you and 1 Sm 28:16
The **L** has done to you as he spoke 1 Sm 28:17
for the **L** has torn the kingdom out 1 Sm 28:17
the voice of the **L** and did not carry 1 Sm 28:18
therefore the **L** has done this thing to 1 Sm 28:18
the **L** will give Israel also with you 1 Sm 28:19
The **L** will give the army of Israel 1 Sm 28:19
this fellow reconcile himself to his **l**? 1 Sm 29:4
David and said to him, "As the **L** lives, 1 Sm 29:6
against the enemies of my **l** the king?" 1 Sm 29:8
the servants of your **l** who came with 1 Sm 29:10
strengthened himself in the **L** his God. 1 Sm 30:6
And David inquired of the **L**, "Shall I 1 Sm 30:8
with what the **L** has given us. 1 Sm 30:23
the spoil of the enemies of the **L**." 1 Sm 30:26
I have brought them here to my **l**." 2 Sm 1:10
the people of the **L** and for the house 2 Sm 1:12
After this David inquired of the **L**, 2 Sm 2:1
cities of Judah?" And the **L** said to him, 2 Sm 2:1
to them, "May you be blessed by the **L**, 2 Sm 2:5
loyalty to Saul your **l** and buried him. 2 Sm 2:5
Now may the **L** show steadfast love and 2 Sm 2:6
and be valiant, for Saul your **l** is dead, 2 Sm 2:7
for David what the **L** has sworn to him, 2 Sm 3:9
about, for the **L** has promised David, 2 Sm 3:18
will gather all Israel to my **l** the king, 2 Sm 3:21
guiltless before the **L** for the blood 2 Sm 3:28
The **L** repay the evildoer according to 2 Sm 3:39
The **L** has avenged my lord the king 2 Sm 4:8
LORD has avenged my **l** the king this 2 Sm 4:8

Rimmon the Beerothite, "As the **L** lives, 2 Sm 4:9
And the **L** said to you, 'You shall be 2 Sm 5:2
with them at Hebron before the **L**, 2 Sm 5:3
became greater and greater, for the **L**, 2 Sm 5:10
knew that the **L** had established him 2 Sm 5:12
And David inquired of the **L**, "Shall I 2 Sm 5:19
my hand?" And the **L** said to David, 2 Sm 5:19
"The **L** has burst through my 2 Sm 5:20
And when David inquired of the **L**, he 2 Sm 5:23
for then the **L** has gone out before you 2 Sm 5:24
David did as the **L** commanded him, 2 Sm 5:25
by the name of the **L** of hosts who sits 2 Sm 6:2
Israel were making merry before the **L**, 2 Sm 6:5
the anger of the **L** was kindled against 2 Sm 6:7
angry because the **L** had burst forth 2 Sm 6:8
And David was afraid of the **L** that day, 2 Sm 6:9
can the ark of the **L** come to me?" 2 Sm 6:9
take the ark of the **L** into the city of 2 Sm 6:10
the ark of the **L** remained in the house 2 Sm 6:11
and the **L** blessed Obed-edom and all 2 Sm 6:11
"The **L** has blessed the household of 2 Sm 6:12
the ark of the **L** had gone six steps, 2 Sm 6:13
David danced before the **L** with all his 2 Sm 6:14
the ark of the **L** with shouting and 2 Sm 6:15
As the ark of the **L** came into the city 2 Sm 6:16
leaping and dancing before the **L**, 2 Sm 6:16
in the ark of the **L** and set it in its 2 Sm 6:17
and peace offerings before the **L**. 2 Sm 6:17
people in the name of the **L** of hosts 2 Sm 6:18
said to Michal, "It was before the **L**, 2 Sm 6:21
the people of the **L**—and I will make 2 Sm 6:21
—and I will make merry before the **L**. 2 Sm 6:21
his house and the **L** had given him rest 2 Sm 7:1
is in your heart, for the **L** is with you." 2 Sm 7:3
the word of the **L** came to Nathan, 2 Sm 7:4
tell my servant David, 'Thus says the **L**: 2 Sm 7:5
David, 'Thus says the **L** of hosts, 2 Sm 7:8
the **L** declares to you that the LORD 2 Sm 7:11
to you that the **L** will make you a 2 Sm 7:11
went in and sat before the **L** and said, 2 Sm 7:18
LORD and said, "Who am I, O **L** GOD, 2 Sm 7:18
a small thing in your eyes, O **L** GOD. 2 Sm 7:19
is instruction for mankind, O **L** GOD! 2 Sm 7:19
For you know your servant, O **L** GOD! 2 Sm 7:20
Therefore you are great, O **L** God. For 2 Sm 7:22
And you, O **L**, became their God. 2 Sm 7:24
And now, O **L** God, confirm forever 2 Sm 7:25
'The **L** of hosts is God over Israel,' 2 Sm 7:26
For you, O **L** of hosts, the God of 2 Sm 7:27
And now, O **L** GOD, you are God, and 2 Sm 7:28
For you, O **L** GOD, have spoken, and 2 Sm 7:29
And the **L** gave victory to David 2 Sm 8:6
also King David dedicated to the **L**, 2 Sm 8:11
And the **L** gave victory to David 2 Sm 8:14
to all that my **l** the king commands 2 Sm 9:11
the Ammonites said to Hanun their **l**, 2 Sm 10:3
and may the **L** do what seems good 2 Sm 10:12
house with all the servants of his **l**, 2 Sm 11:9
and my **l** Joab and the servants of 2 Sm 11:11
the servants of my **l** are camping in 2 Sm 11:11
his couch with the servants of his **l**, 2 Sm 11:13
that David had done displeased the **L**. 2 Sm 11:27
And the **L** sent Nathan to David. He 2 Sm 12:1
and he said to Nathan, "As the **L** lives, 2 Sm 12:5
Thus says the **L**, the God of Israel, 'I 2 Sm 12:7
have you despised the word of the **L**, 2 Sm 12:9
Thus says the **L**, 'Behold, I will raise 2 Sm 12:11
sinned against the **L**." And Nathan 2 Sm 12:13
"The **L** also has put away your sin; 2 Sm 12:13
deed you have utterly scorned the **L**, 2 Sm 12:14
And the **L** afflicted the child that 2 Sm 12:15
the house of the **L** and worshiped. 2 Sm 12:20
knows whether the **L** will be 2 Sm 12:22
name Solomon. And the **L** loved him 2 Sm 12:24
his name Jedidiah, because of the **L**. 2 Sm 12:25
"Let not my **l** suppose that they have 2 Sm 13:32
therefore let not my **l** the king so 2 Sm 13:33
"On me be the guilt, my **l** the king, 2 Sm 14:9
let the king invoke the **L** your God, 2 Sm 14:11
destroyed." He said, "As the **L** lives, 2 Sm 14:11
a word to my **l** the king." He said, 2 Sm 14:12
say this to my **l** the king because the 2 Sm 14:15
'The word of my **l** the king will set 2 Sm 14:17
for my **l** the king is like the angel of 2 Sm 14:17
evil. The **L** your God be with you!" 2 Sm 14:17
said, "Let my **l** the king speak." 2 Sm 14:18
"As surely as you live, my **l** the king, 2 Sm 14:19
anything that my **l** the king has 2 Sm 14:19
But my **l** has wisdom like the 2 Sm 14:20
favor in your sight, my **l** the king, 2 Sm 14:22
my vow, which I have vowed to the **L**, 2 Sm 15:7
'If the **L** will indeed bring me back to 2 Sm 15:8
then I will offer worship to the **L**.'" 2 Sm 15:8
do whatever my **l** the king decides." 2 Sm 15:15
and may the **L** show steadfast love 2 Sm 15:20

answered the king, "As the **L** lives, 2 Sm 15:21
LORD lives, and as my **l** the king lives, 2 Sm 15:21
wherever my **l** the king shall be, 2 Sm 15:21
If I find favor in the eyes of the **L**, he 2 Sm 15:25
Absalom." And David said, "O **L**, 2 Sm 15:31
favor in your sight, my **l** the king." 2 Sm 16:4
The **L** has avenged on you all the 2 Sm 16:8
and the **L** has given the kingdom into 2 Sm 16:8
this dead dog curse my **l** the king? 2 Sm 16:9
is cursing because the **L** has said to 2 Sm 16:10
him curse, for the **L** has told him to. 2 Sm 16:11
It may be that the **L** will look on the 2 Sm 16:12
and that the **L** will repay me with 2 Sm 16:12
for whom the **L** and this people and 2 Sm 16:18
Ahithophel." For the **L** had ordained 2 Sm 17:14
so that the **L** might bring harm 2 Sm 17:14
the king that the **L** has delivered him 2 Sm 18:19
and said, "Blessed be the **L** your God, 2 Sm 18:28
their hand against my **l** the king." 2 Sm 18:28
said, "Good news for my **l** the king! 2 Sm 18:31
For the **L** has delivered you this day 2 Sm 18:31
the enemies of my **l** the king and all 2 Sm 18:32
to your servants, for I swear by the **L**, 2 Sm 19:7
"Let not my **l** hold me guilty or 2 Sm 19:19
on the day my **l** the king left 2 Sm 19:19
come down to meet my **l** the king." 2 Sm 19:20
He answered, "My **l**, O king, my 2 Sm 19:26
your servant to my **l** the king. 2 Sm 19:27
But my **l** the king is like the angel of 2 Sm 19:27
to death before my **l** the king, 2 Sm 19:28
since my **l** the king has come safely 2 Sm 19:30
an added burden to my **l** the king? 2 Sm 19:35
Let him go over with my **l** the king, 2 Sm 19:37
swallow up the heritage of the **L**? 2 Sm 20:19
And David sought the face of the **L**. 2 Sm 21:1
And the **L** said, "There is bloodguilt 2 Sm 21:1
you may bless the heritage of the **L**?" 2 Sm 21:3
hang them before the **L** at Gibeah of 2 Sm 21:6
the chosen of the **L**." And the king 2 Sm 21:6
the oath of the **L** that was between 2 Sm 21:7
them on the mountain before the **L**, 2 Sm 21:9
David spoke to the **L** the words of this 2 Sm 22:1
day when the **L** delivered him from 2 Sm 22:1
"The **L** is my rock and my fortress 2 Sm 22:2
I call upon the **L**, who is worthy to be 2 Sm 22:4
"In my distress I called upon the **L**; to 2 Sm 22:7
The **L** thundered from heaven, and 2 Sm 22:14
were laid bare, at the rebuke of the **L**, 2 Sm 22:16
calamity, but the **L** was my support. 2 Sm 22:19
"The **L** dealt with me according to 2 Sm 22:21
the ways of the **L** and have not 2 Sm 22:22
And the **L** has rewarded me 2 Sm 22:25
For you are my lamp, O **L**, and my 2 Sm 22:29
perfect; the word of the **L** proves true; 2 Sm 22:31
"For who is God, but the **L**? And who 2 Sm 22:32
they cried to the **L**, but he did not 2 Sm 22:42
"The **L** lives, and blessed be my 2 Sm 22:47
"For this I will praise you, O **L**, 2 Sm 22:50
"The Spirit of the **L** speaks by me; his 2 Sm 23:2
And the **L** brought about a great 2 Sm 23:10
and the **L** worked a great victory. 2 Sm 23:12
drink of it. He poured it out to the **L** 2 Sm 23:16
and said, "Far be it from me, O **L**, 2 Sm 23:17
the anger of the **L** was kindled against 2 Sm 24:1
"May the **L** your God add to the people 2 Sm 24:3
while the eyes of my **l** the king still see 2 Sm 24:3
but why does my **l** the king delight in 2 Sm 24:3
And David said to the **L**, "I have 2 Sm 24:10
But now, O **L**, please take away the 2 Sm 24:10
the word of the **L** came to the prophet 2 Sm 24:11
and say to David, 'Thus says the **L**, 2 Sm 24:12
Let us fall into the hand of the **L**, for 2 Sm 24:14
So the **L** sent a pestilence on Israel 2 Sm 24:15
the **L** relented from the calamity and 2 Sm 24:16
the angel of the **L** was by the 2 Sm 24:16
David spoke to the **L** when he saw 2 Sm 24:17
an altar to the **L** on the threshing 2 Sm 24:18
at Gad's word, as the **L** commanded. 2 Sm 24:19
"Why has my **l** the king come to his 2 Sm 24:21
in order to build an altar to the **L**, 2 Sm 24:21
"Let my **l** the king take and offer up 2 Sm 24:22
king, "The **L** your God accept you." 2 Sm 24:23
burnt offerings to the **L** my God that 2 Sm 24:24
an altar to the **L** and offered burnt 2 Sm 24:25
So the **L** responded to the plea for the 2 Sm 24:25
woman be sought for my **l** the king, 1 Kgs 1:2
that my **l** the king may be warm." 1 Kgs 1:2
king and David our **l** does not know 1 Kgs 1:11
to him, 'Did you not, my **l** the king, 1 Kgs 1:13
She said to him, "My **l**, you swore to 1 Kgs 1:17
to your servant by the **L** your God, 1 Kgs 1:17
is king, although you, my **l** the king, 1 Kgs 1:18
And now, my **l** the king, the eyes of 1 Kgs 1:20
the throne of my **l** the king after him. 1 Kgs 1:20
when my **l** the king sleeps with his 1 Kgs 1:21

And Nathan said, "My **l** the king,	1 Kgs 1:24
brought about by my **l** the king and	1 Kgs 1:27
the throne of my **l** the king after	1 Kgs 1:27
king swore, saying, "As the **L** lives,	1 Kgs 1:29
as I swore to you by the **L**, the God of	1 Kgs 1:30
"May my **l** King David live forever!"	1 Kgs 1:31
servants of your **l** and have Solomon	1 Kgs 1:33
May the **L**, the God of my lord the	1 Kgs 1:36
the LORD, the God of my **l** the king,	1 Kgs 1:36
As the **L** has been with my lord the	1 Kgs 1:37
the LORD has been with my **l** the king,	1 Kgs 1:37
than the throne of my **l** King David."	1 Kgs 1:37
for our **l** King David has made	1 Kgs 1:43
to congratulate our **l** King David,	1 Kgs 1:47
the king also said, 'Blessed be the **L**,	1 Kgs 1:48
and keep the charge of the **L** your God,	1 Kgs 2:3
that the **L** may establish his word that	1 Kgs 2:4
at the Jordan, I swore to him by the **L**,	1 Kgs 2:8
brother's, for it was his from the **L**.	1 Kgs 2:15
Then King Solomon swore by the **L**,	1 Kgs 2:23
Now therefore as the **L** lives, who has	1 Kgs 2:24
the ark of the **L** GOD before David my	1 Kgs 2:26
Abiathar from being priest to the **L**,	1 Kgs 2:27
the word of the **L** that he had spoken	1 Kgs 2:27
to the tent of the **L** and caught hold of	1 Kgs 2:28
"Joab has fled to the tent of the **L**,	1 Kgs 2:29
to the tent of the **L** and said to him,	1 Kgs 2:30
The **L** will bring back his bloody	1 Kgs 2:32
be peace from the **L** forevermore."	1 Kgs 2:33
as my **l** the king has said, so will your	1 Kgs 2:38
swear by the **L** and solemnly warn	1 Kgs 2:42
oath to the **L** and the commandment	1 Kgs 2:43
So the **L** will bring back your harm	1 Kgs 2:44
be established before the **L** forever."	1 Kgs 2:45
the house of the **L** and the wall around	1 Kgs 3:1
yet been built for the name of the **L**.	1 Kgs 3:2
Solomon loved the **L**, walking in the	1 Kgs 3:3
At Gibeon the **L** appeared to Solomon	1 Kgs 3:5
And now, O **L** my God, you have made	1 Kgs 3:7
It pleased the **L** that Solomon had	1 Kgs 3:10
the ark of the covenant of the **L**,	1 Kgs 3:15
The one woman said, "Oh, my **l**, this	1 Kgs 3:17
heart yearned for her son, "Oh, my **l**,	1 Kgs 3:26
the name of the **L** his God because of	1 Kgs 5:3
until the **L** put them under the soles of	1 Kgs 5:3
But now the **L** my God has given me	1 Kgs 5:4
a house for the name of the **L** my God,	1 Kgs 5:5
God, as the **L** said to David my father,	1 Kgs 5:5
and said, "Blessed be the **L** this day,	1 Kgs 5:7
And the **L** gave Solomon wisdom, as	1 Kgs 5:12
he began to build the house of the **L**.	1 Kgs 6:1
built for the **L** was sixty cubits	1 Kgs 6:2
the word of the **L** came to Solomon,	1 Kgs 6:11
there the ark of the covenant of the **L**.	1 Kgs 6:19
of the house of the **L** was laid,	1 Kgs 6:37
the house of the **L** and the vestibule of	1 Kgs 7:12
King Solomon on the house of the **L**:	1 Kgs 7:40
all these vessels in the house of the **L**,	1 Kgs 7:45
vessels that were in the house of the **L**:	1 Kgs 7:48
on the house of the **L** was finished.	1 Kgs 7:51
in the treasuries of the house of the **L**.	1 Kgs 7:51
of the covenant of the **L** out of the city	1 Kgs 8:1
And they brought up the ark of the **L**,	1 Kgs 8:4
of the covenant of the **L** to its place in	1 Kgs 8:6
where the **L** made a covenant with the	1 Kgs 8:9
a cloud filled the house of the **L**,	1 Kgs 8:10
the glory of the **L** filled the house of	1 Kgs 8:11
of the LORD filled the house of the **L**.	1 Kgs 8:11
"The **L** has said that he would dwell	1 Kgs 8:12
And he said, "Blessed be the **L**, the	1 Kgs 8:15
build a house for the name of the **L**,	1 Kgs 8:17
But the **L** said to David my father,	1 Kgs 8:18
Now the **L** has fulfilled his promise	1 Kgs 8:20
throne of Israel, as the **L** promised,	1 Kgs 8:20
built the house for the name of the **L**,	1 Kgs 8:20
the covenant of the **L** that he made	1 Kgs 8:21
the altar of the **L** in the presence of	1 Kgs 8:22
and said, "O **L**, God of Israel, there is	1 Kgs 8:23
Now therefore, O **L**, God of Israel,	1 Kgs 8:25
servant and to his plea, O **L** my God,	1 Kgs 8:28
they pray to the **L** toward the city that	1 Kgs 8:44
our fathers out of Egypt, O **L** GOD."	1 Kgs 8:53
all this prayer and plea to the **L**,	1 Kgs 8:54
arose from before the altar of the **L**,	1 Kgs 8:54
"Blessed be the **L** who has given rest	1 Kgs 8:56
The **L** our God be with us, as he was	1 Kgs 8:57
which I have pleaded before the **L**,	1 Kgs 8:59
be near to the **L** our God day and	1 Kgs 8:59
the earth may know that the **L** is God;	1 Kgs 8:60
be wholly true to the **L** our God,	1 Kgs 8:61
him, offered sacrifice before the **L**.	1 Kgs 8:62
offerings to the **L** 22,000 oxen and	1 Kgs 8:63
of Israel dedicated the house of the **L**.	1 Kgs 8:63
that was before the house of the **L**,	1 Kgs 8:64
that was before the **L** was too small to	1 Kgs 8:64
Brook of Egypt, before the **L** our God,	1 Kgs 8:65
the goodness that the **L** had shown to	1 Kgs 8:66
the house of the **L** and the king's house	1 Kgs 9:1
the **L** appeared to Solomon a second	1 Kgs 9:2
And the **L** said to him, "I have heard	1 Kgs 9:3
'Why has the **L** done thus to this land	1 Kgs 9:8
they abandoned the **L** their God who	1 Kgs 9:9
Therefore the **L** has brought all this	1 Kgs 9:9
the house of the **L** and the king's	1 Kgs 9:10
the house of the **L** and his own house	1 Kgs 9:15
on the altar that he built to the **L**,	1 Kgs 9:25
making offerings with it before the **L**.	1 Kgs 9:25
concerning the name of the **L**,	1 Kgs 10:1
that he offered at the house of the **L**,	1 Kgs 10:5
Blessed be the **L** your God, who has	1 Kgs 10:9
Because the **L** loved Israel forever, he	1 Kgs 10:9
the house of the **L** and for the king's	1 Kgs 10:12
concerning which the **L** had said to	1 Kgs 11:2
was not wholly true to the **L** his God,	1 Kgs 11:4
the sight of the **L** and did not wholly	1 Kgs 11:6
LORD and did not wholly follow the **L**,	1 Kgs 11:6
And the **L** was angry with Solomon,	1 Kgs 11:9
heart had turned away from the **L**,	1 Kgs 11:9
not keep what the **L** commanded.	1 Kgs 11:10
Therefore the **L** said to Solomon,	1 Kgs 11:11
And the **L** raised up an adversary	1 Kgs 11:14
ten pieces, for thus says the **L**,	1 Kgs 11:31
about by the **L** that he might	1 Kgs 12:15
which the **L** spoke by Ahijah the	1 Kgs 12:15
'Thus says the **L**, You shall not go	1 Kgs 12:24
the word of the **L** and went home	1 Kgs 12:24
according to the word of the **L**.	1 Kgs 12:24
in the temple of the **L** at Jerusalem,	1 Kgs 12:27
this people will turn again to their **l**,	1 Kgs 12:27
Judah by the word of the **L** to Bethel.	1 Kgs 13:1
altar by the word of the **L** and said,	1 Kgs 13:2
said, "O altar, altar, thus says the **L**:	1 Kgs 13:2
is the sign that the **L** has spoken:	1 Kgs 13:3
of God had given by the word of the **L**.	1 Kgs 13:5
now the favor of the **L** your God,	1 Kgs 13:6
And the man of God entreated the **L**,	1 Kgs 13:6
commanded me by the word of the **L**,	1 Kgs 13:9
was said to me by the word of the **L**,	1 Kgs 13:17
spoke to me by the word of the **L**,	1 Kgs 13:18
the word of the **L** came to the	1 Kgs 13:20
came from Judah, "Thus says the **L**,	1 Kgs 13:21
the word of the **L** and have not kept	1 Kgs 13:21
command that the **L** your God	1 Kgs 13:21
who disobeyed the word of the **L**;	1 Kgs 13:26
therefore the **L** has given him to the	1 Kgs 13:26
to the word that the **L** spoke to him."	1 Kgs 13:26
the word of the **L** against the altar in	1 Kgs 13:32
And the **L** said to Ahijah, "Behold, the	1 Kgs 14:5
Go, tell Jeroboam, 'Thus says the **L**,	1 Kgs 14:7
shall eat, for the **L** has spoken it."'	1 Kgs 14:11
found something pleasing to the **L**,	1 Kgs 14:13
the **L** will raise up for himself a king	1 Kgs 14:14
the **L** will strike Israel as a reed is	1 Kgs 14:15
Asherim, provoking the **L** to anger.	1 Kgs 14:15
him, according to the word of the **L**,	1 Kgs 14:18
the city that the **L** had chosen out of	1 Kgs 14:21
what was evil in the sight of the **L**,	1 Kgs 14:22
nations that the **L** drove out before	1 Kgs 14:24
the house of the **L** and the treasures	1 Kgs 14:26
king went into the house of the **L**,	1 Kgs 14:28
was not wholly true to the **L** his God,	1 Kgs 15:3
for David's sake the **L** his God gave	1 Kgs 15:4
in the eyes of the **L** and did not turn	1 Kgs 15:5
what was right in the eyes of the **L**,	1 Kgs 15:11
was wholly true to the **L** all his days.	1 Kgs 15:14
the house of the **L** the sacred gifts of	1 Kgs 15:15
the house of the **L** and the treasures	1 Kgs 15:18
the sight of the **L** and walked in the	1 Kgs 15:26
to the word of the **L** that he spoke by	1 Kgs 15:29
anger to which he provoked the **L**,	1 Kgs 15:30
the sight of the **L** and walked in the	1 Kgs 15:34
the word of the **L** came to Jehu the	1 Kgs 16:1
the word of the **L** came by the prophet	1 Kgs 16:7
evil that he did in the sight of the **L**,	1 Kgs 16:7
according to the word of the **L**,	1 Kgs 16:12
provoking the **L** God of Israel to	1 Kgs 16:13
doing evil in the sight of the **L**,	1 Kgs 16:19
what was evil in the sight of the **L**,	1 Kgs 16:25
made Israel to sin, provoking the **L**,	1 Kgs 16:26
of Omri did evil in the sight of the **L**,	1 Kgs 16:30
Ahab did more to provoke the **L**, the	1 Kgs 16:33
according to the word of the **L**,	1 Kgs 16:34
"As the **L** the God of Israel lives,	1 Kgs 17:1
And the word of the **L** came to him,	1 Kgs 17:2
did according to the word of the **L**.	1 Kgs 17:5
Then the word of the **L** came to him,	1 Kgs 17:8
she said, "As the **L** your God lives,	1 Kgs 17:12
For thus says the **L** the God of Israel,	1 Kgs 17:14
the day that the **L** sends rain upon	1 Kgs 17:14
to the word of the **L** that he spoke by	1 Kgs 17:16
And he cried to the **L**, "O LORD my	1 Kgs 17:20
he cried to the LORD, "O **L** my God,	1 Kgs 17:20
child three times and cried to the **L**,	1 Kgs 17:21
and cried to the LORD, "O **L** my God,	1 Kgs 17:21
And the **L** listened to the voice of	1 Kgs 17:22
the word of the **L** in your mouth is	1 Kgs 17:24
days the word of the **L** came to Elijah,	1 Kgs 18:1
(Now Obadiah feared the **L** greatly,	1 Kgs 18:3
Jezebel cut off the prophets of the **L**,	1 Kgs 18:4
face and said, "Is it you, my **l** Elijah?"	1 Kgs 18:7
Go, tell your **l**, 'Behold, Elijah is	1 Kgs 18:8
As the **L** your God lives, there is no	1 Kgs 18:10
or kingdom where my **l** has not sent	1 Kgs 18:10
And now you say, 'Go, tell your **l**,	1 Kgs 18:11
the Spirit of the **L** will carry you I	1 Kgs 18:12
have feared the **L** from my youth.	1 Kgs 18:12
it not been told my **l** what I did when	1 Kgs 18:13
Jezebel killed the prophets of the **L**,	1 Kgs 18:13
And now you say, 'Go, tell your **l**,	1 Kgs 18:14
Elijah said, "As the **L** of hosts lives,	1 Kgs 18:15
of the **L** and followed	1 Kgs 18:18
different opinions? If the **L** is God,	1 Kgs 18:21
I only, am left a prophet of the **L**,	1 Kgs 18:22
I will call upon the name of the **L**,	1 Kgs 18:24
the altar of the **L** that had been	1 Kgs 18:30
to whom the word of the **L** came,	1 Kgs 18:31
built an altar in the name of the **L**.	1 Kgs 18:32
prophet came near and said, "O **L**,	1 Kgs 18:36
Answer me, O **L**, answer me, that	1 Kgs 18:37
this people may know that you, O **L**,	1 Kgs 18:37
the fire of the **L** fell and consumed	1 Kgs 18:38
fell on their faces and said, "The **L**,	1 Kgs 18:39
and said, "The LORD, he is God; the **L**,	1 Kgs 18:39
And the hand of the **L** was on Elijah,	1 Kgs 18:46
now, O **L**, take away my life, for I am	1 Kgs 19:4
the angel of the **L** came again a	1 Kgs 19:7
the word of the **L** came to him,	1 Kgs 19:9
"I have been very jealous for the **L**,	1 Kgs 19:10
mount before the **L**." And behold,	1 Kgs 19:11
LORD." And behold, the **L** passed by,	1 Kgs 19:11
in pieces the rocks before the **L**,	1 Kgs 19:11
LORD, but the **L** was not in the wind.	1 Kgs 19:11
but the **L** was not in the earthquake.	1 Kgs 19:11
a fire, but the **L** was not in the fire.	1 Kgs 19:12
"I have been very jealous for the **L**,	1 Kgs 19:14
And the **L** said to him, "Go, return	1 Kgs 19:15
of Israel answered, "As you say, my **l**,	1 Kgs 20:4
of Ben-hadad, "Tell my **l** the king,	1 Kgs 20:9
of Israel and said, "Thus says the **L**,	1 Kgs 20:13
you shall know that I am the **L**."	1 Kgs 20:13
whom?" He said, "Thus says the **L**,	1 Kgs 20:14
the king of Israel, "Thus says the **L**,	1 Kgs 20:28
"The **L** is a god of the hills but he is	1 Kgs 20:28
you shall know that I am the **L**.'"	1 Kgs 20:28
his fellow at the command of the **L**,	1 Kgs 20:35
have not obeyed the voice of the **L**,	1 Kgs 20:36
he said to him, "Thus says the **L**,	1 Kgs 20:42
"The **L** forbid that I should give you	1 Kgs 21:3
the word of the **L** came to Elijah the	1 Kgs 21:17
shall say to him, 'Thus says the **L**,	1 Kgs 21:19
shall say to him, 'Thus says the **L**:	1 Kgs 21:19
do what is evil in the sight of the **L**.	1 Kgs 21:20
And of Jezebel the **L** also said, 'The	1 Kgs 21:23
evil in the sight of the **L** like Ahab,	1 Kgs 21:25
whom the **L** cast out before the	1 Kgs 21:26
the word of the **L** came to Elijah the	1 Kgs 21:28
"Inquire first for the word of the **L**."	1 Kgs 22:5
for the **L** will give it into the hand of	1 Kgs 22:6
another prophet of the **L** of whom we	1 Kgs 22:7
by whom we may inquire of the **L**,	1 Kgs 22:8
of iron and said, "Thus says the **L**,	1 Kgs 22:11
the **L** will give it into the hand of the	1 Kgs 22:12
But Micaiah said, "As the **L** lives,	1 Kgs 22:14
the LORD lives, what the **L** says to me,	1 Kgs 22:14
the **L** will give it into the hand of the	1 Kgs 22:15
but the truth in the name of the **L**?"	1 Kgs 22:16
And the **L** said, 'These have no	1 Kgs 22:17
"Therefore hear the word of the **L**:	1 Kgs 22:19
I saw the **L** sitting on his throne, and	1 Kgs 22:19
and the **L** said, 'Who will entice	1 Kgs 22:20
forward and stood before the **L**,	1 Kgs 22:21
And the **L** said to him, 'By what	1 Kgs 22:22
the **L** has put a lying spirit in the	1 Kgs 22:23
the **L** has declared disaster for you."	1 Kgs 22:23
did the Spirit of the **L** go from me to	1 Kgs 22:24
the **L** has not spoken by me." And	1 Kgs 22:28
the word of the **L** that he had	1 Kgs 22:38
what was right in the sight of the **L**.	1 Kgs 22:43
the sight of the **L** and walked in the	1 Kgs 22:52
worshiped him and provoked the **L**,	1 Kgs 22:53
But the angel of the **L** said to Elijah the	2 Kgs 1:3
Now therefore thus says the **L**, You	2 Kgs 1:4
you, and say to him, Thus says the **L**,	2 Kgs 1:6
Then the angel of the **L** said to Elijah,	2 Kgs 1:15
and said to him, "Thus says the **L**,	2 Kgs 1:16

the word of the **L** that Elijah had	2 Kgs 1:17
Now when the **L** was about to take	2 Kgs 2:1
for the **L** has sent me as far as Bethel."	2 Kgs 2:2
But Elisha said, "As the **L** lives,	2 Kgs 2:2
know that today the **L** will take away	2 Kgs 2:3
for the **L** has sent me to Jericho." But	2 Kgs 2:4
to Jericho." But he said, "As the **L** lives,	2 Kgs 2:4
know that today the **L** will take away	2 Kgs 2:5
for the **L** has sent me to the Jordan."	2 Kgs 2:6
Jordan." But he said, "As the **L** lives,	2 Kgs 2:6
the water, saying, "Where is the **L**,	2 Kgs 2:14
the Spirit of the **L** has caught him up	2 Kgs 2:16
of this city is pleasant, as my **l** sees,	2 Kgs 2:19
salt in it and said, "Thus says the **L**,	2 Kgs 2:21
he cursed them in the name of the **L**.	2 Kgs 2:24
did what was evil in the sight of the **L**,	2 Kgs 3:2
The **L** has called these three kings to	2 Kgs 3:10
"Is there no prophet of the **L** here,	2 Kgs 3:11
may inquire of the **L**?" Then one of	2 Kgs 3:11
"The word of the **L** is with him." So	2 Kgs 3:12
it is the **L** who has called these three	2 Kgs 3:13
Elisha said, "As the **L** of hosts lives,	2 Kgs 3:14
the hand of the **L** came upon him.	2 Kgs 3:15
And he said, "Thus says the **L**, 'I will	2 Kgs 3:16
For thus says the **L**, 'You shall not see	2 Kgs 3:17
is a light thing in the sight of the **L**.	2 Kgs 3:18
know that your servant feared the **L**,	2 Kgs 4:1
a son." And she said, "No, my **l**,	2 Kgs 4:16
and the **L** has hidden it from me and	2 Kgs 4:27
she said, "Did I ask my **l** for a son?	2 Kgs 4:28
"As the **L** lives and as you yourself	2 Kgs 4:30
the two of them and prayed to the **L**.	2 Kgs 4:33
that they may eat, for thus says the **L**,	2 Kgs 4:43
left, according to the word of the **L**.	2 Kgs 4:44
by him the **L** had given victory	2 Kgs 5:1
"Would that my **l** were with the	2 Kgs 5:3
So Naaman went in and told his **l**,	2 Kgs 5:4
call upon the name of the **L** his God,	2 Kgs 5:11
But he said, "As the **L** lives, before	2 Kgs 5:16
or sacrifice to any god but the **L**.	2 Kgs 5:17
matter may the **L** pardon your	2 Kgs 5:18
the **L** pardon your servant in this	2 Kgs 5:18
As the **L** lives, I will run after him	2 Kgs 5:20
one of his servants said, "None, my **l**,	2 Kgs 6:12
Then Elisha prayed and said, "O **L**,	2 Kgs 6:17
may see." So the **L** opened the eyes of	2 Kgs 6:17
him, Elisha prayed to the **L** and said,	2 Kgs 6:18
entered Samaria, Elisha said, "O **L**,	2 Kgs 6:20
may see." So the **L** opened their eyes	2 Kgs 6:20
cried out to him, saying, "Help, my **l**,	2 Kgs 6:26
he said, "If the **L** will not help you,	2 Kgs 6:27
and said, "This trouble is from the **L**!	2 Kgs 6:33
should I wait for the **L** any longer?"	2 Kgs 6:33
Elisha said, "Hear the word of the **L**:	2 Kgs 7:1
thus says the **L**, Tomorrow about this	2 Kgs 7:1
"If the **L** himself should make	2 Kgs 7:2
For the **L** had made the army of the	2 Kgs 7:6
according to the word of the **L**.	2 Kgs 7:16
"If the **L** himself should make	2 Kgs 7:19
can, for the **L** has called for a famine,	2 Kgs 8:1
And Gehazi said, "My **l**, O king, here is	2 Kgs 8:5
and inquire of the **L** through him,	2 Kgs 8:8
but the **L** has shown me that he shall	2 Kgs 8:10
"Why does my **l** weep?" He answered,	2 Kgs 8:12
"The **L** has shown me that you are to	2 Kgs 8:13
did what was evil in the sight of the **L**.	2 Kgs 8:18
Yet the **L** was not willing to destroy	2 Kgs 8:19
did what was evil in the sight of the **L**,	2 Kgs 8:27
on his head and say, 'Thus says the **L**,	2 Kgs 9:3
"Thus says the **L** the God of Israel,	2 Kgs 9:6
you king over the people of the **L**,	2 Kgs 9:6
the blood of all the servants of the **L**.	2 Kgs 9:7
spoke to me, saying, 'Thus says the **L**,	2 Kgs 9:12
how the **L** made this pronouncement	2 Kgs 9:25
sons—declares the **L**—I will repay	2 Kgs 9:26
accordance with the word of the **L**."	2 Kgs 9:26
he said, "This is the word of the **L**,	2 Kgs 9:36
earth nothing of the word of the **L**,	2 Kgs 10:10
which the **L** spoke concerning the	2 Kgs 10:10
for the **L** has done what he said by	2 Kgs 10:10
see my zeal for the **L**." So he had him	2 Kgs 10:16
to the word of the **L** that he spoke to	2 Kgs 10:17
no servant of the **L** here among you,	2 Kgs 10:23
And the **L** said to Jehu, "Because you	2 Kgs 10:30
in the law of the **L** the God of Israel	2 Kgs 10:31
In those days the **L** began to cut off	2 Kgs 10:32
years, hidden in the house of the **L**,	2 Kgs 11:3
come to him in the house of the **L**.	2 Kgs 11:4
under oath in the house of the **L**,	2 Kgs 11:4
the house of the **L** on behalf of the	2 Kgs 11:7
which were in the house of the **L**.	2 Kgs 11:10
into the house of the **L** to the people.	2 Kgs 11:13
put to death in the house of the **L**."	2 Kgs 11:15
covenant between the **L** and the	2 Kgs 11:17
watchmen over the house of the **L**.	2 Kgs 11:18
king down from the house of the **L**,	2 Kgs 11:19
right in the eyes of the **L** all his days,	2 Kgs 12:2
is brought into the house of the **L**,	2 Kgs 12:4
him to bring into the house of the **L**,	2 Kgs 12:4
side as one entered the house of the **L**.	2 Kgs 12:9
was brought into the house of the **L**.	2 Kgs 12:9
that was found in the house of the **L**.	2 Kgs 12:10
the oversight of the house of the **L**.	2 Kgs 12:11
who worked on the house of the **L**,	2 Kgs 12:11
repairs on the house of the **L**,	2 Kgs 12:12
the house of the **L** basins of silver,	2 Kgs 12:13
was brought into the house of the **L**,	2 Kgs 12:13
repairing the house of the **L** with it.	2 Kgs 12:14
not brought into the house of the **L**;	2 Kgs 12:16
the house of the **L** and of the king's	2 Kgs 12:18
the sight of the **L** and followed the	2 Kgs 13:2
anger of the **L** was kindled against	2 Kgs 13:3
Jehoahaz sought the favor of the **L**,	2 Kgs 13:4
of the LORD, and the **L** listened to him,	2 Kgs 13:4
(Therefore the **L** gave Israel a savior,	2 Kgs 13:5
what was evil in the sight of the **L**.	2 Kgs 13:11
But the **L** was gracious to them and	2 Kgs 13:23
what was right in the eyes of the **L**,	2 Kgs 14:3
of Moses, where the **L** commanded,	2 Kgs 14:6
the house of the **L** and in the	2 Kgs 14:14
what was evil in the sight of the **L**.	2 Kgs 14:24
according to the word of the **L**,	2 Kgs 14:25
For the **L** saw that the affliction of	2 Kgs 14:26
But the **L** had not said that he would	2 Kgs 14:27
what was right in the eyes of the **L**,	2 Kgs 15:3
And the **L** touched the king, so that	2 Kgs 15:5
did what was evil in the sight of the **L**,	2 Kgs 15:9
the promise of the **L** that he gave to	2 Kgs 15:12
what was evil in the sight of the **L**.	2 Kgs 15:18
what was evil in the sight of the **L**.	2 Kgs 15:24
what was evil in the sight of the **L**.	2 Kgs 15:28
what was right in the eyes of the **L**,	2 Kgs 15:34
the upper gate of the house of the **L**.	2 Kgs 15:35
In those days the **L** began to send	2 Kgs 15:37
was right in the eyes of the **L** his God,	2 Kgs 16:2
nations whom the **L** drove out before	2 Kgs 16:3
the house of the **L** and in the	2 Kgs 16:8
was before the **L** he removed from	2 Kgs 16:14
his altar and the house of the **L**,	2 Kgs 16:14
to go around the house of the **L**,	2 Kgs 16:18
did what was evil in the sight of the **L**,	2 Kgs 17:2
had sinned against the **L** their God,	2 Kgs 17:7
nations whom the **L** drove out before	2 Kgs 17:8
secretly against the **L** their God	2 Kgs 17:9
did whom the **L** carried away before	2 Kgs 17:11
things, provoking the **L** to anger,	2 Kgs 17:11
of which the **L** had said to them,	2 Kgs 17:12
Yet the **L** warned Israel and Judah	2 Kgs 17:13
did not believe in the **L** their God.	2 Kgs 17:14
whom the **L** had commanded	2 Kgs 17:15
commandments of the **L** their God,	2 Kgs 17:16
to do evil in the sight of the **L**,	2 Kgs 17:17
Therefore the **L** was very angry with	2 Kgs 17:18
commandments of the **L** their God,	2 Kgs 17:19
And the **L** rejected all the	2 Kgs 17:20
from following the **L** and made	2 Kgs 17:21
until the **L** removed Israel out of his	2 Kgs 17:23
there, they did not fear the **L**.	2 Kgs 17:25
Therefore the **L** sent lions among	2 Kgs 17:25
them how they should fear the **L**.	2 Kgs 17:28
also feared the **L** and appointed from	2 Kgs 17:32
So they feared the **L** but also served	2 Kgs 17:33
They do not fear the **L**, and they do	2 Kgs 17:34
that the **L** commanded the	2 Kgs 17:34
The **L** made a covenant with them	2 Kgs 17:35
but you shall fear the **L**, who	2 Kgs 17:36
but you shall fear the **L** your God,	2 Kgs 17:39
nations feared the **L** and also served	2 Kgs 17:41
what was right in the eyes of the **L**,	2 Kgs 18:3
He trusted in the **L** the God of Israel,	2 Kgs 18:5
For he held fast to the **L**. He did not	2 Kgs 18:6
that the **L** commanded Moses.	2 Kgs 18:6
And the **L** was with him; wherever he	2 Kgs 18:7
the voice of the **L** their God but	2 Kgs 18:12
the servant of the **L** commanded.	2 Kgs 18:12
the house of the **L** and in the	2 Kgs 18:15
the temple of the **L** and from the	2 Kgs 18:16
"We trust in the **L** our God," is it not	2 Kgs 18:22
is it without the **L** that I have come	2 Kgs 18:25
The **L** said to me, Go up against this	2 Kgs 18:25
make you trust in the **L** by saying,	2 Kgs 18:30
saying, The **L** will surely deliver us,	2 Kgs 18:30
you by saying, The **L** will deliver us.	2 Kgs 18:32
that the **L** should deliver Jerusalem	2 Kgs 18:35
and went into the house of the **L**.	2 Kgs 19:1
may be that the **L** your God heard all	2 Kgs 19:4
the words that the **L** your God has	2 Kgs 19:4
"Say to your master, 'Thus says the **L**:	2 Kgs 19:6
the house of the **L** and spread it	2 Kgs 19:14
the LORD and spread it before the **L**.	2 Kgs 19:14
prayed before the **L** and said:	2 Kgs 19:15
"O **L** the God of Israel, who is	2 Kgs 19:15
Incline your ear, O **L**, and hear; open	2 Kgs 19:16
hear; open your eyes, O **L**, and see;	2 Kgs 19:16
Truly, O **L**, the kings of Assyria	2 Kgs 19:17
So now, O **L** our God, save us, please,	2 Kgs 19:19
the earth may know that you, O **L**,	2 Kgs 19:19
Hezekiah, saying, "Thus says the **L**,	2 Kgs 19:20
word that the **L** has spoken	2 Kgs 19:21
messengers you have mocked the **L**,	2 Kgs 19:23
The zeal of the **L** will do this.	2 Kgs 19:31
thus says the **L** concerning the king	2 Kgs 19:32
come into this city, declares the **L**.	2 Kgs 19:33
the angel of the **L** went out and	2 Kgs 19:35
and said to him, "Thus says the **L**,	2 Kgs 20:1
face to the wall and prayed to the **L**,	2 Kgs 20:2
"Now, O **L**, please remember how I	2 Kgs 20:3
court, the word of the **L** came to him:	2 Kgs 20:4
leader of my people, Thus says the **L**,	2 Kgs 20:5
you shall go up to the house of the **L**,	2 Kgs 20:5
be the sign that the **L** will heal me,	2 Kgs 20:8
the house of the **L** on the third day?"	2 Kgs 20:8
shall be the sign to you from the **L**,	2 Kgs 20:9
that the **L** will do the thing that he	2 Kgs 20:9
Isaiah the prophet called to the **L**,	2 Kgs 20:11
to Hezekiah, "Hear the word of the **L**:	2 Kgs 20:16
Nothing shall be left, says the **L**.	2 Kgs 20:17
"The word of the **L** that you have	2 Kgs 20:19
did what was evil in the sight of the **L**,	2 Kgs 21:2
nations whom the **L** drove out before	2 Kgs 21:2
he built altars in the house of the **L**,	2 Kgs 21:4
of the LORD, of which the **L** had said,	2 Kgs 21:4
the two courts of the house of the **L**.	2 Kgs 21:5
He did much evil in the sight of the **L**,	2 Kgs 21:6
house of which the **L** said to David	2 Kgs 21:7
done whom the **L** destroyed before the	2 Kgs 21:9
And the **L** said by his servants the	2 Kgs 21:10
therefore thus says the **L**, the God of	2 Kgs 21:12
what was evil in the sight of the **L**.	2 Kgs 21:16
what was evil in the sight of the **L**,	2 Kgs 21:20
He abandoned the **L**, the God of his	2 Kgs 21:22
and did not walk in the way of the **L**.	2 Kgs 21:22
in the eyes of the **L** and walked in all	2 Kgs 22:2
the secretary, to the house of the **L**,	2 Kgs 22:3
been brought into the house of the **L**,	2 Kgs 22:4
the oversight of the house of the **L**,	2 Kgs 22:5
who are at the house of the **L**,	2 Kgs 22:5
the house of the **L**." And Hilkiah gave	2 Kgs 22:8
the oversight of the house of the **L**."	2 Kgs 22:9
"Go, inquire of the **L** for me, and for	2 Kgs 22:13
the wrath of the **L** that is kindled	2 Kgs 22:13
she said to them, "Thus says the **L**,	2 Kgs 22:15
Thus says the **L**, behold, I will bring	2 Kgs 22:16
who sent you to inquire of the **L**,	2 Kgs 22:18
you say to him, Thus says the **L**,	2 Kgs 22:18
you humbled yourself before the **L**,	2 Kgs 22:19
I also have heard you, declares the **L**.	2 Kgs 22:19
king went up to the house of the **L**,	2 Kgs 23:2
had been found in the house of the **L**.	2 Kgs 23:2
and made a covenant before the **L**,	2 Kgs 23:3
to walk after the **L** and to keep his	2 Kgs 23:3
the temple of the **L** all the vessels	2 Kgs 23:4
the Asherah from the house of the **L**,	2 Kgs 23:6
who were in the house of the **L**,	2 Kgs 23:7
up to the altar of the **L** in Jerusalem,	2 Kgs 23:9
at the entrance to the house of the **L**,	2 Kgs 23:11
the two courts of the house of the **L**,	2 Kgs 23:12
to the word of the **L** that the man of	2 Kgs 23:16
had made, provoking the **L** to anger.	2 Kgs 23:19
the Passover to the **L** your God,	2 Kgs 23:21
was kept to the **L** in Jerusalem.	2 Kgs 23:23
priest found in the house of the **L**.	2 Kgs 23:24
who turned to the **L** with all his	2 Kgs 23:25
Still the **L** did not turn from the	2 Kgs 23:26
And the **L** said, "I will remove Judah	2 Kgs 23:27
what was evil in the sight of the **L**,	2 Kgs 23:32
what was evil in the sight of the **L**,	2 Kgs 23:37
And the **L** sent against him bands of	2 Kgs 24:2
to the word of the **L** that he spoke by	2 Kgs 24:2
upon Judah at the command of the **L**,	2 Kgs 24:3
blood, and the **L** would not pardon.	2 Kgs 24:4
did what was evil in the sight of the **L**,	2 Kgs 24:9
the house of the **L** and the treasures	2 Kgs 24:13
vessels of gold in the temple of the **L**,	2 Kgs 24:13
had made, as the **L** had foretold.	2 Kgs 24:13
what was evil in the sight of the **L**,	2 Kgs 24:19
of the anger of the **L** it came to the	2 Kgs 24:20
the house of the **L** and the king's	2 Kgs 25:9
that were in the house of the **L**,	2 Kgs 25:13
sea that were in the house of the **L**,	2 Kgs 25:13
had made for the house of the **L**,	2 Kgs 25:16
firstborn, was evil in the sight of the **L**,	1 Chr 2:3
into exile when the **L** sent Judah and	1 Chr 6:15
the house of the **L** after the ark rested	1 Chr 6:31
built the house of the **L** in Jerusalem,	1 Chr 6:32

been in charge of the camp of the **L**,	1 Chr 9:19
in time past; the **L** was with him.	1 Chr 9:20
of the gates of the house of the **L**,	1 Chr 9:23
broke faith with the **L** in that he did	1 Chr 10:13
did not keep the command of the **L**,	1 Chr 10:13
did not seek guidance from the **L**.	1 Chr 10:14
Therefore the **L** put him to death	1 Chr 10:14
And the **L** your God said to you, 'You	1 Chr 11:2
with them at Hebron before the **L**.	1 Chr 11:3
to the word of the **L** by Samuel.	1 Chr 11:3
for the **L** of hosts was with him.	1 Chr 11:9
the word of the **L** concerning Israel.	1 Chr 11:10
And the **L** saved them by a great	1 Chr 11:14
drink it. He poured it out to the **L**	1 Chr 11:18
him, according to the word of the **L**.	1 Chr 12:23
good to you and from the **L** our God,	1 Chr 13:2
the name of the **L** who sits enthroned	1 Chr 13:6
anger of the **L** was kindled against	1 Chr 13:10
angry because the **L** had broken	1 Chr 13:11
And the **L** blessed the household of	1 Chr 13:14
knew that the **L** had established him	1 Chr 14:2
my hand?" And the **L** said to him,	1 Chr 14:10
and the **L** brought the fear of him	1 Chr 14:17
for the **L** had chosen them to carry	1 Chr 15:2
the ark of the **L** and to minister to	1 Chr 15:2
bring up the ark of the **L** to its place,	1 Chr 15:3
you may bring up the ark of the **L**,	1 Chr 15:12
the **L** our God broke out against us,	1 Chr 15:13
to bring up the ark of the **L**,	1 Chr 15:14
according to the word of the **L**.	1 Chr 15:15
covenant of the **L** from the house	1 Chr 15:25
the ark of the covenant of the **L**,	1 Chr 15:26
the covenant of the **L** with shouting,	1 Chr 15:28
the covenant of the **L** came to the	1 Chr 15:29
the people in the name of the **L**	1 Chr 16:2
as ministers before the ark of the **L**,	1 Chr 16:4
invoke, to thank, and to praise the **L**,	1 Chr 16:4
be sung to the **L** by Asaph and his	1 Chr 16:7
Oh give thanks to the **L**; call upon	1 Chr 16:8
of those who seek the **L** rejoice!	1 Chr 16:10
Seek the **L** and his strength; seek his	1 Chr 16:11
He is the **L** our God; his judgments	1 Chr 16:14
Sing to the **L**, all the earth! Tell of	1 Chr 16:23
For great is the **L**, and greatly to be	1 Chr 16:25
idols, but the **L** made the heavens.	1 Chr 16:26
Ascribe to the **L**, O clans of the	1 Chr 16:28
ascribe to the **L** glory and strength!	1 Chr 16:28
Ascribe to the **L** the glory due his	1 Chr 16:29
Worship the **L** in the splendor of	1 Chr 16:29
among the nations, "The **L** reigns!"	1 Chr 16:31
of the forest sing for joy before the **L**,	1 Chr 16:33
Oh give thanks to the **L**, for he is	1 Chr 16:34
Blessed be the **L**, the God of Israel,	1 Chr 16:36
said, "Amen!" and praised the **L**.	1 Chr 16:36
covenant of the **L** to minister	1 Chr 16:37
the tabernacle of the **L** in the high	1 Chr 16:39
burnt offerings to the **L** on the altar	1 Chr 16:40
Law of the **L** that he commanded	1 Chr 16:40
named to give thanks to the **L**,	1 Chr 16:41
the covenant of the **L** is under a tent."	1 Chr 17:1
the word of the **L** came to Nathan,	1 Chr 17:3
my servant David, 'Thus says the **L**:	1 Chr 17:4
David, 'Thus says the **L** of hosts,	1 Chr 17:7
to you that the **L** will build you a	1 Chr 17:10
in and sat before the **L** and said,	1 Chr 17:16
LORD and said, "Who am I, O **L** God,	1 Chr 17:16
me future generations, O **L** God!	1 Chr 17:17
For your servant's sake, O **L**, and	1 Chr 17:19
There is none like you, O **L**, and	1 Chr 17:20
be your people forever, and you, O **L**,	1 Chr 17:22
And now, O **L**, let the word that you	1 Chr 17:23
forever, saying, 'The **L** of hosts,	1 Chr 17:24
And now, O **L**, you are God, and you	1 Chr 17:26
forever before you, for it is you, O **L**,	1 Chr 17:27
And the **L** gave victory to David	1 Chr 18:6
also King David dedicated to the **L**,	1 Chr 18:11
And the **L** gave victory to David	1 Chr 18:13
and may the **L** do what seems good	1 Chr 19:13
"May the **L** add to his people a	1 Chr 21:3
Are they not, my **l** the king, all of	1 Chr 21:3
Why then should my **l** require this?	1 Chr 21:3
And the **L** spoke to Gad, David's seer,	1 Chr 21:9
and say to David, 'Thus says the **L**,	1 Chr 21:10
and said to him, "Thus says the **L**,	1 Chr 21:11
else three days of the sword of the **L**,	1 Chr 21:12
of the **L** destroying throughout	1 Chr 21:12
Let me fall into the hand of the **L**,	1 Chr 21:13
So the **L** sent a pestilence on Israel,	1 Chr 21:14
he was about to destroy it, the **L** saw,	1 Chr 21:15
the angel of the **L** was standing by	1 Chr 21:15
angel of the **L** standing between	1 Chr 21:16
Please let your hand, O **L** my God,	1 Chr 21:17
angel of the **L** had commanded Gad	1 Chr 21:18
an altar to the **L** on the threshing	1 Chr 21:18
he had spoken in the name of the **L**.	1 Chr 21:19
on it an altar to the **L**—give it to me	1 Chr 21:22
and let my **l** the king do what seems	1 Chr 21:23
will not take for the **L** what is yours,	1 Chr 21:24
altar to the **L** and presented burnt	1 Chr 21:26
peace offerings and called on the **L**,	1 Chr 21:26
and the **L** answered him with fire	1 Chr 21:26
Then the **L** commanded the angel,	1 Chr 21:27
saw that the **L** had answered him	1 Chr 21:28
For the tabernacle of the **L**, which	1 Chr 21:29
of the sword of the angel of the **L**.	1 Chr 21:30
the house of the **L** God and here the	1 Chr 22:1
built for the **L** must be exceedingly	1 Chr 22:5
him to build a house for the **L**,	1 Chr 22:6
a house to the name of the **L** my God.	1 Chr 22:7
But the word of the **L** came to me,	1 Chr 22:8
"Now, my son, the **L** be with you, so	1 Chr 22:11
the house of the **L** your God,	1 Chr 22:11
may the **L** grant you discretion and	1 Chr 22:12
may keep the law of the **L** your God.	1 Chr 22:12
rules that the **L** commanded Moses	1 Chr 22:13
the house of the **L** 100,000 talents of	1 Chr 22:14
and work! The **L** be with you!"	1 Chr 22:16
"Is not the **L** your God with you?	1 Chr 22:18
subdued before the **L** and his people.	1 Chr 22:18
and heart to seek the **L** your God.	1 Chr 22:19
build the sanctuary of the **L** God,	1 Chr 22:19
the covenant of the **L** and the holy	1 Chr 22:19
a house built for the name of the **L**."	1 Chr 22:19
of the work in the house of the **L**,	1 Chr 23:4
praises to the **L** with the instruments	1 Chr 23:5
offerings before the **L** and minister	1 Chr 23:13
for the service of the house of the **L**.	1 Chr 23:24
For David said, "The **L**, the God of	1 Chr 23:25
for the service of the house of the **L**,	1 Chr 23:28
thanking and praising the **L**,	1 Chr 23:30
were offered to the **L** on Sabbaths,	1 Chr 23:31
of them, regularly before the **L**.	1 Chr 23:31
for the service of the house of the **L**.	1 Chr 23:32
the house of the **L** according to the	1 Chr 24:19
as the **L** God of Israel had	1 Chr 24:19
in thanksgiving and praise to the **L**.	1 Chr 25:3
in the house of the **L** with cymbals,	1 Chr 25:6
who were trained in singing to the **L**,	1 Chr 25:7
ministering in the house of the **L**.	1 Chr 26:12
the treasuries of the house of the **L**.	1 Chr 26:22
maintenance of the house of the **L**.	1 Chr 26:27
the work of the **L** and for the service	1 Chr 26:30
for the **L** had promised to make	1 Chr 27:23
the covenant of the **L** and for the	1 Chr 28:2
Yet the **L** God of Israel chose me from	1 Chr 28:4
my sons (for the **L** has given me	1 Chr 28:5
of the kingdom of the **L** over Israel.	1 Chr 28:5
of all Israel, the assembly of the **L**,	1 Chr 28:8
commandments of the **L** your God,	1 Chr 28:8
for the **L** searches all hearts and	1 Chr 28:9
for the **L** has chosen you to build a	1 Chr 28:10
for the courts of the house of the **L**,	1 Chr 28:12
of the service in the house of the **L**;	1 Chr 28:13
for the service in the house of the **L**,	1 Chr 28:13
the ark of the covenant of the **L**.	1 Chr 28:18
in writing from the hand of the **L**,	1 Chr 28:19
do not be dismayed, for the **L** God,	1 Chr 28:20
of the house of the **L** is finished.	1 Chr 28:20
will not be for man but for the **L** God.	1 Chr 29:1
consecrating himself today to the **L**?"	1 Chr 29:5
to the treasury of the house of the **L**,	1 Chr 29:8
heart they had offered freely to the **L**.	1 Chr 29:9
David blessed the **L** in the presence	1 Chr 29:10
"Blessed are you, O **L**, the God of	1 Chr 29:10
Yours, O **L**, is the greatness and the	1 Chr 29:11
Yours is the kingdom, O **L**, and you	1 Chr 29:11
O **L** our God, all this abundance	1 Chr 29:16
O **L**, the God of Abraham, Isaac,	1 Chr 29:18
"Bless the **L** your God." And all the	1 Chr 29:20
And all the assembly blessed the **L**,	1 Chr 29:20
paid homage to the **L** and to the	1 Chr 29:20
And they offered sacrifices to the **L**,	1 Chr 29:21
day offered burnt offerings to the **L**,	1 Chr 29:21
and drank before the **L** on that day	1 Chr 29:22
anointed him as prince for the **L**,	1 Chr 29:22
the throne of the **L** as king in place	1 Chr 29:23
And the **L** made Solomon very great	1 Chr 29:25
and the **L** his God was with him and	2 Chr 1:1
the servant of the **L** had made in the	2 Chr 1:3
there before the tabernacle of the **L**.	2 Chr 1:5
there to the bronze altar before the **L**,	2 Chr 1:6
O **L** God, let your word to David my	2 Chr 1:9
to build a temple for the name of the **L**,	2 Chr 2:1
the name of the **L** my God and	2 Chr 2:4
the appointed feasts of the **L** our God,	2 Chr 2:4
"Because the **L** loves his people,	2 Chr 2:11
said, "Blessed be the **L** God of Israel,	2 Chr 2:12
a temple for the **L** and a royal palace	2 Chr 2:12
craftsmen, the craftsmen of my **l**,	2 Chr 2:14
and wine, of which my **l** has spoken,	2 Chr 2:15
the house of the **L** in Jerusalem on	2 Chr 3:1
where the **L** had appeared to David his	2 Chr 3:1
King Solomon for the house of the **L**.	2 Chr 4:16
did for the house of the **L** was finished.	2 Chr 5:1
of the covenant of the **L** out of the city	2 Chr 5:2
of the covenant of the **L** to its place,	2 Chr 5:7
where the **L** made a covenant with	2 Chr 5:10
in praise and thanksgiving to the **L**),	2 Chr 5:13
instruments, in praise to the **L**,	2 Chr 5:13
the house, the house of the **L**,	2 Chr 5:13
the glory of the **L** filled the house of	2 Chr 5:14
"The **L** has said that he would dwell in	2 Chr 6:1
And he said, "Blessed be the **L**, the God	2 Chr 6:4
to build a house for the name of the **L**,	2 Chr 6:7
But the **L** said to David my father,	2 Chr 6:8
Now the **L** has fulfilled his promise	2 Chr 6:10
throne of Israel, as the **L** promised,	2 Chr 6:10
built the house for the name of the **L**,	2 Chr 6:10
the covenant of the **L** that he made	2 Chr 6:11
the altar of the **L** in the presence of	2 Chr 6:12
and said, "O **L**, God of Israel, there is	2 Chr 6:14
Now therefore, O **L**, God of Israel,	2 Chr 6:16
Now therefore, O **L**, God of Israel, let	2 Chr 6:17
servant and to his plea, O **L** my God,	2 Chr 6:19
"And now arise, O **L** God, and go to	2 Chr 6:41
Let your priests, O **L** God, be clothed	2 Chr 6:41
O **L** God, do not turn away the face of	2 Chr 6:42
and the glory of the **L** filled the temple.	2 Chr 7:1
could not enter the house of the **L**,	2 Chr 7:2
the glory of the **L** filled the LORD'S	2 Chr 7:2
and the glory of the **L** on the temple,	2 Chr 7:3
worshiped and gave thanks to the **L**,	2 Chr 7:3
people offered sacrifice before the **L**.	2 Chr 7:4
for music to the **L** that King David	2 Chr 7:6
giving thanks to the **L**—for his	2 Chr 7:6
that was before the house of the **L**,	2 Chr 7:7
prosperity that the **L** had granted to	2 Chr 7:10
the house of the **L** and the king's	2 Chr 7:11
in the house of the **L** and in his own	2 Chr 7:11
Then the **L** appeared to Solomon in	2 Chr 7:12
'Why has the **L** done thus to this	2 Chr 7:21
say, 'Because they abandoned the **L**,	2 Chr 7:22
the house of the **L** and his own house,	2 Chr 8:1
the ark of the **L** has come are holy."	2 Chr 8:11
burnt offerings to the **L** on the altar	2 Chr 8:12
on the altar of the **L** that he had built	2 Chr 8:12
of the house of the **L** was laid until it	2 Chr 8:16
So the house of the **L** was completed.	2 Chr 8:16
that he offered at the house of the **L**,	2 Chr 9:4
Blessed be the **L** your God, who has	2 Chr 9:8
his throne as king for the **L** your God!	2 Chr 9:8
the house of the **L** and for the king's	2 Chr 9:11
by God that the **L** might fulfill his	2 Chr 10:15
the word of the **L** came to Shemaiah	2 Chr 11:2
'Thus says the **L**, You shall not go up	2 Chr 11:4
the word of the **L** and returned and	2 Chr 11:4
out from serving as priests of the **L**,	2 Chr 11:14
hearts to seek the **L** God of Israel	2 Chr 11:16
to Jerusalem to sacrifice to the **L**,	2 Chr 11:16
he abandoned the law of the **L**,	2 Chr 12:1
they had been unfaithful to the **L**,	2 Chr 12:2
and said to them, "Thus says the **L**,	2 Chr 12:5
and said, "The **L** is righteous."	2 Chr 12:6
When the **L** saw that they humbled	2 Chr 12:7
the word of the **L** came to Shemaiah:	2 Chr 12:7
the house of the **L** and the treasures	2 Chr 12:9
king went into the house of the **L**,	2 Chr 12:11
the wrath of the **L** turned from him,	2 Chr 12:12
the city that the **L** had chosen out of	2 Chr 12:13
he did not set his heart to seek the **L**.	2 Chr 12:14
to know that the **L** God of Israel gave	2 Chr 13:5
rose up and rebelled against his **l**,	2 Chr 13:6
the kingdom of the **L** in the hand of	2 Chr 13:8
not driven out the priests of the **L**,	2 Chr 13:9
But as for us, the **L** is our God, and	2 Chr 13:10
ministering to the **L** who are sons	2 Chr 13:10
offer to the **L** every morning and	2 Chr 13:11
we keep the charge of the **L** our God,	2 Chr 13:11
of Israel, do not fight against the **L**,	2 Chr 13:12
And they cried to the **L**, and the	2 Chr 13:14
because they relied on the **L**,	2 Chr 13:18
And the **L** struck him down, and he	2 Chr 13:20
and right in the eyes of the **L** his God.	2 Chr 14:2
and commanded Judah to seek the **L**,	2 Chr 14:4
those years, for the **L** gave him peace.	2 Chr 14:6
we have sought the **L** our God.	2 Chr 14:7
And Asa cried to the **L** his God, "O	2 Chr 14:11
Asa cried to the LORD his God, "O **L**,	2 Chr 14:11
Help us, O **L** our God, for we rely on	2 Chr 14:11
come against this multitude. O **L**,	2 Chr 14:11
So the **L** defeated the Ethiopians	2 Chr 14:12
broken before the **L** and his army.	2 Chr 14:13
for the fear of the **L** was upon them.	2 Chr 14:14
The **L** is with you while you are with	2 Chr 15:2
in their distress they turned to the **L**,	2 Chr 15:4

the altar of the **L** that was in front 2 Chr 15:8
of the vestibule of the house of the **L**. 2 Chr 15:8
they saw that the **L** his God was with 2 Chr 15:9
They sacrificed to the **L** on that day 2 Chr 15:11
into a covenant to seek the **L**, 2 Chr 15:12
that whoever would not seek the **L**, 2 Chr 15:13
an oath to the **L** with a loud voice 2 Chr 15:14
and the **L** gave them rest all around. 2 Chr 15:15
the house of the **L** and the king's 2 Chr 16:2
and did not rely on the **L** your God, 2 Chr 16:7
Yet because you relied on the **L**, he 2 Chr 16:8
For the eyes of the **L** run to and fro 2 Chr 16:9
in his disease he did not seek the **L**, 2 Chr 16:12
The **L** was with Jehoshaphat, 2 Chr 17:3
Therefore the **L** established the 2 Chr 17:5
was courageous in the ways of the **L**. 2 Chr 17:6
Book of the Law of the **L** with them. 2 Chr 17:9
the fear of the **L** fell upon all the 2 Chr 17:10
a volunteer for the service of the **L**, 2 Chr 17:16
"Inquire first for the word of the **L**." 2 Chr 18:4
another prophet of the **L** of whom we 2 Chr 18:6
by whom we may inquire of the **L**, 2 Chr 18:7
of iron and said, "Thus says the **L**, 2 Chr 18:10
The **L** will give it into the hand of 2 Chr 18:11
But Micaiah said, "As the **L** lives, 2 Chr 18:13
but the truth in the name of the **L**?" 2 Chr 18:15
And the **L** said, 'These have no 2 Chr 18:16
"Therefore hear the word of the **L**: 2 Chr 18:18
I saw the **L** sitting on his throne, 2 Chr 18:18
And the **L** said, 'Who will entice 2 Chr 18:19
forward and stood before the **L**, 2 Chr 18:20
And the **L** said to him, 'By what 2 Chr 18:20
the **L** has put a lying spirit in the 2 Chr 18:22
The **L** has declared disaster 2 Chr 18:22
did the Spirit of the **L** go from me to 2 Chr 18:23
the **L** has not spoken by me." And 2 Chr 18:27
cried out, and the **L** helped him; 2 Chr 18:31
and love those who hate the **L**? 2 Chr 19:2
has gone out against you from the **L**. 2 Chr 19:2
and brought them back to the **L**, 2 Chr 19:4
you judge not for man but for the **L**. 2 Chr 19:6
then, let the fear of the **L** be upon you. 2 Chr 19:7
is no injustice with the **L** our God, 2 Chr 19:7
give judgment for the **L** and to decide 2 Chr 19:8
you shall do in the fear of the **L**, 2 Chr 19:9
guilt before the **L** and wrath may 2 Chr 19:10
is over you in all matters of the **L**; 2 Chr 19:11
and may the **L** be with the upright!" 2 Chr 19:11
afraid and set his face to seek the **L**, 2 Chr 20:3
assembled to seek help from the **L**; 2 Chr 20:4
of Judah they came to seek the **L**. 2 Chr 20:4
and Jerusalem, in the house of the **L**, 2 Chr 20:5
and said, "O **L**, God of our fathers, are 2 Chr 20:6
all Judah stood before the **L**, 2 Chr 20:13
Spirit of the **L** came upon Jahaziel 2 Chr 20:14
Thus says the **L** to you, 'Do not be 2 Chr 20:15
salvation of the **L** on your behalf, 2 Chr 20:17
them, and the **L** will be with you." 2 Chr 20:17
of Jerusalem fell down before the **L**, 2 Chr 20:18
before the LORD, worshiping the **L**. 2 Chr 20:18
Korahites, stood up to praise the **L**, 2 Chr 20:19
Believe in the **L** your God, and you 2 Chr 20:20
to sing to the **L** and praise him in 2 Chr 20:21
and say, "Give thanks to the **L**, 2 Chr 20:21
the **L** set an ambush against the 2 Chr 20:22
for there they blessed the **L**. 2 Chr 20:26
for the **L** had made them rejoice 2 Chr 20:27
and trumpets, to the house of the **L**. 2 Chr 20:28
heard that the **L** had fought against 2 Chr 20:29
what was right in the sight of the **L**. 2 Chr 20:32
the **L** will destroy what you have 2 Chr 20:37
did what was evil in the sight of the **L**. 2 Chr 21:6
Yet the **L** was not willing to destroy 2 Chr 21:7
rule, because he had forsaken the **L**, 2 Chr 21:10
prophet, saying, "Thus says the **L**, 2 Chr 21:12
the **L** will bring a great plague on 2 Chr 21:14
And the **L** stirred up against 2 Chr 21:16
after all this the **L** struck him in his 2 Chr 21:18
did what was evil in the sight of the **L**, 2 Chr 22:4
whom the **L** had anointed to destroy 2 Chr 22:7
who sought the **L** with all his heart." 2 Chr 22:9
as the **L** spoke concerning the sons of 2 Chr 23:3
be in the courts of the house of the **L**. 2 Chr 23:5
the house of the **L** except the priests 2 Chr 23:6
people shall keep the charge of the **L**. 2 Chr 23:6
into the house of the **L** to the people. 2 Chr 23:12
her to death in the house of the **L**." 2 Chr 23:14
house of the **L** under the direction 2 Chr 23:18
to be in charge of the house of the **L**, 2 Chr 23:18
to offer burnt offerings to the **L**, 2 Chr 23:18
of the house of the **L** so that no one 2 Chr 23:19
king down from the house of the **L**, 2 Chr 23:20
in the eyes of the **L** all the days of 2 Chr 24:2
decided to restore the house of the **L**. 2 Chr 24:4
levied by Moses, the servant of the **L**, 2 Chr 24:6
of the house of the **L** for the Baals. 2 Chr 24:7
outside the gate of the house of the **L**. 2 Chr 24:8
bring in for the **L** the tax that Moses 2 Chr 24:9
of the work of the house of the **L**, 2 Chr 24:12
to restore the house of the **L**, 2 Chr 24:12
bronze to repair the house of the **L**. 2 Chr 24:12
made utensils for the house of the **L**, 2 Chr 24:14
the house of the **L** regularly all the 2 Chr 24:14
they abandoned the house of the **L**, 2 Chr 24:18
them to bring them back to the **L**. 2 Chr 24:19
break the commandments of the **L**, 2 Chr 24:20
Because you have forsaken the **L**, he 2 Chr 24:20
in the court of the house of the **L**. 2 Chr 24:21
he said, "May the **L** see and avenge!" 2 Chr 24:22
the **L** delivered into their hand a 2 Chr 24:24
because Judah had forsaken the **L**, 2 Chr 24:24
what was right in the eyes of the **L**, 2 Chr 25:2
of Moses, where the **L** commanded, 2 Chr 25:4
with you, for the **L** is not with Israel, 2 Chr 25:7
"The **L** is able to give you much 2 Chr 25:9
Therefore the **L** was angry with 2 Chr 25:15
turned away from the **L** they made a 2 Chr 25:27
what was right in the eyes of the **L**, 2 Chr 26:4
God, and as long as he sought the **L**, 2 Chr 26:5
was unfaithful to the **L** his God and 2 Chr 26:16
the temple of the **L** to burn incense 2 Chr 26:16
eighty priests of the **L** who were men 2 Chr 26:17
Uzziah, to burn incense to the **L**, 2 Chr 26:18
you no honor from the **L** God." 2 Chr 26:18
of the priests in the house of the **L**, 2 Chr 26:19
out, because the **L** had struck him. 2 Chr 26:20
excluded from the house of the **L**. 2 Chr 26:21
the eyes of the **L** according to all that 2 Chr 27:2
he did not enter the temple of the **L**. 2 Chr 27:2
the house of the **L** and did much 2 Chr 27:3
his ways before the **L** his God. 2 Chr 27:6
do what was right in the eyes of the **L**, 2 Chr 28:1
nations whom the **L** drove out before 2 Chr 28:3
Therefore the **L** his God gave him 2 Chr 28:5
because they had forsaken the **L**, 2 Chr 28:6
But a prophet of the **L** was there, 2 Chr 28:9
said to them, "Behold, because the **L**, 2 Chr 28:9
your own against the **L** your God? 2 Chr 28:10
fierce wrath of the **L** is upon you." 2 Chr 28:11
us guilt against the **L** in addition to 2 Chr 28:13
For the **L** humbled Judah because 2 Chr 28:19
had been very unfaithful to the **L**. 2 Chr 28:19
the house of the **L** and the house of 2 Chr 28:21
more faithless to the **L**—this same 2 Chr 28:22
up the doors of the house of the **L**, 2 Chr 28:24
gods, provoking to anger the **L**, 2 Chr 28:25
what was right in the eyes of the **L**, 2 Chr 29:2
the house of the **L** and repaired them. 2 Chr 29:3
and consecrate the house of the **L**, 2 Chr 29:5
was evil in the sight of the **L** our God. 2 Chr 29:6
habitation of the **L** and turned their 2 Chr 29:6
the wrath of the **L** came on Judah 2 Chr 29:8
to make a covenant with the **L**, 2 Chr 29:10
for the **L** has chosen you to stand in 2 Chr 29:11
commanded, by the words of the **L**, 2 Chr 29:15
LORD, to cleanse the house of the **L**. 2 Chr 29:15
of the house of the **L** to cleanse it, 2 Chr 29:16
the temple of the **L** into the court of 2 Chr 29:16
into the court of the house of the **L**. 2 Chr 29:16
they came to the vestibule of the **L**. 2 Chr 29:17
they consecrated the house of the **L**, 2 Chr 29:17
have cleansed all the house of the **L**, 2 Chr 29:18
they are before the altar of the **L**." 2 Chr 29:19
and went up to the house of the **L**, 2 Chr 29:20
to offer them on the altar of the **L**. 2 Chr 29:21
in the house of the **L** with cymbals, 2 Chr 29:25
was from the **L** through his 2 Chr 29:25
began, the song to the **L** began also, 2 Chr 29:27
sing praises to the **L** with the words 2 Chr 29:30
consecrated yourselves to the **L**. 2 Chr 29:31
house of the **L**." And the assembly 2 Chr 29:31
were for a burnt offering to the **L**. 2 Chr 29:32
of the house of the **L** was restored. 2 Chr 29:35
the house of the **L** at Jerusalem to 2 Chr 30:1
to keep the Passover to the **L**, 2 Chr 30:1
come and keep the Passover to the **L**, 2 Chr 30:5
"O people of Israel, return to the **L**, 2 Chr 30:6
were faithless to the **L** God of their 2 Chr 30:7
yield yourselves to the **L** and come to 2 Chr 30:8
forever, and serve the **L** your God, 2 Chr 30:8
For if you return to the **L**, your 2 Chr 30:9
For the **L** your God is gracious and 2 Chr 30:9
commanded by the word of the **L**. 2 Chr 30:12
offerings into the house of the **L**. 2 Chr 30:15
not clean, to consecrate it to the **L**. 2 Chr 30:17
"May the good **L** pardon everyone 2 Chr 30:18
who sets his heart to seek God, the **L**, 2 Chr 30:19
And the **L** heard Hezekiah and 2 Chr 30:20
the priests praised the **L** day by day, 2 Chr 30:21
with all their might to the **L**. 2 Chr 30:21
good skill in the service of the **L**. 2 Chr 30:22
and giving thanks to the **L**, 2 Chr 30:22
the camp of the **L** and to give thanks 2 Chr 31:2
as it is written in the Law of the **L**. 2 Chr 31:3
give themselves to the Law of the **L**. 2 Chr 31:4
had been dedicated to the **L** their God, 2 Chr 31:6
they blessed the **L** and his people 2 Chr 31:8
into the house of the **L**, 2 Chr 31:10
left, for the **L** has blessed his people, 2 Chr 31:10
chambers in the house of the **L**, 2 Chr 31:11
reserved for the **L** and the most 2 Chr 31:14
the house of the **L** as the duty of 2 Chr 31:16
and faithful before the **L** his God. 2 Chr 31:20
of flesh, but with us is the **L** our God, 2 Chr 32:8
"The **L** our God will deliver us from 2 Chr 32:11
more against the **L** GOD and against 2 Chr 32:16
letters to cast contempt on the **L**, 2 Chr 32:17
And the **L** sent an angel, who cut off 2 Chr 32:21
So the **L** saved Hezekiah and the 2 Chr 32:22
gifts to the **L** to Jerusalem and 2 Chr 32:23
of death, and he prayed to the **L**, 2 Chr 32:24
the wrath of the **L** did not come 2 Chr 32:26
did what was evil in the sight of the **L**, 2 Chr 33:2
nations whom the **L** drove out before 2 Chr 33:2
he built altars in the house of the **L**, 2 Chr 33:4
of the LORD, of which the **L** had said, 2 Chr 33:4
the two courts of the house of the **L**. 2 Chr 33:5
He did much evil in the sight of the **L**, 2 Chr 33:6
nations whom the **L** destroyed before 2 Chr 33:9
The **L** spoke to Manasseh and to his 2 Chr 33:10
Therefore the **L** brought upon them 2 Chr 33:11
the favor of the **L** his God and 2 Chr 33:12
Manasseh knew that the **L** was God. 2 Chr 33:13
and the idol from the house of the **L**, 2 Chr 33:15
the house of the **L** and in Jerusalem, 2 Chr 33:15
the altar of the **L** and offered on it 2 Chr 33:16
he commanded Judah to serve the **L**, 2 Chr 33:16
places, but only to the **L** their God. 2 Chr 33:17
spoke to him in the name of the **L**, 2 Chr 33:18
what was evil in the sight of the **L**, 2 Chr 33:22
not humble himself before the **L**, 2 Chr 33:23
what was right in the eyes of the **L**, 2 Chr 34:2
to repair the house of the **L** his God. 2 Chr 34:8
were working in the house of the **L**. 2 Chr 34:10
the house of the **L** gave it for 2 Chr 34:10
brought into the house of the **L**, 2 Chr 34:14
Law of the **L** given through Moses. 2 Chr 34:14
house of the **L**." And Hilkiah gave 2 Chr 34:15
the house of the **L** and have given it 2 Chr 34:17
inquire of the **L** for me and for those 2 Chr 34:21
the wrath of the **L** that is poured out 2 Chr 34:21
have not kept the word of the **L**, 2 Chr 34:21
she said to them, "Thus says the **L**, 2 Chr 34:23
Thus says the **L**, behold, I will bring 2 Chr 34:24
who sent you to inquire of the **L**, 2 Chr 34:26
you say to him, Thus says the **L**, 2 Chr 34:26
also have heard you, declares the **L**. 2 Chr 34:27
king went up to the house of the **L**, 2 Chr 34:30
been found in the house of the **L**. 2 Chr 34:30
and made a covenant before the **L**, 2 Chr 34:31
to walk after the **L** and to keep his 2 Chr 34:31
in Israel serve the **L** their God. 2 Chr 34:33
not turn away from following the **L**, 2 Chr 34:33
kept a Passover to the **L** in Jerusalem. 2 Chr 35:1
in the service of the house of the **L**. 2 Chr 35:2
all Israel and who were holy to the **L**, 2 Chr 35:3
Now serve the **L** your God and his 2 Chr 35:3
to the word of the **L** by Moses." 2 Chr 35:6
of the lay people, to offer to the **L**, 2 Chr 35:12
service of the **L** was prepared that 2 Chr 35:16
burnt offerings on the altar of the **L**, 2 Chr 35:16
what is written in the Law of the **L**, 2 Chr 35:26
was evil in the sight of the **L** his God. 2 Chr 36:5
the house of the **L** to Babylon and put 2 Chr 36:7
did what was evil in the sight of the **L**. 2 Chr 36:9
vessels of the house of the **L**, 2 Chr 36:10
evil in the sight of the **L** his God. 2 Chr 36:12
who spoke from the mouth of the **L**. 2 Chr 36:12
his heart against turning to the **L**, 2 Chr 36:13
the house of the **L** that he had made 2 Chr 36:14
The **L**, the God of their fathers, sent 2 Chr 36:15
the wrath of the **L** rose against his 2 Chr 36:16
the treasures of the house of the **L**, 2 Chr 36:18
the word of the **L** by the mouth of 2 Chr 36:21
the word of the **L** by the mouth of 2 Chr 36:22
the **L** stirred up the spirit of Cyrus 2 Chr 36:22
says Cyrus king of Persia, 'The **L**, 2 Chr 36:23
may the **L** his God be with him. 2 Chr 36:23
that the word of the **L** by the mouth of Ezr 1:1
the **L** stirred up the spirit of Cyrus king Ezr 1:1
"Thus says Cyrus king of Persia: The **L**, Ezr 1:2
in Judah, and rebuild the house of the **L**, Ezr 1:3
the house of the **L** that is in Jerusalem. Ezr 1:5
house of the **L** that Nebuchadnezzar had Ezr 1:7
the house of the **L** that is in Jerusalem, Ezr 2:68

they offered burnt offerings on it to the **L**, Ezr 3:3
and at all the appointed feasts of the **L**, Ezr 3:5
who made a freewill offering to the **L**. Ezr 3:5
began to offer burnt offerings to the **L**. Ezr 3:6
of the temple of the **L** was not yet laid. Ezr 3:6
supervise the work of the house of the **L**. Ezr 3:8
the foundation of the temple of the **L**, Ezr 3:10
of Asaph, with cymbals, to praise the **L**, Ezr 3:10
praising and giving thanks to the **L**, Ezr 3:11
a great shout when they praised the **L**, Ezr 3:11
of the house of the **L** was laid. Ezr 3:11
exiles were building a temple to the **L**, Ezr 4:1
but we alone will build to the **L**, the God Ezr 4:3
the peoples of the land to worship the **L**, Ezr 6:21
for the **L** had made them joyful and had Ezr 6:22
Law of Moses that the **L** the God of Israel Ezr 7:6
for the hand of the **L** his God was on him. Ezr 7:6
set his heart to study the Law of the **L**, Ezr 7:10
commandments of the **L** and his Ezr 7:11
Blessed be the **L**, the God of our fathers, Ezr 7:27
the house of the **L** that is in Jerusalem, Ezr 7:27
for the hand of the **L** my God was on Ezr 7:28
I said to them, "You are holy to the **L**, Ezr 8:28
the gold are a freewill offering to the **L**, Ezr 8:28
the chambers of the house of the **L**." Ezr 8:29
All this was a burnt offering to the **L**. Ezr 8:35
spread out my hands to the **L** my God, Ezr 9:5
favor has been shown by the **L** our God, Ezr 9:8
O **L** the God of Israel, you are just, for we Ezr 9:15
to the counsel of my **l** and of those who Ezr 10:3
Now then make confession to the **L**, Ezr 10:11
And I said, "O **L** God of heaven, the great Neh 1:5
O **L**, let your ear be attentive to the Neh 1:11
nobles would not stoop to serve their **L**. Neh 3:5
Remember the **L**, who is great and Neh 4:14
said "Amen" and praised the **L**. Neh 5:13
Moses that the **L** had commanded Neh 8:1
And Ezra blessed the **L**, the great God, Neh 8:6
and worshiped the **L** with their faces Neh 8:6
"This day is holy to the **L** your God; Neh 8:9
ready, for this day is holy to our **L**. Neh 8:10
for the joy of the **L** is your strength." Neh 8:10
the Law that the **L** had commanded by Neh 8:14
of the Law of the **L** their God for a Neh 9:3
and worshiped the **L** their God. Neh 9:3
with a loud voice to the **L** their God. Neh 9:4
up and bless the **L** your God from Neh 9:5
"You are the **L**, you alone. You have Neh 9:6
You are the **L**, the God who chose Neh 9:7
commandments of the **L** our Lord Neh 10:29
of the LORD our **L** and his rules and Neh 10:29
to burn on the altar of the **L** our God, Neh 10:34
year by year, to the house of the **L**; Neh 10:35
came to present themselves before the **L**, Jb 1:6
The **L** said to Satan, "From where have Jb 1:7
come?" Satan answered the **L** and said, Jb 1:7
And the **L** said to Satan, "Have you Jb 1:8
Then Satan answered the **L** and said, Jb 1:9
And the **L** said to Satan, "Behold, all that Jb 1:12
went out from the presence of the **L**. Jb 1:12
and naked shall I return. The **L** gave, Jb 1:21
LORD gave, and the **L** has taken away; Jb 1:21
away; blessed be the name of the **L**." Jb 1:21
came to present themselves before the **L**, Jb 2:1
them to present himself before the **L**. Jb 2:1
And the **L** said to Satan, "From where Jb 2:2
come?" Satan answered the **L** and said, Jb 2:2
And the **L** said to Satan, "Have you Jb 2:3
Then Satan answered the **L** and said, Jb 2:4
And the **L** said to Satan, "Behold, he is in Jb 2:6
the presence of the **L** and struck Job with Jb 2:7
that the hand of the **L** has done this? Jb 12:9
he said to man, 'Behold, the fear of the **L**, Jb 28:28
Then the **L** answered Job out of the Jb 38:1
And the **L** said to Job: Jb 40:1
Then Job answered the **L** and said: Jb 40:3
Then the **L** answered Job out of the Jb 40:6
Then Job answered the **L** and said: Jb 42:1
After the **L** had spoken these words to Jb 42:7
Job, the **L** said to Eliphaz the Temanite: Jb 42:7
went and did what the **L** had told them, Jb 42:9
them, and the **L** accepted Job's prayer. Jb 42:9
And the **L** restored the fortunes of Job, Jb 42:10
And the **L** gave Job twice as much as he Jb 42:10
the evil that the **L** had brought upon Jb 42:11
And the **L** blessed the latter days of Job Jb 42:12
but his delight is in the law of the **L**, and Ps 1:2
for the **L** knows the way of the righteous, Ps 1:6
against the **L** and against his anointed, Ps 2:2
laughs; the **L** holds them in derision. Ps 2:4
The **L** said to me, "You are my Son; Ps 2:7
Serve the **L** with fear, and rejoice with Ps 2:11
O **L**, how many are my foes! Many are Ps 3:1
But you, O **L**, are a shield about me, my Ps 3:3
I cried aloud to the **L**, and he answered me Ps 3:4
slept; I woke again, for the **L** sustained me. Ps 3:5
Arise, O **L**! Save me, O my God! For you Ps 3:7
Salvation belongs to the **L**; your blessing Ps 3:8
But know that the **L** has set apart the Ps 4:3
himself; the **L** hears when I call to him. Ps 4:3
sacrifices, and put your trust in the **L**. Ps 4:5
up the light of your face upon us, O **L**!" Ps 4:6
for you alone, O **L**, make me dwell in Ps 4:8
Give ear to my words, O **L**; consider my Ps 5:1
O **L**, in the morning you hear my voice; in Ps 5:3
the **L** abhors the bloodthirsty and Ps 5:6
Lead me, O **L**, in your righteousness Ps 5:8
For you bless the righteous, O **L**; you Ps 5:12
O **L**, rebuke me not in your anger, nor Ps 6:1
Be gracious to me, O **L**, for I am Ps 6:2
heal me, O **L**, for my bones are troubled. Ps 6:2
troubled. But you, O **L**—how long? Ps 6:3
Turn, O **L**, deliver my life; save me for the Ps 6:4
for the **L** has heard the sound of my Ps 6:8
The **L** has heard my plea; the LORD accepts Ps 6:9
heard my plea; the **L** accepts my prayer. Ps 6:9
he sang to the **L** concerning the words of Ps 7:T
O **L** my God, in you do I take refuge; save Ps 7:1
O **L** my God, if I have done this, if there is Ps 7:3
Arise, O **L**, in your anger; lift yourself up Ps 7:6
The **L** judges the peoples; judge me, O Ps 7:8
judge me, O **L**, according to my Ps 7:8
I will give to the **L** the thanks due to his Ps 7:17
I will sing praise to the name of the **L**, Ps 7:17
O **L**, our Lord, how majestic is your name Ps 8:1
O LORD, our **L**, how majestic is your name Ps 8:1
O **L**, our Lord, how majestic is your name Ps 8:9
O LORD, our **L**, how majestic is your name Ps 8:9
give thanks to the **L** with my whole heart; Ps 9:1
But the **L** sits enthroned forever; he has Ps 9:7
The **L** is a stronghold for the oppressed, a Ps 9:9
name put their trust in you, for you, O **L**, Ps 9:10
Sing praises to the **L**, who sits enthroned Ps 9:11
Be gracious to me, O **L**! See my affliction Ps 9:13
The **L** has made himself known; he has Ps 9:16
Arise, O **L**! Let not man prevail; let the Ps 9:19
Put them in fear, O **L**! Let the nations Ps 9:20
Why, O **L**, do you stand afar off? Why do Ps 10:1
for gain curses and renounces the **L**. Ps 10:3
Arise, O **L**; O God, lift up your hand; Ps 10:12
The **L** is king forever and ever; the Ps 10:16
O **L**, you hear the desire of the afflicted; Ps 10:17
In the **L** I take refuge; how can you say to Ps 11:1
The **L** is in his holy temple; the LORD'S Ps 11:4
The **L** tests the righteous, but his soul Ps 11:5
For the **L** is righteous; he loves righteous Ps 11:7
Save, O **L**, for the godly one is gone; for Ps 12:1
May the **L** cut off all flattering lips, the Ps 12:3
needy groan, I will now arise," says the **L**; Ps 12:5
The words of the **L** are pure words, like Ps 12:6
You, O **L**, will keep them; you will guard Ps 12:7
How long, O **L**? Will you forget me Ps 13:1
Consider and answer me, O **L** my God; Ps 13:3
I will sing to the **L**, because he has dealt Ps 13:6
The **L** looks down from heaven on the Ps 14:2
eat bread and do not call upon the **L**? Ps 14:4
plans of the poor, but the **L** is his refuge. Ps 14:6
When the **L** restores the fortunes of his Ps 14:7
O **L**, who shall sojourn in your tent? Ps 15:1
but who honors those who fear the **L**; Ps 15:4
I say to the **L**, "You are my Lord; I have Ps 16:2
I say to the LORD, "You are my **L**; I have Ps 16:2
The **L** is my chosen portion and my cup; Ps 16:5
I bless the **L** who gives me counsel; in the Ps 16:7
I have set the **L** always before me; Ps 16:8
Hear a just cause, O **L**; attend to my cry! Ps 17:1
Arise, O **L**! Confront him, subdue him! Ps 17:13
from men by your hand, O **L**, from Ps 17:14
A Psalm of David, the servant of the **L**, Ps 18:T
of this song to the **L** on the day when the Ps 18:T
the day when the **L** rescued him from Ps 18:T
I love you, O **L**, my strength. Ps 18:1
The **L** is my rock and my fortress and Ps 18:2
I call upon the **L**, who is worthy to be Ps 18:3
In my distress I called upon the **L**; to my Ps 18:6
The **L** also thundered in the heavens, Ps 18:13
were laid bare at your rebuke, O **L**, Ps 18:15
calamity, but the **L** was my support. Ps 18:18
The **L** dealt with me according to my Ps 18:20
For I have kept the ways of the **L**, and Ps 18:21
So the **L** has rewarded me according to Ps 18:24
the **L** my God lightens my darkness. Ps 18:28
is perfect; the word of the **L** proves true; Ps 18:30
For who is God, but the **L**? And who is a Ps 18:31
they cried to the **L**, but he did not Ps 18:41
The **L** lives, and blessed be my rock, Ps 18:46
For this I will praise you, O **L**, among Ps 18:49
The law of the **L** is perfect, reviving the Ps 19:7
the testimony of the **L** is sure, making Ps 19:7
the precepts of the **L** are right, rejoicing Ps 19:8
the commandment of the **L** is pure, Ps 19:8
the fear of the **L** is clean, enduring Ps 19:9
the rules of the **L** are true, and righteous Ps 19:9
heart be acceptable in your sight, O **L**, Ps 19:14
May the **L** answer you in the day of Ps 20:1
May the **L** fulfill all your petitions! Ps 20:5
I know that the **L** saves his anointed; Ps 20:6
we trust in the name of the **L** our God. Ps 20:7
O **L**, save the king! May he answer us Ps 20:9
O **L**, in your strength the king rejoices, Ps 21:1
For the king trusts in the **L**, and through Ps 21:7
The **L** will swallow them up in his Ps 21:9
Be exalted, O **L**, in your strength! We Ps 21:13
"He trusts in the **L**; let him deliver him; Ps 22:8
But you, O **L**, do not be far off! O you Ps 22:19
You who fear the **L**, praise him! All you Ps 22:23
those who seek him shall praise the **L**! Ps 22:26
earth shall remember and turn to the **L**, Ps 22:27
For kingship belongs to the **L**, and he Ps 22:28
be told of the **L** to the coming Ps 22:30
The **L** is my shepherd; I shall not want. Ps 23:1
I shall dwell in the house of the **L** forever. Ps 23:6
Who shall ascend the hill of the **L**? And Ps 24:3
blessing from the **L** and righteousness Ps 24:5
Who is this King of glory? The **L**, strong Ps 24:8
The LORD, strong and mighty, the **L**, Ps 24:8
The **L** of hosts, he is the King of glory! Ps 24:10
To you, O **L**, I lift up my soul. Ps 25:1
Make me to know your ways, O **L**; teach Ps 25:4
Remember your mercy, O **L**, and your Ps 25:6
me, for the sake of your goodness, O **L**! Ps 25:7
Good and upright is the **L**; therefore he Ps 25:8
the paths of the **L** are steadfast love and Ps 25:10
For your name's sake, O **L**, pardon my Ps 25:11
Who is the man who fears the **L**? Him Ps 25:12
The friendship of the **L** is for those who Ps 25:14
My eyes are ever toward the **L**, for he Ps 25:15
Vindicate me, O **L**, for I have walked in Ps 26:1
I have trusted in the **L** without wavering. Ps 26:1
Prove me, O **L**, and try me; test my heart Ps 26:2
and go around your altar, O **L**, Ps 26:6
O **L**, I love the habitation of your house Ps 26:8
in the great assembly I will bless the **L**. Ps 26:12
The **L** is my light and my salvation; Ps 27:1
The **L** is the stronghold of my life; of Ps 27:1
One thing have I asked of the **L**, that will Ps 27:4
in the house of the **L** all the days of my Ps 27:4
the beauty of the **L** and to inquire in Ps 27:4
joy; I will sing and make melody to the **L**. Ps 27:6
Hear, O **L**, when I cry aloud; be gracious Ps 27:7
says to you, "Your face, **L**, do I seek." Ps 27:8
forsaken me, but the **L** will take me in. Ps 27:10
Teach me your way, O **L**, and lead me Ps 27:11
the goodness of the **L** in the land of Ps 27:13
Wait for the **L**; be strong, and let your Ps 27:14
your heart take courage; wait for the **L**! Ps 27:14
To you, O **L**, I call; my rock, be not deaf Ps 28:1
regard the works of the **L** or the work of Ps 28:5
Blessed be the **L**! for he has heard the Ps 28:6
The **L** is my strength and my shield; in Ps 28:7
The **L** is the strength of his people; he is Ps 28:8
Ascribe to the **L**, O heavenly beings, Ps 29:1
ascribe to the **L** glory and strength. Ps 29:1
Ascribe to the **L** the glory due his name; Ps 29:2
worship the **L** in the splendor of holiness. Ps 29:2
The voice of the **L** is over the waters; the Ps 29:3
the God of glory thunders, the **L**, over Ps 29:3
The voice of the **L** is powerful; the voice Ps 29:4
the voice of the **L** is full of majesty. Ps 29:4
The voice of the **L** breaks the cedars; the Ps 29:5
the **L** breaks the cedars of Lebanon. Ps 29:5
The voice of the **L** flashes forth flames of Ps 29:7
The voice of the **L** shakes the wilderness; Ps 29:8
the **L** shakes the wilderness of Kadesh. Ps 29:8
The voice of the **L** makes the deer give Ps 29:9
The **L** sits enthroned over the flood; the Ps 29:10
the **L** sits enthroned as king forever. Ps 29:10
May the **L** give strength to his people! Ps 29:11
May the **L** bless his people with peace! Ps 29:11
I will extol you, O **L**, for you have drawn Ps 30:1
O **L** my God, I cried to you for help, and Ps 30:2
O **L**, you have brought up my soul from Ps 30:3
Sing praises to the **L**, O you his saints, Ps 30:4
By your favor, O **L**, you made my Ps 30:7
To you, O **L**, I cry, and to the Lord I plead Ps 30:8
LORD, I cry, and to the **L** I plead for mercy: Ps 30:8
Hear, O **L**, and be merciful to me! O Ps 30:10
O LORD, and be merciful to me! O **L**, Ps 30:10
O **L** my God, I will give thanks to you Ps 30:12
In you, O **L**, do I take refuge; let me never Ps 31:1
you have redeemed me, O **L**, faithful God. Ps 31:5
to worthless idols, but I trust in the **L**. Ps 31:6
Be gracious to me, O **L**, for I am in Ps 31:9
But I trust in you, O **L**; I say, "You are Ps 31:14
O **L**, let me not be put to shame, for I Ps 31:17

Blessed be the **L**, for he has wondrously Ps 31:21
Love the **L**, all you his saints! The LORD Ps 31:23
The **L** preserves the faithful but Ps 31:23
courage, all you who wait for the **L**! Ps 31:24
against whom the **L** counts no iniquity, Ps 32:2
transgressions to the **L**," and you forgave Ps 32:5
surrounds the one who trusts in the **L**. Ps 32:10
Be glad in the **L**, and rejoice, O Ps 32:11
Shout for joy in the **L**, O you righteous! Ps 33:1
Give thanks to the **L** with the lyre; make Ps 33:2
For the word of the **L** is upright, and all Ps 33:4
earth is full of the steadfast love of the **L**. Ps 33:5
the word of the **L** the heavens were made, Ps 33:6
Let all the earth fear the **L**; let all the Ps 33:8
The **L** brings the counsel of the nations Ps 33:10
The counsel of the **L** stands forever, the Ps 33:11
Blessed is the nation whose God is the **L**, Ps 33:12
The **L** looks down from heaven; he sees Ps 33:13
the eye of the **L** is on those who fear Ps 33:18
Our soul waits for the **L**; he is our help Ps 33:20
Let your steadfast love, O **L**, be upon us, Ps 33:22
I will bless the **L** at all times; his praise Ps 34:1
My soul makes its boast in the **L**; let the Ps 34:2
Oh, magnify the **L** with me, and let us Ps 34:3
I sought the **L**, and he answered me and Ps 34:4
and the **L** heard him and saved him out Ps 34:6
angel of the **L** encamps around those Ps 34:7
Oh, taste and see that the **L** is good! Ps 34:8
Oh, fear the **L**, you his saints, for those Ps 34:9
those who seek the **L** lack no good Ps 34:10
to me; I will teach you the fear of the **L**. Ps 34:11
The eyes of the **L** are toward the Ps 34:15
The face of the **L** is against those who Ps 34:16
the **L** hears and delivers them out of all Ps 34:17
The **L** is near to the brokenhearted and Ps 34:18
but the **L** delivers him out of them all. Ps 34:19
The **L** redeems the life of his servants; Ps 34:22
Contend, O **L**, with those who contend Ps 35:1
the angel of the **L** driving them away! Ps 35:5
with the angel of the **L** pursuing them! Ps 35:6
Then my soul will rejoice in the **L**, Ps 35:9
All my bones shall say, "O **L**, who is Ps 35:10
How long, O **L**, will you look on? Ps 35:17
You have seen, O **L**; be not silent! O Ps 35:22
be not silent! O **L**, be not far from me! Ps 35:22
for my cause, my God and my **L**! Ps 35:23
Vindicate me, O **L**, my God, according Ps 35:24
glad and say evermore, "Great is the **L**, Ps 35:27
Of David, the servant of the **L**. Ps 36:T
Your steadfast love, O **L**, extends to the Ps 36:5
great deep; man and beast you save, O **L**. Ps 36:6
Trust in the **L**, and do good; dwell in the Ps 37:3
Delight yourself in the **L**, and he will give Ps 37:4
Commit your way to the **L**; trust in him, Ps 37:5
Be still before the **L** and wait patiently for Ps 37:7
who wait for the **L** shall inherit the land. Ps 37:9
but the **L** laughs at the wicked, for he Ps 37:13
but the **L** upholds the righteous. Ps 37:17
The **L** knows the days of the blameless, Ps 37:18
the enemies of the **L** are like the glory of Ps 37:20
those blessed by the **L** shall inherit the Ps 37:22
steps of a man are established by the **L**, Ps 37:23
headlong, for the **L** upholds his hand. Ps 37:24
For the **L** loves justice; he will not Ps 37:28
The **L** will not abandon him to his Ps 37:33
Wait for the **L** and keep his way, and he Ps 37:34
salvation of the righteous is from the **L**; Ps 37:39
The **L** helps them and delivers them; he Ps 37:40
O **L**, rebuke me not in your anger, nor Ps 38:1
O **L**, all my longing is before you; my Ps 38:9
But for you, O **L**, do I wait; it is you, O Ps 38:15
it is you, O **L** my God, who will answer. Ps 38:15
Do not forsake me, O **L**! O my God, be Ps 38:21
Make haste to help me, O **L**, my Ps 38:22
"O **L**, make me know my end and what Ps 39:4
"And now, O **L**, for what do I wait? My Ps 39:7
"Hear my prayer, O **L**, and give ear to Ps 39:12
I waited patiently for the **L**; he inclined to Ps 40:1
see and fear, and put their trust in the **L**. Ps 40:3
is the man who makes the **L** his trust, Ps 40:4
You have multiplied, O **L** my God, your Ps 40:5
not restrained my lips, as you know, O **L**. Ps 40:9
As for you, O **L**, you will not restrain Ps 40:11
Be pleased, O **L**, to deliver me! O LORD, Ps 40:13
Be pleased, O LORD, to deliver me! O **L**, Ps 40:13
say continually, "Great is the **L**!" Ps 40:16
needy, but the **L** takes thought for me. Ps 40:17
In the day of trouble the **L** delivers him; Ps 41:1
the **L** protects him and keeps him alive; Ps 41:2
The **L** sustains him on his sickbed; in Ps 41:3
As for me, I said, "O **L**, be gracious to me; Ps 41:4
But you, O **L**, be gracious to me, and Ps 41:10
Blessed be the **L**, the God of Israel, from Ps 41:13
By day the **L** commands his steadfast Ps 42:8
Awake! Why are you sleeping, O **L**? Ps 44:23
beauty. Since he is your **l**, bow to him. Ps 45:11
The **L** of hosts is with us; the God of Ps 46:7
Come, behold the works of the **L**, how he Ps 46:8
The **L** of hosts is with us; the God of Ps 46:11
For the **L**, the Most High, is to be feared, a Ps 47:2
shout, the **L** with the sound of a trumpet. Ps 47:5
Great is the **L** and greatly to be praised in Ps 48:1
have we seen in the city of the **L** of hosts, Ps 48:8
The Mighty One, God the **L**, speaks and Ps 50:1
O **L**, open my lips, and my mouth will Ps 51:15
helper; the **L** is the upholder of my life. Ps 54:4
I will give thanks to your name, O **L**, for Ps 54:6
Destroy, O **L**, divide their tongues; for I Ps 55:9
But I call to God, and the **L** will save me. Ps 55:16
Cast your burden on the **L**, and he will Ps 55:22
In God, whose word I praise, in the **L**, Ps 56:10
I will give thanks to you, O **L**, among the Ps 57:9
out the fangs of the young lions, O **L**! Ps 58:6
For no transgression or sin of mine, O **L**, Ps 59:3
You, **L** God of hosts, are God of Israel. Ps 59:5
But you, O **L**, laugh at them; you hold all Ps 59:8
your power and bring them down, O **L**, Ps 59:11
and that to you, O **L**, belongs steadfast Ps 62:12
one rejoice in the **L** and take refuge in Ps 64:10
my heart, the **L** would not have listened. Ps 66:18
through the deserts; his name is the **L**; Ps 68:4
The **L** gives the word; the women who Ps 68:11
yes, where the **L** will dwell forever? Ps 68:16
upon thousands; the **L** is among them; Ps 68:17
that the **L** God may dwell there. Ps 68:18
Blessed be the **L**, who daily bears us up; Ps 68:19
is a God of salvation, and to GOD, the **L**, Ps 68:20
The **L** said, "I will bring them back Ps 68:22
God in the great congregation, the **L**, Ps 68:26
sing to God; sing praises to the **L**, Selah Ps 68:32
to shame through me, O **L** GOD of hosts; Ps 69:6
But as for me, my prayer is to you, O **L**. Ps 69:13
Answer me, O **L**, for your steadfast love Ps 69:16
This will please the **L** more than an ox Ps 69:31
For the **L** hears the needy and does not Ps 69:33
Make haste, O God, to deliver me! O **L**, Ps 70:1
You are my help and my deliverer; O **L**, Ps 70:5
In you, O **L**, do I take refuge; let me never Ps 71:1
For you, O **L**, are my hope, my trust, O Ps 71:5
you, O Lord, are my hope, my trust, O **L**, Ps 71:5
mighty deeds of the **L** GOD I will come; Ps 71:16
Blessed be the **L**, the God of Israel, who Ps 72:18
Like a dream when one awakes, O **L**, Ps 73:20
I have made the **L** GOD my refuge, that I Ps 73:28
Remember this, O **L**, how the enemy Ps 74:18
in the hand of the **L** there is a cup with Ps 75:8
your vows to the **L** your God and Ps 76:11
In the day of my trouble I seek the **L**; in Ps 77:2
"Will the **L** spurn forever, and never Ps 77:7
I will remember the deeds of the **L**; yes, I Ps 77:11
generation the glorious deeds of the **L**, Ps 78:4
Therefore, when the **L** heard, he was Ps 78:21
Then the **L** awoke as from sleep, like a Ps 78:65
How long, O **L**? Will you be angry Ps 79:5
with which they have taunted you, O **L**! Ps 79:12
O **L** God of hosts, how long will you be Ps 80:4
Restore us, O **L** God of hosts! let your Ps 80:19
I am the **L** your God, who brought you Ps 81:10
who hate the **L** would cringe toward Ps 81:15
that they may seek your name, O **L**. Ps 83:16
that you alone, whose name is the **L**, Ps 83:18
is your dwelling place, O **L** of hosts! Ps 84:1
longs, yes, faints for the courts of the **L**; Ps 84:2
her young, at your altars, O **L** of hosts, Ps 84:3
O **L** God of hosts, hear my prayer; give Ps 84:8
For the **L** God is a sun and shield; the Ps 84:11
shield; the **L** bestows favor and honor. Ps 84:11
O **L** of hosts, blessed is the one who Ps 84:12
L, you were favorable to your land; you Ps 85:1
Show us your steadfast love, O **L**, and Ps 85:7
Let me hear what God the **L** will speak, Ps 85:8
Yes, the **L** will give what is good, and Ps 85:12
Incline your ear, O **L**, and answer me, for Ps 86:1
Be gracious to me, O **L**, for to you do I cry Ps 86:3
the soul of your servant, for to you, O **L**, Ps 86:4
For you, O **L**, are good and forgiving, Ps 86:5
Give ear, O **L**, to my prayer; listen to my Ps 86:6
is none like you among the gods, O **L**, Ps 86:8
shall come and worship before you, O **L**, Ps 86:9
Teach me your way, O **L**, that I may Ps 86:11
I give thanks to you, O **L** my God, with Ps 86:12
But you, O **L**, are a God merciful and Ps 86:15
L, have helped me and comforted me. Ps 86:17
the **L** loves the gates of Zion more than Ps 87:2
The **L** records as he registers the peoples, Ps 87:6
O **L**, God of my salvation; I cry out day Ps 88:1
Every day I call upon you, O **L**; I spread Ps 88:9
But I, O **L**, cry to you; in the morning Ps 88:13
O **L**, why do you cast my soul away? Ps 88:14
I will sing of the steadfast love of the **L**, Ps 89:1
the heavens praise your wonders, O **L**, Ps 89:5
in the skies can be compared to the **L**? Ps 89:6
among the heavenly beings is like the **L**, Ps 89:6
O **L** God of hosts, who is mighty as you Ps 89:8
of hosts, who is mighty as you are, O **L**, Ps 89:8
know the festal shout, who walk, O **L**, Ps 89:15
For our shield belongs to the **L**, our Ps 89:18
How long, O **L**? Will you hide yourself Ps 89:46
L, where is your steadfast love of old, Ps 89:49
Remember, O **L**, how your servants are Ps 89:50
with which your enemies mock, O **L**, Ps 89:51
Blessed be the **L** forever! Amen and Ps 89:52
L, you have been our dwelling place in Ps 90:1
Return, O **L**! How long? Have pity on Ps 90:13
Let the favor of the **L** our God be upon Ps 90:17
I will say to the **L**, "My refuge and my Ps 91:2
you have made the **L** your dwelling place Ps 91:9
It is good to give thanks to the **L**, to sing Ps 92:1
For you, O **L**, have made me glad by Ps 92:4
How great are your works, O **L**! Your Ps 92:5
but you, O **L**, are on high forever. Ps 92:8
For behold, your enemies, O **L**, for Ps 92:9
They are planted in the house of the **L**; Ps 92:13
to declare that the **L** is upright; he is my Ps 92:15
The **L** reigns; he is robed in majesty; the Ps 93:1
he is robed in majesty; the **L** is robed; Ps 93:1
The floods have lifted up, O **L**, the floods Ps 93:3
waves of the sea, the **L** on high is mighty! Ps 93:4
holiness befits your house, O **L**, Ps 93:5
O **L**, God of vengeance, O God of Ps 94:1
O **L**, how long shall the wicked, how Ps 94:3
They crush your people, O **L**, and afflict Ps 94:5
and they say, "The **L** does not see; the Ps 94:7
the **L**—knows the thoughts of man, Ps 94:11
is the man whom you discipline, O **L**, Ps 94:12
For the **L** will not forsake his people; he Ps 94:14
If the **L** had not been my help, my soul Ps 94:17
"My foot slips," your steadfast love, O **L**, Ps 94:18
But the **L** has become my stronghold, Ps 94:22
the **L** our God will wipe them out. Ps 94:23
Oh come, let us sing to the **L**; let us make Ps 95:1
For the **L** is a great God, and a great King Ps 95:3
let us kneel before the **L**, our Maker! Ps 95:6
Oh sing to the **L** a new song; sing to the Ps 96:1
a new song; sing to the **L**, all the earth! Ps 96:1
Sing to the **L**, bless his name; tell of his Ps 96:2
For great is the **L**, and greatly to be Ps 96:4
idols, but the **L** made the heavens. Ps 96:5
Ascribe to the **L**, O families of the Ps 96:7
ascribe to the **L** glory and strength! Ps 96:7
Ascribe to the **L** the glory due his name; Ps 96:8
Worship the **L** in the splendor of Ps 96:9
Say among the nations, "The **L** reigns! Ps 96:10
before the **L**, for he comes, for he comes Ps 96:13
The **L** reigns, let the earth rejoice; let the Ps 97:1
mountains melt like wax before the **L**, Ps 97:5
the LORD, before the **L** of all the earth. Ps 97:5
rejoice, because of your judgments, O **L**. Ps 97:8
For you, O **L**, are most high over all the Ps 97:9
O you who love the **L**, hate evil! He Ps 97:10
Rejoice in the **L**, O you righteous, and Ps 97:12
Oh sing to the **L** a new song, for he has Ps 98:1
The **L** has made known his salvation; he Ps 98:2
Make a joyful noise to the **L**, all the Ps 98:4
Sing praises to the **L** with the lyre, with Ps 98:5
a joyful noise before the King, the **L**! Ps 98:6
before the **L**, for he comes to judge the Ps 98:9
The **L** reigns; let the peoples tremble! He Ps 99:1
The **L** is great in Zion; he is exalted over Ps 99:2
Exalt the **L** our God; worship at his Ps 99:5
They called to the **L**, and he answered Ps 99:6
O **L** our God, you answered them; you Ps 99:8
Exalt the **L** our God, and worship at his Ps 99:9
mountain; for the **L** our God is holy! Ps 99:9
Make a joyful noise to the **L**, all the Ps 100:1
Serve the **L** with gladness! Come into Ps 100:2
Know that the **L**, he is God! It is he who Ps 100:3
For the **L** is good; his steadfast love Ps 100:5
justice; to you, O **L**, I will make music. Ps 101:1
all the evildoers from the city of the **L**. Ps 101:8
pours out his complaint before the **L**. Ps 102:T
Hear my prayer, O **L**; let my cry come to Ps 102:1
But you, O **L**, are enthroned forever; Ps 102:12
Nations will fear the name of the **L**, Ps 102:15
For the **L** builds up Zion; he appears Ps 102:16
yet to be created may praise the **L**: Ps 102:18
from heaven the **L** looked at the earth, Ps 102:19
may declare in Zion the name of the **L**, Ps 102:21
and kingdoms, to worship the **L**. Ps 102:22
Bless the **L**, O my soul, and all that is Ps 103:1
Bless the **L**, O my soul, and forget not Ps 103:2
The **L** works righteousness and justice Ps 103:6
The **L** is merciful and gracious, slow to Ps 103:8
so the **L** shows compassion to those Ps 103:13
love of the **L** is from everlasting Ps 103:17

The **L** has established his throne in Ps 103:19
Bless the **L**, O you his angels, you Ps 103:20
Bless the **L**, all his hosts, his ministers, Ps 103:21
Bless the **L**, all his works, in all places Ps 103:22
his dominion. Bless the **L**, O my soul! Ps 103:22
Bless the **L**, O my soul! O LORD my God, Ps 104:1
soul! O **L** my God, you are very great! Ps 104:1
trees of the **L** are watered abundantly, Ps 104:16
O **L**, how manifold are your works! In Ps 104:24
May the glory of the **L** endure forever; Ps 104:31
may the **L** rejoice in his works, Ps 104:31
I will sing to the **L** as long as I live; I Ps 104:33
pleasing to him, for I rejoice in the **L**. Ps 104:34
be no more! Bless the **L**, O my soul! Ps 104:35
the LORD, O my soul! Praise the **L**! Ps 104:35
Oh give thanks to the **L**; call upon his Ps 105:1
hearts of those who seek the **L** rejoice! Ps 105:3
Seek the **L** and his strength; seek his Ps 105:4
He is the **L** our God; his judgments are Ps 105:7
to pass, the word of the **L** tested him. Ps 105:19
he made him **l** of his house and ruler Ps 105:21
And the **L** made his people very Ps 105:24
and observe his laws. Praise the **L**! Ps 105:45
Praise the **L**! Oh give thanks to the Ps 106:1
Oh give thanks to the **L**, for he is good, Ps 106:1
can utter the mighty deeds of the **L**, Ps 106:2
Remember me, O **L**, when you show Ps 106:4
and Aaron, the holy one of the **L**, Ps 106:16
and did not obey the voice of the **L**. Ps 106:25
they provoked the **L** to anger with Ps 106:29
peoples, as the **L** commanded them, Ps 106:34
the anger of the **L** was kindled against Ps 106:40
Save us, O **L** our God, and gather us Ps 106:47
Blessed be the **L**, the God of Israel, Ps 106:48
the people say, "Amen!" Praise the **L**! Ps 106:48
Oh give thanks to the **L**, for he is good, Ps 107:1
Let the redeemed of the **L** say so, whom Ps 107:2
they cried to the **L** in their trouble, Ps 107:6
Let them thank the **L** for his steadfast Ps 107:8
they cried to the **L** in their trouble, Ps 107:13
Let them thank the **L** for his steadfast Ps 107:15
they cried to the **L** in their trouble, Ps 107:19
Let them thank the **L** for his steadfast Ps 107:21
they saw the deeds of the **L**, his Ps 107:24
they cried to the **L** in their trouble, Ps 107:28
Let them thank the **L** for his steadfast Ps 107:31
consider the steadfast love of the **L**. Ps 107:43
I will give thanks to you, O **L**, among Ps 108:3
fathers be remembered before the **L**, Ps 109:14
Let them be before the **L** continually, Ps 109:15
the reward of my accusers from the **L**, Ps 109:20
But you, O GOD my **L**, deal on my Ps 109:21
Help me, O **L** my God! Save me Ps 109:26
is your hand; you, O **L**, have done it! Ps 109:27
I will give great thanks to the **L**; Ps 109:30
The **L** says to my Lord: "Sit at my right Ps 110:1
The LORD says to my **L**: "Sit at my right Ps 110:1
The **L** sends forth from Zion your Ps 110:2
The **L** has sworn and will not change Ps 110:4
The **L** is at your right hand; he will Ps 110:5
Praise the **L**! I will give thanks to the Ps 111:1
give thanks to the **L** with my whole Ps 111:1
Great are the works of the **L**, studied by Ps 111:2
the **L** is gracious and merciful. Ps 111:4
The fear of the **L** is the beginning of Ps 111:10
Praise the **L**! Blessed is the man who Ps 112:1
Blessed is the man who fears the **L**, who Ps 112:1
his heart is firm, trusting in the **L**. Ps 112:7
Praise the **L**! Praise, O servants of the Ps 113:1
Praise, O servants of the **L**, praise the Ps 113:1
of the LORD, praise the name of the **L**! Ps 113:1
the name of the **L** from this time forth Ps 113:2
the name of the **L** is to be praised! Ps 113:3
The **L** is high above all nations, and his Ps 113:4
Who is like the **L** our God, who is Ps 113:5
joyous mother of children. Praise the **L**! Ps 113:9
O earth, at the presence of the **L**, Ps 114:7
Not to us, O **L**, not to us, but to your Ps 115:1
O Israel, trust in the **L**! He is their help Ps 115:9
O house of Aaron, trust in the **L**! He is Ps 115:10
You who fear the **L**, trust in the LORD! Ps 115:11
You who fear the LORD, trust in the **L**! Ps 115:11
The **L** has remembered us; he will Ps 115:12
he will bless those who fear the **L**, both Ps 115:13
May the **L** give you increase, you and Ps 115:14
May you be blessed by the **L**, who Ps 115:15
The dead do not praise the **L**, nor do Ps 115:17
we will bless the **L** from this time forth Ps 115:18
forth and forevermore. Praise the **L**! Ps 115:18
I love the **L**, because he has heard my Ps 116:1
Then I called on the name of the **L**: "O Ps 116:4
I called on the name of the LORD: "O **L**, Ps 116:4
Gracious is the **L**, and righteous; our Ps 116:5
The **L** preserves the simple; when I was Ps 116:6
for the **L** has dealt bountifully with Ps 116:7
I will walk before the **L** in the land of Ps 116:9
I render to the **L** for all his benefits Ps 116:12
and call on the name of the **L**, Ps 116:13
my vows to the **L** in the presence of Ps 116:14
in the sight of the **L** is the death of his Ps 116:15
O **L**, I am your servant; I am your Ps 116:16
and call on the name of the **L**. Ps 116:17
my vows to the **L** in the presence of Ps 116:18
in the courts of the house of the **L**, in Ps 116:19
your midst, O Jerusalem. Praise the **L**! Ps 116:19
Praise the **L**, all nations! Extol him, all Ps 117:1
faithfulness of the **L** endures forever. Ps 117:2
the LORD endures forever. Praise the **L**! Ps 117:2
Oh give thanks to the **L**, for he is good; Ps 118:1
Let those who fear the **L** say, "His Ps 118:4
Out of my distress I called on the **L**; the Ps 118:5
the **L** answered me and set me free. Ps 118:5
The **L** is on my side; I will not fear. Ps 118:6
The **L** is on my side as my helper; I Ps 118:7
to take refuge in the **L** than to trust in Ps 118:8
to take refuge in the **L** than to trust in Ps 118:9
in the name of the **L** I cut them off! Ps 118:10
in the name of the **L** I cut them off! Ps 118:11
in the name of the **L** I cut them off! Ps 118:12
that I was falling, but the **L** helped me. Ps 118:13
The **L** is my strength and my song; he Ps 118:14
right hand of the **L** does valiantly, Ps 118:15
the right hand of the **L** exalts, the right Ps 118:16
the right hand of the **L** does valiantly!" Ps 118:16
live, and recount the deeds of the **L**. Ps 118:17
The **L** has disciplined me severely, but Ps 118:18
them and give thanks to the **L**. Ps 118:19
This is the gate of the **L**; the righteous Ps 118:20
This is the day that the **L** has made; let Ps 118:24
Save us, we pray, O **L**! O LORD, we pray, Ps 118:25
Save us, we pray, O LORD! O **L**, we pray, Ps 118:25
is he who comes in the name of the **L**! Ps 118:26
We bless you from the house of the **L**. Ps 118:26
The **L** is God, and he has made his Ps 118:27
Oh give thanks to the **L**, for he is good; Ps 118:29
who walk in the law of the **L**! Ps 119:1
Blessed are you, O **L**; teach me your Ps 119:12
I cling to your testimonies, O **L**; let me Ps 119:31
Teach me, O **L**, the way of your Ps 119:33
your steadfast love come to me, O **L**, Ps 119:41
rules from of old, I take comfort, O **L**. Ps 119:52
your name in the night, O **L**, Ps 119:55
The **L** is my portion; I promise to keep Ps 119:57
The earth, O **L**, is full of your steadfast Ps 119:64
have dealt well with your servant, O **L**, Ps 119:65
I know, O **L**, that your rules are Ps 119:75
Forever, O **L**, your word is firmly fixed Ps 119:89
give me life, O **L**, according to your Ps 119:107
my freewill offerings of praise, O **L**, Ps 119:108
It is time for the **L** to act, for your law Ps 119:126
Righteous are you, O **L**, and right are Ps 119:137
whole heart I cry; answer me, O **L**! Ps 119:145
according to your steadfast love; O **L**, Ps 119:149
But you are near, O **L**, and all your Ps 119:151
Great is your mercy, O **L**; give me life Ps 119:156
I hope for your salvation, O **L**, and I Ps 119:166
Let my cry come before you, O **L**; Ps 119:169
I long for your salvation, O **L**, and Ps 119:174
In my distress I called to the **L**, and he Ps 120:1
Deliver me, O **L**, from lying lips, from a Ps 120:2
My help comes from the **L**, who made Ps 121:2
The **L** is your keeper; the LORD is your Ps 121:5
the **L** is your shade on your right hand. Ps 121:5
The **L** will keep you from all evil; he Ps 121:7
The **L** will keep your going out and Ps 121:8
to me, "Let us go to the house of the **L**!" Ps 122:1
the tribes go up, the tribes of the **L**, Ps 122:4
to give thanks to the name of the **L**. Ps 122:4
the sake of the house of the **L** our God, Ps 122:9
so our eyes look to the **L** our God, Ps 123:2
Have mercy upon us, O **L**, have mercy Ps 123:3
it had not been the **L** who was on our Ps 124:1
it had not been the **L** who was on our Ps 124:2
Blessed be the **L**, who has not given us Ps 124:6
Our help is in the name of the **L**, who Ps 124:8
who trust in the **L** are like Mount Zion, Ps 125:1
so the **L** surrounds his people, Ps 125:2
Do good, O **L**, to those who are good, Ps 125:4
their crooked ways the **L** will lead away Ps 125:5
When the **L** restored the fortunes of Ps 126:1
"The **L** has done great things for them." Ps 126:2
The **L** has done great things for us; we Ps 126:3
Restore our fortunes, O **L**, like streams Ps 126:4
Unless the **L** builds the house, those Ps 127:1
Unless the **L** watches over the city, the Ps 127:1
children are a heritage from the **L**, Ps 127:3
Blessed is everyone who fears the **L**, who Ps 128:1
the man be blessed who fears the **L**. Ps 128:4
The **L** bless you from Zion! May you Ps 128:5
The **L** is righteous; he has cut the cords Ps 129:4
"The blessing of the **L** be upon you! Ps 129:8
We bless you in the name of the **L**!" Ps 129:8
Out of the depths I cry to you, O **L**! Ps 130:1
O **L**, hear my voice! Let your ears be Ps 130:2
If you, O **L**, should mark iniquities, O Ps 130:3
O LORD, should mark iniquities, O **L**, Ps 130:3
I wait for the **L**, my soul waits, and in Ps 130:5
waits for the **L** more than watchmen Ps 130:6
O Israel, hope in the **L**! For with the Ps 130:7
For with the **L** there is steadfast love, Ps 130:7
O **L**, my heart is not lifted up; my eyes Ps 131:1
hope in the **L** from this time forth and Ps 131:3
Remember, O **L**, in David's favor, all the Ps 132:1
how he swore to the **L** and vowed to the Ps 132:2
until I find a place for the **L**, a dwelling Ps 132:5
Arise, O **L**, and go to your resting place, Ps 132:8
The **L** swore to David a sure oath from Ps 132:11
For the **L** has chosen Zion; he has Ps 132:13
For there the **L** has commanded the Ps 133:3
Come, bless the **L**, all you servants of Ps 134:1
bless the LORD, all you servants of the **L**, Ps 134:1
stand by night in the house of the **L**! Ps 134:1
hands to the holy place and bless the **L**! Ps 134:2
May the **L** bless you from Zion, he who Ps 134:3
Praise the **L**! Praise the name of the Ps 135:1
Praise the name of the **L**, give praise, O Ps 135:1
LORD, give praise, O servants of the **L**, Ps 135:1
who stand in the house of the **L**, in the Ps 135:2
Praise the **L**, for the LORD is good; sing to Ps 135:3
Praise the LORD, for the **L** is good; sing to Ps 135:3
For the **L** has chosen Jacob for himself, Ps 135:4
For I know that the **L** is great, and that Ps 135:5
great, and that our **L** is above all gods. Ps 135:5
Whatever the **L** pleases, he does, in Ps 135:6
Your name, O **L**, endures forever, your Ps 135:13
endures forever, your renown, O **L**, Ps 135:13
For the **L** will vindicate his people and Ps 135:14
O house of Israel, bless the **L**! O house Ps 135:19
LORD! O house of Aaron, bless the **L**! Ps 135:19
O house of Levi, bless the **L**! You who Ps 135:20
You who fear the **L**, bless the LORD! Ps 135:20
You who fear the LORD, bless the **L**! Ps 135:20
Blessed be the **L** from Zion, he who Ps 135:21
who dwells in Jerusalem! Praise the **L**! Ps 135:21
Give thanks to the **L**, for he is good, for Ps 136:1
Give thanks to the **L** of lords, for his Ps 136:3
Remember, O **L**, against the Edomites Ps 137:7
I give you thanks, O **L**, with my whole Ps 138:1
of the earth shall give you thanks, O **L**, Ps 138:4
and they shall sing of the ways of the **L**, Ps 138:5
the LORD, for great is the glory of the **L**. Ps 138:5
For though the **L** is high, he regards the Ps 138:6
The **L** will fulfill his purpose for me; Ps 138:8
your steadfast love, O **L**, endures Ps 138:8
O **L**, you have searched me and known Ps 139:1
a word is on my tongue, behold, O **L**, Ps 139:4
Do I not hate those who hate you, O **L**? Ps 139:21
Deliver me, O **L**, from evil men; preserve Ps 140:1
Guard me, O **L**, from the hands of the Ps 140:4
I say to the **L**, You are my God; give ear Ps 140:6
to the voice of my pleas for mercy, O **L**! Ps 140:6
O **L**, my Lord, the strength of my Ps 140:7
O LORD, my **L**, the strength of my Ps 140:7
Grant not, O **L**, the desires of the Ps 140:8
I know that the **L** will maintain the Ps 140:12
O **L**, I call upon you; hasten to me! Give Ps 141:1
Set a guard, O **L**, over my mouth; keep Ps 141:3
my eyes are toward you, O GOD, my **L**; Ps 141:8
With my voice I cry out to the **L**; with Ps 142:1
my voice I plead for mercy to the **L**. Ps 142:1
I cry to you, O **L**; I say, "You are my Ps 142:5
Hear my prayer, O **L**; give ear to my Ps 143:1
Answer me quickly, O **L**! My spirit Ps 143:7
Deliver me from my enemies, O **L**! I Ps 143:9
For your name's sake, O **L**, preserve Ps 143:11
Blessed be the **L**, my rock, who trains Ps 144:1
O **L**, what is man that you regard him, Ps 144:3
Bow your heavens, O **L**, and come Ps 144:5
are the people whose God is the **L**! Ps 144:15
Great is the **L**, and greatly to be praised, Ps 145:3
The **L** is gracious and merciful, slow to Ps 145:8
The **L** is good to all, and his mercy is Ps 145:9
works shall give thanks to you, O **L**, Ps 145:10
[The **L** is faithful in all his words and Ps 145:13
The **L** upholds all who are falling and Ps 145:14
The **L** is righteous in all his ways and Ps 145:17
The **L** is near to all who call on him, Ps 145:18
The **L** preserves all who love him, but Ps 145:20
mouth will speak the praise of the **L**, Ps 145:21
Praise the **L**! Praise the LORD, O my Ps 146:1
the LORD! Praise the **L**, O my soul! Ps 146:1
I will praise the **L** as long as I live; I will Ps 146:2
of Jacob, whose hope is in the **L** his God, Ps 146:5
hungry. The **L** sets the prisoners free; Ps 146:7
the **L** opens the eyes of the blind. The Ps 146:8

Context	Reference
The **L** lifts up those who are bowed	Ps 146:8
bowed down; the **L** loves the righteous.	Ps 146:8
The **L** watches over the sojourners; he	Ps 146:9
The **L** will reign forever, your God, O	Ps 146:10
Zion, to all generations. Praise the **L**!	Ps 146:10
Praise the **L**! For it is good to sing	Ps 147:1
The **L** builds up Jerusalem; he gathers	Ps 147:2
Great is our **L**, and abundant in power;	Ps 147:5
The **L** lifts up the humble; he casts the	Ps 147:6
Sing to the **L** with thanksgiving; make	Ps 147:7
but the **L** takes pleasure in those who	Ps 147:11
Praise the **L**, O Jerusalem! Praise your	Ps 147:12
do not know his rules. Praise the **L**!	Ps 147:20
Praise the **L**! Praise the LORD from the	Ps 148:1
Praise the **L** from the heavens; praise	Ps 148:1
Let them praise the name of the **L**! For	Ps 148:5
Praise the **L** from the earth, you great	Ps 148:7
Let them praise the name of the **L**, for	Ps 148:13
who are near to him. Praise the **L**!	Ps 148:14
Praise the **L**! Sing to the LORD a new	Ps 149:1
the LORD! Sing to the **L** a new song,	Ps 149:1
For the **L** takes pleasure in his people;	Ps 149:4
for all his godly ones. Praise the **L**!	Ps 149:9
Praise the **L**! Praise God in his	Ps 150:1
everything that has breath praise the **L**!	Ps 150:6
breath praise the LORD! Praise the **L**!	Ps 150:6
The fear of the **L** is the beginning of	Prv 1:7
and did not choose the fear of the **L**,	Prv 1:29
the fear of the **L** and find the knowledge	Prv 2:5
For the **L** gives wisdom; from his mouth	Prv 2:6
Trust in the **L** with all your heart, and do	Prv 3:5
eyes; fear the **L**, and turn away from evil.	Prv 3:7
Honor the **L** with your wealth and with	Prv 3:9
for the **L** reproves him whom he loves,	Prv 3:12
The **L** by wisdom founded the earth; by	Prv 3:19
for the **L** will be your confidence and	Prv 3:26
person is an abomination to the **L**,	Prv 3:32
man's ways are before the eyes of the **L**,	Prv 5:21
There are six things that the **L** hates,	Prv 6:16
The fear of the **L** is hatred of evil. Pride	Prv 8:13
"The **L** possessed me at the beginning	Prv 8:22
finds life and obtains favor from the **L**,	Prv 8:35
The fear of the **L** is the beginning of	Prv 9:10
The **L** does not let the righteous go	Prv 10:3
The blessing of the **L** makes rich, and	Prv 10:22
The fear of the **L** prolongs life, but the	Prv 10:27
The way of the **L** is a stronghold to the	Prv 10:29
balance is an abomination to the **L**,	Prv 11:1
heart are an abomination to the **L**,	Prv 11:20
A good man obtains favor from the **L**,	Prv 12:2
lips are an abomination to the **L**,	Prv 12:22
walks in uprightness fears the **L**,	Prv 14:2
the fear of the **L** one has strong	Prv 14:26
The fear of the **L** is a fountain of life,	Prv 14:27
The eyes of the **L** are in every place,	Prv 15:3
the wicked is an abomination to the **L**,	Prv 15:8
the wicked is an abomination to the **L**,	Prv 15:9
and Abaddon lie open before the **L**;	Prv 15:11
the fear of the **L** than great treasure	Prv 15:16
The **L** tears down the house of the	Prv 15:25
wicked are an abomination to the **L**,	Prv 15:26
The **L** is far from the wicked, but he	Prv 15:29
The fear of the **L** is instruction in	Prv 15:33
the answer of the tongue is from the **L**.	Prv 16:1
own eyes, but the **L** weighs the spirit.	Prv 16:2
Commit your work to the **L**, and your	Prv 16:3
The **L** has made everything for its	Prv 16:4
in heart is an abomination to the **L**;	Prv 16:5
the fear of the **L** one turns away from	Prv 16:6
When a man's ways please the **L**, he	Prv 16:7
his way, but the **L** establishes his steps.	Prv 16:9
and blessed is he who trusts in the **L**.	Prv 16:20
but its every decision is from the **L**.	Prv 16:33
is for gold, and the **L** tests hearts.	Prv 17:3
both alike an abomination to the **L**.	Prv 17:15
The name of the **L** is a strong tower;	Prv 18:10
thing and obtains favor from the **L**.	Prv 18:22
to ruin, his heart rages against the **L**.	Prv 19:3
but a prudent wife is from the **L**.	Prv 19:14
is generous to the poor lends to the **L**,	Prv 19:17
is the purpose of the **L** that will stand.	Prv 19:21
The fear of the **L** leads to life, and	Prv 19:23
both alike an abomination to the **L**.	Prv 20:10
seeing eye, the **L** has made them both.	Prv 20:12
wait for the **L**, and he will deliver you.	Prv 20:22
weights are an abomination to the **L**,	Prv 20:23
A man's steps are from the **L**; how	Prv 20:24
The spirit of man is the lamp of the **L**,	Prv 20:27
is a stream of water in the hand of the **L**;	Prv 21:1
own eyes, but the **L** weighs the heart.	Prv 21:2
more acceptable to the **L** than sacrifice.	Prv 21:3
no counsel can avail against the **L**.	Prv 21:30
battle, but the victory belongs to the **L**.	Prv 21:31
together; the **L** is the maker of them all.	Prv 22:2
and fear of the **L** is riches and honor	Prv 22:4
The eyes of the **L** keep watch over	Prv 22:12
he with whom the **L** is angry will fall	Prv 22:14
That your trust may be in the **L**, I	Prv 22:19
for the **L** will plead their cause and rob	Prv 22:23
in the fear of the **L** all the day.	Prv 23:17
lest the **L** see it and be displeased, and	Prv 24:18
My son, fear the **L** and the king, and	Prv 24:21
on his head, and the **L** will reward you.	Prv 25:22
who seek the **L** understand it	Prv 28:5
is the one who fears the **L** always,	Prv 28:14
who trusts in the **L** will be enriched.	Prv 28:25
the **L** gives light to the eyes of both.	Prv 29:13
but whoever trusts in the **L** is safe.	Prv 29:25
but it is from the **L** that a man gets	Prv 29:26
"Who is the **L**?" or lest I be poor and	Prv 30:9
woman who fears the **L** is to be	Prv 31:30
are flashes of fire, the very flame of the **L**.	Sg 8:6
and give ear, O earth; for the **L** has spoken:	Is 1:2
They have forsaken the **L**, they have	Is 1:4
If the **L** of hosts had not left us a few	Is 1:9
Hear the word of the **L**, you rulers of	Is 1:10
says the **L**; I have had enough of burnt	Is 1:11
now, let us reason together, says the **L**:	Is 1:18
for the mouth of the **L** has spoken."	Is 1:20
Therefore the **L** declares, the LORD of	Is 1:24
the Lord declares, the **L** of hosts,	Is 1:24
who forsake the **L** shall be consumed.	Is 1:28
of the house of the **L** shall be established as	Is 2:2
let us go up to the mountain of the **L**,	Is 2:3
law, and the word of the **L** from Jerusalem.	Is 2:3
come, let us walk in the light of the **L**.	Is 2:5
in the dust from before the terror of the **L**,	Is 2:10
and the **L** alone will be exalted in that	Is 2:11
For the **L** of hosts has a day against all	Is 2:12
and the **L** alone will be exalted in that	Is 2:17
ground, from before the terror of the **L**,	Is 2:19
the cliffs, from before the terror of the **L**,	Is 2:21
the **L** GOD of hosts is taking away from	Is 3:1
speech and their deeds are against the **L**,	Is 3:8
The **L** has taken his place to contend; he	Is 3:13
The **L** will enter into judgment with the	Is 3:14
of the poor?" declares the **L** GOD of hosts.	Is 3:15
The **L** said: Because the daughters of Zion	Is 3:16
therefore the **L** will strike with a scab the	Is 3:17
and the **L** will lay bare their secret parts.	Is 3:17
In that day the **L** will take away the finery	Is 3:18
the branch of the **L** shall be beautiful and	Is 4:2
when the **L** shall have washed away the	Is 4:4
Then the **L** will create over the whole site	Is 4:5
For the vineyard of the **L** of hosts is the	Is 5:7
The **L** of hosts has sworn in my hearing:	Is 5:9
but they do not regard the deeds of the **L**,	Is 5:12
But the **L** of hosts is exalted in justice, and	Is 5:16
have rejected the law of the **L** of hosts,	Is 5:24
the anger of the **L** was kindled against his	Is 5:25
died I saw the **L** sitting upon a throne,	Is 6:1
and said: "Holy, holy, holy is the **L** of hosts;	Is 6:3
eyes have seen the King, the **L** of hosts!"	Is 6:5
And I heard the voice of the **L** saying,	Is 6:8
I said, "How long, O **L**?" And he said:	Is 6:11
and the **L** removes people far away, and	Is 6:12
And the **L** said to Isaiah, "Go out to meet	Is 7:3
thus says the **L** GOD: "It shall not stand,	Is 7:7
Again the **L** spoke to Ahaz,	Is 7:10
"Ask a sign of the **L** your God; let it be	Is 7:11
ask, and I will not put the **L** to the test."	Is 7:12
Therefore the **L** himself will give you a	Is 7:14
The **L** will bring upon you and upon	Is 7:17
In that day the **L** will whistle for the fly	Is 7:18
In that day the **L** will shave with a razor	Is 7:20
Then the **L** said to me, "Take a large tablet	Is 8:1
Then the **L** said to me, "Call his name	Is 8:3
The **L** spoke to me again:	Is 8:5
the **L** is bringing up against them the	Is 8:7
For the **L** spoke thus to me with his	Is 8:11
But the **L** of hosts, him you shall regard	Is 8:13
I will wait for the **L**, who is hiding his face	Is 8:17
the children whom the **L** has given me	Is 8:18
and portents in Israel from the **L** of hosts,	Is 8:18
The zeal of the **L** of hosts will do this.	Is 9:7
The **L** has sent a word against Jacob, and it	Is 9:8
But the **L** raises the adversaries of Rezin	Is 9:11
struck them, nor inquire of the **L** of hosts.	Is 9:13
So the **L** cut off from Israel head and tail,	Is 9:14
Therefore the **L** does not rejoice over their	Is 9:17
the wrath of the **L** of hosts the land	Is 9:19
When the **L** has finished all his work on	Is 10:12
Therefore the **L** GOD of hosts will send	Is 10:16
of his fruitful land the **L** will destroy,	Is 10:18
who struck them, but will lean on the **L**,	Is 10:20
For the **L** GOD of hosts will make a full	Is 10:23
Therefore thus says the **L** GOD of hosts:	Is 10:24
And the **L** of hosts will wield against	Is 10:26
the **L** GOD of hosts will lop the boughs	Is 10:33
the Spirit of the **L** shall rest upon him,	Is 11:2
Spirit of knowledge and the fear of the **L**.	Is 11:2
his delight shall be in the fear of the **L**.	Is 11:3
the knowledge of the **L** as the waters cover	Is 11:9
In that day the **L** will extend his hand yet	Is 11:11
And the **L** will utterly destroy the tongue	Is 11:15
"I will give thanks to you, O **L**, for though	Is 12:1
for the **L** GOD is my strength and my	Is 12:2
"Give thanks to the **L**, call upon his	Is 12:4
"Sing praises to the **L**, for he has done	Is 12:5
The **L** of hosts is mustering a host for	Is 13:4
the **L** and the weapons of his indignation,	Is 13:5
Wail, for the day of the **L** is near; as	Is 13:6
Behold, the day of the **L** comes, cruel,	Is 13:9
at the wrath of the **L** of hosts in the day	Is 13:13
For the **L** will have compassion on Jacob	Is 14:1
When the **L** has given you rest from your	Is 14:3
The **L** has broken the staff of the wicked,	Is 14:5
against them," declares the **L** of hosts,	Is 14:22
descendants and posterity," says the **L**.	Is 14:22
of destruction," declares the **L** of hosts.	Is 14:23
The **L** of hosts has sworn: "As I have	Is 14:24
For the **L** of hosts has purposed, and	Is 14:27
"The **L** has founded Zion, and in her the	Is 14:32
word that the **L** spoke concerning Moab	Is 16:13
But now the **L** has spoken, saying, "In	Is 16:14
children of Israel, declares the **L** of hosts.	Is 17:3
of a fruit tree, declares the **L** God of Israel.	Is 17:6
For thus the **L** said to me: "I will quietly	Is 18:4
will be brought to the **L** of hosts from a	Is 18:7
the place of the name of the **L** of hosts.	Is 18:7
the **L** is riding on a swift cloud and comes	Is 19:1
over them, declares the **L** GOD of hosts.	Is 19:4
might know what the **L** of hosts has	Is 19:12
The **L** has mingled within her a spirit of	Is 19:14
the hand that the **L** of hosts shakes over	Is 19:16
the purpose that the **L** of hosts has	Is 19:17
and swear allegiance to the **L** of hosts.	Is 19:18
be an altar to the **L** in the midst of the	Is 19:19
Egypt, and a pillar to the **L** at its border.	Is 19:19
and a witness to the **L** of hosts in the	Is 19:20
they cry to the **L** because of oppressors,	Is 19:20
And the **L** will make himself known to	Is 19:21
Egyptians will know the **L** in that day	Is 19:21
make vows to the **L** and perform them.	Is 19:21
And the **L** will strike Egypt, striking and	Is 19:22
healing, and they will return to the **L**,	Is 19:22
whom the **L** of hosts has blessed, saying,	Is 19:25
at that time the **L** spoke by Isaiah the son	Is 20:2
Then the **L** said, "As my servant Isaiah	Is 20:3
For thus the **L** said to me: "Go, set a	Is 21:6
"Upon a watchtower I stand, O **L**,	Is 21:8
what I have heard from the **L** of hosts,	Is 21:10
For thus the **L** said to me, "Within a	Is 21:16
of the sons of Kedar will be few, for the **L**,	Is 21:17
For the **L** GOD of hosts has a day of	Is 22:5
In that day the **L** GOD of hosts called for	Is 22:12
The **L** of hosts has revealed himself in	Is 22:14
until you die," says the **L** GOD of hosts.	Is 22:14
Thus says the **L** GOD of hosts, "Come, go	Is 22:15
the **L** will hurl you away violently,	Is 22:17
In that day, declares the **L** of hosts, the	Is 22:25
it will be cut off, for the **L** has spoken."	Is 22:25
The **L** of hosts has purposed it, to defile	Is 23:9
the **L** has given command concerning	Is 23:11
of seventy years, the **L** will visit Tyre,	Is 23:17
and her wages will be holy to the **L**.	Is 23:18
for those who dwell before the **L**.	Is 23:18
the **L** will empty the earth and make it	Is 24:1
plundered; for the **L** has spoken this word.	Is 24:3
the majesty of the **L** they shout from the	Is 24:14
Therefore in the east give glory to the **L**;	Is 24:15
the sea, give glory to the name of the **L**,	Is 24:15
On that day the **L** will punish the host of	Is 24:21
for the **L** of hosts reigns on Mount Zion	Is 24:23
O **L**, you are my God; I will exalt you; I	Is 25:1
On this mountain the **L** of hosts will	Is 25:6
and the **L** GOD will wipe away tears from	Is 25:8
from all the earth, for the **L** has spoken.	Is 25:8
This is the **L**; we have waited for him; let	Is 25:9
For the hand of the **L** will rest on this	Is 25:10
but the **L** will lay low his pompous pride	Is 25:11
Trust in the **L** forever, for the LORD GOD is	Is 26:4
for the **L** GOD is an everlasting rock.	Is 26:4
In the path of your judgments, O **L**, we	Is 26:8
and does not see the majesty of the **L**.	Is 26:10
O **L**, your hand is lifted up, but they do	Is 26:11
O **L**, you will ordain peace for us; you	Is 26:12
O **L** our God, other lords besides you	Is 26:13
But you have increased the nation, O **L**,	Is 26:15
O **L**, in distress they sought you; they	Is 26:16
birth, so were we because of you, O **L**;	Is 26:17
the **L** is coming out from his place to	Is 26:21
In that day the **L** with his hard and great	Is 27:1
I, the **L**, am its keeper; every moment I	Is 27:3
Brook of Egypt the **L** will thresh out the	Is 27:12

come and worship the **L** on the holy Is 27:13
the **L** has one who is mighty and strong; Is 28:2
In that day the **L** of hosts will be a crown Is 28:5
a foreign tongue the **L** will speak to this Is 28:11
And the word of the **L** will be to them Is 28:13
Therefore hear the word of the **L**, you Is 28:14
therefore thus says the **L** GOD, "Behold, I Is 28:16
For the **L** will rise up as on Mount Is 28:21
of destruction from the **L** GOD of hosts Is 28:22
This also comes from the **L** of hosts; he Is 28:29
be visited by the **L** of hosts with thunder Is 29:6
For the **L** has poured out upon you a Is 29:10
And the **L** said: "Because this people Is 29:13
who hide deep from the **L** your counsel, Is 29:15
meek shall obtain fresh joy in the **L**, Is 29:19
Therefore thus says the **L**, who redeemed Is 29:22
"Ah, stubborn children," declares the **L**, Is 30:1
unwilling to hear the instruction of the **L**; Is 30:9
For thus said the **L** GOD, the Holy One of Is 30:15
Therefore the **L** waits to be gracious to Is 30:18
For the **L** is a God of justice; blessed are Is 30:18
And though the **L** give you the bread of Is 30:20
the day when the **L** binds up the Is 30:26
the name of the **L** comes from afar, Is 30:27
the flute to go to the mountain of the **L**, Is 30:29
And the **L** will cause his majestic voice Is 30:30
be terror-stricken at the voice of the **L**, Is 30:31
appointed staff that the **L** lays on them Is 30:32
the breath of the **L**, like a stream of Is 30:33
to the Holy One of Israel or consult the **L**! Is 31:1
When the **L** stretches out his hand, the Is 31:3
For thus the **L** said to me, "As a lion or a Is 31:4
so the **L** of hosts will come down to fight Is 31:4
so the **L** of hosts will protect Jerusalem; Is 31:5
the standard in panic," declares the **L**, Is 31:9
to utter error concerning the **L**, Is 32:6
O **L**, be gracious to us; we wait for you. Be Is 33:2
The **L** is exalted, for he dwells on high; he Is 33:5
the fear of the **L** is Zion's treasure. Is 33:6
"Now I will arise," says the **L**, "now I will Is 33:10
But there the **L** in majesty will be for us Is 33:21
For the **L** is our judge; the LORD is our Is 33:22
LORD is our judge; the **L** is our lawgiver; Is 33:22
LORD is our lawgiver; the **L** is our king; Is 33:22
For the **L** is enraged against all the Is 34:2
The **L** has a sword; it is sated with blood; Is 34:6
For the **L** has a sacrifice in Bozrah, a Is 34:6
For the **L** has a day of vengeance, a year Is 34:8
Seek and read from the book of the **L**: Is 34:16
For the mouth of the **L** has commanded, Is 34:16
They shall see the glory of the **L**, the Is 35:2
the ransomed of the **L** shall return and Is 35:10
"We trust in the **L** our God," is it not he Is 36:7
is it without the **L** that I have come up Is 36:10
The **L** said to me, Go up against this Is 36:10
make you trust in the **L** by saying, Is 36:15
by saying, "The **L** will surely deliver us. Is 36:15
"The **L** will deliver us." Has any of the Is 36:18
that the **L** should deliver Jerusalem out Is 36:20
and went into the house of the **L**. Is 37:1
It may be that the **L** your God will hear Is 37:4
the words that the **L** your God has heard; Is 37:4
"Say to your master, 'Thus says the **L**: Is 37:6
Hezekiah went up to the house of the **L**, Is 37:14
of the LORD, and spread it before the **L**. Is 37:14
And Hezekiah prayed to the **L**: Is 37:15
"O **L** of hosts, God of Israel, who is Is 37:16
Incline your ear, O **L**, and hear; open Is 37:17
and hear; open your eyes, O **L**, and see; Is 37:17
Truly, O **L**, the kings of Assyria have Is 37:18
So now, O **L** our God, save us from his Is 37:20
may know that you alone are the **L**." Is 37:20
to Hezekiah, saying, "Thus says the **L**, Is 37:21
word that the **L** has spoken concerning Is 37:22
your servants you have mocked the **L**, Is 37:24
The zeal of the **L** of hosts will do this. Is 37:32
thus says the **L** concerning the king Is 37:33
not come into this city, declares the **L**. Is 37:34
the angel of the **L** went out and struck Is 37:36
to him, and said to him, "Thus says the **L**: Is 38:1
his face to the wall and prayed to the **L**, Is 38:2
and said, "Please, O **L**, remember how I Is 38:3
Then the word of the **L** came to Isaiah: Is 38:4
"Go and say to Hezekiah, Thus says the **L**, Is 38:5
"This shall be the sign to you from the **L**, Is 38:7
that the **L** will do this thing that he has Is 38:7
I said, I shall not see the **L**, the LORD in Is 38:11
the LORD, the **L** in the land of the living; Is 38:11
are weary with looking upward. O **L**, Is 38:14
O **L**, by these things men live, and in all Is 38:16
The **L** will save me, and we will play my Is 38:20
days of our lives, at the house of the **L**. Is 38:20
that I shall go up to the house of the **L**?" Is 38:22
"Hear the word of the **L** of hosts: Is 39:5
Babylon. Nothing shall be left, says the **L**. Is 39:6

"The word of the **L** that you have spoken Is 39:8
the wilderness prepare the way of the **L**; Is 40:3
And the glory of the **L** shall be revealed, Is 40:5
for the mouth of the **L** has spoken." Is 40:5
when the breath of the **L** blows on it; Is 40:7
Behold, the **L** GOD comes with might, Is 40:10
Who has measured the Spirit of the **L**, or Is 40:13
O Israel, "My way is hidden from the **L**, Is 40:27
The **L** is the everlasting God, the Creator Is 40:28
who wait for the **L** shall renew their Is 40:31
I, the **L**, the first, and with the last; I am Is 41:4
For I, the **L** your God, hold your right Is 41:13
the one who helps you, declares the **L**; Is 41:14
And you shall rejoice in the **L**; in the Is 41:16
with thirst, I the **L** will answer them; Is 41:17
that the hand of the **L** has done this, Is 41:20
Set forth your case, says the **L**; bring Is 41:21
Thus says God, the **L**, who created the Is 42:5
"I am the **L**; I have called you in Is 42:6
I am the **L**; that is my name; my glory I Is 42:8
Sing to the **L** a new song, his praise from Is 42:10
Let them give glory to the **L**, and declare Is 42:12
The **L** goes out like a mighty man, like a Is 42:13
one, or blind as the servant of the **L**? Is 42:19
The **L** was pleased, for his righteousness' Is 42:21
Was it not the **L**, against whom we have Is 42:24
But now thus says the **L**, he who created Is 43:1
For I am the **L** your God, the Holy One of Is 43:3
"You are my witnesses," declares the **L**, Is 43:10
I, I am the **L**, and besides me there is no Is 43:11
you are my witnesses," declares the **L**, Is 43:12
Thus says the **L**, your Redeemer, the Is 43:14
I am the **L**, your Holy One, the Creator of Is 43:15
Thus says the **L**, who makes a way in Is 43:16
Thus says the **L** who made you, who Is 44:2
Thus says the **L**, the King of Israel and Is 44:6
of Israel and his Redeemer, the **L** of hosts: Is 44:6
Sing, O heavens, for the **L** has done it; Is 44:23
For the **L** has redeemed Jacob, and will Is 44:23
Thus says the **L**, your Redeemer, who Is 44:24
"I am the **L**, who made all things, who Is 44:24
Thus says the **L** to his anointed, to Cyrus, Is 45:1
that you may know that it is I, the **L**, Is 45:3
I am the **L**, and there is no other, besides Is 45:5
me; I am the **L**, and there is no other. Is 45:6
and create calamity, I am the **L**, Is 45:7
both to sprout; I the **L** have created it. Is 45:8
Thus says the **L**, the Holy One of Israel, Is 45:11
for price or reward," says the **L** of hosts. Is 45:13
Thus says the **L**: "The wealth of Egypt Is 45:14
saved by the **L** with everlasting Is 45:17
For thus says the **L**, who created the Is 45:18
"I am the **L**, and there is no other. Is 45:18
I the **L** speak the truth; I declare what is Is 45:19
declared it of old? Was it not I, the **L**? Is 45:21
"Only in the **L**, it shall be said of me, are Is 45:24
In the **L** all the offspring of Israel shall Is 45:25
Our Redeemer—the **L** of hosts is his Is 47:4
by the name of the **L** and confess the God Is 48:1
God of Israel; the **L** of hosts is his name. Is 48:2
The **L** loves him; he shall perform his Is 48:14
there." And now the **L** GOD has sent me, Is 48:16
Thus says the **L**, your Redeemer, the Is 48:17
"I am the **L** your God, who teaches you Is 48:17
"The **L** has redeemed his servant Jacob!" Is 48:20
"There is no peace," says the **L**, "for the Is 48:22
The **L** called me from the womb, from Is 49:1
yet surely my right is with the **L**, and my Is 49:4
And now the **L** says, he who formed me Is 49:5
for I am honored in the eyes of the **L**, Is 49:5
Thus says the **L**, the Redeemer of Israel Is 49:7
because of the **L**, who is faithful, the Holy Is 49:7
Thus says the **L**: "In a time of favor I have Is 49:8
for the **L** has comforted his people and Is 49:13
But Zion said, "The **L** has forsaken me; Is 49:14
forsaken me; my **L** has forgotten me." Is 49:14
As I live, declares the **L**, you shall put Is 49:18
Thus says the **L** GOD: "Behold, I will lift Is 49:22
Then you will know that I am the **L**; Is 49:23
For thus says the **L**: "Even the captives Is 49:25
shall know that I am the **L** your Savior, Is 49:26
Thus says the **L**: "Where is your mother's Is 50:1
The **L** GOD has given me the tongue of Is 50:4
The **L** GOD has opened my ear, and I was Is 50:5
But the **L** GOD helps me; therefore I have Is 50:7
Behold, the **L** GOD helps me; who will Is 50:9
among you fears the **L** and obeys the Is 50:10
in the name of the **L** and rely on his God. Is 50:10
righteousness, you who seek the **L**: Is 51:1
For the **L** comforts Zion; he comforts all Is 51:3
Eden, her desert like the garden of the **L**; Is 51:3
awake, put on strength, O arm of the **L**; Is 51:9
the ransomed of the **L** shall return and Is 51:11
and have forgotten the **L**, your Maker, Is 51:13
I am the **L** your God, who stirs up the sea Is 51:15

its waves roar—the **L** of hosts is his Is 51:15
from the hand of the **L** the cup of his Is 51:17
they are full of the wrath of the **L**, the Is 51:20
Thus says your **L**, the LORD, your God Is 51:22
Thus says your Lord, the **L**, your God Is 51:22
For thus says the **L**: "You were sold for Is 52:3
For thus says the **L** GOD: "My people went Is 52:4
what have I here," declares the **L**, Is 52:5
Their rulers wail," declares the **L**, "and Is 52:5
to eye they see the return of the **L** to Zion. Is 52:8
for the **L** has comforted his people; Is 52:9
The **L** has bared his holy arm before the Is 52:10
you who bear the vessels of the **L**. Is 52:11
go in flight, for the **L** will go before you, Is 52:12
has the arm of the **L** been revealed? Is 53:1
and the **L** has laid on him the iniquity of Is 53:6
Yet it was the will of the **L** to crush him; Is 53:10
the will of the **L** shall prosper in his Is 53:10
of her who is married," says the **L**. Is 54:1
your husband, the **L** of hosts is his name; Is 54:5
For the **L** has called you like a wife Is 54:6
will have compassion on you," says the **L**, Is 54:8
peace shall not be removed," says the **L**, Is 54:10
your children shall be taught by the **L**, Is 54:13
servants of the **L** and their vindication Is 54:17
vindication from me, declares the **L**." Is 54:17
run to you, because of the **L** your God, Is 55:5
"Seek the **L** while he may be found; call Is 55:6
let him return to the **L**, that he may have Is 55:7
are your ways my ways, declares the **L**. Is 55:8
and it shall make a name for the **L**, an Is 55:13
Thus says the **L**: "Keep justice, and do Is 56:1
who has joined himself to the **L** say, Is 56:3
"The **L** will surely separate me from his Is 56:3
For thus says the **L**: "To the eunuchs who Is 56:4
foreigners who join themselves to the **L**, Is 56:6
minister to him, to love the name of the **L**, Is 56:6
The **L** GOD, who gathers the outcasts of Is 56:8
to the far and to the near," says the **L**, Is 57:19
this a fast, and a day acceptable to the **L**? Is 58:5
the glory of the **L** shall be your rear Is 58:8
you shall call, and the **L** will answer; Is 58:9
And the **L** will guide you continually Is 58:11
and the holy day of the **L** honorable; Is 58:13
then you shall take delight in the **L**, and Is 58:14
for the mouth of the **L** has spoken." Is 58:14
transgressing, and denying the **L**, and Is 59:13
The **L** saw it, and it displeased him that Is 59:15
fear the name of the **L** from the west, Is 59:19
stream, which the wind of the **L** drives. Is 59:19
turn from transgression," declares the **L**. Is 59:20
is my covenant with them," says the **L**: Is 59:21
of your children's offspring," says the **L**, Is 59:21
and the glory of the **L** has risen upon you. Is 60:1
but the **L** will arise upon you, and his Is 60:2
bring good news, the praises of the **L**. Is 60:6
them, for the name of the **L** your God, Is 60:9
they shall call you the City of the **L**, the Is 60:14
and you shall know that I, the **L**, am Is 60:16
but the **L** will be your everlasting light, Is 60:19
for the **L** will be your everlasting light, Is 60:20
one a mighty nation; I am the **L**; Is 60:22
The Spirit of the **L** GOD is upon me, Is 61:1
because the **L** has anointed me to bring Is 61:1
of righteousness, the planting of the **L**, Is 61:3
you shall be called the priests of the **L**; Is 61:6
For I the **L** love justice; I hate robbery and Is 61:8
they are an offspring the **L** has blessed. Is 61:9
I will greatly rejoice in the **L**; my soul Is 61:10
so the **L** GOD will cause righteousness Is 61:11
name that the mouth of the **L** will give. Is 62:2
be a crown of beauty in the hand of the **L**, Is 62:3
for the **L** delights in you, and your land Is 62:4
You who put the **L** in remembrance, take Is 62:6
The **L** has sworn by his right hand and Is 62:8
who garner it shall eat it and praise the **L**, Is 62:9
the **L** has proclaimed to the end of the Is 62:11
The Holy People, The Redeemed of the **L**; Is 62:12
I will recount the steadfast love of the **L**, Is 63:7
love of the LORD, the praises of the **L**, Is 63:7
according to all that the **L** has granted us, Is 63:7
valley, the Spirit of the **L** gave them rest. Is 63:14
you, O **L**, are our Father, our Redeemer Is 63:16
O **L**, why do you make us wander from Is 63:17
But now, O **L**, you are our Father; we are Is 64:8
Be not so terribly angry, O **L**, and Is 64:9
restrain yourself at these things, O **L**? Is 64:12
fathers' iniquities together, says the **L**; Is 65:7
Thus says the **L**: "As the new wine is Is 65:8
But you who forsake the **L**, who forget Is 65:11
Therefore thus says the **L** GOD: "Behold, Is 65:13
and the **L** GOD will put you to death, Is 65:15
be the offspring of the blessed of the **L**, Is 65:23
in all my holy mountain," says the **L**. Is 65:25
Thus says the **L**: "Heaven is my throne, Is 66:1

all these things came to be, declares the **L**. Is 66:2
Hear the word of the **L**, you who tremble Is 66:5
sake have said, 'Let the **L** be glorified, Is 66:5
The sound of the **L**, rendering Is 66:6
and not cause to bring forth?" says the **L**; Is 66:9
For thus says the **L**: "Behold, I will Is 66:12
and the hand of the **L** shall be known to Is 66:14
"For behold, the **L** will come in fire, and Is 66:15
by fire will the **L** enter into judgment, Is 66:16
and those slain by the **L** shall be many. Is 66:16
come to an end together, declares the **L**. Is 66:17
all the nations as an offering to the **L**, Is 66:20
holy mountain Jerusalem, says the **L**, Is 66:20
in a clean vessel to the house of the **L**. Is 66:20
for priests and for Levites, says the **L**. Is 66:21
shall remain before me, says the **L**, Is 66:22
to worship before me, declares the **L**. Is 66:23
whom the word of the **L** came in the days Jer 1:2
Now the word of the **L** came to me, Jer 1:4
Then I said, "Ah, **L** GOD! Behold, I do not Jer 1:6
But the **L** said to me, "Do not say, 'I am Jer 1:7
with you to deliver you, declares the **L**." Jer 1:8
Then the **L** put out his hand and touched Jer 1:9
And the **L** said to me, "Behold, I have put Jer 1:9
And the word of the **L** came to me, Jer 1:11
Then the **L** said to me, "You have seen Jer 1:12
The word of the **L** came to me a second Jer 1:13
Then the **L** said to me, "Out of the north Jer 1:14
kingdoms of the north, declares the **L**, Jer 1:15
you, for I am with you, declares the **L**, Jer 1:19
The word of the **L** came to me, saying, Jer 2:1
the hearing of Jerusalem, Thus says the **L**, Jer 2:2
Israel was holy to the **L**, the firstfruits of Jer 2:3
disaster came upon them, declares the **L**." Jer 2:3
Hear the word of the **L**, O house of Jacob, Jer 2:4
Thus says the **L**: "What wrong did your Jer 2:5
'Where is the **L** who brought us up from Jer 2:6
The priests did not say, 'Where is the **L**?' Jer 2:8
I still contend with you, declares the **L**, Jer 2:9
be utterly desolate, declares the **L**, Jer 2:12
yourself by forsaking the **L** your God, Jer 2:17
bitter for you to forsake the **L** your God; Jer 2:19
is not in you, declares the **L** GOD of hosts. Jer 2:19
is still before me, declares the **L** GOD. Jer 2:22
transgressed against me, declares the **L**. Jer 2:29
O generation, behold the word of the **L**. Jer 2:31
for the **L** has rejected those in whom you Jer 2:37
would you return to me? declares the **L**. Jer 3:1
The **L** said to me in the days of King Jer 3:6
heart, but in pretense, declares the **L**." Jer 3:10
And the **L** said to me, "Faithless Israel Jer 3:11
"'Return, faithless Israel, declares the **L**. Jer 3:12
anger, for I am merciful, declares the **L**; Jer 3:12
you rebelled against the **L** your God and Jer 3:13
not obeyed my voice, declares the **L**. Jer 3:13
O faithless children, declares the **L**; Jer 3:14
in the land, in those days, declares the **L**, Jer 3:16
the covenant of the **L**." It shall not come Jer 3:16
shall be called the throne of the **L**, Jer 3:17
it, to the presence of the **L** in Jerusalem, Jer 3:17
to me, O house of Israel, declares the **L**.'" Jer 3:20
way; they have forgotten the **L** their God. Jer 3:21
come to you, for you are the **L** our God. Jer 3:22
Truly in the **L** our God is the salvation Jer 3:23
we have sinned against the **L** our God, Jer 3:25
not obeyed the voice of the **L** our God." Jer 3:25
"If you return, O Israel, declares the **L**, to Jer 4:1
and if you swear, 'As the **L** lives,' in truth, Jer 4:2
For thus says the **L** to the men of Judah Jer 4:3
Circumcise yourselves to the **L**; remove Jer 4:4
fierce anger of the **L** has not turned back Jer 4:8
"In that day, declares the **L**, courage shall Jer 4:9
Then I said, "Ah, **L** GOD, surely you have Jer 4:10
has rebelled against me, declares the **L**. Jer 4:17
its cities were laid in ruins before the **L**, Jer 4:26
For thus says the **L**, "The whole land Jer 4:27
say, "As the **L** lives," yet they swear falsely. Jer 5:2
O **L**, do not your eyes look for truth? You Jer 5:3
for they do not know the way of the **L**, the Jer 5:4
to them, for they know the way of the **L**, Jer 5:5
declares the **L**; and shall I not avenge Jer 5:9
utterly treacherous to me, declares the **L**. Jer 5:11
spoken falsely of the **L** and have said, Jer 5:12
Therefore thus says the **L**, the God of Jer 5:14
afar, O house of Israel, declares the **L**. Jer 5:15
"But even in those days, declares the **L**, I Jer 5:18
'Why has the **L** our God done all these Jer 5:19
declares the **L**; Do you not tremble Jer 5:22
in their hearts, 'Let us fear the **L** our God, Jer 5:24
declares the **L**, and shall I not avenge Jer 5:29
For thus says the **L** of hosts: "Cut down Jer 6:6
Thus says the **L** of hosts: "They shall Jer 6:9
the word of the **L** is to them an object of Jer 6:10
Therefore I am full of the wrath of the **L**; Jer 6:11
inhabitants of the land," declares the **L**. Jer 6:12

they shall be overthrown," says the **L**. Jer 6:15
Thus says the **L**: "Stand by the roads, Jer 6:16
Therefore thus says the **L**: 'Behold, I will Jer 6:21
Thus says the **L**: "Behold, a people is Jer 6:22
are called, for the **L** has rejected them." Jer 6:30
word that came to Jeremiah from the **L**: Jer 7:1
this word, and say, Hear the word of the **L**, Jer 7:2
who enter these gates to worship the **L**. Jer 7:2
Thus says the **L** of hosts, the God of Israel: Jer 7:3
'This is the temple of the **L**, the temple of Jer 7:4
the temple of the LORD, the temple of the **L**, Jer 7:4
the temple of the LORD, the temple of the **L**.' Jer 7:4
I myself have seen it, declares the **L**. Jer 7:11
done all these things, declares the **L**, Jer 7:13
it I whom they provoke? declares the **L**. Jer 7:19
Therefore thus says the **L** GOD: behold, Jer 7:20
Thus says the **L** of hosts, the God of Jer 7:21
did not obey the voice of the **L** their God, Jer 7:28
for the **L** has rejected and forsaken the Jer 7:29
done evil in my sight, declares the **L**. Jer 7:30
the days are coming, declares the **L**, Jer 7:32
"At that time, declares the **L**, the bones of Jer 8:1
have driven them, declares the **L** of hosts. Jer 8:3
"You shall say to them, Thus says the **L**: Jer 8:4
but my people know not the rules of the **L**. Jer 8:7
are wise, and the law of the **L** is with us'? Jer 8:8
they have rejected the word of the **L**, Jer 8:9
they shall be overthrown, says the **L**. Jer 8:12
I would gather them, declares the **L**, Jer 8:13
for the **L** our God has doomed us to Jer 8:14
because we have sinned against the **L**. Jer 8:14
they shall bite you," declares the **L**. Jer 8:17
of the land: "Is the **L** not in Zion? Jer 8:19
and they do not know me, declares the **L**. Jer 9:3
they refuse to know me, declares the **L**. Jer 9:6
Therefore thus says the **L** of hosts: Jer 9:7
declares the **L**, and shall I not avenge Jer 9:9
whom has the mouth of the **L** spoken, Jer 9:12
And the **L** says: "Because they have Jer 9:13
Therefore thus says the **L** of hosts, the Jer 9:15
Thus says the **L** of hosts: "Consider, and Jer 9:17
Hear, O women, the word of the **L**, and let Jer 9:20
Speak, "Thus declares the **L**: 'The dead Jer 9:22
Thus says the **L**: "Let not the wise man Jer 9:23
that I am the **L** who practices steadfast Jer 9:24
in these things I delight, declares the **L**." Jer 9:24
the days are coming, declares the **L**, Jer 9:25
Hear the word that the **L** speaks to you, O Jer 10:1
Thus says the **L**: "Learn not the way of Jer 10:2
There is none like you, O **L**; you are Jer 10:6
But the **L** is the true God; he is the Jer 10:10
inheritance; the **L** of hosts is his name. Jer 10:16
For thus says the **L**: "Behold, I am Jer 10:18
are stupid and do not inquire of the **L**; Jer 10:21
I know, O **L**, that the way of man is not Jer 10:23
Correct me, O **L**, but in justice; not in Jer 10:24
word that came to Jeremiah from the **L**: Jer 11:1
You shall say to them, Thus says the **L**, Jer 11:3
this day." Then I answered, "So be it, **L**." Jer 11:5
And the **L** said to me, "Proclaim all these Jer 11:6
Again the **L** said to me, "A conspiracy Jer 11:9
Therefore, thus says the **L**, behold, I am Jer 11:11
The **L** once called you 'a green olive Jer 11:16
The **L** of hosts, who planted you, has Jer 11:17
The **L** made it known to me and I Jer 11:18
But, O **L** of hosts, who judges Jer 11:20
thus says the **L** concerning the men Jer 11:21
"Do not prophesy in the name of the **L**, Jer 11:21
therefore thus says the **L** of hosts: Jer 11:22
Righteous are you, O **L**, when I complain Jer 12:1
But you, O **L**, know me; you see me, and Jer 12:3
the sword of the **L** devours from one Jer 12:12
because of the fierce anger of the **L**." Jer 12:13
Thus says the **L** concerning all my evil Jer 12:14
to swear by my name, 'As the **L** lives,' Jer 12:16
it up and destroy it, declares the **L**." Jer 12:17
Thus says the **L** to me, "Go and buy a Jer 13:1
loincloth according to the word of the **L**, Jer 13:2
And the word of the **L** came to me a Jer 13:3
the Euphrates, as the **L** commanded me. Jer 13:5
And after many days the **L** said to me, Jer 13:6
Then the word of the **L** came to me: Jer 13:8
"Thus says the **L**: Even so will I spoil the Jer 13:9
of Judah cling to me, declares the **L**, Jer 13:11
'Thus says the **L**, the God of Israel, Jer 13:12
you shall say to them, 'Thus says the **L**: Jer 13:13
and sons together, declares the **L**. Jer 13:14
ear; be not proud, for the **L** has spoken. Jer 13:15
Give glory to the **L** your God before he Jer 13:16
measured out to you, declares the **L**, Jer 13:25
The word of the **L** that came to Jeremiah Jer 14:1
our iniquities testify against us, act, O **L**, Jer 14:7
Yet you, O **L**, are in the midst of us, and Jer 14:9
Thus says the **L** concerning this Jer 14:10
therefore the **L** does not accept them; Jer 14:10

The **L** said to me: "Do not pray for the Jer 14:11
"Ah, **L** GOD, behold, the prophets say to Jer 14:13
And the **L** said to me: "The prophets are Jer 14:14
thus says the **L** concerning the Jer 14:15
We acknowledge our wickedness, O **L**, Jer 14:20
showers? Are you not he, O **L** our God? Jer 14:22
Then the **L** said to me, "Though Moses Jer 15:1
you shall say to them, 'Thus says the **L**: Jer 15:2
four kinds of destroyers, declares the **L**: Jer 15:3
You have rejected me, declares the **L**; Jer 15:6
before their enemies, declares the **L**." Jer 15:9
The **L** said, "Have I not set you free for Jer 15:11
O **L**, you know; remember me and visit Jer 15:15
for I am called by your name, O **L**, Jer 15:16
Therefore thus says the **L**: "If you Jer 15:19
you and deliver you, declares the **L**. Jer 15:20
The word of the **L** came to me: Jer 16:1
For thus says the **L** concerning the sons Jer 16:3
"For thus says the **L**: Do not enter the Jer 16:5
steadfast love and mercy, declares the **L**. Jer 16:5
For thus says the **L** of hosts, the God of Jer 16:9
'Why has the **L** pronounced all this Jer 16:10
committed against the **L** our God?' Jer 16:10
have forsaken me, declares the **L**, Jer 16:11
the days are coming, declares the **L**, Jer 16:14
'As the **L** lives who brought up the Jer 16:14
but 'As the **L** lives who brought up the Jer 16:15
for many fishers, declares the **L**, Jer 16:16
O **L**, my strength and my stronghold, Jer 16:19
shall know that my name is the **L**." Jer 16:21
Thus says the **L**: "Cursed is the man Jer 17:5
whose heart turns away from the **L**. Jer 17:5
"Blessed is the man who trusts in the **L**, Jer 17:7
trusts in the LORD, whose trust is the **L**. Jer 17:7
"I the **L** search the heart and test the Jer 17:10
O **L**, the hope of Israel, all who forsake Jer 17:13
the earth, for they have forsaken the **L**, Jer 17:13
Heal me, O **L**, and I shall be healed; save Jer 17:14
say to me, "Where is the word of the **L**? Jer 17:15
Thus said the **L** to me: "Go and stand in Jer 17:19
'Hear the word of the **L**, you kings of Jer 17:20
Thus says the **L**: Take care for the sake Jer 17:21
"But if you listen to me, declares the **L**, Jer 17:24
thank offerings to the house of the **L**. Jer 17:26
word that came to Jeremiah from the **L**: Jer 18:1
Then the word of the **L** came to me: Jer 18:5
as this potter has done? declares the **L**. Jer 18:6
'Thus says the **L**, behold, I am shaping Jer 18:11
"Therefore thus says the **L**: Ask among Jer 18:13
Hear me, O **L**, and listen to the voice of Jer 18:19
Yet you, O **L**, know all their plotting to Jer 18:23
Thus says the **L**, "Go, buy a potter's Jer 19:1
You shall say, 'Hear the word of the **L**, O Jer 19:3
Thus says the **L** of hosts, the God of Jer 19:3
behold, days are coming, declares the **L**, Jer 19:6
say to them, 'Thus says the **L** of hosts: Jer 19:11
will I do to this place, declares the **L**, Jer 19:12
where the **L** had sent him to prophesy, Jer 19:14
"Thus says the **L** of hosts, the God of Jer 19:15
was chief officer in the house of the **L**, Jer 20:1
Benjamin Gate of the house of the **L**. Jer 20:2
"The **L** does not call your name Jer 20:3
For thus says the **L**: Behold, I will make Jer 20:4
O **L**, you have deceived me, and I was Jer 20:7
For the word of the **L** has become for me Jer 20:8
But the **L** is with me as a dread warrior; Jer 20:11
O **L** of hosts, who tests the righteous, Jer 20:12
Sing to the **L**; praise the LORD! For he Jer 20:13
Sing to the LORD; praise the **L**! For he Jer 20:13
cities that the **L** overthrew without pity; Jer 20:16
word that came to Jeremiah from the **L**, Jer 21:1
"Inquire of the **L** for us, for Jer 21:2
Perhaps the **L** will deal with us Jer 21:2
shall say to Zedekiah, 'Thus says the **L**, Jer 21:4
Afterward, declares the **L**, I will give Jer 21:7
people you shall say: 'Thus says the **L**: Jer 21:8
harm and not for good, declares the **L**: Jer 21:10
of Judah say, 'Hear the word of the **L**, Jer 21:11
Thus says the **L**: "'Execute justice in Jer 21:12
O rock of the plain, declares the **L**; Jer 21:13
to the fruit of your deeds, declares the **L**; Jer 21:14
Thus says the **L**: "Go down to the house Jer 22:1
and say, 'Hear the word of the **L**, O King Jer 22:2
Thus says the **L**: Do justice and Jer 22:3
words, I swear by myself, declares the **L**, Jer 22:5
thus says the **L** concerning the house Jer 22:6
"Why has the **L** dealt thus with this Jer 22:8
the covenant of the **L** their God and Jer 22:9
thus says the **L** concerning Shallum Jer 22:11
Is not this to know me? declares the **L**. Jer 22:16
thus says the **L** concerning Jehoiakim Jer 22:18
lament for him, saying, 'Ah, **l**!' or 'Ah, Jer 22:18
"As I live, declares the **L**, though Jer 22:24
land, land, land, hear the word of the **L**! Jer 22:29
Thus says the **L**: "Write this man down Jer 22:30

the sheep of my pasture!" declares the **L**. Jer 23:1
Therefore thus says the **L**, the God of Jer 23:2
to you for your evil deeds, declares the **L**. Jer 23:2
shall any be missing, declares the **L**. Jer 23:4
the days are coming, declares the **L**, Jer 23:5
be called: 'The **L** is our righteousness.' Jer 23:6
the days are coming, declares the **L**, Jer 23:7
'As the **L** lives who brought up the Jer 23:7
but 'As the **L** lives who brought up and Jer 23:8
because of the **L** and because of his holy Jer 23:9
I have found their evil, declares the **L**. Jer 23:11
of their punishment, declares the **L**. Jer 23:12
thus says the **L** of hosts concerning Jer 23:15
Thus says the **L** of hosts: "Do not listen Jer 23:16
minds, not from the mouth of the **L**. Jer 23:16
to those who despise the word of the **L**, Jer 23:17
in the council of the **L** to see and to Jer 23:18
Behold, the storm of the **L**! Wrath has Jer 23:19
The anger of the **L** will not turn back Jer 23:20
"Am I a God at hand, declares the **L**, Jer 23:23
so that I cannot see him? declares the **L**. Jer 23:24
fill heaven and earth? declares the **L**. Jer 23:24
in common with wheat? declares the **L**. Jer 23:28
Is not my word like fire, declares the **L**, Jer 23:29
am against the prophets, declares the **L**, Jer 23:30
am against the prophets, declares the **L**, Jer 23:31
tongues and declare, 'declares the **L**.' Jer 23:31
prophesy lying dreams, declares the **L**, Jer 23:32
profit this people at all, declares the **L**. Jer 23:32
asks you, 'What is the burden of the **L**?' Jer 23:33
and I will cast you off, declares the **L**.' Jer 23:33
people who says, 'The burden of the **L**,' Jer 23:34
brother, 'What has the **L** answered?' Jer 23:35
answered?' or 'What has the **L** spoken?' Jer 23:35
'the burden of the **L**' you shall mention Jer 23:36
words of the living God, the **L** of hosts, Jer 23:36
'What has the **L** answered you?' Jer 23:37
you?' or 'What has the **L** spoken?' Jer 23:37
But if you say, 'The burden of the **L**,' Jer 23:38
burden of the LORD,' thus says the **L**, Jer 23:38
"The burden of the **L**," when I sent to Jer 23:38
shall not say, 'The burden of the **L**,'" Jer 23:38
to Babylon, the **L** showed me this vision: Jer 24:1
of figs placed before the temple of the **L**. Jer 24:1
And the **L** said to me, "What do you see, Jer 24:3
Then the word of the **L** came to me: Jer 24:4
"Thus says the **L**, the God of Israel: Like Jer 24:5
them a heart to know that I am the **L**, Jer 24:7
"But thus says the **L**: Like the bad figs Jer 24:8
day, the word of the **L** has come to me, Jer 25:3
although the **L** persistently sent to you Jer 25:4
the land that the **L** has given to you Jer 25:5
have not listened to me, declares the **L**, Jer 25:7
"Therefore thus says the **L** of hosts: Jer 25:8
all the tribes of the north, declares the **L**, Jer 25:9
for their iniquity, declares the **L**, Jer 25:12
Thus the **L**, the God of Israel, said to Jer 25:15
nations to whom the **L** sent me drink it: Jer 25:17
say to them, 'Thus says the **L** of hosts, Jer 25:27
say to them, 'Thus says the **L** of hosts: Jer 25:28
of the earth, declares the **L** of hosts.' Jer 25:29
"'The **L** will roar from on high, and Jer 25:30
for the **L** has an indictment against the Jer 25:31
he will put to the sword, declares the **L**.' Jer 25:31
"Thus says the **L** of hosts: Behold, Jer 25:32
those pierced by the **L** on that day shall Jer 25:33
For the **L** is laying waste their pasture, Jer 25:36
because of the fierce anger of the **L**. Jer 25:37
of Judah, this word came from the **L**: Jer 26:1
"Thus says the **L**: Stand in the court of Jer 26:2
in the house of the **L** all the words that I Jer 26:2
You shall say to them, 'Thus says the **L**: Jer 26:4
these words in the house of the **L**. Jer 26:7
all that the **L** had commanded him Jer 26:8
you prophesied in the name of the **L**, Jer 26:9
around Jeremiah in the house of the **L**. Jer 26:9
to the house of the **L** and took their seat Jer 26:10
of the New Gate of the house of the **L**. Jer 26:10
"The **L** sent me to prophesy against this Jer 26:12
and obey the voice of the **L** your God, Jer 26:13
and the **L** will relent of the disaster that Jer 26:13
for in truth the **L** sent me to you to Jer 26:15
to us in the name of the **L** our God." Jer 26:16
'Thus says the **L** of hosts, "'Zion shall Jer 26:18
he not fear the **L** and entreat the favor Jer 26:19
the LORD and entreat the favor of the **L**, Jer 26:19
and did not the **L** relent of the disaster Jer 26:19
who prophesied in the name of the **L**, Jer 26:20
this word came to Jeremiah from the **L**. Jer 27:1
Thus the **L** said to me: "Make yourself Jer 27:2
'Thus says the **L** of hosts, the God of Jer 27:4
and with pestilence, declares the **L**, Jer 27:8
it and dwell there, declares the **L**."'" Jer 27:11
as the **L** has spoken concerning any Jer 27:13
I have not sent them, declares the **L**, but Jer 27:15
this people, saying, "Thus says the **L**: Jer 27:16
and if the word of the **L** is with them, Jer 27:18
let them intercede with the **L** of hosts, Jer 27:18
that are left in the house of the **L**, Jer 27:18
For thus says the **L** of hosts concerning Jer 27:19
thus says the **L** of hosts, the God of Jer 27:21
that are left in the house of the **L**, Jer 27:21
day when I visit them, declares the **L**. Jer 27:22
spoke to me in the house of the **L**, Jer 28:1
"Thus says the **L** of hosts, the God of Jer 28:2
who went to Babylon, declares the **L**, Jer 28:4
who were standing in the house of the **L**, Jer 28:5
Jeremiah said, "Amen! May the **L** do so; Jer 28:6
may the **L** make the words that you have Jer 28:6
Babylon the vessels of the house of the **L**, Jer 28:6
be known that the **L** has truly sent the Jer 28:9
all the people, saying, "Thus says the **L**: Jer 28:11
the word of the **L** came to Jeremiah: Jer 28:12
"Go, tell Hananiah, 'Thus says the **L**: Jer 28:13
For thus says the **L** of hosts, the God of Jer 28:14
Hananiah, the **L** has not sent you, Jer 28:15
Therefore thus says the **L**: 'Behold, I Jer 28:16
have uttered rebellion against the **L**.'" Jer 28:16
"Thus says the **L** of hosts, the God of Jer 29:4
into exile, and pray to the **L** on its behalf, Jer 29:7
For thus says the **L** of hosts, the God of Jer 29:8
I did not send them, declares the **L**. Jer 29:9
"For thus says the **L**: When seventy Jer 29:10
the plans I have for you, declares the **L**, Jer 29:11
I will be found by you, declares the **L**, Jer 29:14
where I have driven you, declares the **L**, Jer 29:14
'The **L** has raised up prophets for us in Jer 29:15
thus says the **L** concerning the king Jer 29:16
'Thus says the **L** of hosts, behold, I am Jer 29:17
attention to my words, declares the **L**, Jer 29:19
you would not listen, declares the **L**.' Jer 29:19
Hear the word of the **L**, all you exiles Jer 29:20
'Thus says the **L** of hosts, the God of Jer 29:21
"The **L** make you like Zedekiah and Jer 29:22
and I am witness, declares the **L**."' Jer 29:23
"Thus says the **L** of hosts, the God of Jer 29:25
'The **L** has made you priest instead of Jer 29:26
the house of the **L** over every madman Jer 29:26
the word of the **L** came to Jeremiah: Jer 29:30
'Thus says the **L** concerning Shemaiah Jer 29:31
therefore thus says the **L**: Behold, I will Jer 29:32
I will do to my people, declares the **L**, Jer 29:32
he has spoken rebellion against the **L**.'" Jer 29:32
word that came to Jeremiah from the **L**: Jer 30:1
"Thus says the **L**, the God of Israel: Jer 30:2
behold, days are coming, declares the **L**, Jer 30:3
my people, Israel and Judah, says the **L**, Jer 30:3
words that the **L** spoke concerning Israel Jer 30:4
"Thus says the **L**: We have heard a cry Jer 30:5
pass in that day, declares the **L** of hosts, Jer 30:8
they shall serve the **L** their God and Jer 30:9
not, O Jacob my servant, declares the **L**, Jer 30:10
am with you to save you, declares the **L**; Jer 30:11
"For thus says the **L**: Your hurt is Jer 30:12
your wounds I will heal, declares the **L**, Jer 30:17
"Thus says the **L**: Behold, I will restore Jer 30:18
himself to approach me? declares the **L**. Jer 30:21
Behold the storm of the **L**! Wrath has Jer 30:23
fierce anger of the **L** will not turn back Jer 30:24
"At that time, declares the **L**, I will be the Jer 31:1
Thus says the **L**: "The people who Jer 31:2
the **L** appeared to him from far away. I Jer 31:3
let us go up to Zion, to the **L** our God.'" Jer 31:6
For thus says the **L**: "Sing aloud with Jer 31:7
proclaim, give praise, and say, 'O **L**, save Jer 31:7
"Hear the word of the **L**, O nations, and Jer 31:10
For the **L** has ransomed Jacob and has Jer 31:11
be radiant over the goodness of the **L**, Jer 31:12
with my goodness, declares the **L**." Jer 31:14
Thus says the **L**: "A voice is heard in Jer 31:15
Thus says the **L**: "Keep your voice from Jer 31:16
a reward for your work, declares the **L**, Jer 31:16
is hope for your future, declares the **L**, Jer 31:17
be restored, for you are the **L** my God. Jer 31:18
have mercy on him, declares the **L**. Jer 31:20
For the **L** has created a new thing on Jer 31:22
Thus says the **L** of hosts, the God of Jer 31:23
"'The **L** bless you, O habitation of Jer 31:23
the days are coming, declares the **L**, Jer 31:27
to build and to plant, declares the **L**. Jer 31:28
the days are coming, declares the **L**, Jer 31:31
I was their husband, declares the **L**. Jer 31:32
of Israel after those days, declares the **L**: Jer 31:33
each his brother, saying, 'Know the **L**,' Jer 31:34
of them to the greatest, declares the **L**. Jer 31:34
Thus says the **L**, who gives the sun for Jer 31:35
its waves roar—the **L** of hosts is his Jer 31:35
departs from before me, declares the **L**, Jer 31:36
Thus says the **L**: "If the heavens above Jer 31:37
all that they have done, declares the **L**." Jer 31:37
the days are coming, declares the **L**, Jer 31:38
be rebuilt for the **L** from the tower of Jer 31:38
toward the east, shall be sacred to the **L**. Jer 31:40
to Jeremiah from the **L** in the tenth year Jer 32:1
you prophesy and say, 'Thus says the **L**: Jer 32:3
remain until I visit him, declares the **L**. Jer 32:5
said, "The word of the **L** came to me: Jer 32:6
in accordance with the word of the **L**, Jer 32:8
I knew that this was the word of the **L**. Jer 32:8
'Thus says the **L** of hosts, the God of Jer 32:14
For thus says the **L** of hosts, the God of Jer 32:15
the son of Neriah, I prayed to the **L**, Jer 32:16
'Ah, **L** GOD! It is you who has made the Jer 32:17
God, whose name is the **L** of hosts, Jer 32:18
Yet you, O **L** GOD, have said to me, "Buy Jer 32:25
The word of the **L** came to Jeremiah: Jer 32:26
"Behold, I am the **L**, the God of all flesh. Jer 32:27
Therefore, thus says the **L**: Behold, I am Jer 32:28
the work of their hands, declares the **L**. Jer 32:30
"Now therefore thus says the **L**, the God Jer 32:36
"For thus says the **L**: Just as I have Jer 32:42
restore their fortunes, declares the **L**." Jer 32:44
The word of the **L** came to Jeremiah a Jer 33:1
"Thus says the **L** who made the earth, Jer 33:2
the **L** who formed it to establish it—the Jer 33:2
it to establish it—the **L** is his name: Jer 33:2
For thus says the **L**, the God of Israel, Jer 33:4
"Thus says the **L**: In this place of which Jer 33:10
thank offerings to the house of the **L**: Jer 33:11
"'Give thanks to the **L** of hosts, for the Jer 33:11
to the LORD of hosts, for the **L** is good, Jer 33:11
of the land as at first, says the **L**. Jer 33:11
"Thus says the **L** of hosts: In this place Jer 33:12
of the one who counts them, says the **L**. Jer 33:13
the days are coming, declares the **L**, Jer 33:14
be called: 'The **L** is our righteousness.' Jer 33:16
"For thus says the **L**: David shall never Jer 33:17
The word of the **L** came to Jeremiah: Jer 33:19
"Thus says the **L**: If you can break my Jer 33:20
The word of the **L** came to Jeremiah: Jer 33:23
'The **L** has rejected the two clans that Jer 33:24
Thus says the **L**: If I have not Jer 33:25
word that came to Jeremiah from the **L**, Jer 34:1
"Thus says the **L**, the God of Israel: Go Jer 34:2
Judah and say to him, 'Thus says the **L**: Jer 34:2
Yet hear the word of the **L**, O Zedekiah Jer 34:4
Thus says the **L** concerning you: 'You Jer 34:4
"Alas, **l**!"' For I have spoken the word, Jer 34:5
I have spoken the word, declares the **L**." Jer 34:5
word that came to Jeremiah from the **L**, Jer 34:8
The word of the **L** came to Jeremiah Jer 34:12
the LORD came to Jeremiah from the **L**: Jer 34:12
"Thus says the **L**, the God of Israel: I Jer 34:13
"Therefore, thus says the **L**: You have Jer 34:17
and to famine, declares the **L**. Jer 34:17
Behold, I will command, declares the **L**, Jer 34:22
to Jeremiah from the **L** in the days of Jer 35:1
and bring them to the house of the **L**, Jer 35:2
to the house of the **L** into the chamber of Jer 35:4
the word of the **L** came to Jeremiah: Jer 35:12
"Thus says the **L** of hosts, the God of Jer 35:13
and listen to my words? declares the **L**. Jer 35:13
Therefore, thus says the **L**, the God of Jer 35:17
said, "Thus says the **L** of hosts, Jer 35:18
therefore thus says the **L** of hosts, the Jer 35:19
this word came to Jeremiah from the **L**: Jer 36:1
all the words of the **L** that he had spoken Jer 36:4
banned from going to the house of the **L**, Jer 36:5
the words of the **L** from the scroll that Jer 36:6
plea for mercy will come before the **L**, Jer 36:7
wrath that the **L** has pronounced Jer 36:7
the words of the **L** in the LORD'S house. Jer 36:8
Jerusalem proclaimed a fast before the **L**. Jer 36:9
from the scroll, in the house of the **L**, Jer 36:10
all the words of the **L** from the scroll, Jer 36:11
the prophet, but the **L** hid them. Jer 36:26
the word of the **L** came to Jeremiah: Jer 36:27
Judah you shall say, 'Thus says the **L**, Jer 36:29
thus says the **L** concerning Jehoiakim Jer 36:30
the words of the **L** that he spoke through Jer 37:2
"Please pray for us to the **L** our God." Jer 37:3
the word of the **L** came to Jeremiah the Jer 37:6
"Thus says the **L**, God of Israel: Thus Jer 37:7
Thus says the **L**, Do not deceive Jer 37:9
any word from the **L**?" Jeremiah said, Jer 37:17
Now hear, please, O my **l** the king: let Jer 37:20
"Thus says the **L**: He who stays in this Jer 38:2
Thus says the **L**: This city shall surely Jer 38:3
"My **l** the king, these men have done evil Jer 38:9
third entrance of the temple of the **L**. Jer 38:14
secretly to Jeremiah, "As the **L** lives, Jer 38:16
said to Zedekiah, "Thus says the **L**, Jer 38:17
now the voice of the **L** in what I say to Jer 38:20
the vision which the **L** has shown to Jer 38:21
The word of the **L** came to Jeremiah Jer 39:15

Ethiopian, 'Thus says the **L** of hosts, Jer 39:16
deliver you on that day, declares the **L**, Jer 39:17
put your trust in me, declares the **L**.'" Jer 39:18
Jeremiah from the **L** after Nebuzaradan Jer 40:1
"The **L** your God pronounced this Jer 40:2
The **L** has brought it about, and has Jer 40:3
you sinned against the **L** and did not Jer 40:3
incense to present at the temple of the **L**. Jer 41:5
you, and pray to the **L** your God for us, Jer 42:2
that the **L** your God may show us the Jer 42:3
will pray to the **L** your God according to Jer 42:4
and whatever the **L** answers you I will Jer 42:4
"May the **L** be a true and faithful witness Jer 42:5
word with which the **L** your God sends Jer 42:5
obey the voice of the **L** our God to whom Jer 42:6
we obey the voice of the **L** our God." Jer 42:6
days the word of the **L** came to Jeremiah. Jer 42:7
and said to them, "Thus says the **L**, the Jer 42:9
Do not fear him, declares the **L**, for I am Jer 42:11
disobeying the voice of the **L** your God Jer 42:13
then hear the word of the **L**, O remnant Jer 42:15
Thus says the **L** of hosts, the God of Jer 42:15
"For thus says the **L** of hosts, the God of Jer 42:18
The **L** has said to you, O remnant of Jer 42:19
For you sent me to the **L** your God, Jer 42:20
saying, 'Pray for us to the **L** our God, Jer 42:20
and whatever the **L** our God says Jer 42:20
the voice of the **L** your God in anything Jer 42:21
people all these words of the **L** their God, Jer 43:1
with which the **L** their God had sent him Jer 43:1
The **L** our God did not send you to say, Jer 43:2
the people did not obey the voice of the **L**, Jer 43:4
for they did not obey the voice of the **L**. Jer 43:7
the word of the **L** came to Jeremiah in Jer 43:8
say to them, 'Thus says the **L** of hosts, Jer 43:10
"Thus says the **L** of hosts, the God of Jer 44:2
And now thus says the **L** God of hosts, Jer 44:7
"Therefore thus says the **L** of hosts, the Jer 44:11
have spoken to us in the name of the **L**, Jer 44:16
the land, did not the **L** remember them? Jer 44:21
The **L** could no longer bear your evil Jer 44:22
you sinned against the **L** and did not Jer 44:23
obey the voice of the **L** or walk in his Jer 44:23
all the women, "Hear the word of the **L**, Jer 44:24
Thus says the **L** of hosts, the God of Jer 44:25
Therefore hear the word of the **L**, all Jer 44:26
sworn by my great name, says the **L**, Jer 44:26
of Egypt, saying, 'As the **L** GOD lives.' Jer 44:26
shall be the sign to you, declares the **L**, Jer 44:29
Thus says the **L**, behold, I will give Jer 44:30
"Thus says the **L**, the God of Israel, to Jer 45:2
For the **L** has added sorrow to my pain. Jer 45:3
shall you say to him, Thus says the **L**: Jer 45:4
disaster upon all flesh, declares the **L**. Jer 45:5
The word of the **L** that came to Jeremiah Jer 46:1
—terror on every side! declares the **L**. Jer 46:5
day is the day of the **L** GOD of hosts, Jer 46:10
For the **L** GOD of hosts holds a sacrifice Jer 46:10
The word that the **L** spoke to Jeremiah Jer 46:13
stand because the **L** thrust them down. Jer 46:15
the King, whose name is the **L** of hosts, Jer 46:18
cut down her forest, declares the **L**, Jer 46:23
The **L** of hosts, the God of Israel, said: Jer 46:25
as in the days of old, declares the **L**. Jer 46:26
not, O Jacob my servant, declares the **L**, Jer 46:28
The word of the **L** that came to Jeremiah Jer 47:1
"Thus says the **L**: Behold, waters are Jer 47:2
For the **L** is destroying the Philistines, Jer 47:4
Ah, sword of the **L**! How long till you are Jer 47:6
it be quiet when the **L** has given it a Jer 47:7
Thus says the **L** of hosts, the God of Jer 48:1
shall be destroyed, as the **L** has spoken. Jer 48:8
does the work of the **L** with slackness, Jer 48:10
the days are coming, declares the **L**, Jer 48:12
the King, whose name is the **L** of hosts. Jer 48:15
and his arm is broken, declares the **L**. Jer 48:25
he magnified himself against the **L**, Jer 48:26
I know his insolence, declares the **L**; his Jer 48:30
to an end in Moab, declares the **L**, Jer 48:35
for which no one cares, declares the **L**. Jer 48:38
For thus says the **L**: "Behold, one shall Jer 48:40
he magnified himself against the **L**. Jer 48:42
O inhabitant of Moab! declares the **L**. Jer 48:43
of their punishment, declares the **L**. Jer 48:44
declares the **L**." Thus far is the Jer 48:47
Thus says the **L**: "Has Israel no sons? Jer 49:1
the days are coming, declares the **L**, Jer 49:2
those who dispossessed him, says the **L**. Jer 49:2
upon you, declares the **L** GOD of hosts, Jer 49:5
of the Ammonites, declares the **L**." Jer 49:6
Thus says the **L** of hosts: "Is wisdom no Jer 49:7
For thus says the **L**: "If those who did Jer 49:12
I have sworn by myself, declares the **L**, Jer 49:13
I have heard a message from the **L**, and Jer 49:14
you down from there, declares the **L**. Jer 49:16
cities were overthrown, says the **L**, Jer 49:18
the plan that the **L** has made against Jer 49:20
in that day, declares the **L** of hosts. Jer 49:26
Thus says the **L**: "Rise up, advance Jer 49:28
O inhabitants of Hazor! declares the **L**. Jer 49:30
that dwells securely, declares the **L**, Jer 49:31
from every side of them, declares the **L**. Jer 49:32
The word of the **L** that came to Jer 49:34
Thus says the **L** of hosts: "Behold, I will Jer 49:35
them, my fierce anger, declares the **L**. Jer 49:37
their king and officials, declares the **L**. Jer 49:38
the fortunes of Elam, declares the **L**." Jer 49:39
word that the **L** spoke concerning Jer 50:1
days and in that time, declares the **L**, Jer 50:4
and they shall seek the **L** their God. Jer 50:4
join ourselves to the **L** in an everlasting Jer 50:5
for they have sinned against the **L**, Jer 50:7
their habitation of righteousness, the **L**, Jer 50:7
her shall be sated, declares the **L**. Jer 50:10
of the wrath of the **L** she shall not be Jer 50:13
for she has sinned against the **L**. Jer 50:14
For this is the vengeance of the **L**: take Jer 50:15
Therefore, thus says the **L** of hosts, the Jer 50:18
days and in that time, declares the **L**, Jer 50:20
them to destruction, declares the **L**, Jer 50:21
and caught, because you opposed the **L**. Jer 50:24
The **L** has opened his armory and Jer 50:25
for the **L** GOD of hosts has a work to do Jer 50:25
in Zion the vengeance of the **L** our God, Jer 50:28
For she has proudly defied the **L**, the Jer 50:29
be destroyed on that day, declares the **L**. Jer 50:30
proud one, declares the **L** GOD of hosts, Jer 50:31
"Thus says the **L** of hosts: The people of Jer 50:33
is strong; the **L** of hosts is his name. Jer 50:34
against the Chaldeans, declares the **L**, Jer 50:35
their neighboring cities, declares the **L**, Jer 50:40
the plan that the **L** has made against Jer 50:45
Thus says the **L**: "Behold, I will stir up Jer 51:1
forsaken by their God, the **L** of hosts, Jer 51:5
The **L** has brought about our Jer 51:10
in Zion the work of the **L** our God. Jer 51:10
The **L** has stirred up the spirit of the Jer 51:11
it, for that is the vengeance of the **L**, Jer 51:11
for the **L** has both planned and done Jer 51:12
The **L** of hosts has sworn by himself: Jer 51:14
inheritance; the **L** of hosts is his name. Jer 51:19
they have done in Zion, declares the **L**. Jer 51:24
O destroying mountain, declares the **L**, Jer 51:25
be a perpetual waste, declares the **L**. Jer 51:26
For thus says the **L** of hosts, the God of Jer 51:33
Therefore thus says the **L**: "Behold, I Jer 51:36
sleep and not wake, declares the **L**. Jer 51:39
his life from the fierce anger of the **L**! Jer 51:45
them out of the north, declares the **L**. Jer 51:48
Remember the **L** from far away, and let Jer 51:50
the days are coming, declares the **L**, Jer 51:52
from me against her, declares the **L**. Jer 51:53
For the **L** is laying Babylon waste and Jer 51:55
pieces, for the **L** is a God of recompense; Jer 51:56
the King, whose name is the **L** of hosts. Jer 51:57
"Thus says the **L** of hosts: The broad Jer 51:58
and say, 'O **L**, you have said Jer 51:62
he did what was evil in the sight of the **L**, Jer 52:2
of the anger of the **L** things came to the Jer 52:3
And he burned the house of the **L**, and Jer 52:13
bronze that were in the house of the **L**, Jer 52:17
sea that were in the house of the **L**, Jer 52:17
king had made for the house of the **L**, Jer 52:20
because the **L** has afflicted her for the Lam 1:5
she has no comforter. "O **L**, behold my Lam 1:9
"Look, O **L**, and see, for I am despised." Lam 1:11
which the **L** inflicted on the day of his Lam 1:12
the **L** gave me into the hands of those Lam 1:14
"The **L** rejected all my mighty men in Lam 1:15
the **L** has trodden as in a winepress the Lam 1:15
the **L** has commanded against Jacob Lam 1:17
"The **L** is in the right, for I have Lam 1:18
"Look, O **L**, for I am in distress; my Lam 1:20
How the **L** in his anger has set the Lam 2:1
The **L** has swallowed up without mercy Lam 2:2
The **L** has become like an enemy; he Lam 2:5
the **L** has made Zion forget festival and Lam 2:6
The **L** has scorned his altar, disowned Lam 2:7
in the house of the **L** as on the day of Lam 2:7
The **L** determined to lay in ruins the Lam 2:8
her prophets find no vision from the **L**. Lam 2:9
The **L** has done what he purposed; he Lam 2:17
Their heart cried to the **L**. O wall of the Lam 2:18
like water before the presence of the **L**! Lam 2:19
Look, O **L**, and see! With whom have Lam 2:20
be killed in the sanctuary of the **L**? Lam 2:20
of the anger of the **L** no one escaped or Lam 2:22
perished; so has my hope from the **L**." Lam 3:18
steadfast love of the **L** never ceases; Lam 3:22
"The **L** is my portion," says my soul, Lam 3:24
The **L** is good to those who wait for Lam 3:25
wait quietly for the salvation of the **L**. Lam 3:26
For the **L** will not cast off forever, Lam 3:31
in his lawsuit, the **L** does not approve. Lam 3:36
pass, unless the **L** has commanded it? Lam 3:37
our ways, and return to the **L**! Lam 3:40
until the **L** from heaven looks down Lam 3:50
"I called on your name, O **L**, from the Lam 3:55
"You have taken up my cause, O **L**; Lam 3:58
have seen the wrong done to me, O **L**; Lam 3:59
"You have heard their taunts, O **L**, all Lam 3:61
"You will repay them, O **L**, according Lam 3:64
them from under your heavens, O **L**." Lam 3:66
The **L** gave full vent to his wrath; he Lam 4:11
The **L** himself has scattered them; he Lam 4:16
Remember, O **L**, what has befallen us; Lam 5:1
But you, O **L**, reign forever; your Lam 5:19
Restore us to yourself, O **L**, that we Lam 5:21
the word of the **L** came to Ezekiel the Ezk 1:3
the hand of the **L** was upon him there. Ezk 1:3
of the likeness of the glory of the **L**. Ezk 1:28
shall say to them, 'Thus says the **L** GOD.' Ezk 2:4
and say to them, 'Thus says the **L** GOD,' Ezk 3:11
be the glory of the **L** from its place!" Ezk 3:12
the hand of the **L** being strong upon Ezk 3:14
days, the word of the **L** came to me: Ezk 3:16
the hand of the **L** was upon me there. Ezk 3:22
behold, the glory of the **L** stood there, Ezk 3:23
say to them, 'Thus says the **L** GOD.' Ezk 3:27
And the **L** said, "Thus shall the people Ezk 4:13
Then I said, "Ah, **L** GOD! Behold, I have Ezk 4:14
"Thus says the **L** GOD: This is Jerusalem. Ezk 5:5
Therefore thus says the **L** GOD: Because Ezk 5:7
therefore thus says the **L** GOD: Behold, I, Ezk 5:8
Therefore, as I live, declares the **L** GOD, Ezk 5:11
know that I am the **L**—that I have Ezk 5:13
and with furious rebukes—I am the **L**, Ezk 5:15
upon you. I am the **L**; I have spoken." Ezk 5:17
The word of the **L** came to me: Ezk 6:1
of Israel, hear the word of the **L** GOD! Ezk 6:3
Thus says the **L** GOD to the mountains Ezk 6:3
and you shall know that I am the **L**. Ezk 6:7
And they shall know that I am the **L**. I Ezk 6:10
Thus says the **L** GOD: "Clap your hands Ezk 6:11
And you shall know that I am the **L**, Ezk 6:13
Then they will know that I am the **L**." Ezk 6:14
The word of the **L** came to me: Ezk 7:1
thus says the **L** GOD to the land of Israel: Ezk 7:2
Then you will know that I am the **L**. Ezk 7:4
"Thus says the **L** GOD: Disaster after Ezk 7:5
Then you will know that I am the **L**, Ezk 7:9
them in the day of the wrath of the **L**. Ezk 7:19
and they shall know that I am the **L**." Ezk 7:27
the hand of the **L** GOD fell upon me there. Ezk 8:1
For they say, 'The **L** does not see us, the Ezk 8:12
see us, the **L** has forsaken the land.'" Ezk 8:12
of the north gate of the house of the **L**, Ezk 8:14
the inner court of the house of the **L**. Ezk 8:16
at the entrance of the temple of the **L**, Ezk 8:16
with their backs to the temple of the **L**, Ezk 8:16
And the **L** said to him, "Pass through the Ezk 9:4
fell upon my face, and cried, "Ah, **L** GOD! Ezk 9:8
they say, 'The **L** has forsaken the land, Ezk 9:9
the land, and the **L** does not see.' Ezk 9:9
And the glory of the **L** went up from the Ezk 10:4
the brightness of the glory of the **L**. Ezk 10:4
the glory of the **L** went out from the Ezk 10:18
of the east gate of the house of the **L**, Ezk 10:19
me to the east gate of the house of the **L**, Ezk 11:1
And the Spirit of the **L** fell upon me, Ezk 11:5
he said to me, "Say, Thus says the **L**: Ezk 11:5
Therefore thus says the **L** GOD: Your Ezk 11:7
the sword upon you, declares the **L** GOD. Ezk 11:8
and you shall know that I am the **L**. Ezk 11:10
and you shall know that I am the **L**. Ezk 11:12
a loud voice and said, "Ah, **L** GOD! Ezk 11:13
And the word of the **L** came to me: Ezk 11:14
have said, 'Go far from the **L**; Ezk 11:15
Therefore say, 'Thus says the **L** GOD: Ezk 11:16
Therefore say, 'Thus says the **L** GOD: I Ezk 11:17
their own heads, declares the **L** GOD." Ezk 11:21
the glory of the **L** went up from the Ezk 11:23
the things that the **L** had shown me. Ezk 11:25
The word of the **L** came to me: Ezk 12:1
morning the word of the **L** came to me: Ezk 12:8
Say to them, 'Thus says the **L** GOD: Ezk 12:10
And they shall know that I am the **L**, Ezk 12:15
go, and may know that I am the **L**." Ezk 12:16
And the word of the **L** came to me: Ezk 12:17
Thus says the **L** GOD concerning the Ezk 12:19
and you shall know that I am the **L**." Ezk 12:20
And the word of the **L** came to me: Ezk 12:21
them therefore, 'Thus says the **L** GOD: Ezk 12:23
For I am the **L**; I will speak the word Ezk 12:25
and perform it, declares the **L** GOD." Ezk 12:25

And the word of the **L** came to me: Ezk 12:26
say to them, Thus says the **L** GOD: Ezk 12:28
will be performed, declares the **L** GOD." Ezk 12:28
The word of the **L** came to me: Ezk 13:1
own hearts: 'Hear the word of the **L**!' Ezk 13:2
Thus says the **L** GOD, Woe to the Ezk 13:3
stand in battle in the day of the **L**. Ezk 13:5
They say, 'Declares the **L**,' when the Ezk 13:6
LORD,' when the **L** has not sent them, Ezk 13:6
you have said, 'Declares the **L**,' Ezk 13:7
Therefore thus says the **L** GOD: Ezk 13:8
I am against you, declares the **L** GOD. Ezk 13:8
you shall know that I am the **L** GOD. Ezk 13:9
Therefore thus says the **L** GOD: I will Ezk 13:13
it, and you shall know that I am the **L**. Ezk 13:14
there was no peace, declares the **L** GOD. Ezk 13:16
and say, Thus says the **L** GOD: Woe to Ezk 13:18
"Therefore thus says the **L** GOD: Ezk 13:20
and you shall know that I am the **L**. Ezk 13:21
And you shall know that I am the **L**." Ezk 13:23
And the word of the **L** came to me: Ezk 14:2
and say to them, Thus says the **L** GOD: Ezk 14:4
I the **L** will answer him as he comes Ezk 14:4
house of Israel, Thus says the **L** GOD: Ezk 14:6
him, I the **L** will answer him myself. Ezk 14:7
and you shall know that I am the **L**. Ezk 14:8
is deceived and speaks a word, I, the **L**, Ezk 14:9
may be their God, declares the **L** GOD." Ezk 14:11
And the word of the **L** came to me: Ezk 14:12
righteousness, declares the **L** GOD. Ezk 14:14
were in it, as I live, declares the **L** GOD, Ezk 14:16
were in it, as I live, declares the **L** GOD, Ezk 14:18
were in it, as I live, declares the **L** GOD, Ezk 14:20
"For thus says the **L** GOD: How much Ezk 14:21
I have done in it, declares the **L** GOD." Ezk 14:23
And the word of the **L** came to me: Ezk 15:1
Therefore thus says the **L** GOD: Like the Ezk 15:6
and you will know that I am the **L**, Ezk 15:7
acted faithlessly, declares the **L** GOD." Ezk 15:8
Again the word of the **L** came to me: Ezk 16:1
say, Thus says the **L** GOD to Jerusalem: Ezk 16:3
covenant with you, declares the **L** GOD, Ezk 16:8
bestowed on you, declares the **L** GOD. Ezk 16:14
and so it was, declares the **L** GOD. Ezk 16:19
(woe, woe to you! declares the **L** GOD), Ezk 16:23
is your heart, declares the **L** GOD, Ezk 16:30
O prostitute, hear the word of the **L**: Ezk 16:35
Thus says the **L** GOD, Because your Ezk 16:36
upon your head, declares the **L** GOD. Ezk 16:43
As I live, declares the **L** GOD, your Ezk 16:48
your abominations, declares the **L**. Ezk 16:58
"For thus says the **L** GOD: I will deal Ezk 16:59
and you shall know that I am the **L**, Ezk 16:62
you have done, declares the **L** GOD." Ezk 16:63
The word of the **L** came to me: Ezk 17:1
say, Thus says the **L** GOD: A great eagle Ezk 17:3
"Say, Thus says the **L** GOD: Will it Ezk 17:9
Then the word of the **L** came to me: Ezk 17:11
"As I live, declares the **L** GOD, surely in Ezk 17:16
Therefore thus says the **L** GOD: As I Ezk 17:19
and you shall know that I am the **L**; Ezk 17:21
Thus says the **L** GOD: "I myself will Ezk 17:22
of the field shall know that I am the **L**; Ezk 17:24
I am the **L**; I have spoken, and I will do Ezk 17:24
The word of the **L** came to me: Ezk 18:1
As I live, declares the **L** GOD, this Ezk 18:3
he shall surely live, declares the **L** GOD. Ezk 18:9
of the wicked, declares the **L** GOD, Ezk 18:23
you say, 'The way of the **L** is not just.' Ezk 18:25
says, 'The way of the **L** is not just.' Ezk 18:29
to his ways, declares the **L** GOD. Ezk 18:30
death of anyone, declares the **L** GOD; Ezk 18:32
elders of Israel came to inquire of the **L**, Ezk 20:1
And the word of the **L** came to me: Ezk 20:2
and say to them, Thus says the **L** GOD, Ezk 20:3
As I live, declares the **L** GOD, I will not Ezk 20:3
and say to them, Thus says the **L** GOD: Ezk 20:5
to them, saying, I am the **L** your God. Ezk 20:5
the idols of Egypt; I am the **L** your God. Ezk 20:7
that I am the **L** who sanctifies them. Ezk 20:12
I am the **L** your God; walk in my Ezk 20:19
may know that I am the **L** your God. Ezk 20:20
that they might know that I am the **L**. Ezk 20:26
and say to them, Thus says the **L** GOD: Ezk 20:27
house of Israel, Thus says the **L** GOD: Ezk 20:30
As I live, declares the **L** GOD, I will not Ezk 20:31
"As I live, declares the **L** GOD, surely Ezk 20:33
with you, declares the **L** GOD. Ezk 20:36
Then you will know that I am the **L**. Ezk 20:38
O house of Israel, thus says the **L** GOD: Ezk 20:39
height of Israel, declares the **L** GOD, Ezk 20:40
And you shall know that I am the **L**, Ezk 20:42
And you shall know that I am the **L**, Ezk 20:44
O house of Israel, declares the **L** GOD." Ezk 20:44
And the word of the **L** came to me: Ezk 20:45
of the Negeb, Hear the word of the **L**: Ezk 20:47
Thus says the **L** GOD, Behold, I will Ezk 20:47
shall see that I the **L** have kindled it; Ezk 20:48
Then I said, "Ah, **L** GOD! They are Ezk 20:49
The word of the **L** came to me: Ezk 21:1
to the land of Israel, Thus says the **L**: Ezk 21:3
all flesh shall know that I am the **L**. Ezk 21:5
it will be fulfilled,'" declares the **L** GOD. Ezk 21:7
And the word of the **L** came to me: Ezk 21:8
prophesy and say, Thus says the **L**; Ezk 21:9
despise the rod?" declares the **L** GOD. Ezk 21:13
satisfy my fury; I the **L** have spoken." Ezk 21:17
The word of the **L** came to me again: Ezk 21:18
"Therefore thus says the **L** GOD: Ezk 21:24
thus says the **L** GOD: Remove the Ezk 21:26
Thus says the **L** GOD concerning the Ezk 21:28
remembered, for I the **L** have spoken." Ezk 21:32
And the word of the **L** came to me, Ezk 22:1
You shall say, Thus says the **L** GOD: A Ezk 22:3
have forgotten, declares the **L** GOD. Ezk 22:12
deal with you? I the **L** have spoken, Ezk 22:14
and you shall know that I am the **L**." Ezk 22:16
And the word of the **L** came to me: Ezk 22:17
Therefore thus says the **L** GOD: Ezk 22:19
it, and you shall know that I am the **L**; Ezk 22:22
And the word of the **L** came to me: Ezk 22:23
them, saying, 'Thus says the **L** GOD,' Ezk 22:28
Lord GOD,' when the **L** has not spoken. Ezk 22:28
upon their heads, declares the **L** GOD." Ezk 22:31
The word of the **L** came to me: Ezk 23:1
O Oholibah, thus says the **L** GOD: Ezk 23:22
"For thus says the **L** GOD: Behold, I Ezk 23:28
Thus says the **L** GOD: "You shall Ezk 23:32
for I have spoken, declares the **L** GOD. Ezk 23:34
Therefore thus says the **L** GOD: Ezk 23:35
The **L** said to me: "Son of man, will Ezk 23:36
For thus says the **L** GOD: "Bring up a Ezk 23:46
you shall know that I am the **L** GOD." Ezk 23:49
month, the word of the **L** came to me: Ezk 24:1
and say to them, Thus says the **L** GOD: Ezk 24:3
"Therefore thus says the **L** GOD: Woe to Ezk 24:6
Therefore thus says the **L** GOD: Woe to Ezk 24:9
I am the **L**. I have spoken; it shall Ezk 24:14
will be judged, declares the **L** GOD." Ezk 24:14
The word of the **L** came to me: Ezk 24:15
them, "The word of the **L** came to me: Ezk 24:20
house of Israel, Thus says the **L** GOD: Ezk 24:21
you will know that I am the **L** GOD.' Ezk 24:24
and they will know that I am the **L**." Ezk 24:27
The word of the **L** came to me: Ezk 25:1
Hear the word of the **L** GOD: Ezk 25:3
Thus says the **L** GOD, Because you said, Ezk 25:3
Then you will know that I am the **L**. Ezk 25:5
For thus says the **L** GOD: Because you Ezk 25:6
Then you will know that I am the **L**. Ezk 25:7
"Thus says the **L** GOD: Because Moab Ezk 25:8
Then they will know that I am the **L**. Ezk 25:11
"Thus says the **L** GOD: Because Edom Ezk 25:12
therefore thus says the **L** GOD, I will Ezk 25:13
my vengeance, declares the **L** GOD. Ezk 25:14
"Thus says the **L** GOD: Because the Ezk 25:15
therefore thus says the **L** GOD, Behold, Ezk 25:16
Then they will know that I am the **L**, Ezk 25:17
month, the word of the **L** came to me: Ezk 26:1
therefore thus says the **L** GOD: Behold, I Ezk 26:3
for I have spoken, declares the **L** GOD. Ezk 26:5
Then they will know that I am the **L**. Ezk 26:6
"For thus says the **L** GOD: Behold, I will Ezk 26:7
shall never be rebuilt, for I am the **L**; Ezk 26:14
I have spoken, declares the **L** GOD. Ezk 26:14
"Thus says the **L** GOD to Tyre: Will Ezk 26:15
"For thus says the **L** GOD: When I Ezk 26:19
be found again, declares the **L** GOD." Ezk 26:21
The word of the **L** came to me: Ezk 27:1
many coastlands, thus says the **L** GOD: Ezk 27:3
The word of the **L** came to me: Ezk 28:1
prince of Tyre, Thus says the **L** GOD: Ezk 28:2
therefore thus says the **L** GOD: Because Ezk 28:6
for I have spoken, declares the **L** GOD." Ezk 28:10
the word of the **L** came to me: Ezk 28:11
and say to him, Thus says the **L** GOD: Ezk 28:12
The word of the **L** came to me: Ezk 28:20
and say, Thus says the **L** GOD: Ezk 28:22
that I am the **L** when I execute Ezk 28:22
Then they will know that I am the **L**. Ezk 28:23
they will know that I am the **L** GOD. Ezk 28:24
"Thus says the **L** GOD: When I gather Ezk 28:25
will know that I am the **L** their God." Ezk 28:26
month, the word of the **L** came to me: Ezk 29:1
speak, and say, Thus says the **L** GOD: Ezk 29:3
of Egypt shall know that I am the **L**. Ezk 29:6
Therefore thus says the **L** GOD: Behold, I Ezk 29:8
Then they will know that I am the **L**. Ezk 29:9
"For thus says the **L** GOD: At the end of Ezk 29:13
they will know that I am the **L** GOD." Ezk 29:16
month, the word of the **L** came to me: Ezk 29:17
Therefore thus says the **L** GOD: Behold, Ezk 29:19
worked for me, declares the **L** GOD. Ezk 29:20
Then they will know that I am the **L**." Ezk 29:21
The word of the **L** came to me: Ezk 30:1
and say, Thus says the **L** GOD: Ezk 30:2
the day is near, the day of the **L** is near; Ezk 30:3
"Thus says the **L**: Those who support Ezk 30:6
her by the sword, declares the **L** GOD. Ezk 30:6
Then they will know that I am the **L**, Ezk 30:8
"Thus says the **L** GOD: "I will put an Ezk 30:10
by the hand of foreigners; I am the **L**; Ezk 30:12
"Thus says the **L** GOD: "I will destroy Ezk 30:13
Then they will know that I am the **L**." Ezk 30:19
month, the word of the **L** came to me: Ezk 30:20
Therefore thus says the **L** GOD: Behold, Ezk 30:22
Then they shall know that I am the **L**, Ezk 30:25
Then they will know that I am the **L**." Ezk 30:26
month, the word of the **L** came to me: Ezk 31:1
"Therefore thus says the **L** GOD: Ezk 31:10
"Thus says the **L** GOD: On the day the Ezk 31:15
all his multitude, declares the **L** GOD." Ezk 31:18
month, the word of the **L** came to me: Ezk 32:1
Thus says the **L** GOD: I will throw my Ezk 32:3
on your land, declares the **L** GOD. Ezk 32:8
"For thus says the **L** GOD: The sword Ezk 32:11
to run like oil, declares the **L** GOD. Ezk 32:14
it, then they will know that I am the **L**. Ezk 32:15
they chant it, declares the **L** GOD." Ezk 32:16
month, the word of the **L** came to me: Ezk 32:17
slain by the sword, declares the **L** GOD. Ezk 32:31
all his multitude, declares the **L** GOD." Ezk 32:32
The word of the **L** came to me: Ezk 33:1
to them, As I live, declares the **L** GOD, Ezk 33:11
say, 'The way of the **L** is not just,' Ezk 33:17
you say, 'The way of the **L** is not just.' Ezk 33:20
the hand of the **L** had been upon me Ezk 33:22
The word of the **L** came to me: Ezk 33:23
say to them, Thus says the **L** GOD: Ezk 33:25
Say this to them, Thus says the **L** GOD: Ezk 33:27
Then they will know that I am the **L**, Ezk 33:29
the word is that comes from the **L**.' Ezk 33:30
The word of the **L** came to me: Ezk 34:1
to the shepherds, Thus says the **L** GOD: Ezk 34:2
you shepherds, hear the word of the **L**: Ezk 34:7
As I live, declares the **L** GOD, surely Ezk 34:8
you shepherds, hear the word of the **L**: Ezk 34:9
Thus says the **L** GOD, Behold, I am Ezk 34:10
"For thus says the **L** GOD: Behold, I, I Ezk 34:11
them lie down, declares the **L** GOD. Ezk 34:15
for you, my flock, thus says the **L** GOD: Ezk 34:17
thus says the **L** GOD to them: Ezk 34:20
And I, the **L**, will be their God, and my Ezk 34:24
them. I am the **L**; I have spoken. Ezk 34:24
And they shall know that I am the **L**, Ezk 34:27
that I am the **L** their God with them, Ezk 34:30
are my people, declares the **L** GOD. Ezk 34:30
I am your God, declares the **L** GOD." Ezk 34:31
The word of the **L** came to me: Ezk 35:1
and say to it, Thus says the **L** GOD: Ezk 35:3
and you shall know that I am the **L**. Ezk 35:4
therefore, as I live, declares the **L** GOD, I Ezk 35:6
Then you will know that I am the **L**. Ezk 35:9
of them'—although the **L** was there— Ezk 35:10
therefore, as I live, declares the **L** GOD, I Ezk 35:11
And you shall know that I am the **L**. "I Ezk 35:12
Thus says the **L** GOD: While the whole Ezk 35:14
Then they will know that I am the **L**. Ezk 35:15
of Israel, hear the word of the **L**. Ezk 36:1
Thus says the **L** GOD: Because the Ezk 36:2
and say, Thus says the **L** GOD: Ezk 36:3
of Israel, hear the word of the **L** GOD: Ezk 36:4
Thus says the **L** GOD to the mountains Ezk 36:4
therefore thus says the **L** GOD: Surely I Ezk 36:5
and valleys, Thus says the **L** GOD: Ezk 36:6
Therefore thus says the **L** GOD: I swear Ezk 36:7
Then you will know that I am the **L**. Ezk 36:11
Thus says the **L** GOD: Because they say Ezk 36:13
nation of children, declares the **L** GOD. Ezk 36:14
to stumble, declares the **L** GOD." Ezk 36:15
The word of the **L** came to me: Ezk 36:16
of them, 'These are the people of the **L**, Ezk 36:20
house of Israel, Thus says the **L** GOD: Ezk 36:22
the nations will know that I am the **L**, Ezk 36:23
that I am the LORD, declares the **L** GOD, Ezk 36:23
sake that I will act, declares the **L** GOD; Ezk 36:32
"Thus says the **L** GOD: On the day that Ezk 36:33
you shall know that I am the **L**; Ezk 36:36
I am the **L**; I have spoken, and I will do Ezk 36:36
"Thus says the **L** GOD: This also I will Ezk 36:37
Then they will know that I am the **L**." Ezk 36:38
The hand of the **L** was upon me, and he Ezk 37:1
in the Spirit of the **L** and set me down in Ezk 37:1
bones live?" And I answered, "O **L** GOD, Ezk 37:3
O dry bones, hear the word of the **L**. Ezk 37:4

Thus says the **L** GOD to these bones: Ezk 37:5
and you shall know that I am the **L**." Ezk 37:6
say to the breath, Thus says the **L** GOD: Ezk 37:9
and say to them, Thus says the **L** GOD: Ezk 37:12
And you shall know that I am the **L**, Ezk 37:13
Then you shall know that I am the **L**; Ezk 37:14
and I will do it, declares the **L**." Ezk 37:14
The word of the **L** came to me: Ezk 37:15
say to them, Thus says the **L** GOD: Ezk 37:19
say to them, Thus says the **L** GOD: Ezk 37:21
that I am the **L** who sanctifies Israel, Ezk 37:28
The word of the **L** came to me: Ezk 38:1
and say, Thus says the **L** GOD: Behold, I Ezk 38:3
"Thus says the **L** GOD: On that day, Ezk 38:10
and say to Gog, Thus says the **L** GOD: Ezk 38:14
"Thus says the **L** GOD: Are you he of Ezk 38:17
the land of Israel, declares the **L** GOD, Ezk 38:18
all my mountains, declares the **L** GOD. Ezk 38:21
Then they will know that I am the **L**. Ezk 38:23
Gog and say, Thus says the **L** GOD: Ezk 39:1
for I have spoken, declares the **L** GOD. Ezk 39:5
and they shall know that I am the **L**. Ezk 39:6
the nations shall know that I am the **L**, Ezk 39:7
be brought about, declares the **L** GOD. Ezk 39:8
plundered them, declares the **L** GOD. Ezk 39:10
I show my glory, declares the **L** GOD. Ezk 39:13
you, son of man, thus says the **L** GOD: Ezk 39:17
kinds of warriors,' declares the **L** GOD. Ezk 39:20
shall know that I am the **L** their God, Ezk 39:22
"Therefore thus says the **L** GOD: Now I Ezk 39:25
shall know that I am the **L** their God, Ezk 39:28
house of Israel, declares the **L** GOD." Ezk 39:29
day, the hand of the **L** was upon me, Ezk 40:1
come near to the **L** to minister to him. Ezk 40:46
"This is the table that is before the **L**." Ezk 41:22
who approach the **L** shall eat the Ezk 42:13
the glory of the **L** entered the temple by Ezk 43:4
the glory of the **L** filled the temple. Ezk 43:5
me, "Son of man, thus says the **L** GOD: Ezk 43:18
to minister to me, declares the **L** GOD, Ezk 43:19
You shall present them before the **L**, Ezk 43:24
them up as a burnt offering to the **L**. Ezk 43:24
I will accept you, declares the **L** GOD." Ezk 43:27
And the **L** said to me, "This gate shall Ezk 44:2
and no one shall enter by it, for the **L**, Ezk 44:2
may sit in it to eat bread before the **L**. Ezk 44:3
the glory of the **L** filled the temple of the Ezk 44:4
of the LORD filled the temple of the **L**. Ezk 44:4
And the **L** said to me, "Son of man, Ezk 44:5
of the temple of the **L** and all its laws. Ezk 44:5
house of Israel, Thus says the **L** GOD: Ezk 44:6
"Thus says the **L** GOD: No foreigner, Ezk 44:9
concerning them, declares the **L** GOD, Ezk 44:12
fat and the blood, declares the **L** GOD. Ezk 44:15
his sin offering, declares the **L** GOD. Ezk 44:27
shall set apart for the **L** a portion of the Ezk 45:1
and approach the **L** to minister to Ezk 45:4
"Thus says the **L** GOD: Enough, O Ezk 45:9
of my people, declares the **L** GOD. Ezk 45:9
for them, declares the **L** GOD. Ezk 45:15
"Thus says the **L** GOD: In the first Ezk 45:18
offering to the **L** seven young bulls Ezk 45:23
"Thus says the **L** GOD: The gate of the Ezk 46:1
that gate before the **L** on the Sabbaths Ezk 46:3
prince offers to the **L** on the Sabbath Ezk 46:4
land come before the **L** at the appointed Ezk 46:9
offerings as a freewill offering to the **L**, Ezk 46:12
for a burnt offering to the **L** daily; Ezk 46:13
the flour, as a grain offering to the **L**. Ezk 46:14
"Thus says the **L** GOD: If the prince Ezk 46:16
Thus says the **L** GOD: "This is the Ezk 47:13
his inheritance, declares the **L** GOD. Ezk 47:23
set apart for the **L** shall be 25,000 Ezk 48:9
the sanctuary of the **L** in the midst of Ezk 48:10
of the land, for it is holy to the **L**. Ezk 48:14
are their portions, declares the **L** GOD. Ezk 48:29
that time on shall be, The **L** is there." Ezk 48:35
And the **L** gave Jehoiakim king of Judah Dn 1:2
said to Daniel, "I fear my **l** the king, Dn 1:10
your God is God of gods and **L** of kings, Dn 2:47
Belteshazzar answered and said, "My **l**, Dn 4:19
which has come upon my **l** the king, Dn 4:24
up yourself against the **L** of heaven. Dn 5:23
the word of the **L** to Jeremiah the prophet, Dn 9:2
Then I turned my face to the **L** God, Dn 9:3
I prayed to the **L** my God and made Dn 9:4
God and made confession, saying, "O **L**, Dn 9:4
To you, O **L**, belongs righteousness, but Dn 9:7
To us, O **L**, belongs open shame, to our Dn 9:8
To the **L** our God belong mercy and Dn 9:9
the voice of the **L** our God by walking Dn 9:10
not entreated the favor of the **L** our God, Dn 9:13
Therefore the **L** has kept ready the Dn 9:14
for the **L** our God is righteous in all the Dn 9:14
And now, O **L** our God, who brought Dn 9:15
"O **L**, according to all your righteous Dn 9:16
for mercy, and for your own sake, O **L**, Dn 9:17
O **L**, hear; O Lord, forgive. O Lord, pay Dn 9:19
O Lord, hear; O **L**, forgive. O Lord, pay Dn 9:19
O Lord, forgive. O **L**, pay attention and Dn 9:19
my plea before the **L** my God for the Dn 9:20
to him who stood before me, "O my **l**, Dn 10:16
can my lord's servant talk with my **l**? Dn 10:17
strengthened and said, "Let my **l** speak, Dn 10:19
Then I said, "O my **l**, what shall be the Dn 12:8
The word of the **L** that came to Hosea, Hos 1:1
When the **L** first spoke through Hosea, Hos 1:2
through Hosea, the **L** said to Hosea, Hos 1:2
great whoredom by forsaking the **L**." Hos 1:2
And the **L** said to him, "Call his name Hos 1:4
And the **L** said to him, "Call her name Hos 1:6
and I will save them by the **L** their God. Hos 1:7
And the **L** said, "Call his name Not My Hos 1:9
her lovers and forgot me, declares the **L**. Hos 2:13
"And in that day, declares the **L**, you Hos 2:16
faithfulness. And you shall know the **L**. Hos 2:20
in that day I will answer, declares the **L**, Hos 2:21
And the **L** said to me, "Go again, love a Hos 3:1
even as the **L** loves the children of Israel, Hos 3:1
shall return and seek the **L** their God, Hos 3:5
come in fear to the **L** and to his goodness Hos 3:5
Hear the word of the **L**, O children of Hos 4:1
for the **L** has a controversy with the Hos 4:1
they have forsaken the **L** to cherish Hos 4:10
and swear not, "As the **L** lives." Hos 4:15
can the **L** now feed them like a lamb in Hos 4:16
is within them, and they know not the **L**. Hos 5:4
and herds they shall go to seek the **L**, Hos 5:6
They have dealt faithlessly with the **L**; Hos 5:7
"Come, let us return to the **L**; for he has Hos 6:1
us know; let us press on to know the **L**; Hos 6:3
they do not return to the **L** their God, Hos 7:10
like a vulture is over the house of the **L**, Hos 8:1
eat it, but the **L** does not accept them. Hos 8:13
shall not remain in the land of the **L**, Hos 9:3
not pour drink offerings of wine to the **L**, Hos 9:4
it shall not come to the house of the **L**. Hos 9:4
and on the day of the feast of the **L**? Hos 9:5
Give them, O **L**—what will you give? Hos 9:14
The **L** will break down their altars and Hos 10:2
have no king, for we do not fear the **L**; Hos 10:3
ground, for it is the time to seek the **L**, Hos 10:12
They shall go after the **L**; he will roar Hos 11:10
them to their homes, declares the **L**. Hos 11:11
The **L** has an indictment against Judah Hos 12:2
the **L**, the God of hosts, the LORD is his Hos 12:5
of hosts, the **L** is his memorial name: Hos 12:5
I am the **L** your God from the land of Hos 12:9
By a prophet the **L** brought Israel up Hos 12:13
so his **L** will leave his bloodguilt on Hos 12:14
But I am the **L** your God from the land Hos 13:4
the east wind, the wind of the **L**, Hos 13:15
Return, O Israel, to the **L** your God, for Hos 14:1
with you words and return to the **L**; Hos 14:2
for the ways of the **L** are right, and the Hos 14:9
The word of the **L** that came to Joel, the son Jl 1:1
offering are cut off from the house of the **L**. Jl 1:9
The priests mourn, the ministers of the **L**. Jl 1:9
of the land to the house of the **L** your God, Jl 1:14
of the LORD your God, and cry out to the **L**. Jl 1:14
For the day of the **L** is near, and as Jl 1:15
To you, O **L**, I call. For fire has devoured Jl 1:19
tremble, for the day of the **L** is coming; Jl 2:1
The **L** utters his voice before his army, for Jl 2:11
For the day of the **L** is great and very Jl 2:11
"Yet even now," declares the **L**, "return to Jl 2:12
and not your garments." Return to the **L**, Jl 2:13
and a drink offering for the **L** your God? Jl 2:14
altar let the priests, the ministers of the **L**, Jl 2:17
weep and say, "Spare your people, O **L**, Jl 2:17
Then the **L** became jealous for his land Jl 2:18
The **L** answered and said to his people, Jl 2:19
rejoice, for the **L** has done great things! Jl 2:21
of Zion, and rejoice in the **L** your God, Jl 2:23
and praise the name of the **L** your God, Jl 2:26
and that I am the **L** your God and there is Jl 2:27
great and awesome day of the **L** comes. Jl 2:31
calls on the name of the **L** shall be saved. Jl 2:32
be those who escape, as the **L** has said, Jl 2:32
shall be those whom the **L** calls. Jl 2:32
to a nation far away, for the **L** has spoken." Jl 3:8
there. Bring down your warriors, O **L**. Jl 3:11
For the day of the **L** is near in the valley of Jl 3:14
The **L** roars from Zion, and utters his Jl 3:16
But the **L** is a refuge to his people, a Jl 3:16
you shall know that I am the **L** your God, Jl 3:17
the house of the **L** and water the Valley Jl 3:18
not avenged, for the **L** dwells in Zion." Jl 3:21
"The **L** roars from Zion and utters his Am 1:2
Thus says the **L**: "For three Am 1:3
shall go into exile to Kir," says the **L**. Am 1:5
Thus says the **L**: "For three Am 1:6
Philistines shall perish," says the **L** GOD. Am 1:8
Thus says the **L**: "For three Am 1:9
Thus says the **L**: "For three Am 1:11
Thus says the **L**: "For three Am 1:13
he and his princes together," says the **L**. Am 1:15
Thus says the **L**: "For three Am 2:1
kill all its princes with him," says the **L**. Am 2:3
Thus says the **L**: "For three Am 2:4
they have rejected the law of the **L**, Am 2:4
Thus says the **L**: "For three Am 2:6
so, O people of Israel?" declares the **L**. Am 2:11
away naked in that day," declares the **L**. Am 2:16
this word that the **L** has spoken against Am 3:1
come to a city, unless the **L** has done it? Am 3:6
"For the **L** GOD does nothing without Am 3:7
The **L** GOD has spoken; who can but Am 3:8
know how to do right," declares the **L**, Am 3:10
Therefore thus says the **L** GOD: "An Am 3:11
Thus says the **L**: "As the shepherd Am 3:12
the house of Jacob," declares the **L** GOD, Am 3:13
shall come to an end," declares the **L**. Am 3:15
The **L** GOD has sworn by his holiness Am 4:2
be cast out into Harmon," declares the **L**. Am 4:3
O people of Israel!" declares the **L** GOD. Am 4:5
you did not return to me," declares the **L**. Am 4:6
you did not return to me," declares the **L**. Am 4:8
you did not return to me," declares the **L**. Am 4:9
did not return to me," declares the **L**. Am 4:10
did not return to me," declares the **L**. Am 4:11
on the heights of the earth—the **L**, Am 4:13
For thus says the **L** GOD: "The city that Am 5:3
For thus says the **L** to the house of Israel: Am 5:4
Seek the **L** and live, lest he break out like Am 5:6
surface of the earth, the **L** is his name; Am 5:8
and so the **L**, the God of hosts, will be Am 5:14
it may be that the **L**, the God of hosts, Am 5:15
Therefore thus says the **L**, the God of Am 5:16
says the LORD, the God of hosts, the **L**: Am 5:16
pass through your midst," says the **L**. Am 5:17
Woe to you who desire the day of the **L**! Am 5:18
Why would you have the day of the **L**? Am 5:18
Is not the day of the **L** darkness, and not Am 5:20
exile beyond Damascus," says the **L**, Am 5:27
The **L** GOD has sworn by himself, Am 6:8
has sworn by himself, declares the **L**, Am 6:8
must not mention the name of the **L**." Am 6:10
For behold, the **L** commands, and the Am 6:11
O house of Israel," declares the **L**, Am 6:14
This is what the **L** GOD showed me: Am 7:1
the grass of the land, I said, "O **L** GOD, Am 7:2
The **L** relented concerning this; "It shall Am 7:3
this; "It shall not be," said the **L**. Am 7:3
This is what the **L** GOD showed me: Am 7:4
the **L** GOD was calling for a judgment by Am 7:4
Then I said, "O **L** GOD, please cease! How Am 7:5
The **L** relented concerning this; "This Am 7:6
"This also shall not be," said the **L** GOD. Am 7:6
the **L** was standing beside a wall built Am 7:7
And the **L** said to me, "Amos, what do Am 7:8
I said, "A plumb line." Then the **L** said, Am 7:8
But the **L** took me from following the Am 7:15
the flock, and the **L** said to me, Am 7:15
Now therefore hear the word of the **L**. Am 7:16
Therefore thus says the **L**: "'Your wife Am 7:17
This is what the **L** GOD showed me: Am 8:1
of summer fruit." Then the **L** said to me, Am 8:2
wailings in that day," declares the **L** GOD. Am 8:3
The **L** has sworn by the pride of Jacob: Am 8:7
"And on that day," declares the **L** GOD, "I Am 8:9
days are coming," declares the **L** GOD, Am 8:11
water, but of hearing the words of the **L**. Am 8:11
run to and fro, to seek the word of the **L**, Am 8:12
I saw the **L** standing beside the altar, and Am 9:1
The **L** GOD of hosts, he who touches the Am 9:5
surface of the earth—the **L** is his name. Am 9:6
to me, O people of Israel?" declares the **L**. Am 9:7
the eyes of the **L** GOD are upon the sinful Am 9:8
the house of Jacob," declares the **L**. Am 9:8
name," declares the **L** who does this. Am 9:12
the days are coming," declares the **L**, Am 9:13
have given them," says the **L** your God. Am 9:15
Thus says the **L** GOD concerning Edom: Ob 1:1
We have heard a report from the **L**, and a Ob 1:1
I will bring you down, declares the **L**. Ob 1:4
Will I not on that day, declares the **L**, Ob 1:8
For the day of the **L** is near upon all the Ob 1:15
the house of Esau, for the **L** has spoken. Ob 1:18
Now the word of the **L** came to Jonah the Jon 1:1
to Tarshish from the presence of the **L**. Jon 1:3
away from the presence of the **L**. Jon 1:3
But the **L** hurled a great wind upon the Jon 1:4
to them, "I am a Hebrew, and I fear the **L**, Jon 1:9
was fleeing from the presence of the **L**, Jon 1:10

Therefore they called out to the **L**, "O	Jon 1:14
they called out to the LORD, "O **L**,	Jon 1:14
not on us innocent blood, for you, O **L**,	Jon 1:14
Then the men feared the **L** exceedingly,	Jon 1:16
a sacrifice to the **L** and made vows.	Jon 1:16
And the **L** appointed a great fish to	Jon 1:17
Jonah prayed to the **L** his God from the	Jon 2:1
saying, "I called out to the **L**, out of my	Jon 2:2
up my life from the pit, O **L** my God.	Jon 2:6
was fainting away, I remembered the **L**,	Jon 2:7
I will pay. Salvation belongs to the **L**!"	Jon 2:9
And the **L** spoke to the fish, and it	Jon 2:10
Then the word of the **L** came to Jonah the	Jon 3:1
Nineveh, according to the word of the **L**.	Jon 3:3
And he prayed to the **L** and said, "O LORD,	Jon 4:2
And he prayed to the LORD and said, "O **L**,	Jon 4:2
Therefore now, O **L**, please take my life	Jon 4:3
And the **L** said, "Do you do well to be	Jon 4:4
Now the **L** God appointed a plant and	Jon 4:6
And the **L** said, "You pity the plant, for	Jon 4:10
The word of the **L** that came to Micah of	Mi 1:1
and let the **L** GOD be a witness against	Mi 1:2
against you, the **L** from his holy temple.	Mi 1:2
behold, the **L** is coming out of his place,	Mi 1:3
has come down from the **L** to the gate of	Mi 1:12
Therefore thus says the **L**: behold, against	Mi 2:3
the line by lot in the assembly of the **L**.	Mi 2:5
of Jacob? Has the **L** grown impatient?	Mi 2:7
on before them, the **L** at their head.	Mi 2:13
Then they will cry to the **L**, but he will	Mi 3:4
Thus says the **L** concerning the prophets	Mi 3:5
filled with power, with the Spirit of the **L**,	Mi 3:8
yet they lean on the **L** and say, "Is not the	Mi 3:11
and say, "Is not the **L** in the midst of us?	Mi 3:11
the house of the **L** shall be established as	Mi 4:1
let us go up to the mountain of the **L**,	Mi 4:2
and the word of the **L** from Jerusalem.	Mi 4:2
the mouth of the **L** of hosts has spoken.	Mi 4:4
in the name of the **L** our God forever and	Mi 4:5
In that day, declares the **L**, I will assemble	Mi 4:6
and the **L** will reign over them in Mount	Mi 4:7
there the **L** will redeem you from the	Mi 4:10
they do not know the thoughts of the **L**;	Mi 4:12
and shall devote their gain to the **L**, their	Mi 4:13
their wealth to the **L** of the whole earth.	Mi 4:13
his flock in the strength of the **L**,	Mi 5:4
the majesty of the name of the **L** his God.	Mi 5:4
of many peoples like dew from the **L**,	Mi 5:7
And in that day, declares the **L**, I will cut	Mi 5:10
Hear what the **L** says: Arise, plead your	Mi 6:1
you mountains, the indictment of the **L**,	Mi 6:2
for the **L** has an indictment against his	Mi 6:2
you may know the saving acts of the **L**."	Mi 6:5
"With what shall I come before the **L**,	Mi 6:6
Will the **L** be pleased with thousands of	Mi 6:7
and what does the **L** require of you but to	Mi 6:8
The voice of the **L** cries to the city—and it	Mi 6:9
But as for me, I will look to the **L**; I will	Mi 7:7
sit in darkness, the **L** will be a light to me.	Mi 7:8
the indignation of the **L** because I have	Mi 7:9
"Where is the **L** your God?" My eyes will	Mi 7:10
shall turn in dread to the **L** our God,	Mi 7:17
The **L** is a jealous and avenging God; the	Na 1:2
God; the **L** is avenging and wrathful;	Na 1:2
the **L** takes vengeance on his adversaries	Na 1:2
The **L** is slow to anger and great in power,	Na 1:3
and the **L** will by no means clear the	Na 1:3
The **L** is good, a stronghold in the day of	Na 1:7
What do you plot against the **L**? He will	Na 1:9
came one who plotted evil against the **L**,	Na 1:11
Thus says the **L**, "Though they are at	Na 1:12
The **L** has given commandment about	Na 1:14
For the **L** is restoring the majesty of	Na 2:2
I am against you, declares the **L** of hosts,	Na 2:13
I am against you, declares the **L** of hosts,	Na 3:5
O **L**, how long shall I cry for help, and	Hab 1:2
you not from everlasting, O **L** my God,	Hab 1:12
We shall not die. O **L**, you have	Hab 1:12
And the **L** answered me: "Write the	Hab 2:2
is it not from the **L** of hosts that peoples	Hab 2:13
of the glory of the **L** as the waters cover	Hab 2:14
But the **L** is in his holy temple; let all	Hab 2:20
O **L**, I have heard the report of you, and	Hab 3:2
the report of you, and your work, O **L**,	Hab 3:2
Was your wrath against the rivers, O **L**?	Hab 3:8
yet I will rejoice in the **L**; I will take joy	Hab 3:18
GOD, the **L**, is my strength; he makes	Hab 3:19
The word of the **L** that came to	Zep 1:1
the face of the earth," declares the **L**.	Zep 1:2
the face of the earth," declares the **L**.	Zep 1:3
and swear to the **L** and yet swear by	Zep 1:5
have turned back from following the **L**,	Zep 1:6
who do not seek the **L** or inquire of him."	Zep 1:6
Be silent before the **L** GOD! For the day of	Zep 1:7
For the day of the **L** is near; the LORD has	Zep 1:7
the **L** has prepared a sacrifice and	Zep 1:7
"On that day," declares the **L**, "a cry will	Zep 1:10
in their hearts, 'The **L** will not do good,	Zep 1:12
The great day of the **L** is near, near and	Zep 1:14
the sound of the day of the **L** is bitter;	Zep 1:14
because they have sinned against the **L**;	Zep 1:17
them on the day of the wrath of the **L**.	Zep 1:18
upon you the burning anger of the **L**,	Zep 2:2
upon you the day of the anger of the **L**.	Zep 2:2
Seek the **L**, all you humble of the land,	Zep 2:3
hidden on the day of the anger of the **L**.	Zep 2:3
The word of the **L** is against you, O	Zep 2:5
For the **L** their God will be mindful of	Zep 2:7
as I live," declares the **L** of hosts,	Zep 2:9
against the people of the **L** of hosts.	Zep 2:10
The **L** will be awesome against them;	Zep 2:11
She does not trust in the **L**; she does not	Zep 3:2
The **L** within her is righteous; he does no	Zep 3:5
"Therefore wait for me," declares the **L**,	Zep 3:8
the name of the **L** and serve him with	Zep 3:9
shall seek refuge in the name of the **L**,	Zep 3:12
The **L** has taken away the judgments	Zep 3:15
The King of Israel, the **L**, is in your	Zep 3:15
The **L** your God is in your midst, a	Zep 3:17
fortunes before your eyes," says the **L**.	Zep 3:20
the word of the **L** came by the hand of	Hg 1:1
"Thus says the **L** of hosts: These people	Hg 1:2
yet come to rebuild the house of the **L**."	Hg 1:2
Then the word of the **L** came by the hand	Hg 1:3
Now, therefore, thus says the **L** of hosts:	Hg 1:5
"Thus says the **L** of hosts: Consider your	Hg 1:7
it and that I may be glorified, says the **L**.	Hg 1:8
it away. Why? declares the **L** of hosts.	Hg 1:9
obeyed the voice of the **L** their God,	Hg 1:12
prophet, as the **L** their God had sent him.	Hg 1:12
sent him. And the people feared the **L**.	Hg 1:12
Then Haggai, the messenger of the **L**,	Hg 1:13
message, "I am with you, declares the **L**."	Hg 1:13
And the **L** stirred up the spirit of	Hg 1:14
worked on the house of the **L** of hosts,	Hg 1:14
the word of the **L** came by the hand of	Hg 2:1
be strong, O Zerubbabel, declares the **L**.	Hg 2:4
all you people of the land, declares the **L**.	Hg 2:4
for I am with you, declares the **L** of hosts,	Hg 2:4
For thus says the **L** of hosts: Yet once	Hg 2:6
this house with glory, says the **L** of hosts.	Hg 2:7
the gold is mine, declares the **L** of hosts.	Hg 2:8
than the former, says the **L** of hosts.	Hg 2:9
I will give peace, declares the **L** of hosts.'"	Hg 2:9
the word of the **L** came by Haggai the	Hg 2:10
"Thus says the **L** of hosts: Ask the	Hg 2:11
this nation before me, declares the **L**,	Hg 2:14
placed upon stone in the temple of the **L**,	Hg 2:15
you did not turn to me, declares the **L**.	Hg 2:17
The word of the **L** came a second time to	Hg 2:20
On that day, declares the **L** of hosts, I	Hg 2:23
the son of Shealtiel, declares the **L**,	Hg 2:23
chosen you, declares the **L** of hosts."	Hg 2:23
the word of the **L** came to the prophet	Zec 1:1
"The **L** was very angry with your fathers.	Zec 1:2
say to them, Thus declares the **L** of hosts:	Zec 1:3
Return to me, says the **L** of hosts, and I	Zec 1:3
I will return to you, says the **L** of hosts.	Zec 1:3
cried out, 'Thus says the **L** of hosts,	Zec 1:4
or pay attention to me, declares the **L**.	Zec 1:4
As the **L** of hosts purposed to deal with us	Zec 1:6
the word of the **L** came to the prophet	Zec 1:7
Then I said, 'What are these, my **l**?' The	Zec 1:9
are they whom the **L** has sent to patrol	Zec 1:10
the angel of the **L** who was standing	Zec 1:11
Then the angel of the **L** said, 'O LORD of	Zec 1:12
the angel of the LORD said, 'O **L** of hosts,	Zec 1:12
And the **L** answered gracious and	Zec 1:13
me, 'Cry out, Thus says the **L** of hosts:	Zec 1:14
Therefore, thus says the **L**, I have	Zec 1:16
be built in it, declares the **L** of hosts,	Zec 1:16
Cry out again, Thus says the **L** of hosts:	Zec 1:17
and the **L** will again comfort Zion and	Zec 1:17
Then the **L** showed me four craftsmen.	Zec 1:20
a wall of fire all around, declares the **L**,	Zec 2:5
the land of the north, declares the **L**.	Zec 2:6
four winds of the heavens, declares the **L**.	Zec 2:6
For thus said the **L** of hosts, after his	Zec 2:8
will know that the **L** of hosts has sent	Zec 2:9
will dwell in your midst, declares the **L**.	Zec 2:10
join themselves to the **L** in that day,	Zec 2:11
shall know that the **L** of hosts has sent	Zec 2:11
And the **L** will inherit Judah as his	Zec 2:12
Be silent, all flesh, before the **L**, for he	Zec 2:13
priest standing before the angel of the **L**,	Zec 3:1
And the **L** said to Satan, "The LORD	Zec 3:2
LORD said to Satan, "The **L** rebuke you,	Zec 3:2
The **L** who has chosen Jerusalem rebuke	Zec 3:2
And the angel of the **L** was standing by.	Zec 3:5
angel of the **L** solemnly assured Joshua,	Zec 3:6
"Thus says the **L** of hosts: If you will	Zec 3:7
its inscription, declares the **L** of hosts,	Zec 3:9
In that day, declares the **L** of hosts,	Zec 3:10
talked with me, "What are these, my **l**?"	Zec 4:4
know what these are?" I said, "No, my **l**."	Zec 4:5
"This is the word of the **L** to Zerubbabel:	Zec 4:6
but by my Spirit, says the **L** of hosts.	Zec 4:6
Then the word of the **L** came to me,	Zec 4:8
will know that the **L** of hosts has sent	Zec 4:9
"These seven are the eyes of the **L**,	Zec 4:10
what these are?" I said, "No, my **l**."	Zec 4:13
who stand by the **L** of the whole earth."	Zec 4:14
I will send it out, declares the **L** of hosts,	Zec 5:4
talked with me, "What are these, my **l**?"	Zec 6:4
themselves before the **L** of all the	Zec 6:5
And the word of the **L** came to me:	Zec 6:9
say to him, 'Thus says the **L** of hosts,	Zec 6:12
and he shall build the temple of the **L**.	Zec 6:12
the temple of the **L** and shall bear royal	Zec 6:13
in the temple of the **L** as a reminder to	Zec 6:14
and help to build the temple of the **L**.	Zec 6:15
shall know that the **L** of hosts has sent	Zec 6:15
obey the voice of the **L** your God."	Zec 6:15
the word of the **L** came to Zechariah on	Zec 7:1
their men to entreat the favor of the **L**,	Zec 7:2
of the house of the **L** of hosts and the	Zec 7:3
Then the word of the **L** of hosts came to	Zec 7:4
the words that the **L** proclaimed by the	Zec 7:7
the word of the **L** came to Zechariah,	Zec 7:8
"Thus says the **L** of hosts, Render true	Zec 7:9
the words that the **L** of hosts had sent	Zec 7:12
great anger came from the **L** of hosts.	Zec 7:12
I would not hear," says the **L** of hosts,	Zec 7:13
And the word of the **L** of hosts came,	Zec 8:1
"Thus says the **L** of hosts: I am jealous	Zec 8:2
Thus says the **L**: I have returned to Zion	Zec 8:3
city, and the mountain of the **L** of hosts,	Zec 8:3
Thus says the **L** of hosts: Old men and	Zec 8:4
Thus says the **L** of hosts: If it is	Zec 8:6
in my sight, declares the **L** of hosts?	Zec 8:6
Thus says the **L** of hosts: behold, I will	Zec 8:7
Thus says the **L** of hosts: "Let your	Zec 8:9
of the house of the **L** of hosts was laid,	Zec 8:9
the former days, declares the **L** of hosts.	Zec 8:11
For thus says the **L** of hosts: "As I	Zec 8:14
and I did not relent, says the **L** of hosts,	Zec 8:14
all these things I hate, declares the **L**."	Zec 8:17
And the word of the **L** of hosts came to	Zec 8:18
"Thus says the **L** of hosts: The fast of	Zec 8:19
"Thus says the **L** of hosts: Peoples shall	Zec 8:20
entreat the favor of the **L** and to seek the	Zec 8:21
of the LORD and to seek the **L** of hosts;	Zec 8:21
come to seek the **L** of hosts in Jerusalem	Zec 8:22
and to entreat the favor of the **L**.	Zec 8:22
Thus says the **L** of hosts: In those days	Zec 8:23
of the word of the **L** is against the land of	Zec 9:1
For the **L** has an eye on mankind and on	Zec 9:1
the **L** will strip her of her possessions and	Zec 9:4
Then the **L** will appear over them, and	Zec 9:14
the **L** GOD will sound the trumpet and	Zec 9:14
The **L** of hosts will protect them, and	Zec 9:15
On that day the **L** their God will save	Zec 9:16
Ask rain from the **L** in the season of the	Zec 10:1
from the **L** who makes the storm	Zec 10:1
for the **L** of hosts cares for his flock, the	Zec 10:3
shall fight because the **L** is with them,	Zec 10:5
for I am the **L** their God and I will	Zec 10:6
glad; their hearts shall rejoice in the **L**.	Zec 10:7
I will make them strong in the **L**, and	Zec 10:12
walk in his name," declares the **L**.	Zec 10:12
Thus said the **L** my God: "Become	Zec 11:4
who sell them say, 'Blessed be the **L**,	Zec 11:5
inhabitants of this land, declares the **L**.	Zec 11:6
me, knew that it was the word of the **L**.	Zec 11:11
Then the **L** said to me, "Throw it to the	Zec 11:13
threw them into the house of the **L**,	Zec 11:13
Then the **L** said to me, "Take once	Zec 11:15
of the word of the **L** concerning Israel:	Zec 12:1
Thus declares the **L**, who stretched out	Zec 12:1
On that day, declares the **L**, I will strike	Zec 12:4
have strength through the **L** of hosts,	Zec 12:5
"And the **L** will give salvation to the	Zec 12:7
On that day the **L** will protect the	Zec 12:8
shall be like God, like the angel of the **L**,	Zec 12:8
on that day, declares the **L** of hosts,	Zec 13:2
for you speak lies in the name of the **L**.'	Zec 13:3
next to me," declares the **L** of hosts.	Zec 13:7
In the whole land, declares the **L**, two	Zec 13:8
and they will say, 'The **L** is my God.'"	Zec 13:9
Behold, a day is coming for the **L**, when	Zec 14:1
Then the **L** will go out and fight against	Zec 14:3
Then the **L** my God will come, and all	Zec 14:5
a unique day, which is known to the **L**,	Zec 14:7
And the **L** will be king over all the	Zec 14:9
On that day the **L** will be one and his	Zec 14:9

plague with which the **L** will strike all Zec 14:12
great panic from the **L** shall fall on Zec 14:13
to worship the King, the **L** of hosts, Zec 14:16
to worship the King, the **L** of hosts, Zec 14:17
with which the **L** afflicts the nations Zec 14:18
"Holy to the **L**." And the pots in the Zec 14:20
in the house of the **L** shall be as the Zec 14:20
Judah shall be holy to the **L** of hosts, Zec 14:21
in the house of the **L** of hosts on that Zec 14:21
of the word of the **L** to Israel by Malachi. Mal 1:1
"I have loved you," says the **L**. But you Mal 1:2
Esau Jacob's brother?" declares the **L**. Mal 1:2
rebuild the ruins," the **L** of hosts says, Mal 1:4
with whom the **L** is angry forever.'" Mal 1:4
"Great is the **L** beyond the border of Mal 1:5
says the **L** of hosts to you, O priests, who Mal 1:6
or show you favor? says the **L** of hosts. Mal 1:8
favor to any of you? says the **L** of hosts. Mal 1:9
no pleasure in you, says the **L** of hosts, Mal 1:10
among the nations, says the **L** of hosts. Mal 1:11
and you snort at it, says the **L** of hosts. Mal 1:13
that from your hand? says the **L**. Mal 1:13
sacrifices to the **L** what is blemished. Mal 1:14
I am a great King, says the **L** of hosts, Mal 1:14
honor to my name, says the **L** of hosts, Mal 2:2
with Levi may stand, says the **L** of hosts. Mal 2:4
for he is the messenger of the **L** of hosts. Mal 2:7
the covenant of Levi, says the **L** of hosts, Mal 2:8
has profaned the sanctuary of the **L**, Mal 2:11
May the **L** cut off from the tents of Mal 2:12
brings an offering to the **L** of hosts! Mal 2:12
not?" Because the **L** was witness Mal 2:14
who hates and divorces, says the **L**, Mal 2:16
with violence, says the **L** of hosts. Mal 2:16
have wearied the **L** with your words. Mal 2:17
does evil is good in the sight of the **L**, Mal 2:17
And the **L** whom you seek will suddenly Mal 3:1
behold, he is coming, says the **L** of hosts. Mal 3:1
offerings in righteousness to the **L**. Mal 3:3
will be pleasing to the **L** as in the days of Mal 3:4
and do not fear me, says the **L** of hosts. Mal 3:5
"For I the **L** do not change; therefore Mal 3:6
I will return to you, says the **L** of hosts. Mal 3:7
put me to the test, says the **L** of hosts, Mal 3:10
not fail to bear, says the **L** of hosts. Mal 3:11
be a land of delight, says the **L** of hosts. Mal 3:12
have been hard against me, says the **L**. Mal 3:13
as in mourning before the **L** of hosts? Mal 3:14
those who feared the **L** spoke with one Mal 3:16
The **L** paid attention and heard them, Mal 3:16
who feared the **L** and esteemed his Mal 3:16
shall be mine, says the **L** of hosts, Mal 3:17
shall set them ablaze, says the **L** of hosts, Mal 4:1
the day when I act, says the **L** of hosts. Mal 4:3
great and awesome day of the **L** comes. Mal 4:5
an angel of the **L** appeared to him in a Mt 1:20
to fulfill what the **L** had spoken by the Mt 1:22
as the angel of the **L** commanded him: Mt 1:24
an angel of the **L** appeared to Joseph in a Mt 2:13
to fulfill what the **L** had spoken by the Mt 2:15
an angel of the **L** appeared in a dream to Mt 2:19
the wilderness: 'Prepare the way of the **L**; Mt 3:3
'You shall not put the **L** your God to the Mt 4:7
"'You shall worship the **L** your God and Mt 4:10
shall perform to the **L** what you have Mt 5:33
"Not everyone who says to me, '**L**, Lord,' Mt 7:21
L,' will enter the kingdom of heaven, Mt 7:21
that day many will say to me, '**L**, Lord, Mt 7:22
L, did we not prophesy in your name, Mt 7:22
knelt before him, saying, "**L**, if you will, Mt 8:2
"**L**, my servant is lying paralyzed at Mt 8:6
"**L**, I am not worthy to have you come Mt 8:8
"**L**, let me first go and bury my father." Mt 8:21
saying, "Save us, **L**; we are perishing." Mt 8:25
to do this?" They said to him, "Yes, **L**." Mt 9:28
pray earnestly to the **L** of the harvest to Mt 9:38
you, Father, **L** of heaven and earth, Mt 11:25
For the Son of Man is **l** of the Sabbath." Mt 12:8
And Peter answered him, "**L**, if it is you, Mt 14:28
to sink he cried out, "**L**, save me." Mt 14:30
was crying, "Have mercy on me, O **L**, Mt 15:22
knelt before him, saying, "**L**, help me." Mt 15:25
L, yet even the dogs eat the crumbs that Mt 15:27
L! This shall never happen to you." Mt 16:22
to Jesus, "**L**, it is good that we are here. Mt 17:4
said, "**L**, have mercy on my son, for he Mt 17:15
"**L**, how often will my brother sin Mt 18:21
the rulers of the Gentiles **l** it over them, Mt 20:25
they cried out, "**L**, have mercy on us, Mt 20:30
out all the more, "**L**, have mercy on us, Mt 20:31
said to him, "**L**, let our eyes be opened." Mt 20:33
you, you shall say, 'The **L** needs them,' Mt 21:3
is he who comes in the name of the **L**! Mt 21:9
"You shall love the **L** your God with all Mt 22:37
that David, in the Spirit, calls him **L**, Mt 22:43
"'The **L** said to my Lord, Sit at my right Mt 22:44
"'The Lord said to my **L**, Sit at my right Mt 22:44
If then David calls him **L**, how is he his Mt 22:45
is he who comes in the name of the **L**.'" Mt 23:39
know on what day your **L** is coming. Mt 24:42
virgins came also, saying, '**L**, lord, Mt 25:11
came also, saying, 'Lord, **l**, open to us.' Mt 25:11
'**L**, when did we see you hungry and Mt 25:37
'**L**, when did we see you hungry or Mt 25:44
say to him one after another, "Is it I, **L**?" Mt 26:22
the potter's field, as the **L** directed me." Mt 27:10
an angel of the **L** descended from heaven Mt 28:2
'Prepare the way of the **L**, make his paths Mk 1:3
Son of Man is **l** even of the Sabbath." Mk 2:28
them how much the **L** has done for Mk 5:19
L; yet even the dogs under the table eat Mk 7:28
rulers of the Gentiles **l** it over them, Mk 10:42
'The **L** has need of it and will send it Mk 11:3
is he who comes in the name of the **L**! Mk 11:9
Israel: The **L** our God, the Lord is one. Mk 12:29
Israel: The Lord our God, the **L** is one. Mk 12:29
you shall love the **L** your God with all Mk 12:30
declared, "'The **L** said to my Lord, Mk 12:36
declared, "'The Lord said to my **L**, Mk 12:36
David himself calls him **L**. So how is Mk 12:37
And if the **L** had not cut short the Mk 13:20
So then the **L** Jesus, after he had Mk 16:19
while the **L** worked with them and Mk 16:20
the commandments and statutes of the **L**. Lk 1:6
the temple of the **L** and burn incense. Lk 1:9
an angel of the **L** standing on the right Lk 1:11
for he will be great before the **L**. And he Lk 1:15
the children of Israel to the **L** their God, Lk 1:16
make ready for the **L** a people prepared." Lk 1:17
"Thus the **L** has done for me in the days Lk 1:25
O favored one, the **L** is with you!" Lk 1:28
And the **L** God will give to him the Lk 1:32
said, "Behold, I am the servant of the **L**; Lk 1:38
the mother of my **L** should come to me? Lk 1:43
of what was spoken to her from the **L**." Lk 1:45
Mary said, "My soul magnifies the **L**, Lk 1:46
heard that the **L** had shown great Lk 1:58
be?" For the hand of the **L** was with him. Lk 1:66
"Blessed be the **L** God of Israel, for he has Lk 1:68
will go before the **L** to prepare his ways, Lk 1:76
And an angel of the **L** appeared to them, Lk 2:9
the glory of the **L** shone around them, Lk 2:9
of David a Savior, who is Christ the **L**. Lk 2:11
which the **L** has made known to us." Lk 2:15
up to Jerusalem to present him to the **L** Lk 2:22
(as it is written in the Law of the **L**, Lk 2:23
the womb shall be called holy to the **L**") Lk 2:23
to what is said in the Law of the **L**, Lk 2:24
"**L**, now you are letting your servant Lk 2:29
according to the Law of the **L**, Lk 2:39
'Prepare the way of the **L**, make his paths Lk 3:4
"'You shall worship the **L** your God, Lk 4:8
'You shall not put the **L** your God to the Lk 4:12
"The Spirit of the **L** is upon me, because Lk 4:18
from me, for I am a sinful man, O **L**." Lk 5:8
his face and begged him, "**L**, if you will, Lk 5:12
And the power of the **L** was with him to Lk 5:17
"The Son of Man is **l** of the Sabbath." Lk 6:5
"Why do you call me '**L**, Lord,' and not Lk 6:46
me 'Lord, **L**,' and not do what I tell you? Lk 6:46
saying to him, "**L**, do not trouble yourself, Lk 7:6
And when the **L** saw her, he had Lk 7:13
his disciples to him, sent them to the **L**, Lk 7:19
"**L**, do you want us to tell fire to come Lk 9:54
"**L**, let me first go and bury my father." Lk 9:59
L, but let me first say farewell to those at Lk 9:61
After this the **L** appointed seventy-two Lk 10:1
pray earnestly to the **L** of the harvest to Lk 10:2
"**L**, even the demons are subject to us Lk 10:17
you, Father, **L** of heaven and earth, Lk 10:21
"You shall love the **L** your God with all Lk 10:27
"**L**, do you not care that my sister has Lk 10:40
But the **L** answered her, "Martha, Lk 10:41
said to him, "**L**, teach us to pray, Lk 11:1
And the **L** said to him, "Now you Lk 11:39
"**L**, are you telling this parable for us or Lk 12:41
And the **L** said, "Who then is the Lk 12:42
Then the **L** answered him, "You Lk 13:15
"**L**, will those who are saved be few?" Lk 13:23
at the door, saying, '**L**, open to us,' Lk 13:25
is he who comes in the name of the **L**!'" Lk 13:35
The apostles said to the **L**, "Increase our Lk 17:5
And the **L** said, "If you had faith like a Lk 17:6
to him, "Where, **L**?" He said to them, Lk 17:37
And the **L** said, "Hear what the Lk 18:6
He said, "**L**, let me recover my sight." Lk 18:41
And Zacchaeus stood and said to the **L**, Lk 19:8
L, the half of my goods I give to the poor. Lk 19:8
'**L**, your mina has made ten minas' Lk 19:16
'**L**, your mina has made five minas.' Lk 19:18
came, saying, '**L**, here is your mina, Lk 19:20
they said to him, '**L**, he has ten minas!' Lk 19:25
shall say this: 'The **L** has need of it.'" Lk 19:31
And they said, "The **L** has need of it." Lk 19:34
King who comes in the name of the **L**! Lk 19:38
where he calls the **L** the God of Lk 20:37
of Psalms, "'The **L** said to my Lord, Lk 20:42
of Psalms, "'The Lord said to my **L**, Lk 20:42
David thus calls him **L**, so how is he Lk 20:44
"**L**, I am ready to go with you both to Lk 22:33
L, here are two swords." And he said to Lk 22:38
"**L**, shall we strike with the sword?" Lk 22:49
And the **L** turned and looked at Peter. Lk 22:61
Peter remembered the saying of the **L**, Lk 22:61
they did not find the body of the **L** Jesus. Lk 24:3
saying, "The **L** has risen indeed, and Lk 24:34
'Make straight the way of the **L**,' Jn 1:23
the bread after the **L** had given thanks. Jn 6:23
answered him, "**L**, to whom shall we go? Jn 6:68
She said, "No one, **L**." And Jesus said, Jn 8:11
"**L**, I believe," and he worshiped him. Jn 9:38
who anointed the **L** with ointment and Jn 11:2
him, saying, "**L**, he whom you love is ill." Jn 11:3
said to him, "**L**, if he has fallen asleep, Jn 11:12
said to Jesus, "**L**, if you had been here, Jn 11:21
"Yes, **L**; I believe that you are the Christ, Jn 11:27
saying to him, "**L**, if you had been here, Jn 11:32
They said to him, "**L**, come and see." Jn 11:34
"**L**, by this time there will be an odor, Jn 11:39
is he who comes in the name of the **L**, Jn 12:13
"**L**, who has believed what he heard Jn 12:38
has the arm of the **L** been revealed?" Jn 12:38
said to him, "**L**, do you wash my feet?" Jn 13:6
"**L**, not my feet only but also my hands Jn 13:9
You call me Teacher and **L**, and you Jn 13:13
If I then, your **L** and Teacher, have Jn 13:14
against Jesus, said to him, "**L**, who is it?" Jn 13:25
"**L**, where are you going?" Jesus Jn 13:36
him, "**L**, why can I not follow you now? Jn 13:37
"**L**, we do not know where you are going. Jn 14:5
said to him, "**L**, show us the Father, Jn 14:8
"**L**, how is it that you will manifest Jn 14:22
"They have taken the **L** out of the tomb, Jn 20:2
to them, "They have taken away my **L**, Jn 20:13
"I have seen the **L**"—and that he had Jn 20:18
disciples were glad when they saw the **L**. Jn 20:20
"We have seen the **L**." But he said to Jn 20:25
answered him, "My **L** and my God!" Jn 20:28
"It is the **L**!" When Simon Peter heard Jn 21:7
Simon Peter heard that it was the **L**, Jn 21:7
are you?" They knew it was the **L**. Jn 21:12
L; you know that I love you." He said to Jn 21:15
L; you know that I love you." He said to Jn 21:16
said to him, "**L**, you know everything; Jn 21:17
"**L**, who is it that is going to betray Jn 21:20
said to Jesus, "**L**, what about this man?" Jn 21:21
"**L**, will you at this time restore the Acts 1:6
the time that the **L** Jesus went in and Acts 1:21
"You, **L**, who know the hearts of all, Acts 1:24
to blood, before the day of the **L** comes, Acts 2:20
upon the name of the **L** shall be saved.' Acts 2:21
him, "'I saw the **L** always before me, Acts 2:25
himself says, "'The **L** said to my Lord, Acts 2:34
himself says, "'The Lord said to my **L**, Acts 2:34
God has made him both **L** and Christ, Acts 2:36
everyone whom the **L** our God calls to Acts 2:39
And the **L** added to their number day Acts 2:47
may come from the presence of the **L**, Acts 3:20
'The **L** God will raise up for you a Acts 3:22
together to God and said, "Sovereign **L**, Acts 4:24
against the **L** and against his Acts 4:26
L, look upon their threats and grant to Acts 4:29
to the resurrection of the **L** Jesus, Acts 4:33
agreed together to test the Spirit of the **L**? Acts 5:9
than ever believers were added to the **L**, Acts 5:14
an angel of the **L** opened the prison Acts 5:19
to look, there came the voice of the **L**: Acts 7:31
Then the **L** said to him, 'Take off the Acts 7:33
will you build for me, says the **L**, Acts 7:49
Stephen, he called out, "**L** Jesus, Acts 7:59
"**L**, do not hold this sin against them." Acts 7:60
baptized in the name of the **L** Jesus. Acts 8:16
of yours, and pray to the **L** that, Acts 8:22
Simon answered, "Pray for me to the **L**, Acts 8:24
testified and spoken the word of the **L**, Acts 8:25
Now an angel of the **L** said to Philip, Acts 8:26
the Spirit of the **L** carried Philip away, Acts 8:39
murder against the disciples of the **L**, Acts 9:1
he said, "Who are you, **L**?" And he said, Acts 9:5
The **L** said to him in a vision, Acts 9:10
"Ananias." And he said, "Here I am, **L**." Acts 9:10
And the **L** said to him, "Rise and go to Acts 9:11
"**L**, I have heard from many about this Acts 9:13
But the **L** said to him, "Go, for he is a Acts 9:15
the **L** Jesus who appeared to you on the Acts 9:17

how on the road he had seen the **L**,	Acts 9:27
preaching boldly in the name of the **L**.	Acts 9:28
in the fear of the **L** and in the comfort	Acts 9:31
saw him, and they turned to the **L**.	Acts 9:35
all Joppa, and many believed in the **L**.	Acts 9:42
"What is it, **L**?" And he said to him,	Acts 10:4
L; for I have never eaten anything	Acts 10:14
have been commanded by the **L**."	Acts 10:33
through Jesus Christ (he is **L** of all),	Acts 10:36
L; for nothing common or unclean	Acts 11:8
And I remembered the word of the **L**,	Acts 11:16
we believed in the **L** Jesus Christ,	Acts 11:17
Hellenists also, preaching the **L** Jesus.	Acts 11:20
And the hand of the **L** was with them,	Acts 11:21
number who believed turned to the **L**.	Acts 11:21
faithful to the **L** with steadfast	Acts 11:23
many people were added to the **L**.	Acts 11:24
an angel of the **L** stood next to him,	Acts 12:7
am sure that the **L** has sent his angel	Acts 12:11
to them how the **L** had brought him	Acts 12:17
an angel of the **L** struck him down,	Acts 12:23
were worshiping the **L** and fasting,	Acts 13:2
crooked the straight paths of the **L**?	Acts 13:10
behold, the hand of the **L** is upon you,	Acts 13:11
astonished at the teaching of the **L**.	Acts 13:12
gathered to hear the word of the **L**.	Acts 13:44
For so the **L** has commanded us,	Acts 13:47
and glorifying the word of the **L**,	Acts 13:48
word of the **L** was spreading	Acts 13:49
a long time, speaking boldly for the **L**,	Acts 14:3
them to the **L** in whom they	Acts 14:23
through the grace of the **L** Jesus,	Acts 15:11
remnant of mankind may seek the **L**,	Acts 15:17
are called by my name, says the **L**,	Acts 15:17
for the sake of our **L** Jesus Christ.	Acts 15:26
and preaching the word of the **L**,	Acts 15:35
we proclaimed the word of the **L**,	Acts 15:36
by the brothers to the grace of the **L**.	Acts 15:40
The **L** opened her heart to pay	Acts 16:14
have judged me to be faithful to the **L**,	Acts 16:15
And they said, "Believe in the **L** Jesus,	Acts 16:31
spoke the word of the **L** to him and to	Acts 16:32
in it, being **L** of heaven and earth,	Acts 17:24
of the synagogue, believed in the **L**,	Acts 18:8
And the **L** said to Paul one night in a	Acts 18:9
been instructed in the way of the **L**.	Acts 18:25
baptized in the name of the **L** Jesus.	Acts 19:5
of Asia heard the word of the **L**,	Acts 19:10
the name of the **L** Jesus over those	Acts 19:13
the name of the **L** Jesus was extolled.	Acts 19:17
word of the **L** continued to increase	Acts 19:20
serving the **L** with all humility and	Acts 20:19
and of faith in our **L** Jesus Christ.	Acts 20:21
that I received from the **L** Jesus,	Acts 20:24
remember the words of the **L** Jesus,	Acts 20:35
for the name of the **L** Jesus."	Acts 21:13
said, "Let the will of the **L** be done."	Acts 21:14
'Who are you, **L**?' And he said to me,	Acts 22:8
I do, **L**?' And the Lord said to me,	Acts 22:10
And the **L** said to me, 'Rise, and go	Acts 22:10
'**L**, they themselves know that in one	Acts 22:19
following night the **L** stood by him	Acts 23:11
definite to write to my **l** about him.	Acts 25:26
'Who are you, **L**?' And the Lord said,	Acts 26:15
And the **L** said, 'I am Jesus whom you	Acts 26:15
teaching about the **L** Jesus Christ	Acts 28:31
from the dead, Jesus Christ our **L**,	Rom 1:4
God our Father and the **L** Jesus Christ.	Rom 1:7
against whom the **L** will not count	Rom 4:8
who raised from the dead Jesus our **L**,	Rom 4:24
with God through our **L** Jesus Christ.	Rom 5:1
in God through our **L** Jesus Christ,	Rom 5:11
eternal life through Jesus Christ our **L**.	Rom 5:21
is eternal life in Christ Jesus our **L**.	Rom 6:23
be to God through Jesus Christ our **L**!	Rom 7:25
the love of God in Christ Jesus our **L**.	Rom 8:39
for the **L** will carry out his sentence	Rom 9:28
"If the **L** of hosts had not left us	Rom 9:29
mouth that Jesus is **L** and believe in	Rom 10:9
the same **L** is Lord of all, bestowing	Rom 10:12
the same Lord is **L** of all, bestowing	Rom 10:12
on the name of the **L** will be saved."	Rom 10:13
"**L**, who has believed what he has	Rom 10:16
"**L**, they have killed your prophets,	Rom 11:3
who has known the mind of the **L**,	Rom 11:34
zeal, be fervent in spirit, serve the **L**.	Rom 12:11
is mine, I will repay, says the **L**."	Rom 12:19
But put on the **L** Jesus Christ, and	Rom 13:14
for the **L** is able to make him stand.	Rom 14:4
the day, observes it in honor of the **L**.	Rom 14:6
one who eats, eats in honor of the **L**,	Rom 14:6
in honor of the **L** and gives thanks to	Rom 14:6
If we live, we live to the **L**, and if we die,	Rom 14:8
the Lord, and if we die, we die to the **L**.	Rom 14:8
that he might be **L** both of the dead	Rom 14:9
for it is written, "As I live, says the **L**,	Rom 14:11
persuaded in the **L** Jesus that nothing	Rom 14:14
God and Father of our **L** Jesus Christ.	Rom 15:6
And again, "Praise the **L**, all you	Rom 15:11
by our **L** Jesus Christ and by the love	Rom 15:30
welcome her in the **L** in a way worthy	Rom 16:2
Greet Ampliatus, my beloved in the **L**.	Rom 16:8
Greet those in the **L** who belong to	Rom 16:11
Greet those workers in the **L**,	Rom 16:12
Persis, who has worked hard in the **L**.	Rom 16:12
Greet Rufus, chosen in the **L**; also his	Rom 16:13
persons do not serve our **L** Christ,	Rom 16:18
The grace of our **L** Jesus Christ be	Rom 16:20
wrote this letter, greet you in the **L**.	Rom 16:22
upon the name of our **L** Jesus Christ,	1 Cor 1:2
Jesus Christ, both their **L** and ours:	1 Cor 1:2
God our Father and the **L** Jesus Christ.	1 Cor 1:3
for the revealing of our **L** Jesus Christ,	1 Cor 1:7
in the day of our **L** Jesus Christ.	1 Cor 1:8
of his Son, Jesus Christ our **L**.	1 Cor 1:9
by the name of our **L** Jesus Christ,	1 Cor 1:10
the one who boasts, boast in the **L**."	1 Cor 1:31
not have crucified the **L** of glory.	1 Cor 2:8
the mind of the **L** so as to instruct	1 Cor 2:16
you believed, as the **L** assigned to each.	1 Cor 3:5
"The **L** knows the thoughts of the	1 Cor 3:20
acquitted. It is the **L** who judges me.	1 Cor 4:4
before the time, before the **L** comes,	1 Cor 4:5
beloved and faithful child in the **L**,	1 Cor 4:17
I will come to you soon, if the **L** wills,	1 Cor 4:19
the name of the **L** Jesus and my spirit	1 Cor 5:4
present, with the power of our **L** Jesus,	1 Cor 5:4
spirit may be saved in the day of the **L**.	1 Cor 5:5
the name of the **L** Jesus Christ and by	1 Cor 6:11
for sexual immorality, but for the **L**,	1 Cor 6:13
for the Lord, and the **L** for the body.	1 Cor 6:13
And God raised the **L** and will also	1 Cor 6:14
is joined to the **L** becomes one spirit	1 Cor 6:17
I give this charge (not I, but the **L**):	1 Cor 7:10
not the **L**) that if any brother has a	1 Cor 7:12
the life that the **L** has assigned to	1 Cor 7:17
who was called in the **L** as a slave is a	1 Cor 7:22
Lord as a slave is a freedman of the **L**.	1 Cor 7:22
I have no command from the **L**,	1 Cor 7:25
is anxious about the things of the **L**,	1 Cor 7:32
of the Lord, how to please the **L**.	1 Cor 7:32
is anxious about the things of the **L**,	1 Cor 7:34
your undivided devotion to the **L**.	1 Cor 7:35
to whom she wishes, only in the **L**.	1 Cor 7:39
and for whom we exist, and one **L**,	1 Cor 8:6
apostle? Have I not seen Jesus our **L**?	1 Cor 9:1
not you my workmanship in the **L**?	1 Cor 9:1
are the seal of my apostleship in the **L**.	1 Cor 9:2
and the brothers of the **L** and Cephas?	1 Cor 9:5
the **L** commanded that those who	1 Cor 9:14
drink the cup of the **L** and the cup of	1 Cor 10:21
of the table of the **L** and the table of	1 Cor 10:21
Shall we provoke the **L** to jealousy?	1 Cor 10:22
in the **L** woman is not independent	1 Cor 11:11
I received from the **L** what I also	1 Cor 11:23
that the **L** Jesus on the night when	1 Cor 11:23
the cup of the **L** in an unworthy	1 Cor 11:27
the body and blood of the **L**.	1 Cor 11:27
But when we are judged by the **L**, we	1 Cor 11:32
can say "Jesus is **L**" except in the Holy	1 Cor 12:3
varieties of service, but the same **L**;	1 Cor 12:5
will not listen to me, says the **L**."	1 Cor 14:21
to you are a command of the **L**.	1 Cor 14:37
which I have in Christ Jesus our **L**,	1 Cor 15:31
victory through our **L** Jesus Christ.	1 Cor 15:57
abounding in the work of the **L**,	1 Cor 15:58
knowing that in the **L** your labor is	1 Cor 15:58
some time with you, if the **L** permits.	1 Cor 16:7
for he is doing the work of the **L**,	1 Cor 16:10
send you hearty greetings in the **L**.	1 Cor 16:19
If anyone has no love for the **L**, let	1 Cor 16:22
Lord, let him be accursed. Our **L**,	1 Cor 16:22
The grace of the **L** Jesus be with you.	1 Cor 16:23
God our Father and the **L** Jesus Christ.	2 Cor 1:2
God and Father of our **L** Jesus Christ,	2 Cor 1:3
the day of our **L** Jesus you will boast	2 Cor 1:14
Not that we **l** it over your faith, but	2 Cor 1:24
a door was opened for me in the **L**,	2 Cor 2:12
But when one turns to the **L**, the veil	2 Cor 3:16
Now the **L** is the Spirit, and where the	2 Cor 3:17
Spirit, and where the Spirit of the **L** is,	2 Cor 3:17
face, beholding the glory of the **L**,	2 Cor 3:18
this comes from the **L** who is the	2 Cor 3:18
is not ourselves, but Jesus Christ as **L**,	2 Cor 4:5
he who raised the **L** Jesus will raise us	2 Cor 4:14
in the body we are away from the **L**,	2 Cor 5:6
from the body and at home with the **L**.	2 Cor 5:8
Therefore, knowing the fear of the **L**,	2 Cor 5:11
be separate from them, says the **L**,	2 Cor 6:17
to me, says the **L** Almighty."	2 Cor 6:18
themselves first to the **L** and then by	2 Cor 8:5
know the grace of our **L** Jesus Christ,	2 Cor 8:9
the glory of the **L** himself and to show	2 Cor 8:19
which the **L** gave for building you up	2 Cor 10:8
the one who boasts, boast in the **L**."	2 Cor 10:17
but the one whom the **L** commends.	2 Cor 10:18
The God and Father of the **L** Jesus,	2 Cor 11:31
on to visions and revelations of the **L**.	2 Cor 12:1
times I pleaded with the **L** about this,	2 Cor 12:8
authority that the **L** has given me	2 Cor 13:10
The grace of the **L** Jesus Christ and	2 Cor 13:14
God our Father and the **L** Jesus Christ,	Gal 1:3
have confidence in the **L** that you will	Gal 5:10
except in the cross of our **L** Jesus Christ,	Gal 6:14
The grace of our **L** Jesus Christ be with	Gal 6:18
God our Father and the **L** Jesus Christ.	Eph 1:2
God and Father of our **L** Jesus Christ,	Eph 1:3
your faith in the **L** Jesus and your love	Eph 1:15
that the God of our **L** Jesus Christ, the	Eph 1:17
grows into a holy temple in the **L**.	Eph 2:21
he has realized in Christ Jesus our **L**,	Eph 3:11
I therefore, a prisoner for the **L**, urge you	Eph 4:1
one **L**, one faith, one baptism,	Eph 4:5
Now this I say and testify in the **L**, that	Eph 4:17
darkness, but now you are light in the **L**.	Eph 5:8
try to discern what is pleasing to the **L**.	Eph 5:10
understand what the will of the **L** is.	Eph 5:17
making melody to the **L** with all your	Eph 5:19
in the name of our **L** Jesus Christ,	Eph 5:20
to your own husbands, as to the **L**.	Eph 5:22
Children, obey your parents in the **L**, for	Eph 6:1
the discipline and instruction of the **L**.	Eph 6:4
a good will as to the **L** and not to man,	Eph 6:7
this he will receive back from the **L**,	Eph 6:8
be strong in the **L** and in the strength	Eph 6:10
faithful minister in the **L** will tell you	Eph 6:21
God the Father and the **L** Jesus Christ.	Eph 6:23
all who love our **L** Jesus Christ with	Eph 6:24
God our Father and the **L** Jesus Christ.	Phil 1:2
confident in the **L** by my	Phil 1:14
tongue confess that Jesus Christ is **L**,	Phil 2:11
I hope in the **L** Jesus to send Timothy	Phil 2:19
I trust in the **L** that shortly I myself	Phil 2:24
So receive him in the **L** with all joy,	Phil 2:29
Finally, my brothers, rejoice in the **L**.	Phil 3:1
worth of knowing Christ Jesus my **L**.	Phil 3:8
it we await a Savior, the **L** Jesus Christ,	Phil 3:20
joy and crown, stand firm thus in the **L**,	Phil 4:1
and I entreat Syntyche to agree in the **L**.	Phil 4:2
Rejoice in the **L** always; again I will say,	Phil 4:4
be known to everyone. The **L** is at hand;	Phil 4:5
I rejoiced in the **L** greatly that now at	Phil 4:10
The grace of the **L** Jesus Christ be with	Phil 4:23
God, the Father of our **L** Jesus Christ,	Col 1:3
as to walk in a manner worthy of the **L**,	Col 1:10
as you received Christ Jesus the **L**,	Col 2:6
as the **L** has forgiven you, so you also	Col 3:13
everything in the name of the **L** Jesus,	Col 3:17
to your husbands, as is fitting in the **L**.	Col 3:18
in everything, for this pleases the **L**.	Col 3:20
with sincerity of heart, fearing the **L**.	Col 3:22
heartily, as for the **L** and not for men,	Col 3:23
that from the **L** you will receive	Col 3:24
reward. You are serving the **L** Christ.	Col 3:24
minister and fellow servant in the **L**.	Col 4:7
that you have received in the **L**."	Col 4:17
the Father and the **L** Jesus Christ:	1 Thes 1:1
of hope in our **L** Jesus Christ.	1 Thes 1:3
became imitators of us and of the **L**,	1 Thes 1:6
the word of the **L** sounded forth from	1 Thes 1:8
who killed both the **L** Jesus and the	1 Thes 2:15
of boasting before our **L** Jesus at his	1 Thes 2:19
live, if you are standing fast in the **L**.	1 Thes 3:8
and Father himself, and our **L** Jesus,	1 Thes 3:11
and may the **L** make you increase	1 Thes 3:12
the coming of our **L** Jesus with all	1 Thes 3:13
we ask and urge you in the **L** Jesus,	1 Thes 4:1
we gave you through the **L** Jesus.	1 Thes 4:2
because the **L** is an avenger in all	1 Thes 4:6
declare to you by a word from the **L**,	1 Thes 4:15
are left until the coming of the **L**,	1 Thes 4:15
For the **L** himself will descend from	1 Thes 4:16
in the clouds to meet the **L** in the air,	1 Thes 4:17
and so we will always be with the **L**.	1 Thes 4:17
that the day of the **L** will come like a	1 Thes 5:2
salvation through our **L** Jesus Christ,	1 Thes 5:9
you in the **L** and admonish you,	1 Thes 5:12
at the coming of our **L** Jesus Christ.	1 Thes 5:23
under oath before the **L** to have this	1 Thes 5:27
The grace of our **L** Jesus Christ be	1 Thes 5:28
our Father and the **L** Jesus Christ:	2 Thes 1:1
our Father and the **L** Jesus Christ.	2 Thes 1:2
when the **L** Jesus is revealed from	2 Thes 1:7
do not obey the gospel of our **L** Jesus.	2 Thes 1:8
the presence of the **L** and from the	2 Thes 1:9

the name of our **L** Jesus may be 2 Thes 1:12
of our God and the **L** Jesus Christ. 2 Thes 1:12
the coming of our **L** Jesus Christ and 2 Thes 2:1
effect that the day of the **L** has come. 2 Thes 2:2
whom the **L** Jesus will kill with the 2 Thes 2:8
for you, brothers beloved by the **L**, 2 Thes 2:13
the glory of our **L** Jesus Christ. 2 Thes 2:14
Now may our **L** Jesus Christ 2 Thes 2:16
the word of the **L** may speed ahead 2 Thes 3:1
But the **L** is faithful. He will establish 2 Thes 3:3
have confidence in the **L** about you, 2 Thes 3:4
May the **L** direct your hearts to the 2 Thes 3:5
in the name of our **L** Jesus Christ, 2 Thes 3:6
encourage in the **L** Jesus Christ to 2 Thes 3:12
Now may the **L** of peace himself 2 Thes 3:16
in every way. The **L** be with you all. 2 Thes 3:16
The grace of our **L** Jesus Christ be 2 Thes 3:18
God the Father and Christ Jesus our **L**. 1 Tm 1:2
given me strength, Christ Jesus our **L**, 1 Tm 1:12
the grace of our **L** overflowed for me 1 Tm 1:14
sound words of our **L** Jesus Christ and 1 Tm 6:3
the appearing of our **L** Jesus Christ, 1 Tm 6:14
the King of kings and **L** of lords, 1 Tm 6:15
God the Father and Christ Jesus our **L**. 2 Tm 1:2
ashamed of the testimony about our **L**, 2 Tm 1:8
May the **L** grant mercy to the 2 Tm 1:16
may the **L** grant him to find mercy 2 Tm 1:18
to find mercy from the **L** on that Day! 2 Tm 1:18
for the **L** will give you understanding 2 Tm 2:7
"The **L** knows those who are his," 2 Tm 2:19
name of the **L** depart from iniquity." 2 Tm 2:19
who call on the **L** from a pure heart. 2 Tm 2:22
yet from them all the **L** rescued me. 2 Tm 3:11
crown of righteousness, which the **L**, 2 Tm 4:8
the **L** will repay him according to his 2 Tm 4:14
But the **L** stood by me and 2 Tm 4:17
The **L** will rescue me from every evil 2 Tm 4:18
The **L** be with your spirit. Grace be 2 Tm 4:22
God our Father and the **L** Jesus Christ. Phlm 1:3
you have toward the **L** Jesus and all the Phlm 1:5
to you, both in the flesh and in the **L**. Phlm 1:16
want some benefit from you in the **L**. Phlm 1:20
The grace of the **L** Jesus Christ be Phlm 1:25
L, laid the foundation of the earth in Heb 1:10
It was declared at first by the **L**, and it Heb 2:3
evident that our **L** was descended from Heb 7:14
"The **L** has sworn and will not change Heb 7:21
places, in the true tent that the **L** set up, Heb 8:2
the days are coming, declares the **L**, Heb 8:8
no concern for them, declares the **L**. Heb 8:9
of Israel after those days, declares the **L**: Heb 8:10
one his brother, saying, 'Know the **L**,' Heb 8:11
them after those days, declares the **L**: Heb 10:16
again, "The **L** will judge his people." Heb 10:30
regard lightly the discipline of the **L**, Heb 12:5
For the **L** disciplines the one he loves, Heb 12:6
without which no one will see the **L**. Heb 12:14
confidently say, "The **L** is my helper; Heb 13:6
again from the dead our **L** Jesus, Heb 13:20
a servant of God and of the **L** Jesus Christ, Jas 1:1
that he will receive anything from the **L**; Jas 1:7
you hold the faith in our **L** Jesus Christ, Jas 2:1
in our Lord Jesus Christ, the **L** of glory. Jas 2:1
With it we bless our **L** and Father, and Jas 3:9
Humble yourselves before the **L**, and he Jas 4:10
Instead you ought to say, "If the **L** wills, Jas 4:15
have reached the ears of the **L** of hosts. Jas 5:4
brothers, until the coming of the **L**. Jas 5:7
hearts, for the coming of the **L** is at hand. Jas 5:8
who spoke in the name of the **L**. Jas 5:10
and you have seen the purpose of the **L**, Jas 5:11
how the **L** is compassionate and Jas 5:11
him with oil in the name of the **L**. Jas 5:14
who is sick, and the **L** will raise him up. Jas 5:15
God and Father of our **L** Jesus Christ! 1 Pt 1:3
the word of the **L** remains forever." And 1 Pt 1:25
indeed you have tasted that the **L** is good. 1 Pt 2:3
Sarah obeyed Abraham, calling him **l**. 1 Pt 3:6
the eyes of the **L** are on the righteous, 1 Pt 3:12
the face of the **L** is against those who 1 Pt 3:12
your hearts regard Christ the **L** as holy, 1 Pt 3:15
the knowledge of God and of Jesus our **L**. 2 Pt 1:2
in the knowledge of our **L** Jesus Christ. 2 Pt 1:8
kingdom of our **L** and Savior Jesus 2 Pt 1:11
as our **L** Jesus Christ made clear to me. 2 Pt 1:14
and coming of our **L** Jesus Christ, 2 Pt 1:16
then the **L** knows how to rescue the 2 Pt 2:9
judgment against them before the **L**. 2 Pt 2:11
knowledge of our **L** and Savior Jesus 2 Pt 2:20
commandment of the **L** and Savior 2 Pt 3:2
that with the **L** one day is as a thousand 2 Pt 3:8
The **L** is not slow to fulfill his promise 2 Pt 3:9
But the day of the **L** will come like a 2 Pt 3:10
the patience of our **L** as salvation, 2 Pt 3:15
knowledge of our **L** and Savior Jesus 2 Pt 3:18
and deny our only Master and **L**, Jude 1:4
but said, "The **L** rebuke you." Jude 1:9
the **L** came with ten thousands of his Jude 1:14
of the apostles of our **L** Jesus Christ. Jude 1:17
the mercy of our **L** Jesus Christ that Jude 1:21
our Savior, through Jesus Christ our **L**, Jude 1:25
Alpha and the Omega," says the **L** God, Rv 1:8
"Holy, holy, holy, is the **L** God Almighty, Rv 4:8
"Worthy are you, our **L** and God, to Rv 4:11
out with a loud voice, "O Sovereign **L**, Rv 6:10
that stand before the **L** of the earth. Rv 11:4
and Egypt, where their **L** was crucified. Rv 11:8
the kingdom of our **L** and of his Christ, Rv 11:15
give thanks to you, **L** God Almighty, Rv 11:17
who die in the **L** from now on." "Blessed Rv 14:13
are your deeds, O **L** God the Almighty! Rv 15:3
Who will not fear, O **L**, and glorify your Rv 15:4
altar saying, "Yes, **L** God the Almighty, Rv 16:7
for he is **L** of lords and King of kings, Rv 17:14
for mighty is the **L** God who has judged Rv 18:8
For the **L** our God the Almighty reigns. Rv 19:6
written, King of kings and **L** of lords. Rv 19:16
its temple is the **L** God the Almighty Rv 21:22
or sun, for the **L** God will be their light, Rv 22:5
And the **L**, the God of the spirits of the Rv 22:6
coming soon." Amen. Come, **L** Jesus! Rv 22:20
The grace of the **L** Jesus be with all. Rv 22:21

LORD'S (136)

steal silver or gold from your **l** house? Gn 44:8
die, and we also will be my **l** servants." Gn 44:9
behold, we are my **l** servants, both we Gn 44:16
your servant speak a word in my **l** ears, Gn 44:18
spent. The herds of livestock are my **l**. Gn 47:18
you may know that the earth is the **L**. Ex 9:29
shall eat it in haste. It is the **L** Passover. Ex 12:11
say, 'It is the sacrifice of the **L** Passover, Ex 12:27
animals that are males shall be the **L**. Ex 13:12
and upward, shall give the **L** offering. Ex 30:14
when you give the **L** offering to make Ex 30:15
camp and said, "Who is on the **L** side? Ex 32:26
heart, let him bring the **L** contribution: Ex 35:5
and brought the **L** contribution to be Ex 35:21
brought it as the **L** contribution. Ex 35:24
is a most holy part of the **L** food offerings. Lv 2:3
a most holy part of the **L** food offerings. Lv 2:10
with a pleasing aroma. All fat is the **L**. Lv 3:16
any of the **L** commandments about Lv 4:2
that by the **L** commandments ought not Lv 4:13
that by the **L** commandments ought not Lv 4:27
the altar, on top of the **L** food offerings. Lv 4:35
this on the altar, on the **L** food offerings; Lv 5:12
that by the **L** commandments ought not Lv 5:17
generations, from the **L** food offerings. Lv 6:18
sacrifice of the **L** peace offerings while Lv 7:20
the sacrifice of the **L** peace offerings, Lv 7:21
hands shall bring the **L** food offerings. Lv 7:30
and of his sons from the **L** food offerings, Lv 7:35
that is left of the **L** food offerings, Lv 10:12
sons' due, from the **L** food offerings, Lv 10:13
For they offer the **L** food offerings, the Lv 21:6
come near to offer the **L** food offerings; Lv 21:21
the month at twilight, is the **L** Passover. Lv 23:5
besides the **L** Sabbaths and besides Lv 23:38
holy portion out of the **L** food offerings, Lv 24:9
dedicate; whether ox or sheep, it is the **L**. Lv 27:26
land or of the fruit of the trees, is the **L**; Lv 27:30
kept from bringing the **L** offering at its Nm 9:7
did not bring the **L** offering at its Nm 9:13
to Moses, "Is the **L** hand shortened? Nm 11:23
that all the **L** people were prophets, Nm 11:29
shall give the **L** contribution to Nm 18:28
of the first month is the **L** Passover, Nm 28:16
to execute the **L** vengeance on Midian. Nm 31:3
and the **L** tribute of sheep was 675. Nm 31:37
36,000, of which the **L** tribute was 72. Nm 31:38
30,500, of which the **L** tribute was 61. Nm 31:39
of which the **L** tribute was 32 persons. Nm 31:40
And we have brought the **L** offering, Nm 31:50
And the **L** anger was kindled on that Nm 32:10
And the **L** anger was kindled against Nm 32:13
because the **L** release has been Dt 15:2
They shall eat the **L** food offerings as Dt 18:1
But the **L** portion is his people, Jacob his Dt 32:9
the commander of the **L** army said to Jos 5:15
For it was the **L** doing to harden their Jos 11:20
pass over into the **L** land where the Jos 22:19
land where the **L** tabernacle stands, Jos 22:19
from the Ammonites shall be the **L**, Jgs 11:31
For the pillars of the earth are the **L**, 1 Sm 2:8
"Surely the **L** anointed is before him." 1 Sm 16:6
For the battle is the **L**, and he will 1 Sm 17:47
me and fight the **L** battles." For Saul 1 Sm 18:17
this thing to my lord, the **L** anointed, 1 Sm 24:6
him, seeing he is the **L** anointed." 1 Sm 24:6
my lord, for he is the **L** anointed.' 1 Sm 24:10
hand against the **L** anointed and be 1 Sm 26:9
out my hand against the **L** anointed. 1 Sm 26:11
watch over your lord, the **L** anointed. 1 Sm 26:16
out my hand against the **L** anointed. 1 Sm 26:23
your hand to destroy the **L** anointed?" 2 Sm 1:14
saying, 'I have killed the **L** anointed.'" 2 Sm 1:16
because he cursed the **L** anointed?" 2 Sm 19:21
Take your **l** servants and pursue him, 2 Sm 20:6
men of the **L** prophets by fifties 1 Kgs 18:13
that they should be the **L** people, 2 Kgs 11:17
he said, "The **L** arrow of victory, 2 Kgs 13:17
the king, all of them my **l** servants? 1 Chr 21:3
the glory of the LORD filled the **L** house. 2 Chr 7:2
that they should be the **L** people. 2 Chr 23:16
holy temple; the **L** throne is in heaven; Ps 11:4
The earth is the **L** and the fullness Ps 24:1
The heavens are the **L** heavens, but Ps 115:16
This is the **L** doing; it is marvelous in Ps 118:23
shall we sing the **L** song in a foreign Ps 137:4
do not despise the **L** discipline or be Prv 3:11
The **L** curse is on the house of the Prv 3:33
A just balance and scales are the **L**; all Prv 16:11
possess them in the **L** land as male and Is 14:2
has received from the **L** hand double for Is 40:2
This one will say, 'I am the **L**,' another Is 44:5
another will write on his hand, 'The **L**,' Is 44:5
Behold, the **L** hand is not shortened, that Is 59:1
to proclaim the year of the **L** favor, and Is 61:2
her branches, for they are not the **L**. Jer 5:10
"Stand in the gate of the **L** house, and Jer 7:2
because the **L** flock has been taken Jer 13:17
in the court of the **L** house and said to Jer 19:14
So I took the cup from the **L** hand, and Jer 25:17
Stand in the court of the **L** house, and Jer 26:2
the vessels of the **L** house will now Jer 27:16
this place all the vessels of the **L** house, Jer 28:3
the people in the **L** house you shall read Jer 36:6
the words of the LORD in the **L** house. Jer 36:8
entry of the New Gate of the **L** house. Jer 36:10
for this is the time of the **L** vengeance, Jer 51:6
Babylon was a golden cup in the **L** hand, Jer 51:7
for the **L** purposes against Babylon Jer 51:29
into the holy places of the **L** house.' Jer 51:51
breath of our nostrils, the **L** anointed, Lam 4:20
How can my **l** servant talk with my Dn 10:17
Esau, and the kingdom shall be the **L**. Ob 1:21
The cup in the **L** right hand will come Hab 2:16
on the day of the **L** sacrifice—"I will Zep 1:8
spoke to the people with the **L** message, Hg 1:13
the foundation of the **L** temple was laid, Hg 2:18
By saying that the **L** table may be Mal 1:7
you say that the **L** table is polluted, Mal 1:12
do. You cover the **L** altar with tears, Mal 2:13
this was the **L** doing, and it is Mt 21:42
this was the **L** doing, and it is Mk 12:11
death before he had seen the **L** Christ. Lk 2:26
to proclaim the year of the **L** favor." Lk 4:19
who sat at the **L** feet and listened to his Lk 10:39
we live or whether we die, we are the **L**. Rom 14:8
who by the **L** mercy is trustworthy. 1 Cor 7:25
For "the earth is the **L**, and the 1 Cor 10:26
it is not the **L** supper that you eat. 1 Cor 11:20
you proclaim the **L** death until he 1 Cor 11:26
not only in the **L** sight but also in 2 Cor 8:21
say not with the **L** authority but as a 2 Cor 11:17
apostles except James the **L** brother. Gal 1:19
And the **L** servant must not be 2 Tm 2:24
Be subject for the **L** sake to every 1 Pt 2:13
I was in the Spirit on the **L** day, and I Rv 1:10

LORDED (1)

Even their servants **l** it over the people. Neh 5:15

LORDLY (1)

to the potter"—the **l** price at which I Zec 11:13

LORDS (41)

and said, "My **l**, please turn aside to your Gn 19:2
And Lot said to them, "Oh, no, my **l**. Gn 19:18
your God is God of gods and Lord of **l**, Dt 10:17
the five **l** of the Philistines and all the Jgs 3:3
And the **l** of the Philistines came up to Jgs 16:5
Then the **l** of the Philistines brought up Jgs 16:8
sent and called the **l** of the Philistines, Jgs 16:18
his heart." Then the **l** of the Philistines Jgs 16:18
Now the **l** of the Philistines gathered to Jgs 16:23
All the **l** of the Philistines were there, Jgs 16:27
house fell upon the **l** and upon all the Jgs 16:30
together all the **l** of the Philistines 1 Sm 5:8
together all the **l** of the Philistines 1 Sm 5:11
the number of the **l** of the Philistines, 1 Sm 6:4
plague was on all of you and on your **l**. 1 Sm 6:4
and the **l** of the Philistines went after 1 Sm 6:12
And when the five **l** of the Philistines 1 Sm 6:16
the Philistines belonging to the five **l**, 1 Sm 6:18
the **l** of the Philistines went up against 1 Sm 7:7
As the **l** of the Philistines were passing 1 Sm 29:2

the **l** do not approve of you. 1 Sm 29:6
not displease the **l** of the Philistines." 1 Sm 29:7
his counselors and his **l** and all Israel Ezr 8:25
Give thanks to the Lord of **l**, for his Ps 136:3
the **l** of the nations have struck down its Is 16:8
other **l** besides you have ruled over us, Is 26:13
out, and roll in ashes, you **l** of the flock, Jer 25:34
nor escape for the **l** of the flock. Jer 25:35
and the wail of the **l** of the flock! Jer 25:36
My counselors and my **l** sought me, and Dn 4:36
for a thousand of his **l** and drank wine in Dn 5:1
be brought, that the king and his **l**, Dn 5:2
God in Jerusalem, and the king and his **l**, Dn 5:3
color changed, and his **l** were perplexed. Dn 5:9
of the words of the king and his **l**, Dn 5:10
in before you, and you and your **l**, Dn 5:23
own signet and with the signet of his **l**, Dn 6:17
there are many "gods" and many "**l**"— 1 Cor 8:5
the King of kings and Lord of **l**, 1 Tm 6:15
for he is Lord of **l** and King of kings, Rv 17:14
written, King of kings and Lord of **l**. Rv 19:16

LORDSHIP (1)
of the Gentiles exercise **l** over them, Lk 22:25

LOSE (20)
and you **l** your life with the lives of Jgs 18:25
alive, and not **l** some of the animals." 1 Kgs 18:5
do not **l** sight of these—keep sound Prv 3:21
a time to seek, and a time to **l**; a time to Eccl 3:6
is better that you **l** one of your members Mt 5:29
is better that you **l** one of your members Mt 5:30
Whoever finds his life will **l** it, and Mt 10:39
you, he will by no means **l** his reward." Mt 10:42
For whoever would save his life will **l** it, Mt 16:25
For whoever would save his life will **l** it, Mk 8:35
to Christ will by no means **l** his reward. Mk 9:41
For whoever would save his life will **l** it, Lk 9:24
seeks to preserve his life will **l** it, Lk 17:33
ought always to pray and not **l** heart. Lk 18:1
that I should **l** nothing of all that he has Jn 6:39
by the mercy of God, we do not **l** heart. 2 Cor 4:1
So we do not **l** heart. Though our 2 Cor 4:16
I ask you not to **l** heart over what I am Eph 3:13
lawless people and **l** your own stability. 2 Pt 3:17
that you may not **l** what we have worked 2 Jn 1:8

LOSES (9)
your brother's, which he **l** and you find; Dt 22:3
and whoever **l** his life for my sake will Mt 10:39
but whoever **l** his life for my sake will Mt 16:25
but whoever **l** his life for my sake and Mk 8:35
but whoever **l** his life for my sake will Lk 9:24
whole world and **l** or forfeits himself? Lk 9:25
having ten silver coins, if she **l** one coin, Lk 15:8
it, but whoever **l** his life will keep it. Lk 17:33
Whoever loves his life **l** it, and whoever Jn 12:25

LOSS (16)
bring to you. I bore the **l** of it myself. Gn 31:39
only he shall pay for the **l** of his time, Ex 21:19
and the **l** there was great on that day, 2 Sm 18:7
to be compared with the **l** to the king." Est 7:4
sit as a widow or know the **l** of children": Is 47:8
the **l** of children and widowhood shall Is 47:9
so that the king might suffer no **l**. Dn 6:2
Being at a **l** how to investigate these Acts 25:20
will be with injury and much **l**, Acts 27:10
Crete and incurred this injury and **l**. Acts 27:21
there will be no **l** of life among you, Acts 27:22
work is burned up, he will suffer **l**, 1 Cor 3:15
so that you suffered no **l** through us. 2 Cor 7:9
had, I counted as **l** for the sake of Christ. Phil 3:7
I count everything as **l** because of the Phil 3:8
I have suffered the **l** of all things and Phil 3:8

LOST (39)
for a cloak, or for any kind of **l** thing, Ex 22:9
or has found something **l** and lied about Lv 6:3
to him or the **l** thing that he found Lv 6:4
or with any **l** thing of your brother's, Dt 22:3
of the people of Dan was **l** to them, Jos 19:47
donkeys of Kish, Saul's father, were **l**. 1 Sm 9:3
donkeys that were **l** three days ago, 1 Sm 9:20
Foreigners **l** heart and came 2 Sm 22:46
army like the army that you have **l**, 1 Kgs 20:25
all way of escape will be **l** to them, and Jb 11:20
Foreigners **l** heart and came trembling Ps 18:45
I have gone astray like a **l** sheep; seek Ps 119:176
and those riches were **l** in a bad Eccl 5:14
and not one among them has **l** its young. Sg 4:2
not one among them has **l** its young. Sg 6:6
For I am **l**; for I am a man of unclean lips, Is 6:5
and those who were **l** in the land of Is 27:13
"My people have been **l** sheep. Their Jer 50:6
closed over my head; I said, 'I am **l**.' Lam 3:54
she waited in vain, that her hope was **l**, Ezk 19:5
back, the **l** you have not sought, Ezk 34:4
I will seek the **l**, and I will bring back Ezk 34:16
bones are dried up, and our hope is **l**; Ezk 37:11
salt of the earth, but if salt has **l** its taste, Mt 5:13
but go rather to the **l** sheep of the house Mt 10:6
was sent only to the **l** sheep of the house Mt 15:24
is good, but if the salt has **l** its saltiness, Mk 9:50
"Salt is good, but if salt has **l** its taste, Lk 14:34
a hundred sheep, if he has **l** one of them, Lk 15:4
country, and go after the one that is **l**, Lk 15:4
for I have found my sheep that was **l**.' Lk 15:6
for I have found the coin that I had **l**.' Lk 15:9
is alive again; he was **l**, and is found.' Lk 15:24
and is alive; he was **l**, and is found.'" Lk 15:32
of Man came to seek and to save the **l**." Lk 19:10
fragments, that nothing may be **l**." Jn 6:12
one of them has been **l** except the son of Jn 17:12
whom you gave me I have **l** not one." Jn 18:9
and your splendors are **l** to you, Rv 18:14

LOT (94)
and Haran; and Haran fathered **L**. Gn 11:27
Abram his son and **L** the son of Haran, Gn 11:31
had told him, and **L** went with him. Gn 12:4
Sarai his wife, and **L** his brother's son, Gn 12:5
and all that he had, and **L** with him, Gn 13:1
And **L**, who went with Abram, also had Gn 13:5
Then Abram said to **L**, "Let there be no Gn 13:8
And **L** lifted up his eyes and saw that Gn 13:10
So **L** chose for himself all the Jordan Gn 13:11
Jordan Valley, and **L** journeyed east. Gn 13:11
while **L** settled among the cities of the Gn 13:12
after **L** had separated from him, Gn 13:14
They also took **L**, the son of Abram's Gn 14:12
back his kinsman **L** with his Gn 14:16
and **L** was sitting in the gate of Sodom. Gn 19:1
When **L** saw them, he rose to meet them Gn 19:1
And they called to **L**, "Where are the Gn 19:5
L went out to the men at the entrance, Gn 19:6
they pressed hard against the man **L**, Gn 19:9
hands and brought **L** into the house Gn 19:10
Then the men said to **L**, "Have you Gn 19:12
So **L** went out and said to his Gn 19:14
morning dawned, the angels urged **L**, Gn 19:15
And **L** said to them, "Oh, no, my lords. Gn 19:18
on the earth when **L** came to Zoar. Gn 19:23
Abraham and sent **L** out of the Gn 19:29
the cities in which **L** had lived. Gn 19:29
Now **L** went up out of Zoar and lived in Gn 19:30
the daughters of **L** became pregnant Gn 19:36
one **l** for the LORD and the other lot for Lv 16:8
lot for the LORD and the other **l** for Azazel. Lv 16:8
the goat on which the **l** fell for the LORD Lv 16:9
goat on which the **l** fell for Azazel shall Lv 16:10
But the land shall be divided by **l**. Nm 26:55
divided according to **l** between the Nm 26:56
the land by **l** according to your Nm 33:54
Wherever the **l** falls for anyone, that Nm 33:54
is the land that you shall inherit by **l**, Nm 34:13
land for inheritance by **l** to the people Nm 36:2
away from the **l** of our inheritance. Nm 36:3
Ar to the people of **L** for a possession.' Dt 2:9
given it to the sons of **L** for a possession.' Dt 2:19
the LORD takes by **l** shall come near by Jos 7:14
Their inheritance was by **l**, just as the Jos 14:2
given me but one **l** and one portion as Jos 17:14
The **l** of the tribe of the people of Jos 18:11
The second **l** came out for Simeon, for Jos 19:1
The third **l** came up for the people of Jos 19:10
The fourth **l** came out for Issachar, for Jos 19:17
The fifth **l** came out for the tribe of the Jos 19:24
The sixth **l** came out for the people of Jos 19:32
The seventh **l** came out for the tribe of Jos 19:40
Israel distributed by **l** at Shiloh before Jos 19:51
The **l** came out for the clans of the Jos 21:4
the priest received by **l** from the tribes of Jos 21:4
Kohathites received by **l** from the clans Jos 21:5
Gershonites received by **l** from the clans Jos 21:6
people of Israel gave by **l** to the Levites, Jos 21:8
of Levi; since the **l** fell to them first. Jos 21:10
to Gibeah: we will go up against it by **l**, Jgs 20:9
the tribe of Benjamin was taken by **l**. 1 Sm 10:20
clan of the Matrites was taken by **l**; 1 Sm 10:21
Saul the son of Kish was taken by **l**. 1 Sm 10:21
"Cast the **l** between me and my son 1 Sm 14:42
Kohathites, for theirs was the first **l**, 1 Chr 6:54
Kohathites were given by **l** out of the 1 Chr 6:61
They gave by **l** out of the tribes of 1 Chr 6:65
They divided them by **l**, all alike, for 1 Chr 24:5
The first **l** fell to Jehoiarib, the second 1 Chr 24:7
The first **l** fell for Asaph to Joseph; the 1 Chr 25:9
The **l** for the east fell to Shelemiah. 1 Chr 26:14
and his **l** came out for the north. 1 Chr 26:14
portion and my cup; you hold my **l**. Ps 16:5
are the strong arm of the children of **L**. Ps 83:8
throw in your **l** among us; we will all Prv 1:14
The **l** is cast into the lap, but its every Prv 16:33
The **l** puts an end to quarrels and Prv 18:18
rejoice in his work, for that is his **l**. Eccl 3:22
God has given him, for this is his **l**. Eccl 5:18
and to accept his **l** and rejoice in his Eccl 5:19
us, and the **l** of those who plunder us. Is 17:14
He has cast the **l** for them; his hand has Is 34:17
is your portion; they, they, are your **l**; Is 57:6
of dishonor they shall rejoice in their **l**; Is 61:7
This is your **l**, the portion I have Jer 13:25
So they cast lots, and the **l** fell on Jonah. Jon 1:7
to cast the line by **l** in the assembly of the Mi 2:5
This shall be their **l** in return for their Zep 2:10
he was chosen by **l** to enter the temple of Lk 1:9
was in the days of **L**—they were eating Lk 17:28
on the day when **L** went out from Lk 17:29
for them, and the **l** fell on Matthias, Acts 1:26
have neither part nor **l** in this matter, Acts 8:21
and if he rescued righteous **L**, greatly 2 Pt 2:7

LOT'S (3)
and the herdsmen of **L** livestock. Gn 13:7
But **L** wife, behind him, looked back, Gn 19:26
Remember **L** wife. Lk 17:32

LOTAN (5)
of the land: **L**, Shobal, Zibeon, Anah, Gn 36:20
The sons of **L** were Hori and Hemam; Gn 36:22
the chiefs **L**, Shobal, Zibeon, Anah, Gn 36:29
L, Shobal, Zibeon, Anah, Dishon, 1 Chr 1:38
The sons of **L**: Hori and Hemam; and 1 Chr 1:39

LOTAN'S (2)
and Hemam; and **L** sister was Timna. Gn 36:22
Hemam; and **L** sister was Timna. 1 Chr 1:39

LOTS (25)
And Aaron shall cast **l** over the two Lv 16:8
And I will cast **l** for you here before the Jos 18:6
And I will cast **l** for you here before the Jos 18:8
and Joshua cast **l** for them in Shiloh Jos 18:10
his younger brother alike, cast **l**, 1 Chr 24:31
And they cast **l** for their duties, small 1 Chr 25:8
And they cast **l** by fathers' houses, 1 Chr 26:13
They cast **l** also for his son 1 Chr 26:14
have likewise cast **l** for the wood Neh 10:34
rest of the people cast **l** to bring one out Neh 11:1
they cast **l**) before Haman day after day; Est 3:7
them, and had cast Pur (that is, cast **l**), Est 9:24
You would even cast **l** over the fatherless, Jb 6:27
them, and for my clothing they cast **l**. Ps 22:18
and have cast **l** for my people, and have Jl 3:3
his gates and cast **l** for Jerusalem, Ob 1:11
said to one another, "Come, let us cast **l**, Jon 1:7
evil has come upon us." So they cast **l**, Jon 1:7
for her honored men **l** were cast, and all Na 3:10
garments among them by casting **l**. Mt 27:35
among them, casting **l** for them, Mk 15:24
do." And they cast **l** to divide his Lk 23:34
but cast **l** for it to see whose it shall be." Jn 19:24
my clothing they cast **l**." So the soldiers Jn 19:24
And they cast **l** for them, and the lot Acts 1:26

LOTUS (2)
Under the **l** plants he lies, in the shelter Jb 40:21
For his shade the **l** trees cover him; the Jb 40:22

LOUD (77)
with me, and I cried out with a **l** voice. Gn 39:14
mountain and a very **l** trumpet blast, Ex 19:16
you shall sound the **l** trumpet on the Lv 25:9
all the congregation raised a **l** cry, Nm 14:1
and the thick darkness, with a **l** voice; Dt 5:22
to all the men of Israel in a **l** voice: Dt 27:14
"Then **l** beat the horses' hoofs with the Jgs 5:22
Samuel, she cried out with a **l** voice. 1 Sm 28:12
face, and the king cried with a **l** voice, 2 Sm 19:4
the assembly of Israel with a **l** voice, 1 Kgs 8:55
called out in a **l** voice in the 2 Kgs 18:28
and made **l** music on harps and 1 Chr 15:28
the LORD with a **l** voice and with 2 Chr 15:14
the God of Israel, with a very **l** voice. 2 Chr 20:19
shouted it with a **l** voice in the 2 Chr 32:18
wept with a **l** voice when they saw the Ezr 3:12
the assembly answered with a **l** voice, Ezr 10:12
and they cried with a **l** voice to the LORD Neh 9:4
and he cried out with a **l** and bitter cry. Est 4:1
skillfully on the strings, with **l** shouts. Ps 33:3
peoples! Shout to God with **l** songs of joy! Ps 47:1
Because of my **l** groaning my bones Ps 102:5
praise him with **l** clashing cymbals! Ps 150:5
She is **l** and wayward; her feet do not Prv 7:11
The woman Folly is **l**; she is seductive Prv 9:13
blesses his neighbor with a **l** voice, Prv 27:14
called out in a **l** voice in the language Is 36:13
they cry in my ears with a **l** voice, Ezk 8:18
Then he cried in my ears with a **l** voice, Ezk 9:1
and cried out with a **l** voice and said, Ezk 11:13
Quarter, a **l** crash from the hills. Zep 1:10

he will exult over you with **l** singing. Zep 3:17
in Ramah, weeping and **l** lamentation, Mt 2:18
out his angels with a **l** trumpet call, Mt 24:31
hour Jesus cried out with a **l** voice, Mt 27:46
out again with a **l** voice and yielded up Mt 27:50
him and crying out with a **l** voice, Mk 1:26
And crying out with a **l** voice, he said, Mk 5:7
ninth hour Jesus cried with a **l** voice, Mk 15:34
And Jesus uttered a **l** cry and breathed Mk 15:37
and she exclaimed with a **l** cry, "Blessed Lk 1:42
demon, and he cried out with a **l** voice, Lk 4:33
down before him and said with a **l** voice, Lk 8:28
back, praising God with a **l** voice; Lk 17:15
and praise God with a **l** voice for all the Lk 19:37
demanding with **l** cries that he should Lk 23:23
Then Jesus, calling out with a **l** voice, Lk 23:46
these things, he cried out with a **l** voice, Jn 11:43
cried out with a **l** voice and stopped Acts 7:57
to his knees he cried out with a **l** voice, Acts 7:60
were possessed, crying with a **l** voice, Acts 8:7
said in a **l** voice, "Stand upright on Acts 14:10
But Paul cried with a **l** voice, "Do not Acts 16:28
his defense, Festus said with a **l** voice, Acts 26:24
and supplications, with **l** cries and tears, Heb 5:7
For, speaking **l** boasts of folly, they 2 Pt 2:18
heard behind me a **l** voice like a trumpet Rv 1:10
a strong angel proclaiming with a **l** voice, Rv 5:2
saying with a **l** voice, "Worthy is the Rv 5:12
They cried out with a **l** voice, "O Rv 6:10
and he called with a **l** voice to the four Rv 7:2
and crying out with a **l** voice, "Salvation Rv 7:10
an eagle crying with a **l** voice as it flew Rv 8:13
and called out with a **l** voice, like a lion Rv 10:3
Then they heard a **l** voice from heaven Rv 11:12
and there were **l** voices in heaven, Rv 11:15
And I heard a **l** voice in heaven, saying, Rv 12:10
waters and like the sound of **l** thunder. Rv 14:2
And he said with a **l** voice, "Fear God Rv 14:7
followed them, saying with a **l** voice, Rv 14:9
calling with a **l** voice to him who sat on Rv 14:15
and he called with a **l** voice to the one Rv 14:18
Then I heard a **l** voice from the temple Rv 16:1
and a **l** voice came out of the temple, Rv 16:17
what seemed to be the **l** voice of a great Rv 19:1
and with a **l** voice he called to all the Rv 19:17
And I heard a **l** voice from the throne Rv 21:3

LOUD-MOUTHED (1)
they are **l** boasters, showing favoritism Jude 1:16

LOUDER (2)
sound of the trumpet grew **l** and louder, Ex 19:19
sound of the trumpet grew louder and **l**, Ex 19:19

LOUDLY (5)
who should play **l** on musical 1 Chr 15:16
roared against him; they have roared **l**. Jer 2:15
The king called **l** to bring in the Dn 5:7
people weeping and wailing **l**. Mk 5:38
and I began to weep **l** because no one was Rv 5:4

LOVE (550)
son, your only son Isaac, whom you **l**, Gn 22:2
and show steadfast **l** to my master Gn 24:12
have shown steadfast **l** to my master." Gn 24:14
forsaken his steadfast **l** and his Gn 24:27
to show steadfast **l** and faithfulness to Gn 24:49
for me delicious food, such as I **l**, Gn 27:4
days because of the **l** he had for her. Gn 29:20
for now my husband will **l** me." Gn 29:32
the deeds of steadfast **l** and all the Gn 32:10
showed him steadfast **l** and gave him Gn 39:21
led in your steadfast **l** the people whom Ex 15:13
but showing steadfast **l** to thousands of Ex 20:6
thousands of those who **l** me and keep Ex 20:6
if the slave plainly says, 'I **l** my master, Ex 21:5
in steadfast **l** and faithfulness, Ex 34:6
keeping steadfast **l** for thousands, Ex 34:7
but you shall **l** your neighbor as Lv 19:18
you, and you shall **l** him as yourself, Lv 19:34
to anger and abounding in steadfast **l**, Nm 14:18
to the greatness of your steadfast **l**, Nm 14:19
but showing steadfast **l** to thousands of Dt 5:10
thousands of those who **l** me and keep Dt 5:10
You shall **l** the LORD your God with all Dt 6:5
that the LORD set his **l** on you and chose Dt 7:7
covenant and steadfast **l** with those who Dt 7:9
love with those who **l** him and keep his Dt 7:9
and the steadfast **l** that he swore Dt 7:12
He will **l** you, bless you, and multiply Dt 7:13
God, to walk in all his ways, to **l** him, Dt 10:12
set his heart in **l** on your fathers and Dt 10:15
L the sojourner, therefore, for you were Dt 10:19
"You shall therefore **l** the LORD your God Dt 11:1
you today, to **l** the LORD your God, Dt 11:13
to know whether you **l** the LORD your Dt 13:3
so that you will **l** the LORD your God with Dt 30:6
commanded you, to **l** the LORD your God, Jos 22:5
therefore, to **l** the LORD your God. Jos 23:11
did not show steadfast **l** to the family of Jgs 8:35
"You only hate me; you do not **l** me. Jgs 14:16
said to him, "How can you say, 'I **l** you,' Jgs 16:15
in you, and all his servants **l** you. 1 Sm 18:22
show me the steadfast **l** of the LORD, 1 Sm 20:14
off your steadfast **l** from my house 1 Sm 20:15
David swear again by his **l** for him, 1 Sm 20:17
your **l** to me was extraordinary, 2 Sm 1:26
surpassing the **l** of women. 2 Sm 1:26
LORD show steadfast **l** and faithfulness 2 Sm 2:6
I keep showing steadfast **l** to the house 2 Sm 3:8
but my steadfast **l** will not depart 2 Sm 7:15
me?" Amnon said to him, "I **l** Tamar, 2 Sm 13:4
was greater than the **l** with which he 2 Sm 13:15
show steadfast **l** and faithfulness 2 Sm 15:20
because you **l** those who hate you and 2 Sm 19:6
hate you and hate those who **l** you. 2 Sm 19:6
and shows steadfast **l** to his anointed, 2 Sm 22:51
great and steadfast **l** to your servant 1 Kgs 3:6
great and steadfast **l** and have given 1 Kgs 3:6
and showing steadfast **l** to your 1 Kgs 8:23
gods." Solomon clung to these in **l**. 1 Kgs 11:2
for his steadfast **l** endures forever! 1 Chr 16:34
for his steadfast **l** endures forever. 1 Chr 16:41
not take my steadfast **l** from him, 1 Chr 17:13
great and steadfast **l** to David my 2 Chr 1:8
for his steadfast **l** endures forever," 2 Chr 5:13
and showing steadfast **l** to your 2 Chr 6:14
Remember your steadfast **l** for David 2 Chr 6:42
for his steadfast **l** endures forever." 2 Chr 7:3
—for his steadfast **l** endures forever— 2 Chr 7:6
help the wicked and **l** those who hate 2 Chr 19:2
for his steadfast **l** endures forever." 2 Chr 20:21
for his steadfast **l** endures forever Ezr 3:11
to me his steadfast **l** before the king and Ezr 7:28
to us his steadfast **l** before the kings of Ezr 9:9
covenant and steadfast **l** with those who Neh 1:5
love with those who **l** him and keep his Neh 1:5
to anger and abounding in steadfast **l**, Neh 9:17
who keeps covenant and steadfast **l**, Neh 9:32
to the greatness of your steadfast **l**. Neh 13:22
have granted me life and steadfast **l**, Jb 10:12
for correction or for his land or for **l**, Jb 37:13
are they the pinions and plumage of **l**? Jb 39:13
How long will you **l** vain words and seek Ps 4:2
the abundance of your steadfast **l**, Ps 5:7
that those who **l** your name may exult in Ps 5:11
save me for the sake of your steadfast **l**. Ps 6:4
But I have trusted in your steadfast **l**; my Ps 13:5
Wondrously show your steadfast **l**, O Ps 17:7
I **l** you, O LORD, my strength. Ps 18:1
and shows steadfast **l** to his anointed, Ps 18:50
and through the steadfast **l** of the Most Ps 21:7
your mercy, O LORD, and your steadfast **l**, Ps 25:6
to your steadfast **l** remember me, Ps 25:7
the LORD are steadfast **l** and faithfulness, Ps 25:10
For your steadfast **l** is before my eyes, Ps 26:3
I **l** the habitation of your house and the Ps 26:8
rejoice and be glad in your steadfast **l**, Ps 31:7
servant; save me in your steadfast **l**! Ps 31:16
shown his steadfast **l** to me when Ps 31:21
L the LORD, all you his saints! The LORD Ps 31:23
but steadfast **l** surrounds the one who Ps 32:10
earth is full of the steadfast **l** of the LORD. Ps 33:5
on those who hope in his steadfast **l**, Ps 33:18
Let your steadfast **l**, O LORD, be upon us, Ps 33:22
Your steadfast **l**, O LORD, extends to the Ps 36:5
How precious is your steadfast **l**, O God! Ps 36:7
continue your steadfast **l** to those who Ps 36:10
concealed your steadfast **l** and your Ps 40:10
your steadfast **l** and your faithfulness Ps 40:11
may those who **l** your salvation say Ps 40:16
day the LORD commands his steadfast **l**, Ps 42:8
us for the sake of your steadfast **l**! Ps 44:26
A Maskil of the Sons of Korah; a **l** song. Ps 45:T
We have thought on your steadfast **l**, O Ps 48:9
me, O God, according to your steadfast **l**; Ps 51:1
The steadfast **l** of God endures all the Ps 52:1
You **l** evil more than good, and lying Ps 52:3
You **l** all words that devour, O deceitful Ps 52:4
trust in the steadfast **l** of God forever and Ps 52:8
out his steadfast **l** and his faithfulness! Ps 57:3
For your steadfast **l** is great to the Ps 57:10
My God in his steadfast **l** will meet me; Ps 59:10
of your steadfast **l** in the morning. Ps 59:16
the God who shows me steadfast **l**. Ps 59:17
appoint steadfast **l** and faithfulness to Ps 61:7
that to you, O Lord, belongs steadfast **l**. Ps 62:12
Because your steadfast **l** is better than Ps 63:3
or removed his steadfast **l** from me! Ps 66:20
of your steadfast **l** answer me in Ps 69:13
me, O LORD, for your steadfast **l** is good; Ps 69:16
and those who **l** his name shall dwell in Ps 69:36
May those who **l** your salvation say Ps 70:4
Has his steadfast **l** forever ceased? Are his Ps 77:8
Show us your steadfast **l**, O LORD, and Ps 85:7
Steadfast **l** and faithfulness meet; Ps 85:10
abounding in steadfast **l** to all who call Ps 86:5
For great is your steadfast **l** toward me; Ps 86:13
in steadfast **l** and faithfulness. Ps 86:15
Is your steadfast **l** declared in the grave, Ps 88:11
I will sing of the steadfast **l** of the LORD, Ps 89:1
said, "Steadfast **l** will be built up forever; Ps 89:2
steadfast **l** and faithfulness go before Ps 89:14
and my steadfast **l** shall be with Ps 89:24
My steadfast **l** I will keep for him Ps 89:28
from him my steadfast **l** or be false to Ps 89:33
Lord, where is your steadfast **l** of old, Ps 89:49
us in the morning with your steadfast **l**, Ps 90:14
"Because he holds fast to me in **l**, I will Ps 91:14
declare your steadfast **l** in the morning, Ps 92:2
"My foot slips," your steadfast **l**, Ps 94:18
O you who **l** the LORD, hate evil! He Ps 97:10
his steadfast **l** and faithfulness Ps 98:3
is good; his steadfast **l** endures forever, Ps 100:5
I will sing of steadfast **l** and justice; to Ps 101:1
crowns you with steadfast **l** and mercy, Ps 103:4
to anger and abounding in steadfast **l**. Ps 103:8
is his steadfast **l** toward those who Ps 103:11
But the steadfast **l** of the LORD is from Ps 103:17
good, for his steadfast **l** endures forever! Ps 106:1
the abundance of your steadfast **l**, Ps 106:7
to the abundance of his steadfast **l**. Ps 106:45
good, for his steadfast **l** endures forever! Ps 107:1
them thank the LORD for his steadfast **l**, Ps 107:8
thank the LORD for his steadfast **l**, Ps 107:15
thank the LORD for his steadfast **l**, Ps 107:21
thank the LORD for his steadfast **l**, Ps 107:31
consider the steadfast **l** of the LORD. Ps 107:43
For your steadfast **l** is great above the Ps 108:4
In return for my **l** they accuse me, but I Ps 109:4
me evil for good, and hatred for my **l**. Ps 109:5
because your steadfast **l** is good, Ps 109:21
Save me according to your steadfast **l**! Ps 109:26
of your steadfast **l** and your Ps 115:1
I **l** the LORD, because he has heard my Ps 116:1
For great is his steadfast **l** toward us, Ps 117:2
good; for his steadfast **l** endures forever! Ps 118:1
say, "His steadfast **l** endures forever." Ps 118:2
say, "His steadfast **l** endures forever." Ps 118:3
say, "His steadfast **l** endures forever." Ps 118:4
for his steadfast **l** endures forever! Ps 118:29
Let your steadfast **l** come to me, O Ps 119:41
in your commandments, which I **l**. Ps 119:47
your commandments, which I **l**, Ps 119:48
earth, O LORD, is full of your steadfast **l**; Ps 119:64
Let your steadfast **l** comfort me Ps 119:76
In your steadfast **l** give me life, that I Ps 119:88
Oh how I **l** your law! It is my Ps 119:97
the double-minded, but I **l** your law. Ps 119:113
dross, therefore I **l** your testimonies. Ps 119:119
servant according to your steadfast **l**, Ps 119:124
Therefore I **l** your commandments Ps 119:127
way with those who **l** your name. Ps 119:132
voice according to your steadfast **l**; Ps 119:149
Consider how I **l** your precepts! Give Ps 119:159
me life according to your steadfast **l**. Ps 119:159
abhor falsehood, but I **l** your law. Ps 119:163
peace have those who **l** your law; Ps 119:165
testimonies; I **l** them exceedingly. Ps 119:167
"May they be secure who **l** you! Ps 122:6
For with the LORD there is steadfast **l**, Ps 130:7
good, for his steadfast **l** endures forever. Ps 136:1
gods, for his steadfast **l** endures forever. Ps 136:2
lords, for his steadfast **l** endures forever; Ps 136:3
for his steadfast **l** endures forever; Ps 136:4
for his steadfast **l** endures forever; Ps 136:5
for his steadfast **l** endures forever; Ps 136:6
for his steadfast **l** endures forever; Ps 136:7
day, for his steadfast **l** endures forever; Ps 136:8
night, for his steadfast **l** endures forever; Ps 136:9
for his steadfast **l** endures forever; Ps 136:10
for his steadfast **l** endures forever; Ps 136:11
arm, for his steadfast **l** endures forever; Ps 136:12
two, for his steadfast **l** endures forever; Ps 136:13
of it, for his steadfast **l** endures forever; Ps 136:14
Sea, for his steadfast **l** endures forever; Ps 136:15
for his steadfast **l** endures forever; Ps 136:16
for his steadfast **l** endures forever; Ps 136:17
for his steadfast **l** endures forever; Ps 136:18
for his steadfast **l** endures forever; Ps 136:19
for his steadfast **l** endures forever; Ps 136:20
for his steadfast **l** endures forever; Ps 136:21
for his steadfast **l** endures forever. Ps 136:22
for his steadfast **l** endures forever; Ps 136:23
foes, for his steadfast **l** endures forever; Ps 136:24
for his steadfast **l** endures forever. Ps 136:25
for his steadfast **l** endures forever. Ps 136:26

for your steadfast **l** and your Ps 138:2
your steadfast **l**, O LORD, endures Ps 138:8
hear in the morning of your steadfast **l**, Ps 143:8
And in your steadfast **l** you will cut off Ps 143:12
he is my steadfast **l** and my fortress, my Ps 144:2
to anger and abounding in steadfast **l**. Ps 145:8
The LORD preserves all who **l** him, but Ps 145:20
in those who hope in his steadfast **l**. Ps 147:11
O simple ones, will you **l** being simple? Prv 1:22
Let not steadfast **l** and faithfulness Prv 3:3
keep you; **l** her, and she will guard you. Prv 4:6
delight; be intoxicated always in her **l**. Prv 5:19
let us take our fill of **l** till morning; Prv 7:18
morning; let us delight ourselves with **l**. Prv 7:18
I **l** those who love me, and those who Prv 8:17
I love those who **l** me, and those who Prv 8:17
an inheritance to those who **l** me, Prv 8:21
himself; all who hate me **l** death." Prv 8:36
reprove a wise man, and he will **l** you. Prv 9:8
stirs up strife, but **l** covers all offenses. Prv 10:12
good meet steadfast **l** and faithfulness. Prv 14:22
dinner of herbs where **l** is than a Prv 15:17
By steadfast **l** and faithfulness iniquity Prv 16:6
Whoever covers an offense seeks **l**, but Prv 17:9
and those who **l** it will eat its fruits. Prv 18:21
What is desired in a man is steadfast **l**, Prv 19:22
a man proclaims his own steadfast **l**, Prv 20:6
L not sleep, lest you come to poverty; Prv 20:13
Steadfast **l** and faithfulness preserve Prv 20:28
and by steadfast **l** his throne is upheld. Prv 20:28
Better is open rebuke than hidden **l**. Prv 27:5
a time to **l**, and a time to hate; a time for Eccl 3:8
Whether it is **l** or hate, man does not Eccl 9:1
Their **l** and their hate and their envy Eccl 9:6
Enjoy life with the wife whom you **l**, all Eccl 9:9
his mouth! For your **l** is better than wine; Sg 1:2
is oil poured out; therefore virgins **l** you. Sg 1:3
you; we will extol your **l** more than wine; Sg 1:4
love more than wine; rightly do they **l** you. Sg 1:4
I compare you, my **l**, to a mare among Sg 1:9
Behold, you are beautiful, my **l**; behold, Sg 1:15
so is my **l** among the young women. Sg 2:2
house, and his banner over me was **l**. Sg 2:4
me with apples, for I am sick with **l**. Sg 2:5
not stir up or awaken **l** until it pleases. Sg 2:7
"Arise, my **l**, my beautiful one, and come Sg 2:10
Arise, my **l**, my beautiful one, and come Sg 2:13
not stir up or awaken **l** until it pleases. Sg 3:5
was inlaid with **l** by the daughters Sg 3:10
Behold, you are beautiful, my **l**, behold, Sg 4:1
You are altogether beautiful, my **l**; there is Sg 4:7
How beautiful is your **l**, my sister, my Sg 4:10
How much better is your **l** than wine, Sg 4:10
Eat, friends, drink, and be drunk with **l**! Sg 5:1
"Open to me, my sister, my **l**, my dove, my Sg 5:2
beloved, that you tell him I am sick with **l**. Sg 5:8
You are beautiful as Tirzah, my **l**, lovely Sg 6:4
are in bloom. There I will give you my **l**. Sg 7:12
not stir up or awaken **l** until it pleases. Sg 8:4
upon your arm, for **l** is strong as death, Sg 8:6
Many waters cannot quench **l**, neither Sg 8:7
If a man offered for **l** all the wealth of his Sg 8:7
for my beloved my **l** song concerning his Is 5:1
a throne will be established in steadfast **l**, Is 16:5
but in **l** you have delivered my life from Is 38:17
in my eyes, and honored, and I **l** you, Is 43:4
but with everlasting **l** I will have Is 54:8
but my steadfast **l** shall not depart from Is 54:10
covenant, my steadfast, sure **l** for David. Is 55:3
minister to him, to **l** the name of the LORD, Is 56:6
For I the LORD **l** justice; I hate robbery and Is 61:8
I will recount the steadfast **l** of the LORD, Is 63:7
to the abundance of his steadfast **l**. Is 63:7
in his **l** and in his pity he redeemed them; Is 63:9
and be glad for her, all you who **l** her; Is 66:10
devotion of your youth, your **l** as a bride, Jer 2:2
well you direct your course to seek **l**! Jer 2:33
my people **l** to have it so, but what will Jer 5:31
I am the LORD who practices steadfast **l**, Jer 9:24
this people, my steadfast **l** and mercy, Jer 16:5
I have loved you with an everlasting **l**; Jer 31:3
You show steadfast **l** to thousands, but Jer 32:18
for his steadfast **l** endures forever!' Jer 33:11
The steadfast **l** of the LORD never Lam 3:22
to the abundance of his steadfast **l**; Lam 3:32
you, behold, you were at the age for **l**, Ezk 16:8
came to her into the bed of **l**, Ezk 23:17
covenant and steadfast **l** with those who Dn 9:4
love with those who **l** him and keep his Dn 9:4
in justice, in steadfast **l** and in mercy. Hos 2:19
l a woman who is loved by another man Hos 3:1
to other gods and **l** cakes of raisins." Hos 3:1
There is no faithfulness or steadfast **l**, Hos 4:1
to whoring; their rulers dearly **l** shame. Hos 4:18
Your **l** is like a morning cloud, like the Hos 6:4

For I desire steadfast **l** and not sacrifice, Hos 6:6
I will **l** them no more; all their princes Hos 9:15
righteousness; reap steadfast **l**; Hos 10:12
cords of kindness, with the bands of **l**, Hos 11:4
God, return, hold fast to **l** and justice, Hos 12:6
heal their apostasy; I will **l** them freely, Hos 14:4
to anger, and abounding in steadfast **l**; Jl 2:13
for so you **l** to do, O people of Israel!" Am 4:5
Hate evil, and **l** good, and establish Am 5:15
idols forsake their hope of steadfast **l**. Jon 2:8
to anger and abounding in steadfast **l**, Jon 4:2
you who hate the good and **l** the evil, who Mi 3:2
of you but to do justice, and to **l** kindness, Mi 6:8
because he delights in steadfast **l**. Mi 7:18
to Jacob and steadfast **l** to Abraham, Mi 7:20
with gladness; he will quiet you by his **l**; Zep 3:17
against one another, and **l** no false oath, Zec 8:17
feasts. Therefore **l** truth and peace. Zec 8:19
'You shall **l** your neighbor and hate Mt 5:43
L your enemies and pray for those who Mt 5:44
For if you **l** those who love you, what Mt 5:46
For if you love those who **l** you, what Mt 5:46
For they **l** to stand and pray in the Mt 6:5
he will hate the one and **l** the other, Mt 6:24
You shall **l** your neighbor as yourself." Mt 19:19
"You shall **l** the Lord your God with all Mt 22:37
You shall **l** your neighbor as yourself. Mt 22:39
and they **l** the place of honor at feasts Mt 23:6
increased, the **l** of many will grow cold. Mt 24:12
And you shall **l** the Lord your God Mk 12:30
'You shall **l** your neighbor as Mk 12:31
And to **l** him with all the heart and Mk 12:33
and to **l** one's neighbor as oneself, Mk 12:33
I say to you who hear, **L** your enemies, Lk 6:27
"If you **l** those who love you, what Lk 6:32
"If you love those who **l** you, what Lk 6:32
For even sinners **l** those who love them. Lk 6:32
For even sinners love those who **l** them. Lk 6:32
But **l** your enemies, and do good, and Lk 6:35
Now which of them will **l** him more?" Lk 7:42
"You shall **l** the Lord your God with all Lk 10:27
and neglect justice and the **l** of God. Lk 11:42
For you **l** the best seat in the Lk 11:43
he will hate the one and **l** the other, Lk 16:13
and **l** greetings in the marketplaces Lk 20:46
you do not have the **l** of God within you. Jn 5:42
God were your Father, you would **l** me, Jn 8:42
him, saying, "Lord, he whom you **l** is ill." Jn 11:3
I give to you, that you **l** one another: Jn 13:34
loved you, you also are to **l** one another. Jn 13:34
disciples, if you have **l** for one another." Jn 13:35
"If you **l** me, you will keep my Jn 14:15
and I will **l** him and manifest myself to Jn 14:21
my word, and my Father will **l** him, Jn 14:23
Whoever does not **l** me does not keep Jn 14:24
the world may know that I **l** the Father. Jn 14:31
me, so have I loved you. Abide in my **l**. Jn 15:9
you will abide in my **l**, Jn 15:10
commandments and abide in his **l**. Jn 15:10
that you **l** one another as I have loved Jn 15:12
Greater **l** has no one than this, that Jn 15:13
you, so that you will **l** one another. Jn 15:17
world, the world would **l** you as its own; Jn 15:19
that the **l** with which you have loved me Jn 17:26
do you **l** me more than these?" He said Jn 21:15
you know that I **l** you." He said to him, Jn 21:15
of John, do you **l** me?" He said to him, Jn 21:16
you know that I **l** you." He said to him, Jn 21:16
do you **l** me?" Peter was grieved because Jn 21:17
time, "Do you **l** me?" and he said to him, Jn 21:17
you know that I **l** you." Jesus said to Jn 21:17
because God's **l** has been poured into Rom 5:5
but God shows his **l** for us in that while Rom 5:8
that for those who **l** God all things Rom 8:28
shall separate us from the **l** of Christ? Rom 8:35
separate us from the **l** of God in Christ Rom 8:39
Let **l** be genuine. Abhor what is evil; Rom 12:9
L one another with brotherly Rom 12:10
one anything, except to **l** each other, Rom 13:8
"You shall **l** your neighbor as Rom 13:9
L does no wrong to a neighbor; Rom 13:10
therefore **l** is the fulfilling of the law. Rom 13:10
eat, you are no longer walking in **l**. Rom 14:15
Jesus Christ and by the **l** of the Spirit, Rom 15:30
has prepared for those who **l** him"— 1 Cor 2:9
rod, or with **l** in a spirit of gentleness? 1 Cor 4:21
"knowledge" puffs up, but **l** builds up. 1 Cor 8:1
of men and of angels, but have not **l**, 1 Cor 13:1
to remove mountains, but have not **l**, 1 Cor 13:2
my body to be burned, but have not **l**, 1 Cor 13:3
L is patient and kind; love does not 1 Cor 13:4
and kind; **l** does not envy or boast; 1 Cor 13:4
L bears all things, believes all things, 1 Cor 13:7
L never ends. As for prophecies, they 1 Cor 13:8
So now faith, hope, and **l** abide, these 1 Cor 13:13

three; but the greatest of these is **l**. 1 Cor 13:13
Pursue **l**, and earnestly desire the 1 Cor 14:1
Let all that you do be done in **l**. 1 Cor 16:14
If anyone has no **l** for the Lord, let 1 Cor 16:22
My **l** be with you all in Christ Jesus. 1 Cor 16:24
you know the abundant **l** that I have 2 Cor 2:4
So I beg you to reaffirm your **l** for him. 2 Cor 2:8
For the **l** of Christ controls us, 2 Cor 5:14
kindness, the Holy Spirit, genuine **l**; 2 Cor 6:6
and in our **l** for you—see that you 2 Cor 8:7
of others that your **l** also is genuine. 2 Cor 8:8
the churches of your **l** and of our 2 Cor 8:24
And why? Because I do not **l** you? 2 Cor 11:11
spent for your souls. If I **l** you more, 2 Cor 12:15
and the God of **l** and peace will be 2 Cor 13:11
Jesus Christ and the **l** of God and the 2 Cor 13:14
but only faith working through **l**. Gal 5:6
flesh, but through **l** serve one another. Gal 5:13
"You shall **l** your neighbor as Gal 5:14
But the fruit of the Spirit is **l**, joy, peace, Gal 5:22
be holy and blameless before him. In **l** Eph 1:4
Lord Jesus and your **l** toward all the Eph 1:15
because of the great **l** with which he Eph 2:4
you, being rooted and grounded in **l**, Eph 3:17
and to know the **l** of Christ that Eph 3:19
patience, bearing with one another in **l**, Eph 4:2
Rather, speaking the truth in **l**, we are Eph 4:15
grow so that it builds itself up in **l**. Eph 4:16
And walk in **l**, as Christ loved us and Eph 5:2
Husbands, **l** your wives, as Christ loved Eph 5:25
way husbands should **l** their wives as Eph 5:28
let each one of you **l** his wife as himself, Eph 5:33
be to the brothers, and **l** with faith, Eph 6:23
be with all who **l** our Lord Jesus Christ Eph 6:24
Lord Jesus Christ with **l** incorruptible. Eph 6:24
prayer that your **l** may abound more Phil 1:9
The latter do it out of **l**, knowing that I Phil 1:16
in Christ, any comfort from **l**, Phil 2:1
of the same mind, having the same **l**, Phil 2:2
my brothers, whom I **l** and long for, Phil 4:1
Jesus and of the **l** that you have for Col 1:4
made known to us your **l** in the Spirit. Col 1:8
be encouraged, being knit together in **l**, Col 2:2
And above all these put on **l**, which Col 3:14
Husbands, **l** your wives, and do not be Col 3:19
and labor of **l** and steadfastness of 1 Thes 1:3
of your faith and **l** and reported that 1 Thes 3:6
and abound in **l** for one another 1 Thes 3:12
concerning brotherly **l** you have 1 Thes 4:9
been taught by God to **l** one another, 1 Thes 4:9
put on the breastplate of faith and **l**, 1 Thes 5:8
very highly in **l** because of their 1 Thes 5:13
and the **l** of every one of you for one 2 Thes 1:3
they refused to **l** the truth and 2 Thes 2:10
your hearts to the **l** of God and to 2 Thes 3:5
of our charge is **l** that issues from a 1 Tm 1:5
with the faith and **l** that are in Christ 1 Tm 1:14
continue in faith and **l** and holiness, 1 Tm 2:15
example in speech, in conduct, in **l**, 1 Tm 4:12
For the **l** of money is a root of all 1 Tm 6:10
godliness, faith, **l**, steadfastness, 1 Tm 6:11
but of power and **l** and self-control. 2 Tm 1:7
in the faith and **l** that are in Christ 2 Tm 1:13
righteousness, faith, **l**, and peace, 2 Tm 2:22
in life, my faith, my patience, my **l**, 2 Tm 3:10
Demas, in **l** with this present world, 2 Tm 4:10
self-controlled, sound in faith, in **l**, Ti 2:2
the young women to **l** their husbands and Ti 2:4
to you. Greet those who **l** us in the faith. Ti 3:15
I hear of your **l** and of the faith Phlm 1:5
much joy and comfort from your **l**, Phlm 1:7
your work and the **l** that you showed Heb 6:10
up one another to **l** and good works, Heb 10:24
Let brotherly **l** continue. Heb 13:1
Keep your life free from **l** of money, and Heb 13:5
God has promised to those who **l** him. Jas 1:12
he has promised to those who **l** him? Jas 2:5
"You shall **l** your neighbor as yourself," Jas 2:8
you have not seen him, you **l** him. 1 Pt 1:8
to the truth for a sincere brotherly **l**, 1 Pt 1:22
l one another earnestly from a pure 1 Pt 1:22
Honor everyone. **L** the brotherhood. 1 Pt 2:17
unity of mind, sympathy, brotherly **l**, 1 Pt 3:8
For "Whoever desires to **l** life and see 1 Pt 3:10
since **l** covers a multitude of sins. 1 Pt 4:8
Greet one another with the kiss of **l**. 1 Pt 5:14
affection, and brotherly affection with **l**. 2 Pt 1:7
in him truly the **l** of God is perfected. 1 Jn 2:5
Do not **l** the world or the things in the 1 Jn 2:15
world, the **l** of the Father is not in him. 1 Jn 2:15
See what kind of **l** the Father has given 1 Jn 3:1
is the one who does not **l** his brother. 1 Jn 3:10
that we should **l** one another. 1 Jn 3:11
into life, because we **l** the brothers. 1 Jn 3:14
Whoever does not **l** abides in death. 1 Jn 3:14

By this we know **l**, that he laid down 1 Jn 3:16
him, how does God's **l** abide in him? 1 Jn 3:17
let us not **l** in word or talk but in deed 1 Jn 3:18
his Son Jesus Christ and **l** one another, 1 Jn 3:23
Beloved, let us **l** one another, for love is 1 Jn 4:7
let us love one another, for **l** is from God, 1 Jn 4:7
Anyone who does not **l** does not know 1 Jn 4:8
does not know God, because God is **l**. 1 Jn 4:8
In this the **l** of God was made manifest 1 Jn 4:9
In this is **l**, not that we have loved God 1 Jn 4:10
us, we also ought to **l** one another. 1 Jn 4:11
has ever seen God; if we **l** one another, 1 Jn 4:12
abides in us and his **l** is perfected in us. 1 Jn 4:12
and to believe the **l** that God has for 1 Jn 4:16
God is **l**, and whoever abides in love 1 Jn 4:16
and whoever abides in **l** abides in God, 1 Jn 4:16
By this is **l** perfected with us, so that we 1 Jn 4:17
There is no fear in **l**, but perfect love 1 Jn 4:18
fear in love, but perfect **l** casts out fear. 1 Jn 4:18
fears has not been perfected in **l**. 1 Jn 4:18
We **l** because he first loved us. 1 Jn 4:19
says, "I **l** God," and hates his brother, 1 Jn 4:20
he who does not **l** his brother whom he 1 Jn 4:20
he has seen cannot **l** God whom he has 1 Jn 4:20
loves God must also **l** his brother. 1 Jn 4:21
we know that we **l** the children of God, 1 Jn 5:2
when we **l** God and obey his 1 Jn 5:2
For this is the **l** of God, that we keep his 1 Jn 5:3
lady and her children, whom I **l** in truth, 2 Jn 1:1
Christ the Father's Son, in truth and **l**. 2 Jn 1:3
the beginning—that we **l** one another. 2 Jn 1:5
And this is **l**, that we walk according to 2 Jn 1:6
to the beloved Gaius, whom I **l** in truth. 3 Jn 1:1
who testified to your **l** before the church. 3 Jn 1:6
mercy, peace, and **l** be multiplied to you. Jude 1:2
These are blemishes on your **l** feasts, Jude 1:12
keep yourselves in the **l** of God, waiting Jude 1:21
you have abandoned the **l** you had at first. Rv 2:4
your **l** and faith and service and patient Rv 2:19
Those whom I **l**, I reprove and discipline, Rv 3:19

LOVE'S (1)
yet for **l** sake I prefer to appeal to you— Phlm 1:9

LOVED (101)
and she became his wife, and he **l** her. Gn 24:67
Isaac **l** Esau because he ate of his Gn 25:28
ate of his game, but Rebekah **l** Jacob. Gn 25:28
delicious food, such as his father **l**. Gn 27:14
Jacob **l** Rachel. And he said, "I will Gn 29:18
also, and he **l** Rachel more than Leah, Gn 29:30
He **l** the young woman and spoke Gn 34:3
Now Israel **l** Joseph more than any other Gn 37:3
saw that their father **l** him more than Gn 37:4
And because he **l** your fathers and chose Dt 4:37
wives, the one **l** and the other unloved, Dt 21:15
and both the **l** and the unloved have Dt 21:15
treat the son of the **l** as the firstborn in Dt 21:16
you, because the LORD your God **l** you. Dt 23:5
Yes, he **l** his people, all his holy ones were Dt 33:3
After this he **l** a woman in the Valley of Jgs 16:4
gave a double portion, because he **l** her, 1 Sm 1:5
his service. And Saul **l** him greatly, 1 Sm 16:21
and Jonathan **l** him as his own soul. 1 Sm 18:1
because he **l** him as his own soul. 1 Sm 18:3
But all Israel and Judah **l** David, for 1 Sm 18:16
Saul's daughter Michal **l** David. 1 Sm 18:20
that Michal, Saul's daughter, **l** him, 1 Sm 18:28
for he **l** him as he loved his own soul. 1 Sm 20:17
for he loved him as he **l** his own soul. 1 Sm 20:17
name Solomon. And the LORD **l** him 2 Sm 12:24
a time Amnon, David's son, **l** her. 2 Sm 13:1
the love with which he had **l** her. 2 Sm 13:15
Solomon **l** the LORD, walking in the 1 Kgs 3:3
of his father, for Hiram always **l** David. 1 Kgs 5:1
Because the LORD **l** Israel forever, he 1 Kgs 10:9
Now King Solomon **l** many foreign 1 Kgs 11:1
Because your God **l** Israel and would 2 Chr 9:8
Rehoboam **l** Maacah the daughter 2 Chr 11:21
in the fertile lands, for he **l** the soil. 2 Chr 26:10
the king **l** Esther more than all the Est 2:17
and those whom I **l** have turned against Jb 19:19
you have **l** righteousness and hated Ps 45:7
He **l** to curse; let curses come upon Ps 109:17
beautiful and pleasant you are, O **l** one, Sg 7:6
yourself with them, you have **l** their bed, Is 57:8
said, 'It is hopeless, for I have **l** foreigners, Jer 2:25
of heaven, which they have **l** and served, Jer 8:2
people: "They have **l** to wander thus; Jer 14:10
I have **l** you with an everlasting love; Jer 31:3
all those you **l** and all those you hated. Ezk 16:37
to tell it to you, for you are greatly **l**. Dn 9:23
he said to me, "O Daniel, man greatly **l**, Dn 10:11
And he said, "O man greatly **l**, fear not, Dn 10:19
a woman who is **l** by another man and Hos 3:1
You have **l** a prostitute's wages on all Hos 9:1
became detestable like the thing they **l**. Hos 9:10
was a trained calf that **l** to thresh, Hos 10:11
When Israel was a child, I **l** him, and Hos 11:1
"I have **l** you," says the LORD. But you Mal 1:2
"How have you **l** us?" "Is not Esau Mal 1:2
declares the LORD. "Yet I have **l** Jacob Mal 1:2
And Jesus, looking at him, **l** him, and Mk 10:21
are many, are forgiven—for she **l** much. Lk 7:47
"For God so **l** the world, that he gave his Jn 3:16
and people **l** the darkness rather than the Jn 3:19
Now Jesus **l** Martha and her sister and Jn 11:5
So the Jews said, "See how he **l** him!" Jn 11:36
for they **l** the glory that comes from Jn 12:43
having **l** his own who were in the world, Jn 13:1
were in the world, he **l** them to the end. Jn 13:1
One of his disciples, whom Jesus **l**, was Jn 13:23
just as I have **l** you, you also are to love Jn 13:34
he who loves me will be **l** by my Father, Jn 14:21
If you **l** me, you would have rejoiced, Jn 14:28
As the Father has **l** me, so have I loved Jn 15:9
the Father has loved me, so have I **l** you. Jn 15:9
you love one another as I have **l** you. Jn 15:12
because you have **l** me and have Jn 16:27
that you sent me and **l** them even as you Jn 17:23
me and loved them even as you **l** me. Jn 17:23
given me because you **l** me before the Jn 17:24
with which you have **l** me may be in Jn 17:26
the disciple whom he **l** standing nearby, Jn 19:26
the other disciple, the one whom Jesus **l**, Jn 20:2
disciple whom Jesus **l** therefore said to Jn 21:7
disciple whom Jesus **l** following them, Jn 21:20
in Rome who are **l** by God and called Rom 1:7
conquerors through him who **l** us. Rom 8:37
As it is written, "Jacob I **l**, but Esau I Rom 9:13
If I love you more, am I to be **l** less? 2 Cor 12:15
God, who **l** me and gave himself for me. Gal 2:20
of the great love with which he **l** us, Eph 2:4
as Christ **l** us and gave himself up for Eph 5:2
as Christ **l** the church and gave Eph 5:25
For we know, brothers **l** by God, that 1 Thes 1:4
who **l** us and gave us eternal 2 Thes 2:16
also to all who have **l** his appearing. 2 Tm 4:8
You have **l** righteousness and hated Heb 1:9
of Beor, who **l** gain from wrongdoing, 2 Pt 2:15
not that we have **l** God but that he 1 Jn 4:10
loved God but that he **l** us and sent his 1 Jn 4:10
Beloved, if God so **l** us, we also ought to 1 Jn 4:11
We love because he first **l** us. 1 Jn 4:19
feet and they will learn that I have **l** you. Rv 3:9
for they **l** not their lives even unto Rv 12:11

LOVELY (14)
How **l** are your tents, O Jacob, your Nm 24:5
"Saul and Jonathan, beloved and **l**! In 2 Sm 1:23
her beauty, for she was **l** to look at. Est 1:11
a beautiful figure and was **l** to look at, Est 2:7
How **l** is your dwelling place, O LORD of Ps 84:1
a **l** deer, a graceful doe. Let her breasts Prv 5:19
I am very dark, but **l**, O daughters of Sg 1:5
Your cheeks are **l** with ornaments, your Sg 1:10
for your voice is sweet, and your face is **l**. Sg 2:14
like a scarlet thread, and your mouth is **l**. Sg 4:3
as Tirzah, my love, **l** as Jerusalem, Sg 6:4
The **l** and delicately bred I will destroy, Jer 6:2
"In that day the **l** virgins and the young Am 8:13
is just, whatever is pure, whatever is **l**, Phil 4:8

LOVER (3)
therefore hear this, you **l** of pleasures, Is 47:8
not quarrelsome, not a **l** of money. 1 Tm 3:3
but hospitable, a **l** of good, self-controlled, Ti 1:8

LOVERS (25)
You have played the whore with many **l**; Jer 3:1
you have sat awaiting **l** like an Arab in Jer 3:2
Your **l** despise you; they seek your life. Jer 4:30
Abarim, for all your **l** are destroyed. Jer 22:20
and your **l** shall go into captivity; Jer 22:22
All your **l** have forgotten you; they care Jer 30:14
among all her **l** she has none to Lam 1:2
"I called to my **l**, but they deceived me; Lam 1:19
but you gave your gifts to all your **l**, Ezk 16:33
in your whorings with your **l**, Ezk 16:36
will gather all your **l** with whom you Ezk 16:37
and she lusted after her **l** the Assyrians, Ezk 23:5
I delivered her into the hands of her **l**, Ezk 23:9
up against you your **l** from whom you Ezk 23:22
For she said, 'I will go after my **l**, who Hos 2:5
She shall pursue her **l** but not overtake Hos 2:7
her lewdness in the sight of her **l**, Hos 2:10
my wages, which my **l** have given me.' Hos 2:12
and went after her **l** and forgot me, Hos 2:13
wandering alone; Ephraim has hired **l**. Hos 8:9
The Pharisees, who were **l** of money, Lk 16:14
For people will be **l** of self, lovers of 2 Tm 3:2
people will be lovers of self, **l** of money, 2 Tm 3:2
l of pleasure rather than lovers of God, 2 Tm 3:4
lovers of pleasure rather than **l** of God, 2 Tm 3:4

LOVES (70)
food for your father, such as he **l**. Gn 27:9
children, and his father **l** him.' Gn 44:20
it is because the LORD **l** you and is keeping Dt 7:8
and the widow, and **l** the sojourner, Dt 10:18
because he **l** you and your household, Dt 15:16
age, for your daughter-in-law who **l** you, Ru 4:15
"Because the LORD **l** his people, 2 Chr 2:11
the wicked and the one who **l** violence. Ps 11:5
LORD is righteous; he **l** righteous deeds; Ps 11:7
He **l** righteousness and justice; the earth Ps 33:5
there who desires life and **l** many days, Ps 34:12
For the LORD **l** justice; he will not Ps 37:28
for us, the pride of Jacob whom he **l**. Ps 47:4
tribe of Judah, Mount Zion, which he **l**. Ps 78:68
the LORD **l** the gates of Zion more than all Ps 87:2
The King in his might **l** justice. You Ps 99:4
is well tried, and your servant **l** it. Ps 119:140
bowed down; the LORD **l** the righteous. Ps 146:8
for the LORD reproves him whom he **l**, as Prv 3:12
Whoever **l** discipline loves knowledge, Prv 12:1
Whoever loves discipline **l** knowledge, Prv 12:1
but he who **l** him is diligent to Prv 13:24
but he **l** him who pursues Prv 15:9
and he **l** him who speaks what is right. Prv 16:13
A friend **l** at all times, and a brother is Prv 17:17
Whoever **l** transgression loves strife; Prv 17:19
Whoever loves transgression **l** strife; Prv 17:19
Whoever gets sense **l** his own soul; he Prv 19:8
Whoever **l** pleasure will be a poor Prv 21:17
he who **l** wine and oil will not be rich. Prv 21:17
He who **l** purity of heart, and whose Prv 22:11
He who **l** wisdom makes his father glad, Prv 29:3
He who **l** money will not be satisfied Eccl 5:10
nor he who **l** wealth with his income; Eccl 5:10
Tell me, you whom my soul **l**, where you Sg 1:7
by night I sought him whom my soul **l**; Sg 3:1
squares; I will seek him whom my soul **l**. Sg 3:2
"Have you seen him whom my soul **l**?" Sg 3:3
them when I found him whom my soul **l**. Sg 3:4
Everyone **l** a bribe and runs after gifts. Is 1:23
The LORD **l** him; he shall perform his Is 48:14
even as the LORD **l** the children of Israel, Hos 3:1
are false balances, he **l** to oppress. Hos 12:7
the sanctuary of the LORD, which he **l**, Mal 2:11
Whoever **l** father or mother more than Mt 10:37
and whoever **l** son or daughter more Mt 10:37
for he **l** our nation, and he is the one who Lk 7:5
But he who is forgiven little, **l** little." Lk 7:47
The Father **l** the Son and has given all Jn 3:35
For the Father **l** the Son and shows him Jn 5:20
For this reason the Father **l** me, because Jn 10:17
Whoever **l** his life loses it, and whoever Jn 12:25
and keeps them, he it is who **l** me. Jn 14:21
And he who **l** me will be loved by my Jn 14:21
Jesus answered him, "If anyone **l** me, he Jn 14:23
for the Father himself **l** you, because Jn 16:27
for the one who **l** another has fulfilled Rom 13:8
But if anyone **l** God, he is known by 1 Cor 8:3
compulsion, for God **l** a cheerful giver. 2 Cor 9:7
bodies. He who **l** his wife loves himself. Eph 5:28
bodies. He who loves his wife **l** himself. Eph 5:28
For the Lord disciplines the one he **l**, Heb 12:6
Whoever **l** his brother abides in the 1 Jn 2:10
in the world. If anyone **l** the world, 1 Jn 2:15
and whoever **l** has been born of God and 1 Jn 4:7
whoever **l** God must also love his 1 Jn 4:21
and everyone who **l** the Father loves 1 Jn 5:1
who loves the Father **l** whoever has been 1 Jn 5:1
To him who **l** us and has freed us from Rv 1:5
and everyone who **l** and practices Rv 22:15

LOVESICK (1)
"How **l** is your heart, declares the Lord Ezk 16:30

LOVING (8)
you to do, **l** the LORD your God, Dt 11:22
by **l** the LORD your God and by walking Dt 19:9
you today, by **l** the LORD your God, Dt 30:16
l the LORD your God, obeying his voice Dt 30:20
dreaming, lying down, **l** to slumber. Is 56:10
without self-control, brutal, not **l** good, 2 Tm 3:3
when the goodness and **l** kindness of God Ti 3:4
Above all, keep **l** one another earnestly, 1 Pt 4:8

LOW (54)
was brought very **l** because of Midian. Jgs 6:6
You have brought me very **l**, and you Jgs 11:35
makes rich; he brings **l** and he exalts. 1 Sm 2:7
the fire the sound of a **l** whisper. 1 Kgs 19:12
to their husbands, high and **l** alike." Est 1:20
he has grass, or the ox **l** over his fodder? Jb 6:5
But a man dies and is laid **l**; man Jb 14:10
they are brought **l**, and he perceives it Jb 14:21
they are brought **l** and gathered up like Jb 24:24

proud and bring him **l** and tread down Jb 40:12
false; he is laid **l** even at the sight of him. Jb 41:9
both **l** and high, rich and poor together! Ps 49:2
Those of **l** estate are but a breath; those Ps 62:9
of them and laid **l** the young men of Ps 78:31
to meet us, for we are brought very **l**. Ps 79:8
and were brought **l** through their Ps 106:43
and brought **l** through oppression, Ps 107:39
when I was brought **l**, he saved me. Ps 116:6
he who remembered us in our **l** estate, Ps 136:23
to my cry, for I am brought very **l**! Ps 142:6
for many a victim has she laid **l**, and all Prv 7:26
One's pride will bring him **l**, but he Prv 29:23
places, and the rich sit in a **l** place. Eccl 10:6
—when the sound of the grinding is **l**, Eccl 12:4
the daughters of song are brought **l**— Eccl 12:4
and each one is brought **l**—do not forgive Is 2:9
haughty looks of man shall be brought **l**, Is 2:11
is lifted up—and it shall be brought **l**; Is 2:12
the lofty pride of men shall be brought **l**, Is 2:17
is humbled, and each one is brought **l**, Is 5:15
and the eyes of the haughty are brought **l**. Is 5:15
down, and the lofty will be brought **l**. Is 10:33
and lay **l** the pompous pride of the Is 13:11
of Lebanon, saying, 'Since you were laid **l**, Is 14:8
the ground, you who laid the nations **l**! Is 14:12
day the glory of Jacob will be brought **l**, Is 17:4
the LORD will lay **l** his pompous pride Is 25:11
of his walls he will bring down, lay **l**, Is 25:12
He lays it **l**, lays it low to the ground, casts Is 26:5
He lays it low, lays it **l** to the ground, casts Is 26:5
And you will be brought **l**; from the earth Is 29:4
down, and the city will be utterly laid **l**. Is 32:19
and every mountain and hill be made **l**; Is 40:4
you shall come bending **l** to you, Is 60:14
and became a **l** spreading vine, Ezk 17:6
I bring **l** the high tree, and make high Ezk 17:24
the high tree, and make high the **l** tree, Ezk 17:24
Exalt that which is **l**, and bring low Ezk 21:26
low, and bring **l** that which is exalted. Ezk 21:26
scattered; the everlasting hills sank **l**. Hab 3:6
The pride of Assyria shall be laid **l**, Zec 10:11
every mountain and hill shall be made **l**, Lk 3:5
God chose what is **l** and despised in 1 Cor 1:28
I know how to be brought **l**, and I Phil 4:12

LOWER (25)
Make it with **l**, second, and third decks. Gn 6:16
them in front to the **l** part of the two Ex 28:27
them in front to the **l** part of the two Ex 39:20
and you shall come down **l** and lower. Dt 28:43
and you shall come down lower and **l**. Dt 28:43
to the **l** end of the Sea of Chinnereth, Jos 13:27
her the upper springs and the **l** springs. Jos 15:19
as far as the territory of **L** Beth-horon, Jos 16:3
that lies south of **L** Beth-horon. Jos 18:13
her the upper springs and the **l** springs. Jgs 1:15
rebuilt Gezer) and **L** Beth-horon 1 Kgs 9:17
who built both **L** and Upper 1 Chr 7:24
Upper Beth-horon and **L** Beth-horon, 2 Chr 8:5
hard as a stone, hard as the **l** millstone. Jb 41:24
made him a little **l** than the heavenly Ps 8:5
here," than to be put **l** in the presence of Prv 25:7
You collected the waters of the **l** pool, Is 22:9
of the gates. This was the **l** pavement. Ezk 40:18
the inner front of the **l** gate to the outer Ezk 40:19
than from the **l** and middle chambers Ezk 42:5
ground more than the **l** and the middle Ezk 42:6
the base on the ground to the **l** ledge, Ezk 43:14
also descended into the **l** parts of the Eph 4:9
him for a little while **l** than the angels; Heb 2:7
a little while was made **l** than the angels, Heb 2:9

LOWERED (4)
Then each man quickly **l** his sack to Gn 44:11
prevailed, and whenever he **l** his hand, Ex 17:11
aground on the Syrtis, they **l** the gear, Acts 27:17
and had **l** the ship's boat into the sea Acts 27:30

LOWERING (1)
opening in the wall, **l** him in a basket. Acts 9:25

LOWEST (6)
The **l** story was five cubits broad, the 1 Kgs 6:6
The entrance for the **l** story was on the 1 Kgs 6:8
So in the **l** parts of the space behind the Neh 4:13
one went up from the **l** story to the top Ezk 41:7
begin with shame to take the **l** place. Lk 14:9
you are invited, go and sit in the **l** place, Lk 14:10

LOWING (3)
along one highway, **l** as they went. 1 Sm 6:12
in my ears and the **l** of the oxen that I 1 Sm 15:14
through, and the **l** of cattle is not heard; Jer 9:10

LOWLAND (10)
hill country and in the **l** and in the Negeb Dt 1:7
country and in the **l** all along the coast Jos 9:1
and the Negeb and the **l** and the slopes, Jos 10:40
south of Chinneroth, and in the **l**, Jos 11:2
of Goshen and the **l** and the Arabah Jos 11:16
and the hill country of Israel and its **l** Jos 11:16
in the hill country, in the **l**, in the Jos 12:8
And in the **l**, Eshtaol, Zorah, Ashnah, Jos 15:33
hill country, in the Negeb, and in the **l**. Jgs 1:9
and the South and the **l** were inhabited?" Zec 7:7

LOWLIEST (1)
he will and sets over it the **l** of men.' Dn 4:17

LOWLY (16)
he sets on high those who are **l**, and those Jb 5:11
'It is because of pride'; but he saves the **l**. Jb 22:29
the LORD is high, he regards the **l**, Ps 138:6
Better to be **l** and have a servant than to Prv 12:9
better to be of a **l** spirit with the poor Prv 16:19
but he who is **l** in spirit will obtain Prv 29:23
him who is of a contrite and **l** spirit, Is 57:15
lowly spirit, to revive the spirit of the **l**, Is 57:15
"Take a **l** seat, for your beautiful crown Jer 13:18
and there they shall be a **l** kingdom. Ezk 29:14
It shall be the most **l** of the kingdoms, Ezk 29:15
in your midst a people humble and **l**. Zep 3:12
from me, for I am gentle and **l** in heart, Mt 11:29
be haughty, but associate with the **l**. Rom 12:16
who will transform our **l** body to be Phil 3:21
Let the **l** brother boast in his exaltation, Jas 1:9

LOYALLY (3)
"I will deal **l** with Hanun the son of 2 Sm 10:2
as his father dealt **l** with me." So 2 Sm 10:2
But deal **l** with the sons of Barzillai the 1 Kgs 2:7

LOYALTY (3)
because you showed this **l** to Saul your 2 Sm 2:5
"Is this your **l** to your friend? 2 Sm 16:17
for with such **l** they met me when I fled 1 Kgs 2:7

LUCIUS (2)
who was called Niger, **L** of Cyrene, Acts 13:1
so do **L** and Jason and Sosipater, my Rom 16:21

LUD (6)
Asshur, Arpachshad, **L**, and Aram. Gn 10:22
Asshur, Arpachshad, **L**, and Aram. 1 Chr 1:17
to the nations, to Tarshish, Pul, and **L**, Is 66:19
and Put who handle the shield, men of **L**, Jer 46:9
"Persia and **L** and Put were in your Ezk 27:10
Cush, and Put, and **L**, and all Arabia, Ezk 30:5

LUDIM (2)
Egypt fathered **L**, Anamim, Lehabim, Gn 10:13
Egypt fathered **L**, Anamim, 1 Chr 1:11

LUHITH (2)
For at the ascent of **L** they go up weeping; Is 15:5
at the ascent of **L** they go up weeping; Jer 48:5

LUKE (3)
L the beloved physician greets you, as Col 4:14
L alone is with me. Get Mark and 2 Tm 4:11
do Mark, Aristarchus, Demas, and **L**, Phlm 1:24

LUKEWARM (1)
So, because you are **l**, and neither hot Rv 3:16

LUMP (5)
out of the same **l** one vessel for Rom 9:21
as firstfruits is holy, so is the whole **l**, Rom 11:16
that a little leaven leavens the whole **l**? 1 Cor 5:6
the old leaven that you may be a new **l**, 1 Cor 5:7
A little leaven leavens the whole **l**. Gal 5:9

LURED (1)
tempted when he is **l** and enticed by his Jas 1:14

LURK (3)
They stir up strife, they **l**; they watch my Ps 56:6
people; they **l** like fowlers lying in wait. Jer 5:26
like a leopard I will **l** beside the way. Hos 13:7

LURKING (2)
note of all the **l** places where he 1 Sm 23:23
to tear, as a young lion **l** in ambush. Ps 17:12

LURKS (2)
he **l** in ambush like a lion in his thicket; Ps 10:9
thicket; he **l** that he may seize the poor; Ps 10:9

LUSH (1)
He is a **l** plant before the sun, and his Jb 8:16

LUST (10)
underfoot those who **l** after tribute; Ps 68:30
treacherous are taken captive by their **l**. Prv 11:6
you who burn with **l** among the oaks, Is 57:5
the wind! Who can restrain her **l**? Jer 2:24
Because your **l** was poured out and Ezk 16:36
poured out their whoring **l** upon her. Ezk 23:8
her sister in her **l** and in her whoring, Ezk 23:11
they defiled her with their whoring **l**. Ezk 23:17
in the passion of **l** like the Gentiles 1 Thes 4:5
who indulge in the **l** of defiling passion 2 Pt 2:10

LUSTED (6)
and she **l** after her lovers the Assyrians, Ezk 23:5
the idols of everyone after whom she **l**. Ezk 23:7
of the Assyrians, after whom she **l**. Ezk 23:9
She **l** after the Assyrians, governors Ezk 23:12
she **l** after them and sent messengers Ezk 23:16
and **l** after her paramours there, Ezk 23:20

LUSTFUL (4)
with the Egyptians, your **l** neighbors, Ezk 16:26
for with **l** talk in their mouths they Ezk 33:31
like one who sings **l** songs with a Ezk 33:32
at a woman with **l** intent has already Mt 5:28

LUSTS (1)
gave them up in the **l** of their hearts to Rom 1:24

LUSTY (1)
They were well-fed, **l** stallions, each Jer 5:8

LUTE (2)
to the music of the **l** and the harp, to the Ps 92:3
sound; praise him with **l** and harp! Ps 150:3

LUXURIANT (1)
Israel is a **l** vine that yields its fruit. The Hos 10:1

LUXURIOUS (1)
rich from the power of her **l** living." Rv 18:3

LUXURIOUSLY (1)
Saul, who clothed you **l** in scarlet, 2 Sm 1:24

LUXURY (6)
It is not fitting for a fool to live in **l**, Prv 19:10
for by them he lives in **l**, and his food is Hab 1:16
clothing and live in **l** are in kings' Lk 7:25
on the earth in **l** and in self-indulgence. Jas 5:5
As she glorified herself and lived in **l**, so Rv 18:7
immorality and lived in **l** with her, Rv 18:9

LUZ (8)
the name of the city was **L** at the first. Gn 28:19
And Jacob came to **L** (that is, Bethel), Gn 35:6
appeared to me at **L** in the land of Gn 48:3
Then going from Bethel to **L**, it passes Jos 16:2
along southward in the direction of **L**, Jos 18:13
of Luz, to the shoulder of **L** (that is, Jos 18:13
the name of the city was formerly **L**.) Jgs 1:23
and built a city and called its name **L**. Jgs 1:26

LYCAONIA (1)
fled to Lystra and Derbe, cities of **L**, Acts 14:6

LYCAONIAN (1)
lifted up their voices, saying in **L**, Acts 14:11

LYCIA (1)
and Pamphylia, we came to Myra in **L**. Acts 27:5

LYDDA (3)
down also to the saints who lived at **L**. Acts 9:32
all the residents of **L** and Sharon saw Acts 9:35
Since **L** was near Joppa, the disciples, Acts 9:38

LYDIA (2)
who heard us was a woman named **L**, Acts 16:14
went out of the prison and visited **L**. Acts 16:40

LYE (3)
with snow and cleanse my hands with **l**, Jb 9:30
your dross as with **l** and remove all your Is 1:25
you wash yourself with **l** and use much Jer 2:22

LYING (73)
behold, three flocks of sheep **l** beside it, Gn 29:2
in Israel by **l** with Jacob's daughter, Gn 34:7
labor at it and pay no regard to **l** words." Ex 5:9
one who hates you **l** down under its Ex 23:5
Bamoth to the valley **l** in the region of Nm 21:20
who has known man by **l** with him. Nm 31:17
not known man by **l** with him keep Nm 31:18
had not known man by **l** with him. Nm 31:35
or hurled something at him, **l** in wait, Nm 35:20
anything on him without **l** in wait Nm 35:22
is found slain, **l** in the open country, Dt 21:1
"If a man is found **l** with the wife of Dt 22:22
ground while he was **l** fast asleep from Jgs 4:21
Now she had men **l** in ambush in an Jgs 16:9
And the men **l** in ambush were Jgs 16:12
there was his concubine **l** at the door of Jgs 19:27
had not known a man by **l** with him, Jgs 21:12
not see, was **l** down in his own place. 1 Sm 3:2
and Samuel was **l** down in the temple 1 Sm 3:3
both his hands were **l** cut off on the 1 Sm 5:4
Saul was **l** within the encampment, 1 Sm 26:5
Amnon's house, where he was **l** down. 2 Sm 13:8
and will be a **l** spirit in the mouth of 1 Kgs 22:22
LORD has put a **l** spirit in the mouth 1 Kgs 22:23
he saw the child **l** dead on his bed. 2 Kgs 4:32
and will be a **l** spirit in the mouth of 2 Chr 18:21
LORD has put a **l** spirit in the mouth 2 Chr 18:22
were dead bodies **l** on the ground; 2 Chr 20:24
Let the **l** lips be mute, which speak Ps 31:18

and **l** more than speaking what is right. Ps 52:3
speaking against me with **l** tongues. Ps 109:2
Deliver me, O LORD, from **l** lips, from a Ps 120:2
my path and my **l** down and are Ps 139:3
haughty eyes, a **l** tongue, and hands Prv 6:17
one who conceals hatred has **l** lips, Prv 10:18
but a **l** tongue is but for a moment. Prv 12:19
L lips are an abomination to the LORD, Prv 12:22
of treasures by a **l** tongue is a fleeting Prv 21:6
A **l** tongue hates its victims, and a Prv 26:28
Remove far from me falsehood and **l**; Prv 30:8
they are a rebellious people, **l** children, Is 30:9
schemes to ruin the poor with **l** words, Is 32:7
they cannot bark, dreaming, **l** down, Is 56:10
and uttering from the heart **l** words. Is 59:13
people; they lurk like fowlers **l** in wait. Jer 5:26
the **l** pen of the scribes has made it into a Jer 8:8
They are prophesying to you a **l** vision, Jer 14:14
against those who prophesy **l** dreams, Jer 23:32
spoken in my name **l** words that I did Jer 29:23
He is a bear **l** in wait for me, a lion in Lam 3:10
seen false visions and **l** divinations. Ezk 13:6
a false vision and uttered a **l** divination, Ezk 13:7
uttered falsehood and seen **l** visions, Ezk 13:8
visions and who give **l** divinations. Ezk 13:9
not live, by your **l** to my people, Ezk 13:19
have agreed to speak **l** and corrupt words Dn 2:9
there is swearing, **l**, murder, stealing, Hos 4:2
"Lord, my servant is **l** paralyzed at home, Mt 8:6
he saw his mother-in-law **l** sick with a Mt 8:14
brought to him a paralytic, **l** on a bed. Mt 9:2
and found the child **l** in bed and the Mk 7:30
in swaddling cloths and **l** in a manger." Lk 2:12
and Joseph, and the baby **l** in a manger. Lk 2:16
what he had been **l** on and went home, Lk 5:25
l in wait for him, to catch him in Lk 11:54
When Jesus saw him **l** there and knew Jn 5:6
to look in, he saw the linen cloths **l** there, Jn 20:5
the tomb. He saw the linen cloths **l** there, Jn 20:6
not **l** with the linen cloths but folded up Jn 20:7
of their men are **l** in ambush for him, Acts 23:21
the truth in Christ—I am not **l**; Rom 9:1
forever, knows that I am not **l**. 2 Cor 11:31
(I am telling the truth, I am not **l**), 1 Tm 2:7

LYRE (29)
of all those who play the **l** and pipe. Gn 4:21
and songs, with tambourine and **l**? Gn 31:27
tambourine, flute, and **l** before them, 1 Sm 10:5
man who is skillful in playing the **l**, 1 Sm 16:16
David took the **l** and played it with 1 Sm 16:23
house while David was playing the **l**, 1 Sm 18:10
hand. And David was playing the **l**. 1 Sm 19:9
with the **l** in thanksgiving 1 Chr 25:3
the tambourine and the **l** and rejoice to Jb 21:12
My **l** is turned to mourning, and my Jb 30:31
Give thanks to the LORD with the **l**; make Ps 33:2
joy, and I will praise you with the **l**, Ps 43:4
will solve my riddle to the music of the **l**. Ps 49:4
Awake, my glory! Awake, O harp and **l**! I Ps 57:8
I will sing praises to you with the **l**, O Ps 71:22
tambourine, the sweet **l** with the harp. Ps 81:2
lute and the harp, to the melody of the **l**. Ps 92:3
Sing praises to the LORD with the **l**, with Ps 98:5
lyre, with the **l** and the sound of melody! Ps 98:5
Awake, O harp and **l**! I will awake the Ps 108:2
make melody to our God on the **l**! Ps 147:7
melody to him with tambourine and **l**! Ps 149:3
They have **l** and harp, tambourine and Is 5:12
my inner parts moan like a **l** for Moab, Is 16:11
has ceased, the mirth of the **l** is stilled. Is 24:8
hear the sound of the horn, pipe, **l**, trigon, Dn 3:5
the sound of the horn, pipe, **l**, trigon, Dn 3:7
the sound of the horn, pipe, **l**, trigon, Dn 3:10
the sound of the horn, pipe, **l**, trigon, Dn 3:15

LYRES (17)
with songs and **l** and harps and 2 Sm 6:5
also **l** and harps for the singers. 1 Kgs 10:12
with song and **l** and harps and 1 Chr 13:8
on harps and **l** and cymbals, 1 Chr 15:16
were to lead with **l** according to the 1 Chr 15:21
made loud music on harps and **l**. 1 Chr 15:28
Jeiel, who were to play harps and **l**; 1 Chr 16:5
of Jeduthun, who prophesied with **l**, 1 Chr 25:1
and **l** for the service of the house of 1 Chr 25:6
linen, with cymbals, harps, and **l**, 2 Chr 5:12
l also and harps for the singers. 2 Chr 9:11
with harps and **l** and trumpets, 2 Chr 20:28
the LORD with cymbals, harps, and **l**, 2 Chr 29:25
singing, with cymbals, harps, and **l**. Neh 12:27
On the willows there we hung up our **l**. Ps 137:2
be to the sound of tambourines and **l**. Is 30:32
the sound of your **l** shall be heard no Ezk 26:13

LYSANIAS (1)
Trachonitis, and **L** tetrarch of Abilene, Lk 3:1

LYSIAS (2)
"Claudius **L**, to his Excellency the Acts 23:26
"When **L** the tribune comes down, Acts 24:22

LYSTRA (6)
learned of it and fled to **L** and Derbe, Acts 14:6
Now at **L** there was a man sitting who Acts 14:8
they returned to **L** and to Iconium Acts 14:21
Paul came also to Derbe and to **L**. A Acts 16:1
of by the brothers at **L** and Iconium. Acts 16:2
and at **L**—which persecutions I 2 Tm 3:11

M

MAACAH (22)
bore Tebah, Gaham, Tahash, and **M**. Gn 22:24
Absalom the son of **M** the daughter of 2 Sm 3:3
and the king of **M** with 1,000 men, 2 Sm 10:6
of Tob and **M** were by themselves 2 Sm 10:8
Eliphelet the son of Ahasbai of **M**, 2 Sm 23:34
ran away to Achish, son of **M**, 1 Kgs 2:39
mother's name was **M** the daughter 1 Kgs 15:2
mother's name was **M** the daughter 1 Kgs 15:10
He also removed **M** his mother from 1 Kgs 15:13
M, Caleb's concubine, bore Sheber 1 Chr 2:48
third, Absalom, whose mother was **M**, 1 Chr 3:2
The name of his sister was **M**. 1 Chr 7:15
And **M** the wife of Machir bore a son, 1 Chr 7:16
and the name of his wife was **M**. 1 Chr 8:29
Jeiel, and the name of his wife was **M**, 1 Chr 9:35
Hanan the son of **M**, and Joshaphat 1 Chr 11:43
and the king of **M** with his army, 1 Chr 19:7
Shephatiah the son of **M**; 1 Chr 27:16
After her he took **M** the daughter of 2 Chr 11:20
Rehoboam loved **M** the daughter of 2 Chr 11:21
Abijah the son of **M** as chief prince 2 Chr 11:22
Even **M**, his mother, King Asa 2 Chr 15:16

MAACATH (1)
but Geshur and **M** dwell in the midst of Jos 13:13

MAACATHITE (3)
and Jaazaniah the son of the **M**. 2 Kgs 25:23
the Garmite and Eshtemoa the **M**. 1 Chr 4:19
Netophathite, Jezaniah the son of the **M**, Jer 40:8

MAACATHITES (4)
the border of the Geshurites and the **M**, Dt 3:14
boundary of the Geshurites and the **M**, Jos 12:5
and the region of the Geshurites and **M**, Jos 13:11
not drive out the Geshurites or the **M**, Jos 13:13

MAADAI (1)
Of the sons of Bani: **M**, Amram, Uel, Ezr 10:34

MAADIAH (1)
Mijamin, **M**, Bilgah, Neh 12:5

MAAI (1)
Azarel, Milalai, Gilalai, **M**, Nethanel, Neh 12:36

MAARATH (1)
M, Beth-anoth, and Eltekon: six cities Jos 15:59

MAAREH-GEBA (1)
rushed out of their place from **M**. Jgs 20:33

MAASAI (1)
of Malchijah, and **M** the son of Adiel, 1 Chr 9:12

MAASEIAH (23)
Eliab, Benaiah, **M**, Mattithiah, 1 Chr 15:18
M, and Benaiah were to play harps 1 Chr 15:20
the son of Obed, **M** the son of Adaiah, 2 Chr 23:1
Jeiel the secretary and **M** the officer, 2 Chr 26:11
killed **M** the king's son and Azrikam 2 Chr 28:7
and **M** the governor of the city, 2 Chr 34:8
M, Eliezer, Jarib, and Gedaliah, some Ezr 10:18
M, Elijah, Shemaiah, Jehiel, and Ezr 10:21
Elioenai, **M**, Ishmael, Nethanel, Ezr 10:22
Adna, Chelal, Benaiah, **M**, Mattaniah, Ezr 10:30
After them Azariah the son of **M**, son Neh 3:23
Hilkiah, and **M** on his right hand, Neh 8:4
Akkub, Shabbethai, Hodiah, **M**, Kelita, Neh 8:7
Rehum, Hashabnah, **M**, Neh 10:25
and **M** the son of Baruch, son of Neh 11:5
of Pedaiah, son of Kolaiah, son of **M**, Neh 11:7
the priests Eliakim, **M**, Miniamin, Neh 12:41
and **M**, Shemaiah, Eleazar, Uzzi, Neh 12:42
and Zephaniah the priest, the son of **M**, Jer 21:1
of Kolaiah and Zedekiah the son of **M**, Jer 29:21
to Zephaniah the son of **M** the priest, Jer 29:25
above the chamber of **M** the son of Jer 35:4
and Zephaniah the priest, the son of **M**, Jer 37:3

MAATH (1)
the son of **M**, the son of Mattathias, the Lk 3:26

MAAZ (1)
of Jerahmeel: **M**, Jamin, and Eker. 1 Chr 2:27

MAAZIAH (2)
to Delaiah, the twenty-fourth to **M**. 1 Chr 24:18
M, Bilgai, Shemaiah; these are the Neh 10:8

MACEDONIA (24)
night: a man of **M** was standing there, Acts 16:9
saying, "Come over to **M** and help us." Acts 16:9
we sought to go on into **M**, Acts 16:10
of the district of **M** and a Roman Acts 16:12
Silas and Timothy arrived from **M**, Acts 18:5
to pass through **M** and Achaia and Acts 19:21
And having sent into **M** two of his Acts 19:22
he said farewell and departed for **M**. Acts 20:1
Syria, he decided to return through **M**. Acts 20:3
For **M** and Achaia have been pleased Rom 15:26
visit you after passing through **M**, 1 Cor 16:5
for I intend to pass through **M**, 1 Cor 16:5
I wanted to visit you on my way to **M**, 2 Cor 1:16
back to you from **M** and have you 2 Cor 1:16
took leave of them and went on to **M**. 2 Cor 2:13
For even when we came into **M**, our 2 Cor 7:5
been given among the churches of **M**, 2 Cor 8:1
I boast about you to the people of **M**, 2 Cor 9:2
who came from **M** supplied my need. 2 Cor 11:9
beginning of the gospel, when I left **M**, Phil 4:15
all the believers in **M** and in Achaia. 1 Thes 1:7
forth from you in **M** and Achaia, 1 Thes 1:8
to all the brothers throughout **M**. 1 Thes 4:10
As I urged you when I was going to **M**, 1 Tm 1:3

MACEDONIAN (1)
Aristarchus, a **M** from Thessalonica. Acts 27:2

MACEDONIANS (2)
M who were Paul's companions in Acts 19:29
if some **M** come with me and find that 2 Cor 9:4

MACHBANNAI (1)
Jeremiah tenth, **M** eleventh. 1 Chr 12:13

MACHBENAH (1)
Sheva the father of **M** and the father 1 Chr 2:49

MACHI (1)
the tribe of Gad, Geuel the son of **M**. Nm 13:15

MACHIR (22)
The children also of **M** the son of Gn 50:23
The sons of Manasseh: of **M**, the clan Nm 26:29
and **M** was the father of Gilead; Nm 26:29
son of Hepher, son of Gilead, son of **M**, Nm 27:1
And the sons of **M** the son of Nm 32:39
Moses gave Gilead to **M** the son of Nm 32:40
of the people of Gilead the son of **M**, Nm 36:1
To **M** I gave Gilead, Dt 3:15
to the people of **M** the son of Manasseh Jos 13:31
of the people of **M** according to their Jos 13:31
To **M** the firstborn of Manasseh, the Jos 17:1
son of Hepher, son of Gilead, son of **M**, Jos 17:3
from **M** marched down the Jgs 5:14
is in the house of **M** the son of Ammiel, 2 Sm 9:4
from the house of **M** the son of 2 Sm 9:5
and **M** the son of Ammiel from 2 Sm 17:27
to the daughter of **M** the father of 1 Chr 2:21
All these were descendants of **M**, the 1 Chr 2:23
bore; she bore **M** the father of Gilead. 1 Chr 7:14
And **M** took a wife for Huppim and 1 Chr 7:15
Maacah the wife of **M** bore a son, 1 Chr 7:16
were the sons of Gilead the son of **M**, 1 Chr 7:17

MACHIRITES (1)
of Machir, the clan of the **M**; Nm 26:29

MACHNADEBAI (1)
M, Shashai, Sharai, Ezr 10:40

MACHPELAH (6)
that he may give me the cave of **M**, Gn 23:9
So the field of Ephron in **M**, which was Gn 23:17
of the field of **M** east of Mamre (that Gn 23:19
his sons buried him in the cave of **M**, Gn 25:9
in the cave that is in the field at **M**, to Gn 49:30
him in the cave of the field at **M**, Gn 50:13

MAD (7)
that you are driven **m** by the sights that Dt 28:34
"Behold, you see the man is **m**. 1 Sm 21:14
Why did this **m** fellow come to you?" 2 Kgs 9:11
of laughter, "It is **m**," and of pleasure, Eccl 2:2
of images, and they are **m** over idols. Jer 50:38
her wine; therefore the nations went **m**. Jer 51:7
the man of the spirit is **m**, because of Hos 9:7

MADAI (2)
Gomer, Magog, **M**, Javan, Tubal, Gn 10:2
Gomer, Magog, **M**, Javan, Tubal, 1 Chr 1:5

MADE (1279)
And God **m** the expanse and separated the Gn 1:7
And God **m** the two great lights—the Gn 1:16
And God **m** the beasts of the earth Gn 1:25
And God saw everything that he had **m**, Gn 1:31

blessed the seventh day and **m** it holy, Gn 2:3
that the LORD God **m** the earth and the Gn 2:4
ground the LORD God **m** to spring up Gn 2:9
from the man he **m** into a woman and Gn 2:22
of the field that the LORD God had **m**. Gn 3:1
together and **m** themselves loincloths. Gn 3:7
And the LORD God **m** for Adam and for Gn 3:21
man, he **m** him in the likeness of God. Gn 5:1
sorry that he had **m** man on the earth, Gn 6:6
for I am sorry that I have **m** them." Gn 6:7
living thing that I have **m** I will blot out Gn 7:4
And God **m** a wind blow over the earth, Gn 8:1
the window of the ark that he had **m** Gn 8:6
shed, for God **m** man in his own image. Gn 9:6
the place where he had **m** an altar at the Gn 13:4
these kings **m** war with Bera king of Gn 14:2
you should say, 'I have **m** Abram rich.' Gn 14:23
that day the LORD **m** a covenant with Gn 15:18
for I have **m** you the father of a Gn 17:5
And he **m** them a feast and baked Gn 19:3
So they **m** their father drink wine that Gn 19:33
So they **m** their father drink wine that Gn 19:35
Sarah said, "God has **m** laughter for me; Gn 21:6
And Abraham **m** a great feast on the Gn 21:8
and the two men **m** a covenant. Gn 21:27
So they **m** a covenant at Beersheba. Gn 21:32
throughout its whole area, was **m** over Gn 23:17
that is in it were **m** over to Abraham as Gn 23:20
And he **m** the camels kneel down Gn 24:11
My master **m** me swear, saying, 'You Gn 24:37
"For now the LORD has **m** room for us, Gn 26:22
So he **m** them a feast, and they ate and Gn 26:30
and they **m** life bitter for Isaac and Gn 26:35
"Behold, I have **m** him lord over you, Gn 27:37
Then Jacob **m** a vow, saying, "If God Gn 28:20
all the people of the place and **m** a feast. Gn 29:22
anointed a pillar and **m** a vow to me. Gn 31:13
And they took stones and **m** a heap, Gn 31:46
himself a house and **m** booths for his Gn 33:17
And he **m** him a robe of many colors. Gn 37:3
breach you have **m** for yourself!" Gn 38:29
and he **m** him overseer of his house and Gn 39:4
the time that he **m** him overseer in his Gn 39:5
whatever he did, the LORD **m** it succeed. Gn 39:23
he **m** a feast for all his servants and Gn 40:20
And he **m** him ride in his second Gn 41:43
"God has **m** me forget all my hardship Gn 41:51
"For God has **m** me fruitful in the land Gn 41:52
him when Joseph **m** himself known to Gn 45:1
He has **m** me a father to Pharaoh, and Gn 45:8
Joseph, God has **m** me lord of all Egypt. Gn 45:9
he **m** servants of them from one end of Gn 47:21
So Joseph **m** it a statute concerning the Gn 47:26
his arms were **m** agile by the hands of Gn 49:24
My father **m** me swear, saying, 'I am Gn 50:5
bury your father, as he **m** you swear." Gn 50:6
and he **m** a mourning for his father Gn 50:10
Then Joseph **m** the sons of Israel swear, Gn 50:25
So they ruthlessly **m** the people of Israel Ex 1:13
and **m** their lives bitter with hard Ex 1:14
work they ruthlessly **m** them work as Ex 1:14
for him a basket **m** of bulrushes and Ex 2:3
"Who **m** you a prince and a judge over Ex 2:14
said to him, "Who has **m** man's mouth? Ex 4:11
of bricks that they **m** in the past you Ex 5:8
because you have **m** us stink in the Ex 5:21
"See, I have **m** you like God to Pharaoh, Ex 7:1
their secret arts and **m** frogs come up on Ex 8:7
for Joseph had **m** the sons of Israel Ex 13:19
So he **m** ready his chariot and took his Ex 14:6
wind all night and **m** the sea dry land, Ex 14:21
which you have **m** for your abode, Ex 15:17
Then Moses **m** Israel set out from the Ex 15:22
There the LORD **m** for them a statute Ex 15:25
taste of it was like wafers **m** with honey. Ex 16:31
of all Israel and **m** them heads over the Ex 18:25
six days the LORD **m** heaven and earth, Ex 20:11
blessed the Sabbath day and **m** it holy. Ex 20:11
that the LORD has **m** with you in Ex 24:8
lampstand shall be **m** of hammered Ex 25:31
three cups **m** like almond blossoms, Ex 25:33
and three cups **m** like almond Ex 25:33
be four cups **m** like almond blossoms, Ex 25:34
It shall be **m**, with all these utensils, out Ex 25:39
It shall be **m** with cherubim skillfully Ex 26:31
you on the mountain, so shall it be **m**. Ex 27:8
band on it shall be **m** like it and be of Ex 28:8
bread and one cake of bread **m** with oil, Ex 29:23
which atonement was **m** at their Ex 29:33
six days the LORD **m** heaven and earth, Ex 31:17
with a graving tool and **m** a golden calf. Ex 32:4
And Aaron **m** proclamation and said, Ex 32:5
They have **m** for themselves a golden Ex 32:8
calf that they had **m** and burned it with Ex 32:20
on the water and **m** the people of Israel Ex 32:20
They have **m** for themselves gods of Ex 32:31
on the people, because they **m** the calf, Ex 32:35
made the calf, the one that Aaron **m**. Ex 32:35
these words I have **m** a covenant with Ex 34:27
among the workmen **m** the tabernacle Ex 36:8
They were **m** of fine twined linen and Ex 36:8
He **m** loops of blue on the edge of the Ex 36:11
Likewise he **m** them on the edge of the Ex 36:11
He **m** fifty loops on the one curtain, and Ex 36:12
and he **m** fifty loops on the edge of the Ex 36:12
And he **m** fifty clasps of gold, and Ex 36:13
He also **m** curtains of goats' hair for a Ex 36:14
the tabernacle. He **m** eleven curtains. Ex 36:14
And he **m** fifty loops on the edge of the Ex 36:17
And he **m** fifty clasps of bronze to Ex 36:18
And he **m** for the tent a covering of Ex 36:19
Then he **m** the upright frames for the Ex 36:20
frames for the tabernacle he **m** thus: Ex 36:23
And he **m** forty bases of silver under Ex 36:24
on the north side, he **m** twenty frames Ex 36:25
tabernacle westward he **m** six frames. Ex 36:27
He **m** two frames for corners of the Ex 36:28
He **m** two of them this way for the two Ex 36:29
He **m** bars of acacia wood, five for the Ex 36:31
And he **m** the middle bar to run from Ex 36:33
and **m** their rings of gold for holders for Ex 36:34
He **m** the veil of blue and purple and Ex 36:35
skillfully worked into it he **m** it. Ex 36:35
And for it he **m** four pillars of acacia Ex 36:36
He also **m** a screen for the entrance of Ex 36:37
Bezalel **m** the ark of acacia wood. Two Ex 37:1
and **m** a molding of gold around it. Ex 37:2
And he **m** poles of acacia wood and Ex 37:4
And he **m** a mercy seat of pure gold. Two Ex 37:6
And he **m** two cherubim of gold. He Ex 37:7
He **m** them of hammered work on the Ex 37:7
the mercy seat he **m** the cherubim on its Ex 37:8
He also **m** the table of acacia wood. Ex 37:10
and **m** a molding of gold around it. Ex 37:11
And he **m** a rim around it a Ex 37:12
and **m** a molding of gold around the Ex 37:12
He **m** the poles of acacia wood to carry Ex 37:15
And he **m** the vessels of pure gold that Ex 37:16
He also **m** the lampstand of pure gold. Ex 37:17
He **m** the lampstand of hammered Ex 37:17
three cups **m** like almond blossoms, Ex 37:19
and three cups **m** like almond Ex 37:19
were four cups **m** like almond Ex 37:20
And he **m** its seven lamps and its tongs Ex 37:23
He **m** it and all its utensils out of a Ex 37:24
He **m** the altar of incense of acacia Ex 37:25
And he **m** a molding of gold around it, Ex 37:26
and **m** two rings of gold on it under its Ex 37:27
And he **m** the poles of acacia wood and Ex 37:28
He **m** the holy anointing oil also, and Ex 37:29
He **m** the altar of burnt offering of Ex 38:1
He **m** horns for it on its four corners. Its Ex 38:2
And he **m** all the utensils of the altar, the Ex 38:3
fire pans. He **m** all its utensils of bronze. Ex 38:3
And he **m** for the altar a grating, a Ex 38:4
He **m** the poles of acacia wood and Ex 38:6
with them. He **m** it hollow, with boards. Ex 38:7
He **m** the basin of bronze and its stand of Ex 38:8
And he **m** the court. For the south side Ex 38:9
m all that the LORD commanded Moses; Ex 38:22
the 1,775 shekels he **m** hooks for the Ex 38:28
their capitals and **m** fillets for them. Ex 38:28
with it he **m** the bases for the entrance Ex 38:30
scarlet yarns they **m** finely woven Ex 39:1
They **m** the holy garments for Aaron, as Ex 39:1
He **m** the ephod of gold, blue and purple Ex 39:2
They **m** for the ephod attaching Ex 39:4
it was of one piece with it and **m** like it, Ex 39:5
They **m** the onyx stones, enclosed in Ex 39:6
He **m** the breastpiece, in skilled work, in Ex 39:8
They **m** the breastpiece doubled, a span Ex 39:9
And they **m** on the breastpiece twisted Ex 39:15
And they **m** two settings of gold filigree Ex 39:16
Then they **m** two rings of gold, and put Ex 39:19
And they **m** two rings of gold, and Ex 39:20
He also **m** the robe of the ephod woven Ex 39:22
the robe they **m** pomegranates of blue Ex 39:24
They also **m** bells of pure gold, and put Ex 39:25
They also **m** the coats, woven of fine Ex 39:27
They **m** the plate of the holy crown of Ex 39:30
a pan, it shall be **m** of fine flour with oil. Lv 2:7
grain offering that is **m** of these things to Lv 2:8
bring to the LORD shall be **m** with leaven, Lv 2:11
he has committed is **m** known to him, Lv 4:23
he has committed is **m** known to him, Lv 4:28
the mistake that he **m** unintentionally, Lv 5:18
It shall be **m** with oil on a griddle. You Lv 6:21
food offering may be **m** to the LORD shall Lv 7:25
or in a skin or in anything **m** of skin, Lv 13:48
or the woof or in any article **m** of skin, Lv 13:49
or any article **m** of skin that is diseased, Lv 13:52
or the woof or in any article **m** of skin, Lv 13:53
or the woof, or in any article **m** of skin, Lv 13:57
or any article **m** of skin from which Lv 13:58
or the woof, or in any article **m** of skin, Lv 13:59
out and has **m** atonement for himself Lv 16:17
"And when he has **m** an end of atoning Lv 16:20
day shall atonement be **m** for you to Lv 16:30
atonement may be **m** for the people Lv 16:34
a garment of cloth **m** of two kinds of Lv 19:19
her freedom, a distinction shall be **m**. Lv 19:20
he has **m** naked her fountain, Lv 20:18
which he may be **m** unclean or a person Lv 22:5
be waved, **m** of two tenths of an ephah. Lv 23:17
may know that I **m** the people of Israel Lv 23:43
of your yoke and **m** you walk erect. Lv 26:13
laws that the LORD **m** between him and Lv 26:46
then he shall be **m** to stand before the Lv 27:8
deduction shall be **m** from the Lv 27:18
restitution may be **m** for the wrong, Nm 5:8
with which atonement is **m** for him. Nm 5:8
And when he has **m** her drink the Nm 5:27
shall drink no vinegar **m** from wine or Nm 6:3
the chief of Issachar, **m** an offering. Nm 7:18
shown Moses, so he **m** the lampstand. Nm 8:4
and Aaron **m** atonement for them to Nm 8:21
and boiled it in pots and **m** cakes of it. Nm 11:8
who returned and **m** all the Nm 14:36
it had not been **m** clear what should Nm 15:34
let them be **m** into hammered plates Nm 16:38
the incense and **m** atonement for the Nm 16:47
charge of the contributions **m** to me, Nm 18:8
And why have you **m** us come up out Nm 20:5
So Moses **m** a bronze serpent and set it Nm 21:9
He has **m** his sons fugitives, and his Nm 21:29
"Because you have **m** a fool of me. Nm 22:29
for his God and **m** atonement for the Nm 25:13
took Joshua and **m** him stand before Nm 27:22
Her husband has **m** them void, and Nm 30:12
and he **m** them wander in the Nm 32:13
no atonement can be **m** for the land Nm 35:33
Our brothers have **m** our hearts melt, Dt 1:28
his spirit and **m** his heart obstinate, Dt 2:30
LORD your God, which he **m** with you, Dt 4:23
The LORD our God **m** a covenant with us Dt 5:2
of the covenant that the LORD **m** with you, Dt 9:9
they have **m** themselves a metal image.' Dt 9:12
You had **m** yourselves a golden calf. Dt 9:16
the sinful thing, the calf that you had **m**, Dt 9:21
So I **m** an ark of acacia wood, and cut Dt 10:3
put the tablets in the ark that I had **m**. Dt 10:5
LORD your God has **m** you as numerous Dt 10:22
how he **m** the water of the Red Sea flow Dt 11:4
high above all nations that he has **m**, Dt 26:19
a thing **m** by the hands of a craftsman, Dt 27:15
covenant that he had **m** with them at Dt 29:1
with which the LORD has **m** it sick— Dt 29:22
which he **m** with them when he Dt 29:25
my covenant that I have **m** with them. Dt 31:16
you, who **m** you and established you? Dt 32:6
He **m** him ride on the high places of the Dt 32:13
drank foaming wine **m** from the blood Dt 32:14
he forsook God who **m** him and scoffed Dt 32:15
They have **m** me jealous with what is Dt 32:21
oath of yours that you have **m** us swear. Jos 2:17
to your oath that you have **m** us swear." Jos 2:20
So Joshua **m** flint knives and Jos 5:3
Joshua burned Ai and **m** it forever a Jos 8:28
and went and **m** ready provisions and Jos 9:4
And Joshua **m** peace with them and Jos 9:15
peace with them and **m** a covenant with Jos 9:15
days after they had **m** a covenant with Jos 9:16
But Joshua **m** them that day cutters of Jos 9:27
of Gibeon had **m** peace with Israel Jos 10:1
For it has **m** peace with Joshua and with Jos 10:4
against Gibeon and **m** war against it. Jos 10:5
Joshua **m** war a long time with all Jos 11:18
not a city that **m** peace with the people Jos 11:19
who went up with me **m** the heart of the Jos 14:8
day but have been **m** to do forced Jos 16:10
Then allotment was **m** to the people of Jos 17:1
And allotments were **m** to the rest of the Jos 17:2
that the LORD had **m** to the house of Jos 21:45
For the LORD has **m** the Jordan a Jos 22:25
altar of the LORD, which our fathers **m**, Jos 22:28
of Canaan, and **m** his offspring many. Jos 24:3
and the Egyptians and **m** the sea come Jos 24:7
So Joshua **m** a covenant with the Jos 24:25
And Ehud **m** for himself a sword with Jgs 3:16
the people of Israel **m** for themselves the Jgs 6:2
And Gideon **m** an ephod of it and put it Jgs 8:27
the Baals and **m** Baal-berith their god. Jgs 8:33
and they went and **m** Abimelech king, Jgs 9:6
integrity when you **m** Abimelech king, Jgs 9:16
on one stone, and have **m** Abimelech, Jgs 9:18

And God also **m** all the evil of the men of Jgs 9:57
time the Ammonites **m** war against Jgs 11:4
when the Ammonites **m** war against Jgs 11:5
and the people **m** him head and leader Jgs 11:11
And Jephthah **m** a vow to the LORD and Jgs 11:30
according to his vow that he had **m**. Jgs 11:39
encamped in Judah and **m** a raid on Jgs 15:9
And she **m** them tight with the pin and Jgs 16:14
She **m** him sleep on her knees. And she Jgs 16:19
They **m** him stand between the pillars. Jgs 16:25
who **m** it into a carved image and a Jgs 17:4
and he **m** an ephod and household gods, Jgs 17:5
take my gods that I **m** and the priest, Jgs 18:24
people of Dan took what Micah had **m**, Jgs 18:27
set up Micah's carved image that he **m**, Jgs 18:31
the girl's father, **m** him stay, Jgs 19:4
seized his concubine and **m** her go out Jgs 19:25
was that when they **m** a great cloud of Jgs 20:38
because the LORD had **m** a breach in Jgs 21:15
You have **m** this last kindness greater Ru 3:10
petition that you have **m** to him." 1 Sm 1:17
me my petition that I **m** to him. 1 Sm 1:27
old, he **m** his sons judges over Israel. 1 Sm 8:1
and there they **m** Saul king before 1 Sm 11:15
to me and have **m** a king over you. 1 Sm 12:1
out of Egypt and **m** them dwell in this 1 Sm 12:8
Jonathan and his armor-bearer **m**, 1 Sm 14:14
"I regret that I have **m** Saul king, for 1 Sm 15:11
your sword has **m** women childless, 1 Sm 15:33
that he had **m** Saul king over 1 Sm 15:35
called Abinadab and **m** him pass 1 Sm 16:8
Then Jesse **m** Shammah pass by. And 1 Sm 16:9
And Jesse **m** seven of his sons pass 1 Sm 16:10
Then Jonathan **m** a covenant with 1 Sm 18:3
his presence and **m** him a 1 Sm 18:13
And Jonathan **m** a covenant with 1 Sm 20:16
And Jonathan **m** David swear again 1 Sm 20:17
I have **m** an appointment with the 1 Sm 21:2
in their hands and **m** marks on the 1 Sm 21:13
the two of them **m** a covenant before 1 Sm 23:18
the Philistines have **m** a raid against 1 Sm 23:27
Then Abigail **m** haste and took two 1 Sm 25:18
and have **m** a great mistake." 1 Sm 26:21
men went up and **m** raids against the 1 Sm 27:8
"Where have you **m** a raid today?" 1 Sm 27:10
"He has **m** himself an utter stench to 1 Sm 27:12
the Amalekites had **m** a raid against 1 Sm 30:1
We had **m** a raid against the Negeb 1 Sm 30:14
And he **m** it a statute and a rule for 1 Sm 30:25
and he **m** him king over Gilead and the 2 Sm 2:9
David **m** a feast for Abner and the 2 Sm 3:20
and King David **m** a covenant with 2 Sm 5:3
kingdom shall be **m** sure forever 2 Sm 7:16
have **m** this revelation to your 2 Sm 7:27
And David **m** a name for himself 2 Sm 8:13
they **m** peace with Israel and became 2 Sm 10:19
and drank, so that he **m** him drunk. 2 Sm 11:13
and iron axes and **m** them toil at the 2 Sm 12:31
tormented that he **m** himself ill 2 Sm 13:2
and kneaded it and **m** cakes in his 2 Sm 13:8
cakes she had **m** and brought them 2 Sm 13:10
the people have **m** me afraid, 2 Sm 14:15
that you have **m** yourself a stench 2 Sm 16:21
For you have **m** it clear today that 2 Sm 19:6
He **m** darkness around him his 2 Sm 22:12
refuge and has **m** my way blameless. 2 Sm 22:33
He **m** my feet like the feet of a deer 2 Sm 22:34
and your gentleness **m** me great. 2 Sm 22:36
you **m** those who rise against me 2 Sm 22:40
You **m** my enemies turn their backs 2 Sm 22:41
For he has **m** with me an everlasting 2 Sm 23:5
King David has **m** Solomon king, 1 Kgs 1:43
father, and who has **m** me a house, 1 Kgs 2:24
Solomon **m** a marriage alliance with 1 Kgs 3:1
he sacrificed and **m** offerings at the 1 Kgs 3:3
you have **m** your servant king in place 1 Kgs 3:7
and **m** a feast for all his servants. 1 Kgs 3:15
and the two of them **m** a treaty. 1 Kgs 5:12
And he **m** for the house windows with 1 Kgs 6:4
And he **m** side chambers all around. 1 Kgs 6:5
of the house he **m** offsets on the wall 1 Kgs 6:6
and he **m** the ceiling of the house of 1 Kgs 6:9
inner sanctuary he **m** two cherubim 1 Kgs 6:23
inner sanctuary he **m** doors of 1 Kgs 6:31
So also he **m** for the entrance to the 1 Kgs 6:33
And he **m** the Hall of Pillars; its length 1 Kgs 7:6
And he **m** the Hall of the Throne 1 Kgs 7:7
Solomon also **m** a house like this hall 1 Kgs 7:8
All these were **m** of costly stones, cut 1 Kgs 7:9
He also **m** two capitals of cast bronze 1 Kgs 7:16
Likewise he **m** pomegranates in two 1 Kgs 7:18
Then he **m** the sea of cast metal. It 1 Kgs 7:23
and its brim was **m** like the brim of a 1 Kgs 7:26
He also **m** the ten stands of bronze. 1 Kgs 7:27
was round, as a pedestal is **m**, 1 Kgs 7:31
The wheels were **m** like a chariot 1 Kgs 7:33
this manner he **m** the ten stands. 1 Kgs 7:37
And he **m** ten basins of bronze. Each 1 Kgs 7:38
Hiram also **m** the pots, the shovels, 1 Kgs 7:40
which Hiram **m** for King Solomon, 1 Kgs 7:45
So Solomon **m** all the vessels that 1 Kgs 7:48
where the LORD **m** a covenant with the 1 Kgs 8:9
has fulfilled his promise that he **m**. 1 Kgs 8:20
the LORD that he **m** with our fathers, 1 Kgs 8:21
his neighbor and is **m** to take an oath 1 Kgs 8:31
whatever plea is **m** by any man or by 1 Kgs 8:38
plea, which you have **m** before me. 1 Kgs 9:3
people of Israel Solomon **m** no slaves. 1 Kgs 9:22
Israel forever, he has **m** you king, 1 Kgs 10:9
And the king **m** of the almug wood 1 Kgs 10:12
King Solomon **m** 200 large shields 1 Kgs 10:16
And he **m** 300 shields of beaten gold; 1 Kgs 10:17
The king also **m** a great ivory 1 Kgs 10:18
of it was never **m** in any kingdom. 1 Kgs 10:20
And the king **m** silver as common 1 Kgs 10:27
and he **m** cedar as plentiful as the 1 Kgs 10:27
who **m** offerings and sacrificed to 1 Kgs 11:8
and lived there and **m** him king in 1 Kgs 11:24
"Your father **m** our yoke heavy. Now 1 Kgs 12:4
you, 'Your father **m** our yoke heavy, 1 Kgs 12:10
"My father **m** your yoke heavy, 1 Kgs 12:14
the assembly and **m** him king over 1 Kgs 12:20
took counsel and **m** two calves of 1 Kgs 12:28
He also **m** temples on high places 1 Kgs 12:31
sacrificing to the calves that he **m**. 1 Kgs 12:32
of the high places that he had **m**. 1 Kgs 12:32
altar that he had **m** in Bethel on the 1 Kgs 12:33
but **m** priests for the high places 1 Kgs 13:33
the people and **m** you leader over 1 Kgs 14:7
have gone and **m** for yourself other 1 Kgs 14:9
because they have **m** their Asherim, 1 Kgs 14:15
he sinned and **m** Israel to sin." 1 Kgs 14:16
shields of gold that Solomon had **m**, 1 Kgs 14:26
and King Rehoboam **m** in their 1 Kgs 14:27
all the idols that his fathers had **m**. 1 Kgs 15:12
because she had **m** an abominable 1 Kgs 15:13
Then King Asa **m** a proclamation 1 Kgs 15:22
in his sin which he **m** Israel to sin. 1 Kgs 15:26
sinned and that he **m** Israel to sin, 1 Kgs 15:30
in his sin which he **m** Israel to sin. 1 Kgs 15:34
of the dust and **m** you leader over my 1 Kgs 16:2
Jeroboam and have **m** my people 1 Kgs 16:2
and which they **m** Israel to sin, 1 Kgs 16:13
king." Therefore all Israel **m** Omri, 1 Kgs 16:16
and the conspiracy that he **m**, 1 Kgs 16:20
in the sins that he **m** Israel to sin, 1 Kgs 16:26
And Ahab **m** an Asherah. Ahab did 1 Kgs 16:33
around the altar that they had **m**. 1 Kgs 18:26
And he **m** a trench about the altar, 1 Kgs 18:32
terms." So he **m** a covenant with 1 Kgs 20:34
because you have **m** Israel to sin. 1 Kgs 21:22
son of Chenaanah **m** for himself 1 Kgs 22:11
still sacrificed and **m** offerings on 1 Kgs 22:43
Jehoshaphat also **m** peace with the 1 Kgs 22:44
Jehoshaphat **m** ships of Tarshish to 1 Kgs 22:48
son of Nebat, who **m** Israel to sin. 1 Kgs 22:52
the pillar of Baal that his father had **m**. 2 Kgs 3:2
son of Nebat, which he **m** Israel to sin; 2 Kgs 3:3
when they had **m** a circuitous march 2 Kgs 3:9
threw it in there and **m** the iron float. 2 Kgs 6:6
For the Lord had **m** the army of the 2 Kgs 7:6
ready." And they **m** ready his chariot. 2 Kgs 9:21
how the LORD **m** this pronouncement 2 Kgs 9:25
soon as he had **m** an end of offering 2 Kgs 10:25
Baal, and **m** it a latrine to this day. 2 Kgs 10:27
which he **m** Israel to sin—that is, 2 Kgs 10:29
Jeroboam, which he **m** Israel to sin. 2 Kgs 10:31
And he **m** a covenant with them and 2 Kgs 11:4
And Jehoiada **m** a covenant between 2 Kgs 11:17
the priests had **m** no repairs on the 2 Kgs 12:6
But there were not **m** for the house 2 Kgs 12:13
servants arose and **m** a conspiracy 2 Kgs 12:20
of Nebat, which he **m** Israel to sin; 2 Kgs 13:2
Jeroboam, which he **m** Israel to sin, 2 Kgs 13:6
destroyed them and **m** them like the 2 Kgs 13:7
of Nebat, which he **m** Israel to sin, 2 Kgs 13:11
Aphek until you have **m** an end of 2 Kgs 13:17
Syria until you had **m** an end of it, 2 Kgs 13:19
still sacrificed and **m** offerings on the 2 Kgs 14:4
And they **m** a conspiracy against 2 Kgs 14:19
and **m** him king instead of his 2 Kgs 14:21
of Nebat, which he **m** Israel to sin. 2 Kgs 14:24
still sacrificed and **m** offerings on the 2 Kgs 15:4
of Nebat, which he **m** Israel to sin. 2 Kgs 15:9
and the conspiracy that he **m**, 2 Kgs 15:15
of Nebat, which he **m** Israel to sin. 2 Kgs 15:18
of Nebat, which he **m** Israel to sin. 2 Kgs 15:24
of Nebat, which he **m** Israel to sin. 2 Kgs 15:28
son of Elah **m** a conspiracy against 2 Kgs 15:30
still sacrificed and **m** offerings on 2 Kgs 15:35
he sacrificed and **m** offerings on the 2 Kgs 16:4
Damascus, so Uriah the priest **m** it, 2 Kgs 16:11
and there they **m** offerings on all the 2 Kgs 17:11
covenant that he **m** with their 2 Kgs 17:15
and **m** for themselves metal images 2 Kgs 17:16
and they **m** an Asherah and 2 Kgs 17:16
they **m** Jeroboam the son of Nebat 2 Kgs 17:21
the LORD and **m** them commit great 2 Kgs 17:21
But every nation still **m** gods of its 2 Kgs 17:29
places that the Samaritans had **m**, 2 Kgs 17:29
men of Babylon **m** Succoth-benoth, 2 Kgs 17:30
the men of Cuth **m** Nergal, 2 Kgs 17:30
the men of Hamath **m** Ashima, 2 Kgs 17:30
and the Avvites **m** Nibhaz and 2 Kgs 17:31
The LORD **m** a covenant with them 2 Kgs 17:35
covenant that I have **m** with you. 2 Kgs 17:38
the bronze serpent that Moses had **m**, 2 Kgs 18:4
people of Israel had **m** offerings to it 2 Kgs 18:4
earth; you have **m** heaven and earth. 2 Kgs 19:15
might and how he **m** the pool and 2 Kgs 20:20
altars for Baal and **m** an Asherah, 2 Kgs 21:3
Asherah that he had **m** he set in the 2 Kgs 21:7
and has **m** Judah also to sin with his 2 Kgs 21:11
the sin that he **m** Judah to sin so 2 Kgs 21:16
people of the land **m** Josiah his son 2 Kgs 21:24
me and have **m** offerings to other 2 Kgs 22:17
by the pillar and **m** a covenant before 2 Kgs 23:3
of the LORD all the vessels **m** for Baal, 2 Kgs 23:4
where the priests had **m** offerings, 2 Kgs 23:8
which the kings of Judah had **m**, 2 Kgs 23:12
that Manasseh had **m** in the two 2 Kgs 23:12
son of Nebat, who **m** Israel to sin, 2 Kgs 23:15
which kings of Israel had **m**, 2 Kgs 23:19
and **m** him king in his father's 2 Kgs 23:30
And Pharaoh Neco **m** Eliakim the 2 Kgs 23:34
Solomon king of Israel had **m**, 2 Kgs 24:13
the king of Babylon **m** Mattaniah, 2 Kgs 24:17
Then a breach was **m** in the city, and 2 Kgs 25:4
that Solomon had **m** for the house 2 Kgs 25:16
and his sons **m** offerings on the 1 Chr 6:49
and David **m** a covenant with them 1 Chr 11:3
received them and **m** them officers 1 Chr 12:18
brothers had **m** preparation for 1 Chr 12:39
Philistines had come and **m** a raid in 1 Chr 14:9
the Philistines yet again **m** a raid in 1 Chr 14:13
and **m** loud music on harps and 1 Chr 15:28
covenant that he **m** with Abraham, 1 Chr 16:16
idols, but the LORD **m** the heavens. 1 Chr 16:26
And you **m** your people Israel to be 1 Chr 17:22
With it Solomon **m** the bronze sea 1 Chr 18:8
they **m** peace with David and 1 Chr 19:19
which Moses had **m** in the 1 Chr 21:29
he **m** Solomon his son king over 1 Chr 23:1
that I have **m** for praise." 1 Chr 23:5
firstborn, his father **m** him chief), 1 Chr 26:10
reign search was **m** and men of 1 Chr 26:31
and I **m** preparations for building. 1 Chr 28:2
altar of incense **m** of refined gold, 1 Chr 28:18
All this he **m** clear to me in writing 1 Chr 28:19
of fathers' houses **m** their freewill 1 Chr 29:6
for which I have **m** provision." 1 Chr 29:19
And they **m** Solomon the son of 1 Chr 29:22
And the LORD **m** Solomon very great 1 Chr 29:25
with him and **m** him exceedingly 2 Chr 1:1
of the LORD had **m** in the wilderness, 2 Chr 1:3
the son of Uri, son of Hur, had **m**, 2 Chr 1:5
and have **m** me king in his place. 2 Chr 1:8
for you have **m** me king over a people 2 Chr 1:9
people over whom I have **m** you king, 2 Chr 1:11
And the king **m** silver and gold as 2 Chr 1:15
and he **m** cedar as plentiful as the 2 Chr 1:15
he has **m** you king over them." 2 Chr 2:11
of Israel, who **m** heaven and earth, 2 Chr 2:12
fine gold and **m** palms and chains 2 Chr 3:5
And he **m** the Most Holy Place. Its 2 Chr 3:8
Holy Place he **m** two cherubim of 2 Chr 3:10
And he **m** the veil of blue and purple 2 Chr 3:14
the house he **m** two pillars thirty-five 2 Chr 3:15
He **m** chains like a necklace and put 2 Chr 3:16
and he **m** a hundred pomegranates 2 Chr 3:16
He **m** an altar of bronze, twenty cubits 2 Chr 4:1
Then he **m** the sea of cast metal. It was 2 Chr 4:2
And its brim was **m** like the brim of a 2 Chr 4:5
He also **m** ten basins in which to 2 Chr 4:6
And he **m** ten golden lampstands as 2 Chr 4:7
He also **m** ten tables and placed them 2 Chr 4:8
And he **m** a hundred basins of gold. 2 Chr 4:8
He **m** the court of the priests and the 2 Chr 4:9
Hiram also **m** the pots, the shovels, 2 Chr 4:11
He **m** the stands also, and the basins 2 Chr 4:14
for these Huram-abi **m** of burnished 2 Chr 4:16
Solomon **m** all these things in great 2 Chr 4:18
So Solomon **m** all the vessels that 2 Chr 4:19
that the cherubim **m** a covering 2 Chr 5:8
where the LORD **m** a covenant with 2 Chr 5:10

has fulfilled his promise that he **m**. 2 Chr 6:10
the LORD that he **m** with the people of 2 Chr 6:11
Solomon had **m** a bronze platform 2 Chr 6:13
his neighbor and is **m** to take an 2 Chr 6:22
whatever plea is **m** by any man or by 2 Chr 6:29
King David had **m** for giving thanks 2 Chr 7:6
altar Solomon had **m** could not hold 2 Chr 7:7
to the prayer that is **m** in this place. 2 Chr 7:15
of Israel Solomon **m** no slaves for 2 Chr 8:9
forever, he has **m** you king over them, 2 Chr 9:8
And the king **m** from the algum 2 Chr 9:11
King Solomon **m** 200 large shields of 2 Chr 9:15
And he **m** 300 shields of beaten gold; 2 Chr 9:16
The king also **m** a great ivory throne 2 Chr 9:17
like it was ever **m** for any kingdom. 2 Chr 9:19
And the king **m** silver as common in 2 Chr 9:27
and he **m** cedar as plentiful as the 2 Chr 9:27
"Your father **m** our yoke heavy. Now 2 Chr 10:4
you, 'Your father **m** our yoke heavy, 2 Chr 10:10
"My father **m** your yoke heavy, 2 Chr 10:14
He **m** the fortresses strong, and put 2 Chr 11:11
the cities and **m** them very strong. 2 Chr 11:12
and for the calves that he had **m**. 2 Chr 11:15
three years they **m** Rehoboam the 2 Chr 11:17
shields of gold that Solomon had **m**, 2 Chr 12:9
and King Rehoboam **m** in their 2 Chr 12:10
calves that Jeroboam **m** you for gods. 2 Chr 13:8
and **m** priests for yourselves like the 2 Chr 13:9
because she had **m** a detestable 2 Chr 15:16
and they **m** a very great fire in his 2 Chr 16:14
and they **m** no war against 2 Chr 17:10
and he **m** a marriage alliance with 2 Chr 18:1
son of Chenaanah **m** for himself 2 Chr 18:10
and when they had **m** an end of the 2 Chr 20:23
the LORD had **m** them rejoice over 2 Chr 20:27
what you have **m**." And the ships 2 Chr 20:37
covenant that he had **m** with David, 2 Chr 21:7
he **m** high places in the hill country 2 Chr 21:11
into whoredom and **m** Judah go 2 Chr 21:11
His people **m** no fire in his honor, 2 Chr 21:19
like the fires **m** for his fathers. 2 Chr 21:19
of Jerusalem **m** Ahaziah his 2 Chr 22:1
all the assembly **m** a covenant with 2 Chr 23:3
And Jehoiada **m** a covenant 2 Chr 23:16
and they **m** a chest and set it outside 2 Chr 24:8
proclamation was **m** throughout 2 Chr 24:9
and with it were **m** utensils for the 2 Chr 24:14
"Have we **m** you a royal counselor? 2 Chr 25:16
the LORD they **m** a conspiracy 2 Chr 25:27
and **m** him king instead of his father 2 Chr 26:1
sought the LORD, God **m** him prosper. 2 Chr 26:5
He went out and **m** war against the 2 Chr 26:6
in the muster **m** by Jeiel the 2 Chr 26:11
In Jerusalem he **m** engines, invented 2 Chr 26:15
He even **m** metal images for the 2 Chr 28:2
and he **m** offerings in the Valley of 2 Chr 28:3
he sacrificed and **m** offerings on the 2 Chr 28:4
the Philistines had **m** raids on the 2 Chr 28:18
for he had **m** Judah act sinfully and 2 Chr 28:19
and he **m** himself altars in every 2 Chr 28:24
city of Judah he **m** high places to 2 Chr 28:25
and he has **m** them an object of 2 Chr 29:8
we have **m** ready and consecrated, 2 Chr 29:19
slaughtered them and **m** a sin 2 Chr 29:24
offering should be **m** for all Israel. 2 Chr 29:24
so that he **m** them a desolation, 2 Chr 30:7
He also **m** weapons and shields in 2 Chr 32:5
and he **m** for himself treasuries for 2 Chr 32:27
altars to the Baals, and **m** Asherahs, 2 Chr 33:3
the idol that he had **m** he set in the 2 Chr 33:7
that Manasseh his father had **m**, 2 Chr 33:22
people of the land **m** Josiah his son 2 Chr 33:25
and he **m** dust of them and scattered 2 Chr 34:4
me and have **m** offerings to other 2 Chr 34:25
his place and **m** a covenant before 2 Chr 34:31
Then he **m** all who were present in 2 Chr 34:32
people of Israel and **m** all who were 2 Chr 34:33
They **m** these a rule in Israel; 2 Chr 35:25
son of Josiah and **m** him king in his 2 Chr 36:1
king of Egypt **m** Eliakim his brother 2 Chr 36:4
and **m** his brother Zedekiah king 2 Chr 36:10
who had **m** him swear by God. 2 Chr 36:13
that he had **m** holy in Jerusalem. 2 Chr 36:14
so that he **m** a proclamation 2 Chr 36:22
so that he **m** a proclamation throughout Ezr 1:1
m freewill offerings for the house of Ezr 2:68
of everyone who **m** a freewill offering Ezr 3:5
Jeshua the son of Jozadak **m** a beginning, Ezr 3:8
people of Judah and **m** them afraid to Ezr 4:4
that search may be **m** in the book of Ezr 4:15
And I **m** a decree, and search has been Ezr 4:19
I made a decree, and search has been **m**, Ezr 4:19
and sedition have been **m** in it. Ezr 4:19
a decree that these men be **m** to cease, Ezr 4:21
not rebuilt, until a decree is **m** by me. Ezr 4:21

and by force and power **m** them cease. Ezr 4:23
Cyrus the king **m** a decree that this Ezr 5:13
whom he had **m** governor; Ezr 5:14
let search be **m** in the royal archives Ezr 5:17
Then Darius the king **m** a decree, and Ezr 6:1
a decree, and search was **m** in Babylonia, Ezr 6:1
it, and his house shall be **m** a dunghill. Ezr 6:11
for the LORD had **m** them joyful and had Ezr 6:22
While Ezra prayed and **m** confession, Ezr 10:1
Ezra arose and **m** the leading priests Ezr 10:5
proclamation was **m** throughout Judah Ezr 10:7
called the priests and **m** them swear to Neh 5:12
that they had **m** for the purpose. Neh 8:4
brought them and **m** booths for Neh 8:16
from the captivity **m** booths and lived Neh 8:17
of it they **m** confession and worshiped Neh 9:3
You have **m** heaven, the heaven of Neh 9:6
and **m** with him the covenant to give to Neh 9:8
And you **m** a name for yourself, as it is Neh 9:10
and you **m** known to them your holy Neh 9:14
when they had **m** for themselves a Neh 9:18
of their enemies, who **m** them suffer. Neh 9:27
for God had **m** them rejoice with Neh 12:43
And I **m** them take oath in the name Neh 13:25
and God **m** him king over all Israel. Neh 13:26
foreign women **m** even him to sin. Neh 13:26
queen's behavior will be **m** known to all Est 1:17
So when the decree **m** by the king is Est 1:20
Esther had not **m** known her people or Est 2:10
on her head and **m** her queen instead of Est 2:17
Esther had not **m** known her kindred or Est 2:20
as they had **m** known to him the people Est 3:6
"Let a gallows fifty cubits high be **m**, Est 5:14
Haman, and he had the gallows **m**. Est 5:14
day they rested and **m** that a day of Est 9:17
formed three groups and **m** a raid on the Jb 1:17
They **m** an appointment together to Jb 2:11
and you have **m** firm the feeble knees. Jb 4:4
trembling, which **m** all my bones shake. Jb 4:14
Why have you **m** me your mark? Jb 7:20
who **m** the Bear and Orion, the Pleiades Jb 9:9
Your hands fashioned and **m** me, and Jb 10:8
Remember that you have **m** me like clay; Jb 10:9
out; he has **m** desolate all my company. Jb 16:7
"He has **m** me a byword of the peoples, Jb 17:6
God has **m** my heart faint; the Jb 23:16
By his wind the heavens were **m** fair; his Jb 26:13
the Almighty, who has **m** my soul bitter, Jb 27:2
No mention shall be **m** of coral or of Jb 28:18
when he **m** a decree for the rain and a Jb 28:26
of the unrighteous and **m** him drop his Jb 29:17
"I have **m** a covenant with my eyes; how Jb 31:1
Did not he who **m** me in the womb Jb 31:15
"If I have **m** gold my trust or called fine Jb 31:24
without payment and **m** its owners Jb 31:39
The Spirit of God has **m** me, and the Jb 33:4
that all men whom he **m** may know it. Jb 37:7
when I **m** clouds its garment and thick Jb 38:9
because God has **m** her forget wisdom Jb 39:17
Behemoth, which I **m** as I made you; Jb 40:15
Behemoth, which I made as I **m** you; Jb 40:15
let him who **m** him bring near his Jb 40:19
His back is **m** of rows of shields, shut Jb 41:15
out, and falls into the hole that he has **m**. Ps 7:15
Yet you have **m** him a little lower than the Ps 8:5
nations; you have **m** the wicked perish; Ps 9:5
nations have sunk in the pit that they **m**; Ps 9:15
The LORD has **m** himself known; he has Ps 9:16
He **m** darkness his covering, his Ps 18:11
with strength and **m** my way Ps 18:32
He **m** my feet like the feet of a deer and Ps 18:33
me, and your gentleness **m** me great. Ps 18:35
you **m** those who rise against me sink Ps 18:39
You **m** my enemies turn their backs to Ps 18:40
you **m** me the head of the nations; Ps 18:43
you **m** me trust you at my mother's Ps 22:9
LORD, you **m** my mountain stand strong; Ps 30:7
the word of the LORD the heavens were **m**, Ps 33:6
you have **m** my days a few Ps 39:5
You have **m** us turn back from the foe, Ps 44:10
You have **m** us like sheep for slaughter Ps 44:11
You have **m** us the taunt of our Ps 44:13
You have **m** us a byword among the Ps 44:14
citadels God has **m** himself known as Ps 48:3
who **m** a covenant with me by Ps 50:5
You have **m** the land to quake; you have Ps 60:2
You have **m** your people see hard things; Ps 60:3
given us wine to drink that **m** us stagger. Ps 60:3
When I **m** sackcloth my clothing, I Ps 69:11
You who have **m** me see many troubles Ps 71:20
May prayer be **m** for him continually, Ps 72:15
I have **m** the Lord GOD my refuge, that I Ps 73:28
earth; you have **m** summer and winter. Ps 74:17
Then my spirit **m** a diligent search: Ps 77:6
you have **m** known your might among Ps 77:14

it, and **m** the waters stand like a heap. Ps 78:13
He **m** streams come out of the rock and Ps 78:16
So he **m** their days vanish like a breath, Ps 78:33
He **m** a path for his anger; he did not Ps 78:50
and their widows **m** no lamentation. Ps 78:64
son whom you **m** strong for yourself. Ps 80:15
whom you have **m** strong for yourself! Ps 80:17
He **m** it a decree in Joseph when he went Ps 81:5
the nations you have **m** shall come and Ps 86:9
me; you have **m** me a horror to them. Ps 88:8
"I have **m** a covenant with my chosen Ps 89:3
foes; you have **m** all his enemies rejoice. Ps 89:42
and you have not **m** him stand in Ps 89:43
You have **m** his splendor to cease and Ps 89:44
Because you have **m** the LORD your Ps 91:9
O LORD, have **m** me glad by your work; Ps 92:4
The sea is his, for he **m** it, and his hands Ps 95:5
idols, but the LORD **m** the heavens. Ps 96:5
The LORD has **m** known his salvation; he Ps 98:2
It is he who **m** us, and we are his; we are Ps 100:3
He **m** known his ways to Moses, his Ps 103:7
He **m** the moon to mark the seasons; Ps 104:19
In wisdom have you **m** them all; the Ps 104:24
the covenant that he **m** with Abraham, Ps 105:9
he **m** him lord of his house and ruler Ps 105:21
And the LORD **m** his people very Ps 105:24
very fruitful and **m** them stronger Ps 105:24
sent darkness, and **m** the land dark; Ps 105:28
They **m** a calf in Horeb and worshiped Ps 106:19
for they **m** his spirit bitter, and he Ps 106:33
He **m** the storm be still, and the waves Ps 107:29
by the LORD, who **m** heaven and earth! Ps 115:15
This is the day that the LORD has **m**; let Ps 118:24
and he has **m** his light to shine upon Ps 118:27
in which you have **m** me hope. Ps 119:49
Your hands have **m** and fashioned Ps 119:73
They have almost **m** an end of me on Ps 119:87
the LORD, who **m** heaven and earth. Ps 121:2
of the LORD, who **m** heaven and earth. Ps 124:8
my back; they **m** long their furrows." Ps 129:3
from Zion, he who **m** heaven and earth! Ps 134:3
who by understanding **m** the heavens, Ps 136:5
to him who **m** the great lights, for his Ps 136:7
and **m** Israel pass through the midst of Ps 136:14
for I am fearfully and wonderfully **m**. Ps 139:14
you, when I was being **m** in secret, Ps 139:15
he has **m** me sit in darkness like those Ps 143:3
and his mercy is over all that he has **m**. Ps 145:9
who **m** heaven and earth, the sea, and Ps 146:6
unless they have **m** someone stumble. Prv 4:16
before he had **m** the earth with its fields, Prv 8:26
when he **m** firm the skies above, when Prv 8:28
The LORD has **m** everything for its Prv 16:4
Who can say, "I have **m** my heart pure; Prv 20:9
seeing eye, the LORD has **m** them both. Prv 20:12
The horse is **m** ready for the day of Prv 21:31
I have **m** them known to you today, Prv 22:19
is crooked cannot be **m** straight, Eccl 1:15
I **m** great works. I built houses and Eccl 2:4
I **m** myself gardens and parks, and Eccl 2:5
I **m** myself pools from which to water Eccl 2:6
He has **m** everything beautiful in its Eccl 3:11
by sadness of face the heart is **m** glad. Eccl 7:3
straight what he has **m** crooked? Eccl 7:13
God has **m** the one as well as the other, Eccl 7:14
I found, that God **m** man upright, Eccl 7:29
Bread is **m** for laughter, and wine Eccl 10:19
they **m** me keeper of the vineyards, but Sg 1:6
King Solomon **m** himself a carriage from Sg 3:9
He **m** its posts of silver, its back of gold, Sg 3:10
hands, to what their own fingers have **m**. Is 2:8
which they **m** for themselves to worship, Is 2:20
and you are **m** to dwell alone in the midst Is 5:8
latter time he has **m** glorious the way of Is 9:1
let this be **m** known in all the earth. Is 12:5
service with which you were **m** to serve, Is 14:3
this the man who **m** the earth tremble, Is 14:16
who **m** the world like a desert and Is 14:17
not look on what his own fingers have **m**, Is 17:8
of her tribes have **m** Egypt stagger. Is 19:13
You **m** a reservoir between the two walls Is 22:11
her palaces bare, they **m** her a ruin. Is 23:13
For you have **m** the city a heap, the Is 25:2
therefore he who **m** them will not have Is 27:11
"We have **m** a covenant with death, Is 28:15
to us, for we have **m** lies our refuge, Is 28:15
not scoff, lest your bonds be **m** strong; Is 28:22
that the thing **m** should say of its Is 29:16
indeed, for the king it is **m** ready, its pyre Is 30:33
is made ready, its pyre **m** deep and wide, Is 30:33
your hands have sinfully **m** for you. Is 31:7
the earth; you have **m** heaven and earth. Is 37:16
and every mountain and hill be **m** low; Is 40:4
consult, and who **m** him understand? Is 40:14
for my glory, whom I formed and **m**." Is 43:7

Thus says the LORD who **m** you, who	Is 44:2
"I am the LORD, who **m** all things, who	Is 44:24
I **m** the earth and created man on it; it	Is 45:12
the earth and **m** it (he established	Is 45:18
I have **m**, and I will bear; I will carry and	Is 46:4
on the aged you **m** your yoke exceedingly	Is 47:6
he **m** water flow for them from the rock;	Is 48:21
He **m** my mouth like a sharp sword; in	Is 49:2
he hid me; he **m** me a polished arrow;	Is 49:2
who **m** the depths of the sea a way for the	Is 51:10
of the son of man who is **m** like grass,	Is 51:12
and you have **m** your back like the	Is 51:23
And they **m** his grave with the wicked	Is 53:9
Behold, I **m** him a witness to the peoples, a	Is 55:4
have gone up to it, you have **m** it wide;	Is 57:8
and you have **m** a covenant for yourself	Is 57:8
before me, and the breath of life that I **m**.	Is 57:16
your iniquities have **m** a separation	Is 59:2
paths; they have **m** their roads crooked;	Is 59:8
of Israel, because he has **m** you beautiful.	Is 60:9
I **m** them drunk in my wrath, and I	Is 63:6
and have **m** us melt in the hand of our	Is 64:7
because they **m** offerings on the	Is 65:7
All these things my hand has **m**, and so	Is 66:2
They have **m** offerings to other gods and	Jer 1:16
defiled my land and **m** my heritage an	Jer 2:7
They have **m** his land a waste; his cities	Jer 2:15
are your gods that you **m** for yourself?	Jer 2:28
or missed; it shall not be **m** again.	Jer 3:16
They have **m** their faces harder than	Jer 5:3
"I have **m** you a tester of metals among	Jer 6:27
where I **m** my name dwell at first,	Jer 7:12
lying pen of the scribes has **m** it into a lie.	Jer 8:8
It is he who **m** the earth by his power,	Jer 10:12
covenant that I **m** with their fathers.	Jer 11:10
The LORD **m** it known to me and I	Jer 11:18
they have **m** my pleasant portion a	Jer 12:10
They have **m** it a desolation; desolate, it	Jer 12:11
The whole land is **m** desolate, but no	Jer 12:11
so I **m** the whole house of Israel and the	Jer 13:11
long will it be before you are **m** clean?"	Jer 13:27
I have **m** their widows more in number	Jer 15:8
I have **m** anguish and terror fall upon	Jer 15:8
they **m** them stumble in their ways, in	Jer 18:15
and **m** all the nations to whom the	Jer 25:17
my outstretched arm have **m** the earth,	Jer 27:5
but you have **m** in their place bars of	Jer 28:13
and you have **m** this people trust in a	Jer 28:15
'The LORD has **m** you priest instead of	Jer 29:26
send him, and has **m** you trust in a lie,	Jer 29:31
the covenant that I **m** with their fathers	Jer 31:32
is you who has **m** the heavens and the	Jer 32:17
and have **m** a name for yourself,	Jer 32:20
Therefore you have **m** all this disaster	Jer 32:23
roofs offerings have been **m** to Baal and	Jer 32:29
"Thus says the LORD who **m** the earth,	Jer 33:2
fulfill the promise I **m** to the house of	Jer 33:14
King Zedekiah had **m** a covenant with	Jer 34:8
I myself **m** a covenant with your	Jer 34:13
and you **m** a covenant before me in the	Jer 34:15
of the covenant that they **m** before me,	Jer 34:18
king of Babylon **m** king in the	Jer 37:1
secretary, for it had been **m** a prison.	Jer 37:15
"As the LORD lives, who **m** our souls,	Jer 38:16
'I **m** a humble plea to the king that he	Jer 38:26
the month, a breach was **m** in the city.	Jer 39:2
that King Asa had **m** for defense against	Jer 41:9
of Babylon had **m** governor over the	Jer 41:18
their wives had **m** offerings to other	Jer 44:15
"When we **m** offerings to the queen of	Jer 44:19
approval that we **m** cakes for her	Jer 44:19
is because you **m** offerings and	Jer 44:23
perform our vows that we have **m**,	Jer 44:25
He **m** many stumble, and they fell, and	Jer 46:16
is destroyed; her little ones have **m** a cry.	Jer 48:4
I have **m** the wine cease from the	Jer 48:33
that the LORD has **m** against Edom and	Jer 49:20
king of Babylon has **m** a plan against	Jer 49:30
that the LORD has **m** against Babylon,	Jer 50:45
"It is he who **m** the earth by his power,	Jer 51:15
me; he has **m** me an empty vessel;	Jer 51:34
Then a breach was **m** in the city, and all	Jer 52:7
Solomon the king had **m** for the house	Jer 52:20
fire; into my bones he **m** it descend;	Lam 1:13
the LORD has **m** Zion forget festival and	Lam 2:6
he has **m** the enemy rejoice over you	Lam 2:17
He has **m** my flesh and my skin waste	Lam 3:4
he has **m** me dwell in darkness like the	Lam 3:6
escape; he has **m** my chains heavy;	Lam 3:7
of stones; he has **m** my paths crooked.	Lam 3:9
me to pieces; he has **m** me desolate;	Lam 3:11
He has **m** my teeth grind on gravel,	Lam 3:16
on gravel, and **m** me cower in ashes;	Lam 3:16
You have **m** us scum and garbage	Lam 3:45
I have **m** your face as hard as their faces,	Ezk 3:8
than flint have I **m** your forehead.	Ezk 3:9
I have **m** you a watchman for the	Ezk 3:17
the trumpet and **m** everything ready,	Ezk 7:14
and they **m** their abominable images	Ezk 7:20
for I have **m** you a sign for the house of	Ezk 12:6
they ravage it, and it be **m** desolate,	Ezk 14:15
I **m** you flourish like a plant of the field.	Ezk 16:7
I **m** my vow to you and entered into a	Ezk 16:8
your garments and **m** for yourself	Ezk 16:16
and **m** for yourself images of men,	Ezk 16:17
vaulted chamber and **m** yourself a	Ezk 16:24
lofty place and **m** your beauty an	Ezk 16:25
and have **m** your sisters appear	Ezk 16:51
for you have **m** your sisters appear	Ezk 16:52
royal offspring and **m** a covenant	Ezk 17:13
the king dwells who **m** him king,	Ezk 17:16
of her cubs and **m** him a young lion.	Ezk 19:5
in whose sight I **m** myself known to	Ezk 20:9
my statutes and **m** known to them	Ezk 20:11
Ah, it is **m** like lightning; it is taken	Ezk 21:15
Because you have **m** your guilt to be	Ezk 21:24
defiled by the idols that you have **m**,	Ezk 22:4
Therefore I have **m** you a reproach to	Ezk 22:4
at the dishonest gain that you have **m**,	Ezk 22:13
they have **m** many widows in her	Ezk 22:25
They have **m** no distinction between	Ezk 22:26
land of Israel when it was **m** desolate,	Ezk 25:3
when slaughter is **m** in your midst?	Ezk 26:15
your builders **m** perfect your beauty.	Ezk 27:4
They **m** all your planks of fir trees	Ezk 27:5
Of oaks of Bashan they **m** your oars;	Ezk 27:6
they **m** your deck of pines from the	Ezk 27:6
around; they **m** perfect your beauty.	Ezk 27:11
bound with cords and **m** secure.	Ezk 27:24
understanding you have **m** wealth for	Ezk 28:4
'My Nile is my own; I **m** it for myself.'	Ezk 29:3
you broke and **m** all their loins to	Ezk 29:7
you said, 'The Nile is mine, and I **m** it,'	Ezk 29:9
king of Babylon **m** his army labor	Ezk 29:18
Every head was **m** bald, and every	Ezk 29:18
the deep **m** it grow tall, making its	Ezk 31:4
birds of the heavens **m** their nests in its	Ezk 31:6
I **m** it beautiful in the mass of its	Ezk 31:9
I **m** the nations quake at the sound of	Ezk 31:16
They have **m** her a bed among the	Ezk 32:25
I have **m** a watchman for the house of	Ezk 33:7
when I have **m** the land a desolation	Ezk 33:29
Precisely because they **m** you desolate	Ezk 36:3
with hearths **m** at the bottom of the	Ezk 46:23
urgent?" Then Arioch **m** the matter	Dn 2:15
to his house and **m** the matter known to	Dn 2:17
and have now **m** known to me what we	Dn 2:23
for you have **m** known to us the king's	Dn 2:23
and he has **m** known to King	Dn 2:28
who reveals mysteries **m** known to you	Dn 2:29
interpretation may be **m** known to the	Dn 2:30
A great God has **m** known to the king	Dn 2:45
and **m** him ruler over the whole	Dn 2:48
Daniel **m** a request of the king, and he	Dn 2:49
King Nebuchadnezzar **m** an image of	Dn 3:1
You, O king, have **m** a decree, that every	Dn 3:10
and worship the image that I have **m**,	Dn 3:15
I saw a dream that **m** me afraid. As I lay	Dn 4:5
So I **m** a decree that all the wise men of	Dn 4:6
You shall be **m** to eat grass like an ox,	Dn 4:25
And you shall be **m** to eat grass like an	Dn 4:32
King Belshazzar **m** a great feast for a	Dn 5:1
father the king—**m** him chief of the	Dn 5:11
and his mind was **m** like that of a beast,	Dn 5:21
and a proclamation was **m** about him,	Dn 5:29
from the ground and **m** to stand on two	Dn 7:4
So he told me and **m** known to me the	Dn 7:16
this horn **m** war with the saints and	Dn 7:21
But he touched me and **m** me stand up.	Dn 8:18
who was **m** king over the realm of the	Dn 9:1
to the LORD my God and **m** confession,	Dn 9:4
hand, and have **m** a name for yourself,	Dn 9:15
He **m** me understand, speaking with me	Dn 9:22
that an alliance is **m** with him he shall	Dn 11:23
may be refined, purified, and **m** white,	Dn 11:35
to the report **m** to their congregation.	Hos 7:12
They **m** kings, but not through me.	Hos 8:4
silver and gold they **m** idols for their	Hos 8:4
For it is from Israel; a craftsman **m** it; it	Hos 8:6
idols skillfully **m** of their silver,	Hos 13:2
it down; their branches are **m** white.	Jl 1:7
"But you **m** the Nazirites drink wine,	Am 2:12
and I **m** the stench of your camp go up	Am 4:10
He who **m** the Pleiades and Orion, and	Am 5:8
your images that you **m** for yourselves,	Am 5:26
high places of Isaac shall be **m** desolate,	Am 7:9
heaven, who **m** the sea and the dry land."	Jon 1:9
a sacrifice to the LORD and **m** vows.	Jon 1:16
That is why I **m** haste to flee to Tarshish;	Jon 4:2
east of the city and **m** a booth for himself	Jon 4:5
appointed a plant and **m** it come up over	Jon 4:6
because they have **m** their deeds evil.	Mi 3:4
my people and **m** boasts against their	Zep 2:8
their cities have been **m** desolate,	Zep 3:6
the covenant that I **m** with you when you	Hg 2:5
They **m** their hearts diamond-hard lest	Zec 7:12
and the pleasant land was **m** desolate."	Zec 7:14
my bow; I have **m** Ephraim its arrow.	Zec 9:13
covenant that I had **m** with all the	Zec 11:10
from the garment, and a worse tear is **m**.	Mt 9:16
touch his garment, I will be **m** well."	Mt 9:21
your faith has **m** you well." And	Mt 9:22
And instantly the woman was **m** well.	Mt 9:22
Immediately he **m** the disciples get into	Mt 14:22
as many as touched it were **m** well.	Mt 14:36
your tradition you have **m** void the word	Mt 15:6
all that he had, and payment to be **m**.	Mt 18:25
from the beginning **m** them male and	Mt 19:4
who have been **m** eunuchs by men,	Mt 19:12
who have **m** themselves eunuchs	Mt 19:12
and you have **m** them equal to us who	Mt 20:12
the temple that has **m** the gold sacred?	Mt 23:17
with them, and he **m** five talents more.	Mt 25:16
had the two talents **m** two talents more.	Mt 25:17
talents; here I have **m** five talents more.'	Mt 25:20
talents; here I have **m** two talents more.'	Mt 25:22
the tomb to be **m** secure until the third	Mt 27:64
So they went and **m** the tomb secure by	Mt 27:66
leprosy left him, and he was **m** clean.	Mk 1:42
him, and when they had **m** an opening,	Mk 2:4
new from the old, and a worse tear is **m**.	Mk 2:21
the grainfields, and as they **m** their way,	Mk 2:23
to them, "The Sabbath was **m** for man,	Mk 2:27
is hidden except to be **m** manifest;	Mk 4:22
so that she may be **m** well and live."	Mk 5:23
even his garments, I will be **m** well."	Mk 5:28
"Daughter, your faith has **m** you well;	Mk 5:34
Immediately he **m** his disciples get into	Mk 6:45
And as many as touched it were **m** well.	Mk 6:56
'God **m** them male and female.'	Mk 10:6
your faith has **m** you well." And	Mk 10:52
But you have **m** it a den of robbers."	Mk 11:17
this temple that is **m** with hands,	Mk 14:58
build another, not **m** with hands.'"	Mk 14:58
he remained silent and **m** no answer.	Mk 14:61
But Jesus **m** no further answer, so that	Mk 15:5
And they **m** signs to his father,	Lk 1:62
which the Lord has **m** known to us."	Lk 2:15
they **m** known the saying that had been	Lk 2:17
every mountain and hill shall be **m** low,	Lk 3:5
And Levi **m** him a great feast in his	Lk 5:29
is hidden that will not be **m** manifest,	Lk 8:17
"Daughter, your faith has **m** you well;	Lk 8:48
Did not he who **m** the outside make the	Lk 11:40
who **m** me a judge or arbitrator over	Lk 12:14
and immediately she was **m** straight,	Lk 13:13
birds of the air **m** nests in its	Lk 13:19
your way; your faith has **m** you well."	Lk 17:19
your sight; your faith has **m** you well."	Lk 18:42
your mina has **m** ten minas more.'	Lk 19:16
'Lord, your mina has **m** five minas.'	Lk 19:18
but you have **m** it a den of robbers."	Lk 19:46
at some length, but he **m** no answer.	Lk 23:9
All things were **m** through him, and	Jn 1:3
him was not any thing **m** that was made.	Jn 1:3
him was not any thing made that was **m**.	Jn 1:3
and the world was **m** through him,	Jn 1:10
the Father's side, he has **m** him known.	Jn 1:18
Galilee, where he had **m** the water wine.	Jn 4:46
on the Sabbath I **m** a man's whole body	Jn 7:23
on the ground and **m** mud with the saliva.	Jn 9:6
man called Jesus **m** mud and anointed	Jn 9:11
Sabbath day when Jesus **m** the mud and	Jn 9:14
that day on they **m** plans to put him	Jn 11:53
of expensive ointment **m** from pure nard,	Jn 12:3
So the chief priests **m** plans to put	Jn 12:10
my Father I have **m** known to you.	Jn 15:15
I **m** known to them your name, and I	Jn 17:26
and officers had **m** a charcoal fire,	Jn 18:18
die because he has **m** himself the Son of	Jn 19:7
You have **m** known to me the paths of	Acts 2:28
certain that God has **m** him both Lord	Acts 2:36
his feet and ankles were **m** strong.	Acts 3:7
power or piety we have **m** him walk?	Acts 3:12
his name—has **m** this man strong	Acts 3:16
covenant that God **m** with your	Acts 3:25
who **m** the heaven and the earth and	Acts 4:24
who **m** him ruler over Egypt and over	Acts 7:10
second visit Joseph **m** himself known	Acts 7:13
'Who **m** you a ruler and a judge over	Acts 7:27
'Who **m** you a ruler and a judge?'	Acts 7:35
And they **m** a calf in those days, and	Acts 7:41
the images that you **m** to worship;	Acts 7:43
does not dwell in houses **m** by hands,	Acts 7:48
Stephen and **m** great lamentation	Acts 8:2

the man who **m** havoc in Jerusalem Acts 9:21
garments that Dorcas **m** while she was Acts 9:39
time, "What God has **m** clean, Acts 10:15
having **m** inquiry for Simon's house, Acts 10:17
the third day and **m** him to appear, Acts 10:40
from heaven, 'What God has **m** clean, Acts 11:9
prayer for him was **m** to God by the Acts 12:5
our fathers and **m** the people great Acts 13:17
"'I have **m** you a light for the Gentiles, Acts 13:47
an attempt was **m** by both Gentiles Acts 14:5
seeing that he had faith to be **m** well, Acts 14:9
who **m** the heaven and the earth and Acts 14:15
that city and had **m** many disciples, Acts 14:21
the early days God **m** a choice among Acts 15:7
and he **m** no distinction between us Acts 15:9
we **m** a direct voyage to Samothrace, Acts 16:11
The God who **m** the world and Acts 17:24
does not live in temples **m** by man, Acts 17:24
And he **m** from one man every Acts 17:26
the Jews **m** a united attack on Paul Acts 18:12
who **m** silver shrines of Artemis, Acts 19:24
saying that gods **m** with hands are Acts 19:26
when a plot was **m** against him by the Acts 20:3
the Holy Spirit has **m** you overseers, Acts 20:28
the Jews **m** a plot and bound Acts 23:12
than forty who **m** this conspiracy. Acts 23:13
reforms are being **m** for this nation, Acts 24:2
they came together here, I **m** no delay, Acts 25:17
out his hand and **m** his defense: Acts 26:1
hope in the promise **m** by God to our Acts 26:6
to the wind they **m** for the beach. Acts 27:40
And from there we **m** a circuit and Acts 28:13
after Paul had **m** one statement: Acts 28:25
world, in the things that have been **m**. Rom 1:20
"I have **m** you the father of many Rom 4:17
No distrust **m** him waver concerning Rom 4:20
the many were **m** sinners, Rom 5:19
the many will be **m** righteous. Rom 5:19
"Why have you **m** me like this?" Rom 9:20
writings has been **m** known to all Rom 16:26
Has not God **m** foolish the wisdom of 1 Cor 1:20
whom God **m** our wisdom and our 1 Cor 1:30
husband is **m** holy because 1 Cor 7:14
unbelieving wife is **m** holy because 1 Cor 7:14
we have not **m** use of this right, 1 Cor 9:12
But I have **m** no use of any of these 1 Cor 9:15
all, I have **m** myself a servant to all, 1 Cor 9:19
For man was not **m** from woman, 1 Cor 11:8
for as woman was **m** from man, so 1 Cor 11:12
free—and all were **m** to drink of one 1 Cor 12:13
If a revelation is **m** to another sitting 1 Cor 14:30
so also in Christ shall all be **m** alive. 1 Cor 15:22
because they have **m** up for your 1 Cor 16:17
For I **m** up my mind not to make 2 Cor 2:1
those who should have **m** me rejoice, 2 Cor 2:3
who has **m** us competent to be 2 Cor 3:6
from God, a house not **m** with hands, 2 Cor 5:1
For our sake he **m** him to be sin who 2 Cor 5:21
For even if I **m** you grieve with my 2 Cor 7:8
whatever boasts I **m** to him about 2 Cor 7:14
must give as he has **m** up his mind, 2 Cor 9:7
every way we have **m** this plain to 2 Cor 11:6
I am not weak? Who is **m** to fall, 2 Cor 11:29
my power is **m** perfect in weakness." 2 Cor 12:9
the promises were **m** to Abraham and Gal 3:16
to whom the promise had been **m**, Gal 3:19
is always good to be **m** much of for a Gal 4:18
m us alive together with Christ—by Eph 2:5
which is **m** in the flesh by hands— Eph 2:11
who has **m** us both one and has Eph 2:14
how the mystery was **m** known to me by Eph 3:3
which was not **m** known to the sons of Eph 3:5
this gospel I was **m** a minister according Eph 3:7
God might now be **m** known to the Eph 3:10
but **m** himself nothing, taking the form Phil 2:7
Christ Jesus has **m** me his own. Phil 3:12
not consider that I have **m** it my own. Phil 3:13
let your requests be **m** known to God. Phil 4:6
and has **m** known to us your love in the Col 1:8
with a circumcision **m** without hands, Col 2:11
flesh, God **m** alive together with him, Col 2:13
we could have **m** demands as apostles 1 Thes 2:6
prophecies previously **m** about you, 1 Tm 1:18
some have **m** shipwreck of their 1 Tm 1:19
and thanksgivings be **m** for all people, 1 Tm 2:1
for it is **m** holy by the word of God and 1 Tm 4:5
about which you **m** the good 1 Tm 6:12
before Pontius Pilate **m** the good 1 Tm 6:13
You **m** him for a little while lower than Heb 2:7
a little while was **m** lower than the Heb 2:9
he had to be **m** like his brothers in Heb 2:17
not exalt himself to be **m** a high priest, Heb 5:5
And being **m** perfect, he became the Heb 5:9
For when God **m** a promise to Heb 6:13
(for the law **m** nothing perfect); but on Heb 7:19
became priests were **m** such without Heb 7:20
but this one was **m** a priest with an Heb 7:21
a Son who has been **m** perfect forever. Heb 7:28
the covenant that I **m** with their fathers Heb 8:9
These preparations having thus been **m**, Heb 9:6
more perfect tent (not **m** with hands, Heb 9:11
of the one who **m** it must be Heb 9:16
as long as the one who **m** it is alive. Heb 9:17
not into holy places **m** with hands, Heb 9:24
enemies should be **m** a footstool for Heb 10:13
is seen was not **m** out of things that Heb 11:3
m mention of the exodus of the Heb 11:22
sword, were **m** strong out of weakness, Heb 11:34
from us they should not be **m** perfect. Heb 11:40
voice whose words **m** the hearers beg Heb 12:19
the spirits of the righteous **m** perfect, Heb 12:23
things that have been **m**—in order Heb 12:27
you not then **m** distinctions among Jas 2:4
curse people who are **m** in the likeness of Jas 3:9
the spirit that he has **m** to dwell in us"? Jas 4:5
the world but was **m** manifest in the 1 Pt 1:20
in the flesh but **m** alive in the spirit, 1 Pt 3:18
as our Lord Jesus Christ **m** clear to me. 2 Pt 1:14
myths when we **m** known to you 2 Pt 1:16
the life was **m** manifest, and we have 1 Jn 1:2
the Father and was **m** manifest to us— 1 Jn 1:2
is the promise that he **m** to us—eternal 1 Jn 2:25
love of God was **m** manifest among us, 1 Jn 4:9
does not believe God has **m** him a liar, 1 Jn 5:10
He **m** it known by sending his angel to Rv 1:1
and **m** us a kingdom, priests to his God Rv 1:6
and you have **m** them a kingdom and Rv 5:10
washed their robes and **m** them white in Rv 7:14
the water, because it had been **m** bitter. Rv 8:11
I had eaten it my stomach was **m** bitter. Rv 10:10
worship him who **m** heaven and earth, Rv 14:7
she who **m** all nations drink the wine of Rv 14:8
and the earth was **m** bright with his Rv 18:1
come, and his Bride has **m** herself ready; Rv 19:7
each of the gates **m** of a single pearl, Rv 21:21

MADLY (1)
The chariots race **m** through the streets; Na 2:4

MADMAN (4)
to behave as a **m** in my presence? 1 Sm 21:15
Like a **m** who throws firebrands, Prv 26:18
the LORD over every **m** who prophesies, Jer 29:26
am talking like a **m**—with far 2 Cor 11:23

MADMANNAH (2)
Ziklag, **M**, Sansannah, Jos 15:31
She also bore Shaaph the father of **M**, 1 Chr 2:49

MADMEN (2)
Do I lack **m**, that you have brought 1 Sm 21:15
You also, O **M**, shall be brought to Jer 48:2

MADMENAH (1)
M is in flight; the inhabitants of Gebim Is 10:31

MADNESS (9)
strike you with **m** and blindness and Dt 28:28
wisdom and to know **m** and folly. Eccl 1:17
to consider wisdom and **m** and folly. Eccl 2:12
oppression drives the wise into **m**, Eccl 7:7
of folly and the foolishness that is **m**. Eccl 7:25
and **m** is in their hearts while they live, Eccl 9:3
and the end of his talk is evil **m**. Eccl 10:13
horse with panic, and its rider with **m**. Zec 12:4
voice and restrained the prophet's **m**. 2 Pt 2:16

MADON (2)
heard of this, he sent to Jobab king of **M**, Jos 11:1
the king of **M**, one; the king of Hazor, Jos 12:19

MAGADAN (1)
the boat and went to the region of **M**. Mt 15:39

MAGBISH (1)
The sons of **M**, 156. Ezr 2:30

MAGDALENE (12)
whom were Mary **M** and Mary the Mt 27:56
Mary **M** and the other Mary were there, Mt 27:61
Mary **M** and the other Mary went to see Mt 28:1
distance, among whom were Mary **M**, Mk 15:40
Mary **M** and Mary the mother of Joses Mk 15:47
Mary **M** and Mary the mother of James Mk 16:1
the week, he appeared first to Mary **M**, Mk 16:9
Mary, called **M**, from whom seven Lk 8:2
Now it was Mary **M** and Joanna and Lk 24:10
Mary the wife of Clopas, and Mary **M**. Jn 19:25
of the week Mary **M** came to the tomb Jn 20:1
Mary **M** went and announced to the Jn 20:18

MAGDIEL (2)
M, and Iram; these are the chiefs of Gn 36:43
M, and Iram; these are the chiefs of 1 Chr 1:54

MAGGOT (1)
how much less man, who is a **m**, and the Jb 25:6

MAGGOTS (1)
m are laid as a bed beneath you, and Is 14:11

MAGIC (6)
A bribe is like a **m** stone in the eyes of Prv 17:8
the women who sew **m** bands upon all Ezk 13:18
am against your **m** bands with which Ezk 13:20
had previously practiced **m** in the city Acts 8:9
time he had amazed them with his **m**. Acts 8:11
who had practiced **m** arts brought Acts 19:19

MAGICIAN (4)
and the skillful **m** and the expert Is 3:3
a thing of any **m** or enchanter or Dn 2:10
Paphos, they came upon a certain **m**, Acts 13:6
But Elymas the **m** (for that is the Acts 13:8

MAGICIANS (15)
and called for all the **m** of Egypt and all Gn 41:8
And I told it to the **m**, but there was no Gn 41:24
the sorcerers, and they, the **m** of Egypt, Ex 7:11
But the **m** of Egypt did the same by their Ex 7:22
But the **m** did the same by their secret arts Ex 8:7
The **m** tried by their secret arts to Ex 8:18
Then the **m** said to Pharaoh, "This is the Ex 8:19
And the **m** could not stand before Moses Ex 9:11
boils came upon the **m** and upon all the Ex 9:11
than all the **m** and enchanters that Dn 1:20
Then the king commanded that the **m**, Dn 2:2
m, or astrologers can show to the king Dn 2:27
Then the **m**, the enchanters, the Dn 4:7
"O Belteshazzar, chief of the **m**, because I Dn 4:9
the king—made him chief of the **m**, Dn 5:11

MAGISTRATE (1)
you go with your accuser before the **m**, Lk 12:58

MAGISTRATES (8)
appoint **m** and judges who may judge Ezr 7:25
the treasurers, the justices, the **m**, Dn 3:2
the treasurers, the justices, the **m**, Dn 3:3
they had brought them to the **m**, Acts 16:20
and the **m** tore the garments off them Acts 16:22
it was day, the **m** sent the police, Acts 16:35
"The **m** have sent to let you go. Acts 16:36
police reported these words to the **m**, Acts 16:38

MAGNIFICENCE (1)
she may even be deposed from her **m**, Acts 19:27

MAGNIFICENT (2)
for the LORD must be exceedingly **m**, 1 Chr 22:5
the Lord comes, the great and **m** day. Acts 2:20

MAGNIFIED (5)
And your name will be **m** forever, 2 Sm 7:26
will be established and **m** forever, 1 Chr 17:24
because he **m** himself against the LORD, Jer 48:26
because he **m** himself against the LORD. Jer 48:42
And you **m** yourselves against me Ezk 35:13

MAGNIFIES (1)
And Mary said, "My soul **m** the Lord, Lk 1:46

MAGNIFY (9)
If indeed you **m** yourselves against me Jb 19:5
Oh, **m** the LORD with me, and let us exalt Ps 34:3
dishonor who **m** themselves against Ps 35:26
a song; I will **m** him with thanksgiving. Ps 69:30
or the saw **m** itself against him who Is 10:15
sake, to **m** his law and make it glorious. Is 42:21
exalt himself and **m** himself above Dn 11:36
god, for he shall **m** himself above all. Dn 11:37
to the Gentiles, I **m** my ministry Rom 11:13

MAGOG (5)
Gomer, **M**, Madai, Javan, Tubal, Gn 10:2
Gomer, **M**, Madai, Javan, Tubal, 1 Chr 1:5
your face toward Gog, of the land of **M**, Ezk 38:2
I will send fire on **M** and on those who Ezk 39:6
the four corners of the earth, Gog and **M**, Rv 20:8

MAGPIASH (1)
M, Meshullam, Hezir, Neh 10:20

MAHALAB (1)
and it ends at the sea; **M**, Achzib, Jos 19:29

MAHALALEEL (1)
of Enoch, the son of Jared, the son of **M**, Lk 3:37

MAHALALEL (7)
Kenan had lived 70 years, he fathered **M**. Gn 5:12
lived after he fathered **M** 840 years and Gn 5:13
When **M** had lived 65 years, he fathered Gn 5:15
M lived after he fathered Jared 830 years Gn 5:16
Thus all the days of **M** were 895 years, Gn 5:17
Kenan, **M**, Jared; 1 Chr 1:2
Amariah, son of Shephatiah, son of **M**, Neh 11:4

MAHALATH (4)
he had, **M** the daughter of Ishmael, Gn 28:9
took as wife **M** the daughter of 2 Chr 11:18
To the choirmaster: according to **M**. A Ps 53:T

choirmaster: according to **M** Leannoth. Ps 88:T

MAHANAIM (13)
So he called the name of that place **M**. Gn 32:2
and from **M** to the territory of Debir, Jos 13:26
Their region extended from **M**, Jos 13:30
manslayer, **M** with its pasturelands, Jos 21:38
of Saul and brought him over to **M**, 2 Sm 2:8
of Saul, went out from **M** to Gibeon. 2 Sm 2:12
the whole morning, they came to **M**. 2 Sm 2:29
Then David came to **M**. And 2 Sm 17:24
When David came to **M**, Shobi the 2 Sm 17:27
king with food while he stayed at **M**, 2 Sm 19:32
curse on the day when I went to **M**. 1 Kgs 2:8
Ahinadab the son of Iddo, in **M**; 1 Kgs 4:14
M with its pasturelands, 1 Chr 6:80

MAHANEH-DAN (2)
of the LORD began to stir him in **M**, Jgs 13:25
that place is called **M** to this day; Jgs 18:12

MAHARAI (3)
the Ahohite, **M** of Netophah, 2 Sm 23:28
M of Netophah, Heled the son of 1 Chr 11:30
tenth month, was **M** of Netophah, 1 Chr 27:13

MAHATH (3)
of Zuph, son of Elkanah, son of **M**, 1 Chr 6:35
Levites arose, **M** the son of Amasai, 2 Chr 29:12
M, and Benaiah were overseers 2 Chr 31:13

MAHAVITE (1)
Eliel the **M**, and Jeribai, and 1 Chr 11:46

MAHAZIOTH (2)
Joshbekashah, Mallothi, Hothir, **M**. 1 Chr 25:4
to the twenty-third, to **M**, his sons 1 Chr 25:30

MAHER-SHALAL-HASH-BAZ (2)
in common characters, 'Belonging to **M**.' Is 8:1
the LORD said to me, "Call his name **M**; Is 8:3

MAHLAH (5)
the daughters of Zelophehad were **M**, Nm 26:33
M, Noah, Hoglah, Milcah, and Tirzah. Nm 27:1
for **M**, Tirzah, Hoglah, Milcah, and Nm 36:11
M, Noah, Hoglah, Milcah, and Tirzah. Jos 17:3
bore Ishhod, Abiezer and **M**. 1 Chr 7:18

MAHLI (12)
The sons of Merari: **M** and Mushi. These Ex 6:19
of Merari by their clans: **M** and Mushi. Nm 3:20
The sons of Merari: **M** and Mushi. 1 Chr 6:19
M, Libni his son, Shimei his son, 1 Chr 6:29
son of **M**, son of Mushi, son of 1 Chr 6:47
The sons of Merari: **M** and Mushi. 1 Chr 23:21
The sons of **M**: Eleazar and Kish. 1 Chr 23:21
M, Eder, and Jeremoth, three. 1 Chr 23:23
The sons of Merari: **M** and Mushi. 1 Chr 24:26
Of **M**: Eleazar, who had no sons. 1 Chr 24:28
of Mushi: **M**, Eder, and Jerimoth. 1 Chr 24:30
of the sons of **M** the son of Levi, Ezr 8:18

MAHLITES (2)
the clan of the **M** and the clan of Nm 3:33
of the Hebronites, the clan of the **M**, Nm 26:58

MAHLON (4)
of his two sons were **M** and Chilion. Ru 1:2
and both **M** and Chilion died, so that the Ru 1:5
all that belonged to Chilion and to **M**. Ru 4:9
Also Ruth the Moabite, the widow of **M**, I Ru 4:10

MAHOL (1)
Calcol, and Darda, the sons of **M**, 1 Kgs 4:31

MAHSEIAH (2)
to Baruch the son of Neriah son of **M**, Jer 32:12
Seraiah the son of Neriah, son of **M**, Jer 51:59

MAID (1)
as with the **m**, so with her mistress; Is 24:2

MAIDEN (1)
a **m** whom no man had known. Gn 24:16

MAIDENS (3)
Young men and **m** together, old men Ps 148:12
her household and portions for her **m**. Prv 31:15
old men outright, young men and **m**, Ezk 9:6

MAIDSERVANT (5)
the cause of my manservant or my **m**, Jb 31:13
servant, and save the son of your **m**. Ps 86:16
I am your servant, the son of your **m**. Ps 116:16
as the eyes of a **m** to the hand of her Ps 123:2
and a **m** when she displaces her Prv 30:23

MAIDSERVANTS (1)
in my house and my **m** count me as a Jb 19:15

MAIL (4)
and he was armed with a coat of **m**, 1 Sm 17:5
and clothed him with a coat of **m**, 1 Sm 17:38
shields, spears, helmets, coats of **m**, 2 Chr 26:14
spears, shields, bows, and coats of **m**. Neh 4:16

MAIMED (1)
young or heal the **m** or nourish the Zec 11:16

MAIN (4)
the **m** encampment that was north of Jos 8:13
the men in the **m** ambush was that Jgs 20:38
and Moab and the **m** part of the Dn 11:41
Go therefore to the **m** roads and invite to Mt 22:9

MAINLAND (2)
her daughters on the **m** shall be killed Ezk 26:6
the sword your daughters on the **m**. Ezk 26:8

MAINSTAY (1)
the bow of Elam, the **m** of their might. Jer 49:35

MAINTAIN (11)
poor and cannot **m** himself with you, Lv 25:35
and their plea, and **m** their cause. 1 Kgs 8:45
and their plea, and **m** their cause 1 Kgs 8:49
and may he **m** the cause of his 1 Kgs 8:59
and their plea, and **m** their cause. 2 Chr 6:35
and **m** their cause and forgive your 2 Chr 6:39
m the right of the afflicted and the Ps 82:3
that the LORD will **m** the cause of the Ps 140:12
of his iniquity, none can **m** his life. Ezk 7:13
in everything and **m** the traditions 1 Cor 11:2
eager to **m** the unity of the Spirit in the Eph 4:3

MAINTAINED (1)
For you have **m** my just cause; you have Ps 9:4

MAINTAINS (1)
the proud but **m** the widow's Prv 15:25

MAINTENANCE (2)
gifts for the **m** of the house 1 Chr 26:27
your household and **m** for your girls. Prv 27:27

MAJESTIC (13)
Who is like you, **m** in holiness, Ex 15:11
he thunders with his **m** voice, and he Jb 37:4
the locust? His **m** snorting is terrifying. Jb 39:20
how **m** is your name in all the earth! Ps 8:1
how **m** is your name in all the earth! Ps 8:9
more **m** than the mountains of prey. Ps 76:4
axe, and Lebanon will fall by the **M** One. Is 10:34
LORD will cause his **m** voice to be heard Is 30:30
with oars can go, nor **m** ship can pass. Is 33:21
through, I will make you **m** forever, Is 60:15
her and the daughters of **m** nations, Ezk 32:18
make them like his **m** steed in battle. Zec 10:3
was borne to him by the **M** Glory, 2 Pt 1:17

MAJESTY (44)
greatness of your **m** you overthrow your Ex 15:7
A firstborn bull—he has **m**, and his Dt 33:17
your help, through the skies in his **m**. Dt 33:26
Splendor and **m** are before him; 1 Chr 16:27
the glory and the victory and the **m**, 1 Chr 29:11
on him such royal **m** as had not 1 Chr 29:25
Will not his **m** terrify you, and the Jb 13:11
God, and I could not have faced his **m**. Jb 31:23
God is clothed with awesome **m**. Jb 37:22
"Adorn yourself with **m** and dignity; Jb 40:10
splendor and **m** you bestow on him. Ps 21:5
the voice of the LORD is full of **m**. Ps 29:4
O mighty one, in your splendor and **m**! Ps 45:3
In your **m** ride out victoriously for the Ps 45:4
power to God, whose **m** is over Israel, Ps 68:34
The LORD reigns; he is robed in **m**; the Ps 93:1
Splendor and **m** are before him; strength Ps 96:6
You are clothed with splendor and **m**, Ps 104:1
Full of splendor and **m** is his work, and Ps 111:3
On the glorious splendor of your **m**, Ps 145:5
his **m** is above earth and heaven. Ps 148:13
the LORD, and from the splendor of his **m**. Is 2:10
the LORD, and from the splendor of his **m**, Is 2:19
the LORD, and from the splendor of his **m**, Is 2:21
over the **m** of the LORD they shout from Is 24:14
and does not see the **m** of the LORD. Is 26:10
But there the LORD in **m** will be for us a Is 33:21
given to it, the **m** of Carmel and Sharon. Is 35:2
the glory of the LORD, the **m** of our God. Is 35:2
he had no form or **m** that we should look Is 53:2
him, saying, 'Ah, lord!' or 'Ah, his **m**!' Jer 22:18
of Zion all her **m** has departed. Lam 1:6
residence and for the glory of my **m**?" Dn 4:30
my **m** and splendor returned to me. Dn 4:36
and greatness and glory and **m**. Dn 5:18
person to whom royal **m** has not been Dn 11:21
in the **m** of the name of the LORD his God. Mi 5:4
the LORD is restoring the **m** of Jacob as the Na 2:2
the majesty of Jacob as the **m** of Israel, Na 2:2
And all were astonished at the **m** of God. Lk 9:43
down at the right hand of the **M** on high, Heb 1:3
hand of the throne of the **M** in heaven, Heb 8:1
but we were eyewitnesses of his **m**. 2 Pt 1:16
our Lord, be glory, **m**, dominion, Jude 1:25

MAJORITY (4)
of whom the **m** had to that point 1 Chr 12:29
For a **m** of the people, many of them 2 Chr 30:18
the **m** decided to put out to sea from Acts 27:12
this punishment by the **m** is enough, 2 Cor 2:6

MAKAZ (1)
Ben-deker, in **M**, Shaalbim, 1 Kgs 4:9

MAKE (1050)
God said, "Let us **m** man in our image, Gn 1:26
alone; I will **m** him a helper fit for him." Gn 2:18
the tree was to be desired to **m** one wise, Gn 3:6
"I have determined to **m** an end of all Gn 6:13
M yourself an ark of gopher wood. Gn 6:14
M rooms in the ark, and cover it inside Gn 6:14
This is how you are to **m** it: the length of Gn 6:15
M a roof for the ark, and finish it to a Gn 6:16
M it with lower, second, and third decks. Gn 6:16
the covenant that I **m** between me and Gn 9:12
to one another, "Come, let us **m** bricks, Gn 11:3
and let us **m** a name for ourselves, Gn 11:4
And I will **m** of you a great nation, and I Gn 12:2
I will bless you and **m** your name great, Gn 12:2
I will **m** your offspring as the dust of Gn 13:16
that I may **m** my covenant between me Gn 17:2
I will **m** you exceedingly fruitful, and I Gn 17:6
fruitful, and I will **m** you into nations, Gn 17:6
him and will **m** him fruitful and Gn 17:20
and I will **m** him into a great nation. Gn 17:20
of fine flour! Knead it, and **m** cakes." Gn 18:6
Come, let us **m** our father drink wine, Gn 19:32
Let us **m** him drink wine tonight also. Gn 19:34
And I will **m** a nation of the son of the Gn 21:13
for I will **m** him into a great nation." Gn 21:18
that I may **m** you swear by the LORD, the Gn 24:3
us, and let us **m** a covenant with you, Gn 26:28
bless you and **m** you fruitful and Gn 28:3
Come now, let us **m** a covenant, you Gn 31:44
and **m** your offspring as the sand of the Gn 32:12
M marriages with us. Give your Gn 34:9
M an altar there to the God who Gn 35:1
so that I may **m** there an altar to the God Gn 35:3
him on the journey that you are to **m**, Gn 42:38
and slaughter an animal and **m** ready, Gn 43:16
fall upon us to **m** us servants and seize Gn 43:18
"**M** everyone go out from me." So no one Gn 45:1
for there I will **m** you into a great Gn 46:3
I will **m** you fruitful and multiply you, Gn 48:4
and I will **m** of you a company of Gn 48:4
'God **m** you as Ephraim and as Gn 48:20
and you **m** them rest from their Ex 5:5
longer give the people straw to **m** bricks, Ex 5:7
servants, yet they say to us, '**M** bricks!' Ex 5:16
LORD I did not **m** myself known to them. Ex 6:3
and **m** frogs come up on the land of Ex 8:5
But the LORD will **m** a distinction between Ex 9:4
can eat you shall **m** your count for the Ex 12:4
and I **m** them know the statutes of God Ex 18:16
and **m** them know the way in which Ex 18:20
"You shall not **m** for yourself a carved Ex 20:4
You shall not **m** gods of silver to be Ex 20:23
nor shall you **m** for yourselves gods of Ex 20:23
of earth you shall **m** for me and Ex 20:24
If you **m** me an altar of stone, you shall Ex 20:25
the owner of the pit shall **m** restoration. Ex 21:34
he shall **m** restitution from the best in Ex 22:5
started the fire shall **m** full restitution. Ex 22:6
the oath, and he shall not **m** restitution. Ex 22:11
him, he shall **m** restitution to its owner. Ex 22:12
He shall not **m** restitution for what has Ex 22:13
with it, he shall **m** full restitution. Ex 22:14
was with it, he shall not **m** restitution; Ex 22:15
bride-price for her and **m** her his wife. Ex 22:16
and **m** no mention of the names of Ex 23:13
and I will **m** all your enemies turn their Ex 23:27
You shall **m** no covenant with them Ex 23:32
land, lest they **m** you sin against me; Ex 23:33
And let them **m** me a sanctuary, that I Ex 25:8
and of all its furniture, so you shall **m** it. Ex 25:9
"They shall **m** an ark of acacia wood. Ex 25:10
and you shall **m** on it a molding of gold Ex 25:11
You shall **m** poles of acacia wood and Ex 25:13
"You shall **m** a mercy seat of pure gold. Ex 25:17
And you shall **m** two cherubim of gold; Ex 25:18
of hammered work shall you **m** them, Ex 25:18
M one cherub on the one end, and one Ex 25:19
seat shall you **m** the cherubim on Ex 25:19
"You shall **m** a table of acacia wood. Ex 25:23
with pure gold and **m** a molding of gold Ex 25:24
And you shall **m** a rim around it a Ex 25:25
And you shall **m** for it four rings of Ex 25:26
You shall **m** the poles of acacia wood, Ex 25:28
And you shall **m** its plates and dishes Ex 25:29
you shall **m** them of pure gold. Ex 25:29
"You shall **m** a lampstand of pure gold. Ex 25:31

You shall **m** seven lamps for it. And the	Ex 25:37
And see that you **m** them after the	Ex 25:40
you shall **m** the tabernacle with ten	Ex 26:1
you shall **m** them with cherubim	Ex 26:1
And you shall **m** loops of blue on the	Ex 26:4
Likewise you shall **m** loops on the edge	Ex 26:4
Fifty loops you shall **m** on the one	Ex 26:5
and fifty loops you shall **m** on the edge of	Ex 26:5
And you shall **m** fifty clasps of gold, and	Ex 26:6
"You shall also **m** curtains of goats' hair	Ex 26:7
tabernacle; eleven curtains shall you **m**.	Ex 26:7
You shall **m** fifty loops on the edge of	Ex 26:10
"You shall **m** fifty clasps of bronze, and	Ex 26:11
And you shall **m** for the tent a covering	Ex 26:14
"You shall **m** upright frames for the	Ex 26:15
You shall **m** the frames for the	Ex 26:18
of silver you shall **m** under the twenty	Ex 26:19
westward you shall **m** six frames.	Ex 26:22
And you shall **m** two frames for	Ex 26:23
"You shall **m** bars of acacia wood, five	Ex 26:26
with gold and shall **m** their rings of	Ex 26:29
"And you shall **m** a veil of blue and	Ex 26:31
"You shall **m** a screen for the entrance	Ex 26:36
And you shall **m** for the screen five	Ex 26:37
"You shall **m** the altar of acacia wood,	Ex 27:1
And you shall **m** horns for it on its four	Ex 27:2
You shall **m** pots for it to receive its	Ex 27:3
You shall **m** all its utensils of bronze.	Ex 27:3
You shall also **m** for it a grating, a	Ex 27:4
the net you shall **m** four bronze rings at	Ex 27:4
And you shall **m** poles for the altar, poles	Ex 27:6
You shall **m** it hollow, with boards. As it	Ex 27:8
"You shall **m** the court of the	Ex 27:9
And you shall **m** holy garments for	Ex 28:2
that they **m** Aaron's garments to	Ex 28:3
are the garments that they shall **m**:	Ex 28:4
They shall **m** holy garments for Aaron	Ex 28:4
"And they shall **m** the ephod of gold, of	Ex 28:6
You shall **m** settings of gold filigree,	Ex 28:13
"You shall **m** a breastpiece of	Ex 28:15
of the ephod you shall **m** it—of gold,	Ex 28:15
and fine twined linen shall you **m** it.	Ex 28:15
You shall **m** for the breastpiece twisted	Ex 28:22
And you shall **m** for the breastpiece	Ex 28:23
You shall **m** two rings of gold, and put	Ex 28:26
And you shall **m** two rings of gold, and	Ex 28:27
"You shall **m** the robe of the ephod all	Ex 28:31
hem you shall **m** pomegranates of blue	Ex 28:33
"You shall **m** a plate of pure gold and	Ex 28:36
and you shall **m** a turban of fine linen,	Ex 28:39
and you shall **m** a sash embroidered	Ex 28:39
sons you shall **m** coats and sashes	Ex 28:40
You shall **m** them for glory and	Ex 28:40
You shall **m** for them linen	Ex 28:42
You shall **m** them of fine wheat flour.	Ex 29:2
the altar, when you **m** atonement for it,	Ex 29:36
days you shall **m** atonement for the	Ex 29:37
"You shall **m** an altar on which to burn	Ex 30:1
incense; you shall **m** it of acacia wood.	Ex 30:1
And you shall **m** a molding of gold	Ex 30:3
And you shall **m** two golden rings for it.	Ex 30:4
two opposite sides of it you shall **m** them,	Ex 30:4
You shall **m** the poles of acacia wood	Ex 30:5
Aaron shall **m** atonement on its horns	Ex 30:10
atonement he shall **m** atonement for it	Ex 30:10
LORD'S offering to **m** atonement for	Ex 30:15
so as to **m** atonement for your lives."	Ex 30:16
"You shall also **m** a basin of bronze,	Ex 30:18
And you shall **m** of these a sacred	Ex 30:25
and you shall **m** no other like it in	Ex 30:32
and **m** an incense blended as by the	Ex 30:35
that you shall **m** according to its	Ex 30:37
you shall not **m** for yourselves.	Ex 30:37
that they may **m** all that I have	Ex 31:6
"Up, **m** us gods who shall go before us.	Ex 32:1
in order that I may **m** a great nation of	Ex 32:10
me, '**M** us gods who shall go before us.	Ex 32:23
perhaps I can **m** atonement for your	Ex 32:30
"I will **m** all my goodness pass before	Ex 33:19
lest you **m** a covenant with the	Ex 34:12
lest you **m** a covenant with the	Ex 34:15
after their gods and **m** your sons whore	Ex 34:16
"You shall not **m** for yourself any gods	Ex 34:17
among you come and **m** all that the	Ex 35:10
Everyone who could **m** a contribution	Ex 35:24
accepted for him to **m** atonement for him.	Lv 1:4
the priest shall **m** atonement for them,	Lv 4:20
So the priest shall **m** atonement for him	Lv 4:26
the priest shall **m** atonement for him,	Lv 4:31
the priest shall **m** atonement for him	Lv 4:35
And the priest shall **m** atonement for him	Lv 5:6
the priest shall **m** atonement for him	Lv 5:10
the priest shall **m** atonement for him	Lv 5:13
He shall also **m** restitution for what he	Lv 5:16
the priest shall **m** atonement for him	Lv 5:16
the priest shall **m** atonement for him	Lv 5:18
And the priest shall **m** atonement for him	Lv 6:7
tent of meeting to **m** atonement in the	Lv 6:30
and consecrated it to **m** atonement for it.	Lv 8:15
to be done to **m** atonement for you.	Lv 8:34
burnt offering and **m** atonement for	Lv 9:7
of the people and **m** atonement for them,	Lv 9:7
to **m** atonement for them before the	Lv 10:17
You shall not **m** yourselves detestable	Lv 11:43
to **m** a distinction between the unclean	Lv 11:47
the LORD and **m** atonement for her.	Lv 12:7
the priest shall **m** atonement for her,	Lv 12:8
the priest shall **m** atonement for him	Lv 14:18
to **m** atonement for him who is to be	Lv 14:19
the priest shall **m** atonement for him,	Lv 14:20
to be waved, to **m** atonement for him,	Lv 14:21
to **m** atonement for him before the	Lv 14:29
the priest shall **m** atonement before the	Lv 14:31
So he shall **m** atonement for the house,	Lv 14:53
the priest shall **m** atonement for him	Lv 15:15
the priest shall **m** atonement for her	Lv 15:30
himself and shall **m** atonement for	Lv 16:6
before the LORD to **m** atonement over it,	Lv 16:10
and shall **m** atonement for himself and	Lv 16:11
Thus he shall **m** atonement for the	Lv 16:16
time he enters to **m** atonement in the	Lv 16:17
before the LORD and **m** atonement for it,	Lv 16:18
the people and **m** atonement for	Lv 16:24
was brought in to **m** atonement in the	Lv 16:27
in his father's place shall **m** atonement,	Lv 16:32
He shall **m** atonement for the holy	Lv 16:33
and he shall **m** atonement for the tent	Lv 16:33
and he shall **m** atonement for the	Lv 16:33
on the altar to **m** atonement for your	Lv 17:11
wife and so **m** yourself unclean with	Lv 18:20
animal and so **m** yourself unclean	Lv 18:23
"Do not **m** yourselves unclean by any	Lv 18:24
vomit you out when you **m** it unclean,	Lv 18:28
and never to **m** yourselves unclean by	Lv 18:30
turn to idols or **m** for yourselves any	Lv 19:4
the priest shall **m** atonement for him	Lv 19:22
You shall not **m** any cuts on your body	Lv 19:28
and so **m** yourselves unclean by them:	Lv 19:31
to **m** my sanctuary unclean and to	Lv 20:3
for that is to **m** naked one's relative;	Lv 20:19
You shall not **m** yourselves detestable	Lv 20:25
'No one shall **m** himself unclean for the	Lv 21:1
for her he may **m** himself unclean).	Lv 21:3
He shall not **m** himself unclean as a	Lv 21:4
They shall not **m** bald patches on their	Lv 21:5
beards, nor **m** any cuts on their body.	Lv 21:5
dead bodies nor **m** himself unclean,	Lv 21:11
beasts, and so **m** himself unclean by it:	Lv 22:8
And you shall **m** proclamation on the	Lv 23:21
to **m** atonement for you before the LORD	Lv 23:28
takes an animal's life shall **m** it good,	Lv 24:18
kills an animal shall **m** it good,	Lv 24:21
And if you **m** a sale to your neighbor or	Lv 25:14
you shall not **m** him serve as a slave:	Lv 25:39
You may **m** slaves of them, but over	Lv 25:46
"You shall not **m** idols for yourselves or	Lv 26:1
lie down, and none shall **m** you afraid.	Lv 26:6
turn to you and **m** you fruitful and	Lv 26:9
clear out the old to **m** way for the new.	Lv 26:10
I will **m** my dwelling among you, and	Lv 26:11
the eyes and **m** the heart ache.	Lv 26:16
and I will **m** your heavens like iron and	Lv 26:19
your livestock and **m** you few in	Lv 26:22
waste and will **m** your sanctuaries	Lv 26:31
humbled and they **m** amends for their	Lv 26:41
and they shall **m** amends for their	Lv 26:43
not exchange it or **m** a substitute for it,	Lv 27:10
twenty gerahs shall **m** a shekel.	Lv 27:25
neither shall he **m** a substitute for it;	Lv 27:33
And he shall **m** full restitution for his	Nm 5:7
Then the priest shall **m** her take an	Nm 5:19
then' (let the priest **m** the woman take	Nm 5:21
the woman) 'the LORD **m** you a curse	Nm 5:21
your bowels and **m** your womb swell	Nm 5:22
And he shall **m** the woman drink the	Nm 5:24
and afterward shall **m** the woman	Nm 5:26
if they die, shall he **m** himself unclean,	Nm 6:7
offering, and **m** atonement for him,	Nm 6:11
the LORD **m** his face to shine upon you	Nm 6:25
to the LORD to **m** atonement for the	Nm 8:12
of meeting and to **m** atonement for the	Nm 8:19
"**M** two silver trumpets. Of hammered	Nm 10:2
Of hammered work you shall **m** them,	Nm 10:2
I the LORD **m** myself known to him in a	Nm 12:6
and I will **m** of you a nation greater	Nm 14:12
I swore that I would **m** you dwell,	Nm 14:30
to **m** a pleasing aroma to the LORD,	Nm 15:3
the priest shall **m** atonement for all	Nm 15:25
the priest shall **m** atonement before	Nm 15:28
to **m** atonement for him,	Nm 15:28
and tell them to **m** tassels on the	Nm 15:38
you must also **m** yourself a prince	Nm 16:13
congregation and **m** atonement for	Nm 16:46
Thus I will **m** to cease from me the	Nm 17:5
that you may **m** an end of their	Nm 17:10
"**M** a fiery serpent and set it on a pole,	Nm 21:8
M him stand before Eleazar the priest	Nm 27:19
sin offering, to **m** atonement for you.	Nm 28:22
male goat, to **m** atonement for you.	Nm 28:30
a sin offering, to **m** atonement for you;	Nm 29:5
or her husband may **m** void.	Nm 30:13
to **m** atonement for ourselves before	Nm 31:50
m you a thousand times as many as you	Dt 1:11
M them known to your children and your	Dt 4:9
made with you, and **m** a carved image,	Dt 4:23
our fathers did the LORD **m** this covenant,	Dt 5:3
"'You shall not **m** for yourself a carved	Dt 5:8
You shall **m** no covenant with them and	Dt 7:2
You may not **m** an end of them at once,	Dt 7:22
and you shall **m** their name perish from	Dt 7:24
that he might **m** you know that man does	Dt 8:3
them out and **m** them perish quickly,	Dt 9:3
And I will **m** of you a nation mightier	Dt 9:14
on the mountain and **m** an ark of wood.	Dt 10:1
his name and **m** his habitation there.	Dt 12:5
will choose, to **m** his name dwell there,	Dt 12:11
to **m** you leave the way in which the	Dt 13:5
shall inquire and **m** search and ask	Dt 13:14
not cut yourselves or **m** any baldness on	Dt 14:1
will choose, to **m** his name dwell there,	Dt 14:23
will choose, to **m** his name dwell there.	Dt 16:2
will choose, to **m** his name dwell in it,	Dt 16:6
will choose, to **m** his name dwell there.	Dt 16:11
of the LORD your God that you shall **m**.	Dt 16:21
lest he **m** the heart of his fellows melt	Dt 20:8
you shall **m** a parapet for your roof,	Dt 22:8
"You shall **m** yourself tassels on the	Dt 22:12
"If you **m** a vow to the LORD your God,	Dt 23:21
"When you **m** your neighbor a loan of	Dt 24:10
man to whom you **m** the loan shall	Dt 24:11
will choose, to **m** his name to dwell there.	Dt 26:2
"And you shall **m** response before the	Dt 26:5
And the LORD will **m** you abound in	Dt 28:11
And the LORD will **m** you the head and	Dt 28:13
The LORD will **m** the pestilence stick to	Dt 28:21
The LORD will **m** the rain of your land	Dt 28:24
that you should never **m** again;	Dt 28:68
commanded Moses to **m** with the people	Dt 29:1
And he will **m** you more prosperous and	Dt 30:5
your God will **m** you abundantly	Dt 30:9
So I will **m** them jealous with those who	Dt 32:21
is no god besides me; I kill and I **m** alive;	Dt 32:39
I will **m** my arrows drunk with blood,	Dt 32:42
then you will **m** your way prosperous,	Jos 1:8
"**M** flint knives and circumcise the sons	Jos 5:2
And when they **m** a long blast with the	Jos 6:5
shall not shout or **m** your voice heard,	Jos 6:10
the devoted things and **m** the camp of	Jos 6:18
Do not **m** the whole people toil up there,	Jos 7:3
country, so now **m** a covenant with us."	Jos 9:6
then how can we **m** a covenant with	Jos 9:7
Come now, **m** a covenant with us."'	Jos 9:11
at Shiloh to **m** war against them.	Jos 22:12
against the LORD or **m** us as rebels by	Jos 22:19
your children might **m** our children	Jos 22:25
among you or **m** mention of the	Jos 23:7
among you and **m** marriages with	Jos 23:12
and you shall **m** no covenant with the	Jgs 2:2
I will **m** melody to the LORD, the God of	Jgs 5:3
said to them, "Let me **m** a request of you:	Jgs 8:24
to **m** a carved image and a metal image.	Jgs 17:3
but do not **m** yourself known to the man	Ru 3:3
May the LORD **m** the woman, who is	Ru 4:11
the ash heap to **m** them sit with princes	1 Sm 2:8
his mother used to **m** for him a little	1 Sm 2:19
So you must **m** images of your tumors	1 Sm 6:5
and to **m** his implements of war and	1 Sm 8:12
their voice and **m** them a king."	1 Sm 8:22
that I may **m** known to you the word	1 Sm 9:27
said to Nahash, "**M** a treaty with us,	1 Sm 11:1
this condition I will **m** a treaty with	1 Sm 11:2
pleased the LORD to **m** you a people	1 Sm 12:22
the Hebrews **m** themselves swords	1 Sm 13:19
his daughter and **m** his father's	1 Sm 17:25
Saul thought to **m** David fall by	1 Sm 18:25
will he **m** you all commanders of	1 Sm 22:7
Go, **m** yet more sure. Know and see	1 Sm 23:22
the LORD will certainly **m** my lord a	1 Sm 25:28
I will **m** you my bodyguard for life."	1 Sm 28:2
M your covenant with me, and	2 Sm 3:12
"Good; I will **m** a covenant with you.	2 Sm 3:13
that they may **m** a covenant with you,	2 Sm 3:21
—and I will **m** merry before the LORD.	2 Sm 6:21
I will **m** myself yet more contemptible	2 Sm 6:22
And I will **m** for you a great name, like	2 Sm 7:9

you that the LORD will **m** you a house. 2 Sm 7:11
greatness, to **m** your servant know it. 2 Sm 7:21
sister Tamar come and **m** a couple of 2 Sm 13:6
shall I today **m** you wander about 2 Sm 15:20
And how shall I **m** atonement, that 2 Sm 21:3
the crooked you **m** yourself seem 2 Sm 22:27
and **m** his throne greater than the 1 Kgs 1:37
'May your God **m** the name of 1 Kgs 1:47
and **m** his throne greater than your 1 Kgs 1:47
now I have one request to **m** of you; 1 Kgs 2:16
"I have one small request to **m** of you; 1 Kgs 2:20
the king said to her, "**M** your request, 1 Kgs 2:20
"Did I not **m** you swear by the LORD 1 Kgs 2:42
Each man had to **m** provision for one 1 Kgs 4:7
and I will **m** it into rafts to go by sea to 1 Kgs 5:9
but I will **m** him ruler all the days of 1 Kgs 11:34
come to Shechem to **m** him king. 1 Kgs 12:1
went up to the altar to **m** offerings. 1 Kgs 12:33
standing by the altar to **m** offerings. 1 Kgs 13:1
high places who **m** offerings on you, 1 Kgs 13:2
and I will **m** your house like the 1 Kgs 16:3
the son of Ginath, to **m** him king, 1 Kgs 16:21
But first **m** me a little cake of it and 1 Kgs 17:13
and afterward **m** something for 1 Kgs 17:13
if I do not **m** your life as the life of one 1 Kgs 19:2
And I will **m** your house like the 1 Kgs 21:22
times shall I **m** you swear that 1 Kgs 22:16
'I will **m** this dry streambed full of 2 Kgs 3:16
Let us **m** a small room on the roof 2 Kgs 4:10
said, "Am I God, to kill and to **m** alive, 2 Kgs 5:7
and let us **m** a place for us to dwell 2 Kgs 6:2
LORD himself should **m** windows in 2 Kgs 7:2
LORD himself should **m** windows in 2 Kgs 7:19
son of Ahab to **m** war against Hazael 2 Kgs 8:28
And I will **m** the house of Ahab like 2 Kgs 9:9
"**M** ready." And they made ready his 2 Kgs 9:21
tell us. We will not **m** anyone king. 2 Kgs 10:5
to sacrifice and **m** offerings on the 2 Kgs 12:3
m a wager with my master the king 2 Kgs 18:23
Do not let Hezekiah **m** you trust in 2 Kgs 18:30
'**M** your peace with me and come 2 Kgs 18:31
and I will **m** him fall by the sword in 2 Kgs 19:7
had ordained to **m** offerings in the 2 Kgs 23:5
Place, and to **m** atonement for Israel, 1 Chr 6:49
with all Israel, to **m** him king, 1 Chr 11:10
named to come and **m** David king. 1 Chr 12:31
full intent to **m** David king over 1 Chr 12:38
of a single mind to **m** David king. 1 Chr 12:38
m known his deeds among the 1 Chr 16:8
And I will **m** for you a name, like the 1 Chr 17:8
I will therefore **m** preparation for it." 1 Chr 22:5
forever should **m** offerings before 1 Chr 23:13
had promised to **m** Israel as many 1 Chr 27:23
pleasure in me to **m** me king over all 1 Chr 28:4
hand it is to **m** great and to give 1 Chr 29:12
as a place to **m** offerings before him? 2 Chr 2:6
as overseers to **m** the people work. 2 Chr 2:18
and singers to **m** themselves heard in 2 Chr 5:13
and I will **m** it a proverb and a 2 Chr 7:20
come to Shechem to **m** him king. 2 Chr 10:1
for he intended to **m** him king. 2 Chr 11:22
as not to **m** a complete destruction. 2 Chr 12:12
times shall I **m** you swear that 2 Chr 18:15
of Israel to **m** war against Hazael 2 Chr 22:5
who could **m** war with mighty 2 Chr 26:13
high places to **m** offerings to other 2 Chr 28:25
in my heart to **m** a covenant with 2 Chr 29:10
his ministers and **m** offerings to 2 Chr 29:11
altar, to **m** atonement for all Israel. 2 Chr 29:24
they decreed to **m** a proclamation 2 Chr 30:5
did not **m** return according 2 Chr 32:25
We **m** known to the king that if this Ezr 4:16
Therefore **m** a decree that these men be Ezr 4:21
I **m** a decree regarding what you shall do Ezr 6:8
Also I **m** a decree that if anyone alters Ezr 6:11
is in Jerusalem. I Darius **m** a decree; Ezr 6:12
I **m** a decree that anyone of the people of Ezr 7:13
seven counselors to **m** inquiries about Ezr 7:14
m a decree to all the treasurers in the Ezr 7:21
Therefore let us **m** a covenant with our Ezr 10:3
Now then **m** confession to the LORD, Ezr 10:11
chosen, to **m** my name dwell there.' Neh 1:9
give me timber to **m** beams for the gates Neh 2:8
"The God of heaven will **m** us prosper, Neh 2:20
prophets who wanted to **m** me afraid. Neh 6:14
Tobiah sent letters to **m** me afraid. Neh 6:19
send portions and to **m** great rejoicing, Neh 8:12
and other leafy trees to **m** booths, Neh 8:15
mercies you did not **m** an end of them Neh 9:31
of all this we **m** a firm covenant in Neh 9:38
sin offerings to **m** atonement for Neh 10:33
had commanded her not to **m** it known. Est 2:10
that they should **m** them days of Est 9:22
Have I said, '**M** me a gift'? Or, 'From your Jb 6:22
m me understand how I have gone Jb 6:24

is man, that you **m** so much of him, Jb 7:17
lie down, and none will **m** you afraid; Jb 11:19
M me know my transgression and my Jb 13:23
things against me and **m** me inherit the Jb 13:26
They **m** night into day; 'The light,' they Jb 17:12
as my house, if I **m** my bed in darkness, Jb 17:13
against me and **m** my disgrace an Jb 19:5
to him if you **m** your ways blameless? Jb 22:3
You will **m** your prayer to him, and he Jb 22:27
the olive rows of the wicked they **m** oil; Jb 24:11
you **m** me ride on it, and you toss me Jb 30:22
he who made me in the womb **m** him? Jb 31:15
to his ways he will **m** it befall him. Jb 34:11
Will he then **m** repayment to suit you, Jb 34:33
question you, and you **m** it known to me. Jb 38:3
and to **m** the ground sprout with grass? Jb 38:27
Do you **m** him leap like the locust? His Jb 39:20
question you, and you **m** it known to me. Jb 40:7
Will he **m** many pleas to you? Will he Jb 41:3
Will he **m** a covenant with you to take Jb 41:4
The arrow cannot **m** him flee; for him Jb 41:28
you, and you **m** it known to me.' Jb 42:4
and I will **m** the nations your heritage, Ps 2:8
you alone, O LORD, **m** me dwell in safety. Ps 4:8
enemies; **m** your way straight before me. Ps 5:8
M them bear their guilt, O God; let them Ps 5:10
You **m** known to me the path of life; in Ps 16:11
the crooked you **m** yourself seem Ps 18:26
For you **m** him most blessed forever; you Ps 21:6
you **m** him glad with the joy of your Ps 21:6
You will **m** them as a blazing oven when Ps 21:9
see me mock me; they **m** mouths at me; Ps 22:7
M me to know your ways, O LORD; teach Ps 25:4
joy; I will sing and **m** melody to the LORD. Ps 27:6
M your face shine on your servant; save Ps 31:16
m melody to him with the harp of ten Ps 33:2
M haste to help me, O Lord, my Ps 38:22
m me know my end and what is the Ps 39:4
Do not **m** me the scorn of the fool! Ps 39:8
deliver me! O LORD, **m** haste to help me! Ps 40:13
stringed instruments **m** you glad; Ps 45:8
you will **m** them princes in all the Ps 45:16
a river whose streams **m** glad the city of Ps 46:4
man who would not **m** God his refuge, Ps 52:7
is steadfast! I will sing and **m** melody! Ps 57:7
no fault of mine, they run and **m** ready. Ps 59:4
m them totter by your power and bring Ps 59:11
You **m** the going out of the morning and Ps 65:8
I will **m** an offering of bulls and goats. Ps 66:15
us and bless us and **m** his face to shine Ps 67:1
and the drunkards **m** songs about me. Ps 69:12
I am in distress; **m** haste to answer me. Ps 69:17
and **m** their loins tremble continually. Ps 69:23
M haste, O God, to deliver me! O LORD, Ps 70:1
deliver me! O LORD, **m** haste to help me! Ps 70:1
me; O my God, **m** haste to help me! Ps 71:12
slippery places; you **m** them fall to ruin. Ps 73:18
M your vows to the LORD your God and Ps 76:11
You **m** us an object of contention for Ps 80:6
For behold, your enemies **m** an uproar; Ps 83:2
accord; against you they **m** a covenant— Ps 83:5
M their nobles like Oreb and Zeeb, all Ps 83:11
O my God, **m** them like whirling dust, Ps 83:13
the Valley of Baca they **m** it a place of Ps 84:6
go before him and **m** his footsteps a Ps 85:13
mouth I will **m** known your faithfulness Ps 89:1
And I will **m** him the firstborn, the Ps 89:27
M us glad for as many days as you have Ps 90:15
let us **m** a joyful noise to the rock of our Ps 95:1
let us **m** a joyful noise to him with songs Ps 95:2
who **m** their boast in worthless idols; Ps 97:7
M a joyful noise to the LORD, all the earth; Ps 98:4
sound of the horn **m** a joyful noise Ps 98:6
M a joyful noise to the LORD, all the Ps 100:1
justice; to you, O LORD, I will **m** music. Ps 101:1
You **m** springs gush forth in the Ps 104:10
oil to **m** his face shine and bread to Ps 104:15
You **m** darkness, and it is night, when Ps 104:20
m known his deeds among the peoples! Ps 105:1
that he might **m** known his mighty Ps 106:8
them that he would **m** them fall in the Ps 106:26
and would **m** their offspring fall Ps 106:27
I will sing and **m** melody with all my Ps 108:1
until I **m** your enemies your footstool." Ps 110:1
to **m** them sit with princes, with the Ps 113:8
and they do not **m** a sound in their Ps 115:7
Those who **m** them become like them; Ps 115:8
M me understand the way of your Ps 119:27
M your face shine upon your Ps 119:135
law; nothing can **m** them stumble. Ps 119:165
There I will **m** a horn to sprout for Ps 132:17
Those who **m** them become like them, Ps 135:18
If I **m** my bed in Sheol, you are there! Ps 139:8
They **m** their tongue sharp as a Ps 140:3
M me know the way I should go, for to Ps 143:8

to **m** known to the children of man Ps 145:12
m melody to our God on the lyre! Ps 147:7
to evil, and they **m** haste to shed blood. Prv 1:16
you; I will **m** my words known to you. Prv 1:23
him, and he will **m** straight your paths. Prv 3:6
plans, feet that **m** haste to run to evil, Prv 6:18
To **m** an apt answer is a joy to a man, Prv 15:23
strokes **m** clean the innermost parts. Prv 20:30
to **m** you know what is right and true, Prv 22:21
M no friendship with a man given to Prv 22:24
Oil and perfume **m** the heart glad, and Prv 27:9
Be wise, my son, and **m** my heart glad, Prv 27:11
yet they **m** their homes in the cliffs; Prv 30:26
who can **m** straight what he has made Eccl 7:13
and do not **m** yourself too wise. Eccl 7:16
Dead flies **m** the perfumer's ointment Eccl 10:1
flock, where you **m** it lie down at noon; Sg 1:7
We will **m** for you ornaments of gold, Sg 1:11
M haste, my beloved, and be like a Sg 8:14
even though you **m** many prayers, I will Is 1:15
Wash yourselves; **m** yourselves clean; Is 1:16
And I will **m** boys their princes, and Is 3:4
you shall not **m** me leader of the people." Is 3:7
I will **m** it a waste; it shall not be pruned or Is 5:6
M the heart of this people dull, and their Is 6:10
and that they may **m** the fatherless their Is 10:2
the Lord GOD of hosts will **m** a full end, Is 10:23
m known his deeds among the peoples, Is 12:4
to **m** the land a desolation and to destroy Is 13:9
I will **m** people more rare than fine gold, Is 13:12
Therefore I will **m** the heavens tremble, Is 13:13
no shepherds will **m** their flocks lie Is 13:20
I will **m** myself like the Most High.' Is 14:14
"And I will **m** it a possession of the Is 14:23
m your shade like night at the height of Is 16:3
lie down, and none will **m** them afraid. Is 17:2
though you **m** them grow on the day Is 17:11
and **m** them blossom in the morning Is 17:11
and they will **m** Egypt stagger in all its Is 19:14
And the LORD will **m** himself known to Is 19:21
and they will **m** vows to the LORD and Is 19:21
M sweet melody; sing many songs, that Is 23:16
will empty the earth and **m** it desolate, Is 24:1
the LORD of hosts will **m** for all peoples a Is 25:6
you **m** level the way of the righteous. Is 26:7
my protection, let them **m** peace with me, Is 27:5
with me, let them **m** peace with me." Is 27:5
women come and **m** a fire of them. Is 27:11
And I will **m** justice the line, and Is 28:17
say of its maker, "He did not **m** me"; Is 29:16
who by a word **m** a man out to be an Is 29:21
but not mine, and who **m** an alliance, Is 30:1
strip, and **m** yourselves bare, and tie Is 32:11
weak hands, and **m** firm the feeble knees. Is 35:3
m a wager with my master the king of Is 36:8
Do not let Hezekiah **m** you trust in the Is 36:15
M your peace with me and come out to Is 36:16
and I will **m** him fall by the sword in his Is 37:7
that you should **m** fortified cities crash Is 37:26
I will **m** the shadow cast by the declining Is 38:8
Oh restore me to health and **m** me live! Is 38:16
m straight in the desert a highway for our Is 40:3
Behold, I **m** of you a threshing sledge, Is 41:15
and you shall **m** the hills like chaff; Is 41:15
I will **m** the wilderness a pool of water, Is 41:18
up his voice, or **m** it heard in the street; Is 42:2
to magnify his law and **m** it glorious. Is 42:21
I will **m** a way in the wilderness and Is 43:19
And shall I **m** the rest of it an Is 44:19
I **m** well-being and create calamity, Is 45:7
and I will **m** all his ways level; Is 45:13
whom will you liken me and **m** me equal, Is 46:5
at the new moons **m** known what shall Is 47:13
I will **m** you as a light for the nations, Is 49:6
And I will **m** all my mountains a road, Is 49:11
Your builders **m** haste; your destroyers Is 49:17
for me; **m** room for me to dwell in.' Is 49:20
I will **m** your oppressors eat their own Is 49:26
I dry up the sea, I **m** the rivers a desert; Is 50:2
with blackness and **m** sackcloth their Is 50:3
m many to be accounted righteous, Is 53:11
I will **m** your pinnacles of agate, your Is 54:12
and I will **m** with you an everlasting Is 55:3
and it shall **m** a name for the LORD, an Is 55:13
and **m** them joyful in my house of prayer; Is 56:7
yours this day will not **m** your voice to be Is 58:4
scorched places and **m** your bones Is 58:11
and I will **m** you ride on the heights of Is 58:14
not cover themselves with what they **m**. Is 59:6
and I will **m** the place of my feet Is 60:13
through, I will **m** you majestic forever, Is 60:15
I will **m** your overseers peace and your Is 60:17
and I will **m** an everlasting covenant with Is 61:8
waters before them to **m** for himself an Is 63:12
to **m** for yourself a glorious name. Is 63:14

why do you **m** us wander from your Is 63:17
water to boil—to **m** your name known to Is 64:2
new earth that I **m** shall remain before Is 66:22
I, behold, I **m** you this day a fortified city, Jer 1:18
out from his place to **m** your land a waste; Jer 4:7
a desolation; yet I will not **m** a full end. Jer 4:27
rows and destroy, but **m** not a full end; Jer 5:10
the LORD, I will not **m** a full end of you. Jer 5:18
cause of the fatherless, to **m** it prosper, Jer 5:28
you in disgust, lest I **m** you a desolation, Jer 6:8
m mourning as for an only son, most Jer 6:26
swear falsely, **m** offerings to Baal, Jer 7:9
to **m** cakes for the queen of heaven. Jer 7:18
I will **m** Jerusalem a heap of ruins, a lair Jer 9:11
and I will **m** the cities of Judah a Jer 9:11
let them **m** haste and raise a wailing Jer 9:18
gods who did not **m** the heavens and Jer 10:11
the north country to **m** the cities of Jer 10:22
to the gods to whom they **m** offerings, Jer 11:12
to shame, altars to **m** offerings to Baal. Jer 11:13
And I will **m** them a horror to all the Jer 15:4
I will **m** you serve your enemies in a Jer 15:14
And I will **m** you to this people a Jer 15:20
or cut himself or **m** himself bald for Jer 16:6
Can man **m** for himself gods? Such are Jer 16:20
behold, I will **m** them know, Jer 16:21
this once I will **m** them know my Jer 16:21
and I will **m** you serve your enemies in a Jer 17:4
me; they **m** offerings to false gods; Jer 18:15
"Come, let us **m** plots against Jeremiah, Jer 18:18
in this place I will **m** void the plans of Jer 19:7
And I will **m** this city a horror, a thing to Jer 19:8
And I will **m** them eat the flesh of their Jer 19:9
I will **m** you a terror to yourself and to Jer 20:4
deeds and will **m** him withdraw from Jer 21:2
Lebanon, yet surely I will **m** you a desert, Jer 22:6
who think to **m** my people forget my Jer 23:27
I will **m** them a horror to all the Jer 24:9
to destruction, and **m** them a horror, Jer 25:9
and great kings shall **m** slaves even of Jer 25:14
and **m** all the nations to whom I send Jer 25:15
to **m** them a desolation and a waste, Jer 25:18
then I will **m** this house like Shiloh, and Jer 26:6
and I will **m** this city a curse for all the Jer 26:6
"**M** yourself straps and yoke-bars, and Jer 27:2
and great kings shall **m** him their slave. Jer 27:7
may the LORD **m** the words that you have Jer 28:6
and I will **m** them like vile figs that are Jer 29:17
and will **m** them a horror to all the Jer 29:18
"The LORD **m** you like Zedekiah and Jer 29:22
foreigners shall no more **m** a servant of Jer 30:8
and ease, and none shall **m** him afraid. Jer 30:10
I will **m** a full end of all the nations Jer 30:11
you, but of you I will not **m** a full end. Jer 30:11
and all who prey on you I will **m** a prey. Jer 30:16
shall not be few; I will **m** them honored, Jer 30:19
I will **m** him draw near, and he shall Jer 30:21
I will **m** them walk by brooks of water, Jer 31:9
for yourself; **m** yourself guideposts; Jer 31:21
when I will **m** a new covenant with the Jer 31:31
covenant that I will **m** with the house Jer 31:33
place, and I will **m** them dwell in safety. Jer 32:37
I will **m** with them an everlasting Jer 32:40
were torn down to **m** a defense against Jer 33:4
offerings, and to **m** sacrifices forever." Jer 33:18
in Jerusalem to **m** a proclamation of Jer 34:8
I will **m** you a horror to all the Jer 34:17
I will **m** them like the calf that they cut Jer 34:18
I will **m** the cities of Judah a desolation Jer 34:22
that they went to **m** offerings and serve Jer 44:3
from their evil and **m** no offerings to Jer 44:5
m offerings to the queen of heaven and Jer 44:17
to **m** offerings to the queen of heaven Jer 44:25
and ease, and none shall **m** him afraid. Jer 46:27
I will **m** a full end of all the nations to Jer 46:28
you, but of you I will not **m** a full end. Jer 46:28
"**M** him drunk, because he magnified Jer 48:26
I will **m** you small among the nations, Jer 49:15
Though you **m** your nest as high as the Jer 49:16
I will suddenly **m** him run away from Jer 49:19
which shall **m** her land a desolation, Jer 50:3
I will suddenly **m** them run away from Jer 50:44
walls of Babylon; **m** the watch strong; Jer 51:12
crags, and **m** you a burnt mountain. Jer 51:25
to **m** the land of Babylon a desolation, Jer 51:29
dry up her sea and **m** her fountain dry, Jer 51:36
them a feast and **m** them drunk, Jer 51:39
I will **m** drunk her officials and her Jer 51:57
And I will **m** your tongue cling to the Ezk 3:26
a single vessel and **m** your bread from Ezk 4:9
I will **m** you a desolation and an object Ezk 5:14
against them and **m** the land desolate Ezk 6:14
Therefore I **m** it an unclean thing to Ezk 7:20
Will you **m** a full end of the remnant Ezk 11:13
I will **m** a stormy wind break out in Ezk 13:13

hailstones in wrath to **m** a full end. Ezk 13:13
and **m** veils for the heads of persons of Ezk 13:18
I will **m** him a sign and a byword and Ezk 14:8
Is wood taken from it to **m** anything? Ezk 15:3
And I will **m** the land desolate, because Ezk 15:8
m known to Jerusalem her Ezk 16:2
I will **m** you stop playing the whore, Ezk 16:41
the high tree, and **m** high the low tree, Ezk 17:24
green tree, and **m** the dry tree flourish. Ezk 17:24
and **m** yourselves a new heart and a Ezk 18:31
the wilderness, to **m** a full end of them. Ezk 20:13
did not destroy them or **m** a full end of Ezk 20:17
I will **m** you pass under the rod, and I Ezk 20:37
And **m** a signpost; make it at the head Ezk 21:19
m it at the head of the way to a city. Ezk 21:19
A ruin, ruin, ruin I will **m** it. This also Ezk 21:27
interest and profit and **m** gain of your Ezk 22:12
and **m** them an object of terror and a Ezk 23:46
bloody city! I also will **m** the pile great. Ezk 24:9
aloud; **m** no mourning for the dead. Ezk 24:17
among you and **m** their dwellings in Ezk 25:4
I will **m** Rabbah a pasture for camels Ezk 25:5
the peoples and will **m** you perish out of Ezk 25:7
And I will **m** it desolate; from Teman Ezk 25:13
soil from her and **m** her a bare rock. Ezk 26:4
I will **m** you a bare rock. You shall be Ezk 26:14
When I **m** you a city laid waste, like Ezk 26:19
then I will **m** you go down with those Ezk 26:20
and I will **m** you to dwell in the world Ezk 26:20
cedar from Lebanon to **m** a mast for Ezk 27:5
they **m** themselves bald for you and Ezk 27:31
though you **m** your heart like the heart Ezk 28:2
Because you **m** your heart like the Ezk 28:6
and **m** the fish of your streams stick to Ezk 29:4
and I will **m** the land of Egypt an utter Ezk 29:10
And I will **m** the land of Egypt a Ezk 29:12
And I will **m** them so small that they Ezk 29:15
I will **m** Pathros a desolation and will Ezk 30:14
and I will **m** the sword fall from his Ezk 30:22
the heavens and **m** their stars dark; Ezk 32:7
lights of heaven will I **m** dark over you, Ezk 32:8
I will **m** many peoples appalled at you, Ezk 32:10
Then I will **m** their waters clear, and Ezk 32:14
When I **m** the land of Egypt desolate, Ezk 32:15
them, and **m** him their watchman, Ezk 33:2
And I will **m** the land a desolation and Ezk 33:28
and I myself will **m** them lie down, Ezk 34:15
"I will **m** with them a covenant of Ezk 34:25
And I will **m** them and the places all Ezk 34:26
and none shall **m** them afraid. Ezk 34:28
and I will **m** you a desolation and a Ezk 35:3
I will **m** Mount Seir a waste and a Ezk 35:7
I will **m** you a perpetual desolation, and Ezk 35:9
And I will **m** myself known among Ezk 35:11
earth rejoices, I will **m** you desolate. Ezk 35:14
that they might **m** its pasturelands a Ezk 36:5
the grain and **m** it abundant and Ezk 36:29
I will **m** the fruit of the tree and the Ezk 36:30
stick of Judah, and **m** them one stick, Ezk 37:19
And I will **m** them one nation in the Ezk 37:22
I will **m** a covenant of peace with Ezk 37:26
my holiness and **m** myself known in Ezk 38:23
and will **m** your arrows drop out of Ezk 39:3
holy name I will **m** known in the midst Ezk 39:7
will go out and **m** fires of the weapons Ezk 39:9
and they will **m** fires of them for seven Ezk 39:9
for they will **m** their fires of the Ezk 39:10
months they will **m** their search. Ezk 39:14
their land with none to **m** them afraid, Ezk 39:26
to **m** a separation between the holy Ezk 42:20
m known to them the design of the Ezk 43:11
and **m** known to them as well all its Ezk 43:11
the altar and **m** atonement for it. Ezk 43:20
days shall they **m** atonement for the Ezk 43:26
"This is the offering that you shall **m**: Ezk 45:13
offerings, to **m** atonement for them, Ezk 45:15
to **m** atonement on behalf of the Ezk 45:17
so you shall **m** atonement for the Ezk 45:20
he shall **m** the same provision for sin Ezk 45:25
if you do not **m** known to me the dream Dn 2:5
if you do not **m** the dream known to me, Dn 2:9
a man who will **m** known to the king Dn 2:25
"Are you able to **m** known to me the Dn 2:26
Therefore I **m** a decree: Any people, Dn 3:29
that they might **m** known to me the Dn 4:6
but they could not **m** known to me its Dn 4:7
are not able to **m** known to me the Dn 4:18
read the writing or **m** known to the king Dn 5:8
read this writing and **m** known to me its Dn 5:15
read the writing and **m** known to me its Dn 5:16
to the king and **m** known to him the Dn 5:17
I **m** a decree, that in all my royal Dn 6:26
m this man understand the vision." Dn 8:16
I will **m** known to you what shall be at Dn 8:19
cunning he shall **m** deceit prosper Dn 8:25

m your face to shine upon your Dn 9:17
And he shall **m** a strong covenant with Dn 9:27
and came to **m** you understand what is Dn 10:14
some years they shall **m** an alliance, Dn 11:6
king of the north to **m** an agreement. Dn 11:6
the people shall **m** many understand, Dn 11:33
He shall **m** them rulers over many and Dn 11:39
themselves and **m** themselves white Dn 12:10
I strip her naked and **m** her as in the day Hos 2:3
was born, and **m** her like a wilderness, Hos 2:3
and **m** her like a parched land, Hos 2:3
I will **m** them a forest, and the beasts of Hos 2:12
her her vineyards and **m** the Valley of Hos 2:15
And I will **m** for them a covenant on Hos 2:18
and I will **m** you lie down in safety. Hos 2:18
tribes of Israel I **m** known what is sure. Hos 5:9
By their evil they **m** the king glad, and Hos 7:3
with empty oaths they **m** covenants; Hos 10:4
Israel? How can I **m** you like Admah? Hos 11:8
they **m** a covenant with Assyria, and Hos 12:1
I will again **m** you dwell in tents, as in Hos 12:9
and **m** for themselves metal images, Hos 13:2
LORD, and **m** not your heritage a reproach, Jl 2:17
I will no more **m** you a reproach among Jl 2:19
that we may **m** the ephah small and the Am 8:5
"I will **m** the sun go down at noon and Am 8:9
I will **m** it like the mourning for an Am 8:10
and they shall **m** gardens and eat their Am 9:14
I will **m** you small among the nations; Ob 1:2
did not labor, nor did you **m** it grow, Jon 4:10
Therefore I will **m** Samaria a heap in the Mi 1:6
I will **m** lamentation like the jackals, and Mi 1:8
M yourselves bald and cut off your hair, Mi 1:16
m yourselves as bald as the eagle, for Mi 1:16
who detest justice and **m** crooked all that Mi 3:9
fig tree, and no one shall **m** them afraid, Mi 4:4
and the lame I will **m** the remnant, and Mi 4:7
of Zion, for I will **m** your horn iron, Mi 4:13
iron, and I will **m** your hoofs bronze; Mi 4:13
counsels, that I may **m** you a desolation, Mi 6:16
flood he will **m** a complete end Na 1:8
He will **m** a complete end; trouble will Na 1:9
the metal image. I will **m** your grave, Na 1:14
and I will **m** nations look at your Na 3:5
with contempt and **m** you a spectacle. Na 3:6
Why do you **m** me see iniquity, and Hab 1:3
You **m** mankind like the fish of the Hab 1:14
m it plain on tablets, so he may run Hab 2:2
those awake who will **m** you tremble? Hab 2:7
out your wrath and **m** them drunk, Hab 2:15
it; in the midst of the years **m** it known; Hab 3:2
sudden end he will **m** of all the Zep 1:18
and he will **m** Nineveh a desolation, Zep 2:13
they were eager to **m** all their deeds Zep 3:7
down, and none shall **m** them afraid." Zep 3:13
for I will **m** you renowned and praised Zep 3:20
the LORD, and **m** you like a signet ring, Hg 2:23
them silver and gold, and **m** a crown, Zec 6:11
that are true and **m** for peace; Zec 8:16
Grain shall **m** the young men flourish, Zec 9:17
and will **m** them like his majestic steed Zec 10:3
I will **m** them strong in the LORD, and Zec 10:12
I am about to **m** Jerusalem a cup of Zec 12:2
that day I will **m** Jerusalem a heavy Zec 12:3
"On that day I will **m** the clans of Judah Zec 12:6
and so I **m** you despised and abased Mal 2:9
Did he not **m** them one, with a portion Mal 2:15
the day when I **m** up my treasured Mal 3:17
way of the Lord; **m** his paths straight.'" Mt 3:3
me, and I will **m** you fishers of men." Mt 4:19
for you cannot **m** one hair white or Mt 5:36
"Lord, if you will, you can **m** me clean." Mt 8:2
ordered them not to **m** him known. Mt 12:16
"Either **m** the tree good and its fruit Mt 12:33
or **m** the tree bad and its fruit bad, Mt 12:33
the air come and **m** nests in its Mt 13:32
If you wish, I will **m** three tents here, one Mt 17:4
prayer,' but you **m** it a den of robbers." Mt 21:13
For they **m** their phylacteries broad and Mt 23:5
sea and land to **m** a single proselyte, Mt 23:15
you **m** him twice as much a child of Mt 23:15
and said, "Have you no answer to **m**? Mt 26:62
soldiers. Go, **m** it as secure as you can." Mt 27:65
Go therefore and **m** disciples of all Mt 28:19
way of the Lord, **m** his paths straight,'" Mk 1:3
and I will **m** you become fishers of Mk 1:17
him, "If you will, you can **m** me clean." Mk 1:40
ordered them not to **m** him known. Mk 3:12
of the air can **m** nests in its shade." Mk 4:32
that we are here. Let us **m** three tents, Mk 9:5
saltiness, how will you **m** it salty again? Mk 9:50
and for a pretense **m** long prayers. Mk 12:40
small copper coins, which **m** a penny. Mk 12:42
Jesus, "Have you no answer to **m**? Mk 14:60
asked him, "Have you no answer to **m**? Mk 15:4

to **m** ready for the Lord a people Lk 1:17
the way of the Lord, **m** his paths straight. Lk 3:4
"Lord, if you will, you can **m** me clean." Lk 5:12
and **m** an offering for your cleansing, Lk 5:14
"Can you **m** wedding guests fast while Lk 5:34
that we are here. Let us **m** three tents, Lk 9:33
Samaritans, to **m** preparations for him. Lk 9:52
made the outside **m** the inside also? Lk 11:40
m an effort to settle with him on the Lk 12:58
But they all alike began to **m** excuses. Lk 14:18
m friends for yourselves by means of Lk 16:9
on this day the things that **m** for peace! Lk 19:42
until I **m** your enemies your footstool.' Lk 20:43
and for a pretense **m** long prayers. Lk 20:47
'**M** straight the way of the Lord,' Jn 1:23
do not **m** my Father's house a house of Jn 2:16
and take him by force to **m** him king, Jn 6:15
died! Who do you **m** yourself out to be?" Jn 8:53
you, being a man, **m** yourself God." Jn 10:33
come to him and **m** our home with Jn 14:23
and I will continue to **m** it known, Jn 17:26
you will **m** me full of gladness with Acts 2:28
until I **m** your enemies your footstool.' Acts 2:35
'**M** for us gods who will go before us. Acts 7:40
spoke to Moses directed him to **m** it, Acts 7:44
Did not my hand **m** all these things?' Acts 7:50
rise and **m** your bed." And Acts 9:34
wanted to **m** a defense to the crowd. Acts 19:33
the defense that I now **m** before you." Acts 22:1
'**M** haste and get out of Jerusalem Acts 22:18
nation, I cheerfully **m** my defense. Acts 24:10
before you and to **m** an accusation, Acts 24:19
had opportunity to **m** his defense Acts 25:16
I am going to **m** my defense today Acts 26:2
and tried to **m** them blaspheme, Acts 26:11
overboard first and **m** for the land, Acts 27:43
The purpose was to **m** him the father Rom 4:11
and to **m** him the father of the Rom 4:12
bodies, to **m** you obey their passions. Rom 6:12
to **m** out of the same lump one vessel Rom 9:21
his wrath and to **m** known his power, Rom 9:22
in order to **m** known the riches of his Rom 9:23
"I will **m** you jealous of those who are Rom 10:19
a foolish nation I will **m** you angry." Rom 10:19
the Gentiles, so as to **m** Israel jealous. Rom 11:11
order somehow to **m** my fellow Jews Rom 11:14
and **m** no provision for the flesh, Rom 13:14
for the Lord is able to **m** him stand. Rom 14:4
for anyone to **m** another stumble by Rom 14:20
and thus I **m** it my ambition to Rom 15:20
been pleased to **m** some contribution Rom 15:26
write these things to **m** you ashamed, 1 Cor 4:14
of Christ and **m** them members of 1 Cor 6:15
meat, lest I **m** my brother stumble. 1 Cor 8:13
so as not to **m** full use of my right in 1 Cor 9:18
body," that would not **m** it any less a 1 Cor 12:15
body," that would not **m** it any less a 1 Cor 12:16
But that was to **m** us rely not on 2 Cor 1:9
Do I **m** my plans according to the 2 Cor 1:17
mind not to **m** another painful visit 2 Cor 2:1
who is there to **m** me glad but the one 2 Cor 2:2
away, we **m** it our aim to please him. 2 Cor 5:9
"I will **m** my dwelling among them 2 Cor 6:16
M room in your hearts for us. We 2 Cor 7:2
God is able to **m** all grace abound to 2 Cor 9:8
in order to **m** sure I was not running or Gal 2:2
by God, so as to **m** the promise void. Gal 3:17
They **m** much of you, but for no good Gal 4:17
out, that you may **m** much of them. Gal 4:17
those who want to **m** a good showing in Gal 6:12
perfect, but I press on to **m** it my own, Phil 3:12
you, to **m** the word of God fully known, Col 1:25
them God chose to **m** known how great Col 1:27
that I may **m** it clear, which is how I Col 4:4
may the Lord **m** you increase and 1 Thes 3:12
that our God may **m** you worthy of 2 Thes 1:11
which they **m** confident assertions. 1 Tm 1:7
household and to **m** some return to 1 Tm 5:4
which are able to **m** you wise for 2 Tm 3:15
right hand until I **m** your enemies a Heb 1:13
should **m** the founder of their salvation Heb 2:10
to **m** propitiation for the sins of the Heb 2:17
always lives to **m** intercession for Heb 7:25
"See that you **m** everything according to Heb 8:5
covenant that I will **m** with the house Heb 8:10
year, **m** perfect those who draw near. Heb 10:1
covenant that I will **m** with them after Heb 10:16
people who speak thus **m** it clear that Heb 11:14
and **m** straight paths for your feet, so Heb 12:13
is sown in peace by those who **m** peace. Jas 3:18
a year there and trade and **m** a profit"— Jas 4:13
always being prepared to **m** a defense to 1 Pt 3:15
m every effort to supplement your faith 2 Pt 1:5
more diligent to **m** your calling and 2 Pt 1:10
And I will **m** every effort so that after 2 Pt 1:15
we have not sinned, we **m** him a liar, 1 Jn 1:10
I will **m** those of the synagogue of Satan Rv 3:9
I will **m** them come and bow down before Rv 3:9
I will **m** him a pillar in the temple of my Rv 3:12
it will **m** your stomach bitter, but in Rv 10:9
the bottomless pit will **m** war on them Rv 11:7
over them and **m** merry and exchange Rv 11:10
and went off to **m** war on the rest Rv 12:17
it was allowed to **m** war on the saints Rv 13:7
telling them to **m** an image for the Rv 13:14
to **m** her drain the cup of the wine of Rv 16:19
They will **m** war on the Lamb, and the Rv 17:14
They will **m** her desolate and naked, Rv 17:16
armies gathered to **m** war against him Rv 19:19

MAKER (17)

Can a man be pure before his **M**? Jb 4:17
else my **M** would soon take me away. Jb 32:22
But none says, 'Where is God my **M**, Jb 35:10
afar and ascribe righteousness to my **M**. Jb 36:3
let us kneel before the LORD, our **M**! Ps 95:6
Let Israel be glad in his **M**; let the Ps 149:2
oppresses a poor man insults his **M**, Prv 14:31
Whoever mocks the poor insults his **M**; Prv 17:5
together; the LORD is the **m** of them all. Prv 22:2
In that day man will look to his **M**, and Is 17:7
that the thing made should say of its **m**, Is 29:16
and have forgotten the LORD, your **M**, Is 51:13
For your **M** is your husband, the LORD of Is 54:5
of me, 'Is he not a **m** of parables?'" Ezk 20:49
has forgotten his **M** and built palaces, Hos 8:14
is an idol when its **m** has shaped it, Hab 2:18
For its **m** trusts in his own creation Hab 2:18

MAKERS (1)

the **m** of idols go in confusion together. Is 45:16

MAKES (144)

Who **m** him mute, or deaf, or seeing, or Ex 4:11
that the LORD **m** a distinction between Ex 11:7
Whoever **m** any like it to use as Ex 30:38
The priest who **m** atonement with it shall Lv 7:7
is the blood that **m** atonement by the Lv 17:11
If anyone **m** a special vow to the LORD Lv 27:2
when the LORD **m** your thigh fall away Nm 5:21
a man or a woman **m** a special vow, Nm 6:2
LORD for the person who **m** a mistake, Nm 15:28
then he **m** void her vow that was on Nm 30:8
But if her husband **m** them null and Nm 30:12
But if he **m** them null and void after Nm 30:15
nations that the LORD **m** to perish before Dt 8:20
But if it **m** no peace with you, but Dt 20:12
peace with you, but **m** war against you, Dt 20:12
against the city that **m** war with you, Dt 20:20
be the man who **m** a carved or cast Dt 27:15
The LORD **m** poor and makes rich; he 1 Sm 2:7
The LORD makes poor and **m** rich; he 1 Sm 2:7
me when my son **m** a covenant with 1 Sm 22:8
like rain that **m** grass to sprout from 2 Sm 23:4
away stripped, and judges he **m** fools. Jb 12:17
He **m** nations great, and he destroys Jb 12:23
of the earth and **m** them wander in a Jb 12:24
and he **m** them stagger like a drunken Jb 12:25
with God; he **m** peace in his high heaven. Jb 25:2
like a booth that a watchman **m**. Jb 27:18
When he **m** inquiry, what shall I Jb 31:14
of the Almighty, that **m** him understand. Jb 32:8
of the earth and **m** us wiser than the Jb 35:11
eagle mounts up and **m** his nest on Jb 39:27
On the rock he dwells and **m** his home, Jb 39:28
He **m** his tail stiff like a cedar; the Jb 40:17
He **m** the deep boil like a pot; he makes Jb 41:31
pot; he **m** the sea like a pot of ointment. Jb 41:31
He **m** a pit, digging it out, and falls into Ps 7:15
lips, the tongue that **m** great boasts, Ps 12:3
He **m** me lie down in green pastures. He Ps 23:2
and he **m** known to them his covenant. Ps 25:14
He **m** Lebanon to skip like a calf, and Ps 29:6
voice of the LORD **m** the deer give birth Ps 29:9
My soul **m** its boast in the LORD; let the Ps 34:2
is the man who **m** the LORD his trust, Ps 40:4
He **m** wars cease to the end of the earth; Ps 46:9
the waters; he **m** the clouds his chariot; Ps 104:3
he **m** his messengers winds, his Ps 104:4
on princes and **m** them wander in Ps 107:40
of affliction and **m** their families like Ps 107:41
Your commandment **m** me wiser Ps 119:98
He it is who **m** the clouds rise at the end Ps 135:7
who **m** lightnings for the rain and Ps 135:7
the earth; he **m** grass grow on the hills. Ps 147:8
He **m** peace in your borders; he fills Ps 147:14
he **m** his wind blow and the waters Ps 147:18
For jealousy **m** a man furious, and he Prv 6:34
of Solomon. A wise son **m** a glad father, Prv 10:1
but the hand of the diligent **m** rich. Prv 10:4
but he who **m** his ways crooked will be Prv 10:9
The blessing of the LORD **m** rich, and Prv 10:22
down, but a good word **m** him glad. Prv 12:25
Hope deferred **m** the heart sick, but a Prv 13:12
to the flesh, but envy **m** the bones rot. Prv 14:30
but it **m** itself known even in the Prv 14:33
A glad heart **m** a cheerful face, but by Prv 15:13
A wise son **m** a glad father, but a Prv 15:20
he **m** even his enemies to be at peace Prv 16:7
of the wise **m** his speech judicious Prv 16:23
he who **m** his door high seeks Prv 17:19
A man's gift **m** room for him and Prv 18:16
and whoever **m** haste with his feet Prv 19:2
Good sense **m** one slow to anger, and it Prv 19:11
Even a child **m** himself known by his Prv 20:11
He who loves wisdom **m** his father glad, Prv 29:3
with strength and **m** her arms strong. Prv 31:17
She **m** bed coverings for herself; her Prv 31:22
She **m** linen garments and sells them; Prv 31:24
A man's wisdom **m** his face shine, Eccl 8:1
the work of God who **m** everything. Eccl 11:5
when he **m** all the stones of the altars like Is 27:9
the father **m** known to the children your Is 38:19
and **m** the rulers of the earth as Is 40:23
he **m** them like dust with his sword, like Is 41:2
says the LORD, who **m** a way in the sea, Is 43:16
Also he **m** a god and worships it; he Is 44:15
he **m** it an idol and falls down before it. Is 44:15
And the rest of it he **m** into a god, his Is 44:17
the signs of liars and **m** fools of diviners, Is 44:25
men back and **m** their knowledge Is 44:25
hire a goldsmith, and he **m** it into a god; Is 46:6
waste places and **m** her wilderness like Is 51:3
when his soul **m** an offering for sin, he Is 53:10
and **m** intercession for the Is 53:12
who departs from evil **m** himself a prey. Is 59:15
he establishes Jerusalem and **m** it a praise Is 62:7
he who **m** a memorial offering of Is 66:3
and he **m** the mist rise from the ends of Jer 10:13
He **m** lightning for the rain, and he Jer 10:13
it into gloom and **m** it deep darkness. Jer 13:16
trusts in man and **m** flesh his strength, Jer 17:5
who **m** his neighbor serve him for Jer 22:13
"She **m** a sound like a serpent gliding Jer 46:22
the high place and **m** offerings to his Jer 48:35
and he **m** the mist rise from the ends of Jer 51:16
He **m** lightning for the rain, and he Jer 51:16
come, and that **m** idols to defile herself! Ezk 22:3
If the prince **m** a gift to any of his sons Ezk 46:16
But if he **m** a gift out of his Ezk 46:17
that whoever **m** petition to any god or Dn 6:7
that anyone who **m** petition to any god Dn 6:12
but **m** his petition three times a day." Dn 6:13
the transgression that **m** desolate, Dn 8:13
shall come one who **m** desolate, Dn 9:27
up the abomination that **m** desolate. Dn 11:31
the abomination that **m** desolate is set Dn 12:11
thought, who **m** the morning darkness, Am 4:13
who **m** destruction flash forth against Am 5:9
He rebukes the sea and **m** it dry; he dries Na 1:4
to his net and **m** offerings to his Hab 1:16
to him who **m** his neighbors drink Hab 2:15
creation when he **m** speechless idols! Hab 2:18
strength; he **m** my feet like the deer's; Hab 3:19
he **m** me tread on my high places. Hab 3:19
from the LORD who **m** the storm clouds, Zec 10:1
immorality, **m** her commit adultery. Mt 5:32
For he **m** his sun rise on the evil and on Mt 5:45
gift or the altar that **m** the gift sacred? Mt 23:19
He even **m** the deaf hear and the mute Mk 7:37
for he has a spirit that **m** him mute. Mk 9:17
Everyone who **m** himself a king Jn 19:12
says the Lord, who **m** these things Acts 15:17
let us pursue what **m** for peace and Rom 14:19
if food **m** my brother stumble, 1 Cor 8:13
bear it if someone **m** slaves of you, 2 Cor 11:20
(what they were **m** no difference to Gal 2:6
m the body grow so that it builds itself Eph 4:16
angels he says, "He **m** his angels winds, Heb 1:7
This **m** Jesus the guarantor of a better Heb 7:22
covenant, he **m** the first one obsolete. Heb 8:13
friend of the world **m** himself an enemy Jas 4:4
Everyone who **m** a practice of sinning 1 Jn 3:4
Whoever **m** a practice of sinning is of 1 Jn 3:8
one born of God **m** a practice of sinning, 1 Jn 3:9
and **m** the earth and its inhabitants Rv 13:12
in righteousness he judges and **m** war. Rv 19:11

MAKHELOTH (2)

out from Haradah and camped at **M**. Nm 33:25
they set out from **M** and camped at Nm 33:26

MAKING (80)

trouble on me by **m** me stink to the Gn 34:30
all your task of **m** bricks today and Ex 5:14
he said, "Behold, I am **m** a covenant. Ex 34:10
your daughter by **m** her a prostitute, Lv 19:29
you act corruptly by **m** a carved image Dt 4:16

you act corruptly by **m** a carved image Dt 4:25
m war against it in order to take it, Dt 20:19
the LORD your God is **m** with you today, Dt 29:12
alone that I am **m** this sworn covenant, Dt 29:14
spoke no more of **m** war against them Jos 22:33
and you do me wrong by **m** war on me. Jgs 11:27
As they were **m** their hearts merry, Jgs 19:22
Abner was **m** himself strong in the 2 Sm 3:6
house of Israel were **m** merry before the 2 Sm 6:5
m himself a name and doing for them 2 Sm 7:23
a line, **m** them lie down on the ground. 2 Sm 8:2
and skill for **m** any work in bronze. 1 Kgs 7:14
m offerings with it before the LORD. 1 Kgs 9:25
he committed, **m** Israel to sin. 1 Kgs 16:19
quarried stone for **m** repairs on the 2 Kgs 12:12
was entrusted with **m** the flat cakes. 1 Chr 9:31
in **m** known all these great things. 1 Chr 17:19
m for yourself a name for great and 1 Chr 17:21
them, **m** offerings to them. 2 Chr 25:14
m that a day of feasting and gladness. Est 9:18
weapons, **m** his arrows fiery shafts. Ps 7:13
of the LORD is sure, **m** wise the simple; Ps 19:7
my feet upon a rock, **m** my steps secure. Ps 40:2
m her the joyous mother of children. Ps 113:9
m melody to him with tambourine and Ps 149:3
m your ear attentive to wisdom and Prv 2:2
holy," and to reflect only after **m** vows. Prv 20:25
Of **m** many books there is no end, Eccl 12:12
to him who forms it, 'What are you **m**?' Is 45:9
the earth, **m** it bring forth and sprout, Is 55:10
in gardens and **m** offerings on bricks; Is 65:3
I am **m** my words in your mouth a fire, Jer 5:14
me to anger by **m** offerings to Baal." Jer 11:17
the vessel he was **m** of clay was spoiled Jer 18:4
m their land a horror, a thing to be Jer 18:16
profaned this place by **m** offerings in it Jer 19:4
inhabitants, **m** this city like Topheth. Jer 19:12
son is born to you," **m** him very glad. Jer 20:15
king of Babylon is **m** war against us. Jer 21:2
LORD, **m** the land an everlasting waste. Jer 25:12
m offerings to other gods in the land of Jer 44:8
since we left off **m** offerings to the Jer 44:18
LORD'S hand, **m** all the earth drunken; Jer 51:7
and **m** your lofty place in every Ezk 16:31
m myself known to them in the land of Ezk 20:5
piece after piece, without **m** any choice. Ezk 24:6
m its rivers flow around the place of its Ezk 31:4
m you rule over them all—you are the Dn 2:38
and found Daniel **m** petition and plea Dn 6:11
m you desolate because of your sins. Mi 6:13
players and the crowd **m** a commotion, Mt 9:23
"Why are you **m** a commotion and Mk 5:39
that they were **m** headway painfully, Mk 6:48
thus **m** void the word of God by your Mk 7:13
And he kept **m** signs to them and Lk 1:22
And **m** a whip of cords, he drove them all Jn 2:15
that Jesus was **m** and baptizing more Jn 4:1
own Father, **m** himself equal with God. Jn 5:18
me to go with them, **m** no distinction. Acts 11:12
you not stop **m** crooked the straight Acts 13:10
of my mind and **m** me captive to the Rom 7:23
Christ, God **m** his appeal through us. 2 Cor 5:20
rejoicing; as poor, yet **m** many rich; 2 Cor 6:10
m known to us the mystery of his will, Eph 1:9
man in place of the two, so **m** peace, Eph 2:15
m the best use of the time, because the Eph 5:16
singing and **m** melody to the Lord with Eph 5:19
m supplication for all the saints, Eph 6:18
mine for you all **m** my prayer with joy, Phil 1:4
m peace by the blood of his cross. Col 1:20
outsiders, **m** the best use of the time. Col 4:5
After **m** purification for sins, he sat Heb 1:3
m them an example of what is going to 2 Pt 2:6
even **m** fire come down from heaven to Rv 13:13
I am **m** all things new." Also he said, Rv 21:5

MAKKEDAH (9)
struck them as far as Azekah and **M**. Jos 10:10
and hid themselves in the cave at **M**. Jos 10:16
been found, hidden in the cave at **M**." Jos 10:17
safe to Joshua in the camp at **M**. Jos 10:21
As for **M**, Joshua captured it on that Jos 10:28
did to the king of **M** just as he had done Jos 10:28
him passed on from **M** to Libnah and Jos 10:29
the king of **M**, one; the king of Bethel, Jos 12:16
Beth-dagon, Naamah, and **M**: Jos 15:41

MALACHI (1)
of the word of the LORD to Israel by **M**. Mal 1:1

MALCAM (1)
his wife: Jobab, Zibia, Mesha, **M**, 1 Chr 8:9

MALCHI-SHUA (5)
of Saul were Jonathan, Ishvi, and **M**. 1 Sm 14:49
down Jonathan and Abinadab and **M**, 1 Sm 31:2
M, Abinadab and Eshbaal; 1 Chr 8:33
fathered Jonathan, **M**, Abinadab, 1 Chr 9:39
Jonathan and Abinadab and **M**, 1 Chr 10:2

MALCHIAH (3)
the son of **M** and Zephaniah the Jer 21:1
Pashhur the son of **M** heard the words Jer 38:1
and cast him into the cistern of **M**, Jer 38:6

MALCHIEL (3)
And the sons of Beriah: Heber and **M**. Gn 46:17
Heber, the clan of the Heberites; of **M**, Nm 26:45
Heber, and **M**, who fathered Birzaith. 1 Chr 7:31

MALCHIELITES (1)
of Malchiel, the clan of the **M**. Nm 26:45

MALCHIJAH (12)
Michael, son of Baaseiah, son of **M**, 1 Chr 6:40
Jeroham, son of Pashhur, son of **M**, 1 Chr 9:12
the fifth to **M**, the sixth to Mijamin, 1 Chr 24:9
Ramiah, Izziah, **M**, Mijamin, Eleazar, Ezr 10:25
Eliezer, Isshijah, **M**, Shemaiah, Ezr 10:31
M the son of Harim and Hasshub the Neh 3:11
M the son of Rechab, ruler of the Neh 3:14
After him **M**, one of the goldsmiths, Neh 3:31
and Pedaiah, Mishael, **M**, Hashum, Neh 8:4
Pashhur, Amariah, **M**, Neh 10:3
Zechariah, son of Pashhur, son of **M**, Neh 11:12
Eleazar, Uzzi, Jehohanan, **M**, Elam, Neh 12:42

MALCHIRAM (1)
M, Pedaiah, Shenazzar, Jekamiah, 1 Chr 3:18

MALCHUS (1)
right ear. (The servant's name was **M**.) Jn 18:10

MALCONTENTS (1)
m, following their own sinful desires; Jude 1:16

MALE (218)
him; **m** and female he created them. Gn 1:27
M and female he created them, and he Gn 5:2
with you. They shall be **m** and female. Gn 6:19
of all clean animals, the **m** and his mate, Gn 7:2
that are not clean, the **m** and his mate, Gn 7:2
birds of the heavens also, **m** and female, Gn 7:3
two and two, **m** and female, went into the Gn 7:9
that entered, **m** and female of all flesh, Gn 7:16
and he had sheep, oxen, **m** donkeys, Gn 12:16
sheep, oxen, male donkeys, **m** servants, Gn 12:16
Every **m** among you shall be Gn 17:10
Every **m** throughout your generations, Gn 17:12
Any uncircumcised **m** who is not Gn 17:14
every **m** among the men of Abraham's Gn 17:23
and **m** servants and female servants, Gn 20:14
gold, **m** servants and female servants, Gn 24:35
Laban removed the **m** goats that were Gn 30:35
female servants and **m** servants, Gn 30:43
have oxen, donkeys, flocks, **m** servants, Gn 32:5
female goats and twenty **m** goats, Gn 32:14
female donkeys and ten **m** donkeys. Gn 32:15
we are by every **m** among you being Gn 34:15
people—when every **m** among us is Gn 34:22
and every **m** was circumcised, Gn 34:24
them, but let the **m** children live. Ex 1:17
done this, and let the **m** children live?" Ex 1:18
shall be without blemish, a **m** a year old. Ex 12:5
son, or your daughter, your **m** servant, Ex 20:10
your neighbor's wife, or his **m** servant, Ex 20:17
she shall not go out as the **m** slaves do. Ex 21:7
a man strikes his slave, **m** or female, Ex 21:20
strikes the eye of his slave, **m** or female, Ex 21:26
out the tooth of his slave, **m** or female, Ex 21:27
If the ox gores a slave, **m** or female, the Ex 21:32
womb are mine, all your **m** livestock, Ex 34:19
herd, he shall offer a **m** without blemish. Lv 1:3
he shall bring a **m** without blemish, Lv 1:10
an animal from the herd, **m** or female, Lv 3:1
is an animal from the flock, **m** or female, Lv 3:6
his offering a goat, a **m** without blemish, Lv 4:23
Every **m** among the children of Aaron Lv 6:18
Every **m** among the priests may eat of it; Lv 6:29
Every **m** among the priests may eat of it. It Lv 7:6
of Israel, 'Take a **m** goat for a sin offering, Lv 9:3
a woman conceives and bears a **m** child, Lv 12:2
who bears a child, either **m** or female. Lv 12:7
shall take two **m** lambs without Lv 14:10
take one of the **m** lambs and offer it Lv 14:12
he shall take one **m** lamb for a guilt Lv 14:21
that is, for anyone, **m** or female, Lv 15:33
the people of Israel two **m** goats for a sin Lv 16:5
shall not lie with a **m** as with a woman; Lv 18:22
a man lies with a **m** as with a woman, Lv 20:13
you it shall be a **m** without blemish, Lv 22:19
you shall offer a **m** lamb a year old Lv 23:12
And you shall offer one **m** goat for a sin Lv 23:19
and two **m** lambs a year old as a Lv 23:19
and for your **m** and female slaves Lv 25:6
As for your **m** and female slaves whom Lv 25:44
you may buy **m** and female slaves Lv 25:44
the valuation of a **m** from twenty years Lv 27:3
shall be for a **m** twenty shekels, Lv 27:5
shall be for a **m** five shekels of silver, Lv 27:6
the valuation for a **m** shall be fifteen Lv 27:7
to the number of names, every **m**, Nm 1:2
every **m** from twenty years old and Nm 1:20
every **m** from twenty years old and Nm 1:22
every **m** from a month old and upward Nm 3:15
above the number of the **m** Levites, Nm 3:46
You shall put out both **m** and female, Nm 5:3
separation and bring a **m** lamb a year Nm 6:12
one **m** lamb a year old without Nm 6:14
herd, one ram, one **m** lamb a year old, Nm 7:15
one **m** goat for a sin offering; Nm 7:16
two oxen, five rams, five **m** goats, Nm 7:17
goats, and five **m** lambs a year old. Nm 7:17
herd, one ram, one **m** lamb a year old, Nm 7:21
one **m** goat for a sin offering; Nm 7:22
two oxen, five rams, five **m** goats, Nm 7:23
goats, and five **m** lambs a year old. Nm 7:23
herd, one ram, one **m** lamb a year old, Nm 7:27
one **m** goat for a sin offering; Nm 7:28
two oxen, five rams, five **m** goats, Nm 7:29
goats, and five **m** lambs a year old. Nm 7:29
herd, one ram, one **m** lamb a year old, Nm 7:33
one **m** goat for a sin offering; Nm 7:34
two oxen, five rams, five **m** goats, Nm 7:35
goats, and five **m** lambs a year old. Nm 7:35
herd, one ram, one **m** lamb a year old, Nm 7:39
one **m** goat for a sin offering; Nm 7:40
two oxen, five rams, five **m** goats, Nm 7:41
goats, and five **m** lambs a year old. Nm 7:41
herd, one ram, one **m** lamb a year old, Nm 7:45
one **m** goat for a sin offering; Nm 7:46
two oxen, five rams, five **m** goats, Nm 7:47
goats, and five **m** lambs a year old. Nm 7:47
herd, one ram, one **m** lamb a year old, Nm 7:51
one **m** goat for a sin offering; Nm 7:52
two oxen, five rams, five **m** goats, Nm 7:53
goats, and five **m** lambs a year old. Nm 7:53
herd, one ram, one **m** lamb a year old, Nm 7:57
one **m** goat for a sin offering; Nm 7:58
two oxen, five rams, five **m** goats, Nm 7:59
goats, and five **m** lambs a year old. Nm 7:59
herd, one ram, one **m** lamb a year old, Nm 7:63
one **m** goat for a sin offering; Nm 7:64
two oxen, five rams, five **m** goats, Nm 7:65
goats, and five **m** lambs a year old. Nm 7:65
herd, one ram, one **m** lamb a year old, Nm 7:69
one **m** goat for a sin offering; Nm 7:70
two oxen, five rams, five **m** goats, Nm 7:71
goats, and five **m** lambs a year old. Nm 7:71
herd, one ram, one **m** lamb a year old, Nm 7:75
one **m** goat for a sin offering; Nm 7:76
two oxen, five rams, five **m** goats, Nm 7:77
goats, and five **m** lambs a year old. Nm 7:77
herd, one ram, one **m** lamb a year old, Nm 7:81
one **m** goat for a sin offering; Nm 7:82
two oxen, five rams, five **m** goats, Nm 7:83
goats, and five **m** lambs a year old. Nm 7:83
rams, twelve **m** lambs a year old, Nm 7:87
and twelve **m** goats for a sin offering; Nm 7:87
bulls, the rams sixty, the **m** goats sixty, Nm 7:88
sixty, the **m** lambs a year old sixty. Nm 7:88
rule, and one **m** goat for a sin offering. Nm 15:24
it. Every **m** may eat it; it is holy to you. Nm 18:10
every **m** from a month old and Nm 26:62
two **m** lambs a year old without Nm 28:3
two **m** lambs a year old without Nm 28:9
seven **m** lambs a year old without Nm 28:11
Also one **m** goat for a sin offering to Nm 28:15
ram, and seven **m** lambs a year old; Nm 28:19
also one **m** goat for a sin offering, to Nm 28:22
one ram, seven **m** lambs a year old; Nm 28:27
with one **m** goat, to make atonement Nm 28:30
seven **m** lambs a year old without Nm 29:2
with one **m** goat for a sin offering, to Nm 29:5
one ram, seven **m** lambs a year old: Nm 29:8
also one **m** goat for a sin offering, Nm 29:11
rams, fourteen **m** lambs a year old; Nm 29:13
also one **m** goat for a sin offering, Nm 29:16
fourteen **m** lambs a year old without Nm 29:17
also one **m** goat for a sin offering, Nm 29:19
fourteen **m** lambs a year old without Nm 29:20
also one **m** goat for a sin offering, Nm 29:22
fourteen **m** lambs a year old without Nm 29:23
also one **m** goat for a sin offering, Nm 29:25
fourteen **m** lambs a year old without Nm 29:26
also one **m** goat for a sin offering; Nm 29:28
fourteen **m** lambs a year old without Nm 29:29
also one **m** goat for a sin offering; Nm 29:31
fourteen **m** lambs a year old without Nm 29:32
also one **m** goat for a sin offering; Nm 29:34
seven **m** lambs a year old without Nm 29:36
also one **m** goat for a sin offering; Nm 29:38

Moses, and killed every **m**. Nm 31:7
kill every **m** among the little ones, Nm 31:17
of any figure, the likeness of **m** or female, Dt 4:16
your daughter or your **m** servant or your Dt 5:14
that your **m** servant and your female Dt 5:14
house, his field, or his **m** servant, Dt 5:21
There shall not be **m** or female barren Dt 7:14
your **m** servants and your female Dt 12:12
your **m** servant and your female Dt 12:18
your **m** servant and your female Dt 16:11
your **m** servant and your female Dt 16:14
are crushed or whose **m** organ is cut off Dt 23:1
to your enemies as **m** and female slaves, Dt 28:68
These were the **m** descendants of Jos 17:2
every **m** and every woman that has Jgs 21:11
has lain with a **m** you shall devote to Jgs 21:11
will take your **m** servants and female 1 Sm 8:16
so much as one **m** of all who belong 1 Sm 25:22
left to Nabal so much as one **m**." 1 Sm 25:34
he struck down every **m** in Edom 1 Kgs 11:15
he had cut off every **m** in Edom). 1 Kgs 11:16
will cut off from Jeroboam every **m**, 1 Kgs 14:10
there were also **m** cult prostitutes in 1 Kgs 14:24
put away the **m** cult prostitutes out 1 Kgs 15:12
leave him a single **m** of his relatives 1 Kgs 16:11
and will cut off from Ahab every **m**, 1 Kgs 21:21
remnant of the **m** cult prostitutes 1 Kgs 22:46
m servants and female servants? 2 Kgs 5:26
and I will cut off from Ahab every **m**, 2 Kgs 9:8
houses of the **m** cult prostitutes who 2 Kgs 23:7
Judah and Jerusalem, **m** and female, 2 Chr 28:10
and seven **m** goats for a sin offering 2 Chr 29:21
portions to every **m** among the 2 Chr 31:19
besides their **m** and female servants, of Ezr 2:65
and they had 200 **m** and female singers. Ezr 2:65
a sin offering for all Israel 12 **m** goats, Ezr 6:17
and as a sin offering twelve **m** goats. Ezr 8:35
besides their **m** and female servants, of Neh 7:67
they had 245 singers, **m** and female. Neh 7:67
I bought **m** and female slaves, and had Eccl 2:7
in the LORD'S land as **m** and female slaves. Is 14:2
set free his Hebrew slaves, **m** and female, Jer 34:9
would set free his slave, **m** or female, Jer 34:10
and took back the **m** and female slaves Jer 34:11
you took back his **m** and female slaves, Jer 34:16
and be as **m** goats before the flock. Jer 50:8
to the slaughter, like rams and **m** goats. Jer 51:40
and sheep, between rams and **m** goats. Ezk 34:17
shall offer a **m** goat without blemish Ezk 43:22
shall provide daily a **m** goat for a sin Ezk 43:25
and a **m** goat daily for a sin offering. Ezk 45:23
a **m** goat came from the west across the Dn 8:5
Even on the **m** and female servants in Jl 2:29
be the cheat who has a **m** in his flock, Mal 1:14
killed all the **m** children in Bethlehem Mt 2:16
beginning made them **m** and female, Mt 19:4
'God made them **m** and female.' Mk 10:6
"Every **m** who first opens the womb Lk 2:23
to beat the **m** and female servants, Lk 12:45
even on my **m** servants and female Acts 2:18
nor free, there is neither **m** nor female, Gal 3:28
She gave birth to a **m** child, one who is Rv 12:5
who had given birth to the **m** child. Rv 12:13

MALES (17)
while it felt secure and killed all the **m**. Gn 34:25
the LORD, let all his **m** be circumcised. Ex 12:48
your animals that are **m** shall be the Ex 13:12
to the LORD all the **m** that first open the Ex 13:15
year shall all your **m** appear before the Ex 23:17
year shall all your **m** appear before the Ex 34:23
number of all the **m** from a month old Nm 3:22
According to the number of all the **m**, Nm 3:28
number of all the **m** from a month old Nm 3:34
all the **m** from a month old and Nm 3:39
"List all the firstborn **m** of the people of Nm 3:40
And all the firstborn **m**, according to Nm 3:43
"All the firstborn **m** that are born of Dt 15:19
a year all your **m** shall appear before Dt 16:16
you shall put all its **m** to the sword, Dt 20:13
all the **m** of the people who came out of Jos 5:4
m from three years old and upward 2 Chr 31:16

MALICE (11)
My enemies say of me in **m**, "When will Ps 41:5
They scoff and speak with **m**; loftily they Ps 73:8
with all the **m** within your soul Ezk 25:6
and took vengeance with **m** of soul to Ezk 25:15
But Jesus, aware of their **m**, said, "Why Mt 22:18
covetousness, **m**. They are full of envy, Rom 1:29
the old leaven, the leaven of **m** and evil, 1 Cor 5:8
put away from you, along with all **m**. Eph 4:31
anger, wrath, **m**, slander, and obscene Col 3:8
passing our days in **m** and envy, Ti 3:3
So put away all **m** and all deceit and 1 Pt 2:1

MALICIOUS (4)
with a wicked man to be a **m** witness. Ex 23:1
If a **m** witness arises to accuse a person Dt 19:16
M witnesses rise up; they ask me of Ps 35:11
They speak against you with **m** intent; Ps 139:20

MALICIOUSLY (2)
came forward and **m** accused the Jews. Dn 3:8
men who had **m** accused Daniel were Dn 6:24

MALICIOUSNESS (1)
strife, deceit, **m**. They are gossips, Rom 1:29

MALIGN (2)
much more will they **m** those of his Mt 10:25
flood of debauchery, and they **m** you; 1 Pt 4:4

MALLET (1)
and her right hand to the workmen's **m**; Jgs 5:26

MALLOTHI (2)
Joshbekashah, **M**, Hothir, 1 Chr 25:4
to the nineteenth, to **M**, his sons and 1 Chr 25:26

MALLOW (1)
or is there any taste in the juice of the **m**? Jb 6:6

MALLUCH (6)
son of Kishi, son of Abdi, son of **M**, 1 Chr 6:44
of Bani were Meshullam, **M**, Adaiah, Ezr 10:29
Benjamin, **M**, and Shemariah. Ezr 10:32
Hattush, Shebaniah, **M**, Neh 10:4
M, Harim, Baanah. Neh 10:27
Amariah, **M**, Hattush, Neh 12:2

MALLUCHI (1)
of **M**, Jonathan; of Shebaniah, Joseph; Neh 12:14

MALTA (1)
learned that the island was called **M**. Acts 28:1

MAMRE (10)
and came and settled by the oaks of **M**, Gn 13:18
living by the oaks of **M** the Amorite, Gn 14:13
Aner, Eshcol, and **M** take their share." Gn 14:24
LORD appeared to him by the oaks of **M**, Gn 18:1
which was to the east of **M**, Gn 23:17
field of Machpelah east of **M** (that is, Gn 23:19
the son of Zohar the Hittite, east of **M**, Gn 25:9
Jacob came to his father Isaac at **M**, Gn 35:27
the field at Machpelah, to the east of **M**, Gn 49:30
the field at Machpelah, to the east of **M**, Gn 50:13

MAN (2018)
God said, "Let us make **m** in our image, Gn 1:26
So God created **m** in his own image, in Gn 1:27
and there was no **m** to work the ground, Gn 2:5
LORD God formed the **m** of dust from the Gn 2:7
life, and the **m** became a living creature. Gn 2:7
there he put the **m** whom he had formed. Gn 2:8
LORD God took the **m** and put him in Gn 2:15
And the LORD God commanded the **m**, Gn 2:16
is not good that the **m** should be alone; Gn 2:18
brought them to the **m** to see what he Gn 2:19
And whatever the **m** called every living Gn 2:19
The **m** gave names to all livestock and Gn 2:20
caused a deep sleep to fall upon the **m**, Gn 2:21
had taken from the **m** he made into a Gn 2:22
into a woman and brought her to the **m**. Gn 2:22
Then the **m** said, "This at last is bone of Gn 2:23
because she was taken out of **M**." Gn 2:23
Therefore a **m** shall leave his father and Gn 2:24
And the **m** and his wife were both naked Gn 2:25
and the **m** and his wife hid themselves Gn 3:8
LORD God called to the **m** and said to him, Gn 3:9
The **m** said, "The woman whom you Gn 3:12
The **m** called his wife's name Eve, Gn 3:20
the **m** has become like one of us in Gn 3:22
He drove out the **m**, and at the east of the Gn 3:24
"I have gotten a **m** with the help of the Gn 4:1
I have killed a **m** for wounding me, a Gn 4:23
me, a young **m** for striking me. Gn 4:23
When God created **m**, he made him in Gn 5:1
them and named them **M** when they were Gn 5:2
When **m** began to multiply on the face of Gn 6:1
that the daughters of **m** were attractive. Gn 6:2
"My Spirit shall not abide in **m** forever, Gn 6:3
to the daughters of **m** and they bore Gn 6:4
that the wickedness of **m** was great in the Gn 6:5
sorry that he had made **m** on the earth, Gn 6:6
"I will blot out **m** whom I have created Gn 6:7
m and animals and creeping things and Gn 6:7
Noah was a righteous **m**, blameless in Gn 6:9
m and animals and creeping things and Gn 7:23
again curse the ground because of **m**, Gn 8:21
every beast I will require it and from **m**. Gn 9:5
From his fellow **m** I will require a Gn 9:5
will require a reckoning for the life of **m**. Gn 9:5
"Whoever sheds the blood of **m**, by man Gn 9:6
of man, by **m** shall his blood be shed, Gn 9:6
shed, for God made **m** in his own image. Gn 9:6
Noah began to be a **m** of the soil, and he Gn 9:20
was the first on earth to be a mighty **m**. Gn 10:8
which the children of **m** had built. Gn 11:5
to him: "This **m** shall not be your heir; Gn 15:4
He shall be a wild donkey of a **m**, his Gn 16:12
child be born to a **m** who is a hundred Gn 17:17
and good, and gave it to a young **m**, Gn 18:7
and old, all the people to the last **m**, Gn 19:4
daughters who have not known any **m**. Gn 19:8
they pressed hard against the **m** Lot, Gn 19:9
and there is not a **m** on earth to come Gn 19:31
you are a dead **m** because of the woman Gn 20:3
a maiden whom no **m** had known. Gn 24:16
The **m** gazed at her in silence to learn Gn 24:21
the **m** took a gold ring weighing a half Gn 24:22
The **m** bowed his head and worshiped Gn 24:26
Laban ran out toward the **m**, to the Gn 24:29
"Thus the **m** spoke to me," he went to Gn 24:30
man spoke to me," he went to the **m**. Gn 24:30
So the **m** came to the house and Gn 24:32
"Will you go with this **m**?" She said, Gn 24:58
rode on the camels and followed the **m**. Gn 24:61
said to the servant, "Who is that **m**, Gn 24:65
good old age, an old **m** and full of years, Gn 25:8
was a skillful hunter, a **m** of the field, Gn 25:27
of the field, while Jacob was a quiet **m**, Gn 25:27
"Whoever touches this **m** or his wife Gn 26:11
and the **m** became rich, and gained Gn 26:13
"Behold, my brother Esau is a hairy **m**, Gn 27:11
is a hairy man, and I am a smooth **m**. Gn 27:11
that I should give her to any other **m**; Gn 29:19
Thus the **m** increased greatly and had Gn 30:43
And a **m** wrestled with him until the Gn 32:24
When the **m** saw that he did not Gn 32:25
And the young **m** did not delay to do Gn 34:19
And a **m** found him wandering in the Gn 37:15
in the fields. And the **m** asked him, Gn 37:15
And the **m** said, "They have gone Gn 37:17
"By the **m** to whom these belong, Gn 38:25
Joseph, and he became a successful **m**, Gn 39:2
interpretation to each **m** according to Gn 41:12
select a discerning and wise **m**, Gn 41:33
servants, "Can we find a **m** like this, Gn 41:38
We are all sons of one **m**. We are Gn 42:11
the sons of one **m** in the land of Gn 42:13
"The **m**, the lord of the land, spoke Gn 42:30
Then the **m**, the lord of the land, said to Gn 42:33
to him, "The **m** solemnly warned us, Gn 43:3
we will not go down, for the **m** said to us, Gn 43:5
as to tell the **m** that you had another Gn 43:6
"The **m** questioned us carefully about Gn 43:7
and carry a present down to the **m**, Gn 43:11
brother, and arise, go again to the **m**. Gn 43:13
grant you mercy before the **m**, Gn 43:14
The **m** did as Joseph told him and Gn 43:17
And when the **m** had brought the men Gn 43:24
well, the old **m** of whom you spoke? Gn 43:27
Then each **m** quickly lowered his sack Gn 44:11
ground, and each **m** opened his sack. Gn 44:11
and every **m** loaded his donkey, Gn 44:13
not know that a **m** like me can indeed Gn 44:15
Only the **m** in whose hand the cup was Gn 44:17
my lord, 'We have a father, an old **m**, Gn 44:20
Now a **m** from the house of Levi went and Ex 2:1
And he said to the **m** in the wrong, Ex 2:13
where is he? Why have you left the **m**? Ex 2:20
Moses was content to dwell with the **m**, Ex 2:21
For each **m** cast down his staff, and they Ex 7:12
and there were gnats on **m** and beast. Ex 8:17
not. So there were gnats on **m** and beast. Ex 8:18
out in sores on **m** and beast throughout Ex 9:9
breaking out in sores on **m** and beast. Ex 9:10
for every **m** and beast that is in the field Ex 9:19
on **m** and beast and every plant of the Ex 9:22
all the land of Egypt, both **m** and beast. Ex 9:25
"How long shall this **m** be a snare to us? Ex 10:7
every **m** of his neighbor and every Ex 11:2
the **m** Moses was very great in the land Ex 11:3
of the people of Israel, either **m** or beast, Ex 11:7
of this month every **m** shall take a lamb Ex 12:3
in the land of Egypt, both **m** and beast; Ex 12:12
people of Israel, both of **m** and of beast, Ex 13:2
Every firstborn of **m** among your sons Ex 13:13
the firstborn of **m** and the firstborn Ex 13:15
The LORD is a **m** of war; the LORD is his Ex 15:3
whether beast or **m**, he shall not live.' Ex 19:13
"When a **m** sells his daughter as a slave, Ex 21:7
"Whoever strikes a **m** so that he dies Ex 21:12
But if a **m** willfully attacks another to Ex 21:14
"Whoever steals a **m** and sells him, and Ex 21:16
with his fist and the **m** does not die but Ex 21:18
then if the **m** rises again and walks Ex 21:19
"When a **m** strikes his slave, male or Ex 21:20
"When a **m** strikes the eye of his slave, Ex 21:26
"When an ox gores a **m** or a woman to Ex 21:28

kept it in, and it kills a **m** or a woman, Ex 21:29
"When a **m** opens a pit, or when a man Ex 21:33
or when a **m** digs a pit and does not Ex 21:33
"If a **m** steals an ox or a sheep, and kills Ex 22:1
"If a **m** causes a field or vineyard to be Ex 22:5
"If a **m** gives to his neighbor money or Ex 22:7
"If a **m** gives to his neighbor a donkey Ex 22:10
"If a **m** borrows anything of his Ex 22:14
"If a **m** seduces a virgin who is not Ex 22:16
hands with a wicked **m** to be a Ex 23:1
you be partial to a poor **m** in his lawsuit. Ex 23:3
From every **m** whose heart moves him Ex 25:2
the **m** who brought us up out of the land Ex 32:1
the **m** who brought us up out of the Ex 32:23
face to face, as a **m** speaks to his friend. Ex 33:11
Joshua the son of Nun, a young **m**, Ex 33:11
face, for **m** shall not see me and live." Ex 33:20
every **m** dedicating an offering of gold Ex 35:22
"Let no **m** or woman do anything more Ex 36:6
"When a **m** is afflicted with a leprous Lv 13:9
"When a **m** or woman has a disease on Lv 13:29
"When a **m** or a woman has spots on Lv 13:38
he is a leprous **m**, he is unclean. The Lv 13:44
him shall set the **m** who is to be Lv 14:11
When any **m** has a discharge from his Lv 15:2
"If a **m** has an emission of semen, he Lv 15:16
If a **m** lies with a woman and has an Lv 15:18
And if any **m** lies with her and her Lv 15:24
and for the **m** who lies with a woman Lv 15:33
by the hand of a **m** who is in readiness. Lv 16:21
bloodguilt shall be imputed to that **m**. Lv 17:4
and that **m** shall be cut off from among Lv 17:4
that **m** shall be cut off from his people. Lv 17:9
"If a **m** lies sexually with a woman who Lv 19:20
assigned to another **m** and not yet Lv 19:20
head and honor the face of an old **m**, Lv 19:32
my face against that **m** and will cut him Lv 20:3
their eyes to that **m** when he gives one Lv 20:4
my face against that **m** and against his Lv 20:5
"If a **m** commits adultery with the wife Lv 20:10
If a **m** lies with his father's wife, he has Lv 20:11
If a **m** lies with his daughter-in-law, Lv 20:12
If a **m** lies with a male as with a Lv 20:13
If a **m** takes a woman and her mother Lv 20:14
If a **m** lies with an animal, he shall Lv 20:15
"If a **m** takes his sister, a daughter of Lv 20:17
If a **m** lies with a woman during her Lv 20:18
If a **m** lies with his uncle's wife, he has Lv 20:20
If a **m** takes his brother's wife, it is Lv 20:21
"A **m** or a woman who is a medium or Lv 20:27
shall draw near, a **m** blind or lame, Lv 21:18
or a **m** who has an injured foot or an Lv 21:19
or a dwarf or a **m** with a defect in his Lv 21:20
No **m** of the offspring of Aaron the Lv 21:21
with the dead or a **m** who has had an Lv 22:4
woman's son and a **m** of Israel fought Lv 24:10
If a **m** has no one to redeem it and then Lv 25:26
the balance to the **m** to whom he sold Lv 25:27
"If a **m** sells a dwelling house in a Lv 25:29
"When a **m** dedicates his house as a Lv 27:14
"If a **m** dedicates to the LORD part of the Lv 27:16
or if he has sold the field to another **m**, Lv 27:20
and the **m** shall give the valuation on Lv 27:23
to the LORD, no **m** may dedicate; Lv 27:26
devoted thing that a **m** devotes to the Lv 27:28
that he has, whether **m** or beast, Lv 27:28
If a **m** wishes to redeem some of his Lv 27:31
shall be with you a **m** from each tribe, Nm 1:4
each **m** being the head of the house of Nm 1:4
and upward, every **m** able to go to war: Nm 1:26
and upward, every **m** able to go to war: Nm 1:28
and upward, every **m** able to go to war: Nm 1:30
and upward, every **m** able to go to war: Nm 1:32
and upward, every **m** able to go to war: Nm 1:34
and upward, every **m** able to go to war: Nm 1:36
and upward, every **m** able to go to war: Nm 1:38
and upward, every **m** able to go to war: Nm 1:40
and upward, every **m** able to go to war: Nm 1:42
every **m** able to go to war in Israel— Nm 1:45
each **m** in his own camp and each Nm 1:52
own camp and each **m** by his own Nm 1:52
in Israel, both of **m** and of beast. Nm 3:13
When a **m** or woman commits any of Nm 5:6
But if the **m** has no next of kin to whom Nm 5:8
if a **m** lies with her sexually, and it is Nm 5:13
then the **m** shall bring his wife to the Nm 5:15
saying, 'If no **m** has lain with you, Nm 5:19
and some **m** other than your husband Nm 5:20
jealousy comes over a **m** and he is Nm 5:30
The **m** shall be free from iniquity, but Nm 5:31
When either a **m** or a woman makes a Nm 6:2
"And if any **m** dies very suddenly beside Nm 6:9
to each **m** according to his service." Nm 7:5
Israel are mine, both of **m** and of beast. Nm 8:17
time; that **m** shall bear his sin. Nm 9:13

And a young **m** ran and told Moses, Nm 11:27
Now the **m** Moses was very meek, more Nm 12:3
of their fathers you shall send a **m**, Nm 13:2
Now if you kill this people as one **m**, Nm 14:15
they found a **m** gathering sticks on Nm 15:32
Moses, "The **m** shall be put to death; Nm 15:35
and the **m** whom the LORD chooses Nm 16:7
So every **m** took his censer and put Nm 16:18
the spirits of all flesh, shall one **m** sin, Nm 16:22
the staff of the **m** whom I choose shall Nm 17:5
they looked, and each **m** took his staff. Nm 17:9
womb of all flesh, whether **m** or beast, Nm 18:15
the firstborn of **m** you shall redeem, Nm 18:15
And a **m** who is clean shall gather up Nm 19:9
"If the **m** who is unclean does not Nm 19:20
God is not **m**, that he should lie, or a Nm 23:19
man, that he should lie, or a son of **m**, Nm 23:19
the oracle of the **m** whose eye is opened, Nm 24:3
the oracle of the **m** whose eye is Nm 24:15
and went after the **m** of Israel into the Nm 25:8
the **m** of Israel and the woman through Nm 25:8
The name of the slain **m** of Israel, Nm 25:14
saying, 'If a **m** dies and has no son, Nm 27:8
appoint a **m** over the congregation Nm 27:16
son of Nun, a **m** in whom is the Spirit, Nm 27:18
If a **m** vows a vow to the LORD, or swears Nm 30:2
Moses about a **m** and his wife Nm 30:16
the plunder, both of **m** and of beast. Nm 31:11
who has known **m** by lying with Nm 31:17
who have not known **m** by lying with Nm 31:18
was taken, both of **m** and of beast, Nm 31:26
who had not known **m** by lying with Nm 31:35
and there is not a **m** missing from us. Nm 31:49
LORD'S offering, what each **m** found, Nm 31:50
and every armed **m** of you will pass Nm 32:21
over, every **m** who is armed for war, Nm 32:27
every **m** who is armed to battle before Nm 32:29
righteously between a **m** and his brother Dt 1:16
men from you, one **m** from each tribe. Dt 1:23
God carried you, as a **m** carries his son, Dt 1:31
the day that God created **m** on the earth, Dt 4:32
seen God speak with **m** and man still Dt 5:24
God speak with man and **m** still live. Dt 5:24
make you know that **m** does not live by Dt 8:3
but **m** lives by every word that comes Dt 8:3
your heart that, as a **m** disciplines his son, Dt 8:5
a Hebrew **m** or a Hebrew woman, Dt 15:12
Every **m** shall give as he is able, Dt 16:17
a **m** or woman who does what is evil in Dt 17:2
to your gates that **m** or woman who has Dt 17:5
you shall stone that **m** or woman to Dt 17:5
The **m** who acts presumptuously by Dt 17:12
your God, or the judge, that **m** shall die. Dt 17:12
though the **m** did not deserve to die, Dt 19:6
'Is there any **m** who has built a new Dt 20:5
in the battle and another **m** dedicate it. Dt 20:5
And is there any **m** who has planted a Dt 20:6
the battle and another **m** enjoy its fruit. Dt 20:6
And is there any **m** who has betrothed a Dt 20:7
die in the battle and another **m** take her.' Dt 20:7
'Is there any **m** who is fearful and Dt 20:8
nearest to the slain **m** shall take a heifer Dt 21:3
nearest to the slain **m** shall wash their Dt 21:6
"If a **m** has two wives, the one loved and Dt 21:15
"If a **m** has a stubborn and rebellious Dt 21:18
"And if a **m** has committed a crime Dt 21:22
day, for a hanged **m** is cursed by God. Dt 21:23
nor shall a **m** put on a woman's cloak, Dt 22:5
"If any **m** takes a wife and goes in to her Dt 22:13
'I gave my daughter to this **m** to marry, Dt 22:16
city shall take the **m** and whip him, Dt 22:18
"If a **m** is found lying with the wife of Dt 22:22
found lying with the wife of another **m**, Dt 22:22
die, the **m** who lay with the woman, Dt 22:22
and a **m** meets her in the city and lies Dt 22:23
and the **m** because he violated his Dt 22:24
the open country a **m** meets a young Dt 22:25
and the **m** seizes her and lies with her, Dt 22:25
then only the **m** who lay with her shall Dt 22:25
that of a **m** attacking and murdering Dt 22:26
"If a **m** meets a virgin who is not Dt 22:28
then the **m** who lay with her shall give Dt 22:29
"A **m** shall not take his father's wife, so Dt 22:30
"If any **m** among you becomes unclean Dt 23:10
"When a **m** takes a wife and marries her, Dt 24:1
and the latter **m** hates her and writes her Dt 24:3
out of his house, or if the latter **m** dies, Dt 24:3
"When a **m** is newly married, he shall Dt 24:5
"If a **m** is found stealing one of his Dt 24:7
and the **m** to whom you make the loan Dt 24:11
And if he is a poor **m**, you shall not Dt 24:12
then if the guilty **m** deserves to be beaten, Dt 25:2
wife of the dead **m** shall not be married Dt 25:5
And if the **m** does not wish to take his Dt 25:7
it be done to the **m** who does not build up Dt 25:9

"'Cursed be the **m** who makes a carved Dt 27:15
who misleads a blind **m** on the road.' Dt 27:18
a wife, but another **m** shall ravish her. Dt 28:30
The **m** who is the most tender and Dt 28:54
be among you a **m** or woman or clan Dt 29:18
his jealousy will smoke against that **m**, Dt 29:20
terror, for young **m** and woman alike, Dt 32:25
nursing child with the **m** of gray hairs. Dt 32:25
with which Moses the **m** of God blessed Dt 33:1
No **m** shall be able to stand before you all Jos 1:5
no spirit left in any **m** because of you, Jos 2:11
the tribes of Israel, from each tribe a **m**. Jos 3:12
from the people, from each tribe a **m**, Jos 4:2
he had appointed, a **m** from each tribe. Jos 4:4
a **m** was standing before him with his Jos 5:13
the city, every **m** straight before him, Jos 6:20
the LORD be the **m** who rises up and Jos 6:26
LORD takes shall come near **m** by man. Jos 7:14
LORD takes shall come near man by **m**. Jos 7:14
the clan of the Zerahites **m** by man, Jos 7:17
the clan of the Zerahites man by **m**, Jos 7:17
brought near his household **m** by man, Jos 7:18
brought near his household man by **m**, Jos 7:18
Not a **m** was left in Ai or Bethel who did Jos 8:17
upon which no **m** has wielded an iron Jos 8:31
Not a **m** of them shall stand before you." Jos 10:8
when the LORD obeyed the voice of a **m**, Jos 10:14
Not a **m** moved his tongue against any Jos 10:21
But every **m** they struck with the edge Jos 11:14
said to Moses the **m** of God in Jos 14:6
was the greatest **m** among the Jos 14:15
and Bashan, because he was a **m** of war. Jos 17:1
no **m** has been able to stand before you Jos 23:9
One **m** of you puts to flight a thousand, Jos 23:10
away, every **m** to his inheritance. Jos 24:28
And the spies saw a **m** coming out of the Jgs 1:24
but they let the **m** and all his family go. Jgs 1:25
And the **m** went to the land of the Jgs 1:26
Gera, the Benjaminite, a left-handed **m**. Jgs 3:15
of Moab. Now Eglon was a very fat **m**. Jgs 3:17
able-bodied men; not a **m** escaped. Jgs 3:29
the edge of the sword; not a **m** was left. Jgs 4:16
tent, and if any **m** comes and asks you, Jgs 4:20
will show you the **m** whom you are Jgs 4:22
A womb or two for every **m**; spoil of Jgs 5:30
LORD is with you, O mighty **m** of valor." Jgs 6:12
shall strike the Midianites as one **m**." Jgs 6:16
let all the others go every **m** to his home." Jgs 7:7
all the rest of Israel every **m** to his tent, Jgs 7:8
a **m** was telling a dream to his comrade. Jgs 7:13
of Gideon the son of Joash, a **m** of Israel; Jgs 7:14
Every **m** stood in his place around the Jgs 7:21
he captured a young **m** of Succoth and Jgs 8:14
them!" But the young **m** did not draw Jgs 8:20
afraid, because he was still a young **m**. Jgs 8:20
yourself and fall upon us, for as the **m** is, Jgs 8:21
and every **m** threw in it the earrings of Jgs 8:25
to the young **m** his armor-bearer and Jgs 9:54
And his young **m** thrust him through, Jgs 9:54
of Puah, son of Dodo, a **m** of Issachar, Jgs 10:1
"Who is the **m** who will begin to fight Jgs 10:18
She had never known a **m**, and it Jgs 11:39
There was a certain **m** of Zorah, of the Jgs 13:2
her husband, "A **m** of God came to me, Jgs 13:6
please let the **m** of God whom you sent Jgs 13:8
the **m** who came to me the other day Jgs 13:10
and came to the **m** and said to him, Jgs 13:11
"Are you the **m** who spoke to this Jgs 13:11
And the young **m** grew, and the LORD Jgs 13:24
companion, who had been his best **m**. Jgs 14:20
become weak and be like any other **m**." Jgs 16:7
weak and be like any other **m**." Jgs 16:11
weak and be like any other **m**." Jgs 16:13
weak and be like any other **m**." Jgs 16:17
And she called a **m** and had him shave Jgs 16:19
said to the young **m** who held him by Jgs 16:26
There was a **m** of the hill country of Jgs 17:1
And the **m** Micah had a shrine, and he Jgs 17:5
there was a young **m** of Bethlehem in Jgs 17:7
And the **m** departed from the town of Jgs 17:8
Levite was content to dwell with the **m**, Jgs 17:11
and the young **m** became to him like Jgs 17:11
and the young **m** became his priest, Jgs 17:12
you to be priest to the house of one **m**, Jgs 18:19
And the girl's father said to the **m**, "Be Jgs 19:6
And when the **m** rose up to go, his Jgs 19:7
And when the **m** and his concubine and Jgs 19:9
But the **m** would not spend the night. Jgs 19:10
And he said to his young **m**, "Come Jgs 19:13
an old **m** was coming from his work in Jgs 19:16
The **m** was from the hill country of Jgs 19:16
And the old **m** said, "Where are you Jgs 19:17
and the young **m** with your servants. Jgs 19:19
And the old **m** said, "Peace be to you; I Jgs 19:20
And they said to the old **m**, the master Jgs 19:22

"Bring out the **m** who came into your	Jgs 19:22
And the **m**, the master of the house,	Jgs 19:23
since this **m** has come into my house,	Jgs 19:23
but against this **m** do not do this	Jgs 19:24
So the **m** seized his concubine and	Jgs 19:25
and the **m** rose up and went away to his	Jgs 19:28
assembled as one **m** to the LORD	Jgs 20:1
And all the people arose as one **m**,	Jgs 20:8
against the city, united as one **m**.	Jgs 20:11
had not known a **m** by lying with him,	Jgs 21:12
and snatch each **m** his wife from	Jgs 21:21
not take for each **m** of them his wife	Jgs 21:22
time, every **m** to his tribe and family,	Jgs 21:24
from there every **m** to his inheritance.	Jgs 21:24
and a **m** of Bethlehem in Judah went to	Ru 1:1
The name of the **m** was Elimelech and	Ru 1:2
a worthy **m** of the clan of Elimelech,	Ru 2:1
said to his young **m** who was in charge	Ru 2:5
Blessed be the **m** who took notice of	Ru 2:19
to her, "The **m** is a close relative of ours,	Ru 2:20
yourself known to the **m** until he has	Ru 3:3
At midnight the **m** was startled and	Ru 3:8
told her all that the **m** had done for her,	Ru 3:16
for the **m** will not rest but will settle the	Ru 3:18
a certain **m** of Ramathaim-zophim	1 Sm 1:1
Now this **m** used to go up year by year	1 Sm 1:3
The **m** Elkanah and all his house	1 Sm 1:21
for not by might shall a **m** prevail.	1 Sm 2:9
that when any **m** offered sacrifice,	1 Sm 2:13
and say to the **m** who was sacrificing,	1 Sm 2:15
And if the **m** said to him, "Let them	1 Sm 2:16
And the young **m** Samuel grew in the	1 Sm 2:21
If someone sins against a **m**, God will	1 Sm 2:25
Now the young **m** Samuel continued	1 Sm 2:26
favor with the LORD and also with **m**.	1 Sm 2:26
And there came a **m** of God to Eli and	1 Sm 2:27
will not be an old **m** in your house.	1 Sm 2:31
not be an old **m** in your house forever.	1 Sm 2:32
Now the young **m** Samuel was	1 Sm 3:1
that the LORD was calling the young **m**.	1 Sm 3:8
and they fled, every **m** to his home.	1 Sm 4:10
A **m** of Benjamin ran from the battle	1 Sm 4:12
And when the **m** came into the city	1 Sm 4:13
uproar?" Then the **m** hurried and	1 Sm 4:14
And the **m** said to Eli, "I am he who	1 Sm 4:16
he died, for the **m** was old and heavy.	1 Sm 4:18
men of Israel, "Go every **m** to his city."	1 Sm 8:22
There was a **m** of Benjamin whose	1 Sm 9:1
Aphiah, a Benjaminite, a **m** of wealth.	1 Sm 9:1
name was Saul, a handsome young **m**.	1 Sm 9:2
There was not a **m** among the people of	1 Sm 9:2
"Behold, there is a **m** of God in this city,	1 Sm 9:6
and he is a **m** who is held in honor;	1 Sm 9:6
if we go, what can we bring the **m**?	1 Sm 9:7
is no present to bring to the **m** of God.	1 Sm 9:7
I will give it to the **m** of God to tell us	1 Sm 9:8
when a **m** went to inquire of God,	1 Sm 9:9
to the city where the **m** of God was.	1 Sm 9:10
will send to you a **m** from the land of	1 Sm 9:16
"Here is the **m** of whom I spoke to	1 Sm 9:17
and his young **m** and brought them	1 Sm 9:22
them and be turned into another **m**.	1 Sm 10:6
And a **m** of the place answered, "And	1 Sm 10:12
"Is there a **m** still to come?" and the	1 Sm 10:22
"How can this **m** save us?" And they	1 Sm 10:27
people, and they came out as one **m**.	1 Sm 11:7
"Not a **m** shall be put to death this	1 Sm 11:13
he sent home, every **m** to his tent.	1 Sm 13:2
has sought out a **m** after his own	1 Sm 13:14
said to the young **m** who carried his	1 Sm 14:1
said to the young **m** who carried his	1 Sm 14:6
"Cursed be the **m** who eats food until	1 Sm 14:24
'Cursed be the **m** who eats food this	1 Sm 14:28
'Let every **m** bring his ox or his	1 Sm 14:34
us not leave a **m** of them." And they	1 Sm 14:36
there was not a **m** among all the	1 Sm 14:39
And when Saul saw any strong **m**, or	1 Sm 14:52
any strong man, or any valiant **m**,	1 Sm 14:52
them, but kill both **m** and woman,	1 Sm 15:3
lie or have regret, for he is not a **m**,	1 Sm 15:29
For the LORD sees not as **m** sees: man	1 Sm 16:7
m looks on the outward appearance,	1 Sm 16:7
you to seek out a **m** who is skillful in	1 Sm 16:16
"Provide for me a **m** who can play	1 Sm 16:17
is skillful in playing, a **m** of valor,	1 Sm 16:18
playing, a man of valor, a **m** of war,	1 Sm 16:18
in speech, and a **m** of good presence,	1 Sm 16:18
of Saul? Choose a **m** for yourselves,	1 Sm 17:8
Give me a **m**, that we may fight	1 Sm 17:10
days of Saul the **m** was already old	1 Sm 17:12
men of Israel, when they saw the **m**,	1 Sm 17:24
you seen this **m** who has come	1 Sm 17:25
will enrich the **m** who kills him	1 Sm 17:25
be done for the **m** who kills this	1 Sm 17:26
it be done to the **m** who kills him."	1 Sm 17:27
and he has been a **m** of war from his	1 Sm 17:33
young **m**?" And David answered,	1 Sm 17:58
I am a poor **m** and have no	1 Sm 18:23
And behold, I will send the young **m**,	1 Sm 20:21
If I say to the young **m**, 'Look, the	1 Sm 20:21
Now a certain **m** of the servants of	1 Sm 21:7
"Behold, you see the **m** is mad.	1 Sm 21:14
both **m** and woman, child and	1 Sm 22:19
For if a **m** finds his enemy, will he let	1 Sm 24:19
And there was a **m** in Maon whose	1 Sm 25:2
The **m** was very rich; he had three	1 Sm 25:2
Now the name of the **m** was Nabal,	1 Sm 25:3
but the **m** was harsh and badly	1 Sm 25:3
"Every **m** strap on his sword!" And	1 Sm 25:13
sword!" And every **m** of them	1 Sm 25:13
such a worthless **m** that one cannot	1 Sm 25:17
No **m** saw it or knew it, nor did any	1 Sm 26:12
said to Abner, "Are you not a **m**?	1 Sm 26:15
LORD rewards every **m** for his	1 Sm 26:23
his men, every **m** with his household,	1 Sm 27:3
would leave neither **m** nor woman	1 Sm 27:9
would leave neither **m** nor woman	1 Sm 27:11
she said, "An old **m** is coming up,	1 Sm 28:14
said to him, "Send the **m** back,	1 Sm 29:4
He said, "I am a young **m** of Egypt,	1 Sm 30:13
day, and not a **m** of them escaped,	1 Sm 30:17
except that each **m** may lead away	1 Sm 30:22
behold, a **m** came from Saul's camp,	2 Sm 1:2
said to the young **m** who told him,	2 Sm 1:5
And the young **m** who told him said,	2 Sm 1:6
said to the young **m** who told him,	2 Sm 1:13
prince and a great **m** has fallen this	2 Sm 3:38
of Rimmon a **m** of Benjamin from	2 Sm 4:2
have killed a righteous **m** in his own	2 Sm 4:11
The rich **m** had very many flocks	2 Sm 12:2
but the poor **m** had nothing but one	2 Sm 12:3
there came a traveler to the rich **m**,	2 Sm 12:4
prepared it for the **m** who had come to	2 Sm 12:4
was greatly kindled against the **m**,	2 Sm 12:5
the **m** who has done this deserves to	2 Sm 12:5
said to David, "You are the **m**!	2 Sm 12:7
And Jonadab was a very crafty **m**.	2 Sm 13:3
called the young **m** who served him	2 Sm 13:17
And the young **m** who kept the	2 Sm 13:34
'Give up the **m** who struck his	2 Sm 14:7
the hand of the **m** who would destroy	2 Sm 14:16
bring back the young **m** Absalom."	2 Sm 14:21
And when any **m** had a dispute to	2 Sm 15:2
but there is no **m** designated by the	2 Sm 15:3
Then every **m** with a dispute or cause	2 Sm 15:4
And whenever a **m** came near to pay	2 Sm 15:5
there came out a **m** of the family of	2 Sm 16:5
"Get out, get out, you **m** of blood,	2 Sm 16:7
you man of blood, you worthless **m**!	2 Sm 16:7
is on you, for you are a **m** of blood."	2 Sm 16:8
You seek the life of only one **m**, and	2 Sm 17:3
Then even the valiant **m**, whose	2 Sm 17:10
that your father is a mighty **m**,	2 Sm 17:10
But a young **m** saw them and told	2 Sm 17:18
to the house of a **m** at Bahurim,	2 Sm 17:18
the son of a **m** named Ithra the	2 Sm 17:25
with the young **m** Absalom." And all	2 Sm 18:5
And a certain **m** saw it and told Joab,	2 Sm 18:10
Joab said to the **m** who told him,	2 Sm 18:11
But the **m** said to Joab, "Even if I felt	2 Sm 18:12
sake protect the young **m** Absalom.'	2 Sm 18:12
looked, he saw a **m** running alone.	2 Sm 18:24
watchman saw another **m** running.	2 Sm 18:26
another **m** running alone!" The	2 Sm 18:26
"He is a good **m** and comes with	2 Sm 18:27
the young **m** Absalom?" Ahimaaz	2 Sm 18:29
with the young **m** Absalom?" And	2 Sm 18:32
you for evil be like that young **m**."	2 Sm 18:32
not a **m** will stay with you this night,	2 Sm 19:7
Israel had fled every **m** to his own	2 Sm 19:8
of all the men of Judah as one **m**,	2 Sm 19:14
Barzillai was a very aged **m**, eighty	2 Sm 19:32
for he was a very wealthy **m**.	2 Sm 19:32
happened to be there a worthless **m**,	2 Sm 20:1
of Jesse; every **m** to his tents, O Israel!"	2 Sm 20:1
And when the **m** saw that all the	2 Sm 20:12
But a **m** of the hill country of	2 Sm 20:21
from the city, every **m** to his home.	2 Sm 20:22
for us to put any **m** to death in Israel."	2 Sm 21:4
"The **m** who consumed us and	2 Sm 21:5
where there was a **m** of great stature,	2 Sm 21:20
with the blameless **m** you show	2 Sm 22:26
the oracle of the **m** who was raised on	2 Sm 23:1
but the **m** who touches them arms	2 Sm 23:7
Jehoiada was a valiant **m** of Kabzeel,	2 Sm 23:20
down an Egyptian, a handsome **m**.	2 Sm 23:21
let me not fall into the hand of **m**."	2 Sm 24:14
so?" He was also a very handsome **m**,	1 Kgs 1:6
you are a worthy **m** and bring good	1 Kgs 1:42
"If he will show himself a worthy **m**,	1 Kgs 1:52
Be strong, and show yourself a **m**,	1 Kgs 2:2
shall not lack a **m** on the throne of	1 Kgs 2:4
him guiltless, for you are a wise **m**.	1 Kgs 2:9
Each **m** had to make provision for one	1 Kgs 4:7
every **m** under his vine and under his	1 Kgs 4:25
and his father was a **m** of Tyre,	1 Kgs 7:14
shall not lack a **m** to sit before me	1 Kgs 8:25
"If a **m** sins against his neighbor and	1 Kgs 8:31
plea is made by any **m** or by all your	1 Kgs 8:38
shall not lack a **m** on the throne of	1 Kgs 9:5
The **m** Jeroboam was very able, and	1 Kgs 11:28
that the young **m** was industrious	1 Kgs 11:28
came to Shemaiah the **m** of God:	1 Kgs 12:22
Every **m** return to his home, for this	1 Kgs 12:24
a **m** of God came out of Judah by the	1 Kgs 13:1
And the **m** cried against the altar by	1 Kgs 13:2
heard the saying of the **m** of God,	1 Kgs 13:4
the sign that the **m** of God had given	1 Kgs 13:5
And the king said to the **m** of God,	1 Kgs 13:6
to me." And the **m** of God entreated	1 Kgs 13:6
And the king said to the **m** of God,	1 Kgs 13:7
And the **m** of God said to the king, "If	1 Kgs 13:8
him all that the **m** of God had done	1 Kgs 13:11
the way that the **m** of God who came	1 Kgs 13:12
he went after the **m** of God and	1 Kgs 13:14
"Are you the **m** of God who came	1 Kgs 13:14
he cried to the **m** of God who came	1 Kgs 13:21
"It is the **m** of God who disobeyed	1 Kgs 13:26
up the body of the **m** of God and laid	1 Kgs 13:29
grave in which the **m** of God is	1 Kgs 13:31
as a **m** burns up dung until it is all	1 Kgs 14:10
have you against me, O **m** of God?	1 Kgs 17:18
I know that you are a **m** of God,	1 Kgs 17:24
see how this **m** is seeking trouble,	1 Kgs 20:7
And each struck down his **m**. The	1 Kgs 20:20
And a **m** of God came near and said	1 Kgs 20:28
And a certain **m** of the sons of the	1 Kgs 20:35
please." But the **m** refused to strike	1 Kgs 20:35
Then he found another **m** and said,	1 Kgs 20:37
please." And the **m** struck him—	1 Kgs 20:37
turned and brought a **m** to me and	1 Kgs 20:39
man to me and said, 'Guard this **m**;	1 Kgs 20:39
of your hand the **m** whom I had	1 Kgs 20:42
"There is yet one **m** by whom we may	1 Kgs 22:8
But a certain **m** drew his bow at	1 Kgs 22:34
the army, "Every **m** to his city,	1 Kgs 22:36
city, and every **m** to his country!"	1 Kgs 22:36
to him, "There came a **m** to meet us,	2 Kgs 1:6
"What kind of **m** was he who came to	2 Kgs 1:7
of a hill, and said to him, "O **m** of God,	2 Kgs 1:9
captain of fifty, "If I am a **m** of God,	2 Kgs 1:10
and said to him, "O **m** of God,	2 Kgs 1:11
answered them, "If I am a **m** of God,	2 Kgs 1:12
and entreated him, "O **m** of God,	2 Kgs 1:13
piece of land every **m** threw a stone	2 Kgs 3:25
She came and told the **m** of God, and	2 Kgs 4:7
that this is a holy **m** of God who is	2 Kgs 4:9
she said, "No, my lord, O **m** of God;	2 Kgs 4:16
on the bed of the **m** of God and shut	2 Kgs 4:21
quickly go to the **m** of God and come	2 Kgs 4:22
and came to the **m** of God at Mount	2 Kgs 4:25
When the **m** of God saw her coming,	2 Kgs 4:25
to the mountain to the **m** of God,	2 Kgs 4:27
But the **m** of God said, "Leave her	2 Kgs 4:27
the stew, they cried out, "O **m** of God,	2 Kgs 4:40
A **m** came from Baal-shalishah,	2 Kgs 4:42
bringing the **m** of God bread of the	2 Kgs 4:42
was a great **m** with his master and in	2 Kgs 5:1
He was a mighty **m** of valor, but he	2 Kgs 5:1
that this **m** sends word to me to cure a	2 Kgs 5:7
word to me to cure a **m** of his leprosy?	2 Kgs 5:7
But when Elisha the **m** of God heard	2 Kgs 5:8
to the word of the **m** of God,	2 Kgs 5:14
Then he returned to the **m** of God, he	2 Kgs 5:15
the servant of Elisha the **m** of God,	2 Kgs 5:20
heart go when the **m** turned from his	2 Kgs 5:26
Then the **m** of God said, "Where did it	2 Kgs 6:6
But the **m** of God sent word to the king	2 Kgs 6:9
place about which the **m** of God told	2 Kgs 6:10
the servant of the **m** of God rose early	2 Kgs 6:15
LORD opened the eyes of the young **m**,	2 Kgs 6:17
bring you to the **m** whom you seek."	2 Kgs 6:19
had dispatched a **m** from his	2 Kgs 6:32
the king leaned said to the **m** of God,	2 Kgs 7:2
as the **m** of God had said when the	2 Kgs 7:17
For when the **m** of God had said to	2 Kgs 7:18
captain had answered the **m** of God,	2 Kgs 7:19
according to the word of the **m** of God.	2 Kgs 8:2
Gehazi the servant of the **m** of God,	2 Kgs 8:4
him, "The **m** of God has come here,"	2 Kgs 8:7
with you and go to meet the **m** of God,	2 Kgs 8:8
embarrassed. And the **m** of God wept.	2 Kgs 8:11
So the young **m**, the servant of the	2 Kgs 9:4
And the young **m** poured the oil on his	2 Kgs 9:6
Then in haste every **m** of them took	2 Kgs 9:13

So a **m** on horseback went to meet 2 Kgs 9:18
there was not a **m** left who did not 2 Kgs 10:21
"The **m** who allows any of those 2 Kgs 10:24
let not a **m** escape." So when they 2 Kgs 10:25
every **m** with his weapons in his 2 Kgs 11:11
for which each **m** is assessed— 2 Kgs 12:4
Then the **m** of God was angry with 2 Kgs 13:19
And as a **m** was being buried, 2 Kgs 13:21
was seen and the **m** was thrown into 2 Kgs 13:21
as soon as the **m** touched the bones 2 Kgs 13:21
Israel, and every **m** fled to his home. 2 Kgs 14:12
fifty shekels of silver from every **m**, 2 Kgs 15:20
the hand of any **m** who leans on it. 2 Kgs 18:21
'Tell the **m** who sent you to me, 2 Kgs 22:15
LORD that the **m** of God proclaimed, 2 Kgs 23:16
the tomb of the **m** of God who came 2 Kgs 23:17
let no **m** move his bones." So they let 2 Kgs 23:18
the first on earth to be a mighty **m**. 1 Chr 1:10
was a valiant **m** of Kabzeel, 1 Chr 11:22
an Egyptian, a **m** of great stature, 1 Chr 11:23
a mighty **m** among the thirty and a 1 Chr 12:4
Zadok, a young **m** mighty in valor, 1 Chr 12:28
where there was a **m** of great stature, 1 Chr 20:6
not let me fall into the hand of **m**." 1 Chr 21:13
born to you who shall be a **m** of rest. 1 Chr 22:9
sons of Moses the **m** of God were 1 Chr 23:14
who was a mighty **m** of the thirty 1 Chr 27:6
being a **m** of understanding and a 1 Chr 27:32
for you are a **m** of war and have shed 1 Chr 28:3
be every willing **m** who has skill 1 Chr 28:21
will not be for **m** but for the LORD 1 Chr 29:1
So now send me a **m** skilled to work in 2 Chr 2:7
"Now I have sent a skilled **m**, who 2 Chr 2:13
Dan, and his father was a **m** of Tyre. 2 Chr 2:14
and I chose no **m** as prince over my 2 Chr 6:5
shall not lack a **m** to sit before me 2 Chr 6:16
indeed dwell with **m** on the earth? 2 Chr 6:18
"If a **m** sins against his neighbor and 2 Chr 6:22
plea is made by any **m** or by all your 2 Chr 6:29
shall not lack a **m** to rule Israel.' 2 Chr 7:18
for so David the **m** of God had 2 Chr 8:14
came to Shemaiah the **m** of God: 2 Chr 11:2
Return every **m** to his home, for this 2 Chr 11:4
God; let not **m** prevail against you." 2 Chr 14:11
whether young or old, **m** or woman. 2 Chr 15:13
Eliada, a mighty **m** of valor, with 2 Chr 17:17
"There is yet one **m** by whom we 2 Chr 18:7
But a certain **m** drew his bow at 2 Chr 18:33
you judge not for **m** but for the LORD. 2 Chr 19:6
every **m** of Judah and Jerusalem, 2 Chr 20:27
every **m** with his weapon in his 2 Chr 23:10
But a **m** of God came to him and 2 Chr 25:7
And Amaziah said to the **m** of God, 2 Chr 25:9
of Israel?" The **m** of God answered, 2 Chr 25:9
Israel, and every **m** fled to his home. 2 Chr 25:22
And Zichri, a mighty **m** of Ephraim, 2 Chr 28:7
to the Law of Moses the **m** of God. 2 Chr 30:16
their cities, every **m** to his possession. 2 Chr 31:1
'Tell the **m** who sent you to me, 2 Chr 34:23
compassion on young **m** or virgin, 2 Chr 36:17
young man or virgin, old **m** or aged. 2 Chr 36:17
people gathered as one **m** to Jerusalem. Ezr 3:1
written in the Law of Moses the **m** of God. Ezr 3:2
a **m** learned in matters of the Ezr 7:11
the leading **m** at the place Casiphia, Ezr 8:17
us, they brought us a **m** of discretion, Ezr 8:18
the sight of this **m**." Now I was Neh 1:11
The **m** who sounded the trumpet was Neh 4:18
"Let every **m** and his servant pass the Neh 4:22
God shake out every **m** from his house Neh 5:13
said, "Should such a **m** as I run away? Neh 6:11
And what **m** such as I could go into Neh 6:11
faithful and God-fearing **m** than many. Neh 7:2
people gathered as one **m** into the square Neh 8:1
of David the **m** of God, Neh 12:24
instruments of David the **m** of God. Neh 12:36
staff of his palace to do as each **m** desired. Est 1:8
that every **m** be master in his own Est 1:22
know that if any **m** or woman goes to Est 4:11
be done to the **m** whom the king delights Est 6:6
"For the **m** whom the king delights to Est 6:7
Let them dress the **m** whom the king Est 6:9
be done to the **m** whom the king delights Est 6:9
be done to the **m** whom the king Est 6:11
for the **m** Mordecai grew more and more Est 9:4
There was a **m** in the land of Uz whose Jb 1:1
and that **m** was blameless and upright, Jb 1:1
so that this **m** was the greatest of all the Jb 1:3
on the earth, a blameless and upright **m**, Jb 1:8
on the earth, a blameless and upright **m**, Jb 2:3
All that a **m** has he will give for his life. Jb 2:4
and the night that said, 'A **m** is conceived.' Jb 3:3
is light given to a **m** whose way is hidden, Jb 3:23
'Can mortal **m** be in the right before Jb 4:17
God? Can a **m** be pure before his Maker? Jb 4:17
but **m** is born to trouble as the sparks fly Jb 5:7
the speech of a despairing **m** is wind? Jb 6:26
"Has not **m** a hard service on earth, and Jb 7:1
What is **m**, that you make so much of Jb 7:17
God will not reject a blameless **m**, Jb 8:20
But how can a **m** be in the right before Jb 9:2
For he is not a **m**, as I am, that I might Jb 9:32
you eyes of flesh? Do you see as **m** sees? Jb 10:4
Are your days as the days of **m**, or your Jb 10:5
and a **m** full of talk be judged right? Jb 11:2
But a stupid **m** will get understanding Jb 11:12
when a wild donkey's colt is born a **m**! Jb 11:12
he answered me, a just and blameless **m**, Jb 12:4
if he shuts a **m** in, none can open. Jb 12:14
makes them stagger like a drunken **m**. Jb 12:25
you deceive him, as one deceives a **m**? Jb 13:9
M wastes away like a rotten thing, like a Jb 13:28
"**M** who is born of a woman is few of Jb 14:1
But a **m** dies and is laid low; man Jb 14:10
m breathes his last, and where is he? Jb 14:10
so a **m** lies down and rises not again; till Jb 14:12
If a **m** dies, shall he live again? All the Jb 14:14
the earth; so you destroy the hope of **m**. Jb 14:19
"Should a wise **m** answer with windy Jb 15:2
"Are you the first **m** who was born? Or Jb 15:7
What is **m**, that he can be pure? Or he Jb 15:14
a **m** who drinks injustice like water! Jb 15:16
The wicked **m** writhes in pain all his Jb 15:20
would argue the case of a **m** with God, Jb 16:21
as a son of **m** does with his neighbor. Jb 16:21
I shall not find a wise **m** among you. Jb 17:10
from of old, since **m** was placed on earth, Jb 20:4
As for me, is my complaint against **m**? Jb 21:4
that the evil **m** is spared in the day of Jb 21:30
"Can a **m** be profitable to God? Surely he Jb 22:2
The **m** with power possessed the land, Jb 22:8
the land, and the favored **m** lived in it. Jb 22:8
There an upright **m** could argue with Jb 23:7
they glean the vineyard of the wicked **m**. Jb 24:6
How then can **m** be in the right before Jb 25:4
how much less **m**, who is a maggot, and Jb 25:6
man, who is a maggot, and the son of **m**, Jb 25:6
is the portion of a wicked **m** with God, Jb 27:13
M puts an end to darkness and searches Jb 28:3
"**M** puts his hand to the flinty rock and Jb 28:9
M does not know its worth, and it is not Jb 28:13
And he said to **m**, 'Behold, the fear of the Jb 28:28
But it is the spirit in **m**, the breath of the Jb 32:8
God may vanquish him, not a **m**.' Jb 32:13
show partiality to any **m** or use flattery Jb 32:21
answer you, for God is greater than **m**. Jb 33:12
in two, though **m** does not perceive it. Jb 33:14
that he may turn **m** aside from his deed Jb 33:17
his deed and conceal pride from a **m**; Jb 33:17
"**M** is also rebuked with pain on his bed Jb 33:19
to declare to **m** what is right for him, Jb 33:23
then **m** prays to God, and he accepts Jb 33:26
and he restores to **m** his righteousness. Jb 33:26
things, twice, three times, with a **m**, Jb 33:29
What **m** is like Job, who drinks up Jb 34:7
'It profits a **m** nothing that he should Jb 34:9
to the work of a **m** he will repay him, Jb 34:11
together, and **m** would return to dust. Jb 34:15
one,' and to nobles, 'Wicked **m**,' Jb 34:18
"For his eyes are on the ways of a **m**, Jb 34:21
has no need to consider a **m** further, Jb 34:23
him, whether it be a nation or a **m**? Jb 34:29
that a godless **m** should not reign, that Jb 34:30
and the wise **m** who hears me will say: Jb 34:34
wickedness concerns a **m** like yourself, Jb 35:8
and your righteousness a son of **m**. Jb 35:8
has looked on it; **m** beholds it from afar. Jb 36:25
He seals up the hand of every **m**, that all Jb 37:7
Did a **m** ever wish that he would be Jb 37:20
Dress for action like a **m**; I will question Jb 38:3
to bring rain on a land where no **m** is, Jb 38:26
is, on the desert in which there is no **m**, Jb 38:26
"Dress for action like a **m**; I will question Jb 40:7
Behold, the hope of a **m** is false; he is laid Jb 41:9
And Job died, an old **m**, and full of days. Jb 42:17
Blessed is the **m** who walks not in the Ps 1:1
abhors the bloodthirsty and deceitful **m**. Ps 5:6
If a **m** does not repent, God will whet his Ps 7:12
the wicked **m** conceives evil and is Ps 7:14
what is **m** that you are mindful of him, Ps 8:4
and the son of **m** that you care for him? Ps 8:4
Let not **m** prevail; let the nations be Ps 9:19
so that **m** who is of the earth may strike Ps 10:18
see, his eyelids test, the children of **m**. Ps 11:4
vanished from among the children of **m**. Ps 12:1
is exalted among the children of **m**. Ps 12:8
down from heaven on the children of **m**, Ps 14:2
With regard to the works of **m**, by the Ps 17:4
with the blameless **m** you show Ps 18:25
you rescued me from the **m** of violence. Ps 18:48
his chamber, and, like a strong **m**, Ps 19:5
from among the children of **m**. Ps 21:10
But I am a worm and not a **m**, scorned Ps 22:6
Who is the **m** who fears the LORD? Him Ps 25:12
Blessed is the **m** against whom the LORD Ps 32:2
heaven; he sees all the children of **m**; Ps 33:13
This poor **m** cried, and the LORD heard Ps 34:6
Blessed is the **m** who takes refuge in Ps 34:8
What **m** is there who desires life and Ps 34:12
great deep; **m** and beast you save, O LORD. Ps 36:6
over the **m** who carries out evil devices! Ps 37:7
The steps of a **m** are established by the Ps 37:23
I have seen a wicked, ruthless **m**, Ps 37:35
for there is a future for the **m** of peace. Ps 37:37
But I am like a deaf **m**; I do not hear, Ps 38:13
like a mute **m** who does not open his Ps 38:13
have become like a **m** who does not Ps 38:14
Surely a **m** goes about as a shadow! Ps 39:6
m heaps up wealth and does not know Ps 39:6
you discipline a **m** with rebukes for Ps 39:11
Blessed is the **m** who makes the LORD his Ps 40:4
the deceitful and unjust **m** deliver me! Ps 43:1
Truly no **m** can ransom another, or give Ps 49:7
M in his pomp will not remain; he is Ps 49:12
Be not afraid when a **m** becomes rich, Ps 49:16
M in his pomp yet without Ps 49:20
Why do you boast of evil, O mighty **m**? Ps 52:1
"See the **m** who would not make God his Ps 52:7
on the children of **m** to see if there Ps 53:2
But it is you, a **m**, my equal, my Ps 55:13
to me, O God, for **m** tramples on me; Ps 56:1
not be afraid. What can **m** do to me? Ps 56:11
amid fiery beasts—the children of **m**, Ps 57:4
you judge the children of **m** uprightly? Ps 58:1
the foe, for vain is the salvation of **m**! Ps 60:11
will all of you attack a **m** to batter him, Ps 62:3
will render to a **m** according to his Ps 62:12
inward mind and heart of a **m** are deep! Ps 64:6
in his deeds toward the children of **m**. Ps 66:5
the grasp of the unjust and cruel **m**. Ps 71:4
Surely the wrath of **m** shall praise you; Ps 76:10
M ate of the bread of the angels; he sent Ps 78:25
like a strong **m** shouting because of Ps 78:65
hand be on the **m** of your right hand, Ps 80:17
the son of **m** whom you have made Ps 80:17
to the pit; I am a **m** who has no strength, Ps 88:4
you have created all the children of **m**! Ps 89:47
What **m** can live and never see death? Ps 89:48
A Prayer of Moses, the **m** of God. Ps 90:T
You return **m** to dust and say, "Return, O Ps 90:3
dust and say, "Return, O children of **m**!" Ps 90:3
The stupid **m** cannot know; the fool Ps 92:6
He who teaches **m** knowledge— Ps 94:10
the LORD—knows the thoughts of **m**, Ps 94:11
Blessed is the **m** whom you discipline, Ps 94:12
As for **m**, his days are like grass; he Ps 103:15
livestock and plants for **m** to cultivate, Ps 104:14
and wine to gladden the heart of **m**, oil Ps 104:15
M goes out to his work and to his Ps 104:23
he had sent a **m** ahead of them, Joseph, Ps 105:17
the foe, for vain is the salvation of **m**! Ps 108:12
Appoint a wicked **m** against him; let an Ps 109:6
Blessed is the **m** who fears the LORD, Ps 112:1
is well with the **m** who deals generously Ps 112:5
The wicked **m** sees it and is angry; he Ps 112:10
he has given to the children of **m**. Ps 115:16
I will not fear. What can **m** do to me? Ps 118:6
refuge in the LORD than to trust in **m**. Ps 118:8
How can a young **m** keep his way pure? Ps 119:9
Blessed is the **m** who fills his quiver Ps 127:5
thus shall the **m** be blessed who fears Ps 128:4
of Egypt, both of **m** and of beast; Ps 135:8
evil hunt down the violent **m** speedily! Ps 140:11
Let a righteous **m** strike me—it is a Ps 141:5
O LORD, what is **m** that you regard him, Ps 144:3
or the son of **m** that you think of him? Ps 144:3
M is like a breath; his days are like a Ps 144:4
the children of **m** your mighty deeds, Ps 145:12
not your trust in princes, in a son of **m**, Ps 146:3
nor his pleasure in the legs of a **m**, Ps 147:10
good success in the sight of God and **m**. Prv 3:4
Do not contend with a **m** for no reason, Prv 3:30
Do not envy a **m** of violence and do not Prv 3:31
a robber, and want like an armed **m**. Prv 6:11
A worthless person, a wicked **m**, goes Prv 6:12
Can a **m** carry fire next to his chest and Prv 6:27
For jealousy makes a **m** furious, and he Prv 6:34
the youths, a young **m** lacking sense, Prv 7:7
I call, and my cry is to the children of **m**. Prv 8:4
and delighting in the children of **m**. Prv 8:31
who reproves a wicked **m** incurs injury. Prv 9:7
reprove a wise **m**, and he will love you. Prv 9:8
Give instruction to a wise **m**, and he will Prv 9:9
teach a righteous **m**, and he will increase Prv 9:9
is pleasure to a **m** of understanding. Prv 10:23

mouth the godless **m** would destroy his Prv 11:9
but a **m** of understanding remains Prv 11:12
A **m** who is kind benefits himself, but Prv 11:17
himself, but a cruel **m** hurts himself. Prv 11:17
A good **m** obtains favor from the LORD, Prv 12:2
but a **m** of evil devices he condemns. Prv 12:2
A **m** is commended according to his Prv 12:8
to play the great **m** and lack bread. Prv 12:9
An evil **m** is ensnared by the Prv 12:13
of his mouth a **m** is satisfied with Prv 12:14
eyes, but a wise **m** listens to advice. Prv 12:15
A prudent **m** conceals knowledge, but Prv 12:23
but the diligent **m** will get precious Prv 12:27
of his mouth a **m** eats what is good, Prv 13:2
wealth, but a poor **m** hears no threat. Prv 13:8
A good **m** leaves an inheritance to his Prv 13:22
is easy for a **m** of understanding. Prv 14:6
There is a way that seems right to a **m**, Prv 14:12
and a good **m** will be filled with the Prv 14:14
A **m** of quick temper acts foolishly, Prv 14:17
and a **m** of evil devices is hated. Prv 14:17
oppresses a poor **m** insults his Maker, Prv 14:31
in the heart of a **m** of understanding, Prv 14:33
more the hearts of the children of **m**! Prv 15:11
A hot-tempered **m** stirs up strife, but Prv 15:18
but a foolish **m** despises his mother. Prv 15:20
but a **m** of understanding walks Prv 15:21
To make an apt answer is a joy to a **m**, Prv 15:23
The plans of the heart belong to **m**, but Prv 16:1
All the ways of a **m** are pure in his own Prv 16:2
The heart of **m** plans his way, but the Prv 16:9
of death, and a wise **m** will appease it. Prv 16:14
There is a way that seems right to a **m**, Prv 16:25
A worthless **m** plots evil, and his Prv 16:27
A dishonest **m** spreads strife, and a Prv 16:28
A **m** of violence entices his neighbor Prv 16:29
deeper into a **m** of understanding than Prv 17:10
An evil **m** seeks only rebellion, and a Prv 17:11
Let a **m** meet a she-bear robbed of her Prv 17:12
A **m** of crooked heart does not Prv 17:20
a fine on a righteous **m** is not good, Prv 17:26
a cool spirit is a **m** of understanding. Prv 17:27
the righteous **m** runs into it and is Prv 18:10
A **m** of many companions may come Prv 18:24
but a poor **m** is deserted by his friend. Prv 19:4
Many seek the favor of a generous **m**, Prv 19:6
is a friend to a **m** who gives gifts. Prv 19:6
A **m** of great wrath will pay the Prv 19:19
are the plans in the mind of a **m**, Prv 19:21
is desired in a **m** is steadfast love, Prv 19:22
love, and a poor **m** is better than a liar. Prv 19:22
reprove a **m** of understanding, Prv 19:25
is an honor for a **m** to keep aloof from Prv 20:3
but a **m** of understanding will draw it Prv 20:5
Many a **m** proclaims his own steadfast Prv 20:6
love, but a faithful **m** who can find? Prv 20:6
Bread gained by deceit is sweet to a **m**, Prv 20:17
how then can **m** understand his way? Prv 20:24
The spirit of **m** is the lamp of the LORD, Prv 20:27
Every way of a **m** is right in his own Prv 21:2
when a wise **m** is instructed, he gains Prv 21:11
loves pleasure will be a poor **m**; Prv 21:17
dwelling, but a foolish **m** devours it. Prv 21:20
A wise **m** scales the city of the mighty Prv 21:22
haughty **m** who acts with arrogant Prv 21:24
the word of a **m** who hears will endure. Prv 21:28
A wicked **m** puts on a bold face, but Prv 21:29
no friendship with a **m** given to anger, Prv 22:24
to anger, nor go with a wrathful **m**, Prv 22:24
Do you see a **m** skillful in his work? Prv 22:29
not eat the bread of a **m** who is stingy; Prv 23:6
A wise **m** is full of strength, and a man Prv 24:5
and a **m** of knowledge enhances his Prv 24:5
will he not repay **m** according to his Prv 24:12
as a wicked **m** against the dwelling Prv 24:15
for the evil **m** has no future; the lamp Prv 24:20
I will pay the **m** back for what he has Prv 24:29
by the vineyard of a **m** lacking sense, Prv 24:30
a robber, and want like an armed **m**. Prv 24:34
without rain is a **m** who boasts of a Prv 25:14
A **m** who bears false witness against Prv 25:18
in a treacherous **m** in time of Prv 25:19
is a righteous **m** who gives way Prv 25:26
A **m** without self-control is like a city Prv 25:28
Do you see a **m** who is wise in his own Prv 26:12
is the **m** who deceives his neighbor Prv 26:19
is a quarrelsome **m** for kindling strife. Prv 26:21
from its nest is a **m** who strays from his Prv 27:8
iron, and one **m** sharpens another. Prv 27:17
so the heart of **m** reflects the man. Prv 27:19
so the heart of man reflects the **m**. Prv 27:19
and never satisfied are the eyes of **m**. Prv 27:20
gold, and a **m** is tested by his praise. Prv 27:21
but with a **m** of understanding and Prv 28:2
A poor **m** who oppresses the poor is a Prv 28:3
Better is a poor **m** who walks in his Prv 28:6
integrity than a rich **m** who is crooked Prv 28:6
A rich **m** is wise in his own eyes, but a Prv 28:11
but a poor **m** who has understanding Prv 28:11
A faithful **m** will abound with Prv 28:20
for a piece of bread a **m** will do wrong. Prv 28:21
A stingy **m** hastens after wealth and Prv 28:22
Whoever rebukes a **m** will afterward Prv 28:23
is a companion to a **m** who destroys. Prv 28:24
A greedy **m** stirs up strife, but the one Prv 28:25
A **m** who flatters his neighbor spreads a Prv 29:5
An evil **m** is ensnared in his Prv 29:6
but a righteous **m** sings and rejoices. Prv 29:6
A righteous **m** knows the rights of the Prv 29:7
a wicked **m** does not understand such Prv 29:7
If a wise **m** has an argument with a Prv 29:9
but a wise **m** quietly holds it back. Prv 29:11
The poor **m** and the oppressor meet Prv 29:13
Do you see a **m** who is hasty in his Prv 29:20
A **m** of wrath stirs up strife, and one Prv 29:22
The fear of **m** lays a snare, but Prv 29:25
is from the LORD that a **m** gets justice. Prv 29:26
An unjust **m** is an abomination to the Prv 29:27
The oracle. The **m** declares, I am weary, Prv 30:1
Surely I am too stupid to be a **m**. I have Prv 30:2
I have not the understanding of a **m**. Prv 30:2
seas, and the way of a **m** with a virgin. Prv 30:19
What does **m** gain by all the toil at Eccl 1:3
full of weariness; a **m** cannot utter it; Eccl 1:8
to the children of **m** to be busy with. Eccl 1:13
for the children of **m** to do under Eccl 2:3
the delight of the children of **m**. Eccl 2:8
For what can the **m** do who comes Eccl 2:12
leave it to the **m** who will come after Eccl 2:18
What has a **m** from all the toil and Eccl 2:22
to the children of **m** to be busy with. Eccl 3:10
in all his toil—this is God's gift to **m**. Eccl 3:13
to the children of **m** that God is testing Eccl 3:18
to the children of **m** and what happens Eccl 3:19
and **m** has no advantage over the Eccl 3:19
the spirit of **m** goes upward and Eccl 3:21
better than that a **m** should rejoice in Eccl 3:22
And though a **m** might prevail against Eccl 4:12
a **m** to whom God gives wealth, Eccl 6:2
If a **m** fathers a hundred children and Eccl 6:3
All the toil of **m** is for his mouth, yet his Eccl 6:7
advantage has the wise **m** over the fool? Eccl 6:8
what does the poor **m** have who knows Eccl 6:8
named, and it is known what **m** is, Eccl 6:10
and what is the advantage to **m**? Eccl 6:11
what is good for **m** while he lives the Eccl 6:12
For who can tell **m** what will be after Eccl 6:12
It is better for a **m** to hear the rebuke of Eccl 7:5
so that **m** may not find out anything Eccl 7:14
There is a righteous **m** who perishes in Eccl 7:15
there is a wicked **m** who prolongs his Eccl 7:15
strength to the wise **m** more than ten Eccl 7:19
is not a righteous **m** on earth who does Eccl 7:20
One **m** among a thousand I found, but Eccl 7:28
I found, that God made **m** upright, Eccl 7:29
No **m** has power to retain the spirit, or Eccl 8:8
when **m** had power over man to his Eccl 8:9
man had power over **m** to his hurt. Eccl 8:9
heart of the children of **m** is fully set to Eccl 8:11
for **m** has no good thing under the sun Eccl 8:15
that **m** cannot find out the work that Eccl 8:17
However much **m** may toil in seeking, Eccl 8:17
Even though a wise **m** claims to know, Eccl 8:17
it is love or hate, **m** does not know; Eccl 9:1
of the children of **m** are full of evil, Eccl 9:3
For **m** does not know his time. Like Eccl 9:12
so the children of **m** are snared at an Eccl 9:12
there was found in it a poor, wise **m**, Eccl 9:15
Yet no one remembered that poor **m**. Eccl 9:15
though no **m** knows what is to be, Eccl 10:14
Rejoice, O young **m**, in your youth, Eccl 11:9
because **m** is going to his eternal Eccl 12:5
for this is the whole duty of **m**. Eccl 12:13
If a **m** offered for love all the wealth of his Sg 8:7
So **m** is humbled, and each one is brought Is 2:9
The haughty looks of **m** shall be brought Is 2:11
the haughtiness of **m** shall be humbled, Is 2:17
Stop regarding **m** in whose nostrils is Is 2:22
the mighty **m** and the soldier, the judge Is 3:2
the captain of fifty and the **m** of rank, the Is 3:3
For a **m** will take hold of his brother in the Is 3:6
shall take hold of one **m** in that day, Is 4:1
M is humbled, and each one is brought Is 5:15
for I am a **m** of unclean lips, and I dwell in Is 6:5
In that day a **m** will keep alive a young Is 7:21
bow and arrows a **m** will come there, Is 7:24
the elder and honored **m** is the head, and Is 9:15
it will be as when a sick **m** wastes away. Is 10:18
'Is this the **m** who made the earth Is 14:16
In that day **m** will look to his Maker, and Is 17:7
as a drunken **m** staggers in his vomit. Is 19:14
you away violently, O you strong **m**. Is 22:17
The earth staggers like a drunken **m**; it Is 24:20
As when a hungry **m** dreams he is eating Is 29:8
as when a thirsty **m** dreams he is Is 29:8
by a word make a **m** out to be an Is 29:21
The Egyptians are **m**, and not God, and Is 31:3
Assyrian shall fall by a sword, not of **m**; Is 31:8
and a sword, not of **m**, shall devour him; Is 31:8
are despised; there is no regard for **m**. Is 33:8
then shall the lame **m** leap like a deer, Is 35:6
pierce the hand of any **m** who leans on it. Is 36:6
I shall look on **m** no more among the Is 38:11
or what **m** shows him his counsel? Is 40:13
The LORD goes out like a mighty **m**, like Is 42:13
man, like a **m** of war he stirs up his zeal; Is 42:13
He shapes it into the figure of a **m**, with Is 44:13
figure of a man, with the beauty of a **m**, Is 44:13
Then it becomes fuel for a **m**. He takes a Is 44:15
I made the earth and created **m** on it; it Is 45:12
the **m** of my counsel from a far country. Is 46:11
Why, when I came, was there no **m**; why, Is 50:2
fear not the reproach of **m**, nor be Is 51:7
you that you are afraid of **m** who dies, Is 51:12
of the son of **m** who is made like grass, Is 51:12
a **m** of sorrows, and acquainted with Is 53:3
wicked and with a rich **m** in his death, Is 53:9
and the unrighteous **m** his thoughts; Is 55:7
Blessed is the **m** who does this, and the Is 56:2
this, and the son of **m** who holds it fast, Is 56:2
The righteous **m** perishes, and no one Is 57:1
For the righteous **m** is taken away from Is 57:1
He saw that there was no **m**, and Is 59:16
For as a young **m** marries a young Is 62:5
or an old **m** who does not fill out his Is 65:20
for the young **m** shall die a hundred Is 65:20
an ox is like one who kills a **m**; Is 66:3
none passes through, where no **m** dwells?' Jer 2:6
"If a **m** divorces his wife and she goes Jer 3:1
I looked, and behold, there was no **m**, Jer 4:25
are forsaken, and no **m** dwells in them. Jer 4:29
her squares to see if you can find a **m**, Jer 5:1
on horses, set in array as a **m** for battle, Jer 6:23
out on this place, upon **m** and beast, Jer 7:20
no **m** relents of his evil, saying, 'What Jer 8:6
Who is the **m** so wise that he can Jer 9:12
"Let not the wise **m** boast in his wisdom, Jer 9:23
let not the mighty **m** boast in his might, Jer 9:23
let not the rich **m** boast in his riches, Jer 9:23
Every **m** is stupid and without Jer 10:14
that the way of **m** is not in himself, Jer 10:23
that it is not in **m** who walks to direct Jer 10:23
Cursed be the **m** who does not hear the Jer 11:3
made desolate, but no **m** lays it to heart. Jer 12:11
the loincloth clings to the waist of a **m**, Jer 13:11
Why should you be like a **m** confused, Jer 14:9
a **m** of strife and contention to the Jer 15:10
Can **m** make for himself gods? Such Jer 16:20
"Cursed is the **m** who trusts in man and Jer 17:5
man who trusts in **m** and makes flesh Jer 17:5
"Blessed is the **m** who trusts in the LORD, Jer 17:7
to give every **m** according to his ways, Jer 17:10
Cursed be the **m** who brought the news Jer 20:15
Let that **m** be like the cities that the Jer 20:16
of this city, both **m** and beast. Jer 21:6
and every **m** will say to his neighbor, Jer 22:8
Is this **m** Coniah a despised, broken Jer 22:28
"Write this **m** down as childless, a man Jer 22:30
a **m** who shall not succeed in his days, Jer 22:30
I am like a drunken **m**, like a man Jer 23:9
man, like a **m** overcome by wine, Jer 23:9
Can a **m** hide himself in secret places Jer 23:24
I will punish that **m** and his household. Jer 23:34
"This **m** deserves the sentence of death, Jer 26:11
"This **m** does not deserve the sentence Jer 26:16
There was another **m** who prophesied Jer 26:20
Ask now, and see, can a **m** bear a child? Jer 30:6
then do I see every **m** with his hands on Jer 30:6
on the earth: a woman encircles a **m**." Jer 31:22
Judah with the seed of **m** and the seed of Jer 31:27
Each **m** who eats sour grapes, his teeth Jer 31:30
to all the ways of the children of **m**, Jer 32:19
'It is a desolation, without **m** or beast; Jer 32:43
say, 'It is a waste without **m** or beast,' Jer 33:10
without **m** or inhabitant or beast, Jer 33:10
place that is waste, without **m** or beast, Jer 33:12
David shall never lack a **m** to sit on the Jer 33:17
shall never lack a **m** in my presence to Jer 33:18
Hanan the son of Igdaliah, the **m** of God, Jer 35:4
shall never lack a **m** to stand before Jer 35:19
and will cut off from it **m** and beast?" Jer 36:29
only wounded men, every **m** in his tent, Jer 37:10
to the king, "Let this **m** be put to death, Jer 38:4
For this **m** is not seeking the welfare of Jer 38:4
to cut off from you **m** and woman, Jer 44:7

by the mouth of any **m** of Judah in all Jer 44:26
driven out, every **m** straight before him, Jer 49:5
says the LORD, no **m** shall dwell there, Jer 49:18
dwell there, no **m** shall sojourn in her. Jer 49:18
waste; no **m** shall dwell there; Jer 49:33
dwell there; no **m** shall sojourn in her." Jer 49:33
in it; both **m** and beast shall flee away. Jer 50:3
the LORD, so no **m** shall dwell there, Jer 50:40
and no son of **m** shall sojourn in her. Jer 50:40
arrayed as a **m** for battle against you, Jer 50:42
Every **m** is stupid and without Jer 51:17
you I break in pieces **m** and woman; Jer 51:22
in pieces the old **m** and the youth; Jer 51:22
in pieces the young **m** and the young Jer 51:22
and through which no son of **m** passes. Jer 51:43
shall dwell in it, neither **m** nor beast, Jer 51:62
faint like a wounded **m** in the streets of Lam 2:12
I am the **m** who has seen affliction Lam 3:1
It is good for a **m** that he bear the yoke Lam 3:27
to deny a **m** justice in the presence of Lam 3:35
to subvert a **m** in his lawsuit, the Lord Lam 3:36
Why should a living **m** complain, a Lam 3:39
should a living man complain, a **m**, Lam 3:39
And he said to me, "Son of **m**, stand on Ezk 2:1
And he said to me, "Son of **m**, I send you Ezk 2:3
And you, son of **m**, be not afraid of them, Ezk 2:6
"But you, son of **m**, hear what I say to Ezk 2:8
And he said to me, "Son of **m**, eat Ezk 3:1
And he said to me, "Son of **m**, feed your Ezk 3:3
And he said to me, "Son of **m**, go to the Ezk 3:4
Moreover, he said to me, "Son of **m**, all Ezk 3:10
"Son of **m**, I have made you a Ezk 3:17
And you, O son of **m**, behold, cords will Ezk 3:25
"And you, son of **m**, take a brick and lay Ezk 4:1
Moreover, he said to me, "Son of **m**, Ezk 4:16
"And you, O son of **m**, take a sharp Ezk 5:1
"Son of **m**, set your face toward the Ezk 6:2
"And you, O son of **m**, thus says the Lord Ezk 7:2
a form that had the appearance of a **m**. Ezk 8:2
Then he said to me, "Son of **m**, lift up Ezk 8:5
And he said to me, "Son of **m**, do you see Ezk 8:6
Then he said to me, "Son of **m**, dig in the Ezk 8:8
Then he said to me, "Son of **m**, have Ezk 8:12
to me, "Have you seen this, O son of **m**? Ezk 8:15
to me, "Have you seen this, O son of **m**? Ezk 8:17
and with them was a **m** clothed in linen, Ezk 9:2
And he called to the **m** clothed in linen, Ezk 9:3
And behold, the **m** clothed in linen, Ezk 9:11
And he said to the **m** clothed in linen, Ezk 10:2
side of the house, when the **m** went in, Ezk 10:3
he commanded the **m** clothed in linen, Ezk 10:6
the hands of the **m** clothed in linen, Ezk 10:7
And he said to me, "Son of **m**, these are Ezk 11:2
against them, prophesy, O son of **m**." Ezk 11:4
"Son of **m**, your brothers, even your Ezk 11:15
"Son of **m**, you dwell in the midst of a Ezk 12:2
As for you, son of **m**, prepare for Ezk 12:3
"Son of **m**, has not the house of Israel, Ezk 12:9
"Son of **m**, eat your bread with Ezk 12:18
"Son of **m**, what is this proverb that Ezk 12:22
"Son of **m**, behold, they of the house of Ezk 12:27
"Son of **m**, prophesy against the Ezk 13:2
"And you, son of **m**, set your face Ezk 13:17
"Son of **m**, these men have taken their Ezk 14:3
And I will set my face against that **m**; I Ezk 14:8
"Son of **m**, when a land sins against Ezk 14:13
it, and cut off from it **m** and beast, Ezk 14:13
land, and I cut off from it **m** and beast, Ezk 14:17
blood, to cut off from it **m** and beast, Ezk 14:19
to cut off from it **m** and beast! Ezk 14:21
"Son of **m**, how does the wood of the Ezk 15:2
"Son of **m**, make known to Jerusalem Ezk 16:2
"Son of **m**, propound a riddle, and Ezk 17:2
"If a **m** is righteous and does what is Ezk 18:5
true justice between **m** and man, Ezk 18:8
true justice between man and **m**, Ezk 18:8
"Now suppose this **m** fathers a son Ezk 18:14
"Son of **m**, speak to the elders of Israel, Ezk 20:3
Will you judge them, son of **m**, will Ezk 20:4
"Therefore, son of **m**, speak to the Ezk 20:27
"Son of **m**, set your face toward the Ezk 20:46
"Son of **m**, set your face toward Ezk 21:2
"As for you, son of **m**, groan; with Ezk 21:6
"Son of **m**, prophesy and say, Thus says Ezk 21:9
Cry out and wail, son of **m**, for it is Ezk 21:12
"As for you, son of **m**, prophesy. Clap Ezk 21:14
"As for you, son of **m**, mark two ways Ezk 21:19
"And you, son of **m**, prophesy, and Ezk 21:28
"And you, son of **m**, will you judge, will Ezk 22:2
"Son of **m**, the house of Israel has Ezk 22:18
"Son of **m**, say to her, You are a land Ezk 22:24
I sought for a **m** among them who Ezk 22:30
"Son of **m**, there were two women, the Ezk 23:2
"Son of **m**, will you judge Oholah and Ezk 23:36
"Son of **m**, write down the name of this Ezk 24:2

"Son of **m**, behold, I am about to take Ezk 24:16
"As for you, son of **m**, surely on the Ezk 24:25
"Son of **m**, set your face toward the Ezk 25:2
Edom and cut off from it **m** and beast. Ezk 25:13
"Son of **m**, because Tyre said Ezk 26:2
"Now you, son of **m**, raise a Ezk 27:2
"Son of **m**, say to the prince of Tyre, Ezk 28:2
heart of the seas,' yet you are but a **m**, Ezk 28:2
who kill you, though you are but a **m**, Ezk 28:9
"Son of **m**, raise a lamentation over Ezk 28:12
"Son of **m**, set your face toward Sidon, Ezk 28:21
"Son of **m**, set your face against Ezk 29:2
and will cut off from you **m** and beast, Ezk 29:8
No foot of **m** shall pass through it, Ezk 29:11
"Son of **m**, Nebuchadnezzar king of Ezk 29:18
"Son of **m**, prophesy, and say, Thus Ezk 30:2
"Son of **m**, I have broken the arm of Ezk 30:21
him like a **m** mortally wounded. Ezk 30:24
"Son of **m**, say to Pharaoh king of Ezk 31:2
below, among the children of **m**, Ezk 31:14
"Son of **m**, raise a lamentation over Ezk 32:2
and no foot of **m** shall trouble them Ezk 32:13
"Son of **m**, wail over the multitude of Ezk 32:18
"Son of **m**, speak to your people and say Ezk 33:2
of the land take a **m** from among them, Ezk 33:2
"So you, son of **m**, I have made a Ezk 33:7
"And you, son of **m**, say to the house Ezk 33:10
"And you, son of **m**, say to your Ezk 33:12
by the time the **m** came to me in Ezk 33:22
"Son of **m**, the inhabitants of these Ezk 33:24
saying, 'Abraham was only one **m**, Ezk 33:24
"As for you, son of **m**, your people who Ezk 33:30
"Son of **m**, prophesy against the Ezk 34:2
"Son of **m**, set your face against Mount Ezk 35:2
"And you, son of **m**, prophesy to the Ezk 36:1
I will multiply on you **m** and beast, Ezk 36:11
"Son of **m**, when the house of Israel Ezk 36:17
And he said to me, "Son of **m**, can these Ezk 37:3
prophesy, son of **m**, and say to the Ezk 37:9
Then he said to me, "Son of **m**, these Ezk 37:11
"Son of **m**, take a stick and write on it, Ezk 37:16
"Son of **m**, set your face toward Gog, of Ezk 38:2
"Therefore, son of **m**, prophesy, and Ezk 38:14
"And you, son of **m**, prophesy against Ezk 39:1
"As for you, son of **m**, thus says the Ezk 39:17
there was a **m** whose appearance was Ezk 40:3
And the **m** said to me, "Son of man, Ezk 40:4
And the man said to me, "Son of **m**, Ezk 40:4
While the **m** was standing beside me, I Ezk 43:6
and he said to me, "Son of **m**, this is the Ezk 43:7
"As for you, son of **m**, describe to the Ezk 43:10
And he said to me, "Son of **m**, thus Ezk 43:18
And the LORD said to me, "Son of **m**, Ezk 44:5
the **m** measured a thousand cubits, Ezk 47:3
And he said to me, "Son of **m**, have you Ezk 47:6
"There is not a **m** on earth who can Dn 2:10
exiles from Judah a **m** who will make Dn 2:25
wherever they dwell, the children of **m**, Dn 2:38
that every **m** who hears the sound of the Dn 3:10
There is a **m** in your kingdom in whom Dn 5:11
petition to any god or **m** for thirty days, Dn 6:7
to any god or **m** within thirty days Dn 6:12
and made to stand on two feet like a **m**, Dn 7:4
man, and the mind of a **m** was given to it. Dn 7:4
in this horn were eyes like the eyes of a **m**, Dn 7:8
heaven there came one like a son of **m**, Dn 7:13
me one having the appearance of a **m**. Dn 8:15
make this **m** understand the vision." Dn 8:16
he said to me, "Understand, O son of **m**, Dn 8:17
I was speaking in prayer, the **m** Gabriel, Dn 9:21
and behold, a **m** clothed in linen, Dn 10:5
said to me, "O Daniel, **m** greatly loved, Dn 10:11
of the children of **m** touched my lips. Dn 10:16
the appearance of a **m** touched me and Dn 10:18
And he said, "O **m** greatly loved, fear Dn 10:19
someone said to the **m** clothed in linen, Dn 12:6
And I heard the **m** clothed in linen, who Dn 12:7
is loved by another **m** and is an Hos 3:1
play the whore, or belong to another **m**; Hos 3:3
As robbers lie in wait for a **m**, so the Hos 6:9
the **m** of the spirit is mad, because of Hos 9:7
for I am God and not a **m**, the Holy One Hos 11:9
gladness dries up from the children of **m**. Jl 1:12
a **m** and his father go in to the same girl, Am 2:7
and declares to **m** what is his thought, Am 4:13
as if a **m** fled from a lion, and a bear Am 5:19
so that every **m** from Mount Esau will be Ob 1:9
and his nobles: Let neither **m** nor beast, Jon 3:7
but let **m** and beast be covered with Jon 3:8
away; they oppress a **m** and his house, Mi 2:2
and his house, a **m** and his inheritance. Mi 2:2
If a **m** should go about and utter wind Mi 2:11
they shall sit every **m** under his vine and Mi 4:4
which delay not for a **m** nor wait for the Mi 5:7
for a man nor wait for the children of **m**. Mi 5:7

He has told you, O **m**, what is good; and Mi 6:8
Shall I acquit the **m** with wicked scales Mi 6:11
and the great **m** utters the evil desire of Mi 7:3
M the ramparts; watch the road; dress for Na 2:1
swallows up the **m** more righteous Hab 1:13
an arrogant **m** who is never at rest. Hab 2:5
for the blood of **m** and violence to the Hab 2:8
for the blood of **m** and violence to the Hab 2:17
"I will sweep away **m** and beast; I will Zep 1:3
bitter; the mighty **m** cries aloud there. Zep 1:14
have been made desolate, without a **m**, Zep 3:6
ground brings forth, on **m** and beast, Hg 1:11
and behold, a **m** riding on a red horse! Zec 1:8
So the **m** who was standing among the Zec 1:10
a **m** with a measuring line in his hand! Zec 2:1
said to him, "Run, say to that young **m**, Zec 2:4
like a **m** who is awakened out of his Zec 4:1
the **m** whose name is the Branch: Zec 6:12
was no wage for **m** or any wage for Zec 8:10
for I set every **m** against his neighbor. Zec 8:10
and formed the spirit of **m** within him: Zec 12:1
the soil, for a **m** sold me in my youth.' Zec 13:5
against the **m** who stands next to me," Zec 13:7
any descendant of the **m** who does this, Mal 2:12
"For the **m** who hates and divorces, Mal 2:16
Will **m** rob God? Yet you are robbing Mal 3:8
spare them as a **m** spares his son who Mal 3:17
being a just **m** and unwilling to put her Mt 1:19
written, "'**M** shall not live by bread alone, Mt 4:4
be like a wise **m** who built his house Mt 7:24
be like a foolish **m** who built his house Mt 7:26
For I too am a **m** under authority, with Mt 8:9
but the Son of **M** has nowhere to lay his Mt 8:20
saying, "What sort of **m** is this, Mt 8:27
to themselves, "This **m** is blaspheming." Mt 9:3
that the Son of **M** has authority on earth Mt 9:6
he saw a **m** called Matthew sitting at the Mt 9:9
a demon-oppressed **m** who was mute Mt 9:32
had been cast out, the mute **m** spoke. Mt 9:33
of Israel before the Son of **M** comes. Mt 10:23
have come to set a **m** against his father, Mt 10:35
out to see? A **m** dressed in soft clothing? Mt 11:8
The Son of **M** came eating and Mt 11:19
For the Son of **M** is lord of the Sabbath." Mt 12:8
And a **m** was there with a withered Mt 12:10
much more value is a **m** than a sheep! Mt 12:12
Then he said to the **m**, "Stretch out Mt 12:13
your hand." And the **m** stretched it out, Mt 12:13
Then a demon-oppressed **m** who was Mt 12:22
him, so that the **m** spoke and saw. Mt 12:22
demons, that this **m** casts out demons." Mt 12:24
unless he first binds the strong **m**? Mt 12:29
against the Son of **M** will be forgiven, Mt 12:32
so will the Son of **M** be three days and Mt 12:40
But he replied to the **m** who told him, Mt 12:48
be compared to a **m** who sowed good Mt 13:24
mustard seed that a **m** took and sowed Mt 13:31
who sows the good seed is the Son of **M**. Mt 13:37
The Son of **M** will send his angels, and Mt 13:41
field, which a **m** found and covered up. Mt 13:44
"Where did this **m** get this wisdom and Mt 13:54
Where then did this **m** get all these Mt 13:56
do people say that the Son of **M** is?" Mt 16:13
things of God, but on the things of **m**." Mt 16:23
what will it profit a **m** if he gains the Mt 16:26
Or what shall a **m** give in return for his Mt 16:26
For the Son of **M** is going to come with Mt 16:27
see the Son of **M** coming in his Mt 16:28
until the Son of **M** is raised from the Mt 17:9
also the Son of **M** will certainly suffer Mt 17:12
to the crowd, a **m** came up to him and, Mt 17:14
"The Son of **M** is about to be delivered Mt 17:22
If a **m** has a hundred sheep and one of Mt 18:12
'Therefore a **m** shall leave his father and Mt 19:5
has joined together, let not **m** separate." Mt 19:6
"If such is the case of a **m** with his wife, Mt 19:10
And behold, a **m** came up to him, Mt 19:16
The young **m** said to him, "All these I Mt 19:20
When the young **m** heard this he went Mt 19:22
and said, "With **m** this is impossible, Mt 19:26
when the Son of **M** will sit on his Mt 19:28
And the Son of **M** will be delivered over Mt 20:18
even as the Son of **M** came not to be Mt 20:28
heaven or from **m**?" And they Mt 21:25
But if we say, 'From **m**,' we are afraid of Mt 21:26
do you think? A **m** had two sons. Mt 21:28
he saw there a **m** who had no wedding Mt 22:11
said, 'If a **m** dies having no children, Mt 22:24
And call no **m** your father on earth, for Mt 23:9
so will be the coming of the Son of **M**. Mt 24:27
in heaven the sign of the Son of **M**, Mt 24:30
see the Son of **M** coming on the clouds Mt 24:30
so will be the coming of the Son of **M**. Mt 24:37
so will be the coming of the Son of **M**. Mt 24:39
for the Son of **M** is coming at an hour Mt 24:44

it will be like a **m** going on a journey, Mt 25:14
'Master, I knew you to be a hard **m**, Mt 25:24
"When the Son of **M** comes in his Mt 25:31
and the Son of **M** will be delivered up to Mt 26:2
the city to a certain **m** and say to him, Mt 26:18
The Son of **M** goes as it is written of Mt 26:24
but woe to that **m** by whom the Son of Mt 26:24
by whom the Son of **M** is betrayed! Mt 26:24
been better for that **m** if he had not Mt 26:24
and the Son of **M** is betrayed into the Mt 26:45
saying, "The one I will kiss is the **m**; Mt 26:48
and said, "This **m** said, 'I am able to Mt 26:61
will see the Son of **M** seated at the right Mt 26:64
"This **m** was with Jesus of Nazareth." Mt 26:71
it with an oath: "I do not know the **m**." Mt 26:72
not know the **m**." And immediately the Mt 26:74
nothing to do with that righteous **m**, Mt 27:19
went out, they found a **m** of Cyrene, Mt 27:32
They compelled this **m** to carry his Mt 27:32
it, said, "This **m** is calling Elijah." Mt 27:47
there came a rich **m** from Arimathea, Mt 27:57
their synagogue a **m** with an unclean Mk 1:23
"Why does this **m** speak like that? He is Mk 2:7
that the Son of **M** has authority on Mk 2:10
to them, "The Sabbath was made for **m**, Mk 2:27
made for man, not **m** for the Sabbath. Mk 2:27
So the Son of **M** is lord even of the Mk 2:28
and a **m** was there with a withered hand. Mk 3:1
he said to the **m** with the withered hand, Mk 3:3
hardness of heart, and said to the **m**, Mk 3:5
unless he first binds the strong **m**. Mk 3:27
sins will be forgiven the children of **m**, Mk 3:28
God is as if a **m** should scatter seed on Mk 4:26
of the tombs a **m** with an unclean spirit. Mk 5:2
was saying to him, "Come out of the **m**, Mk 5:8
Jesus and saw the demon-possessed **m**, Mk 5:15
to the demon-possessed **m** and to the Mk 5:16
the **m** who had been possessed with Mk 5:18
"Where did this **m** get these things? Mk 6:2
that he was a righteous and holy **m**, Mk 6:20
'If a **m** tells his father or his mother, Mk 7:11
For from within, out of the heart of **m**, Mk 7:21
brought to him a **m** who was deaf and Mk 7:32
to him a blind **m** and begged him to Mk 8:22
he took the blind **m** by the hand and Mk 8:23
that the Son of **M** must suffer many Mk 8:31
things of God, but on the things of **m**." Mk 8:33
what does it profit a **m** to gain the whole Mk 8:36
For what can a **m** give in return for his Mk 8:37
will the Son of **M** also be ashamed Mk 8:38
until the Son of **M** had risen from the Mk 9:9
of the Son of **M** that he should suffer Mk 9:12
"The Son of **M** is going to be delivered Mk 9:31
"Is it lawful for a **m** to divorce his wife?" Mk 10:2
"Moses allowed a **m** to write a Mk 10:4
'Therefore a **m** shall leave his father Mk 10:7
has joined together, let not **m** separate." Mk 10:9
a **m** ran up and knelt before him and Mk 10:17
and said, "With **m** it is impossible, Mk 10:27
and the Son of **M** will be delivered over Mk 10:33
For even the Son of **M** came not to be Mk 10:45
him." And they called the blind **m**, Mk 10:49
for you?" And the blind **m** said to him, Mk 10:51
of John from heaven or from **m**? Mk 11:30
'From **m**'?"—they were afraid of the Mk 11:32
"A **m** planted a vineyard and put a Mk 12:1
the **m** must take the widow and raise Mk 12:19
see the Son of **M** coming in clouds Mk 13:26
It is like a **m** going on a journey, when Mk 13:34
and a **m** carrying a jar of water will Mk 14:13
For the Son of **M** goes as it is written of Mk 14:21
but woe to that **m** by whom the Son of Mk 14:21
by whom the Son of **M** is betrayed! Mk 14:21
been better for that **m** if he had not Mk 14:21
The Son of **M** is betrayed into the Mk 14:41
saying, "The one I will kiss is the **m**. Mk 14:44
And a young **m** followed him, with Mk 14:51
will see the Son of **M** seated at the right Mk 14:62
bystanders, "This **m** is one of them." Mk 14:69
do not know this **m** of whom you Mk 14:71
there was a **m** called Barabbas. Mk 15:7
shall I do with the **m** you call the King Mk 15:12
"Truly this **m** was the Son of God!" Mk 15:39
they saw a young **m** sitting on the right Mk 16:5
For I am an old **m**, and my wife is Lk 1:18
virgin betrothed to a **m** whose name was Lk 1:27
Now there was a **m** in Jerusalem, whose Lk 2:25
and this **m** was righteous and devout, Lk 2:25
in stature and in favor with God and **m**. Lk 2:52
written, '**M** shall not live by bread alone.'" Lk 4:4
synagogue there was a **m** who had the Lk 4:33
"Depart from me, for I am a sinful **m**, Lk 5:8
the cities, there came a **m** full of leprosy. Lk 5:12
on a bed a **m** who was paralyzed, Lk 5:18
he said, "**M**, your sins are forgiven you." Lk 5:20
that the Son of **M** has authority on earth Lk 5:24
—he said to the **m** who was paralyzed— Lk 5:24
"The Son of **M** is lord of the Sabbath." Lk 6:5
and a **m** was there whose right hand was Lk 6:6
he said to the **m** with the withered hand, Lk 6:8
as evil, on account of the Son of **M**! Lk 6:22
"Can a blind **m** lead a blind man? Lk 6:39
"Can a blind man lead a blind **m**? Lk 6:39
he is like a **m** building a house, who dug Lk 6:48
do them is like a **m** who built a house Lk 6:49
For I too am a **m** set under authority, Lk 7:8
a **m** who had died was being carried out, Lk 7:12
And he said, "Young **m**, I say to you, Lk 7:14
And the dead **m** sat up and began to Lk 7:15
out to see? A **m** dressed in soft clothing? Lk 7:25
The Son of **M** has come eating and Lk 7:34
said to himself, "If this **m** were a prophet, Lk 7:39
there met him a **m** from the city who Lk 8:27
the unclean spirit to come out of the **m**. Lk 8:29
came out of the **m** and entered the pigs, Lk 8:33
Jesus and found the **m** from whom the Lk 8:35
how the demon-possessed **m** had been Lk 8:36
The **m** from whom the demons had Lk 8:38
And there came a **m** named Jairus, who Lk 8:41
"The Son of **M** must suffer many things Lk 9:22
what does it profit a **m** if he gains the Lk 9:25
will the Son of **M** be ashamed when he Lk 9:26
behold, a **m** from the crowd cried out, Lk 9:38
The Son of **M** is about to be delivered Lk 9:44
but the Son of **M** has nowhere to lay his Lk 9:58
"A **m** was going down from Jerusalem Lk 10:30
a neighbor to the **m** who fell among Lk 10:36
had gone out, the mute **m** spoke, Lk 11:14
When a strong **m**, fully armed, guards Lk 11:21
will the Son of **M** be to this generation. Lk 11:30
the Son of **M** also will acknowledge Lk 12:8
against the Son of **M** will be forgiven, Lk 12:10
"**M**, who made me a judge or arbitrator Lk 12:14
land of a rich **m** produced plentifully, Lk 12:16
for the Son of **M** is coming at an hour Lk 12:40
"A **m** had a fig tree planted in his Lk 13:6
mustard seed that a **m** took and sowed Lk 13:19
there was a **m** before him who had Lk 14:2
said also to the **m** who had invited him, Lk 14:12
"A **m** once gave a great banquet and Lk 14:16
'This **m** began to build and was not Lk 14:30
"This **m** receives sinners and eats with Lk 15:2
"What **m** of you, having a hundred Lk 15:4
"There was a **m** who had two sons. Lk 15:11
"There was a rich **m** who had a Lk 16:1
to him that this **m** was wasting his Lk 16:1
"There was a rich **m** who was clothed Lk 16:19
gate was laid a poor **m** named Lazarus, Lk 16:20
The poor **m** died and was carried by Lk 16:22
The rich **m** also died and was buried, Lk 16:22
to see one of the days of the Son of **M**, Lk 17:22
so will the Son of **M** be in his day. Lk 17:24
so will it be in the days of the Son of **M**. Lk 17:26
the day when the Son of **M** is revealed. Lk 17:30
who neither feared God nor respected **m**. Lk 18:2
I neither fear God nor respect **m**, Lk 18:4
Nevertheless, when the Son of **M** comes, Lk 18:8
this **m** went down to his house Lk 18:14
about the Son of **M** by the prophets will Lk 18:31
a blind **m** was sitting by the roadside Lk 18:35
And there was a **m** named Zacchaeus. Lk 19:2
to be the guest of a **m** who is a sinner." Lk 19:7
For the Son of **M** came to seek and to Lk 19:10
do not want this **m** to reign over us.' Lk 19:14
of you, because you are a severe **m**. Lk 19:21
You knew that I was a severe **m**, taking Lk 19:22
of John from heaven or from **m**?" Lk 20:4
But if we say, 'From **m**,' all the people Lk 20:6
"A **m** planted a vineyard and let it out to Lk 20:9
the **m** must take the widow and raise Lk 20:28
will see the Son of **M** coming in a cloud Lk 21:27
and to stand before the Son of **M**." Lk 21:36
a **m** carrying a jar of water will meet Lk 22:10
For the Son of **M** goes as it has been Lk 22:22
but woe to that **m** by whom he is Lk 22:22
came a crowd, and the **m** called Judas, Lk 22:47
you betray the Son of **M** with a kiss?" Lk 22:48
him, said, "This **m** also was with him." Lk 22:56
of them." But Peter said, "**M**, I am not." Lk 22:58
"Certainly this **m** also was with him, Lk 22:59
"**M**, I do not know what you are talking Lk 22:60
now on the Son of **M** shall be seated at Lk 22:69
"We found this **m** misleading our Lk 23:2
the crowds, "I find no guilt in this **m**." Lk 23:4
he asked whether the **m** was a Galilean. Lk 23:6
"You brought me this **m** as one who Lk 23:14
I did not find this **m** guilty of any of Lk 23:14
cried out together, "Away with this **m**, Lk 23:18
a **m** who had been thrown into prison Lk 23:19
He released the **m** who had been Lk 23:25
but this **m** has done nothing wrong." Lk 23:41
"Certainly this **m** was innocent!" Lk 23:47
Now there was a **m** named Joseph, Lk 23:50
of the council, a good and righteous **m**, Lk 23:50
This **m** went to Pilate and asked for the Lk 23:52
that the Son of **M** must be delivered into Lk 24:7
a **m** who was a prophet mighty in deed Lk 24:19
There was a **m** sent from God, whose Jn 1:6
of the will of the flesh nor of the will of **m**, Jn 1:13
'After me comes a **m** who ranks before Jn 1:30
and descending on the Son of **M**." Jn 1:51
needed no one to bear witness about **m**, Jn 2:25
for he himself knew what was in **m**. Jn 2:25
Now there was a **m** of the Pharisees Jn 3:1
This **m** came to Jesus by night and said to Jn 3:2
"How can a **m** be born when he is old? Jn 3:4
descended from heaven, the Son of **M**. Jn 3:13
so must the Son of **M** be lifted up, Jn 3:14
see a **m** who told me all that I ever did. Jn 4:29
When this **m** heard that Jesus had come Jn 4:47
son will live." The **m** believed the word Jn 4:50
One **m** was there who had been an invalid Jn 5:5
The sick **m** answered him, "Sir, I have no Jn 5:7
And at once the **m** was healed, and he took Jn 5:9
Jews said to the **m** who had been healed, Jn 5:10
answered them, "The **m** who healed me, Jn 5:11
man who healed me, that **m** said to me, Jn 5:11
him, "Who is the **m** who said to you, Jn 5:12
Now the **m** who had been healed did not Jn 5:13
The **m** went away and told the Jews that Jn 5:15
judgment, because he is the Son of **M**. Jn 5:27
the testimony that I receive is from **m**, Jn 5:34
life, which the Son of **M** will give to you. Jn 6:27
"How can this **m** give us his flesh to eat?" Jn 6:52
flesh of the Son of **M** and drink his blood, Jn 6:53
to see the Son of **M** ascending to where he Jn 6:62
some said, "He is a good **m**," others said, Jn 7:12
"How is it that this **m** has learning, Jn 7:15
and you circumcise a **m** on the Sabbath. Jn 7:22
the Sabbath a **m** receives circumcision, Jn 7:23
"Is not this the **m** whom they seek to kill? Jn 7:25
But we know where this **m** comes from, Jn 7:27
he do more signs than this **m** has done?" Jn 7:31
"Where does this **m** intend to go that we Jn 7:35
"No one ever spoke like this **m**!" Jn 7:46
our law judge a **m** without first giving Jn 7:51
"When you have lifted up the Son of **M**, Jn 8:28
a **m** who has told you the truth that I Jn 8:40
he passed by, he saw a **m** blind from birth. Jn 9:1
"Rabbi, who sinned, this **m** or his parents, Jn 9:2
answered, "It was not that this **m** sinned, Jn 9:3
"Is this not the **m** who used to sit and Jn 9:8
is like him." He kept saying, "I am the **m**." Jn 9:9
"The **m** called Jesus made mud and Jn 9:11
to the Pharisees the **m** who had formerly Jn 9:13
Pharisees said, "This **m** is not from God, Jn 9:16
"How can a **m** who is a sinner do such Jn 9:16
So they said again to the blind **m**, "What Jn 9:17
the parents of the **m** who had received his Jn 9:18
time they called the **m** who had been Jn 9:24
to God. We know that this **m** is a sinner." Jn 9:24
has spoken to Moses, but as for this **m**, Jn 9:29
The **m** answered, "Why, this is an Jn 9:30
opened the eyes of a **m** born blind. Jn 9:32
If this **m** were not from God, he could do Jn 9:33
he said, "Do you believe in the Son of **M**?" Jn 9:35
way, that **m** is a thief and a robber. Jn 10:1
for blasphemy, because you, being a **m**, Jn 10:33
that John said about this **m** was true." Jn 10:41
Now a certain **m** was ill, Lazarus of Jn 11:1
eyes of the blind **m** also have kept this Jn 11:37
also have kept this **m** from dying?" Jn 11:37
stone." Martha, the sister of the dead **m**, Jn 11:39
The **m** who had died came out, his Jn 11:44
to do? For this **m** performs many signs. Jn 11:47
for you that one **m** should die for the Jn 11:50
come for the Son of **M** to be glorified. Jn 12:23
say that the Son of **M** must be lifted up? Jn 12:34
be lifted up? Who is this Son of **M**?" Jn 12:34
glory that comes from **m** more than the Jn 12:43
said, "Now is the Son of **M** glorified, Jn 13:31
be expedient that one **m** should die for Jn 18:14
a relative of the **m** whose ear Peter had Jn 18:26
do you bring against this **m**?" Jn 18:29
him, "If this **m** were not doing evil, Jn 18:30
I should release one **m** for you at the Jn 18:39
They cried out again, "Not this **m**, but Jn 18:40
robe. Pilate said to them, "Behold the **m**!" Jn 19:5
the Jews cried out, "If you release this **m**, Jn 19:12
of the Jews,' but rather, 'This **m** said, Jn 19:21
to Jesus, "Lord, what about this **m**?" Jn 21:21
(Now this **m** bought a field with the Acts 1:18
a **m** attested to you by God with Acts 2:22
And a **m** lame from birth was being Acts 3:2
—has made this **m** strong whom you Acts 3:16

has given the **m** this perfect health Acts 3:16
a good deed done to a crippled **m**, Acts 4:9
by what means this **m** has been healed, Acts 4:9
—by him this **m** is standing before Acts 4:10
But seeing the **m** who was healed Acts 4:14
For the **m** on whom this sign of Acts 4:22
But a **m** named Ananias, with his wife Acts 5:1
if this plan or this undertaking is of **m**, Acts 5:38
a **m** full of faith and of the Holy Spirit, Acts 6:5
"This **m** never ceases to speak words Acts 6:13
defended the oppressed **m** and avenged Acts 7:24
But the **m** who was wronging his Acts 7:27
—this **m** God sent as both ruler and Acts 7:35
This **m** led them out, performing Acts 7:36
and the Son of **M** standing at the right Acts 7:56
at the feet of a young **m** named Saul. Acts 7:58
But there was a **m** named Simon, who Acts 8:9
"This **m** is the power of God that is Acts 8:10
Judas look for a **m** of Tarsus named Acts 9:11
in a vision a **m** named Ananias come Acts 9:12
I have heard from many about this **m**, Acts 9:13
"Is not this the **m** who made havoc in Acts 9:21
There he found a **m** named Aeneas, Acts 9:33
there was a **m** named Cornelius, Acts 10:1
a devout **m** who feared God with all his Acts 10:2
an upright and God-fearing **m**, Acts 10:22
up, saying, "Stand up; I too am a **m**." Acts 10:26
a **m** stood before me in bright Acts 10:30
for he was a good **m**, full of the Holy Acts 11:24
"The voice of a god, and not of a **m**!" Acts 12:22
Sergius Paulus, a **m** of intelligence, Acts 13:7
of Kish, a **m** of the tribe of Benjamin, Acts 13:21
the son of Jesse a **m** after my heart, Acts 13:22
that through this **m** forgiveness of Acts 13:38
Lystra there was a **m** sitting who could Acts 14:8
a **m** of Macedonia was standing there, Acts 16:9
does not live in temples made by **m**, Acts 17:24
he made from one **m** every nation of Acts 17:26
by the art and imagination of **m**. Acts 17:29
righteousness by a **m** whom he has Acts 17:31
the house of a **m** named Titius Justus, Acts 18:7
"This **m** is persuading people to Acts 18:13
He was an eloquent **m**, competent in Acts 18:24
And the **m** in whom was the evil Acts 19:16
For a **m** named Demetrius, a Acts 19:24
And a young **m** named Eutychus, Acts 20:9
will bind the **m** who owns this Acts 21:11
This is the **m** who is teaching Acts 21:28
a devout **m** according to the law, Acts 22:12
for you to flog a **m** who is a Roman Acts 22:25
to do? For this **m** is a Roman citizen." Acts 22:26
"We find nothing wrong in this **m**. Acts 23:9
"Take this young **m** to the tribune, Acts 23:17
me to bring this young **m** to you, Acts 23:18
the tribune dismissed the young **m**, Acts 23:22
This **m** was seized by the Jews and Acts 23:27
there would be a plot against the **m**, Acts 23:30
For we have found this **m** a plague, Acts 24:5
conscience toward both God and **m**. Acts 24:16
there is anything wrong about the **m**, Acts 25:5
"There is a **m** left prisoner by Felix, Acts 25:14
and ordered the **m** to be brought. Acts 25:17
to hear the **m** myself." "Tomorrow," Acts 25:22
you see this **m** about whom the Acts 25:24
"This **m** is doing nothing to deserve Acts 26:31
"This **m** could have been set free if he Acts 26:32
"No doubt this **m** is a murderer. Acts 28:4
belonging to the chief **m** of the island, Acts 28:7
resembling mortal **m** and birds Rom 1:23
Therefore you have no excuse, O **m**, Rom 2:1
O **m**—you who judge those who do Rom 2:3
if a **m** who is uncircumcised keeps the Rom 2:26
praise is not from **m** but from God. Rom 2:29
blessed is the **m** against whom the Lord Rom 4:8
came into the world through one **m**, Rom 5:12
of that one **m** Jesus Christ abounded Rom 5:15
death reigned through that one **m**, Rom 5:17
in life through the one **m** Jesus Christ. Rom 5:17
lives with another **m** while her Rom 7:3
if she marries another **m** she is not an Rom 7:3
Wretched **m** that I am! Who will Rom 7:24
had conceived children by one **m**, Rom 9:10
But who are you, O **m**, to answer back Rom 9:20
heard, nor the heart of **m** imagined, 1 Cor 2:9
pagans, for a **m** has his father's wife. 1 Cor 5:1
are to deliver this **m** to Satan for the 1 Cor 5:5
"It is good for a **m** not to have sexual 1 Cor 7:1
each **m** should have his own wife and 1 Cor 7:2
The unmarried **m** is anxious about 1 Cor 7:32
But the married **m** is anxious about 1 Cor 7:33
you that is not common to **m**. 1 Cor 10:13
that the head of every **m** is Christ, 1 Cor 11:3
Every **m** who prays or prophesies 1 Cor 11:4
For a **m** ought not to cover his head, 1 Cor 11:7
of God, but woman is the glory of **m**. 1 Cor 11:7
For **m** was not made from woman, 1 Cor 11:8
from woman, but woman from **m**. 1 Cor 11:8
Neither was **m** created for woman, 1 Cor 11:9
for woman, but woman for **m**. 1 Cor 11:9
is not independent of **m** nor man of 1 Cor 11:11
of man nor **m** of woman; 1 Cor 11:11
for as woman was made from **m**, so 1 Cor 11:12
man, so **m** is now born of woman. 1 Cor 11:12
you that if a **m** wears long hair it 1 Cor 11:14
When I became a **m**, I gave up 1 Cor 13:11
For as by a **m** came death, by a man 1 Cor 15:21
by a **m** has come also the 1 Cor 15:21
"The first **m** Adam became a living 1 Cor 15:45
The first **m** was from the earth, a 1 Cor 15:47
was from the earth, a **m** of dust; 1 Cor 15:47
dust; the second **m** is from heaven. 1 Cor 15:47
As was the **m** of dust, so also are 1 Cor 15:48
the dust, and as is the **m** of heaven, 1 Cor 15:48
borne the image of the **m** of dust, 1 Cor 15:49
bear the image of the **m** of heaven. 1 Cor 15:49
sight but also in the sight of **m**. 2 Cor 8:21
I know a **m** in Christ who fourteen 2 Cor 12:2
I know that this **m** was caught up 2 Cor 12:3
be told, which **m** may not utter. 2 Cor 12:4
On behalf of this **m** I will boast, but 2 Cor 12:5
apostle—not from men nor through **m**, Gal 1:1
am I now seeking the approval of **m**, Gal 1:10
or of God? Or am I trying to please **m**? Gal 1:10
If I were still trying to please **m**, I would Gal 1:10
For I did not receive it from any **m**, nor Gal 1:12
along with Abraham, the **m** of faith. Gal 3:9
again to every **m** who accepts Gal 5:3
in himself one new **m** in place of the Eph 2:15
"Therefore a **m** shall leave his father Eph 5:31
a good will as to the Lord and not to **m**, Eph 6:7
gospel, so we speak, not to please **m**, 1 Thes 2:4
this, disregards not **m** but God, 1 Thes 4:8
and the **m** of lawlessness is revealed, 2 Thes 2:3
God and men, the **m** Christ Jesus, 1 Tm 2:5
or to exercise authority over a **m**; 1 Tm 2:12
rebuke an older **m** but encourage him 1 Tm 5:1
But as for you, O **m** of God, flee these 1 Tm 6:11
that the **m** of God may be competent, 2 Tm 3:17
an old **m** and now a prisoner also for Phlm 1:9
been testified somewhere, "What is **m**, Heb 2:6
you are mindful of him, or the son of **m**, Heb 2:6
See how great this **m** was to whom Heb 7:4
But this **m** who does not have his Heb 7:6
the true tent that the Lord set up, not **m**. Heb 8:2
just as it is appointed for **m** to die once, Heb 9:27
Therefore from one **m**, and him as Heb 11:12
I will not fear; what can **m** do to me?" Heb 13:6
he is a double-minded **m**, unstable in all Jas 1:8
So also will the rich **m** fade away in the Jas 1:11
Blessed is the **m** who remains steadfast Jas 1:12
for the anger of **m** does not produce the Jas 1:20
he is like a **m** who looks intently at his Jas 1:23
For if a **m** wearing a gold ring and fine Jas 2:2
and a poor **m** in shabby clothing also Jas 2:2
good place," while you say to the poor **m**, Jas 2:3
But you have dishonored the poor **m**. Are Jas 2:6
in what he says, he is a perfect **m**, Jas 3:2
Elijah was a **m** with a nature like ours, Jas 5:17
was ever produced by the will of **m**, 2 Pt 1:21
as that righteous **m** lived among them 2 Pt 2:8
of the lampstands one like a son of **m**, Rv 1:13
third living creature with the face of a **m**, Rv 4:7
of the beast, for it is the number of a **m**, Rv 13:18
seated on the cloud one like a son of **m**, Rv 14:14
had never been since **m** was on the Rv 16:18
the dwelling place of God is with **m**. Rv 21:3

MAN'S (86)
for the intention of **m** heart is evil from Gn 8:21
you have taken, for she is a **m** wife." Gn 20:3
Now then, return the **m** wife, for he is a Gn 20:7
and to replace every **m** money in his Gn 42:25
every **m** bundle of money was in his Gn 42:35
and there was each **m** money in the Gn 43:21
and put each **m** money in the mouth of Gn 44:1
we cannot see the **m** face unless our Gn 44:26
said to him, "Who has made **m** mouth? Ex 4:11
If it gores a **m** son or daughter, he shall Ex 21:31
"When one **m** ox butts another's, so Ex 21:35
loose and it feeds in another **m** field, Ex 22:5
safe, and it is stolen from the **m** house, Ex 22:7
who offers any **m** burnt offering shall Lv 7:8
"If a **m** hair falls out from his head, he Lv 13:40
And if a **m** hair falls out from his Lv 13:41
If any **m** wife goes astray and breaks Nm 5:12
staffs. Write each **m** name on his staff, Nm 17:2
"A woman shall not wear a **m** garment, Dt 22:5
if she goes and becomes another **m** wife, Dt 24:2
the LORD set every **m** sword against his Jgs 7:22
the door of the **m** house where her Jgs 19:26
"The **m** name with whom I worked Ru 2:19
or taken anything from any **m** hand." 1 Sm 12:4
"Let no **m** heart fail because of him. 1 Sm 17:32
took the poor **m** lamb and prepared 2 Sm 12:4
little cloud like a **m** hand is rising 1 Kgs 18:44
money that a **m** heart prompts him 2 Kgs 12:4
days of man, or your years as a **m** years, Jb 10:5
This is the wicked **m** portion from God, Jb 20:29
'He will answer none of **m** words'? Jb 33:13
and bread to strengthen **m** heart. Ps 104:15
Redeem me from **m** oppression, that I Ps 119:134
For a **m** ways are before the eyes of the Prv 5:21
A rich **m** wealth is his strong city; the Prv 10:15
the work of a **m** hand comes back to Prv 12:14
Anxiety in a **m** heart weighs him Prv 12:25
The ransom of a **m** life is his wealth, Prv 13:8
When a **m** ways please the LORD, he Prv 16:7
The words of a **m** mouth are deep Prv 18:4
A rich **m** wealth is his strong city, and Prv 18:11
Before destruction a **m** heart is Prv 18:12
A **m** spirit will endure sickness, but a Prv 18:14
A **m** gift makes room for him and Prv 18:16
the fruit of a **m** mouth his stomach is Prv 18:20
When a **m** folly brings his way to ruin, Prv 19:3
All a poor **m** brothers hate him; how Prv 19:7
The purpose in a **m** heart is like deep Prv 20:5
Take a **m** garment when he has put Prv 20:16
A **m** steps are from the LORD; how then Prv 20:24
and oil are in a wise **m** dwelling, Prv 21:20
Like a lame **m** legs, which hang Prv 26:7
Take a **m** garment when he has put Prv 27:13
Also, he has put eternity into **m** heart, Eccl 3:11
work come from a **m** envy of his Eccl 4:4
A **m** wisdom makes his face shine, and Eccl 8:1
although **m** trouble lies heavy on him. Eccl 8:6
though the poor **m** wisdom is despised Eccl 9:16
A wise **m** heart inclines him to the Eccl 10:2
words of a wise **m** mouth win him Eccl 10:12
from him and becomes another **m** wife, Jer 3:1
for the burden is every **m** own word, Jer 23:36
Every **m** sword will be against his Ezk 38:21
measuring reed in the **m** hand was six Ezk 40:5
Let his mind be changed from a **m**, and Dn 4:16
And I heard a **m** voice between the Dn 8:16
"O LORD, let us not perish for this **m** life, Jon 1:14
a **m** enemies are the men of his own Mi 7:6
enter a strong **m** house and plunder Mt 12:29
saying, "I am innocent of this **m** blood; Mt 27:24
enter a strong **m** house and plunder Mk 3:27
us that if a **m** brother dies and leaves Mk 12:19
with what fell from the rich **m** table. Lk 16:21
wrote for us that if a **m** brother dies, Lk 20:28
Sabbath I made a **m** whole body well? Jn 7:23
Then he anointed the **m** eyes with the Jn 9:6
also are not one of this **m** disciples, Jn 18:17
intend to bring this **m** blood upon us." Acts 5:28
me, and we entered the **m** house. Acts 11:12
Of this **m** offspring God has brought Acts 13:23
if many died through one **m** trespass, Rom 5:15
is not like the result of that one **m** sin. Rom 5:16
If, because of one **m** trespass, death Rom 5:17
by the one **m** disobedience the many Rom 5:19
so by the one **m** obedience the many Rom 5:19
was preached by me is not **m** gospel. Gal 1:11

MAN-MADE (1)
even with a **m** covenant, no one annuls Gal 3:15

MANAEN (1)
M a member of the court of Herod the Acts 13:1

MANAGE (3)
He must **m** his own household well, 1 Tm 3:4
know how to **m** his own household, 1 Tm 3:5
bear children, **m** their households, 1 Tm 5:14

MANAGED (1)
we **m** with difficulty to secure the Acts 27:16

MANAGEMENT (3)
Turn in the account of your **m**, for you Lk 16:2
master is taking the **m** away from me? Lk 16:3
do, so that when I am removed from **m**, Lk 16:4

MANAGER (6)
the wife of Chuza, Herod's household **m**, Lk 8:3
"Who then is the faithful and wise **m**, Lk 12:42
"There was a rich man who had a **m**, Lk 16:1
for you can no longer be **m**.' Lk 16:2
And the **m** said to himself, 'What shall I Lk 16:3
commended the dishonest **m** for his Lk 16:8

MANAGERS (1)
is under guardians and **m** until the date Gal 4:2

MANAGING (1)
m their children and their own 1 Tm 3:12

MANAHATH (3)
Alvan, **M**, Ebal, Shepho, and Onam. Gn 36:23
Alvan, **M**, Ebal, Shepho, and Onam. 1 Chr 1:40

and they were carried into exile to **M**): 1 Chr 8:6

MANAHATHITES (1)
Atroth-beth-joab and half of the **M**, 1 Chr 2:54

MANASSEH (144)
called the name of the firstborn **M**. Gn 41:51
of Egypt were born **M** and Ephraim, Gn 46:20
with him his two sons, **M** and Ephraim. Gn 48:1
Ephraim and **M** shall be mine, as Gn 48:5
and **M** in his left hand toward Israel's Gn 48:13
and his left hand on the head of **M**, Gn 48:14
his hands (for **M** was the firstborn). Gn 48:14
as Ephraim and as **M**.'" Thus he put Gn 48:20
Thus he put Ephraim before **M**. Gn 48:20
Machir the son of **M** were counted as Gn 50:23
the son of Ammihud, and from **M**, Nm 1:10
Of the people of **M**, their generations, Nm 1:34
listed of the tribe of **M** were 32,200. Nm 1:35
And next to him shall be the tribe of **M**, Nm 2:20
of the people of **M** being Gamaliel the Nm 2:20
Pedahzur, the chief of the people of **M**: Nm 7:54
of the people of **M** was Gamaliel the Nm 10:23
of Joseph (that is, from the tribe of **M**), Nm 13:11
to their clans: **M** and Ephraim. Nm 26:28
The sons of **M**: of Machir, the clan of Nm 26:29
These are the clans of **M**, and those Nm 26:34
son of Gilead, son of Machir, son of **M**, Nm 27:1
from the clans of **M** the son of Joseph. Nm 27:1
to the half-tribe of **M** the son of Nm 32:33
Machir the son of **M** went to Gilead Nm 32:39
gave Gilead to Machir the son of **M**, Nm 32:40
Jair the son of **M** went and captured Nm 32:41
and also the half-tribe of **M**. Nm 34:14
of the tribe of the people of **M** a chief, Nm 34:23
of Gilead the son of Machir, son of **M**, Nm 36:1
of the people of **M** the son of Joseph, Nm 36:12
of Argob, I gave to the half-tribe of **M**. Dt 3:13
and they are the thousands of **M**." Dt 33:17
all Naphtali, the land of Ephraim and **M**, Dt 34:2
and the half-tribe of **M** Joshua said, Jos 1:12
the half-tribe of **M** passed over armed Jos 4:12
and the Gadites and the half-tribe of **M**. Jos 12:6
the nine tribes and half the tribe of **M**." Jos 13:7
of the tribe of **M** the Reubenites and the Jos 13:8
an inheritance to the half-tribe of **M**. Jos 13:29
of the people of **M** according to their Jos 13:29
of Machir the son of **M** for the half of Jos 13:31
Joseph were two tribes, **M** and Ephraim. Jos 14:4
The people of Joseph, **M** and Ephraim, Jos 16:4
allotment was made to the people of **M**, Jos 17:1
To Machir the firstborn of **M**, the father Jos 17:1
the rest of the people of **M** by their clans, Jos 17:2
the male descendants of **M** the son of Jos 17:2
son of Gilead, son of Machir, son of **M**, Jos 17:3
Thus there fell to **M** ten portions, besides Jos 17:5
the daughters of **M** received an Jos 17:6
was allotted to the rest of the people of **M**. Jos 17:6
The territory of **M** reached from Asher Jos 17:7
The land of Tappuah belonged to **M**, Jos 17:8
on the boundary of **M** belonged to the Jos 17:8
of the brook, among the cities of **M**, Jos 17:9
Then the boundary of **M** goes on the Jos 17:9
and in Asher **M** had Beth-shean and Jos 17:11
Yet the people of **M** could not take Jos 17:12
the house of Joseph, to Ephraim and **M**, Jos 17:17
half the tribe of **M** have received their Jos 18:7
Golan in Bashan, from the tribe of **M**. Jos 20:8
the tribe of Dan and the half-tribe of **M**, Jos 21:5
and from the half-tribe of **M** in Bashan, Jos 21:6
and out of the half-tribe of **M**, Taanach Jos 21:25
were given out of the half-tribe of **M**, Jos 21:27
and the Gadites and the half-tribe of **M**, Jos 22:1
half of the tribe of **M** Moses had given a Jos 22:7
and the half-tribe of **M** returned home, Jos 22:9
and the half-tribe of **M** built there an Jos 22:10
and the half-tribe of **M** have built the Jos 22:11
people of Gad and the half-tribe of **M**, Jos 22:13
people of Gad, and the half-tribe of **M**, Jos 22:15
and the half-tribe of **M** said in answer Jos 22:21
of Gad and the people of **M** spoke, Jos 22:30
the people of Gad and the people of **M**, Jos 22:31
M did not drive out the inhabitants of Jgs 1:27
Behold, my clan is the weakest in **M**, Jgs 6:15
he sent messengers throughout all **M**, Jgs 6:35
and from Asher and from all **M**, Jgs 7:23
through Gilead and **M** and passed on Jgs 11:29
in the midst of Ephraim and **M**." Jgs 12:4
had the villages of Jair the son of **M**, 1 Kgs 4:13
and **M** his son reigned in his place. 2 Kgs 20:21
M was twelve years old when he 2 Kgs 21:1
and **M** led them astray to do more evil 2 Kgs 21:9
"Because **M** king of Judah has 2 Kgs 21:11
M shed very much innocent blood, 2 Kgs 21:16
rest of the acts of **M** and all that he 2 Kgs 21:17
And **M** slept with his fathers and 2 Kgs 21:18
the LORD, as **M** his father had done. 2 Kgs 21:20
and the altars that **M** had made in 2 Kgs 23:12
with which **M** had provoked 2 Kgs 23:26
out of his sight, for the sins of **M**, 2 Kgs 24:3
his son, Hezekiah his son, **M** his son, 1 Chr 3:13
the half-tribe of **M** had valiant men 1 Chr 5:18
of the half-tribe of **M** lived in the 1 Chr 5:23
the Gadites, and the half-tribe of **M**, 1 Chr 5:26
out of the half-tribe, the half of **M**, 1 Chr 6:61
Asher, Naphtali and **M** in Bashan. 1 Chr 6:62
and out of the half-tribe of **M**, Aner 1 Chr 6:70
out of the clan of the half-tribe of **M**: 1 Chr 6:71
The sons of **M**: Asriel, whom his 1 Chr 7:14
of Gilead the son of Machir, son of **M**. 1 Chr 7:17
Ephraim, and **M** lived in Jerusalem: 1 Chr 9:3
of the men of **M** deserted to David 1 Chr 12:19
these men of **M** deserted to him: 1 Chr 12:20
Zillethai, chiefs of thousands in **M**. 1 Chr 12:20
Of the half-tribe of **M** 18,000, who 1 Chr 12:31
the half-tribe of **M** from beyond the 1 Chr 12:37
for the half-tribe of **M**, Joel the son 1 Chr 27:20
for the half-tribe of **M** in Gilead, 1 Chr 27:21
M, and Simeon who were residing 2 Chr 15:9
wrote letters also to Ephraim and **M**, 2 Chr 30:1
the country of Ephraim and **M**, 2 Chr 30:10
However, some men of Asher, of **M**, 2 Chr 30:11
of them from Ephraim, **M**, Issachar, 2 Chr 30:18
Benjamin, and in Ephraim and **M**, 2 Chr 31:1
And **M** his son reigned in his place. 2 Chr 32:33
M was twelve years old when he 2 Chr 33:1
M led Judah and the inhabitants of 2 Chr 33:9
The LORD spoke to **M** and to his 2 Chr 33:10
who captured **M** with hooks and 2 Chr 33:11
Then **M** knew that the LORD was 2 Chr 33:13
Now the rest of the acts of **M**, and 2 Chr 33:18
So **M** slept with his fathers, and they 2 Chr 33:20
the LORD, as **M** his father had done. 2 Chr 33:22
all the images that **M** his father had 2 Chr 33:22
as **M** his father had humbled 2 Chr 33:23
And in the cities of **M**, Ephraim, and 2 Chr 34:6
had collected from **M** and Ephraim 2 Chr 34:9
Mattaniah, Bezalel, Binnui, and **M**. Ezr 10:30
Eliphelet, Jeremai, **M**, and Shimei. Ezr 10:33
Gilead is mine; **M** is mine; Ephraim is Ps 60:7
Before Ephraim and Benjamin and **M**, Ps 80:2
Gilead is mine; **M** is mine; Ephraim is Ps 108:8
M devours Ephraim, and Ephraim Is 9:21
Ephraim, and Ephraim devours **M**; Is 9:21
earth because of what **M** the son of Jer 15:4
the east side to the west, **M**, one portion. Ezk 48:4
Adjoining the territory of **M**, from the Ezk 48:5
and Hezekiah the father of **M**, and Mt 1:10
of Manasseh, and **M** the father of Amos, Mt 1:10
of Naphtali, 12,000 from the tribe of **M**, Rv 7:6

MANASSEH'S (2)
it from Ephraim's head to **M** head. Gn 48:17
and that to the north being **M**, Jos 17:10

MANASSITE (1)
Jair the **M** took all the region of Argob, Dt 3:14

MANASSITES (6)
Gadites, and Golan in Bashan for the **M**. Dt 4:43
the Gadites, and the half-tribe of the **M**. Dt 29:8
within the inheritance of the **M**, Jos 16:9
and the Reubenites, and the **M**, 2 Kgs 10:33
also in possession of the **M**, 1 Chr 7:29
half-tribe of the **M** for everything 1 Chr 26:32

MANDRAKES (6)
Reuben went and found **m** in the field Gn 30:14
"Please give me some of your son's **m**." Gn 30:14
away my son's **m** also?" Rachel said, Gn 30:15
tonight in exchange for your son's **m**." Gn 30:15
you with my son's **m**." So he lay with Gn 30:16
The **m** give forth fragrance, and beside Sg 7:13

MANE (1)
Do you clothe his neck with a **m**? Jb 39:19

MANGER (6)
you? Will he spend the night at your **m**? Jb 39:9
there are no oxen, the **m** is clean, Prv 14:4
in swaddling cloths and laid him in a **m**, Lk 2:7
in swaddling cloths and lying in a **m**." Lk 2:12
and Joseph, and the baby lying in a **m**. Lk 2:16
his donkey from the **m** and lead it Lk 13:15

MANHOOD (2)
heel, and in his **m** he strove with God. Hos 12:3
of the Son of God, to mature **m**, Eph 4:13

MANIFEST (13)
And I will **m** my holiness among you Ezk 20:41
and I will **m** my glory in your midst. Ezk 28:22
in her and **m** my holiness in Ezk 28:22
and **m** my holiness in them in the Ezk 28:25
nothing is hidden except to be made **m**; Mk 4:22
is hidden that will not be made **m**, Lk 8:17
I will love him and **m** myself to him." Jn 14:21
how is it that you will **m** yourself to us, Jn 14:22
each one's work will become **m**, for 1 Cor 3:13
world but was made **m** in the last times 1 Pt 1:20
the life was made **m**, and we have seen it, 1 Jn 1:2
with the Father and was made **m** to us— 1 Jn 1:2
the love of God was made **m** among us, 1 Jn 4:9

MANIFESTATION (1)
each is given the **m** of the Spirit for 1 Cor 12:7

MANIFESTATIONS (1)
you are eager for **m** of the Spirit, 1 Cor 14:12

MANIFESTED (8)
did at Cana in Galilee, and **m** his glory. Jn 2:11
"I have **m** your name to the people whom Jn 17:6
of God has been **m** apart from the law, Rom 3:21
of Jesus may also be **m** in our bodies. 2 Cor 4:10
Jesus also may be **m** in our mortal 2 Cor 4:11
He was **m** in the flesh, vindicated by 1 Tm 3:16
now has been **m** through the 2 Tm 1:10
at the proper time **m** in his word through Ti 1:3

MANIFOLD (3)
wisdom! For he is **m** in understanding. Jb 11:6
O LORD, how **m** are your works! In Ps 104:24
the church the **m** wisdom of God Eph 3:10

MANKIND (51)
that swarm on the earth, and all **m**. Gn 7:21
is to be devoted for destruction from **m**, Lv 27:29
if they are visited by the fate of all **m**, Nm 16:29
their inheritance, when he divided **m**, Dt 32:8
to come, and this is instruction for **m**, 2 Sm 7:19
the hearts of all the children of **m**), 1 Kgs 8:39
know the hearts of the children of **m**, 2 Chr 6:30
what do I do to you, you watcher of **m**? Jb 7:20
living thing and the breath of all **m**. Jb 12:10
all **m** follows after him, and those who Jb 21:33
they hang in the air, far away from **m**; Jb 28:4
All **m** has looked on it; man beholds it Jb 36:25
pour down and drop on **m** abundantly. Jb 36:28
scorned by **m** and despised by the people. Ps 22:6
in you, in the sight of the children of **m**! Ps 31:19
The children of **m** take refuge in the Ps 36:7
Surely all **m** stands as a mere breath! Ps 39:5
to him; surely all **m** is a mere breath! Ps 39:11
M will say, "Surely there is a reward for Ps 58:11
Then all **m** fears; they tell what God has Ps 64:9
they are not stricken like the rest of **m**. Ps 73:5
the tent where he dwelt among **m**, Ps 78:60
I said in my alarm, "All **m** are liars." Ps 116:11
and increases the traitors among **m**. Prv 23:28
and the scoffer is an abomination to **m**. Prv 24:9
the earth, the needy from among **m**. Prv 30:14
under the sun, and it lies heavy on **m**: Eccl 6:1
of feasting, for this is the end of all **m**, Eccl 7:2
In that day **m** will cast away their idols of Is 2:20
fine gold, and **m** than the gold of Ophir. Is 13:12
and the poor among **m** shall exult in the Is 29:19
form beyond that of the children of **m**— Is 52:14
to this day in Israel and among all **m**, Jer 32:20
among the nations, despised among **m**. Jer 49:15
driven from among the children of **m**, Dn 5:21
rules the kingdom of **m** and sets over it Dn 5:21
and there is no one upright among **m**; Mi 7:2
You make **m** like the fish of the sea, Hab 1:14
I will cut off **m** from the face of the Zep 1:3
I will bring distress on **m**, so that they Zep 1:17
LORD has an eye on **m** and on all the Zec 9:1
that the remnant of **m** may seek the Acts 15:17
himself gives to all **m** life and breath Acts 17:25
man every nation of **m** to live on all Acts 17:26
children of wrath, like the rest of **m**. Eph 2:3
and displease God and oppose all **m** 1 Thes 2:15
can be tamed and has been tamed by **m**, Jas 3:7
year, were released to kill a third of **m**. Rv 9:15
three plagues a third of **m** was killed, Rv 9:18
The rest of **m**, who were not killed by Rv 9:20
been redeemed from **m** as firstfruits for Rv 14:4

MANNA (17)
the house of Israel called its name **m**. Ex 16:31
"Take a jar, and put an omer of **m** in it, Ex 16:33
people of Israel ate the **m** forty years, Ex 16:35
They ate the **m** till they came to the Ex 16:35
is nothing at all but this **m** to look at." Nm 11:6
Now the **m** was like coriander seed, Nm 11:7
camp in the night, the **m** fell with it. Nm 11:9
and let you hunger and fed you with **m**, Dt 8:3
the wilderness with **m** that your fathers Dt 8:16
And the **m** ceased the day after they ate Jos 5:12
there was no longer **m** for the people of Jos 5:12
not withhold your **m** from their Neh 9:20
rained down on them **m** to eat and gave Ps 78:24
Our fathers ate the **m** in the wilderness; Jn 6:31
Your fathers ate the **m** in the wilderness, Jn 6:49

which was a golden urn holding the **m**, Heb 9:4
I will give some of the hidden **m**, Rv 2:17

MANNER (28)
in to us after the **m** of all the earth. Gn 19:31
In this **m** you shall eat it: with your belt Ex 12:11
And this is the **m** of the release: every Dt 15:2
the city in the same **m** seven times. Jos 6:15
true, what is to be the child's **m** of life, Jgs 13:12
in security, after the **m** of the Sidonians, Jgs 18:7
and this was the **m** of attesting in Israel. Ru 4:7
After this **m** he made the ten stands. 1 Kgs 7:37
after the **m** of the nations from 2 Kgs 17:33
they do according to the former **m**. 2 Kgs 17:34
did according to their former **m**. 2 Kgs 17:40
and I answered them in the same **m**. Neh 6:4
and they who dwell in it will die in like **m**; Is 51:6
king of Judah I spoke in like **m**: Jer 27:12
yourselves after the **m** of your fathers Ezk 20:30
you a pestilence after the **m** of Egypt; Am 4:10
and Lazarus in like **m** bad things; Lk 16:25
according to the strict **m** of the law of Acts 22:3
"My **m** of life from my youth, spent Acts 26:4
filled with all **m** of unrighteousness, Rom 1:29
in an unworthy **m** will be guilty 1 Cor 11:27
you to walk in a **m** worthy of the calling Eph 4:1
belongs to your former **m** of life and is Eph 4:22
Only let your **m** of life be worthy of the Phil 1:27
so as to walk in a **m** worthy of the Lord, Col 1:10
you to walk in a **m** worthy of God, 1 Thes 2:12
on their journey in a **m** worthy of God. 3 Jn 1:6
Yet in like **m** these people also, relying Jude 1:8

MANOAH (18)
tribe of the Danites, whose name was **M**. Jgs 13:2
Then **M** prayed to the LORD and said, "O Jgs 13:8
And God listened to the voice of **M**, and Jgs 13:9
But **M** her husband was not with her. Jgs 13:9
And **M** arose and went after his wife Jgs 13:11
And **M** said, "Now when your words Jgs 13:12
And the angel of the LORD said to **M**, "Of Jgs 13:13
M said to the angel of the LORD, "Please Jgs 13:15
And the angel of the LORD said to **M**, "If Jgs 13:16
to the LORD." (For **M** did not know that Jgs 13:16
And **M** said to the angel of the LORD, Jgs 13:17
So **M** took the young goat with the Jgs 13:19
and **M** and his wife were watching. Jgs 13:19
Now **M** and his wife were watching, Jgs 13:20
appeared no more to **M** and to his wife. Jgs 13:21
Then **M** knew that he was the angel of Jgs 13:21
And **M** said to his wife, "We shall Jgs 13:22
Eshtaol in the tomb of **M** his father. Jgs 16:31

MANSERVANT (1)
the cause of my **m** or my maidservant, Jb 31:13

MANSLAYER (20)
where you shall permit the **m** to flee, Nm 35:6
that the **m** who kills any person Nm 35:11
that the **m** may not die until he stands Nm 35:12
judge between the **m** and the avenger Nm 35:24
shall rescue the **m** from the hand Nm 35:25
But if the **m** shall at any time go Nm 35:26
and the avenger of blood kills the **m**, Nm 35:27
the high priest the **m** may return to Nm 35:28
that the **m** might flee there, anyone who Dt 4:42
so that any **m** can flee to them. Dt 19:3
"This is the provision for the **m**, who by Dt 19:4
anger pursue the **m** and overtake him, Dt 19:6
that the **m** who strikes any person Jos 20:3
shall not give up the **m** into his hand, Jos 20:5
Then the **m** may return to his own town Jos 20:6
Hebron, the city of refuge for the **m**, Jos 21:13
Shechem, the city of refuge for the **m**, Jos 21:21
the city of refuge for the **m**, Jos 21:27
the city of refuge for the **m**, Jos 21:32
the city of refuge for the **m**, Jos 21:38

MANTLES (1)
the festal robes, the **m**, the cloaks, and the Is 3:22

MANURE (2)
also, until I dig around it and put on **m**. Lk 13:8
use either for the soil or for the **m** pile. Lk 14:35

MANY (551)
with you, as **m** as came out of the ark; Gn 9:10
And Abraham sojourned **m** days in Gn 21:34
of flocks and herds and **m** servants, Gn 26:14
And he made him a robe of **m** colors. Gn 37:3
robe, the robe of **m** colors that he wore. Gn 37:23
sent the robe of **m** colors and brought Gn 37:32
loins and mourned for his son **m** days. Gn 37:34
and to keep alive for you **m** survivors. Gn 45:7
"How **m** are the days of the years of your Gn 47:8
for that is how **m** are required for Gn 50:3
bring it about that **m** people should be Gn 50:20
of Israel are too **m** and too mighty for Ex 1:9
During those **m** days the king of Egypt Ex 2:23
"Behold, the people of the land are now **m**, Ex 5:5
the LORD to look and **m** of them perish. Ex 19:21
shall not fall in with the **m** to do evil, Ex 23:2
witness in a lawsuit, siding with the **m**, Ex 23:2
on all fours, or whatever has **m** feet, Lv 11:42
has a discharge of blood for **m** days, Lv 15:25
If the years are **m**, you shall increase Lv 25:16
If there are still **m** years left, he shall Lv 25:51
continued over the tabernacle **m** days, Nm 9:19
or weak, whether they are few or **m**, Nm 13:18
As **m** as you offer, so shall you do Nm 15:12
do with each one, as **m** as there are. Nm 15:12
people, so that **m** people of Israel died. Nm 21:6
of the people, because they were **m**. Nm 22:3
and his seed shall be in **m** waters; Nm 24:7
from the larger tribes you shall take **m**, Nm 35:8
a thousand times as **m** as you are and Dt 1:11
So you remained at Kadesh **m** days, the Dt 1:46
And for **m** days we traveled around Dt 2:1
lived there, a people great and **m**, Dt 2:10
a people great and **m**, and tall as the Dt 2:21
bars, besides very **m** unwalled villages. Dt 3:5
it, and clears away **m** nations before you, Dt 7:1
you, and you shall lend to **m** nations, Dt 15:6
and you shall rule over **m** nations, Dt 15:6
must not acquire **m** horses for himself Dt 17:16
to Egypt in order to acquire **m** horses, Dt 17:16
shall not acquire **m** wives for himself, Dt 17:17
eat your fill of grapes, as **m** as you wish, Dt 23:24
And you shall lend to **m** nations, but Dt 28:12
And **m** evils and troubles will come Dt 31:17
And when **m** evils and troubles have Dt 31:21
old; consider the years of **m** generations; Dt 32:7
with very **m** horses and chariots. Jos 11:4
forsaken your brothers these **m** days, Jos 22:3
of Canaan, and made his offspring **m**. Jos 24:3
people with you are too **m** for me to give Jgs 7:2
said to Gideon, "The people are still too **m**. Jgs 7:4
his own offspring, for he had **m** wives. Jgs 8:30
And **m** fell wounded, up to the entrance Jgs 9:40
our country, who has killed **m** of us." Jgs 16:24
but she who has **m** children is forlorn. 1 Sm 2:5
the LORD from saving by **m** or by few." 1 Sm 14:6
There are **m** servants these days who 1 Sm 25:10
You will do **m** things and will 1 Sm 26:25
and also **m** of the people have fallen 2 Sm 1:4
man had very **m** flocks and herds, 2 Sm 12:2
m people were coming from the road 2 Sm 13:34
has been mourning **m** days for the 2 Sm 14:2
"How **m** years have I still to live, 2 Sm 19:34
took me; he drew me out of **m** waters. 2 Sm 22:17
a hundred times as **m** as they are, 2 Sm 24:3
So Shimei lived in Jerusalem **m** days. 1 Kgs 2:38
too **m** to be numbered or counted for 1 Kgs 3:8
and Israel were as **m** as the sand by 1 Kgs 4:20
because there were so **m** of them; 1 Kgs 7:47
sacrificing so **m** sheep and oxen that 1 Kgs 8:5
Solomon loved **m** foreign women, 1 Kgs 11:1
and her household ate for **m** days. 1 Kgs 17:15
After **m** days the word of the LORD 1 Kgs 18:1
and prepare it first, for you are **m**, 1 Kgs 18:25
"How **m** times shall I make you 1 Kgs 22:16
of your mother Jezebel are so **m**?" 2 Kgs 9:22
'With my **m** chariots I have gone up 2 Kgs 19:23
his brothers did not have **m** children, 1 Chr 4:27
For **m** fell, because the war was of 1 Chr 5:22
36,000, for they had **m** wives and sons. 1 Chr 7:4
their father mourned **m** days, 1 Chr 7:22
having **m** sons and grandsons, 1 Chr 8:40
a hundred times as **m** as they are! 1 Chr 21:3
and Beriah did not have **m** sons, 1 Chr 23:11
the sons of Rehabiah were very **m**. 1 Chr 23:17
to make Israel as **m** as the stars of 1 Chr 27:23
LORD has given me **m** sons) he has 1 Chr 28:5
sacrificing so **m** sheep and oxen that 2 Chr 5:6
army with very **m** chariots and 2 Chr 16:8
"How **m** times shall I make you 2 Chr 18:15
and of the **m** oracles against him 2 Chr 24:27
wilderness and cut out **m** cisterns, 2 Chr 26:10
And **m** people came together in 2 Chr 30:13
For there were **m** in the assembly 2 Chr 30:17
people, **m** of them from Ephraim, 2 Chr 30:18
A great **m** people were gathered, and 2 Chr 32:4
And **m** brought gifts to the LORD to 2 Chr 32:23
But **m** of the priests and Levites and Ezr 3:12
laid, though **m** shouted aloud for joy, Ezr 3:12
the house that was built **m** years ago, Ezr 5:11
But the people are **m**, and it is a time of Ezr 10:13
our sons and our daughters, we are **m**. Neh 5:2
of Judah sent **m** letters to Tobiah, Neh 6:17
For **m** in Judah were bound by oath to Neh 6:18
faithful and God-fearing man than **m**. Neh 7:2
and **m** times you delivered them Neh 9:29
M years you bore with them and Neh 9:30
Among the **m** nations there was no Neh 13:26
and pomp of his greatness for **m** days, Est 1:4
and when **m** young women were Est 2:8
and **m** of them lay in sackcloth and Est 4:3
And **m** from the peoples of the country Est 8:17
500 female donkeys, and very **m** servants, Jb 1:3
Behold, you have instructed **m**, and you Jb 4:3
also that your offspring shall be **m**, Jb 5:25
you afraid; **m** will court your favor. Jb 11:19
How **m** are my iniquities and my sins? Jb 13:23
"I have heard **m** such things; miserable Jb 16:2
me, and **m** such things are in his mind. Jb 23:14
days speak, and **m** years teach wisdom.' Jb 32:7
Will he make **m** pleas to you? Will he Jb 41:3
O LORD, how **m** are my foes! Many are Ps 3:1
are my foes! **M** are rising against me; Ps 3:1
m are saying of my soul, there is no Ps 3:2
not be afraid of **m** thousands of people Ps 3:6
There are **m** who say, "Who will show us Ps 4:6
he took me; he drew me out of **m** waters. Ps 18:16
M bulls encompass me; strong bulls of Ps 22:12
Consider how **m** are my foes, and with Ps 25:19
glory thunders, the LORD, over **m** waters. Ps 29:3
hear the whispering of **m**—terror on Ps 31:13
M are the sorrows of the wicked, but Ps 32:10
there who desires life and loves **m** days, Ps 34:12
M are the afflictions of the righteous, Ps 34:19
has than the abundance of **m** wicked. Ps 37:16
and **m** are those who hate me Ps 38:19
M will see and fear, and put their trust in Ps 40:3
I wage, for **m** are arrayed against me. Ps 55:18
all day long, for **m** attack me proudly. Ps 56:2
I have been as a portent to **m**, but you are Ps 71:7
made me see **m** troubles and calamities Ps 71:20
heart the insults of all the **m** nations, Ps 89:50
Make us glad for as **m** days as you have Ps 90:15
and for as **m** years as we have seen evil. Ps 90:15
Mightier than the thunders of **m** waters, Ps 93:4
When the cares of my heart are **m**, Ps 94:19
rejoice; let the **m** coastlands be glad! Ps 97:1
M times he delivered them, but they Ps 106:43
M are my persecutors and my Ps 119:157
who struck down **m** nations and Ps 135:10
me and deliver me from the **m** waters, Ps 144:7
that the years of your life may be **m**. Prv 4:10
for **m** a victim has she laid low, and all Prv 7:26
When words are **m**, transgression is Prv 10:19
The lips of the righteous feed **m**, but Prv 10:21
neighbor, but the rich has **m** friends. Prv 14:20
fail, but with **m** advisers they succeed. Prv 15:22
A man of **m** companions may come Prv 18:24
Wealth brings **m** new friends, but a Prv 19:4
M seek the favor of a generous man, Prv 19:6
M are the plans in the mind of a man, Prv 19:21
M a man proclaims his own steadfast Prv 20:6
a land transgresses, it has **m** rulers, Prv 28:2
who hides his eyes will get **m** a curse. Prv 28:27
M seek the face of a ruler, but it is Prv 29:26
"**M** women have done excellently, but Prv 31:29
men and women, and **m** concubines, Eccl 2:8
and a fool's voice with **m** words. Eccl 5:3
dreams increase and words grow **m**, Eccl 5:7
a hundred children and lives **m** years, Eccl 6:3
so that the days of his years are **m**, Eccl 6:3
heart knows that **m** times you have Eccl 7:22
but they have sought out **m** schemes. Eccl 7:29
folly is set in **m** high places, and the Eccl 10:6
waters, for you will find it after **m** days. Eccl 11:1
So if a person lives **m** years, let him Eccl 11:8
that the days of darkness will be **m**. Eccl 11:8
and arranging **m** proverbs with Eccl 12:9
Of making **m** books there is no end, Eccl 12:12
M waters cannot quench love, neither can Sg 8:7
even though you make **m** prayers, I will Is 1:15
and **m** peoples shall come, and say: "Come, Is 2:3
and shall decide disputes for **m** peoples; Is 2:4
"Surely **m** houses shall be desolate, large Is 5:9
the forsaken places are **m** in the midst of Is 6:12
the waters of the River, mighty and **m**, Is 8:7
And **m** shall stumble on it. They shall Is 8:15
Ah, the thunder of **m** peoples; they Is 17:12
roar like the roaring of **m** waters, Is 17:13
the breaches of the city of David were **m**. Is 22:9
And on **m** waters your revenue was the Is 23:3
Make sweet melody; sing **m** songs, that Is 23:16
and after **m** days they will be punished. Is 24:22
because they are **m** and in horsemen Is 31:1
With my **m** chariots I have gone up the Is 37:24
He sees **m** things, but does not observe Is 42:20
in spite of your **m** sorceries and the great Is 47:9
enchantments and your **m** sorceries, Is 47:12
You are wearied with your **m** counsels; Is 47:13
As **m** were astonished at you— Is 52:14
so shall he sprinkle **m** nations; kings Is 52:15
make **m** to be accounted righteous, Is 53:11
I will divide him a portion with the **m**, Is 53:12

yet he bore the sin of **m**, and makes Is 53:12
up the foundations of **m** generations; Is 58:12
cities, the devastations of **m** generations. Is 61:4
and those slain by the LORD shall be **m**. Is 66:16
for as **m** as your cities are your gods, O Jer 2:28
You have played the whore with **m** lovers; Jer 3:1
because their transgressions are **m**, Jer 5:6
gods have become as **m** as your cities, Jer 11:13
and as **m** as the streets of Jerusalem are Jer 11:13
house, when she has done **m** vile deeds? Jer 11:15
M shepherds have destroyed my Jer 12:10
And after **m** days the LORD said to me, Jer 13:6
name's sake; for our backslidings are **m**; Jer 14:7
"Behold, I am sending for **m** fishers, Jer 16:16
afterward I will send for **m** hunters, Jer 16:16
For I hear **m** whispering. Terror is on Jer 20:10
"'And **m** nations will pass by this city, Jer 22:8
For **m** nations and great kings shall Jer 25:14
Then **m** nations and great kings shall Jer 27:7
and pestilence against **m** countries and Jer 28:8
that you may live **m** days in the land Jer 35:7
And **m** similar words were added to Jer 36:32
cells and remained there **m** days, Jer 37:16
In vain you have used **m** medicines; Jer 46:11
He made **m** stumble, and they fell, and Jer 46:16
mighty nation and **m** kings are Jer 50:41
O you who dwell by **m** waters, rich in Jer 51:13
I will fill you with men, as **m** as locusts, Jer 51:14
Their waves roar like **m** waters; the Jer 51:55
for my groans are **m**, and my heart is Lam 1:22
why do you forsake us for so **m** days? Lam 5:20
their wings like the sound of **m** waters, Ezk 1:24
not to **m** peoples of foreign speech and a Ezk 3:6
that he sees is for **m** days from now, Ezk 12:27
upon you in the sight of **m** women. Ezk 16:41
pinions, rich in plumage of **m** colors, Ezk 17:3
take a strong arm or **m** people to pull it Ezk 17:9
and siege walls built to cut off **m** lives. Ezk 17:17
hearts may melt, and **m** stumble. Ezk 21:15
they have made **m** widows in her Ezk 22:25
will bring up **m** nations against you, Ezk 26:3
horsemen and a host of **m** soldiers. Ezk 26:7
horses will be so **m** that their dust will Ezk 26:10
of the peoples to **m** coastlands, Ezk 27:3
M coastlands were your own special Ezk 27:15
from the seas, you satisfied **m** peoples; Ezk 27:33
its rivers, and **m** waters were stopped. Ezk 31:15
net over you with a host of **m** peoples, Ezk 32:3
"I will trouble the hearts of **m** peoples, Ezk 32:9
I will make **m** peoples appalled at you, Ezk 32:10
all its beasts from beside **m** waters; Ezk 32:13
possession of the land; but we are **m**; Ezk 33:24
there were very **m** on the surface of the Ezk 37:2
all his hordes—**m** peoples are with you. Ezk 38:6
After **m** days you will be mustered. In Ezk 38:8
were gathered from **m** peoples upon the Ezk 38:8
your hordes, and **m** peoples with you. Ezk 38:9
north, you and **m** peoples with you, Ezk 38:15
his hordes and the **m** peoples who are Ezk 38:22
known in the eyes of **m** nations. Ezk 38:23
my holiness in the sight of **m** nations. Ezk 39:27
coming was like the sound of **m** waters, Ezk 43:2
of the river very **m** trees on the one Ezk 47:7
will live, and there will be very **m** fish. Ezk 47:9
Its fish will be of very **m** kinds, like Ezk 47:10
Daniel high honors and **m** great gifts, Dn 2:48
Without warning he shall destroy **m**. Dn 8:25
vision, for it refers to **m** days from now." Dn 8:26
a strong covenant with **m** for one week, Dn 9:27
"In those times **m** shall rise against the Dn 11:14
and shall capture **m** of them, Dn 11:18
away, and **m** shall fall down slain. Dn 11:26
the people shall make **m** understand, Dn 11:33
And **m** shall join themselves to them Dn 11:34
them rulers over **m** and shall divide Dn 11:39
and horsemen, and with **m** ships. Dn 11:40
to destroy and devote **m** to destruction. Dn 11:44
And **m** of those who sleep in the dust of Dn 12:2
and those who turn **m** to righteousness, Dn 12:3
M shall run to and fro, and knowledge Dn 12:4
M shall purify themselves and make Dn 12:10
"You must dwell as mine for **m** days. Hos 3:3
of Israel shall dwell **m** days without king Hos 3:4
your **m** gardens and your vineyards, Am 4:9
I know how **m** are your transgressions Am 5:12
"So **m** dead bodies!" "They are thrown Am 8:3
and **m** nations shall come, and say: Mi 4:2
He shall judge between **m** peoples, and Mi 4:3
Now **m** nations are assembled against Mi 4:11
you shall beat in pieces **m** peoples; Mi 4:13
in the midst of **m** peoples like dew from Mi 5:7
the nations, in the midst of **m** peoples, Mi 5:8
they are at full strength and **m**, Na 1:12
Because you have plundered **m** nations, Hab 2:8
your house by cutting off **m** peoples; Hab 2:10
from your bow, calling for **m** arrows. Hab 3:9
And **m** nations shall join themselves to Zec 2:11
month, as I have done for so **m** years?" Zec 7:3
come, even the inhabitants of **m** cities. Zec 8:20
M peoples and strong nations shall Zec 8:22
they shall be as **m** as they were before. Zec 10:8
and he turned **m** from iniquity. Mal 2:6
You have caused **m** to stumble by your Mal 2:8
But when he saw **m** of the Pharisees and Mt 3:7
that they will be heard for their **m** words. Mt 6:7
and those who enter by it are **m**. Mt 7:13
On that day **m** will say to me, 'Lord, Mt 7:22
and do **m** mighty works in your name?' Mt 7:22
m will come from east and west and Mt 8:11
brought to him **m** who were oppressed Mt 8:16
Now a herd of **m** pigs was feeding at Mt 8:30
m tax collectors and sinners came and Mt 9:10
are of more value than **m** sparrows. Mt 10:31
And **m** followed him, and he healed Mt 12:15
And he told them **m** things in parables, Mt 13:3
m prophets and righteous people Mt 13:17
he did not do **m** mighty works there, Mt 13:58
And as **m** as touched it were made well. Mt 14:36
the crippled, the mute, and **m** others, Mt 15:30
"How **m** loaves do you have?" They Mt 15:34
and how **m** baskets you gathered? Mt 16:9
and how **m** baskets you gathered? Mt 16:10
Jerusalem and suffer **m** things from Mt 16:21
I forgive him? As **m** as seven times?" Mt 18:21
But **m** who are first will be last, and the Mt 19:30
and to give his life as a ransom for **m**." Mt 20:28
to the wedding feast as **m** as you find.' Mt 22:9
For **m** are called, but few are chosen." Mt 22:14
For **m** will come in my name, saying, 'I Mt 24:5
the Christ,' and they will lead **m** astray. Mt 24:5
And then **m** will fall away and betray Mt 24:10
And **m** false prophets will arise and Mt 24:11
prophets will arise and lead **m** astray. Mt 24:11
increased, the love of **m** will grow cold. Mt 24:12
is poured out for **m** for the forgiveness Mt 26:28
though **m** false witnesses came Mt 26:60
you not hear how **m** things they testify Mt 27:13
And **m** bodies of the saints who had Mt 27:52
into the holy city and appeared to **m**. Mt 27:53
There were also **m** women there, Mt 27:55
And he healed **m** who were sick with Mk 1:34
diseases, and cast out **m** demons. Mk 1:34
And **m** were gathered together, so that Mk 2:2
m tax collectors and sinners were Mk 2:15
for there were **m** who followed him. Mk 2:15
for he had healed **m**, so that all who had Mk 3:10
was teaching them **m** things in parables, Mk 4:2
With **m** such parables he spoke the Mk 4:33
"My name is Legion, for we are **m**." Mk 5:9
suffered much under **m** physicians, Mk 5:26
and **m** who heard him were astonished, Mk 6:2
they cast out **m** demons and anointed Mk 6:13
and anointed with oil **m** who were sick Mk 6:13
rest a while." For **m** were coming and Mk 6:31
Now **m** saw them going and recognized Mk 6:33
And he began to teach them **m** things. Mk 6:34
to them, "How **m** loaves do you have? Mk 6:38
And as **m** as touched it were made well. Mk 6:56
And there are **m** other traditions that Mk 7:4
down. And **m** such things you do." Mk 7:13
"How **m** loaves do you have?" They said, Mk 8:5
how **m** baskets full of broken pieces did Mk 8:19
how **m** baskets full of broken pieces did Mk 8:20
of Man must suffer **m** things and be Mk 8:31
that he should suffer **m** things and be Mk 9:12
But **m** who are first will be last, and Mk 10:31
and to give his life as a ransom for **m**." Mk 10:45
And **m** rebuked him, telling him to be Mk 10:48
And **m** spread their cloaks on the road, Mk 11:8
And so with **m** others: some they beat, Mk 12:5
box. **M** rich people put in large sums. Mk 12:41
M will come in my name, saying, 'I am Mk 13:6
'I am he!' and they will lead **m** astray. Mk 13:6
covenant, which is poured out for **m**. Mk 14:24
For **m** bore false witness against him, Mk 14:56
chief priests accused him of **m** things. Mk 15:3
See how **m** charges they bring against Mk 15:4
there were also **m** other women who Mk 15:41
Inasmuch as **m** have undertaken to Lk 1:1
gladness, and **m** will rejoice at his birth, Lk 1:14
And he will turn **m** of the children of Lk 1:16
for the fall and rising of **m** in Israel, Lk 2:34
so that thoughts from **m** hearts may be Lk 2:35
So with **m** other exhortations he Lk 3:18
there were **m** widows in Israel in the Lk 4:25
And there were **m** lepers in Israel in the Lk 4:27
And demons also came out of **m**, crying, Lk 4:41
that hour he healed **m** people of diseases Lk 7:21
and on **m** who were blind he bestowed Lk 7:21
I tell you, her sins, which are **m**, Lk 7:47
manager, and Susanna, and **m** others, Lk 8:3
man. (For **m** a time it had seized him. Lk 8:29
"Legion," for **m** demons had entered Lk 8:30
of Man must suffer **m** things and be Lk 9:22
I tell you that **m** prophets and kings Lk 10:24
anxious and troubled about **m** things, Lk 10:41
provoke him to speak about **m** things, Lk 11:53
when so **m** thousands of the people had Lk 12:1
you are of more value than **m** sparrows. Lk 12:7
have ample goods laid up for **m** years; Lk 12:19
enter through the narrow door. For **m**, Lk 13:24
gave a great banquet and invited **m**. Lk 14:16
Not **m** days later, the younger son Lk 15:13
'How **m** of my father's hired servants Lk 15:17
'Look, these **m** years I have served you, Lk 15:29
first he must suffer **m** things and be Lk 17:25
who will not receive **m** times more in Lk 18:30
For **m** will come in my name, saying, 'I Lk 21:8
And they said **m** other things against Lk 22:65
m believed in his name when they saw Jn 2:23
M Samaritans from that town believed Jn 4:39
And **m** more believed because of his Jn 4:41
and two fish, but what are they for so **m**?" Jn 6:9
When **m** of his disciples heard it, they Jn 6:60
After this **m** of his disciples turned back Jn 6:66
Yet **m** of the people believed in him. They Jn 7:31
saying these things, **m** believed in him. Jn 8:30
M of them said, "He has a demon, and is Jn 10:20
"I have shown you **m** good works from Jn 10:32
And **m** came to him. And they said, Jn 10:41
And **m** believed in him there. Jn 10:42
and **m** of the Jews had come to Martha Jn 11:19
M of the Jews therefore, who had come Jn 11:45
to do? For this man performs **m** signs. Jn 11:47
and **m** went up from the country to Jn 11:55
on account of him **m** of the Jews were Jn 12:11
he had done so **m** signs before them, Jn 12:37
m even of the authorities believed in Jn 12:42
In my Father's house are **m** rooms. If it Jn 14:2
"I still have **m** things to say to you, but Jn 16:12
M of the Jews read this inscription, for Jn 19:20
Now Jesus did **m** other signs in the Jn 20:30
And although there were so **m**, the net Jn 21:11
Now there are also **m** other things that Jn 21:25
alive after his suffering by **m** proofs, Acts 1:3
the Holy Spirit not **m** days from now." Acts 1:5
And with **m** other words he bore Acts 2:40
and **m** wonders and signs were being Acts 2:43
But **m** of those who had heard the word Acts 4:4
for as **m** as were owners of lands or Acts 4:34
Now **m** signs and wonders were Acts 5:12
and a great **m** of the priests became Acts 6:7
came out of **m** who were possessed, Acts 8:7
and **m** who were paralyzed or lame were Acts 8:7
the gospel to **m** villages of the Acts 8:25
I have heard from **m** about this man, Acts 9:13
When **m** days had passed, the Jews Acts 9:23
all Joppa, and **m** believed in the Lord. Acts 9:42
stayed in Joppa for **m** days with one Acts 9:43
in and found **m** persons gathered. Acts 10:27
And a great **m** people were added to Acts 11:24
church and taught a great **m** people. Acts 11:26
where **m** were gathered together and Acts 12:12
and for **m** days he appeared to those Acts 13:31
m Jews and devout converts to Acts 13:43
and as **m** as were appointed to eternal Acts 13:48
that city and had made **m** disciples, Acts 14:21
that through **m** tribulations we Acts 14:22
the brothers with **m** words. Acts 15:32
word of the Lord, with **m** others also. Acts 15:35
And this she kept doing for **m** days. Acts 16:18
they had inflicted **m** blows upon Acts 16:23
as did a great **m** of the devout Greeks Acts 17:4
M of them therefore believed, with Acts 17:12
And **m** of the Corinthians hearing Acts 18:8
for I have **m** in this city who are my Acts 18:10
Paul stayed **m** days longer and then Acts 18:18
Also **m** of those who were now Acts 19:18
and turned away a great **m** people, Acts 19:26
There were **m** lamps in the upper Acts 20:8
While we were staying for **m** days, a Acts 21:10
how **m** thousands there are among Acts 21:20
"Knowing that for **m** years you have Acts 24:10
bringing **m** and serious charges Acts 25:7
And as they stayed there **m** days, Acts 25:14
I ought to do **m** things in opposing the Acts 26:9
not only locked up **m** of the saints in Acts 26:10
sun nor stars appeared for **m** days, Acts 27:20
you the father of **m** nations"—in the Rom 4:17
become the father of **m** nations, Rom 4:18
For if **m** died through one man's Rom 5:15
one man Jesus Christ abounded for **m**. Rom 5:15
gift following **m** trespasses brought Rom 5:16
man's disobedience the **m** were made Rom 5:19
man's obedience the **m** will be made Rom 5:19

be the firstborn among **m** brothers. Rom 8:29
as in one body we have **m** members, Rom 12:4
so we, though **m**, are one body in Rom 12:5
I have longed for **m** years to come to Rom 15:23
been a patron of **m** and of myself as Rom 16:2
not **m** of you were wise according to 1 Cor 1:26
standards, not **m** were powerful, 1 Cor 1:26
powerful, not **m** were of noble birth. 1 Cor 1:26
in Christ, you do not have **m** fathers. 1 Cor 4:15
as indeed there are **m** "gods" and many 1 Cor 8:5
there are many "gods" and **m** "lords"— 1 Cor 8:5
bread, we who are **m** are one body, 1 Cor 10:17
my own advantage, but that of **m**, 1 Cor 10:33
That is why **m** of you are weak and 1 Cor 11:30
body is one and has **m** members, 1 Cor 12:12
the members of the body, though **m**, 1 Cor 12:12
not consist of one member but of **m**. 1 Cor 12:14
As it is, there are **m** parts, yet one 1 Cor 12:20
are doubtless **m** different languages 1 Cor 14:10
to me, and there are **m** adversaries. 1 Cor 16:9
so that **m** will give thanks on our 2 Cor 1:11
granted us through the prayers of **m**. 2 Cor 1:11
and anguish of heart and with **m** tears, 2 Cor 2:4
For we are not, like so **m**, peddlers of 2 Cor 2:17
as poor, yet making **m** rich; 2 Cor 6:10
and found earnest in **m** matters, 2 Cor 8:22
overflowing in **m** thanksgivings to 2 Cor 9:12
Since **m** boast according to the 2 Cor 11:18
through **m** a sleepless night, 2 Cor 11:27
have to mourn over **m** of those who 2 Cor 12:21
in Judaism beyond **m** of my own Gal 1:14
Did you suffer so **m** things in vain—if Gal 3:4
say, "And to offsprings," referring to **m**, Gal 3:16
For as **m** of you as were baptized into Gal 3:27
For **m**, of whom I have often told you Phil 3:18
into **m** senseless and harmful desires 1 Tm 6:9
pierced themselves with **m** pangs. 1 Tm 6:10
in the presence of **m** witnesses. 1 Tm 6:12
the presence of **m** witnesses entrust to 2 Tm 2:2
For there are **m** who are insubordinate, Ti 1:10
Long ago, at **m** times and in many ways, Heb 1:1
Long ago, at many times and in **m** ways, Heb 1:1
exist, in bringing **m** sons to glory, Heb 2:10
The former priests were **m** in number, Heb 7:23
been offered once to bear the sins of **m**, Heb 9:28
born descendants as **m** as the stars Heb 11:12
heaven and as **m** as the innumerable Heb 11:12
trouble, and by it **m** become defiled; Heb 12:15
Not **m** of you should become teachers, Jas 3:1
For we all stumble in **m** ways, and if Jas 3:2
And **m** will follow their sensuality, and 2 Pt 2:2
so now **m** antichrists have come. 1 Jn 2:18
for **m** false prophets have gone out into 1 Jn 4:1
For **m** deceivers have gone out into the 2 Jn 1:7
his voice was like the roar of **m** waters. Rv 1:15
and the elders the voice of **m** angels, Rv 5:11
and **m** people died from the water, Rv 8:11
like the noise of **m** chariots with horses Rv 9:9
again prophesy about **m** peoples and Rv 10:11
like the roar of **m** waters and like the Rv 14:2
prostitute who is seated on **m** waters, Rv 17:1
like the roar of **m** waters and like the Rv 19:6
of fire, and on his head are **m** diadems, Rv 19:12

MANY-COLORED (1)
In **m** robes she is led to the king, with Ps 45:14

MANY-PEAKED (2)
mountain of Bashan; O **m** mountain, Ps 68:15
you look with hatred, O **m** mountain, Ps 68:16

MAOCH (1)
with him, to Achish the son of **M**, 1 Sm 27:2

MAON (7)
M, Carmel, Ziph, Juttah, Jos 15:55
his men were in the wilderness of **M**, 1 Sm 23:24
and lived in the wilderness of **M**. 1 Sm 23:25
after David in the wilderness of **M**. 1 Sm 23:25
was a man in **M** whose business was 1 Sm 25:2
M; and Maon fathered Beth-zur. 1 Chr 2:45
Maon; and **M** fathered Beth-zur. 1 Chr 2:45

MAONITES (1)
Amalekites and the **M** oppressed you, Jgs 10:12

MAR (1)
on your temples or **m** the edges of your Lv 19:27

MARA (1)
call me **M**, for the Almighty has dealt Ru 1:20

MARAH (5)
When they came to **M**, they could not Ex 15:23
drink the water of **M** because it was Ex 15:23
it was bitter; therefore it was named **M**. Ex 15:23
wilderness of Etham and camped at **M**. Nm 33:8
they set out from **M** and came to Elim; Nm 33:9

MARAUDING (2)
and became leader of a **m** band, 1 Kgs 11:24
a **m** band was seen and the man was 2 Kgs 13:21

MARBLE (4)
all sorts of precious stones and **m**. 1 Chr 29:2
and purple to silver rods and **m** pillars, Est 1:6
m, mother-of-pearl and precious stones. Est 1:6
of costly wood, bronze, iron and **m**, Rv 18:12

MARCH (19)
They shall set out first on the **m**. Nm 2:9
They shall set out third on the **m**. Nm 2:24
was the order of **m** of the people of Nm 10:28
set out on the **m** till Miriam was Nm 12:15
You shall **m** around the city, all the men Jos 6:3
seventh day you shall **m** around the city Jos 6:4
M around the city and let the armed men Jos 6:7
Kishon. **M** on, my soul, with might! Jgs 5:21
right that you should **m** out and in 1 Sm 29:6
way shall we **m**?" Jehoram answered, 2 Kgs 3:8
made a circuitous **m** of seven days, 2 Kgs 3:9
no king, yet all of them **m** in rank; Prv 30:27
briers to battle! I would **m** against them, Is 27:4
for her enemies **m** in force and come Jer 46:22
They **m** each on his way; they do not Jl 2:7
who **m** through the breadth of the earth, Hab 1:6
a guard, so that none shall **m** to and fro; Zec 9:8
no oppressor shall again **m** over them, Zec 9:8
the trumpet and will **m** forth in the Zec 9:14

MARCHED (18)
the second day they **m** around the city Jos 6:14
and **m** around the city in the same Jos 6:15
that day that they **m** around the city Jos 6:15
having **m** up all night from Gilgal. Jos 10:9
Whenever they **m** out, the hand of the Jgs 2:15
when you **m** from the region of Edom, Jgs 5:4
down to the gates **m** the people of the Jgs 5:11
Then down **m** the remnant of the noble; Jgs 5:13
people of the LORD **m** down for me Jgs 5:13
their root they **m** down into the Jgs 5:14
from Machir **m** down the commanders, Jgs 5:14
And Joab and his men **m** all night, 2 Sm 2:32
while all the army **m** out by hundreds 2 Sm 18:4
So King Jehoram **m** out of Samaria at 2 Kgs 3:6
king of Assyria **m** up against 2 Kgs 16:9
when you **m** through the wilderness, Ps 68:7
You **m** through the earth in fury; you Hab 3:12
And they **m** up over the broad plain of Rv 20:9

MARCHES (1)
not jostle one another; each **m** in his path; Jl 2:8

MARCHING (7)
the Egyptians were **m** after them, Ex 14:10
the Jordan, and **m** the whole morning, 2 Sm 2:29
you hear the sound of **m** in the tops of 2 Sm 5:24
m through the gate of the guards to 2 Kgs 11:19
hear the sound of **m** in the tops of 1 Chr 14:15
m through the upper gate to the 2 Chr 23:20
m in the greatness of his strength? Is 63:1

MARE (1)
love, to a **m** among Pharaoh's chariots. Sg 1:9

MAREAL (1)
and on to **M** and touches Dabbesheth, Jos 19:11

MARESHAH (9)
Keilah, Achzib, and **M**: nine cities with Jos 15:44
M his firstborn, who fathered Ziph. 1 Chr 2:42
fathered Ziph. The son of **M**: Hebron. 1 Chr 2:42
of Lecah, Laadah the father of **M**, 1 Chr 4:21
Gath, **M**, Ziph, 2 Chr 11:8
300 chariots, and came as far as **M**. 2 Chr 14:9
in the Valley of Zephathah at **M**. 2 Chr 14:10
Dodavahu of **M** prophesied against 2 Chr 20:37
a conqueror to you, inhabitants of **M**; Mi 1:15

MARINERS (4)
of the sea with their **m** were in you to Ezk 27:9
merchandise, your **m** and your pilots, Ezk 27:27
The **m** and all the pilots of the sea Ezk 27:29
Then the **m** were afraid, and each cried Jon 1:5

MARITAL (1)
her food, her clothing, or her **m** rights. Ex 21:10

MARK (33)
And the LORD put a **m** on Cain, Gn 4:15
It shall be as a **m** on your hand or Ex 13:16
the side of it, as though I shot at a **m**. 1 Sm 20:20
"**M** when Amnon's heart is merry 2 Sm 13:28
elders of the land and said, "**M**, now, 1 Kgs 20:7
Why have you made me your **m**? Jb 7:20
and commands it to strike the **m**. Jb 36:32
M the blameless and behold the Ps 37:37
"**M** this, then, you who forget God, lest I Ps 50:22
He made the moon to **m** the seasons; Ps 104:19
If you, O LORD, should **m** iniquities, O Ps 130:3
and put a **m** on the foreheads of the men Ezk 9:4
but touch no one on whom is the **m**. Ezk 9:6
m two ways for the sword of the king Ezk 21:19
M a way for the sword to come to Ezk 21:20
LORD said to me, "Son of man, **m** well, Ezk 44:5
And **m** well the entrance to the temple Ezk 44:5
I see in his hands the **m** of the nails, Jn 20:25
place my finger into the **m** of the nails, Jn 20:25
of John whose other name was **M**, Acts 12:12
them John, whose other name was **M**. Acts 12:25
to take with them John called **M**. Acts 15:37
Barnabas took **M** with him and Acts 15:39
and **M** the cousin of Barnabas Col 4:10
Get **M** and bring him with you, for he 2 Tm 4:11
and so do **M**, Aristarchus, Demas, Phlm 1:24
sends you greetings, and so does **M**, 1 Pt 5:13
can buy or sell unless he has the **m**, Rv 13:17
image and receives a **m** on his forehead Rv 14:9
whoever receives the **m** of its name." Rv 14:11
people who bore the **m** of the beast and Rv 16:2
who had received the **m** of the beast Rv 19:20
had not received its **m** on their foreheads Rv 20:4

MARKED (5)
and **m** them for destruction to this 1 Chr 4:41
of darkness, and he is **m** for the sword. Jb 15:22
when he **m** out the foundations of the Prv 8:29
of his hand and **m** off the heavens with Is 40:12
to be **m** on the right hand or the Rv 13:16

MARKERS (1)
"Set up road **m** for yourself; make Jer 31:21

MARKET (3)
now in the street, now in the **m**, and at Prv 7:12
In your **m** these traded with you in Ezk 27:24
in the meat **m** without raising any 1 Cor 10:25

MARKETPLACE (6)
and fraud do not depart from its **m**. Ps 55:11
he saw others standing idle in the **m**, Mt 20:3
and when they come from the **m**, they do Mk 7:4
children sitting in the **m** and calling to Lk 7:32
them into the **m** before the rulers. Acts 16:19
and in the **m** every day with those Acts 17:17

MARKETPLACES (6)
children sitting in the **m** and calling to Mt 11:16
and greetings in the **m** and being called Mt 23:7
the sick in the **m** and implored him Mk 6:56
long robes and like greetings in the **m** Mk 12:38
the synagogues and greetings in the **m**. Lk 11:43
love greetings in the **m** and the best Lk 20:46

MARKETS (2)
the street, in the **m** she raises her voice; Prv 1:20
coastlands were your own special **m**; Ezk 27:15

MARKS (5)
hands and made **m** on the doors 1 Sm 21:13
a line; he **m** it out with a pencil. Is 44:13
it with planes and **m** it with a compass. Is 44:13
to remove the **m** of circumcision. 1 Cor 7:18
for I bear on my body the **m** of Jesus. Gal 6:17

MAROTH (1)
the inhabitants of **M** wait anxiously for Mi 1:12

MARRED (1)
at you—his appearance was so **m**, Is 52:14

MARRIAGE (27)
she had not been given to him in **m**. Gn 38:14
And he gave him in **m** Asenath, the Gn 41:45
daughters he gave in **m** outside his clan, Jgs 12:9
give his daughter in **m** to Benjamin." Jgs 21:1
Solomon made a **m** alliance with 1 Kgs 3:1
daughter whom he had taken in **m**. 1 Kgs 7:8
shall not enter into **m** with them, 1 Kgs 11:2
he gave him in **m** the sister of his 1 Kgs 11:19
gave his daughter in **m** to Jarha his 1 Chr 2:35
he made a **m** alliance with Ahab. 2 Chr 18:1
their young women had no **m** song. Ps 78:63
sons, and give your daughters in **m**, Jer 29:6
so they will mix with one another in **m**, Dn 2:43
they neither marry nor are given in **m**, Mt 22:30
drinking, marrying and giving in **m**, Mt 24:38
ready went in with him to the **m** feast, Mt 25:10
they neither marry nor are given in **m**, Mk 12:25
and marrying and being given in **m**, Lk 17:27
of this age marry and are given in **m**, Lk 20:34
dead neither marry nor are given in **m**, Lk 20:35
dies she is released from the law of **m**. Rom 7:2
he who refrains from **m** will do even 1 Cor 7:38
who forbid **m** and require abstinence 1 Tm 4:3
Let **m** be held in honor among all, and Heb 13:4
all, and let the **m** bed be undefiled, Heb 13:4
glory, for the **m** of the Lamb has come, Rv 19:7
are invited to the **m** supper of the Lamb." Rv 19:9

MARRIAGES (2)
Make **m** with us. Give your daughters to Gn 34:9
among you and make **m** with them, Jos 23:12

MARRIED (33)
if he comes in **m**, then his wife shall go Ex 21:3
not engaged to be **m** and lies with her, Ex 22:16
the Cushite woman whom he had **m**, Nm 12:1
for he had **m** a Cushite woman. Nm 12:1
But if they are **m** to any of the sons of Nm 36:3
were **m** to sons of their father's Nm 36:11
They were **m** into the clans of the Nm 36:12
"When a man is newly **m**, he shall not Dt 24:5
man shall not be **m** outside the family to Dt 25:5
who had **m** Abigal the daughter of 2 Sm 17:25
Azubah died, Caleb **m** Ephrath, 1 Chr 2:19
whom he **m** when he was sixty years 1 Chr 2:21
of Pharaoh, whom Mered **m**; 1 Chr 4:17
kinsmen, the sons of Kish, **m** them. 1 Chr 23:22
God and have **m** foreign women from Ezr 10:2
broken faith and **m** foreign women, Ezr 10:10
the men who had **m** foreign women. Ezr 10:17
the priests who had **m** foreign women: Ezr 10:18
All these had **m** foreign women, and Ezr 10:44
Jews who had **m** women of Ashdod, Neh 13:23
but a **m** woman hunts down a precious Prv 6:26
children of her who is **m**," says the LORD. Is 54:1
My Delight Is in Her, and your land **M**; Is 62:4
delights in you, and your land shall be **m**. Is 62:4
and has **m** the daughter of a foreign Mal 2:11
among us. The first **m** and died, Mt 22:25
Philip's wife, because he had **m** her. Mk 6:17
And another said, 'I have **m** a wife, and Lk 14:20
Thus a **m** woman is bound by law to Rom 7:2
To the **m** I give this charge (not I, but 1 Cor 7:10
But the **m** man is anxious about 1 Cor 7:33
But the **m** woman is anxious about 1 Cor 7:34
is free to be **m** to whom she wishes, 1 Cor 7:39

MARRIES (14)
If Jacob **m** one of the Hittite women Gn 27:46
If a priest's daughter **m** a layman, she Lv 22:12
If she **m** a husband, while under her Nm 30:6
"When a man takes a wife and **m** her, if Dt 24:1
For as a young man **m** a young woman, Is 62:5
And whoever **m** a divorced woman Mt 5:32
for sexual immorality, and **m** another, Mt 19:9
his wife and **m** another commits Mk 10:11
divorces her husband and **m** another, Mk 10:12
his wife and **m** another commits Lk 16:18
and he who **m** a woman divorced from Lk 16:18
and if she **m** another man she is not an Rom 7:3
sinned, and if a betrothed woman **m**, 1 Cor 7:28
So then he who **m** his betrothed does 1 Cor 7:38

MARROW (3)
of milk and the **m** of his bones moist. Jb 21:24
of well-aged wine, of rich food full of **m**, Is 25:6
of soul and of spirit, of joints and of **m**, Heb 4:12

MARRY (24)
who were to **m** his daughters, Gn 19:14
They shall not **m** a prostitute or a Lv 21:7
neither shall they **m** a woman divorced Lv 21:7
or a prostitute, these he shall not **m**. Lv 21:14
of the tribe into which they **m**. Nm 36:3
of the tribe into which they **m**, Nm 36:4
'Let them **m** whom they think best, Nm 36:6
only they shall **m** within the clan of Nm 36:6
'I gave my daughter to this man to **m**, Dt 22:16
young woman, so shall your sons **m** you, Is 62:5
They shall not **m** a widow or a Ezk 44:22
man with his wife, it is better not to **m**." Mt 19:10
his brother must **m** the widow and Mt 22:24
resurrection they neither **m** nor are Mt 22:30
they neither **m** nor are given in Mk 12:25
sons of this age **m** and are given in Lk 20:34
from the dead neither **m** nor are given Lk 20:35
exercise self-control, they should **m**. 1 Cor 7:9
For it is better to **m** than to be aflame 1 Cor 7:9
But if you do **m**, you have not sinned, 1 Cor 7:28
Yet those who **m** will have worldly 1 Cor 7:28
as he wishes: let them **m**—it is no sin. 1 Cor 7:36
away from Christ, they desire to **m** 1 Tm 5:11
So I would have younger widows **m**, 1 Tm 5:14

MARRYING (4)
Would you therefore refrain from **m**? Ru 1:13
our God by **m** foreign women?" Neh 13:27
drinking, **m** and giving in marriage, Mt 24:38
and drinking and **m** and being given Lk 17:27

MARSENA (1)
Tarshish, Meres, **M**, and Memucan, Est 1:14

MARSH (2)
"Can papyrus grow where there is no **m**? Jb 8:11
in the shelter of the reeds and in the **m**. Jb 40:21

MARSHAL (1)
Ashkenaz; appoint a **m** against her; Jer 51:27

MARSHES (2)
been seized, the **m** are burned with fire, Jer 51:32
its swamps and **m** will not become Ezk 47:11

MARTHA (13)
a woman named **M** welcomed him Lk 10:38
But **M** was distracted with much Lk 10:40
the Lord answered her, "**M**, Martha, Lk 10:41
M, you are anxious and troubled about Lk 10:41
the village of Mary and her sister **M**. Jn 11:1
Now Jesus loved **M** and her sister and Jn 11:5
Jews had come to **M** and Mary to Jn 11:19
So when **M** heard that Jesus was Jn 11:20
M said to Jesus, "Lord, if you had been Jn 11:21
M said to him, "I know that he will rise Jn 11:24
still in the place where **M** had met him. Jn 11:30
Jesus said, "Take away the stone." **M**, Jn 11:39
M served, and Lazarus was one of those Jn 12:2

MARTYRS (1)
of the saints, the blood of the **m** of Jesus. Rv 17:6

MARVEL (6)
Do not **m** that I said to you, 'You must be Jn 3:7
will he show him, so that you may **m**. Jn 5:20
Do not **m** at this, for an hour is coming Jn 5:28
them, "I did one deed, and you all **m** at it. Jn 7:21
the angel said to me, "Why do you **m**? Rv 17:7
of the world will **m** to see the beast, Rv 17:8

MARVELED (18)
he **m** and said to those who followed Mt 8:10
And the men **m**, saying, "What sort of Mt 8:27
And the crowds **m**, saying, "Never was Mt 9:33
When the disciples saw it, they **m**, Mt 21:20
When they heard it, they **m**. And they Mt 22:22
had done for him, and everyone **m**. Mk 5:20
And he **m** because of their unbelief. And Mk 6:6
that are God's." And they **m** at him. Mk 12:17
father and his mother **m** at what was Lk 2:33
well of him and **m** at the gracious words Lk 4:22
Jesus heard these things, he **m** at him, Lk 7:9
And they were afraid, and they **m**, Lk 8:25
the mute man spoke, and the people **m**. Lk 11:14
They **m** that he was talking with a Jn 4:27
The Jews therefore **m**, saying, "How is it Jn 7:15
and to be **m** at among all who have 2 Thes 1:10
and the whole earth **m** as they followed Rv 13:3
of Jesus. When I saw her, I **m** greatly. Rv 17:6

MARVELING (4)
while they were all **m** at everything he Lk 9:43
but **m** at his answer they became Lk 20:26
and he went home **m** at what had Lk 24:12
still disbelieved for joy and were **m**, Lk 24:41

MARVELOUS (13)
his **m** works among all the peoples! 1 Chr 16:24
unsearchable, **m** things without number: Jb 5:9
out, and **m** things beyond number. Jb 9:10
his **m** works among all the peoples! Ps 96:3
a new song, for he has done **m** things! Ps 98:1
is the LORD'S doing; it is **m** in our eyes. Ps 118:23
with things too great and too **m** for me. Ps 131:1
of Egypt, I will show them **m** things. Mi 7:15
If it is **m** in the sight of the remnant of Zec 8:6
days, should it also be **m** in my sight, Zec 8:6
Lord's doing, and it is **m** in our eyes'? Mt 21:42
Lord's doing, and it is **m** in our eyes'?" Mk 12:11
you out of darkness into his **m** light. 1 Pt 2:9

MARVELOUSLY (1)
spread far, for he was **m** helped, 2 Chr 26:15

MARVELS (2)
Before all your people I will do **m**, such Ex 34:10
signs in Egypt and his **m** in the fields of Ps 78:43

MARY (54)
the father of Joseph the husband of **M**, Mt 1:16
When his mother **M** had been betrothed Mt 1:18
David, do not fear to take **M** as your wife, Mt 1:20
they saw the child with **M** his mother, Mt 2:11
son? Is not his mother called **M**? Mt 13:55
among whom were **M** Magdalene and Mt 27:56
Mary Magdalene and **M** the mother of Mt 27:56
M Magdalene and the other Mary were Mt 27:61
Magdalene and the other **M** were there, Mt 27:61
M Magdalene and the other Mary went Mt 28:1
Magdalene and the other **M** went to see Mt 28:1
the son of **M** and brother of James and Mk 6:3
among whom were **M** Magdalene, Mk 15:40
and **M** the mother of James the Mk 15:40
M Magdalene and Mary the mother of Mk 15:47
Mary Magdalene and **M** the mother of Mk 15:47
M Magdalene and Mary the mother of Mk 16:1
Mary Magdalene and **M** the mother of Mk 16:1
week, he appeared first to **M** Magdalene, Mk 16:9
of David. And the virgin's name was **M**. Lk 1:27
M, for you have found favor with God. Lk 1:30
And **M** said to the angel, "How will this Lk 1:34
And **M** said, "Behold, I am the servant of Lk 1:38
In those days **M** arose and went with Lk 1:39
when Elizabeth heard the greeting of **M**, Lk 1:41
And **M** said, "My soul magnifies the Lk 1:46
And **M** remained with her about three Lk 1:56
to be registered with **M**, his betrothed, Lk 2:5
with haste and found **M** and Joseph, Lk 2:16
But **M** treasured up all these things, Lk 2:19
blessed them and said to **M** his mother, Lk 2:34
M, called Magdalene, from whom seven Lk 8:2
And she had a sister called **M**, who sat Lk 10:39
M has chosen the good portion, which Lk 10:42
Now it was **M** Magdalene and Joanna Lk 24:10
and Joanna and **M** the mother of Lk 24:10
the village of **M** and her sister Martha. Jn 11:1
It was **M** who anointed the Lord with Jn 11:2
come to Martha and **M** to console them Jn 11:19
but **M** remained seated in the house. Jn 11:20
this, she went and called her sister **M**, Jn 11:28
her, saw **M** rise quickly and go out, Jn 11:31
Now when **M** came to where Jesus was Jn 11:32
who had come with **M** and had seen Jn 11:45
M therefore took a pound of expensive Jn 12:3
his mother's sister, **M** the wife of Clopas, Jn 19:25
the wife of Clopas, and **M** Magdalene. Jn 19:25
day of the week **M** Magdalene came to Jn 20:1
But **M** stood weeping outside the tomb, Jn 20:11
"**M**." She turned and said to him in Jn 20:16
M Magdalene went and announced to Jn 20:18
with the women and **M** the mother of Acts 1:14
this, he went to the house of **M**, Acts 12:12
Greet **M**, who has worked hard for Rom 16:6

MASH (1)
sons of Aram: Uz, Hul, Gether, and **M**. Gn 10:23

MASHAL (1)
M with its pasturelands, Abdon with 1 Chr 6:74

MASKIL (13)
A **M** of David. Ps 32:T
choirmaster. A **M** of the Sons of Korah. Ps 42:T
choirmaster. A **M** of the Sons of Korah. Ps 44:T
A **M** of the Sons of Korah; a love song. Ps 45:T
A **M** of David, when Doeg, the Edomite, Ps 52:T
according to Mahalath. A **M** of David. Ps 53:T
A **M** of David, when the Ziphites went Ps 54:T
stringed instruments. A **M** of David. Ps 55:T
A **M** of Asaph. Ps 74:T
A **M** of Asaph. Ps 78:T
Leannoth. A **M** of Heman the Ezrahite. Ps 88:T
A **M** of Ethan the Ezrahite. Ps 89:T
A **M** of David, when he was in the cave. Ps 142:T

MASONRY (1)
of the four courts was a row of **m**, Ezk 46:23

MASONS (7)
also carpenters and **m** who built 2 Sm 5:11
and to the **m** and the stonecutters, as 2 Kgs 12:12
and to the builders, and to the **m**), 2 Kgs 22:6
also **m** and carpenters to build a 1 Chr 14:1
stonecutters, **m**, carpenters, and all 1 Chr 22:15
and they hired **m** and carpenters to 2 Chr 24:12
gave money to the **m** and the carpenters, Ezr 3:7

MASREKAH (2)
and Samlah of **M** reigned in his place. Gn 36:36
and Samlah of **M** reigned in his 1 Chr 1:47

MASS (4)
they **m** themselves together against me. Jb 16:10
dust runs into a **m** and the clods stick Jb 38:38
its height with the **m** of its branches. Ezk 19:11
it beautiful in the **m** of its branches, Ezk 31:9

MASSA (2)
Mishma, Dumah, **M**, Gn 25:14
Mishma, Dumah, **M**, Hadad, Tema, 1 Chr 1:30

MASSAH (5)
the name of the place **M** and Meribah, Ex 17:7
God to the test, as you tested him at **M**. Dt 6:16
and at **M** and at Kibroth-hattaavah you Dt 9:22
to your godly one, whom you tested at **M**, Dt 33:8
as on the day at **M** in the wilderness, Ps 95:8

MAST (3)
sea, like one who lies on the top of a **m**. Prv 23:34
they cannot hold the **m** firm in its place Is 33:23
from Lebanon to make a **m** for you. Ezk 27:5

MASTER (152)
thigh of Abraham his **m** and swore to Gn 24:9
all sorts of choice gifts from his **m**; Gn 24:10
said, "O LORD, God of my **m** Abraham, Gn 24:12
show steadfast love to my **m** Abraham. Gn 24:12
have shown steadfast love to my **m**." Gn 24:14

break faith in the **m** of the devoted Jos 22:20
to Micah, "What is the **m** with you, Jgs 18:23
you ask me, 'What is the **m** with you?'" Jgs 18:24
until you learn how the **m** turns out, Ru 3:18
will not rest but will settle the **m** today." Ru 3:18
But about the **m** of the kingdom, 1 Sm 10:16
they reported the **m** in the ears of the 1 Sm 11:4
yourself when the **m** was in hand, 1 Sm 20:19
And as for the **m** of which you and I 1 Sm 20:23
Jonathan and David knew the **m**. 1 Sm 20:39
charged me with a **m** and said to me, 1 Sm 21:2
anything of the **m** about which I 1 Sm 21:2
Who would listen to you in this **m**? 1 Sm 30:24
Joab, 'Do not let this **m** trouble you, 2 Sm 11:25
then are you angry over this **m**? 2 Sm 19:42
at Abel,' and so they settled a **m**. 2 Sm 20:18
"It is not a **m** of silver or gold between 2 Sm 21:4
you desire in the **m** of cedar and 1 Kgs 5:8
except in the **m** of Uriah the Hittite. 1 Kgs 15:5
In this **m** may the LORD pardon your 2 Kgs 5:18
LORD pardon your servant in this **m**." 2 Kgs 5:18
broke faith in the **m** of the devoted 1 Chr 2:7
concerning any **m** and concerning 2 Chr 8:15
And so in the **m** of the envoys of the 2 Chr 32:31
And take care not to be slack in this **m**. Ezr 4:22
the king send us his pleasure in this **m**." Ezr 5:17
because of this **m** and because of Ezr 10:9
we have greatly transgressed in this **m**. Ezr 10:13
our God over this **m** is turned away Ezr 10:14
they sat down to examine the **m**; Ezr 10:16
and of what they had faced in this **m**, Est 9:26
If it is a **m** of justice, who can summon Jb 9:19
and, 'The root of the **m** is found in him,' Jb 19:28
You will decide on a **m**, and it will be Jb 22:28
who repeats a **m** separates close friends. Prv 17:9
and a time for every **m** under heaven: Eccl 3:1
a time for every **m** and for every work. Eccl 3:17
do not be amazed at the **m**, Eccl 5:8
or some winged creature tell the **m**. Eccl 10:20
The end of the **m**; all has been heard. Eccl 12:13
Were your whorings so small a **m** Ezk 16:20
So he listened to them in this **m**, and Dn 1:14
And in every **m** of wisdom and Dn 1:20
Arioch made the **m** known to Daniel. Dn 2:15
and made the **m** known to Hananiah, Dn 2:17
have made known to us the king's **m**." Dn 2:23
have no need to answer you in this **m**. Dn 3:16
not show the interpretation of the **m**. Dn 5:15
This is the interpretation of the **m**: Dn 5:26
the dream and told the sum of the **m**. Dn 7:1
"Here is the end of the **m**. As for me, Dn 7:28
changed, but I kept the **m** in my heart." Dn 7:28
So they kept the **m** to themselves, Mk 9:10
asked him again about this **m**. Mk 10:10
have neither part nor lot in this **m**, Acts 8:21
gathered together to consider this **m**. Acts 15:6
"If it were a **m** of wrongdoing or Acts 18:14
since it is a **m** of questions about Acts 18:15
and circumcision is a **m** of the heart, Rom 2:29
God is not a **m** of eating and Rom 14:17
proved yourselves innocent in the **m**. 2 Cor 7:11
And in this **m** I give my judgment: 2 Cor 8:10
burdened, but that as a **m** of fairness 2 Cor 8:13
you may not prove vain in this **m**, 2 Cor 9:3
and wrong his brother in this **m**, 1 Thes 4:6

MATTERS (11)
king in all **m** concerning the 1 Chr 27:1
is over you in all **m** of the LORD; 2 Chr 19:11
house of Judah, in all the king's **m**, 2 Chr 19:11
man learned in **m** of the Ezr 7:11
side in all **m** concerning the people. Neh 11:24
neglected the weightier **m** of the law: Mt 23:23
more, then, **m** pertaining to this life! 1 Cor 6:3
Now concerning the **m** about which 1 Cor 7:1
tested and found earnest in many **m**, 2 Cor 8:22
blaspheming about **m** of which they 2 Pt 2:12
when he speaks in them of these **m**. 2 Pt 3:16

MATTHAN (2)
of Eleazar, and Eleazar the father of **M**, Mt 1:15
of Matthan, and **M** the father of Jacob, Mt 1:15

MATTHAT (2)
the son of **M**, the son of Levi, the son of Lk 3:24
of Eliezer, the son of Jorim, the son of **M**, Lk 3:29

MATTHEW (5)
he saw a man called **M** sitting at the tax Mt 9:9
Thomas and **M** the tax collector; Mt 10:3
and Philip, and Bartholomew, and **M**, Mk 3:18
and **M**, and Thomas, and James the son Lk 6:15
and Thomas, Bartholomew and **M**, Acts 1:13

MATTHIAS (2)
who was also called Justus, and **M**. Acts 1:23
cast lots for them, and the lot fell on **M**, Acts 1:26

MATTITHIAH (8)
and **M**, one of the Levites, the 1 Chr 9:31
Benaiah, Maaseiah, **M**, Eliphelehu, 1 Chr 15:18
but **M**, Eliphelehu, Mikneiah, 1 Chr 15:21
Jeiel, Shemiramoth, Jehiel, **M**, Eliab, 1 Chr 16:5
Jeshaiah, Shimei, Hashabiah, and **M**, 1 Chr 25:3
M, his sons and his brothers, 1 Chr 25:21
Jeiel, **M**, Zabad, Zebina, Jaddai, Joel, Ezr 10:43
And beside him stood **M**, Shema, Neh 8:4

MATTOCK (1)
to sharpen his plowshare, his **m**, 1 Sm 13:20

MATTOCKS (1)
for the plowshares and for the **m**, 1 Sm 13:21

MATURE (8)
of life, and their fruit does not **m**. Lk 8:14
Yet among the **m** we do impart 1 Cor 2:6
in evil, but in your thinking be **m**. 1 Cor 14:20
of the Son of God, to **m** manhood, Eph 4:13
those of us who are **m** think this way, Phil 3:15
we may present everyone **m** in Christ. Col 1:28
you may stand **m** and fully assured Col 4:12
But solid food is for the **m**, for those Heb 5:14

MATURITY (1)
doctrine of Christ and go on to **m**, Heb 6:1

MAXIMS (1)
Your **m** are proverbs of ashes; your Jb 13:12

MAZZAROTH (1)
you lead forth the **M** in their season, Jb 38:32

ME-JARKON (1)
and **M** and Rakkon with the territory Jos 19:46

MEADOW (1)
was like a young palm planted in a **m**; Hos 9:13

MEADOWS (2)
the **m** clothe themselves with flocks, Ps 65:13
with **m** for shepherds and folds for Zep 2:6

MEAGER (2)
and feed him **m** rations of bread 1 Kgs 22:27
feed him with **m** rations of bread 2 Chr 18:26

MEAL (6)
not the son of Jesse come to the **m**, 1 Sm 20:27
cors of fine flour and sixty cors of **m**, 1 Kgs 4:22
wheat of Minnith, **m**, honey, Ezk 27:17
the lamb and the **m** offering and the Ezk 46:15
one goes ahead with his own **m**. 1 Cor 11:21
who sold his birthright for a single **m**. Heb 12:16

MEALTIME (1)
And at **m** Boaz said to her, "Come here Ru 2:14

MEAN (34)
"What do you **m** by all this company Gn 33:8
Do you **m** to kill me as you killed the Ex 2:14
you, 'What do you **m** by this service?' Ex 12:26
your son asks you, 'What does this **m**?' Ex 13:14
to come, 'What do those stones **m** to you?' Jos 4:6
to come, 'What do these stones **m**?' Jos 4:21
of the Hebrews **m**?" And when they 1 Sm 4:6
does this uproar in the city **m**?" 1 Kgs 1:41
What do you **m** by crushing my people, Is 3:15
What do you **m** that you have gone up, Is 22:1
what do you **m** that you dress in scarlet, Jer 4:30
you not know what these things **m**? Ezk 17:12
"What do you **m** by repeating this Ezk 18:2
not tell us what these things **m** for us, Ezk 24:19
you not tell us what you **m** by these?' Ezk 37:18
came and said to him, "What do you **m**, Jon 1:6
saying, "I do not know what you **m**." Mt 26:70
this rising from the dead might **m**. Mk 9:10
understand what you **m**." And he went Mk 14:68
What does he **m** by saying, 'You will Jn 7:36
"What does he **m** by 'a little while'? Jn 16:18
to one another, "What does this **m**?" Acts 2:12
the vision that he had seen might **m**, Acts 10:17
know therefore what these things **m**." Acts 17:20
more will their full inclusion **m**! Rom 11:12
will their acceptance **m** but life from Rom 11:15
What I **m** is that each one of you 1 Cor 1:12
This is what I **m**, brothers: the 1 Cor 7:29
I do not **m** your conscience, but his. 1 Cor 10:29
what do people **m** by being baptized 1 Cor 15:29
I do not **m** that others should be eased 2 Cor 8:13
This is what I **m**: the law, which came Gal 3:17
I **m** that the heir, as long as he is a child, Gal 4:1
ascended," what does it **m** but that he Eph 4:9

MEANING (6)
"What is the **m** of these seven ewe Gn 21:29
'What is the **m** of the testimonies and the Dt 6:20
(for that is the **m** of his name) opposed Acts 13:8
not at all **m** the sexually immoral of 1 Cor 5:10
in the world, and none is without **m**, 1 Cor 14:10
I do not know the **m** of the language, 1 Cor 14:11

MEANS (66)
of Pharaoh's dream **m** that the thing Gn 41:32
on them, you shall by no **m** reduce it, Ex 5:8
shall by no **m** reduce your number Ex 5:19
but who will by no **m** clear the guilty, Ex 34:7
and finds sufficient **m** to redeem it, Lv 25:26
if he has not sufficient **m** to recover it, Lv 25:28
And if he is not redeemed by these **m**, Lv 25:54
but he will by no **m** clear the guilty, Nm 14:18
and by what **m** we may overpower him, Jgs 16:5
but by all **m** return him a guilt 1 Sm 6:3
and he devises **m** so that the 2 Sm 14:14
wilderness, but by all **m** pass over, 2 Sm 17:16
and by no **m** put him to death." But 1 Kgs 3:26
and by no **m** put him to death; 1 Kgs 3:27
this man; if by any **m** he is missing, 1 Kgs 20:39
the LORD said to him, 'By what **m**?' 1 Kgs 22:22
the LORD said to him, 'By what **m**?' 2 Chr 18:20
I will by no **m** leave you unpunished. Jer 30:11
I will by no **m** leave you unpunished." Jer 46:28
the LORD will by no **m** clear the guilty. Na 1:3
call his name Immanuel" (which **m**, Mt 1:23
are by no **m** least among the rulers of Mt 2:6
Go and learn what this **m**, 'I desire Mt 9:13
you, he will by no **m** lose his reward." Mt 10:42
And if you had known what this **m**, 'I Mt 12:7
called Golgotha (which **m** Place of a Mt 27:33
said to her, "Talitha cumi," which **m**, Mk 5:41
to Christ will by no **m** lose his reward. Mk 9:41
called Golgotha (which **m** Place of a Mk 15:22
Eloi, lema sabachthani?" which **m**, Mk 15:34
who provided for them out of their **m**. Lk 8:3
for yourselves by **m** of unrighteous Lk 16:9
to him, "Rabbi" (which **m** Teacher), Jn 1:38
found the Messiah" (which **m** Christ). Jn 1:41
shall be called Cephas" (which **m** Peter). Jn 1:42
in the pool of Siloam" (which **m** Sent). Jn 9:7
"Rabboni!" (which **m** Teacher). Jn 20:16
by what **m** this man has been healed, Acts 4:9
apostles Barnabas (which **m** son of Acts 4:36
Tabitha, which, translated, **m** Dorcas. Acts 9:36
But Peter said, "By no **m**, Lord; for I Acts 10:14
But I said, 'By no **m**, Lord; for nothing Acts 11:8
By no **m**! Let God be true though every Rom 3:4
By no **m**! For then how could God Rom 3:6
the law by this faith? By no **m**! Rom 3:31
By no **m**! How can we who died to sin Rom 6:2
under law but under grace? By no **m**! Rom 6:15
we say? That the law is sin? By no **m**! Rom 7:7
then, bring death to me? By no **m**! Rom 7:13
This **m** that it is not the children of the Rom 9:8
injustice on God's part? By no **m**! Rom 9:14
has God rejected his people? By no **m**! Rom 11:1
order that they might fall? By no **m**! Rom 11:11
Now if their trespass **m** riches for the Rom 11:12
and if their failure **m** riches for the Rom 11:12
if their rejection **m** the reconciliation Rom 11:15
that by all **m** I might save some. 1 Cor 9:22
For they gave according to their **m**, as 2 Cor 8:3
as I can testify, and beyond their **m**, 2 Cor 8:3
the flesh, that **m** fruitful labor for me. Phil 1:22
that by any **m** possible I may attain Phil 3:11
that godliness is a **m** of gain. 1 Tm 6:5
not by **m** of the blood of goats and Heb 9:12
and calves but by **m** of his own blood, Heb 9:12
and that by **m** of these the world that 2 Pt 3:6
heads, and by **m** of them they wound. Rv 9:19

MEANT (14)
As for you, you **m** evil against me, but Gn 50:20
evil against me, but God **m** it for good, Gn 50:20
to him as he had **m** to do to his brother. Dt 19:19
to him, "If the LORD had **m** to kill us, Jgs 13:23
They **m** to kill me, and they violated my Jgs 20:5
on the sea. He **m** to pass by them, Mk 6:48
disciples asked him what this parable **m**, Lk 8:9
and asked what these things **m**. Lk 15:26
going by, he inquired what this **m**. Lk 18:36
they thought that he **m** taking rest in Jn 11:13
asking yourselves, what I **m** by saying, Jn 16:19
that God's kindness is **m** to lead you to Rom 2:4
"Food is **m** for the stomach and the 1 Cor 6:13
body is not **m** for sexual immorality, 1 Cor 6:13

MEANTIME (1)
In the **m**, when so many thousands of Lk 12:1

MEANWHILE (3)
M the Midianites had sold him in Gn 37:36
M all Judah stood before the LORD, 2 Chr 20:13
M the disciples were urging him, saying, Jn 4:31

MEARAH (1)
and **M** that belongs to the Sidonians, Jos 13:4

MEASURE (51)
sand of the sea, until he ceased to **m** it, Gn 41:49
And you shall **m**, outside the city, on Nm 35:5

You shall **m** the distances and divide Dt 19:3
and they shall **m** the distance to the Dt 21:2
have, a full and fair **m** you shall have, Dt 25:15
and understanding beyond **m**, 1 Kgs 4:29
had the same **m** and the same 1 Kgs 6:25
of costly stones, cut according to **m**, 1 Kgs 7:9
of the same **m** and the same form. 1 Kgs 7:37
Its **m** is longer than the earth and Jb 11:9
and apportioned the waters by **m**, Jb 28:25
my end and what is the **m** of my days; Ps 39:4
and given them tears to drink in full **m**. Ps 80:5
power; his understanding is beyond **m**. Ps 147:5
appetite and opened its mouth beyond **m**, Is 5:14
M by measure, by exile you contended Is 27:8
Measure by **m**, by exile you contended Is 27:8
the earth in a **m** and weighed the Is 40:12
shall come upon you in full **m**, Is 47:9
will be like this day, great beyond **m**." Is 56:12
I will **m** into their bosom payment for Is 65:7
I will discipline you in just **m**, and I Jer 30:11
I will discipline you in just **m**, and I Jer 46:28
And water you shall drink by **m**, the Ezk 4:11
shall drink water by **m** and in dismay. Ezk 4:16
iniquities; and they shall **m** the plan. Ezk 43:10
district you shall **m** off a section Ezk 45:3
and the bath shall be of the same **m**, Ezk 45:11
the homer shall be the standard **m**. Ezk 45:11
side, which is to be 4,500 cubits by **m**, Ezk 48:30
side, which is to be 4,500 cubits by **m**, Ezk 48:33
and the scant **m** that is accursed? Mi 6:10
And he said to me, "To **m** Jerusalem, Zec 2:2
and with the **m** you use it will be Mt 7:2
Fill up, then, the **m** of your fathers. Mt 23:32
to what you hear: with the **m** you use, Mk 4:24
And they were astonished beyond **m**, Mk 7:37
give, and it will be given to you. Good **m**, Lk 6:38
For with the **m** you use it will be Lk 6:38
of God, for he gives the Spirit without **m**. Jn 3:34
might become sinful beyond **m**. Rom 7:13
each according to the **m** of faith that Rom 12:3
but in some **m**—not to put it too 2 Cor 2:5
But when they **m** themselves by one 2 Cor 10:12
of us according to the **m** of Christ's gift. Eph 4:7
to the **m** of the stature of the fullness of Eph 4:13
always to fill up the **m** of their sins. 1 Thes 2:16
"Rise and **m** the temple of God and the Rv 11:1
but do not **m** the court outside the Rv 11:2
give her a like **m** of torment and Rv 18:7
rod of gold to **m** the city and its Rv 21:15

MEASURED (60)
to measure it, for it could not be **m**. Gn 41:49
But when they **m** it with an omer, Ex 16:18
and he **m** out six measures of barley and Ru 3:15
defeated Moab and he **m** them with a 2 Sm 8:2
Two lines he **m** to be put to death, and 2 Sm 8:2
The other cherub also **m** ten cubits; 1 Kgs 6:25
of twelve cubits **m** its circumference. 1 Kgs 7:15
of thirty cubits **m** its circumference. 1 Kgs 7:23
baths, each basin **m** four cubits, 1 Kgs 7:38
of thirty cubits **m** its circumference. 2 Chr 4:2
Who has **m** the waters in the hollow of Is 40:12
Who has **m** the Spirit of the LORD, or Is 40:13
lot, the portion I have **m** out to you, Jer 13:25
"If the heavens above can be **m**, and the Jer 31:37
and the sands of the sea cannot be **m**, Jer 33:22
So he **m** the thickness of the wall, one Ezk 40:5
steps, and **m** the threshold of the gate, Ezk 40:6
Then he **m** the vestibule of the gateway, Ezk 40:8
Then he **m** the vestibule of the gateway, Ezk 40:9
Then he **m** the width of the opening of Ezk 40:11
Then he **m** the gate from the ceiling of Ezk 40:13
He **m** also the vestibule, twenty cubits. Ezk 40:14
Then he **m** the distance from the Ezk 40:19
court, he **m** its length and its breadth. Ezk 40:20
And he **m** from gate to gate, a hundred Ezk 40:23
And he **m** its jambs and its vestibule; Ezk 40:24
And he **m** from gate to gate toward the Ezk 40:27
south gate, and he **m** the south gate. Ezk 40:28
on the east side, and he **m** the gate. Ezk 40:32
me to the north gate, and he **m** it. Ezk 40:35
And he **m** the court, a hundred cubits Ezk 40:47
of the temple and **m** the jambs of the Ezk 40:48
me to the nave and **m** the jambs. Ezk 41:1
And he **m** the length of the nave, forty Ezk 41:2
the inner room and **m** the jambs of the Ezk 41:3
And he **m** the length of the room, Ezk 41:4
Then he **m** the wall of the temple, six Ezk 41:5
of the side chambers **m** a full reed of Ezk 41:8
Then he **m** the temple, a hundred Ezk 41:13
Then he **m** the length of the building Ezk 41:15
inside and outside, was a **m** pattern. Ezk 41:17
and **m** the temple area all around. Ezk 42:15
He **m** the east side with the measuring Ezk 42:16
He **m** the north side, 500 cubits by the Ezk 42:17
He **m** the south side, 500 cubits by the Ezk 42:18
Then he turned to the west side and **m**, Ezk 42:19
He **m** it on the four sides. It had a wall Ezk 42:20
And from this **m** district you shall Ezk 45:3
as the fixed portion of oil, **m** in baths, Ezk 45:14
hand, the man **m** a thousand cubits, Ezk 47:3
Again he **m** a thousand, and led me Ezk 47:4
was knee-deep. Again he **m** a thousand, Ezk 47:4
Again he **m** a thousand, and it was a Ezk 47:5
sea, which cannot be **m** or numbered. Hos 1:10
He stood and **m** the earth; he looked and Hab 3:6
the measure you use it will be **m** to you. Mt 7:2
measure you use, it will be **m** to you, Mk 4:24
you use it will be **m** back to you." Lk 6:38
And he **m** the city with his rod, 12,000 Rv 21:16
He also **m** its wall, 144 cubits by Rv 21:17

MEASUREMENT (3)
costly stones, cut according to **m**, 1 Kgs 7:11
its wall, 144 cubits by human **m**, Rv 21:17
which is also an angel's **m**. Rv 21:17

MEASUREMENTS (4)
These are Solomon's **m** for building 2 Chr 3:3
Who determined its **m**—surely you Jb 38:5
"These are the **m** of the altar by cubits Ezk 43:13
and these shall be its **m**: the north side Ezk 48:16

MEASURES (12)
in **m** of length or weight or quantity. Lv 19:35
not have in your house two kinds of **m**, Dt 25:14
he measured out six **m** of barley and put Ru 3:15
"These six **m** of barley he gave to me, Ru 3:17
oil, and all **m** of quantity or size. 1 Chr 23:29
weights and unequal **m** are both alike Prv 20:10
When one came to a heap of twenty **m**, Hg 2:16
one came to the wine vat to draw fifty **m**, Hg 2:16
took and hid in three **m** of flour, Mt 13:33
took and hid in three **m** of flour, Lk 13:21
He said, 'A hundred **m** of oil.' He said to Lk 16:6
owe?' He said, 'A hundred **m** of wheat.' Lk 16:7

MEASURING (19)
over Jerusalem the **m** line of 2 Kgs 21:13
Their **m** line goes out through all the Ps 19:4
And the **m** line shall go out farther, Jer 31:39
of Zion; he stretched out the **m** line; Lam 2:8
a linen cord and a **m** reed in his hand. Ezk 40:3
the length of the **m** reed in the man's Ezk 40:5
when he had finished **m** the interior of Ezk 42:15
the east side with the **m** reed, Ezk 42:16
500 cubits by the **m** reed all around. Ezk 42:16
500 cubits by the **m** reed all around. Ezk 42:17
south side, 500 cubits by the **m** reed. Ezk 42:18
measured, 500 cubits by the **m** reed. Ezk 42:19
on eastward with a **m** line in his hand, Ezk 47:3
have an allotment **m** 25,000 cubits on Ezk 48:10
land shall be divided up with a **m** line; Am 7:17
and the **m** line shall be stretched out Zec 1:16
behold, a man with a **m** line in his hand! Zec 2:1
Then I was given a **m** rod like a staff, Rv 11:1
spoke with me had a **m** rod of gold to Rv 21:15

MEAT (48)
when we sat by the **m** pots and ate bread Ex 16:3
gives you in the evening **m** to eat and in Ex 16:8
to them, 'At twilight you shall eat **m**, Ex 16:12
and said, "Oh that we had **m** to eat! Nm 11:4
Where am I to get **m** to give to all this Nm 11:13
weep before me and say, 'Give us **m**, Nm 11:13
for tomorrow, and you shall eat **m**, Nm 11:18
saying, "Who will give us **m** to eat? Nm 11:18
Therefore the LORD will give you **m**, Nm 11:18
and you have said, 'I will give them **m**, Nm 11:21
While the **m** was yet between their Nm 11:33
may slaughter and eat **m** within any of Dt 12:15
you, and you say, 'I will eat **m**,' Dt 12:20
'I will eat meat,' because you crave **m**, Dt 12:20
you may eat **m** whenever you desire. Dt 12:20
The **m** he put in a basket, and the broth Jgs 6:19
"Take the **m** and the unleavened cakes, Jgs 6:20
and touched the **m** and the unleavened Jgs 6:21
would come, while the **m** was boiling, 1 Sm 2:13
"Give **m** for the priest to roast, 1 Sm 2:15
will not accept boiled **m** from you but 1 Sm 2:15
my water and my **m** that I have 1 Sm 25:11
a cake of bread, a portion of **m**, 2 Sm 6:19
him bread and **m** in the morning, 1 Kgs 17:6
and bread and **m** in the evening, 1 Kgs 17:6
each a loaf of bread, a portion of **m**, 1 Chr 16:3
that has not been filled with his **m**?' Jb 31:31
give bread or provide **m** for his people?" Ps 78:20
he rained **m** on them like dust, winged Ps 78:27
or among gluttonous eaters of **m**, Prv 23:20
They slice **m** on the right, but are still Is 9:20
Over the half he eats **m**; he roasts it and Is 44:16
on its coals; I roasted **m** and have eaten. Is 44:19
and broth of tainted **m** is in their vessels; Is 65:4
nor has tainted **m** come into my Ezk 4:14
city is the cauldron, and we are the **m**.' Ezk 11:3
laid in the midst of it, they are the **m**, Ezk 11:7
nor shall you be the **m** in the midst of Ezk 11:11
put in it the pieces of **m**, all the good Ezk 24:4
logs, kindle the fire, boil the **m** well, Ezk 24:10
no **m** or wine entered my mouth, Dn 10:3
offerings, they sacrifice **m** and eat it, Hos 8:13
pieces and chop them up like **m** in a pot, Mi 3:3
'If someone carries holy **m** in the fold of Hg 2:12
them and boil the **m** of the sacrifice in Zec 14:21
is good not to eat **m** or drink wine or Rom 14:21
brother stumble, I will never eat **m**, 1 Cor 8:13
sold in the **m** market without 1 Cor 10:25

MEBUNNAI (1)
of Anathoth, **M** the Hushathite, 2 Sm 23:27

MECHERATHITE (1)
Hepher the **M**, Ahijah the Pelonite, 1 Chr 11:36

MECONAH (1)
in Ziklag, in **M** and its villages, Neh 11:28

MEDAD (2)
named Eldad, and the other named **M**, Nm 11:26
"Eldad and **M** are prophesying in the Nm 11:27

MEDAN (2)
bore him Zimran, Jokshan, **M**, Midian, Gn 25:2
bore Zimran, Jokshan, **M**, Midian, 1 Chr 1:32

MEDDLER (1)
or a thief or an evildoer or as a **m**. 1 Pt 4:15

MEDDLES (1)
Whoever **m** in a quarrel not his own Prv 26:17

MEDE (3)
And Darius the **M** received the Dn 5:31
the son of Ahasuerus, by descent a **M**, Dn 9:1
for me, in the first year of Darius the **M**, Dn 11:1

MEDEBA (5)
as Nophah; fire spread as far as **M**." Nm 21:30
all the tableland of **M** as far as Dibon; Jos 13:9
the valley, and all the tableland by **M**; Jos 13:16
who came and encamped before **M**. 1 Chr 19:7
weep; over Nebo and over **M** Moab wails. Is 15:2

MEDES (11)
of Gozan, and in the cities of the **M**. 2 Kgs 17:6
of Gozan, and in the cities of the **M**, 2 Kgs 18:11
of the Persians and the **M** so that it may Est 1:19
I am stirring up the **M** against them, Is 13:17
up the spirit of the kings of the **M**, Jer 51:11
for war against her, the kings of the **M**, Jer 51:28
and given to the **M** and Persians." Dn 5:28
to the law of the **M** and the Persians, Dn 6:8
to the law of the **M** and Persians, Dn 6:12
is a law of the **M** and Persians that no Dn 6:15
Parthians and **M** and Elamites and Acts 2:9

MEDIA (8)
the capital that is in the province of **M**, Ezr 6:2
army of Persia and **M** and the nobles and Est 1:3
the seven princes of Persia and **M**, Est 1:14
women of Persia and **M** who have heard Est 1:18
of the kings of **M** and Persia? Est 10:2
Go up, O Elam; lay siege, O **M**; all the Is 21:2
kings of Elam, and all the kings of **M**; Jer 25:25
these are the kings of **M** and Persia. Dn 8:20

MEDIATE (1)
against a man, God will **m** for him, 1 Sm 2:25

MEDIATES (1)
the old as the covenant he **m** is better, Heb 8:6

MEDIATOR (4)
If there be for him an angel, a **m**, one of Jb 33:23
and there is one **m** between God and 1 Tm 2:5
Therefore he is the **m** of a new Heb 9:15
and to Jesus, the **m** of a new covenant, Heb 12:24

MEDIATORS (1)
and your **m** transgressed against me. Is 43:27

MEDICINE (2)
A joyful heart is good **m**, but a Prv 17:22
your cause, no **m** for your wound, Jer 30:13

MEDICINES (1)
In vain you have used many **m**; there is Jer 46:11

MEDITATE (16)
Isaac went out to **m** in the field toward Gn 24:63
but you shall **m** on it day and night, Jos 1:8
speak of ruin and **m** treachery all day Ps 38:12
and **m** on you in the watches of the Ps 63:6
God, I moan; when I **m**, my spirit faints. Ps 77:3
let me **m** in my heart." Then my spirit Ps 77:6
work, and **m** on your mighty deeds. Ps 77:12
I will **m** on your precepts and fix my Ps 119:15
your servant will **m** on your statutes. Ps 119:23
and I will **m** on your wondrous works. Ps 119:27

I love, and I will **m** on your statutes. Ps 119:48
as for me, I will **m** on your precepts. Ps 119:78
night, that I may **m** on your promise. Ps 119:148
of old; I **m** on all that you have done; Ps 143:5
and on your wondrous works, I will **m**. Ps 145:5
minds not to **m** beforehand how to Lk 21:14

MEDITATES (1)
LORD, and on his law he **m** day and night. Ps 1:2

MEDITATION (6)
fear of God and hindering **m** before God. Jb 15:4
of my mouth and the **m** of my heart be Ps 19:14
the **m** of my heart shall be Ps 49:3
May my **m** be pleasing to him, for I Ps 104:34
I love your law! It is my **m** all the day. Ps 119:97
for your testimonies are my **m**. Ps 119:99

MEDIUM (5)
a woman who is a **m** or a wizard shall Lv 20:27
or a charmer or a **m** or a wizard or a Dt 18:11
"Seek out for me a woman who is a **m**, 1 Sm 28:7
him, "Behold, there is a **m** at En-dor." 1 Sm 28:7
of the LORD, and also consulted a **m**, 1 Chr 10:13

MEDIUMS (9)
"Do not turn to **m** or wizards; do not Lv 19:31
"If a person turns to **m** and wizards, Lv 20:6
had put the **m** and the necromancers 1 Sm 28:3
cut off the **m** and the necromancers 1 Sm 28:9
and dealt with **m** and with wizards. 2 Kgs 21:6
put away the **m** and the 2 Kgs 23:24
and dealt with **m** and with wizards. 2 Chr 33:6
"Inquire of the **m** and the necromancers Is 8:19
and the **m** and the necromancers; Is 19:3

MEEK (5)
Now the man Moses was very **m**, more Nm 12:3
But the **m** shall inherit the land and Ps 37:11
decide with equity for the **m** of the earth; Is 11:4
The **m** shall obtain fresh joy in the Is 29:19
"Blessed are the **m**, for they shall inherit Mt 5:5

MEEKNESS (5)
cause of truth and **m** and righteousness; Ps 45:4
by the **m** and gentleness of Christ—I 2 Cor 10:1
kindness, humility, **m**, and patience, Col 3:12
and receive with **m** the implanted word, Jas 1:21
show his works in the **m** of wisdom. Jas 3:13

MEET (141)
Sodom went out to **m** him at the Valley Gn 14:17
the tent door to **m** them and bowed Gn 18:2
he rose to **m** them and bowed himself Gn 19:1
the servant ran to **m** her and said, Gn 24:17
in the field to **m** us?" The servant said, Gn 24:65
he ran to **m** him and embraced him Gn 29:13
Leah went out to **m** him and said, Gn 30:16
Esau, and he is coming to **m** you, Gn 32:6
But Esau ran to **m** him and embraced Gn 33:4
and went up to **m** Israel his father in Gn 46:29
Behold, he is coming out to **m** you, and Ex 4:14
into the wilderness to **m** Moses." So he Ex 4:27
Stand on the bank of the Nile to **m** him, Ex 7:15
went out to **m** his father-in-law and Ex 18:7
the people out of the camp to **m** God, Ex 19:17
"If you **m** your enemy's ox or his donkey Ex 23:4
There I will **m** with you, and from Ex 25:22
the LORD, where I will **m** with you, Ex 29:42
There I will **m** with the people of Israel, Ex 29:43
the testimony, where I will **m** with you. Ex 30:6
of meeting where I shall **m** with you. Ex 30:36
the testimony, where I **m** with you. Nm 17:4
he went out to **m** him at the city of Nm 22:36
Perhaps the LORD will come to **m** me, Nm 23:3
while I **m** the LORD over there." Nm 23:15
congregation went to **m** them outside Nm 31:13
because they did not **m** you with bread Dt 23:4
toward the Arabah to **m** Israel in battle. Jos 8:14
the journey and go to **m** them and say to Jos 9:11
to **m** you by the river Kishon with his Jgs 4:7
Jael came out to **m** Sisera and said to Jgs 4:18
Jael went out to **m** him and said to him, Jgs 4:22
Naphtali, and they went up to **m** them. Jgs 6:35
of my house to **m** me when I return Jgs 11:31
came out to **m** him with tambourines Jgs 11:34
Philistines came shouting to **m** him. Jgs 15:14
saw him, he came with joy to **m** him. Jgs 19:3
up, for you will **m** him immediately." 1 Sm 9:13
you will **m** two men by Rachel's tomb 1 Sm 10:2
up to God at Bethel will **m** you there, 1 Sm 10:3
you will **m** a group of prophets 1 Sm 10:5
Now when these signs **m** you, do what 1 Sm 10:7
Saul went out to **m** him and greet 1 Sm 13:10
went up after Saul to **m** the army; 1 Sm 13:15
Samuel rose early to **m** Saul in the 1 Sm 15:12
city came to **m** him trembling and 1 Sm 16:4
and came and drew near to **m** David, 1 Sm 17:48
the battle line to **m** the Philistine. 1 Sm 17:48
singing and dancing, to **m** King Saul, 1 Sm 18:6
came to **m** David trembling 1 Sm 21:1
who sent you this day to **m** me! 1 Sm 25:32
you had hurried and come to **m** me, 1 Sm 25:34
they went out to **m** David and to 1 Sm 30:21
meet David and to **m** the people who 1 Sm 30:21
of Saul came out to **m** David and said, 2 Sm 6:20
it was told David, he sent to **m** them, 2 Sm 10:5
the Archite came to **m** him with his 2 Sm 15:32
Absalom happened to **m** the servants 2 Sm 18:9
came to Gilgal to **m** the king and to 2 Sm 19:15
the men of Judah to **m** King David. 2 Sm 19:16
to come down to **m** my lord the 2 Sm 19:20
of Saul came down to **m** the king. 2 Sm 19:24
he came to Jerusalem to **m** the king, 2 Sm 19:25
is in Gibeon, Amasa came to **m** them. 2 Sm 20:8
he came down to **m** me at the Jordan, 1 Kgs 2:8
the king rose to **m** her and bowed 1 Kgs 2:19
And you shall **m** my wishes by 1 Kgs 5:9
So Obadiah went to **m** Ahab, and 1 Kgs 18:16
him. And Ahab went to **m** Elijah. 1 Kgs 18:16
go down to **m** Ahab king of Israel, 1 Kgs 21:18
go up to **m** the messengers of the king 2 Kgs 1:3
to him, "There came a man to **m** us, 2 Kgs 1:6
he who came to **m** you and told you 2 Kgs 1:7
And they came to **m** him and bowed 2 Kgs 2:15
Run at once to **m** her and say to her, 2 Kgs 4:26
If you **m** anyone, do not greet him, 2 Kgs 4:29
he returned to **m** him and told 2 Kgs 4:31
from the chariot to **m** him and said, 2 Kgs 5:21
turned from his chariot to **m** you? 2 Kgs 5:26
with you and go to **m** the man of God, 2 Kgs 8:8
So Hazael went to **m** him, and took a 2 Kgs 8:9
a horseman and send to **m** them, 2 Kgs 9:17
horseback went to **m** him and said, 2 Kgs 9:18
in his chariot, and went to **m** Jehu, 2 Kgs 9:21
son of Rechab coming to **m** him. 2 Kgs 10:15
Damascus to **m** Tiglath-pileser 2 Kgs 16:10
King Josiah went to **m** him, and 2 Kgs 23:29
David went out to **m** them and said 1 Chr 12:17
men, he sent messengers to **m** them, 1 Chr 19:5
And Asa went out to **m** him, and 2 Chr 14:10
and he went out to **m** Asa and said to 2 Chr 15:2
seer went out to **m** him and said to 2 Chr 19:2
out with Jehoram to **m** Jehu the son 2 Chr 22:7
he went out to **m** the army that came 2 Chr 28:9
and Josiah went out to **m** him. 2 Chr 35:20
and let us **m** together at Hakkephirim Neh 6:2
"Let us **m** together in the house of God, Neh 6:10
for they did not **m** the people of Israel Neh 13:2
They **m** with darkness in the daytime Jb 5:14
still; days of affliction come to **m** me. Jb 30:27
strength; he goes out to **m** the weapons. Jb 39:21
all generations I shall not **m** adversity." Ps 10:6
For you **m** him with rich blessings; you Ps 21:3
ready. Awake, come to **m** me, and see! Ps 59:4
My God in his steadfast love will **m** me; Ps 59:10
your compassion come speedily to **m** us, Ps 79:8
Steadfast love and faithfulness **m**; Ps 85:10
so now I have come out to **m** you, to Prv 7:15
there you do not **m** words of knowledge. Prv 14:7
who devise good **m** steadfast love and Prv 14:22
Let a man **m** a she-bear robbed of her Prv 17:12
The rich and the poor **m** together; the Prv 22:2
man and the oppressor **m** together; Prv 29:13
the LORD said to Isaiah, "Go out to **m** Ahaz, Is 7:3
is stirred up to **m** you when you come; Is 14:9
m the fugitive with bread, O inhabitants Is 21:14
And wild animals shall **m** with hyenas; Is 34:14
You **m** him who joyfully works Is 64:5
May their men **m** death by pestilence, Jer 18:21
came out from Mizpah to **m** them, Jer 41:6
One runner runs to **m** another, and one Jer 51:31
and one messenger to **m** another, Jer 51:31
on earth who can **m** the king's demand, Dn 2:10
together, unless they have agreed to **m**? Am 3:3
do this to you, prepare to **m** your God, Am 4:12
'Disaster shall not overtake or **m** us.' Am 9:10
another angel came forward to **m** him Zec 2:3
behold, all the city came out to **m** Jesus, Mt 8:34
lamps and went to **m** the bridegroom. Mt 25:1
is the bridegroom! Come out to **m** him.' Mt 25:6
carrying a jar of water will **m** you. Mk 14:13
ten thousand to **m** him who comes Lk 14:31
carrying a jar of water will **m** you. Lk 22:10
of palm trees and went out to **m** him, Jn 12:13
the crowd went to **m** him was that they Jn 12:18
chief priests and all the council to **m**, Acts 22:30
Appius and Three Taverns to **m** us. Acts 28:15
—unless indeed you fail to **m** the test! 2 Cor 13:5
in the clouds to **m** the Lord in the 1 Thes 4:17
not neglecting to **m** together, as is the Heb 10:25
when you **m** trials of various kinds, Jas 1:2

MEETING (150)
In the tent of **m**, outside the veil that is Ex 27:21
go into the tent of **m** or when they come Ex 28:43
of the tent of **m** and wash them with Ex 29:4
bring the bull before the tent of **m**. Ex 29:10
LORD at the entrance of the tent of **m**, Ex 29:11
into the tent of **m** to minister in the Ex 29:30
basket in the entrance of the tent of **m**. Ex 29:32
of the tent of **m** before the LORD, Ex 29:42
consecrate the tent of **m** and the altar. Ex 29:44
give it for the service of the tent of **m**, Ex 30:16
it between the tent of **m** and the altar, Ex 30:18
When they go into the tent of **m**, or Ex 30:20
anoint the tent of **m** and the ark of Ex 30:26
in the tent of **m** where I shall meet Ex 30:36
the tent of **m**, and the ark of the Ex 31:7
the camp, and he called it the tent of **m**. Ex 33:7
the LORD would go out to the tent of **m**, Ex 33:7
to be used for the tent of **m**, Ex 35:21
in the entrance of the tent of **m**. Ex 38:8
bases for the entrance of the tent of **m**, Ex 38:30
of the tent of **m** was finished, Ex 39:32
of the tabernacle, for the tent of **m**; Ex 39:40
erect the tabernacle of the tent of **m**. Ex 40:2
door of the tabernacle of the tent of **m**, Ex 40:6
between the tent of **m** and the altar, Ex 40:7
of the tent of **m** and shall wash them Ex 40:12
He put the table in the tent of **m**, on the Ex 40:22
He put the lampstand in the tent of **m**, Ex 40:24
altar in the tent of **m** before the veil, Ex 40:26
of the tabernacle of the tent of **m**, Ex 40:29
between the tent of **m** and the altar, Ex 40:30
When they went into the tent of **m**, and Ex 40:32
Then the cloud covered the tent of **m**, Ex 40:34
enter the tent of **m** because the cloud Ex 40:35
and spoke to him from the tent of **m**, Lv 1:1
bring it to the entrance of the tent of **m**, Lv 1:3
that is at the entrance of the tent of **m**. Lv 1:5
and kill it at the entrance of the tent of **m**, Lv 3:2
and kill it in front of the tent of **m**; Lv 3:8
head and kill it in front of the tent of **m**, Lv 3:13
of the tent of **m** before the LORD and Lv 4:4
of the bull and bring it into the tent of **m**, Lv 4:5
before the LORD that is in the tent of **m**, Lv 4:7
that is at the entrance of the tent of **m**. Lv 4:7
and bring it in front of the tent of **m**. Lv 4:14
of the blood of the bull into the tent of **m**, Lv 4:16
that is in the tent of **m** before the LORD, Lv 4:18
that is at the entrance of the tent of **m**. Lv 4:18
the court of the tent of **m** they shall eat it. Lv 6:16
be eaten, in the court of the tent of **m**. Lv 6:26
into the tent of **m** to make atonement in Lv 6:30
at the entrance of the tent of **m**." Lv 8:3
assembled at the entrance of the tent of **m**. Lv 8:4
the flesh at the entrance of the tent of **m**, Lv 8:31
entrance of the tent of **m** for seven days, Lv 8:33
of the tent of **m** you shall remain day Lv 8:35
commanded in front of the tent of **m**, Lv 9:5
and Aaron went into the tent of **m**, Lv 9:23
go outside the entrance of the tent of **m**, Lv 10:7
with you, when you go into the tent of **m**, Lv 10:9
entrance of the tent of **m** a lamb a year Lv 12:6
LORD, at the entrance of the tent of **m**. Lv 14:11
priest, to the entrance of the tent of **m**, Lv 14:23
of the tent of **m** and give them to Lv 15:14
priest, to the entrance of the tent of **m**. Lv 15:29
the LORD at the entrance of the tent of **m**. Lv 16:7
And so he shall do for the tent of **m**, Lv 16:16
be in the tent of **m** from the time he Lv 16:17
Place and the tent of **m** and the altar, Lv 16:20
into the tent of **m** and shall take off Lv 16:23
for the tent of **m** and for the altar, Lv 16:33
entrance of the tent of **m** to offer it as a Lv 17:4
the priest at the entrance of the tent of **m**, Lv 17:5
of the tent of **m** and burn the fat Lv 17:6
entrance of the tent of **m** to offer it to the Lv 17:9
LORD, to the entrance of the tent of **m**, Lv 19:21
the veil of the testimony, in the tent of **m**, Lv 24:3
the wilderness of Sinai, in the tent of **m**, Nm 1:1
camp facing the tent of **m** on every side. Nm 2:2
"Then the tent of **m** shall set out, with Nm 2:17
whole congregation before the tent of **m**, Nm 3:7
all the furnishings of the tent of **m**, Nm 3:8
the tent of **m** involved the tabernacle, Nm 3:25
screen for the entrance of the tent of **m**, Nm 3:25
before the tent of **m** toward the sunrise, Nm 3:38
on duty, to do the work in the tent of **m**. Nm 4:3
of the sons of Kohath in the tent of **m**: Nm 4:4
things of the tent of **m** that the sons of Nm 4:15
to do duty, to do service in the tent of **m**. Nm 4:23
and the tent of **m** with its covering and Nm 4:25
screen for the entrance of the tent of **m** Nm 4:25
sons of the Gershonites in the tent of **m**, Nm 4:28
duty, to do the service of the tent of **m**. Nm 4:30
whole of their service in the tent of **m**: Nm 4:31
whole of their service in the tent of **m**, Nm 4:33
on duty, for service in the tent of **m**; Nm 4:35

all who served in the tent of **m**, Nm 4:37
on duty for service in the tent of **m**— Nm 4:39
all who served in the tent of **m**, Nm 4:41
on duty, for service in the tent of **m**— Nm 4:43
of bearing burdens in the tent of **m**, Nm 4:47
priest to the entrance of the tent of **m**, Nm 6:10
to the entrance of the tent of **m**, Nm 6:13
of the tent of **m** and shall take the Nm 6:18
be used in the service of the tent of **m**, Nm 7:5
into the tent of **m** to speak with the Nm 7:89
before the tent of **m** and assemble the Nm 8:9
shall go in to serve at the tent of **m**, Nm 8:15
at the tent of **m** and to make atonement Nm 8:19
in the tent of **m** before Aaron and his Nm 8:22
do duty in the service of the tent of **m**. Nm 8:24
in the tent of **m** by keeping guard, Nm 8:26
to you at the entrance of the tent of **m**. Nm 10:3
them, and bring them to the tent of **m**, Nm 11:16
to the tent of **m**." And the three of them Nm 12:4
at the tent of **m** to all the people Nm 14:10
of the tent of **m** with Moses and Nm 16:18
them at the entrance of the tent of **m**. Nm 16:19
they turned toward the tent of **m**. Nm 16:42
came to the front of the tent of **m**, Nm 16:43
Moses at the entrance of the tent of **m**, Nm 16:50
in the tent of **m** before the testimony, Nm 17:4
over the tent of **m** for all the service Nm 18:4
LORD, to do the service of the tent of **m**. Nm 18:6
they do, their service in the tent of **m**, Nm 18:21
Israel do not come near the tent of **m**, Nm 18:22
shall do the service of the tent of **m**, Nm 18:23
for your service in the tent of **m**. Nm 18:31
the front of the tent of **m** seven times. Nm 19:4
of the tent of **m** and fell on their Nm 20:6
in the entrance of the tent of **m**. Nm 25:6
at the entrance of the tent of **m**, Nm 27:2
and brought it into the tent of **m**, Nm 31:54
and present yourselves in the tent of **m**, Dt 31:14
presented themselves in the tent of **m**. Dt 31:14
at Shiloh and set up the tent of **m** there. Jos 18:1
LORD, at the entrance of the tent of **m**. Jos 19:51
at the entrance to the tent of **m**. 1 Sm 2:22
up the ark of the LORD, the tent of **m**, 1 Kgs 8:4
of the tent of **m** until Solomon built 1 Chr 6:32
at the entrance of the tent of **m**. 1 Chr 9:21
of the tent of **m** and the sanctuary, 1 Chr 23:32
was at Gibeon, for the tent of **m** of God, 2 Chr 1:3
the LORD, which was at the tent of **m**, 2 Chr 1:6
at Gibeon, from before the tent of **m**, 2 Chr 1:13
they brought up the ark, the tent of **m**, 2 Chr 5:5
have roared in the midst of your **m** place; Ps 74:4
they burned all the **m** places of God in Ps 74:8
like a garden, laid in ruins his **m** place; Lam 2:6
And after the **m** of the synagogue Acts 13:43

MEETS (8)
Esau my brother **m** you and asks Gn 32:17
when he **m** him, he shall put him to Nm 35:19
murderer to death when he **m** him. Nm 35:21
and a man **m** her in the city and lies Dt 22:23
country a man **m** a young woman Dt 22:25
"If a man **m** a virgin who is not Dt 22:28
And behold, the woman **m** him, dressed Prv 7:10
the east whom victory **m** at every step? Is 41:2

MEGIDDO (12)
of Taanach, one; the king of **M**, one; Jos 12:21
the inhabitants of **M** and its villages; Jos 17:11
or the inhabitants of **M** and its villages, Jgs 1:27
at Taanach, by the waters of **M**; Jgs 5:19
M, and all Beth-shean that is beside 1 Kgs 4:12
and Hazor and **M** and Gezer 1 Kgs 9:15
And he fled to **M** and died there. 2 Kgs 9:27
and Pharaoh Neco killed him at **M**, 2 Kgs 23:29
a chariot from **M** and brought him 2 Kgs 23:30
and its towns, **M** and its towns, 1 Chr 7:29
but came to fight in the plain of **M**. 2 Chr 35:22
for Hadad-rimmon in the plain of **M**. Zec 12:11

MEHETABEL (3)
his wife's name was **M**, the daughter of Gn 36:39
and his wife's name was **M**, the 1 Chr 1:50
Shemaiah the son of Delaiah, son of **M**, Neh 6:10

MEHIDA (2)
the sons of Bazluth, the sons of **M**, the Ezr 2:52
the sons of Bazlith, the sons of **M**, the Neh 7:54

MEHIR (1)
the brother of Shuhah, fathered **M**, 1 Chr 4:11

MEHOLATHITE (2)
was given to Adriel the **M** for a wife. 1 Sm 18:19
to Adriel the son of Barzillai the **M**; 2 Sm 21:8

MEHUJAEL (2)
was born Irad, and Irad fathered **M**, Gn 4:18
Mehujael, and **M** fathered Methushael, Gn 4:18

MEHUMAN (1)
merry with wine, he commanded **M**, Est 1:10

MELATIAH (1)
to them repaired **M** the Gibeonite and Neh 3:7

MELCHI (2)
of Matthat, the son of Levi, the son of **M**, Lk 3:24
the son of **M**, the son of Addi, the son of Lk 3:28

MELCHIZEDEK (10)
And **M** king of Salem brought out Gn 14:18
are a priest forever after the order of **M**." Ps 110:4
are a priest forever, after the order of **M**." Heb 5:6
God a high priest after the order of **M**. Heb 5:10
high priest forever after the order of **M**. Heb 6:20
For this **M**, king of Salem, priest of the Heb 7:1
loins of his ancestor when **M** met him. Heb 7:10
priest to arise after the order of **M**, Heb 7:11
priest arises in the likeness of **M**, Heb 7:15
a priest forever, after the order of **M**." Heb 7:17

MELEA (1)
the son of **M**, the son of Menna, the son Lk 3:31

MELECH (2)
Micah: Pithon, **M**, Tarea, and Ahaz. 1 Chr 8:35
Micah: Pithon, **M**, Tahrea, and Ahaz. 1 Chr 9:41

MELODY (12)
I will sing; I will make **m** to the LORD, Jgs 5:3
joy; I will sing and make **m** to the LORD. Ps 27:6
make **m** to him with the harp of ten Ps 33:2
is steadfast! I will sing and make **m**! Ps 57:7
the lute and the harp, to the **m** of the lyre. Ps 92:3
lyre, with the lyre and the sound of **m**! Ps 98:5
will sing and make **m** with all my Ps 108:1
make **m** to our God on the lyre! Ps 147:7
making **m** to him with tambourine Ps 149:3
Make sweet **m**; sing many songs, that Is 23:16
to the **m** of your harps I will not listen. Am 5:23
singing and making **m** to the Lord Eph 5:19

MELONS (1)
cost nothing, the cucumbers, the **m**, Nm 11:5

MELT (21)
Our brothers have made our hearts **m**, Dt 1:28
the heart of his fellows **m** like his own.' Dt 20:8
of the land **m** away before you. Jos 2:9
of the land **m** away because of Jos 2:24
with me made the heart of the people **m**; Jos 14:8
of a lion, will utterly **m** with fear, 2 Sm 17:10
When they **m**, they disappear; when it is Jb 6:17
The mountains **m** like wax before the Ps 97:5
be feeble, and every human heart will **m**. Is 13:7
O city; **m** in fear, O Philistia, all of you! Is 14:31
of the Egyptians will **m** within them. Is 19:1
and have made us **m** in the hand of our Is 64:7
they **m** in fear, they are troubled like Jer 49:23
Every heart will **m**, and all hands will Ezk 21:7
that their hearts may **m**, and many Ezk 21:15
to blow the fire on it in order to **m** it, Ezk 22:20
and I will put you in and **m** you. Ezk 22:20
And the mountains will **m** under him, Mi 1:4
quake before him; the hills **m**; Na 1:5
Hearts **m** and knees tremble; anguish is Na 2:10
heavenly bodies will **m** as they burn! 2 Pt 3:12

MELTED (12)
inhabitants of Canaan have **m** away. Ex 15:15
eat; but when the sun grew hot, it **m**. Ex 16:21
as soon as we heard it, our hearts **m**, Jos 2:11
their hearts **m** and there was no longer Jos 5:1
hearts of the people **m** and became as Jos 7:5
fire, and his bonds **m** off his hands. Jgs 15:14
is like wax; it is **m** within my breast; Ps 22:14
their courage **m** away in their evil Ps 107:26
and you shall be **m** in the midst of it. Ezk 22:21
As silver is **m** in a furnace, so you Ezk 22:22
so you shall be **m** in the midst of it, Ezk 22:22
that its uncleanness may be **m** in it, Ezk 24:11

MELTS (8)
totter; he utters his voice, the earth **m**. Ps 46:6
drive them away; as wax **m** before fire, Ps 68:2
he gnashes his teeth and **m** away; Ps 112:10
My soul **m** away for sorrow; Ps 119:28
He sends out his word, and **m** them; he Ps 147:18
squares everyone wails and **m** in tears. Is 15:3
hosts, he who touches the earth and it **m**, Am 9:5
river gates are opened; the palace **m** away; Na 2:6

MEMBER (11)
and a **m** of my household will be my Gn 15:3
you or to a **m** of the stranger's clan, Lv 25:47
a respected **m** of the Council, Mk 15:43
Arimathea. He was a **m** of the council, Lk 23:50
Manaen a **m** of the court of Herod the Acts 13:1
a **m** of the tribe of Benjamin. Rom 11:1
not consist of one **m** but of many. 1 Cor 12:14
If all were a single **m**, where would 1 Cor 12:19
If one **m** suffers, all suffer together; if 1 Cor 12:26
suffer together; if one **m** is honored, 1 Cor 12:26
So also the tongue is a small **m**, yet it Jas 3:5

MEMBERS (30)
and all the **m** of his household, Gn 36:6
The **m** of the half-tribe of Manasseh 1 Chr 5:23
and all my **m** are like a shadow. Jb 17:7
whose **m** were like those of donkeys, Ezk 23:20
lose one of your **m** than that your whole Mt 5:29
lose one of your **m** than that your whole Mt 5:30
Do not present your **m** to sin as Rom 6:13
and your **m** to God as instruments for Rom 6:13
you once presented your **m** as slaves to Rom 6:19
so now present your **m** as slaves to Rom 6:19
were at work in our **m** to bear fruit for Rom 7:5
I see in my **m** another law waging war Rom 7:23
to the law of sin that dwells in my **m**. Rom 7:23
For as in one body we have many **m**, Rom 12:4
and the **m** do not all have the same Rom 12:4
and individually **m** one of another. Rom 12:5
that your bodies are **m** of Christ? 1 Cor 6:15
I then take the **m** of Christ and make 1 Cor 6:15
and make them **m** of a prostitute? 1 Cor 6:15
as the body is one and has many **m**, 1 Cor 12:12
members, and all the **m** of the body, 1 Cor 12:12
is, God arranged the **m** in the body, 1 Cor 12:18
but that the **m** may have the same 1 Cor 12:25
of Christ and individually **m** of it. 1 Cor 12:27
with the saints and **m** of the household Eph 2:19
are fellow heirs, **m** of the same body, Eph 3:6
neighbor, for we are **m** one of another. Eph 4:25
because we are **m** of his body. Eph 5:30
and especially for **m** of his household, 1 Tm 5:8
The tongue is set among our **m**, staining Jas 3:6

MEMORABLE (1)
gave orders to bring the book of **m** deeds, Est 6:1

MEMORIAL (19)
"This day shall be for you a **m** day, and Ex 12:14
hand and as a **m** between your eyes, Ex 13:9
"Write this as a **m** in a book and recite Ex 17:14
burn this as its **m** portion on the altar, Lv 2:2
the grain offering its **m** portion and burn Lv 2:9
shall burn as its **m** portion some of the Lv 2:16
of it as its **m** portion and burn this Lv 5:12
burn this as its **m** portion on the altar, Lv 6:15
a **m** proclaimed with blast of trumpets, Lv 23:24
with the bread as a **m** portion as a food Lv 24:7
of the grain offering, as its **m** portion, Nm 5:26
as a **m** for the people of Israel before Nm 31:54
be to the people of Israel a **m** forever." Jos 4:7
A Psalm of David, for the **m** offering. Ps 38:T
Of David, for the **m** offering. Ps 70:T
and the doorpost you have set up your **m**; Is 57:8
who makes a **m** offering of frankincense, Is 66:3
God of hosts, the LORD is his **m** name: Hos 12:5
alms have ascended as a **m** before God. Acts 10:4

MEMORY (11)
utterly blot out the **m** of Amalek from Ex 17:14
shall blot out the **m** of Amalek from Dt 25:19
I will wipe them from human **m**," Dt 32:26
His **m** perishes from the earth, and he Jb 18:17
out; the very **m** of them has perished. Ps 9:6
to cut off the **m** of them from the earth. Ps 34:16
he may cut off the **m** of them from the Ps 109:15
The **m** of the righteous is a blessing, Prv 10:7
reward, for the **m** of them is forgotten. Eccl 9:5
has done will also be told in **m** of her." Mt 26:13
she has done will be told in **m** of her." Mk 14:9

MEMPHIS (8)
fools, and the princes of **M** are deluded; Is 19:13
the men of **M** and Tahpanhes have Jer 2:16
of Egypt, at Migdol, at Tahpanhes, at **M**, Jer 44:1
proclaim in **M** and Tahpanhes; Jer 46:14
For **M** shall become a waste, a ruin, Jer 46:19
and put an end to the images in **M**; Ezk 30:13
and **M** shall face enemies by day. Ezk 30:16
shall gather them; **M** shall bury them. Hos 9:6

MEMUCAN (3)
Tarshish, Meres, Marsena, and **M**, Est 1:14
Then **M** said in the presence of the king Est 1:16
princes, and the king did as **M** proposed. Est 1:21

MEN (1339)
These were the mighty **m** who were of Gn 6:4
men who were of old, the **m** of renown. Gn 6:4
Pharaoh gave **m** orders concerning Gn 12:20
Now the **m** of Sodom were wicked, Gn 13:13
captive, he led forth his trained **m**, Gn 14:14
but what the young **m** have eaten, Gn 14:24
the share of the **m** who went with me. Gn 14:24
male among the **m** of Abraham's Gn 17:23
And all the **m** of his house, those born Gn 17:27

three **m** were standing in front of him.	Gn 18:2
Then the **m** set out from there, and	Gn 18:16
So the **m** turned from there and went	Gn 18:22
before they lay down, the **m** of the city,	Gn 19:4
the men of the city, the **m** of Sodom,	Gn 19:4
"Where are the **m** who came to you	Gn 19:5
Lot went out to the **m** at the entrance,	Gn 19:6
Only do nothing to these **m**, for they	Gn 19:8
But the **m** reached out their hands and	Gn 19:10
with blindness the **m** who were at	Gn 19:11
Then the **m** said to Lot, "Have you	Gn 19:12
So the **m** seized him and his wife and	Gn 19:16
And the **m** were very much afraid.	Gn 20:8
and the two **m** made a covenant.	Gn 21:27
and took two of his young **m** with him,	Gn 22:3
Then Abraham said to his young **m**,	Gn 22:5
So Abraham returned to his young **m**,	Gn 22:19
the daughters of the **m** of the city are	Gn 24:13
the feet of the **m** who were with him.	Gn 24:32
And he and the **m** who were with him	Gn 24:54
and Abraham's servant and his **m**.	Gn 24:59
When the **m** of the place asked him	Gn 26:7
"lest the **m** of the place should kill me	Gn 26:7
there are four hundred **m** with him."	Gn 32:6
you have striven with God and with **m**,	Gn 32:28
coming, and four hundred **m** with him.	Gn 33:1
and the **m** were indignant and very	Gn 34:7
city and spoke to the **m** of their city,	Gn 34:20
"These **m** are at peace with us; let them	Gn 34:21
this condition will the **m** agree to dwell	Gn 34:22
And he asked the **m** of the place,	Gn 38:21
Also, the **m** of the place said, 'No cult	Gn 38:22
and none of the **m** of the house was	Gn 39:11
she called to the **m** of her household	Gn 39:14
magicians of Egypt and all its wise **m**.	Gn 41:8
all sons of one man. We are honest **m**.	Gn 42:11
if you are honest **m**, let one of your	Gn 42:19
But we said to him, 'We are honest **m**;	Gn 42:31
I shall know that you are honest **m**:	Gn 42:33
that you are not spies but honest **m**,	Gn 42:34
So the **m** took this present, and they	Gn 43:15
his house, "Bring the **m** into the house,	Gn 43:16
for the **m** are to dine with me at noon."	Gn 43:16
and brought the **m** to Joseph's house.	Gn 43:17
And the **m** were afraid because they	Gn 43:18
had brought the **m** into Joseph's house	Gn 43:24
And the **m** looked at one another in	Gn 43:33
the **m** were sent away with their	Gn 44:3
to his steward, "Up, follow after the **m**,	Gn 44:4
And the **m** are shepherds, for they have	Gn 46:32
he took five **m** and presented them	Gn 47:2
if you know any able **m** among them,	Gn 47:6
For in their anger they killed **m**, and in	Gn 49:6
for all the **m** who were seeking your life	Ex 4:19
be laid on the **m** that they may labor	Ex 5:9
summoned the wise **m** and the sorcerers,	Ex 7:11
Let the **m** go, that they may serve the	Ex 10:7
Go, the **m** among you, and serve the	Ex 10:11
about six hundred thousand **m** on foot,	Ex 12:37
Moses said to Joshua, "Choose for us **m**,	Ex 17:9
look for able **m** from all the people,	Ex 18:21
from all the people, **m** who fear God,	Ex 18:21
and place such **m** over the people as	Ex 18:21
Moses chose able **m** out of all Israel	Ex 18:25
"When **m** quarrel and one strikes the	Ex 21:18
"When **m** strive together and hit a	Ex 21:22
And he sent young **m** of the people of	Ex 24:5
his hand on the chief **m** of the people of	Ex 24:11
And I have given to all able **m** ability,	Ex 31:6
about three thousand **m** of the people	Ex 32:28
So they came, both **m** and women. All	Ex 35:22
All the **m** and women, the people of	Ex 35:29
years old and upward, for 603,550 **m**.	Ex 38:26
the names of the **m** who shall assist you.	Nm 1:5
and Aaron took these **m** who had been	Nm 1:17
the help of the chiefs of Israel, twelve **m**,	Nm 1:44
there were certain **m** who were unclean	Nm 9:6
And those **m** said to him, "We are	Nm 9:7
"Gather for me seventy **m** of the elders	Nm 11:16
he gathered seventy **m** of the elders	Nm 11:24
Now two **m** remained in the camp,	Nm 11:26
"Send **m** to spy out the land of Canaan,	Nm 13:2
all of them **m** who were heads of the	Nm 13:3
the names of the **m** whom Moses sent	Nm 13:16
Then the **m** who had gone up with	Nm 13:31
none of the **m** who have seen my	Nm 14:22
And the **m** whom Moses sent to spy	Nm 14:36
the **m** who brought up a bad report of	Nm 14:37
Of those **m** who went to spy out the	Nm 14:38
son of Peleth, sons of Reuben, took **m**.	Nm 16:1
from the assembly, well-known **m**.	Nm 16:2
Will you put out the eyes of these **m**?	Nm 16:14
from the tents of these wicked **m**,	Nm 16:26
If these **m** die as all men die, or if they	Nm 16:29
If these men die as all **m** die, or if they	Nm 16:29
know that these **m** have despised the	Nm 16:30
consumed the 250 **m** offering the	Nm 16:35
censers of these **m** who have sinned	Nm 16:38
and said, "Who are these **m** with you?"	Nm 22:9
him, "If the **m** have come to call you,	Nm 22:20
LORD said to Balaam, "Go with the **m**,	Nm 22:35
kill those of his **m** who have yoked	Nm 25:5
died, when the fire devoured 250 **m**,	Nm 26:10
"Arm **m** from among you for the war,	Nm 31:3
priest said to the **m** in the army who	Nm 31:21
a tribute from the **m** of war who went	Nm 31:28
from that of the **m** who had served in	Nm 31:42
have counted the **m** of war who	Nm 31:49
(The **m** in the army had each taken	Nm 31:53
'Surely none of the **m** who came up	Nm 32:11
fathers' place, a brood of sinful **m**,	Nm 32:14
the names of the **m** who shall divide	Nm 34:17
These are the names of the **m**: Of the	Nm 34:19
These are the **m** whom the LORD	Nm 34:29
wise, understanding, and experienced **m**,	Dt 1:13
of your tribes, wise and experienced **m**,	Dt 1:15
me and said, 'Let us send **m** before us,	Dt 1:22
to me, and I took twelve **m** from you,	Dt 1:23
'Not one of these **m** of this evil	Dt 1:35
entire generation, that is, the **m** of war,	Dt 2:14
as soon as all the **m** of war had perished	Dt 2:16
to destruction every city, **m**, women,	Dt 2:34
to destruction every city, **m**, women,	Dt 3:6
All your **m** of valor shall cross over	Dt 3:18
among you all the **m** who followed the	Dt 4:3
landmark, which the **m** of old have set,	Dt 19:14
Then all the **m** of the city shall stone	Dt 21:21
and the **m** of her city shall stone her to	Dt 22:21
is a dispute between **m** and they come	Dt 25:1
"When **m** fight with one another and	Dt 25:11
shall declare to all the **m** of Israel in a	Dt 27:14
and your officers, all the **m** of Israel,	Dt 29:10
Assemble the people, **m**, women, and	Dt 31:12
live, and not die, but let his **m** be few."	Dt 33:6
but all the **m** of valor among you shall	Jos 1:14
of Nun sent two **m** secretly from Shittim	Jos 2:1
m of Israel have come here tonight to	Jos 2:2
"Bring out the **m** who have come to you,	Jos 2:3
had taken the two **m** and hidden them.	Jos 2:4
And she said, "True, the **m** came to me,	Jos 2:4
to be closed at dark, the **m** went out.	Jos 2:5
out. I do not know where the **m** went.	Jos 2:5
So the **m** pursued after them on the way	Jos 2:7
Before the **m** lay down, she came up to	Jos 2:8
and said to the **m**, "I know that the LORD	Jos 2:9
And the **m** said to her, "Our life for	Jos 2:14
The **m** said to her, "We will be guiltless	Jos 2:17
Then the two **m** returned. They came	Jos 2:23
therefore take twelve **m** from the tribes	Jos 3:12
"Take twelve **m** from the people, from	Jos 4:2
called the twelve **m** from the people	Jos 4:4
who came out of Egypt, all the **m** of war,	Jos 5:4
the **m** of war who came out of Egypt,	Jos 5:6
with its king and mighty **m** of valor.	Jos 6:2
all the **m** of war going around the city	Jos 6:3
and let the armed **m** pass on before the	Jos 6:7
The armed **m** were walking before the	Jos 6:9
And the armed **m** were walking before	Jos 6:13
city to destruction, both **m** and women,	Jos 6:21
But to the two **m** who had spied out the	Jos 6:22
So the young **m** who had been spies	Jos 6:23
Joshua sent **m** from Jericho to Ai, which	Jos 7:2
the land." And the **m** went up and spied	Jos 7:2
two or three thousand **m** go up and	Jos 7:3
So about 3,000 **m** went up there from the	Jos 7:4
people. And they fled before the **m** of Ai,	Jos 7:4
and the **m** of Ai killed about thirty-six of	Jos 7:5
thirty-six of their **m** and chased them	Jos 7:5
Take all the fighting **m** with you, and	Jos 8:1
and all the fighting **m** arose to go up	Jos 8:3
chose 30,000 mighty **m** of valor and	Jos 8:3
And all the fighting **m** who were with	Jos 8:11
He took about 5,000 **m** and set them in	Jos 8:12
he and all his people, the **m** of the city,	Jos 8:14
And the **m** in the ambush rose quickly	Jos 8:19
So when the **m** of Ai looked back,	Jos 8:20
back and struck down the **m** of Ai.	Jos 8:21
who fell that day, both **m** and women,	Jos 8:25
and said to him and to the **m** of Israel,	Jos 9:6
But the **m** of Israel said to the Hivites,	Jos 9:7
So the **m** took some of their provisions,	Jos 9:14
than Ai, and all its **m** were warriors.	Jos 10:2
And the **m** of Gibeon sent to Joshua at	Jos 10:6
with him, and all the mighty **m** of valor.	Jos 10:7
of the cave and set **m** by it to guard	Jos 10:18
summoned all the **m** of Israel and	Jos 10:24
to the chiefs of the **m** of war who had	Jos 10:24
Provide three **m** from each tribe, and I	Jos 18:4
So the **m** arose and went, and Joshua	Jos 18:8
So the **m** went and passed up and down	Jos 18:9
And the **m** of Judah fought against	Jgs 1:8
And afterward the **m** of Judah went down	Jgs 1:9
the Moabites, all strong, able-bodied **m**;	Jgs 3:29
you, 'Go, gather your **m** at Mount Tabor,	Jgs 4:6
And 10,000 **m** went up at his heels, and	Jgs 4:10
iron, and all the **m** who were with him,	Jgs 4:13
Tabor with 10,000 **m** following him.	Jgs 4:14
So Gideon took ten **m** of his servants	Jgs 6:27
of his family and the **m** of the town to do	Jgs 6:27
When the **m** of the town rose early in	Jgs 6:28
Then the **m** of the town said to Joash,	Jgs 6:30
their hands to their mouths, was 300 **m**,	Jgs 7:6
"With the 300 **m** who lapped I will save	Jgs 7:7
man to his tent, but retained the 300 **m**.	Jgs 7:8
outposts of the armed **m** who were in the	Jgs 7:11
divided the 300 **m** into three companies	Jgs 7:16
and the hundred **m** who were with	Jgs 7:19
And the **m** of Israel were called out from	Jgs 7:23
Jordan." So all the **m** of Ephraim were	Jgs 7:24
Then the **m** of Ephraim said to him,	Jgs 8:1
he and the 300 **m** who were with him,	Jgs 8:4
So he said to the **m** of Succoth, "Please	Jgs 8:5
and the **m** of Penuel answered him as the	Jgs 8:8
answered him as the **m** of Succoth had	Jgs 8:8
And he said to the **m** of Penuel, "When I	Jgs 8:9
with their army, about 15,000 **m**,	Jgs 8:10
there had fallen 120,000 **m** who drew the	Jgs 8:10
and elders of Succoth, seventy-seven **m**.	Jgs 8:14
he came to the **m** of Succoth and said,	Jgs 8:15
bread to your **m** who are exhausted?'"	Jgs 8:15
with them taught the **m** of Succoth a	Jgs 8:16
of Penuel and killed the **m** of the city.	Jgs 8:17
"Where are the **m** whom you killed at	Jgs 8:18
Then the **m** of Israel said to Gideon,	Jgs 8:22
the sons of Jerubbaal, seventy **m**,	Jgs 9:5
by which gods and **m** are honored,	Jgs 9:9
that cheers God and **m** and go hold sway	Jgs 9:13
killed his sons, seventy **m** on one stone,	Jgs 9:18
killed them, and on the **m** of Shechem,	Jgs 9:24
of Shechem put **m** in ambush against	Jgs 9:25
Serve the **m** of Hamor the father of	Jgs 9:28
Abimelech and all the **m** who were with	Jgs 9:34
the shadow of the mountains for **m**."	Jgs 9:36
he said to the **m** who were with him,	Jgs 9:48
also died, about 1,000 **m** and women.	Jgs 9:49
and all the **m** and women and all the	Jgs 9:51
And when the **m** of Israel saw that	Jgs 9:55
the evil of the **m** of Shechem return on	Jgs 9:57
The **m** of Ephraim were called to arms,	Jgs 12:1
gathered all the **m** of Gilead and	Jgs 12:4
And the **m** of Gilead struck Ephraim,	Jgs 12:4
"Let me go over," the **m** of Gilead said to	Jgs 12:5
there, for so the young **m** used to do.	Jgs 14:10
And the **m** of the city said to him on	Jgs 14:18
and struck down thirty **m** of the town	Jgs 14:19
And the **m** of Judah said, "Why have	Jgs 15:10
Then 3,000 **m** of Judah went down to	Jgs 15:11
took it, and with it he struck 1,000 **m**.	Jgs 15:15
have I struck down a thousand **m**."	Jgs 15:16
Now she had **m** lying in ambush in an	Jgs 16:9
Samson!" And the **m** lying in ambush	Jgs 16:12
the house was full of **m** and women.	Jgs 16:27
there were about 3,000 **m** and women,	Jgs 16:27
Dan sent five able **m** from the whole	Jgs 18:2
Then the five **m** departed and came to	Jgs 18:7
So 600 **m** of the tribe of Dan, armed	Jgs 18:11
Then the five **m** who had gone to scout	Jgs 18:14
Now the 600 **m** of the Danites, armed	Jgs 18:16
And the five **m** who had gone to scout	Jgs 18:17
with the 600 **m** armed with weapons	Jgs 18:17
the **m** who were in the houses near	Jgs 18:22
The **m** of the place were Benjaminites.	Jgs 19:16
hearts merry, behold, the **m** of the city,	Jgs 19:22
But the **m** would not listen to him. So	Jgs 19:25
400,000 **m** on foot that drew the sword.	Jgs 20:2
we will take ten **m** of a hundred	Jgs 20:10
So all the **m** of Israel gathered against	Jgs 20:11
tribes of Israel sent **m** through all the	Jgs 20:12
Now therefore give up the **m**, the	Jgs 20:13
on that day 26,000 **m** who drew the	Jgs 20:15
Gibeah, who mustered 700 chosen **m**.	Jgs 20:15
were 700 chosen **m** who were	Jgs 20:16
And the **m** of Israel, apart from	Jgs 20:17
mustered 400,000 **m** who drew the	Jgs 20:17
drew the sword; all these were **m** of war.	Jgs 20:17
And the **m** of Israel went out to fight	Jgs 20:20
and the **m** of Israel drew up the battle	Jgs 20:20
on that day 22,000 **m** of the Israelites.	Jgs 20:21
But the people, the **m** of Israel, took	Jgs 20:22
and destroyed 18,000 **m** of the people of	Jgs 20:25
All these were **m** who drew the sword.	Jgs 20:25
So Israel set **m** in ambush around	Jgs 20:29
open country, about thirty **m** of Israel.	Jgs 20:31
And all the **m** of Israel rose up out of	Jgs 20:33
and the **m** of Israel who were in	Jgs 20:33

Gibeah 10,000 chosen **m** out of all	Jgs 20:34
Israel destroyed 25,100 **m** of Benjamin	Jgs 20:35
All these were **m** who drew the sword.	Jgs 20:35
The **m** of Israel gave ground to	Jgs 20:36
they trusted the **m** in ambush whom	Jgs 20:36
Then the **m** in ambush hurried and	Jgs 20:37
the **m** in ambush moved out and	Jgs 20:37
signal between the **m** of Israel and	Jgs 20:38
of Israel and the **m** in the main	Jgs 20:38
the **m** of Israel should turn in battle.	Jgs 20:39
strike and kill about thirty **m** of Israel.	Jgs 20:39
Then the **m** of Israel turned, and the	Jgs 20:41
and the **m** of Benjamin were dismayed,	Jgs 20:41
their backs before the **m** of Israel in the	Jgs 20:42
Eighteen thousand **m** of Benjamin fell,	Jgs 20:44
of Benjamin fell, all of them **m** of valor.	Jgs 20:44
Five thousand **m** of them were cut	Jgs 20:45
and 2,000 **m** of them were struck down.	Jgs 20:45
Benjamin were 25,000 **m** who drew the	Jgs 20:46
drew the sword, all of them **m** of valor.	Jgs 20:46
But 600 **m** turned and fled toward the	Jgs 20:47
And the **m** of Israel turned back	Jgs 20:48
m and beasts and all that they found.	Jgs 20:48
Now the **m** of Israel had sworn at	Jgs 21:1
of their bravest **m** there and	Jgs 21:10
not charged the young **m** not to touch	Ru 2:9
drink what the young **m** have drawn."	Ru 2:9
to glean, Boaz instructed his young **m**,	Ru 2:15
close by my young **m** until they have	Ru 2:21
that you have not gone after young **m**,	Ru 3:10
And he took ten **m** of the elders of the city	Ru 4:2
Now the sons of Eli were worthless **m**.	1 Sm 2:12
sin of the young **m** was very great in	1 Sm 2:17
for the **m** treated the offering of the	1 Sm 2:17
house shall die by the sword of **m**.	1 Sm 2:33
about four thousand **m** on the field	1 Sm 4:2
Take courage, and be **m**, O Philistines,	1 Sm 4:9
they have been to you; be **m** and fight."	1 Sm 4:9
And when the **m** of Ashdod saw how	1 Sm 5:7
panic, and he afflicted the **m** of the city,	1 Sm 5:9
The **m** who did not die were struck	1 Sm 5:12
The **m** did so, and took two milk cows	1 Sm 6:10
And the **m** of Beth-shemesh offered	1 Sm 6:15
some of the **m** of Beth-shemesh,	1 Sm 6:19
He struck seventy **m** of them, and the	1 Sm 6:19
Then the **m** of Beth-shemesh said,	1 Sm 6:20
And the **m** of Kiriath-jearim came and	1 Sm 7:1
And the **m** of Israel went out from	1 Sm 7:11
of your young **m** and your donkeys,	1 Sm 8:16
Samuel then said to the **m** of Israel,	1 Sm 8:22
"Take one of the young **m** with you,	1 Sm 9:3
will meet two **m** by Rachel's tomb	1 Sm 10:2
Three **m** going up to God at Bethel	1 Sm 10:3
and with him went **m** of valor whose	1 Sm 10:26
and all the **m** of Jabesh said to	1 Sm 11:1
told him the news of the **m** of Jabesh.	1 Sm 11:5
and the **m** of Judah thirty thousand.	1 Sm 11:8
you say to the **m** of Jabesh-gilead:	1 Sm 11:9
came and told the **m** of Jabesh,	1 Sm 11:9
Therefore the **m** of Jabesh said,	1 Sm 11:10
Bring the **m**, that we may put them	1 Sm 11:12
Saul and all the **m** of Israel rejoiced	1 Sm 11:15
Saul chose three thousand **m** of Israel.	1 Sm 13:2
When the **m** of Israel saw that they	1 Sm 13:6
with him, about six hundred **m**.	1 Sm 13:15
with him were about six hundred **m**,	1 Sm 14:2
"Behold, we will cross over to the **m**,	1 Sm 14:8
And the **m** of the garrison hailed	1 Sm 14:12
killed about twenty **m** within as it	1 Sm 14:14
when all the **m** of Israel who had	1 Sm 14:22
And the **m** of Israel had been hard	1 Sm 14:24
two hundred thousand **m** on foot,	1 Sm 15:4
on foot, and ten thousand **m** of Judah.	1 Sm 15:4
One of the young **m** answered,	1 Sm 16:18
And Saul and the **m** of Israel were	1 Sm 17:2
they and all the **m** of Israel were in	1 Sm 17:19
All the **m** of Israel, when they saw	1 Sm 17:24
And the **m** of Israel said, "Have you	1 Sm 17:25
David said to the **m** who stood by	1 Sm 17:26
heard when he spoke to the **m**.	1 Sm 17:28
And the **m** of Israel and Judah rose	1 Sm 17:52
so that Saul set him over the **m** of war.	1 Sm 18:5
arose and went, along with his **m**,	1 Sm 18:27
with the young **m** for such and	1 Sm 21:2
if the young **m** have kept themselves	1 Sm 21:4
vessels of the young **m** are holy even	1 Sm 21:5
were with him about four hundred **m**.	1 Sm 22:2
and the **m** who were with him.	1 Sm 22:6
But David's **m** said to him, "Behold,	1 Sm 23:3
And David and his **m** went to Keilah	1 Sm 23:5
to Keilah, to besiege David and his **m**.	1 Sm 23:8
Will the **m** of Keilah surrender me	1 Sm 23:11
"Will the **m** of Keilah surrender me	1 Sm 23:12
me and my **m** into the hand	1 Sm 23:12
Then David and his **m**, who were	1 Sm 23:13
Now David and his **m** were in the	1 Sm 23:24
And Saul and his **m** went to seek	1 Sm 23:25
and David and his **m** on the other	1 Sm 23:26
As Saul and his **m** were closing in	1 Sm 23:26
on David and his **m** to capture them,	1 Sm 23:26
three thousand chosen **m** out of all	1 Sm 24:2
to seek David and his **m** in front of the	1 Sm 24:2
Now David and his **m** were sitting in	1 Sm 24:3
And the **m** of David said to him, "Here	1 Sm 24:4
He said to his **m**, "The LORD forbid	1 Sm 24:6
David persuaded his **m** with these	1 Sm 24:7
you listen to the words of **m** who say,	1 Sm 24:9
but David and his **m** went up to the	1 Sm 24:22
So David sent ten young **m**. And	1 Sm 25:5
And David said to the young **m**, "Go	1 Sm 25:5
Ask your young **m**, and they will tell	1 Sm 25:8
let my young **m** find favor in	1 Sm 25:8
When David's young **m** came, they	1 Sm 25:9
and give it to **m** who come from I	1 Sm 25:11
So David's young **m** turned away	1 Sm 25:12
And David said to his **m**, "Every	1 Sm 25:13
about four hundred **m** went up after	1 Sm 25:13
But one of the young **m** told Abigail,	1 Sm 25:14
Yet the **m** were very good to us, and	1 Sm 25:15
And she said to her young **m**, "Go on	1 Sm 25:19
David and his **m** came down toward	1 Sm 25:20
did not see the young **m** of my lord,	1 Sm 25:25
given to the young **m** who follow my	1 Sm 25:27
If **m** rise up to pursue you and to	1 Sm 25:29
three thousand chosen **m** of Israel to	1 Sm 26:2
he accept an offering, but if it is **m**,	1 Sm 26:19
one of the young **m** come over and	1 Sm 26:22
and the six hundred **m** who were with	1 Sm 27:2
with Achish at Gath, he and his **m**,	1 Sm 27:3
Now David and his **m** went up and	1 Sm 27:8
that you and your **m** are to go out	1 Sm 28:1
and went, he and two **m** with him.	1 Sm 28:8
and David and his **m** were passing on	1 Sm 29:2
it not be with the heads of the **m** here?	1 Sm 29:4
set out with his **m** early in the	1 Sm 29:11
David and his **m** came to Ziklag	1 Sm 30:1
when David and his **m** came to the	1 Sm 30:3
and the six hundred **m** who were with	1 Sm 30:9
pursued, he and four hundred **m**.	1 Sm 30:10
except four hundred young **m**,	1 Sm 30:17
to the two hundred **m** who had been	1 Sm 30:21
fellows among the **m** who had gone	1 Sm 30:22
where David and his **m** had roamed.	1 Sm 30:31
and the **m** of Israel fled before the	1 Sm 31:1
and his armor-bearer, and all his **m**,	1 Sm 31:6
And when the **m** of Israel who were on	1 Sm 31:7
Jordan saw that the **m** of Israel had	1 Sm 31:7
all the valiant **m** arose and went all	1 Sm 31:12
so did all the **m** who were with him.	2 Sm 1:11
called one of the young **m** and said,	2 Sm 1:15
David brought up his **m** who were with	2 Sm 2:3
And the **m** of Judah came, and there	2 Sm 2:4
"It was the **m** of Jabesh-gilead who	2 Sm 2:4
messengers to the **m** of Jabesh-gilead	2 Sm 2:5
"Let the young **m** arise and compete	2 Sm 2:14
And Abner and the **m** of Israel were	2 Sm 2:17
one of the young **m** and take his	2 Sm 2:21
surely the **m** would not have given up	2 Sm 2:27
and all the **m** stopped and pursued	2 Sm 2:28
And Abner and his **m** went all that	2 Sm 2:29
servants nineteen **m** besides Asahel.	2 Sm 2:30
down of Benjamin 360 of Abner's **m**.	2 Sm 2:31
Joab and his **m** marched all night,	2 Sm 2:32
came with twenty **m** to David at	2 Sm 3:20
for Abner and the **m** who were with	2 Sm 3:20
though anointed king. These **m**,	2 Sm 3:39
son had two **m** who were captains	2 Sm 4:2
when wicked **m** have killed a	2 Sm 4:11
And David commanded his young **m**,	2 Sm 4:12
the king and his **m** went to Jerusalem	2 Sm 5:6
David and his **m** carried them away.	2 Sm 5:21
gathered all the chosen **m** of Israel,	2 Sm 6:1
of Israel, both **m** and women,	2 Sm 6:19
And violent **m** shall afflict them no	2 Sm 7:10
will discipline him with the rod of **m**,	2 Sm 7:14
men, with the stripes of the sons of **m**,	2 Sm 7:14
struck down 22,000 **m** of the Syrians.	2 Sm 8:5
them, for the **m** were greatly ashamed.	2 Sm 10:5
and the king of Maacah with 1,000 **m**,	2 Sm 10:6
with 1,000 men, and the **m** of Tob,	2 Sm 10:6
men, and the men of Tob, 12,000 **m**.	2 Sm 10:6
Joab and all the host of the mighty **m**.	2 Sm 10:7
of Rehob and the **m** of Tob and	2 Sm 10:8
some of the best **m** of Israel and	2 Sm 10:9
The rest of his **m** he put in the	2 Sm 10:10
of the Syrians the **m** of 700 chariots,	2 Sm 10:18
where he knew there were valiant **m**.	2 Sm 11:16
And the **m** of the city came out and	2 Sm 11:17
"The **m** gained an advantage over us	2 Sm 11:23
"There were two **m** in a certain city,	2 Sm 12:1
all the young **m** the king's sons,	2 Sm 13:32
horses, and fifty **m** to run before him.	2 Sm 15:1
stole the hearts of the **m** of Israel.	2 Sm 15:6
went two hundred **m** from Jerusalem	2 Sm 15:11
"The hearts of the **m** of Israel have	2 Sm 15:13
on with all his **m** and all the little	2 Sm 15:22
summer fruit for the young **m** to eat,	2 Sm 16:2
and all the mighty **m** were on his	2 Sm 16:6
So David and his **m** went on the	2 Sm 16:13
and all the people, the **m** of Israel,	2 Sm 16:15
people and all the **m** of Israel have	2 Sm 16:18
"Let me choose twelve thousand **m**,	2 Sm 17:1
father and his **m** are mighty men,	2 Sm 17:8
father and his men are mighty **m**,	2 Sm 17:8
who are with him are valiant **m**.	2 Sm 17:10
him and all the **m** with him not one	2 Sm 17:12
Absalom and all the **m** of Israel said,	2 Sm 17:14
gone, the **m** came up out of the well,	2 Sm 17:21
the Jordan with all the **m** of Israel.	2 Sm 17:24
David mustered the **m** who were with	2 Sm 18:1
And the king said to the **m**, "I myself	2 Sm 18:2
But the **m** said, "You shall not go out.	2 Sm 18:3
And the **m** of Israel were defeated there	2 Sm 18:7
great on that day, twenty thousand **m**.	2 Sm 18:7
And ten young **m**, Joab's	2 Sm 18:15
delivered up the **m** who raised their	2 Sm 18:28
the heart of all the **m** of Judah as one	2 Sm 19:14
come down with the **m** of Judah to	2 Sm 19:16
were a thousand **m** from Benjamin.	2 Sm 19:17
house were but **m** doomed to death	2 Sm 19:28
voice of singing **m** and singing	2 Sm 19:35
Then all the **m** of Israel came to the	2 Sm 19:41
our brothers the **m** of Judah stolen	2 Sm 19:41
and all David's **m** with him?"	2 Sm 19:41
All the **m** of Judah answered the men	2 Sm 19:42
of Judah answered the **m** of Israel,	2 Sm 19:42
And the **m** of Israel answered the	2 Sm 19:43
of Israel answered the **m** of Judah,	2 Sm 19:43
the words of the **m** of Judah were	2 Sm 19:43
than the words of the **m** of Israel.	2 Sm 19:43
So all the **m** of Israel withdrew from	2 Sm 20:2
But the **m** of Judah followed their	2 Sm 20:2
"Call the **m** of Judah together to me	2 Sm 20:4
after him Joab's **m** and the	2 Sm 20:7
the Pelethites, and all the mighty **m**.	2 Sm 20:7
one of Joab's young **m** took his stand	2 Sm 20:11
And all the **m** who were with Joab	2 Sm 20:15
from the **m** of Jabesh-gilead,	2 Sm 21:12
Then David's **m** swore to him, "You	2 Sm 21:17
you delivered me from **m** of violence.	2 Sm 22:49
When one rules justly over **m**, ruling	2 Sm 23:3
But worthless **m** are all like thorns	2 Sm 23:6
of the mighty **m** whom David had:	2 Sm 23:8
the three mighty **m** was Eleazar the	2 Sm 23:9
battle, and the **m** of Israel withdrew.	2 Sm 23:9
and the **m** returned after him only to	2 Sm 23:10
and the **m** fled from the Philistines.	2 Sm 23:11
of the thirty chief **m** went down and	2 Sm 23:13
the three mighty **m** broke through	2 Sm 23:16
the blood of the **m** who went at the	2 Sm 23:17
These things the three mighty **m** did.	2 Sm 23:17
against three hundred **m** and killed	2 Sm 23:18
a name beside the three mighty **m**.	2 Sm 23:22
were 800,000 valiant **m** who drew the	2 Sm 24:9
and the **m** of Judah were 500,000.	2 Sm 24:9
from Dan to Beersheba 70,000 **m**.	2 Sm 24:15
and fifty **m** to run before him.	1 Kgs 1:5
and David's mighty **m** were not with	1 Kgs 1:8
or the mighty **m** or Solomon his	1 Kgs 1:10
the sword two **m** more righteous and	1 Kgs 2:32
For he was wiser than all other **m**,	1 Kgs 4:31
and the draft numbered 30,000 **m**.	1 Kgs 5:13
builders and the **m** of Gebal did	1 Kgs 5:18
And all the **m** of Israel assembled to	1 Kgs 8:2
Happy are your **m**! Happy are your	1 Kgs 10:8
Paran and took **m** with them from	1 Kgs 11:18
And he gathered **m** about him and	1 Kgs 11:24
took counsel with the old **m**,	1 Kgs 12:6
counsel that the old **m** gave him and	1 Kgs 12:8
with the young **m** who had grown	1 Kgs 12:8
And the young **m** who had grown	1 Kgs 12:10
that the old **m** had given him,	1 Kgs 12:13
to the counsel of the young **m**,	1 Kgs 12:14
m passed by and saw the body	1 Kgs 13:25
I hid a hundred **m** of the LORD'S	1 Kgs 18:13
LORD, but Baal's prophets are 450 **m**.	1 Kgs 18:22
in the booths, he said to his **m**,	1 Kgs 20:12
"**M** are coming out from Samaria."	1 Kgs 20:17
fell upon 27,000 **m** who were left.	1 Kgs 20:30
Now the **m** were watching for a	1 Kgs 20:33
set two worthless **m** opposite him,	1 Kgs 21:10
And the **m** of his city, the elders and	1 Kgs 21:11
the two worthless **m** came in and	1 Kgs 21:13
And the worthless **m** brought a	1 Kgs 21:13
together, about four hundred **m**,	1 Kgs 22:6

him a captain of fifty **m** with his fifty. 2 Kgs 1:9
captain of fifty **m** with his fifty. 2 Kgs 1:11
captains of fifty **m** with their fifties, 2 Kgs 1:14
Fifty **m** of the sons of the prophets also 2 Kgs 2:7
are with your servants fifty strong **m**. 2 Kgs 2:16
"Send." They sent therefore fifty **m**. 2 Kgs 2:17
Now the **m** of the city said to Elisha, 2 Kgs 2:19
they poured out some for the **m** to eat. 2 Kgs 4:40
and said, "Pour some out for the **m**, 2 Kgs 4:41
And Elisha said, "Give to the **m**, that 2 Kgs 4:42
before a hundred **m**?" So he repeated, 2 Kgs 4:43
So he repeated, "Give them to the **m**, 2 Kgs 4:43
of Ephraim two young **m** of the sons 2 Kgs 5:22
in the house, and he sent the **m** away, 2 Kgs 5:24
"O LORD, open the eyes of these **m**, 2 Kgs 6:20
there were four **m** who were lepers 2 Kgs 7:3
"Let some **m** take five of the 2 Kgs 7:13
kill their young **m** with the sword 2 Kgs 8:12
were with the great **m** of the city, 2 Kgs 10:6
all his great **m** and his close friends 2 Kgs 10:11
had stationed eighty **m** outside and 2 Kgs 10:24
they each brought his **m** who were to 2 Kgs 11:9
accounting from the **m** into whose 2 Kgs 12:15
that is, from all the wealthy **m**, 2 Kgs 15:20
him with fifty **m** of the people 2 Kgs 15:25
Syria and drove the **m** of Judah from 2 Kgs 16:6
The **m** of Babylon made 2 Kgs 17:30
the **m** of Cuth made Nergal, 2 Kgs 17:30
the **m** of Hamath made Ashima, 2 Kgs 17:30
and not to the **m** sitting on the wall, 2 Kgs 18:27
said to him, "What did these **m** say? 2 Kgs 20:14
with him all the **m** of Judah and all 2 Kgs 23:2
their places with the bones of **m**. 2 Kgs 23:14
that I see?" And the **m** of the city told 2 Kgs 23:17
and all the mighty **m** of valor, 2 Kgs 24:14
and the chief **m** of the land he took 2 Kgs 24:15
to Babylon all the **m** of valor, 2 Kgs 24:16
and all the **m** of war fled by night by 2 Kgs 25:4
been in command of the **m** of war, 2 Kgs 25:19
and five **m** of the king's council 2 Kgs 25:19
and sixty **m** of the people of the land 2 Kgs 25:19
captains and their **m** heard that the 2 Kgs 25:23
came with their **m** to Gedaliah at 2 Kgs 25:23
Gedaliah swore to them and their **m**, 2 Kgs 25:24
came with ten **m** and struck down 2 Kgs 25:25
Ir-nahash. These are the **m** of Recah. 1 Chr 4:12
and Jokim, and the **m** of Cozeba, and 1 Chr 4:22
clan multiply like the **m** of Judah. 1 Chr 4:27
five hundred **m** of the Simeonites, 1 Chr 4:42
had valiant **m** who carried 1 Chr 5:18
2,000 donkeys, and 100,000 **m** alive. 1 Chr 5:21
Jahdiel, mighty warriors, famous **m**, 1 Chr 5:24
These are the **m** whom David put in 1 Chr 6:31
These are the **m** who served and their 1 Chr 6:33
Isshiah, all five of them were chief **m**. 1 Chr 7:3
whom the **m** of Gath who were born 1 Chr 7:21
All of these were **m** of Asher, heads of 1 Chr 7:40
for service in war, was 26,000 **m**. 1 Chr 7:40
to their generations, chief **m**. 1 Chr 8:28
of Ulam were **m** who were mighty 1 Chr 8:40
mighty **m** for the work of the service 1 Chr 9:13
and the **m** of Israel fled before the 1 Chr 10:1
And when all the **m** of Israel who 1 Chr 10:7
all the valiant **m** arose and took 1 Chr 10:12
are the chiefs of David's mighty **m**, 1 Chr 11:10
is an account of David's mighty **m**: 1 Chr 11:11
the three mighty **m** was Eleazar the 1 Chr 11:12
and the **m** fled from the Philistines. 1 Chr 11:13
of the thirty chief **m** went down to 1 Chr 11:15
the three mighty **m** broke through 1 Chr 11:18
I drink the lifeblood of these **m**? 1 Chr 11:19
things did the three mighty **m**. 1 Chr 11:19
spear against 300 **m** and killed 1 Chr 11:20
a name beside the three mighty **m**. 1 Chr 11:24
The mighty **m** were Asahel the 1 Chr 11:26
Now these are the **m** who came to 1 Chr 12:1
among the mighty **m** who helped 1 Chr 12:1
for a hundred **m** and the greatest 1 Chr 12:14
These are the **m** who crossed the 1 Chr 12:15
And some of the **m** of Benjamin and 1 Chr 12:16
Some of the **m** of Manasseh deserted 1 Chr 12:19
these **m** of Manasseh deserted to 1 Chr 12:20
they were all mighty **m** of valor and 1 Chr 12:21
from day to day **m** came to David to 1 Chr 12:22
The **m** of Judah bearing shield and 1 Chr 12:24
mighty **m** of valor for war, 1 Chr 12:25
20,800, mighty **m** of valor, 1 Chr 12:30
famous **m** in their fathers' houses. 1 Chr 12:30
m who had understanding of the 1 Chr 12:32
whom were 37,000 **m** armed with 1 Chr 12:34
the Danites 28,600 **m** equipped for 1 Chr 12:35
120,000 **m** armed with all the 1 Chr 12:37
All these, **m** of war, arrayed in battle 1 Chr 12:38
to all Israel, both **m** and women, 1 Chr 16:3
And violent **m** shall waste them no 1 Chr 17:9

struck down 22,000 **m** of the Syrians. 1 Chr 18:5
David was told concerning the **m**, 1 Chr 19:5
for the **m** were greatly ashamed. 1 Chr 19:5
and all the army of the mighty **m**. 1 Chr 19:8
some of the best **m** of Israel and 1 Chr 19:10
The rest of his **m** he put in the 1 Chr 19:11
the Syrians the **m** of 7,000 chariots 1 Chr 19:18
there were 1,100,000 **m** who drew the 1 Chr 21:5
on Israel, and 70,000 **m** of Israel fell. 1 Chr 21:14
and the total was 38,000 **m**. 1 Chr 23:3
Since more chief **m** were found 1 Chr 24:4
for they were **m** of great ability. 1 Chr 26:6
whose brothers were able **m**, 1 Chr 26:7
able **m** qualified for the service; 1 Chr 26:8
had sons and brothers, able **m**, 1 Chr 26:9
corresponding to their chief **m**, 1 Chr 26:12
and his brothers, 1,700 **m** of ability, 1 Chr 26:30
was made and **m** of great ability 1 Chr 26:31
and his brothers, 2,700 **m** of ability, 1 Chr 26:32
the mighty **m** and all the seasoned 1 Chr 28:1
All the leaders and the mighty **m**, 1 Chr 29:24
Solomon assigned 70,000 **m** to bear 2 Chr 2:2
And all the **m** of Israel assembled 2 Chr 5:3
took counsel with the old **m**, 2 Chr 10:6
the counsel that the old **m** gave him, 2 Chr 10:8
with the young **m** who had grown 2 Chr 10:8
And the young **m** who had grown 2 Chr 10:10
forsaking the counsel of the old **m**, 2 Chr 10:13
to the counsel of the young **m**, 2 Chr 10:14
having an army of valiant **m** of war, 2 Chr 13:3
men of war, 400,000 chosen **m**. 2 Chr 13:3
Then the **m** of Judah raised the 2 Chr 13:15
And when the **m** of Judah shouted, 2 Chr 13:15
The **m** of Israel fled before Judah, 2 Chr 13:16
fell slain of Israel 500,000 chosen **m**. 2 Chr 13:17
Thus the **m** of Israel were subdued 2 Chr 13:18
time, and the **m** of Judah prevailed, 2 Chr 13:18
and 280,000 **m** from Benjamin that 2 Chr 14:8
All these were mighty **m** of valor. 2 Chr 14:8
of a million **m** and 300 chariots, 2 Chr 14:9
The **m** of Judah carried away very 2 Chr 14:13
He had soldiers, mighty **m** of valor, 2 Chr 17:13
with 300,000 mighty **m** of valor; 2 Chr 17:14
with 200,000 mighty **m** of valor. 2 Chr 17:16
with 200,000 **m** armed with bow 2 Chr 17:17
prophets together, four hundred **m**, 2 Chr 18:5
Some **m** came and told Jehoshaphat, 2 Chr 20:2
the **m** of Ammon and Moab and 2 Chr 20:10
ambush against the **m** of Ammon, 2 Chr 20:22
For the **m** of Ammon and Moab 2 Chr 20:23
for the band of **m** that came with the 2 Chr 22:1
and they each brought his **m**, 2 Chr 23:8
of the Syrians had come with few **m**, 2 Chr 24:24
Amaziah assembled the **m** of Judah 2 Chr 25:5
that they were 300,000 choice **m**, 2 Chr 25:5
also 100,000 mighty **m** of valor from 2 Chr 25:6
and struck down 10,000 **m** of Seir. 2 Chr 25:11
The **m** of Judah captured another 2 Chr 25:12
But the **m** of the army whom 2 Chr 25:13
the gods of the **m** of Seir and set 2 Chr 25:14
houses of mighty **m** of valor was 2 Chr 26:12
engines, invented by skillful **m**, 2 Chr 26:15
of the LORD who were **m** of valor, 2 Chr 26:17
in one day, all of them **m** of valor, 2 Chr 28:6
The **m** of Israel took captive 200,000 2 Chr 28:8
chiefs also of the **m** of Ephraim, 2 Chr 28:12
So the armed **m** left the captives and 2 Chr 28:14
And the **m** who have been 2 Chr 28:15
However, some **m** of Asher, of 2 Chr 30:11
there were **m** in the several cities 2 Chr 31:19
officers and his mighty **m** to stop the 2 Chr 32:3
And the **m** did the work faithfully. 2 Chr 34:12
with all the **m** of Judah and the 2 Chr 34:30
all the singing **m** and singing 2 Chr 35:25
killed their young **m** with the sword 2 Chr 36:17
be assisted by the **m** of his place with Ezr 1:4
The number of the **m** of the people of Ezr 2:2
The **m** of Netophah, 56. Ezr 2:22
The **m** of Anathoth, 128. Ezr 2:23
The **m** of Michmas, 122. Ezr 2:27
The **m** of Bethel and Ai, 223. Ezr 2:28
old **m** who had seen the first house, Ezr 3:12
the officials, the Persians, the **m** of Erech, Ezr 4:9
of Erech, the Babylonians, the **m** of Susa, Ezr 4:9
the **m** of the province Beyond the River, Ezr 4:11
a decree that these **m** be made to cease, Ezr 4:21
the names of the **m** who are building this Ezr 5:4
to be paid to these **m** in full and without Ezr 6:8
and I gathered leading **m** from Israel to Ezr 7:28
with whom were registered 150 **m**. Ezr 8:3
son of Zerahiah, and with him 200 **m**. Ezr 8:4
the son of Jahaziel, and with him 300 **m**. Ezr 8:5
the son of Jonathan, and with him 50 **m**. Ezr 8:6
the son of Athaliah, and with him 70 **m**. Ezr 8:7
the son of Michael, and with him 80 **m**. Ezr 8:8

the son of Jehiel, and with him 218 **m**. Ezr 8:9
son of Josiphiah, and with him 160 **m**. Ezr 8:10
the son of Bebai, and with him 28 **m**. Ezr 8:11
son of Hakkatan, and with him 110 **m**. Ezr 8:12
and Shemaiah, and with them 60 **m**. Ezr 8:13
Uthai and Zaccur, and with them 70 **m**. Ezr 8:14
Zechariah, and Meshullam, leading **m**, Ezr 8:16
and Elnathan, who were **m** of insight, Ezr 8:16
officials and chief **m** has been foremost." Ezr 9:2
of God, a very great assembly of **m**, Ezr 10:1
Then all the **m** of Judah and Benjamin Ezr 10:9
Ezra the priest selected **m**, heads of Ezr 10:16
end of all the **m** who had married Ezr 10:17
came with certain **m** from Judah. Neh 1:2
in the night, I and a few **m** with me. Neh 2:12
And next to him the **m** of Jericho built. Neh 3:2
the **m** of Gibeon and of Mizpah, Neh 3:7
as far as the house of the mighty **m**. Neh 3:16
priests, the **m** of the surrounding area, Neh 3:22
my servants nor the **m** of the guard Neh 4:23
for other **m** have our fields and our Neh 5:5
there were at my table 150 **m**, Neh 5:17
The number of the **m** of the people of Neh 7:7
The **m** of Bethlehem and Netophah, Neh 7:26
The **m** of Anathoth, 128. Neh 7:27
The **m** of Beth-azmaveth, 42. Neh 7:28
The **m** of Kiriath-jearim, Chephirah, Neh 7:29
The **m** of Ramah and Geba, 621. Neh 7:30
The **m** of Michmas, 122. Neh 7:31
The **m** of Bethel and Ai, 123. Neh 7:32
The **m** of the other Nebo, 52. Neh 7:33
both **m** and women and all who could Neh 8:2
the presence of the **m** and the women Neh 8:3
blessed all the **m** who willingly offered Neh 11:2
lived in Jerusalem were 468 valiant **m**. Neh 11:6
and his brothers, **m** of valor, 928. Neh 11:8
their brothers, mighty **m** of valor, Neh 11:14
On that day **m** were appointed over Neh 12:44
said to the wise **m** who knew the times Est 1:13
the **m** next to him being Carshena, Est 1:14
the king's young **m** who attended him Est 2:2
the **m** were both hanged on the gallows. Est 2:23
The king's young **m** who attended him Est 6:3
And the king's young **m** told him, Est 6:5
Then his wise **m** and his wife Zeresh Est 6:13
sold merely as slaves, **m** and women, Est 7:4
itself the Jews killed and destroyed 500 **m**, Est 9:6
killed and destroyed 500 **m** and also the Est 9:12
of Adar and they killed 300 **m** in Susa, Est 9:15
of the night, when deep sleep falls on **m**, Jb 4:13
Should your babble silence **m**, and when Jb 11:3
For he knows worthless **m**; when he Jb 11:11
(what wise **m** have told, without hiding Jb 15:18
M have gaped at me with their mouth; Jb 16:10
and I am one before whom **m** spit. Jb 17:6
to the old way that wicked **m** have trod? Jb 22:15
the young **m** saw me and withdrew, and Jb 29:8
"**M** listened to me and waited and kept Jb 29:21
laugh at me, **m** who are younger than I, Jb 30:1
of their hands, **m** whose vigor is gone? Jb 30:2
if the **m** of my tent have not said, 'Who Jb 31:31
So these three **m** ceased to answer Job, Jb 32:1
no answer in the mouth of these three **m**, Jb 32:5
of the night, when deep sleep falls on **m**, Jb 33:15
opens the ears of **m** and terrifies them Jb 33:16
He sings before **m** and says: 'I sinned Jb 33:27
"Hear my words, you wise **m**, and give Jb 34:2
with evildoers and walks with wicked **m**? Jb 34:8
hear me, you **m** of understanding: Jb 34:10
M of understanding will say to me, and Jb 34:34
end, because he answers like wicked **m**. Jb 34:36
answer, because of the pride of evil **m**. Jb 35:12
extol his work, of which **m** have sung. Jb 36:24
that all **m** whom he made may know it. Jb 37:7
Therefore **m** fear him; he does not Jb 37:24
O **m**, how long shall my honor be turned Ps 4:2
the nations know that they are but **m**! Ps 9:20
from **m** by your hand, O LORD, from Ps 17:14
from **m** of the world whose portion is in Ps 17:14
I do not sit with **m** of falsehood, nor do I Ps 26:4
sinners, nor my life with bloodthirsty **m**, Ps 26:9
you hide them from the plots of **m**; Ps 31:20
are the most handsome of the sons of **m**; Ps 45:2
against me; ruthless **m** seek my life; Ps 54:3
m of blood and treachery shall not live Ps 55:23
when Saul sent **m** to watch his house in Ps 59:T
evil, and save me from bloodthirsty **m**. Ps 59:2
my life; fierce **m** stir up strife against me. Ps 59:3
you let **m** ride over our heads; we went Ps 66:12
though you **m** lie among the sheepfolds Ps 68:13
train and receiving gifts among **m**, Ps 68:18
all the **m** of war were unable to use their Ps 76:5
and laid low the young **m** of Israel. Ps 78:31
Fire devoured their young **m**, and their Ps 78:63
nevertheless, like **m** you shall die, and Ps 82:7

insolent **m** have risen up against me; Ps 86:14
a band of ruthless **m** seek my life, and Ps 86:14
When **m** in the camp were jealous of Ps 106:16
wondrous works to the children of **m**! Ps 107:8
wondrous works to the children of **m**! Ps 107:15
wondrous works to the children of **m**! Ps 107:21
staggered like drunken **m** and were at Ps 107:27
wondrous works to the children of **m**! Ps 107:31
O God! O **m** of blood, depart from me! Ps 139:19
Deliver me, O LORD, from evil **m**; Ps 140:1
evil men; preserve me from violent **m**, Ps 140:1
preserve me from violent **m**, who have Ps 140:4
in company with **m** who work iniquity, Ps 141:4
Young **m** and maidens together, old Ps 148:12
maidens together, old **m** and children! Ps 148:12
but these **m** lie in wait for their own Prv 1:18
way of evil, from **m** of perverted speech, Prv 2:12
m whose paths are crooked, and who Prv 2:15
"To you, O **m**, I call, and my cry is to the Prv 8:4
gets honor, and violent **m** get riches. Prv 11:16
glory of young **m** is their strength, Prv 20:29
the splendor of old **m** is their gray Prv 20:29
he will not stand before obscure **m**. Prv 22:29
Be not envious of evil **m**, nor desire to Prv 24:1
Solomon which the **m** of Hezekiah Prv 25:1
eyes than seven **m** who can answer Prv 26:16
Evil **m** do not understand justice, but Prv 28:5
Bloodthirsty **m** hate one who is Prv 29:10
I got singers, both **m** and women, and Eccl 2:8
There was a little city with few **m** in it, Eccl 9:14
tremble, and the strong **m** are bent, Eccl 12:3
so is my beloved among the young **m**. Sg 2:3
Around it are sixty mighty **m**, some of the Sg 3:7
men, some of the mighty **m** of Israel, Sg 3:7
the lofty pride of **m** shall be humbled, Is 2:11
the lofty pride of **m** shall be brought low, Is 2:17
Your **m** shall fall by the sword and your Is 3:25
the sword and your mighty **m** in battle. Is 3:25
inhabitants of Jerusalem and **m** of Judah, Is 5:3
and the **m** of Judah are his pleasant Is 5:7
knowledge; their honored **m** go hungry, Is 5:13
and valiant **m** in mixing strong drink, Is 5:22
Is it too little for you to weary **m**, that you Is 7:13
Lord does not rejoice over their young **m**, Is 9:17
summoned my mighty **m** to execute my Is 13:3
Their bows will slaughter the young **m**; Is 13:18
therefore the armed **m** of Moab cry aloud; Is 15:4
Where then are your wise **m**? Let them Is 19:12
archers of the mighty **m** of the sons of Is 21:17
neither reared young **m** nor brought up Is 23:4
the earth are scorched, and few **m** are left. Is 24:6
When **m** give it to one who can read, Is 29:11
of me is a commandment taught by **m**, Is 29:13
the wisdom of their wise **m** shall perish, Is 29:14
of their discerning **m** shall be hidden." Is 29:14
and his young **m** shall be put to forced Is 31:8
you, and not to the **m** sitting on the wall, Is 36:12
with which the young **m** of the king of Is 37:6
O Lord, by these things **m** live, and in all Is 38:16
and said to him, "What did these **m** say? Is 39:3
and young **m** shall fall exhausted; Is 40:30
not, you worm Jacob, you **m** of Israel! Is 41:14
and I love you, I give **m** in return for you, Is 43:4
who turns wise **m** back and makes their Is 44:25
of Cush, and the Sabeans, **m** of stature, Is 45:14
He was despised and rejected by **m**; a man Is 53:3
as one from whom **m** hide their faces he Is 53:3
devout **m** are taken away, while no one Is 57:1
m will not cover themselves with what Is 59:6
those in full vigor we are like dead **m**. Is 59:10
dead bodies of the **m** who have rebelled Is 66:24
the **m** of Memphis and Tahpanhes have Jer 2:16
the LORD to the **m** of Judah and Jerusalem: Jer 4:3
O **m** of Judah and inhabitants of Jer 4:4
For wicked **m** are found among my Jer 5:26
in wait. They set a trap; they catch **m**. Jer 5:26
and upon the gatherings of young **m**, Jer 6:11
all you **m** of Judah who enter these gates Jer 7:2
them, Thus says the LORD: When **m** fall, Jer 8:4
The wise **m** shall be put to shame; they Jer 8:9
adulterers, a company of treacherous **m**. Jer 9:2
and the young **m** from the squares. Jer 9:21
'The dead bodies of **m** shall fall like Jer 9:22
purple; they are all the work of skilled **m**. Jer 10:9
and speak to the **m** of Judah and the Jer 11:2
exists among the **m** of Judah and Jer 11:9
LORD concerning the **m** of Anathoth, Jer 11:21
The young **m** shall die by the sword, Jer 11:22
bring disaster upon the **m** of Anathoth, Jer 11:23
"If you have raced with **m** on foot, and Jer 12:5
the mothers of young **m** a destroyer at Jer 15:8
the **m** of Judah and the inhabitants of Jer 17:25
say to the **m** of Judah and the Jer 18:11
May their **m** meet death by pestilence, Jer 18:21
in the sight of the **m** who go with you, Jer 19:10

M shall bury in Topheth because there Jer 19:11
Jehoiakim sent to Egypt certain **m**, Jer 26:22
with the **m** and animals that are on the Jer 27:5
and the young **m** and the old shall be Jer 31:13
the **m** of Judah and the inhabitants of Jer 32:32
the dead bodies of **m** whom I shall strike Jer 33:5
And the **m** who transgressed my Jer 34:18
hearing of all the **m** of Judah who come Jer 36:6
remained of them only wounded **m**, Jer 37:10
these **m** have done evil in all that they Jer 38:9
"Take three **m** with you from here, Jer 38:10
Ebed-melech took the **m** with him and Jer 38:11
the hand of these **m** who seek your life." Jer 38:16
into the hand of the **m** of whom you are Jer 39:17
open country and their **m** heard that the Jer 40:7
the land and had committed to him **m**, Jer 40:7
son of the Maacathite, they and their **m**. Jer 40:8
of Shaphan, swore to them and their **m**, Jer 40:9
came with ten **m** to Gedaliah the son of Jer 41:1
Nethaniah and the ten **m** with him rose Jer 41:2
eighty **m** arrived from Shechem and Jer 41:5
Nethaniah and the **m** with him Jer 41:7
But there were ten **m** among them who Jer 41:8
the bodies of the **m** whom he had struck Jer 41:9
they took all their **m** and went to fight Jer 41:12
escaped from Johanan with eight **m**, Jer 41:15
All the **m** who set their faces to go to Jer 42:17
and all the insolent **m** said to Jeremiah, Jer 43:2
the **m**, the women, the children, the Jer 43:6
in the sight of the **m** of Judah, Jer 43:9
Then all the **m** who knew that their Jer 44:15
said to all the people, **m** and women, Jer 44:20
All the **m** of Judah who are in the land Jer 44:27
m of Cush and Put who handle the Jer 46:9
Put who handle the shield, **m** of Lud, Jer 46:9
M shall cry out, and every inhabitant of Jer 47:2
'We are heroes and mighty **m** of war'? Jer 48:14
of his young **m** have gone down Jer 48:15
for the **m** of Kir-hareseth I mourn. Jer 48:31
like a flute for the **m** of Kir-hareseth. Jer 48:36
Therefore her young **m** shall fall in her Jer 49:26
from them, and **m** shall cry to them: Jer 49:29
Therefore her young **m** shall fall in her Jer 50:30
against her officials and her wise **m**! Jer 50:35
Spare not her young **m**; devote to Jer 51:3
Surely I will fill you with **m**, as many Jer 51:14
drunk her officials and her wise **m**, Jer 51:57
and all the **m** of war fled and went out Jer 52:7
had been in command of the **m** of war, Jer 52:25
war, and seven **m** of the king's council, Jer 52:25
and sixty **m** of the people of the land, Jer 52:25
rejected all my mighty **m** in my midst; Lam 1:15
against me to crush my young **m**; Lam 1:15
and my young **m** have gone into Lam 1:18
and my young **m** have fallen by Lam 2:21
afflict or grieve the children of **m**. Lam 3:33
Young **m** are compelled to grind at the Lam 5:13
The old **m** have left the city gate, the Lam 5:14
the city gate, the young **m** their music. Lam 5:14
them stood seventy **m** of the elders Ezk 8:11
and the altar, were about twenty-five **m**, Ezk 8:16
six **m** came from the direction of the Ezk 9:2
the foreheads of the **m** who sigh and Ezk 9:4
Kill old **m** outright, young men and Ezk 9:6
men outright, young **m** and maidens, Ezk 9:6
of the gateway there were twenty-five **m**. Ezk 11:1
these are the **m** who devise iniquity and Ezk 11:2
these **m** have taken their idols into Ezk 14:3
even if these three **m**, Noah, Daniel, Ezk 14:14
even if these three **m** were in it, as I Ezk 14:16
though these three **m** were in it, as I Ezk 14:18
and made for yourself images of **m**, Ezk 16:17
M give gifts to all prostitutes, but you Ezk 16:33
under oath (the chief **m** of the land he Ezk 17:13
learned to catch prey; he devoured **m**. Ezk 19:3
learned to catch prey; he devoured **m**, Ezk 19:6
you into the hands of brutish **m**, Ezk 21:31
There are **m** in you who slander to shed Ezk 22:9
In you **m** uncover their fathers' Ezk 22:10
all of them desirable young **m**, Ezk 23:6
the choicest **m** of Assyria all of them, Ezk 23:7
for in her youth **m** had lain with her Ezk 23:8
horses, all of them desirable young **m**. Ezk 23:12
She saw **m** portrayed on the wall, the Ezk 23:14
with them, desirable young **m**, Ezk 23:23
all of them, officers and **m** of renown, Ezk 23:23
They even sent for **m** to come from Ezk 23:40
and with **m** of the common sort Ezk 23:42
in to her, as **m** go in to a prostitute. Ezk 23:44
But righteous **m** shall pass judgment Ezk 23:45
your lips, nor eat the bread of **m**." Ezk 24:17
cover your lips, nor eat the bread of **m**. Ezk 24:22
enters your gates as **m** enter a city that Ezk 26:10
your skilled **m**, O Tyre, were in you; Ezk 27:8
of Gebal and her skilled **m** were in you, Ezk 27:9

were in your army as your **m** of war. Ezk 27:10
M of Arvad and Helech were on your Ezk 27:11
and **m** of Gamad were in your towers. Ezk 27:11
The **m** of Dedan traded with you. Ezk 27:15
and all your **m** of war who are in you, Ezk 27:27
The young **m** of On and of Pi-beseth Ezk 30:17
terror of the mighty **m** was in the land Ezk 32:27
will set apart **m** to travel through Ezk 39:14
with mighty **m** and all kinds of Ezk 39:20
that all the wise **m** of Babylon be Dn 2:12
and the wise **m** were about to be killed; Dn 2:13
gone out to kill the wise **m** of Babylon. Dn 2:14
with the rest of the wise **m** of Babylon. Dn 2:18
to destroy the wise **m** of Babylon. Dn 2:24
"Do not destroy the wise **m** of Babylon; Dn 2:24
answered the king and said, "No wise **m**, Dn 2:27
prefect over all the wise **m** of Babylon. Dn 2:48
Meshach, and Abednego. These **m**, Dn 3:12
they brought these **m** before the king. Dn 3:13
some of the mighty **m** of his army to Dn 3:20
Then these **m** were bound in their Dn 3:21
the fire killed those **m** who took up Dn 3:22
And these three **m**, Shadrach, Meshach, Dn 3:23
we not cast three **m** bound into the Dn 3:24
and said, "But I see four **m** unbound, Dn 3:25
any power over the bodies of those **m**. Dn 3:27
that all the wise **m** of Babylon should be Dn 4:6
rules the kingdom of **m** and gives it to Dn 4:17
he will and sets over it the lowliest of **m**.' Dn 4:17
because all the wise **m** of my kingdom Dn 4:18
that you shall be driven from among **m**, Dn 4:25
rules the kingdom of **m** and gives it to Dn 4:25
and you shall be driven from among **m**, Dn 4:32
rules the kingdom of **m** and gives it to Dn 4:32
was driven from among **m** and ate grass Dn 4:33
king declared to the wise **m** of Babylon, Dn 5:7
Then all the king's wise **m** came in, but Dn 5:8
Now the wise **m**, the enchanters, have Dn 5:15
Then these **m** said, "We shall not find Dn 6:5
Then these **m** came by agreement and Dn 6:11
Then these **m** came by agreement to the Dn 6:15
and those **m** who had maliciously Dn 6:24
and destroy mighty **m** and the people Dn 8:24
shame, as at this day, to the **m** of Judah, Dn 9:7
for the **m** who were with me did not see Dn 10:7
for the **m** themselves go aside with Hos 4:14
your old **m** shall dream dreams, Jl 2:28
and your young **m** shall see visions. Jl 2:28
Consecrate for war; stir up the mighty **m**. Jl 3:9
Let all the **m** of war draw near; let them Jl 3:9
some of your young **m** for Nazirites. Am 2:11
I killed your young **m** with the sword, Am 4:10
the notable **m** of the first of the nations, Am 6:1
And if ten **m** remain in one house, they Am 6:9
virgins and the young **m** shall faint for Am 8:13
the LORD, destroy the wise **m** out of Edom, Ob 1:8
And your mighty **m** shall be dismayed, O Ob 1:9
Then the **m** were exceedingly afraid and Jon 1:10
have done!" For the **m** knew that he was Jon 1:10
the **m** rowed hard to get back to dry Jon 1:13
Then the **m** feared the LORD exceedingly, Jon 1:16
in its pasture, a noisy multitude of **m**. Mi 2:12
seven shepherds and eight princes of **m**; Mi 5:5
Your rich **m** are full of violence; your Mi 6:12
man's enemies are the **m** of his own Mi 7:6
The shield of his mighty **m** is red; his Na 2:3
street; for her honored **m** lots were cast, Na 3:10
and all her great **m** were bound in Na 3:10
by like the wind and go on, guilty **m**, Hab 1:11
will punish the **m** who are complacent, Zep 1:12
Her prophets are fickle, treacherous **m**; Zep 3:4
before you, for they are **m** who are a sign: Zec 3:8
Regem-melech and their **m** to entreat the Zec 7:2
Old **m** and old women shall again sit in Zec 8:4
In those days ten **m** from the nations of Zec 8:23
shall make the young **m** flourish, Zec 9:17
They shall be like mighty **m** in battle, Zec 10:5
wise **m** from the east came to Jerusalem, Mt 2:1
summoned the wise **m** secretly and Mt 2:7
that he had been tricked by the wise **m**, Mt 2:16
that he had ascertained from the wise **m**. Mt 2:16
me, and I will make you fishers of **m**." Mt 4:19
And the **m** marveled, saying, "What sort Mt 8:27
two demon-possessed **m** met him, Mt 8:28
happened to the demon-possessed **m**. Mt 8:33
God, who had given such authority to **m**. Mt 9:8
from there, two blind **m** followed him, Mt 9:27
the house, the blind **m** came to him, Mt 9:28
Beware of **m**, for they will deliver you Mt 10:17
who acknowledges me before **m**, Mt 10:32
but whoever denies me before **m**, I also Mt 10:33
The **m** of Nineveh will rise up at the Mt 12:41
but while his **m** were sleeping, his Mt 13:25
m drew it ashore and sat down and Mt 13:48
who ate were about five thousand **m**, Mt 14:21

And when the **m** of that place Mt 14:35
as doctrines the commandments of **m**.'" Mt 15:9
Those who ate were four thousand **m**, Mt 15:38
to be delivered into the hands of **m**, Mt 17:22
who have been made eunuchs by **m**, Mt 19:12
there were two blind **m** sitting by the Mt 20:30
You blind **m**! For which is greater, the Mt 23:19
you prophets and wise **m** and scribes, Mt 23:34
Then two **m** will be in the field; one Mt 24:40
is it that these **m** testify against you?" Mt 26:62
trembled and became like dead **m**. Mt 28:4
I will make you become fishers of **m**." Mk 1:17
to him a paralytic carried by four **m**. Mk 2:3
and the leading **m** of Galilee. Mk 6:21
ate the loaves were five thousand **m**. Mk 6:44
as doctrines the commandments of **m**.' Mk 7:7
of God and hold to the tradition of **m**." Mk 7:8
And he looked up and said, "I see **m**, but Mk 8:24
to be delivered into the hands of **m**, Mk 9:31
is it that these **m** testify against you?" Mk 14:60
from now on you will be catching **m**." Lk 5:10
some **m** were bringing on a bed a man Lk 5:18
And when the **m** had come to him, they Lk 7:20
For there were about five thousand **m**. Lk 9:14
behold, two **m** were talking with him, Lk 9:30
glory and the two **m** who stood with Lk 9:32
And as the **m** were parting from him, Lk 9:33
to be delivered into the hands of **m**." Lk 9:44
judgment with the **m** of this generation Lk 11:31
The **m** of Nineveh will rise up at the Lk 11:32
who acknowledges me before **m**, Lk 12:8
who denies me before **m** will be denied Lk 12:9
and be like **m** who are waiting for their Lk 12:36
none of those **m** who were invited shall Lk 14:24
those who justify yourselves before **m**, Lk 16:15
is exalted among **m** is an abomination Lk 16:15
"Two **m** went up into the temple to Lk 18:10
I thank you that I am not like other **m**, Lk 18:11
is impossible with **m** is possible with Lk 18:27
and the principal **m** of the people Lk 19:47
Now the **m** who were holding Jesus in Lk 22:63
two **m** stood by them in dazzling Lk 24:4
faces to the ground, the **m** said to them, Lk 24:5
the hands of sinful **m** and be crucified Lk 24:7
was life, and the life was the light of **m**. Jn 1:4
grass in the place. So the **m** sat down, Jn 6:10
that the testimony of two **m** is true. Jn 8:17
am he. So, if you seek me, let these **m** go." Jn 18:8
two **m** stood by them in white robes, Acts 1:10
and said, "**M** of Galilee, why do you Acts 1:11
one of the **m** who have accompanied Acts 1:21
—one of these **m** must become with us Acts 1:22
devout **m** from every nation under Acts 2:5
"**M** of Judea and all who dwell in Acts 2:14
For these **m** are not drunk, as you Acts 2:15
and your young **m** shall see visions, Acts 2:17
and your old **m** shall dream dreams; Acts 2:17
"**M** of Israel, hear these words: Jesus of Acts 2:22
and killed by the hands of lawless **m**. Acts 2:23
"**M** of Israel, why do you wonder at Acts 3:12
the number of the **m** came to about five Acts 4:4
heaven given among **m** by which we Acts 4:12
they were uneducated, common **m**, Acts 4:13
"What shall we do with these **m**? Acts 4:16
You have not lied to **m** but to God." Acts 5:4
The young **m** rose and wrapped him up Acts 5:6
When the young **m** came in they Acts 5:10
multitudes of both **m** and women, Acts 5:14
The **m** whom you put in prison are Acts 5:25
"We must obey God rather than **m**. Acts 5:29
orders to put the **m** outside for a little Acts 5:34
And he said to them, "**M** of Israel, take Acts 5:35
what you are about to do with these **m**. Acts 5:35
to be somebody, and a number of **m**, Acts 5:36
keep away from these **m** and let them Acts 5:38
among you seven **m** of good repute, Acts 6:3
they secretly instigated **m** who said, Acts 6:11
them, saying, '**M**, you are brothers. Acts 7:26
Devout **m** buried Stephen and made Acts 8:2
he dragged off **m** and women and Acts 8:3
were baptized, both **m** and women. Acts 8:12
belonging to the Way, **m** or women, Acts 9:2
The **m** who were traveling with him Acts 9:7
Peter was there, sent two **m** to him, Acts 9:38
And now send **m** to Joppa and bring Acts 10:5
the **m** who were sent by Cornelius, Acts 10:17
"Behold, three **m** are looking for you. Acts 10:19
Peter went down to the **m** and said, Acts 10:21
went to uncircumcised **m** and ate with Acts 11:3
very moment three **m** arrived at the Acts 11:11
of them, **m** of Cyprus and Cyrene, Acts 11:20
"**M** of Israel and you who fear God, Acts 13:16
and the leading **m** of the city, Acts 13:50
down to us in the likeness of **m**!" Acts 14:11
"**M**, why are you doing these things? Acts 14:15
We also are **m**, of like nature with Acts 14:15
But some **m** came down from Judea Acts 15:1
to choose **m** from among them and Acts 15:22
Silas, leading **m** among the brothers, Acts 15:22
to choose **m** and send them to you Acts 15:25
m who have risked their lives for the Acts 15:26
"These **m** are servants of the Most Acts 16:17
they said, "These **m** are Jews, Acts 16:20
the police, saying, "Let those **m** go." Acts 16:35
m who are Roman citizens, Acts 16:37
taking some wicked **m** of the rabble, Acts 17:5
"These **m** who have turned the world Acts 17:6
women of high standing as well as **m**. Acts 17:12
"**M** of Athens, I perceive that in every Acts 17:22
But some **m** joined him and believed, Acts 17:34
There were about twelve **m** in all. Acts 19:7
"**M**, you know that from this Acts 19:25
the crowd, he said, "**M** of Ephesus, Acts 19:35
have brought these **m** here who are Acts 19:37
selves will arise **m** speaking twisted Acts 20:30
We have four **m** who are under a Acts 21:23
take these **m** and purify yourself Acts 21:24
Then Paul took the **m**, and the next Acts 21:26
crying out, "**M** of Israel, help! This is Acts 21:28
the four thousand **m** of the Assassins Acts 21:38
to prison both **m** and women, Acts 22:4
than forty of their **m** are lying in Acts 23:21
which these **m** themselves accept, Acts 24:15
else let these **m** themselves say what Acts 24:20
priests and the principal **m** of the Jews Acts 25:2
"let the **m** of authority among you go Acts 25:5
and the prominent **m** of the city. Acts 25:23
"**M**, you should have listened to me Acts 27:21
m, for I have faith in God that it will Acts 27:25
"Unless these **m** stay in the ship, Acts 27:31
and unrighteousness of **m**, Rom 1:18
and the **m** likewise gave up natural Rom 1:27
m committing shameless acts with Rom 1:27
shameless acts with **m** and receiving Rom 1:27
judges the secrets of **m** by Christ Jesus. Rom 2:16
spread to all **m** because all sinned Rom 5:12
led to condemnation for all **m**, Rom 5:18
leads to justification and life for all **m**. Rom 5:18
myself seven thousand **m** who have Rom 11:4
to God and approved by **m**. Rom 14:18
foolishness of God is wiser than **m**, 1 Cor 1:25
weakness of God is stronger than **m**. 1 Cor 1:25
in the wisdom of **m** but in the power 1 Cor 2:5
So let no one boast in **m**. For all 1 Cor 3:21
as last of all, like **m** sentenced to death, 1 Cor 4:9
to the world, to angels, and to **m**. 1 Cor 4:9
nor **m** who practice homosexuality, 1 Cor 6:9
a price; do not become slaves of **m**. 1 Cor 7:23
in the tongues of **m** and of angels, 1 Cor 13:1
a tongue speaks not to **m** but to God; 1 Cor 14:2
stand firm in the faith, act like **m**, 1 Cor 16:13
yours. Give recognition to such **m**. 1 Cor 16:18
of God's word, but as **m** of sincerity, 2 Cor 2:17
of our boasting about you to these **m**. 2 Cor 8:24
For such **m** are false apostles, 2 Cor 11:13
apostle—not from **m** nor through man, Gal 1:1
For before certain **m** came from James, Gal 2:12
to the sons of **m** in other generations as Eph 3:5
host of captives, and he gave gifts to **m**." Eph 4:8
servant, being born in the likeness of **m**. Phil 2:7
Lord with all joy, and honor such **m**, Phil 2:29
heartily, as for the Lord and not for **m**, Col 3:23
are the only **m** of the circumcision Col 4:11
know what kind of **m** we proved to be 1 Thes 1:5
not as the word of **m** but as what it 1 Thes 2:13
be delivered from wicked and evil **m**. 2 Thes 3:2
m who practice homosexuality, 1 Tm 1:10
is one mediator between God and **m**, 1 Tm 2:5
that in every place the **m** should pray, 1 Tm 2:8
father. Treat younger **m** like brothers, 1 Tm 5:1
The sins of some **m** are conspicuous, 1 Tm 5:24
entrust to faithful **m** who will be 2 Tm 2:2
so these **m** also oppose the truth, 2 Tm 3:8
m corrupted in mind and disqualified 2 Tm 3:8
plain to all, as was that of those two **m**. 2 Tm 3:9
Older **m** are to be sober-minded, dignified, Ti 2:2
urge the younger **m** to be self-controlled. Ti 2:6
chosen from among **m** is appointed to Heb 5:1
to act on behalf of **m** in relation to God, Heb 5:1
one case tithes are received by mortal **m**, Heb 7:8
the law appoints **m** in their weakness Heb 7:28
living stone rejected by **m** but in the 1 Pt 2:4
but **m** spoke from God as they were 2 Pt 1:21
I am writing to you, young **m**, because 1 Jn 2:13
I write to you, young **m**, because you 1 Jn 2:14
If we receive the testimony of **m**, the 1 Jn 5:9
earth, so that **m** should slay one another, Rv 6:4
And all shipmasters and seafaring **m**, Rv 18:17
flesh of captains, the flesh of mighty **m**, Rv 19:18
and their riders, and the flesh of all **m**, Rv 19:18

MEN'S (4)
his house, "Fill the **m** sacks with food, Gn 44:1
not gods, but the work of **m** hands, 2 Kgs 19:18
which are the work of **m** hands. 2 Chr 32:19
were no gods, but the work of **m** hands, Is 37:19

MENAHEM (8)
Then **M** the son of Gadi came up 2 Kgs 15:14
At that time **M** sacked Tiphsah and 2 Kgs 15:16
M the son of Gadi began to reign 2 Kgs 15:17
and **M** gave Pul a thousand talents 2 Kgs 15:19
M exacted the money from Israel, 2 Kgs 15:20
rest of the deeds of **M** and all that he 2 Kgs 15:21
And **M** slept with his fathers, and 2 Kgs 15:22
the son of **M** began to reign 2 Kgs 15:23

MEND (1)
Now therefore **m** your ways and your Jer 26:13

MENDED (2)
and wineskins, worn-out and torn and **m**, Jos 9:4
potter's vessel, so that it can never be **m**. Jer 19:11

MENDING (2)
with Zebedee their father, **m** their nets, Mt 4:21
who were in their boat **m** the nets. Mk 1:19

MENE (3)
inscribed: **M**, MENE, TEKEL, and PARSIN. Dn 5:25
inscribed: MENE, **M**, TEKEL, and PARSIN. Dn 5:25
M, God has numbered the days of your Dn 5:26

MENNA (1)
the son of Melea, the son of **M**, the son of Lk 3:31

MENSTRUAL (11)
shall be in her **m** impurity for seven Lv 15:19
she lies during her **m** impurity shall be Lv 15:20
her and her **m** impurity comes upon Lv 15:24
days, not at the time of her **m** impurity, Lv 15:25
in the uncleanness of her **m** impurity. Lv 15:26
her who is unwell with her **m** impurity, Lv 15:33
while she is in her **m** uncleanness. Lv 18:19
woman during her **m** period and Lv 20:18
a woman in her time of **m** impurity, Ezk 18:6
who are unclean in their **m** impurity. Ezk 22:10
of a woman in her **m** impurity. Ezk 36:17

MENSTRUATION (2)
As at the time of her **m**, she shall be Lv 12:2
shall be unclean two weeks, as in her **m**. Lv 12:5

MENTION (10)
me the kindness to **m** me to Pharaoh, Gn 40:14
and make no **m** of the names of other Ex 23:13
among you or make **m** of the names of Jos 23:7
No **m** shall be made of coral or of Jb 28:18
who know me I **m** Rahab and Babylon; Ps 87:4
If I say, "I will not **m** him, or speak any Jer 20:9
of the LORD' you shall **m** no more, Jer 23:36
We must not **m** the name of the LORD." Am 6:10
of his Son, that without ceasing I **m** you Rom 1:9
made **m** of the exodus of the Israelites Heb 11:22

MENTIONED (8)
gave the following cities **m** by name, Jos 21:9
As soon as he **m** the ark of God, Eli 1 Sm 4:18
these **m** by name were princes in 1 Chr 4:38
these cities that are **m** by name. 1 Chr 6:65
who have been **m** by name rose 2 Chr 28:15
the Levites. These were all **m** by name. Ezr 8:20
Leave out nothing that you have **m**." Est 6:10
to whom it is **m** will fear because of Is 19:17

MENTIONING (1)
constantly **m** you in our prayers, 1 Thes 1:2

MENUHOTH (1)
had other sons: Haroeh, half of the **M**. 1 Chr 2:52

MEONOTHAI (2)
the sons of Othniel: Hathath and **M**. 1 Chr 4:13
M fathered Ophrah; and Seraiah 1 Chr 4:14

MEPHAATH (4)
and Jahaz, and Kedemoth, and **M**, Jos 13:18
and **M** with its pasturelands—four Jos 21:37
and **M** with its pasturelands; 1 Chr 6:79
upon Holon, and Jahzah, and **M**, Jer 48:21

MEPHIBOSHETH (14)
became lame. And his name was **M**. 2 Sm 4:4
And **M** the son of Jonathan, son of 2 Sm 9:6
And David said, "**M**!" And he answered, 2 Sm 9:6
But **M** your master's grandson shall 2 Sm 9:10
your servant do." So **M** ate at David's 2 Sm 9:11
And **M** had a young son, whose name 2 Sm 9:12
So **M** lived in Jerusalem, for he ate 2 Sm 9:13
Ziba the servant of **M** met him, 2 Sm 16:1
all that belonged to **M** is now yours." 2 Sm 16:4
And **M** the son of Saul came down to 2 Sm 19:24
"Why did you not go with me, **M**?" 2 Sm 19:25
And **M** said to the king, "Oh, let him 2 Sm 19:30
But the king spared **M**, the son of 2 Sm 21:7

saying, "Jesus, Master, have **m** on us." Lk 17:13
"Jesus, Son of David, have **m** on me!" Lk 18:38
more, "Son of David, have **m** on me!" Lk 18:39
"I will have **m** on whom I have mercy, Rom 9:15
"I will have mercy on whom I have **m**, Rom 9:15
or exertion, but on God, who has **m**. Rom 9:16
So then he has **m** on whomever he Rom 9:18
the riches of his glory for vessels of **m**, Rom 9:23
now have received **m** because of their Rom 11:30
order that by the **m** shown to you Rom 11:31
to you they also may now receive **m**. Rom 11:31
that he may have **m** on all. Rom 11:32
the one who does acts of **m**, with Rom 12:8
Gentiles might glorify God for his **m**. Rom 15:9
who by the Lord's **m** is trustworthy. 1 Cor 7:25
having this ministry by the **m** of God, 2 Cor 4:1
this rule, peace and **m** be upon them, Gal 6:16
But God, being rich in **m**, because of the Eph 2:4
But God had **m** on him, and not only Phil 2:27
m, and peace from God the Father and 1 Tm 1:2
But I received **m** because I had acted 1 Tm 1:13
But I received **m** for this reason, that 1 Tm 1:16
m, and peace from God the Father and 2 Tm 1:2
the Lord grant **m** to the household 2 Tm 1:16
grant him to find **m** from the Lord on 2 Tm 1:18
but according to his own **m**, Ti 3:5
that we may receive **m** and find grace Heb 4:16
of glory overshadowing the **m** seat. Heb 9:5
Moses dies without **m** on the evidence Heb 10:28
For judgment is without **m** to one who Jas 2:13
mercy to one who has shown no **m**. Jas 2:13
no mercy. **M** triumphs over judgment. Jas 2:13
open to reason, full of **m** and good fruits, Jas 3:17
According to his great **m**, he has caused 1 Pt 1:3
once you had not received **m**, but now 1 Pt 2:10
mercy, but now you have received **m**. 1 Pt 2:10
Grace, **m**, and peace will be with us, 2 Jn 1:3
May **m**, peace, and love be multiplied to Jude 1:2
waiting for the **m** of our Lord Jesus Jude 1:21
And have **m** on those who doubt; Jude 1:22
to others show **m** with fear, hating Jude 1:23

MERE (7)
you think that **m** words are strategy 2 Kgs 18:20
all mankind stands as a **m** breath! Ps 39:5
him; surely all mankind is a **m** breath! Ps 39:11
but **m** talk tends only to poverty. Prv 14:23
By **m** words a servant is not Prv 29:19
Do you think that **m** words are strategy Is 36:5
They utter **m** words; with empty oaths Hos 10:4

MERED (2)
of Ezrah: Jether, **M**, Epher, and Jalon. 1 Chr 4:17
of Pharaoh, whom **M** married; 1 Chr 4:17

MERELY (6)
If we had been sold **m** as slaves, men and Est 7:4
who are circumcised **m** in the flesh Jer 9:25
of hosts that peoples labor **m** for fire, Hab 2:13
one is a Jew who is **m** one outwardly, Rom 2:28
who are not **m** circumcised but who Rom 4:12
are you not being **m** human? 1 Cor 3:4

MEREMOTH (6)
weighed into the hands of **M** the priest, Ezr 8:33
Vaniah, **M**, Eliashib, Ezr 10:36
And next to them **M** the son of Uriah, Neh 3:4
After him **M** the son of Uriah, son of Neh 3:21
Harim, **M**, Obadiah, Neh 10:5
Shecaniah, Rehum, **M**, Neh 12:3

MERES (1)
Admatha, Tarshish, **M**, Marsena, Est 1:14

MERIB-BAAL (4)
and the son of Jonathan was **M**; and 1 Chr 8:34
and **M** was the father of Micah. 1 Chr 8:34
And the son of Jonathan was **M**, and 1 Chr 9:40
Merib-baal, and **M** fathered Micah. 1 Chr 9:40

MERIBAH (8)
the name of the place Massah and **M**, Ex 17:7
These are the waters of **M**, where the Nm 20:13
my command at the waters of **M**. Nm 20:24
are the waters of **M** of Kadesh in the Nm 27:14
whom you quarreled at the waters of **M**; Dt 33:8
thunder; I tested you at the waters of **M**. Ps 81:7
do not harden your hearts, as at **M**, as on Ps 95:8
They angered him at the waters of **M**, Ps 106:32

MERIBAH-KADESH (3)
of the people of Israel at the waters of **M**, Dt 32:51
from Tamar as far as the waters of **M**, Ezk 47:19
run from Tamar to the waters of **M**, Ezk 48:28

MERODACH (1)
Bel is put to shame, **M** is dismayed. Jer 50:2

MERODACH-BALADAN (2)
At that time **M** the son of Baladan, 2 Kgs 20:12
At that time **M** the son of Baladan, king Is 39:1

MEROM (2)
at the waters of **M** to fight with Israel. Jos 11:5
by the waters of **M** and fell upon them. Jos 11:7

MERONOTHITE (2)
the donkeys was Jehdeiah the **M**. 1 Chr 27:30
the Gibeonite and Jadon the **M**, Neh 3:7

MEROZ (1)
"Curse **M**, says the angel of the LORD, Jgs 5:23

MERRY (16)
And they drank and were **m** with him. Gn 43:34
And when their hearts were **m**, they Jgs 16:25
the night, and let your heart be **m**." Jgs 19:6
Lodge here and let your heart be **m**, and Jgs 19:9
As they were making their hearts **m**, Jgs 19:22
eaten and drunk, and his heart was **m**, Ru 3:7
Nabal's heart was **m** within him, 1 Sm 25:36
Israel were making **m** before the LORD, 2 Sm 6:5
—and I will make **m** before the LORD. 2 Sm 6:21
when Amnon's heart is **m** with wine, 2 Sm 13:28
the heart of the king was **m** with wine, Est 1:10
and drink your wine with a **m** heart, Eccl 9:7
the young men and the old shall be **m**. Jer 31:13
them drunk, that they may become **m**, Jer 51:39
for many years; relax, eat, drink, be **m**.' Lk 12:19
them and make **m** and exchange Rv 11:10

MERRY-HEARTED (1)
the vine languishes, all the **m** sigh. Is 24:7

MERRYMAKERS (1)
and shall go forth in the dance of the **m**. Jer 31:4

MESH (1)
by his own feet, and he walks on its **m**. Jb 18:8

MESHA (3)
lived extended from **M** in the direction Gn 10:30
Now **M** king of Moab was a sheep 2 Kgs 3:4
his wife: Jobab, Zibia, **M**, Malcam, 1 Chr 8:9

MESHACH (15)
he called Shadrach, Mishael he called **M**, Dn 1:7
M, and Abednego over the affairs of the Dn 2:49
Babylon: Shadrach, **M**, and Abednego. Dn 3:12
M, and Abednego be brought. Dn 3:13
it true, O Shadrach, **M**, and Abednego, Dn 3:14
M, and Abednego answered and said to Dn 3:16
against Shadrach, **M**, and Abednego. Dn 3:19
to bind Shadrach, **M**, and Abednego, Dn 3:20
took up Shadrach, **M**, and Abednego. Dn 3:22
three men, Shadrach, **M**, and Abednego, Dn 3:23
declared, "Shadrach, **M**, and Abednego, Dn 3:26
M, and Abednego came out from the Dn 3:26
the God of Shadrach, **M**, and Abednego, Dn 3:28
M, and Abednego shall be torn limb Dn 3:29
M, and Abednego in the province of Dn 3:30

MESHECH (8)
Madai, Javan, Tubal, **M**, and Tiras. Gn 10:2
Madai, Javan, Tubal, **M**, and Tiras. 1 Chr 1:5
of Aram: Uz, Hul, Gether, and **M**. 1 Chr 1:17
Woe to me, that I sojourn in **M**, that I Ps 120:5
Javan, Tubal, and **M** traded with you; Ezk 27:13
the chief prince of **M** and Tubal, Ezk 38:2
O Gog, chief prince of **M** and Tubal. Ezk 38:3
O Gog, chief prince of **M** and Tubal. Ezk 39:1

MESHECH-TUBAL (1)
"**M** is there, and all her multitude, her Ezk 32:26

MESHELEMIAH (4)
the son of **M** was gatekeeper at 1 Chr 9:21
of the Korahites, **M** the son of Kore, of 1 Chr 26:1
And **M** had sons: Zechariah the 1 Chr 26:2
And **M** had sons and brothers, able 1 Chr 26:9

MESHEZABEL (3)
the son of Berechiah, son of **M** repaired. Neh 3:4
M, Zadok, Jaddua, Neh 10:21
And Pethahiah the son of **M**, of the Neh 11:24

MESHILLEMITH (1)
son of Meshullam, son of **M**, 1 Chr 9:12

MESHILLEMOTH (2)
of Johanan, Berechiah the son of **M**, 2 Chr 28:12
son of Azarel, son of Ahzai, son of **M**, Neh 11:13

MESHOBAB (1)
M, Jamlech, Joshah the son of 1 Chr 4:34

MESHULLAM (25)
the son of Azaliah, son of **M**, 2 Kgs 22:3
M and Hananiah, and Shelomith 1 Chr 3:19
Michael, **M**, Sheba, Jorai, Jacan, Zia 1 Chr 5:13
Zebadiah, **M**, Hizki, Heber, 1 Chr 8:17
Sallu the son of **M**, son of Hodaviah, 1 Chr 9:7
Michri, and **M** the son of Shephatiah, 1 Chr 9:8
Azariah the son of Hilkiah, son of **M**, 1 Chr 9:11
of Adiel, son of Jahzerah, son of **M**, 1 Chr 9:12
of Merari, and Zechariah and **M**, 2 Chr 34:12
Elnathan, Nathan, Zechariah, and **M**, Ezr 8:16
and **M** and Shabbethai the Levite Ezr 10:15
Of the sons of Bani were **M**, Malluch, Ezr 10:29
And next to them **M** the son of Neh 3:4
son of Paseah and **M** the son of Neh 3:6
After him **M** the son of Berechiah Neh 3:30
taken the daughter of **M** the son of Neh 6:18
Zechariah, and **M** on his left hand. Neh 8:4
M, Abijah, Mijamin, Neh 10:7
Magpiash, **M**, Hezir, Neh 10:20
Sallu the son of **M**, son of Joed, son of Neh 11:7
Seraiah the son of Hilkiah, son of **M**, Neh 11:11
of Ezra, **M**; of Amariah, Jehohanan; Neh 12:13
of Iddo, Zechariah; of Ginnethon, **M**; Neh 12:16
Bakbukiah, Obadiah, **M**, Talmon, Neh 12:25
and Azariah, Ezra, **M**, Neh 12:33

MESHULLEMETH (1)
mother's name was **M** the daughter 2 Kgs 21:19

MESOPOTAMIA (7)
he arose and went to **M** to the city of Gn 24:10
the son of Beor from Pethor of **M**, Dt 23:4
hand of Cushan-rishathaim king of **M**. Jgs 3:8
Cushan-rishathaim king of **M** into his Jgs 3:10
hire chariots and horsemen from **M**, 1 Chr 19:6
Medes and Elamites and residents of **M**, Acts 2:9
our father Abraham when he was in **M**, Acts 7:2

MESSAGE (26)
So they sent a **m** to Joseph, saying, Gn 50:16
to Balaam and gave him Balak's **m**. Nm 22:7
and said, "I have a secret **m** for you, Jgs 3:19
"I have a **m** from God for you." And he Jgs 3:20
and sent a **m** by Nathan the prophet. 2 Sm 12:25
King David sent this **m** to Zadok and 2 Sm 19:11
"I have heard the **m** that you have sent 1 Kgs 5:8
Ben-hadad heard this **m** as he was 1 Kgs 20:12
Whoever sends a **m** by the hand of a Prv 26:6
and to whom will he explain the **m**? Is 28:9
will be sheer terror to understand the **m**. Is 28:19
I have heard a **m** from the LORD, and an Jer 49:14
call out against it the **m** that I tell you." Jon 3:2
spoke to the people with the LORD'S **m**, Hg 1:13
confirmed the **m** by accompanying Mk 16:20
declare to you a **m** by which you will Acts 11:14
of the synagogue sent a **m** to them, Acts 13:15
has been sent the **m** of this salvation. Acts 13:26
my speech and my **m** were not in 1 Cor 2:4
to us the **m** of reconciliation. 2 Cor 5:19
for he strongly opposed our **m**. 2 Tm 4:15
through me the **m** might be fully 2 Tm 4:17
For since the **m** declared by angels Heb 2:2
but the **m** they heard did not benefit Heb 4:2
This is the **m** we have heard from him 1 Jn 1:5
For this is the **m** that you have heard 1 Jn 3:11

MESSAGES (1)
beg that no further **m** be spoken to Heb 12:19

MESSENGER (35)
a **m** came to Saul, saying, "Hurry 1 Sm 23:27
And he instructed the **m**, "When 2 Sm 11:19
So the **m** went and came and told 2 Sm 11:22
The **m** said to David, "The men 2 Sm 11:23
David said to the **m**, "Thus shall you 2 Sm 11:25
And a **m** came to David, saying, 2 Sm 15:13
Then Jezebel sent a **m** to Elijah, 1 Kgs 19:2
And the **m** who went to summon 1 Kgs 22:13
And Elisha sent a **m** to him, saying, 2 Kgs 5:10
but before the **m** arrived Elisha said 2 Kgs 6:32
Look, when the **m** comes, shut the 2 Kgs 6:32
the **m** came down to him and said, 2 Kgs 6:33
saying, "The **m** reached them, 2 Kgs 9:18
When the **m** came and told him, 2 Kgs 10:8
And the **m** who went to summon 2 Chr 18:12
and there came a **m** to Job and said, "The Jb 1:14
A wicked **m** falls into trouble, but a Prv 13:17
A king's wrath is a **m** of death, and a Prv 16:14
and a cruel **m** will be sent against Prv 17:11
harvest is a faithful **m** to those who Prv 25:13
do not say before the **m** that it was a Eccl 5:6
servant, or deaf as my **m** whom I send? Is 42:19
another, and one **m** to meet another, Jer 51:31
from afar, to whom a **m** was sent; Ezk 23:40
and a **m** has been sent among the Ob 1:1
Then Haggai, the **m** of the LORD, spoke to Hg 1:13
for he is the **m** of the LORD of hosts. Mal 2:7
I send my **m** and he will prepare the way Mal 3:1
and the **m** of the covenant in whom you Mal 3:1
"Behold, I send my **m** before your face, Mt 11:10
"Behold, I send my **m** before your face, Mk 1:2
"Behold, I send my **m** before your face, Lk 7:27
nor is a **m** greater than the one who sent Jn 13:16
the flesh, a **m** of Satan to harass me, 2 Cor 12:7
and your **m** and minister to my need, Phil 2:25

MESSENGERS (81)
And Jacob sent **m** before him to Esau Gn 32:3
And the **m** returned to Jacob, saying, Gn 32:6
Moses sent **m** from Kadesh to the Nm 20:14
Then Israel sent **m** to Sihon king of Nm 21:21
sent **m** to Balaam the son of Beor at Nm 22:5
I not tell your **m** whom you sent to Nm 24:12
"So I sent **m** from the wilderness of Dt 2:26
because she hid the **m** whom we sent. Jos 6:17
she hid the **m** whom Joshua sent Jos 6:25
So Joshua sent **m**, and they ran to the Jos 7:22
And he sent **m** throughout all Jgs 6:35
And he sent **m** to Asher, Zebulun, and Jgs 6:35
Gideon sent **m** throughout all the hill Jgs 7:24
And he sent **m** to Abimelech secretly, Jgs 9:31
Then Jephthah sent **m** to the king of Jgs 11:12
answered the **m** of Jephthah, Jgs 11:13
Jephthah again sent **m** to the king of Jgs 11:14
Israel then sent **m** to the king of Edom, Jgs 11:17
Israel then sent **m** to Sihon king of the Jgs 11:19
So they sent **m** to the inhabitants of 1 Sm 6:21
that we may send **m** through all the 1 Sm 11:3
When the **m** came to Gibeah of Saul, 1 Sm 11:4
territory of Israel by the hand of **m**, 1 Sm 11:7
And they said to the **m** who had come, 1 Sm 11:9
deliverance.'" When the **m** came and 1 Sm 11:9
Therefore Saul sent **m** to Jesse and 1 Sm 16:19
Saul sent **m** to David's house to 1 Sm 19:11
And when Saul sent **m** to take David, 1 Sm 19:14
Then Saul sent the **m** to see David, 1 Sm 19:15
And when the **m** came in, behold, 1 Sm 19:16
Then Saul sent **m** to take David, and 1 Sm 19:20
of God came upon the **m** of Saul, 1 Sm 19:20
it was told Saul, he sent other **m**, 1 Sm 19:21
And Saul sent **m** again the third 1 Sm 19:21
David sent **m** out of the wilderness to 1 Sm 25:14
She followed the **m** of David and 1 Sm 25:42
armor and sent **m** throughout the 1 Sm 31:9
David sent **m** to the men of 2 Sm 2:5
And Abner sent **m** to David on his 2 Sm 3:12
Then David sent **m** to Ish-bosheth, 2 Sm 3:14
presence, he sent **m** after Abner, 2 Sm 3:26
Hiram king of Tyre sent **m** to David, 2 Sm 5:11
So David sent **m** and took her, and she 2 Sm 11:4
And Joab sent **m** to David and said, 2 Sm 12:27
sent secret **m** throughout all 2 Sm 15:10
And he sent **m** into the city to Ahab 1 Kgs 20:2
The **m** came again and said, "Thus 1 Kgs 20:5
So he said to the **m** of Ben-hadad, 1 Kgs 20:9
do.'" And the **m** departed and brought 1 Kgs 20:9
so he sent **m**, telling them, "Go, inquire 2 Kgs 1:2
go up to meet the **m** of the king of 2 Kgs 1:3
The **m** returned to the king, and he 2 Kgs 1:5
you have sent **m** to inquire of 2 Kgs 1:16
And the **m** returned and told the 2 Kgs 7:15
Then Amaziah sent **m** to Jehoash the 2 Kgs 14:8
So Ahaz sent **m** to Tiglath-pileser 2 Kgs 16:7
in Hoshea, for he had sent **m** to So, 2 Kgs 17:4
you." So he sent **m** again to Hezekiah, 2 Kgs 19:9
from the hand of the **m** and read it; 2 Kgs 19:14
By your **m** you have mocked the 2 Kgs 19:23
and sent **m** throughout the land of 1 Chr 10:9
Hiram king of Tyre sent **m** to David, 1 Chr 14:1
me." So David sent **m** to console him 1 Chr 19:2
the men, he sent **m** to meet them, 1 Chr 19:5
they sent **m** and brought out the 1 Chr 19:16
sent persistently to them by his **m**, 2 Chr 36:15
they kept mocking the **m** of God, 2 Chr 36:16
And I sent **m** to them, saying, "I am Neh 6:3
he makes his **m** winds, his ministers a Ps 104:4
will one answer the **m** of the nation? Is 14:32
Go, you swift **m**, to a nation, tall and Is 18:2
when he heard it, he sent **m** to Hezekiah, Is 37:9
the letter from the hand of the **m**, Is 37:14
servant and fulfills the counsel of his **m**, Is 44:26
after them and sent **m** to them in Ezk 23:16
"On that day **m** shall go out from me in Ezk 30:9
the voice of your **m** shall no longer be Na 2:13
When John's **m** had gone, Jesus began Lk 7:24
And he sent **m** ahead of him, who went Lk 9:52
brothers, they are **m** of the churches, 2 Cor 8:23
when she received the **m** and sent them Jas 2:25

MESSIAH (2)
have found the **M**" (which means Jn 1:41
"I know that **M** is coming (he who is Jn 4:25

MET (45)
his way, and the angels of God **m** him. Gn 32:1
company that I **m**?" Jacob answered, Gn 33:8
the God of the Hebrews, has **m** with us; Ex 3:18
the way the LORD **m** him and sought to Ex 4:24
So he went and **m** him at the mountain Ex 4:27
"The God of the Hebrews has **m** with us. Ex 5:3
They **m** Moses and Aaron, who were Ex 5:20
all the hardship that we have **m**: Nm 20:14
and God **m** Balaam. And Balaam said Nm 23:4
And the LORD **m** Balaam and put a Nm 23:16
because he **m** her in the open country, Dt 22:27
they **m** young women coming out to 1 Sm 9:11
behold, a group of prophets **m** him, 1 Sm 10:10
down toward her, and she **m** them. 1 Sm 25:20
David went out and **m** them at the 2 Sm 2:13
the servant of Mephibosheth **m** him, 2 Sm 16:1
with such loyalty they **m** me when I 1 Kgs 2:7
went away a lion **m** him on the road 1 Kgs 13:24
on the way, behold, Elijah **m** him. 1 Kgs 18:7
a lion **m** him and struck him down. 1 Kgs 20:36
and **m** him at the property of Naboth 2 Kgs 9:21
Jehu **m** the relatives of Ahaziah 2 Kgs 10:13
he **m** Jehonadab the son of Rechab 2 Kgs 10:15
he **m** the princes of Judah and the 2 Chr 22:8
As he **m** them, he said to them, "Come in Jer 41:6
He **m** God at Bethel, and there God Hos 12:4
fled from a lion, and a bear **m** him, Am 5:19
two demon-possessed men **m** him, Mt 8:28
And behold, Jesus **m** them and said, Mt 28:9
immediately there **m** him out of the Mk 5:2
there **m** him a man from the city who Lk 8:27
the mountain, a great crowd **m** him. Lk 9:37
a village, he was **m** by ten lepers, Lk 17:12
his servants **m** him and told him that his Jn 4:51
Jesus was coming, she went and **m** him, Jn 11:20
in the place where Martha had **m** him. Jn 11:30
for Jesus often **m** there with his disciples. Jn 18:2
Cornelius **m** him and fell down at his Acts 10:25
a whole year they **m** with the church Acts 11:26
we were **m** by a slave girl who had a Acts 16:16
And when he **m** us at Assos, we took Acts 20:14
before the accused **m** the accusers Acts 25:16
we may appear to have **m** the test, 2 Cor 13:7
m Abraham returning from the Heb 7:1
ancestor when Melchizedek **m** him. Heb 7:10

METAL (34)
make for yourself any gods of cast **m**. Ex 34:17
make for yourselves any gods of cast **m**: Lv 19:4
destroy all their **m** images and Nm 33:52
they have made themselves a **m** image.' Dt 9:12
who makes a carved or cast **m** image, Dt 27:15
to make a carved image and a **m** image. Jgs 17:3
it into a carved image and a **m** image. Jgs 17:4
gods, a carved image, and a **m** image? Jgs 18:14
the household gods, and the **m** image, Jgs 18:17
the household gods, and the **m** image, Jgs 18:18
Then he made the sea of cast **m**. It 1 Kgs 7:23
for yourself other gods and **m** images, 1 Kgs 14:9
made for themselves **m** images of 2 Kgs 17:16
the craftsmen and the **m** workers, 2 Kgs 24:16
Then he made the sea of cast **m**. It was 2 Chr 4:2
He even made **m** images for the 2 Chr 28:2
and the carved and the **m** images. 2 Chr 34:3
and the carved and the **m** images, 2 Chr 34:4
out the skies, hard as a cast **m** mirror? Jb 37:18
in Horeb and worshiped a **m** image. Ps 106:19
silver and your gold-plated **m** images. Is 30:22
their **m** images are empty wind. Is 41:29
in carved idols, who say to **m** images, Is 42:17
image and my **m** image commanded Is 48:5
the craftsmen, and the **m** workers, Jer 24:1
and the **m** workers had departed from Jer 29:2
midst of the fire, as it were gleaming **m**. Ezk 1:4
his waist I saw as it were gleaming **m**, Ezk 1:27
of brightness, like gleaming **m**. Ezk 8:2
their gods with their **m** images and their Dn 11:8
and make for themselves **m** images, Hos 13:2
off the carved image and the **m** image. Na 1:14
come with flashing **m** on the day Na 2:3
its maker has shaped it, a **m** image, Hab 2:18

METALS (1)
you a tester of **m** among my people, Jer 6:27

METHEG-AMMAH (1)
and David took **M** out of the hand of 2 Sm 8:1

METHUSELAH (7)
Enoch had lived 65 years, he fathered **M**. Gn 5:21
God after he fathered **M** 300 years and Gn 5:22
When **M** had lived 187 years, he Gn 5:25
M lived after he fathered Lamech 782 Gn 5:26
Thus all the days of **M** were 969 years, Gn 5:27
Enoch, **M**, Lamech; 1 Chr 1:3
the son of **M**, the son of Enoch, the son Lk 3:37

METHUSHAEL (2)
Mehujael, and Mehujael fathered **M**, Gn 4:18
Methushael, and **M** fathered Lamech. Gn 4:18

MEUNIM (2)
the sons of Asnah, the sons of **M**, the Ezr 2:50
the sons of Besai, the sons of **M**, the Neh 7:52

MEUNITES (3)
their tents and the **M** who were found 1 Chr 4:41
and with them some of the **M**, 2 Chr 20:1
lived in Gurbaal and against the **M**. 2 Chr 26:7

MEZAHAB (2)
the daughter of Matred, daughter of **M**. Gn 36:39
of Matred, the daughter of **M**. 1 Chr 1:50

MEZOBAITE (1)
Eliel, and Obed, and Jaasiel the **M**. 1 Chr 11:47

MIBHAR (1)
of Nathan, **M** the son of Hagri, 1 Chr 11:38

MIBSAM (3)
of Ishmael; and Kedar, Adbeel, **M**, Gn 25:13
Nebaioth, and Kedar, Adbeel, **M**, 1 Chr 1:29
Shallum was his son, **M** his son, 1 Chr 4:25

MIBZAR (2)
Kenaz, Teman, **M**, Gn 36:42
Kenaz, Teman, **M**, 1 Chr 1:53

MICA (5)
had a young son, whose name was **M**. 2 Sm 9:12
Galal and Mattaniah the son of **M**, 1 Chr 9:15
M, Rehob, Hashabiah, Neh 10:11
and Mattaniah the son of **M**, son of Neh 11:17
son of Mattaniah, son of **M**, Neh 11:22

MICAH (30)
of Ephraim, whose name was **M**. Jgs 17:1
image. And it was in the house of **M**. Jgs 17:4
And the man **M** had a shrine, and he Jgs 17:5
country of Ephraim to the house of **M**. Jgs 17:8
And **M** said to him, "Where do you Jgs 17:9
And **M** said to him, "Stay with me, and Jgs 17:10
And **M** ordained the Levite, and the Jgs 17:12
his priest, and was in the house of **M**. Jgs 17:12
Then **M** said, "Now I know that the Jgs 17:13
country of Ephraim, to the house of **M**, Jgs 18:2
When they were by the house of **M**, they Jgs 18:3
to them, "This is how **M** dealt with me: Jgs 18:4
Ephraim, and came to the house of **M**. Jgs 18:13
of the young Levite, at the home of **M**, Jgs 18:15
gone a distance from the home of **M**, Jgs 18:22
Dan, who turned around and said to **M**, Jgs 18:23
And when **M** saw that they were too Jgs 18:26
people of Dan took what **M** had made, Jgs 18:27
M his son, Reaiah his son, Baal his 1 Chr 5:5
and Merib-baal was the father of **M**. 1 Chr 8:34
The sons of **M**: Pithon, Melech, 1 Chr 8:35
and Merib-baal fathered **M**. 1 Chr 9:40
The sons of **M**: Pithon, Melech, 1 Chr 9:41
M the chief and Isshiah the second. 1 Chr 23:20
of Uzziel, **M**; of the sons of Micah, 1 Chr 24:24
Micah; of the sons of **M**, Shamir. 1 Chr 24:24
The brother of **M**, Isshiah; of the 1 Chr 24:25
of Shaphan, Abdon the son of **M**, 2 Chr 34:20
"**M** of Moresheth prophesied in the days Jer 26:18
LORD that came to **M** of Moresheth in the Mi 1:1

MICAH'S (3)
these went into **M** house and took Jgs 18:18
in the houses near **M** house were called Jgs 18:22
So they set up **M** carved image that he Jgs 18:31

MICAIAH (27)
of the LORD, **M** the son of Imlah, 1 Kgs 22:8
"Bring quickly **M** the son of Imlah." 1 Kgs 22:9
went to summon **M** said to him, 1 Kgs 22:13
But **M** said, "As the LORD lives, what 1 Kgs 22:14
"**M**, shall we go to Ramoth-gilead to 1 Kgs 22:15
And **M** said, "Therefore hear the 1 Kgs 22:19
near and struck **M** on the cheek 1 Kgs 22:24
And **M** said, "Behold, you shall see 1 Kgs 22:25
And the king of Israel said, "Seize **M**, 1 Kgs 22:26
And **M** said, "If you return in peace, 1 Kgs 22:28
Shaphan, and Achbor the son of **M**, 2 Kgs 22:12
mother's name was **M** the daughter 2 Chr 13:2
Zechariah, Nethanel, and **M**, 2 Chr 17:7
of the LORD, **M** the son of Imlah; 2 Chr 18:7
"Bring quickly **M** the son of Imlah." 2 Chr 18:8
went to summon **M** said to him, 2 Chr 18:12
But **M** said, "As the LORD lives, what 2 Chr 18:13
"**M**, shall we go to Ramoth-gilead to 2 Chr 18:14
And **M** said, "Therefore hear the 2 Chr 18:18
near and struck **M** on the cheek 2 Chr 18:23
And **M** said, "Behold, you shall see 2 Chr 18:24
"Seize **M** and take him back to 2 Chr 18:25
And **M** said, "If you return in peace, 2 Chr 18:27
son of Mattaniah, son of **M**, Neh 12:35
Maaseiah, Miniamin, **M**, Elioenai, Neh 12:41
When **M** the son of Gemariah, son of Jer 36:11
And **M** told them all the words that he Jer 36:13

MICE (5)
"Five golden tumors and five golden **m**, 1 Sm 6:4
and images of your **m** that ravage the 1 Sm 6:5
box with the golden **m** and the images 1 Sm 6:11
and the golden **m**, according to the 1 Sm 6:18
pig's flesh and the abomination and **m**, Is 66:17

MICHAEL (15)
tribe of Asher, Sethur the son of **M**; Nm 13:13
M, Meshullam, Sheba, Jorai, Jacan, 1 Chr 5:13
son of Jaroah, son of Gilead, son of **M**, 1 Chr 5:14
son of **M**, son of Baaseiah, son of 1 Chr 6:40
M, Obadiah, Joel, and Isshiah, all five 1 Chr 7:3
M, Ishpah, and Joha were sons of 1 Chr 8:16
Adnah, Jozabad, Jediael, **M**, Jozabad, 1 Chr 12:20
for Issachar, Omri the son of **M**; 1 Chr 27:18
Azariah, **M**, and Shephatiah; 2 Chr 21:2
of Shephatiah, Zebadiah the son of **M**, Ezr 8:8
withstood me twenty-one days, but **M**, Dn 10:13
by my side against these except **M**, Dn 10:21
"At that time shall arise **M**, the great Dn 12:1
But when the archangel **M**, contending Jude 1:9
M and his angels fighting against the Rv 12:7

MICHAL (17)
and the name of the younger **M**. 1 Sm 14:49
Now Saul's daughter **M** loved David. 1 Sm 18:20
gave him his daughter **M** for a wife. 1 Sm 18:27
the LORD was with David, and that **M**, 1 Sm 18:28
kill him in the morning. But **M**, 1 Sm 19:11
So **M** let David down through the 1 Sm 19:12
M took an image and laid it on the 1 Sm 19:13
Saul said to **M**, "Why have you 1 Sm 19:17
has escaped?" And **M** answered Saul, 1 Sm 19:17
Saul had given **M** his daughter, 1 Sm 25:44
see my face unless you first bring **M**, 2 Sm 3:13
son, saying, "Give me my wife **M**, 2 Sm 3:14
M the daughter of Saul looked out of 2 Sm 6:16
But **M** the daughter of Saul came out 2 Sm 6:20
And David said to **M**, "It was before 2 Sm 6:21
And **M** the daughter of Saul had no 2 Sm 6:23
M the daughter of Saul looked out 1 Chr 15:29

MICHMAS (2)
The men of **M**, 122. Ezr 2:27
The men of **M**, 122. Neh 7:31

MICHMASH (9)
were with Saul in **M** and the hill 1 Sm 13:2
They came up and encamped in **M**, to 1 Sm 13:5
the Philistines had mustered at **M**, 1 Sm 13:11
but the Philistines encamped in **M**. 1 Sm 13:16
Philistines went out to the pass of **M**. 1 Sm 13:23
crag rose on the north in front of **M**, 1 Sm 14:5
that day from **M** to Aijalon. 1 Sm 14:31
also lived from Geba onward, at **M**, Neh 11:31
Migron; at **M** he stores his baggage; Is 10:28

MICHMETHATH (2)
from there to the sea. On the north is **M**. Jos 16:6
of Manasseh reached from Asher to **M**, Jos 17:7

MICHRI (1)
Elah the son of Uzzi, son of **M**, 1 Chr 9:8

MIDCOURSE (1)
He has broken my strength in **m**; he Ps 102:23

MIDDAY (3)
And as **m** passed, they raved on 1 Kgs 18:29
Gate from early morning until **m**, Neh 8:3
At **m**, O king, I saw on the way a light Acts 26:13

MIDDIN (1)
wilderness, Beth-arabah, **M**, Secacah, Jos 15:61

MIDDLE (32)
The **m** bar, halfway up the frames, Ex 26:28
an opening for the head in the **m** of it, Ex 28:32
And he made the **m** bar to run from Ex 36:33
cubits, the city being in the **m**. Nm 35:5
with the **m** of the valley as a border, Dt 3:16
and from the **m** of the valley as far as the Jos 12:2
and the city that is in the **m** of the valley, Jos 13:9
the city that is in the **m** of the valley, Jos 13:16
camp at the beginning of the **m** watch, Jgs 7:19
grasped the two **m** pillars on which Jgs 16:29
and cut off their garments in the **m**, 2 Sm 10:4
the city that is in the **m** of the valley, 2 Sm 24:5
broad, the **m** one was six cubits broad, 1 Kgs 6:6
one went up by stairs to the **m** story, 1 Kgs 6:8
and from the **m** story to the third. 1 Kgs 6:8
each other in the **m** of the house. 1 Kgs 6:27
king consecrated the **m** of the court 1 Kgs 8:64
Isaiah had gone out of the **m** court, 2 Kgs 20:4
and cut off their garments in the **m**, 1 Chr 19:4
Solomon consecrated the **m** of the 2 Chr 7:7
I said, In the **m** of my days I must depart; Is 38:10
of Babylon came and sat in the **m** gate: Jer 39:3
ends of it, and the **m** of it is charred, Ezk 15:4
and set me down in the **m** of the valley; Ezk 37:1
to the top story through the **m** story. Ezk 41:7
from the lower and **m** chambers of the Ezk 42:5
more than the lower and the **m** ones. Ezk 42:6
of silver, its **m** and thighs of bronze, Dn 2:32
a fire in the **m** of the courtyard and Lk 22:55
About the **m** of the feast Jesus went up Jn 7:14
burst open in the **m** and all his bowels Acts 1:18
through the **m** of the street of the city; Rv 22:2

MIDIAN (51)
Zimran, Jokshan, Medan, **M**, Ishbak, Gn 25:2
The sons of **M** were Ephah, Epher, Gn 25:4
who defeated **M** in the country of Gn 36:35
Pharaoh and stayed in the land of **M**. Ex 2:15
the priest of **M** had seven daughters, Ex 2:16
of his father-in-law, Jethro, the priest of **M**, Ex 3:1
And the LORD said to Moses in **M**, "Go Ex 4:19
Jethro, the priest of **M**, Moses' Ex 18:1
And Moab said to the elders of **M**, Nm 22:4
and the elders of **M** departed with the Nm 22:7
tribal head of a father's house in **M**. Nm 25:15
Cozbi, the daughter of the chief of **M**, Nm 25:18
they may go against **M** to execute the Nm 31:3
to execute the LORD'S vengeance on **M**. Nm 31:3
They warred against **M**, as the LORD Nm 31:7
killed the kings of **M** with the rest of Nm 31:8
Zur, Hur, and Reba, the five kings of **M**. Nm 31:8
captive the women of **M** and their little Nm 31:9
Moses defeated with the leaders of **M**, Jos 13:21
gave them into the hand of **M** seven years. Jgs 6:1
And the hand of **M** overpowered Israel, Jgs 6:2
and because of **M** the people of Israel Jgs 6:2
was brought very low because of **M**. Jgs 6:6
us and given us into the hand of **M**." Jgs 6:13
and save Israel from the hand of **M**; Jgs 6:14
And the camp of **M** was north of them, Jgs 7:1
And the camp of **M** was below him in the Jgs 7:8
into the camp of **M** and came to the Jgs 7:13
given into his hand **M** and all the Jgs 7:14
has given the host of **M** into your hand." Jgs 7:15
all Manasseh, and they pursued after **M**. Jgs 7:23
And they captured the two princes of **M**, Jgs 7:25
Then they pursued **M**, and they brought Jgs 7:25
went to fight with **M**?" And they accused Jgs 8:1
given into your hands the princes of **M**, Jgs 8:3
Zebah and Zalmunna, the kings of **M**." Jgs 8:5
them and captured the two kings of **M**, Jgs 8:12
you have saved us from the hand of **M**." Jgs 8:22
garments worn by the kings of **M**, Jgs 8:26
So **M** was subdued before the people of Jgs 8:28
and delivered you from the hand of **M**, Jgs 9:17
They set out from **M** and came to 1 Kgs 11:18
Zimran, Jokshan, Medan, **M**, Ishbak, 1 Chr 1:32
The sons of **M**: Ephah, Epher, 1 Chr 1:33
who defeated **M** in the country of 1 Chr 1:46
Do to them as you did to **M**, as to Sisera Ps 83:9
you have broken as on the day of **M**. Is 9:4
as when he struck **M** at the rock of Is 10:26
you, the young camels of **M** and Ephah; Is 60:6
curtains of the land of **M** did tremble. Hab 3:7
and became an exile in the land of **M**, Acts 7:29

MIDIANITE (5)
Then **M** traders passed by. And they Gn 37:28
said to Hobab the son of Reuel the **M**, Nm 10:29
came and brought a **M** woman to his Nm 25:6
who was killed with the **M** woman, Nm 25:14
the name of the **M** woman who was Nm 25:15

MIDIANITES (12)
Meanwhile the **M** had sold him in Gn 37:36
"Harass the **M** and strike them down, Nm 25:17
"Avenge the people of Israel on the **M**. Nm 31:2
the **M** and the Amalekites and the people Jgs 6:3
cried out to the LORD on account of the **M**, Jgs 6:7
in the winepress to hide it from the **M**. Jgs 6:11
and you shall strike the **M** as one man." Jgs 6:16
Now all the **M** and the Amalekites and Jgs 6:33
for me to give the **M** into their hand, Jgs 7:2
save you and give the **M** into your hand, Jgs 7:7
And the **M** and the Amalekites and all Jgs 7:12
down against the **M** and capture the Jgs 7:24

MIDNIGHT (14)
About **m** I will go out in the midst of Ex 11:4
At **m** the LORD struck down all the Ex 12:29
But Samson lay till **m**, and at midnight Jgs 16:3
and at **m** he arose and took hold of the Jgs 16:3
At **m** the man was startled and turned Ru 3:8
And she arose at **m** and took my son 1 Kgs 3:20
at **m** the people are shaken and pass Jb 34:20
At **m** I rise to praise you, because of Ps 119:62
But at **m** there was a cry, 'Here is the Mt 25:6
will come, in the evening, or at **m**, Mk 13:35
will go to him at **m** and say to him, Lk 11:5
About **m** Paul and Silas were praying Acts 16:25
and he prolonged his speech until **m**. Acts 20:7
about **m** the sailors suspected that Acts 27:27

MIDST (265)
be an expanse in the **m** of the waters, Gn 1:6
The tree of life was in the **m** of the garden, Gn 2:9
of the tree that is in the **m** of the garden, Gn 3:3
Lot out of the **m** of the overthrow when Gn 19:29
into a multitude in the **m** of the earth." Gn 48:16
in a flame of fire out of the **m** of a bush. Ex 3:2
that I am the LORD in the **m** of the earth. Ex 8:22
continually in the **m** of the hail, Ex 9:24
midnight I will go out in the **m** of Egypt, Ex 11:4
of Israel went into the **m** of the sea on Ex 14:22
went in after them into the **m** of the sea, Ex 14:23
the Egyptians into the **m** of the sea. Ex 14:27
on dry ground in the **m** of the sea. Ex 15:19
to Moses out of the **m** of the cloud. Ex 24:16
a sanctuary, that I may dwell in their **m**. Ex 25:8
please let the Lord go in the **m** of us, Ex 34:9
go, lest it become a snare in your **m**. Ex 34:12
my tabernacle that is in their **m**." Lv 15:31
them in the **m** of their uncleannesses. Lv 16:16
of the Levites in the **m** of the camps; Nm 2:17
their camp, in the **m** of which I dwell." Nm 5:3
O LORD, are in the **m** of this people. Nm 14:14
perished from the **m** of the assembly. Nm 16:33
away from the **m** of this Nm 16:45
and ran into the **m** of the assembly. Nm 16:47
be cut off from the **m** of the assembly, Nm 19:20
and passed through the **m** of the sea Nm 33:8
you live, in the **m** of which I dwell, Nm 35:34
LORD dwell in the **m** of the people of Nm 35:34
go up or fight, for I am not in your **m**, Dt 1:42
LORD spoke to you out of the **m** of the fire. Dt 4:12
to you at Horeb out of the **m** of the fire, Dt 4:15
of a god speaking out of the **m** of the fire, Dt 4:33
himself from the **m** of another nation, Dt 4:34
heard his words out of the **m** of the fire. Dt 4:36
at the mountain, out of the **m** of the fire, Dt 5:4
at the mountain out of the **m** of the fire, Dt 5:22
the voice out of the **m** of the darkness, Dt 5:23
heard his voice out of the **m** of the fire. Dt 5:24
God speaking out of the **m** of fire as we Dt 5:26
your God in your **m** is a jealous God, Dt 6:15
for the LORD your God is in your **m**, Dt 7:21
the mountain out of the **m** of the fire on Dt 9:10
the mountain out of the **m** of the fire on Dt 10:4
that followed them, in the **m** of all Israel. Dt 11:6
So you shall purge the evil from your **m**. Dt 13:5
all its spoil into the **m** of its open square Dt 13:16
So you shall purge the evil from your **m**. Dt 17:7
you shall purge the evil from your **m**. Dt 19:19
innocent blood in the **m** of your people Dt 21:8
the guilt of innocent blood from your **m**, Dt 21:9
you shall purge the evil from your **m**, Dt 21:21
you shall purge the evil from your **m**. Dt 22:21
you shall purge the evil from your **m**. Dt 22:24
your God walks in the **m** of your camp, Dt 23:14
He shall dwell with you, in your **m**, in Dt 23:16
So you shall purge the evil from your **m**. Dt 24:7
we came through the **m** of the nations Dt 29:16
faith with me in the **m** of the people of Dt 32:51
me as holy in the **m** of the people of Dt 32:51
"Pass through the **m** of the camp and Jos 1:11
on dry ground in the **m** of the Jordan, Jos 3:17
from here out of the **m** of the Jordan, Jos 4:3
LORD your God into the **m** of the Jordan, Jos 4:5
twelve stones out of the **m** of the Jordan, Jos 4:8
up twelve stones in the **m** of the Jordan, Jos 4:9
ark stood in the **m** of the Jordan until Jos 4:10
LORD came up from the **m** of the Jordan, Jos 4:18
"There are devoted things in your **m**, Jos 7:13
them, so they were in the **m** of Israel, Jos 8:22
sun stopped in the **m** of heaven and did Jos 10:13
Maacath dwell in the **m** of Israel to this Jos 13:13
have lived in the **m** of Ephraim to this Jos 16:10
was in the **m** of the inheritance Jos 19:1
inheritance in the **m** of their Jos 19:9
the Levites in the **m** of the possession of Jos 21:41
we know that the LORD is in our **m**, Jos 22:31
Egypt with what I did in the **m** of it, Jos 24:5
in the **m** of Ephraim and Manasseh." Jgs 12:4
cities were destroying them in their **m**. Jgs 20:42
they came into the **m** of the camp in 1 Sm 11:11
him in the **m** of his brothers. 1 Sm 16:13
have fallen in the **m** of the battle! 2 Sm 1:25
him aside into the **m** of the gate to 2 Sm 3:27
they came into the **m** of the house as 2 Sm 4:6
his stand in the **m** of the plot and 2 Sm 23:12
servant is in the **m** of your people 1 Kgs 3:8
from the **m** of the iron furnace). 1 Kgs 8:51
went out into the **m** of the battle, 1 Kgs 20:39
they were in the **m** of Samaria. 2 Kgs 6:20
his stand in the **m** of the plot and 1 Chr 11:14
of Asaph, in the **m** of the assembly. 2 Chr 20:14
they went through the **m** of the sea on Neh 9:11
ashes, and went out into the **m** of the city, Est 4:1
in the **m** of the congregation I will Ps 22:22
God is in the **m** of her; she shall not be Ps 46:5
love, O God, in the **m** of your temple. Ps 48:9
ruin is in its **m**; oppression and fraud Ps 55:11
My soul is in the **m** of lions; I lie down Ps 57:4

have roared in the **m** of your meeting Ps 74:4
working salvation in the **m** of the earth. Ps 74:12
he let them fall in the **m** of their camp, Ps 78:28
in the **m** of the gods he holds judgment: Ps 82:1
me not away in the **m** of my days— Ps 102:24
will praise him in the **m** of the throng. Ps 109:30
scepter. Rule in the **m** of your enemies! Ps 110:2
of the house of the LORD, in your **m**, Ps 116:19
who in your **m**, O Egypt, sent signs and Ps 135:9
made Israel pass through the **m** of it, Ps 136:14
Though I walk in the **m** of trouble, you Ps 138:7
itself known even in the **m** of fools. Prv 14:33
one who lies down in the **m** of the sea, Prv 23:34
of Jerusalem from its **m** by a spirit of Is 4:4
he built a watchtower in the **m** of it, and Is 5:2
made to dwell alone in the **m** of the land. Is 5:8
were as refuse in the **m** of the streets. Is 5:25
and I dwell in the **m** of a people of unclean Is 6:5
places are many in the **m** of the land. Is 6:12
up the son of Tabeel as king in the **m** of it," Is 7:6
end, as decreed, in the **m** of all the earth. Is 10:23
for great in your **m** is the Holy One of Is 12:6
to the LORD in the **m** of the land of Egypt, Is 19:19
Assyria, a blessing in the **m** of the earth, Is 19:24
it shall be in the **m** of the earth among Is 24:13
out his hands in the **m** of it as a Is 25:11
the work of my hands, in his **m**, Is 29:23
and fountains in the **m** of the valleys. Is 41:18
unclean thing; go out from the **m** of her; Is 52:11
If you take away the yoke from your **m**, Is 58:9
their descendants in the **m** of the peoples; Is 61:9
he who put in the **m** of them his Holy Is 63:11
into the gardens, following one in the **m**, Is 66:17
of Benjamin, from the **m** of Jerusalem! Jer 6:1
shall be built up in the **m** of my people. Jer 12:16
Yet you, O LORD, are in the **m** of us, and Jer 14:9
in the **m** of his days they will leave him, Jer 17:11
them together into the **m** of this city. Jer 21:4
ruler shall come out from their **m**; Jer 30:21
infant and child, from the **m** of Judah, Jer 44:7
hired soldiers in her **m** are like fattened Jer 46:21
"Flee from the **m** of Babylon, and go out Jer 50:8
against all the foreign troops in her **m**, Jer 50:37
"Flee from the **m** of Babylon; let every Jer 51:6
"Go out of the **m** of her, my people! Let Jer 51:45
all her slain shall fall in the **m** of her. Jer 51:47
and cast it into the **m** of the Euphrates, Jer 51:63
who were found in the **m** of the city. Jer 52:25
overtaken her in the **m** of her distress. Lam 1:3
rejected all my mighty men in my **m**; Lam 1:15
who shed in the **m** of her the blood of Lam 4:13
continually, and in the **m** of the fire, Ezk 1:4
And from the **m** of it came the likeness Ezk 1:5
shall burn in the fire in the **m** of the city, Ezk 5:2
and cast them into the **m** of the fire and Ezk 5:4
judgments in your **m** in the sight Ezk 5:8
fathers shall eat their sons in your **m**, Ezk 5:10
be consumed with famine in your **m**; Ezk 5:12
And the slain shall fall in your **m**, and Ezk 6:7
while your abominations are in your **m**. Ezk 7:4
while your abominations are in your **m**. Ezk 7:9
whom you have laid in the **m** of it, Ezk 11:7
you shall be brought out of the **m** of it. Ezk 11:7
And I will bring you out of the **m** of it, Ezk 11:9
shall you be the meat in the **m** of it. Ezk 11:11
went up from the **m** of the city and Ezk 11:23
you dwell in the **m** of a rebellious Ezk 12:2
it falls, you shall perish in the **m** of it. Ezk 13:14
cut him off from the **m** of my people, Ezk 14:8
destroy him from the **m** of my people Ezk 14:9
restore your own fortunes in their **m**, Ezk 16:53
in the **m** of young lions she reared her Ezk 19:2
against them in the **m** of the land of Ezk 20:8
blood shall be in the **m** of the land. Ezk 21:32
A city that sheds blood in her **m**, so Ezk 22:3
sojourner suffers extortion in your **m**; Ezk 22:7
they commit lewdness in your **m**. Ezk 22:9
at the blood that has been in your **m**. Ezk 22:13
gather you into the **m** of Jerusalem. Ezk 22:19
and you shall be melted in the **m** of it. Ezk 22:21
so you shall be melted in the **m** of it, Ezk 22:22
her prophets in her **m** is like a roaring Ezk 22:25
have made many widows in her **m**. Ezk 22:25
Her princes in her **m** are like wolves Ezk 22:27
For the blood she has shed is in her **m**; Ezk 24:7
and make their dwellings in your **m**. Ezk 25:4
She shall be in the **m** of the sea a place Ezk 26:5
they will cast into the **m** of the waters. Ezk 26:12
when slaughter is made in your **m**? Ezk 26:15
with all your crew that is in your **m**, Ezk 27:27
like one destroyed in the **m** of the sea? Ezk 27:32
your crew in your **m** have sunk with Ezk 27:34
in the **m** of the stones of fire you Ezk 28:14
were filled with violence in your **m**, Ezk 28:16
from the **m** of the stones of fire. Ezk 28:16
so I brought fire out from your **m**; Ezk 28:18
I will manifest my glory in your **m**. Ezk 28:22
and the slain shall fall in her **m**, by Ezk 28:23
dragon that lies in the **m** of his streams, Ezk 29:3
you up out of the **m** of your streams, Ezk 29:4
desolation in the **m** of desolated Ezk 29:12
desolated in the **m** of desolated Ezk 30:7
cities shall be in the **m** of cities that are Ezk 30:7
their helpers, out of the **m** of Sheol: Ezk 32:21
my sanctuary in their **m** forevermore. Ezk 37:26
sanctuary is in their **m** forevermore." Ezk 37:28
make known in the **m** of my people Ezk 39:7
I will dwell in the **m** of the people of Ezk 43:7
me, and I will dwell in their **m** forever. Ezk 43:9
west, with the sanctuary in the **m** of it. Ezk 48:8
sanctuary of the LORD in the **m** of it. Ezk 48:10
In the **m** of it shall be the city, Ezk 48:15
of the temple shall be in its **m**. Ezk 48:21
which are in the **m** of that which Ezk 48:22
unbound, walking in the **m** of the fire, Dn 3:25
and behold, a tree in the **m** of the earth, Dn 4:10
not a man, the Holy One in your **m**, Hos 11:9
shall know that I am in the **m** of Israel, Jl 2:27
I will cut off the ruler from its **m**, and Am 2:3
within her, and the oppressed in her **m**." Am 3:9
pass through your **m**," says the LORD. Am 5:17
flock and calves from the **m** of the stall, Am 6:4
plumb line in the **m** of my people Israel; Am 7:8
against you in the **m** of the house of Am 7:10
and say, "Is not the LORD in the **m** of us? Mi 3:11
shall be in the **m** of many peoples like Mi 5:7
the nations, in the **m** of many peoples, Mi 5:8
in a forest in the **m** of a garden land; Mi 7:14
your troops are women in your **m**. Na 3:13
In the **m** of the years revive it; in the Hab 3:2
it; in the **m** of the years make it known; Hab 3:2
Herds shall lie down in her **m**, all kinds Zep 2:14
remove from your **m** your proudly Zep 3:11
will leave in your **m** a people humble Zep 3:12
King of Israel, the LORD, is in your **m**; Zep 3:15
The LORD your God is in your **m**, a Zep 3:17
of Egypt. My Spirit remains in your **m**. Hg 2:5
LORD, and I will be the glory in her **m**.'" Zec 2:5
I come and I will dwell in your **m**, Zec 2:10
And I will dwell in your **m**, and you Zec 2:11
and will dwell in the **m** of Jerusalem, Zec 8:3
them to dwell in the **m** of Jerusalem. Zec 8:8
like a blazing pot in the **m** of wood, Zec 12:6
from you will be divided in your **m**. Zec 14:1
you out as sheep in the **m** of wolves, Mt 10:16
a child, he put him in the **m** of them Mt 18:2
a child and put him in the **m** of them, Mk 9:36
stood up in the **m** and asked Jesus, Mk 14:60
But passing through their **m**, he went Lk 4:30
had thrown him down in their **m**, Lk 4:35
through the tiles into the **m** before Jesus. Lk 5:19
you out as lambs in the **m** of wolves. Lk 10:3
the kingdom of God is in the **m** of you." Lk 17:21
in adultery, and placing her in the **m** Jn 8:3
that God did through him in your **m**, Acts 2:22
And when they had set them in the **m**, Acts 4:7
standing in the **m** of the Areopagus, Acts 17:22
So Paul went out from their **m**. Acts 17:33
Therefore go out from their **m**, and 2 Cor 6:17
without blemish in the **m** of a crooked Phil 2:15
of God in the **m** of much conflict. 1 Thes 2:2
in the **m** of the congregation I will sing Heb 2:12
man fade away in the **m** of his pursuits. Jas 1:11
and in the **m** of the lampstands one like Rv 1:13
be a voice in the **m** of the four living Rv 6:6
For the Lamb in the **m** of the throne will Rv 7:17

MIDWIFE (4)
was at its hardest, the **m** said to her, Gn 35:17
and the **m** took and tied a scarlet Gn 38:28
"When you serve as **m** to the Hebrew Ex 1:16
give birth before the **m** comes to them." Ex 1:19

MIDWIVES (6)
the king of Egypt said to the Hebrew **m**, Ex 1:15
But the **m** feared God and did not do as Ex 1:17
of Egypt called the **m** and said to them, Ex 1:18
The **m** said to Pharaoh, "Because the Ex 1:19
So God dealt well with the **m**. And the Ex 1:20
And because the **m** feared God, he gave Ex 1:21

MIGDAL-EL (1)
Yiron, **M**, Horem, Beth-anath, and Jos 19:38

MIGDAL-GAD (1)
Zenan, Hadashah, **M**, Jos 15:37

MIGDOL (6)
of Pi-hahiroth, between **M** and the sea, Ex 14:2
and they camped before **M**. Nm 33:7
who lived in the land of Egypt, at **M**, Jer 44:1
"Declare in Egypt, and proclaim in **M**; Jer 46:14
and desolation, from **M** to Syene, Ezk 29:10
from **M** to Syene they shall fall within Ezk 30:6

MIGHT (345)
"Oh that Ishmael **m** live before you!" Gn 17:18
One of the people **m** easily have lain Gn 26:10
that they **m** breed among the sticks, Gn 30:41
so that I **m** have sent you away with Gn 31:27
on him"—that he **m** rescue him out of Gn 37:22
he feared that harm **m** happen to him. Gn 42:4
"Reuben, you are my firstborn, my **m**, Gn 49:3
that they **m** travel by day and by night. Ex 13:21
of Egypt that I **m** dwell among them. Ex 29:46
so that he **m** bestow a blessing upon Ex 32:29
tent together that it **m** be a single Ex 36:18
the opening, so that it **m** not tear. Ex 39:23
of the nations, that I **m** be their God: Lv 26:45
people in your **m** from among them, Nm 14:13
that he **m** give him into your hand, Dt 2:30
that you **m** do them in the land that you Dt 4:14
that you **m** know that the LORD is God; Dt 4:35
hear his voice, that he **m** discipline you. Dt 4:36
that the manslayer **m** flee there, anyone Dt 4:42
that it **m** go well with them and with Dt 5:29
with all your soul and with all your **m**. Dt 6:5
that he **m** bring us in and give us the Dt 6:23
good always, that he **m** preserve us alive, Dt 6:24
in the wilderness, that he **m** humble you, Dt 8:2
that he **m** make you know that man does Dt 8:3
that he **m** humble you and test you, Dt 8:16
'My power and the **m** of my hand have Dt 8:17
so that he **m** not die by the hand of the Jos 20:9
to come your children **m** say to our Jos 22:24
So your children **m** make our children Jos 22:25
of the people of Israel **m** know war, Jgs 3:2
Kishon. March on, my soul, with **m**! Jgs 5:21
as he rises in his **m**." And the land had Jgs 5:31
"Go in this **m** of yours and save Israel Jgs 6:14
the seventy sons of Jerubbaal **m** come, Jgs 9:24
strength lies, and how you **m** be bound, Jgs 16:6
Please tell me how you **m** be bound." Jgs 16:10
Tell me how you **m** be bound." And he Jgs 16:13
for not by **m** shall a man prevail. 1 Sm 2:9
that you **m** eat with the guests." So 1 Sm 9:24
that he **m** become the king's 1 Sm 18:27
that he **m** kill him in the morning. 1 Sm 19:11
danced before the LORD with all his **m**. 2 Sm 6:14
with a dispute or cause **m** come to me, 2 Sm 15:4
so that the LORD **m** bring harm upon 2 Sm 17:14
a house, that my name **m** be there. 1 Kgs 8:16
the LORD that he **m** fulfill his word, 1 Kgs 12:15
that he **m** permit no one to go out or 1 Kgs 15:17
rest of all the acts of Asa, all his **m**, 1 Kgs 15:23
Baasha and what he did, and his **m**, 1 Kgs 16:5
he did, and the **m** that he showed, 1 Kgs 16:27
And he asked that he **m** die, saying, 1 Kgs 19:4
and his **m** that he showed, 1 Kgs 22:45
and all that he did, and all his **m**, 2 Kgs 10:34
and all that he did, and his **m**, 2 Kgs 13:8
and the **m** with which he fought 2 Kgs 13:12
of Jehoash that he did, and his **m**, 2 Kgs 14:15
and all that he did, and his **m**, 2 Kgs 14:28
that he **m** help him to confirm his 2 Kgs 15:19
Hezekiah and all his **m** and how he 2 Kgs 20:20
that they **m** provoke me to anger 2 Kgs 22:17
that no one **m** burn his son or his 2 Kgs 23:10
that he **m** establish the words of the 2 Kgs 23:24
with all his soul and with all his **m**, 2 Kgs 23:25
that he **m** not reign in Jerusalem, 2 Kgs 23:33
and that your hand **m** be with me, 1 Chr 4:10
harm so that it **m** not bring me 1 Chr 4:10
rejoicing before God with all their **m**, 1 Chr 13:8
In your hand are power and **m**, and 1 Chr 29:12
his rule and his **m** and of the 1 Chr 29:30
a house, that my name **m** be there, 2 Chr 6:5
place, you and the ark of your **m**. 2 Chr 6:41
God that the LORD **m** fulfill his word, 2 Chr 10:15
that he **m** permit no one to go out or 2 Chr 16:1
In your hand are power and **m**, so 2 Chr 20:6
in order that he **m** give them into 2 Chr 25:20
singing with all their **m** to the LORD. 2 Chr 30:21
that they **m** give themselves to the 2 Chr 31:4
in order that they **m** take the city. 2 Chr 32:18
that they **m** provoke me to anger 2 Chr 34:25
that they **m** distribute them 2 Chr 35:12
mouth of Jeremiah **m** be fulfilled, 2 Chr 36:22
by the mouth of Jeremiah **m** be fulfilled, Ezr 1:1
that we **m** write down the names of their Ezr 5:10
that we **m** humble ourselves before our Ezr 8:21
that they **m** do with them as they Neh 9:24
that no load **m** be brought in on the Neh 13:19
so that he **m** take off his sackcloth, Est 4:4
that he **m** show it to Esther and explain it Est 4:8
people or province that **m** attack them, Est 8:11
And all the acts of his power and **m**, and Est 10:2
"Oh that I **m** have my request, and that Jb 6:8
not a man, as I am, that I **m** answer him, Jb 9:32

us, who **m** lay his hand on us both. Jb 9:33
"With God are wisdom and **m**; he has Jb 12:13
Oh, that I knew where I **m** find him, that Jb 23:3
find him, that I **m** come even to his seat! Jb 23:3
with the **m** of your hand you persecute Jb 30:21
that it **m** take hold of the skirts of the Jb 38:13
"Do you give the horse his **m**? Do you Jb 39:19
crushed, sink down, and fall by his **m**. Ps 10:10
heaven with the saving **m** of his right Ps 20:6
and by its great **m** it cannot rescue. Ps 33:17
your name, and vindicate me by your **m**. Ps 54:1
the mountains, being girded with **m**; Ps 65:6
who rules by his **m** forever, whose eyes Ps 66:7
I proclaim your **m** to another Ps 71:18
You divided the sea by your **m**; you Ps 74:13
made known your **m** among the Ps 77:14
the glorious deeds of the LORD, and his **m**, Ps 78:4
that the next generation **m** know them, Ps 78:6
stir up your **m** and come to save us! Ps 80:2
The King in his **m** loves justice. You Ps 99:4
so that they **m** not again cover the Ps 104:9
that they **m** keep his statutes and Ps 105:45
that he **m** make known his mighty Ps 106:8
my heart, that I **m** not sin against you. Ps 119:11
afflicted, that I **m** learn your statutes. Ps 119:71
place, you and the ark of your **m**. Ps 132:8
shall speak of the **m** of your awesome Ps 145:6
so that the waters **m** not transgress his Prv 8:29
a man of knowledge enhances his **m**, Prv 24:5
till I **m** see what was good for the Eccl 2:3
though a man **m** prevail against one Eccl 4:12
hand finds to do, do it with your **m**, Eccl 9:10
But I say that wisdom is better than **m**, Eccl 9:16
the Spirit of counsel and **m**, Is 11:2
turned away, that you **m** comfort me. Is 12:1
tell you that they **m** know what the LORD Is 19:12
have waited for him, that he **m** save us. Is 25:9
you who are near, acknowledge my **m**. Is 33:13
Behold, the Lord GOD comes with **m**, and Is 40:10
all by name, by the greatness of his **m**, Is 40:26
who has no **m** he increases strength. Is 40:29
it from the beginning, that we **m** know, Is 41:26
know, and beforehand, that we **m** say, Is 41:26
the heat of his anger and the **m** of battle; Is 42:25
myself that they **m** declare my praise. Is 43:21
and that Israel **m** be gathered to him— Is 49:5
that I **m** bless him and multiply him. Is 51:2
work of my hands, that I **m** be glorified. Is 60:21
Where are your zeal and your **m**? Is 63:15
that the mountains **m** quake at your Is 64:1
and that the nations **m** tremble at your Is 64:2
that I **m** weep day and night for the slain Jer 9:1
that I **m** leave my people and go away Jer 9:2
let not the mighty man boast in his **m**, Jer 9:23
are great, and your name is great in **m**. Jer 10:6
LORD, that they **m** be for me a people, Jer 13:11
make them know my power and my **m**, Jer 16:21
that they **m** not hear and receive Jer 17:23
course is evil, and their **m** is not right. Jer 23:10
that you **m** provoke me to anger with the Jer 25:7
bow of Elam, the mainstay of their **m**. Jer 49:35
down in fierce anger all the **m** of Israel; Lam 2:3
you and exalted the **m** of your foes. Lam 2:17
that it **m** stand in battle in the day of Ezk 13:5
where it was planted, that he **m** water it. Ezk 17:7
that it **m** produce branches and bear Ezk 17:8
that the kingdom **m** be humble and Ezk 17:14
and keep his covenant that it **m** stand. Ezk 17:14
that they **m** give him horses and a Ezk 17:15
that they **m** know that I am the LORD Ezk 20:12
firstborn, that I **m** devastate them. Ezk 20:26
I did it that they **m** know that I am the Ezk 20:26
fall, and her proud **m** shall come down; Ezk 30:6
and her proud **m** shall come to an end Ezk 30:18
who for all their **m** are laid with those Ezk 32:29
the terror that they caused by their **m**; Ezk 32:30
and her proud **m** shall come to an Ezk 33:28
that they **m** make its pasturelands a Ezk 36:5
here in order that I **m** show it to you. Ezk 40:4
that he **m** show the interpretation to the Dn 2:16
and his companions **m** not be destroyed Dn 2:18
ever, to whom belong wisdom and **m**. Dn 2:20
for you have given me wisdom and **m**, Dn 2:23
the kingdom, the power, and the **m**, Dn 2:37
that they **m** make known to me the Dn 4:6
and his concubines **m** drink from them. Dn 5:2
so that the king **m** suffer no loss. Dn 6:2
that nothing **m** be changed concerning Dn 6:17
that they **m** enlarge their border. Am 1:13
Jonah, that it **m** be a shade over his head, Jon 4:6
And he asked that he **m** die and said, "It Jon 4:8
Spirit of the LORD, and with justice and **m**, Mi 3:8
shall see and be ashamed of all their **m**; Mi 7:16
guilty men, whose own **m** is their god!" Hab 1:11
Not by **m**, nor by power, but by my Zec 4:6
stopped their ears that they **m** not hear. Zec 7:11
was laid, that the temple **m** be built. Zec 8:9
that you **m** not kindle fire on my altar Mal 1:10
spoken by the prophets **m** be fulfilled: Mt 2:23
by the prophet Isaiah **m** be fulfilled: Mt 4:14
—so that they **m** accuse him. Mt 12:10
an oath to give her whatever she **m** ask. Mt 14:7
him that they **m** only touch the Mt 14:36
to him that he **m** lay his hands on Mt 19:13
of the prophets **m** be fulfilled." Then Mt 26:56
against Jesus that they **m** put him to Mt 26:59
the Sabbath, so that they **m** accuse him. Mk 3:2
apostles) so that they **m** be with him Mk 3:14
be with him and he **m** send them out to Mk 3:14
begged him that he **m** be with him. Mk 5:18
him that they **m** touch even the Mk 6:56
what this rising from the dead **m** mean. Mk 9:10
to him that he **m** touch them, Mk 10:13
possible, the hour **m** pass from him. Mk 14:35
so that they **m** go and anoint him. Mk 16:1
discern what sort of greeting this **m** be. Lk 1:29
our enemies, **m** serve him without fear, Lk 1:74
John, whether he **m** be the Christ, Lk 3:15
so that they **m** find a reason to accuse Lk 6:7
one another what they **m** do to Jesus. Lk 6:11
had gone begged that he **m** be with him, Lk 8:38
them, so that they **m** not perceive it. Lk 9:45
to catch him in something he **m** say. Lk 11:54
that I **m** celebrate with my friends. Lk 15:29
infants to him that he **m** touch them. Lk 18:15
that he **m** know what they had gained Lk 19:15
at my coming I **m** have collected it Lk 19:23
that they **m** catch him in something Lk 20:20
and officers how he **m** betray him to Lk 22:4
have you, that he **m** sift you like wheat, Lk 22:31
the light, that all **m** believe through him. Jn 1:7
water, that he **m** be revealed to Israel." Jn 1:31
order that the world **m** be saved through Jn 3:17
that they **m** have some charge to bring Jn 8:6
the works of God **m** be displayed in him. Jn 9:3
them know, so that they **m** arrest him. Jn 11:57
by the prophet Isaiah **m** be fulfilled: Jn 12:38
that the Scripture **m** be fulfilled. Jn 17:12
that I **m** not be delivered over to the Jn 18:36
Pilate that their legs **m** be broken and Jn 19:31
broken and that they **m** be taken away. Jn 19:31
place that the Scripture **m** be fulfilled: Jn 19:36
asked Pilate that he **m** take away the Jn 19:38
at least his shadow **m** fall on some of Acts 5:15
You **m** even be found opposing God!" Acts 5:39
for them that they **m** receive the Holy Acts 8:15
he **m** bring them bound to Jerusalem. Acts 9:2
on him so that he **m** regain his sight." Acts 9:12
the vision that he had seen **m** mean, Acts 10:17
that these things **m** be told them Acts 13:42
the hope that they **m** feel their way Acts 17:27
so that he **m** not have to spend time Acts 20:16
hear me this day **m** become such as I Acts 26:29
And fearing that we **m** run on the Acts 27:29
so that he **m** be just and the justifier of Rom 3:26
grace also **m** reign through Rom 5:21
we too **m** walk in newness of life. Rom 6:4
the body of sin **m** be brought to Rom 6:6
in order that sin **m** be shown to be sin, Rom 7:13
the commandment **m** become sinful Rom 7:13
requirement of the law **m** be fulfilled in Rom 8:4
in order that he **m** be the firstborn Rom 8:29
God's purpose of election **m** continue, Rom 9:11
up, that I **m** show my power in you, Rom 9:17
that my name **m** be proclaimed in Rom 9:17
stumble in order that they **m** fall? Rom 11:11
broken off so that I **m** be grafted in." Rom 11:19
a gift to him that he **m** be repaid?" Rom 11:35
that he **m** be Lord both of the dead and Rom 14:9
of the Scriptures we **m** have hope. Rom 15:4
that the Gentiles **m** glorify God for Rom 15:9
that no human being **m** boast in the 1 Cor 1:29
that your faith **m** not rest in the 1 Cor 2:5
that we **m** understand the things 1 Cor 2:12
so that we **m** share the rule with you! 1 Cor 4:8
to all, that I **m** win more of them. 1 Cor 9:19
the law) that I **m** win those under the 1 Cor 9:20
of Christ) that I **m** win those outside 1 Cor 9:21
became weak, that I **m** win the weak. 1 Cor 9:22
that by all means I **m** save some. 1 Cor 9:22
that we **m** not desire evil as they did. 1 Cor 10:6
so that you **m** have a second 2 Cor 1:15
when I came I **m** not suffer pain from 2 Cor 2:3
that I **m** test you and know whether 2 Cor 2:9
so that the Israelites **m** not gaze at the 2 Cor 3:13
that those who live **m** no longer live 2 Cor 5:15
in him we **m** become the 2 Cor 5:21
earnestness for us **m** be revealed to 2 Cor 7:12
you by his poverty **m** become rich. 2 Cor 8:9
myself so that you **m** be exalted, 2 Cor 11:7
in order that I **m** preach him among Gal 1:16
so that they **m** bring us into slavery— Gal 2:4
truth of the gospel **m** be preserved for Gal 2:5
I died to the law, so that I **m** live to God. Gal 2:19
the blessing of Abraham **m** come to the Gal 3:14
so that we **m** receive the promised Spirit Gal 3:14
faith in Jesus Christ **m** be given to those Gal 3:22
in order that we **m** be justified by faith. Gal 3:24
so that we **m** receive adoption as sons. Gal 4:5
to hope in Christ **m** be to the praise Eph 1:12
to the working of his great **m** Eph 1:19
coming ages he **m** show the Eph 2:7
that he **m** create in himself one new Eph 2:15
and **m** reconcile us both to God in one Eph 2:16
wisdom of God **m** now be made Eph 3:10
the heavens, that he **m** fill all things.) Eph 4:10
that he **m** sanctify her, having Eph 5:26
so that he **m** present the church to Eph 5:27
that she **m** be holy and without Eph 5:27
the Lord and in the strength of his **m**. Eph 6:10
all power, according to his glorious **m**, Col 1:11
that in everything he **m** be preeminent. Col 1:18
that we **m** not be a burden to any of 1 Thes 2:9
the Gentiles that they **m** be saved— 1 Thes 2:16
awake or asleep we **m** live with him. 1 Thes 5:10
the Lord and from the glory of his **m**, 2 Thes 1:9
that we **m** not be a burden to any of 2 Thes 3:8
Jesus Christ **m** display his perfect 1 Tm 1:16
me the message **m** be fully 2 Tm 4:17
and all the Gentiles **m** hear it. 2 Tm 4:17
so that you **m** put what remained into Ti 1:5
his grace we **m** become heirs according Ti 3:7
in order that he **m** serve me on your Phlm 1:13
order that your goodness **m** not be by Phlm 1:14
that you **m** have him back forever, Phlm 1:15
grace of God he **m** taste death for Heb 2:9
through death he **m** destroy the one Heb 2:14
so that he **m** become a merciful and Heb 2:17
fled for refuge **m** have strong Heb 6:18
One **m** even say that Levi himself, who Heb 7:9
of the firstborn **m** not touch them. Heb 11:28
so that they **m** rise again to a better Heb 11:35
he prayed fervently that it **m** not rain, Jas 5:17
so that you **m** follow in his steps. 1 Pt 2:21
that we **m** die to sin and live to 1 Pt 2:24
that he **m** bring us to God, 1 Pt 3:18
they **m** live in the spirit the way God 1 Pt 4:6
angels, though greater in **m** and power, 2 Pt 2:11
that it **m** become plain that they all are 1 Jn 2:19
world, so that we **m** live through him. 1 Jn 4:9
so that they **m** eat food sacrificed to idols Rv 2:14
and wisdom and **m** and honor and Rv 5:12
and glory and **m** forever and ever!" Rv 5:13
that no wind **m** blow on earth or sea or Rv 7:1
honor and power and **m** be to our God Rv 7:12
that a third of their light **m** be darkened, Rv 8:12
third of the day **m** be kept from shining, Rv 8:12
when she bore her child he **m** devour it. Rv 12:4
eagle so that she **m** fly from the serpent Rv 12:14
image of the beast **m** even speak and Rv 13:15
even speak and **m** cause those who Rv 13:15
so that he **m** not deceive the nations any Rv 20:3

MIGHTIER (12)

from us, for you are much **m** than we." Gn 26:16
a nation greater and **m** than they." Nm 14:12
nations greater and **m** than yourselves, Dt 4:38
more numerous and **m** than yourselves, Dt 7:1
nations greater and **m** than yourselves, Dt 9:1
of you a nation **m** and greater than they.' Dt 9:14
nations greater and **m** than yourselves. Dt 11:23
M than the thunders of many waters, Ps 93:4
waters, **m** than the waves of the sea, Ps 93:4
he who is coming after me is **m** than I, Mt 3:11
"After me comes he who is **m** than I, Mk 1:7
water, but he who is **m** than I is coming, Lk 3:16

MIGHTIEST (1)

which is **m** among beasts and does Prv 30:30

MIGHTILY (4)

the waters prevailed so **m** on the earth Gn 7:19
voice; he will roar **m** against his fold, Jer 25:30
and let them call out **m** to God. Jon 3:8
continued to increase and prevail **m**. Acts 19:20

MIGHTY (262)

These were the **m** men who were of old, Gn 6:4
he was the first on earth to be a **m** man. Gn 10:8
He was a **m** hunter before the LORD. Gn 10:9
"Like Nimrod a **m** hunter before the Gn 10:9
surely become a great and **m** nation, Gn 18:18
"With **m** wrestlings I have wrestled with Gn 30:8
the hands of the **M** One of Jacob (from Gn 49:24
your father are **m** beyond the blessings Gn 49:26
of Israel are too many and too **m** for us. Ex 1:9
you go unless compelled by a **m** hand. Ex 3:19

they sank like lead in the **m** waters. Ex 15:10
with great power and with a **m** hand? Ex 32:11
for me, since they are too **m** for me. Nm 22:6
your greatness and your **m** hand. Dt 3:24
can do such works and **m** acts as yours? Dt 3:24
by a **m** hand and an outstretched arm, Dt 4:34
from there with a **m** hand and an Dt 5:15
brought us out of Egypt with a **m** hand. Dt 6:21
you out with a **m** hand and redeemed you Dt 7:8
saw, the signs, the wonders, the **m** hand, Dt 7:19
brought out of Egypt with a **m** hand. Dt 9:26
gods and Lord of lords, the great, the **m**, Dt 10:17
his **m** hand and his outstretched arm, Dt 11:2
a nation, great, **m**, and populous. Dt 26:5
of Egypt with a **m** hand and an Dt 26:8
and for all the **m** power and all the great Dt 34:12
know that the hand of the LORD is **m**, Jos 4:24
hand, with its king and **m** men of valor. Jos 6:2
And Joshua chose 30,000 **m** men of valor Jos 8:3
with him, and all the **m** men of valor. Jos 10:7
"The **M** One, God, the LORD! The Jos 22:22
One, God, the LORD! The **M** One, Jos 22:22
marched down for me against the **m**. Jgs 5:13
to the help of the LORD against the **m**. Jgs 5:23
LORD is with you, O **m** man of valor." Jgs 6:12
Jephthah the Gileadite was a **m** warrior, Jgs 11:1
The bows of the **m** are broken, but the 1 Sm 2:4
the camp, all Israel gave a **m** shout, 1 Sm 4:5
us from the power of these **m** gods? 1 Sm 4:8
thundered with a **m** sound that day 1 Sm 7:10
high places! How the **m** have fallen! 2 Sm 1:19
there the shield of the **m** was defiled, 2 Sm 1:21
of the slain, from the fat of the **m**, 2 Sm 1:22
"How the **m** have fallen in the midst 2 Sm 1:25
"How the **m** have fallen, and the 2 Sm 1:27
Joab and all the host of the **m** men. 2 Sm 10:7
people and all the **m** men were on his 2 Sm 16:6
your father and his men are **m** men, 2 Sm 17:8
knows that your father is a **m** man, 2 Sm 17:10
and the Pelethites, and all the **m** men. 2 Sm 20:7
hated me, for they were too **m** for me. 2 Sm 22:18
the names of the **m** men whom David 2 Sm 23:8
among the three **m** men was Eleazar 2 Sm 23:9
Then the three **m** men broke 2 Sm 23:16
it. These things the three **m** men did. 2 Sm 23:17
won a name beside the three **m** men. 2 Sm 23:22
and Rei and David's **m** men were not 1 Kgs 1:8
or Benaiah or the **m** men or Solomon 1 Kgs 1:10
of your great name and your **m** hand, 1 Kgs 8:42
to Syria. He was a **m** man of valor, 2 Kgs 5:1
officials and all the **m** men of valor, 2 Kgs 24:14
was the first on earth to be a **m** man. 1 Chr 1:10
Hodaviah, and Jahdiel, **m** warriors, 1 Chr 5:24
Tola, **m** warriors of their generations, 1 Chr 7:2
were in all 87,000 **m** warriors, 1 Chr 7:5
heads of fathers' houses, **m** warriors. 1 Chr 7:7
of their fathers' houses, **m** warriors, 1 Chr 7:9
of their fathers' houses, **m** warriors, 1 Chr 7:11
houses, approved, **m** warriors, 1 Chr 7:40
were men who were **m** warriors, 1 Chr 8:40
m men for the work of the service of 1 Chr 9:13
are the chiefs of David's **m** men, 1 Chr 11:10
is an account of David's **m** men: 1 Chr 11:11
among the three **m** men was 1 Chr 11:12
Then the three **m** men broke 1 Chr 11:18
These things did the three **m** men. 1 Chr 11:19
a name beside the three **m** men. 1 Chr 11:24
The **m** men were Asahel the brother 1 Chr 11:26
were among the **m** men who helped 1 Chr 12:1
a **m** man among the thirty and a 1 Chr 12:4
in the wilderness **m** and experienced 1 Chr 12:8
for they were all **m** men of valor and 1 Chr 12:21
Simeonites, **m** men of valor for war, 1 Chr 12:25
Zadok, a young man **m** in valor, 1 Chr 12:28
20,800, **m** men of valor, 1 Chr 12:30
Joab and all the army of the **m** men. 1 Chr 19:8
Benaiah who was a **m** man of the 1 Chr 27:6
the **m** men and all the seasoned 1 Chr 28:1
All the leaders and the **m** men, and 1 Chr 29:24
name and your **m** hand and your 2 Chr 6:32
with 800,000 chosen **m** warriors. 2 Chr 13:3
But Abijah grew **m**. And he took 2 Chr 13:21
bows. All these were **m** men of valor. 2 Chr 14:8
help, between the **m** and the weak. 2 Chr 14:11
He had soldiers, **m** men of valor, in 2 Chr 17:13
with 300,000 **m** men of valor; 2 Chr 17:14
LORD, with 200,000 **m** men of valor. 2 Chr 17:16
Eliada, a **m** man of valor, with 2 Chr 17:17
He hired also 100,000 **m** men of valor 2 Chr 25:6
of fathers' houses of **m** men of valor 2 Chr 26:12
who could make war with **m** power, 2 Chr 26:13
So Jotham became **m**, because he 2 Chr 27:6
And Zichri, a **m** man of Ephraim, 2 Chr 28:7
his officers and his **m** men to stop the 2 Chr 32:3
off all the **m** warriors and 2 Chr 32:21
And **m** kings have been over Jerusalem, Ezr 4:20
and before all the king's **m** officers. Ezr 7:28
and as far as the house of the **m** men. Neh 3:16
the depths, as a stone into **m** waters. Neh 9:11
therefore, our God, the great, the **m**, Neh 9:32
and their brothers, **m** men of valor, Neh 11:14
their mouth and from the hand of the **m**. Jb 5:15
He is wise in heart and **m** in strength Jb 9:4
it is a contest of strength, behold, he is **m**! Jb 9:19
away stripped and overthrows the **m**. Jb 12:19
live, reach old age, and grow **m** in power? Jb 21:7
prolongs the life of the **m** by his power; Jb 24:22
condemn him who is righteous and **m**, Jb 34:17
and the **m** are taken away by no Jb 34:20
He shatters the **m** without investigation Jb 34:24
call for help because of the arm of the **m**. Jb 35:9
"Behold, God is **m**, and does not despise Jb 36:5
he is **m** in strength of understanding. Jb 36:5
to the downpour, his **m** downpour. Jb 37:6
his limbs, or his **m** strength, Jb 41:12
he raises himself up the **m** are afraid; Jb 41:25
hated me, for they were too **m** for me. Ps 18:17
The LORD, strong and **m**, the LORD, Ps 24:8
strong and mighty, the LORD, **m** in battle! Ps 24:8
in the **m** throng I will praise you. Ps 35:18
But my foes are vigorous, they are **m**, Ps 38:19
Gird your sword on your thigh, O **m** one, Ps 45:3
The **M** One, God the LORD, speaks and Ps 50:1
devouring fire, around him a **m** tempest. Ps 50:3
Why do you boast of evil, O **m** man? Ps 52:1
my salvation and my glory; my **m** rock, Ps 62:7
he sends out his voice, his **m** voice. Ps 68:33
m are those who would destroy me, those Ps 69:4
With the **m** deeds of the Lord GOD I will Ps 71:16
work, and meditate on your **m** deeds. Ps 77:12
shade, the **m** cedars with its branches. Ps 80:10
O LORD God of hosts, who is **m** as you are, Ps 89:8
your enemies with your **m** arm. Ps 89:10
You have a **m** arm; strong is your Ps 89:13
"I have granted help to one who is **m**; Ps 89:19
waves of the sea, the LORD on high is **m**! Ps 93:4
angels, you **m** ones who do his word, Ps 103:20
Who can utter the **m** deeds of the LORD, Ps 106:2
he might make known his **m** power. Ps 106:8
sends forth from Zion your **m** scepter. Ps 110:2
His offspring will be **m** in the land; the Ps 112:2
LORD and vowed to the **M** One of Jacob, Ps 132:2
dwelling place for the **M** One of Jacob." Ps 132:5
many nations and killed **m** kings, Ps 135:10
and killed **m** kings, for his steadfast Ps 136:18
another, and shall declare your **m** acts. Ps 145:4
to the children of man your **m** deeds, Ps 145:12
praise him in his **m** heavens! Ps 150:1
Praise him for his **m** deeds; praise him Ps 150:2
low, and all her slain are a **m** throng. Prv 7:26
is slow to anger is better than the **m**, Prv 16:32
the city of the **m** and brings down the Prv 21:22
the rock badgers are a people not **m**, Prv 30:26
Around it are sixty **m** men, some of the Sg 3:7
mighty men, some of the **m** men of Israel, Sg 3:7
the LORD of hosts, the **M** One of Israel: Is 1:24
the **m** man and the soldier, the judge and Is 3:2
by the sword and your **m** men in battle. Is 3:25
them the waters of the River, **m** and many, Is 8:7
be called Wonderful Counselor, **M** God, Is 9:6
the remnant of Jacob, to the **m** God. Is 10:21
have summoned my **m** men to execute Is 13:3
they roar like the roaring of **m** waters! Is 17:12
near and far, a nation **m** and conquering, Is 18:2
near and far, a nation **m** and conquering, Is 18:7
of the archers of the **m** men of the sons Is 21:17
the Lord has one who is **m** and strong; Is 28:2
a destroying tempest, like a storm of **m**, Is 28:2
them, and young steers with the **m** bulls. Is 34:7
The LORD goes out like a **m** man, like a Is 42:13
he shows himself **m** against his foes. Is 42:13
a way in the sea, a path in the **m** waters, Is 43:16
Can the prey be taken from the **m**, or the Is 49:24
the captives of the **m** shall be taken, Is 49:25
your Redeemer, the **M** One of Jacob." Is 49:26
The dogs have a **m** appetite; they never Is 56:11
and your Redeemer, the **M** One of Jacob. Is 60:16
a clan, and the smallest one a **m** nation; Is 60:22
by his right hand and by his **m** arm: Is 62:8
I, speaking in righteousness, **m** to save." Is 63:1
an open tomb; they are all **m** warriors. Jer 5:16
let not the **m** man boast in his might, Jer 9:23
like a **m** warrior who cannot save? Jer 14:9
after them, O great and **m** God, Jer 32:18
great in counsel and **m** in deed, whose Jer 32:19
Why are your **m** ones face down? They Jer 46:15
say, 'We are heroes and **m** men of war'? Jer 48:14
say, 'How the **m** scepter is broken, the Jer 48:17
a **m** nation and many kings are Jer 50:41
Babylon waste and stilling her **m** voice. Jer 51:55
Lord rejected all my **m** men in my Lam 1:15
Pharaoh with his **m** army and great Ezk 17:17
surely with a **m** hand and an Ezk 20:33
with a **m** hand and an outstretched Ezk 20:34
and your **m** pillars will fall to the Ezk 26:11
city renowned, who was **m** on the sea; Ezk 26:17
the hand of a **m** one of the nations. Ezk 31:11
to fall by the swords of **m** ones, Ezk 32:12
The **m** chiefs shall speak of them, Ezk 32:21
And they do not lie with the **m**, the Ezk 32:27
for the terror of the **m** men was in the Ezk 32:27
on horses, a great host, a **m** army. Ezk 38:15
You shall eat the flesh of the **m**, and Ezk 39:18
with **m** men and all kinds of Ezk 39:20
image, **m** and of exceeding brightness, Dn 2:31
ordered some of the **m** men of his army Dn 3:20
great are his signs, how **m** his wonders! Dn 4:3
I have built by my **m** power as a royal Dn 4:30
and destroy **m** men and the people who Dn 8:24
out of the land of Egypt with a **m** hand, Dn 9:15
Then a **m** king shall arise, who shall Dn 11:3
with an exceedingly great and **m** army, Dn 11:25
Consecrate for war; stir up the **m** men. Jl 3:9
strength, nor shall the **m** save his life; Am 2:14
of heart among the **m** shall flee away Am 2:16
And your **m** men shall be dismayed, O Ob 1:9
sea, and there was a **m** tempest on the sea, Jon 1:4
The shield of his **m** men is red; his Na 2:3
your horses, the surging of **m** waters. Hab 3:15
is bitter; the **m** man cries aloud there. Zep 1:14
is in your midst, a **m** one who will save; Zep 3:17
They shall be like **m** men in battle, Zec 10:5
shall become like a **m** warrior, Zec 10:7
and do many **m** works in your name?' Mt 7:22
where most of his **m** works had been Mt 11:20
For if the **m** works done in you had Mt 11:21
For if the **m** works done in you had Mt 11:23
get this wisdom and these **m** works? Mt 13:54
he did not do many **m** works there, Mt 13:58
How are such **m** works done by his Mk 6:2
And he could do no **m** work there, except Mk 6:5
no one who does a **m** work in my name Mk 9:39
for he who is **m** has done great things Lk 1:49
brought down the **m** from their thrones Lk 1:52
For if the **m** works done in you had Lk 10:13
voice for all the **m** works that they had Lk 19:37
who was a prophet **m** in deed and word Lk 24:19
heaven a sound like a **m** rushing wind, Acts 2:2
our own tongues the **m** works of God." Acts 2:11
by God with **m** works and wonders Acts 2:22
and he was **m** in his words and deeds. Acts 7:22
signs and wonders and **m** works. 2 Cor 12:12
from heaven with his **m** angels 2 Thes 1:7
out of weakness, became **m** in war, Heb 11:34
under the **m** hand of God so that at the 1 Pt 5:6
I saw another **m** angel coming down Rv 10:1
And he called out with a **m** voice, Rv 18:2
for **m** is the Lord God who has judged Rv 18:8
You great city, you **m** city, Babylon! Rv 18:10
Then a **m** angel took up a stone like a Rv 18:21
and like the sound of **m** peals of thunder, Rv 19:6
flesh of captains, the flesh of **m** men, Rv 19:18

MIGRATED (1)
And as people **m** from the east, they Gn 11:2

MIGRON (2)
Gibeah in the pomegranate cave at **M**. 1 Sm 14:2
to Aiath; he has passed through **M**; Is 10:28

MIJAMIN (4)
the fifth to Malchijah, the sixth to **M**, 1 Chr 24:9
Izziah, Malchijah, **M**, Eleazar, Ezr 10:25
Meshullam, Abijah, **M**, Neh 10:7
M, Maadiah, Bilgah, Neh 12:5

MIKLOTH (3)
and **M** (he fathered Shimeah). Now 1 Chr 8:32
Gedor, Ahio, Zechariah, and **M**; 1 Chr 9:37
and **M** was the father of Shimeam; 1 Chr 9:38

MIKNEIAH (2)
Mattithiah, Eliphelehu, and **M**, 1 Chr 15:18
Eliphelehu, **M**, Obed-edom, 1 Chr 15:21

MIKTAM (6)
A **M** of David. Ps 16:T
A **M** of David, when the Philistines Ps 56:T
A **M** of David, when he fled from Saul, in Ps 57:T
to Do Not Destroy. A **M** of David. Ps 58:T
A **M** of David, when Saul sent men to Ps 59:T
A **M** of David; for instruction; when he Ps 60:T

MILALAI (1)
Shemaiah, Azarel, **M**, Gilalai, Neh 12:36

MILCAH (11)
M, the daughter of Haran the father of Gn 11:29
of Haran the father of **M** and Iscah. Gn 11:29
M also has borne children to your Gn 22:20

These eight **M** bore to Nahor, Gn 22:23
who was born to Bethuel the son of **M**, Gn 24:15
the daughter of Bethuel the son of **M**, Gn 24:24
Nahor's son, whom **M** bore to him.' Gn 24:47
Noah, Hoglah, **M**, and Tirzah. Nm 26:33
Mahlah, Noah, Hoglah, **M**, and Tirzah. Nm 27:1
Tirzah, Hoglah, **M**, and Noah, Nm 36:11
Mahlah, Noah, Hoglah, **M**, and Tirzah. Jos 17:3

MILCOM (6)
and after **M** the abomination of the 1 Kgs 11:5
and **M** the god of the Ammonites, 1 Kgs 11:33
and for **M** the abomination of the 2 Kgs 23:13
Why then has **M** dispossessed Gad, and Jer 49:1
For **M** shall go into exile, with his priests Jer 49:3
swear to the LORD and yet swear by **M**, Zep 1:5

MILDEW (5)
drought and with blight and with **m**. Dt 28:22
pestilence or blight or **m** or locust or 1 Kgs 8:37
pestilence or blight or **m** or locust or 2 Chr 6:28
"I struck you with blight and **m**; your Am 4:9
with blight and with **m** and with hail, Hg 2:17

MILE (1)
And if anyone forces you to go one **m**, go Mt 5:41

MILES (4)
you to go one mile, go with him two **m**. Mt 5:41
about seven **m** from Jerusalem, Lk 24:13
they had rowed about three or four **m**, Jn 6:19
was near Jerusalem, about two **m** off, Jn 11:18

MILETUS (3)
and the day after that we went to **M**. Acts 20:15
Now from **M** he sent to Ephesus and Acts 20:17
I left Trophimus, who was ill, at **M**. 2 Tm 4:20

MILITARY (2)
his nobles and **m** commanders and the Mk 6:21
hall with the **m** tribunes and the Acts 25:23

MILK (49)
he took curds and **m** and the calf that Gn 18:8
wine, and his teeth whiter than **m**. Gn 49:12
land, a land flowing with **m** and honey, Ex 3:8
a land flowing with **m** and honey."' Ex 3:17
you, a land flowing with **m** and honey, Ex 13:5
not boil a young goat in its mother's **m**. Ex 23:19
up to a land flowing with **m** and honey; Ex 33:3
boil a young goat in its mother's **m**." Ex 34:26
a land flowing with **m** and honey.' Lv 20:24
It flows with **m** and honey, and this is Nm 13:27
us, a land that flows with **m** and honey. Nm 14:8
of a land flowing with **m** and honey, Nm 16:13
a land flowing with **m** and honey, Nm 16:14
you, in a land flowing with **m** and honey. Dt 6:3
a land flowing with **m** and honey. Dt 11:9
not boil a young goat in its mother's **m**. Dt 14:21
land, a land flowing with **m** and honey. Dt 26:9
a land flowing with **m** and honey.' Dt 26:15
you, a land flowing with **m** and honey, Dt 27:3
the land flowing with **m** and honey, Dt 31:20
from the herd, and **m** from the flock, Dt 32:14
to us, a land flowing with **m** and honey. Jos 5:6
she opened a skin of **m** and gave him a Jgs 4:19
He asked water and she gave him **m**; she Jgs 5:25
new cart and two **m** cows on which 1 Sm 6:7
and took two **m** cows and yoked them 1 Sm 6:10
pour me out like **m** and curdle me like Jb 10:10
his pails full of **m** and the marrow of Jb 21:24
will be enough goats' **m** for your food, Prv 27:27
For pressing **m** produces curds, Prv 30:33
honey and **m** are under your tongue; Sg 4:11
my honey, I drank my wine with my **m**. Sg 5:1
beside streams of water, bathed in **m**, Sg 5:12
of the abundance of **m** that they give, Is 7:22
Those who are weaned from the **m**, those Is 28:9
buy wine and **m** without money and Is 55:1
You shall suck the **m** of nations; you Is 60:16
them a land flowing with **m** and honey, Jer 11:5
a land flowing with **m** and honey. Jer 32:22
were purer than snow, whiter than **m**; Lam 4:7
a land flowing with **m** and honey, Ezk 20:6
a land flowing with **m** and honey, Ezk 20:15
fruit, and they shall drink your **m**. Ezk 25:4
wine, and the hills shall flow with **m**, Jl 3:18
I fed you with **m**, not solid food, for you 1 Cor 3:2
a flock without getting some of the **m**? 1 Cor 9:7
of God. You need **m**, not solid food, Heb 5:12
who lives on **m** is unskilled in Heb 5:13
infants, long for the pure spiritual **m**, 1 Pt 2:2

MILKING (1)
thirty **m** camels and their calves, forty Gn 32:15

MILL (5)
one shall take a **m** or an upper millstone Dt 24:6
And he ground at the **m** in the prison. Jgs 16:21
men are compelled to grind at the **m**, Lam 5:13
Two women will be grinding at the **m**; Mt 24:41
and the sound of the **m** will be heard in Rv 18:22

MILLET (1)
barley, beans and lentils, **m** and emmer, Ezk 4:9

MILLION (2)
talents of gold, a **m** talents of silver, 1 Chr 22:14
an army of a **m** men and 300 2 Chr 14:9

MILLO (7)
the city all around from the **M** inward. 2 Sm 5:9
own house and the **M** and the wall of 1 Kgs 9:15
built for her. Then he built the **M**. 1 Kgs 9:24
Solomon built the **M**, and closed up 1 Kgs 11:27
down Joash in the house of **M**, 2 Kgs 12:20
around from the **M** in complete 1 Chr 11:8
and he strengthened the **M** in the city 2 Chr 32:5

MILLSTONE (8)
shall take a mill or an upper **m** in pledge, Dt 24:6
threw an upper **m** on Abimelech's head Jgs 9:53
cast an upper **m** on him from 2 Sm 11:21
is hard as a stone, hard as the lower **m**. Jb 41:24
to have a great **m** fastened around his Mt 18:6
him if a great **m** were hung around his Mk 9:42
for him if a **m** were hung around his Lk 17:2
a stone like a great **m** and threw it into Rv 18:21

MILLSTONES (2)
Take the **m** and grind flour, put off your Is 47:2
the grinding of the **m** and the light of Jer 25:10

MINA (5)
plus fifteen shekels shall be your **m**. Ezk 45:12
your **m** has made ten minas more.' Lk 19:16
'Lord, your **m** has made five minas.' Lk 19:18
came, saying, 'Lord, here is your **m**, Lk 19:20
who stood by, 'Take the **m** from him, Lk 19:24

MINAS (10)
three **m** of gold went into each 1 Kgs 10:17
61,000 darics of gold, 5,000 **m** of silver, Ezr 2:69
priests' garments and 500 **m** of silver. Neh 7:70
darics of gold and 2,200 **m** of silver. Neh 7:71
20,000 darics of gold, 2,000 **m** of silver, Neh 7:72
ten of his servants, he gave them ten **m**, Lk 19:13
your mina has made ten **m** more.' Lk 19:16
'Lord, your mina has made five **m**.' Lk 19:18
give it to the one who has the ten **m**.' Lk 19:24
they said to him, 'Lord, he has ten **m**!' Lk 19:25

MINCING (1)
with their eyes, **m** along as they go, Is 3:16

MIND (112)
but his father kept the saying in **m**. Gn 37:11
Look, you have some evil purpose in **m**. Ex 10:10
the **m** of Pharaoh and his servants was Ex 14:5
craftsman in whose **m** the LORD had Ex 36:2
of man, that he should change his **m**. Nm 23:19
that they had such a **m** as this always, Dt 5:29
and blindness and confusion of **m**, Dt 28:28
you call them to **m** among all the Dt 30:1
to what is in my heart and in my **m**. 1 Sm 2:35
and will tell you all that is on your **m**. 1 Sm 9:19
days ago, do not set your **m** on them, 1 Sm 9:20
an understanding **m** to govern 1 Kgs 3:9
I give you a wise and discerning **m**, 1 Kgs 3:12
and breadth of **m** like the sand on the 1 Kgs 4:29
repent with all their **m** and with all 1 Kgs 8:48
she told him all that was on her **m**. 1 Kgs 10:2
which God had put into his **m**. 1 Kgs 10:24
And the **m** of the king of Syria was 2 Kgs 6:11
were of a single **m** to make David 1 Chr 12:38
Now set your **m** and heart to seek 1 Chr 22:19
a whole heart and with a willing **m**, 1 Chr 28:9
all that he had in **m** for the courts of 1 Chr 28:12
repent with all their **m** and with all 2 Chr 6:38
she told him all that was on her **m**. 2 Chr 9:1
which God had put into his **m**. 2 Chr 9:23
height, for the people had a **m** to work. Neh 4:6
are inventing them out of your own **m**." Neh 6:8
me, and many such things are in his **m**. Jb 23:14
parts or given understanding to the **m**? Jb 38:36
and try me; test my heart and my **m**. Ps 26:2
search." For the inward **m** and heart of a Ps 64:6
has sworn and will not change his **m**, Ps 110:4
sense, but one of twisted **m** is despised. Prv 12:8
Many are the plans in the **m** of a man, Prv 19:21
Whoever trusts in his own **m** is a fool, Prv 28:26
in perfect peace whose **m** is stayed on you, Is 26:3
this and stand firm, recall it to **m**, Is 46:8
not be remembered or come into **m**. Is 65:17
shall not come to **m** or be remembered Jer 3:16
command, nor did it come into my **m**. Jer 7:31
who tests the heart and the **m**, Jer 11:20
LORD search the heart and test the **m**, Jer 17:10
or decree, nor did it come into my **m**— Jer 19:5
who sees the heart and the **m**, Jer 20:12
accomplished the intentions of his **m**. Jer 30:24
them, nor did it enter into my **m**, Jer 32:35
them? Did it not come into his **m**? Jer 44:21
and let Jerusalem come into your **m**: Jer 51:50
But this I call to **m**, and therefore I Lam 3:21
the things that come into your **m**. Ezk 11:5
is in your **m** shall never happen Ezk 20:32
day, thoughts will come into your **m**, Ezk 38:10
you may know the thoughts of your **m**. Dn 2:30
Let his **m** be changed from a man's, and Dn 4:16
and let a beast's **m** be given to him; Dn 4:16
and his **m** was made like that of a beast, Dn 5:21
and set his **m** to deliver Daniel. Dn 6:14
man, and the **m** of a man was given to it. Dn 7:4
and in his own **m** he shall become Dn 8:25
are not setting your **m** on the things of Mt 16:23
afterward he changed his **m** and went. Mt 21:29
with all your soul and with all your **m**. Mt 22:37
he changed his **m** and brought back the Mt 27:3
they were saying, "He is out of his **m**." Mk 3:21
sitting there, clothed and in his right **m**, Mk 5:15
are not setting your **m** on the things of Mk 8:33
and with all your **m** and with all your Mk 12:30
feet of Jesus, clothed and in his right **m**, Lk 8:35
all your strength and with all your **m**, Lk 10:27
are out of your **m**." But she kept Acts 12:15
voice, "Paul, you are out of your **m**; Acts 26:24
is driving you out of your **m**." Acts 26:24
But Paul said, "I am not out of my **m**, Acts 26:25
up to a debased **m** to do what ought Rom 1:28
the law of my **m** and making me Rom 7:23
serve the law of God with my **m**, Rom 7:25
To set the **m** on the flesh is death, but to Rom 8:6
but to set the **m** on the Spirit is life and Rom 8:6
For the **m** that is set on the flesh is Rom 8:7
knows what is the **m** of the Spirit, Rom 8:27
who has known the **m** of the Lord, Rom 11:34
transformed by the renewal of your **m**, Rom 12:2
be fully convinced in his own **m**. Rom 14:5
united in the same **m** and the same 1 Cor 1:10
has understood the **m** of the Lord 1 Cor 2:16
him?" But we have the **m** of Christ. 1 Cor 2:16
spirit prays but my **m** is unfruitful. 1 Cor 14:14
but I will pray with my **m** also; 1 Cor 14:15
but I will sing with my **m** also. 1 Cor 14:15
five words with my **m** in order to 1 Cor 14:19
I made up my **m** not to make another 2 Cor 2:1
if we are in our right **m**, it is for you. 2 Cor 5:13
must give as he has made up his **m**, 2 Cor 9:7
out the desires of the body and the **m**, Eph 2:3
with one **m** striving side by side for the Phil 1:27
my joy by being of the same **m**, Phil 2:2
love, being in full accord and of one **m**. Phil 2:2
Have this **m** among yourselves, which Phil 2:5
once were alienated and hostile in **m**, Col 1:21
up without reason by his sensuous **m**, Col 2:18
quietly, and to **m** your own affairs, 1 Thes 4:11
be quickly shaken in **m** or alarmed, 2 Thes 2:2
who are depraved in **m** and deprived of 1 Tm 6:5
men corrupted in **m** and disqualified 2 Tm 3:8
has sworn and will not change his **m**, Heb 7:21
Finally, all of you, have unity of **m**, 1 Pt 3:8
love, a tender heart, and a humble **m**. 1 Pt 3:8
stirring up your sincere **m** by way of 2 Pt 3:1
that I am he who searches **m** and heart, Rv 2:23
This calls for a **m** with wisdom: the Rv 17:9
These are of one **m** and hand over their Rv 17:13
by being of one **m** and handing over Rv 17:17

MINDFUL (6)
obey and were not **m** of the wonders Neh 9:17
what is man that you are **m** of him, and Ps 8:4
For he who avenges blood is **m** of them; Ps 9:12
their God will be **m** of them and restore Zep 2:7
"What is man, that you are **m** of him, Heb 2:6
is a gracious thing, when, **m** of God, 1 Pt 2:19

MINDS (25)
people change their **m** when they see Ex 13:17
you who test the **m** and hearts, Ps 7:9
and the deceit of their own **m**. Jer 14:14
They speak visions of their own **m**, not Jer 23:16
who prophesy out of their own **m**. Ezk 13:17
afterward change your **m** and believe Mt 21:32
it therefore in your **m** not to meditate Lk 21:14
he opened their **m** to understand the Lk 24:45
and poisoned their **m** against the Acts 14:2
you with words, unsettling your **m**, Acts 15:24
they changed their **m** and said that he Acts 28:6
to the flesh set their **m** on the things of Rom 8:5
to the Spirit set their **m** on the things of Rom 8:5
not say that you are out of your **m**? 1 Cor 14:23
But their **m** were hardened. For to 2 Cor 3:14
has blinded the **m** of the unbelievers, 2 Cor 4:4
Gentiles do, in the futility of their **m**. Eph 4:17
to be renewed in the spirit of your **m**, Eph 4:23

shame, with **m** set on earthly things. Phil 3:19
your hearts and your **m** in Christ Jesus. Phil 4:7
Set your **m** on things that are above, not Col 3:2
but both their **m** and their consciences Ti 1:15
I will put my laws into their **m**, and Heb 8:10
hearts, and write them on their **m**," Heb 10:16
preparing your **m** for action, 1 Pt 1:13

MINE (1) [Noun]
"Surely there is a **m** for silver, and a place Jb 28:1

MINGLE (1)
ashes like bread and **m** tears with my Ps 102:9

MINGLED (4)
seah of fine flour **m** with a fourth of Ex 29:40
The LORD has **m** within her a spirit of Is 19:14
blood Pilate had **m** with their sacrifices. Lk 13:1
to be a sea of glass **m** with fire—and also Rv 15:2

MINIAMIN (3)
Eden, **M**, Jeshua, Shemaiah, 2 Chr 31:15
of Abijah, Zichri; of **M**, of Moadiah, Neh 12:17
Eliakim, Maaseiah, **M**, Micaiah, Neh 12:41

MINISTER (51)
near the altar to **m** in the Holy Place, Ex 28:43
tent of meeting to **m** in the Holy Place, Ex 29:30
or when they come near the altar to **m**, Ex 30:20
the priest, that they may **m** to him. Nm 3:6
of meeting, as they **m** at the tabernacle. Nm 3:7
of Israel as they **m** at the tabernacle. Nm 3:8
sanctuary with which the priests **m**, Nm 3:31
They **m** to their brothers in the tent of Nm 8:26
before the congregation to **m** to them, Nm 16:9
may join you and **m** to you while you Nm 18:2
stand before the LORD to **m** to him and to Dt 10:8
priest who stands to **m** there before the Dt 17:12
tribes to stand and **m** in the name of Dt 18:5
Levites who stand to **m** there before the Dt 18:7
God has chosen them to **m** to him and to Dt 21:5
could not stand to **m** because of the 1 Kgs 8:11
of the LORD and to **m** to him forever. 1 Chr 15:2
of the LORD to **m** regularly before the 1 Chr 16:37
before the LORD and **m** to him and 1 Chr 23:13
could not stand to **m** because of the 2 Chr 5:14
to **m** to him and to be his ministers 2 Chr 29:11
to **m** in the gates of the camp of the 2 Chr 31:2
to the priests who **m** in the house of Neh 10:36
are, as well as the priests who **m**, Neh 10:39
the way that is blameless shall **m** to me. Ps 101:6
join themselves to the LORD, to **m** to him, Is 56:6
you; the rams of Nebaioth shall **m** to you; Is 60:7
walls, and their kings shall **m** to you; Is 60:10
and the Levitical priests who **m** to me." Jer 33:22
come near to the LORD to **m** to him. Ezk 40:46
there the garments in which they **m**, Ezk 42:14
who draw near to me to **m** to me, Ezk 43:19
stand before the people, to **m** to them. Ezk 44:11
me, shall come near to me to **m** to me. Ezk 44:15
shall approach my table, to **m** to me, Ezk 44:16
while they **m** at the gates of the inner Ezk 44:17
inner court, to **m** in the Holy Place, Ezk 44:27
who **m** in the sanctuary and approach Ezk 45:4
and approach the LORD to **m** to him, Ezk 45:4
be for the Levites who **m** at the temple, Ezk 45:5
where those who **m** at the temple Ezk 46:24
or in prison, and did not **m** to you?' Mt 25:44
to be a **m** of Christ Jesus to the Rom 15:16
I was made a **m** according to the gift Eph 3:7
brother and faithful **m** in the Lord Eph 6:21
and your messenger and **m** to my need, Phil 2:25
He is a faithful **m** of Christ on your Col 1:7
and of which I, Paul, became a **m**. Col 1:23
which I became a **m** according to the Col 1:25
brother and faithful **m** and fellow Col 4:7
a **m** in the holy places, in the true tent Heb 8:2

MINISTERED (10)
ministering women who **m** in the Ex 38:8
And his son Eleazar **m** as priest in his Dt 10:6
of Aaron, **m** before it in those days), Jgs 20:28
And the boy **m** to the LORD in the 1 Sm 2:11
They **m** with song before the 1 Chr 6:32
the priests and the Levites who **m**. Neh 12:44
Because they **m** to them before their Ezk 44:12
they followed him and **m** to him, Mk 15:41
that these hands **m** to my necessities Acts 20:34
act of grace that is being **m** by us, 2 Cor 8:19

MINISTERING (16)
worked garments for **m** in the Holy Ex 35:19
mirrors of the **m** women who ministered Ex 38:8
garments, for **m** in the Holy Place. Ex 39:1
around the hem of the robe for **m**, Ex 39:26
worked garments for **m** in the Holy Ex 39:41
Samuel was **m** before the LORD, a boy 1 Sm 2:18
young man Samuel was **m** to the LORD 1 Sm 3:1
did, **m** in the house of the LORD. 1 Chr 26:12
We have priests **m** to the LORD who 2 Chr 13:10
LORD except the priests and **m** Levites. 2 Chr 23:6
of the temple and **m** in the temple. Ezk 44:11
which they have been **m** and lay them Ezk 44:19
behold, angels came and were **m** to him. Mt 4:11
followed Jesus from Galilee, **m** to him, Mt 27:55
animals, and the angels were **m** to him. Mk 1:13
Are they not all **m** spirits sent out to Heb 1:14

MINISTERS (18)
And it shall be on Aaron when he **m**, Ex 28:35
and **m** in the name of the LORD his God, Dt 18:7
of the Levites as **m** before the ark of 1 Chr 16:4
and to be his **m** and make offerings 2 Chr 29:11
to send us **m** for the house of our God. Ezr 8:17
Bless the LORD, all his hosts, his **m**, Ps 103:21
messengers winds, his **m** a flaming fire. Ps 104:4
shall speak of you as the **m** of our God; Is 61:6
with the Levitical priests my **m**. Jer 33:21
They shall be **m** in my sanctuary, Ezk 44:11
LORD. The priests mourn, the **m** of the LORD. Jl 1:9
lament, O priests; wail, O **m** of the altar. Jl 1:13
the night in sackcloth, O **m** of my God! Jl 1:13
the altar let the priests, the **m** of the LORD, Jl 2:17
were eyewitnesses and **m** of the word Lk 1:2
taxes, for the authorities are **m** of God, Rom 13:6
us competent to be **m** of a new 2 Cor 3:6
angels winds, and his **m** a flame of fire." Heb 1:7

MINISTRY (26)
to do the service of **m** and the service of Nm 4:47
David offered praises by their **m**; 2 Chr 7:6
of praise and **m** before the priests 2 Chr 8:14
Jesus, when he began his **m**, was about Lk 3:23
and was allotted his share in this **m**." Acts 1:17
place in this **m** and apostleship from Acts 1:25
to prayer and to the **m** of the word." Acts 6:4
my course and the **m** that I received Acts 20:24
among the Gentiles through his **m**. Acts 21:19
to the Gentiles, I magnify my **m** Rom 11:13
I have fulfilled the **m** of the gospel of Rom 15:19
Now if the **m** of death, carved in letters 2 Cor 3:7
will not the **m** of the Spirit have even 2 Cor 3:8
was glory in the **m** of condemnation, 2 Cor 3:9
the **m** of righteousness must far exceed 2 Cor 3:9
having this **m** by the mercy of God, 2 Cor 4:1
and gave us the **m** of reconciliation; 2 Cor 5:18
no fault may be found with our **m**, 2 Cor 6:3
write to you about the **m** for the saints, 2 Cor 9:1
For the **m** of this service is not only 2 Cor 9:12
for his apostolic **m** to the circumcised Gal 2:8
to equip the saints for the work of **m**, Eph 4:12
that you fulfill the **m** that you have Col 4:17
work of an evangelist, fulfill your **m**. 2 Tm 4:5
you, for he is very useful to me for **m**. 2 Tm 4:11
Christ has obtained a **m** that is as much Heb 8:6

MINNI (1)
kingdoms, Ararat, **M**, and Ashkenaz; Jer 51:27

MINNITH (2)
from Aroer to the neighborhood of **M**, Jgs 11:33
for your merchandise wheat of **M**, Ezk 27:17

MINT (2)
For you tithe **m** and dill and cumin, Mt 23:23
For you tithe **m** and rue and every Lk 11:42

MIRACLE (1)
you, 'Prove yourselves by working a **m**,' Ex 7:9

MIRACLES (11)
before Pharaoh all the **m** that I have put Ex 4:21
his **m** and the judgments he uttered, 1 Chr 16:12
works that he has done, his **m**, Ps 105:5
signs among them and **m** in the land Ps 105:27
seeing signs and great **m** performed, Acts 8:13
was doing extraordinary **m** by the Acts 19:11
to another the working of **m**, to 1 Cor 12:10
prophets, third teachers, then **m**, 1 Cor 12:28
Are all teachers? Do all work **m**? 1 Cor 12:29
to you and works **m** among you do so Gal 3:5
and wonders and various **m** and by gifts Heb 2:4

MIRACULOUS (2)
that is why these **m** powers are at work Mt 14:2
That is why these **m** powers are at work Mk 6:14

MIRE (10)
them down like the **m** of the streets. 2 Sm 22:43
God has cast me into the **m**, and I have Jb 30:19
like a threshing sledge on the **m**. Jb 41:30
I cast them out like the **m** of the streets. Ps 18:42
I sink in deep **m**, where there is no Ps 69:2
Deliver me from sinking in the **m**; let Ps 69:14
tread them down like the **m** of the streets. Is 10:6
quiet, and its waters toss up **m** and dirt. Is 57:20
trampled down like the **m** of the streets. Mi 7:10
herself, returns to wallow in the **m**." 2 Pt 2:22

MIRIAM (15)
Then **M** the prophetess, the sister of Ex 15:20
And **M** sang to them: "Sing to the LORD, Ex 15:21
M and Aaron spoke against Moses Nm 12:1
said to Moses and to Aaron and **M**, Nm 12:4
of the tent and called Aaron and **M**, Nm 12:5
over the tent, behold, **M** was leprous, Nm 12:10
And Aaron turned toward **M**, and Nm 12:10
So **M** was shut outside the camp seven Nm 12:15
on the march till **M** was brought in Nm 12:15
And **M** died there and was buried there. Nm 20:1
Aaron and Moses and **M** their sister. Nm 26:59
LORD your God did to **M** on the way as Dt 24:9
and she conceived and bore **M**, 1 Chr 4:17
of Amram: Aaron, Moses, and **M**. 1 Chr 6:3
I sent before you Moses, Aaron, and **M**. Mi 6:4

MIRMAH (1)
Jeuz, Sachia, and **M**. These were his 1 Chr 8:10

MIRROR (3)
out the skies, hard as a cast metal **m**? Jb 37:18
For now we see in a **m** dimly, but 1 Cor 13:12
looks intently at his natural face in a **m**. Jas 1:23

MIRRORS (2)
from the **m** of the ministering women Ex 38:8
the **m**, the linen garments, the turbans, Is 3:23

MIRTH (10)
have sent you away with **m** and songs, Gn 31:27
songs, and our tormentors, **m**, saying, Ps 137:3
the heart of fools is in the house of **m**. Eccl 7:4
The **m** of the tambourines is stilled, the Is 24:8
has ceased, the **m** of the lyre is stilled. Is 24:8
Jerusalem the voice of **m** and the voice of Jer 7:34
the voice of **m** and the voice of gladness, Jer 16:9
them the voice of **m** and the voice of Jer 25:10
the voice of **m** and the voice of Jer 33:11
And I will put an end to all her **m**, her Hos 2:11

MIRY (2)
the pit of destruction, out of the **m** bog, Ps 40:2
Let them be cast into fire, into **m** pits, Ps 140:10

MISCARRIAGE (1)
neither death nor **m** shall come from 2 Kgs 2:21

MISCARRIED (1)
and your female goats have not **m**, Gn 31:38

MISCARRY (2)
None shall **m** or be barren in your Ex 23:26
fail; their cow calves and does not **m**. Jb 21:10

MISCARRYING (1)
Give them a **m** womb and dry breasts. Hos 9:14

MISCHIEF (7)
and is pregnant with **m** and gives birth Ps 7:14
His **m** returns upon his own head, and Ps 7:16
under his tongue are **m** and iniquity. Ps 10:7
you do see, for you note **m** and vexation, Ps 10:14
evil against you, though they devise **m**, Ps 21:11
let the **m** of their lips overwhelm them! Ps 140:9
they conceive **m** and give birth to Is 59:4

MISCHIEVOUS (1)
lips, and a liar gives ear to a **m** tongue. Prv 17:4

MISCONDUCT (2)
and accuses her of **m** and brings a bad Dt 22:14
and behold, he has accused her of **m**, Dt 22:17

MISERABLE (2)
such things; **m** comforters are you all. Jb 16:2
those wretches to a **m** death and let out Mt 21:41

MISERIES (1)
and howl for the **m** that are coming upon Jas 5:1

MISERY (7)
became impatient over the **m** of Israel. Jgs 10:16
"Why is light given to him who is in **m**, Jb 3:20
and nights of **m** are apportioned to me. Jb 7:3
You will forget your **m**; you will Jb 11:16
of everyone in **m** will come against Jb 20:22
and remember their **m** no more. Prv 31:7
in their paths are ruin and **m**, Rom 3:16

MISFORTUNE (5)
He has not beheld **m** in Jacob, nor has Nm 23:21
side. There is neither adversary nor **m**. 1 Kgs 5:4
who is at ease there is contempt for **m**; Jb 12:5
day of your brother in the day of his **m**; Ob 1:12
long time and saw no **m** come to him, Acts 28:6

MISFORTUNES (1)
the hearing of the LORD about their **m**, Nm 11:1

MISHAEL (8)
sons of Uzziel: **M**, Elzaphan, and Sithri. Ex 6:22
And Moses called **M** and Elzaphan, the Lv 10:4
right hand, and Pedaiah, **M**, Malchijah, Neh 8:4
M, and Azariah of the tribe of Judah. Dn 1:6

called Shadrach, **M** he called Meshach, Dn 1:7
over Daniel, Hananiah, **M**, and Azariah, Dn 1:11
like Daniel, Hananiah, **M**, and Azariah. Dn 1:19
known to Hananiah, **M**, and Azariah, Dn 2:17

MISHAL (2)
Allammelech, Amad, and **M**. On the Jos 19:26
tribe of Asher, **M** with its pasturelands, Jos 21:30

MISHAM (1)
Eber, **M**, and Shemed, who built Ono 1 Chr 8:12

MISHAP (1)
suffering no **m** or failure in bearing; Ps 144:14

MISHMA (4)
M, Dumah, Massa, Gn 25:14
M, Dumah, Massa, Hadad, Tema, 1 Chr 1:30
his son, Mibsam his son, **M** his son. 1 Chr 4:25
The sons of **M**: Hammuel his son, 1 Chr 4:26

MISHMANNAH (1)
M fourth, Jeremiah fifth, 1 Chr 12:10

MISHRAITES (1)
the Shumathites, and the **M**; 1 Chr 2:53

MISLEAD (3)
deceive you or **m** you in this 2 Chr 32:15
your guides **m** you and they have Is 3:12
Beware lest Hezekiah **m** you by saying, Is 36:18

MISLEADING (4)
Is not Hezekiah **m** you, that he may 2 Chr 32:11
for you oracles that are false and **m**. Lam 2:14
"We found this man **m** our nation and Lk 23:2
this man as one who was **m** the people. Lk 23:14

MISLEADS (3)
be anyone who **m** a blind man Dt 27:18
Hezekiah when he **m** you by saying, 2 Kgs 18:32
Whoever **m** the upright into an evil Prv 28:10

MISLED (1)
because they have **m** my people, Ezk 13:10

MISPAR (1)
Reelaiah, Mordecai, Bilshan, **M**, Bigvai, Ezr 2:2

MISPERETH (1)
Mordecai, Bilshan, **M**, Bigvai, Neh 7:7

MISREPHOTH-MAIM (2)
them as far as Great Sidon and **M**, Jos 11:8
of the hill country from Lebanon to **M**, Jos 13:6

MISREPRESENTING (1)
We are even found to be **m** God, 1 Cor 15:15

MISS (3)
could sling a stone at a hair and not **m**. Jgs 20:16
and we did not **m** anything when we 1 Sm 25:15
shall inspect your fold and **m** nothing. Jb 5:24

MISSED (4)
is the new moon, and you will be **m**, 1 Sm 20:18
and they **m** nothing all the time they 1 Sm 25:7
so that nothing was **m** of all that 1 Sm 25:21
come to mind or be remembered or **m**; Jer 3:16

MISSES (2)
If your father **m** me at all, then say, 1 Sm 20:6
makes haste with his feet **m** his way. Prv 19:2

MISSING (10)
with your God be **m** from your grain Lv 2:13
and there is not a man **m** from us. Nm 31:49
Nothing was **m**, whether small or 1 Sm 30:19
there were **m** from David's servants 2 Sm 2:30
if by any means he is **m**, your life 1 Kgs 20:39
Let none be **m**, for I have a great 2 Kgs 10:19
Whoever is **m** shall not live." But 2 Kgs 10:19
of the LORD: Not one of these shall be **m**; Is 34:16
he is strong in power not one is **m**. Is 40:26
nor be dismayed, neither shall any be **m**, Jer 23:4

MISSION (4)
manner of life, and what is his **m**?" Jgs 13:12
the LORD sent you on a **m** and said, 1 Sm 15:18
have gone on the **m** on which the 1 Sm 15:20
in their boasted **m** they work on 2 Cor 11:12

MIST (9)
and a **m** was going up from the land and Gn 2:6
drops of water; they distill his **m** in rain, Jb 36:27
fire and hail, snow and **m**, stormy wind Ps 148:8
like a cloud and your sins like **m**; Is 44:22
and he makes the **m** rise from the ends Jer 10:13
and he makes the **m** rise from the ends Jer 51:16
be like the morning **m** or like the dew Hos 13:3
a time." Immediately **m** and darkness Acts 13:11
For you are a **m** that appears for a little Jas 4:14

MISTAKE (8)
for him for the **m** that he made Lv 5:18
shall be forgiven, because it was a **m**, Nm 15:25
offering before the LORD for their **m**. Nm 15:25
population was involved in the **m**. Nm 15:26
LORD for the person who makes a **m**, Nm 15:28
"You **m** the shadow of the mountains Jgs 9:36
foolishly, and have made a great **m**." 1 Sm 26:21
before the messenger that it was a **m**. Eccl 5:6

MISTREAT (5)
You shall not **m** any widow or Ex 22:22
If you do **m** them, and they cry out to Ex 22:23
and **m** me." But his armor-bearer 1 Sm 31:4
come and **m** me." But 1 Chr 10:4
rulers, to **m** them and to stone them, Acts 14:5

MISTREATED (3)
rather to be **m** with the people Heb 11:25
and goats, destitute, afflicted, **m**— Heb 11:37
with them, and those who are **m**, Heb 13:3

MISTRESS (11)
she looked with contempt on her **m**. Gn 16:4
said, "I am fleeing from my **m** Sarai." Gn 16:8
"Return to your **m** and submit to her." Gn 16:9
of the woman, the **m** of the house, 1 Kgs 17:17
She said to her **m**, "Would that my 2 Kgs 5:3
of a maidservant to the hand of her **m**, Ps 123:2
when she displaces her **m**. Prv 30:23
master; as with the maid, so with her **m**; Is 24:2
no more be called the **m** of kingdoms. Is 47:5
"I shall be **m** forever," so that you did not Is 47:7
its **m** is stripped; she is carried off, her Na 2:7

MISTS (1)
waterless springs and **m** driven by a 2 Pt 2:17

MISUNDERSTAND (1)
enemy, lest their adversaries should **m**, Dt 32:27

MITHKAH (2)
set out from Terah and camped at **M**. Nm 33:28
they set out from **M** and camped at Nm 33:29

MITHNITE (1)
of Maacah, and Joshaphat the **M**, 1 Chr 11:43

MITHREDATH (2)
these out in charge of **M** the treasurer, Ezr 1:8
Bishlam and **M** and Tabeel and the rest Ezr 4:7

MITYLENE (1)
we took him on board and went to **M**. Acts 20:14

MIX (5)
that you may not **m** with these nations Jos 23:7
boil the meat well, **m** in the spices, Ezk 24:10
so they will **m** with one another in Dn 2:43
just as iron does not **m** with clay. Dn 2:43
m a double portion for her in the cup Rv 18:6

MIXED (59)
A **m** multitude also went up with them, Ex 12:38
bread, unleavened cakes **m** with oil, Ex 29:2
loaves of fine flour **m** with oil or Lv 2:4
be of fine flour unleavened, **m** with oil. Lv 2:5
You shall bring it well **m**, in baked Lv 6:21
every grain offering, **m** with oil or dry, Lv 7:10
sacrifice unleavened loaves **m** with oil, Lv 7:12
and loaves of fine flour well **m** with oil. Lv 7:12
the LORD, and a grain offering **m** with oil, Lv 9:4
of an ephah of fine flour **m** with oil, Lv 14:10
an ephah of fine flour **m** with oil for a Lv 14:21
of an ephah of fine flour **m** with oil, Lv 23:13
bread, loaves of fine flour **m** with oil, Nm 6:15
them full of fine flour **m** with oil for a Nm 7:13
them full of fine flour **m** with oil for a Nm 7:19
them full of fine flour **m** with oil for a Nm 7:25
them full of fine flour **m** with oil for a Nm 7:31
them full of fine flour **m** with oil for a Nm 7:37
them full of fine flour **m** with oil for a Nm 7:43
them full of fine flour **m** with oil for a Nm 7:49
them full of fine flour **m** with oil for a Nm 7:55
them full of fine flour **m** with oil for a Nm 7:61
them full of fine flour **m** with oil for a Nm 7:67
them full of fine flour **m** with oil for a Nm 7:73
them full of fine flour **m** with oil for a Nm 7:79
its grain offering of fine flour **m** with oil, Nm 8:8
flour, **m** with a quarter of a hin of oil; Nm 15:4
an ephah of fine flour **m** with a third of Nm 15:6
of fine flour, **m** with half a hin of oil. Nm 15:9
m with a quarter of a hin of beaten oil. Nm 28:5
flour for a grain offering, **m** with oil, Nm 28:9
flour for a grain offering, **m** with oil, Nm 28:12
flour for a grain offering, **m** with oil, Nm 28:12
a tenth of fine flour **m** with oil as a Nm 28:13
grain offering of fine flour **m** with oil; Nm 28:20
grain offering of fine flour **m** with oil, Nm 28:28
grain offering of fine flour **m** with oil, Nm 29:3
shall be of fine flour **m** with oil, Nm 29:9
grain offering of fine flour **m** with oil, Nm 29:14
cloth of wool and linen **m** together. Dt 22:11
offering, the offering **m** with oil, 1 Chr 23:29
the holy race has **m** itself with the Ezr 9:2
there is a cup with foaming wine, well **m**, Ps 75:8
but they **m** with the nations and Ps 106:35
her beasts; she has **m** her wine; Prv 9:2
bread and drink of the wine I have **m**. Prv 9:5
over wine; those who go to try **m** wine. Prv 23:30
a rounded bowl that never lacks **m** wine. Sg 7:2
dross, your best wine **m** with water. Is 1:22
and fill cups of **m** wine for Destiny, Is 65:11
and all the **m** tribes among them; all Jer 25:20
the kings of the **m** tribes who dwell in Jer 25:24
as you saw iron **m** with the soft clay. Dn 2:41
As you saw the iron **m** with soft clay, so Dn 2:43
a **m** people shall dwell in Ashdod, and I Zec 9:6
offered him wine to drink, **m** with gall, Mt 27:34
they offered him wine **m** with myrrh, Mk 15:23
there followed hail and fire, **m** with blood, Rv 8:7
double portion for her in the cup she **m**. Rv 18:6

MIXES (1)
Ephraim **m** himself with the peoples; Hos 7:8

MIXING (2)
priests, prepared the **m** of the spices, 1 Chr 9:30
wine, and valiant men in **m** strong drink, Is 5:22

MIXTURE (1)
came bringing a **m** of myrrh and aloes, Jn 19:39

MIZAR (1)
Jordan and of Hermon, from Mount **M**. Ps 42:6

MIZPAH (42)
and **M**, for he said, "The LORD watch Gn 31:49
Hivites under Hermon in the land of **M**. Jos 11:3
together, and they encamped at **M**. Jgs 10:17
all his words before the LORD at **M**. Jgs 11:11
and passed on to **M** of Gilead, Jgs 11:29
and from **M** of Gilead he passed on to Jgs 11:29
Then Jephthah came to his home at **M**. Jgs 11:34
assembled as one man to the LORD at **M**. Jgs 20:1
the people of Israel had gone up to **M**.) Jgs 20:3
Now the men of Israel had sworn at **M**, Jgs 21:1
who did not come up to the LORD to **M**, Jgs 21:5
come up to the LORD to **M**?" And behold, Jgs 21:8
Samuel said, "Gather all Israel at **M**, 1 Sm 7:5
So they gathered at **M** and drew water 1 Sm 7:6
Samuel judged the people of Israel at **M**. 1 Sm 7:6
the people of Israel had gathered at **M**, 1 Sm 7:7
went out from **M** and pursued the 1 Sm 7:11
set it up between **M** and Shen and 1 Sm 7:12
year by year to Bethel, Gilgal, and **M**. 1 Sm 7:16
the people together to the LORD at **M**. 1 Sm 10:17
Asa built Geba of Benjamin and **M**. 1 Kgs 15:22
with their men to Gedaliah at **M**, 2 Kgs 25:23
Chaldeans who were with him at **M**. 2 Kgs 25:25
and with them he built Geba and **M**. 2 Chr 16:6
the men of Gibeon and of **M**, Neh 3:7
of Col-hozeh, ruler of the district of **M**, Neh 3:15
him Ezer the son of Jeshua, ruler of **M**, Neh 3:19
to Gedaliah the son of Ahikam, at **M**, Jer 40:6
went to Gedaliah at **M**—Ishmael the son Jer 40:8
As for me, I will dwell at **M**, to represent Jer 40:10
to the land of Judah, to Gedaliah at **M**. Jer 40:12
open country came to Gedaliah at **M** Jer 40:13
Kareah spoke secretly to Gedaliah at **M**, Jer 40:15
to Gedaliah the son of Ahikam, at **M**. Jer 41:1
As they ate bread together there at **M**, Jer 41:1
Judeans who were with Gedaliah at **M**, Jer 41:3
came out from **M** to meet them, Jer 41:6
all the rest of the people who were in **M**, Jer 41:10
and all the people who were left at **M**, Jer 41:10
away captive from **M** turned around Jer 41:14
with him took from **M** all the rest of Jer 41:16
have been a snare at **M** and a net spread Hos 5:1

MIZPEH (4)
and eastward as far as the Valley of **M**. Jos 11:8
Dilean, **M**, Joktheel, Jos 15:38
M, Chephirah, Mozah, Jos 18:26
David went from there to **M** of Moab. 1 Sm 22:3

MIZZAH (3)
Nahath, Zerah, Shammah, and **M**. Gn 36:13
Nahath, Zerah, Shammah, and **M**; Gn 36:17
Nahath, Zerah, Shammah, and **M**. 1 Chr 1:37

MNASON (1)
us to the house of **M** of Cyprus, Acts 21:16

MOAB (170)
bore a son and called his name **M**. Gn 19:37
defeated Midian in the country of **M**, Gn 36:35
trembling seizes the leaders of **M**; Ex 15:15
in the wilderness that is opposite **M**, Nm 21:11
for the Arnon is the border of **M**, Nm 21:13
Moab, between **M** and the Amorites. Nm 21:13
of Ar, and leans to the border of **M**." Nm 21:15
lying in the region of **M** by the top of Nm 21:20
the former king of **M** and taken all Nm 21:26
It devoured Ar of **M**, and swallowed Nm 21:28

Woe to you, O **M**! You are undone, O Nm 21:29
in the plains of **M** beyond the Jordan at Nm 22:1
And **M** was in great dread of the people, Nm 22:3
M was overcome with fear of the people Nm 22:3
And **M** said to the elders of Midian, Nm 22:4
Zippor, who was king of **M** at that time, Nm 22:4
So the elders of **M** and the elders of Nm 22:7
the princes of **M** stayed with Balaam. Nm 22:8
"Balak the son of Zippor, king of **M**, Nm 22:10
So the princes of **M** rose and went to Nm 22:14
and went with the princes of **M**. Nm 22:21
went out to meet him at the city of **M**, Nm 22:36
the princes of **M** were standing beside Nm 23:6
the king of **M** from the eastern Nm 23:7
and the princes of **M** with him. Nm 23:17
the forehead of **M** and break down Nm 24:17
to whore with the daughters of **M**. Nm 25:1
in the plains of **M** by the Jordan at Nm 26:3
in the plains of **M** by the Jordan at Nm 26:63
on the plains of **M** by the Jordan at Nm 31:12
at Iye-abarim, in the territory of **M**. Nm 33:44
in the plains of **M** by the Jordan at Nm 33:48
far as Abel-shittim in the plains of **M**. Nm 33:49
in the plains of **M** by the Jordan at Nm 33:50
in the plains of **M** by the Jordan at Nm 35:1
in the plains of **M** by the Jordan at Nm 36:13
Beyond the Jordan, in the land of **M**, Dt 1:5
in the direction of the wilderness of **M**. Dt 2:8
'Do not harass **M** or contend with them in Dt 2:9
you are to cross the border of **M** at Ar. Dt 2:18
with the people of Israel in the land of **M**, Dt 29:1
Mount Nebo, which is in the land of **M**, Dt 32:49
up from the plains of **M** to Mount Nebo, Dt 34:1
of the LORD died there in the land of **M**, Dt 34:5
in the land of **M** opposite Beth-peor; Dt 34:6
for Moses in the plains of **M** thirty days. Dt 34:8
Moses distributed in the plains of **M**, Jos 13:32
Balak the son of Zippor, king of **M**, Jos 24:9
Eglon the king of **M** against Israel, Jgs 3:12
Eglon the king of **M** eighteen years. Jgs 3:14
tribute by him to Eglon the king of **M**. Jgs 3:15
presented the tribute to Eglon king of **M**. Jgs 3:17
So **M** was subdued that day under the Jgs 3:30
of Syria, the gods of Sidon, the gods of **M**, Jgs 10:6
take away the land of **M** or the land of Jgs 11:15
And they sent also to the king of **M**, but Jgs 11:17
and the land of **M** and arrived on the Jgs 11:18
of the land of **M** and camped on the Jgs 11:18
they did not enter the territory of **M**, Jgs 11:18
for the Arnon was the boundary of **M**. Jgs 11:18
Balak the son of Zippor, king of **M**? Jgs 11:25
went to sojourn in the country of **M**, Ru 1:1
the country of **M** and remained there. Ru 1:2
to return from the country of **M**, Ru 1:6
heard in the fields of **M** that the LORD had Ru 1:6
who returned from the country of **M**. Ru 1:22
back with Naomi from the country of **M**. Ru 2:6
has come back from the country of **M**, Ru 4:3
and into the hand of the king of **M**. 1 Sm 12:9
his enemies on every side, against **M**, 1 Sm 14:47
went from there to Mizpeh of **M**. 1 Sm 22:3
And he said to the king of **M**, "Please 1 Sm 22:3
And he left them with the king of **M**, 1 Sm 22:4
And he defeated **M** and he measured 2 Sm 8:2
from Edom, **M**, the Ammonites, the 2 Sm 8:12
He struck down two ariels of **M**. 2 Sm 23:20
for Chemosh the abomination of **M**, 1 Kgs 11:7
Sidonians, Chemosh the god of **M**, 1 Kgs 11:33
of Ahab, **M** rebelled against Israel. 2 Kgs 1:1
Now Mesha king of **M** was a sheep 2 Kgs 3:4
the king of **M** rebelled against the king 2 Kgs 3:5
"The king of **M** has rebelled against 2 Kgs 3:7
me to battle against **M**?" And he said, 2 Kgs 3:7
to give them into the hand of **M**." 2 Kgs 3:10
to give them into the hand of **M**." 2 Kgs 3:13
down. Now then, **M**, to the spoil!" 2 Kgs 3:23
When the king of **M** saw that the 2 Kgs 3:26
for Chemosh the abomination of **M**, 2 Kgs 23:13
defeated Midian in the country of **M**, 1 Chr 1:46
who ruled in **M** and returned to 1 Chr 4:22
in the country of **M** after he had sent 1 Chr 8:8
He struck down two heroes of **M**. 1 Chr 11:22
And he defeated **M**, and the Moabites 1 Chr 18:2
from Edom, **M**, the Ammonites, 1 Chr 18:11
of Ammon and **M** and Mount Seir, 2 Chr 20:10
of Ammon, **M**, and Mount Seir, 2 Chr 20:22
of Ammon and **M** rose against the 2 Chr 20:23
women of Ashdod, Ammon, and **M**. Neh 13:23
M is my washbasin; upon Edom I cast Ps 60:8
and the Ishmaelites, **M** and the Hagrites, Ps 83:6
M is my washbasin; upon Edom I cast Ps 108:9
put out their hand against Edom and **M**, Is 11:14
An oracle concerning **M**. Because Ar of Is 15:1
Because Ar of **M** is laid waste in a night, Is 15:1
is laid waste in a night, **M** is undone; Is 15:1
because Kir of **M** is laid waste in a night, Is 15:1
is laid waste in a night, **M** is undone. Is 15:1
over Nebo and over Medeba **M** wails. Is 15:2
therefore the armed men of **M** cry aloud; Is 15:4
My heart cries out for **M**; her fugitives flee Is 15:5
For a cry has gone around the land of **M**; Is 15:8
more, a lion for those of **M** who escape, Is 15:9
so are the daughters of **M** at the fords of Is 16:2
let the outcasts of **M** sojourn among you; Is 16:4
heard of the pride of **M**—how proud he is! Is 16:6
Therefore let **M** wail for Moab, let Is 16:7
Therefore let Moab wail for **M**, let Is 16:7
my inner parts moan like a lyre for **M**, Is 16:11
And when **M** presents himself, when he Is 16:12
LORD spoke concerning **M** in the past. Is 16:13
the glory of **M** will be brought into Is 16:14
and **M** shall be trampled down in his Is 25:10
M, and all who dwell in the desert who Jer 9:26
Edom, **M**, and the sons of Ammon; Jer 25:21
word to the king of Edom, the king of **M**, Jer 27:3
Judeans who were in **M** and among the Jer 40:11
Concerning **M**. Thus says the LORD of Jer 48:1
the renown of **M** is no more. In Heshbon Jer 48:2
M is destroyed; her little ones have made Jer 48:4
"Give wings to **M**, for she would fly Jer 48:9
"**M** has been at ease from his youth and Jer 48:11
Then **M** shall be ashamed of Chemosh, Jer 48:13
The destroyer of **M** and his cities has Jer 48:15
The calamity of **M** is near at hand, and Jer 48:16
For the destroyer of **M** has come up Jer 48:18
M is put to shame, for it is broken; wail Jer 48:20
beside the Arnon, that **M** is laid waste. Jer 48:20
and all the cities of the land of **M**, Jer 48:24
The horn of **M** is cut off, and his arm is Jer 48:25
so that **M** shall wallow in his vomit, Jer 48:26
dwell in the rock, O inhabitants of **M**! Jer 48:28
heard of the pride of **M**—he is very Jer 48:29
Therefore I wail for **M**; I cry out for all Jer 48:31
I wail for Moab; I cry out for all **M**; Jer 48:31
taken away from the fruitful land of **M**; Jer 48:33
And I will bring to an end in **M**, Jer 48:35
my heart moans for **M** like a flute, Jer 48:36
all the housetops of **M** and in the Jer 48:38
for I have broken **M** like a vessel for Jer 48:38
How **M** has turned his back in shame! Jer 48:39
So **M** has become a derision and a Jer 48:39
eagle and spread his wings against **M**; Jer 48:40
of the warriors of **M** shall be in that Jer 48:41
M shall be destroyed and be no longer a Jer 48:42
are before you, O inhabitant of **M**! Jer 48:43
For I will bring these things upon **M**, Jer 48:44
it has destroyed the forehead of **M**, the Jer 48:45
Woe to you, O **M**! The people of Jer 48:46
restore the fortunes of **M** in the latter Jer 48:47
LORD." Thus far is the judgment on **M**. Jer 48:47
Because **M** and Seir said, 'Behold, the Ezk 25:8
lay open the flank of **M** from the cities, Ezk 25:9
and I will execute judgments upon **M**. Ezk 25:11
Edom and **M** and the main part of the Dn 11:41
"For three transgressions of **M**, and for Am 2:1
So I will send a fire upon **M**, and it shall Am 2:2
of Kerioth, and **M** shall die amid uproar, Am 2:2
remember what Balak king of **M** devised, Mi 6:5
heard the taunts of **M** and the revilings Zep 2:8
of Israel, "**M** shall become like Sodom, Zep 2:9

MOABITE (12)
"No Ammonite or **M** may enter the Dt 23:3
These took **M** wives; the name of the one Ru 1:4
and Ruth the **M** her daughter-in-law Ru 1:22
And Ruth the **M** said to Naomi, "Let me Ru 2:2
answered, "She is the young **M** woman, Ru 2:6
And Ruth the **M** said, "Besides, he said to Ru 2:21
of Naomi, you also acquire Ruth the **M**, Ru 4:5
Also Ruth the **M**, the widow of Mahlon, I Ru 4:10
M, Ammonite, Edomite, Sidonian, 1 Kgs 11:1
sons of Elnaam, and Ithmah the **M**, 1 Chr 11:46
the son of Shimrith the **M**. 2 Chr 24:26
no Ammonite or **M** should ever enter Neh 13:1

MOABITES (17)
He is the father of the **M** to this day. Gn 19:37
as Rephaim, but the **M** call them Emim. Dt 2:11
live in Seir and the **M** who live in Ar did Dt 2:29
your enemies the **M** into your hand." Jgs 3:28
the Jordan against the **M** and did not Jgs 3:28
killed at that time about 10,000 of the **M**, Jgs 3:29
And the **M** became servants to David 2 Sm 8:2
will also give the **M** into your hand, 2 Kgs 3:18
When all the **M** heard that the kings 2 Kgs 3:21
the **M** saw the water opposite them as 2 Kgs 3:22
the Israelites rose and struck the **M**, 2 Kgs 3:24
forward, striking the **M** as they went. 2 Kgs 3:24
Now bands of **M** used to invade the 2 Kgs 13:20
and bands of the **M** and bands of the 2 Kgs 24:2
and the **M** became servants to David 1 Chr 18:2
After this the **M** and Ammonites, and 2 Chr 20:1
the Jebusites, the Ammonites, the **M**, Ezr 9:1

MOADIAH (1)
Zichri; of Miniamin, of **M**, Piltai; Neh 12:17

MOAN (8)
I am restless in my complaint and I **m**, Ps 55:2
at noon I utter my complaint and **m**, Ps 55:17
When I remember God, I **m**; when I Ps 77:3
Therefore my inner parts **m** like a lyre Is 16:11
or a crane I chirp; I **m** like a dove. Is 38:14
like bears; we **m** and moan like doves; Is 59:11
like bears; we moan and **m** like doves; Is 59:11
a taunt song against you and **m** bitterly, Mi 2:4

MOANING (4)
I am weary with my **m**; every night I flood Ps 6:6
and there shall be **m** and lamentation, Is 29:2
like doves of the valleys, all of them **m**, Ezk 7:16
m like doves and beating their breasts. Na 2:7

MOANS (2)
Therefore my heart **m** for Moab like a Jer 48:36
and my heart **m** like a flute for the men Jer 48:36

MOAT (1)
be built again with squares and **m**, Dn 9:25

MOB (2)
men of the rabble, they formed a **m**, Acts 17:5
for the **m** of the people followed, Acts 21:36

MOCK (14)
Assyria has sent to **m** the living God, 2 Kgs 19:4
he has sent to **m** the living God. 2 Kgs 19:16
babble silence men, and when you **m**, Jb 11:3
will speak, and after I have spoken, **m** on. Jb 21:3
All who see me **m** me; they make Ps 22:7
with which your enemies **m**, O LORD, Ps 89:51
with which they **m** the footsteps of your Ps 89:51
I will **m** when terror strikes you, Prv 1:26
Fools **m** at the guilt offering, but the Prv 14:9
of Assyria has sent to **m** the living God, Is 37:4
which he has sent to **m** the living God. Is 37:17
those who are far from you will **m** you; Ezk 22:5
And they will **m** him and spit on him, Mk 10:34
to finish, all who see it begin to **m** him, Lk 14:29

MOCKED (23)
you have **m** me and told me lies. Jgs 16:10
"Until now you have **m** me and told Jgs 16:13
You have **m** me these three times, and Jgs 16:15
And at noon Elijah **m** them, saying, 1 Kgs 18:27
"Whom have you **m** and reviled? 2 Kgs 19:22
messengers you have **m** the Lord, 2 Kgs 19:23
laughed them to scorn and **m** them. 2 Chr 30:10
m and derided by those around us. Ps 79:4
O Lord, how your servants are **m**, Ps 89:50
"'Whom have you **m** and reviled? Is 37:23
By your servants you have **m** the Lord, Is 37:24
over her; they **m** at her downfall. Lam 1:7
the Gentiles to be **m** and flogged and Mt 20:19
And kneeling before him, they **m** him, Mt 27:29
And when they had **m** him, they Mt 27:31
with the scribes and elders, **m** him, Mt 27:41
And when they had **m** him, they Mk 15:20
priests with the scribes **m** him to one Mk 15:31
and will be **m** and shamefully treated Lk 18:32
treated him with contempt and **m** him. Lk 23:11
The soldiers also **m** him, coming up Lk 23:36
the resurrection of the dead, some **m**. Acts 17:32
God is not **m**, for whatever one sows, that Gal 6:7

MOCKER (1)
Wine is a **m**, strong drink a brawler, Prv 20:1

MOCKERS (3)
Surely there are **m** about me, and my eye Jb 17:2
like profane **m** at a feast, they gnash at Ps 35:16
wine; he stretched out his hand with **m**. Hos 7:5

MOCKERY (1)
nations, and a **m** to all the countries. Ezk 22:4

MOCKING (6)
I shall seem to be **m** him and bring a Gn 27:12
But they kept **m** the messengers of 2 Chr 36:16
Whom are you **m**? Against whom do you Is 57:4
Jesus in custody were **m** him as they Lk 22:63
But others **m** said, "They are filled Acts 2:13
Others suffered **m** and flogging, and Heb 11:36

MOCKS (6)
he **m** at the calamity of the innocent. Jb 9:23
are glad; the innocent one **m** at them, Jb 22:19
Whoever **m** the poor insults his Maker; Prv 17:5
A worthless witness **m** at justice, and Prv 19:28
The eye that **m** a father and scorns to Prv 30:17
all the day; everyone **m** me. Jer 20:7

MODEL (2)
to Uriah the priest a **m** of the altar, 2 Kgs 16:10

in all respects to be a **m** of good works, Ti 2:7

MODESTY (2)
parts are treated with greater **m**, 1 Cor 12:23
apparel, with **m** and self-control, 1 Tm 2:9

MOIST (2)
the sweeping away of **m** and dry alike. Dt 29:19
of milk and the marrow of his bones **m**. Jb 21:24

MOISTEN (1)
one third of a hin of oil to **m** the flour, Ezk 46:14

MOISTURE (2)
He loads the thick cloud with **m**; the Jb 37:11
up, it withered away, because it had no **m**. Lk 8:6

MOLADAH (4)
Amam, Shema, **M**, Jos 15:26
their inheritance Beersheba, Sheba, **M**, Jos 19:2
lived in Beersheba, **M**, Hazar-shual, 1 Chr 4:28
in Jeshua and in **M** and Beth-pelet, Neh 11:26

MOLD (1)
the mortar; take hold of the brick **m**! Na 3:14

MOLDED (1)
Will what is **m** say to its molder, Rom 9:20

MOLDER (1)
Will what is molded say to its **m**, Rom 9:20

MOLDING (10)
shall make on it a **m** of gold around it. Ex 25:11
gold and make a **m** of gold around it. Ex 25:24
wide, and a **m** of gold around the rim. Ex 25:25
you shall make a **m** of gold around it. Ex 30:3
Under its **m** on two opposite sides of it Ex 30:4
outside, and made a **m** of gold around it. Ex 37:2
gold, and made a **m** of gold around it. Ex 37:11
and made a **m** of gold around the rim. Ex 37:12
And he made a **m** of gold around it, Ex 37:26
two rings of gold on it under its **m**, Ex 37:27

MOLE (1)
that swarm on the ground: the **m** rat, Lv 11:29

MOLECH (8)
any of your children to offer them to **M**, Lv 18:21
of his children to **M** shall surely be put Lv 20:2
he has given one of his children to **M**, Lv 20:3
when he gives one of his children to **M**, Lv 20:4
all who follow him in whoring after **M**. Lv 20:5
and for **M** the abomination of the 1 Kgs 11:7
or his daughter as an offering to **M**. 2 Kgs 23:10
offer up their sons and daughters to **M**, Jer 32:35

MOLES (1)
to worship, to the **m** and to the bats, Is 2:20

MOLID (1)
and she bore him Ahban and **M**. 1 Chr 2:29

MOLOCH (1)
took up the tent of **M** and the star of Acts 7:43

MOMENT (29)
if for a single **m** I should go up among Ex 33:5
to look on the holy things even for a **m**, Nm 4:20
that I may consume them in a **m**." Nm 16:21
consume them in a **m**." And they fell Nm 16:45
now for a brief **m** favor has been shown Ezr 9:8
every morning and test him every **m**? Jb 7:18
and the joy of the godless but for a **m**? Jb 20:5
In a **m** they die; at midnight the people Jb 34:20
turn back and be put to shame in a **m**. Ps 6:10
For his anger is but for a **m**, and his Ps 30:5
How they are destroyed in a **m**, swept Ps 73:19
in a **m** he will be broken beyond Prv 6:15
but a lying tongue is but for a **m**. Prv 12:19
the LORD, am its keeper; every **m** I water it. Is 27:3
two things shall come to you in a **m**, Is 47:9
For a brief **m** I deserted you, but with Is 54:7
overflowing anger for a **m** I hid my face Is 54:8
a nation be brought forth in one **m**? Is 66:8
tents are laid waste, my curtains in a **m**. Jer 4:20
Sodom, which was overthrown in a **m**, Lam 4:6
and tremble every **m** and be appalled Ezk 26:16
They shall tremble every **m**, every one Ezk 32:10
the servant was healed at that very **m**. Mt 8:13
And from that **m** he sought an Mt 26:16
the kingdoms of the world in a **m** of time, Lk 4:5
at that very **m** three men arrived at Acts 11:11
in a **m**, in the twinkling of an eye, at 1 Cor 15:52
did not yield in submission even for a **m**, Gal 2:5
For the **m** all discipline seems painful Heb 12:11

MOMENTARY (1)
For this slight **m** affliction is 2 Cor 4:17

MONEY (135)
bought with your **m** from any Gn 17:12
and he who is bought with your **m**, Gn 17:13
in his house or bought with his **m**, Gn 17:23
those bought with **m** from a foreigner, Gn 17:27
us, and he has indeed devoured our **m**. Gn 31:15
a hundred pieces of **m** the piece of land Gn 33:19
to replace every man's **m** in his sack, Gn 42:25
he saw his **m** in the mouth of his sack. Gn 42:27
brothers, "My **m** has been put back; Gn 42:28
every man's bundle of **m** was in his Gn 42:35
their father saw their bundles of **m**, Gn 42:35
Take double the **m** with you. Carry Gn 43:12
back with you the **m** that was returned Gn 43:12
and they took double the **m** with them, Gn 43:15
and they said, "It is because of the **m**, Gn 43:18
there was each man's **m** in the mouth Gn 43:21
of his sack, our **m** in full weight. Gn 43:21
have brought other **m** down with us Gn 43:22
know who put our **m** in our sacks." Gn 43:22
I received your **m**." Then he brought Gn 43:23
and put each man's **m** in the mouth of Gn 44:1
with his **m** for the grain." And he did as Gn 44:2
the **m** that we found in the mouths of Gn 44:8
gathered up all the **m** that was found Gn 47:14
Joseph brought the **m** into Pharaoh's Gn 47:14
And when the **m** was all spent in the Gn 47:15
before your eyes? For our **m** is gone." Gn 47:15
for your livestock, if your **m** is gone." Gn 47:16
from my lord that our **m** is all spent. Gn 47:18
slave that is bought for **m** may eat of it Ex 12:44
out for nothing, without payment of **m**. Ex 21:11
not to be avenged, for the slave is his **m**. Ex 21:21
He shall give **m** to its owner, Ex 21:34
gives to his neighbor **m** or goods to keep Ex 22:7
he shall pay **m** equal to the bride-price Ex 22:17
"If you lend **m** to any of my people with Ex 22:25
take the atonement **m** from the people Ex 30:16
buys a slave as his property for **m**, Lv 22:11
shall not lend him your **m** at interest, Lv 25:37
and give the **m** to Aaron and his sons Nm 3:48
took the redemption **m** from those who Nm 3:49
of the people of Israel he took the **m**, Nm 3:50
gave the redemption **m** to Aaron and Nm 3:51
shall purchase food from them for **m**, Dt 2:6
you shall also buy water of them for **m**, Dt 2:6
You shall sell me food for **m**, that I may Dt 2:28
that I may eat, and give me water for **m**, Dt 2:28
shall turn it into **m** and bind up the Dt 14:25
and bind up the **m** in your hand and Dt 14:25
and spend the **m** for whatever you Dt 14:26
But you shall not sell her for **m**, nor Dt 21:14
on loans to your brother, interest on **m**, Dt 23:19
of Shechem for a hundred pieces of **m**. Jos 24:32
her and brought the **m** in their hands. Jgs 16:18
So when he restored the **m** to his mother, Jgs 17:4
to you, I will give you its value in **m**." 1 Kgs 21:2
to him, 'Give me your vineyard for **m**, 1 Kgs 21:6
which he refused to give you for **m**, 1 Kgs 21:15
it a time to accept **m** and garments, 2 Kgs 5:26
"All the **m** of the holy things that is 2 Kgs 12:4
the **m** for which each man is assessed 2 Kgs 12:4
assessed—the **m** from the assessment 2 Kgs 12:4
persons—and the **m** that a man's 2 Kgs 12:4
take no more **m** from your donors, 2 Kgs 12:7
take no more **m** from the people, 2 Kgs 12:8
in it all the **m** that was brought into 2 Kgs 12:9
that there was much **m** in the chest, 2 Kgs 12:10
and counted the **m** that was found 2 Kgs 12:10
would give the **m** that was weighed 2 Kgs 12:11
from the **m** that was brought into 2 Kgs 12:13
hand they delivered the **m** to pay out 2 Kgs 12:15
The **m** from the guilt offerings and 2 Kgs 12:16
offerings and the **m** from the sin 2 Kgs 12:16
exacted the **m** from Israel, 2 Kgs 15:20
he may count the **m** that has been 2 Kgs 22:4
from them for the **m** that is delivered 2 Kgs 22:7
emptied out the **m** that was found 2 Kgs 22:9
land to give the **m** according to the 2 Kgs 23:35
gather from all Israel **m** to repair the 2 Chr 24:5
saw that there was much **m** in it, 2 Chr 24:11
day, and collected **m** in abundance. 2 Chr 24:11
the rest of the **m** before the king and 2 Chr 24:14
and gave him the **m** that had been 2 Chr 34:9
bringing out the **m** that had been 2 Chr 34:14
emptied out the **m** that was found 2 Chr 34:17
So they gave **m** to the masons and the Ezr 3:7
With this **m**, then, you shall with all Ezr 7:17
"We have borrowed **m** for the king's tax Neh 5:4
are lending them **m** and grain. Neh 5:10
their houses, and the percentage of **m**, Neh 5:11
said to Haman, "The **m** is given to you, Est 3:11
the exact sum of **m** that Haman had Est 4:7
gave him a piece of **m** and a ring of Jb 42:11
not put out his **m** at interest and does Ps 15:5
he took a bag of **m** with him; at full Prv 7:20
should a fool have **m** in his hand to Prv 17:16
He who loves **m** will not be satisfied Eccl 5:10
money will not be satisfied with **m**, Eccl 5:10
of wisdom is like the protection of **m**, Eccl 7:12
life, and **m** answers everything. Eccl 10:19
have not bought me sweet cane with **m**, Is 43:24
and you shall be redeemed without **m**." Is 52:3
and he who has no **m**, come, buy and eat! Is 55:1
and milk without **m** and without price. Is 55:1
do you spend your **m** for that which is Is 55:2
cousin, and weighed out the **m** to him, Jer 32:9
witnesses, and weighed the **m** on scales. Jer 32:10
"Buy the field for **m** and get witnesses" Jer 32:25
Fields shall be bought for **m**, and deeds Jer 32:44
its prophets practice divination for **m**; Mi 3:11
the other. You cannot serve God and **m**. Mt 6:24
in the ground and hid his master's **m**. Mt 25:18
have invested my **m** with the bankers, Mt 25:27
into the treasury, since it is blood **m**." Mt 27:6
a sufficient sum of **m** to the soldiers Mt 28:12
So they took the **m** and did as they were Mt 28:15
—no bread, no bag, no **m** in their belts— Mk 6:8
the people putting **m** into the offering Mk 12:41
were glad and promised to give him **m**. Mk 14:11
"Do not extort **m** from anyone by Lk 3:14
no staff, nor bag, nor bread, nor **m**; Lk 9:3
other. You cannot serve God and **m**." Lk 16:13
The Pharisees, who were lovers of **m**, Lk 16:14
he had given the **m** to be called to Lk 19:15
did you not put my **m** in the bank, Lk 19:23
were glad, and agreed to give him **m**. Lk 22:5
him and brought the **m** and laid it at Acts 4:37
the apostles' hands, he offered them **m**, Acts 8:18
could obtain the gift of God with **m**! Acts 8:20
they had taken **m** as security from Acts 17:9
time he hoped that **m** would be given Acts 24:26
not quarrelsome, not a lover of **m**. 1 Tm 3:3
For the love of **m** is a root of all kinds 1 Tm 6:10
people will be lovers of self, lovers of **m**, 2 Tm 3:2
Keep your life free from love of **m**, and Heb 13:5

MONEY-CHANGERS (4)
the tables of the **m** and the seats of Mt 21:12
the tables of the **m** and the seats of Mk 11:15
and pigeons, and the **m** sitting there. Jn 2:14
the coins of the **m** and overturned their Jn 2:15

MONEYBAG (5)
Carry no **m**, no knapsack, no sandals, Lk 10:4
you out with no **m** or knapsack or Lk 22:35
now let the one who has a **m** take it, Lk 22:36
having charge of the **m** he used to help Jn 12:6
thought that, because Judas had the **m**, Jn 13:29

MONEYBAGS (1)
Provide yourselves with **m** that do not Lk 12:33

MONEYLENDER (2)
poor, you shall not be like a **m** to him, Ex 22:25
"A certain **m** had two debtors. One owed Lk 7:41

MONITOR (1)
the gecko, the **m** lizard, the lizard, the Lv 11:30

MONSTER (2)
Am I the sea, or a sea **m**, that you set a Jb 7:12
vessel; he has swallowed me like a **m**; Jer 51:34

MONSTERS (1)
the heads of the sea **m** on the waters. Ps 74:13

MONTH (247)
year of Noah's life, in the second **m**, Gn 7:11
month, on the seventeenth day of the **m**, Gn 7:11
and in the seventh **m**, on the seventeenth Gn 8:4
month, on the seventeenth day of the **m**, Gn 8:4
continued to abate until the tenth **m**; Gn 8:5
in the tenth **m**, on the first day of the Gn 8:5
the tenth month, on the first day of the **m**, Gn 8:5
six hundred and first year, in the first **m**, Gn 8:13
in the first month, the first day of the **m**, Gn 8:13
In the second **m**, on the twenty-seventh Gn 8:14
on the twenty-seventh day of the **m**, Gn 8:14
flesh!" And he stayed with him a **m**. Gn 29:14
"This **m** shall be for you the beginning Ex 12:2
It shall be the first **m** of the year for you. Ex 12:2
tenth day of this **m** every man shall take Ex 12:3
keep it until the fourteenth day of this **m**, Ex 12:6
In the first **m**, from the fourteenth day Ex 12:18
the fourteenth day of the **m** at evening, Ex 12:18
the twenty-first day of the **m** at evening. Ex 12:18
Today, in the **m** of Abib, you are going Ex 13:4
you shall keep this service in this **m**. Ex 13:5
day of the second **m** after they had Ex 16:1
at the appointed time in the **m** of Abib, Ex 23:15
at the time appointed in the **m** Abib, Ex 34:18
for in the **m** Abib you came out from Ex 34:18
first day of the first **m** you shall erect the Ex 40:2
In the first **m** in the second year, on the Ex 40:17
second year, on the first day of the **m**, Ex 40:17
to you forever that in the seventh **m**, Lv 16:29
month, on the tenth day of the **m**, Lv 16:29
In the first **m**, on the fourteenth day of Lv 23:5
the fourteenth day of the **m** at twilight, Lv 23:5

day of the same **m** is the Feast of Lv 23:6
of Israel, saying, In the seventh **m**, Lv 23:24
month, on the first day of the **m**, Lv 23:24
day of this seventh **m** is the Day of Lv 23:27
day of the **m** beginning at evening, Lv 23:32
day of this seventh **m** and for seven Lv 23:34
"On the fifteenth day of the seventh **m**, Lv 23:39
you shall celebrate it in the seventh **m**. Lv 23:41
on the tenth day of the seventh **m**. Lv 25:9
the person is from a **m** old up to five Lv 27:6
on the first day of the second **m**, Nm 1:1
and on the first day of the second **m**, Nm 1:18
every male from a **m** old and upward Nm 3:15
the males from a **m** old and upward Nm 3:22
the males, from a **m** old and upward, Nm 3:28
the males from a **m** old and upward Nm 3:34
all the males from a **m** old and upward, Nm 3:39
of Israel, from a **m** old and upward, Nm 3:40
from a **m** old and upward as listed were Nm 3:43
in the first **m** of the second year after Nm 9:1
On the fourteenth day of this **m**, at Nm 9:3
they kept the Passover in the first **m**, Nm 9:5
month, on the fourteenth day of the **m**, Nm 9:5
In the second **m** on the fourteenth day Nm 9:11
Whether it was two days, or a **m**, or a Nm 9:22
In the second year, in the second **m**, Nm 10:11
month, on the twentieth day of the **m**, Nm 10:11
but a whole **m**, until it comes out at Nm 11:20
meat, that they may eat a whole **m**!' Nm 11:21
price (at a **m** old you shall Nm 18:16
into the wilderness of Zin in the first **m**, Nm 20:1
every male from a **m** old and upward. Nm 26:62
offering of each **m** throughout the Nm 28:14
day of the first **m** is the LORD'S Nm 28:16
on the fifteenth day of this **m** is a feast. Nm 28:17
day of the seventh **m** you shall have a Nm 29:1
day of this seventh **m** you shall have a Nm 29:7
day of the seventh **m** you shall have a Nm 29:12
set out from Rameses in the first **m**, Nm 33:3
on the fifteenth day of the first **m**. Nm 33:3
of Egypt, on the first day of the fifth **m**. Nm 33:38
year, on the first day of the eleventh **m**, Dt 1:3
"Observe the **m** of Abib and keep the Dt 16:1
for in the **m** of Abib the LORD your God Dt 16:1
her father and her mother a full **m**. Dt 21:13
Jordan on the tenth day of the first **m**, Jos 4:19
fourteenth day of the **m** in the evening Jos 5:10
ate no food the second day of the **m**, 1 Sm 20:34
make provision for one **m** in the year. 1 Kgs 4:7
Solomon's table, each one in his **m**. 1 Kgs 4:27
to Lebanon, 10,000 a **m** in shifts. 1 Kgs 5:14
They would be a **m** in Lebanon and 1 Kgs 5:14
reign over Israel, in the **m** of Ziv, 1 Kgs 6:1
month of Ziv, which is the second **m**, 1 Kgs 6:1
of the LORD was laid, in the **m** of Ziv. 1 Kgs 6:37
in the eleventh year, in the **m** of Bul, 1 Kgs 6:38
month of Bul, which is the eighth **m**, 1 Kgs 6:38
at the feast in the **m** Ethanim, 1 Kgs 8:2
Ethanim, which is the seventh **m**. 1 Kgs 8:2
day of the eighth **m** like the feast 1 Kgs 12:32
on the fifteenth day in the eighth **m**, 1 Kgs 12:33
in the **m** that he had devised from 1 Kgs 12:33
and he reigned one **m** in Samaria. 2 Kgs 15:13
year of his reign, in the tenth **m**, 2 Kgs 25:1
month, on the tenth day of the **m**, 2 Kgs 25:1
day of the fourth **m** the famine was so 2 Kgs 25:3
In the fifth **m**, on the seventh day of 2 Kgs 25:8
seventh day of the **m**—that was the 2 Kgs 25:8
But in the seventh **m**, Ishmael the 2 Kgs 25:25
king of Judah, in the twelfth **m**, 2 Kgs 25:27
on the twenty-seventh day of the **m**, 2 Kgs 25:27
crossed the Jordan in the first **m**, 1 Chr 12:15
m after month throughout the year, 1 Chr 27:1
month after **m** throughout the year, 1 Chr 27:1
of the first division in the first **m**; 1 Chr 27:2
He served for the first **m**. 1 Chr 27:3
of the division of the second **m**; 1 Chr 27:4
third commander, for the third **m**, 1 Chr 27:5
of Joab was fourth, for the fourth **m**, 1 Chr 27:7
The fifth commander, for the fifth **m**, 1 Chr 27:8
Sixth, for the sixth **m**, was Ira, the son 1 Chr 27:9
Seventh, for the seventh **m**, was 1 Chr 27:10
Eighth, for the eighth **m**, was 1 Chr 27:11
Ninth, for the ninth **m**, was Abiezer 1 Chr 27:12
Tenth, for the tenth **m**, was 1 Chr 27:13
Eleventh, for the eleventh **m**, was 1 Chr 27:14
Twelfth, for the twelfth **m**, was 1 Chr 27:15
build in the second **m** of the fourth 2 Chr 3:2
at the feast that is in the seventh **m**. 2 Chr 5:3
day of the seventh **m** he sent the 2 Chr 7:10
in the third **m** of the fifteenth 2 Chr 15:10
first year of his reign, in the first **m**, 2 Chr 29:3
on the first day of the first **m**, 2 Chr 29:17
eighth day of the **m** they came to the 2 Chr 29:17
day of the first **m** they finished. 2 Chr 29:17
keep the Passover in the second **m**— 2 Chr 30:2
Unleavened Bread in the second **m**, 2 Chr 30:13
the fourteenth day of the second **m**. 2 Chr 30:15
In the third **m** they began to pile up 2 Chr 31:7
and finished them in the seventh **m**. 2 Chr 31:7
on the fourteenth day of the first **m**. 2 Chr 35:1
When the seventh **m** came, and the Ezr 3:1
day of the seventh **m** they began to offer Ezr 3:6
of God at Jerusalem, in the second **m**, Ezr 3:8
on the third day of the **m** of Adar, Ezr 6:15
On the fourteenth day of the first **m**, the Ezr 6:19
And he came to Jerusalem in the fifth **m**, Ezr 7:8
first day of the first **m** he began to go up Ezr 7:9
day of the fifth **m** he came to Jerusalem, Ezr 7:9
Ahava on the twelfth day of the first **m**, Ezr 8:31
It was the ninth **m**, on the twentieth day Ezr 10:9
month, on the twentieth day of the **m**. Ezr 10:9
day of the tenth **m** they sat down to Ezr 10:16
day of the first **m** they had come to Ezr 10:17
Now it happened in the **m** of Chislev, in Neh 1:1
In the **m** of Nisan, in the twentieth year Neh 2:1
on the twenty-fifth day of the **m** Elul, Neh 6:15
And when the seventh **m** had come, Neh 7:73
heard, on the first day of the seventh **m**. Neh 8:2
during the feast of the seventh **m**, Neh 8:14
twenty-fourth day of this **m** the people of Neh 9:1
into his royal palace in the tenth **m**, Est 2:16
tenth month, which is the **m** of Tebeth, Est 2:16
In the first **m**, which is the month of Est 3:7
the first month, which is the **m** of Nisan, Est 3:7
and they cast it **m** after month till the Est 3:7
cast it month after **m** till the twelfth Est 3:7
it month after month till the twelfth **m**, Est 3:7
twelfth month, which is the **m** of Adar. Est 3:7
on the thirteenth day of the first **m**, Est 3:12
day, the thirteenth day of the twelfth **m**, Est 3:13
twelfth month, which is the **m** of Adar, Est 3:13
summoned at that time, in the third **m**, Est 8:9
the third month, which is the **m** of Sivan, Est 8:9
on the thirteenth day of the twelfth **m**, Est 8:12
twelfth month, which is the **m** of Adar. Est 8:12
Now in the twelfth **m**, which is the Est 9:1
twelfth month, which is the **m** of Adar, Est 9:1
fourteenth day of the **m** of Adar and Est 9:15
on the thirteenth day of the **m** of Adar, Est 9:17
the fourteenth day of the **m** of Adar as a Est 9:19
fourteenth day of the **m** Adar and also Est 9:21
and as the **m** that had been turned for Est 9:22
the captivity of Jerusalem in the fifth **m**. Jer 1:3
themselves; in her **m** they will find her. Jer 2:24
Judah, in the fifth **m** of the fourth year, Jer 28:1
In that same year, in the seventh **m**, the Jer 28:17
of Josiah, king of Judah, in the ninth **m**, Jer 36:9
It was the ninth **m**, and the king was Jer 36:22
Zedekiah king of Judah, in the tenth **m**, Jer 39:1
year of Zedekiah, in the fourth **m**, Jer 39:2
fourth month, on the ninth day of the **m**, Jer 39:2
In the seventh **m**, Ishmael the son of Jer 41:1
ninth year of his reign, in the tenth **m**, Jer 52:4
tenth month, on the tenth day of the **m**, Jer 52:4
day of the fourth **m** the famine was so Jer 52:6
In the fifth **m**, on the tenth day of the Jer 52:12
the tenth day of the **m**—that was the Jer 52:12
king of Judah, in the twelfth **m**, Jer 52:31
on the twenty-fifth day of the **m**, Jer 52:31
In the thirtieth year, in the fourth **m**, on Ezk 1:1
fourth month, on the fifth day of the **m**, Ezk 1:1
the fifth day of the **m** (it was the fifth Ezk 1:2
In the sixth year, in the sixth **m**, on the Ezk 8:1
sixth month, on the fifth day of the **m**, Ezk 8:1
In the seventh year, in the fifth **m**, on Ezk 20:1
fifth month, on the tenth day of the **m**, Ezk 20:1
In the ninth year, in the tenth **m**, on the Ezk 24:1
tenth month, on the tenth day of the **m**, Ezk 24:1
eleventh year, on the first day of the **m**, Ezk 26:1
In the tenth year, in the tenth **m**, on the Ezk 29:1
month, on the twelfth day of the **m**, Ezk 29:1
the twenty-seventh year, in the first **m**, Ezk 29:17
first month, on the first day of the **m**, Ezk 29:17
In the eleventh year, in the first **m**, on Ezk 30:20
month, on the seventh day of the **m**, Ezk 30:20
In the eleventh year, in the third **m**, on Ezk 31:1
third month, on the first day of the **m**, Ezk 31:1
In the twelfth year, in the twelfth **m**, on Ezk 32:1
twelfth month, on the first day of the **m**, Ezk 32:1
In the twelfth year, in the twelfth **m**, Ezk 32:17
month, on the fifteenth day of the **m**, Ezk 32:17
year of our exile, in the tenth **m**, Ezk 33:21
tenth month, on the fifth day of the **m**, Ezk 33:21
of the year, on the tenth day of the **m**, Ezk 40:1
In the first **m**, on the first day of the Ezk 45:18
first month, on the first day of the **m**, Ezk 45:18
seventh day of the **m** for anyone who Ezk 45:20
"In the first **m**, on the fourteenth day Ezk 45:21
on the fourteenth day of the **m**, Ezk 45:21
In the seventh **m**, on the fifteenth day Ezk 45:25
fifteenth day of the **m** and for the Ezk 45:25
but they will bear fresh fruit every **m**, Ezk 47:12
On the twenty-fourth day of the first **m**, Dn 10:4
year of Darius the king, in the sixth **m**, Hg 1:1
the sixth month, on the first day of the **m**, Hg 1:1
on the twenty-fourth day of the **m**, in the Hg 1:15
day of the month, in the sixth **m**, Hg 1:15
In the seventh **m**, on the twenty-first day Hg 2:1
month, on the twenty-first day of the **m**, Hg 2:1
the twenty-fourth day of the ninth **m**, Hg 2:10
the twenty-fourth day of the ninth **m**. Hg 2:18
on the twenty-fourth day of the **m**, Hg 2:20
In the eighth **m**, in the second year of Zec 1:1
the twenty-fourth day of the eleventh **m**, Zec 1:7
month, which is the **m** of Shebat, Zec 1:7
on the fourth day of the ninth **m**, Zec 7:1
I weep and abstain in the fifth **m**, Zec 7:3
mourned in the fifth **m** and in the Zec 7:5
The fast of the fourth **m** and the fast of Zec 8:19
In one **m** I destroyed the three Zec 11:8
In the sixth **m** the angel Gabriel was Lk 1:26
and this is the sixth **m** with her who was Lk 1:36
prepared for the hour, the day, the **m**, Rv 9:15
kinds of fruit, yielding its fruit each **m**. Rv 22:2

MONTHS (58)
About three **m** later Judah was told, Gn 38:24
he was a fine child, she hid him three **m**. Ex 2:2
shall be for you the beginning of **m**. Ex 12:2
and at the beginnings of your **m**, Nm 10:10
"At the beginnings of your **m**, you Nm 28:11
month throughout the **m** of the year. Nm 28:14
of the sun and the rich yield of the **m**, Dt 33:14
leave me alone two **m**, that I may go up Jgs 11:37
"Go." Then he sent her away for two **m**, Jgs 11:38
And at the end of two **m**, she returned Jgs 11:39
in Judah, and was there some four **m**. Jgs 19:2
at the rock of Rimmon four **m**. Jgs 20:47
the country of the Philistines seven **m**. 1 Sm 6:1
the Philistines was a year and four **m**. 1 Sm 27:7
of Judah was seven years and six **m**. 2 Sm 2:11
over Judah seven years and six **m**, 2 Sm 5:5
of Obed-edom the Gittite three **m**, 2 Sm 6:11
at the end of nine **m** and twenty days. 2 Sm 24:8
will you flee three **m** before your foes 2 Sm 24:13
in Lebanon and two **m** at home. 1 Kgs 5:14
and all Israel remained there six **m**, 1 Kgs 11:16
reigned over Israel in Samaria six **m**. 2 Kgs 15:8
he reigned three **m** in Jerusalem. 2 Kgs 23:31
and he reigned three **m** in Jerusalem. 2 Kgs 24:8
he reigned for seven years and six **m**. 1 Chr 3:4
of Obed-edom in his house three **m**. 1 Chr 13:14
or three **m** of devastation by your 1 Chr 21:12
and he reigned three **m** in Jerusalem. 2 Chr 36:2
and he reigned three **m** and ten days 2 Chr 36:9
after being twelve **m** under the Est 2:12
six **m** with oil of myrrh and six months Est 2:12
of myrrh and six **m** with spices and Est 2:12
let it not come into the number of the **m**. Jb 3:6
so I am allotted **m** of emptiness, and Jb 7:3
and the number of his **m** is with you, Jb 14:5
when the number of their **m** is cut off? Jb 21:21
"Oh, that I were as in the **m** of old, as in Jb 29:2
Can you number the **m** that they fulfill, Jb 39:2
For seven **m** the house of Israel will be Ezk 39:12
the end of seven **m** they will make Ezk 39:14
the end of twelve **m** he was walking on Dn 4:29
there were yet three **m** to the harvest; Am 4:7
and for five **m** she kept herself hidden, Lk 1:24
with her about three **m** and returned to Lk 1:56
were shut up three years and six **m**, Lk 4:25
Do you not say, 'There are yet four **m**, Jn 4:35
brought up for three **m** in his father's Acts 7:20
And he stayed a year and six **m**, Acts 18:11
and for three **m** spoke boldly, Acts 19:8
There he spent three **m**, and when a Acts 20:3
After three **m** we set sail in a ship that Acts 28:11
observe days and **m** and seasons and Gal 4:10
was hidden for three **m** by his parents, Heb 11:23
for three years and six **m** it did not rain Jas 5:17
were allowed to torment them for five **m**, Rv 9:5
to hurt people for five **m** is in their tails. Rv 9:10
trample the holy city for forty-two **m**. Rv 11:2
to exercise authority for forty-two **m**. Rv 13:5

MONUMENT (5)
he set up a **m** for himself and turned 1 Sm 15:12
it is called Absalom's **m** to this day. 2 Sm 18:18
"What is that **m** that I see?" And the 2 Kgs 23:17
to set up his **m** at the river Euphrates. 1 Chr 18:3
within my walls a **m** and a name better Is 56:5

MONUMENTS (1)
and decorate the **m** of the righteous, Mt 23:29

MOON (59)
Behold, the sun, the **m**, and eleven stars Gn 37:9
On the third new **m** after the people of Ex 19:1
the burnt offering of the new **m**, Nm 29:6
you see the sun and the **m** and the stars, Dt 4:19
or the sun or the **m** or any of the host of Dt 17:3
"Sun, stand still at Gibeon, and **m**, Jos 10:12
the sun stood still, and the **m** stopped, Jos 10:13
"Behold, tomorrow is the new **m**, 1 Sm 20:5
to him, "Tomorrow is the new **m**, 1 Sm 20:18
And when the new **m** came, the king 1 Sm 20:24
second day, the day after the new **m**, 1 Sm 20:27
It is neither new **m** nor Sabbath." She 2 Kgs 4:23
sun and the **m** and the constellations 2 Kgs 23:5
the offerings at the new **m** and at all the Ezr 3:5
Behold, even the **m** is not bright, and the Jb 25:5
the face of the full **m** and spreads over it Jb 26:9
it shone, or the **m** moving in splendor, Jb 31:26
work of your fingers, the **m** and the stars, Ps 8:3
the sun endures, and as long as the **m**, Ps 72:5
and peace abound, till the **m** be no more! Ps 72:7
Blow the trumpet at the new **m**, at the Ps 81:3
trumpet at the new moon, at the full **m**, Ps 81:3
Like the **m** it shall be established Ps 89:37
He made the **m** to mark the seasons; Ps 104:19
strike you by day, nor the **m** by night. Ps 121:6
the **m** and stars to rule over the night, Ps 136:9
Praise him, sun and **m**, praise him, all Ps 148:3
him; at full **m** he will come home." Prv 7:20
the light and the **m** and the stars are Eccl 12:2
down like the dawn, beautiful as the **m**, Sg 6:10
New **m** and Sabbath and the calling of Is 1:13
rising, and the **m** will not shed its light. Is 13:10
Then the **m** will be confounded and the Is 24:23
the light of the **m** will be as the light of Is 30:26
brightness shall the **m** give you light; Is 60:19
go down, nor your **m** withdraw itself; Is 60:20
From new **m** to new moon, and from Is 66:23
From new moon to new **m**, and from Is 66:23
before the sun and the **m** and all the host Jer 8:2
the fixed order of the **m** and the stars for Jer 31:35
cloud, and the **m** shall not give its light. Ezk 32:7
the day of the new **m** it shall be opened. Ezk 46:1
the day of the new **m** he shall offer a Ezk 46:6
Now the new **m** shall devour them with Hos 5:7
The sun and the **m** are darkened, and the Jl 2:10
be turned to darkness, and the **m** to blood, Jl 2:31
The sun and the **m** are darkened, and the Jl 3:15
saying, "When will the new **m** be over, Am 8:5
The sun and **m** stood still in their Hab 3:11
and the **m** will not give its light, Mt 24:29
and the **m** will not give its light, Mk 13:24
will be signs in sun and **m** and stars, Lk 21:25
turned to darkness and the **m** to blood, Acts 2:20
the sun, and another glory of the **m**, 1 Cor 15:41
to a festival or a new **m** or a Sabbath. Col 2:16
sackcloth, the full **m** became like blood, Rv 6:12
the sun was struck, and a third of the **m**, Rv 8:12
with the sun, with the **m** under her feet, Rv 12:1
has no need of sun or **m** to shine on it, Rv 21:23

MOONS (10)
on Sabbaths, new **m** and feast days, 1 Chr 23:31
and the new **m** and the appointed 2 Chr 2:4
Moses for the Sabbaths, the new **m**, 2 Chr 8:13
for the Sabbaths, the new **m**, 2 Chr 31:3
offering, the Sabbaths, the new **m**, Neh 10:33
Your new **m** and your appointed feasts Is 1:14
who at the new **m** make known what Is 47:13
offerings, at the feasts, the new **m**, Ezk 45:17
on the Sabbaths and on the new **m**. Ezk 46:3
to all her mirth, her feasts, her new **m**, Hos 2:11

MOORED (1)
land at Gennesaret and **m** to the shore. Mk 6:53

MORALS (1)
"Bad company ruins good **m**." 1 Cor 15:33

MORDECAI (60)
Seraiah, Reelaiah, **M**, Bilshan, Ezr 2:2
Raamiah, Nahamani, **M**, Bilshan, Neh 7:7
in Susa the citadel whose name was **M**, Est 2:5
died, **M** took her as his own daughter. Est 2:7
for **M** had commanded her not to make Est 2:10
And every day **M** walked in front of the Est 2:11
the daughter of Abihail the uncle of **M**, Est 2:15
time, **M** was sitting at the king's gate. Est 2:19
her people, as **M** had commanded her, Est 2:20
for Esther obeyed **M** just as when she Est 2:20
days, as **M** was sitting at the king's gate, Est 2:21
And this came to the knowledge of **M**, Est 2:22
Esther told the king in the name of **M**. Est 2:22
But **M** did not bow down or pay homage. Est 3:2
who were at the king's gate said to **M**, Est 3:3
when Haman saw that **M** did not bow Est 3:5
he disdained to lay hands on **M** alone. Est 3:6
had made known to him the people of **M**, Est 3:6
to destroy all the Jews, the people of **M**, Est 3:6
When **M** learned all that had been done, Est 4:1
M tore his clothes and put on sackcloth Est 4:1
She sent garments to clothe **M**, so that he Est 4:4
ordered him to go to **M** to learn what this Est 4:5
Hathach went out to **M** in the open Est 4:6
and **M** told him all that had happened to Est 4:7
M also gave him a copy of the written Est 4:8
went and told Esther what **M** had said. Est 4:9
commanded him to go to **M** and say, Est 4:10
And they told **M** what Esther had said. Est 4:12
Then **M** told them to reply to Esther, Est 4:13
Then Esther told them to reply to **M**, Est 4:15
M then went away and did everything as Est 4:17
But when Haman saw **M** in the king's Est 5:9
him, he was filled with wrath against **M**. Est 5:9
so long as I see **M** the Jew sitting at the Est 5:13
tell the king to have **M** hanged upon it. Est 5:14
was found written how **M** had told about Est 6:2
has been bestowed on **M** for this?" The Est 6:3
the king about having **M** hanged on the Est 6:4
and do so to **M** the Jew who sits at the Est 6:10
and he dressed **M** and led him through Est 6:11
Then **M** returned to the king's gate. But Est 6:12
and his wife Zeresh said to him, "If **M**, Est 6:13
gallows that Haman has prepared for **M**, Est 7:9
the gallows that he had prepared for **M**. Est 7:10
And **M** came before the king, for Esther Est 8:1
had taken from Haman, and gave it to **M**. Est 8:2
And Esther set **M** over the house of Est 8:2
said to Queen Esther and to **M** the Jew, Est 8:7
to all that **M** commanded concerning the Est 8:9
Then **M** went out from the presence of Est 8:15
Jews, for the fear of **M** had fallen on them. Est 9:3
For **M** was great in the king's house, and Est 9:4
for the man **M** grew more and more Est 9:4
And **M** recorded these things and sent Est 9:20
to do, and what **M** had written to them. Est 9:23
and **M** the Jew gave full written Est 9:29
as **M** the Jew and Queen Esther Est 9:31
the full account of the high honor of **M**, Est 10:2
For **M** the Jew was second in rank to Est 10:3

MORDECAI'S (1)
to see whether **M** words would stand, Est 3:4

MORE (554)
Now the serpent was **m** crafty than any Gn 3:1
and gained **m** and more until he Gn 26:13
gained more and **m** until he became Gn 26:13
also, and he loved Rachel **m** than Leah, Gn 29:30
Israel loved Joseph **m** than any other Gn 37:3
their father loved him **m** than all his Gn 37:4
to his brothers they hated him even **m**. Gn 37:5
they hated him even **m** for his dreams Gn 37:8
and said, "She is **m** righteous than I, Gn 38:26
day with our father, and one is no **m**." Gn 42:13
One is no **m**, and the youngest is this Gn 42:32
Joseph is no **m**, and Simeon is no more, Gn 42:36
Joseph is no more, and Simeon is no **m**, Gn 42:36
But the **m** they were oppressed, the more Ex 1:12
the **m** they multiplied and the more they Ex 1:12
multiplied and the **m** they spread Ex 1:12
will cease, and there will be no **m** hail, Ex 9:29
"Yet one plague **m** I will bring upon Ex 11:1
so. They gathered, some **m**, some less. Ex 16:17
The rich shall not give **m**, and the poor Ex 30:15
people bring much **m** than enough for Ex 36:5
woman do anything **m** for the Ex 36:6
was sufficient to do all the work, and **m**. Ex 36:7
they shall no **m** sacrifice their sacrifices Lv 17:7
the duty of the service and serve no **m**. Nm 8:25
m than all people who were on the face Nm 12:3
pass through on foot, nothing **m**." Nm 20:19
m in number and more honorable Nm 22:15
in number and **m** honorable than Nm 22:15
of the LORD my God to do less or **m**. Nm 22:18
I may know what **m** the LORD will say Nm 22:19
to increase still **m** the fierce anger of Nm 32:14
with a loud voice; and he added no **m**. Dt 5:22
the voice of the LORD our God any **m**, Dt 5:25
seven nations **m** numerous and mightier Dt 7:1
not because you were **m** in number than Dt 7:7
my God or see this great fire any **m**, Dt 18:16
stripes may be given him, but not **m**, Dt 25:3
on to beat him with **m** stripes than these, Dt 25:3
will make you **m** prosperous and Dt 30:5
the LORD. How much **m** after my death! Dt 31:27
I will be with you no **m**, unless you Jos 7:12
There were **m** who died because of the Jos 10:11
God and spoke no **m** of making war Jos 22:33
back and were **m** corrupt than their Jgs 2:19
against me; let me speak just once **m**. Jgs 6:39
let me test just once **m** with the fleece. Jgs 6:39
Israel, and they raised their heads no **m**. Jgs 8:28
gods; therefore I will save you no **m**. Jgs 10:13
LORD appeared no **m** to Manoah and Jgs 13:21
her younger sister **m** beautiful than Jgs 15:2
at his death were **m** than those whom Jgs 16:30
we go out once **m** to battle against our Jgs 20:28
do so to me and **m** also if anything but Ru 1:17
to go with her, she said no **m**. Ru 1:18
you, who is **m** to you than seven sons, Ru 4:15
sad? Am I not **m** to you than ten sons?" 1 Sm 1:8
Talk no **m** so very proudly, let not 1 Sm 2:3
do so to you and **m** also if you hide 1 Sm 3:17
people of Israel **m** handsome than he. 1 Sm 9:2
Philistines increased **m** and more. 1 Sm 14:19
Philistines increased more and **m**. 1 Sm 14:19
said, "God do so to me and **m** also; 1 Sm 14:44
and what **m** can he have but the 1 Sm 18:8
Saul was even **m** afraid of David. So 1 Sm 18:29
out David had **m** success than all 1 Sm 18:30
do so to Jonathan and **m** also if I do 1 Sm 20:13
How much **m** today will their vessels 1 Sm 21:5
how much **m** then if we go to Keilah 1 Sm 23:3
Go, make yet **m** sure. Know and see 1 Sm 23:22
David, "You are **m** righteous than I, 1 Sm 24:17
to the enemies of David and **m** also, 1 Sm 25:22
David, for I will no **m** do you harm, 1 Sm 26:21
from me and answers me no **m**, 1 Sm 28:15
until they had no **m** strength to weep. 1 Sm 30:4
men stopped and pursued Israel no **m**, 2 Sm 2:28
God do so to Abner and **m** also, if I do 2 Sm 3:9
saying, "God do so to me and **m** also, 2 Sm 3:35
sons of Zeruiah, are **m** severe than I. 2 Sm 3:39
How much **m**, when wicked men 2 Sm 4:11
And David took **m** concubines and 2 Sm 5:13
and **m** sons and daughters were born 2 Sm 5:13
myself yet **m** contemptible than 2 Sm 6:22
own place and be disturbed no **m**. 2 Sm 7:10
violent men shall afflict them no **m**, 2 Sm 7:10
And what **m** can David say to you? 2 Sm 7:20
little, I would add to you as much **m**. 2 Sm 12:8
that the avenger of blood kill no **m**, 2 Sm 14:11
how much **m** now may this 2 Sm 16:11
the forest devoured **m** people that day 2 Sm 18:8
God do so to me and **m** also, if you 2 Sm 19:13
"Why speak any **m** of your affairs? 2 Sm 19:29
in David also we have **m** than you. 2 Sm 19:43
will do us **m** harm than Absalom. 2 Sm 20:6
name of Solomon **m** famous than 1 Kgs 1:47
do so to me and **m** also if this word 1 Kgs 2:23
sword two men **m** righteous and 1 Kgs 2:32
LORD, there was no **m** breath in her. 1 Kgs 10:5
m than all that their fathers had 1 Kgs 14:22
and did **m** evil than all who were 1 Kgs 16:25
m than all who were before him. 1 Kgs 16:30
Ahab did **m** to provoke the LORD, the 1 Kgs 16:33
may the gods do to me and **m** also, 1 Kgs 19:2
"The gods do so to me and **m** also, 1 Kgs 20:10
horsemen!" And he saw him no **m**. 2 Kgs 2:12
saved himself there **m** than once or 2 Kgs 6:10
are with us are **m** than those who are 2 Kgs 6:16
"May God do so to me and **m** also, 2 Kgs 6:31
they found no **m** of her than the skull 2 Kgs 9:35
therefore take no **m** money from 2 Kgs 12:7
should take no **m** money from the 2 Kgs 12:8
an army of **m** than fifty horsemen 2 Kgs 13:7
them astray to do **m** evil than the 2 Kgs 21:9
and has done things **m** evil than all 2 Kgs 21:11
Jabez was **m** honorable than his 1 Chr 4:9
And David took **m** wives in 1 Chr 14:3
and David fathered **m** sons and 1 Chr 14:3
own place and be disturbed no **m**. 1 Chr 17:9
violent men shall waste them no **m**, 1 Chr 17:9
And what **m** can David say to you 1 Chr 17:18
to save the Ammonites any **m**. 1 Chr 19:19
Since **m** chief men were found 1 Chr 24:4
LORD, there was no **m** breath in her. 2 Chr 9:4
And there was no **m** war until the 2 Chr 15:19
until they could carry no **m**. 2 Chr 20:25
able to give you much **m** than this." 2 Chr 25:9
he became yet **m** faithless to the 2 Chr 28:22
the Levites were **m** upright in heart 2 Chr 29:34
for there are **m** with us than with 2 Chr 32:7
servants said still **m** against the 2 Chr 32:16
and I will no **m** remove the foot of 2 Chr 33:8
to do **m** evil than the nations whom 2 Chr 33:9
Amon incurred guilt **m** and more. 2 Chr 33:23
Amon incurred guilt more and **m**. 2 Chr 33:23
for he was a **m** faithful and God-fearing Neh 7:2
you are bringing **m** wrath on Israel Neh 13:18
the king loved Esther **m** than all the Est 2:17
favor in his sight **m** than all the virgins, Est 2:17
you will escape any **m** than all the other Est 4:13
the king delight to honor **m** than me?" Est 6:6
man Mordecai grew **m** and more Est 9:4
Mordecai grew more and **m** powerful. Est 9:4
and dig for it **m** than for hidden Jb 3:21

how much **m** those who dwell in houses Jb 4:19
of him who sees me will behold me no **m**; Jb 7:8
he returns no **m** to his house, nor does Jb 7:10
and the tent of the wicked will be no **m**." Jb 8:22
the heavens are no **m** he will not awake Jb 14:12
The eye that saw him will see him no **m**, Jb 20:9
nor will his place any **m** behold him. Jb 20:9
words of his mouth **m** than my portion Jb 23:12
He goes to bed rich, but will do so no **m**; Jb 27:19
"They are dismayed; they answer no **m**; Jb 32:15
they stand there, and answer no **m**? Jb 32:16
nor regards the rich **m** than the poor, Jb 34:19
punishment; I will not offend any **m**; Jb 34:31
if I have done iniquity, I will do it no **m**'? Jb 34:32
who teaches us **m** than the beasts of the Jb 35:11
latter days of Job **m** than his beginning. Jb 42:12
You have put **m** joy in my heart than they Ps 4:7
is of the earth may strike terror no **m**. Ps 10:18
M to be desired are they than gold, even Ps 19:10
them down and build them up no **m**. Ps 28:5
a little while, the wicked will be no **m**; Ps 37:10
passed away, and behold, he was no **m**; Ps 37:36
again, before I depart and am no **m**!" Ps 39:13
of them, yet they are **m** than can be told. Ps 40:5
they are **m** than the hairs of my head; Ps 40:12
You love evil **m** than good, and lying Ps 52:3
and lying **m** than speaking what is right. Ps 52:3
consume them till they are no **m**, that Ps 59:13
M in number than the hairs of my head Ps 69:4
will please the LORD **m** than an ox or Ps 69:31
and will praise you yet **m** and more. Ps 71:14
and will praise you yet more and **m**. Ps 71:14
peace abound, till the moon be no **m**! Ps 72:7
m majestic than the mountains of prey. Ps 76:4
Yet they sinned still **m** against him, Ps 78:17
name of Israel be remembered no **m**!" Ps 83:4
the gates of Zion **m** than all the dwelling Ps 87:2
like those whom you remember no **m**, Ps 88:5
it is gone, and its place knows it no **m**. Ps 103:16
the earth, and let the wicked be no **m**! Ps 104:35
I have **m** understanding than all my Ps 119:99
I understand **m** than the aged, for I Ps 119:100
you, and what **m** shall be done to you, Ps 120:3
for we have had **m** than enough of Ps 123:3
Our soul has had **m** than enough of the Ps 123:4
for the Lord **m** than watchmen for Ps 130:6
m than watchmen for the morning. Ps 130:6
count them, they are **m** than the sand. Ps 139:18
into fire, into miry pits, no **m** to rise! Ps 140:10
She is **m** precious than jewels, and Prv 3:15
the tempest passes, the wicked is no **m**, Prv 10:25
how much **m** the wicked and the Prv 11:31
wicked are overthrown and are no **m**, Prv 12:7
how much **m** the hearts of the Prv 15:11
brother offended is **m** unyielding than Prv 18:19
how much **m** do his friends go far from Prv 19:7
and justice is **m** acceptable to the Prv 21:3
how much **m** when he brings it with Prv 21:27
There is **m** hope for a fool than for Prv 26:12
will afterward find **m** favor than he Prv 28:23
There is **m** hope for a fool than for Prv 29:20
and remember their misery no **m**. Prv 31:7
She is far **m** precious than jewels. Prv 31:10
m than any who had been before me in Eccl 2:7
saw that there is **m** gain in wisdom Eccl 2:13
as there is **m** gain in light than in Eccl 2:13
are already dead **m** fortunate than the Eccl 4:2
The **m** words, the more vanity, and Eccl 6:11
The more words, the **m** vanity, and Eccl 6:11
to the wise man **m** than ten rulers who Eccl 7:19
I find something **m** bitter than death: Eccl 7:26
nothing, and they have no **m** reward, Eccl 9:5
forever they have no **m** share in all that Eccl 9:6
the edge, he must use **m** strength, Eccl 10:10
you; we will extol your love **m** than wine; Sg 1:4
is your beloved **m** than another beloved, Sg 5:9
is your beloved **m** than another beloved, Sg 5:9
Bring no **m** vain offerings; incense is an Is 1:13
What **m** was there to do for my vineyard, Is 5:4
add field to field, until there is no **m** room, Is 5:8
of Jacob will no **m** lean on him who Is 10:20
I will make people **m** rare than fine gold, Is 13:12
the vegetation fails, the greenery is no **m**. Is 15:6
for I will bring upon Dibon even **m**, a Is 15:9
the oppressor is no **m** and destruction has Is 16:4
terror! Before morning, they are no **m**! Is 17:14
will be driven away, and will be no **m**. Is 19:7
"You will no **m** exult, O oppressed virgin Is 23:12
No **m** do they drink wine with singing; Is 24:9
ruin; the foreigners' palace is a city no **m**; Is 25:2
shed on it, and will no **m** cover its slain. Is 26:21
"Jacob shall no **m** be ashamed, no more Is 29:22
ashamed, no **m** shall his face grow pale. Is 29:22
let us hear no **m** about the Holy One of Is 30:11
Zion, in Jerusalem; you shall weep no **m**. Is 30:19
The fool will no **m** be called noble, nor Is 32:5
In little **m** than a year you will shudder, Is 32:10
You will see no **m** the insolent people, Is 33:19
on man no **m** among the inhabitants Is 38:11
For you shall no **m** be called tender and Is 47:1
for you shall no **m** be called the mistress Is 47:5
bowl of my wrath you shall drink no **m**; Is 51:22
for there shall no **m** come into you the Is 52:1
desolate one will be **m** than the children Is 54:1
widowhood you will remember no **m**. Is 54:4
of Noah should no **m** go over the earth, Is 54:9
Violence shall no **m** be heard in your Is 60:18
sun shall be no **m** your light by day, Is 60:19
Your sun shall no **m** go down, nor your Is 60:20
You shall no **m** be termed Forsaken, and Is 62:4
your land shall no **m** be termed Desolate, Is 62:4
no **m** shall be heard in it the sound of Is 65:19
No **m** shall there be in it an infant who Is 65:20
'We are free, we will come no **m** to you'? Jer 2:31
has shown herself **m** righteous than Jer 3:11
declares the LORD, they shall no **m** say, Jer 3:16
they shall no **m** stubbornly follow their Jer 3:17
when it will no **m** be called Topheth, Jer 7:32
that his name be remembered no **m**." Jer 11:19
made their widows **m** in number than Jer 15:8
this place shall no **m** be called Topheth, Jer 19:6
or speak any **m** in his name," there is in Jer 20:9
he shall return no **m** to see his native Jer 22:10
this place: "He shall return here no **m**, Jer 22:11
care for them, and they shall fear no **m**, Jer 23:4
of the LORD' you shall mention no **m**, Jer 23:36
be drunk and vomit, fall and rise no **m**, Jer 25:27
foreigners shall no **m** make a servant Jer 30:8
garden, and they shall languish no **m**. Jer 31:12
her children, because they are no **m**." Jer 31:15
"Once **m** they shall use these words in Jer 31:23
and I will remember their sin no **m**." Jer 31:34
a taunt. You shall see this place no **m**. Jer 42:18
my name shall no **m** be invoked by the Jer 44:26
because they are **m** numerous than Jer 46:23
the renown of Moab is no **m**. In Jer 48:2
M than for Jazer I weep for you, O vine Jer 48:32
of hosts: "Is wisdom no **m** in Teman? Jer 49:7
and his neighbors; and he is no **m**. Jer 49:10
'Thus shall Babylon sink, to rise no **m**, Jer 51:64
the law is no **m**, and her prophets find Lam 2:9
their bodies were **m** ruddy than coral, Lam 4:7
them; he will regard them no **m**; Lam 4:16
Our fathers sinned, and are no **m**; and Lam 5:7
by doing wickedness **m** than the Ezk 5:6
against my statutes **m** than the Ezk 5:6
Because you are **m** turbulent than the Ezk 5:7
and when I bring **m** and more famine Ezk 5:16
I bring more and **m** famine upon you Ezk 5:16
and they shall no **m** use it as a Ezk 12:23
there shall be no **m** any false vision or Ezk 12:24
and I will say to you, The wall is no **m**, Ezk 13:15
they shall be no **m** in your hand as Ezk 13:21
you shall no **m** see false visions Ezk 13:23
of Israel may no **m** go astray from me, Ezk 14:11
How much **m** when I send upon Ezk 14:21
you shall also give payment no **m**. Ezk 16:41
I will be calm and will no **m** be angry. Ezk 16:42
time you were **m** corrupt than they Ezk 16:47
have committed **m** abominations Ezk 16:51
which you acted **m** abominably than Ezk 16:52
they, they are **m** in the right than you. Ezk 16:52
this proverb shall no **m** be used by you Ezk 18:3
his voice should no **m** be heard on the Ezk 19:9
you shall no **m** profane with your Ezk 20:39
You shall be no **m** remembered, for I Ezk 21:32
and she became **m** corrupt than her Ezk 23:11
be remembered no **m** among the Ezk 25:10
of your lyres shall be heard no **m**. Ezk 26:13
a dreadful end, and you shall be no **m**. Ezk 26:21
end and shall be no **m** forever.'" Ezk 27:36
end and shall be no **m** forever." Ezk 28:19
there shall be no **m** a brier to prick Ezk 28:24
They shall no **m** be a prey to the Ezk 34:28
they shall no **m** be consumed with Ezk 34:29
and will do **m** good to you than ever Ezk 36:11
the galleries took **m** away from them Ezk 42:5
from the ground **m** than the lower Ezk 42:6
of Israel shall no **m** defile my holy Ezk 43:7
princes shall no **m** oppress my people, Ezk 45:8
wisdom that I have **m** than all the Dn 2:30
heated seven times **m** than it was Dn 3:19
and still **m** greatness was added to me. Dn 4:36
three **m** kings shall arise in Persia, Dn 11:2
for I will no **m** have mercy on the house Hos 1:6
shall be remembered by name no **m**. Hos 2:17
The **m** they increased, the more they Hos 4:7
increased, the **m** they sinned against me; Hos 4:7
I will love them no **m**; all their princes Hos 9:15
The **m** his fruit increased, the more Hos 10:1
fruit increased, the **m** altars he built; Hos 10:1
The **m** they were called, the more they Hos 11:2
they were called, the **m** they went away; Hos 11:2
And now they sin **m** and more, and Hos 13:2
And now they sin more and **m**, and Hos 13:2
and we will say no **m**, 'Our God,' to the Hos 14:3
and I will no **m** make you a reproach Jl 2:19
"Fallen, no **m** to rise, is the virgin Israel; Am 5:2
the sea grew **m** and more tempestuous. Jon 1:11
the sea grew more and **m** tempestuous. Jon 1:11
the sea grew **m** and more tempestuous Jon 1:13
grew more and **m** tempestuous against Jon 1:13
which there are **m** than 120,000 persons Jon 4:11
you shall have no **m** tellers of fortunes; Mi 5:12
you shall bow down no **m** to the work of Mi 5:13
afflicted you, I will afflict you no **m**. Na 1:12
"No **m** shall your name be perpetuated; Na 1:14
increased your merchants **m** than the Na 3:16
m fierce than the evening wolves; Hab 1:8
up the man **m** righteous than he? Hab 1:13
For all the traders are no **m**; all who Zep 1:11
But all the **m** they were eager to make all Zep 3:7
Yet once **m**, in a little while, I will shake Hg 2:6
"Take once **m** the equipment of a Zec 11:15
so that they shall be remembered no **m**. Zec 13:2
you a blessing until there is no **m** need. Mal 3:10
Then once **m** you shall see the Mal 3:18
to be comforted, because they are no **m**." Mt 2:18
anything **m** than this comes from evil. Mt 5:37
what **m** are you doing than others? Mt 5:47
Is not life **m** than food, and the body Mt 6:25
food, and the body **m** than clothing? Mt 6:25
them. Are you not of **m** value than they? Mt 6:26
oven, will he not much **m** clothe you, Mt 6:30
how much **m** will your Father who is in Mt 7:11
it will be **m** bearable on the day of Mt 10:15
how much **m** will they malign those of Mt 10:25
you are of **m** value than many Mt 10:31
loves father or mother **m** than me is Mt 10:37
loves son or daughter **m** than me is not Mt 10:37
Yes, I tell you, and **m** than a prophet. Mt 11:9
it will be **m** bearable on the day of Mt 11:22
that it will be **m** tolerable on the day Mt 11:24
Of how much **m** value is a man than a Mt 12:12
it seven other spirits **m** evil than itself, Mt 12:45
to the one who has, **m** will be given, Mt 13:12
he rejoices over it **m** than over the Mt 18:13
they thought they would receive **m**, Mt 20:10
be silent, but they cried out all the **m**, Mt 20:31
he sent other servants, **m** than the first. Mt 21:36
dare to ask him any **m** questions. Mt 22:46
with them, and he made five talents **m**. Mt 25:16
had the two talents made two talents **m**. Mt 25:17
came forward, bringing five talents **m**, Mt 25:20
here I have made five talents **m**.' Mt 25:20
here I have made two talents **m**.' Mt 25:22
to everyone who has will **m** be given, Mt 25:29
at once send me **m** than twelve legions Mt 26:53
he done?" But they shouted all the **m**, Mt 27:23
together, so that there was no **m** room, Mk 2:2
to you, and still **m** will be added to you. Mk 4:24
For to the one who has, **m** will be given, Mk 4:25
But the **m** he charged them, the more Mk 7:36
the **m** zealously they proclaimed it. Mk 7:36
But he cried out all the **m**, "Son of Mk 10:48
is much **m** than all whole burnt Mk 12:33
one dared to ask him any **m** questions. Mk 12:34
widow has put in **m** than all those Mk 12:43
been sold for **m** than three hundred Mk 14:5
he done?" But they shouted all the **m**, Mk 15:14
"Collect no **m** than you are authorized Lk 3:13
But now even **m** the report about him Lk 5:15
Yes, I tell you, and **m** than a prophet. Lk 7:26
Now which of them will love him **m**?" Lk 7:42
for to the one who has, **m** will be given, Lk 8:18
do not trouble the Teacher any **m**." Lk 8:49
"We have no **m** than five loaves and two Lk 9:13
it will be **m** bearable on that day for Lk 10:12
But it will be **m** bearable in the Lk 10:14
of him, and whatever **m** you spend, Lk 10:35
how much **m** will the heavenly Father Lk 11:13
seven other spirits **m** evil than itself, Lk 11:26
after that have nothing **m** that they can Lk 12:4
you are of **m** value than many sparrows. Lk 12:7
For life is **m** than food, and the body Lk 12:23
food, and the body **m** than clothing. Lk 12:23
Of how much **m** value are you than Lk 12:24
oven, how much **m** will he clothe you, Lk 12:28
much, they will demand the **m**. Lk 12:48
lest someone **m** distinguished than you Lk 14:8
there will be **m** joy in heaven over one Lk 15:7
hired servants have **m** than enough Lk 15:17
of this world are **m** shrewd in dealing Lk 16:8
not receive many times **m** in this time, Lk 18:30
But he cried out all the **m**, "Son of Lk 18:39

your mina has made ten minas **m**.’ Lk 19:16
to everyone who has, **m** will be given, Lk 19:26
widow has put in **m** than all of them. Lk 21:3
in an agony he prayed **m** earnestly; Lk 22:44
“No **m** of this!” And he touched his ear Lk 22:51
Pilate addressed them once **m**, desiring Lk 23:20
making and baptizing **m** disciples than Jn 4:1
And many **m** believed because of his Jn 4:41
Sin no **m**, that nothing worse may Jn 5:14
Jews were seeking all the **m** to kill him, Jn 5:18
will he do **m** signs than this man has Jn 7:31
And once **m** he bent down and wrote on Jn 8:8
you; go, and from now on sin no **m**.”]] Jn 8:11
that comes from man **m** than the glory Jn 12:43
while and the world will see me no **m**, Jn 14:19
fruit he prunes, that it may bear **m** fruit. Jn 15:2
this statement, he was even **m** afraid. Jn 19:8
do you love me **m** than these?” He said Jn 21:15
them to speak no **m** to anyone in this Acts 4:17
was performed was **m** than forty years Acts 4:22
And **m** than ever believers were added Acts 5:14
away, and the eunuch saw him no **m**, Acts 8:39
Saul increased all the **m** in strength, Acts 9:22
dead, no **m** to return to corruption, Acts 13:34
these Jews were **m** noble than those Acts 17:11
to him the way of God **m** accurately. Acts 18:26
‘It is **m** blessed to give than to Acts 20:35
language, they became even **m** quiet. Acts 22:2
There were **m** than forty who made Acts 23:13
to determine his case **m** exactly. Acts 23:15
to inquire somewhat **m** closely about Acts 23:20
for **m** than forty of their men are Acts 23:21
that it is not **m** than twelve days since Acts 24:11
among them not **m** than eight or Acts 25:6
the centurion paid **m** attention to the Acts 27:11
M than that, we rejoice in our Rom 5:3
much **m** shall we be saved by him Rom 5:9
God by the death of his Son, much **m**, Rom 5:10
M than that, we also rejoice in God Rom 5:11
much **m** have the grace of God and Rom 5:15
much **m** will those who receive the Rom 5:17
increased, grace abounded all the **m**, Rom 5:20
lawlessness leading to **m** lawlessness, Rom 6:19
is the one who died—**m** than that, Rom 8:34
things we are **m** than conquerors Rom 8:37
how much **m** will their full Rom 11:12
olive tree, how much **m** will these, Rom 11:24
to think of himself **m** highly than he Rom 12:3
How much **m**, then, matters 1 Cor 6:3
claim on you, do not we even **m**? 1 Cor 9:12
to all, that I might win **m** of them. 1 Cor 9:19
which our **m** presentable parts do 1 Cor 12:24
show you a still **m** excellent way. 1 Cor 12:31
in tongues, but even **m** to prophesy. 1 Cor 14:5
I speak in tongues **m** than all of you. 1 Cor 14:18
he appeared to **m** than five hundred 1 Cor 15:6
of the Spirit have even **m** glory? 2 Cor 3:8
much **m** will what is permanent 2 Cor 3:11
grace extends to **m** and more people 2 Cor 4:15
extends to more and **m** people it may 2 Cor 4:15
zeal for me, so that I rejoiced still **m**. 2 Cor 7:7
we rejoiced still **m** at the joy of Titus, 2 Cor 7:13
but who is now **m** earnest than ever 2 Cor 8:22
labors, far **m** imprisonments, 2 Cor 11:23
no one may think **m** of me than he 2 Cor 12:6
will boast all the **m** gladly of my 2 Cor 12:9
If I love you **m**, am I to be loved less? 2 Cor 12:15
an intermediary implies **m** than one, Gal 3:20
whose slaves you want to be once **m**? Gal 4:9
desolate one will be **m** than those of the Gal 4:27
able to do far **m** abundantly than all Eph 3:20
your love may abound **m** and more, Phil 1:9
your love may abound more and **m**, Phil 1:9
are much **m** bold to speak the word Phil 1:14
in the flesh is **m** necessary on your Phil 1:24
count others **m** significant than Phil 2:3
presence but much **m** in my absence, Phil 2:12
I am the **m** eager to send him, Phil 2:28
for confidence in the flesh, I have **m**: Phil 3:4
I have received full payment, and **m**. I Phil 4:18
we endeavored the **m** eagerly and 1 Thes 2:17
are doing, that you do so **m** and more. 1 Thes 4:1
are doing, that you do so more and **m**. 1 Thes 4:1
brothers, to do this **m** and more, 1 Thes 4:10
brothers, to do this more and **m**, 1 Thes 4:10
lead people into **m** and more 2 Tm 2:16
people into more and **m** ungodliness, 2 Tm 2:16
twice, have nothing **m** to do with him, Ti 3:10
longer as a slave but **m** than a slave, Phlm 1:16
to me, but how much **m** to you, Phlm 1:16
that you will do even **m** than I say. Phlm 1:21
has inherited is **m** excellent than theirs. Heb 1:4
counted worthy of **m** glory than Moses Heb 3:3
Moses—as much **m** glory as the builder Heb 3:3
of a house has **m** honor than the house Heb 3:3
desired to show **m** convincingly to the Heb 6:17
This becomes even **m** evident when Heb 7:15
that is as much **m** excellent than the old Heb 8:6
and I will remember their sins no **m**.” Heb 8:12
the greater and **m** perfect tent (not Heb 9:11
how much **m** will the blood of Christ, Heb 9:14
sins and their lawless deeds no **m**.” Heb 10:17
and all the **m** as you see the Day Heb 10:25
to God a **m** acceptable sacrifice than Heb 11:4
And what **m** shall I say? For time Heb 11:32
Shall we not much **m** be subject to the Heb 12:9
“Yet once **m** I will shake not only the Heb 12:26
“Yet once **m**,” indicates the removal Heb 12:27
I urge you the **m** earnestly to do this Heb 13:19
But he gives **m** grace. Therefore it says, Jas 4:6
of your faith—**m** precious than gold 1 Pt 1:7
be all the **m** diligent to make your 2 Pt 1:10
And we have something **m** sure, the 2 Pt 1:19
one of the elders said to me, “Weep no **m**; Rv 5:5
They shall hunger no **m**, neither thirst Rv 7:16
is in it, that there would be no **m** delay, Rv 10:6
with violence, and will be found no **m**; Rv 18:21
trumpeters, will be heard in you no **m**, Rv 18:22
of any craft will be found in you no **m**, Rv 18:22
of the mill will be heard in you no **m**, Rv 18:22
light of a lamp will shine in you no **m**, Rv 18:23
and bride will be heard in you no **m**, Rv 18:23
Once **m** they cried out, “Hallelujah! The Rv 19:3
had passed away, and the sea was no **m**. Rv 21:1
from their eyes, and death shall be no **m**, Rv 21:4
And night will be no **m**. They will need Rv 22:5

MOREH (3)

to the place at Shechem, to the oak of **M**. Gn 12:6
opposite Gilgal, beside the oak of **M**? Dt 11:30
was north of them, by the hill of **M**, Jgs 7:1

MOREOVER (76)

I will bless her, and **m**, I will give you a Gn 17:16
M, his concubine, whose name was Gn 22:24
a present sent to my lord Esau. And **m**, Gn 32:18
‘**M**, your servant Jacob is behind us.’” Gn 32:20
M, she is pregnant by immorality.” Gn 38:24
M, Pharaoh said to Joseph, “I am Gn 41:44
M, all the earth came to Egypt to Gn 41:57
M, I have given to you rather than to Gn 48:22
I do not know the LORD, and **m**, I will not Ex 5:2
M, I have heard the groaning of the people Ex 6:5
M, the man Moses was very great in the Ex 11:3
M, look for able men from all the Ex 18:21
“**M**, you shall make the tabernacle with Ex 26:1
M, you shall eat no blood whatever, Lv 7:26
M, whoever enters the house while it is Lv 14:46
M, you have not brought us into a Nm 16:14
“**M**, you shall speak and say to the Nm 18:26
M, you shall accept no ransom for the Nm 35:31
M, the LORD your God will send hornets Dt 7:20
sacred portion out of my house, and **m**, Dt 26:13
M, before the fat was burned, the 1 Sm 2:15
M, as for me, far be it from me that I 1 Sm 12:23
M, the LORD will give Israel also with 1 Sm 28:19
M, the LORD declares to you that the 2 Sm 7:11
m, I have taken the city of waters. 2 Sm 12:27
M, Ahithophel said to Absalom, “Let 2 Sm 17:1
M, the king’s servants came to 1 Kgs 1:47
“**M**, you also know what Joab the son 1 Kgs 2:5
M, each stand had four bronze 1 Kgs 7:30
M, the fleet of Hiram, which 1 Kgs 10:11
M, the LORD will raise up for himself 1 Kgs 14:14
M, the word of the LORD came by the 1 Kgs 16:7
M, is it without the LORD that I have 2 Kgs 18:25
M, Manasseh shed very much 2 Kgs 21:16
M, the altar at Bethel, the high place 2 Kgs 23:15
M, Josiah put away the mediums 2 Kgs 23:24
M, I declare to you that the LORD will 1 Chr 17:10
M, in addition to all that I have 1 Chr 29:3
M, the bronze altar that Bezalel the 2 Chr 1:5
M, the servants of Hiram and the 2 Chr 9:10
M, conditions were good in Judah. 2 Chr 12:12
M, in Jerusalem Jehoshaphat 2 Chr 19:8
M, he made high places in the hill 2 Chr 21:11
M, Uzziah built towers in Jerusalem 2 Chr 26:9
M, Uzziah had an army of soldiers, 2 Chr 26:11
M, he built cities in the hill country 2 Chr 27:4
M, I make a decree regarding what you Ezr 6:8
M, I and my brothers and my servants Neh 5:10
M, from the time that I was appointed Neh 5:14
M, there were at my table 150 men, Neh 5:17
M, in those days the nobles of Judah Neh 6:17
“**M**, the gallows that Haman has prepared Est 7:9
M, by them is your servant warned; in Ps 19:11
M, I saw under the sun that in the Eccl 3:16
M, all his days he eats in darkness in Eccl 5:17
M, it has not seen the sun or known Eccl 6:5
M, the light of the moon will be as the Is 30:26
M, is it without the LORD that I have Is 36:10
M, the men of Memphis and Tahpanhes Jer 2:16
M, I will give all the wealth of the city, all Jer 20:5
M, I will banish from them the voice of Jer 25:10
M, he said to me, “Son of man, all my Ezk 3:10
M, he said to me, “Son of man, behold, I Ezk 4:16
M, I will make you a desolation and an Ezk 5:14
M, I gave them my Sabbaths, as a sign Ezk 20:12
M, I swore to them in the wilderness Ezk 20:15
M, I swore to them in the wilderness Ezk 20:23
M, I gave them statutes that were not Ezk 20:25
M, this they have done to me: they Ezk 23:38
M, the word of the LORD came to me: Ezk 28:11
“**M**, wine is a traitor, an arrogant man Hab 2:5
M, even the dogs came and licked his Lk 16:21
M, some women of our company Lk 24:22
M, he even brought Greeks into the Acts 21:28
M, it is required of stewards that they 1 Cor 4:2
M, he must be well thought of by 1 Tm 3:7

MORESHETH (2)

“Micah of **M** prophesied in the days of Jer 26:18
that came to Micah of **M** in the days of Mi 1:1

MORESHETH-GATH (1)

you shall give parting gifts to **M**; Mi 1:14

MORIAH (2)

whom you love, and go to the land of **M**, Gn 22:2
of the LORD in Jerusalem on Mount **M**, 2 Chr 3:1

MORNING (232)

And there was evening and there was **m**, Gn 1:5
And there was evening and there was **m**, Gn 1:8
And there was evening and there was **m**, Gn 1:13
And there was evening and there was **m**, Gn 1:19
And there was evening and there was **m**, Gn 1:23
And there was evening and there was **m**, Gn 1:31
As **m** dawned, the angels urged Lot, Gn 19:15
went early in the **m** to the place where Gn 19:27
rose early in the **m** and called all his Gn 20:8
rose early in the **m** and took bread and Gn 21:14
So Abraham rose early in the **m**, Gn 22:3
When they arose in the **m**, he said, Gn 24:54
In the **m** they rose early and exchanged Gn 26:31
So early in the **m** Jacob took the stone Gn 28:18
And in the **m**, behold, it was Leah! And Gn 29:25
Early in the **m** Laban arose and kissed Gn 31:55
When Joseph came to them in the **m**, he Gn 40:6
So in the **m** his spirit was troubled, and Gn 41:8
As soon as the **m** was light, the men Gn 44:3
in the **m** devouring the prey and at Gn 49:27
Go to Pharaoh in the **m**, as he is going Ex 7:15
up early in the **m** and present yourself to Ex 8:20
up early in the **m** and present yourself Ex 9:13
When it was **m**, the east wind had Ex 10:13
shall let none of it remain until the **m**; Ex 12:10
remains until the **m** you shall burn. Ex 12:10
out of the door of his house until the **m**. Ex 12:22
And in the **m** watch the LORD in the Ex 14:24
normal course when the **m** appeared. Ex 14:27
and in the **m** you shall see the glory of Ex 16:7
to eat and in the **m** bread to the full, Ex 16:8
and in the **m** you shall be filled with Ex 16:12
and in the **m** dew lay around the camp. Ex 16:13
no one leave any of it over till the **m**.” Ex 16:19
Some left part of it till the **m**, and it bred Ex 16:20
M by morning they gathered it, each as Ex 16:21
Morning by **m** they gathered it, each as Ex 16:21
left over lay aside to be kept till the **m**.’” Ex 16:23
So they laid it aside till the **m**, as Moses Ex 16:24
around Moses from **m** till evening. Ex 18:13
around you from **m** till evening?” Ex 18:14
On the **m** of the third day there were Ex 19:16
the fat of my feast remain until the **m**. Ex 23:18
He rose early in the **m** and built an altar Ex 24:4
it from evening to **m** before the LORD. Ex 27:21
or of the bread remain until the **m**, Ex 29:34
One lamb you shall offer in the **m**, and Ex 29:39
and its drink offering, as in the **m**, Ex 29:41
Every **m** when he dresses the lamps he Ex 30:7
Be ready by the **m**, and come up in the Ex 34:2
and come up in the **m** to Mount Sinai, Ex 34:2
he rose early in the **m** and went up on Ex 34:4
of the Passover remain until the **m**. Ex 34:25
bringing him freewill offerings every **m**, Ex 36:3
hearth on the altar all night until the **m**, Lv 6:9
priest shall burn wood on it every **m**, Lv 6:12
half of it in the **m** and half in the Lv 6:20
He shall not leave any of it until the **m**. Lv 7:15
altar, besides the burnt offering of the **m**. Lv 9:17
remain with you all night until the **m**. Lv 19:13
day; you shall leave none of it until **m**: Lv 22:30
it from evening to **m** before the LORD Lv 24:3
They shall leave none of it until the **m**, Nm 9:12
like the appearance of fire until **m**. Nm 9:15
cloud remained from evening until **m**. Nm 9:21
And when the cloud lifted in the **m**, Nm 9:21

rose early in the **m** and went up to Nm 14:40
"In the **m** the LORD will show who is Nm 16:5
Balaam rose in the **m** and said to the Nm 22:13
Balaam rose in the **m** and saddled his Nm 22:21
And in the **m** Balak took Balaam and Nm 22:41
The one lamb you shall offer in the **m**, Nm 28:4
Like the grain offering of the **m**, and Nm 28:8
besides the burnt offering of the **m**, Nm 28:23
of the first day remain all night until **m**. Dt 16:4
And in the **m** you shall turn and go to Dt 16:7
In the **m** you shall say, 'If only it were Dt 28:67
you shall say, 'If only it were **m**!' Dt 28:67
rose early in the **m** and they set out Jos 3:1
Then Joshua rose early in the **m**, and the Jos 6:12
In the **m** therefore you shall be brought Jos 7:14
rose early in the **m** and brought Israel Jos 7:16
arose early in the **m** and mustered the Jos 8:10
the men of the town rose early in the **m**, Jgs 6:28
for him shall be put to death by **m**. Jgs 6:31
he rose early next **m** and squeezed the Jgs 6:38
Then in the **m**, as soon as the sun is up, Jgs 9:33
"Let us wait till the light of the **m**; Jgs 16:2
the fourth day they arose early in the **m**, Jgs 19:5
day he arose early in the **m** to depart. Jgs 19:8
arise early in the **m** for your journey, Jgs 19:9
and abused her all night until the **m**. Jgs 19:25
And as **m** appeared, the woman came Jgs 19:26
And her master rose up in the **m**, and Jgs 19:27
rose in the **m** and encamped against Jgs 20:19
has continued from early **m** until now, Ru 2:7
Remain tonight, and in the **m**, if he will Ru 3:13
I will redeem you. Lie down until the **m**." Ru 3:13
So she lay at his feet until the **m**, but Ru 3:14
early in the **m** and worshiped before 1 Sm 1:19
Samuel lay until **m**; then he opened 1 Sm 3:15
But when they rose early on the next **m**, 1 Sm 5:4
and in the **m** I will let you go and will 1 Sm 9:19
the camp in the **m** watch and struck 1 Sm 11:11
and plunder them until the **m** light; 1 Sm 14:36
rose early to meet Saul in the **m**. 1 Sm 15:12
and took his stand, **m** and evening. 1 Sm 17:16
rose early in the **m** and left the sheep 1 Sm 17:20
Therefore be on your guard in the **m**. 1 Sm 19:2
that he might kill him in the **m**. 1 Sm 19:11
In the **m** Jonathan went out into the 1 Sm 20:35
if by **m** I leave so much as one male 1 Sm 25:22
truly by **m** there had not been left to 1 Sm 25:34
him nothing at all until the **m** light. 1 Sm 25:36
In the **m**, when the wine had gone 1 Sm 25:37
rise early in the **m** with the servants 1 Sm 29:10
with you, and start early in the **m**, 1 Sm 29:10
men early in the **m** to return to the 1 Sm 29:11
pursuit of their brothers until the **m**." 2 Sm 2:27
Jordan, and marching the whole **m**, 2 Sm 2:29
In the **m** David wrote a letter to Joab 2 Sm 11:14
are you so haggard **m** after morning? 2 Sm 13:4
are you so haggard morning after **m**? 2 Sm 13:4
he dawns on them like the **m** light, 2 Sm 23:4
sun shining forth on a cloudless **m**, 2 Sm 23:4
And when David arose in the **m**, the 2 Sm 24:11
Israel from the **m** until the appointed 2 Sm 24:15
I rose in the **m** to nurse my child, 1 Kgs 3:21
I looked at him closely in the **m**, 1 Kgs 3:21
him bread and meat in the **m**, 1 Kgs 17:6
name of Baal from **m** until noon, 1 Kgs 18:26
The next **m**, about the time of 2 Kgs 3:20
rose early in the **m** and the sun shone 2 Kgs 3:22
God rose early in the **m** and went out, 2 Kgs 6:15
are silent and wait until the **m** light, 2 Kgs 7:9
the entrance of the gate until the **m**." 2 Kgs 10:8
Then in the **m**, when he went out, he 2 Kgs 10:9
altar burn the **m** burnt offering and 2 Kgs 16:15
when people arose early in the **m**, 2 Kgs 19:35
had charge of opening it every **m**. 1 Chr 9:27
offering regularly **m** and evening, 1 Chr 16:40
And they were to stand every **m**, 1 Chr 23:30
for burnt offerings **m** and evening, 2 Chr 2:4
the LORD every **m** and every evening 2 Chr 13:11
rose early in the **m** and went out 2 Chr 20:20
the burnt offerings of **m** and evening, 2 Chr 31:3
the LORD, burnt offerings **m** and evening. Ezr 3:3
Water Gate from early **m** until midday, Neh 8:3
and in the **m** she would return to the Est 2:14
and in the **m** tell the king to have Est 5:14
rise early in the **m** and offer burnt Jb 1:5
but have none, nor see the eyelids of the **m**, Jb 3:9
Between **m** and evening they are beaten Jb 4:20
visit him every **m** and test him every Jb 7:18
its darkness will be like the **m**. Jb 11:17
For deep darkness is **m** to all of them; Jb 24:17
when the **m** stars sang together and all Jb 38:7
you commanded the **m** since your days Jb 38:12
O LORD, in the **m** you hear my voice; in the Ps 5:3
in the **m** I prepare a sacrifice for you and Ps 5:3
for the night, but joy comes with the **m**. Ps 30:5
moved; God will help her when **m** dawns. Ps 46:5
upright shall rule over them in the **m**. Ps 49:14
Evening and **m** and at noon I utter my Ps 55:17
aloud of your steadfast love in the **m**. Ps 59:16
the going out of the **m** and the evening to Ps 65:8
been stricken and rebuked every **m**. Ps 73:14
in the **m** my prayer comes before you. Ps 88:13
like grass that is renewed in the **m**: Ps 90:5
in the **m** it flourishes and is renewed; in Ps 90:6
Satisfy us in the **m** with your steadfast Ps 90:14
to declare your steadfast love in the **m**, Ps 92:2
M by morning I will destroy all the Ps 101:8
Morning by **m** I will destroy all the Ps 101:8
from the womb of the **m**, the dew of Ps 110:3
Lord more than watchmen for the **m**, Ps 130:6
more than watchmen for the **m**. Ps 130:6
take the wings of the **m** and dwell in the Ps 139:9
me hear in the **m** of your steadfast love, Ps 143:8
Come, let us take our fill of love till **m**; Prv 7:18
a loud voice, rising early in the **m**, Prv 27:14
and your princes feast in the **m**! Eccl 10:16
In the **m** sow your seed, and at evening Eccl 11:6
Woe to those who rise early in the **m**, that Is 5:11
them blossom in the **m** that you sow, Is 17:11
evening time, behold, terror! Before **m**, Is 17:14
says: "**M** comes, and also the night. Is 21:12
for **m** by morning it will pass through, Is 28:19
for morning by **m** it will pass through, Is 28:19
Be our arm every **m**, our salvation in the Is 33:2
And when people arose early in the **m**, Is 37:36
I calmed myself until **m**; like a lion he Is 38:13
M by morning he awakens; he awakens Is 50:4
who is weary. Morning by **m** he awakens; Is 50:4
hear a cry in the **m** and an alarm at Jer 20:16
"'Execute justice in the **m**, and deliver Jer 21:12
they are new every **m**; great is your Lam 3:23
In the **m** the word of the LORD came to Ezk 12:8
So I spoke to the people in the **m**, and Ezk 24:18
And on the next **m** I did as I was Ezk 24:18
time the man came to me in the **m**, Ezk 33:22
m by morning you shall provide it. Ezk 46:13
morning by **m** you shall provide it. Ezk 46:13
grain offering with it **m** by morning, Ezk 46:14
grain offering with it morning by **m**, Ezk 46:14
oil shall be provided, **m** by morning, Ezk 46:15
oil shall be provided, morning by **m**, Ezk 46:15
Your love is like a **m** cloud, like the dew Hos 6:4
in the **m** it blazes like a flaming fire. Hos 7:6
they shall be like the **m** mist or like the Hos 13:3
bring your sacrifices every **m**, your Am 4:4
thought, who makes the **m** darkness, Am 4:13
darkness into the **m** and darkens the Am 5:8
When the **m** dawns, they perform it, Mi 2:1
wolves that leave nothing till the **m**. Zep 3:3
every **m** he shows forth his justice; Zep 3:5
And in the **m**, 'It will be stormy today, Mt 16:3
out early in the **m** to hire laborers for Mt 20:1
In the **m**, as he was returning to the Mt 21:18
When **m** came, all the chief priests and Mt 27:1
And rising very early in the **m**, while it Mk 1:35
As they passed by in the **m**, they saw Mk 11:20
or when the cock crows, or in the **m**— Mk 13:35
And as soon as it was **m**, the chief Mk 15:1
And early in the **m** all the people came Lk 21:38
They were at the tomb early in the **m**, Lk 24:22
Early in the **m** he came again to the Jn 8:2
governor's headquarters. It was early **m**. Jn 18:28
From **m** till evening he expounded to Acts 28:23
day dawns and the **m** star rises in your 2 Pt 1:19
And I will give him the **m** star. Rv 2:28
of David, the bright **m** star." Rv 22:16

MORNINGS (2)
said to me, "For 2,300 evenings and **m**. Dn 8:14
the evenings and the **m** that has been Dn 8:26

MORSEL (13)
while I bring a **m** of bread, that you Gn 18:5
your heart with a **m** of bread, Jgs 19:5
bread and dip your **m** in the wine." So Ru 2:14
places, that I may eat a **m** of bread."'" 1 Sm 2:36
Let me set a **m** of bread before you; 1 Sm 28:22
to eat of his **m** and drink from his 2 Sm 12:3
"Bring me a **m** of bread in your 1 Kgs 17:11
or have eaten my **m** alone, and the Jb 31:17
Better is a dry **m** with quiet than a Prv 17:1
whom I will give this **m** of bread when I Jn 13:26
dipped it." So when he had dipped the **m**, Jn 13:26
Then after he had taken the **m**, Satan Jn 13:27
So, after receiving the **m** of bread, he Jn 13:30

MORSELS (3)
of a whisperer are like delicious **m**; Prv 18:8
will vomit up the **m** that you have Prv 23:8
of a whisperer are like delicious **m**; Prv 26:22

MORTAL (12)
'Can **m** man be in the right before God? Jb 4:17
for images resembling **m** man and Rom 1:23
sin therefore reign in your **m** bodies, Rom 6:12
give life to your **m** bodies through his Rom 8:11
and this **m** body must put on 1 Cor 15:53
and the **m** puts on immortality, 1 Cor 15:54
may be manifested in our **m** flesh. 2 Cor 4:11
so that what is **m** may be swallowed 2 Cor 5:4
one case tithes are received by **m** men, Heb 7:8
of its heads seemed to have a **m** wound, Rv 13:3
wound, but its **m** wound was healed, Rv 13:3
first beast, whose **m** wound was healed. Rv 13:12

MORTALLY (1)
before him like a man **m** wounded. Ezk 30:24

MORTAR (7)
had brick for stone, and bitumen for **m**. Gn 11:3
bitter with hard service, in **m** and brick, Ex 1:14
Crush a fool in a **m** with a pestle along Prv 27:22
he shall trample on rulers as on **m**, as Is 41:25
hide them in the **m** in the pavement that Jer 43:9
your forts; go into the clay; tread the **m**; Na 3:14
Wail, O inhabitants of the **M**! For all Zep 1:11

MORTARS (1)
or beat it in **m** and boiled it in Nm 11:8

MORTGAGING (1)
those who said, "We are **m** our fields, Neh 5:3

MOSAIC (1)
and silver on a **m** pavement of porphyry, Est 1:6

MOSERAH (1)
from Beeroth Bene-jaakan to **M**. Dt 10:6

MOSEROTH (2)
from Hashmonah and camped at **M**. Nm 33:30
they set out from **M** and camped at Nm 33:31

MOSES (834)
She named him **M**, "Because," she said, Ex 2:10
One day, when **M** had grown up, he went Ex 2:11
the Egyptian?" Then **M** was afraid, Ex 2:14
Pharaoh heard of it, he sought to kill **M**. Ex 2:15
But **M** fled from Pharaoh and stayed in Ex 2:15
away, but **M** stood up and saved them, Ex 2:17
And **M** was content to dwell with the Ex 2:21
and he gave **M** his daughter Zipporah. Ex 2:21
Now **M** was keeping the flock of his Ex 3:1
And **M** said, "I will turn aside to see this Ex 3:3
out of the bush, "**M**, Moses!" And he said, Ex 3:4
out of the bush, "Moses, **M**!" And he said, Ex 3:4
the God of Jacob." And **M** hid his face, Ex 3:6
But **M** said to God, "Who am I that I Ex 3:11
Then **M** said to God, "If I come to the Ex 3:13
God said to **M**, "I AM WHO I AM." And he Ex 3:14
God also said to **M**, "Say this to the Ex 3:15
Then **M** answered, "But behold, they will Ex 4:1
it became a serpent, and **M** ran from it. Ex 4:3
But the LORD said to **M**, "Put out your Ex 4:4
But **M** said to the LORD, "Oh, my Lord, I Ex 4:10
LORD was kindled against **M** and he said, Ex 4:14
M went back to Jethro his father-in-law Ex 4:18
they are still alive." And Jethro said to **M**, Ex 4:18
And the LORD said to **M** in Midian, "Go Ex 4:19
So **M** took his wife and his sons and had Ex 4:20
And **M** took the staff of God in his hand. Ex 4:20
And the LORD said to **M**, "When you go Ex 4:21
the wilderness to meet **M**." So he went Ex 4:27
And **M** told Aaron all the words of the Ex 4:28
Then **M** and Aaron went and gathered Ex 4:29
LORD had spoken to **M** and did the signs Ex 4:30
Afterward **M** and Aaron went and said to Ex 5:1
of Egypt said to them, "**M** and Aaron, Ex 5:4
They met **M** and Aaron, who were Ex 5:20
Then **M** turned to the LORD and said, "O Ex 5:22
But the LORD said to **M**, "Now you shall Ex 6:1
God spoke to **M** and said to him, "I am the Ex 6:2
M spoke thus to the people of Israel, but Ex 6:9
of Israel, but they did not listen to **M**, Ex 6:9
So the LORD said to **M**, Ex 6:10
But **M** said to the LORD, "Behold, the Ex 6:12
the LORD spoke to **M** and Aaron and gave Ex 6:13
sister, and she bore him Aaron and **M**, Ex 6:20
are the Aaron and **M** to whom the LORD Ex 6:26
from Egypt, this **M** and this Aaron. Ex 6:27
when the LORD spoke to **M** in the land of Ex 6:28
the LORD said to **M**, "I am the LORD; tell Ex 6:29
But **M** said to the LORD, "Behold, I am of Ex 6:30
And the LORD said to **M**, "See, I have made Ex 7:1
M and Aaron did so; they did just as the Ex 7:6
Now **M** was eighty years old, and Aaron Ex 7:7
Then the LORD said to **M** and Aaron, Ex 7:8
So **M** and Aaron went to Pharaoh and Ex 7:10
Then the LORD said to **M**, "Pharaoh's Ex 7:14
And the LORD said to **M**, "Say to Aaron, Ex 7:19
M and Aaron did as the LORD Ex 7:20

Then the LORD said to **M**, "Go in to Ex 8:1
And the LORD said to **M**, "Say to Aaron, Ex 8:5
Then Pharaoh called **M** and Aaron and Ex 8:8
M said to Pharaoh, "Be pleased to Ex 8:9
And he said, "Tomorrow." **M** said, "Be it Ex 8:10
So **M** and Aaron went out from Ex 8:12
and **M** cried to the LORD about the frogs, Ex 8:12
the LORD did according to the word of **M**. Ex 8:13
Then the LORD said to **M**, "Say to Aaron, Ex 8:16
Then the LORD said to **M**, "Rise up early Ex 8:20
Then Pharaoh called **M** and Aaron and Ex 8:25
But **M** said, "It would not be right to do Ex 8:26
Then **M** said, "Behold, I am going out Ex 8:29
So **M** went out from Pharaoh and prayed Ex 8:30
And the LORD did as **M** asked, and Ex 8:31
Then the LORD said to **M**, "Go in to Ex 9:1
And the LORD said to **M** and Aaron, "Take Ex 9:8
and let **M** throw them in the air in the Ex 9:8
And **M** threw it in the air, and it became Ex 9:10
could not stand before **M** because of the Ex 9:11
to them, as the LORD had spoken to **M**. Ex 9:12
Then the LORD said to **M**, "Rise up early Ex 9:13
Then the LORD said to **M**, "Stretch out Ex 9:22
Then **M** stretched out his staff toward Ex 9:23
sent and called **M** and Aaron and Ex 9:27
M said to him, "As soon as I have gone Ex 9:29
So **M** went out of the city from Pharaoh Ex 9:33
just as the LORD had spoken through **M**. Ex 9:35
Then the LORD said to **M**, "Go in to Ex 10:1
So **M** and Aaron went in to Pharaoh and Ex 10:3
So **M** and Aaron were brought back to Ex 10:8
M said, "We will go with our young and Ex 10:9
Then the LORD said to **M**, "Stretch out Ex 10:12
So **M** stretched out his staff over the Ex 10:13
Pharaoh hastily called **M** and Aaron Ex 10:16
Then the LORD said to **M**, "Stretch out Ex 10:21
So **M** stretched out his hand toward Ex 10:22
Then Pharaoh called **M** and said, "Go, Ex 10:24
But **M** said, "You must also let us have Ex 10:25
M said, "As you say! I will not see your Ex 10:29
The LORD said to **M**, "Yet one plague Ex 11:1
the man **M** was very great in the land of Ex 11:3
So **M** said, "Thus says the LORD: About Ex 11:4
Then the LORD said to **M**, "Pharaoh will Ex 11:9
M and Aaron did all these wonders Ex 11:10
The LORD said to **M** and Aaron in the Ex 12:1
Then **M** called all the elders of Israel Ex 12:21
LORD had commanded **M** and Aaron, Ex 12:28
Then he summoned **M** and Aaron by Ex 12:31
of Israel had also done as **M** told them, Ex 12:35
And the LORD said to **M** and Aaron, Ex 12:43
as the LORD commanded **M** and Aaron. Ex 12:50
The LORD said to **M**, Ex 13:1
Then **M** said to the people, "Remember Ex 13:3
M took the bones of Joseph with him, Ex 13:19
Then the LORD said to **M**, Ex 14:1
They said to **M**, "Is it because there are Ex 14:11
And **M** said to the people, "Fear not, Ex 14:13
The LORD said to **M**, "Why do you cry Ex 14:15
Then **M** stretched out his hand over the Ex 14:21
Then the LORD said to **M**, "Stretch out Ex 14:26
So **M** stretched out his hand over the Ex 14:27
in the LORD and in his servant **M**. Ex 14:31
Then **M** and the people of Israel sang Ex 15:1
Then **M** made Israel set out from the Ex 15:22
And the people grumbled against **M**, Ex 15:24
Israel grumbled against **M** and Aaron in Ex 16:2
Then the LORD said to **M**, "Behold, I am Ex 16:4
So **M** and Aaron said to all the people of Ex 16:6
And **M** said, "When the LORD gives you Ex 16:8
Then **M** said to Aaron, "Say to the whole Ex 16:9
And the LORD said to **M**, Ex 16:11
And **M** said to them, "It is the bread Ex 16:15
And **M** said to them, "Let no one leave Ex 16:19
But they did not listen to **M**. Some left Ex 16:20
stank. And **M** was angry with them. Ex 16:20
of the congregation came and told **M**, Ex 16:22
the morning, as **M** commanded them, Ex 16:24
M said, "Eat it today, for today is a Ex 16:25
And the LORD said to **M**, "How long will Ex 16:28
M said, "This is what the LORD has Ex 16:32
And **M** said to Aaron, "Take a jar, and Ex 16:33
As the LORD commanded **M**, so Aaron Ex 16:34
the people quarreled with **M** and said, Ex 17:2
us water to drink." And **M** said to them, Ex 17:2
the people grumbled against **M** and said, Ex 17:3
So **M** cried to the LORD, "What shall I do Ex 17:4
And the LORD said to **M**, "Pass on before Ex 17:5
and the people will drink." And **M** did so, Ex 17:6
So **M** said to Joshua, "Choose for us men, Ex 17:9
So Joshua did as **M** told him, and Ex 17:10
and fought with Amalek, while **M**, Ex 17:10
Whenever **M** held up his hand, Israel Ex 17:11
Then the LORD said to **M**, "Write this as Ex 17:14
And **M** built an altar and called the Ex 17:15

God had done for **M** and for Israel his Ex 18:1
and his wife to **M** in the wilderness Ex 18:5
And when he sent word to **M**, "I, your Ex 18:6
M went out to meet his father-in-law and Ex 18:7
Then **M** told his father-in-law all that Ex 18:8
The next day **M** sat to judge the people, Ex 18:13
people stood around **M** from morning Ex 18:13
And **M** said to his father-in-law, Ex 18:15
So **M** listened to the voice of his Ex 18:24
M chose able men out of all Israel and Ex 18:25
Any hard case they brought to **M**, but Ex 18:26
Then **M** let his father-in-law depart, Ex 18:27
while **M** went up to God. The LORD called Ex 19:3
So **M** came and called the elders of the Ex 19:7
we will do." And **M** reported the words of Ex 19:8
And the LORD said to **M**, "Behold, I am Ex 19:9
you forever." When **M** told the words Ex 19:9
the LORD said to **M**, "Go to the people Ex 19:10
So **M** went down from the mountain to Ex 19:14
Then **M** brought the people out of the Ex 19:17
grew louder and louder, **M** spoke, Ex 19:19
And the LORD called **M** to the top of the Ex 19:20
top of the mountain, and **M** went up. Ex 19:20
And the LORD said to **M**, "Go down and Ex 19:21
And **M** said to the LORD, "The people Ex 19:23
So **M** went down to the people and told Ex 19:25
and said to **M**, "You speak to us, and we Ex 20:19
M said to the people, "Do not fear, for Ex 20:20
while **M** drew near to the thick Ex 20:21
And the LORD said to **M**, "Thus you Ex 20:22
Then he said to **M**, "Come up to the Ex 24:1
M alone shall come near to the LORD, but Ex 24:2
M came and told the people all the words Ex 24:3
And **M** wrote down all the words of the Ex 24:4
And **M** took half of the blood and put it Ex 24:6
And **M** took the blood and threw it on Ex 24:8
Then **M** and Aaron, Nadab, and Abihu, Ex 24:9
The LORD said to **M**, "Come up to me on Ex 24:12
So **M** rose with his assistant Joshua, Ex 24:13
and **M** went up into the mountain of Ex 24:13
Then **M** went up on the mountain, and Ex 24:15
day he called to **M** out of the midst Ex 24:16
M entered the cloud and went up on the Ex 24:18
And **M** was on the mountain forty days Ex 24:18
The LORD said to **M**, Ex 25:1
The LORD said to **M**, Ex 30:11
The LORD said to **M**, Ex 30:17
The LORD said to **M**, Ex 30:22
The LORD said to **M**, Ex 30:34
The LORD said to **M**, Ex 31:1
And the LORD said to **M**, Ex 31:12
And he gave to **M**, when he had Ex 31:18
the people saw that **M** delayed to come Ex 32:1
As for this **M**, the man who brought us Ex 32:1
And the LORD said to **M**, "Go down, for Ex 32:7
And the LORD said to **M**, "I have seen this Ex 32:9
But **M** implored the LORD his God and Ex 32:11
Then **M** turned and went down from Ex 32:15
the people as they shouted, he said to **M**, Ex 32:17
And **M** said to Aaron, "What did this Ex 32:21
As for this **M**, the man who brought us Ex 32:23
And when **M** saw that the people had Ex 32:25
then **M** stood in the gate of the camp Ex 32:26
of Levi did according to the word of **M**. Ex 32:28
And **M** said, "Today you have been Ex 32:29
The next day **M** said to the people, "You Ex 32:30
So **M** returned to the LORD and said, Ex 32:31
But the LORD said to **M**, "Whoever has Ex 32:33
The LORD said to **M**, "Depart; go up from Ex 33:1
For the LORD had said to **M**, "Say to the Ex 33:5
Now **M** used to take the tent and pitch it Ex 33:7
Whenever **M** went out to the tent, all the Ex 33:8
and watch **M** until he had gone into the Ex 33:8
When **M** entered the tent, the pillar of Ex 33:9
tent, and the LORD would speak with **M**. Ex 33:9
the LORD used to speak to **M** face to face, Ex 33:11
When **M** turned again into the camp, Ex 33:11
M said to the LORD, "See, you say to me, Ex 33:12
And the LORD said to **M**, "This very Ex 33:17
M said, "Please show me your glory." Ex 33:18
The LORD said to **M**, "Cut for yourself Ex 34:1
So **M** cut two tablets of stone like the Ex 34:4
And **M** quickly bowed his head toward Ex 34:8
And the LORD said to **M**, "Write these Ex 34:27
When **M** came down from Mount Ex 34:29
M did not know that the skin of his Ex 34:29
and all the people of Israel saw **M**, Ex 34:30
But **M** called to them, and Aaron and Ex 34:31
to him, and **M** talked with them. Ex 34:31
And when **M** had finished speaking Ex 34:33
Whenever **M** went in before the LORD to Ex 34:34
people of Israel would see the face of **M**, Ex 34:35
And **M** would put the veil over his face Ex 34:35
M assembled all the congregation of the Ex 35:1
M said to all the congregation of the Ex 35:4

Israel departed from the presence of **M**. Ex 35:20
LORD had commanded by **M** to be done Ex 35:29
Then **M** said to the people of Israel, "See, Ex 35:30
And **M** called Bezalel and Oholiab and Ex 36:2
they received from **M** all the Ex 36:3
and said to **M**, "The people bring much Ex 36:5
So **M** gave command, and word was Ex 36:6
recorded at the commandment of **M**, Ex 38:21
made all that the LORD commanded **M**; Ex 38:22
Aaron, as the LORD had commanded **M**. Ex 39:1
linen, as the LORD had commanded **M**. Ex 39:5
of Israel, as the LORD had commanded **M**. Ex 39:7
ephod, as the LORD had commanded **M**. Ex 39:21
as the LORD had commanded **M**. Ex 39:26
as the LORD had commanded **M**. Ex 39:29
above, as the LORD had commanded **M**. Ex 39:31
to all that the LORD had commanded **M**; Ex 39:32
they brought the tabernacle to **M**, Ex 39:33
to all that the LORD had commanded **M**, Ex 39:42
And **M** saw all the work, and behold, Ex 39:43
had they done it. Then **M** blessed them. Ex 39:43
The LORD spoke to **M**, saying, Ex 40:1
This **M** did; according to all that the Ex 40:16
M erected the tabernacle. He laid its Ex 40:18
over it, as the LORD had commanded **M**. Ex 40:19
as the LORD had commanded **M**. Ex 40:21
LORD, as the LORD had commanded **M**. Ex 40:23
LORD, as the LORD had commanded **M**. Ex 40:25
on it, as the LORD had commanded **M**. Ex 40:27
as the LORD had commanded **M**. Ex 40:29
with which **M** and Aaron and his sons Ex 40:31
washed, as the LORD commanded **M**. Ex 40:32
of the court. So **M** finished the work. Ex 40:33
And **M** was not able to enter the tent of Ex 40:35
The LORD called **M** and spoke to him from Lv 1:1
And the LORD spoke to **M**, saying, Lv 4:1
The LORD spoke to **M**, saying, Lv 5:14
The LORD spoke to **M**, saying, Lv 6:1
The LORD spoke to **M**, saying, Lv 6:8
The LORD spoke to **M**, saying, Lv 6:19
The LORD spoke to **M**, saying, Lv 6:24
The LORD spoke to **M**, saying, Lv 7:22
The LORD spoke to **M**, saying, Lv 7:28
the LORD commanded **M** on Mount Lv 7:38
The LORD spoke to **M**, saying, Lv 8:1
And **M** did as the LORD commanded him, Lv 8:4
And **M** said to the congregation, "This is Lv 8:5
And **M** brought Aaron and his sons and Lv 8:6
holy crown, as the LORD commanded **M**. Lv 8:9
Then **M** took the anointing oil and Lv 8:10
And **M** brought Aaron's sons and Lv 8:13
on them, as the LORD commanded **M**. Lv 8:13
And he killed it, and **M** took the blood, Lv 8:15
fat, and **M** burned them on the altar. Lv 8:16
the camp, as the LORD commanded **M**. Lv 8:17
and **M** threw the blood against the sides Lv 8:19
and **M** burned the head and the pieces Lv 8:20
and **M** burned the whole ram on the Lv 8:21
for the LORD, as the LORD commanded **M**. Lv 8:21
and **M** took some of its blood and put it Lv 8:23
and **M** put some of the blood on the Lv 8:24
And **M** threw the blood against the sides Lv 8:24
Then **M** took them from their hands Lv 8:28
And **M** took the breast and waved it for a Lv 8:29
ordination, as the LORD commanded **M**. Lv 8:29
Then **M** took some of the anointing oil Lv 8:30
And **M** said to Aaron and his sons, "Boil Lv 8:31
things that the LORD commanded by **M**. Lv 8:36
On the eighth day **M** called Aaron and his Lv 9:1
they brought what **M** commanded in Lv 9:5
And **M** said, "This is the thing that the Lv 9:6
Then **M** said to Aaron, "Draw near to the Lv 9:7
on the altar, as the LORD commanded **M**. Lv 9:10
before the LORD, as **M** commanded. Lv 9:21
And **M** and Aaron went into the tent of Lv 9:23
Then **M** said to Aaron, "This is what the Lv 10:3
And **M** called Mishael and Elzaphan, the Lv 10:4
coats out of the camp, as **M** had said. Lv 10:5
And **M** said to Aaron and to Eleazar and Lv 10:6
And they did according to the word of **M**. Lv 10:7
the LORD has spoken to them by **M**." Lv 10:11
M spoke to Aaron and to Eleazar and Lv 10:12
Now **M** diligently inquired about the Lv 10:16
And Aaron said to **M**, "Behold, today Lv 10:19
And when **M** heard that, he approved. Lv 10:20
And the LORD spoke to **M** and Aaron, Lv 11:1
The LORD spoke to **M**, saying, Lv 12:1
The LORD spoke to **M** and Aaron, saying, Lv 13:1
The LORD spoke to **M**, saying, Lv 14:1
The LORD spoke to **M** and Aaron, Lv 14:33
The LORD spoke to **M** and Aaron, saying, Lv 15:1
The LORD spoke to **M** after the death of Lv 16:1
and the LORD said to **M**, "Tell Aaron your Lv 16:2
of all their sins." And **M** did as the LORD Lv 16:34
And the LORD spoke to **M**, saying, Lv 17:1

And the LORD spoke to **M**, saying,	Lv 18:1
And the LORD spoke to **M**, saying,	Lv 19:1
The LORD spoke to **M**, saying,	Lv 20:1
And the LORD said to **M**, "Speak to the	Lv 21:1
And the LORD spoke to **M**, saying,	Lv 21:16
So **M** spoke to Aaron and to his sons	Lv 21:24
And the LORD spoke to **M**, saying,	Lv 22:1
And the LORD spoke to **M**, saying,	Lv 22:17
And the LORD spoke to **M**, saying,	Lv 22:26
The LORD spoke to **M**, saying,	Lv 23:1
And the LORD spoke to **M**, saying,	Lv 23:9
And the LORD spoke to **M**, saying,	Lv 23:23
And the LORD spoke to **M**, saying,	Lv 23:26
And the LORD spoke to **M**, saying,	Lv 23:33
Thus **M** declared to the people of Israel	Lv 23:44
The LORD spoke to **M**, saying,	Lv 24:1
cursed. Then they brought him to **M**.	Lv 24:11
Then the LORD spoke to **M**, saying,	Lv 24:13
So **M** spoke to the people of Israel, and	Lv 24:23
of Israel did as the LORD commanded **M**.	Lv 24:23
The LORD spoke to **M** on Mount Sinai,	Lv 25:1
of Israel through **M** on Mount Sinai.	Lv 26:46
The LORD spoke to **M**, saying,	Lv 27:1
the LORD commanded **M** for the people	Lv 27:34
The LORD spoke to **M** in the wilderness of	Nm 1:1
M and Aaron took these men who had	Nm 1:17
as the LORD commanded **M**. So he listed	Nm 1:19
whom **M** and Aaron listed with the	Nm 1:44
For the LORD spoke to **M**, saying,	Nm 1:48
to all that the LORD commanded **M**.	Nm 1:54
The LORD spoke to **M** and Aaron, saying,	Nm 2:1
of Israel, as the LORD commanded **M**.	Nm 2:33
to all that the LORD commanded **M**,	Nm 2:34
generations of Aaron and **M** at the time	Nm 3:1
the LORD spoke with **M** on Mount Sinai.	Nm 3:1
And the LORD spoke to **M**, saying,	Nm 3:5
And the LORD spoke to **M**, saying,	Nm 3:11
the LORD spoke to **M** in the wilderness	Nm 3:14
So **M** listed them according to the word	Nm 3:16
were **M** and Aaron and his sons,	Nm 3:38
whom **M** and Aaron listed at the	Nm 3:39
And the LORD said to **M**, "List all the	Nm 3:40
So **M** listed all the firstborn among the	Nm 3:42
And the LORD spoke to **M**, saying,	Nm 3:44
So **M** took the redemption money from	Nm 3:49
And **M** gave the redemption money to	Nm 3:51
of the LORD, as the LORD commanded **M**.	Nm 3:51
The LORD spoke to **M** and Aaron, saying,	Nm 4:1
The LORD spoke to **M** and Aaron,	Nm 4:17
The LORD spoke to **M**, saying,	Nm 4:21
And **M** and Aaron and the chiefs of the	Nm 4:34
whom **M** and Aaron listed according	Nm 4:37
the commandment of the LORD by **M**.	Nm 4:37
whom **M** and Aaron listed according	Nm 4:41
whom **M** and Aaron listed according	Nm 4:45
the commandment of the LORD by **M**.	Nm 4:45
whom **M** and Aaron and the chiefs of	Nm 4:46
of the LORD through **M** they were listed,	Nm 4:49
by him, as the LORD commanded **M**.	Nm 4:49
The LORD spoke to **M**, saying,	Nm 5:1
as the LORD said to **M**, so the people of	Nm 5:4
And the LORD spoke to **M**, saying,	Nm 5:5
And the LORD spoke to **M**, saying,	Nm 5:11
And the LORD spoke to **M**, saying,	Nm 6:1
The LORD spoke to **M**, saying,	Nm 6:22
On the day when **M** had finished setting	Nm 7:1
Then the LORD said to **M**,	Nm 7:4
So **M** took the wagons and the oxen and	Nm 7:6
And the LORD said to **M**, "They shall	Nm 7:11
And when **M** went into the tent of	Nm 7:89
Now the LORD spoke to **M**, saying,	Nm 8:1
lampstand, as the LORD commanded **M**.	Nm 8:3
the pattern that the LORD had shown **M**,	Nm 8:4
And the LORD spoke to **M**, saying,	Nm 8:5
Thus did **M** and Aaron and all the	Nm 8:20
LORD commanded **M** concerning the	Nm 8:20
had commanded **M** concerning the	Nm 8:22
And the LORD spoke to **M**, saying,	Nm 8:23
the LORD spoke to **M** in the wilderness of	Nm 9:1
So **M** told the people of Israel that they	Nm 9:4
to all that the LORD commanded **M**,	Nm 9:5
and they came before **M** and Aaron on	Nm 9:6
And **M** said to them, "Wait, that I may	Nm 9:8
The LORD spoke to **M**, saying,	Nm 9:9
at the command of the LORD by **M**.	Nm 9:23
The LORD spoke to **M**, saying,	Nm 10:1
at the command of the LORD by **M**.	Nm 10:13
And **M** said to Hobab the son of Reuel	Nm 10:29
And whenever the ark set out, **M** said,	Nm 10:35
Then the people cried out to **M**, and	Nm 11:2
out to Moses, and **M** prayed to the LORD,	Nm 11:2
M heard the people weeping	Nm 11:10
blazed hotly, and **M** was displeased.	Nm 11:10
M said to the LORD, "Why have you	Nm 11:11
Then the LORD said to **M**, "Gather for	Nm 11:16
But **M** said, "The people among	Nm 11:21
And the LORD said to **M**, "Is the LORD'S	Nm 11:23
So **M** went out and told the people the	Nm 11:24
And a young man ran and told **M**,	Nm 11:27
the assistant of **M** from his youth,	Nm 11:28
from his youth, said, "My lord **M**,	Nm 11:28
But **M** said to him, "Are you jealous	Nm 11:29
And **M** and the elders of Israel	Nm 11:30
Aaron spoke against **M** because of the	Nm 12:1
LORD indeed spoken only through **M**?	Nm 12:2
Now the man **M** was very meek, more	Nm 12:3
the LORD said to **M** and to Aaron and	Nm 12:4
Not so with my servant **M**. He is	Nm 12:7
afraid to speak against my servant **M**?"	Nm 12:8
And Aaron said to **M**, "Oh, my lord,	Nm 12:11
And **M** cried to the LORD, "O God,	Nm 12:13
But the LORD said to **M**, "If her father	Nm 12:14
The LORD spoke to **M**, saying,	Nm 13:1
So **M** sent them from the wilderness of	Nm 13:3
of the men whom **M** sent to spy out	Nm 13:16
And **M** called Hoshea the son of Nun	Nm 13:16
M sent them to spy out the land of	Nm 13:17
And they came to **M** and Aaron and	Nm 13:26
quieted the people before **M** and said,	Nm 13:30
Israel grumbled against **M** and Aaron.	Nm 14:2
Then **M** and Aaron fell on their faces	Nm 14:5
And the LORD said to **M**, "How long	Nm 14:11
But **M** said to the LORD, "Then the	Nm 14:13
the LORD spoke to **M** and to Aaron,	Nm 14:26
And the men whom **M** sent to spy out	Nm 14:36
When **M** told these words to all the	Nm 14:39
But **M** said, "Why now are you	Nm 14:41
of the LORD nor **M** departed out of the	Nm 14:44
The LORD spoke to **M**, saying,	Nm 15:1
The LORD spoke to **M**, saying,	Nm 15:17
that the LORD has spoken to **M**,	Nm 15:22
the LORD has commanded you by **M**,	Nm 15:23
brought him to **M** and Aaron and	Nm 15:33
And the LORD said to **M**, "The man	Nm 15:35
stones, as the LORD commanded **M**.	Nm 15:36
The LORD said to **M**,	Nm 15:37
And they rose up before **M**, with a	Nm 16:2
together against **M** and against	Nm 16:3
When **M** heard it, he fell on his face,	Nm 16:4
And **M** said to Korah, "Hear now, you	Nm 16:8
And **M** sent to call Dathan and	Nm 16:12
And **M** was very angry and said to the	Nm 16:15
And **M** said to Korah, "Be present, you	Nm 16:16
the tent of meeting with **M** and Aaron.	Nm 16:18
the LORD spoke to **M** and to Aaron,	Nm 16:20
And the LORD spoke to **M**, saying,	Nm 16:23
Then **M** rose and went to Dathan and	Nm 16:25
And **M** said, "Hereby you shall know	Nm 16:28
Then the LORD spoke to **M**, saying,	Nm 16:36
—as the LORD said to him through **M**.	Nm 16:40
grumbled against **M** and against	Nm 16:41
had assembled against **M** and against	Nm 16:42
And **M** and Aaron came to the front	Nm 16:43
and the LORD spoke to **M**, saying,	Nm 16:44
And **M** said to Aaron, "Take your	Nm 16:46
Aaron took it as **M** said and ran into	Nm 16:47
Aaron returned to **M** at the entrance	Nm 16:50
The LORD spoke to **M**, saying,	Nm 17:1
M spoke to the people of Israel. And all	Nm 17:6
And **M** deposited the staffs before the	Nm 17:7
On the next day **M** went into the tent of	Nm 17:8
Then **M** brought out all the staffs from	Nm 17:9
And the LORD said to **M**, "Put back the	Nm 17:10
Thus did **M**; as the LORD commanded	Nm 17:11
And the people of Israel said to **M**,	Nm 17:12
And the LORD spoke to **M**, saying,	Nm 18:25
Now the LORD spoke to **M** and to Aaron,	Nm 19:1
together against **M** and against	Nm 20:2
the people quarreled with **M** and said,	Nm 20:3
Then **M** and Aaron went from the	Nm 20:6
and the LORD spoke to **M**, saying,	Nm 20:7
And **M** took the staff from before the	Nm 20:9
Then **M** and Aaron gathered the	Nm 20:10
And **M** lifted up his hand and struck	Nm 20:11
And the LORD said to **M** and Aaron,	Nm 20:12
M sent messengers from Kadesh to	Nm 20:14
the LORD said to **M** and Aaron at	Nm 20:23
M did as the LORD commanded. And	Nm 20:27
And **M** stripped Aaron of his	Nm 20:28
Then **M** and Eleazar came down from	Nm 20:28
spoke against God and against **M**,	Nm 21:5
And the people came to **M** and said,	Nm 21:7
serpents from us." So **M** prayed for the	Nm 21:7
And the LORD said to **M**, "Make a fiery	Nm 21:8
So **M** made a bronze serpent and set it	Nm 21:9
the well of which the LORD said to **M**,	Nm 21:16
And **M** sent to spy out Jazer, and they	Nm 21:32
But the LORD said to **M**, "Do not fear	Nm 21:34
And the LORD said to **M**, "Take all the	Nm 25:4
And **M** said to the judges of Israel,	Nm 25:5
in the sight of **M** and in the sight of the	Nm 25:6
And the LORD said to **M**,	Nm 25:10
And the LORD spoke to **M**, saying,	Nm 25:16
the LORD said to **M** and to Eleazar the	Nm 26:1
And **M** and Eleazar the priest spoke	Nm 26:3
upward," as the LORD commanded **M**.	Nm 26:4
who contended against **M** and Aaron	Nm 26:9
The LORD spoke to **M**, saying,	Nm 26:52
Amram Aaron and **M** and Miriam	Nm 26:59
were those listed by **M** and Eleazar the	Nm 26:63
of those listed by **M** and Aaron the	Nm 26:64
they stood before **M** and before Eleazar	Nm 27:2
M brought their case before the LORD.	Nm 27:5
And the LORD said to **M**,	Nm 27:6
rule, as the LORD commanded **M**.'"	Nm 27:11
The LORD said to **M**, "Go up into this	Nm 27:12
M spoke to the LORD, saying,	Nm 27:15
So the LORD said to **M**, "Take Joshua	Nm 27:18
And **M** did as the LORD commanded	Nm 27:22
him as the LORD directed through **M**.	Nm 27:23
The LORD spoke to **M**, saying,	Nm 28:1
So **M** told the people of Israel	Nm 29:40
just as the LORD had commanded **M**.	Nm 29:40
M spoke to the heads of the tribes of the	Nm 30:1
the LORD commanded **M** about a man	Nm 30:16
The LORD spoke to **M**, saying,	Nm 31:1
So **M** spoke to the people, saying, "Arm	Nm 31:3
And **M** sent them to the war, a	Nm 31:6
Midian, as the LORD commanded **M**,	Nm 31:7
and the plunder and the spoil to **M**,	Nm 31:12
M and Eleazar the priest and all the	Nm 31:13
And **M** was angry with the officers of	Nm 31:14
M said to them, "Have you let all the	Nm 31:15
law that the LORD has commanded **M**:	Nm 31:21
The LORD said to **M**,	Nm 31:25
And **M** and Eleazar the priest did as	Nm 31:31
priest did as the LORD commanded **M**.	Nm 31:31
And **M** gave the tribute, which was	Nm 31:41
the priest, as the LORD commanded **M**.	Nm 31:41
which **M** separated from that of the	Nm 31:42
people of Israel's half **M** took one of	Nm 31:47
the LORD, as the LORD commanded **M**.	Nm 31:47
of hundreds, came near to **M**	Nm 31:48
and said to **M**, "Your servants have	Nm 31:49
And **M** and Eleazar the priest received	Nm 31:51
And **M** and Eleazar the priest received	Nm 31:54
came and said to **M** and to Eleazar the	Nm 32:2
But **M** said to the people of Gad and to	Nm 32:6
So **M** said to them, "If you will do this,	Nm 32:20
and the people of Reuben said to **M**,	Nm 32:25
So **M** gave command concerning	Nm 32:28
And **M** said to them, "If the people of	Nm 32:29
And **M** gave to them, to the people of	Nm 32:33
And **M** gave Gilead to Machir the son	Nm 32:40
under the leadership of **M** and Aaron.	Nm 33:1
M wrote down their starting places,	Nm 33:2
the LORD spoke to **M** in the plains of	Nm 33:50
The LORD spoke to **M**, saying,	Nm 34:1
M commanded the people of Israel,	Nm 34:13
The LORD spoke to **M**, saying,	Nm 34:16
The LORD spoke to **M** in the plains of	Nm 35:1
And the LORD spoke to **M**, saying,	Nm 35:9
near and spoke before **M** and before the	Nm 36:1
And **M** commanded the people of Israel	Nm 36:5
did as the LORD commanded **M**,	Nm 36:10
LORD commanded through **M** to the	Nm 36:13
are the words that **M** spoke to all Israel	Dt 1:1
M spoke to the people of Israel according	Dt 1:3
of Moab, **M** undertook to explain this law,	Dt 1:5
Then **M** set apart three cities in the east	Dt 4:41
is the law that **M** set before the people	Dt 4:44
which **M** spoke to the people of Israel	Dt 4:45
whom **M** and the people of Israel defeated	Dt 4:46
And **M** summoned all Israel and said to	Dt 5:1
Now **M** and the elders of Israel	Dt 27:1
Then **M** and the Levitical priests said to	Dt 27:9
That day **M** charged the people, saying,	Dt 27:11
the LORD commanded **M** to make with	Dt 29:1
And **M** summoned all Israel and said to	Dt 29:2
So **M** continued to speak these words to	Dt 31:1
Then **M** summoned Joshua and said to	Dt 31:7
Then **M** wrote this law and gave it to the	Dt 31:9
And **M** commanded them, "At the end	Dt 31:10
And the LORD said to **M**, "Behold, the	Dt 31:14
commission him." And **M** and Joshua	Dt 31:14
And the LORD said to **M**, "Behold, you	Dt 31:16
So **M** wrote this song the same day and	Dt 31:22
When **M** had finished writing the	Dt 31:24
M commanded the Levites who carried	Dt 31:25
Then **M** spoke the words of this song	Dt 31:30
M came and recited all the words of this	Dt 32:44
And when **M** had finished speaking all	Dt 32:45
That very day the LORD spoke to **M**,	Dt 32:48
the blessing with which **M** the man of	Dt 33:1
when **M** commanded us a law, as a	Dt 33:4

Then **M** went up from the plains of	Dt 34:1
So **M** the servant of the LORD died there in	Dt 34:5
M was 120 years old when he died. His	Dt 34:7
of Israel wept for **M** in the plains of	Dt 34:8
and mourning for **M** were ended.	Dt 34:8
for **M** had laid his hands on him.	Dt 34:9
and did as the LORD had commanded **M**.	Dt 34:9
arisen a prophet since in Israel like **M**,	Dt 34:10
deeds of terror that **M** did in the sight	Dt 34:12
After the death of **M** the servant of the	Jos 1:1
"**M** my servant is dead. Now therefore	Jos 1:2
have given to you, just as I promised to **M**.	Jos 1:3
Just as I was with **M**, so I will be with you.	Jos 1:5
the law that **M** my servant commanded	Jos 1:7
the word that **M** the servant of	Jos 1:13
in the land that **M** gave you beyond the	Jos 1:14
the land that **M** the servant of the LORD	Jos 1:15
Just as we obeyed **M** in all things, so we	Jos 1:17
your God be with you, as he was with **M**!	Jos 1:17
that they may know that, as I was with **M**,	Jos 3:7
to all that **M** had commanded Joshua.	Jos 4:10
the people of Israel, as **M** had told them.	Jos 4:12
him just as they had stood in awe of **M**,	Jos 4:14
just as **M** the servant of the LORD had	Jos 8:31
it is written in the Book of the Law of **M**,	Jos 8:31
on the stones a copy of the law of **M**,	Jos 8:32
just as **M** the servant of the LORD had	Jos 8:33
of all that **M** commanded that Joshua	Jos 8:35
commanded his servant **M** to give you	Jos 9:24
just as **M** the servant of the LORD had	Jos 11:12
LORD had commanded **M** his servant,	Jos 11:15
his servant, so **M** commanded Joshua,	Jos 11:15
of all that the LORD had commanded **M**.	Jos 11:15
just as the LORD commanded **M**.	Jos 11:20
to all that the LORD had spoken to **M**.	Jos 11:23
M, the servant of the LORD, and the	Jos 12:6
And **M** the servant of the LORD gave their	Jos 12:6
their inheritance, which **M** gave them,	Jos 13:8
as **M** the servant of the LORD gave them:	Jos 13:8
these **M** had struck and driven out.	Jos 13:12
of Levi alone **M** gave no inheritance.	Jos 13:14
And **M** gave an inheritance to the tribe	Jos 13:15
whom **M** defeated with the leaders of	Jos 13:21
M gave an inheritance also to the tribe	Jos 13:24
And **M** gave an inheritance to the	Jos 13:29
the inheritances that **M** distributed in	Jos 13:32
the tribe of Levi **M** gave no inheritance;	Jos 13:33
by the hand of **M** for the nine and	Jos 14:2
For **M** had given an inheritance to the	Jos 14:3
of Israel did as the LORD commanded **M**;	Jos 14:5
what the LORD said to **M** the man of God	Jos 14:6
forty years old when **M** the servant of the	Jos 14:7
And **M** swore on that day, saying,	Jos 14:9
that the LORD spoke this word to **M**,	Jos 14:10
as I was in the day that **M** sent me;	Jos 14:11
"The LORD commanded **M** to give us an	Jos 17:4
which **M** the servant of the LORD gave	Jos 18:7
of which I spoke to you through **M**,	Jos 20:2
LORD commanded through **M** that we be	Jos 21:2
the LORD had commanded through **M**.	Jos 21:8
have kept all that **M** the servant of the	Jos 22:2
which **M** the servant of the LORD gave	Jos 22:4
and the law that **M** the servant of the	Jos 22:5
the tribe of Manasseh **M** had given a	Jos 22:7
by command of the LORD through **M**.	Jos 22:9
is written in the Book of the Law of **M**,	Jos 23:6
And I sent **M** and Aaron, and I plagued	Jos 24:5
was given to Caleb, as **M** had said.	Jgs 1:20
their fathers by the hand of **M**.	Jgs 3:4
of Hobab the father-in-law of **M**,	Jgs 4:11
the son of Gershom, son of **M**,	Jgs 18:30
who appointed **M** and Aaron and	1 Sm 12:6
LORD and the LORD sent **M** and Aaron,	1 Sm 12:8
as it is written in the Law of **M**,	1 Kgs 2:3
tablets of stone that **M** put there at	1 Kgs 8:9
declared through **M** your servant,	1 Kgs 8:53
which he spoke by **M** his servant.	1 Kgs 8:56
written in the Book of the Law of **M**,	2 Kgs 14:6
the bronze serpent that **M** had made,	2 Kgs 18:4
that the LORD commanded **M**.	2 Kgs 18:6
even all that **M** the servant of the	2 Kgs 18:12
my servant **M** commanded them."	2 Kgs 21:8
according to all the Law of **M**,	2 Kgs 23:25
of Amram: Aaron, **M**, and Miriam.	1 Chr 6:3
according to all that **M** the servant of	1 Chr 6:49
as **M** had commanded according to	1 Chr 15:15
which **M** had made in the	1 Chr 21:29
the LORD commanded **M** for Israel.	1 Chr 22:13
The sons of Amram: Aaron and **M**.	1 Chr 23:13
But the sons of **M** the man of God	1 Chr 23:14
The sons of **M**: Gershom and	1 Chr 23:15
the son of Gershom, son of **M**,	1 Chr 26:24
which **M** the servant of the LORD had	2 Chr 1:3
the two tablets that **M** put there at	2 Chr 5:10
the commandment of **M** for the	2 Chr 8:13
as it is written in the Law of **M**,	2 Chr 23:18
and Jerusalem the tax levied by **M**,	2 Chr 24:6
LORD the tax that **M** the servant of	2 Chr 24:9
written in the Law, in the Book of **M**,	2 Chr 25:4
to the Law of **M** the man of God.	2 Chr 30:16
and the rules given through **M**."	2 Chr 33:8
Law of the LORD given through **M**.	2 Chr 34:14
to the word of the LORD by **M**."	2 Chr 35:6
as it is written in the Book of **M**.	2 Chr 35:12
written in the Law of **M** the man of God.	Ezr 3:2
as it is written in the Book of **M**.	Ezr 6:18
skilled in the Law of **M** that the LORD the	Ezr 7:6
that you commanded your servant **M**.	Neh 1:7
that you commanded your servant **M**,	Neh 1:8
Book of the Law of **M** that the LORD had	Neh 8:1
had commanded by **M** that the people	Neh 8:14
statutes and a law by **M** your servant.	Neh 9:14
that was given by **M** the servant of	Neh 10:29
from the Book of **M** in the hearing of	Neh 13:1
a flock by the hand of **M** and Aaron.	Ps 77:20
A Prayer of **M**, the man of God.	Ps 90:T
M and Aaron were among his priests,	Ps 99:6
He made known his ways to **M**, his acts	Ps 103:7
He sent **M**, his servant, and Aaron,	Ps 105:26
camp were jealous of **M** and Aaron,	Ps 106:16
he would destroy them—had not **M**,	Ps 106:23
it went ill with **M** on their account,	Ps 106:32
the days of old, of **M** and his people.	Is 63:11
arm to go at the right hand of **M**,	Is 63:12
"Though **M** and Samuel stood before	Jer 15:1
in the Law of **M** the servant of God	Dn 9:11
As it is written in the Law of **M**, all this	Dn 9:13
house of slavery, and I sent before you **M**,	Mi 6:4
"Remember the law of my servant **M**,	Mal 4:4
and offer the gift that **M** commanded,	Mt 8:4
there appeared to them **M** and Elijah,	Mt 17:3
you and one for **M** and one for Elijah."	Mt 17:4
"Why then did **M** command one to give	Mt 19:7
your hardness of heart **M** allowed you to	Mt 19:8
saying, "Teacher, **M** said, 'If a man dies	Mt 22:24
your cleansing what **M** commanded,	Mk 1:44
For **M** said, 'Honor your father and	Mk 7:10
there appeared to them Elijah with **M**,	Mk 9:4
you and one for **M** and one for Elijah."	Mk 9:5
them, "What did **M** command you?"	Mk 10:3
"**M** allowed a man to write a certificate	Mk 10:4
M wrote for us that if a man's brother	Mk 12:19
have you not read in the book of **M**,	Mk 12:26
purification according to the Law of **M**,	Lk 2:22
for your cleansing, as **M** commanded,	Lk 5:14
were talking with him, **M** and Elijah,	Lk 9:30
you and one for **M** and one for Elijah"	Lk 9:33
said, 'They have **M** and the Prophets;	Lk 16:29
'If they do not hear **M** and the Prophets,	Lk 16:31
M wrote for us that if a man's brother	Lk 20:28
the dead are raised, even **M** showed,	Lk 20:37
And beginning with **M** and all the	Lk 24:27
in the Law of **M** and the Prophets and	Lk 24:44
For the law was given through **M**; grace	Jn 1:17
found him of whom **M** in the Law and	Jn 1:45
And as **M** lifted up the serpent in the	Jn 3:14
M, on whom you have set your hope.	Jn 5:45
If you believed **M**, you would believe me;	Jn 5:46
it was not **M** who gave you the bread	Jn 6:32
Has not **M** given you the law? Yet none of	Jn 7:19
M gave you circumcision (not that it is	Jn 7:22
you circumcision (not that it is from **M**,	Jn 7:22
so that the law of **M** may not be broken,	Jn 7:23
Now in the Law **M** commanded us to	Jn 8:5
are his disciple, but we are disciples of **M**.	Jn 9:28
We know that God has spoken to **M**, but	Jn 9:29
M said, 'The Lord God will raise up for	Acts 3:22
words against **M** and God."	Acts 6:11
the customs that **M** delivered to us."	Acts 6:14
At this time **M** was born; and he was	Acts 7:20
And **M** was instructed in all the	Acts 7:22
At this retort **M** fled and became an	Acts 7:29
When **M** saw it, he was amazed at the	Acts 7:31
And **M** trembled and did not dare to	Acts 7:32
"This **M**, whom they rejected, saying,	Acts 7:35
This is the **M** who said to the Israelites,	Acts 7:37
As for this **M** who led us out from the	Acts 7:40
he who spoke to **M** directed him to	Acts 7:44
could not be freed by the law of **M**.	Acts 13:39
according to the custom of **M**,	Acts 15:1
to order them to keep the law of **M**."	Acts 15:5
from ancient generations **M** has had	Acts 15:21
are among the Gentiles to forsake **M**,	Acts 21:21
the prophets and **M** said would come	Acts 26:22
from the Law of **M** and from the	Acts 28:23
Yet death reigned from Adam to **M**,	Rom 5:14
For he says to **M**, "I will have mercy	Rom 9:15
For **M** writes about the righteousness	Rom 10:5
Israel not understand? First **M** says,	Rom 10:19
For it is written in the Law of **M**, "You	1 Cor 9:9
all were baptized into **M** in the cloud	1 Cor 10:2
not like **M**, who would put a veil over	2 Cor 3:13
to this day whenever **M** is read a veil	2 Cor 3:15
Just as Jannes and Jambres opposed **M**,	2 Tm 3:8
just as **M** also was faithful in all God's	Heb 3:2
of more glory than **M**—as much more	Heb 3:3
Now **M** was faithful in all God's house	Heb 3:5
it not all those who left Egypt led by **M**?	Heb 3:16
with that tribe **M** said nothing about	Heb 7:14
For when **M** was about to erect the tent,	Heb 8:5
had been declared by **M** to all the	Heb 9:19
aside the law of **M** dies without mercy	Heb 10:28
By faith **M**, when he was born, was	Heb 11:23
By faith **M**, when he was grown up,	Heb 11:24
so terrifying was the sight that **M** said,	Heb 12:21
was disputing about the body of **M**,	Jude 1:9
And they sing the song of **M**, the servant	Rv 15:3

MOSES' (18)

foreskin and touched **M** feet with it	Ex 4:25
But **M** hands grew weary, so they took	Ex 17:12
the priest of Midian, **M** father-in-law,	Ex 18:1
Now Jethro, **M** father-in-law, had taken	Ex 18:2
had taken Zipporah, **M** wife,	Ex 18:2
Jethro, **M** father-in-law, came with his	Ex 18:5
And Jethro, **M** father-in-law, brought a	Ex 18:12
eat bread with **M** father-in-law before	Ex 18:12
When **M** father-in-law saw all that he	Ex 18:14
M father-in-law said to him, "What	Ex 18:17
and the dancing, **M** anger burned hot,	Ex 32:19
that the skin of **M** face was shining.	Ex 34:35
It was **M** portion of the ram of	Lv 8:29
Reuel the Midianite, **M** father-in-law,	Nm 10:29
to Joshua the son of Nun, **M** assistant,	Jos 1:1
of the Kenite, **M** father-in-law,	Jgs 1:16
scribes and the Pharisees sit on **M** seat,	Mt 23:2
could not gaze at **M** face because of its	2 Cor 3:7

MOST (150)

wine. (He was priest of God **M** High.)	Gn 14:18
"Blessed be Abram by God **M** High,	Gn 14:19
and blessed be God **M** High, who has	Gn 14:20
my hand to the LORD, God **M** High,	Gn 14:22
Now he was the **m** honored of all his	Gn 34:19
you the Holy Place from the **M** Holy.	Ex 26:33
of the testimony in the **M** Holy Place.	Ex 26:34
it, and the altar shall be **m** holy.	Ex 29:37
generations. It is **m** holy to the LORD."	Ex 30:10
them, that they may be **m** holy.	Ex 30:29
with you. It shall be **m** holy for you.	Ex 30:36
so that the altar may become **m** holy.	Ex 40:10
it is a **m** holy part of the LORD'S food	Lv 2:3
it is a **m** holy part of the LORD'S food	Lv 2:10
It is a thing **m** holy, like the sin offering	Lv 6:17
be killed before the LORD; it is **m** holy.	Lv 6:25
the priests may eat of it; it is **m** holy.	Lv 6:29
is the law of the guilt offering. It is **m** holy.	Lv 7:1
shall be eaten in a holy place. It is **m** holy.	Lv 7:6
beside the altar, for it is **m** holy.	Lv 10:12
since it is a thing **m** holy and has been	Lv 10:17
belongs to the priest; it is **m** holy.	Lv 14:13
both of the **m** holy and of the holy	Lv 21:22
it is for him a **m** holy portion out of the	Lv 24:9
every devoted thing is **m** holy to the	Lv 27:28
in the tent of meeting: the **m** holy things.	Nm 4:4
they come near to the **m** holy things:	Nm 4:19
shall be yours of the **m** holy things,	Nm 18:9
shall be **m** holy to you and to your	Nm 18:9
In a **m** holy place shall you eat it.	Nm 18:10
knows the knowledge of the **M** High,	Nm 24:16
man who is the **m** tender and refined	Dt 28:54
The **m** tender and refined woman	Dt 28:56
When the **M** High gave to the nations	Dt 32:8
he said, "**M** blessed of sons be Asher;	Dt 33:24
"**M** blessed of women be Jael, the wife of	Jgs 5:24
of tent-dwelling women **m** blessed.	Jgs 5:24
one another, David weeping the **m**.	1 Sm 20:41
and the **M** High uttered his voice.	2 Sm 22:14
He was the **m** renowned of the thirty	2 Sm 23:19
inner sanctuary, as the **M** Holy Place.	1 Kgs 6:16
part of the house, the **M** Holy Place,	1 Kgs 7:50
of the house, in the **M** Holy Place,	1 Kgs 8:6
lodging place, its **m** fruitful forest.	2 Kgs 19:23
for all the work of the **M** Holy Place,	1 Chr 6:49
He was the **m** renowned of the thirty	1 Chr 11:21
apart to dedicate the **m** holy things,	1 Chr 23:13
And he made the **M** Holy Place. Its	2 Chr 3:8
In the **M** Holy Place he made two	2 Chr 3:10
inner doors to the **M** Holy Place and	2 Chr 4:22
of the house, in the **M** Holy Place,	2 Chr 5:7
the LORD and the **m** holy offerings.	2 Chr 31:14
were not to partake of the **m** holy food,	Ezr 2:63
to partake of the **m** holy food until a	Neh 7:65
to one of the king's **m** noble officials.	Est 6:9
to the name of the LORD, the **M** High.	Ps 7:17
I will sing praise to your name, O **M** High.	Ps 9:2

and the **M** High uttered his voice, Ps 18:13
For you make him **m** blessed forever; Ps 21:6
steadfast love of the **M** High he shall not Ps 21:7
hands toward your **m** holy sanctuary. Ps 28:2
You are the **m** handsome of the sons of Ps 45:2
God, the holy habitation of the **M** High. Ps 46:4
For the LORD, the **M** High, is to be feared, Ps 47:2
and perform your vows to the **M** High, Ps 50:14
I cry out to God **M** High, to God who Ps 57:2
Is there knowledge in the **M** High?" Ps 73:11
years of the right hand of the **M** High." Ps 77:10
rebelling against the **M** High in the Ps 78:17
rock, the **M** High God their redeemer. Ps 78:35
rebelled against the **M** High God and Ps 78:56
I said, "You are gods, sons of the **M** High, Ps 82:6
LORD, are the **M** High over all the earth. Ps 83:18
for the **M** High himself will establish Ps 87:5
in the shelter of the **M** High will abide in Ps 91:1
LORD your dwelling place—the **M** High, Ps 91:9
to sing praises to your name, O **M** High; Ps 92:1
O LORD, are **m** high over all the earth; Ps 97:9
spurned the counsel of the **M** High. Ps 107:11
not know, O **m** beautiful among women, Sg 1:8
beloved, O **m** beautiful among women? Sg 5:9
His mouth is **m** sweet, and he is Sg 5:16
gone, O **m** beautiful among women? Sg 6:1
I will make myself like the **M** High.' Is 14:14
its remotest height, its **m** fruitful forest. Is 37:24
a heritage **m** beautiful of all nations. Jer 3:19
as for an only son, **m** bitter lamentation, Jer 6:26
justice in the presence of the **M** High, Lam 3:35
the mouth of the **M** High that good Lam 3:38
and honey, the **m** glorious of all lands. Ezk 20:6
and honey, the **m** glorious of all lands, Ezk 20:15
you, the **m** ruthless of the nations; Ezk 28:7
It shall be the **m** lowly of the Ezk 29:15
with him, the **m** ruthless of nations, Ezk 30:11
Foreigners, the **m** ruthless of nations, Ezk 31:12
all of them **m** ruthless of nations. Ezk 32:12
said to me, "This is the **M** Holy Place." Ezk 41:4
LORD shall eat the **m** holy offerings. Ezk 42:13
they shall put the **m** holy offerings— Ezk 42:13
mountain all around shall be **m** holy. Ezk 43:12
things and the things that are **m** holy, Ezk 44:13
be the sanctuary, the **M** Holy Place. Ezk 45:3
portion of the land, a **m** holy place, Ezk 48:12
Abednego, servants of the **M** High God, Dn 3:26
and wonders that the **M** High God has Dn 4:2
may know that the **M** High rules the Dn 4:17
It is a decree of the **M** High, which has Dn 4:24
you know that the **M** High rules the Dn 4:25
you know that the **M** High rules the Dn 4:32
to me, and I blessed the **M** High, Dn 4:34
the **M** High God gave Nebuchadnezzar Dn 5:18
he knew that the **M** High God rules the Dn 5:21
the saints of the **M** High shall receive Dn 7:18
was given for the saints of the **M** High, Dn 7:22
shall speak words against the **M** High, Dn 7:25
shall wear out the saints of the **M** High, Dn 7:25
to the people of the saints of the **M** High; Dn 7:27
prophet, and to anoint a **m** holy place. Dn 9:24
and though they call out to the **M** High, Hos 11:7
the **m** upright of them a thorn hedge. Mi 7:4
the cities where **m** of his mighty Mt 11:20
M of the crowd spread their cloaks on Mt 21:8
with me, Jesus, Son of the **M** High God? Mk 5:7
like a corpse, so that **m** of them said, Mk 9:26
commandment is the **m** important of Mk 12:28
Jesus answered, "The **m** important is, Mk 12:29
account for you, **m** excellent Theophilus, Lk 1:3
and will be called the Son of the **M** High. Lk 1:32
power of the **M** High will overshadow Lk 1:35
will be called the prophet of the **M** High; Lk 1:76
and you will be sons of the **M** High, Lk 6:35
with me, Jesus, Son of the **M** High God? Lk 8:28
Yet the **M** High does not dwell in Acts 7:48
men are servants of the **M** High God, Acts 16:17
and **m** of them did not know why Acts 19:32
being sorrowful **m** of all because of Acts 20:38
by your foresight, **m** excellent Felix, Acts 24:2
out of my mind, **m** excellent Festus, Acts 26:25
with **m** of them God was not pleased, 1 Cor 10:5
let there be only two or at **m** three, 1 Cor 14:27
at one time, **m** of whom are still alive, 1 Cor 15:6
we are of all people **m** to be pitied. 1 Cor 15:19
your zeal has stirred up **m** of them. 2 Cor 9:2
I will **m** gladly spend and be spent 2 Cor 12:15
And **m** of the brothers, having become Phil 1:14
as we pray **m** earnestly night and 1 Thes 3:10
king of Salem, priest of the **M** High God, Heb 7:1
second section called the **M** Holy Place, Heb 9:3
yourselves up in your **m** holy faith; Jude 1:20
of God, its radiance like a **m** rare jewel, Rv 21:11

MOTH (8)

in the dust, who are crushed like the **m**. Jb 4:19
you consume like a **m** what is dear to Ps 39:11
like a garment; the **m** will eat them up. Is 50:9
For the **m** will eat them up like a Is 51:8
But I am like a **m** to Ephraim, and like Hos 5:12
where **m** and rust destroy and where Mt 6:19
where neither **m** nor rust destroys and Mt 6:20
no thief approaches and no **m** destroys. Lk 12:33

MOTH'S (1)

He builds his house like a **m**, like a Jb 27:18

MOTH-EATEN (2)

a rotten thing, like a garment that is **m**. Jb 13:28
have rotted and your garments are **m**. Jas 5:2

MOTHER (229)

his father and his **m** and hold fast to Gn 2:24
Eve, because she was the **m** of all living. Gn 3:20
though not the daughter of my **m**, Gn 20:12
and his **m** took a wife for him from the Gn 21:21
and to her **m** costly ornaments. Gn 24:53
Her brother and her **m** said, "Let the Gn 24:55
tent of Sarah his **m** and took Rebekah, Gn 24:67
But Jacob said to Rebekah his **m**, Gn 27:11
His **m** said to him, "Let your curse be Gn 27:13
took them and brought them to his **m**, Gn 27:14
and his **m** prepared delicious food, Gn 27:14
of Rebekah, Jacob's and Esau's **m**. Gn 28:5
his father and his **m** and gone to Gn 28:7
field and brought them to his **m** Leah. Gn 30:14
Shall I and your **m** and your brothers Gn 37:10
So the girl went and called the child's **m**. Ex 2:8
"Honor your father and your **m**, that Ex 20:12
his father or his **m** shall be put to Ex 21:15
his father or his **m** shall be put to Ex 21:17
sheep: seven days it shall be with its **m**; Ex 22:30
which is the nakedness of your **m**; Lv 18:7
she is your **m**, you shall not uncover her Lv 18:7
of you shall revere his **m** and his father, Lv 19:3
his father or his **m** shall surely be put Lv 20:9
death; he has cursed his father or his **m**; Lv 20:9
a man takes a woman and her **m** also, Lv 20:14
of his father or a daughter of his **m**, Lv 20:17
except for his closest relatives, his **m**, his Lv 21:2
even for his father or for his **m**. Lv 21:11
it shall remain seven days with its **m**, Lv 22:27
Not even for his father or for his **m**, for Nm 6:7
"'Honor your father and your **m**, as the Dt 5:16
"If your brother, the son of your **m**, or Dt 13:6
her father and her **m** a full month. Dt 21:13
voice of his father or the voice of his **m**, Dt 21:18
his father and his **m** shall take hold of Dt 21:19
or eggs and the **m** sitting on the young Dt 22:6
you shall not take the **m** with the young. Dt 22:6
You shall let the **m** go, but the young Dt 22:7
woman and her **m** shall take and Dt 22:15
who dishonors his father or his **m**.' Dt 27:16
of his father or the daughter of his **m**.' Dt 27:22
who said of his father and **m**, 'I regard Dt 33:9
you will save alive my father and **m**, Jos 2:13
into your house your father and **m**, Jos 2:18
and her father and **m** and brothers and Jos 6:23
I arose; I, Deborah, arose as a **m** in Israel. Jgs 5:7
the **m** of Sisera wailed through the Jgs 5:28
were my brothers, the sons of my **m**. Jgs 8:19
he came up and told his father and **m**, Jgs 14:2
But his father and **m** said to him, "Is Jgs 14:3
His father and **m** did not know that it Jgs 14:4
down with his father and **m** to Timnah, Jgs 14:5
his father or his **m** what he had done. Jgs 14:6
to his father and **m** and gave some to Jgs 14:9
I have not told my father nor my **m**, Jgs 14:16
And he said to his **m**, "The 1,100 pieces Jgs 17:2
I took it." And his **m** said, "Blessed be Jgs 17:2
the 1,100 pieces of silver to his **m**. Jgs 17:3
And his **m** said, "I dedicate the silver to Jgs 17:3
So when he restored the money to his **m**, Jgs 17:4
his **m** took 200 pieces of silver and gave Jgs 17:4
left your father and **m** and your native Ru 2:11
And his **m** used to make for him a 1 Sm 2:19
so shall your **m** be childless among 1 Sm 15:33
let my father and my **m** stay with you, 1 Sm 22:3
Nahash, sister of Zeruiah, Joab's **m**. 2 Sm 17:25
the grave of my father and my **m**. 2 Sm 19:37
to destroy a city that is a **m** in Israel. 2 Sm 20:19
said to Bathsheba the **m** of Solomon, 1 Kgs 1:11
to Bathsheba the **m** of Solomon. 1 Kgs 2:13
had a seat brought for the king's **m**, 1 Kgs 2:19
to her, "Make your request, my **m**, 1 Kgs 2:20
King Solomon answered his **m**, "And 1 Kgs 2:22
put him to death; she is his **m**." 1 Kgs 3:27
removed Maacah his **m** from being 1 Kgs 15:13
from being queen **m** because she 1 Kgs 15:13
house and delivered him to his **m**. 1 Kgs 17:23
"Let me kiss my father and my **m**, 1 Kgs 19:20
in the way of his **m** and in the way 1 Kgs 22:52
though not like his father and **m**, 2 Kgs 3:2
the prophets of your **m**." But the king 2 Kgs 3:13
to his servant, "Carry him to his **m**." 2 Kgs 4:19
lifted him and brought him to his **m**, 2 Kgs 4:20
Then the **m** of the child said, "As the 2 Kgs 4:30
the sorceries of your **m** Jezebel are so 2 Kgs 9:22
and the sons of the queen **m**." 2 Kgs 10:13
when Athaliah the **m** of Ahaziah saw 2 Kgs 11:1
himself and his **m** and his servants 2 Kgs 24:12
The king's **m**, the king's wives, his 2 Kgs 24:15
was Atarah; she was the **m** of Onam. 1 Chr 2:26
Absalom, whose **m** was Maacah, 1 Chr 3:2
Adonijah, whose **m** was Haggith; 1 Chr 3:2
and his **m** called his name Jabez, 1 Chr 4:9
Even Maacah, his **m**, King Asa 2 Chr 15:16
from being queen **m** because she 2 Chr 15:16
for his **m** was his counselor in doing 2 Chr 22:3
when Athaliah the **m** of Ahaziah 2 Chr 22:10
uncle, for she had neither father nor **m**. Est 2:7
at, and when her father and her **m** died, Est 2:7
are my father,' and to the worm, 'My **m**,' Jb 17:14
a stench to the children of my own **m**. Jb 19:17
my father and my **m** have forsaken me, Ps 27:10
as one who laments his **m**, I bowed Ps 35:14
and in sin did my **m** conceive me. Ps 51:5
let not the sin of his **m** be blotted out! Ps 109:14
making her the joyous **m** of children. Ps 113:9
my soul, like a weaned child with its **m**; Ps 131:2
tender, the only one in the sight of my **m**, Prv 4:3
but a foolish son is a sorrow to his **m**. Prv 10:1
but a foolish man despises his **m**. Prv 15:20
and chases away his **m** is a son who Prv 19:26
If one curses his father or his **m**, his Prv 20:20
do not despise your **m** when she is old. Prv 23:22
Let your father and **m** be glad; let her Prv 23:25
robs his father or his **m** and says, Prv 28:24
left to himself brings shame to his **m**. Prv 29:15
scorns to obey a **m** will be picked out Prv 30:17
An oracle that his **m** taught him: Prv 31:1
with which his **m** crowned him on Sg 3:11
one, is the only one, the only one of her **m**, Sg 6:9
into the house of my **m**—she who used to Sg 8:2
There your **m** was in labor with you; Sg 8:5
knows how to cry 'My father' or 'My **m**,' Is 8:4
the body of my **m** he named my name. Is 49:1
your transgressions your **m** was sent Is 50:1
As one whom his **m** comforts, so I will Is 66:13
Say to the king and the queen **m**: "Take Jer 13:18
Woe is me, my **m**, that you bore me, a Jer 15:10
to drink for his father or his **m**. Jer 16:7
The day when my **m** bore me, let it not Jer 20:14
so my **m** would have been my grave, Jer 20:17
hurl you and the **m** who bore you into Jer 22:26
after King Jeconiah and the queen **m**, Jer 29:2
your **m** shall be utterly shamed, and Jer 50:12
was an Amorite and your **m** a Hittite. Ezk 16:3
use this proverb about you: 'Like **m**, Ezk 16:44
You are the daughter of your **m**, who Ezk 16:45
Your **m** was a Hittite and your father Ezk 16:45
and say: What was your **m**? A lioness! Ezk 19:2
Your **m** was like a vine in a vineyard Ezk 19:10
Father and **m** are treated with Ezk 22:7
two women, the daughters of one **m**. Ezk 23:2
However, for father or **m**, for son or Ezk 44:25
"Plead with your **m**, plead—for she is Hos 2:2
For their **m** has played the whore; she Hos 2:5
you by night; and I will destroy your **m**. Hos 4:5
the daughter rises up against her **m**, Mi 7:6
his father and **m** who bore him will say Zec 13:3
And his father and **m** who bore him Zec 13:3
When his **m** Mary had been betrothed Mt 1:18
they saw the child with Mary his **m**, Mt 2:11
and said, "Rise, take the child and his **m**, Mt 2:13
the child and his **m** by night and Mt 2:14
take the child and his **m** and go to the Mt 2:20
took the child and his **m** and went to the Mt 2:21
father, and a daughter against her **m**, Mt 10:35
loves father or **m** more than me Mt 10:37
his **m** and his brothers stood outside, Mt 12:46
the man who told him, "Who is my **m**, Mt 12:48
said, "Here are my **m** and my brothers! Mt 12:49
is my brother and sister and **m**." Mt 12:50
son? Is not his **m** called Mary? Mt 13:55
Prompted by her **m**, she said, "Give me Mt 14:8
to the girl, and she brought it to her **m**. Mt 14:11
'Honor your father and your **m**,' Mt 15:4
reviles father or **m** must surely die.' Mt 15:4
say, 'If anyone tells his father or his **m**, Mt 15:5
his father and his **m** and hold fast to Mt 19:5
Honor your father and **m**, and, You Mt 19:19
sisters or father or **m** or children or Mt 19:29
Then the **m** of the sons of Zebedee Mt 20:20
and Mary the **m** of James and Mt 27:56
and Joseph and the **m** of the sons of Mt 27:56
And his **m** and his brothers came, and Mk 3:31
"Your **m** and your brothers are outside, Mk 3:32

"Who are my **m** and my brothers?" Mk 3:33
said, "Here are my **m** and my brothers! Mk 3:34
he is my brother and sister and **m**." Mk 3:35
the child's father and **m** and those who Mk 5:40
And she went out and said to her **m**, Mk 6:24
to the girl, and the girl gave it to her **m**. Mk 6:28
said, 'Honor your father and your **m**'; Mk 7:10
reviles father or **m** must surely die.' Mk 7:10
say, 'If a man tells his father or his **m**, Mk 7:11
him to do anything for his father or **m**, Mk 7:12
leave his father and **m** and hold fast to Mk 10:7
defraud, Honor your father and **m**.'" Mk 10:19
brothers or sisters or **m** or father or Mk 10:29
and Mary the **m** of James the younger Mk 15:40
and Mary the **m** of Joses saw Mk 15:47
and Mary the **m** of James and Mk 16:1
to me that the **m** of my Lord should Lk 1:43
but his **m** answered, "No; he shall be Lk 1:60
his father and his **m** marveled at what Lk 2:33
blessed them and said to Mary his **m**, Lk 2:34
And his **m** said to him, "Son, why have Lk 2:48
And his **m** treasured up all these things Lk 2:51
being carried out, the only son of his **m**, Lk 7:12
to speak, and Jesus gave him to his **m**. Lk 7:15
Then his **m** and his brothers came to Lk 8:19
"Your **m** and your brothers are Lk 8:20
"My **m** and my brothers are those who Lk 8:21
James, and the father and **m** of the child. Lk 8:51
m against daughter and daughter Lk 12:53
daughter and daughter against **m**, Lk 12:53
his own father and **m** and wife and Lk 14:26
witness, Honor your father and **m**.'" Lk 18:20
Joanna and Mary the **m** of James and Lk 24:10
in Galilee, and the **m** of Jesus was there. Jn 2:1
wine ran out, the **m** of Jesus said to him, Jn 2:3
His **m** said to the servants, "Do whatever Jn 2:5
with his **m** and his brothers and his Jn 2:12
of Joseph, whose father and **m** we know? Jn 6:42
of Jesus were his **m** and his mother's Jn 19:25
When Jesus saw his **m** and the disciple Jn 19:26
loved standing nearby, he said to his **m**, Jn 19:26
your **m**!" And from that hour the Jn 19:27
the women and Mary the **m** of Jesus, Acts 1:14
the **m** of John whose other name was Acts 12:12
also his **m**, who has been a mother to Rom 16:13
who has been a **m** to me as well. Rom 16:13
above is free, and she is our **m**. Gal 4:26
leave his father and **m** and hold fast to Eph 5:31
"Honor your father and **m**" (this is the Eph 6:2
like a nursing **m** taking care of her 1 Thes 2:7
Lois and your **m** Eunice and now, 2 Tm 1:5
He is without father or **m** or genealogy, Heb 7:3
m of prostitutes and of earth's Rv 17:5

MOTHER'S (73)
and told her **m** household about these Gn 24:28
Isaac was comforted after his **m** death. Gn 24:67
and may your **m** sons bow down to Gn 27:29
to the house of Bethuel your **m** father, Gn 28:2
the daughters of Laban your **m** brother. Gn 28:2
the daughter of Laban his **m** brother, Gn 29:10
and the sheep of Laban his **m** brother, Gn 29:10
the flock of Laban his **m** brother. Gn 29:10
saw his brother Benjamin, his **m** son, Gn 43:29
and he alone is left of his **m** children, Gn 44:20
not boil a young goat in its **m** milk. Ex 23:19
not boil a young goat in its **m** milk." Ex 34:26
father's daughter or your **m** daughter, Lv 18:9
the nakedness of your **m** sister, Lv 18:13
sister, for she is your **m** relative. Lv 18:13
the nakedness of your **m** sister or of Lv 20:19
His **m** name was Shelomith, the Lv 24:11
when he comes out of his **m** womb." Nm 12:12
not boil a young goat in its **m** milk. Dt 14:21
to Shechem to his **m** relatives and said to Jgs 9:1
and to the whole clan of his **m** family, Jgs 9:1
And his **m** relatives spoke all these words Jgs 9:3
a Nazirite to God from my **m** womb. Jgs 16:17
"Go, return each of you to her **m** house. Ru 1:8
to the shame of your **m** nakedness? 1 Sm 20:30
whose **m** name was Zeruah, 1 Kgs 11:26
His **m** name was Naamah the 1 Kgs 14:21
His **m** name was Naamah the 1 Kgs 14:31
His **m** name was Maacah the 1 Kgs 15:2
His **m** name was Maacah the 1 Kgs 15:10
His **m** name was Azubah the 1 Kgs 22:42
His **m** name was Athaliah; she was a 2 Kgs 8:26
His **m** name was Zibiah of 2 Kgs 12:1
His **m** name was Jehoaddin of 2 Kgs 14:2
His **m** name was Jecoliah of 2 Kgs 15:2
His **m** name was Jerusha the 2 Kgs 15:33
His **m** name was Abi the daughter of 2 Kgs 18:2
His **m** name was Hephzibah. 2 Kgs 21:1
His **m** name was Meshullemeth the 2 Kgs 21:19
His **m** name was Jedidah the 2 Kgs 22:1
His **m** name was Hamutal the 2 Kgs 23:31
His **m** name was Zebidah the 2 Kgs 23:36
His **m** name was Nehushta the 2 Kgs 24:8
His **m** name was Hamutal the 2 Kgs 24:18
His **m** name was Naamah the 2 Chr 12:13
His **m** name was Micaiah the 2 Chr 13:2
His **m** name was Azubah the 2 Chr 20:31
His **m** name was Athaliah, the 2 Chr 22:2
His **m** name was Zibiah of 2 Chr 24:1
His **m** name was Jehoaddan of 2 Chr 25:1
His **m** name was Jecoliah of 2 Chr 26:3
His **m** name was Jerushah the 2 Chr 27:1
His **m** name was Abijah the 2 Chr 29:1
said, "Naked I came from my **m** womb, Jb 1:21
it did not shut the doors of my **m** womb, Jb 3:10
and from my **m** womb I guided the Jb 31:18
you made me trust you at my **m** breasts. Ps 22:9
and from my **m** womb you have been Ps 22:10
brother; you slander your own **m** son. Ps 50:20
to my brothers, an alien to my **m** sons. Ps 69:8
are he who took me from my **m** womb. Ps 71:6
knitted me together in my **m** womb. Ps 139:13
and forsake not your **m** teaching, Prv 1:8
and forsake not your **m** teaching. Prv 6:20
he came from his **m** womb he shall go Eccl 5:15
My **m** sons were angry with me; they Sg 1:6
I had brought him into my **m** house, Sg 3:4
to me who nursed at my **m** breasts! Sg 8:1
"Where is your **m** certificate of divorce, Is 50:1
His **m** name was Hamutal the daughter Jer 52:1
the Holy Spirit, even from his **m** womb. Lk 1:15
second time into his **m** womb and be Jn 3:4
Jesus were his mother and his **m** sister, Jn 19:25

MOTHER-IN-LAW (18)
be anyone who lies with his **m**.' Dt 27:23
And Orpah kissed her **m**, but Ruth Ru 1:14
have done for your **m** since the death of Ru 2:11
city. Her **m** saw what she had gleaned. Ru 2:18
And her **m** said to her, "Where did you Ru 2:19
So she told her **m** with whom she had Ru 2:19
harvests. And she lived with her **m**. Ru 2:23
Then Naomi her **m** said to her, "My Ru 3:1
did just as her **m** had commanded her. Ru 3:6
And when she came to her **m**, she said, Ru 3:16
not go back empty-handed to your **m**.'" Ru 3:17
the daughter-in-law against her **m**; Mi 7:6
he saw his **m** lying sick with a fever. Mt 8:14
and a daughter-in-law against her **m**. Mt 10:35
Now Simon's **m** lay ill with a fever, and Mk 1:30
Now Simon's **m** was ill with a high Lk 4:38
m against her daughter-in-law and Lk 12:53
and daughter-in-law against **m**." Lk 12:53

MOTHER-OF-PEARL (1)
marble, **m** and precious stones. Est 1:6

MOTHERS (11)
attack me, the **m** with the children. Gn 32:11
their fathers and do not bless their **m**. Prv 30:11
and their queens your nursing **m**. Is 49:23
brought against the **m** of young men Jer 15:8
and concerning the **m** who bore them Jer 16:3
They cry to their **m**, "Where is bread Lam 2:12
fatherless; our **m** are like widows. Lam 5:3
m were dashed in pieces with their Hos 10:14
and sisters and **m** and children and Mk 10:30
those who strike their fathers and **m**, 1 Tm 1:9
older women like **m**, younger women 1 Tm 5:2

MOTHERS' (1)
life is poured out on their **m** bosom. Lam 2:12

MOTIONED (2)
so Simon Peter **m** to him to ask Jesus of Jn 13:24
steps, **m** with his hand to the people. Acts 21:40

MOTIONING (3)
But **m** to them with his hand to be Acts 12:17
stood up, and **m** with his hand said: Acts 13:16
And Alexander, **m** with his hand, Acts 19:33

MOTTLED (2)
the flock were striped, spotted, and **m**. Gn 31:10
the flock are striped, spotted, and **m**, Gn 31:12

MOUND (8)
They cast up a **m** against the city, 2 Sm 20:15
shield or cast up a siege **m** against it. 2 Kgs 19:32
a shield or cast up a siege **m** against it. Is 37:33
trees; cast up a siege **m** against Jerusalem. Jer 6:6
the city shall be rebuilt on its **m**, and Jer 30:18
it shall become a desolate **m**, and its Jer 49:2
against it, and cast up a **m** against it. Ezk 4:2
you and throw up a **m** against you, Ezk 26:8

MOUNDS (6)
cities that stood on **m** did Israel burn, Jos 11:13
of spices, **m** of sweet-smelling herbs. Sg 5:13
the siege **m** have come up to the city to Jer 32:24
against the siege **m** and against the Jer 33:4
when **m** are cast up and siege walls Ezk 17:17
rams against the gates, to cast up **m**, Ezk 21:22

MOUNT (157)
"On the **m** of the LORD it shall be Gn 22:14
will come down on **M** Sinai in the sight Ex 19:11
Now **M** Sinai was wrapped in smoke Ex 19:18
The LORD came down on **M** Sinai, to the Ex 19:20
people cannot come up to **M** Sinai, Ex 19:23
The glory of the LORD dwelt on **M** Sinai, Ex 24:16
speaking with him on **M** Sinai, Ex 31:18
their ornaments, from **M** Horeb onward. Ex 33:6
and come up in the morning to **M** Sinai, Ex 34:2
in the morning and went up on **M** Sinai, Ex 34:4
Moses came down from **M** Sinai, Ex 34:29
LORD had spoken with him in **M** Sinai. Ex 34:32
the LORD commanded Moses on **M** Sinai, Lv 7:38
The LORD spoke to Moses on **M** Sinai, Lv 25:1
of Israel through Moses on **M** Sinai. Lv 26:46
for the people of Israel on **M** Sinai. Lv 27:34
the LORD spoke with Moses on **M** Sinai. Nm 3:1
set out from the **m** of the LORD three Nm 10:33
whole congregation, came to **M** Hor. Nm 20:22
said to Moses and Aaron at **M** Hor, Nm 20:23
his son and bring them up to **M** Hor. Nm 20:25
And they went up **M** Hor in the sight Nm 20:27
From **M** Hor they set out by the way to Nm 21:4
which was ordained at **M** Sinai for a Nm 28:6
and camped at **M** Shepher. Nm 33:23
set out from **M** Shepher and camped Nm 33:24
from Kadesh and camped at **M** Hor, Nm 33:37
the priest went up **M** Hor at the Nm 33:38
123 years old when he died on **M** Hor. Nm 33:39
they set out from **M** Hor and camped Nm 33:41
Sea you shall draw a line to **M** Hor. Nm 34:7
From **M** Hor you shall draw a line to Nm 34:8
by the way of **M** Seir to Kadesh-barnea. Dt 1:2
for many days we traveled around **M** Seir. Dt 2:1
because I have given **M** Seir to Esau as a Dt 2:5
the Valley of the Arnon to **M** Hermon Dt 3:8
of the Arnon, as far as **M** Sirion (that is, Dt 4:48
set the blessing on **M** Gerizim and the Dt 11:29
Gerizim and the curse on **M** Ebal. Dt 11:29
I command you today, on **M** Ebal, Dt 27:4
these shall stand on **M** Gerizim to bless Dt 27:12
these shall stand on **M** Ebal for the Dt 27:13
this mountain of the Abarim, **M** Nebo, Dt 32:49
your brother died in **M** Hor and was Dt 32:50
upon us; he shone forth from **M** Paran; Dt 33:2
up from the plains of Moab to **M** Nebo, Dt 34:1
to the LORD, the God of Israel, on **M** Ebal, Jos 8:30
them in front of **M** Gerizim and half of Jos 8:33
and half of them in front of **M** Ebal, Jos 8:33
from **M** Halak, which rises toward Seir, Jos 11:17
Valley of Lebanon below **M** Hermon. Jos 11:17
the Valley of the Arnon to **M** Hermon, Jos 12:1
and ruled over **M** Hermon and Salecah Jos 12:5
in the Valley of Lebanon to **M** Halak, Jos 12:7
from Baal-gad below **M** Hermon to Jos 13:5
and Maacathites, and all **M** Hermon, Jos 13:11
and from there to the cities of **M** Ephron. Jos 15:9
circles west of Baalah to **M** Seir, Jos 15:10
northern shoulder of **M** Jearim (that is, Jos 15:10
and passes along to **M** Baalah and goes Jos 15:11
persisted in dwelling in **M** Heres, Jgs 1:35
and the Hivites who lived on **M** Lebanon, Jgs 3:3
from **M** Baal-hermon as far as Jgs 3:3
you, 'Go, gather your men at **M** Tabor, Jgs 4:6
of Abinoam had gone up to **M** Tabor, Jgs 4:12
went down from **M** Tabor with 10,000 Jgs 4:14
hurry away from **M** Gilead.'" Then Jgs 7:3
stood on top of **M** Gerizim and cried Jgs 9:7
And Abimelech went up to **M** Zalmon, Jgs 9:48
Philistines and fell slain on **M** Gilboa. 1 Sm 31:1
and his three sons fallen on **M** Gilboa. 1 Sm 31:8
chance I happened to be on **M** Gilboa, 2 Sm 1:6
went up the ascent of the **M** of Olives, 2 Sm 15:30
Rehoboam hurried to **m** his chariot 1 Kgs 12:18
gather all Israel to me at **M** Carmel, 1 Kgs 18:19
the prophets together at **M** Carmel. 1 Kgs 18:20
went up to the top of **M** Carmel. 1 Kgs 18:42
forty nights to Horeb, the **m** of God. 1 Kgs 19:8
and stand on the **m** before the LORD." 1 Kgs 19:11
From there he went on to **M** Carmel, 2 Kgs 2:25
came to the man of God at **M** Carmel. 2 Kgs 4:25
and out of **M** Zion a band of 2 Kgs 19:31
to the south of the **m** of corruption, 2 Kgs 23:13
he saw the tombs there on the **m**. 2 Kgs 23:16
of the Simeonites, went to **M** Seir, 1 Chr 4:42
Baal-hermon, Senir, and **M** Hermon. 1 Chr 5:23
and fell slain on **M** Gilboa. 1 Chr 10:1
and his sons fallen on **M** Gilboa. 1 Chr 10:8
of the LORD in Jerusalem on **M** Moriah, 2 Chr 3:1
stood up on **M** Zemaraim that is 2 Chr 13:4
of Ammon and Moab and **M** Seir, 2 Chr 20:10
men of Ammon, Moab, and **M** Seir, 2 Chr 20:22

against the inhabitants of **M** Seir, 2 Chr 20:23
You came down on **M** Sinai and spoke Neh 9:13
Though his height **m** up to the heavens, Jb 20:6
of Jordan and of Hermon, from **M** Mizar. Ps 42:6
is the joy of all the earth, **M** Zion, Ps 48:2
Let **M** Zion be glad! Let the daughters of Ps 48:11
at the **m** that God desired for his abode, Ps 68:16
of your heritage! Remember **M** Zion, Ps 74:2
but he chose the tribe of Judah, **M** Zion, Ps 78:68
On the holy **m** stands the city he Ps 87:1
who trust in the LORD are like **M** Zion, Ps 125:1
over the whole site of **M** Zion and over her Is 4:5
it, but could not yet **m** an attack against it. Is 7:1
the LORD of hosts, who dwells on **M** Zion. Is 8:18
all his work on **M** Zion and on Is 10:12
shake his fist at the **m** of the daughter of Is 10:32
I will sit on the **m** of assembly in the far Is 14:13
desert, to the **m** of the daughter of Zion. Is 16:1
whose land the rivers divide, to **M** Zion, Is 18:7
of hosts reigns on **M** Zion and in Is 24:23
the LORD will rise up as on **M** Perazim; Is 28:21
the nations be that fight against **M** Zion. Is 29:8
come down to fight on **M** Zion and on its Is 31:4
and out of **M** Zion a band of survivors. Is 37:32
they shall **m** up with wings like eagles; Is 40:31
proclaims trouble from **M** Ephraim. Jer 4:15
Harness the horses; **m**, O horsemen! Jer 46:4
one shall **m** up and fly swiftly like an Jer 49:22
Though Babylon should **m** up to Jer 51:53
for **M** Zion which lies desolate; jackals Lam 5:18
up their wings to **m** up from the earth, Ezk 10:16
of man, set your face against **M** Seir, Ezk 35:2
Behold, I am against you, **M** Seir, and I Ezk 35:3
I will make **M** Seir a waste and a Ezk 35:7
you shall be desolate, **M** Seir, and all Ezk 35:15
For in **M** Zion and in Jerusalem there Jl 2:32
and understanding out of **M** Esau? Ob 1:8
that every man from **M** Esau will be cut Ob 1:9
But in **M** Zion there shall be those who Ob 1:17
of the Negeb shall possess **M** Esau, Ob 1:19
shall go up to **M** Zion to rule Mount Ob 1:21
go up to Mount Zion to rule **M** Esau, Ob 1:21
reign over them in **M** Zion from this time Mi 4:7
and the Holy One from **M** Paran. Hab 3:3
shall stand on the **M** of Olives that lies Zec 14:4
and the **M** of Olives shall be split in two Zec 14:4
half of the **M** shall move northward, Zec 14:4
came to Bethphage, to the **M** of Olives, Mt 21:1
As he sat on the **M** of Olives, the Mt 24:3
hymn, they went out to the **M** of Olives. Mt 26:30
and Bethany, at the **M** of Olives, Mk 11:1
as he sat on the **M** of Olives opposite the Mk 13:3
they went out to the **M** of Olives. Mk 14:26
Bethany, at the **m** that is called Olivet, Lk 19:29
on the way down the **M** of Olives—the Lk 19:37
out and lodged on the **m** called Olivet. Lk 21:37
as was his custom, to the **M** of Olives, Lk 22:39
but Jesus went to the **M** of Olives. Jn 8:1
to Jerusalem from the **m** called Olivet, Acts 1:12
to him in the wilderness of **M** Sinai, Acts 7:30
the angel who spoke to him at **M** Sinai, Acts 7:38
One is from **M** Sinai, bearing children Gal 4:24
Now Hagar is **M** Sinai in Arabia; she Gal 4:25
you have come to **M** Zion and to the Heb 12:22
and behold, on **M** Zion stood the Lamb, Rv 14:1

MOUNTAIN (175)
to your brothers one **m** slope that I Gn 48:22
and came to Horeb, the **m** of God. Ex 3:1
of Egypt, you shall serve God on this **m**." Ex 3:12
and met him at the **m** of God and kissed Ex 4:27
in and plant them on your own **m**, Ex 15:17
where he was encamped at the **m** of God. Ex 18:5
There Israel encamped before the **m**, Ex 19:2
The LORD called to him out of the **m**, Ex 19:3
to go up into the **m** or touch the edge of Ex 19:12
Whoever touches the **m** shall be put to Ex 19:12
blast, they shall come up to the **m**." Ex 19:13
went down from the **m** to the people Ex 19:14
a thick cloud on the **m** and a very loud Ex 19:16
took their stand at the foot of the **m**. Ex 19:17
kiln, and the whole **m** trembled greatly. Ex 19:18
on Mount Sinai, to the top of the **m**. Ex 19:20
LORD called Moses to the top of the **m**, Ex 19:20
limits around the **m** and consecrate Ex 19:23
of the trumpet and the **m** smoking, Ex 20:18
and built an altar at the foot of the **m**, Ex 24:4
up to me on the **m** and wait there, Ex 24:12
and Moses went up into the **m** of God. Ex 24:13
Then Moses went up on the **m**, and the Ex 24:15
and the cloud covered the **m**. Ex 24:15
on the top of the **m** in the sight of the Ex 24:17
the cloud and went up on the **m**. Ex 24:18
Moses was on the **m** forty days and Ex 24:18
which is being shown you on the **m**. Ex 25:40
for it that you were shown on the **m**. Ex 26:30
As it has been shown you on the **m**, so Ex 27:8
delayed to come down from the **m**, Ex 32:1
went down from the **m** with the two Ex 32:15
and broke them at the foot of the **m**. Ex 32:19
yourself there to me on the top of the **m**. Ex 34:2
let no one be seen throughout all the **m**. Ex 34:3
flocks or herds graze opposite that **m**." Ex 34:3
his hand as he came down from the **m**, Ex 34:29
Aaron died there on the top of the **m**. Nm 20:28
and Eleazar came down from the **m**. Nm 20:28
"Go up into this **m** of Abarim and see Nm 27:12
'You have stayed long enough at this **m**. Dt 1:6
traveling around this **m** country long Dt 2:3
came near and stood at the foot of the **m**, Dt 4:11
while the **m** burned with fire to the heart Dt 4:11
LORD spoke with you face to face at the **m**, Dt 5:4
the fire, and you did not go up into the **m**. Dt 5:5
your assembly at the **m** out of the midst Dt 5:22
while the **m** was burning with fire, Dt 5:23
I went up the **m** to receive the tablets Dt 9:9
I remained on the **m** forty days and forty Dt 9:9
with you on the **m** out of the midst Dt 9:10
So I turned and came down from the **m**, Dt 9:15
and the **m** was burning with fire. Dt 9:15
the brook that ran down from the **m**. Dt 9:21
up to me on the **m** and make an ark of Dt 10:1
and went up the **m** with the two tablets Dt 10:3
spoken to you on the **m** out of the midst Dt 10:4
came down from the **m** and put the Dt 10:5
"I myself stayed on the **m**, as at the first Dt 10:10
the ibex, the antelope, and the **m** sheep. Dt 14:5
"Go up this **m** of the Abarim, Mount Dt 32:49
And die on the **m** which you go up, and Dt 32:50
They shall call peoples to their **m**; there Dt 33:19
to the top of the **m** that lies over against Jos 15:8
from the top of the **m** to the spring of the Jos 15:9
on the **m** that lies south of Lower Jos 18:13
side southward from the **m** that lies to Jos 18:14
the border of the **m** that overlooks the Jos 18:16
of Ephraim, north of the **m** of Gaash. Jos 24:30
of Ephraim, north of the **m** of Gaash. Jgs 2:9
Philistines stood on the **m** on the one 1 Sm 17:3
Israel stood on the **m** on the other side, 1 Sm 17:3
Saul went on one side of the **m**, and 1 Sm 23:26
his men on the other side of the **m**. 1 Sm 23:26
came down under cover of the **m**, 1 Sm 25:20
behind him by the side of the **m**. 2 Sm 13:34
them on the **m** before the LORD, 2 Sm 21:9
on the **m** east of Jerusalem. 1 Kgs 11:7
cast him upon some **m** or into some 2 Kgs 2:16
she came to the **m** to the man of 2 Kgs 4:27
the **m** was full of horses and chariots 2 Kgs 6:17
had built on the **m** of the house of 2 Chr 33:15
"But the **m** falls and crumbles away, Jb 14:18
you know when the **m** goats give birth? Jb 39:1
to my soul, "Flee like a bird to your **m**, Ps 11:1
O LORD, you made my **m** stand strong; Ps 30:7
in the city of our God! His holy **m**, Ps 48:1
O **m** of God, mountain of Bashan; O Ps 68:15
O mountain of God, **m** of Bashan; O Ps 68:15
O many-peaked **m**, mountain of Ps 68:15
many-peaked mountain, **m** of Bashan! Ps 68:15
look with hatred, O many-peaked **m**, Ps 68:16
to the **m** which his right hand had won. Ps 78:54
our God, and worship at his holy **m**; Ps 99:9
will go away to the **m** of myrrh and the Sg 4:6
the latter days that the **m** of the house of Is 2:2
"Come, let us go up to the **m** of the LORD, to Is 2:3
not hurt or destroy in all my holy **m**; Is 11:9
On this **m** the LORD of hosts will make for Is 25:6
swallow up on this **m** the covering that is Is 25:7
the hand of the LORD will rest on this **m**, Is 25:10
the LORD on the holy **m** at Jerusalem. Is 27:13
are left like a flagstaff on the top of a **m**, Is 30:17
And on every lofty **m** and every high hill Is 30:25
of the flute to go to the **m** of the LORD, Is 30:29
up, and every **m** and hill be made low; Is 40:4
Get you up to a high **m**, O Zion, herald of Is 40:9
these I will bring to my holy **m**, and Is 56:7
On a high and lofty **m** you have set your Is 57:7
the land and shall inherit my holy **m**. Is 57:13
forsake the LORD, who forget my holy **m**, Is 65:11
destroy in all my holy **m**," says the LORD. Is 65:25
dromedaries, to my holy **m** Jerusalem, Is 66:20
hunt them from every **m** and every hill, Jer 16:16
Do the **m** waters run dry, the cold Jer 18:14
and the **m** of the house a wooded Jer 26:18
From **m** to hill they have gone. Jer 50:6
I am against you, O destroying **m**, Jer 51:25
the crags, and make you a burnt **m**. Jer 51:25
city and stood on the **m** that is on the Ezk 11:23
will plant it on a high and lofty **m**. Ezk 17:22
On the **m** height of Israel will I plant Ezk 17:23
"For on my holy **m**, the mountain Ezk 20:40
holy mountain, the **m** height of Israel, Ezk 20:40
you; you were on the holy **m** of God; Ezk 28:14
as a profane thing from the **m** of God, Ezk 28:16
and on the **m** heights of Israel shall be Ezk 34:14
and set me down on a very high **m**, Ezk 40:2
on the top of the **m** all around shall be Ezk 43:12
image became a great **m** and filled the Dn 2:35
was cut from a **m** by no human hand, Dn 2:45
the sea and the glorious holy **m**. Dn 11:45
in Zion; sound an alarm on my holy **m**! Jl 2:1
your God, who dwells in Zion, my holy **m**. Jl 3:17
of Bashan, who are on the **m** of Samaria, Am 4:1
who feel secure on the **m** of Samaria, Am 6:1
For as you have drunk on my holy **m**, Ob 1:16
and the **m** of the house a wooded height. Mi 3:12
the latter days that the **m** of the house of Mi 4:1
"Come, let us go up to the **m** of the LORD, Mi 4:2
sea to sea and from **m** to mountain. Mi 7:12
sea to sea and from mountain to **m**. Mi 7:12
no longer be haughty in my holy **m**. Zep 3:11
Who are you, O great **m**? Before Zec 4:7
city, and the **m** of the LORD of hosts, Zec 8:3
of the LORD of hosts, the holy **m**. Zec 8:3
him to a very high **m** and showed him all Mt 4:8
Seeing the crowds, he went up on the **m**, Mt 5:1
When he came down from the **m**, great Mt 8:1
went up on the **m** by himself to pray. Mt 14:23
went up on the **m** and sat down there. Mt 15:29
led them up a high **m** by themselves. Mt 17:1
And as they were coming down the **m**, Mt 17:9
of mustard seed, you will say to this **m**, Mt 17:20
fig tree, but even if you say to this **m**, Mt 21:21
to the **m** to which Jesus had directed Mt 28:16
he went up on the **m** and called to him Mk 3:13
of them, he went up on the **m** to pray. Mk 6:46
and led them up a high **m** by themselves. Mk 9:2
And as they were coming down the **m**, he Mk 9:9
I say to you, whoever says to this **m**, Mk 11:23
and every **m** and hill shall be made low, Lk 3:5
these days he went out to the **m** to pray, Lk 6:12
and James and went up on the **m** to pray. Lk 9:28
when they had come down from the **m**, Lk 9:37
Our fathers worshiped on this **m**, but Jn 4:20
when neither on this **m** nor in Jerusalem Jn 4:21
Jesus went up on the **m**, and there he sat Jn 6:3
withdrew again to the **m** by himself. Jn 6:15
pattern that was shown you on the **m**." Heb 8:5
given, "If even a beast touches the **m**, Heb 12:20
for we were with him on the holy **m**. 2 Pt 1:18
and every **m** and island was removed Rv 6:14
trumpet, and something like a great **m**, Rv 8:8
away in the Spirit to a great, high **m**, Rv 21:10

MOUNTAINS (160)
that all the high **m** under the whole Gn 7:19
The waters prevailed above the **m**, Gn 7:20
the ark came to rest on the **m** of Ararat. Gn 8:4
of the month, the tops of the **m** were seen. Gn 8:5
offering on one of the **m** of which I shall Gn 22:2
kill them in the **m** and to consume Ex 32:12
the king of Moab from the eastern **m**: Nm 23:7
and camped in the **m** of Abarim, Nm 33:47
set out from the **m** of Abarim and Nm 33:48
on the high **m** and on the hills and Dt 12:2
sets on fire the foundations of the **m**. Dt 32:22
of the ancient **m** and the abundance Dt 33:15
The **m** quaked before the LORD, even Sinai Jgs 5:5
dens that are in the **m** and the caves and Jgs 6:2
mistake the shadow of the **m** for men." Jgs 9:36
up and down on the **m** and weep for my Jgs 11:37
and wept for her virginity on the **m**. Jgs 11:38
one who hunts a partridge in the **m**." 1 Sm 26:20
"You **m** of Gilboa, let there be no dew 2 Sm 1:21
strong wind tore the **m** and broke in 1 Kgs 19:11
"I saw all Israel scattered on the **m**, 1 Kgs 22:17
I have gone up the heights of the **m**, 2 Kgs 19:23
were swift as gazelles upon the **m**: 1 Chr 12:8
"I saw all Israel scattered on the **m**, 2 Chr 18:16
he who removes **m**, and they know it not, Jb 9:5
with the rain of the **m** and cling to the Jb 24:8
flinty rock and overturns **m** by the roots. Jb 28:9
He ranges the **m** as his pasture, and he Jb 39:8
For the **m** yield food for him where all Jb 40:20
also of the **m** trembled and quaked, Ps 18:7
Your righteousness is like the **m** of God; Ps 36:6
though the **m** be moved into the heart of Ps 46:2
though the **m** tremble at its swelling. Ps 46:3
who by his strength established the **m**, Ps 65:6
Let the **m** bear prosperity for the people, Ps 72:3
land; on the tops of the **m** may it wave; Ps 72:16
you, more majestic than the **m** of prey. Ps 76:4
The **m** were covered with its shade, the Ps 80:10
forest, as the flame sets the **m** ablaze, Ps 83:14
Before the **m** were brought forth, or ever Ps 90:2
earth; the heights of the **m** are his also. Ps 95:4
The **m** melt like wax before the LORD, Ps 97:5
garment; the waters stood above the **m**. Ps 104:6

The **m** rose, the valleys sank down to Ps 104:8
your lofty abode you water the **m**; Ps 104:13
The high **m** are for the wild goats; the Ps 104:18
who touches the **m** and they smoke! Ps 104:32
The **m** skipped like rams, the hills like Ps 114:4
O **m**, that you skip like rams? O hills, Ps 114:6
As the **m** surround Jerusalem, so the Ps 125:2
Hermon, which falls on the **m** of Zion! Ps 133:3
Touch the **m** so that they smoke! Ps 144:5
M and all hills, fruit trees and all Ps 148:9
Before the **m** had been shaped, before Prv 8:25
the vegetation of the **m** is gathered, Prv 27:25
Behold, he comes, leaping over the **m**, Sg 2:8
like a gazelle or a young stag on cleft **m**. Sg 2:17
the dens of lions, from the **m** of leopards. Sg 4:8
or a young stag on the **m** of spices. Sg 8:14
be established as the highest of the **m**, Is 2:2
against all the lofty **m**, and against all the Is 2:14
and struck them, and the **m** quaked; Is 5:25
a tumult is on the **m** as of a great Is 13:4
and on my **m** trample him underfoot; Is 14:25
like chaff on the **m** before the wind and Is 17:13
earth, when a signal is raised on the **m**, Is 18:3
birds of prey of the **m** and to the beasts of Is 18:6
down of walls and a shouting to the **m**. Is 22:5
rise; the **m** shall flow with their blood. Is 34:3
I have gone up the heights of the **m**, Is 37:24
and weighed the **m** in scales and Is 40:12
you shall thresh the **m** and crush them, Is 41:15
joy, let them shout from the top of the **m**. Is 42:11
I will lay waste **m** and hills, and dry up Is 42:15
break forth into singing, O **m**, O forest, Is 44:23
And I will make all my **m** a road, and Is 49:11
O earth; break forth, O **m**, into singing! Is 49:13
How beautiful upon the **m** are the feet of Is 52:7
For the **m** may depart and the hills be Is 54:10
the **m** and the hills before you shall Is 55:12
that the **m** might quake at your presence Is 64:1
down, the **m** quaked at your presence. Is 64:3
made offerings on the **m** and insulted me Is 65:7
and from Judah possessors of my **m**; Is 65:9
hills are a delusion, the orgies on the **m**. Jer 3:23
I looked on the **m**, and behold, they were Jer 4:24
take up weeping and wailing for the **m**, Jer 9:10
your feet stumble on the twilight **m**, Jer 13:16
on the **m** in the open country. Your Jer 17:3
plant vineyards on the **m** of Samaria; Jer 31:5
Tabor among the **m** and like Carmel Jer 46:18
astray, turning them away on the **m**. Jer 50:6
the heavens; they chased us on the **m**; Lam 4:19
set your face toward the **m** of Israel, Ezk 6:2
and say, You **m** of Israel, hear the word Ezk 6:3
says the Lord GOD to the **m** and the hills, Ezk 6:3
and not of joyful shouting on the **m**. Ezk 7:7
survivors escape, they will be on the **m**, Ezk 7:16
does not eat upon the **m** or lift up his Ezk 18:6
things), who even eats upon the **m**, Ezk 18:11
does not eat upon the **m** or lift up his Ezk 18:15
no more be heard on the **m** of Israel. Ezk 19:9
and people in you who eat on the **m**; Ezk 22:9
On the **m** and in all the valleys its Ezk 31:12
your flesh upon the **m** and fill the Ezk 32:5
land even to the **m** with your flowing Ezk 32:6
and the **m** of Israel shall be so desolate Ezk 33:28
wandered over all the **m** and on every Ezk 34:6
And I will feed them on the **m** of Israel, Ezk 34:13
they shall feed on the **m** of Israel. Ezk 34:14
And I will fill its **m** with the slain. On Ezk 35:8
you uttered against the **m** of Israel, Ezk 35:12
son of man, prophesy to the **m** of Israel, Ezk 36:1
of Israel, and say, O **m** of Israel, Ezk 36:1
therefore, O **m** of Israel, hear the word Ezk 36:4
the Lord GOD to the **m** and the hills, Ezk 36:4
of Israel, and say to the **m** and hills, Ezk 36:6
"But you, O **m** of Israel, shall shoot Ezk 36:8
nation in the land, on the **m** of Israel. Ezk 37:22
many peoples upon the **m** of Israel, Ezk 38:8
And the **m** shall be thrown down, and Ezk 38:20
a sword against Gog on all my **m**, Ezk 38:21
and lead you against the **m** of Israel. Ezk 39:2
You shall fall on the **m** of Israel, you Ezk 39:4
sacrificial feast on the **m** of Israel, Ezk 39:17
the tops of the **m** and burn offerings on Hos 4:13
their altars, and they shall say to the **m**, Hos 10:8
is spread upon the **m** a great and powerful Jl 2:2
of chariots, they leap on the tops of the **m**, Jl 2:5
in that day the **m** shall drip sweet wine, Jl 3:18
yourselves on the **m** of Samaria, Am 3:9
he who forms the **m** and creates the Am 4:13
the **m** shall drip sweet wine, and all the Am 9:13
at the roots of the **m**. I went down to the Jon 2:6
And the **m** will melt under him, and the Mi 1:4
be established as the highest of the **m**, Mi 4:1
Arise, plead your case before the **m**, and Mi 6:1
Hear, you **m**, the indictment of the LORD, Mi 6:2
The **m** quake before him; the hills melt; Na 1:5
Behold, upon the **m**, the feet of him who Na 1:15
are scattered on the **m** with none to Na 3:18
then the eternal **m** were scattered; Hab 3:6
The **m** saw you and writhed; the Hab 3:10
chariots came out from between two **m**. Zec 6:1
And the **m** were mountains of bronze. Zec 6:1
And the mountains were **m** of bronze. Zec 6:1
you shall flee to the valley of my **m**, Zec 14:5
the valley of the **m** shall reach to Azal. Zec 14:5
the ninety-nine on the **m** and go in Mt 18:12
let those who are in Judea flee to the **m**. Mt 24:16
tombs and on the **m** he was always Mk 5:5
let those who are in Judea flee to the **m**. Mk 13:14
let those who are in Judea flee to the **m**, Lk 21:21
Then they will begin to say to the **m**, Lk 23:30
if I have all faith, so as to remove **m**, 1 Cor 13:2
—wandering about in deserts and **m**, Heb 11:38
the caves and among the rocks of the **m**, Rv 6:15
calling to the **m** and rocks, "Fall on us Rv 6:16
fled away, and no **m** were to be found. Rv 16:20
seven heads are seven **m** on which the Rv 17:9

MOUNTAINTOPS (3)
men in ambush against him on the **m**, Jgs 9:25
down from the **m**!" And Zebul said Jgs 9:36
altars, on every high hill, on all the **m**, Ezk 6:13

MOUNTED (17)
hurried and rose and **m** a donkey, 1 Sm 25:42
young men, who **m** camels and fled. 1 Sm 30:17
arose, and each **m** his mule and fled. 2 Sm 13:29
the donkey for him and he **m** it. 1 Kgs 13:13
Then Jehu **m** his chariot and went to 2 Kgs 9:16
Rehoboam quickly **m** his chariot 2 Chr 10:18
and our guilt has **m** up to the heavens. Ezr 9:6
sent the letters by **m** couriers riding on Est 8:10
m on their swift horses that were used in Est 8:14
They **m** up to heaven; they went down Ps 107:26
And the cherubim **m** up. These were Ezk 10:15
these stood still, and when they **m** up, Ezk 10:17
mounted up, these **m** up with them, Ezk 10:17
up their wings and **m** up from the Ezk 10:19
is he, humble and **m** on a donkey, Zec 9:9
to you, humble, and **m** on a donkey, Mt 21:5
The number of **m** troops was twice ten Rv 9:16

MOUNTS (2)
that the eagle **m** up and makes Jb 39:27
Also provide **m** for Paul to ride and Acts 23:24

MOURN (39)
Abraham went in to **m** for Sarah and to Gn 23:2
on sackcloth and **m** before Abner." 2 Sm 3:31
to the city to **m** and to bury him. 1 Kgs 13:29
And all Israel shall **m** for him and 1 Kgs 14:13
do not **m** or weep." For all the people Neh 8:9
and those who **m** are lifted to safety. Jb 5:11
laugh; a time to **m**, and a time to dance; Eccl 3:4
And her gates shall lament and **m**; empty, Is 3:26
M, utterly stricken, for the raisin cakes of Is 16:7
The fishermen will **m** and lament, all Is 19:8
of our God; to comfort all who **m**; Is 61:2
to grant to those who **m** in Zion—to give Is 61:3
with her in joy, all you who **m** over her; Is 66:10
"For this the earth shall **m**, and the Jer 4:28
of my people is my heart wounded; I **m**, Jer 8:21
long will the land **m** and the grass of Jer 12:4
Moab; for the men of Kir-hareseth I **m**. Jer 48:31
The roads to Zion **m**, for none come to Lam 1:4
not the buyer rejoice, nor the seller **m**, Ezk 7:12
yet you shall not **m** or weep, nor shall Ezk 24:16
you shall not **m** or weep, but you shall Ezk 24:23
the calf of Beth-aven. Its people **m** for it, Hos 10:5
The priests **m**, the ministers of the LORD. Jl 1:9
the pastures of the shepherds **m**, and the Am 1:2
and everyone **m** who dwells in it, Am 8:8
and it melts, and all who dwell in it **m**, Am 9:5
those of you who **m** for the festival, Zep 3:18
have pierced, they shall **m** for him, Zec 12:10
The land shall **m**, each family by Zec 12:12
"Blessed are those who **m**, for they shall Mt 5:4
"Can the wedding guests **m** as long as Mt 9:15
we sang a dirge, and you did not **m**.' Mt 11:17
then all the tribes of the earth will **m**, Mt 24:30
laugh now, for you shall **m** and weep. Lk 6:25
arrogant! Ought you not rather to **m**? 1 Cor 5:2
and those who **m** as though they were 1 Cor 7:30
I may have to **m** over many of those 2 Cor 12:21
Be wretched and **m** and weep. Let your Jas 4:9
of the earth weep and **m** for her, Rv 18:11

MOURNED (16)
on his loins and **m** for his son many Gn 37:34
heard this disastrous word, they **m**, Ex 33:4
people of Israel, the people **m** greatly. Nm 14:39
and the people **m** because the LORD 1 Sm 6:19
all Israel assembled and **m** for him, 1 Sm 25:1
and all Israel had **m** for him and 1 Sm 28:3
And they **m** and wept and fasted until 2 Sm 1:12
And David **m** for his son day after 2 Sm 13:37
own grave. And they **m** over him, 1 Kgs 13:30
all Israel buried him and **m** for him, 1 Kgs 14:18
Ephraim their father **m** many days, 1 Chr 7:22
Judah and Jerusalem **m** for Josiah. 2 Chr 35:24
I sat down and wept and **m** for days, Neh 1:4
When you fasted and **m** in the fifth Zec 7:5
been with him, as they **m** and wept. Mk 16:10
dust on their heads as they wept and **m**, Rv 18:19

MOURNER (2)
"Pretend to be a **m** and put on 2 Sm 14:2
No one shall break bread for the **m**, to Jer 16:7

MOURNERS (3)
his troops, like one who comforts **m**. Jb 29:25
home, and the **m** go about the streets— Eccl 12:5
and restore comfort to him and his **m**, Is 57:18

MOURNERS' (1)
It shall be like **m** bread to them; all who Hos 9:4

MOURNING (56)
"The days of **m** for my father are Gn 27:41
son, **m**." Thus his father wept for him. Gn 37:35
and he made a **m** for his father seven Gn 50:10
saw the **m** on the threshing floor of Gn 50:11
is a grievous **m** by the Egyptians." Gn 50:11
not eaten of the tithe while I was **m**, Dt 26:14
days of weeping and **m** for Moses were Dt 34:8
And when the **m** was over, David 2 Sm 11:27
a mourner and put on **m** garments. 2 Sm 14:2
who has been **m** many days for 2 Sm 14:2
king is weeping and **m** for Absalom." 2 Sm 19:1
day was turned into **m** for all the 2 Sm 19:2
for he was **m** over the faithlessness of Ezr 10:6
there was great **m** among the Jews, Est 4:3
his house, **m** and with his head covered. Est 6:12
gladness and from **m** into a holiday; Est 9:22
My lyre is turned to **m**, and my pipe to Jb 30:31
have turned for me my **m** into dancing; Ps 30:11
his mother, I bowed down in **m**. Ps 35:14
and prostrate; all the day I go about **m**. Ps 38:6
Why do I go **m** because of the oppression Ps 42:9
do I go about **m** because of the Ps 43:2
to go to the house of **m** than to go to the Eccl 7:2
heart of the wise is in the house of **m**, Eccl 7:4
GOD of hosts called for weeping and **m**, Is 22:12
light, and your days of **m** shall be ended. Is 60:20
of ashes, the oil of gladness instead of **m**, Is 61:3
make **m** as for an only son, most bitter Jer 6:26
and call for the **m** women to come; Jer 9:17
Do not enter the house of **m**, or go to Jer 16:5
I will turn their **m** into joy; I will Jer 31:13
daughter of Judah **m** and lamentation. Lam 2:5
our dancing has been turned to **m**. Lam 5:15
it words of lamentation and **m** and woe. Ezk 2:10
not aloud; make no **m** for the dead. Ezk 24:17
in bitterness of soul, with bitter **m**. Ezk 27:31
cedar went down to Sheol I caused **m**; Ezk 31:15
days I, Daniel, was **m** for three weeks. Dn 10:2
with fasting, with weeping, and with **m**; Jl 2:12
call the farmers to **m** and to wailing Am 5:16
turn your feasts into **m** and all your Am 8:10
will make it like the **m** for an only son Am 8:10
like the jackals, and **m** like the ostriches. Mi 1:8
On that day the **m** in Jerusalem will be Zec 12:11
great as the **m** for Hadad-rimmon in Zec 12:11
of walking as in **m** before the LORD of Mal 3:14
And all were weeping and **m** for her, but Lk 8:52
women who were **m** and lamenting for Lk 23:27
mourn as though they were not **m**, 1 Cor 7:30
as he told us of your longing, your **m**, 2 Cor 7:7
laughter be turned to **m** and your joy to Jas 4:9
her a like measure of torment and **m**, Rv 18:7
I am no widow, and **m** I shall never see.' Rv 18:7
in a single day, death and **m** and famine, Rv 18:8
of her torment, weeping and **m** aloud, Rv 18:15
neither shall there be **m** nor crying nor Rv 21:4

MOURNS (11)
own body, and he **m** only for himself." Jb 14:22
The earth **m** and withers; the world Is 24:4
The wine **m**, the vine languishes, all the Is 24:7
The land **m** and languishes; Lebanon is Is 33:9
it a desolation; desolate, it **m** to me. Jer 12:11
"Judah **m** and her gates languish; her Jer 14:2
because of the curse the land **m**, and Jer 23:10
The king **m**, the prince is wrapped in Ezk 7:27
Therefore the land **m**, and all who dwell Hos 4:3
The fields are destroyed, the ground **m**, Jl 1:10
for him, as one **m** for an only child, Zec 12:10

MOUSE (1)
the mole rat, the **m**, the great lizard of Lv 11:29

MOUTH (350)
which has opened its **m** to receive your Gn 4:11
in her **m** was a freshly plucked olive Gn 8:11
The stone on the well's **m** was large, Gn 29:2
roll the stone from the **m** of the well and Gn 29:3
back in its place over the **m** of the well. Gn 29:3
the stone is rolled from the **m** of the well; Gn 29:8
from the well's **m** and watered the Gn 29:10
he saw his money in the **m** of his sack. Gn 42:27
here it is in the **m** of my sack!" At this Gn 42:28
was returned in the **m** of your sacks. Gn 43:12
man's money in the **m** of his sack, Gn 43:21
each man's money in the **m** of his sack, Gn 44:1
in the **m** of the sack of the youngest, Gn 44:2
see, that it is my **m** that speaks to you. Gn 45:12
said to him, "Who has made man's **m**? Ex 4:11
will be with your **m** and teach you what Ex 4:12
speak to him and put the words in his **m**, Ex 4:15
will be with your **m** and with his mouth Ex 4:15
mouth and with his **m** and will teach Ex 4:15
to the people, and he shall be your **m**, Ex 4:16
the law of the LORD may be in your **m**. Ex 13:9
With him I speak **m** to mouth, clearly, Nm 12:8
With him I speak mouth to **m**, clearly, Nm 12:8
ground opens its **m** and swallows Nm 16:30
earth opened its **m** and swallowed Nm 16:32
the LORD opened the **m** of the donkey, Nm 22:28
The word that God puts in my **m**, that Nm 22:38
put a word in Balaam's **m** and said, Nm 23:5
speak what the LORD puts in my **m**?" Nm 23:12
and put a word in his **m** and said, Nm 23:16
earth opened its **m** and swallowed Nm 26:10
to all that proceeds out of his **m**. Nm 30:2
word that comes from the **m** of the LORD. Dt 8:3
earth opened its **m** and swallowed them Dt 11:6
And I will put my words in his **m**, and Dt 18:18
what you have promised with your **m**. Dt 23:23
you. It is in your **m** and in your heart, Dt 30:14
and let the earth hear the words of my **m**. Dt 32:1
of the Law shall not depart from your **m**, Jos 1:8
neither shall any word go out of your **m**, Jos 6:10
large stones against the **m** of the cave Jos 10:18
"Open the **m** of the cave and bring Jos 10:22
large stones against the **m** of the cave, Jos 10:27
is the Salt Sea, to the **m** of the Jordan. Jos 15:5
the bay of the sea at the **m** of the Jordan. Jos 15:5
So according to the **m** of the LORD he Jos 17:4
said to him, "Where is your **m** now, Jgs 9:38
For I have opened my **m** to the LORD, Jgs 11:35
you have opened your **m** to the LORD; Jgs 11:36
to what has gone out of your **m**, Jgs 11:36
your hand on your **m** and come with Jgs 18:19
before the LORD, Eli observed her **m**. 1 Sm 1:12
My **m** derides my enemies, because I 1 Sm 2:1
let not arrogance come from your **m**; 1 Sm 2:3
but no one put his hand to his **m**, 1 Sm 14:26
and put his hand to his **m**, 1 Sm 14:27
him and delivered it out of his **m**. 1 Sm 17:35
for your own **m** has testified against 2 Sm 1:16
him." So Joab put the words in her **m**. 2 Sm 14:3
these words in the **m** of your servant. 2 Sm 14:19
over the well's **m** and scattered grain 2 Sm 17:19
is news in his **m**." And he drew 2 Sm 18:25
and devouring fire from his **m**; 2 Sm 22:9
he promised with his **m** to David my 1 Kgs 8:15
You spoke with your **m**, and with 1 Kgs 8:24
word of the LORD in your **m** is truth." 1 Kgs 17:24
and every **m** that has not kissed 1 Kgs 19:18
lying spirit in the **m** of all his 1 Kgs 22:22
lying spirit in the **m** of all these your 1 Kgs 22:23
child, putting his **m** on his mouth, 2 Kgs 4:34
child, putting his mouth on his **m**, 2 Kgs 4:34
in your nose and my bit in your **m**, 2 Kgs 19:28
he promised with his **m** to David my 2 Chr 6:4
You spoke with your **m**, and with 2 Chr 6:15
lying spirit in the **m** of all his 2 Chr 18:21
lying spirit in the **m** of these your 2 Chr 18:22
words of Neco from the **m** of God, 2 Chr 35:22
who spoke from the **m** of the LORD. 2 Chr 36:12
of the LORD by the **m** of Jeremiah, 2 Chr 36:21
LORD by the **m** of Jeremiah might 2 Chr 36:22
the LORD by the **m** of Jeremiah might be Ezr 1:1
manna from their **m** and gave them Neh 9:20
As the word left the **m** of the king, Est 7:8
this Job opened his **m** and cursed the day Jb 3:1
the sword of their **m** and from the hand Jb 5:15
have hope, and injustice shuts her **m**. Jb 5:16
"Therefore I will not restrain my **m**; I will Jb 7:11
and the words of your **m** be a great wind? Jb 8:2
He will yet fill your **m** with laughter, and Jb 8:21
right, my own **m** would condemn me; Jb 9:20
For your iniquity teaches your **m**, and Jb 15:5
Your own **m** condemns you, and not I; Jb 15:6
and bring such words out of your **m**? Jb 15:13
by the breath of his **m** he will depart. Jb 15:30
I could strengthen you with my **m**, and Jb 16:5
Men have gaped at me with their **m**; Jb 16:10
plead with him with my **m** for mercy. Jb 19:16
"Though evil is sweet in his **m**, though Jb 20:12
is loath to let it go and holds it in his **m**, Jb 20:13
appalled, and lay your hand over your **m**. Jb 21:5
Receive instruction from his **m**, and lay Jb 22:22
him and fill my **m** with arguments. Jb 23:4
the words of his **m** more than my Jb 23:12
talking and laid their hand on their **m**; Jb 29:9
their tongue stuck to the roof of their **m**. Jb 29:10
enticed, and my **m** has kissed my hand, Jb 31:27
(I have not let my **m** sin by asking for Jb 31:30
no answer in the **m** of these three men, Jb 32:5
Behold, I open my **m**; the tongue in my Jb 33:2
my mouth; the tongue in my **m** speaks. Jb 33:2
Job opens his **m** in empty talk; he Jb 35:16
the rumbling that comes from his **m**. Jb 37:2
I answer you? I lay my hand on my **m**. Jb 40:4
though Jordan rushes against his **m**. Jb 40:23
Out of his **m** go flaming torches; sparks Jb 41:19
and a flame comes forth from his **m**. Jb 41:21
For there is no truth in their **m**; their Ps 5:9
Out of the **m** of babes and infants, you Ps 8:2
His **m** is filled with cursing and deceit Ps 10:7
purposed that my **m** will not transgress. Ps 17:3
nostrils, and devouring fire from his **m**; Ps 18:8
the words of my **m** and the meditation Ps 19:14
Save me from the **m** of the lion! You Ps 22:21
and by the breath of his **m** all their host. Ps 33:6
his praise shall continually be in my **m**. Ps 34:1
The words of his **m** are trouble and Ps 36:3
The **m** of the righteous utters wisdom, Ps 37:30
a mute man who does not open his **m**. Ps 38:13
hear, and in whose **m** are no rebukes. Ps 38:14
I will guard my **m** with a muzzle, so long Ps 39:1
I do not open my **m**, for it is you who Ps 39:9
He put a new song in my **m**, a song of Ps 40:3
My **m** shall speak wisdom; the Ps 49:3
"You give your **m** free rein for evil, and Ps 50:19
lips, and my **m** will declare your praise. Ps 51:15
my prayer; give ear to the words of my **m**. Ps 54:2
and my **m** will praise you with joyful Ps 63:5
lips uttered and my **m** promised when I Ps 66:14
I cried to him with my **m**, and high Ps 66:17
me up, or the pit close its **m** over me. Ps 69:15
My **m** is filled with your praise, and with Ps 71:8
My **m** will tell of your righteous acts, of Ps 71:15
incline your ears to the words of my **m**! Ps 78:1
I will open my **m** in a parable; I will utter Ps 78:2
Open your **m** wide, and I will fill it. Ps 81:10
with my **m** I will make known your Ps 89:1
glad, and all wickedness shuts its **m**. Ps 107:42
With my **m** I will give great thanks to Ps 109:30
lips I declare all the rules of your **m**. Ps 119:13
the word of truth utterly out of my **m**, Ps 119:43
The law of your **m** is better to me than Ps 119:72
I may keep the testimonies of your **m**. Ps 119:88
taste, sweeter than honey to my **m**! Ps 119:103
I open my **m** and pant, because I long Ps 119:131
Then our **m** was filled with laughter, Ps 126:2
my tongue stick to the roof of my **m**, Ps 137:6
they have heard the words of your **m**, Ps 138:4
Set a guard, O LORD, over my **m**; keep Ps 141:3
bones be scattered at the **m** of Sheol. Ps 141:7
My **m** will speak the praise of the LORD, Ps 145:21
from his **m** come knowledge and Prv 2:6
not turn away from the words of my **m**. Prv 4:5
do not depart from the words of my **m**. Prv 5:7
if you are snared in the words of your **m**, Prv 6:2
mouth, caught in the words of your **m**, Prv 6:2
and be attentive to the words of my **m**. Prv 7:24
for my **m** will utter truth; wickedness is Prv 8:7
All the words of my **m** are righteous; Prv 8:8
but the **m** of the wicked conceals Prv 10:6
The **m** of the righteous is a fountain of Prv 10:11
but the **m** of the wicked conceals Prv 10:11
but the **m** of a fool brings ruin near. Prv 10:14
The **m** of the righteous brings forth Prv 10:31
is acceptable, but the **m** of the wicked, Prv 10:32
With his **m** the godless man would Prv 11:9
but by the **m** of the wicked it is Prv 11:11
but the **m** of the upright delivers them. Prv 12:6
the fruit of his **m** a man is satisfied Prv 12:14
the fruit of his **m** a man eats what Prv 13:2
Whoever guards his **m** preserves his Prv 13:3
By the **m** of a fool comes a rod for his Prv 14:3
but the **m** of the wicked pours out evil Prv 15:28
king; his **m** does not sin in judgment. Prv 16:10
works for him; his **m** urges him on. Prv 16:26
words of a man's **m** are deep waters; Prv 18:4
into a fight, and his **m** invites a beating. Prv 18:6
A fool's **m** is his ruin, and his lips are a Prv 18:7
fruit of a man's **m** his stomach is Prv 18:20
will not even bring it back to his **m**. Prv 19:24
and the **m** of the wicked devours Prv 19:28
but afterward his **m** will be full of Prv 20:17
Whoever keeps his **m** and his tongue Prv 21:23
The **m** of forbidden women is a deep Prv 22:14
fool; in the gate he does not open his **m**. Prv 24:7
useless, is a proverb in the **m** of fools. Prv 26:7
drunkard is a proverb in the **m** of fools. Prv 26:9
him out to bring it back to his **m**. Prv 26:15
and a flattering **m** works ruin. Prv 26:28
praise you, and not your own **m**; Prv 27:2
she eats and wipes her **m** and says, "I Prv 30:20
evil, put your hand on your **m**. Prv 30:32
Open your **m** for the mute, for the Prv 31:8
Open your **m**, judge righteously, defend Prv 31:9
She opens her **m** with wisdom, and the Prv 31:26
Be not rash with your **m**, nor let your Eccl 5:2
Let not your **m** lead you into sin, and do Eccl 5:6
All the toil of man is for his **m**, yet his Eccl 6:7
of a wise man's **m** win him favor, Eccl 10:12
of the words of his **m** is foolishness, Eccl 10:13
Let him kiss me with the kisses of his **m**! Sg 1:2
like a scarlet thread, and your **m** is lovely. Sg 4:3
His **m** is most sweet, and he is altogether Sg 5:16
and your **m** like the best wine. It goes Sg 7:9
sword; for the **m** of the LORD has spoken." Is 1:20
and opened its **m** beyond measure, Is 5:14
And he touched my **m** and said: "Behold, Is 6:7
on the west devour Israel with open **m**. Is 9:12
and an evildoer, and every **m** speaks folly. Is 9:17
a wing or opened the **m** or chirped." Is 10:14
strike the earth with the rod of his **m**, Is 11:4
draw near with their **m** and honor me Is 29:13
For the **m** of the LORD has commanded, Is 34:16
in your nose and my bit in your **m**, Is 37:29
for the **m** of the LORD has spoken." Is 40:5
from my **m** has gone out in Is 45:23
went out from my **m** and I announced Is 48:3
He made my **m** like a sharp sword; in the Is 49:2
my words in your **m** and covered you in Is 51:16
he was afflicted, yet he opened not his **m**; Is 53:7
shearers is silent, so he opened not his **m**. Is 53:7
and there was no deceit in his **m**. Is 53:9
my word be that goes out from my **m**; Is 55:11
do you open your **m** wide and stick out Is 57:4
for the **m** of the LORD has spoken." Is 58:14
and my words that I have put in your **m**, Is 59:21
mouth, shall not depart out of your **m**, Is 59:21
mouth, or out of the **m** of your offspring, Is 59:21
or out of the **m** of your children's Is 59:21
a new name that the **m** of the LORD will Is 62:2
LORD put out his hand and touched my **m**. Jer 1:9
"Behold, I have put my words in your **m**. Jer 1:9
I am making my words in your **m** a fire, Jer 5:14
with his **m** each speaks peace to his Jer 9:8
To whom has the **m** of the LORD spoken, Jer 9:12
let your ear receive the word of his **m**; Jer 9:20
are near in their **m** and far from their Jer 12:2
is worthless, you shall be as my **m**. Jer 15:19
own minds, not from the **m** of the LORD. Jer 23:16
be invoked by the **m** of any man of Jer 44:26
nests in the sides of the **m** of a gorge. Jer 48:28
take out of his **m** what he has Jer 51:44
let him put his **m** in the dust—there Lam 3:29
Is it not from the **m** of the Most High Lam 3:38
sticks to the roof of its **m** for thirst; Lam 4:4
open your **m** and eat what I give you." Ezk 2:8
So I opened my **m**, and he gave me this Ezk 3:2
it, and it was in my **m** as sweet as honey. Ezk 3:3
you hear a word from my **m**, Ezk 3:17
your tongue cling to the roof of your **m**, Ezk 3:26
I speak with you, I will open your **m**, Ezk 3:27
nor has tainted meat come into my **m**." Ezk 4:14
a byword in your **m** in the day of Ezk 16:56
never open your **m** again because of Ezk 16:63
rams, to open the **m** with murder, Ezk 21:22
On that day your **m** will be opened to Ezk 24:27
you hear a word from my **m**, Ezk 33:7
he had opened my **m** by the time the Ezk 33:22
in the morning, so my **m** was opened, Ezk 33:22
yourselves against me with your **m**, Ezk 35:13
the words were still in the king's **m**, Dn 4:31
brought and laid on the **m** of the den, Dn 6:17
It had three ribs in its **m** between its teeth; Dn 7:5
of a man, and a **m** speaking great things. Dn 7:8
had eyes and a **m** that spoke great Dn 7:20
no meat or wine entered my **m**, Dn 10:3
lips. Then I opened my **m** and spoke. Dn 10:16
the names of the Baals from her **m**, Hos 2:17
I have slain them by the words of my **m**, Hos 6:5
the sweet wine, for it is cut off from your **m**. Jl 1:5
shepherd rescues from the **m** of the lion Am 3:12
for the **m** of the LORD of hosts has spoken. Mi 4:4
and their tongue is deceitful in their **m**. Mi 6:12
the doors of your **m** from her who lies Mi 7:5
shaken they fall into the **m** of the eater. Na 3:12

be found in their **m** a deceitful tongue. Zep 3:13
these words from the **m** of the prophets Zec 8:9
I will take away its blood from its **m**, and Zec 9:7
True instruction was in his **m**, and no Mal 2:6
should seek instruction from his **m**, Mal 2:7
word that comes from the **m** of God.'" Mt 4:4
And he opened his **m** and taught them, Mt 5:2
abundance of the heart the **m** speaks. Mt 12:34
prophet: "I will open my **m** in parables; Mt 13:35
what goes into the **m** that defiles a Mt 15:11
a person, but what comes out of the **m**; Mt 15:11
goes into the **m** passes into the Mt 15:17
comes out of the **m** proceeds from the Mt 15:18
when you open its **m** you will find a Mt 17:27
"'Out of the **m** of infants and nursing Mt 21:16
and rolled about, foaming at the **m**. Mk 9:20
And immediately his **m** was opened and Lk 1:64
he spoke by the **m** of his holy prophets Lk 1:70
words that were coming from his **m**. Lk 4:22
abundance of the heart his **m** speaks. Lk 6:45
him so that he foams at the **m**; Lk 9:39
for I will give you a **m** and wisdom, Lk 21:15
a hyssop branch and held it to his **m**. Jn 19:29
beforehand by the **m** of David Acts 1:16
God foretold by the **m** of all the Acts 3:18
God spoke by the **m** of his holy Acts 3:21
who through the **m** of our father Acts 4:25
shearer is silent, so he opens not his **m**. Acts 8:32
Then Philip opened his **m**, and Acts 8:35
So Peter opened his **m** and said: Acts 10:34
or unclean has ever entered my **m**.' Acts 11:8
that by my **m** the Gentiles should hear Acts 15:7
you the same things by word of **m**. Acts 15:27
when Paul was about to open his **m**, Acts 18:14
One and to hear a voice from his **m**; Acts 22:14
stood by him to strike him on the **m**. Acts 23:2
"Their **m** is full of curses and Rom 3:14
law, so that every **m** may be stopped, Rom 3:19
in your **m** and in your heart" (that is, Rom 10:8
you confess with your **m** that Jesus is Rom 10:9
and with the **m** one confesses and is Rom 10:10
in opening my **m** boldly to proclaim Eph 6:19
slander, and obscene talk from your **m**. Col 3:8
the breath of his **m** and bring to 2 Thes 2:8
it. So I was rescued from the lion's **m**. 2 Tm 4:17
From the same **m** come blessing and Jas 3:10
sin, neither was deceit found in his **m**. 1 Pt 2:22
from his **m** came a sharp two-edged Rv 1:16
against them with the sword of my **m**. Rv 2:16
hot nor cold, I will spit you out of my **m**. Rv 3:16
but in your **m** it will be sweet as honey." Rv 10:9
It was sweet as honey in my **m**, but Rv 10:10
pours from their **m** and consumes their Rv 11:5
a river out of his **m** after the woman, Rv 12:15
earth opened its **m** and swallowed the Rv 12:16
that the dragon had poured from his **m**. Rv 12:16
bear's, and its **m** was like a lion's mouth. Rv 13:2
bear's, and its mouth was like a lion's **m**. Rv 13:2
was given a **m** uttering haughty and Rv 13:5
It opened its **m** to utter blasphemies Rv 13:6
and in their **m** no lie was found, for they Rv 14:5
coming out of the **m** of the dragon and Rv 16:13
and out of the **m** of the beast and Rv 16:13
and out of the **m** of the false prophet, Rv 16:13
From his **m** comes a sharp sword with Rv 19:15
that came from the **m** of him who was Rv 19:21

MOUTHS (40)
that we found in the **m** of our sacks we Gn 44:8
Put it in their **m**, that this song may be Dt 31:19
unforgotten in the **m** of their offspring). Dt 31:21
lapped, putting their hands to their **m**, Jgs 7:6
and they opened their **m** as for the Jb 29:23
with their **m** they speak arrogantly. Ps 17:10
see me mock me; they make **m** at me; Ps 22:7
they open wide their **m** at me, like a Ps 22:13
They open wide their **m** against me; Ps 35:21
O God, break the teeth in their **m**; tear Ps 58:6
bellowing with their **m** with swords in Ps 59:7
For the sin of their **m**, the words of their Ps 59:12
They bless with their **m**, but inwardly Ps 62:4
exult, for the **m** of liars will be stopped. Ps 63:11
They set their **m** against the heavens, Ps 73:9
while the food was still in their **m**, Ps 78:30
But they flattered him with their **m**; Ps 78:36
wicked and deceitful **m** are opened Ps 109:2
They have **m**, but do not speak; eyes, Ps 115:5
They have **m**, but do not speak; they Ps 135:16
nor is there any breath in their **m**. Ps 135:17
whose **m** speak lies and whose right Ps 144:8
whose **m** speak lies and whose right Ps 144:11
but the **m** of fools pour out folly. Prv 15:2
but the **m** of fools feed on folly. Prv 15:14
shall shut their **m** because of him; Is 52:15
your wives have declared with your **m**, Jer 44:25
our enemies open their **m** against us; Lam 3:46
with lustful talk in their **m** they act; Ezk 33:31
I will rescue my sheep from their **m**, Ezk 34:10
sent his angel and shut the lions' **m**, Dn 6:22
him who puts nothing into their **m**. Mi 3:5
they shall lay their hands on their **m**; Mi 7:16
and their tongues will rot in their **m**. Zec 14:12
corrupting talk come out of your **m**, Eph 4:29
promises, stopped the **m** of lions, Heb 11:33
we put bits into the **m** of horses so that Jas 3:3
smoke and sulfur came out of their **m**. Rv 9:17
and sulfur coming out of their **m**. Rv 9:18
the horses is in their **m** and in their tails, Rv 9:19

MOVE (19)
father's hand to **m** it from Ephraim's Gn 48:17
"You shall not **m** your neighbor's Dt 19:14
let no man **m** his bones." So they let 2 Kgs 23:18
he could not **m** about freely because 1 Chr 12:1
Some **m** landmarks; they seize flocks Jb 24:2
it, and all that **m** in the field feed on it. Ps 80:13
Do not **m** the ancient landmark that Prv 22:28
Do not **m** an ancient landmark or Prv 23:10
all the living who **m** about under the Eccl 4:15
to set up an idol that will not **m**. Is 40:20
it stands there; it cannot **m** from its place. Is 46:7
hammer and nails so that it cannot **m**. Jer 10:4
like those who **m** the landmark; Hos 5:10
half of the Mount shall **m** northward, Zec 14:4
this mountain, '**M** from here to there,' Mt 17:20
'Move from here to there,' and it will **m**, Mt 17:20
are not willing to **m** them with their Mt 23:4
may say to you, 'Friend, **m** up higher.' Lk 14:10
him we live and **m** and have our Acts 17:28

MOVED (46)
And all flesh died that **m** on the earth, Gn 7:21
From there he **m** to the hill country on Gn 12:8
cities of the valley and **m** his tent as far Gn 13:12
So Abram **m** his tent and came and Gn 13:18
And he **m** from there and dug another Gn 26:22
And they **m** on from Succoth and Ex 13:20
the host of Israel **m** and went behind Ex 14:19
the pillar of cloud **m** from before them Ex 14:19
the people of Israel **m** on from the Ex 17:1
him, and everyone whose spirit **m** him, Ex 35:21
whose heart **m** them to bring anything Ex 35:29
Not a man **m** his tongue against any of Jos 10:21
For the LORD was **m** to pity by their Jgs 2:18
the son of Ebed **m** into Shechem with Jgs 9:26
the men in ambush **m** out and struck Jgs 20:37
only her lips **m**, and her voice was not 1 Sm 1:13
And the Philistine **m** forward and 1 Sm 17:41
places where I have **m** with all the 2 Sm 7:7
the king was deeply **m** and went up 2 Sm 18:33
is established; it shall never be **m**. 1 Chr 16:30
places where I have **m** with all Israel, 1 Chr 17:6
and God was **m** by his entreaty and 2 Chr 33:13
and how God was **m** by his entreaty, 2 Chr 33:19
He says in his heart, "I shall not be **m**; Ps 10:6
who does these things shall never be **m**. Ps 15:5
love of the Most High he shall not be **m**. Ps 21:7
in my prosperity, "I shall never be **m**." Ps 30:6
the mountains be **m** into the heart Ps 46:2
is in the midst of her; she shall not be **m**; Ps 46:5
will never permit the righteous to be **m**. Ps 55:22
they **m** him to jealousy with their idols. Ps 78:58
world is established; it shall never be **m**. Ps 93:1
world is established; it shall never be **m**; Ps 96:10
so that it should never be **m**. Ps 104:5
For the righteous will never be **m**; he Ps 112:6
He will not let your foot be **m**; he who Ps 121:3
like Mount Zion, which cannot be **m**, Ps 125:1
root of the righteous will never be **m**. Prv 12:3
there was none that **m** a wing or opened Is 10:14
it with nails so that it cannot be **m**. Is 41:7
quaking, and all the hills **m** to and fro. Jer 4:24
the king of the south, **m** with rage, Dn 11:11
M with pity, he stretched out his hand Mk 1:41
he was deeply **m** in his spirit and greatly Jn 11:33
Then Jesus, deeply **m** again, came to the Jn 11:38
that no one be **m** by these afflictions. 1 Thes 3:3

MOVES (9)
and every living creature that **m**, Gn 1:21
every living thing that **m** on the earth." Gn 1:28
bird, everything that **m** on the earth, Gn 8:19
every man whose heart **m** him you shall Ex 25:2
living creature that **m** through the Lv 11:46
be anyone who **m** his neighbor's Dt 27:17
passes by me, and I see him not; he **m** on, Jb 9:11
hills, and all that **m** in the field is mine. Ps 50:11
the seas and everything that **m** in them. Ps 69:34

MOVING (4)
Every **m** thing that lives shall be food for Gn 9:3
but I have been **m** about in a tent for 2 Sm 7:6
it shone, or the moon **m** in splendor, Jb 31:26
the appearance of torches **m** to and fro Ezk 1:13

MOWED (1)
wages of the laborers who **m** your fields, Jas 5:4

MOWINGS (1)
was the latter growth after the king's **m**. Am 7:1

MOWN (1)
he be like rain that falls on the **m** grass, Ps 72:6

MOZA (5)
bore Haran, **M**, and Gazez; 1 Chr 2:46
and Zimri. Zimri fathered **M**. 1 Chr 8:36
M fathered Binea; Raphah was his 1 Chr 8:37
and Zimri. And Zimri fathered **M**. 1 Chr 9:42
M fathered Binea, and Rephaiah was 1 Chr 9:43

MOZAH (1)
Mizpeh, Chephirah, **M**, Jos 18:26

MUCH (200)
things. And the men were very **m** afraid. Gn 20:8
us, for you are **m** mightier than we." Gn 26:16
was five times as **m** as any of theirs. Gn 43:34
sacks with food, as **m** as they can carry, Gn 44:1
up with them, and very **m** livestock, Ex 12:38
will be twice as **m** as they gather daily." Ex 16:5
it, each one of you, as **m** as he can eat. Ex 16:16
whoever gathered **m** had nothing left Ex 16:18
of them gathered as **m** as he could eat. Ex 16:18
gathered it, each as **m** as he could eat; Ex 16:21
day they gathered twice as **m** bread, Ex 16:22
of sweet-smelling cinnamon half as **m**, Ex 30:23
"The people bring **m** more than enough Ex 36:5
if he is poor and cannot afford so **m**, Lv 14:21
not so **m** as for the sole of the foot to tread Dt 2:5
that you have **m** livestock) shall remain Dt 3:19
any of your towns, as **m** as you desire, Dt 12:15
You shall carry **m** seed into the field Dt 28:38
the LORD. How **m** more after my death! Dt 31:27
there remains yet very **m** land to possess. Jos 13:1
to your tents with **m** wealth and with Jos 22:8
much wealth and with very **m** livestock, Jos 22:8
bronze, and iron, and with **m** clothing. Jos 22:8
and then take as **m** as you wish," he 1 Sm 2:16
How **m** better if the people had eaten 1 Sm 14:30
fled from him and were **m** afraid. 1 Sm 17:24
Saul's son, delighted **m** in David. 1 Sm 19:1
How **m** more today will their vessels 1 Sm 21:5
to heart and was **m** afraid of Achish 1 Sm 21:12
nothing of all this, **m** or little." 1 Sm 22:15
how **m** more then if we go to Keilah 1 Sm 23:3
morning I leave so **m** as one male of 1 Sm 25:22
been left to Nabal so **m** as one male." 1 Sm 25:34
a raid, bringing **m** spoil with them. 2 Sm 3:22
How **m** more, when wicked men have 2 Sm 4:11
King David took very **m** bronze. 2 Sm 8:8
little, I would add to you as **m** more. 2 Sm 12:8
was no one so **m** to be praised for 2 Sm 14:25
how **m** more now may this 2 Sm 16:11
how **m** less this house that I have 1 Kgs 8:27
timber and gold, as **m** as he desired, 1 Kgs 9:11
spices and very **m** gold and precious 1 Kgs 10:2
and mules, so **m** year by year. 1 Kgs 10:25
a little, but Jehu will serve him **m**. 2 Kgs 10:18
saw that there was **m** money in the 2 Kgs 12:10
He did **m** evil in the sight of the LORD, 2 Kgs 21:6
shed very **m** innocent blood, 2 Kgs 21:16
'You have shed **m** blood and have 1 Chr 22:8
you have shed so **m** blood before me 1 Chr 22:8
weighing, for there is so **m** of it; 1 Chr 22:14
how **m** less this house that I have 2 Chr 6:18
spices and very **m** gold and precious 2 Chr 9:1
horses, and mules, so **m** year by year. 2 Chr 9:24
of Judah carried away very **m** spoil. 2 Chr 14:13
for there was **m** plunder in them. 2 Chr 14:14
days in taking the spoil, it was so **m**. 2 Chr 20:25
saw that there was **m** money in it, 2 Chr 24:11
is able to give you **m** more than this." 2 Chr 25:9
people in them and took **m** spoil. 2 Chr 25:13
the LORD and did **m** building on the 2 Chr 27:3
They also took **m** spoil from them 2 Chr 28:8
of Assyria come and find **m** water?" 2 Chr 32:4
How **m** less will your God deliver 2 Chr 32:15
He did **m** evil in the sight of the LORD, 2 Chr 33:6
and salt without prescribing how **m**. Ezr 7:22
of the heart." Then I was very **m** afraid. Neh 2:2
is failing. There is too **m** rubble. Neh 4:10
how **m** more those who dwell in houses Jb 4:19
is man, that you make so **m** of him, Jb 7:17
how **m** less one who is abominable and Jb 15:16
and if I forbear, how **m** of it leaves me? Jb 16:6
how **m** less man, who is a maggot, and Jb 25:6
or because my hand had found **m**, Jb 31:25
How **m** less when you say that you do Jb 35:14
does not take **m** note of transgression, Jb 35:15
gave Job twice as **m** as he had before. Jb 42:10

are they than gold, even **m** fine gold; Ps 19:10
testimonies I delight as **m** as in all Ps 119:14
With **m** seductive speech she persuades Prv 7:21
how **m** more the wicked and the Prv 11:31
ground of the poor would yield **m** food, Prv 13:23
of the righteous there is **m** treasure, Prv 15:6
how **m** more the hearts of the children Prv 15:11
How **m** better to get wisdom than gold! Prv 16:16
how **m** more do his friends go far from Prv 19:7
m less for a slave to rule over princes. Prv 19:10
how **m** more when he brings it with Prv 21:27
It is not good to eat **m** honey, nor is it Prv 25:27
to anger causes **m** transgression. Prv 29:22
For in **m** wisdom is much vexation, Eccl 1:18
For in much wisdom is **m** vexation, Eccl 1:18
For a dream comes with **m** business, Eccl 5:3
of a laborer, whether he eats little or **m**, Eccl 5:12
in darkness in **m** vexation and Eccl 5:17
For he will not **m** remember the days Eccl 5:20
However **m** man may toil in seeking, Eccl 8:17
war, but one sinner destroys **m** good. Eccl 9:18
and **m** study is a weariness of the Eccl 12:12
How **m** better is your love than wine, and Sg 4:10
wash yourself with lye and use **m** soap, Jer 2:22
How **m** you go about, changing your Jer 2:36
How **m** more when I send upon Ezk 14:21
it was used for nothing. How **m** less, Ezk 15:5
eagle with great wings and **m** plumage, Ezk 17:7
and held in derision, for it contains **m**; Ezk 23:32
the lambs shall be as **m** as he is able, Ezk 46:5
and with the lambs as **m** as he is able, Ezk 46:7
with the lambs as **m** as one is able Ezk 46:11
was **m** distressed and set his mind to Dn 6:14
and it was told, 'Arise, devour **m** flesh.' Dn 7:5
hand from their left, and also **m** cattle?" Jon 4:11
You have sown **m**, and harvested little. Hg 1:6
You looked for **m**, and behold, it came to Hg 1:9
the oven, will he not **m** more clothe you, Mt 6:30
how **m** more will your Father who is in Mt 7:11
how **m** more will they malign those of Mt 10:25
Of how **m** more value is a man than a Mt 12:12
ground, where they did not have **m** soil, Mt 13:5
make him twice as **m** a child of hell Mt 23:15
over a little; I will set you over **m**. Mt 25:21
over a little; I will set you over **m**. Mt 25:23
for I have suffered **m** because of him Mt 27:19
ground, where it did not have **m** soil, Mk 4:5
and tell them how **m** the Lord has done Mk 5:19
in the Decapolis how **m** Jesus had done Mk 5:20
who had suffered **m** under many Mk 5:26
is **m** more than all whole burnt Mk 12:33
many, are forgiven—for she loved **m**. Lk 7:47
and declare how **m** God has done for Lk 8:39
the whole city how **m** Jesus had done for Lk 8:39
Martha was distracted with **m** serving. Lk 10:40
how **m** more will the heavenly Father Lk 11:13
Of how **m** more value are you than the Lk 12:24
oven, how **m** more will he clothe you, Lk 12:28
Everyone to whom **m** was given, of Lk 12:48
was given, of him **m** will be required, Lk 12:48
from him to whom they entrusted **m**, Lk 12:48
first, 'How **m** do you owe my master?' Lk 16:5
to another, 'And how **m** do you owe?' Lk 16:7
in a very little is also faithful in **m**, Lk 16:10
in a very little is also dishonest in **m**. Lk 16:10
down." Now there was **m** grass in the Jn 6:10
So also the fish, as **m** as they wanted. Jn 6:11
And there was **m** muttering about him Jn 7:12
I have **m** to say about you and much to Jn 8:26
much to say about you and **m** to judge, Jn 8:26
alone; but if it dies, it bears **m** fruit. Jn 12:24
I will no longer talk **m** with you, for the Jn 14:30
and I in him, he it is that bears **m** fruit, Jn 15:5
that you bear **m** fruit and so prove to be Jn 15:8
sold the land for so **m**." And she said, Acts 5:8
so much." And she said, "Yes, for so **m**." Acts 5:8
So there was **m** joy in that city. Acts 8:8
how **m** evil he has done to your saints Acts 9:13
will show him how **m** he must suffer Acts 9:16
And after there had been **m** debate, Acts 15:7
brought her owners **m** gain by Acts 16:16
had given them **m** encouragement, Acts 20:2
And there was **m** weeping on the part Acts 20:37
"Since through you we enjoy **m** peace, Acts 24:2
Since **m** time had passed, and the Acts 27:9
will be with injury and **m** loss, Acts 27:10
M in every way. To begin with, the Jews Rom 3:2
m more shall we be saved by him from Rom 5:9
God by the death of his Son, **m** more, Rom 5:10
m more have the grace of God and the Rom 5:15
m more will those who receive the Rom 5:17
has endured with **m** patience vessels of Rom 9:22
how **m** more will their full inclusion Rom 11:12
olive tree, how **m** more will these, Rom 11:24
and in fear and **m** trembling, 1 Cor 2:3
we are to judge angels? How **m** more, 1 Cor 6:3
is it too **m** if we reap material things 1 Cor 9:11
to you out of **m** affliction and anguish 2 Cor 2:4
m more will what is permanent have 2 Cor 3:11
"Whoever gathered **m** had nothing 2 Cor 8:15
I boast a little too **m** of our authority, 2 Cor 10:8
They make **m** of you, but for no good Gal 4:17
you out, that you may make **m** of them. Gal 4:17
always good to be made **m** of for a good Gal 4:18
are **m** more bold to speak the word Phil 1:14
in my presence but **m** more in my Phil 2:12
you received the word in **m** affliction, 1 Thes 1:6
of God in the midst of **m** conflict. 1 Thes 2:2
not addicted to **m** wine, 1 Tm 3:8
not slanderers or slaves to **m** wine. Ti 2:3
For I have derived **m** joy and comfort Phlm 1:7
to me, but how **m** more to you, Phlm 1:16
having become as **m** superior to angels Heb 1:4
we must pay **m** closer attention to Heb 2:1
than Moses—as **m** more glory as the Heb 3:3
About this we have **m** to say, and it is Heb 5:11
that is as **m** more excellent than Heb 8:6
how **m** more will the blood of Christ, Heb 9:14
How **m** worse punishment, do you Heb 10:29
Shall we not **m** more be subject to the Heb 12:9
m less will we escape if we reject him Heb 12:25
Though I have **m** to write to you, I 2 Jn 1:12
I had **m** to write to you, but I would 3 Jn 1:13
and he was given **m** incense to offer with Rv 8:3

MUD (10)

was no water in the cistern, but only **m**, Jer 38:6
only mud, and Jeremiah sank in the **m**. Jer 38:6
now that your feet are sunk in the **m**, Jer 38:22
and fine gold like the **m** of the streets. Zec 9:3
trampling the foe in the **m** of the streets; Zec 10:5
the ground and made **m** with the saliva. Jn 9:6
he anointed the man's eyes with the **m** Jn 9:6
called Jesus made **m** and anointed my Jn 9:11
when Jesus made the **m** and opened his Jn 9:14
he said to them, "He put **m** on my eyes, Jn 9:15

MUDDIED (2)

Like a **m** spring or a polluted fountain Prv 25:26
what you have **m** with your feet? Ezk 34:19

MUDDY (1)

that you must **m** the rest of the water Ezk 34:18

MULBERRY (1)

seed, you could say to this **m** tree, Lk 17:6

MULE (8)

and each mounted his **m** and fled. 2 Sm 13:29
Absalom was riding on his **m**, and 2 Sm 18:9
and the **m** went under the thick 2 Sm 18:9
while the **m** that was under him went 2 Sm 18:9
Solomon my son ride on my own **m**, 1 Kgs 1:33
on King David's **m** and brought him 1 Kgs 1:38
they had him ride on the king's **m**. 1 Kgs 1:44
Be not like a horse or a **m**, without Ps 32:9

MULES (9)

myrrh, spices, horses, and **m**, 1 Kgs 10:25
and save the horses and **m** alive, 1 Kgs 18:5
on camels and on **m** and on oxen, 1 Chr 12:40
myrrh, spices, horses, and **m**, 2 Chr 9:24
Their horses were 736, their **m** were 245, Ezr 2:66
Their horses were 736, their **m** 245, Neh 7:68
in litters and on **m** and on dromedaries, Is 66:20
war horses, and **m** for your wares. Ezk 27:14
plague shall fall on the horses, the **m**, Zec 14:15

MULES' (1)

to your servant two **m** load of earth, 2 Kgs 5:17

MULTIPLIED (35)

in it, and were fruitful and **m** greatly. Gn 47:27
they **m** and grew exceedingly strong, so Ex 1:7
the more they **m** and the more they Ex 1:12
And the people **m** and grew very strong. Ex 1:20
my wonders may be **m** in the land of Ex 11:9
The LORD your God has **m** you, and Dt 1:10
silver and gold is **m** and all that you Dt 8:13
is multiplied and all that you have is **m**, Dt 8:13
your children may be **m** in the land Dt 11:21
their livestock had **m** in the land 1 Chr 5:9
You **m** their children as the stars of Neh 9:23
If his children are **m**, it is for the sword, Jb 27:14
And if your transgressions are **m**, what Jb 35:6
You have **m**, O LORD my God, your Ps 40:5
For by me your days will be **m**, and Prv 9:11
You have **m** the nation; you have Is 9:3
to the king with oil and **m** your perfumes; Is 57:9
our transgressions are **m** before you, Is 59:12
And when you have **m** and increased in Jer 3:16
and he has **m** in the daughter of Judah Lam 2:5
You have **m** your slain in this city and Ezk 11:6
You **m** your whoring also with the Ezk 16:29
mouth, and **m** your words against me; Ezk 35:13
dwell in all the earth: Peace be **m** to you! Dn 4:1
in all the earth: "Peace be **m** to you. Dn 6:25
Because Ephraim has **m** altars for Hos 8:11
and Judah has **m** fortified cities; Hos 8:14
it was I who **m** visions, and through Hos 12:10
of the disciples **m** greatly in Jerusalem, Acts 6:7
the people increased and **m** in Egypt Acts 7:17
in the comfort of the Holy Spirit, it **m**. Acts 9:31
But the word of God increased and **m**. Acts 12:24
blood: May grace and peace be **m** to you. 1 Pt 1:2
May grace and peace be **m** to you in the 2 Pt 1:2
May mercy, peace, and love be **m** to you. Jude 1:2

MULTIPLIES (5)

a tempest and **m** my wounds without Jb 9:17
among us and **m** his words against Jb 34:37
talk; he **m** words without knowledge." Jb 35:16
Whoever **m** his wealth by interest and Prv 28:8
A fool **m** words, though no man Eccl 10:14

MULTIPLY (50)

"Be fruitful and **m** and fill the waters in Gn 1:22
the seas, and let birds **m** on the earth." Gn 1:22
"Be fruitful and **m** and fill the earth and Gn 1:28
"I will surely **m** your pain in Gn 3:16
When man began to **m** on the face of the Gn 6:1
and be fruitful and **m** on the earth." Gn 8:17
"Be fruitful and **m** and fill the earth. Gn 9:1
And you, be fruitful and **m**, teem on the Gn 9:7
multiply, teem on the earth and **m** in it." Gn 9:7
"I will surely **m** your offspring so that Gn 16:10
me and you, and may **m** you greatly." Gn 17:2
make him fruitful and **m** him greatly. Gn 17:20
and I will surely **m** your offspring as Gn 22:17
I will **m** your offspring as the stars of Gn 26:4
will bless you and **m** your offspring for Gn 26:24
you and make you fruitful and **m** you, Gn 28:3
am God Almighty: be fruitful and **m**. Gn 35:11
I will make you fruitful and **m** you, Gn 48:4
us deal shrewdly with them, lest they **m**, Ex 1:10
and though I **m** my signs and wonders in Ex 7:3
and the wild beasts **m** against you. Ex 23:29
'I will **m** your offspring as the stars of Ex 32:13
make you fruitful and **m** you and will Lv 26:9
with you, and that you may **m** greatly, Dt 6:3
He will love you, bless you, and **m** you. Dt 7:13
be careful to do, that you may live and **m**, Dt 8:1
your herds and flocks **m** and your silver Dt 8:13
have compassion on you and **m** you, Dt 13:17
his rules, then you shall live and **m**, Dt 30:16
did all their clan **m** like the men of 1 Chr 4:27
nest, and I shall **m** my days as the sand, Jb 29:18
those who run after another god shall **m**; Ps 16:4
By his blessing they **m** greatly, and he Ps 107:38
he will refuse though you **m** gifts. Prv 6:35
him, that I might bless him and **m** him. Is 51:2
fold, and they shall be fruitful and **m**. Jer 23:3
daughters; **m** there, and do not decrease. Jer 29:6
I will **m** them, and they shall not be Jer 30:19
so I will **m** the offspring of David my Jer 33:22
And I will **m** people on you, the whole Ezk 36:10
And I will **m** on you man and beast, Ezk 36:11
and they shall **m** and be fruitful. Ezk 36:11
set them in their land and **m** them, Ezk 37:26
they shall play the whore, but not **m**, Hos 4:10
long; they **m** falsehood and violence; Hos 12:1
to Gilgal, and **m** transgression; Am 4:4
M yourselves like the locust; multiply Na 3:15
like the locust; **m** like the grasshopper! Na 3:15
food will supply and **m** your seed for 2 Cor 9:10
"Surely I will bless you and **m** you." Heb 6:14

MULTIPLYING (3)

delight in doing you good and **m** you, Dt 28:63
to any passerby and **m** your whoring. Ezk 16:25
lustful neighbors, **m** your whoring, Ezk 16:26

MULTITUDE (75)

that they cannot be numbered for **m**." Gn 16:10
you shall be the father of a **m** of nations. Gn 17:4
made you the father of a **m** of nations. Gn 17:5
which cannot be numbered for **m**.'" Gn 32:12
let them grow into a **m** in the midst of Gn 48:16
shall become a **m** of nations." Gn 48:19
A mixed **m** also went up with them, Ex 12:38
like the sand on the seashore in **m**. 1 Sm 13:5
the **m** was dispersing here and there. 1 Sm 14:16
all the people, the whole **m** of Israel, 2 Sm 6:19
as the sand by the sea for **m**, 2 Sm 17:11
to be numbered or counted for **m**. 1 Kgs 3:8
Have you seen all this great **m**? 1 Kgs 20:13
give all this great **m** into your hand, 1 Kgs 20:28
fare like the whole **m** of Israel who 2 Kgs 7:13
together with the rest of the **m**, 2 Kgs 25:11
you are a great **m** and have with you 2 Chr 13:8
name we have come against this **m**. 2 Chr 14:11
"A great **m** is coming against you 2 Chr 20:2

and popular with the **m** of his brothers, Est 10:3
"Should a **m** of words go unanswered, Jb 11:2
because I stood in great fear of the **m**, Jb 31:34
"Because of the **m** of oppressions people Jb 35:9
and songs of praise, a **m** keeping festival. Ps 42:4
In a **m** of people is the glory of a king, Prv 14:28
"What to me is the **m** of your sacrifices? Is 1:11
and their **m** is parched with thirst. Is 5:13
of Jerusalem and her **m** will go down, Is 5:14
is on the mountains as of a great **m**! Is 13:4
into contempt, in spite of all his great **m**, Is 16:14
But the **m** of your foreign foes shall be Is 29:5
and the **m** of the ruthless like passing Is 29:5
And the **m** of all the nations that fight Is 29:7
so shall the **m** of all the nations be that Is 29:8
A **m** of camels shall cover you, the young Is 60:6
her for the **m** of her transgressions; Lam 1:5
mourn, for wrath is upon all their **m**. Ezk 7:12
For the vision concerns all their **m**; it Ezk 7:13
battle, for my wrath is upon all their **m**. Ezk 7:14
as he comes with the **m** of his idols, Ezk 14:4
sound of a carefree **m** was with her; Ezk 23:42
By the **m** of your iniquities, in the Ezk 28:18
of Egypt, and cut off the **m** of Thebes. Ezk 30:15
to Pharaoh king of Egypt and to his **m**: Ezk 31:2
"This is Pharaoh and all his **m**, Ezk 31:18
I will cause your **m** to fall by the Ezk 32:12
of Egypt, and all its **m** shall perish. Ezk 32:12
over Egypt, and over all her **m**, shall Ezk 32:16
"Son of man, wail over the **m** of Egypt, Ezk 32:18
there, and all her **m** around her grave; Ezk 32:24
a bed among the slain with all her **m**, Ezk 32:25
is there, and all her **m**, Ezk 32:26
he will be comforted for all his **m**, Ezk 32:31
by the sword, Pharaoh and all his **m**, Ezk 32:32
there Gog and all his **m** will be buried. Ezk 39:11
of his words like the sound of a **m**. Dn 10:6
war and assemble a **m** of great forces, Dn 11:10
And he shall raise a great **m**, but it Dn 11:11
And when the **m** is taken away, his Dn 11:12
king of the north shall again raise a **m**, Dn 11:13
way and in the **m** of your warriors, Hos 10:13
a flock in its pasture, a noisy **m** of men. Mi 2:12
because of the **m** of people and livestock Zec 2:4
And the whole **m** of the people were Lk 1:10
with the angel a **m** of the heavenly host Lk 2:13
disciples and a great **m** of people from Lk 6:17
Olives—the whole **m** of his disciples Lk 19:37
followed him a great **m** of the people Lk 23:27
In these lay a **m** of invalids—blind, lame, Jn 5:3
And at this sound the **m** came together, Acts 2:6
from death and will cover a **m** of sins. Jas 5:20
earnestly, since love covers a **m** of sins. 1 Pt 4:8
a great **m** that no one could number, Rv 7:9
be the loud voice of a great **m** in heaven, Rv 19:1
what seemed to be the voice of a great **m**, Rv 19:6

MULTITUDES (5)
sword; drag her away, and all her **m**. Ezk 32:20
M, multitudes, in the valley of decision! Jl 3:14
Multitudes, **m**, in the valley of decision! Jl 3:14
the Lord, **m** of both men and women, Acts 5:14
are peoples and **m** and nations and Rv 17:15

MUPPIM (1)
Gera, Naaman, Ehi, Rosh, **M**, Huppim, Gn 46:21

MURDER (24)
"You shall not **m**. Ex 20:13
"'You shall not **m**. Dt 5:17
and the sojourner, and **m** the fatherless; Ps 94:6
Will you steal, **m**, commit adultery, Jer 7:9
On the day after the **m** of Gedaliah, Jer 41:4
rams, to open the mouth with **m**, Ezk 21:22
there is swearing, lying, **m**, stealing, and Hos 4:2
together; they **m** on the way to Shechem; Hos 6:9
said to those of old, 'You shall not **m**; Mt 5:21
heart come evil thoughts, **m**, adultery, Mt 15:19
And Jesus said, "You shall not **m**, Mt 19:18
sexual immorality, theft, **m**, adultery, Mk 7:21
'Do not **m**, Do not commit adultery, Mk 10:19
who had committed **m** in the Mk 15:7
'Do not commit adultery, Do not **m**, Do Lk 18:20
started in the city and for **m**. Lk 23:19
into prison for insurrection and **m**, Lk 23:25
breathing threats and **m** against the Acts 9:1
They are full of envy, **m**, strife, deceit, Rom 1:29
commit adultery, You shall not **m**, Rom 13:9
"Do not **m**." If you do not commit Jas 2:11
If you do not commit adultery but do **m**, Jas 2:11
You desire and do not have, so you **m**. Jas 4:2
his brother. And why did he **m** him? 1 Jn 3:12

MURDERED (6)
the husband of the woman who was **m**, Jgs 20:4
are sons of those who **m** the prophets. Mt 23:31
whom you **m** between the sanctuary Mt 23:35
whom you have now betrayed and **m**, Acts 7:52
you have **m** the righteous person. Jas 5:6
was of the evil one and **m** his brother. 1 Jn 3:12

MURDERER (20)
iron object, so that he died, he is a **m**. Nm 35:16
The **m** shall be put to death. Nm 35:16
cause death, and he died, he is a **m**. Nm 35:17
The **m** shall be put to death. Nm 35:17
cause death, and he died, he is a **m**. Nm 35:18
The **m** shall be put to death. Nm 35:18
shall himself put the **m** to death; Nm 35:19
blow shall be put to death. He is a **m**. Nm 35:21
blood shall put the **m** to death when Nm 35:21
the **m** shall be put to death on the Nm 35:30
accept no ransom for the life of a **m**, Nm 35:31
you see how this **m** has sent to take 2 Kgs 6:32
peace, you Zimri, **m** of your master?" 2 Kgs 9:31
The **m** rises before it is light, that he Jb 24:14
desires. He was a **m** from the beginning, Jn 8:44
and asked for a **m** to be granted to you, Acts 3:14
another, "No doubt this man is a **m**. Acts 28:4
of you suffer as a **m** or a thief or an 1 Pt 4:15
Everyone who hates his brother is a **m**, 1 Jn 3:15
you know that no **m** has eternal life 1 Jn 3:15

MURDERERS (7)
not put to death the children of the **m**, 2 Kgs 14:6
Righteousness lodged in her, but now **m**. Is 1:21
"Woe is me! I am fainting before **m**." Jer 4:31
and destroyed those **m** and burned their Mt 22:7
strike their fathers and mothers, for **m**, 1 Tm 1:9
the faithless, the detestable, as for **m**, Rv 21:8
sexually immoral and **m** and idolaters, Rv 22:15

MURDERING (1)
a man attacking and **m** his neighbor, Dt 22:26

MURDERS (3)
in hiding places he **m** the innocent. Ps 10:8
and whoever **m** will be liable to Mt 5:21
they repent of their **m** or their sorceries Rv 9:21

MURMUR (1)
and those who **m** will accept Is 29:24

MURMURED (3)
And you **m** in your tents and said, Dt 1:27
all the congregation **m** against the Jos 9:18
They **m** in their tents, and did not Ps 106:25

MUSCLES (1)
and his power in the **m** of his belly. Jb 40:16

MUSE (1)
Your heart will **m** on the terror: "Where Is 33:18

MUSED (1)
As I **m**, the fire burned; then I spoke with Ps 39:3

MUSHI (8)
The sons of Merari: Mahli and **M**. These Ex 6:19
of Merari by their clans: Mahli and **M**. Nm 3:20
The sons of Merari: Mahli and **M**. 1 Chr 6:19
son of Mahli, son of **M**, son of Merari, 1 Chr 6:47
The sons of Merari: Mahli and **M**. 1 Chr 23:21
The sons of **M**: Mahli, Eder, and 1 Chr 23:23
The sons of Merari: Mahli and **M**. 1 Chr 24:26
The sons of **M**: Mahli, Eder, and 1 Chr 24:30

MUSHITES (2)
of the Mahlites and the clan of the **M**: Nm 3:33
of the Mahlites, the clan of the **M**, Nm 26:58

MUSIC (20)
leader of the Levites in **m**, 1 Chr 15:22
in music, should direct the **m**, 1 Chr 15:22
the leader of the **m** of the singers. 1 Chr 15:27
and made loud **m** on harps and 1 Chr 15:28
cymbals for the **m** and instruments 1 Chr 16:42
their father in the **m** in the house of 1 Chr 25:6
with the instruments for **m** to the LORD 2 Chr 7:6
were skillful with instruments of **m**, 2 Chr 34:12
I will solve my riddle to the **m** of the lyre. Ps 49:4
to the **m** of the lute and the harp, to the Ps 92:3
justice; to you, O LORD, I will make **m**. Ps 101:1
will play my **m** on stringed instruments Is 38:20
the city gate, the young men their **m**. Lam 5:14
And I will stop the **m** of your songs, Ezk 26:13
harp, bagpipe, and every kind of **m**, Dn 3:5
harp, bagpipe, and every kind of **m**, Dn 3:7
harp, bagpipe, and every kind of **m**, Dn 3:10
harp, bagpipe, and every kind of **m**, Dn 3:15
invent for themselves instruments of **m**, Am 6:5
to the house, he heard **m** and dancing. Lk 15:25

MUSICAL (5)
songs of joy, and with **m** instruments. 1 Sm 18:6
play loudly on **m** instruments, 1 Chr 15:16
cymbals and other **m** instruments, 2 Chr 5:13
with their **m** instruments leading 2 Chr 23:13
with the **m** instruments of David the Neh 12:36

MUSICIAN (2)
now bring me a **m**." And when the 2 Kgs 3:15
a musician." And when the **m** played, 2 Kgs 3:15

MUSICIANS (3)
To the sound of **m** at the watering Jgs 5:11
the singers in front, the **m** last, between Ps 68:25
and the sound of harpists and **m**, of Rv 18:22

MUSING (1)
Either he is **m**, or he is relieving 1 Kgs 18:27

MUST (215)
desire is for you, but you **m** rule over it." Gn 4:7
her, 'This is the kindness you **m** do me: Gn 20:13
M I then take your son back to the land Gn 24:5
only you **m** not take my son back Gn 24:8
"You **m** not take a wife from the Gn 28:1
"You **m** not take a wife from the Gn 28:6
him and said, "You **m** come in to me, Gn 30:16
for such a thing **m** not be done. Gn 34:7
father Israel said to them, "If it **m** be so, Gn 43:11
You **m** tell my father of all my honor Gn 45:13
the time drew near that Israel **m** die, Gn 47:29
but you **m** still deliver the same number Ex 5:18
We **m** go three days' journey into the Ex 8:27
only you **m** not go very far away. Ex 8:28
herds, for we **m** hold a feast to the LORD." Ex 10:9
"You **m** also let us have sacrifices and Ex 10:25
Our livestock also **m** go with us; not a Ex 10:26
for we **m** take of them to serve the LORD Ex 10:26
know with what we **m** serve the LORD Ex 10:26
way in which they **m** walk and what Ex 18:20
they must walk and what they **m** do. Ex 18:20
It **m** be put into water, and it shall be Lv 11:32
The priest **m** pronounce him unclean; Lv 13:44
be forbidden to you; it **m** not be eaten. Lv 19:23
the flock, to be accepted it **m** be perfect; Lv 22:21
but they **m** not touch the holy things, Nm 4:15
that you **m** also make yourself a Nm 16:13
puts in my mouth, that **m** I speak." Nm 22:38
"**M** I not take care to speak what the Nm 23:12
'All that the LORD says, that I **m** do'?" Nm 23:26
You **m** wash your clothes on the Nm 31:24
For he **m** remain in his city of refuge Nm 35:28
the way by which we **m** go up and the Dt 1:22
For I **m** die in this land; I must not go Dt 4:22
in this land; I **m** not go over the Jordan. Dt 4:22
then you **m** devote them to complete Dt 7:2
Only he **m** not acquire many horses for Dt 17:16
you, therefore your camp **m** be holy, Dt 23:14
the days approach when you **m** die. Dt 31:14
that you too **m** turn away this day Jos 22:18
that you **m** go to take a wife from the Jgs 14:3
"There **m** be an inheritance for the Jgs 21:17
'You **m** not go back empty-handed to Ru 3:17
he would say, "No, you **m** give it now, 1 Sm 2:16
the God of Israel **m** not remain with us, 1 Sm 5:7
So you **m** make images of your tumors 1 Sm 6:5
comes, since he **m** bless the sacrifice; 1 Sm 9:13
We **m** all die; we are like water 2 Sm 14:14
he is asleep and **m** be awakened." 1 Kgs 18:27
for the LORD **m** be exceedingly 1 Chr 22:5
I have provided. To these you **m** add. 1 Chr 22:14
"It is so; we **m** do as you have said. Ezr 10:12
to us ten times, "You **m** return to us." Neh 4:12
him; I **m** appeal for mercy to my accuser. Jb 9:15
I **m** plead with him with my mouth for Jb 19:16
In the gullies of the torrents they **m** dwell, Jb 30:6
I **m** speak, that I may find relief; I must Jb 32:20
find relief; I **m** open my lips and answer. Jb 32:20
For you **m** choose, and not I; therefore Jb 34:33
How long **m** I take counsel in my soul Ps 13:2
which **m** be curbed with bit and bridle, Ps 32:9
and the stupid alike **m** perish and leave Ps 49:10
I **m** perform my vows to you, O God; I Ps 56:12
lies. What I did not steal **m** I now restore? Ps 69:4
How long **m** your servant endure? Ps 119:84
I awake? I **m** have another drink." Prv 23:35
seeing that I **m** leave it to the man who Eccl 2:18
and skill **m** leave everything Eccl 2:21
is vanity; but God is the one you **m** fear. Eccl 5:7
the edge, he **m** use more strength, Eccl 10:10
In the middle of my days I **m** depart; Is 38:10
How long **m** I see the standard and hear Jer 4:21
This is the city that **m** be punished; there Jer 6:6
this is an affliction, and I **m** bear it." Jer 10:19
says the LORD of hosts: You **m** drink! Jer 25:28
years each of you **m** set free the fellow Jer 34:14
you **m** set him free from your service.' Jer 34:14
"We **m** report all these words to the Jer 36:16
not deserve to drink the cup **m** drink it, Jer 49:12
not go unpunished, but you **m** drink. Jer 49:12
Babylon **m** fall for the slain of Israel, Jer 51:49
We **m** pay for the water we drink; the Lam 5:4
we drink; the wood we get **m** be bought. Lam 5:4
sight, as those do who **m** go into exile. Ezk 12:4

you yourself **m** bear the consequences Ezk 23:35
that you **m** tread down with your feet Ezk 34:18
that you **m** muddy the rest of the Ezk 34:18
And **m** my sheep eat what you have Ezk 34:19
m pass before the end of the desolations Dn 9:2
"You **m** dwell as mine for many days. Hos 3:3
but Ephraim **m** lead his children out to Hos 9:13
is false; now they **m** bear their guilt. Hos 10:2
Ephraim to the yoke; Judah **m** plow; Hos 10:11
plow; Jacob **m** harrow for himself. Hos 10:11
We **m** not mention the name of the Am 6:10
and Israel **m** go into exile away from Am 7:11
You therefore **m** be perfect, as your Mt 5:48
pray, you **m** not be like the hypocrites. Mt 6:5
reviles father or mother **m** surely die.' Mt 15:4
his disciples that he **m** go to Jerusalem Mt 16:21
scribes say that first Elijah **m** come?" Mt 17:10
what good deed **m** I do to have eternal Mt 19:16
be great among you **m** be your servant, Mt 20:26
be first among you **m** be your slave, Mt 20:27
his brother **m** marry the widow and Mt 22:24
are not alarmed, for this **m** take place, Mt 24:6
Therefore you also **m** be ready, for the Mt 24:44
said to him, "Even if I **m** die with you, Mt 26:35
Scriptures be fulfilled, that it **m** be so?" Mt 26:54
reviles father or mother **m** surely die.' Mk 7:10
the Son of Man **m** suffer many things Mk 8:31
scribes say that first Elijah **m** come?" Mk 9:11
he **m** be last of all and servant of all." Mk 9:35
what **m** I do to inherit eternal life?" Mk 10:17
great among you **m** be your servant, Mk 10:43
be first among you **m** be slave of all. Mk 10:44
the man **m** take the widow and raise Mk 12:19
This **m** take place, but the end is not Mk 13:7
And the gospel **m** first be proclaimed Mk 13:10
said emphatically, "If I **m** die with you, Mk 14:31
And he **m** not drink wine or strong Lk 1:15
you not know that I **m** be in my Father's Lk 2:49
"I **m** preach the good news of the Lk 4:43
But new wine **m** be put into fresh Lk 5:38
"The Son of Man **m** suffer many things Lk 9:22
You also **m** be ready, for the Son of Lk 12:40
I **m** go on my way today and tomorrow Lk 13:33
a field, and I **m** go out and see it. Lk 14:18
saying, 'I repent,' you **m** forgive him." Lk 17:4
But first he **m** suffer many things and Lk 17:25
what **m** I do to inherit eternal life?" Lk 18:18
down, for I **m** stay at your house today." Lk 19:5
the man **m** take the widow and raise up Lk 20:28
for these things **m** first take place, Lk 21:9
you that this Scripture **m** be fulfilled in Lk 22:37
the Son of Man **m** be delivered into the Lk 24:7
and the Psalms **m** be fulfilled." Lk 24:44
that I said to you, 'You **m** be born again.' Jn 3:7
so **m** the Son of Man be lifted up, Jn 3:14
He **m** increase, but I must decrease." Jn 3:30
He must increase, but I **m** decrease." Jn 3:30
who worship him **m** worship in spirit Jn 4:24
Then they said to him, "What **m** we do, Jn 6:28
We **m** work the works of him who sent Jn 9:4
I **m** bring them also, and they will listen Jn 10:16
If anyone serves me, he **m** follow me; Jn 12:26
say that the Son of Man **m** be lifted up? Jn 12:34
is written in their Law **m** be fulfilled: Jn 15:25
Scripture, that he **m** rise from the dead. Jn 20:9
one of these men **m** become with us a Acts 1:22
whom heaven **m** receive until the time Acts 3:21
among men by which we **m** be saved." Acts 4:12
you rather than to God, you **m** judge, Acts 4:19
"We **m** obey God rather than men. Acts 5:29
him how much he **m** suffer for the Acts 9:16
many tribulations we **m** enter the Acts 14:22
said, "Sirs, what **m** I do to be saved?" Acts 16:30
I have been there, I **m** also see Rome." Acts 19:21
in this way we **m** help the weak and Acts 20:35
so you **m** testify also in Rome." Acts 23:11
that the Christ **m** suffer and that, by Acts 26:23
Paul; you **m** stand before Caesar. Acts 27:24
But we **m** run aground on some Acts 27:26
say that one **m** not commit adultery, Rom 2:22
So you also **m** consider yourselves Rom 6:11
Therefore one **m** be in subjection, not Rom 13:5
We **m** not indulge in sexual 1 Cor 10:8
We **m** not put Christ to the test, as 1 Cor 10:9
for there **m** be factions among you 1 Cor 11:19
For he **m** reign until he has put all 1 Cor 15:25
this perishable body **m** put on the 1 Cor 15:53
this mortal body **m** put on 1 Cor 15:53
You also **m** help us by prayer, so that 2 Cor 1:11
ministry of righteousness **m** far exceed 2 Cor 3:9
For we **m** all appear before the 2 Cor 5:10
Each one **m** give as he has made up 2 Cor 9:7
To my shame, I **m** say, we were too 2 Cor 11:21
If I **m** boast, I will boast of the things 2 Cor 11:30
I **m** go on boasting. Though there is 2 Cor 12:1
Every charge **m** be established by the 2 Cor 13:1
is taught the word **m** share all good Gal 6:6
that you **m** no longer walk as the Eph 4:17
impurity or covetousness **m** not even be Eph 5:3
But now you **m** put them all away: Col 3:8
has forgiven you, so you also **m** forgive. Col 3:13
Therefore an overseer **m** be above 1 Tm 3:2
He **m** manage his own household well, 1 Tm 3:4
He **m** not be a recent convert, or he 1 Tm 3:6
he **m** be well thought of by outsiders, 1 Tm 3:7
Deacons likewise **m** be dignified, not 1 Tm 3:8
They **m** hold the mystery of the faith 1 Tm 3:9
Their wives likewise **m** be dignified, 1 Tm 3:11
have believing masters **m** not be 1 Tm 6:2
rather they **m** serve all the better since 1 Tm 6:2
the Lord's servant **m** not be 2 Tm 2:24
as God's steward, **m** be above reproach. Ti 1:7
He **m** not be arrogant or quick-tempered Ti 1:7
He **m** hold firm to the trustworthy word as Ti 1:9
They **m** be silenced, since they are Ti 1:11
Therefore we **m** pay much closer Heb 2:1
of him to whom we **m** give account. Heb 4:13
the one who made it **m** be established. Heb 9:16
draw near to God **m** believe that he Heb 11:6
For that person **m** not suppose that he Jas 1:7
whoever loves God **m** also love his 1 Jn 4:21
But you **m** remember, beloved, the Jude 1:17
the things that **m** soon take place. Rv 1:1
will show you what **m** take place after Rv 4:1
"You **m** again prophesy about many Rv 10:11
sword, with the sword **m** he be slain. Rv 13:10
he does come he **m** remain only a little Rv 17:10
but he said to me, "You **m** not do that! Rv 19:10
After that he **m** be released for a little Rv 20:3
his servants what **m** soon take place." Rv 22:6
but he said to me, "You **m** not do that! I Rv 22:9

MUSTARD (5)
is like a grain of **m** seed that a man Mt 13:31
if you have faith like a grain of **m** seed, Mt 17:20
It is like a grain of **m** seed, which, when Mk 4:31
is like a grain of **m** seed that a man Lk 13:19
"If you had faith like a grain of **m** seed, Lk 17:6

MUSTER (5)
and **m** an army like the army that 1 Kgs 20:25
This was the **m** of them by fathers' 2 Chr 17:14
the numbers in the **m** made by Jeiel 2 Chr 26:11
of the merchants, opposite the **M** Gate, Neh 3:31
Now **m** your troops, O daughter of troops; Mi 5:1

MUSTERED (20)
in the morning and **m** the people and Jos 8:10
the people of Benjamin **m** out of their Jgs 20:15
of Gibeah, who **m** 700 chosen men. Jgs 20:15
m 400,000 men who drew the sword; Jgs 20:17
For when the people were **m**, behold, not Jgs 21:9
When he **m** them at Bezek, the people 1 Sm 11:8
And the Philistines **m** to fight with 1 Sm 13:5
the Philistines had **m** at Michmash, 1 Sm 13:11
Then David **m** the men who were 2 Sm 18:1
Then he **m** the servants of the 1 Kgs 20:15
And after them he **m** all the people 1 Kgs 20:15
Ben-hadad **m** the Syrians and went 1 Kgs 20:26
of Israel were **m** and were 1 Kgs 20:27
Samaria at that time and **m** all Israel. 2 Kgs 3:6
king of Syria **m** his entire army 2 Kgs 6:24
of the army who **m** the people of the 2 Kgs 25:19
the Ammonites were **m** from their 1 Chr 19:7
He **m** those twenty years old and 2 Chr 25:5
of the army who **m** the people of the Jer 52:25
After many days you will be **m**. In the Ezk 38:8

MUSTERING (1)
The LORD of hosts is **m** a host for battle. Is 13:4

MUSTERS (1)
flashing metal on the day he **m** them; Na 2:3

MUTE (23)
Who makes him **m**, or deaf, or seeing, or Ex 4:11
Let the lying lips be **m**, which speak Ps 31:18
like a **m** man who does not open his Ps 38:13
I was **m** and silent; I held my peace to no Ps 39:2
I am **m**; I do not open my mouth, for it is Ps 39:9
Open your mouth for the **m**, for the Prv 31:8
deer, and the tongue of the **m** sing for joy. Is 35:6
that you shall be **m** and unable to Ezk 3:26
you shall speak and be no longer **m**. Ezk 24:27
was opened, and I was no longer **m**. Ezk 33:22
my face toward the ground and was **m**. Dn 10:15
man who was **m** was brought to Mt 9:32
had been cast out, the **m** man spoke. Mt 9:33
who was blind and **m** was brought to Mt 12:22
the lame, the blind, the crippled, the **m**, Mt 15:30
when they saw the **m** speaking, Mt 15:31
makes the deaf hear and the **m** speak." Mk 7:37
for he has a spirit that makes him **m**. Mk 9:17
saying to it, "You **m** and deaf spirit, Mk 9:25
making signs to them and remained **m**. Lk 1:22
was casting out a demon that was **m**. Lk 11:14
demon had gone out, the **m** man spoke, Lk 11:14
pagans you were led astray to **m** idols, 1 Cor 12:2

MUTH-LABBEN (1)
To the choirmaster: according to **M**. A Ps 9:T

MUTILATE (1)
look out for those who **m** the flesh. Phil 3:2

MUTILATED (2)
or one who has a **m** face or a limb too Lv 21:18
blind or disabled or **m** or having a Lv 22:22

MUTILATION (1)
a blemish in them, because of their **m**, Lv 22:25

MUTTER (1)
who chirp and **m**," should not a Is 8:19

MUTTERING (2)
there was much **m** about him among Jn 7:12
heard the crowd **m** these things about Jn 7:32

MUTTERS (1)
spoken lies; your tongue **m** wickedness. Is 59:3

MUTUAL (1)
for peace and for **m** upbuilding. Rom 14:19

MUTUALLY (1)
that we may be **m** encouraged by each Rom 1:12

MUZZLE (4)
"You shall not **m** an ox when it is Dt 25:4
I will guard my mouth with a **m**, so long Ps 39:1
"You shall not **m** an ox when it treads 1 Cor 9:9
"You shall not **m** an ox when it 1 Tm 5:18

MYRA (1)
Pamphylia, we came to **M** in Lycia. Acts 27:5

MYRIADS (2)
numbering **m** of myriads and Rv 5:11
myriads of **m** and thousands Rv 5:11

MYRRH (20)
camels bearing gum, balm, and **m**, Gn 37:25
a little honey, gum, **m**, pistachio nuts, Gn 43:11
finest spices: of liquid **m** 500 shekels, Ex 30:23
silver and gold, garments, **m**, spices, 1 Kgs 10:25
and of gold, garments, **m**, spices, 2 Chr 9:24
months with oil of **m** and six months Est 2:12
are all fragrant with **m** and aloes and Ps 45:8
I have perfumed my bed with **m**, aloes, Prv 7:17
to me a sachet of **m** that lies between my Sg 1:13
perfumed with **m** and frankincense, Sg 3:6
away to the mountain of **m** and the hill of Sg 4:6
all trees of frankincense, **m** and aloes, Sg 4:14
my bride, I gathered my **m** with my spice, Sg 5:1
beloved, and my hands dripped with **m**, Sg 5:5
with myrrh, my fingers with liquid **m**, Sg 5:5
His lips are lilies, dripping liquid **m**. Sg 5:13
him gifts, gold and frankincense and **m**. Mt 2:11
they offered him wine mixed with **m**, Mk 15:23
bringing a mixture of **m** and aloes, Jn 19:39
spice, incense, **m**, frankincense, Rv 18:13

MYRTLE (6)
branches of olive, wild olive, **m**, palm, Neh 8:15
wilderness the cedar, the acacia, the **m**, Is 41:19
instead of the brier shall come up the **m**; Is 55:13
was standing among the **m** trees in the Zec 1:8
standing among the **m** trees answered, Zec 1:10
who was standing among the **m** trees, Zec 1:11

MYSIA (2)
And when they had come up to **M**, Acts 16:7
So, passing by **M**, they went down to Acts 16:8

MYSTERIES (6)
there is a God in heaven who reveals **m**, Dn 2:28
and he who reveals **m** made known to Dn 2:29
and Lord of kings, and a revealer of **m**, Dn 2:47
of Christ and stewards of the **m** of God. 1 Cor 4:1
and understand all **m** and all 1 Cor 13:2
him, but he utters **m** in the Spirit. 1 Cor 14:2

MYSTERY (27)
the God of heaven concerning this **m**, Dn 2:18
Then the **m** was revealed to Daniel in a Dn 2:19
to the king the **m** that the king has Dn 2:27
for me, this **m** has been revealed to me, Dn 2:30
for you have been able to reveal this **m**." Dn 2:47
in you and that no **m** is too difficult for Dn 4:9
I want you to understand this **m**, Rom 11:25
the revelation of the **m** that was kept Rom 16:25
Behold! I tell you a **m**. We shall not 1 Cor 15:51
making known to us the **m** of his will, Eph 1:9
how the **m** was made known to me by Eph 3:3
perceive my insight into the **m** of Christ, Eph 3:4
This **m** is that the Gentiles are fellow Eph 3:6
is the plan of the **m** hidden for ages in Eph 3:9

This **m** is profound, and I am saying Eph 5:32
boldly to proclaim the **m** of the gospel, Eph 6:19
the **m** hidden for ages and generations Col 1:26
are the riches of the glory of this **m**, Col 1:27
and the knowledge of God's **m**, Col 2:2
for the word, to declare the **m** of Christ, Col 4:3
For the **m** of lawlessness is already at 2 Thes 2:7
They must hold the **m** of the faith with 1 Tm 3:9
we confess, is the **m** of godliness: 1 Tm 3:16
As for the **m** of the seven stars that you Rv 1:20
angel, the **m** of God would be fulfilled, Rv 10:7
her forehead was written a name of **m**: Rv 17:5
I will tell you the **m** of the woman, and of Rv 17:7

MYTHS (5)
devote themselves to **m** and endless 1 Tm 1:4
nothing to do with irreverent, silly **m**. 1 Tm 4:7
to the truth and wander off into **m**. 2 Tm 4:4
themselves to Jewish **m** and the Ti 1:14
follow cleverly devised **m** when we 2 Pt 1:16

N

NAAM (1)
son of Jephunneh: Iru, Elah, and **N**; 1 Chr 4:15

NAAMAH (5)
iron. The sister of Tubal-cain was **N**. Gn 4:22
Beth-dagon, **N**, and Makkedah: Jos 15:41
name was **N** the Ammonite. 1 Kgs 14:21
name was **N** the Ammonite. 1 Kgs 14:31
name was **N** the Ammonite. 2 Chr 12:13

NAAMAN (18)
Bela, Becher, Ashbel, Gera, **N**, Ehi, Gn 46:21
And the sons of Bela were Ard and **N**: Nm 26:40
of Ard, the clan of the Ardites; of **N**, Nm 26:40
N, commander of the army of the king 2 Kgs 5:1
So **N** went in and told his lord, "Thus 2 Kgs 5:4
that I have sent to you **N** my servant, 2 Kgs 5:6
So **N** came with his horses and 2 Kgs 5:9
But **N** was angry and went away, 2 Kgs 5:11
Then **N** said, "If not, please let there 2 Kgs 5:17
in peace." But when **N** had gone from 2 Kgs 5:19
master has spared this **N** the Syrian, 2 Kgs 5:20
So Gehazi followed **N**. And when 2 Kgs 5:21
And when **N** saw someone running 2 Kgs 5:21
And **N** said, "Be pleased to accept two 2 Kgs 5:23
the leprosy of **N** shall cling to 2 Kgs 5:27
Abishua, **N**, Ahoah, 1 Chr 8:4
N, Ahijah, and Gera, that is, Heglam, 1 Chr 8:7
was cleansed, but only **N** the Syrian." Lk 4:27

NAAMAN'S (1)
she worked in the service of **N** wife. 2 Kgs 5:2

NAAMATHITE (4)
Bildad the Shuhite, and Zophar the **N**. Jb 2:11
Then Zophar the **N** answered and said: Jb 11:1
Then Zophar the **N** answered and said: Jb 20:1
Shuhite and Zophar the **N** went and did Jb 42:9

NAAMITES (1)
Ardites; of Naaman, the clan of the **N**. Nm 26:40

NAARAH (4)
down from Janoah to Ataroth and to **N**, Jos 16:7
of Tekoa, had two wives, Helah and **N**; 1 Chr 4:5
N bore him Ahuzzam, Hepher, 1 Chr 4:6
These were the sons of **N**. 1 Chr 4:6

NAARAI (1)
Hezro of Carmel, **N** the son of Ezbai, 1 Chr 11:37

NAARAN (1)
and its towns, and to the east **N**, 1 Chr 7:28

NABAL (19)
Now the name of the man was **N**, and 1 Sm 25:3
the wilderness that **N** was shearing 1 Sm 25:4
and go to **N** and greet him in my 1 Sm 25:5
they said all this to **N** in the name of 1 Sm 25:9
And **N** answered David's servants, 1 Sm 25:10
But she did not tell her husband **N**. 1 Sm 25:19
fellow, **N**, for as his name is, 1 Sm 25:25
N is his name, and folly is with him. 1 Sm 25:25
seek to do evil to my lord be as **N**. 1 Sm 25:26
not been left to **N** so much as one 1 Sm 25:34
And Abigail came to **N**, and behold, 1 Sm 25:36
when the wine had gone out of **N**, 1 Sm 25:37
ten days later the LORD struck **N**, 1 Sm 25:38
When David heard that **N** was dead, 1 Sm 25:39
the insult I received at the hand of **N**, 1 Sm 25:39
returned the evil of **N** on his own 1 Sm 25:39
Abigail the widow of **N** of Carmel. 1 Sm 30:5
and Abigail the widow of **N** of Carmel. 2 Sm 2:2
of Abigail the widow of **N** of Carmel; 2 Sm 3:3

NABAL'S (3)
the young men told Abigail, **N** wife, 1 Sm 25:14
And **N** heart was merry within him, 1 Sm 25:36
and Abigail of Carmel, **N** widow. 1 Sm 27:3

NABOTH (22)
Now **N** the Jezreelite had a vineyard 1 Kgs 21:1
And after this Ahab said to **N**, "Give 1 Kgs 21:2
But **N** said to Ahab, "The LORD forbid 1 Kgs 21:3
because of what **N** the Jezreelite had 1 Kgs 21:4
I spoke to **N** the Jezreelite and 1 Kgs 21:6
you the vineyard of **N** the Jezreelite." 1 Kgs 21:7
leaders who lived with **N** in his city. 1 Kgs 21:8
and set **N** at the head of the people. 1 Kgs 21:9
a fast and set **N** at the head of 1 Kgs 21:12
a charge against **N** in the presence 1 Kgs 21:13
"**N** cursed God and the king." So 1 Kgs 21:13
Jezebel, saying, "**N** has been stoned; 1 Kgs 21:14
Jezebel heard that **N** had been 1 Kgs 21:15
of the vineyard of **N** the Jezreelite, 1 Kgs 21:15
you for money, for **N** is not alive, 1 Kgs 21:15
as Ahab heard that **N** was dead, 1 Kgs 21:16
to the vineyard of **N** the Jezreelite, 1 Kgs 21:16
behold, he is in the vineyard of **N**, 1 Kgs 21:18
up the blood of **N** shall dogs lick 1 Kgs 21:19
him at the property of **N** the Jezreelite. 2 Kgs 9:21
ground belonging to **N** the Jezreelite. 2 Kgs 9:25
the blood of **N** and the blood 2 Kgs 9:26

NACON (1)
they came to the threshing floor of **N**, 2 Sm 6:6

NADAB (20)
sister of Nahshon, and she bore him **N**, Ex 6:23
the LORD, you and Aaron, **N**, and Abihu, Ex 24:1
Then Moses and Aaron, **N**, and Abihu, Ex 24:9
Aaron and Aaron's sons, **N** and Abihu, Ex 28:1
Now **N** and Abihu, the sons of Aaron, Lv 10:1
N the firstborn, and Abihu, Eleazar, and Nm 3:2
But **N** and Abihu died before the LORD Nm 3:4
And to Aaron were born **N**, Abihu, Nm 26:60
But **N** and Abihu died when they Nm 26:61
and **N** his son reigned in his place. 1 Kgs 14:20
N the son of Jeroboam began to 1 Kgs 15:25
for **N** and all Israel were laying siege 1 Kgs 15:27
rest of the acts of **N** and all that he 1 Kgs 15:31
sons of Shammai: **N** and Abishur. 1 Chr 2:28
The sons of **N**: Seled and Appaim; 1 Chr 2:30
N, Abihu, Eleazar, and Ithamar. 1 Chr 6:3
son: Abdon, then Zur, Kish, Baal, **N**, 1 Chr 8:30
Abdon, then Zur, Kish, Baal, Ner, **N**, 1 Chr 9:36
N, Abihu, Eleazar, and Ithamar. 1 Chr 24:1
But **N** and Abihu died before their 1 Chr 24:2

NAGGAI (1)
of Nahum, the son of Esli, the son of **N**, Lk 3:25

NAHALAL (2)
and Kattath, **N**, Shimron, Idalah, and Jos 19:15
N with its pasturelands—four cities; Jos 21:35

NAHALIEL (2)
and from Mattanah to **N**, and from Nm 21:19
to Nahaliel, and from **N** to Bamoth, Nm 21:19

NAHALOL (1)
of Kitron, or the inhabitants of **N**, Jgs 1:30

NAHAM (1)
of the wife of Hodiah, the sister of **N**, 1 Chr 4:19

NAHAMANI (1)
Azariah, Raamiah, **N**, Mordecai, Neh 7:7

NAHARAI (2)
Zelek the Ammonite, **N** of Beeroth, 2 Sm 23:37
Zelek the Ammonite, **N** of Beeroth, 1 Chr 11:39

NAHASH (9)
Then **N** the Ammonite went up and 1 Sm 11:1
and all the men of Jabesh said to **N**, 1 Sm 11:1
But **N** the Ammonite said to them, 1 Sm 11:2
when you saw that **N** the king of the 1 Sm 12:12
deal loyally with Hanun the son of **N**, 2 Sm 10:2
married Abigal the daughter of **N**, 2 Sm 17:25
Shobi the son of **N** from Rabbah of 2 Sm 17:27
Now after this **N** the king of the 1 Chr 19:1
deal kindly with Hanun the son of **N**, 1 Chr 19:2

NAHATH (5)
N, Zerah, Shammah, and Mizzah. Gn 36:13
the chiefs **N**, Zerah, Shammah, and Gn 36:17
N, Zerah, Shammah, and Mizzah. 1 Chr 1:37
his son, Zophai his son, **N** his son, 1 Chr 6:26
while Jehiel, Azaziah, **N**, Asahel, 2 Chr 31:13

NAHBI (1)
tribe of Naphtali, **N** the son of Vophsi; Nm 13:14

NAHOR (17)
Serug had lived 30 years, he fathered **N**. Gn 11:22
lived after he fathered **N** 200 years and Gn 11:23
When **N** had lived 29 years, he Gn 11:24
And **N** lived after he fathered Terah Gn 11:25
he fathered Abram, **N**, and Haran. Gn 11:26
Terah fathered Abram, **N**, and Haran; Gn 11:27
And Abram and **N** took wives. The Gn 11:29
has borne children to your brother **N**: Gn 22:20
These eight Milcah bore to **N**, Gn 22:23
went to Mesopotamia to the city of **N**. Gn 24:10
the son of Milcah, the wife of **N**, Gn 24:15
son of Milcah, whom she bore to **N**." Gn 24:24
know Laban the son of **N**?" They said, Gn 29:5
God of Abraham and the God of **N**, Gn 31:53
Terah, the father of Abraham and of **N**; Jos 24:2
Serug, **N**, Terah; 1 Chr 1:26
the son of Terah, the son of **N**, Lk 3:34

NAHOR'S (2)
wife was Sarai, and the name of **N** wife, Gn 11:29
said, 'The daughter of Bethuel, **N** son, Gn 24:47

NAHSHON (13)
of Amminadab and the sister of **N**, Ex 6:23
from Judah, **N** the son of Amminadab; Nm 1:7
people of Judah being **N** the son of Nm 2:3
the first day was **N** the son of Nm 7:12
was the offering of **N** the son of Nm 7:17
over their company was **N** the son of Nm 10:14
Amminadab fathered **N**, Nahshon Ru 4:20
fathered Nahshon, **N** fathered Salmon, Ru 4:20
and Amminadab fathered **N**, 1 Chr 2:10
N fathered Salmon, Salmon fathered 1 Chr 2:11
and Amminadab the father of **N**, Mt 1:4
of Nahshon, and **N** the father of Salmon, Mt 1:4
son of Boaz, the son of Sala, the son of **N**, Lk 3:32

NAHUM (2)
The book of the vision of **N** of Elkosh. Na 1:1
the son of Amos, the son of **N**, Lk 3:25

NAILING (1)
This he set aside, **n** it to the cross. Col 2:14

NAILS (9)
she shall shave her head and pare her **n**. Dt 21:12
quantities of iron for **n** for the doors 1 Chr 22:3
of gold for the **n** was fifty shekels. 2 Chr 3:9
and like **n** firmly fixed are the Eccl 12:11
they strengthen it with **n** so that it cannot Is 41:7
it with hammer and **n** so that it cannot Jer 10:4
and his **n** were like birds' claws. Dn 4:33
I see in his hands the mark of the **n**, Jn 20:25
place my finger into the mark of the **n**, Jn 20:25

NAIN (1)
afterward he went to a town called **N**, Lk 7:11

NAIOTH (6)
he and Samuel went and lived at **N**. 1 Sm 19:18
"Behold, David is at **N** in Ramah." 1 Sm 19:19
"Behold, they are at **N** in Ramah." 1 Sm 19:22
And he went there to **N** in Ramah. 1 Sm 19:23
until he came to **N** in Ramah. 1 Sm 19:23
David fled from **N** in Ramah and 1 Sm 20:1

NAIVE (1)
they deceive the hearts of the **n**. Rom 16:18

NAKED (40)
his wife were both **n** and were not Gn 2:25
opened, and they knew that they were **n**. Gn 3:7
and I was afraid, because I was **n**, Gn 3:10
He said, "Who told you that you were **n**? Gn 3:11
undergarments to cover their **n** flesh. Ex 28:42
he has made **n** her fountain, Lv 20:18
for that is to make **n** one's relative; Lv 20:19
before Samuel and lay **n** all that day 1 Sm 19:24
all who were **n** among them. 2 Chr 28:15
"**N** I came from my mother's womb, Jb 1:21
my mother's womb, and **n** shall I return. Jb 1:21
and stripped the **n** of their clothing. Jb 22:6
They lie all night **n**, without clothing, Jb 24:7
They go about **n**, without clothing; Jb 24:10
Sheol is **n** before God, and Abaddon has Jb 26:6
womb he shall go again, **n** as he came, Eccl 5:15
and he did so, walking **n** and barefoot. Is 20:2
Isaiah has walked **n** and barefoot for Is 20:3
the young and the old, **n** and barefoot, Is 20:4
when you see the **n**, to cover him, and not Is 58:7
had grown; yet you were **n** and bare. Ezk 16:7
youth, when you were **n** and bare, Ezk 16:22
jewels and leave you **n** and bare. Ezk 16:39
and covers the **n** with a garment, Ezk 18:7
and covers the **n** with a garment, Ezk 18:16
your labor and leave you **n** and bare, Ezk 23:29
lest I strip her **n** and make her as in the Hos 2:3
mighty shall flee away **n** in that day," Am 2:16
lament and wail; I will go stripped and **n**; Mi 1:8
I was **n** and you clothed me, I was sick Mt 25:36
and welcome you, or **n** and clothe you? Mt 25:38
me, **n** and you did not clothe me, Mt 25:43
thirsty or a stranger or **n** or sick or in Mt 25:44

he left the linen cloth and ran away **n**. Mk 14:52
fled out of that house **n** and wounded. Acts 19:16
putting it on we may not be found **n**. 2 Cor 5:3
but all are **n** and exposed to the eyes of Heb 4:13
are wretched, pitiable, poor, blind, and **n**. Rv 3:17
may not go about **n** and be seen Rv 16:15
They will make her desolate and **n**, and Rv 17:16

NAKEDNESS (58)

saw the **n** of his father and told his two Gn 9:22
and covered the **n** of their father. Gn 9:23
and they did not see their father's **n**. Gn 9:23
you have come to see the **n** of the land." Gn 42:9
it is the **n** of the land that you have Gn 42:12
altar, that your **n** be not exposed on it.' Ex 20:26
one of his close relatives to uncover **n**. Lv 18:6
shall not uncover the **n** of your father, Lv 18:7
father, which is the **n** of your mother; Lv 18:7
mother, you shall not uncover her **n**. Lv 18:7
shall not uncover the **n** of your father's Lv 18:8
of your father's wife; it is your father's **n**. Lv 18:8
shall not uncover the **n** of your sister, Lv 18:9
shall not uncover the **n** of your son's Lv 18:10
for their **n** is your own nakedness. Lv 18:10
for their nakedness is your own **n**. Lv 18:10
shall not uncover the **n** of your father's Lv 18:11
shall not uncover the **n** of your father's Lv 18:12
not uncover the **n** of your mother's Lv 18:13
shall not uncover the **n** of your father's Lv 18:14
not uncover the **n** of your Lv 18:15
son's wife, you shall not uncover her **n**. Lv 18:15
not uncover the **n** of your brother's Lv 18:16
brother's wife; it is your brother's **n**. Lv 18:16
shall not uncover the **n** of a woman Lv 18:17
daughter's daughter to uncover her **n**; Lv 18:17
uncovering her **n** while her sister is Lv 18:18
woman to uncover her **n** while she is in Lv 18:19
wife, he has uncovered his father's **n**; Lv 20:11
daughter of his mother, and sees her **n**, Lv 20:17
sees her nakedness, and she sees his **n**, Lv 20:17
He has uncovered his sister's **n**, and he Lv 20:17
menstrual period and uncovers her **n**, Lv 20:18
not uncover the **n** of your mother's Lv 20:19
wife, he has uncovered his uncle's **n**; Lv 20:20
He has uncovered his brother's **n**; they Lv 20:21
that he does not uncover his father's **n**. Dt 22:30
he has uncovered his father's **n**.' Dt 27:20
against you, in hunger and thirst, in **n**, Dt 28:48
to the shame of your mother's **n**? 1 Sm 20:30
with buttocks uncovered, the **n** of Egypt. Is 20:4
Your **n** shall be uncovered, and your Is 47:3
loved their bed, you have looked on **n**. Is 57:8
her despise her, for they have seen her **n**; Lam 1:8
garment over you and covered your **n**; Ezk 16:8
out and your **n** uncovered in your Ezk 16:36
side and will uncover your **n** to them, Ezk 16:37
to them, that they may see all your **n**. Ezk 16:37
In you men uncover their fathers' **n**; Ezk 22:10
These uncovered her **n**; they seized her Ezk 23:10
whoring so openly and flaunted her **n**, Ezk 23:18
and the **n** of your whoring shall be Ezk 23:29
and my flax, which were to cover her **n**. Hos 2:9
inhabitants of Shaphir, in **n** and shame; Mi 1:11
nations look at your **n** and kingdoms at Na 3:5
them drunk, in order to gaze at their **n**! Hab 2:15
or persecution, or famine, or **n**, Rom 8:35
the shame of your **n** may not be seen, Rv 3:18

NAME (912)

The **n** of the first is the Pishon. It is the Gn 2:11
The **n** of the second river is the Gihon. It Gn 2:13
And the **n** of the third river is the Tigris, Gn 2:14
every living creature, that was its **n**. Gn 2:19
The man called his wife's **n** Eve, Gn 3:20
he called the **n** of the city after the name Gn 4:17
name of the city after the **n** of his son, Gn 4:17
The **n** of the one was Adah, and the Gn 4:19
was Adah, and the **n** of the other Zillah. Gn 4:19
His brother's **n** was Jubal; he was the Gn 4:21
and she bore a son and called his **n** Seth, Gn 4:25
was born, and he called his **n** Enosh. Gn 4:26
began to call upon the **n** of the LORD. Gn 4:26
and called his **n** Noah, saying, "Out of Gn 5:29
the **n** of the one was Peleg, for in his Gn 10:25
and his brother's **n** was Joktan. Gn 10:25
and let us make a **n** for ourselves, Gn 11:4
Therefore its **n** was called Babel, Gn 11:9
The **n** of Abram's wife was Sarai, and Gn 11:29
was Sarai, and the **n** of Nahor's wife, Gn 11:29
I will bless you and make your **n** great, Gn 12:2
LORD and called upon the **n** of the LORD. Gn 12:8
Abram called upon the **n** of the LORD. Gn 13:4
Egyptian servant whose **n** was Hagar. Gn 16:1
You shall call his **n** Ishmael, because Gn 16:11
So she called the **n** of the LORD who Gn 16:13
son, and Abram called the **n** of his son, Gn 16:15

longer shall your **n** be called Abram, Gn 17:5
Abram, but your **n** shall be Abraham, Gn 17:5
wife, you shall not call her **n** Sarai, Gn 17:15
name Sarai, but Sarah shall be her **n**. Gn 17:15
a son, and you shall call his **n** Isaac. Gn 17:19
there." Therefore the **n** of the city Gn 19:22
bore a son and called his **n** Moab. Gn 19:37
bore a son and called his **n** Ben-ammi. Gn 19:38
Abraham called the **n** of his son who Gn 21:3
and called there on the **n** of the LORD, Gn 21:33
So Abraham called the **n** of that place, Gn 22:14
his concubine, whose **n** was Reumah, Gn 22:24
had a brother whose **n** was Laban. Gn 24:29
another wife, whose **n** was Keturah. Gn 25:1
hairy cloak, so they called his **n** Esau. Gn 25:25
Esau's heel, so his **n** was called Jacob. Gn 25:26
(Therefore his **n** was called Gn 25:30
So he called the **n** of the well Esek, Gn 26:20
over that also, so he called its **n** Sitnah. Gn 26:21
So he called its **n** Rehoboth, saying, Gn 26:22
and called upon the **n** of the LORD and Gn 26:25
therefore the **n** of the city is Beersheba Gn 26:33
He called the **n** of that place Bethel, but Gn 28:19
but the **n** of the city was Luz at the Gn 28:19
The **n** of the older was Leah, and the Gn 29:16
and the **n** of the younger was Rachel. Gn 29:16
a son, and she called his **n** Reuben, Gn 29:32
son also." And she called his **n** Simeon. Gn 29:33
sons." Therefore his **n** was called Levi. Gn 29:34
Therefore she called his **n** Judah. Gn 29:35
a son." Therefore she called his **n** Dan. Gn 30:6
prevailed." So she called his **n** Naphtali. Gn 30:8
has come!" so she called his **n** Gad. Gn 30:11
me happy." So she called his **n** Asher. Gn 30:13
husband." So she called his **n** Issachar. Gn 30:18
six sons." So she called his **n** Zebulun. Gn 30:20
a daughter and called her **n** Dinah. Gn 30:21
And she called his **n** Joseph, saying, Gn 30:24
N your wages, and I will give it." Gn 30:28
So he called the **n** of that place Gn 32:2
to him, "What is your **n**?" And he said, Gn 32:27
"Your **n** shall no longer be called Gn 32:28
"Please tell me your **n**." But he said, Gn 32:29
that you ask my **n**?" And there he Gn 32:29
So Jacob called the **n** of the place Gn 32:30
Therefore the **n** of the place is called Gn 33:17
Bethel. So he called its **n** Allon-bacuth. Gn 35:8
And God said to him, "Your **n** is Jacob; Gn 35:10
no longer shall your **n** be called Jacob, Gn 35:10
Israel shall be your **n**." So he called his Gn 35:10
your name." So he called his **n** Israel. Gn 35:10
So Jacob called the **n** of the place where Gn 35:15
was dying), she called his **n** Ben-oni; Gn 35:18
the **n** of his city being Dinhabah. Gn 36:32
his place, the **n** of his city being Avith. Gn 36:35
his place, the **n** of his city being Pau; Gn 36:39
being Pau; his wife's **n** was Mehetabel, Gn 36:39
certain Adullamite, whose **n** was Hirah. Gn 38:1
a certain Canaanite whose **n** was Shua. Gn 38:2
and bore a son, and he called his **n** Er. Gn 38:3
bore a son, and she called his **n** Onan. Gn 38:4
bore a son, and she called his **n** Shelah. Gn 38:5
Er his firstborn, and her **n** was Tamar. Gn 38:6
yourself!" Therefore his **n** was called Gn 38:29
his hand, and his **n** was called Zerah. Gn 38:30
called Joseph's **n** Zaphenath-paneah. Gn 41:45
Joseph called the **n** of the firstborn Gn 41:51
The **n** of the second he called Ephraim, Gn 41:52
be called by the **n** of their brothers in Gn 48:6
and in them let my **n** be carried on, Gn 48:16
and the **n** of my fathers Abraham and Gn 48:16
to a son, and he called his **n** Gershom, Ex 2:22
to you,' and they ask me, 'What is his **n**?' Ex 3:13
This is my **n** forever, and thus I am to be Ex 3:15
I came to Pharaoh to speak in your **n**, Ex 5:23
but by my **n** the LORD I did not make Ex 6:3
so that my **n** may be proclaimed in all Ex 9:16
LORD is a man of war; the LORD is his **n**. Ex 15:3
the house of Israel called its **n** manna. Ex 16:31
And he called the **n** of the place Massah Ex 17:7
built an altar and called the **n** of it, Ex 17:15
The **n** of the one was Gershom (for he Ex 18:3
and the **n** of the other, Eliezer (for he Ex 18:4
shall not take the **n** of the LORD your Ex 20:7
him guiltless who takes his **n** in vain. Ex 20:7
where I cause my **n** to be remembered I Ex 20:24
your transgression, for my **n** is in him. Ex 23:21
like signets, each engraved with its **n**, Ex 28:21
I have called by **n** Bezalel the son of Uri, Ex 31:2
Yet you have said, 'I know you by **n**, Ex 33:12
in my sight, and I know you by **n**." Ex 33:17
proclaim before you my **n** 'The LORD.' Ex 33:19
there, and proclaimed the **n** of the LORD. Ex 34:5
god, for the LORD, whose **n** is Jealous, Ex 34:14
LORD has called by **n** Bezalel the son of Ex 35:30

like signets, each engraved with its **n**, Ex 39:14
and so profane the **n** of your God: Lv 18:21
You shall not swear by my **n** falsely, Lv 19:12
and so profane the **n** of your God: Lv 19:12
unclean and to profane my holy **n**. Lv 20:3
God and not profane the **n** of their God. Lv 21:6
so that they do not profane my holy **n**: Lv 22:2
And you shall not profane my holy **n**, Lv 22:32
woman's son blasphemed the **N**, Lv 24:11
Moses. His mother's **n** was Shelomith, Lv 24:11
Whoever blasphemes the **n** of the LORD Lv 24:16
the native, when he blasphemes the **N**, Lv 24:16
you shall list by **n** the objects that they Nm 4:32
shall they put my **n** upon the people of Nm 6:27
So the **n** of that place was called Nm 11:3
Therefore the **n** of that place was Nm 11:34
staffs. Write each man's **n** on his staff, Nm 17:2
and write Aaron's **n** on the staff of Levi. Nm 17:3
So the **n** of the place was called Nm 21:3
The **n** of the slain man of Israel, who Nm 25:14
And the **n** of the Midianite woman Nm 25:15
And the **n** of the daughter of Asher Nm 26:46
The **n** of Amram's wife was Jochebed Nm 26:59
Why should the **n** of our father be Nm 27:4
and called it Nobah, after his own **n**. Nm 32:42
and called the villages after his own **n**, Dt 3:14
shall not take the **n** of the LORD your Dt 5:11
him guiltless who takes his **n** in vain. Dt 5:11
shall serve and by his **n** you shall swear. Dt 6:13
shall make their **n** perish from under Dt 7:24
and blot out their **n** from under heaven. Dt 9:14
to minister to him and to bless in his **n**, Dt 10:8
to him, and by his **n** you shall swear. Dt 10:20
gods and destroy their **n** out of that place. Dt 12:3
tribes to put his **n** and make his Dt 12:5
will choose, to make his **n** dwell there, Dt 12:11
will choose to put his **n** there is too far Dt 12:21
will choose, to make his **n** dwell there, Dt 14:23
your God chooses, to set his **n** there, Dt 14:24
will choose, to make his **n** dwell there. Dt 16:2
will choose, to make his **n** dwell in it, Dt 16:6
will choose, to make his **n** dwell there. Dt 16:11
stand and minister in the **n** of the LORD, Dt 18:5
and ministers in the **n** of the LORD his Dt 18:7
my words that he shall speak in my **n**, Dt 18:19
speak a word in my **n** that I have not Dt 18:20
or who speaks in the **n** of other gods, Dt 18:20
a prophet speaks in the **n** of the LORD, Dt 18:22
to him and to bless in the **n** of the LORD, Dt 21:5
and brings a bad **n** upon her, Dt 22:14
has brought a bad **n** upon a virgin of Dt 22:19
shall succeed to the **n** of his dead Dt 25:6
that his **n** may not be blotted out of Dt 25:6
to perpetuate his brother's **n** in Israel; Dt 25:7
And the **n** of his house shall be called Dt 25:10
will choose, to make his **n** to dwell there. Dt 26:2
that you are called by the **n** of the LORD, Dt 28:10
may fear this glorious and awesome **n**, Dt 28:58
will blot out his **n** from under heaven. Dt 29:20
For I will proclaim the **n** of the LORD; Dt 32:3
of a prostitute whose **n** was Rahab and Jos 2:1
from you." And so the **n** of that place is Jos 5:9
us and cut off our **n** from the earth. Jos 7:9
And what will you do for your great **n**?" Jos 7:9
to this day the **n** of that place is called Jos 7:26
because of the **n** of the LORD your God. Jos 9:9
Now the **n** of Hebron formerly was Jos 14:15
Now the **n** of Debir formerly was Jos 15:15
Dan, after the **n** of Dan their ancestor. Jos 19:47
the following cities mentioned by **n**, Jos 21:9
in Hebron (now the **n** of Hebron was Jgs 1:10
The **n** of Debir was formerly Jgs 1:11
So the **n** of the city was called Hormah. Jgs 1:17
(Now the **n** of the city was formerly Jgs 1:23
and built a city and called its **n** Luz. Jgs 1:26
its name Luz. That is its **n** to this day. Jgs 1:26
And they called the **n** of that place Jgs 2:5
a son, and he called his **n** Abimelech. Jgs 8:31
of the Danites, whose **n** was Manoah. Jgs 13:2
was from, and he did not tell me his **n**, Jgs 13:6
the angel of the LORD, "What is your **n**, Jgs 13:17
said to him, "Why do you ask my **n**, Jgs 13:18
bore a son and called his **n** Samson. Jgs 13:24
Therefore the **n** of it was called Jgs 15:19
Valley of Sorek, whose **n** was Delilah. Jgs 16:4
of Ephraim, whose **n** was Micah. Jgs 17:1
Dan, after the **n** of Dan their ancestor, Jgs 18:29
but the **n** of the city was Laish at the Jgs 18:29
The **n** of the man was Elimelech and the Ru 1:2
was Elimelech and the **n** of his wife Ru 1:2
the **n** of the one was Orpah and the name Ru 1:4
was Orpah and the **n** of the other Ruth. Ru 1:4
the clan of Elimelech, whose **n** was Boaz. Ru 2:1
"The man's **n** with whom I worked Ru 2:19
in order to perpetuate the **n** of the dead in Ru 4:5

to perpetuate the **n** of the dead in his	Ru 4:10
that the **n** of the dead may not be cut off	Ru 4:10
and may his **n** be renowned in Israel!	Ru 4:14
of the neighborhood gave him a **n**,	Ru 4:17
of Ephraim whose **n** was Elkanah the	1 Sm 1:1
The **n** of the one was Hannah, and the	1 Sm 1:2
was Hannah, and the **n** of the other,	1 Sm 1:2
a son, and she called his **n** Samuel,	1 Sm 1:20
and Shen and called its **n** Ebenezer;	1 Sm 7:12
The **n** of his firstborn son was Joel, and	1 Sm 8:2
son was Joel, and the **n** of his second,	1 Sm 8:2
a man of Benjamin whose **n** was Kish,	1 Sm 9:1
And he had a son whose **n** was Saul, a	1 Sm 9:2
The **n** of the one was Bozez, and the	1 Sm 14:4
Bozez, and the **n** of the other Seneh.	1 Sm 14:4
the **n** of the firstborn was Merab,	1 Sm 14:49
and the **n** of the younger Michal.	1 Sm 14:49
And the **n** of Saul's wife was	1 Sm 14:50
And the **n** of the commander of his	1 Sm 14:50
the Philistine of Gath, Goliath by **n**,	1 Sm 17:23
come to you in the **n** of the LORD of	1 Sm 17:45
so that his **n** was highly esteemed.	1 Sm 18:30
sworn both of us in the **n** of the LORD,	1 Sm 20:42
His **n** was Doeg the Edomite, the chief	1 Sm 21:7
will not destroy my **n** out of my	1 Sm 24:21
Now the **n** of the man was Nabal, and	1 Sm 25:3
Nabal, and the **n** of his wife Abigail.	1 Sm 25:3
go to Nabal and greet him in my **n**.	1 Sm 25:5
all this to Nabal in the **n** of David,	1 Sm 25:9
fellow, Nabal, for as his **n** is,	1 Sm 25:25
Nabal is his **n**, and folly is with him.	1 Sm 25:25
up for me whomever I shall **n** to you."	1 Sm 28:8
had a concubine whose **n** was Rizpah,	2 Sm 3:7
the **n** of the one was Baanah, and the	2 Sm 4:2
Baanah, and the **n** of the other Rechab,	2 Sm 4:2
lame. And his **n** was Mephibosheth.	2 Sm 4:4
flood." Therefore the **n** of that place	2 Sm 5:20
which is called by the **n** of the LORD of	2 Sm 6:2
the people in the **n** of the LORD of	2 Sm 6:18
And I will make for you a great **n**, like	2 Sm 7:9
like the **n** of the great ones of the earth.	2 Sm 7:9
He shall build a house for my **n**, and I	2 Sm 7:13
making himself a **n** and doing for	2 Sm 7:23
And your **n** will be magnified forever,	2 Sm 7:26
And David made a **n** for himself when	2 Sm 8:13
of the house of Saul whose **n** was Ziba,	2 Sm 9:2
had a young son, whose **n** was Mica.	2 Sm 9:12
a son, and he called his **n** Solomon.	2 Sm 12:24
So he called his **n** Jedidiah, because	2 Sm 12:25
the city and it be called by my **n**."	2 Sm 12:28
beautiful sister, whose **n** was Tamar.	2 Sm 13:1
had a friend, whose **n** was Jonadab,	2 Sm 13:3
my husband neither **n** nor remnant	2 Sm 14:7
one daughter whose **n** was Tamar.	2 Sm 14:27
house of Saul, whose **n** was Shimei,	2 Sm 16:5
to keep my **n** in remembrance." He	2 Sm 18:18
He called the pillar after his own **n**,	2 Sm 18:18
a worthless man, whose **n** was Sheba,	2 Sm 20:1
nations, and sing praises to your **n**.	2 Sm 22:50
them and won a **n** beside the three.	2 Sm 23:18
and won a **n** beside the three mighty	2 Sm 23:22
God make the **n** of Solomon more	1 Kgs 1:47
had yet been built for the **n** of the LORD.	1 Kgs 3:2
build a house for the **n** of the LORD his	1 Kgs 5:3
build a house for the **n** of the LORD my	1 Kgs 5:5
place, shall build the house for my **n**.'	1 Kgs 5:5
on the south and called its **n** Jachin,	1 Kgs 7:21
on the north and called its **n** Boaz.	1 Kgs 7:21
a house, that my **n** might be there.	1 Kgs 8:16
to build a house for the **n** of the LORD,	1 Kgs 8:17
your heart to build a house for my **n**,	1 Kgs 8:18
you shall build the house for my **n**.'	1 Kgs 8:19
built the house for the **n** of the LORD,	1 Kgs 8:20
you have said, 'My **n** shall be there,'	1 Kgs 8:29
and acknowledge your **n** and pray	1 Kgs 8:33
and acknowledge your **n** and turn	1 Kgs 8:35
hear of your great **n** and your mighty	1 Kgs 8:42
earth may know your **n** and fear you,	1 Kgs 8:43
that I have built is called by your **n**.	1 Kgs 8:43
the house that I have built for your **n**.	1 Kgs 8:44
the house that I have built for your **n**,	1 Kgs 8:48
built, by putting my **n** there forever.	1 Kgs 9:3
have consecrated for my **n** I will cast	1 Kgs 9:7
Solomon concerning the **n** of the	1 Kgs 10:1
whose mother's **n** was Zeruah,	1 Kgs 11:26
where I have chosen to put my **n**.	1 Kgs 11:36
to the house of David, Josiah by **n**,	1 Kgs 13:2
the tribes of Israel, to put his **n** there.	1 Kgs 14:21
His mother's **n** was Naamah the	1 Kgs 14:21
His mother's **n** was Naamah the	1 Kgs 14:31
His mother's **n** was Maacah the	1 Kgs 15:2
His mother's **n** was Maacah the	1 Kgs 15:10
hill and called the **n** of the city that	1 Kgs 16:24
built Samaria, after the **n** of Shemer,	1 Kgs 16:24
you call upon the **n** of your god,	1 Kgs 18:24
I will call upon the **n** of the LORD,	1 Kgs 18:24
and call upon the **n** of your god,	1 Kgs 18:25
and called upon the **n** of Baal from	1 Kgs 18:26
saying, "Israel shall be your **n**,"	1 Kgs 18:31
he built an altar in the **n** of the LORD.	1 Kgs 18:32
letters in Ahab's **n** and sealed them	1 Kgs 21:8
but the truth in the **n** of the LORD?"	1 Kgs 22:16
His mother's **n** was Azubah the	1 Kgs 22:42
he cursed them in the **n** of the LORD.	2 Kgs 2:24
and call upon the **n** of the LORD his	2 Kgs 5:11
His mother's **n** was Athaliah;	2 Kgs 8:26
His mother's **n** was Zibiah of	2 Kgs 12:1
His mother's **n** was Jehoaddin of	2 Kgs 14:2
it Joktheel, which is its **n** to this day.	2 Kgs 14:7
would blot out the **n** of Israel from	2 Kgs 14:27
His mother's **n** was Jecoliah of	2 Kgs 15:2
His mother's **n** was Jerusha the	2 Kgs 15:33
His mother's **n** was Abi the daughter	2 Kgs 18:2
His mother's **n** was Hephzibah.	2 Kgs 21:1
said, "In Jerusalem will I put my **n**."	2 Kgs 21:4
of Israel, I will put my **n** forever.	2 Kgs 21:7
His mother's **n** was Meshullemeth	2 Kgs 21:19
His mother's **n** was Jedidah the	2 Kgs 22:1
of which I said, My **n** shall be there."	2 Kgs 23:27
His mother's **n** was Hamutal the	2 Kgs 23:31
and changed his **n** to Jehoiakim.	2 Kgs 23:34
His mother's **n** was Zebidah the	2 Kgs 23:36
His mother's **n** was Nehushta the	2 Kgs 24:8
and changed his **n** to Zedekiah.	2 Kgs 24:17
His mother's **n** was Hamutal the	2 Kgs 24:18
the **n** of the one was Peleg (for in his	1 Chr 1:19
and his brother's **n** was Joktan.	1 Chr 1:19
the **n** of his city being Dinhabah.	1 Chr 1:43
place, the **n** of his city being Avith.	1 Chr 1:46
his place, the **n** of his city being Pai;	1 Chr 1:50
and his wife's **n** was Mehetabel, the	1 Chr 1:50
another wife, whose **n** was Atarah;	1 Chr 2:26
The **n** of Abishur's wife was Abihail,	1 Chr 2:29
an Egyptian slave whose **n** was Jarha.	1 Chr 2:34
and the **n** of their sister was	1 Chr 4:3
and his mother called his **n** Jabez,	1 Chr 4:9
these mentioned by **n** were princes in	1 Chr 4:38
These, registered by **n**, came in the	1 Chr 4:41
these cities that are mentioned by **n**.	1 Chr 6:65
The **n** of his sister was Maacah.	1 Chr 7:15
And the **n** of the second was	1 Chr 7:15
a son, and she called his **n** Peresh;	1 Chr 7:16
and the **n** of his brother was Sheresh;	1 Chr 7:16
And he called his **n** Beriah, because	1 Chr 7:23
and the **n** of his wife was Maacah.	1 Chr 8:29
and the **n** of his wife was Maacah,	1 Chr 9:35
them and won a **n** beside the three.	1 Chr 11:20
and won a **n** beside the three	1 Chr 11:24
is called by the **n** of the LORD who	1 Chr 13:6
flood." Therefore the **n** of that place	1 Chr 14:11
blessed the people in the **n** of the LORD	1 Chr 16:2
thanks to the LORD; call upon his **n**;	1 Chr 16:8
Glory in his holy **n**; let the hearts of	1 Chr 16:10
to the LORD the glory due his **n**;	1 Chr 16:29
we may give thanks to your holy **n**,	1 Chr 16:35
And I will make for you a **n**, like the	1 Chr 17:8
like the **n** of the great ones of the	1 Chr 17:8
for yourself a **n** for great and	1 Chr 17:21
and your **n** will be established and	1 Chr 17:24
he had spoken in the **n** of the LORD.	1 Chr 21:19
build a house to the **n** of the LORD my	1 Chr 22:7
You shall not build a house to my **n**,	1 Chr 22:8
For his **n** shall be Solomon, and I	1 Chr 22:9
He shall build a house for my **n**. He	1 Chr 22:10
a house built for the **n** of the LORD."	1 Chr 22:19
blessings in his **n** forever.	1 Chr 23:13
may not build a house for my **n**,	1 Chr 28:3
our God, and praise your glorious **n**.	1 Chr 29:13
for your holy **n** comes from your	1 Chr 29:16
to build a temple for the **n** of the LORD,	2 Chr 2:1
build a house for the **n** of the LORD my	2 Chr 2:4
a house, that my **n** might be there,	2 Chr 6:5
Jerusalem that my **n** may be there,	2 Chr 6:6
to build a house for the **n** of the LORD,	2 Chr 6:7
your heart to build a house for my **n**,	2 Chr 6:8
to you shall build the house for my **n**.'	2 Chr 6:9
built the house for the **n** of the LORD,	2 Chr 6:10
you have promised to set your **n**,	2 Chr 6:20
and acknowledge your **n** and pray	2 Chr 6:24
and acknowledge your **n** and turn	2 Chr 6:26
sake of your great **n** and your mighty	2 Chr 6:32
earth may know your **n** and fear you,	2 Chr 6:33
that I have built is called by your **n**.	2 Chr 6:33
the house that I have built for your **n**,	2 Chr 6:34
the house that I have built for your **n**,	2 Chr 6:38
called by my **n** humble themselves,	2 Chr 7:14
this house that my **n** may be there	2 Chr 7:16
that I have consecrated for my **n**,	2 Chr 7:20
the tribes of Israel to put his **n** there.	2 Chr 12:13
His mother's **n** was Naamah the	2 Chr 12:13
His mother's **n** was Micaiah the	2 Chr 13:2
and in your **n** we have come against	2 Chr 14:11
but the truth in the **n** of the LORD?"	2 Chr 18:15
for you in it a sanctuary for your **n**,	2 Chr 20:8
you—for your **n** is in this house	2 Chr 20:9
Therefore the **n** of that place has	2 Chr 20:26
His mother's **n** was Azubah the	2 Chr 20:31
His mother's **n** was Athaliah,	2 Chr 22:2
His mother's **n** was Zibiah of	2 Chr 24:1
His mother's **n** was Jehoaddan of	2 Chr 25:1
His mother's **n** was Jecoliah of	2 Chr 26:3
His mother's **n** was Jerushah the	2 Chr 27:1
LORD was there, whose **n** was Oded,	2 Chr 28:9
been mentioned by **n** rose and took	2 Chr 28:15
His mother's **n** was Abijah the	2 Chr 29:1
were designated by **n** to distribute	2 Chr 31:19
"In Jerusalem shall my **n** be forever."	2 Chr 33:4
of Israel, I will put my **n** forever,	2 Chr 33:7
spoke to him in the **n** of the LORD,	2 Chr 33:18
and changed his **n** to Jehoiakim.	2 Chr 36:4
the Gileadite, and was called by their **n**).	Ezr 2:61
in the **n** of the God of Israel who was over	Ezr 5:1
to one whose **n** was Sheshbazzar,	Ezr 5:14
who has caused his **n** to dwell there	Ezr 6:12
Levites. These were all mentioned by **n**.	Ezr 8:20
houses, each of them designated by **n**.	Ezr 10:16
have chosen, to make my **n** dwell there.'	Neh 1:9
servants who delight to fear your **n**,	Neh 1:11
could give me a bad **n** in order to taunt	Neh 6:13
Gileadite and was called by their **n**).	Neh 7:63
Blessed be your glorious **n**, which is	Neh 9:5
and gave him the **n** Abraham.	Neh 9:7
And you made a **n** for yourself, as it is	Neh 9:10
made them take oath in the **n** of God,	Neh 13:25
Susa the citadel whose **n** was Mordecai,	Est 2:5
in her and she was summoned by **n**.	Est 2:14
told the king in the **n** of Mordecai.	Est 2:22
was written in the **n** of King Ahasuerus	Est 3:12
regard to the Jews, in the **n** of the king,	Est 8:8
an edict written in the **n** of the king and	Est 8:8
he wrote in the **n** of King Ahasuerus	Est 8:10
a man in the land of Uz whose **n** was Job,	Jb 1:1
taken away; blessed be the **n** of the LORD."	Jb 1:21
the earth, and he has no **n** in the street.	Jb 18:17
And he called the **n** of the first daughter	Jb 42:14
and the **n** of the second Keziah,	Jb 42:14
and the **n** of the third Keren-happuch.	Jb 42:14
those who love your **n** may exult in you.	Ps 5:11
and I will sing praise to the **n** of the LORD,	Ps 7:17
how majestic is your **n** in all the earth!	Ps 8:1
how majestic is your **n** in all the earth!	Ps 8:9
I will sing praise to your **n**, O Most High.	Ps 9:2
have blotted out their **n** forever and ever.	Ps 9:5
those who know your **n** put their trust in	Ps 9:10
among the nations, and sing to your **n**.	Ps 18:49
May the **n** of the God of Jacob protect	Ps 20:1
and in the **n** of our God set up our	Ps 20:5
but we trust in the **n** of the LORD our God.	Ps 20:7
I will tell of your **n** to my brothers; in	Ps 22:22
Ascribe to the LORD the glory due his **n**;	Ps 29:2
his saints, and give thanks to his holy **n**.	Ps 30:4
in him, because we trust in his holy **n**.	Ps 33:21
with me, and let us exalt his **n** together!	Ps 34:3
"When will he die and his **n** perish?"	Ps 41:5
through your **n** we tread down those who	Ps 44:5
we will give thanks to your **n** forever.	Ps 44:8
If we had forgotten the **n** of our God or	Ps 44:20
I will cause your **n** to be remembered in	Ps 45:17
As your **n**, O God, so your praise	Ps 48:10
I will wait for your **n**, for it is good, in the	Ps 52:9
O God, save me, by your **n**, and vindicate	Ps 54:1
I will give thanks to your **n**, O LORD, for it	Ps 54:6
me the heritage of those who fear your **n**.	Ps 61:5
So will I ever sing praises to your **n**, as I	Ps 61:8
as I live; in your **n** I will lift up my hands.	Ps 63:4
sing the glory of his **n**; give to him	Ps 66:2
to you; they sing praises to your **n**." Selah	Ps 66:4
Sing to God, sing praises to his **n**; lift up a	Ps 68:4
through the deserts; his **n** is the LORD;	Ps 68:4
I will praise the **n** of God with a song; I	Ps 69:30
those who love his **n** shall dwell in it.	Ps 69:36
May his **n** endure forever, his fame	Ps 72:17
Blessed be his glorious **n** forever; may	Ps 72:19
profaned the dwelling place of your **n**,	Ps 74:7
Is the enemy to revile your **n** forever?	Ps 74:10
and a foolish people reviles your **n**.	Ps 74:18
let the poor and needy praise your **n**.	Ps 74:21
O God; we give thanks, for your **n** is near.	Ps 75:1
God is known; his **n** is great in Israel.	Ps 76:1
kingdoms that do not call upon your **n**!	Ps 79:6
of our salvation, for the glory of your **n**;	Ps 79:9
us life, and we will call upon your **n**!	Ps 80:18
let the **n** of Israel be remembered no	Ps 83:4
with shame, that they may seek your **n**,	Ps 83:16
that you alone, whose **n** is the LORD,	Ps 83:18

you, O Lord, and shall glorify your **n**. Ps 86:9
truth; unite my heart to fear your **n**. Ps 86:11
heart, and I will glorify your **n** forever. Ps 86:12
and Hermon joyously praise your **n**. Ps 89:12
who exult in your **n** all the day and in Ps 89:16
and in my **n** shall his horn be exalted. Ps 89:24
protect him, because he knows my **n**. Ps 91:14
to the LORD, to sing praises to your **n**, Ps 92:1
Sing to the LORD, bless his **n**; tell of his Ps 96:2
Ascribe to the LORD the glory due his **n**; Ps 96:8
and give thanks to his holy **n**! Ps 97:12
them praise your great and awesome **n**! Ps 99:3
was among those who called upon his **n**. Ps 99:6
praise! Give thanks to him; bless his **n**! Ps 100:4
who deride me use my **n** for a curse. Ps 102:8
Nations will fear the **n** of the LORD, and Ps 102:15
may declare in Zion the **n** of the LORD, Ps 102:21
all that is within me, bless his holy **n**! Ps 103:1
give thanks to the LORD; call upon his **n**; Ps 105:1
Glory in his holy **n**; let the hearts of Ps 105:3
thanks to your holy **n** and glory in Ps 106:47
may his **n** be blotted out in the second Ps 109:13
forever. Holy and awesome is his **n**! Ps 111:9
of the LORD, praise the **n** of the LORD! Ps 113:1
Blessed be the **n** of the LORD from this Ps 113:2
the **n** of the LORD is to be praised! Ps 113:3
LORD, not to us, but to your **n** give glory, Ps 115:1
Then I called on the **n** of the LORD: "O Ps 116:4
salvation and call on the **n** of the LORD, Ps 116:13
and call on the **n** of the LORD. Ps 116:17
me; in the **n** of the LORD I cut them off! Ps 118:10
side; in the **n** of the LORD I cut them off! Ps 118:11
in the **n** of the LORD I cut them off! Ps 118:12
is he who comes in the **n** of the LORD! Ps 118:26
I remember your **n** in the night, O Ps 119:55
your way with those who love your **n**. Ps 119:132
to give thanks to the **n** of the LORD. Ps 122:4
Our help is in the **n** of the LORD, who Ps 124:8
you! We bless you in the **n** of the LORD!" Ps 129:8
Praise the **n** of the LORD, give praise, O Ps 135:1
is good; sing to his **n**, for it is pleasant! Ps 135:3
Your **n**, O LORD, endures forever, your Ps 135:13
give thanks to your **n** for your steadfast Ps 138:2
above all things your **n** and your word. Ps 138:2
your enemies take your **n** in vain! Ps 139:20
righteous shall give thanks to your **n**; Ps 140:13
that I may give thanks to your **n**! Ps 142:7
King, and bless your **n** forever and ever. Ps 145:1
you and praise your **n** forever and ever. Ps 145:2
flesh bless his holy **n** forever and ever. Ps 145:21
Let them praise the **n** of the LORD! For Ps 148:5
Let them praise the **n** of the LORD, for Ps 148:13
of the LORD, for his **n** alone is exalted; Ps 148:13
Let them praise his **n** with dancing, Ps 149:3
but the **n** of the wicked will rot. Prv 10:7
The **n** of the LORD is a strong tower; the Prv 18:10
"Scoffer" is the **n** of the arrogant, Prv 21:24
A good **n** is to be chosen rather than Prv 22:1
What is his **n**, and what is his son's Prv 30:4
is his name, and what is his son's **n**? Prv 30:4
and steal and profane the **n** of my God. Prv 30:9
and in darkness its **n** is covered. Eccl 6:4
A good **n** is better than precious Eccl 7:1
oils are fragrant; your **n** is oil poured out; Sg 1:3
clothes, only let us be called by your **n**; Is 4:1
a son, and shall call his **n** Immanuel. Is 7:14
to me, "Call his **n** Maher-shalal-hashbaz; Is 8:3
and his **n** shall be called Wonderful Is 9:6
"Give thanks to the LORD, call upon his **n**, Is 12:4
the peoples, proclaim that his **n** is exalted. Is 12:4
cut off from Babylon **n** and remnant, Is 14:22
the place of the **n** of the LORD of hosts. Is 18:7
of the sea, give glory to the **n** of the LORD, Is 24:15
I will praise your **n**, for you have done Is 25:1
your **n** and remembrance are the desire Is 26:8
but your **n** alone we bring to Is 26:13
in his midst, they will sanctify my **n**; Is 29:23
the **n** of the LORD comes from afar, Is 30:27
host by number, calling them all by **n**, Is 40:26
of the sun, and he shall call upon my **n**; Is 41:25
I am the LORD; that is my **n**; my glory I Is 42:8
you; I have called you by **n**, you are mine. Is 43:1
everyone who is called by my **n**, whom I Is 43:7
another will call on the **n** of Jacob, Is 44:5
and **n** himself by the name of Israel." Is 44:5
and name himself by the **n** of Israel." Is 44:5
the God of Israel, who call you by your **n**. Is 45:3
Israel my chosen, I call you by your **n**, Is 45:4
chosen, I call you by your name, I **n** you, Is 45:4
LORD of hosts is his **n**—is the Holy One Is 47:4
of Jacob, who are called by the **n** of Israel, Is 48:1
who swear by the **n** of the LORD and Is 48:1
God of Israel; the LORD of hosts is his **n**. Is 48:2
do it, for how should my **n** be profaned? Is 48:11
their **n** would never be cut off or Is 48:19

the body of my mother he named my **n**. Is 49:1
no light trust in the **n** of the LORD and Is 50:10
waves roar—the LORD of hosts is his **n**. Is 51:15
continually all the day my **n** is despised. Is 52:5
Therefore my people shall know my **n**. Is 52:6
your husband, the LORD of hosts is his **n**; Is 54:5
and it shall make a **n** for the LORD, an Is 55:13
a monument and a **n** better than sons Is 56:5
give them an everlasting **n** that shall not Is 56:5
minister to him, to love the **n** of the LORD, Is 56:6
who inhabits eternity, whose **n** is Holy: Is 57:15
So they shall fear the **n** of the LORD from Is 59:19
with them, for the **n** of the LORD your God, Is 60:9
be called by a new **n** that the mouth of Is 62:2
to make for himself an everlasting **n**, Is 63:12
people, to make for yourself a glorious **n**. Is 63:14
our Redeemer from of old is your **n**. Is 63:16
like those who are not called by your **n**. Is 63:19
to make your **n** known to your adversaries, Is 64:2
There is no one who calls upon your **n**, Is 64:7
to a nation that was not called by my **n**. Is 65:1
You shall leave your **n** to my chosen for Is 65:15
his servants he will call by another **n**. Is 65:15
shall your offspring and your **n** remain. Is 66:22
in this house, which is called by my **n**, Jer 7:10
Has this house, which is called by my **n**, Jer 7:11
Shiloh, where I made my **n** dwell at first, Jer 7:12
do to the house that is called by my **n**, Jer 7:14
in the house that is called by my **n**, Jer 7:30
are great, and your **n** is great in might. Jer 10:6
inheritance; the LORD of hosts is his **n**. Jer 10:16
on the peoples that call not on your **n**, Jer 10:25
that his **n** be remembered no more." Jer 11:19
"Do not prophesy in the **n** of the LORD, Jer 11:21
ways of my people, to swear by my **n**, Jer 12:16
that they might be for me a people, a **n**, Jer 13:11
midst of us, and we are called by your **n**; Jer 14:9
prophets are prophesying lies in my **n**. Jer 14:14
who prophesy in my **n** although I did Jer 14:15
of my heart, for I am called by your **n**, Jer 15:16
they shall know that my **n** is the LORD." Jer 16:21
"The LORD does not call your **n** Pashhur, Jer 20:3
speak any more in his **n**," there is in my Jer 20:9
And this is the **n** by which he will be Jer 23:6
have said who prophesy lies in my **n**, Jer 23:25
my people forget my **n** by their dreams Jer 23:27
as their fathers forgot my **n** for Baal? Jer 23:27
at the city that is called by my **n**, Jer 25:29
have you prophesied in the **n** of the LORD, Jer 26:9
spoken to us in the **n** of the LORD our Jer 26:16
who prophesied in the **n** of the LORD, Jer 26:20
they are prophesying falsely in my **n**, Jer 27:15
they are prophesying to you in my **n**; Jer 29:9
are prophesying a lie to you in my **n**: Jer 29:21
have spoken in my **n** lying words that I Jer 29:23
sent letters in your **n** to all the people Jer 29:25
waves roar—the LORD of hosts is his **n**: Jer 31:35
God, whose **n** is the LORD of hosts, Jer 32:18
and have made a **n** for yourself, Jer 32:20
in the house that is called by my **n**, Jer 32:34
it to establish it—the LORD is his **n**: Jer 33:2
And this city shall be to me a **n** of joy, a Jer 33:9
And this is the **n** by which it will be Jer 33:16
me in the house that is called by my **n**, Jer 34:15
and profaned my **n** when each of Jer 34:16
have spoken to us in the **n** of the LORD, Jer 44:16
Behold, I have sworn by my great **n**, Jer 44:26
that my **n** shall no more be invoked by Jer 44:26
Call the **n** of Pharaoh, king of Egypt, Jer 46:17
the King, whose **n** is the LORD of hosts, Jer 46:18
the King, whose **n** is the LORD of hosts. Jer 48:15
around him, and all who know his **n**; Jer 48:17
is strong; the LORD of hosts is his **n**. Jer 50:34
inheritance; the LORD of hosts is his **n**. Jer 51:19
the King, whose **n** is the LORD of hosts. Jer 51:57
His mother's **n** was Hamutal the Jer 52:1
"I called on your **n**, O LORD, from the Lam 3:55
But I acted for the sake of my **n**, that it Ezk 20:9
But I acted for the sake of my **n**, that it Ezk 20:14
hand and acted for the sake of my **n**, Ezk 20:22
So its **n** is called Bamah to this day.) Ezk 20:29
but my holy **n** you shall no more Ezk 20:39
you will mock you; your **n** is defiled; Ezk 22:5
Oholah was the **n** of the elder and Ezk 23:4
elder and Oholibah the **n** of her sister. Ezk 23:4
of man, write down the **n** of this day, Ezk 24:2
they came, they profaned my holy **n**, Ezk 36:20
But I had concern for my holy **n**, Ezk 36:21
to act, but for the sake of my holy **n**, Ezk 36:22
vindicate the holiness of my great **n**, Ezk 36:23
"And my holy **n** I will make known in Ezk 39:7
not let my holy **n** be profaned anymore. Ezk 39:7
(Hamonah is also the **n** of the city.) Ezk 39:16
and I will be jealous for my holy **n**. Ezk 39:25
of Israel shall no more defile my holy **n**, Ezk 43:7

defiled my holy **n** by their Ezk 43:8
And the **n** of the city from that time Ezk 48:35
"Blessed be the **n** of God forever and Dn 2:20
to Daniel, whose **n** was Belteshazzar, Dn 2:26
named Belteshazzar after the **n** of my god, Dn 4:8
Then Daniel, whose **n** was Belteshazzar, Dn 4:19
who spoke in your **n** to our kings, Dn 9:6
hand, and have made a **n** for yourself, Dn 9:15
and the city that is called by your **n**. Dn 9:18
and your people are called by your **n**." Dn 9:19
everyone whose **n** shall be found written Dn 12:1
the LORD said to him, "Call his **n** Jezreel, Hos 1:4
LORD said to him, "Call her **n** No Mercy, Hos 1:6
the LORD said, "Call his **n** Not My People, Hos 1:9
shall be remembered by **n** no more. Hos 2:17
of hosts, the LORD is his memorial **n**: Hos 12:5
and praise the **n** of the LORD your God, Jl 2:26
who calls on the **n** of the LORD shall Jl 2:32
same girl, so that my holy **n** is profaned; Am 2:7
the LORD, the God of hosts, is his **n**! Am 4:13
the surface of the earth, the LORD is his **n**; Am 5:8
the LORD, whose **n** is the God of hosts. Am 5:27
must not mention the **n** of the LORD." Am 6:10
surface of the earth—the LORD is his **n**. Am 9:6
are called by my **n**," declares the LORD Am 9:12
the peoples walk each in the **n** of its god, Mi 4:5
we will walk in the **n** of the LORD our God Mi 4:5
in the majesty of the **n** of the LORD his Mi 5:4
and it is sound wisdom to fear your **n**: Mi 6:9
"No more shall your **n** be perpetuated; Na 1:14
of Baal and the **n** of the idolatrous priests Zep 1:4
may call upon the **n** of the LORD and Zep 3:9
shall seek refuge in the **n** of the LORD, Zep 3:12
of him who swears falsely by my **n**. Zec 5:4
the man whose **n** is the Branch: Zec 6:12
shall walk in his **n**," declares the LORD. Zec 10:12
for you speak lies in the **n** of the LORD.' Zec 13:3
They will call upon my **n**, and I will Zec 13:9
day the LORD will be one and his **n** one. Zec 14:9
to you, O priests, who despise my **n**. Mal 1:6
you say, 'How have we despised your **n**?' Mal 1:6
to its setting my **n** will be great among Mal 1:11
place incense will be offered to my **n**, Mal 1:11
For my **n** will be great among the Mal 1:11
and my **n** will be feared among the Mal 1:14
take it to heart to give honor to my **n**, Mal 2:2
he feared me. He stood in awe of my **n**. Mal 2:5
feared the LORD and esteemed his **n**. Mal 3:16
But for you who fear my **n**, the sun of Mal 4:2
a son, and you shall call his **n** Jesus, Mt 1:21
shall call his **n** Immanuel" (which Mt 1:23
birth to a son. And he called his **n** Jesus. Mt 1:25
Father in heaven, hallowed be your **n**. Mt 6:9
Lord, did we not prophesy in your **n**, Mt 7:22
name, and cast out demons in your **n**, Mt 7:22
and do many mighty works in your **n**?' Mt 7:22
and in his **n** the Gentiles will hope." Mt 12:21
one such child in my **n** receives me, Mt 18:5
two or three are gathered in my **n**, Mt 18:20
is he who comes in the **n** of the Lord! Mt 21:9
is he who comes in the **n** of the Lord.'" Mt 23:39
For many will come in my **n**, saying, 'I Mt 24:5
the high priest, whose **n** was Caiaphas, Mt 26:3
the twelve, whose **n** was Judas Iscariot, Mt 26:14
found a man of Cyrene, Simon by **n**. Mt 27:32
baptizing them in the **n** of the Father Mt 28:19
Simon (to whom he gave the **n** Peter); Mk 3:16
(to whom he gave the **n** Boanerges, Mk 3:17
asked him, "What is your **n**?" He replied, Mk 5:9
your name?" He replied, "My **n** is Legion, Mk 5:9
the rulers of the synagogue, Jairus by **n**, Mk 5:22
of it, for Jesus' **n** had become known. Mk 6:14
one such child in my **n** receives me, Mk 9:37
someone casting out demons in your **n**, Mk 9:38
mighty work in my **n** will be able soon Mk 9:39
is he who comes in the **n** of the Lord! Mk 11:9
Many will come in my **n**, saying, 'I am Mk 13:6
in my **n** they will cast out demons; Mk 16:17
of Aaron, and her **n** was Elizabeth. Lk 1:5
you a son, and you shall call his **n** John. Lk 1:13
betrothed to a man whose **n** was Joseph, Lk 1:27
of David. And the virgin's **n** was Mary. Lk 1:27
a son, and you shall call his **n** Jesus. Lk 1:31
great things for me, and holy is his **n**. Lk 1:49
of your relatives is called by this **n**." Lk 1:61
"His **n** is John." And they all wondered. Lk 1:63
the **n** given by the angel before he was Lk 2:21
man in Jerusalem, whose **n** was Simeon, Lk 2:25
and revile you and spurn your **n** as evil, Lk 6:22
him, "What is your **n**?" And he said, Lk 8:30
receives this child in my **n** receives me, Lk 9:48
someone casting out demons in your **n**, Lk 9:49
demons are subject to us in your **n**!" Lk 10:17
pray, say: "Father, hallowed be your **n**. Lk 11:2
is he who comes in the **n** of the Lord!'" Lk 13:35

King who comes in the **n** of the Lord! Lk 19:38
For many will come in my **n**, saying, 'I Lk 21:8
be proclaimed in his **n** to all nations, Lk 24:47
a man sent from God, whose **n** was John. Jn 1:6
did receive him, who believed in his **n**, Jn 1:12
many believed in his **n** when they saw Jn 2:23
has not believed in the **n** of the only Son Jn 3:18
I have come in my Father's **n**, and you do Jn 5:43
If another comes in his own **n**, you will Jn 5:43
his own sheep by **n** and leads them out. Jn 10:3
do in my Father's **n** bear witness about Jn 10:25
is he who comes in the **n** of the Lord, Jn 12:13
glorify your **n**." Then a voice came Jn 12:28
Whatever you ask in my **n**, this I will Jn 14:13
If you ask me anything in my **n**, I will Jn 14:14
whom the Father will send in my **n**, Jn 14:26
whatever you ask the Father in my **n**, Jn 15:16
they will do to you on account of my **n**, Jn 15:21
whatever you ask of the Father in my **n**, Jn 16:23
now you have asked nothing in my **n**. Jn 16:24
In that day you will ask in my **n**, and I Jn 16:26
"I have manifested your **n** to the people Jn 17:6
Holy Father, keep them in your **n**, Jn 17:11
I was with them, I kept them in your **n**, Jn 17:12
I made known to them your **n**, and I Jn 17:26
ear. (The servant's **n** was Malchus.) Jn 18:10
by believing you may have life in his **n**. Jn 20:31
who calls upon the **n** of the Lord shall Acts 2:21
one of you in the **n** of Jesus Christ for Acts 2:38
In the **n** of Jesus Christ of Nazareth, rise Acts 3:6
And his **n**—by faith in his name—has Acts 3:16
—by faith in his **n**—has made this Acts 3:16
power or by what **n** did you do this?" Acts 4:7
of Israel that by the **n** of Jesus Christ of Acts 4:10
there is no other **n** under heaven given Acts 4:12
to speak no more to anyone in this **n**." Acts 4:17
speak or teach at all in the **n** of Jesus. Acts 4:18
performed through the **n** of your holy Acts 4:30
charged you not to teach in this **n**, Acts 5:28
them not to speak in the **n** of Jesus, Acts 5:40
worthy to suffer dishonor for the **n**. Acts 5:41
of God and the **n** of Jesus Christ, Acts 8:12
been baptized in the **n** of the Lord Acts 8:16
priests to bind all who call on your **n**." Acts 9:14
mine to carry my **n** before the Gentiles Acts 9:15
he must suffer for the sake of my **n**." Acts 9:16
of those who called upon this **n**? Acts 9:21
had preached boldly in the **n** of Jesus. Acts 9:27
preaching boldly in the **n** of the Lord. Acts 9:28
forgiveness of sins through his **n**." Acts 10:43
to be baptized in the **n** of Jesus Christ. Acts 10:48
of John whose other **n** was Mark, Acts 12:12
them John, whose other **n** was Mark. Acts 12:25
is the meaning of his **n**) opposed them, Acts 13:8
to take from them a people for his **n**. Acts 15:14
the Gentiles who are called by my **n**, Acts 15:17
you in the **n** of Jesus Christ Acts 16:18
were baptized in the **n** of the Lord Acts 19:5
undertook to invoke the **n** of the Lord Acts 19:13
and the **n** of the Lord Jesus was Acts 19:17
in Jerusalem for the **n** of the Lord Acts 21:13
away your sins, calling on his **n**.' Acts 22:16
things in opposing the **n** of Jesus of Acts 26:9
the sake of his **n** among all the nations, Rom 1:5
"The **n** of God is blasphemed among Rom 2:24
and that my **n** might be proclaimed in Rom 9:17
who calls on the **n** of the Lord will Rom 10:13
the Gentiles, and sing to your **n**." Rom 15:9
place call upon the **n** of our Lord Jesus 1 Cor 1:2
by the **n** of our Lord Jesus Christ, 1 Cor 1:10
were you baptized in the **n** of Paul? 1 Cor 1:13
say that you were baptized in my **n**. 1 Cor 1:15
are assembled in the **n** of the Lord 1 Cor 5:4
anyone who bears the **n** of brother if 1 Cor 5:11
were justified in the **n** of the Lord 1 Cor 6:11
and above every **n** that is named, Eph 1:21
the Father in the **n** of our Lord Jesus Eph 5:20
bestowed on him the **n** that is above Phil 2:9
on him the name that is above every **n**, Phil 2:9
so that at the **n** of Jesus every knee Phil 2:10
do everything in the **n** of the Lord Jesus, Col 3:17
so that the **n** of our Lord Jesus may 2 Thes 1:12
in the **n** of our Lord Jesus Christ, 2 Thes 3:6
so that the **n** of God and the teaching 1 Tm 6:1
who names the **n** of the Lord 2 Tm 2:19
to angels as the **n** he has inherited is Heb 1:4
"I will tell of your **n** to my brothers; Heb 2:12
He is first, by translation of his **n**, king Heb 7:2
fruit of lips that acknowledge his **n**. Heb 13:15
blaspheme the honorable **n** by which Jas 2:7
prophets who spoke in the **n** of the Lord. Jas 5:10
him with oil in the **n** of the Lord. Jas 5:14
If you are insulted for the **n** of Christ, 1 Pt 4:14
but let him glorify God in that **n**. 1 Pt 4:16
that we believe in the **n** of his Son Jesus 1 Jn 3:23
you who believe in the **n** of the Son of 1 Jn 5:13
they have gone out for the sake of the **n**, 3 Jn 1:7
Yet you hold fast my **n**, and you did not Rv 2:13
with a new **n** written on the stone that no Rv 2:17
I will never blot his **n** out of the book of Rv 3:5
I will confess his **n** before my Father and Rv 3:5
kept my word and have not denied my **n**. Rv 3:8
and I will write on him the **n** of my God, Rv 3:12
my God, and the **n** of the city of my God, Rv 3:12
God out of heaven, and my own new **n**. Rv 3:12
And its rider's **n** was Death, and Hades Rv 6:8
The **n** of the star is Wormwood. A third Rv 8:11
His **n** in Hebrew is Abaddon, and in Rv 9:11
and saints, and those who fear your **n**, Rv 11:18
blaspheming his **n** and his dwelling, Rv 13:6
everyone whose **n** has not been written Rv 13:8
the **n** of the beast or the number of its Rv 13:17
of the beast or the number of its **n**. Rv 13:17
144,000 who had his **n** and his Father's Rv 14:1
name and his Father's **n** written on their Rv 14:1
whoever receives the mark of its **n**." Rv 14:11
and its image and the number of its **n**, Rv 15:2
will not fear, O Lord, and glorify your **n**? Rv 15:4
and they cursed the **n** of God who had Rv 16:9
her forehead was written a **n** of mystery: Rv 17:5
and he has a **n** written that no one Rv 19:12
and the **n** by which he is called is The Rv 19:13
and on his thigh he has a **n** written, Rv 19:16
And if anyone's **n** was not found Rv 20:15
face, and his **n** will be on their foreheads. Rv 22:4

NAME'S (22)
his people, for his great **n** sake, 1 Sm 12:22
from a far country for your **n** sake 1 Kgs 8:41
in paths of righteousness for his **n** sake. Ps 23:3
For your **n** sake, O LORD, pardon my Ps 25:11
and for your **n** sake you lead me and Ps 31:3
and atone for our sins, for your **n** sake! Ps 79:9
Yet he saved them for his **n** sake, that Ps 106:8
deal on my behalf for your **n** sake; Ps 109:21
For your **n** sake, O LORD, preserve my Ps 143:11
"For my **n** sake I defer my anger, for the Is 48:9
and cast you out for my **n** sake have said, Is 66:5
against us, act, O LORD, for your **n** sake; Jer 14:7
Do not spurn us, for your **n** sake; do not Jer 14:21
when I deal with you for my **n** sake, Ezk 20:44
you will be hated by all for my **n** sake. Mt 10:22
or children or lands, for my **n** sake, Mt 19:29
be hated by all nations for my **n** sake. Mt 24:9
you will be hated by all for my **n** sake. Mk 13:13
kings and governors for my **n** sake. Lk 21:12
You will be hated by all for my **n** sake. Lk 21:17
your sins are forgiven for his **n** sake. 1 Jn 2:12
patiently and bearing up for my **n** sake, Rv 2:3

NAMED (82)
he blessed them and **n** them Man when Gn 5:2
likeness, after his image, and **n** him Seth. Gn 5:3
Isaac shall your offspring be **n**. Gn 21:12
silver that he had **n** in the hearing of Gn 23:16
of Ishmael, **n** in the order of their birth: Gn 25:13
Esau said, "Is he not rightly **n** Jacob? Gn 27:36
me today." Therefore he **n** it Galeed, Gn 31:48
the place was **n** Abel-mizraim; Gn 50:11
one of whom was **n** Shiphrah and the Ex 1:15
She **n** him Moses, "Because," she said, "I Ex 2:10
it was bitter; therefore it was **n** Marah. Ex 15:23
Aaron took these men who had been **n**, Nm 1:17
remained in the camp, one **n** Eldad, Nm 11:26
named Eldad, and the other **n** Medad, Nm 11:26
And they **n** the city Dan, after the name Jgs 18:29
born to Naomi." They **n** him Obed. Ru 4:17
And she **n** the child Ichabod, saying, 1 Sm 4:21
Philistines a champion **n** Goliath of 1 Sm 17:4
of Bethlehem in Judah, **n** Jesse, 1 Sm 17:12
the son of Ahitub, **n** Abiathar, 1 Sm 22:20
son of a man **n** Ithra the Ishmaelite, 2 Sm 17:25
children of Jacob, whom he **n** Israel. 2 Kgs 17:34
who were expressly **n** to come and 1 Chr 12:31
chosen and expressly **n** to give 1 Chr 16:41
man of God were **n** among the tribe 1 Chr 23:14
has come to be has already been **n**, Eccl 6:10
offspring of evildoers nevermore be **n**! Is 14:20
the body of my mother he **n** my name. Is 49:1
a sentry there **n** Irijah the son of Jer 37:13
of the city being **n** after the tribes of Ezk 48:31
—he who was **n** Belteshazzar after the Dn 4:8
Daniel, whom the king **n** Belteshazzar. Dn 5:12
to Daniel, who was **n** Belteshazzar. Dn 10:1
And I took two staffs, one I **n** Favor, the Zec 11:7
one I named Favor, the other I **n** Union. Zec 11:7
a rich man from Arimathea, **n** Joseph, Mt 27:57
(whom he also **n** apostles) so that Mk 3:14
of Judea, there was a priest **n** Zechariah, Lk 1:5
from God to a city of Galilee **n** Nazareth, Lk 1:26
went out and saw a tax collector **n** Levi, Lk 5:27
from them twelve, whom he **n** apostles: Lk 6:13
Simon, whom he **n** Peter, and Andrew Lk 6:14
And there came a man **n** Jairus, who Lk 8:41
And a woman **n** Martha welcomed Lk 10:38
gate was laid a poor man **n** Lazarus, Lk 16:20
And there was a man **n** Zacchaeus. He Lk 19:2
Now there was a man **n** Joseph, from Lk 23:50
were going to a village **n** Emmaus, Lk 24:13
Then one of them, **n** Cleopas, answered Lk 24:18
was a man of the Pharisees **n** Nicodemus, Jn 3:1
But a man **n** Ananias, with his wife Acts 5:1
a Pharisee in the council **n** Gamaliel, Acts 5:34
at the feet of a young man **n** Saul. Acts 7:58
But there was a man **n** Simon, who had Acts 8:9
a disciple at Damascus **n** Ananias. Acts 9:10
Judas look for a man of Tarsus **n** Saul, Acts 9:11
a vision a man **n** Ananias come in Acts 9:12
There he found a man **n** Aeneas, Acts 9:33
was in Joppa a disciple **n** Tabitha, Acts 9:36
there was a man **n** Cornelius, Acts 10:1
And one of them **n** Agabus stood up Acts 11:28
a servant girl **n** Rhoda came to Acts 12:13
a Jewish false prophet **n** Bar-Jesus. Acts 13:6
A disciple was there, **n** Timothy, the Acts 16:1
who heard us was a woman **n** Lydia, Acts 16:14
and a woman **n** Damaris and others Acts 17:34
And he found a Jew **n** Aquila, a native Acts 18:2
to the house of a man **n** Titius Justus, Acts 18:7
Now a Jew **n** Apollos, a native of Acts 18:24
Jewish high priest **n** Sceva were doing Acts 19:14
For a man **n** Demetrius, a Acts 19:24
And a young man **n** Eutychus, sitting Acts 20:9
a prophet **n** Agabus came down from Acts 21:10
of the Augustan Cohort **n** Julius. Acts 27:1
the chief man of the island, **n** Publius, Acts 28:7
Isaac shall your offspring be **n**." Rom 9:7
not where Christ has already been **n**, Rom 15:20
and above every name that is **n**, Eph 1:21
family in heaven and on earth is **n**, Eph 3:15
must not even be **n** among you, Eph 5:3
rather than one **n** after the order of Heb 7:11
Isaac shall your offspring be **n**." Heb 11:18

NAMELESS (1)
A senseless, a **n** brood, they have been Jb 30:8

NAMELY (16)
of Joseph, **n**, of the people of Ephraim, Nm 1:32
n, Ishmael the son of Nethaniah, 2 Kgs 25:23
them into exile, **n**, the Reubenites, 1 Chr 5:26
hand, **n**, Asaph the son of Berechiah, 1 Chr 6:39
of their fathers' houses, **n** of Tola, 1 Chr 7:2
n the sons of Jeshua and Joab, Ezr 2:6
The sons of Ater, **n** of Hezekiah, 98. Ezr 2:16
n, to send us ministers for the house of Ezr 8:17
n Sherebiah with his sons and Ezr 8:18
n the sons of Jeshua and Joab, Neh 7:11
The sons of Ater, **n** of Hezekiah, 98. Neh 7:21
sons of Jedaiah, **n** the house of Jeshua, Neh 7:39
n of Kadmiel of the sons of Hodevah, Neh 7:43
desolations of Jerusalem, **n**, seventy years. Dn 9:2
n, his eternal power and divine nature, Rom 1:20
was made lower than the angels, **n** Jesus, Heb 2:9

NAMES (91)
The man gave **n** to all livestock and to Gn 2:20
These are the **n** of the sons of Ishmael, Gn 25:13
sons of Ishmael and these are their **n**, Gn 25:16
he gave them the **n** that his father had Gn 26:18
These are the **n** of Esau's sons: Eliphaz Gn 36:10
These are the **n** of the chiefs of Esau, Gn 36:40
and their dwelling places, by their **n**: Gn 36:40
Now these are the **n** of the descendants Gn 46:8
These are the **n** of the sons of Israel who Ex 1:1
These are the **n** of the sons of Levi Ex 6:16
no mention of the **n** of other gods, Ex 23:13
and engrave on them the **n** of the sons of Ex 28:9
six of their **n** on the one stone, and the Ex 28:10
and the **n** of the remaining six on the Ex 28:10
the two stones with the **n** of the sons of Ex 28:11
shall bear their **n** before the LORD Ex 28:12
stones with their **n** according to the Ex 28:21
names according to the **n** of the sons of Ex 28:21
So Aaron shall bear the **n** of the sons of Ex 28:29
according to the **n** of the sons of Israel. Ex 39:6
stones with their **n** according to the Ex 39:14
names according to the **n** of the sons of Ex 39:14
houses, according to the number of **n**, Nm 1:2
And these are the **n** of the men who shall Nm 1:5
to the number of **n** from twenty years Nm 1:18
houses, according to the number of **n**, Nm 1:20
listed, according to the number of **n**, Nm 1:22
according to the number of the **n**, Nm 1:24
houses, according to the number of **n**, Nm 1:26
houses, according to the number of **n**, Nm 1:28
houses, according to the number of **n**, Nm 1:30
houses, according to the number of **n**, Nm 1:32

houses, according to the number of **n**, Nm 1:34
houses, according to the number of **n**, Nm 1:36
houses, according to the number of **n**, Nm 1:38
houses, according to the number of **n**, Nm 1:40
houses, according to the number of **n**, Nm 1:42
These are the **n** of the sons of Aaron: Nm 3:2
These are the **n** of the sons of Aaron, the Nm 3:3
these were the sons of Levi by their **n**: Nm 3:17
And these are the **n** of the sons of Nm 3:18
upward, taking the number of their **n**. Nm 3:40
males, according to the number of **n**, Nm 3:43
And these were their **n**: From the tribe Nm 13:4
These were the **n** of the men whom Nm 13:16
And the **n** of the daughters of Nm 26:33
according to the number of **n**. Nm 26:53
According to the **n** of the tribes of Nm 26:55
The **n** of his daughters were: Mahlah, Nm 27:1
Baal-meon (their **n** were changed), Nm 32:38
And they gave other **n** to the cities Nm 32:38
"These are the **n** of the men who shall Nm 34:17
These are the **n** of the men: Of the Nm 34:19
and these are the **n** of his daughters: Jos 17:3
make mention of the **n** of their gods or Jos 23:7
and the **n** of his two sons were Mahlon Ru 1:2
And the **n** of his two daughters were 1 Sm 14:49
And the **n** of his three sons who went 1 Sm 17:13
And these are the **n** of those who were 2 Sm 5:14
These are the **n** of the mighty men 2 Sm 23:8
These were their **n**: Ben-hur, in the hill 1 Kgs 4:8
And these are the **n** of the sons of 1 Chr 6:17
had six sons, and these are their **n**: 1 Chr 8:38
had six sons and these are their **n**: 1 Chr 9:44
These are the **n** of the children born 1 Chr 14:4
number of the **n** of the individuals 1 Chr 23:24
"What are the **n** of the men who are Ezr 5:4
We also asked them their **n**, for your Ezr 5:10
might write down the **n** of their leaders. Ezr 5:10
who came later, their **n** being Eliphelet, Ezr 8:13
document are the **n** of our princes, Neh 9:38
the seals are the **n** of Nehemiah the Neh 10:1
not pour out or take their **n** on my lips. Ps 16:4
they called lands by their own **n**. Ps 49:11
the stars; he gives to all of them their **n**. Ps 147:4
As for their **n**, Oholah is Samaria, and Ezk 23:4
"These are the **n** of the tribes: Ezk 48:1
the chief of the eunuchs gave them **n**: Dn 1:7
I will remove the **n** of the Baals from Hos 2:17
I will cut off the **n** of the idols from the Zec 13:2
The **n** of the twelve apostles are these: Mt 10:2
but rejoice that your **n** are written in Lk 10:20
about words and **n** and your own Acts 18:15
workers, whose **n** are in the book of life. Phil 4:3
"Let everyone who **n** the name of the 2 Tm 2:19
Yet you have still a few **n** in Sardis, people Rv 3:4
horns and blasphemous **n** on its heads. Rv 13:1
beast that was full of blasphemous **n**, Rv 17:3
dwellers on earth whose **n** have not been Rv 17:8
on the gates the **n** of the twelve tribes Rv 21:12
them were the twelve **n** of the twelve Rv 21:14

NAOMI (22)
Elimelech and the name of his wife **N**, Ru 1:2
But Elimelech, the husband of **N**, died, Ru 1:3
But **N** said to her two daughters-in-law, Ru 1:8
But **N** said, "Turn back, my daughters; Ru 1:11
And when **N** saw that she was Ru 1:18
them. And the women said, "Is this **N**?" Ru 1:19
She said to them, "Do not call me **N**; call Ru 1:20
Why call me **N**, when the LORD has Ru 1:21
So **N** returned, and Ruth the Moabite Ru 1:22
Now **N** had a relative of her husband's, a Ru 2:1
And Ruth the Moabite said to **N**, "Let me Ru 2:2
who came back with **N** from the country Ru 2:6
And **N** said to her daughter-in-law, Ru 2:20
living or the dead!" **N** also said to her, Ru 2:20
And **N** said to Ruth, her Ru 2:22
Then **N** her mother-in-law said to her, Ru 3:1
"**N**, who has come back from the Ru 4:3
day you buy the field from the hand of **N**, Ru 4:5
from the hand of **N** all that belonged to Ru 4:9
Then the women said to **N**, "Blessed be Ru 4:14
Then **N** took the child and laid him on Ru 4:16
has been born to **N**." They named him Ru 4:17

NAPHATH (1)
Megiddo and its villages; the third is **N**. Jos 17:11

NAPHATH-DOR (2)
the king of Dor in **N**, one; the king of Jos 12:23
in all **N** (he had Taphath the 1 Kgs 4:11

NAPHISH (3)
Hadad, Tema, Jetur, **N**, and Kedemah. Gn 25:15
Jetur, **N**, and Kedemah. These are the 1 Chr 1:31
the Hagrites, Jetur, **N**, and Nodab. 1 Chr 5:19

NAPHOTH-DOR (1)
in the lowland, and in **N** on the west, Jos 11:2

NAPHTALI (53)
prevailed." So she called his name **N**. Gn 30:8
Bilhah, Rachel's servant: Dan and **N**. Gn 35:25
The sons of **N**: Jahzeel, Guni, Jezer, and Gn 46:24
"**N** is a doe let loose that bears Gn 49:21
Dan and **N**, Gad and Asher. Ex 1:4
from **N**, Ahira the son of Enan." Nm 1:15
Of the people of **N**, their generations, by Nm 1:42
listed of the tribe of **N** were 53,400. Nm 1:43
Then the tribe of **N**, the chief of the Nm 2:29
of the people of **N** being Ahira the son Nm 2:29
of Enan, the chief of the people of **N**: Nm 7:78
of the people of **N** was Ahira the son Nm 10:27
from the tribe of **N**, Nahbi the son of Nm 13:14
The sons of **N** according to their Nm 26:48
are the clans of **N** according to their Nm 26:50
Of the tribe of the people of **N** a chief, Nm 34:28
Gad, Asher, Zebulun, Dan, and **N**. Dt 27:13
And of **N** he said, "O Naphtali, sated Dt 33:23
And of Naphtali he said, "O **N**, sated Dt 33:23
all **N**, the land of Ephraim and Dt 34:2
sixth lot came out for the people of **N**, Jos 19:32
people of Naphtali, for the people of **N**, Jos 19:32
of the people of **N** according to their Jos 19:39
in Galilee in the hill country of **N**, Jos 20:7
the tribe of Asher, from the tribe of **N**, Jos 21:6
and out of the tribe of **N**, Kedesh in Jos 21:32
N did not drive out the inhabitants of Jgs 1:33
from the people of **N** and the people of Jgs 4:6
called out Zebulun and **N** to Kedesh. Jgs 4:10
death; **N**, too, on the heights of the field. Jgs 5:18
messengers to Asher, Zebulun, and **N**, Jgs 6:35
were called out from **N** and from Asher Jgs 7:23
in **N** (he had taken Basemath the 1 Kgs 4:15
the son of a widow of the tribe of **N**, 1 Kgs 7:14
Chinneroth, with all the land of **N**. 1 Kgs 15:20
Gilead, and Galilee, all the land of **N**, 2 Kgs 15:29
Dan, Joseph, Benjamin, **N**, Gad, and 1 Chr 2:2
Asher, **N** and Manasseh in Bashan. 1 Chr 6:62
and out of the tribe of **N**: Kedesh in 1 Chr 6:76
The sons of **N**: Jahziel, Guni, Jezer 1 Chr 7:13
Of **N** 1,000 commanders with 1 Chr 12:34
far as Issachar and Zebulun and **N**, 1 Chr 12:40
Ishmaiah the son of Obadiah; for **N**, 1 Chr 27:19
and all the store cities of **N**. 2 Chr 16:4
and Simeon, and as far as **N**, 2 Chr 34:6
princes of Zebulun, the princes of **N**. Ps 68:27
the land of Zebulun and the land of **N**, Is 9:1
the east side to the west, **N**, one portion. Ezk 48:3
Adjoining the territory of **N**, from the Ezk 48:4
the gate of Asher, and the gate of **N**. Ezk 48:34
sea, in the territory of Zebulun and **N**, Mt 4:13
"The land of Zebulun and the land of **N**, Mt 4:15
tribe of Asher, 12,000 from the tribe of **N**, Rv 7:6

NAPHTUHIM (2)
Ludim, Anamim, Lehabim, **N**, Gn 10:13
Ludim, Anamim, Lehabim, **N**, 1 Chr 1:11

NARCISSUS (1)
Lord who belong to the family of **N**. Rom 16:11

NARD (5)
his couch, my **n** gave forth its fragrance. Sg 1:12
with all choicest fruits, henna with **n**, Sg 4:13
n and saffron, calamus and cinnamon, Sg 4:14
alabaster flask of ointment of pure **n**, Mk 14:3
of expensive ointment made from pure **n**, Jn 12:3

NARRATIVE (1)
undertaken to compile a **n** of the things Lk 1:1

NARROW (12)
LORD stood in a **n** path between the Nm 22:24
went ahead and stood in a **n** place, Nm 22:26
country of Ephraim is too **n** for you." Jos 17:15
is a deep pit; an adulteress is a **n** well. Prv 23:27
and the covering too **n** to wrap oneself Is 28:20
you will be too **n** for your inhabitants, Is 49:19
in your ears: 'The place is too **n** for me; Is 49:20
thresholds and the **n** windows and the Ezk 41:16
And there were **n** windows and palm Ezk 41:26
"Enter by the **n** gate. For the gate is wide Mt 7:13
For the gate is **n** and the way is hard that Mt 7:14
"Strive to enter through the **n** door. For Lk 13:24

NARROWER (1)
Now the upper chambers were **n**, for Ezk 42:5

NARROWING (1)
n inwards toward the side rooms and Ezk 40:16

NATHAN (43)
Shammua, Shobab, **N**, Solomon, 2 Sm 5:14
the king said to **N** the prophet, "See 2 Sm 7:2
And **N** said to the king, "Go, do all that 2 Sm 7:3
night the word of the LORD came to **N**, 2 Sm 7:4
with all this vision, **N** spoke to David. 2 Sm 7:17
And the LORD sent **N** to David. He 2 Sm 12:1
against the man, and he said to **N**, 2 Sm 12:5
N said to David, "You are the man! 2 Sm 12:7
David said to **N**, "I have sinned 2 Sm 12:13
the LORD." And **N** said to David, 2 Sm 12:13
Then **N** went to his house. And the 2 Sm 12:15
and sent a message by **N** the prophet. 2 Sm 12:25
Igal the son of **N** of Zobah, Bani the 2 Sm 23:36
son of Jehoiada and **N** the prophet and 1 Kgs 1:8
he did not invite **N** the prophet or 1 Kgs 1:10
Then **N** said to Bathsheba the 1 Kgs 1:11
with the king, **N** the prophet came in. 1 Kgs 1:22
"Here is **N** the prophet." And when he 1 Kgs 1:23
And **N** said, "My lord the king, have 1 Kgs 1:24
to me Zadok the priest, **N** the prophet, 1 Kgs 1:32
the priest and **N** the prophet there 1 Kgs 1:34
So Zadok the priest, **N** the prophet, 1 Kgs 1:38
him Zadok the priest, **N** the prophet, 1 Kgs 1:44
the priest and **N** the prophet have 1 Kgs 1:45
Azariah the son of **N** was over the 1 Kgs 4:5
Zabud the son of **N** was priest and 1 Kgs 4:5
Attai fathered **N**, and Nathan 1 Chr 2:36
Nathan, and **N** fathered Zabad. 1 Chr 2:36
Shimea, Shobab, **N** and Solomon, 1 Chr 3:5
Joel the brother of **N**, Mibhar the 1 Chr 11:38
Shammua, Shobab, **N**, Solomon, 1 Chr 14:4
house, David said to **N** the prophet, 1 Chr 17:1
And **N** said to David, "Do all that is 1 Chr 17:2
night the word of the LORD came to **N**, 1 Chr 17:3
all this vision, **N** spoke to David. 1 Chr 17:15
in the Chronicles of **N** the prophet, 1 Chr 29:29
in the history of **N** the prophet, 2 Chr 9:29
the king's seer and of **N** the prophet, 2 Chr 29:25
Jarib, Elnathan, **N**, Zechariah, Ezr 8:16
Shelemiah, **N**, Adaiah, Ezr 10:39
David, when **N** the prophet went to him, Ps 51:T
the family of the house of **N** by itself, Zec 12:12
the son of Mattatha, the son of **N**, Lk 3:31

NATHAN-MELECH (1)
the chamber of **N** the chamberlain, 2 Kgs 23:11

NATHANAEL (6)
Philip found **N** and said to him, "We Jn 1:45
N said to him, "Can anything good come Jn 1:46
Jesus saw **N** coming toward him and Jn 1:47
N said to him, "How do you know me?" Jn 1:48
N answered him, "Rabbi, you are the Son Jn 1:49
(called the Twin), **N** of Cana in Galilee, Jn 21:2

NATION (155)
And I will make of you a great **n**, and I Gn 12:2
judgment on the **n** that they serve, Gn 15:14
and I will make him into a great **n**. Gn 17:20
surely become a great and mighty **n**, Gn 18:18
And I will make a **n** of the son of the Gn 21:13
for I will make him into a great **n**." Gn 21:18
A **n** and a company of nations shall Gn 35:11
for there I will make you into a great **n**. Gn 46:3
all the land of Egypt since it became a **n**. Ex 9:24
to me a kingdom of priests and a holy **n**. Ex 19:6
that I may make a great **n** of you." Ex 32:10
Consider too that this **n** is your people." Ex 33:13
created in all the earth or in any **n**. Ex 34:10
it vomited out the **n** that was before Lv 18:28
the customs of the **n** that I am driving Lv 20:23
make of you a **n** greater and mightier Nm 14:12
'Surely this great **n** is a wise and Dt 4:6
For what great **n** is there that has a god so Dt 4:7
And what great **n** is there, that has Dt 4:8
to go and take a **n** for himself from the Dt 4:34
for himself from the midst of another **n**, Dt 4:34
make of you a **n** mightier and greater Dt 9:14
few in number, and there he became a **n**, Dt 26:5
A **n** that you have not known shall eat Dt 28:33
set over you to a **n** that neither you nor Dt 28:36
LORD will bring a **n** against you from Dt 28:49
a **n** whose language you do not Dt 28:49
a hard-faced **n** who shall not respect the Dt 28:50
provoke them to anger with a foolish **n**. Dt 32:21
"For they are a **n** void of counsel, and Dt 32:28
until all the **n** finished passing over Jos 3:17
When all the **n** had finished passing over Jos 4:1
years in the wilderness, until all the **n**, Jos 5:6
of the whole **n** was finished, Jos 5:8
until the **n** took vengeance on their Jos 10:13
the one **n** on earth whom God went to 2 Sm 7:23
yourself from Egypt, a **n** and its gods? 2 Sm 7:23
there is no **n** or kingdom where my 1 Kgs 18:10
take an oath of the kingdom or **n**, 1 Kgs 18:10
But every **n** still made gods of its 2 Kgs 17:29
every **n** in the cities in which they 2 Kgs 17:29
wandering from **n** to nation, from 1 Chr 16:20
wandering from nation to **n**, from 1 Chr 16:20
the one **n** on earth whom God went 1 Chr 17:21
N was crushed by nation and city by 2 Chr 15:6
Nation was crushed by **n** and city by 2 Chr 15:6
no god of any **n** or kingdom has 2 Chr 32:15
behold him, whether it be a **n** or a man? Jb 34:29

Blessed is the **n** whose God is the LORD, Ps 33:12
say, "Come, let us wipe them out as a **n**; Ps 83:4
wandering from **n** to nation, from one Ps 105:13
wandering from nation to **n**, from one Ps 105:13
I may rejoice in the gladness of your **n**, Ps 106:5
He has not dealt thus with any other **n**; Ps 147:20
Righteousness exalts a **n**, but sin is a Prv 14:34
Ah, sinful **n**, a people laden with iniquity, Is 1:4
n shall not lift up sword against nation, Is 2:4
nation shall not lift up sword against **n**, Is 2:4
You have multiplied the **n**; you have Is 9:3
Against a godless **n** I send him, and Is 10:6
will one answer the messengers of the **n**? Is 14:32
Go, you swift messengers, to a **n**, tall and Is 18:2
near and far, a **n** mighty and conquering, Is 18:2
near and far, a **n** mighty and conquering, Is 18:7
that the righteous **n** that keeps faith may Is 26:2
But you have increased the **n**, O LORD, Is 26:15
O LORD, you have increased the **n**; Is 26:15
to one deeply despised, abhorred by the **n**, Is 49:7
me, my people, and give ear to me, my **n**; Is 51:4
you shall call a **n** that you do not know, Is 55:5
and a **n** that did not know you shall run Is 55:5
if they were a **n** that did righteousness Is 58:2
For the **n** and kingdom that will not Is 60:12
a clan, and the smallest one a mighty **n**; Is 60:22
here am I," to a **n** that was not called by Is 65:1
Shall a **n** be brought forth in one Is 66:8
Has a **n** changed its gods, even though Jer 2:11
I not avenge myself on a **n** such as this? Jer 5:9
I am bringing against you a **n** from afar, Jer 5:15
It is an enduring **n**; it is an ancient Jer 5:15
it is an ancient **n**, a nation whose Jer 5:15
a **n** whose language you do not know, Jer 5:15
I not avenge myself on a **n** such as this?" Jer 5:29
a great **n** is stirring from the farthest Jer 6:22
'This is the **n** that did not obey the voice Jer 7:28
I not avenge myself on a **n** such as this? Jer 9:9
But if any **n** will not listen, then I will Jer 12:17
I declare concerning a **n** or a kingdom, Jer 18:7
and if that **n**, concerning which I have Jer 18:8
I declare concerning a **n** or a kingdom Jer 18:9
punish the king of Babylon and that **n**, Jer 25:12
disaster is going forth from **n** to nation, Jer 25:32
disaster is going forth from nation to **n**, Jer 25:32
"'"But if any **n** or kingdom will not serve Jer 27:8
I will punish that **n** with the sword, Jer 27:8
But any **n** that will bring its neck Jer 27:11
spoken concerning any **n** that will not Jer 27:13
from being a **n** before me forever." Jer 31:36
they are no longer a **n** in their sight. Jer 33:24
'Come, let us cut her off from being a **n**!' Jer 48:2
"Rise up, advance against a **n** at ease, Jer 49:31
there shall be no **n** to which those Jer 49:36
out of the north a **n** has come up against Jer 50:3
a mighty **n** and many kings are Jer 50:41
we watched for a **n** which could not Lam 4:17
and you bereave your **n** of children,' Ezk 36:13
no longer bereave your **n** of children, Ezk 36:14
no longer cause your **n** to stumble, Ezk 36:15
I will make them one **n** in the land, Ezk 37:22
n, or language that speaks anything Dn 3:29
four kingdoms shall arise from his **n**, Dn 8:22
been since there was a **n** till that time. Dn 12:1
For a **n** has come up against my land, Jl 1:6
sell them to the Sabeans, to a **n** far away, Jl 3:8
behold, I will raise up against you a **n**, Am 6:14
n shall not lift up sword against nation, Mi 4:3
nation shall not lift up sword against **n**, Mi 4:3
and those who were cast off, a strong **n**; Mi 4:7
the Chaldeans, that bitter and hasty **n**, Hab 1:6
together, yes, gather, O shameless **n**, Zep 2:1
of the seacoast, you **n** of the Cherethites! Zep 2:5
survivors of my **n** shall possess them." Zep 2:9
this people, and with this **n** before me, Hg 2:14
you are robbing me, the whole **n** of you. Mal 3:9
For **n** will rise against nation, and Mt 24:7
For nation will rise against **n**, and Mt 24:7
For **n** will rise against nation, and Mk 13:8
For nation will rise against **n**, and Mk 13:8
for he loves our **n**, and he is the one who Lk 7:5
to them, "**N** will rise against nation, Lk 21:10
to them, "Nation will rise against **n**, Lk 21:10
man misleading our **n** and forbidding Lk 23:2
take away both our place and our **n**." Jn 11:48
not that the whole **n** should perish." Jn 11:50
that Jesus would die for the **n**, Jn 11:51
and not for the **n** only, but also to Jn 11:52
Your own **n** and the chief priests have Jn 18:35
devout men from every **n** under heaven. Acts 2:5
'But I will judge the **n** that they serve,' Acts 7:7
well spoken of by the whole Jewish **n**, Acts 10:22
with or to visit anyone of another **n**, Acts 10:28
but in every **n** anyone who fears him Acts 10:35
from one man every **n** of mankind to Acts 17:26
reforms are being made for this **n**, Acts 24:2
you have been a judge over this **n**, Acts 24:10
bring alms to my **n** and to present Acts 24:17
among my own **n** and in Jerusalem, Acts 26:4
had no charge to bring against my **n**. Acts 28:19
you jealous of those who are not a **n**; Rom 10:19
with a foolish **n** I will make you Rom 10:19
race, a royal priesthood, a holy **n**, 1 Pt 2:9
tribe and language and people and **n**, Rv 5:9
that no one could number, from every **n**, Rv 7:9
tribe and people and language and **n**, Rv 13:7
to every **n** and tribe and language and Rv 14:6

NATIONS (490)

own language, by their clans, in their **n**. Gn 10:5
languages, their lands, and their **n**. Gn 10:20
languages, their lands, and their **n**. Gn 10:31
to their genealogies, in their **n**, Gn 10:32
and from these the **n** spread abroad on Gn 10:32
shall be the father of a multitude of **n**. Gn 17:4
made you the father of a multitude of **n**. Gn 17:5
fruitful, and I will make you into **n**, Gn 17:6
will bless her, and she shall become **n**; Gn 17:16
and all the **n** of the earth shall be Gn 18:18
offspring shall all the **n** of the earth be Gn 22:18
said to her, "Two **n** are in your womb, Gn 25:23
your offspring all the **n** of the earth Gn 26:4
serve you, and **n** bow down to you. Gn 27:29
and a company of **n** shall come from Gn 35:11
shall become a multitude of **n**." Gn 48:19
I will cast out **n** before you and enlarge Ex 34:24
for by all these the **n** I am driving out Lv 18:24
from among the **n** that are around Lv 25:44
And I will scatter you among the **n**, and Lv 26:33
And you shall perish among the **n**, and Lv 26:38
of the land of Egypt in the sight of the **n**, Lv 26:45
then the **n** who have heard your fame Nm 14:15
and not counting itself among the **n**! Nm 23:9
he shall eat up the **n**, his adversaries, Nm 24:8
"Amalek was the first among the **n**, Nm 24:20
in number among the **n** where the LORD Dt 4:27
out before you **n** greater and mightier Dt 4:38
of it, and clears away many **n** before you, Dt 7:1
seven **n** more numerous and mightier Dt 7:1
in your heart, 'These **n** are greater than I. Dt 7:17
will clear away these **n** before you little Dt 7:22
Like the **n** that the LORD makes to perish Dt 8:20
go in to dispossess **n** greater and mightier Dt 9:1
the wickedness of these **n** that the LORD is Dt 9:4
the wickedness of these **n** the LORD your Dt 9:5
will drive out all these **n** before you, Dt 11:23
you will dispossess **n** greater and Dt 11:23
the places where the **n** whom you shall Dt 12:2
off before you the **n** whom you go in Dt 12:29
'How did these **n** serve their gods? Dt 12:30
you, and you shall lend to many **n**, Dt 15:6
borrow, and you shall rule over many **n**, Dt 15:6
me, like all the **n** that are around me,' Dt 17:14
the abominable practices of those **n**. Dt 18:9
for these **n**, which you are about to Dt 18:14
God cuts off the **n** whose land the LORD Dt 19:1
you, which are not cities of the **n** here. Dt 20:15
honor high above all **n** that he has Dt 26:19
set you high above all the **n** of the earth. Dt 28:1
And you shall lend to many **n**, but you Dt 28:12
And among these **n** you shall find no Dt 28:65
the midst of the **n** through which you Dt 29:16
God to go and serve the gods of those **n**. Dt 29:18
all the **n** will say, 'Why has the LORD Dt 29:24
mind among all the **n** where the LORD Dt 30:1
He will destroy these **n** before you, so that Dt 31:3
High gave to the **n** their inheritance, Dt 32:8
has done to all these **n** for your sake, Jos 23:3
for your tribes those **n** that remain, Jos 23:4
along with all the **n** that I have already Jos 23:4
mix with these **n** remaining among you Jos 23:7
out before you great and strong **n**. Jos 23:9
remnant of these **n** remaining among Jos 23:12
no longer drive out these **n** before you, Jos 23:13
them any of the **n** that Joshua left when Jgs 2:21
So the LORD left those **n**, not driving Jgs 2:23
Now these are the **n** that the LORD left, to Jgs 3:1
These are the **n**: the five lords of the Jgs 3:3
for us a king to judge us like all the **n**." 1 Sm 8:5
that we also may be like all the **n**, and 1 Sm 8:20
dedicated from all the **n** he subdued, 2 Sm 8:11
you kept me as the head of the **n**; 2 Sm 22:44
will praise you, O LORD, among the **n**, 2 Sm 22:50
fame was in all the surrounding **n**. 1 Kgs 4:31
And people of all **n** came to hear the 1 Kgs 4:34
from the **n** concerning which the 1 Kgs 11:2
abominations of the **n** that the LORD 1 Kgs 14:24
practices of the **n** whom the LORD 2 Kgs 16:3
the customs of the **n** whom the LORD 2 Kgs 17:8
as the **n** did whom the LORD carried 2 Kgs 17:11
they followed the **n** that were around 2 Kgs 17:15
"The **n** that you have carried away 2 Kgs 17:26
manner of the **n** from among whom 2 Kgs 17:33
So these **n** feared the LORD and also 2 Kgs 17:41
the gods of the **n** ever delivered his 2 Kgs 18:33
the gods of the **n** delivered them, 2 Kgs 19:12
the **n** that my fathers destroyed, 2 Kgs 19:12
have laid waste the **n** and their lands 2 Kgs 19:17
practices of the **n** whom the LORD 2 Kgs 21:2
more evil than the **n** had done whom 2 Kgs 21:9
brought the fear of him upon all **n**. 1 Chr 14:17
Declare his glory among the **n**, his 1 Chr 16:24
and let them say among the **n**, 1 Chr 16:31
and deliver us from among the **n**, 1 Chr 16:35
in driving out **n** before your people 1 Chr 17:21
he had carried off from all the **n**, 1 Chr 18:11
rule over all the kingdoms of the **n**. 2 Chr 20:6
abominations of the **n** whom the 2 Chr 28:3
the gods of the **n** of those lands at 2 Chr 32:13
the gods of those **n** that my fathers 2 Chr 32:14
the gods of the **n** of the lands who 2 Chr 32:17
the sight of all **n** from that time 2 Chr 32:23
abominations of the **n** whom the 2 Chr 33:2
more evil than the **n** whom the LORD 2 Chr 33:9
all the abominations of the **n**. 2 Chr 36:14
and the rest of the **n** whom the great and Ezr 4:10
brothers who have been sold to the **n**, Neh 5:8
prevent the taunts of the **n** our enemies? Neh 5:9
to us from the **n** that were around us. Neh 5:17
was written, "It is reported among the **n**, Neh 6:6
all the **n** around us were afraid and fell Neh 6:16
Among the many **n** there was no Neh 13:26
He makes **n** great, and he destroys them; Jb 12:23
he enlarges **n**, and leads them away. Jb 12:23
Why do the **n** rage and the peoples plot in Ps 2:1
of me, and I will make the **n** your heritage, Ps 2:8
You have rebuked the **n**; you have made Ps 9:5
The **n** have sunk in the pit that they Ps 9:15
return to Sheol, all the **n** that forget God. Ps 9:17
prevail; let the **n** be judged before you! Ps 9:19
Let the **n** know that they are but men! Ps 9:20
and ever; the **n** perish from his land. Ps 10:16
people; you made me the head of the **n**; Ps 18:43
I will praise you, O LORD, among the **n**, Ps 18:49
families of the **n** shall worship before Ps 22:27
to the LORD, and he rules over the **n**. Ps 22:28
brings the counsel of the **n** to nothing; Ps 33:10
you with your own hand drove out the **n**, Ps 44:2
and have scattered us among the **n**. Ps 44:11
have made us a byword among the **n**, Ps 44:14
therefore **n** will praise you forever and Ps 45:17
The **n** rage, the kingdoms totter; he Ps 46:6
I will be exalted among the **n**, I will be Ps 46:10
peoples under us, and **n** under our feet. Ps 47:3
God reigns over the **n**; God sits on his Ps 47:8
I will sing praises to you among the **n**. Ps 57:9
Rouse yourself to punish all the **n**; spare Ps 59:5
at them; you hold all the **n** in derision. Ps 59:8
eyes keep watch on the **n**—let not the Ps 66:7
earth, your saving power among all **n**. Ps 67:2
Let the **n** be glad and sing for joy, for you Ps 67:4
with equity and guide the **n** upon earth. Ps 67:4
fall down before him, all **n** serve him! Ps 72:11
blessed in him, all **n** call him blessed! Ps 72:17
He drove out **n** before them; he Ps 78:55
the **n** have come into your inheritance; Ps 79:1
your anger on the **n** that do not know Ps 79:6
Why should the **n** say, "Where is their Ps 79:10
be known among the **n** before our eyes! Ps 79:10
Egypt; you drove out the **n** and planted it. Ps 80:8
the earth; for you shall inherit all the **n**! Ps 82:8
All the **n** you have made shall come and Ps 86:9
my heart the insults of all the many **n**, Ps 89:50
He who disciplines the **n**, does he not Ps 94:10
Declare his glory among the **n**, his Ps 96:3
Say among the **n**, "The LORD reigns! Ps 96:10
his righteousness in the sight of the **n**. Ps 98:2
N will fear the name of the LORD, and Ps 102:15
And he gave them the lands of the **n**, Ps 105:44
make their offspring fall among the **n**, Ps 106:27
they mixed with the **n** and learned to Ps 106:35
he gave them into the hand of the **n**, so Ps 106:41
God, and gather us from among the **n**, Ps 106:47
I will sing praises to you among the **n**. Ps 108:3
He will execute judgment among the **n**, Ps 110:6
in giving them the inheritance of the **n**. Ps 111:6
The LORD is high above all **n**, and his Ps 113:4
Why should the **n** say, "Where is their Ps 115:2
Praise the LORD, all **n**! Extol him, all Ps 117:1
All **n** surrounded me; in the name of Ps 118:10
then they said among the **n**, "The LORD Ps 126:2
struck down many **n** and killed Ps 135:10
The idols of the **n** are silver and gold, Ps 135:15
vengeance on the **n** and punishments Ps 149:7
be cursed by peoples, abhorred by **n**, Prv 24:24
the hills; and all the **n** shall flow to it, Is 2:2

He shall judge between the **n**, and shall Is 2:4
He will raise a signal for **n** afar off, and Is 5:26
land beyond the Jordan, Galilee of the **n**. Is 9:1
heart to destroy, and to cut off **n** not a few; Is 10:7
the peoples—of him shall the **n** inquire, Is 11:10
a signal for the **n** and will assemble the Is 11:12
of kingdoms, of **n** gathering together! Is 13:4
that ruled the **n** in anger with Is 14:6
their thrones all who were kings of the **n**. Is 14:9
to the ground, you who laid the **n** low! Is 14:12
All the kings of the **n** lie in glory, each Is 14:18
hand that is stretched out over all the **n**. Is 14:26
the lords of the **n** have struck down its Is 16:8
Ah, the roar of **n**; they roar like the Is 17:12
The **n** roar like the roaring of many Is 17:13
the Nile; you were the merchant of the **n**. Is 23:3
be in the midst of the earth among the **n**, Is 24:13
you; cities of ruthless **n** will fear you. Is 25:3
peoples, the veil that is spread over all **n**. Is 25:7
multitude of all the **n** that fight against Is 29:7
multitude of all the **n** be that fight Is 29:8
to sift the **n** with the sieve of destruction, Is 30:28
when you lift yourself up, **n** are scattered, Is 33:3
Draw near, O **n**, to hear, and listen, Is 34:1
For the LORD is enraged against all the **n**, Is 34:2
of the gods of the **n** delivered his land out Is 36:18
Have the gods of the **n** delivered them, Is 37:12
them, the **n** that my fathers destroyed, Is 37:12
have laid waste all the **n** and their lands, Is 37:18
the **n** are like a drop from a bucket, Is 40:15
All the **n** are as nothing before him, they Is 40:17
He gives up **n** before him, so that he Is 41:2
him; he will bring forth justice to the **n**. Is 42:1
a covenant for the people, a light for the **n**, Is 42:6
All the **n** gather together, and the peoples Is 43:9
to subdue **n** before him and to loose the Is 45:1
near together, you survivors of the **n**! Is 45:20
I will make you as a light for the **n**, that Is 49:6
"Behold, I will lift up my hand to the **n**, Is 49:22
his holy arm before the eyes of all the **n**, Is 52:10
so shall he sprinkle many **n**; kings shall Is 52:15
will possess the **n** and will people Is 54:3
And **n** shall come to your light, and Is 60:3
the wealth of the **n** shall come to you. Is 60:5
may bring to you the wealth of the **n**, Is 60:11
those **n** shall be utterly laid waste. Is 60:12
You shall suck the milk of **n**; you shall Is 60:16
you shall eat the wealth of the **n**, and in Is 61:6
offspring shall be known among the **n**, Is 61:9
and praise to sprout up before all the **n**. Is 61:11
The **n** shall see your righteousness, and Is 62:2
and that the **n** might tremble at your Is 64:2
the glory of the **n** like an overflowing Is 66:12
is coming to gather all **n** and tongues. Is 66:18
from them I will send survivors to the **n**, Is 66:19
shall declare my glory among the **n**. Is 66:19
brothers from all the **n** as an offering to Is 66:20
you; I appointed you a prophet to the **n**." Jer 1:5
you this day over **n** and over kingdoms, Jer 1:10
of the LORD, and all **n** shall gather to it, Jer 3:17
land, a heritage most beautiful of all **n**. Jer 3:19
then **n** shall bless themselves in him, Jer 4:2
his thicket, a destroyer of **n** has set out; Jer 4:7
Warn the **n** that he is coming; Jer 4:16
Therefore hear, O **n**, and know, O Jer 6:18
them among the **n** whom neither they Jer 9:16
hair, for all these **n** are uncircumcised, Jer 9:26
"Learn not the way of the **n**, nor be Jer 10:2
heavens because the **n** are dismayed at Jer 10:2
would not fear you, O King of the **n**? Jer 10:7
the wise ones of the **n** and in all their Jer 10:7
and the **n** cannot endure his Jer 10:10
your wrath on the **n** that know you not, Jer 10:25
false gods of the **n** that can bring rain? Jer 14:22
to you shall the **n** come from the ends Jer 16:19
Ask among the **n**, Who has heard the Jer 18:13
"'And many **n** will pass by this city, and Jer 22:8
and against all these surrounding **n**. Jer 25:9
and these **n** shall serve the king of Jer 25:11
Jeremiah prophesied against all the **n**. Jer 25:13
For many **n** and great kings shall Jer 25:14
and make all the **n** to whom I send you Jer 25:15
and made all the **n** to whom the LORD Jer 25:17
LORD has an indictment against the **n**; Jer 25:31
city a curse for all the **n** of the earth.'" Jer 26:6
All the **n** shall serve him and his son Jer 27:7
Then many **n** and great kings shall Jer 27:7
neck of all the **n** within two years." But Jer 28:11
the neck of all these **n** an iron yoke to Jer 28:14
you from all the **n** and all the places Jer 29:14
reproach among all the **n** where I have Jer 29:18
end of all the **n** among whom I Jer 30:11
and raise shouts for the chief of the **n**; Jer 31:7
"Hear the word of the LORD, O **n**, and Jer 31:10
a glory before all the **n** of the earth who Jer 33:9
against Israel and Judah and all the **n**, Jer 36:2
Judah from all the **n** to which they had Jer 43:5
and a taunt among all the **n** of the earth? Jer 44:8
Jeremiah the prophet concerning the **n**. Jer 46:1
The **n** have heard of your shame, and Jer 46:12
full end of all the **n** to which I have Jer 46:28
an envoy has been sent among the **n**: Jer 49:14
I will make you small among the **n**, Jer 49:15
"Declare among the **n** and proclaim, set Jer 50:2
against Babylon a gathering of great **n**, Jer 50:9
Behold, she shall be the last of the **n**, a Jer 50:12
has become a horror among the **n**! Jer 50:23
her cry shall be heard among the **n**." Jer 50:46
earth drunken; the **n** drank of her wine; Jer 51:7
of her wine; therefore the **n** went mad. Jer 51:7
of war: with you I break **n** in pieces; Jer 51:20
earth; blow the trumpet among the **n**; Jer 51:27
prepare the **n** for war against her; Jer 51:27
Prepare the **n** for war against her, the Jer 51:28
has become a horror among the **n**! Jer 51:41
The **n** shall no longer flow to him; the Jer 51:44
and the **n** weary themselves only for Jer 51:58
she who was great among the **n**! Lam 1:1
she dwells now among the **n**, but finds Lam 1:3
she has seen the **n** enter her sanctuary, Lam 1:10
her king and princes are among the **n**; Lam 2:9
people said among the **n**, "They shall Lam 4:15
shadow we shall live among the **n**." Lam 4:20
you to the people of Israel, to **n** of rebels, Ezk 2:3
among the **n** where I will drive them." Ezk 4:13
I have set her in the center of the **n**, with Ezk 5:5
by doing wickedness more than the **n**, Ezk 5:6
more turbulent than the **n** that are all Ezk 5:7
to the rules of the **n** that are all around Ezk 5:7
in your midst in the sight of the **n**. Ezk 5:8
reproach among the **n** all around you Ezk 5:14
and a horror, to the **n** all around you, Ezk 5:15
you have among the **n** some who escape Ezk 6:8
me among the **n** where they are Ezk 6:9
the worst of the **n** to take possession of Ezk 7:24
the rules of the **n** that are around Ezk 11:12
I removed them far off among the **n**, Ezk 11:16
them among the **n** and scatter them Ezk 12:15
among the **n** where they Ezk 12:16
forth among the **n** because of your Ezk 16:14
The **n** heard about him; he was caught Ezk 19:4
Then the **n** set against him from Ezk 19:8
the sight of the **n** among whom they Ezk 20:9
not be profaned in the sight of the **n**, Ezk 20:14
not be profaned in the sight of the **n**, Ezk 20:22
them among the **n** and disperse them Ezk 20:23
—the thought, 'Let us be like the **n**, Ezk 20:32
among you in the sight of the **n**. Ezk 20:41
I have made you a reproach to the **n**, Ezk 22:4
you among the **n** and disperse you Ezk 22:15
your own doing in the sight of the **n**, Ezk 22:16
whore with the **n** and defiled yourself Ezk 23:30
will hand you over as plunder to the **n**. Ezk 25:7
house of Judah is like all the other **n**,' Ezk 25:8
be remembered no more among the **n**, Ezk 25:10
and will bring up many **n** against you, Ezk 26:3
she shall become plunder for the **n**, Ezk 26:5
upon you, the most ruthless of the **n**; Ezk 28:7
holiness in them in the sight of the **n**, Ezk 28:25
scatter the Egyptians among the **n**, Ezk 29:12
never again exalt itself above the **n**. Ezk 29:15
they will never again rule over the **n**. Ezk 29:15
day of clouds, a time of doom for the **n**. Ezk 30:3
with him, the most ruthless of **n**, Ezk 30:11
Egyptians among the **n** and disperse Ezk 30:23
Egyptians among the **n** and disperse Ezk 30:26
and under its shadow lived all great **n**. Ezk 31:6
into the hand of a mighty one of the **n**. Ezk 31:11
Foreigners, the most ruthless of **n**, Ezk 31:12
I made the **n** quake at the sound of its Ezk 31:16
lived under its shadow among the **n**. Ezk 31:17
"You consider yourself a lion of the **n**, Ezk 32:2
I bring your destruction among the **n**, Ezk 32:9
ones, all of them most ruthless of **n**. Ezk 32:12
the daughters of the **n** shall chant it; Ezk 32:16
her and the daughters of majestic **n**, Ezk 32:18
They shall no more be a prey to the **n**, Ezk 34:28
no longer suffer the reproach of the **n**. Ezk 34:29
'These two **n** and these two countries Ezk 35:10
the possession of the rest of the **n**, Ezk 36:3
derision to the rest of the **n** all around, Ezk 36:4
the rest of the **n** and against all Edom, Ezk 36:5
you have suffered the reproach of the **n**. Ezk 36:6
I swear that the **n** that are all around Ezk 36:7
hear anymore the reproach of the **n**, Ezk 36:15
I scattered them among the **n**, and Ezk 36:19
But when they came to the **n**, Ezk 36:20
profaned among the **n** to which they Ezk 36:21
profaned among the **n** to which you Ezk 36:22
has been profaned among the **n**, Ezk 36:23
And the **n** will know that I am the Ezk 36:23
take you from the **n** and gather you Ezk 36:24
the disgrace of famine among the **n**. Ezk 36:30
Then the **n** that are left all around you Ezk 36:36
Israel from the **n** among which they Ezk 37:21
all, and they shall be no longer two **n**, Ezk 37:22
Then the **n** will know that I am the Ezk 37:28
people who were gathered from the **n**, Ezk 38:12
my land, that the **n** may know me, Ezk 38:16
myself known in the eyes of many **n**. Ezk 38:23
And the **n** shall know that I am the Ezk 39:7
"And I will set my glory among the **n**, Ezk 39:21
and all the **n** shall see my judgment Ezk 39:21
And the **n** shall know that the house Ezk 39:23
my holiness in the sight of many **n**. Ezk 39:27
exile among the **n** and then assembled Ezk 39:28
remaining among the **n** anymore. Ezk 39:28
O peoples, **n**, and languages, Dn 3:4
n, and languages fell down and Dn 3:7
to all peoples, **n**, and languages, Dn 4:1
n, and languages trembled and feared Dn 5:19
n, and languages that dwell in all the Dn 6:25
n, and languages should serve him; Dn 7:14
they are among the **n** as a useless vessel. Hos 8:8
Though they hire allies among the **n**, I Hos 8:10
they shall be wanderers among the **n**. Hos 9:17
and **n** shall be gathered against them Hos 10:10
a reproach, a byword among the **n**. Jl 2:17
more make you a reproach among the **n**. Jl 2:19
I will gather all the **n** and bring them down Jl 3:2
them among the **n** and have divided Jl 3:2
Proclaim this among the **n**: Consecrate for Jl 3:9
Hasten and come, all you surrounding **n**, Jl 3:11
Let the **n** stir themselves up and come up Jl 3:12
I will sit to judge all the surrounding **n**. Jl 3:12
the notable men of the first of the **n**, Am 6:1
Israel among all the **n** as one shakes Am 9:9
of Edom and all the **n** who are called by Am 9:12
a messenger has been sent among the **n**: Ob 1:1
I will make you small among the **n**; Ob 1:2
day of the LORD is near upon all the **n**. Ob 1:15
so all the **n** shall drink continually; Ob 1:16
and many **n** shall come, and say: "Come, Mi 4:2
and shall decide for strong **n** afar off; Mi 4:3
Now many **n** are assembled against Mi 4:11
remnant of Jacob shall be among the **n**, Mi 5:8
execute vengeance on the **n** that did not Mi 5:15
The **n** shall see and be ashamed of all Mi 7:16
who betrays **n** with her whorings, Na 3:4
and I will make **n** look at your nakedness Na 3:5
"Look among the **n**, and see; wonder Hab 1:5
net and mercilessly killing **n** forever? Hab 1:17
gathers for himself all **n** and collects as Hab 2:5
Because you have plundered many **n**, Hab 2:8
and **n** weary themselves for nothing? Hab 2:13
the earth; he looked and shook the **n**; Hab 3:6
in fury; you threshed the **n** in anger. Hab 3:12
each in its place, all the lands of the **n**. Zep 2:11
"I have cut off **n**; their battlements are in Zep 3:6
For my decision is to gather **n**, to Zep 3:8
And I will shake all **n**, so that the Hg 2:7
that the treasures of all **n** shall come in, Hg 2:7
the strength of the kingdoms of the **n**, Hg 2:22
exceedingly angry with the **n** that are at Zec 1:15
the horns of the **n** who lifted up their Zec 1:21
sent me to the **n** who plundered you, Zec 2:8
And many **n** shall join themselves to Zec 2:11
among all the **n** that they had Zec 7:14
been a byword of cursing among the **n**, Zec 8:13
peoples and strong **n** shall come to Zec 8:22
ten men from the **n** of every tongue Zec 8:23
off, and he shall speak peace to the **n**; Zec 9:10
Though I scattered them among the **n**, Zec 10:9
And all the **n** of the earth will gather Zec 12:3
to destroy all the **n** that come against Zec 12:9
gather all the **n** against Jerusalem to Zec 14:2
and fight against those **n** as when he Zec 14:3
all the surrounding **n** shall be Zec 14:14
survives of all the **n** that have come Zec 14:16
the LORD afflicts the **n** that do not go Zec 14:18
punishment to all the **n** that do not go Zec 14:19
my name will be great among the **n**, Mal 1:11
my name will be great among the **n**, Mal 1:11
my name will be feared among the **n**. Mal 1:14
Then all **n** will call you blessed, for Mal 3:12
be hated by all **n** for my name's sake. Mt 24:9
the whole world as a testimony to all **n**, Mt 24:14
Before him will be gathered all the **n**, Mt 25:32
therefore and make disciples of all **n**, Mt 28:19
called a house of prayer for all the **n**'? Mk 11:17
must first be proclaimed to all **n**. Mk 13:10
For all the **n** of the world seek after Lk 12:30
sword and be led captive among all **n**, Lk 21:24
earth distress of **n** in perplexity because Lk 21:25
be proclaimed in his name to all **n**, Lk 24:47

they dispossessed the **n** that God drove Acts 7:45
after destroying seven **n** in the land Acts 13:19
he allowed all the **n** to walk in their Acts 14:16
the sake of his name among all the **n**, Rom 1:5
the father of many **n**"—in the Rom 4:17
should become the father of many **n**, Rom 4:18
has been made known to all **n**, Rom 16:26
"In you shall all the **n** be blessed." Gal 3:8
by angels, proclaimed among the **n**, 1 Tm 3:16
to him I will give authority over the **n**, Rv 2:26
many peoples and **n** and languages and Rv 10:11
leave that out, for it is given over to the **n**, Rv 11:2
tribes and languages and **n** will gaze at Rv 11:9
The **n** raged, but your wrath came, and Rv 11:18
who is to rule all the **n** with a rod of iron, Rv 12:5
she who made all **n** drink the wine of the Rv 14:8
and true are your ways, O King of the **n**! Rv 15:3
All **n** will come and worship you, for Rv 15:4
three parts, and the cities of the **n** fell, Rv 16:19
and multitudes and **n** and languages. Rv 17:15
For all **n** have drunk the wine of the Rv 18:3
and all **n** were deceived by your Rv 18:23
sword with which to strike down the **n**, Rv 19:15
he might not deceive the **n** any longer, Rv 20:3
come out to deceive the **n** that are at the Rv 20:8
By its light will the **n** walk, and the Rv 21:24
into it the glory and the honor of the **n**. Rv 21:26
of the tree were for the healing of the **n**. Rv 22:2

NATIVE (25)
he is a sojourner or a **n** of the land. Ex 12:19
keep it; he shall be as a **n** of the land. Ex 12:48
one law for the **n** and for the stranger Ex 12:49
either the **n** or the stranger who Lv 16:29
beasts, whether he is a **n** or a sojourner, Lv 17:15
either the **n** or the stranger who Lv 18:26
sojourns with you as the **n** among you, Lv 19:34
All **n** Israelites shall dwell in booths, Lv 23:42
The sojourner as well as the **n**, when he Lv 24:16
rule for the sojourner and for the **n**, Lv 24:22
both for the sojourner and for the **n**." Nm 9:14
Every **n** Israelite shall do these things Nm 15:13
for him who is **n** among the people of Nm 15:29
hand, whether he is **n** or a sojourner, Nm 15:30
all Israel, sojourner as well as **n** born, Jos 8:33
and mother and your **n** land and came Ru 2:11
and from the gate of his **n** place. Ru 4:10
shall return no more to see his **n** land. Jer 22:10
of Babylonians whose **n** land was Ezk 23:15
hear, each of us in his own **n** language? Acts 2:8
a Levite, a **n** of Cyprus, Acts 4:36
a Jew named Aquila, a **n** of Pontus, Acts 18:2
named Apollos, a **n** of Alexandria, Acts 18:24
The **n** people showed us unusual Acts 28:2
When the **n** people saw the creature Acts 28:4

NATIVE-BORN (1)
shall be to you as **n** children of Israel. Ezk 47:22

NATURAL (10)
women exchanged **n** relations for Rom 1:26
likewise gave up **n** relations with Rom 1:27
terms, because of your **n** limitations. Rom 6:19
if God did not spare the **n** branches, Rom 11:21
more will these, the **n** branches, Rom 11:24
The **n** person does not accept the 1 Cor 2:14
It is sown a **n** body; it is raised a 1 Cor 15:44
If there is a **n** body, there is also a 1 Cor 15:44
the spiritual that is first but the **n**, 1 Cor 15:46
looks intently at his **n** face in a mirror. Jas 1:23

NATURALLY (2)
was killed with a sword or who died **n**, Nm 19:16
shall not eat anything that has died **n**. Dt 14:21

NATURE (14)
We also are men, of like **n** with you, Acts 14:15
his eternal power and divine **n**, Rom 1:20
for those that are contrary to **n**; Rom 1:26
the law, by **n** do what the law requires, Rom 2:14
from what is by **n** a wild olive tree, Rom 11:24
olive tree, and grafted, contrary to **n**, Rom 11:24
Does not **n** itself teach you that if a 1 Cor 11:14
Though our outer **n** is wasting away, 2 Cor 4:16
our inner **n** is being renewed day by 2 Cor 4:16
enslaved to those that by **n** are not gods. Gal 4:8
mind, and were by **n** children of wrath, Eph 2:3
of God and the exact imprint of his **n**, Heb 1:3
Elijah was a man with a **n** like ours, and Jas 5:17
may become partakers of the divine **n**, 2 Pt 1:4

NAVE (18)
in front of the **n** of the house was 1 Kgs 6:3
both the **n** and the inner sanctuary. 1 Kgs 6:5
the **n** in front of the inner sanctuary, 1 Kgs 6:17
entrance to the **n** doorposts of 1 Kgs 6:33
for the doors of the **n** of the temple. 1 Kgs 7:50
in front of the **n** of the house was 2 Chr 3:4
The **n** he lined with cypress and 2 Chr 3:5
stood on their feet, facing the **n**. 2 Chr 3:13
the doors of the **n** of the temple were 2 Chr 4:22
brought me to the **n** and measured the Ezk 41:1
And he measured the length of the **n**, Ezk 41:2
its breadth, twenty cubits, across the **n**. Ezk 41:4
The inside of the **n** and the vestibules Ezk 41:15
carved; similarly the wall of the **n**. Ezk 41:20
The doorposts of the **n** were squared, Ezk 41:21
The **n** and the Holy Place had each a Ezk 41:23
doors of the **n** were carved cherubim Ezk 41:25
those opposite the **n** were a hundred Ezk 42:8

NAVEL (1)
Your **n** is a rounded bowl that never lacks Sg 7:2

NAZARENE (2)
be fulfilled: "He shall be called a **N**." Mt 2:23
and said, "You also were with the **N**, Mk 14:67

NAZARENES (1)
and is a ringleader of the sect of the **N**. Acts 24:5

NAZARETH (28)
And he went and lived in a city called **N**, Mt 2:23
And leaving **N** he went and lived in Mt 4:13
is the prophet Jesus, from **N** of Galilee." Mt 21:11
"This man was with Jesus of **N**." Mt 26:71
days Jesus came from **N** of Galilee and Mk 1:9
have you to do with us, Jesus of **N**? Mk 1:24
when he heard that it was Jesus of **N**, Mk 10:47
You seek Jesus of **N**, who was crucified. Mk 16:6
from God to a city of Galilee named **N**, Lk 1:26
went up from Galilee, from the town of **N**, Lk 2:4
into Galilee, to their own town of **N**. Lk 2:39
and came to **N** and was submissive Lk 2:51
And he came to **N**, where he had been Lk 4:16
have you to do with us, Jesus of **N**? Lk 4:34
told him, "Jesus of **N** is passing by." Lk 18:37
said to him, "Concerning Jesus of **N**, Lk 24:19
and also the prophets wrote, Jesus of **N**, Jn 1:45
good come out of **N**?" Philip said to him, Jn 1:46
him, "Jesus of **N**." Jesus said to them, Jn 18:5
do you seek?" And they said, "Jesus of **N**." Jn 18:7
It read, "Jesus of **N**, the King of the Jews." Jn 19:19
Jesus of **N**, a man attested to you by Acts 2:22
In the name of Jesus Christ of **N**, rise up Acts 3:6
that by the name of Jesus Christ of **N**, Acts 4:10
that this Jesus of **N** will destroy this Acts 6:14
anointed Jesus of **N** with the Holy Acts 10:38
And he said to me, 'I am Jesus of **N**, Acts 22:8
in opposing the name of Jesus of **N**. Acts 26:9

NAZIRITE (11)
makes a special vow, the vow of a **N**, Nm 6:2
"And this is the law for the **N**, when the Nm 6:13
And the **N** shall shave his consecrated Nm 6:18
shall put them on the hands of the **N**, Nm 6:19
And after that the **N** may drink wine. Nm 6:20
"This is the law of the **N**. But if he vows Nm 6:21
offering to the LORD above his **N** vow, Nm 6:21
do in addition to the law of the **N**." Nm 6:21
the child shall be a **N** to God from the Jgs 13:5
the child shall be a **N** to God from the Jgs 13:7
for I have been a **N** to God from my Jgs 16:17

NAZIRITES (2)
and some of your young men for **N**. Am 2:11
"But you made the **N** drink wine, and Am 2:12

NEAH (1)
on to Rimmon it bends toward **N**, Jos 19:13

NEAPOLIS (1)
and the following day to **N**, Acts 16:11

NEAR (306)
Then Abraham drew **n** and said, "Will Gn 18:23
Lot, and drew **n** to break the door down. Gn 19:9
Behold, this city is **n** enough to flee to, Gn 19:20
Isaac said to Jacob, "Please come **n**, Gn 27:21
So Jacob went **n** to Isaac his father, Gn 27:22
Then he said, "Bring it **n** to me, that I Gn 27:25
bless you." So he brought it **n** to him, Gn 27:25
said to him, "Come **n** and kiss me, Gn 27:26
So he came **n** and kissed him. And Gn 27:27
Jacob came **n** and rolled the stone Gn 29:10
times, until he came **n** to his brother. Gn 33:3
Then the servants drew **n**, they and their Gn 33:6
her children drew **n** and bowed down. Gn 33:7
And last Joseph and Rachel drew **n**, and Gn 33:7
the terebinth tree that was **n** Shechem. Gn 35:4
pasture their father's flock **n** Shechem. Gn 37:12
and before he came **n** to them they Gn 37:18
said to his brothers, "Come **n** to me, Gn 45:4
near to me, please." And they came **n**. Gn 45:4
land of Goshen, and you shall be **n** me, Gn 45:10
when the time drew **n** that Israel must Gn 47:29
So Joseph brought them **n** him, and he Gn 48:10
right hand, and brought them **n** him. Gn 48:13
Then he said, "Do not come **n**; take your Ex 3:5
Then he may come **n** and keep it; he Ex 12:48
of the Philistines, although that was **n**. Ex 13:17
When Pharaoh drew **n**, the people of Ex 14:10
without one coming **n** the other all Ex 14:20
people of Israel, 'Come **n** before the LORD, Ex 16:9
for the third day; do not go **n** a woman." Ex 19:15
the priests who come **n** to the LORD Ex 19:22
while Moses drew **n** to the thick Ex 20:21
of the house shall come **n** to God to show Ex 22:8
Moses alone shall come **n** to the LORD, Ex 24:2
LORD, but the others shall not come **n**, Ex 24:2
"Then bring **n** to you Aaron your Ex 28:1
or when they come **n** the altar to Ex 28:43
or when they come **n** the altar to Ex 30:20
as soon as he came **n** the camp and saw Ex 32:19
and they were afraid to come **n** him. Ex 34:30
all the people of Israel came **n**, Ex 34:32
the congregation drew **n** and stood before Lv 9:5
"Draw **n** to the altar and offer your sin Lv 9:7
So Aaron drew **n** to the altar and killed Lv 9:8
'Among those who are **n** me I will be Lv 10:3
of Aaron, and said to them, "Come **n**; Lv 10:4
So they came **n** and carried them in Lv 10:5
when they drew **n** before the LORD and Lv 16:1
virgin sister (who is **n** to him because Lv 21:3
one who has a blemish shall draw **n**, Lv 21:18
a blemish shall come **n** to offer the Lv 21:21
he shall not come **n** to offer the bread of Lv 21:21
And if any outsider comes **n**, he shall Nm 1:51
"Bring the tribe of Levi **n**, and set them Nm 3:6
But if any outsider comes **n**, he shall be Nm 3:10
any outsider who came **n** was to be put Nm 3:38
die when they come **n** to the most holy Nm 4:19
priest shall bring her **n** and set her Nm 5:16
the LORD he shall not go **n** a dead body. Nm 6:6
people of Israel come **n** the sanctuary." Nm 8:19
of Zin to Rehob, **n** Lebo-hamath. Nm 13:21
is holy, and will bring him **n** to him. Nm 16:5
he chooses he will bring **n** to him. Nm 16:5
of Israel, to bring you **n** to himself, Nm 16:9
and that he has brought you **n** him, Nm 16:10
should draw **n** to burn incense before Nm 16:40
Everyone who comes **n**, who comes Nm 17:13
who comes **n** to the tabernacle of the Nm 17:13
but shall not come **n** to the vessels of Nm 18:3
tent, and no outsider shall come **n** you. Nm 18:4
any outsider who comes **n** shall be put Nm 18:7
Israel do not come **n** the tent of Nm 18:22
which is **n** the River in the land of the Nm 22:5
but not now; I behold him, but not **n**: Nm 24:17
Then drew **n** the daughters of Nm 27:1
of hundreds, came **n** to Moses Nm 31:48
Then they came **n** to him and said, Nm 32:16
came **n** and spoke before Moses and Nm 36:1
Then all of you came **n** me and said, 'Let Dt 1:22
the sons of Ammon you did not draw **n**, Dt 2:37
there that has a god so **n** to it as the LORD Dt 4:7
And you came **n** and stood at the foot of Dt 4:11
burning with fire, you came **n** to me, Dt 5:23
Go **n** and hear all that the LORD our God Dt 5:27
you, whether **n** you or far off from you, Dt 13:7
seventh year, the year of release is **n**,' Dt 15:9
And when you draw **n** to the battle, the Dt 20:2
you are drawing **n** for battle against Dt 20:3
"When you draw **n** to a city to fight Dt 20:10
if he does not live **n** you and you do not Dt 22:2
this woman, and when I came **n** her, Dt 22:14
of the one draws **n** to rescue her Dt 25:11
But the word is very **n** you. It is in your Dt 30:14
Do not come **n** it, in order that you may Jos 3:4
from Jericho to Ai, which is **n** Beth-aven, Jos 7:2
you shall be brought **n** by your tribes. Jos 7:14
LORD takes by lot shall come **n** by clans. Jos 7:14
LORD takes shall come **n** by households. Jos 7:14
LORD takes shall come **n** man by man. Jos 7:14
and brought Israel **n** tribe by tribe, Jos 7:16
And he brought **n** the clans of Judah, Jos 7:17
And he brought **n** the clan of the Jos 7:17
And he brought **n** his household man Jos 7:18
went up and drew **n** before the city and Jos 8:11
alive, and brought him **n** to Joshua. Jos 8:23
war who had gone with him, "Come **n**; Jos 10:24
Then they came **n** and put their Jos 10:24
Judah, which lies in the Negeb **n** Arad, Jgs 1:16
back at the idols **n** Gilgal and said, Jgs 3:19
oak in Zaanannim, which is **n** Kedesh. Jgs 4:11
against it and drew **n** to the door of Jgs 9:52
in the houses **n** Micah's house were Jgs 18:22
When they were **n** Jebus, the day was Jgs 19:11
"Come and let us draw **n** to one of these Jgs 19:13
the sun went down on them **n** Gibeah, Jgs 19:14
"Shall we again draw **n** to fight against Jgs 20:23
of Israel came **n** against the people Jgs 20:24
the Philistines drew **n** to attack Israel. 1 Sm 7:10

brought all the tribes of Israel **n**, 1 Sm 10:20
the tribe of Benjamin **n** by its clans, 1 Sm 10:21
said, "Let us draw **n** to God here." 1 Sm 14:36
moved forward and came **n** to David, 1 Sm 17:41
and came and drew **n** to meet David, 1 Sm 17:48
when David came **n** to the people 1 Sm 30:21
with him drew **n** to battle against 2 Sm 10:13
did you go so **n** the city to fight? 2 Sm 11:20
Why did you go so **n** the wall?' 2 Sm 11:21
she brought them **n** him to eat, 2 Sm 13:11
at Baal-hazor, which is **n** Ephraim, 2 Sm 13:23
a man came **n** to pay homage 2 Sm 15:5
die in my own city **n** the grave of my 2 Sm 19:37
And he came **n** her, and the woman 2 Sm 20:17
When David's time to die drew **n**, he 1 Kgs 2:1
to the land of the enemy, far off or **n**, 1 Kgs 8:46
be **n** to the LORD our God day and 1 Kgs 8:59
which is **n** Eloth on the shore of the 1 Kgs 9:26
And Elijah came **n** to all the people 1 Kgs 18:21
"Come **n** to me." And all the people 1 Kgs 18:30
And all the people came **n** to him. 1 Kgs 18:30
Elijah the prophet came **n** and said, 1 Kgs 18:36
a prophet came **n** to Ahab king of 1 Kgs 20:13
the prophet came **n** to the king 1 Kgs 20:22
a man of God came **n** and said to the 1 Kgs 20:28
garden, because it is **n** my house, 1 Kgs 21:2
of Chenaanah came **n** and struck 1 Kgs 22:24
were at Jericho drew **n** to Elisha and 2 Kgs 2:5
But his servants came **n** and said to 2 Kgs 5:13
Then the king drew **n** to the altar 2 Kgs 16:12
with him drew **n** before the Syrians 1 Chr 19:14
away captive to a land far or **n**, 2 Chr 6:36
of Chenaanah came **n** and struck 2 Chr 18:23
Arabians who are **n** the Ethiopians. 2 Chr 21:16
yourselves to the LORD. Come **n**; 2 Chr 29:31
the Jews who lived **n** them came from Neh 4:12
of King Ahasuerus, both **n** and far, Est 9:20
light,' they say, 'is **n** to the darkness.' Jb 17:12
His soul draws **n** the pit, and his life to Jb 33:22
him who made him bring **n** his sword! Jb 40:19
Who would come **n** him with a bridle? Jb 41:13
One is so **n** to another that no air can Jb 41:16
Be not far from me, for trouble is **n**, and Ps 22:11
bit and bridle, or it will not stay **n** you. Ps 32:9
The LORD is **n** to the brokenhearted and Ps 34:18
is the one you choose and bring **n**, Ps 65:4
Draw **n** to my soul, redeem me; ransom Ps 69:18
But for me it is good to be **n** God; I have Ps 73:28
God; we give thanks, for your name is **n**. Ps 75:1
Surely his salvation is **n** to those who Ps 85:9
of troubles, and my life draws **n** to Sheol. Ps 88:3
right hand, but it will not come **n** you. Ps 91:7
befall you, no plague come **n** your tent. Ps 91:10
and they drew **n** to the gates of death. Ps 107:18
They draw **n** who persecute me with Ps 119:150
But you are **n**, O LORD, and all your Ps 119:151
The LORD is **n** to all who call on him, Ps 145:18
the people of Israel who are **n** to him. Ps 148:14
and do not go **n** the door of her house, Prv 5:8
passing along the street **n** her corner, Prv 7:8
but the mouth of a fool brings ruin **n**. Prv 10:14
a neighbor who is **n** than a brother Prv 27:10
To draw **n** to listen is better than to offer Eccl 5:1
and the years draw **n** of which you will Eccl 12:1
counsel of the Holy One of Israel draw **n**, Is 5:19
Wail, for the day of the LORD is **n**; as Is 13:6
and smooth, to a people feared **n** and far, Is 18:2
smooth, from a people feared **n** and far, Is 18:7
her pangs when she is **n** to giving birth, Is 26:17
this people draw **n** with their mouth Is 29:13
and you who are **n**, acknowledge my Is 33:13
Draw **n**, O nations, to hear, and give Is 34:1
let us together draw **n** for judgment. Is 41:1
tremble; they have drawn **n** and come. Is 41:5
yourselves and come; draw **n** together, Is 45:20
I bring **n** my righteousness; it is not far Is 46:13
Draw **n** to me, hear this: from the Is 48:16
He who vindicates me is **n**. Who will Is 50:8
is my adversary? Let him come **n** to me. Is 50:8
My righteousness draws **n**, my salvation Is 51:5
from terror, for it shall not come **n** you. Is 54:14
be found; call upon him while he is **n**; Is 55:6
But you, draw **n**, sons of the sorceress, Is 57:3
to the far and to the **n**," says the LORD, Is 57:19
judgments; they delight to draw **n** to God. Is 58:2
say, "Keep to yourself, do not come **n** me, Is 65:5
you are **n** in their mouth and far from Jer 12:2
all the kings of the north, far and **n**, one Jer 25:26
I will make him draw **n**, and he shall Jer 30:21
which was **n** the chamber of the Jer 35:4
at Geruth Chimham **n** Bethlehem, Jer 41:17
from the least to the greatest, came **n** Jer 42:1
The calamity of Moab is **n** at hand, Jer 48:16
the cities of the land of Moab, far and **n**. Jer 48:24
You came **n** when I called on you; you Lam 3:57
walk in our streets; our end drew **n**; Lam 4:18
and he who is **n** shall fall by the sword, Ezk 6:12
the day is **n**, a day of tumult, and not of Ezk 7:7
"Bring **n** the executioners of the city, Ezk 9:1
say, 'The time is not **n** to build houses. Ezk 11:3
But say to them, The days are **n**, and Ezk 12:23
and you have brought your days **n**, Ezk 22:4
Those who are **n** and those who are far Ezk 22:5
For the day is **n**, the day of the LORD is Ezk 30:3
the day is near, the day of the LORD is **n**; Ezk 30:3
of Levi may come **n** to the LORD to Ezk 40:46
before they go **n** to that which Ezk 42:14
who draw **n** to me to minister to me, Ezk 43:19
They shall not come **n** to me, to serve Ezk 44:13
nor come **n** any of my holy things Ezk 44:13
shall come **n** to me to minister to me. Ezk 44:15
defile themselves by going **n** to a dead Ezk 44:25
Then Nebuchadnezzar came **n** to the Dn 3:26
Then they came **n** and said before the Dn 6:12
As he came **n** to the den where Daniel Dn 6:20
So he came **n** where I stood. And when Dn 8:17
those who are **n** and those who are far Dn 9:7
For the day of the LORD is **n**, and as Jl 1:15
for the day of the LORD is coming; it is **n**, Jl 2:1
Let all the men of war draw **n**; let them Jl 3:9
day of the LORD is **n** in the valley of Jl 3:14
of disaster and bring **n** the seat of Am 6:3
day of the LORD is **n** upon all the nations. Ob 1:15
For the day of the LORD is **n**; the LORD has Zep 1:7
The great day of the LORD is **n**, near and Zep 1:14
the LORD is near, **n** and hastening fast; Zep 1:14
the LORD; she does not draw **n** to her God. Zep 3:2
"Then I will draw **n** to you for judgment. Mal 3:5
Now when they drew **n** to Jerusalem and Mt 21:1
When the season for fruit drew **n**, he Mt 21:34
its leaves, you know that summer is **n**. Mt 24:32
all these things, you know that he is **n**, Mt 24:33
they could not get **n** him because of the Mk 2:4
Now when they drew **n** to Jerusalem, to Mk 11:1
its leaves, you know that summer is **n**. Mk 13:28
taking place, you know that he is **n**, Mk 13:29
As he drew **n** to the gate of the town, Lk 7:12
When the days drew **n** for him to be Lk 9:51
kingdom of God has come **n** to you.' Lk 10:9
that the kingdom of God has come **n**.' Lk 10:11
sinners were all drawing **n** to hear him. Lk 15:1
as he came and drew **n** to the house, Lk 15:25
As he drew **n** to Jericho, a blind man Lk 18:35
And when he came **n**, he asked him, Lk 18:40
because he was **n** to Jerusalem, Lk 19:11
When he drew **n** to Bethphage and Lk 19:29
As he was drawing **n**—already on the Lk 19:37
And when he drew **n** and saw the city, Lk 19:41
know that its desolation has come **n**. Lk 21:20
your redemption is drawing **n**." Lk 21:28
know that the summer is already **n**. Lk 21:30
know that the kingdom of God is **n**. Lk 21:31
the Feast of Unleavened Bread drew **n**, Lk 22:1
them. He drew **n** to Jesus to kiss him, Lk 22:47
Jesus himself drew **n** and went with Lk 24:15
So they drew **n** to the village to which Lk 24:28
also was baptizing at Aenon **n** Salim, Jn 3:23
n the field that Jacob had given to his son Jn 4:5
on the sea and coming **n** the boat, Jn 6:19
from Tiberias came **n** the place where Jn 6:23
Some of the Pharisees **n** him heard these Jn 9:40
Bethany was **n** Jerusalem, about two Jn 11:18
there to the region **n** the wilderness, Jn 11:54
Jesus was crucified was **n** the city, Jn 19:20
called Olivet, which is **n** Jerusalem, Acts 1:12
"But as the time of the promise drew **n**, Acts 7:17
at the sight, and as he drew **n** to look, Acts 7:31
Since Lydda was **n** Joppa, the disciples, Acts 9:38
on my way and drew **n** to Damascus, Acts 22:6
ready to kill him before he comes **n**." Acts 23:15
Havens, **n** which was the city of Lasea. Acts 27:8
"The word is **n** you, in your mouth Rom 10:8
beatings, and often **n** death. 2 Cor 11:23
off have been brought **n** by the blood Eph 2:13
far off and peace to those who were **n**. Eph 2:17
Indeed he was ill, **n** to death. But God Phil 2:27
with confidence draw **n** to the throne Heb 4:16
it is worthless and **n** to being cursed, Heb 6:8
through which we draw **n** to God. Heb 7:19
those who draw **n** to God through Heb 7:25
year, make perfect those who draw **n**. Heb 10:1
let us draw **n** with a true heart in full Heb 10:22
more as you see the Day drawing **n**. Heb 10:25
for whoever would draw **n** to God must Heb 11:6
Draw **n** to God, and he will draw near to Jas 4:8
near to God, and he will draw **n** to you. Jas 4:8
keep what is written in it, for the time is **n**. Rv 1:3
prophecy of this book, for the time is **n**. Rv 22:10

NEARBY (1)
the disciple whom he loved standing **n**, Jn 19:26

NEARER (4)
Yet there is a redeemer **n** than I. Ru 3:12
mouth." And he drew **n** and nearer. 2 Sm 18:25
mouth." And he drew nearer and **n**. 2 Sm 18:25
For salvation is **n** to us now than Rom 13:11

NEAREST (6)
then he and his **n** neighbor shall take Ex 12:4
then his **n** redeemer shall come and Lv 25:25
inheritance to the **n** kinsman of his Nm 27:11
of the city that is **n** to the slain man shall Dt 21:3
the elders of that city **n** to the slain man Dt 21:6
my plague, and my **n** kin stand far off. Ps 38:11

NEARIAH (3)
Igal, Bariah, **N**, and Shaphat, 1 Chr 3:22
The sons of **N**: Elioenai, Hizkiah, and 1 Chr 3:23
their leaders Pelatiah, **N**, Rephaiah, 1 Chr 4:42

NEARING (1)
suspected that they were **n** land. Acts 27:27

NEARLY (3)
were near Jebus, the day was **n** over, Jgs 19:11
almost stumbled, my steps had **n** slipped. Ps 73:2
for he **n** died for the work of Christ, Phil 2:30

NEARSIGHTED (1)
these qualities is so **n** that he is blind, 2 Pt 1:9

NEBAI (1)
Hariph, Anathoth, **N**, Neh 10:19

NEBAIOTH (5)
their birth: **N**, the firstborn of Ishmael; Gn 25:13
Ishmael, Abraham's son, the sister of **N**. Gn 28:9
Ishmael's daughter, the sister of **N**. Gn 36:3
firstborn of Ishmael, **N**, and Kedar, 1 Chr 1:29
you; the rams of **N** shall minister to you; Is 60:7

NEBALLAT (1)
Hadid, Zeboim, **N**, Neh 11:34

NEBAT (25)
Jeroboam the son of **N**, an 1 Kgs 11:26
Jeroboam the son of **N** heard of it (for 1 Kgs 12:2
Shilonite to Jeroboam the son of **N**. 1 Kgs 12:15
year of King Jeroboam the son of **N**, 1 Kgs 15:1
the house of Jeroboam the son of **N**. 1 Kgs 16:3
the way of Jeroboam the son of **N**, 1 Kgs 16:26
in the sins of Jeroboam the son of **N**, 1 Kgs 16:31
the house of Jeroboam the son of **N**, 1 Kgs 21:22
in the way of Jeroboam the son of **N**, 1 Kgs 22:52
to the sin of Jeroboam the son of **N**, 2 Kgs 3:3
the house of Jeroboam the son of **N**, 2 Kgs 9:9
the sins of Jeroboam the son of **N**, 2 Kgs 10:29
the sins of Jeroboam the son of **N**, 2 Kgs 13:2
the sins of Jeroboam the son of **N**, 2 Kgs 13:11
the sins of Jeroboam the son of **N**, 2 Kgs 14:24
the sins of Jeroboam the son of **N**, 2 Kgs 15:9
the sins of Jeroboam the son of **N**, 2 Kgs 15:18
the sins of Jeroboam the son of **N**, 2 Kgs 15:24
the sins of Jeroboam the son of **N**, 2 Kgs 15:28
made Jeroboam the son of **N** king. 2 Kgs 17:21
erected by Jeroboam the son of **N**, 2 Kgs 23:15
concerning Jeroboam the son of **N**? 2 Chr 9:29
Jeroboam the son of **N** heard of it (for 2 Chr 10:2
Shilonite to Jeroboam the son of **N**. 2 Chr 10:15
Yet Jeroboam the son of **N**, a servant 2 Chr 13:6

NEBO (13)
Heshbon, Elealeh, Sebam, **N**, and Beon, Nm 32:3
N, and Baal-meon (their names were Nm 32:38
the mountains of Abarim, before **N**. Nm 33:47
mountain of the Abarim, Mount **N**, Dt 32:49
up from the plains of Moab to Mount **N**, Dt 34:1
in Aroer, as far as **N** and Baal-meon. 1 Chr 5:8
The sons of **N**, 52. Ezr 2:29
Of the sons of **N**: Jeiel, Mattithiah, Ezr 10:43
The men of the other **N**, 52. Neh 7:33
over **N** and over Medeba Moab wails. Is 15:2
Bel bows down; **N** stoops; their idols are Is 46:1
of Israel: "Woe to **N**, for it is laid waste! Jer 48:1
and Dibon, and **N**, and Jer 48:22

NEBUCHADNEZZAR (91)
his days, **N** king of Babylon came up, 2 Kgs 24:1
the servants of **N** king of Babylon 2 Kgs 24:10
And **N** king of Babylon came to the 2 Kgs 24:11
N king of Babylon came with all his 2 Kgs 25:1
was the nineteenth year of King **N**, 2 Kgs 25:8
whom **N** king of Babylon had left, 2 Kgs 25:22
into exile by the hand of **N**. 1 Chr 6:15
him came up **N** king of Babylon 2 Chr 36:6
N also carried part of the vessels of 2 Chr 36:7
of the year King **N** sent and brought 2 Chr 36:10
He also rebelled against King **N**, 2 Chr 36:13
of the LORD that **N** had carried away from Ezr 1:7
of those exiles whom **N** the king of Ezr 2:1
into the hand of **N** king of Babylon, Ezr 5:12
which **N** had taken out of the temple Ezr 5:14

which **N** took out of the temple that is in Ezr 6:5
of those exiles whom **N** the king of Neh 7:6
whom **N** king of Babylon had carried Est 2:6
for **N** king of Babylon is making war Jer 21:2
into the hand of **N** king of Babylon and Jer 21:7
into the hand of **N** king of Babylon and Jer 22:25
After **N** king of Babylon had taken into Jer 24:1
was the first year of **N** king of Babylon), Jer 25:1
the LORD, and for **N** the king of Babylon, Jer 25:9
given all these lands into the hand of **N**, Jer 27:6
will not serve this **N** king of Babylon, Jer 27:8
which **N** king of Babylon did not take Jer 27:20
which **N** king of Babylon took away Jer 28:3
break the yoke of **N** king of Babylon Jer 28:11
iron yoke to serve **N** king of Babylon, Jer 28:14
whom **N** had taken into exile from Jer 29:1
sent to Babylon to **N** king of Babylon. Jer 29:3
into the hand of **N** king of Babylon, Jer 29:21
which was the eighteenth year of **N**. Jer 32:1
into the hand of **N** king of Babylon, Jer 32:28
when **N** king of Babylon and all his Jer 34:1
But when **N** king of Babylon came up Jer 35:11
whom **N** king of Babylon made king in Jer 37:1
N king of Babylon and all his army Jer 39:1
brought him up to **N** king of Babylon, Jer 39:5
N king of Babylon gave command Jer 39:11
will send and take **N** the king of Jer 43:10
into the hand of **N** king of Babylon, Jer 44:30
Carchemish and which **N** king of Jer 46:2
the coming of **N** king of Babylon Jer 46:13
into the hand of **N** king of Babylon and Jer 46:26
of Hazor that **N** king of Babylon Jer 49:28
For **N** king of Babylon has made a Jer 49:30
and now at last **N** king of Babylon has Jer 50:17
"**N** the king of Babylon has devoured Jer 51:34
N king of Babylon came with all his Jer 52:4
that was the nineteenth year of King **N**, Jer 52:12
the people whom **N** carried away Jer 52:28
eighteenth year of **N** he carried away Jer 52:29
in the twenty-third year of **N**, Jer 52:30
from the north **N** king of Babylon, Ezk 26:7
N king of Babylon made his army Ezk 29:18
land of Egypt to **N** king of Babylon; Ezk 29:19
by the hand of **N** king of Babylon. Ezk 30:10
N king of Babylon came to Jerusalem Dn 1:1
the eunuchs brought them in before **N**. Dn 1:18
In the second year of the reign of **N**, Dn 2:1
reign of Nebuchadnezzar, **N** had dreams; Dn 2:1
made known to King **N** what will be in Dn 2:28
Then King **N** fell upon his face and paid Dn 2:46
King **N** made an image of gold, whose Dn 3:1
Then King **N** sent to gather the satraps, Dn 3:2
of the image that King **N** had set up. Dn 3:2
of the image that King **N** had set up. Dn 3:3
stood before the image that **N** had set up. Dn 3:3
the golden image that King **N** has set up. Dn 3:5
the golden image that King **N** had set up. Dn 3:7
They declared to King **N**, "O king, live Dn 3:9
Then **N** in furious rage commanded Dn 3:13
N answered and said to them, "Is it true, Dn 3:14
answered and said to the king, "O **N**, Dn 3:16
Then **N** was filled with fury, and the Dn 3:19
Then King **N** was astonished and rose Dn 3:24
Then **N** came near to the door of the Dn 3:26
N answered and said, "Blessed be the Dn 3:28
King **N** to all peoples, nations, and Dn 4:1
N, was at ease in my house and Dn 4:4
This dream I, King **N**, saw. And you, O Dn 4:18
All this came upon King **N**. Dn 4:28
fell a voice from heaven, "O King **N**, Dn 4:31
the word was fulfilled against **N**. Dn 4:33
of the days I, **N**, lifted my eyes to heaven, Dn 4:34
N, praise and extol and honor the King Dn 4:37
and of silver that **N** his father had taken Dn 5:2
gods were found in him, and King **N**, Dn 5:11
High God gave **N** your father kingship Dn 5:18

NEBUSHAZBAN (1)
captain of the guard, **N** the Rab-saris, Jer 39:13

NEBUZARADAN (15)
king of Babylon—**N**, 2 Kgs 25:8
N the captain of the guard carried 2 Kgs 25:11
And **N** the captain of the guard took 2 Kgs 25:20
Then **N**, the captain of the guard, Jer 39:9
N, the captain of the guard, left in the Jer 39:10
concerning Jeremiah through **N**, Jer 39:11
So **N** the captain of the guard, Jer 39:13
from the LORD after **N** the captain of the Jer 40:1
who were left at Mizpah, whom **N**, Jer 41:10
and every person whom **N** the captain of Jer 43:6
king of Babylon—**N** the captain of the Jer 52:12
And **N** the captain of the guard carried Jer 52:15
But **N** the captain of the guard left Jer 52:16
And **N** the captain of the guard took Jer 52:26
N the captain of the guard carried Jer 52:30

NECESSARILY (1)
there is **n** a change in the law as well. Heb 7:12

NECESSARY (13)
to sin! For it is **n** that temptations come, Mt 18:7
but one thing is **n**. Mary has chosen Lk 10:42
Was it not **n** that the Christ should Lk 24:26
"It was **n** that the word of God be Acts 13:46
"It is **n** to circumcise them and to Acts 15:5
proving that it was **n** for the Christ to Acts 17:3
So I thought it **n** to urge the brothers to 2 Cor 9:5
in the flesh is more **n** on your account. Phil 1:24
I have thought it **n** to send to you Phil 2:25
thus it is **n** for this priest also to have Heb 8:3
Thus it was **n** for the copies of the Heb 9:23
though now for a little while, if **n**, 1 Pt 1:6
I found it **n** to write appealing to you to Jude 1:3

NECESSITIES (1)
ministered to my **n** and to those Acts 20:34

NECESSITY (2)
being under no **n** but having his 1 Cor 7:37
for boasting. For **n** is laid upon me. 1 Cor 9:16

NECK (64)
hands and on the smooth part of his **n**. Gn 27:16
you shall break his yoke from your **n**." Gn 27:40
him and fell on his **n** and kissed him, Gn 33:4
linen and put a gold chain about his **n**. Gn 41:42
his brother Benjamin's **n** and wept, Gn 45:14
wept, and Benjamin wept upon his **n**. Gn 45:14
him and fell on his **n** and wept on his Gn 46:29
neck and wept on his **n** a good while. Gn 46:29
hand shall be on the **n** of your enemies; Gn 49:8
will not redeem it you shall break its **n**. Ex 13:13
will not redeem it you shall break its **n**. Ex 34:20
its head from its **n** but shall not sever Lv 5:8
shall break the heifer's **n** there in the Dt 21:4
over the heifer whose **n** was broken in Dt 21:6
of iron on your **n** until he has destroyed Dt 28:48
work embroidered for the **n** as spoil?' Jgs 5:30
and his **n** was broken and he died, 1 Sm 4:18
He stiffened his **n** and hardened his 2 Chr 36:13
and stiffened their **n** and did not Neh 9:16
they stiffened their **n** and appointed a Neh 9:17
and stiffened their **n** and would not Neh 9:29
he seized me by the **n** and dashed me to Jb 16:12
Do you clothe his **n** with a mane? Jb 39:19
In his **n** abides strength, and terror Jb 41:22
For the waters have come up to my **n**. Ps 69:1
horn on high, or speak with haughty **n**.'" Ps 75:5
his **n** was put in a collar of iron; Ps 105:18
for your head and pendants for your **n**. Prv 1:9
forsake you; bind them around your **n**; Prv 3:3
your soul and adornment for your **n**. Prv 3:22
heart always; tie them around your **n**. Prv 6:21
who is often reproved, yet stiffens his **n**, Prv 29:1
ornaments, your **n** with strings of jewels. Sg 1:10
Your **n** is like the tower of David, built in Sg 4:4
Your **n** is like an ivory tower. Your eyes Sg 7:4
and pass on, reaching even to the **n**, Is 8:8
shoulder, and his yoke from your **n**; Is 10:27
stream that reaches up to the **n**; Is 30:28
and your **n** is an iron sinew and your Is 48:4
loose the bonds from your **n**, O captive Is 52:2
a lamb, like one who breaks a dog's **n**; Is 66:3
or incline their ear, but stiffened their **n**. Jer 7:26
incline their ear, but stiffened their **n**, Jer 17:23
it, because they have stiffened their **n**, Jer 19:15
and yoke-bars, and put them on your **n**. Jer 27:2
and put its **n** under the yoke of the king Jer 27:8
that will bring its **n** under the yoke of Jer 27:11
yoke-bars from the **n** of Jeremiah the Jer 28:10
of Babylon from the **n** of all the nations Jer 28:11
from off the **n** of Jeremiah the Jer 28:12
have put upon the **n** of all these nations Jer 28:14
to put him in the stocks and **n** irons. Jer 29:26
I will break his yoke from off your **n**, Jer 30:8
together; they were set upon my **n**; Lam 1:14
on your wrists and a chain on your **n**. Ezk 16:11
of gold around his **n** and shall be the Dn 5:7
of gold around your **n** and shall be the Dn 5:16
a chain of gold was put around his **n**, Dn 5:29
loved to thresh, and I spared her fair **n**; Hos 10:11
laying him bare from thigh to **n**. Hab 3:13
fastened around his **n** and to be Mt 18:6
were hung around his **n** and he were Mk 9:42
were hung around his **n** and he were Lk 17:2
a yoke on the **n** of the disciples that Acts 15:10

NECKLACE (3)
made chains like a **n** and put them 2 Chr 3:16
Therefore pride is their **n**; violence Ps 73:6
of your eyes, with one jewel of your **n**. Sg 4:9

NECKS (10)
your feet on the **n** of these kings." Then Jos 10:24
came near and put their feet on their **n**. Jos 10:24
that were on the **n** of their camels. Jgs 8:21
that were around the **n** of their camels. Jgs 8:26
haughty and walk with outstretched **n**, Is 3:16
"Bring your **n** under the yoke of the Jer 27:12
Our pursuers are at our **n**; we are weary; Lam 5:5
place you on the **n** of the profane Ezk 21:29
from which you cannot remove your **n**, Mi 2:3
who risked their **n** for my life, to Rom 16:4

NECO (9)
his days Pharaoh **N** king of Egypt 2 Kgs 23:29
and Pharaoh **N** killed him at 2 Kgs 23:29
And Pharaoh **N** put him in bonds 2 Kgs 23:33
And Pharaoh **N** made Eliakim the 2 Kgs 23:34
assessment, to give it to Pharaoh **N**. 2 Kgs 23:35
N king of Egypt went up to fight at 2 Chr 35:20
to the words of **N** from the mouth of 2 Chr 35:22
But **N** took Jehoahaz his brother and 2 Chr 36:4
Concerning the army of Pharaoh **N**, Jer 46:2

NECROMANCER (1)
or a medium or a wizard or a **n**, Dt 18:11

NECROMANCERS (5)
the mediums and the **n** out of the 1 Sm 28:3
the mediums and the **n** from the land. 1 Sm 28:9
mediums and the **n** and the 2 Kgs 23:24
the mediums and the **n** who chirp and Is 8:19
the sorcerers, and the mediums and the **n**; Is 19:3

NECTAR (1)
Your lips drip **n**, my bride; honey and Sg 4:11

NEDABIAH (1)
Jekamiah, Hoshama and **N**; 1 Chr 3:18

NEED (73)
me." But he said, "What **n** is there? Gn 33:15
the priest **n** not seek for the yellow hair; Lv 13:36
to him and lend him sufficient for his **n**, Dt 15:8
You **n** not be afraid of him. Dt 18:22
the house wherever any **n** of repairs is 2 Kgs 12:5
the Levites no longer **n** to carry the 1 Chr 23:26
timber you **n** from Lebanon 2 Chr 2:16
You will not **n** to fight in this battle. 2 Chr 20:17
You **n** not carry it on your shoulders. 2 Chr 35:3
They did not **n** to depart from their 2 Chr 35:15
calamity; they **n** no one to help them. Jb 30:13
Behold, no fear of me **n** terrify you; my Jb 33:7
For God has no **n** to consider a man Jb 34:23
None who seek her **n** weary themselves; Jer 2:24
by the king according to his daily **n**, Jer 52:34
that they will not **n** to take wood out Ezk 39:10
we have no **n** to answer you in this Dn 3:16
you a blessing until there is no more **n**. Mal 3:10
him, saying, "I **n** to be baptized by you, Mt 3:14
Father knows what you **n** before you ask Mt 6:8
Father knows that you **n** them all. Mt 6:32
who are well have no **n** of a physician, Mt 9:12
But Jesus said, "They **n** not go away; Mt 14:16
he **n** not honor his father.' So for the Mt 15:6
What further witnesses do we **n**? Mt 26:65
who are well have no **n** of a physician, Mk 2:17
did, when he was in **n** and was hungry, Mk 2:25
'The Lord has **n** of it and will send it Mk 11:3
said, "What further witnesses do we **n**? Mk 14:63
who are well have no **n** of a physician, Lk 5:31
and cured those who had **n** of healing. Lk 9:11
your Father knows that you **n** them. Lk 12:30
righteous persons who **n** no repentance. Lk 15:7
that country, and he began to be in **n**. Lk 15:14
shall say this: 'The Lord has **n** of it.'" Lk 19:31
And they said, "The Lord has **n** of it." Lk 19:34
said, "What further testimony do we **n**? Lk 22:71
We **n** to give an answer to those who sent Jn 1:22
one who has bathed does not **n** to wash, Jn 13:10
"Buy what we **n** for the feast," or that he Jn 13:29
things and do not **n** anyone to question Jn 16:30
the proceeds to all, as any had **n**. Acts 2:45
it was distributed to each as any had **n**. Acts 4:35
her in whatever she may **n** from you, Rom 16:2
since then you would **n** to go out of 1 Cor 5:10
"I have no **n** of you," nor again the 1 Cor 12:21
head to the feet, "I have no **n** of you." 1 Cor 12:21
Or do we **n**, as some do, letters of 2 Cor 3:1
present time should supply their **n**, 2 Cor 8:14
their abundance may supply your **n**, 2 Cor 8:14
when I was with you and was in **n**, 2 Cor 11:9
from Macedonia supplied my **n**. 2 Cor 11:9
something to share with anyone in **n**. Eph 4:28
your messenger and minister to my **n**, Phil 2:25
Not that I am speaking of being in **n**, Phil 4:11
plenty and hunger, abundance and **n**. Phil 4:12
will supply every **n** of yours according Phil 4:19
so that we **n** not say anything. 1 Thes 1:8
love you have no **n** for anyone to 1 Thes 4:9
you have no **n** to have anything 1 Thes 5:1

worker who has no **n** to be ashamed, 2 Tm 2:15
works, so as to help cases of urgent **n**, Ti 3:14
and find grace to help in time of **n**. Heb 4:16
you **n** someone to teach you again the Heb 5:12
of the oracles of God. You **n** milk, Heb 5:12
what further **n** would there have been Heb 7:11
He has no **n**, like those high priests, to Heb 7:27
For you have **n** of endurance, so that Heb 10:36
and you have no **n** that anyone should 1 Jn 2:27
world's goods and sees his brother in **n**, 1 Jn 3:17
rich, I have prospered, and I **n** nothing, Rv 3:17
And the city has no **n** of sun or moon Rv 21:23
They will **n** no light of lamp or sun, for Rv 22:5

NEEDED (5)
And whatever is **n**—bulls, rams, or sheep Ezr 6:9
and **n** no one to bear witness about man, Jn 2:25
hands, as though he **n** anything, Acts 17:25
sail, they put on board whatever we **n**. Acts 28:10
giving them the things **n** for the body, Jas 2:16

NEEDFUL (1)
feed me with the food that is **n** for me, Prv 30:8

NEEDLE (3)
through the eye of a **n** than for a rich Mt 19:24
through the eye of a **n** than for a rich Mk 10:25
through the eye of a **n** than for a rich Lk 18:25

NEEDLEWORK (6)
fine twined linen, embroidered with **n**. Ex 26:36
fine twined linen, embroidered with **n**. Ex 27:16
shall make a sash embroidered with **n**. Ex 28:39
fine twined linen, embroidered with **n**, Ex 36:37
was embroidered with **n** in blue and Ex 38:18
and scarlet yarns, embroidered with **n**, Ex 39:29

NEEDS (9)
But what everyone **n** to eat, that alone Ex 12:16
they shall do all that **n** to be done with Nm 4:26
the king, according to his daily **n**, 2 Kgs 25:30
to you, you shall say, 'The Lord **n** them,' Mt 21:3
he will rise and give him whatever he **n**. Lk 11:8
be prevented from attending to his **n**. Acts 24:23
Contribute to the **n** of the saints and Rom 12:13
not only supplying the **n** of the saints, 2 Cor 9:12
sent me help for my **n** once and again. Phil 4:16

NEEDY (54)
to your brother, to the **n** and to the poor, Dt 15:11
a hired servant who is poor and **n**, Dt 24:14
he lifts the **n** from the ash heap to 1 Sm 2:8
But he saves the **n** from the sword of their Jb 5:15
is light, that he may kill the poor and **n**, Jb 24:14
I was a father to the **n**, and I searched Jb 29:16
Was not my soul grieved for the **n**? Jb 30:25
of clothing, or the **n** without covering, Jb 31:19
For the **n** shall not always be forgotten, Ps 9:18
poor are plundered, because the **n** groan, Ps 12:5
the poor and **n** from him who robs Ps 35:10
bows to bring down the poor and **n**, Ps 37:14
As for me, I am poor and **n**, but the Ps 40:17
goodness, O God, you provided for the **n**. Ps 68:10
the LORD hears the **n** and does not Ps 69:33
But I am poor and **n**; hasten to me, O Ps 70:5
give deliverance to the children of the **n**, Ps 72:4
For he delivers the **n** when he calls, the Ps 72:12
He has pity on the weak and the **n**, and Ps 72:13
the needy, and saves the lives of the **n**. Ps 72:13
let the poor and **n** praise your name. Ps 74:21
Rescue the weak and the **n**; deliver them Ps 82:4
and answer me, for I am poor and **n**. Ps 86:1
he raises up the **n** out of affliction and Ps 107:41
the poor and **n** and the brokenhearted, Ps 109:16
For I am poor and **n**, and my heart is Ps 109:22
he stands at the right hand of the **n**, Ps 109:31
dust and lifts the **n** from the ash heap, Ps 113:7
and will execute justice for the **n**. Ps 140:12
who is generous to the **n** honors him. Prv 14:31
earth, the **n** from among mankind. Prv 30:14
defend the rights of the poor and **n**. Prv 31:9
and reaches out her hands to the **n**. Prv 31:20
to turn aside the **n** from justice and to rob Is 10:2
will graze, and the **n** lie down in safety; Is 14:30
poor, a stronghold to the **n** in his distress, Is 25:4
it, the feet of the poor, the steps of the **n**." Is 26:6
even when the plea of the **n** is right. Is 32:7
When the poor and **n** seek water, and Is 41:17
they do not defend the rights of the **n**. Jer 5:28
the life of the **n** from the hand of Jer 20:13
He judged the cause of the poor and **n**; Jer 22:16
ease, but did not aid the poor and **n**. Ezk 16:49
oppresses the poor and **n**, commits Ezk 18:12
They have oppressed the poor and **n**, Ezk 22:29
silver, and the **n** for a pair of sandals— Am 2:6
who oppress the poor, who crush the **n**, Am 4:1
a bribe, and turn aside the **n** in the gate. Am 5:12
who trample on the **n** and bring the poor Am 8:4
poor for silver and the **n** for a pair of Am 8:6
"Thus, when you give to the **n**, sound no Mt 6:2
But when you give to the **n**, do not let Mt 6:3
Sell your possessions, and give to the **n**. Lk 12:33
was not a **n** person among them, Acts 4:34

NEGEB (40)
journeyed on, still going toward the **N**. Gn 12:9
he had, and Lot with him, into the **N**. Gn 13:1
journeyed on from the **N** as far as Bethel Gn 13:3
the territory of the **N** and lived between Gn 20:1
and was dwelling in the **N**. Gn 24:62
"Go up into the **N** and go up into the Nm 13:17
went up into the **N** and came to Nm 13:22
Amalekites dwell in the land of the **N**. Nm 13:29
the king of Arad, who lived in the **N**, Nm 21:1
who lived in the **N** in the land of Nm 33:40
lowland and in the **N** and by the seacoast, Dt 1:7
the **N**, and the Plain, that is, the Valley of Dt 34:3
hill country and the **N** and the lowland Jos 10:40
country and all the **N** and all the land Jos 11:16
slopes, in the wilderness, and in the **N**, Jos 12:8
you have given me the land of the **N**, Jos 15:19
as far as Baalath-beer, Ramah of the **N**. Jos 19:8
who lived in the hill country, in the **N**, Jgs 1:9
you have set me in the land of the **N**, Jgs 1:15
of Judah, which lies in the **N** near Arad, Jgs 1:16
say, "Against the **N** of Judah," or, 1 Sm 27:10
"Against the **N** of the Jerahmeelites," 1 Sm 27:10
or, "Against the **N** of the Kenites." 1 Sm 27:10
raid against the **N** and against Ziklag. 1 Sm 30:1
raid against the **N** of the Cherethites 1 Sm 30:14
to Judah and against the **N** of Caleb, 1 Sm 30:14
those in Bethel, in Ramoth of the **N**, 1 Sm 30:27
went out to the **N** of Judah at 2 Sm 24:7
the Shephelah and the **N** of Judah, 2 Chr 28:18
fortunes, O LORD, like streams in the **N**! Ps 126:4
As whirlwinds in the **N** sweep on, it Is 21:1
An oracle on the beasts of the **N**. Is 30:6
The cities of the **N** are shut up, with Jer 13:19
from the hill country, and from the **N**, Jer 17:26
Shephelah, and in the cities of the **N**; Jer 32:44
Shephelah, and in the cities of the **N**, Jer 33:13
against the forest land in the **N**. Ezk 20:46
Say to the forest of the **N**, Hear the Ezk 20:47
Those of the **N** shall possess Mount Ob 1:19
shall possess the cities of the **N**. Ob 1:20

NEGLECT (9)
care that you do not **n** the Levite as long Dt 12:19
And you shall not **n** the Levite who is Dt 14:27
We will not **n** the house of our God." Neh 10:39
instruction and be wise, and do not **n** it. Prv 8:33
herb, and **n** justice and the love of God. Lk 11:42
Do not **n** the gift you have, which was 1 Tm 4:14
we escape if we **n** such a great salvation? Heb 2:3
Do not **n** to show hospitality to Heb 13:2
Do not **n** to do good and to share what Heb 13:16

NEGLECTED (2)
and have **n** the weightier matters of the Mt 23:23
their widows were being **n** in the daily Acts 6:1

NEGLECTING (3)
to have done, without **n** the others. Mt 23:23
to have done, without **n** the others. Lk 11:42
not **n** to meet together, as is the habit Heb 10:25

NEGLIGENT (1)
My sons, do not now be **n**, for the 2 Chr 29:11

NEHELAM (3)
To Shemaiah of **N** you shall say: Jer 29:24
the LORD concerning Shemaiah of **N**: Jer 29:31
punish Shemaiah of **N** and his Jer 29:32

NEHEMIAH (8)
with Zerubbabel, Jeshua, **N**, Seraiah, Ezr 2:2
The words of **N** the son of Hacaliah. Neh 1:1
After him **N** the son of Azbuk, ruler of Neh 3:16
with Zerubbabel, Jeshua, **N**, Azariah, Neh 7:7
And **N**, who was the governor, and Ezra Neh 8:9
seals are the names of **N** the governor, Neh 10:1
in the days of **N** the governor and of Neh 12:26
in the days of **N** gave the daily Neh 12:47

NEHUM (1)
Bilshan, Mispereth, Bigvai, **N**, Baanah. Neh 7:7

NEHUSHTA (1)
mother's name was **N** the daughter of 2 Kgs 24:8

NEHUSHTAN (1)
made offerings to it (it was called **N**). 2 Kgs 18:4

NEIEL (1)
northward to Beth-emek and **N**. Jos 19:27

NEIGH (1)
in the pasture, and **n** like stallions, Jer 50:11

NEIGHBOR (105)
but each woman shall ask of her **n**, and Ex 3:22
every man of his **n** and every woman of Ex 11:2
his neighbor and every woman of her **n**, Ex 11:2
and his nearest **n** shall take according Ex 12:4
not bear false witness against your **n**. Ex 20:16
a man gives to his **n** money or goods to Ex 22:7
God condemns shall pay double to his **n**. Ex 22:9
a man gives to his **n** a donkey or an ox Ex 22:10
"If a man borrows anything of his **n**, Ex 22:14
and his companion and his **n**.'" Ex 32:27
the LORD by deceiving his **n** in a matter of Lv 6:2
robbery, or if he has oppressed his **n** Lv 6:2
shall not oppress your **n** or rob him. Lv 19:13
righteousness shall you judge your **n**. Lv 19:15
not stand up against the life of your **n**: Lv 19:16
you shall reason frankly with your **n**, Lv 19:17
but you shall love your **n** as yourself: Lv 19:18
adultery with the wife of his **n**, Lv 20:10
If anyone injures his **n**, as he has done Lv 24:19
make a sale to your **n** or buy from your Lv 25:14
to your neighbor or buy from your **n**, Lv 25:14
You shall pay your **n** according to the Lv 25:15
anyone who kills his **n** unintentionally, Dt 4:42
not bear false witness against your **n**. Dt 5:20
shall release what he has lent to his **n**. Dt 15:2
He shall not exact it of his **n**, his brother, Dt 15:2
kills his **n** unintentionally without Dt 19:4
into the forest with his **n** to cut wood, Dt 19:5
handle and strikes his **n** so that he dies Dt 19:5
since he had not hated his **n** in the past. Dt 19:6
if anyone hates his **n** and lies in wait Dt 19:11
a man attacking and murdering his **n**, Dt 22:26
"When you make your **n** a loan of any Dt 24:10
who strikes down his **n** in secret.' Dt 27:24
because he struck his **n** unknowingly, Jos 20:5
day and has given it to a **n** of yours, 1 Sm 15:28
of your hand and given it to your **n**, 1 Sm 28:17
your eyes and give them to your **n**, 2 Sm 12:11
man sins against his **n** and is made 1 Kgs 8:31
man sins against his **n** and is made 2 Chr 6:22
God, as a son of man does with his **n**. Jb 16:21
Everyone utters lies to his **n**; with Ps 12:2
with his tongue and does no evil to his **n**, Ps 15:3
Whoever slanders his **n** secretly I will Ps 101:5
Do not say to your **n**, "Go, and come Prv 3:28
Do not plan evil against your **n**, who Prv 3:29
if you have put up security for your **n**, Prv 6:1
you have come into the hand of your **n**: Prv 6:3
hasten, and plead urgently with your **n**. Prv 6:3
the godless man would destroy his **n**, Prv 11:9
Whoever belittles his **n** lacks sense, Prv 11:12
who is righteous is a guide to his **n**, Prv 12:26
The poor is disliked even by his **n**, but Prv 14:20
Whoever despises his **n** is a sinner, Prv 14:21
of violence entices his **n** and leads him Prv 16:29
up security in the presence of his **n**. Prv 17:18
evil; his **n** finds no mercy in his eyes. Prv 21:10
witness against your **n** without cause, Prv 24:28
end, when your **n** puts you to shame? Prv 25:8
Argue your case with your **n** himself, Prv 25:9
false witness against his **n** is like a war Prv 25:18
the man who deceives his **n** and says, Prv 26:19
Better is a **n** who is near than a Prv 27:10
Whoever blesses his **n** with a loud Prv 27:14
man who flatters his **n** spreads a net for Prv 29:5
work come from a man's envy of his **n**. Eccl 4:4
every one his fellow and every one his **n**; Is 3:5
against another and each against his **n**, Is 19:2
Everyone helps his **n** and says to his Is 41:6
sons together, **n** and friend shall perish.'" Jer 6:21
Let everyone beware of his **n**, and put no Jer 9:4
and every **n** goes about as a slanderer. Jer 9:4
Everyone deceives his **n**, and no one Jer 9:5
his mouth each speaks peace to his **n**, Jer 9:8
a lament, and each to her **n** a dirge. Jer 9:20
eat the flesh of his **n** in the siege and in Jer 19:9
this city, and every man will say to his **n**, Jer 22:8
who makes his **n** serve him for nothing Jer 22:13
every one to his **n** and every one to his Jer 23:35
each one teach his **n** and each his Jer 31:34
by proclaiming liberty, each to his **n**, Jer 34:15
every one to his brother and to his **n**; Jer 34:17
Put no trust in a **n**; have no confidence in Mi 7:5
you will invite his **n** to come under his Zec 3:10
in, for I set every man against his **n**. Zec 8:10
of them to fall into the hand of his **n**, Zec 11:6
'You shall love your **n** and hate your Mt 5:43
and, You shall love your **n** as yourself." Mt 19:19
it: You shall love your **n** as yourself. Mt 22:39
'You shall love your **n** as yourself.' Mk 12:31
strength, and to love one's **n** as oneself, Mk 12:33
all your mind, and your **n** as yourself." Lk 10:27
said to Jesus, "And who is my **n**?" Lk 10:29
proved to be a **n** to the man who fell Lk 10:36

NER (16)
of his army was Abner the son of **N**, 1 Sm 14:50
and **N** the father of Abner was the 1 Sm 14:51
Saul lay, with Abner the son of **N**, 1 Sm 26:5
the army, and to Abner the son of **N**, 1 Sm 26:14
But Abner the son of **N**, commander of 2 Sm 2:8
Abner the son of **N**, and the servants 2 Sm 2:12
"Abner the son of **N** came to the king, 2 Sm 3:23
Abner the son of **N** came to deceive 2 Sm 3:25
for the blood of Abner the son of **N**. 2 Sm 3:28
to put to death Abner the son of **N**. 2 Sm 3:37
armies of Israel, Abner the son of **N**, 1 Kgs 2:5
than himself, Abner the son of **N**, 1 Kgs 2:32
N was the father of Kish, Kish of 1 Chr 8:33
then Zur, Kish, Baal, **N**, Nadab, 1 Chr 9:36
N fathered Kish, Kish fathered Saul, 1 Chr 9:39
Abner the son of **N** and Joab the son 1 Chr 26:28

NEREUS (1)
Philologus, Julia, **N** and his sister, Rom 16:15

NERGAL (1)
the men of Cuth made **N**, 2 Kgs 17:30

NERGAL-SAR-EZER (3)
N, Samgar-nebu, Sar-sekim the Jer 39:3
the Rab-saris, **N** the Rab-mag, Jer 39:3
the Rab-saris, **N** the Rab-mag, Jer 39:13

NERI (1)
the son of Shealtiel, the son of **N**, Lk 3:27

NERIAH (10)
Baruch the son of **N** son of Mahseiah, Jer 32:12
of purchase to Baruch the son of **N**, Jer 32:16
Jeremiah called Baruch the son of **N**, Jer 36:4
Baruch the son of **N** did all that Jer 36:8
Baruch the son of **N** took the scroll in Jer 36:14
it to Baruch the scribe, the son of **N**, Jer 36:32
Baruch the son of **N** has set you against Jer 43:3
the prophet and Baruch the son of **N**. Jer 43:6
prophet spoke to Baruch the son of **N**, Jer 45:1
commanded Seraiah the son of **N**, Jer 51:59

NEST (13)
place, and your **n** is set in the rock. Nm 24:21
you come across a bird's **n** in any tree or Dt 22:6
Like an eagle that stirs up its **n**, that Dt 32:11
Then I thought, 'I shall die in my **n**, and Jb 29:18
mounts up and makes his **n** on high? Jb 39:27
a home, and the swallow a **n** for herself, Ps 84:3
bird that strays from its **n** is a man who Prv 27:8
has found like a **n** the wealth of the Is 10:14
Like fleeing birds, like a scattered **n**, so Is 16:2
Though you make your **n** as high as Jer 49:16
its branches birds of every sort will **n**. Ezk 17:23
though your **n** is set among the stars, Ob 1:4
gain for his house, to set his **n** on high, Hab 2:9

NESTED (1)
of Lebanon, **n** among the cedars, Jer 22:23

NESTS (9)
In them the birds build their **n**; the Ps 104:17
There the owl **n** and lays and hatches Is 34:15
Be like the dove that **n** in the sides of the Jer 48:28
the heavens made their **n** in its boughs; Ezk 31:6
have holes, and birds of the air have **n**, Mt 8:20
air come and make **n** in its branches." Mt 13:32
of the air can make **n** in its shade." Mk 4:32
have holes, and birds of the air have **n**, Lk 9:58
of the air made **n** in its branches." Lk 13:19

NET (35)
and on the **n** you shall make four Ex 27:4
altar so that the **n** extends halfway down Ex 27:5
For he is cast into a **n** by his own feet, Jb 18:8
in the wrong and closed his **n** about me. Jb 19:6
in the **n** that they hid their own foot has Ps 9:15
the poor when he draws him into his **n**. Ps 10:9
for he will pluck my feet out of the **n**. Ps 25:15
take me out of the **n** they have hidden for Ps 31:4
without cause they hid their **n** for me; Ps 35:7
And let the **n** that he hid ensnare him; let Ps 35:8
They set a **n** for my steps; my soul was Ps 57:6
You brought us into the **n**; you laid a Ps 66:11
and with cords they have spread a **n**; Ps 140:5
For in vain is a **n** spread in the sight of Prv 1:17
his neighbor spreads a **n** for his feet. Prv 29:5
Like fish that are taken in an evil **n**, Eccl 9:12
of every street like an antelope in a **n**; Is 51:20
it descend; he spread a **n** for my feet; Lam 1:13
And I will spread my **n** over him, and Ezk 12:13
I will spread my **n** over him, and he Ezk 17:20
every side; they spread their **n** over him; Ezk 19:8
I will throw my **n** over you with a host Ezk 32:3
at Mizpah and a **n** spread upon Tabor. Hos 5:1
they go, I will spread over them my **n**; Hos 7:12
blood, and each hunts the other with a **n**. Mi 7:2
a hook; he drags them out with his **n**; Hab 1:15
sacrifices to his **n** and makes offerings Hab 1:16
on emptying his **n** and mercilessly Hab 1:17
his brother, casting a **n** into the sea, Mt 4:18
heaven is like a **n** that was thrown into Mt 13:47
of Simon casting a **n** into the sea, Mk 1:16
"Cast the **n** on the right side of the boat, Jn 21:6
in the boat, dragging the **n** full of fish, Jn 21:8
went aboard and hauled the **n** ashore, Jn 21:11
there were so many, the **n** was not torn. Jn 21:11

NETAIM (1)
were inhabitants of **N** and Gederah. 1 Chr 4:23

NETHANEL (14)
from Issachar, **N** the son of Zuar; Nm 1:8
people of Issachar being **N** the son of Nm 2:5
On the second day **N** the son of Zuar, Nm 7:18
was the offering of **N** the son of Zuar. Nm 7:23
people of Issachar was **N** the son of Nm 10:15
N the fourth, Raddai the fifth, 1 Chr 2:14
Shebaniah, Joshaphat, **N**, Amasai, 1 Chr 15:24
the scribe Shemaiah, the son of **N**, 1 Chr 24:6
third, Sachar the fourth, **N** the fifth, 1 Chr 26:4
Zechariah, **N**, and Micaiah, 2 Chr 17:7
and Shemaiah and **N** his brothers, 2 Chr 35:9
Maaseiah, Ishmael, **N**, Jozabad, Ezr 10:22
of Hilkiah, Hashabiah; of Jedaiah, **N**. Neh 12:21
Milalai, Gilalai, Maai, **N**, Judah, Neh 12:36

NETHANIAH (20)
namely, Ishmael the son of **N**, 2 Kgs 25:23
month, Ishmael the son of **N**, 2 Kgs 25:25
Zaccur, Joseph, **N**, and Asharelah, 1 Chr 25:2
the fifth to **N**, his sons and his 1 Chr 25:12
the Levites, Shemaiah, **N**, Zebadiah, 2 Chr 17:8
all the officials sent Jehudi the son of **N**, Jer 36:14
at Mizpah—Ishmael the son of **N**, Jer 40:8
Ishmael the son of **N** to take your life?" Jer 40:14
and strike down Ishmael the son of **N**, Jer 40:15
seventh month, Ishmael the son of **N**, Jer 41:1
Ishmael the son of **N** and the ten men Jer 41:2
Ishmael the son of **N** came out from Jer 41:6
Ishmael the son of **N** and the men with Jer 41:7
Ishmael the son of **N** filled it with the Jer 41:9
Ishmael the son of **N** took them captive Jer 41:10
evil that Ishmael the son of **N** had done, Jer 41:11
to fight against Ishmael the son of **N**. Jer 41:12
the son of **N** escaped from Johanan Jer 41:15
recovered from Ishmael the son of **N**, Jer 41:16
Ishmael the son of **N** had struck down Jer 41:18

NETOPHAH (7)
Zalmon the Ahohite, Maharai of **N**, 2 Sm 23:28
Heleb the son of Baanah of **N**, Ittai 2 Sm 23:29
Maharai of **N**, Heled the son of 1 Chr 11:30
Heled the son of Baanah of **N**, 1 Chr 11:30
the tenth month, was Maharai of **N**, 1 Chr 27:13
The men of **N**, 56. Ezr 2:22
The men of Bethlehem and **N**, 188. Neh 7:26

NETOPHATHITE (3)
the son of Tanhumeth the **N**, 2 Kgs 25:23
twelfth month, was Heldai the **N**, 1 Chr 27:15
of Tanhumeth, the sons of Ephai the **N**, Jer 40:8

NETOPHATHITES (3)
Bethlehem, the **N**, Atroth-beth-joab 1 Chr 2:54
who lived in the villages of the **N**. 1 Chr 9:16
and from the villages of the **N**; Neh 12:28

NETS (14)
Let the wicked fall into their own **n**, Ps 141:10
woman whose heart is snares and **n**, Eccl 7:26
will languish who spread **n** on the water. Is 19:8
of the sea a place for the spreading of **n**, Ezk 26:5
shall be a place for the spreading of **n**. Ezk 26:14
it will be a place for the spreading of **n**. Ezk 47:10
they left their **n** and followed him. Mt 4:20
Zebedee their father, mending their **n**, Mt 4:21
they left their **n** and followed him. Mk 1:18
who were in their boat mending the **n**. Mk 1:19
out of them and were washing their **n**. Lk 5:2
the deep and let down your **n** for a catch." Lk 5:4
But at your word I will let down the **n**." Lk 5:5
of fish, and their **n** were breaking. Lk 5:6

NETTLES (5)
bray; under the **n** they huddle together. Jb 30:7
the ground was covered with **n**, and its Prv 24:31
n and thistles in its fortresses. Is 34:13
N shall possess their precious things of Hos 9:6
a land possessed by **n** and salt pits, Zep 2:9

NETWORK (4)
also make for it a grating, a **n** of bronze, Ex 27:4
for the altar a grating, a **n** of bronze, Ex 38:4
A **n** and pomegranates, all of bronze, Jer 52:22
were a hundred upon the **n** all around. Jer 52:23

NEVER (205)
"I will **n** again curse the ground Gn 8:21
that **n** again shall all flesh be cut off by Gn 9:11
and **n** again shall there be a flood to Gn 9:11
And the waters shall **n** again become a Gn 9:15
such as I had **n** seen in all the land of Gn 41:19
men. Your servants have **n** been spies." Gn 42:11
are honest men; we have **n** been spies. Gn 42:31
to pieces, and I have **n** seen him since. Gn 44:28
to Joseph, "I **n** expected to see your face; Gn 48:11
such as **n** has been in Egypt from the Ex 9:18
such as had **n** been in all the land of Ex 9:24
swarm of locusts as had **n** been before, Ex 10:14
take care **n** to see my face again, for on Ex 10:28
land of Egypt, such as there has **n** been, Ex 11:6
you see today, you shall **n** see again. Ex 14:13
So keep my charge **n** to practice any of Lv 18:30
and **n** to make yourselves unclean by Lv 18:30
that there may **n** again be wrath on the Nm 18:5
and on which a yoke has **n** come. Nm 19:2
hear and fear and **n** again do any such Dt 13:11
For there will **n** cease to be poor in the Dt 15:11
'You shall **n** return that way again.' Dt 17:16
and shall **n** again commit any such Dt 19:20
a heifer that has **n** been worked and that Dt 21:3
that you should **n** make again; Dt 28:68
no gods, to gods they had **n** known, Dt 32:17
whom your fathers had **n** dreaded. Dt 32:17
some of you shall **n** be anything but Jos 9:23
'I will **n** break my covenant with you, Jgs 2:1
She had **n** known a man, and it Jgs 11:39
"A razor has **n** come upon my head, Jgs 16:17
"Such a thing has **n** happened or been Jgs 19:30
on which there has **n** come a yoke, 1 Sm 6:7
the house of Joab **n** be without one 2 Sm 3:29
the sword shall **n** depart from your 2 Sm 12:10
me, and he shall **n** touch you again." 2 Sm 14:10
His father had **n** at any time displeased 1 Kgs 1:6
N again came such an abundance 1 Kgs 10:10
like of it was **n** made in any 1 Kgs 10:20
for he **n** prophesies good concerning 1 Kgs 22:8
is established; it shall **n** be moved. 1 Chr 16:30
There **n** was seen the like of them 2 Chr 9:11
for he **n** prophesies good concerning 2 Chr 18:7
and **n** seek their peace or prosperity, Ezr 9:12
that Vashti is **n** again to come before Est 1:19
days of Purim should **n** fall into disuse Est 9:28
child, as infants who **n** see the light? Jb 3:16
is a breath; my eye will **n** again see good. Jb 7:7
will deny him, saying, 'I have **n** seen you.' Jb 8:18
of soul, **n** having tasted of prosperity. Jb 21:25
do those who know him **n** see his days? Jb 24:1
inward parts are in turmoil and **n** still; Jb 30:27
he has hidden his face, he will **n** see it." Ps 10:11
who does these things shall **n** be moved. Ps 15:5
in my prosperity, "I shall **n** be moved." Ps 30:6
do I take refuge; let me **n** be put to shame; Ps 31:1
and their faces shall **n** be ashamed. Ps 34:5
of their life is costly and can **n** suffice, Ps 49:8
should live on forever and **n** see the pit. Ps 49:9
his fathers, who will **n** again see light. Ps 49:19
he will **n** permit the righteous to be Ps 55:22
the stillborn child who **n** sees the sun. Ps 58:8
I take refuge; let me **n** be put to shame! Ps 71:1
spurn forever, and **n** again be favorable? Ps 77:7
What man can live and **n** see death? Ps 89:48
world is established; it shall **n** be moved. Ps 93:1
is established; it shall **n** be moved; Ps 96:10
so that it should **n** be moved. Ps 104:5
For the righteous will **n** be moved; he Ps 112:6
I will **n** forget your precepts, for by Ps 119:93
The righteous will **n** be removed, but Prv 10:30
root of the righteous will **n** be moved. Prv 12:3
Sheol and Abaddon are **n** satisfied, Prv 27:20
and **n** satisfied are the eyes of man. Prv 27:20
Three things are **n** satisfied; four never Prv 30:15
things are never satisfied; four **n** say, Prv 30:15
womb, the land **n** satisfied with water, Prv 30:16
with water, and the fire that **n** says, Prv 30:16
and his eyes are **n** satisfied with riches, Eccl 4:8
satisfied with riches, so that he **n** asks, Eccl 4:8
on earth who does good and **n** sins. Eccl 7:20
a rounded bowl that **n** lacks mixed wine. Sg 7:2
It will **n** be inhabited or lived in for all Is 13:20
is a city no more; it will **n** be rebuilt. Is 25:2
tent, whose stakes will **n** be plucked up, Is 33:20
before today you have **n** heard of them, Is 48:7
You have **n** heard, you have never Is 48:8
have never heard, you have **n** known, Is 48:8
their name would **n** be cut off or Is 48:19
my righteousness will **n** be dismayed. Is 51:6
a mighty appetite; they **n** have enough. Is 56:11
and all the night they shall **n** be silent. Is 62:6
like those over whom you have **n** ruled, Is 63:19
vessel, so that it can **n** be mended. Jer 19:11
eternal dishonor will **n** be forgotten. Jer 20:11
die, and he shall **n** see this land again." Jer 22:12

David shall **n** lack a man to sit on the Jer 33:17
the Levitical priests shall **n** lack a man Jer 33:18
son of Rechab shall **n** lack a man to Jer 35:19
covenant that will **n** be forgotten.' Jer 50:5
She shall **n** again have people, nor be Jer 50:39
The steadfast love of the LORD **n** ceases; Lam 3:22
ceases; his mercies **n** come to an end; Lam 3:22
GOD! Behold, I have **n** defiled myself. Ezk 4:14
up till now I have **n** eaten what died of Ezk 4:14
I will do with you what I have **n** yet done, Ezk 5:9
and the like of which I will **n** do again. Ezk 5:9
The like has **n** been, nor ever shall be. Ezk 16:16
and **n** open your mouth again Ezk 16:63
in your mind shall **n** happen—the Ezk 20:32
of nets. You shall **n** be rebuilt, Ezk 26:14
sought for, you will **n** be found again, Ezk 26:21
and **n** again exalt itself above the Ezk 29:15
small that they will **n** again rule over Ezk 29:15
And it shall **n** again be the reliance of Ezk 29:16
that you may **n** again suffer the Ezk 36:30
up a kingdom that shall **n** be destroyed, Dn 2:44
his kingdom shall **n** be destroyed, and Dn 6:26
such as **n** has been since there was a Dn 12:1
their like has **n** been before, nor will be Jl 2:2
And my people shall **n** again be put to Jl 2:26
And my people shall **n** again be put to Jl 2:27
and strangers shall **n** again pass through Jl 3:17
people Israel; I will **n** again pass by them; Am 7:8
but **n** again prophesy at Bethel, for it is Am 7:13
people Israel; I will **n** again pass by them. Am 8:2
"Surely I will **n** forget any of their deeds. Am 8:7
lives,' they shall fall, and **n** rise again." Am 8:14
and they shall **n** again be uprooted out Am 9:15
and shall be as though they had **n** been. Ob 1:16
for **n** again shall the worthless pass Na 1:15
is paralyzed, and justice **n** goes forth. Hab 1:4
an arrogant man who is **n** at rest. Hab 2:5
as Sheol; like death he has **n** enough. Hab 2:5
your midst; you shall **n** again fear evil. Zep 3:15
You eat, but you **n** have enough; you Hg 1:6
you drink, but you **n** have your fill. Hg 1:6
for there shall **n** again be a decree of Zec 14:11
you will **n** enter the kingdom of heaven. Mt 5:20
you will **n** get out until you have paid Mt 5:26
will I declare to them, 'I **n** knew you; Mt 7:23
"**N** was anything like this seen in Mt 9:33
will indeed hear but **n** understand, Mt 13:14
and you will indeed see but **n** perceive. Mt 13:14
you, Lord! This shall **n** happen to you." Mt 16:22
you will **n** enter the kingdom of heaven. Mt 18:3
over the ninety-nine that **n** went astray. Mt 18:13
have you **n** read, "'Out of the mouth of Mt 21:16
"Have you **n** read in the Scriptures: Mt 21:42
the world until now, no, and **n** will be. Mt 24:21
because of you, I will **n** fall away." Mt 26:33
saying, "We **n** saw anything like this!" Mk 2:12
them, "Have you **n** read what David did, Mk 2:25
the Holy Spirit **n** has forgiveness, Mk 3:29
out of him and **n** enter him again." Mk 9:25
God created until now, and **n** will be. Mk 13:19
you will **n** get out until you have paid Lk 12:59
you, and I **n** disobeyed your command, Lk 15:29
yet you **n** gave me a young goat, Lk 15:29
and the wombs that **n** bore and the Lk 23:29
bore and the breasts that **n** nursed!' Lk 23:29
I will give him will **n** be thirsty forever. Jn 4:14
His voice you have **n** heard, his form you Jn 5:37
never heard, his form you have **n** seen, Jn 5:37
whoever believes in me shall **n** thirst. Jn 6:35
whoever comes to me I will **n** cast out. Jn 6:37
has learning, when he has **n** studied?" Jn 7:15
of Abraham and have **n** been enslaved to Jn 8:33
keeps my word, he will **n** see death." Jn 8:51
keeps my word, he will **n** taste death.' Jn 8:52
N since the world began has it been Jn 9:32
them eternal life, and they will **n** perish, Jn 10:28
who lives and believes in me shall **n** die. Jn 11:26
"You shall **n** wash my feet." Jesus Jn 13:8
my hand into his side, I will **n** believe." Jn 20:25
"This man **n** ceases to speak words Acts 6:13
for I have **n** eaten anything that is Acts 10:14
crippled from birth and had **n** walked. Acts 14:8
will indeed hear but **n** understand, Acts 28:26
you will indeed see but **n** perceive. Acts 28:26
raised from the dead will **n** die again; Rom 6:9
in him of whom they have **n** heard? Rom 10:14
with the lowly. **N** be conceited. Rom 12:16
Beloved, **n** avenge yourselves, but Rom 12:19
but rather decide **n** to put a Rom 14:13
"Those who have **n** been told of him Rom 15:21
those who have **n** heard will Rom 15:21
them members of a prostitute? **N**! 1 Cor 6:15
brother stumble, I will **n** eat meat, 1 Cor 8:13
Love **n** ends. As for prophecies, they 1 Cor 13:8
For we **n** came with words of flattery, 1 Thes 2:5
always learning and **n** able to arrive at 2 Tm 3:7
hope of eternal life, which God, who **n** lies, Ti 1:2
the true form of these realities, it can **n**, Heb 10:1
which can **n** take away sins. Heb 10:11
"I will **n** leave you nor forsake you." Heb 13:5
practice these qualities you will **n** fall. 2 Pt 1:10
been better for them **n** to have known 2 Pt 2:21
and I will **n** blot his name out of the book Rv 3:5
N shall he go out of it, and I will write on Rv 3:12
and day and night they **n** cease to say, Rv 4:8
such as there had **n** been since man Rv 16:18
no widow, and mourning I shall **n** see.' Rv 18:7
are lost to you, **n** to be found again!" Rv 18:14
and its gates will **n** be shut by day— Rv 21:25

NEVER-ENDING (1)

malice of soul to destroy in **n** enmity, Ezk 25:15

NEVERMORE (1)

the offspring of evildoers **n** be named! Is 14:20

NEVERTHELESS (53)

N, his younger brother shall be greater Gn 48:19
N, in the day when I visit, I will visit Ex 32:34
N, among those that chew the cud or Lv 11:4
N, a spring or a cistern holding water Lv 11:36
N, the firstborn of man you shall Nm 18:15
N, Kain shall be burned when Nm 24:22
N, those who died by the plague were Nm 25:9
N, it shall also be purified with the Nm 31:23
N, the inhabitants of Beth-shemesh and Jgs 1:33
N, the road on which you are going will Jgs 4:9
N, the lords do not approve of you. 1 Sm 29:6
N, the commanders of the Philistines 1 Sm 29:9
N, David took the stronghold of Zion, 2 Sm 5:7
N, because by this deed you have 2 Sm 12:14
N, you shall not build the house, but 1 Kgs 8:19
N, I will not take the whole 1 Kgs 11:34
N, for David's sake the LORD his God 1 Kgs 15:4
N, the heart of Asa was wholly true 1 Kgs 15:14
N I will send my servants to you 1 Kgs 20:6
N, he clung to the sin of Jeroboam the 2 Kgs 3:3
N, the high places were not taken 2 Kgs 12:3
N, they did not depart from the sins of 2 Kgs 13:6
N, the high places were not taken 2 Kgs 15:4
N, the high places were not 2 Kgs 15:35
N, David took the stronghold of Zion, 1 Chr 11:5
N, it is not you who shall build the 2 Chr 6:9
N, they shall be servants to him, that 2 Chr 12:8
N, the heart of Asa was wholly true 2 Chr 15:17
N, some good is found in you, for you 2 Chr 19:3
N, the people still sacrificed at the 2 Chr 33:17
N, Josiah did not turn away from 2 Chr 35:22
"**N**, they were disobedient and rebelled Neh 9:26
N, in your great mercies you did not Neh 9:31
N, foreign women made even him to Neh 13:26
N, Haman restrained himself and went Est 5:10
N, I am continually with you; you hold Ps 73:23
n, like men you shall die, and fall like Ps 82:7
N, he looked upon their distress, when Ps 106:44
N, my eye spared them, and I did not Ezk 20:17
N, I will read the writing to the king and Dn 5:17
N, the men rowed hard to get back to Jon 1:13
n, not as I will, but as you will." Mt 26:39
N know this, that the kingdom of God Lk 10:11
N, do not rejoice in this, that the spirits Lk 10:20
N, I must go on my way today and Lk 13:33
N, when the Son of Man comes, will he Lk 18:8
N, not my will, but yours, be done." Lk 22:42
N, many even of the authorities Jn 12:42
N, I tell you the truth: it is to your Jn 16:7
N, we have not made use of this right, 1 Cor 9:12
N, with most of them God was not 1 Cor 10:5
N, in the Lord woman is not 1 Cor 11:11
N, in church I would rather speak 1 Cor 14:19

NEW (143)

Now there arose a **n** king over Egypt, who Ex 1:8
On the third **n** moon after the people of Ex 19:1
ears, roasted with fire, crushed **n** grain. Lv 2:14
a grain offering of **n** grain to the LORD. Lv 23:16
clear out the old to make way for the **n**. Lv 26:10
But if the LORD creates something **n**, Nm 16:30
a grain offering of **n** grain to the LORD Nm 28:26
the burnt offering of the **n** moon, Nm 29:6
who has built a **n** house and has not Dt 20:5
"When you build a **n** house, you shall Dt 22:8
to **n** gods that had come recently, Dt 32:17
These wineskins were **n** when we filled Jos 9:13
When **n** gods were chosen, then war was Jgs 5:8
him with two **n** ropes and brought Jgs 15:13
they bind me with **n** ropes that have Jgs 16:11
So Delilah took **n** ropes and bound Jgs 16:12
take and prepare a **n** cart and two milk 1 Sm 6:7
"Behold, tomorrow is the **n** moon, 1 Sm 20:5
to him, "Tomorrow is the **n** moon, 1 Sm 20:18
And when the **n** moon came, the 1 Sm 20:24
second day, the day after the **n** moon, 1 Sm 20:27
ark of God on a **n** cart and brought it 2 Sm 6:3
of Abinadab, were driving the **n** cart, 2 Sm 6:3
and who was armed with a **n** sword, 2 Sm 21:16
had dressed himself in a **n** garment, 1 Kgs 11:29
laid hold of the **n** garment that was 1 Kgs 11:30
He said, "Bring me a **n** bowl, and put 2 Kgs 2:20
It is neither **n** moon nor Sabbath." 2 Kgs 4:23
carried the ark of God on a **n** cart, 1 Chr 13:7
Sabbaths, **n** moons and feast days, 1 Chr 23:31
the Sabbaths and the **n** moons and the 2 Chr 2:4
Moses for the Sabbaths, the **n** moons, 2 Chr 8:13
house of the LORD, before the **n** court, 2 Chr 20:5
for the Sabbaths, the **n** moons, 2 Chr 31:3
the offerings at the **n** moon and at all the Ezr 3:5
offering, the Sabbaths, the **n** moons, Neh 10:33
me, and my bow ever **n** in my hand.' Jb 29:20
no vent; like **n** wineskins ready to burst. Jb 32:19
Sing to him a **n** song; play skillfully on Ps 33:3
He put a **n** song in my mouth, a song of Ps 40:3
Blow the trumpet at the **n** moon, at the Ps 81:3
Oh sing to the LORD a **n** song; sing to the Ps 96:1
Oh sing to the LORD a **n** song, for he has Ps 98:1
I will sing a **n** song to you, O God; upon Ps 144:9
Sing to the LORD a **n** song, his praise in Ps 149:1
Wealth brings many **n** friends, but a Prv 19:4
is gone and the **n** growth appears and Prv 27:25
and there is nothing **n** under the sun. Eccl 1:9
of which it is said, "See, this is **n**"? Eccl 1:10
are all choice fruits, **n** as well as old, Sg 7:13
N moon and Sabbath and the calling of Is 1:13
Your **n** moons and your appointed feasts Is 1:14
of you a threshing sledge, **n**, sharp, Is 41:15
come to pass, and **n** things I now declare; Is 42:9
Sing to the LORD a **n** song, his praise Is 42:10
Behold, I am doing a **n** thing; now it Is 43:19
who at the **n** moons make known what Is 47:13
time forth I announce to you **n** things, Is 48:6
you found **n** life for your strength, and Is 57:10
be called by a **n** name that the mouth Is 62:2
"As the **n** wine is found in the cluster, and Is 65:8
I create **n** heavens and a new earth, Is 65:17
I create new heavens and a **n** earth, Is 65:17
"For as the **n** heavens and the new earth Is 66:22
new heavens and the **n** earth that I make Is 66:22
From **n** moon to new moon, and from Is 66:23
From new moon to **n** moon, and from Is 66:23
in the entry of the **N** Gate of the house Jer 26:10
LORD has created a **n** thing on the earth: Jer 31:22
I will make a **n** covenant with the Jer 31:31
at the entry of the **N** Gate of the LORD'S Jer 36:10
they are **n** every morning; great is Lam 3:23
and a **n** spirit I will put within them. Ezk 11:19
and make yourselves a **n** heart and a Ezk 18:31
yourselves a new heart and a **n** spirit! Ezk 18:31
And I will give you a **n** heart, and a Ezk 36:26
and a **n** spirit I will put within you. Ezk 36:26
offerings, at the feasts, the **n** moons, Ezk 45:17
on the day of the **n** moon it shall be Ezk 46:1
on the Sabbaths and on the **n** moons. Ezk 46:3
On the day of the **n** moon he shall offer Ezk 46:6
all her mirth, her feasts, her **n** moons, Hos 2:11
whoredom, wine, and **n** wine, which Hos 4:11
Now the **n** moon shall devour them with Hos 5:7
them, and the **n** wine shall fail them. Hos 9:2
saying, "When will the **n** moon be over, Am 8:5
and the hills, on the grain, the **n** wine, Hg 1:11
flourish, and **n** wine the young women. Zec 9:17
Neither is **n** wine put into old wineskins. Mt 9:17
But **n** wine is put into fresh wineskins, Mt 9:17
his treasure what is **n** and what is old." Mt 13:52
"Truly, I say to you, in the **n** world, Mt 19:28
day when I drink it **n** with you in my Mt 26:29
and laid it in his own **n** tomb, which Mt 27:60
is this? A **n** teaching with authority! Mk 1:27
tears away from it, the **n** from the old, Mk 2:21
And no one puts **n** wine into old Mk 2:22
But **n** wine is for fresh wineskins." Mk 2:22
when I drink it **n** in the kingdom of Mk 14:25
demons; they will speak in **n** tongues; Mk 16:17
a piece from a **n** garment and puts it Lk 5:36
If he does, he will tear the **n**, and the Lk 5:36
the piece from the **n** will not match the Lk 5:36
And no one puts **n** wine into old Lk 5:37
the **n** wine will burst the skins and it Lk 5:37
But **n** wine must be put into fresh Lk 5:38
no one after drinking old wine desires **n**, Lk 5:39
for you is the **n** covenant in my blood. Lk 22:20
A **n** commandment I give to you, that Jn 13:34
and in the garden a **n** tomb in which no Jn 19:41
said, "They are filled with **n** wine." Acts 2:13
we know what this **n** teaching is that Acts 17:19
telling or hearing something **n**. Acts 17:21
code but in the **n** life of the Spirit. Rom 7:6
old leaven that you may be a **n** lump, 1 Cor 5:7

"This cup is the **n** covenant in my 1 Cor 11:25
to be ministers of a **n** covenant, 2 Cor 3:6
is in Christ, he is a **n** creation. 2 Cor 5:17
passed away; behold, the **n** has come. 2 Cor 5:17
nor uncircumcision, but a **n** creation. Gal 6:15
create in himself one **n** man in place of Eph 2:15
and to put on the **n** self, created after Eph 4:24
to a festival or a **n** moon or a Sabbath. Col 2:16
and have put on the **n** self, which is Col 3:10
I will establish a **n** covenant with the Heb 8:8
In speaking of a **n** covenant, he makes Heb 8:13
he is the mediator of a **n** covenant, Heb 9:15
by the **n** and living way that he Heb 10:20
to Jesus, the mediator of a **n** covenant, Heb 12:24
we are waiting for **n** heavens and a new 2 Pt 3:13
new heavens and a **n** earth in which 2 Pt 3:13
I am writing you no **n** commandment, 1 Jn 2:7
it is a **n** commandment that I am 1 Jn 2:8
I were writing you a **n** commandment, 2 Jn 1:5
with a **n** name written on the stone that Rv 2:17
of the city of my God, the **n** Jerusalem, Rv 3:12
God out of heaven, and my own **n** name. Rv 3:12
And they sang a **n** song, saying, "Worthy Rv 5:9
they were singing a **n** song before the Rv 14:3
Then I saw a **n** heaven and a new earth, Rv 21:1
Then I saw a new heaven and a **n** earth, Rv 21:1
And I saw the holy city, **n** Jerusalem, Rv 21:2
I am making all things **n**." Also he said, Rv 21:5

NEWBORN (2)
field forsakes her **n** fawn because there Jer 14:5
Like **n** infants, long for the pure 1 Pt 2:2

NEWLY (1)
"When a man is **n** married, he shall not Dt 24:5

NEWNESS (1)
Father, we too might walk in **n** of life. Rom 6:4

NEWS (70)
as Laban heard the **n** about Jacob, Gn 29:13
man came into the city and told the **n**, 1 Sm 4:13
who brought the **n** answered and said, 1 Sm 4:17
when she heard the **n** that the ark of 1 Sm 4:19
So they told him the **n** of the men of 1 Sm 11:5
nor woman alive to bring **n** to Gath, 1 Sm 27:11
to carry the good **n** to the house of 1 Sm 31:9
years old when the **n** about Saul and 2 Sm 4:4
and thought he was bringing good **n**, 2 Sm 4:10
was the reward I gave him for his **n**. 2 Sm 4:10
David all the **n** about the fighting. 2 Sm 11:18
telling all the **n** about the fighting 2 Sm 11:19
were on the way, **n** came to David, 2 Sm 13:30
me run and carry **n** to the king that 2 Sm 18:19
him, "You are not to carry **n** today. 2 Sm 18:20
You may carry **n** another day, but 2 Sm 18:20
day, but today you shall carry no **n**, 2 Sm 18:20
you will have no reward for the **n**?" 2 Sm 18:22
there is **n** in his mouth." And he 2 Sm 18:25
The king said, "He also brings **n**." 2 Sm 18:26
a good man and comes with good **n**." 2 Sm 18:27
said, "Good **n** for my lord the king! 2 Sm 18:31
are a worthy man and bring good **n**." 1 Kgs 1:42
When the **n** came to Joab—for Joab 1 Kgs 2:28
charged with unbearable **n** for you. 1 Kgs 14:6
right. This day is a day of good **n**. 2 Kgs 7:9
the city to go and tell the **n** in Jezreel." 2 Kgs 9:15
to carry the good **n** to their idols and 1 Chr 10:9
have told the glad **n** of deliverance in the Ps 40:9
women who announce the **n** are a great Ps 68:11
He is not afraid of bad **n**; his heart is Ps 112:7
heart, and good **n** refreshes the bones. Prv 15:30
soul, so is good **n** from a far country. Prv 25:25
high mountain, O Zion, herald of good **n**; Is 40:9
strength, O Jerusalem, herald of good **n**; Is 40:9
I give to Jerusalem a herald of good **n**. Is 41:27
are the feet of him who brings good **n**, Is 52:7
peace, who brings good **n** of happiness, Is 52:7
frankincense, and shall bring good **n**, Is 60:6
anointed me to bring good **n** to the poor; Is 61:1
man who brought the **n** to my father, Jer 20:15
Jerusalem heard **n** about them, Jer 37:5
confounded, for they have heard bad **n**; Jer 49:23
say, 'Because of the **n** that it is coming. Ezk 21:7
will come to you to report to you the **n**. Ezk 24:26
But **n** from the east and the north shall Dn 11:44
the feet of him who brings good **n**, Na 1:15
All who hear the **n** about you clap their Na 3:19
the poor have good **n** preached to them. Mt 11:5
talk freely about it, and to spread the **n**, Mk 1:45
to you and to bring you this good **n**. Lk 1:19
I bring you good **n** of a great joy that Lk 2:10
he preached good **n** to the people. Lk 3:18
me to proclaim good **n** to the poor. Lk 4:18
must preach the good **n** of the kingdom Lk 4:43
the poor have good **n** preached to them. Lk 7:22
and bringing the good **n** of the kingdom Lk 8:1
since then the good **n** of the kingdom Lk 16:16
he preached good **n** about the Acts 8:12
he told him the good **n** about Jesus. Acts 8:35
preaching good **n** of peace through Acts 10:36
bring you the good **n** that what God Acts 13:32
with you, and we bring you good **n**, Acts 14:15
feet of those who preach the good **n**!" Rom 10:15
that I too may be cheered by **n** of you. Phil 2:19
brought us the good **n** of your faith 1 Thes 3:6
For good **n** came to us just as to them, Heb 4:2
received the good **n** failed to enter Heb 4:6
who preached the good **n** to you by the 1 Pt 1:12
word is the good **n** that was preached to 1 Pt 1:25

NEXT (108)
shall bear to you at this time **n** year." Gn 17:21
return to you about this time **n** year, Gn 18:10
return to you about this time **n** year, Gn 18:14
The **n** day, the firstborn said to the Gn 19:34
When he went out the **n** day, behold, two Ex 2:13
And the **n** day the LORD did this thing. All Ex 9:6
The **n** day Moses sat to judge the people, Ex 18:13
two bases under the **n** frame for its two Ex 26:19
and two bases under the **n** frame. Ex 26:21
on its inside edge **n** to the ephod. Ex 28:26
rose up early the **n** day and offered burnt Ex 32:6
The **n** day Moses said to the people, Ex 32:30
two bases under the **n** frame for its two Ex 36:24
frame and two bases under the **n** frame. Ex 36:26
on its inside edge **n** to the ephod. Ex 39:19
and on the **n** day what remains of it Lv 7:16
Those to camp **n** to him shall be the Nm 2:5
And those to camp **n** to him shall be Nm 2:12
And **n** to him shall be the tribe of Nm 2:20
And those to camp **n** to him shall be Nm 2:27
if the man has no **n** of kin to whom Nm 5:8
day and all night and all the **n** day, Nm 11:32
But on the **n** day all the congregation Nm 16:41
On the **n** day Moses went into the tent Nm 17:8
And the **n** generation, your children Dt 29:22
he rose early **n** morning and squeezed Jgs 6:38
And the **n** day the people rose early and Jgs 21:4
people of Ashdod rose early the **n** day, 1 Sm 5:3
when they rose early on the **n** morning, 1 Sm 5:4
And the **n** day Saul put the people in 1 Sm 11:11
firstborn, and **n** to him Abinadab, 1 Sm 17:13
The **n** day a harmful spirit from God 1 Sm 18:10
over Israel, and I shall be **n** to you. 1 Sm 23:17
until the evening of the **n** day, 1 Sm 30:17
The **n** day, when the Philistines came 1 Sm 31:8
in Jerusalem that day and the **n**. 2 Sm 11:12
"See, Joab's field is **n** to mine, 2 Sm 14:30
And **n** to him among the three 2 Sm 23:9
And **n** to him was Shammah, the 2 Sm 23:11
and he was born **n** after Absalom. 1 Kgs 1:6
The **n** morning, about the time of 2 Kgs 3:20
this season, about this time **n** year, 2 Kgs 4:16
And on the **n** day I said to her, 'Give 2 Kgs 6:29
But the **n** day he took the bed cloth 2 Kgs 8:15
The **n** day, when the Philistines 1 Chr 10:8
And **n** to him among the three 1 Chr 11:12
and on the **n** day offered burnt 1 Chr 29:21
and **n** to him Jehohanan the 2 Chr 17:15
and **n** to him Amasiah the son of 2 Chr 17:16
and **n** to him Jehozabad with 2 Chr 17:18
and Elkanah the **n** in authority to 2 Chr 28:7
And **n** to him the men of Jericho built. Neh 3:2
And **n** to them Zaccur the son of Imri Neh 3:2
And **n** to them Meremoth the son of Neh 3:4
And **n** to them Meshullam the son of Neh 3:4
And **n** to them Zadok the son of Baana Neh 3:4
And **n** to them the Tekoites repaired, Neh 3:5
And **n** to them repaired Melatiah the Neh 3:7
N to them Uzziel the son of Harhaiah, Neh 3:8
N to him Hananiah, one of the Neh 3:8
N to them Rephaiah the son of Hur, Neh 3:9
N to them Jedaiah the son of Neh 3:10
And **n** to him Hattush the son of Neh 3:10
N to him Shallum the son of Neh 3:12
N to him Hashabiah, ruler of half the Neh 3:17
N to him Ezer the son of Jeshua, ruler Neh 3:19
the men **n** to him being Carshena, Est 1:14
that you may tell the **n** generation Ps 48:13
that the **n** generation might know them, Ps 78:6
Can a man carry fire **n** to his chest and Prv 6:27
The **n** day, when Pashhur released Jer 20:3
And on the **n** morning I did as I was Ezk 24:18
But when dawn came up the **n** day, God Jon 4:7
the man who stands **n** to me," declares Zec 13:7
persecute you in one town, flee to the **n**, Mt 10:23
N day, that is, after the day of Mt 27:62
to them, "Let us go on to the **n** towns, Mk 1:38
On the **n** day, when they had come down Lk 9:37
And the **n** day he took out two denarii Lk 10:35
Then if it should bear fruit **n** year, well Lk 13:9
The **n** day he saw Jesus coming toward Jn 1:29
The **n** day again John was standing with Jn 1:35
The **n** day Jesus decided to go to Galilee. Jn 1:43
On the **n** day the crowd that remained on Jn 6:22
The **n** day the large crowd that had Jn 12:12
put them in custody until the **n** day, Acts 4:3
On the **n** day their rulers and elders and Acts 4:5
The **n** day, as they were on their Acts 10:9
The **n** day he rose and went away Acts 10:23
an angel of the Lord stood **n** to him, Acts 12:7
might be told them the **n** Sabbath. Acts 13:42
The **n** Sabbath almost the whole city Acts 13:44
and on the **n** day he went on with Acts 14:20
His house was **n** door to the Acts 18:7
one place to the **n** through the region Acts 18:23
them, intending to depart on the **n** day, Acts 20:7
the **n** day we touched at Samos; Acts 20:15
course to Cos, and the **n** day to Rhodes, Acts 21:1
On the **n** day we departed and came to Acts 21:8
and the **n** day he purified himself Acts 21:26
But on the **n** day, desiring to know Acts 22:30
And on the **n** day they returned to the Acts 23:32
And the **n** day he took his seat on the Acts 25:6
but on the **n** day took my seat on the Acts 25:17
So on the **n** day Agrippa and Bernice Acts 25:23
The **n** day we put in at Sidon. And Acts 27:3
they began the **n** day to jettison the Acts 27:18
"About this time **n** year I will return Rom 9:9

NEZIAH (2)
the sons of **N**, and the sons of Hatipha. Ezr 2:54
the sons of **N**, the sons of Hatipha. Neh 7:56

NEZIB (1)
Iphtah, Ashnah, **N**, Jos 15:43

NIBHAZ (1)
and the Avvites made **N** and Tartak; 2 Kgs 17:31

NIBSHAN (1)
N, the City of Salt, and Engedi: six Jos 15:62

NICANOR (1)
and Philip, and Prochorus, and **N**, Acts 6:5

NICODEMUS (5)
was a man of the Pharisees named **N**, Jn 3:1
N said to him, "How can a man be born Jn 3:4
N said to him, "How can these things be?" Jn 3:9
N, who had gone to him before, and who Jn 7:50
N also, who earlier had come to Jesus Jn 19:39

NICOLAITANS (2)
you hate the works of the **N**, which I also Rv 2:6
some who hold the teaching of the **N**. Rv 2:15

NICOLAUS (1)
and Timon, and Parmenas, and **N**, Acts 6:5

NICOPOLIS (1)
to you, do your best to come to me at **N**, Ti 3:12

NIGER (1)
Barnabas, Simeon who was called **N**, Acts 13:1

NIGHT (307)
light Day, and the darkness he called **N**. Gn 1:5
heavens to separate the day from the **n**. Gn 1:14
lesser light to rule the **n**—and the stars. Gn 1:16
to rule over the day and over the **n**, and Gn 1:18
heat, summer and winter, day and **n**, Gn 8:22
divided his forces against them by **n**, Gn 14:15
house and spend the **n** and wash your Gn 19:2
we will spend the **n** in the town square." Gn 19:2
made their father drink wine that **n**. Gn 19:33
"Behold, I lay last **n** with my father. Gn 19:34
their father drink wine that **n** also. Gn 19:35
in a dream by **n** and said to him, Gn 20:3
father's house for us to spend the **n**?" Gn 24:23
and fodder, and room to spend the **n**." Gn 24:25
and drank, and they spent the **n** there. Gn 24:54
appeared to him the same **n** and said, Gn 26:24
a certain place and stayed there that **n**, Gn 28:11
mandrakes." So he lay with her that **n**. Gn 30:16
in a dream by **n** and said to him, Gn 31:24
God of your father spoke to me last **n**, Gn 31:29
it, whether stolen by day or stolen by **n**. Gn 31:39
heat consumed me, and the cold by **n**, Gn 31:40
of my hands and rebuked you last **n**." Gn 31:42
bread and spent the **n** in the hill Gn 31:54
So he stayed there that **n**, and from Gn 32:13
he himself stayed that **n** in the camp. Gn 32:21
The same **n** he arose and took his two Gn 32:22
And one **n** they both dreamed—the Gn 40:5
we dreamed on the same **n**, he and I, Gn 41:11
to Israel in visions of the **n** and said, Gn 46:2
the land all that day and all that **n**. Ex 10:13
They shall eat the flesh that **n**, roasted Ex 12:8
pass through the land of Egypt that **n**, Ex 12:12
And Pharaoh rose up in the **n**, he and Ex 12:30
Moses and Aaron by **n** and said, Ex 12:31
It was a **n** of watching by the LORD, to Ex 12:42

so this same **n** is a night of watching Ex 12:42
same night is a **n** of watching kept to Ex 12:42
and by **n** in a pillar of fire to give them Ex 13:21
that they might travel by day and by **n**. Ex 13:21
pillar of fire by **n** did not depart from Ex 13:22
it lit up the **n** without one coming near Ex 14:20
one coming near the other all **n**. Ex 14:20
strong east wind all **n** and made the sea Ex 14:21
by day, and fire was in it by **n**, Ex 40:38
on the altar all **n** until the morning, Lv 6:9
shall remain day and **n** for seven days, Lv 8:35
with you all **n** until the morning. Lv 19:13
by day and the appearance of fire by **n**. Nm 9:16
out, or if it continued for a day and a **n**, Nm 9:21
the dew fell upon the camp in the **n**, Nm 11:9
all that day and all **n** and all the next Nm 11:32
a loud cry, and the people wept that **n**. Nm 14:1
by day and in a pillar of fire by **n**. Nm 14:14
came to Balaam at **n** and said to him, Nm 22:20
in fire by **n** and in the cloud by day, Dt 1:33
your God brought you out of Egypt by **n**. Dt 16:1
the first day remain all **n** until morning. Dt 16:4
body shall not remain all **n** on the tree, Dt 21:23
N and day you shall be in dread and Dt 28:66
but you shall meditate on it day and **n**, Jos 1:8
the camp and spent the **n** in the camp. Jos 6:11
men of valor and sent them out by **n**. Jos 8:3
Joshua spent that **n** among the people. Jos 8:9
But Joshua spent that **n** in the valley. Jos 8:13
having marched up all **n** from Gilgal. Jos 10:9
That **n** the LORD said to him, "Take your Jgs 6:25
of the town to do it by day, he did it by **n**. Jgs 6:27
And God did so that **n**; and it was dry on Jgs 6:40
That same **n** the LORD said to him, "Arise, Jgs 7:9
Now therefore, go by **n**, you and the Jgs 9:32
him rose up by **n** and set an ambush Jgs 9:34
an ambush for him all **n** at the gate of Jgs 16:2
They kept quiet all **n**, saying, "Let us Jgs 16:2
they ate and drank and spent the **n** there. Jgs 19:4
to the man, "Be pleased to spend the **n**, Jgs 19:6
him, till he spent the **n** there again. Jgs 19:7
toward evening. Please, spend the **n**. Jgs 19:9
But the man would not spend the **n**. He Jgs 19:10
of the Jebusites and spend the **n** in it." Jgs 19:11
places and spend the **n** at Gibeah or at Jgs 19:13
to go in and spend the **n** at Gibeah. Jgs 19:15
them into his house to spend the **n**. Jgs 19:15
Only, do not spend the **n** in the square." Jgs 19:20
abused her all **n** until the morning. Jgs 19:25
I and my concubine, to spend the **n**. Jgs 20:4
surrounded the house against me by **n**. Jgs 20:5
have a husband this **n** and should bear Ru 1:12
with him that **n** and they 1 Sm 14:34
the Philistines by **n** and plunder 1 Sm 14:36
angry, and he cried to the LORD all **n**. 1 Sm 15:11
said to me this **n**." And he said to 1 Sm 15:16
And David fled and escaped that **n**. 1 Sm 19:10
lay naked all that day and all that **n**. 1 Sm 19:24
a wall to us both by **n** and by day, 1 Sm 25:16
and Abishai went to the army by **n**. 1 Sm 26:7
And they came to the woman by **n**. 1 Sm 28:8
had eaten nothing all day and all **n**. 1 Sm 28:20
they rose and went away that **n**. 1 Sm 28:25
arose and went all **n** and took the 1 Sm 31:12
went all that **n** through the Arabah. 2 Sm 2:29
And Joab and his men marched all **n**, 2 Sm 2:32
went by the way of the Arabah all **n**, 2 Sm 4:7
But that same **n** the word of the LORD 2 Sm 7:4
went in and lay all **n** on the ground. 2 Sm 12:16
will not spend the **n** with the people. 2 Sm 17:8
not a man will stay with you this **n**, 2 Sm 19:7
by day, or the beasts of the field by **n**. 2 Sm 21:10
appeared to Solomon in a dream by **n**, 1 Kgs 3:5
And this woman's son died in the **n**, 1 Kgs 3:19
eyes may be open **n** and day toward 1 Kgs 8:29
near to the LORD our God day and **n**, 1 Kgs 8:59
they came by **n** and surrounded the 2 Kgs 6:14
the king rose in the **n** and said to his 2 Kgs 7:12
with all his chariots and rose by **n**, 2 Kgs 8:21
And that **n** the angel of the LORD 2 Kgs 19:35
men of war fled by **n** by the way of 2 Kgs 25:4
for they were on duty day and **n**. 1 Chr 9:33
But that same **n** the word of the LORD 1 Chr 17:3
In that **n** God appeared to Solomon, 2 Chr 1:7
be open day and **n** toward this house, 2 Chr 6:20
to Solomon in the **n** and said to him: 2 Chr 7:12
and he rose by **n** and struck the 2 Chr 21:9
offerings and the fat parts until **n**; 2 Chr 35:14
son of Eliashib, where he spent the **n**, Ezr 10:6
before you day and **n** for the people of Neh 1:6
Then I arose in the **n**, I and a few men Neh 2:12
I went out by **n** by the Valley Gate to Neh 2:13
I went up in the **n** by the valley and Neh 2:15
as a protection against them day and **n**. Neh 4:9
servant pass the **n** within Jerusalem, Neh 4:22
a guard for us by **n** and may labor by Neh 4:22
They are coming to kill you by **n**." Neh 6:10
pillar of fire in the **n** to light for them Neh 9:12
the pillar of fire by **n** to light for them Neh 9:19
not eat or drink for three days, **n** or day. Est 4:16
On that **n** the king could not sleep. And Est 6:1
on which I was born, and the **n** that said, Jb 3:3
That **n**—let thick darkness seize it! Let it Jb 3:6
Behold, let that **n** be barren; let no joyful Jb 3:7
Amid thoughts from visions of the **n**, Jb 4:13
and grope at noonday as in the **n**. Jb 5:14
say, 'When shall I arise?' But the **n** is long, Jb 7:4
They make **n** into day; 'The light,' they Jb 17:12
will be chased away like a vision of the **n**. Jb 20:8
They lie all **n** naked, without clothing, Jb 24:7
and needy, and in the **n** he is like a thief. Jb 24:14
in the **n** a whirlwind carries him off. Jb 27:20
with the dew all **n** on my branches, Jb 29:19
the dry ground by **n** in waste and Jb 30:3
The **n** racks my bones, and the pain Jb 30:17
In a dream, in a vision of the **n**, when Jb 33:15
their works, he overturns them in the **n**, Jb 34:25
my Maker, who gives songs in the **n**, Jb 35:10
Do not long for the **n**, when peoples Jb 36:20
Will he spend the **n** at your manger? Jb 39:9
and on his law he meditates day and **n**. Ps 1:2
every **n** I flood my bed with tears; Ps 6:6
in the **n** also my heart instructs me. Ps 16:7
tried my heart, you have visited me by **n**, Ps 17:3
and **n** to night reveals knowledge. Ps 19:2
and night to **n** reveals knowledge. Ps 19:2
by day, but you do not answer, and by **n**, Ps 22:2
Weeping may tarry for the **n**, but joy Ps 30:5
For day and **n** your hand was heavy Ps 32:4
My tears have been my food day and **n**, Ps 42:3
love, and at **n** his song is with me, Ps 42:8
Day and **n** they go around it on its Ps 55:10
meditate on you in the watches of the **n**; Ps 63:6
Yours is the day, yours also the **n**; you Ps 74:16
in the **n** my hand is stretched out Ps 77:2
"Let me remember my song in the **n**; Ps 77:6
a cloud, and all the **n** with a fiery light. Ps 78:14
salvation; I cry out day and **n** before you. Ps 88:1
when it is past, or as a watch in the **n**. Ps 90:4
You will not fear the terror of the **n**, nor Ps 91:5
the morning, and your faithfulness by **n**, Ps 92:2
You make darkness, and it is **n**, when Ps 104:20
a covering, and fire to give light by **n**. Ps 105:39
I remember your name in the **n**, O Ps 119:55
awake before the watches of the **n**, Ps 119:148
strike you by day, nor the moon by **n**. Ps 121:6
who stand by **n** in the house of the Ps 134:1
the moon and stars to rule over the **n**, Ps 136:9
me, and the light about me be **n**," Ps 139:11
the **n** is bright as the day, for darkness Ps 139:12
evening, at the time of **n** and darkness. Prv 7:9
while it is yet **n** and provides food for Prv 31:15
Her lamp does not go out at **n**. Prv 31:18
Even in the **n** his heart does not rest. Eccl 2:23
how neither day nor **n** do one's eyes see Eccl 8:16
On my bed by **n** I sought him whom my Sg 3:1
his sword at his thigh, against terror by **n**. Sg 3:8
dew, my locks with the drops of the **n**." Sg 5:2
and the shining of a flaming fire by **n**; Is 4:5
the pass; at Geba they lodge for the **n**; Is 10:29
Because Ar of Moab is laid waste in a **n**, Is 15:1
because Kir of Moab is laid waste in a **n**, Is 15:1
make your shade like **n** at the height of Is 16:3
Seir, "Watchman, what time of the **n**? Is 21:11
night? Watchman, what time of the **n**?" Is 21:11
says: "Morning comes, and also the **n**. Is 21:12
My soul yearns for you in the **n**; my spirit Is 26:9
Lest anyone punish it, I keep it **n** and day; Is 27:3
it will pass through, by day and by **n**; Is 28:19
shall be like a dream, a vision of the **n**. Is 29:7
a song as in the **n** when a holy feast is Is 30:29
N and day it shall not be quenched; its Is 34:10
there the **n** bird settles and finds for Is 34:14
from day to **n** you bring me to an end; Is 38:12
from day to **n** you bring me to an end. Is 38:13
day and **n** they shall not be shut, that Is 60:11
the day and all the **n** they shall never be Is 62:6
tombs, and spend the **n** in secret places; Is 65:4
let us attack by **n** and destroy her Jer 6:5
I might weep day and **n** for the slain of the Jer 9:1
traveler who turns aside to tarry for a **n**? Jer 14:8
my eyes run down with tears **n** and day, Jer 14:17
you shall serve other gods day and **n**, Jer 16:13
of the moon and the stars for light by **n**, Jer 31:35
the day and my covenant with the **n**, Jer 33:20
so that day and **n** will not come at their Jer 33:20
covenant with day and **n** and the fixed Jer 33:25
to the heat by day and the frost by **n**. Jer 36:30
out of the city at **n** by way of the king's Jer 39:4
If thieves came by **n**, would they not Jer 49:9
out from the city by **n** by the way of a Jer 52:7
She weeps bitterly in the **n**, with tears Lam 1:2
stream down like a torrent day and **n**! Lam 2:18
"Arise, cry out in the **n**, at the Lam 2:19
at the beginning of the **n** watches! Lam 2:19
revealed to Daniel in a vision of the **n**. Dn 2:19
That very **n** Belshazzar the Chaldean Dn 5:30
to his palace and spent the **n** fasting; Dn 6:18
Daniel declared, "I saw in my vision by **n**, Dn 7:2
After this I saw in the **n** visions, and Dn 7:7
I saw in the **n** visions, and behold, with Dn 7:13
also shall stumble with you by **n**; Hos 4:5
their intrigue; all **n** their anger smolders; Hos 7:6
Go in, pass the **n** in sackcloth, O Jl 1:13
the morning and darkens the day into **n**, Am 5:8
if plunderers came by **n**—how you have Ob 1:5
into being in a **n** and perished in a Jon 4:10
being in a night and perished in a **n**. Jon 4:10
Therefore it shall be **n** to you, without Mi 3:6
"I saw in the **n**, and behold, a man riding Zec 1:8
is known to the LORD, neither day nor **n**, Zec 14:7
and his mother by **n** and departed to Mt 2:14
fourth watch of the **n** he came to them, Mt 14:25
what part of the **n** the thief was Mt 24:43
will all fall away because of me this **n**. Mt 26:31
to him, "Truly, I tell you, this very **n**, Mt 26:34
'His disciples came by **n** and stole him Mt 28:13
He sleeps and rises **n** and day, and the Mk 4:27
N and day among the tombs and on the Mk 5:5
fourth watch of the **n** he came to them, Mk 6:48
to him, "Truly, I tell you, this very **n**, Mk 14:30
field, keeping watch over their flock by **n**. Lk 2:8
with fasting and prayer **n** and day. Lk 2:37
"Master, we toiled all **n** and took nothing! Lk 5:5
and all **n** he continued in prayer to God. Lk 6:12
This **n** your soul is required of you, Lk 12:20
in that **n** there will be two in one bed. Lk 17:34
to his elect, who cry to him day and **n**? Lk 18:7
but at **n** he went out and lodged on the Lk 21:37
man came to Jesus by **n** and said to him, Jn 3:2
day; **n** is coming, when no one can work. Jn 9:4
But if anyone walks in the **n**, he Jn 11:10
he immediately went out. And it was **n**. Jn 13:30
who earlier had come to Jesus by **n**, Jn 19:39
the boat, but that **n** they caught nothing. Jn 21:3
But during the **n** an angel of the Lord Acts 5:19
the gates day and **n** in order to kill Acts 9:24
disciples took him by **n** and let him Acts 9:25
about to bring him out, on that very **n**, Acts 12:6
And a vision appeared to Paul in the **n**: Acts 16:9
same hour of the **n** and washed their Acts 16:33
Paul and Silas away by **n** to Berea, Acts 17:10
the Lord said to Paul one **n** in a vision, Acts 18:9
I did not cease **n** or day to admonish Acts 20:31
The following **n** the Lord stood by Acts 23:11
as Caesarea at the third hour of the **n**. Acts 23:23
and brought him by **n** to Antipatris. Acts 23:31
as they earnestly worship **n** and day. Acts 26:7
For this very **n** there stood before me Acts 27:23
When the fourteenth **n** had come, as Acts 27:27
The **n** is far gone; the day is at hand. Rom 13:12
Lord Jesus on the **n** when he was 1 Cor 11:23
a **n** and a day I was adrift at sea; 2 Cor 11:25
through many a sleepless **n**, 2 Cor 11:27
labor and toil: we worked **n** and day, 1 Thes 2:9
pray most earnestly **n** and day that 1 Thes 3:10
Lord will come like a thief in the **n**. 1 Thes 5:2
are not of the **n** or of the darkness. 1 Thes 5:5
For those who sleep, sleep at **n**, and 1 Thes 5:7
those who get drunk, are drunk at **n**. 1 Thes 5:7
toil and labor we worked **n** and day, 2 Thes 3:8
supplications and prayers **n** and day, 1 Tm 5:5
constantly in my prayers **n** and day. 2 Tm 1:3
and day and **n** they never cease to say, Rv 4:8
and serve him day and **n** in his temple; Rv 7:15
shining, and likewise a third of the **n**. Rv 8:12
them day and **n** before our God. Rv 12:10
ever, and they have no rest, day or **n**, Rv 14:11
tormented day and **n** forever and ever. Rv 20:10
by day—and there will be no **n** there. Rv 21:25
And **n** will be no more. They will need Rv 22:5

NIGHTHAWK (2)

the ostrich, the **n**, the sea gull, the hawk Lv 11:16
the ostrich, the **n**, the sea gull, the hawk Dt 14:15

NIGHTS (19)

rain on the earth forty days and forty **n**, Gn 7:4
upon the earth forty days and forty **n**. Gn 7:12
on the mountain forty days and forty **n**. Ex 24:18
with the LORD forty days and forty **n**. Ex 34:28
on the mountain forty days and forty **n**. Dt 9:9
forty days and forty **n** the LORD gave me Dt 9:11
the LORD as before, forty days and forty **n**. Dt 9:18
the LORD for these forty days and forty **n**, Dt 9:25
at the first time, forty days and forty **n**, Dt 10:10

water for three days and three **n**. 1 Sm 30:12
food forty days and forty **n** to Horeb, 1 Kgs 19:8
on the ground seven days and seven **n**, Jb 2:13
and **n** of misery are apportioned to me. Jb 7:3
and at my post I am stationed whole **n**. Is 21:8
belly of the fish three days and three **n**. Jon 1:17
And after fasting forty days and forty **n**, Mt 4:2
three days and three **n** in the belly of Mt 12:40
be three days and three **n** in the heart of Mt 12:40
riots, labors, sleepless **n**, 2 Cor 6:5

NILE (46)
dreamed that he was standing by the **N**, Gn 41:1
up out of the **N** seven cows attractive Gn 41:2
thin, came up out of the **N** after them, Gn 41:3
by the other cows on the bank of the **N**. Gn 41:3
I was standing on the banks of the **N**. Gn 41:17
came up out of the **N** and fed in the Gn 41:18
to the Hebrews you shall cast into the **N**, Ex 1:22
some water from the **N** and pour it on Ex 4:9
shall take from the **N** will become blood Ex 4:9
Stand on the bank of the **N** to meet him, Ex 7:15
I will strike the water that is in the **N**, Ex 7:17
The fish in the **N** shall die, and the Nile Ex 7:18
the Nile shall die, and the **N** will stink, Ex 7:18
weary of drinking water from the **N**."'" Ex 7:18
the staff and struck the water in the **N**, Ex 7:20
all the water in the **N** turned into blood. Ex 7:20
And the fish in the **N** died, and the Nile Ex 7:21
the fish in the Nile died, and the **N** stank, Ex 7:21
could not drink water from the **N**. Ex 7:21
Egyptians dug along the **N** for water to Ex 7:24
they could not drink the water of the **N**. Ex 7:24
passed after the LORD had struck the **N**. Ex 7:25
The **N** shall swarm with frogs that shall Ex 8:3
your houses and be left only in the **N**." Ex 8:9
people. They shall be left only in the **N**." Ex 8:11
the staff with which you struck the **N**, Ex 17:5
all Israel from the **N** of Egypt to 1 Chr 13:5
branches of Egypt's **N** will diminish and Is 19:6
There will be bare places by the **N**, on the Is 19:7
places by the Nile, on the brink of the **N**, Is 19:7
all that is sown by the **N** will be parched, Is 19:7
and lament, all who cast a hook in the **N**; Is 19:8
the grain of Shihor, the harvest of the **N**; Is 23:3
Cross over your land like the **N**, O Is 23:10
to Egypt to drink the waters of the **N**? Jer 2:18
"Who is this, rising like the **N**, like Jer 46:7
Egypt rises like the **N**, like rivers whose Jer 46:8
streams, that says, 'My **N** is my own; Ezk 29:3
"Because you said, 'The **N** is mine, and Ezk 29:9
I will dry up the **N** and will sell the Ezk 30:12
dwells in it, and all of it rise like the **N**, Am 8:8
and sink again, like the **N** of Egypt?" Am 8:8
in it mourn, and all of it rises like the **N**, Am 9:5
and sinks again, like the **N** of Egypt; Am 9:5
you better than Thebes that sat by the **N**, Na 3:8
the depths of the **N** shall be dried up. Zec 10:11

NIMRAH (1)
"Ataroth, Dibon, Jazer, **N**, Heshbon, Nm 32:3

NIMRIM (2)
the waters of **N** are a desolation; the grass Is 15:6
For the waters of **N** also have become Jer 48:34

NIMROD (4)
Cush fathered **N**; he was the first on Gn 10:8
"Like **N** a mighty hunter before the Gn 10:9
Cush fathered **N**. He was the first on 1 Chr 1:10
sword, and the land of **N** at its entrances; Mi 5:6

NIMSHI (5)
Jehu the son of **N** you shall anoint 1 Kgs 19:16
Jehu the son of Jehoshaphat, son of **N**. 2 Kgs 9:2
the son of **N** conspired against Joram. 2 Kgs 9:14
like the driving of Jehu the son of **N**, 2 Kgs 9:20
Jehoram to meet Jehu the son of **N**, 2 Chr 22:7

NINE (13)
"On the fifth day **n** bulls, two rams, Nm 29:26
to give to the **n** tribes and to the Nm 34:13
N cubits was its length, and four cubits Dt 3:11
an inheritance to the **n** tribes and half Jos 13:7
of Moses for the **n** and one-half tribes. Jos 14:2
Mareshah: **n** cities with their villages. Jos 15:44
and Zior: **n** cities with their villages. Jos 15:54
with its pasturelands—**n** cities out of Jos 21:16
at the end of **n** months and twenty 2 Sm 24:8
over Israel, and he reigned **n** years. 2 Kgs 17:1
Elishama, Eliada, and Eliphelet, **n**. 1 Chr 3:8
while **n** out of ten remained in the Neh 11:1
not ten cleansed? Where are the **n**? Lk 17:17

NINETEEN (2)
and Beth-shemesh—**n** cities with their Jos 19:38
from David's servants **n** men besides 2 Sm 2:30

NINETEENTH (4)
—that was the **n** year of King 2 Kgs 25:8
the **n** to Pethahiah, the twentieth to 1 Chr 24:16
to the **n**, to Mallothi, his sons and 1 Chr 25:26
—that was the **n** year of King Jer 52:12

NINETY (2)
Shall Sarah, who is **n** years old, bear a Gn 17:17
all around, and its length **n** cubits. Ezk 41:12

NINETY-EIGHT (1)
Now Eli was **n** years old and his eyes 1 Sm 4:15

NINETY-NINE (6)
When Abram was **n** years old the LORD Gn 17:1
Abraham was **n** years old when he was Gn 17:24
he not leave the **n** on the mountains Mt 18:12
more than over the **n** that never went Mt 18:13
does not leave the **n** in the open country, Lk 15:4
repents than over **n** righteous persons Lk 15:7

NINETY-SIX (2)
Israel, twelve bulls for all Israel, **n** rams, Ezr 8:35
There were **n** pomegranates on the Jer 52:23

NINEVEH (20)
land he went into Assyria and built **N**, Gn 10:11
Resen between **N** and Calah; that is the Gn 10:12
and went home and lived at **N**. 2 Kgs 19:36
and returned home and lived at **N**. Is 37:37
"Arise, go to **N**, that great city, and call Jon 1:2
"Arise, go to **N**, that great city, and call Jon 3:2
So Jonah arose and went to **N**, according Jon 3:3
Now **N** was an exceedingly great city, Jon 3:3
forty days, and **N** shall be overthrown!" Jon 3:4
And the people of **N** believed God. They Jon 3:5
The word reached the king of **N**, and he Jon 3:6
proclamation and published through **N**, Jon 3:7
And should not I pity **N**, that great city, Jon 4:11
An oracle concerning **N**. The book of the Na 1:1
N is like a pool whose waters run away. Na 2:8
shrink from you and say, Wasted is **N**; Na 3:7
and he will make **N** a desolation, Zep 2:13
The men of **N** will rise up at the Mt 12:41
Jonah became a sign to the people of **N**, Lk 11:30
The men of **N** will rise up at the Lk 11:32

NINTH (33)
On the **n** day of the month beginning Lv 23:32
you shall eat the old until the **n** year, Lv 25:22
On the **n** day Abidan the son of Nm 7:60
In the **n** year of Hoshea, the king of 2 Kgs 17:6
which was the **n** year of Hoshea 2 Kgs 18:10
And in the **n** year of his reign, in the 2 Kgs 25:1
On the **n** day of the fourth month the 2 Kgs 25:3
Johanan eighth, Elzabad **n**, 1 Chr 12:12
the **n** to Jeshua, the tenth to 1 Chr 24:11
the **n** to Mattaniah, his sons and his 1 Chr 25:16
N, for the ninth month, was Abiezer 1 Chr 27:12
Ninth, for the **n** month, was Abiezer 1 Chr 27:12
It was the **n** month, on the twentieth day Ezr 10:9
of Josiah, king of Judah, in the **n** month, Jer 36:9
It was the **n** month, and the king was Jer 36:22
In the **n** year of Zedekiah king of Judah, Jer 39:1
month, on the **n** day of the month, Jer 39:2
And in the **n** year of his reign, in the Jer 52:4
On the **n** day of the fourth month the Jer 52:6
In the **n** year, in the tenth month, on Ezk 24:1
the twenty-fourth day of the **n** month, Hg 2:10
the twenty-fourth day of the **n** month. Hg 2:18
on the fourth day of the **n** month, Zec 7:1
about the sixth hour and the **n** hour, Mt 20:5
over all the land until the **n** hour. Mt 27:45
And about the **n** hour Jesus cried out Mt 27:46
over the whole land until the **n** hour. Mk 15:33
And at the **n** hour Jesus cried with a Mk 15:34
over the whole land until the **n** hour, Lk 23:44
temple at the hour of prayer, the **n** hour. Acts 3:1
About the **n** hour of the day he saw Acts 10:3
praying in my house at the **n** hour, Acts 10:30
chrysolite, the eighth beryl, the **n** topaz, Rv 21:20

NISAN (2)
In the month of **N**, in the twentieth year Neh 2:1
the first month, which is the month of **N**, Est 3:7

NISROCH (2)
in the house of **N** his god, 2 Kgs 19:37
worshiping in the house of **N** his god, Is 37:38

NOADIAH (2)
son of Jeshua and **N** the son of Binnui. Ezr 8:33
and also the prophetess **N** and the rest Neh 6:14

NOAH (55)
and called his name **N**, saying, "Out of Gn 5:29
lived after he fathered **N** 595 years and Gn 5:30
After **N** was 500 years old, Noah Gn 5:32
was 500 years old, **N** fathered Shem, Gn 5:32
But **N** found favor in the eyes of the LORD. Gn 6:8
These are the generations of **N**. Noah was Gn 6:9
N was a righteous man, blameless in his Gn 6:9
in his generation. **N** walked with God. Gn 6:9
And **N** had three sons, Shem, Ham, and Gn 6:10
And God said to **N**, "I have determined Gn 6:13
N did this; he did all that God Gn 6:22
Then the LORD said to **N**, "Go into the ark, Gn 7:1
And **N** did all that the LORD had Gn 7:5
N was six hundred years old when the Gn 7:6
And **N** and his sons and his wife and his Gn 7:7
and female, went into the ark with **N**, Gn 7:9
with Noah, as God had commanded **N**. Gn 7:9
On the very same day **N** and his sons, Gn 7:13
They went into the ark with **N**, two and Gn 7:15
Only **N** was left, and those who were Gn 7:23
But God remembered **N** and all the Gn 8:1
end of forty days **N** opened the window of Gn 8:6
So **N** knew that the waters had subsided Gn 8:11
And **N** removed the covering of the ark Gn 8:13
Then God said to **N**, Gn 8:15
So **N** went out, and his sons and his wife Gn 8:18
Then **N** built an altar to the LORD and Gn 8:20
And God blessed **N** and his sons and said Gn 9:1
Then God said to **N** and to his sons with Gn 9:8
God said to **N**, "This is the sign of the Gn 9:17
The sons of **N** who went forth from the Gn 9:18
These three were the sons of **N**, and Gn 9:19
N began to be a man of the soil, and he Gn 9:20
When **N** awoke from his wine and Gn 9:24
After the flood **N** lived 350 years. Gn 9:28
All the days of **N** were 950 years, and he Gn 9:29
are the generations of the sons of **N**, Gn 10:1
These are the clans of the sons of **N**, Gn 10:32
Zelophehad were Mahlah, **N**, Hoglah, Nm 26:33
Mahlah, **N**, Hoglah, Milcah, and Nm 27:1
Tirzah, Hoglah, Milcah, and **N**, Nm 36:11
Mahlah, **N**, Hoglah, Milcah, and Jos 17:3
N, Shem, Ham, and Japheth. 1 Chr 1:4
"This is like the days of **N** to me: as I Is 54:9
that the waters of **N** should no more go Is 54:9
even if these three men, **N**, Daniel, and Ezk 14:14
even if **N**, Daniel, and Job were in it, as Ezk 14:20
As were the days of **N**, so will be the Mt 24:37
until the day when **N** entered the ark, Mt 24:38
Arphaxad, the son of Shem, the son of **N**, Lk 3:36
Just as it was in the days of **N**, so will it Lk 17:26
until the day when **N** entered the ark, Lk 17:27
By faith **N**, being warned by God Heb 11:7
God's patience waited in the days of **N**, 1 Pt 3:20
the ancient world, but preserved **N**, 2 Pt 2:5

NOAH'S (2)
In the six hundredth year of **N** life, in Gn 7:11
and **N** wife and the three wives of his Gn 7:13

NOB (6)
David came to **N** to Ahimelech the 1 Sm 21:1
"I saw the son of Jesse coming to **N**, 1 Sm 22:9
house, the priests who were at **N**, 1 Sm 22:11
And **N**, the city of the priests, he put 1 Sm 22:19
Anathoth, **N**, Ananiah, Neh 11:32
This very day he will halt at **N**; he will Is 10:32

NOBAH (3)
And **N** went and captured Kenath and Nm 32:42
and its villages, and called it **N**, Nm 32:42
tent dwellers east of **N** and Jogbehah and Jgs 8:11

NOBILITY (3)
when your king is the son of the **n**, Eccl 10:17
and the **n** of Jerusalem and her multitude Is 5:14
both of the royal family and of the **n**, Dn 1:3

NOBLE (18)
down marched the remnant of the **n**; Jgs 5:13
the great and **n** Osnappar deported and Ezr 4:10
This very day the **n** women of Persia Est 1:18
over to one of the king's most **n** officials. Est 6:9
Hear, for I will speak **n** things, and from Prv 8:6
to strike the **n** for their uprightness. Prv 17:26
to be put lower in the presence of a **n**. Prv 25:7
are your feet in sandals, O **n** daughter! Sg 7:1
The fool will no more be called **n**, nor the Is 32:5
But he who is **n** plans noble things, and Is 32:8
But he who is noble plans **n** things, and Is 32:8
noble things, and on **n** things he stands. Is 32:8
and bear fruit and become a **n** vine. Ezk 17:8
produce fruit and become a **n** cedar. Ezk 17:23
was adorned with **n** stones and offerings, Lk 21:5
these Jews were more **n** than those in Acts 17:11
powerful, not many were of **n** birth. 1 Cor 1:26
office of overseer, he desires a **n** task. 1 Tm 3:1

NOBLE'S (1)
she brought him curds in a **n** bowl. Jgs 5:25

NOBLEMAN (1)
"A **n** went into a far country to receive Lk 19:12

NOBLES (26)
dug, that the **n** of the people delved, Nm 21:18
And he took the captains, the **n**, the 2 Chr 23:20
not yet told the Jews, the priests, the **n**, Neh 2:16

but their **n** would not stoop to serve Neh 3:5
and said to the **n** and to the officials Neh 4:14
And I said to the **n** and to the officials Neh 4:19
charges against the **n** and the officials. Neh 5:7
in those days the **n** of Judah sent many Neh 6:17
heart to assemble the **n** and the officials Neh 7:5
join with their brothers, their **n**, and Neh 10:29
Then I confronted the **n** of Judah and Neh 13:17
and Media and the **n** and governors of the Est 1:3
the voice of the **n** was hushed, and their Jb 29:10
says to a king, 'Worthless one,' and to **n**, Jb 34:18
N shall come from Egypt; Cush shall Ps 68:31
Make their **n** like Oreb and Zeeb, all Ps 83:11
with chains and their **n** with fetters of Ps 149:8
by me princes rule, and **n**, all who Prv 8:16
hand for them to enter the gates of the **n**. Is 13:2
Its **n**—there is no one there to call it a Is 34:12
Her **n** send their servants for water; they Jer 14:3
and all the **n** of Judah and Jerusalem— Jer 27:20
Babylon slaughtered all the **n** of Judah. Jer 39:6
"By the decree of the king and his **n**: Jon 3:7
O king of Assyria; your **n** slumber. Na 3:18
banquet for his **n** and military Mk 6:21

NOCTURNAL (1)
unclean because of a **n** emission, Dt 23:10

NOD (1)
of the LORD and settled in the land of **N**, Gn 4:16

NODAB (1)
the Hagrites, Jetur, Naphish, and **N**. 1 Chr 5:19

NODDED (1)
when the governor had **n** to him to Acts 24:10

NOGAH (2)
N, Nepheg, Japhia, 1 Chr 3:7
N, Nepheg, Japhia, 1 Chr 14:6

NOHAH (2)
trod them down from **N** as far as Jgs 20:43
N the fourth, and Rapha the fifth. 1 Chr 8:2

NOISE (27)
When Joshua heard the **n** of the people Ex 32:17
"There is a **n** of war in the camp." Ex 32:17
Philistines heard the **n** of the shouting, 1 Sm 4:6
so that the earth was split by their **n**. 1 Kgs 1:40
This is the **n** that you have heard. 1 Kgs 1:45
Athaliah heard the **n** of the guard 2 Kgs 11:13
Athaliah heard the **n** of the people 2 Chr 23:12
because of the **n** of the enemy, because of Ps 55:3
let us make a joyful **n** to the rock of our Ps 95:1
let us make a joyful **n** to him with songs Ps 95:2
Make a joyful **n** to the LORD, all the earth; Ps 98:4
horn make a joyful **n** before the King, Ps 98:6
Make a joyful **n** to the LORD, all the Ps 100:1
is stilled, the **n** of the jubilant has ceased, Is 24:8
place. You subdue the **n** of the foreigners; Is 25:5
and with earthquake and great **n**, Is 29:6
by their shouting or daunted at their **n**, Is 31:4
At the tumultuous **n** peoples flee; when Is 33:3
At the **n** of horseman and archer every Jer 4:29
At the **n** of the stamping of the hoofs of Jer 47:3
The **n** of battle is in the land, and great Jer 50:22
The **n** of great destruction from the Jer 51:54
waters; the **n** of their voice is raised, Jer 51:55
will shake at the **n** of the horsemen Ezk 26:10
away from me the **n** of your songs; Am 5:23
and the **n** of their wings was like the noise Rv 9:9
wings was like the **n** of many chariots Rv 9:9

NOISY (4)
at the head of the **n** streets she cries out; Prv 1:21
Egypt, '**N** one who lets the hour go by.' Jer 46:17
in its pasture, a **n** multitude of men. Mi 2:12
I am a **n** gong or a clanging cymbal. 1 Cor 13:1

NOMADS (1)
and **n** shall eat among the ruins of the Is 5:17

NONE (263)
N of us will withhold from you his Gn 23:6
This is **n** other than the house of God, Gn 28:17
to do his work and **n** of the men of the Gn 39:11
but there was **n** who could interpret Gn 41:8
there is **n** so discerning and wise as Gn 41:39
may know that there is **n** like me in all Ex 9:14
And you shall let **n** of it remain until Ex 12:10
N of you shall go out of the door of his Ex 12:22
I will put **n** of the diseases on you that I Ex 15:26
which is a Sabbath, there will be **n**." Ex 16:26
went out to gather, but they found **n**. Ex 16:27
N shall appear before me Ex 23:15
N shall miscarry or be barren in your Ex 23:26
And **n** shall appear before me Ex 34:20
"**N** of you shall approach any one of his Lv 18:6
rules and do **n** of these abominations, Lv 18:26
N of your offspring throughout their Lv 21:17
N of the offspring of Aaron who has a Lv 22:4
you shall leave **n** of it until morning: Lv 22:30
lie down, and **n** shall make you afraid. Lv 26:6
and you shall flee when **n** pursues you. Lv 26:17
and they shall fall when **n** pursues. Lv 26:36
if to escape a sword, though **n** pursues. Lv 26:37
But to the sons of Kohath he gave **n**, Nm 7:9
They shall leave **n** of it until the Nm 9:12
n of the men who have seen my glory Nm 14:22
And **n** of those who despised me shall Nm 14:23
'Surely **n** of the men who came up out Nm 32:11
n except Caleb the son of Jephunneh Nm 32:12
and **n** of the evil diseases of Egypt, Dt 7:15
N of the devoted things shall stick to Dt 13:17
n of his descendants may enter the Dt 23:2
n of them may enter the assembly of the Dt 23:3
"**N** of the daughters of Israel shall be a Dt 23:17
and **n** of the sons of Israel shall be a Dt 23:17
power is gone and there is **n** remaining, Dt 32:36
and there is **n** that can deliver out of my Dt 32:39
"There is **n** like God, O Jeshurun, who Dt 33:26
n like him for all the signs and the Dt 34:11
of Israel. **N** went out, and none came in. Jos 6:1
of Israel. None went out, and **n** came in. Jos 6:1
until there was left **n** that survived or Jos 8:22
every person in it; he left **n** remaining. Jos 10:28
person in it; he left **n** remaining in it. Jos 10:30
his people, until he left **n** remaining. Jos 10:33
He left **n** remaining, as he had done to Jos 10:37
every person in it; he left **n** remaining. Jos 10:39
He left **n** remaining, but devoted to Jos 10:40
struck them until he left **n** remaining. Jos 11:8
there was **n** left that breathed. Jos 11:11
But **n** of the cities that stood on Jos 11:13
There was **n** of the Anakim left in the Jos 11:22
man, saying, "**N** of us will go to his tent, Jgs 20:8
tent, and **n** of us will return to his house. Jgs 20:8
"There is **n** holy like the LORD; there is 1 Sm 2:2
like the LORD; there is **n** besides you; 1 Sm 2:2
with him and let **n** of his words fall 1 Sm 3:19
There is **n** like him among all the 1 Sm 10:24
on my enemies." So **n** of the people 1 Sm 14:24
for there is **n** but that here." And 1 Sm 21:9
And David said, "There is **n** like that; 1 Sm 21:9
N of you is sorry for me or discloses to 1 Sm 22:8
For there is **n** like you, and there is no 2 Sm 7:22
They looked, but there was **n** to save; 2 Sm 22:42
so that **n** like you has been before 1 Kgs 3:12
been before you and **n** like you shall 1 Kgs 3:12
N were of silver; silver was not 1 Kgs 10:21
There was **n** that followed the house 1 Kgs 12:20
to all Judah, **n** was exempt, 1 Kgs 15:22
(There was **n** who sold himself to do 1 Kgs 21:25
I will receive **n**." And he urged him to 2 Kgs 5:16
one of his servants said, "**N**, my lord, 2 Kgs 6:12
and **n** shall bury her." Then he 2 Kgs 9:10
until he left him **n** remaining. 2 Kgs 10:11
persons, and he spared **n** of them. 2 Kgs 10:14
Let **n** be missing, for I have a great 2 Kgs 10:19
was very bitter, for there was **n** left, 2 Kgs 14:26
free, and there was **n** to help Israel. 2 Kgs 14:26
N was left but the tribe of Judah 2 Kgs 17:18
so that there was **n** like him among 2 Kgs 18:5
N remained, except the poorest 2 Kgs 24:14
There is **n** like you, O LORD, and 1 Chr 17:20
such as **n** of the kings had who were 2 Chr 1:12
and **n** after you shall have the like." 2 Chr 1:12
"O LORD, there is **n** like you to help, 2 Chr 14:11
fell until **n** remained alive, 2 Chr 14:13
so that **n** is able to withstand you. 2 Chr 20:6
lying on the ground; **n** had escaped. 2 Chr 20:24
N of the kings of Israel had kept 2 Chr 35:18
I found there **n** of the sons of Levi. Ezr 8:15
for **n** can stand before you because of Ezr 9:15
me, **n** of us took off our clothes; Neh 4:23
Job, that there is **n** like him on the earth, Jb 1:8
Job, that there is **n** like him on the earth, Jb 2:3
let it hope for light, but have **n**, nor see the Jb 3:9
and there is **n** to deliver out of your Jb 10:7
lie down, and **n** will make you afraid; Jb 11:19
If he tears down, **n** can rebuild; if he Jb 12:14
if he shuts a man in, **n** can open. Jb 12:14
cities, in houses that **n** should inhabit, Jb 15:28
In his tent dwells that which is **n** of his; Jb 18:15
the fatherless who had **n** to help him. Jb 29:12
there was **n** among you who refuted Job Jb 32:12
'He will answer **n** of man's words'? Jb 33:13
But **n** says, 'Where is God my Maker, Jb 35:10
rending it in pieces, with **n** to deliver. Ps 7:2
wickedness to account till you find **n**. Ps 10:15
deeds, there is **n** who does good. Ps 14:1
there is **n** who does good, not even one. Ps 14:3
cried for help, but there was **n** to save; Ps 18:41
trouble is near, and there is **n** to help. Ps 22:11
n who wait for you shall be put to Ps 25:3
n of those who take refuge in him will Ps 34:22
toward us; **n** can compare with you! Ps 40:5
tear you apart, and there be **n** to deliver! Ps 50:22
iniquity; there is **n** who does good. Ps 53:1
there is **n** who does good, not even one. Ps 53:3
spare **n** of those who treacherously plot Ps 59:5
I looked for pity, but there was **n**, and Ps 69:20
none, and for comforters, but I found **n**. Ps 69:20
seize him, for there is **n** to deliver him." Ps 71:11
and there is **n** among us who knows how Ps 74:9
There is **n** like you among the gods, O Ps 86:8
and there was **n** among his tribes who Ps 105:37
labor; they fell down, with **n** to help. Ps 107:12
Let there be **n** to extend kindness to Ps 109:12
me, when as yet there were **n** of them. Ps 139:16
see: there is **n** who takes notice of me; Ps 142:4
and would have **n** of my reproof, Prv 1:25
would have **n** of my counsel and Prv 1:30
n who go to her come back, nor do they Prv 2:19
n who touches her will go unpunished. Prv 6:29
I would kiss you, and **n** would despise me. Sg 8:1
burn together, with **n** to quench them. Is 1:31
N is weary, none stumbles, none Is 5:27
None is weary, **n** stumbles, none Is 5:27
none stumbles, **n** slumbers or sleeps, Is 5:27
prey; they carry it off, and **n** can rescue. Is 5:29
and there was **n** that moved a wing or Is 10:14
or like sheep with **n** to gather them, Is 13:14
lie down, and **n** will make them afraid. Is 17:2
He shall open, and **n** shall shut; and he Is 22:22
and he shall shut, and **n** shall open. Is 22:22
house is shut up so that **n** can enter. Is 24:10
you traitor, whom **n** has betrayed! Is 33:1
n shall pass through it forever and ever. Is 34:10
be missing; **n** shall be without her mate. Is 34:16
and needy seek water, and there is **n**, Is 41:17
There was **n** who declared it, none who Is 41:26
none who declared it, **n** who proclaimed, Is 41:26
proclaimed, **n** who heard your words. Is 41:26
have become plunder with **n** to rescue, Is 42:22
with none to rescue, spoil with **n** to say, Is 42:22
there is **n** who can deliver from my Is 43:13
from the west, that there is **n** besides me; Is 45:6
God and a Savior; there is **n** besides me. Is 45:21
no other; I am God, and there is **n** like me, Is 46:9
There is **n** to guide her among all the Is 51:18
there is **n** to take her by the hand among Is 51:18
doves; we hope for justice, but there is **n**; Is 59:11
darkness, in a land that **n** passes through, Jer 2:6
N who seek her need weary themselves; Jer 2:24
like fire, and burn with **n** to quench it, Jer 4:4
the earth, and **n** will frighten them away. Jer 7:33
the reaper, and **n** shall gather them.'" Jer 9:22
There is **n** like you, O LORD; you are Jer 10:6
in all their kingdoms there is **n** like you. Jer 10:7
and **n** of them shall be left. For I will Jer 11:23
are shut up, with **n** to open them; Jer 13:19
sword, with **n** to bury them—them, Jer 14:16
like fire, and burn with **n** to quench it, Jer 21:12
for **n** of his offspring shall succeed in Jer 22:30
That day is so great there is **n** like it; it is Jer 30:7
and ease, and **n** shall make him afraid. Jer 30:10
There is **n** to uphold your cause, no Jer 30:13
been kept, and they drink **n** to this day, Jer 35:14
He shall have **n** to sit on the throne of Jer 36:30
so that **n** of the remnant of Judah who Jer 44:14
and ease, and **n** shall make him afraid. Jer 46:27
him, with **n** to gather the fugitives. Jer 49:5
land a desolation, and **n** shall dwell in it; Jer 50:3
sought in Israel, and there shall be **n**. Jer 50:20
And sin in Judah, and **n** shall be found, Jer 50:20
and fall, with **n** to raise him up, Jer 50:32
all her lovers she has **n** to comfort her; Lam 1:2
Zion mourn, for **n** come to the festival; Lam 1:4
of the foe, and there was **n** to help her, Lam 1:7
hands, but there is **n** to comfort her; Lam 1:17
there is **n** to deliver us from their hand. Lam 5:8
N of them shall remain, nor their Ezk 7:11
of his iniquity, **n** can maintain his life. Ezk 7:13
everything ready, but **n** goes to battle, Ezk 7:14
will seek peace, but there shall be **n**. Ezk 7:25
N of my words will be delayed any Ezk 12:28
he himself did **n** of these things), Ezk 18:11
N of the transgressions that he has Ezk 18:22
N of the righteous deeds that he has Ezk 18:24
N of them cast away the detestable Ezk 20:8
I should not destroy it, but I found **n**. Ezk 22:30
n of his righteous deeds shall be Ezk 33:13
N of the sins that he has committed Ezk 33:16
so desolate that **n** will pass through. Ezk 33:28
earth, with **n** to search or seek for them. Ezk 34:6
and **n** shall make them afraid. Ezk 34:28
in their land with **n** to make them Ezk 39:26
I will leave **n** of them remaining Ezk 39:28
so that **n** of my people shall be Ezk 46:18
among all of them **n** was found like Dn 1:19

and **n** can stay his hand or say to him, Dn 4:35
there is **n** who contends by my side Dn 10:21
he wills, and **n** shall stand before him. Dn 11:16
come to his end, with **n** to help him. Dn 11:45
And **n** of the wicked shall understand, Dn 12:10
Yet let no one contend, and let **n** accuse, Hos 4:4
fallen, and **n** of them calls upon me. Hos 7:7
I will bereave them till **n** is left. Hos 9:12
I am the LORD your God and there is **n** else. Jl 2:27
on her land, with **n** to raise her up." Am 5:2
it devour, with **n** to quench it for Bethel, Am 5:6
Therefore you will have **n** to cast the line Mi 2:5
tears in pieces, and there is **n** to deliver. Mi 5:8
"Halt! Halt!" they cry, but **n** turns back. Na 2:8
where his cubs were, with **n** to disturb? Na 2:11
the mountains with **n** to gather them. Na 3:18
down, and **n** shall make them afraid." Zep 3:13
and let **n** of you devise evil against Zec 7:10
a guard, so that **n** shall march to and fro; Zec 9:8
and I will deliver **n** from their hand." Zec 11:6
and let **n** of you be faithless to the wife Mal 2:15
places seeking rest, but finds **n**. Mt 12:43
but they found **n**, though many false Mt 26:60
to put him to death, but they found **n**. Mk 14:55
"**N** of your relatives is called by this Lk 1:61
tunics is to share with him who has **n**, Lk 3:11
Elijah was sent to **n** of them but only Lk 4:26
Elisha, and **n** of them was cleansed, Lk 4:27
those born of women **n** is greater than Lk 7:28
seeking rest, and finding **n** it says, Lk 11:24
he came seeking fruit on it and found **n**. Lk 13:6
seeking fruit on this fig tree, and I find **n**. Lk 13:7
n of those men who were invited shall Lk 14:24
able, and **n** may cross from there to us.' Lk 16:26
But they understood **n** of these things. Lk 18:34
which **n** of your adversaries will be Lk 21:15
you the law? Yet **n** of you keeps the law. Jn 7:19
him who sent me, and **n** of you asks me, Jn 16:5
have breakfast." Now **n** of the disciples Jn 21:12
N of the rest dared join them, but the Acts 5:13
I know that **n** of you among whom I Acts 20:25
and that **n** of his friends should be Acts 24:23
I am persuaded that **n** of these things Acts 26:26
and **n** of the brothers coming here Acts 28:21
is written: "**N** is righteous, no, not one; Rom 3:10
For **n** of us lives to himself, and none Rom 14:7
to himself, and **n** of us dies to himself. Rom 14:7
God that I baptized **n** of you except 1 Cor 1:14
N of the rulers of this age understood 1 Cor 2:8
that **n** of you may be puffed up in 1 Cor 4:6
have wives live as though they had **n**, 1 Cor 7:29
world, and **n** is without meaning, 1 Cor 14:10
But I saw **n** of the other apostles except Gal 1:19
is called "today," that **n** of you may be Heb 3:13
But let **n** of you suffer as a murderer or 1 Pt 4:15

NONSENSE (2)
For the household gods utter **n**, and the Zec 10:2
is doing, talking wicked **n** against us. 3 Jn 1:10

NOON (15)
for the men are to dine with me at **n**." Gn 43:16
the present for Joseph's coming at **n**, Gn 43:25
name of Baal from morning until **n**, 1 Kgs 18:26
And at **n** Elijah mocked them, 1 Kgs 18:27
And they went out at **n**, while 1 Kgs 20:16
mother, the child sat on her lap till **n**, 2 Kgs 4:20
and morning and at **n** I utter my Ps 55:17
flock, where you make it lie down at **n**; Sg 1:7
your shade like night at the height of **n**; Is 16:3
we stumble at **n** as in the twilight, Is 59:10
against her; arise, and let us attack at **n**! Jer 6:4
cry in the morning and an alarm at **n**, Jer 20:16
sun go down at **n** and darken the earth Am 8:9
Ashdod's people shall be driven out at **n**, Zep 2:4
about **n** a great light from heaven Acts 22:6

NOONDAY (8)
and you shall grope at **n**, as the blind Dt 28:29
Ish-bosheth as he was taking his **n** rest. 2 Sm 4:5
daytime and grope at **n** as in the night. Jb 5:14
your life will be brighter than the **n**; Jb 11:17
as the light, and your justice as the **n**. Ps 37:6
nor the destruction that wastes at **n**. Ps 91:6
darkness and your gloom be as the **n**. Is 58:10
mothers of young men a destroyer at **n**; Jer 15:8

NOPHAH (1)
and we laid waste as far as **N**; Nm 21:30

NORMAL (1)
sea returned to its **n** course when the Ex 14:27

NORTH (149)
them to Hobah, **n** of Damascus. Gn 14:15
the east and to the **n** and to the south, Gn 28:14
tabernacle, on the **n** side twenty frames, Ex 26:20
you shall put the table on the **n** side. Ex 26:35
its length on the **n** side there shall be Ex 27:11
side of the tabernacle, on the **n** side, Ex 36:25
And for the **n** side there were hangings Ex 38:11
meeting, on the **n** side of the tabernacle, Ex 40:22
shall kill it on the **n** side of the altar Lv 1:11
"On the **n** side shall be the standard of Nm 2:25
to camp on the **n** side of the tabernacle. Nm 3:35
and on the **n** side two thousand cubits, Nm 35:5
city and encamped on the **n** side of Ai, Jos 8:11
encampment that was **n** of the city Jos 8:13
the boundary on the **n** side runs from Jos 15:5
and passes along **n** of Beth-arabah. Jos 15:6
to the shoulder of the hill **n** of Ekron, Jos 15:11
to the sea. On the **n** is Michmethath. Jos 16:6
Manasseh goes on the **n** side of the Jos 17:9
and that to the **n** being Manasseh's, Jos 17:10
On the **n** Asher is reached, and on the Jos 17:10
continue in their territory on the **n**. Jos 18:5
On the **n** side their boundary began at Jos 18:12
goes up to the shoulder **n** of Jericho, Jos 18:12
which is at the **n** end of the Valley of Jos 18:16
passing on to the **n** of the shoulder of Jos 18:18
passes on to the **n** of the shoulder of Jos 18:19
then on the **n** the boundary turns Jos 19:14
Then it continues in the **n** to Cabul, Jos 19:27
Ephraim, **n** of the mountain of Gaash. Jos 24:30
of Ephraim, **n** of the mountain of Gaash. Jgs 2:9
And the camp of Midian was **n** of them, Jgs 7:1
the LORD at Shiloh, which is **n** of Bethel, Jgs 21:19
crag rose on the **n** in front of 1 Sm 14:5
the pillar on the **n** and called its 1 Kgs 7:21
stood on twelve oxen, three facing **n**, 1 Kgs 7:25
and five on the **n** side of the house. 1 Kgs 7:39
on the south side and five on the **n**, 1 Kgs 7:49
the house to the **n** side of the house, 2 Kgs 11:11
and put it on the **n** side of his altar. 2 Kgs 16:14
the four sides, east, west, **n**, and south. 1 Chr 9:24
and his lot came out for the **n**. 1 Chr 26:14
six each day, on the **n** four each day, 1 Chr 26:17
one on the south, the other on the **n**; 2 Chr 3:17
called Jachin, and that on the **n** Boaz. 2 Chr 3:17
It stood on twelve oxen, three facing **n**, 2 Chr 4:4
the south side, and five on the **n** side. 2 Chr 4:6
five on the south side and five on the **n**. 2 Chr 4:7
five on the south side and five on the **n**. 2 Chr 4:8
the house to the **n** side of the house, 2 Chr 23:10
those who gave thanks went to the **n**, Neh 12:38
He stretches out the **n** over the void and Jb 26:7
Out of the **n** comes golden splendor; Jb 37:22
of all the earth, Mount Zion, in the far **n**, Ps 48:2
The **n** and the south, you have created Ps 89:12
the west, from the **n** and from the south. Ps 107:3
The **n** wind brings forth rain, and a Prv 25:23
to the south and goes around to the **n**; Eccl 1:6
if a tree falls to the south or to the **n**, Eccl 11:3
Awake, O **n** wind, and come, O south Sg 4:16
of assembly in the far reaches of the **n**; Is 14:13
For smoke comes out of the **n**, and there Is 14:31
I stirred up one from the **n**, and he has Is 41:25
I will say to the **n**, Give up, and to the Is 43:6
these from the **n** and from the west, Is 49:12
a boiling pot, facing away from the **n**." Jer 1:13
"Out of the **n** disaster shall be let loose Jer 1:14
all the tribes of the kingdoms of the **n**, Jer 1:15
and proclaim these words toward the **n**, Jer 3:12
from the land of the **n** to the land that I Jer 3:18
stay not, for I bring disaster from the **n**, Jer 4:6
for disaster looms out of the **n**, Jer 6:1
a people is coming from the **n** country, Jer 6:22
out of the **n** country to make Jer 10:22
and see those who come from the **n**. Jer 13:20
Can one break iron, iron from the **n**, Jer 15:12
of Israel out of the **n** country and out of Jer 16:15
of Israel out of the **n** country and out of Jer 23:8
I will send for all the tribes of the **n**, Jer 25:9
all the kings of the **n**, far and near, one Jer 25:26
them from the **n** country and gather Jer 31:8
in the **n** by the river Euphrates they have Jer 46:6
a sacrifice in the **n** country by the river Jer 46:10
biting fly from the **n** has come upon Jer 46:20
into the hand of a people from the **n**." Jer 46:24
Behold, waters are rising out of the **n**, Jer 47:2
"For out of the **n** a nation has come up Jer 50:3
of great nations, from the **n** country. Jer 50:9
"Behold, a people comes from the **n**; a Jer 50:41
shall come against them out of the **n**, Jer 51:48
behold, a stormy wind came out of the **n**, Ezk 1:4
gateway of the inner court that faces **n**, Ezk 8:3
eyes now toward the **n**." So I lifted up Ezk 8:5
So I lifted up my eyes toward the **n**, Ezk 8:5
the north, and behold, **n** of the altar gate, Ezk 8:5
the entrance of the **n** gate of the house Ezk 8:14
of the upper gate, which faces **n**, Ezk 9:2
with her daughters to the **n** of you; Ezk 16:46
from south to **n** shall be scorched Ezk 20:47
against all flesh from south to **n**. Ezk 21:4
you from the **n** with chariots and Ezk 23:24
Tyre from the **n** Nebuchadnezzar king Ezk 26:7
"The princes of the **n** are there, all of Ezk 32:30
uttermost parts of the **n** with all his Ezk 38:6
out of the uttermost parts of the **n**, Ezk 38:15
up from the uttermost parts of the **n**, Ezk 39:2
on the east side and on the **n** side. Ezk 40:19
As for the gate that faced toward the **n**, Ezk 40:20
And opposite the gate on the **n**, as on Ezk 40:23
Then he brought me to the **n** gate, and Ezk 40:35
goes up to the entrance of the **n** gate, Ezk 40:40
at the side of the **n** gate facing south, Ezk 40:44
at the side of the south gate facing **n**. Ezk 40:44
the chamber that faces **n** is for the Ezk 40:46
the free space, one door toward the **n**, Ezk 41:11
out into the outer court, toward the **n**, Ezk 42:1
and opposite the building on the **n**. Ezk 42:1
whose door faced **n** was a hundred Ezk 42:2
long, and their doors were on the **n**. Ezk 42:4
similar to the chambers on the **n**, Ezk 42:11
"The **n** chambers and the south Ezk 42:13
He measured the **n** side, 500 cubits by Ezk 42:17
me by way of the **n** gate to the front of Ezk 44:4
who enters by the **n** gate to worship Ezk 46:9
south gate shall go out by the **n** gate: Ezk 46:9
to the **n** row of the holy chambers for Ezk 46:19
out by way of the **n** gate and led me Ezk 47:2
On the **n** side, from the Great Sea by Ezk 47:15
with the border of Hamath to the **n**. Ezk 47:17
to the north. This shall be the **n** side. Ezk 47:17
the **n** side 4,500 cubits, the south side Ezk 48:16
have open land: on the **n** 250 cubits, Ezk 48:17
On the **n** side, which is to be 4,500 Ezk 48:30
the king of the **n** to make an agreement. Dn 11:6
enter the fortress of the king of the **n**, Dn 11:7
refrain from attacking the king of the **n**. Dn 11:8
out and fight with the king of the **n**. Dn 11:11
the king of the **n** shall again raise a Dn 11:13
the king of the **n** shall come and throw Dn 11:15
the king of the **n** shall rush upon him Dn 11:40
the east and the **n** shall alarm him, Dn 11:44
from sea to sea, and from **n** to east; Am 8:12
hand against the **n** and destroy Assyria, Zep 2:13
Flee from the land of the **n**, declares the Zec 2:6
black horses goes toward the **n** country, Zec 6:6
who go toward the **n** country have set Zec 6:8
set my Spirit at rest in the **n** country." Zec 6:8
east and west, and from **n** and south, Lk 13:29
the east three gates, on the **n** three gates, Rv 21:13

NORTHEASTER (1)
a tempestuous wind, called the **n**, Acts 27:14

NORTHERLY (1)
it bends in a **n** direction going on to Jos 18:17

NORTHERN (10)
"This shall be your **n** border: from the Nm 34:7
This shall be your **n** border. Nm 34:9
kings who were in the **n** hill country, Jos 11:2
at the **n** end of the Valley of Rephaim. Jos 15:8
along to the **n** shoulder of Mount Jos 15:10
boundary ends at the **n** bay of the Salt Jos 18:19
is on the **n** border of Damascus, Ezk 47:17
Beginning at the **n** extreme, beside the Ezk 48:1
(which is on the **n** border of Damascus Ezk 48:1
25,000 cubits on the **n** side, Ezk 48:10

NORTHERNER (1)
"I will remove the **n** far from you, and Jl 2:20

NORTHWARD (8)
n and southward and eastward and Gn 13:14
mountain country long enough. Turn **n** Dt 2:3
eyes westward and **n** and southward and Dt 3:27
of Egypt, **n** to the boundary of Ekron, Jos 13:3
from the Valley of Achor, and so **n**, Jos 15:7
Valley of Iphtahel **n** to Beth-emek and Jos 19:27
westward and **n** and southward. Dn 8:4
one half of the Mount shall move **n**, Zec 14:4

NORTHWEST (1)
Crete, facing both southwest and **n**, Acts 27:12

NOSE (11)
the ring on her **n** and the bracelets on Gn 24:47
my hook in your **n** and my bit in 2 Kgs 19:28
by his eyes, or pierce his **n** with a snare? Jb 40:24
put a rope in his **n** or pierce his jaw with Jb 41:2
curds, pressing the **n** produces blood, Prv 30:33
Your **n** is like a tower of Lebanon, which Sg 7:4
the signet rings and **n** rings; Is 3:21
put my hook in your **n** and my bit in Is 37:29
Behold, they put the branch to their **n**. Ezk 8:17
a ring on your **n** and earrings in your Ezk 16:12
shall cut off your **n** and your ears, Ezk 23:25

NOSES (1)
but do not hear; **n**, but do not smell. Ps 115:6

NOSTRILS (14)
and breathed into his **n** the breath of life, Gn 2:7
dry land in whose **n** was the breath of Gn 7:22
At the blast of your **n** the waters piled up; Ex 15:8
out at your **n** and becomes loathsome Nm 11:20
Smoke went up from his **n**, and 2 Sm 22:9
at the blast of the breath of his **n**. 2 Sm 22:16
is in me, and the spirit of God is in my **n**, Jb 27:3
Out of his **n** comes forth smoke, as Jb 41:20
Smoke went up from his **n**, and Ps 18:8
at the blast of the breath of your **n**. Ps 18:15
Stop regarding man in whose **n** is breath, Is 2:22
holy for you." These are a smoke in my **n**, Is 65:5
The breath of our **n**, the LORD'S Lam 4:20
stench of your camp go up into your **n**; Am 4:10

NOTABLE (2)
the **n** men of the first of the nations, Am 6:1
For that a **n** sign has been performed Acts 4:16

NOTE (6)
See therefore and take **n** of all the 1 Sm 23:23
does not take much **n** of transgression, Jb 35:15
do see, for you **n** mischief and vexation, Ps 10:14
the streets of Jerusalem, look and take **n**! Jer 5:1
N then the kindness and the severity Rom 11:22
in this letter, take **n** of that person, 2 Thes 3:14

NOTED (1)
'I have **n** what Amalek did to Israel in 1 Sm 15:2

NOTES (1)
or the harp, do not give distinct **n**, 1 Cor 14:7

NOTHING (297)
And **n** that they propose to do will now Gn 11:6
I will take **n** but what the young men Gn 14:24
Only do **n** to these men, for they have Gn 19:8
for I can do **n** till you arrive there." Gn 19:22
have done to you **n** but good and have Gn 26:29
should you therefore serve me for **n**? Gn 29:15
also I have done **n** that they should put Gn 40:15
There is **n** left in the sight of my lord Gn 47:18
so that **n** of all that belongs to the people Ex 9:4
You shall eat **n** leavened; in all your Ex 12:20
whoever gathered much had **n** left over, Ex 16:18
in the seventh he shall go out free, for **n**. Ex 21:2
things for her, she shall go out for **n**, Ex 21:11
If he has **n**, then he shall be sold for his Ex 22:3
he shall eat **n** that is produced Nm 6:4
the fish we ate in Egypt that cost **n**, Nm 11:5
and there is **n** at all but this manna to Nm 11:6
wicked men, and touch **n** of theirs, Nm 16:26
only pass through on foot, **n** more." Nm 20:19
'Let **n** hinder you from coming to me, Nm 22:16
you have done **n** but bless them." Nm 23:11
has bound herself and says **n** to her, Nm 30:4
hears of it and says **n** to her on the day Nm 30:7
heard of it and said **n** to her and did Nm 30:11
if her husband says **n** to her from day Nm 30:14
because he said **n** to her on the day Nm 30:14
has been with you. You have lacked **n**.'" Dt 2:7
scarcity, in which you will lack **n**, Dt 8:9
your poor brother, and you give him **n**, Dt 15:9
you shall save alive **n** that breathes, Dt 20:16
But you shall do **n** to the young Dt 22:26
he is eating, because he has **n** else left, Dt 28:55
and salt, **n** sown and nothing growing, Dt 29:23
and salt, nothing sown and **n** growing, Dt 29:23
searched all along the way and found **n**. Jos 2:22
He left **n** undone of all that the LORD Jos 11:15
wine or strong drink, and eat **n** unclean, Jgs 13:4
wine or strong drink, and eat **n** unclean, Jgs 13:7
and although he had **n** in his hand, Jgs 14:6
lacking **n** that is in the earth and Jgs 18:7
it is very good. And will you do **n**? Jgs 18:9
him everything and hid **n** from him. 1 Sm 3:18
us! For **n** like this has happened before. 1 Sm 4:7
for **n** can hinder the LORD from saving 1 Sm 14:6
my father does **n** either great or small 1 Sm 20:2
But the boy knew **n**. Only Jonathan 1 Sm 20:39
your servant has known **n** of all this, 1 Sm 22:15
and they missed **n** all the time they 1 Sm 25:7
so that **n** was missed of all that 1 Sm 25:21
So she told him **n** at all until the 1 Sm 25:36
There is **n** better for me than that I 1 Sm 27:1
for he had eaten **n** all day and all 1 Sm 28:20
For I have found **n** wrong in you from 1 Sm 29:6
N was missing, whether small or 1 Sm 30:19
the poor man had **n** but one little ewe 2 Sm 12:3
went in their innocence and knew **n**. 2 Sm 15:11
grain on it, and **n** was known of it. 2 Sm 17:19
life (and there is **n** hidden from the 2 Sm 18:13
and servants are **n** to you, 2 Sm 19:6
do you say **n** about bringing the 2 Sm 19:10
that cost me **n**." So David bought 2 Sm 24:24
in his month. They let **n** be lacking. 1 Kgs 4:27
There was **n** in the ark except the two 1 Kgs 8:9
there was **n** hidden from the king 1 Kgs 10:3
LORD your God lives, I have **n** baked, 1 Kgs 17:12
and said, "There is **n**." And he said, 1 Kgs 18:43
you speak to me **n** but the truth in 1 Kgs 22:16
"Your servant has **n** in the house 2 Kgs 4:2
n but the horses tied and the donkeys 2 Kgs 7:10
fall to the earth **n** of the word of 2 Kgs 10:10
There was **n** in his house or in all 2 Kgs 20:13
there is **n** in my storehouses that I 2 Kgs 20:15
N shall be left, says the LORD. 2 Kgs 20:17
burnt offerings that cost me **n**." 1 Chr 21:24
There was **n** in the ark except the two 2 Chr 5:10
There was **n** hidden from Solomon 2 Chr 9:2
N like it was ever made for any 2 Chr 9:19
you speak to me **n** but the truth in 2 Chr 18:15
Israel there had been **n** like this in 2 Chr 30:26
"You have **n** to do with us in building a Ezr 4:3
This is **n** but sadness of the heart." Neh 2:2
restore these and require **n** from them. Neh 5:12
portions to anyone who has **n** ready, Neh 8:10
in the wilderness, and they lacked **n**. Neh 9:21
she asked for **n** except what Hegai the Est 2:15
Yet all this is worth **n** to me, so long as I Est 5:13
him said, "**N** has been done for him." Est 6:3
Leave out **n** that you have mentioned." Est 6:10
you shall inspect your fold and miss **n**. Jb 5:24
For you have now become **n**; you see my Jb 6:21
For we are but of yesterday and know **n**, Jb 8:9
There was **n** left after he had eaten; Jb 20:21
There is **n** left of your answers but Jb 21:34
of your brothers for **n** and stripped the Jb 22:6
and show that there is **n** in what I say?" Jb 24:25
over the void and hangs the earth on **n**. Jb 26:7
'It profits a man **n** that he should take Jb 34:9
you have tested me, and you will find **n**; Ps 17:3
them, and there is **n** hidden from its heat. Ps 19:6
brings the counsel of the nations to **n**; Ps 33:10
and my lifetime is as **n** before you. Ps 39:5
Surely for **n** they are in turmoil; man Ps 39:6
For when he dies he will carry **n** away; Ps 49:17
And there is **n** on earth that I desire Ps 73:25
be far from me; I will know **n** of evil. Ps 101:4
your law; **n** can make them stumble. Ps 119:165
and **n** you desire can compare with her. Prv 3:15
there is **n** twisted or crooked in them. Prv 8:8
is loud; she is seductive and knows **n**. Prv 9:13
soul of the sluggard craves and gets **n**, Prv 13:4
One pretends to be rich, yet has **n**; Prv 13:7
By insolence comes **n** but strife, but Prv 13:10
he will seek at harvest and have **n**. Prv 20:4
If you have **n** with which to pay, why Prv 22:27
life; he hears the curse, but discloses **n**. Prv 29:24
done, and there is **n** new under the sun. Eccl 1:9
and there was **n** to be gained under the Eccl 2:11
There is **n** better for a person than that Eccl 2:24
that there is **n** better for them Eccl 3:12
n can be added to it, nor anything Eccl 3:14
I saw that there is **n** better than that a Eccl 3:22
of a son, but he has **n** in his hand. Eccl 5:14
and shall take **n** for his toil that he Eccl 5:15
so that he lacks **n** of all that he desires, Eccl 6:2
that they will die, but the dead know **n**, Eccl 9:5
counsel together, but it will come to **n**; Is 8:10
N remains but to crouch among the Is 10:4
And there will be **n** for Egypt that head Is 19:15
ruthless shall come to **n** and the scoffer Is 29:20
kingdom, and all its princes shall be **n**. Is 34:12
There was **n** in his house or in all his Is 39:2
There is **n** in my storehouses that I did Is 39:4
to Babylon. **N** shall be left, says the LORD. Is 39:6
All the nations are as **n** before him, they Is 40:17
by him as less than **n** and emptiness. Is 40:17
who brings princes to **n**, and makes the Is 40:23
you shall be as **n** and shall perish. Is 41:11
who war against you shall be as **n** at all. Is 41:12
Behold, you are **n**, and your work is less Is 41:24
nothing, and your work is less than **n**; Is 41:24
they are all a delusion; their works are **n**; Is 41:29
All who fashion idols are **n**, and the Is 44:9
or casts an idol that is profitable for **n**? Is 44:10
you suddenly, of which you know **n**. Is 47:11
I have spent my strength for **n** and vanity; Is 49:4
"You were sold for **n**, and you shall be Is 52:3
and the Assyrian oppressed them for **n**. Is 52:4
that my people are taken away for **n**? Is 52:5
of the LORD and have said, 'He will do **n**; Jer 5:12
there is **n** but oppression within her. Jer 6:6
in your anger, lest you bring me to **n**. Jer 10:24
have tired themselves out but profit **n**. Jer 12:13
loincloth was spoiled; it was good for **n**. Jer 13:7
like this loincloth, which is good for **n**. Jer 13:10
"Our fathers have inherited **n** but lies, Jer 16:19
neighbor serve him for **n** and does not Jer 22:13
have forgotten you; they care **n** for you; Jer 30:14
arm! **N** is too hard for you. Jer 32:17
They did **n** of all you commanded Jer 32:23
of Judah have done **n** but evil in my Jer 32:30
of Israel have done **n** but provoke me to Jer 32:30
for the king can do **n** against you." Jer 38:5
ask you a question; hide **n** from me." Jer 38:14
hide **n** from us and we will not put you Jer 38:25
some of the poor people who owned **n**, Jer 39:10
tell you. I will keep **n** back from you." Jer 42:4
the squares there is **n** but lamentation, Jer 48:38
her to destruction; let **n** be left of her. Jer 50:26
The peoples labor for **n**, and the Jer 51:58
will cut it off, so that **n** shall dwell in it, Jer 51:62
"Is it **n** to you, all you who pass by? Lam 1:12
long, and every vision comes to **n**'? Ezk 12:22
their own spirit, and have seen **n**! Ezk 13:3
when it was whole, it was used for **n**. Ezk 15:5
They shall have **n** of wool on them, Ezk 44:17
of the earth are accounted as **n**, Dn 4:35
that **n** might be changed concerning Dn 6:17
one shall be cut off and shall have **n**. Dn 9:26
in Gilead, they shall surely come to **n**: Hos 12:11
a desolate wilderness, and **n** escapes them. Jl 2:3
cry out from his den, if he has taken **n**? Am 3:4
from the ground, when it has taken **n**? Am 3:5
Lord GOD does **n** without revealing his Am 3:7
into exile, and Bethel shall come to **n**." Am 5:5
him who puts **n** into their mouths. Mi 3:5
and nations weary themselves for **n**? Hab 2:13
wolves that leave **n** till the morning. Zep 3:3
you see it now? Is it not as **n** in your eyes? Hg 2:3
and the olive tree have yielded **n**. Hg 2:19
to him, "See that you say **n** to anyone, Mt 8:4
for **n** is covered that will not be Mt 10:26
he said **n** to them without a parable. Mt 13:34
me now three days and have **n** to eat. Mt 15:32
and **n** will be impossible for you." Mt 17:20
went to it and found **n** on it but only Mt 21:19
'If anyone swears by the temple, it is **n**, Mt 23:16
'If anyone swears by the altar, it is **n**, Mt 23:18
"Have **n** to do with that righteous man, Mt 27:19
when Pilate saw that he was gaining **n**, Mt 27:24
to him, "See that you say **n** to anyone, Mk 1:44
For **n** is hidden except to be made Mk 4:22
charged them to take **n** for their journey Mk 6:8
There is **n** outside a person that by Mk 7:15
had gathered, and they had **n** to eat, Mk 8:1
me now three days and have **n** to eat. Mk 8:2
he came to it, he found **n** but leaves, Mk 11:13
with **n** but a linen cloth about his Mk 14:51
seized them, and they said **n** to anyone, Mk 16:8
For **n** will be impossible with God." Lk 1:37
the devil. And he ate **n** during those days. Lk 4:2
"Master, we toiled all night and took **n**! Lk 5:5
do good, and lend, expecting **n** in return, Lk 6:35
For **n** is hidden that will not be made Lk 8:17
said to them, "Take **n** for your journey, Lk 9:3
of the enemy, and **n** shall hurt you. Lk 10:19
journey, and I have **n** to set before him'; Lk 11:6
N is covered up that will not be revealed, Lk 12:2
and after that have **n** more that they can Lk 12:4
you lack anything?" They said, "**N**." Lk 22:35
n deserving death has been done by Lk 23:15
deeds; but this man has done **n** wrong." Lk 23:41
him, "Sir, you have **n** to draw water with, Jn 4:11
more, that **n** worse may happen to you." Jn 5:14
you, the Son can do **n** of his own accord, Jn 5:19
"I can do **n** on my own. As I hear, I judge, Jn 5:30
leftover fragments, that **n** may be lost." Jn 6:12
that I should lose **n** of all that he has Jn 6:39
speaking openly, and they say **n** to him! Jn 7:26
he, and that I do **n** on my own authority, Jn 8:28
and has **n** to do with the truth, Jn 8:44
"If I glorify myself, my glory is **n**. Jn 8:54
man were not from God, he could do **n**." Jn 9:33
a hired hand and cares **n** for the sheep. Jn 10:13
year, said to them, "You know **n** at all. Jn 11:49
"You see that you are gaining **n**. Jn 12:19
fruit, for apart from me you can do **n**. Jn 15:5
In that day you will ask **n** of me. Truly, Jn 16:23
now you have asked **n** in my name. Jn 16:24
come together. I have said **n** in secret. Jn 18:20
the boat, but that night they caught **n**. Jn 21:3
them, they had **n** to say in opposition. Acts 4:14
him were dispersed and came to **n**. Acts 5:36
that **n** of what you have said may Acts 8:24
his eyes were opened, he saw **n**. Acts 9:8
for **n** common or unclean has ever Acts 11:8
spend their time in **n** except telling or Acts 17:21
Artemis may be counted as **n**, Acts 19:27
you ought to be quiet and do **n** rash. Acts 19:36
know that there is **n** in what they Acts 21:24
"We find **n** wrong in this man. Acts 23:9
but charged with **n** deserving death Acts 23:29
But if there is **n** to their charges Acts 25:11
that he had done **n** deserving death. Acts 25:25

But I have **n** definite to write to my Acts 25:26
saying **n** but what the prophets and Acts 26:22
"This man is doing **n** to deserve death Acts 26:31
and without food, having taken **n**. Acts 27:33
I had done **n** against our people Acts 28:17
the body of sin might be brought to **n**, Rom 6:6
For I know that **n** good dwells in me, Rom 7:18
born and had done **n** either good or Rom 9:11
the Lord Jesus that **n** is unclean in Rom 14:14
are not, to bring to **n** things that are, 1 Cor 1:28
I decided to know **n** among you except 1 Cor 2:2
and humiliate those who have **n**? 1 Cor 11:22
mountains, but have not love, I am **n**. 1 Cor 13:2
burned, but have not love, I gain **n**. 1 Cor 13:3
as having **n**, yet possessing 2 Cor 6:10
gathered much had **n** left over, 2 Cor 8:15
be humiliated—to say **n** of you—for 2 Cor 9:4
Though there is **n** to be gained by it, I 2 Cor 12:1
super-apostles, even though I am **n**. 2 Cor 12:11
who seemed influential added **n** to me. Gal 2:6
thinks he is something, when he is **n**, Gal 6:3
Do **n** from rivalry or conceit, but in Phil 2:3
but made himself **n**, taking the form of Phil 2:7
and bring to **n** by the appearance 2 Thes 2:8
person, and have **n** to do with him, 2 Thes 3:14
and **n** is to be rejected if it is received 1 Tm 4:4
Have **n** to do with irreverent, silly 1 Tm 4:7
prejudging, doing **n** from partiality. 1 Tm 5:21
up with conceit and understands **n**. 1 Tm 6:4
for we brought **n** into the world, and 1 Tm 6:7
Have **n** to do with foolish, ignorant 2 Tm 2:23
to the defiled and unbelieving, **n** is pure; Ti 1:15
to shame, having **n** evil to say about us. Ti 2:8
then twice, have **n** more to do with him, Ti 3:10
on their way; see that they lack **n**. Ti 3:13
preferred to do **n** without your Phlm 1:14
repay it—to say **n** of your owing me Phlm 1:19
to him, he left **n** outside his control. Heb 2:8
that tribe Moses said **n** about priests. Heb 7:14
(for the law made **n** perfect); but on the Heb 7:19
be perfect and complete, lacking in **n**. Jas 1:4
the name, accepting **n** from the Gentiles. 3 Jn 1:7
I am rich, I have prospered, and I need **n**, Rv 3:17
But **n** unclean will ever enter it, nor Rv 21:27

NOTHINGS (1)
will you comfort me with empty **n**? Jb 21:34

NOTICE (9)
your eyes, that you should take **n** of me, Ru 2:10
be the man who took **n** of you." So she Ru 2:19
And all the people took **n** of it, and it 2 Sm 3:36
see: there is none who takes **n** of me; Ps 142:4
but do not **n** the log that is in your own Mt 7:3
but do not **n** the log that is in your own Lk 6:41
giving **n** when the days of Acts 21:26
give **n** to the tribune to bring him Acts 23:15
of these things has escaped his **n**, Acts 26:26

NOTICED (2)
when he **n** how they chose the places of Lk 14:7
land, but they **n** a bay with a beach, Acts 27:39

NOTIFY (1)
We also **n** you that it shall not be Ezr 7:24

NOTORIOUS (1)
had then a **n** prisoner called Barabbas. Mt 27:16

NOURISH (1)
or heal the maimed or **n** the healthy, Zec 11:16

NOURISHED (4)
The waters **n** it; the deep made it grow Ezk 31:4
n and knit together through its joints Col 2:19
in which she is to be **n** for 1,260 days. Rv 12:6
the place where she is to be **n** for a time, Rv 12:14

NOURISHER (1)
a restorer of life and a **n** of your old age, Ru 4:15

NOURISHES (2)
He plants a cedar and the rain **n** it. Is 44:14
his own flesh, but **n** and cherishes it, Eph 5:29

NOURISHING (1)
now share in the **n** root of the olive Rom 11:17

NOWHERE (5)
And he said, "Your servant went **n**." 2 Kgs 5:25
the Son of Man has **n** to lay his head." Mt 8:20
"Go **n** among the Gentiles and enter no Mt 10:5
the Son of Man has **n** to lay his head." Lk 9:58
I do, for I have **n** to store my crops?' Lk 12:17

NULL (3)
husband makes them **n** and void on Nm 30:12
if he makes them **n** and void after he Nm 30:15
faith is **n** and the promise is void. Rom 4:14

NULLIFY (2)
their faithlessness **n** the faithfulness Rom 3:3
I do not **n** the grace of God, for if Gal 2:21

NUMB (1)
of Egypt." And his heart became **n**, Gn 45:26

NUMBER (162)
"Look toward heaven, and **n** the stars, Gn 15:5
if you are able to **n** them." Then he said Gn 15:5
according to the **n** of their dependents. Gn 47:12
But the **n** of bricks that they made in the Ex 5:8
must still deliver the same **n** of bricks." Ex 5:18
by no means reduce your **n** of bricks, Ex 5:19
shall take according to the **n** of persons; Ex 12:4
according to the **n** of the persons that Ex 16:16
land; I will fulfill the **n** of your days. Ex 23:26
his life to the LORD when you **n** them, Ex 30:12
plague among them when you **n** them. Ex 30:12
And their pillars were four in **n**. Their Ex 38:19
according to the **n** of years after Lv 25:15
you according to the **n** of years for Lv 25:15
for it is the **n** of the crops that he is Lv 25:16
his sale shall vary with the **n** of years. Lv 25:50
your livestock and make you few in **n**, Lv 26:22
houses, according to the **n** of names, Nm 1:2
according to the **n** of names from Nm 1:18
houses, according to the **n** of names, Nm 1:20
listed, according to the **n** of names, Nm 1:22
according to the **n** of the names, Nm 1:24
houses, according to the **n** of names, Nm 1:26
houses, according to the **n** of names, Nm 1:28
houses, according to the **n** of names, Nm 1:30
houses, according to the **n** of names, Nm 1:32
houses, according to the **n** of names, Nm 1:34
houses, according to the **n** of names, Nm 1:36
houses, according to the **n** of names, Nm 1:38
houses, according to the **n** of names, Nm 1:40
houses, according to the **n** of names, Nm 1:42
listing according to the **n** of all the Nm 3:22
According to the **n** of all the males, Nm 3:28
listing according to the **n** of all the Nm 3:34
upward, taking the **n** of their names. Nm 3:40
males, according to the **n** of names, Nm 3:43
over and above the **n** of the male Nm 3:46
whom I am **n** six hundred thousand Nm 11:21
in this wilderness, and of all your **n**, Nm 14:29
According to the **n** of the days in Nm 14:34
Moses, with a **n** of the people of Israel, Nm 16:2
more in **n** and more honorable than Nm 22:15
dust of Jacob or **n** the fourth part of Nm 23:10
according to the **n** of names. Nm 26:53
of Gad had a very great **n** of livestock. Nm 32:1
be left few in **n** among the nations where Dt 4:27
you were more in **n** than any other people Dt 7:7
his presence with a **n** of stripes in Dt 25:2
into Egypt and sojourned there, few in **n**, Dt 26:5
of heaven, you shall be left few in **n**, Dt 28:62
peoples according to the **n** of the sons of Dt 32:8
according to the **n** of the tribes of the Jos 4:5
according to the **n** of the tribes of the Jos 4:8
in **n** like the sand that is on the seashore, Jos 11:4
come like locusts in **n**—both they and Jgs 6:5
And the **n** of those who lapped, putting Jgs 7:6
and their camels were without **n**, Jgs 7:12
able men from the whole **n** of their tribe, Jgs 18:2
took their wives, according to their **n**, Jgs 21:23
according to the **n** of the lords of the 1 Sm 6:4
according to the **n** of all the cities of 1 Sm 6:18
were given in full **n** to the king, 1 Sm 18:27
And the **n** of the days that David lived 1 Sm 27:7
Then they arose and passed over by **n**, 2 Sm 2:15
toes on each foot, twenty-four in **n**, 2 Sm 21:20
saying, "Go, **n** Israel and Judah." 2 Sm 24:1
Dan to Beersheba, and **n** the people, 2 Sm 24:2
that I may know the **n** of the people." 2 Sm 24:2
of the king to **n** the people of Israel. 2 Sm 24:4
according to the **n** of the tribes of 1 Kgs 18:31
their **n** in the days of David being 1 Chr 7:2
Their **n** enrolled by genealogies, for 1 Chr 7:40
When you were few in **n**, and of 1 Chr 16:19
toes on each foot, twenty-four in **n**, 1 Chr 20:6
Israel and incited David to **n** Israel. 1 Chr 21:1
of the army, "Go, **n** Israel, 1 Chr 21:2
a report, that I may know their **n**." 1 Chr 21:2
who gave command to **n** the people? 1 Chr 21:17
and cedar timbers without **n**, for the 1 Chr 22:4
all kinds of craftsmen without **n**, 1 Chr 22:15
according to the **n** of the names 1 Chr 23:24
according to the **n** required of them, 1 Chr 23:31
The **n** of them along with their 1 Chr 25:7
This is the **n** of the people of Israel, 1 Chr 27:1
and the **n** was not entered in the 1 Chr 27:24
people were without **n** who came 2 Chr 12:3
The whole **n** of the heads of fathers' 2 Chr 26:12
took captive a great **n** of his people 2 Chr 28:5
The **n** of the burnt offerings that the 2 Chr 29:32
Besides the great **n** of burnt 2 Chr 29:35
themselves in sufficient **n**, 2 Chr 30:3
from the flock to the **n** of 30,000, 2 Chr 35:7
And this was the **n** of them: 30 basins of Ezr 1:9
The **n** of the men of the people of Israel: Ezr 2:2
burnt offerings by **n** according to the Ezr 3:4
according to the **n** of the tribes of Israel. Ezr 6:17
The **n** of the men of the people of Israel: Neh 7:7
splendor of his riches, the **n** of his sons, Est 5:11
That very day the **n** of those killed in Est 9:11
offerings according to the **n** of them all. Jb 1:5
let it not come into the **n** of the months. Jb 3:6
marvelous things without **n**: Jb 5:9
out, and marvelous things beyond **n**. Jb 9:10
and the **n** of his months is with you, Jb 14:5
For then you would **n** my steps; you Jb 14:16
when the **n** of their months is cut off? Jb 21:21
Is there any **n** to his armies? Upon whom Jb 25:3
not he see my ways and **n** all my steps? Jb 31:4
not; the **n** of his years is unsearchable. Jb 36:26
then, and the **n** of your days is great! Jb 38:21
Who can **n** the clouds by wisdom? Or Jb 38:37
Can you **n** the months that they fulfill, Jb 39:2
evils have encompassed me beyond **n**; Ps 40:12
Zion, go around her, **n** her towers, Ps 48:12
More in **n** than the hairs of my head are Ps 69:4
day, for their **n** is past my knowledge. Ps 71:15
So teach us to **n** our days that we may Ps 90:12
When they were few in **n**, of little Ps 105:12
came, young locusts without **n**, Ps 105:34
He determines the **n** of the stars; he Ps 147:4
eighty concubines, and virgins without **n**. Sg 6:8
He who brings out their host by **n**, Is 40:26
people have forgotten me days without **n**. Jer 2:32
their widows more in **n** than the sand of Jer 15:8
of Egypt to the land of Judah, few in **n**; Jer 44:28
than locusts; they are without **n**. Jer 46:23
This is the **n** of the people whom Jer 52:28
For the **n** of the days that you lie on it, Ezk 4:4
For I assign to you a **n** of days, 390 days, Ezk 4:5
equal to the **n** of the years of their Ezk 4:5
During the **n** of days that you lie on your Ezk 4:9
from these a small **n** and bind them in Ezk 5:3
perceived in the books the **n** of years that, Dn 9:2
Yet the **n** of the children of Israel shall Hos 1:10
against my land, powerful and beyond **n**; Jl 1:6
done this, they enclosed a large **n** of fish, Lk 5:6
Iscariot, who was of the **n** of the twelve. Lk 22:3
men sat down, about five thousand in **n**. Jn 6:10
Lord added to their **n** day by day those Acts 2:47
and the **n** of the men came to about five Acts 4:4
Now the full **n** of those who believed Acts 4:32
to be somebody, and a **n** of men, Acts 5:36
when the disciples were increasing in **n**, Acts 6:1
summoned the full **n** of the disciples Acts 6:2
and the **n** of the disciples multiplied Acts 6:7
and a great **n** who believed turned to Acts 11:21
a way that a great **n** of both Jews and Acts 14:1
And a **n** of those who had practiced Acts 19:19
sailed slowly for a **n** of days and Acts 27:7
"Though the **n** of the sons of Israel be Rom 9:27
The former priests were many in **n**, Heb 7:23
until the **n** of their fellow servants and Rv 6:11
And I heard the **n** of the sealed, 144,000, Rv 7:4
a great multitude that no one could **n**, Rv 7:9
The **n** of mounted troops was twice ten Rv 9:16
times ten thousand; I heard their **n**. Rv 9:16
name of the beast or the **n** of its name. Rv 13:17
understanding calculate the **n** of the Rv 13:18
of the beast, for it is the **n** of a man, Rv 13:18
the number of a man, and his **n** is 666. Rv 13:18
and its image and the **n** of its name, Rv 15:2
battle; their **n** is like the sand of the sea. Rv 20:8

NUMBERED (25)
that they cannot be **n** for multitude." Gn 16:10
sea, which cannot be **n** for multitude.'" Gn 32:12
sons and his daughters **n** thirty-three. Gn 46:15
Each one who is **n** in the census shall Ex 30:13
Everyone who is **n** in the census, from Ex 30:14
gone out in the army, **n** 337,500 sheep, Nm 31:36
And Saul **n** the people who were 1 Sm 13:15
the people and **n** them in Telaim, 1 Sm 15:4
struck him after he had **n** the people. 2 Sm 24:10
too many to be **n** or counted for 1 Kgs 3:8
all Israel, and the draft **n** 30,000 men. 1 Kgs 5:13
that they could not be counted or **n**. 1 Kgs 8:5
thirty years old and upward, were **n**, 1 Chr 23:3
of Levi were **n** from twenty years 1 Chr 23:27
that they could not be counted or **n**. 2 Chr 5:6
death and was **n** with the transgressors; Is 53:12
of heaven cannot be **n** and the sands of Jer 33:22
our days were **n**, for our end had come. Lam 4:18
God has **n** the days of your kingdom Dn 5:26
sea, which cannot be measured or **n**. Hos 1:10
even the hairs of your head are all **n**. Mt 10:30
even the hairs of your head are all **n**. Lk 12:7

'And he was **n** with the transgressors.' Lk 22:37
For he was **n** among us and was Acts 1:17
and he was **n** with the eleven apostles. Acts 1:26

NUMBERING (6)
gave the sum of the **n** of the people to 2 Sm 24:9
gave the sum of the **n** of the people to 1 Chr 21:5
include Levi and Benjamin in the **n**, 1 Chr 21:6
the year, each division **n** 24,000: 1 Chr 27:1
and the herd, **n** about two thousand, Mk 5:13
n myriads of myriads and thousands of Rv 5:11

NUMBERS (8)
My **n** are few, and if they gather Gn 34:30
These are the **n** of the divisions of 1 Chr 12:23
for great **n** had deserted to him from 2 Chr 15:9
they found among them, in great **n**, 2 Chr 20:25
according to the **n** in the muster 2 Chr 26:11
consecrated themselves in great **n**. 2 Chr 30:24
the faith, and they increased in **n** daily. Acts 16:5
to him at his lodging in greater **n**. Acts 28:23

NUMEROUS (12)
you are today as **n** as the stars of heaven. Dt 1:10
seven nations more **n** and mightier than Dt 7:1
lest the wild beasts grow too **n** for you. Dt 7:22
God has made you as **n** as the stars of Dt 10:22
Whereas you were as **n** as the stars of Dt 28:62
more prosperous and **n** than your Dt 30:5
inheritance, although I am a **n** people, Jos 17:14
said to them, "If you are a **n** people, Jos 17:15
"You are a **n** people and have great Jos 17:17
They were very **n** from Bashan to 1 Chr 5:23
king over a people as **n** as the dust of 2 Chr 1:9
because they are more **n** than locusts; Jer 46:23

NUN (30)
his assistant Joshua the son of **N**, Ex 33:11
And Joshua the son of **N**, the assistant Nm 11:28
tribe of Ephraim, Hoshea the son of **N**; Nm 13:8
called Hoshea the son of **N** Joshua. Nm 13:16
Joshua the son of **N** and Caleb the son Nm 14:6
Jephunneh and Joshua the son of **N**. Nm 14:30
Joshua the son of **N** and Caleb the son Nm 14:38
Jephunneh and Joshua the son of **N**. Nm 26:65
to Moses, "Take Joshua the son of **N**, Nm 27:18
the Kenizzite and Joshua the son of **N**, Nm 32:12
Joshua the son of **N** and to the heads Nm 32:28
the priest and Joshua the son of **N**. Nm 34:17
Joshua the son of **N**, who stands before Dt 1:38
Joshua the son of **N** and said, Dt 31:23
the people, he and Joshua the son of **N**. Dt 32:44
And Joshua the son of **N** was full of the Dt 34:9
LORD, the LORD said to Joshua the son of **N**, Jos 1:1
Joshua the son of **N** sent two men secretly Jos 2:1
over and came to Joshua the son of **N**, Jos 2:23
Joshua the son of **N** called the priests and Jos 6:6
and Joshua the son of **N** and the heads of Jos 14:1
Joshua the son of **N** and the leaders and Jos 17:4
among them to Joshua the son of **N**. Jos 19:49
Joshua the son of **N** and the heads of Jos 19:51
to Joshua the son of **N** and to the heads Jos 21:1
After these things Joshua the son of **N**, Jos 24:29
And Joshua the son of **N**, the servant of Jgs 2:8
he spoke by Joshua the son of **N**. 1 Kgs 16:34
N his son, Joshua his son. 1 Chr 7:27
of Jeshua the son of **N** to that day the Neh 8:17

NURSE (17)
Abraham that Sarah would **n** children? Gn 21:7
away Rebekah their sister and her **n**, Gn 24:59
And Deborah, Rebekah's **n**, died, and Gn 35:8
and call you a **n** from the Hebrew women Ex 2:7
the Hebrew women to **n** the child for Ex 2:7
"Take this child away and **n** him for me, Ex 2:9
as a **n** carries a nursing child,' Nm 11:12
laid him on her lap and became his **n**. Ru 4:16
Jezreel, and his **n** took him up and fled, 2 Sm 4:4
I rose in the morning to **n** my child, 1 Kgs 3:21
she put him and his **n** in a bedroom. 2 Kgs 11:2
put him and his **n** in a bedroom. 2 Chr 22:11
me? Or why the breasts, that I should **n**? Jb 3:12
you shall **n** at the breast of kings; Is 60:16
that you may **n** and be satisfied from Is 66:11
and you shall **n**, you shall be carried Is 66:12
they **n** their young, but the daughter of Lam 4:3

NURSED (5)
So the woman took the child and **n** him. Ex 2:9
woman remained and **n** her son until 1 Sm 1:23
brother to me who **n** at my mother's Sg 8:1
you, and the breasts at which you **n**!" Lk 11:27
bore and the breasts that never **n**!' Lk 23:29

NURSING (15)
and that the **n** flocks and herds are a Gn 33:13
bosom, as a nurse carries a **n** child,' Nm 11:12
the **n** child with the man of gray hairs. Dt 32:25
So Samuel took a **n** lamb and offered it 1 Sm 7:9
from following the **n** ewes he brought Ps 78:71
The **n** child shall play over the hole of the Is 11:8
"Can a woman forget her **n** child, that Is 49:15
and their queens your **n** mothers. Is 49:23
The tongue of the **n** infant sticks to the Lam 4:4
elders; gather the children, even **n** infants. Jl 2:16
of infants and **n** babies you have Mt 21:16
for those who are **n** infants in those Mt 24:19
for those who are **n** infants in those Mk 13:17
for those who are **n** infants in those Lk 21:23
like a **n** mother taking care of her 1 Thes 2:7

NUT (1)
I went down to the **n** orchard to look at Sg 6:11

NUTS (1)
little honey, gum, myrrh, pistachio **n**, Gn 43:11

NYMPHA (1)
and to **N** and the church in her house. Col 4:15

O

OAK (18)
the place at Shechem, to the **o** of Moreh. Gn 12:6
she was buried under an **o** below Bethel. Gn 35:8
opposite Gilgal, beside the **o** of Moreh? Dt 11:30
Heleph, from the **o** in Zaanannim, Jos 19:33
tent as far away as the **o** in Zaanannim, Jgs 4:11
king, by the **o** of the pillar at Shechem. Jgs 9:6
from the direction of the Diviners' **O**." Jgs 9:37
further and come to the **o** of Tabor. 1 Sm 10:3
and his head caught fast in the **o**, 2 Sm 18:9
I saw Absalom hanging in an **o**." 2 Sm 18:10
while he was still alive in the **o**. 2 Sm 18:14
and found him sitting under an **o**. 1 Kgs 13:14
bones under the **o** in Jabesh and 1 Chr 10:12
you shall be like an **o** whose leaf withers, Is 1:30
be burned again, like a terebinth or an **o**, Is 6:13
a cypress tree or an **o** and lets it grow Is 44:14
green tree, and under every leafy **o**, Ezk 6:13
burn offerings on the hills, under **o**, Hos 4:13

OAKS (10)
came and settled by the **o** of Mamre, Gn 13:18
was living by the **o** of Mamre the Gn 14:13
appeared to him by the **o** of Mamre, Gn 18:1
be ashamed of the **o** that you desired; Is 1:29
lifted up; and against all the **o** of Bashan; Is 2:13
you who burn with lust among the **o**, Is 57:5
they may be called **o** of righteousness, Is 61:3
Of **o** of Bashan they made your oars; Ezk 27:6
cedars and who was as strong as the **o**; Am 2:9
Wail, **o** of Bashan, for the thick forest Zec 11:2

OAR (1)
their ships come all who handle the **o**. Ezk 27:29

OARS (2)
streams, where no galley with **o** can go, Is 33:21
Of oaks of Bashan they made your **o**; Ezk 27:6

OATH (74)
because there both of them swore an **o**. Gn 21:31
you will be free from this **o** of mine; Gn 24:8
Then you will be free from my **o**, when Gn 24:41
her to you, you will be free from my **o**.' Gn 24:41
and I will establish the **o** that I swore to Gn 26:3
an **o** by the LORD shall be between them Ex 22:11
The owner shall accept the **o**, and he Ex 22:11
utters with his lips a rash **o** to do evil or to Lv 5:4
good, any sort of rash **o** that people swear, Lv 5:4
the priest shall make her take an **o**, Nm 5:19
the woman take the **o** of the curse, Nm 5:21
a curse and an **o** among your people, Nm 5:21
or swears an **o** to bind himself by a Nm 30:2
bound herself by a pledge with an **o**, Nm 30:10
and any binding **o** to afflict herself, Nm 30:13
you and is keeping the **o** that he swore to Dt 7:8
with respect to this **o** of yours that you Jos 2:17
with respect to your **o** that you have Jos 2:20
Joshua laid an **o** on them at that time, Jos 6:26
because of the **o** that we swore to them." Jos 9:20
taken a great **o** concerning him who Jgs 21:5
so Saul had laid an **o** on the people, 1 Sm 14:24
mouth, for the people feared the **o**. 1 Sm 14:26
father charge the people with the **o**, 1 Sm 14:27
strictly charged the people with an **o**, 1 Sm 14:28
die." And the king gave him his **o**. 2 Sm 19:23
because of the **o** of the LORD that was 2 Sm 21:7
you not kept your **o** to the LORD and 1 Kgs 2:43
made to take an **o** and comes and 1 Kgs 8:31
and swears his **o** before your altar 1 Kgs 8:31
he would take an **o** of the kingdom 1 Kgs 18:10
and put them under **o** in the house of 2 Kgs 11:4
made to take an **o** and comes and 2 Chr 6:22
and swears his **o** before your altar 2 Chr 6:22
They swore an **o** to the LORD with a 2 Chr 15:14
And all Judah rejoiced over the **o**, 2 Chr 15:15
and all Israel take **o** that they would do Ezr 10:5
do as had been said. So they took the **o**. Ezr 10:5
in Judah were bound by **o** to him, Neh 6:18
into a curse and an **o** to walk in God's Neh 10:29
I made them take **o** in the name of Neh 13:25
I have sworn an **o** and confirmed it, Ps 119:106
to David a sure **o** from which he will Ps 132:11
command, because of God's **o** to him. Eccl 8:2
he who swears is as he who shuns an **o**. Eccl 9:2
and he who takes an **o** in the land shall Is 65:16
that I may confirm the **o** that I swore to Jer 11:5
by famine, and they shall become an **o**, Jer 44:12
have despised the **o** in breaking the Ezk 16:59
putting him under **o** (the chief men of Ezk 17:13
made him king, whose **o** he despised, Ezk 17:16
He despised the **o** in breaking the Ezk 17:18
I live, surely it is my **o** that he despised, Ezk 17:19
And the curse and **o** that are written in Dn 9:11
against one another, and love no false **o**, Zec 8:17
But I say to you, Do not take an **o** at all, Mt 5:34
And do not take an **o** by your head, for Mt 5:36
he promised with an **o** to give her Mt 14:7
of the temple, he is bound by his **o**.' Mt 23:16
is on the altar, he is bound by his **o**.' Mt 23:18
And again he denied it with an **o**: "I do Mt 26:72
the **o** that he swore to our father Lk 1:73
had sworn with an **o** to him that he Acts 2:30
themselves by an **o** neither to eat Acts 23:12
bound ourselves by an **o** to taste no Acts 23:14
themselves by an **o** neither to eat Acts 23:21
I put you under **o** before the Lord to 1 Thes 5:27
all their disputes an **o** is final for Heb 6:16
his purpose, he guaranteed it with an **o**, Heb 6:17
And it was not without an **o**. For those Heb 7:20
priests were made such without an **o**, Heb 7:20
made a priest with an **o** by the one who Heb 7:21
as high priests, but the word of the **o**, Heb 7:28
by heaven or by earth or by any other **o**, Jas 5:12

OATHS (5)
they rose early and exchanged **o**. Gn 26:31
They have sworn solemn **o**, but he Ezk 21:23
with empty **o** they make covenants; Hos 10:4
but because of his **o** and his guests he Mt 14:9
but because of his **o** and his guests he Mk 6:26

OBADIAH (21)
And Ahab called **O**, who was over the 1 Kgs 18:3
(Now **O** feared the LORD greatly, 1 Kgs 18:3
O took a hundred prophets and hid 1 Kgs 18:4
And Ahab said to **O**, "Go through the 1 Kgs 18:5
and **O** went in another direction by 1 Kgs 18:6
And as **O** was on the way, behold, 1 Kgs 18:7
And **O** recognized him and fell on his 1 Kgs 18:7
So **O** went to meet Ahab, and told 1 Kgs 18:16
Rephaiah, his son Arnan, his son **O**, 1 Chr 3:21
Michael, **O**, Joel, and Isshiah, all five of 1 Chr 7:3
Ishmael, Sheariah, **O**, and Hanan. 1 Chr 8:38
and **O** the son of Shemaiah, son of 1 Chr 9:16
Ishmael, Sheariah, **O**, and Hanan; 1 Chr 9:44
Ezer the chief, **O** second, Eliab third, 1 Chr 12:9
for Zebulun, Ishmaiah the son of **O**; 1 Chr 27:19
his officials, Ben-hail, **O**, Zechariah, 2 Chr 17:7
were set Jahath and **O** the Levites, 2 Chr 34:12
Of the sons of Joab, **O** the son of Jehiel, Ezr 8:9
Harim, Meremoth, **O**, Neh 10:5
Bakbukiah, **O**, Meshullam, Neh 12:25
The vision of **O**. Thus says the Lord GOD Ob 1:1

OBAL (2)
O, Abimael, Sheba, Gn 10:28
O, Abimael, Sheba, 1 Chr 1:22

OBED (13)
born to Naomi." They named him **O**. Ru 4:17
Salmon fathered Boaz, Boaz fathered **O**, Ru 4:21
O fathered Jesse, and Jesse fathered Ru 4:22
Boaz fathered **O**, Obed fathered Jesse. 1 Chr 2:12
Boaz fathered Obed, **O** fathered Jesse. 1 Chr 2:12
Ephlal, and Ephlal fathered **O**. 1 Chr 2:37
O fathered Jehu, and Jehu fathered 1 Chr 2:38
Eliel, and **O**, and Jaasiel the 1 Chr 11:47
Othni, Rephael, **O** and Elzabad, 1 Chr 26:7
of Jehohanan, Azariah the son of **O**, 2 Chr 23:1
Rahab, and Boaz the father of **O** by Ruth, Mt 1:5
of Obed by Ruth, and **O** the father of Jesse, Mt 1:5
the son of Jesse, the son of **O**, the son of Lk 3:32

OBED-EDOM (19)
it aside to the house of **O** the Gittite. 2 Sm 6:10
in the house of **O** the Gittite three 2 Sm 6:11
and the LORD blessed **O** and all his 2 Sm 6:11
the household of **O** and all that 2 Sm 6:12
God from the house of **O** to the city of 2 Sm 6:12
it aside to the house of **O** the Gittite. 1 Chr 13:13

the household of **O** in his house 1 Chr 13:14
the household of **O** and all that 1 Chr 13:14
and the gatekeepers **O** and Jeiel. 1 Chr 15:18
Eliphelehu, Mikneiah, **O**, Jeiel, 1 Chr 15:21
O and Jehiah were to be gatekeepers 1 Chr 15:24
from the house of **O** with rejoicing. 1 Chr 15:25
Eliab, Benaiah, **O**, and Jeiel, 1 Chr 16:5
and also **O** and his sixty-eight 1 Chr 16:38
his sixty-eight brothers, while **O**, 1 Chr 16:38
And **O** had sons: Shemaiah the 1 Chr 26:4
of the sons of **O** with their sons and 1 Chr 26:8
for the service; sixty-two of **O**. 1 Chr 26:8
in the house of God, in the care of **O**. 2 Chr 25:24

OBED-EDOM'S (1)
O came out for the south, and to his 1 Chr 26:15

OBEDIENCE (13)
and to him shall be the **o** of the peoples. Gn 49:10
to bring about the **o** of faith for the Rom 1:5
by the one man's **o** the many will be Rom 5:19
of sin, which leads to death, or of **o**, Rom 6:16
bring the Gentiles to **o**—by word and Rom 15:18
For your **o** is known to all, so that I Rom 16:19
God, to bring about the **o** of faith— Rom 16:26
as he remembers the **o** of you all, 2 Cor 7:15
when your **o** is complete. 2 Cor 10:6
Confident of your **o**, I write to you, Phlm 1:21
he learned **o** through what he suffered. Heb 5:8
for **o** to Jesus Christ and for sprinkling 1 Pt 1:2
your souls by your **o** to the truth for 1 Pt 1:22

OBEDIENT (9)
has spoken we will do, and we will be **o**." Ex 24:7
If you are willing and **o**, you shall eat the Is 1:19
of the priests became **o** to the faith. Acts 6:7
yourselves to anyone as **o** slaves, Rom 6:16
of sin have become **o** from the heart to Rom 6:17
know whether you are **o** in everything. 2 Cor 2:9
himself by becoming **o** to the point Phil 2:8
to rulers and authorities, to be **o**, Ti 3:1
As **o** children, do not be conformed to 1 Pt 1:14

OBELISKS (1)
He shall break the **o** of Heliopolis, Jer 43:13

OBEY (113)
my son, **o** my voice as I command you. Gn 27:8
only **o** my voice, and go, bring them to Gn 27:13
Now therefore, my son, **o** my voice. Gn 27:43
that I should **o** his voice and let Israel go? Ex 5:2
Now **o** my voice; I will give you advice, Ex 18:19
if you will indeed **o** my voice and keep Ex 19:5
attention to him and **o** his voice; Ex 23:21
"But if you carefully **o** his voice and do Ex 23:22
of the people of Israel may **o**. Nm 27:20
to the LORD your God and **o** his voice. Dt 4:30
because you would not **o** the voice of the Dt 8:20
and did not believe him or **o** his voice. Dt 9:23
you will indeed **o** my commandments Dt 11:13
if you **o** the commandments of the LORD Dt 11:27
if you do not **o** the commandments of Dt 11:28
Be careful to **o** all these words that I Dt 12:28
his commandments and **o** his voice, Dt 13:4
if you **o** the voice of the LORD your God, Dt 13:18
if only you will strictly **o** the voice of the Dt 15:5
son who will not **o** the voice of his Dt 21:18
and rebellious; he will not **o** our voice; Dt 21:20
and his rules, and will **o** his voice. Dt 26:17
You shall therefore **o** the voice of the Dt 27:10
"And if you faithfully **o** the voice of the Dt 28:1
if you **o** the voice of the LORD your God. Dt 28:2
if you **o** the commandments of the LORD Dt 28:13
"But if you will not **o** the voice of the Dt 28:15
because you did not **o** the voice of the Dt 28:45
because you did not **o** the voice of the Dt 28:62
and **o** his voice in all that I command Dt 30:2
And you shall again **o** the voice of the Dt 30:8
when you **o** the voice of the LORD your Dt 30:10
If you **o** the commandments of the LORD Dt 30:16
Moses in all things, so we will **o** you. Jos 1:17
because they did not **o** the voice of the Jos 5:6
we will serve, and his voice we will **o**." Jos 24:24
Israel would **o** the commandments Jgs 3:4
"**O** the voice of the people in all that 1 Sm 8:7
Now then, **o** their voice; only you shall 1 Sm 8:9
the people refused to **o** the voice of 1 Sm 8:19
"**O** their voice and make them a 1 Sm 8:22
and serve him and **o** his voice and 1 Sm 12:14
But if you will not **o** the voice of the 1 Sm 12:15
then did you not **o** the voice of the 1 Sm 15:19
Behold, to **o** is better than sacrifice, 1 Sm 15:22
Because you did not **o** the voice of 1 Sm 28:18
therefore, you also **o** your servant. 1 Sm 28:22
to me, 'What you say is good; I will **o**.' 1 Kgs 2:42
in my statutes and **o** my rules and 1 Kgs 6:12
my side, and if you are ready to **o** me, 2 Kgs 10:6
because they did not **o** the voice of 2 Kgs 18:12
Whoever will not **o** the law of your God Ezr 7:26
and did not **o** your commandments. Neh 9:16
They refused to **o** and were not Neh 9:17
and did not **o** your commandments, Neh 9:29
stiffened their neck and would not **o**. Neh 9:29
and did not **o** the voice of the LORD. Ps 106:25
father and scorns to **o** a mother will be Prv 30:17
Moab, and the Ammonites shall **o** them. Is 11:14
walk, and whose law they would not **o**? Is 42:24
'**O** my voice, and I will be your God, and Jer 7:23
But they did not **o** or incline their ear, Jer 7:24
the nation that did not **o** the voice of the Jer 7:28
even to this day, saying, **O** my voice. Jer 11:7
Yet they did not **o** or incline their ear, Jer 11:8
For if you will indeed **o** this word, then Jer 22:4
But if you will not **o** these words, I swear Jer 22:5
and **o** the voice of the LORD your God, Jer 26:13
But they did not **o** your voice or walk in Jer 32:23
O now the voice of the LORD in what I Jer 38:20
against the LORD and did not **o** his voice, Jer 40:3
we will **o** the voice of the LORD our God to Jer 42:6
well with us when we **o** the voice of the Jer 42:6
all the people did not **o** the voice of the Jer 43:4
for they did not **o** the voice of the LORD. Jer 43:7
the LORD and did not **o** the voice of the Jer 44:23
and keep my rules and **o** them. Ezk 11:20
statutes, and be careful to **o** my rules, Ezk 20:19
and were not careful to **o** my rules, Ezk 20:21
statutes and be careful to **o** my rules. Ezk 36:27
rules and be careful to **o** my statutes. Ezk 37:24
all dominions shall serve and **o** them.' Dn 7:27
turned aside, refusing to **o** your voice. Dn 9:11
vengeance on the nations that did not **o**. Mi 5:15
if you will diligently **o** the voice of the Zec 6:15
is this, that even winds and sea **o** him?" Mt 8:27
the unclean spirits, and they **o** him." Mk 1:27
is this, that even wind and sea **o** him?" Mk 4:41
even winds and water, and they **o** him?" Lk 8:25
planted in the sea,' and it would **o** you. Lk 17:6
whoever does not **o** the Son shall not see Jn 3:36
"We must **o** God rather than men. Acts 5:29
God has given to those who **o** him." Acts 5:32
Our fathers refused to **o** him, but Acts 7:39
are self-seeking and do not **o** the truth, Rom 2:8
obey the truth, but **o** unrighteousness, Rom 2:8
indeed is of value if you **o** the law, Rom 2:25
bodies, to make you **o** their passions. Rom 6:12
you are slaves of the one whom you **o**, Rom 6:16
every thought captive to **o** Christ, 2 Cor 10:5
Children, **o** your parents in the Lord, for Eph 6:1
o your earthly masters with fear and Eph 6:5
Children, **o** your parents in everything, Col 3:20
o in everything those who are your Col 3:22
those who do not **o** the gospel of our 2 Thes 1:8
If anyone does not **o** what we say in 2 Thes 3:14
of eternal salvation to all who **o** him, Heb 5:9
O your leaders and submit to them, Heb 13:17
the mouths of horses so that they **o** us, Jas 3:3
so that even if some do not **o** the word, 1 Pt 3:1
because they formerly did not **o**, when 1 Pt 3:20
those who do not **o** the gospel of God? 1 Pt 4:17
we love God and **o** his commandments. 1 Jn 5:2

OBEYED (51)
blessed, because you have **o** my voice." Gn 22:18
because Abraham **o** my voice and kept Gn 26:5
and that Jacob had **o** his father and his Gn 28:7
wilderness. But so far, you have not **o**." Ex 7:16
ten times and have not **o** my voice, Nm 14:22
And the LORD **o** the voice of Israel and Nm 21:3
I have **o** the voice of the LORD my God. Dt 26:14
So the people of Israel **o** him and did as Dt 34:9
Just as we **o** Moses in all things, so we Jos 1:17
when the LORD **o** the voice of a man, Jos 10:14
you and have **o** my voice in Jos 22:2
their altars.' But you have not **o** my voice. Jgs 2:2
who had **o** the commandments of the Jgs 2:17
their fathers and have not **o** my voice, Jgs 2:20
dwell.' But you have not **o** my voice." Jgs 6:10
I have **o** your voice in all that you 1 Sm 12:1
"I have **o** the voice of the LORD. 1 Sm 15:20
I feared the people and **o** their voice. 1 Sm 15:24
See, I have **o** your voice, and I have 1 Sm 25:35
"Behold, your servant has **o** you. 1 Sm 28:21
soon as they heard of me, they **o** me. 2 Sm 22:45
"Because you have not **o** the voice of 1 Kgs 20:36
They neither listened nor **o**. 2 Kgs 18:12
our fathers have not **o** the words of 2 Kgs 22:13
he prospered, and all Israel **o** him. 1 Chr 29:23
for Esther **o** Mordecai just as when she Est 2:20
As soon as they heard of me they **o** me; Ps 18:44
tree, and that you have not **o** my voice, Jer 3:13
and we have not **o** the voice of the LORD Jer 3:25
and have not **o** my voice or walked in Jer 9:13
youth, that you have not **o** my voice. Jer 22:21
hosts: Because you have not **o** my words, Jer 25:8
And they **o**, all the officials and all the Jer 34:10
again. They **o** and set them free. Jer 34:10
You have not **o** me by proclaiming Jer 34:17
We have **o** the voice of Jonadab the son Jer 35:8
in tents and have **o** and done all that Jer 35:10
for they have **o** their father's command. Jer 35:14
them, but this people has not **o** me. Jer 35:16
Because you have **o** the command of Jer 35:18
but you have not **o** the voice of the LORD Jer 42:21
not walked in my statutes or **o** my rules, Ezk 5:7
walked in my statutes, nor **o** my rules, Ezk 11:12
because they had not **o** my rules, but Ezk 20:24
and have not **o** the voice of the LORD our Dn 9:10
has done, and we have not **o** his voice. Dn 9:14
people, **o** the voice of the LORD their God, Hg 1:12
But they have not all **o** the gospel. For Rom 10:16
my beloved, as you have always **o**, Phil 2:12
By faith Abraham **o** when he was Heb 11:8
as Sarah **o** Abraham, calling him lord. 1 Pt 3:6

OBEYING (5)
presumptuously by not **o** the priest who Dt 17:12
o his voice and holding fast to him, Dt 30:20
as in **o** the voice of the LORD? 1 Sm 15:22
do his word, **o** the voice of his word! Ps 103:20
Who hindered you from **o** the truth? Gal 5:7

OBEYS (2)
you fears the LORD and **o** the voice of his Is 50:10
takes no interest or profit, **o** my rules, Ezk 18:17

OBIL (1)
the camels was **O** the Ishmaelite; 1 Chr 27:30

OBJECT (12)
if he struck him down with an iron **o**, Nm 35:16
he has made them an **o** of horror, 2 Chr 29:8
and an **o** of dread to my acquaintances; Ps 31:11
You make us an **o** of contention for our Ps 80:6
I am an **o** of scorn to my accusers; Ps 109:25
word of the LORD is to them an **o** of scorn; Jer 6:10
the **o** of their taunts all day long. Lam 3:14
their rising; I am the **o** of their taunts. Lam 3:63
desolation and an **o** of reproach among Ezk 5:14
you have become an **o** of reproach for Ezk 16:57
and make them an **o** of terror and a Ezk 23:46
every so-called god or **o** of worship, 2 Thes 2:4

OBJECTED (1)
But because the Jews **o**, I was Acts 28:19

OBJECTION (1)
when I was sent for, I came without **o**. Acts 10:29

OBJECTS (3)
rings and armlets, all sorts of gold **o**, Ex 35:22
list by name the **o** that they are Nm 4:32
and observed the **o** of your worship, Acts 17:23

OBLATION (2)
until the time of the offering of the **o**, 1 Kgs 18:29
at the time of the offering of the **o**, 1 Kgs 18:36

OBLIGATE (1)
We **o** ourselves to bring the firstfruits Neh 10:35

OBLIGATED (7)
in their villages were **o** to come in 1 Chr 9:25
the Jews firmly **o** themselves and their Est 9:27
the Jew and Queen Esther **o** them, Est 9:31
and as they had **o** themselves and their Est 9:31
For children are not **o** to save up for 2 Cor 12:14
circumcision that he is **o** to keep the Gal 5:3
of this he is **o** to offer sacrifice for Heb 5:3

OBLIGATION (4)
return and be free of **o** to the LORD and Nm 32:22
take on ourselves the **o** to give yearly Neh 10:32
I am under **o** both to Greeks and to Rom 1:14
are strong have an **o** to bear with the Rom 15:1

OBLIGED (1)
the land shall be **o** to give this offering Ezk 45:16

OBLIGING (1)
o them to keep the fourteenth day of the Est 9:21

OBOTH (4)
of Israel set out and camped in **O**. Nm 21:10
they set out from **O** and camped at Nm 21:11
set out from Punon and camped at **O**. Nm 33:43
they set out from **O** and camped at Nm 33:44

OBSCENE (1)
slander, and **o** talk from your mouth. Col 3:8

OBSCURE (3)
kings; he will not stand before **o** men. Prv 22:29
the people of an **o** speech that you Is 33:19
in Cilicia, a citizen of no **o** city. Acts 21:39

OBSERVANCE (2)
to them for **o** the decisions that Acts 16:4
you yourself also live in **o** of the law. Acts 21:24

OBSERVE (33)
And you shall **o** the Feast of Ex 12:17
Therefore you shall **o** this day, Ex 12:17
You shall **o** this rite as a statute for you Ex 12:24
"**O** what I command you this day. Ex 34:11
You shall **o** the Feast of Weeks, the Ex 34:22
And you shall **o** all my statutes and all Lv 19:37
you shall **o** a day of solemn rest, Lv 23:24
my statutes and **o** my commandments Lv 26:3
and do not **o** all these Nm 15:22
"'**O** the Sabbath day, to keep it holy, as Dt 5:12
"**O** the month of Abib and keep the Dt 16:1
you shall be careful to **o** these statutes. Dt 16:12
very careful to **o** the commandment and Jos 22:5
All that I commanded her let her **o**." Jgs 13:14
he lies down, **o** the place where he lies. Ru 3:4
But Amasa did not **o** the sword that 2 Sm 20:10
you are careful to **o** the statutes and 1 Chr 22:13
o and seek out all the 1 Chr 28:8
and to **o** and do all the Neh 10:29
birth? Do you **o** the calving of the does? Jb 39:1
might keep his statutes and **o** his laws. Ps 105:45
Blessed are they who **o** justice, who do Ps 106:3
keep your law and **o** it with my whole Ps 119:34
me, that I may **o** your testimonies. Ps 119:146
a ruler, **o** carefully what is before you, Prv 23:1
heart, and let your eyes **o** my ways. Prv 23:26
sees many things, but does not **o** them; Is 42:20
has been careful to **o** all my statutes, Ezk 18:19
so that they may **o** all its laws and all Ezk 43:11
so practice and **o** whatever they tell you Mt 23:3
teaching them to **o** all that I have Mt 28:20
are many other traditions that they **o**, Mk 7:4
You **o** days and months and seasons Gal 4:10

OBSERVED (11)
"I have **o** you and what has been done to Ex 3:16
forever to be **o** throughout their Ex 27:21
For they **o** your word and kept your Dt 33:9
before the LORD, Eli **o** her mouth. 1 Sm 1:12
of Purim should be **o** at their appointed Est 9:31
All this I **o** while applying my heart to Eccl 8:9
"Have you not **o** that these people are Jer 33:24
who eat the king's food be **o** by you, Dn 1:13
of God is not coming with signs to be **o**, Lk 17:20
I **o** animals and beasts of prey and Acts 11:6
I passed along and **o** the objects of Acts 17:23

OBSERVES (5)
hearts of them all and **o** all their deeds. Ps 33:15
The Righteous One **o** the house of the Prv 21:12
He who **o** the wind will not sow, and he Eccl 11:4
The one who **o** the day, observes it in Rom 14:6
the day, **o** it in honor of the Lord. Rom 14:6

OBSERVING (1)
o the Sabbath throughout their Ex 31:16

OBSOLETE (2)
new covenant, he makes the first one **o**. Heb 8:13
what is becoming **o** and growing old Heb 8:13

OBSTACLE (2)
rather than put an **o** in the way of 1 Cor 9:12
We put no **o** in anyone's way, so that 2 Cor 6:3

OBSTACLES (1)
divisions and create **o** contrary to the Rom 16:17

OBSTINATE (2)
hardened his spirit and made his heart **o**, Dt 2:30
Because I know that you are **o**, and your Is 48:4

OBSTRUCTION (1)
remove every **o** from my people's way." Is 57:14

OBTAIN (18)
be that I shall **o** children by her." And Gn 16:2
the one who understands **o** guidance, Prv 1:5
and forsakes them will **o** mercy. Prv 28:13
he who is lowly in spirit will **o** honor. Prv 29:23
The meek shall **o** fresh joy in the LORD, Is 29:19
they shall **o** gladness and joy, and Is 35:10
they shall **o** gladness and joy, and Is 51:11
without warning and **o** the kingdom Dn 11:21
you thought you could **o** the gift of Acts 8:20
bondage to decay and **o** the freedom of Rom 8:21
Israel failed to **o** what it was seeking. Rom 11:7
the prize? So run that you may **o** it. 1 Cor 9:24
but to **o** salvation through our Lord 1 Thes 5:9
so that you may **o** the glory of our 2 Thes 2:14
they also may **o** the salvation that 2 Tm 2:10
that no one fails to **o** the grace of God; Heb 12:15
You covet and cannot **o**, so you fight and Jas 4:2
were called, that you may **o** a blessing. 1 Pt 3:9

OBTAINED (11)
the people of Simeon **o** an inheritance in Jos 19:9
God, which he **o** with his own blood. Acts 20:28
that they had **o** their purpose, Acts 27:13
him we have also **o** access by faith into Rom 5:2
The elect **o** it, but the rest were Rom 11:7
In him we have **o** an inheritance, Eph 1:11
that I have already **o** this or am already Phil 3:12
having patiently waited, **o** the promise. Heb 6:15
Christ has **o** a ministry that is as much Heb 8:6
enforced justice, **o** promises, Heb 11:33
To those who have **o** a faith of equal 2 Pt 1:1

OBTAINING (1)
o the outcome of your faith, the 1 Pt 1:9

OBTAINS (3)
me finds life and **o** favor from the LORD, Prv 8:35
A good man **o** favor from the LORD, but Prv 12:2
a good thing and **o** favor from the Prv 18:22

OCCASION (4)
On one **o**, while the crowd was pressing in Lk 5:1
as is good for building up, as fits the **o**, Eph 4:29
give the adversary no **o** for slander. 1 Tm 5:14
there would have been no **o** to look for a Heb 8:7

OCCASIONED (1)
I have **o** the death of all the persons 1 Sm 22:22

OCCASIONS (1)
Behold, he finds **o** against me, he counts Jb 33:10

OCCUPATION (3)
calls you and says, 'What is your **o**?' Gn 46:33
"What is your **o**?" And they said to Gn 47:3
evil has come upon us. What is your **o**? Jon 1:8

OCCUPIED (2)
because God keeps him **o** with joy in Eccl 5:20
Macedonia, Paul was **o** with the word, Acts 18:5

OCCUPY (5)
said, "Let us go up at once and **o** it, Nm 13:30
possession, that you may **o** his land.' Dt 2:31
and they also **o** the land that the LORD Dt 3:20
house that I shall **o**." And the king Neh 2:8
I do not **o** myself with things too great Ps 131:1

OCCUR (1)
of famine that are to **o** in the land of Gn 41:36

OCCURRED (6)
years, which **o** in the land of Egypt, Gn 41:48
years of plenty that **o** in the land of Gn 41:53
And this **o** because the people of 2 Kgs 17:7
gain the mastery over them, the reverse **o**: Est 9:1
believed, when he saw what had **o**, Acts 13:12
since a death has **o** that redeems them Heb 9:15

OCHRAN (5)
from Asher, Pagiel the son of **O**; Nm 1:13
of Asher being Pagiel the son of **O**, Nm 2:27
On the eleventh day Pagiel the son of **O**, Nm 7:72
was the offering of Pagiel the son of **O**. Nm 7:77
of Asher was Pagiel the son of **O**. Nm 10:26

ODED (3)
God came upon Azariah the son of **O**, 2 Chr 15:1
the prophecy of Azariah the son of **O**, 2 Chr 15:8
LORD was there, whose name was **O**, 2 Chr 28:9

ODOR (1)
"Lord, by this time there will be an **o**, Jn 11:39

OFF (420)
the waters were dried from **o** the earth. Gn 8:13
shall all flesh be cut **o** by the waters of Gn 9:11
earth, and they left **o** building the city. Gn 11:8
foreskin shall be cut **o** from his people; Gn 17:14
sat down opposite him a good way **o**, Gn 21:16
she took **o** her widow's garments and Gn 38:14
and taking **o** her veil she put on the Gn 38:19
take your sandals **o** your feet, for the place Ex 3:5
a flint and cut **o** her son's foreskin and Ex 4:25
that the frogs be cut **o** from you and your Ex 8:9
would have been cut **o** from the earth. Ex 9:15
that person shall be cut **o** from Israel. Ex 12:15
will be cut **o** from the congregation Ex 12:19
and trembled, and they stood far **o** Ex 20:18
The people stood far **o**, while Moses Ex 20:21
shall be cut **o** from his people.'" Ex 30:33
shall be cut **o** from his people." Ex 30:38
soul shall be cut **o** from among his Ex 31:14
"Take **o** the rings of gold that are in the Ex 32:2
So all the people took **o** the rings of gold Ex 32:3
them, 'Let any who have gold take it **o**.' Ex 32:24
So now take **o** your ornaments, that I Ex 33:5
it outside the camp, far **o** from the camp, Ex 33:7
the altar and wring **o** its head and burn Lv 1:15
whole fat tail, cut **o** close to the backbone, Lv 3:9
Then he shall take **o** his garments and Lv 6:11
person shall be cut **o** from his people. Lv 7:20
person shall be cut **o** from his people." Lv 7:21
the LORD shall be cut **o** from his people. Lv 7:25
person shall be cut **o** from his people." Lv 7:27
his clothes and shave **o** all his hair and Lv 14:8
day he shall shave **o** all his hair from Lv 14:9
eyebrows. He shall shave **o** all his hair, Lv 14:9
that they scrape **o** they shall pour Lv 14:41
and shall take **o** the linen garments Lv 16:23
man shall be cut **o** from among his Lv 17:4
that man shall be cut **o** from his people. Lv 17:9
and will cut him **o** from among his Lv 17:10
blood. Whoever eats it shall be cut **o**. Lv 17:14
them shall be cut **o** from among their Lv 18:29
person shall be cut **o** from his people. Lv 19:8
You shall not round **o** the hair on your Lv 19:27
and will cut him **o** from among his Lv 20:3
and will cut them **o** from among their Lv 20:5
and will cut him **o** from among his Lv 20:6
and they shall be cut **o** in the sight of Lv 20:17
them shall be cut **o** from among their Lv 20:18
nor shave **o** the edges of their beards, Lv 21:5
person shall be cut **o** from my presence: Lv 22:3
very day shall be cut **o** from his people. Lv 23:29
book and wash them **o** into the water Nm 5:23
person shall be cut **o** from his people Nm 9:13
person shall be cut **o** from among his Nm 15:30
that person shall be utterly cut **o**; Nm 15:31
put fire on it from **o** the altar and lay Nm 16:46
that person shall be cut **o** from Israel; Nm 19:13
person shall be cut **o** from the midst Nm 19:20
and he destroy you from **o** the face of the Dt 6:15
you will perish quickly **o** the good land Dt 11:17
LORD your God cuts **o** before you the Dt 12:29
you, whether near you or far **o** from you, Dt 13:7
LORD your God cuts **o** the nations whose Dt 19:1
And she shall take **o** the clothes in Dt 21:13
male organ is cut **o** shall enter the Dt 23:1
and pull his sandal **o** his foot and spit Dt 25:9
of him who had his sandal pulled **o**.' Dt 25:10
then you shall cut **o** her hand. Your eye Dt 25:12
faint and weary, and cut **o** your tail, Dt 25:18
he has consumed you **o** the land that Dt 28:21
with the oil, for your olives shall drop **o**. Dt 28:40
you shall be plucked **o** the land that Dt 28:63
your sandals have not worn **o** your feet. Dt 29:5
not too hard for you, neither is it far **o**. Dt 30:11
like a lion; he tears **o** arm and scalp. Dt 33:20
the Jordan shall be cut **o** from flowing, Jos 3:13
the Salt Sea, were completely cut **o**. Jos 3:16
of the Jordan were cut **o** before the ark of Jos 4:7
the waters of the Jordan were cut **o**. Jos 4:7
"Take **o** your sandals from your feet, Jos 5:15
surround us and cut **o** our name from Jos 7:9
that time and cut **o** the Anakim from Jos 11:21
And she got **o** her donkey, and Caleb Jos 15:18
long will you put **o** going in to take Jos 18:3
all the nations that I have already cut **o**, Jos 23:4
you perish from **o** this good ground Jos 23:13
destroyed you from **o** this good land Jos 23:15
perish quickly from **o** the good land Jos 23:16
caught him and cut **o** his thumbs and Jgs 1:6
and their big toes cut **o** used to pick up Jgs 1:7
fire, and his bonds melted **o** his hands. Jgs 15:14
he snapped the ropes **o** his arms like a Jgs 16:12
and had him shave **o** the seven locks of Jgs 16:19
"One tribe is cut **o** from Israel this day. Jgs 21:6
from the dancers whom they carried **o**. Jgs 21:23
the one drew **o** his sandal and gave it to Ru 4:7
"Buy it for yourself," he drew **o** his sandal. Ru 4:8
may not be cut **o** from among his Ru 4:10
the wicked shall be cut **o** in darkness, 1 Sm 2:9
when I will cut **o** your strength and 1 Sm 2:31
I shall not cut **o** from my altar shall 1 Sm 2:33
were lying cut **o** on the threshold. 1 Sm 5:4
lighten his hand from **o** you and your 1 Sm 6:5
Then send it **o** and let it go its way 1 Sm 6:8
tested them." So David put them **o**. 1 Sm 17:39
you down and cut **o** your head. 1 Sm 17:46
killed him and cut **o** his head with it. 1 Sm 17:51
And he too stripped **o** his clothes, 1 Sm 19:24
and do not cut **o** your steadfast love 1 Sm 20:15
when the LORD cuts **o** every one of the 1 Sm 20:15
arose and stealthily cut **o** a corner of 1 Sm 24:4
because he had cut **o** a corner of 1 Sm 24:5
fact that I cut **o** the corner of your 1 Sm 24:11
you will not cut **o** my offspring after 1 Sm 24:21
side and stood far **o** on the top of 1 Sm 26:13
how he has cut **o** the mediums and 1 Sm 28:9
but carried them **o** and went their 1 Sm 30:2
So they cut **o** his head and stripped off 1 Sm 31:9
his head and stripped **o** his armor and 1 Sm 31:9
killed them and cut **o** their hands and 2 Sm 4:12
the lame will ward you **o**"—thinking, 2 Sm 5:6
went and have cut **o** all your enemies 2 Sm 7:9
servants and shaved **o** half the beard 2 Sm 10:4
of each and cut **o** their garments in 2 Sm 10:4
Let me go over and take **o** his head." 2 Sm 16:9
his donkey and went **o** home to his 2 Sm 17:23
And they cut **o** the head of Sheba the 2 Sm 20:22
to the land of the enemy, far **o** or near, 1 Kgs 8:46

then I will cut **o** Israel from the land 1 Kgs 9:7
until he had cut **o** every male in 1 Kgs 11:16
so as to cut it **o** and to destroy it 1 Kgs 13:34
and will cut **o** from Jeroboam every 1 Kgs 14:10
Israel who shall cut **o** the house of 1 Kgs 14:14
when Jezebel cut **o** the prophets of 1 Kgs 18:4
himself like he who takes it **o**.'" 1 Kgs 20:11
and will cut **o** from Ahab every 1 Kgs 21:21
their raids had carried **o** a little girl 2 Kgs 5:2
he cut **o** a stick and threw it in there 2 Kgs 6:6
murderer has sent to take **o** my head? 2 Kgs 6:32
and they carried **o** silver and gold and 2 Kgs 7:8
tent and carried **o** things from it 2 Kgs 7:8
and I will cut **o** from Ahab every male, 2 Kgs 9:8
LORD began to cut **o** parts of Israel. 2 Kgs 10:32
those who come **o** duty on the 2 Kgs 11:5
who were to go **o** duty on the 2 Kgs 11:9
And King Ahaz cut **o** the frames of 2 Kgs 16:17
down the sea from **o** the bronze oxen 2 Kgs 16:17
and I will cast **o** this city that I have 2 Kgs 23:27
and carried **o** all the treasures of the 2 Kgs 24:13
So Jehoiachin put **o** his prison 2 Kgs 25:29
They carried **o** their livestock: 50,000 1 Chr 5:21
gone and have cut **o** all your enemies 1 Chr 17:8
that he had carried **o** from all the 1 Chr 18:11
them and cut **o** their garments in 1 Chr 19:4
him, he will cast you **o** forever. 1 Chr 28:9
they were to rinse **o** what was used for 2 Chr 4:6
and Levites who come **o** duty on the 2 Chr 23:4
who were to go **o** duty on the 2 Chr 23:8
who cut **o** all the mighty warriors 2 Chr 32:21
me, none of us took **o** our clothes; Neh 4:23
so that he might take **o** his sackcloth, Est 4:4
And the king took **o** his signet ring, Est 8:2
perished? Or where were the upright cut **o**? Jb 4:7
he would let loose his hand and cut me **o**! Jb 6:9
my complaint, I will put **o** my sad face, Jb 9:27
He will shake **o** his unripe grape like the Jb 15:33
and cast **o** his blossom like the olive Jb 15:33
my plans are broken **o**, the desires of Jb 17:11
dragged **o** in the day of God's wrath. Jb 20:28
the number of their months is cut **o**? Jb 21:21
'Surely our adversaries are cut **o**, Jb 22:20
They thrust the poor **o** the road; the poor Jb 24:4
they are cut **o** like the heads of grain. Jb 24:24
hope of the godless when God cuts him **o**, Jb 27:8
in the night a whirlwind carries him **o**. Jb 27:20
they have cast **o** restraint in my Jb 30:11
I too was pinched **o** from a piece of clay. Jb 33:6
I? How am I better **o** than if I had sinned?' Jb 35:3
out the prey; his eyes behold it afar **o**. Jb 39:29
Who can strip **o** his outer garment? Jb 41:13
Why, O LORD, do you stand afar **o**? Why Ps 10:1
May the LORD cut **o** all flattering lips, the Ps 12:3
But you, O LORD, do not be far **o**! O you Ps 22:19
Cast me not **o**; forsake me not, O God of Ps 27:9
Do not drag me **o** with the wicked, with Ps 28:3
"I am cut **o** from your sight." But you Ps 31:22
to cut **o** the memory of them from the Ps 34:16
For the evildoers shall be cut **o**, but those Ps 37:9
but those cursed by him shall be cut **o**. Ps 37:22
children of the wicked shall be cut **o**. Ps 37:28
will look on when the wicked are cut **o**. Ps 37:34
the future of the wicked shall be cut **o**. Ps 37:38
plague, and my nearest kin stand far **o**. Ps 38:11
Do not cast me **o** in the time of old age; Ps 71:9
O God, why do you cast us **o** forever? Ps 74:1
All the horns of the wicked I will cut **o**, Ps 75:10
who cuts **o** the spirit of princes, who is Ps 76:12
more, for they are cut **o** from your hand. Ps 88:5
But now you have cast **o** and rejected; Ps 89:38
cutting **o** all the evildoers from the city Ps 101:8
May his posterity be cut **o**; may his Ps 109:13
that he may cut **o** the memory of them Ps 109:15
evening; I am shaken **o** like a locust. Ps 109:23
in the name of the LORD I cut them **o**! Ps 118:10
in the name of the LORD I cut them **o**! Ps 118:11
in the name of the LORD I cut them **o**! Ps 118:12
love you will cut **o** my enemies, Ps 143:12
the wicked will be cut **o** from the land, Prv 2:22
but the perverse tongue will be cut **o**. Prv 10:31
and your hope will not be cut **o**. Prv 23:18
and your hope will not be cut **o**. Prv 24:14
is like one who takes **o** a garment on a Prv 25:20
hand of a fool cuts **o** his own feet and Prv 26:6
vision the people cast **o** restraint, Prv 29:18
to devour the poor from **o** the earth, Prv 30:14
that a stillborn child is better **o** than he. Eccl 6:3
That which has been is far **o**, and deep, Eccl 7:24
perfumer's ointment give **o** a stench; Eccl 10:1
I had put **o** my garment; how could I put it Sg 5:3
He will raise a signal for nations afar **o**, Is 5:26
prey; they carry it **o**, and none can rescue. Is 5:29
So the LORD cut **o** from Israel head and Is 9:14
to destroy, and to cut **o** nations not a few; Is 10:7
those who harass Judah shall be cut **o**; Is 11:13
"and will cut **o** from Babylon name and Is 14:22
he cuts **o** the shoots with pruning hooks, Is 18:5
branches he lops **o** and clears away. Is 18:5
your waist and take **o** your sandals from Is 20:2
and the load that was on it will be cut **o**, Is 22:25
all who watch to do evil shall be cut **o**, Is 29:20
Bashan and Carmel shake **o** their leaves. Is 33:9
Hear, you who are far **o**, what I have Is 33:13
up my life; he cuts me **o** from the loom; Is 38:12
hand and marked **o** the heavens with Is 40:12
the tempest carries them **o** like stubble. Is 40:24
I have chosen you and not cast you **o**"; Is 41:9
it is not far **o**, and my salvation will not Is 46:13
and grind flour, put **o** your veil, Is 47:2
flour, put off your veil, strip **o** your robe, Is 47:2
it for you, that I may not cut you **o**. Is 48:9
would never be cut **o** or destroyed from Is 48:19
that he was cut **o** out of the land Is 53:8
like a wife of youth when she is cast **o**," Is 54:6
everlasting sign that shall not be cut **o**." Is 55:13
everlasting name that shall not be cut **o**. Is 56:5
you sent your envoys far **o**, and sent down Is 57:9
The wind will carry them **o**, a breath Is 57:13
back, and righteousness stands afar **o**; Is 59:14
and Javan, to the coastlands afar **o**, Is 66:19
has perished; it is cut **o** from their lips. Jer 7:28
"'Cut **o** your hair and cast it away; raise Jer 7:29
cutting **o** the children from the streets Jer 9:21
let us cut him **o** from the land of the Jer 11:19
my right hand, yet I would tear you **o** Jer 22:24
declares the LORD, and not a God afar **o**? Jer 23:23
are the burden, and I will cast you **o**, Jer 23:33
the yoke-bars from **o** the neck of Jer 28:12
I will break his yoke from **o** your neck, Jer 30:8
then I will cast **o** all the offspring of Jer 31:37
king would cut them **o** with a knife Jer 36:23
and will cut **o** from it man and beast?" Jer 36:29
to cut **o** from you man and woman, Jer 44:7
you may be cut **o** and become a curse Jer 44:8
you for harm, to cut **o** all Judah. Jer 44:11
But since we left **o** making offerings to Jer 44:18
to cut **o** from Tyre and Sidon every Jer 47:4
let us cut her **o** from being a nation!' Jer 48:2
The horn of Moab is cut **o**, and his arm Jer 48:25
head is shaved and every beard cut **o**. Jer 48:37
Cut **o** from Babylon the sower, and the Jer 50:16
his life! Be not cut **o** in her punishment, Jer 51:6
this place that you will cut it **o**, Jer 51:62
So Jehoiachin put **o** his prison Jer 52:33
For the Lord will not cast **o** forever, Lam 3:31
He who is far **o** shall die of pestilence, Ezk 6:12
removed them far **o** among the Ezk 11:16
now, and he prophesies of times far **o**.' Ezk 12:27
also I will tear **o** and deliver my people Ezk 13:21
byword and cut him **o** from the midst Ezk 14:8
it, and cut **o** from it man and beast, Ezk 14:13
and I cut **o** from it man and beast, Ezk 14:17
blood, to cut **o** from it man and beast, Ezk 14:19
to cut **o** from it man and beast! Ezk 14:21
water and washed **o** your blood from Ezk 16:9
He broke **o** the topmost of its young Ezk 17:4
not pull up its roots and cut **o** its fruit, Ezk 17:9
siege walls built to cut **o** many lives. Ezk 17:17
I will break **o** from the topmost of its Ezk 17:22
they were stripped **o** and withered. Ezk 19:12
sheath and will cut **o** from you both Ezk 21:3
Because I will cut **o** from you both Ezk 21:4
the turban and take **o** the crown. Ezk 21:26
They shall cut **o** your nose and your Ezk 23:25
I will cut you **o** from the peoples and Ezk 25:7
against Edom and cut **o** from it man Ezk 25:13
and I will cut **o** the Cherethites and Ezk 25:16
robes and strip **o** their embroidered Ezk 26:16
and will cut **o** from you man and beast, Ezk 29:8
and he shall carry **o** its wealth and Ezk 29:19
and cut **o** the multitude of Thebes. Ezk 30:15
and I will cut **o** from it all who come Ezk 35:7
our hope is lost; we are clean cut **o**.' Ezk 37:11
to seize spoil and carry **o** plunder, to Ezk 38:12
your hosts to carry **o** plunder, Ezk 38:13
And **o** to the side, on the outside as one Ezk 40:40
and **o** to the other side of the vestibule Ezk 40:40
they shall put **o** the garments in Ezk 44:19
you shall measure **o** a section 25,000 Ezk 45:3
down the tree and lop **o** its branches, Dn 4:14
strip **o** its leaves and scatter its fruit. Dn 4:14
break **o** your sins by practicing Dn 4:27
as I looked its wings were plucked **o**, Dn 7:4
one shall be cut **o** and shall have Dn 9:26
He shall also carry **o** to Egypt their gods Dn 11:8
I will carry **o**, and no one shall rescue. Hos 5:14
king of Israel shall be utterly cut **o**. Hos 10:15
sweet wine, for it is cut **o** from your mouth. Jl 1:5
it has stripped **o** their bark and thrown it Jl 1:7
drink offering are cut **o** from the house of Jl 1:9
Is not the food cut **o** before our eyes, joy Jl 1:16
and cut **o** the inhabitants from the Am 1:5
I will cut **o** the inhabitants from Am 1:8
with the sword and cast **o** all pity, Am 1:11
I will cut **o** the ruler from its midst, and Am 2:3
the altar shall be cut **o** and fall to the Am 3:14
Mount Esau will be cut **o** by slaughter. Ob 1:9
you, and you shall be cut **o** forever. Ob 1:10
that strangers carried **o** his wealth and Ob 1:11
at the crossroads to cut **o** his fugitives; Ob 1:14
yourselves bald and cut **o** your hair, Mi 1:16
tear the skin from **o** my people and their Mi 3:2
people and their flesh from **o** their bones, Mi 3:2
people, and flay their skin from **o** them, Mi 3:3
and shall decide for strong nations afar **o**; Mi 4:3
the remnant, and those who were cast **o**, Mi 4:7
and all your enemies shall be cut **o**. Mi 5:9
I will cut **o** your horses from among you Mi 5:10
and I will cut **o** the cities of your land Mi 5:11
and I will cut **o** sorceries from your Mi 5:12
and I will cut **o** your carved images and Mi 5:13
break his yoke from **o** you and will Na 1:13
gods I will cut **o** the carved image and Na 1:14
pass through you; he is utterly cut **o**. Na 1:15
she is carried **o**, her slave girls lamenting, Na 2:7
I will cut **o** your prey from the earth, Na 2:13
devour you; the sword will cut you **o**. Na 3:15
your house by cutting **o** many peoples; Hab 2:10
the flock be cut **o** from the fold and Hab 3:17
I will cut **o** mankind from the face of the Zep 1:3
and I will cut **o** from this place the Zep 1:4
more; all who weigh out silver are cut **o**. Zep 1:11
"I have cut **o** nations; their battlements Zep 3:6
would not be cut **o** according to all that Zep 3:7
those who are far **o** shall come and help Zec 6:15
and I will cut **o** the pride of Philistia. Zec 9:6
I will cut **o** the chariot from Ephraim Zec 9:10
and the battle bow shall be cut **o**, and Zec 9:10
the fat ones, tearing **o** even their hoofs. Zec 11:16
I will cut **o** the names of the idols from Zec 13:2
two thirds shall be cut **o** and perish, Zec 13:8
people shall not be cut **o** from the city. Zec 14:2
May the LORD cut **o** from the tents of Mal 2:12
you to sin, cut it **o** and throw it away. Mt 5:30
shake **o** the dust from your feet when Mt 10:14
you to sin, cut it **o** and throw it away. Mt 18:8
But they paid no attention and went **o**, Mt 22:5
of the high priest and cut **o** his ear. Mt 26:51
shake **o** the dust that is on your feet as a Mk 6:11
if your hand causes you to sin, cut it **o**. Mk 9:43
if your foot causes you to sin, cut it **o**. Mk 9:45
And throwing **o** his cloak, he sprang Mk 10:50
of the high priest and cut **o** his ear. Mk 14:47
leave that town shake **o** the dust from Lk 9:5
clings to our feet we wipe **o** against you. Lk 10:11
not, while the other is yet a great way **o**, Lk 14:32
But while he was still a long way **o**, his Lk 15:20
and saw Abraham far **o** and Lazarus at Lk 16:23
But the tax collector, standing far **o**, Lk 18:13
the high priest and cut **o** his right ear. Lk 22:50
was near Jerusalem, about two miles **o**, Jn 11:18
priest's servant and cut **o** his right ear. Jn 18:10
of the man whose ear Peter had cut **o**, Jn 18:26
the land, but about a hundred yards **o**. Jn 21:8
your children and for all who are far **o**, Acts 2:39
'Take **o** the sandals from your feet, Acts 7:33
he dragged **o** men and women and Acts 8:3
to Caesarea and sent him **o** to Tarsus. Acts 9:30
And the chains fell **o** his hands. Acts 12:7
their hands on them and sent them **o**. Acts 13:3
But they shook **o** the dust from their Acts 13:51
So when they were sent **o**, they went Acts 15:30
they were sent **o** in peace by the Acts 15:33
tore the garments **o** them and gave Acts 16:22
immediately sent Paul **o** on his way Acts 17:14
shouting and throwing **o** their cloaks Acts 22:23
knowledge of the Way, put them **o**, Acts 24:22
and arrived with difficulty **o** Cnidus, Acts 27:7
sailed under the lee of Crete **o** Salmone. Acts 27:7
So they cast **o** the anchors and left Acts 27:40
shook **o** the creature into the fire and Acts 28:5
What then? Are we Jews any better **o**? Rom 3:9
accursed and cut **o** from Christ for Rom 9:3
some of the branches were broken **o**, Rom 11:17
"Branches were broken **o** so that I Rom 11:19
They were broken **o** because of their Rom 11:20
Otherwise you too will be cut **o**. Rom 11:22
then let us cast **o** the works of Rom 13:12
We are no worse **o** if we do not eat, and 1 Cor 8:8
we do not eat, and no better **o** if we do. 1 Cor 8:8
for a wife to cut **o** her hair or shave 1 Cor 11:6
who once were far **o** have been brought Eph 2:13
you who were far **o** and peace to those Eph 2:17
to put **o** your old self, which belongs to Eph 4:22

by putting **o** the body of the flesh, Col 2:11
that you have put **o** the old self with Col 3:9
to the truth and wander **o** into myths. 2 Tm 4:4
know that the putting **o** of my body 2 Pt 1:14
the woman and went **o** to make war on Rv 12:17
They will stand far **o**, in fear of her Rv 18:10
wealth from her, will stand far **o**, Rv 18:15
all whose trade is on the sea, stood far **o** Rv 18:17

OFFEND (1)
punishment; I will not **o** any more; Jb 34:31

OFFENDED (5)
A brother **o** is more unyielding than a Prv 18:19
and has grievously **o** in taking Ezk 25:12
blessed is the one who is not **o** by me." Mt 11:6
the Pharisees were **o** when they heard Mt 15:12
blessed is the one who is not **o** by me." Lk 7:23

OFFENDER (1)
by a word make a man out to be an **o**, Is 29:21

OFFENDERS (2)
my son Solomon will be counted **o**." 1 Kgs 1:21
that they were worse **o** than all the Lk 13:4

OFFENSE (17)
Jacob said to Laban, "What is my **o**? Gn 31:36
baker committed an **o** against their lord Gn 40:1
in connection with any **o** that he has Dt 19:15
has committed no **o** punishable by Dt 22:26
number of stripes in proportion to his **o**. Dt 25:2
Whoever covers an **o** seeks love, but he Prv 17:9
and it is his glory to overlook an **o**. Prv 19:11
sanctuary and a stone of **o** and a rock of Is 8:14
And they took **o** at him. But Jesus said Mt 13:57
However, not to give **o** to them, go to the Mt 17:27
here with us?" And they took **o** at him. Mk 6:3
this, said to them, "Do you take **o** at this? Jn 6:61
Caesar have I committed any **o**." Acts 25:8
a stone of stumbling, and a rock of **o**; Rom 9:33
Give no **o** to Jews or to Greeks or to 1 Cor 10:32
In that case the **o** of the cross has been Gal 5:11
and a rock of **o**." They stumble because 1 Pt 2:8

OFFENSES (3)
to Pharaoh, "I remember my **o** today. Gn 41:9
stirs up strife, but love covers all **o**. Prv 10:12
for calmness will lay great **o** to rest. Eccl 10:4

OFFER (201)
and **o** him there as a burnt offering on Gn 22:2
cry, 'Let us go and **o** sacrifice to our God.' Ex 5:8
shall not delay to **o** from the fullness of Ex 22:29
"You shall not **o** the blood of my Ex 23:18
and every day you shall **o** a bull as a Ex 29:36
this is what you shall **o** on the altar: Ex 29:38
One lamb you shall **o** in the morning, Ex 29:39
the other lamb you shall **o** at twilight. Ex 29:39
The other lamb you shall **o** at twilight, Ex 29:41
and shall **o** with it a grain offering and Ex 29:41
You shall not **o** unauthorized incense Ex 30:9
"You shall not **o** the blood of my Ex 34:25
herd, he shall **o** a male without blemish. Lv 1:3
And the priest shall **o** all of it and burn it Lv 1:13
with all your offerings you shall **o** salt. Lv 2:13
"If you **o** a grain offering of firstfruits to Lv 2:14
you shall **o** for the grain offering of your Lv 2:14
he shall **o** it without blemish before the Lv 3:1
he shall **o** the fat covering the entrails and Lv 3:3
or female, he shall **o** it without blemish. Lv 3:6
offering, then he shall **o** it before the LORD, Lv 3:7
peace offering he shall **o** as a food offering Lv 3:9
a goat, then he shall **o** it before the LORD Lv 3:12
Then he shall **o** from it, as his offering Lv 3:14
then he shall **o** for the sin that he has Lv 4:3
the assembly shall **o** a bull from the Lv 4:14
who shall **o** first the one for the sin Lv 5:8
Then he shall **o** the second for a burnt Lv 5:10
sons of Aaron shall **o** it before the LORD Lv 6:14
and his sons shall **o** to the LORD on Lv 6:20
and **o** it for a pleasing aroma to the LORD. Lv 6:21
shall **o** it to the LORD as decreed forever. Lv 6:22
offerings that one may **o** to the LORD. Lv 7:11
then he shall **o** with the thanksgiving Lv 7:12
from it he shall **o** one loaf from each Lv 7:14
blemish, and **o** them before the LORD. Lv 9:2
to the altar and **o** your sin offering and Lv 9:7
and he shall **o** it before the LORD and Lv 12:7
of the male lambs and **o** it for a guilt Lv 14:12
The priest shall **o** the sin offering, to Lv 14:19
the priest shall **o** the burnt offering Lv 14:20
And he shall **o**, of the turtledoves or Lv 14:30
"Aaron shall **o** the bull as a sin offering Lv 16:6
and come out and **o** his burnt offering Lv 16:24
of the tent of meeting to **o** it as a gift to Lv 17:4
of the tent of meeting to **o** it to the LORD, Lv 17:9
of your children to **o** them to Molech, Lv 18:21
"When you **o** a sacrifice of peace Lv 19:5
you shall **o** it so that you may be Lv 19:5
eaten the same day you **o** it or on the day Lv 19:6
For they **o** the LORD'S food offerings, the Lv 21:6
may approach to **o** the bread of Lv 21:17
shall come near to **o** the LORD'S food Lv 21:21
not come near to **o** the bread of his Lv 21:21
offerings that they **o** to the LORD, Lv 22:18
You shall not **o** anything that has a Lv 22:20
or scabs you shall not **o** to the LORD or Lv 22:22
torn or cut you shall not **o** to the LORD; Lv 22:24
neither shall you **o** as the bread of your Lv 22:25
you shall **o** a male lamb a year old Lv 23:12
And you shall **o** one male goat for a sin Lv 23:19
and the priest shall **o** one for a sin Nm 6:11
before the LORD and **o** his sin offering Nm 6:16
and he shall **o** the ram as a sacrifice of Nm 6:17
The priest shall **o** also its grain offering Nm 6:17
to Moses, "They shall **o** their offerings, Nm 7:11
and Aaron shall **o** the Levites before Nm 8:11
and you shall **o** the one for a sin Nm 8:12
and shall **o** them as a wave offering to Nm 8:13
and you **o** to the LORD from the herd or Nm 15:3
brings his offering shall **o** to the LORD a Nm 15:4
and you shall **o** with the burnt Nm 15:5
you shall **o** for a grain offering two Nm 15:6
drink offering you shall **o** a third of a Nm 15:7
And when you **o** a bull as a burnt Nm 15:8
then one shall **o** with the bull a grain Nm 15:9
And you shall **o** for the drink offering Nm 15:10
As many as you **o**, so shall you do Nm 15:12
and he wishes to **o** a food offering, Nm 15:14
the congregation shall **o** one bull Nm 15:24
he shall **o** a female goat a year old for Nm 15:27
or beast, which they **o** to the LORD, Nm 18:15
you shall be careful to **o** to me at its Nm 28:2
offering that you shall **o** to the LORD: Nm 28:3
one lamb you shall **o** in the morning, Nm 28:4
the other lamb you shall **o** at twilight; Nm 28:4
The other lamb you shall **o** at twilight. Nm 28:8
you shall **o** it as a food offering, Nm 28:8
you shall **o** a burnt offering to the Nm 28:11
but **o** a food offering, a burnt offering Nm 28:19
of an ephah shall you **o** for a bull, Nm 28:20
a tenth shall you **o** for each of the Nm 28:21
You shall **o** these besides the burnt Nm 28:23
In the same way you shall **o** daily, for Nm 28:24
when you **o** a grain offering of new Nm 28:26
but **o** a burnt offering, with a pleasing Nm 28:27
you shall **o** them and their drink Nm 28:31
and you shall **o** a burnt offering, for a Nm 29:2
but you shall **o** a burnt offering to the Nm 29:8
And you shall **o** a burnt offering, a Nm 29:13
but you shall **o** a burnt offering, a Nm 29:36
"These you shall **o** to the LORD at your Nm 29:39
that you do not **o** your burnt offerings Dt 12:13
there you shall **o** your burnt offerings, Dt 12:14
and **o** your burnt offerings, the flesh Dt 12:27
And you shall **o** the Passover sacrifice to Dt 16:2
You may not **o** the Passover sacrifice Dt 16:5
there you shall **o** the Passover sacrifice, Dt 16:6
to fight against it, **o** terms of peace to it. Dt 20:10
And you shall **o** burnt offerings on it to Dt 27:6
and there you shall **o** yourselves for sale Dt 28:68
mountain; there they **o** right sacrifices; Dt 33:19
we did so to **o** burnt offerings or grain Jos 22:23
take the second bull and **o** it as a burnt Jgs 6:26
and I will **o** it up for a burnt offering." Jgs 11:31
then **o** it to the LORD." (For Manoah did Jgs 13:16
Philistines gathered to **o** a great Jgs 16:23
his house went up to **o** to the LORD the 1 Sm 1:21
her husband to **o** the yearly sacrifice. 1 Sm 2:19
to you to **o** burnt offerings and 1 Sm 10:8
then I will **o** worship to the LORD.'" 2 Sm 15:8
says the LORD, Three things I **o** you. 2 Sm 24:12
the king take and **o** up what seems 2 Sm 24:22
I will not **o** burnt offerings to the 2 Sm 24:24
Solomon used to **o** a thousand burnt 1 Kgs 3:4
Solomon used to **o** up burnt offerings 1 Kgs 9:25
people go up to **o** sacrifices in the 1 Kgs 12:27
servant will not **o** burnt offering or 2 Kgs 5:17
I have a great sacrifice to **o** to Baal. 2 Kgs 10:19
went in to **o** sacrifices and burnt 2 Kgs 10:24
to **o** burnt offerings to the LORD on 1 Chr 16:40
says the LORD, Three things I **o** you; 1 Chr 21:10
nor **o** burnt offerings that cost me 1 Chr 21:24
and 4,000 shall **o** praises to the LORD 1 Chr 23:5
Who then will **o** willingly, 1 Chr 29:5
should be able thus to **o** willingly? 1 Chr 29:14
They **o** to the LORD every morning 2 Chr 13:11
to **o** burnt offerings to the LORD, 2 Chr 23:18
sons of Aaron to **o** them on the altar 2 Chr 29:21
of the lay people, to **o** to the LORD, 2 Chr 35:12
Passover and to **o** burnt offerings 2 Chr 35:16
God of Israel, to **o** burnt offerings on it, Ezr 3:2
month they began to **o** burnt offerings to Ezr 3:6
that they may **o** pleasing sacrifices to Ezr 6:10
and you shall **o** them on the altar of the Ezr 7:17
the morning and **o** burnt offerings Jb 1:5
Or, 'From your wealth **o** a bribe for me'? Jb 6:22
my servant Job and **o** up a burnt offering Jb 42:8
O right sacrifices, and put your trust in Ps 4:5
and I will **o** in his tent sacrifices with Ps 27:6
everyone who is godly **o** prayer to you at Ps 32:6
O to God a sacrifice of thanksgiving, Ps 50:14
I will **o** to you burnt offerings of Ps 66:15
And let them **o** sacrifices of Ps 107:22
Your people will **o** themselves freely on Ps 110:3
I will **o** to you the sacrifice of Ps 116:17
"I had to **o** sacrifices, and today I have Prv 7:14
is better than to **o** the sacrifice of fools, Eccl 5:1
bed, and there you went up to **o** sacrifice. Is 57:7
and though they **o** burnt offering and Jer 14:12
to **o** up their sons and daughters to Jer 32:35
in my presence to **o** burnt offerings, Jer 33:18
chambers; then **o** them wine to drink." Jer 35:2
Even jackals **o** the breast; they nurse Lam 4:3
your gifts and **o** up your children Ezk 20:31
second day you shall **o** a male goat Ezk 43:22
you shall **o** a bull from the herd Ezk 43:23
salt on them and **o** them up as a Ezk 43:24
onward the priests shall **o** on the altar Ezk 43:27
my temple, when you **o** to me my food, Ezk 44:7
stand before me to **o** me the fat and Ezk 44:15
Holy Place, he shall **o** his sin offering, Ezk 44:27
The priests shall **o** his burnt offering Ezk 46:2
new moon he shall **o** a bull from the Ezk 46:6
And he shall **o** his burnt offering or Ezk 46:12
"Those who **o** human sacrifice kiss Hos 13:2
o a sacrifice of thanksgiving of that Am 4:5
Even though you **o** me your burnt Am 5:22
Sabbath, that we may **o** wheat for sale, Am 8:5
And what they **o** there is unclean. Hg 2:14
When you **o** blind animals in sacrifice, Mal 1:8
And when you **o** those that are lame or Mal 1:8
brother, and then come and **o** your gift. Mt 5:24
to the priest and **o** the gift that Moses Mt 8:4
to the priest and **o** for your cleansing Mk 1:44
and to **o** a sacrifice according to what is Lk 2:24
disciples of John fast often and **o** prayers, Lk 5:33
you on the cheek, **o** the other also, Lk 6:29
and wanted to **o** sacrifice with the Acts 14:13
pagans sacrifice they **o** to demons 1 Cor 10:20
to God, to **o** gifts and sacrifices for sins. Heb 5:1
he is obligated to **o** sacrifice for his own Heb 5:3
those high priests, to **o** sacrifices daily, Heb 7:27
is appointed to **o** gifts and sacrifices; Heb 8:3
this priest also to have something to **o**. Heb 8:3
there are priests who **o** gifts according to Heb 8:4
Nor was it to **o** himself repeatedly, as Heb 9:25
and thus let us **o** to God acceptable Heb 12:28
let us continually **o** up a sacrifice Heb 13:15
to **o** spiritual sacrifices acceptable to 1 Pt 2:5
given much incense to **o** with the prayers Rv 8:3

OFFERED (120)
clean bird and **o** burnt offerings on Gn 8:20
and took the ram and **o** it up as a Gn 22:13
and Jacob **o** a sacrifice in the hill Gn 31:54
and **o** sacrifices to the God of his father Gn 46:1
who **o** burnt offerings and sacrificed Ex 24:5
the next day and **o** burnt offerings and Ex 32:6
bronze that was **o** was seventy talents Ex 38:29
and **o** on it the burnt offering and the Ex 40:29
but they shall not be **o** on the altar for a Lv 2:12
And all its fat shall be **o**, the fat tail, the fat Lv 7:3
skin of the burnt offering that he has **o**. Lv 7:8
people and killed it and **o** it as a sin Lv 9:15
the burnt offering and **o** it according to Lv 9:16
on it and **o** unauthorized fire before Lv 10:1
today they have **o** their sin offering and Lv 10:19
animal that may be **o** as an offering to Lv 27:9
that may not be **o** as an offering to Lv 27:11
LORD when they **o** unauthorized fire Nm 3:4
And the chiefs **o** offerings for the Nm 7:10
and the chiefs **o** their offering before Nm 7:10
He who **o** his offering the first day was Nm 7:12
He **o** for his offering one silver plate Nm 7:19
have cleansed them and **o** them as a Nm 8:15
and Aaron **o** them as a wave offering Nm 8:21
altar, for they **o** them before the LORD, Nm 16:38
which those who were burned had **o**, Nm 16:39
'When you have **o** from it the best of Nm 18:30
And Balak and Balaam **o** on each altar Nm 23:2
altars and I have **o** on each altar a Nm 23:4
built seven altars and **o** a bull and a Nm 23:14
and **o** a bull and a ram on each altar. Nm 23:30
died when they **o** unauthorized fire Nm 26:61
it shall be **o** besides the regular burnt Nm 28:15
It shall be **o** besides the regular burnt Nm 28:24
I was unclean, or **o** any of it to the dead. Dt 26:14
iron tool." And they **o** on it burnt Jos 8:31

that the people **o** themselves willingly, Jgs 5:2
of Israel who **o** themselves willingly Jgs 5:9
the second bull was **o** on the altar that Jgs 6:28
and **o** it on the rock to the LORD, Jgs 13:19
and **o** burnt offerings and peace Jgs 20:26
there an altar and **o** burnt offerings and Jgs 21:4
was that when any man **o** sacrifice, 1 Sm 2:13
wood of the cart and **o** the cows as a 1 Sm 6:14
of Beth-shemesh **o** burnt offerings 1 Sm 6:15
a nursing lamb and **o** it as a whole 1 Sm 7:9
offerings." And he **o** the burnt 1 Sm 13:9
myself, and **o** the burnt offering." 1 Sm 13:12
And David **o** burnt offerings and 2 Sm 6:17
the LORD and **o** burnt offerings and 2 Sm 24:25
and **o** up burnt offerings and peace 1 Kgs 3:15
with him, **o** sacrifice before the LORD. 1 Kgs 8:62
Solomon **o** as peace offerings to the 1 Kgs 8:63
for there he **o** the burnt offering and 1 Kgs 8:64
burnt offerings that he **o** at the house 1 Kgs 10:5
and he **o** sacrifices on the altar. 1 Kgs 12:32
in his place and **o** him for a burnt 2 Kgs 3:27
and **o** no tribute to the king of 2 Kgs 17:4
and they **o** burnt offerings and peace 1 Chr 16:1
burnt offerings were **o** to the LORD 1 Chr 23:31
whole heart they had **o** freely to the 1 Chr 29:9
heart I have freely **o** all these things, 1 Chr 29:17
And they **o** sacrifices to the LORD, 1 Chr 29:21
on the next day **o** burnt offerings to 1 Chr 29:21
and **o** a thousand burnt offerings on 2 Chr 1:6
and all the people **o** sacrifice before the 2 Chr 7:4
King Solomon **o** as a sacrifice 22,000 2 Chr 7:5
—whenever David **o** praises by their 2 Chr 7:6
for there he **o** the burnt offering and 2 Chr 7:7
Then Solomon **o** up burnt offerings 2 Chr 8:12
burnt offerings that he **o** at the house 2 Chr 9:4
And they **o** burnt offerings in the 2 Chr 24:14
burned incense or **o** burnt offerings 2 Chr 29:7
the burnt offering be **o** on the altar. 2 Chr 29:27
of the LORD and **o** on it sacrifices of 2 Chr 33:16
costly wares, besides all that was freely **o**. Ezr 1:6
and they **o** burnt offerings on it to the Ezr 3:3
and **o** the daily burnt offerings by Ezr 3:4
rebuilt, the place where sacrifices were **o**, Ezr 6:3
They **o** at the dedication of this house of Ezr 6:17
his counselors have freely **o** to the God Ezr 7:15
lords and all Israel there present had **o**. Ezr 8:25
o burnt offerings to the God of Israel, Ezr 8:35
the men who willingly **o** to live in Neh 11:2
And they **o** great sacrifices that day Neh 12:43
then bulls will be **o** on your altar. Ps 51:19
of Peor, and ate sacrifices **o** to the dead; Ps 106:28
If a man **o** for love all the wealth of his Sg 8:7
roofs offerings have been **o** to all the Jer 19:13
the offerings that you **o** in the cities of Jer 44:21
wherever they **o** pleasing aroma to all Ezk 6:13
there they **o** their sacrifices and there Ezk 20:28
and they have even **o** up to them for Ezk 23:37
an offering and incense be **o** up to him. Dn 2:46
and they **o** a sacrifice to the LORD and Jon 1:16
place incense will be **o** to my name, Mal 1:11
opening their treasures, they **o** him gifts, Mt 2:11
they **o** him wine to drink, mixed with Mt 27:34
And they **o** him wine mixed with Mk 15:23
and **o** a sacrifice to the idol and were Acts 7:41
the apostles' hands, he **o** them money, Acts 8:18
If the dough **o** as firstfruits is holy, so Rom 11:16
Now concerning food **o** to idols: we 1 Cor 8:1
as to the eating of food **o** to idols, 1 Cor 8:4
idols, eat food as really **o** to an idol, 1 Cor 8:7
is weak, to eat food **o** to idols? 1 Cor 8:10
That food **o** to idols is anything, or 1 Cor 10:19
"This has been **o** in sacrifice," then 1 Cor 10:28
Jesus **o** up prayers and supplications, Heb 5:7
this once for all when he **o** up himself. Heb 7:27
and sacrifices are **o** that cannot perfect Heb 9:9
the eternal Spirit **o** himself without Heb 9:14
having been **o** once to bear the sins of Heb 9:28
that are continually **o** every year, Heb 10:1
would they not have ceased to be **o**, Heb 10:2
offerings" (these are **o** according to the Heb 10:8
But when Christ had **o** for all time a Heb 10:12
By faith Abel **o** to God a more Heb 11:4
when he was tested, **o** up Isaac, Heb 11:17
by works when he **o** up his son Isaac Jas 2:21

OFFERING (772)
brought to the LORD an **o** of the fruit of Gn 4:3
the LORD had regard for Abel and his **o**, Gn 4:4
but for Cain and his **o** he had no regard. Gn 4:5
him there as a burnt **o** on one of the Gn 22:2
wood for the burnt **o** and arose and went Gn 22:3
the wood of the burnt **o** and laid it on Gn 22:6
but where is the lamb for a burnt **o**?" Gn 22:7
for himself the lamb for a burnt **o**, Gn 22:8
it up as a burnt **o** instead of his son. Gn 22:13
poured out a drink **o** on it and poured Gn 35:14
brought a burnt **o** and sacrifices to Ex 18:12
with fire outside the camp; it is a sin **o**. Ex 29:14
on the altar. It is a burnt **o** to the LORD. Ex 29:18
a pleasing aroma, a food **o** to the LORD. Ex 29:18
wave them for a wave **o** before the LORD. Ex 29:24
them on the altar on top of the burnt **o**, Ex 29:25
the LORD. It is a food **o** to the LORD. Ex 29:25
wave it for a wave **o** before the LORD, Ex 29:26
breast of the wave **o** that is waved and Ex 29:27
offer a bull as a sin **o** for atonement. Ex 29:36
a fourth of a hin of wine for a drink **o**. Ex 29:40
with it a grain **o** and its drink offering, Ex 29:41
with it a grain offering and its drink **o**, Ex 29:41
a pleasing aroma, a food **o** to the LORD. Ex 29:41
a regular burnt **o** throughout your Ex 29:42
a regular incense **o** before the LORD Ex 30:8
unauthorized incense on it, or a burnt **o**, Ex 30:9
on it, or a burnt offering, or a grain **o**, Ex 30:9
and you shall not pour a drink **o** on it. Ex 30:9
blood of the sin **o** of atonement he shall Ex 30:10
half a shekel as an **o** to the LORD. Ex 30:13
old and upward, shall give the LORD'S **o**. Ex 30:14
give the LORD'S **o** to make atonement Ex 30:15
minister, to burn a food **o** to the LORD, Ex 30:20
the altar of burnt **o** with all its utensils Ex 30:28
the altar of burnt **o** with all its utensils, Ex 31:9
the altar of burnt **o**, with its grating of Ex 35:16
every man dedicating an **o** of gold to Ex 35:22
brought it as a freewill **o** to the LORD. Ex 35:29
the altar of burnt **o** of acacia wood. Ex 38:1
of the sanctuary, the gold from the **o**, Ex 38:24
set the altar of burnt **o** before the door of Ex 40:6
the altar of burnt **o** and all its utensils, Ex 40:10
the altar of burnt **o** at the entrance of Ex 40:29
on it the burnt **o** and the grain offering, Ex 40:29
on it the burnt offering and the grain **o**, Ex 40:29
any one of you brings an **o** to the LORD, Lv 1:2
you shall bring your **o** of livestock from Lv 1:2
"If his **o** is a burnt offering from the herd, Lv 1:3
"If his offering is a burnt **o** from the herd, Lv 1:3
lay his hand on the head of the burnt **o**, Lv 1:4
he shall flay the burnt **o** and cut it into Lv 1:6
burn all of it on the altar, as a burnt **o**, Lv 1:9
a food **o** with a pleasing aroma to the Lv 1:9
"If his gift for a burnt **o** is from the flock, Lv 1:10
it is a burnt **o**, a food offering with a Lv 1:13
a food **o** with a pleasing aroma to the Lv 1:13
"If his **o** to the LORD is a burnt offering of Lv 1:14
offering to the LORD is a burnt **o** of birds, Lv 1:14
he shall bring his **o** of turtledoves or Lv 1:14
It is a burnt **o**, a food offering with a Lv 1:17
a food **o** with a pleasing aroma to the Lv 1:17
anyone brings a grain **o** as an offering to Lv 2:1
a grain offering as an **o** to the LORD, Lv 2:1
to the LORD, his **o** shall be of fine flour. Lv 2:1
a food **o** with a pleasing aroma to the Lv 2:2
the rest of the grain **o** shall be for Aaron Lv 2:3
you bring a grain **o** baked in the oven Lv 2:4
a grain offering baked in the oven as an **o**, Lv 2:4
And if your **o** is a grain offering baked on Lv 2:5
offering is a grain **o** baked on a griddle, Lv 2:5
in pieces and pour oil on it; it is a grain **o**. Lv 2:6
And if your **o** is a grain offering cooked in Lv 2:7
your offering is a grain **o** cooked in a pan, Lv 2:7
shall bring the grain **o** that is made of Lv 2:8
from the grain **o** its memorial portion Lv 2:9
a food **o** with a pleasing aroma to the Lv 2:9
the rest of the grain **o** shall be for Aaron Lv 2:10
"No grain **o** that you bring to the LORD Lv 2:11
nor any honey as a food **o** to the LORD. Lv 2:11
As an **o** of firstfruits you may bring Lv 2:12
your God be missing from your grain **o**; Lv 2:13
"If you offer a grain **o** of firstfruits to the Lv 2:14
offer for the grain **o** of your firstfruits Lv 2:14
lay frankincense on it; it is a grain **o**. Lv 2:15
frankincense; it is a food **o** to the LORD. Lv 2:16
"If his **o** is a sacrifice of peace offering, if Lv 3:1
"If his offering is a sacrifice of peace **o**, if Lv 3:1
hand on the head of his **o** and kill it at the Lv 3:2
And from the sacrifice of the peace **o**, as a Lv 3:3
the peace offering, as a food **o** to the LORD, Lv 3:3
burn it on the altar on top of the burnt **o**, Lv 3:5
it is a food **o** with a pleasing aroma to the Lv 3:5
"If his **o** for a sacrifice of peace offering to Lv 3:6
for a sacrifice of peace **o** to the LORD is an Lv 3:6
If he offers a lamb for his **o**, then he shall Lv 3:7
lay his hand on the head of his **o**, and kill Lv 3:8
sacrifice of the peace **o** he shall offer as Lv 3:9
he shall offer as a food **o** to the LORD its fat; Lv 3:9
on the altar as a food **o** to the LORD. Lv 3:11
"If his **o** is a goat, then he shall offer it Lv 3:12
it, as his **o** for a food offering to the LORD, Lv 3:14
it, as his offering for a food **o** to the LORD, Lv 3:14
altar as a food **o** with a pleasing aroma. Lv 3:16
without blemish to the LORD for a sin **o**. Lv 4:3
of the altar of burnt **o** that is at the Lv 4:7
the bull of the sin **o** he shall remove from Lv 4:8
shall burn them on the altar of burnt **o**. Lv 4:10
the herd for a sin **o** and bring it in front Lv 4:14
of the altar of burnt **o** that is at the Lv 4:18
As he did with the bull of the sin **o**, so Lv 4:20
first bull; it is the sin **o** for the assembly. Lv 4:21
to him, he shall bring as his **o** a goat, Lv 4:23
they kill the burnt **o** before the LORD; Lv 4:24
offering before the LORD; it is a sin **o**. Lv 4:24
the blood of the sin **o** with his finger and Lv 4:25
of the altar of burnt **o** and pour out the Lv 4:25
blood at the base of the altar of burnt **o**. Lv 4:25
to him, he shall bring for his **o** a goat, Lv 4:28
the head of the sin **o** and kill the sin Lv 4:29
offering and kill the sin **o** in the place of Lv 4:29
the sin offering in the place of burnt **o**. Lv 4:29
of the altar of burnt **o** and pour out all Lv 4:30
brings a lamb as his **o** for a sin offering, Lv 4:32
brings a lamb as his offering for a sin **o**, Lv 4:32
on the head of the sin **o** and kill it for a Lv 4:33
kill it for a sin **o** in the place where they Lv 4:33
in the place where they kill the burnt **o**. Lv 4:33
the blood of the sin **o** with his finger and Lv 4:34
of the altar of burnt **o** and pour out all Lv 4:34
the flock, a lamb or a goat, for a sin **o**. Lv 5:6
one for a sin **o** and the other for a burnt Lv 5:7
a sin offering and the other for a burnt **o**. Lv 5:7
who shall offer first the one for the sin **o**. Lv 5:8
of the blood of the sin **o** on the side of the Lv 5:9
out at the base of the altar; it is a sin **o**. Lv 5:9
second for a burnt **o** according to the Lv 5:10
he shall bring as his **o** for the sin that he Lv 5:11
tenth of an ephah of fine flour for a sin **o**. Lv 5:11
no frankincense on it, for it is a sin **o**. Lv 5:11
on the LORD'S food offerings; it is a sin **o**. Lv 5:12
shall be for the priest, as in the grain **o**." Lv 5:13
the shekel of the sanctuary, for a guilt **o**. Lv 5:15
for him with the ram of the guilt **o**, Lv 5:16
the flock, or its equivalent for a guilt **o**, Lv 5:18
It is a guilt **o**; he has indeed incurred Lv 5:19
of the flock, or its equivalent for a guilt **o**. Lv 6:6
saying, This is the law of the burnt **o**. Lv 6:9
The burnt **o** shall be on the hearth on the Lv 6:9
has reduced the burnt **o** on the altar and Lv 6:10
shall arrange the burnt **o** on it and shall Lv 6:12
"And this is the law of the grain **o**. The Lv 6:14
fine flour of the grain **o** and its oil and Lv 6:15
that is on the grain **o** and burn this as its Lv 6:15
holy, like the sin **o** and the guilt offering. Lv 6:17
holy, like the sin offering and the guilt **o**. Lv 6:17
"This is the **o** that Aaron and his sons Lv 6:20
ephah of fine flour as a regular grain **o**, Lv 6:20
mixed, in baked pieces like a grain **o**, Lv 6:21
Every grain **o** of a priest shall be wholly Lv 6:23
sons, saying, This is the law of the sin **o**. Lv 6:25
place where the burnt **o** is killed shall Lv 6:25
killed shall the sin **o** be killed before the Lv 6:25
But no sin **o** shall be eaten from which Lv 6:30
"This is the law of the guilt **o**. It is most Lv 7:1
they kill the burnt **o** they shall kill the Lv 7:2
burnt offering they shall kill the guilt **o**, Lv 7:2
them on the altar as a food **o** to the LORD; Lv 7:5
a food offering to the LORD; it is a guilt **o**. Lv 7:5
The guilt **o** is just like the sin offering; Lv 7:7
The guilt offering is just like the sin **o**; Lv 7:7
offers any man's burnt **o** shall have for Lv 7:8
the skin of the burnt **o** that he has offered. Lv 7:8
And every grain **o** baked in the oven and Lv 7:9
And every grain **o**, mixed with oil or dry, Lv 7:10
he shall bring his **o** with loaves of Lv 7:13
it he shall offer one loaf from each **o**, Lv 7:14
shall be eaten on the day of his **o**. Lv 7:15
if the sacrifice of his **o** is a vow offering Lv 7:16
offering is a vow **o** or a freewill offering, Lv 7:16
offering is a vow offering or a freewill **o**, Lv 7:16
the sacrifice of his peace **o** is eaten on the Lv 7:18
of which a food **o** may be made to Lv 7:25
LORD shall bring his **o** to the LORD from Lv 7:29
be waved as a wave **o** before the LORD. Lv 7:30
This is the law of the burnt **o**, of the Lv 7:37
law of the burnt offering, of the grain **o**, Lv 7:37
of the grain offering, of the sin **o**, Lv 7:37
offering, of the sin offering, of the guilt **o**, Lv 7:37
of the guilt offering, of the ordination **o**, Lv 7:37
ordination offering, and of the peace **o**, Lv 7:37
the bull of the sin **o** and the two rams and Lv 8:2
Then he brought the bull of the sin **o**, Lv 8:14
on the head of the bull of the sin **o**. Lv 8:14
he presented the ram of the burnt **o**, Lv 8:18
It was a burnt **o** with a pleasing aroma, Lv 8:21
a pleasing aroma, a food **o** for the LORD, Lv 8:21
waved them as a wave **o** before the LORD. Lv 8:27
them on the altar with the burnt **o**. Lv 8:28
was an ordination **o** with a pleasing Lv 8:28

a pleasing aroma, a food **o** to the LORD. Lv 8:28
waved it for a wave **o** before the LORD. Lv 8:29
a bull calf for a sin **o** and a ram for a Lv 9:2
for a sin offering and a ram for a burnt **o**, Lv 9:2
of Israel, 'Take a male goat for a sin **o**, Lv 9:3
a year old without blemish, for a burnt **o**, Lv 9:3
the LORD, and a grain **o** mixed with oil, Lv 9:4
and offer your sin **o** and your burnt Lv 9:7
and your burnt **o** and make atonement Lv 9:7
and bring the **o** of the people and make Lv 9:7
to the altar and killed the calf of the sin **o**, Lv 9:8
the liver from the sin **o** he burned on the Lv 9:10
Then he killed the burnt **o**, and Aaron's Lv 9:12
And they handed the burnt **o** to him, Lv 9:13
them with the burnt **o** on the altar. Lv 9:14
he presented the people's **o** and took the Lv 9:15
the goat of the sin **o** that was for the Lv 9:15
and killed it and offered it as a sin **o**, Lv 9:15
he presented the burnt **o** and offered it Lv 9:16
And he presented the grain **o**, took a Lv 9:17
besides the burnt **o** of the morning. Lv 9:17
waved for a wave **o** before the LORD, Lv 9:21
he came down from **o** the sin offering Lv 9:22
from offering the sin **o** and the burnt Lv 9:22
offering and the burnt **o** and the peace Lv 9:22
consumed the burnt **o** and the pieces Lv 9:24
"Take the grain **o** that is left of the Lv 10:12
to wave for a wave **o** before the LORD, Lv 10:15
inquired about the goat of the sin **o**, Lv 10:16
you not eaten the sin **o** in the place of Lv 10:17
have offered their sin **o** and their burnt Lv 10:19
and their burnt **o** before the LORD, Lv 10:19
If I had eaten the sin **o** today, would the Lv 10:19
meeting a lamb a year old for a burnt **o**, Lv 12:6
and a pigeon or a turtledove for a sin **o**, Lv 12:6
one for a burnt **o** and the other for a sin Lv 12:8
a burnt offering and the other for a sin **o**. Lv 12:8
and a grain **o** of three tenths of an Lv 14:10
the male lambs and offer it for a guilt **o**, Lv 14:12
wave them for a wave **o** before the LORD. Lv 14:12
they kill the sin **o** and the burnt Lv 14:13
kill the sin offering and the burnt **o**, Lv 14:13
For the guilt **o**, like the sin offering, Lv 14:13
For the guilt offering, like the sin **o**, Lv 14:13
take some of the blood of the guilt **o**, Lv 14:14
foot, on top of the blood of the guilt **o**. Lv 14:17
The priest shall offer the sin **o**, to make Lv 14:19
And afterward he shall kill the burnt **o**. Lv 14:19
shall offer the burnt **o** and the grain Lv 14:20
offering and the grain **o** on the altar. Lv 14:20
male lamb for a guilt **o** to be waved, Lv 14:21
fine flour mixed with oil for a grain **o**, Lv 14:21
one shall be a sin **o** and the other a Lv 14:22
a sin offering and the other a burnt **o**. Lv 14:22
the lamb of the guilt **o** and the log of Lv 14:24
wave them for a wave **o** before the LORD. Lv 14:24
he shall kill the lamb of the guilt **o**. Lv 14:25
the blood of the guilt **o** and put it on the Lv 14:25
where the blood of the guilt **o** was put. Lv 14:28
one for a sin **o** and the other for a burnt Lv 14:31
sin offering and the other for a burnt **o**, Lv 14:31
a burnt offering, along with a grain **o**. Lv 14:31
one for a sin **o** and the other for a burnt Lv 15:15
sin offering and the other for a burnt **o**. Lv 15:15
use one for a sin **o** and the other for a Lv 15:30
sin offering and the other for a burnt **o**. Lv 15:30
from the herd for a sin **o** and a ram for a Lv 16:3
a sin offering and a ram for a burnt **o**. Lv 16:3
of Israel two male goats for a sin **o**, Lv 16:5
a sin offering, and one ram for a burnt **o**. Lv 16:5
the bull as a sin **o** for himself and shall Lv 16:6
lot fell for the LORD and use it as a sin **o**, Lv 16:9
present the bull as a sin **o** for himself, Lv 16:11
shall kill the bull as a sin **o** for himself. Lv 16:11
the goat of the sin **o** that is for the Lv 16:15
and offer his burnt **o** and the burnt Lv 16:24
offering and the burnt **o** of the people Lv 16:24
the fat of the sin **o** he shall burn on the Lv 16:25
the bull for the sin **o** and the goat for Lv 16:27
sin offering and the goat for the sin **o**, Lv 16:27
them, who offers a burnt **o** or sacrifice Lv 17:8
the tent of meeting, a ram for a guilt **o**. Lv 19:21
ram of the guilt **o** before the LORD for Lv 19:22
shall be holy, an **o** of praise to the LORD. Lv 19:24
Israel presents a burnt **o** as his offering, Lv 22:18
Israel presents a burnt offering as his **o**, Lv 22:18
vow or as a freewill **o** from the herd or Lv 22:21
to the LORD as a food **o** on the altar. Lv 22:22
too long or too short for a freewill **o**, Lv 22:23
but for a vow **o** it cannot be accepted. Lv 22:23
be acceptable as a food **o** to the LORD. Lv 22:27
you shall present a food **o** to the LORD for Lv 23:8
blemish as a burnt **o** to the LORD. Lv 23:12
And the grain **o** with it shall be two Lv 23:13
a food **o** to the LORD with a pleasing Lv 23:13
and the drink **o** with it shall be of wine, Lv 23:13
you have brought the **o** of your God: Lv 23:14
you brought the sheaf of the wave **o**. Lv 23:15
shall present a grain **o** of new grain to Lv 23:16
They shall be a burnt **o** to the LORD, Lv 23:18
with their grain **o** and their drink Lv 23:18
a food **o** with a pleasing aroma to the Lv 23:18
shall offer one male goat for a sin **o**, Lv 23:19
firstfruits as a wave **o** before the LORD, Lv 23:20
you shall present a food **o** to the LORD." Lv 23:25
and present a food **o** to the LORD. Lv 23:27
and present a food **o** to the LORD. Lv 23:36
memorial portion as a food **o** to the LORD. Lv 24:7
that may be offered as an **o** to the LORD, Lv 27:9
may not be offered as an **o** to the LORD, Lv 27:11
bowls, and the flagons for the drink **o**; Nm 4:7
fragrant incense, the regular grain **o**, Nm 4:16
priest and bring the **o** required of her, Nm 5:15
on it, for it is a grain **o** of jealousy, Nm 5:15
of jealousy, a grain **o** of remembrance, Nm 5:15
her hands the grain **o** of remembrance, Nm 5:18
which is the grain **o** of jealousy. Nm 5:18
shall take the grain **o** of jealousy out of Nm 5:25
shall wave the grain **o** before the LORD Nm 5:25
shall take a handful of the grain **o**, Nm 5:26
offer one for a sin **o** and the other for a Nm 6:11
sin offering and the other for a burnt **o**, Nm 6:11
a male lamb a year old for a guilt **o**. Nm 6:12
year old without blemish for a burnt **o**, Nm 6:14
a year old without blemish as a sin **o**, Nm 6:14
one ram without blemish as a peace **o**, Nm 6:14
and their grain **o** and their drink Nm 6:15
and offer his sin **o** and his burnt Nm 6:16
offer his sin offering and his burnt **o**, Nm 6:16
as a sacrifice of peace **o** to the LORD, Nm 6:17
offer also its grain **o** and its drink Nm 6:17
also its grain offering and its drink **o**. Nm 6:17
is under the sacrifice of the peace **o**. Nm 6:18
wave them for a wave **o** before the LORD. Nm 6:20
But if he vows an **o** to the LORD above Nm 6:21
chiefs offered their **o** before the altar. Nm 7:10
He who offered his **o** the first day was Nm 7:12
And his **o** was one silver plate whose Nm 7:13
fine flour mixed with oil for a grain **o**; Nm 7:13
male lamb a year old, for a burnt **o**; Nm 7:15
one male goat for a sin **o**; Nm 7:16
This was the **o** of Nahshon the son of Nm 7:17
Zuar, the chief of Issachar, made an **o**. Nm 7:18
He offered for his **o** one silver plate Nm 7:19
fine flour mixed with oil for a grain **o**; Nm 7:19
male lamb a year old, for a burnt **o**; Nm 7:21
one male goat for a sin **o**; Nm 7:22
This was the **o** of Nethanel the son of Nm 7:23
his **o** was one silver plate whose weight Nm 7:25
fine flour mixed with oil for a grain **o**; Nm 7:25
male lamb a year old, for a burnt **o**; Nm 7:27
one male goat for a sin **o**; Nm 7:28
This was the **o** of Eliab the son of Nm 7:29
his **o** was one silver plate whose weight Nm 7:31
fine flour mixed with oil for a grain **o**; Nm 7:31
male lamb a year old, for a burnt **o**; Nm 7:33
one male goat for a sin **o**; Nm 7:34
This was the **o** of Elizur the son of Nm 7:35
his **o** was one silver plate whose weight Nm 7:37
fine flour mixed with oil for a grain **o**; Nm 7:37
male lamb a year old, for a burnt **o**; Nm 7:39
one male goat for a sin **o**; Nm 7:40
This was the **o** of Shelumiel the son of Nm 7:41
his **o** was one silver plate whose weight Nm 7:43
fine flour mixed with oil for a grain **o**; Nm 7:43
male lamb a year old, for a burnt **o**; Nm 7:45
one male goat for a sin **o**; Nm 7:46
This was the **o** of Eliasaph the son of Nm 7:47
his **o** was one silver plate whose weight Nm 7:49
fine flour mixed with oil for a grain **o**; Nm 7:49
male lamb a year old, for a burnt **o**; Nm 7:51
one male goat for a sin **o**; Nm 7:52
This was the **o** of Elishama the son of Nm 7:53
his **o** was one silver plate whose weight Nm 7:55
fine flour mixed with oil for a grain **o**; Nm 7:55
male lamb a year old, for a burnt **o**; Nm 7:57
one male goat for a sin **o**; Nm 7:58
This was the **o** of Gamaliel the son of Nm 7:59
his **o** was one silver plate whose weight Nm 7:61
fine flour mixed with oil for a grain **o**; Nm 7:61
male lamb a year old, for a burnt **o**; Nm 7:63
one male goat for a sin **o**; Nm 7:64
This was the **o** of Abidan the son of Nm 7:65
his **o** was one silver plate whose weight Nm 7:67
fine flour mixed with oil for a grain **o**; Nm 7:67
male lamb a year old, for a burnt **o**; Nm 7:69
one male goat for a sin **o**; Nm 7:70
This was the **o** of Ahiezer the son of Nm 7:71
his **o** was one silver plate whose weight Nm 7:73
fine flour mixed with oil for a grain **o**; Nm 7:73
male lamb a year old, for a burnt **o**; Nm 7:75
one male goat for a sin **o**; Nm 7:76
This was the **o** of Pagiel the son of Nm 7:77
his **o** was one silver plate whose weight Nm 7:79
fine flour mixed with oil for a grain **o**; Nm 7:79
male lamb a year old, for a burnt **o**; Nm 7:81
one male goat for a sin **o**; Nm 7:82
This was the **o** of Ahira the son of Nm 7:83
This was the dedication **o** for the altar Nm 7:84
the cattle for the burnt **o** twelve bulls, Nm 7:87
lambs a year old, with their grain **o**; Nm 7:87
and twelve male goats for a sin **o**; Nm 7:87
This was the dedication **o** for the altar Nm 7:88
herd and its grain **o** of fine flour mixed Nm 8:8
another bull from the herd for a sin **o**. Nm 8:8
the LORD as a wave **o** from the people of Nm 8:11
the one for a sin **o** and the other for a Nm 8:12
the other for a burnt **o** to the LORD to Nm 8:12
shall offer them as a wave **o** to the LORD. Nm 8:13
them and offered them as a wave **o**. Nm 8:15
them as a wave **o** before the LORD, Nm 8:21
bringing the LORD'S **o** at its appointed Nm 9:7
not bring the LORD'S **o** at its appointed Nm 9:13
the flock a food **o** or a burnt offering Nm 15:3
food offering or a burnt **o** or a sacrifice, Nm 15:3
or as a freewill **o** or at your appointed Nm 15:3
he who brings his **o** shall offer to the Nm 15:4
to the LORD a grain **o** of a tenth of an Nm 15:4
and you shall offer with the burnt **o**, or Nm 15:5
of wine for the drink **o** for each lamb. Nm 15:5
shall offer for a grain **o** two tenths of an Nm 15:6
And for the drink **o** you shall offer a Nm 15:7
offer a bull as a burnt **o** or sacrifice, Nm 15:8
the bull a grain **o** of three tenths of Nm 15:9
shall offer for the drink **o** half a hin of Nm 15:10
offering half a hin of wine, as a food **o**, Nm 15:10
in this way, in **o** a food offering, Nm 15:13
in this way, in offering a food **o**, Nm 15:13
you, and he wishes to offer a food **o**, Nm 15:14
one bull from the herd for a burnt **o**, Nm 15:24
with its grain **o** and its drink offering, Nm 15:24
with its grain offering and its drink **o**, Nm 15:24
the rule, and one male goat for a sin **o**. Nm 15:24
and they have brought their **o**, Nm 15:25
their offering, a food **o** to the LORD, Nm 15:25
and their sin **o** before the LORD for Nm 15:25
a female goat a year old for a sin **o**. Nm 15:27
to the LORD, "Do not respect their **o**. Nm 16:15
consumed the 250 men **o** the incense. Nm 16:35
every **o** of theirs, every grain offering of Nm 18:9
every grain **o** of theirs and every sin Nm 18:9
theirs and every sin **o** of theirs and Nm 18:9
of theirs and every guilt **o** of theirs, Nm 18:9
and shall burn their fat as a food **o**, Nm 18:17
of the people of Israel; it is a sin **o**. Nm 19:9
take some ashes of the burnt sin **o**, Nm 19:17
to Balak, "Stand beside your burnt **o**, Nm 23:3
were standing beside his burnt **o**. Nm 23:6
"Stand here beside your burnt **o**, Nm 23:15
he was standing beside his burnt **o**, Nm 23:17
people of Israel and say to them, 'My **o**, Nm 28:2
This is the food **o** that you shall offer to Nm 28:3
blemish, day by day, as a regular **o**. Nm 28:3
of an ephah of fine flour for a grain **o**, Nm 28:5
It is a regular burnt **o**, which was Nm 28:6
a pleasing aroma, a food **o** to the LORD. Nm 28:6
Its drink **o** shall be a quarter of a hin Nm 28:7
pour out a drink **o** of strong drink to Nm 28:7
Like the grain **o** of the morning, Nm 28:8
of the morning, and like its drink **o**, Nm 28:8
offering, you shall offer it as a food **o**, Nm 28:8
of an ephah of fine flour for a grain **o**, Nm 28:9
mixed with oil, and its drink **o**: Nm 28:9
this is the burnt **o** of every Sabbath, Nm 28:10
the regular burnt **o** and its drink Nm 28:10
regular burnt offering and its drink **o**. Nm 28:10
you shall offer a burnt **o** to the LORD: Nm 28:11
of an ephah of fine flour for a grain **o**, Nm 28:12
two tenths of fine flour for a grain **o**, Nm 28:12
with oil as a grain **o** for every lamb; Nm 28:13
for a burnt **o** with a pleasing aroma, a Nm 28:13
a pleasing aroma, a food **o** to the LORD. Nm 28:13
This is the burnt **o** of each month Nm 28:14
one male goat for a sin **o** to the LORD; Nm 28:15
the regular burnt **o** and its drink Nm 28:15
regular burnt offering and its drink **o**. Nm 28:15
but offer a food **o**, a burnt offering to Nm 28:19
a food offering, a burnt **o** to the LORD: Nm 28:19
also their grain **o** of fine flour mixed Nm 28:20
also one male goat for a sin **o**, to make Nm 28:22
besides the burnt **o** of the morning, Nm 28:23
which is for a regular burnt **o**. Nm 28:23
for seven days, the food of a food **o**, Nm 28:24
the regular burnt **o** and its drink Nm 28:24
regular burnt offering and its drink **o**. Nm 28:24

you offer a grain **o** of new grain to Nm 28:26
but offer a burnt **o**, with a pleasing Nm 28:27
also their grain **o** of fine flour mixed Nm 28:28
the regular burnt **o** and its grain Nm 28:31
regular burnt offering and its grain **o**, Nm 28:31
shall offer them and their drink **o**. Nm 28:31
and you shall offer a burnt **o**, for a Nm 29:2
also their grain **o** of fine flour mixed Nm 29:3
with one male goat for a sin **o**, to make Nm 29:5
besides the burnt **o** of the new moon, Nm 29:6
of the new moon, and its grain **o**, Nm 29:6
and the regular burnt **o** and its grain Nm 29:6
regular burnt offering and its grain **o**, Nm 29:6
its grain offering, and their drink **o**, Nm 29:6
a pleasing aroma, a food **o** to the LORD. Nm 29:6
you shall offer a burnt **o** to the LORD, Nm 29:8
And their grain **o** shall be of fine flour Nm 29:9
also one male goat for a sin **o**, besides Nm 29:11
besides the sin **o** of atonement, Nm 29:11
and the regular burnt **o** and its grain Nm 29:11
regular burnt offering and its grain **o**, Nm 29:11
And you shall offer a burnt **o**, a food Nm 29:13
shall offer a burnt offering, a food **o**, Nm 29:13
and their grain **o** of fine flour mixed Nm 29:14
also one male goat for a sin **o**, besides Nm 29:16
offering, besides the regular burnt **o**, Nm 29:16
its grain **o** and its drink offering. Nm 29:16
its grain offering and its drink **o**. Nm 29:16
with the grain **o** and the drink Nm 29:18
also one male goat for a sin **o**, besides Nm 29:19
the regular burnt **o** and its grain Nm 29:19
regular burnt offering and its grain **o**, Nm 29:19
with the grain **o** and the drink Nm 29:21
also one male goat for a sin **o**, besides Nm 29:22
the regular burnt **o** and its grain Nm 29:22
offering and its grain **o** and its drink Nm 29:22
and its grain offering and its drink **o**. Nm 29:22
with the grain **o** and the drink Nm 29:24
also one male goat for a sin **o**, besides Nm 29:25
offering, besides the regular burnt **o**, Nm 29:25
its grain **o** and its drink offering. Nm 29:25
its grain offering and its drink **o**. Nm 29:25
with the grain **o** and the drink Nm 29:27
also one male goat for a sin **o**; besides Nm 29:28
the regular burnt **o** and its grain Nm 29:28
offering and its grain **o** and its drink Nm 29:28
and its grain offering and its drink **o**. Nm 29:28
with the grain **o** and the drink Nm 29:30
also one male goat for a sin **o**; besides Nm 29:31
besides the regular burnt **o**, its grain Nm 29:31
the regular burnt offering, its grain **o**, Nm 29:31
with the grain **o** and the drink Nm 29:33
also one male goat for a sin **o**; besides Nm 29:34
besides the regular burnt **o**, its grain Nm 29:34
the regular burnt offering, its grain **o**, Nm 29:34
its grain offering, and its drink **o**. Nm 29:34
but you shall offer a burnt **o**, a food Nm 29:36
shall offer a burnt offering, a food **o**, Nm 29:36
and the grain **o** and the drink Nm 29:37
also one male goat for a sin **o**; besides Nm 29:38
the regular burnt **o** and its grain Nm 29:38
offering and its grain **o** and its drink Nm 29:38
and its grain offering and its drink **o**. Nm 29:38
And we have brought the LORD'S **o**, Nm 31:50
as a whole burnt **o** to the LORD your Dt 13:16
tribute of a freewill **o** from your hand, Dt 16:10
from the people, from those **o** a sacrifice, Dt 18:3
burns his son or his daughter as an **o**, Dt 18:10
and drank the wine of their drink **o**? Dt 32:38
us now build an altar, not for burnt **o**, Jos 22:26
LORD by building an altar for burnt **o**, Jos 22:29
an altar for burnt offering, grain **o**, Jos 22:29
offer it as a burnt **o** with the wood of the Jgs 6:26
and I will offer it up for a burnt **o**." Jgs 11:31
But if you prepare a burnt **o**, then offer Jgs 13:16
took the young goat with the grain **o**, Jgs 13:19
have accepted a burnt **o** and a grain Jgs 13:23
offering and a grain **o** at our hands, Jgs 13:23
the men treated the **o** of the LORD with 1 Sm 2:17
choicest parts of every **o** of my people 1 Sm 2:29
atoned for by sacrifice or **o** forever." 1 Sm 3:14
but by all means return him a guilt **o**. 1 Sm 6:3
"What is the guilt **o** that we shall 1 Sm 6:4
you are returning to him as a guilt **o**. 1 Sm 6:8
the cows as a burnt **o** to the LORD. 1 Sm 6:14
returned as a guilt **o** to the LORD: 1 Sm 6:17
it as a whole burnt **o** to the LORD. 1 Sm 7:9
As Samuel was **o** up the burnt 1 Sm 7:10
Samuel was offering up the burnt **o**, 1 Sm 7:10
said, "Bring the burnt **o** here to me, 1 Sm 13:9
offerings." And he offered the burnt **o**. 1 Sm 13:9
he had finished **o** the burnt offering, 1 Sm 13:10
he had finished offering the burnt **o**, 1 Sm 13:10
myself, and offered the burnt **o**." 1 Sm 13:12
up against me, may he accept an **o**, 1 Sm 26:19
David had finished **o** the burnt 2 Sm 6:18
while Absalom was **o** the sacrifices, 2 Sm 15:12
for the burnt **o** and the threshing 2 Sm 24:22
as Solomon finished **o** all this prayer 1 Kgs 8:54
he offered the burnt **o** and the grain 1 Kgs 8:64
offering and the grain **o** and the fat 1 Kgs 8:64
to receive the burnt **o** and the grain 1 Kgs 8:64
offering and the grain **o** and the fat 1 Kgs 8:64
the time of the **o** of the oblation, 1 Kgs 18:29
it on the burnt **o** and on the wood." 1 Kgs 18:33
at the time of the **o** of the oblation, 1 Kgs 18:36
consumed the burnt **o** and the wood 1 Kgs 18:38
about the time of **o** the sacrifice, 2 Kgs 3:20
offered him for a burnt **o** on the wall. 2 Kgs 3:27
will not offer burnt **o** or sacrifice to 2 Kgs 5:17
made an end of **o** the burnt offering, 2 Kgs 10:25
made an end of offering the burnt **o**, 2 Kgs 10:25
He even burned his son as an **o**, 2 Kgs 16:3
burned his burnt **o** and his grain 2 Kgs 16:13
and his grain **o** and poured his 2 Kgs 16:13
poured his drink **o** and threw the 2 Kgs 16:13
the morning burnt **o** and the 2 Kgs 16:15
the evening grain **o** and the king's 2 Kgs 16:15
and the king's burnt **o** and his grain 2 Kgs 16:15
burnt offering and his grain **o**, 2 Kgs 16:15
with the burnt **o** of all the people of 2 Kgs 16:15
and their grain **o** and their drink 2 Kgs 16:15
grain offering and their drink **o**. 2 Kgs 16:15
blood of the burnt **o** and all the 2 Kgs 16:15
son as an **o** and used fortune-telling 2 Kgs 21:6
or his daughter as an **o** to Molech. 2 Kgs 23:10
the altar of burnt **o** and on the altar 1 Chr 6:49
David had finished **o** the burnt 1 Chr 16:2
bring an **o** and come before him! 1 Chr 16:29
altar of burnt **o** regularly morning 1 Chr 16:40
wood and the wheat for a grain **o**; 1 Chr 21:23
heaven upon the altar of burnt **o**. 1 Chr 21:26
the altar of burnt **o** were at that time 1 Chr 21:29
here the altar of burnt **o** for Israel." 1 Chr 22:1
showbread, the flour for the grain **o**, 1 Chr 23:29
of unleavened bread, the baked **o**, 1 Chr 23:29
baked offering, the **o** mixed with oil, 1 Chr 23:29
here, **o** freely and joyously to you. 1 Chr 29:17
off what was used for the burnt **o**, 2 Chr 4:6
consumed the burnt **o** and the 2 Chr 7:1
he offered the burnt **o** and the fat of 2 Chr 7:7
not hold the burnt **o** and the grain 2 Chr 7:7
offering and the grain **o** and the fat. 2 Chr 7:7
o according to the commandment of 2 Chr 8:13
and burned his sons as an **o**, 2 Chr 28:3
the altar of burnt **o** and all its 2 Chr 29:18
goats for a sin **o** for the kingdom 2 Chr 29:21
goats for the sin **o** were brought to 2 Chr 29:23
and made a sin **o** with their blood 2 Chr 29:24
that the burnt **o** and the sin 2 Chr 29:24
and the sin **o** should be made 2 Chr 29:24
that the burnt **o** be offered on 2 Chr 29:27
And when the burnt **o** began, the 2 Chr 29:27
until the burnt **o** was finished. 2 Chr 29:28
When the **o** was finished, the king 2 Chr 29:29
these were for a burnt **o** to the LORD. 2 Chr 29:32
his sons as an **o** in the Valley of 2 Chr 33:6
of Aaron were **o** the burnt offerings 2 Chr 35:14
who made a freewill **o** to the LORD. Ezr 3:5
and as a sin **o** for all Israel 12 male Ezr 6:17
the **o** for the house of our God that the Ezr 8:25
and the gold are a freewill **o** to the LORD, Ezr 8:28
lambs, and as a sin **o** twelve male goats. Ezr 8:35
goats. All this was a burnt **o** to the LORD. Ezr 8:35
and their guilt **o** was a ram of the flock Ezr 10:19
the showbread, the regular grain **o**, Neh 10:33
grain offering, the regular burnt **o**, Neh 10:33
have likewise cast lots for the wood **o**, Neh 10:34
they had previously put the grain **o**, Neh 13:5
with the grain **o** and the frankincense. Neh 13:9
for the wood **o** at appointed times, Neh 13:31
Job and offer up a burnt **o** for yourselves. Jb 42:8
A Psalm of David, for the memorial **o**. Ps 38:T
Sacrifice and **o** you have not desired, but Ps 40:6
Burnt offering and sin **o** you have not Ps 40:6
Burnt offering and sin **o** you have not Ps 40:6
you will not be pleased with a burnt **o**. Ps 51:16
With a freewill **o** I will sacrifice to you; I Ps 54:6
I will make an **o** of bulls and goats. Ps 66:15
Of David, for the memorial **o**. Ps 70:T
bring an **o**, and come into his courts! Ps 96:8
Fools mock at the guilt **o**, but the Prv 14:9
day and worship with sacrifice and **o**, Is 19:21
nor are its beasts enough for a burnt **o**. Is 40:16
impoverished for an **o** chooses wood Is 40:20
when his soul makes an **o** for sin, he Is 53:10
to them you have poured out a drink **o**, Is 57:6
offering, you have brought a grain **o**. Is 57:6
he who presents a grain **o**, like one who Is 66:3
makes a memorial **o** of frankincense, Is 66:3
from all the nations as an **o** to the LORD, Is 66:20
Israelites bring their grain **o** in a clean Is 66:20
they offer burnt **o** and grain offering, Jer 14:12
they offer burnt offering and grain **o**, Jer 14:12
them up as an **o** by fire to them? Ezk 16:21
o yourself to any passerby and Ezk 16:25
very gifts in their **o** up all their Ezk 20:26
presented the provocation of their **o**; Ezk 20:28
where the burnt **o** was to be washed. Ezk 40:38
on which the burnt **o** and the sin Ezk 40:39
offering and the sin **o** and the guilt Ezk 40:39
offering and the guilt **o** were to be Ezk 40:39
tables of hewn stone for the burnt **o**, Ezk 40:42
tables the flesh of the **o** was to be laid. Ezk 40:43
the most holy offerings—the grain **o**, Ezk 42:13
—the grain offering, the sin **o**, Ezk 42:13
the sin offering, and the guilt **o**, Ezk 42:13
it is erected for **o** burnt offerings upon Ezk 43:18
GOD, a bull from the herd for a sin **o**. Ezk 43:19
shall also take the bull of the sin **o**, Ezk 43:21
male goat without blemish for a sin **o**; Ezk 43:22
offer them up as a burnt **o** to the LORD. Ezk 43:24
provide daily a male goat for a sin **o**; Ezk 43:25
slaughter the burnt **o** and the Ezk 44:11
the Holy Place, he shall offer his sin **o**, Ezk 44:27
They shall eat the grain **o**, the sin Ezk 44:29
shall eat the grain offering, the sin **o**, Ezk 44:29
the sin offering, and the guilt **o**, Ezk 44:29
and every **o** of all kinds from all your Ezk 44:30
"This is the **o** that you shall make: Ezk 45:13
watering places of Israel for grain **o**, Ezk 45:15
of Israel for grain offering, burnt **o**, Ezk 45:15
obliged to give this **o** to the prince in Ezk 45:16
the blood of the sin **o** and put it on the Ezk 45:19
of the land a young bull for a sin **o**. Ezk 45:22
provide as a burnt **o** to the LORD seven Ezk 45:23
days; and a male goat daily for a sin **o**. Ezk 45:23
provide as a grain **o** an ephah for each Ezk 45:24
shall offer his burnt **o** and his peace Ezk 46:2
The burnt **o** that the prince offers to the Ezk 46:4
And the grain **o** with the ram shall be Ezk 46:5
and the grain **o** with the lambs shall be Ezk 46:5
As a grain **o** he shall provide an ephah Ezk 46:7
the grain **o** with a young bull shall be Ezk 46:11
When the prince provides a freewill **o**, Ezk 46:12
either a burnt **o** or peace offerings as a Ezk 46:12
offerings as a freewill **o** to the LORD, Ezk 46:12
shall offer his burnt **o** or his peace Ezk 46:12
blemish for a burnt **o** to the LORD Ezk 46:13
provide a grain **o** with it morning Ezk 46:14
the flour, as a grain **o** to the LORD. Ezk 46:14
lamb and the meal **o** and the oil shall Ezk 46:15
by morning, for a regular burnt **o**. Ezk 46:15
shall boil the guilt **o** and the sin Ezk 46:20
boil the guilt offering and the sin **o**, Ezk 46:20
and where they shall bake the grain **o**, Ezk 46:20
commanded that an **o** and incense be Dn 2:46
the regular burnt **o** was taken away Dn 8:11
the regular burnt **o** because of Dn 8:12
vision concerning the regular burnt **o**, Dn 8:13
he shall put an end to sacrifice and **o**. Dn 9:27
shall take away the regular burnt **o**. Dn 11:31
that the regular burnt **o** is taken away Dn 12:11
The grain **o** and the drink offering are cut Jl 1:9
offering and the drink **o** are cut off from Jl 1:9
Because grain **o** and drink offering are Jl 1:13
offering and drink **o** are withheld from Jl 1:13
a grain **o** and a drink offering for the LORD Jl 2:14
offering and a drink **o** for the LORD your Jl 2:14
of my dispersed ones, shall bring my **o**. Zep 3:10
By **o** polluted food upon my altar. But Mal 1:7
I will not accept an **o** from your hand. Mal 1:10
be offered to my name, and a pure **o**. Mal 1:11
or sick, and this you bring as your **o**! Mal 1:13
who brings an **o** to the LORD of hosts! Mal 2:12
no longer regards the **o** or accepts it Mal 2:13
Then the **o** of Judah and Jerusalem will Mal 3:4
So if you are **o** your gift at the altar and Mt 5:23
people putting money into the **o** box. Mk 12:41
who are contributing to the **o** box. Mk 12:43
and make an **o** for your cleansing, Lk 5:14
rich putting their gifts into the **o** box, Lk 21:1
him, coming up and **o** him sour wine Lk 23:36
kills you will think he is **o** service to God. Jn 16:2
the people from **o** sacrifice to them. Acts 14:18
fulfilled and the **o** presented for each Acts 21:26
so that the **o** of the Gentiles may be Rom 15:16
for us, a fragrant **o** and sacrifice to God. Eph 5:2
out as a drink **o** upon the sacrificial Phil 2:17
upon the sacrificial **o** of your faith, Phil 2:17
the gifts you sent, a fragrant **o**, Phil 4:18
already being poured out as a drink **o**, 2 Tm 4:6
sanctified through the **o** of the body Heb 10:10
o repeatedly the same sacrifices, Heb 10:11
For by a single **o** he has perfected for Heb 10:14

these, there is no longer any **o** for sin. Heb 10:18
was in the act of **o** up his only son, Heb 11:17

OFFERINGS (361)
bird and offered burnt **o** on the altar. Gn 8:20
for the **o** we shall sacrifice to the LORD Ex 8:26
If we sacrifice **o** abominable to the Ex 8:26
also let us have sacrifices and burnt **o**, Ex 10:25
on it your burnt **o** and your peace Ex 20:24
your burnt offerings and your peace **o**, Ex 20:24
who offered burnt **o** and sacrificed peace Ex 24:5
and sacrificed peace **o** of oxen to Ex 24:5
and bowls with which to pour drink **o**; Ex 25:29
the people of Israel from their peace **o**, Ex 29:28
and offered burnt **o** and brought peace Ex 32:6
burnt offerings and brought peace **o**. Ex 32:6
bringing him freewill **o** every morning, Ex 36:3
flagons with which to pour drink **o**. Ex 37:16
it is a most holy part of the LORD'S food **o**. Lv 2:3
it is a most holy part of the LORD'S food **o**. Lv 2:10
shall season all your grain **o** with salt. Lv 2:13
with all your **o** you shall offer salt. Lv 2:13
the ox of the sacrifice of the peace **o**); Lv 4:10
like the fat of the sacrifice of peace **o**. Lv 4:26
as the fat is removed from the peace **o**, Lv 4:31
is removed from the sacrifice of peace **o**, Lv 4:35
it on the altar, on top of the LORD'S food **o**. Lv 4:35
this on the altar, on the LORD'S food **o**; Lv 5:12
shall burn on it the fat of the peace **o**. Lv 6:12
given it as their portion of my food **o**. Lv 6:17
your generations, from the LORD'S food **o**. Lv 6:18
the sacrifice of peace **o** that one may Lv 7:11
of his peace **o** for thanksgiving he Lv 7:13
who throws the blood of the peace **o**. Lv 7:14
of his peace **o** for thanksgiving shall Lv 7:15
the LORD'S peace **o** while an uncleanness Lv 7:20
from the sacrifice of the LORD'S peace **o**, Lv 7:21
sacrifice of his peace **o** to the LORD shall Lv 7:29
LORD from the sacrifice of his peace **o**. Lv 7:29
own hands shall bring the LORD'S food **o**. Lv 7:30
from the sacrifice of your peace **o**. Lv 7:32
the blood of the peace **o** and the fat shall Lv 7:33
out of the sacrifices of their peace **o**, Lv 7:34
and of his sons from the LORD'S food **o**, Lv 7:35
of Israel to bring their **o** to the LORD, Lv 7:38
that is in the basket of ordination **o**, Lv 8:31
and an ox and a ram for peace **o**, to Lv 9:4
the sacrifice of peace **o** for the people. Lv 9:18
and the burnt offering and the peace **o**. Lv 9:22
offering that is left of the LORD'S food **o**, Lv 10:12
your sons' due, from the LORD'S food **o**, Lv 10:13
sacrifices of the peace **o** of the people of Lv 10:14
bring with the food **o** of the fat pieces Lv 10:15
cannot afford the **o** for his cleansing." Lv 14:32
them as sacrifices of peace **o** to the LORD. Lv 17:5
offer a sacrifice of peace **o** to the LORD, Lv 19:5
For they offer the LORD'S food **o**, the bread Lv 21:6
come near to offer the LORD'S food **o**; Lv 21:21
their vows or freewill **o** that they offer to Lv 22:18
a sacrifice of peace **o** to the LORD to Lv 22:21
their grain offering and their drink **o**, Lv 23:18
a year old as a sacrifice of peace **o**. Lv 23:19
you shall present food **o** to the LORD. Lv 23:36
for presenting to the LORD food **o**, Lv 23:37
offerings, burnt **o** and grain offerings, Lv 23:37
offerings, burnt offerings and grain **o**, Lv 23:37
grain offerings, sacrifices and drink **o**, Lv 23:37
besides all your vow **o** and besides all Lv 23:38
offerings and besides all your freewill **o**, Lv 23:38
holy portion out of the LORD'S food **o**, Lv 24:9
their grain offering and their drink **o**. Nm 6:15
and brought their **o** before the LORD, six Nm 7:3
the chiefs offered **o** for the dedication Nm 7:10
said to Moses, "They shall offer their **o**, Nm 7:11
and for the sacrifice of peace **o**, two Nm 7:17
and for the sacrifice of peace **o**, two Nm 7:23
and for the sacrifice of peace **o**, two Nm 7:29
and for the sacrifice of peace **o**, two Nm 7:35
and for the sacrifice of peace **o**, two Nm 7:41
and for the sacrifice of peace **o**, two Nm 7:47
and for the sacrifice of peace **o**, two Nm 7:53
and for the sacrifice of peace **o**, two Nm 7:59
and for the sacrifice of peace **o**, two Nm 7:65
and for the sacrifice of peace **o**, two Nm 7:71
and for the sacrifice of peace **o**, two Nm 7:77
and for the sacrifice of peace **o**, two Nm 7:83
sacrifice of peace **o** twenty-four bulls, Nm 7:88
over your burnt **o** and over the Nm 10:10
over the sacrifices of your peace **o**. Nm 10:10
fulfill a vow or for peace **o** to the LORD, Nm 15:8
all the wave **o** of the people of Israel. Nm 18:11
'My offering, my food for my food **o**, Nm 28:2
Their drink **o** shall be half a hin of Nm 28:14
its grain offering, and their drink **o**. Nm 29:11
offering and the drink **o** for the bulls, Nm 29:18
its grain offering, and their drink **o**. Nm 29:19
offering and the drink **o** for the bulls, Nm 29:21
offering and the drink **o** for the bulls, Nm 29:24
offering and the drink **o** for the bulls, Nm 29:27
offering and the drink **o** for the bulls, Nm 29:30
its grain offering, and its drink **o**. Nm 29:31
offering and the drink **o** for the bulls, Nm 29:33
offering and the drink **o** for the bull, Nm 29:37
to your vow **o** and your freewill Nm 29:39
vow offerings and your freewill **o**, Nm 29:39
freewill offerings, for your burnt **o**, Nm 29:39
burnt offerings, and for your grain **o**, Nm 29:39
grain offerings, and for your drink **o**, Nm 29:39
drink offerings, and for your peace **o**." Nm 29:39
bring your burnt **o** and your sacrifices, Dt 12:6
that you present, your vow **o**, Dt 12:6
your vow offerings, your freewill **o**, Dt 12:6
your burnt **o** and your sacrifices, your Dt 12:11
all your finest vow **o** that you vow to Dt 12:11
not offer your burnt **o** at any place that Dt 12:13
there you shall offer your burnt **o**, Dt 12:14
or any of your vow **o** that you vow, Dt 12:17
or your freewill **o** or the contribution Dt 12:17
that are due from you, and your vow **o**, Dt 12:26
and offer your burnt **o**, the flesh and the Dt 12:27
eat the LORD'S food **o** as their inheritance. Dt 18:1
And you shall offer burnt **o** on it to the Dt 27:6
you shall sacrifice peace **o** and shall eat Dt 27:7
you and whole burnt **o** on your altar. Dt 33:10
they offered on it burnt **o** to the LORD and Jos 8:31
to the LORD and sacrificed peace **o**. Jos 8:31
The **o** by fire to the LORD God of Israel Jos 13:14
so to offer burnt **o** or grain offerings or Jos 22:23
offerings or grain **o** or peace offerings Jos 22:23
or grain offerings or peace **o** on it, Jos 22:23
with our burnt **o** and sacrifices and Jos 22:27
offerings and sacrifices and peace **o**, Jos 22:27
our fathers made, not for burnt **o**, Jos 22:28
and offered burnt **o** and peace offerings Jgs 20:26
offerings and peace **o** before the LORD. Jgs 20:26
and offered burnt **o** and peace offerings. Jgs 21:4
and offered burnt offerings and peace **o**. Jgs 21:4
your father all my **o** by fire from the 1 Sm 2:28
sacrifices and my **o** that I 1 Sm 2:29
offered burnt **o** and sacrificed 1 Sm 6:15
you to offer burnt **o** and to sacrifice 1 Sm 10:8
offerings and to sacrifice peace **o**. 1 Sm 10:8
they sacrificed peace **o** before the 1 Sm 11:15
and the peace **o**." And he offered the 1 Sm 13:9
delight in burnt **o** and sacrifices, 1 Sm 15:22
dew or rain upon you, nor fields of **o**! 2 Sm 1:21
David offered burnt **o** and peace 2 Sm 6:17
offerings and peace **o** before the LORD. 2 Sm 6:17
offering the burnt **o** and the peace 2 Sm 6:18
the burnt offerings and the peace **o**, 2 Sm 6:18
will not offer burnt **o** to the LORD my 2 Sm 24:24
and offered burnt **o** and peace 2 Sm 24:25
offered burnt offerings and peace **o**. 2 Sm 24:25
he sacrificed and made **o** at the high 1 Kgs 3:3
offer a thousand burnt **o** on that altar. 1 Kgs 3:4
offered up burnt **o** and peace 1 Kgs 3:15
up burnt offerings and peace **o**, 1 Kgs 3:15
offered as peace **o** to the LORD 1 Kgs 8:63
and the fat pieces of the peace **o**, 1 Kgs 8:64
and the fat pieces of the peace **o**. 1 Kgs 8:64
offer up burnt **o** and peace offerings 1 Kgs 9:25
offerings and peace **o** on the altar 1 Kgs 9:25
making **o** with it before the LORD. 1 Kgs 9:25
and his burnt **o** that he offered at the 1 Kgs 10:5
who made **o** and sacrificed to their 1 Kgs 11:8
and went up to the altar to make **o**. 1 Kgs 12:33
was standing by the altar to make **o**. 1 Kgs 13:1
the high places who make **o** on you, 1 Kgs 13:2
sacrificed and made **o** on the high 1 Kgs 22:43
in to offer sacrifices and burnt **o**. 2 Kgs 10:24
to sacrifice and make **o** on the high 2 Kgs 12:3
from the guilt **o** and the money 2 Kgs 12:16
from the sin **o** was not brought 2 Kgs 12:16
sacrificed and made **o** on the high 2 Kgs 14:4
sacrificed and made **o** on the high 2 Kgs 15:4
sacrificed and made **o** on the high 2 Kgs 15:35
he sacrificed and made **o** on the high 2 Kgs 16:4
the blood of his peace **o** on the altar. 2 Kgs 16:13
and there they made **o** on all the 2 Kgs 17:11
their daughters as **o** and used 2 Kgs 17:17
of Israel had made **o** to it (it was 2 Kgs 18:4
me and have made **o** to other gods, 2 Kgs 22:17
had ordained to make **o** in the high 2 Kgs 23:5
places where the priests had made **o**, 2 Kgs 23:8
and his sons made **o** on the altar of 1 Chr 6:49
they offered burnt **o** and peace 1 Chr 16:1
offerings and peace **o** before God. 1 Chr 16:1
offering the burnt **o** and the peace 1 Chr 16:2
the burnt offerings and the peace **o**, 1 Chr 16:2
to offer burnt **o** to the LORD on the 1 Chr 16:40
oxen for burnt **o** and the threshing 1 Chr 21:23
nor offer burnt **o** that cost me 1 Chr 21:24
and presented burnt **o** and peace 1 Chr 21:26
offerings and peace **o** and called on 1 Chr 21:26
forever should make **o** before the 1 Chr 23:13
and whenever burnt **o** were offered 1 Chr 23:31
fathers' houses made their freewill **o**, 1 Chr 29:6
next day offered burnt **o** to the LORD, 1 Chr 29:21
and 1,000 lambs, with their drink **o**, 1 Chr 29:21
and offered a thousand burnt **o** on it. 2 Chr 1:6
and for burnt **o** morning and evening, 2 Chr 2:4
as a place to make **o** before him? 2 Chr 2:6
offering and the fat of the peace **o**, 2 Chr 7:7
offered up burnt **o** to the LORD 2 Chr 8:12
and his burnt **o** that he offered at the 2 Chr 9:4
every evening burnt **o** and incense 2 Chr 13:11
LORD, to offer burnt **o** to the LORD, 2 Chr 23:18
for the service and for the burnt **o**, 2 Chr 24:14
they offered burnt **o** in the house 2 Chr 24:14
worshiped them, making **o** to them. 2 Chr 25:14
and he made **o** in the Valley of the 2 Chr 28:3
he sacrificed and made **o** on the high 2 Chr 28:4
high places to make **o** to other gods, 2 Chr 28:25
incense or offered burnt **o** in the Holy 2 Chr 29:7
his ministers and make **o** to him." 2 Chr 29:11
sacrifices and thank **o** to the house 2 Chr 29:31
brought sacrifices and thank **o**, 2 Chr 29:31
of a willing heart brought burnt **o**. 2 Chr 29:31
of the burnt **o** that the assembly 2 Chr 29:32
And the consecrated **o** were 600 2 Chr 29:33
and could not flay all the burnt **o**, 2 Chr 29:34
the great number of burnt **o**, 2 Chr 29:35
there was the fat of the peace **o**, 2 Chr 29:35
there were the drink **o** for the burnt 2 Chr 29:35
the drink offerings for the burnt **o**. 2 Chr 29:35
and brought burnt **o** into the house 2 Chr 30:15
sacrificing peace **o** and giving 2 Chr 30:22
1,000 bulls and 7,000 sheep for **o**, 2 Chr 30:24
for burnt **o** and peace offerings, 2 Chr 31:2
for burnt offerings and peace **o**, 2 Chr 31:2
own possessions was for the burnt **o**: 2 Chr 31:3
the burnt **o** of morning and evening, 2 Chr 31:3
and the burnt **o** for the Sabbaths, 2 Chr 31:3
gate, was over the freewill **o** to God, 2 Chr 31:14
for the LORD and the most holy **o**. 2 Chr 31:14
sacrifices of peace **o** and of 2 Chr 33:16
me and have made **o** to other gods, 2 Chr 34:25
as Passover **o** for all who were 2 Chr 35:7
for the Passover **o** 2,600 Passover 2 Chr 35:8
for the Passover **o** 5,000 lambs and 2 Chr 35:9
set aside the burnt **o** that they might 2 Chr 35:12
and they boiled the holy **o** in pots, in 2 Chr 35:13
were offering the burnt **o** and the fat 2 Chr 35:14
and to offer burnt **o** on the altar of 2 Chr 35:16
besides freewill **o** for the house of God Ezr 1:4
made freewill **o** for the house of God, Ezr 2:68
of the God of Israel, to offer burnt **o** on it, Ezr 3:2
and they offered burnt **o** on it to the LORD, Ezr 3:3
the LORD, burnt **o** morning and evening. Ezr 3:3
the daily burnt **o** by number according Ezr 3:4
and after that the regular burnt **o**, the Ezr 3:5
the **o** at the new moon and at all the Ezr 3:5
and the **o** of everyone who made a Ezr 3:5
they began to offer burnt **o** to the LORD. Ezr 3:6
or sheep for burnt **o** to the God of heaven, Ezr 6:9
and with the freewill **o** of the people and Ezr 7:16
with their grain **o** and their drink Ezr 7:17
their grain offerings and their drink **o**, Ezr 7:17
offered burnt **o** to the God of Israel, Ezr 8:35
and the sin **o** to make atonement for Neh 10:33
and offer burnt **o** according to the Jb 1:5
their drink **o** of blood I will not pour out Ps 16:4
he remember all your **o** and regard with Ps 20:3
your burnt **o** are continually before me. Ps 50:8
in burnt **o** and whole burnt offerings; Ps 51:19
in burnt offerings and whole burnt **o**; Ps 51:19
you, O God; I will render thank **o** to you. Ps 56:12
come into your house with burnt **o**; Ps 66:13
offer to you burnt **o** of fattened animals, Ps 66:15
Accept my freewill **o** of praise, O Ps 119:108
had enough of burnt **o** of rams and the Is 1:11
Bring no more vain **o**; incense is an Is 1:13
not brought me your sheep for burnt **o**, Is 43:23
I have not burdened you with **o**, or Is 43:23
their burnt **o** and their sacrifices will be Is 56:7
in gardens and making **o** on bricks; Is 65:3
because they made **o** on the mountains Is 65:7
They have made **o** to other gods and Jer 1:16
Your burnt **o** are not acceptable, nor Jer 6:20
adultery, swear falsely, make **o** to Baal, Jer 7:9
And they pour out drink **o** to other gods, Jer 7:18
"Add your burnt **o** to your sacrifices, Jer 7:21
them concerning burnt **o** and sacrifices. Jer 7:22
cry to the gods to whom they make **o**, Jer 11:12
up to shame, altars to make **o** to Baal. Jer 11:13
me to anger by making **o** to Baal." Jer 11:17

bringing burnt **o** and sacrifices, Jer 17:26
sacrifices, grain **o** and frankincense, Jer 17:26
and bringing thank **o** to the house of Jer 17:26
forgotten me; they make **o** to false gods; Jer 18:15
this place by making **o** in it to other Jer 19:4
their sons in the fire as burnt **o** to Baal, Jer 19:5
on whose roofs **o** have been offered Jer 19:13
and drink **o** have been poured out to Jer 19:13
on whose roofs **o** have been made Jer 32:29
to Baal and drink **o** have been poured Jer 32:29
as they bring thank **o** to the house of Jer 33:11
a man in my presence to offer burnt **o**, Jer 33:18
offer burnt offerings, to burn grain **o**, Jer 33:18
bringing grain **o** and incense to present Jer 41:5
they went to make **o** and serve other gods Jer 44:3
their evil and make no **o** to other gods. Jer 44:5
making **o** to other gods in the land of Jer 44:8
their wives had made **o** to other gods, Jer 44:15
make **o** to the queen of heaven and Jer 44:17
of heaven and pour out drink **o** to her, Jer 44:17
we left off making **o** to the queen of Jer 44:18
heaven and pouring out drink **o** to her, Jer 44:18
"When we made **o** to the queen of Jer 44:19
heaven and poured out drink **o** to her, Jer 44:19
image and poured out drink **o** to her?" Jer 44:19
"As for the **o** that you offered in the Jer 44:21
because you made **o** and because you Jer 44:23
to make **o** to the queen of heaven and to Jer 44:25
heaven and to pour out drink **o** to her.' Jer 44:25
the high place and makes **o** to his god. Jer 48:35
for incense and the bowls for drink **o**. Jer 52:19
there they poured out their drink **o**. Ezk 20:28
of your gifts, with all your sacred **o**. Ezk 20:40
which the burnt **o** and the sacrifices Ezk 40:42
the LORD shall eat the most holy **o**. Ezk 42:13
put the most holy **o**—the grain Ezk 42:13
for offering burnt **o** upon it and Ezk 43:18
the altar your burnt **o** and your peace Ezk 43:27
burnt offerings and your peace **o**, Ezk 43:27
offering of all kinds from all your **o**, Ezk 44:30
offering, burnt offering, and peace **o**, Ezk 45:15
prince's duty to furnish the burnt **o**, Ezk 45:17
to furnish the burnt offerings, grain **o**, Ezk 45:17
offerings, grain offerings, and drink **o**, Ezk 45:17
he shall provide the sin **o**, grain Ezk 45:17
shall provide the sin offerings, grain **o**, Ezk 45:17
sin offerings, grain offerings, burnt **o**, Ezk 45:17
offerings, burnt offerings, and peace **o**, Ezk 45:17
make the same provision for sin **o**, Ezk 45:25
provision for sin offerings, burnt **o**, Ezk 45:25
offerings, burnt offerings, and grain **o**, Ezk 45:25
offer his burnt offering and his peace **o**, Ezk 46:2
burnt offering or peace **o** as a freewill Ezk 46:12
offering or his peace **o** as he does on Ezk 46:12
Baals when she burned **o** to them and Hos 2:13
the mountains and burn **o** on the hills, Hos 4:13
knowledge of God rather than burnt **o**. Hos 6:6
As for my sacrificial **o**, they sacrifice Hos 8:13
shall not pour drink **o** of wine to the Hos 9:4
to the Baals and burning **o** to idols. Hos 11:2
is leavened, and proclaim freewill **o**, Am 4:5
me your burnt **o** and grain offerings, Am 5:22
me your burnt offerings and grain **o**, Am 5:22
and the peace **o** of your fattened Am 5:22
to me sacrifices and **o** during the forty Am 5:25
Shall I come before him with burnt **o**, Mi 6:6
to his net and makes **o** to his dragnet; Hab 1:16
dung on your faces, the dung of your **o**, Mal 2:3
and they will bring **o** in righteousness to Mal 3:3
than all whole burnt **o** and sacrifices." Mk 12:33
it was adorned with noble stones and **o**, Lk 21:5
alms to my nation and to present **o**. Acts 24:17
at the altar share in the sacrificial **o**? 1 Cor 9:13
"Sacrifices and **o** you have not desired, Heb 10:5
in burnt **o** and sin offerings you have Heb 10:6
offerings and sin **o** you have taken Heb 10:6
in sacrifices and **o** and burnt offerings Heb 10:8
offerings and burnt **o** and sin Heb 10:8
offerings and sin **o**" (these are offered Heb 10:8

OFFERS (21)
offering, if he **o** an animal from the herd, Lv 3:1
If he **o** a lamb for his offering, then he Lv 3:7
The priest who **o** it for sin shall eat it. In Lv 6:26
And the priest who **o** any man's burnt Lv 7:8
griddle shall belong to the priest who **o** it. Lv 7:9
If he **o** it for a thanksgiving, then he Lv 7:12
eaten on the day that he **o** his sacrifice, Lv 7:16
day, he who **o** it shall not be accepted, Lv 7:18
Whoever **o** the sacrifice of his peace Lv 7:29
the sons of Aaron **o** the blood of the Lv 7:33
them, who **o** a burnt offering or sacrifice Lv 17:8
him, for he **o** the bread of your God. Lv 21:8
And when anyone **o** a sacrifice of peace Lv 22:21
that your servant **o** toward this place. 1 Kgs 8:29
that your servant **o** toward this place. 2 Chr 6:20
who freely **o** to go to Jerusalem, Ezr 7:13
The one who **o** thanksgiving as his Ps 50:23
grain offering, like one who **o** pig's blood; Is 66:3
him who **o** sacrifice in the high place Jer 48:35
offering that the prince **o** to the LORD on Ezk 46:4
which he **o** for himself and for the Heb 9:7

OFFICE (12)
up your head and restore you to your **o**, Gn 40:13
I was restored to my **o**, and the baker Gn 41:13
to the judge who is in **o** in those days, Dt 17:9
the judges who are in **o** in those days. Dt 19:17
the priest who is in **o** at that time and say Dt 26:3
established them in their **o** of trust. 1 Chr 9:22
his days be few; may another take his **o**! Ps 109:8
I will thrust you from your **o**, and you Is 22:19
in it'; and "'Let another take his **o**.' Acts 1:20
If anyone aspires to the **o** of overseer, 1 Tm 3:1
receive the priestly **o** have a Heb 7:5
by death from continuing in **o**, Heb 7:23

OFFICER (19)
in Egypt to Potiphar, an **o** of Pharaoh, Gn 37:36
to Egypt, and Potiphar, an **o** of Pharaoh, Gn 39:1
son of Jerubbaal, and is not Zebul his **o**? Jgs 9:28
of Israel summoned an **o** and said, 1 Kgs 22:9
city he took an **o** who had been in 2 Kgs 25:19
the chief **o** of the house of God; 1 Chr 9:11
Eleazar was the chief **o** over them in 1 Chr 9:20
was chief **o** in charge of the 1 Chr 26:24
Eliezer the son of Zichri was chief **o**; 1 Chr 27:16
of Israel summoned an **o** and said, 2 Chr 18:8
secretary and the **o** of the chief 2 Chr 24:11
the secretary and Maaseiah the **o**, 2 Chr 26:11
The chief **o** in charge of them was 2 Chr 31:12
and Azariah the chief **o** of the house 2 Chr 31:13
Without having any chief, **o**, or ruler, Prv 6:7
who was chief **o** in the house of the LORD, Jer 20:1
the city he took an **o** who had been in Jer 52:25
and the judge hand you over to the **o**, Lk 12:58
the officer, and the **o** put you in prison. Lk 12:58

OFFICERS (71)
And Pharaoh was angry with his two **o**, Gn 40:2
So he asked Pharaoh's **o** who were with Gn 40:7
chariots of Egypt with **o** over all of them. Ex 14:7
and his chosen **o** were sunk in the Red Ex 15:4
elders of the people and **o** over them, Nm 11:16
was angry with the **o** of the army, Nm 31:14
Then the **o** who were over the Nm 31:48
of fifties, commanders of tens, and **o**, Dt 1:15
shall appoint judges and **o** in all your Dt 16:18
Then the **o** shall speak to the people, Dt 20:5
And the **o** shall speak further to the Dt 20:8
And when the **o** have finished speaking Dt 20:9
of your tribes, your elders, and your **o**, Dt 29:10
all the elders of your tribes and your **o**, Dt 31:28
Joshua commanded the **o** of the people, Jos 1:10
of three days the **o** went through the Jos 3:2
with their elders and **o** and their judges, Jos 8:33
its elders and heads, its judges and **o**, Jos 23:2
the heads, the judges, and the **o** of Israel. Jos 24:1
and give it to his **o** and to his servants. 1 Sm 8:15
the son of Nathan was over the **o**; 1 Kgs 4:5
Solomon had twelve **o** over all Israel, 1 Kgs 4:7
And those **o** supplied provisions for 1 Kgs 4:27
Solomon's 3,300 chief **o** who were 1 Kgs 5:16
These were the chief **o** who were over 1 Kgs 9:23
to the hands of the **o** of the guard, 1 Kgs 14:27
Jehu said to the guard and to the **o**, 2 Kgs 10:25
the guard and the **o** cast them out 2 Kgs 10:25
These Gadites were **o** of the army; 1 Chr 12:14
and made them **o** of his troops. 1 Chr 12:18
the LORD, 6,000 shall be **o** and judges, 1 Chr 23:4
for there were sacred **o** and officers of 1 Chr 24:5
sacred officers and **o** of God among 1 Chr 24:5
houses and the **o** of the thousands 1 Chr 26:26
duties for Israel, as **o** and judges. 1 Chr 26:29
and their **o** who served the king in all 1 Chr 27:1
the **o** of the divisions that served the 1 Chr 28:1
also the **o** and all the people will be 1 Chr 28:21
and the **o** over the king's work. 1 Chr 29:6
they were soldiers, and his **o**, the 2 Chr 8:9
were the chief **o** of King Solomon, 2 Chr 8:10
to the hands of the **o** of the guard, 2 Chr 12:10
and the Levites will serve you as **o**. 2 Chr 19:11
to the king's **o** by the Levites, 2 Chr 24:11
he planned with his **o** and his mighty 2 Chr 32:3
and commanders and **o** in the 2 Chr 32:21
Jehiel, the chief **o** of the house of God, 2 Chr 35:8
All the **o** of the priests and the people 2 Chr 36:14
and before all the king's mighty **o**. Ezr 7:28
had sent with me **o** of the army and Neh 2:9
let the king appoint **o** in all the provinces Est 2:3
and his **o** desert the standard in panic," Is 31:9
all the rest of the **o** of the king of Jer 39:3
and all the chief **o** of the king of Jer 39:13
family, one of the chief **o** of the king, Jer 41:1
king of Babylon and his **o**. Jer 46:26
of them having the appearance of **o**, Ezk 23:15
all of them, **o** and men of renown, Ezk 23:23
He remembers his **o**; they stumble as Na 2:5
the chief priests and **o** how he might Lk 22:4
the chief priests and **o** of the temple and Lk 22:52
priests and Pharisees sent **o** to arrest him. Jn 7:32
The **o** then came to the chief priests and Jn 7:45
The **o** answered, "No one ever spoke like Jn 7:46
of soldiers and some **o** from the chief Jn 18:3
their captain and the **o** of the Jews Jn 18:12
Now the servants and **o** had made a Jn 18:18
one of the **o** standing by struck Jesus Jn 18:22
the chief priests and the **o** saw him, Jn 19:6
But when the **o** came, they did not find Acts 5:22
captain with the **o** went and brought Acts 5:26

OFFICES (4)
the Levites for their **o** of praise and 2 Chr 8:14
their service according to their **o**, 2 Chr 31:16
upward was according to their **o**, 2 Chr 31:17
priests to their **o** and encouraged 2 Chr 35:2

OFFICIAL (5)
So the king appointed an **o** for her, 2 Kgs 8:6
for the high **o** is watched by a higher, Eccl 5:8
there was an **o** whose son was Jn 4:46
The **o** said to him, "Sir, come down Jn 4:49
a eunuch, a court **o** of Candace, Acts 8:27

OFFICIALS (96)
And the **o** of Succoth said, "Are the hands Jgs 8:6
down for him the **o** and elders of Jgs 8:14
sons, and all the royal **o** of Judah, 1 Kgs 1:9
and these were his high **o**: Azariah the 1 Kgs 4:2
were the soldiers, they were his **o**, 1 Kgs 9:22
food of his table, the seating of his **o**, 1 Kgs 10:5
servants and his **o** and his palace 2 Kgs 24:12
and his officials and his palace **o**. 2 Kgs 24:12
Jerusalem and all the **o** and all the 2 Kgs 24:14
mother, the king's wives, his **o**, 2 Kgs 24:15
be afraid because of the Chaldean **o**. 2 Kgs 25:24
sons were the chief **o** in the service 1 Chr 18:17
at Jerusalem all the **o** of Israel, 1 Chr 28:1
officials of Israel, the **o** of the tribes, 1 Chr 28:1
his sons, together with the palace **o**, 1 Chr 28:1
food of his table, the seating of his **o**, 2 Chr 9:4
third year of his reign he sent his **o**, 2 Chr 17:7
early and gathered the **o** of the city 2 Chr 29:20
king and the **o** commanded the 2 Chr 29:30
were scribes and **o** and gatekeepers. 2 Chr 34:13
And his **o** contributed willingly to 2 Chr 35:8
the judges, the governors, the **o**, Ezr 4:9
whom David and his **o** had set apart to Ezr 8:20
been done, the **o** approached me and said, Ezr 9:1
the hand of the **o** and chief men has Ezr 9:2
by order of the **o** and the elders all his Ezr 10:8
Let our **o** stand for the whole Ezr 10:14
And the **o** did not know where I had Neh 2:16
the Jews, the priests, the nobles, the **o**, Neh 2:16
the nobles and to the **o** and to the rest Neh 4:14
the nobles and to the **o** and to the rest Neh 4:19
charges against the nobles and the **o**. Neh 5:7
were at my table 150 men, Jews and **o**, Neh 5:17
the nobles and the **o** and the people to Neh 7:5
God, and I and half of the **o** with me; Neh 12:40
So I confronted the **o** and said, "Why Neh 13:11
he gave a feast for all his **o** and servants. Est 1:3
in the presence of the king and the **o**, Est 1:16
also against all the **o** and all the peoples Est 1:16
will say the same to all the king's **o**, Est 1:18
a great feast for all his **o** and servants; Est 2:18
throne above all the **o** who were with Est 3:1
provinces and to the **o** of all the peoples, Est 3:12
him above the **o** and the servants Est 5:11
over to one of the king's most noble **o**. Est 6:9
the governors and the **o** of the provinces Est 8:9
All the **o** of the provinces and the satraps Est 9:3
to falsehood, all his **o** will be wicked. Prv 29:12
For though his **o** are at Zoan and his Is 30:4
land, against the kings of Judah, its **o**, Jer 1:18
they, their kings, their **o**, their priests, Jer 2:26
LORD, courage shall fail both king and **o**. Jer 4:9
of the kings of Judah, the bones of its **o**, Jer 8:1
and on horses, they and their **o**, Jer 17:25
of Judah, together with the **o** of Judah, Jer 24:1
I treat Zedekiah the king of Judah, his **o**, Jer 24:8
and the cities of Judah, its kings and **o**, Jer 25:18
king of Egypt, his servants, his **o**, Jer 25:19
When the **o** of Judah heard these Jer 26:10
the prophets said to the **o** and to all the Jer 26:11
spoke to all the **o** and all the people, Jer 26:12
Then the **o** and all the people said to the Jer 26:16
with all his warriors and all the **o**, Jer 26:21
eunuchs, the **o** of Judah and Jerusalem, Jer 29:2
me to anger—their kings and their **o**, Jer 32:32

all the **o** and all the people who had Jer 34:10
the **o** of Judah, the officials of Jer 34:19
officials of Judah, the **o** of Jerusalem, Jer 34:19
king of Judah and his **o** I will give into Jer 34:21
which was near the chamber of the **o**, Jer 35:4
and all the **o** were sitting there: Jer 36:12
the son of Hananiah, and all the **o**. Jer 36:12
Then all the **o** sent Jehudi the son of Jer 36:14
Then the **o** said to Baruch, "Go and Jer 36:19
king and all the **o** who stood beside the Jer 36:21
Jeremiah and brought him to the **o**. Jer 37:14
And the **o** were enraged at Jeremiah, Jer 37:15
Then the **o** said to the king, "Let this Jer 38:4
will surrender to the **o** of the king of Jer 38:17
do not surrender to the **o** of the king of Jer 38:18
being led out to the **o** of the king of Jer 38:22
If the **o** hear that I have spoken with Jer 38:25
Then all the **o** came to Jeremiah and Jer 38:27
Then all the **o** of the king of Babylon Jer 39:3
and our fathers, our kings and our **o**, Jer 44:17
your fathers, your kings and your **o**, Jer 44:21
go into exile with his priests and his **o**. Jer 48:7
go into exile, with his priests and his **o**. Jer 49:3
in Elam and destroy their king and **o**, Jer 49:38
and against her **o** and her wise men! Jer 50:35
will make drunk her **o** and her wise Jer 51:57
also slaughtered all the **o** of Judah at Jer 52:10
and all the **o** of the provinces to come to Dn 3:2
and all the **o** of the provinces gathered for Dn 3:3
"I will punish the **o** and the king's sons Zep 1:8
Her **o** within her are roaring lions; her Zep 3:3

OFFSETS (2)
of the house he made **o** on the wall in 1 Kgs 6:6
There were **o** all around the wall of the Ezk 41:6

OFFSPRING (171)
and between your **o** and her offspring; Gn 3:15
and between your offspring and her **o**; Gn 3:15
for me another **o** instead of Abel, Gn 4:25
to keep their **o** alive on the face of all the Gn 7:3
covenant with you and your **o** after you, Gn 9:9
"To your **o** I will give this land." So he Gn 12:7
I will give to you and to your **o** forever. Gn 13:15
I will make your **o** as the dust of the Gn 13:16
the earth, your **o** also can be counted. Gn 13:16
said, "Behold, you have given me no **o**, Gn 15:3
he said to him, "So shall your **o** be." Gn 15:5
certain that your **o** will be sojourners Gn 15:13
saying, "To your **o** I give this land, Gn 15:18
will surely multiply your **o** so that they Gn 16:10
you and your **o** after you throughout Gn 17:7
to be God to you and to your **o** after you. Gn 17:7
to you and to your **o** after you the land Gn 17:8
you and your **o** after you throughout Gn 17:9
me and you and your **o** after you: Gn 17:10
any foreigner who is not of your **o**, Gn 17:12
covenant for his **o** after him. Gn 17:19
we may preserve **o** from our father." Gn 19:32
we may preserve **o** from our father." Gn 19:34
through Isaac shall your **o** be named. Gn 21:12
woman also, because he is your **o**." Gn 21:13
will surely multiply your **o** as the stars Gn 22:17
And your **o** shall possess the gate of his Gn 22:17
and in your **o** shall all the nations of Gn 22:18
to me, 'To your **o** I will give this land,' Gn 24:7
and may your **o** possess the gate of Gn 24:60
to you and to your **o** I will give all these Gn 26:3
I will multiply your **o** as the stars of Gn 26:4
and will give to your **o** all these lands. Gn 26:4
And in your **o** all the nations of the Gn 26:4
and multiply your **o** for my servant Gn 26:24
to you and to your **o** with you, Gn 28:4
you lie I will give to you and to your **o**. Gn 28:13
Your **o** shall be like the dust of the Gn 28:14
in you and your **o** shall all the families Gn 28:14
and make your **o** as the sand of the sea, Gn 32:12
I will give the land to your **o** after you." Gn 35:12
to her, and raise up **o** for your brother." Gn 38:8
Onan knew that the **o** would not be his. Gn 38:9
so as not to give **o** to his brother. Gn 38:9
into Egypt, Jacob and all his **o** with him, Gn 46:6
All his **o** he brought with him into Gn 46:7
give this land to your **o** after you for an Gn 48:4
behold, God has let me see your **o** also." Gn 48:11
and his **o** shall become a multitude of Gn 48:19
forever for him and for his **o** after him. Ex 28:43
and to his **o** throughout their Ex 30:21
'I will multiply your **o** as the stars of Ex 32:13
I have promised I will give to your **o**, Ex 32:13
Jacob, saying, 'To your **o** I will give it.' Ex 33:1
not profane his **o** among his people, Lv 21:15
None of your **o** throughout their Lv 21:17
No man of the **o** of Aaron the priest Lv 21:21
of all your **o** throughout your Lv 22:3
None of the **o** of Aaron who has a Lv 22:4
LORD for you and for your **o** with you." Nm 18:19
to give to them and to their **o** after them.' Dt 1:8
fathers and chose their **o** after them and Dt 4:37
fathers and chose their **o** after them, Dt 10:15
fathers to give to them and to their **o**, Dt 11:9
wonder against you and your **o** forever. Dt 28:46
It shall eat the **o** of your cattle and the Dt 28:51
and your **o** extraordinary afflictions, Dt 28:59
your heart and the heart of your **o**, Dt 30:6
life, that you and your **o** may live, Dt 30:19
unforgotten in the mouths of their **o**). Dt 31:21
and to Jacob, 'I will give it to your **o**.' Dt 34:4
land of Canaan, and made his **o** many. Jos 24:3
Gideon had seventy sons, his own **o**, Jgs 8:30
because of the **o** that the LORD will give Ru 4:12
and between my **o** and your 1 Sm 20:42
between my offspring and your **o**, 1 Sm 20:42
you will not cut off my **o** after me, 1 Sm 24:21
the king this day on Saul and on his **o**." 2 Sm 4:8
I will raise up your **o** after you, 2 Sm 7:12
anointed, to David and his **o** forever." 2 Sm 22:51
I will afflict the **o** of David because 1 Kgs 11:39
O **o** of Israel his servant, sons of 1 Chr 16:13
I will raise up your **o** after you, 1 Chr 17:11
covenant to give to his **o** the land of the Neh 9:8
themselves and their **o** and all who Est 9:27
had obligated themselves and their **o**, Est 9:31
know also that your **o** shall be many, Jb 5:25
Their **o** are established in their presence, Jb 21:8
when they crouch, bring forth their **o**, Jb 39:3
his anointed, to David and his **o** forever. Ps 18:50
and their **o** from among the children of Ps 21:10
the LORD, praise him! All you **o** of Jacob, Ps 22:23
stand in awe of him, all you **o** of Israel! Ps 22:23
and his **o** shall inherit the land. Ps 25:13
the **o** of his servants shall inherit it, and Ps 69:36
'I will establish your **o** forever, and build Ps 89:4
I will establish his **o** forever and his Ps 89:29
His **o** shall endure forever, his throne as Ps 89:36
their **o** shall be established before you. Ps 102:28
O **o** of Abraham, his servant, children Ps 105:6
would make their **o** fall among the Ps 106:27
His **o** will be mighty in the land; the Ps 112:2
but the **o** of the righteous will be Prv 11:21
a people laden with iniquity, **o** of evildoers, Is 1:4
"May the **o** of evildoers nevermore be Is 14:20
of his father's house, the **o** and issue, Is 22:24
whom I have chosen, the **o** of Abraham, Is 41:8
I will bring your **o** from the east, and Is 43:5
I will pour my Spirit upon your **o**, and my Is 44:3
I did not say to the **o** of Jacob, 'Seek me Is 45:19
In the LORD all the **o** of Israel shall be Is 45:25
your **o** would have been like the sand, Is 48:19
an offering for sin, he shall see his **o**; Is 53:10
and your **o** will possess the nations and Is 54:3
o of the adulterer and the loose woman. Is 57:3
children of transgression, the **o** of deceit, Is 57:4
mouth, or out of the mouth of your **o**, Is 59:21
of your children's **o**," says the LORD, Is 59:21
Their **o** shall be known among the Is 61:9
that they are an **o** the LORD has blessed. Is 61:9
I will bring forth **o** from Jacob, and from Is 65:9
for they shall be the **o** of the blessed of Is 65:23
so shall your **o** and your name remain Is 66:22
all your kinsmen, all the **o** of Ephraim. Jer 7:15
for none of his **o** shall succeed in Jer 22:30
brought up and led the **o** of the house of Jer 23:8
and your **o** from the land of their Jer 30:10
then shall the **o** of Israel cease from Jer 31:36
will cast off all the **o** of Israel for all that Jer 31:37
I will multiply the **o** of David my Jer 33:22
I will reject the **o** of Jacob and David Jer 33:26
not choose one of his **o** to rule over the Jer 33:26
to rule over the **o** of Abraham, Jer 33:26
punish him and his **o** and his servants Jer 36:31
and your **o** from the land of their Jer 46:27
one of the royal **o** and made a Ezk 17:13
I swore to the **o** of the house of Jacob, Ezk 20:5
only virgins of the **o** of the house of Ezk 44:22
Behold, I will rebuke your **o**, and spread Mal 2:3
was the one God seeking? Godly **o**. Mal 2:15
widow and raise up **o** for his brother. Mk 12:19
took a wife, and when he died left no **o**. Mk 12:20
took her, and died, leaving no **o**. Mk 12:21
And the seven left no **o**. Last of all the Mk 12:22
to Abraham and to his **o** forever." Lk 1:55
widow and raise up **o** for his brother. Lk 20:28
the Christ comes from the **o** of David, Jn 7:42
"We are **o** of Abraham and have never Jn 8:33
I know that you are **o** of Abraham; yet Jn 8:37
'And in your **o** shall all the families of Acts 3:25
as a possession and to his **o** after him, Acts 7:5
effect—that his **o** would be sojourners Acts 7:6
Of this man's **o** God has brought to Acts 13:23
have said, "'For we are indeed his **o**.' Acts 17:28
Being then God's **o**, we ought not to Acts 17:29
to Abraham and his **o** that he would Rom 4:13
be guaranteed to all his **o**—not only to Rom 4:16
he had been told, "So shall your **o** be." Rom 4:18
of Abraham because they are his **o**, Rom 9:7
Isaac shall your **o** be named." Rom 9:7
of the promise are counted as **o**. Rom 9:8
"If the Lord of hosts had not left us **o**, Rom 9:29
So am I. Are they **o** of Abraham? 2 Cor 11:22
were made to Abraham and to his **o**. Gal 3:16
to one, "And to your **o**," who is Christ. Gal 3:16
until the **o** should come to whom the Gal 3:19
are Christ's, then you are Abraham's **o**, Gal 3:29
risen from the dead, the **o** of David, 2 Tm 2:8
helps, but he helps the **o** of Abraham. Heb 2:16
Isaac shall your **o** be named." Heb 11:18
off to make war on the rest of her **o**, Rv 12:17

OFFSPRINGS (1)
not say, "And to **o**," referring to many, Gal 3:16

OFTEN (35)
As **o** as she went up to the house of the 1 Sm 1:7
and as **o** as they came out David had 1 Sm 18:30
for Hadadezer had **o** been at war with 2 Sm 8:10
And as **o** as the king went into the 1 Kgs 14:28
for Hadadezer had **o** been at war 1 Chr 18:10
And as **o** as the king went into the 2 Chr 12:11
had not kept it as **o** as prescribed. 2 Chr 30:5
"How **o** is it that the lamp of the wicked Jb 21:17
he restrained his anger **o** and did not Ps 78:38
How **o** they rebelled against him in the Ps 78:40
He who is **o** reproved, yet stiffens his Prv 29:1
As **o** as it passes through it will take you; Is 28:19
For as **o** as I speak against him, I do Jer 31:20
For **o** he falls into the fire, and often Mt 17:15
falls into the fire, and **o** into the water. Mt 17:15
how **o** will my brother sin against me, Mt 18:21
How **o** would I have gathered your Mt 23:37
for he had **o** been bound with shackles Mk 5:4
And it has **o** cast him into fire and into Mk 9:22
disciples of John fast **o** and offer prayers, Lk 5:33
How **o** would I have gathered your Lk 13:34
for Jesus **o** met there with his disciples. Jn 18:2
he sent for him **o** and conversed with Acts 24:26
And I punished them **o** in all the Acts 26:11
that I have **o** intended to come to you Rom 1:13
why I have so **o** been hindered from Rom 15:22
Do this, as **o** as you drink it, in 1 Cor 11:25
For as **o** as you eat this bread and 1 Cor 11:26
whom we have **o** tested and found 2 Cor 8:22
beatings, and **o** near death. 2 Cor 11:23
in hunger and thirst, **o** without food, 2 Cor 11:27
of whom I have **o** told you and now tell Phil 3:18
for he **o** refreshed me and was not 2 Tm 1:16
that has drunk the rain that **o** falls on it, Heb 6:7
every kind of plague, as **o** as they desire. Rv 11:6

OG (22)
And **O** the king of Bashan came out Nm 21:33
the kingdom of **O** king of Bashan, Nm 32:33
in Heshbon, and **O** the king of Bashan, Dt 1:4
And **O** the king of Bashan came out Dt 3:1
LORD our God gave into our hand **O** also, Dt 3:3
of Argob, the kingdom of **O** in Bashan. Dt 3:4
cities of the kingdom of **O** in Bashan. Dt 3:10
(For only **O** the king of Bashan was left Dt 3:11
and all Bashan, the kingdom of **O**, Dt 3:13
possession of his land and the land of **O**, Dt 4:47
king of Heshbon and **O** the king of Dt 29:7
will do to them as he did to Sihon and **O**, Dt 31:4
were beyond the Jordan, to Sihon and **O**, Jos 2:10
of Heshbon, and to **O** king of Bashan, Jos 9:10
and **O** king of Bashan, one of the Jos 12:4
all the kingdom of **O** in Bashan, who Jos 13:12
whole kingdom of **O** king of Bashan, Jos 13:30
cities of the kingdom of **O** in Bashan. Jos 13:31
Amorites and of **O** king of Bashan. 1 Kgs 4:19
and the land of **O** king of Bashan. Neh 9:22
Sihon, king of the Amorites, and **O**, Ps 135:11
and **O**, king of Bashan, for his Ps 136:20

OHAD (2)
Jemuel, Jamin, **O**, Jachin, Zohar, and Gn 46:10
Jemuel, Jamin, **O**, Jachin, Zohar, and Ex 6:15

OHEL (1)
and Hashubah, **O**, Berechiah, 1 Chr 3:20

OHOLAH (5)
O was the name of the elder and Ezk 23:4
As for their names, **O** is Samaria, and Ezk 23:4
"**O** played the whore while she was Ezk 23:5
man, will you judge **O** and Oholibah? Ezk 23:36
they went in to **O** and to Oholibah, Ezk 23:44

OHOLIAB (5)
behold, I have appointed with him **O**, Ex 31:6
both him and **O** the son of Ahisamach Ex 35:34

"Bezalel and **O** and every craftsman in Ex 36:1
called Bezalel and **O** and every Ex 36:2
and with him was **O** the son of Ex 38:23

OHOLIBAH (6)
of the elder and **O** the name of her Ezk 23:4
Oholah is Samaria, and **O** is Jerusalem. Ezk 23:4
"Her sister **O** saw this, and she became Ezk 23:11
Therefore, O **O**, thus says the Lord Ezk 23:22
of man, will you judge Oholah and **O**? Ezk 23:36
Thus they went in to Oholah and to **O**, Ezk 23:44

OHOLIBAMAH (8)
O the daughter of Anah the daughter of Gn 36:2
and **O** bore Jeush, Jalam, and Korah. Gn 36:5
are the sons of **O** the daughter of Anah Gn 36:14
These are the sons of **O**, Esau's wife: the Gn 36:18
the chiefs born of **O** the daughter of Gn 36:18
Dishon and **O** the daughter of Anah. Gn 36:25
O, Elah, Pinon, Gn 36:41
O, Elah, Pinon, 1 Chr 1:52

OIL (211)
for a pillar and poured **o** on the top of Gn 28:18
drink offering on it and poured **o** on it. Gn 35:14
o for the lamps, spices for the anointing Ex 25:6
spices for the anointing **o** and for the Ex 25:6
to you pure beaten olive **o** for the light, Ex 27:20
bread, unleavened cakes mixed with **o**, Ex 29:2
and unleavened wafers smeared with **o**. Ex 29:2
shall take the anointing **o** and pour it on Ex 29:7
is on the altar, and of the anointing **o**, Ex 29:21
and one cake of bread made with **o**, Ex 29:23
with a fourth of a hin of beaten **o**, Ex 29:40
of the sanctuary, and a hin of olive **o**. Ex 30:24
a sacred anointing **o** blended as by Ex 30:25
it shall be a holy anointing **o**. Ex 30:25
my holy anointing **o** throughout your Ex 30:31
and the anointing **o** and the fragrant Ex 31:11
o for the light, spices for the anointing Ex 35:8
spices for the anointing **o** and for the Ex 35:8
and its lamps, and the **o** for the light; Ex 35:14
and the anointing **o** and the fragrant Ex 35:15
and spices and **o** for the light, and for Ex 35:28
oil for the light, and for the anointing **o**, Ex 35:28
He made the holy anointing **o** also, and Ex 37:29
all its utensils, and the **o** for the light; Ex 39:37
the anointing **o** and the fragrant Ex 39:38
take the anointing **o** and anoint the Ex 40:9
He shall pour **o** on it and put Lv 2:1
from it a handful of the fine flour and **o**, Lv 2:2
flour mixed with **o** or unleavened wafers Lv 2:4
oil or unleavened wafers smeared with **o**. Lv 2:4
be of fine flour unleavened, mixed with **o**. Lv 2:5
shall break it in pieces and pour **o** on it; Lv 2:6
a pan, it shall be made of fine flour with **o**. Lv 2:7
And you shall put **o** on it and lay Lv 2:15
grain and some of the **o** with all of its Lv 2:16
He shall put no **o** on it and shall put no Lv 5:11
grain offering and its **o** and all the Lv 6:15
It shall be made with **o** on a griddle. You Lv 6:21
every grain offering, mixed with **o** or dry, Lv 7:10
unleavened loaves mixed with **o**, Lv 7:12
oil, unleavened wafers smeared with **o**, Lv 7:12
loaves of fine flour well mixed with **o**. Lv 7:12
and the anointing **o** and the bull Lv 8:2
took the anointing **o** and anointed the Lv 8:10
some of the anointing **o** on Aaron's head Lv 8:12
loaf of bread with **o** and one wafer and Lv 8:26
some of the anointing **o** and of the blood Lv 8:30
LORD, and a grain offering mixed with **o**, Lv 9:4
for the anointing **o** of the LORD is upon Lv 10:7
of an ephah of fine flour mixed with **o**, Lv 14:10
flour mixed with oil, and one log of **o**. Lv 14:10
a guilt offering, along with the log of **o**, Lv 14:12
some of the log of **o** and pour it into the Lv 14:15
his right finger in the **o** that is in his Lv 14:16
and sprinkle some **o** with his finger Lv 14:16
And some of the **o** that remains in his Lv 14:17
And the rest of the **o** that is in the Lv 14:18
fine flour mixed with **o** for a grain Lv 14:21
oil for a grain offering, and a log of **o**; Lv 14:21
of the guilt offering and the log of **o**, Lv 14:24
pour some of the **o** into the palm of Lv 14:26
right finger some of the **o** that is in his Lv 14:27
shall put some of the **o** that is in his Lv 14:28
And the rest of the **o** that is in the Lv 14:29
head the anointing **o** is poured and Lv 21:10
of the anointing **o** of his God Lv 21:12
of an ephah of fine flour mixed with **o**, Lv 23:13
to bring you pure **o** from beaten olives Lv 24:2
and all the vessels for **o** with which it is Nm 4:9
shall have charge of the **o** for the light, Nm 4:16
grain offering, and the anointing **o**, Nm 4:16
He shall pour no **o** on it and put no Nm 5:15
bread, loaves of fine flour mixed with **o**, Nm 6:15
and unleavened wafers smeared with **o**, Nm 6:15
fine flour mixed with **o** for a grain Nm 7:13
fine flour mixed with **o** for a grain Nm 7:19
fine flour mixed with **o** for a grain Nm 7:25
fine flour mixed with **o** for a grain Nm 7:31
fine flour mixed with **o** for a grain Nm 7:37
fine flour mixed with **o** for a grain Nm 7:43
fine flour mixed with **o** for a grain Nm 7:49
fine flour mixed with **o** for a grain Nm 7:55
fine flour mixed with **o** for a grain Nm 7:61
fine flour mixed with **o** for a grain Nm 7:67
fine flour mixed with **o** for a grain Nm 7:73
fine flour mixed with **o** for a grain Nm 7:79
grain offering of fine flour mixed with **o**, Nm 8:8
like the taste of cakes baked with **o**. Nm 11:8
mixed with a quarter of a hin of **o**; Nm 15:4
flour mixed with a third of a hin of **o**. Nm 15:6
of fine flour, mixed with half a hin of **o**. Nm 15:9
All the best of the **o** and all the best of Nm 18:12
with a quarter of a hin of beaten **o**. Nm 28:5
flour for a grain offering, mixed with **o**, Nm 28:9
for a grain offering, mixed with **o**, Nm 28:12
for a grain offering, mixed with **o**, Nm 28:12
fine flour mixed with **o** as a grain Nm 28:13
offering of fine flour mixed with **o**; Nm 28:20
offering of fine flour mixed with **o**, Nm 28:28
offering of fine flour mixed with **o**, Nm 29:3
shall be of fine flour mixed with **o**, Nm 29:9
offering of fine flour mixed with **o**, Nm 29:14
who was anointed with the holy **o**. Nm 35:25
your grain and your wine and your **o**, Dt 7:13
your grain and your wine and your **o**. Dt 11:14
your grain or of your wine or of your **o**, Dt 12:17
your grain, of your wine, and of your **o**, Dt 14:23
of your grain, of your wine and of your **o**, Dt 18:4
shall not anoint yourself with the **o**, Dt 28:40
shall not leave you grain, wine, or **o**, Dt 28:51
of the rock, and **o** out of the flinty rock. Dt 32:13
brothers, and let him dip his foot in **o**. Dt 33:24
took a flask of **o** and poured it on 1 Sm 10:1
Israel? Fill your horn with **o**, and go. 1 Sm 16:1
took the horn of **o** and anointed him 1 Sm 16:13
the shield of Saul, not anointed with **o**. 2 Sm 1:21
Do not anoint yourself with **o**, but 2 Sm 14:2
took the horn of **o** from the tent and 1 Kgs 1:39
and 20,000 cors of beaten **o**. 1 Kgs 5:11
flour in a jar and a little **o** in a jug. 1 Kgs 17:12
and the jug of **o** shall not be empty, 1 Kgs 17:14
did the jug of **o** become empty, 1 Kgs 17:16
nothing in the house except a jar of **o**." 2 Kgs 4:2
another." Then the **o** stopped flowing. 2 Kgs 4:6
said, "Go, sell the **o** and pay your debts, 2 Kgs 4:7
and take this flask of **o** in your hand, 2 Kgs 9:1
Then take the flask of **o** and pour it on 2 Kgs 9:3
young man poured the **o** on his head, 2 Kgs 9:6
the gold, the spices, the precious **o**, 2 Kgs 20:13
over the fine flour, the wine, the **o**, 1 Chr 9:29
clusters of raisins, and wine and **o**, 1 Chr 12:40
offering, the offering mixed with **o**, 1 Chr 23:29
and over the stores of **o** was Joash. 1 Chr 27:28
baths of wine, and 20,000 baths of **o**." 2 Chr 2:10
the wheat and barley, **o** and wine, 2 Chr 2:15
and stores of food, **o**, and wine. 2 Chr 11:11
the firstfruits of grain, wine, **o**, honey, 2 Chr 31:5
for the yield of grain, wine, and **o**; 2 Chr 32:28
and **o** to the Sidonians and the Tyrians to Ezr 3:7
the God of heaven, wheat, salt, wine, or **o**, Ezr 6:9
wheat, 100 baths of wine, 100 baths of **o**, Ezr 7:22
and **o** that you have been exacting Neh 5:11
fruit of every tree, the wine and the **o**, Neh 10:37
of grain, wine, and **o** to the chambers, Neh 10:39
and the tithes of grain, wine, and **o**, Neh 13:5
wine, and **o** into the storehouses. Neh 13:12
six months with **o** of myrrh and six Est 2:12
olive rows of the wicked they make **o**; Jb 24:11
the rock poured out for me streams of **o**! Jb 29:6
my enemies; you anoint my head with **o**; Ps 23:5
you with the **o** of gladness beyond Ps 45:7
his words were softer than **o**, yet they Ps 55:21
with my holy **o** I have anointed him, Ps 89:20
ox; you have poured over me fresh **o**. Ps 92:10
o to make his face shine and bread to Ps 104:15
body like water, like **o** into his bones! Ps 109:18
It is like the precious **o** on the head, Ps 133:2
let him rebuke me—it is **o** for my head; Ps 141:5
and her speech is smoother than **o**, Prv 5:3
who loves wine and **o** will not be rich. Prv 21:17
Precious treasure and **o** are in a wise Prv 21:20
O and perfume make the heart glad, Prv 27:9
wind or to grasp **o** in one's right hand. Prv 27:16
Let not **o** be lacking on your head. Eccl 9:8
are fragrant; your name is **o** poured out; Sg 1:3
pressed out or bound up or softened with **o**. Is 1:6
they drink. Arise, O princes; **o** the shield! Is 21:5
silver, the gold, the spices, the precious **o**, Is 39:2
to the king with **o** and multiplied your Is 57:9
the **o** of gladness instead of mourning, Is 61:3
over the grain, the wine, and the **o**, Jer 31:12
gather wine and summer fruits and **o**, Jer 40:10
o, and honey hidden in the fields." So he Jer 41:8
from you and anointed you with **o**. Ezk 16:9
You ate fine flour and honey and **o**. Ezk 16:13
and set my **o** and my incense before Ezk 16:18
with fine flour and **o** and honey—you Ezk 16:19
you had placed my incense and my **o**. Ezk 23:41
of Minnith, meal, honey, **o**, and balm. Ezk 27:17
and cause their rivers to run like **o**, Ezk 32:14
and as the fixed portion of **o**, measured Ezk 45:14
ram, and a hin of **o** to each ephah. Ezk 45:24
and grain offerings, and for the **o**. Ezk 45:25
together with a hin of **o** to each ephah. Ezk 46:5
together with a hin of **o** to each ephah. Ezk 46:7
together with a hin of **o** to an ephah. Ezk 46:11
third of a hin of **o** to moisten the flour, Ezk 46:14
offering and the **o** shall be provided, Ezk 46:15
wool and my flax, my **o** and my drink.' Hos 2:5
gave her the grain, the wine, and the **o**, Hos 2:8
answer the grain, the wine, and the **o**, Hos 2:22
with Assyria, and **o** is carried to Egypt. Hos 12:1
the wine dries up, the **o** languishes. Jl 1:10
I am sending to you grain, wine, and **o**, Jl 2:19
the vats shall overflow with wine and **o**. Jl 2:24
of rams, with ten thousands of rivers of **o**? Mi 6:7
olives, but not anoint yourselves with **o**; Mi 6:15
hills, on the grain, the new wine, the **o**, Hg 1:11
or stew or wine or **o** or any kind of food, Hg 2:12
which the golden **o** is poured out?" Zec 4:12
their lamps, they took no **o** with them, Mt 25:3
wise took flasks of **o** with their lamps. Mt 25:4
said to the wise, 'Give us some of your **o**, Mt 25:8
and anointed with **o** many who were Mk 6:13
You did not anoint my head with **o**, but Lk 7:46
up his wounds, pouring on **o** and wine. Lk 10:34
He said, 'A hundred measures of **o**.' He Lk 16:6
you with the **o** of gladness beyond Heb 1:9
anointing him with **o** in the name of the Jas 5:14
and do not harm the **o** and wine!" Rv 6:6
frankincense, wine, **o**, fine flour, Rv 18:13

OILS (3)
your anointing **o** are fragrant; your name Sg 1:3
the fragrance of your **o** than any spice! Sg 4:10
and anoint themselves with the finest **o**, Am 6:6

OINTMENT (14)
a pot; he makes the sea like a pot of **o**. Jb 41:31
A good name is better than precious **o**, Eccl 7:1
flies make the perfumer's **o** give off a Eccl 10:1
an alabaster flask of very expensive **o**, Mt 26:7
In pouring this **o** on my body, she has Mt 26:12
an alabaster flask of **o** of pure nard, Mk 14:3
"Why was the **o** wasted like that? Mk 14:4
For this **o** could have been sold for Mk 14:5
house, brought an alabaster flask of **o**, Lk 7:37
his feet and anointed them with the **o**. Lk 7:38
oil, but she has anointed my feet with **o**. Lk 7:46
anointed the Lord with **o** and wiped his Jn 11:2
a pound of expensive **o** made from pure Jn 12:3
"Why was this **o** not sold for three Jn 12:5

OINTMENTS (2)
months with spices and **o** for women— Est 2:12
returned and prepared spices and **o**. Lk 23:56

OLD (391)
After Noah was 500 years **o**, Noah Gn 5:32
were the mighty men who were of **o**, Gn 6:4
was six hundred years **o** when the flood of Gn 7:6
When Shem was 100 years **o**, he Gn 11:10
was seventy-five years **o** when he Gn 12:4
to him, "Bring me a heifer three years **o**, Gn 15:9
years old, a female goat three years **o**, Gn 15:9
goat three years old, a ram three years **o**, Gn 15:9
you shall be buried in a good **o** age. Gn 15:15
was eighty-six years **o** when Hagar Gn 16:16
was ninety-nine years **o** the LORD Gn 17:1
who is eight days **o** among you shall Gn 17:12
to a man who is a hundred years **o**? Gn 17:17
Shall Sarah, who is ninety years **o**, Gn 17:17
was ninety-nine years **o** when he was Gn 17:24
son was thirteen years **o** when he was Gn 17:25
Now Abraham and Sarah were **o**, Gn 18:11
"After I am worn out, and my lord is **o**, Gn 18:12
I indeed bear a child, now that I am **o**?' Gn 18:13
the men of Sodom, both young and **o**, Gn 19:4
said to the younger, "Our father is **o**, Gn 19:31
Abraham a son in his **o** age at the time Gn 21:2
his son Isaac when he was eight days **o**, Gn 21:4
was a hundred years **o** when his son Gn 21:5
Yet I have borne him a son in his **o** age." Gn 21:7
Now Abraham was **o**, well advanced in Gn 24:1
a son to my master when she was **o**, Gn 24:36
his last and died in a good **o** age, Gn 25:8

good old age, an **o** man and full of years, Gn 25:8
Isaac was forty years **o** when he took Gn 25:20
Isaac was sixty years **o** when she bore Gn 25:26
When Esau was forty years **o**, he took Gn 26:34
When Isaac was **o** and his eyes were Gn 27:1
He said, "Behold, I am **o**; I do not know Gn 27:2
to his people, **o** and full of days. Gn 35:29
Joseph, being seventeen years **o**, was Gn 37:2
because he was the son of his **o** age. Gn 37:3
was thirty years **o** when he entered Gn 41:46
well, the **o** man of whom you spoke? Gn 43:27
my lord, 'We have a father, an **o** man, Gn 44:20
a young brother, the child of his **o** age. Gn 44:20
So Joseph died, being 110 years **o**. They Gn 50:26
Now Moses was eighty years **o**, and Aaron Ex 7:7
years old, and Aaron eighty-three years **o**, Ex 7:7
"We will go with our young and our **o**. Ex 10:9
be without blemish, a male a year **o**. Ex 12:5
two lambs a year **o** day by day Ex 29:38
from twenty years **o** and upward, Ex 30:14
from twenty years **o** and upward, Ex 38:26
a lamb, both a year **o** without blemish, Lv 9:3
a lamb a year **o** for a burnt offering, Lv 12:6
ewe lamb a year **o** without blemish, Lv 14:10
head and honor the face of an **o** man, Lv 19:32
male lamb a year **o** without blemish as Lv 23:12
seven lambs a year **o** without blemish, Lv 23:18
male lambs a year **o** as a sacrifice of Lv 23:19
you will be eating some of the **o** crop; Lv 25:22
you shall eat the **o** until the ninth year, Lv 25:22
You shall eat **o** store long kept, and you Lv 26:10
shall clear out the **o** to make way for Lv 26:10
male from twenty years **o** up to sixty Lv 27:3
up to sixty years **o** shall be fifty shekels Lv 27:3
is from five years **o** up to twenty years Lv 27:5
from five years old up to twenty years **o**, Lv 27:5
person is from a month **o** up to five years Lv 27:6
is from a month old up to five years **o**, Lv 27:6
And if the person is sixty years **o** or over, Lv 27:7
From twenty years **o** and upward, all in Nm 1:3
from twenty years **o** and upward, Nm 1:18
male from twenty years **o** and upward, Nm 1:20
male from twenty years **o** and upward, Nm 1:22
from twenty years **o** and upward, Nm 1:24
from twenty years **o** and upward, Nm 1:26
from twenty years **o** and upward, Nm 1:28
from twenty years **o** and upward, Nm 1:30
from twenty years **o** and upward, Nm 1:32
from twenty years **o** and upward, Nm 1:34
from twenty years **o** and upward, Nm 1:36
from twenty years **o** and upward, Nm 1:38
from twenty years **o** and upward, Nm 1:40
from twenty years **o** and upward, Nm 1:42
from twenty years **o** and upward, Nm 1:45
male from a month **o** and upward you Nm 3:15
males from a month **o** and upward was Nm 3:22
males, from a month **o** and upward, Nm 3:28
males from a month **o** and upward was Nm 3:34
the males from a month **o** and upward, Nm 3:39
of Israel, from a month **o** and upward, Nm 3:40
from a month **o** and upward as listed Nm 3:43
from thirty years **o** up to fifty years old, Nm 4:3
from thirty years old up to fifty years **o**, Nm 4:3
From thirty years **o** up to fifty years Nm 4:23
thirty years old up to fifty years **o**, Nm 4:23
From thirty years **o** up to fifty years Nm 4:30
thirty years old up to fifty years **o**, Nm 4:30
from thirty years **o** up to fifty years old, Nm 4:35
from thirty years old up to fifty years **o**, Nm 4:35
from thirty years **o** up to fifty years old, Nm 4:39
from thirty years old up to fifty years **o**, Nm 4:39
from thirty years **o** up to fifty years old, Nm 4:43
from thirty years old up to fifty years **o**, Nm 4:43
from thirty years **o** up to fifty years old, Nm 4:47
from thirty years old up to fifty years **o**, Nm 4:47
male lamb a year **o** for a guilt offering. Nm 6:12
lamb a year **o** without blemish for Nm 6:14
ewe lamb a year **o** without blemish as Nm 6:14
herd, one ram, one male lamb a year **o**, Nm 7:15
goats, and five male lambs a year **o**. Nm 7:17
herd, one ram, one male lamb a year **o**, Nm 7:21
goats, and five male lambs a year **o**. Nm 7:23
herd, one ram, one male lamb a year **o**, Nm 7:27
goats, and five male lambs a year **o**. Nm 7:29
herd, one ram, one male lamb a year **o**, Nm 7:33
goats, and five male lambs a year **o**. Nm 7:35
herd, one ram, one male lamb a year **o**, Nm 7:39
goats, and five male lambs a year **o**. Nm 7:41
herd, one ram, one male lamb a year **o**, Nm 7:45
goats, and five male lambs a year **o**. Nm 7:47
herd, one ram, one male lamb a year **o**, Nm 7:51
goats, and five male lambs a year **o**. Nm 7:53
herd, one ram, one male lamb a year **o**, Nm 7:57
goats, and five male lambs a year **o**. Nm 7:59
herd, one ram, one male lamb a year **o**, Nm 7:63
goats, and five male lambs a year **o**. Nm 7:65
herd, one ram, one male lamb a year **o**, Nm 7:69
goats, and five male lambs a year **o**. Nm 7:71
herd, one ram, one male lamb a year **o**, Nm 7:75
goats, and five male lambs a year **o**. Nm 7:77
herd, one ram, one male lamb a year **o**, Nm 7:81
goats, and five male lambs a year **o**. Nm 7:83
rams, twelve male lambs a year **o**, Nm 7:87
sixty, the male lambs a year **o** sixty. Nm 7:88
from twenty-five years **o** and upward Nm 8:24
from twenty years **o** and upward, Nm 14:29
female goat a year **o** for a sin offering. Nm 15:27
price (at a month **o** you shall redeem Nm 18:16
Israel, from twenty years **o** and upward, Nm 26:2
from twenty years **o** and upward," as Nm 26:4
male from a month **o** and upward. Nm 26:62
male lambs a year **o** without blemish, Nm 28:3
male lambs a year **o** without blemish, Nm 28:9
male lambs a year **o** without blemish; Nm 28:11
ram, and seven male lambs a year **o**; Nm 28:19
one ram, seven male lambs a year **o**; Nm 28:27
male lambs a year **o** without blemish; Nm 29:2
one ram, seven male lambs a year **o**: Nm 29:8
rams, fourteen male lambs a year **o**; Nm 29:13
male lambs a year **o** without blemish, Nm 29:17
male lambs a year **o** without blemish, Nm 29:20
male lambs a year **o** without blemish, Nm 29:23
male lambs a year **o** without blemish, Nm 29:26
male lambs a year **o** without blemish, Nm 29:29
male lambs a year **o** without blemish, Nm 29:32
male lambs a year **o** without blemish, Nm 29:36
from twenty years **o** and upward, Nm 32:11
Aaron was 123 years **o** when he died Nm 33:39
children, and have grown **o** in the land, Dt 4:25
landmark, which the men of **o** have set, Dt 19:14
shall not respect the **o** or show mercy to Dt 28:50
he said to them, "I am 120 years **o** today. Dt 31:2
Remember the days of **o**; consider the Dt 32:7
Moses was 120 years **o** when he died. His Dt 34:7
both men and women, young and **o**, Jos 6:21
Now Joshua was **o** and advanced in Jos 13:1
him, "You are **o** and advanced in years, Jos 13:1
I was forty years **o** when Moses the Jos 14:7
I am this day eighty-five years **o**. Jos 14:10
and Joshua was **o** and well advanced in Jos 23:1
"I am now **o** and well advanced in years. Jos 23:2
of the LORD, died, being 110 years **o**. Jos 24:29
bull, and the second bull seven years **o**, Jgs 6:25
died in a good **o** age and was buried Jgs 8:32
an **o** man was coming from his work Jgs 19:16
square of the city. And the **o** man said, Jgs 19:17
And the **o** man said, "Peace be to you; I Jgs 19:20
And they said to the **o** man, the master Jgs 19:22
way, for I am too **o** to have a husband. Ru 1:12
of life and a nourisher of your **o** age, Ru 4:15
Now Eli was very **o**, and he kept 1 Sm 2:22
will not be an **o** man in your house. 1 Sm 2:31
shall not be an **o** man in your house 1 Sm 2:32
was ninety-eight years **o** and his eyes 1 Sm 4:15
he died, for the man was **o** and heavy. 1 Sm 4:18
the men of the city, both young and **o**, 1 Sm 5:9
When Samuel became **o**, he made his 1 Sm 8:1
you are **o** and your sons do not walk in 1 Sm 8:5
before you, and I am **o** and gray; 1 Sm 12:2
Saul was … years **o** when he began to 1 Sm 13:1
man was already **o** and advanced in 1 Sm 17:12
the inhabitants of the land from of **o**, 1 Sm 27:8
she said, "An **o** man is coming up, 1 Sm 28:14
was forty years **o** when he began to 2 Sm 2:10
He was five years **o** when the news 2 Sm 4:4
was thirty years **o** when he began 2 Sm 5:4
was a very aged man, eighty years **o**. 2 Sm 19:32
I am this day eighty years **o**. Can I 2 Sm 19:35
King David was **o** and advanced in 1 Kgs 1:1
chamber (now the king was very **o**, 1 Kgs 1:15
when Solomon was **o** his wives 1 Kgs 11:4
took counsel with the **o** men, 1 Kgs 12:6
the counsel that the **o** men gave him 1 Kgs 12:8
counsel that the **o** men had given 1 Kgs 12:13
Now an **o** prophet lived in Bethel. 1 Kgs 13:11
in the city where the **o** prophet lived. 1 Kgs 13:25
was forty-one years **o** when he 1 Kgs 14:21
But in his **o** age he was diseased in 1 Kgs 15:23
was thirty-five years **o** when he 1 Kgs 22:42
has no son, and her husband is **o**." 2 Kgs 4:14
was thirty-two years **o** when he 2 Kgs 8:17
was twenty-two years **o** when he 2 Kgs 8:26
was seven years **o** when he began 2 Kgs 11:21
was twenty-five years **o** when he 2 Kgs 14:2
Azariah, who was sixteen years **o**, 2 Kgs 14:21
He was sixteen years **o** when he began 2 Kgs 15:2
was twenty-five years **o** when he 2 Kgs 15:33
was twenty years **o** when he began 2 Kgs 16:2
was twenty-five years **o** when he 2 Kgs 18:2
planned from days of **o** what now I 2 Kgs 19:25
was twelve years **o** when he began 2 Kgs 21:1
was twenty-two years **o** when he 2 Kgs 21:19
was eight years **o** when he began 2 Kgs 22:1
was twenty-three years **o** when he 2 Kgs 23:31
was twenty-five years **o** when he 2 Kgs 23:36
was eighteen years **o** when he became 2 Kgs 24:8
was twenty-one years **o** when he 2 Kgs 24:18
married when he was sixty years **o**, 1 Chr 2:21
When David was **o** and full of days, 1 Chr 23:1
Levites, thirty years **o** and upward, 1 Chr 23:3
from twenty years **o** and upward 1 Chr 23:24
from twenty years **o** and upward. 1 Chr 23:27
the length, in cubits of the **o** standard, 2 Chr 3:3
took counsel with the **o** men, 2 Chr 10:6
the counsel that the **o** men gave him, 2 Chr 10:8
forsaking the counsel of the **o** men, 2 Chr 10:13
was forty-one years **o** when he 2 Chr 12:13
be put to death, whether young or **o**, 2 Chr 15:13
was thirty-five years **o** when he 2 Chr 20:31
was thirty-two years **o** when he 2 Chr 21:5
was thirty-two years **o** when he 2 Chr 21:20
was twenty-two years **o** when he 2 Chr 22:2
was seven years **o** when he began 2 Chr 24:1
But Jehoiada grew **o** and full of days, 2 Chr 24:15
died. He was 130 years **o** at his death. 2 Chr 24:15
was twenty-five years **o** when he 2 Chr 25:1
those twenty years **o** and upward, 2 Chr 25:5
took Uzziah, who was sixteen years **o**, 2 Chr 26:1
was sixteen years **o** when he began 2 Chr 26:3
was twenty-five years **o** when he 2 Chr 27:1
was twenty-five years **o** when he 2 Chr 27:8
was twenty years **o** when he began 2 Chr 28:1
when he was twenty-five years **o**, 2 Chr 29:1
to their brothers, **o** and young alike, 2 Chr 31:15
from three years **o** and upward— 2 Chr 31:16
from twenty years **o** and upward 2 Chr 31:17
was twelve years **o** when he began 2 Chr 33:1
was twenty-two years **o** when he 2 Chr 33:21
was eight years **o** when he began 2 Chr 34:1
was twenty-three years **o** when he 2 Chr 36:2
was twenty-five years **o** when he 2 Chr 36:5
was eight years **o** when he became 2 Chr 36:9
was twenty-one years **o** when he 2 Chr 36:11
man or virgin, **o** man or aged. 2 Chr 36:17
Levites, from twenty years **o** and upward, Ezr 3:8
o men who had seen the first house, Ezr 3:12
sedition was stirred up in it from of **o**. Ezr 4:15
this city from of **o** has risen against Ezr 4:19
and to annihilate all Jews, young and **o**, Est 3:13
shall come to your grave in ripe **o** age, Jb 5:26
Though its root grow **o** in the earth, and Jb 14:8
Do you not know this from of **o**, since Jb 20:4
Why do the wicked live, reach **o** age, and Jb 21:7
you keep to the **o** way that wicked men Jb 22:15
"Oh, that I were as in the months of **o**, as Jb 29:2
It is not the **o** who are wise, nor the aged Jb 32:9
And Job died, an **o** man, and full of Jb 42:17
love, for they have been from of **o**. Ps 25:6
I have been young, and now am **o**, yet I Ps 37:25
performed in their days, in the days of **o**: Ps 44:1
them, he who is enthroned from of **o**, Ps 55:19
Do not cast me off in the time of **o** age; Ps 71:9
So even to **o** age and gray hairs, O God, Ps 71:18
which you have purchased of **o**, Ps 74:2
Yet God my King is from of **o**, working Ps 74:12
I consider the days of **o**, the years long Ps 77:5
yes, I will remember your wonders of **o**. Ps 77:11
I will utter dark sayings from of **o**, Ps 78:2
Of **o** you spoke in a vision to your godly Ps 89:19
Lord, where is your steadfast love of **o**, Ps 89:49
They still bear fruit in **o** age; they are Ps 92:14
Your throne is established from of **o**; you Ps 93:2
Of **o** you laid the foundation of the Ps 102:25
When I think of your rules from of **o**, I Ps 119:52
I remember the days of **o**; I meditate on Ps 143:5
together, **o** men and children! Ps 148:12
of his work, the first of his acts of **o**. Prv 8:22
but the splendor of **o** men is their gray Prv 20:29
even when he is **o** he will not depart Prv 22:6
not despise your mother when she is **o**. Prv 23:22
wise youth than an **o** and foolish king Eccl 4:13
are all choice fruits, new as well as **o**, Sg 7:13
Cushite exiles, both the young and the **o**, Is 20:4
the two walls for the water of the **o** pool. Is 22:11
city whose origin is from days of **o**, Is 23:7
done wonderful things, plans formed of **o**, Is 25:1
planned from days of **o** what now I Is 37:26
things, nor consider the things of **o**. Is 43:18
I not told you from of **o** and declared it? Is 44:8
told this long ago? Who declared it of **o**? Is 45:21
even to your **o** age I am he, and to gray Is 46:4
remember the former things of **o**; for I am Is 46:9
"The former things I declared of **o**; they Is 48:3
I declared them to you from of **o**, before Is 48:5
from of **o** your ear has not been opened. Is 48:8

awake, as in days of **o**, the generations of Is 51:9
up and carried them all the days of **o**. Is 63:9
Then he remembered the days of **o**, of Is 63:11
our Redeemer from of **o** is your name. Is 63:16
From of **o** no one has heard or perceived Is 64:4
or an **o** man who does not fill out his Is 65:20
young man shall die a hundred years **o**, Is 65:20
a hundred years **o** shall be accursed. Is 65:20
that I gave of **o** to your fathers forever. Jer 7:7
and your fathers from of **o** and forever. Jer 25:5
children shall be as they were of **o**, Jer 30:20
young men and the **o** shall be merry. Jer 31:13
took from there **o** rags and worn-out Jer 38:11
shall be inhabited as in the days of **o**, Jer 46:26
break in pieces the **o** man and the Jer 51:22
was twenty-one years **o** when he became Jer 52:1
things that were hers from days of **o**. Lam 1:7
of the streets lie the young and the **o**; Lam 2:21
The **o** men have left the city gate, the Lam 5:14
be restored! Renew our days as of **o**— Lam 5:21
Kill **o** men outright, young men and Ezk 9:6
go down to the pit, to the people of **o**, Ezk 26:20
world below, among ruins from of **o**, Ezk 26:20
a lamb a year **o** without blemish for a Ezk 46:13
kingdom, being about sixty-two years **o**. Dn 5:31
your **o** men shall dream dreams, Jl 2:28
ruins and rebuild it as in the days of **o**, Am 9:11
ruler in Israel, whose origin is from of **o**, Mi 5:2
burnt offerings, with calves a year **o**? Mi 6:6
in Bashan and Gilead as in the days of **o**. Mi 7:14
sworn to our fathers from the days of **o**. Mi 7:20
O men and old women shall again sit in Zec 8:4
Old men and **o** women shall again sit in Zec 8:4
as in the days of **o** and as in former Mal 3:4
region who were two years **o** or under, Mt 2:16
have heard that it was said to those of **o**, Mt 5:21
have heard that it was said to those of **o**, Mt 5:33
of unshrunk cloth on an **o** garment, Mt 9:16
is new wine put into **o** wineskins. Mt 9:17
his treasure what is new and what is **o**." Mt 13:52
of unshrunk cloth on an **o** garment. Mk 2:21
tears away from it, the new from the **o**, Mk 2:21
no one puts new wine into **o** wineskins. Mk 2:22
a prophet, like one of the prophets of **o**." Mk 6:15
For I am an **o** man, and my wife is Lk 1:18
relative Elizabeth in her **o** age has also Lk 1:36
mouth of his holy prophets from of **o**, Lk 1:70
And when he was twelve years **o**, they Lk 2:42
garment and puts it on an **o** garment. Lk 5:36
piece from the new will not match the **o**. Lk 5:36
no one puts new wine into **o** wineskins. Lk 5:37
one after drinking **o** wine desires new, Lk 5:39
desires new, for he says, 'The **o** is good.'" Lk 5:39
that one of the prophets of **o** had risen. Lk 9:8
that one of the prophets of **o** has risen." Lk 9:19
with moneybags that do not grow **o**, Lk 12:33
"How can a man be born when he is **o**? Jn 3:4
said to him, "You are not yet fifty years **o**, Jn 8:57
you wanted, but when you are **o**, Jn 21:18
and your **o** men shall dream dreams; Acts 2:17
was more than forty years **o**. Acts 4:22
"When he was forty years **o**, it came Acts 7:23
known from of **o**.' Acts 15:18
he was about a hundred years **o**), Rom 4:19
We know that our **o** self was crucified Rom 6:6
serve not under the **o** written code but Rom 7:6
Cleanse out the **o** leaven that you may 1 Cor 5:7
the festival, not with the **o** leaven, 1 Cor 5:8
day, when they read the **o** covenant, 2 Cor 3:14
The **o** has passed away; behold, the 2 Cor 5:17
to put off your **o** self, which belongs to Eph 4:22
have put off the **o** self with its practices Col 3:9
an **o** man and now a prisoner also for Phlm 1:9
excellent than the **o** as the covenant Heb 8:6
obsolete and growing **o** is ready to Heb 8:13
the people of **o** received their Heb 11:2
but an **o** commandment that you had 1 Jn 2:7
The **o** commandment is the word that 1 Jn 2:7

OLDER (16)
other, the **o** shall serve the younger." Gn 25:23
he called Esau his **o** son and said to Gn 27:1
the best garments of Esau her **o** son, Gn 27:15
the words of Esau her **o** son were told to Gn 27:42
The name of the **o** was Leah, and the Gn 29:16
kingdom, for he is my **o** brother, 1 Kgs 2:22
to the camp had killed all the **o** sons. 2 Chr 22:1
aged are among us, **o** than your father. Jb 15:10
speak to Job because they were **o** than he. Jb 32:4
"Now his **o** son was in the field, and as Lk 15:25
one by one, beginning with the **o** ones, Jn 8:9
told, "The **o** will serve the younger." Rom 9:12
not rebuke an **o** man but encourage 1 Tm 5:1
o women like mothers, younger 1 Tm 5:2
O men are to be sober-minded, dignified, Ti 2:2
O women likewise are to be reverent in Ti 2:3

OLDEST (7)
to his servant, the **o** of his household, Gn 24:2
The three **o** sons of Jesse had 1 Sm 17:13
on armor, from the youngest to the **o**, 2 Kgs 3:21
Then he took his **o** son who was to 2 Kgs 3:27
he could not be enrolled as the **o** son; 1 Chr 5:1
drinking wine in their **o** brother's house, Jb 1:13
drinking wine in their **o** brother's house, Jb 1:18

OLIVE (41)
her mouth was a freshly plucked **o** leaf. Gn 8:11
vineyard, and with your **o** orchard. Ex 23:11
to you pure beaten **o** oil for the light, Ex 27:20
of the sanctuary, and a hin of **o** oil. Ex 30:24
and vineyards and **o** trees that you did Dt 6:11
pomegranates, a land of **o** trees and honey, Dt 8:8
When you beat your **o** trees, you shall Dt 24:20
You shall have **o** trees throughout all Dt 28:40
of vineyards and **o** orchards that you Jos 24:13
over them, and they said to the **o** tree, Jgs 9:8
But the **o** tree said to them, 'Shall I leave Jgs 9:9
grain, as well as the **o** orchards. Jgs 15:5
and vineyards and **o** orchards and 1 Sm 8:14
garments, **o** orchards and vineyards, 2 Kgs 5:26
a land of **o** trees and honey, 2 Kgs 18:32
Over the **o** and sycamore trees in the 1 Chr 27:28
fields, their vineyards, their **o** orchards, Neh 5:11
to the hills and bring branches of **o**, Neh 8:15
and bring branches of olive, wild **o**, Neh 8:15
o orchards and fruit trees in Neh 9:25
and cast off his blossom like the **o** tree. Jb 15:33
among the **o** rows of the wicked they Jb 24:11
I am like a green **o** tree in the house of Ps 52:8
will be like **o** shoots around your Ps 128:3
as when an **o** tree is beaten—two or three Is 17:6
the nations, as when an **o** tree is beaten, Is 24:13
cedar, the acacia, the myrtle, and the **o**. Is 41:19
LORD once called you 'a green **o** tree, Jer 11:16
his beauty shall be like the **o**, and his Hos 14:6
fig trees and your **o** trees the locust Am 4:9
the produce of the **o** fail and the fields Hab 3:17
and the **o** tree have yielded nothing. Hg 2:19
And there are two **o** trees by it, one on the Zec 4:3
"What are these two **o** trees on the right Zec 4:11
are these two branches of the **o** trees, Zec 4:12
off, and you, although a wild **o** shoot, Rom 11:17
in the nourishing root of the **o** tree, Rom 11:17
from what is by nature a wild **o** tree, Rom 11:24
to nature, into a cultivated **o** tree, Rom 11:24
be grafted back into their own **o** tree. Rom 11:24
These are the two **o** trees and the two Rv 11:4

OLIVES (16)
you pure oil from beaten **o** for the lamp, Lv 24:2
with the oil, for your **o** shall drop off. Dt 28:40
up the ascent of the Mount of **O**, 2 Sm 15:30
you shall tread **o**, but not anoint Mi 6:15
on the Mount of **O** that lies before Zec 14:4
and the Mount of **O** shall be split in two Zec 14:4
came to Bethphage, to the Mount of **O**, Mt 21:1
As he sat on the Mount of **O**, the Mt 24:3
hymn, they went out to the Mount of **O**. Mt 26:30
and Bethany, at the Mount of **O**, Mk 11:1
on the Mount of **O** opposite the temple, Mk 13:3
they went out to the Mount of **O**. Mk 14:26
down the Mount of **O**—the whole Lk 19:37
as was his custom, to the Mount of **O**, Lk 22:39
but Jesus went to the Mount of **O**. Jn 8:1
Can a fig tree, my brothers, bear **o**, or a Jas 3:12

OLIVET (3)
Bethany, at the mount that is called **O**, Lk 19:29
out and lodged on the mount called **O**. Lk 21:37
to Jerusalem from the mount called **O**, Acts 1:12

OLIVEWOOD (4)
he made two cherubim of **o**, 1 Kgs 6:23
inner sanctuary he made doors of **o**; 1 Kgs 6:31
the two doors of **o** with carvings of 1 Kgs 6:32
entrance to the nave doorposts of **o**, 1 Kgs 6:33

OLYMPAS (1)
Julia, Nereus and his sister, and **O**, Rom 16:15

OMAR (3)
sons of Eliphaz were Teman, **O**, Zepho, Gn 36:11
the chiefs Teman, **O**, Zepho, Kenaz, Gn 36:15
Teman, **O**, Zepho, Gatam, Kenaz, and 1 Chr 1:36

OMEGA (3)
the Alpha and the **O**," says the Lord God, Rv 1:8
I am the Alpha and the **O**, the beginning Rv 21:6
I am the Alpha and the **O**, the first and Rv 22:13

OMENS (6)
shall not interpret **o** or tell fortunes. Lv 19:26
not go, as at other times, to look for **o**, Nm 24:1
or tells fortunes or interprets **o**, Dt 18:10
used divination and **o** and sold 2 Kgs 17:17
used fortune-telling and **o** and dealt 2 Kgs 21:6
fortune-telling and **o** and sorcery, 2 Chr 33:6

OMER (5)
You shall each take an **o**, according to Ex 16:16
But when they measured it with an **o**, Ex 16:18
'Let an **o** of it be kept throughout your Ex 16:32
a jar, and put an **o** of manna in it, Ex 16:33
(An **o** is the tenth part of an ephah.) Ex 16:36

OMERS (1)
twice as much bread, two **o** each. Ex 16:22

OMRI (18)
king." Therefore all Israel made **O**, 1 Kgs 16:16
So **O** went up from Gibbethon, and 1 Kgs 16:17
him king, and half followed **O**. 1 Kgs 16:21
people who followed **O** overcame the 1 Kgs 16:22
So Tibni died, and **O** became king. 1 Kgs 16:22
Judah, **O** began to reign over Israel, 1 Kgs 16:23
O did what was evil in the sight of 1 Kgs 16:25
the rest of the acts of **O** that he did, 1 Kgs 16:27
And **O** slept with his fathers and was 1 Kgs 16:28
Ahab the son of **O** began to reign 1 Kgs 16:29
the son of **O** reigned over Israel 1 Kgs 16:29
Ahab the son of **O** did evil in the 1 Kgs 16:30
a granddaughter of **O** king of Israel. 2 Kgs 8:26
Joash, Eliezer, Elioenai, **O**, Jeremoth, 1 Chr 7:8
Uthai the son of Ammihud, son of **O**, 1 Chr 9:4
for Issachar, **O** the son of Michael; 1 Chr 27:18
Athaliah, the granddaughter of **O**. 2 Chr 22:2
For you have kept the statutes of **O**, and Mi 6:16

ON (5) [Proper Noun]
the daughter of Potiphera priest of **O**. Gn 41:45
the daughter of Potiphera priest of **O**, Gn 41:50
daughter of Potiphera the priest of **O**, Gn 46:20
sons of Eliab, and **O** the son of Peleth, Nm 16:1
The young men of **O** and of Pi-beseth Ezk 30:17

ONAM (4)
Manahath, Ebal, Shepho, and **O**. Gn 36:23
Manahath, Ebal, Shepho, and **O**. 1 Chr 1:40
was Atarah; she was the mother of **O**. 1 Chr 2:26
The sons of **O**: Shammai and Jada. 1 Chr 2:28

ONAN (8)
bore a son, and she called his name **O**. Gn 38:4
Then Judah said to **O**, "Go in to your Gn 38:8
But **O** knew that the offspring would not Gn 38:9
Er, **O**, Shelah, Perez, and Zerah (but Er Gn 46:12
Zerah (but Er and **O** died in the land Gn 46:12
The sons of Judah were Er and **O**; and Nm 26:19
and Er and **O** died in the land of Nm 26:19
The sons of Judah: Er, **O** and Shelah; 1 Chr 2:3

ONCE (112)
and I will speak again but this **o**. Gn 18:32
O when Jacob was cooking stew, Esau Gn 25:29
forgive my sin, please, only this **o**, Ex 10:17
make atonement on its horns **o** a year. Ex 30:10
make atonement for it **o** in the year Ex 30:10
the people of Israel **o** in the year Lv 16:34
will treat me like this, kill me at **o**, Nm 11:15
said, "Let us go up at **o** and occupy it, Nm 13:30
O again Balak sent princes, more in Nm 22:15
You may not make an end of them at **o**, Dt 7:22
the men of war going around the city **o**. Jos 6:3
LORD to circle the city, going about it **o**. Jos 6:11
day they marched around the city **o**, Jos 6:14
against me; let me speak just **o** more. Jgs 6:39
let me test just **o** more with the fleece. Jgs 6:39
The trees **o** went out to anoint a king over Jgs 9:8
and please strengthen me only this **o**, Jgs 16:28
"Shall we go out **o** more to battle Jgs 20:28
Then Saul fell at **o** full length on the 1 Sm 28:20
Go in at **o** to King David, and say to 1 Kgs 1:13
O every three years the fleet of ships 1 Kgs 10:22
Run at **o** to meet her and say to her, 'Is 2 Kgs 4:26
again and walked **o** back and forth 2 Kgs 4:35
O when the king of Syria was warring 2 Kgs 6:8
himself there more than **o** or twice. 2 Kgs 6:10
O every three years the ships of 2 Chr 9:21
lodged outside Jerusalem **o** or twice. Neh 13:20
could not answer him **o** in a thousand Jb 9:3
I have spoken **o**, and I will not answer; Jb 40:5
O God has spoken; twice have I heard Ps 62:11
stand before you when **o** your anger is Ps 76:7
O for all I have sworn by my holiness; I Ps 89:35
All at **o** he follows her, as an ox goes to Prv 7:22
The vexation of a fool is known at **o**, Prv 12:16
The LORD **o** called you 'a green olive Jer 11:16
this **o** I will make them know my Jer 16:21
"**O** more they shall use these words in Jer 31:23
Those who **o** feasted on delicacies Lam 4:5
thus says the LORD of hosts: Yet **o** more, Hg 2:6
'Let us go at **o** to entreat the favor of the Zec 8:21
"Take **o** more the equipment of a Zec 11:15
Then **o** more you shall see the Mal 3:18
needs them,' and he will send them at **o**." Mt 21:3

again!" And the fig tree withered at **o**. Mt 21:19
"How did the fig tree wither at **o**?" Mt 21:20
five talents went at **o** and traded with Mt 25:16
And he came up to Jesus at **o** and said, Mt 26:49
and he will at **o** send me more than Mt 26:53
And one of them at **o** ran and took a Mt 27:48
And at **o** his fame spread everywhere Mk 1:28
charged him and sent him away at **o**, Mk 1:43
grain is ripe, at **o** he puts in the sickle, Mk 4:29
you to give me at **o** the head of John the Mk 6:25
came, he went up to him at **o** and said, Mk 14:45
her spirit returned, and she got up at **o**. Lk 8:55
door to him at **o** when he comes and Lk 12:36
a cloud rising in the west, you say at **o**, Lk 12:54
When **o** the master of the house has Lk 13:25
"A man **o** gave a great banquet and Lk 14:16
field, 'Come at **o** and recline at table'? Lk 17:7
take place, but the end will not be at **o**." Lk 21:9
Pilate addressed them **o** more, desiring Lk 23:20
And at **o** the man was healed, and he took Jn 5:9
And **o** more he bent down and wrote on Jn 8:8
him in himself, and glorify him at **o**. Jn 13:32
denied it, and at **o** a rooster crowed. Jn 18:27
and at **o** there came out blood and Jn 19:34
the thing was taken up at **o** to heaven. Acts 10:16
So I sent for you at **o**, and you have Acts 10:33
and he was baptized at **o**, he and all Acts 16:33
temple, and at **o** the gates were shut. Acts 21:30
He at **o** took soldiers and centurions Acts 21:32
the man, I sent him to you at **o**, Acts 23:30
death he died he died to sin, **o** for all, Rom 6:10
that you who were **o** slaves of sin have Rom 6:17
just as you **o** presented your members Rom 6:19
I was **o** alive apart from the law, but Rom 7:9
o I have enjoyed your company for a Rom 15:24
what **o** had glory has come to have 2 Cor 3:10
Even though we **o** regarded Christ 2 Cor 5:16
beaten with rods. **O** I was stoned. 2 Cor 11:25
the faith he **o** tried to destroy." Gal 1:23
it or adds to it **o** it has been ratified. Gal 3:15
whose slaves you want to be **o** more? Gal 4:9
in which you **o** walked, following the Eph 2:2
among whom we all **o** lived in the Eph 2:3
Christ Jesus you who **o** were far off Eph 2:13
sent me help for my needs **o** and again. Phil 4:16
who **o** were alienated and hostile in Col 1:21
In these you too **o** walked, when you were Col 3:7
For we ourselves were **o** foolish, Ti 3:3
after warning him **o** and then twice, Ti 3:10
those who have **o** been enlightened, Heb 6:4
they are crucifying **o** again the Son Heb 6:6
since he did this **o** for all when he Heb 7:27
the high priest goes, and he but **o** a year, Heb 9:7
he entered **o** for all into the holy places, Heb 9:12
he has appeared **o** for all at the end of Heb 9:26
just as it is appointed for man to die **o**, Heb 9:27
having been offered **o** to bear the sins Heb 9:28
worshipers, having **o** been cleansed, Heb 10:2
of the body of Jesus Christ **o** for all. Heb 10:10
"Yet **o** more I will shake not only the Heb 12:26
"Yet **o** more," indicates the removal of Heb 12:27
goes away and at **o** forgets what he was Jas 1:24
O you were not a people, but now you 1 Pt 2:10
o you had not received mercy, but now 1 Pt 2:10
For Christ also suffered **o** for sins, the 1 Pt 3:18
the faith that was **o** for all delivered to Jude 1:3
you, although you **o** fully knew it, Jude 1:5
At **o** I was in the Spirit, and behold, a Rv 4:2
O more they cried out, "Hallelujah! The Rv 19:3

ONE (2460)

heavens be gathered together into **o** place, Gn 1:9
It is the **o** that flowed around the whole Gn 2:11
It is the **o** that flowed around the whole Gn 2:13
and while he slept took **o** of his ribs and Gn 2:21
his wife, and they shall become **o** flesh. Gn 2:24
the tree was to be desired to make **o** wise, Gn 3:6
man has become like **o** of us in Gn 3:22
The name of the **o** was Adah, and the Gn 4:19
LORD has cursed this **o** shall bring us Gn 5:29
the name of the **o** was Peleg, for in his Gn 10:25
the whole earth had **o** language and the Gn 11:1
And they said to **o** another, "Come, let Gn 11:3
the LORD said, "Behold, they are **o** people, Gn 11:6
people, and they have all **o** language, Gn 11:6
not understand **o** another's speech." Gn 11:7
so that if **o** can count the dust of the Gn 13:16
Then **o** who had escaped came and Gn 14:13
And as they brought them out, **o** said, Gn 19:17
enough to flee to, and it is a little **o**. Gn 19:20
Let me escape there—is it not a little **o**? Gn 19:20
she put the child under **o** of the bushes. Gn 21:15
a burnt offering on **o** of the mountains Gn 22:2
let her be the **o** whom you have Gn 24:14
the **o** shall be stronger than the other, Gn 25:23
O of the people might easily have lain Gn 26:10
to his father, "Have you but **o** blessing, Gn 27:38
I be bereft of you both in **o** day?" Gn 27:45
If Jacob marries **o** of the Hittite women Gn 27:46
like these, **o** of the women of the land, Gn 27:46
your wife from there **o** of the daughters Gn 28:2
Taking **o** of the stones of the place, he Gn 28:11
Complete the week of this **o**, and we Gn 29:27
Every **o** that is not speckled and spotted Gn 30:33
spotted, every **o** that had white on it, Gn 30:35
when we are out of **o** another's sight. Gn 31:49
daughters, although no **o** is with us, Gn 31:50
Esau comes to the **o** camp and attacks Gn 32:8
If they are driven hard for **o** day, all the Gn 33:13
our sister to **o** who is uncircumcised, Gn 34:14
dwell with you and become **o** people. Gn 34:16
with us to become **o** people—when Gn 34:22
They said to **o** another, "Here comes Gn 37:19
him and throw him into **o** of the pits. Gn 37:20
she was in labor, **o** put out a hand, Gn 38:28
hand, saying, "This **o** came out first." Gn 38:28
But **o** day, when he went into the house Gn 39:11
was done there, he was the **o** who did it. Gn 39:22
And **o** night they both dreamed—the Gn 40:5
and there is no **o** to interpret them." And Gn 40:8
and good, were growing on **o** stalk. Gn 41:5
and there is no **o** who can interpret it. Gn 41:15
eaten them no **o** would have known Gn 41:21
dream seven ears growing on **o** stalk, Gn 41:22
but there was no **o** who could explain Gn 41:24
"The dreams of Pharaoh are **o**; Gn 41:25
ears are seven years; the dreams are **o**. Gn 41:26
without your consent no **o** shall lift up Gn 41:44
sons, "Why do you look at **o** another?" Gn 42:1
He was the **o** who sold to all the people of Gn 42:6
We are all sons of **o** man. We are Gn 42:11
the sons of **o** man in the land of Gn 42:13
day with our father, and **o** is no more." Gn 42:13
Send **o** of you, and let him bring your Gn 42:16
let **o** of your brothers remain confined Gn 42:19
Then they said to **o** another, "In truth Gn 42:21
And as **o** of them opened his sack to Gn 42:27
they turned trembling to **o** another, Gn 42:28
O is no more, and the youngest is this Gn 42:32
leave **o** of your brothers with me, and Gn 42:33
is dead, and he is the only **o** left. Gn 42:38
men looked at **o** another in Gn 43:33
O left me, and I said, Surely he has Gn 44:28
If you take this **o** also from me, and Gn 44:29
from me." So no **o** stayed with him Gn 45:1
servants of them from **o** end of Egypt to Gn 47:21
since this **o** is the firstborn, put your Gn 48:18
to your brothers **o** mountain slope that Gn 48:22
judge his people as **o** of the tribes of Gn 49:16
hands of the Mighty **O** of Jacob (from Gn 49:24
o of whom was named Shiphrah and the Ex 1:15
said, "This is **o** of the Hebrews' children." Ex 2:6
O day, when Moses had grown up, he Ex 2:11
beating a Hebrew, **o** of his people. Ex 2:11
this way and that, and seeing no **o**, Ex 2:12
took as his wife **o** of the daughters of Ex 6:25
know that there is no **o** like the LORD our Ex 8:10
and from his people; not **o** remained. Ex 8:31
but not **o** of the livestock of the people of Ex 9:6
not **o** of the livestock of Israel was dead. Ex 9:7
of the land, so that no **o** can see the land. Ex 10:5
They did not see **o** another, nor did Ex 10:23
"Yet **o** plague more I will bring upon Ex 11:1
It shall be eaten in **o** house; you shall Ex 12:46
There shall be **o** law for the native and Ex 12:49
up the night without **o** coming near the Ex 14:20
into the sea, not **o** of them remained. Ex 14:28
of Israel saw it, they said to **o** another, Ex 16:15
'Gather of it, each **o** of you, as much as Ex 16:16
"Let no **o** leave any of it over till the Ex 16:19
let no **o** go out of his place on the Ex 16:29
Hur held up his hands, **o** on one side, Ex 17:12
Hur held up his hands, one on **o** side, Ex 17:12
The name of the **o** was Gershom (for he Ex 18:3
I decide between **o** person and another, Ex 18:16
men quarrel and **o** strikes the other Ex 21:18
the **o** who hit her shall surely be fined, Ex 21:22
"When **o** man's ox butts another's, so Ex 21:35
any kind of lost thing, of which **o** says, Ex 22:9
The **o** whom God condemns shall pay Ex 22:9
see the donkey of **o** who hates you lying Ex 23:5
them out from before you in **o** year, Ex 23:29
people answered with **o** voice and said, Ex 24:3
its four feet, two rings on the **o** side of it, Ex 25:12
Make **o** cherub on the one end, and one Ex 25:19
Make one cherub on the **o** end, and one Ex 25:19
one end, and **o** cherub on the other end. Ex 25:19
Of **o** piece with the mercy seat shall you Ex 25:19
their wings, their faces **o** to another; Ex 25:20
its flowers shall be of **o** piece with it. Ex 25:31
of the lampstand out of **o** side of it and Ex 25:32
with calyx and flower, on **o** branch, Ex 25:33
and a calyx of **o** piece with it under Ex 25:35
branches shall be of **o** piece with it, Ex 25:36
curtains shall be coupled to **o** another, Ex 26:3
curtains shall be coupled to **o** another. Ex 26:3
loops you shall make on the **o** curtain, Ex 26:5
set; the loops shall be opposite **o** another. Ex 26:5
and couple the curtains **o** to the other Ex 26:6
of the curtain that is outermost in **o** set, Ex 26:10
of the curtains, the cubit on the **o** side, Ex 26:13
two bases under **o** frame for its two Ex 26:19
of silver, two bases under **o** frame, Ex 26:21
two bases under **o** frame, and two bases Ex 26:25
the frames of the **o** side of the Ex 26:26
its horns shall be of **o** piece with it, and Ex 27:2
linen a hundred cubits long for **o** side. Ex 27:9
The hangings for the **o** side of the gate Ex 27:14
be made like it and be of **o** piece with it, Ex 28:8
six of their names on the **o** stone, and Ex 28:10
Take **o** bull of the herd and two rams Ex 29:1
shall put them in **o** basket and bring Ex 29:3
"Then you shall take **o** of the rams, and Ex 29:15
and **o** loaf of bread and one cake of Ex 29:23
loaf of bread and **o** cake of bread made Ex 29:23
and **o** wafer out of the basket of Ex 29:23
O lamb you shall offer in the morning, Ex 29:39
Its horns shall be of **o** piece with it. Ex 30:2
Each **o** who is numbered in the census Ex 30:13
each **o** at the cost of his son and of his Ex 32:29
made the calf, the **o** that Aaron made. Ex 32:35
and no **o** put on his ornaments. Ex 33:4
No **o** shall come up with you, and let no Ex 34:3
and let no **o** be seen throughout all the Ex 34:3
no **o** shall covet your land, when you Ex 34:24
And every **o** who possessed blue or Ex 35:23
And every **o** who possessed acacia wood Ex 35:24
He coupled five curtains to **o** another, Ex 36:10
five curtains he coupled to **o** another. Ex 36:10
He made fifty loops on the **o** curtain, Ex 36:12
set. The loops were opposite **o** another. Ex 36:12
and coupled the curtains **o** to the other Ex 36:13
of the outermost curtain of the **o** set, Ex 36:17
two bases under **o** frame for its two Ex 36:24
two bases under **o** frame and two bases Ex 36:26
the frames of the **o** side of the Ex 36:31
two rings on its **o** side and two rings on Ex 37:3
o cherub on the one end, and one Ex 37:8
one cherub on the **o** end, and one Ex 37:8
one end, and **o** cherub on the other end. Ex 37:8
Of **o** piece with the mercy seat he made Ex 37:8
their wings, with their faces **o** to another; Ex 37:9
and its flowers were of **o** piece with it. Ex 37:17
of the lampstand out of **o** side of it and Ex 37:18
with calyx and flower, on **o** branch, Ex 37:19
and a calyx of **o** piece with it under Ex 37:21
their branches were of **o** piece with it. Ex 37:22
height. Its horns were of **o** piece with it. Ex 37:25
Its horns were of **o** piece with it, and he Ex 38:2
The hangings for **o** side of the gate were Ex 38:14
band on it was of **o** piece with it and Ex 39:5
When any **o** of you brings an offering to Lv 1:2
not to be done, and does any **o** of them, Lv 4:2
and they do any **o** of the things that by Lv 4:13
doing unintentionally any **o** of all the Lv 4:22
in doing any **o** of the things Lv 4:27
may be with which **o** becomes unclean, Lv 5:3
o for a sin offering and the other for a Lv 5:7
shall offer first the **o** for the sin offering. Lv 5:8
has committed in any **o** of these things, Lv 5:13
of the things that **o** may do and thereby Lv 6:7
And **o** shall take from it a handful of the Lv 6:15
the sin offering; there is **o** law for them. Lv 7:7
of peace offerings that **o** may offer to the Lv 7:11
it he shall offer **o** loaf from each offering, Lv 7:14
itself and the fat of **o** that is torn by Lv 7:24
the LORD he took **o** unleavened loaf and Lv 8:26
one unleavened loaf and **o** loaf of bread Lv 8:26
bread with oil and **o** wafer and placed Lv 8:26
offered it as a sin offering, like the first **o**. Lv 9:15
o for a burnt offering and the other for a Lv 12:8
Aaron the priest or to **o** of his sons the Lv 13:2
the spot remains in **o** place and does Lv 13:23
the spot remains in **o** place and does Lv 13:28
command them to kill **o** of the birds in Lv 14:5
and **o** ewe lamb a year old without Lv 14:10
flour mixed with oil, and **o** log of oil. Lv 14:10
the priest shall take **o** of the male Lv 14:12
then he shall take **o** male lamb for a Lv 14:21
The **o** shall be a sin offering and the Lv 14:22
o for a sin offering and the other for a Lv 14:31
and shall kill **o** of the birds in an Lv 14:50
bed on which the **o** with the discharge Lv 15:4
on which the **o** with the discharge Lv 15:6
the body of the **o** with the discharge Lv 15:7
And if the **o** with the discharge spits on Lv 15:8

saddle on which the **o** with the discharge Lv 15:9
Anyone whom the **o** with the discharge Lv 15:11
vessel that the **o** with the discharge Lv 15:12
"And when the **o** with a discharge is Lv 15:13
o for a sin offering and the other for a Lv 15:15
the priest shall use **o** for a sin offering Lv 15:30
offering, and **o** ram for a burnt offering. Lv 16:5
o lot for the LORD and the other lot for Lv 16:8
No **o** may be in the tent of meeting Lv 16:17
If any **o** of the house of Israel kills an ox Lv 17:3
say to them, Any **o** of the house of Israel, Lv 17:8
"If any **o** of the house of Israel or of the Lv 17:10
"Any **o** also of the people of Israel, or of Lv 17:13
you shall approach any **o** of his close Lv 18:6
Every **o** of you shall revere his mother Lv 19:3
falsely; you shall not lie to **o** another. Lv 19:11
Any **o** of the people of Israel or of the Lv 20:2
because he has given **o** of his children to Lv 20:3
man when he gives **o** of his children to Lv 20:4
'No **o** shall make himself unclean for Lv 21:1
For no **o** who has a blemish shall draw Lv 21:18
or **o** who has a mutilated face or a limb Lv 21:18
'If any **o** of all your offspring throughout Lv 22:3
When any **o** of the house of Israel or of Lv 22:18
ox or a sheep and her young in **o** day. Lv 22:28
and **o** bull from the herd and two rams. Lv 23:18
And you shall offer **o** male goat for a Lv 23:19
out of the camp the **o** who cursed, Lv 24:14
of the camp the **o** who had cursed and Lv 24:23
you shall not wrong **o** another. Lv 25:14
You shall not wrong **o** another, but Lv 25:17
If a man has no **o** to redeem it and then Lv 25:26
And if **o** of the Levites exercises his Lv 25:33
not rule, **o** over another ruthlessly. Lv 25:46
O of his brothers may redeem him, Lv 25:48
they shall flee as **o** flees from the sword, Lv 26:36
They shall stumble over **o** another, as Lv 26:37
in fact substitute **o** animal for another, Lv 27:10
No **o** devoted, who is to be devoted for Lv 27:29
O shall not differentiate between good Lv 27:33
and so they set out, each **o** in his clan, Nm 2:34
each **o** with his task of serving or Nm 4:49
Each **o** shall keep his holy donations: Nm 5:10
the priest shall offer **o** for a sin offering Nm 6:11
o male lamb a year old without Nm 6:14
and **o** ewe lamb a year old without Nm 6:14
and **o** ram without blemish as a peace Nm 6:14
and **o** unleavened loaf out of the basket Nm 6:19
of the basket and **o** unleavened wafer, Nm 6:19
two of the chiefs, and for each **o** an ox. Nm 7:3
offer their offerings, **o** chief each day, Nm 7:11
his offering was **o** silver plate whose Nm 7:13
shekels, **o** silver basin of 70 shekels, Nm 7:13
o golden dish of 10 shekels, full of Nm 7:14
o bull from the herd, one ram, one Nm 7:15
one bull from the herd, **o** ram, one Nm 7:15
herd, one ram, **o** male lamb a year old, Nm 7:15
o male goat for a sin offering; Nm 7:16
for his offering **o** silver plate whose Nm 7:19
shekels, **o** silver basin of 70 shekels, Nm 7:19
o golden dish of 10 shekels, full of Nm 7:20
o bull from the herd, one ram, one Nm 7:21
one bull from the herd, **o** ram, one Nm 7:21
herd, one ram, **o** male lamb a year old, Nm 7:21
o male goat for a sin offering; Nm 7:22
his offering was **o** silver plate whose Nm 7:25
shekels, **o** silver basin of 70 shekels, Nm 7:25
o golden dish of 10 shekels, full of Nm 7:26
o bull from the herd, one ram, one Nm 7:27
one bull from the herd, **o** ram, one Nm 7:27
herd, one ram, **o** male lamb a year old, Nm 7:27
o male goat for a sin offering; Nm 7:28
his offering was **o** silver plate whose Nm 7:31
shekels, **o** silver basin of 70 shekels, Nm 7:31
o golden dish of 10 shekels, full of Nm 7:32
o bull from the herd, one ram, one Nm 7:33
one bull from the herd, **o** ram, one Nm 7:33
herd, one ram, **o** male lamb a year old, Nm 7:33
o male goat for a sin offering; Nm 7:34
his offering was **o** silver plate whose Nm 7:37
shekels, **o** silver basin of 70 shekels, Nm 7:37
o golden dish of 10 shekels, full of Nm 7:38
o bull from the herd, one ram, one Nm 7:39
one bull from the herd, **o** ram, one Nm 7:39
herd, one ram, **o** male lamb a year old, Nm 7:39
o male goat for a sin offering; Nm 7:40
his offering was **o** silver plate whose Nm 7:43
shekels, **o** silver basin of 70 shekels, Nm 7:43
o golden dish of 10 shekels, full of Nm 7:44
o bull from the herd, one ram, one Nm 7:45
one bull from the herd, **o** ram, one Nm 7:45
herd, one ram, **o** male lamb a year old, Nm 7:45
o male goat for a sin offering; Nm 7:46
his offering was **o** silver plate whose Nm 7:49
shekels, **o** silver basin of 70 shekels, Nm 7:49
o golden dish of 10 shekels, full of Nm 7:50
o bull from the herd, one ram, one Nm 7:51
one bull from the herd, **o** ram, one Nm 7:51
herd, one ram, **o** male lamb a year old, Nm 7:51
o male goat for a sin offering; Nm 7:52
his offering was **o** silver plate whose Nm 7:55
shekels, **o** silver basin of 70 shekels, Nm 7:55
o golden dish of 10 shekels, full of Nm 7:56
o bull from the herd, one ram, one Nm 7:57
one bull from the herd, **o** ram, one Nm 7:57
herd, one ram, **o** male lamb a year old, Nm 7:57
o male goat for a sin offering; Nm 7:58
his offering was **o** silver plate whose Nm 7:61
shekels, **o** silver basin of 70 shekels, Nm 7:61
o golden dish of 10 shekels, full of Nm 7:62
o bull from the herd, one ram, one Nm 7:63
one bull from the herd, **o** ram, one Nm 7:63
herd, one ram, **o** male lamb a year old, Nm 7:63
o male goat for a sin offering; Nm 7:64
his offering was **o** silver plate whose Nm 7:67
shekels, **o** silver basin of 70 shekels, Nm 7:67
o golden dish of 10 shekels, full of Nm 7:68
o bull from the herd, one ram, one Nm 7:69
one bull from the herd, **o** ram, one Nm 7:69
herd, one ram, **o** male lamb a year old, Nm 7:69
o male goat for a sin offering; Nm 7:70
his offering was **o** silver plate whose Nm 7:73
shekels, **o** silver basin of 70 shekels, Nm 7:73
o golden dish of 10 shekels, full of Nm 7:74
o bull from the herd, one ram, one Nm 7:75
one bull from the herd, **o** ram, one Nm 7:75
herd, one ram, **o** male lamb a year old, Nm 7:75
o male goat for a sin offering; Nm 7:76
his offering was **o** silver plate whose Nm 7:79
shekels, **o** silver basin of 70 shekels, Nm 7:79
o golden dish of 10 shekels, full of Nm 7:80
o bull from the herd, one ram, one Nm 7:81
one bull from the herd, **o** ram, one Nm 7:81
herd, one ram, **o** male lamb a year old, Nm 7:81
o male goat for a sin offering; Nm 7:82
you shall offer the **o** for a sin offering Nm 8:12
If any **o** of you or of your descendants Nm 9:10
You shall have **o** statute, both for the Nm 9:14
But if they blow only **o**, then the chiefs, Nm 10:4
You shall not eat just **o** day, or two Nm 11:19
in the camp, **o** named Eldad, Nm 11:26
Let her not be as **o** dead, whose flesh is Nm 12:12
a man, every **o** a chief among them." Nm 13:2
And they said to **o** another, "Let us Nm 14:4
Now if you kill this people as **o** man, Nm 14:15
not **o** shall come into the land where I Nm 14:30
then **o** shall offer with the bull a grain Nm 15:9
you offer, so shall you do with each **o**, Nm 15:12
there shall be **o** statute for you and for Nm 15:15
O law and one rule shall be for you Nm 15:16
One law and **o** rule shall be for you Nm 15:16
congregation shall offer **o** bull from Nm 15:24
and **o** male goat for a sin offering. Nm 15:24
"If **o** person sins unintentionally, he Nm 15:27
You shall have **o** law for him who Nm 15:29
congregation are holy, every **o** of them, Nm 16:3
The **o** whom he chooses he will bring Nm 16:5
the LORD chooses shall be the holy **o**. Nm 16:7
I have not taken **o** donkey from them, Nm 16:15
and I have not harmed **o** of them." Nm 16:15
And let every **o** of you take his censer Nm 16:17
and every **o** of you bring before the Nm 16:17
the spirits of all flesh, shall **o** man sin, Nm 16:22
them staffs, **o** for each fathers' house, Nm 17:2
For there shall be **o** staff for the head of Nm 17:3
chiefs gave him staffs, **o** for each chief, Nm 17:6
The **o** who burns the heifer shall wash Nm 19:8
And the **o** who gathers the ashes of the Nm 19:10
The **o** who sprinkles the water for Nm 19:21
and the **o** who touches the water for Nm 19:21
And **o** from Jacob shall exercise Nm 24:19
o of the people of Israel came and Nm 25:6
these there was not **o** of those listed by Nm 26:64
in the wilderness." Not **o** of them was Nm 26:65
The **o** lamb you shall offer in the Nm 28:4
two bulls from the herd, **o** ram, seven Nm 28:11
offering, mixed with oil, for the **o** ram; Nm 28:12
Also **o** male goat for a sin offering to Nm 28:15
two bulls from the herd, **o** ram, and Nm 28:19
also **o** male goat for a sin offering, to Nm 28:22
two bulls from the herd, **o** ram, seven Nm 28:27
for each bull, two tenths for **o** ram, Nm 28:28
with **o** male goat, to make atonement Nm 28:30
o bull from the herd, one ram, seven Nm 29:2
one bull from the herd, **o** ram, seven Nm 29:2
and **o** tenth for each of the seven Nm 29:4
with **o** male goat for a sin offering, to Nm 29:5
o bull from the herd, one ram, seven Nm 29:8
one bull from the herd, **o** ram, seven Nm 29:8
for the bull, two tenths for the **o** ram, Nm 29:9
also **o** male goat for a sin offering, Nm 29:11
also **o** male goat for a sin offering, Nm 29:16
also **o** male goat for a sin offering, Nm 29:19
also **o** male goat for a sin offering, Nm 29:22
also **o** male goat for a sin offering, Nm 29:25
also **o** male goat for a sin offering; Nm 29:28
also **o** male goat for a sin offering; Nm 29:31
also **o** male goat for a sin offering; Nm 29:34
o bull, one ram, seven male lambs a Nm 29:36
one bull, **o** ram, seven male lambs a Nm 29:36
also **o** male goat for a sin offering; Nm 29:38
out to battle, **o** out of five hundred, Nm 31:28
half you shall take **o** drawn out of Nm 31:30
Israel's half Moses took **o** of every 50, Nm 31:47
You shall take **o** chief from every Nm 34:18
to death on the testimony of **o** witness. Nm 35:30
by the blood of the **o** who shed it. Nm 35:33
be transferred from **o** tribe to another, Nm 36:7
for every **o** of the people of Israel shall Nm 36:7
Israel shall be wife to **o** of the clan of Nm 36:8
so that every **o** of the people of Israel Nm 36:8
be transferred from **o** tribe to another, Nm 36:9
men from you, **o** man from each tribe. Dt 1:23
'Not **o** of these men of this evil Dt 1:35
And every **o** of you fastened on his Dt 1:41
and ask from **o** end of heaven to the Dt 4:32
he may flee to **o** of these cities and save Dt 4:42
O Israel: The LORD our God, the LORD is **o**. Dt 6:4
will not be slack with **o** who hates him. Dt 7:10
No **o** shall be able to stand against you Dt 7:24
No **o** shall be able to stand against you. Dt 11:25
the LORD will choose in **o** of your tribes, Dt 12:14
from the **o** end of the earth to the other, Dt 13:7
"If you hear in **o** of your cities, which Dt 13:12
o of your brothers should become poor, Dt 15:7
or of three witnesses the **o** who is to die Dt 17:6
put to death on the evidence of **o** witness. Dt 17:6
requiring decision between **o** kind of Dt 17:8
o kind of legal right and another, Dt 17:8
or **o** kind of assault and another, Dt 17:8
O from among your brothers you shall Dt 17:15
—he may flee to **o** of these cities and live, Dt 19:5
he dies, and he flees into **o** of these cities, Dt 19:11
the **o** loved and the other unloved, Dt 21:15
for help there was no **o** to rescue her. Dt 22:27
"No **o** whose testicles are crushed or Dt 23:1
"No **o** born of a forbidden union may Dt 23:2
he shall choose within **o** of your towns, Dt 23:16
shall be free at home **o** year to be happy Dt 24:5
"No **o** shall take a mill or an upper Dt 24:6
a man is found stealing **o** of his brothers, Dt 24:7
whether he is **o** of your brothers or one Dt 24:14
of your brothers or **o** of the sojourners Dt 24:14
Each **o** shall be put to death for his own Dt 24:16
if **o** should go on to beat him with more Dt 25:3
and **o** of them dies and has no son, Dt 25:5
men fight with **o** another and the Dt 25:11
the wife of the **o** draws near to rescue Dt 25:11
come out against you **o** way and flee Dt 28:7
You shall go out **o** way against them Dt 28:25
there shall be no **o** to frighten them Dt 28:26
and there shall be no **o** to help you. Dt 28:29
but there shall be no **o** to help you. Dt 28:31
from **o** end of the earth to the other, Dt 28:64
from the **o** who chops your wood to the Dt 29:11
your wood to the **o** who draws your Dt 29:11
o who, when he hears the words of this Dt 29:19
How could **o** have chased a thousand, Dt 32:30
and your Urim to your godly **o**, Dt 33:8
but no **o** knows the place of his burial to Dt 34:6
down from above shall stand in **o** heap." Jos 3:13
gathered together as **o** to fight against Jos 9:2
was a great city, like **o** of the royal cities, Jos 10:2
all these kings and their land at **o** time, Jos 10:42
o of the remnant of the Rephaim, Jos 12:4
the king of Jericho, **o**; the king of Ai, Jos 12:9
the king of Ai, which is beside Bethel, **o**; Jos 12:9
of Jerusalem, **o**; the king of Hebron, Jos 12:10
Jerusalem, one; the king of Hebron, **o**; Jos 12:10
of Jarmuth, **o**; the king of Lachish, Jos 12:11
of Jarmuth, one; the king of Lachish, **o**; Jos 12:11
the king of Eglon, **o**; the king of Gezer, Jos 12:12
king of Eglon, one; the king of Gezer, **o**; Jos 12:12
the king of Debir, **o**; the king of Geder, Jos 12:13
king of Debir, one; the king of Geder, **o**; Jos 12:13
king of Hormah, **o**; the king of Arad, Jos 12:14
of Hormah, one; the king of Arad, **o**; Jos 12:14
of Libnah, **o**; the king of Adullam, Jos 12:15
of Libnah, one; the king of Adullam, **o**; Jos 12:15
of Makkedah, **o**; the king of Bethel, Jos 12:16
of Makkedah, one; the king of Bethel, **o**; Jos 12:16
king of Tappuah, **o**; the king of Hepher, Jos 12:17
of Tappuah, one; the king of Hepher, **o**; Jos 12:17
king of Aphek, **o**; the king of Lasharon, Jos 12:18
of Aphek, one; the king of Lasharon, **o**; Jos 12:18

king of Madon, **o**; the king of Hazor, Jos 12:19
of Madon, one; the king of Hazor, **o**; Jos 12:19
o; the king of Achshaph, Jos 12:20
one; the king of Achshaph, **o**; Jos 12:20
of Taanach, **o**; the king of Megiddo, Jos 12:21
Taanach, one; the king of Megiddo, **o**; Jos 12:21
o; the king of Jokneam in Carmel, Jos 12:22
one; the king of Jokneam in Carmel, **o**; Jos 12:22
o; the king of Goiim in Galilee, Jos 12:23
one; the king of Goiim in Galilee, **o**; Jos 12:23
the king of Tirzah, **o**: in all, thirty-one Jos 12:24
of Beor, the **o** who practiced divination, Jos 13:22
you given me but **o** lot and one portion Jos 17:14
but one lot and **o** portion as an Jos 17:14
You shall not have **o** allotment only, Jos 17:17
He shall flee to **o** of these cities and shall Jos 20:4
o of the clans of the Kohathites who Jos 21:10
o of the clans of the Levites, Jos 21:27
Not **o** of all their enemies had Jos 21:44
Not **o** word of all the good promises Jos 21:45
Now to the **o** half of the tribe of Jos 22:7
o from each of the tribal families of Jos 22:14
every **o** of them the head of a family Jos 22:14
"The Mighty **O**, God, the LORD! The Jos 22:22
the LORD! The Mighty **O**, God, the LORD! Jos 22:22
O man of you puts to flight a thousand, Jos 23:10
that not **o** word has failed of all the Jos 23:14
to pass for you; not **o** of them has failed. Jos 23:14
shall strike the Midianites as **o** man." Jgs 6:16
And they said to **o** another, "Who has Jgs 6:29
I say to you, 'This **o** shall go with you,' Jgs 7:4
say to you, 'This **o** shall not go with you,' Jgs 7:4
"Every **o** who laps the water with his Jgs 7:5
every **o** who kneels down to drink." Jgs 7:5
Every **o** of them resembled the son of a Jgs 8:18
every **o** of you give me the earrings from Jgs 8:24
rule over you, or that **o** rule over you?' Jgs 9:2
of Jerubbaal, seventy men, on **o** stone. Jgs 9:5
killed his sons, seventy men on **o** stone, Jgs 9:18
and **o** company is coming from the Jgs 9:37
So every **o** of the people cut down his Jgs 9:49
the leaders of Gilead, said to **o** another, Jgs 10:18
the LORD, to the **o** who works wonders, Jgs 13:19
at Timnah he saw **o** of the daughters of Jgs 14:1
"I saw **o** of the daughters of the Jgs 14:2
the lion in pieces as **o** tears a young goat. Jgs 14:6
be bound, that **o** could subdue you." Jgs 16:6
right hand on the **o** and his left hand Jgs 16:29
gods, and ordained **o** of his sons, Jgs 17:5
man became to him like **o** of his sons. Jgs 17:11
you to be priest to the house of **o** man, Jgs 18:19
let us draw near to **o** of these places and Jgs 19:13
for no **o** took them into his house to Jgs 19:15
but no **o** has taken me into his house. Jgs 19:18
congregation assembled as **o** man to the Jgs 20:1
And all the people arose as **o** man, Jgs 20:8
against the city, united as **o** man. Jgs 20:11
every **o** could sling a stone at a hair Jgs 20:16
o of which goes up to Bethel and the Jgs 20:31
"No **o** of us shall give his daughter in Jgs 21:1
today there should be **o** tribe lacking in Jgs 21:3
"**O** tribe is cut off from Israel this day. Jgs 21:6
"What **o** is there of the tribes of Israel Jgs 21:8
no **o** had come to the camp from Jgs 21:8
not **o** of the inhabitants of Jabesh-gilead Jgs 21:9
the name of the **o** was Orpah and the Ru 1:4
go to glean in another field or leave this **o**, Ru 2:8
though I am not **o** of your servants." Ru 2:13
relative of ours, **o** of our redeemers." Ru 2:20
but arose before **o** could recognize Ru 3:14
for there is no **o** besides you to redeem it, Ru 4:4
the **o** drew off his sandal and gave it to the Ru 4:7
The name of the **o** was Hannah, and 1 Sm 1:2
The only **o** of you whom I shall not 1 Sm 2:33
"Please put me in **o** of the priests' 1 Sm 2:36
of Beth-shemesh along **o** highway, 1 Sm 6:12
o for Ashdod, one for Gaza, one for 1 Sm 6:17
one for Ashdod, **o** for Gaza, one for 1 Sm 6:17
Ashdod, one for Gaza, **o** for Ashkelon, 1 Sm 6:17
Gaza, one for Ashkelon, **o** for Gath, 1 Sm 6:17
Ashkelon, one for Gath, **o** for Ekron, 1 Sm 6:17
"Take **o** of the young men with you, 1 Sm 9:3
there, **o** carrying three young goats, 1 Sm 10:3
the people said to **o** another, 1 Sm 10:11
the people away, each **o** to his home. 1 Sm 10:25
Then, if there is no **o** to save us, we 1 Sm 11:3
people, and they came out as **o** man. 1 Sm 11:7
O company turned toward Ophrah, 1 Sm 13:17
But every **o** of the Israelites went 1 Sm 13:20
O day Jonathan the son of Saul said to 1 Sm 14:1
a rocky crag on the **o** side and a rocky 1 Sm 14:4
The name of the **o** was Bozez, and the 1 Sm 14:4
The **o** crag rose on the north in front 1 Sm 14:5
but no **o** put his hand to his mouth, 1 Sm 14:26
Then **o** of the people said, "Your 1 Sm 14:28
the blood.'" So every **o** of the people 1 Sm 14:34
to all Israel, "You shall be on **o** side, 1 Sm 14:40
there shall not **o** hair of his head fall 1 Sm 14:45
"Neither has the LORD chosen this **o**." 1 Sm 16:8
"Neither has the LORD chosen this **o**." 1 Sm 16:9
O of the young men answered, 1 Sm 16:18
stood on the mountain on the **o** side, 1 Sm 17:3
Philistine shall be like **o** of them, 1 Sm 17:36
the women sang to **o** another as they 1 Sm 18:7
are Samuel and David?" And **o** said, 1 Sm 19:22
LORD cuts off every **o** of the enemies 1 Sm 20:15
And they kissed **o** another and wept 1 Sm 20:41
another and wept with **o** another, 1 Sm 20:41
are you alone, and no **o** with you?" 1 Sm 21:1
'Let no **o** know anything of the matter 1 Sm 21:2
they not sing to **o** another of him in 1 Sm 21:11
of Jesse give every **o** of you fields and 1 Sm 22:7
No **o** discloses to me when my son 1 Sm 22:8
But **o** of the sons of Ahimelech the 1 Sm 22:20
Saul went on **o** side of the mountain, 1 Sm 23:26
But **o** of the young men told Abigail, 1 Sm 25:14
worthless man that **o** cannot speak 1 Sm 25:17
I leave so much as **o** male of all who 1 Sm 25:22
left to Nabal so much as **o** male." 1 Sm 25:34
to the earth with **o** stroke of the spear, 1 Sm 26:8
For **o** of the people came in to destroy 1 Sm 26:15
a single flea like **o** who hunts a 1 Sm 26:20
Let **o** of the young men come over 1 Sm 26:22
"Now I shall perish **o** day by the hand 1 Sm 27:1
be given me in **o** of the country towns, 1 Sm 27:5
they sing to **o** another in dances, 1 Sm 29:5
They killed no **o**, but carried them off 1 Sm 30:2
Then David called **o** of the young 2 Sm 1:15
down, the **o** on the one side of the pool, 2 Sm 2:13
down, the one on the **o** side of the pool, 2 Sm 2:13
and seize **o** of the young men and take 2 Sm 2:21
Abner and became **o** group and took 2 Sm 2:25
But **o** thing I require of you; that is, 2 Sm 3:13
Joab never be without **o** who has a 2 Sm 3:29
as **o** falls before the wicked you have 2 Sm 3:34
the name of the **o** was Baanah, and the 2 Sm 4:2
when **o** told me, 'Behold, Saul is dead,' 2 Sm 4:10
meat, and a cake of raisins to each **o**. 2 Sm 6:19
as **o** of the vulgar fellows shamelessly 2 Sm 6:20
the **o** nation on earth whom God went 2 Sm 7:23
to death, and **o** full line to be spared. 2 Sm 8:2
David's table, like **o** of the king's sons. 2 Sm 9:11
It happened, late **o** afternoon, when 2 Sm 11:2
about the woman. And **o** said, 2 Sm 11:3
sword devours now **o** and now 2 Sm 11:25
city, the **o** rich and the other poor. 2 Sm 12:1
had nothing but **o** little ewe lamb, 2 Sm 12:3
was unwilling to take **o** of his own 2 Sm 12:4
you would be as **o** of the outrageous 2 Sm 13:13
sons, and not **o** of them is left." 2 Sm 13:30
they quarreled with **o** another in the 2 Sm 14:6
field. There was no **o** to separate them, 2 Sm 14:6
and **o** struck the other and killed him. 2 Sm 14:6
not **o** hair of your son shall fall to 2 Sm 14:11
bring his banished **o** home again. 2 Sm 14:13
that the banished **o** will not remain 2 Sm 14:14
o cannot turn to the right hand or to 2 Sm 14:19
Israel there was no **o** so much to be 2 Sm 14:25
and **o** daughter whose name was 2 Sm 14:27
gave was as if **o** consulted the word 2 Sm 16:23
You seek the life of only **o** man, and 2 Sm 17:3
has hidden himself in **o** of the pits or 2 Sm 17:9
the men with him not **o** will be left. 2 Sm 17:12
By daybreak not **o** was left who had 2 Sm 17:22
o third under the command of Joab, 2 Sm 18:2
o third under the command of 2 Sm 18:2
and **o** third under the command of 2 Sm 18:2
all Israel fled every **o** to his own 2 Sm 18:17
of all the men of Judah as **o** man, 2 Sm 19:14
And **o** of Joab's young men took his 2 Sm 20:11
I am **o** of those who are peaceable 2 Sm 20:19
o of the descendants of the giants, 2 Sm 21:16
who was **o** of the descendants of the 2 Sm 21:18
When **o** rules justly over men, ruling 2 Sm 23:3
hundred whom he killed at **o** time. 2 Sm 23:8
brother of Joab was **o** of the thirty; 2 Sm 23:24
Choose **o** of them, that I may do it to 2 Sm 24:12
not **o** of his hairs shall fall to the 1 Kgs 1:52
And now I have **o** request to make of 1 Kgs 2:16
"I have **o** small request to make of 1 Kgs 2:20
The **o** woman said, "Oh, my lord, this 1 Kgs 3:17
There was no **o** else with us in the 1 Kgs 3:18
Then the king said, "The **o** says, 1 Kgs 3:23
is dead, and my son is the living **o**.'" 1 Kgs 3:23
and give half to the **o** and half to the 1 Kgs 3:25
to make provision for **o** month in the 1 Kgs 4:7
And there was **o** governor who was 1 Kgs 4:19
Solomon's provision for **o** day was 1 Kgs 4:22
table, each **o** in his month. 1 Kgs 4:27
that there is no **o** among us who 1 Kgs 5:6
the middle **o** was six cubits broad, 1 Kgs 6:6
and **o** went up by stairs to the middle 1 Kgs 6:8
was the length of **o** wing of the 1 Kgs 6:24
cubits from the tip of **o** wing to the tip 1 Kgs 6:24
The height of **o** cherub was ten 1 Kgs 6:26
that a wing of **o** touched the one wall, 1 Kgs 6:27
that a wing of one touched the **o** wall, 1 Kgs 6:27
two leaves of the **o** door were folding, 1 Kgs 6:34
of cut stone and **o** course of cedar 1 Kgs 6:36
cubits was the height of **o** pillar, 1 Kgs 7:15
The height of the **o** capital was five 1 Kgs 7:16
a lattice for the **o** capital and a lattice 1 Kgs 7:17
rows around the **o** latticework to 1 Kgs 7:18
crown that projected upward **o** cubit. 1 Kgs 7:31
the wheels were of **o** piece with the 1 Kgs 7:32
The supports were of **o** piece with the 1 Kgs 7:34
and its panels were of **o** piece with it. 1 Kgs 7:35
and the **o** sea, and the twelve oxen 1 Kgs 7:44
—for there is no **o** who does not sin— 1 Kgs 8:46
Not **o** word has failed of all his good 1 Kgs 8:56
came to Solomon in **o** year was 666 1 Kgs 10:14
o on each end of a step on the six 1 Kgs 10:20
Every **o** of them brought his present, 1 Kgs 10:25
but I will give **o** tribe to your son, 1 Kgs 11:13
(but he shall have **o** tribe, for the 1 Kgs 11:32
Yet to his son I will give **o** tribe, that 1 Kgs 11:36
And he set **o** in Bethel, and the other 1 Kgs 12:29
went as far as Dan to be before **o**. 1 Kgs 12:30
he might permit no **o** to go out or 1 Kgs 15:17
of Jeroboam not **o** that breathed, 1 Kgs 15:29
Ahab went in **o** direction by himself, 1 Kgs 18:6
let them choose **o** bull for 1 Kgs 18:23
"Choose for yourselves **o** bull and 1 Kgs 18:25
was no voice, and no **o** answered. 1 Kgs 18:26
there was no voice. No **o** answered; 1 Kgs 18:29
one answered; no **o** paid attention. 1 Kgs 18:29
let not **o** of them escape." And they 1 Kgs 18:40
life as the life of **o** of them by this 1 Kgs 19:2
And the **o** who escapes from the 1 Kgs 19:17
and the **o** who escapes from the 1 Kgs 19:17
encamped opposite **o** another seven 1 Kgs 20:29
100,000 foot soldiers in **o** day. 1 Kgs 20:29
recognized him as **o** of the prophets. 1 Kgs 20:41
"There is yet **o** man by whom we 1 Kgs 22:8
the prophets with **o** accord are 1 Kgs 22:13
word be like the word of **o** of them, 1 Kgs 22:13
And **o** said one thing, and another 1 Kgs 22:20
And one said **o** thing, and another 1 Kgs 22:20
was parted to the **o** side and to the 2 Kgs 2:8
was parted to the **o** side and to the 2 Kgs 2:14
of the LORD?" Then **o** of the king of 2 Kgs 3:11
together and struck **o** another down. 2 Kgs 3:23
Now the wife of **o** of the sons of the 2 Kgs 4:1
all these vessels. And when **o** is full, 2 Kgs 4:4
O day Elisha went on to Shunem, 2 Kgs 4:8
O day he came there, and he turned 2 Kgs 4:11
he went out **o** day to his father among 2 Kgs 4:18
"Send me **o** of the servants and one of 2 Kgs 4:22
of the servants and **o** of the donkeys, 2 Kgs 4:22
O of them went out into the field to 2 Kgs 4:39
Now the Syrians on **o** of their raids 2 Kgs 5:2
Then **o** of them said, "Be pleased to go 2 Kgs 6:3
But as **o** was felling a log, his axe head 2 Kgs 6:5
And **o** of his servants said, "None, my 2 Kgs 6:12
And they said to **o** another, "Why are 2 Kgs 7:3
Syrians, behold, there was no **o** there. 2 Kgs 7:5
army, so that they said to **o** another, 2 Kgs 7:6
Then they said to **o** another, "We are 2 Kgs 7:9
there was no **o** to be seen or heard 2 Kgs 7:10
And **o** of his servants said, "Let some 2 Kgs 7:13
and he reigned **o** year in Jerusalem. 2 Kgs 8:26
Elisha the prophet called **o** of the sons 2 Kgs 9:1
then let no **o** slip out of the city to go 2 Kgs 9:15
of Jezreel, so that no **o** can say, 2 Kgs 9:37
Baal was filled from **o** end to the 2 Kgs 10:21
o third of you, those who come off 2 Kgs 11:5
the right side as **o** entered the house of 2 Kgs 12:9
But each **o** shall die for his own sin." 2 Kgs 14:6
let us look **o** another in the face." 2 Kgs 14:8
of Judah faced **o** another in battle 2 Kgs 14:11
and he reigned **o** month in Samaria. 2 Kgs 15:13
"Send there **o** of the priests whom 2 Kgs 17:27
So **o** of the priests whom they had 2 Kgs 17:28
Then each **o** of you will eat of his 2 Kgs 18:31
vine, and each **o** of his own fig tree, 2 Kgs 18:31
and each **o** of you will drink the 2 Kgs 18:31
Against the Holy **O** of Israel! 2 Kgs 19:22
wipe Jerusalem as **o** wipes a dish, 2 Kgs 21:13
filled Jerusalem from **o** end to 2 Kgs 21:16
that no **o** might burn his son or his 2 Kgs 23:10
As for the two pillars, the **o** sea, and 2 Kgs 25:16
height of the **o** pillar was eighteen 2 Kgs 25:17
the name of the **o** was Peleg (for in 1 Chr 1:19
and Mattithiah, **o** of the Levites, the 1 Chr 9:31
300 whom he killed at **o** time. 1 Chr 11:11

David said that no **o** but the Levites 1 Chr 15:2
from **o** kingdom to another people, 1 Chr 16:20
he allowed no **o** to oppress them; he 1 Chr 16:21
after you, **o** of your own sons, 1 Chr 17:11
the **o** nation on earth whom God 1 Chr 17:21
who was **o** of the descendants of the 1 Chr 20:4
choose **o** of them, that I may do it to 1 Chr 21:10
o father's house being chosen for 1 Chr 24:6
for Eleazar and **o** chosen for Ithamar. 1 Chr 24:6
Judah, Elihu, **o** of David's brothers; 1 Chr 27:18
o wing of the one, of five cubits, 2 Chr 3:11
one wing of the **o**, of five cubits, 2 Chr 3:11
and of this cherub, **o** wing, of five 2 Chr 3:12
in front of the temple, **o** on the south, 2 Chr 3:17
and the **o** sea, and the twelve oxen 2 Chr 4:15
—for there is no **o** who does not sin— 2 Chr 6:36
away the face of your anointed **o**! 2 Chr 6:42
came to Solomon in **o** year was 666 2 Chr 9:13
o on each end of a step on the six 2 Chr 9:19
Every **o** of them brought his present, 2 Chr 9:24
he might permit no **o** to go out or 2 Chr 16:1
"There is yet **o** man by whom we 2 Chr 18:7
the prophets with **o** accord are 2 Chr 18:12
word be like the word of **o** of them, 2 Chr 18:12
And **o** said one thing, and another 2 Chr 18:19
And one said **o** thing, and another 2 Chr 18:19
they all helped to destroy **o** another. 2 Chr 20:23
and he reigned **o** year in Jerusalem. 2 Chr 22:2
of Ahaziah had no **o** able to rule the 2 Chr 22:9
Sabbath, **o** third shall be gatekeepers, 2 Chr 23:4
and **o** third shall be at the king's 2 Chr 23:5
the king's house and **o** third at the 2 Chr 23:5
Let no **o** enter the house of the LORD 2 Chr 23:6
LORD so that no **o** should enter who 2 Chr 23:19
but each **o** shall die for his own sin." 2 Chr 25:4
let us look **o** another in the face." 2 Chr 25:17
of Judah faced **o** another in battle 2 Chr 25:21
o of the king's commanders. 2 Chr 26:11
killed 120,000 from Judah in **o** day, 2 Chr 28:6
Judah to give them **o** heart to do 2 Chr 30:12
"Before **o** altar you shall worship, 2 Chr 32:12
people gathered as **o** man to Jerusalem. Ezr 3:1
were delivered to **o** whose name was Ezr 5:14
of great stones and **o** layer of timber. Ezr 6:4
Nor is this a task for **o** day or for two, Ezr 10:13
that Hanani, **o** of my brothers, came Neh 1:2
And I told no **o** what my God had put Neh 2:12
with me but the **o** on which I rode. Neh 2:12
to him Hananiah, **o** of the perfumers, Neh 3:8
each **o** opposite his own house. Neh 3:28
him Malchijah, **o** of the goldsmiths, Neh 3:31
on the work with **o** hand and held his Neh 4:17
on the wall, far from **o** another. Neh 4:19
for each day was **o** ox and six choice Neh 5:18
the people gathered as **o** man into the Neh 8:1
people cast lots to bring **o** out of ten to Neh 11:1
of Judah, every **o** in his inheritance. Neh 11:20
O went to the south on the wall to the Neh 12:31
And **o** of the sons of Jehoiada, the son Neh 13:28
and old, women and children, in **o** day, Est 3:13
for no **o** was allowed to enter the king's Est 4:2
for Hathach, **o** of the king's eunuchs, Est 4:5
there is but **o** law—to be put to death, Est 4:11
except the **o** to whom the king holds out Est 4:11
Queen Esther let no **o** but me come with Est 5:12
be handed over to **o** of the king's most Est 6:9
o of the eunuchs in attendance on the Est 7:9
on **o** day throughout all the provinces of Est 8:12
And no **o** could stand against them, for Est 9:2
they send gifts of food to **o** another. Est 9:19
gifts of food to **o** another and gifts to Est 9:22
o who feared God and turned away from Jb 1:1
a feast in the house of each **o** on his day, Jb 1:4
"You speak as **o** of the foolish women Jb 2:10
nights, and no **o** spoke a word to him, Jb 2:13
"If **o** ventures a word with you, will you be Jb 4:2
the gate, and there is no **o** to deliver them. Jb 5:4
blessed is the **o** whom God reproves; Jb 5:17
I have not denied the words of the Holy **O**. Jb 6:10
If **o** wished to contend with him, one could Jb 9:3
o could not answer him once in a Jb 9:3
It is all **o**; therefore I say, He destroys both Jb 9:22
when you mock, shall no **o** shame you? Jb 11:3
In the thought of **o** who is at ease there is Jb 12:5
you deceive him, as **o** deceives a man? Jb 13:9
your eyes on such a **o** and bring me into Jb 14:3
thing out of an unclean? There is not **o**. Jb 14:4
how much less **o** who is abominable Jb 15:16
and I am **o** before whom men spit. Jb 17:6
O dies in his full vigor, being wholly at Jb 21:23
are glad; the innocent **o** mocks at them, Jb 22:19
He delivers even the **o** who is not Jb 22:30
help; yet God charges no **o** with wrong. Jb 24:12
troops, like **o** who comforts mourners. Jb 29:25
calamity; they need no **o** to help them. Jb 30:13

"Yet does not **o** in a heap of ruins Jb 30:24
And did not **o** fashion us in the womb? Jb 31:15
Oh, that I had **o** to hear me! (Here is my Jb 31:35
For God speaks in **o** way, and in two, Jb 33:14
an angel, a mediator, **o** of the thousand, Jb 33:23
Shall **o** who hates justice govern? Will Jb 34:17
who says to a king, 'Worthless **o**,' and to Jb 34:18
o who is perfect in knowledge is with Jb 36:4
"And now no **o** looks on the light when Jb 37:21
Can **o** take him by his eyes, or pierce Jb 40:24
No **o** is so fierce that he dares to stir him Jb 41:10
O is so near to another that no air can Jb 41:16
They are joined **o** to another; they clasp Jb 41:17
o would think the deep to be Jb 41:32
and the **o** greedy for gain curses and Ps 10:3
the wicked and the **o** who loves violence. Ps 11:5
Save, O LORD, for the godly **o** is gone; for Ps 12:1
there is none who does good, not even **o**. Ps 14:3
Sheol, or let your holy **o** see corruption. Ps 16:10
even the **o** who could not keep himself Ps 22:29
O thing have I asked of the LORD, that Ps 27:4
I have been forgotten like **o** who is dead; Ps 31:12
abundantly repays the **o** who acts in Ps 31:23
Blessed is the **o** whose transgression is Ps 32:1
love surrounds the **o** who trusts in Ps 32:10
all his bones; not **o** of them is broken. Ps 34:20
as **o** who laments his mother, I bowed Ps 35:14
not yourself over the **o** who prospers in Ps 37:7
Blessed is the **o** who considers the poor! Ps 41:1
And when **o** comes to see me, he utters Ps 41:6
your sword on your thigh, O mighty **o**, Ps 45:3
The Mighty **O**, God the LORD, speaks and Ps 50:1
you thought that I was **o** like yourself. Ps 50:21
The **o** who offers thanksgiving as his Ps 50:23
to **o** who orders his way rightly I will Ps 50:23
there is none who does good, not even **o**. Ps 53:3
Let the righteous **o** rejoice in the LORD Ps 64:10
Blessed is the **o** you choose and bring Ps 65:4
the **o** who by his strength established the Ps 65:6
down rain, before God, the **O** of Sinai, Ps 68:8
Israel—he is the **o** who gives power and Ps 68:35
a desolation; let no **o** dwell in their tents. Ps 69:25
to you with the lyre, O Holy **O** of Israel. Ps 71:22
Like a dream when **o** awakes, O Lord, Ps 73:20
putting down **o** and lifting up another. Ps 75:7
and provoked the Holy **O** of Israel. Ps 78:41
and there was no **o** to bury them. Ps 79:3
For they conspire with **o** accord; against Ps 83:5
each **o** appears before God in Zion. Ps 84:7
hosts, blessed is the **o** who trusts in you! Ps 84:12
with Cush—"This **o** was born there," Ps 87:4
"This **o** and that one were born in her"; Ps 87:5
"This one and that **o** were born in her"; Ps 87:5
peoples, "This **o** was born there." Selah Ps 87:6
like **o** set loose among the dead, like the Ps 88:5
made a covenant with my chosen **o**; Ps 89:3
LORD, our king to the Holy **O** of Israel. Ps 89:18
you spoke in a vision to your godly **o**, Ps 89:19
"I have granted help to **o** who is mighty; Ps 89:19
I have exalted **o** chosen from the people. Ps 89:19
No **o** who practices deceit shall dwell in Ps 101:7
no **o** who utters lies shall continue Ps 101:7
A Prayer of **o** afflicted, when he is faint Ps 102:T
from **o** kingdom to another people, Ps 105:13
he allowed no **o** to oppress them; he Ps 105:14
adversaries; not **o** of them was left. Ps 106:11
and Aaron, the holy **o** of the LORD, Ps 106:16
them—had not Moses, his chosen **o**, Ps 106:23
and every **o** of your righteous rules Ps 119:160
at your word like **o** who finds great Ps 119:162
and vowed to the Mighty **O** of Jacob, Ps 132:2
place for the Mighty **O** of Jacob." Ps 132:5
turn away the face of your anointed **o**. Ps 132:10
"**O** of the sons of your body I will set Ps 132:11
saying, "Sing us **o** of the songs of Zion!" Ps 137:3
book were written, every **o** of them, Ps 139:16
As when **o** plows and breaks up the Ps 141:7
remains to me; no **o** cares for my soul. Ps 142:4
for no **o** living is righteous before you. Ps 143:2
O generation shall commend your Ps 145:4
and the **o** who understands obtain Prv 1:5
among us; we will all have **o** purse"— Prv 1:14
out my hand and no **o** has heeded, Prv 1:24
Blessed is the **o** who finds wisdom, and Prv 3:13
and the **o** who gets understanding, Prv 3:13
the only **o** in the sight of my mother, Prv 4:3
and **o** who sows discord among Prv 6:19
Or can **o** walk on hot coals and his feet Prv 6:28
Blessed is the **o** who listens to me, Prv 8:34
the knowledge of the Holy **O** is insight. Prv 9:10
The **o** who conceals hatred has lying Prv 10:18
but **o** who sows righteousness gets a Prv 11:18
O gives freely, yet grows all the richer; Prv 11:24
and **o** who waters will himself be Prv 11:25
No **o** is established by wickedness, but Prv 12:3

sense, but **o** of twisted mind is despised. Prv 12:8
There is **o** whose rash words are like Prv 12:18
O who is righteous is a guide to his Prv 12:26
O pretends to be rich, yet has nothing; Prv 13:7
that **o** may turn away from the snares Prv 13:14
O who is wise is cautious and turns Prv 14:16
but **o** who breathes out lies is Prv 14:25
of the LORD **o** has strong confidence, Prv 14:26
that **o** may turn away from the snares Prv 14:27
wrath falls on **o** who acts shamefully. Prv 14:35
fear of the LORD **o** turns away from evil. Prv 16:6
the inheritance as **o** of the brothers. Prv 17:2
stone in the eyes of the **o** who gives it; Prv 17:8
O who lacks sense gives a pledge and Prv 17:18
and **o** with a dishonest tongue falls Prv 17:20
If **o** gives an answer before he hears, it Prv 18:13
The **o** who states his case first seems Prv 18:17
in his integrity than **o** who is crooked Prv 19:1
Good sense makes **o** slow to anger, and Prv 19:11
If **o** curses his father or his mother, his Prv 20:20
The Righteous **O** observes the house of Prv 21:12
O who wanders from the way of good Prv 21:16
Be not **o** of those who give pledges, who Prv 22:26
for he is like **o** who is inwardly Prv 23:7
You will be like **o** who lies down in the Prv 23:34
like **o** who lies on the top of a mast. Prv 23:34
a heavy heart is like **o** who takes off a Prv 25:20
Like **o** who binds the stone in the sling Prv 26:8
in the sling is **o** who gives honor to Prv 26:8
who wounds everyone is **o** who hires a Prv 26:10
his own is like **o** who takes a passing Prv 26:17
O who is full loathes honey, but to one Prv 27:7
but to **o** who is hungry everything Prv 27:7
iron, and **o** man sharpens another. Prv 27:17
The wicked flee when no **o** pursues, but Prv 28:1
The **o** who keeps the law is a son with Prv 28:7
If **o** turns away his ear from hearing the Prv 28:9
Blessed is the **o** who fears the LORD Prv 28:14
If **o** is burdened with the blood of Prv 28:17
fugitive until death; let no **o** help him. Prv 28:17
but the **o** who trusts in the LORD will Prv 28:25
Bloodthirsty men hate **o** who is Prv 29:10
and **o** given to anger causes much Prv 29:22
but **o** whose way is straight is an Prv 29:27
nor have I knowledge of the Holy **O**. Prv 30:3
strong drink to the **o** who is perishing, Prv 31:6
For to the **o** who pleases him God has Eccl 2:26
only to give to **o** who pleases God. Eccl 2:26
to the beasts is the same; as **o** dies, Eccl 3:19
All go to **o** place. All are from the dust, Eccl 3:20
and they had no **o** to comfort them! Eccl 4:1
and there was no **o** to comfort them. Eccl 4:1
o person who has no other, either son or Eccl 4:8
Two are better than **o**, because they Eccl 4:9
For if they fall, **o** will lift up his fellow. Eccl 4:10
but how can **o** keep warm alone? Eccl 4:11
might prevail against **o** who is alone, Eccl 4:12
vanity; but God is the **o** you must fear. Eccl 5:7
the toil with which **o** toils under the Eccl 5:18
no good—do not all go to the **o** place? Eccl 6:6
able to dispute with **o** stronger than he. Eccl 6:10
God has made the **o** as well as the Eccl 7:14
for the **o** who fears God shall come out Eccl 7:18
while adding **o** thing to another to find Eccl 7:27
O man among a thousand I found, but Eccl 7:28
Yet no **o** remembered that poor man. Eccl 9:15
war, but **o** sinner destroys much good. Eccl 9:18
and **o** does not sharpen the edge, Eccl 10:10
but wisdom helps **o** to succeed. Eccl 10:10
and **o** rises up at the sound of a bird, Eccl 12:4
they are given by **o** Shepherd. Eccl 12:11
should I be like **o** who veils herself beside Sg 1:7
"Arise, my love, my beautiful **o**, and Sg 2:10
Arise, my love, my beautiful **o**, and come Sg 2:13
and not **o** among them has lost its young. Sg 4:2
captivated my heart with **o** glance of your Sg 4:9
your eyes, with **o** jewel of your necklace. Sg 4:9
my sister, my love, my dove, my perfect **o**, Sg 5:2
not **o** among them has lost its young. Sg 6:6
My dove, my perfect **o**, is the only one, the Sg 6:9
My dove, my perfect one, is the only **o**, the Sg 6:9
is the only one, the only **o** of her mother, Sg 6:9
beautiful and pleasant you are, O loved **o**, Sg 7:6
I was in his eyes as **o** who finds peace. Sg 8:10
each **o** was to bring for its fruit a Sg 8:11
they have despised the Holy **O** of Israel, Is 1:4
the LORD of hosts, the Mighty **O** of Israel: Is 1:24
and each **o** is brought low—do not forgive Is 2:9
And the people will oppress **o** another, Is 3:5
every **o** his fellow and every one his Is 3:5
one his fellow and every **o** his neighbor; Is 3:5
shall take hold of **o** man in that day, Is 4:1
acres of vineyard shall yield but **o** bath, Is 5:10
is humbled, and each **o** is brought low, Is 5:15
counsel of the Holy **O** of Israel draw near, Is 5:19

despised the word of the Holy **O** of Israel. Is 5:24
And if **o** looks to the land, behold, Is 5:30
And **o** called to another and said: "Holy, Is 6:3
Then **o** of the seraphim flew to me, having Is 6:6
and tail, palm branch and reed in **o** day— Is 9:14
like fuel for the fire; no **o** spares another. Is 9:19
and as **o** gathers eggs that have been Is 10:14
become a fire, and his Holy **O** a flame, Is 10:17
devour his thorns and briers in **o** day. Is 10:17
lean on the LORD, the Holy **O** of Israel, Is 10:20
and Lebanon will fall by the Majestic **O**. Is 10:34
in your midst is the Holy **O** of Israel." Is 12:6
They will look aghast at **o** another; their Is 13:8
What will **o** answer the messengers of Is 14:32
the tent of David **o** who judges and seeks Is 16:5
and as when **o** gleans the ears of grain in Is 17:5
his eyes will look on the Holy **O** of Israel. Is 17:7
O of these will be called the City of Is 19:18
O my threshed and winnowed **o**, what I Is 21:10
O is calling to me from Seir, Is 21:11
for seventy years, like the days of **o** king. Is 23:15
of praise, of glory to the Righteous **O**. Is 24:16
grain, and you will be gleaned **o** by one, Is 27:12
grain, and you will be gleaned one by **o**, Is 27:12
the Lord has **o** who is mighty and strong; Is 28:2
I am the **o** who has laid as a foundation Is 28:16
Does **o** crush grain for bread? No, he Is 28:28
When men give it to **o** who can read, Is 29:11
they give the book to **o** who cannot read, Is 29:12
shall exult in the Holy **O** of Israel. Is 29:19
will sanctify the Holy **O** of Jacob and Is 29:23
no more about the Holy **O** of Israel." Is 30:11
Therefore thus says the Holy **O** of Israel, Is 30:12
said the Lord GOD, the Holy **O** of Israel, Is 30:15
A thousand shall flee at the threat of **o**; Is 30:17
as when **o** sets out to the sound of the Is 30:29
not look to the Holy **O** of Israel or consult Is 31:1
Its nobles—there is no **o** there to call it a Is 34:12
are gathered, each **o** with her mate. Is 34:15
the LORD: Not **o** of these shall be missing; Is 34:16
Then each **o** of you will eat of his own Is 36:16
own vine, and each **o** of his own fig tree, Is 36:16
and each **o** of you will drink the water of Is 36:16
heights? Against the Holy **O** of Israel! Is 37:23
I should be like him? says the Holy **O**. Is 40:25
he is strong in power not **o** is missing. Is 40:26
Who stirred up **o** from the east whom Is 41:2
"Fear not, I am the **o** who helps you." Is 41:13
men of Israel! I am the **o** who helps you, Is 41:14
your Redeemer is the Holy **O** of Israel. Is 41:14
in the Holy **O** of Israel you shall glory. Is 41:16
this, the Holy **O** of Israel has created it. Is 41:20
I stirred up **o** from the north, and he has Is 41:25
But when I look there is no **o**; among Is 41:28
Who is blind as my dedicated **o**, or Is 42:19
the LORD your God, the Holy **O** of Israel, Is 43:3
your Redeemer, the Holy **O** of Israel: Is 43:14
I am the LORD, your Holy **O**, the Creator Is 43:15
This **o** will say, 'I am the LORD'S,' another Is 44:5
No **o** considers, nor is there knowledge Is 44:19
Thus says the LORD, the Holy **O** of Israel, Is 45:11
One of Israel, and the **o** who formed him: Is 45:11
If **o** cries to it, it does not answer or save Is 46:7
will take vengeance, and I will spare no **o**. Is 47:3
hosts is his name—is the Holy **O** of Israel. Is 47:4
heart, "I am, and there is no **o** besides me; Is 47:8
shall come to you in a moment, in **o** day; Is 47:9
wickedness, you said, "No **o** sees me"; Is 47:10
"I am, and there is no **o** besides me." Is 47:10
own direction; there is no **o** to save you. Is 47:15
your Redeemer, the Holy **O** of Israel: Is 48:17
the Redeemer of Israel and his Holy **O**, Is 49:7
and his Holy One, to **o** deeply despised, Is 49:7
LORD, who is faithful, the Holy **O** of Israel, Is 49:7
your Redeemer, the Mighty **O** of Jacob." Is 49:26
when I called, was there no **o** to answer? Is 50:2
you; for he was but **o** when I called him, Is 51:2
and as **o** from whom men hide their faces Is 53:3
we have turned every **o** to his own way; Is 53:6
by his knowledge shall the righteous **o**, Is 53:11
"Sing, O barren **o**, who did not bear; Is 54:1
children of the desolate **o** will be more Is 54:1
and the Holy **O** of Israel is your Redeemer, Is 54:5
"O afflicted **o**, storm-tossed and not Is 54:11
your God, and of the Holy **O** of Israel, Is 55:5
way, each to his own gain, **o** and all. Is 56:11
man perishes, and no **o** lays it to heart; Is 57:1
are taken away, while no **o** understands. Is 57:1
For thus says the **O** who is high and Is 57:15
No **o** enters suit justly; no one goes to law Is 59:4
suit justly; no **o** goes to law honestly; Is 59:4
and from **o** that is crushed a viper is Is 59:5
no **o** who treads on them knows peace. Is 59:8
that there was no **o** to intercede; Is 59:16
your God, and for the Holy **O** of Israel, Is 60:9
the LORD, the Zion of the Holy **O** of Israel. Is 60:14
and hated, with no **o** passing through, Is 60:15
your Redeemer, the Mighty **O** of Jacob. Is 60:16
The least **o** shall become a clan, and the Is 60:22
and the smallest **o** a mighty nation; Is 60:22
and from the peoples no **o** was with me; Is 63:3
I looked, but there was no **o** to help; I was Is 63:5
appalled, but there was no **o** to uphold; Is 63:5
From of old no **o** has heard or perceived Is 64:4
have all become like **o** who is unclean, Is 64:6
There is no **o** who calls upon your name, Is 64:7
But this is the **o** to whom I will look: he Is 66:2
an ox is like **o** who kills a man; Is 66:3
a lamb, like **o** who breaks a dog's neck; Is 66:3
offering, like **o** who offers pig's blood; Is 66:3
frankincense, like **o** who blesses an idol. Is 66:3
because when I called, no **o** answered, Is 66:4
things? Shall a land be born in **o** day? Is 66:8
a nation be brought forth in **o** moment? Is 66:8
As **o** whom his mother comforts, so I Is 66:13
the gardens, following **o** in the midst, Is 66:17
o of the priests who were in Anathoth in Jer 1:1
and every **o** shall set his throne at the Jer 1:15
you seen what she did, that faithless **o**, Jer 3:6
for all the adulteries of that faithless **o**, Jer 3:8
o from a city and two from a family, Jer 3:14
And you, O desolate **o**, what do you Jer 4:30
anguish as of **o** giving birth to her first Jer 4:31
a man, **o** who does justice and seeks truth, Jer 5:1
you truly execute justice **o** with another, Jer 7:5
If **o** turns away, does he not return? Jer 8:4
his neighbor, and no **o** speaks the truth; Jer 9:5
laid waste so that no **o** passes through, Jer 9:10
wilderness, so that no **o** passes through? Jer 9:12
for he is the **o** who formed all things, Jer 10:16
there is no **o** to spread my tent again Jer 10:20
the LORD devours from **o** end of the land Jer 12:12
And I will dash them **o** against another, Jer 13:14
Can **o** break iron, iron from the north, Jer 15:12
and no **o** shall lament for them or cut Jer 16:6
No **o** shall break bread for the mourner, Jer 16:7
every **o** of you follows his stubborn, Jer 16:12
Return, every **o** from his evil way, and Jer 18:11
and will every **o** act according to the Jer 18:12
this city, as **o** breaks a potter's vessel, Jer 19:11
broken pot, a vessel no **o** cares for? Jer 22:28
so that no **o** turns from his evil; Jer 23:14
by their dreams that they tell **o** another, Jer 23:27
who steal my words from **o** another. Jer 23:30
"When **o** of this people, or a prophet or Jer 23:33
priest, or **o** of the people who says, Jer 23:34
every **o** to his neighbor and every one to Jer 23:35
his neighbor and every **o** to his brother, Jer 23:35
O basket had very good figs, like Jer 24:2
saying, 'Turn now, every **o** of you, from Jer 25:5
the north, far and near, **o** after another, Jer 25:26
day shall extend from **o** end of the earth Jer 25:33
and every **o** turn from his evil way, Jer 26:3
I am the **o** who knows, and I am Jer 29:23
and all your foes, every **o** of them, Jer 30:16
'It is Zion, for whom no **o** cares!' Jer 30:17
Their prince shall be **o** of themselves; Jer 30:21
longer shall each **o** teach his neighbor Jer 31:34
rewarding each **o** according to his Jer 32:19
I will give them **o** heart and one way, Jer 32:39
I will give them one heart and **o** way, Jer 32:39
the hands of the **o** who counts them, Jer 33:13
and will not choose **o** of his offspring to Jer 33:26
female, so that no **o** should enslave a Jew, Jer 34:9
every **o** to his brother and to his Jer 34:17
of the LORD, into **o** of the chambers; Jer 35:2
'Turn now every **o** of you from his evil Jer 35:15
so that every **o** may turn from his evil Jer 36:3
and that every **o** will turn from his evil Jer 36:7
words, they turned **o** to another in fear. Jer 36:16
and let no **o** know where you are." Jer 36:19
"Let no **o** know of these words, Jer 38:24
of Nethaniah, and no **o** will know it. Jer 40:15
family, **o** of the chief officers of the king, Jer 41:1
a desolation, and no **o** dwells in them, Jer 44:2
and they fell, and they said **o** to another, Jer 46:16
'Noisy **o** who lets the hour go by.' Jer 46:17
like Carmel by the sea, shall **o** come. Jer 46:18
no **o** treads them with shouts of joy; Jer 48:33
like a vessel for which no **o** cares, Jer 48:38
o shall fly swiftly like an eagle and Jer 48:40
o shall mount up and fly swiftly like an Jer 49:22
and the **o** who handles the sickle in Jer 50:16
every **o** shall turn to his own people, Jer 50:16
and every **o** shall flee to his own land. Jer 50:16
Encamp around her; let no **o** escape. Jer 50:29
defied the LORD, the Holy **O** of Israel. Jer 50:29
"Behold, I am against you, O proud **o**, Jer 50:31
The proud **o** shall stumble and fall, Jer 50:32
full of guilt against the Holy **O** of Israel. Jer 51:5
of Babylon; let every **o** save his life! Jer 51:6
for he is the **o** who formed all things, Jer 51:19
O runner runs to meet another, and Jer 51:31
and **o** messenger to meet another, Jer 51:31
a desert, a land in which no **o** dwells, Jer 51:43
Let every **o** save his life from the fierce Jer 51:45
a report comes in **o** year and afterward Jer 51:46
As for the two pillars, the **o** sea, the Jer 52:20
the height of the **o** pillar was eighteen Jer 52:21
The height of the **o** capital was five Jer 52:22
is far from me, **o** to revive my spirit; Lam 1:16
yet there is no **o** to comfort me. Lam 1:21
of the LORD no **o** escaped or survived; Lam 2:22
It is good that **o** should wait quietly for Lam 3:26
give his cheek to the **o** who strikes, Lam 3:30
beg for food, but no **o** gives to them. Lam 4:4
with blood that no **o** was able to touch Lam 4:14
their wings touched **o** another. Each one Ezk 1:9
Each **o** of them went straight forward, Ezk 1:9
o for each of the four of them. Ezk 1:15
out straight, **o** toward another. Ezk 1:23
and I heard the voice of **o** speaking. Ezk 1:28
creatures as they touched **o** another, Ezk 3:13
you cannot turn from **o** side to the other, Ezk 4:8
water, and look at **o** another in dismay, Ezk 4:17
moaning, each **o** over his iniquity. Ezk 7:16
but touch no **o** on whom is the mark. Ezk 9:6
the cherubim, **o** beside each cherub, Ezk 10:9
And every **o** had four faces: the first Ezk 10:14
Each **o** of them went straight forward. Ezk 10:22
And I will give them **o** heart, and a Ezk 11:19
Any **o** of the house of Israel who takes Ezk 14:4
For any **o** of the house of Israel, or of Ezk 14:7
so that no **o** may pass through Ezk 14:15
No **o** solicited you to play the whore, Ezk 16:34
And he took **o** of the royal offspring Ezk 17:13
Can **o** escape who does such things? Ezk 17:15
topmost of its young twigs a tender **o**, Ezk 17:22
Israel, every **o** according to his ways, Ezk 18:30
And she brought up **o** of her cubs; he Ezk 19:3
your eyes feast on, every **o** of you, Ezk 20:7
Go serve every **o** of you his idols, now Ezk 20:39
And you, O profane wicked **o**, prince Ezk 21:25
the **o** to whom judgment belongs, Ezk 21:27
in you, every **o** according to his power, Ezk 22:6
O commits abomination with his Ezk 22:11
As **o** gathers silver and bronze and Ezk 22:20
two women, the daughters of **o** mother. Ezk 23:2
Take the choicest **o** of the flock; pile the Ezk 24:5
iniquities and groan to **o** another. Ezk 24:23
like **o** destroyed in the midst of the Ezk 27:32
strong arm and the **o** that was broken, Ezk 30:22
the hand of a mighty **o** of the nations. Ezk 31:11
every moment, every **o** for his own life, Ezk 32:10
sword comes and takes any **o** of them, Ezk 33:6
If I say to the wicked, O wicked **o**, you Ezk 33:8
saying, 'Abraham was only **o** man, Ezk 33:24
doors of the houses, say to **o** another, Ezk 33:30
are to them like **o** who sings lustful Ezk 33:32
I will set up over them **o** shepherd, Ezk 34:23
And join them **o** to another into one Ezk 37:17
join them one to another into **o** stick, Ezk 37:17
that they may become **o** in your hand. Ezk 37:17
of Judah, and make them **o** stick, Ezk 37:19
stick, that they may be **o** in my hand. Ezk 37:19
I will make them **o** nation in the land, Ezk 37:22
And **o** king shall be king over them Ezk 37:22
and they shall all have **o** shepherd. Ezk 37:24
that I am the LORD, the Holy **O** in Israel. Ezk 39:7
the thickness of the wall, **o** reed; Ezk 40:5
wall, one reed; and the height, **o** reed. Ezk 40:5
the threshold of the gate, **o** reed deep. Ezk 40:6
rooms, **o** reed long and one reed broad; Ezk 40:7
rooms, one reed long and **o** reed broad; Ezk 40:7
of the gate at the inner end, **o** reed. Ezk 40:7
of the gateway, on the inside, **o** reed. Ezk 40:8
the side rooms, **o** cubit on either side. Ezk 40:12
the ceiling of the **o** side room to the Ezk 40:13
trees on its jambs, **o** on either side. Ezk 40:26
on the outside as **o** goes up to the Ezk 40:40
and a half broad, and **o** cubit high, Ezk 40:42
o at the side of the north gate facing Ezk 40:44
beside the jambs, **o** on either side. Ezk 40:49
were in three stories, **o** over another, Ezk 41:6
and so **o** went up from the lowest story Ezk 41:7
the free space, **o** door toward the north, Ezk 41:11
face toward the palm tree on the **o** side, Ezk 41:19
as **o** enters them from the outer court. Ezk 42:9
wall on the east as **o** enters them. Ezk 42:12
I heard **o** speaking to me out of the Ezk 43:6
its base shall be **o** cubit high and one Ezk 43:13
be one cubit high and **o** cubit broad, Ezk 43:13
with a rim of **o** span around its edge. Ezk 43:13
two cubits, with a breadth of **o** cubit; Ezk 43:14
four cubits, with a breadth of **o** cubit; Ezk 43:14

broad, and its base **o** cubit all around. Ezk 43:17
be opened, and no **o** shall enter by it, Ezk 44:2
in length to **o** of the tribal Ezk 45:7
the bath containing **o** tenth of a Ezk 45:11
and the ephah **o** tenth of a homer; Ezk 45:11
o sixth of an ephah from each homer Ezk 45:13
and **o** sixth of an ephah from each Ezk 45:13
o tenth of a bath from each cor (the Ezk 45:14
And **o** sheep from every flock of two Ezk 45:15
no **o** shall return by way of the gate by Ezk 46:9
the lambs as much as **o** is able to give, Ezk 46:11
by morning, **o** sixth of an ephah, Ezk 46:14
and **o** third of a hin of oil to moisten Ezk 46:14
of his inheritance to **o** of his servants, Ezk 46:17
many trees on the **o** side and on the Ezk 47:7
the east side to the west, Dan, **o** portion. Ezk 48:1
east side to the west, Asher, **o** portion. Ezk 48:2
side to the west, Naphtali, **o** portion. Ezk 48:3
side to the west, Manasseh, **o** portion. Ezk 48:4
side to the west, Ephraim, **o** portion. Ezk 48:5
east side to the west, Reuben, **o** portion. Ezk 48:6
east side to the west, Judah, **o** portion. Ezk 48:7
in length equal to **o** of the tribal Ezk 48:8
side to the west, Benjamin, **o** portion. Ezk 48:23
east side to the west, Simeon, **o** portion. Ezk 48:24
side to the west, Issachar, **o** portion. Ezk 48:25
side to the west, Zebulun, **o** portion. Ezk 48:26
the east side to the west, Gad, **o** portion. Ezk 48:27
to me, there is but **o** sentence for you. Dn 2:9
and no **o** can show it to the king except Dn 2:11
will mix with **o** another in marriage, Dn 2:43
in bed, and behold, a watcher, a holy **o**, Dn 4:13
the king saw a watcher, a holy **o**, Dn 4:23
are that Daniel, **o** of the exiles of Judah, Dn 5:13
three presidents, of whom Daniel was **o**, Dn 6:2
who is **o** of the exiles from Judah, Dn 6:13
out of the sea, different from **o** another. Dn 7:3
And behold, another beast, a second **o**, Dn 7:5
one, like a bear. It was raised up on **o** side. Dn 7:5
up among them another horn, a little **o**, Dn 7:8
of heaven there came **o** like a son of Dn 7:13
and his kingdom **o** that shall not be Dn 7:14
I approached **o** of those who stood there Dn 7:16
high, but **o** was higher than the other, Dn 8:3
the other, and the higher **o** came up last. Dn 8:3
and there was no **o** who could rescue Dn 8:4
And there was no **o** who could rescue the Dn 8:7
Out of **o** of them came a little horn, Dn 8:9
Then I heard a holy **o** speaking, and Dn 8:13
and another holy **o** said to the one who Dn 8:13
holy one said to the **o** who spoke, Dn 8:13
stood before me **o** having the Dn 8:15
of bold face, **o** who understands riddles, Dn 8:23
to the coming of an anointed **o**, Dn 9:25
an anointed **o** shall be cut off and shall Dn 9:26
strong covenant with many for **o** week, Dn 9:27
abominations shall come **o** who makes Dn 9:27
but Michael, **o** of the chief princes, Dn 10:13
o in the likeness of the children of man Dn 10:16
Again **o** having the appearance of a Dn 10:18
but **o** of his princes shall be stronger Dn 11:5
branch from her roots **o** shall arise in Dn 11:7
arise in his place **o** who shall send an Dn 11:20
fathers, or to the **o** beloved by women. Dn 11:37
o on this bank of the stream and one on Dn 12:5
of the stream and **o** on that bank of Dn 12:5
shall appoint for themselves **o** head. Hos 1:11
and no **o** shall rescue her out of my Hos 2:10
Yet let no **o** contend, and let none Hos 4:4
I will carry off, and no **o** shall rescue. Hos 5:14
O like a vulture is over the house of the Hos 8:1
became to them as **o** who eases the Hos 11:4
not a man, the Holy **O** in your midst, Hos 11:9
with God and is faithful to the Holy **O**. Hos 11:12
They do not jostle **o** another; each marches Jl 2:8
the breaches, each **o** straight ahead; Am 4:3
I would send rain on **o** city, and send no Am 4:7
o field would have rain, and the field on Am 4:7
And if ten men remain in **o** house, they Am 6:9
the **o** who anoints him for burial, Am 6:10
on rocks? Does **o** plow there with oxen? Am 6:12
the sword; not **o** of them shall flee away; Am 9:1
flee away; not **o** of them shall escape. Am 9:1
all the nations as **o** shakes with a sieve, Am 9:9
for Jerusalem, you were like **o** of them. Ob 1:11
And they said to **o** another, "Come, let us Jon 1:7
thus they preach—"**o** should not preach Mi 2:6
fig tree, and no **o** shall make them afraid, Mi 4:4
shall come forth for me **o** who is to be Mi 5:2
there is no **o** upright among mankind; Mi 7:2
From you came **o** who plotted evil Na 1:11
fly away; no **o** knows where they are. Na 3:17
O LORD my God, my Holy **O**? Hab 1:12
and the Holy **O** from Mount Paran. Hab 3:3
and there is no **o** else." What a Zep 2:15
their streets so that no **o** walks in them; Zep 3:6
of the LORD and serve him with **o** accord. Zep 3:9
your midst, a mighty **o** who will save; Zep 3:17
You clothe yourselves, but no **o** is warm. Hg 1:6
When **o** came to a heap of twenty Hg 2:16
When **o** came to the wine vat to draw Hg 2:16
every **o** by the sword of his brother. Hg 2:22
Judah, so that no **o** raised his head. Zec 1:21
every **o** of you will invite his neighbor Zec 3:10
o on the right of the bowl and the other Zec 4:3
out according to what is on **o** side, Zec 5:3
show kindness and mercy to **o** another, Zec 7:9
desolate, so that no **o** went to and fro, Zec 7:14
shall do: Speak the truth to **o** another; Zec 8:16
evil in your hearts against **o** another, Zec 8:17
The inhabitants of **o** city shall go to Zec 8:21
And I took two staffs, **o** I named Favor, Zec 11:7
In **o** month I destroyed the three Zec 11:8
are left devour the flesh of **o** another." Zec 11:9
him, as **o** mourns for an only child, Zec 12:10
over him, as **o** weeps over a firstborn. Zec 12:10
And if **o** asks him, 'What are these Zec 13:6
perish, and **o** third shall be left alive. Zec 13:8
fire, and refine them as **o** refines silver, Zec 13:9
so that **o** half of the Mount shall move Zec 14:4
the LORD will be **o** and his name one. Zec 14:9
the LORD will be one and his name **o**. Zec 14:9
the hand of the **o** will be raised against Zec 14:13
Oh that there were **o** among you who Mal 1:10
covenant with him was **o** of life and Mal 2:5
Have we not all **o** Father? Has not one Mal 2:10
one Father? Has not **o** God created us? Mal 2:10
Why then are we faithless to **o** another, Mal 2:10
Did he not make them **o**, with a portion Mal 2:15
And what was the **o** God seeking? Mal 2:15
feared the LORD spoke with **o** another. Mal 3:16
between **o** who serves God and one who Mal 3:18
who serves God and **o** who does not Mal 3:18
"The voice of **o** crying in the wilderness: Mt 3:3
Therefore whoever relaxes **o** of the least Mt 5:19
better that you lose **o** of your members Mt 5:29
better that you lose **o** of your members Mt 5:30
for you cannot make **o** hair white or Mt 5:36
say to you, Do not resist the **o** who is evil. Mt 5:39
And if anyone forces you to go **o** mile, go Mt 5:41
Give to the **o** who begs from you, and do Mt 5:42
do not refuse the **o** who would borrow Mt 5:42
"No **o** can serve two masters, for either Mt 6:24
he will hate the **o** and love the other, Mt 6:24
be devoted to the **o** and despise the other. Mt 6:24
his glory was not arrayed like **o** of these. Mt 6:29
asks receives, and the **o** who seeks finds, Mt 7:8
and to the **o** who knocks it will be opened. Mt 7:8
Or which **o** of you, if his son asks him for Mt 7:9
but the **o** who does the will of my Father Mt 7:21
teaching them as **o** who had authority, Mt 7:29
And I say to **o**, 'Go,' and he goes, and to Mt 8:9
with no **o** in Israel have I found such Mt 8:10
so fierce that no **o** could pass that way. Mt 8:28
No **o** puts a piece of unshrunk cloth on Mt 9:16
them, "See that no **o** knows about it." Mt 9:30
But the **o** who endures to the end will Mt 10:22
When they persecute you in **o** town, Mt 10:23
And not **o** of them will fall to the Mt 10:29
The **o** who receives a prophet because Mt 10:41
and the **o** who receives a righteous Mt 10:41
And whoever gives **o** of these little ones Mt 10:42
to him, "Are you the **o** who is to come, Mt 11:3
And blessed is the **o** who is not offended Mt 11:6
there has arisen no **o** greater than John Mt 11:11
Yet the **o** who is least in the kingdom of Mt 11:11
and no **o** knows the Son except the Mt 11:27
and no **o** knows the Father except the Mt 11:27
"Which **o** of you who has a sheep, Mt 12:11
For to the **o** who has, more will be Mt 13:12
but from the **o** who has not, Mt 13:12
the evil **o** comes and snatches away Mt 13:19
this is the **o** who hears the word and Mt 13:20
this is the **o** who hears the word, Mt 13:22
this is the **o** who hears the word and Mt 13:23
and yields, in **o** case a hundredfold, Mt 13:23
"The **o** who sows the good seed is the Mt 13:37
The weeds are the sons of the evil **o**, Mt 13:38
who, on finding **o** pearl of great value, Mt 13:46
others Jeremiah or **o** of the prophets." Mt 16:14
the disciples to tell no **o** that he was the Mt 16:20
o for you and one for Moses and one for Mt 17:4
one for you and **o** for Moses and one for Mt 17:4
you and one for Moses and **o** for Elijah." Mt 17:4
their eyes, they saw no **o** but Jesus only. Mt 17:8
commanded them, "Tell no **o** the vision, Mt 17:9
"Whoever receives **o** such child in my Mt 18:5
but whoever causes **o** of these little ones Mt 18:6
but woe to the **o** by whom the Mt 18:7
you to enter life with **o** eye than with two Mt 18:9
you do not despise **o** of these little ones. Mt 18:10
a hundred sheep and **o** of them has Mt 18:12
go in search of the **o** that went astray? Mt 18:12
is in heaven that **o** of these little ones Mt 18:14
take **o** or two others along with you, Mt 18:16
o was brought to him who owed him Mt 18:24
he found **o** of his fellow servants who Mt 18:28
Father will do to every **o** of you, Mt 18:35
his wife, and they shall become **o** flesh'? Mt 19:5
So they are no longer two but **o** flesh. Mt 19:6
then did Moses command **o** to give a Mt 19:7
Let the **o** who is able to receive this Mt 19:12
is good? There is only **o** who is good. Mt 19:17
said to him, 'Because no **o** has hired us.' Mt 20:7
saying, 'These last worked only **o** hour, Mt 20:12
But he replied to **o** of them, 'Friend, I Mt 20:13
o at your right hand and one at your Mt 20:21
at your right hand and **o** at your left, Mt 20:21
them, "I also will ask you **o** question, Mt 21:24
tenants took his servants and beat **o**, Mt 21:35
And the **o** who falls on this stone will Mt 21:44
no attention and went off, **o** to his farm, Mt 22:5
And **o** of them, a lawyer, asked him a Mt 22:35
And no **o** was able to answer him a Mt 22:46
be called rabbi, for you have **o** teacher, Mt 23:8
father on earth, for you have **o** Father, Mt 23:9
instructors, for you have **o** instructor, Mt 23:10
not be left here **o** stone upon another Mt 24:2
them, "See that no **o** leads you astray. Mt 24:4
away and betray **o** another and hate Mt 24:10
betray one another and hate **o** another. Mt 24:10
But the **o** who endures to the end will Mt 24:13
Let the **o** who is on the housetop not go Mt 24:17
and let the **o** who is in the field not turn Mt 24:18
from **o** end of heaven to the other. Mt 24:31
that day and hour no **o** knows, Mt 24:36
in the field; **o** will be taken and one left. Mt 24:40
in the field; one will be taken and **o** left. Mt 24:40
at the mill; **o** will be taken and one left. Mt 24:41
at the mill; one will be taken and **o** left. Mt 24:41
To **o** he gave five talents, to another Mt 25:15
talents, to another two, to another **o**, Mt 25:15
who had received the **o** talent went and Mt 25:18
had received the **o** talent came forward, Mt 25:24
But from the **o** who has not, Mt 25:29
will separate people **o** from another as Mt 25:32
as you did it to **o** of the least of these my Mt 25:40
did not do it to **o** of the least of these, Mt 25:45
Then **o** of the twelve, whose name was Mt 26:14
I say to you, **o** of you will betray me." Mt 26:21
began to say to him **o** after another, Mt 26:22
could you not watch with me **o** hour? Mt 26:40
speaking, Judas came, **o** of the twelve, Mt 26:47
saying, "The **o** I will kiss is the man; Mt 26:48
o of those who were with Jesus Mt 26:51
Peter, "Certainly you too are **o** of them, Mt 26:73
the crowd any **o** prisoner whom they Mt 27:15
him, **o** on the right and one on the left. Mt 27:38
him, one on the right and **o** on the left. Mt 27:38
And **o** of them at once ran and took a Mt 27:48
the voice of **o** crying in the wilderness: Mk 1:3
he taught them as **o** who had authority, Mk 1:22
who you are—the Holy **O** of God." Mk 1:24
No **o** sews a piece of unshrunk cloth on Mk 2:21
And no **o** puts new wine into old Mk 2:22
O Sabbath he was going through the Mk 2:23
But no **o** can enter a strong man's Mk 3:27
For to the **o** who has, more will be Mk 4:25
be given, and from the **o** who has not, Mk 4:25
with great fear and said to **o** another, Mk 4:41
And no **o** could bind him anymore, not Mk 5:3
No **o** had the strength to subdue him. Mk 5:4
man, the **o** who had had the legion, Mk 5:15
Then came **o** of the rulers of the Mk 5:22
And he allowed no **o** to follow him Mk 5:37
them that no **o** should know this, Mk 5:43
a prophet, like **o** of the prophets of old." Mk 6:15
And Jesus charged them to tell no **o**. But Mk 7:36
"How can **o** feed these people with bread Mk 8:4
and they had only **o** loaf with them in Mk 8:14
began discussing with **o** another the Mk 8:16
Elijah; and others, **o** of the prophets." Mk 8:28
charged them to tell no **o** about him. Mk 8:30
as no **o** on earth could bleach them. Mk 9:3
o for you and one for Moses and one for Mk 9:5
one for you and **o** for Moses and one for Mk 9:5
you and one for Moses and **o** for Elijah." Mk 9:5
them to tell no **o** what they had seen, Mk 9:9
things are possible for **o** who believes." Mk 9:23
had argued with **o** another about who Mk 9:34
"Whoever receives **o** such child in my Mk 9:37
for no **o** who does a mighty work in my Mk 9:39
For the **o** who is not against us is for us. Mk 9:40
"Whoever causes **o** of these little ones Mk 9:42
kingdom of God with **o** eye than with Mk 9:47

and be at peace with **o** another." Mk 9:50
and they shall become **o** flesh.' So they Mk 10:8
So they are no longer two but **o** flesh. Mk 10:8
good? No **o** is good except God alone. Mk 10:18
and said to him, "You lack **o** thing: Mk 10:21
there is no **o** who has left house or Mk 10:29
o at your right hand and one at your Mk 10:37
at your right hand and **o** at your left, Mk 10:37
a colt tied, on which no **o** has ever sat. Mk 11:2
"May no **o** ever eat fruit from you Mk 11:14
to them, "I will ask you **o** question; Mk 11:29
And they discussed it with **o** another, Mk 11:31
He had still **o** other, a beloved son. Mk 12:6
But those tenants said to **o** another, Mk 12:7
And they brought **o**. And he said to Mk 12:16
And **o** of the scribes came up and Mk 12:28
heard them disputing with **o** another, Mk 12:28
Israel: The Lord our God, the Lord is **o**. Mk 12:29
You have truly said that he is **o**, and Mk 12:32
And after that no **o** dared to ask him Mk 12:34
temple, **o** of his disciples said to him, Mk 13:1
not be left here **o** stone upon another Mk 13:2
to them, "See that no **o** leads you astray. Mk 13:5
But the **o** who endures to the end will Mk 13:13
Let the **o** who is on the housetop not go Mk 13:15
and let the **o** who is in the field not Mk 13:16
that day or that hour, no **o** knows, Mk 13:32
Judas Iscariot, who was **o** of the twelve, Mk 14:10
I say to you, **o** of you will betray me, Mk 14:18
betray me, **o** who is eating with me." Mk 14:18
and to say to him **o** after another, Mk 14:19
He said to them, "It is **o** of the twelve, Mk 14:20
o who is dipping bread into the dish Mk 14:20
asleep? Could you not watch **o** hour? Mk 14:37
speaking, Judas came, **o** of the twelve, Mk 14:43
saying, "The **o** I will kiss is the man. Mk 14:44
But **o** of those who stood by drew his Mk 14:47
o of the servant girls of the high priest Mk 14:66
bystanders, "This man is **o** of them." Mk 14:69
to Peter, "Certainly you are **o** of them, Mk 14:70
to release for them **o** prisoner for whom Mk 15:6
o on his right and one on his left. Mk 15:27
one on his right and **o** on his left. Mk 15:27
the scribes mocked him to **o** another, Mk 15:31
And they were saying to **o** another, Mk 16:3
to her and said, "Greetings, O favored **o**, Lk 1:28
heaven, the shepherds said to **o** another, Lk 2:15
"The voice of **o** crying in the wilderness: Lk 3:4
know who you are—the Holy **O** of God." Lk 4:34
were all amazed and said to **o** another, Lk 4:36
his hands on every **o** of them and healed Lk 4:40
On **o** occasion, while the crowd was Lk 5:1
Getting into **o** of the boats, which was Lk 5:3
While he was in **o** of the cities, there Lk 5:12
And he charged him to tell no **o**, but "go Lk 5:14
On **o** of those days, as he was teaching, Lk 5:17
"No **o** tears a piece from a new garment Lk 5:36
And no **o** puts new wine into old Lk 5:37
And no **o** after drinking old wine desires Lk 5:39
and discussed with **o** another what they Lk 6:11
To **o** who strikes you on the cheek, offer Lk 6:29
and from **o** who takes away your cloak Lk 6:29
and from **o** who takes away your goods Lk 6:30
But the **o** who hears and does not do Lk 6:49
and he is the **o** who built us our Lk 7:5
under me: and I say to **o**, 'Go,' and he goes; Lk 7:8
saying, "Are you the **o** who is to come, Lk 7:19
saying, 'Are you the **o** who is to come, Lk 7:20
And blessed is the **o** who is not offended Lk 7:23
Yet the **o** who is least in the kingdom of Lk 7:28
marketplace and calling to **o** another, Lk 7:32
O of the Pharisees asked him to eat with Lk 7:36
O owed five hundred denarii, and the Lk 7:41
Simon answered, "The **o**, I suppose, for Lk 7:43
"No **o** after lighting a lamp covers it Lk 8:16
then how you hear, for to the **o** who has, Lk 8:18
be given, and from the **o** who has not, Lk 8:18
O day he got into a boat with his Lk 8:22
and they marveled, saying to **o** another, Lk 8:25
he allowed no **o** to enter with him, Lk 8:51
them to tell no **o** what had happened. Lk 8:56
and by others that **o** of the prophets of old Lk 9:8
that **o** of the prophets of old has risen." Lk 9:19
commanded them to tell this to no **o**, Lk 9:21
o for you and one for Moses and one for Lk 9:33
one for you and **o** for Moses and one for Lk 9:33
one for Moses and **o** for Elijah"—not Lk 9:33
saying, "This is my Son, my Chosen **O**; Lk 9:35
silent and told no **o** in those days Lk 9:36
among you all is the **o** who is great." Lk 9:48
for the **o** who is not against you is for Lk 9:50
"No **o** who puts his hand to the plow and Lk 9:62
no sandals, and greet no **o** on the road. Lk 10:4
"The **o** who hears you hears me, and Lk 10:16
and the **o** who rejects you rejects me, Lk 10:16

and the **o** who rejects me rejects him Lk 10:16
and no **o** knows who the Son is except Lk 10:22
"The **o** who showed him mercy." And Lk 10:37
but **o** thing is necessary. Mary has Lk 10:42
finished, **o** of his disciples said to him, Lk 11:1
receives, and the **o** who seeks finds, Lk 11:10
and to the **o** who knocks it will be Lk 11:10
but when **o** stronger than he attacks Lk 11:22
"No **o** after lighting a lamp puts it in a Lk 11:33
O of the lawyers answered him, Lk 11:45
the burdens with **o** of your fingers. Lk 11:46
that they were trampling **o** another, Lk 12:1
And not **o** of them is forgotten before Lk 12:6
but the **o** who denies me before men will Lk 12:9
but the **o** who blasphemes against the Lk 12:10
So is the **o** who lays up treasure for Lk 12:21
glory was not arrayed like **o** of these. Lk 12:27
But the **o** who did not know, and did Lk 12:48
from now on in **o** house there will be Lk 12:52
he was teaching in **o** of the synagogues Lk 13:10
O Sabbath, when he went to dine at the Lk 14:1
When **o** of those who reclined at table Lk 14:15
any **o** of you who does not renounce all Lk 14:33
a hundred sheep, if he has lost **o** of them, Lk 15:4
country, and go after the **o** that is lost, Lk 15:4
joy in heaven over **o** sinner who repents Lk 15:7
ten silver coins, if she loses **o** coin, Lk 15:8
of God over **o** sinner who repents." Lk 15:10
hired himself out to **o** of the citizens of Lk 15:15
pigs ate, and no **o** gave him anything. Lk 15:16
Treat me as **o** of your hired servants."' Lk 15:19
And he called **o** of the servants and Lk 15:26
his master's debtors **o** by one, Lk 16:5
his master's debtors one by **o**, Lk 16:5
"**O** who is faithful in a very little is also Lk 16:10
and **o** who is dishonest in a very little is Lk 16:10
he will hate the **o** and love the other, Lk 16:13
be devoted to the **o** and despise the Lk 16:13
to pass away than for **o** dot of the Law Lk 16:17
but woe to the **o** through whom they Lk 17:1
that he should cause **o** of these little ones Lk 17:2
"Will any **o** of you who has a servant Lk 17:7
Then **o** of them, when he saw that he Lk 17:15
Was no **o** found to return and give Lk 17:18
you will desire to see **o** of the days of the Lk 17:22
up the sky from **o** side to the other, Lk 17:24
day, let the **o** who is on the housetop, Lk 17:31
and likewise let the **o** who is in the field Lk 17:31
in that night there will be two in **o** bed. Lk 17:34
bed. **O** will be taken and the other left. Lk 17:34
O will be taken and the other left." Lk 17:35
o a Pharisee and the other a tax Lk 18:10
but the **o** who humbles himself will be Lk 18:14
good? No **o** is good except God alone. Lk 18:19
he said to him, "**O** thing you still lack. Lk 18:22
there is no **o** who has left house or wife Lk 18:29
and give it to the **o** who has the ten Lk 19:24
be given, but from the **o** who has not, Lk 19:26
colt tied, on which no **o** has ever yet sat. Lk 19:30
will not leave **o** stone upon another Lk 19:44
O day, as Jesus was teaching the people Lk 20:1
And they discussed it with **o** another, Lk 20:5
This **o** also they wounded and cast out. Lk 20:12
not be left here **o** stone upon another Lk 21:6
And they began to question **o** another, Lk 22:23
and the leader as **o** who serves. Lk 22:26
o who reclines at table or one who Lk 22:27
who reclines at table or **o** who serves? Lk 22:27
Is it not the **o** who reclines at table? Lk 22:27
I am among you as the **o** who serves. Lk 22:27
"But now let the **o** who has a Lk 22:36
And let the **o** who has no sword sell his Lk 22:36
has no sword sell his cloak and buy **o**. Lk 22:36
the man called Judas, **o** of the twelve, Lk 22:47
And **o** of them struck the servant of the Lk 22:50
"You also are **o** of them." But Peter Lk 22:58
me this man as **o** who was misleading Lk 23:14
away, they seized **o** Simon of Cyrene, Lk 23:26
o on his right and one on his left. Lk 23:33
one on his right and **o** on his left. Lk 23:33
he is the Christ of God, his Chosen **O**!" Lk 23:35
O of the criminals who were hanged Lk 23:39
where no **o** had ever yet been laid. Lk 23:53
Then **o** of them, named Cleopas, Lk 24:18
that he was the **o** to redeem Israel. Lk 24:21
No **o** has ever seen God; the only God, Jn 1:18
"I am the voice of **o** crying out in the Jn 1:23
but among you stands **o** you do not Jn 1:26
O of the two who heard John speak and Jn 1:40
and needed no **o** to bear witness about Jn 2:25
for no **o** can do these signs that you do Jn 3:2
unless **o** is born again he cannot see the Jn 3:3
unless **o** is born of water and the Spirit, Jn 3:5
No **o** has ascended into heaven except he Jn 3:13
cannot receive even **o** thing unless it Jn 3:27

The **o** who has the bride is the Jn 3:29
heard, yet no **o** receives his testimony. Jn 3:32
and the **o** you now have is not your Jn 4:18
was talking with a woman, but no **o** said, Jn 4:27
So the disciples said to **o** another, "Has Jn 4:33
Already the **o** who reaps is receiving Jn 4:36
holds true, '**O** sows and another reaps.' Jn 4:37
O man was there who had been an invalid Jn 5:5
I have no **o** to put me into the pool when Jn 5:7
The Father judges no **o**, but has given all Jn 5:22
do not believe the **o** whom he has sent. Jn 5:38
you receive glory from **o** another and do Jn 5:44
There is **o** who accuses you: Moses, on Jn 5:45
O of his disciples, Andrew, Simon Peter's Jn 6:8
that there had been only **o** boat there, Jn 6:22
No **o** can come to me unless the Father Jn 6:44
so that **o** may eat of it and not die. Jn 6:50
I told you that no **o** can come to me Jn 6:65
to know, that you are the Holy **O** of God." Jn 6:69
the Twelve? And yet **o** of you is a devil." Jn 6:70
of Simon Iscariot, for he, **o** of the Twelve, Jn 6:71
For no **o** works in secret if he seeks to be Jn 7:4
fear of the Jews no **o** spoke openly of him. Jn 7:13
The **o** who speaks on his own authority Jn 7:18
but the **o** who seeks the glory of him who Jn 7:18
Jesus answered them, "I did **o** deed, and Jn 7:21
no **o** will know where he comes from." Jn 7:27
arrest him, but no **o** laid a hand on him, Jn 7:30
The Jews said to **o** another, "Where does Jn 7:35
arrest him, but no **o** laid hands on him. Jn 7:44
"No **o** ever spoke like this man!" Jn 7:46
to him before, and who was **o** of them, Jn 7:50
they heard it, they went away **o** by one, Jn 8:9
they heard it, they went away one by **o**, Jn 8:9
are they? Has no **o** condemned you?" Jn 8:10
She said, "No **o**, Lord." And Jesus said, Jn 8:11
judge according to the flesh; I judge no **o**. Jn 8:15
I am the **o** who bears witness about Jn 8:18
in the temple; but no **o** arrested him, Jn 8:20
We have **o** Father—even God." Jn 8:41
Which **o** of you convicts me of sin? If I Jn 8:46
there is **O** who seeks it, and he is the Jn 8:50
night is coming, when no **o** can work. Jn 9:4
O thing I do know, that though I was Jn 9:25
So there will be **o** flock, one shepherd. Jn 10:16
So there will be one flock, **o** shepherd. Jn 10:16
No **o** takes it from me, but I lay it down Jn 10:18
not the words of **o** who is oppressed by Jn 10:21
and no **o** will snatch them out of my Jn 10:28
and no **o** is able to snatch them out of Jn 10:29
I and the Father are **o**." Jn 10:30
But **o** of them, Caiaphas, who was high Jn 11:49
better for you that **o** man should die for Jn 11:50
also to gather into **o** the children of God Jn 11:52
Jesus and saying to **o** another as they Jn 11:56
and Lazarus was **o** of those reclining Jn 12:2
o of his disciples (he who was about to Jn 12:4
So the Pharisees said to **o** another, "You Jn 12:19
The **o** who walks in the darkness does Jn 12:35
The **o** who rejects me and does not Jn 12:48
"The **o** who has bathed does not need to Jn 13:10
you are clean, but not every **o** of you." Jn 13:10
you also ought to wash **o** another's feet. Jn 13:14
greater than the **o** who sent him. Jn 13:16
whoever receives the **o** I send receives Jn 13:20
receives me receives the **o** who sent me." Jn 13:20
I say to you, **o** of you will betray me." Jn 13:21
The disciples looked at **o** another, Jn 13:22
O of his disciples, whom Jesus loved, Jn 13:23
Now no **o** at the table knew why he said Jn 13:28
I give to you, that you love **o** another: Jn 13:34
you, you also are to love **o** another. Jn 13:34
if you have love for **o** another." Jn 13:35
No **o** comes to the Father except through Jn 14:6
that you love **o** another as I have loved Jn 15:12
Greater love has no **o** than this, that Jn 15:13
you, so that you will love **o** another. Jn 15:17
them the works that no **o** else did, Jn 15:24
some of his disciples said to **o** another, Jn 16:17
and no **o** will take your joy from you. Jn 16:22
you have given me, that they may be **o**, Jn 17:11
that they may be one, even as we are **o**. Jn 17:11
and not **o** of them has been lost except Jn 17:12
but that you keep them from the evil **o**. Jn 17:15
that they may all be **o**, just as you, Jn 17:21
that they may be **o** even as we are one, Jn 17:22
that they may be one even as we are **o**, Jn 17:22
me, that they may become perfectly **o**, Jn 17:23
whom you gave me I have lost not **o**." Jn 18:9
be expedient that **o** man should die Jn 18:14
"You also are not **o** of this man's Jn 18:17
o of the officers standing by struck Jn 18:22
him, "You also are not **o** of his disciples, Jn 18:25
O of the servants of the high priest, a Jn 18:26
that I should release **o** man for you at Jn 18:39

with him two others, **o** on either side,	Jn 19:18
into four parts, **o** part for each soldier;	Jn 19:23
woven in **o** piece from top to bottom,	Jn 19:23
so they said to **o** another, "Let us not	Jn 19:24
But **o** of the soldiers pierced his side	Jn 19:34
"Not **o** of his bones will be broken."	Jn 19:36
tomb in which no **o** had yet been laid.	Jn 19:41
other disciple, the **o** whom Jesus loved,	Jn 20:2
lain, **o** at the head and one at the feet.	Jn 20:12
lain, one at the head and **o** at the feet.	Jn 20:12
Now Thomas, **o** of the Twelve, called	Jn 20:24
the **o** who had been reclining at table	Jn 21:20
Were every **o** of them to be written, I	Jn 21:25
All these with **o** accord were devoting	Acts 1:14
and let there be no **o** to dwell in it';	Acts 1:20
So **o** of the men who have	Acts 1:21
up from us—**o** of these men must	Acts 1:22
show which **o** of these two you have	Acts 1:24
arrived, they were all together in **o** place.	Acts 2:1
to them and rested on each **o** of them.	Acts 2:3
because each **o** was hearing them speak	Acts 2:6
and perplexed, saying to **o** another,	Acts 2:12
or let your Holy **O** see corruption.	Acts 2:27
that he would set **o** of his descendants	Acts 2:30
and be baptized every **o** of you in the	Acts 2:38
recognized him as the **o** who sat at the	Acts 3:10
you denied the Holy and Righteous **O**,	Acts 3:14
you by turning every **o** of you from	Acts 3:26
And there is salvation in no **o** else, for	Acts 4:12
they conferred with **o** another,	Acts 4:15
who believed were of **o** heart and soul,	Acts 4:32
and no **o** said that any of the things	Acts 4:32
we opened them we found no **o** inside."	Acts 5:23
And seeing **o** of them being wronged,	Acts 7:24
This is the **o** who was in the	Acts 7:38
the coming of the Righteous **O**,	Acts 7:52
the crowds with **o** accord paid attention	Acts 8:6
hearing the voice but seeing no **o**.	Acts 9:7
in Joppa for many days with **o** Simon,	Acts 9:43
to Joppa and bring **o** Simon who is	Acts 10:5
He is lodging with **o** Simon, a tanner,	Acts 10:6
said, "I am the **o** you are looking for.	Acts 10:21
that he is the **o** appointed by God to	Acts 10:42
speaking the word to no **o** except Jews.	Acts 11:19
And **o** of them named Agabus stood	Acts 11:28
they went out and went along **o** street,	Acts 12:10
and they came to him with **o** accord,	Acts 12:20
No, but behold, after me **o** is coming,	Acts 13:25
not let your Holy **O** see corruption.'	Acts 13:35
not believe, even if **o** tells it to you.'"	Acts 13:41
good to us, having come to **o** accord,	Acts 15:25
take with them **o** who had withdrawn	Acts 15:38
O who heard us was a woman named	Acts 16:14
he made from **o** man every nation	Acts 17:26
is actually not far from each **o** of us,	Acts 17:27
Lord said to Paul **o** night in a vision,	Acts 18:9
and no **o** will attack you to harm	Acts 18:10
departed and went from **o** place to the	Acts 18:23
to believe in the **o** who was to come	Acts 19:4
Now some cried out **o** thing, some	Acts 19:32
hours they all cried out with **o** voice,	Acts 19:34
bring charges against **o** another.	Acts 19:38
and said farewell to **o** another. Then	Acts 21:6
and stayed with them for **o** day.	Acts 21:7
the evangelist, who was **o** of the seven,	Acts 21:8
he related **o** by one the things that	Acts 21:19
he related one by **o** the things that	Acts 21:19
offering presented for each **o** of them.	Acts 21:26
in the crowd were shouting **o** thing,	Acts 21:34
the voice of the **o** who was speaking to	Acts 22:9
"And **o** Ananias, a devout man	Acts 22:12
to see the Righteous **O** and to hear a	Acts 22:14
know that in **o** synagogue after	Acts 22:19
Paul perceived that **o** part were	Acts 23:6
Paul called **o** of the centurions and	Acts 23:17
"Tell no **o** that you have informed me	Acts 23:22
elders and a spokesman, **o** Tertullus.	Acts 24:1
o who stirs up riots among all the Jews	Acts 24:5
other than this **o** thing that I cried	Acts 24:21
me, no **o** can give me up to them.	Acts 25:11
withdrawn, they said to **o** another,	Acts 26:31
from his hand, they said to **o** another,	Acts 28:4
And after **o** day a south wind sprang	Acts 28:13
after Paul had made **o** statement:	Acts 28:25
consumed with passion for **o** another,	Rom 1:27
O man, every **o** of you who judges.	Rom 2:1
will render to each **o** according to his	Rom 2:6
You who say that **o** must not commit	Rom 2:22
For no **o** is a Jew who is merely one	Rom 2:28
is a Jew who is merely **o** outwardly,	Rom 2:28
But a Jew is **o** inwardly, and	Rom 2:29
God be true though every **o** were a liar,	Rom 3:4
written: "None is righteous, no, not **o**;	Rom 3:10
no **o** understands; no one seeks for	Rom 3:11
one understands; no **o** seeks for God.	Rom 3:11
no **o** does good, not even one."	Rom 3:12
no one does good, not even **o**."	Rom 3:12
the justifier of the **o** who has faith in	Rom 3:26
For we hold that **o** is justified by faith	Rom 3:28
since God is **o**. He will justify the	Rom 3:30
Now to the **o** who works, his wages are	Rom 4:4
And to the **o** who does not work but	Rom 4:5
the blessing of the **o** to whom God	Rom 4:6
but also to the **o** who shares the faith	Rom 4:16
For **o** will scarcely die for a righteous	Rom 5:7
for a good person **o** would dare even to	Rom 5:7
came into the world through **o** man,	Rom 5:12
was a type of the **o** who was to come.	Rom 5:14
many died through **o** man's trespass,	Rom 5:15
the grace of that **o** man Jesus Christ	Rom 5:15
not like the result of that **o** man's sin.	Rom 5:16
judgment following **o** trespass	Rom 5:16
If, because of **o** man's trespass, death	Rom 5:17
death reigned through that **o** man,	Rom 5:17
in life through the **o** man Jesus Christ.	Rom 5:17
as **o** trespass led to condemnation for	Rom 5:18
so **o** act of righteousness leads to	Rom 5:18
For as by the **o** man's disobedience the	Rom 5:19
so by the **o** man's obedience the many	Rom 5:19
For **o** who has died has been set free	Rom 6:7
are slaves of the **o** whom you obey,	Rom 6:16
Christ Jesus is the **o** who died—more	Rom 8:34
had conceived children by **o** man,	Rom 9:10
of the same lump **o** vessel for honored	Rom 9:21
For with the heart **o** believes and is	Rom 10:10
with the mouth **o** confesses and is	Rom 10:10
as you were at **o** time disobedient to	Rom 11:30
For as in **o** body we have many	Rom 12:4
though many, are **o** body in Christ,	Rom 12:5
individually members **o** of another.	Rom 12:5
the **o** who teaches, in his teaching;	Rom 12:7
the **o** who exhorts, in his exhortation;	Rom 12:8
the **o** who contributes, in generosity;	Rom 12:8
generosity; the **o** who leads, with zeal;	Rom 12:8
the **o** who does acts of mercy, with	Rom 12:8
Love **o** another with brotherly	Rom 12:10
Outdo **o** another in showing honor.	Rom 12:10
Live in harmony with **o** another. Do	Rom 12:16
Repay no **o** evil for evil, but give	Rom 12:17
no fear of the **o** who is in authority?	Rom 13:3
Therefore **o** must be in subjection, not	Rom 13:5
Owe no **o** anything, except to love each	Rom 13:8
for the **o** who loves another has	Rom 13:8
As for the **o** who is weak in faith,	Rom 14:1
O person believes he may eat	Rom 14:2
Let not the **o** who eats despise the one	Rom 14:3
who eats despise the **o** who abstains,	Rom 14:3
and let not the **o** who abstains pass	Rom 14:3
pass judgment on the **o** who eats,	Rom 14:3
O person esteems one day as better	Rom 14:5
One person esteems **o** day as better	Rom 14:5
Each **o** should be fully convinced in	Rom 14:5
The **o** who observes the day, observes	Rom 14:6
The **o** who eats, eats in honor of the	Rom 14:6
to God, while the **o** who abstains,	Rom 14:6
pass judgment on **o** another any	Rom 14:13
do not destroy the **o** for whom Christ	Rom 14:15
Blessed is the **o** who has no reason to	Rom 14:22
live in such harmony with **o** another,	Rom 15:5
you may with **o** voice glorify the	Rom 15:6
Therefore welcome **o** another as	Rom 15:7
and able to instruct **o** another.	Rom 15:14
Greet **o** another with a holy kiss. All	Rom 16:16
I mean is that each **o** of you says,	1 Cor 1:12
so that no **o** may say that you were	1 Cor 1:15
Where is the **o** who is wise? Where is	1 Cor 1:20
as it is written, "Let the **o** who boasts,	1 Cor 1:31
So also no **o** comprehends the	1 Cor 2:11
but is himself to be judged by no **o**.	1 Cor 2:15
For when **o** says, "I follow Paul," and	1 Cor 3:4
who plants and he who waters are **o**,	1 Cor 3:8
Let each **o** take care how he builds	1 Cor 3:10
For no **o** can lay a foundation other	1 Cor 3:11
what sort of work each **o** has done.	1 Cor 3:13
Let no **o** deceive himself. If anyone	1 Cor 3:18
So let no **o** boast in men. For all	1 Cor 3:21
This is how **o** should regard us, as	1 Cor 4:1
Then each **o** will receive his	1 Cor 4:5
puffed up in favor of **o** against another.	1 Cor 4:6
judgment on the **o** who did such	1 Cor 5:3
—not even to eat with such a **o**.	1 Cor 5:11
When **o** of you has a grievance	1 Cor 6:1
that there is no **o** among you wise	1 Cor 6:5
at all with **o** another is already	1 Cor 6:7
God will destroy both **o** and the other.	1 Cor 6:13
a prostitute becomes **o** body with	1 Cor 6:16
"The two will become **o** flesh."	1 Cor 6:16
the Lord becomes **o** spirit with him.	1 Cor 6:17
Do not deprive **o** another, except	1 Cor 7:5
God, **o** of one kind and one of another.	1 Cor 7:7
God, one of **o** kind and one of another.	1 Cor 7:7
God, one of one kind and **o** of another.	1 Cor 7:7
Each **o** should remain in the	1 Cor 7:20
give my judgment as **o** who by the	1 Cor 7:25
and that "there is no God but **o**."	1 Cor 8:4
yet for us there is **o** God, the Father,	1 Cor 8:6
and for whom we exist, and **o** Lord,	1 Cor 8:6
law I became as **o** under the law	1 Cor 9:20
law I became as **o** outside the law	1 Cor 9:21
but only **o** receives the prize?	1 Cor 9:24
I do not box as **o** beating the air.	1 Cor 9:26
Because there is **o** bread, we who are	1 Cor 10:17
bread, we who are many are **o** body,	1 Cor 10:17
for we all partake of the **o** bread.	1 Cor 10:17
Let no **o** seek his own good, but the	1 Cor 10:24
If **o** of the unbelievers invites you to	1 Cor 10:27
the sake of the **o** who informed you,	1 Cor 10:28
each **o** goes ahead with his own	1 Cor 11:21
O goes hungry, another gets drunk.	1 Cor 11:21
together to eat, wait for **o** another—	1 Cor 11:33
understand that no **o** speaking in the	1 Cor 12:3
is accursed!" and no **o** can say "Jesus	1 Cor 12:3
To **o** is given through the Spirit the	1 Cor 12:8
gifts of healing by the **o** Spirit,	1 Cor 12:9
are empowered by **o** and the same	1 Cor 12:11
apportions to each **o** individually as	1 Cor 12:11
as the body is **o** and has many	1 Cor 12:12
the body, though many, are **o** body,	1 Cor 12:12
For in **o** Spirit we were all baptized	1 Cor 12:13
were all baptized into **o** body—Jews	1 Cor 12:13
all were made to drink of **o** Spirit.	1 Cor 12:13
does not consist of **o** member but of	1 Cor 12:14
in the body, each **o** of them,	1 Cor 12:18
is, there are many parts, yet **o** body.	1 Cor 12:20
have the same care for **o** another.	1 Cor 12:25
If **o** member suffers, all suffer	1 Cor 12:26
if **o** member is honored, all rejoice	1 Cor 12:26
For **o** who speaks in a tongue speaks	1 Cor 14:2
but to God; for no **o** understands him,	1 Cor 14:2
the **o** who prophesies speaks to people	1 Cor 14:3
The **o** who speaks in a tongue builds	1 Cor 14:4
but the **o** who prophesies builds up	1 Cor 14:4
The **o** who prophesies is greater than	1 Cor 14:5
is greater than the **o** who speaks in	1 Cor 14:5
o who speaks in a tongue should	1 Cor 14:13
come together, each **o** has a hymn,	1 Cor 14:26
But if there is no **o** to interpret, let	1 Cor 14:28
For you can all prophesy **o** by one,	1 Cor 14:31
For you can all prophesy one by **o**,	1 Cor 14:31
than five hundred brothers at **o** time,	1 Cor 15:6
Last of all, as to **o** untimely born, he	1 Cor 15:8
but there is **o** kind for humans,	1 Cor 15:39
glory of the heavenly is of **o** kind,	1 Cor 15:40
There is **o** glory of the sun, and	1 Cor 15:41
So let no **o** despise him. Help him on	1 Cor 16:11
Greet **o** another with a holy kiss.	1 Cor 16:20
me glad but the **o** whom I have	2 Cor 2:2
For such a **o**, this punishment by the	2 Cor 2:6
to **o** a fragrance from death to death,	2 Cor 2:16
But when **o** turns to the Lord, the veil	2 Cor 3:16
same image from **o** degree of glory	2 Cor 3:18
so that each **o** may receive what is	2 Cor 5:10
that **o** has died for all, therefore all	2 Cor 5:14
we regard no **o** according to the flesh.	2 Cor 5:16
We have wronged no **o**, we have	2 Cor 7:2
no one, we have corrupted no **o**,	2 Cor 7:2
one, we have taken advantage of no **o**.	2 Cor 7:2
the sake of the **o** who did the wrong,	2 Cor 7:12
the sake of the **o** who suffered the	2 Cor 7:12
course so that no **o** should blame us	2 Cor 8:20
Each **o** must give as he has made up	2 Cor 9:7
themselves by **o** another and	2 Cor 10:12
compare themselves with **o** another,	2 Cor 10:12
"Let the **o** who boasts, boast in the	2 Cor 10:17
is not the **o** who commends himself	2 Cor 10:18
but the **o** whom the Lord	2 Cor 10:18
you, for I betrothed you to **o** husband,	2 Cor 11:2
Jesus than the **o** we proclaimed,	2 Cor 11:4
spirit from the **o** you received,	2 Cor 11:4
gospel from the **o** you accepted,	2 Cor 11:4
I repeat, let no **o** think me foolish.	2 Cor 11:16
I am a better **o**—I am talking like a	2 Cor 11:23
of the Jews the forty lashes less **o**.	2 Cor 11:24
so that no **o** may think more of me	2 Cor 12:6
for restoration, comfort **o** another,	2 Cor 13:11
one another, agree with **o** another,	2 Cor 13:11
Greet **o** another with a holy kiss.	2 Cor 13:12
not that there is another **o**, but there are	Gal 1:7
gospel contrary to the **o** we preached to	Gal 1:8
a gospel contrary to the **o** you received,	Gal 1:9
works of the law no **o** will be justified.	Gal 2:16
is evident that no **o** is justified before	Gal 3:11
rather "The **o** who does them shall live	Gal 3:12
no **o** annuls it or adds to it once it has	Gal 3:15
referring to many, but referring to **o**,	Gal 3:16

an intermediary implies more than **o**, Gal 3:20
implies more than one, but God is **o**. Gal 3:20
female, for you are all **o** in Christ Jesus. Gal 3:28
o by a slave woman and one by a free Gal 4:22
a slave woman and a **o** by a free woman. Gal 4:22
O is from Mount Sinai, bearing Gal 4:24
"Rejoice, O barren **o** who does not bear; Gal 4:27
children of the desolate **o** will be more Gal 4:27
than those of the **o** who has a Gal 4:27
and the **o** who is troubling you will Gal 5:10
flesh, but through love serve **o** another. Gal 5:13
For the whole law is fulfilled in **o** word: Gal 5:14
But if you bite and devour **o** another, Gal 5:15
you are not consumed by **o** another. Gal 5:15
conceited, provoking **o** another, Gal 5:26
one another, envying **o** another. Gal 5:26
Bear **o** another's burdens, and so fulfill Gal 6:2
But let each **o** test his own work, and Gal 6:4
O who is taught the word must share all Gal 6:6
all good things with the **o** who teaches. Gal 6:6
God is not mocked, for whatever **o** sows, Gal 6:7
For the **o** who sows to his own flesh will Gal 6:8
but the **o** who sows to the Spirit will from Gal 6:8
From now on let no **o** cause me trouble, Gal 6:17
in this age but also in the **o** to come. Eph 1:21
result of works, so that no **o** may boast. Eph 2:9
remember that at **o** time you Gentiles Eph 2:11
has made us both **o** and has broken Eph 2:14
might create in himself **o** new man in Eph 2:15
both to God in **o** body through the Eph 2:16
both have access in **o** Spirit to the Eph 2:18
patience, bearing with **o** another in love, Eph 4:2
There is **o** body and one Spirit—just as Eph 4:4
There is one body and **o** Spirit—just as Eph 4:4
were called to the **o** hope that belongs to Eph 4:4
o Lord, one faith, one baptism, Eph 4:5
one Lord, **o** faith, one baptism, Eph 4:5
one Lord, one faith, **o** baptism, Eph 4:5
o God and Father of all, who is over all Eph 4:6
was given to each **o** of us according to Eph 4:7
descended is the **o** who also ascended Eph 4:10
let each **o** of you speak the truth with Eph 4:25
for we are members **o** of another. Eph 4:25
Be kind to **o** another, tenderhearted, Eph 4:32
tenderhearted, forgiving **o** another, Eph 4:32
Let no **o** deceive you with empty words, Eph 5:6
for at **o** time you were darkness, but now Eph 5:8
addressing **o** another in psalms and Eph 5:19
submitting to **o** another out of Eph 5:21
For no **o** ever hated his own flesh, but Eph 5:29
wife, and the two shall become **o** flesh." Eph 5:31
let each **o** of you love his wife as Eph 5:33
all the flaming darts of the evil **o**; Eph 6:16
that you are standing firm in **o** spirit, Phil 1:27
with **o** mind striving side by side for Phil 1:27
love, being in full accord and of **o** mind. Phil 2:2
For I have no **o** like him, who will be Phil 2:20
But **o** thing I do: forgetting what lies Phil 3:13
in order that no **o** may delude you with Col 2:4
See to it that no **o** takes you captive by Col 2:8
Therefore let no **o** pass judgment on Col 2:16
Let no **o** disqualify you, insisting on Col 2:18
Do not lie to **o** another, seeing that you Col 3:9
bearing with **o** another and, if one has a Col 3:13
if **o** has a complaint against another, Col 3:13
which indeed you were called in **o** body. Col 3:15
and admonishing **o** another in Col 3:16
and beloved brother, who is **o** of you. Col 4:9
Epaphras, who is **o** of you, a servant of Col 4:12
we exhorted each **o** of you and 1 Thes 2:12
that no **o** be moved by these 1 Thes 3:3
abound in love for **o** another and for 1 Thes 3:12
that each **o** of you know how to 1 Thes 4:4
that no **o** transgress and wrong his 1 Thes 4:6
been taught by God to love **o** another, 1 Thes 4:9
outsiders and be dependent on no **o**. 1 Thes 4:12
Therefore encourage **o** another with 1 Thes 4:18
Therefore encourage **o** another and 1 Thes 5:11
one another and build **o** another up, 1 Thes 5:11
See that no **o** repays anyone evil for 1 Thes 5:15
to do good to **o** another and to 1 Thes 5:15
and the love of every **o** of you for one 2 Thes 1:3
of you for **o** another is increasing. 2 Thes 1:3
Let no **o** deceive you in any way. For 2 Thes 2:3
then the lawless **o** will be revealed, 2 Thes 2:8
coming of the lawless **o** is by the 2 Thes 2:9
you and guard you against the evil **o**. 2 Thes 3:3
the law is good, if **o** uses it lawfully, 1 Tm 1:8
For there is **o** God, and there is one 1 Tm 2:5
and there is **o** mediator between God 1 Tm 2:5
above reproach, the husband of **o** wife, 1 Tm 3:2
each be the husband of **o** wife, 1 Tm 3:12
may know how **o** ought to behave 1 Tm 3:15
Let no **o** despise you for your youth, 1 Tm 4:12
having been the wife of **o** husband, 1 Tm 5:9

whom no **o** has ever seen or can see. 1 Tm 6:16
aim is to please the **o** who enlisted him. 2 Tm 2:4
present yourself to God as **o** approved, 2 Tm 2:15
my first defense no **o** came to stand 2 Tm 4:16
is above reproach, the husband of **o** wife, Ti 1:6
O of the Cretans, a prophet of their own, Ti 1:12
all authority. Let no **o** disregard you. Ti 2:15
to speak evil of no **o**, to avoid quarreling, Ti 3:2
hated by others and hating **o** another. Ti 3:3
who are sanctified all have **o** origin. Heb 2:11
he might destroy the **o** who has the Heb 2:14
But exhort **o** another every day, as long Heb 3:13
so that no **o** may fall by the same sort Heb 4:11
but **o** who in every respect has been Heb 4:15
And no **o** takes this honor for himself, Heb 5:4
And we desire each **o** of you to show the Heb 6:11
since he had no **o** greater by whom to Heb 6:13
In the **o** case tithes are received by Heb 7:8
by **o** of whom it is testified that he lives. Heb 7:8
O might even say that Levi himself, who Heb 7:9
rather than **o** named after the order of Heb 7:11
For the **o** of whom these things are Heb 7:13
from which no **o** has ever served at the Heb 7:13
On the **o** hand, a former Heb 7:18
but this **o** was made a priest with an Heb 7:21
with an oath by the **o** who said to him: Heb 7:21
o who is seated at the right hand of the Heb 8:1
each **o** his neighbor and each one his Heb 8:11
his neighbor and each **o** his brother, Heb 8:11
covenant, he makes the first **o** obsolete. Heb 8:13
the death of the **o** who made it must be Heb 9:16
force as long as the **o** who made it is Heb 9:17
how to stir up **o** another to love and Heb 10:24
of some, but encouraging **o** another, Heb 10:25
be deserved by the **o** who has spurned Heb 10:29
a better possession and an abiding **o**. Heb 10:34
and the coming **o** will come and will Heb 10:37
but my righteous **o** shall live by faith, Heb 10:38
Therefore from **o** man, and him as Heb 11:12
a better country, that is, a heavenly **o**. Heb 11:16
For the Lord disciplines the **o** he loves, Heb 12:6
without which no **o** will see the Heb 12:14
See to it that no **o** fails to obtain the Heb 12:15
that no **o** is sexually immoral or Heb 12:16
for the **o** who doubts is like a wave of the Jas 1:6
Let no **o** say when he is tempted, "I am Jas 1:13
with evil, and he himself tempts no **o**. Jas 1:13
But the **o** who looks into the perfect law, Jas 1:25
pay attention to the **o** who wears the fine Jas 2:3
law but fails in **o** point has become Jas 2:10
is without mercy to **o** who has shown no Jas 2:13
and **o** of you says to them, "Go in peace, Jas 2:16
You believe that God is **o**; you do well. Jas 2:19
Do not speak evil against **o** another, Jas 4:11
The **o** who speaks against a brother or Jas 4:11
There is only **o** lawgiver and judge, he Jas 4:12
Do not grumble against **o** another, Jas 5:9
of faith will save the **o** who is sick, Jas 5:15
confess your sins to **o** another and pray Jas 5:16
to one another and pray for **o** another, Jas 5:16
love **o** another earnestly from a pure 1 Pt 1:22
o endures sorrows while suffering 1 Pt 2:19
all, keep loving **o** another earnestly, 1 Pt 4:8
Show hospitality to **o** another without 1 Pt 4:9
received a gift, use it to serve **o** another, 1 Pt 4:10
speaks, as **o** who speaks oracles of God; 1 Pt 4:11
as **o** who serves by the strength that 1 Pt 4:11
of you, with humility toward **o** another, 1 Pt 5:5
Greet **o** another with the kiss of love. 1 Pt 5:14
But do not overlook this **o** fact, beloved, 2 Pt 3:8
that with the Lord **o** day is as a thousand 2 Pt 3:8
years, and a thousand years as **o** day. 2 Pt 3:8
light, we have fellowship with **o** another, 1 Jn 1:7
because you have overcome the evil **o**. 1 Jn 2:13
you, and you have overcome the evil **o**. 1 Jn 2:14
you have been anointed by the Holy **O**, 1 Jn 2:20
No **o** who denies the Son has the 1 Jn 2:23
No **o** who abides in him keeps on 1 Jn 3:6
no **o** who keeps on sinning has either 1 Jn 3:6
Little children, let no **o** deceive you. 1 Jn 3:7
No **o** born of God makes a practice of 1 Jn 3:9
nor is the **o** who does not love his 1 Jn 3:10
that we should love **o** another. 1 Jn 3:11
was of the evil **o** and murdered his 1 Jn 3:12
Son Jesus Christ and love **o** another, 1 Jn 3:23
Beloved, let us love **o** another, for love is 1 Jn 4:7
us, we also ought to love **o** another. 1 Jn 4:11
No **o** has ever seen God; if we love one 1 Jn 4:12
if we love **o** another, God abides in us 1 Jn 4:12
the world except the **o** who believes that 1 Jn 5:5
And the Spirit is the **o** who testifies, 1 Jn 5:6
I do not say that **o** should pray for that. 1 Jn 5:16
him, and the evil **o** does not touch him. 1 Jn 5:18
world lies in the power of the evil **o**. 1 Jn 5:19
but the **o** we have had from the 2 Jn 1:5

the beginning—that we love **o** another. 2 Jn 1:5
Such a **o** is the deceiver and the 2 Jn 1:7
you. Greet the friends, every **o** of them. 3 Jn 1:15
Blessed is the **o** who reads aloud the words Rv 1:3
midst of the lampstands **o** like a son of Rv 1:13
and the living **o**. I died, and behold I am Rv 1:18
To the **o** who conquers I will grant to eat Rv 2:7
The **o** who conquers will not be hurt by Rv 2:11
To the **o** who conquers I will give some Rv 2:17
the stone that no **o** knows except the one Rv 2:17
one knows except the **o** who receives it.' Rv 2:17
The **o** who conquers and who keeps my Rv 2:26
The **o** who conquers will be clothed thus Rv 3:5
'The words of the holy **o**, the true one, who Rv 3:7
'The words of the holy one, the true **o**, who Rv 3:7
of David, who opens and no **o** will shut, Rv 3:7
one will shut, who shuts and no **o** opens. Rv 3:7
an open door, which no **o** is able to shut. Rv 3:8
have, so that no **o** may seize your crown. Rv 3:11
The **o** who conquers, I will make him a Rv 3:12
The **o** who conquers, I will grant him to Rv 3:21
in heaven, with **o** seated on the throne. Rv 4:2
And no **o** in heaven or on earth or under Rv 5:3
loudly because no **o** was found worthy Rv 5:4
And **o** of the elders said to me, "Weep no Rv 5:5
when the Lamb opened **o** of the seven Rv 6:1
and I heard **o** of the four living creatures Rv 6:1
earth, so that men should slay **o** another, Rv 6:4
great multitude that no **o** could number, Rv 7:9
Then **o** of the elders addressed me, Rv 7:13
o who is to rule all the nations with a rod Rv 12:5
O of its heads seemed to have a mortal Rv 13:3
so that no **o** can buy or sell unless he Rv 13:17
let the **o** who has understanding Rv 13:18
No **o** could learn that song except the Rv 14:3
and seated on the cloud **o** like a son of Rv 14:14
a loud voice to the **o** who had the sharp Rv 14:18
And **o** of the four living creatures gave to Rv 15:7
and no **o** could enter the sanctuary until Rv 15:8
of the waters say, "Just are you, O Holy **O**, Rv 16:5
thief! Blessed is the **o** who stays awake, Rv 16:15
about **o** hundred pounds each, Rv 16:21
Then **o** of the seven angels who had the Rv 17:1
kings, five of whom have fallen, **o** is, Rv 17:10
to receive authority as kings for **o** hour, Rv 17:12
These are of **o** mind and hand over Rv 17:13
by being of **o** mind and handing Rv 17:17
since no **o** buys their cargo anymore, Rv 18:11
The **o** sitting on it is called Faithful Rv 19:11
written that no **o** knows but himself. Rv 19:12
and holy is the **o** who shares in the Rv 20:6
and they were judged, each **o** of them, Rv 20:13
The **o** who conquers will have this Rv 21:7
Then came **o** of the seven angels who Rv 21:9
And the **o** who spoke with me had a Rv 21:15
Blessed is the **o** who keeps the words of Rv 22:7
am the **o** who heard and saw these Rv 22:8
"Come." And let the **o** who hears say, Rv 22:17
"Come." And let the **o** who is thirsty Rv 22:17
let the **o** who desires take the water of Rv 22:17

ONE'S (16)
is in the skin of **o** body a boil and it Lv 13:18
for that is to make naked **o** relative; Lv 20:19
which were on **o** left at the gate of the 2 Kgs 23:8
And he departed with no **o** regret. 2 Chr 21:20
of a warrior are the children of **o** youth. Ps 127:4
nor is it glorious to seek **o** own glory. Prv 25:27
wind or to grasp oil in **o** right hand. Prv 27:16
O pride will bring him low, but he Prv 29:23
day nor night do **o** eyes see sleep, Eccl 8:16
And when **o** relative, the one who Am 6:10
it lawful to divorce **o** wife for any Mt 19:3
and to love **o** neighbor as oneself, Mk 12:33
for **o** life does not consist in the Lk 12:15
I coveted no **o** silver or gold or Acts 20:33
each **o** work will become manifest, 1 Cor 3:13
impartially according to each **o** deeds, 1 Pt 1:17

ONE-FIFTH (1)
the land and take **o** of the produce of Gn 41:34

ONE-HALF (2)
hand of Moses for the nine and **o** tribes. Jos 14:2
to the two and **o** tribes beyond the Jos 14:3

ONES (116)
wealth, all their little **o** and their wives, Gn 34:29
both we and you and also our little **o**. Gn 43:8
Egypt for your little **o** and for your Gn 45:19
carried Jacob their father, their little **o**, Gn 46:5
and as food for your little **o**." Gn 47:24
and your little **o**." Thus he comforted Gn 50:21
LORD your God. But which **o** are to go?" Ex 10:8
you, if ever I let you and your little **o** go! Ex 10:10
your little **o** also may go with you; Ex 10:24
These were the **o** chosen from the Nm 1:16

wives and our little **o** will become a Nm 14:3
But your little **o**, who you said would Nm 14:31
wives, their sons, and their little **o**. Nm 16:27
the women of Midian and their little **o**, Nm 31:9
kill every male among the little **o**, Nm 31:17
livestock, and cities for our little **o**, Nm 32:16
And our little **o** shall live in the Nm 32:17
cities for your little **o** and folds for Nm 32:24
Our little **o**, our wives, our livestock, Nm 32:26
And as for your little **o**, who you said Dt 1:39
Only your wives, your little **o**, and your Dt 3:19
But these are the **o** that you shall not Dt 14:12
but the women and the little **o**, the Dt 20:14
with young **o** or eggs and the mother Dt 22:6
your little **o**, your wives, and the Dt 29:11
the people, men, women, and little **o**, Dt 31:12
came from the ten thousands of holy **o**, Dt 33:2
people, all his holy **o** were in his hand; Dt 33:3
Your wives, your little **o**, and your Jos 1:14
of Israel, and the women, and the little **o**, Jos 8:35
putting the little **o** and the livestock Jgs 18:21
sword; also the women and the little **o**. Jgs 21:10
"He will guard the feet of his faithful **o**, 1 Sm 2:9
like the name of the great **o** of the earth. 2 Sm 7:9
and all the little **o** who were with 2 Sm 15:22
in pieces their little **o** and rip open 2 Kgs 8:12
servant, sons of Jacob, his chosen **o**! 1 Chr 16:13
saying, "Touch not my anointed **o**, 1 Chr 16:22
the name of the great **o** of the earth. 1 Chr 17:8
before the LORD, with their little **o**, 2 Chr 20:13
of rubbish, and burned **o** at that?" Neh 4:2
To which of the holy **o** will you turn? Jb 5:1
Behold, God puts no trust in his holy **o**, Jb 15:15
when its young **o** cry to God for help, Jb 38:41
Their young **o** become strong; they grow Jb 39:4
His young **o** suck up blood, and where Jb 39:30
in the land, they are the excellent **o**, Ps 16:3
"Gather to me my faithful **o**, who made a Ps 50:5
That your beloved **o** may be delivered, Ps 60:5
together against your treasured **o**. Ps 83:3
in the assembly of the holy **o**! Ps 89:5
to be feared in the council of the holy **o**, Ps 89:7
angels, you mighty **o** who do his word, Ps 103:20
children of Jacob, his chosen **o**! Ps 105:6
saying, "Touch not my anointed **o**, do Ps 105:15
with joy, his chosen **o** with singing. Ps 105:43
upon the prosperity of your chosen **o**, Ps 106:5
That your beloved **o** may be delivered, Ps 108:6
You rebuke the insolent, accursed **o**, Ps 119:21
who takes your little **o** and dashes them Ps 137:9
This is honor for all his godly **o**. Ps 149:9
"How long, O simple **o**, will you love Prv 1:22
O simple **o**, learn prudence; O fools, learn Prv 8:5
and there are yet higher **o** over them. Eccl 5:8
have commanded my consecrated **o**, Is 13:3
execute my anger, my proudly exulting **o**. Is 13:3
are at ease, shudder, you complacent **o**; Is 32:11
among all the wise **o** of the nations and Jer 10:7
Why are your mighty **o** face down? Jer 46:15
is destroyed; her little **o** have made a cry. Jer 48:4
Even the little **o** of the flock shall be Jer 49:20
Surely the little **o** of their flock shall be Jer 50:45
to fall by the swords of mighty **o**, Ezk 32:12
with the wool, you slaughter the fat **o**, Ezk 34:3
more than the lower and the middle **o**. Ezk 42:6
the decision by the word of the holy **o**, Dn 4:17
he shall be different from the former **o**, Dn 7:24
their little **o** shall be dashed in pieces, Hos 13:16
the daughter of my dispersed **o**, Zep 3:10
your midst your proudly exultant **o**, Zep 3:11
are the two anointed **o** who stand by the Zec 4:14
north country, the white **o** go after them, Zec 6:6
and the dappled **o** go toward the south Zec 6:6
but devours the flesh of the fat **o**, Zec 11:16
I will turn my hand against the little **o**. Zec 13:7
will come, and all the holy **o** with him. Zec 14:5
gives one of these little **o** even a cup of Mt 10:42
one of these little **o** who believe in me Mt 18:6
you do not despise one of these little **o**. Mt 18:10
that one of these little **o** should perish. Mt 18:14
to him, "Which **o**?" And Jesus said, Mt 19:18
and their great **o** exercise authority Mt 20:25
And these are the **o** along the path, Mk 4:15
And these are the **o** sown on rocky Mk 4:16
ones sown on rocky ground: the **o** who, Mk 4:16
others are the **o** sown among thorns. Mk 4:18
good soil are the **o** who hear the word Mk 4:20
one of these little **o** who believe in me Mk 9:42
and their great **o** exercise authority Mk 10:42
The **o** along the path are those who have Lk 8:12
And the **o** on the rock are those who, Lk 8:13
tear down my barns and build larger **o**, Lk 12:18
should cause one of these little **o** to sin. Lk 17:2
And he said to them, "O foolish **o**, and Lk 24:25
one by one, beginning with the older **o**, Jn 8:9
Or are you the only **o** it has reached? 1 Cor 14:36
Put on then, as God's chosen **o**, holy Col 3:12
Are not the rich the **o** who oppress you, Jas 2:6
you, and the **o** who drag you into court? Jas 2:6
Are they not the **o** who blaspheme the Jas 2:7
as they blaspheme the glorious **o**, 2 Pt 2:10
and blaspheme the glorious **o**. Jude 1:8
came with ten thousands of his holy **o**, Jude 1:14
earth and the great **o** and the generals Rv 6:15
"These are the **o** coming out of the great Rv 7:14
merchants were the great **o** of the earth, Rv 18:23

ONESELF (5)

For the bed is too short to stretch **o** on, Is 28:20
the covering too narrow to wrap **o** in. Is 28:20
No coal for warming **o** is this, no fire to Is 47:14
and to love one's neighbor as **o**, Mk 12:33
and to keep **o** unstained from the world. Jas 1:27

ONESIMUS (2)

and with him **O**, our faithful and Col 4:9
O, whose father I became in my Phlm 1:10

ONESIPHORUS (2)

grant mercy to the household of **O**, 2 Tm 1:16
and Aquila, and the household of **O**. 2 Tm 4:19

ONIONS (1)

the melons, the leeks, the **o**, Nm 11:5

ONLY (335)

of his heart was **o** evil continually. Gn 6:5
O Noah was left, and those who were Gn 7:23
and this is **o** the beginning of what they Gn 11:6
O do nothing to these men, for they have Gn 19:8
said, "Take your son, your **o** son Isaac, Gn 22:2
not withheld your son, your **o** son, Gn 22:12
not withheld your son, your **o** son, Gn 22:16
o you must not take my son back Gn 24:8
o obey my voice, and go, bring them to Gn 27:13
for with **o** my staff I crossed this Gn 32:10
O give me the young woman to be my Gn 34:12
O on this condition will we agree with Gn 34:15
O on this condition will the men agree Gn 34:22
O let us agree with them, and they will Gn 34:23
O remember me, when it is well with Gn 40:14
O as regards the throne will I be greater Gn 41:40
brother is dead, and he is the **o** one left. Gn 42:38
They had gone **o** a short distance from Gn 44:4
O the man in whose hand the cup was Gn 44:17
O the land of the priests he did not buy, Gn 47:22
O their children, their flocks, and their Gn 50:8
and your houses and be left **o** in the Nile." Ex 8:9
people. They shall be left **o** in the Nile." Ex 8:11
o you must not go very far away. Ex 8:28
O let not Pharaoh cheat again by not Ex 8:29
O in the land of Goshen, where the Ex 9:26
forgive my sin, please, **o** this once, Ex 10:17
the LORD your God **o** to remove this Ex 10:17
o let your flocks and your herds Ex 10:24
for you, and you have **o** to be silent." Ex 14:14
o he shall pay for the loss of his time, Ex 21:19
for that is his **o** covering, and it is his Ex 22:27
him clean; it is **o** an eruption. Lv 13:6
"**O** the tribe of Levi you shall not list, Nm 1:49
But if they blow **o** one, then the chiefs, Nm 10:4
LORD indeed spoken **o** through Moses? Nm 12:2
O do not rebel against the LORD. And do Nm 14:9
o Joshua the son of Nun and Caleb Nm 14:38
Let me **o** pass through on foot, Nm 20:19
with them; but **o** do what I tell you." Nm 22:20
but speak **o** the word that I tell you." Nm 22:35
You shall see **o** a fraction of them and Nm 23:13
o the gold, the silver, the bronze, the Nm 31:22
o they shall marry within the clan of Nm 36:6
your land. I will go **o** by the road; Dt 2:27
drink. **O** let me pass through on foot, Dt 2:28
O the livestock we took as spoil for Dt 2:35
O to the land of the sons of Ammon you Dt 2:37
(For **o** Og the king of Bashan was left of Dt 3:11
O your wives, your little ones, and your Dt 3:19
you have **o** begun to show your servant Dt 3:24
"**O** take care, and keep your soul Dt 4:9
but saw no form; there was **o** a voice. Dt 4:12
O you shall not eat the blood; you shall Dt 12:16
O be sure that you do not eat the blood, Dt 12:23
if **o** you will strictly obey the voice of the Dt 15:5
O you shall not eat its blood; you shall Dt 15:23
Justice, and **o** justice, you shall follow, Dt 16:20
O he must not acquire many horses for Dt 17:16
O on the evidence of two witnesses or of Dt 19:15
O the trees that you know are not trees Dt 20:20
then **o** the man who lay with her shall Dt 22:25
and you shall **o** go up and not down, Dt 28:13
you shall be **o** oppressed and robbed Dt 28:29
you shall be **o** oppressed and crushed Dt 28:33
you shall say, 'If **o** it were evening!' Dt 28:67
you shall say, 'If **o** it were morning!' Dt 28:67
O be strong and very courageous, being Jos 1:7
O may the LORD your God be with you, Jos 1:17
to death. **O** be strong and courageous." Jos 1:18
It was **o** on that day that they marched Jos 6:15
O Rahab the prostitute and all who are Jos 6:17
O the silver and gold, and the vessels of Jos 6:24
O its spoil and its livestock you shall take Jos 8:2
O the livestock and the spoil of that city Jos 8:27
O in Gaza, in Gath, and in Ashdod did Jos 11:22
O allot the land to Israel for an Jos 13:6
in the land, but **o** cities to dwell in, Jos 14:4
had no sons, but **o** daughters, Jos 17:3
You shall not have one allotment **o**, Jos 17:17
O be very careful to observe the Jos 22:5
O do not rebel against the LORD or Jos 22:19
It was **o** in order that the generations of Jgs 3:2
Please let it be dry on the fleece **o**, and on Jgs 6:39
and it was dry on the fleece **o**, and on all Jgs 6:40
to you. **O** please deliver us this day." Jgs 10:15
She was his **o** child; besides her he had Jgs 11:34
over him and said, "You **o** hate me; Jgs 14:16
we will **o** bind you and give you into Jgs 15:13
and please strengthen me **o** this once, Jgs 16:28
O, do not spend the night in the Jgs 19:20
o her lips moved, and her voice was 1 Sm 1:13
o, may the LORD establish his word." 1 Sm 1:23
boiled meat from you but **o** raw." 1 Sm 2:15
The **o** one of you whom I shall not cut 1 Sm 2:33
O the trunk of Dagon was left to him. 1 Sm 5:4
your heart to the LORD and serve him **o**, 1 Sm 7:3
Ashtaroth, and they served the LORD **o**. 1 Sm 7:4
o you shall solemnly warn them and 1 Sm 8:9
O fear the LORD and serve him 1 Sm 12:24
O be valiant for me and fight the 1 Sm 18:17
O Jonathan and David knew the 1 Sm 20:39
You came **o** yesterday, and shall I 2 Sm 15:20
will flee. I will strike down **o** the king, 2 Sm 17:2
You seek the life of **o** one man, and all 2 Sm 17:3
men returned after him **o** to strip the 2 Sm 23:10
o he sacrificed and made offerings at 1 Kgs 3:3
the house; **o** we two were in the house. 1 Kgs 3:18
if **o** your sons pay close attention to 1 Kgs 8:25
to all his ways (for you, you **o**, 1 Kgs 8:39
he said to him, "**O** let me depart." 1 Kgs 11:22
of David but the tribe of Judah **o**. 1 Kgs 12:20
doing **o** that which was right in my 1 Kgs 14:8
for he **o** of Jeroboam shall come to 1 Kgs 14:13
o a handful of flour in a jar and a 1 Kgs 17:12
Elijah said to the people, "I, even I **o**, 1 Kgs 18:22
with the sword, and I, even I **o**, 1 Kgs 19:10
with the sword, and I, even I **o**, 1 Kgs 19:14
great, but **o** with the king of Israel." 1 Kgs 22:31
till **o** its stones were left in 2 Kgs 3:25
O consider, and see how he is seeking a 2 Kgs 5:7
you, but **o** the worshipers of Baal." 2 Kgs 10:23
strike down Syria **o** three times." 2 Kgs 13:19
was left but the tribe of Judah **o**. 2 Kgs 17:18
if **o** they will be careful to do 2 Kgs 21:8
Sheshan had no sons, **o** daughters, 1 Chr 2:34
O, may the LORD grant you 1 Chr 22:12
having no sons, but **o** daughters; 1 Chr 23:22
if **o** your sons pay close attention to 2 Chr 6:16
to all his ways, for you, you **o**, 2 Chr 6:30
great, but **o** with the king of Israel." 2 Chr 18:30
if **o** they will be careful to do all that I 2 Chr 33:8
places, but **o** to the LORD their God. 2 Chr 33:17
O Jonathan the son of Asahel and Ezr 10:15
"Not **o** against the king has Queen Est 1:16
O against him do not stretch out your Jb 1:12
he is in your hand; **o** spare his life." Jb 2:6
O grant me two things, then I will not Jb 13:20
He feels **o** the pain of his own body, and Jb 14:22
body, and he mourns **o** for himself." Jb 14:22
me; I stand, and you **o** look at me. Jb 30:20
wrath! Fret not yourself; it tends **o** to evil. Ps 37:8
I said, "**O** let them not rejoice over me, Ps 38:16
Against you, you **o**, have I sinned and Ps 51:4
He **o** is my rock and my salvation, my Ps 62:2
They **o** plan to thrust him down from Ps 62:4
He **o** is my rock and my salvation, my Ps 62:6
You will **o** look with your eyes and see Ps 91:8
the **o** one in the sight of my mother, Prv 4:3
price of a prostitute is **o** a loaf of bread, Prv 6:26
desire of the righteous ends **o** in good; Prv 11:23
he should give, and **o** suffers want. Prv 11:24
profit, but mere talk tends **o** to poverty. Prv 14:23
An evil man seeks **o** rebellion, and a Prv 17:11
but **o** in expressing his opinion. Prv 18:2
him, you will **o** have to do it again. Prv 19:19
and to reflect **o** after making vows. Prv 20:25
who is hasty comes **o** to poverty. Prv 21:5
to the rich, will **o** come to poverty. Prv 22:16
found honey, eat **o** enough for you, Prv 25:16
neighbor and says, "I am **o** joking!" Prv 26:19
with a fool, the fool **o** rages and laughs, Prv 29:9

king? **O** what has already been done. Eccl 2:12
o to give to one who pleases God. Eccl 2:26
My dove, my perfect one, is the **o** one, the Sg 6:9
is the only one, the **o** one of her mother, Sg 6:9
clothes, **o** let us be called by your name; Is 4:1
the sea, **o** a remnant of them will return. Is 10:22
shame, and the craftsmen are **o** human. Is 44:11
"**O** in the LORD, it shall be said of me, are Is 45:24
you fast **o** to quarrel and to fight and to Is 58:4
know how to speak, for I am **o** a youth." Jer 1:6
said to me, "Do not say, 'I am **o** a youth'; Jer 1:7
O acknowledge your guilt, that you Jer 3:13
Then I said, "These are **o** the poor; they Jer 5:4
make mourning as for an **o** son, most Jer 6:26
'We are delivered!'—**o** to go on doing all Jer 7:10
eyes and heart **o** for your dishonest Jer 22:17
O know for certain that if you put me Jer 26:15
for these were the **o** fortified cities of Jer 34:7
remained of them **o** wounded men, Jer 37:10
was no water in the cistern, but **o** mud, Jer 38:6
they not destroy **o** enough for Jer 49:9
nations weary themselves **o** for fire." Jer 51:58
Not **o** did you walk in their ways and Ezk 16:47
saying, 'Abraham was **o** one man, Ezk 33:24
with **o** a wall between me and them. Ezk 43:8
O the prince may sit in it to eat bread Ezk 44:3
but **o** virgins of the offspring of the Ezk 44:22
against strongholds, but **o** for a time. Dn 11:24
their bread shall be for their hunger **o**; Hos 9:4
"You **o** have I known of all the families Am 3:2
the mourning for an **o** son and the end Am 8:10
they not steal **o** enough for themselves? Ob 1:5
for him, as one mourns for an **o** child, Zec 12:10
Evildoers not **o** prosper but they put Mal 3:15
your God and him **o** shall you serve.'" Mt 4:10
And if you greet **o** your brothers, what Mt 5:47
come under my roof, but **o** say the word, Mt 8:8
said to herself, "If I **o** touch his garment, Mt 9:21
who were with him, but **o** for the priests? Mt 12:4
heard it, they said, "It is **o** by Beelzebul, Mt 12:24
"We have **o** five loaves here and two Mt 14:17
him that they might **o** touch the fringe Mt 14:36
"I was sent **o** to the lost sheep of the Mt 15:24
their eyes, they saw no one but Jesus **o**. Mt 17:8
saying, but **o** those to whom it is given. Mt 19:11
is good? There is **o** one who is good. Mt 19:17
o with difficulty will a rich person Mt 19:23
saying, 'These last worked **o** one hour, Mt 20:12
it and found nothing on it but **o** leaves. Mt 21:19
you will not **o** do what has been done to Mt 21:21
heaven, nor the Son, but the Father **o**. Mt 24:36
the synagogue, "Do not fear, **o** believe." Mk 5:36
and they had **o** one loaf with them in Mk 8:14
saw anyone with them but Jesus **o**. Mk 9:8
heaven, nor the Son, but **o** the Father. Mk 13:32
your God, and him **o** shall you serve.'" Lk 4:8
sent to none of them but **o** to Zarephath, Lk 4:26
cleansed, but **o** Naaman the Syrian." Lk 4:27
carried out, the **o** son of his mother, Lk 7:12
for he had an **o** daughter, about twelve Lk 8:42
not fear; **o** believe, and she will be well." Lk 8:50
to look at my son, for he is my **o** child. Lk 9:38
we have **o** done what was our duty.'" Lk 17:10
"Are you the **o** visitor to Jerusalem who Lk 24:18
glory as of the **o** Son from the Father, Jn 1:14
No one has ever seen God; the **o** God, who Jn 1:18
so loved the world, that he gave his **o** Son, Jn 3:16
believed in the name of the **o** Son of God. Jn 3:18
did not baptize, but **o** his disciples), Jn 4:2
because not **o** was he breaking the Jn 5:18
but **o** what he sees the Father doing. Jn 5:19
the glory that comes from the **o** God? Jn 5:44
saw that there had been **o** one boat there, Jn 6:22
The thief comes **o** to steal and kill and Jn 10:10
and not for the nation **o**, but also to Jn 11:52
not **o** on account of him but also to see Jn 12:9
not my feet **o** but also my hands and my Jn 13:9
life, that they know you the **o** true God, Jn 17:3
"I do not ask for these **o**, but also for Jn 17:20
since it is **o** the third hour of the day. Acts 2:15
the proceeds and brought **o** a part of it Acts 5:2
but they had **o** been baptized in the Acts 8:16
though he knew **o** the baptism of Acts 18:25
and hear that not **o** in Ephesus but in Acts 19:26
there is danger not **o** that this trade of Acts 19:27
if **o** I may finish my course and the Acts 20:24
I am ready not **o** to be imprisoned but Acts 21:13
I not **o** locked up many of the saints Acts 26:10
to God that not **o** you but also all Acts 26:29
loss, not **o** of the cargo and the ship, Acts 27:10
of life among you, but **o** of the ship. Acts 27:22
they not **o** do them but give approval Rom 1:32
Or is God the God of Jews **o**? Is he not Rom 3:29
this blessing then **o** for the Rom 4:9
his offspring—not **o** to the adherent of Rom 4:16
is binding on a person **o** as long as he Rom 7:1
And not **o** the creation, but we Rom 8:23
And not **o** so, but also when Rebecca Rom 9:10
not from the Jews **o** but also from the Rom 9:24
sea, **o** a remnant of them will be saved, Rom 9:27
not **o** to avoid God's wrath but also for Rom 13:5
the weak person eats **o** vegetables. Rom 14:2
to whom not **o** I give thanks but all Rom 16:4
to the **o** wise God be glory Rom 16:27
the flesh and behaving **o** in a human 1 Cor 3:3
but **o** God who gives the growth. 1 Cor 3:7
will be saved, but **o** as through fire. 1 Cor 3:15
O let each person lead the life that the 1 Cor 7:17
to whom she wishes, **o** in the Lord. 1 Cor 7:39
Or is it **o** Barnabas and I who have no 1 Cor 9:6
compete, but **o** one receives the prize? 1 Cor 9:24
let there be **o** two or at most three, 1 Cor 14:27
Or are you the **o** ones it has reached? 1 Cor 14:36
If in this life **o** we have hoped in 1 Cor 15:19
because **o** through Christ is it taken 2 Cor 3:14
it is veiled **o** to those who are perishing. 2 Cor 4:3
and not **o** by his coming but also by 2 Cor 7:7
letter grieved you, though **o** for a while. 2 Cor 7:8
year ago started not **o** to do this work 2 Cor 8:10
For he not **o** accepted our appeal, but 2 Cor 8:17
And not **o** that, but he has been 2 Cor 8:19
what is honorable not **o** in the Lord's 2 Cor 8:21
service is not **o** supplying the needs 2 Cor 9:12
but will boast **o** with regard to the 2 Cor 10:13
against the truth, but **o** for the truth. 2 Cor 13:8
They **o** were hearing it said, "He who Gal 1:23
O, they asked us to remember the poor, Gal 2:10
Let me ask you **o** this: Did you receive Gal 3:2
and not **o** when I am present with you, Gal 4:18
but **o** faith working through love. Gal 5:6
O do not use your freedom as an Gal 5:13
and **o** in order that they may not be Gal 6:12
not **o** in this age but also in the one to Eph 1:21
but **o** such as is good for building up, Eph 4:29
O that in every way, whether in Phil 1:18
O let your manner of life be worthy of Phil 1:27
Christ you should not **o** believe in him Phil 1:29
of you look not **o** to his own interests, Phil 2:4
not **o** as in my presence but much Phil 2:12
him, and not **o** on him but on me also, Phil 2:27
O let us hold true to what we have Phil 3:16
in giving and receiving, except you **o**. Phil 4:15
These are the **o** men of the Col 4:11
our gospel came to you not **o** in word, 1 Thes 1:5
For not **o** has the word of the Lord 1 Thes 1:8
share with you not **o** the gospel of 1 Thes 2:8
O he who now restrains it will do so 2 Thes 2:7
ages, immortal, invisible, the **o** God, 1 Tm 1:17
from house to house, and not **o** idlers, 1 Tm 5:13
(No longer drink **o** water, but use a 1 Tm 5:23
he who is the blessed and **o** Sovereign, 1 Tm 6:15
does no good, but **o** ruins the hearers. 2 Tm 2:14
house there are not **o** vessels of gold 2 Tm 2:20
and not **o** to me but also to all who 2 Tm 4:8
for himself, but **o** when called by God, Heb 5:4
but into the second **o** the high priest Heb 9:7
but deal **o** with food and drink and Heb 9:10
For a will takes effect **o** at death, since Heb 9:17
was in the act of offering up his **o** son, Heb 11:17
I will shake not **o** the earth but also Heb 12:26
be doers of the word, and not hearers **o**, Jas 1:22
There is **o** one lawgiver and judge, he Jas 4:12
not **o** to the good and gentle but also to 1 Pt 2:18
and not for ours **o** but also for the sins of 1 Jn 2:2
that God sent his **o** Son into the world, 1 Jn 4:9
not by the water **o** but by the water and 1 Jn 5:6
whom I love in truth, and not **o** I, 2 Jn 1:1
and deny our **o** Master and Lord, Jude 1:4
to the **o** God, our Savior, through Jesus Jude 1:25
O hold fast what you have until I come. Rv 2:25
but **o** those people who do not have the Rv 9:4
come he must remain **o** a little while. Rv 17:10
but **o** those who are written in the Rv 21:27

ONO (5)
who built **O** and Lod with its towns, 1 Chr 8:12
The sons of Lod, Hadid, and **O**, 725. Ezr 2:33
in the plain of **O**." But they intended to Neh 6:2
The sons of Lod, Hadid, and **O**, 721. Neh 7:37
Lod, and **O**, the valley of craftsmen. Neh 11:35

ONTO (2)
leaders of Judah up **o** the wall and Neh 12:31
Behold, I will throw her **o** a sickbed, and Rv 2:22

ONWARD (7)
their ornaments, from Mount Horeb **o**. Ex 33:6
and **o** throughout your generations, Nm 15:23
sight of all nations from that time **o**. 2 Chr 32:23
of Benjamin also lived from Geba **o**, Neh 11:31
from the eighth day **o** the priests shall Ezk 43:27
Now then, consider from this day **o**. Hg 2:15
Consider from this day **o**, from the Hg 2:18

ONYCHA (1)
Moses, "Take sweet spices, stacte, and **o**, Ex 30:34

ONYX (12)
is good; bdellium and **o** stone are there. Gn 2:12
o stones, and stones for setting, for the Ex 25:7
You shall take two **o** stones, and engrave Ex 28:9
and the fourth row a beryl, an **o**, and a Ex 28:20
and **o** stones and stones for setting, for Ex 35:9
the leaders brought **o** stones and stones Ex 35:27
They made the **o** stones, enclosed in Ex 39:6
and the fourth row, a beryl, an **o**, and a Ex 39:13
great quantities of **o** and stones for 1 Chr 29:2
gold of Ophir, in precious **o** or sapphire. Jb 28:16
and diamond, beryl, **o**, and jasper, Ezk 28:13
the fifth **o**, the sixth carnelian, the Rv 21:20

OPEN (180)
with us, and the land shall be **o** to you. Gn 34:10
is the first to **o** the womb among the Ex 13:2
all the males that first **o** the womb, Ex 13:15
All that **o** the womb are mine, all your Ex 34:19
He shall tear it **o** by its wings, but shall Lv 1:17
let the living bird go into the **o** field. Lv 14:7
go out of the city into the **o** country. Lv 14:53
that they sacrifice in the **o** field, Lv 17:5
Instead of all who **o** the womb, the Nm 8:16
And every **o** vessel that has no cover Nm 19:15
Whoever in the **o** field touches Nm 19:16
the midst of its **o** square and burn the Dt 13:16
but you shall **o** your hand to him and Dt 15:8
'You shall **o** wide your hand to your Dt 15:11
is found slain, lying in the **o** country, Dt 21:1
"But if in the **o** country a man meets a Dt 22:25
because he met her in the **o** country, Dt 22:27
The LORD will **o** to you his good Dt 28:12
They left the city **o** and pursued Israel. Jos 8:17
of Ai in the **o** wilderness where they Jos 8:24
"**O** the mouth of the cave and bring Jos 10:22
when he still did not **o** the doors of the Jgs 3:25
And God split **o** the hollow place that is Jgs 15:19
and sat down in the **o** square of the city, Jgs 19:15
the traveler in the **o** square of the city. Jgs 19:17
other to Gibeah, and in the **o** country, Jgs 20:31
Egyptian in the **o** country and 1 Sm 30:11
were by themselves in the **o** country. 2 Sm 10:8
of my lord are camping in the **o** field. 2 Sm 11:11
in the form of gourds and **o** flowers. 1 Kgs 6:18
and palm trees and **o** flowers, 1 Kgs 6:29
cherubim, palm trees, and **o** flowers. 1 Kgs 6:32
and palm trees and **o** flowers, 1 Kgs 6:35
your eyes may be **o** night and day 1 Kgs 8:29
Let your eyes be **o** to the plea of your 1 Kgs 8:52
of them were alone in the **o** country. 1 Kgs 11:29
who dies in the **o** country the birds 1 Kgs 14:11
who dies in the **o** country the birds 1 Kgs 21:24
please **o** his eyes that he may see." So 2 Kgs 6:17
said, "O LORD, **o** the eyes of these men, 2 Kgs 6:20
to hide themselves in the **o** country, 2 Kgs 7:12
ones and rip **o** their pregnant 2 Kgs 8:12
Then **o** the door and flee; do not 2 Kgs 9:3
"**O** the window eastward," and he 2 Kgs 13:17
on, because they did not **o** it to him. 2 Kgs 15:16
and he ripped **o** all the women in it 2 Kgs 15:16
hear; **o** your eyes, O LORD, and see; 2 Kgs 19:16
were by themselves in the **o** country. 1 Chr 19:9
your eyes may be **o** day and night 2 Chr 6:20
let your eyes be **o** and your ears 2 Chr 6:40
my eyes will be **o** and my ears 2 Chr 7:15
people sat in the **o** square before the Ezr 10:9
heavy rain; we cannot stand in the **o**. Ezr 10:13
let your ear be attentive and your eyes **o**, Neh 1:6
the space behind the wall, in **o** places, Neh 4:13
to me with an **o** letter in his hand. Neh 6:5
out to Mordecai in the **o** square of the city Est 4:6
God would speak and **o** his lips to you, Jb 11:5
if he shuts a man in, none can **o**. Jb 12:14
And do you **o** your eyes on such a one Jb 14:3
He slashes **o** my kidneys and does not Jb 16:13
and the cloud is not split **o** under them. Jb 26:8
find relief; I must **o** my lips and answer. Jb 32:20
Behold, I **o** my mouth; the tongue in my Jb 33:2
become strong; they grow up in the **o**; Jb 39:4
Who can **o** the doors of his face? Jb 41:14
is destruction; their throat is an **o** grave; Ps 5:9
they **o** wide their mouths at me, like a Ps 22:13
They **o** wide their mouths against me; Ps 35:21
a mute man who does not **o** his mouth. Ps 38:13
I do not **o** my mouth, for it is you who Ps 39:9
desired, but you have given me an **o** ear. Ps 40:6
O Lord, **o** my lips, and my mouth will Ps 51:15
the land to quake; you have torn it **o**; Ps 60:2
You split **o** springs and brooks; you Ps 74:15
You hold my eyelids **o**; I am so troubled Ps 77:4
I will **o** my mouth in a parable; I will Ps 78:2

O your mouth wide, and I will fill it. Ps 81:10
gather it up; when you **o** your hand, Ps 104:28
O to me the gates of righteousness, Ps 118:19
O my eyes, that I may behold Ps 119:18
I **o** my mouth and pant, because I Ps 119:131
You **o** your hand; you satisfy the Ps 145:16
by his knowledge the deeps broke **o**, Prv 3:20
and Abaddon lie **o** before the LORD; Prv 15:11
o your eyes, and you will have plenty Prv 20:13
in the gate he does not **o** his mouth. Prv 24:7
Better is **o** rebuke than hidden love. Prv 27:5
O your mouth for the mute, for the Prv 31:8
O your mouth, judge righteously, Prv 31:9
"**O** to me, my sister, my love, my dove, my Sg 5:2
I arose to **o** to my beloved, and my hands Sg 5:5
on the west devour Israel with **o** mouth. Is 9:12
He shall **o**, and none shall shut; and he Is 22:22
and he shall shut, and none shall **o**. Is 22:22
O the gates, that the righteous nation that Is 26:2
does he continually **o** and harrow his Is 28:24
and hear; **o** your eyes, O LORD, and see; Is 37:17
I will **o** rivers on the bare heights, and Is 41:18
to **o** the eyes that are blind, to bring out Is 42:7
his ears are **o**, but he does not hear. Is 42:20
to **o** doors before him that gates may not Is 45:1
let the earth **o**, that salvation and Is 45:8
Against whom do you **o** your mouth wide Is 57:4
Your gates shall be **o** continually; day Is 60:11
Their quiver is like an **o** tomb; they are Jer 5:16
men shall fall like dung upon the **o** field, Jer 9:22
are shut up, with none to **o** them; Jer 13:19
on the mountains in the **o** country. Jer 17:3
terms and conditions and the **o** copy. Jer 32:11
sealed deed of purchase and this **o** deed, Jer 32:14
whose eyes are **o** to all the ways of the Jer 32:19
the forces in the **o** country and their Jer 40:7
the forces in the **o** country came to Jer 40:13
her from every quarter; **o** her granaries; Jer 50:26
"All our enemies **o** their mouths Lam 3:46
o your mouth and eat what I give you." Ezk 2:8
I speak with you, I will **o** your mouth, Ezk 3:27
but you were cast out on the **o** field, Ezk 16:5
and never **o** your mouth again Ezk 16:63
rams, to **o** the mouth with murder, Ezk 21:22
therefore I will lay **o** the flank of Moab Ezk 25:9
peoples is broken; it has swung **o** to me. Ezk 26:2
you shall fall on the **o** field, and not be Ezk 29:5
and I will **o** your lips among them. Ezk 29:21
on the **o** field I will fling you, and will Ezk 32:4
and whoever is in the **o** field I will give Ezk 33:27
I will **o** your graves and raise you Ezk 37:12
I am the LORD, when I **o** your graves, Ezk 37:13
You shall fall in the **o** field, for I have Ezk 39:5
fifty cubits for an **o** space around it. Ezk 45:2
city, for dwellings and for **o** country. Ezk 48:15
And the city shall have **o** land: on the Ezk 48:17
his upper chamber **o** toward Jerusalem. Dn 6:10
righteousness, but to us **o** shame, Dn 9:7
To us, O Lord, belongs **o** shame, to our Dn 9:8
O your eyes and see our desolations, and Dn 9:18
I will tear **o** their breast, and there I will Hos 13:8
a lion, as a wild beast would rip them **o**. Hos 13:8
and their pregnant women ripped **o**. Hos 13:16
they have ripped **o** pregnant women in Am 1:13
under him, and the valleys will split **o**, Mi 1:4
make Samaria a heap in the **o** country, Mi 1:6
from the city and dwell in the **o** country; Mi 4:10
of your land are wide **o** to your enemies; Na 3:13
O your doors, O Lebanon, that the fire Zec 11:1
the house of Judah I will keep my eyes **o**, Zec 12:4
if I will not **o** the windows of heaven for Mal 3:10
"I will **o** my mouth in parables; Mt 13:35
and when you **o** its mouth you will Mt 17:27
came also, saying, 'Lord, lord, **o** to us.' Mt 25:11
so that they may **o** the door to him at Lk 12:36
at the door, saying, 'Lord, **o** to us,' Lk 13:25
leave the ninety-nine in the **o** country, Lk 15:4
he do to you? How did he **o** your eyes?" Jn 9:26
Can a demon **o** the eyes of the blind?" Jn 10:21
headlong he burst **o** in the middle Acts 1:18
her joy she did not **o** the gate but ran Acts 12:14
and saw that the prison doors were **o**, Acts 16:27
when Paul was about to **o** his mouth, Acts 18:14
against anyone, the courts are **o**, Acts 19:38
to **o** their eyes, so that they may turn Acts 26:18
had sailed across the **o** sea along the Acts 27:5
"Their throat is an **o** grave; they use Rom 3:13
but by the **o** statement of the truth we 2 Cor 4:2
you, Corinthians; our heart is wide **o**. 2 Cor 6:11
authorities and put them to **o** shame, Col 2:15
that God may **o** to us a door for the word, Col 4:3
are believers and not **o** to the charge of Ti 1:6
pure, then peaceable, gentle, **o** to reason, Jas 3:17
and his ears are **o** to their prayer. 1 Pt 3:12
Behold, I have set before you an **o** door, Rv 3:8
and behold, a door standing **o** in heaven! Rv 4:1
"Who is worthy to **o** the scroll and break Rv 5:2
the earth was able to **o** the scroll or to Rv 5:3
one was found worthy to **o** the scroll or to Rv 5:4
so that he can **o** the scroll and its seven Rv 5:5
are you to take the scroll and to **o** its seals, Rv 5:9
He had a little scroll **o** in his hand. And Rv 10:2
take the scroll that is **o** in the hand of the Rv 10:8

OPENED (125)

that when you eat of it your eyes will be **o**, Gn 3:5
Then the eyes of both were **o**, and they Gn 3:7
which has **o** its mouth to receive your Gn 4:11
and the windows of the heavens were **o**. Gn 7:11
of forty days Noah **o** the window of the Gn 8:6
Then God **o** her eyes, and she saw a Gn 21:19
that Leah was hated, he **o** her womb, Gn 29:31
God listened to her and **o** her womb. Gn 30:22
Joseph **o** all the storehouses and sold to Gn 41:56
And as one of them **o** his sack to give Gn 42:27
to the lodging place we **o** our sacks, Gn 43:21
the ground, and each man **o** his sack. Gn 44:11
When she **o** it, she saw the child, and Ex 2:6
And the earth **o** its mouth and Nm 16:32
Then the LORD **o** the mouth of the Nm 22:28
Then the LORD **o** the eyes of Balaam, Nm 22:31
the oracle of the man whose eye is **o**, Nm 24:3
the oracle of the man whose eye is **o**, Nm 24:15
and the earth **o** its mouth and Nm 26:10
how the earth **o** its mouth and swallowed Dt 11:6
chamber, they took the key and **o** them, Jgs 3:25
I am thirsty." So she **o** a skin of milk Jgs 4:19
For I have **o** my mouth to the LORD, and Jgs 11:35
you have **o** your mouth to the LORD; Jgs 11:36
and when he **o** the doors of the house Jgs 19:27
then he **o** the doors of the house of the 1 Sm 3:15
seven times, and the child **o** his eyes. 2 Kgs 4:35
may see." So the LORD **o** the eyes of the 2 Kgs 6:17
see." So the LORD **o** their eyes and they 2 Kgs 6:20
bury her." Then he **o** the door and 2 Kgs 9:10
the window eastward," and he **o** it. 2 Kgs 13:17
he **o** the doors of the house of the 2 Chr 29:3
gates of Jerusalem be **o** until the sun is Neh 7:3
And Ezra **o** the book in the sight of all Neh 8:5
people, and as he **o** it all the people stood. Neh 8:5
they should not be **o** until after the Neh 13:19
After this Job **o** his mouth and cursed the Jb 3:1
and they **o** their mouths as for the Jb 29:23
street; I have **o** my doors to the traveler), Jb 31:32
the skies above and **o** the doors of Ps 78:23
He **o** the rock, and water gushed out; it Ps 105:41
the earth **o** and swallowed up Dathan, Ps 106:17
and deceitful mouths are **o** against me, Ps 109:2
I **o** to my beloved, but my beloved had Sg 5:6
grape blossoms have **o** and the Sg 7:12
its appetite and **o** its mouth beyond Is 5:14
moved a wing or **o** the mouth or Is 10:14
For the windows of heaven are **o**, and the Is 24:18
Then the eyes of the blind shall be **o**, and Is 35:5
from of old your ear has not been **o**. Is 48:8
The Lord GOD has **o** my ear, and I was not Is 50:5
he was afflicted, yet he **o** not his mouth; Is 53:7
shearers is silent, so he **o** not his mouth. Is 53:7
The LORD has **o** his armory and Jer 50:25
by the Chebar canal, the heavens were **o**, Ezk 1:1
So I **o** my mouth, and he gave me this Ezk 3:2
your mouth will be **o** to the fugitive, Ezk 24:27
and he had **o** my mouth by the time Ezk 33:22
in the morning, so my mouth was **o**, Ezk 33:22
of the side chambers **o** on the free Ezk 41:11
it shall not be **o**, and no one shall enter Ezk 44:2
but on the Sabbath day it shall be **o**, Ezk 46:1
the day of the new moon it shall be **o**. Ezk 46:1
the gate facing east shall be **o** for him. Ezk 46:12
sat in judgment, and the books were **o**. Dn 7:10
lips. Then I **o** my mouth and spoke. Dn 10:16
The river gates are **o**; the palace melts Na 2:6
shall be a fountain **o** for the house of Zec 13:1
and behold, the heavens were **o** to him, Mt 3:16
And he **o** his mouth and taught them, Mt 5:2
will find; knock, and it will be **o** to you. Mt 7:7
and to the one who knocks it will be **o**. Mt 7:8
And their eyes were **o**. And Jesus sternly Mt 9:30
said to him, "Lord, let our eyes be **o**." Mt 20:33
The tombs also were **o**. And many Mt 27:52
to him, "Ephphatha," that is, "Be **o**." Mk 7:34
And his ears were **o**, his tongue was Mk 7:35
on his eyes again; and he **o** his eyes, Mk 8:25
his mouth was **o** and his tongue Lk 1:64
and was praying, the heavens were **o**, Lk 3:21
will find; knock, and it will be **o** to you. Lk 11:9
and to the one who knocks it will be **o**. Lk 11:10
And their eyes were **o**, and they Lk 24:31
road, while he **o** to us the Scriptures?" Lk 24:32
Then he **o** their minds to understand Lk 24:45
truly, I say to you, you will see heaven **o**, Jn 1:51
to him, "Then how were your eyes **o**?" Jn 9:10
when Jesus made the mud and **o** his eyes. Jn 9:14
him, since he has **o** your eyes?" He said, Jn 9:17
know, nor do we know who **o** his eyes. Jn 9:21
he comes from, and yet he **o** my eyes. Jn 9:30
it been heard that anyone **o** the eyes of a Jn 9:32
"Could not he who **o** the eyes of the Jn 11:37
angel of the Lord **o** the prison doors Acts 5:19
but when we **o** them we found no one Acts 5:23
he said, "Behold, I see the heavens **o**, Acts 7:56
Then Philip **o** his mouth, and Acts 8:35
ground, and although his eyes were **o**, Acts 9:8
"Tabitha, arise." And she **o** her eyes, Acts 9:40
saw the heavens **o** and something Acts 10:11
So Peter **o** his mouth and said: "Truly Acts 10:34
It **o** for them of its own accord, and Acts 12:10
knocking, and when they **o**, Acts 12:16
and how he had **o** a door of faith to Acts 14:27
The Lord **o** her heart to pay attention Acts 16:14
And immediately all the doors were **o**, Acts 16:26
door for effective work has **o** to me, 1 Cor 16:9
though a door was **o** for me in the 2 Cor 2:12
holy places is not yet **o** as long as the Heb 9:8
living way that he **o** for us through Heb 10:20
watched when the Lamb **o** one of the Rv 6:1
When he **o** the second seal, I heard the Rv 6:3
When he **o** the third seal, I heard the third Rv 6:5
When he **o** the fourth seal, I heard the Rv 6:7
When he **o** the fifth seal, I saw under the Rv 6:9
When he **o** the sixth seal, I looked, and Rv 6:12
When the Lamb **o** the seventh seal, there Rv 8:1
He **o** the shaft of the bottomless pit, and Rv 9:2
Then God's temple in heaven was **o**, Rv 11:19
and the earth **o** its mouth and Rv 12:16
It **o** its mouth to utter blasphemies Rv 13:6
of the tent of witness in heaven was **o**, Rv 15:5
Then I saw heaven **o**, and behold, a Rv 19:11
before the throne, and books were **o**. Rv 20:12
Then another book was **o**, which is the Rv 20:12

OPENING (21)

It shall have an **o** for the head in the Ex 28:32
it, with a woven binding around the **o**, Ex 28:32
the opening, like the **o** in a garment, Ex 28:32
and the **o** of the robe in it was like the Ex 39:23
robe in it was like the **o** in a garment, Ex 39:23
garment, with a binding around the **o**, Ex 39:23
he said to her, "Stand at the **o** of the tent, Jgs 4:20
Its **o** was within a crown that 1 Kgs 7:31
Its **o** was round, as a pedestal is made, 1 Kgs 7:31
At its **o** there were carvings, and its 1 Kgs 7:31
had charge of **o** it every morning. 1 Chr 9:27
and the **o** of the prison to those who are Is 61:1
the width of the **o** of the gateway, Ezk 40:11
present himself at the **o** of the womb. Hos 13:13
thrust down the leaden weight on its **o**. Zec 5:8
Then, **o** their treasures, they offered him Mt 2:11
he saw the heavens **o** and the Spirit Mk 1:10
him, and when they had made an **o**, Mk 2:4
let him down through an **o** in the wall, Acts 9:25
given to me in **o** my mouth boldly to Eph 6:19
forth from the same **o** both fresh and Jas 3:11

OPENINGS (1)

cubits; the **o** faced each other. Ezk 40:13

OPENLY (7)

on her whoring so **o** and flaunted her Ezk 23:18
Jesus could no longer **o** enter a town, Mk 1:45
works in secret if he seeks to be known **o**. Jn 7:4
for fear of the Jews no one spoke **o** of him. Jn 7:13
And here he is, speaking **o**, and they say Jn 7:26
no longer walked **o** among the Jews, Jn 11:54
him, "I have spoken **o** to the world. Jn 18:20

OPENS (23)

to the LORD all that first **o** the womb. Ex 13:12
"When a man **o** a pit, or when a man Ex 21:33
every firstborn who **o** the womb Nm 3:12
and the ground **o** its mouth and Nm 16:30
Everything that **o** the womb of all Nm 18:15
to you peaceably and it **o** to you, Dt 20:11
he **o** his eyes, and his wealth is gone. Jb 27:19
He **o** shafts in a valley away from where Jb 28:4
then he **o** the ears of men and terrifies Jb 33:16
Job **o** his mouth in empty talk; he Jb 35:16
He **o** their ears to instruction and Jb 36:10
by their affliction and **o** their ear by Jb 36:15
the LORD **o** the eyes of the blind. The Ps 146:8
he who **o** wide his lips comes to ruin. Prv 13:3
She **o** her hand to the poor and reaches Prv 31:20
She **o** her mouth with wisdom, and the Prv 31:26
He who **o** the breach goes up before Mi 2:13
"Every male who first **o** the womb shall Lk 2:23
To him the gatekeeper **o**. The sheep hear Jn 10:3
shearer is silent, so he **o** not his mouth. Acts 8:32
key of David, who **o** and no one will shut, Rv 3:7

no one will shut, who shuts and no one **o**. Rv 3:7
If anyone hears my voice and **o** the door, Rv 3:20

OPHEL (5)
did much building on the wall of **O**. 2 Chr 27:3
Fish Gate, and carried it around **O**, 2 Chr 33:14
servants living on **O** repaired to a Neh 3:26
projecting tower as far as the wall of **O**. Neh 3:27
But the temple servants lived on **O**; Neh 11:21

OPHIR (13)
O, Havilah, and Jobab; all these were Gn 10:29
they went to **O** and brought from 1 Kgs 9:28
Hiram, which brought gold from **O**, 1 Kgs 10:11
brought from **O** a very great 1 Kgs 10:11
ships of Tarshish to go to **O** for gold, 1 Kgs 22:48
O, Havilah, and Jobab; all these were 1 Chr 1:23
3,000 talents of gold, of the gold of **O**, 1 Chr 29:4
and they went to **O** together with the 2 Chr 8:18
Solomon, who brought gold from **O**, 2 Chr 9:10
and gold of **O** among the stones of the Jb 22:24
It cannot be valued in the gold of **O**, in Jb 28:16
right hand stands the queen in gold of **O**. Ps 45:9
gold, and mankind than the gold of **O**. Is 13:12

OPHNI (1)
O, Geba—twelve cities with their Jos 18:24

OPHRAH (8)
Avvim, Parah, **O**, Jos 18:23
came and sat under the terebinth at **O**, Jgs 6:11
To this day it still stands at **O**, which Jgs 6:24
an ephod of it and put it in his city, in **O**. Jgs 8:27
of Joash his father, at **O** of the Abiezrites. Jgs 8:32
his father's house at **O** and killed his Jgs 9:5
One company turned toward **O**, to 1 Sm 13:17
Meonothai fathered **O**; and Seraiah 1 Chr 4:14

OPINION (7)
timid and afraid to declare my **o** to you. Jb 32:6
'Listen to me; let me also declare my **o**.' Jb 32:10
with my share; I also will declare my **o**. Jb 32:17
but only in expressing his **o**. Prv 18:2
and you do not care about anyone's **o**, Mt 22:16
true and do not care about anyone's **o**. Mk 12:14
and every lofty **o** raised against the 2 Cor 10:5

OPINIONS (2)
go limping between two different **o**? 1 Kgs 18:21
him, but not to quarrel over **o**. Rom 14:1

OPPONENT (3)
And each caught his **o** by the head 2 Sm 2:16
persecutor, and insolent **o**. 1 Tm 1:13
so that an **o** may be put to shame, Ti 2:8

OPPONENT'S (1)
and thrust his sword in his **o** side, 2 Sm 2:16

OPPONENTS (2)
not frightened in anything by your **o**. Phil 1:28
correcting his **o** with gentleness. God 2 Tm 2:25

OPPORTUNE (1)
he departed from him until an **o** time. Lk 4:13

OPPORTUNITY (17)
was seeking an **o** against the Philistines. Jgs 14:4
moment he sought an **o** to betray him. Mt 26:16
But an **o** came when Herod on his Mk 6:21
And he sought an **o** to betray him. Mk 14:11
This will be your **o** to bear witness. Lk 21:13
and sought an **o** to betray him Lk 22:6
When I get an **o** I will summon you." Acts 24:25
to face and had **o** to make his defense Acts 25:16
seizing an **o** through the Rom 7:8
seizing an **o** through the Rom 7:11
your freedom, avail yourself of the **o**. 1 Cor 7:21
now. He will come when he has **o**. 1 Cor 16:12
use your freedom as an **o** for the flesh, Gal 5:13
So then, as we have **o**, let us do good to Gal 6:10
and give no **o** to the devil. Eph 4:27
concerned for me, but you had no **o**. Phil 4:10
out, they would have had **o** to return. Heb 11:15

OPPOSE (4)
have come out to **o** you because your Nm 22:32
said nothing to her and did not **o** her, Nm 30:11
displease God and **o** all mankind 1 Thes 2:15
Moses, so these men also **o** the truth, 2 Tm 3:8

OPPOSED (10)
forgive her, because her father **o** her. Nm 30:5
and Jahzeiah the son of Tikvah **o** this, Ezr 10:15
and caught, because you **o** the LORD. Jer 50:24
of many in Israel, and for a sign that is **o** Lk 2:34
is the meaning of his name) **o** them, Acts 13:8
And when they **o** and reviled him, he Acts 18:6
came to Antioch, I **o** him to his face, Gal 2:11
the flesh, for these are **o** to each other, Gal 5:17
Just as Jannes and Jambres **o** Moses, so 2 Tm 3:8
for he strongly **o** our message. 2 Tm 4:15

OPPOSES (6)
But if her father **o** her on the day that Nm 30:5
husband comes to hear of it, he **o** her, Nm 30:8
who makes himself a king **o** Caesar." Jn 19:12
who **o** and exalts himself against 2 Thes 2:4
Therefore it says, "God **o** the proud, but Jas 4:6
for "God **o** the proud but gives grace to 1 Pt 5:5

OPPOSING (4)
did to Israel in **o** them on the way 1 Sm 15:2
me to hurry. Cease **o** God, 2 Chr 35:21
might even be found **o** God!" So they Acts 5:39
do many things in **o** the name of Jesus Acts 26:9

OPPOSITE (71)
went and sat down **o** him a good way Gn 21:16
of the child." And as she sat **o** him, Gn 21:16
which is **o** Egypt in the direction of Gn 25:18
set; the loops shall be **o** one another. Ex 26:5
south side of the tabernacle **o** the table, Ex 26:35
its molding on two **o** sides of it you Ex 30:4
flocks or herds graze **o** that mountain." Ex 34:3
set. The loops were **o** one another. Ex 36:12
it under its molding, on two **o** sides of it, Ex 37:27
o the table on the south side of the Ex 40:24
in the wilderness that is **o** Moab, Nm 21:11
the earth, and they are dwelling **o** me. Nm 22:5
in the wilderness, in the Arabah **o** Suph, Dt 1:1
So we remained in the valley **o** Beth-peor. Dt 3:29
the Jordan in the valley **o** Beth-peor, Dt 4:46
who live in the Arabah, **o** Gilgal, Dt 11:30
which is in the land of Moab, **o** Jericho, Dt 32:49
to the top of Pisgah, which is **o** Jericho. Dt 34:1
valley in the land of Moab **o** Beth-peor; Dt 34:6
off. And the people passed over **o** Jericho. Jos 3:16
stood on **o** sides of the ark before the Jos 8:33
which is **o** the ascent of Adummim, Jos 15:7
that lies to the south, **o** Beth-horon, Jos 18:14
which is **o** the ascent of Adummim. Jos 18:17
departed and arrived **o** Jebus (that is, Jgs 19:10
Nohah as far as **o** Gibeah on the east. Jgs 20:43
Jonathan sat **o**, and Abner sat by 1 Sm 20:25
come against them **o** the balsam 2 Sm 5:23
on the hillside **o** him and cursed 2 Sm 16:13
and window **o** window in three tiers. 1 Kgs 7:4
and window was **o** window in three 1 Kgs 7:5
And they encamped **o** one another 1 Kgs 20:29
And set two worthless men **o** him, 1 Kgs 21:10
men came in and sat **o** him. 1 Kgs 21:13
who were at Jericho saw him **o** them, 2 Kgs 2:15
Moabites saw the water **o** them as red 2 Kgs 3:22
break through, **o** the king of Edom, 2 Kgs 3:26
these also lived **o** their kinsmen in 1 Chr 8:32
these also lived **o** their kinsmen in 1 Chr 9:38
come against them **o** the balsam 1 Chr 14:14
o them the priests sounded trumpets, 2 Chr 7:6
son of Harumaph repaired **o** his house. Neh 3:10
repaired to a point **o** the tombs of Neh 3:16
repaired another section **o** the ascent to Neh 3:19
and Hasshub repaired **o** their house. Neh 3:23
son of Uzai repaired **o** the buttress and Neh 3:25
repaired to a point **o** the Water Gate on Neh 3:26
repaired another section **o** the great Neh 3:27
repaired, each one **o** his own house. Neh 3:28
of Immer repaired **o** his own house. Neh 3:29
of Berechiah repaired **o** his chamber. Neh 3:30
of the merchants, **o** the Muster Gate, Neh 3:31
and their brothers stood **o** them in the Neh 12:9
with their brothers who stood **o** them, Neh 12:24
inside the throne room **o** the entrance to Est 5:1
And **o** the gate on the north, as on the Ezk 40:23
the three of them, **o** the threshold, Ezk 41:16
chambers that were **o** the separate yard Ezk 42:1
the separate yard and **o** the building on Ezk 42:1
toward the outer court, **o** the chambers, Ezk 42:7
while those **o** the nave were a hundred Ezk 42:8
o the yard and opposite the building, Ezk 42:10
opposite the yard and **o** the building, Ezk 42:10
the south chambers **o** the yard are Ezk 42:13
boundary to a point **o** Lebo-hamath. Ezk 47:20
of the king's palace, **o** the lampstand. Dn 5:5
Mary were there, sitting **o** the tomb. Mt 27:61
And he sat down **o** the treasury and Mk 12:41
sat on the Mount of Olives **o** the temple, Mk 13:3
of the Gerasenes, which is **o** Galilee. Lk 8:26
we came the following day **o** Chios; Acts 20:15

OPPOSITION (1)
them, they had nothing to say in **o**. Acts 4:14

OPPRESS (24)
If you **o** my daughters, or if you take Gn 31:50
with which the Egyptians **o** them. Ex 3:9
shall not wrong a sojourner or **o** him, Ex 22:21
"You shall not **o** a sojourner. You know Ex 23:9
"You shall not **o** your neighbor or rob Lv 19:13
"You shall not **o** a hired servant who is Dt 24:14
he allowed no one to **o** them; he 1 Chr 16:21
Does it seem good to you to **o**, to despise Jb 10:3
he allowed no one to **o** them; he Ps 105:14
of good; let not the insolent **o** me. Ps 119:122
And the people will **o** one another, every Is 3:5
own pleasure, and **o** all your workers. Is 58:3
if you do not **o** the sojourner, the Jer 7:6
me, and I will punish all who **o** them. Jer 30:20
does not **o** anyone, but restores to the Ezk 18:7
does not **o** anyone, exacts no pledge, Ezk 18:16
my princes shall no more **o** my people, Ezk 45:8
hands are false balances, he loves to **o**. Hos 12:7
mountain of Samaria, who **o** the poor, Am 4:1
"and they shall **o** you from Am 6:14
they **o** a man and his house, a man and Mi 2:2
do not **o** the widow, the fatherless, the Zec 7:10
against those who **o** the hired worker in Mal 3:5
Are not the rich the ones who **o** you, and Jas 2:6

OPPRESSED (40)
But the more they were **o**, the more they Ex 1:12
robbery, or if he has **o** his neighbor Lv 6:2
shall be only **o** and robbed continually, Dt 28:29
shall be only **o** and crushed Dt 28:33
of those who afflicted and **o** them. Jgs 2:18
of iron and he **o** the people of Israel Jgs 4:3
and from the hand of all who **o** you, Jgs 6:9
and they crushed and **o** the people of Jgs 10:8
For eighteen years they **o** all the people Jgs 10:8
Amalekites and the Maonites **o** you, Jgs 10:12
have I defrauded? Whom have I **o**? 1 Sm 12:3
not defrauded us or **o** us or taken 1 Sm 12:4
into Egypt, and the Egyptians **o** them, 1 Sm 12:8
Israel, how the king of Syria **o** them. 2 Kgs 13:4
Hazael king of Syria **o** Israel all the 2 Kgs 13:22
The LORD is a stronghold for the **o**, a Ps 9:9
to do justice to the fatherless and the **o**, Ps 10:18
and justice for all who are **o**. Ps 103:6
Their enemies **o** them, and they were Ps 106:42
who executes justice for the **o**, who Ps 146:7
And behold, the tears of the **o**, and they Eccl 4:1
captors, and rule over those who **o** them. Is 14:2
exult, O **o** virgin daughter of Sidon; Is 23:12
O Lord, I am **o**; be my pledge of safety! Is 38:14
and the Assyrian **o** them for nothing. Is 52:4
He was **o**, and he was afflicted, yet he Is 53:7
the straps of the yoke, to let the **o** go free, Is 58:6
The people of Israel are **o**, and the Jer 50:33
They have **o** the poor and needy, and Ezk 22:29
iniquities by showing mercy to the **o**, Dn 4:27
Ephraim is **o**, crushed in judgment, Hos 5:11
within her, and the **o** in her midst." Am 3:9
diseases and pains, those **o** by demons, Mt 4:24
to him many who were **o** by demons, Mt 8:16
my daughter is severely **o** by a demon." Mt 15:22
him all who were sick or **o** by demons. Mk 1:32
blind, to set at liberty those who are **o**, Lk 4:18
the words of one who is **o** by a demon. Jn 10:21
he defended the **o** man and avenged Acts 7:24
healing all who were **o** by the devil, Acts 10:38

OPPRESSES (6)
land against the adversary who **o** you, Nm 10:9
on me; all day long an attacker **o** me; Ps 56:1
Whoever **o** a poor man insults his Prv 14:31
Whoever **o** the poor to increase his Prv 22:16
A poor man who **o** the poor is a beating Prv 28:3
o the poor and needy, commits Ezk 18:12

OPPRESSING (2)
of all the kingdoms that were **o** you.' 1 Sm 10:18
who is rebellious and defiled, the **o** city! Zep 3:1

OPPRESSION (27)
have also seen the **o** with which the Ex 3:9
or what he got by **o** or the deposit that was Lv 6:4
saw our affliction, our toil, and our **o**. Dt 26:7
to him, for he saw the **o** of Israel, 2 Kgs 13:4
is filled with cursing and deceit and **o**; Ps 10:7
because of the **o** of the enemy?" Ps 42:9
because of the **o** of the enemy? Ps 43:2
Why do you forget our affliction and **o**? Ps 44:24
enemy, because of the **o** of the wicked. Ps 55:3
o and fraud do not depart from its Ps 55:11
From **o** and violence he redeems their Ps 72:14
with malice; loftily they threaten **o**. Ps 73:8
and brought low through **o**, Ps 107:39
Redeem me from man's **o**, that I may Ps 119:134
see in a province the **o** of the poor and Eccl 5:8
Surely **o** drives the wise into madness, Eccl 7:7
learn to do good; seek justice, correct **o**; Is 1:17
and the writers who keep writing **o**, Is 10:1
and trust in **o** and perverseness and Is 30:12
By **o** and judgment he was taken away; Is 53:8
you shall be far from **o**, for you shall not Is 54:14
our God, speaking **o** and revolt, Is 59:13
there is nothing but **o** within her. Jer 6:6

Heaping **o** upon oppression, and deceit Jer 9:6
Heaping oppression upon **o**, and deceit Jer 9:6
and for practicing **o** and violence." Jer 22:17
Put away violence and **o**, and execute Ezk 45:9

OPPRESSIONS (3)
of the multitude of **o** people cry out; Jb 35:9
I saw all the **o** that are done under Eccl 4:1
uprightly, who despises the gain of **o**, Is 33:15

OPPRESSOR (14)
children of the needy, and crush the **o**! Ps 72:4
who lacks understanding is a cruel **o**, Prv 28:16
The poor man and the **o** meet together; Prv 29:13
the staff for his shoulder, the rod of his **o**, Is 9:4
king of Babylon: "How the **o** has ceased, Is 14:4
When the **o** is no more and destruction Is 16:4
all the day because of the wrath of the **o**, Is 51:13
destroy? And where is the wrath of the **o**? Is 51:13
the hand of the **o** him who has been Jer 21:12
the hand of the **o** him who has been Jer 22:3
a waste because of the sword of the **o**, Jer 25:38
birth, because of the sword of the **o**.' Jer 46:16
because of the sword of the **o**, every one Jer 50:16
no **o** shall again march over them, for Zec 9:8

OPPRESSORS (7)
and the heritage that **o** receive from the Jb 27:13
and right; do not leave me to my **o**. Ps 119:121
On the side of their **o** there was power, Eccl 4:1
My people—infants are their **o**, and Is 3:12
When they cry to the LORD because of **o**, Is 19:20
I will make your **o** eat their own flesh, Is 49:26
at that time I will deal with all your **o**. Zep 3:19

ORACLE (26)
said, "The **o** of Balaam the son of Beor, Nm 24:3
the **o** of the man whose eye is opened, Nm 24:3
the **o** of him who hears the words of Nm 24:4
"The **o** of Balaam the son of Beor, Nm 24:15
the **o** of the man whose eye is opened, Nm 24:15
the **o** of him who hears the words of Nm 24:16
The **o** of David, the son of Jesse, the 2 Sm 23:1
the **o** of the man who was raised on 2 Sm 23:1
An **o** is on the lips of a king; his Prv 16:10
The words of Agur son of Jakeh. The **o**. Prv 30:1
An **o** that his mother taught him: Prv 31:1
The **o** concerning Babylon which Isaiah Is 13:1
year that King Ahaz died came this **o**: Is 14:28
An **o** concerning Moab. Because Ar of Is 15:1
An **o** concerning Damascus. Behold, Is 17:1
An **o** concerning Egypt. Behold, the LORD Is 19:1
The **o** concerning the wilderness of the Is 21:1
The **o** concerning Dumah. One is Is 21:11
The **o** concerning Arabia. In the Is 21:13
The **o** concerning the valley of vision. Is 22:1
The **o** concerning Tyre. Wail, O ships of Is 23:1
An **o** on the beasts of the Negeb. Through Is 30:6
This **o** concerns the prince in Ezk 12:10
An **o** concerning Nineveh. The book of Na 1:1
The **o** that Habakkuk the prophet saw. Hab 1:1
The **o** of the word of the LORD to Israel by Mal 1:1

ORACLES (7)
and of the many **o** against him and 2 Chr 24:27
have seen for you **o** that are false and Lam 2:14
and their walking staff gives them **o**. Hos 4:12
He received living **o** to give to us. Acts 7:38
Jews were entrusted with the **o** of God. Rom 3:2
the basic principles of the **o** of God. Heb 5:12
speaks, as one who speaks **o** of God; 1 Pt 4:11

ORATION (1)
throne, and delivered an **o** to them. Acts 12:21

ORCHARD (3)
your vineyard, and with your olive **o**. Ex 23:11
shoots are an **o** of pomegranates with Sg 4:13
went down to the nut **o** to look at the Sg 6:11

ORCHARDS (6)
of vineyards and olive **o** that you did Jos 24:13
the standing grain, as well as the olive **o**. Jgs 15:5
vineyards and olive **o** and give them 1 Sm 8:14
and garments, olive **o** and vineyards, 2 Kgs 5:26
fields, their vineyards, their olive **o**, Neh 5:11
olive **o** and fruit trees in abundance. Neh 9:25

ORDAIN (6)
anoint them and **o** them and Ex 28:41
Thus you shall **o** Aaron and his sons. Ex 29:9
Through seven days shall you **o** them, Ex 29:35
for it will take seven days to **o** you. Lv 8:33
my King, O God; **o** salvation for Jacob! Ps 44:4
O LORD, you will **o** peace for us; you have Is 26:12

ORDAINED (12)
be anointed in them and **o** in them. Ex 29:29
"Today you have been **o** for the service Ex 32:29
priests, whom he **o** to serve as priests. Nm 3:3
which was **o** at Mount Sinai for a Nm 28:6
household gods, and **o** one of his sons, Jgs 17:5
And Micah **o** the Levite, and the young Jgs 17:12
For the LORD had **o** to defeat the good 2 Sm 17:14
he **o** to be priests of the high places. 1 Kgs 13:33
of Judah had **o** to make offerings 2 Kgs 23:5
LORD our God, as **o** forever for Israel. 2 Chr 2:4
But it was **o** by God that the downfall 2 Chr 22:7
LORD, you have **o** them as a judgment, Hab 1:12

ORDER (141)
laid the wood in **o** and bound Isaac his Gn 22:9
Ishmael, named in the **o** of their birth: Gn 25:13
in **o** that I may find favor in your Gn 32:5
all my people shall **o** themselves as you Gn 41:40
in **o** that you may dwell in the land of Gn 46:34
the other stone, in the **o** of their birth. Ex 28:10
in **o** that I may make a great nation of Ex 32:10
I may know you in **o** to find favor in Ex 33:13
This was the **o** of march of the people Nm 10:28
return to Egypt in **o** to acquire many Dt 17:16
making war against it in **o** to take it, Dt 20:19
of flax that she had laid in **o** on the roof. Jos 2:6
in **o** that you may know the way you Jos 3:4
in **o** that they should be devoted to Jos 11:20
in **o** to test Israel by them, whether they Jgs 2:22
It was only in **o** that the generations of the Jgs 3:2
here, with stones laid in due **o**. Jgs 6:26
in **o** to perpetuate the name of the dead in Ru 4:5
In **o** to change the course of things 2 Sm 14:20
his house in **o** and hanged himself, 2 Sm 17:23
in **o** to build an altar to the LORD, 2 Sm 24:21
costly stones in **o** to lay the 1 Kgs 5:17
on the wall in **o** that the supporting 1 Kgs 6:6
in **o** that all the peoples of the earth 1 Kgs 8:43
put the wood in **o** and cut the bull 1 Kgs 18:33
"O man of God, this is the king's **o**, 2 Kgs 1:11
it with cunning in **o** to destroy the 2 Kgs 10:19
says the LORD, 'Set your house in **o**, 2 Kgs 20:1
priests of the second **o** and the keepers 2 Kgs 23:4
their service according to their **o**. 1 Chr 6:32
men of war, arrayed in battle **o**, 1 Chr 12:38
them their brothers of the second **o**, 1 Chr 15:18
Heman were under the **o** of the king. 1 Chr 25:6
in **o** that all the peoples of the earth 2 Chr 6:33
singing, according to the **o** of David. 2 Chr 23:18
in **o** that he might give them into 2 Chr 25:20
in **o** that his fierce anger may turn 2 Chr 29:10
in **o** that they might take the city. 2 Chr 32:18
in **o** to test him and to know all that 2 Chr 32:31
disguised himself in **o** to fight with 2 Chr 35:22
in **o** that search may be made in the Ezr 4:15
by **o** of the officials and the elders all his Ezr 10:8
give me a bad name in **o** to taunt me. Neh 6:13
Ezra the scribe in **o** to study the words Neh 8:13
had warned them in **o** to turn them Neh 9:26
you warned them in **o** to turn them Neh 9:29
in **o** to show the peoples and the princes Est 1:11
the king, let a royal **o** go out from him, Est 1:19
So when the king's **o** and his edict were Est 2:8
in **o** to see whether Mordecai's words Est 3:4
went out hurriedly by **o** of the king, Est 3:15
let an **o** be written to revoke the letters Est 8:5
like deep shadow without any **o**, Jb 10:22
if you can; set your words in **o** before me; Jb 33:5
men to watch his house in **o** to kill him. Ps 59:T
forever after the **o** of Melchizedek." Ps 110:4
evil way, in **o** to keep your word. Ps 119:101
Set your house in **o**, for you shall die, you Is 38:1
by day and the fixed **o** of the moon and Jer 31:35
"If this fixed **o** departs from before me, Jer 31:36
night and the fixed **o** of heaven and Jer 33:25
in **o** that you may know that my words Jer 44:29
his wicked way, in **o** to save his life, Ezk 3:18
to blow the fire on it in **o** to melt it, Ezk 22:20
All this is in **o** that no trees by the Ezk 31:14
them, in **o** to cleanse the land. Ezk 39:12
were brought here in **o** that I might Ezk 40:4
in **o** not to bring them out into the Ezk 46:20
but in **o** that the interpretation may be Dn 2:30
Because the king's **o** was urgent and the Dn 3:22
lift themselves up in **o** to fulfill the Dn 11:14
to the Greeks in **o** to remove them far Jl 3:6
drunk, in **o** to gaze at their nakedness! Hab 2:15
not put on a hairy cloak in **o** to deceive, Zec 13:4
before other people in **o** to be seen by Mt 6:1
the house empty, swept, and put in **o**. Mt 12:44
and plotted together in **o** to arrest Jesus Mt 26:4
Therefore **o** the tomb to be made Mt 27:64
of God in **o** to establish your Mk 7:9
came up and in **o** to test him asked, Mk 10:2
the chief priests in **o** to betray him to Mk 14:10
it finds the house swept and put in **o**. Lk 11:25
in **o** that those who would pass from Lk 16:26
but in **o** that the world might be saved Jn 3:17
But in **o** that it may spread no further Acts 4:17
gates day and night in **o** to kill him, Acts 9:24
began and explained it to them in **o**: Acts 11:4
them and to **o** them to keep Acts 15:5
Having received this **o**, he put them Acts 16:24
to the law you **o** me to be struck?" Acts 23:3
in **o** that I may reap some harvest Rom 1:13
in **o** that the promise may rest on Rom 4:16
him by baptism into death, in **o** that, Rom 6:4
crucified with him in **o** that the body of Rom 6:6
in **o** that we may bear fruit for God. Rom 7:4
in **o** that sin might be shown to be sin, Rom 7:13
in **o** that the righteous requirement of Rom 8:4
suffer with him in **o** that we may also Rom 8:17
in **o** that he might be the firstborn Rom 8:29
or bad—in **o** that God's purpose of Rom 9:11
in **o** to make known the riches of his Rom 9:23
did they stumble in **o** that they might Rom 11:11
in **o** somehow to make my fellow Rom 11:14
now been disobedient in **o** that by the Rom 11:31
in **o** to confirm the promises given to Rom 15:8
and in **o** that the Gentiles might Rom 15:9
but to promote good **o** and to secure 1 Cor 7:35
I became as a Jew, in **o** to win Jews. 1 Cor 9:20
among you in **o** that those who 1 Cor 11:19
my mind in **o** to instruct others, 1 Cor 14:19
should be done decently and in **o**. 1 Cor 14:40
But each in his own **o**: Christ the 1 Cor 15:23
but in **o** that your earnestness for us 2 Cor 7:12
support from them in **o** to serve you. 2 Cor 11:8
in **o** to undermine the claim of those 2 Cor 11:12
city of Damascus in **o** to seize me, 2 Cor 11:32
in **o** that I might preach him among Gal 1:16
in **o** to make sure I was not running or Gal 2:2
in **o** to be justified by faith in Christ Gal 2:16
in **o** that we might be justified by faith. Gal 3:24
and only in **o** that they may not be Gal 6:12
as rubbish, in **o** that I may gain Christ Phil 3:8
in **o** to present you holy and blameless Col 1:22
I say this in **o** that no one may delude Col 2:4
to see your good **o** and the firmness of Col 2:5
in **o** that all may be condemned 2 Thes 2:12
that you might put what remained into **o**, Ti 1:5
in **o** that he might serve me on your Phlm 1:13
your consent in **o** that your goodness Phlm 1:14
forever, after the **o** of Melchizedek." Heb 5:6
a high priest after the **o** of Melchizedek. Heb 5:10
forever after the **o** of Melchizedek. Heb 6:20
to arise after the **o** of Melchizedek, Heb 7:11
than one named after the **o** of Aaron? Heb 7:11
forever, after the **o** of Melchizedek." Heb 7:17
abolishes the first in **o** to establish the Heb 10:9
could not endure the **o** that was given, Heb 12:20
been made—in **o** that the things that Heb 12:27
outside the gate in **o** to sanctify the Heb 13:12
earnestly to do this in **o** that I may be Heb 13:19
God supplies—in **o** that in everything 1 Pt 4:11

ORDERED (26)
And the king **o** Joab and Abishai and 2 Sm 18:5
covenant, **o** in all things and secure. 2 Sm 23:5
And Jehu **o**, "Sanctify a solemn 2 Kgs 10:20
because he **o** his ways before the 2 Chr 27:6
diligence what Darius the king had **o**. Ezr 6:13
and **o** him to go to Mordecai to learn Est 4:5
and did everything as Esther had **o** him. Est 4:17
And Jeremiah **o** Baruch, saying, "I am Jer 36:5
Jeremiah the prophet **o** him about Jer 36:8
He **o** the furnace heated seven times Dn 3:19
And he **o** some of the mighty men of his Dn 3:20
and **o** them not to make him known. Mt 12:16
Then he **o** the crowds to sit down on Mt 14:19
not pay, his master **o** him to be sold, Mt 18:25
Then Pilate **o** it to be given to him. Mt 27:58
And he strictly **o** them not to make him Mk 3:12
he **o** these servants to whom he had Lk 19:15
staying with them he **o** them not to Acts 1:4
the sentries and **o** that they should Acts 12:19
and arrested him and **o** him to be Acts 21:33
he **o** him to be brought into the Acts 21:34
the tribune **o** him to be brought into Acts 22:24
on the tribunal and **o** Paul to be Acts 25:6
on the tribunal and **o** the man to be Acts 25:17
I **o** him to be held until I could send Acts 25:21
He **o** those who could swim to jump Acts 27:43

ORDERING (2)
o the jailer to keep them safely. Acts 16:23
o his accusers also to state before you Acts 23:30

ORDERLY (1)
time past, to write an **o** account for you, Lk 1:3

ORDERS (18)
Pharaoh gave men **o** concerning him, Gn 12:20
And Joseph gave **o** to fill their bags Gn 42:25
the LORD to battle, as my lord **o**." Nm 32:27
and I will give **o** concerning you." 2 Sm 14:8
when the king gave **o** to all the 2 Sm 18:5

Then I gave **o**, and they cleansed the Neh 13:9
be shut and gave **o** that they should Neh 13:19
For the king had given **o** to all the staff of Est 1:8
And he gave **o** to bring the book of Est 6:1
he gave **o** in writing that his evil plan Est 9:25
to one who **o** his way rightly I will show Ps 50:23
So King Zedekiah gave **o**, and they Jer 37:21
he gave **o** to go over to the other side. Mt 8:18
an executioner with **o** to bring John's Mk 6:27
the Pharisees had given **o** that if anyone Jn 11:57
stood up and gave **o** to put the men Acts 5:34
off them and gave **o** to beat them with Acts 16:22
Then he gave **o** to the centurion that Acts 24:23

ORDINANCE (2)
should establish an **o** and enforce an Dn 6:7
that no injunction or **o** that the king Dn 6:15

ORDINANCES (3)
Do you know the **o** of the heavens? Can Jb 38:33
Lord GOD: These are the **o** for the altar: Ezk 43:18
the law of commandments and **o**, Eph 2:15

ORDINARY (14)
be poured on the body of an **o** person, Ex 30:32
you shall not do any **o** work. Lv 23:7
you shall not do any **o** work." Lv 23:8
You shall not do any **o** work. Lv 23:21
You shall not do any **o** work, Lv 23:25
you shall not do any **o** work. Lv 23:35
you shall not do any **o** work. Lv 23:36
You shall not do any **o** work, Nm 28:18
You shall not do any **o** work. Nm 28:25
You shall not do any **o** work, Nm 28:26
You shall not do any **o** work. Nm 29:1
You shall not do any **o** work, Nm 29:12
You shall not do any **o** work, Nm 29:35
are holy even when it is an **o** journey. 1 Sm 21:5

ORDINATION (13)
and the right thigh (for it is a ram of **o**), Ex 29:22
of the ram of Aaron's **o** and wave it for Ex 29:26
that is contributed from the ram of **o**, Ex 29:27
shall take the ram of **o** and boil its flesh Ex 29:31
was made at their **o** and consecration, Ex 29:33
of the flesh for the **o** or of the bread Ex 29:34
of the guilt offering, of the **o** offering, Lv 7:37
he presented the other ram, the ram of **o**, Lv 8:22
This was an **o** offering with a pleasing Lv 8:28
It was Moses' portion of the ram of **o**, as Lv 8:29
bread that is in the basket of **o** offerings, Lv 8:31
until the days of your **o** are completed, Lv 8:33
Whoever comes for **o** with a young 2 Chr 13:9

ORE (2)
earth, and copper is smelted from the **o**. Jb 28:2
the farthest limit the **o** in gloom and deep Jb 28:3

OREB (7)
the two princes of Midian, **O** and Zeeb. Jgs 7:25
They killed **O** at the rock of Oreb, and Jgs 7:25
They killed Oreb at the rock of **O**, and Jgs 7:25
brought the heads of **O** and Zeeb to Jgs 7:25
hands the princes of Midian, **O** and Zeeb. Jgs 8:3
Make their nobles like **O** and Zeeb, all Ps 83:11
when he struck Midian at the rock of **O**. Is 10:26

OREN (1)
Ram, his firstborn, Bunah, **O**, Ozem, 1 Chr 2:25

ORGAN (1)
crushed or whose male **o** is cut off shall Dt 23:1

ORGANIZED (4)
And David **o** them in divisions 1 Chr 23:6
David **o** them according to the 1 Chr 24:3
they **o** them under sixteen heads of 1 Chr 24:4
Levites whom David had **o** to be in 2 Chr 23:18

ORGIES (4)
are a delusion, the **o** on the mountains. Jer 3:23
daytime, not in **o** and drunkenness, Rom 13:13
drunkenness, **o**, and things like these. Gal 5:21
drunkenness, **o**, drinking parties, 1 Pt 4:3

ORIGIN (6)
your exultant city whose **o** is from days of Is 23:7
Your **o** and your birth are of the land of Ezk 16:3
you were created, in the land of your **o**, Ezk 21:30
the land of Pathros, the land of their **o**, Ezk 29:14
be ruler in Israel, whose **o** is from of old, Mi 5:2
those who are sanctified all have one **o**. Heb 2:11

ORIGINAL (1)
we hold our **o** confidence firm to Heb 3:14

ORION (3)
who made the Bear and **O**, the Pleiades Jb 9:9
of the Pleiades or loose the cords of **O**? Jb 38:31
He who made the Pleiades and **O**, and Am 5:8

ORNAMENT (3)
a gold ring or an **o** of gold is a wise Prv 25:12
LORD, you shall put them all on as an **o**; Is 49:18
His beautiful **o** they used for pride, and Ezk 7:20

ORNAMENTS (13)
her brother and to her mother costly **o**. Gn 24:53
they mourned, and no one put on his **o**. Ex 33:4
So now take off your **o**, that I may know Ex 33:5
of Israel stripped themselves of their **o**, Ex 33:6
he took the crescent **o** that were on the Jgs 8:21
besides the crescent **o** and the pendants Jgs 8:26
who put **o** of gold on your apparel. 2 Sm 1:24
Your cheeks are lovely with **o**, your neck Sg 1:10
We will make for you **o** of gold, studded Sg 1:11
Can a virgin forget her **o**, or a bride her Jer 2:32
that you adorn yourself with **o** of gold, Jer 4:30
I adorned you with **o** and put bracelets Ezk 16:11
eyes, and adorned yourself with **o**. Ezk 23:40

ORNAN (11)
the threshing floor of **O** the Jebusite. 1 Chr 21:15
the threshing floor of **O** the Jebusite. 1 Chr 21:18
Now **O** was threshing wheat. He 1 Chr 21:20
As David came to **O**, Ornan looked 1 Chr 21:21
O looked and saw David and went 1 Chr 21:21
And David said to **O**, "Give me the 1 Chr 21:22
Then **O** said to David, "Take it, and 1 Chr 21:23
But King David said to **O**, "No, but I 1 Chr 21:24
So David paid **O** 600 shekels of gold 1 Chr 21:25
the threshing floor of **O** the Jebusite, 1 Chr 21:28
the threshing floor of **O** the Jebusite. 2 Chr 3:1

ORPAH (2)
name of the one was **O** and the name of Ru 1:4
And **O** kissed her mother-in-law, but Ru 1:14

ORPHAN (1)
of our hands. In you the **o** finds mercy." Hos 14:3

ORPHANS (3)
We have become **o**, fatherless; our Lam 5:3
"I will not leave you as **o**; I will come to Jn 14:18
to visit **o** and widows in their affliction, Jas 1:27

OSNAPPAR (1)
great and noble **O** deported and settled Ezr 4:10

OSTRICH (3)
the **o**, the nighthawk, the sea gull, the Lv 11:16
the **o**, the nighthawk, the sea gull, the Dt 14:15
"The wings of the **o** wave proudly, but Jb 39:13

OSTRICHES (7)
of jackals and a companion of **o**. Jb 30:29
there **o** will dwell, and there wild goats Is 13:21
be the haunt of jackals, an abode for **o**. Is 34:13
will honor me, the jackals and the **o**, Is 43:20
in Babylon, and **o** shall dwell in her. Jer 50:39
cruel, like the **o** in the wilderness. Lam 4:3
like the jackals, and mourning like the **o**. Mi 1:8

OTHER (420)
more crafty than any **o** beast of the field Gn 3:1
was Adah, and the name of the **o** Zillah. Gn 4:19
years; and he had **o** sons and daughters. Gn 5:4
807 years and had **o** sons and daughters. Gn 5:7
815 years and had **o** sons and daughters. Gn 5:10
840 years and had **o** sons and daughters. Gn 5:13
830 years and had **o** sons and daughters. Gn 5:16
800 years and had **o** sons and daughters. Gn 5:19
300 years and had **o** sons and daughters. Gn 5:22
782 years and had **o** sons and daughters. Gn 5:26
595 years and had **o** sons and daughters. Gn 5:30
years and had **o** sons and daughters. Gn 11:11
years and had **o** sons and daughters. Gn 11:13
years and had **o** sons and daughters. Gn 11:15
years and had **o** sons and daughters. Gn 11:17
years and had **o** sons and daughters. Gn 11:19
years and had **o** sons and daughters. Gn 11:21
years and had **o** sons and daughters. Gn 11:23
years and had **o** sons and daughters. Gn 11:25
east. Thus they separated from each **o**. Gn 13:11
and laid each half over against the **o**. Gn 15:10
the one shall be stronger than the **o**, Gn 25:23
This is none **o** than the house of God, Gn 28:17
that I should give her to any **o** man; Gn 29:19
we will give you the **o** also in return for Gn 29:27
Joseph more than any **o** of his sons, Gn 37:3
And behold, seven **o** cows, ugly and Gn 41:3
and stood by the **o** cows on the bank of Gn 41:3
Seven **o** cows came up after them, poor Gn 41:19
send back your **o** brother and Gn 43:14
we have brought **o** money down with Gn 43:22
of them from one end of Egypt to the **o**. Gn 47:21
was named Shiphrah and the **o** Puah, Ex 1:15
chariots and all the **o** chariots of Egypt Ex 14:7
one coming near the **o** all night. Ex 14:20
on one side, and the **o** on the other side. Ex 17:12
on one side, and the other on the **o** side. Ex 17:12
and the name of the **o**, Eliezer (for he Ex 18:4
And they asked each **o** of their welfare Ex 18:7
"You shall have no **o** gods before me. Ex 20:3
and one strikes the **o** with a stone or Ex 21:18
to any god, **o** than the LORD alone, Ex 22:20
no mention of the names of **o** gods, Ex 23:13
of it, and two rings on the **o** side of it. Ex 25:12
one end, and one cherub on the **o** end. Ex 25:19
of the lampstand out of the **o** side of it; Ex 25:32
on the **o** branch—so for the six Ex 25:33
and the **o** five curtains shall be coupled Ex 26:3
the curtains one to the **o** with the clasps, Ex 26:6
the one side, and the cubit on the **o** side, Ex 26:13
the frames of the **o** side of the Ex 26:27
On the **o** side the hangings shall be Ex 27:15
of the remaining six on the **o** stone, Ex 28:10
"You shall take the **o** ram, and Aaron Ex 29:19
and the **o** lamb you shall offer at Ex 29:39
The **o** lamb you shall offer at twilight, Ex 29:41
you shall make no **o** like it in Ex 30:32
from every **o** people on the face of the Ex 33:16
(for you shall worship no **o** god, for the Ex 34:14
and the **o** five curtains he coupled to Ex 36:10
the curtains one to the **o** with clasps. Ex 36:13
on the edge of the **o** connecting curtain. Ex 36:17
the frames of the **o** side of the Ex 36:32
on its one side and two rings on its **o** side. Ex 37:3
one end, and one cherub on the **o** end. Ex 37:8
of the lampstand out of the **o** side of it; Ex 37:18
on the **o** branch—so for the six Ex 37:19
And so for the **o** side. On both sides of Ex 38:15
sin offering and the **o** for a burnt offering. Lv 5:7
and put on **o** garments and carry Lv 6:11
torn by beasts may be put to any **o** use, Lv 7:24
Then he presented the **o** ram, the ram of Lv 8:22
But all **o** winged insects that have four Lv 11:23
burnt offering and the **o** for a sin Lv 12:8
sin offering and the **o** a burnt offering. Lv 14:22
sin offering and the **o** for a burnt Lv 14:31
Then they shall take **o** stones and put Lv 14:42
and he shall take **o** plaster and plaster Lv 14:42
sin offering and the **o** for a burnt Lv 15:15
sin offering and the **o** for a burnt Lv 15:30
lot for the LORD and the **o** lot for Azazel. Lv 16:8
and some man **o** than your husband Nm 5:20
sin offering and the **o** for a burnt Nm 6:11
sin offering and the **o** for a burnt Nm 8:12
Eldad, and the **o** named Medad, Nm 11:26
side and a day's journey on the **o** side, Nm 11:31
and camped on the **o** side of the Nm 21:13
bless Israel, he did not go, as at **o** times, Nm 24:1
and the **o** lamb you shall offer at Nm 28:4
The **o** lamb you shall offer at twilight. Nm 28:8
with them on the **o** side of the Jordan Nm 32:19
And they gave **o** names to the cities Nm 32:38
of the sons of the **o** tribes of the people Nm 36:3
and ask from one end of heaven to the **o**, Dt 4:32
LORD is God; there is no **o** besides him. Dt 4:35
and on the earth beneath; there is no **o**. Dt 4:39
"'You shall have no **o** gods before me. Dt 5:7
You shall not go after **o** gods, the gods of Dt 6:14
sons from following me, to serve **o** gods. Dt 7:4
in number than any **o** people that the Dt 7:7
God and go after **o** gods and serve them Dt 8:19
turn aside and serve **o** gods and worship Dt 11:16
to go after **o** gods that you have not Dt 11:28
and if he says, 'Let us go after **o** gods,' Dt 13:2
saying, 'Let us go and serve **o** gods,' Dt 13:6
from the one end of the earth to the **o**, Dt 13:7
city, saying, 'Let us go and serve **o** gods,' Dt 13:13
gone and served **o** gods and worshiped Dt 17:3
or who speaks in the name of **o** gods, Dt 18:20
you shall add three **o** cities to these three, Dt 19:9
wives, the one loved and the **o** unloved, Dt 21:15
army or be liable for any **o** public duty. Dt 24:5
the left, to go after **o** gods to serve them. Dt 28:14
there you shall serve **o** gods of wood and Dt 28:36
from one end of the earth to the **o**, Dt 28:64
there you shall serve **o** gods of wood and Dt 28:64
went and served **o** gods and worshiped Dt 29:26
away to worship **o** gods and serve Dt 30:17
because they have turned to **o** gods. Dt 31:18
they will turn to **o** gods and serve them, Dt 31:20
With the **o** half of the tribe of Manasseh Jos 13:8
which is on the **o** side of the Jordan, Jos 17:5
goes in the **o** direction eastward toward Jos 19:12
gave you on the **o** side of the Jordan. Jos 22:4
but to the **o** half Joshua had given a Jos 22:7
for yourselves an altar **o** than the altar Jos 22:19
o than the altar of the LORD our God Jos 22:29
and go and serve **o** gods and bow down Jos 23:16
and of Nahor; and they served **o** gods. Jos 24:2
who lived on the **o** side of the Jordan. Jos 24:8
should forsake the LORD to serve **o** gods, Jos 24:16
They went after **o** gods, from among the Jgs 2:12
for they whored after **o** gods and bowed Jgs 2:17
than their fathers, going after **o** gods, Jgs 2:19

"This is no **o** than the sword of Gideon Jgs 7:14
have forsaken me and served **o** gods; Jgs 10:13
and camped on the **o** side of the Arnon. Jgs 11:18
came to me the **o** day has appeared to Jgs 13:10
become weak and be like any **o** man." Jgs 16:7
become weak and be like any **o** man." Jgs 16:11
become weak and be like any **o** man." Jgs 16:13
become weak and be like any **o** man." Jgs 16:17
go out as at **o** times and shake myself Jgs 16:20
on the one and his left hand on the **o**. Jgs 16:29
in array against Gibeah, as at **o** times. Jgs 20:30
And as at **o** times they began to strike Jgs 20:31
goes up to Bethel and the **o** to Gibeah, Jgs 20:31
was Orpah and the name of the **o** Ruth. Ru 1:4
drew off his sandal and gave it to the **o**, Ru 4:7
was Hannah, and the name of the **o**, 1 Sm 1:2
came and stood, calling as at **o** times, 1 Sm 3:10
day, forsaking me and serving **o** gods, 1 Sm 8:8
garrison on the **o** side." But he 1 Sm 14:1
side and a rocky crag on the **o** side. 1 Sm 14:4
Bozez, and the name of the **o** Seneh. 1 Sm 14:4
and the **o** on the south in front of 1 Sm 14:5
will be on the **o** side." And the people 1 Sm 14:40
stood on the mountain on the **o** side, 1 Sm 17:3
was told Saul, he sent **o** messengers, 1 Sm 19:21
king sat on his seat, as at **o** times, 1 Sm 20:25
his men on the **o** side of the 1 Sm 23:26
went over to the **o** side and stood far 1 Sm 26:13
of the LORD, saying, 'Go, serve **o** gods.' 1 Sm 26:19
and put on **o** garments and went, 1 Sm 28:8
who were on the **o** side of the valley 1 Sm 31:7
and the **o** on the other side of the pool. 2 Sm 2:13
and the other on the **o** side of the pool. 2 Sm 2:13
Baanah, and the name of the **o** Rechab, 2 Sm 4:2
city, the one rich and the **o** poor. 2 Sm 12:1
is greater than the **o** that you did to 2 Sm 13:16
and one struck the **o** and killed him. 2 Sm 14:6
in one of the pits or in some **o** place. 2 Sm 17:9
On the **o** hand, if I had dealt 2 Sm 18:13
so that no **o** king shall compare with 1 Kgs 3:13
But the **o** woman said, "No, the living 1 Kgs 3:22
your son is dead'; and the **o** says, 'No; 1 Kgs 3:23
give half to the one and half to the **o**." 1 Kgs 3:25
put him to death." But the **o** said, 1 Kgs 3:26
as far as the **o** side of Jokmeam; 1 Kgs 4:12
For he was wiser than all **o** men, 1 Kgs 4:31
the length of the **o** wing of the 1 Kgs 6:24
the tip of one wing to the tip of the **o**. 1 Kgs 6:24
The **o** cherub also measured ten 1 Kgs 6:25
and so was that of the **o** cherub. 1 Kgs 6:26
a wing of the **o** cherub touched the 1 Kgs 6:27
the other cherub touched the **o** wall; 1 Kgs 6:27
their **o** wings touched each other in 1 Kgs 6:27
wings touched each **o** in the middle 1 Kgs 6:27
two leaves of the **o** door were folding. 1 Kgs 6:34
dwell, in the **o** court back of the hall, 1 Kgs 7:8
the height of the **o** capital was five 1 Kgs 7:16
capital and a lattice for the **o** capital. 1 Kgs 7:17
he did the same with the **o** capital. 1 Kgs 7:18
all around, and so with the **o** capital. 1 Kgs 7:20
that the LORD is God; there is no **o**. 1 Kgs 8:60
but go and serve **o** gods and worship 1 Kgs 9:6
and laid hold on **o** gods and worshiped 1 Kgs 9:9
turned away his heart after **o** gods, 1 Kgs 11:4
that he should not go after **o** gods. 1 Kgs 11:10
in Bethel, and the **o** he put in Dan. 1 Kgs 12:29
made for yourself **o** gods and metal 1 Kgs 14:9
I will prepare the **o** bull and lay it 1 Kgs 18:23
was parted to the one side and to the **o**, 2 Kgs 2:8
was parted to the one side and to the **o**, 2 Kgs 2:14
Baal was filled from one end to the **o**. 2 Kgs 10:21
the priest and the **o** priests and said to 2 Kgs 12:7
king of Egypt, and had feared **o** gods 2 Kgs 17:7
"You shall not fear **o** gods or bow 2 Kgs 17:35
to do. You shall not fear **o** gods, 2 Kgs 17:37
with you. You shall not fear **o** gods, 2 Kgs 17:38
and have made offerings to **o** gods, 2 Kgs 22:17
father of Kiriath-jearim had **o** sons: 1 Chr 2:52
of the temple free from **o** service, 1 Chr 9:33
Eliezer had no **o** sons, but the sons 1 Chr 23:17
the wall of the house, and its **o** wing, 2 Chr 3:11
touched the wing of the **o** cherub; 2 Chr 3:11
the wall of the house, and the **o** wing, 2 Chr 3:12
one on the south, the **o** on the north; 2 Chr 3:17
cymbals and **o** musical instruments, 2 Chr 5:13
and go and serve **o** gods and worship 2 Chr 7:19
laid hold on **o** gods and worshiped 2 Chr 7:22
yourselves like the peoples of **o** lands? 2 Chr 13:9
places to make offerings to **o** gods, 2 Chr 28:25
so until **o** priests had consecrated 2 Chr 29:34
done to all the peoples of **o** lands? 2 Chr 32:13
and have made offerings to **o** gods, 2 Chr 34:25
"What have we to do with each **o**, 2 Chr 35:21
410 bowls of silver, and 1,000 **o** vessels; Ezr 1:10
The sons of the **o** Elam, 1,254. Ezr 2:31

or **o** servants of this house of God. Ezr 7:24
hand and held his weapon with the **o**. Neh 4:17
for **o** men have our fields and our Neh 5:5
The men of the **o** Nebo, 52. Neh 7:33
The sons of the **o** Elam, 1,254. Neh 7:34
palm, and **o** leafy trees to make booths, Neh 8:15
out of ten remained in the **o** towns. Neh 11:1
The **o** choir of those who gave thanks Neh 12:38
are different from those of every **o** people, Est 3:8
will escape any more than all the **o** Jews. Est 4:13
cut down, they wither before any **o** plant. Jb 8:12
they clasp each **o** and cannot be Jb 41:17
righteousness and peace kiss each **o**. Ps 85:10
has not dealt thus with any **o** nation; Ps 147:20
until the **o** comes and examines him. Prv 18:17
is the same; as one dies, so dies the **o**. Eccl 3:19
one person who has no **o**, either son or Eccl 4:8
God has made the one as well as the **o**, Eccl 7:14
o lords besides you have ruled over us, Is 26:13
my glory I give to no **o**, nor my praise to Is 42:8
I am the LORD, and there is no **o**, besides Is 45:5
me; I am the LORD, and there is no **o**. Is 45:6
'Surely God is in you, and there is no **o**, Is 45:14
"I am the LORD, and there is no **o**. Is 45:18
And there is no **o** god besides me, a Is 45:21
earth! For I am God, and there is no **o**. Is 45:22
of old; for I am God, and there is no **o**; Is 46:9
made offerings to **o** gods and worshiped Jer 1:16
you do not go after **o** gods to your own Jer 7:6
and go after **o** gods that you have not Jer 7:9
they pour out drink offerings to **o** gods, Jer 7:18
They have gone after **o** gods to serve Jer 11:10
from one end of the land to the **o**; Jer 12:12
and have gone after **o** gods to serve Jer 13:10
and have gone after **o** gods and have Jer 16:11
there you shall serve **o** gods day and Jer 16:13
offerings in it to **o** gods whom neither Jer 19:4
been poured out to **o** gods—shall be Jer 19:13
God and worshiped **o** gods and served Jer 22:9
figs, but the **o** basket had very bad figs, Jer 24:2
Do not go after **o** gods to serve and Jer 25:6
from one end of the earth to the **o**. Jer 25:33
have been poured out to **o** gods, Jer 32:29
and do not go after **o** gods to serve them, Jer 35:15
in Edom and in **o** lands heard that the Jer 40:11
offerings and serve **o** gods that they Jer 44:3
evil and make no offerings to **o** gods. Jer 44:5
making offerings to **o** gods in the land of Jer 44:8
wives had made offerings to **o** gods, Jer 44:15
you cannot turn from one side to the **o**, Ezk 4:8
were different from **o** women in your Ezk 16:34
house of Judah is like all the **o** nations,' Ezk 25:8
one side room to the ceiling of the **o**, Ezk 40:13
cubits; the openings faced each **o**. Ezk 40:13
and off to the **o** side of the vestibule of Ezk 40:40
the **o** at the side of the south gate Ezk 40:44
o chambers was a breadth of twenty Ezk 41:10
lion toward the palm tree on the **o** side. Ezk 41:19
shall put on **o** garments before they Ezk 42:14
And they shall put on **o** garments, lest Ezk 44:19
many trees on the one side and on the **o**. Ezk 47:7
tunics, their hats, and their **o** garments, Dn 3:21
for there is no **o** god who is able to Dn 3:29
above all the **o** presidents and satraps, Dn 6:3
and the **o** horn that came up and before Dn 7:20
were high, but one was higher than the **o**, Dn 8:3
He shall not pay attention to any **o** god, Dn 11:37
though they turn to **o** gods and love Hos 3:1
blood, and each hunts the **o** with a net. Mi 7:2
the right of the bowl and the **o** on its left." Zec 4:3
out according to what is on the **o** side. Zec 5:3
I named Favor, the **o** I named Union. Zec 11:7
northward, and the **o** half southward. Zec 14:4
be raised against the hand of the **o**. Zec 14:13
on from there he saw two **o** brothers, Mt 4:21
the right cheek, turn to him the **o** also. Mt 5:39
your righteousness before **o** people in Mt 6:1
either he will hate the one and love the **o**, Mt 6:24
be devoted to the one and despise the **o**. Mt 6:24
he gave orders to go over to the **o** side. Mt 8:18
And when he came to the **o** side, to the Mt 8:28
and it was restored, healthy like the **o**. Mt 12:13
brings with it seven **o** spirits more evil Mt 12:45
O seeds fell on rocky ground, where they Mt 13:5
O seeds fell among thorns, and the Mt 13:7
O seeds fell on good soil and produced Mt 13:8
boat and go before him to the **o** side, Mt 14:22
When the disciples reached the **o** side, Mt 16:5
And he went to the **o** son and said the Mt 21:30
Again he sent **o** servants, more than Mt 21:36
out the vineyard to **o** tenants who will Mt 21:41
Again he sent **o** servants, saying, 'Tell Mt 22:4
winds, from one end of heaven to the **o**. Mt 24:31
Afterward the **o** virgins came also, Mt 25:11
Magdalene and the **o** Mary were there, Mt 27:61

Mary Magdalene and the **o** Mary went to Mt 28:1
O seed fell on rocky ground, where it did Mk 4:5
O seed fell among thorns, and the thorns Mk 4:7
And **o** seeds fell into good soil and Mk 4:8
and the desires for **o** things enter in and Mk 4:19
to them, "Let us go across to the **o** side." Mk 4:35
as he was. And **o** boats were with him. Mk 4:36
They came to the **o** side of the sea, to the Mk 5:1
crossed again in the boat to the **o** side, Mk 5:21
the boat and go before him to the **o** side, Mk 6:45
there are many **o** traditions that they Mk 7:4
the boat again, and went to the **o** side. Mk 8:13
He had still one **o**, a beloved son. Mk 12:6
There is no **o** commandment greater Mk 12:31
is one, and there is no **o** besides him. Mk 12:32
were also many **o** women who came Mk 15:41
So with many **o** exhortations he Lk 3:18
kingdom of God to the **o** towns as well; Lk 4:43
their partners in the **o** boat to come and Lk 5:7
strikes you on the cheek, offer the **o** also, Lk 6:29
five hundred denarii, and the **o** fifty. Lk 7:41
us go across to the **o** side of the lake." So Lk 8:22
he saw him he passed by on the **o** side. Lk 10:31
and saw him, passed by on the **o** side. Lk 10:32
and brings seven **o** spirits more evil Lk 11:26
worse sinners than all the **o** Galileans, Lk 13:2
if not, while the **o** is yet a great way off, Lk 14:32
he will hate the one and love the **o**, Lk 16:13
be devoted to the one and despise the **o**. Lk 16:13
lights up the sky from one side to the **o**, Lk 17:24
bed. One will be taken and the **o** left. Lk 17:34
One will be taken and the **o** left." Lk 17:35
one a Pharisee and the **o** a tax collector. Lk 18:10
I thank you that I am not like **o** men, Lk 18:11
to his house justified, rather than the **o**. Lk 18:14
they said many **o** things against him, Lk 22:65
friends with each **o** that very day, Lk 23:12
they had been at enmity with each **o**. Lk 23:12
But the **o** rebuked him, saying, "Do Lk 23:40
of James and the **o** women with them Lk 24:10
talking with each **o** about all these Lk 24:14
are holding with each **o** as you walk?" Lk 24:17
They said to each **o**, "Did not our Lk 24:32
Jesus went away to the **o** side of the Sea of Jn 6:1
that remained on the **o** side of the sea Jn 6:22
O boats from Tiberias came near the Jn 6:23
they found him on the **o** side of the sea, Jn 6:25
And I have **o** sheep that are not of this Jn 10:16
So the **o** disciple, who was known to the Jn 18:16
and of the **o** who had been crucified Jn 19:32
went to Simon Peter and the **o** disciple, Jn 20:2
So Peter went out with the **o** disciple, and Jn 20:3
but the **o** disciple outran Peter and Jn 20:4
Then the **o** disciple, who had reached the Jn 20:8
So the **o** disciples told him, "We have Jn 20:25
Now Jesus did many **o** signs in the Jn 20:30
The **o** disciples came in the boat, Jn 21:8
there are also many **o** things that Jesus Jn 21:25
began to speak in **o** tongues as the Spirit Acts 2:4
And with many **o** words he bore Acts 2:40
for there is no **o** name under heaven Acts 4:12
brothers. Why do you wrong each **o**?' Acts 7:26
showing tunics and **o** garments that Acts 9:39
of John whose **o** name was Mark, Acts 12:12
them John, whose **o** name was Mark. Acts 12:25
so that they separated from each **o**. Acts 15:39
were Sadducees and the **o** Pharisees, Acts 23:6
o than this one thing that I cried out Acts 24:21
Paul and some **o** prisoners to a Acts 27:1
no one anything, except to love each **o**, Rom 13:8
not covet," and any **o** commandment, Rom 13:9
lay a foundation **o** than that which 1 Cor 3:11
God will destroy both one and the **o**. 1 Cor 6:13
Every **o** sin a person commits is 1 Cor 6:18
as do the **o** apostles and the brothers of 1 Cor 9:5
About the **o** things I will give 1 Cor 11:34
On the **o** hand, the one who 1 Cor 14:3
but the **o** person is not being built 1 Cor 14:17
perhaps of wheat or of some **o** grain. 1 Cor 15:37
him to visit you with the **o** brothers, 1 Cor 16:12
to you anything **o** than what you 2 Cor 1:13
to the **o** a fragrance from life to life. 2 Cor 2:16
I robbed **o** churches by accepting 2 Cor 11:8
And, apart from **o** things, there is 2 Cor 11:28
saw none of the **o** apostles except James Gal 1:19
that you will take no **o** view than mine, Gal 5:10
the flesh, for these are opposed to each **o**, Gal 5:17
sons of men in **o** generations as it has Eph 3:5
against another, forgiving each **o**; Col 3:13
by mortal men, but in the **o** case, Heb 7:8
but on the **o** hand, a better hope is Heb 7:19
by heaven or by earth or by any **o** oath, Jas 5:12
destruction, as they do the **o** Scriptures. 2 Pt 3:16
I say, I do not lay on you any **o** burden. Rv 2:24
the blasts of the **o** trumpets that the three Rv 8:13

fallen, one is, the **o** has not yet come, Rv 17:10

OTHER'S (1)
mutually encouraged by each **o** faith, Rom 1:12

OTHERS (130)
came to buy among the **o** who came, Gn 42:5
the LORD, but the **o** shall not come near, Ex 24:2
And the **o** came out from the city Jos 8:22
and let all the **o** go every man to his Jgs 7:7
O of them were appointed over the 1 Chr 9:29
O, of the sons of the priests, prepared 1 Chr 9:30
his way, and out of the soil **o** will spring. Jb 8:19
brought low and gathered up like all **o**; Jb 24:24
for another, and let **o** bow down on her. Jb 31:10
my transgressions as **o** do by hiding Jb 31:33
investigation and sets **o** in their place. Jb 34:24
must perish and leave their wealth to **o**. Ps 49:10
They are not in trouble as **o** are; they are Ps 73:5
give your honor to **o** and your years to Prv 5:9
he who rejects reproof leads **o** astray. Prv 10:17
times you have yourself cursed **o**. Eccl 7:22
"I will gather yet **o** to him besides those Is 56:8
Their houses shall be turned over to **o**, Jer 6:12
give their wives to **o** and their fields to Jer 8:10
the son of Achbor and **o** with him, Jer 26:22
And to the **o** he said in my hearing, Ezk 9:5
the **o** followed without turning as they Ezk 10:11
they had the same size as the **o**. Ezk 40:24
all around, like the windows of the **o**. Ezk 40:25
gate. It was of the same size as the **o**. Ezk 40:28
were of the same size as the **o**, Ezk 40:29
gate. It was of the same size as the **o**. Ezk 40:32
were of the same size as the **o**, Ezk 40:33
it. It had the same size as the **o**. Ezk 40:35
were of the same size as the **o**, Ezk 40:36
but you have set **o** to keep my charge Ezk 44:8
broken, in place of which four **o** arose, Dn 8:22
be plucked up and go to **o** besides these. Dn 11:4
Daniel, looked, and behold, two **o** stood, Dn 12:5
"Blessed are you when **o** revile you and Mt 5:11
same way, let your light shine before **o**, Mt 5:16
commandments and teaches **o** to do the Mt 5:19
what more are you doing than **o**? Mt 5:47
the streets, that they may be praised by **o**. Mt 6:2
street corners, that they may be seen by **o**. Mt 6:5
For if you forgive **o** their trespasses, your Mt 6:14
if you do not forgive **o** their trespasses, Mt 6:15
faces that their fasting may be seen by **o**. Mt 6:16
not be seen by **o** but by your Father Mt 6:18
whatever you wish that **o** would do to Mt 7:12
the crippled, the mute, and many **o**, Mt 15:30
say John the Baptist, **o** say Elijah, Mt 16:14
and **o** Jeremiah or one of the prophets." Mt 16:14
toll or tax? From their sons or from **o**?" Mt 17:25
he said, "From **o**," Jesus said to him, Mt 17:26
take one or two **o** along with you, Mt 18:16
third hour he saw **o** standing idle in the Mt 20:3
hour he went out and found **o** standing. Mt 20:6
and **o** cut branches from the trees and Mt 21:8
They do all their deeds to be seen by **o**. Mt 23:5
and being called rabbi by **o**. Mt 23:7
to have done, without neglecting the **o**. Mt 23:23
also outwardly appear righteous to **o**, Mt 23:28
"He saved **o**; he cannot save himself. He Mt 27:42
But the **o** said, "Wait, let us see whether Mt 27:49
And **o** are the ones sown among thorns. Mk 4:18
But **o** said, "He is Elijah." And others Mk 6:15
others said, "He is Elijah." And **o** said, Mk 6:15
told him, "John the Baptist; and **o** say, Mk 8:28
and others say, Elijah; and **o**, one of the Mk 8:28
and **o** spread leafy branches that they Mk 11:8
And so with many **o**: some they beat, Mk 12:5
the tenants and give the vineyard to **o**. Mk 12:9
to one another, saying, "He saved **o**; Mk 15:31
of tax collectors and **o** reclining at table Lk 5:29
And as you wish that **o** would do to you, Lk 6:31
manager, and Susanna, and many **o**, Lk 8:3
of God, but for **o** they are in parables, Lk 8:10
and by **o** that one of the prophets of old Lk 9:8
answered, "John the Baptist. But **o** say, Lk 9:19
But others say, Elijah, and **o**, that one of Lk 9:19
Lord appointed seventy-two **o** and sent Lk 10:1
while **o**, to test him, kept seeking from Lk 11:16
to have done, without neglecting the **o**. Lk 11:42
offenders than all the **o** who lived in Lk 13:4
righteous, and treated **o** with contempt: Lk 18:9
the vineyard to **o**." When they heard Lk 20:16
Two **o**, who were criminals, were led Lk 23:32
scoffed at him, saying, "He saved **o**; Lk 23:35
O have labored, and you have entered Jn 4:38
some said, "He is a good man," **o** said, Jn 7:12
O said, "This is the Christ." But some Jn 7:41
Some said, "It is he." **O** said, "No, but he is Jn 9:9
he does not keep the Sabbath." But **o** said, Jn 9:16
O said, "These are not the words of one Jn 10:21
O said, "An angel has spoken to him." Jn 12:29
accord, or did **o** say it to you about me?" Jn 18:34
they crucified him, and with him two **o**, Jn 19:18
and two **o** of his disciples were together. Jn 21:2
But **o** mocking said, "They are filled Acts 2:13
be sojourners in a land belonging to **o**, Acts 7:6
and some of the **o** were appointed to go Acts 15:2
word of the Lord, with many **o** also. Acts 15:35
this babbler wish to say?" **O** said, Acts 17:18
of the dead, some mocked. But **o** said, Acts 17:32
named Damaris and **o** with them. Acts 17:34
by what he said, but **o** disbelieved. Acts 28:24
you then who teach **o**, do you not Rom 2:21
in among the **o** and now share Rom 11:17
If to **o** I am not an apostle, at least I am 1 Cor 9:2
If **o** share this rightful claim on you, 1 Cor 9:12
after preaching to **o** I myself should 1 Cor 9:27
with my mind in order to instruct **o**, 1 Cor 14:19
and let the **o** weigh what is said. 1 Cor 14:29
the fear of the Lord, we persuade **o**. 2 Cor 5:11
by the earnestness of **o** that your love 2 Cor 8:8
do not mean that **o** should be eased 2 Cor 8:13
contribution for them and for all **o**, 2 Cor 9:13
beyond limit in the labors of **o**. 2 Cor 10:15
those who sinned before and all the **o**, 2 Cor 13:2
envy and rivalry, but **o** from good will. Phil 1:15
in humility count **o** more significant Phil 2:3
interests, but also to the interests of **o**. Phil 2:4
people, whether from you or from **o**, 1 Thes 2:6
may not grieve as **o** do who have no 1 Thes 4:13
So then let us not sleep, as **o** do, but let 1 Thes 5:6
hands, nor take part in the sins of **o**; 1 Tm 5:22
but the sins of **o** appear later. 1 Tm 5:24
men who will be able to teach **o** also. 2 Tm 2:2
envy, hated by **o** and hating one another. Ti 3:3
O suffered mocking and flogging, and Heb 11:36
a herald of righteousness, with seven **o**, 2 Pt 2:5
save **o** by snatching them out of the Jude 1:23
to **o** show mercy with fear, hating even Jude 1:23
her back as she herself has paid back **o**, Rv 18:6

OTHERWISE (12)
O it will come to pass, when my lord 1 Kgs 1:21
ate the Passover **o** than as 2 Chr 30:18
and do not join with those who do **o**, Prv 24:21
O, when he has laid a foundation and Lk 14:29
o grace would no longer be grace. Rom 11:6
kindness. **O** you too will be cut off. Rom 11:22
O your children would be unclean, 1 Cor 7:14
O, if you give thanks with your 1 Cor 14:16
O, what do people mean by being 1 Cor 15:29
O, if some Macedonians come with me 2 Cor 9:4
way, and if in anything you think **o**, Phil 3:15
O, would they not have ceased to be Heb 10:2

OTHNI (1)
O, Rephael, Obed and Elzabad, whose 1 Chr 26:7

OTHNIEL (7)
And **O** the son of Kenaz, the brother of Jos 15:17
And **O** the son of Kenaz, Caleb's Jgs 1:13
who saved them, **O** the son of Kenaz, Jgs 3:9
years. Then **O** the son of Kenaz died. Jgs 3:11
The sons of Kenaz: **O** and Seraiah; 1 Chr 4:13
and Seraiah; and the sons of **O**: 1 Chr 4:13
was Heldai the Netophathite, of **O**; 1 Chr 27:15

OUGHT (54)
done to me things that **o** not to be done." Gn 20:9
the LORD'S commandments **o** not to be Lv 4:13
of the LORD his God **o** not to be done, Lv 4:22
the LORD'S commandments **o** not to be Lv 4:27
the LORD'S commandments **o** not to be Lv 5:17
You certainly **o** to have eaten it in the Lv 10:18
will know what you **o** to do to him, 1 Kgs 2:9
times, to know what Israel **o** to do, 1 Chr 12:32
O you not to know that the LORD God 2 Chr 13:5
O you not to walk in the fear of our God Neh 5:9
These you **o** to have done, without Mt 23:23
Then you **o** to have invested my money Mt 25:27
standing where it **o** not to be Mk 13:14
These you **o** to have done, without Lk 11:42
in that very hour what you **o** to say." Lk 12:12
six days in which work **o** to be done. Lk 13:14
And **o** not this woman, a daughter of Lk 13:16
the effect that they **o** always to pray and Lk 18:1
is the place where people **o** to worship." Jn 4:20
you also **o** to wash one another's feet. Jn 13:14
to that law he **o** to die because he Jn 19:7
we **o** not to think that the divine Acts 17:29
you **o** to be quiet and do nothing Acts 19:36
they **o** to be here before you and to Acts 24:19
tribunal, where I **o** to be tried. Acts 25:10
shouting that he **o** not to live any Acts 25:24
was convinced that I **o** to do many Acts 26:9
mind to do what **o** not to be done. Rom 1:28
do not know what to pray for as we **o**, Rom 8:26
more highly than he **o** to think, Rom 12:3
they **o** also to be of service to them in Rom 15:27
arrogant! **O** you not rather to mourn? 1 Cor 5:2
he does not yet know as he **o** to know. 1 Cor 8:2
For a man **o** not to cover his head, 1 Cor 11:7
is why a wife **o** to have a symbol 1 Cor 11:10
for I **o** to have been commended by 2 Cor 12:11
I may declare it boldly, as I **o** to speak. Eph 6:20
make it clear, which is how I **o** to speak. Col 4:4
may know how you **o** to answer each Col 4:6
from us how you **o** to live and to 1 Thes 4:1
We **o** always to give thanks to God 2 Thes 1:3
But we **o** always to give thanks to 2 Thes 2:13
know how you **o** to imitate us, 2 Thes 3:7
may know how one **o** to behave in 1 Tm 3:15
hard-working farmer who **o** to have 2 Tm 2:6
shameful gain what they **o** not to teach. Ti 1:11
by this time you **o** to be teachers, Heb 5:12
My brothers, these things **o** not to be so. Jas 3:10
Instead you **o** to say, "If the Lord wills, Jas 4:15
what sort of people **o** you to be in lives 2 Pt 3:11
says he abides in him **o** to walk in the 1 Jn 2:6
and we **o** to lay down our lives for the 1 Jn 3:16
loved us, we also **o** to love one another. 1 Jn 4:11
Therefore we **o** to support people like 3 Jn 1:8

OUTCAST (3)
banished one will not remain an **o**. 2 Sm 14:14
because they have called you an **o**: Jer 30:17
I will save the lame and gather the **o**, Zep 3:19

OUTCASTS (5)
If your **o** are in the uttermost parts of Dt 30:4
up Jerusalem; he gathers the **o** of Israel. Ps 147:2
night at the height of noon; shelter the **o**; Is 16:3
let the **o** of Moab sojourn among you; be Is 16:4
The Lord GOD, who gathers the **o** of Israel, Is 56:8

OUTCOME (6)
them, that we may know their **o**; Is 41:22
what shall be the **o** of these things?" Dn 12:8
not gaze at the **o** of what was being 2 Cor 3:13
Consider the **o** of their way of life, and Heb 13:7
obtaining the **o** of your faith, the 1 Pt 1:9
what will be the **o** for those who do not 1 Pt 4:17

OUTCRY (9)
"Because the **o** against Sodom and Gn 18:20
according to the **o** that has come Gn 18:21
because the **o** against its people has Gn 19:13
When Eli heard the sound of the **o**, he 1 Sm 4:14
there arose a great **o** of the people and Neh 5:1
when I heard their **o** and these words. Neh 5:6
for righteousness, but behold, an **o**! Is 5:7
There is an **o** in the streets for lack of Is 24:11
"From the **o** at Heshbon even to Jer 48:34

OUTDO (1)
O one another in showing honor. Rom 12:10

OUTDOORS (2)
rises again and walks **o** with his staff, Ex 21:19
O the sword shall bereave, and indoors Dt 32:25

OUTER (32)
flowers, in the inner and **o** rooms. 1 Kgs 6:29
with gold in the inner and **o** rooms. 1 Kgs 6:30
the house and the **o** entrance for the 2 Kgs 16:18
Afterward he built an **o** wall for the 2 Chr 33:14
had just entered the **o** court of the king's Est 6:4
Who can strip off his **o** garment? Who Jb 41:13
was heard as far as the **o** court, Ezk 10:5
Then he brought me into the **o** court. Ezk 40:17
lower gate to the **o** front of the inner Ezk 40:19
the north, belonging to the **o** court, Ezk 40:20
Its vestibule faced the **o** court, and Ezk 40:31
Its vestibule faced the **o** court, and it Ezk 40:34
Its vestibule faced the **o** court, and it Ezk 40:37
The thickness of the **o** wall of the side Ezk 41:9
Then he led me out into the **o** court, Ezk 42:1
pavement that belonged to the **o** court, Ezk 42:3
to the chambers, toward the **o** court, Ezk 42:7
the chambers on the **o** court were fifty Ezk 42:8
as one enters them from the **o** court. Ezk 42:9
of it into the **o** court without laying Ezk 42:14
me back to the **o** gate of the sanctuary, Ezk 44:1
go out into the **o** court to the people, Ezk 44:19
them out into the **o** court and so Ezk 46:20
me out to the **o** court and led me Ezk 46:21
the outside to the **o** gate that faces Ezk 47:2
will be thrown into the **o** darkness. Mt 8:12
foot and cast him into the **o** darkness. Mt 22:13
worthless servant into the **o** darkness. Mt 25:30
He laid aside his **o** garments, and taking Jn 13:4
and put on his **o** garments and resumed Jn 13:12
it was the Lord, he put on his **o** garment, Jn 21:7
Though our **o** nature is wasting 2 Cor 4:16

OUTERMOST (7)
on the edge of the **o** curtain in the first Ex 26:4

on the edge of the **o** curtain in the second Ex 26:4
edge of the curtain that is **o** in one set, Ex 26:10
of the curtain that is **o** in the second set. Ex 26:10
on the edge of the **o** curtain of the first Ex 36:11
the edge of the **o** curtain of the second Ex 36:11
on the edge of the **o** curtain of the one Ex 36:17

OUTFLOW (1)
harvest and from the **o** of your presses. Ex 22:29

OUTLAY (1)
and for any **o** for the repairs of the 2 Kgs 12:12

OUTLET (1)
closed the upper **o** of the waters 2 Chr 32:30

OUTLIVED (2)
of the elders who **o** Joshua and had Jos 24:31
all the days of the elders who **o** Joshua, Jgs 2:7

OUTLYING (1)
and consumed some **o** parts of the Nm 11:1

OUTPOSTS (1)
his servant to the **o** of the armed men Jgs 7:11

OUTPOURED (1)
the avenging of the **o** blood of your Ps 79:10

OUTPOURING (1)
of Israel in the **o** of your wrath on Ezk 9:8

OUTRAGE (2)
committed abomination and **o** in Israel. Jgs 20:6
for all the **o** that they have committed Jgs 20:10

OUTRAGED (1)
and has **o** the Spirit of grace? Heb 10:29

OUTRAGEOUS (7)
he had done an **o** thing in Israel by Gn 34:7
she has done an **o** thing in Israel by Dt 22:21
he has done an **o** thing in Israel.'" Jos 7:15
this man do not do this **o** thing." Jgs 19:24
done in Israel; do not do this **o** thing. 2 Sm 13:12
be as one of the **o** fools in Israel. 2 Sm 13:13
they have done an **o** thing in Israel, Jer 29:23

OUTRAN (2)
way of the plain, and **o** the Cushite. 2 Sm 18:23
but the other disciple **o** Peter and reached Jn 20:4

OUTRIGHT (1)
Kill old men **o**, young men and maidens, Ezk 9:6

OUTSIDE (118)
of his father and told his two brothers **o**. Gn 9:22
And he brought him **o** and said, "Look Gn 15:5
him out and set him **o** the city. Gn 19:16
the camels kneel down **o** the city by Gn 24:11
of the LORD. Why do you stand **o**? Gn 24:31
not take any of the flesh **o** the house, Ex 12:46
gold, inside and **o** shall you overlay it, Ex 25:11
And you shall set the table **o** the veil, Ex 26:35
o the veil that is before the testimony, Ex 27:21
you shall burn with fire **o** the camp; Ex 29:14
to take the tent and pitch it **o** the camp, Ex 33:7
tent of meeting, which was **o** the camp. Ex 33:7
overlaid it with pure gold inside and **o**, Ex 37:2
north side of the tabernacle, **o** the veil, Ex 40:22
bull—he shall carry **o** the camp to a Lv 4:12
shall carry the bull **o** the camp and Lv 4:21
and carry the ashes **o** the camp to a Lv 6:11
dung he burned up with fire **o** the camp, Lv 8:17
you shall not go **o** the entrance of the Lv 8:33
skin he burned up with fire **o** the camp. Lv 9:11
And do not go **o** the entrance of the tent Lv 10:7
alone. His dwelling shall be **o** the camp. Lv 13:46
the camp, but live **o** his tent seven days. Lv 14:8
them into an unclean place **o** the city. Lv 14:40
pour out in an unclean place **o** the city. Lv 14:41
Holy Place, shall be carried **o** the camp. Lv 16:27
a goat in the camp, or kills it **o** the camp, Lv 17:3
O the veil of the testimony, in the tent of Lv 24:3
and female, putting them **o** the camp, Nm 5:3
Israel did so, and put them **o** the camp; Nm 5:4
Let her be shut **o** the camp seven days, Nm 12:14
So Miriam was shut **o** the camp seven Nm 12:15
stone him with stones **o** the camp." Nm 15:35
brought him **o** the camp Nm 15:36
it shall be taken **o** the camp and Nm 19:3
heifer and deposit them **o** the camp in a Nm 19:9
went to meet them **o** the camp. Nm 31:13
Encamp **o** the camp seven days. Nm 31:19
And you shall measure, **o** the city, on Nm 35:5
blood finds him **o** the boundaries of Nm 35:27
emission, then he shall go **o** the camp. Dt 23:10
"You shall have a place **o** the camp, Dt 23:12
your tools, and when you sit down **o**, Dt 23:13
You shall stand **o**, and the man to Dt 24:11
shall not be married **o** the family to a Dt 25:5
shut up inside and **o** because of the people Jos 6:1
relatives and put them **o** the camp of Jos 6:23
he gave in marriage **o** his clan, Jgs 12:9
he brought in from **o** for his sons. Jgs 12:9
For around the **o** of the house he made 1 Kgs 6:6
and from the **o** to the great court. 1 Kgs 7:9
but they could not be seen from **o**. 1 Kgs 8:8
So they took him **o** the city and 1 Kgs 21:13
Then he said, "Go **o**, borrow vessels 2 Kgs 4:3
had stationed eighty men **o** and said, 2 Kgs 10:24
He burned them **o** Jerusalem in the 2 Kgs 23:4
the house of the LORD, **o** Jerusalem, 2 Kgs 23:6
but they could not be seen from **o**. 2 Chr 5:9
a chest and set it **o** the gate of the 2 Chr 24:8
of the springs that were **o** the city; 2 Chr 32:3
it, and **o** it he built another wall, 2 Chr 32:5
and he threw them **o** of the city. 2 Chr 33:15
who were over the **o** work of the house Neh 11:16
of wares lodged **o** Jerusalem once or Neh 13:20
them, "Why do you lodge **o** the wall? Neh 13:21
The sluggard says, "There is a lion **o**! I Prv 22:13
Prepare your work **o**; get everything Prv 24:27
If I found you **o**, I would kiss you, and Sg 8:1
who are besieging you **o** the walls. Jer 21:4
wall all around the **o** of the temple area, Ezk 40:5
on the **o** as one goes up to the entrance Ezk 40:40
On the **o** of the inner gateway there Ezk 40:44
even to the inner room, and on the **o**. Ezk 41:17
all the walls all around, inside and **o**, Ezk 41:17
of wood in front of the vestibule **o**. Ezk 41:25
there was a wall **o** parallel to the Ezk 42:7
to the temple, **o** the sacred area. Ezk 43:21
by the vestibule of the gate from **o**, Ezk 46:2
led me around on the **o** to the outer gate Ezk 47:2
thief breaks in, and the bandits raid **o**. Hos 7:1
But when the crowd had been put **o**, he Mt 9:25
his mother and his brothers stood **o**, Mt 12:46
For you clean the **o** of the cup and the Mt 23:25
the plate, that the **o** also may be clean. Mt 23:26
Peter was sitting **o** in the courtyard. Mt 26:69
and standing **o** they sent to him and Mk 3:31
"Your mother and your brothers are **o**, Mk 3:32
but for those **o** everything is in Mk 4:11
he put them all **o** and took the child's Mk 5:40
There is nothing **o** a person that by Mk 7:15
into a person from **o** cannot defile him, Mk 7:18
found a colt tied at a door **o** in the street, Mk 11:4
the people were praying **o** at the hour of Lk 1:10
and your brothers are standing **o**, Lk 8:20
you Pharisees cleanse the **o** of the cup Lk 11:39
he who made the **o** make the inside Lk 11:40
you begin to stand **o** and to knock at Lk 13:25
but Peter stood **o** at the door. So the Jn 18:16
So Pilate went **o** to them and said, Jn 18:29
he went back **o** to the Jews and told Jn 18:38
But Mary stood weeping **o** the tomb, Jn 20:11
to put the men **o** for a little while. Acts 5:34
But Peter put them all **o**, and knelt Acts 9:40
Sabbath day we went **o** the gate to the Acts 16:13
us until we were **o** the city. Acts 21:5
God judges those **o**. "Purge the evil 1 Cor 5:13
sin a person commits is **o** the body, 1 Cor 6:18
To those **o** the law I became as one 1 Cor 9:21
I became as one **o** the law (not being 1 Cor 9:21
the law (not being **o** the law of God 1 Cor 9:21
that I might win those **o** the law. 1 Cor 9:21
to him, he left nothing **o** his control. Heb 2:8
for sin are burned **o** the camp. Heb 13:11
So Jesus also suffered **o** the gate in Heb 13:12
let us go to him **o** the camp and bear Heb 13:13
do not measure the court **o** the temple; Rv 11:2
the winepress was trodden **o** the city, Rv 14:20
O are the dogs and sorcerers and the Rv 22:15

OUTSIDER (10)
but an **o** shall not eat of them, Ex 29:33
any of it on an **o** shall be cut off from Ex 30:33
And if any **o** comes near, he shall be Nm 1:51
But if any **o** comes near, he shall be put Nm 3:10
And any **o** who came near was to be Nm 3:38
to the people of Israel, so that no **o**, Nm 16:40
the tent, and no **o** shall come near you. Nm 18:4
and any **o** who comes near shall be put Nm 18:7
the position of an **o** say "Amen" to 1 Cor 14:16
and an unbeliever or **o** enters, 1 Cor 14:24

OUTSIDERS (5)
For what have I to do with judging **o**? 1 Cor 5:12
tongues, and **o** or unbelievers enter, 1 Cor 14:23
Conduct yourselves wisely toward **o**, Col 4:5
live properly before **o** and be 1 Thes 4:12
he must be well thought of by **o**, 1 Tm 3:7

OUTSKIRTS (6)
side begins at the **o** of Kiriath-jearim. Jos 18:15
When I come to the **o** of the camp, do as Jgs 7:17
with him came to the **o** of the camp at Jgs 7:19
were going down to the **o** of the city, 1 Sm 9:27
was staying in the **o** of Gibeah in the 1 Sm 14:2
Behold, these are but the **o** of his ways, Jb 26:14

OUTSPREAD (1)
and its **o** wings will fill the breadth of your Is 8:8

OUTSTRETCHED (19)
redeem you with an **o** arm and with great Ex 6:6
by war, by a mighty hand and an **o** arm, Dt 4:34
there with a mighty hand and an **o** arm. Dt 5:15
the mighty hand, and the **o** arm, Dt 7:19
by your great power and by your **o** arm.' Dt 9:29
his mighty hand and his **o** arm, Dt 11:2
Egypt with a mighty hand and an **o** arm, Dt 26:8
mighty hand, and of your **o** arm), 1 Kgs 8:42
knelt with hands **o** toward heaven. 1 Kgs 8:54
with great power and with an **o** arm. 2 Kgs 17:36
your mighty hand and your **o** arm, 2 Chr 6:32
with a strong hand and an **o** arm, for Ps 136:12
Zion are haughty and walk with **o** necks, Is 3:16
against you with **o** hand and strong Jer 21:5
great power and my **o** arm have made Jer 27:5
your great power and by your **o** arm! Jer 32:17
with a strong hand and **o** arm, Jer 32:21
mighty hand and an **o** arm and with Ezk 20:33
with a mighty hand and an **o** arm, Ezk 20:34

OUTWARD (4)
wall of the city **o** a thousand cubits all Nm 35:4
man looks on the **o** appearance, but 1 Sm 16:7
nor is circumcision **o** and physical. Rom 2:28
who boast about **o** appearance and 2 Cor 5:12

OUTWARDLY (3)
tombs, which **o** appear beautiful, Mt 23:27
So you also **o** appear righteous to Mt 23:28
no one is a Jew who is merely one **o**, Rom 2:28

OUTWEIGHS (1)
so a little folly **o** wisdom and honor. Eccl 10:1

OUTWIT (1)
The enemy shall not **o** him; the wicked Ps 89:22

OUTWITTED (1)
so that we would not be **o** by Satan; 2 Cor 2:11

OVEN (12)
offering baked in the **o** as an offering, Lv 2:4
offering baked in the **o** and all that is Lv 7:9
Whether **o** or stove, it shall be broken Lv 11:35
bread in a single **o** and shall dole out Lv 26:26
them as a blazing **o** when you appear. Ps 21:9
is hot as an **o** with the burning heat Lam 5:10
are like a heated **o** whose baker ceases to Hos 7:4
with hearts like an **o** they approach their Hos 7:6
All of them are hot as an **o**, and they Hos 7:7
the day is coming, burning like an **o**, Mal 4:1
alive and tomorrow is thrown into the **o**, Mt 6:30
and tomorrow is thrown into the **o**, Lk 12:28

OVENS (3)
and into your **o** and your kneading Ex 8:3
section and the Tower of the **O**. Neh 3:11
on the wall, above the Tower of the **O**, Neh 12:38

OVERBOARD (2)
the ship's tackle **o** with their own Acts 27:19
could swim to jump **o** first and make Acts 27:43

OVERCAME (1)
who followed Omri **o** the people who 1 Kgs 16:22

OVERCOME (20)
occupy it, for we are well able to **o** it." Nm 13:30
Moab was **o** with fear of the people of Nm 22:3
They had **o** Ziklag and burned it with 1 Sm 30:1
you will not **o** him but will surely fall Est 6:13
of the rich valley of those **o** with wine! Is 28:1
then we can **o** him and take our Jer 20:10
will stumble; they will not **o** me. Jer 20:11
a drunken man, like a man **o** by wine, Jer 23:9
was **o** and lay sick for some days. Dn 8:27
were immediately **o** with amazement. Mk 5:42
darkness, and the darkness has not **o** it. Jn 1:5
But take heart; I have **o** the world." Jn 16:33
still longer. And being **o** by sleep, Acts 20:9
Do not be **o** by evil, but overcome Rom 12:21
by evil, but **o** evil with good. Rom 12:21
are again entangled in them and **o**, 2 Pt 2:20
men, because you have **o** the evil one. 1 Jn 2:13
in you, and you have **o** the evil one. 1 Jn 2:14
you are from God and have **o** them, 1 Jn 4:4
is the victory that has **o** the world—our 1 Jn 5:4

OVERCOMES (4)
than he attacks him and **o** him, Lk 11:22
of corruption. For whatever **o** a person, 2 Pt 2:19
who has been born of God **o** the world. 1 Jn 5:4
Who is it that **o** the world except the one 1 Jn 5:5

OVEREXTENDING (1)
For we are not **o** ourselves, as 2 Cor 10:14

OVERWHELMED (4)
And Joshua **o** Amalek and his people Ex 17:13
not afraid, but the sea **o** their enemies. Ps 78:53
And I sat there **o** among them seven Ezk 3:15
or he may be **o** by excessive sorrow. 2 Cor 2:7

OVERWHELMING (3)
Wrath is cruel, anger is **o**, but who can Prv 27:4
when the **o** whip passes through it will Is 28:15
when the **o** scourge passes through, you Is 28:18

OVERWHELMS (2)
around you, and sudden terror **o** you, Jb 22:10
come upon me, and horror **o** me. Ps 55:5

OWE (5)
to choke him, saying, 'Pay what you **o**.' Mt 18:28
first, 'How much do you **o** my master?' Lk 16:5
to another, 'And how much do you **o**?' Lk 16:7
O no one anything, except to love each Rom 13:8
to do it, and indeed they **o** it to them. Rom 15:27

OWED (8)
to him who **o** him ten thousand Mt 18:24
fellow servants who **o** him a hundred Mt 18:28
One **o** five hundred denarii, and the Lk 7:41
Pay to all what is **o** to them: taxes to Rom 13:7
taxes to whom taxes are **o**, revenue to Rom 13:7
owed, revenue to whom revenue is **o**, Rom 13:7
is owed, respect to whom respect is **o**, Rom 13:7
is owed, honor to whom honor is **o**. Rom 13:7

OWES (1)
you at all, or **o** you anything, Phlm 1:18

OWING (1)
say nothing of your **o** me even your Phlm 1:19

OWL (13)
the little **o**, the cormorant, the Lv 11:17
owl, the cormorant, the short-eared **o**, Lv 11:17
the barn **o**, the tawny owl, the carrion Lv 11:18
the barn owl, the tawny **o**, the carrion Lv 11:18
the little **o** and the short-eared owl, the Dt 14:16
the little owl and the short-eared **o**, the Dt 14:16
owl and the short-eared owl, the barn **o** Dt 14:16
and the tawny **o**, the carrion vulture Dt 14:17
I am like a desert **o** of the wilderness, Ps 102:6
wilderness, like an **o** of the waste places; Ps 102:6
it, the **o** and the raven shall dwell in it. Is 34:11
There the **o** nests and lays and hatches Is 34:15
even the **o** and the hedgehog shall lodge Zep 2:14

OWN (592)
yielding seed according to their **o** kinds, Gn 1:12
So God created man in his **o** image, in Gn 1:27
years, he fathered a son in his **o** likeness, Gn 5:3
shed, for God made man in his **o** image. Gn 9:6
in their lands, each with his **o** language, Gn 10:5
heir; your very **o** son shall be your heir." Gn 15:4
I may go to my **o** home and country. Gn 30:25
I provide for my **o** household also?" Gn 30:30
He put his **o** droves apart and did not Gn 30:40
kings shall come from your **o** body. Gn 35:11
our **o** flesh." And his brothers listened Gn 37:27
"Let her keep the things as her **o**, Gn 38:23
in the prison—each his **o** dream, Gn 40:5
each dream with its **o** interpretation. Gn 40:5
a dream with its **o** interpretation. Gn 41:11
Egypt, who were his **o** descendants, Gn 46:26
and four fifths shall be your **o**, Gn 47:24
Manasseh were counted as Joseph's **o**. Gn 50:23
beaten; but the fault is in your **o** people." Ex 5:16
in and plant them on your **o** mountain, Ex 15:17
and he went away to his **o** country. Ex 18:27
from the best in his **o** field and in his Ex 22:5
in his own field and in his **o** vineyard. Ex 22:5
to whom you swore by your **o** self, Ex 32:13
His **o** hands shall bring the LORD'S food Lv 7:30
pour it into the palm of his **o** left hand Lv 14:15
the oil into the palm of his **o** left hand, Lv 14:26
their nakedness is your **o** nakedness. Lv 18:10
against the sons of your **o** people, Lv 19:18
take as his wife a virgin of his **o** people, Lv 21:14
and go back to his **o** clan and return to Lv 25:41
each man in his **o** camp and each man Nm 1:52
camp and each man by his **o** standard. Nm 1:52
shall camp each by his **o** standard, Nm 2:2
I consecrated for my **o** all the firstborn Nm 3:13
I will depart to my **o** land and to my Nm 10:30
to follow after your **o** heart and your Nm 15:39
after your own heart and your **o** eyes, Nm 15:39
that it has not been of my **o** accord. Nm 16:28
princes of Balak, "Go to your **o** land, Nm 22:13
any power of my **o** to speak anything? Nm 22:38
Therefore now flee to your **o** place. I Nm 24:11
to do either good or bad of my **o** will. Nm 24:13
of Korah, but died for his **o** sin. Nm 27:3
and called it Nobah, after his **o** name. Nm 32:42
shall hold on to its **o** inheritance.'" Nm 36:9
and called the villages after his **o** name, Dt 3:14
Egypt, to be a people of his **o** inheritance, Dt 4:20
you out of Egypt with his **o** presence, Dt 4:37
doing whatever is right in his **o** eyes, Dt 12:8
who is as your **o** soul entices you Dt 13:6
and an army larger than your **o**, Dt 20:1
the heart of his fellows melt like his **o**.' Dt 20:8
one shall be put to death for his **o** sin. Dt 24:16
street, his blood shall be on his **o** head, Jos 2:19
and put them among their **o** belongings. Jos 7:11
may return to his **o** town and his own Jos 20:6
return to his own town and his **o** home, Jos 20:6
their **o** land of which they had possessed Jos 22:9
him in his **o** inheritance at Jos 24:30
and their **o** daughters they gave to their Jgs 3:6
me, saying, 'My **o** hand has saved me.' Jgs 7:2
of Joash went and lived in his **o** house. Jgs 8:29
Gideon had seventy sons, his **o** offspring, Jgs 8:30
did what was right in his **o** eyes. Jgs 17:6
did what was right in his **o** eyes. Jgs 21:25
for myself, lest I impair my **o** inheritance. Ru 4:6
not see, was lying down in his **o** place. 1 Sm 3:2
of Israel, and let it return to its **o** place, 1 Sm 5:11
If it goes up on the way to its **o** land, to 1 Sm 6:9
sought out a man after his **o** heart, 1 Sm 13:14
the Philistines went to their **o** place. 1 Sm 14:46
you are little in your **o** eyes, 1 Sm 15:17
and Jonathan loved him as his **o** soul. 1 Sm 18:1
because he loved him as his **o** soul. 1 Sm 18:3
he loved him as he loved his **o** soul. 1 Sm 20:17
the son of Jesse to your **o** shame, 1 Sm 20:30
and from saving with your **o** hand, 1 Sm 25:26
avenging myself with my **o** hand! 1 Sm 25:33
of Nabal on his **o** head." Then David 1 Sm 25:39
and buried him in Ramah, his **o** city. 1 Sm 28:3
Saul took his **o** sword and fell 1 Sm 31:4
for your **o** mouth has testified against 2 Sm 1:16
righteous man in his **o** house on his 2 Sm 4:11
may dwell in their **o** place and be 2 Sm 7:10
and according to your **o** heart, 2 Sm 7:21
to take one of his **o** flock or herd to 2 Sm 12:4
evil against you out of your **o** house. 2 Sm 12:11
He then went to his **o** house. 2 Sm 12:20
"Let him dwell apart in his **o** house; 2 Sm 14:24
lived apart in his **o** house and did not 2 Sm 14:24
"Behold, my **o** son seeks my life; 2 Sm 16:11
and went off home to his **o** city. 2 Sm 17:23
Israel fled every one to his **o** home. 2 Sm 18:17
He called the pillar after his **o** name, 2 Sm 18:18
had fled every man to his **o** home. 2 Sm 19:8
I may die in my **o** city near the grave 2 Sm 19:37
him, and he returned to his **o** home. 2 Sm 19:39
and killed him with his **o** spear. 2 Sm 23:21
you may save your **o** life and the life 1 Kgs 1:12
Solomon my son ride on my **o** mule, 1 Kgs 1:33
throne this day, my **o** eyes seeing it.'" 1 Kgs 1:48
and rose, and each went his **o** way. 1 Kgs 1:49
back his bloody deeds on his **o** head, 1 Kgs 2:32
was buried in his **o** house in the 1 Kgs 2:34
Your blood shall be on your **o** head." 1 Kgs 2:37
"You know in your **o** heart all the 1 Kgs 2:44
back your harm on your **o** head. 1 Kgs 2:44
finished building his **o** house and the 1 Kgs 3:1
was building his **o** house thirteen 1 Kgs 7:1
His **o** house where he was to dwell, in 1 Kgs 7:8
bringing his conduct on his **o** head, 1 Kgs 8:32
affliction of his **o** heart and 1 Kgs 8:38
the LORD and his **o** house and the 1 Kgs 9:15
of David to her **o** house that Solomon 1 Kgs 9:24
I heard in my **o** land of your words 1 Kgs 10:6
I came and my **o** eyes had seen it. 1 Kgs 10:7
went back to her **o** land with her 1 Kgs 10:13
in marriage the sister of his **o** wife, 1 Kgs 11:19
that I may go to my **o** country." 1 Kgs 11:21
to go to your **o** country?" And he 1 Kgs 11:22
Look now to your **o** house, David." 1 Kgs 12:16
that he had devised from his **o** heart. 1 Kgs 12:33
And he laid the body in his **o** grave. 1 Kgs 13:30
of his father and his **o** sacred gifts, 1 Kgs 15:15
he lodged, and laid him on his **o** bed. 1 Kgs 17:19
shall dogs lick your **o** blood."'" 1 Kgs 21:19
took hold of his **o** clothes and tore 2 Kgs 2:12
him and returned to their **o** land. 2 Kgs 3:27
"I dwell among my **o** people." 2 Kgs 4:13
said, "You shall see it with your **o** eyes, 2 Kgs 7:2
"You shall see it with your **o** eyes, 2 Kgs 7:19
of Judah and set up a king of their **o**. 2 Kgs 8:20
had dedicated, and his **o** sacred gifts, 2 Kgs 12:18
But each one shall die for his **o** sin." 2 Kgs 14:6
exiled from their **o** land to Assyria 2 Kgs 17:23
made gods of its **o** and put them in 2 Kgs 17:29
the LORD but also served their **o** gods, 2 Kgs 17:33
you to eat their **o** dung and to drink 2 Kgs 18:27
dung and to drink their **o** urine?" 2 Kgs 18:27
each one of you will eat of his **o** vine, 2 Kgs 18:31
vine, and each one of his **o** fig tree, 2 Kgs 18:31
will drink the water of his **o** cistern, 2 Kgs 18:31
you away to a land like your **o** land, 2 Kgs 18:32
a rumor and return to his **o** land, 2 Kgs 19:7
him fall by the sword in his **o** land.'" 2 Kgs 19:7
for my **o** sake and for the sake of my 2 Kgs 19:34
this city for my **o** sake and for my 2 Kgs 20:6
And some of your **o** sons, who shall 2 Kgs 20:18
and buried him in his **o** tomb. 2 Kgs 23:30
Saul took his **o** sword and fell 1 Chr 10:4
and killed him with his **o** spear. 1 Chr 11:23
from his **o** fathers' house. 1 Chr 12:28
may dwell in their **o** place and be 1 Chr 17:9
after you, one of your **o** sons, 1 Chr 17:11
LORD, and according to your **o** heart, 1 Chr 17:19
a treasure of my **o** of gold and silver, 1 Chr 29:3
and of your **o** have we given you. 1 Chr 29:14
from your hand and is all your **o**. 1 Chr 29:16
bringing his conduct on his **o** head, 2 Chr 6:23
each knowing his **o** affliction and 2 Chr 6:29
affliction and his **o** sorrow and 2 Chr 6:29
and in his **o** house he successfully 2 Chr 7:11
the house of the LORD and his **o** house, 2 Chr 8:1
I heard in my **o** land of your words 2 Chr 9:5
until I came and my **o** eyes had seen it. 2 Chr 9:6
went back to her **o** land with her 2 Chr 9:12
Look now to your **o** house, David." 2 Chr 10:16
he appointed his **o** priests for the 2 Chr 11:15
of his father and his **o** sacred gifts, 2 Chr 15:18
of Judah and set up a king of their **o**. 2 Chr 21:8
but each one shall die for his **o** sin." 2 Chr 25:4
not deliver their **o** people from your 2 Chr 25:15
not sins of your **o** against the LORD 2 Chr 28:10
hissing, as you see with your **o** eyes. 2 Chr 29:8
king from his **o** possessions was for 2 Chr 31:3
with shame of face to his **o** land. 2 Chr 32:21
some of his **o** sons struck him down 2 Chr 32:21
Jerusalem and Judah, each to his **o** town. Ezr 2:1
Ananiah repaired beside his **o** house. Neh 3:23
repaired, each one opposite his **o** house. Neh 3:28
of Immer repaired opposite his **o** house. Neh 3:29
their taunt on their **o** heads and give Neh 4:4
are inventing them out of your **o** mind." Neh 6:8
afraid and fell greatly in their **o** esteem, Neh 6:16
and some in front of their **o** homes." Neh 7:3
Even in their **o** kingdom, enjoying Neh 9:35
every province in its **o** script and to Est 1:22
and to every people in its **o** language, Est 1:22
be master in his **o** household and speak Est 1:22
Mordecai took her as his **o** daughter. Est 2:7
who had taken her as his **o** daughter, Est 2:15
every province in its **o** script and every Est 3:12
script and every people in its **o** language. Est 3:12
in my **o** house?" As the word left the Est 7:8
each province in its **o** script and to each Est 8:9
and to each people in its **o** language, Est 8:9
the Jews should return on his **o** head, Est 9:25
him, they came each from his **o** place, Jb 2:11
He catches the wise in their **o** craftiness, Jb 5:13
right, my **o** mouth would condemn me; Jb 9:20
a pit, and my **o** clothes will abhor me. Jb 9:31
He feels only the pain of his **o** body, and Jb 14:22
Your **o** mouth condemns you, and not I; Jb 15:6
and not I; your **o** lips testify against you. Jb 15:6
and his **o** schemes throw him down. Jb 18:7
For he is cast into a net by his **o** feet, and Jb 18:8
a stench to the children of my **o** mother. Jb 19:17
he will perish forever like his **o** dung; Jb 20:7
Let their **o** eyes see their destruction, Jb 21:20
because he was righteous in his **o** eyes. Jb 32:1
any who are wise in their **o** conceit." Jb 37:24
to you that your **o** right hand can save Jb 40:14
ponder in your **o** hearts on your beds, and Ps 4:4
O God; let them fall by their **o** counsels; Ps 5:10
His mischief returns upon his **o** head, Ps 7:16
and on his **o** skull his violence descends. Ps 7:16
that they hid their **o** foot has been Ps 9:15
are snared in the work of their **o** hands. Ps 9:16
who swears to his **o** hurt and does not Ps 15:4
flatters himself in his **o** eyes that his Ps 36:2
their sword shall enter their **o** heart, Ps 37:15
you with your **o** hand drove out the Ps 44:2
for not by their **o** sword did they win the Ps 44:3
the land, nor did their **o** arm save them, Ps 44:3
they called lands by their **o** names. Ps 49:11
you slander your **o** mother's son. Ps 50:20
and sought refuge in his **o** destruction!" Ps 52:7
with their **o** tongues turned against Ps 64:8
Let their **o** table before them become a Ps 69:22
does not despise his **o** people who are Ps 69:33
place; they set up their **o** signs for signs. Ps 74:4
hearts, to follow their **o** counsels. Ps 81:12
be wrapped in their **o** shame as in a Ps 109:29
for himself, Israel as his **o** possession. Ps 135:4
Let the wicked fall into their **o** nets, Ps 141:10

these men lie in wait for their **o** blood; Prv 1:18
they set an ambush for their **o** lives. Prv 1:18
and have their fill of their **o** devices. Prv 1:31
do not lean on your **o** understanding. Prv 3:5
Be not wise in your **o** eyes; fear the LORD, Prv 3:7
Drink water from your **o** cistern, Prv 5:15
cistern, flowing water from your **o** well. Prv 5:15
the wicked falls by his **o** wickedness. Prv 11:5
troubles his **o** household will Prv 11:29
The way of a fool is right in his **o** eyes, Prv 12:15
but folly with her **o** hands tears it down. Prv 14:1
The heart knows its **o** bitterness, and Prv 14:10
unjust gain troubles his **o** household, Prv 15:27
the ways of a man are pure in his **o** eyes, Prv 16:2
isolates himself seeks his **o** desire; Prv 18:1
Whoever gets sense loves his **o** soul; he Prv 19:8
a man proclaims his **o** steadfast love, Prv 20:6
way of a man is right in his **o** eyes, Prv 21:2
the poor to increase his **o** wealth, Prv 22:16
nor is it glorious to seek one's **o** glory. Prv 25:27
to his folly, lest he be wise in his **o** eyes. Prv 26:5
fool cuts off his **o** feet and drinks Prv 26:6
see a man who is wise in his **o** eyes? Prv 26:12
is wiser in his **o** eyes than seven men Prv 26:16
in a quarrel not his **o** is like one who Prv 26:17
praise you, and not your **o** mouth; Prv 27:2
mouth; a stranger, and not your **o** lips. Prv 27:2
into an evil way will fall into his **o** pit, Prv 28:10
A rich man is wise in his **o** eyes, but a Prv 28:11
Whoever trusts in his **o** mind is a fool, Prv 28:26
The partner of a thief hates his **o** life; Prv 29:24
are clean in their **o** eyes but are not Prv 30:12
fool folds his hands and eats his **o** flesh. Eccl 4:5
though in his **o** kingdom he had been Eccl 4:14
but my **o** vineyard I have not kept! Sg 1:6
My vineyard, my very **o**, is before me; Sg 8:12
hands, to what their **o** fingers have made. Is 2:8
"We will eat our **o** bread and wear our own Is 4:1
eat our own bread and wear our **o** clothes, Is 4:1
Woe to those who are wise in their **o** eyes, Is 5:21
own eyes, and shrewd in their **o** sight! Is 5:21
each devours the flesh of his **o** arm, Is 9:20
them, each will turn to his **o** people, Is 13:14
people, and each will flee to his **o** land. Is 13:14
Israel, and will set them in their **o** land, Is 14:1
nations lie in glory, each in his **o** tomb; Is 14:18
not look on what his **o** fingers have made, Is 17:8
you to eat their **o** dung and drink their Is 36:12
own dung and drink their **o** urine?" Is 36:12
each one of you will eat of his **o** vine, Is 36:16
own vine, and each one of his **o** fig tree, Is 36:16
you will drink the water of his **o** cistern, Is 36:16
take you away to a land like your **o** land, Is 36:17
hear a rumor and return to his **o** land, Is 37:7
him fall by the sword in his **o** land.'" Is 37:7
for my **o** sake and for the sake of my Is 37:35
And some of your **o** sons, who will come Is 39:7
out your transgressions for my **o** sake, Is 43:25
wander about each in his **o** direction; Is 47:15
For my **o** sake, for my own sake, I do it, Is 48:11
For my own sake, for my **o** sake, I do it, Is 48:11
make your oppressors eat their **o** flesh, Is 49:26
be drunk with their **o** blood as with Is 49:26
we have turned every one to his **o** way; Is 53:6
they have all turned to their **o** way, each Is 56:11
to their own way, each to his **o** gain, Is 56:11
on backsliding in the way of his **o** heart. Is 57:17
day of your fast you seek your **o** pleasure, Is 58:3
not to hide yourself from your **o** flesh? Is 58:7
if you honor it, not going your **o** ways, Is 58:13
own ways, or seeking your **o** pleasure, Is 58:13
then his **o** arm brought him salvation, Is 59:16
so my **o** arm brought me salvation, and Is 63:5
that is not good, following their **o** devices; Is 65:2
These have chosen their **o** ways, and their Is 66:3
worshiped the works of their **o** hands. Jer 1:16
your **o** sword devoured your prophets Jer 2:30
will give you shepherds after my **o** heart, Jer 3:15
stubbornly follow their **o** evil heart. Jer 3:17
do not go after other gods to your **o** harm, Jer 7:6
Is it not themselves, to their **o** shame? Jer 7:19
but walked in their **o** counsels and the Jer 7:24
Everyone turns to his **o** course, like a Jer 8:6
stubbornly followed their **o** hearts and Jer 9:14
stubbornly follow their **o** heart and Jer 13:10
and the deceit of their **o** minds. Jer 14:14
them back to their **o** land that I gave Jer 16:15
We will follow our **o** plans, and will Jer 18:12
Then they shall dwell in their **o** land." Jer 23:8
They speak visions of their **o** minds, Jer 23:16
who stubbornly follows his **o** heart, Jer 23:17
who prophesy the deceit of their **o** heart, Jer 23:26
for the burden is every man's **o** word, Jer 23:36
the work of your hands to your **o** harm. Jer 25:7
as you have heard with your **o** ears." Jer 26:11
until the time of his **o** land comes. Jer 27:7
and serve him, I will leave on its **o** land, Jer 27:11
shall come back to their **o** country. Jer 31:17
But everyone shall die for his **o** sin. Jer 31:30
for their **o** good and the good of their Jer 32:39
is about to return to Egypt, to its **o** land. Jer 37:7
you and let you remain in your **o** land. Jer 42:12
Judah, the evil of their wives, your **o** evil, Jer 44:9
us go back to our **o** people and to the Jer 46:16
every one shall turn to his **o** people, Jer 50:16
and every one shall flee to his **o** land. Jer 50:16
her, and let us go each to his **o** country, Jer 51:9
women have boiled their **o** children; Lam 4:10
be loathsome in their **o** sight for the evils Ezk 6:9
bring their deeds upon their **o** heads, Ezk 11:21
dug through the wall with my **o** hands. Ezk 12:7
those who prophesy from their **o** hearts: Ezk 13:2
prophets who follow their **o** spirit, Ezk 13:3
who prophesy out of their **o** minds. Ezk 13:17
people and keep your **o** souls alive? Ezk 13:18
would deliver but their **o** lives by their Ezk 14:14
would deliver but their **o** lives by their Ezk 14:20
I will restore your **o** fortunes in their Ezk 16:53
be profaned by your **o** doing in the Ezk 22:16
were your **o** special markets; Ezk 27:15
shall dwell in their **o** land that I gave Ezk 28:25
his streams, that says, 'My Nile is my **o**; Ezk 29:3
every moment, every one for his **o** life, Ezk 32:10
his blood shall be upon his **o** head. Ezk 33:4
when it is their **o** way that is not just. Ezk 33:17
and will bring them into their **o** land. Ezk 34:13
house of Israel lived in their **o** land, Ezk 36:17
and bring you into your **o** land. Ezk 36:24
and I will place you in your **o** land. Ezk 37:14
and bring them to their **o** land. Ezk 37:21
assembled them into their **o** land. Ezk 39:28
their inheritance out of his **o** property, Ezk 46:18
than the youths who are of your **o** age? Dn 1:10
and worship any god except their **o** God. Dn 3:28
sealed it with his **o** signet and with the Dn 6:17
shall be great—but not by his **o** power; Dn 8:24
and in his **o** mind he shall become Dn 8:25
his pleas for mercy, and for your **o** sake, Dn 9:17
Delay not, for your **o** sake, O my God, Dn 9:19
the south but shall return to his **o** land. Dn 11:9
violent among your **o** people shall lift Dn 11:14
toward the fortresses of his **o** land, Dn 11:19
work his will and return to his **o** land. Dn 11:28
they made idols for their **o** destruction. Hos 8:4
have trusted in your **o** way and in the Hos 10:13
them because of their **o** counsels. Hos 11:6
your payment on your **o** head swiftly and Jl 3:4
to remove them far from their **o** border. Jl 3:6
I will return your payment on your **o** head. Jl 3:7
not by our **o** strength captured Am 6:13
your deeds shall return on your **o** head. Ob 1:15
Jacob shall possess their **o** possessions. Ob 1:17
enemies are the men of his **o** house. Mi 7:6
the earth, to seize dwellings not their **o**. Hab 1:6
men, whose **o** might is their god!" Hab 1:11
and collects as his **o** all peoples." Hab 2:5
up what is not his **o**—for how long? Hab 2:6
maker trusts in his **o** creation when he Hab 2:18
pierced with his **o** arrows the heads Hab 3:14
of you busies himself with his **o** house. Hg 1:9
over them, for now I see with my **o** eyes. Zec 9:8
and their **o** shepherds have no pity on Zec 11:5
Your **o** eyes shall see this, and you shall Mal 1:5
departed to their **o** country by another Mt 2:12
Sufficient for the day is its **o** trouble. Mt 6:34
do not notice the log that is in your **o** eye? Mt 7:3
eye,' when there is the log in your **o** eye? Mt 7:4
first take the log out of your **o** eye, Mt 7:5
and leave the dead to bury their **o** dead." Mt 8:22
he crossed over and came to his **o** city. Mt 9:1
will be those of his **o** household. Mt 10:36
his hometown and in his **o** household." Mt 13:57
received what was my **o** with interest. Mt 25:27
robe and put his **o** clothes on him and Mt 27:31
and laid it in his **o** new tomb, which he Mt 27:60
privately to his **o** disciples he explained Mk 4:34
his relatives and in his **o** household." Mk 6:4
cloak and put his **o** clothes on him. Mk 15:20
went to be registered, each to his **o** town. Lk 2:3
will pierce through your **o** soul also), Lk 2:35
into Galilee, to their **o** town of Nazareth. Lk 2:39
not notice the log that is in your **o** eye? Lk 6:41
do not see the log that is in your **o** eye? Lk 6:42
first take the log out of your **o** eye, Lk 6:42
for each tree is known by its **o** fruit. For Lk 6:44
"Leave the dead to bury their **o** dead. Lk 9:60
set him on his **o** animal and brought Lk 10:34
man, fully armed, guards his **o** palace, Lk 11:21
does not hate his **o** father and mother Lk 14:26
and sisters, yes, and even his **o** life, Lk 14:26
does not bear his **o** cross and come Lk 14:27
dealing with their **o** generation than the Lk 16:8
who will give you that which is your **o**? Lk 16:12
'I will condemn you with your **o** words, Lk 19:22
have heard it ourselves from his **o** lips." Lk 22:71
He came to his **o**, and his own people did Jn 1:11
and his **o** people did not receive him. Jn 1:11
He first found his **o** brother Simon and Jn 1:41
has no honor in his **o** hometown.) Jn 4:44
but he was even calling God his **o** Father, Jn 5:18
the Son can do nothing of his **o** accord, Jn 5:19
"I can do nothing on my **o**. As I hear, I Jn 5:30
because I seek not my **o** will but the will Jn 5:30
If another comes in his **o** name, you will Jn 5:43
not to do my **o** will but the will of him Jn 6:38
I am speaking on my **o** authority. Jn 7:17
who speaks on his **o** authority seeks his Jn 7:18
on his own authority seeks his **o** glory, Jn 7:18
But I have not come of my **o** accord. Jn 7:28
[[They went each to his **o** house, Jn 7:53
and that I do nothing on my **o** authority, Jn 8:28
I came not of my **o** accord, but he sent Jn 8:42
he lies, he speaks out of his **o** character, Jn 8:44
Yet I do not seek my **o** glory; there is One Jn 8:50
and he calls his **o** sheep by name and Jn 10:3
When he has brought out all his **o**, he Jn 10:4
a shepherd, who does not **o** the sheep, Jn 10:12
I know my **o** and my own know me, Jn 10:14
I know my own and my **o** know me, Jn 10:14
me, but I lay it down of my **o** accord. Jn 10:18
He did not say this of his **o** accord, but Jn 11:51
I have not spoken on my **o** authority, Jn 12:49
having loved his **o** who were in the world, Jn 13:1
to you I do not speak on my **o** authority, Jn 14:10
world, the world would love you as its **o**; Jn 15:19
for he will not speak on his **o** authority, Jn 16:13
will be scattered, each to his **o** home, Jn 16:32
glorify me in your **o** presence with the Jn 17:5
judge him by your **o** law." The Jews said Jn 18:31
"Do you say this of your **o** accord, Jn 18:34
Your **o** nation and the chief priests have Jn 18:35
and he went out, bearing his **o** cross, to Jn 19:17
the disciple took her to his **o** home. Jn 19:27
the Father has fixed by his **o** authority. Acts 1:7
called in their **o** language Akeldama, Acts 1:19
Judas turned aside to go to his **o** place." Acts 1:25
hearing them speak in his **o** language. Acts 2:6
each of us in his **o** native language? Acts 2:8
telling in our **o** tongues the mighty Acts 2:11
as though by our **o** power or piety we Acts 3:12
things that belonged to him was his **o**, Acts 4:32
unsold, did it not remain your **o**? Acts 5:4
him and brought him up as her **o** son. Acts 7:21
It opened for them of its **o** accord, and Acts 12:10
purpose of God in his **o** generation, Acts 13:36
the nations to walk in their **o** ways. Acts 14:16
even some of your **o** poets have said, Acts 17:28
them, "Your blood be on your **o** heads! Acts 18:6
words and names and your **o** law, Acts 18:15
which he obtained with his **o** blood. Acts 20:28
from among your **o** selves will arise Acts 20:30
belt and bound his **o** feet and hands Acts 21:11
him about their **o** religion and about Acts 25:19
beginning among my **o** nation and in Acts 26:4
tackle overboard with their **o** hands. Acts 27:19
two whole years at his **o** expense, Acts 28:30
faith when he considered his **o** body, Rom 4:19
I do not understand my **o** actions. For Rom 7:15
By sending his **o** Son in the likeness of Rom 8:3
did not spare his **o** Son but gave him Rom 8:32
God, and seeking to establish their **o**, Rom 10:3
be grafted back into their **o** olive tree. Rom 11:24
Lest you be wise in your **o** conceits, I Rom 11:25
It is before his **o** master that he stands Rom 14:4
be fully convinced in his **o** mind. Rom 14:5
our Lord Christ, but their **o** appetites, Rom 16:18
we labor, working with our **o** hands. 1 Cor 4:12
and defraud—even your **o** brothers! 1 Cor 6:8
person sins against his **o** body. 1 Cor 6:18
have from God? You are not your **o**, 1 Cor 6:19
man should have his **o** wife and each 1 Cor 7:2
wife and each woman her **o** husband. 1 Cor 7:2
not have authority over her **o** body, 1 Cor 7:4
not have authority over his **o** body, 1 Cor 7:4
But each has his **o** gift from God, one 1 Cor 7:7
I say this for your **o** benefit, not to lay 1 Cor 7:35
serves as a soldier at his **o** expense? 1 Cor 9:7
For if I do this of my **o** will, I have a 1 Cor 9:17
I have a reward, but not of my **o** will, 1 Cor 9:17
Let no one seek his **o** good, but the 1 Cor 10:24
I do, not seeking my **o** advantage, 1 Cor 10:33
one goes ahead with his **o** meal. 1 Cor 11:21
It does not insist on its **o** way; it is not 1 Cor 13:5
But each in his **o** order: Christ the 1 Cor 15:23
and to each kind of seed its **o** body. 1 Cor 15:38

write this greeting with my **o** hand. 1 Cor 16:21
are restricted in your **o** affections. 2 Cor 6:12
And besides our **o** comfort, we 2 Cor 7:13
beyond their means, of their **o** free will, 2 Cor 8:3
he is going to you of his **o** accord. 2 Cor 8:17
robbers, danger from my **o** people, 2 Cor 11:26
but on my **o** behalf I will not boast, 2 Cor 12:5
beyond many of my **o** age among my Gal 1:14
But let each one test his **o** work, and then Gal 6:4
For each will have to bear his **o** load. Gal 6:5
one who sows to his **o** flesh will from the Gal 6:8
I am writing to you with my **o** hand. Gal 6:11
And this is not your **o** doing; it is the gift Eph 2:8
doing honest work with his **o** hands, Eph 4:28
Wives, submit to your **o** husbands, as Eph 5:22
love their wives as their **o** bodies. Eph 5:28
For no one ever hated his **o** flesh, but Eph 5:29
of you look not only to his **o** interests, Phil 2:4
work out your **o** salvation with fear Phil 2:12
They all seek their **o** interests, not Phil 2:21
righteousness of my **o** that comes from Phil 3:9
perfect, but I press on to make it my **o**, Phil 3:12
Christ Jesus has made me his **o**. Phil 3:12
not consider that I have made it my **o**. Phil 3:13
write this greeting with my **o** hand. Col 4:18
mother taking care of her **o** children. 1 Thes 2:7
gospel of God but also our **o** selves, 1 Thes 2:8
you into his **o** kingdom and glory. 1 Thes 2:12
things from your **o** countrymen as 1 Thes 2:14
how to control his **o** body in holiness 1 Thes 4:4
quietly, and to mind your **o** affairs, 1 Thes 4:11
quietly and to earn their **o** living. 2 Thes 3:12
write this greeting with my **o** hand. 2 Thes 3:17
He must manage his **o** household well, 1 Tm 3:4
know how to manage his **o** household, 1 Tm 3:5
children and their **o** households well. 1 Tm 3:12
godliness to their **o** household and to 1 Tm 5:4
slaves regard their **o** masters as worthy 1 Tm 6:1
because of his **o** purpose and grace, 2 Tm 1:9
teachers to suit their **o** passions, 2 Tm 4:3
One of the Cretans, a prophet of their **o**, Ti 1:12
kind, and submissive to their **o** husbands, Ti 2:5
submissive to their **o** masters in Ti 2:9
a people for his **o** possession who are Ti 2:14
but according to his **o** mercy, Ti 3:5
compulsion but of your **o** free will. Phlm 1:14
I, Paul, write this with my **o** hand: I Phlm 1:19
of your owing me even your **o** self. Phlm 1:19
to offer sacrifice for his **o** sins just as he Heb 5:3
of God to their **o** harm and holding him Heb 6:6
first for his **o** sins and then for those of Heb 7:27
calves but by means of his **o** blood, Heb 9:12
places every year with blood not his **o**, Heb 9:25
the people through his **o** blood. Heb 13:12
he is lured and enticed by his **o** desire. Jas 1:14
Of his **o** will he brought us forth by the Jas 1:18
nation, a people for his **o** possession, 1 Pt 2:9
wives, be subject to your **o** husbands, 1 Pt 3:1
called us to his **o** glory and excellence, 2 Pt 1:3
from someone's **o** interpretation. 2 Pt 1:20
was rebuked for his **o** transgression; 2 Pt 2:16
"The dog returns to its **o** vomit, and the 2 Pt 2:22
scoffing, following their **o** sinful desires. 2 Pt 3:3
unstable twist to their **o** destruction, 2 Pt 3:16
lawless people and lose your **o** stability. 2 Pt 3:17
Because his **o** deeds were evil and his 1 Jn 3:12
stay within their **o** position of authority, Jude 1:6
casting up the foam of their **o** shame; Jude 1:13
following their **o** sinful desires; Jude 1:16
following their **o** ungodly passions." Jude 1:18
God out of heaven, and my **o** new name. Rv 3:12

OWNED (1)
some of the poor people who **o** nothing, Jer 39:10

OWNER (24)
but the **o** of the ox shall not be liable. Ex 21:28
and its **o** has been warned but has not Ex 21:29
and its **o** also shall be put to death. Ex 21:29
the **o** shall give to their master thirty Ex 21:32
the **o** of the pit shall make restoration. Ex 21:34
He shall give money to its **o**, and the Ex 21:34
in the past, and its **o** has not kept it in, Ex 21:36
the **o** of the house shall come near to Ex 22:8
The **o** shall accept the oath, and he Ex 22:11
him, he shall make restitution to its **o**. Ex 22:12
injured or dies, the **o** not being with it, Ex 22:14
If the **o** was with it, he shall not make Ex 22:15
time he was with his **o** shall be rated as Lv 25:50
the name of Shemer, the **o** of the hill. 1 Kgs 16:24
what advantage has their **o** but to see Eccl 5:11
riches were kept by their **o** to his hurt, Eccl 5:13
The ox knows its **o**, and the donkey its Is 1:3
the **o** of the vineyard said to his foreman, Mt 20:8
When therefore the **o** of the vineyard Mt 21:40
What will the **o** of the vineyard do? He Mk 12:9
Then the **o** of the vineyard said, 'What Lk 20:13
What then will the **o** of the vineyard do Lk 20:15
the pilot and to the **o** of the ship than Acts 27:11
a slave, though he is the **o** of everything, Gal 4:1

OWNERS (5)
and made its **o** breathe their last, Jb 31:39
untying the colt, its **o** said to them, Lk 19:33
as many as were **o** of lands or houses Acts 4:34
and brought her **o** much gain by Acts 16:16
But when her **o** saw that their hope of Acts 16:19

OWNS (3)
me the cave of Machpelah, which he **o**; Gn 23:9
then he who **o** the house shall come Lv 14:35
bind the man who **o** this belt and Acts 21:11

OX (79)
servant, or his female servant, or his **o**, Ex 20:17
"When an **o** gores a man or a woman Ex 21:28
a woman to death, the **o** shall be stoned, Ex 21:28
the owner of the **o** shall not be liable. Ex 21:28
But if the **o** has been accustomed to Ex 21:29
man or a woman, the **o** shall be stoned, Ex 21:29
If the **o** gores a slave, male or female, Ex 21:32
of silver, and the **o** shall be stoned. Ex 21:32
it, and an **o** or a donkey falls into it, Ex 21:33
"When one man's **o** butts another's, so Ex 21:35
shall sell the live **o** and share its price, Ex 21:35
known that the **o** has been accustomed Ex 21:36
not kept it in, he shall repay **o** for ox, Ex 21:36
not kept it in, he shall repay ox for **o**, Ex 21:36
"If a man steals an **o** or a sheep, and kills Ex 22:1
sells it, he shall repay five oxen for an **o**, Ex 22:1
whether it is an **o** or a donkey or a sheep, Ex 22:4
breach of trust, whether it is for an **o**, Ex 22:9
neighbor a donkey or an **o** or a sheep or Ex 22:10
you meet your enemy's **o** or his donkey Ex 23:4
that your **o** and your donkey may have Ex 23:12
are taken from the **o** of the sacrifice of Lv 4:10
You shall eat no fat, of **o** or sheep or goat. Lv 7:23
and an **o** and a ram for peace offerings, to Lv 9:4
Then he killed the **o** and the ram, the Lv 9:18
But the fat pieces of the **o** and of the ram, Lv 9:19
house of Israel kills an **o** or a lamb or a Lv 17:3
"When an **o** or sheep or goat is born, it Lv 22:27
you shall not kill an **o** or a sheep and Lv 22:28
whether **o** or sheep, it is the LORD'S. Lv 27:26
two of the chiefs, and for each one an **o**. Nm 7:3
as the **o** licks up the grass of the field." Nm 22:4
for them like the horns of the wild **o**. Nm 23:22
is for him like the horns of the wild **o**; Nm 24:8
or your **o** or your donkey or any of your Dt 5:14
servant, or his female servant, his **o**, Dt 5:21
are the animals you may eat: the **o**, Dt 14:4
the LORD your God an **o** or a sheep in Dt 17:1
a sacrifice, whether an **o** or a sheep: Dt 18:3
not see your brother's **o** or his sheep Dt 22:1
brother's donkey or his **o** fallen down by Dt 22:4
not plow with an **o** and a donkey Dt 22:10
shall not muzzle an **o** when it is treading Dt 25:4
Your **o** shall be slaughtered before your Dt 28:31
and his horns are the horns of a wild **o**; Dt 33:17
in Israel and no sheep or **o** or donkey. Jgs 6:4
his anointed. Whose **o** have I taken? 1 Sm 12:3
every man bring his **o** or his sheep 1 Sm 14:34
people brought his **o** with him that 1 Sm 14:34
woman, child and infant, **o** and sheep, 1 Sm 15:3
and infant, **o**, donkey and sheep, 1 Sm 22:19
he sacrificed an **o** and a fattened 2 Sm 6:13
each day was one **o** and six choice Neh 5:18
he has grass, or the **o** low over his fodder? Jb 6:5
they take the widow's **o** for a pledge. Jb 24:3
"Is the wild **o** willing to serve you? Will Jb 39:9
as I made you; he eats grass like an **o**. Jb 40:15
a calf, and Sirion like a young wild **o**. Ps 29:6
the LORD more than an **o** or a bull with Ps 69:31
exalted my horn like that of the wild **o**; Ps 92:10
for the image of an **o** that eats grass. Ps 106:20
her, as an **o** goes to the slaughter, Prv 7:22
crops come by the strength of the **o**. Prv 14:4
is than a fattened **o** and hatred with it. Prv 15:17
The **o** knows its owner, and the donkey its Is 1:3
and the lion shall eat straw like the **o**. Is 11:7
let the feet of the **o** and the donkey range Is 32:20
the lion shall eat straw like the **o**, and Is 65:25
"He who slaughters an **o** is like one who Is 66:3
four had the face of an **o** on the left side, Ezk 1:10
You shall be made to eat grass like an **o**, Dn 4:25
you shall be made to eat grass like an **o**, Dn 4:32
among men and ate grass like an **o**, Dn 4:33
He was fed grass like an **o**, and his body Dn 5:21
the Sabbath untie his **o** or his donkey Lk 13:15
having a son or an **o** that has fallen into Lk 14:5
shall not muzzle an **o** when it treads 1 Cor 9:9
shall not muzzle an **o** when it treads 1 Tm 5:18
lion, the second living creature like an **o**, Rv 4:7

OXEN (86)
and he had sheep, **o**, male donkeys, Gn 12:16
Then Abimelech took sheep and **o**, Gn 20:14
took sheep and **o** and gave them Gn 21:27
I have **o**, donkeys, flocks, male servants, Gn 32:5
in their willfulness they hamstrung **o**. Gn 49:6
peace offerings, your sheep and your **o**. Ex 20:24
or sells it, he shall repay five **o** for an ox, Ex 22:1
the same with your **o** and with your Ex 22:30
peace offerings of **o** to the LORD. Ex 24:5
before the LORD, six wagons and twelve **o**, Nm 7:3
the wagons and the **o** and gave them to Nm 7:6
Two wagons and four **o** he gave to the Nm 7:7
four wagons and eight **o** he gave to the Nm 7:8
the sacrifice of peace offerings, two **o**, Nm 7:17
the sacrifice of peace offerings, two **o**, Nm 7:23
the sacrifice of peace offerings, two **o**, Nm 7:29
the sacrifice of peace offerings, two **o**, Nm 7:35
the sacrifice of peace offerings, two **o**, Nm 7:41
the sacrifice of peace offerings, two **o**, Nm 7:47
the sacrifice of peace offerings, two **o**, Nm 7:53
the sacrifice of peace offerings, two **o**, Nm 7:59
the sacrifice of peace offerings, two **o**, Nm 7:65
the sacrifice of peace offerings, two **o**, Nm 7:71
the sacrifice of peace offerings, two **o**, Nm 7:77
the sacrifice of peace offerings, two **o**, Nm 7:83
And Balak sacrificed **o** and sheep, and Nm 22:40
people and of the **o** and of the donkeys Nm 31:28
out of every fifty, of the people, of the **o**, Nm 31:30
whatever you desire—**o** or sheep or Dt 14:26
and women, young and old, **o**, sheep, Jos 6:21
daughters and his **o** and donkeys and Jos 7:24
coming from the field behind the **o**. 1 Sm 11:5
He took a yoke of **o** and cut them in 1 Sm 11:7
it be done to his **o**!" Then the dread of 1 Sm 11:7
and took sheep and **o** and calves and 1 Sm 14:32
sheep and of the **o** and of the fattened 1 Sm 15:9
and the lowing of the **o** that I hear?" 1 Sm 15:14
sheep and of the **o** to sacrifice to the 1 Sm 15:15
people took of the spoil, sheep and **o**, 1 Sm 15:21
but would take away the sheep, the **o**, 1 Sm 27:9
and took hold of it, for the **o** stumbled. 2 Sm 6:6
Here are the **o** for the burnt offering 2 Sm 24:22
and the yokes of the **o** for the wood. 2 Sm 24:22
floor and the **o** for fifty shekels 2 Sm 24:24
o, and fattened cattle by the Serpent's 1 Kgs 1:9
He has sacrificed **o**, fattened cattle, 1 Kgs 1:19
down this day and has sacrificed **o**, 1 Kgs 1:25
ten fat **o**, and twenty pasture-fed 1 Kgs 4:23
It stood on twelve **o**, three facing 1 Kgs 7:25
frames were lions, **o**, and cherubim. 1 Kgs 7:29
above and below the lions and **o**, 1 Kgs 7:29
and the twelve **o** underneath the sea. 1 Kgs 7:44
so many sheep and **o** that they could 1 Kgs 8:5
the LORD 22,000 **o** and 120,000 sheep. 1 Kgs 8:63
with twelve yoke of **o** in front of 1 Kgs 19:19
And he left the **o** and ran after Elijah 1 Kgs 19:20
the yoke of **o** and sacrificed them 1 Kgs 19:21
with the yokes of the **o** and gave it to 1 Kgs 19:21
orchards and vineyards, sheep and **o**, 2 Kgs 5:26
off the bronze **o** that were under 2 Kgs 16:17
on camels and on mules and on **o**, 1 Chr 12:40
and wine and oil, **o** and sheep, 1 Chr 12:40
hold of the ark, for the **o** stumbled. 1 Chr 13:9
I give the **o** for burnt offerings and 1 Chr 21:23
It stood on twelve **o**, three facing north, 2 Chr 4:4
sea, and the twelve **o** underneath it. 2 Chr 4:15
so many sheep and **o** that they could 2 Chr 5:6
a sacrifice 22,000 **o** and 120,000 sheep. 2 Chr 7:5
had brought 700 **o** and 7,000 sheep. 2 Chr 15:11
of sheep and **o** for him and 2 Chr 18:2
7,000 sheep, 3,000 camels, 500 yoke of **o**, Jb 1:3
"The **o** were plowing and the donkeys Jb 1:14
sheep, 6,000 camels, 1,000 yoke of **o**, Jb 42:12
all sheep and **o**, and also the beasts of the Ps 8:7
me from the horns of the wild **o**! Ps 22:21
Where there are no **o**, the manger is Prv 14:4
killing **o** and slaughtering sheep, Is 22:13
and the **o** and the donkeys that work the Is 30:24
Wild **o** shall fall with them, and young Is 34:7
on rocks? Does one plow there with **o**? Am 6:12
my **o** and my fat calves have been Mt 22:4
said, 'I have bought five yoke of **o**, Lk 14:19
those who were selling **o** and sheep and Jn 2:14
out of the temple, with the sheep and **o**. Jn 2:15
brought **o** and garlands to the gates Acts 14:13
grain." Is it for **o** that God is 1 Cor 9:9

OXGOAD (1)
killed 600 of the Philistines with an **o**, Jgs 3:31

OZEM (2)
O the sixth, David the seventh. 1 Chr 2:15
Bunah, Oren, **O**, and Ahijah. 1 Chr 2:25

OZNI (1)
of **O**, the clan of the Oznites; of Eri, the Nm 26:16

OZNITES (1)
of Ozni, the clan of the **O**; of Eri, the Nm 26:16

P

PAARAI (1)
Hezro of Carmel, **P** the Arbite, 2 Sm 23:35

PACE (3)
at the **p** of the livestock that are ahead Gn 33:14
of me and at the **p** of the children, Gn 33:14
do not slacken the **p** for me unless I 2 Kgs 4:24

PACT (1)
said, let there be a sworn **p** between us, Gn 26:28

PADDAN (1)
As for me, when I came from **P**, to my Gn 48:7

PADDAN-ARAM (10)
daughter of Bethuel the Aramean of **P**, Gn 25:20
go to **P** to the house of Bethuel your Gn 28:2
And he went to **P**, to Laban, the son of Gn 28:5
and sent him away to **P** to take a wife Gn 28:6
his father and his mother and gone to **P**. Gn 28:7
possession that he had acquired in **P**, Gn 31:18
the land of Canaan, on his way from **P**, Gn 33:18
to Jacob again, when he came from **P**, Gn 35:9
of Jacob who were born to him in **P**. Gn 35:26
of Leah, whom she bore to Jacob in **P**, Gn 46:15

PADON (2)
of Keros, the sons of Siaha, the sons of **P**, Ezr 2:44
of Keros, the sons of Sia, the sons of **P**, Neh 7:47

PAGANS (3)
that is not tolerated even among **p**, 1 Cor 5:1
imply that what **p** sacrifice they 1 Cor 10:20
that when you were **p** you were led 1 Cor 12:2

PAGIEL (5)
from Asher, **P** the son of Ochran; Nm 1:13
people of Asher being **P** the son of Nm 2:27
On the eleventh day **P** the son of Nm 7:72
was the offering of **P** the son of Ochran. Nm 7:77
people of Asher was **P** the son of Nm 10:26

PAHATH-MOAB (6)
The sons of **P**, namely the sons of Jeshua Ezr 2:6
Of the sons of **P**, Eliehoenai the son of Ezr 8:4
Of the sons of **P**: Adna, Chelal, Ezr 10:30
the son of **P** repaired another section Neh 3:11
The sons of **P**, namely the sons of Neh 7:11
people: Parosh, **P**, Elam, Zattu, Bani, Neh 10:14

PAI (1)
place, the name of his city being **P**; 1 Chr 1:50

PAID (49)
keeper of the prison **p** no attention to Gn 39:23
his face to the earth and **p** homage. 1 Sm 24:8
his face to the ground and **p** homage. 1 Sm 28:14
he fell to the ground and **p** homage. 2 Sm 1:2
for whom I **p** the bridal price of a 2 Sm 3:14
and fell on his face and **p** homage. 2 Sm 9:6
And he **p** homage and said, "What is 2 Sm 9:8
to the ground and **p** homage and said, 2 Sm 14:4
the ground and **p** homage and 2 Sm 14:22
went out and **p** homage to the 2 Sm 24:20
Bathsheba bowed and **p** homage to 1 Kgs 1:16
to the ground and **p** homage to the 1 Kgs 1:31
And he came and **p** homage to King 1 Kgs 1:53
one answered; no one **p** attention. 1 Kgs 18:29
And they **p** it out to the carpenters 2 Kgs 12:11
became his vassal and **p** him tribute. 2 Kgs 17:3
threshing floor and **p** homage to 1 Chr 21:21
So David **p** Ornan 600 shekels of 1 Chr 21:25
their heads and **p** homage to the 1 Chr 29:20
of Judah came and **p** homage to the 2 Chr 24:17
The Ammonites **p** tribute to Uzziah, 2 Chr 26:8
The Ammonites **p** him the same 2 Chr 27:5
his people, but they **p** no attention. 2 Chr 33:10
whom tribute, custom, and toll were **p**. Ezr 4:20
Let the cost be **p** from the royal treasury. Ezr 6:4
The cost is to be **p** to these men in full Ezr 6:8
kept your law or **p** attention to your Neh 9:34
bowed down and **p** homage to Haman, Est 3:2
It will be **p** in full before his time, and Jb 15:32
sacrifices, and today I have **p** my vows; Prv 7:14
Oh that you had **p** attention to my Is 48:18
because they have not **p** attention to my Jer 6:19
I have **p** attention and listened, but they Jer 8:6
or who has **p** attention to his word and Jer 23:18
upon his face and **p** homage to Daniel, Dn 2:46
So he **p** the fare and went on board, to go Jon 1:3
The LORD **p** attention and heard them, Mal 3:16
get out until you have **p** the last penny. Mt 5:26
But they **p** no attention and went off, one Mt 22:5
to you?" And they **p** him thirty pieces Mt 26:15
out until you have **p** the very last Lk 12:59
with one accord **p** attention to what Acts 8:6
They all **p** attention to him, from the Acts 8:10
And they **p** attention to him because Acts 8:11
But Gallio **p** no attention to any of Acts 18:17
But the centurion **p** more attention to Acts 27:11
the wrongdoer will be **p** back for the Col 3:25
tithes, **p** tithes through Abraham, Heb 7:9
back as she herself has **p** back others, Rv 18:6

PAILS (1)
his **p** full of milk and the marrow of his Jb 21:24

PAIN (38)
surely multiply your **p** in childbearing; Gn 3:16
in **p** you shall bring forth children. Gn 3:16
in **p** you shall eat of it all the days of Gn 3:17
shall enter into her and cause bitter **p**. Nm 5:24
shall enter into her and cause bitter **p**, Nm 5:27
saying, "Because I bore him in **p**." 1 Chr 4:9
not bring me **p**!" And God granted 1 Chr 4:10
I would even exult in **p** unsparing, for I Jb 6:10
He feels only the **p** of his own body, and Jb 14:22
wicked man writhes in **p** all his days, Jb 15:20
solace of my lips would assuage your **p**. Jb 16:5
"If I speak, my **p** is not assuaged, and if I Jb 16:6
and the **p** that gnaws me takes no rest. Jb 30:17
is also rebuked with **p** on his bed and Jb 33:19
ready to fall, and my **p** is ever before me. Ps 38:17
and they recount the **p** of those you Ps 69:26
But I am afflicted and in **p**; let your Ps 69:29
and put away **p** from your body, Eccl 11:10
you rest from your **p** and turmoil and the Is 14:3
away in a day of grief and incurable **p**. Is 17:11
you shall cry out for **p** of heart and shall Is 65:14
before her **p** came upon her she delivered Is 66:7
My anguish, my anguish! I writhe in **p**! Jer 4:19
hold of us, **p** as of a woman in labor. Jer 6:24
Why is my **p** unceasing, my wound Jer 15:18
upon you, **p** as of a woman in labor!" Jer 22:23
over your hurt? Your **p** is incurable. Jer 30:15
For the LORD has added sorrow to my **p**. Jer 45:3
seized him, **p** as of a woman in labor. Jer 50:43
Take balm for her **p**; perhaps she may Jer 51:8
The land trembles and writhes in **p**, for Jer 51:29
that **p** seized you like a woman in labor? Mi 4:9
For if I cause you **p**, who is there to 2 Cor 2:2
I might not suffer **p** from those who 2 Cor 2:3
not to cause you **p** but to let you know 2 Cor 2:4
Now if anyone has caused **p**, he has 2 Cor 2:5
the God of heaven for their **p** and sores. Rv 16:11
be mourning nor crying nor **p** anymore, Rv 21:4

PAINED (1)
me glad but the one whom I have **p**? 2 Cor 2:2

PAINFUL (4)
work and from the **p** toil of our hands." Gn 5:29
not to make another **p** visit to you. 2 Cor 2:1
all discipline seems **p** rather than Heb 12:11
and harmful and **p** sores came upon the Rv 16:2

PAINFULLY (1)
saw that they were making headway **p**, Mk 6:48

PAINS (13)
gave birth, for her **p** came upon her. 1 Sm 4:19
With great **p** I have provided for the 1 Chr 22:14
That God distributes **p** in his anger? Jb 21:17
the heart of a woman in her birth **p**; Jer 48:41
the heart of a woman in her birth **p**." Jer 49:22
reason of the vision **p** have come upon Dn 10:16
afflicted with various diseases and **p**, Mt 4:24
are but the beginning of the birth **p**. Mt 24:8
are but the beginning of the birth **p**. Mk 13:8
So I always take **p** to have a clear Acts 24:16
together in the **p** of childbirth until Rom 8:22
upon them as labor **p** come upon a 1 Thes 5:3
crying out in birth **p** and the agony of Rv 12:2

PAINT (1)
gold, that you enlarge your eyes with **p**? Jer 4:30

PAINTED (2)
And she **p** her eyes and adorned her 2 Kgs 9:30
them you bathed yourself, **p** your eyes, Ezk 23:40

PAINTING (1)
it with cedar and **p** it with vermilion. Jer 22:14

PAIR (8)
and a **p** of the animals that are not clean, Gn 7:2
with it under each **p** of the six branches Ex 25:35
with it under each **p** of the six branches Ex 37:21
and put a torch between each **p** of tails. Jgs 15:4
silver, and the needy for a **p** of sandals— Am 2:6
and the needy for a **p** of sandals and sell Am 8:6
the Law of the Lord, "a **p** of turtledoves, Lk 2:24
And its rider had a **p** of scales in his hand. Rv 6:5

PAIRS (4)
Take with you seven **p** of all clean Gn 7:2
and seven **p** of the birds of the heavens Gn 7:3
When he sees riders, horsemen in **p**, Is 21:7
riders, horsemen in **p**!" And he answered, Is 21:9

PALACE (44)
Ahishar was in charge of the **p**; and 1 Kgs 4:6
beside the **p** of Ahab king of Samaria. 1 Kgs 21:1
So he who was over the **p**, and he who 2 Kgs 10:5
behind the guards) shall guard the **p**. 2 Kgs 11:6
be eunuchs in the **p** of the king of 2 Kgs 20:18
and his officials and his **p** officials. 2 Kgs 24:12
his sons, together with the **p** officials, 1 Chr 28:1
for the **p** will not be for man but for 1 Chr 29:1
he may build the **p** for which I have 1 Chr 29:19
of the LORD, and a royal **p** for himself. 2 Chr 2:1
for the LORD and a royal **p** for himself. 2 Chr 2:12
commander of the **p** and Elkanah 2 Chr 28:7
and put them in his **p** in Babylon. 2 Chr 36:7
eat the salt of the **p** and it is not fitting Ezr 4:14
in the court of the garden of the king's **p**. Est 1:5
to all the staff of his **p** to do as each man Est 1:8
the women in the **p** that belonged to King Est 1:9
taken into the king's **p** and put in Est 2:8
chosen young women from the king's **p**, Est 2:9
with her from the harem to the king's **p**. Est 2:13
Ahasuerus into his royal **p** in the tenth Est 2:16
that in the king's **p** you will escape any Est 4:13
stood in the inner court of the king's **p**, Est 5:1
room opposite the entrance to the **p**. Est 5:1
outer court of the king's **p** to speak to the Est 6:4
and went into the **p** garden, Est 7:7
king returned from the **p** garden to the Est 7:8
led along as they enter the **p** of the king. Ps 45:15
pillars cut for the structure of a **p**; Ps 144:12
a ruin; the foreigners' **p** is a city no more; Is 25:2
For the **p** is forsaken, the populous city Is 32:14
shall be eunuchs in the **p** of the king of Is 39:7
and the **p** shall stand where it used to Jer 30:18
guard that was in the **p** of the king of Jer 32:2
entrance to Pharaoh's **p** in Tahpanhes, Jer 43:9
and competent to stand in the king's **p**, Dn 1:4
ease in my house and prospering in my **p**. Dn 4:4
on the roof of the royal **p** of Babylon, Dn 4:29
on the plaster of the wall of the king's **p**, Dn 5:5
king went to his **p** and spent the night Dn 6:18
river gates are opened; the **p** melts away; Na 2:6
people gathered in the **p** of the high Mt 26:3
led him away inside the **p** (that is, Mk 15:16
man, fully armed, guards his own **p**, Lk 11:21

PALACES (12)
and burned all its **p** with fire and 2 Chr 36:19
From ivory **p** stringed instruments Ps 45:8
take in your hands, yet it is in kings' **p**. Prv 30:28
its towers, and jackals in the pleasant **p**; Is 13:22
siege towers, they stripped her **p** bare, Is 23:13
let us attack by night and destroy her **p**!" Jer 6:5
it has entered our **p**, cutting off the Jer 9:21
it shall devour the **p** of Jerusalem and Jer 17:27
up Israel; he has swallowed up all its **p**; Lam 2:5
hand of the enemy the walls of her **p**; Lam 2:7
has forgotten his Maker and built **p**, Hos 8:14
comes into our land and treads in our **p**, Mi 5:5

PALAL (1)
P the son of Uzai repaired opposite the Neh 3:25

PALATE (3)
Cannot my **p** discern the cause of Jb 6:30
the ear test words as the **p** tastes food? Jb 12:11
for the ear tests words as the **p** tastes food. Jb 34:3

PALATIAL (1)
he shall pitch his **p** tents between the Dn 11:45

PALE (5)
ashamed, no more shall his face grow **p**. Is 29:22
in labor? Why has every face turned **p**? Jer 30:6
peoples are in anguish; all faces grow **p**. Jl 2:6
anguish is in all loins; all faces grow **p**! Na 2:10
And I looked, and behold, a **p** horse! And Rv 6:8

PALLU (5)
Reuben: Hanoch, **P**, Hezron, and Carmi. Gn 46:9
of Israel: Hanoch, **P**, Hezron, and Carmi; Ex 6:14
the clan of the Hanochites; of **P**, Nm 26:5
And the sons of **P**: Eliab. Nm 26:8
Israel: Hanoch, **P**, Hezron, and Carmi. 1 Chr 5:3

PALLUITES (1)
Hanochites; of Pallu, the clan of the **P**; Nm 26:5

PALM (37)
springs of water and seventy **p** trees, Ex 15:27
and pour it into the **p** of his own left Lv 14:15
of the oil into the **p** of his own left hand, Lv 14:26
branches of **p** trees and boughs of leafy Lv 23:40
Like **p** groves that stretch afar, like Nm 24:6

springs of water and seventy **p** trees, Nm 33:9
is, the Valley of Jericho the city of **p** trees, Dt 34:3
to sit under the **p** of Deborah between Jgs 4:5
of cherubim and **p** trees and open 1 Kgs 6:29
with carvings of cherubim, **p** trees, 1 Kgs 6:32
on the cherubim and on the **p** trees. 1 Kgs 6:32
carved cherubim and **p** trees and 1 Kgs 6:35
carved cherubim, lions, and **p** trees, 1 Kgs 7:36
at Jericho, the city of **p** trees. 2 Chr 28:15
p, and other leafy trees to make booths, Neh 8:15
flourish like the **p** tree and grow Ps 92:12
Your stature is like a **p** tree, and your Sg 7:7
I say I will climb the **p** tree and lay hold of Sg 7:8
and tail, **p** branch and reed in one day— Is 9:14
Egypt that head or tail, **p** branch or reed, Is 19:15
inside, and on the jambs were **p** trees. Ezk 40:16
and its **p** trees were of the same size as Ezk 40:22
them, and it had **p** trees on its jambs, Ezk 40:26
court, and **p** trees were on its jambs, Ezk 40:31
court, and it had **p** trees on its jambs, Ezk 40:34
court, and it had **p** trees on its jambs, Ezk 40:37
It was carved of cherubim and **p** trees, Ezk 41:18
a **p** tree between cherub and cherub. Ezk 41:18
human face toward the **p** tree on the Ezk 41:19
young lion toward the **p** tree on the Ezk 41:19
cherubim and **p** trees were carved; Ezk 41:20
were carved cherubim and **p** trees, Ezk 41:25
narrow windows and **p** trees on either Ezk 41:26
was like a young **p** planted in a Hos 9:13
Pomegranate, **p**, and apple, all the trees of Jl 1:12
they took branches of **p** trees and went Jn 12:13
robes, with **p** branches in their hands, Rv 7:9

PALMS (7)
put all these on the **p** of Aaron and on Ex 29:24
of Aaron and on the **p** of his sons, Ex 29:24
from the city of **p** into the wilderness of Jgs 1:16
And they took possession of the city of **p**. Jgs 3:13
and the feet and the **p** of her hands. 2 Kgs 9:35
fine gold and made **p** and chains on it. 2 Chr 3:5
engraved you on the **p** of my hands; Is 49:16

PALTI (2)
tribe of Benjamin, **P** the son of Raphu; Nm 13:9
David's wife, to **P** the son of Laish, 1 Sm 25:44

PALTIEL (2)
of Issachar a chief, **P** the son of Azzan. Nm 34:26
her from her husband **P** the son of 2 Sm 3:15

PALTITE (1)
Helez the **P**, Ira the son of Ikkesh of 2 Sm 23:26

PAMPERS (1)
Whoever **p** his servant from Prv 29:21

PAMPHYLIA (5)
Phrygia and **P**, Egypt and the parts of Acts 2:10
from Paphos and came to Perga in **P**. Acts 13:13
through Pisidia and came to **P**. Acts 14:24
from them in **P** and had not Acts 15:38
sea along the coast of Cilicia and **P**, Acts 27:5

PAN (4)
offering is a grain offering cooked in a **p**, Lv 2:7
that is prepared on a **p** or a griddle shall Lv 7:9
thrust it into the **p** or kettle or 1 Sm 2:14
And she took the **p** and emptied it out 2 Sm 13:9

PANELED (2)
were **p** with wood all around, Ezk 41:16
you yourselves to dwell in your **p** houses, Hg 1:4

PANELING (1)
p it with cedar and painting it with Jer 22:14

PANELS (7)
they had **p**, and the panels were set in 1 Kgs 7:28
and the **p** were set in the frames, 1 Kgs 7:28
and on the **p** that were set in the 1 Kgs 7:29
were carvings, and its **p** were square, 1 Kgs 7:31
four wheels were underneath the **p**. 1 Kgs 7:32
its stays and its **p** were of one piece 1 Kgs 7:35
the surfaces of its stays and on its **p**, 1 Kgs 7:36

PANGS (13)
p have seized the inhabitants of Ex 15:14
cause of grief or **p** of conscience for 1 Sm 25:31
For they have no **p** until death; their Ps 73:4
me; the **p** of Sheol laid hold on me; Ps 116:3
be dismayed: **p** and agony will seize them; Is 13:8
p have seized me, like the pangs of a Is 21:3
seized me, like the **p** of a woman in labor; Is 21:3
and cries out in her **p** when she is near Is 26:17
Will not **p** take hold of you like those of Jer 13:21
will be pitied when **p** come upon you, Jer 22:23
The **p** of childbirth come for him, but Hos 13:13
raised him up, loosing the **p** of death, Acts 2:24
and pierced themselves with many **p**. 1 Tm 6:10

PANIC (18)
and threw the Egyptian forces into a **p**, Ex 14:24
I will visit you with **p**, with wasting Lv 26:16
Do not fear or **p** or be in dread of them, Dt 20:3
LORD threw them into a **p** before Israel, Jos 10:10
and he threw all the army into a **p**. Jgs 8:12
against the city, causing a very great **p**, 1 Sm 5:9
was a deathly **p** throughout the whole 1 Sm 5:11
And there was a **p** in the camp, in the 1 Sm 14:15
quaked, and it became a very great **p**. 1 Sm 14:15
discouraged and throw him into a **p**, 2 Sm 17:2
it, they were astounded; they were in **p**; Ps 48:5
the standard in **p**," declares the LORD, Is 31:9
We have heard a cry of **p**, of terror, and Jer 30:5
she turned to flee, and **p** seized her; Jer 49:24
with fire, and the soldiers are in **p**. Jer 51:32
p and pitfall have come upon us, Lam 3:47
the LORD, I will strike every horse with **p**, Zec 12:4
that day a great **p** from the LORD shall Zec 14:13

PANS (8)
shovels and basins and forks and fire **p**. Ex 27:3
the basins, the forks, and the fire **p**. Ex 38:3
are used for the service there, the fire **p**, Nm 4:14
basins, dishes for incense, and fire **p**, 1 Kgs 7:50
the fire **p** also and the bowls. What 2 Kgs 25:15
basins, dishes for incense, and fire **p**, 2 Chr 4:22
in pots, in cauldrons, and in **p**, 2 Chr 35:13
bowls and the fire **p** and the basins and Jer 52:19

PANT (5)
thorns, and the thirsty **p** after his wealth. Jb 5:5
I open my mouth and **p**, because I Ps 119:131
like a woman in labor; I will gasp and **p**. Is 42:14
bare heights; they **p** for air like jackals; Jer 14:6
beasts of the field **p** for you because the Jl 1:20

PANTS (2)
As a deer **p** for flowing streams, so pants Ps 42:1
flowing streams, so **p** my soul for you, Ps 42:1

PAPER (1)
you, I would rather not use **p** and ink. 2 Jn 1:12

PAPHOS (2)
through the whole island as far as **P**, Acts 13:6
set sail from **P** and came to Acts 13:13

PAPYRUS (2)
"Can **p** grow where there is no marsh? Jb 8:11
by the sea, in vessels of **p** on the waters! Is 18:2

PARABLE (32)
I will open my mouth in a **p**; I will utter Ps 78:2
and speak a **p** to the house of Israel; Ezk 17:2
And utter a **p** to the rebellious house Ezk 24:3
"Hear then the **p** of the sower: Mt 13:18
He put another **p** before them, saying, Mt 13:24
He put another **p** before them, saying, Mt 13:31
He told them another **p**. "The kingdom Mt 13:33
he said nothing to them without a **p**. Mt 13:34
"Explain to us the **p** of the weeds of the Mt 13:36
Peter said to him, "Explain the **p** to us." Mt 15:15
"Hear another **p**. There was a master of Mt 21:33
to them, "Do you not understand this **p**? Mk 4:13
of God, or what **p** shall we use for it? Mk 4:30
He did not speak to them without a **p**, Mk 4:34
his disciples asked him about the **p**. Mk 7:17
that he had told the **p** against them. Mk 12:12
He also told them a **p**: "No one tears a Lk 5:36
He also told them a **p**: "Can a blind man Lk 6:39
after town came to him, he said in a **p**: Lk 8:4
disciples asked him what this **p** meant, Lk 8:9
Now the **p** is this: The seed is the word of Lk 8:11
And he told them a **p**, saying, "The Lk 12:16
are you telling this **p** for us or for all?" Lk 12:41
And he told this **p**: "A man had a fig tree Lk 13:6
Now he told a **p** to those who were Lk 14:7
So he told them this **p**: Lk 15:3
And he told them a **p** to the effect that Lk 18:1
He also told this **p** to some who trusted Lk 18:9
these things, he proceeded to tell a **p**, Lk 19:11
And he began to tell the people this **p**: "A Lk 20:9
that he had told this **p** against them, Lk 20:19
And he told them a **p**: "Look at the fig Lk 21:29

PARABLES (18)
saying of me, 'Is he not a maker of **p**?'" Ezk 20:49
and through the prophets gave **p**. Hos 12:10
And he told them many things in **p**, Mt 13:3
"Why do you speak to them in **p**?" Mt 13:10
This is why I speak to them in **p**, Mt 13:13
things Jesus said to the crowds in **p**; Mt 13:34
prophet: "I will open my mouth in **p**; Mt 13:35
And when Jesus had finished these **p**, Mt 13:53
priests and the Pharisees heard his **p**, Mt 21:45
And again Jesus spoke to them in **p**, Mt 22:1
them to him and said to them in **p**, Mk 3:23
he was teaching them many things in **p**, Mk 4:2
with the twelve asked him about the **p**. Mk 4:10
but for those outside everything is in **p**, Mk 4:11
How then will you understand all the **p**? Mk 4:13
With many such **p** he spoke the word Mk 4:33
And he began to speak to them in **p**. "A Mk 12:1
of God, but for others they are in **p**, Lk 8:10

PARADISE (3)
to you, today you will be with me in **P**." Lk 23:43
was caught up into **p**—whether in 2 Cor 12:3
of the tree of life, which is in the **p** of God.' Rv 2:7

PARAH (1)
Avvim, **P**, Ophrah, Jos 18:23

PARALLEL (2)
was a wall outside **p** to the chambers, Ezk 42:7
west border, **p** to the tribal portions, Ezk 48:21

PARALYTIC (8)
behold, some people brought to him a **p**, Mt 9:2
Jesus saw their faith, he said to the **p**, Mt 9:2
sins"—he then said to the **p**—"Rise, Mt 9:6
bringing to him a **p** carried by four men. Mk 2:3
they let down the bed on which the **p** lay. Mk 2:4
Jesus saw their faith, he said to the **p**, Mk 2:5
Which is easier, to say to the **p**, 'Your Mk 2:9
earth to forgive sins"—he said to the **p**— Mk 2:10

PARALYTICS (1)
oppressed by demons, epileptics, and **p**, Mt 4:24

PARALYZED (8)
of the people of the land are **p** by terror. Ezk 7:27
So the law is **p**, and justice never goes Hab 1:4
"Lord, my servant is lying **p** at home, Mt 8:6
bringing on a bed a man who was **p**, Lk 5:18
to the man who was **p**—"I say to you, Lk 5:24
multitude of invalids—blind, lame, and **p**. Jn 5:3
and many who were **p** or lame were Acts 8:7
bedridden for eight years, who was **p**. Acts 9:33

PARAMOURS (1)
and lusted after her **p** there, whose Ezk 23:20

PARAN (11)
He lived in the wilderness of **P**, and his Gn 21:21
settled down in the wilderness of **P**. Nm 10:12
and camped in the wilderness of **P**. Nm 12:16
sent them from the wilderness of **P**, Nm 13:3
people of Israel in the wilderness of **P**, Nm 13:26
opposite Suph, between **P** and Tophel, Dt 1:1
upon us; he shone forth from Mount **P**; Dt 33:2
and went down to the wilderness of **P**. 1 Sm 25:1
and came to **P** and took men 1 Kgs 11:18
men with them from **P** and came to 1 Kgs 11:18
and the Holy One from Mount **P**. Hab 3:3

PARAPET (1)
house, you shall make a **p** for your roof, Dt 22:8

PARCEL (1)
is selling the **p** of land that belonged to Ru 4:3

PARCHED (18)
neither bread nor grain **p** or fresh until Lv 23:14
the land, unleavened cakes and **p** grain. Jos 5:11
brothers an ephah of this **p** grain, 1 Sm 17:17
and five seahs of **p** grain and a 1 Sm 25:18
vessels, wheat, barley, flour, **p** grain, 2 Sm 17:28
but the rebellious dwell in a **p** land. Ps 68:6
with my crying out; my throat is **p**. Ps 69:3
of water, a **p** land into springs of water. Ps 107:35
my soul thirsts for you like a **p** land. Ps 143:6
and their multitude is **p** with thirst. Is 5:13
dried up, and the river will be dry and **p**, Is 19:5
and all that is sown by the Nile will be **p**, Is 19:7
is none, and their tongue is **p** with thirst, Is 41:17
shall dwell in the **p** places of the Jer 17:6
your glory, and sit on the **p** ground, Jer 48:18
a wilderness, and make her like a **p** land, Hos 2:3
shall dry up; his spring shall be **p**; Hos 13:15
and drive him into a **p** and desolate land, Jl 2:20

PARCHMENTS (1)
also the books, and above all the **p**. 2 Tm 4:13

PARDON (14)
for he will not **p** your transgression, Ex 23:21
people, and **p** our iniquity and our sin, Ex 34:9
Please **p** the iniquity of this people, Nm 14:19
please **p** my sin and return with me 1 Sm 15:25
matter may the LORD **p** your servant: 2 Kgs 5:18
the LORD **p** your servant in this 2 Kgs 5:18
blood, and the LORD would not **p**. 2 Kgs 24:4
"May the good LORD **p** everyone 2 Chr 30:18
Why do you not **p** my transgression and Jb 7:21
your name's sake, O LORD, **p** my guilt, Ps 25:11
and to our God, for he will abundantly **p**. Is 55:7
justice and seeks truth, that I may **p** her. Jer 5:1
"How can I **p** you? Your children have Jer 5:7
for I will **p** those whom I leave as a Jer 50:20

PARDONED (2)
Then the LORD said, "I have **p**, Nm 14:20
warfare is ended, that her iniquity is **p**, Is 40:2

out of the uttermost **p** of the north, Ezk 38:15
up from the uttermost **p** of the north, Ezk 39:2
come into the richest **p** of the province, Dn 11:24
who is in the innermost **p** of the house, Am 6:10
garments and divided them into four **p**, Jn 19:23
Egypt and the **p** of Libya belonging to Acts 2:10
As it is, there are many **p**, yet one 1 Cor 12:20
the **p** of the body that seem to be 1 Cor 12:22
and on those **p** of the body that we 1 Cor 12:23
and our unpresentable **p** are treated 1 Cor 12:23
our more presentable **p** do not 1 Cor 12:24
descended into the lower **p** of the earth? Eph 4:9
The great city was split into three **p**, Rv 16:19

PARTY (7)
him (that is, the **p** of the Sadducees), Acts 5:17
the circumcision **p** criticized him, Acts 11:2
who belonged to the **p** of the Pharisees Acts 15:5
scribes of the Pharisees' **p** stood up and Acts 23:9
to the strictest **p** of our religion Acts 26:5
himself, fearing the circumcision **p**. Gal 2:12
especially those of the circumcision **p**. Ti 1:10

PARUAH (1)
Jehoshaphat the son of **P**, in Issachar; 1 Kgs 4:17

PARVAIM (1)
stones. The gold was gold of **P**. 2 Chr 3:6

PAS-DAMMIM (1)
with David at **P** when the 1 Chr 11:13

PASACH (1)
of Japhlet: **P**, Bimhal, and Ashvath. 1 Chr 7:33

PASEAH (4)
Beth-rapha, **P**, and Tehinnah, 1 Chr 4:12
the sons of Uzza, the sons of **P**, the sons Ezr 2:49
Joiada the son of **P** and Meshullam the Neh 3:6
the sons of Uzza, the sons of **P**, Neh 7:51

PASHHUR (14)
Adaiah the son of Jeroham, son of **P**, 1 Chr 9:12
The sons of **P**, 1,247. Ezr 2:38
Of the sons of **P**: Elioenai, Maaseiah, Ezr 10:22
The sons of **P**, 1,247. Neh 7:41
P, Amariah, Malchijah, Neh 10:3
of Amzi, son of Zechariah, son of **P**, Neh 11:12
Now **P** the priest, the son of Immer, who Jer 20:1
Then **P** beat Jeremiah the prophet, and Jer 20:2
when **P** released Jeremiah from the Jer 20:3
"The LORD does not call your name **P**, Jer 20:3
you, **P**, and all who dwell in your house, Jer 20:6
Zedekiah sent to him **P** the son of Jer 21:1
the son of Mattan, Gedaliah the son of **P**, Jer 38:1
and **P** the son of Malchiah heard the Jer 38:1

PASS (207)
in your sight, do not **p** by your servant. Gn 18:3
and after that you may **p** on—since you Gn 18:5
let me **p** through all your flock today, Gn 30:32
that I will not **p** over this heap to you, Gn 31:52
and you will not **p** over this heap and Gn 31:52
"**P** on ahead of me and put a space Gn 32:16
Let my lord **p** on ahead of his servant, Gn 33:14
For I will **p** through the land of Egypt Ex 12:12
when I see the blood, I will **p** over you, Ex 12:13
For the LORD will **p** through to strike Ex 12:23
the LORD will **p** over the door and will Ex 12:23
as a stone, till your people, O LORD, **p** by, Ex 15:16
till the people **p** by whom you have Ex 15:16
said to Moses, "**P** on before the people, Ex 17:5
make all my goodness **p** before you and Ex 33:19
of all that **p** under the herdsman's Lv 27:32
brings the curse **p** into your bowels Nm 5:22
Please let us **p** through your land. We Nm 20:17
We will not **p** through field or Nm 20:17
said to him, "You shall not **p** through, Nm 20:18
for it. Let me only **p** through on foot, Nm 20:19
"You shall not **p** through." And Edom Nm 20:20
"Let me **p** through your land. We will Nm 21:22
allow Israel to **p** through his territory. Nm 21:23
the fire, you shall **p** through the fire, Nm 31:23
the fire, you shall **p** through the water. Nm 31:23
man of you will **p** over the Jordan Nm 32:21
but your servants will **p** over, every Nm 32:27
will **p** with you over the Jordan and Nm 32:29
if they will not **p** over with you armed, Nm 32:30
We will **p** over armed before the LORD Nm 32:32
When you **p** over the Jordan into the Nm 33:51
to Hazar-addar, and **p** along to Azmon. Nm 34:4
"You are about to **p** through the territory Dt 2:4
'Let me **p** through your land. I will go Dt 2:27
drink. Only let me **p** through on foot, Dt 2:28
of Heshbon would not let us **p** by him, Dt 2:30
or wonder that he tells you comes to **p**, Dt 13:2
word does not come to **p** or come true, Dt 18:22
"**P** through the midst of the camp and Jos 1:11
days you are to **p** over this Jordan to Jos 1:11
among you shall **p** over armed before Jos 1:14
of the covenant and **p** on before the Jos 3:6
from their tents to **p** over the Jordan with Jos 3:14
"**P** on before the ark of the LORD your God Jos 4:5
and let the armed men **p** on before the ark Jos 6:7
house of Israel had failed; all came to **p**. Jos 21:45
p over into the LORD'S land where the Jos 22:19
All have come to **p** for you; not one of Jos 23:14
and did not allow anyone to **p** over. Jgs 3:28
'Please let us **p** through your land,' Jgs 11:17
'Please let us **p** through your land to Jgs 11:19
trust Israel to **p** through his territory, Jgs 11:20
of Israel, but we will **p** on to Gibeah." Jgs 19:12
"Tell the servant to **p** on before us, 1 Sm 9:27
And all these signs came to **p** that day. 1 Sm 10:9
went out to the **p** of Michmash. 1 Sm 13:23
and made him **p** before Samuel. 1 Sm 16:8
Then Jesse made Shammah **p** by. And 1 Sm 16:9
seven of his sons **p** before Samuel. 1 Sm 16:10
p on." So Ittai the Gittite passed on 2 Sm 15:22
wilderness, but by all means **p** over, 2 Sm 17:16
Otherwise it will come to **p**, when my 1 Kgs 1:21
of Samaria shall surely come to **p**." 1 Kgs 13:32
land between them to **p** through it. 1 Kgs 18:6
"Beware that you do not **p** this place, 2 Kgs 6:9
generation." And so it came to **p**.) 2 Kgs 15:12
days of old what now I bring to **p**, 2 Kgs 19:25
they may let me **p** through until I come Neh 2:7
for the animal that was under me to **p**. Neh 2:14
and his servant **p** the night within Neh 4:22
as torrential streams that **p** away, Jb 6:15
appointed his limits that he cannot **p**, Jb 14:5
has walled up my way, so that I cannot **p**, Jb 19:8
the people are shaken and **p** away, Jb 34:20
refuge, till the storms of destruction **p** by. Ps 57:1
the sea and let them **p** through it, Ps 78:13
so that all who **p** along the way pluck Ps 80:12
All who **p** by plunder him; he has Ps 89:41
For all our days **p** away under your Ps 90:9
For my days **p** away like smoke, and Ps 102:3
them like a robe, and they will **p** away, Ps 102:26
set a boundary that they may not **p**, Ps 104:9
until what he had said came to **p**, the Ps 105:19
nor do those who **p** by say, "The Ps 129:8
and made Israel **p** through the midst Ps 136:14
into their own nets, while I **p** by safely. Ps 141:10
gave a decree, and it shall not **p** away. Ps 148:6
not go on it; turn away from it and **p** on. Prv 4:15
calling to those who **p** by, who are Prv 9:15
he who purses his lips brings evil to **p**. Prv 16:30
It shall come to **p** in the latter days that the Is 2:2
And the idols shall utterly **p** away. Is 2:18
shall not stand, and it shall not come to **p**. Is 7:7
on into Judah, it will overflow and **p** on, Is 8:8
They will **p** through the land, greatly Is 8:21
they have crossed over the **p**; at Geba Is 10:29
morning by morning it will **p** through, Is 28:19
His rock shall **p** away in terror, and his Is 31:9
oars can go, nor majestic ship can **p**. Is 33:21
none shall **p** through it forever and ever. Is 34:10
Holiness; the unclean shall not **p** over it. Is 35:8
from days of old what now I bring to **p**, Is 37:26
Behold, the former things have come to **p**, Is 42:9
When you **p** through the waters, I will be Is 43:2
I have spoken, and I will bring it to **p**; I Is 46:11
uncover your legs, **p** through the rivers. Is 47:2
suddenly I did them and they came to **p**. Is 48:3
before they came to **p** I announced them Is 48:5
the sea a way for the redeemed to **p** over? Is 51:10
to you, 'Bow down, that we may **p** over'; Is 51:23
and like the street for them to **p** over." Is 51:23
sea, a perpetual barrier that it cannot **p**; Jer 5:22
though they roar, they cannot **p** over it. Jer 5:22
like a grape-gatherer **p** your hand again Jer 6:9
And it shall come to **p**, if they will Jer 12:16
"'And many nations will **p** by this city, Jer 22:8
the word of that prophet comes to **p**, Jer 28:9
"And it shall come to **p** in that day, Jer 30:8
And it shall come to **p** that as I have Jer 31:28
What you spoke has come to **p**, and Jer 32:24
flocks shall again **p** under the hands of Jer 33:13
"Is it nothing to you, all you who **p** by? Lam 1:12
All who **p** along the way clap their Lam 2:15
Who has spoken and it came to **p**, Lam 3:37
cloud so that no prayer can **p** through. Lam 3:44
of Uz; but to you also the cup shall **p**; Lam 4:21
a barber's razor and **p** it over your head Ezk 5:1
you and in the sight of all who **p** by. Ezk 5:14
and blood shall **p** through you, Ezk 5:17
LORD said to him, "**P** through the city, Ezk 9:4
hearing, "**P** through the city after him, Ezk 9:5
And it came to **p**, while I was Ezk 11:13
wild beasts to **p** through the land, Ezk 14:15
that no one may **p** through because of Ezk 14:15
say, Let a sword **p** through the land, Ezk 14:17
I will make you **p** under the rod, and I Ezk 20:37
righteous men shall **p** judgment on Ezk 23:45
I have spoken; it shall come to **p**; I will Ezk 24:14
No foot of man shall **p** through it, and Ezk 29:11
and no foot of beast shall **p** through it; Ezk 29:11
so desolate that none will **p** through. Ezk 33:28
was a river that I could not **p** through, Ezk 47:5
and let seven periods of time **p** over him. Dn 4:16
till seven periods of time **p** over him,' Dn 4:23
seven periods of time shall **p** over you, Dn 4:25
seven periods of time shall **p** over you, Dn 4:32
dominion, which shall not **p** away, Dn 7:14
must **p** before the end of the desolations Dn 9:2
coming and overflow and **p** through, Dn 11:10
and shall overflow and **p** through. Dn 11:40
Go in, **p** the night in sackcloth, O Jl 1:13
"And it shall come to **p** afterward, that I Jl 2:28
it shall come to **p** that everyone who calls Jl 2:32
strangers shall never again **p** through it. Jl 3:17
for I will **p** through your midst," says Am 5:17
P over to Calneh, and see, and from there Am 6:2
stretch themselves out shall **p** away." Am 6:7
Israel; I will never again **p** by them; Am 7:8
Israel; I will never again **p** by them. Am 8:2
P on your way, inhabitants of Shaphir, Mi 1:11
robe from those who **p** by trustingly with Mi 2:8
they break through and **p** the gate, Mi 2:13
It shall come to **p** in the latter days that Mi 4:1
they will be cut down and **p** away. Na 1:12
shall the worthless **p** through you; Na 1:15
And this shall come to **p**, if you will Zec 6:15
He shall **p** through the sea of troubles Zec 10:11
to you, until heaven and earth **p** away, Mt 5:18
will **p** from the Law until all is Mt 5:18
so fierce that no one could **p** that way. Mt 8:28
generation will not **p** away until all Mt 24:34
Heaven and earth will **p** away, but my Mt 24:35
away, but my words will not **p** away. Mt 24:35
if it be possible, let this cup **p** from me; Mt 26:39
if this cannot **p** unless I drink it, Mt 26:42
on the sea. He meant to **p** by them, Mk 6:48
that what he says will come to **p**, Mk 11:23
generation will not **p** away until all Mk 13:30
Heaven and earth will **p** away, but my Mk 13:31
away, but my words will not **p** away. Mk 13:31
possible, the hour might **p** from him. Mk 14:35
heaven and earth to **p** away than for Lk 16:17
that those who would **p** from here to Lk 16:26
see him, for he was about to **p** that way. Lk 19:4
generation will not **p** away until all Lk 21:32
Heaven and earth will **p** away, but my Lk 21:33
away, but my words will not **p** away. Lk 21:33
And he had to **p** through Samaria. Jn 4:4
it shall come to **p** that everyone who Acts 2:21
the Spirit to **p** through Macedonia Acts 19:21
and Moses said would come to **p**: Acts 26:22
one who abstains **p** judgment on the Rom 14:3
Who are you to **p** judgment on the Rom 14:4
Why do you **p** judgment on your Rom 14:10
let us not **p** judgment on one Rom 14:13
no reason to **p** judgment on himself Rom 14:22
of this age, who are doomed to **p** away. 1 Cor 2:6
As for prophecies, they will **p** away; as 1 Cor 13:8
as for knowledge, it will **p** away. 1 Cor 13:8
comes, the partial will **p** away. 1 Cor 13:10
then shall come to **p** the saying that 1 Cor 15:54
for I intend to **p** through Macedonia, 1 Cor 16:5
Therefore let no one **p** judgment on you Col 2:16
affliction, just as it has come to **p**, 1 Thes 3:4
like a flower of the grass he will **p** away. Jas 1:10
then the heavens will **p** away with a 2 Pt 3:10

PASSAGE (9)
to give Israel **p** through his territory, Nm 20:21
before the chambers was a **p** inward, Ezk 42:4
with a **p** in front of them. They were Ezk 42:11
an entrance at the beginning of the **p**, Ezk 42:12
the **p** before the corresponding wall on Ezk 42:12
of Moses, in the **p** about the bush, Mk 12:26
Moses showed, in the **p** about the bush, Lk 20:37
Now the **p** of the Scripture that he was Acts 8:32
And again in this **p** he said, "They shall Heb 4:5

PASSED (122)
Abram **p** through the land to the place Gn 12:6
a flaming torch **p** between these pieces. Gn 15:17
So the present **p** on ahead of him, and Gn 32:21
The sun rose upon him as he **p** Penuel, Gn 32:31
Then Midianite traders **p** by. And they Gn 37:28
Seven full days **p** after the LORD had Ex 7:25
for he **p** over the houses of the people of Ex 12:27
you with my hand until I have **p** by. Ex 33:22
The LORD **p** before him and proclaimed, Ex 34:6
land, which we **p** through to spy it out, Nm 14:7
until we have **p** through your Nm 20:17
until we have **p** through your Nm 21:22
before Hahiroth and **p** through the Nm 33:8

be careful to do what has **p** your lips, Dt 23:23
of the nations through which you **p**. Dt 29:16
from the hills and **p** over and came to Jos 2:23
Israel, and lodged there before they **p** over. Jos 3:1
go, for you have not **p** this way before." Jos 3:4
And the people **p** over opposite Jericho. Jos 3:16
When it **p** over the Jordan, the waters of Jos 4:7
Joshua. The people **p** over in haste. Jos 4:10
LORD and the priests **p** over before the Jos 4:11
half-tribe of Manasseh **p** over armed Jos 4:12
40,000 ready for war **p** over before the Jos 4:13
'Israel **p** over this Jordan on dry ground.' Jos 4:22
of the Jordan for you until you **p** over, Jos 4:23
which he dried up for us until we **p** over, Jos 4:23
Israel with him **p** on from Makkedah Jos 10:29
all Israel with him **p** on from Libnah Jos 10:31
all Israel with him **p** on from Lachish Jos 10:34
So the men went and **p** up and down in Jos 18:9
all the peoples through whom we **p**. Jos 24:17
and he **p** beyond the idols and escaped to Jgs 3:26
they robbed all who **p** by them along Jgs 9:25
and he **p** through Gilead and Jgs 11:29
and Manasseh and **p** on to Mizpah Jgs 11:29
Mizpah of Gilead he **p** on to the Jgs 11:29
And they **p** on from there to the hill Jgs 18:13
So they **p** on and went their way. And Jgs 19:14
reapers, and he **p** to her roasted grain. Ru 2:14
lodged at Kiriath-jearim, a long time **p**, 1 Sm 7:2
And he **p** through the hill country of 1 Sm 9:4
of Ephraim and **p** through the land 1 Sm 9:4
And they **p** through the land of 1 Sm 9:4
Then they **p** through the land of 1 Sm 9:4
on before us, and when he has **p** on, 1 Sm 9:27
And the battle **p** beyond Beth-aven. 1 Sm 14:23
and turned and **p** on and went 1 Sm 15:12
they arose and **p** over by number, 2 Sm 2:15
And all his servants **p** by him, and 2 Sm 15:18
him from Gath, **p** on before the king. 2 Sm 15:18
So Ittai the Gittite **p** on with all his 2 Sm 15:22
wept aloud as all the people **p** by, 2 Sm 15:23
and all the people **p** on toward the 2 Sm 15:23
the people had all **p** out of the city. 2 Sm 15:24
When David had **p** a little beyond the 2 Sm 16:1
And Sheba **p** through all the tribes 2 Sm 20:14
men **p** by and saw the body thrown 1 Kgs 13:25
And as midday **p**, they raved on 1 Kgs 18:29
LORD." And behold, the LORD **p** by, 1 Kgs 19:11
Elijah **p** by him and cast his cloak 1 Kgs 19:19
And as the king **p**, he cried to the 1 Kgs 20:39
So whenever he **p** that way, he would 2 Kgs 4:8
Then Joram **p** over to Zair with all 2 Kgs 8:21
beast of Lebanon **p** by and trampled 2 Kgs 14:9
Riblah, and they **p** sentence on him. 2 Kgs 25:6
Then Jehoram **p** over with his 2 Chr 21:9
beast of Lebanon **p** by and trampled 2 Chr 25:18
remember it as waters that have **p** away. Jb 11:16
given, and no stranger **p** among them). Jb 15:19
not trodden it; the lion has not **p** over it. Jb 28:8
and my prosperity has **p** away like a Jb 30:15
when the wind has **p** and cleared them. Jb 37:21
But he **p** away, and behold, he was no Ps 37:36
land; they **p** through the river on foot. Ps 66:6
I **p** by the field of a sluggard, by the Prv 24:30
Scarcely had I **p** them when I found him Sg 3:4
to Aiath; he has **p** through Migron; Is 10:28
shoots spread abroad and **p** over the sea. Is 16:8
for a little while until the fury has **p** by. Is 26:20
I gave them has **p** away from them." Jer 8:13
cut in two and **p** between its parts— Jer 34:18
of the land who **p** between the parts of Jer 34:19
of Hamath; and he **p** sentence on him. Jer 39:5
Your branches **p** over the sea, reached Jer 48:32
of Hamath, and he **p** sentence on him. Jer 52:9
"And when I **p** by you and saw you Ezk 16:6
"When I **p** by you again and saw you, Ezk 16:8
that it was in the sight of all who **p** by. Ezk 36:34
in, a river that could not be **p** through. Ezk 47:5
your waves and your billows **p** over me. Jon 2:3
As Jesus **p** on from there, he saw a man Mt 9:9
And as Jesus **p** on from there, two blind Mt 9:27
And those who **p** by derided him, Mt 27:39
And as he **p** by, he saw Levi the son of Mk 2:14
on from there and **p** through Galilee. Mk 9:30
As they **p** by in the morning, they saw Mk 11:20
And those who **p** by derided him, Mk 15:29
when he saw him he **p** by on the other Lk 10:31
and saw him, **p** by on the other side. Lk 10:32
judgment, but has **p** from death to life. Jn 5:24
As he **p** by, he saw a man blind from Jn 9:1
"Now when forty years had **p**, an angel Acts 7:30
and as he **p** through he preached the Acts 8:40
When many days had **p**, the Jews Acts 9:23
When they had **p** the first and the Acts 12:10
Then they **p** through Pisidia and Acts 14:24
they **p** through both Phoenicia and Acts 15:3
when they had **p** through Amphipolis Acts 17:1
For as I **p** along and observed the Acts 17:23
Paul **p** through the inland country Acts 19:1
Now when some days had **p**, Agrippa Acts 25:13
Since much time had **p**, and the Acts 27:9
forbearance he had **p** over former sins. Rom 3:25
the cloud, and all **p** through the sea, 1 Cor 10:1
The old has **p** away; behold, the new 2 Cor 5:17
priest who has **p** through the heavens, Heb 4:14
know that we have **p** out of death into 1 Jn 3:14
The first woe has **p**; behold, two woes are Rv 9:12
The second woe has **p**; behold, the third Rv 11:14
heaven and the first earth had **p** away, Rv 21:1
for the former things have **p** away." Rv 21:4

PASSERBY (3)

and lavished your whorings on any **p**; Ezk 16:15
yourself to any **p** and multiplying Ezk 16:25
And they compelled a **p**, Simon of Mk 15:21

PASSES (40)

and while my glory **p** by I will put you Ex 33:22
the ascent of Akrabbim, **p** along to Zin, Jos 15:3
p along to Azmon, goes out by the Brook Jos 15:4
up to Beth-hoglah and **p** along north of Jos 15:6
And the boundary **p** along to the waters Jos 15:7
p along to the northern shoulder of Jos 15:10
to Beth-shemesh and **p** along by Jos 15:10
to Shikkeron and **p** along to Mount Jos 15:11
from Bethel to Luz, it **p** along to Ataroth, Jos 16:2
Taanath-shiloh and **p** along beyond Jos 16:6
there the boundary **p** along southward Jos 18:13
Then the boundary **p** on to the north of Jos 18:19
From there it **p** along on the east Jos 19:13
Within the **p**, by which Jonathan 1 Sm 14:4
Behold, he **p** by me, and I see him not; he Jb 9:11
If he **p** through and imprisons and Jb 11:10
prevail forever against him, and he **p**; Jb 14:20
sea, whatever **p** along the paths of the seas. Ps 8:8
a wind that **p** and comes not again. Ps 78:39
for the wind **p** over it, and it is gone, Ps 103:16
When the tempest **p**, the wicked is no Prv 10:25
vain life, which he **p** like a shadow? Eccl 6:12
the overwhelming whip **p** through it Is 28:15
the overwhelming scourge **p** through, Is 28:18
As often as it **p** through it will take you; Is 28:19
He pursues them and **p** on safely, by Is 41:3
darkness, in a land that none **p** through, Jer 2:6
are laid waste so that no one **p** through, Jer 9:10
a wilderness, so that no one **p** through? Jer 9:12
Everyone who **p** by it is horrified and Jer 18:16
Everyone who **p** by it will be horrified Jer 19:8
Everyone who **p** by it will be horrified Jer 49:17
everyone who **p** by Babylon shall be Jer 50:13
and through which no son of man **p**. Jer 51:43
Their king **p** on before them, the LORD at Mi 2:13
—before the day **p** away like chaff— Zep 2:2
Everyone who **p** by her hisses and Zep 2:15
it **p** through waterless places seeking Mt 12:43
goes into the mouth **p** into the stomach Mt 15:17
it **p** through waterless places seeking Lk 11:24

PASSING (37)

of all the earth is **p** over before you into Jos 3:11
and all Israel was **p** over on dry ground Jos 3:17
all the nation finished **p** over the Jordan. Jos 3:17
the nation had finished **p** over the Jordan, Jos 4:1
when all the people had finished **p** over, Jos 4:11
and **p** on to the north of the shoulder of Jos 18:18
"We are **p** from Bethlehem in Judah to Jgs 19:18
the Philistines were **p** on by hundreds 1 Sm 29:2
and his men were **p** on in the rear 1 Sm 29:2
Everyone **p** by it will be astonished 1 Kgs 9:8
of God who is continually **p** our way. 2 Kgs 4:9
king of Israel was **p** by on the wall, 2 Kgs 6:26
clothes—now he was **p** by on the wall 2 Kgs 6:30
everyone **p** by will be astonished and 2 Chr 7:21
a breath; his days are like a **p** shadow. Ps 144:4
p along the street near her corner, taking Prv 7:8
is one who hires a **p** fool or drunkard. Prv 26:10
like one who takes a **p** dog by the ears. Prv 26:17
the multitude of the ruthless like **p** chaff. Is 29:5
and hated, with no one **p** through, Is 60:15
are on the sea are dismayed at your **p**.' Ezk 26:18
iniquity and **p** over transgression Mi 7:18
when they heard that Jesus was **p** by, Mt 20:30
P alongside the Sea of Galilee, he saw Mk 1:16
But **p** through their midst, he went Lk 4:30
Jerusalem he was **p** along between Lk 17:11
told him, "Jesus of Nazareth is **p** by." Lk 18:37
He entered Jericho and was **p** through. Lk 19:1
So, **p** by Mysia, they went down to Acts 16:8
For in **p** judgment on another you Rom 2:1
I hope to see you in **p** as I go to Spain, Rom 15:24
present form of this world is **p** away. 1 Cor 7:31
visit you after **p** through Macedonia, 1 Cor 16:5
I do not want to see you now just in **p**. 1 Cor 16:7
pleasures, **p** our days in malice and envy, Ti 3:3
because the darkness is **p** away and the 1 Jn 2:8
And the world is **p** away along with its 1 Jn 2:17

PASSION (7)

were consumed with **p** for one Rom 1:27
to marry than to be aflame with **p**. 1 Cor 7:9
immorality, impurity, **p**, evil desire, Col 3:5
not in the **p** of lust like the Gentiles 1 Thes 4:5
lust of defiling **p** and despise authority. 2 Pt 2:10
the wine of the **p** of her sexual Rv 14:8
the wine of the **p** of her sexual Rv 18:3

PASSIONS (20)

God gave them up to dishonorable **p**. Rom 1:26
bodies, to make you obey their **p**. Rom 6:12
we were living in the flesh, our sinful **p**, Rom 7:5
his betrothed, if his **p** are strong, 1 Cor 7:36
crucified the flesh with its **p** and desires. Gal 5:24
we all once lived in the **p** of our flesh, Eph 2:3
for when their **p** draw them away 1 Tm 5:11
So flee youthful **p** and pursue 2 Tm 2:22
with sins and led astray by various **p**, 2 Tm 3:6
teachers to suit their own **p**, 2 Tm 4:3
to renounce ungodliness and worldly **p**, Ti 2:12
astray, slaves to various **p** and pleasures, Ti 3:3
this, that your **p** are at war within you? Jas 4:1
you ask wrongly, to spend it on your **p**. Jas 4:3
be conformed to the **p** of your former 1 Pt 1:14
exiles to abstain from the **p** of the flesh, 1 Pt 2:11
no longer for human **p** but for the will 1 Pt 4:2
do, living in sensuality, **p**, drunkenness, 1 Pt 4:3
they entice by sensual **p** of the flesh 2 Pt 2:18
following their own ungodly **p**." Jude 1:18

PASSOVER (79)

shall eat it in haste. It is the LORD'S **P**. Ex 12:11
to your clans, and kill the **P** lamb. Ex 12:21
say, 'It is the sacrifice of the LORD'S **P**, Ex 12:27
and Aaron, "This is the statute of the **P**: Ex 12:43
you and would keep the **P** to the LORD, Ex 12:48
the Feast of the **P** remain until the Ex 34:25
of the month at twilight, is the LORD'S **P**. Lv 23:5
of Israel keep the **P** at its appointed time. Nm 9:2
of Israel that they should keep the **P**. Nm 9:4
And they kept the **P** in the first month, Nm 9:5
they could not keep the **P** on that day, Nm 9:6
he shall still keep the **P** to the LORD. Nm 9:10
the statute for the **P** they shall keep it. Nm 9:12
is not on a journey fails to keep the **P**, Nm 9:13
you and would keep the **P** to the LORD, Nm 9:14
the statute of the **P** and according to its Nm 9:14
day of the first month is the LORD'S **P**, Nm 28:16
On the day after the **P**, the people of Nm 33:3
of Abib and keep the **P** to the LORD your Dt 16:1
you shall offer the **P** sacrifice to the LORD Dt 16:2
may not offer the **P** sacrifice within any Dt 16:5
in it, there you shall offer the **P** sacrifice, Dt 16:6
they kept the **P** on the fourteenth day of Jos 5:10
And the day after the **P**, on that very day, Jos 5:11
"Keep the **P** to the LORD your God, 2 Kgs 23:21
For no such **P** had been kept since 2 Kgs 23:22
of King Josiah this **P** was kept to the 2 Kgs 23:23
at Jerusalem to keep the **P** to the LORD, 2 Chr 30:1
counsel to keep the **P** in the second 2 Chr 30:2
come and keep the **P** to the LORD, 2 Chr 30:5
they slaughtered the **P** lamb on the 2 Chr 30:15
to slaughter the **P** lamb for 2 Chr 30:17
yet they ate the **P** otherwise than as 2 Chr 30:18
Josiah kept a **P** to the LORD in 2 Chr 35:1
they slaughtered the **P** lamb on the 2 Chr 35:1
And slaughter the **P** lamb, and 2 Chr 35:6
as **P** offerings for all who were 2 Chr 35:7
priests for the **P** offerings 2,600 2 Chr 35:8
Passover offerings 2,600 **P** lambs and 2 Chr 35:8
Levites for the **P** offerings 5,000 2 Chr 35:9
And they slaughtered the **P** lamb, 2 Chr 35:11
they roasted the **P** lamb with fire 2 Chr 35:13
to keep the **P** and to offer burnt 2 Chr 35:16
were present kept the **P** at that time, 2 Chr 35:17
No **P** like it had been kept in Israel 2 Chr 35:18
had kept such a **P** as was kept by 2 Chr 35:18
the reign of Josiah this **P** was kept. 2 Chr 35:19
month, the returned exiles kept the **P**. Ezr 6:19
So they slaughtered the **P** lamb for all Ezr 6:20
you shall celebrate the Feast of the **P**, Ezk 45:21
that after two days the **P** is coming, Mt 26:2
have us prepare for you to eat the **P**?" Mt 26:17
I will keep the **P** at your house with my Mt 26:18
directed them, and they prepared the **P**. Mt 26:19
two days before the **P** and the Feast of Mk 14:1
when they sacrificed the **P** lamb, Mk 14:12
us go and prepare for you to eat the **P**?" Mk 14:12
I may eat the **P** with my disciples?' Mk 14:14
told them, and they prepared the **P**. Mk 14:16
every year at the Feast of the **P**. Lk 2:41
Bread drew near, which is called the **P**. Lk 22:1

on which the **P** lamb had to be Lk 22:7
saying, "Go and prepare the **P** for us, Lk 22:8
I may eat the **P** with my disciples?' Lk 22:11
had told them, and they prepared the **P**. Lk 22:13
desired to eat this **P** with you before I Lk 22:15
The **P** of the Jews was at hand, and Jesus Jn 2:13
when he was in Jerusalem at the **P** Feast, Jn 2:23
Now the **P**, the feast of the Jews, was at Jn 6:4
Now the **P** of the Jews was at hand, and Jn 11:55
Jerusalem before the **P** to purify Jn 11:55
Six days before the **P**, Jesus therefore Jn 12:1
Now before the Feast of the **P**, when Jesus Jn 13:1
not be defiled, but could eat the **P**. Jn 18:28
should release one man for you at the **P**. Jn 18:39
it was the day of Preparation of the **P**. Jn 19:14
intending after the **P** to bring him out Acts 12:4
For Christ, our **P** lamb, has been 1 Cor 5:7
faith he kept the **P** and sprinkled the Heb 11:28

PAST (32)
the days of weeping for him were **p**, Gn 50:4
either in the **p** or since you have spoken Ex 4:10
people straw to make bricks, as in the **p**; Ex 5:7
they made in the **p** you shall impose on Ex 5:8
bricks today and yesterday, as in the **p**?" Ex 5:14
has been accustomed to gore in the **p**, Ex 21:29
has been accustomed to gore in the **p**, Ex 21:36
"For ask now of the days that are **p**, Dt 4:32
being at enmity with him in time **p**; Dt 4:42
without having hated him in the **p**— Dt 19:4
he had not hated his neighbor in the **p**. Dt 19:6
and did not hate him in the **p**. Jos 20:5
"Surely the bitterness of death is **p**." 1 Sm 15:32
"For some time **p** you have been 2 Sm 3:17
In times **p**, when Saul was king over us, 2 Sm 5:2
been your father's servant in time **p**, 2 Sm 15:34
the chief officer over them in time **p**; 1 Chr 9:20
In times **p**, even when Saul was king, 1 Chr 11:2
A spirit glided **p** my face; the hair of my Jb 4:15
conceal me until your wrath be **p**, Jb 14:13
My days are **p**; my plans are broken off, Jb 17:11
for their number is **p** my knowledge. Ps 71:15
sight are but as yesterday when it is **p**, Ps 90:4
for behold, the winter is **p**; the rain is Sg 2:11
LORD spoke concerning Moab in the **p**. Is 16:13
"The harvest is **p**, the summer is ended, Jer 8:20
When the Sabbath was **p**, Mary Mk 16:1
all things closely for some time **p**, Lk 1:3
In **p** generations he allowed all the Acts 14:16
Paul had decided to sail **p** Ephesus, Acts 20:16
even when she was **p** the age, Heb 11:11
The time that is **p** suffices for doing 1 Pt 4:3

PASTORS (1)
the evangelists, the **p** and teachers, Eph 4:11

PASTURE (39)
Water the sheep and go, **p** them." Gn 29:7
I will again **p** your flock and keep it: Gn 30:31
brothers went to **p** their father's flock Gn 37:12
for there is no **p** for your servants' Gn 47:4
the LORD of hosts, I took you from the **p**, 2 Sm 7:8
of the valley, to seek **p** for their flocks, 1 Chr 4:39
where they found rich, good **p**, and 1 Chr 4:40
because there was **p** there for their 1 Chr 4:41
LORD of hosts, I took you from the **p**, 1 Chr 17:7
landmarks; they seize flocks and **p** them. Jb 24:2
He ranges the mountains as his **p**, and he Jb 39:8
anger smoke against the sheep of your **p**? Ps 74:1
But we your people, the sheep of your **p**, Ps 79:13
is our God, and we are the people of his **p**, Ps 95:7
we are his people, and the sheep of his **p**. Ps 100:3
my soul loves, where you **p** your flock, Sg 1:7
and **p** your young goats beside the Sg 1:8
Then shall the lambs graze as in their **p**, Is 5:17
a joy of wild donkeys, a **p** of flocks; Is 32:14
ways; on all bare heights shall be their **p**; Is 49:9
Sharon shall become a **p** for flocks, and Is 65:10
her; they shall **p**, each in his place. Jer 6:3
the sheep of my **p**!" declares the LORD. Jer 23:1
For the LORD is laying waste their **p**, Jer 25:36
of the Jordan against a perennial **p**, Jer 49:19
though you frolic like a heifer in the **p**, Jer 50:11
I will restore Israel to his **p**, and he shall Jer 50:19
of the Jordan against a perennial **p**, Jer 50:44
have become like deer that find no **p**; Lam 1:6
will make Rabbah a **p** for camels and Ezk 25:5
I will feed them with good **p**, and on Ezk 34:14
and on rich **p** they shall feed on the Ezk 34:14
enough for you to feed on the good **p**, Ezk 34:18
down with your feet the rest of your **p**; Ezk 34:18
are my sheep, human sheep of my **p**, Ezk 34:31
feed them like a lamb in a broad **p**? Hos 4:16
perplexed because there is no **p** for them; Jl 1:18
like sheep in a fold, like a flock in its **p**, Mi 2:12
saved and will go in and out and find **p**. Jn 10:9

PASTURE-FED (1)
ten fat oxen, and twenty **p** cattle, a 1 Kgs 4:23

PASTURED (3)
and Jacob **p** the rest of Laban's flock. Gn 30:36
as he **p** the donkeys of Zibeon his Gn 36:24
Over the herds that **p** in Sharon was 1 Chr 27:29

PASTURELAND (2)
But the fields of **p** belonging to their Lv 25:34
belong to them as **p** for their cities. Nm 35:5

PASTURELANDS (107)
give to the Levites **p** around the cities. Nm 35:2
and their **p** shall be for their cattle and Nm 35:3
The **p** of the cities, which you shall Nm 35:4
shall be forty-eight, with their **p**. Nm 35:7
with their **p** for their livestock and their Jos 14:4
in, along with their **p** for our livestock." Jos 21:2
the following cities and **p** out of their Jos 21:3
These cities and their **p** the people of Jos 21:8
of Judah, along with the **p** around it. Jos 21:11
of refuge for the manslayer, with its **p**, Jos 21:13
its pasturelands, Libnah with its **p**, Jos 21:13
Jattir with its **p**, Eshtemoa with its Jos 21:14
its pasturelands, Eshtemoa with its **p**, Jos 21:14
Holon with its **p**, Debir with its Jos 21:15
with its pasturelands, Debir with its **p**, Jos 21:15
Ain with its **p**, Juttah with its Jos 21:16
with its pasturelands, Juttah with its **p**, Jos 21:16
Beth-shemesh with its **p**—nine cities Jos 21:16
tribe of Benjamin, Gibeon with its **p**, Jos 21:17
with its pasturelands, Geba with its **p**, Jos 21:17
Anathoth with its **p**, and Almon with Jos 21:18
and Almon with its **p**—four cities. Jos 21:18
were in all thirteen cities with their **p**. Jos 21:19
with its **p** in the hill country of Jos 21:21
country of Ephraim, Gezer with its **p**, Jos 21:21
Kibzaim with its **p**, Beth-horon with its Jos 21:22
Beth-horon with its **p**—four cities; Jos 21:22
out of the tribe of Dan, Elteke with its **p**, Jos 21:23
its pasturelands, Gibbethon with its **p**, Jos 21:23
Aijalon with its **p**, Gath-rimmon with Jos 21:24
Gath-rimmon with its **p**—four cities; Jos 21:24
of Manasseh, Taanach with its **p**, Jos 21:25
Gath-rimmon with its **p**—two cities. Jos 21:25
Kohathites were ten in all with their **p**. Jos 21:26
Manasseh, Golan in Bashan with its **p**, Jos 21:27
and Beeshterah with its **p**—two cities; Jos 21:27
the tribe of Issachar, Kishion with its **p**, Jos 21:28
its pasturelands, Daberath with its **p**, Jos 21:28
Jarmuth with its **p**, En-gannim with its Jos 21:29
En-gannim with its **p**—four cities; Jos 21:29
of the tribe of Asher, Mishal with its **p**, Jos 21:30
with its pasturelands, Abdon with its **p**, Jos 21:30
Helkath with its **p**, and Rehob with its Jos 21:31
and Rehob with its **p**—four cities; Jos 21:31
Naphtali, Kedesh in Galilee with its **p**, Jos 21:32
manslayer, Hammoth-dor with its **p**, Jos 21:32
and Kartan with its **p**—three cities. Jos 21:32
were in all thirteen cities with their **p**. Jos 21:33
tribe of Zebulun, Jokneam with its **p**, Jos 21:34
with its pasturelands, Kartah with its **p**, Jos 21:34
Dimnah with its **p**, Nahalal with its Jos 21:35
Nahalal with its **p**—four cities; Jos 21:35
of the tribe of Reuben, Bezer with its **p**, Jos 21:36
with its pasturelands, Jahaz with its **p**, Jos 21:36
Kedemoth with its **p**, and Mephaath Jos 21:37
and Mephaath with its **p**—four cities; Jos 21:37
of Gad, Ramoth in Gilead with its **p**, Jos 21:38
the manslayer, Mahanaim with its **p**, Jos 21:38
Heshbon with its **p**, Jazer with its Jos 21:39
Jazer with its **p**—four cities in all. Jos 21:39
in all forty-eight cities with their **p**. Jos 21:41
These cities each had its **p** around it. So Jos 21:42
and in all the **p** of Sharon to their 1 Chr 5:16
land of Judah and its surrounding **p**, 1 Chr 6:55
Hebron, Libnah with its **p**, Jattir, 1 Chr 6:57
Jattir, Eshtemoa with its **p**, 1 Chr 6:57
Hilen with its **p**, Debir with its 1 Chr 6:58
its pasturelands, Debir with its **p**, 1 Chr 6:58
Ashan with its **p**, and Beth-shemesh 1 Chr 6:59
and Beth-shemesh with its **p**; 1 Chr 6:59
of Benjamin, Gibeon, Geba with its **p**, 1 Chr 6:60
its pasturelands, Alemeth with its **p**, 1 Chr 6:60
and Anathoth with its **p**. 1 Chr 6:60
the Levites the cities with their **p**. 1 Chr 6:64
Shechem with its **p** in the hill 1 Chr 6:67
country of Ephraim, Gezer with its **p**, 1 Chr 6:67
Jokmeam with its **p**, Beth-horon with 1 Chr 6:68
pasturelands, Beth-horon with its **p**, 1 Chr 6:68
Aijalon with its **p**, Gath-rimmon 1 Chr 6:69
Gath-rimmon with its **p**, 1 Chr 6:69
of Manasseh, Aner with its **p**, 1 Chr 6:70
pasturelands, and Bileam with its **p**, 1 Chr 6:70
Bashan with its **p** and Ashtaroth 1 Chr 6:71
and Ashtaroth with its **p**; 1 Chr 6:71
Kedesh with its **p**, Daberath with its 1 Chr 6:72
its pasturelands, Daberath with its **p**, 1 Chr 6:72
Ramoth with its **p**, and Anem with its 1 Chr 6:73
pasturelands, and Anem with its **p**; 1 Chr 6:73
Mashal with its **p**, Abdon with its 1 Chr 6:74
its pasturelands, Abdon with its **p**, 1 Chr 6:74
Hukok with its **p**, and Rehob with its 1 Chr 6:75
pasturelands, and Rehob with its **p**; 1 Chr 6:75
Kedesh in Galilee with its **p**, 1 Chr 6:76
its pasturelands, Hammon with its **p**, 1 Chr 6:76
and Kiriathaim with its **p**. 1 Chr 6:76
Rimmono with its **p**, Tabor with its 1 Chr 6:77
its pasturelands, Tabor with its **p**, 1 Chr 6:77
Bezer in the wilderness with its **p**, 1 Chr 6:78
its pasturelands, Jahzah with its **p**, 1 Chr 6:78
Kedemoth with its **p**, and Mephaath 1 Chr 6:79
and Mephaath with its **p**; 1 Chr 6:79
Ramoth in Gilead with its **p**, 1 Chr 6:80
pasturelands, Mahanaim with its **p**, 1 Chr 6:80
Heshbon with its **p**, and Jazer with its 1 Chr 6:81
its pasturelands, and Jazer with its **p**. 1 Chr 6:81
and Levites in the cities that have **p**, 1 Chr 13:2
that they might make its **p** a prey. Ezk 36:5

PASTURES (13)
He makes me lie down in green **p**. He Ps 23:2
of the LORD are like the glory of the **p**; Ps 37:20
The **p** of the wilderness overflow, the Ps 65:12
for ourselves of the **p** of God." Ps 83:12
on all the thornbushes, and on all the **p**. Is 7:19
day your livestock will graze in large **p**, Is 30:23
a lamentation for the **p** of the wilderness, Jer 9:10
and the **p** of the wilderness are dried up. Jer 23:10
fire has devoured the **p** of the wilderness, Jl 1:19
fire has devoured the **p** of the wilderness. Jl 1:20
field, for the **p** of the wilderness are green; Jl 2:22
the **p** of the shepherds mourn, and the Am 1:2
And you, O seacoast, shall be **p**, with Zep 2:6

PASTURING (3)
old, was **p** the flock with his brothers. Gn 37:2
"Are not your brothers **p** the flock at Gn 37:13
me, please, where they are **p** the flock." Gn 37:16

PATARA (1)
day to Rhodes, and from there to **P**. Acts 21:1

PATCH (2)
for the **p** tears away from the garment, Mt 9:16
If he does, the **p** tears away from it, the Mk 2:21

PATCHED (1)
with worn-out, **p** sandals on their feet, Jos 9:5

PATCHES (1)
shall not make bald **p** on their heads, Lv 21:5

PATE (1)
on the **p** of him who is prince among Dt 33:16

PATH (37)
a serpent in the way, a viper by the **p**, Gn 49:17
in a narrow **p** between the vineyards, Nm 22:24
in the ground, a trap for him in the **p**. Jb 18:10
"That **p** no bird of prey knows, and the Jb 28:7
They break up my **p**; they promote my Jb 30:13
You make known to me the **p** of life; in Ps 16:11
me on a level **p** because of my enemies. Ps 27:11
This is the **p** of those who have foolish Ps 49:13
the sea, your **p** through the great waters; Ps 77:19
He made a **p** for his anger; he did not Ps 78:50
me in the **p** of your commandments, Ps 119:35
a lamp to my feet and a light to my **p**. Ps 119:105
You search out my **p** and my lying Ps 139:3
In the **p** where I walk they have hidden Ps 142:3
and justice and equity, every good **p**; Prv 2:9
Do not enter the **p** of the wicked, and do Prv 4:14
But the **p** of the righteous is like the Prv 4:18
Ponder the **p** of your feet; then all your Prv 4:26
to death; her steps follow the **p** to Sheol; Prv 5:5
she does not ponder the **p** of life; her ways Prv 5:6
heeds instruction is on the **p** to life, Prv 10:17
In the **p** of righteousness is life, and in Prv 12:28
but the **p** of the upright is a level Prv 15:19
The **p** of life leads upward for the Prv 15:24
The **p** of the righteous is level; you make Is 26:7
In the **p** of your judgments, O LORD, we Is 26:8
leave the way, turn aside from the **p**, let Is 30:11
Who taught him the **p** of justice, and Is 40:14
way in the sea, a **p** in the mighty waters, Is 43:16
in a straight **p** in which they shall not Jer 31:9
jostle one another; each marches in his **p**; Jl 2:8
as he sowed, some seeds fell along the **p**, Mt 13:4
This is what was sown along the **p**. Mt 13:19
as he sowed, some seed fell along the **p**, Mk 4:4
And these are the ones along the **p**, Mk 4:15
some fell along the **p** and was trampled Lk 8:5
The ones along the **p** are those who have Lk 8:12

PATHLESS (1)
and makes them wander in a **p** waste. Jb 12:24

PATHROS (5)
from Assyria, from Egypt, from **P**, Is 11:11
at Memphis, and in the land of **P**, Jer 44:1
the people who lived in **P** in the land of Jer 44:15
and bring them back to the land of **P**, Ezk 29:14
I will make **P** a desolation and will set Ezk 30:14

PATHRUSIM (2)
P, Casluhim (from whom the Gn 10:14
P, Casluhim (from whom the 1 Chr 1:12

PATHS (42)
Such are the **p** of all who forget God; the Jb 8:13
feet in the stocks and watch all my **p**; Jb 13:27
pass, and he has set darkness upon my **p**. Jb 19:8
with its ways, and do not stay in its **p**. Jb 24:13
feet in the stocks and watches all my **p**.' Jb 33:11
that you may discern the **p** to its home? Jb 38:20
whatever passes along the **p** of the seas. Ps 8:8
My steps have held fast to your **p**; my feet Ps 17:5
He leads me in **p** of righteousness for his Ps 23:3
your ways, O LORD; teach me your **p**. Ps 25:4
All the **p** of the LORD are steadfast love Ps 25:10
them; hold back your foot from their **p**, Prv 1:15
guarding the **p** of justice and watching Prv 2:8
who forsake the **p** of uprightness to Prv 2:13
men whose **p** are crooked, and who are Prv 2:15
down to death, and her **p** to the departed; Prv 2:18
back, nor do they regain the **p** of life. Prv 2:19
good and keep to the **p** of the righteous. Prv 2:20
him, and he will make straight your **p**. Prv 3:6
of pleasantness, and all her **p** are peace. Prv 3:17
I have led you in the **p** of uprightness. Prv 4:11
of the LORD, and he ponders all his **p**. Prv 5:21
to her ways; do not stray into her **p**, Prv 7:25
way of righteousness, in the **p** of justice, Prv 8:20
we may walk in his **p**." For out of Zion Is 2:3
have swallowed up the course of your **p**. Is 3:12
on safely, by **p** his feet have not trod. Is 41:3
in **p** that they have not known I will Is 42:16
know, and there is no justice in their **p**; Is 59:8
and look, and ask for the ancient **p**, Jer 6:16
to them like slippery **p** in the darkness, Jer 23:12
of stones; he has made my **p** crooked. Lam 3:9
her, so that she cannot find her **p**. Hos 2:6
on his way; they do not swerve from their **p**. Jl 2:7
we may walk in his **p**." For out of Zion Mi 4:2
the way of the Lord; make his **p** straight.'" Mt 3:3
way of the Lord, make his **p** straight,'" Mk 1:3
the way of the Lord, make his **p** straight. Lk 3:4
have made known to me the **p** of life; Acts 2:28
crooked the straight **p** of the Lord? Acts 13:10
in their **p** are ruin and misery, Rom 3:16
and make straight **p** for your feet, so Heb 12:13

PATHWAY (1)
is life, and in its **p** there is no death. Prv 12:28

PATIENCE (21)
With **p** a ruler may be persuaded, and Prv 25:15
knees, imploring him, 'Have **p** with me, Mt 18:26
and pleaded with him, 'Have **p** with me, Mt 18:29
and good heart, and bear fruit with **p**. Lk 8:15
of his kindness and forbearance and **p**, Rom 2:4
to those who by **p** in well-doing seek for Rom 2:7
we do not see, we wait for it with **p**. Rom 8:25
endured with much **p** vessels of wrath Rom 9:22
by purity, knowledge, **p**, kindness, the 2 Cor 6:6
among you with utmost **p**, 2 Cor 12:12
the Spirit is love, joy, peace, **p**, kindness, Gal 5:22
with all humility and gentleness, with **p**, Eph 4:2
might, for all endurance and **p** with joy, Col 1:11
kindness, humility, meekness, and **p**, Col 3:12
display his perfect **p** as an example 1 Tm 1:16
my aim in life, my faith, my **p**, 2 Tm 3:10
exhort, with complete **p** and teaching. 2 Tm 4:2
through faith and **p** inherit the Heb 6:12
As an example of suffering and **p**, Jas 5:10
when God's **p** waited in the days of 1 Pt 3:20
And count the **p** of our Lord as 2 Pt 3:15

PATIENT (13)
And what is my end, that I should be **p**? Jb 6:11
and the **p** in spirit is better than the Eccl 7:8
Rejoice in hope, be **p** in tribulation, Rom 12:12
Love is **p** and kind; love does not envy 1 Cor 13:4
help the weak, be **p** with them all. 1 Thes 5:14
Be **p**, therefore, brothers, until the coming Jas 5:7
fruit of the earth, being **p** about it, Jas 5:7
You also, be **p**. Establish your hearts, for Jas 5:8
count slowness, but is **p** toward you, 2 Pt 3:9
kingdom and the **p** endurance that are Rv 1:9
works, your toil and your **p** endurance, Rv 2:2
and faith and service and **p** endurance, Rv 2:19
have kept my word about **p** endurance, Rv 3:10

PATIENTLY (7)
still before the LORD and wait **p** for him; Ps 37:7
I waited **p** for the LORD; he inclined to me Ps 40:1
Therefore I beg you to listen to me **p**. Acts 26:3
experience when you **p** endure the 2 Cor 1:6
able to teach, **p** enduring evil, 2 Tm 2:24
And thus Abraham, having **p** waited, Heb 6:15
know you are enduring **p** and bearing up Rv 2:3

PATMOS (1)
on the island called **P** on account of the Rv 1:9

PATRIARCH (2)
confidence about the **p** David that he Acts 2:29
to whom Abraham the **p** gave a tenth of Heb 7:4

PATRIARCHS (4)
of Jacob, and Jacob of the twelve **p**. Acts 7:8
"And the **p**, jealous of Joseph, sold him Acts 7:9
To them belong the **p**, and from their Rom 9:5
to confirm the promises given to the **p**, Rom 15:8

PATRIMONY (1)
what he receives from the sale of his **p**. Dt 18:8

PATROBAS (1)
Phlegon, Hermes, **P**, Hermas, Rom 16:14

PATROL (3)
whom the LORD has sent to **p** the earth.' Zec 1:10
they were impatient to go and **p** the earth. Zec 6:7
p the earth." So they patrolled the earth. Zec 6:7

PATROLLED (2)
trees, and said, 'We have **p** the earth, Zec 1:11
"Go, patrol the earth." So they **p** the earth. Zec 6:7

PATRON (1)
for she has been a **p** of many and of Rom 16:2

PATTERN (8)
you concerning the **p** of the tabernacle, Ex 25:9
you make them after the **p** for them, Ex 25:40
according to the **p** that the LORD had Nm 8:4
priest a model of the altar, and its **p**, 2 Kgs 16:10
inside and outside, was a measured **p**. Ezk 41:17
it, according to the **p** that he had seen. Acts 7:44
Follow the **p** of the sound words that 2 Tm 1:13
according to the **p** that was shown Heb 8:5

PAU (1)
his place, the name of his city being **P**; Gn 36:39

PAUL (161)
But Saul, who was also called **P**, filled Acts 13:9
Now **P** and his companions set sail Acts 13:13
So **P** stood up, and motioning with Acts 13:16
to Judaism followed **P** and Barnabas, Acts 13:43
to contradict what was spoken by **P**, Acts 13:45
And **P** and Barnabas spoke out Acts 13:46
persecution against **P** and Barnabas, Acts 13:50
He listened to **P** speaking. And Paul, Acts 14:9
He listened to Paul speaking. And **P**, Acts 14:9
the crowds saw what **P** had done, Acts 14:11
Barnabas they called Zeus, and **P**, Acts 14:12
apostles Barnabas and **P** heard of it, Acts 14:14
they stoned **P** and dragged him out of Acts 14:19
And after **P** and Barnabas had no Acts 15:2
P and Barnabas and some of the Acts 15:2
to Barnabas and **P** as they related Acts 15:12
to Antioch with **P** and Barnabas. Acts 15:22
with our beloved Barnabas and **P**, Acts 15:25
But **P** and Barnabas remained in Acts 15:35
after some days **P** said to Barnabas, Acts 15:36
But **P** thought best not to take with Acts 15:38
but **P** chose Silas and departed, Acts 15:40
P came also to Derbe and to Lystra. A Acts 16:1
P wanted Timothy to accompany Acts 16:3
a vision appeared to **P** in the night: Acts 16:9
And when **P** had seen the vision, Acts 16:10
pay attention to what was said by **P**. Acts 16:14
She followed **P** and us, crying out, Acts 16:17
P, having become greatly annoyed, Acts 16:18
they seized **P** and Silas and dragged Acts 16:19
About midnight **P** and Silas were Acts 16:25
But **P** cried with a loud voice, "Do not Acts 16:28
fear he fell down before **P** and Silas. Acts 16:29
the jailer reported these words to **P**, Acts 16:36
But **P** said to them, "They have Acts 16:37
And **P** went in, as was his custom, and Acts 17:2
were persuaded and joined **P** and Silas, Acts 17:4
immediately sent **P** and Silas Acts 17:10
was proclaimed by **P** at Berea also, Acts 17:13
brothers immediately sent **P** off on Acts 17:14
who conducted **P** brought him Acts 17:15
Now while **P** was waiting for them at Acts 17:16
So **P**, standing in the midst of the Acts 17:22
So **P** went out from their midst. Acts 17:33
After this **P** left Athens and went to Acts 18:1
P was occupied with the word, Acts 18:5
Corinthians hearing **P** believed and Acts 18:8
And the Lord said to **P** one night in a Acts 18:9
united attack on **P** and brought him Acts 18:12
But when **P** was about to open his Acts 18:14
P stayed many days longer and then Acts 18:18
P passed through the inland country Acts 19:1
And **P** said, "John baptized with the Acts 19:4
And when **P** had laid his hands on Acts 19:6
miracles by the hands of **P**, Acts 19:11
by the Jesus, whom **P** proclaims." Acts 19:13
"Jesus I know, and **P** I recognize, Acts 19:15
after these events **P** resolved in the Acts 19:21
all of Asia this **P** has persuaded and Acts 19:26
But when **P** wished to go in among Acts 19:30
uproar ceased, **P** sent for the disciples, Acts 20:1
to break bread, **P** talked with them, Acts 20:7
a deep sleep as **P** talked still longer. Acts 20:9
But **P** went down and bent over him, Acts 20:10
And when **P** had gone up and had Acts 20:11
intending to take **P** aboard there, Acts 20:13
For **P** had decided to sail past Acts 20:16
all; they embraced **P** and kissed him, Acts 20:37
Spirit they were telling **P** not to go on Acts 21:4
Then **P** answered, "What are you Acts 21:13
On the following day **P** went in with Acts 21:18
Then **P** took the men, and the next Acts 21:26
they supposed that **P** had brought Acts 21:29
They seized **P** and dragged him out of Acts 21:30
the soldiers, they stopped beating **P**. Acts 21:32
As **P** was about to be brought into Acts 21:37
P replied, "I am a Jew, from Tarsus in Acts 21:39
permission, **P**, standing on the steps, Acts 21:40
P said to the centurion who was Acts 22:25
citizenship for a large sum." **P** said, Acts 22:28
for he realized that **P** was a Roman Acts 22:29
and he brought **P** down and set him Acts 22:30
looking intently at the council, **P** said, Acts 23:1
Then **P** said to him, "God is going to Acts 23:3
And **P** said, "I did not know, brothers, Acts 23:5
Now when **P** perceived that one part Acts 23:6
afraid that **P** would be torn to pieces Acts 23:10
to eat nor drink till they had killed **P**. Acts 23:12
to taste no food till we have killed **P**. Acts 23:14
and entered the barracks and told **P**. Acts 23:16
P called one of the centurions and Acts 23:17
"**P** the prisoner called me and asked Acts 23:18
ask you to bring **P** down to the Acts 23:20
Also provide mounts for **P** to ride and Acts 23:24
took **P** and brought him by night to Acts 23:31
they presented **P** also before him. Acts 23:33
the governor their case against **P**. Acts 24:1
had nodded to him to speak, **P** replied: Acts 24:10
and he sent for **P** and heard him Acts 24:24
that money would be given him by **P**. Acts 24:26
the Jews a favor, Felix left **P** in prison. Acts 24:27
the Jews laid out their case against **P**, Acts 25:2
as a favor against **P** that he summon Acts 25:3
Festus replied that **P** was being kept at Acts 25:4
tribunal and ordered **P** to be brought. Acts 25:6
P argued in his defense, "Neither Acts 25:8
to do the Jews a favor, said to **P**, Acts 25:9
But **P** said, "I am standing before Acts 25:10
dead, but whom **P** asserted to be alive. Acts 25:19
But when **P** had appealed to be kept Acts 25:21
of Festus, **P** was brought in. Acts 25:23
So Agrippa said to **P**, "You have Acts 26:1
for yourself." Then **P** stretched out his Acts 26:1
voice, "**P**, you are out of your mind; Acts 26:24
But **P** said, "I am not out of my mind, Acts 26:25
And Agrippa said to **P**, "In a short Acts 26:28
And **P** said, "Whether short or long, I Acts 26:29
they delivered **P** and some other Acts 27:1
And Julius treated **P** kindly and gave Acts 27:3
Fast was already over, **P** advised them, Acts 27:9
owner of the ship than to what **P** said. Acts 27:11
P stood up among them and said, Acts 27:21
P; you must stand before Caesar. Acts 27:24
P said to the centurion and the Acts 27:31
P urged them all to take some food, Acts 27:33
But the centurion, wishing to save **P**, Acts 27:43
When **P** had gathered a bundle of Acts 28:3
And **P** visited him and prayed, and Acts 28:8
P thanked God and took courage. Acts 28:15
P was allowed to stay by himself, Acts 28:16
they departed after **P** had made one Acts 28:25
P, a servant of Christ Jesus, called to be Rom 1:1
P, called by the will of God to be an 1 Cor 1:1
"I follow **P**," or "I follow Apollos," or 1 Cor 1:12
divided? Was **P** crucified for you? 1 Cor 1:13
were you baptized in the name of **P**? 1 Cor 1:13
one says, "I follow **P**," and another, 1 Cor 3:4
What then is Apollos? What is **P**? 1 Cor 3:5
whether **P** or Apollos or Cephas or 1 Cor 3:22
P, write this greeting with my own 1 Cor 16:21
P, an apostle of Christ Jesus by the will 2 Cor 1:1
I, **P**, myself entreat you, by the 2 Cor 10:1

P, an apostle—not from men nor Gal 1:1
P, say to you that if you accept Gal 5:2
P, an apostle of Christ Jesus by the will Eph 1:1
P, a prisoner for Christ Jesus on behalf Eph 3:1
P and Timothy, servants of Christ Jesus, Phil 1:1
P, an apostle of Christ Jesus by the will of Col 1:1
and of which I, **P**, became a minister. Col 1:23
P, write this greeting with my own Col 4:18
P, Silvanus, and Timothy, To the 1 Thes 1:1
P, again and again—but Satan 1 Thes 2:18
P, Silvanus, and Timothy, To the 2 Thes 1:1
P, write this greeting with my own 2 Thes 3:17
P, an apostle of Christ Jesus by 1 Tm 1:1
P, an apostle of Christ Jesus by the will 2 Tm 1:1
P, a servant of God and an apostle of Jesus Ti 1:1
P, a prisoner for Christ Jesus, and Phlm 1:1
P, an old man and now a prisoner also Phlm 1:9
I, **P**, write this with my own hand: I Phlm 1:19
as our beloved brother **P** also wrote to 2 Pt 3:15

PAUL'S (4)
who were **P** companions in Acts 19:29
he took **P** belt and bound his own feet Acts 21:11
Now the son of **P** sister heard of their Acts 23:16
Festus laid **P** case before the king, Acts 25:14

PAULUS (1)
He was with the proconsul, Sergius **P**, Acts 13:7

PAVEMENT (10)
his feet as it were a **p** of sapphire stone, Ex 24:10
ground on the **p** and worshiped and 2 Chr 7:3
and silver on a mosaic **p** of porphyry, Est 1:6
in the mortar in the **p** that is at the Jer 43:9
behold, there were chambers and a **p**, Ezk 40:17
court. Thirty chambers faced the **p**. Ezk 40:17
And the **p** ran along the side of the Ezk 40:18
of the gates. This was the lower **p**. Ezk 40:18
and facing the **p** that belonged to the Ezk 42:3
seat at a place called The Stone **P**, Jn 19:13

PAVILION (1)
of the clouds, the thunderings of his **p**? Jb 36:29

PAW (2)
delivered me from the **p** of the lion 1 Sm 17:37
lion and from the **p** of the bear will 1 Sm 17:37

PAWS (2)
And all that walk on their **p**, among the Lv 11:27
He **p** in the valley and exults in his Jb 39:21

PAY (94)
will hate us and **p** us back for all Gn 50:15
may labor at it and **p** no regard to lying Ex 5:9
but whoever did not **p** attention to the Ex 9:21
only he shall **p** for the loss of his time, Ex 21:19
and he shall **p** as the judges determine. Ex 21:22
is harm, then you shall **p** life for life, Ex 21:23
be bloodguilt for him. He shall surely **p**. Ex 22:3
or a donkey or a sheep, he shall **p** double. Ex 22:4
if the thief is found, he shall **p** double. Ex 22:7
God condemns shall **p** double to his Ex 22:9
he shall **p** money equal to the Ex 22:17
"**P** attention to all that I have said to Ex 23:13
P careful attention to him and obey his Ex 23:21
You shall **p** your neighbor according Lv 25:15
he sold it and **p** back the balance to Lv 25:27
he shall **p** proportionately for his Lv 25:51
shall calculate and **p** for his Lv 25:52
if someone is too poor to **p** the valuation, Lv 27:8
I and my livestock, then I will **p** for it. Nm 20:19
the yearly sacrifice and to **p** his vow. 1 Sm 1:21
But she did not answer or **p** attention. 1 Sm 4:20
a man came near to **p** homage to him, 2 Sm 15:5
king, "Please let me go and **p** my vow, 2 Sm 15:7
yours." And Ziba said, "I **p** homage; 2 Sm 16:4
'If your sons **p** close attention to their 1 Kgs 2:4
and I will **p** you for your servants such 1 Kgs 5:6
if only your sons **p** close attention to 1 Kgs 8:25
or else you shall **p** a talent of silver.' 1 Kgs 20:39
said, "Go, sell the oil and **p** your debts, 2 Kgs 4:7
delivered the money to **p** out to the 2 Kgs 12:15
if only your sons **p** close attention to 2 Chr 6:16
but they would not **p** attention. 2 Chr 24:19
walls finished, they will not **p** tribute, Ezr 4:13
Mordecai did not bow down or **p** homage. Est 3:2
did not bow down or **p** homage to him, Est 3:5
and I will **p** 10,000 talents of silver into Est 3:9
Haman had promised to **p** into the king's Est 4:7
Let him **p** it out to them, that they may Jb 21:19
will hear you, and you will **p** your vows. Jb 22:27
power? No; he would **p** attention to me. Jb 23:6
P attention, O Job, listen to me; be silent, Jb 33:31
I hate those who **p** regard to worthless Ps 31:6
wicked borrows but does not **p** back, Ps 37:21
I will **p** my vows to the LORD in the Ps 116:14
I will **p** my vows to the LORD in the Ps 116:18
but if he is caught, he will **p** sevenfold; Prv 6:31
man of great wrath will **p** the penalty, Prv 19:19
If you have nothing with which to **p**, Prv 22:27
I will **p** the man back for what he has Prv 24:29
no pleasure in fools. **P** what you vow. Eccl 5:4
than that you should vow and not **p**. Eccl 5:5
and all who work for **p** will be grieved. Is 19:10
'**P** attention to the sound of the trumpet!' Jer 6:17
But they said, 'We will not **p** attention.' Jer 6:17
and let us not **p** attention to any of his Jer 18:18
because they did not **p** attention to my Jer 29:19
We must **p** for the water we drink; the Lam 5:4
anything from Tyre to **p** for the labor Ezk 29:18
men, O king, **p** no attention to you; Dn 3:12
forgive. O Lord, **p** attention and act. Dn 9:19
turn back and **p** attention to those Dn 11:30
He shall **p** no attention to the gods of Dn 11:37
He shall not **p** attention to any other Dn 11:37
O priests! **P** attention, O house of Israel! Hos 5:1
and we will **p** with bulls the vows of our Hos 14:2
Those who **p** regard to vain idols forsake Jon 2:8
to you; what I have vowed I will **p**. Jon 2:9
p attention, O earth, and all that is in it, Mi 1:2
they did not hear or **p** attention to me, Zec 1:4
they refused to **p** attention and turned Zec 7:11
received without paying; give without **p**. Mt 10:8
said, "Does your teacher not **p** the tax?" Mt 17:24
And since he could not **p**, his master Mt 18:25
with me, and I will **p** you everything.' Mt 18:26
to choke him, saying, '**P** what you owe.' Mt 18:28
patience with me, and I will **p** you.' Mt 18:29
in prison until he should **p** the debt. Mt 18:30
jailers, until he should **p** all his debt. Mt 18:34
the laborers and **p** them their wages, Mt 20:8
Is it lawful to **p** taxes to Caesar, or not?" Mt 22:17
to them, "**P** attention to what you hear: Mk 4:24
Is it lawful to **p** taxes to Caesar, or not? Mk 12:14
Should we **p** them, or should we not?" Mk 12:14
When they could not **p**, he cancelled the Lk 7:42
P attention to yourselves! If your Lk 17:3
her heart to **p** attention to what Acts 16:14
P careful attention to yourselves and Acts 20:28
along with them and **p** their expenses, Acts 21:24
For the same reason you also **p** taxes, Rom 13:6
P to all what is owed to them: taxes to Rom 13:7
Therefore we must **p** much closer Heb 2:1
and if you **p** attention to the one who Jas 2:3
you will do well to **p** attention as to a 2 Pt 1:19
P her back as she herself has paid back Rv 18:6

PAYING (6)
"When you have finished **p** all the tithe Dt 26:12
you vow a vow to God, do not delay **p** it, Eccl 5:4
Are you **p** me back for something? Jl 3:4
If you are **p** me back, I will return your Jl 3:4
You received without **p**; give without Mt 10:8
we eat anyone's bread without **p** for it, 2 Thes 3:8

PAYMENT (16)
go out for nothing, without **p** of money. Ex 21:11
of the LORD your God in **p** for any vow, Dt 23:18
himself, for emptiness will be his **p**. Jb 15:31
eaten its yield without **p** and made its Jb 31:39
into their bosom **p** for their former Is 65:7
a prostitute, because you scorned **p**. Ezk 16:31
you to play the whore, and you gave **p**, Ezk 16:34
payment, while no **p** was given to you; Ezk 16:34
and you shall also give **p** no more. Ezk 16:41
they brought you in **p** ivory tusks and Ezk 27:15
of Egypt as his **p** for which he labored, Ezk 29:20
I will return your **p** on your own head Jl 3:4
and I will return your **p** on your own head. Jl 3:7
and all that he had, and **p** to be made. Mt 18:25
I have received full **p**, and more. I am Phil 4:18
the spring of the water of life without **p**. Rv 21:6

PAYS (1)
exiles from Judah, **p** no attention to you, Dn 6:13

PEACE (367)
you shall go to your fathers in **p**; Gn 15:15
but good and have sent you away in **p**. Gn 26:29
way, and they departed from him in **p**. Gn 26:31
I come again to my father's house in **p**, Gn 28:21
so Jacob held his **p** until they came. Gn 34:5
"These men are at **p** with us; let them Gn 34:21
He replied, "**P** to you, do not be afraid. Gn 43:23
as for you, go up in **p** to your father." Gn 44:17
And Jethro said to Moses, "Go in **p**." Ex 4:18
people also will go to their place in **p**." Ex 18:23
burnt offerings and your **p** offerings, Ex 20:24
offerings and sacrificed **p** offerings of Ex 24:5
people of Israel from their **p** offerings, Ex 29:28
burnt offerings and brought **p** offerings. Ex 32:6
"If his offering is a sacrifice of **p** offering, Lv 3:1
And from the sacrifice of the **p** offering, as Lv 3:3
for a sacrifice of **p** offering to the LORD Lv 3:6
the sacrifice of the **p** offering he shall offer Lv 3:9
the ox of the sacrifice of the **p** offerings); Lv 4:10
like the fat of the sacrifice of **p** offerings. Lv 4:26
the fat is removed from the **p** offerings, Lv 4:31
from the sacrifice of **p** offerings, Lv 4:35
shall burn on it the fat of the **p** offerings. Lv 6:12
of the sacrifice of **p** offerings that one Lv 7:11
sacrifice of his **p** offerings for Lv 7:13
who throws the blood of the **p** offerings. Lv 7:14
sacrifice of his **p** offerings for Lv 7:15
the sacrifice of his **p** offering is eaten on Lv 7:18
of the LORD'S **p** offerings while an Lv 7:20
the sacrifice of the LORD'S **p** offerings, Lv 7:21
the sacrifice of his **p** offerings to the LORD Lv 7:29
LORD from the sacrifice of his **p** offerings. Lv 7:29
from the sacrifice of your **p** offerings. Lv 7:32
the blood of the **p** offerings and the fat Lv 7:33
out of the sacrifices of their **p** offerings, Lv 7:34
ordination offering, and of the **p** offering, Lv 7:37
and an ox and a ram for **p** offerings, to Lv 9:4
the sacrifice of **p** offerings for the people. Lv 9:18
the burnt offering and the **p** offerings. Lv 9:22
will be glorified.'" And Aaron held his **p**. Lv 10:3
the sacrifices of the **p** offerings of the Lv 10:14
them as sacrifices of **p** offerings to the Lv 17:5
offer a sacrifice of **p** offerings to the LORD, Lv 19:5
offers a sacrifice of **p** offerings to the Lv 22:21
a year old as a sacrifice of **p** offerings. Lv 23:19
I will give **p** in the land, and you shall lie Lv 26:6
ram without blemish as a **p** offering, Nm 6:14
as a sacrifice of **p** offering to the LORD, Nm 6:17
is under the sacrifice of the **p** offering. Nm 6:18
countenance upon you and give you **p**. Nm 6:26
and for the sacrifice of **p** offerings, two Nm 7:17
and for the sacrifice of **p** offerings, two Nm 7:23
and for the sacrifice of **p** offerings, two Nm 7:29
and for the sacrifice of **p** offerings, two Nm 7:35
and for the sacrifice of **p** offerings, two Nm 7:41
and for the sacrifice of **p** offerings, two Nm 7:47
and for the sacrifice of **p** offerings, two Nm 7:53
and for the sacrifice of **p** offerings, two Nm 7:59
and for the sacrifice of **p** offerings, two Nm 7:65
and for the sacrifice of **p** offerings, two Nm 7:71
and for the sacrifice of **p** offerings, two Nm 7:77
and for the sacrifice of **p** offerings, two Nm 7:83
the sacrifice of **p** offerings twenty-four Nm 7:88
over the sacrifices of your **p** offerings. Nm 10:10
a vow or for **p** offerings to the LORD, Nm 15:8
I give to him my covenant of **p**, Nm 25:12
offerings, and for your **p** offerings." Nm 29:39
the king of Heshbon, with words of **p**, Dt 2:26
to fight against it, offer terms of **p** to it. Dt 20:10
But if it makes no **p** with you, but Dt 20:12
shall not seek their **p** or their prosperity Dt 23:6
you shall sacrifice **p** offerings and shall Dt 27:7
to the LORD and sacrificed **p** offerings. Jos 8:31
And Joshua made **p** with them and Jos 9:15
of Gibeon had made **p** with Israel and Jos 10:1
For it has made **p** with Joshua and with Jos 10:4
a city that made **p** with the people of Jos 11:19
or grain offerings or **p** offerings on it, Jos 22:23
offerings and sacrifices and **p** offerings, Jos 22:27
for there was **p** between Jabin the king of Jgs 4:17
But the LORD said to him, "**P** be to you. Jgs 6:23
to the LORD and called it, The LORD is **P**. Jgs 6:24
men of Penuel, "When I come again in **p**, Jgs 8:9
I return in **p** from the Ammonites Jgs 11:31
And the priest said to them, "Go in **p**. Jgs 18:6
And the old man said, "**P** be to you; I Jgs 19:20
burnt offerings and **p** offerings before Jgs 20:26
offered burnt offerings and **p** offerings. Jgs 21:4
of Rimmon and proclaimed **p** to them. Jgs 21:13
Then Eli answered, "Go in **p**, and the 1 Sm 1:17
There was **p** also between Israel and 1 Sm 7:14
offerings and to sacrifice **p** offerings. 1 Sm 10:8
him no present. But he held his **p**. 1 Sm 10:27
they sacrificed **p** offerings before 1 Sm 11:15
and the **p** offerings." And he offered 1 Sm 13:9
Jonathan said to David, "Go in **p**, 1 Sm 20:42
'**P** be to you, and peace be to your 1 Sm 25:6
be to you, and **p** be to your house, 1 Sm 25:6
house, and **p** be to all that you have. 1 Sm 25:6
to her, "Go up in **p** to your house. 1 Sm 25:35
sent Abner away, and he went in **p**. 2 Sm 3:21
sent him away, and he had gone in **p**. 2 Sm 3:22
has let him go, and he has gone in **p**." 2 Sm 3:23
burnt offerings and **p** offerings before 2 Sm 6:17
burnt offerings and the **p** offerings, 2 Sm 6:18
they made **p** with Israel and became 2 Sm 10:19
you? Now hold your **p**, my sister. 2 Sm 13:20
"Go in **p**." So he arose and went to 2 Sm 15:9
Go back to the city in **p**, with your 2 Sm 15:27
man, and all the people will be at **p**." 2 Sm 17:3
burnt offerings and **p** offerings. 2 Sm 24:25
avenging in time of **p** for blood that 1 Kgs 2:5
let his gray head go down to Sheol in **p**. 1 Kgs 2:6

throne there shall be **p** from the LORD 1 Kgs 2:33
up burnt offerings and **p** offerings, 1 Kgs 3:15
And he had **p** on all sides around 1 Kgs 4:24
And there was **p** between Hiram and 1 Kgs 5:12
Solomon offered as **p** offerings to the 1 Kgs 8:63
and the fat pieces of the **p** offerings, 1 Kgs 8:64
and the fat pieces of the **p** offerings. 1 Kgs 8:64
burnt offerings and **p** offerings on the 1 Kgs 9:25
He said, "If they have come out for **p**, 1 Kgs 20:18
let each return to his home in **p**.'" 1 Kgs 22:17
bread and water, until I come in **p**."'" 1 Kgs 22:27
Micaiah said, "If you return in **p**, 1 Kgs 22:28
Jehoshaphat also made **p** with the 1 Kgs 22:44
"Go in **p**." But when Naaman had 2 Kgs 5:19
meet them, and let him say, 'Is it **p**?'" 2 Kgs 9:17
says the king, 'Is it **p**?'" And Jehu said, 2 Kgs 9:18
said, "What do you have to do with **p**? 2 Kgs 9:18
has said, 'Is it **p**?'" And Jehu answered, 2 Kgs 9:19
"What do you have to do with **p**? 2 Kgs 9:19
when Joram saw Jehu, he said, "Is it **p**, 2 Kgs 9:22
He answered, "What **p** can there be, 2 Kgs 9:22
Jehu entered the gate, she said, "Is it **p**, 2 Kgs 9:31
the blood of his **p** offerings on the 2 Kgs 16:13
'Make your **p** with me and come out 2 Kgs 18:31
if there will be **p** and security in my 2 Kgs 20:19
shall be gathered to your grave in **p**, 2 Kgs 22:20
P, peace to you, and peace to your 1 Chr 12:18
Peace, **p** to you, and peace to your 1 Chr 12:18
peace to you, and **p** to your helpers! 1 Chr 12:18
offerings and **p** offerings before 1 Chr 16:1
burnt offerings and the **p** offerings, 1 Chr 16:2
they made **p** with David and 1 Chr 19:19
burnt offerings and **p** offerings and 1 Chr 21:26
and I will give **p** and quiet to Israel in 1 Chr 22:9
he not given you **p** on every side? 1 Chr 22:18
offering and the fat of the **p** offerings, 2 Chr 7:7
those years, for the LORD gave him **p**. 2 Chr 14:6
he has given us **p** on every side." So 2 Chr 14:7
times there was no **p** to him who 2 Chr 15:5
let each return to his home in **p**.'" 2 Chr 18:16
bread and water until I return in **p**.'" 2 Chr 18:26
Micaiah said, "If you return in **p**, 2 Chr 18:27
there was the fat of the **p** offerings, 2 Chr 29:35
sacrificing **p** offerings and giving 2 Chr 30:22
for burnt offerings and **p** offerings, 2 Chr 31:2
on it sacrifices of **p** offerings and of 2 Chr 33:16
shall be gathered to your grave in **p**, 2 Chr 34:28
as follows: "To Darius the king, all **p**. Ezr 5:7
Law of the God of heaven. **P**. And now Ezr 7:12
and never seek their **p** or prosperity, Ezr 9:12
of Ahasuerus, in words of **p** and truth, Est 9:30
his people and spoke **p** to all his people. Est 10:3
beasts of the field shall be at **p** with you. Jb 5:23
You shall know that your tent is at **p**, Jb 5:24
The tents of robbers are at **p**, and those Jb 12:6
and in **p** they go down to Sheol. Jb 21:13
"Agree with God, and be at **p**; thereby Jb 22:21
with God; he makes **p** in his high heaven. Jb 25:2
In **p** I will both lie down and sleep; for you Ps 4:8
who speak **p** with their neighbors while Ps 28:3
May the LORD bless his people with **p**! Ps 29:11
evil and do good; seek **p** and pursue it. Ps 34:14
For they do not speak **p**, but against Ps 35:20
and delight themselves in abundant **p**. Ps 37:11
for there is a future for the man of **p**. Ps 37:37
mute and silent; I held my **p** to no avail, Ps 39:2
to my cry; hold not your **p** at my tears! Ps 39:12
and when they are at **p**, let it become a Ps 69:22
the righteous flourish, and **p** abound, Ps 72:7
do not hold your **p** or be still, O God! Ps 83:1
speak, for he will speak **p** to his people, Ps 85:8
righteousness and **p** kiss each other. Ps 85:10
Great **p** have those who love your Ps 119:165
my dwelling among those who hate **p**. Ps 120:6
I am for **p**, but when I speak, they are Ps 120:7
Pray for the **p** of Jerusalem! "May they Ps 122:6
P be within your walls and security Ps 122:7
sake I will say, "**P** be within you!" Ps 122:8
away with evildoers! **P** be upon Israel! Ps 125:5
children's children! **P** be upon Israel! Ps 128:6
He makes **p** in your borders; he fills Ps 147:14
and years of life and **p** they will add to Prv 3:2
of pleasantness, and all her paths are **p**. Prv 3:17
evil, but those who plan **p** have joy. Prv 12:20
even his enemies to be at **p** with him. Prv 16:7
to hate; a time for war, and a time for **p**. Eccl 3:8
then I was in his eyes as one who finds **p**. Sg 8:10
God, Everlasting Father, Prince of **P**. Is 9:6
of his government and of **p** there will be no Is 9:7
keep him in perfect **p** whose mind is Is 26:3
O LORD, you will ordain **p** for us; you Is 26:12
my protection, let them make **p** with me, Is 27:5
peace with me, let them make **p** with me." Is 27:5
And the effect of righteousness will be **p**, Is 32:17
the streets; the envoys of **p** weep bitterly. Is 33:7
Make your **p** with me and come out to Is 36:16
"There will be **p** and security in my Is 39:8
For a long time I have held my **p**; I have Is 42:14
Then your **p** would have been like a Is 48:18
"There is no **p**," says the LORD, "for the Is 48:22
who brings good news, who publishes **p**, Is 52:7
was the chastisement that brought us **p**, Is 53:5
and my covenant of **p** shall not be Is 54:10
and great shall be the **p** of your children. Is 54:13
shall go out in joy and be led forth in **p**; Is 55:12
he enters into **p**; they rest in their beds Is 57:2
Have I not held my **p**, even for a long Is 57:11
P, peace, to the far and to the near," says Is 57:19
p, to the far and to the near," says the Is 57:19
There is no **p**," says my God, "for the Is 57:21
The way of **p** they do not know, and there Is 59:8
no one who treads on them knows **p**. Is 59:8
make your overseers **p** and your Is 60:17
I will extend **p** to her like a river, Is 66:12
of my people lightly, saying, '**P**, peace,' Jer 6:14
saying, 'Peace, **p**,' when there is no peace. Jer 6:14
saying, 'Peace, peace,' when there is no **p**. Jer 6:14
of my people lightly, saying, '**P**, peace,' Jer 8:11
saying, 'Peace, **p**,' when there is no peace. Jer 8:11
saying, 'Peace, peace,' when there is no **p**. Jer 8:11
We looked for **p**, but no good came; for a Jer 8:15
his mouth each speaks **p** to his neighbor, Jer 9:8
of the land to the other; no flesh has **p**. Jer 12:12
I will give you assured **p** in this place.'" Jer 14:13
We looked for **p**, but no good came; for Jer 14:19
I have taken away my **p** from this people, Jer 16:5
As for the prophet who prophesies **p**, Jer 28:9
heard a cry of panic, of terror, and no **p**. Jer 30:5
You shall die in **p**. And as spices were Jer 34:5
and he shall go away from there in **p**. Jer 43:12
my soul is bereft of **p**; I have forgotten Lam 3:17
When anguish comes, they will seek **p**, Ezk 7:25
saying, '**P**,' when there is no peace, Ezk 13:10
saying, 'Peace,' when there is no **p**, Ezk 13:10
Jerusalem and saw visions of **p** for her, Ezk 13:16
of peace for her, when there was no **p**, Ezk 13:16
them a covenant of **p** and banish wild Ezk 34:25
I will make a covenant of **p** with them. Ezk 37:26
burnt offerings and your **p** offerings, Ezk 43:27
burnt offering, and **p** offerings, Ezk 45:15
burnt offerings, and **p** offerings, Ezk 45:17
his burnt offering and his **p** offerings, Ezk 46:2
a burnt offering or **p** offerings as a Ezk 46:12
burnt offering or his **p** offerings as he Ezk 46:12
in all the earth: **P** be multiplied to you! Dn 4:1
in all the earth: "**P** be multiplied to you. Dn 6:25
greatly loved, fear not, **p** be with you; Dn 10:19
and the **p** offerings of your fattened Am 5:22
those at **p** with you have deceived you; Ob 1:7
who cry "**P**" when they have something Mi 3:5
And he shall be their **p**. When the Mi 5:5
brings good news, who publishes **p**! Na 1:15
And in this place I will give **p**, declares the Hg 2:9
and the counsel of **p** shall be between Zec 6:13
For there shall be a sowing of **p**. The Zec 8:12
judgments that are true and make for **p**; Zec 8:16
feasts. Therefore love truth and **p**. Zec 8:19
off, and he shall speak **p** to the nations; Zec 9:10
covenant with him was one of life and **p**, Mal 2:5
walked with me in **p** and uprightness, Mal 2:6
is worthy, let your **p** come upon it, Mt 10:13
is not worthy, let your **p** return to you. Mt 10:13
that I have come to bring **p** to the earth. Mt 10:34
I have not come to bring **p**, but a Mt 10:34
sea, "**P**! Be still!" And the wind ceased, Mk 4:39
go in **p**, and be healed of your disease." Mk 5:34
and be at **p** with one another." Mk 9:50
to guide our feet into the way of **p**." Lk 1:79
and on earth **p** among those with whom Lk 2:14
you are letting your servant depart in **p**, Lk 2:29
"Your faith has saved you; go in **p**." Lk 7:50
your faith has made you well; go in **p**." Lk 8:48
you enter, first say, '**P** be to this house!' Lk 10:5
And if a son of **p** is there, your peace will Lk 10:6
peace is there, your **p** will rest upon him. Lk 10:6
that I have come to give **p** on earth? Lk 12:51
a delegation and asks for terms of **p**. Lk 14:32
P in heaven and glory in the highest!" Lk 19:38
on this day the things that make for **p**! Lk 19:42
them, and said to them, "**P** to you!" Lk 24:36
P I leave with you; my peace I give to Jn 14:27
I leave with you; my **p** I give to you. Jn 14:27
to you, that in me you may have **p**. Jn 16:33
them and said to them, "**P** be with you." Jn 20:19
said to them again, "**P** be with you. Jn 20:21
among them and said, "**P** be with you." Jn 20:26
and Samaria had **p** and was being Acts 9:31
good news of **p** through Jesus Christ Acts 10:36
king's chamberlain, they asked for **p**, Acts 12:20
were sent off in **p** by the brothers to Acts 15:33
Therefore come out now and go in **p**." Acts 16:36
"Since through you we enjoy much **p**, Acts 24:2
Grace to you and **p** from God our Rom 1:7
and honor and **p** for everyone who Rom 2:10
and the way of **p** they have not Rom 3:17
we have **p** with God through our Lord Rom 5:1
to set the mind on the Spirit is life and **p**. Rom 8:6
but of righteousness and **p** and joy in Rom 14:17
what makes for **p** and for mutual Rom 14:19
you with all joy and **p** in believing, Rom 15:13
May the God of **p** be with you all. Rom 15:33
The God of **p** will soon crush Satan Rom 16:20
Grace to you and **p** from God our 1 Cor 1:3
not enslaved. God has called you to **p**. 1 Cor 7:15
is not a God of confusion but of **p**. 1 Cor 14:33
Help him on his way in **p**, that he 1 Cor 16:11
Grace to you and **p** from God our 2 Cor 1:2
agree with one another, live in **p**; 2 Cor 13:11
God of love and **p** will be with you. 2 Cor 13:11
Grace to you and **p** from God our Father Gal 1:3
fruit of the Spirit is love, joy, **p**, patience, Gal 5:22
this rule, **p** and mercy be upon them, Gal 6:16
Grace to you and **p** from God our Father Eph 1:2
For he himself is our **p**, who has made Eph 2:14
man in place of the two, so making **p**, Eph 2:15
he came and preached **p** to you who Eph 2:17
were far off and **p** to those who were Eph 2:17
the unity of the Spirit in the bond of **p**. Eph 4:3
the readiness given by the gospel of **p**. Eph 6:15
P be to the brothers, and love with Eph 6:23
Grace to you and **p** from God our Father Phil 1:2
And the **p** of God, which surpasses all Phil 4:7
and the God of **p** will be with you. Phil 4:9
Grace to you and **p** from God our Father. Col 1:2
making **p** by the blood of his cross. Col 1:20
And let the **p** of Christ rule in your Col 3:15
Lord Jesus Christ: Grace to you and **p**. 1 Thes 1:1
"There is **p** and security," then 1 Thes 5:3
work. Be at **p** among yourselves. 1 Thes 5:13
the God of **p** himself sanctify you 1 Thes 5:23
Grace to you and **p** from God our 2 Thes 1:2
may the Lord of **p** himself give you 2 Thes 3:16
peace himself give you **p** at all times 2 Thes 3:16
and **p** from God the Father and Christ 1 Tm 1:2
and **p** from God the Father and Christ 2 Tm 1:2
righteousness, faith, love, and **p**, 2 Tm 2:22
Grace and **p** from God the Father and Ti 1:4
Grace to you and **p** from God our Phlm 1:3
is also king of Salem, that is, king of **p**. Heb 7:2
Strive for **p** with everyone, and for the Heb 12:14
may the God of **p** who brought again Heb 13:20
and one of you says to them, "Go in **p**, be Jas 2:16
righteousness is sown in **p** by those who Jas 3:18
is sown in peace by those who make **p**. Jas 3:18
May grace and **p** be multiplied to you. 1 Pt 1:2
do good; let him seek **p** and pursue it. 1 Pt 3:11
love. **P** to all of you who are in Christ. 1 Pt 5:14
May grace and **p** be multiplied to you in 2 Pt 1:2
him without spot or blemish, and at **p**. 2 Pt 3:14
Grace, mercy, and **p** will be with us, 2 Jn 1:3
P be to you. The friends greet you. 3 Jn 1:15
mercy, **p**, and love be multiplied to you. Jude 1:2
Grace to you and **p** from him who is and Rv 1:4
was permitted to take **p** from the earth, Rv 6:4

PEACEABLE (2)
of those who are **p** and faithful in 2 Sm 20:19
wisdom from above is first pure, then **p**, Jas 3:17

PEACEABLY (6)
if it responds to you **p** and it opens to Dt 20:11
the Jordan; now therefore restore it **p**." Jgs 11:13
trembling and said, "Do you come **p**?" 1 Sm 16:4
"**P**; I have come to sacrifice to the 1 Sm 16:5
and go **p**, that you may not displease 1 Sm 29:7
as it depends on you, live **p** with all. Rom 12:18

PEACEFUL (5)
the land was very broad, quiet, and **p**, 1 Chr 4:40
My people will abide in a **p** habitation, Is 32:18
and the **p** folds are devastated because Jer 25:37
that we may lead a **p** and quiet life, 1 Tm 2:2
it yields the **p** fruit of righteousness Heb 12:11

PEACEFULLY (3)
him and could not speak **p** to him. Gn 37:4
she said, "Do you come **p**?" He said, 1 Kgs 2:13
you come peacefully?" He said, "**P**." 1 Kgs 2:13

PEACEMAKERS (1)
"Blessed are the **p**, for they shall be called Mt 5:9

PEACOCKS (2)
gold, silver, ivory, apes, and **p**. 1 Kgs 10:22
gold, silver, ivory, apes, and **p**. 2 Chr 9:21

PEAK (2)
Depart from the **p** of Amana, from the Sg 4:8
Amana, from the **p** of Senir and Hermon, Sg 4:8

PEALS (5)
and rumblings and **p** of thunder, Rv 4:5
on the earth, and there were **p** of thunder, Rv 8:5
of lightning, rumblings, **p** of thunder, Rv 11:19
of lightning, rumblings, **p** of thunder, Rv 16:18
like the sound of mighty **p** of thunder, Rv 19:6

PEARL (2)
who, on finding one **p** of great value, Mt 13:46
each of the gates made of a single **p**, Rv 21:21

PEARLS (8)
crystal; the price of wisdom is above **p**. Jb 28:18
holy, and do not throw your **p** before pigs, Mt 7:6
is like a merchant in search of fine **p**, Mt 13:45
hair and gold or **p** or costly attire, 1 Tm 2:9
and adorned with gold and jewels and **p**, Rv 17:4
of gold, silver, jewels, **p**, fine linen, Rv 18:12
with gold, with jewels, and with **p**! Rv 18:16
And the twelve gates were twelve **p**, each Rv 21:21

PEBBLE (2)
until not even a **p** is to be found 2 Sm 17:13
a sieve, but no **p** shall fall to the earth. Am 9:9

PEDAHEL (1)
a chief, **P** the son of Ammihud. Nm 34:28

PEDAHZUR (5)
from Manasseh, Gamaliel the son of **P**; Nm 1:10
Manasseh being Gamaliel the son of **P**, Nm 2:20
the eighth day Gamaliel the son of **P**, Nm 7:54
the offering of Gamaliel the son of **P**. Nm 7:59
Manasseh was Gamaliel the son of **P**. Nm 10:23

PEDAIAH (8)
the daughter of **P** of Rumah. 2 Kgs 23:36
Malchiram, **P**, Shenazzar, Jekamiah, 1 Chr 3:18
and the sons of **P**: Zerubbabel and 1 Chr 3:19
of Manasseh, Joel the son of **P**; 1 Chr 27:20
guard. After him **P** the son of Parosh Neh 3:25
and Maaseiah on his right hand, and **P**, Neh 8:4
of Meshullam, son of Joed, son of **P**, Neh 11:7
Zadok the scribe, and **P** of the Levites, Neh 13:13

PEDDLERS (1)
are not, like so many, **p** of God's word, 2 Cor 2:17

PEDESTAL (2)
Its opening was round, as a **p** is made, 1 Kgs 7:31
were under it and put it on a stone **p**. 2 Kgs 16:17

PEELED (2)
trees, and **p** white streaks in them, Gn 30:37
the sticks that he had **p** in front of the Gn 30:38

PEERED (1)
"Out of the window she **p**, the mother of Jgs 5:28

PEG (8)
But Jael the wife of Heber took a tent **p**, Jgs 4:21
him and drove the **p** into his temple Jgs 4:21
Sisera dead, with the tent **p** in his temple. Jgs 4:22
hand to the tent **p** and her right hand Jgs 5:26
will fasten him like a **p** in a secure place, Is 22:23
the **p** that was fastened in a secure place Is 22:25
Do people take a **p** from it to hang any Ezk 15:3
the cornerstone, from him the tent **p**, Zec 10:4

PEGS (10)
and all its **p** and all the pegs of the Ex 27:19
all its pegs and all the **p** of the court, Ex 27:19
the **p** of the tabernacle and the pegs of Ex 35:18
of the tabernacle and the **p** of the court, Ex 35:18
And all the **p** for the tabernacle and for Ex 38:20
of the court, all the **p** of the tabernacle, Ex 38:31
and all the **p** around the court. Ex 38:31
the gate of the court, its cords, and its **p**; Ex 39:40
court, with their bases and **p** and cords. Nm 3:37
the court with their bases, **p**, and cords, Nm 4:32

PEKAH (11)
And **P** the son of Remaliah, his 2 Kgs 15:25
P the son of Remaliah began to 2 Kgs 15:27
In the days of **P** king of Israel, 2 Kgs 15:29
a conspiracy against **P** the son of 2 Kgs 15:30
rest of the acts of **P** and all that he 2 Kgs 15:31
the second year of **P** the son of 2 Kgs 15:32
king of Syria and **P** the son of 2 Kgs 15:37
the seventeenth year of **P** the son of 2 Kgs 16:1
king of Syria and **P** the son of 2 Kgs 16:5
For **P** the son of Remaliah killed 2 Chr 28:6
king of Syria and **P** the son of Remaliah Is 7:1

PEKAHIAH (3)
and **P** his son reigned in his place. 2 Kgs 15:22
P the son of Menahem began to 2 Kgs 15:23
rest of the deeds of **P** and all that he 2 Kgs 15:26

PEKOD (2)
and against the inhabitants of **P**. Jer 50:21
the Chaldeans, **P** and Shoa and Koa, Ezk 23:23

PELAIAH (3)
Hodaviah, Eliashib, **P**, Akkub, 1 Chr 3:24
Azariah, Jozabad, Hanan, **P**, the Levites, Neh 8:7
Shebaniah, Hodiah, Kelita, **P**, Hanan, Neh 10:10

PELALIAH (1)
Adaiah the son of Jeroham, son of **P**, Neh 11:12

PELATIAH (5)
P and Jeshaiah, his son Rephaiah, his 1 Chr 3:21
Mount Seir, having as their leaders **P**, 1 Chr 4:42
P, Hanan, Anaiah, Neh 10:22
son of Azzur, and **P** the son of Benaiah, Ezk 11:1
that **P** the son of Benaiah died. Ezk 11:13

PELEG (8)
the name of the one was **P**, for in his Gn 10:25
Eber had lived 34 years, he fathered **P**. Gn 11:16
lived after he fathered **P** 430 years and Gn 11:17
When **P** had lived 30 years, he fathered Gn 11:18
And **P** lived after he fathered Reu 209 Gn 11:19
of the one was **P** (for in his days 1 Chr 1:19
Eber, **P**, Reu; 1 Chr 1:25
son of Serug, the son of Reu, the son of **P**, Lk 3:35

PELET (2)
Regem, Jotham, Geshan, **P**, Ephah, 1 Chr 2:47
also Jeziel and **P**, the sons of 1 Chr 12:3

PELETH (2)
the sons of Eliab, and On the son of **P**, Nm 16:1
The sons of Jonathan: **P** and Zaza. 1 Chr 2:33

PELETHITES (7)
was over the Cherethites and the **P**, 2 Sm 8:18
and all the Cherethites, and all the **P**, 2 Sm 15:18
men and the Cherethites and the **P**, 2 Sm 20:7
of the Cherethites and the **P**; 2 Sm 20:23
Cherethites and the **P** went down and 1 Kgs 1:38
and the Cherethites and the **P**. 1 Kgs 1:44
was over the Cherethites and the **P**; 1 Chr 18:17

PELONITE (3)
Shammoth of Harod, Helez the **P**, 1 Chr 11:27
the Mecherathite, Ahijah the **P**, 1 Chr 11:36
the seventh month, was Helez the **P**, 1 Chr 27:10

PELUSIUM (2)
And I will pour out my wrath on **P**, Ezk 30:15
fire to Egypt; **P** shall be in great agony; Ezk 30:16

PEN (5)
that with an iron **p** and lead they were Jb 19:24
my tongue is like the **p** of a ready scribe. Ps 45:1
the lying **p** of the scribes has made it into Jer 8:8
sin of Judah is written with a **p** of iron; Jer 17:1
I would rather not write with **p** and ink. 3 Jn 1:13

PENALTY (6)
A man of great wrath will pay the **p**, Prv 19:19
You bear the **p** of your lewdness and Ezk 16:58
you shall bear the **p** for your sinful Ezk 23:49
no reason for the death **p** in my case. Acts 28:18
in themselves the due **p** for their error. Rom 1:27
who is troubling you will bear the **p**, Gal 5:10

PENCIL (1)
stretches a line; he marks it out with a **p**. Is 44:13

PENDANTS (3)
ornaments and the **p** and the purple Jgs 8:26
for your head and **p** for your neck. Prv 1:9
the **p**, the bracelets, and the scarves; Is 3:19

PENIEL (1)
Jacob called the name of the place **P**, Gn 32:30

PENINNAH (3)
other, **P**. And Peninnah had children, 1 Sm 1:2
And **P** had children, but Hannah had 1 Sm 1:2
would give portions to **P** his wife and to 1 Sm 1:4

PENITENT (1)
because your heart was **p**, and you 2 Kgs 22:19

PENNIES (1)
Are not five sparrows sold for two **p**? Lk 12:6

PENNY (4)
get out until you have paid the last **p**. Mt 5:26
Are not two sparrows sold for a **p**? And Mt 10:29
small copper coins, which make a **p**. Mk 12:42
out until you have paid the very last **p**." Lk 12:59

PENTECOST (3)
When the day of **P** arrived, they were all Acts 2:1
Jerusalem, if possible, on the day of **P**. Acts 20:16
But I will stay in Ephesus until **P**, 1 Cor 16:8

PENUEL (8)
The sun rose upon him as he passed **P**, Gn 32:31
And from there he went up to **P**, and Jgs 8:8
and the men of **P** answered him as the Jgs 8:8
And he said to the men of **P**, "When I Jgs 8:9
down the tower of **P** and killed the men Jgs 8:17
he went out from there and built **P**. 1 Kgs 12:25

and **P** fathered Gedor, and Ezer 1 Chr 4:4
and **P** were the sons of Shashak. 1 Chr 8:25

PEOPLE'S (12)
he presented the **p** offering and took Lv 9:15
who hate him and cleanses his **p** land." Dt 32:43
shout from the sound of the **p** weeping, Ezr 3:13
will you be angry with your **p** prayers? Ps 80:4
every obstruction from my **p** way." Is 57:14
"Go and stand in the **P** Gate, by which Jer 17:19
thrown out and trampled under **p** feet. Mt 5:13
For this **p** heart has grown dull, and Mt 13:15
to bear, and lay them on **p** shoulders, Mt 23:4
shut the kingdom of heaven in **p** faces. Mt 23:13
are full of dead **p** bones and all Mt 23:27
For this **p** heart has grown dull, and Acts 28:27

PEOPLE-PLEASERS (2)
not by the way of eye-service, as **p**, but as Eph 6:6
masters, not by way of eye-service, as **p**, Col 3:22

PEOPLES (234)
these the coastland **p** spread in their Gn 10:5
kings of **p** shall come from her." Gn 17:16
and two **p** from within you shall be Gn 25:23
Let **p** serve you, and nations bow down Gn 27:29
that you may become a company of **p**. Gn 28:3
of you a company of **p** and will give this Gn 48:4
to him shall be the obedience of the **p**. Gn 49:10
The **p** have heard; they tremble; pangs Ex 15:14
be my treasured possession among all **p**, Ex 19:5
who have separated you from the **p**. Lv 20:24
and have separated you from the **p**, Lv 20:26
fear of you on the **p** who are under the Dt 2:25
your understanding in the sight of the **p**, Dt 4:6
allotted to all the **p** under the whole Dt 4:19
the LORD will scatter you among the **p**, Dt 4:27
the gods of the **p** who are around you, Dt 6:14
out of all the **p** who are on the face of the Dt 7:6
chose you, for you were the fewest of all **p**, Dt 7:7
You shall be blessed above all **p**. There Dt 7:14
shall consume all the **p** that the LORD Dt 7:16
God do to all the **p** of whom you are Dt 7:19
offspring after them, you above all **p**, Dt 10:15
of the gods of the **p** who are around you, Dt 13:7
out of all the **p** who are on the face of the Dt 14:2
the cities of these **p** that the LORD your Dt 20:16
And all the **p** of the earth shall see that Dt 28:10
byword among all the **p** where the LORD Dt 28:37
the LORD will scatter you among all **p**, Dt 28:64
again from all the **p** where the LORD your Dt 30:3
the borders of the **p** according to the Dt 32:8
with them he shall gore the **p**, all of Dt 33:17
They shall call **p** to their mountain; Dt 33:19
so that all the **p** of the earth may know Jos 4:24
and among all the **p** through whom we Jos 24:17
the LORD drove out before us all the **p**, Jos 24:18
the gods of the **p** who were around them, Jgs 2:12
and brought down **p** under me, 2 Sm 22:48
order that all the **p** of the earth may 1 Kgs 8:43
from among all the **p** of the earth to 1 Kgs 8:53
that all the **p** of the earth may know 1 Kgs 8:60
a proverb and a byword among all **p**. 1 Kgs 9:7
me." And he said, "Hear, all you **p**!" 1 Kgs 22:28
after the gods of the **p** of the land, 1 Chr 5:25
make known his deeds among the **p**! 1 Chr 16:8
marvelous works among all the **p**! 1 Chr 16:24
For all the gods of the **p** are idols, 1 Chr 16:26
Ascribe to the LORD, O clans of the **p**, 1 Chr 16:28
order that all the **p** of the earth may 2 Chr 6:33
a proverb and a byword among all **p**. 2 Chr 7:20
yourselves like the **p** of other lands? 2 Chr 13:9
me." And he said, "Hear, all you **p**!" 2 Chr 18:27
have done to all the **p** of other lands? 2 Chr 32:13
of the gods of the **p** of the earth, 2 Chr 32:19
on them because of the **p** of the lands, Ezr 3:3
the uncleanness of the **p** of the land to Ezr 6:21
themselves from the **p** of the lands Ezr 9:1
has mixed itself with the **p** of the lands. Ezr 9:2
with the impurity of the **p** of the lands, Ezr 9:11
intermarry with the **p** who practice Ezr 9:14
foreign women from the **p** of the land, Ezr 10:2
yourselves from the **p** of the land Ezr 10:11
I will scatter you among the **p**, Neh 1:8
them kingdoms and **p** and allotted to Neh 9:22
with their kings and the **p** of the land, Neh 9:24
into the hand of the **p** of the lands. Neh 9:30
themselves from the **p** of the lands Neh 10:28
our daughters to the **p** of the land or Neh 10:30
And if the **p** of the land bring in goods Neh 10:31
order to show the **p** and the princes her Est 1:11
the officials and all the **p** who are in all Est 1:16
and dispersed among the **p** in all the Est 3:8
provinces and to the officials of all the **p**, Est 3:12
proclamation to all the **p** to be ready for Est 3:14
being publicly displayed to all **p**, Est 8:13
And many from the **p** of the country Est 8:17

for the fear of them had fallen on all **p**. Est 9:2
"He has made me a byword of the **p**, and I Jb 17:6
the night, when **p** vanish in their place. Jb 36:20
For by these he judges **p**; he gives food Jb 36:31
do the nations rage and the **p** plot in vain? Ps 2:1
the assembly of the **p** be gathered about Ps 7:7
The LORD judges the **p**; judge me, O LORD, Ps 7:8
he judges the **p** with uprightness. Ps 9:8
in Zion! Tell among the **p** his deeds! Ps 9:11
vengeance and subdued **p** under me, Ps 18:47
nothing; he frustrates the plans of the **p**. Ps 33:10
you afflicted the **p**, but them you set free; Ps 44:2
nations, a laughingstock among the **p**. Ps 44:14
the king's enemies; the **p** fall under you. Ps 45:5
Clap your hands, all **p**! Shout to God Ps 47:1
He subdued **p** under us, and nations Ps 47:3
The princes of the **p** gather as the people Ps 47:9
Hear this, all **p**! Give ear, all inhabitants Ps 49:1
escape? In wrath cast down the **p**, O God! Ps 56:7
give thanks to you, O Lord, among the **p**; Ps 57:9
of their waves, the tumult of the **p**, Ps 65:7
Bless our God, O **p**; let the sound of his Ps 66:8
Let the **p** praise you, O God; let all the Ps 67:3
praise you, O God; let all the **p** praise you! Ps 67:3
for you judge the **p** with equity and guide Ps 67:4
Let the **p** praise you, O God; let all the Ps 67:5
praise you, O God; let all the **p** praise you! Ps 67:5
herd of bulls with the calves of the **p**. Ps 68:30
tribute; scatter the **p** who delight in war. Ps 68:30
made known your might among the **p**. Ps 77:14
The LORD records as he registers the **p**, Ps 87:6
his marvelous works among all the **p**! Ps 96:3
all the gods of the **p** are worthless idols, Ps 96:5
Ascribe to the LORD, O families of the **p**, Ps 96:7
moved; he will judge the **p** with equity." Ps 96:10
and the **p** in his faithfulness. Ps 96:13
righteousness, and all the **p** see his glory. Ps 97:6
righteousness, and the **p** with equity. Ps 98:9
The LORD reigns; let the **p** tremble! He sits Ps 99:1
great in Zion; he is exalted over all the **p**. Ps 99:2
when **p** gather together, and Ps 102:22
make known his deeds among the **p**! Ps 105:1
him; the ruler of the **p** set him free; Ps 105:20
They did not destroy the **p**, as the LORD Ps 106:34
thanks to you, O LORD, among the **p**; Ps 108:3
the LORD, all nations! Extol him, all **p**! Ps 117:1
I take refuge, who subdues **p** under me. Ps 144:2
Kings of the earth and all **p**, princes Ps 148:11
the nations and punishments on the **p**, Ps 149:7
are in the right," will be cursed by **p**, Prv 24:24
and many **p** shall come, and say: "Come, Is 2:3
and shall decide disputes for many **p**; Is 2:4
his place to contend; he stands to judge **p**. Is 3:13
Be broken, you **p**, and be shattered; give Is 8:9
I remove the boundaries of **p**, and Is 10:13
has found like a nest the wealth of the **p**; Is 10:14
as a signal for the **p**—of him shall the Is 11:10
make known his deeds among the **p**, Is 12:4
And the **p** will take them and bring them Is 14:2
that struck the **p** in wrath with Is 14:6
Ah, the thunder of many **p**; they thunder Is 17:12
Therefore strong **p** will glorify you; cities Is 25:3
hosts will make for all **p** a feast of rich Is 25:6
the covering that is cast over all **p**, Is 25:7
on the jaws of the **p** a bridle that leads Is 30:28
At the tumultuous noise **p** flee; when you Is 33:3
And the **p** will be as if burned to lime, Is 33:12
nations, to hear, and give attention, O **p**! Is 34:1
coastlands; let the **p** renew their strength; Is 41:1
for you, **p** in exchange for your life. Is 43:4
gather together, and the **p** assemble. Is 43:9
and give attention, you **p** from afar. Is 49:1
the nations, and raise my signal to the **p**; Is 49:22
I will set my justice for a light to the **p**. Is 51:4
gone out, and my arms will judge the **p**; Is 51:5
Behold, I made him a witness to the **p**, a Is 55:4
a leader and commander for the **p**. Is 55:4
shall be called a house of prayer for all **p**." Is 56:7
cover the earth, and thick darkness the **p**; Is 60:2
their descendants in the midst of the **p**; Is 61:9
it of stones; lift up a signal over the **p**. Is 62:10
and from the **p** no one was with me; Is 63:3
I trampled down the **p** in my anger; I Is 63:6
for the customs of the **p** are vanity. A tree Jer 10:3
and on the **p** that call not on your Jer 10:25
and all the **p** were fighting against Jer 34:1
The **p** labor for nothing, and the Jer 51:58
but hear, all you **p**, and see my Lam 1:18
become the laughingstock of all **p**, Lam 3:14
us scum and garbage among the **p**. Lam 3:45
not to many **p** of foreign speech and a Ezk 3:6
you from the **p** and assemble you Ezk 11:17
you out from the **p** and gather you out Ezk 20:34
bring you into the wilderness of the **p**, Ezk 20:35
you out from the **p** and gather you out Ezk 20:41
chariots and wagons and a host of **p**. Ezk 23:24
you off from the **p** and will make you Ezk 25:7
'Aha, the gate of the **p** is broken; Ezk 26:2
merchant of the **p** to many coastlands, Ezk 27:3
from the seas, you satisfied many **p**; Ezk 27:33
merchants among the **p** hiss at you; Ezk 27:36
know you among the **p** are appalled at Ezk 28:19
of Israel from the **p** among whom they Ezk 28:25
Egyptians from the **p** among whom Ezk 29:13
and all the **p** of the earth have gone Ezk 31:12
my net over you with a host of many **p**, Ezk 32:3
"I will trouble the hearts of many **p**, Ezk 32:9
I will make many **p** appalled at you, Ezk 32:10
them out from the **p** and gather them Ezk 34:13
the disgrace of the **p** and no longer Ezk 36:15
all his hordes—many **p** are with you. Ezk 38:6
gathered from many **p** upon the Ezk 38:8
brought out from the **p** and now dwell Ezk 38:8
all your hordes, and many **p** with you. Ezk 38:9
the north, you and many **p** with you, Ezk 38:15
hordes and the many **p** who are with Ezk 38:22
your hordes and the **p** who are with Ezk 39:4
back from the **p** and gathered them Ezk 39:27
aloud, "You are commanded, O **p**, Dn 3:4
as soon as all the **p** heard the sound of the Dn 3:7
and every kind of music, all the **p**, Dn 3:7
King Nebuchadnezzar to all **p**, nations, Dn 4:1
of the greatness that he gave him, all **p**, Dn 5:19
Then King Darius wrote to all the **p**, Dn 6:25
and glory and a kingdom, that all **p**, Dn 7:14
Ephraim mixes himself with the **p**; Hos 7:8
Exult not like the **p**; for you have played Hos 9:1
Before them **p** are in anguish; all faces Jl 2:6
Why should they say among the **p**, Jl 2:17
Hear, you **p**, all of you; pay attention, O Mi 1:2
up above the hills; and **p** shall flow to it, Mi 4:1
He shall judge between many **p**, and shall Mi 4:3
For all the **p** walk each in the name of its Mi 4:5
bronze; you shall beat in pieces many **p**; Mi 4:13
in the midst of many **p** like dew from the Mi 5:7
the nations, in the midst of many **p**, Mi 5:8
her whorings, and **p** with her charms. Na 3:4
nations and collects as his own all **p**." Hab 2:5
the remnant of the **p** shall plunder you, Hab 2:8
for your house by cutting off many **p**; Hab 2:10
LORD of hosts that **p** labor merely for Hab 2:13
the speech of the **p** to a pure speech, Zep 3:9
praised among all the **p** of the earth, Zep 3:20
P shall yet come, even the inhabitants Zec 8:20
Many **p** and strong nations shall come Zec 8:22
that I had made with all the **p**. Zec 11:10
of staggering to all the surrounding **p**. Zec 12:2
Jerusalem a heavy stone for all the **p**. Zec 12:3
every horse of the **p** with blindness. Zec 12:4
and to the left all the surrounding **p**, Zec 12:6
will strike all the **p** that wage war Zec 14:12
have prepared in the presence of all **p**, Lk 2:31
Gentiles rage, and the **p** plot in vain? Acts 4:25
with the Gentiles and the **p** of Israel, Acts 4:27
Gentiles, and let all the **p** extol him." Rom 15:11
from all tribes and **p** and languages, Rv 7:9
prophesy about many **p** and nations Rv 10:11
days some from the **p** and tribes and Rv 11:9
are **p** and multitudes and nations and Rv 17:15

PEOPLES' (1)
possession of the fruit of the **p** toil, Ps 105:44

PEOR (9)
So Balak took Balaam to the top of **P**, Nm 23:28
So Israel yoked himself to Baal of **P**. Nm 25:3
have yoked themselves to Baal of **P**." Nm 25:5
they beguiled you in the matter of **P**, Nm 25:18
day of the plague on account of **P**." Nm 25:18
against the LORD in the incident of **P**, Nm 31:16
all the men who followed the Baal of **P**. Dt 4:3
of the sin at **P** from which even yet Jos 22:17
they yoked themselves to the Baal of **P**, Ps 106:28

PER (1)
you shall take five shekels **p** head; you Nm 3:47

PERAZIM (1)
For the LORD will rise up as on Mount **P**; Is 28:21

PERCEIVE (18)
him not; he moves on, but I do not **p** him. Jb 9:11
there, and backward, but I do not **p** him; Jb 23:8
and in two, though man does not **p** it. Jb 33:14
does not see; the God of Jacob does not **p**." Ps 94:7
does not he who weighs the heart **p** it? Prv 24:12
understand; keep on seeing, but do not **p**.' Is 6:9
now it springs forth, do you not **p** it? Is 43:19
and you will indeed see but never **p**. Mt 13:14
Do you not yet **p**? Do you not remember Mt 16:9
so that "they may indeed see but not **p**, Mk 4:12
bread? Do you not yet **p** or understand? Mk 8:17
for I **p** that power has gone out from Lk 8:46
from them, so that they might not **p** it. Lk 9:45
to him, "Sir, I **p** that you are a prophet. Jn 4:19
I **p** that in every way you are very Acts 17:22
I **p** that the voyage will be with injury Acts 27:10
and you will indeed see but never **p**. Acts 28:26
you can **p** my insight into the mystery Eph 3:4

PERCEIVED (21)
Then Gideon **p** that he was the angel of Jgs 6:22
called me." Then Eli **p** that the LORD 1 Sm 3:8
because they **p** that the wisdom of 1 Kgs 3:28
for they **p** that this work had been Neh 6:16
the simple, I have **p** among the youths, Prv 7:7
I **p** that this also is but a striving after Eccl 1:17
And yet I **p** that the same event Eccl 2:14
I **p** that there is nothing better for them Eccl 3:12
I **p** that whatever God does endures Eccl 3:14
of old no one has heard or **p** by the ear, Is 64:4
p in the books the number of years that, Dn 9:2
they **p** that he was speaking about Mt 21:45
for they **p** that he had told the parable Mk 12:12
For he **p** that it was out of envy that Mk 15:10
When Jesus **p** their thoughts, he Lk 5:22
for they **p** that he had told this parable Lk 20:19
But he **p** their craftiness, and said to Lk 20:23
John, and **p** that they were uneducated, Acts 4:13
Now when Paul **p** that one part were Acts 23:6
and divine nature, have been clearly **p**, Rom 1:20
pillars, **p** the grace that was given to me, Gal 2:9

PERCEIVES (2)
it; they are brought low, and he **p** it not. Jb 14:21
She **p** that her merchandise is Prv 31:18

PERCEIVING (3)
p in his spirit that they thus questioned Mk 2:8
p in himself that power had gone out Mk 5:30
P then that they were about to come and Jn 6:15

PERCENTAGE (1)
and their houses, and the **p** of money, Neh 5:11

PERENNIAL (2)
jungle of the Jordan against a **p** pasture, Jer 49:19
of the Jordan against a **p** pasture, Jer 50:44

PERES (1)
P, your kingdom is divided and given to Dn 5:28

PERESH (1)
a son, and she called his name **P**; 1 Chr 7:16

PEREZ (18)
Therefore his name was called **P**. Gn 38:29
P, and Zerah (but Er and Onan died in Gn 46:12
and the sons of **P** were Hezron and Gn 46:12
the clan of the Shelanites; of **P**, Nm 26:20
And the sons of **P** were: of Hezron, the Nm 26:21
may your house be like the house of **P**, Ru 4:12
Now these are the generations of **P**: Perez Ru 4:18
generations of Perez: **P** fathered Hezron, Ru 4:18
Tamar also bore him **P** and Zerah. 1 Chr 2:4
The sons of **P**: Hezron and Hamul. 1 Chr 2:5
P, Hezron, Carmi, Hur, and Shobal. 1 Chr 4:1
from the sons of **P** the son of Judah. 1 Chr 9:4
was a descendant of **P** and was chief 1 Chr 27:3
son of Mahalalel, of the sons of **P**; Neh 11:4
All the sons of **P** who lived in Neh 11:6
Judah the father of **P** and Zerah by Mt 1:3
by Tamar, and **P** the father of Hezron, Mt 1:3
of Arni, the son of Hezron, the son of **P**, Lk 3:33

PEREZ-UZZA (1)
that place is called **P** to this day. 1 Chr 13:11

PEREZ-UZZAH (1)
And that place is called **P**, to this day. 2 Sm 6:8

PEREZITES (1)
Shelanites; of Perez, the clan of the **P**; Nm 26:20

PERFECT (41)
the flock, to be accepted it must be **p**; Lv 22:21
"The Rock, his work is **p**, for all his ways Dt 32:4
This God—his way is **p**; the word of 2 Sm 22:31
one who is **p** in knowledge is with you. Jb 36:4
works of him who is **p** in knowledge, Jb 37:16
This God—his way is **p**; the word of the Ps 18:30
The law of the LORD is **p**, reviving the Ps 19:7
me, my sister, my love, my dove, my **p** one, Sg 5:2
My dove, my **p** one, is the only one, the Sg 6:9
You keep him in **p** peace whose mind is Is 26:3
for it was **p** through the splendor that I Ezk 16:14
Tyre, you have said, 'I am **p** in beauty.' Ezk 27:3
your builders made **p** your beauty. Ezk 27:4
all around; they made **p** your beauty. Ezk 27:11
full of wisdom and **p** in beauty. Ezk 28:12
You therefore must be **p**, as your Mt 5:48
be perfect, as your heavenly Father is **p**. Mt 5:48
Jesus said to him, "If you would be **p**, Mt 19:21
given the man this **p** health in the Acts 3:16
what is good and acceptable and **p**. Rom 12:2

but when the **p** comes, the partial 1 Cor 13:10
because I have **p** confidence in you. 2 Cor 7:16
power is made **p** in weakness." 2 Cor 12:9
already obtained this or am already **p**, Phil 3:12
everything together in **p** harmony. Col 3:14
might display his **p** patience as an 1 Tm 1:16
and to show **p** courtesy toward all people. Ti 3:2
of their salvation **p** through suffering. Heb 2:10
And being made **p**, he became the Heb 5:9
(for the law made nothing **p**); but on Heb 7:19
a Son who has been made **p** forever. Heb 7:28
offered that cannot **p** the conscience of Heb 9:9
the greater and more **p** tent (not made Heb 9:11
year, make **p** those who draw near. Heb 10:1
from us they should not be made **p**. Heb 11:40
to the spirits of the righteous made **p**, Heb 12:23
effect, that you may be **p** and complete, Jas 1:4
good gift and every **p** gift is from above, Jas 1:17
But the one who looks into the **p** law, the Jas 1:25
stumble in what he says, he is a **p** man, Jas 3:2
no fear in love, but **p** love casts out fear. 1 Jn 4:18

PERFECTED (6)
Spirit, are you now being **p** by the flesh? Gal 3:3
single offering he has **p** for all time Heb 10:14
word, in him truly the love of God is **p**. 1 Jn 2:5
God abides in us and his love is **p** in us. 1 Jn 4:12
By this is love **p** with us, so that we may 1 Jn 4:17
whoever fears has not been **p** in love. 1 Jn 4:18

PERFECTER (1)
to Jesus, the founder and **p** of our faith, Heb 12:2

PERFECTION (5)
Out of Zion, the **p** of beauty, God shines Ps 50:2
I have seen a limit to all **p**, but your Ps 119:96
the city that was called the **p** of beauty, Lam 2:15
"You were the signet of **p**, full of Ezk 28:12
Now if **p** had been attainable through Heb 7:11

PERFECTLY (1)
you in me, that they may become **p** one, Jn 17:23

PERFORM (29)
to your brother's wife and **p** the duty of a Gn 38:8
statutes and keep my rules and **p** them, Lv 25:18
which he commanded you to **p**, Dt 4:13
her as his wife and **p** the duty of a Dt 25:5
he will not **p** the duty of a husband's Dt 25:7
that we do **p** the service of the LORD in Jos 22:27
that the king will **p** the request of his 2 Sm 14:15
to **p** the words of this covenant that 2 Kgs 23:3
to **p** the words of the covenant that 2 Chr 34:31
my vows I will **p** before those who fear Ps 22:25
and **p** your vows to the Most High, Ps 50:14
I must **p** my vows to you, O God; I will Ps 56:12
your name, as I **p** my vows day after day. Ps 61:8
burnt offerings; I will **p** my vows to you, Ps 66:13
vows to the LORD your God and **p** them; Ps 76:11
my heart to **p** your statutes forever, Ps 119:112
will make vows to the LORD and **p** them. Is 19:21
he shall **p** his purpose on Babylon, and Is 48:14
for I am watching over my word to **p** it." Jer 1:12
'We will surely **p** our vows that we have Jer 44:25
confirm your vows and **p** your vows! Jer 44:25
house, I will speak the word and **p** it, Ezk 12:25
terms of an agreement and **p** them. Dn 11:17
When the morning dawns, they **p** it, Mi 2:1
but shall **p** to the Lord what you have Mt 5:33
will arise and **p** great signs and Mt 24:24
will arise and **p** signs and wonders, Mk 13:22
cast out demons and **p** cures today and Lk 13:32
and believe you? What work do you **p**? Jn 6:30

PERFORMED (24)
of the LORD that he **p** for you and for 1 Sm 12:7
and has not **p** my commandments." 1 Sm 15:11
I have **p** the commandment of the 1 Sm 15:13
and they **p** their service according to 1 Chr 6:32
and **p** signs and wonders against Neh 9:10
of the wonders that you **p** among them, Neh 9:17
And they **p** the service of their God Neh 12:45
because she has not **p** the command of Est 1:15
told us, what deeds you **p** in their days, Ps 44:1
God, in Zion, and to you shall vows be **p**. Ps 65:1
of their fathers he **p** wonders in the land Ps 78:12
when he **p** his signs in Egypt and his Ps 78:43
They **p** his signs among them and Ps 105:27
to be **p** with faithfulness and Ps 111:8
Who has **p** and done this, calling the Is 41:4
word that I will speak, and it will be **p**. Ezk 12:25
but the word that I speak will be **p**, Ezk 12:28
for the labor that he had **p** against her. Ezk 29:18
when they had **p** everything according Lk 2:39
sign has been **p** through them is Acts 4:16
sign of healing was **p** was more than Acts 4:22
and wonders are **p** through the name Acts 4:30
And seeing signs and great miracles **p**, Acts 8:13
true apostle were **p** among you with 2 Cor 12:12

PERFORMING (6)
seven days, **p** what the LORD has charged, Lv 8:35
testimonies, and your statutes, **p** all, 1 Chr 29:19
p wonders and signs in Egypt and at Acts 7:36
p deeds in keeping with their Acts 26:20
the first section, **p** their ritual duties, Heb 9:6
For they are demonic spirits, **p** signs, Rv 16:14

PERFORMS (2)
we to do? For this man **p** many signs. Jn 11:47
It **p** great signs, even making fire come Rv 13:13

PERFUME (5)
like it to use as **p** shall be cut off from Ex 30:38
Oil and **p** make the heart glad, and the Prv 27:9
the armlets, the sashes, the **p** boxes, Is 3:20
Instead of **p** there will be rottenness; and Is 3:24
was filled with the fragrance of the **p**. Jn 12:3

PERFUMED (2)
I have **p** my bed with myrrh, aloes, and Prv 7:17
smoke, **p** with myrrh and frankincense, Sg 3:6

PERFUMER (3)
anointing oil blended as by the **p**; Ex 30:25
make an incense blended as by the **p**, Ex 30:35
fragrant incense, blended as by the **p**. Ex 37:29

PERFUMER'S (2)
kinds of spices prepared by the **p** art, 2 Chr 16:14
Dead flies make the **p** ointment give off Eccl 10:1

PERFUMERS (2)
your daughters to be **p** and cooks and 1 Sm 8:13
Next to him Hananiah, one of the **p**, Neh 3:8

PERFUMES (1)
the king with oil and multiplied your **p**; Is 57:9

PERGA (3)
Paphos and came to **P** in Pamphylia. Acts 13:13
they went on from **P** and came to Acts 13:14
when they had spoken the word in **P**, Acts 14:25

PERGAMUM (2)
to Smyrna and to **P** and to Thyatira and Rv 1:11
to the angel of the church in **P** write: Rv 2:12

PERHAPS (34)
"**P** the woman may not be willing to Gn 24:5
'**P** the woman will not follow me.' Gn 24:39
P my father will feel me, and I shall Gn 27:12
shall see his face. **P** he will accept me." Gn 32:20
of your sacks. **P** it was an oversight. Gn 43:12
p I can make atonement for your sin." Ex 32:30
P I shall be able to defeat them and Nm 22:6
P I shall be able to fight against them Nm 22:11
P the LORD will come to meet me, and Nm 23:3
P it will please God that you may Nm 23:27
said to the Hivites, "**P** you live among us; Jos 9:7
P he will lighten his hand from off you 1 Sm 6:5
P he can tell us the way we should go." 1 Sm 9:6
P we may find grass and save the 1 Kgs 18:5
or **p** he is asleep and must be 1 Kgs 18:27
of Israel. **P** he will spare your life." 1 Kgs 20:31
youth; **p** you may be able to succeed; Is 47:12
to succeed; **p** you may inspire terror. Is 47:12
"**P** he will be deceived; then we can Jer 20:10
P the LORD will deal with us according to Jer 21:2
balm for her pain; **p** she may be healed. Jer 51:8
P they will understand, though they are Ezk 12:3
that there may **p** be a lengthening of Dn 4:27
P the god will give a thought to us, that Jon 1:6
p you may be hidden on the day of the Zep 2:3
beloved son; **p** they will respect him.' Lk 20:13
righteous person—though **p** for a good Rom 5:7
except **p** by agreement for a limited 1 Cor 7:5
p of wheat or of some other grain. 1 Cor 15:37
and **p** I will stay with you or even 1 Cor 16:6
For I fear that **p** when I come I may 2 Cor 12:20
you wish—that **p** there may be 2 Cor 12:20
God may **p** grant them repentance 2 Tm 2:25
For this **p** is why he was parted from Phlm 1:15

PERIDA (1)
the sons of Sophereth, the sons of **P**, Neh 7:57

PERIL (3)
"At **p** to our heads he will desert to 1 Chr 12:19
We get our bread at the **p** of our lives, Lam 5:9
He delivered us from such a deadly **p**, 2 Cor 1:10

PERIOD (4)
during her menstrual **p** and uncovers Lv 20:18
But the previous **p** shall be void, Nm 6:12
was the regular **p** of their beautifying, Est 2:12
they asked him to stay for a longer **p**, Acts 18:20

PERIODS (5)
and let seven **p** of time pass over him. Dn 4:16
field, till seven **p** of time pass over him,' Dn 4:23
and seven **p** of time shall pass over you, Dn 4:25
and seven **p** of time shall pass over you, Dn 4:32
having determined allotted **p** and the Acts 17:26

PERISH (108)
land may not **p** through the famine." Gn 41:36
to the LORD to look and many of them **p**. Ex 19:21
And you shall **p** among the nations, Lv 26:38
of Israel said to Moses, "Behold, we **p**, Nm 17:12
of the LORD, shall die. Are we all to **p**?" Nm 17:13
you will soon utterly **p** from the land Dt 4:26
make their name **p** from under heaven. Dt 7:24
warn you today that you shall surely **p**. Dt 8:19
that the LORD makes to **p** before you, Dt 8:20
to perish before you, so shall you **p**, Dt 8:20
drive them out and make them **p** quickly, Dt 9:3
and you will **p** quickly off the good land Dt 11:17
are destroyed and **p** quickly on account Dt 28:20
They shall pursue you until you **p**. Dt 28:22
flock, until they have caused you to **p**. Dt 28:51
to you today, that you shall surely **p**. Dt 30:18
And he did not **p** alone for his Jos 22:20
until you **p** from off this good ground Jos 23:13
and you shall **p** quickly from off the Jos 23:16
"So may all your enemies **p**, O LORD! But Jgs 5:31
or he will go down into battle and **p**. 1 Sm 26:10
"Now I shall **p** one day by the hand of 1 Sm 27:1
For the whole house of Ahab shall **p**, 2 Kgs 9:8
but you and your father's house will **p**. Est 4:14
though it is against the law, and if I **p**, Est 4:16
it is against the law, and if I perish, I **p**." Est 4:16
"Let the day **p** on which I was born, and Jb 3:3
By the breath of God they **p**, and by the Jb 4:9
they **p** forever without anyone regarding Jb 4:20
course; they go up into the waste and **p**. Jb 6:18
forget God; the hope of the godless shall **p**. Jb 8:13
he will **p** forever like his own dung; those Jb 20:7
him who was about to **p** came upon me, Jb 29:13
I have seen anyone **p** for lack of Jb 31:19
all flesh would **p** together, and man Jb 34:15
they **p** by the sword and die without Jb 36:12
but the way of the wicked will **p**. Ps 1:6
lest he be angry, and you **p** in the way, Ps 2:12
they stumble and **p** before your presence. Ps 9:3
the nations; you have made the wicked **p**; Ps 9:5
the hope of the poor shall not **p** forever. Ps 9:18
and ever; the nations **p** from his land. Ps 10:16
But the wicked will **p**; the enemies of the Ps 37:20
"When will he die and his name **p**?" Ps 41:5
the stupid alike must **p** and leave their Ps 49:10
not remain; he is like the beasts that **p**. Ps 49:12
understanding is like the beasts that **p**. Ps 49:20
fire, so the wicked shall **p** before God! Ps 68:2
those who are far from you shall **p**; Ps 73:27
may they **p** at the rebuke of your face! Ps 80:16
forever; let them **p** in disgrace, Ps 83:17
O LORD, for behold, your enemies shall **p**; Ps 92:9
They will **p**, but you will remain; they Ps 102:26
away; the desire of the wicked will **p**! Ps 112:10
the earth; on that very day his plans **p**. Ps 146:4
the expectation of the wicked will **p**. Prv 10:28
When the wicked dies, his hope will **p**, Prv 11:7
when the wicked **p** there are shouts Prv 11:10
and he who breathes out lies will **p**. Prv 19:9
A false witness will **p**, but the word of a Prv 21:28
hide themselves, but when they **p**, Prv 28:28
the wisdom of their wise men shall **p**, Is 29:14
will fall, and they will all **p** together. Is 31:3
you shall be as nothing and shall **p**. Is 41:11
kingdom that will not serve you shall **p**; Is 60:12
together, neighbor and friend shall **p**.'" Jer 6:21
us go into the fortified cities and **p** there, Jer 8:14
has doomed us to **p** and has given us Jer 8:14
and the earth shall **p** from the earth Jer 10:11
time of their punishment they shall **p**. Jer 10:15
They shall **p** by the sword and by Jer 16:4
for the law shall not **p** from the priest, Jer 18:18
and I will drive you out, and you will **p**. Jer 27:10
that I will drive you out and you will **p**, Jer 27:15
and the remnant of Judah would **p**?" Jer 40:15
the valley shall **p**, and the plain shall be Jer 48:8
time of their punishment they shall **p**. Jer 51:18
feasted on delicacies **p** in the streets; Lam 4:5
it falls, you shall **p** in the midst of it, Ezk 13:14
and will make you **p** out of the Ezk 25:7
of Egypt, and all its multitude shall **p**. Ezk 32:12
Samaria's king shall **p** like a twig on Hos 10:7
of the Philistines shall **p**," says the Lord Am 1:8
Flight shall **p** from the swift, and the Am 2:14
house, and the houses of ivory shall **p**, Am 3:15
give a thought to us, that we may not **p**." Jon 1:6
"O LORD, let us not **p** for this man's life, Jon 1:14
his fierce anger, so that we may not **p**." Jon 3:9
The king shall **p** from Gaza; Ashkelon Zec 9:5
LORD, two thirds shall be cut off and **p**, Zec 13:8
that one of these little ones should **p**. Mt 18:14
who take the sword will **p** by the sword. Mt 26:52

you repent, you will all likewise **p**. Lk 13:3
you repent, you will all likewise **p**." Lk 13:5
a prophet should **p** away from Lk 13:33
bread, but I **p** here with hunger! Lk 15:17
But not a hair of your head will **p**. Lk 21:18
in him should not **p** but have eternal life. Jn 3:16
them eternal life, and they will never **p**, Jn 10:28
not that the whole nation should **p**." Jn 11:50
to him, "May your silver **p** with you, Acts 8:20
you scoffers, be astounded and **p**; Acts 13:41
not a hair is to **p** from the head of any Acts 27:34
the law will also **p** without the law, Rom 2:12
to things that all **p** as they are used) Col 2:22
they will **p**, but you remain; they will Heb 1:11
the prostitute did not **p** with those who Heb 11:31
you, not wishing that any should **p**, 2 Pt 3:9

PERISHABLE (7)
They do it to receive a **p** wreath, but 1 Cor 9:25
What is sown is **p**; what is raised is 1 Cor 15:42
nor does the **p** inherit the 1 Cor 15:50
For this **p** body must put on the 1 Cor 15:53
When the **p** puts on the 1 Cor 15:54
not with **p** things such as silver or gold, 1 Pt 1:18
not of **p** seed but of imperishable, 1 Pt 1:23

PERISHED (32)
and they **p** from the midst of the Nm 16:33
that we had **p** when our brothers Nm 20:3
when our brothers **p** before the LORD! Nm 20:3
congregation saw that Aaron had **p**, Nm 20:29
p; and we laid waste as far as Nophah; Nm 21:30
is, the men of war, had **p** from the camp, Dt 2:14
them from the camp, until they had **p**. Dt 2:15
the men of war had **p** and were dead from Dt 2:16
p, because they did not obey the voice of Jos 5:6
fallen, and the weapons of war **p**!" 2 Sm 1:27
and the seven of them **p** together. 2 Sm 21:9
of Israel who have already **p**. 2 Kgs 7:13
who that was innocent ever **p**? Jb 4:7
out; the very memory of them has **p**. Ps 9:6
I would have **p** in my affliction. Ps 119:92
their hate and their envy have already **p**, Eccl 9:6
did not accept discipline; truth has **p**; Jer 7:28
has come upon Gaza; Ashkelon has **p**. Jer 47:5
the riches they gained have **p**. Jer 48:36
Has counsel **p** from the prudent? Jer 49:7
my priests and elders **p** in the city, Lam 1:19
so I say, "My endurance has **p**; so has Lam 3:18
you and say to you, "'How you have **p**, Ezk 26:17
because the harvest of the field has **p**. Jl 1:11
into being in a night and **p** in a night. Jon 4:10
Has your counselor **p**, that pain seized Mi 4:9
The godly has **p** from the earth, and there Mi 7:2
who **p** between the altar and the Lk 11:51
He too **p**, and all who followed him Acts 5:37
have fallen asleep in Christ have **p**. 1 Cor 15:18
existed was deluged with water and **p**. 2 Pt 3:6
Balaam's error and **p** in Korah's Jude 1:11

PERISHES (9)
The strong lion **p** for lack of prey, and Jb 4:11
His memory **p** from the earth, and he Jb 18:17
and the expectation of wealth **p** too. Prv 11:7
righteous man who **p** in his Eccl 7:15
The righteous man **p**, and no one lays it Is 57:1
while the law **p** from the priest and Ezk 7:26
Do not labor for the food that **p**, but for Jn 6:27
grass; its flower falls, and its beauty **p**. Jas 1:11
precious than gold that **p** though it is 1 Pt 1:7

PERISHING (9)
the pit, his life from **p** by the sword. Jb 33:18
Give strong drink to the one who is **p**, Prv 31:6
him, saying, "Save us, Lord; we are **p**." Mt 8:25
do you not care that we are **p**?" Mk 4:38
we are **p**!" And he awoke and rebuked Lk 8:24
of the cross is folly to those who are **p**, 1 Cor 1:18
saved and among those who are **p**, 2 Cor 2:15
it is veiled only to those who are **p**. 2 Cor 4:3
deception for those who are **p**, 2 Thes 2:10

PERIZZITE (1)
the Hittite, the Amorite, the **P**, Neh 9:8

PERIZZITES (22)
Canaanites and the **P** were dwelling in Gn 13:7
the Hittites, the **P**, the Rephaim, Gn 15:20
of the land, the Canaanites and the **P**. Gn 34:30
the Hittites, the Amorites, the **P**, Ex 3:8
the Hittites, the Amorites, the **P**, Ex 3:17
Hittites and the **P** and the Canaanites, Ex 23:23
the Amorites, the Hittites, the **P**, Ex 33:2
the Canaanites, the Hittites, the **P**, Ex 34:11
the Amorites, the Canaanites, the **P**, Dt 7:1
the Amorites, the Canaanites and the **P**, Dt 20:17
the Hittites, the Hivites, the **P**, Jos 3:10
the Amorites, the Canaanites, the **P**, Jos 9:1
the west, the Amorites, the Hittites, the **P**, Jos 11:3
the Amorites, the Canaanites, the **P**, Jos 12:8
in the land of the **P** and the Rephaim, Jos 17:15
you, and also the Amorites, the **P**, Jos 24:11
the Canaanites and the **P** into their hand, Jgs 1:4
and defeated the Canaanites and the **P**. Jgs 1:5
the Hittites, the Amorites, the **P**, Jgs 3:5
left of the Amorites, the Hittites, the **P**, 1 Kgs 9:20
left of the Hittites, the Amorites, the **P**, 2 Chr 8:7
from the Canaanites, the Hittites, the **P**, Ezr 9:1

PERJURERS (1)
p, and whatever else is contrary to 1 Tm 1:10

PERMANENT (1)
much more will what is **p** have glory. 2 Cor 3:11

PERMANENTLY (2)
you, or anyone is living **p** among you, Nm 15:14
but he holds his priesthood **p**, because Heb 7:24

PERMISSION (5)
So he gave them **p**. And the unclean Mk 5:13
let them enter these. So he gave them **p**. Lk 8:32
the body of Jesus, and Pilate gave him **p**. Jn 19:38
And when he had given him **p**, Paul, Acts 21:40
"You have **p** to speak for yourself." Acts 26:1

PERMIT (14)
But God did not **p** him to harm me. Gn 31:7
And why did you not **p** me to kiss my Gn 31:28
"You shall not **p** a sorceress to live. Ex 22:18
where you shall **p** the manslayer to flee, Nm 35:6
words and did not **p** them to attack 1 Sm 24:7
that he might **p** no one to go out or 1 Kgs 15:17
that he might **p** no one to go out or 2 Chr 16:1
he will never **p** the righteous to be Ps 55:22
Their deeds do not **p** them to return to Hos 5:4
And he would not **p** the demons to Mk 1:34
And he did not **p** him but said to him, Mk 5:19
then you no longer **p** him to do Mk 7:12
beg you, **p** me to speak to the people." Acts 21:39
I do not **p** a woman to teach or to 1 Tm 2:12

PERMITS (2)
some time with you, if the Lord **p**. 1 Cor 16:7
And this we will do if God **p**. Heb 6:3

PERMITTED (2)
For they are not **p** to speak, but 1 Cor 14:34
Its rider was **p** to take peace from the Rv 6:4

PERPETUAL (23)
and his sons as a **p** due from the people Ex 29:28
them to a **p** priesthood throughout Ex 40:15
sons, as a **p** due from the people of Israel. Lv 7:34
It is a **p** due throughout their Lv 7:36
out of the LORD'S food offerings, a **p** due." Lv 24:9
to you for a **p** statute throughout your Nm 10:8
a portion and to your sons as a **p** due. Nm 18:8
and daughters with you, as a **p** due. Nm 18:11
and daughters with you, as a **p** due. Nm 18:19
It shall be a **p** statute throughout your Nm 18:23
this shall be a **p** statute for the people Nm 19:10
him the covenant of a **p** priesthood, Nm 25:13
Direct your steps to the **p** ruins; the Ps 74:3
the sea, a **p** barrier that it cannot pass; Jer 5:22
this people turned away in **p** backsliding? Jer 8:5
you everlasting reproach and **p** shame, Jer 23:40
and all her cities shall be **p** wastes." Jer 49:13
foundation, but you shall be a **p** waste, Jer 51:26
then sleep a **p** sleep and not wake, Jer 51:39
they shall sleep a **p** sleep and not wake, Jer 51:57
Because you cherished **p** enmity and Ezk 35:5
I will make you a **p** desolation, and Ezk 35:9
offering to the LORD. This is a **p** statute. Ezk 46:14

PERPETUALLY (1)
cast off all pity, and his anger tore **p**, Am 1:11

PERPETUATE (3)
brother refuses to **p** his brother's name Dt 25:7
in order to **p** the name of the dead in his Ru 4:5
to **p** the name of the dead in his Ru 4:10

PERPETUATED (1)
you: "No more shall your name be **p**; Na 1:14

PERPETUITY (2)
"The land shall not be sold in **p**, for the Lv 25:23
city shall belong in **p** to the buyer, Lv 25:30

PERPLEXED (10)
his color changed, and his lords were **p**. Dn 5:9
herds of cattle are **p** because there is no Jl 1:18
When he heard him, he was greatly **p**, Mk 6:20
all that was happening, and he was **p**, Lk 9:7
While they were **p** about this, behold, Lk 24:4
And all were amazed and **p**, saying to Acts 2:12
words, they were greatly **p** about them, Acts 5:24
while Peter was inwardly **p** as to what Acts 10:17
crushed; **p**, but not driven to despair; 2 Cor 4:8
change my tone, for I am **p** about you. Gal 4:20

PERPLEXITY (1)
distress of nations in **p** because of the Lk 21:25

PERSECUTE (17)
with the might of your hand you **p** me. Jb 30:21
For they **p** him whom you have struck Ps 69:26
When will you judge those who **p** me? Ps 119:84
are sure; they **p** me with falsehood; Ps 119:86
They draw near who **p** me with evil Ps 119:150
Princes **p** me without cause, but my Ps 119:161
Let those be put to shame who **p** me, Jer 17:18
others revile you and **p** you and utter all Mt 5:11
enemies and pray for those who **p** you, Mt 5:44
When they **p** you in one town, flee to Mt 10:23
in your synagogues and **p** from town to Mt 23:34
some of whom they will kill and **p**,' Lk 11:49
will lay their hands on you and **p** you, Lk 21:12
they persecuted me, they will also **p** you. Jn 15:20
of the prophets did not your fathers **p**? Acts 7:52
Bless those who **p** you; bless and do Rom 12:14
"He who used to **p** us is now preaching Gal 1:23

PERSECUTED (14)
on your foes and enemies who **p** you. Dt 30:7
those who are **p** for righteousness' sake, Mt 5:10
for so they **p** the prophets who were Mt 5:12
If they **p** me, they will also persecute Jn 15:20
I **p** this Way to the death, binding and Acts 22:4
fury against them I **p** them even to Acts 26:11
When reviled, we bless; when **p**, we 1 Cor 4:12
because I **p** the church of God. 1 Cor 15:9
p, but not forsaken; struck down, but 2 Cor 4:9
how I **p** the church of God violently and Gal 1:13
according to the flesh **p** him who was Gal 4:29
circumcision, why am I still being **p**? Gal 5:11
that they may not be **p** for the cross of Gal 6:12
a godly life in Christ Jesus will be **p**, 2 Tm 3:12

PERSECUTING (7)
And this was why the Jews were **p** Jesus, Jn 5:16
to him, "Saul, Saul, why are you **p** me?" Acts 9:4
he said, "I am Jesus, whom you are **p**. Acts 9:5
to me, 'Saul, Saul, why are you **p** me?' Acts 22:7
Jesus of Nazareth, whom you are **p**.' Acts 22:8
'Saul, Saul, why are you **p** me? Acts 26:14
said, 'I am Jesus whom you are **p**. Acts 26:15

PERSECUTION (7)
the nations in anger with unrelenting **p**. Is 14:6
when tribulation or **p** arises on Mt 13:21
when tribulation or **p** arises on Mk 4:17
that day a great **p** against the church in Acts 8:1
because of the **p** that arose over Acts 11:19
stirred up **p** against Paul and Acts 13:50
Shall tribulation, or distress, or **p**, or Rom 8:35

PERSECUTIONS (5)
and children and lands, with **p**, Mk 10:30
hardships, **p**, and calamities. 2 Cor 12:10
faith in all your **p** and in the 2 Thes 1:4
my **p** and sufferings that happened to 2 Tm 3:11
and at Lystra—which **p** I endured; 2 Tm 3:11

PERSECUTOR (2)
as to zeal, a **p** of the church; as to Phil 3:6
p, and insolent opponent. 1 Tm 1:13

PERSECUTORS (5)
hand of my enemies and from my **p**! Ps 31:15
Many are my **p** and my adversaries, Ps 119:157
Deliver me from my **p**, for they are too Ps 142:6
and take vengeance for me on my **p**. Jer 15:15
warrior; therefore my **p** will stumble; Jer 20:11

PERSEVERANCE (1)
To that end keep alert with all **p**, Eph 6:18

PERSEVERED (1)
I also **p** in the work on this wall, and Neh 5:16

PERSEVERES (1)
the perfect law, the law of liberty, and **p**, Jas 1:25

PERSIA (29)
establishment of the kingdom of **P**, 2 Chr 36:20
in the first year of Cyrus king of **P**, 2 Chr 36:22
up the spirit of Cyrus king of **P**, 2 Chr 36:22
"Thus says Cyrus king of **P**, 'The 2 Chr 36:23
In the first year of Cyrus king of **P**, that Ezr 1:1
stirred up the spirit of Cyrus king of **P**, Ezr 1:1
"Thus says Cyrus king of **P**: The LORD, Ezr 1:2
Cyrus king of **P** brought these out in Ezr 1:8
that they had from Cyrus king of **P**. Ezr 3:7
Cyrus the king of **P** has commanded us." Ezr 4:3
purpose, all the days of Cyrus king of **P**, Ezr 4:5
even until the reign of Darius king of **P**. Ezr 4:5
associates wrote to Artaxerxes king of **P**. Ezr 4:7
year of the reign of Darius king of **P**. Ezr 4:24
and Darius and Artaxerxes king of **P**; Ezr 6:14
this, in the reign of Artaxerxes king of **P**, Ezr 7:1

us his steadfast love before the kings of **P**, Ezr 9:9
The army of **P** and Media and the nobles Est 1:3
the seven princes of **P** and Media, Est 1:14
the noble women of **P** and Media who Est 1:18
Chronicles of the kings of Media and **P**? Est 10:2
"**P** and Lud and Put were in your Ezk 27:10
P, Cush, and Put are with them, all of Ezk 38:5
these are the kings of Media and **P**. Dn 8:20
of Cyrus king of **P** a word was revealed Dn 10:1
the kingdom of **P** withstood me Dn 10:13
for I was left there with the kings of **P**, Dn 10:13
return to fight against the prince of **P**; Dn 10:20
three more kings shall arise in **P**, Dn 11:2

PERSIAN (2)
priests in the reign of Darius the **P**. Neh 12:22
of Darius and the reign of Cyrus the **P**. Dn 6:28

PERSIANS (6)
judges, the governors, the officials, the **P**, Ezr 4:9
the laws of the **P** and the Medes so Est 1:19
is divided and given to the Medes and **P**." Dn 5:28
to the law of the Medes and the **P**, Dn 6:8
according to the law of the Medes and **P**, Dn 6:12
of the Medes and **P** that no injunction Dn 6:15

PERSIS (1)
Greet the beloved **P**, who has worked Rom 16:12

PERSIST (2)
P in this, for by so doing you will 1 Tm 4:16
As for those who **p** in sin, rebuke 1 Tm 5:20

PERSISTED (3)
but the Canaanites **p** in dwelling in Jos 17:12
for the Canaanites **p** in dwelling in that Jgs 1:27
The Amorites **p** in dwelling in Mount Jgs 1:35

PERSISTENT (3)
skin, the disease is a **p** leprous disease; Lv 13:51
is diseased, for it is a **p** leprous disease. Lv 13:52
it is a **p** leprous disease in the house; Lv 14:44

PERSISTENTLY (11)
sent **p** to them by his messengers, 2 Chr 36:15
when I spoke to you **p** you did not listen, Jer 7:13
I have **p** sent all my servants the Jer 7:25
out of the land of Egypt, warning them **p**, Jer 11:7
come to me, and I have spoken **p** to you, Jer 25:3
although the LORD **p** sent to you all his Jer 25:4
that I **p** sent to you by my servants the Jer 29:19
And though I have taught them **p**, they Jer 32:33
I have spoken to you **p**, but you have Jer 35:14
servants the prophets, sending them **p**, Jer 35:15
Yet I **p** sent to you all my servants the Jer 44:4

PERSISTS (1)
call him and speak to him, and if he **p**, Dt 25:8

PERSON (168)
day, that **p** shall be cut off from Israel. Ex 12:15
that **p** will be cut off from the Ex 12:19
But no uncircumcised **p** shall eat of it. Ex 12:48
and I decide between one **p** and another, Ex 18:16
be poured on the body of an ordinary **p**, Ex 30:32
but the **p** who eats of the flesh of the Lv 7:20
that **p** shall be cut off from his people. Lv 7:20
that **p** shall be cut off from his people." Lv 7:21
For every **p** who eats of the fat of an Lv 7:25
that **p** shall be cut off from his people." Lv 7:27
"When a **p** has on the skin of his body a Lv 13:2
shut up the diseased **p** for seven days. Lv 13:4
skin of the diseased **p** from head to foot, Lv 13:12
shall pronounce the diseased **p** clean; Lv 13:17
shall shut up the **p** with the itching Lv 13:31
shall shut up the **p** with the itching Lv 13:33
"The leprous **p** who has the disease Lv 13:45
the law of the leprous **p** for the day of his Lv 14:2
leprous disease is healed in the leprous **p**, Lv 14:3
my face against that **p** who eats blood Lv 17:10
Israel, No **p** among you shall eat blood, Lv 17:12
And every **p** who eats what dies of itself Lv 17:15
statutes and my rules; if a **p** does them, Lv 18:5
and that **p** shall be cut off from his Lv 19:8
"If a **p** turns to mediums and wizards, Lv 20:6
my face against that **p** and will cut him Lv 20:6
that **p** shall be cut off from my presence: Lv 22:3
made unclean or a **p** from whom he Lv 22:5
the **p** who touches such a thing shall be Lv 22:6
"A lay **p** shall not eat of a holy thing; no Lv 22:10
father's food; yet no lay **p** shall eat of it. Lv 22:13
that **p** I will destroy from among his Lv 23:30
he has given a **p** shall be given to Lv 24:20
and whoever kills a **p** shall be put to Lv 24:21
If the **p** is a female, the valuation shall be Lv 27:4
If the **p** is from five years old up to twenty Lv 27:5
If the **p** is from a month old up to five Lv 27:6
And if the **p** is sixty years old or over, Lv 27:7
the LORD, and that **p** realizes his guilt, Nm 5:6
that **p** shall be cut off from his people Nm 9:13
"If one **p** sins unintentionally, he Nm 15:27
the LORD for the **p** who makes a Nm 15:28
But the **p** who does anything with a Nm 15:30
and that **p** shall be cut off from Nm 15:30
that **p** shall be utterly cut off; Nm 15:31
dead body of any **p** shall be unclean Nm 19:11
Whoever touches a dead **p**, the body Nm 19:13
and that **p** shall be cut off from Israel; Nm 19:13
Then a clean **p** shall take hyssop and Nm 19:18
And the clean **p** shall sprinkle it on Nm 19:19
that **p** shall be cut off from the midst Nm 19:20
whatever the unclean **p** touches shall Nm 19:22
you has killed any **p** and whoever has Nm 31:19
who kills any **p** without intent may Nm 35:11
who kills any **p** without intent may Nm 35:15
"If anyone kills a **p**, the murderer Nm 35:30
But no **p** shall be put to death on the Nm 35:30
a **p** shall not be put to death on the Dt 17:6
not suffice against a **p** for any crime or Dt 19:15
arises to accuse a **p** of wrongdoing, Dt 19:16
He devoted to destruction every **p** in it; Jos 10:28
the edge of the sword, and every **p** in it; Jos 10:30
the edge of the sword, and every **p** in it, Jos 10:32
And he devoted every **p** in it to Jos 10:35
its king and its towns, and every **p** in it. Jos 10:37
it to destruction and every **p** in it. Jos 10:37
and devoted to destruction every **p** in it; Jos 10:39
who strikes any **p** without intent or Jos 20:3
who killed a **p** without intent could Jos 20:9
and that you go to battle in **p**. 2 Sm 17:11
your rules, which if a **p** does them, Neh 9:29
to any man or use flattery toward any **p**. Jb 32:21
in whose eyes a vile **p** is despised, but Ps 15:4
for the devious **p** is an abomination to Prv 3:32
A worthless **p**, a wicked man, goes Prv 6:12
an evil **p** will not go unpunished, Prv 11:21
Better is a poor **p** who walks in his Prv 19:1
sleep, and an idle **p** will suffer hunger. Prv 19:15
The wise **p** has his eyes in his head, Eccl 2:14
because sometimes a **p** who has toiled Eccl 2:21
nothing better for a **p** than that he Eccl 2:24
one **p** who has no other, either son or Eccl 4:8
So if a **p** lives many years, let him Eccl 11:8
I choose, a day for a **p** to humble himself? Is 58:5
and every **p** whom Nebuzaradan the Jer 43:6
that wicked **p** shall die for his iniquity, Ezk 3:18
if a righteous **p** turns from his Ezk 3:20
if you warn the righteous **p** not to sin, Ezk 3:21
"But if a wicked **p** turns away from all Ezk 18:21
when a righteous **p** turns away from Ezk 18:24
abominations that the wicked **p** does, Ezk 18:24
When a righteous **p** turns away from Ezk 18:26
when a wicked **p** turns away from the Ezk 18:27
my rules, by which, if a **p** does them, Ezk 20:11
my rules, by which, if a **p** does them, Ezk 20:13
my rules, by which, if a **p** does them, Ezk 20:21
that **p** is taken away in his iniquity, Ezk 33:6
that wicked **p** shall die in his iniquity, Ezk 33:8
his way, that **p** shall die in his iniquity, Ezk 33:9
themselves by going near to a dead **p**. Ezk 44:25
arise a contemptible **p** to whom royal Dn 11:21
receives a righteous **p** because he is Mt 10:41
he is a righteous **p** will receive a Mt 10:41
The good **p** out of his good treasure Mt 12:35
and the evil **p** out of his evil treasure Mt 12:35
the unclean spirit has gone out of a **p**, Mt 12:43
the last state of that **p** is worse than the Mt 12:45
goes into the mouth that defiles a **p**, Mt 15:11
out of the mouth; this defiles a **p**." Mt 15:11
from the heart, and this defiles a **p**. Mt 15:18
These are what defile a **p**. But to eat Mt 15:20
he will repay each **p** according to what Mt 16:27
will a rich **p** enter the kingdom Mt 19:23
than for a rich **p** to enter the kingdom Mt 19:24
is nothing outside a **p** that by going Mk 7:15
come out of a **p** are what defile him." Mk 7:15
goes into a **p** from outside cannot Mk 7:18
comes out of a **p** is what defiles him. Mk 7:20
come from within, and they defile a **p**." Mk 7:23
than for a rich **p** to enter the kingdom Mk 10:25
The good **p** out of the good treasure of Lk 6:45
and the evil **p** out of his evil treasure Lk 6:45
the unclean spirit has gone out of a **p**, Lk 11:24
the last state of that **p** is worse than the Lk 11:26
say to you, 'Give your place to this **p**,' Lk 14:9
than for a rich **p** to enter the kingdom Lk 18:25
"A **p** cannot receive even one thing Jn 3:27
There was not a needy **p** among them, Acts 4:34
not call any **p** common or unclean. Acts 10:28
die for a righteous **p**—though perhaps Rom 5:7
perhaps for a good **p** one would dare Rom 5:7
law is binding on a **p** only as long as he Rom 7:1
the **p** who does the commandments Rom 10:5
Let every **p** be subject to the governing Rom 13:1
One **p** believes he may eat anything, Rom 14:2
while the weak **p** eats only vegetables. Rom 14:2
One **p** esteems one day as better than Rom 14:5
thoughts except the spirit of that **p**, 1 Cor 2:11
The natural **p** does not accept the 1 Cor 2:14
The spiritual **p** judges all things, but 1 Cor 2:15
"Purge the evil **p** from among you." 1 Cor 5:13
other sin a **p** commits is outside 1 Cor 6:18
the sexually immoral **p** sins against 1 Cor 6:18
Only let each **p** lead the life that the 1 Cor 7:17
it is good for a **p** to remain as he is. 1 Cor 7:26
knowledge this weak **p** is destroyed, 1 Cor 8:11
Let a **p** examine himself, then, and 1 Cor 11:28
but the other **p** is not being built up. 1 Cor 14:17
You foolish **p**! What you sow does 1 Cor 15:36
acceptable according to what a **p** has, 2 Cor 8:12
Let such a **p** understand that what 2 Cor 10:11
was still unknown in **p** to the churches Gal 1:22
yet we know that a **p** is not justified by Gal 2:16
know how you ought to answer each **p**. Col 4:6
for a short time, in **p** not in heart, 1 Thes 2:17
say in this letter, take note of that **p**, 2 Thes 3:14
As for a **p** who stirs up division, after Ti 3:10
knowing that such a **p** is warped and Ti 3:11
For that **p** must not suppose that he will Jas 1:7
But each **p** is tempted when he is lured Jas 1:14
let every **p** be quick to hear, slow to Jas 1:19
Do you want to be shown, you foolish **p**, Jas 2:20
You see that a **p** is justified by works Jas 2:24
you have murdered the righteous **p**. Jas 5:6
prayer of a righteous **p** has great power Jas 5:16
inquiring what **p** or time the Spirit of 1 Pt 1:11
adorning be the hidden **p** of the heart 1 Pt 3:4
For whatever overcomes a **p**, to that he 2 Pt 2:19

PERSON'S (4)
And a **p** enemies will be those of his Mt 10:36
will receive a righteous **p** reward. Mt 10:41
who knows a **p** thoughts except the 1 Cor 2:11
his heart, this **p** religion is worthless. Jas 1:26

PERSONS (44)
Sodom said to Abram, "Give me the **p**, Gn 14:21
and these she bore to Jacob—sixteen **p**. Gn 46:18
were born to Jacob—fourteen **p** in all. Gn 46:22
these she bore to Jacob—seven **p** in all. Gn 46:25
All the **p** belonging to Jacob who came Gn 46:26
sons' wives, were sixty-six **p** in all. Gn 46:26
All the **p** of the house of Jacob who Gn 46:27
the descendants of Jacob were seventy **p**; Ex 1:5
shall take according to the number of **p**; Ex 12:4
to the number of the **p** that each of you Ex 16:16
the **p** who do them shall be cut off from Lv 18:29
to the LORD involving the valuation of **p**, Lv 27:2
and on the **p** who were there Nm 19:18
and 32,000 **p** in all, women who had Nm 31:35
The **p** were 16,000, of which the LORD'S Nm 31:40
of which the LORD'S tribute was 32 **p**. Nm 31:40
and 16,000 **p**— Nm 31:46
of every 50, both of **p** and of beasts, Nm 31:47
fathers went down to Egypt seventy **p**, Dt 10:22
been invited, who were about thirty **p**. 1 Sm 9:22
that day eighty-five **p** who wore the 1 Sm 22:18
death of all the **p** of your father's 1 Sm 22:22
time." Now the king's sons, seventy **p**, 2 Kgs 10:6
sons and slaughtered them, seventy **p**, 2 Kgs 10:7
at the pit of Beth-eked, forty-two **p**, 2 Kgs 10:14
from the assessment of **p**—and the 2 Kgs 12:4
away captive from Jerusalem 832 **p**; Jer 52:29
away captive of the Judeans 745 **p**; Jer 52:30
745 persons; all the **p** were 4,600. Jer 52:30
veils for the heads of **p** of every stature, Ezk 13:18
are more than 120,000 **p** who do not Jon 4:11
over ninety-nine righteous **p** who need Lk 15:7
brothers (the company of **p** was in all Acts 1:15
all his kindred, seventy-five **p** in all. Acts 7:14
went in and found many **p** gathered. Acts 10:27
have heard that some **p** have gone out Acts 15:24
with the Jews and the devout **p**, Acts 17:17
(We were in all 276 **p** in the ship.) Acts 27:37
For such **p** do not serve our Lord Rom 16:18
Now such **p** we command and 2 Thes 3:12
you may charge certain **p** not to teach 1 Tm 1:3
Certain **p**, by swerving from these, 1 Tm 1:6
sprinkling of defiled **p** with the blood Heb 9:13
in which a few, that is, eight **p**, 1 Pt 3:20

PERSUADE (4)
the people came to **p** David to eat 2 Sm 3:35
and tried to **p** Jews and Greeks. Acts 18:4
a short time would you **p** me to be a Acts 26:28
the fear of the Lord, we **p** others. 2 Cor 5:11

PERSUADED (11)
So David **p** his men with these words 1 Sm 24:7
With patience a ruler may be **p**, and a Prv 25:15
priests and the elders **p** the crowd to ask Mt 27:20
one accord, and having **p** Blastus, Acts 12:20

Iconium, and having **p** the crowds, Acts 14:19
some of them were **p** and joined Paul Acts 17:4
Asia this Paul has **p** and turned away Acts 19:26
And since he would not be **p**, we Acts 21:14
But do not be **p** by them, for more Acts 23:21
For I am **p** that none of these things Acts 26:26
I know and am **p** in the Lord Jesus Rom 14:14

PERSUADES (1)
much seductive speech she **p** him; Prv 7:21

PERSUADING (2)
"This man is **p** people to worship God Acts 18:13
reasoning and **p** them about the Acts 19:8

PERSUASION (1)
This **p** is not from him who calls you. Gal 5:8

PERSUASIVENESS (2)
and sweetness of speech increases **p**. Prv 16:21
speech judicious and adds **p** to his lips. Prv 16:23

PERTAIN (1)
us all things that **p** to life and godliness, 2 Pt 1:3

PERTAINING (2)
Manassites for everything **p** to God 1 Chr 26:32
more, then, matters **p** to this life! 1 Cor 6:3

PERUDA (1)
the sons of Hassophereth, the sons of **P**, Ezr 2:55

PERVERSE (8)
you because your way is **p** before me. Nm 22:32
end will be, For they are a **p** generation, Dt 32:20
and he said to him, "You son of a **p**, 1 Sm 20:30
I am blameless, he would prove me **p**. Jb 9:20
A **p** heart shall be far from me; I will Ps 101:4
but the **p** tongue will be cut off. Prv 10:31
the mouth of the wicked, what is **p**. Prv 10:32
things, and your heart utter **p** things. Prv 23:33

PERVERSELY (2)
and have acted **p** and wickedly,' 1 Kgs 8:47
and have acted **p** and wickedly,' 2 Chr 6:37

PERVERSENESS (3)
in doing evil and delight in the **p** of evil, Prv 2:14
a tree of life, but **p** in it breaks the spirit. Prv 15:4
trust in oppression and **p** and rely on Is 30:12

PERVERSION (2)
herself to an animal to lie with it: it is **p**. Lv 18:23
be put to death; they have committed **p**; Lv 20:12

PERVERT (11)
siding with the many, so as to **p** justice, Ex 23:2
"You shall not **p** the justice due to your Ex 23:6
You shall not **p** justice. You shall not Dt 16:19
"You shall not **p** the justice due to the Dt 24:17
Does God **p** justice? Or does the Almighty Jb 8:3
justice? Or does the Almighty **p** the right? Jb 8:3
and the Almighty will not **p** justice. Jb 34:12
bribe in secret to **p** the ways of justice. Prv 17:23
has been decreed and **p** the rights of all Prv 31:5
and you **p** the words of the living God, Jer 23:36
who **p** the grace of our God into Jude 1:4

PERVERTED (7)
gain. They took bribes and **p** justice. 1 Sm 8:3
and says: 'I sinned and **p** what was right, Jb 33:27
the way of evil, from men of **p** speech, Prv 2:12
with **p** heart devises evil, continually Prv 6:14
and the way of evil and **p** speech I hate. Prv 8:13
sons because they have **p** their way; Jer 3:21
the righteous; so justice goes forth **p**. Hab 1:4

PERVERTS (1)
be anyone who **p** the justice due Dt 27:19

PESTILENCE (54)
he fall upon us with **p** or with the sword." Ex 5:3
and struck you and your people with **p**, Ex 9:15
your cities, I will send **p** among you, Lv 26:25
them with the **p** and disinherit them, Nm 14:12
LORD will make the **p** stick to you until Dt 28:21
devoured by plague and poisonous **p**; Dt 32:24
there be three days' **p** in your land? 2 Sm 24:13
the LORD sent a **p** on Israel from the 2 Sm 24:15
if there is **p** or blight or mildew or 1 Kgs 8:37
the sword of the LORD, **p** on the land, 1 Chr 21:12
So the LORD sent a **p** on Israel, and 1 Chr 21:14
if there is **p** or blight or mildew or 2 Chr 6:28
the land, or send **p** among my people, 2 Chr 7:13
upon us, the sword, judgment, or **p**, 2 Chr 20:9
Those who survive him the **p** buries, Jb 27:15
snare of the fowler and from the deadly **p**. Ps 91:3
nor the **p** that stalks in darkness, nor the Ps 91:6
by the sword, by famine, and by **p**." Jer 14:12
"'Those who are for **p**, to pestilence, and Jer 15:2
"Those who are for pestilence, to **p**, and Jer 15:2
May their men meet death by **p**, their Jer 18:21
and beast. They shall die of a great **p**. Jer 21:6
the people in this city who survive the **p**, Jer 21:7
die by the sword, by famine, and by **p**, Jer 21:9
send sword, famine, and **p** upon them, Jer 24:10
with the sword, with famine, and with **p**, Jer 27:8
die by the sword, by famine, and by **p**, Jer 27:13
and **p** against many countries and great Jer 28:8
sending on them sword, famine, and **p**, Jer 29:17
pursue them with sword, famine, and **p**, Jer 29:18
sword and famine and **p** the city is Jer 32:24
by sword, by famine, and by **p**': Jer 32:36
to you liberty to the sword, to **p**, Jer 34:17
die by the sword, by famine, and by **p**, Jer 38:2
die by the sword, by famine, and by **p**. Jer 42:17
and by **p** in the place where you desire Jer 42:22
giving over to the **p** those who are Jer 43:11
those who are doomed to the **p**, Jer 43:11
the sword, with famine, and with **p**, Jer 44:13
you shall die of **p** and be consumed Ezk 5:12
P and blood shall pass through you, Ezk 5:17
fall by the sword, by famine, and by **p**. Ezk 6:11
He who is far off shall die of **p**, and he Ezk 6:12
is without; **p** and famine are within. Ezk 7:15
who is in the city famine and **p** devour. Ezk 7:15
from the sword, from famine and **p**, Ezk 12:16
"Or if I send a **p** into that land and Ezk 14:19
sword, famine, wild beasts, and **p**, Ezk 14:21
for I will send **p** into her, and blood Ezk 28:23
and in caves shall die by **p**. Ezk 33:27
With **p** and bloodshed I will enter into Ezk 38:22
sent among you a **p** after the manner of Am 4:10
Before him went **p**, and plague followed Hab 3:5
with famine and with **p** and by wild Rv 6:8

PESTILENCES (1)
and in various places famines and **p**. Lk 21:11

PESTLE (1)
a mortar with a **p** along with crushed Prv 27:22

PETER (152)
Simon (who is called **P**) and Andrew his Mt 4:18
first, Simon, who is called **P**, and Mt 10:2
And **P** answered him, "Lord, if it is you, Mt 14:28
"Come." So **P** got out of the boat and Mt 14:29
But **P** said to him, "Explain the parable Mt 15:15
Simon **P** replied, "You are the Christ, Mt 16:16
And I tell you, you are **P**, and on this Mt 16:18
And **P** took him aside and began to Mt 16:22
But he turned and said to **P**, "Get Mt 16:23
days Jesus took with him **P** and James, Mt 17:1
And **P** said to Jesus, "Lord, it is good that Mt 17:4
half-shekel tax went up to **P** and said, Mt 17:24
Then **P** came up and said to him, Mt 18:21
Then **P** said in reply, "See, we have left Mt 19:27
P answered him, "Though they all fall Mt 26:33
P said to him, "Even if I must die with Mt 26:35
And taking with him **P** and the two Mt 26:37
And he said to **P**, "So, could you not Mt 26:40
And **P** was following him at a distance, Mt 26:58
Now **P** was sitting outside in the Mt 26:69
the bystanders came up and said to **P**, Mt 26:73
And **P** remembered the saying of Jesus, Mt 26:75
Simon (to whom he gave the name **P**); Mk 3:16
to follow him except **P** and James and Mk 5:37
do you say that I am?" **P** answered him, Mk 8:29
And **P** took him aside and began to Mk 8:32
his disciples, he rebuked **P** and said, Mk 8:33
Jesus took with him **P** and James and Mk 9:2
And **P** said to Jesus, "Rabbi, it is good Mk 9:5
P began to say to him, "See, we have Mk 10:28
And **P** remembered and said to him, Mk 11:21
P and James and John and Andrew Mk 13:3
P said to him, "Even though they all Mk 14:29
he took with him **P** and James and Mk 14:33
found them sleeping, and he said to **P**, Mk 14:37
And **P** had followed him at a distance, Mk 14:54
And as **P** was below in the courtyard, Mk 14:66
and seeing **P** warming himself, she Mk 14:67
while the bystanders again said to **P**, Mk 14:70
And **P** remembered how Jesus had Mk 14:72
tell his disciples and **P** that he is going Mk 16:7
But when Simon **P** saw it, he fell down at Lk 5:8
Simon, whom he named **P**, and Andrew Lk 6:14
touched me?" When all denied it, **P** said, Lk 8:45
with him, except **P** and John and James, Lk 8:51
do you say that I am?" And **P** answered, Lk 9:20
he took with him **P** and John and James Lk 9:28
Now **P** and those who were with him Lk 9:32
were parting from him, **P** said to Jesus, Lk 9:33
P said, "Lord, are you telling this Lk 12:41
And **P** said, "See, we have left our Lk 18:28
So Jesus sent **P** and John, saying, "Go Lk 22:8
P said to him, "Lord, I am ready to go Lk 22:33
P, the rooster will not crow this day, Lk 22:34
and **P** was following at a distance. Lk 22:54
together, **P** sat down among them. Lk 22:55
"You also are one of them." But **P** said, Lk 22:58
But **P** said, "Man, I do not know what Lk 22:60
And the Lord turned and looked at **P**. Lk 22:61
And **P** remembered the saying of the Lk 22:61
But **P** rose and ran to the tomb; Lk 24:12
be called Cephas" (which means **P**). Jn 1:42
Bethsaida, the city of Andrew and **P**. Jn 1:44
Simon **P** answered him, "Lord, to whom Jn 6:68
He came to Simon **P**, who said to him, Jn 13:6
P said to him, "You shall never wash my Jn 13:8
Simon **P** said to him, "Lord, not my feet Jn 13:9
so Simon **P** motioned to him to ask Jn 13:24
Simon **P** said to him, "Lord, where are Jn 13:36
P said to him, "Lord, why can I not Jn 13:37
Then Simon **P**, having a sword, drew it Jn 18:10
So Jesus said to **P**, "Put your sword into Jn 18:11
Simon **P** followed Jesus, and so did Jn 18:15
but **P** stood outside at the door. So the Jn 18:16
watch at the door, and brought **P** in. Jn 18:16
The servant girl at the door said to **P**, Jn 18:17
P also was with them, standing and Jn 18:18
Now Simon **P** was standing and Jn 18:25
of the man whose ear **P** had cut off, Jn 18:26
P again denied it, and at once a rooster Jn 18:27
and went to Simon **P** and the other Jn 20:2
So **P** went out with the other disciple, and Jn 20:3
other disciple outran **P** and reached the Jn 20:4
Then Simon **P** came, following him, and Jn 20:6
Simon **P**, Thomas (called the Twin), Jn 21:2
Simon **P** said to them, "I am going Jn 21:3
whom Jesus loved therefore said to **P**, Jn 21:7
the Lord!" When Simon **P** heard that it Jn 21:7
So Simon **P** went aboard and hauled the Jn 21:11
breakfast, Jesus said to Simon **P**, Jn 21:15
do you love me?" **P** was grieved because Jn 21:17
P turned and saw the disciple whom Jn 21:20
When **P** saw him, he said to Jesus, Jn 21:21
P and John and James and Andrew, Acts 1:13
In those days **P** stood up among the Acts 1:15
But **P**, standing with the eleven, lifted Acts 2:14
and said to **P** and the rest of the Acts 2:37
And **P** said to them, "Repent and be Acts 2:38
Now **P** and John were going up to the Acts 3:1
Seeing **P** and John about to go into the Acts 3:3
And **P** directed his gaze at him, as did Acts 3:4
But **P** said, "I have no silver and gold, Acts 3:6
While he clung to **P** and John, all the Acts 3:11
And when **P** saw it he addressed the Acts 3:12
Then **P**, filled with the Holy Spirit, said Acts 4:8
they saw the boldness of **P** and John, Acts 4:13
But **P** and John answered them, Acts 4:19
But **P** said, "Ananias, why has Satan Acts 5:3
And **P** said to her, "Tell me whether you Acts 5:8
But **P** said to her, "How is it that you Acts 5:9
that as **P** came by at least his shadow Acts 5:15
But **P** and the apostles answered, "We Acts 5:29
of God, they sent to them **P** and John, Acts 8:14
But **P** said to him, "May your silver Acts 8:20
Now as **P** went here and there among Acts 9:32
And **P** said to him, "Aeneas, Jesus Acts 9:34
the disciples, hearing that **P** was there, Acts 9:38
So **P** rose and went with them. And Acts 9:39
But **P** put them all outside, and knelt Acts 9:40
eyes, and when she saw **P** she sat up. Acts 9:40
and bring one Simon who is called **P**. Acts 10:5
P went up on the housetop about the Acts 10:9
a voice to him: "Rise, **P**; kill and eat." Acts 10:13
But **P** said, "By no means, Lord; for I Acts 10:14
Now while **P** was inwardly perplexed Acts 10:17
who was called **P** was lodging there. Acts 10:18
And while **P** was pondering the Acts 10:19
And **P** went down to the men and Acts 10:21
When **P** entered, Cornelius met him Acts 10:25
But **P** lifted him up, saying, "Stand Acts 10:26
and ask for Simon who is called **P**. Acts 10:32
So **P** opened his mouth and said: Acts 10:34
While **P** was still saying these things, Acts 10:44
who had come with **P** were amazed, Acts 10:45
and extolling God. Then **P** declared, Acts 10:46
So when **P** went up to Jerusalem, the Acts 11:2
But **P** began and explained it to them Acts 11:4
saying to me, 'Rise, **P**; kill and eat.' Acts 11:7
and bring Simon who is called **P**; Acts 11:13
the Jews, he proceeded to arrest **P** also. Acts 12:3
So **P** was kept in prison, but earnest Acts 12:5
P was sleeping between two soldiers, Acts 12:6
He struck **P** on the side and woke him, Acts 12:7
When **P** came to himself, he said, Acts 12:11
and reported that **P** was standing at Acts 12:14
But **P** continued knocking, and Acts 12:16
soldiers over what had become of **P**. Acts 12:18
debate, **P** stood up and said to them, Acts 15:7
just as **P** had been entrusted with the Gal 2:7
who worked through **P** for his apostolic Gal 2:8
P, an apostle of Jesus Christ, To those 1 Pt 1:1
Simeon **P**, a servant and apostle of Jesus 2 Pt 1:1

PETER'S (4)
And when Jesus entered **P** house, he saw Mt 8:14
Jesus was Andrew, Simon **P** brother. Jn 1:40
of his disciples, Andrew, Simon **P** brother, Jn 6:8
Recognizing **P** voice, in her joy she Acts 12:14

PETHAHIAH (4)
the nineteenth to **P**, the twentieth to 1 Chr 24:16
Kelaiah (that is, Kelita), **P**, Judah, Ezr 10:23
Sherebiah, Hodiah, Shebaniah, and **P**, Neh 9:5
And **P** the son of Meshezabel, of the Neh 11:24

PETHOR (2)
to Balaam the son of Beor at **P**, Nm 22:5
the son of Beor from **P** of Mesopotamia, Dt 23:4

PETHUEL (1)
of the LORD that came to Joel, the son of **P**: Jl 1:1

PETITION (8)
of Israel grant your **p** that you have 1 Sm 1:17
has granted me my **p** that I made to 1 Sm 1:27
this woman for the **p** she asked of the 1 Sm 2:20
voice, and I have granted your **p**." 1 Sm 25:35
that whoever makes **p** to any god or man Dn 6:7
found Daniel making **p** and plea before Dn 6:11
that anyone who makes **p** to any god or Dn 6:12
but makes his **p** three times a day." Dn 6:13

PETITIONED (1)
whom the whole Jewish people **p** me, Acts 25:24

PETITIONS (1)
banners! May the LORD fulfill all your **p**! Ps 20:5

PEULLETHAI (1)
Issachar the seventh, **P** the eighth, 1 Chr 26:5

PHANTOMS (1)
rouse yourself, you despise them as **p**. Ps 73:20

PHANUEL (1)
a prophetess, Anna, the daughter of **P**, Lk 2:36

PHARAOH (234)
And when the princes of **P** saw her, Gn 12:15
Pharaoh saw her, they praised her to **P**. Gn 12:15
But the LORD afflicted **P** and his house Gn 12:17
So **P** called Abram and said, "What is Gn 12:18
And **P** gave men orders concerning Gn 12:20
in Egypt to Potiphar, an officer of **P**, Gn 37:36
to Egypt, and Potiphar, an officer of **P**, Gn 39:1
And **P** was angry with his two officers, Gn 40:2
In three days **P** will lift up your head Gn 40:13
me the kindness to mention me to **P**, Gn 40:14
there were all sorts of baked food for **P**, Gn 40:17
In three days **P** will lift up your head— Gn 40:19
P dreamed that he was standing by the Gn 41:1
attractive, plump cows. And **P** awoke. Gn 41:4
the seven plump, full ears. And **P** awoke, Gn 41:7
P told them his dreams, but there was Gn 41:8
was none who could interpret them to **P**. Gn 41:8
Then the chief cupbearer said to **P**, "I Gn 41:9
When **P** was angry with his servants Gn 41:10
Then **P** sent and called Joseph, and Gn 41:14
his clothes, he came in before **P**. Gn 41:14
And **P** said to Joseph, "I have had a Gn 41:15
Joseph answered **P**, "It is not in me; God Gn 41:16
God will give **P** a favorable answer." Gn 41:16
Then **P** said to Joseph, "Behold, in my Gn 41:17
Then Joseph said to **P**, "The dreams of Gn 41:25
to Pharaoh, "The dreams of **P** are one; Gn 41:25
God has revealed to **P** what he is about Gn 41:25
It is as I told **P**; God has shown to Gn 41:28
God has shown to **P** what he is about Gn 41:28
Now therefore let **P** select a discerning Gn 41:33
Let **P** proceed to appoint overseers over Gn 41:34
under the authority of **P** for food in the Gn 41:35
This proposal pleased **P** and all his Gn 41:37
And **P** said to his servants, "Can we Gn 41:38
Then **P** said to Joseph, "Since God has Gn 41:39
And **P** said to Joseph, "See, I have set Gn 41:41
Then **P** took his signet ring from his Gn 41:42
Moreover, **P** said to Joseph, "I am Gn 41:44
Pharaoh said to Joseph, "I am **P**, Gn 41:44
And **P** called Joseph's name Gn 41:45
entered the service of **P** king of Egypt. Gn 41:46
the presence of **P** and went through Gn 41:46
the people cried to **P** for bread. Gn 41:55
P said to all the Egyptians, "Go to Gn 41:55
by the life of **P**, you shall not go from Gn 42:15
Or else, by the life of **P**, surely you are Gn 42:16
servant, for you are like **P** himself. Gn 44:18
heard it, and the household of **P** heard it. Gn 45:2
He has made me a father to **P**, and lord Gn 45:8
come," it pleased **P** and his servants. Gn 45:16
And **P** said to Joseph, "Say to your Gn 45:17
according to the command of **P**, Gn 45:21
in the wagons that **P** had sent to carry Gn 46:5
will go up and tell **P** and will say to Gn 46:31
When **P** calls you and says, 'What is Gn 46:33
So Joseph went in and told **P**, "My father Gn 47:1
took five men and presented them to **P**. Gn 47:2
P said to his brothers, "What is your Gn 47:3
is your occupation?" And they said to **P**, Gn 47:3
They said to **P**, "We have come to Gn 47:4
Then **P** said to Joseph, "Your father and Gn 47:5
Jacob his father and stood him before **P**, Gn 47:7
before Pharaoh, and Jacob blessed **P**. Gn 47:7
And **P** said to Jacob, "How many are the Gn 47:8
And Jacob said to **P**, "The days of the Gn 47:9
And Jacob blessed **P** and went out Gn 47:10
and went out from the presence of **P**. Gn 47:10
of Rameses, as **P** had commanded. Gn 47:11
we with our land will be servants to **P**. Gn 47:19
bought all the land of Egypt for **P**, Gn 47:20
a fixed allowance from **P** and lived on Gn 47:22
on the allowance that **P** gave them; Gn 47:22
day bought you and your land for **P**. Gn 47:23
the harvests you shall give a fifth to **P**, Gn 47:24
my lord, we will be servants to **P**." Gn 47:25
to this day, that **P** should have the fifth; Gn 47:26
past, Joseph spoke to the household of **P**, Gn 50:4
your eyes, please speak in the ears of **P**, Gn 50:4
And **P** answered, "Go up, and bury your Gn 50:6
With him went up all the servants of **P**, Gn 50:7
They built for **P** store cities, Pithom and Ex 1:11
The midwives said to **P**, "Because the Ex 1:19
Then **P** commanded all his people, Ex 1:22
Now the daughter of **P** came down to Ex 2:5
When **P** heard of it, he sought to kill Ex 2:15
But Moses fled from **P** and stayed in the Ex 2:15
I will send you to **P** that you may bring Ex 3:10
I should go to **P** and bring the children Ex 3:11
that you do before **P** all the miracles that Ex 4:21
Then you shall say to **P**, 'Thus says the Ex 4:22
Moses and Aaron went and said to **P**, Ex 5:1
But **P** said, "Who is the LORD, that I Ex 5:2
And **P** said, "Behold, the people of the land Ex 5:5
The same day **P** commanded the Ex 5:6
out and said to the people, "Thus says **P**, Ex 5:10
the people of Israel came and cried to **P**, Ex 5:15
for them, as they came out from **P**; Ex 5:20
stink in the sight of **P** and his servants, Ex 5:21
For since I came to **P** to speak in your Ex 5:23
"Now you shall see what I will do to **P**; Ex 6:1
tell **P** king of Egypt to let the people of Ex 6:11
to me. How then shall **P** listen to me, Ex 6:12
of Israel and about **P** king of Egypt: Ex 6:13
they who spoke to **P** king of Egypt about Ex 6:27
tell **P** king of Egypt all that I say to you." Ex 6:29
lips. How will **P** listen to me?" Ex 6:30
"See, I have made you like God to **P**, Ex 7:1
brother Aaron shall tell **P** to let the people Ex 7:2
P will not listen to you. Then I will lay my Ex 7:4
years old, when they spoke to **P**. Ex 7:7
"When **P** says to you, 'Prove yourselves Ex 7:9
'Take your staff and cast it down before **P**, Ex 7:9
and Aaron went to **P** and did just as Ex 7:10
down his staff before **P** and his servants, Ex 7:10
Then **P** summoned the wise men and Ex 7:11
Go to **P** in the morning, as he is going Ex 7:15
In the sight of **P** and in the sight of his Ex 7:20
P turned and went into his house, and he Ex 7:23
said to Moses, "Go in to **P** and say to him, Ex 8:1
Then **P** called Moses and Aaron and said, Ex 8:8
Moses said to **P**, "Be pleased to command Ex 8:9
So Moses and Aaron went out from **P**, Ex 8:12
about the frogs, as he had agreed with **P**. Ex 8:12
But when **P** saw that there was a respite, Ex 8:15
Then the magicians said to **P**, "This is Ex 8:19
the morning and present yourself to **P**, Ex 8:20
into the house of **P** and into his servants' Ex 8:24
Then **P** called Moses and Aaron and Ex 8:25
So **P** said, "I will let you go to sacrifice to Ex 8:28
the swarms of flies may depart from **P**, Ex 8:29
Only let not **P** cheat again by not letting Ex 8:29
Moses went out from **P** and prayed to the Ex 8:30
and removed the swarms of flies from **P**, Ex 8:31
But **P** hardened his heart this time also, Ex 8:32
said to Moses, "Go in to **P** and say to him, Ex 9:1
And **P** sent, and behold, not one of the Ex 9:7
But the heart of **P** was hardened, and he Ex 9:7
throw them in the air in the sight of **P**. Ex 9:8
soot from the kiln and stood before **P**. Ex 9:10
But the LORD hardened the heart of **P**, Ex 9:12
and present yourself before **P** and say to Ex 9:13
the servants of **P** hurried his slaves Ex 9:20
Then **P** sent and called Moses and Ex 9:27
of the city from **P** and stretched out his Ex 9:33
But when **P** saw that the rain and the Ex 9:34
So the heart of **P** was hardened, and he Ex 9:35
Then the LORD said to Moses, "Go in to **P**, Ex 10:1
and Aaron went in to **P** and said to him, Ex 10:3
Then he turned and went out from **P**. Ex 10:6
and Aaron were brought back to **P**. Ex 10:8
Then **P** hastily called Moses and Aaron Ex 10:16
he went out from **P** and pleaded with Ex 10:18
Then **P** called Moses and said, "Go, Ex 10:24
Then **P** said to him, "Get away from Ex 10:28
I will bring upon **P** and upon Egypt. Ex 11:1
from the firstborn of **P** who sits on his Ex 11:5
And he went out from **P** in hot anger. Ex 11:8
said to Moses, "**P** will not listen to you, Ex 11:9
Aaron did all these wonders before **P**, Ex 11:10
from the firstborn of **P** who sat on his Ex 12:29
And **P** rose up in the night, he and all Ex 12:30
For when **P** stubbornly refused to let us Ex 13:15
When **P** let the people go, God did not Ex 13:17
For **P** will say of the people of Israel, Ex 14:3
I will get glory over **P** and all his host, Ex 14:4
the mind of **P** and his servants was Ex 14:5
hardened the heart of **P** king of Egypt, Ex 14:8
When **P** drew near, the people of Israel Ex 14:10
I will get glory over **P** and all his host, Ex 14:17
LORD, when I have gotten glory over **P**, Ex 14:18
all the host of **P** that had followed them Ex 14:28
when the horses of **P** with his chariots Ex 15:19
and delivered me from the sword of **P**"). Ex 18:4
LORD had done to **P** and to the Egyptians Ex 18:8
of the hand of **P** and has delivered the Ex 18:10
against Egypt and against **P** and all his Dt 6:22
slavery, from the hand of **P** king of Egypt. Dt 7:8
LORD your God did to **P** and to all Egypt, Dt 7:18
he did in Egypt to **P** the king of Egypt Dt 11:3
to **P** and to all his servants and to all his Dt 29:2
to **P** and to all his servants and to all his Dt 34:11
in Egypt subject to the house of **P**? 1 Sm 2:27
the Egyptians and **P** hardened their 1 Sm 6:6
marriage alliance with **P** king of 1 Kgs 3:1
(**P** king of Egypt had gone up and 1 Kgs 9:16
women, along with the daughter of **P**: 1 Kgs 11:1
came to Egypt, to **P** king of Egypt, 1 Kgs 11:18
found great favor in the sight of **P**, 1 Kgs 11:19
house among the sons of **P**. 1 Kgs 11:20
the army was dead, Hadad said to **P**, 1 Kgs 11:21
But **P** said to him, "What have you 1 Kgs 11:22
under the hand of **P** king of Egypt, 2 Kgs 17:7
Such is **P** king of Egypt to all who 2 Kgs 18:21
In his days **P** Neco king of Egypt 2 Kgs 23:29
and **P** Neco killed him at Megiddo, 2 Kgs 23:29
And **P** Neco put him in bonds at 2 Kgs 23:33
And **P** Neco made Eliakim the son 2 Kgs 23:34
gave the silver and the gold to **P**, 2 Kgs 23:35
according to the command of **P**. 2 Kgs 23:35
his assessment, to give it to **P** Neco. 2 Kgs 23:35
the sons of Bithiah, the daughter of **P**, 1 Chr 4:17
and wonders against **P** and all his Neh 9:10
signs and wonders against **P** and all his Ps 135:9
but overthrew **P** and his host in the Ps 136:15
wisest counselors of **P** give stupid Is 19:11
How can you say to **P**, "I am a son of the Is 19:11
in the protection of **P** and to seek shelter Is 30:2
shall the protection of **P** turn to your Is 30:3
Such is **P** king of Egypt to all who trust in Is 36:6
P king of Egypt, his servants, his Jer 25:19
The army of **P** had come out of Egypt. Jer 37:5
I will give **P** Hophra king of Egypt into Jer 44:30
Concerning the army of **P** Neco, king of Jer 46:2
Call the name of **P**, king of Egypt, Jer 46:17
and **P** and Egypt and her gods and her Jer 46:25
upon **P** and those who trust in him. Jer 46:25
Philistines, before **P** struck down Gaza. Jer 47:1
P with his mighty army and great Ezk 17:17
set your face against **P** king of Egypt, Ezk 29:2
I am against you, **P** king of Egypt, Ezk 29:3
broken the arm of **P** king of Egypt, Ezk 30:21
I am against **P** king of Egypt and will Ezk 30:22
hand, but I will break the arms of **P**, Ezk 30:24
Babylon, but the arms of **P** shall fall. Ezk 30:25
say to **P** king of Egypt and to his Ezk 31:2
"This is **P** and all his multitude, Ezk 31:18
a lamentation over **P** king of Egypt Ezk 32:2
"When **P** sees them, he will be Ezk 32:31
all his multitude, **P** and all his army, Ezk 32:31
by the sword, **P** and all his multitude, Ezk 32:32
gave him favor and wisdom before **P**, Acts 7:10
Joseph's family became known to **P**. Acts 7:13
For the Scripture says to **P**, "For this Rom 9:17

PHARAOH'S (46)
the woman was taken into **P** house. Gn 12:15
So he asked **P** officers who were with Gn 40:7
P cup was in my hand, and I took the Gn 40:11
pressed them into **P** cup and placed Gn 40:11
cup and placed the cup in **P** hand." Gn 40:11
and you shall place **P** cup in his hand Gn 40:13
the third day, which was **P** birthday, Gn 40:20
and he placed the cup in **P** hand. Gn 40:21
the doubling of **P** dream means that Gn 41:32
When the report was heard in **P** house, Gn 45:16
brought the money into **P** house. Gn 47:14

severe on them. The land became **P**. Gn 47:20
of the priests alone did not become **P**. Gn 47:26
Then his sister said to **P** daughter, "Shall I Ex 2:7
And **P** daughter said to her, "Go." So the Ex 2:8
And **P** daughter said to her, "Take this Ex 2:9
grew up, she brought him to **P** daughter, Ex 2:10
whom **P** taskmasters had set over them, Ex 5:14
But I will harden **P** heart, and though I Ex 7:3
Still **P** heart was hardened, and he would Ex 7:13
LORD said to Moses, "**P** heart is hardened; Ex 7:14
So **P** heart remained hardened, and he Ex 7:22
of God." But **P** heart was hardened, Ex 8:19
Then **P** servants said to him, "How long Ex 10:7
they were driven out from **P** presence. Ex 10:11
But the LORD hardened **P** heart, and he Ex 10:20
But the LORD hardened **P** heart, and he Ex 10:27
in the sight of **P** servants and in the sight Ex 11:3
and the LORD hardened **P** heart, Ex 11:10
And I will harden **P** heart, and he will Ex 14:4
all **P** horses and chariots and his Ex 14:9
into the midst of the sea, all **P** horses, Ex 14:23
"**P** chariots and his host he cast into the Ex 15:4
to your son, 'We were **P** slaves in Egypt. Dt 6:21
He took **P** daughter and brought her 1 Kgs 3:1
like this hall for **P** daughter whom he 1 Kgs 7:8
But **P** daughter went up from the city 1 Kgs 9:24
whom Tahpenes weaned in **P** house. 1 Kgs 11:20
Genubath was in **P** house among 1 Kgs 11:20
Solomon brought **P** daughter up 2 Chr 8:11
you, my love, to a mare among **P** chariots. Sg 1:9
P army that came to help you is about to Jer 37:7
Jerusalem at the approach of **P** army, Jer 37:11
the entrance to **P** palace in Tahpanhes, Jer 43:9
P daughter adopted him and brought Acts 7:21
to be called the son of **P** daughter, Heb 11:24

PHARISEE (10)
You blind **P**! First clean the inside of Mt 23:26
Now when the **P** who had invited him Lk 7:39
a **P** asked him to dine with him, Lk 11:37
The **P** was astonished to see that he did Lk 11:38
one a **P** and the other a tax collector. Lk 18:10
The **P**, standing by himself, prayed Lk 18:11
But a **P** in the council named Acts 5:34
out in the council, "Brothers, I am a **P**, Acts 23:6
party of our religion I have lived as a **P**. Acts 26:5
a Hebrew of Hebrews; as to the law, a **P**; Phil 3:5

PHARISEE'S (2)
he went into the **P** house and took his Lk 7:36
he was reclining at table in the **P** house, Lk 7:37

PHARISEES (85)
many of the **P** and Sadducees coming Mt 3:7
exceeds that of the scribes and **P**, Mt 5:20
And when the **P** saw this, they said to his Mt 9:11
him, saying, "Why do we and the **P** fast, Mt 9:14
But the **P** said, "He casts out demons by Mt 9:34
But when the **P** saw it, they said to him, Mt 12:2
But the **P** went out and conspired Mt 12:14
But when the **P** heard it, they said, "It is Mt 12:24
of the scribes and **P** answered him, Mt 12:38
Then **P** and scribes came to Jesus from Mt 15:1
know that the **P** were offended when Mt 15:12
And the **P** and Sadducees came, and to Mt 16:1
of the leaven of the **P** and Sadducees." Mt 16:6
of the leaven of the **P** and Sadducees." Mt 16:11
of the teaching of the **P** and Sadducees. Mt 16:12
And **P** came up to him and tested him Mt 19:3
priests and the **P** heard his parables, Mt 21:45
Then the **P** went and plotted how to Mt 22:15
But when the **P** heard that he had Mt 22:34
Now while the **P** were gathered Mt 22:41
"The scribes and the **P** sit on Moses' Mt 23:2
"But woe to you, scribes and **P**, Mt 23:13
Woe to you, scribes and **P**, hypocrites! Mt 23:15
"Woe to you, scribes and **P**, hypocrites! Mt 23:23
"Woe to you, scribes and **P**, hypocrites! Mt 23:25
"Woe to you, scribes and **P**, hypocrites! Mt 23:27
"Woe to you, scribes and **P**, hypocrites! Mt 23:29
priests and the **P** gathered before Pilate Mt 27:62
And the scribes of the **P**, when they saw Mk 2:16
John's disciples and the **P** were fasting. Mk 2:18
disciples and the disciples of the **P** fast, Mk 2:18
And the **P** were saying to him, "Look, Mk 2:24
The **P** went out and immediately held Mk 3:6
Now when the **P** gathered to him, with Mk 7:1
(For the **P** and all the Jews do not eat Mk 7:3
And the **P** and the scribes asked him, Mk 7:5
The **P** came and began to argue with Mk 8:11
of the leaven of the **P** and the leaven of Mk 8:15
And **P** came up and in order to test him Mk 10:2
to him some of the **P** and some of the Mk 12:13
P and teachers of the law were sitting Lk 5:17
the scribes and the **P** began to question, Lk 5:21
And the **P** and their scribes grumbled at Lk 5:30
prayers, and so do the disciples of the **P**, Lk 5:33
But some of the **P** said, "Why are you Lk 6:2
And the scribes and the **P** watched him, Lk 6:7
but the **P** and the lawyers rejected the Lk 7:30
One of the **P** asked him to eat with him, Lk 7:36
"Now you **P** cleanse the outside of the Lk 11:39
"But woe to you **P**! For you tithe mint Lk 11:42
Woe to you **P**! For you love the best Lk 11:43
the scribes and the **P** began to press Lk 11:53
first, "Beware of the leaven of the **P**, Lk 12:1
that very hour some **P** came and said Lk 13:31
to dine at the house of a ruler of the **P**, Lk 14:1
Jesus responded to the lawyers and **P**, Lk 14:3
And the **P** and the scribes grumbled, Lk 15:2
The **P**, who were lovers of money, Lk 16:14
asked by the **P** when the kingdom Lk 17:20
And some of the **P** in the crowd said to Lk 19:39
(Now they had been sent from the **P**.) Jn 1:24
was a man of the **P** named Nicodemus, Jn 3:1
Jesus learned that the **P** had heard that Jn 4:1
The **P** heard the crowd muttering these Jn 7:32
the chief priests and **P** sent officers to Jn 7:32
then came to the chief priests and **P**, Jn 7:45
The **P** answered them, "Have you also Jn 7:47
the authorities or the **P** believed in him? Jn 7:48
The scribes and the **P** brought a woman Jn 8:3
So the **P** said to him, "You are bearing Jn 8:13
They brought to the **P** the man who had Jn 9:13
So the **P** again asked him how he had Jn 9:15
Some of the **P** said, "This man is not Jn 9:16
Some of the **P** near him heard these Jn 9:40
them went to the **P** and told them what Jn 11:46
priests and the **P** gathered the Council Jn 11:47
chief priests and the **P** had given orders Jn 11:57
So the **P** said to one another, "You see Jn 12:19
but for fear of the **P** they did not confess Jn 12:42
officers from the chief priests and the **P**, Jn 18:3
to the party of the **P** rose up and said, Acts 15:5
part were Sadducees and the other **P**, Acts 23:6
"Brothers, I am a Pharisee, a son of **P**. Acts 23:6
arose between the **P** and the Sadducees, Acts 23:7
spirit, but the **P** acknowledge them all. Acts 23:8

PHARISEES' (1)
the scribes of the **P** party stood up and Acts 23:9

PHARPAR (1)
Are not Abana and **P**, the rivers of 2 Kgs 5:12

PHICOL (3)
Abimelech and **P** the commander Gn 21:22
Abimelech and **P** the commander Gn 21:32
his adviser and **P** the commander of Gn 26:26

PHILADELPHIA (2)
and to Sardis and to **P** and to Laodicea." Rv 1:11
to the angel of the church in **P** write: Rv 3:7

PHILEMON (1)
To **P** our beloved fellow worker Phlm 1:1

PHILETUS (1)
Among them are Hymenaeus and **P**, 2 Tm 2:17

PHILIP (32)
P and Bartholomew; Thomas and Mt 10:3
Andrew, and **P**, and Bartholomew, and Mk 3:18
and his brother **P** tetrarch of the region of Lk 3:1
his brother, and James and John, and **P**, Lk 6:14
He found **P** and said to him, "Follow me." Jn 1:43
Now **P** was from Bethsaida, the city of Jn 1:44
P found Nathanael and said to him, "We Jn 1:45
come out of Nazareth?" **P** said to him, Jn 1:46
Jesus answered him, "Before **P** called you, Jn 1:48
was coming toward him, Jesus said to **P**, Jn 6:5
P answered him, "Two hundred denarii Jn 6:7
So these came to **P**, who was from Jn 12:21
P went and told Andrew; Andrew and Jn 12:22
Andrew and **P** went and told Jesus. Jn 12:22
P said to him, "Lord, show us the Father, Jn 14:8
P? Whoever has seen me has seen the Jn 14:9
James and Andrew, **P** and Thomas, Acts 1:13
of faith and of the Holy Spirit, and **P**, Acts 6:5
P went down to the city of Samaria and Acts 8:5
was being said by **P** when they heard Acts 8:6
when they believed **P** as he preached Acts 8:12
being baptized he continued with **P**. Acts 8:13
Now an angel of the Lord said to **P**, Acts 8:26
And the Spirit said to **P**, "Go over and Acts 8:29
So **P** ran to him and heard him Acts 8:30
me?" And he invited **P** to come up and Acts 8:31
And the eunuch said to **P**, "About Acts 8:34
Then **P** opened his mouth, and Acts 8:35
into the water, **P** and the eunuch, Acts 8:38
the Spirit of the Lord carried **P** away, Acts 8:39
But **P** found himself at Azotus, and as Acts 8:40
entered the house of **P** the evangelist, Acts 21:8

PHILIP'S (2)
the sake of Herodias, his brother **P** wife, Mt 14:3
the sake of Herodias, his brother **P** wife, Mk 6:17

PHILIPPI (6)
came into the district of Caesarea **P**, Mt 16:13
disciples to the villages of Caesarea **P**. Mk 8:27
and from there to **P**, which is a Acts 16:12
we sailed away from **P** after the days of Acts 20:6
the saints in Christ Jesus who are at **P**, Phil 1:1
and been shamefully treated at **P**, 1 Thes 2:2

PHILIPPIANS (1)
And you **P** yourselves know that in the Phil 4:15

PHILISTIA (9)
pangs have seized the inhabitants of **P**. Ex 15:14
cast my shoe; over **P** I shout in triumph." Ps 60:8
Amalek, **P** with the inhabitants of Tyre; Ps 83:7
behold, **P** and Tyre, with Cush—"This Ps 87:4
my shoe; over **P** I shout in triumph." Ps 108:9
Rejoice not, O **P**, all of you, that the rod Is 14:29
out, O city; melt in fear, O **P**, all of you! Is 14:31
O Tyre and Sidon, and all the regions of **P**? Jl 3:4
Ashdod, and I will cut off the pride of **P**. Zec 9:6

PHILISTINE (36)
go over to the **P** garrison on the other 1 Sm 14:1
sought to go over to the **P** garrison, 1 Sm 14:4
Am I not a **P**, and are you not servants 1 Sm 17:8
And the **P** said, "I defy the ranks of 1 Sm 17:10
all Israel heard these words of the **P**, 1 Sm 17:11
forty days the **P** came forward and 1 Sm 17:16
behold, the champion, the **P** of Gath, 1 Sm 17:23
man who kills this **P** and takes away 1 Sm 17:26
For who is this uncircumcised **P**, 1 Sm 17:26
will go and fight with this **P**." 1 Sm 17:32
to go against this **P** to fight with 1 Sm 17:33
and this uncircumcised **P** shall be 1 Sm 17:36
the hand of this **P**." And Saul said to 1 Sm 17:37
his hand, and he approached the **P**. 1 Sm 17:40
And the **P** moved forward and came 1 Sm 17:41
And when the **P** looked and saw 1 Sm 17:42
And the **P** said to David, "Am I a dog, 1 Sm 17:43
sticks?" And the **P** cursed David by 1 Sm 17:43
The **P** said to David, "Come to me, 1 Sm 17:44
Then David said to the **P**, "You come 1 Sm 17:45
When the **P** arose and came and 1 Sm 17:48
toward the battle line to meet the **P**. 1 Sm 17:48
it and struck the **P** on his forehead. 1 Sm 17:49
prevailed over the **P** with a sling 1 Sm 17:50
and struck the **P** and killed him. 1 Sm 17:50
and stood over the **P** and took his 1 Sm 17:51
the head of the **P** and brought it to 1 Sm 17:54
Saul saw David go out against the **P**, 1 Sm 17:55
from the striking down of the **P**, 1 Sm 17:57
with the head of the **P** in his hand. 1 Sm 17:57
returned from striking down the **P**, 1 Sm 18:6
in his hand and he struck down the **P**, 1 Sm 19:5
said, "The sword of Goliath the **P**, 1 Sm 21:9
him the sword of Goliath the **P**." 1 Sm 22:10
and attacked the **P** and killed him. 2 Sm 21:17
struck down the **P** army from 1 Chr 14:16

PHILISTINE'S (1)
every **P** sword was against his fellow, 1 Sm 14:20

PHILISTINES (253)
Casluhim (from whom the **P** came), Gn 10:14
up and returned to the land of the **P**. Gn 21:32
many days in the land of the **P**. Gn 21:34
to Gerar to Abimelech king of the **P**. Gn 26:1
Abimelech king of the **P** looked out of a Gn 26:8
servants, so that the **P** envied him. Gn 26:14
(Now the **P** had stopped and filled with Gn 26:15
which the **P** had stopped after the death Gn 26:18
lead them by way of the land of the **P**, Ex 13:17
from the Red Sea to the Sea of the **P**, Ex 23:31
all the regions of the **P**, and all those of Jos 13:2
there are five rulers of the **P**, those of Jos 13:3
five lords of the **P** and all the Canaanites Jgs 3:3
who killed 600 of the **P** with an oxgoad, Jgs 3:31
of the Ammonites, and the gods of the **P**. Jgs 10:6
into the hand of the **P** and into the hand Jgs 10:7
from the Ammonites and from the **P**? Jgs 10:11
into the hand of the **P** for forty years. Jgs 13:1
to save Israel from the hand of the **P**." Jgs 13:5
he saw one of the daughters of the **P**. Jgs 14:1
one of the daughters of the **P** at Timnah. Jgs 14:2
the uncircumcised **P**?" But Samson Jgs 14:3
seeking an opportunity against the **P**. Jgs 14:4
At that time the **P** ruled over Israel. Jgs 14:4
I shall be innocent in regard to the **P**, Jgs 15:3
the standing grain of the **P** and set fire to Jgs 15:5
Then the **P** said, "Who has done this?" Jgs 15:6
companion." And the **P** came up and Jgs 15:6
Then the **P** came up and encamped in Jgs 15:9
not know that the **P** are rulers over us? Jgs 15:11
the hands of the **P**." And Samson said Jgs 15:12
Lehi, the **P** came shouting to meet him. Jgs 15:14
Israel in the days of the **P** twenty years. Jgs 15:20
And the lords of the **P** came up to her Jgs 16:5

the lords of the **P** brought up to her Jgs 16:8
she said to him, "The **P** are upon you, Jgs 16:9
and said to him, "The **P** are upon you, Jgs 16:12
and said to him, "The **P** are upon you, Jgs 16:14
she sent and called the lords of the **P**, Jgs 16:18
Then the lords of the **P** came up to her Jgs 16:18
And she said, "The **P** are upon you, Jgs 16:20
And the **P** seized him and gouged out Jgs 16:21
the lords of the **P** gathered to offer a Jgs 16:23
All the lords of the **P** were there, and on Jgs 16:27
be avenged on the **P** for my two eyes." Jgs 16:28
me die with the **P**." Then he bowed Jgs 16:30
Israel went out to battle against the **P**. 1 Sm 4:1
and the **P** encamped at Aphek. 1 Sm 4:1
The **P** drew up in line against Israel, 1 Sm 4:2
spread, Israel was defeated by the **P**, 1 Sm 4:2
the LORD defeated us today before the **P**? 1 Sm 4:3
And when the **P** heard the noise of the 1 Sm 4:6
the **P** were afraid, for they said, "A god 1 Sm 4:7
Take courage, and be men, O **P**, lest 1 Sm 4:9
So the **P** fought, and Israel was 1 Sm 4:10
and said, "Israel has fled before the **P**, 1 Sm 4:17
When the **P** captured the ark of God, 1 Sm 5:1
Then the **P** took the ark of God and 1 Sm 5:2
together all the lords of the **P** and said, 1 Sm 5:8
together all the lords of the **P** and said, 1 Sm 5:11
in the country of the **P** seven months. 1 Sm 6:1
And the **P** called for the priests and the 1 Sm 6:2
to the number of the lords of the **P**, 1 Sm 6:4
the lords of the **P** went after them as 1 Sm 6:12
when the five lords of the **P** saw it, 1 Sm 6:16
tumors that the **P** returned as a 1 Sm 6:17
the cities of the **P** belonging to the five 1 Sm 6:18
"The **P** have returned the ark of the 1 Sm 6:21
deliver you out of the hand of the **P**." 1 Sm 7:3
Now when the **P** heard that the people 1 Sm 7:7
the lords of the **P** went up against 1 Sm 7:7
heard of it, they were afraid of the **P**. 1 Sm 7:7
may save us from the hand of the **P**." 1 Sm 7:8
the **P** drew near to attack Israel. 1 Sm 7:10
that day against the **P** and threw them 1 Sm 7:10
and pursued the **P** and struck them, 1 Sm 7:11
So the **P** were subdued and did not 1 Sm 7:13
LORD was against the **P** all the days of 1 Sm 7:13
The cities that the **P** had taken from 1 Sm 7:14
their territory from the hand of the **P**. 1 Sm 7:14
my people from the hand of the **P**. 1 Sm 9:16
where there is a garrison of the **P**. 1 Sm 10:5
of Hazor, and into the hand of the **P**, 1 Sm 12:9
the garrison of the **P** that was at Geba, 1 Sm 13:3
that was at Geba, and the **P** heard of it. 1 Sm 13:3
had defeated the garrison of the **P**, 1 Sm 13:4
Israel had become a stench to the **P**. 1 Sm 13:4
And the **P** mustered to fight with 1 Sm 13:5
and that the **P** had mustered at 1 Sm 13:11
'Now the **P** will come down against 1 Sm 13:12
but the **P** encamped in Michmash. 1 Sm 13:16
camp of the **P** in three companies. 1 Sm 13:17
all the land of Israel, for the **P** said, 1 Sm 13:19
went down to the **P** to sharpen his 1 Sm 13:20
the garrison of the **P** went out to the 1 Sm 13:23
themselves to the garrison of the **P**. 1 Sm 14:11
And the **P** said, "Look, Hebrews are 1 Sm 14:11
camp of the **P** increased more and 1 Sm 14:19
had been with the **P** before that time 1 Sm 14:21
heard that the **P** were fleeing, 1 Sm 14:22
the defeat among the **P** has not been 1 Sm 14:30
struck down the **P** that day from 1 Sm 14:31
go down after the **P** by night and 1 Sm 14:36
of God, "Shall I go down after the **P**? 1 Sm 14:37
Saul went up from pursuing the **P**, 1 Sm 14:46
and the **P** went to their own place. 1 Sm 14:46
kings of Zobah, and against the **P**. 1 Sm 14:47
fighting against the **P** all the days 1 Sm 14:52
Now the **P** gathered their armies for 1 Sm 17:1
drew up in line of battle against the **P**. 1 Sm 17:2
And the **P** stood on the mountain on 1 Sm 17:3
the camp of the **P** a champion named 1 Sm 17:4
valley of Elah, fighting with the **P**. 1 Sm 17:19
And Israel and the **P** drew up for 1 Sm 17:21
the ranks of the **P** and spoke the 1 Sm 17:23
of the host of the **P** this day to the 1 Sm 17:46
When the **P** saw that their 1 Sm 17:51
shout and pursued the **P** as far as 1 Sm 17:52
so that the wounded **P** fell on the way 1 Sm 17:52
came back from chasing the **P**, 1 Sm 17:53
let the hand of the **P** be against him." 1 Sm 18:17
the hand of the **P** may be against 1 Sm 18:21
except a hundred foreskins of the **P**, 1 Sm 18:25
David fall by the hand of the **P**. 1 Sm 18:25
and killed two hundred of the **P**. 1 Sm 18:27
the princes of the **P** came out to 1 Sm 18:30
fought with the **P** and struck them 1 Sm 19:8
the **P** are fighting against Keilah and 1 Sm 23:1
go and attack these **P**?" And the LORD 1 Sm 23:2
and attack the **P** and save Keilah." 1 Sm 23:2
to Keilah against the armies of the **P**?" 1 Sm 23:3
for I will give the **P** into your hand." 1 Sm 23:4
fought with the **P** and brought away 1 Sm 23:5
for the **P** have made a raid against 1 Sm 23:27
after David and went against the **P**. 1 Sm 23:28
Saul returned from following the **P**, 1 Sm 24:1
I should escape to the land of the **P**. 1 Sm 27:1
in the country of the **P** was a year and 1 Sm 27:7
he lived in the country of the **P**. 1 Sm 27:11
those days the **P** gathered their forces 1 Sm 28:1
The **P** assembled and came and 1 Sm 28:4
When Saul saw the army of the **P**, he 1 Sm 28:5
for the **P** are warring against me, 1 Sm 28:15
also with you into the hand of the **P**, 1 Sm 28:19
of Israel also into the hand of the **P**." 1 Sm 28:19
Now the **P** had gathered all their 1 Sm 29:1
the lords of the **P** were passing on by 1 Sm 29:2
the commanders of the **P** said, "What 1 Sm 29:3
said to the commanders of the **P**, 1 Sm 29:3
commanders of the **P** were angry with 1 Sm 29:4
the commanders of the **P** said to him, 1 Sm 29:4
may not displease the lords of the **P**." 1 Sm 29:7
the commanders of the **P** have said, 1 Sm 29:9
to return to the land of the **P**. 1 Sm 29:11
But the **P** went up to Jezreel. 1 Sm 29:11
the land of the **P** and from the land 1 Sm 30:16
Now the **P** fought against Israel, and 1 Sm 31:1
Israel fled before the **P** and fell slain 1 Sm 31:1
And the **P** overtook Saul and his sons, 1 Sm 31:2
and the **P** struck down Jonathan and 1 Sm 31:2
And the **P** came and lived in them. 1 Sm 31:7
when the **P** came to strip the slain, 1 Sm 31:8
throughout the land of the **P**, 1 Sm 31:9
heard what the **P** had done to 1 Sm 31:11
lest the daughters of the **P** rejoice, 2 Sm 1:20
price of a hundred foreskins of the **P**." 2 Sm 3:14
people Israel from the hand of the **P**, 2 Sm 3:18
When the **P** heard that David had 2 Sm 5:17
all the **P** went up to search for David. 2 Sm 5:17
Now the **P** had come and spread out 2 Sm 5:18
the LORD, "Shall I go up against the **P**? 2 Sm 5:19
certainly give the **P** into your hand." 2 Sm 5:19
And the **P** left their idols there, and 2 Sm 5:21
And the **P** came up yet again and 2 Sm 5:22
you to strike down the army of the **P**." 2 Sm 5:24
and struck down the **P** from Geba to 2 Sm 5:25
David defeated the **P** and subdued 2 Sm 8:1
out of the hand of the **P**. 2 Sm 8:1
Edom, Moab, the Ammonites, the **P**, 2 Sm 8:12
and saved us from the hand of the **P**, 2 Sm 19:9
where the **P** had hanged them, 2 Sm 21:12
on the day the **P** killed Saul on 2 Sm 21:12
war again between the **P** and Israel, 2 Sm 21:15
and they fought against the **P**. 2 Sm 21:15
was again war with the **P** at Gob. 2 Sm 21:18
was again war with the **P** at Gob, 2 Sm 21:19
they defied the **P** who were gathered 2 Sm 23:9
struck down the **P** until his hand 2 Sm 23:10
The **P** gathered together at Lehi, 2 Sm 23:11
lentils, and the men fled from the **P**. 2 Sm 23:11
defended it and struck down the **P**, 2 Sm 23:12
when a band of **P** was encamped in 2 Sm 23:13
the garrison of the **P** was then at 2 Sm 23:14
the camp of the **P** and drew water out 2 Sm 23:16
to the land of the **P** and to the border 1 Kgs 4:21
which belonged to the **P**, 1 Kgs 15:27
which belonged to the **P**, 1 Kgs 16:15
in the land of the **P** seven years. 2 Kgs 8:2
returned from the land of the **P**, 2 Kgs 8:3
He struck down the **P** as far as Gaza 2 Kgs 18:8
Casluhim (from whom the **P** came), 1 Chr 1:12
Now the **P** fought against Israel, and 1 Chr 10:1
Israel fled before the **P** and fell slain 1 Chr 10:1
And the **P** overtook Saul and his 1 Chr 10:2
and the **P** struck down Jonathan and 1 Chr 10:2
and the **P** came and lived in them. 1 Chr 10:7
when the **P** came to strip the slain, 1 Chr 10:8
the land of the **P** to carry the good 1 Chr 10:9
heard all that the **P** had done to 1 Chr 10:11
when the **P** were gathered 1 Chr 11:13
barley, and the men fled from the **P**. 1 Chr 11:13
plot and defended it and killed the **P**. 1 Chr 11:14
the army of **P** was encamped in 1 Chr 11:15
the garrison of the **P** was then at 1 Chr 11:16
the camp of the **P** and drew water 1 Chr 11:18
he came with the **P** for the battle 1 Chr 12:19
the rulers of the **P** took counsel and 1 Chr 12:19
When the **P** heard that David had 1 Chr 14:8
all the **P** went up to search for David. 1 Chr 14:8
Now the **P** had come and made a raid 1 Chr 14:9
of God, "Shall I go up against the **P**? 1 Chr 14:10
And the **P** yet again made a raid in 1 Chr 14:13
to strike down the army of the **P**." 1 Chr 14:15
David defeated the **P** and subdued 1 Chr 18:1
its villages out of the hand of the **P**. 1 Chr 18:1
the Ammonites, the **P** and Amalek. 1 Chr 18:11
there arose war with the **P** at Gezer. 1 Chr 20:4
of the giants, and the **P** were subdued. 1 Chr 20:4
And there was again war with the **P**, 1 Chr 20:5
to the land of the **P** and to the border 2 Chr 9:26
Some of the **P** brought Jehoshaphat 2 Chr 17:11
the anger of the **P** and of the 2 Chr 21:16
war against the **P** and broke through 2 Chr 26:6
Ashdod and elsewhere among the **P**. 2 Chr 26:6
him against the **P** and against the 2 Chr 26:7
And the **P** had made raids on the 2 Chr 28:18
of David, when the **P** seized him in Gath. Ps 56:T
the east and of fortune-tellers like the **P**, Is 2:6
on the east and the **P** on the west devour Is 9:12
on the shoulder of the **P** in the west, Is 11:14
kings of the land of the **P** (Ashkelon, Jer 25:20
Jeremiah the prophet concerning the **P**, Jer 47:1
day that is coming to destroy all the **P**, Jer 47:4
For the LORD is destroying the **P**, the Jer 47:4
your enemies, the daughters of the **P**, Ezk 16:27
her, and for the daughters of the **P**, Ezk 16:57
Because the **P** acted revengefully and Ezk 25:15
stretch out my hand against the **P**, Ezk 25:16
the remnant of the **P** shall perish," says Am 1:8
the great; then go down to Gath of the **P**. Am 6:2
and the **P** from Caphtor and the Syrians Am 9:7
shall possess the land of the **P**; Ob 1:19
is against you, O Canaan, land of the **P**; Zep 2:5

PHILOLOGUS (1)
Greet **P**, Julia, Nereus and his sister, Rom 16:15

PHILOSOPHERS (1)
Epicurean and Stoic **p** also conversed Acts 17:18

PHILOSOPHY (1)
takes you captive by **p** and empty deceit, Col 2:8

PHINEHAS (25)
daughters of Putiel, and she bore him **P**. Ex 6:25
When **P** the son of Eleazar, son of Nm 25:7
"**P** the son of Eleazar, son of Aaron the Nm 25:11
together with **P** the son of Eleazar the Nm 31:6
Gilead, **P** the son of Eleazar the priest, Jos 22:13
When **P** the priest and the chiefs of the Jos 22:30
And **P** the son of Eleazar the priest said Jos 22:31
Then **P** the son of Eleazar the priest, Jos 22:32
him at Gibeah, the town of **P** his son, Jos 24:33
and **P** the son of Eleazar, son of Aaron, Jgs 20:28
the two sons of Eli, Hophni and **P**, 1 Sm 1:3
upon your two sons, Hophni and **P**, 1 Sm 2:34
And the two sons of Eli, Hophni and **P**, 1 Sm 4:4
and the two sons of Eli, Hophni and **P**, 1 Sm 4:11
Your two sons also, Hophni and **P**, are 1 Sm 4:17
his daughter-in-law, the wife of **P**, 1 Sm 4:19
Ahitub, Ichabod's brother, son of **P**, 1 Sm 14:3
Eleazar fathered **P**, Phinehas fathered 1 Chr 6:4
Phinehas, **P** fathered Abishua, 1 Chr 6:4
Eleazar his son, **P** his son, Abishua 1 Chr 6:50
And **P** the son of Eleazar was the 1 Chr 9:20
son of Abishua, son of **P**, son of Eleazar, Ezr 7:5
Of the sons of **P**, Gershom. Of the sons of Ezr 8:2
and with him was Eleazar the son of **P**, Ezr 8:33
Then **P** stood up and intervened, and Ps 106:30

PHLEGON (1)
Greet Asyncritus, **P**, Hermes, Rom 16:14

PHOEBE (1)
I commend to you our sister **P**, a Rom 16:1

PHOENICIA (3)
traveled as far as **P** and Cyprus and Acts 11:19
passed through both **P** and Samaria, Acts 15:3
having found a ship crossing to **P**, Acts 21:2

PHOENIX (1)
that somehow they could reach **P**, Acts 27:12

PHRASE (1)
This **p**, "Yet once more," indicates the Heb 12:27

PHRASES (1)
do not heap up empty **p** as the Gentiles do, Mt 6:7

PHRYGIA (3)
P and Pamphylia, Egypt and the parts Acts 2:10
through the region of **P** and Galatia, Acts 16:6
through the region of Galatia and **P**, Acts 18:23

PHYGELUS (1)
among whom are **P** and Hermogenes. 2 Tm 1:15

PHYLACTERIES (1)
For they make their **p** broad and their Mt 23:5

PHYSICAL (1)
nor is circumcision outward and **p**. Rom 2:28

PHYSICALLY (1)
he who is **p** uncircumcised but keeps Rom 2:27

PHYSICIAN (6)
no balm in Gilead? Is there no **p** there? Jer 8:22
"Those who are well have no need of a **p**, Mt 9:12
who are well have no need of a **p**, Mk 2:17
to me this proverb, '**P**, heal yourself.' Lk 4:23
"Those who are well have no need of a **p**, Lk 5:31
Luke the beloved **p** greets you, as does Col 4:14

PHYSICIANS (6)
his servants the **p** to embalm his Gn 50:2
his father. So the **p** embalmed Israel. Gn 50:2
the LORD, but sought help from **p**. 2 Chr 16:12
with lies; worthless **p** are you all. Jb 13:4
who had suffered much under many **p**, Mk 5:26
though she had spent all her living on **p**, Lk 8:43

PI-BESETH (1)
men of On and of **P** shall fall by the Ezk 30:17

PI-HAHIROTH (3)
to turn back and encamp in front of **P**, Ex 14:2
them encamped at the sea, by **P**, Ex 14:9
out from Etham and turned back to **P**, Nm 33:7

PICK (10)
toes cut off used to **p** up scraps under my Jgs 1:7
to him, he said, "**P** up your son." 2 Kgs 4:36
they **p** saltwort and the leaves of bushes, Jb 30:4
And all the **p** of his troops shall fall by Ezk 17:21
"**P** me up and hurl me into the sea; Jon 1:12
—"Rise, **p** up your bed and go home." Mt 9:6
"I say to you, rise, **p** up your bed, and go Mk 2:11
they will **p** up serpents with their Mk 16:18
to you, rise, **p** up your bed and go home." Lk 5:24
p out from among you seven men of Acts 6:3

PICKED (9)
Then she **p** up her son and went out. 2 Kgs 4:37
a mother will be **p** out by the ravens Prv 30:17
So they **p** up Jonah and hurled him into Jon 1:15
he rose and immediately **p** up his bed Mk 2:12
up before them and **p** up what he had Lk 5:25
nor are grapes **p** from a bramble bush. Lk 6:44
And what was left over was **p** up, twelve Lk 9:17
So they **p** up stones to throw at him, but Jn 8:59
The Jews **p** up stones again to stone Jn 10:31

PICKS (2)
with saws and iron **p** and iron axes 2 Sm 12:31
labor with saws and iron **p** and axes. 1 Chr 20:3

PICTURES (1)
in the dark, each in his room of **p**? Ezk 8:12

PIECE (43)
a **p** of land worth four hundred shekels Gn 23:15
pieces of money the **p** of land on which Gn 33:19
Of one **p** with the mercy seat shall you Ex 25:19
and its flowers shall be of one **p** with it. Ex 25:31
and a calyx of one **p** with it under each Ex 25:35
their branches shall be of one **p** with it, Ex 25:36
of it a single **p** of hammered work of Ex 25:36
its horns shall be of one **p** with it, and Ex 27:2
be made like it and be of one **p** with it, Ex 28:8
height. Its horns shall be of one **p** with it. Ex 30:2
Of one **p** with the mercy seat he made the Ex 37:8
and its flowers were of one **p** with it. Ex 37:17
and a calyx of one **p** with it under each Ex 37:21
their branches were of one **p** with it. Ex 37:22
it was a single **p** of hammered work of Ex 37:22
height. Its horns were of one **p** with it. Ex 37:25
Its horns were of one **p** with it, and he Ex 38:2
on it was of one **p** with it and made like Ex 39:5
the burnt offering to him, **p** by piece, Lv 9:13
the burnt offering to him, piece by **p**, Lv 9:13
in the **p** of land that Jacob bought from Jos 24:32
to implore him for a **p** of silver or a 1 Sm 2:36
and they gave him a **p** of a cake of 1 Sm 30:12
wheels were of one **p** with the stands, 1 Kgs 7:32
were of one **p** with the stands. 1 Kgs 7:34
and its panels were of one **p** with it. 1 Kgs 7:35
and ruin every good **p** of land with 2 Kgs 3:19
and on every good **p** of land every 2 Kgs 3:25
And he took a **p** of broken pottery with Jb 2:8
are; I too was pinched off from a **p** of clay. Jb 33:6
of them gave him a **p** of money and a Jb 42:11
but for a **p** of bread a man will do Prv 28:21
Take out of it **p** after piece, without Ezk 24:6
Take out of it piece after **p**, without Ezk 24:6
My people inquire of a **p** of wood, and Hos 4:12
of the lion two legs, or a **p** of an ear, Am 3:12
No one puts a **p** of unshrunk cloth on Mt 9:16
No one sews a **p** of unshrunk cloth on Mk 2:21
"No one tears a **p** from a new garment Lk 5:36
and the **p** from the new will not match Lk 5:36
They gave him a **p** of broiled fish, Lk 24:42
woven in one **p** from top to bottom, Jn 19:23
his wife Sapphira, sold a **p** of property, Acts 5:1

PIECES (143)
flaming torch passed between these **p**. Gn 15:17
your brother a thousand **p** of silver. Gn 20:16
bought for a hundred **p** of money the Gn 33:19
Joseph is without doubt torn to **p**." Gn 37:33
and I said, Surely he has been torn to **p**, Gn 44:28
them and break their pillars in **p**. Ex 23:24
shall have two shoulder **p** attached to its Ex 28:7
stones on the shoulder **p** of the ephod, Ex 28:12
in front to the shoulder **p** of the ephod. Ex 28:25
part of the two shoulder **p** of the ephod, Ex 28:27
Then you shall cut the ram into **p**, and Ex 29:17
and put them with its **p** and its head, Ex 29:17
for the ephod attaching shoulder **p**, Ex 39:4
them on the shoulder **p** of the ephod to Ex 39:7
in front to the shoulder **p** of the ephod. Ex 39:18
part of the two shoulder **p** of the ephod, Ex 39:20
flay the burnt offering and cut it into **p**, Lv 1:6
sons the priests shall arrange the **p**, Lv 1:8
And he shall cut it into **p**, with its head Lv 1:12
You shall break it in **p** and pour oil on it; Lv 2:6
mixed, in baked **p** like a grain offering, Lv 6:21
He cut the ram into **p**, and Moses burned Lv 8:20
burned the head and the **p** and the fat. Lv 8:20
and placed them on the **p** of fat and on Lv 8:26
But the fat **p** of the ox and of the ram, the Lv 9:19
they put the fat **p** on the breasts, and he Lv 9:20
and he burned the fat **p** on the altar, Lv 9:20
the burnt offering and the **p** of fat on the Lv 9:24
food offerings of the fat **p** to wave for a Lv 10:15
oven or stove, it shall be broken in **p**. Lv 11:35
break their bones in **p** and pierce them Nm 24:8
altars and dash in **p** their pillars and chop Dt 7:5
altars and dash in **p** their pillars and Dt 12:3
I would have said, "I will cut them to **p**; I Dt 32:26
of Shechem for a hundred **p** of money. Jos 24:32
two **p** of dyed work embroidered for the Jgs 5:30
they gave him seventy **p** of silver out of Jgs 9:4
he tore the lion in **p** as one tears a young Jgs 14:6
we will each give you 1,100 **p** of silver." Jgs 16:5
"The 1,100 **p** of silver that were taken Jgs 17:2
he restored the 1,100 **p** of silver to his Jgs 17:3
his mother took 200 **p** of silver and gave Jgs 17:4
I will give you ten **p** of silver a year and Jgs 17:10
her, limb by limb, into twelve **p**, Jgs 19:29
and cut her in **p** and sent her Jgs 20:6
of the LORD shall be broken to **p**; 1 Sm 2:10
and cut them in **p** and sent them 1 Sm 11:7
hacked Agag to **p** before the LORD 1 Sm 15:33
glad to give you ten **p** of silver and a 2 Sm 18:11
the weight of a thousand **p** of silver, 2 Sm 18:12
offering and the fat **p** of the peace 1 Kgs 8:64
offering and the fat **p** of the peace 1 Kgs 8:64
was on him, and tore it into twelve **p**. 1 Kgs 11:30
Jeroboam, "Take for yourself ten **p**, 1 Kgs 11:31
and cut it in **p** and lay it on 1 Kgs 18:23
and cut the bull in **p** and laid it on 1 Kgs 18:33
and broke in **p** the rocks before 1 Kgs 19:11
own clothes and tore them in two **p**. 2 Kgs 2:12
sword and dash in **p** their little ones 2 Kgs 8:12
and his images they broke in **p**, 2 Kgs 11:18
And he broke in **p** the bronze serpent 2 Kgs 18:4
down and broke in **p** and cast the 2 Kgs 23:12
And he broke in **p** the pillars and 2 Kgs 23:14
and cut in **p** all the vessels of gold in 2 Kgs 24:13
Chaldeans broke in **p** and carried 2 Kgs 25:13
They were broken in **p**. Nation was 2 Chr 15:6
and his images they broke in **p**, 2 Chr 23:17
rock, and they were all dashed to **p**. 2 Chr 25:12
of God and cut in **p** the vessels of the 2 Chr 28:24
Judah and broke in **p** the pillars and 2 Chr 31:1
And he broke in **p** the Asherim and 2 Chr 34:4
and evening they are beaten to **p**; Jb 4:20
me by the neck and dashed me to **p**; Jb 16:12
me and break me in **p** with words? Jb 19:2
and dash them in **p** like a potter's vessel." Ps 2:9
they tear my soul apart, rending it in **p**, Ps 7:2
than thousands of gold and silver **p**. Ps 119:72
bring for its fruit a thousand **p** of silver. Sg 8:11
Ephraim will be broken to **p** so that it will Is 7:8
will be dashed in **p** before their eyes; Is 13:16
the altars like chalkstones crushed to **p**, Is 27:9
I will break in **p** the doors of bronze and Is 45:2
Was it not you who cut Rahab in **p**, that Is 51:9
who goes out of them shall be torn in **p**, Jer 5:6
a hammer that breaks the rock in **p**? Jer 23:29
his vessels and break his jars in **p**. Jer 48:12
of war: with you I break nations in **p**; Jer 51:20
with you I break in **p** the horse and his Jer 51:21
you I break in **p** the chariot and the Jer 51:21
with you I break in **p** man and woman; Jer 51:22
with you I break in **p** the old man and Jer 51:22
you I break in **p** the young man and Jer 51:22
you I break in **p** the shepherd and his Jer 51:23
you I break in **p** the farmer and his Jer 51:23
I break in **p** governors and Jer 51:23
their bows are broken in **p**, for the LORD Jer 51:56
of the LORD, the Chaldeans broke in **p**, Jer 52:17
turned aside my steps and tore me to **p**; Lam 3:11
handfuls of barley and for **p** of bread, Ezk 13:19
and cut you to **p** with their swords. Ezk 16:40
put in it the **p** of meat, all the good Ezk 24:4
in it the pieces of meat, all the good **p**, Ezk 24:4
of iron and clay, and broke them in **p**. Dn 2:34
the gold, all together were broken in **p**, Dn 2:35
iron breaks to **p** and shatters all Dn 2:40
It shall break in **p** all these kingdoms Dn 2:44
hand, and that it broke in **p** the iron, Dn 2:45
them and broke all their bones in **p**. Dn 6:24
and broke in **p** and stamped what Dn 7:7
and broke in **p** and stamped what Dn 7:19
and trample it down, and break it to **p**. Dn 7:23
calf of Samaria shall be broken to **p**. Hos 8:6
were dashed in **p** with their children. Hos 10:14
their little ones shall be dashed in **p**, Hos 13:16
her carved images shall be beaten to **p**, Mi 1:7
break their bones in **p** and chop them up Mi 3:3
you shall beat in **p** many peoples; Mi 4:13
goes through, treads down and tears in **p**, Mi 5:8
and the rocks are broken into **p** by him. Na 1:6
infants were dashed in **p** at the head of Na 3:10
out as my wages thirty **p** of silver. Zec 11:12
I took the thirty **p** of silver and threw Zec 11:13
baskets full of the broken **p** left over. Mt 14:20
baskets full of the broken **p** left over. Mt 15:37
falls on this stone will be broken to **p**; Mt 21:44
and will cut him in **p** and put him with Mt 24:51
And they paid him thirty **p** of silver. Mt 26:15
brought back the thirty **p** of silver to the Mt 27:3
And throwing down the **p** of silver into Mt 27:5
the chief priests, taking the **p** of silver, Mt 27:6
"And they took the thirty **p** of silver, Mt 27:9
apart, and he broke the shackles in **p**. Mk 5:4
baskets full of broken **p** and of the fish. Mk 6:43
And they took up the broken **p** left over, Mk 8:8
baskets full of broken **p** did you take Mk 8:19
baskets full of broken **p** did you take Mk 8:20
picked up, twelve baskets of broken **p**. Lk 9:17
and will cut him in **p** and put him with Lk 12:46
falls on that stone will be broken to **p**, Lk 20:18
it came to fifty thousand **p** of silver. Acts 19:19
that Paul would be torn to **p** by them, Acts 23:10
the rest on planks or on **p** of the ship. Acts 27:44
as when earthen pots are broken in **p**, Rv 2:27

PIERCE (7)
in pieces and **p** them through with Nm 24:8
which will **p** the hand of any man 2 Kgs 18:21
by his eyes, or **p** his nose with a snare? Jb 40:24
rope in his nose or **p** his jaw with a hook? Jb 41:2
which will **p** the hand of any man who Is 36:6
bore him shall **p** him through when Zec 13:3
(and a sword will **p** through your own Lk 2:35

PIERCED (16)
into the chamber and **p** both of them, Nm 25:8
his head; she shattered and **p** his temple. Jgs 5:26
so that the arrow **p** his heart, 2 Kgs 9:24
fair; his hand **p** the fleeing serpent. Jb 26:13
me; they have **p** my hands and feet— Ps 22:16
with the slain, those **p** by the sword, Is 14:19
cut Rahab in pieces, that **p** the dragon? Is 51:9
the field, behold, those **p** by the sword! Jer 14:18
"And those **p** by the LORD on that day Jer 25:33
away, **p** by lack of the fruits of the field. Lam 4:9
You **p** with his own arrows the heads Hab 3:14
on me, on him whom they have **p**, Zec 12:10
But one of the soldiers **p** his side with a Jn 19:34
will look on him whom they have **p**." Jn 19:37
the faith and **p** themselves with many 1 Tm 6:10
eye will see him, even those who **p** him, Rv 1:7

PIERCES (1)
till an arrow **p** its liver; as a bird rushes Prv 7:23

PIERCING (1)
p to the division of soul and of spirit, Heb 4:12

PIETY (1)
our own power or **p** we have made him Acts 3:12

PIG (2)
And the **p**, because it parts the hoof and Lv 11:7
And the **p**, because it parts the hoof but Dt 14:8

PIG'S (4)
a gold ring in a **p** snout is a beautiful Prv 11:22
who eat **p** flesh, and broth of tainted meat Is 65:4
offering, like one who offers **p** blood; Is 66:3
eating **p** flesh and the abomination and Is 66:17

PIGEON (2)
years old, a turtledove, and a young **p**." Gn 15:9
and a **p** or a turtledove for a sin offering, Lv 12:6

PIGEONS (14)
bring his offering of turtledoves or **p**. Lv 1:14
has committed two turtledoves or two **p**, Lv 5:7
cannot afford two turtledoves or two **p**, Lv 5:11
she shall take two turtledoves or two **p**, Lv 12:8
also two turtledoves or two **p**, Lv 14:22
he shall offer, of the turtledoves or **p**, Lv 14:30
turtledoves or two **p** and come before Lv 15:14
turtledoves or two **p** and bring them Lv 15:29
two turtledoves or two **p** to the priest to Nm 6:10
and the seats of those who sold **p**. Mt 21:12
and the seats of those who sold **p**. Mk 11:15
"a pair of turtledoves, or two young **p**." Lk 2:24
who were selling oxen and sheep and **p**, Jn 2:14
And he told those who sold the **p**, "Take Jn 2:16

PIGS (12)
and do not throw your pearls before **p**, Mt 7:6
a herd of many **p** was feeding at some Mt 8:30
us out, send us away into the herd of **p**." Mt 8:31
So they came out and went into the **p**, Mt 8:32
a great herd of **p** was feeding there on Mk 5:11
begged him, saying, "Send us to the **p**; Mk 5:12
spirits came out, and entered the **p**, Mk 5:13
the demon-possessed man and to the **p**. Mk 5:16
a large herd of **p** was feeding there on Lk 8:32
came out of the man and entered the **p**, Lk 8:33
who sent him into his fields to feed **p**. Lk 15:15
to be fed with the pods that the **p** ate, Lk 15:16

PILATE (56)
delivered him over to **P** the governor. Mt 27:2
Then **P** said to him, "Do you not hear Mt 27:13
they had gathered, **P** said to them, Mt 27:17
P said to them, "Then what shall I do Mt 27:22
So when **P** saw that he was gaining Mt 27:24
He went to **P** and asked for the body of Mt 27:58
Then **P** ordered it to be given to him. Mt 27:58
and the Pharisees gathered before **P** Mt 27:62
P said to them, "You have a guard of Mt 27:65
him away and delivered him over to **P**. Mk 15:1
And **P** asked him, "Are you the King of Mk 15:2
And **P** again asked him, "Have you no Mk 15:4
further answer, so that **P** was amazed. Mk 15:5
up and began to ask **P** to do as he Mk 15:8
And **P** again said to them, "Then what Mk 15:12
And **P** said to them, "Why, what evil Mk 15:14
So **P**, wishing to satisfy the crowd, Mk 15:15
courage and went to **P** and asked for Mk 15:43
P was surprised to hear that he should Mk 15:44
Pontius **P** being governor of Judea, Lk 3:1
Galileans whose blood **P** had mingled Lk 13:1
them arose and brought him before **P**. Lk 23:1
And **P** asked him, "Are you the King of Lk 23:3
Then **P** said to the chief priests and the Lk 23:4
When **P** heard this, he asked whether Lk 23:6
clothing, he sent him back to **P**. Lk 23:11
And Herod and **P** became friends with Lk 23:12
P then called together the chief priests Lk 23:13
P addressed them once more, desiring Lk 23:20
So **P** decided that their demand should Lk 23:24
This man went to **P** and asked for the Lk 23:52
So **P** went outside to them and said, Jn 18:29
P said to them, "Take him yourselves Jn 18:31
So **P** entered his headquarters again and Jn 18:33
P answered, "Am I a Jew? Your own Jn 18:35
Then **P** said to him, "So you are a Jn 18:37
P said to him, "What is truth?" After he Jn 18:38
Then **P** took Jesus and flogged him. Jn 19:1
P went out again and said to them, "See, I Jn 19:4
robe. **P** said to them, "Behold the man!" Jn 19:5
him, crucify him!" **P** said to them, Jn 19:6
When **P** heard this statement, he was Jn 19:8
So **P** said to him, "You will not speak to Jn 19:10
From then on **P** sought to release him, Jn 19:12
So when **P** heard these words, he Jn 19:13
with him, crucify him!" **P** said to them, Jn 19:15
P also wrote an inscription and put it Jn 19:19
So the chief priests of the Jews said to **P**, Jn 19:21
P answered, "What I have written I have Jn 19:22
the Jews asked **P** that their legs might be Jn 19:31
asked **P** that he might take away the Jn 19:38
of Jesus, and **P** gave him permission. Jn 19:38
over and denied in the presence of **P**, Acts 3:13
anointed, both Herod and Pontius **P**, Acts 4:27
they asked **P** to have him executed. Acts 13:28
testimony before Pontius **P** made the 1 Tm 6:13

PILDASH (1)
Chesed, Hazo, **P**, Jidlaph, and Bethuel." Gn 22:22

PILE (10)
you shall set them in two piles, six in a **p**, Lv 24:6
shall put pure frankincense on each **p**, Lv 24:7
month they began to **p** up the heaps, 2 Chr 31:7
like dust, and **p** up clothing like clay, Jb 27:16
he may **p** it up, but the righteous will Jb 27:17
p her up like heaps of grain, and devote Jer 50:26
one of the flock; **p** the logs under it; Ezk 24:5
city! I also will make the **p** great. Ezk 24:9
fortress, for they **p** up earth and take it. Hab 1:10
either for the soil or for the manure **p**. Lk 14:35

PILED (1)
the blast of your nostrils the waters **p** up; Ex 15:8

PILES (1)
And you shall set them in two **p**, six in a Lv 24:6

PILFERING (1)
not **p**, but showing all good faith, so that Ti 2:10

PILHA (1)
Hallohesh, **P**, Shobek, Neh 10:24

PILLAGED (1)
How Esau has been **p**, his treasures Ob 1:6

PILLAR (55)
back, and she became a **p** of salt. Gn 19:26
set it up for a **p** and poured oil on the Gn 28:18
this stone, which I have set up for a **p**, Gn 28:22
where you anointed a **p** and made a Gn 31:13
Jacob took a stone and set it up as a **p**. Gn 31:45
said to Jacob, "See this heap and the **p**, Gn 31:51
heap is a witness, and the **p** is a witness, Gn 31:52
pass over this heap and this **p** to me, Gn 31:52
And Jacob set up a **p** in the place where Gn 35:14
he had spoken with him, a **p** of stone. Gn 35:14
and Jacob set up a **p** over her tomb. It is Gn 35:20
her tomb. It is the **p** of Rachel's tomb, Gn 35:20
them by day in a **p** of cloud to lead Ex 13:21
and by night in a **p** of fire to give them Ex 13:21
The **p** of cloud by day and the pillar of Ex 13:22
cloud by day and the **p** of fire by night Ex 13:22
and the **p** of cloud moved from before Ex 14:19
watch the LORD in the **p** of fire and of Ex 14:24
the **p** of cloud would descend and stand Ex 33:9
the people saw the **p** of cloud standing Ex 33:10
for yourselves or erect an image or **p**, Lv 26:1
came down in a **p** of cloud and stood Nm 12:5
in a **p** of cloud by day and in a pillar Nm 14:14
by day and in a **p** of fire by night. Nm 14:14
And you shall not set up a **p**, which the Dt 16:22
appeared in the tent in a **p** of cloud. Dt 31:15
And the **p** of cloud stood over the Dt 31:15
king, by the oak of the **p** at Shechem. Jgs 9:6
set up for himself the **p** that is in the 2 Sm 18:18
He called the **p** after his own 2 Sm 18:18
cubits was the height of one **p**, 1 Kgs 7:15
fingers. The second **p** was the same. 1 Kgs 7:15
capital that was on the top of the **p**, 1 Kgs 7:18
He set up the **p** on the south and 1 Kgs 7:21
and he set up the **p** on the north and 1 Kgs 7:21
for he put away the **p** of Baal that his 2 Kgs 3:2
they brought out the **p** that was in 2 Kgs 10:26
And they demolished the **p** of Baal, 2 Kgs 10:27
was the king standing by the **p**, 2 Kgs 11:14
king stood by the **p** and made a 2 Kgs 23:3
of the one **p** was eighteen cubits, 2 Kgs 25:17
And the second **p** had the same, 2 Kgs 25:17
standing by his **p** at the entrance, 2 Chr 23:13
By a **p** of cloud you led them in the day, Neh 9:12
and by a **p** of fire in the night to light Neh 9:12
The **p** of cloud to lead them in the way Neh 9:19
nor the **p** of fire by night to light for Neh 9:19
In the **p** of the cloud he spoke to them; Ps 99:7
Egypt, and a **p** to the LORD at its border. Is 19:19
you this day a fortified city, an iron **p**, Jer 1:18
height of the one **p** was eighteen cubits, Jer 52:21
capital. And the second **p** had the same, Jer 52:22
king or prince, without sacrifice or **p**, Hos 3:4
living God, a **p** and buttress of truth. 1 Tm 3:15
I will make him a **p** in the temple of my Rv 3:12

PILLARS (97)
them and break their **p** in pieces. Ex 23:24
at the foot of the mountain, and twelve **p**, Ex 24:4
hang it on four **p** of acacia overlaid Ex 26:32
make for the screen five **p** of acacia, Ex 26:37
Its twenty **p** and their twenty bases Ex 27:10
the hooks of the **p** and their fillets shall Ex 27:10
its **p** twenty and their bases twenty, Ex 27:11
the hooks of the **p** and their fillets shall Ex 27:11
fifty cubits, with ten **p** and ten bases. Ex 27:12
with their three **p** and three bases. Ex 27:14
with their three **p** and three bases. Ex 27:15
It shall have four **p** and with them four Ex 27:16
All the **p** around the court shall be Ex 27:17
altars and break their **p** and cut down Ex 34:13
its hooks and its frames, its bars, its **p**, Ex 35:11
of the court, its **p** and its bases, Ex 35:17
it he made four **p** of acacia and overlaid Ex 36:36
and its five **p** with their hooks. He Ex 36:38
their twenty **p** and their twenty bases Ex 38:10
the hooks of the **p** and their fillets were Ex 38:10
of a hundred cubits, their twenty **p**, Ex 38:11
the hooks of the **p** and their fillets were Ex 38:11
hangings of fifty cubits, their ten **p**, Ex 38:12
the hooks of the **p** and their fillets were Ex 38:12
with their three **p** and three bases. Ex 38:14
with their three **p** and their three bases. Ex 38:15
And the bases for the **p** were of bronze, Ex 38:17
the hooks of the **p** and their fillets were Ex 38:17
and all the **p** of the court were filleted Ex 38:17
And their **p** were four in number. Their Ex 38:19
made hooks for the **p** and overlaid their Ex 38:28
its hooks, its frames, its bars, its **p**, Ex 39:33
the hangings of the court, its **p**, and its Ex 39:40
and put in its poles, and raised up its **p**. Ex 40:18
of the tabernacle, the bars, the **p**, Nm 3:36
also the **p** around the court, with their Nm 3:37
tabernacle, with its bars, **p**, and bases, Nm 4:31
and the **p** around the court with their Nm 4:32
dash in pieces their **p** and chop down their Dt 7:5
dash in pieces their **p** and burn their Dt 12:3
They made him stand between the **p**. Jgs 16:25
"Let me feel the **p** on which the house Jgs 16:26
grasped the two middle **p** on which the Jgs 16:29
For the **p** of the earth are the LORD'S, 1 Sm 2:8
it was built on four rows of cedar **p**, 1 Kgs 7:2
pillars, with cedar beams on the **p**. 1 Kgs 7:2
chambers that were on the forty-five **p**, 1 Kgs 7:3
And he made the Hall of **P**; its length 1 Kgs 7:6
There was a porch in front with **p**, and 1 Kgs 7:6
He cast two **p** of bronze. Eighteen 1 Kgs 7:15
cast bronze to set on the tops of the **p**. 1 Kgs 7:16
for the capitals on the tops of the **p**, 1 Kgs 7:17
the tops of the **p** in the vestibule were 1 Kgs 7:19
were on the two **p** and also above the 1 Kgs 7:20
He set up the **p** at the vestibule of the 1 Kgs 7:21
on the tops of the **p** was lily-work. 1 Kgs 7:22
Thus the work of the **p** was finished. 1 Kgs 7:22
the two **p**, the two bowls of the 1 Kgs 7:41
capitals that were on the tops of the **p**, 1 Kgs 7:41
capitals that were on the tops of the **p**; 1 Kgs 7:41
of the capitals that were on the **p**; 1 Kgs 7:42
high places and **p** and Asherim on 1 Kgs 14:23
up for themselves **p** and Asherim on 2 Kgs 17:10
places and broke the **p** and cut down 2 Kgs 18:4
broke in pieces the **p** and cut down 2 Kgs 23:14
And the **p** of bronze that were in the 2 Kgs 25:13
As for the two **p**, the one sea, and the 2 Kgs 25:16
bronze sea and the **p** and the vessels 1 Chr 18:8
he made two **p** thirty-five cubits 2 Chr 3:15
and put them on the tops of the **p**, 2 Chr 3:16
He set up the **p** in front of the temple, 2 Chr 3:17
the two **p**, the bowls, and the two 2 Chr 4:12
the two capitals on the top of the **p**; 2 Chr 4:12
capitals that were on the top of the **p**; 2 Chr 4:12
of the capitals that were on the **p**. 2 Chr 4:13
and broke down the **p** and cut down 2 Chr 14:3
broke in pieces the **p** and cut down 2 Chr 31:1
and purple to silver rods and marble **p**, Est 1:6
the earth out of its place, and its **p** tremble; Jb 9:6
The **p** of heaven tremble and are Jb 26:11
inhabitants, it is I who keep steady its **p**. Ps 75:3
our daughters like corner **p** cut for the Ps 144:12
her house; she has hewn her seven **p**. Prv 9:1
Those who are the **p** of the land will be Is 19:10
says the LORD of hosts concerning the **p**, Jer 27:19
And the **p** of bronze that were in the Jer 52:17
As for the two **p**, the one sea, the twelve Jer 52:20
As for the **p**, the height of the one pillar Jer 52:21
and your mighty **p** will fall to the Ezk 26:11
And there were **p** beside the jambs, Ezk 40:49
and they had no **p** like the pillars of the Ezk 42:6
had no pillars like the **p** of the courts. Ezk 42:6
country improved, he improved his **p**. Hos 10:1
down their altars and destroy their **p**. Hos 10:2
images and your **p** from among you, Mi 5:13
Cephas and John, who seemed to be **p**, Gal 2:9
like the sun, and his legs like **p** of fire. Rv 10:1

PILLOW (2)
the bed and put a **p** of goats' hair at 1 Sm 19:13
with the **p** of goats' hair at its head. 1 Sm 19:16

PILOT (2)
more attention to the **p** and to the Acts 27:11
rudder wherever the will of the **p** directs. Jas 3:4

PILOTS (4)
O Tyre, were in you; they were your **p**. Ezk 27:8
your mariners and your **p**, Ezk 27:27
cry of your **p** the countryside shakes, Ezk 27:28
mariners and all the **p** of the sea stand Ezk 27:29

PILTAI (1)
Zichri; of Miniamin, of Moadiah, **P**; Neh 12:17

PIN (6)
the web and fasten it tight with the **p**, Jgs 16:13
them tight with the **p** and said to him, Jgs 16:14

from his sleep and pulled away the **p**, Jgs 16:14
"I will **p** David to the wall." But 1 Sm 18:11
And Saul sought to **p** David to the 1 Sm 19:10
Now please let me **p** him to the earth 1 Sm 26:8

PINCHED (1)
are; I too was **p** off from a piece of clay. Jb 33:6

PINE (3)
of our house are cedar; our rafters are **p**. Sg 1:17
the cypress, the plane and the **p** together, Is 41:19
to you, the cypress, the plane, and the **p**, Is 60:13

PINES (1)
made your deck of **p** from the coasts of Ezk 27:6

PINIONS (5)
catching them, bearing them on its **p**, Dt 32:11
but are they the **p** and plumage of love? Jb 39:13
with silver, its **p** with shimmering gold. Ps 68:13
He will cover you with his **p**, and under Ps 91:4
great eagle with great wings and long **p**, Ezk 17:3

PINNACLE (2)
city and set him on the **p** of the temple Mt 4:5
and set him on the **p** of the temple and Lk 4:9

PINNACLES (1)
I will make your **p** of agate, your gates of Is 54:12

PINON (2)
Oholibamah, Elah, **P**, Gn 36:41
Oholibamah, Elah, **P**, 1 Chr 1:52

PIPE (8)
of all those who play the lyre and **p**. Gn 4:21
the lyre and rejoice to the sound of the **p**. Jb 21:12
and my **p** to the voice of those who weep. Jb 30:31
dance; praise him with strings and **p**! Ps 150:4
you hear the sound of the horn, **p**, lyre, Dn 3:5
heard the sound of the horn, **p**, lyre, Dn 3:7
who hears the sound of the horn, **p**, lyre, Dn 3:10
you hear the sound of the horn, **p**, lyre, Dn 3:15

PIPES (2)
went up after him, playing on **p**, 1 Kgs 1:40
beside the two golden **p** from which the Zec 4:12

PIRAM (1)
king of Hebron, to **P** king of Jarmuth, Jos 10:3

PIRATHON (4)
died and was buried at **P** in the land of Jgs 12:15
Benaiah of **P**, Hiddai of the brooks of 2 Sm 23:30
people of Benjamin, Benaiah of **P**, 1 Chr 11:31
eleventh month, was Benaiah of **P**, 1 Chr 27:14

PIRATHONITE (2)
the son of Hillel the **P** judged Israel. Jgs 12:13
son of Hillel the **P** died and was buried Jgs 12:15

PISGAH (8)
by the top of **P** that looks down on Nm 21:20
to the field of Zophim, to the top of **P**, Nm 23:14
Salt Sea, under the slopes of **P** on the east. Dt 3:17
Go up to the top of **P** and lift up your eyes Dt 3:27
Sea of the Arabah, under the slopes of **P**. Dt 4:49
of Moab to Mount Nebo, to the top of **P**, Dt 34:1
southward to the foot of the slopes of **P**; Jos 12:3
and Beth-peor, and the slopes of **P**, and Jos 13:20

PISHON (1)
The name of the first is the **P**. It is the Gn 2:11

PISIDIA (2)
Perga and came to Antioch in **P**. Acts 13:14
they passed through **P** and came to Acts 14:24

PISPA (1)
sons of Jether: Jephunneh, **P**, and Ara. 1 Chr 7:38

PISTACHIO (1)
and a little honey, gum, myrrh, **p** nuts, Gn 43:11

PIT (86)
cast him into this **p** here in the Gn 37:22
they took him and cast him into a **p**. Gn 37:24
The **p** was empty; there was no water in Gn 37:24
Joseph up and lifted him out of the **p**, Gn 37:28
Reuben returned to the **p** and saw that Gn 37:29
and saw that Joseph was not in the **p**, Gn 37:29
that they should put me into the **p**." Gn 40:15
they quickly brought him out of the **p**. Gn 41:14
"When a man opens a **p**, or when a Ex 21:33
when a man digs a **p** and does not cover Ex 21:33
owner of the **p** shall make restoration. Ex 21:34
him into a great **p** in the forest and 2 Sm 18:17
down a lion in a **p** on a day when 2 Sm 23:20
them at the **p** of Beth-eked, 2 Kgs 10:14
down a lion in a **p** on a day when 1 Chr 11:22
yet you will plunge me into a **p**, and my Jb 9:31
if I say to the **p**, 'You are my father,' and Jb 17:14
he keeps back his soul from the **p**, his Jb 33:18
His soul draws near the **p**, and his life to Jb 33:22
him from going down into the **p**; Jb 33:24
my soul from going down into the **p**, Jb 33:28
to bring back his soul from the **p**, that Jb 33:30
He makes a **p**, digging it out, and falls Ps 7:15
have sunk in the **p** that they made; Ps 9:15
become like those who go down to the **p**. Ps 28:1
from among those who go down to the **p**. Ps 30:3
is there in my death, if I go down to the **p**? Ps 30:9
without cause they dug a **p** for my life. Ps 35:7
He drew me up from the **p** of destruction, Ps 40:2
live on forever and never see the **p**. Ps 49:9
them down into the **p** of destruction; Ps 55:23
bowed down. They dug a **p** in my way, Ps 57:6
me up, or the **p** close its mouth over me. Ps 69:15
among those who go down to the **p**; Ps 88:4
You have put me in the depths of the **p**, Ps 88:6
trouble, until a **p** is dug for the wicked. Ps 94:13
who redeems your life from the **p**, who Ps 103:4
lest I be like those who go down to the **p**. Ps 143:7
whole, like those who go down to the **p**; Prv 1:12
mouth of forbidden women is a deep **p**; Prv 22:14
For a prostitute is a deep **p**; an Prv 23:27
Whoever digs a **p** will fall into it, and a Prv 26:27
an evil way will fall into his own **p**, Prv 28:10
He who digs a **p** will fall into it, and a Eccl 10:8
down to Sheol, to the far reaches of the **p**. Is 14:15
who go down to the stones of the **p**, Is 14:19
Terror and the **p** and the snare are upon Is 24:17
sound of the terror shall fall into the **p**, Is 24:18
climbs out of the **p** shall be caught in Is 24:18
be gathered together as prisoners in a **p**; Is 24:22
my life from the **p** of destruction, Is 38:17
who go down to the **p** do not hope for Is 38:18
he shall not die and go down to the **p**, Is 51:14
evil? Yet they have dug a **p** for my life. Jer 18:20
For they have dug a **p** to take me and Jer 18:22
Terror, **p**, and snare are before you, O Jer 48:43
flees from the terror shall fall into the **p**, Jer 48:44
climbs out of the **p** shall be caught in Jer 48:44
me alive into the **p** and cast stones on Lam 3:53
name, O LORD, from the depths of the **p**; Lam 3:55
he was caught in their **p**, and they Ezk 19:4
net over him; he was taken in their **p**. Ezk 19:8
down with those who go down to the **p**, Ezk 26:20
old, with those who go down to the **p**, Ezk 26:20
They shall thrust you down into the **p**, Ezk 28:8
man, with those who go down to the **p**. Ezk 31:14
Sheol with those who go down to the **p**. Ezk 31:16
to those who have gone down to the **p**: Ezk 32:18
are set in the uttermost parts of the **p**; Ezk 32:23
with those who go down to the **p**. Ezk 32:24
with those who go down to the **p**; Ezk 32:25
with those who go down to the **p**. Ezk 32:29
with those who go down to the **p**. Ezk 32:30
yet you brought up my life from the **p**, O Jon 2:6
your prisoners free from the waterless **p**. Zec 9:11
sheep, if it falls into a **p** on the Sabbath, Mt 12:11
lead the blind, both will fall into a **p**." Mt 15:14
it and dug a **p** for the winepress and Mk 12:1
man? Will they not both fall into a **p**? Lk 6:39
the key to the shaft of the bottomless **p**. Rv 9:1
He opened the shaft of the bottomless **p**, Rv 9:2
over them the angel of the bottomless **p**. Rv 9:11
from the bottomless **p** will make war Rv 11:7
rise from the bottomless **p** and go to Rv 17:8
key to the bottomless **p** and a great Rv 20:1
and threw him into the **p**, and shut it Rv 20:3

PITCH (11)
ark, and cover it inside and out with **p**. Gn 6:14
and daubed it with bitumen and **p**. Ex 2:3
and there was **p** darkness in all the land Ex 10:22
to take the tent and **p** it outside the camp, Ex 33:7
people of Israel shall **p** their tents by Nm 1:52
to seek you out a place to **p** your tents, Dt 1:33
no Arab will **p** his tent there; Is 13:20
streams of Edom shall be turned into **p**, Is 34:9
sulfur; her land shall become burning **p**. Is 34:9
her; they shall **p** their tents around her; Jer 6:3
And he shall **p** his palatial tents Dn 11:45

PITCHED (13)
on the east of Bethel and **p** his tent, Gn 12:8
name of the LORD and **p** his tent there. Gn 26:25
Now Jacob had **p** his tent in the hill Gn 31:25
Laban with his kinsmen **p** tents in the Gn 31:25
of land on which he had **p** his tent. Gn 33:19
journeyed on and **p** his tent beyond Gn 35:21
and when the tabernacle is to be **p**, Nm 1:51
and had **p** his tent as far away as the oak Jgs 4:11
inside the tent that David had **p** for it. 2 Sm 6:17
So they **p** a tent for Absalom on the 2 Sm 16:22
for the ark of God and **p** a tent for it. 1 Chr 15:1
inside the tent that David had **p** for it, 1 Chr 16:1
for he had **p** a tent for it in Jerusalem.) 2 Chr 1:4

PITCHER (1)
or the **p** is shattered at the fountain, Eccl 12:6

PITCHERS (1)
I set before the Rechabites **p** full of wine, Jer 35:5

PITFALL (1)
panic and **p** have come upon us, Lam 3:47

PITFALLS (1)
The insolent have dug **p** for me; they Ps 119:85

PITHOM (1)
for Pharaoh store cities, **P** and Raamses. Ex 1:11

PITHON (2)
Micah: **P**, Melech, Tarea, and Ahaz. 1 Chr 8:35
Micah: **P**, Melech, Tahrea, and Ahaz. 1 Chr 9:41

PITIABLE (1)
realizing that you are wretched, **p**, poor, Rv 3:17

PITIED (4)
caused them to be **p** by all those who Ps 106:46
how you will be **p** when pangs come Jer 22:23
No eye **p** you, to do any of these things Ezk 16:5
we are of all people most to be **p**. 1 Cor 15:19

PITS (7)
Valley of Siddim was full of bitumen **p**, Gn 14:10
him and throw him into one of the **p**. Gn 37:20
in one of the **p** or in some other 2 Sm 17:9
Let them be cast into fire, into miry **p**, Ps 140:10
the wilderness, in a land of deserts and **p**, Jer 2:6
anointed, was captured in their **p**, Lam 4:20
a land possessed by nettles and salt **p**, Zep 2:9

PITY (41)
She took **p** on him and said, "This is one Ex 2:6
Your eye shall not **p** them, neither shall Dt 7:16
listen to him, nor shall your eye **p** him, Dt 13:8
Your eye shall not **p** him, but you shall Dt 19:13
Your eye shall not **p**. It shall be life for Dt 19:21
off her hand. Your eye shall have no **p**. Dt 25:12
LORD was moved to **p** by their groaning Jgs 2:18
this thing, and because he had no **p**." 2 Sm 12:6
It hurls at him without **p**; he flees from Jb 27:22
They close their hearts to **p**; with their Ps 17:10
I looked for **p**, but there was none, and Ps 69:20
He has **p** on the weak and the needy, Ps 72:13
How long? Have **p** on your servants! Ps 90:13
You will arise and have **p** on Zion; it is Ps 102:13
her stones dear and have **p** on her dust. Ps 102:14
nor any to **p** his fatherless children! Ps 109:12
the womb; their eyes will not **p** children. Is 13:18
for he who has **p** on them will lead them, Is 49:10
in his love and in his **p** he redeemed them; Is 63:9
I will not **p** or spare or have Jer 13:14
"Who will have **p** on you, O Jerusalem, Jer 15:5
that the LORD overthrew without **p**; Jer 20:16
He shall not **p** them or spare them or Jer 21:7
ago; he has thrown down without **p**; Lam 2:17
of your anger, slaughtering without **p**. Lam 2:21
and pursued us, killing without **p**; Lam 3:43
eye will not spare, and I will have no **p**. Ezk 5:11
eye will not spare you, nor will I have **p**, Ezk 7:4
my eye will not spare, nor will I have **p**. Ezk 7:9
My eye will not spare, nor will I have **p**. Ezk 8:18
shall not spare, and you shall show no **p**. Ezk 9:5
my eye will not spare, nor will I have **p**; Ezk 9:10
for his land and had **p** on his people. Jl 2:18
with the sword and cast off all **p**, Am 1:11
And the LORD said, "You **p** the plant, for Jon 4:10
And should not I **p** Nineveh, that great Jon 4:11
their own shepherds have no **p** on them. Zec 11:5
no longer have **p** on the inhabitants Zec 11:6
And out of **p** for him, the master of that Mt 18:27
And Jesus in **p** touched their eyes, and Mt 20:34
Moved with **p**, he stretched out his hand Mk 1:41

PLACE (847)
heavens be gathered together into one **p**, Gn 1:9
of his ribs and closed up its **p** with flesh. Gn 2:21
But the dove found no **p** to set her foot, Gn 8:9
through the land to the **p** at Shechem, Gn 12:6
far as Bethel to the **p** where his tent had Gn 13:3
to the **p** where he had made an altar at Gn 13:4
and look from the **p** where you are, Gn 13:14
then sweep away the **p** and not spare it Gn 18:24
I will spare the whole **p** for their sake." Gn 18:26
and Abraham returned to his **p**. Gn 18:33
in the city, bring them out of the **p**. Gn 19:12
For we are about to destroy this **p**, Gn 19:13
Get out of this **p**, for the LORD is about Gn 19:14
the morning to the **p** where he had Gn 19:27
There is no fear of God at all in this **p**, Gn 20:11
at every **p** to which we come, say of me, Gn 20:13
Therefore that **p** was called Beersheba, Gn 21:31
and went to the **p** of which God had Gn 22:3
up his eyes and saw the **p** from afar. Gn 22:4
they came to the **p** of which God had Gn 22:9
So Abraham called the name of that **p**, Gn 22:14
me property among you for a burying **p**, Gn 23:4

presence as property for a burying **p**.” Gn 23:9
property for a burying **p** by the Hittites. Gn 23:20
the house and a **p** for the camels.” Gn 24:31
the men of the **p** asked him about his Gn 26:7
the men of the **p** should kill me because Gn 26:7
came to a certain **p** and stayed there Gn 28:11
Taking one of the stones of the **p**, he Gn 28:11
head and lay down in that **p** to sleep. Gn 28:11
and said, “Surely the LORD is in this **p**, Gn 28:16
and said, “How awesome is this **p**! Gn 28:17
He called the name of that **p** Bethel, but Gn 28:19
the stone back in its **p** over the mouth of Gn 29:3
all the people of the **p** and made a feast. Gn 29:22
and he said, “Am I in the **p** of God, Gn 30:2
he called the name of that **p** Mahanaim. Gn 32:2
Jacob called the name of the **p** Peniel, Gn 32:30
the name of the **p** is called Succoth. Gn 33:17
built an altar and called the **p** El-bethel, Gn 35:7
from him in the **p** where he had Gn 35:13
a pillar in the **p** where he had spoken Gn 35:14
the name of the **p** where God had Gn 35:15
son of Zerah of Bozrah reigned in his **p**. Gn 36:33
land of the Temanites reigned in his **p**. Gn 36:34
the country of Moab, reigned in his **p**, Gn 36:35
Samlah of Masrekah reigned in his **p**. Gn 36:36
on the Euphrates reigned in his **p**. Gn 36:37
the son of Achbor reigned in his **p**. Gn 36:38
died, and Hadar reigned in his **p**, Gn 36:39
And he asked the men of the **p**, “Where Gn 38:21
Also, the men of the **p** said, ‘No cult Gn 38:22
the **p** where the king’s prisoners were Gn 39:20
and you shall **p** Pharaoh’s cup in his Gn 40:13
go from this **p** unless your youngest Gn 42:15
give his donkey fodder at the lodging **p**, Gn 42:27
came to the lodging **p** we opened our Gn 43:21
his brother, and he sought a **p** to weep. Gn 43:30
me in their burying **p**.” He answered, Gn 47:30
He saw that a resting **p** was good, and Gn 49:15
the Hittite to possess as a burying **p**. Gn 49:30
Egyptians.” Therefore the **p** was named Gn 50:11
the Hittite to possess as a burying **p**. Gn 50:13
“Do not fear, for am I in the **p** of God? Gn 50:19
for the **p** on which you are standing is Ex 3:5
and honey, to the **p** of the Canaanites, Ex 3:8
At a lodging **p** on the way the LORD met Ex 4:24
anyone rise from his **p** for three days, Ex 10:23
the LORD brought you out from this **p**. Ex 13:3
them on your own mountain, the **p**, Ex 15:17
Remain each of you in his **p**; let no one Ex 16:29
one go out of his **p** on the seventh day.” Ex 16:29
and **p** it before the LORD to be kept Ex 16:33
the name of the **p** Massah and Meribah, Ex 17:7
and **p** such men over the people as Ex 18:21
people also will go to their **p** in peace.” Ex 18:23
In every **p** where I cause my name to be Ex 20:24
appoint for you a **p** to which he may Ex 21:13
bring you to the **p** that I have prepared. Ex 23:20
for you the Holy **P** from the Most Holy. Ex 26:33
of the testimony in the Most Holy **P**. Ex 26:34
his heart, when he goes into the Holy **P**, Ex 28:29
he goes into the Holy **P** before the LORD, Ex 28:35
near the altar to minister in the Holy **P**, Ex 28:43
of meeting to minister in the Holy **P**, Ex 29:30
ordination and boil its flesh in a holy **p**. Ex 29:31
and the fragrant incense for the Holy **P**. Ex 31:11
the people to the **p** about which I have Ex 32:34
there is a **p** by me where you shall Ex 33:21
garments for ministering in the Holy **P**, Ex 35:19
garments, for ministering in the Holy **P**. Ex 39:1
garments for ministering in the Holy **P**, Ex 39:41
and **p** the basin between the tent of Ex 40:7
He put in **p** the screen for the door of the Ex 40:28
altar on the east side, in the **p** for ashes. Lv 1:16
carry outside the camp to a clean **p**, Lv 4:12
and kill it in the **p** where they kill the Lv 4:24
sin offering in the **p** of burnt offering. Lv 4:29
a sin offering in the **p** where they kill the Lv 4:33
the ashes outside the camp to a clean **p**. Lv 6:11
It shall be eaten unleavened in a holy **p**. Lv 6:16
In the **p** where the burnt offering is Lv 6:25
In a holy **p** it shall be eaten, in the court Lv 6:26
on which it was splashed in a holy **p**. Lv 6:27
to make atonement in the Holy **P**; Lv 6:30
In the **p** where they kill the burnt offering Lv 7:2
may eat of it. It shall be eaten in a holy **p**. Lv 7:6
You shall eat it in a holy **p**, because it is Lv 10:13
contributed you shall eat in a clean **p**, Lv 10:14
sin offering in the **p** of the sanctuary, Lv 10:17
and in the **p** of the boil there comes a Lv 13:19
spot remains in one **p** and does not Lv 13:23
spot remains in one **p** and does not Lv 13:28
the lamb in the **p** where they kill the Lv 14:13
offering, in the **p** of the sanctuary. Lv 14:13
in the **p** where the blood of the guilt Lv 14:28
into an unclean **p** outside the city. Lv 14:40
out in an unclean **p** outside the city. Lv 14:41
and put them in the **p** of those stones, Lv 14:42
them out of the city to an unclean **p**. Lv 14:45
any time into the Holy **P** inside the veil, Lv 16:2
way Aaron shall come into the Holy **P**: Lv 16:3
shall make atonement for the Holy **P**, Lv 16:16
in the Holy **P** until he comes Lv 16:17
of atoning for the Holy **P** and the tent of Lv 16:20
went into the Holy **P** and shall leave Lv 16:23
in water in a holy **p** and put on his Lv 16:24
in to make atonement in the Holy **P**, Lv 16:27
in his father’s **p** shall make atonement, Lv 16:32
his sons, and they shall eat it in a holy **p**, Lv 24:9
the woman’s head and **p** in her hands Nm 5:18
and in the **p** where the cloud settled Nm 9:17
setting out for the **p** of which the LORD Nm 10:29
to seek out a resting **p** for them. Nm 10:33
the name of that **p** was called Taberah, Nm 11:3
name of that **p** was called Nm 11:34
That **p** was called the Valley of Nm 13:24
will go up to the **p** that the LORD has Nm 14:40
In a most holy **p** shall you eat it. Every Nm 18:10
And you may eat it in any **p**, you and Nm 18:31
them outside the camp in a clean **p**. Nm 19:9
out of Egypt to bring us to this evil **p**? Nm 20:5
It is no **p** for grain or figs or vines or Nm 20:5
the name of the **p** was called Hormah. Nm 21:3
went ahead and stood in a narrow **p**, Nm 22:26
“Please come with me to another **p**, Nm 23:13
now, I will take you to another **p**. Nm 23:27
Therefore now flee to your own **p**. I Nm 24:11
said, “Enduring is your dwelling **p**, Nm 24:21
Balaam rose and went back to his **p**. Nm 24:25
In the Holy **P** you shall pour out a Nm 28:7
behold, the **p** was a place for livestock. Nm 32:1
behold, the place was a **p** for livestock. Nm 32:1
you have risen in your fathers’ **p**, Nm 32:14
until we have brought them to their **p**. Nm 32:17
that you went until you came to this **p**.’ Dt 1:31
to seek you out a **p** to pitch your tents, Dt 1:33
from before them and settled in their **p**, Dt 2:12
dispossessed them and settled in their **p**, Dt 2:21
and settled in their **p** even to this day. Dt 2:22
destroyed them and settled in their **p**.) Dt 2:23
the land of Egypt until you came to this **p**, Dt 9:7
son Eleazar ministered as priest in his **p**. Dt 10:6
the wilderness, until you came to this **p**, Dt 11:5
Every **p** on which the sole of your foot Dt 11:24
and destroy their name out of that **p**. Dt 12:3
you shall seek the **p** that the LORD your Dt 12:5
then to the **p** that the LORD your God Dt 12:11
burnt offerings at any **p** that you see, Dt 12:13
but at the **p** that the LORD will choose in Dt 12:14
your God in the **p** that the LORD your Dt 12:18
If the **p** that the LORD your God will Dt 12:21
you shall go to the **p** that the LORD will Dt 12:26
your God, in the **p** that he will choose, Dt 14:23
you, because the **p** is too far from you, Dt 14:24
hand and go to the **p** that the LORD your Dt 14:25
year by year at the **p** that the LORD will Dt 15:20
herd, at the **p** that the LORD will choose, Dt 16:2
but at the **p** that the LORD your God will Dt 16:6
and eat it at the **p** that the LORD your God Dt 16:7
at the **p** that the LORD your God will Dt 16:11
your God at the **p** that the LORD will Dt 16:15
your God at the **p** that he will choose: Dt 16:16
and go up to the **p** that the LORD your God Dt 17:8
to you from that **p** that the LORD will Dt 17:10
he desires—to the **p** that the LORD will Dt 18:6
city at the gate of the **p** where he lives, Dt 21:19
“You shall have a **p** outside the camp, Dt 23:12
in the **p** that he shall choose within one Dt 23:16
you shall go to the **p** that the LORD your Dt 26:2
brought us into this **p** and gave us this Dt 26:9
there shall be no resting **p** for the sole of Dt 28:65
And when you came to this **p**, Sihon the Dt 29:7
your God at the **p** that he will choose, Dt 31:11
The eternal God is your dwelling **p**, and Dt 33:27
but no one knows the **p** of his burial to Dt 34:6
Every **p** that the sole of your foot will Jos 1:3
God is providing you a **p** of rest and will Jos 1:13
shall set out from your **p** and follow it. Jos 3:3
from the very **p** where the priests’ feet Jos 4:3
them down in the **p** where you lodge Jos 4:3
with them to the **p** where they lodged and Jos 4:8
in the **p** where the feet of the priests Jos 4:9
returned to their **p** and overflowed all Jos 4:18
children, whom he raised up in their **p**, Jos 5:7
so the name of that **p** is called Gilgal to Jos 5:9
for the **p** where you are standing is Jos 5:15
the name of that **p** is called the Valley Jos 7:26
And they went to the **p** of ambush and lay Jos 8:9
to the appointed **p** toward the Arabah Jos 8:14
the ambush rose quickly out of their **p**, Jos 8:19
this day, in the **p** that he should choose. Jos 9:27
take him into the city and give him a **p**, Jos 20:4
and put in **p** statutes and rules for them Jos 24:25
they called the name of that **p** Bochim. Jgs 2:5
man stood in his **p** around the camp, Jgs 7:21
And that **p** was called Ramath-lehi. Jgs 15:17
split open the hollow **p** that is at Lehi, Jgs 15:19
And they surrounded the **p** and set an Jgs 16:2
to sojourn where he could find a **p**. Jgs 17:8
going to sojourn where I may find a **p**.” Jgs 17:9
you here? What are you doing in this **p**? Jgs 18:3
a **p** where there is no lack of anything Jgs 18:10
this account that **p** is called Jgs 18:12
The men of the **p** were Benjaminites. Jgs 19:16
is this that has taken **p** among you? Jgs 20:12
line in the same **p** where they had Jgs 20:22
up out of their **p** and set themselves in Jgs 20:33
out of their **p** from Maareh-geba. Jgs 20:33
she set out from the **p** where she was with Ru 1:7
he lies down, observe the **p** where he lies. Ru 3:4
and from the gate of his native **p**. Ru 4:10
not see, was lying down in his own **p**. 1 Sm 3:2
So Samuel went and lay down in his **p**. 1 Sm 3:9
took Dagon and put him back in his **p**. 1 Sm 5:3
of Israel, and let it return to its own **p**, 1 Sm 5:11
us with what we shall send it to its **p**.” 1 Sm 6:2
ark of the LORD and **p** it on the cart and 1 Sm 6:8
have a sacrifice today on the high **p**. 1 Sm 9:12
before he goes up to the high **p** to eat. 1 Sm 9:13
them on his way up to the high **p**. 1 Sm 9:14
Go up before me to the high **p**, for 1 Sm 9:19
hall and gave them a **p** at the head of 1 Sm 9:22
down from the high **p** into the city, 1 Sm 9:25
down from the high **p** with harp, 1 Sm 10:5
And a man of the **p** answered, “And 1 Sm 10:12
prophesying, he came to the high **p**. 1 Sm 10:13
Egypt and made them dwell in this **p**. 1 Sm 12:8
you,’ then we will stand still in our **p**, 1 Sm 14:9
the Philistines went to their own **p**. 1 Sm 14:46
Stay in a secret **p** and hide yourself. 1 Sm 19:2
down quickly to the **p** where you hid 1 Sm 20:19
Saul’s side, but David’s **p** was empty. 1 Sm 20:25
the new moon, David’s **p** was empty. 1 Sm 20:27
boy came to the **p** of the arrow that 1 Sm 20:37
the young men for such and such a **p**. 1 Sm 21:2
Know and see the **p** where his foot is, 1 Sm 23:22
Therefore that **p** was called the Rock 1 Sm 23:28
and came to the **p** where Saul had 1 Sm 26:5
And David saw the **p** where Saul lay, 1 Sm 26:5
his way, and Saul returned to his **p**. 1 Sm 26:25
let a **p** be given me in one of the 1 Sm 27:5
may return to the **p** to which you 1 Sm 29:4
Therefore that **p** was called 2 Sm 2:16
who came to the **p** where Asahel had 2 Sm 2:23
name of that **p** is called Baal-perazim. 2 Sm 5:20
And that **p** is called Perez-uzzah, to this 2 Sm 6:8
the ark of the LORD and set it in its **p**, 2 Sm 6:17
I will appoint a **p** for my people Israel 2 Sm 7:10
dwell in their own **p** and be disturbed 2 Sm 7:10
and Hanun his son reigned in his **p**. 2 Sm 10:1
Uriah to the **p** where he knew 2 Sm 11:16
let me see both it and his dwelling **p**. 2 Sm 15:25
of Saul, in whose **p** you have reigned, 2 Sm 16:8
in one of the pits or in some other **p**. 2 Sm 17:9
upon him in some **p** where he is to 2 Sm 17:12
my army from now on in **p** of Joab.’” 2 Sm 19:13
we should have no **p** in all the 2 Sm 21:5
He brought me out into a broad **p**; he 2 Sm 22:20
You gave a wide **p** for my steps under 2 Sm 22:37
he shall sit on my throne in my **p**,’ 1 Kgs 1:30
throne, for he shall be king in my **p**. 1 Kgs 1:35
Jehoiada over the army in **p** of Joab, 1 Kgs 2:35
Zadok the priest in the **p** of Abiathar. 1 Kgs 2:35
go out from there to any **p** whatever. 1 Kgs 2:36
you go out and go to any **p** whatever, 1 Kgs 2:42
there, for that was the great high **p**. 1 Kgs 3:4
your servant king in **p** of David my 1 Kgs 3:7
they brought to the **p** where it was 1 Kgs 4:28
anointed him king in **p** of his father, 1 Kgs 5:1
I will set on your throne in your **p**, 1 Kgs 5:5
rafts to go by sea to the **p** you direct. 1 Kgs 5:9
inner sanctuary, as the Most Holy **P**. 1 Kgs 6:16
part of the house, the Most Holy **P**, 1 Kgs 7:50
the LORD to its **p** in the inner sanctuary 1 Kgs 8:6
of the house, in the Most Holy **P**, 1 Kgs 8:6
out their wings over the **p** of the ark, 1 Kgs 8:7
seen from the Holy **P** before the inner 1 Kgs 8:8
the priests came out of the Holy **P**, 1 Kgs 8:10
house, a **p** for you to dwell in forever.” 1 Kgs 8:13
have risen in the **p** of David my 1 Kgs 8:20
there I have provided a **p** for the ark, 1 Kgs 8:21
house, the **p** of which you have said, 1 Kgs 8:29
that your servant offers toward this **p**. 1 Kgs 8:29
Israel, when they pray toward this **p**. 1 Kgs 8:30
And listen in heaven your dwelling **p**, 1 Kgs 8:30
pray toward this **p** and acknowledge 1 Kgs 8:35

heaven your dwelling **p** and forgive 1 Kgs 8:39
heaven your dwelling **p** and do 1 Kgs 8:43
heaven your dwelling **p** their prayer 1 Kgs 8:49
built a high **p** for Chemosh the 1 Kgs 11:7
Rehoboam his son reigned in his **p**. 1 Kgs 11:43
not eat bread or drink water in this **p**, 1 Kgs 13:8
nor drink water with you in this **p**, 1 Kgs 13:16
drunk water in the **p** of which he 1 Kgs 13:22
and Nadab his son reigned in his **p**. 1 Kgs 14:20
made in their **p** shields of bronze, 1 Kgs 14:27
Abijam his son reigned in his **p**. 1 Kgs 14:31
And Asa his son reigned in his **p**. 1 Kgs 15:8
his son reigned in his **p**. 1 Kgs 15:24
king of Judah and reigned in his **p**. 1 Kgs 15:28
and Elah his son reigned in his **p**. 1 Kgs 16:6
king of Judah, and reigned in his **p**. 1 Kgs 16:10
and Ahab his son reigned in his **p**. 1 Kgs 16:28
shall anoint to be prophet in your **p**. 1 Kgs 19:16
"In the **p** where dogs licked up the 1 Kgs 21:19
Ahaziah his son reigned in his **p**. 1 Kgs 22:40
Jehoram his son reigned in his **p**. 1 Kgs 22:50
became king in his **p** in the second 2 Kgs 1:17
to reign in his **p** and offered him for 2 Kgs 3:27
his hand over the **p** and cure the 2 Kgs 5:11
the **p** where we dwell under your 2 Kgs 6:1
and let us make a **p** for us to dwell 2 Kgs 6:2
it fall?" When he showed him the **p**, 2 Kgs 6:6
such and such a **p** shall be my camp." 2 Kgs 6:8
"Beware that you do not pass this **p**, 2 Kgs 6:9
Israel sent to the **p** about which the 2 Kgs 6:10
And Hazael became king in his **p**. 2 Kgs 8:15
and Ahaziah his son reigned in his **p**. 2 Kgs 8:24
Jehoahaz his son reigned in his **p**. 2 Kgs 10:35
Amaziah his son reigned in his **p**. 2 Kgs 12:21
and Joash his son reigned in his **p**. 2 Kgs 13:9
his son became king in his **p**. 2 Kgs 13:24
Jeroboam his son reigned in his **p**. 2 Kgs 14:16
Zechariah his son reigned in his **p**. 2 Kgs 14:29
and Jotham his son reigned in his **p**. 2 Kgs 15:7
him to death and reigned in his **p**. 2 Kgs 15:10
him to death and reigned in his **p**. 2 Kgs 15:14
Pekahiah his son reigned in his **p**. 2 Kgs 15:22
him to death and reigned in his **p**. 2 Kgs 15:25
him to death and reigned in his **p**, 2 Kgs 15:30
and Ahaz his son reigned in his **p**. 2 Kgs 15:38
from the **p** between his altar and the 2 Kgs 16:14
Hezekiah his son reigned in his **p**. 2 Kgs 16:20
come up against this **p** to destroy it? 2 Kgs 18:25
I entered its farthest lodging **p**, its 2 Kgs 19:23
Esarhaddon his son reigned in his **p**. 2 Kgs 19:37
Manasseh his son reigned in his **p**. 2 Kgs 20:21
and Amon his son reigned in his **p**. 2 Kgs 21:18
made Josiah his son king in his **p**. 2 Kgs 21:24
and Josiah his son reigned in his **p**. 2 Kgs 21:26
disaster upon this **p** and upon its 2 Kgs 22:16
wrath will be kindled against this **p**, 2 Kgs 22:17
I spoke against this **p** and against its 2 Kgs 22:19
bring upon this **p**.'" And they 2 Kgs 22:20
the high **p** erected by Jeroboam the 2 Kgs 23:15
altar with the high **p** he pulled down 2 Kgs 23:15
and made him king in his father's **p**. 2 Kgs 23:30
Josiah king in the **p** of Josiah his 2 Kgs 23:34
Jehoiachin his son reigned in his **p**. 2 Kgs 24:6
Jehoiachin's uncle, king in his **p**, 2 Kgs 24:17
of Zerah of Bozrah reigned in his **p**. 1 Chr 1:44
of the Temanites reigned in his **p**. 1 Chr 1:45
country of Moab, reigned in his **p**, 1 Chr 1:46
of Masrekah reigned in his **p**. 1 Chr 1:47
on the Euphrates reigned in his **p**. 1 Chr 1:48
the son of Achbor, reigned in his **p**. 1 Chr 1:49
died, and Hadad reigned in his **p**, 1 Chr 1:50
to this day, and settled in their **p**, 1 Chr 4:41
they lived in their **p** until the exile. 1 Chr 5:22
for all the work of the Most Holy **P**, 1 Chr 6:49
And that **p** is called Perez-uzza to 1 Chr 13:11
name of that **p** is called 1 Chr 14:11
And he prepared a **p** for the ark of 1 Chr 15:1
bring up the ark of the LORD to its **p**, 1 Chr 15:3
to the **p** that I have prepared for it. 1 Chr 15:12
him; strength and joy are in his **p**. 1 Chr 16:27
LORD in the high **p** that was at 1 Chr 16:39
I will appoint a **p** for my people Israel 1 Chr 17:9
dwell in their own **p** and be disturbed 1 Chr 17:9
died, and his son reigned in his **p**. 1 Chr 19:1
at that time in the high **p** at Gibeon, 1 Chr 21:29
LORD as king in **p** of David his 1 Chr 29:23
Solomon his son reigned in his **p**. 1 Chr 29:28
went to the high **p** that was at Gibeon, 2 Chr 1:3
Kiriath-jearim to the **p** that David had 2 Chr 1:4
and have made me king in his **p**. 2 Chr 1:8
came from the high **p** at Gibeon, 2 Chr 1:13
except as a **p** to make offerings before 2 Chr 2:6
at the **p** that David had appointed, 2 Chr 3:1
And he made the Most Holy **P**. Its 2 Chr 3:8
In the Most Holy **P** he made two 2 Chr 3:10
to the Most Holy **P** and for the doors 2 Chr 4:22
ark of the covenant of the LORD to its **p**, 2 Chr 5:7
of the house, in the Most Holy **P**, 2 Chr 5:7
out their wings over the **p** of the ark, 2 Chr 5:8
seen from the Holy **P** before the inner 2 Chr 5:9
out of the Holy **P** (for all the priests 2 Chr 5:11
house, a **p** for you to dwell in forever." 2 Chr 6:2
have risen in the **p** of David my 2 Chr 6:10
the **p** where you have promised to set 2 Chr 6:20
that your servant offers toward this **p**. 2 Chr 6:20
Israel, when they pray toward this **p**. 2 Chr 6:21
listen from heaven your dwelling **p**, 2 Chr 6:21
pray toward this **p** and acknowledge 2 Chr 6:26
heaven your dwelling **p** and forgive 2 Chr 6:30
heaven your dwelling **p** and do 2 Chr 6:33
heaven your dwelling **p** their prayer 2 Chr 6:39
ears attentive to the prayer of this **p**. 2 Chr 6:40
O LORD God, and go to your resting **p**, 2 Chr 6:41
and have chosen this **p** for myself as 2 Chr 7:12
to the prayer that is made in this **p**. 2 Chr 7:15
Rehoboam his son reigned in his **p**. 2 Chr 9:31
made in their **p** shields of bronze 2 Chr 12:10
and Abijah his son reigned in his **p**. 2 Chr 12:16
And Asa his son reigned in his **p**. 2 Chr 14:1
reigned in his **p** and strengthened 2 Chr 17:1
the name of that **p** has been called 2 Chr 20:26
and Jehoram his son reigned in his **p**. 2 Chr 21:1
his youngest son king in his **p**, 2 Chr 22:1
and take it and return it to its **p**. 2 Chr 24:11
Amaziah his son reigned in his **p**. 2 Chr 24:27
Jotham his son reigned in his **p**. 2 Chr 26:23
and Ahaz his son reigned in his **p**. 2 Chr 27:9
Hezekiah his son reigned in his **p**. 2 Chr 28:27
carry out the filth from the Holy **P**. 2 Chr 29:5
offerings in the Holy **P** to the God of 2 Chr 29:7
Manasseh his son reigned in his **p**. 2 Chr 32:33
and Amon his son reigned in his **p**. 2 Chr 33:20
made Josiah his son king in his **p**. 2 Chr 33:25
disaster upon this **p** and upon its 2 Chr 34:24
poured out on this **p** and will not be 2 Chr 34:25
words against this **p** and its 2 Chr 34:27
bring upon this **p** and its 2 Chr 34:28
king stood in his **p** and made a 2 Chr 34:31
stand in the Holy **P** according to the 2 Chr 35:5
for, the priests stood in their **p**, 2 Chr 35:10
were in their **p** according to the 2 Chr 35:15
king in his father's **p** in Jerusalem. 2 Chr 36:1
Jehoiachin his son reigned in his **p**. 2 Chr 36:8
on his people and on his dwelling **p**. 2 Chr 36:15
each survivor, in whatever **p** he sojourns, Ezr 1:4
by the men of his **p** with silver and gold, Ezr 1:4
They set the altar in its **p**, for fear was on Ezr 3:3
the **p** where sacrifices were offered, Ezr 6:3
temple that is in Jerusalem, each to its **p**. Ezr 6:5
Iddo, the leading man at the **p** Casiphia, Ezr 8:17
the temple servants at the **p** Casiphia, Ezr 8:17
to give us a secure hold within his holy **p**, Ezr 9:8
bring them to the **p** that I have chosen, Neh 1:9
the city, the **p** of my fathers' graves, Neh 2:3
In the **p** where you hear the sound of Neh 4:20
stood up in their **p** and read from the Neh 9:3
While this was taking **p**, I was not in Neh 13:6
young women to the best **p** in the harem. Est 2:9
will rise for the Jews from another **p**, Est 4:14
palace garden to the **p** where they were Est 7:8
him, they came each from his own **p**, Jb 2:11
when it is hot, they vanish from their **p**. Jb 6:17
nor does his **p** know him anymore. Jb 7:10
If he is destroyed from his **p**, then it will Jb 8:18
who shakes the earth out of its **p**, and its Jb 9:6
and the rock is removed from its **p**; Jb 14:18
speak as you do, if you were in my **p**; Jb 16:4
blood, and let my cry find no resting **p**. Jb 16:18
you, or the rock be removed out of its **p**? Jb 18:4
such is the **p** of him who knows not Jb 18:21
nor will his **p** any more behold him. Jb 20:9
he is gone; it sweeps him out of his **p**. Jb 27:21
at him and hisses at him from its **p**. Jb 27:23
silver, and a **p** for gold that they refine. Jb 28:1
Its stones are the **p** of sapphires, and it Jb 28:6
And where is the **p** of understanding? Jb 28:12
And where is the **p** of understanding? Jb 28:20
the way to it, and he knows its **p**. Jb 28:23
investigation and sets others in their **p**. Jb 34:24
for their wickedness in a **p** for all to see, Jb 34:26
distress into a broad **p** where there was Jb 36:16
night, when peoples vanish in their **p**. Jb 36:20
my heart trembles and leaps out of its **p**. Jb 37:1
and caused the dawn to know its **p**, Jb 38:12
of light, and where is the **p** of darkness, Jb 38:19
is the way to the **p** where the light is Jb 38:24
and the salt land for his dwelling **p**? Jb 39:6
and the stars, which you have set in **p**, Ps 8:3
"I will **p** him in the safety for which he Ps 12:5
He brought me out into a broad **p**; he Ps 18:19
You gave a wide **p** for my steps under Ps 18:36
LORD? And who shall stand in his holy **p**? Ps 24:3
your house and the **p** where your glory Ps 26:8
enemy; you have set my feet in a broad **p**. Ps 31:8
You are a hiding **p** for me; you preserve Ps 32:7
though you look carefully at his **p**, he Ps 37:10
broken us in the **p** of jackals and Ps 44:19
In **p** of your fathers shall be your sons; Ps 45:16
consumed in Sheol, with no **p** to dwell. Ps 49:14
is in their dwelling **p** and in their heart. Ps 55:15
brought us out to a **p** of abundance. Ps 66:12
roared in the midst of your meeting **p**; Ps 74:4
profaned the dwelling **p** of your name, Ps 74:7
in Salem, his dwelling **p** in Zion. Ps 76:2
I answered you in the secret **p** of thunder; Ps 81:7
God has taken his **p** in the divine Ps 82:1
How lovely is your dwelling **p**, O LORD of Ps 84:1
of Baca they make it a **p** of springs; Ps 84:6
been our dwelling **p** in all generations. Ps 90:1
the LORD your dwelling **p**—the Most Ps 91:9
it is gone, and its **p** knows it no more. Ps 103:16
sank down to the **p** that you appointed Ps 104:8
and I shall walk in a wide **p**, for I have Ps 119:45
You are my hiding **p** and my shield; I Ps 119:114
until I find a **p** for the LORD, a dwelling Ps 132:5
a dwelling **p** for the Mighty One of Ps 132:5
"Let us go to his dwelling **p**; let us Ps 132:7
Arise, O LORD, and go to your resting **p**, Ps 132:8
he has desired it for his dwelling **p**: Ps 132:13
"This is my resting **p** forever; here I Ps 132:14
hands to the holy **p** and bless the LORD! Ps 134:2
She will **p** on your head a graceful Prv 4:9
The eyes of the LORD are in every **p**, Prv 15:3
presence or stand in the **p** of the great, Prv 25:6
and hastens to the **p** where it rises. Eccl 1:5
to the **p** where the streams flow, there Eccl 1:7
under the sun that in the **p** of justice, Eccl 3:16
and in the **p** of righteousness, Eccl 3:16
All go to one **p**. All are from the dust, Eccl 3:20
youth who was to stand in the king's **p**. Eccl 4:15
no good—do not all go to the one **p**? Eccl 6:6
out of the holy **p** and were praised in Eccl 8:10
There is a vanity that takes **p** on earth, Eccl 8:14
rises against you, do not leave your **p**, Eccl 10:4
high places, and the rich sit in a low **p**. Eccl 10:6
the north, in the **p** where the tree falls, Eccl 11:3
The LORD has taken his **p** to contend; he Is 3:13
In that day every **p** where there used to be Is 7:23
they will become a **p** where cattle are let Is 7:25
down, but we will put cedars in their **p**." Is 9:10
and his resting **p** shall be glorious. Is 11:10
and the earth will be shaken out of its **p**, Is 13:13
will take them and bring them to their **p**, Is 14:2
when he wearies himself on the high **p**, Is 16:12
the **p** of the name of the LORD of hosts. Is 18:7
And I will **p** on his shoulder the key of Is 22:22
I will fasten him like a peg in a secure **p**, Is 22:23
was fastened in a secure **p** will give way, Is 22:25
like heat in a dry **p**. You subdue the noise Is 25:5
Moab shall be trampled down in his **p**, Is 25:10
coming out from his **p** to punish the Is 26:21
wheat in rows and barley in its proper **p**, Is 28:25
and to **p** on the jaws of the peoples a Is 30:28
For a burning **p** has long been prepared; Is 30:33
will be like a hiding **p** from the wind, Is 32:2
the storm, like streams of water in a dry **p**, Is 32:2
his **p** of defense will be the fortresses of Is 33:16
will be for us a **p** of broad rivers and Is 33:21
the mast firm in its **p** or keep the sail Is 33:23
settles and finds for herself a resting **p**. Is 34:14
Esarhaddon his son reigned in his **p**. Is 37:38
shoulders, they carry it, they set it in its **p**, Is 46:7
it stands there; it cannot move from its **p**. Is 46:7
in your ears: 'The **p** is too narrow for me; Is 49:20
"Enlarge the **p** of your tent, and let the Is 54:2
"I dwell in the high and holy **p**, and also Is 57:15
pine, to beautify the **p** of my sanctuary, Is 60:13
and I will make the **p** of my feet glorious. Is 60:13
the Valley of Achor a **p** for herds to lie Is 65:10
build for me, and what is the **p** of my rest? Is 66:1
gone out from his **p** to make your land Jer 4:7
her; they shall pasture, each in his **p**. Jer 6:3
deeds, and I will let you dwell in this **p**. Jer 7:3
widow, or shed innocent blood in this **p**, Jer 7:6
then I will let you dwell in this **p**, in the Jer 7:7
Go now to my **p** that was in Shiloh, Jer 7:12
and to the **p** that I gave to you and to Jer 7:14
my wrath will be poured out on this **p**, Jer 7:20
I had in the desert a travelers' lodging **p**, Jer 9:2
the loincloth from the **p** where I had Jer 13:7
I will give you assured peace in this **p**.'" Jer 14:13
you have sons or daughters in this **p**. Jer 16:2
and daughters who are born in this **p**, Jer 16:3
Behold, I will silence in this **p**, before Jer 16:9
the beginning is the **p** of our sanctuary. Jer 17:12

such disaster upon this **p** that the ears of Jer 19:3
have profaned this **p** by making Jer 19:4
they have filled this **p** with the blood of Jer 19:4
when this **p** shall no more be called Jer 19:6
And in this **p** I will make void the plans Jer 19:7
because there will be no **p** else to bury. Jer 19:11
Thus will I do to this **p**, declares the Jer 19:12
shall be defiled like the **p** of Topheth.'" Jer 19:13
nor shed innocent blood in this **p**. Jer 22:3
father, and who went away from this **p**: Jer 22:11
but in the **p** where they have carried Jer 22:12
have sent away from this **p** to the land of Jer 24:5
body into the burial **p** of the common Jer 26:23
them back and restore them to this **p**." Jer 27:22
will bring back to this **p** all the vessels of Jer 28:3
took away from this **p** and carried to Jer 28:3
bring back to this **p** Jeconiah the son of Jer 28:4
bring back to this **p** from Babylon the Jer 28:6
you have made in their **p** bars of iron. Jer 28:13
promise and bring you back to this **p**. Jer 29:10
you back to the **p** from which I sent Jer 29:14
I will bring them back to this **p**, and I Jer 32:37
In this **p** of which you say, 'It is a waste Jer 33:10
In this **p** that is waste, without man or Jer 33:12
pronounced this disaster against this **p**. Jer 40:2
a taunt. You shall see this **p** no more. Jer 42:18
by pestilence in the **p** where you desire Jer 42:22
LORD, that I will punish you in this **p**, Jer 44:29
in the high **p** and makes offerings Jer 48:35
said concerning this **p** that you will Jer 51:62
the nations, but finds no resting **p**; Lam 1:3
a garden, laid in ruins his meeting **p**; Lam 2:6
be the glory of the LORD from its **p**!" Ezk 3:12
and **p** it as an iron wall between you and Ezk 4:3
and **p** the punishment of the house of Ezk 4:4
And behold, I will **p** cords upon you, so Ezk 4:8
and they shall profane my treasured **p**. Ezk 7:22
an exile from your **p** to another place in Ezk 12:3
your place to another **p** in their sight. Ezk 12:3
yourself a lofty **p** in every square. Ezk 16:24
you built your lofty **p** and made your Ezk 16:25
making your lofty **p** in every square. Ezk 16:31
surely in the **p** where the king dwells Ezk 17:16
What is the high **p** to which you go? Ezk 20:29
lies for you—to **p** you on the necks of Ezk 21:29
In the **p** where you were created, in the Ezk 21:30
midst of the sea a **p** for the spreading of Ezk 26:5
You shall be a **p** for the spreading of Ezk 26:14
rivers flow around the **p** of its planting, Ezk 31:4
live, and I will **p** you in your own land. Ezk 37:14
My dwelling **p** shall be with them, and Ezk 37:27
will come from your **p** out of the Ezk 38:15
will give to Gog a **p** for burial in Israel, Ezk 39:11
said to me, "This is the Most Holy **P**." Ezk 41:4
of the Holy **P** was something Ezk 41:21
nave and the Holy **P** had each a Ezk 41:23
and the guilt offering, for the **p** is holy. Ezk 42:13
When the priests enter the Holy **P**, Ezk 42:14
this is the **p** of my throne and the place Ezk 43:7
of my throne and the **p** of the soles of Ezk 43:7
in the appointed **p** belonging to the Ezk 43:21
the day that he goes into the Holy **P**, Ezk 44:27
inner court, to minister in the Holy **P**, Ezk 44:27
be the sanctuary, the Most Holy **P**. Ezk 45:3
and it shall be a **p** for their houses and Ezk 45:4
houses and a holy **p** for the sanctuary. Ezk 45:4
a **p** was there at the extreme western Ezk 46:19
"This is the **p** where the priests shall Ezk 46:20
it will be a **p** for the spreading of Ezk 47:10
portion of the land, a most holy **p**, Ezk 48:12
and the **p** of his sanctuary was Dn 8:11
broken, in **p** of which four others arose, Dn 8:22
prophet, and to anoint a most holy **p**. Dn 9:24
from her roots one shall arise in his **p**. Dn 11:7
shall arise in his **p** one who shall send Dn 11:20
In his **p** shall arise a contemptible Dn 11:21
stand in your allotted **p** at the end of Dn 12:13
And in the **p** where it was said to them, Hos 1:10
I will return again to my **p**, until they Hos 5:15
stir them up from the **p** to which you have Jl 3:7
I will press you down in your **p**, Am 2:13
behold, the LORD is coming out of his **p**, Mi 1:3
the fire, like waters poured down a steep **p**. Mi 1:4
and what is the high **p** of Judah? Mi 1:5
open country, a **p** for planting vineyards, Mi 1:6
shall take away from you its standing **p**. Mi 1:11
Arise and go, for this is no **p** to rest, Mi 2:10
den, the feeding **p** of the young lions, Na 2:11
stood still in their **p** at the light of Hab 3:11
cut off from this **p** the remnant of Baal Zep 1:4
to him shall bow down, each in its **p**, Zep 2:11
And in this **p** I will give peace, declares Hg 2:9
for he shall branch out from his **p**, and Zec 6:12
Hadrach and Damascus is its resting **p**. Zec 9:1
shall again be inhabited in its **p**, Zec 12:6
of Benjamin to the **p** of the former Zec 14:10
and in every **p** incense will be offered to Mal 1:11
birth of Jesus Christ took **p** in this way. Mt 1:18
All this took **p** to fulfill what the Lord Mt 1:22
to rest over the **p** where the child was. Mt 2:9
reigning over Judea in **p** of his father Mt 2:22
In that **p** there will be weeping and Mt 8:12
In that **p** there will be weeping and Mt 13:42
In that **p** there will be weeping and Mt 13:50
in a boat to a desolate **p** by himself. Mt 14:13
to him and said, "This is a desolate **p**, Mt 14:15
the men of that **p** recognized him, Mt 14:35
in such a desolate **p** to feed so great Mt 15:33
fellow servants saw what had taken **p**, Mt 18:31
to their master all that had taken **p**. Mt 18:31
This took **p** to fulfill what was spoken Mt 21:4
In that **p** there will be weeping and Mt 22:13
and they love the **p** of honor at feasts and Mt 23:6
are not alarmed, for this must take **p**, Mt 24:6
standing in the holy **p** (let the reader Mt 24:15
pass away until all these things take **p**. Mt 24:34
In that **p** there will be weeping and Mt 24:51
In that **p** there will be weeping and Mt 25:30
And he will **p** the sheep on his right, Mt 25:33
with them to a **p** called Gethsemane, Mt 26:36
him, "Put your sword back into its **p**. Mt 26:52
all this has taken **p** that the Scriptures Mt 26:56
potter's field as a burial **p** for strangers. Mt 27:7
came to a **p** called Golgotha (which Mt 27:33
Golgotha (which means **P** of a Skull), Mt 27:33
saw the earthquake and what took **p**, Mt 27:54
as he said. Come, see the **p** where he lay. Mt 28:6
the chief priests all that had taken **p**. Mt 28:11
he departed and went out to a desolate **p**, Mk 1:35
And if any **p** will not receive you and Mk 6:11
yourselves to a desolate **p** and rest a Mk 6:31
the boat to a desolate **p** by themselves. Mk 6:32
to him and said, "This is a desolate **p**, Mk 6:35
with bread here in this desolate **p**?" Mk 8:4
This must take **p**, but the end is not yet. Mk 13:7
when you see these things taking **p**, Mk 13:29
pass away until all these things take **p**. Mk 13:30
they went to a **p** called Gethsemane. Mk 14:32
him to the **p** called Golgotha (which Mk 15:22
Golgotha (which means **P** of a Skull). Mk 15:22
not here. See the **p** where they laid him. Mk 16:6
until the day that these things take **p**, Lk 1:20
because there was no **p** for them in the Lk 2:7
scroll and found the **p** where it was Lk 4:17
went out into every **p** in the surrounding Lk 4:37
he departed and went into a desolate **p**. Lk 4:42
down with them and stood on a level **p**, Lk 6:17
house and took his **p** at the table. Lk 7:36
for we are here in a desolate **p**." Lk 9:12
into every town and **p** where he himself Lk 10:1
when he came to the **p** and saw him, Lk 10:32
Now Jesus was praying in a certain **p**, Lk 11:1
In that **p** there will be weeping and Lk 13:28
feast, do not sit down in a **p** of honor, Lk 14:8
say to you, 'Give your **p** to this person,' Lk 14:9
begin with shame to take the lowest **p**. Lk 14:9
are invited, go and sit in the lowest **p**, Lk 14:10
they also come into this **p** of torment.' Lk 16:28
And when Jesus came to the **p**, he looked Lk 19:5
when these things are about to take **p**?" Lk 21:7
for these things must first take **p**, Lk 21:9
Now when these things begin to take **p**, Lk 21:28
when you see these things taking **p**, Lk 21:31
not pass away until all has taken **p**. Lk 21:32
all these things that are going to take **p**, Lk 21:36
And when he came to the **p**, he said to Lk 22:40
all Judea, from Galilee even to this **p**." Lk 23:5
they came to the **p** that is called The Lk 23:33
the centurion saw what had taken **p**, Lk 23:47
when they saw what had taken **p**, Lk 23:48
These things took **p** in Bethany across Jn 1:28
in Jerusalem is the **p** where people ought Jn 4:20
withdrawn, as there was a crowd in the **p**. Jn 5:13
Now there was much grass in the **p**. Jn 6:10
Tiberias came near the **p** where they had Jn 6:23
me because my word finds no **p** in you. Jn 8:37
Feast of Dedication took **p** at Jerusalem. Jn 10:22
the Jordan to the **p** where John had been Jn 10:40
two days longer in the **p** where he was. Jn 11:6
was still in the **p** where Martha had met Jn 11:30
take away both our **p** and our nation." Jn 11:48
his outer garments and resumed his **p**, Jn 13:12
telling you this now, before it takes **p**, Jn 13:19
when it does take **p** you may believe Jn 13:19
told you that I go to prepare a **p** for you? Jn 14:2
And if I go and prepare a **p** for you, I will Jn 14:3
now I have told you before it takes **p**, Jn 14:29
when it does take **p** you may believe. Jn 14:29
who betrayed him, also knew the **p**, Jn 18:2
judgment seat at a **p** called The Stone Jn 19:13
cross, to the **p** called the place of a skull, Jn 19:17
cross, to the place called the **p** of a skull, Jn 19:17
for the **p** where Jesus was crucified was Jn 19:20
these things took **p** that the Scripture Jn 19:36
Now in the **p** where he was crucified Jn 19:41
linen cloths but folded up in a **p** by itself. Jn 20:7
and **p** my finger into the mark of the Jn 20:25
the nails, and **p** my hand into his side, Jn 20:25
put out your hand, and **p** it in my side. Jn 20:27
out on land, they saw a charcoal fire in **p**, Jn 21:9
to take the **p** in this ministry and Acts 1:25
Judas turned aside to go to his own **p**." Acts 1:25
arrived, they were all together in one **p**. Acts 2:1
your plan had predestined to take **p**. Acts 4:28
the **p** in which they were gathered Acts 4:31
words against this holy **p** and the law, Acts 6:13
will destroy this **p** and will change Acts 6:14
come out and worship me in this **p**.' Acts 7:7
for the **p** where you are standing is Acts 7:33
to find a dwelling **p** for the God of Acts 7:46
the Lord, or what is the **p** of my rest? Acts 7:49
Jerusalem to Gaza." This is a desert **p**. Acts 8:26
the world (this took **p** in the days of Acts 11:28
he departed and went to another **p**. Acts 12:17
we supposed there was a **p** of prayer, Acts 16:13
As we were going to the **p** of prayer, Acts 16:16
the boundaries of their dwelling **p**, Acts 17:26
and went from one **p** to the next Acts 18:23
the people and the law and this **p**. Acts 21:28
temple and has defiled this holy **p**." Acts 21:28
of sins and a **p** among those who are Acts 26:18
we came to a **p** called Fair Havens, Acts 27:8
neighborhood of that **p** were lands Acts 28:7
And when this had taken **p**, the rest of Acts 28:9
"And in the very **p** where it was said to Rom 9:26
those who in every **p** call upon the 1 Cor 1:2
these things took **p** as examples for 1 Cor 10:6
For, in the first **p**, when you come 1 Cor 11:18
it was put in **p** through angels by an Gal 3:19
in himself one new man in **p** of the two, Eph 2:15
together into a dwelling **p** for God by Eph 2:22
nor crude joking, which are out of **p**, Eph 5:4
you of everything that has taken **p** here. Col 4:9
then that in every **p** the men should 1 Tm 2:8
as he says also in another **p**, "You are a Heb 5:6
into the inner **p** behind the curtain, Heb 6:19
for worship and an earthly **p** of holiness. Heb 9:1
of the Presence. It is called the Holy **P**. Heb 9:2
a second section called the Most Holy **P**, Heb 9:3
to go out to a **p** that he was to receive Heb 11:8
sit here in a good **p**," while you say to the Jas 2:3
as to a lamp shining in a dark **p**, 2 Pt 1:19
servants the things that must soon take **p**. Rv 1:1
are and those that are to take **p** after this. Rv 1:19
and remove your lampstand from its **p**, Rv 2:5
show you what must take **p** after this." Rv 4:1
and island was removed from its **p**. Rv 6:14
where she has a **p** prepared by God, Rv 12:6
was no longer any **p** for them in heaven. Rv 12:8
to the **p** where she is to be nourished for Rv 12:14
assembled them at the **p** that in Hebrew Rv 16:16
has become a dwelling **p** for demons, Rv 18:2
fled away, and no **p** was found for them. Rv 20:11
the dwelling **p** of God is with man. Rv 21:3
his servants what must soon take **p**." Rv 22:6

PLACED (31)

garden of Eden he **p** the cherubim and a Gn 3:24
into Pharaoh's cup and **p** the cup in Gn 40:11
and he **p** the cup in Pharaoh's hand. Gn 40:21
the child in it and **p** it among the reeds by Ex 2:3
so Aaron **p** it before the testimony to be Ex 16:34
And he **p** the breastpiece on him, and in Lv 8:8
and one wafer and **p** them on the pieces Lv 8:26
of the people and **p** them around the Nm 11:24
stone, and it was **p** on David's head. 2 Sm 12:30
has established me and **p** me on the 1 Kgs 2:24
And he **p** in Bethel the priests of the 1 Kgs 12:32
away to Assyria and **p** them in Halah, 2 Kgs 17:6
and **p** them in the cities of Samaria 2 Kgs 17:24
have carried away and **p** in the cities 2 Kgs 17:26
stone. And it was **p** on David's head. 1 Chr 20:2
made ten tables and **p** them in the 2 Chr 4:8
He **p** forces in all the fortified cities of 2 Chr 17:2
whom the king had **p** in the fortified 2 Chr 17:19
away from Jerusalem and **p** in the house Ezr 1:7
from of old, since man was **p** on earth, Jb 20:4
I **p** the sand as the boundary for the sea, Jer 5:22
two baskets of figs **p** before the temple of Jer 24:1
man, behold, cords will be **p** upon you, Ezk 3:25
soil. He **p** it beside abundant waters. Ezk 17:5
on which you had **p** my incense and Ezk 23:41
an anointed guardian cherub. I **p** you; Ezk 28:14
to the pit; they are **p** among the slain. Ezk 32:25
and **p** the vessels in the treasury of his Dn 1:2
As I looked, thrones were **p**, and the Dn 7:9

Before stone was **p** upon stone in the Hg 2:15
and refuse to let them be **p** in a tomb, Rv 11:9

PLACES (179)
in the troughs, that is, the watering **p**, Gn 30:38
to their clans and their dwelling **p**, Gn 36:40
to their dwelling **p** in the land Gn 36:43
in all your dwelling **p** you shall eat Ex 12:20
in all your dwelling **p** on the Sabbath Ex 35:3
your generations, in all your dwelling **p**, Lv 3:17
or of animal, in any of your dwelling **p**. Lv 7:26
to the LORD in all your dwelling **p**. Lv 23:3
from your dwelling **p** two loaves of Lv 23:17
all your dwelling **p** throughout your Lv 23:21
your generations in all your dwelling **p**. Lv 23:31
will destroy your high **p** and cut down Lv 26:30
their cities in the **p** where they lived, Nm 31:10
Moses wrote down their starting **p**, Nm 33:2
stages according to their starting **p**. Nm 33:2
images and demolish all their high **p**. Nm 33:52
generations in all your dwelling **p**. Nm 35:29
surely destroy all the **p** where the nations Dt 12:2
him ride on the high **p** of the land, Dt 32:13
they remained in their **p** in the camp Jos 5:8
sound of musicians at the watering **p**, Jgs 5:11
to one of these **p** and spend the night Jgs 19:13
"Please put me in one of the priests' **p**, 1 Sm 2:36
And he judged Israel in all these **p**. 1 Sm 7:16
of all the lurking **p** where he hides, 1 Sm 23:23
for all the **p** where David and his 1 Sm 30:31
O Israel, is slain on your high **p**! 2 Sm 1:19
"Jonathan lies slain on your high **p**. 2 Sm 1:25
In all **p** where I have moved with all the 2 Sm 7:7
people were sacrificing at the high **p**, 1 Kgs 3:2
and made offerings at the high **p**. 1 Kgs 3:3
temples on high **p** and appointed 1 Kgs 12:31
priests of the high **p** that he had 1 Kgs 12:32
of the high **p** who make offerings 1 Kgs 13:2
houses of the high **p** that are in the 1 Kgs 13:32
for the high **p** again from among 1 Kgs 13:33
ordained to be priests of the high **p**. 1 Kgs 13:33
for themselves high **p** and pillars 1 Kgs 14:23
But the high **p** were not taken away. 1 Kgs 15:14
and put commanders in their **p**, 1 Kgs 20:24
Yet the high **p** were not taken away, 1 Kgs 22:43
and made offerings on the high **p**. 1 Kgs 22:43
the high **p** were not taken away; 2 Kgs 12:3
and make offerings on the high **p**. 2 Kgs 12:3
But the high **p** were not removed; the 2 Kgs 14:4
and made offerings on the high **p**. 2 Kgs 14:4
the high **p** were not taken away. 2 Kgs 15:4
and made offerings on the high **p**. 2 Kgs 15:4
the high **p** were not removed. 2 Kgs 15:35
and made offerings on the high **p**. 2 Kgs 15:35
offerings on the high **p** and on the 2 Kgs 16:4
for themselves high **p** in all their 2 Kgs 17:9
made offerings on all the high **p**, 2 Kgs 17:11
of the high **p** that the Samaritans 2 Kgs 17:29
of people as priests of the high **p**, 2 Kgs 17:32
for them in the shrines of the high **p**. 2 Kgs 17:32
He removed the high **p** and broke the 2 Kgs 18:4
he whose high **p** and altars 2 Kgs 18:22
rebuilt the high **p** that Hezekiah his 2 Kgs 21:3
offerings in the high **p** at the cities of 2 Kgs 23:5
defiled the high **p** where the priests 2 Kgs 23:8
broke down the high **p** of the gates 2 Kgs 23:8
priests of the high **p** did not come up 2 Kgs 23:9
king defiled the high **p** that were east 2 Kgs 23:13
and filled their **p** with the bones 2 Kgs 23:14
also of the high **p** that were in the 2 Kgs 23:19
priests of the high **p** who were there, 2 Kgs 23:20
are their dwelling **p** according to 1 Chr 6:54
In all **p** where I have moved with all 1 Chr 17:6
for the **p** to which the ark of the LORD 2 Chr 8:11
to him from all **p** where they lived. 2 Chr 11:13
priests for the high **p** and for the 2 Chr 11:15
and the high **p** and broke down 2 Chr 14:3
of Judah the high **p** and the incense 2 Chr 14:5
But the high **p** were not taken out of 2 Chr 15:17
he took the high **p** and the Asherim 2 Chr 17:6
The high **p**, however, were not taken 2 Chr 20:33
he made high **p** in the hill country 2 Chr 21:11
offerings on the high **p** and on the 2 Chr 28:4
he made high **p** to make offerings 2 Chr 28:25
broke down the high **p** and the altars 2 Chr 31:1
away his high **p** and his altars 2 Chr 32:12
he rebuilt the high **p** that his father 2 Chr 33:3
people still sacrificed at the high **p**, 2 Chr 33:17
which he built high **p** and set up the 2 Chr 33:19
Judah and Jerusalem of the high **p**, 2 Chr 34:3
of the space behind the wall, in open **p**, Neh 4:13
while the people remained in their **p**. Neh 8:7
they sought the Levites in all their **p**, Neh 12:27
in hiding **p** he murders the innocent. Ps 10:8
lines have fallen for me in pleasant **p**; Ps 16:6
their dwelling **p** to all generations, Ps 49:11
Truly you set them in slippery **p**; you Ps 73:18
burned all the meeting **p** of God in the Ps 74:8
for the dark **p** of the land are full of the Ps 74:20
him to anger with their high **p**; Ps 78:58
more than all the dwelling **p** of Jacob. Ps 87:2
wilderness, like an owl of the waste **p**; Ps 102:6
all his works, in all **p** of his dominion. Ps 103:22
to call from the highest **p** in the town, Prv 9:3
takes a seat on the highest **p** of the town, Prv 9:14
folly is set in many high **p**, and the Eccl 10:6
and the forsaken **p** are many in the midst Is 6:12
and to Dibon, to the high **p** to weep; Is 15:2
be like the deserted **p** of the wooded Is 17:9
There will be bare **p** by the Nile, on the Is 19:7
secure dwellings, and in quiet resting **p**. Is 32:18
not he whose high **p** and altars Hezekiah Is 36:7
become level, and the rough **p** a plain. Is 40:4
into light, the rough **p** into level ground. Is 42:16
will go before you and level the exalted **p**, Is 45:2
of darkness and the hoards in secret **p**, Is 45:3
and your desolate **p** and your devastated Is 49:19
comforts all her waste **p** and makes her Is 51:3
into singing, you waste **p** of Jerusalem, Is 52:9
desire in scorched **p** and make your Is 58:11
all our pleasant **p** have become ruins. Is 64:11
in tombs, and spend the night in secret **p**; Is 65:4
they have built the high **p** of Topheth, Jer 7:31
evil family in all the **p** where I have driven Jer 8:3
price of your high **p** for sin throughout Jer 17:3
dwell in the parched **p** of the wilderness, Jer 17:6
of Judah and the **p** around Jerusalem, Jer 17:26
have built the high **p** of Baal to burn Jer 19:5
hide himself in secret **p** so that I cannot Jer 23:24
a curse in all the **p** where I shall drive Jer 24:9
nations and all the **p** where I have Jer 29:14
They built the high **p** of Baal in the Jer 32:35
of Benjamin, in the **p** about Jerusalem, Jer 32:44
of Benjamin, the **p** about Jerusalem, Jer 33:13
returned from all the **p** to which they Jer 40:12
prize of war in all **p** to which you may Jer 45:5
I have uncovered his hiding **p**, and he is Jer 49:10
come into the holy **p** of the LORD'S Jer 51:51
upon you, and I will destroy your high **p**. Ezk 6:3
shall be waste and the high **p** ruined, Ezk 6:6
and waste, in all their dwelling **p**, Ezk 6:14
and their holy **p** shall be profaned. Ezk 7:24
and break down your lofty **p**. Ezk 16:39
of these waste **p** in the land Ezk 33:24
who are in the waste **p** shall fall by the Ezk 33:27
them from all **p** where they have Ezk 34:12
in all the inhabited **p** of the country. Ezk 34:13
make them and the **p** all around my Ezk 34:26
be inhabited and the waste **p** rebuilt. Ezk 36:10
and the waste **p** shall be rebuilt. Ezk 36:33
rebuilt the ruined **p** and replanted that Ezk 36:36
hand against the waste **p** that are now Ezk 38:12
bodies of their kings at their high **p**, Ezk 43:7
from the watering **p** of Israel for grain Ezk 45:15
The high **p** of Aven, the sin of Israel, Hos 10:8
cities, and lack of bread in all your **p**, Am 4:6
the high **p** of Isaac shall be made Am 7:9
and tread upon the high **p** of the earth. Mi 1:3
he makes me tread on my high **p**. Hab 3:19
passes through waterless **p** seeking rest, Mt 12:43
famines and earthquakes in various **p**. Mt 24:7
enter a town, but was out in desolate **p**, Mk 1:45
the synagogues and the **p** of honor at Mk 12:39
There will be earthquakes in various **p**; Mk 13:8
and the rough **p** shall become level ways, Lk 3:5
would withdraw to desolate **p** and pray. Lk 5:16
passes through waterless **p** seeking rest, Lk 11:24
noticed how they chose the **p** of honor, Lk 14:7
the synagogues and the **p** of honor at Lk 20:46
and in various **p** famines and Lk 21:11
of the Jews who were in those **p**, Acts 16:3
spiritual blessing in the heavenly **p**, Eph 1:3
at his right hand in the heavenly **p**, Eph 1:20
him in the heavenly **p** in Christ Jesus, Eph 2:6
and authorities in the heavenly **p**. Eph 3:10
forces of evil in the heavenly **p**. Eph 6:12
a minister in the holy **p**, in the true tent Heb 8:2
the way into the holy **p** is not yet opened Heb 9:8
he entered once for all into the holy **p**, Heb 9:12
not into holy **p** made with hands, Heb 9:24
priest enters the holy **p** every year with Heb 9:25
to enter the holy **p** by the blood of Heb 10:19
brought into the holy **p** by the high Heb 13:11

PLACING (2)
caught in adultery, and **p** her in the midst Jn 8:3
God to the test by **p** a yoke on the Acts 15:10

PLAGUE (44)
I will **p** all your country with frogs. Ex 8:2
with a very severe **p** upon your livestock Ex 9:3
"Yet one **p** more I will bring upon Ex 11:1
and no **p** will befall you to destroy you, Ex 12:13
that there be no **p** among them when Ex 30:12
Then the LORD sent a **p** on the people, Ex 32:35
there may be no **p** among the people of Nm 8:19
down the people with a very great **p**. Nm 11:33
of the land—died by **p** before the LORD. Nm 14:37
out from the LORD; the **p** has begun." Nm 16:46
the **p** had already begun among the Nm 16:47
and the living, and the **p** was stopped. Nm 16:48
those who died in the **p** were 14,700, Nm 16:49
of meeting, when the **p** was stopped. Nm 16:50
Thus the **p** on the people of Israel was Nm 25:8
died by the **p** were twenty-four Nm 25:9
the day of the **p** on account of Peor." Nm 25:18
After the **p**, the LORD said to Moses and Nm 26:1
and so the **p** came among the Nm 31:16
and devoured by **p** and poisonous Dt 32:24
there came a **p** upon the congregation Jos 22:17
with every sort of **p** in the wilderness. 1 Sm 4:8
for the same **p** was on all of you and on 1 Sm 6:4
that the **p** may be averted from the 2 Sm 24:21
and the **p** was averted from Israel. 2 Sm 24:25
in the land at their gates, whatever **p**, 1 Kgs 8:37
do not let the **p** be on your people." 1 Chr 21:17
price—that the **p** may be averted 1 Chr 21:22
in the land at their gates, whatever **p**, 2 Chr 6:28
will bring a great **p** on your people, 2 Chr 21:14
companions stand aloof from my **p**, Ps 38:11
death, but gave their lives over to the **p**. Ps 78:50
to befall you, no **p** come near your tent. Ps 91:10
deeds, and a **p** broke out among them. Ps 106:29
and intervened, and the **p** was stayed. Ps 106:30
pestilence, and **p** followed at his heels. Hab 3:5
this shall be the **p** with which the LORD Zec 14:12
And a **p** like this plague shall fall on Zec 14:15
a plague like this **p** shall fall on the Zec 14:15
there shall be the **p** with which the Zec 14:18
For we have found this man a **p**, one Acts 24:5
to strike the earth with every kind of **p**, Rv 11:6
they cursed God for the **p** of the hail, Rv 16:21
of the hail, because the **p** was so severe. Rv 16:21

PLAGUED (1)
and I **p** Egypt with what I did in the Jos 24:5

PLAGUES (14)
house with great **p** because of Sarai, Gn 12:17
time I will send all my **p** on you yourself, Ex 9:14
Death? O Death, where are your **p**? Hos 13:14
people of diseases and **p** and evil spirits, Lk 7:21
By these three **p** a third of mankind was Rv 9:18
who were not killed by these **p**, Rv 9:20
and amazing, seven angels with seven **p**, Rv 15:1
came the seven angels with the seven **p**, Rv 15:6
sanctuary until the seven **p** of the seven Rv 15:8
of God who had power over these **p**. Rv 16:9
part in her sins, lest you share in her **p**; Rv 18:4
For this reason her **p** will come in a Rv 18:8
full of the seven last **p** and spoke to me, Rv 21:9
add to him the **p** described in this book, Rv 22:18

PLAIN (28)
they found a **p** in the land of Shinar and Gn 11:2
the Negeb, and the **P**, that is, the Valley Dt 34:3
who dwell in the **p** have chariots of Jos 17:16
inhabitants of the **p** because they had Jgs 1:19
not allow them to come down to the **p**. Jgs 1:34
Ahimaaz ran by the way of the **p**, 2 Sm 18:23
In the **p** of the Jordan the king cast 1 Kgs 7:46
let us fight against them in the **p**, 1 Kgs 20:23
we will fight against them in the **p**, 1 Kgs 20:25
In the **p** of the Jordan the king cast 2 Chr 4:17
both in the Shephelah and in the **p**, 2 Chr 26:10
came to fight in the **p** of Megiddo. 2 Chr 35:22
at Hakkephirim in the **p** of Ono." But Neh 6:2
I have given the arid **p** for his home and Jb 39:6
become level, and the rough places a **p**. Is 40:4
of the valley, O rock of the **p**, Jer 21:13
shall perish, and the **p** shall be destroyed, Jer 48:8
He set it up on the **p** of Dura, in the Dn 3:1
"Write the vision; make it **p** on tablets, Hab 2:2
Before Zerubbabel you shall become a **p**. Zec 4:7
Hadad-rimmon in the **p** of Megiddo. Zec 12:11
be turned into a **p** from Geba to Zec 14:10
can be known about God is **p** to them, Rom 1:19
in subjection," it is **p** that he is 1 Cor 15:27
way we have made this **p** to you in all 2 Cor 11:6
very far, for their folly will be **p** to all, 2 Tm 3:9
that it might become **p** that they all are 1 Jn 2:19
up over the broad **p** of the earth and Rv 20:9

PLAINLY (11)
"We see **p** that the LORD has been with Gn 26:28
But if the slave **p** says, 'I love my master, Ex 21:5
stones all the words of this law very **p**." Dt 27:8
"He told us **p** that the donkeys had 1 Sm 10:16
sent to us has been **p** read before me. Ezr 4:18

his tongue was released, and he spoke **p**. Mk 7:35
And he said this **p**. And Peter took him Mk 8:32
If you are the Christ, tell us **p**." Jn 10:24
Then Jesus told them **p**, "Lazarus has Jn 11:14
but will tell you **p** about the Father. Jn 16:25
now you are speaking **p** and not using Jn 16:29

PLAINS (17)
and camped in the **p** of Moab beyond Nm 22:1
with them in the **p** of Moab by the Nm 26:3
of Israel in the **p** of Moab by the Nm 26:63
at the camp on the **p** of Moab by the Nm 31:12
and camped in the **p** of Moab by the Nm 33:48
far as Abel-shittim in the **p** of Moab. Nm 33:49
to Moses in the **p** of Moab by the Nm 33:50
spoke to Moses in the **p** of Moab by the Nm 35:1
of Israel in the **p** of Moab by the Nm 36:13
went up from the **p** of Moab to Mount Dt 34:1
for Moses in the **p** of Moab thirty days. Dt 34:8
the LORD for battle, to the **p** of Jericho. Jos 4:13
in the evening on the **p** of Jericho. Jos 5:10
Moses distributed in the **p** of Moab, Jos 13:32
and overtook him in the **p** of Jericho, 2 Kgs 25:5
overtook Zedekiah in the **p** of Jericho. Jer 39:5
overtook Zedekiah in the **p** of Jericho. Jer 52:8

PLAN (29)
tabernacle according to the **p** for it that Ex 26:30
understands every **p** and thought. 1 Chr 28:9
his son the **p** of the vestibule 1 Chr 28:11
and the **p** of all that he had in mind 1 Chr 28:12
also his **p** for the golden chariot of 1 Chr 28:18
work to be done according to the **p**. 1 Chr 28:19
and the **p** seemed right to the king 2 Chr 30:4
us and that God had frustrated their **p**, Neh 4:15
to avert the evil **p** of Haman the Agagite Est 8:3
writing that his evil **p** that he had Est 9:25
Though they **p** evil against you, though Ps 21:11
They only **p** to thrust him down from Ps 62:4
who **p** evil things in their heart and stir Ps 140:2
Do not **p** evil against your neighbor, Prv 3:29
evil, but those who **p** peace have joy. Prv 12:20
declares the LORD, "who carry out a **p**, Is 30:1
you and devising a **p** against you. Jer 18:11
Therefore hear the **p** that the LORD has Jer 49:20
Babylon has made a **p** against you and Jer 49:30
Therefore hear the **p** that the LORD has Jer 50:45
and they shall measure the **p**. Ezk 43:10
they do not understand his **p**, that he has Mi 4:12
to the definite **p** and foreknowledge of Acts 2:23
hand and your **p** had predestined to Acts 4:28
for if this **p** or this undertaking is of Acts 5:38
The soldiers' **p** was to kill the Acts 27:42
kept them from carrying out their **p**. Acts 27:43
as a **p** for the fullness of time, to unite Eph 1:10
everyone what is the **p** of the mystery Eph 3:9

PLANE (4)
of poplar and almond and **p** trees, Gn 30:37
the cypress, the **p** and the pine together, Is 41:19
shall come to you, the cypress, the **p**, Is 60:13
neither were the **p** trees like its Ezk 31:8

PLANES (1)
He shapes it with **p** and marks it with a Is 44:13

PLANKS (3)
of the house of beams and **p** of cedar. 1 Kgs 6:9
They made all your **p** of fir trees from Ezk 27:5
and the rest on **p** or on pieces of the Acts 27:44

PLANNED (13)
"Why then have you **p** such a thing 2 Sm 14:13
who consumed us and **p** to destroy us, 2 Sm 21:5
I **p** from days of old what now I 2 Kgs 19:25
All that Solomon had **p** to do in the 2 Chr 7:11
he **p** with his officers and his mighty 2 Chr 32:3
men, who have **p** to trip up my feet. Ps 140:4
"As I have **p**, so shall it be, and as I have Is 14:24
who did it, or see him who **p** it long ago. Is 22:11
I **p** from days of old what now I bring to Is 37:26
In Heshbon they **p** disaster against her: Jer 48:2
the LORD has both **p** and done what he Jer 51:12
And the king **p** to set him over the whole Dn 6:3
on which they **p** if possible to run the Acts 27:39

PLANNING (2)
himself about you by **p** to kill you. Gn 27:42
—because they were **p** an ambush to Acts 25:3

PLANS (29)
my **p** are broken off, the desires of my Jb 17:11
You would shame the **p** of the poor, but Ps 14:6
your heart's desire and fulfill all your **p**! Ps 20:4
he frustrates the **p** of the peoples. Ps 33:10
the **p** of his heart to all generations. Ps 33:11
They lay crafty **p** against your people; Ps 83:3
the earth; on that very day his **p** perish. Ps 146:4
a heart that devises wicked **p**, feet that Prv 6:18
Without counsel **p** fail, but with Prv 15:22
The **p** of the heart belong to man, but Prv 16:1
the LORD, and your **p** will be established. Prv 16:3
The heart of man **p** his way, but the Prv 16:9
winks his eyes **p** dishonest things; Prv 16:30
Many are the **p** in the mind of a man, Prv 19:21
P are established by counsel; by wise Prv 20:18
The **p** of the diligent lead surely to Prv 21:5
Whoever **p** to do evil will be called a Prv 24:8
done wonderful things, **p** formed of old, Is 25:1
he **p** wicked schemes to ruin the poor Is 32:7
But he who is noble **p** noble things, and Is 32:8
but in his heart he **p** an ambush for him. Jer 9:8
We will follow our own **p**, and will Jer 18:12
will make void the **p** of Judah and Jer 19:7
For I know the **p** I have for you, Jer 29:11
LORD, **p** for wholeness and not for evil, Jer 29:11
He shall devise **p** against strongholds, Dn 11:24
that day on they made **p** to put him to Jn 11:53
the chief priests made **p** to put Lazarus Jn 12:10
Do I make my **p** according to the 2 Cor 1:17

PLANT (56)
given you every **p** yielding seed that Gn 1:29
have given every green **p** for food." And Gn 1:30
the land and no small **p** of the field had Gn 2:5
man and beast and every **p** of the field, Ex 9:22
hail struck down every **p** of the field and Ex 9:25
of Egypt and eat every **p** in the land, Ex 10:12
remained, neither tree nor **p** of the field, Ex 10:15
bring them in and **p** them on your own Ex 15:17
into the land and **p** any kind of tree Lv 19:23
trees that you did not **p**—and when you Dt 6:11
"You shall not **p** any tree as an Asherah Dt 16:21
not dwell in it. You shall **p** a vineyard, Dt 28:30
You shall **p** vineyards and dress them, Dt 28:39
growing, where no **p** can sprout, Dt 29:23
and olive orchards that you did not **p**.' Jos 24:13
for my people Israel and will **p** them, 2 Sm 7:10
year sow and reap and **p** vineyards, 2 Kgs 19:29
for my people Israel and will **p** them, 1 Chr 17:9
cut down, they wither before any other **p**. Jb 8:12
He is a lush **p** before the sun, and his Jb 8:16
and put out branches like a young **p**. Jb 14:9
they sow fields and **p** vineyards and get Ps 107:37
a time to **p**, and a time to pluck up what Eccl 3:2
though you **p** pleasant plants and sow Is 17:10
them grow on the day that you **p** them, Is 17:11
year sow and reap, and **p** vineyards, Is 37:30
For he grew up before him like a young **p**, Is 53:2
they shall **p** vineyards and eat their fruit. Is 65:21
they shall not **p** and another eat; Is 65:22
and to overthrow, to build and to **p**." Jer 1:10
You **p** them, and they take root; they Jer 12:2
or a kingdom that I will build and **p** it, Jer 18:9
I will **p** them, and not uproot them. Jer 24:6
in them; **p** gardens and eat their produce. Jer 29:5
and **p** gardens and eat their produce."'" Jer 29:28
Again you shall **p** vineyards on the Jer 31:5
the planters shall **p** and shall enjoy the Jer 31:5
will watch over them to build and to **p**, Jer 31:28
and I will **p** them in this land in Jer 32:41
seed; you shall not **p** or have a vineyard; Jer 35:7
I will **p** you, and not pluck you up; Jer 42:10
and **p** battering rams against it all Ezk 4:2
I made you flourish like a **p** of the field. Ezk 16:7
and I myself will **p** it on a high and Ezk 17:22
mountain height of Israel will I **p** it, Ezk 17:23
shall build houses and **p** vineyards. Ezk 28:26
they shall **p** vineyards and drink their Am 9:14
I will **p** them on their land, and they Am 9:15
LORD God appointed a **p** and made it Jon 4:6
was exceedingly glad because of the **p**. Jon 4:6
appointed a worm that attacked the **p**, Jon 4:7
well to be angry for the **p**?" And he said, Jon 4:9
And the LORD said, "You pity the **p**, for Jon 4:10
though they **p** vineyards, they shall not Zep 1:13
"Every **p** that my heavenly Father has Mt 15:13
of the earth or any green **p** or any tree, Rv 9:4

PLANTATIONS (1)
for them renowned **p** so that they Ezk 34:29

PLANTED (37)
And the LORD God **p** a garden in Eden, in Gn 2:8
a man of the soil, and he **p** a vineyard. Gn 9:20
Abraham **p** a tamarisk tree in Gn 21:33
a river, like aloes that the LORD has **p**, Nm 24:6
any man who has **p** a vineyard and has Dt 20:6
For whenever the Israelites **p** crops, the Jgs 6:3
He is like a tree **p** by streams of water that Ps 1:3
drove out the nations, but them you **p**; Ps 44:2
Egypt; you drove out the nations and **p** it. Ps 80:8
the stock that your right hand **p**, and Ps 80:15
They are **p** in the house of the LORD; Ps 92:13
He who **p** the ear, does he not hear? He Ps 94:9
the cedars of Lebanon that he **p**. Ps 104:16
built houses and **p** vineyards for myself. Eccl 2:4
and **p** in them all kinds of fruit trees. Eccl 2:5
plant, and a time to pluck up what is **p**; Eccl 3:2
it of stones, and **p** it with choice vines; Is 5:2
Scarcely are they **p**, scarcely sown, Is 40:24
Yet I **p** you a choice vine, wholly of pure Jer 2:21
The LORD of hosts, who **p** you, has Jer 11:17
He is like a tree **p** by water, that sends out Jer 17:8
and what I have **p** I am plucking up— Jer 45:4
seed of the land and **p** it in fertile soil. Ezk 17:5
him from the bed where it was **p**, Ezk 17:7
It had been **p** on good soil by abundant Ezk 17:8
Behold, it is **p**; will it thrive? Will it Ezk 17:10
a vine in a vineyard **p** by the water, Ezk 19:10
Now it is **p** in the wilderness, in a dry Ezk 19:13
was like a young palm **p** in a meadow; Hos 9:13
in them; you have **p** pleasant vineyards, Am 5:11
Father has not **p** will be rooted Mt 15:13
of a house who **p** a vineyard and put Mt 21:33
"A man **p** a vineyard and put a fence Mk 12:1
"A man had a fig tree **p** in his vineyard, Lk 13:6
tree, 'Be uprooted and **p** in the sea,' Lk 17:6
"A man **p** a vineyard and let it out to Lk 20:9
I **p**, Apollos watered, but God gave the 1 Cor 3:6

PLANTERS (1)
the **p** shall plant and shall enjoy the Jer 31:5

PLANTING (6)
and the men of Judah are his pleasant **p**; Is 5:7
the land forever, the branch of my **p**, Is 60:21
oaks of righteousness, the **p** of the LORD, Is 61:3
its rivers flow around the place of its **p**, Ezk 31:4
the open country, a place for **p** vineyards, Mi 1:6
buying and selling, **p** and building, Lk 17:28

PLANTS (19)
earth sprout vegetation, **p** yielding seed, Gn 1:11
p yielding seed according to their own Gn 1:12
you; and you shall eat the **p** of the field. Gn 3:18
And as I gave you the green **p**, I give you Gn 9:3
and they ate all the **p** in the land and all Ex 10:15
and have become like **p** of the field 2 Kgs 19:26
Under the lotus **p** he lies, in the shelter Jb 40:21
for the livestock and **p** for man to Ps 104:14
in their youth be like **p** full grown, Ps 144:12
the fruit of her hands she **p** a vineyard. Prv 31:16
though you plant pleasant **p** and sow the Is 17:10
and have become like **p** of the field and Is 37:27
He **p** a cedar and the rain nourishes it. Is 44:14
So when the **p** came up and bore grain, Mt 13:26
than all the garden **p** and becomes a Mt 13:32
than all the garden **p** and puts out large Mk 4:32
So neither he who **p** nor he who waters 1 Cor 3:7
He who **p** and he who waters are one, 1 Cor 3:8
Who **p** a vineyard without eating any 1 Cor 9:7

PLASTER (9)
and the **p** that they scrape off they shall Lv 14:41
he shall take other **p** and plaster the Lv 14:42
shall take other plaster and **p** the house. Lv 14:42
and timber and all the **p** of the house, Lv 14:45
up large stones and **p** them with plaster. Dt 27:2
up large stones and plaster them with **p**. Dt 27:2
Ebal, and you shall **p** them with plaster. Dt 27:4
Ebal, and you shall plaster them with **p**. Dt 27:4
appeared and wrote on the **p** of the wall of Dn 5:5

PLASTERED (2)
stones and scraped the house and **p** it, Lv 14:43
in the house after the house was **p**, Lv 14:48

PLATE (18)
"You shall make a **p** of pure gold and Ex 28:36
They made the **p** of the holy crown of Ex 39:30
the turban, in front, he set the golden **p**, Lv 8:9
was one silver **p** whose weight was Nm 7:13
offering one silver **p** whose weight was Nm 7:19
was one silver **p** whose weight was Nm 7:25
was one silver **p** whose weight was Nm 7:31
was one silver **p** whose weight was Nm 7:37
was one silver **p** whose weight was Nm 7:43
was one silver **p** whose weight was Nm 7:49
was one silver **p** whose weight was Nm 7:55
was one silver **p** whose weight was Nm 7:61
was one silver **p** whose weight was Nm 7:67
was one silver **p** whose weight was Nm 7:73
was one silver **p** whose weight was Nm 7:79
each silver **p** weighing 130 shekels and Nm 7:85
clean the outside of the cup and the **p**, Mt 23:25
clean the inside of the cup and the **p**, Mt 23:26

PLATES (5)
you shall make its **p** and dishes for Ex 25:29
the table, its **p** and dishes for incense, Ex 37:16
spread a cloth of blue and put on it the **p**, Nm 4:7
twelve silver **p**, twelve silver basins, Nm 7:84
made into hammered **p** as a covering Nm 16:38

PLATFORM (3)
had made a bronze **p** five cubits long, 2 Chr 6:13

stood on a wooden **p** that they had made Neh 8:4
the temple had a raised **p** all around; Ezk 41:8

PLATTER (4)
the head of John the Baptist here on a **p**." Mt 14:8
was brought on a **p** and given to the Mt 14:11
the head of John the Baptist on a **p**." Mk 6:25
brought his head on a **p** and gave it to Mk 6:28

PLAUSIBLE (2)
were not in **p** words of wisdom, 1 Cor 2:4
one may delude you with **p** arguments. Col 2:4

PLAY (23)
of all those who **p** the lyre and pipe. Gn 4:21
down to eat and drink and rose up to **p**. Ex 32:6
from God is upon you, he will **p** it, 1 Sm 16:16
a man who can **p** well and bring 1 Sm 16:17
singers who should **p** loudly on 1 Chr 15:16
Benaiah were to **p** harps according 1 Chr 15:20
Jeiel, who were to **p** harps and lyres; 1 Chr 16:5
food for him where all the wild beasts **p**. Jb 40:20
Will you **p** with him as with a bird, or Jb 41:5
p skillfully on the strings, with loud Ps 33:3
which you formed to **p** in it. Ps 104:26
upon a ten-stringed harp I will **p** to you, Ps 144:9
a servant than to **p** the great man and Prv 12:9
The nursing child shall **p** over the hole of Is 11:8
and we will **p** my music on stringed Is 38:20
No one solicited you to **p** the whore, Ezk 16:34
You shall not **p** the whore, or belong to Hos 3:3
not be satisfied; they shall **p** the whore, Hos 4:10
they have left their God to **p** the whore. Hos 4:12
Therefore your daughters **p** the whore, Hos 4:13
your daughters when they **p** the whore, Hos 4:14
Though you **p** the whore, O Israel, let Hos 4:15
to eat and drink and rose up to **p**." 1 Cor 10:7

PLAYED (23)
took the lyre and **p** it with his hand. 1 Sm 16:23
And when the musician **p**, 2 Kgs 3:15
acts, and **p** the whore in their deeds. Ps 106:39
You have **p** the whore with many lovers; Jer 3:1
every green tree, and there **p** the whore? Jer 3:6
not fear, but she too went and **p** the whore. Jer 3:8
your beauty and **p** the whore because Ezk 16:15
shrines, and on them **p** the whore. Ezk 16:16
of men, and with them **p** the whore. Ezk 16:17
You also **p** the whore with the Ezk 16:26
You **p** the whore also with the Ezk 16:28
yes, you **p** the whore with them, and Ezk 16:28
They **p** the whore in Egypt; they played Ezk 23:3
Egypt; they **p** the whore in their youth; Ezk 23:3
"Oholah **p** the whore while she was Ezk 23:5
when she **p** the whore in the land of Ezk 23:19
because you **p** the whore with the Ezk 23:30
For their mother has **p** the whore; she Hos 2:5
now, O Ephraim, you have **p** the whore; Hos 5:3
for you have **p** the whore, forsaking your Hos 9:1
"'We **p** the flute for you, and you did Mt 11:17
to one another, "'We **p** the flute for you, Lk 7:32
how will anyone know what is **p**? 1 Cor 14:7

PLAYERS (2)
and saw the flute **p** and the crowd Mt 9:23
musicians, of flute **p** and trumpeters, Rv 18:22

PLAYING (9)
a man who is skillful in **p** the lyre, 1 Sm 16:16
Bethlehemite, who is skillful in **p**, 1 Sm 16:18
his house while David was **p** the lyre, 1 Sm 18:10
in his hand. And David was **p** the lyre. 1 Sm 19:9
people went up after him, **p** on pipes, 1 Kgs 1:40
between them virgins **p** tambourines: Ps 68:25
I will make you stop **p** the whore, and Ezk 16:41
be full of boys and girls **p** in its streets. Zec 8:5
the sound of harpists **p** on their harps, Rv 14:2

PLAYMATES (1)
the marketplaces and calling to their **p**, Mt 11:16

PLAYS (1)
a beautiful voice and **p** well on an Ezk 33:32

PLEA (30)
God responded to the **p** for the land. 2 Sm 21:14
LORD responded to the **p** for the land, 2 Sm 24:25
prayer of your servant and to his **p**, 1 Kgs 8:28
And listen to the **p** of your servant 1 Kgs 8:30
whatever **p** is made by any man or by 1 Kgs 8:38
in heaven their prayer and their **p**, 1 Kgs 8:45
place their prayer and their **p**, 1 Kgs 8:49
be open to the **p** of your servant and 1 Kgs 8:52
servant and to the **p** of your people 1 Kgs 8:52
all this prayer and **p** to the LORD, 1 Kgs 8:54
"I have heard your prayer and your **p**, 1 Kgs 9:3
granted their urgent **p** because they 1 Chr 5:20
prayer of your servant and to his **p**, 2 Chr 6:19
whatever **p** is made by any man or 2 Chr 6:29
from heaven their prayer and their **p**, 2 Chr 6:35
and heard his **p** and brought him 2 Chr 33:13
The LORD has heard my **p**; the LORD Ps 6:9
hide not yourself from my **p** for mercy! Ps 55:1
to my prayer; listen to my **p** for grace. Ps 86:6
Let my **p** come before you; deliver me Ps 119:170
and with an empty **p** turn aside him Is 29:21
even when the **p** of the needy is right. Is 32:7
may be that their **p** for mercy will come Jer 36:7
let my humble **p** come before you and Jer 37:20
'I made a humble **p** to the king that he Jer 38:26
"Let our **p** for mercy come before you, Jer 42:2
me to present your **p** for mercy before Jer 42:9
you heard my **p**, 'Do not close your ear Lam 3:56
making petition and **p** before his God. Dn 6:11
and presenting my **p** before the LORD my Dn 9:20

PLEAD (30)
"**P** with the LORD to take away the frogs Ex 8:8
me when I am to **p** for you and for your Ex 8:9
must not go very far away. **P** for me." Ex 8:28
from you and I will **p** with the LORD that Ex 8:29
P with the LORD, for there has been Ex 9:28
and **p** with the LORD your God only to Ex 10:17
still that I may **p** with you before the 1 Sm 12:7
see to it and **p** my cause and deliver 1 Sm 24:15
name and pray and **p** with you in this 1 Kgs 8:33
and repent and **p** with you in the land 1 Kgs 8:47
name and pray and **p** with you in 2 Chr 6:24
and repent and **p** with you in the land 2 Chr 6:37
to beg his favor and **p** with him on behalf Est 4:8
will seek God and **p** with the Almighty for Jb 8:5
him? Will you **p** the case for God? Jb 13:8
I must **p** with him with my mouth for Jb 19:16
LORD, I cry, and to the Lord I **p** for mercy: Ps 30:8
P my cause and redeem me; give me Ps 119:154
with my voice I **p** for mercy to the LORD. Ps 142:1
and **p** urgently with your neighbor. Prv 6:3
for the LORD will **p** their cause and rob Prv 22:23
he will **p** their cause against you. Prv 23:11
to the fatherless, **p** the widow's cause. Is 1:17
bow down to you. They will **p** with you, Is 45:14
to you; yet I would **p** my case before you. Jer 12:1
He will surely **p** their cause, that he Jer 50:34
I will **p** your cause and take vengeance Jer 51:36
"**P** with your mother, plead—for she is Hos 2:2
your mother, **p**—for she is not my wife, Hos 2:2
Arise, **p** your case before the mountains, Mi 6:1

PLEADED (9)
out from Pharaoh and **p** with the LORD. Ex 10:18
"And I **p** with the LORD at that time, Dt 3:23
with which I have **p** before the LORD, 1 Kgs 8:59
his feet and wept and **p** with him to avert Est 8:3
Have I not **p** for you before the enemy Jer 15:11
servant fell down and **p** with him, Mt 18:29
all that debt because you **p** with me. Mt 18:32
came to Jesus, they **p** with him earnestly, Lk 7:4
Three times I **p** with the Lord about 2 Cor 12:8

PLEADING (1)
the weeping and **p** of Israel's sons Jer 3:21

PLEADINGS (1)
argument and listen to the **p** of my lips. Jb 13:6

PLEADS (2)
your God who **p** the cause of his people: Is 51:22
until he **p** my cause and executes Mi 7:9

PLEAS (18)
And listen to the **p** of your servant 2 Chr 6:21
place their prayer and their **p**, 2 Chr 6:39
Will he make many **p** to you? Will he Jb 41:3
Hear the voice of my **p** for mercy, when I Ps 28:2
he has heard the voice of my **p** for mercy. Ps 28:6
the voice of my **p** for mercy when I Ps 31:22
heard my voice and my **p** for mercy. Ps 116:1
attentive to the voice of my **p** for mercy! Ps 130:2
give ear to the voice of my **p** for mercy, Ps 140:6
O LORD; give ear to my **p** for mercy! Ps 143:1
will listen to their **p** for mercy and heal Is 19:22
they rely on empty **p**, they speak lies, they Is 59:4
and with **p** for mercy I will lead them Jer 31:9
him by prayer and **p** for mercy with Dn 9:3
of your servant and to his **p** for mercy, Dn 9:17
do not present our **p** before you because Dn 9:18
the beginning of your **p** for mercy a Dn 9:23
a spirit of grace and **p** for mercy, Zec 12:10

PLEASANT (31)
up every tree that is **p** to the sight and Gn 2:9
was good, and that the land was **p**, Gn 49:15
Jonathan; very **p** have you been to me; 2 Sm 1:26
I discern what is **p** and what is not? 2 Sm 19:35
"Behold, the situation of this city is **p**, 2 Kgs 2:19
The lines have fallen for me in **p** places; Ps 16:6
Then they despised the **p** land, having Ps 106:24
how good and **p** it is when brothers Ps 133:1
is good; sing to his name, for it is **p**! Ps 135:3
they shall hear my words, for they are **p**. Ps 141:6
for it is **p**, and a song of praise is fitting. Ps 147:1
and knowledge will be **p** to your soul; Prv 2:10
is sweet, and bread eaten in secret is **p**." Prv 9:17
for it will be **p** if you keep them within Prv 22:18
you have eaten, and waste your **p** words. Prv 23:8
are filled with all precious and **p** riches. Prv 24:4
and it is **p** for the eyes to see the sun. Eccl 11:7
How beautiful and **p** you are, O loved one, Sg 7:6
and the men of Judah are his **p** planting; Is 5:7
its towers, and jackals in the **p** palaces; Is 13:22
though you plant **p** plants and sow the Is 17:10
In that day, "A **p** vineyard, sing of it! Is 27:2
Beat your breasts for the **p** fields, for the Is 32:12
and all our **p** places have become ruins. Is 64:11
among my sons, and give you a **p** land, Jer 3:19
they have made my **p** portion a desolate Jer 12:10
and looked, and my sleep was **p** to me. Jer 31:26
your walls and destroy your **p** houses. Ezk 26:12
you have planted **p** vineyards, but you Am 5:11
fro, and the **p** land was made desolate." Zec 7:14
seems painful rather than **p**, Heb 12:11

PLEASANTNESS (2)
days in prosperity, and their years in **p**. Jb 36:11
Her ways are ways of **p**, and all her Prv 3:17

PLEASE (165)
to her as you **p**." Then Sarai dealt Gn 16:6
p turn aside to your servant's house and Gn 19:2
out to you, and do to them as you **p**. Gn 19:8
p grant me success today and show Gn 24:12
'**P** let down your jar that I may drink,' Gn 24:14
"**P** give me a little water to drink from Gn 24:17
"**P** tell me whose daughter you are. Gn 24:23
"**P** give me a little water from your jar Gn 24:43
water.' I said to her, '**P** let me drink.' Gn 24:45
Isaac said to Jacob, "**P** come near, Gn 27:21
women did not **p** Isaac his father, Gn 28:8
"**P** give me some of your son's Gn 30:14
P deliver me from the hand of my Gn 32:11
"**P** tell me your name." But he said, Gn 32:29
p, if I have found favor in your sight, Gn 33:10
P accept my blessing that is brought Gn 33:11
P give her to him to be his wife. Gn 34:8
p, where they are pasturing the flock." Gn 37:16
p identify whether it is your son's robe Gn 37:32
she said, "**P** identify whose these are, Gn 38:25
belong to God? **P** tell them to me." Gn 40:8
and **p** do me the kindness to mention Gn 40:14
p let your servant speak a word in my Gn 44:18
p let your servant remain instead of the Gn 44:33
near to me, **p**." And they came near. Gn 45:4
p let your servants dwell in the land of Gn 47:4
have saved our lives; may it **p** my lord, Gn 47:25
them to me, **p**, that I may bless them." Gn 48:9
eyes, **p** speak in the ears of Pharaoh, Gn 50:4
let me **p** go up and bury my father. Gn 50:5
P forgive the transgression of your Gn 50:17
p forgive the transgression of the Gn 50:17
p let us go a three days' journey into the Ex 3:18
"Oh, my Lord, **p** send someone else." Ex 4:13
"**P** let me go back to my brothers in Ex 4:18
P let us go a three days' journey into the Ex 5:3
forgive my sin, **p**, only this once, Ex 10:17
If she does not **p** her master, who has Ex 21:8
p blot me out of your book that you Ex 32:32
your sight, **p** show me now your ways, Ex 33:13
Moses said, "**P** show me your glory." Ex 33:18
Lord, **p** let the Lord go in the midst of us, Ex 34:9
And he said, "**P** do not leave us, for Nm 10:31
the LORD, "O God, **p** heal her—please." Nm 12:13
the LORD, "O God, please heal her—**p**." Nm 12:13
p let the power of the Lord be great as Nm 14:17
P pardon the iniquity of this people, Nm 14:19
p, from the tents of these wicked men, Nm 16:26
P let us pass through your land. We Nm 20:17
So you, too, **p** stay here tonight, that I Nm 22:19
"**P** come with me to another place, Nm 23:13
Perhaps it will **p** God that you may Nm 23:27
P let me go over and see the good land Dt 3:25
then, **p** swear to me by the LORD that, Jos 2:12
to him, "**P** show us the way into the city, Jgs 1:24
to her, "**P** give me a little water to drink, Jgs 4:19
And Gideon said to him, "**P**, sir, if the Jgs 6:13
And he said to him, "**P**, Lord, how can I Jgs 6:15
P do not depart from here until I come to Jgs 6:18
P let me test just once more with the Jgs 6:39
P let it be dry on the fleece only, and on Jgs 6:39
"**P** give loaves of bread to the people who Jgs 8:5
good to you. Only **p** deliver us this day." Jgs 10:15
'**P** let us pass through your land,' Jgs 11:17
'**P** let us pass through your land to our Jgs 11:19
p let the man of God whom you sent Jgs 13:8
"**P** let us detain you and prepare a Jgs 13:15
beautiful than she? **P** take her instead." Jgs 15:2

"**P** tell me where your great strength lies, Jgs 16:6
P tell me how you might be bound." Jgs 16:10
p remember me and please strengthen Jgs 16:28
remember me and **p** strengthen me Jgs 16:28
p, that we may know whether the Jgs 18:5
toward evening. **P**, spend the night. Jgs 19:9
'**P** let me glean and gather among the Ru 2:7
"**P** put me in one of the priests' places, 1 Sm 2:36
"**P** tell me what Samuel said to you." 1 Sm 10:15
p pardon my sin and return with me 1 Sm 15:25
But should it **p** my father to do you 1 Sm 20:13
"**P** let my father and my mother stay 1 Sm 22:3
p tell your servant." And the LORD 1 Sm 23:11
P give whatever you have at hand to 1 Sm 25:8
P let your servant speak in your ears, 1 Sm 25:24
P forgive the trespass of your 1 Sm 25:28
Now **p** let me pin him to the earth 1 Sm 26:8
Now therefore may it **p** you to bless 2 Sm 7:29
"**P** let my sister Tamar come and 2 Sm 13:6
Now therefore, **p** speak to the king, 2 Sm 13:13
P let the king and his servants go 2 Sm 13:24
p let my brother Amnon go with us." 2 Sm 13:26
"**P** let the king invoke the LORD your 2 Sm 14:11
"**P** let your servant speak a word to 2 Sm 14:12
king, "**P** let me go and pay my vow, 2 Sm 15:7
p turn the counsel of Ahithophel 2 Sm 15:31
P let your servant return, that I may 2 Sm 19:37
p take away the iniquity of your 2 Sm 24:10
P let your hand be against me and 2 Sm 24:17
"**P** ask King Solomon—he will not 1 Kgs 2:17
had given him, they did not **p** him. 1 Kgs 9:12
says, '**P**, let me live.'" And he said, 1 Kgs 20:32
"Strike me, **p**." But the man refused 1 Kgs 20:35
"Strike me, **p**." And the man struck 1 Kgs 20:37
for money, or else, if it **p** you, 1 Kgs 21:6
him, "O man of God, **p** let my life, 2 Kgs 1:13
And Elijah said to Elisha, "**P** stay here, 2 Kgs 2:2
Elijah said to him, "Elisha, **p** stay here, 2 Kgs 2:4
Then Elijah said to him, "**P** stay here, 2 Kgs 2:6
"**P** let there be a double portion of your 2 Kgs 2:9
P let them go and seek your master. 2 Kgs 2:16
p let there be given to your servant 2 Kgs 5:17
P give them a talent of silver and two 2 Kgs 5:22
p open his eyes that he may see." So 2 Kgs 6:17
"**P** strike this people with blindness." 2 Kgs 6:18
"**P** speak to your servants in 2 Kgs 18:26
our God, save us, **p**, from his hand, 2 Kgs 19:19
p remember how I have walked 2 Kgs 20:3
p take away the iniquity of your 1 Chr 21:8
P let your hand, O LORD my God, be 1 Chr 21:17
to this people and **p** them and speak 2 Chr 10:7
bodies and over our livestock as they **p**, Neh 9:37
If it **p** the king, let a royal order go out Est 1:19
If it **p** the king, let it be decreed that they Est 3:9
And Esther said, "If it **p** the king, let the Est 5:4
and if it **p** the king to grant my wish and Est 5:8
in your sight, O king, and if it **p** the king, Est 7:3
And she said, "If it **p** the king, and if I Est 8:5
you may write as you **p** with regard to the Est 8:8
And Esther said, "If it **p** the king, let the Est 9:13
that it would **p** God to crush me, that he Jb 6:9
P turn; let no injustice be done. Turn Jb 6:29
"For inquire, **p**, of bygone ages, and Jb 8:8
This will **p** the LORD more than an ox or Ps 69:31
When a man's ways **p** the LORD, he Prv 16:7
"**P** speak to your servants in Aramaic, Is 36:11
and said, "**P**, O LORD, remember how I Is 38:3
choose the things that **p** me and hold fast Is 56:4
Behold, **p** look, we are all your people. Is 64:9
us, **p**, how did you write all these words? Jer 36:17
"**P** pray for us to the LORD our God." Jer 37:3
Now hear, **p**, O my lord the king: let my Jer 37:20
"**P** let me go and strike down Ishmael Jer 40:15
and their sacrifices shall not **p** him. Hos 9:4
When I **p**, I will discipline them, and Hos 10:10
of the land, I said, "O Lord GOD, **p** forgive! Am 7:2
Then I said, "O Lord GOD, **p** cease! How Am 7:5
now, O LORD, **p** take my life from me, Jon 4:3
go out and see it. **P** have me excused.' Lk 14:18
to examine them. **P** have me excused.' Lk 14:19
him, "**P** come to us without delay." Acts 9:38
who are in the flesh cannot **p** God. Rom 8:8
of the weak, and not to **p** ourselves. Rom 15:1
Let each of us **p** his neighbor for his Rom 15:2
For Christ did not **p** himself, but as it Rom 15:3
things of the Lord, how to **p** the Lord. 1 Cor 7:32
worldly things, how to **p** his wife, 1 Cor 7:33
things, how to **p** her husband. 1 Cor 7:34
as I try to **p** everyone in everything I 1 Cor 10:33
or away, we make it our aim to **p** him. 2 Cor 5:9
or of God? Or am I trying to **p** man? Gal 1:10
If I were still trying to **p** man, I would Gal 1:10
the gospel, so we speak, not to **p** man, 1 Thes 2:4
but to **p** God who tests our hearts. 1 Thes 2:4
how you ought to live and to **p** God, 1 Thes 4:1
his aim is to **p** the one who enlisted 2 Tm 2:4
without faith it is impossible to **p** him, Heb 11:6

PLEASED (51)

Their words **p** Hamor and Hamor's Gn 34:18
This proposal **p** Pharaoh and all his Gn 41:37
have come," it **p** Pharaoh and his Gn 45:16
"Be **p** to command me when I am to plead Ex 8:9
Balaam saw that it **p** the LORD to bless Nm 24:1
said to the man, "Be **p** to spend the night, Jgs 19:6
because it has **p** the LORD to make 1 Sm 12:22
they told Saul, and the thing **p** him. 1 Sm 18:20
it **p** David well to be the king's 1 Sm 18:26
people took notice of it, and it **p** them, 2 Sm 3:36
that the king did **p** all the people. 2 Sm 3:36
were dead today, then you would be **p**. 2 Sm 19:6
It **p** the Lord that Solomon had asked 1 Kgs 3:10
"Be **p** to accept two talents." And he 2 Kgs 5:23
"Be **p** to go with your servants." And he 2 Kgs 6:3
Now you have been **p** to bless the 1 Chr 17:27
will you return?" So it **p** the king to send Neh 2:6
This advice **p** the king and the princes, Est 1:21
queen instead of Vashti." This **p** the king, Est 2:4
And the young woman **p** him and won Est 2:9
king to the feast." This idea **p** Haman, Est 5:14
and did as they **p** to those who hated Est 9:5
"But now, be **p** to look at me, for I will not Jb 6:28
Be **p**, O LORD, to deliver me! O LORD, Ps 40:13
If you see a thief, you are **p** with him, Ps 50:18
you will not be **p** with a burnt offering. Ps 51:16
The LORD was **p**, for his righteousness' Is 42:21
It **p** Darius to set over the kingdom 120 Dn 6:1
power. He did as he **p** and became great. Dn 8:4
for you, O LORD, have done as it **p** you." Jon 1:14
Will the LORD be **p** with thousands of Mi 6:7
beloved Son, with whom I am well **p**." Mt 3:17
beloved with whom my soul is well **p**. Mt 12:18
before the company and **p** Herod, Mt 14:6
my beloved Son, with whom I am well **p**; Mt 17:5
him, but did to him whatever they **p**. Mt 17:12
my beloved Son; with you I am well **p**." Mk 1:11
and danced, she **p** Herod and his guests. Mk 6:22
and they did to him whatever they **p**, Mk 9:13
peace among those with whom he is **p**!" Lk 2:14
my beloved Son; with you I am well **p**." Lk 3:22
what they said **p** the whole gathering, Acts 6:5
and when he saw that it **p** the Jews, he Acts 12:3
Achaia have been **p** to make some Rom 15:26
They were **p** to do it, and indeed they Rom 15:27
it **p** God through the folly of what we 1 Cor 1:21
with most of them God was not **p**, 1 Cor 10:5
was **p** to reveal his Son to me, in order Gal 1:16
all the fullness of God was **p** to dwell, Col 1:19
he was commended as having **p** God. Heb 11:5
beloved Son, with whom I am well **p**," 2 Pt 1:17

PLEASES (16)

is before you; dwell where it **p** you." Gn 20:15
hands on whatever **p** you and take 1 Kgs 20:6
And I said to the king, "If it **p** the king, Neh 2:5
And I said to the king, "If it **p** the king, Neh 2:7
the young woman who **p** the king be Est 2:4
is in the heavens; he does all that he **p**. Ps 115:3
Whatever the LORD **p**, he does, in heaven Ps 135:6
to the one who **p** him God has given Eccl 2:26
only to give to one who **p** God. Eccl 2:26
He who **p** God escapes her, but the Eccl 7:26
an evil cause, for he does whatever he **p**. Eccl 8:3
you not stir up or awaken love until it **p**. Sg 2:7
you not stir up or awaken love until it **p**. Sg 3:5
you not stir up or awaken love until it **p**. Sg 8:4
in everything, for this **p** the Lord. Col 3:20
commandments and do what **p** him. 1 Jn 3:22

PLEASING (58)

when the LORD smelled the **p** aroma, Gn 8:21
It is a **p** aroma, a food offering to the Ex 29:18
offering, as a **p** aroma before the LORD. Ex 29:25
as in the morning, for a **p** aroma, Ex 29:41
a food offering with a **p** aroma to the LORD. Lv 1:9
food offering with a **p** aroma to the LORD. Lv 1:13
food offering with a **p** aroma to the LORD. Lv 1:17
a food offering with a **p** aroma to the LORD. Lv 2:2
a food offering with a **p** aroma to the LORD. Lv 2:9
not be offered on the altar for a **p** aroma. Lv 2:12
a food offering with a **p** aroma to the LORD. Lv 3:5
altar as a food offering with a **p** aroma. Lv 3:16
it on the altar for a **p** aroma to the LORD. Lv 4:31
on the altar, a **p** aroma to the LORD. Lv 6:15
and offer it for a **p** aroma to the LORD. Lv 6:21
It was a burnt offering with a **p** aroma, a Lv 8:21
an ordination offering with a **p** aroma, Lv 8:28
burn the fat for a **p** aroma to the LORD. Lv 17:6
offering to the LORD with a **p** aroma, Lv 23:13
food offering with a **p** aroma to the Lv 23:18
and I will not smell your **p** aromas. Lv 26:31
feasts, to make a **p** aroma to the LORD, Nm 15:3
of a hin of wine, a **p** aroma to the LORD. Nm 15:7
a food offering, a **p** aroma to the LORD. Nm 15:10
offering, with a **p** aroma to the LORD. Nm 15:13
offering, with a **p** aroma to the LORD, Nm 15:14
burnt offering, a **p** aroma to the LORD, Nm 15:24
offering, with a **p** aroma to the LORD. Nm 18:17
for my food offerings, my **p** aroma, Nm 28:2
ordained at Mount Sinai for a **p** aroma, Nm 28:6
offering, with a **p** aroma to the LORD. Nm 28:8
for a burnt offering with a **p** aroma, a Nm 28:13
offering, with a **p** aroma to the LORD. Nm 28:24
offering, with a **p** aroma to the LORD: Nm 28:27
offering, for a **p** aroma to the LORD: Nm 29:2
to the rule for them, for a **p** aroma, Nm 29:6
a burnt offering to the LORD, a **p** aroma: Nm 29:8
offering, with a **p** aroma to the LORD, Nm 29:13
offering, with a **p** aroma to the LORD: Nm 29:36
is found something **p** to the LORD, 1 Kgs 14:13
that they may offer **p** sacrifices to the Ezr 6:10
before the king, and I am **p** in his eyes, Est 8:5
My heart overflows with a **p** theme; I Ps 45:1
May my meditation be **p** to him, for I Ps 104:34
acceptable, nor your sacrifices **p** to me. Jer 6:20
wherever they offered **p** aroma to all Ezk 6:13
—you set before them for a **p** aroma; Ezk 16:19
there they sent up their **p** aromas, and Ezk 20:28
As a **p** aroma I will accept you, when I Ezk 20:41
and Jerusalem will be **p** to the LORD as Mal 3:4
I always do the things that are **p** to him." Jn 8:29
and try to discern what is **p** to the Lord. Eph 5:10
a sacrifice acceptable and **p** to God. Phil 4:18
worthy of the Lord, fully **p** to him, Col 1:10
and it is **p** in the sight of God our 1 Tm 2:3
parents, for this is **p** in the sight of God. 1 Tm 5:4
have, for such sacrifices are **p** to God. Heb 13:16
in us that which is **p** in his sight, Heb 13:21

PLEASURE (42)

out, and my lord is old, shall I have **p**?" Gn 18:12
But if he says, 'I have no **p** in you,' 2 Sm 15:26
the king's household and to do his **p**. 2 Sm 19:18
father's sons he took **p** in me to make 1 Chr 28:4
the heart and have **p** in uprightness. 1 Chr 29:17
the king send us his **p** in this matter." Ezr 5:17
Is it any **p** to the Almighty if you are in Jb 22:3
Do good to Zion in your good **p**; build Ps 51:18
high position. They take **p** in falsehood. Ps 62:4
his princes at his **p** and to teach his Ps 105:22
horse, nor his **p** in the legs of a man, Ps 147:10
but the LORD takes **p** in those who fear Ps 147:11
For the LORD takes **p** in his people; he Ps 149:4
but wisdom is **p** to a man of Prv 10:23
A fool takes no **p** in understanding, but Prv 18:2
Whoever loves **p** will be a poor man; Prv 21:17
heart, "Come now, I will test you with **p**; Eccl 2:1
I said of laughter, "It is mad," and of **p**, Eccl 2:2
I kept my heart from no **p**, for my Eccl 2:10
for my heart found **p** in all my toil, Eccl 2:10
eat and drink and take **p** in all his toil Eccl 3:13
and depriving myself of **p**?" This also is Eccl 4:8
delay paying it, for he has no **p** in fools. Eccl 5:4
you will say, "I have no **p** in them"; Eccl 12:1
the day of your fast you seek your own **p**, Is 58:3
from doing your **p** on my holy day, Is 58:13
your own ways, or seeking your own **p**, Is 58:13
an object of scorn; they take no **p** in it. Jer 6:10
all your lovers with whom you took **p**, Ezk 16:37
Have I any **p** in the death of the Ezk 18:23
For I have no **p** in the death of anyone, Ezk 18:32
I have no **p** in the death of the wicked, Ezk 33:11
that I may take **p** in it and that I may be Hg 1:8
I have no **p** in you, says the LORD of Mal 1:10
is your Father's good **p** to give you the Lk 12:32
both to will and to work for his good **p**. Phil 2:13
truth but had **p** in unrighteousness. 2 Thes 2:12
lovers of **p** rather than lovers of God, 2 Tm 3:4
and sin offerings you have taken no **p**. Heb 10:6
desired nor taken **p** in sacrifices and Heb 10:8
back, my soul has no **p** in him." Heb 10:38
They count it **p** to revel in the daytime. 2 Pt 2:13

PLEASURES (5)

at your right hand are **p** forevermore. Ps 16:11
Now therefore hear this, you lover of **p**, Is 47:8
by the cares and riches and **p** of life, Lk 8:14
astray, slaves to various passions and **p**, Ti 3:3
God than to enjoy the fleeting **p** of sin. Heb 11:25

PLEDGE (36)

And she said, "If you give me a **p**, Gn 38:17
"What **p** shall I give you?" She replied, Gn 38:18
to take back the **p** from the woman's Gn 38:20
I will be a **p** of his safety. From my hand Gn 43:9
your servant became a **p** of safety for Gn 44:32
you take your neighbor's cloak in **p**, Ex 22:26
swears an oath to bind himself by a **p**, Nm 30:2
to the LORD and binds herself by a **p**, Nm 30:3

her vow and of her **p** by which she has Nm 30:4
and every **p** by which she has bound Nm 30:4
no **p** by which she has bound herself Nm 30:5
or bound herself by a **p** with an oath, Nm 30:10
and every **p** by which she bound Nm 30:11
or concerning her **p** of herself shall Nm 30:12
take a mill or an upper millstone in **p**, Dt 24:6
for that would be taking a life in **p**. Dt 24:6
not go into his house to collect his **p**. Dt 24:10
the loan shall bring the **p** out to you. Dt 24:11
a poor man, you shall not sleep in his **p**. Dt 24:12
restore to him the **p** as the sun sets, Dt 24:13
or take a widow's garment in **p**, Dt 24:17
"Lay down a **p** for me with yourself; who Jb 17:3
they take the widow's ox for a **p**. Jb 24:3
and they take a **p** against the poor.) Jb 24:9
Give your servant a **p** of good; let not Ps 119:122
have given your **p** for a stranger, Prv 6:1
hates striking hands in **p** is secure. Prv 11:15
lacks sense gives a **p** and puts up Prv 17:18
and hold it in **p** when he puts up Prv 20:16
and hold it in **p** when he puts up Prv 27:13
Lord, I am oppressed; be my **p** of safety! Is 38:14
anyone, but restores to the debtor his **p**, Ezk 18:7
robbery, does not restore the **p**, Ezk 18:12
does not oppress anyone, exacts no **p**, Ezk 18:16
if the wicked restores the **p**, gives back Ezk 33:15
every altar on garments taken in **p**, Am 2:8

PLEDGED (2)
p their allegiance to King Solomon. 1 Chr 29:24
They **p** themselves to put away their Ezr 10:19

PLEDGES (5)
and her **p** by which she has bound Nm 30:7
vows or all her **p** that are upon her. Nm 30:14
For you have exacted **p** of your brothers Jb 22:6
Be not one of those who give **p**, who Prv 22:26
how long?—and loads himself with **p**!" Hab 2:6

PLEIADES (3)
the **P** and the chambers of the south; Jb 9:9
the chains of the **P** or loose the cords Jb 38:31
He who made the **P** and Orion, and turns Am 5:8

PLENTEOUS (1)
of the ground, which will be rich and **p**. Is 30:23

PLENTIFUL (10)
land of Egypt during the seven **p** years. Gn 41:34
During the seven **p** years the earth Gn 41:47
he made cedar as **p** as the sycamore 1 Kgs 10:27
he made cedar as **p** as the sycamore 2 Chr 1:15
he made cedar as **p** as the sycamore 2 Chr 9:27
love, and with him is **p** redemption. Ps 130:7
I brought you into a **p** land to enjoy its Jer 2:7
he said to his disciples, "The harvest is **p**, Mt 9:37
And he said to them, "The harvest is **p**, Lk 10:2
near Salim, because water was **p** there, Jn 3:23

PLENTIFULLY (2)
and **p** declared sound knowledge! Jb 26:3
"The land of a rich man produced **p**, Lk 12:16

PLENTY (16)
"We have **p** of both straw and fodder, Gn 24:25
of the earth and **p** of grain and wine. Gn 27:28
years of great **p** throughout all the Gn 41:29
and all the **p** will be forgotten in the Gn 41:30
and the **p** will be unknown in the land Gn 41:31
The seven years of **p** that occurred in Gn 41:53
and had enough and have **p** left, 2 Chr 31:10
there will be contempt and wrath in **p**. Est 1:18
then your barns will be filled with **p**, Prv 3:10
works his land will have **p** of bread, Prv 12:11
eyes, and you will have **p** of bread. Prv 20:13
works his land will have **p** of bread, Prv 28:19
pursuits will have **p** of poverty. Prv 28:19
For then we had **p** of food, and Jer 44:17
"You shall eat in **p** and be satisfied, and Jl 2:26
the secret of facing **p** and hunger, Phil 4:12

PLIGHT (1)
courage melted away in their evil **p**; Ps 107:26

PLOT (19)
where there was a **p** of ground full of 2 Sm 23:11
the midst of the **p** and defended it and 2 Sm 23:12
him on the **p** of ground belonging 2 Kgs 9:25
I will repay you on this **p** of ground.' 2 Kgs 9:26
up and throw him on the **p** of ground, 2 Kgs 9:26
There was a **p** of ground full of 1 Chr 11:13
the midst of the **p** and defended it 1 Chr 11:14
the Agagite and the **p** that he had devised Est 8:3
the nations rage and the peoples **p** in vain? Ps 2:1
against me, as they **p** to take my life. Ps 31:13
none of those who treacherously **p** evil. Ps 59:5
do not further their evil **p** or they will be Ps 140:8
Of this a square **p** of 500 by 500 cubits Ezk 45:2
What do you **p** against the LORD? He will Na 1:9
rage, and the peoples **p** in vain? Acts 4:25
but their **p** became known to Saul. Acts 9:24
and when a **p** was made against him Acts 20:3
Jews made a **p** and bound themselves Acts 23:12
there would be a **p** against the man, Acts 23:30

PLOTS (11)
you hide them from the **p** of men; Ps 31:20
He **p** trouble while on his bed; he sets Ps 36:4
The wicked **p** against the righteous and Ps 37:12
Your tongue **p** destruction, like a sharp Ps 52:2
Hide me from the secret **p** of the wicked, Ps 64:2
A worthless man **p** evil, and his speech Prv 16:27
"Come, let us make **p** against Jeremiah, Jer 18:18
their vengeance, all their **p** against me. Lam 3:60
taunts, O LORD, all their **p** against me. Lam 3:61
for **p** shall be devised against him. Dn 11:25
to me through the **p** of the Jews; Acts 20:19

PLOTTED (6)
And they all **p** together to come and Neh 4:8
had **p** against the Jews to destroy them, Est 9:24
you came one who **p** evil against the Na 1:11
Pharisees went and **p** how to entangle Mt 22:15
and **p** together in order to arrest Jesus by Mt 26:4
days had passed, the Jews **p** to kill him, Acts 9:23

PLOTTING (3)
that Saul was **p** harm against him. 1 Sm 23:9
Even though princes sit **p** against me, Ps 119:23
you, O LORD, know all their **p** to kill me. Jer 18:23

PLOW (9)
You shall not **p** with an ox and a Dt 22:10
and some to **p** his ground and to reap 1 Sm 8:12
those who **p** iniquity and sow trouble reap Jb 4:8
The sluggard does not **p** in the autumn; Prv 20:4
he who plows for sowing **p** continually? Is 28:24
Ephraim to the yoke; Judah must **p**; Hos 10:11
on rocks? Does one **p** there with oxen? Am 6:12
puts his hand to the **p** and looks back is Lk 9:62
the plowman should **p** in hope and 1 Cor 9:10

PLOWED (6)
water, which is neither **p** nor sown, Dt 21:4
them, "If you had not **p** with my heifer, Jgs 14:18
The plowers **p** upon my back; they Ps 129:3
of hosts, "'Zion shall be **p** as a field; Jer 26:18
You have **p** iniquity; you have reaped Hos 10:13
because of you Zion shall be **p** as a field; Mi 3:12

PLOWERS (1)
The **p** plowed upon my back; they Ps 129:3

PLOWING (5)
there will be neither **p** nor harvest. Gn 45:6
In **p** time and in harvest you shall rest. Ex 34:21
who was **p** with twelve yoke of oxen 1 Kgs 19:19
"The oxen were **p** and the donkeys Jb 1:14
who has a servant **p** or keeping sheep Lk 17:7

PLOWMAN (2)
"when the **p** shall overtake the reaper Am 9:13
because the **p** should plow in hope 1 Cor 9:10

PLOWMEN (3)
of the land to be vinedressers and **p**. 2 Kgs 25:12
shall be your **p** and vinedressers; Is 61:5
of the land to be vinedressers and **p**. Jer 52:16

PLOWS (2)
As when one **p** and breaks up the earth, Ps 141:7
Does he who **p** for sowing plow Is 28:24

PLOWSHARE (1)
to the Philistines to sharpen his **p**, 1 Sm 13:20

PLOWSHARES (4)
a shekel for the **p** and for the 1 Sm 13:21
and they shall beat their swords into **p**, and Is 2:4
Beat your **p** into swords, and your Jl 3:10
and they shall beat their swords into **p**, Mi 4:3

PLUCK (14)
you may **p** the ears with your hand, Dt 23:25
then I will **p** you up from my land 2 Chr 7:20
LORD, for he will **p** my feet out of the net. Ps 25:15
all who pass along the way **p** its fruit? Ps 80:12
and a time to **p** up what is planted; Eccl 3:2
kingdoms, to **p** up and to break down, Jer 1:10
I will **p** them up from their land, Jer 12:14
and I will **p** up the house of Judah from Jer 12:14
then I will utterly **p** it up and destroy it, Jer 12:17
that I will **p** up and break down and Jer 18:7
watched over them to **p** up and break Jer 31:28
I will plant you, and not **p** you up; Jer 42:10
and they began to **p** heads of grain and Mt 12:1
his disciples began to **p** heads of grain. Mk 2:23

PLUCKED (13)
in her mouth was a freshly **p** olive leaf. Gn 8:11
And you shall be **p** off the land that you Dt 28:63
Is not their tent-cord **p** up within them, Jb 4:21
tent, whose stakes will never be **p** up, Is 33:20
My dwelling is **p** up and removed from Is 38:12
And after I have **p** them up, I will again Jer 12:15
But the vine was **p** up in fury, cast Ezk 19:12
Then as I looked its wings were **p** off, and Dn 7:4
of the first horns were **p** up by the roots. Dn 7:8
for his kingdom shall be **p** up and go to Dn 11:4
were as a brand **p** out of the burning; Am 4:11
you! Is not this a brand **p** from the fire?" Zec 3:2
his disciples **p** and ate some heads of Lk 6:1

PLUCKING (1)
what I have planted I am **p** up—that is, Jer 45:4

PLUMAGE (3)
but are they the pinions and **p** of love? Jb 39:13
long pinions, rich in **p** of many colors, Ezk 17:3
eagle with great wings and much **p**, Ezk 17:7

PLUMB (8)
and the **p** line of the house of Ahab, 2 Kgs 21:13
the line, and righteousness the **p** line; Is 28:17
over it, and the **p** line of emptiness. Is 34:11
beside a wall built with a **p** line, Am 7:7
a plumb line, with a **p** line in his hand. Am 7:7
I said, "A **p** line." Then the Lord said, Am 7:8
I am setting a **p** line in the midst of my Am 7:8
and shall see the **p** line in the hand of Zec 4:10

PLUMP (6)
of the Nile seven cows attractive and **p**, Gn 41:2
cows ate up the seven attractive, **p** cows. Gn 41:4
behold, seven ears of grain, **p** and good, Gn 41:5
the thin ears swallowed up the seven **p**, Gn 41:7
Seven cows, **p** and attractive, came up Gn 41:18
ugly cows ate up the first seven **p** cows, Gn 41:20

PLUNDER (53)
daughters. So you shall **p** the Egyptians." Ex 3:22
ones, and they took as **p** all their cattle, Nm 31:9
and took all the spoil and all the **p**, Nm 31:11
the captives and the **p** and the spoil to Nm 31:12
the count of the **p** that was taken, Nm 31:26
and divide the **p** into two parts Nm 31:27
Now the **p** remaining of the spoil that Nm 31:32
army had each taken **p** for himself.) Nm 31:53
with the **p** of the cities that we captured. Dt 2:35
and the spoil of the cities we took as our **p**. Dt 3:7
spoil, you shall take as **p** for yourselves. Dt 20:14
you shall take as **p** for yourselves. Jos 8:2
spoil of that city Israel took as their **p**, Jos 8:27
the people of Israel took for their **p**. Jos 11:14
by night and **p** them until the 1 Sm 14:36
for there was much **p** in them. 2 Chr 14:14
the month of Adar, and to **p** their goods. Est 3:13
women included, and to **p** their goods, Est 8:11
the Jews, but they laid no hand on the **p**. Est 9:10
in Susa, but they laid no hands on the **p**. Est 9:15
them, but they laid no hands on the **p**. Est 9:16
All who pass by **p** him; he has become Ps 89:41
may strangers **p** the fruits of his toil! Ps 109:11
goods, we shall fill our houses with **p**; Prv 1:13
I command him, to take spoil and seize **p**, Is 10:6
of peoples, and **p** their treasures; Is 10:13
and together they shall **p** the people of Is 11:14
loot us, and the lot of those who **p** us. Is 17:14
they have become **p** with none to rescue, Is 42:22
who shall **p** them and seize them and Jer 20:5
those who **p** you shall be plundered, Jer 30:16
Their camels shall become **p**, their Jer 49:32
all who **p** her shall be sated, declares Jer 50:10
make them an object of terror and a **p**. Ezk 23:46
will hand you over as **p** to the nations. Ezk 25:7
And she shall become **p** for the nations, Ezk 26:5
They will **p** your riches and loot your Ezk 26:12
off its wealth and despoil it and **p** it; Ezk 29:19
to seize spoil and carry off **p**, to turn Ezk 38:12
assembled your hosts to carry off **p**, Ezk 38:13
and **p** those who plundered them, Ezk 39:10
have done, scattering among them **p**, Dn 11:24
sword and flame, by captivity and **p**. Dn 11:33
P the silver, plunder the gold! There is no Na 2:9
Plunder the silver, **p** the gold! There is no Na 2:9
all full of lies and **p**—no end to the prey! Na 3:1
the remnant of the peoples shall **p** you, Hab 2:8
The remnant of my people shall **p** them, Zep 2:9
and they shall become **p** for those who Zec 2:9
a strong man's house and **p** his goods, Mt 12:29
man? Then indeed he may **p** his house. Mt 12:29
a strong man's house and **p** his goods, Mk 3:27
man. Then indeed he may **p** his house. Mk 3:27

PLUNDERED (25)
came upon the slain and **p** the city, Gn 34:27
was in the houses, they captured and **p**. Gn 34:29
they asked. Thus they **p** the Egyptians. Ex 12:36
them over to plunderers, who **p** them. Jgs 2:14
out of the hand of those who **p** them. Jgs 2:16

of the hands of those who **p** them. 1 Sm 14:48
Philistines, and they **p** their camp. 1 Sm 17:53
people went out and **p** the camp of the 2 Kgs 7:16
They **p** all the cities, for there was 2 Chr 14:14
give them up to be **p** in a land where Neh 4:4
friend with evil or **p** my enemy without Ps 7:4
"Because the poor are **p**, because the Ps 12:5
their houses will be **p** and their wives Is 13:16
earth shall be utterly empty and utterly **p**; Is 24:3
But this is a people **p** and looted; they are Is 42:22
those who plunder you shall be **p**, and Jer 30:16
Chaldea shall be **p**; all who plunder her Jer 50:10
all her treasures, that they may be **p**! Jer 50:37
them, and plunder those who **p** them, Ezk 39:10
you, and your strongholds shall be **p**." Am 3:11
for plunderers have **p** them and ruined Na 2:2
Because you have **p** many nations, all Hab 2:8
Their goods shall be **p**, and their houses Zep 1:13
glory sent me to the nations who **p** you, Zec 2:8
taken and the houses **p** and the women Zec 14:2

PLUNDERER (1)
you bring the **p** suddenly upon them! Jer 18:22

PLUNDERERS (6)
Israel, and he gave them over to **p**, Jgs 2:14
and gave them into the hand of **p**, 2 Kgs 17:20
Jacob to the looter, and Israel to the **p**? Is 42:24
though you exult, O **p** of my heritage, Jer 50:11
if **p** came by night—how you have been Ob 1:5
for **p** have plundered them and ruined Na 2:2

PLUNDERING (2)
the lands, to the sword, to captivity, to **p**, Ezr 9:7
joyfully accepted the **p** of your Heb 10:34

PLUNGE (2)
yet you will **p** me into a pit, and my own Jb 9:31
harmful desires that **p** people into ruin 1 Tm 6:9

PLUNGED (1)
and its kingdom was **p** into darkness. Rv 16:10

PLUNGING (1)
like a horse **p** headlong into battle. Jer 8:6

PLUS (2)
twenty shekels **p** twenty-five shekels Ezk 45:12
twenty-five shekels **p** fifteen shekels Ezk 45:12

PLY (1)
prophet and priest **p** their trade through Jer 14:18

POCHERETH-HAZZEBAIM (2)
the sons of Hattil, the sons of **P**, Ezr 2:57
the sons of Hattil, the sons of **P**, Neh 7:59

PODS (1)
to be fed with the **p** that the pigs ate, Lk 15:16

POETS (1)
as even some of your own **p** have said, Acts 17:28

POINT (25)
presence of our kinsmen **p** out what I Gn 31:32
children have come to the **p** of birth, 2 Kgs 19:3
sick and was at the **p** of death. 2 Kgs 20:1
it came to the **p** in Jerusalem and 2 Kgs 24:20
had to that **p** kept their allegiance 1 Chr 12:29
sick and was at the **p** of death, 2 Chr 32:24
repaired to a **p** opposite the tombs of Neh 3:16
repaired to a **p** opposite the Water Neh 3:26
the glittering **p** comes out of his Jb 20:25
children have come to the **p** of birth, and Is 37:3
became sick and was at the **p** of death. Is 38:1
Shall I bring to the **p** of birth and not Is 66:9
with a **p** of diamond it is engraved on the Jer 17:1
things came to the **p** in Jerusalem and Jer 52:3
to a **p** opposite Lebo-hamath. Ezk 47:20
his disciples came to **p** out to him the Mt 24:1
"My little daughter is at the **p** of death. Mk 5:23
who was sick and at the **p** of death, Lk 7:2
heal his son, for he was at the **p** of death. Jn 4:47
At every **p** you have proved 2 Cor 7:11
The **p** is this: whoever sows sparingly 2 Cor 9:6
by becoming obedient to the **p** of death, Phil 2:8
Now the **p** in what we are saying is this: Heb 8:1
yet resisted to the **p** of shedding your Heb 12:4
fails in one **p** has become accountable Jas 2:10

POINTING (1)
yoke from your midst, the **p** of the finger, Is 58:9

POINTS (3)
signals with his feet, **p** with his finger, Prv 6:13
they had certain **p** of dispute with Acts 25:19
But on some **p** I have written to you Rom 15:15

POISON (8)
Gomorrah; their grapes are grapes of **p**; Dt 32:32
their wine is the **p** of serpents and the Dt 32:33
are in me; my spirit drinks their **p**; Jb 6:4
He will suck the **p** of cobras; the tongue Jb 20:16
They gave me **p** for food, and for my Ps 69:21
have turned justice into **p** and the fruit Am 6:12
and if they drink any deadly **p**, it will Mk 16:18
tongue. It is a restless evil, full of deadly **p**. Jas 3:8

POISONED (3)
perish and has given us **p** water to drink, Jer 8:14
food and give them **p** water to drink, Jer 23:15
the Gentiles and **p** their minds against Acts 14:2

POISONOUS (4)
you a root bearing **p** and bitter fruit, Dt 29:18
devoured by plague and **p** pestilence; Dt 32:24
food, and give them **p** water to drink. Jer 9:15
judgment springs up like **p** weeds in the Hos 10:4

POLE (3)
carried it on a **p** between two of them; Nm 13:23
"Make a fiery serpent and set it on a **p**, Nm 21:8
made a bronze serpent and set it on a **p**. Nm 21:9

POLES (39)
You shall make **p** of acacia wood and Ex 25:13
you shall put the **p** into the rings on Ex 25:14
The **p** shall remain in the rings of the Ex 25:15
as holders for the **p** to carry the table. Ex 25:27
You shall make the **p** of acacia wood, Ex 25:28
And you shall make **p** for the altar, poles Ex 27:6
poles for the altar, **p** of acacia wood, Ex 27:6
And the **p** shall be put through the rings, Ex 27:7
so that the **p** are on the two sides of the Ex 27:7
shall be holders for **p** with which to Ex 30:4
You shall make the **p** of acacia wood Ex 30:5
the ark with its **p**, the mercy seat, and Ex 35:12
the table with its **p** and all its utensils, Ex 35:13
and the altar of incense, with its **p**, and Ex 35:15
with its grating of bronze, its **p**, Ex 35:16
And he made **p** of acacia wood and Ex 37:4
and put the **p** into the rings on the sides Ex 37:5
as holders for the **p** to carry the table. Ex 37:14
He made the **p** of acacia wood to carry Ex 37:15
as holders for the **p** with which to carry Ex 37:27
And he made the **p** of acacia wood and Ex 37:28
of the bronze grating as holders for the **p**. Ex 38:5
He made the **p** of acacia wood and Ex 38:6
And he put the **p** through the rings on Ex 38:7
the testimony with its **p** and the mercy Ex 39:35
altar, and its grating of bronze, its **p**, Ex 39:39
and set up its frames, and put in its **p**, Ex 40:18
and put the **p** on the ark and set the Ex 40:20
a cloth all of blue, and shall put in its **p**. Nm 4:6
of goatskin, and shall put in its **p**. Nm 4:8
of goatskin, and shall put in its **p**. Nm 4:11
of goatskin, and shall put in its **p**. Nm 4:14
overshadowed the ark and its **p**. 1 Kgs 8:7
And the **p** were so long that the ends of 1 Kgs 8:8
the ends of the **p** were seen from the 1 Kgs 8:8
of God on their shoulders with the **p**, 1 Chr 15:15
a covering above the ark and its **p**. 2 Chr 5:8
And the **p** were so long that the ends of 2 Chr 5:9
the ends of the **p** were seen from the 2 Chr 5:9

POLICE (2)
it was day, the magistrates sent the **p**, Acts 16:35
The **p** reported these words to the Acts 16:38

POLISH (1)
with your helmets, **p** your spears, Jer 46:4

POLISHED (7)
His body is **p** ivory, bedecked with Sg 5:14
hand he hid me; he made me a **p** arrow; Is 49:2
sword, a sword is sharpened and also **p**, Ezk 21:9
for slaughter, **p** to flash like lightning! Ezk 21:10
So the sword is given to be **p**, that it Ezk 21:11
It is sharpened and **p** to be given into Ezk 21:11
It is **p** to consume and to flash like Ezk 21:28

POLLUTE (1)
You shall not **p** the land in which you Nm 35:33

POLLUTED (12)
And they **p** the house of the LORD 2 Chr 36:14
and the land was **p** with blood. Ps 106:38
muddied spring or a **p** fountain is a Prv 25:26
our righteous deeds are like a **p** garment. Is 64:6
to her? Would not that land be greatly **p**? Jer 3:1
You have **p** the land with your vile Jer 3:2
her whoredom lightly, she **p** the land, Jer 3:9
because they have **p** my land with the Jer 16:18
By offering **p** food upon my altar. But Mal 1:7
altar. But you say, 'How have we **p** you?' Mal 1:7
when you say that the Lord's table is **p**, Mal 1:12
to abstain from the things **p** by idols, Acts 15:20

POLLUTES (1)
which you live, for blood **p** the land, Nm 35:33

POMEGRANATE (10)
a golden bell and a **p**, a golden bell and Ex 28:34
a pomegranate, a golden bell and a **p**, Ex 28:34
a bell and a **p**, a bell and a pomegranate Ex 39:26
a bell and a **p** around the hem of the Ex 39:26
of Gibeah in the **p** cave at Migron. 1 Sm 14:2
are like halves of a **p** behind your veil. Sg 4:3
are like halves of a **p** behind your veil. Sg 6:7
spiced wine to drink, the juice of my **p**. Sg 8:2
P, palm, and apple, all the trees of the field Jl 1:12
Indeed, the vine, the fig tree, the **p**, and Hg 2:19

POMEGRANATES (22)
hem you shall make **p** of blue and Ex 28:33
the robe they made **p** of blue and purple Ex 39:24
the bells between the **p** all around the Ex 39:25
the hem of the robe, between the **p**— Ex 39:25
they also brought some **p** and figs. Nm 13:23
no place for grain or figs or vines or **p**, Nm 20:5
and barley, of vines and fig trees and **p**, Dt 8:8
Likewise he made **p** in two rows 1 Kgs 7:18
were two hundred **p** in two rows 1 Kgs 7:20
and the four hundred **p** for the two 1 Kgs 7:42
two rows of **p** for each latticework, 1 Kgs 7:42
A latticework and **p**, all of bronze, 2 Kgs 25:17
he made a hundred **p** and put them 2 Chr 3:16
and the 400 **p** for the two 2 Chr 4:13
two rows of **p** for each latticework, 2 Chr 4:13
are an orchard of **p** with all choicest Sg 4:13
budded, whether the **p** were in bloom. Sg 6:11
have opened and the **p** are in bloom. Sg 7:12
A network and **p**, all of bronze, were Jer 52:22
the second pillar had the same, with **p**. Jer 52:22
There were ninety-six **p** on the sides; all Jer 52:23
all the **p** were a hundred upon the Jer 52:23

POMP (7)
and the splendor and **p** of his greatness Est 1:4
Man in his **p** will not remain; he is like Ps 49:12
Man in his **p** yet without Ps 49:20
I will put an end to the **p** of the arrogant, Is 13:11
the splendor and **p** of the Chaldeans, Is 13:19
Your **p** is brought down to Sheol, the Is 14:11
and Bernice came with great **p**, Acts 25:23

POMPOUS (3)
and lay low the **p** pride of the ruthless. Is 13:11
it, to defile the **p** pride of all glory, Is 23:9
will lay low his **p** pride together with the Is 25:11

POND (1)
Neither can a salt **p** yield fresh water. Jas 3:12

PONDER (8)
p in your own hearts on your beds, and be Ps 4:4
has brought about and **p** what he has Ps 64:9
I will **p** all your work, and meditate on Ps 77:12
I will **p** the way that is blameless. Oh Ps 101:2
have done; I **p** the work of your hands. Ps 143:5
P the path of your feet; then all your Prv 4:26
she does not **p** the path of life; her ways Prv 5:6
see you will stare at you and **p** over you: Is 14:16

PONDERING (2)
up all these things, **p** them in her heart. Lk 2:19
And while Peter was **p** the vision, the Acts 10:19

PONDERS (2)
eyes of the LORD, and he **p** all his paths. Prv 5:21
heart of the righteous **p** how to answer, Prv 15:28

PONDS (1)
their rivers, their canals, and their **p**, Ex 7:19

PONTIUS (3)
Caesar, **P** Pilate being governor of Judea, Lk 3:1
you anointed, both Herod and **P** Pilate, Acts 4:27
his testimony before **P** Pilate made 1 Tm 6:13

PONTUS (3)
Judea and Cappadocia, **P** and Asia, Acts 2:9
a Jew named Aquila, a native of **P**, Acts 18:2
are elect exiles of the dispersion in **P**, 1 Pt 1:1

POOL (23)
out and met them at the **p** of Gibeon. 2 Sm 2:13
down, the one on the one side of the **p**, 2 Sm 2:13
the other on the other side of the **p**. 2 Sm 2:13
hanged them beside the **p** at Hebron. 2 Sm 4:12
the chariot by the **p** of Samaria, 1 Kgs 22:38
stood by the conduit of the upper **p**, 2 Kgs 18:17
how he made the **p** and the conduit 2 Kgs 20:20
the Fountain Gate and to the King's **P**, Neh 2:14
built the wall of the **P** of Shelah of the Neh 3:15
of David, as far as the artificial **p**, Neh 3:16
who turns the rock into a **p** of water, the Ps 114:8
bathed in milk, sitting beside a full **p**. Sg 5:12
conduit of the upper **p** on the highway to Is 7:3
You collected the waters of the lower **p**, Is 22:9
the two walls for the water of the old **p**. Is 22:11
the burning sand shall become a **p**, and Is 35:7
conduit of the upper **p** on the highway to Is 36:2
I will make the wilderness a **p** of water, Is 41:18
him at the great **p** that is in Gibeon. Jer 41:12
Nineveh is like a **p** whose waters run Na 2:8

there is in Jerusalem by the Sheep Gate a **p**, Jn 5:2
to put me into the **p** when the water is Jn 5:7
wash in the **p** of Siloam" (which means Jn 9:7

POOLS (9)
and their ponds, and all their **p** of water, Ex 7:19
the rivers, over the canals and over the **p**, Ex 8:5
make this dry streambed full of **p**.' 2 Kgs 3:16
the early rain also covers it with **p**. Ps 84:6
He turns a desert into **p** of water, a Ps 107:35
I made myself **p** from which to water Eccl 2:6
Your eyes are **p** in Heshbon, by the gate of Sg 7:4
of the hedgehog, and **p** of water, Is 14:23
the rivers into islands, and dry up the **p**. Is 42:15

POOR (178)
after them, **p** and very ugly and thin, Gn 41:19
to any of my people with you who is **p**, Ex 22:25
you be partial to a **p** man in his lawsuit. Ex 23:3
the justice due to your **p** in his lawsuit. Ex 23:6
that the **p** of your people may eat; Ex 23:11
give more, and the **p** shall not give less, Ex 30:15
"But if he is **p** and cannot afford so Lv 14:21
leave them for the **p** and for the Lv 19:10
not be partial to the **p** or defer to the Lv 19:15
leave them for the **p** and for the Lv 23:22
your brother becomes **p** and sells part Lv 25:25
your brother becomes **p** and cannot Lv 25:35
your brother becomes **p** beside you and Lv 25:39
beside him becomes **p** and sells himself Lv 25:47
if someone is too **p** to pay the valuation, Lv 27:8
and whether the land is rich or **p**, and Nm 13:20
But there will be no **p** among you; for the Dt 15:4
one of your brothers should become **p**, Dt 15:7
shut your hand against your **p** brother, Dt 15:7
eye look grudgingly on your **p** brother, Dt 15:9
will never cease to be **p** in the land. Dt 15:11
your brother, to the needy and to the **p**, Dt 15:11
And if he is a **p** man, you shall not sleep Dt 24:12
a hired servant who is **p** and needy, Dt 24:14
sun sets (for he is **p** and counts on it), Dt 24:15
after young men, whether **p** or rich. Ru 3:10
The LORD makes **p** and makes rich; he 1 Sm 2:7
He raises up the **p** from the dust; he lifts 1 Sm 2:8
since I am a **p** man and have no 1 Sm 18:23
city, the one rich and the other **p**. 2 Sm 12:1
but the **p** man had nothing but one 2 Sm 12:3
but he took the **p** man's lamb and 2 Sm 12:4
of food to one another and gifts to the **p**. Est 9:22
So the **p** have hope, and injustice shuts Jb 5:16
His children will seek the favor of the **p**, Jb 20:10
he has crushed and abandoned the **p**; Jb 20:19
They thrust the **p** off the road; the poor of Jb 24:4
the **p** of the earth all hide themselves. Jb 24:4
donkeys in the desert the **p** go out to their Jb 24:5
and they take a pledge against the **p**.) Jb 24:9
light, that he may kill the **p** and needy, Jb 24:14
because I delivered the **p** who cried for Jb 29:12
withheld anything that the **p** desired, Jb 31:16
nor regards the rich more than the **p**, Jb 34:19
caused the cry of the **p** to come to him, Jb 34:28
the hope of the **p** shall not perish forever. Ps 9:18
arrogance the wicked hotly pursue the **p**; Ps 10:2
thicket; he lurks that he may seize the **p**; Ps 10:9
he seizes the **p** when he draws him into Ps 10:9
"Because the **p** are plundered, because Ps 12:5
You would shame the plans of the **p**, but Ps 14:6
This **p** man cried, and the LORD heard Ps 34:6
delivering the **p** from him who is too Ps 35:10
the **p** and needy from him who robs Ps 35:10
bows to bring down the **p** and needy, Ps 37:14
As for me, I am **p** and needy, but the Ps 40:17
Blessed is the one who considers the **p**! In Ps 41:1
both low and high, rich and **p** together! Ps 49:2
But I am **p** and needy; hasten to me, O Ps 70:5
righteousness, and your **p** with justice! Ps 72:2
he defend the cause of the **p** of the people, Ps 72:4
calls, the **p** and him who has no helper. Ps 72:12
do not forget the life of your **p** forever. Ps 74:19
let the **p** and needy praise your name. Ps 74:21
and answer me, for I am **p** and needy. Ps 86:1
but pursued the **p** and needy and the Ps 109:16
For I am **p** and needy, and my heart is Ps 109:22
distributed freely; he has given to the **p**; Ps 112:9
He raises the **p** from the dust and lifts Ps 113:7
I will satisfy her **p** with bread. Ps 132:15
city; the poverty of the **p** is their ruin. Prv 10:15
another pretends to be **p**, yet has great Prv 13:7
his wealth, but a **p** man hears no threat. Prv 13:8
ground of the **p** would yield much Prv 13:23
The **p** is disliked even by his neighbor, Prv 14:20
blessed is he who is generous to the **p**. Prv 14:21
Whoever oppresses a **p** man insults Prv 14:31
lowly spirit with the **p** than to divide Prv 16:19
Whoever mocks the **p** insults his Prv 17:5
The **p** use entreaties, but the rich Prv 18:23
Better is a **p** person who walks in his Prv 19:1
but a **p** man is deserted by his friend. Prv 19:4
All a **p** man's brothers hate him; how Prv 19:7
is generous to the **p** lends to the LORD, Prv 19:17
love, and a **p** man is better than a liar. Prv 19:22
to the cry of the **p** will himself call out Prv 21:13
loves pleasure will be a **p** man; Prv 21:17
The rich and the **p** meet together; the Prv 22:2
The rich rules over the **p**, and the Prv 22:7
for he shares his bread with the **p**. Prv 22:9
Whoever oppresses the **p** to increase Prv 22:16
Do not rob the **p**, because he is poor, or Prv 22:22
Do not rob the poor, because he is **p**, or Prv 22:22
A **p** man who oppresses the poor is a Prv 28:3
man who oppresses the **p** is a beating Prv 28:3
Better is a **p** man who walks in his Prv 28:6
it for him who is generous to the **p**. Prv 28:8
but a **p** man who has understanding Prv 28:11
bear is a wicked ruler over a **p** people. Prv 28:15
Whoever gives to the **p** will not want, Prv 28:27
man knows the rights of the **p**; Prv 29:7
The **p** man and the oppressor meet Prv 29:13
If a king faithfully judges the **p**, his Prv 29:14
or lest I be **p** and steal and profane Prv 30:9
to devour the **p** from off the earth, Prv 30:14
defend the rights of the **p** and needy. Prv 31:9
her hand to the **p** and reaches out her Prv 31:20
Better was a **p** and wise youth than an Eccl 4:13
his own kingdom he had been born **p**. Eccl 4:14
the oppression of the **p** and the violation Eccl 5:8
And what does the **p** man have who Eccl 6:8
But there was found in it a **p**, wise Eccl 9:15
Yet no one remembered that **p** man. Eccl 9:15
though the **p** man's wisdom is despised Eccl 9:16
the spoil of the **p** is in your houses. Is 3:14
the face of the **p**?" declares the Lord GOD Is 3:15
justice and to rob the **p** of my people of Is 10:2
attention, O Laishah! O **P** Anathoth! Is 10:30
with righteousness he shall judge the **p**, Is 11:4
And the firstborn of the **p** will graze, and Is 14:30
For you have been a stronghold to the **p**, a Is 25:4
The foot tramples it, the feet of the **p**, the Is 26:6
and the **p** among mankind shall exult Is 29:19
schemes to ruin the **p** with lying words, Is 32:7
When the **p** and needy seek water, and Is 41:17
bring the homeless **p** into your house; Is 58:7
anointed me to bring good news to the **p**; Is 61:1
is found the lifeblood of the guiltless **p**; Jer 2:34
Then I said, "These are only the **p**; they Jer 5:4
He judged the cause of the **p** and needy; Jer 22:16
Judah some of the **p** people who owned Jer 39:10
ease, but did not aid the **p** and needy. Ezk 16:49
oppresses the **p** and needy, commits Ezk 18:12
They have oppressed the **p** and needy, Ezk 22:29
trample the head of the **p** into the dust of Am 2:7
of Samaria, who oppress the **p**, Am 4:1
you trample on the **p** and you exact Am 5:11
the needy and bring the **p** of the land to Am 8:4
that we may buy the **p** for silver and the Am 8:6
rejoicing as if to devour the **p** in secret. Hab 3:14
the fatherless, the sojourner, or the **p**, Zec 7:10
"Blessed are the **p** in spirit, for theirs is the Mt 5:3
and the **p** have good news preached to Mt 11:5
sell what you possess and give to the **p**, Mt 19:21
sold for a large sum and given to the **p**." Mt 26:9
For you always have the **p** with you, Mt 26:11
sell all that you have and give to the **p**, Mk 10:21
And a **p** widow came and put in two Mk 12:42
this **p** widow has put in more than all Mk 12:43
and given to the **p**." And they scolded Mk 14:5
For you always have the **p** with you, Mk 14:7
me to proclaim good news to the **p**. Lk 4:18
"Blessed are you who are **p**, for yours is Lk 6:20
the **p** have good news preached to them. Lk 7:22
But when you give a feast, invite the **p**, Lk 14:13
and bring in the **p** and crippled and Lk 14:21
gate was laid a **p** man named Lazarus, Lk 16:20
The **p** man died and was carried by the Lk 16:22
that you have and distribute to the **p**, Lk 18:22
Lord, the half of my goods I give to the **p**. Lk 19:8
and he saw a **p** widow put in two small Lk 21:2
this **p** widow has put in more than all of Lk 21:3
people have drunk freely, then the **p** wine. Jn 2:10
hundred denarii and given to the **p**?" Jn 12:5
this, not because he cared about the **p**, Jn 12:6
The **p** you always have with you, but you Jn 12:8
that he should give something to the **p**. Jn 13:29
contribution for the **p** among the Rom 15:26
sorrowful, yet always rejoicing; as **p**, 2 Cor 6:10
rich, yet for your sake he became **p**, 2 Cor 8:9
distributed freely, he has given to the **p**; 2 Cor 9:9
Only, they asked us to remember the **p**, Gal 2:10
and a **p** man in shabby clothing also Jas 2:2
a good place," while you say to the **p** man, Jas 2:3
chosen those who are **p** in the world to Jas 2:5
But you have dishonored the **p** man. Are Jas 2:6
that you are wretched, pitiable, **p**, blind, Rv 3:17
both small and great, both rich and **p**, Rv 13:16

POOREST (5)
except the **p** people of the land. 2 Kgs 24:14
left some of the **p** of the land to 2 Kgs 25:12
those of the **p** of the land who had not Jer 40:7
captive some of the **p** of the people and Jer 52:15
guard left some of the **p** of the land to be Jer 52:16

POORLY (2)
we are **p** dressed and buffeted and 1 Cor 4:11
or sister is **p** clothed and lacking Jas 2:15

POPLAR (2)
took fresh sticks of **p** and almond and Gn 30:37
the hills, under oak, **p**, and terebinth, Hos 4:13

POPULAR (1)
the Jews and **p** with the multitude Est 10:3

POPULATION (1)
because the whole **p** was involved in Nm 15:26

POPULOUS (2)
became a nation, great, mighty, and **p**. Dt 26:5
palace is forsaken, the **p** city deserted; Is 32:14

PORATHA (1)
and **P** and Adalia and Aridatha Est 9:8

PORCH (3)
went out into the **p** and closed the doors Jgs 3:23
There was a **p** in front with pillars, and 1 Kgs 7:6
of the LORD, between the **p** and the altar, Ezk 8:16

PORCIUS (1)
Felix was succeeded by **P** Festus. Acts 24:27

PORCUPINE (1)
But the hawk and the **p** shall possess it, Is 34:11

PORPHYRY (1)
and silver on a mosaic pavement of **p**, Est 1:6

PORTALS (1)
at the entrance of the **p** she cries aloud: Prv 8:3

PORTENT (2)
I have been as a **p** to many, but you are Ps 71:7
as a sign and a **p** against Egypt and Cush, Is 20:3

PORTENTS (1)
me are signs and **p** in Israel from the Is 8:18

PORTICO (2)
to them in the **p** called Solomon's, Acts 3:11
they were all together in Solomon's **P**. Acts 5:12

PORTION (125)
"Is there any **p** or inheritance left to us Gn 31:14
but Benjamin's **p** was five times as Gn 43:34
go out and gather a day's **p** every day, Ex 16:4
before the LORD, and it shall be your **p**. Ex 29:26
of the priests' **p** that is contributed Ex 29:27
burn this as its memorial **p** on the altar, Lv 2:2
offering its memorial **p** and burn this Lv 2:9
burn as its memorial **p** some of the Lv 2:16
of it as its memorial **p** and burn this on Lv 5:12
burn this as its memorial **p** on the altar, Lv 6:15
given it as their **p** of my food offerings. Lv 6:17
the fat shall have the right thigh for a **p**. Lv 7:33
This is the **p** of Aaron and of his sons Lv 7:35
It was Moses' **p** of the ram of ordination, Lv 8:29
bread as a memorial **p** as a food offering Lv 24:7
for him a most holy **p** out of the LORD'S Lv 24:9
of the grain offering, as its memorial **p**, Nm 5:26
They are a holy **p** for the priest, Nm 6:20
them to you as a **p** and to your sons as Nm 18:8
shall you have any **p** among them. Nm 18:20
I am your **p** and your inheritance Nm 18:20
the **p** of those who had gone out in the Nm 31:36
(All that **p** of Bashan is called the land of Dt 3:13
Levi has no **p** or inheritance with Dt 10:9
since he has no **p** or inheritance with Dt 12:12
for he has no **p** or inheritance with you. Dt 14:27
he has no **p** or inheritance with Dt 14:29
shall have no **p** or inheritance with Dt 18:1
by giving him a double **p** of all that he Dt 21:17
have removed the sacred **p** out of my Dt 26:13
But the LORD'S **p** is his people, Jacob his Dt 32:9
for there a commander's **p** was reserved; Dt 33:21
And no **p** was given to the Levites in the Jos 14:4
son of Jephunneh a **p** among the people Jos 15:13
one lot and one **p** as an inheritance, Jos 17:14
The Levites have no **p** among you, for Jos 18:7
to the people of Israel, to each his **p**. Jos 18:10
Because the **p** of the people of Judah was Jos 19:9
of Gad. You have no **p** in the LORD.' Jos 22:25
to come, "You have no **p** in the LORD."' Jos 22:27
But to Hannah he gave a double **p**, 1 Sm 1:5
to the cook, "Bring the **p** I gave you, 1 Sm 9:23
women, a cake of bread, a **p** of meat, 2 Sm 6:19

and said, “We have no **p** in David, 2 Sm 20:1
king, “What **p** do we have in David? 1 Kgs 12:16
let there be a double **p** of your spirit on 2 Kgs 2:9
to each a loaf of bread, a **p** of meat, 1 Chr 16:3
as your **p** for an inheritance.” 1 Chr 16:18
king, “What **p** have we in David? 2 Chr 10:16
For Ahaz took a **p** from the house of 2 Chr 28:21
Jerusalem to give the **p** due to the 2 Chr 31:4
but you have no **p** or right or claim in Neh 2:20
her with her cosmetics and her **p** of food, Est 2:9
This is the wicked man's **p** from God, Jb 20:29
of his mouth more than my **p** of food. Jb 23:12
the waters; their **p** is cursed in the land; Jb 24:18
“This is the **p** of a wicked man with Jb 27:13
What would be my **p** from God above Jb 31:2
wind shall be the **p** of their cup. Ps 11:6
The LORD is my chosen **p** and my cup; Ps 16:5
men of the world whose **p** is in this life. Ps 17:14
divide up Shechem and **p** out the Vale of Ps 60:6
the sword; they shall be a **p** for jackals. Ps 63:10
dogs may have their **p** from the foe.” Ps 68:23
strength of my heart and my **p** forever. Ps 73:26
Canaan as your **p** for an inheritance.” Ps 105:11
divide up Shechem and **p** out the Valley Ps 108:7
The LORD is my **p**; I promise to keep Ps 119:57
refuge, my **p** in the land of the living.” Ps 142:5
because that is your **p** in life and in Eccl 9:9
Give a **p** to seven, or even to eight, for Eccl 11:2
This is the **p** of those who loot us, and Is 17:14
I will divide him a **p** with the many, Is 53:12
the smooth stones of the valley is your **p**; Is 57:6
of your shame there shall be a double **p**; Is 61:7
their land they shall possess a double **p**; Is 61:7
like these is he who is the **p** of Jacob, Jer 10:16
they have trampled down my **p**; Jer 12:10
made my pleasant **p** a desolate Jer 12:10
lot, the **p** I have measured out to you, Jer 13:25
to receive his **p** there among the Jer 37:12
like these is he who is the **p** of Jacob, Jer 51:19
“The LORD is my **p**,” says my soul, Lam 3:24
your allotted **p** and delivered Ezk 16:27
set apart for the LORD a **p** of the land as a Ezk 45:1
It shall be the holy **p** of the land. It shall Ezk 45:4
“Alongside the **p** set apart as the holy Ezk 45:6
and as the fixed **p** of oil, measured in Ezk 45:14
the east side to the west, Dan, one **p**. Ezk 48:1
the east side to the west, Asher, one **p**. Ezk 48:2
the east side to the west, Naphtali, one **p**. Ezk 48:3
east side to the west, Manasseh, one **p**. Ezk 48:4
the east side to the west, Ephraim, one **p**. Ezk 48:5
the east side to the west, Reuben, one **p**. Ezk 48:6
the east side to the west, Judah, one **p**. Ezk 48:7
shall be the **p** which you shall set apart, Ezk 48:8
The **p** that you shall set apart for the Ezk 48:9
shall be the allotments of the holy **p**: Ezk 48:10
them as a special **p** from the holy Ezk 48:12
portion from the holy **p** of the land, Ezk 48:12
not alienate this choice **p** of the land, Ezk 48:14
alongside the holy **p** shall be 10,000 Ezk 48:18
and it shall be alongside the holy **p**. Ezk 48:18
The whole **p** that you shall set apart Ezk 48:20
the holy **p** together with the property Ezk 48:20
sides of the holy **p** and of the property Ezk 48:21
cubits of the holy **p** to the east border, Ezk 48:21
The holy **p** with the sanctuary of the Ezk 48:21
The **p** of the prince shall lie between Ezk 48:22
east side to the west, Benjamin, one **p**. Ezk 48:23
the east side to the west, Simeon, one **p**. Ezk 48:24
east side to the west, Issachar, one **p**. Ezk 48:25
east side to the west, Zebulun, one **p**. Ezk 48:26
the east side to the west, Gad, one **p**. Ezk 48:27
assigned them a daily **p** of the food that Dn 1:5
Let his **p** be with the beasts in the grass Dn 4:15
and let his **p** be with the beasts of the Dn 4:23
ruined; he changes the **p** of my people; Mi 2:4
inherit Judah as his **p** in the holy land, Zec 2:12
with a **p** of the Spirit in their union? Mal 2:15
Mary has chosen the good **p**, which Lk 10:42
to give them their **p** of food at the Lk 12:42
Or what **p** does a believer share with 2 Cor 6:15
mix a double **p** for her in the cup she Rv 18:6
their **p** will be in the lake that burns Rv 21:8

PORTIONED (1)

his hand has **p** it out to them with the Is 34:17

PORTIONS (19)

firstborn of his flock and of their fat **p**. Gn 4:4
P were taken to them from Joseph's Gn 43:34
then he may have equal **p** to eat, besides Dt 18:8
Thus there fell to Manasseh ten **p**, Jos 17:5
They shall divide it into seven **p**. Judah Jos 18:5
he would give **p** to Peninnah his wife 1 Sm 1:4
to distribute the **p** to their brothers, 2 Chr 31:15
name to distribute **p** to every male 2 Chr 31:19
sweet wine and send **p** to anyone who Neh 8:10
drink and to send **p** and to make great Neh 8:12
gather into them the **p** required by the Neh 12:44
gave the daily **p** for the singers Neh 12:47
found out that the **p** of the Levites had Neh 13:10
her household and **p** for her maidens. Prv 31:15
in length to one of the tribal **p**, Ezk 45:7
of Israel. Joseph shall have two **p**. Ezk 47:13
in length equal to one of the tribal **p**, Ezk 48:8
the west border, parallel to the tribal **p**, Ezk 48:21
tribes of Israel, and these are their **p**, Ezk 48:29

PORTRAYED (3)

further. She saw men **p** on the wall, Ezk 23:14
of the Chaldeans **p** in vermilion, Ezk 23:14
Jesus Christ was publicly **p** as crucified. Gal 3:1

PORTS (1)

about to sail to the **p** along the coast of Acts 27:2

POSITION (7)

restored the chief cupbearer to his **p**, Gn 40:21
camp, so shall they set out, each in **p**, Nm 2:17
Stand firm, hold your **p**, and see the 2 Chr 20:17
king give her royal **p** to another who is Est 1:19
to thrust him down from his high **p**. Ps 62:4
can anyone in the **p** of an outsider 1 Cor 14:16
not stay within their own **p** of authority, Jude 1:6

POSITIONS (3)

“Take your **p**.” And they took their 1 Kgs 20:12
they took their **p** against the city. 1 Kgs 20:12
for kings and all who are in high **p**, 1 Tm 2:2

POSSESS (88)

Chaldeans to give you this land to **p**.” Gn 15:7
GOD, how am I to know that I shall **p** it?” Gn 15:8
And your offspring shall **p** the gate of Gn 22:17
and may your offspring **p** the gate of Gn 24:60
flocks and herds and all that they **p**, Gn 47:1
Ephron the Hittite to **p** as a burying Gn 49:30
Ephron the Hittite to **p** as a burying Gn 50:13
you have increased and **p** the land. Ex 23:30
their land, and I will give it to you to **p**, Lv 20:24
And in all the country you **p**, you shall Lv 25:24
any time the houses in the cities they **p**. Lv 25:32
sold in a city they **p** shall be released in Lv 25:33
went, and his descendants shall **p** it. Nm 14:24
kinsman of his clan, and he shall **p** it. Nm 27:11
for I have given the land to you to **p** it. Nm 33:53
of Israel may **p** the inheritance of Nm 36:8
to them I will give it, and they shall **p** it. Dt 1:39
your God has given you this land to **p**. Dt 3:18
in the land that you are going over to **p**. Dt 4:14
that you are going over the Jordan to **p**. Dt 4:26
in the land that I am giving them to **p**.’ Dt 5:31
live long in the land that you shall **p**. Dt 5:33
land to which you are going over, to **p** it, Dt 6:1
and go in and **p** the land that the LORD Dt 8:1
the LORD has brought me in to **p** this land,’ Dt 9:4
heart are you going in to **p** their land, Dt 9:5
this good land to **p** because of your Dt 9:6
so that they may go in and **p** the land, Dt 10:11
of the land that you are going over to **p**, Dt 11:8
you are going over to **p** is a land of hills Dt 11:11
you. And when you **p** it and live in it, Dt 11:31
God of your fathers, has given you to **p**, Dt 12:1
is giving you for an inheritance to **p**— Dt 15:4
and you **p** it and dwell in it and then Dt 17:14
that the LORD your God is giving you to **p**. Dt 19:2
the LORD your God is giving you to **p**. Dt 19:14
is giving you to **p** someone is found Dt 21:1
is giving you for an inheritance to **p**, Dt 25:19
The cricket shall **p** all your trees and Dt 28:42
your fathers possessed, that you may **p** it. Dt 30:5
are going over the Jordan to enter and **p**. Dt 30:18
that you are going over the Jordan to **p**.” Dt 31:13
that you are going over the Jordan to **p**.” Dt 32:47
of the LORD, **p** the lake and the south.” Dt 33:23
the LORD your God is giving you to **p**.’” Jos 1:11
land of your possession and shall **p** it, Jos 1:15
there remains yet very much land to **p**. Jos 13:1
you shall clear it and **p** it to its farthest Jos 17:18
And you shall **p** their land, just as the Jos 23:5
I gave Esau the hill country of Seir to **p**, Jos 24:4
Will you not **p** what Chemosh your Jgs 11:24
Chemosh your god gives you to **p**? Jgs 11:24
has dispossessed before us, we will **p**. Jgs 11:24
be slow to go, to enter in and **p** the land. Jgs 18:9
that you may **p** this good land and 1 Chr 28:8
them to go in to **p** the land that you Neh 9:15
had told their fathers to enter and **p**. Neh 9:23
and people shall dwell there and **p** it; Ps 69:35
house of Israel will **p** them in the LORD'S Is 14:2
fathers, lest they rise and **p** the earth, Is 14:21
the hawk and the porcupine shall **p** it, Is 34:11
with the line; they shall **p** it forever; Is 34:17
and your offspring will **p** the nations and Is 54:3
refuge in me shall **p** the land and shall Is 57:13
they shall **p** the land forever, the branch Is 60:21
their land they shall **p** a double portion; Is 61:7
my chosen shall **p** it, and my servants Is 65:9
many; the land is surely given us to **p**.’ Ezk 33:24
shed blood; shall you then **p** the land? Ezk 33:25
wife; shall you then **p** the land? Ezk 33:26
And they shall **p** you, and you shall be Ezk 36:12
the kingdom and **p** the kingdom Dn 7:18
Nettles shall **p** their precious things of Hos 9:6
wilderness, to **p** the land of the Amorite. Am 2:10
that they may **p** the remnant of Edom Am 9:12
of Jacob shall **p** their own possessions. Ob 1:17
Those of the Negeb shall **p** Mount Esau, Ob 1:19
of the Shephelah shall **p** the land of the Ob 1:19
they shall **p** the land of Ephraim and the Ob 1:19
Samaria, and Benjamin shall **p** Gilead. Ob 1:19
the people of Israel shall **p** the land of the Ob 1:20
are in Sepharad shall **p** the cities of the Ob 1:20
survivors of my nation shall **p** them.” Zep 2:9
of this people to **p** all these things. Zec 8:12
go, sell what you **p** and give to the poor, Mt 19:21
“all of us **p** knowledge.” This 1 Cor 8:1
However, not all **p** this knowledge. But 1 Cor 8:7
Do all **p** gifts of healing? Do all 1 Cor 12:30

POSSESSED (16)

And every one who **p** blue or purple or Ex 35:23
And every one who **p** acacia wood of Ex 35:24
no survivor left. And they **p** his land. Nm 21:35
you into the land that your fathers **p**, Dt 30:5
which they had **p** themselves by Jos 22:9
the descendants went in and **p** the land, Neh 9:24
He **p** 7,000 sheep, 3,000 camels, 500 yoke of Jb 1:3
The man with power **p** the land, and the Jb 22:8
“The LORD **p** me at the beginning of his Prv 8:22
came when the saints **p** the kingdom. Dn 7:22
a land **p** by nettles and salt pits, Zep 2:9
“He is **p** by Beelzebul,” and “by the Mk 3:22
who had been **p** with demons begged Mk 5:18
little daughter was **p** by an unclean Mk 7:25
at his teaching, for his word **p** authority. Lk 4:32
spirits came out of many who were **p**, Acts 8:7

POSSESSES (1)

every daughter who **p** an inheritance Nm 36:8

POSSESSING (2)

that is in the earth and **p** wealth, Jgs 18:7
as having nothing, yet **p** everything. 2 Cor 6:10

POSSESSION (133)

the land of Canaan, for an everlasting **p**, Gn 17:8
to Abraham as a **p** in the presence of Gn 23:18
that you may take **p** of the land of your Gn 28:4
the livestock in his **p** that he had Gn 31:18
dwelling places in the land of their **p**. Gn 36:43
and gave them a **p** in the land of Gn 47:11
offspring after you for an everlasting **p**.’ Gn 48:4
and to Jacob. I will give it to you for a **p**. Ex 6:8
be my treasured **p** among all peoples, Ex 19:5
him, and anyone found in **p** of him, Ex 21:16
If the stolen beast is found alive in his **p**, Ex 22:4
of Canaan, which I give you for a **p**, Lv 14:34
disease in a house in the land of your **p**, Lv 14:34
the Levites are their **p** among the people Lv 25:33
not be sold, for that is their **p** forever. Lv 25:34
clan and return to the **p** of his fathers. Lv 25:41
sons after you to inherit as a **p** forever. Lv 25:46
to the LORD part of the land that is his **p**, Lv 27:16
devoted. The priest shall be in **p** of it. Lv 27:21
has bought, which is not a part of his **p**, Lv 27:22
to whom the land belongs as a **p**. Lv 27:24
the sword and took **p** of his land from Nm 21:24
Give to us a **p** among our father's Nm 27:4
shall give them **p** of an inheritance Nm 27:7
land be given to your servants for a **p**. Nm 32:5
land shall be your **p** before the LORD. Nm 32:22
give them the land of Gilead for a **p**. Nm 32:29
and the **p** of our inheritance shall Nm 32:32
And you shall take **p** of the land and Nm 33:53
the inheritance of their **p** as cities for Nm 35:2
shall give from the **p** of the people of Nm 35:8
may return to the land of his **p**. Nm 35:28
Go in and take **p** of the land that the LORD Dt 1:8
Go up, take **p**, as the LORD, the God of Dt 1:21
I have given Mount Seir to Esau as a **p**. Dt 2:5
I will not give you any of their land for a **p**, Dt 2:9
I have given Ar to the people of Lot for a **p**.’ Dt 2:9
place, as Israel did to the land of their **p**, Dt 2:12
the land of the people of Ammon as a **p**, Dt 2:19
I have given it to the sons of Lot for a **p**.’ Dt 2:19
Begin to take **p**, and contend with him in Dt 2:24
Begin to take **p**, that you may occupy his Dt 2:31
“When we took **p** of this land at that Dt 3:12
may return to his **p** which I have given Dt 3:20
he shall put them in **p** of the land that Dt 3:28
and go in and take **p** of the land that the Dt 4:1

land that you are entering to take **p** of it. Dt 4:5
go over and take **p** of that good land. Dt 4:22
And they took **p** of his land and the land Dt 4:47
may go in and take **p** of the good land Dt 6:18
land that you are entering to take **p** of it, Dt 7:1
you to be a people for his treasured **p**, Dt 7:6
'Go up and take **p** of the land that I have Dt 9:23
and go in and take **p** of the land that you Dt 11:8
you are entering to take **p** of it is not Dt 11:10
land that you are entering to take **p** of it, Dt 11:29
to go in to take **p** of the land that the Dt 11:31
you to be a people for his treasured **p**, Dt 14:2
that the LORD your God gives you as a **p**, Dt 19:3
land that you are entering to take **p** of it. Dt 23:20
inheritance and have taken **p** of it and Dt 26:1
that you are a people for his treasured **p**, Dt 26:18
land that you are entering to take **p** of it. Dt 28:21
land that you are entering to take **p** of it. Dt 28:63
land that you are entering to take **p** of it. Dt 30:16
them, and you shall put them in **p** of it. Dt 31:7
am giving to the people of Israel for a **p**. Dt 32:49
us a law, as a **p** for the assembly of Jacob. Dt 33:4
to go in to take **p** of the land that the Jos 1:11
and they also take **p** of the land that the Jos 1:15
to the land of your **p** and shall possess it, Jos 1:15
Israel defeated and took **p** of their land Jos 12:1
their land for a **p** to the Reubenites and Jos 12:6
of Israel as a **p** according to their Jos 12:7
could not take **p** of those cities, Jos 17:12
you put off going in to take **p** of the land, Jos 18:3
the sword they took **p** of it and settled Jos 19:47
to Caleb the son of Jephunneh as his **p**. Jos 21:12
in the midst of the **p** of the people of Jos 21:41
And they took **p** of it, and they settled Jos 21:43
your tents in the land where your **p** lies, Jos 22:4
Moses had given a **p** in Bashan, Jos 22:7
had given a **p** beside their brothers Jos 22:7
now, if the land of your **p** is unclean, Jos 22:19
and take for yourselves a **p** among us. Jos 22:19
your hand, and you took **p** of their land, Jos 24:8
Judah, and he took **p** of the hill country, Jgs 1:19
to his inheritance to take **p** of the land. Jgs 2:6
And they took **p** of the city of palms. Jgs 3:13
So Israel took **p** of all the land of the Jgs 11:21
And they took **p** of all the territory of Jgs 11:22
Israel; and are you to take **p** of them? Jgs 11:23
take **p** of the vineyard of Naboth the 1 Kgs 21:15
Naboth the Jezreelite, to take **p** of it. 1 Kgs 21:16
where he has gone to take **p**. 1 Kgs 21:18
and also taken **p**?"' And you shall 1 Kgs 21:19
And they took **p** of Samaria and 2 Kgs 17:24
also in **p** of the Manassites, 1 Chr 7:29
by coming to drive us out of your **p**, 2 Chr 20:11
to their cities, every man to his **p**. 2 Chr 31:1
will then have no **p** in the province Ezr 4:16
that you are entering, to take **p** of it, Ezr 9:11
So they took **p** of the land of Sihon Neh 9:22
and took **p** of houses full of all good Neh 9:25
heritage, and the ends of the earth your **p**. Ps 2:8
apportioned them for a **p** and settled the Ps 78:55
"Let us take **p** for ourselves of the Ps 83:12
and they took **p** of the fruit of the Ps 105:44
Jacob for himself, Israel as his own **p**. Ps 135:4
"And I will make it a **p** of the hedgehog, Is 14:23
Your holy people held **p** for a little while; Is 63:18
their fathers, and they shall take **p** of it." Jer 30:3
for the right of **p** and redemption is Jer 32:8
And they entered and took **p** of it. But Jer 32:23
of the nations to take **p** of their houses. Ezk 7:24
LORD; to us this land is given for a **p**.' Ezk 11:15
you over to the people of the East for a **p**, Ezk 25:4
to the people of the East as a **p**, Ezk 25:10
only one man, yet he got **p** of the land; Ezk 33:24
and we will take **p** of them'—although Ezk 35:10
ancient heights have become our **p**,' Ezk 36:2
so that you became the **p** of the rest of Ezk 36:3
themselves as a **p** with wholehearted Ezk 36:5
and you shall give them no **p** in Israel; Ezk 44:28
no possession in Israel; I am their **p**. Ezk 44:28
the temple, as their **p** for cities to live in. Ezk 45:5
shall become the **p** of the remnant Zep 2:7
day when I make up my treasured **p**, Mal 3:17
it to him as a **p** and to his offspring after Acts 7:5
our inheritance until we acquire **p** of it, Eph 1:14
people for his own **p** who are zealous for Ti 2:14
had a better **p** and an abiding Heb 10:34
a holy nation, a people for his own **p**, 1 Pt 2:9

POSSESSIONS (40)
and all their **p** that they had gathered, Gn 12:5
for their **p** were so great that they could Gn 13:6
enemy took all the **p** of Sodom and Gn 14:11
who was dwelling in Sodom, and his **p**, Gn 14:12
Then he brought back all the **p**, and Gn 14:16
back his kinsman Lot with his **p**, Gn 14:16
they shall come out with great **p**. Gn 15:14
He had **p** of flocks and herds and many Gn 26:14
For their **p** were too great for them to Gn 36:7
And they gained **p** in it, and were Gn 47:27
they shall have **p** among you in the Nm 32:30
when he assigns his **p** as an inheritance Dt 21:16
Their **p** and settlements were Bethel 1 Chr 7:28
dwell again in their **p** in their cities 1 Chr 9:2
your heart, and you have not asked **p**, 2 Chr 1:11
also give you riches, **p**, and honor, 2 Chr 1:12
gifts of silver, gold, and valuable **p**, 2 Chr 21:3
children, your wives, and all your **p**, 2 Chr 21:14
away all the **p** they found that 2 Chr 21:17
king from his own **p** was for the 2 Chr 31:3
for God had given him very great **p**. 2 Chr 32:29
bulls; these were from the king's **p**. 2 Chr 35:7
and his **p** have increased in the land. Jb 1:10
nor will his **p** spread over the earth; Jb 15:29
The **p** of his house will be carried away, Jb 20:28
lord of his house and ruler of all his **p**, Ps 105:21
I had also great **p** of herds and flocks, Eccl 2:7
has given wealth and **p** and power to Eccl 5:19
whom God gives wealth, **p**, and honor, Eccl 6:2
house of Jacob shall possess their own **p**. Ob 1:17
strip her of her **p** and strike down her Zec 9:4
away sorrowful, for he had great **p**. Mt 19:22
to you, he will set him over all his **p**. Mt 24:47
away sorrowful, for he had great **p**. Mk 10:22
not consist in the abundance of his **p**." Lk 12:15
Sell your **p**, and give to the needy. Lk 12:33
to you, he will set him over all his **p**. Lk 12:44
to him that this man was wasting his **p**. Lk 16:1
were selling their **p** and belongings Acts 2:45
the eyes and pride in **p**—is not from the 1 Jn 2:16

POSSESSOR (2)
God Most High, **P** of heaven and earth; Gn 14:19
God Most High, **P** of heaven and earth, Gn 14:22

POSSESSORS (2)
gain; it takes away the life of its **p**. Prv 1:19
and from Judah **p** of my mountains; Is 65:9

POSSIBLE (17)
but with God all things are **p**." Mt 19:26
and wonders, so as to lead astray, if **p**, Mt 24:24
prayed, saying, "My Father, if it be **p**, Mt 26:39
All things are **p** for one who believes." Mk 9:23
God. For all things are **p** with God." Mk 10:27
signs and wonders, to lead astray, if **p**, Mk 13:22
ground and prayed that, if it were **p**, Mk 14:35
"Abba, Father, all things are **p** for you. Mk 14:36
is impossible with men is **p** with God." Lk 18:27
because it was not **p** for him to be held Acts 2:24
of yours, and pray to the Lord that, if **p**, Acts 8:22
Timothy to come to him as soon as **p**, Acts 17:15
was hastening to be at Jerusalem, if **p**, Acts 20:16
which they planned if **p** to run the Acts 27:39
If **p**, so far as it depends on you, live Rom 12:18
For I testify to you that, if **p**, you would Gal 4:15
that by any means **p** I may attain the Phil 3:11

POST (3)
remove the kings, each from his **p**, 1 Kgs 20:24
and at my **p** I am stationed whole nights. Is 21:8
shall take his stand by the **p** of the gate. Ezk 46:2

POSTED (2)
And the priest **p** watchmen over the 2 Kgs 11:18
And Jehoiada **p** watchmen for the 2 Chr 23:18

POSTERITY (6)
or with my descendants or with my **p**, Gn 21:23
He has no **p** or progeny among his Jb 18:19
P shall serve him; it shall be told of the Ps 22:30
May his **p** be cut off; may his name be Ps 109:13
descendants and **p**," says the LORD. Is 14:22
four winds of heaven, but not to his **p**, Dn 11:4

POSTS (6)
of the gate of the city and the two **p**, Jgs 16:3
The priests stood at their **p**; the Levites 2 Chr 7:6
their accustomed **p** according to 2 Chr 30:16
some at their guard **p** and some in front Neh 7:3
He made its **p** of silver, its back of gold, Sg 3:10
and the **p** of the gate of the inner court. Ezk 45:19

POT (23)
a smoking fire **p** and a flaming torch Gn 15:17
in a basket, and the broth he put in a **p**, Jgs 6:19
into the pan or kettle or cauldron or **p**. 1 Sm 2:14
said to his servant, "Set on the large **p**, 2 Kgs 4:38
and cut them up into the **p** of stew, 2 Kgs 4:39
is death in the **p**!" And they could not 2 Kgs 4:40
And he threw it into the **p** and said, 2 Kgs 4:41
eat." And there was no harm in the **p**. 2 Kgs 4:41
from a boiling **p** and burning rushes. Jb 41:20
He makes the deep boil like a **p**; he Jb 41:31
he makes the sea like a **p** of ointment. Jb 41:31
as the crackling of thorns under a **p**, Eccl 7:6
formed him, a **p** among earthen pots! Is 45:9
do you see?" And I said, "I see a boiling **p**, Jer 1:13
this man Coniah a despised, broken **p**, Jer 22:28
a fire burning in the fire **p** before him. Jer 36:22
throw them into the fire in the fire **p**, Jer 36:23
in the fire that was in the fire **p**. Jer 36:23
the Lord GOD: "Set on the **p**, set it on; Ezk 24:3
city, to the **p** whose corrosion is in it, Ezk 24:6
pieces and chop them up like meat in a **p**, Mi 3:3
of Judah like a blazing **p** in the midst of Zec 12:6
And every **p** in Jerusalem and Judah Zec 14:21

POTIPHAR (2)
Midianites had sold him in Egypt to **P**, Gn 37:36
had been brought down to Egypt, and **P**, Gn 39:1

POTIPHERA (3)
Asenath, the daughter of **P** priest of On. Gn 41:45
Asenath, the daughter of **P** priest of On, Gn 41:50
the daughter of **P** the priest of On, Gn 46:20

POTS (18)
we sat by the meat **p** and ate bread to the Ex 16:3
You shall make **p** for it to receive its Ex 27:3
made all the utensils of the altar, the **p**, Ex 38:3
and boiled it in **p** and made cakes of Nm 11:8
Hiram also made the **p**, the shovels, 1 Kgs 7:40
Now the **p**, the shovels, and the 1 Kgs 7:45
they took away the **p** and the shovels 2 Kgs 25:14
Hiram also made the **p**, the shovels, 2 Chr 4:11
The **p**, the shovels, the forks, and all 2 Chr 4:16
they boiled the holy offerings in **p**, 2 Chr 35:13
Sooner than your **p** can feel the heat of Ps 58:9
who formed him, a pot among earthen **p**! Is 45:9
they took away the **p** and the shovels Jer 52:18
basins and the **p** and the lampstands Jer 52:19
how they are regarded as earthen **p**, Lam 4:2
to the LORD." And the **p** in the house of Zec 14:20
of cups and **p** and copper vessels Mk 7:4
as when earthen **p** are broken in pieces, Rv 2:27

POTSHERD (2)
my strength is dried up like a **p**, and my Ps 22:15
Son of Hinnom at the entry of the **P** Gate, Jer 19:2

POTSHERDS (1)
His underparts are like sharp **p**; he Jb 41:30

POTTER (8)
Shall the **p** be regarded as the clay, that Is 29:16
rulers as on mortar, as the **p** treads clay. Is 41:25
Father; we are the clay, and you are our **p**; Is 64:8
vessel, as it seemed good to the **p** to do. Jer 18:4
can I not do with you as this **p** has done? Jer 18:6
"Throw it to the **p**"—the lordly price at Zec 11:13
into the house of the LORD, to the **p**. Zec 11:13
Has the **p** no right over the clay, to Rom 9:21

POTTER'S (12)
and dash them in pieces like a **p** vessel." Ps 2:9
is like that of a **p** vessel that is smashed Is 30:14
"Arise, and go down to the **p** house, and Jer 18:2
So I went down to the **p** house, and there Jer 18:3
of clay was spoiled in the **p** hand, Jer 18:4
Behold, like the clay in the **p** hand, so are Jer 18:6
the LORD, "Go, buy a **p** earthenware flask, Jer 19:1
and this city, as one breaks a **p** vessel, Jer 19:11
as earthen pots, the work of a **p** hands! Lam 4:2
toes, partly of **p** clay and partly of iron, Dn 2:41
bought with them the **p** field as a burial Mt 27:7
and they gave them for the **p** field, as Mt 27:10

POTTERS (1)
These were the **p** who were 1 Chr 4:23

POTTERY (1)
a piece of broken **p** with which to scrape Jb 2:8

POUCH (1)
and put them in his shepherd's **p**. 1 Sm 17:40

POUNCE (1)
Why did you **p** on the spoil and do 1 Sm 15:19

POUNCED (1)
The people **p** on the spoil and took 1 Sm 14:32

POUND (1)
therefore took a **p** of expensive ointment Jn 12:3

POUNDS (2)
aloes, about seventy-five **p** in weight. Jn 19:39
hailstones, about one hundred **p** each, Rv 16:21

POUR (75)
water from the Nile and **p** it on the dry Ex 4:9
bowls with which to **p** drink offerings; Ex 25:29
the anointing oil and **p** it on his head Ex 29:7
of the blood you shall **p** out at the base Ex 29:12
and you shall not **p** a drink offering on Ex 30:9
with which to **p** drink offerings. Ex 37:16
He shall **p** oil on it and put frankincense Lv 2:1
shall break it in pieces and **p** oil on it; Lv 2:6
of the bull he shall **p** out at the base of Lv 4:7
of the blood he shall **p** out at the base of Lv 4:18

of burnt offering and **p** out the rest of Lv 4:25
of burnt offering and **p** out all the rest Lv 4:30
of burnt offering and **p** out all the rest Lv 4:34
of the log of oil and **p** it into the palm of Lv 14:15
And the priest shall **p** some of the oil Lv 14:26
scrape off they shall **p** out in an Lv 14:41
may be eaten shall **p** out its blood and Lv 17:13
He shall **p** no oil on it and put no Nm 5:15
Holy Place you shall **p** out a drink Nm 28:7
you shall **p** it out on the earth like Dt 12:16
you shall **p** it out on the earth like Dt 12:24
you shall **p** it out on the ground like Dt 15:23
and **p** the broth over them." And he did Jgs 6:20
jars with water and **p** it on the burnt 1 Kgs 18:33
and your sons and **p** into all these 2 Kgs 4:4
pot and said, "**P** some out for the men, 2 Kgs 4:41
the flask of oil and **p** it on his head and 2 Kgs 9:3
Did you not **p** me out like milk and Jb 10:10
which the skies **p** down and drop on Jb 36:28
P out the overflowings of your anger, Jb 40:11
of blood I will not **p** out or take their Ps 16:4
things I remember, as I **p** out my soul: Ps 42:4
O people; **p** out your heart before him; Ps 62:8
P out your indignation upon them, and Ps 69:24
P out your anger on the nations that do Ps 79:6
They **p** out their arrogant words; all the Ps 94:4
My lips will **p** forth praise, for you Ps 119:171
I **p** out my complaint before him; I tell Ps 142:2
They shall **p** forth the fame of your Ps 145:7
behold, I will **p** out my spirit to you; Prv 1:23
but the mouths of fools **p** out folly. Prv 15:2
For I will **p** water on the thirsty land, and Is 44:3
I will **p** my Spirit upon your offspring, Is 44:3
if you **p** yourself out for the hungry and Is 58:10
"**P** it out upon the children in the street, Jer 6:11
And they **p** out drink offerings to other Jer 7:18
P out your wrath on the nations that Jer 10:25
For I will **p** out their evil upon them. Jer 14:16
of heaven and **p** out drink offerings Jer 44:17
of heaven and to **p** out drink offerings Jer 44:25
send to him pourers who will **p** him, Jer 48:12
P out your heart like water before the Lam 2:19
Now I will soon **p** out my wrath upon Ezk 7:8
into that land and **p** out my wrath Ezk 14:19
I said I would **p** out my wrath upon Ezk 20:8
I said I would **p** out my wrath upon Ezk 20:13
I said I would **p** out my wrath upon Ezk 20:21
And I will **p** out my indignation upon Ezk 21:31
"Set on the pot, set it on; **p** in water also; Ezk 24:3
she did not **p** it out on the ground to Ezk 24:7
And I will **p** out my wrath on Ezk 30:15
when I **p** out my Spirit upon the house Ezk 39:29
upon them I will **p** out my wrath like Hos 5:10
They shall not **p** drink offerings of wine Hos 9:4
that I will **p** out my Spirit on all flesh; Jl 2:28
in those days I will **p** out my Spirit. Jl 2:29
and I will **p** down her stones into the Mi 1:6
you **p** out your wrath and make them Hab 2:15
to **p** out upon them my indignation, Zep 3:8
"And I will **p** out on the house of David Zec 12:10
of heaven for you and **p** down for you a Mal 3:10
that I will **p** out my Spirit on all flesh, Acts 2:17
in those days I will **p** out my Spirit, Acts 2:18
Does a spring **p** forth from the same Jas 3:11
"Go and **p** out on the earth the seven Rv 16:1

POURED (93)
it up for a pillar and **p** oil on the top of Gn 28:18
He **p** out a drink offering on it and Gn 35:14
a drink offering on it and **p** oil on it. Gn 35:14
and the rain no longer **p** upon the earth. Ex 9:33
It shall not be **p** on the body of an Ex 30:32
And he **p** some of the anointing oil on Lv 8:12
purified the altar and **p** out the blood at Lv 8:15
horns of the altar and **p** out the blood at Lv 9:9
the anointing oil is **p** and who has been Lv 21:10
your sacrifices shall be **p** out on the Dt 12:27
and drew water and **p** it out before the 1 Sm 7:6
a flask of oil and **p** it on his head and 1 Sm 10:1
not drink of it. He **p** it out to the LORD 2 Sm 23:16
ashes that are on it shall be **p** out.'" 1 Kgs 13:3
and the ashes **p** out from the altar, 1 Kgs 13:5
who **p** water on the hands of Elijah." 2 Kgs 3:11
And as she **p** they brought the vessels 2 Kgs 4:5
And they **p** out some for the men to 2 Kgs 4:40
And the young man **p** the oil on his 2 Kgs 9:6
grain offering and **p** his drink 2 Kgs 16:13
not drink it. He **p** it out to the LORD 1 Chr 11:18
shall not be **p** out on Jerusalem 2 Chr 12:7
wrath of the LORD that is **p** out on us, 2 Chr 34:21
my wrath will be **p** out on this place 2 Chr 34:25
and my groanings are **p** out like water. Jb 3:24
and the rock **p** out for me streams of oil! Jb 29:6
"And now my soul is **p** out within me; Jb 30:16
I am **p** out like water, and all my bones Ps 22:14
say, "A deadly thing is **p** out on him; Ps 41:8
sons of men; grace is **p** upon your lips; Ps 45:2
earth quaked, the heavens **p** down rain, Ps 68:8
The clouds **p** out water; the skies gave Ps 77:17
They have **p** out their blood like water Ps 79:3
wild ox; you have **p** over me fresh oil. Ps 92:10
they **p** out innocent blood, the blood of Ps 106:38
oils are fragrant; your name is oil **p** out; Sg 1:3
they **p** out a whispered prayer when your Is 26:16
For the LORD has **p** out upon you a spirit Is 29:10
until the Spirit is **p** upon us from on Is 32:15
So he **p** on him the heat of his anger and Is 42:25
because he **p** out his soul to death and Is 53:12
to them you have **p** out a drink offering, Is 57:6
and I **p** out their lifeblood on the earth." Is 63:6
and my wrath will be **p** out on this place, Jer 7:20
drink offerings have been **p** out to other Jer 19:13
drink offerings have been **p** out to other Jer 32:29
and my wrath were **p** out on the Jer 42:18
so my wrath will be **p** out on you when Jer 42:18
and my anger were **p** out and kindled in Jer 44:6
of heaven and **p** out drink offerings Jer 44:19
her image and **p** out drink offerings Jer 44:19
of Zion; he has **p** out his fury like fire. Lam 2:4
my bile is **p** out to the ground because Lam 2:11
as their life is **p** out on their mothers' Lam 2:12
he **p** out his hot anger, and he kindled Lam 4:11
Because your lust was **p** out and your Ezk 16:36
and there they **p** out their drink Ezk 20:28
arm and with wrath **p** out I will be Ezk 20:33
arm, and with wrath **p** out. Ezk 20:34
I have **p** out my wrath upon you." Ezk 22:22
Therefore I have **p** out my indignation Ezk 22:31
virgin bosom and **p** out their whoring Ezk 23:8
So I **p** out my wrath upon them for the Ezk 36:18
servant of God have been **p** out upon us, Dn 9:11
the decreed end is **p** out on the Dn 9:27
he has **p** down for you abundant rain, the Jl 2:23
the fire, like waters **p** down a steep place. Mi 1:4
of his anger? His wrath is **p** out like fire, Na 1:6
their blood shall be **p** out like dust, and Zep 1:17
from which the golden oil is **p** out?" Zec 4:12
and she **p** it on his head as he reclined at Mt 26:7
which is **p** out for many for the Mt 26:28
broke the flask and **p** it over his head. Mk 14:3
the covenant, which is **p** out for many. Mk 14:24
"This cup that is **p** out for you is the Lk 22:20
And he **p** out the coins of the Jn 2:15
Then he **p** water into a basin and began Jn 13:5
he has **p** out this that you yourselves Acts 2:33
the Holy Spirit was **p** out even on the Acts 10:45
God's love has been **p** into our hearts Rom 5:5
if I am to be **p** out as a drink offering Phil 2:17
I am already being **p** out as a drink 2 Tm 4:6
whom he **p** out on us richly through Jesus Ti 3:6
The serpent **p** water like a river out of Rv 12:15
that the dragon had **p** from his mouth. Rv 12:16
p full strength into the cup of his anger, Rv 14:10
first angel went and **p** out his bowl on Rv 16:2
The second angel **p** out his bowl into the Rv 16:3
The third angel **p** out his bowl into the Rv 16:4
The fourth angel **p** out his bowl on the Rv 16:8
The fifth angel **p** out his bowl on the Rv 16:10
The sixth angel **p** out his bowl on the Rv 16:12
The seventh angel **p** out his bowl into Rv 16:17

POURERS (1)
shall send to him **p** who will pour him, Jer 48:12

POURING (4)
but I have been **p** out my soul before 1 Sm 1:15
of heaven and **p** out drink offerings Jer 44:18
In **p** this ointment on my body, she has Mt 26:12
up his wounds, **p** on oil and wine. Lk 10:34

POURS (11)
He **p** contempt on princes and loosens Jb 12:21
spare; he **p** out my gall on the ground. Jb 16:13
scorn me; my eye **p** out tears to God, Jb 16:20
Day to day **p** out speech, and night to Ps 19:2
wine, well mixed, and he **p** out from it, Ps 75:8
he is faint and **p** out his complaint Ps 102:T
he **p** contempt on princes and makes Ps 107:40
mouth of the wicked **p** out evil things. Prv 15:28
waters of the sea and **p** them out on the Am 5:8
of the sea and **p** them out upon the Am 9:6
fire **p** from their mouth and consumes Rv 11:5

POVERTY (20)
all that you have, do not come to **p**.' Gn 45:11
and **p** will come upon you like a Prv 6:11
A slack hand causes **p**, but the hand of Prv 10:4
city; the **p** of the poor is their ruin. Prv 10:15
P and disgrace come to him who Prv 13:18
is profit, but mere talk tends only to **p**. Prv 14:23
Love not sleep, lest you come to **p**; open Prv 20:13
everyone who is hasty comes only to **p**. Prv 21:5
gives to the rich, will only come to **p**. Prv 22:16
and the glutton will come to **p**, Prv 23:21
and **p** will come upon you like a Prv 24:34
pursuits will have plenty of **p**. Prv 28:19
does not know that **p** will come upon Prv 28:22
and lying; give me neither **p** nor riches; Prv 30:8
and forget their **p** and remember their Prv 31:7
she out of her **p** has put in everything Mk 12:44
but she out of her **p** put in all she had to Lk 21:4
and their extreme **p** have overflowed in 2 Cor 8:2
that you by his **p** might become rich. 2 Cor 8:9
your tribulation and your **p** (but you are Rv 2:9

POWDER (3)
and ground it to **p** and scattered it on Ex 32:20
LORD will make the rain of your land **p**. Dt 28:24
and the images into **p** and cut down 2 Chr 34:7

POWDERS (1)
with all the fragrant **p** of a merchant? Sg 3:6

POWER (233)
Sarai, "Behold, your servant is in your **p**; Gn 16:6
It is in my **p** to do you harm. But the Gn 31:29
in dignity and preeminent in **p**. Gn 49:3
all the miracles that I have put in your **p**. Ex 4:21
I have raised you up, to show you my **p**, Ex 9:16
Israel saw the great **p** that the LORD used Ex 14:31
Your right hand, O LORD, glorious in **p**, Ex 15:6
of Egypt with great **p** and with a mighty Ex 32:11
and I will break the pride of your **p**, and Lv 26:19
you shall have no **p** to stand before Lv 26:37
please let the **p** of the Lord be great as Nm 14:17
Have I now any **p** of my own to speak Nm 22:38
with his own presence, by his great **p**, Dt 4:37
'My **p** and the might of my hand have Dt 8:17
for it is he who gives you **p** to get wealth, Dt 8:18
out by your great **p** and by your Dt 9:29
he sees that their **p** is gone and there Dt 32:36
for all the mighty **p** and all the great Dt 34:12
and they had no **p** to flee this way or Jos 8:20
a numerous people and have great **p**. Jos 17:17
king and exalt the **p** of his anointed." 1 Sm 2:10
and save us from the **p** of our enemies." 1 Sm 4:3
deliver us from the **p** of these mighty 1 Sm 4:8
went to restore his **p** at the river 2 Sm 8:3
soon as the royal **p** was firmly in his 2 Kgs 14:5
to confirm his hold on the royal **p**. 2 Kgs 15:19
of Egypt with great **p** and with an 2 Kgs 17:36
words are strategy and **p** for war? 2 Kgs 18:20
greatness and the **p** and the glory 1 Chr 29:11
In your hand are **p** and might, and 1 Chr 29:12
did not recover his **p** in the days of 2 Chr 13:20
In your hand are **p** and might, so that 2 Chr 20:6
as soon as the royal **p** was firmly his, 2 Chr 25:3
For God has **p** to help or to cast 2 Chr 25:8
could make war with mighty **p**, 2 Chr 26:13
and by force and **p** made them cease. Ezr 4:23
and the **p** of his wrath is against all who Ezr 8:22
redeemed by your great **p** and by your Neh 1:10
enslaved, but it is not in our **p** to help it, Neh 5:5
And all the acts of his **p** and might, and Est 10:2
death, and in war from the **p** of the sword. Jb 5:20
reach old age, and grow mighty in **p**? Jb 21:7
The man with **p** possessed the land, and Jb 22:8
with me in the greatness of his **p**? Jb 23:6
prolongs the life of the mighty by his **p**; Jb 24:22
you have helped him who has no **p**! Jb 26:2
By his **p** he stilled the sea; by his Jb 26:12
thunder of his **p** who can understand?" Jb 26:14
he flees from its **p** in headlong flight. Jb 27:22
Behold, God is exalted in his **p**; who is a Jb 36:22
—we cannot find him; he is great in **p**; Jb 37:23
and his **p** in the muscles of his belly. Jb 40:16
We will sing and praise your **p**. Ps 21:13
my precious life from the **p** of the dog! Ps 22:20
not abandon him to his **p** or let him be Ps 37:33
ransom my soul from the **p** of Sheol, Ps 49:15
them totter by your **p** and bring them Ps 59:11
have I heard this: that **p** belongs to God, Ps 62:11
sanctuary, beholding your **p** and glory. Ps 63:2
shall be given over to the **p** of the sword; Ps 63:10
So great is your **p** that your enemies Ps 66:3
earth, your saving **p** among all nations. Ps 67:2
Summon your **p**, O God, the power, O Ps 68:28
Summon your power, O God, the **p**, O Ps 68:28
Ascribe **p** to God, whose majesty is over Ps 68:34
over Israel, and whose **p** is in the skies. Ps 68:34
the one who gives **p** and strength to his Ps 68:35
generation, your **p** to all those to come. Ps 71:18
in God and did not trust his saving **p**. Ps 78:22
and by his **p** he led out the south wind; Ps 78:26
did not remember his **p** or the day when Ps 78:42
and delivered his **p** to captivity, his Ps 78:61
according to your great **p**, preserve Ps 79:11
can deliver his soul from the **p** of Sheol? Ps 89:48
Who considers the **p** of your anger, and Ps 90:11
and your glorious **p** to their children. Ps 90:16

he might make known his mighty **p**. Ps 106:8
them from the **p** of the enemy. Ps 106:10
brought into subjection under their **p**. Ps 106:42
themselves freely on the day of your **p**, Ps 110:3
has shown his people the **p** of his works, Ps 111:6
of your kingdom and tell of your **p**, Ps 145:11
Great is our Lord, and abundant in **p**; Ps 147:5
it is due, when it is in your **p** to do it. Prv 3:27
and life are in the **p** of the tongue, Prv 18:21
the side of their oppressors there was **p**, Eccl 4:1
and possessions and **p** to enjoy them, Eccl 5:19
God does not give him **p** to enjoy them, Eccl 6:2
No man has **p** to retain the spirit, or Eccl 8:8
the spirit, or **p** over the day of death. Eccl 8:8
when man had **p** over man to his hurt. Eccl 8:9
will lop the boughs with terrifying **p**; Is 10:33
mere words are strategy and **p** for war? Is 36:5
he is strong in **p** not one is missing. Is 40:26
He gives **p** to the faint, and to him who Is 40:29
and the great **p** of your enchantments. Is 47:9
themselves from the **p** of the flame. Is 47:14
cannot redeem? Or have I no **p** to deliver? Is 50:2
It is he who made the earth by his **p**, Jer 10:12
make them know my **p** and my might, Jer 16:21
give them over to the **p** of the sword; Jer 18:21
who by my great **p** and my outstretched Jer 27:5
earth by your great **p** and by your Jer 32:17
"It is he who made the earth by his **p**, Jer 51:15
in you, every one according to his **p**, Ezk 22:6
my sanctuary, the pride of your **p**, Ezk 24:21
people of Israel to the **p** of the sword at Ezk 35:5
of heaven has given the kingdom, the **p**, Dn 2:37
fire had not had any **p** over the bodies of Dn 3:27
built by my mighty **p** as a royal Dn 4:30
saved Daniel from the **p** of the lions." Dn 6:27
was no one who could rescue from his **p**. Dn 8:4
the ram had no **p** to stand before him, Dn 8:7
one who could rescue the ram from his **p**. Dn 8:7
from his nation, but not with his **p**. Dn 8:22
His **p** shall be great—but not by his Dn 8:24
shall be great—but not by his own **p**; Dn 8:24
shall stir up his **p** and his heart against Dn 11:25
the shattering of the **p** of the holy people Dn 12:7
I ransom them from the **p** of Sheol? Hos 13:14
it, because it is in the **p** of their hand. Mi 2:1
But as for me, I am filled with **p**, with the Mi 3:8
The LORD is slow to anger and great in **p**, Na 1:3
from his hand; and there he veiled his **p**. Hab 3:4
Not by might, nor by **p**, but by my Zec 4:6
and strike down her **p** on the sea, Zec 9:4
neither the Scriptures nor the **p** of God. Mt 22:29
of heaven with **p** and great glory. Mt 24:30
the right hand of **P** and coming on the Mt 26:64
in himself that **p** had gone out Mk 5:30
of God after it has come with **p**." Mk 9:1
the Scriptures nor the **p** of God? Mk 12:24
in clouds with great **p** and glory. Mk 13:26
of Man seated at the right hand of **P**, Mk 14:62
before him in the spirit and **p** of Elijah, Lk 1:17
and the **p** of the Most High will Lk 1:35
Jesus returned in the **p** of the Spirit to Lk 4:14
with authority and **p** he commands the Lk 4:36
And the **p** of the Lord was with him to Lk 5:17
for **p** came out from him and healed Lk 6:19
for I perceive that **p** has gone out from Lk 8:46
and gave them **p** and authority over Lk 9:1
and over all the **p** of the enemy, Lk 10:19
in a cloud with **p** and great glory. Lk 21:27
is your hour, and the **p** of darkness." Lk 22:53
at the right hand of the **p** of God." Lk 22:69
you are clothed with **p** from on high." Lk 24:49
But you will receive **p** when the Holy Acts 1:8
though by our own **p** or piety we have Acts 3:12
"By what **p** or by what name did you do Acts 4:7
And with great **p** the apostles were Acts 4:33
And Stephen, full of grace and **p**, was Acts 6:8
"This man is the **p** of God that is called Acts 8:10
saying, "Give me this **p** also, so that Acts 8:19
with the Holy Spirit and with **p**. Acts 10:38
light and from the **p** of Satan to God, Acts 26:18
Son of God in **p** according to the Spirit Rom 1:4
for it is the **p** of God for salvation to Rom 1:16
his eternal **p** and divine nature, Rom 1:20
up, that I might show my **p** in you, Rom 9:17
his wrath and to make known his **p**, Rom 9:22
for God has the **p** to graft them in Rom 11:23
so that by the **p** of the Holy Spirit you Rom 15:13
by the **p** of signs and wonders, by the Rom 15:19
by the **p** of the Spirit of God—so that Rom 15:19
the cross of Christ be emptied of its **p**. 1 Cor 1:17
who are being saved it is the **p** of God. 1 Cor 1:18
Christ the **p** of God and the wisdom of 1 Cor 1:24
in demonstration of the Spirit and of **p**, 1 Cor 2:4
the wisdom of men but in the **p** of God. 1 Cor 2:5
of these arrogant people but their **p**. 1 Cor 4:19
God does not consist in talk but in **p**. 1 Cor 4:20
is present, with the **p** of our Lord Jesus, 1 Cor 5:4
and will also raise us up by his **p**. 1 Cor 6:14
should pray for the **p** to interpret. 1 Cor 14:13
rule and every authority and **p**. 1 Cor 15:24
is sown in weakness; it is raised in **p**. 1 Cor 15:43
is sin, and the **p** of sin is the law. 1 Cor 15:56
that the surpassing **p** belongs to God 2 Cor 4:7
by truthful speech, and the **p** of God; 2 Cor 6:7
but have divine **p** to destroy 2 Cor 10:4
my **p** is made perfect in weakness." 2 Cor 12:9
so that the **p** of Christ may rest upon 2 Cor 12:9
weakness, but lives by the **p** of God. 2 Cor 13:4
we will live with him by the **p** of God. 2 Cor 13:4
greatness of his **p** toward us who Eph 1:19
and authority and **p** and dominion, Eph 1:21
following the prince of the **p** of the air, Eph 2:2
was given me by the working of his **p**. Eph 3:7
be strengthened with **p** through his Eph 3:16
according to the **p** at work within us, Eph 3:20
him and the **p** of his resurrection, Phil 3:10
by the **p** that enables him even to Phil 3:21
May you be strengthened with all **p**, Col 1:11
but also in **p** and in the Holy Spirit 1 Thes 1:5
and every work of faith by his **p**, 2 Thes 1:11
of Satan with all **p** and false signs and 2 Thes 2:9
of fear but of **p** and love and 2 Tm 1:7
suffering for the gospel by the **p** of God, 2 Tm 1:8
of godliness, but denying its **p**. 2 Tm 3:5
the universe by the word of his **p**. Heb 1:3
destroy the one who has the **p** of death, Heb 2:14
but by the **p** of an indestructible life. Heb 7:16
Sarah herself received **p** to conceive, Heb 11:11
quenched the **p** of fire, escaped the Heb 11:34
righteous person has great **p** as it is Jas 5:16
who by God's **p** are being guarded 1 Pt 1:5
His divine **p** has granted to us all things 2 Pt 1:3
known to you the **p** and coming of our 2 Pt 1:16
angels, though greater in might and **p**, 2 Pt 2:11
whole world lies in the **p** of the evil one. 1 Jn 5:19
I know that you have but little **p**, and yet Rv 3:8
God, to receive glory and honor and **p**, Rv 4:11
to receive **p** and wealth and wisdom and Rv 5:12
who had been given **p** to harm earth and Rv 7:2
and honor and **p** and might be Rv 7:12
and they were given **p** like the power of Rv 9:3
given power like the **p** of scorpions of the Rv 9:3
and their **p** to hurt people for five Rv 9:10
For the **p** of the horses is in their mouths Rv 9:19
They have the **p** to shut the sky, that no Rv 11:6
and they have **p** over the waters to turn Rv 11:6
have taken your great **p** and begun to Rv 11:17
salvation and the **p** and the kingdom Rv 12:10
the dragon gave his **p** and his throne and Rv 13:2
from the glory of God and from his **p**, Rv 15:8
of God who had **p** over these plagues. Rv 16:9
who have not yet received royal **p**, Rv 17:12
and hand over their **p** and authority to Rv 17:13
handing over their royal **p** to the beast, Rv 17:17
grown rich from the **p** of her luxurious Rv 18:3
Salvation and glory and **p** belong to our Rv 19:1
Over such the second death has no **p**, Rv 20:6

POWERFUL (13)
man Mordecai grew more and more **p**. Est 9:4
The voice of the LORD is **p**; the voice of the Ps 29:4
and decides between **p** contenders. Prv 18:18
for no great and **p** king has asked such Dn 2:10
canal, and he ran at him in his **p** wrath. Dn 8:6
against my land, **p** and beyond number; Jl 1:6
upon the mountains a great and **p** people; Jl 2:2
stubble, like a **p** army drawn up for battle. Jl 2:5
great; he who executes his word is **p**. Jl 2:11
worldly standards, not many were **p**, 1 Cor 1:26
with you, but is **p** among you. 2 Cor 13:3
through faith in the **p** working of God, Col 2:12
and the generals and the rich and the **p**, Rv 6:15

POWERFULLY (2)
for he **p** refuted the Jews in public, Acts 18:28
his energy that he **p** works within me. Col 1:29

POWERLESS (1)
For we are **p** against this great horde 2 Chr 20:12

POWERS (11)
is why these miraculous **p** are at work Mt 14:2
and the **p** of the heavens will be Mt 24:29
is why these miraculous **p** are at work Mk 6:14
and the **p** in the heavens will be Mk 13:25
For the **p** of the heavens will be shaken. Lk 21:26
present nor things to come, nor **p**, Rom 8:38
And if I have prophetic **p**, and 1 Cor 13:2
against the cosmic **p** over this present Eph 6:12
who have their **p** of discernment Heb 5:14
word of God and the **p** of the age to come, Heb 6:5
and **p** having been subjected to him. 1 Pt 3:22

PRACTICE (31)
man like me can indeed **p** divination?" Gn 44:15
my charge never to **p** any of these Lv 18:30
this has been your **p** and you have 1 Kgs 11:11
the peoples who **p** these abominations? Ezr 9:14
all those who **p** it have a good Ps 111:10
is busy with iniquity, to **p** ungodliness, Is 32:6
see false visions nor **p** divination. Ezk 13:23
its prophets **p** divination for money; Mi 3:11
so **p** and observe whatever they tell you Mt 23:3
they do. For they preach, but do not **p**. Mt 23:3
for us as Romans to accept or **p**." Acts 16:21
that those who **p** such things deserve Rom 1:32
but give approval to those who **p** them. Rom 1:32
you, the judge, **p** the very same things. Rom 2:1
nor men who **p** homosexuality, 1 Cor 6:9
be contentious, we have no such **p**, 1 Cor 11:16
We refuse to **p** cunning or to tamper 2 Cor 4:2
greedy to **p** every kind of impurity. Eph 4:19
heard and seen in me—**p** these things, Phil 4:9
immoral, men who **p** homosexuality, 1 Tm 1:10
P these things, devote yourself to 1 Tm 4:15
trained by constant **p** to distinguish Heb 5:14
there will be disorder and every vile **p**. Jas 3:16
for if you **p** these qualities you will 2 Pt 1:10
darkness, we lie and do not **p** the truth. 1 Jn 1:6
Everyone who makes a **p** of sinning also 1 Jn 3:4
Whoever makes a **p** of sinning is of the 1 Jn 3:8
one born of God makes a **p** of sinning, 1 Jn 3:9
whoever does not **p** righteousness is not 1 Jn 3:10
to idols and **p** sexual immorality. Rv 2:14
my servants to **p** sexual immorality and Rv 2:20

PRACTICED (9)
customs that were **p** before you, Lv 18:30
son of Beor, the one who **p** divination, Jos 13:22
that the kings of Israel had **p**. 2 Kgs 17:8
for his father, because he **p** extortion, Ezk 18:18
the land have **p** extortion and Ezk 22:29
the treachery they have **p** against me, Ezk 39:26
who had previously **p** magic in the city Acts 8:9
those who had **p** magic arts brought Acts 19:19
and sensuality that they have **p**. 2 Cor 12:21

PRACTICES (18)
drinks, and by this that he **p** divination? Gn 44:5
follow the abominable **p** of those Dt 18:9
anyone who **p** divination or tells Dt 18:10
to all their abominable **p** that they have Dt 20:18
drop any of their **p** or their stubborn Jgs 2:19
to the despicable **p** of the nations 2 Kgs 16:3
to the despicable **p** of the nations 2 Kgs 21:2
and not according to the **p** of Israel. 2 Chr 17:4
the people still followed corrupt **p**. 2 Chr 27:2
Esther confirmed these **p** of Purim, Est 9:32
No one who **p** deceit shall dwell in my Ps 101:7
that I am the LORD who **p** steadfast love, Jer 9:24
confessing and divulging their **p**. Acts 19:18
you have put off the old self with its **p** Col 3:9
that everyone who **p** righteousness has 1 Jn 2:29
a practice of sinning also **p** lawlessness; 1 Jn 3:4
Whoever **p** righteousness is righteous, 1 Jn 3:7
everyone who loves and **p** falsehood. Rv 22:15

PRACTICING (3)
and for **p** oppression and violence." Jer 22:17
break off your sins by **p** righteousness, Dn 4:27
"Beware of **p** your righteousness before Mt 6:1

PRAETORIUM (1)
him to be guarded in Herod's **p**. Acts 23:35

PRAISE (207)
"This time I will **p** the LORD." Therefore Gn 29:35
"Judah, your brothers shall **p** you; your Gn 49:8
this is my God, and I will **p** him, my Ex 15:2
be holy, an offering of **p** to the LORD. Lv 19:24
He is your **p**. He is your God, who has Dt 10:21
he will set you in **p** and in fame and in Dt 26:19
the LORD God of Israel and give **p** to him. Jos 7:19
"For this I will **p** you, O LORD, among 2 Sm 22:50
to invoke, to thank, and to **p** the LORD, 1 Chr 16:4
holy name, and glory in your **p**. 1 Chr 16:35
instruments that I have made for **p**." 1 Chr 23:5
in thanksgiving and **p** to the LORD. 1 Chr 25:3
our God, and **p** your glorious name. 1 Chr 29:13
in unison in **p** and thanksgiving to 2 Chr 5:13
instruments, in **p** to the LORD, 2 Chr 5:13
their offices of **p** and ministry before 2 Chr 8:14
Korahites, stood up to **p** the LORD, 2 Chr 20:19
to the LORD and **p** him in holy attire, 2 Chr 20:21
And when they began to sing and **p**, 2 Chr 20:22
of the LORD and to give thanks and **p**. 2 Chr 31:2
of Asaph, with cymbals, to **p** the LORD, Ezr 3:10
is exalted above all blessing and **p**. Neh 9:5
of Asaph, who was the leader of the **p**, Neh 11:17
them, to **p** and to give thanks, Neh 12:24
were songs of **p** and thanksgiving to Neh 12:46

of you; in Sheol who will give you **p**? Ps 6:5
and I will sing **p** to the name of the LORD, Ps 7:17
exult in you; I will sing **p** to your name, Ps 9:2
For this I will **p** you, O LORD, among the Ps 18:49
We will sing and **p** your power. Ps 21:13
midst of the congregation I will **p** you: Ps 22:22
You who fear the LORD, **p** him! All you Ps 22:23
From you comes my **p** in the great Ps 22:25
those who seek him shall **p** the LORD! Ps 22:26
I go down to the pit? Will the dust **p** you? Ps 30:9
glory may sing your **p** and not be silent. Ps 30:12
O you righteous! **P** befits the upright. Ps 33:1
his **p** shall continually be in my mouth. Ps 34:1
in the mighty throng I will **p** you. Ps 35:18
righteousness and of your **p** all the day Ps 35:28
in my mouth, a song of **p** to our God. Ps 40:3
of God with glad shouts and songs of **p**, Ps 42:4
for I shall again **p** him, my salvation Ps 42:5
for I shall again **p** him, my salvation Ps 42:11
joy, and I will **p** you with the lyre, Ps 43:4
for I shall again **p** him, my salvation and Ps 43:5
therefore nations will **p** you forever and Ps 45:17
so your **p** reaches to the ends of the Ps 48:10
and though you get **p** when you do well Ps 49:18
lips, and my mouth will declare your **p**. Ps 51:15
In God, whose word I **p**, in God I trust; I Ps 56:4
In God, whose word I **p**, in the LORD, Ps 56:10
I praise, in the LORD, whose word I **p**, Ps 56:10
love is better than life, my lips will **p** you. Ps 63:3
and my mouth will **p** you with joyful Ps 63:5
P is due to you, O God, in Zion, and to Ps 65:1
of his name; give to him glorious **p**! Ps 66:2
O peoples; let the sound of his **p** be heard, Ps 66:8
mouth, and high **p** was on my tongue. Ps 66:17
Let the peoples **p** you, O God; let all the Ps 67:3
you, O God; let all the peoples **p** you! Ps 67:3
Let the peoples **p** you, O God; let all the Ps 67:5
you, O God; let all the peoples **p** you! Ps 67:5
I will **p** the name of God with a song; I Ps 69:30
Let heaven and earth **p** him, the seas Ps 69:34
womb. My **p** is continually of you. Ps 71:6
My mouth is filled with your **p**, and with Ps 71:8
continually and will **p** you yet more Ps 71:14
I will also **p** you with the harp for your Ps 71:22
let the poor and needy **p** your name. Ps 74:21
Surely the wrath of man shall **p** you; Ps 76:10
to generation we will recount your **p**. Ps 79:13
dwell in your house, ever singing your **p**! Ps 84:4
dead? Do the departed rise up to **p** you? Ps 88:10
Let the heavens **p** your wonders, O LORD, Ps 89:5
and Hermon joyously **p** your name. Ps 89:12
a joyful noise to him with songs of **p**! Ps 95:2
Let them **p** your great and awesome Ps 99:3
thanksgiving, and his courts with **p**! Ps 100:4
yet to be created may **p** the LORD: Ps 102:18
of the LORD, and in Jerusalem his **p**, Ps 102:21
I will sing **p** to my God while I have Ps 104:33
Bless the LORD, O my soul! **P** the LORD! Ps 104:35
and observe his laws. **P** the LORD! Ps 105:45
P the LORD! Oh give thanks to the LORD, Ps 106:1
deeds of the LORD, or declare all his **p**? Ps 106:2
believed his words; they sang his **p**. Ps 106:12
your holy name and glory in your **p**. Ps 106:47
all the people say, "Amen!" **P** the LORD! Ps 106:48
and **p** him in the assembly of the Ps 107:32
Be not silent, O God of my **p**! Ps 109:1
I will **p** him in the midst of the throng. Ps 109:30
P the LORD! I will give thanks to the Ps 111:1
understanding. His **p** endures forever! Ps 111:10
P the LORD! Blessed is the man who Ps 112:1
P the LORD! Praise, O servants of the Ps 113:1
P, O servants of the LORD, praise the Ps 113:1
of the LORD, **p** the name of the LORD! Ps 113:1
joyous mother of children. **P** the LORD! Ps 113:9
The dead do not **p** the LORD, nor do any Ps 115:17
forth and forevermore. **P** the LORD! Ps 115:18
your midst, O Jerusalem. **P** the LORD! Ps 116:19
P the LORD, all nations! Extol him, all Ps 117:1
of the LORD endures forever. **P** the LORD! Ps 117:2
I will **p** you with an upright heart, when Ps 119:7
At midnight I rise to **p** you, because of Ps 119:62
Accept my freewill offerings of **p**, O Ps 119:108
times a day I **p** you for your righteous Ps 119:164
My lips will pour forth **p**, for you Ps 119:171
Let my soul live and **p** you, and let Ps 119:175
P the LORD! Praise the name of the LORD, Ps 135:1
P the name of the LORD, give praise, O Ps 135:1
Praise the name of the LORD, give **p**, O Ps 135:1
P the LORD, for the LORD is good; sing to Ps 135:3
who dwells in Jerusalem! **P** the LORD! Ps 135:21
heart; before the gods I sing your **p**; Ps 138:1
I **p** you, for I am fearfully and Ps 139:14
A Song of **P**. Of David. Ps 145:T
will bless you and **p** your name forever Ps 145:2
My mouth will speak the **p** of the LORD, Ps 145:21
P the LORD! Praise the LORD, O my soul! Ps 146:1
Praise the LORD! **P** the LORD, O my soul! Ps 146:1
I will **p** the LORD as long as I live; I will Ps 146:2
O Zion, to all generations. **P** the LORD! Ps 146:10
P the LORD! For it is good to sing praises Ps 147:1
it is pleasant, and a song of **p** is fitting. Ps 147:1
P the LORD, O Jerusalem! Praise your Ps 147:12
O Jerusalem! **P** your God, O Zion! Ps 147:12
they do not know his rules. **P** the LORD! Ps 147:20
P the LORD! Praise the LORD from the Ps 148:1
P the LORD from the heavens; praise Ps 148:1
from the heavens; **p** him in the heights! Ps 148:1
P him, all his angels; praise him, all his Ps 148:2
him, all his angels; **p** him, all his hosts! Ps 148:2
P him, sun and moon, praise him, all Ps 148:3
Praise him, sun and moon, **p** him, all Ps 148:3
P him, you highest heavens, and you Ps 148:4
Let them **p** the name of the LORD! For he Ps 148:5
P the LORD from the earth, you great sea Ps 148:7
Let them **p** the name of the LORD, for Ps 148:13
horn for his people, **p** for all his saints, Ps 148:14
Israel who are near to him. **P** the LORD! Ps 148:14
P the LORD! Sing to the LORD a new song, Ps 149:1
song, his **p** in the assembly of the godly! Ps 149:1
Let them **p** his name with dancing, Ps 149:3
honor for all his godly ones. **P** the LORD! Ps 149:9
P the LORD! Praise God in his Ps 150:1
P God in his sanctuary; praise him in Ps 150:1
p him in his mighty heavens! Ps 150:1
P him for his mighty deeds; praise him Ps 150:2
p him according to his excellent Ps 150:2
P him with trumpet sound; praise him Ps 150:3
sound; **p** him with lute and harp! Ps 150:3
P him with tambourine and dance; Ps 150:4
and dance; **p** him with strings and pipe! Ps 150:4
P him with sounding cymbals; praise Ps 150:5
p him with loud clashing cymbals! Ps 150:5
everything that has breath **p** the LORD! Ps 150:6
has breath praise the LORD! **P** the LORD! Ps 150:6
Let another **p** you, and not your own Prv 27:2
for gold, and a man is tested by his **p**. Prv 27:21
who forsake the law **p** the wicked, Prv 28:4
and let her works **p** her in the gates. Prv 31:31
the ends of the earth we hear songs of **p**, Is 24:16
I will exalt you; I will **p** your name, for Is 25:1
not thank you; death does not **p** you; Is 38:18
give to no other, nor my **p** to carved idols. Is 42:8
song, his **p** from the end of the earth, Is 42:10
and declare his **p** in the coastlands. Is 42:12
for myself that they might declare my **p**. Is 43:21
for the sake of my **p** I restrain it for you, Is 48:9
your walls Salvation, and your gates **P**. Is 60:18
the garment of **p** instead of a faint spirit; Is 61:3
cause righteousness and **p** to sprout up Is 61:11
Jerusalem and makes it a **p** in the earth. Is 62:7
who garner it shall eat it and **p** the LORD, Is 62:9
might be for me a people, a name, a **p**, Jer 13:11
and I shall be saved, for you are my **p**. Jer 17:14
Sing to the LORD; **p** the LORD! For he has Jer 20:13
proclaim, give **p**, and say, 'O LORD, save Jer 31:7
a **p** and a glory before all the nations of Jer 33:9
is taken, the **p** of the whole earth seized! Jer 51:41
God of my fathers, I give thanks and **p**, Dn 2:23
p and extol and honor the King of Dn 4:37
and **p** the name of the LORD your God, Jl 2:26
heavens, and the earth was full of his **p**. Hab 3:3
their shame into **p** and renown in Zep 3:19
nursing babies you have prepared **p**'?" Mt 21:16
to return and give **p** to God except this Lk 17:18
people, when they saw it, gave **p** to God. Lk 18:43
began to rejoice and **p** God with a loud Lk 19:37
His **p** is not from man but from God. Rom 2:29
"Therefore I will **p** you among the Rom 15:9
And again, "**P** the Lord, all you Rom 15:11
also; I will sing **p** with my spirit, 1 Cor 14:15
and dishonor, through slander and **p**. 2 Cor 6:8
to the **p** of his glorious grace, with Eph 1:6
in Christ might be to the **p** of his glory. Eph 1:12
possession of it, to the **p** of his glory. Eph 1:14
Jesus Christ, to the glory and **p** of God. Phil 1:11
if there is anything worthy of **p**, Phil 4:8
of the congregation I will sing your **p**." Heb 2:12
offer up a sacrifice of **p** to God, Heb 13:15
pray. Is anyone cheerful? Let him sing **p**. Jas 5:13
found to result in **p** and glory and honor 1 Pt 1:7
who do evil and to **p** those who do good. 1 Pt 2:14
throne came a voice saying, "**P** our God, Rv 19:5

PRAISED (24)
saw her, they **p** her to Pharaoh. Gn 12:15
the people saw him, they **p** their god. Jgs 16:24
so much to be **p** for his handsome 2 Sm 14:25
upon the LORD, who is worthy to be **p**, 2 Sm 22:4
great is the LORD, and greatly to be **p**, 1 Chr 16:25
people said, "Amen!" and **p** the LORD. 1 Chr 16:36
and the priests **p** the LORD day 2 Chr 30:21
with a great shout when they **p** the LORD, Ezr 3:11
assembly said "Amen" and **p** the LORD. Neh 5:13
upon the LORD, who is worthy to be **p**, Ps 18:3
LORD and greatly to be **p** in the city of our Ps 48:1
For great is the LORD, and greatly to be **p**; Ps 96:4
setting, the name of the LORD is to be **p**! Ps 113:3
Great is the LORD, and greatly to be **p**, Ps 145:3
a woman who fears the LORD is to be **p**. Prv 31:30
holy place and were **p** in the city where Eccl 8:10
and concubines also, and they **p** her. Sg 6:9
house, where our fathers **p** you, Is 64:11
and **p** and honored him who lives Dn 4:34
They drank wine and **p** the gods of gold Dn 5:4
And you have **p** the gods of silver and Dn 5:23
you renowned and **p** among all the Zep 3:20
the streets, that they may be **p** by others. Mt 6:2
saw what had taken place, he **p** God, Lk 23:47

PRAISES (37)
nations, and sing **p** to your name. 2 Sm 22:50
Sing to him; sing **p** to him; tell of all 1 Chr 16:9
and 4,000 shall offer **p** to the LORD 1 Chr 23:5
whenever David offered **p** by their 2 Chr 7:6
the Levites to sing **p** to the LORD with 2 Chr 29:30
And they sang **p** with gladness, and 2 Chr 29:30
Sing **p** to the LORD, who sits enthroned in Ps 9:11
that I may recount all your **p**, that in the Ps 9:14
are holy, enthroned on the **p** of Israel. Ps 22:3
Sing **p** to the LORD, O you his saints, and Ps 30:4
Sing **p** to God, sing praises! Sing praises Ps 47:6
Sing praises to God, sing **p**! Sing praises Ps 47:6
praises! Sing **p** to our King, sing praises! Ps 47:6
praises! Sing praises to our King, sing **p**! Ps 47:6
of all the earth; sing **p** with a psalm! Ps 47:7
I will sing **p** to you among the nations. Ps 57:9
O my Strength, I will sing **p** to you, for Ps 59:17
So will I ever sing **p** to your name, as I Ps 61:8
earth worships you and sings **p** to you; Ps 66:4
to you; they sing **p** to your name." Selah Ps 66:4
Sing to God, sing **p** to his name; lift up a Ps 68:4
sing to God; sing **p** to the Lord, Selah Ps 68:32
I will sing **p** to you with the lyre, O Holy Ps 71:22
will shout for joy, when I sing **p** to you; Ps 71:23
forever; I will sing **p** to the God of Jacob. Ps 75:9
to the LORD, to sing **p** to your name, Ps 92:1
break forth into joyous song and sing **p**! Ps 98:4
Sing **p** to the LORD with the lyre, with the Ps 98:5
Sing to him, sing **p** to him; tell of all his Ps 105:2
I will sing **p** to you among the nations. Ps 108:3
I will sing **p** to my God while I have my Ps 146:2
For it is good to sing **p** to our God; for it Ps 147:1
Let the high **p** of God be in their throats Ps 149:6
her husband also, and he **p** her: Prv 31:28
"Sing **p** to the LORD, for he has done Is 12:5
shall bring good news, the **p** of the LORD. Is 60:6
love of the LORD, the **p** of the LORD, Is 63:7

PRAISING (10)
morning, thanking and **p** the LORD, 1 Chr 23:30
the people running and **p** the king, 2 Chr 23:12
p and giving thanks to the LORD, Ezr 3:11
of the heavenly host **p** God and saying, Lk 2:13
glorifying and **p** God for all they had Lk 2:20
turned back, **p** God with a loud voice; Lk 17:15
p God and having favor with all the Acts 2:47
them, walking and leaping and **p** God. Acts 3:8
the people saw him walking and **p** God, Acts 3:9
for all were **p** God for what had Acts 4:21

PRAY (95)
he is a prophet, so that he will **p** for you, Gn 20:7
P to the LORD, that he take away the Nm 21:7
and I will **p** to the LORD for you." 1 Sm 7:5
"**P** for your servants to the LORD your 1 Sm 12:19
the LORD by ceasing to **p** for you, 1 Sm 12:23
has found courage to **p** this prayer to 2 Sm 7:27
Israel, when they **p** toward this place. 1 Kgs 8:30
your name and **p** and plead with 1 Kgs 8:33
if they **p** toward this place and 1 Kgs 8:35
and they **p** to the LORD toward the city 1 Kgs 8:44
and **p** to you toward their land, 1 Kgs 8:48
of the LORD your God, and **p** for me, 1 Kgs 13:6
has found courage to **p** before you. 1 Chr 17:25
Israel, when they **p** toward this place. 2 Chr 6:21
your name and **p** and plead with 2 Chr 6:24
if they **p** toward this place and 2 Chr 6:26
and they **p** to you toward this city 2 Chr 6:34
captive, and **p** toward their land, 2 Chr 6:38
and **p** and seek my face and turn 2 Chr 7:14
the God of heaven and **p** for the life of Ezr 6:10
servant that I now **p** before you day and Neh 1:6
what profit do we get if we **p** to him?' Jb 21:15
And my servant Job shall **p** for you, for I Jb 42:8
my King and my God, for to you do I **p**. Ps 5:2
the LORD: "O LORD, I **p**, deliver my soul!" Ps 116:4
Save us, we **p**, O LORD! O LORD, we pray, Ps 118:25
O LORD! O LORD, we **p**, give us success! Ps 118:25

P for the peace of Jerusalem! "May they Ps 122:6
when he comes to his sanctuary to **p**, Is 16:12
"As for you, do not **p** for this people, or Jer 7:16
"Therefore do not **p** for this people, or Jer 11:14
"Do not **p** for the welfare of this people. Jer 14:11
into exile, and **p** to the LORD on its behalf, Jer 29:7
call upon me and come and **p** to me, Jer 29:12
"Please **p** for us to the LORD our God." Jer 37:3
you, and **p** to the LORD your God for us, Jer 42:2
I will **p** to the LORD your God according Jer 42:4
saying, '**P** for us to the LORD our God, Jer 42:20
Love your enemies and **p** for those who Mt 5:44
"And when you **p**, you must not be like Mt 6:5
love to stand and **p** in the synagogues and Mt 6:5
But when you **p**, go into your room and Mt 6:6
shut the door and **p** to your Father who Mt 6:6
"And when you **p**, do not heap up empty Mt 6:7
P then like this: "Our Father in heaven, Mt 6:9
therefore **p** earnestly to the Lord of the Mt 9:38
up on the mountain by himself to **p**. Mt 14:23
he might lay his hands on them and **p**. Mt 19:13
P that your flight may not be in winter Mt 24:20
"Sit here, while I go over there and **p**." Mt 26:36
Watch and **p** that you may not enter Mt 26:41
them, he went up on the mountain to **p**. Mk 6:46
P that it may not happen in winter. Mk 13:18
to his disciples, "Sit here while I **p**." Mk 14:32
Watch and **p** that you may not enter Mk 14:38
would withdraw to desolate places and **p**. Lk 5:16
days he went out to the mountain to **p**, Lk 6:12
curse you, **p** for those who abuse you. Lk 6:28
and went up on the mountain to **p**. Lk 9:28
Therefore **p** earnestly to the Lord of the Lk 10:2
said to him, "Lord, teach us to **p**, Lk 11:1
And he said to them, "When you **p**, say: Lk 11:2
they ought always to **p** and not lose Lk 18:1
"Two men went up into the temple to **p**, Lk 18:10
"**P** that you may not enter into Lk 22:40
Rise and **p** that you may not enter into Lk 22:46
of yours, and **p** to the Lord that, Acts 8:22
Simon answered, "**P** for me to the Lord, Acts 8:24
the housetop about the sixth hour to **p**. Acts 10:9
do not know what to **p** for as we ought, Rom 8:26
proper for a wife to **p** to God with her 1 Cor 11:13
in a tongue should **p** for the power to 1 Cor 14:13
For if I **p** in a tongue, my spirit prays 1 Cor 14:14
I will **p** with my spirit, but I will 1 Cor 14:15
but I will **p** with my mind also; 1 Cor 14:15
while they long for you and **p** for you, 2 Cor 9:14
But we **p** to God that you may not do 2 Cor 13:7
Your restoration is what we **p** for. 2 Cor 13:9
our Lord Jesus Christ, when we **p** for you, Col 1:3
we heard, we have not ceased to **p** for you, Col 1:9
At the same time, **p** also for us, that God Col 4:3
as we **p** most earnestly night and 1 Thes 3:10
p without ceasing, 1 Thes 5:17
Brothers, **p** for us. 1 Thes 5:25
To this end we always **p** for you, that 2 Thes 1:11
Finally, brothers, **p** for us, that the 2 Thes 3:1
that in every place the men should **p**, 1 Tm 2:8
and I **p** that the sharing of your faith Phlm 1:6
P for us, for we are sure that we have a Heb 13:18
among you suffering? Let him **p**. Jas 5:13
of the church, and let them **p** over him, Jas 5:14
to one another and **p** for one another, Jas 5:16
I do not say that one should **p** for that. 1 Jn 5:16
I **p** that all may go well with you and 3 Jn 1:2
most holy faith; **p** in the Holy Spirit; Jude 1:20

PRAYED (56)

Then Abraham **p** to God, and God Gn 20:17
And Isaac **p** to the LORD for his wife, Gn 25:21
out from Pharaoh and **p** to the LORD. Ex 8:30
out to Moses, and Moses **p** to the LORD, Nm 11:2
from us." So Moses **p** for the people. Nm 21:7
And I **p** for Aaron also at the same time. Dt 9:20
And I **p** to the LORD, 'O Lord GOD, destroy Dt 9:26
Then Manoah **p** to the LORD and said, "O Jgs 13:8
was deeply distressed and **p** to the LORD 1 Sm 1:10
For this child I **p**, and the LORD has 1 Sm 1:27
And Hannah **p** and said, "My heart 1 Sm 2:1
to judge us." And Samuel **p** to the LORD. 1 Sm 8:6
the two of them and **p** to the LORD. 2 Kgs 4:33
Then Elisha **p** and said, "O LORD, 2 Kgs 6:17
him, Elisha **p** to the LORD and said, 2 Kgs 6:18
And Hezekiah **p** before the LORD and 2 Kgs 19:15
his face to the wall and **p** to the LORD, 2 Kgs 20:2
For Hezekiah had **p** for them, 2 Chr 30:18
p because of this and cried to 2 Chr 32:20
point of death, and he **p** to the LORD, 2 Chr 32:24
He **p** to him, and God was moved by 2 Chr 33:13
While Ezra **p** and made confession, Ezr 10:1
are you requesting?" So I **p** to the God of Neh 2:4
And we **p** to our God and set a guard as a Neh 4:9
of Job, when he had **p** for his friends. Jb 42:10
I **p** with head bowed on my chest. Ps 35:13
And Hezekiah **p** to the LORD: Is 37:15
Because you have **p** to me concerning Is 37:21
his face to the wall and **p** to the LORD, Is 38:2
the son of Neriah, I **p** to the LORD, Jer 32:16
times a day and **p** and gave thanks Dn 6:10
I **p** to the LORD my God and made Dn 9:4
Then Jonah **p** to the LORD his God from Jon 2:1
And he **p** to the LORD and said, "O LORD, is Jon 4:2
a little farther he fell on his face and **p**, Mt 26:39
the second time, he went away and **p**, Mt 26:42
he went away and **p** for the third time, Mt 26:44
out to a desolate place, and there he **p**. Mk 1:35
he fell on the ground and **p** that, Mk 14:35
And again he went away and **p**, saying Mk 14:39
Pharisee, standing by himself, **p** thus: Lk 18:11
but I have **p** for you that your faith Lk 22:32
a stone's throw, and knelt down and **p**, Lk 22:41
being in an agony he **p** more earnestly; Lk 22:44
And they **p** and said, "You, Lord, who Acts 1:24
And when they had **p**, the place in Acts 4:31
and they **p** and laid their hands on Acts 6:6
who came down and **p** for them that Acts 8:15
all outside, and knelt down and **p**; Acts 9:40
to the people, and **p** continually to God. Acts 10:2
he knelt down and **p** with them all. Acts 20:36
And kneeling down on the beach, we **p** Acts 21:5
from the stern and **p** for day to come. Acts 27:29
And Paul visited him and **p**, and Acts 28:8
and he **p** fervently that it might not rain, Jas 5:17
Then he **p** again, and heaven gave rain, Jas 5:18

PRAYER (114)

And the LORD granted his **p**, and Gn 25:21
found courage to pray this **p** to you. 2 Sm 7:27
have regard to the **p** of your servant 1 Kgs 8:28
cry and to the **p** that your servant 1 Kgs 8:28
may listen to the **p** that your servant 1 Kgs 8:29
whatever **p**, whatever plea is made by 1 Kgs 8:38
hear in heaven their **p** and their plea, 1 Kgs 8:45
dwelling place their **p** and their plea, 1 Kgs 8:49
finished offering all this **p** and plea to 1 Kgs 8:54
"I have heard your **p** and your plea, 1 Kgs 9:3
in accordance with the **p** of Elisha. 2 Kgs 6:18
lift up your **p** for the remnant 2 Kgs 19:4
Your **p** to me about Sennacherib 2 Kgs 19:20
your father: I have heard your **p**; 2 Kgs 20:5
have regard to the **p** of your servant 2 Chr 6:19
cry and to the **p** that your servant 2 Chr 6:19
may listen to the **p** that your servant 2 Chr 6:20
whatever **p**, whatever plea is made by 2 Chr 6:29
from heaven their **p** and their plea, 2 Chr 6:35
dwelling place their **p** and their pleas, 2 Chr 6:39
ears attentive to the **p** of this place. 2 Chr 6:40
As soon as Solomon finished his **p**, fire 2 Chr 7:1
have heard your **p** and have chosen 2 Chr 7:12
ears attentive to the **p** that is made in 2 Chr 7:15
and their **p** came to his holy 2 Chr 30:27
of Manasseh, and his **p** to his God, 2 Chr 33:18
And his **p**, and how God was moved 2 Chr 33:19
to hear the **p** of your servant that I now Neh 1:6
ear be attentive to the **p** of your servant, Neh 1:11
and to the **p** of your servants who Neh 1:11
violence in my hands, and my **p** is pure. Jb 16:17
You will make your **p** to him, and he Jb 22:27
for I will accept his **p** not to deal with you Jb 42:8
told them, and the LORD accepted Job's **p**. Jb 42:9
distress. Be gracious to me and hear my **p**! Ps 4:1
has heard my plea; the LORD accepts my **p**. Ps 6:9
A **P** of David. Ps 17:T
Give ear to my **p** from lips free of deceit! Ps 17:1
everyone who is godly offer **p** to you at a Ps 32:6
"Hear my **p**, O LORD, and give ear to my Ps 39:12
song is with me, a **p** to the God of my life. Ps 42:8
O God, hear my **p**; give ear to the words of Ps 54:2
Give ear to my **p**, O God, and hide not Ps 55:1
Hear my cry, O God, listen to my **p**; Ps 61:1
O you who hears **p**, to you shall all flesh Ps 65:2
he has attended to the voice of my **p**. Ps 66:19
has not rejected my **p** or removed his Ps 66:20
But as for me, my **p** is to you, O LORD. At Ps 69:13
May **p** be made for him continually, Ps 72:15
O LORD God of hosts, hear my **p**; give ear, Ps 84:8
A **P** of David. Ps 86:T
Give ear, O LORD, to my **p**; listen to my Ps 86:6
Let my **p** come before you; incline your Ps 88:2
in the morning my **p** comes before you. Ps 88:13
A **P** of Moses, the man of God. Ps 90:T
A **P** of one afflicted, when he is faint Ps 102:T
Hear my **p**, O LORD; let my cry come to Ps 102:1
he regards the **p** of the destitute and Ps 102:17
destitute and does not despise their **p**. Ps 102:17
they accuse me, but I give myself to **p**. Ps 109:4
forth guilty; let his **p** be counted as sin! Ps 109:7
Let my **p** be counted as incense before Ps 141:2
Yet my **p** is continually against their Ps 141:5
of David, when he was in the cave. A **P**. Ps 142:T
Hear my **p**, O LORD; give ear to my pleas Ps 143:1
but the **p** of the upright is acceptable to Prv 15:8
but he hears the **p** of the righteous. Prv 15:29
the law, even his **p** is an abomination. Prv 28:9
out a whispered **p** when your discipline Is 26:16
therefore lift up your **p** for the remnant Is 37:4
of David your father: I have heard your **p**; Is 38:5
and make them joyful in my house of **p**; Is 56:7
be called a house of **p** for all peoples." Is 56:7
this people, or lift up a cry or **p** for them, Jer 7:16
or lift up a cry or **p** on their behalf, Jer 11:14
call and cry for help, he shuts out my **p**; Lam 3:8
a cloud so that no **p** can pass through. Lam 3:44
seeking him by **p** and pleas for mercy Dn 9:3
listen to the **p** of your servant and to his Dn 9:17
while I was speaking in **p**, the man Dn 9:21
the LORD, and my **p** came to you, Jon 2:7
A **p** of Habakkuk the prophet, Hab 3:1
'My house shall be called a house of **p**,' Mt 21:13
And whatever you ask in **p**, you will Mt 21:22
be driven out by anything but **p**." Mk 9:29
called a house of **p** for all the nations'? Mk 11:17
I tell you, whatever you ask in **p**, Mk 11:24
Zechariah, for your **p** has been heard, Lk 1:13
with fasting and **p** night and day. Lk 2:37
and all night he continued in **p** to God. Lk 6:12
'My house shall be a house of **p**,' Lk 19:46
And when he rose from **p**, he came to Lk 22:45
accord were devoting themselves to **p**, Acts 1:14
going up to the temple at the hour of **p**, Acts 3:1
will devote ourselves to **p** and to the Acts 6:4
your **p** has been heard and your alms Acts 10:31
but earnest **p** for him was made to God Acts 12:5
with **p** and fasting they committed Acts 14:23
we supposed there was a place of **p**, Acts 16:13
As we were going to the place of **p**, we Acts 16:16
my heart's desire and **p** to God for Rom 10:1
in tribulation, be constant in **p**. Rom 12:12
that you may devote yourselves to **p**; 1 Cor 7:5
You also must help us by **p**, so that 2 Cor 1:11
the Spirit, with all **p** and supplication. Eph 6:18
always in every **p** of mine for you all Phil 1:4
mine for you all making my **p** with joy, Phil 1:4
And it is my **p** that your love may Phil 1:9
in everything by **p** and supplication Phil 4:6
Continue steadfastly in **p**, being Col 4:2
is made holy by the word of God and **p**. 1 Tm 4:5
And the **p** of faith will save the one who Jas 5:15
The **p** of a righteous person has great Jas 5:16
and his ears are open to their **p**. 1 Pt 3:12

PRAYERS (26)

The **p** of David, the son of Jesse, are Ps 72:20
will you be angry with your people's **p**? Ps 80:4
even though you make many **p**, I will not Is 1:15
houses and for a pretense make long **p**. Mk 12:40
disciples of John fast often and offer **p**, Lk 5:33
houses and for a pretense make long **p**. Lk 20:47
to the breaking of bread and the **p**. Acts 2:42
"Your **p** and your alms have ascended Acts 10:4
always in my **p**, asking that somehow Rom 1:10
with me in your **p** to God on my Rom 15:30
granted us through the **p** of many. 2 Cor 1:11
for you, remembering you in my **p**, Eph 1:16
know that through your **p** and the help Phil 1:19
struggling on your behalf in his **p**, Col 4:12
constantly mentioning you in our **p**, 1 Thes 1:2
that supplications, **p**, intercessions, 1 Tm 2:1
in supplications and **p** night and day, 1 Tm 5:5
you constantly in my **p** night and day. 2 Tm 1:3
always when I remember you in my **p**, Phlm 1:4
hoping that through your **p** I will be Phlm 1:22
Jesus offered up **p** and supplications, Heb 5:7
life, so that your **p** may not be hindered. 1 Pt 3:7
and sober-minded for the sake of your **p**. 1 Pt 4:7
of incense, which are the **p** of the saints. Rv 5:8
incense to offer with the **p** of all the saints Rv 8:3
of the incense, with the **p** of the saints, Rv 8:4

PRAYING (22)

As she continued **p** before the LORD, 1 Sm 1:12
here in your presence, **p** to the LORD. 1 Sm 1:26
I continued fasting and **p** before the God Neh 1:4
and keep on **p** to a god that cannot save. Is 45:20
While I was speaking and **p**, confessing Dn 9:20
And whenever you stand **p**, forgive, if Mk 11:25
of the people were **p** outside at the hour Lk 1:10
Jesus also had been baptized and was **p**, Lk 3:21
Now it happened that as he was **p** alone, Lk 9:18
And as he was **p**, the appearance of his Lk 9:29
Now Jesus was **p** in a certain place, and Lk 11:1
p that you may have strength to escape Lk 21:36
I am **p** for them. I am not praying for the Jn 17:9
I am not **p** for the world but for those Jn 17:9
Tarsus named Saul, for behold, he is **p**, Acts 9:11
I was **p** in my house at the ninth Acts 10:30

"I was in the city of Joppa **p**, and in a — Acts 11:5
were gathered together and were **p**. — Acts 12:12
Then after fasting and **p** they laid their — Acts 13:3
and Silas were **p** and singing hymns — Acts 16:25
to Jerusalem and was **p** in the temple, — Acts 22:17
p at all times in the Spirit, with all — Eph 6:18

PRAYS (9)
that your servant **p** before you this — 1 Kgs 8:28
he comes and **p** toward this house, — 1 Kgs 8:42
that your servant **p** before you, — 2 Chr 6:19
he comes and **p** toward this house, — 2 Chr 6:32
then man **p** to God, and he accepts him; — Jb 33:26
He **p** to it and says, "Deliver me, for you — Is 44:17
Every man who **p** or prophesies with — 1 Cor 11:4
every wife who **p** or prophesies with — 1 Cor 11:5
my spirit **p** but my mind is — 1 Cor 14:14

PREACH (35)
p against the south, and prophesy — Ezk 20:46
toward Jerusalem and **p** against the — Ezk 21:2
and do not **p** against the house of Isaac.' — Am 7:16
"Do not **p**"—thus they preach—"one — Mi 2:6
preach"—thus they **p**—"one should not — Mi 2:6
"one should not **p** of such things; — Mi 2:6
"I will **p** to you of wine and strong — Mi 2:11
From that time Jesus began to **p**, saying, — Mt 4:17
from there to teach and **p** in their cities. — Mt 11:1
they do. For they **p**, but do not practice. — Mt 23:3
the next towns, that I may **p** there also, — Mk 1:38
him and he might send them out to **p** — Mk 3:14
"I must **p** the good news of the kingdom — Lk 4:43
he commanded us to **p** to the people — Acts 10:42
there they continued to **p** the gospel. — Acts 14:7
had called us to **p** the gospel to them. — Acts 16:10
So I am eager to **p** the gospel to you — Rom 1:15
While you **p** against stealing, — Rom 2:21
how are they to **p** unless they are — Rom 10:15
feet of those who **p** the good news!" — Rom 10:15
make it my ambition to **p** the gospel, — Rom 15:20
send me to baptize but to **p** the gospel, — 1 Cor 1:17
folly of what we **p** to save those who — 1 Cor 1:21
but we **p** Christ crucified, a — 1 Cor 1:23
For if I **p** the gospel, that gives me no — 1 Cor 9:16
me. Woe to me if I do not **p** the gospel! — 1 Cor 9:16
or they, so we **p** and so you believed. — 1 Cor 15:11
came to Troas to **p** the gospel of — 2 Cor 2:12
so that we may **p** the gospel in lands — 2 Cor 10:16
angel from heaven should **p** to you a — Gal 1:8
order that I might **p** him among the — Gal 1:16
But if I, brothers, still **p** circumcision, — Gal 5:11
to **p** to the Gentiles the unsearchable — Eph 3:8
Some indeed **p** Christ from envy and — Phil 1:15
p the word; be ready in season and out — 2 Tm 4:2

PREACHED (22)
and the poor have good news **p** to them. — Mt 11:5
And he **p**, saying, "After me comes he — Mk 1:7
And they went out and **p** everywhere, — Mk 16:20
other exhortations he **p** good news to — Lk 3:18
up, the poor have good news **p** to them. — Lk 7:22
good news of the kingdom of God is **p**, — Lk 16:16
Philip as he **p** good news about — Acts 8:12
he passed through he **p** the gospel to all — Acts 8:40
at Damascus he had **p** boldly in the — Acts 9:27
When they had **p** the gospel to that — Acts 14:21
you, brothers, of the gospel I **p** to you, — 1 Cor 15:1
fast to the word I **p** to you—unless — 1 Cor 15:2
because I **p** God's gospel to you free of — 2 Cor 11:7
a gospel contrary to the one we **p** to you, — Gal 1:8
that the gospel that was **p** by me is not — Gal 1:11
p the gospel beforehand to Abraham, — Gal 3:8
bodily ailment that I **p** the gospel to you — Gal 4:13
And he came and **p** peace to you who — Eph 2:17
offspring of David, as **p** in my gospel, — 2 Tm 2:8
through those who **p** the good news — 1 Pt 1:12
is the good news that was **p** to you. — 1 Pt 1:25
why the gospel was **p** even to those who — 1 Pt 4:6

PREACHER (11)
The words of the **P**, the son of David, — Eccl 1:1
Vanity of vanities, says the **P**, vanity of — Eccl 1:2
I the **P** have been king over Israel in — Eccl 1:12
Behold, this is what I found, says the **P**, — Eccl 7:27
Vanity of vanities, says the **P**; all is — Eccl 12:8
the **P** also taught the people — Eccl 12:9
The **P** sought to find words of delight, — Eccl 12:10
drink," he would be the **p** for this people! — Mi 2:11
seems to be a **p** of foreign divinities"— — Acts 17:18
I was appointed a **p** and an apostle (I — 1 Tm 2:7
I was appointed a **p** and apostle and — 2 Tm 1:11

PREACHING (27)
John the Baptist came **p** in the wilderness — Mt 3:1
it, for they repented at the **p** of Jonah, — Mt 12:41
p in their synagogues and casting out — Mk 1:39
the door. And he was **p** the word to them. — Mk 2:2
And he was **p** in the synagogues of — Lk 4:44
p the gospel and healing everywhere. — Lk 9:6
it, for they repented at the **p** of Jonah, — Lk 11:32
the people in the temple and **p** the gospel, — Lk 20:1
not cease teaching and **p** Jesus as the — Acts 5:42
we should give up **p** the word of God — Acts 6:2
were scattered went about **p** the word. — Acts 8:4
p the gospel to many villages of the — Acts 8:25
p boldly in the name of the Lord. — Acts 9:28
p good news of peace through Jesus — Acts 10:36
to the Hellenists also, **p** the Lord Jesus. — Acts 11:20
teaching and **p** the word of the Lord, — Acts 15:35
—because he was **p** Jesus and the — Acts 17:18
are they to hear without someone **p**? — Rom 10:14
my gospel and the **p** of Jesus Christ, — Rom 16:25
That in my **p** I may present the gospel — 1 Cor 9:18
lest after **p** to others I myself should — 1 Cor 9:27
then our **p** is in vain and your faith — 1 Cor 15:14
the churches for his **p** of the gospel. — 2 Cor 8:18
If anyone is **p** to you a gospel contrary to — Gal 1:9
persecute us is now **p** the faith he once — Gal 1:23
those who labor in **p** and teaching. — 1 Tm 5:17
his word through the **p** with which I have — Ti 1:3

PRECEDE (1)
will not **p** those who have fallen — 1 Thes 4:15

PRECEDED (1)
The prophets who **p** you and me from — Jer 28:8

PRECEPT (8)
For it is **p** upon precept, precept upon — Is 28:10
For it is precept upon **p**, precept upon — Is 28:10
is precept upon precept, **p** upon precept, — Is 28:10
is precept upon precept, precept upon **p**, — Is 28:10
the LORD will be to them **p** upon precept, — Is 28:13
the LORD will be to them precept upon **p**, — Is 28:13
precept upon precept, **p** upon precept, — Is 28:13
precept upon precept, precept upon **p**, — Is 28:13

PRECEPTS (27)
the **p** of the LORD are right, rejoicing the — Ps 19:8
and just; all his **p** are trustworthy; — Ps 111:7
have commanded your **p** to be kept — Ps 119:4
will meditate on your **p** and fix my — Ps 119:15
me understand the way of your **p**, — Ps 119:27
Behold, I long for your **p**; in your — Ps 119:40
a wide place, for I have sought your **p**. — Ps 119:45
fallen to me, that I have kept your **p**. — Ps 119:56
fear you, of those who keep your **p**. — Ps 119:63
but with my whole heart I keep your **p**; — Ps 119:69
as for me, I will meditate on your **p**. — Ps 119:78
earth, but I have not forsaken your **p**. — Ps 119:87
I will never forget your **p**, for by them — Ps 119:93
save me, for I have sought your **p**. — Ps 119:94
more than the aged, for I keep your **p**. — Ps 119:100
Through your **p** I get understanding; — Ps 119:104
me, but I do not stray from your **p**. — Ps 119:110
I consider all your **p** to be right; — Ps 119:128
oppression, that I may keep your **p**. — Ps 119:134
despised, yet I do not forget your **p**. — Ps 119:141
Consider how I love your **p**! Give me — Ps 119:159
I keep your **p** and testimonies, for all — Ps 119:168
to help me, for I have chosen your **p**. — Ps 119:173
for I give you good **p**; do not forsake my — Prv 4:2
and kept all his **p** and done all that — Jer 35:18
uncircumcised keeps the **p** of the law, — Rom 2:26
according to human **p** and teachings? — Col 2:22

PRECINCTS (1)
chamberlain, which was in the **p**. — 2 Kgs 23:11

PRECIOUS (69)
because my life was **p** in your eyes — 1 Sm 26:21
as your life was **p** this day in my — 1 Sm 26:24
so may my life be **p** in the sight of — 1 Sm 26:24
talent of gold, and in it was a **p** stone, — 2 Sm 12:30
and very much gold and **p** stones. — 1 Kgs 10:2
great quantity of spices and **p** stones. — 1 Kgs 10:10
of almug wood and **p** stones. — 1 Kgs 10:11
servants of yours, be **p** in your sight. — 2 Kgs 1:13
now let my life be **p** in your sight." — 2 Kgs 1:14
silver, the gold, the spices, the **p** oil, — 2 Kgs 20:13
talent of gold, and in it was a **p** stone. — 1 Chr 20:2
all sorts of **p** stones and marble. — 1 Chr 29:2
And whoever had **p** stones gave them — 1 Chr 29:8
the house with settings of **p** stones. — 2 Chr 3:6
and very much gold and **p** stones. — 2 Chr 9:1
great quantity of spices, and **p** stones. — 2 Chr 9:9
brought algum wood and **p** stones. — 2 Chr 9:10
goods, clothing, and **p** things, — 2 Chr 20:25
to Jerusalem and **p** things to — 2 Chr 32:23
for silver, for gold, for **p** stones, — 2 Chr 32:27
with the **p** vessels of the house of the — 2 Chr 36:10
fire and destroyed all its **p** vessels. — 2 Chr 36:19
of fine bright bronze as **p** as gold. — Ezr 8:27
marble, mother-of-pearl and **p** stones. — Est 1:6
will be your gold and your **p** silver. — Jb 22:25
the rocks, and his eye sees every **p** thing. — Jb 28:10
the gold of Ophir, in **p** onyx or sapphire. — Jb 28:16
my **p** life from the power of the dog! — Ps 22:20
destruction, my **p** life from the lions! — Ps 35:17
How **p** is your steadfast love, O God! The — Ps 36:7
life, and **p** is their blood in his sight. — Ps 72:14
P in the sight of the LORD is the death — Ps 116:15
It is like the **p** oil on the head, running — Ps 133:2
How **p** to me are your thoughts, O — Ps 139:17
we shall find all **p** goods, we shall fill — Prv 1:13
She is more **p** than jewels, and nothing — Prv 3:15
a married woman hunts down a **p** life. — Prv 6:26
but the diligent man will get **p** wealth. — Prv 12:27
but the lips of knowledge are a **p** jewel. — Prv 20:15
P treasure and oil are in a wise man's — Prv 21:20
are filled with all **p** and pleasant riches. — Prv 24:4
find? She is far more **p** than jewels. — Prv 31:10
A good name is better than **p** ointment, — Eccl 7:1
a stone, a tested stone, a **p** cornerstone, — Is 28:16
the silver, the gold, the spices, the **p** oil, — Is 39:2
Because you are **p** in my eyes, and — Is 43:4
and all your wall of **p** stones. — Is 54:12
If you utter what is **p**, and not what is — Jer 15:19
wandering all the **p** things that were — Lam 1:7
out his hands over all her **p** things; — Lam 1:10
The **p** sons of Zion, worth their weight — Lam 4:2
they have taken treasure and **p** things; — Ezk 22:25
of spices and all **p** stones and gold. — Ezk 27:22
every **p** stone was your covering, — Ezk 28:13
images and their **p** vessels of silver — Dn 11:8
silver, with **p** stones and costly gifts. — Dn 11:38
of silver, and all the **p** things of Egypt, — Dn 11:43
shall possess their **p** things of silver; — Hos 9:6
strip his treasury of every **p** thing. — Hos 13:15
treasure or of the wealth of all **p** things. — Na 2:9
life of any value nor as **p** to myself, — Acts 20:24
foundation with gold, silver, **p** stones, — 1 Cor 3:12
farmer waits for the **p** fruit of the earth, — Jas 5:7
your faith—more **p** than gold that — 1 Pt 1:7
but with the **p** blood of Christ, like that — 1 Pt 1:19
but in the sight of God chosen and **p**, — 1 Pt 2:4
a stone, a cornerstone chosen and **p**, — 1 Pt 2:6
spirit, which in God's sight is very **p**. — 1 Pt 3:4
granted to us his **p** and very great — 2 Pt 1:4

PRECISELY (2)
P because they have misled my — Ezk 13:10
P because they made you desolate and — Ezk 36:3

PREDESTINED (5)
and your plan had **p** to take place. — Acts 4:28
he foreknew he also **p** to be conformed — Rom 8:29
And those whom he **p** he also called, — Rom 8:30
he **p** us for adoption through Jesus — Eph 1:5
having been **p** according to the — Eph 1:11

PREDICTED (4)
proclaimed, who had **p** these things. — 2 Kgs 23:16
from Judah and **p** these things that — 2 Kgs 23:17
And as Isaiah **p**, "If the Lord of hosts — Rom 9:29
indicating when he **p** the sufferings of — 1 Pt 1:11

PREDICTIONS (2)
you should remember the **p** of the holy — 2 Pt 3:2
the **p** of the apostles of our Lord Jesus — Jude 1:17

PREEMINENCE (2)
Unstable as water, you shall not have **p**, — Gn 49:4
neither shall there be **p** among them. — Ezk 7:11

PREEMINENT (3)
p in dignity and preeminent in power. — Gn 49:3
preeminent in dignity and **p** in power. — Gn 49:3
dead, that in everything he might be **p**. — Col 1:18

PREFECT (1)
of Babylon and chief **p** over all the wise — Dn 2:48

PREFECTS (4)
sent to gather the satraps, the **p**, — Dn 3:2
Then the satraps, the **p**, and the — Dn 3:3
And the satraps, the **p**, the governors, — Dn 3:27
of the kingdom, the **p** and the satraps, — Dn 6:7

PREFER (1)
yet for love's sake I **p** to appeal to you— — Phlm 1:9

PREFERENCE (1)
loved as the firstborn in **p** to the son of — Dt 21:16

PREFERRED (2)
Death shall be **p** to life by all the remnant — Jer 8:3
but I **p** to do nothing without your — Phlm 1:14

PREGNANCY (1)
fly away like a bird—no birth, no **p**, — Hos 9:11

PREGNANT (20)
you are **p** and shall bear a son. — Gn 16:11
of Lot became **p** by their father. — Gn 19:36
she is **p** by immorality." And Judah — Gn 38:24
these belong, I am **p**." And she said, — Gn 38:25
men strive together and hit a **p** woman, — Ex 21:22

the wife of Phinehas, was **p**, 1 Sm 4:19
and she sent and told David, "I am **p**." 2 Sm 11:5
ones and rip open their **p** women." 2 Kgs 8:12
open all the women in it who were **p**. 2 Kgs 15:16
conceives evil and is **p** with mischief and Ps 7:14
Like a **p** woman who writhes and cries Is 26:17
we were **p**, we writhed, but we have given Is 26:18
the **p** woman and she who is in labor, Jer 31:8
pieces, and their **p** women ripped open. Hos 13:16
have ripped open **p** women in Gilead, Am 1:13
for women who are **p** and for those who Mt 24:19
for women who are **p** and for those Mk 13:17
for women who are **p** and for those who Lk 21:23
labor pains come upon a **p** woman, 1 Thes 5:3
She was **p** and was crying out in birth Rv 12:2

PREJUDGING (1)
you to keep these rules without **p**, 1 Tm 5:21

PREPARATION (8)
their brothers had made **p** for them. 1 Chr 12:39
I will therefore make **p** for it." So 1 Chr 22:5
Next day, that is, after the day of **P**, the Mt 27:62
had come, since it was the day of **P**, Mk 15:42
It was the day of **P**, and the Sabbath Lk 23:54
Now it was the day of **P** of the Passover. Jn 19:14
Since it was the day of **P**, and so that the Jn 19:31
So because of the Jewish day of **P**, since Jn 19:42

PREPARATIONS (3)
our God, and I made **p** for building. 1 Chr 28:2
of the Samaritans, to make **p** for him. Lk 9:52
These **p** having thus been made, the Heb 9:6

PREPARE (65)
and **p** for me delicious food, such as I Gn 27:4
'Bring me game and **p** for me delicious Gn 27:7
so that I may **p** from them delicious Gn 27:9
day, when they **p** what they bring in, Ex 16:5
and **p** for me here seven bulls and Nm 23:1
here seven altars and **p** for me here Nm 23:29
the people, '**P** your provisions, Jos 1:11
let us detain you and **p** a young goat for Jgs 13:15
your food. But if you **p** a burnt offering, Jgs 13:16
take and **p** a new cart and two milk 1 Sm 6:7
flock or herd to **p** for the guest who 2 Sm 12:4
to eat, and **p** the food in my sight, 2 Sm 13:5
Amnon's house and **p** food for him." 2 Sm 13:7
I may go in and **p** it for myself and 1 Kgs 17:12
And I will **p** the other bull and lay it 1 Kgs 18:23
for yourselves one bull and **p** it first, 1 Kgs 18:25
Ahab, '**P** your chariot and go down, 1 Kgs 18:44
the showbread, to **p** it every Sabbath. 1 Chr 9:32
set stonecutters to **p** dressed stones for 1 Chr 22:2
to **p** timber for me in abundance, for 2 Chr 2:9
commanded them to **p** chambers in 2 Chr 31:11
P yourselves according to your 2 Chr 35:4
yourselves, and **p** for your brothers, 2 Chr 35:6
come to the feast that I will **p** for them, Est 5:8
"If you **p** your heart, you will stretch out Jb 11:13
in the morning I **p** a sacrifice for you and Ps 5:3
You **p** a table before me in the presence Ps 23:5
P your work outside; get everything Prv 24:27
P slaughter for his sons because of the Is 14:21
They **p** the table, they spread the rugs, Is 21:5
"In the wilderness **p** the way of the LORD; Is 40:3
be said, "Build up, build up, **p** the way, Is 57:14
the gates; **p** the way for the people; Is 62:10
"**P** war against her; arise, and let us attack Jer 6:4
I will **p** destroyers against you, each with Jer 22:7
"**P** buckler and shield, and advance for Jer 46:3
P yourselves baggage for exile, O Jer 46:19
set up watchmen; **p** the ambushes; Jer 51:12
p the nations for war against her; Jer 51:27
P the nations for war against her, the Jer 51:28
are inflamed I will **p** them a feast and Jer 51:39
on which you may **p** your bread." Ezk 4:15
man, **p** for yourself an exile's baggage, Ezk 12:3
the Lord GOD, I will **p** you for blood, Ezk 35:6
I will do this to you, **p** to meet your God, Am 4:12
messenger and he will **p** the way before Mal 3:1
in the wilderness: '**P** the way of the Lord; Mt 3:3
face, who will **p** your way before you.' Mt 11:10
body, she has done it to **p** me for burial. Mt 26:12
will you have us **p** for you to eat Mt 26:17
before your face, who will **p** your way, Mk 1:2
'**P** the way of the Lord, make his paths Mk 1:3
you have us go and **p** for you to eat the Mk 14:12
furnished and ready; there **p** for us." Mk 14:15
you will go before the Lord to **p** his ways, Lk 1:76
'**P** the way of the Lord, make his paths Lk 3:4
face, who will **p** your way before you.' Lk 7:27
not rather say to him, '**P** supper for me, Lk 17:8
saying, "Go and **p** the Passover for us, Lk 22:8
to him, "Where will you have us **p** it?" Lk 22:9
large upper room furnished; **p** it there." Lk 22:12
told you that I go to **p** a place for you? Jn 14:2
And if I go and **p** a place for you, I will Jn 14:3
the same time, **p** a guest room for me, Phlm 1:22
to **p** the way for the kings from the east. Rv 16:12

PREPARED (86)
it to a young man, who **p** it quickly. Gn 18:7
and milk and the calf that he had **p**, Gn 18:8
For I have **p** the house and a place for Gn 24:31
and his mother **p** delicious food, Gn 27:14
food and the bread, which she had **p**, Gn 27:17
He also **p** delicious food and brought it Gn 27:31
they **p** the present for Joseph's coming Gn 43:25
Then Joseph **p** his chariot and went up Gn 46:29
to eat, that alone may be **p** by you. Ex 12:16
nor had they **p** any provisions for Ex 12:39
to bring you to the place that I have **p**. Ex 23:20
the oven and all that is **p** on a pan or a Lv 7:9
into his house and **p** a young goat and Jgs 6:19
the woman, and Samson **p** a feast there, Jgs 14:10
early in the morning, and he **p** to go, Jgs 19:5
five sheep already **p** and five seahs 1 Sm 25:18
poor man's lamb and **p** it for the man 2 Sm 12:4
king." And he **p** for himself chariots 1 Kgs 1:5
did the cutting and **p** the timber and 1 Kgs 5:18
built, it was with stone **p** at the quarry, 1 Kgs 6:7
inner sanctuary he **p** in the 1 Kgs 6:19
and they **p** it and called upon the 1 Kgs 18:26
So he **p** for them a great feast, and 2 Kgs 6:23
the priests, **p** the mixing of the spices, 1 Chr 9:30
And he **p** a place for the ark of God 1 Chr 15:1
to its place, which he had **p** for it. 1 Chr 15:3
to the place that I have **p** for it. 1 Chr 15:12
to the place that David had **p** for it, 2 Chr 1:4
kinds of spices **p** by the perfumer's 2 Chr 16:14
And Uzziah **p** for all the army 2 Chr 26:14
because God had **p** for the people, 2 Chr 29:36
house of the LORD, and they **p** them. 2 Chr 31:11
When the service had been **p** for, 2 Chr 35:10
And afterward they **p** for themselves 2 Chr 35:14
so the Levites **p** for themselves and 2 Chr 35:14
brothers the Levites **p** for them. 2 Chr 35:15
service of the LORD was **p** that day, 2 Chr 35:16
this, when Josiah had **p** the temple, 2 Chr 35:20
Now what was **p** at my expense for Neh 5:18
p for Tobiah a large chamber where Neh 13:5
today to a feast that I have **p** for the king." Est 5:4
came to the feast that Esther had **p**. Est 5:5
me come with the king to the feast she **p**. Est 5:12
on the gallows that he had **p** for him. Est 6:4
Haman to the feast that Esther had **p**. Est 6:14
gallows that Haman has **p** for Mordecai, Est 7:9
the gallows that he had **p** for Mordecai. Est 7:10
Behold, I have **p** my case; I know that I Jb 13:18
the city, when I **p** my seat in the square, Jb 29:7
he has **p** for him his deadly weapons, Ps 7:13
provide their grain, for so you have **p** it. Ps 65:9
I have **p** a lamp for my anointed. Ps 132:17
For a burning place has long been **p**; Is 30:33
Say, 'Stand ready and be **p**, for the Jer 46:14
day that you were created they were **p**. Ezk 28:13
the LORD has **p** a sacrifice and Zep 1:7
And when this is **p**, they will set the Zec 5:11
for whom it has been **p** by my Father." Mt 20:23
nursing babies you have **p** praise'?" Mt 21:16
who are invited, See, I have **p** my dinner, Mt 22:4
inherit the kingdom **p** for you from the Mt 25:34
into the eternal fire **p** for the devil and Mt 25:41
directed them, and they **p** the Passover. Mt 26:19
it is for those for whom it has been **p**." Mk 10:40
told them, and they **p** the Passover. Mk 14:16
to make ready for the Lord a people **p**." Lk 1:17
that you have **p** in the presence of all Lk 2:31
of you, and the things you have **p**, Lk 12:20
had told them, and they **p** the Passover. Lk 22:13
they returned and **p** spices and Lk 23:56
the tomb, taking the spices they had **p**. Lk 24:1
vessels of wrath **p** for destruction, Rom 9:22
which he has **p** beforehand for glory— Rom 9:23
what God has **p** for those who love 1 Cor 2:9
He who has **p** us for this very thing is 2 Cor 5:5
good works, which God **p** beforehand, Eph 2:10
For a tent was **p**, the first section, in Heb 9:2
desired, but a body have you **p** for me; Heb 10:5
their God, for he has **p** for them a city. Heb 11:16
always being **p** to make a defense to 1 Pt 3:15
of Noah, while the ark was being **p**, 1 Pt 3:20
had the seven trumpets **p** to blow them. Rv 8:6
the locusts were like horses **p** for battle: Rv 9:7
angels, who had been **p** for the hour, Rv 9:15
where she has a place **p** by God, Rv 12:6
p as a bride adorned for her husband. Rv 21:2

PREPARES (3)
birth to evil, and their womb **p** deceit." Jb 15:35
with clouds; he **p** rain for the earth; Ps 147:8
she **p** her bread in summer and gathers Prv 6:8

PREPARING (6)
p for him a chamber in the courts of Neh 13:7
sacrificial feast that I am **p** for you, Ezk 39:17
sacrificial feast that I am **p** for you. Ezk 39:19
to eat, but while they were **p** it, Acts 10:10
momentary affliction is **p** for us an 2 Cor 4:17
Therefore, **p** your minds for action, 1 Pt 1:13

PRESCRIBED (14)
and for the lambs, in the **p** quantities; Nm 29:18
and for the lambs, in the **p** quantities; Nm 29:21
and for the lambs, in the **p** quantities; Nm 29:24
and for the lambs, in the **p** quantities; Nm 29:27
and for the lambs, in the **p** quantities; Nm 29:30
and for the lambs, in the **p** quantities; Nm 29:33
and for the lambs, in the **p** quantities; Nm 29:37
he made ten golden lampstands as **p**, 2 Chr 4:7
before the inner sanctuary, as **p**; 2 Chr 4:20
for they had not kept it as often as **p**. 2 Chr 30:5
ate the Passover otherwise than as **p**. 2 Chr 30:18
as **p** in the writing of David king of 2 Chr 35:4
Who has **p** for him his way, or who can Jb 36:23
and **p** limits for it and set bars and Jb 38:10

PRESCRIBING (1)
of oil, and salt without **p** how much. Ezr 7:22

PRESENCE (176)
hid themselves from the **p** of the LORD Gn 3:8
went away from the **p** of the LORD and Gn 4:16
Haran died in the **p** of his father Terah Gn 11:28
it to me in your **p** as property for a Gn 23:9
as a possession in the **p** of the Hittites, Gn 23:18
gone out from the **p** of Isaac his father, Gn 27:30
In the **p** of our kinsmen point out what Gn 31:32
went out from the **p** of Pharaoh and Gn 41:46
him, for they were dismayed at his **p**. Gn 45:3
and went out from the **p** of Pharaoh. Gn 47:10
they were driven out from Pharaoh's **p**. Ex 10:11
set the bread of the **P** on the table before Ex 25:30
And he said, "My **p** will go with you, Ex 33:14
to him, "If your **p** will not go with me, Ex 33:15
all its utensils, and the bread of the **P**; Ex 35:13
of Israel departed from the **p** of Moses. Ex 35:20
all its utensils, and the bread of the **P**; Ex 39:36
that person shall be cut off from my **p**: Lv 22:3
of the bread of the **P** they shall spread a Nm 4:7
Aaron went from the **p** of the assembly Nm 20:6
brought you out of Egypt with his own **p**, Dt 4:37
and be beaten in his **p** with a number of Dt 25:2
up to him in the **p** of the elders and pull Dt 25:9
And there, in the **p** of the people of Israel, Jos 8:32
the LORD in his **p** with our burnt Jos 22:27
all his attendants went out from his **p**. Jgs 3:19
'Buy it in the **p** of those sitting here and in Ru 4:4
sitting here and in the **p** of the elders of Ru 4:4
may appear in the **p** of the LORD and 1 Sm 1:22
who was standing here in your **p**, 1 Sm 1:26
to the LORD in the **p** of Eli the priest. 1 Sm 2:11
man Samuel grew in the **p** of the LORD. 1 Sm 2:21
in speech, and a man of good **p**, 1 Sm 16:18
him from his **p** and made him 1 Sm 18:13
to Saul, and he was in his **p** as before. 1 Sm 19:7
no bread there but the bread of the **P**, 1 Sm 21:6
to behave as a madman in my **p**? 1 Sm 21:15
earth away from the **p** of the LORD, 1 Sm 26:20
When Joab came out from David's **p**, 2 Sm 3:26
him, and he ate in his **p** and drank, 2 Sm 11:13
woman out of my **p** and bolt the 2 Sm 13:17
come into my **p**." So Absalom lived 2 Sm 14:24
and did not come into the king's **p**. 2 Sm 14:24
without coming into the king's **p**. 2 Sm 14:28
let me go into the **p** of the king, 2 Sm 14:32
went out from the **p** of the king to 2 Sm 24:4
into the king's **p** and stood before 1 Kgs 1:28
the golden table for the bread of the **P**, 1 Kgs 7:48
the LORD in the **p** of all the assembly 1 Kgs 8:22
earth sought the **p** of Solomon to 1 Kgs 10:24
Naboth in the **p** of the people, 1 Kgs 21:13
So he went out from his **p** a leper, 2 Kgs 5:27
had dispatched a man from his **p**, 2 Kgs 6:32
he cast them from his **p** until now. 2 Kgs 13:23
that he cast them out from his **p**. 2 Kgs 24:20
his strength; seek his **p** continually! 1 Chr 16:11
recorded them in the **p** of the king 1 Chr 24:6
of Aaron, in the **p** of King David, 1 Chr 24:31
the LORD in the **p** of all the assembly. 1 Chr 29:10
altar, the tables for the bread of the **P**, 2 Chr 4:19
the LORD in the **p** of all the assembly 2 Chr 6:12
his knees in the **p** of all the assembly 2 Chr 6:13
the earth sought the **p** of Solomon to 2 Chr 9:23
his forehead in the **p** of the priests in 2 Chr 26:19
has chosen you to stand in his **p**, 2 Chr 29:11
down the altars of the Baals in his **p**, 2 Chr 34:4
king. Now I had not been sad in his **p**. Neh 2:1
And he said in the **p** of his brothers and Neh 4:2
you to anger in the **p** of the builders. Neh 4:5

good deeds in my **p** and reported my Neh 6:19
in the **p** of the men and the women and Neh 8:3
who served in the **p** of King Ahasuerus, Est 1:10
Memucan said in the **p** of the king and Est 1:16
of the chronicles in the **p** of the king. Est 2:23
"Will he even assault the queen in my **p**, Est 7:8
went out from the **p** of the king in Est 8:15
So Satan went out from the **p** of the LORD. Jb 1:12
Satan went out from the **p** of the LORD and Jb 2:7
Their offspring are established in their **p**, Jb 21:8
Therefore I am terrified at his **p**; when I Jb 23:15
me, they have cast off restraint in my **p**. Jb 30:11
Its crashing declares his **p**; the cattle Jb 36:33
they stumble and perish before your **p**. Ps 9:3
of life; in your **p** there is fullness of joy; Ps 16:11
From your **p** let my vindication come! Ps 17:2
make him glad with the joy of your **p**. Ps 21:6
a table before me in the **p** of my enemies; Ps 23:5
the cover of your **p** you hide them from Ps 31:20
so long as the wicked are in my **p**." Ps 39:1
integrity, and set me in your **p** forever. Ps 41:12
Cast me not away from your **p**, and Ps 51:11
name, for it is good, in the **p** of the godly. Ps 52:9
you, our secret sins in the light of your **p**. Ps 90:8
us come into his **p** with thanksgiving; Ps 95:2
gladness! Come into his **p** with singing! Ps 100:2
his strength; seek his **p** continually! Ps 105:4
Tremble, O earth, at the **p** of the Lord, at Ps 114:7
of the Lord, at the **p** of the God of Jacob, Ps 114:7
to the LORD in the **p** of all his people. Ps 116:14
to the LORD in the **p** of all his people, Ps 116:18
Or where shall I flee from your **p**? Ps 139:7
the upright shall dwell in your **p**. Ps 140:13
Leave the **p** of a fool, for there you do Prv 14:7
up security in the **p** of his neighbor. Prv 17:18
away the wicked from the **p** of the king, Prv 25:5
forward in the king's **p** or stand in the Prv 25:6
than to be put lower in the **p** of a noble. Prv 25:7
Be not hasty to go from his **p**. Do not Eccl 8:3
in your very **p** foreigners devour your land; Is 1:7
against the LORD, defying his glorious **p**. Is 3:8
the idols of Egypt will tremble at his **p**, Is 19:1
and the angel of his **p** saved them; Is 63:9
the mountains might quake at your **p**— Is 64:1
that the nations might tremble at your **p**! Is 64:2
down, the mountains quaked at your **p**. Is 64:3
to it, to the **p** of the LORD in Jerusalem, Jer 3:17
remove your detestable things from my **p**, Jer 4:1
you up and cast you away from my **p**, Jer 23:39
in the **p** of the priests and all the people, Jer 28:1
the prophet in the **p** of the priests and Jer 28:5
Hananiah spoke in the **p** of all the Jer 28:11
in the **p** of Hanamel my cousin, Jer 32:12
in the **p** of the witnesses who signed the Jer 32:12
and in the **p** of all the Judeans who were Jer 32:12
I charged Baruch in their **p**, saying, Jer 32:13
a man in my **p** to offer burnt offerings, Jer 33:18
Judah that he cast them out from his **p**. Jer 52:3
like water before the **p** of the Lord! Lam 2:19
man justice in the **p** of the Most High, Lam 3:35
a god,' in the **p** of those who kill you, Ezk 28:9
face of the earth, shall quake at my **p**. Ezk 38:20
"Then from his **p** the hand was sent, Dn 5:24
to flee to Tarshish from the **p** of the LORD. Jon 1:3
to Tarshish, away from the **p** of the LORD. Jon 1:3
he was fleeing from the **p** of the LORD, Jon 1:10
house of God and ate the bread of the **P**, Mt 12:4
high priest, and ate the bread of the **P**, Mk 2:26
am Gabriel, who stands in the **p** of God, Lk 1:19
you have prepared in the **p** of all peoples, Lk 2:31
God and took and ate the bread of the **P**, Lk 6:4
him declared in the **p** of all the people Lk 8:47
to say, 'We ate and drank in your **p**, Lk 13:26
will be honored in the **p** of all who sit at Lk 14:10
were not able in the **p** of the people to Lk 20:26
me in your own **p** with the glory that Jn 17:5
other signs in the **p** of the disciples, Jn 20:30
make me full of gladness with your **p**.' Acts 2:28
over and denied in the **p** of Pilate, Acts 3:13
this perfect health in the **p** of you all. Acts 3:16
may come from the **p** of the Lord, Acts 3:20
Then they left the **p** of the council, Acts 5:41
are all here in the **p** of God to hear all Acts 10:33
thanks to God in the **p** of all he broke Acts 27:35
many nations"—in the **p** of the God in Rom 4:17
being might boast in the **p** of God. 1 Cor 1:29
been for your sake in the **p** of Christ, 2 Cor 2:10
and bring us with you into his **p**. 2 Cor 4:14
and strong, but his bodily **p** is weak, 2 Cor 10:10
not only as in my **p** but much more in Phil 2:12
away from the **p** of the Lord and from 2 Thes 1:9
in sin, rebuke them in the **p** of all, 1 Tm 5:20
In the **p** of God and of Christ Jesus 1 Tm 5:21
confession in the **p** of many 1 Tm 6:12
I charge you in the **p** of God, who 1 Tm 6:13
from me in the **p** of many witnesses 2 Tm 2:2
I charge you in the **p** of God and of 2 Tm 4:1
and the table and the bread of the **P**. Heb 9:2
now to appear in the **p** of God on our Heb 9:24
you blameless before the **p** of his glory Jude 1:24
the throne will shelter them with his **p**. Rv 7:15
the authority of the first beast in its **p**, Rv 13:12
allowed to work in the **p** of the beast it Rv 13:14
and sulfur in the **p** of the holy angels Rv 14:10
holy angels and in the **p** of the Lamb. Rv 14:10
prophet who in its **p** had done the signs Rv 19:20
From his **p** earth and sky fled away, Rv 20:11

PRESENT (129)

him he took a **p** for his brother Esau, Gn 32:13
They are a **p** sent to my lord Esau. Gn 32:18
appease him with the **p** that goes ahead Gn 32:20
So the **p** passed on ahead of him, and Gn 32:21
sight, then accept my **p** from my hand. Gn 33:10
bags, and carry a **p** down to the man, Gn 43:11
So the men took this **p**, and they took Gn 43:15
they prepared the **p** for Joseph's coming Gn 43:25
house to him the **p** that they had with Gn 43:26
the morning and **p** yourself to Pharaoh, Ex 8:20
the morning and **p** yourself before Ex 9:13
and **p** yourself there to me on the top of Ex 34:2
And Aaron shall **p** the goat on which the Lv 16:9
"Aaron shall **p** the bull as a sin offering Lv 16:11
and the altar, he shall **p** the live goat. Lv 16:20
You may **p** a bull or a lamb that has a Lv 22:23
But you shall **p** a food offering to the Lv 23:8
Then you shall **p** a grain offering of Lv 23:16
And you shall **p** with the bread seven Lv 23:18
and you shall **p** a food offering to the Lv 23:25
afflict yourselves and **p** a food offering Lv 23:27
seven days you shall **p** food offerings to Lv 23:36
holy convocation and **p** a food offering Lv 23:36
you shall **p** a contribution to the Nm 15:19
of your dough you shall **p** a loaf as a Nm 15:20
the threshing floor, so shall you **p** it. Nm 15:20
And Moses said to Korah, "Be **p**, you Nm 16:16
that the people of Israel **p** to the LORD I Nm 18:19
which they **p** as a contribution to the Nm 18:24
then you shall **p** a contribution from Nm 18:26
So you shall also **p** a contribution to Nm 18:28
you shall **p** every contribution due to Nm 18:29
tithes and the contribution that you **p**, Dt 12:6
tithes and the contribution that you **p**, Dt 12:11
or the contribution that you **p**, Dt 12:17
Call Joshua and **p** yourselves in the tent Dt 31:14
you and bring out my **p** and set it before Jgs 6:18
and there is no **p** to bring to the man of 1 Sm 9:7
Now therefore **p** yourselves before 1 Sm 10:19
despised him and brought him no **p**. 1 Sm 10:27
the people who were **p** with him, 1 Sm 13:15
people who were **p** with them stayed 1 Sm 13:16
And now let this **p** that your servant 1 Sm 25:27
"Here is a **p** for you from the spoil of 1 Sm 30:26
there followed him a **p** from the king. 2 Sm 11:8
Every one of them brought his **p**, 1 Kgs 10:25
sending to you a **p** of silver and gold. 1 Kgs 15:19
so accept now a **p** from your servant." 2 Kgs 5:15
"Take a **p** with you and go to meet the 2 Kgs 8:8
to meet him, and took a **p** with him, 2 Kgs 8:9
house and sent a **p** to the king of 2 Kgs 16:8
with letters and a **p** to Hezekiah, 2 Kgs 20:12
seen your people, who are **p** here, 1 Chr 29:17
priests who were **p** had consecrated 2 Chr 5:11
Every one of them brought his **p**, 2 Chr 9:24
in addition to our **p** sins and guilt. 2 Chr 28:13
and all who were **p** with him bowed 2 Chr 29:29
Israel who were **p** at Jerusalem kept 2 Chr 30:21
all Israel who were **p** went out to the 2 Chr 31:1
all who were **p** in Jerusalem and 2 Chr 34:32
made all who were **p** in Israel serve 2 Chr 34:33
Passover offerings for all who were **p**, 2 Chr 35:7
Israel who were **p** kept the Passover 2 Chr 35:17
and all Judah and Israel who were **p**, 2 Chr 35:18
lords and all Israel there **p** had offered. Ezr 8:25
the king gave for all the people **p** in Susa, Est 1:5
of God came to **p** themselves before the Jb 1:6
of God came to **p** themselves before the Jb 2:1
came among them to **p** himself before the Jb 2:1
and strength, a very **p** help in trouble. Ps 46:1
envoys with letters and a **p** to Hezekiah, Is 39:1
Declare and **p** your case; let them take Is 45:21
gave him an allowance of food and a **p**, Jer 40:5
offerings and incense to **p** at the temple Jer 41:5
you sent me to **p** your plea for mercy Jer 42:9
When you **p** your gifts and offer up Ezk 20:31
You shall **p** them before the LORD, and Ezk 43:24
For we do not **p** our pleas before you Dn 9:18
time he does not **p** himself at the Hos 13:13
the prophets who were **p** on the day that Zec 8:9
Egypt does not go up and **p** themselves, Zec 14:18
P that to your governor; will he accept Mal 1:8
up to Jerusalem to **p** him to the Lord Lk 2:22
not know how to interpret the **p** time? Lk 12:56
There were some **p** at that very time who Lk 13:1
So in the **p** case I tell you, keep away Acts 5:38
us to James, and all the elders were **p**. Acts 21:18
alms to my nation and to **p** offerings. Acts 24:17
alarmed and said, "Go away for the **p**. Acts 24:25
Agrippa and all who are **p** with us, Acts 25:24
show his righteousness at the **p** time, Rom 3:26
Do not **p** your members to sin as Rom 6:13
but **p** yourselves to God as those who Rom 6:13
that if you **p** yourselves to anyone Rom 6:16
so now **p** your members as slaves to Rom 6:19
the sufferings of this **p** time are not Rom 8:18
nor things **p** nor things to come, Rom 8:38
So too at the **p** time there is a remnant, Rom 11:5
to **p** your bodies as a living sacrifice, Rom 12:1
At **p**, however, I am going to Rom 15:25
life or death or the **p** or the future— 1 Cor 3:22
To the **p** hour we hunger and thirst, 1 Cor 4:11
absent in body, I am **p** in spirit; 1 Cor 5:3
and as if **p**, I have already pronounced 1 Cor 5:3
of the Lord Jesus and my spirit is **p**, 1 Cor 5:4
that in view of the **p** distress it is good 1 Cor 7:26
For the **p** form of this world is 1 Cor 7:31
my preaching I may **p** the gospel free 1 Cor 9:18
abundance at the **p** time should 2 Cor 8:14
you that when I am **p** I may not have 2 Cor 10:2
by letter when absent, we do when **p**. 2 Cor 10:11
to **p** you as a pure virgin to Christ. 2 Cor 11:2
as I did when **p** on my second visit, 2 Cor 13:2
our sins to deliver us from the **p** evil age, Gal 1:4
and not only when I am **p** with you, Gal 4:18
I wish I could be **p** with you now and Gal 4:20
she corresponds to the **p** Jerusalem, for Gal 4:25
so that he might **p** the church to Eph 5:27
cosmic powers over this **p** darkness, Eph 6:12
in order to **p** you holy and blameless Col 1:22
that we may **p** everyone mature in Col 1:28
holds promise for the **p** life and also for 1 Tm 4:8
As for the rich in this **p** age, charge 1 Tm 6:17
Do your best to **p** yourself to God as 2 Tm 2:15
For Demas, in love with this **p** world, 2 Tm 4:10
upright, and godly lives in the **p** age, Ti 2:12
he left nothing outside his control. At **p**, Heb 2:8
(which is symbolic for the **p** age). Heb 9:9
stumbling and to **p** you blameless Jude 1:24

PRESENTABLE (1)

which our more **p** parts do not 1 Cor 12:24

PRESENTED (27)

He **p** himself to him and fell on his Gn 46:29
took five men and **p** them to Pharaoh. Gn 47:2
to the LORD, and when it is **p** to the priest, Lv 2:8
the day they were **p** to serve as priests Lv 7:35
Then he **p** the ram of the burnt offering, Lv 8:18
Then he **p** the other ram, the ram of Lv 8:22
Then he **p** Aaron's sons, and Moses put Lv 8:24
And the sons of Aaron **p** the blood to him, Lv 9:9
Then he **p** the people's offering and took Lv 9:15
And he **p** the burnt offering and offered Lv 9:16
And he **p** the grain offering, took a Lv 9:17
for Azazel shall be **p** alive before the Lv 16:10
contribution that they **p** to the LORD, Nm 31:52
Joshua went and **p** themselves in the Dt 31:14
And they **p** themselves before God. Jos 24:1
And he **p** the tribute to Eglon king of Jgs 3:17
to him under the terebinth and **p** them. Jgs 6:19
p themselves in the assembly of the Jgs 20:2
the LORD and **p** burnt offerings and 1 Chr 21:26
in all Israel **p** themselves to him 2 Chr 11:13
and there they **p** the provocation of Ezk 20:28
Ancient of Days and was **p** before him. Dn 7:13
To them he **p** himself alive after his Acts 1:3
the saints and widows, he **p** her alive. Acts 9:41
and the offering **p** for each one Acts 21:26
they **p** Paul also before him. Acts 23:33
just as you once **p** your members as Rom 6:19

PRESENTING (5)

for **p** to the LORD food offerings, Lv 23:37
when Ehud had finished **p** the tribute, Jgs 3:18
and **p** my plea before the LORD my God Dn 9:20
after **p** themselves before the LORD of all Zec 6:5
this new teaching is that you are **p**? Acts 17:19

PRESENTS (5)

sojourners in Israel **p** a burnt offering Lv 22:18
brought Jehoshaphat **p** and silver 2 Chr 17:11
And when Moab **p** himself, when he Is 16:12
he who **p** a grain offering, like one who Is 66:3
them and make merry and exchange **p**, Rv 11:10

PRESERVE (24)

that we may **p** offspring from our Gn 19:32
that we may **p** offspring from our Gn 19:34
here, for God sent me before you to **p** life. Gn 45:5

me before you to **p** for you a remnant Gn 45:7
good always, that he might **p** us alive, Dt 6:24
that is in them; and you **p** all of them; Neh 9:6
P me, O God, for in you I take refuge. Ps 16:1
May integrity and uprightness **p** me, for Ps 25:21
place for me; you **p** me from trouble; Ps 32:7
and your faithfulness will ever **p** me! Ps 40:11
p my life from dread of the enemy. Ps 64:1
your great power, **p** those doomed to die! Ps 79:11
P my life, for I am godly; save your Ps 86:2
in the midst of trouble, you **p** my life; Ps 138:7
from evil men; **p** me from violent men, Ps 140:1
p me from violent men, who have Ps 140:4
your name's sake, O LORD, **p** my life! Ps 143:11
to **p** you from the evil woman, from the Prv 6:24
but the lips of the wise will **p** them. Prv 14:3
love and faithfulness **p** the king, Prv 20:28
you shall put away, but not **p**, and what Mi 6:14
and what you **p** I will give to the sword. Mi 6:14
Whoever seeks to **p** his life will lose it, Lk 17:33
who have faith and **p** their souls. Heb 10:39

PRESERVED (9)
signs in our sight and **p** us in all the Jos 24:17
He has **p** us and given into our hand 1 Sm 30:23
love, and your care has **p** my spirit. Jb 10:12
They are **p** forever, but the children of Ps 37:28
of Jacob and to bring back the **p** of Israel; Is 49:6
who is left and is **p** shall die of famine. Ezk 6:12
into fresh wineskins, and so both are **p**." Mt 9:17
truth of the gospel might be **p** for you. Gal 2:5
not spare the ancient world, but **p** Noah, 2 Pt 2:5

PRESERVES (7)
The LORD **p** the faithful but abundantly Ps 31:23
He **p** the lives of his saints; he delivers Ps 97:10
The LORD **p** the simple; when I was Ps 116:6
The LORD **p** all who love him, but all Ps 145:20
Whoever guards his mouth **p** his life; Prv 13:3
evil; whoever guards his way **p** his life. Prv 16:17
knowledge is that wisdom **p** the life of Eccl 7:12

PRESIDENTS (5)
and over them three **p**, of whom Daniel Dn 6:2
above all the other **p** and satraps, Dn 6:3
Then the **p** and the satraps sought to find Dn 6:4
Then these **p** and satraps came by Dn 6:6
All the **p** of the kingdom, the prefects and Dn 6:7

PRESS (9)
with a fishhook or **p** down his tongue Jb 41:1
the bent bow, and from the **p** of battle. Is 21:15
a state of siege, and **p** the siege against it. Ezk 4:3
us know; let us **p** on to know the LORD; Hos 6:3
I will **p** you down in your place, Am 2:13
wolves; their horsemen **p** proudly on. Hab 1:8
the Pharisees began to **p** him hard and Lk 11:53
perfect, but I **p** on to make it my own, Phil 3:12
I **p** on toward the goal for the prize of Phil 3:14

PRESSED (22)
But he **p** them strongly; so they turned Gn 19:3
them." Then they **p** hard against the Gn 19:9
the grapes and **p** them into Pharaoh's Gn 40:11
the wall and **p** Balaam's foot against Nm 22:25
The Amorites **p** the people of Dan back Jgs 1:34
the people of Israel **p** harder and harder Jgs 4:24
he told her, because she **p** him hard. Jgs 14:17
And when she **p** him hard with her Jgs 16:16
rose up to go, his father-in-law **p** him, Jgs 19:7
trouble (for the people were hard **p**), 1 Sm 13:6
of Israel had been hard **p** that day, 1 Sm 14:24
The battle **p** hard against Saul, and 1 Sm 31:3
be burdensome to you." He **p** him, 2 Sm 13:25
But Absalom **p** him until he let 2 Sm 13:27
The battle **p** hard against Saul, and 1 Chr 10:3
they are not **p** out or bound up or softened Is 1:6
their breasts were **p** and their virgin Ezk 23:3
your bosom and **p** your young Ezk 23:21
all who had diseases **p** around him to Mk 3:10
Good measure, **p** down, shaken together, Lk 6:38
As Jesus went, the people **p** around him. Lk 8:42
I am hard **p** between the two. My desire Phil 1:23

PRESSES (3)
harvest and from the outflow of your **p**. Ex 22:29
no treader treads out wine in the **p**; Is 16:10
place, as a cart full of sheaves **p** down. Am 2:13

PRESSING (6)
For **p** milk produces curds, pressing Prv 30:33
curds, **p** the nose produces blood, Prv 30:33
blood, and **p** anger produces strife. Prv 30:33
him, "You see the crowd **p** around you, Mk 5:31
while the crowd was **p** in on him to hear Lk 5:1
surround you and are **p** in on you!" Lk 8:45

PRESSURE (2)
you; my **p** will not be heavy upon you. Jb 33:7
there is the daily **p** on me of my 2 Cor 11:28

PRESUME (4)
And do not **p** to say to yourselves, 'We Mt 3:9
Therefore I did not **p** to come to you. But Lk 7:7
Or do you **p** on the riches of his Rom 2:4
he did not **p** to pronounce a Jude 1:9

PRESUMED (1)
But they **p** to go up to the heights of Nm 14:44

PRESUMES (1)
But the prophet who **p** to speak a word Dt 18:20

PRESUMPTION (2)
and **p** is as iniquity and idolatry. 1 Sm 15:23
I know your **p** and the evil of your 1 Sm 17:28

PRESUMPTUOUS (1)
back your servant also from **p** sins; Ps 19:13

PRESUMPTUOUSLY (6)
of the LORD and **p** went up into the Dt 1:43
The man who acts **p** by not obeying the Dt 17:12
shall hear and fear and not act **p** again. Dt 17:13
not spoken; the prophet has spoken it **p**. Dt 18:22
our fathers acted **p** and stiffened their Neh 9:16
Yet they acted **p** and did not obey your Neh 9:29

PRETEND (3)
"Lie down on your bed and **p** to be ill. 2 Sm 13:5
"**P** to be a mourner and put on 2 Sm 14:2
Why do you **p** to be another? 1 Kgs 14:6

PRETENDED (5)
Joshua and all Israel **p** to be beaten Jos 8:15
before them and **p** to be insane 1 Sm 21:13
So Amnon lay down and **p** to be ill. 2 Sm 13:6
came, she **p** to be another woman. 1 Kgs 14:5
him and sent spies, who **p** to be sincere, Lk 20:20

PRETENDS (2)
One **p** to be rich, yet has nothing; Prv 13:7
another **p** to be poor, yet has great Prv 13:7

PRETENSE (5)
to me with her whole heart, but in **p**, Jer 3:10
houses and for a **p** make long prayers. Mk 12:40
houses and for a **p** make long prayers. Lk 20:47
into the sea under **p** of laying out Acts 27:30
in every way, whether in **p** or in truth, Phil 1:18

PRETEXT (1)
nor with a **p** for greed—God is 1 Thes 2:5

PREVAIL (19)
saw that he did not **p** against Jacob, Gn 32:25
for not by might shall a man **p**. 1 Sm 2:9
But if I **p** against him and kill him, 1 Sm 17:9
our God; let not man **p** against you." 2 Chr 14:11
You **p** forever against him, and he Jb 14:20
they **p** against him, like a king ready for Jb 15:24
Let not man **p**; let the nations be judged Ps 9:19
who say, "With our tongue we will **p**, Ps 12:4
When iniquities **p** against me, you atone Ps 65:3
a man might **p** against one who Eccl 4:12
to his sanctuary to pray, he will not **p**. Is 16:12
you, but they shall not **p** against you, Jer 1:19
though the waves toss, they cannot **p**; Jer 5:22
you, but they shall not **p** over you, Jer 15:20
and he shall deal with them and shall **p**. Dn 11:7
tens of thousands, but he shall not **p**. Dn 11:12
the gates of hell shall not **p** against it. Mt 16:18
continued to increase and **p** mightily. Acts 19:20
words, and **p** when you are judged." Rom 3:4

PREVAILED (25)
The waters **p** and increased greatly on Gn 7:18
And the waters **p** so mightily on the Gn 7:19
The waters **p** above the mountains, Gn 7:20
And the waters **p** on the earth 150 days. Gn 7:24
my sister and have **p**." So she called his Gn 30:8
with God and with men, and have **p**." Gn 32:28
Moses held up his hand, Israel **p**, Ex 17:11
he lowered his hand, Amalek **p**. Ex 17:11
his hand **p** over Cushan-rishathaim. Jgs 3:10
So David **p** over the Philistine with a 1 Sm 17:50
the king's word **p** against Joab and 2 Sm 24:4
And when they **p** over them, the 1 Chr 5:20
But the king's word **p** against Joab. 1 Chr 21:4
at that time, and the men of Judah **p**, 2 Chr 13:18
the Ammonites and **p** against them. 2 Chr 27:5
"I have **p** over him," lest my foes rejoice Ps 13:4
youth, yet they have not **p** against me. Ps 129:2
you are stronger than I, and you have **p**. Jer 20:7
have deceived you and **p** against you; Jer 38:22
are desolate, for the enemy has **p**." Lam 1:16
war with the saints and **p** over them, Dn 7:21
He strove with the angel and **p**; he wept Hos 12:4
deceived you; they have **p** against you; Ob 1:7
should be crucified. And their voices **p**. Lk 23:23
house and stay." And she **p** upon us. Acts 16:15

PREVENT (1)
fear of our God to **p** the taunts of the Neh 5:9

PREVENTED (5)
the LORD has **p** me from bearing Gn 16:2
John would have **p** him, saying, "I need Mt 3:14
friends should be **p** from attending to Acts 24:23
to you (but thus far have been **p**), Rom 1:13
because they were **p** by death from Heb 7:23

PREVENTS (1)
What **p** me from being baptized?" Acts 8:36

PREVIOUS (1)
But the **p** period shall be void, because Nm 6:12

PREVIOUSLY (7)
all who knew him **p** saw how he 1 Sm 10:11
where they had **p** put the grain Neh 13:5
thanks before his God, as he had done **p**. Dn 6:10
who had **p** practiced magic in the city Acts 8:9
For they had **p** seen Trophimus the Acts 21:29
not annul a covenant **p** ratified by God, Gal 3:17
with the prophecies **p** made about 1 Tm 1:18

PREY (52)
And when birds of **p** came down on the Gn 15:11
from the **p**, my son, you have gone up. Gn 49:9
morning devouring the **p** and at Gn 49:27
and our little ones will become a **p**. Nm 14:3
ones, who you said would become a **p**, Nm 14:31
it has devoured the **p** and drunk the Nm 23:24
ones, who you said would become a **p**, Dt 1:39
they shall become a **p** and a spoil to 2 Kgs 21:14
The strong lion perishes for lack of **p**, Jb 4:11
of reed, like an eagle swooping on the **p**. Jb 9:26
"That path no bird of **p** knows, and the Jb 28:7
and made him drop his **p** from his teeth. Jb 29:17
"Can you hunt the **p** for the lion, or Jb 38:39
Who provides for the raven its **p**, when Jb 38:41
From there he spies out the **p**; his eyes Jb 39:29
more majestic than the mountains of **p**. Ps 76:4
The young lions roar for their **p**, Ps 104:21
who has not given us as **p** to their teeth! Ps 124:6
they roar; they growl and seize their **p**; Is 5:29
that they may make the fatherless their **p**! Is 10:2
left to the birds of **p** of the mountains and Is 18:6
And the birds of **p** will summer on them, Is 18:6
a lion or a young lion growls over his **p**, Is 31:4
Then **p** and spoil in abundance will be Is 33:23
be divided; even the lame will take the **p**. Is 33:23
calling a bird of **p** from the east, the Is 46:11
Can the **p** be taken from the mighty, or Is 49:24
taken, and the **p** of the tyrant be rescued, Is 49:25
departs from evil makes himself a **p**. Is 59:15
servant? Why then has he become a **p**? Jer 2:14
Are the birds of **p** against her all Jer 12:9
and all who **p** on you I will make a Jer 30:16
all who prey on you I will make a **p**. Jer 30:16
give it into the hands of foreigners for **p**, Ezk 7:21
shall be no more in your hand as **p**, Ezk 13:21
a young lion, and he learned to catch **p**; Ezk 19:3
a young lion, and he learned to catch **p**; Ezk 19:6
is like a roaring lion tearing the **p**; Ezk 22:25
her midst are like wolves tearing the **p**, Ezk 22:27
because my sheep have become a **p**, Ezk 34:8
my flock; they shall no longer be a **p**. Ezk 34:22
shall no more be a **p** to the nations, Ezk 34:28
which have become a **p** and derision to Ezk 36:4
they might make its pasturelands a **p**. Ezk 36:5
give you to birds of **p** of every sort and Ezk 39:4
lion roar in the forest, when he has no **p**? Am 3:4
cubs and strangled **p** for his lionesses; Na 2:12
filled his caves with **p** and his dens with Na 2:12
I will cut off your **p** from the earth, and Na 2:13
full of lies and plunder—no end to the **p**! Na 3:1
"for the day when I rise up to seize the **p**. Zep 3:8
and beasts of **p** and reptiles and Acts 11:6

PRICE (38)
For the full **p** let him give it to me in Gn 23:9
will, hear me: I give the **p** of the field. Gn 23:13
for as great a bride **p** and gift as you Gn 34:12
shall sell the live ox and share its **p**, Ex 21:35
are many, you shall increase the **p**, Lv 25:16
years are few, you shall reduce the **p**, Lv 25:16
and the **p** of his sale shall vary with the Lv 25:50
for his redemption some of his sale **p**. Lv 25:51
he shall add a fifth to the valuation **p**, Lv 27:15
shall calculate the **p** according to the Lv 27:18
he shall add a fifth to its valuation **p**, Lv 27:19
And as the redemption **p** for the 273 of Nm 3:46
sons as the redemption **p** for those who Nm 3:48
And their redemption **p** (at a month Nm 18:16
I paid the bridal **p** of a hundred 2 Sm 3:14
but I will buy it from you for a **p**. 2 Sm 24:24
received them from Kue at a **p**. 1 Kgs 10:28
to me at its full **p**—that the plague 1 Chr 21:22

but I will buy them for the full **p**. 1 Chr 21:24
would buy them from Kue for a **p**. 2 Chr 1:16
and silver cannot be weighed as its **p**. Jb 28:15
crystal; the **p** of wisdom is above pearls. Jb 28:18
a trifle, demanding no high **p** for them. Ps 44:12
another, or give to God the **p** of his life, Ps 49:7
for the **p** of a prostitute is only a loaf of Prv 6:26
clothing, and the goats the **p** of a field. Prv 27:26
not for **p** or reward," says the LORD of Is 45:13
and milk without money and without **p**. Is 55:1
treasures I will give as spoil, without **p**, Jer 15:13
give for spoil as the **p** of your high places Jer 17:3
many and shall divide the land for a **p**. Dn 11:39
for a bribe; its priests teach for a **p**; Mi 3:11
potter"—the lordly **p** at which I was Zec 11:13
the **p** of him on whom a price had been Mt 27:9
of him on whom a **p** had been set by Mt 27:9
for you were bought with a **p**. So 1 Cor 6:20
You were bought with a **p**; do not 1 Cor 7:23
desires take the water of life without **p**. Rv 22:17

PRICED (1)
lordly price at which I was **p** by them. Zec 11:13

PRICK (1)
no more a brier to **p** or a thorn to hurt Ezk 28:24

PRICKED (1)
was embittered, when I was **p** in heart, Ps 73:21

PRIDE (52)
and I will break the **p** of your power, Lv 26:19
himself for the **p** of his heart, 2 Chr 32:26
are humbled you say, 'It is because of **p**'; Jb 22:29
his deed and conceal **p** from a man; Jb 33:17
not answer, because of the **p** of evil men. Jb 35:12
is high; he is king over all the sons of **p**." Jb 41:34
In the **p** of his face the wicked does not Ps 10:4
the righteous in **p** and contempt. Ps 31:18
repays the one who acts in **p**. Ps 31:23
for us, the **p** of Jacob whom he loves. Ps 47:4
their lips, let them be trapped in their **p**. Ps 59:12
Therefore **p** is their necklace; violence Ps 73:6
P and arrogance and the way of evil Prv 8:13
When **p** comes, then comes disgrace, Prv 11:2
P goes before destruction, and a Prv 16:18
man who acts with arrogant **p**. Prv 21:24
One's **p** will bring him low, but he Prv 29:23
and the lofty **p** of men shall be humbled, Is 2:11
and the lofty **p** of men shall be brought Is 2:17
the land shall be the **p** and honor of the Is 4:2
who say in **p** and in arrogance of heart: Is 9:9
lay low the pompous **p** of the ruthless. Is 13:11
We have heard of the **p** of Moab—how Is 16:6
of his arrogance, his **p**, and his insolence; Is 16:6
it, to defile the pompous **p** of all glory, Is 23:9
lay low his pompous **p** together with the Is 25:11
so will I spoil the **p** of Judah and the great Jer 13:9
of Judah and the great **p** of Jerusalem. Jer 13:9
my soul will weep in secret for your **p**; Jer 13:17
We have heard of the **p** of Moab—he is Jer 48:29
he is very proud—of his loftiness, his **p**, Jer 48:29
deceived you, and the **p** of your heart, Jer 49:16
the rod has blossomed; **p** has budded. Ezk 7:10
His beautiful ornament they used for **p**, Ezk 7:20
I will put an end to the **p** of the strong, Ezk 7:24
she and her daughters had **p**, excess of Ezk 16:49
in your mouth in the day of your **p**, Ezk 16:56
my sanctuary, the **p** of your power, Ezk 24:21
shall bring to ruin the **p** of Egypt, Ezk 32:12
and those who walk in **p** he is able to Dn 4:37
The **p** of Israel testifies to his face; Israel Hos 5:5
The **p** of Israel testifies to his face; yet Hos 7:10
"I abhor the **p** of Jacob and hate his Am 6:8
The LORD has sworn by the **p** of Jacob: Am 8:7
The **p** of your heart has deceived you, you Ob 1:3
shall be their lot in return for their **p**, Zep 2:10
and I will cut off the **p** of Philistia. Zec 9:6
The **p** of Assyria shall be laid low, and Zec 10:11
sensuality, envy, slander, **p**, foolishness. Mk 7:22
I protest, brothers, by my **p** in you, 1 Cor 15:31
toward you; I have great **p** in you; 2 Cor 7:4
of the eyes and **p** in possessions—is 1 Jn 2:16

PRIEST (508)
wine. (He was **p** of God Most High.) Gn 14:18
the daughter of Potiphera **p** of On. Gn 41:45
the daughter of Potiphera **p** of On, Gn 41:50
the daughter of Potiphera the **p** of On, Gn 46:20
Now the **p** of Midian had seven Ex 2:16
his father-in-law, Jethro, the **p** of Midian, Ex 3:1
Jethro, the **p** of Midian, Moses' Ex 18:1
The son who succeeds him as **p**, who Ex 29:30
for Aaron the **p** and the garments Ex 31:10
the holy garments for Aaron the **p**, Ex 35:19
of Ithamar the son of Aaron the **p**. Ex 38:21
the holy garments for Aaron the **p**, Ex 39:41
him, that he may serve me as **p**. Ex 40:13
the sons of Aaron the **p** shall put fire on Lv 1:7
And the **p** shall burn all of it on the altar, Lv 1:9
and the **p** shall arrange them on the Lv 1:12
And the **p** shall offer all of it and burn it Lv 1:13
And the **p** shall bring it to the altar and Lv 1:15
And the **p** shall burn it on the altar, on Lv 1:17
and the **p** shall burn this as its memorial Lv 2:2
the LORD, and when it is presented to the **p**, Lv 2:8
And the **p** shall take from the grain Lv 2:9
And the **p** shall burn as its memorial Lv 2:16
And the **p** shall burn it on the altar as a Lv 3:11
And the **p** shall burn them on the altar Lv 3:16
if it is the anointed **p** who sins, thus Lv 4:3
And the anointed **p** shall take some of the Lv 4:5
and the **p** shall dip his finger in the blood Lv 4:6
And the **p** shall put some of the blood on Lv 4:7
and the **p** shall burn them on the altar of Lv 4:10
Then the anointed **p** shall bring some of Lv 4:16
and the **p** shall dip his finger in the Lv 4:17
And the **p** shall make atonement for Lv 4:20
Then the **p** shall take some of the blood Lv 4:25
So the **p** shall make atonement for him Lv 4:26
And the **p** shall take some of its blood Lv 4:30
and the **p** shall burn it on the altar for a Lv 4:31
And the **p** shall make atonement for Lv 4:31
Then the **p** shall take some of the blood Lv 4:34
and the **p** shall burn it on the altar, Lv 4:35
And the **p** shall make atonement for Lv 4:35
And the **p** shall make atonement for him Lv 5:6
He shall bring them to the **p**, who shall Lv 5:8
And the **p** shall make atonement for Lv 5:10
And he shall bring it to the **p**, and the Lv 5:12
and the **p** shall take a handful of it as its Lv 5:12
Thus the **p** shall make atonement for Lv 5:13
And the remainder shall be for the **p**, as Lv 5:13
shall add a fifth to it and give it to the **p**. Lv 5:16
And the **p** shall make atonement for Lv 5:16
shall bring to the **p** a ram without Lv 5:18
and the **p** shall make atonement for him Lv 5:18
shall bring to the **p** as his compensation Lv 6:6
And the **p** shall make atonement for him Lv 6:7
And the **p** shall put on his linen garment Lv 6:10
The **p** shall burn wood on it every Lv 6:12
The **p** from among Aaron's sons, who is Lv 6:22
grain offering of a **p** shall be wholly Lv 6:23
The **p** who offers it for sin shall eat it. In Lv 6:26
The **p** shall burn them on the altar as a Lv 7:5
The **p** who makes atonement with it shall Lv 7:7
And the **p** who offers any man's burnt Lv 7:8
griddle shall belong to the **p** who offers it. Lv 7:9
shall belong to the **p** who throws the Lv 7:14
The **p** shall burn the fat on the altar, but Lv 7:31
shall give to the **p** as a contribution Lv 7:32
them to Aaron the **p** and to his sons, Lv 7:34
she shall bring to the **p** at the entrance of Lv 12:6
And the **p** shall make atonement for her, Lv 12:8
be brought to Aaron the **p** or to one of Lv 13:2
and the **p** shall examine the diseased Lv 13:3
When the **p** has examined him, he shall Lv 13:3
the **p** shall shut up the diseased person Lv 13:4
And the **p** shall examine him on the Lv 13:5
then the **p** shall shut him up for another Lv 13:5
And the **p** shall examine him again on Lv 13:6
then the **p** shall pronounce him clean; Lv 13:6
shown himself to the **p** for his cleansing, Lv 13:7
he shall appear again before the **p**. Lv 13:7
And the **p** shall look, and if the eruption Lv 13:8
then the **p** shall pronounce him Lv 13:8
disease, he shall be brought to the **p**, Lv 13:9
and the **p** shall look. And if there is a Lv 13:10
and the **p** shall pronounce him Lv 13:11
head to foot, so far as the **p** can see, Lv 13:12
then the **p** shall look, and if the leprous Lv 13:13
And the **p** shall examine the raw flesh Lv 13:15
again, then he shall come to the **p**, Lv 13:16
and the **p** shall examine him, and if the Lv 13:17
then the **p** shall pronounce the diseased Lv 13:17
spot, then it shall be shown to the **p**. Lv 13:19
And the **p** shall look, and if it appears Lv 13:20
then the **p** shall pronounce him Lv 13:20
But if the **p** examines it and there is no Lv 13:21
then the **p** shall shut him up seven Lv 13:21
then the **p** shall pronounce him Lv 13:22
and the **p** shall pronounce him clean. Lv 13:23
the **p** shall examine it, and if the hair in Lv 13:25
and the **p** shall pronounce him Lv 13:25
But if the **p** examines it and there is no Lv 13:26
the **p** shall shut him up seven days, Lv 13:26
and the **p** shall examine him the Lv 13:27
then the **p** shall pronounce him Lv 13:27
and the **p** shall pronounce him clean, Lv 13:28
the **p** shall examine the disease. And if Lv 13:30
then the **p** shall pronounce him Lv 13:30
And if the **p** examines the itching Lv 13:31
then the **p** shall shut up the person with Lv 13:31
the seventh day the **p** shall examine the Lv 13:32
and the **p** shall shut up the person with Lv 13:33
the seventh day the **p** shall examine the Lv 13:34
then the **p** shall pronounce him clean. Lv 13:34
then the **p** shall examine him, and if Lv 13:36
the **p** need not seek for the yellow hair; Lv 13:36
and the **p** shall pronounce him clean. Lv 13:37
the **p** shall look, and if the spots on the Lv 13:39
Then the **p** shall examine him, and if Lv 13:43
The **p** must pronounce him unclean; Lv 13:44
disease, and it shall be shown to the **p**. Lv 13:49
And the **p** shall examine the disease Lv 13:50
"And if the **p** examines, and if the Lv 13:53
then the **p** shall command that they Lv 13:54
And the **p** shall examine the diseased Lv 13:55
"But if the **p** examines, and if the Lv 13:56
cleansing. He shall be brought to the **p**, Lv 14:2
and the **p** shall go out of the camp, and Lv 14:3
go out of the camp, and the **p** shall look. Lv 14:3
the **p** shall command them to take for Lv 14:4
And the **p** shall command them to kill Lv 14:5
And the **p** who cleanses him shall set Lv 14:11
And the **p** shall take one of the male Lv 14:12
like the sin offering, belongs to the **p**; Lv 14:13
The **p** shall take some of the blood of Lv 14:14
and the **p** shall put it on the lobe of the Lv 14:14
Then the **p** shall take some of the log of Lv 14:15
in his hand the **p** shall put on the Lv 14:17
Then the **p** shall make atonement for Lv 14:18
The **p** shall offer the sin offering, to Lv 14:19
And the **p** shall offer the burnt offering Lv 14:20
Thus the **p** shall make atonement for Lv 14:20
bring them for his cleansing to the **p**, Lv 14:23
And the **p** shall take the lamb of the Lv 14:24
and the **p** shall wave them for a wave Lv 14:24
And the **p** shall take some of the blood Lv 14:25
And the **p** shall pour some of the oil Lv 14:26
And the **p** shall put some of the oil that Lv 14:28
And the **p** shall make atonement before Lv 14:31
the house shall come and tell the **p**, Lv 14:35
Then the **p** shall command that they Lv 14:36
the house before the **p** goes to examine Lv 14:36
And afterward the **p** shall go in to see Lv 14:36
then the **p** shall go out of the house to Lv 14:38
And the **p** shall come again on the Lv 14:39
then the **p** shall command that they Lv 14:40
then the **p** shall go and look. And if the Lv 14:44
"But if the **p** comes and looks, and if the Lv 14:48
then the **p** shall pronounce the house Lv 14:48
tent of meeting and give them to the **p**. Lv 15:14
And the **p** shall use them, one for a sin Lv 15:15
And the **p** shall make atonement for Lv 15:15
or two pigeons and bring them to the **p**, Lv 15:29
And the **p** shall use one for a sin Lv 15:30
And the **p** shall make atonement for Lv 15:30
And the **p** who is anointed and Lv 16:32
and consecrated as **p** in his father's Lv 16:32
to the **p** at the entrance of the tent of Lv 17:5
And the **p** shall throw the blood on the Lv 17:6
And the **p** shall make atonement for Lv 19:22
her husband, for the **p** is holy to his God. Lv 21:7
And the daughter of any **p**, if she Lv 21:9
"The **p** who is chief among his Lv 21:10
offspring of Aaron the **p** who has a Lv 21:21
foreign guest of the **p** or hired servant Lv 22:10
but if a **p** buys a slave as his property Lv 22:11
to it and give the holy thing to the **p**. Lv 22:14
of the firstfruits of your harvest to the **p**, Lv 23:10
after the Sabbath the **p** shall wave it. Lv 23:11
And the **p** shall wave them with the Lv 23:20
They shall be holy to the LORD for the **p**. Lv 23:20
he shall be made to stand before the **p**, Lv 27:8
the priest, and the **p** shall value him; Lv 27:8
the **p** shall value him according to what Lv 27:8
he shall stand the animal before the **p**, Lv 27:11
and the **p** shall value it as either good or Lv 27:12
as either good or bad; as the **p** values it, Lv 27:12
the **p** shall value it as either good or Lv 27:14
as either good or bad; as the **p** values it, Lv 27:14
then the **p** shall calculate the price Lv 27:18
The **p** shall be in possession of it. Lv 27:21
then the **p** shall calculate the amount Lv 27:23
near, and set them before Aaron the **p**, Nm 3:6
the son of Aaron the **p** was to be chief Nm 3:32
son of Aaron the **p** shall have charge of Nm 4:16
of Ithamar the son of Aaron the **p**. Nm 4:28
of Ithamar the son of Aaron the **p**." Nm 4:33
for wrong shall go to the LORD for the **p**, Nm 5:8
of Israel, which they bring to the **p**, Nm 5:9
anyone gives to the **p** shall be his." Nm 5:10
his wife to the **p** and bring the offering Nm 5:15
"And the **p** shall bring her near and set Nm 5:16
And the **p** shall take holy water in an Nm 5:17
And the **p** shall set the woman before Nm 5:18
in his hand the **p** shall have the water Nm 5:18

Then the **p** shall make her take an Nm 5:19
then' (let the **p** make the woman take Nm 5:21
"Then the **p** shall write these curses in Nm 5:23
And the **p** shall take the grain offering Nm 5:25
And the **p** shall take a handful of the Nm 5:26
and the **p** shall carry out for her all this Nm 5:30
two pigeons to the **p** to the entrance of Nm 6:10
and the **p** shall offer one for a sin Nm 6:11
And the **p** shall bring them before the Nm 6:16
The **p** shall offer also its grain offering Nm 6:17
And the **p** shall take the shoulder of the Nm 6:19
and the **p** shall wave them for a wave Nm 6:20
They are a holy portion for the **p**, Nm 6:20
of Ithamar the son of Aaron the **p**. Nm 7:8
And the **p** shall make atonement for Nm 15:25
And the **p** shall make atonement Nm 15:28
the son of Aaron the **p** to take up the Nm 16:37
So Eleazar the **p** took the bronze Nm 16:39
LORD'S contribution to Aaron the **p**. Nm 18:28
And you shall give it to Eleazar the **p**, Nm 19:3
And Eleazar the **p** shall take some of its Nm 19:4
And the **p** shall take cedarwood and Nm 19:6
Then the **p** shall wash his clothes and Nm 19:7
But the **p** shall be unclean until Nm 19:7
the son of Eleazar, son of Aaron the **p**, Nm 25:7
the son of Eleazar, son of Aaron the **p**, Nm 25:11
and to Eleazar the son of Aaron, the **p**, Nm 26:1
and Eleazar the **p** spoke with them Nm 26:3
listed by Moses and Eleazar the **p**, Nm 26:63
those listed by Moses and Aaron the **p**, Nm 26:64
and before Eleazar the **p** and before the Nm 27:2
stand before Eleazar the **p** and all the Nm 27:19
he shall stand before Eleazar the **p**, Nm 27:21
before Eleazar the **p** and the whole Nm 27:22
with Phinehas the son of Eleazar the **p**, Nm 31:6
spoil to Moses, and to Eleazar the **p**, Nm 31:12
Moses and Eleazar the **p** and all the Nm 31:13
Then Eleazar the **p** said to the men in Nm 31:21
you and Eleazar the **p** and the heads of Nm 31:26
it to Eleazar the **p** as a contribution to Nm 31:29
Moses and Eleazar the **p** did as the Nm 31:31
for the LORD, to Eleazar the **p**, Nm 31:41
and Eleazar the **p** received from them Nm 31:51
and Eleazar the **p** received the gold Nm 31:54
and to Eleazar the **p** and to the chiefs Nm 32:2
them to Eleazar the **p** and to Joshua Nm 32:28
And Aaron the **p** went up Mount Hor Nm 33:38
Eleazar the **p** and Joshua the son of Nm 34:17
death of the high **p** who was anointed Nm 35:25
of refuge until the death of the high **p**, Nm 35:28
of the high **p** the manslayer may Nm 35:28
the land before the death of the high **p**. Nm 35:32
son Eleazar ministered as **p** in his place. Dt 10:6
by not obeying the **p** who stands to Dt 17:12
shall give to the **p** the shoulder and the Dt 18:3
the **p** shall come forward and speak to Dt 20:2
you shall go to the **p** who is in office at Dt 26:3
Then the **p** shall take the basket from Dt 26:4
which Eleazar the **p** and Joshua the son Jos 14:1
approached Eleazar the **p** and Joshua the Jos 17:4
that Eleazar the **p** and Joshua the Jos 19:51
death of him who is high **p** at the time. Jos 20:6
came to Eleazar the **p** and to Joshua the Jos 21:1
of Aaron the **p** received by lot Jos 21:4
of Aaron the **p** they gave Hebron, Jos 21:13
Phinehas the son of Eleazar the **p**, Jos 22:13
When Phinehas the **p** and the chiefs of Jos 22:30
son of Eleazar the **p** said to the people Jos 22:31
Phinehas the son of Eleazar the **p**, Jos 22:32
one of his sons, who became his **p**. Jgs 17:5
with me, and be to me a father and a **p**, Jgs 17:10
and the young man became his **p**, Jgs 17:12
me, because I have a Levite as **p**." Jgs 17:13
has hired me, and I have become his **p**." Jgs 18:4
And the **p** said to them, "Go in peace. Jgs 18:6
while the **p** stood by the entrance of the Jgs 18:17
the metal image, the **p** said to them, Jgs 18:18
with us and be to us a father and a **p**. Jgs 18:19
better for you to be **p** to the house of Jgs 18:19
or to be **p** to a tribe and clan in Israel?" Jgs 18:19
take my gods that I made and the **p**, Jgs 18:24
made, and the **p** who belonged to him, Jgs 18:27
Now Eli the **p** was sitting on the seat 1 Sm 1:9
to the LORD in the presence of Eli the **p**. 1 Sm 2:11
fork brought up the **p** would take for 1 Sm 2:14
"Give meat for the **p** to roast, 1 Sm 2:15
of all the tribes of Israel to be my **p**, 1 Sm 2:28
I will raise up for myself a faithful **p**, 1 Sm 2:35
son of Eli, the **p** of the LORD in Shiloh, 1 Sm 14:3
Now while Saul was talking to the **p**, 1 Sm 14:19
So Saul said to the **p**, "Withdraw 1 Sm 14:19
seems good to you." But the **p** said, 1 Sm 14:36
came to Nob to Ahimelech the **p**. 1 Sm 21:1
And David said to Ahimelech the **p**, 1 Sm 21:2
And the **p** answered David, "I have no 1 Sm 21:4

And David answered the **p**, "Truly 1 Sm 21:5
So the **p** gave him the holy bread, for 1 Sm 21:6
And the **p** said, "The sword of Goliath 1 Sm 21:9
sent to summon Ahimelech the **p**, 1 Sm 22:11
And he said to Abiathar the **p**, "Bring 1 Sm 23:9
And David said to Abiathar the **p**, the 1 Sm 30:7
The king also said to Zadok the **p**, 2 Sm 15:27
and Ira the Jairite was also David's **p**. 2 Sm 20:26
of Zeruiah and with Abiathar the **p**. 1 Kgs 1:7
But Zadok the **p** and Benaiah the son 1 Kgs 1:8
the sons of the king, Abiathar the **p**, 1 Kgs 1:19
of the army, and Abiathar the **p**. 1 Kgs 1:25
me, your servant, and Zadok the **p**, 1 Kgs 1:26
David said, "Call to me Zadok the **p**, 1 Kgs 1:32
And let Zadok the **p** and Nathan the 1 Kgs 1:34
So Zadok the **p**, Nathan the prophet, 1 Kgs 1:38
There Zadok the **p** took the horn of 1 Kgs 1:39
the son of Abiathar the **p** came. 1 Kgs 1:42
king has sent with him Zadok the **p**, 1 Kgs 1:44
And Zadok the **p** and Nathan the 1 Kgs 1:45
side are Abiathar the **p** and Joab the 1 Kgs 2:22
And to Abiathar the **p** the king said, 1 Kgs 2:26
Abiathar from being **p** to the LORD, 1 Kgs 2:27
king put Zadok the **p** in the place of 1 Kgs 2:35
Azariah the son of Zadok was the **p**; 1 Kgs 4:2
son of Nathan was **p** and king's friend; 1 Kgs 4:5
all that Jehoiada the **p** commanded, 2 Kgs 11:9
Sabbath, and came to Jehoiada the **p**. 2 Kgs 11:9
And the **p** gave to the captains the 2 Kgs 11:10
Jehoiada the **p** commanded the 2 Kgs 11:15
who follows her." For the **p** said, 2 Kgs 11:15
killed Mattan the **p** of Baal before 2 Kgs 11:18
And the **p** posted watchmen over the 2 Kgs 11:18
Jehoiada the **p** instructed him. 2 Kgs 12:2
summoned Jehoiada the **p** and the 2 Kgs 12:7
Then Jehoiada the **p** took a chest and 2 Kgs 12:9
and the high **p** came up and 2 Kgs 12:10
sent to Uriah the **p** a model of the 2 Kgs 16:10
And Uriah the **p** built the altar; in 2 Kgs 16:11
Damascus, so Uriah the **p** made it, 2 Kgs 16:11
Ahaz commanded Uriah the **p**, 2 Kgs 16:15
Uriah the **p** did all this, as King 2 Kgs 16:16
"Go up to Hilkiah the high **p**, that he 2 Kgs 22:4
Hilkiah the high **p** said to Shaphan 2 Kgs 22:8
"Hilkiah the **p** has given me a 2 Kgs 22:10
the king commanded Hilkiah the **p**, 2 Kgs 22:12
So Hilkiah the **p**, and Ahikam, and 2 Kgs 22:14
Hilkiah the high **p** and the priests 2 Kgs 23:4
book that Hilkiah the **p** found in the 2 Kgs 23:24
Seraiah the chief **p** and Zephaniah 2 Kgs 25:18
Zephaniah the second **p** and the 2 Kgs 25:18
he who served as **p** in the house that 1 Chr 6:10
he left Zadok the **p** and his brothers 1 Chr 16:39
and Zadok the **p** and Ahimelech the 1 Chr 24:6
the son of Jehoiada the chief **p**; 1 Chr 27:5
prince for the LORD, and Zadok as **p**. 1 Chr 29:22
seven rams becomes a **p** of what are 2 Chr 13:9
without a teaching **p** and without 2 Chr 15:3
Amariah the chief **p** is over you in 2 Chr 19:11
Jehoram and wife of Jehoiada the **p**, 2 Chr 22:11
all that Jehoiada the **p** commanded, 2 Chr 23:8
for Jehoiada the **p** did not dismiss the 2 Chr 23:8
And Jehoiada the **p** gave to the 2 Chr 23:9
Then Jehoiada the **p** brought out 2 Chr 23:14
with the sword." For the **p** said, 2 Chr 23:14
killed Mattan the **p** of Baal before 2 Chr 23:17
LORD all the days of Jehoiada the **p**. 2 Chr 24:2
of the chief **p** would come and 2 Chr 24:11
Zechariah the son of Jehoiada the **p**, 2 Chr 24:20
blood of the son of Jehoiada the **p**, 2 Chr 24:25
But Azariah the **p** went in after him, 2 Chr 26:17
And Azariah the chief **p** and all the 2 Chr 26:20
Azariah the chief **p**, who was of the 2 Chr 31:10
to Hilkiah the high **p** and gave him 2 Chr 34:9
Hilkiah the **p** found the Book of the 2 Chr 34:14
"Hilkiah the **p** has given me a 2 Chr 34:18
there should be a **p** to consult Urim and Ezr 2:63
son of Eleazar, son of Aaron the chief **p**— Ezr 7:5
that King Artaxerxes gave to Ezra the **p**, Ezr 7:11
"Artaxerxes, king of kings, to Ezra the **p**, Ezr 7:12
Whatever Ezra the **p**, the scribe of the Ezr 7:21
into the hands of Meremoth the **p**, Ezr 8:33
And Ezra the **p** stood up and said to Ezr 10:10
exiles did so. Ezra the **p** selected men, Ezr 10:16
Then Eliashib the high **p** rose up with Neh 3:1
of the house of Eliashib the high **p**. Neh 3:20
holy food until a **p** with Urim and Neh 7:65
So Ezra the **p** brought the Law before Neh 8:2
the governor, and Ezra the **p** and scribe, Neh 8:9
And the **p**, the son of Aaron, shall be Neh 10:38
and of Ezra, the **p** and scribe. Neh 12:26
Now before this, Eliashib the **p**, who Neh 13:4
over the storehouses Shelemiah the **p**, Neh 13:13
the son of Eliashib the high **p**, Neh 13:28
"You are a **p** forever after the order of Ps 110:4

Uriah the **p** and Zechariah the son of Is 8:2
shall be, as with the people, so with the **p**; Is 24:2
the **p** and the prophet reel with strong Is 28:7
decks himself like a **p** with a beautiful Is 61:10
and from prophet to **p**, everyone deals Jer 6:13
from prophet to **p**, everyone deals falsely. Jer 8:10
For both prophet and **p** ply their trade Jer 14:18
for the law shall not perish from the **p**, Jer 18:18
Now Pashhur the **p**, the son of Immer, Jer 20:1
son of Malchiah and Zephaniah the **p**, Jer 21:1
"Both prophet and **p** are ungodly; even Jer 23:11
this people, or a prophet or a **p** asks you, Jer 23:33
p, or one of the people who says, Jer 23:34
Zephaniah the son of Maaseiah the **p**, Jer 29:25
has made you **p** instead of Jehoiada Jer 29:26
you priest instead of Jehoiada the **p**, Jer 29:26
Zephaniah the **p** read this letter in the Jer 29:29
son of Shelemiah, and Zephaniah the **p**, Jer 37:3
of the guard took Seraiah the chief **p**, Jer 52:24
priest, and Zephaniah the second **p**, Jer 52:24
indignation has spurned king and **p**. Lam 2:6
Should **p** and prophet be killed in the Lam 2:20
word of the LORD came to Ezekiel the **p**, Ezk 1:3
perishes from the **p** and counsel from Ezk 7:26
not come near to me, to serve me as **p**, Ezk 44:13
No **p** shall drink wine when he enters Ezk 44:21
or a widow who is the widow of a **p**. Ezk 44:22
The **p** shall take some of the blood of Ezk 45:19
for with you is my contention, O **p**. Hos 4:4
I reject you from being a **p** to me. Hos 4:6
And it shall be like people, like **p**; I will Hos 4:9
Then Amaziah the **p** of Bethel sent to Am 7:10
Joshua the son of Jehozadak, the high **p**: Hg 1:1
Joshua the son of Jehozadak, the high **p**, Hg 1:12
Joshua the son of Jehozadak, the high **p**, Hg 1:14
Joshua the son of Jehozadak, the high **p**, Hg 2:2
O Joshua, son of Jehozadak, the high **p**. Hg 2:4
me Joshua the high **p** standing before the Zec 3:1
Hear now, O Joshua the high **p**, you and Zec 3:8
the son of Jehozadak, the high **p**. Zec 6:11
And there shall be a **p** on his throne, Zec 6:13
the lips of a **p** should guard knowledge, Mal 2:7
show yourself to the **p** and offer the gift Mt 8:4
gathered in the palace of the high **p**, Mt 26:3
the servant of the high **p** and cut off his Mt 26:51
Jesus led him to Caiaphas the high **p**, Mt 26:57
as far as the courtyard of the high **p**, Mt 26:58
And the high **p** stood up and said, Mt 26:62
silent. And the high **p** said to him, Mt 26:63
Then the high **p** tore his robes and Mt 26:65
show yourself to the **p** and offer for your Mk 1:44
God, in the time of Abiathar the high **p**, Mk 2:26
servant of the high **p** and cut off his Mk 14:47
And they led Jesus to the high **p**. And Mk 14:53
right into the courtyard of the high **p**. Mk 14:54
And the high **p** stood up in the midst Mk 14:60
Again the high **p** asked him, "Are you Mk 14:61
And the high **p** tore his garments and Mk 14:63
of the servant girls of the high **p** came, Mk 14:66
of Judea, there was a **p** named Zechariah, Lk 1:5
he was serving as **p** before God when his Lk 1:8
one, but "go and show yourself to the **p**, Lk 5:14
Now by chance a **p** was going down Lk 10:31
the servant of the high **p** and cut off his Lk 22:50
Caiaphas, who was high **p** that year, Jn 11:49
but being high **p** that year he Jn 11:51
of Caiaphas, who was high **p** that year. Jn 18:13
that disciple was known to the high **p**, Jn 18:15
with Jesus into the court of the high **p**, Jn 18:15
disciple, who was known to the high **p**, Jn 18:16
The high **p** then questioned Jesus about Jn 18:19
"Is that how you answer the high **p**?" Jn 18:22
sent him bound to Caiaphas the high **p**. Jn 18:24
One of the servants of the high **p**, a Jn 18:26
Annas the high **p** and Caiaphas and Acts 4:6
But the high **p** rose up, and all who Acts 5:17
Now when the high **p** came, and those Acts 5:21
And the high **p** questioned them, Acts 5:27
And the high **p** said, "Are these things Acts 7:1
disciples of the Lord, went to the high **p** Acts 9:1
And the **p** of Zeus, whose temple was Acts 14:13
of a Jewish high **p** named Sceva were Acts 19:14
as the high **p** and the whole council of Acts 22:5
And the high **p** Ananias commanded Acts 23:2
said, "Would you revile God's high **p**?" Acts 23:4
know, brothers, that he was the high **p**, Acts 23:5
days the high **p** Ananias came down Acts 24:1
and faithful high **p** in the service Heb 2:17
the apostle and high **p** of our confession, Heb 3:1
have a great high **p** who has passed Heb 4:14
do not have a high **p** who is unable to Heb 4:15
For every high **p** chosen from among Heb 5:1
not exalt himself to be made a high **p**, Heb 5:5
in another place, "You are a **p** forever, Heb 5:6
by God a high **p** after the order of Heb 5:10

become a high **p** forever after the	Heb 6:20
king of Salem, **p** of the Most High God,	Heb 7:1
the Son of God he continues a **p** forever.	Heb 7:3
have been for another **p** to arise after	Heb 7:11
evident when another **p** arises in the	Heb 7:15
who has become a **p**, not on the basis	Heb 7:16
witnessed of him, "You are a **p** forever,	Heb 7:17
this one was made a **p** with an oath by	Heb 7:21
change his mind, 'You are a **p** forever.'"	Heb 7:21
that we should have such a high **p**,	Heb 7:26
we have such a high **p**, one who is seated	Heb 8:1
For every high **p** is appointed to offer	Heb 8:3
is necessary for this **p** also to have	Heb 8:3
were on earth, he would not be a **p** at all,	Heb 8:4
but into the second only the high **p** goes,	Heb 9:7
appeared as a high **p** of the good things	Heb 9:11
as the high **p** enters the holy places	Heb 9:25
And every **p** stands daily at his	Heb 10:11
we have a great **p** over the house of	Heb 10:21
places by the high **p** as a sacrifice for	Heb 13:11

PRIEST'S (9)

oil that is in the **p** hand he shall put on	Lv 14:18
oil that is in the **p** hand he shall put on	Lv 14:29
If a **p** daughter marries a layman, she	Lv 22:12
But if a **p** daughter is widowed or	Lv 22:13
And the **p** heart was glad. He took the	Jgs 18:20
sacrifice, the **p** servant would come,	1 Sm 2:13
the **p** servant would come and say to	1 Sm 2:15
bringing him into the high **p** house,	Lk 22:54
and struck the high **p** servant and cut	Jn 18:10

PRIESTHOOD (21)

garments to consecrate him for my **p**.	Ex 28:3
And the **p** shall be theirs by a statute	Ex 29:9
to a perpetual **p** throughout their	Ex 40:15
his sons, and they shall guard their **p**.	Nm 3:10
you? And would you seek the **p** also?	Nm 16:10
bear iniquity connected with your **p**.	Nm 18:1
you shall guard your **p** for all that	Nm 18:7
you shall serve. I give your **p** as a gift,	Nm 18:7
him the covenant of a perpetual **p**,	Nm 25:13
for the **p** of the LORD is their heritage.	Jos 18:7
were excluded from the **p** as unclean.	Ezr 2:62
were excluded from the **p** as unclean.	Neh 7:64
have desecrated the **p** and the	Neh 13:29
the covenant of the **p** and the Levites.	Neh 13:29
according to the custom of the **p**, he was	Lk 1:9
during the high **p** of Annas and	Lk 3:2
through the Levitical **p** (for under it	Heb 7:11
For when there is a change in the **p**,	Heb 7:12
but he holds his **p** permanently,	Heb 7:24
up as a spiritual house, to be a holy **p**,	1 Pt 2:5
But you are a chosen race, a royal **p**, a	1 Pt 2:9

PRIESTLY (2)

the Gentiles in the **p** service of the	Rom 15:16
Levi who receive the **p** office have a	Heb 7:5

PRIESTS (412)

Only the land of the **p** he did not buy,	Gn 47:22
for the **p** had a fixed allowance from	Gn 47:22
the land of the **p** alone did not become	Gn 47:26
to me a kingdom of **p** and a holy nation.	Ex 19:6
Also let the **p** who come near to the	Ex 19:22
do not let the **p** and the people break	Ex 19:24
to serve me as **p**—Aaron and Aaron's	Ex 28:1
brother and his sons to serve me as **p**.	Ex 28:4
them, that they may serve me as **p**.	Ex 28:41
them, that they may serve me as **p**.	Ex 29:1
sons I will consecrate to serve me as **p**.	Ex 29:44
them, that they may serve me as **p**.	Ex 30:30
of his sons, for their service as **p**,	Ex 31:10
of his sons, for their service as **p**."	Ex 35:19
of his sons for their service as **p**.	Ex 39:41
father, that they may serve me as **p**.	Ex 40:15
and Aaron's sons the **p** shall bring the	Lv 1:5
And Aaron's sons the **p** shall arrange the	Lv 1:8
and Aaron's sons the **p** shall throw its	Lv 1:11
and bring it to Aaron's sons the **p**. And he	Lv 2:2
and Aaron's sons the **p** shall throw the	Lv 3:2
Every male among the **p** may eat of it; it	Lv 6:29
Every male among the **p** may eat of it. It	Lv 7:6
were presented to serve as **p** of the LORD.	Lv 7:35
the priest or to one of his sons the **p**,	Lv 13:2
make atonement for the **p** and for all	Lv 16:33
the LORD said to Moses, "Speak to the **p**,	Lv 21:1
of the sons of Aaron, the anointed **p**,	Nm 3:3
priests, whom he ordained to serve as **p**.	Nm 3:3
and Ithamar served as **p** in the lifetime	Nm 3:4
sanctuary with which the **p** minister,	Nm 3:31
And the sons of Aaron, the **p**, shall	Nm 10:8
come to the Levitical **p** and to the judge	Dt 17:9
of this law, approved by the Levitical **p**.	Dt 17:18
"The Levitical **p**, all the tribe of Levi,	Dt 18:1
before the **p** and the judges who are in	Dt 19:17
Then the **p**, the sons of Levi, shall come	Dt 21:5
to all that the Levitical **p** shall direct you.	Dt 24:8
Moses and the Levitical **p** said to all	Dt 27:9
Moses wrote this law and gave it to the **p**,	Dt 31:9
your God being carried by the Levitical **p**,	Jos 3:3
And Joshua said to the **p**, "Take up the	Jos 3:6
command the **p** who bear the ark of the	Jos 3:8
of the feet of the **p** bearing the ark of the	Jos 3:13
the Jordan with the **p** bearing the ark of	Jos 3:14
and the feet of the **p** bearing the ark were	Jos 3:15
Now the **p** bearing the ark of the	Jos 3:17
where the feet of the **p** bearing the ark of	Jos 4:9
For the **p** bearing the ark stood in the	Jos 4:10
the LORD and the **p** passed over before the	Jos 4:11
"Command the **p** bearing the ark of the	Jos 4:16
So Joshua commanded the **p**, "Come up	Jos 4:17
And when the **p** bearing the ark of the	Jos 4:18
Seven **p** shall bear seven trumpets of	Jos 6:4
times, and the **p** shall blow the trumpets.	Jos 6:4
son of Nun called the **p** and said to them,	Jos 6:6
and let seven **p** bear seven trumpets	Jos 6:6
the seven **p** bearing the seven trumpets of	Jos 6:8
walking before the **p** who were blowing	Jos 6:9
and the **p** took up the ark of the LORD.	Jos 6:12
And the seven **p** bearing the seven	Jos 6:13
when the **p** had blown the trumpets,	Jos 6:16
before the Levitical **p** who carried the	Jos 8:33
of the descendants of Aaron, the **p**,	Jos 21:19
and his sons were **p** to the tribe of the	Jgs 18:30
and Phinehas, were **p** of the LORD.	1 Sm 1:3
The custom of the **p** with the people	1 Sm 2:13
This is why the **p** of Dagon and all who	1 Sm 5:5
called for the **p** and the diviners	1 Sm 6:2
house, the **p** who were at Nob,	1 Sm 22:11
"Turn and kill the **p** of the LORD,	1 Sm 22:17
their hand to strike the **p** of the LORD.	1 Sm 22:17
turn and strike the **p**." And Doeg the	1 Sm 22:18
turned and struck down the **p**,	1 Sm 22:18
And Nob, the city of the **p**, he put to	1 Sm 22:19
that Saul had killed the **p** of the LORD.	1 Sm 22:21
the son of Abiathar were **p**,	2 Sm 8:17
Pelethites, and David's sons were **p**.	2 Sm 8:18
and Abiathar the **p** with you there?	2 Sm 15:35
tell it to Zadok and Abiathar the **p**.	2 Sm 15:35
said to Zadok and Abiathar the **p**,	2 Sm 17:15
to Zadok and Abiathar the **p**,	2 Sm 19:11
and Zadok and Abiathar were **p**;	2 Sm 20:25
the army; Zadok and Abiathar were **p**;	1 Kgs 4:4
Israel came, and the **p** took up the ark.	1 Kgs 8:3
the **p** and the Levites brought them up.	1 Kgs 8:4
Then the **p** brought the ark of the	1 Kgs 8:6
And when the **p** came out of the Holy	1 Kgs 8:10
so that the **p** could not stand to	1 Kgs 8:11
places and appointed **p** from among	1 Kgs 12:31
placed in Bethel the **p** of the high	1 Kgs 12:32
sacrifice on you the **p** of the high	1 Kgs 13:2
but made **p** for the high places	1 Kgs 13:33
he ordained to be **p** of the high	1 Kgs 13:33
men and his close friends and his **p**,	2 Kgs 10:11
all his worshipers and all his **p**.	2 Kgs 10:19
Jehoash said to the **p**, "All the money	2 Kgs 12:4
let the **p** take, each from his donor,	2 Kgs 12:5
the **p** had made no repairs on the	2 Kgs 12:6
priest and the other **p** and said to	2 Kgs 12:7
So the **p** agreed that they should take	2 Kgs 12:8
And the **p** who guarded the threshold	2 Kgs 12:9
of the LORD; it belonged to the **p**.	2 Kgs 12:16
there one of the **p** whom you carried	2 Kgs 17:27
So one of the **p** whom they had	2 Kgs 17:28
sorts of people as **p** of the high	2 Kgs 17:32
the secretary, and the senior **p**,	2 Kgs 19:2
Jerusalem and the **p** and the prophets,	2 Kgs 23:2
high priest and the **p** of the second	2 Kgs 23:4
And he deposed the **p** whom the kings	2 Kgs 23:5
he brought all the **p** out of the cities	2 Kgs 23:8
places where the **p** had made	2 Kgs 23:8
the **p** of the high places did not come	2 Kgs 23:9
he sacrificed all the **p** of the high	2 Kgs 23:20
in their cities were Israel, the **p**,	1 Chr 9:2
Of the **p**: Jedaiah, Jehoiarib, Jachin,	1 Chr 9:10
Others, of the sons of the **p**, prepared	1 Chr 9:30
as well as to the **p** and Levites in the	1 Chr 13:2
David summoned the **p** Zadok and	1 Chr 15:11
So the **p** and the Levites consecrated	1 Chr 15:14
Benaiah, and Eliezer, the **p**,	1 Chr 15:24
and Jahaziel the **p** were to blow	1 Chr 16:6
his brothers the **p** before the	1 Chr 16:39
the son of Abiathar were **p**;	1 Chr 18:16
of Israel and the **p** and the Levites.	1 Chr 23:2
Eleazar and Ithamar became the **p**.	1 Chr 24:2
fathers' houses of the **p** and of the	1 Chr 24:6
fathers' houses of the **p** and of the	1 Chr 24:31
the divisions of the **p** and of the	1 Chr 28:13
the divisions of the **p** and the Levites	1 Chr 28:21
and the sea was for the **p** to wash in.	2 Chr 4:6
the court of the **p** and the great court	2 Chr 4:9
tent; the Levitical **p** brought them up.	2 Chr 5:5
Then the **p** brought the ark of the	2 Chr 5:7
And when the **p** came out of the Holy	2 Chr 5:11
Place (for all the **p** who were present	2 Chr 5:11
altar with 120 **p** who were	2 Chr 5:12
so that the **p** could not stand to	2 Chr 5:14
Let your **p**, O LORD God, be clothed	2 Chr 6:41
And the **p** could not enter the house of	2 Chr 7:2
The **p** stood at their posts; the Levites	2 Chr 7:6
opposite them the **p** sounded trumpets,	2 Chr 7:6
the divisions of the **p** for their service,	2 Chr 8:14
and ministry before the **p** as the duty	2 Chr 8:14
had commanded the **p** and Levites	2 Chr 8:15
And the **p** and the Levites who were	2 Chr 11:13
out from serving as **p** of the LORD,	2 Chr 11:14
he appointed his own **p** for the high	2 Chr 11:15
you not driven out the **p** of the LORD,	2 Chr 13:9
and made **p** for yourselves like the	2 Chr 13:9
We have **p** ministering to the LORD	2 Chr 13:10
and his **p** with their battle trumpets	2 Chr 13:12
LORD, and the **p** blew the trumpets.	2 Chr 13:14
Levites, the **p** Elishama and Jehoram.	2 Chr 17:8
certain Levites and **p** and heads of	2 Chr 19:8
of you **p** and Levites who come off	2 Chr 23:4
LORD except the **p** and ministering	2 Chr 23:6
of the Levitical **p** and the Levites	2 Chr 23:18
And he gathered the **p** and the Levites	2 Chr 24:5
with eighty **p** of the LORD who were	2 Chr 26:17
but for the **p** the sons of Aaron,	2 Chr 26:18
when he became angry with the **p**,	2 Chr 26:19
the presence of the **p** in the house of	2 Chr 26:19
priest and all the **p** looked at him,	2 Chr 26:20
He brought in the **p** and the Levites	2 Chr 29:4
The **p** went into the inner part of the	2 Chr 29:16
he commanded the **p** the sons of	2 Chr 29:21
and the **p** received the blood and	2 Chr 29:22
and the **p** slaughtered them and	2 Chr 29:24
David, and the **p** with the trumpets.	2 Chr 29:26
But the **p** were too few and could not	2 Chr 29:34
so until other **p** had consecrated	2 Chr 29:34
heart than the **p** in consecrating	2 Chr 29:34
time because the **p** had not	2 Chr 30:3
And the **p** and the Levites were	2 Chr 30:15
The **p** threw the blood that they	2 Chr 30:16
Levites and the **p** praised the LORD	2 Chr 30:21
And the **p** consecrated themselves	2 Chr 30:24
of Judah, and the **p** and the Levites,	2 Chr 30:25
Then the **p** and the Levites arose	2 Chr 30:27
the divisions of the **p** and of the	2 Chr 31:2
to his service, the **p** and the Levites,	2 Chr 31:2
portion due to the **p** and the Levites,	2 Chr 31:4
Hezekiah questioned the **p** and the	2 Chr 31:9
assisting him in the cities of the **p**,	2 Chr 31:15
enrollment of the **p** was according	2 Chr 31:17
And for the sons of Aaron, the **p**,	2 Chr 31:19
male among the **p** and to everyone	2 Chr 31:19
the bones of the **p** on their altars and	2 Chr 34:5
Jerusalem and the **p** and the Levites,	2 Chr 34:30
He appointed the **p** to their offices and	2 Chr 35:2
willingly to the people, to the **p**,	2 Chr 35:8
gave to the **p** for the Passover	2 Chr 35:8
for, the **p** stood in their place,	2 Chr 35:10
and the **p** threw the blood that they	2 Chr 35:11
for themselves and for the **p**,	2 Chr 35:14
because the **p** the sons of Aaron	2 Chr 35:14
themselves and for the **p** the sons of	2 Chr 35:14
by Josiah, and the **p** and the Levites,	2 Chr 35:18
the officers of the **p** and the people	2 Chr 36:14
and Benjamin, and the **p** and the Levites,	Ezr 1:5
The **p**: the sons of Jedaiah, of the house	Ezr 2:36
Also, of the sons of the **p**: the sons of	Ezr 2:61
Now the **p**, the Levites, some of the	Ezr 2:70
the son of Jozadak, with his fellow **p**,	Ezr 3:2
the **p** and the Levites and all who had	Ezr 3:8
the **p** in their vestments came forward	Ezr 3:10
But many of the **p** and Levites and	Ezr 3:12
as the **p** at Jerusalem require—let that be	Ezr 6:9
the people of Israel, the **p** and the Levites,	Ezr 6:16
And they set the **p** in their divisions and	Ezr 6:18
For the **p** and the Levites had purified	Ezr 6:20
all the returned exiles, for their fellow **p**,	Ezr 6:20
of Israel, and some of the **p** and Levites,	Ezr 7:7
of Israel or their **p** or Levites in my	Ezr 7:13
freewill offerings of the people and the **p**,	Ezr 7:16
custom, or toll on anyone of the **p**,	Ezr 7:24
As I reviewed the people and the **p**, I	Ezr 8:15
Then I set apart twelve of the leading **p**:	Ezr 8:24
them before the chief **p** and the Levites	Ezr 8:29
So the **p** and the Levites took over the	Ezr 8:30
of Israel and the **p** and the Levites have	Ezr 9:1
and our **p** have been given into the hand	Ezr 9:7
and made the leading **p** and Levites and	Ezr 10:5
the sons of the **p** who had married	Ezr 10:18
and I had not yet told the Jews, the **p**,	Neh 2:16
priest rose up with his brothers the **p**,	Neh 3:1

After him the **p**, the men of the Neh 3:22
Above the Horse Gate the **p** repaired, Neh 3:28
And I called the **p** and made them Neh 5:12
The **p**: the sons of Jedaiah, namely the Neh 7:39
Also, of the **p**: the sons of Hobaiah, the Neh 7:63
So the **p**, the Levites, the gatekeepers, Neh 7:73
the people, with the **p** and the Levites, Neh 8:13
us, upon our kings, our princes, our **p**, Neh 9:32
Our kings, our princes, our **p**, and our Neh 9:34
of our princes, our Levites, and our **p**." Neh 9:38
Bilgai, Shemaiah; these are the **p**. Neh 10:8
The rest of the people, the **p**, the Neh 10:28
We, the **p**, the Levites, and the people, Neh 10:34
to the **p** who minister in the house of Neh 10:36
tree, the wine and the oil, to the **p**, Neh 10:37
are, as well as the **p** who minister, Neh 10:39
Israel, the **p**, the Levites, the temple Neh 11:3
Of the **p**: Jedaiah the son of Joiarib, Neh 11:10
of Israel, and of the **p** and the Levites, Neh 11:20
These are the **p** and the Levites who Neh 12:1
the chiefs of the **p** and of their brothers Neh 12:7
And in the days of Joiakim were **p**, Neh 12:12
so too were the **p** in the reign of Neh 12:22
And the **p** and the Levites purified Neh 12:30
and the **p** Eliakim, Maaseiah, Neh 12:41
the Law for the **p** and for the Levites Neh 12:44
rejoiced over the **p** and the Levites Neh 12:44
and the contributions for the **p**. Neh 13:5
the duties of the **p** and Levites, Neh 13:30
He leads **p** away stripped and Jb 12:19
Their **p** fell by the sword, and their Ps 78:64
Moses and Aaron were among his **p**, Ps 99:6
Let your **p** be clothed with Ps 132:9
Her **p** I will clothe with salvation, and Ps 132:16
Shebna the secretary, and the senior **p**, Is 37:2
but you shall be called the **p** of the LORD; Is 61:6
also I will take for **p** and for Levites, Is 66:21
one of the **p** who were in Anathoth in the Jer 1:1
the kings of Judah, its officials, its **p**, Jer 1:18
The **p** did not say, 'Where is the LORD?' Jer 2:8
they, their kings, their officials, their **p**, Jer 2:26
The **p** shall be appalled and the prophets Jer 4:9
falsely, and the **p** rule at their direction; Jer 5:31
bones of its officials, the bones of the **p**, Jer 8:1
kings who sit on David's throne, the **p**, Jer 13:13
the people and some of the elders of the **p**, Jer 19:1
The **p** and the prophets and all the people Jer 26:7
then the **p** and the prophets and all the Jer 26:8
Then the **p** and the prophets said to the Jer 26:11
people said to the **p** and the prophets, Jer 26:16
Then I spoke to the **p** and to all this Jer 27:16
the presence of the **p** and all the people, Jer 28:1
in the presence of the **p** and all the people Jer 28:5
elders of the exiles, and to the **p**, Jer 29:1
of Maaseiah the priest, and to all the **p**, Jer 29:25
feast the soul of the **p** with abundance, Jer 31:14
officials, their **p** and their prophets, Jer 32:32
and the Levitical **p** shall never lack a Jer 33:18
with the Levitical **p** my ministers. Jer 33:21
and the Levitical **p** who minister to Jer 33:22
of Jerusalem, the eunuchs, the **p**, Jer 34:19
go into exile with his **p** and his officials. Jer 48:7
go into exile, with his **p** and his officials. Jer 49:3
all her gates are desolate; her **p** groan; Lam 1:4
my **p** and elders perished in the city, Lam 1:19
prophets and the iniquities of her **p**, Lam 4:13
no honor was shown to the **p**, no favor Lam 4:16
Her **p** have done violence to my law Ezk 22:26
south is for the **p** who have charge of Ezk 40:45
north is for the **p** who have charge of Ezk 40:46
where the **p** who approach the LORD Ezk 42:13
When the **p** enter the Holy Place, they Ezk 42:14
give to the Levitical **p** of the family of Ezk 43:19
and the **p** shall sprinkle salt on them Ezk 43:24
eighth day onward the **p** shall offer on Ezk 43:27
"But the Levitical **p**, the sons of Zadok, Ezk 44:15
your offerings, shall belong to the **p**. Ezk 44:30
shall also give to the **p** the first of your Ezk 44:30
The **p** shall not eat of anything, Ezk 44:31
It shall be for the **p**, who minister in the Ezk 45:4
The **p** shall offer his burnt offering and Ezk 46:2
row of the holy chambers for the **p**, Ezk 46:19
the place where the **p** shall boil the Ezk 46:20
the **p** shall have an allotment Ezk 48:10
This shall be for the consecrated **p**, Ezk 48:11
And alongside the territory of the **p**, Ezk 48:13
Hear this, O **p**! Pay attention, O house of Hos 5:1
in wait for a man, so the **p** band together; Hos 6:9
so do its idolatrous **p**—those who Hos 10:5
from the house of the LORD. The **p** mourn, Jl 1:9
Put on sackcloth and lament, O **p**; wail, O Jl 1:13
the vestibule and the altar let the **p**, Jl 2:17
for a bribe; its **p** teach for a price; Mi 3:11
name of the idolatrous **p** along with the Zep 1:4
of the idolatrous priests along with the **p**, Zep 1:4
men; her **p** profane what is holy; Zep 3:4
LORD of hosts: Ask the **p** about the law: Hg 2:11
become holy?'" The **p** answered and Hg 2:12
become unclean?" The **p** answered and Hg 2:13
saying to the **p** of the house of the LORD of Zec 7:3
to all the people of the land and the **p**, Zec 7:5
says the LORD of hosts to you, O **p**, who Mal 1:6
"And now, O **p**, this command is for Mal 2:1
assembling all the chief **p** and scribes of Mt 2:4
who were with him, but only for the **p**? Mt 12:4
on the Sabbath the **p** in the temple Mt 12:5
from the elders and chief **p** and scribes, Mt 16:21
over to the chief **p** and scribes, Mt 20:18
But when the chief **p** and the scribes Mt 21:15
the chief **p** and the elders of the people Mt 21:23
When the chief **p** and the Pharisees Mt 21:45
Then the chief **p** and the elders of the Mt 26:3
was Judas Iscariot, went to the chief **p** Mt 26:14
from the chief **p** and the elders of the Mt 26:47
Now the chief **p** and the whole Council Mt 26:59
all the chief **p** and the elders of the people Mt 27:1
of silver to the chief **p** and the elders, Mt 27:3
But the chief **p**, taking the pieces of Mt 27:6
was accused by the chief **p** and elders, Mt 27:12
Now the chief **p** and the elders Mt 27:20
So also the chief **p**, with the scribes and Mt 27:41
the chief **p** and the Pharisees gathered Mt 27:62
and told the chief **p** all that had taken Mt 28:11
it is not lawful for any but the **p** to eat, Mk 2:26
elders and the chief **p** and the scribes Mk 8:31
over to the chief **p** and the scribes, Mk 10:33
And the chief **p** and the scribes heard Mk 11:18
the chief **p** and the scribes and the Mk 11:27
And the chief **p** and the scribes were Mk 14:1
went to the chief **p** in order to betray Mk 14:10
from the chief **p** and the scribes and Mk 14:43
And all the chief **p** and the elders and Mk 14:53
Now the chief **p** and the whole Mk 14:55
the chief **p** held a consultation with the Mk 15:1
And the chief **p** accused him of many Mk 15:3
that the chief **p** had delivered him Mk 15:10
But the chief **p** stirred up the crowd to Mk 15:11
So also the chief **p** with the scribes Mk 15:31
is not lawful for any but the **p** to eat, Lk 6:4
by the elders and chief **p** and scribes, Lk 9:22
show yourselves to the **p**." And as they Lk 17:14
The chief **p** and the scribes and the Lk 19:47
the chief **p** and the scribes with the Lk 20:1
scribes and the chief **p** sought to lay Lk 20:19
And the chief **p** and the scribes were Lk 22:2
with the chief **p** and officers how Lk 22:4
said to the chief **p** and officers of the Lk 22:52
together, both chief **p** and scribes. Lk 22:66
Pilate said to the chief **p** and the crowds, Lk 23:4
The chief **p** and the scribes stood by, Lk 23:10
together the chief **p** and the rulers Lk 23:13
how our chief **p** and rulers delivered Lk 24:20
when the Jews sent **p** and Levites from Jn 1:19
and the chief **p** and Pharisees sent Jn 7:32
then came to the chief **p** and Pharisees, Jn 7:45
So the chief **p** and the Pharisees Jn 11:47
Now the chief **p** and the Pharisees had Jn 11:57
So the chief **p** made plans to put Jn 12:10
from the chief **p** and the Pharisees, Jn 18:3
and the chief **p** have delivered you Jn 18:35
When the chief **p** and the officers saw Jn 19:6
your King?" The chief **p** answered, Jn 19:15
So the chief **p** of the Jews said to Pilate, Jn 19:21
the **p** and the captain of the temple and Acts 4:1
reported what the chief **p** and the elders Acts 4:23
and the chief **p** heard these words, Acts 5:24
great many of the **p** became obedient to Acts 6:7
authority from the chief **p** to bind all Acts 9:14
bring them bound before the chief **p**?" Acts 9:21
commanded the chief **p** and all the Acts 22:30
went to the chief **p** and elders and Acts 23:14
And the chief **p** and the principal men Acts 25:2
the chief **p** and the elders of the Jews Acts 25:15
receiving authority from the chief **p**, Acts 26:10
and commission of the chief **p**. Acts 26:12
that tribe Moses said nothing about **p**. Heb 7:14
who formerly became **p** were made Heb 7:20
The former **p** were many in number, Heb 7:23
He has no need, like those high **p**, to Heb 7:27
men in their weakness as high **p**, Heb 7:28
since there are **p** who offer gifts Heb 8:4
the **p** go regularly into the first section, Heb 9:6
us a kingdom, **p** to his God and Father, Rv 1:6
made them a kingdom and **p** to our God, Rv 5:10
but they will be **p** of God and of Christ, Rv 20:6

PRIESTS' (9)
the thigh of the **p** portion that is Ex 29:27
this shall be the **p** due from the people, Dt 18:3
very place where the **p** feet stood firmly, Jos 4:3
and the soles of the **p** feet were lifted up Jos 4:18
"Please put me in one of the **p** places, 1 Sm 2:36
minas of silver, and 100 **p** garments. Ezr 2:69
30 **p** garments and 500 minas of silver. Neh 7:70
minas of silver, and 67 **p** garments. Neh 7:72
certain of the **p** sons with trumpets: Neh 12:35

PRIME (1)
as I was in my **p**, when the friendship of Jb 29:4

PRINCE (74)
my lord; you are a **p** of God among us. Gn 23:6
of Hamor the Hivite, the **p** of the land, Gn 34:2
"Who made you a **p** and a judge over us? Ex 2:14
must also make yourself a **p** over us? Nm 16:13
of him who is **p** among his brothers. Dt 33:16
anoint him to be **p** over my people 1 Sm 9:16
anointed you to be **p** over his people 1 Sm 10:1
anointed you to be **p** over his heritage. 1 Sm 10:1
him to be **p** over his people, 1 Sm 13:14
and has appointed you **p** over Israel, 1 Sm 25:30
not know that a **p** and a great man 2 Sm 3:38
Israel, and you shall be **p** over Israel.'" 2 Sm 5:2
house, to appoint me as **p** over Israel, 2 Sm 6:21
that you should be **p** over my people 2 Sm 7:8
Nahshon, **p** of the sons of Judah. 1 Chr 2:10
and you shall be **p** over my people 1 Chr 11:2
The **p** Jehoiada, of the house of 1 Chr 12:27
sheep, to be **p** over my people Israel, 1 Chr 17:7
they anointed him as **p** for the LORD, 1 Chr 29:22
chose no man as **p** over my people 2 Chr 6:5
Maacah as chief **p** among his 2 Chr 11:22
them out to Sheshbazzar the **p** of Judah. Ezr 1:8
you say, 'Where is the house of the **p**? Jb 21:28
steps; like a **p** I would approach him. Jb 31:37
men you shall die, and fall like any **p**." Ps 82:7
king, but without people a **p** is ruined. Prv 14:28
to a fool; still less is false speech to a **p**. Prv 17:7
among the chariots of my kinsman, a **p**. Sg 6:12
God, Everlasting Father, **P** of Peace. Is 9:6
Their **p** shall be one of themselves; Jer 30:21
mourns, the **p** is wrapped in despair, Ezk 7:27
oracle concerns the **p** in Jerusalem Ezk 12:10
And the **p** who is among them shall Ezk 12:12
you, O profane wicked one, **p** of Israel, Ezk 21:25
"Son of man, say to the **p** of Tyre, Thus Ezk 28:2
shall no longer be a **p** from the land of Ezk 30:13
servant David shall be **p** among them. Ezk 34:24
my servant shall be their **p** forever. Ezk 37:25
the chief **p** of Meshech and Tubal, Ezk 38:2
O Gog, chief **p** of Meshech and Tubal. Ezk 38:3
O Gog, chief **p** of Meshech and Tubal. Ezk 39:1
Only the **p** may sit in it to eat bread Ezk 44:3
"And to the **p** shall belong the land on Ezk 45:7
to give this offering to the **p** in Israel. Ezk 45:16
On that day the **p** shall provide for Ezk 45:22
The **p** shall enter by the vestibule of the Ezk 46:2
burnt offering that the **p** offers to the Ezk 46:4
When the **p** enters, he shall enter by the Ezk 46:8
they enter, the **p** shall enter with them, Ezk 46:10
When the **p** provides a freewill Ezk 46:12
If the **p** makes a gift to any of his sons Ezk 46:16
Then it shall revert to the **p**; surely it is Ezk 46:17
The **p** shall not take any of the Ezk 46:18
of the city shall belong to the **p**. Ezk 48:21
tribal portions, it shall belong to the **p**. Ezk 48:21
midst of that which belongs to the **p**. Ezk 48:22
The portion of the **p** shall lie between Ezk 48:22
great, even as great as the **P** of the host. Dn 8:11
even rise up against the **P** of princes, Dn 8:25
to the coming of an anointed one, a **p**, Dn 9:25
And the people of the **p** who is to come Dn 9:26
The **p** of the kingdom of Persia Dn 10:13
return to fight against the **p** of Persia; Dn 10:20
out, behold, the **p** of Greece will come. Dn 10:20
against these except Michael, your **p**. Dn 10:21
and broken, even the **p** of the covenant. Dn 11:22
the great **p** who has charge of your Dn 12:1
dwell many days without king or **p**, Hos 3:4
the **p** and the judge ask for a bribe, and Mi 7:3
casts out demons by the **p** of demons." Mt 9:34
is only by Beelzebul, the **p** of demons, Mt 12:24
Beelzebul," and "by the **p** of demons he Mk 3:22
demons by Beelzebul, the **p** of demons," Lk 11:15
following the **p** of the power of the air, Eph 2:2

PRINCE'S (1)
It shall be the **p** duty to furnish the Ezk 45:17

PRINCES (121)
And when the **p** of Pharaoh saw her, Gn 12:15
He shall father twelve **p**, and I will Gn 17:20
twelve **p** according to their tribes. Gn 25:16
the well that the **p** dug, that the nobles Nm 21:18
to me." So the **p** of Moab stayed with Nm 22:8
morning and said to the **p** of Balak, Nm 22:13
So the **p** of Moab rose and went to Nm 22:14
Once again Balak sent **p**, more in Nm 22:15

donkey and went with the **p** of Moab. Nm 22:21
Balaam went on with the **p** of Balak. Nm 22:35
Balaam and for the **p** who were with Nm 22:40
he and all the **p** of Moab were standing Nm 23:6
offering, and the **p** of Moab with him. Nm 23:17
Zur and Hur and Reba, the **p** of Sihon, Jos 13:21
"Hear, O kings; give ear, O **p**; to the LORD Jgs 5:3
the **p** of Issachar came with Deborah, Jgs 5:15
And they captured the two **p** of Midian, Jgs 7:25
given into your hands the **p** of Midian, Jgs 8:3
make them sit with **p** and inherit a seat 1 Sm 2:8
Then the **p** of the Philistines came 1 Sm 18:30
But the **p** of the Ammonites said to 2 Sm 10:3
to visit the royal **p** and the sons of 2 Kgs 10:13
by name were **p** in their clans, 1 Chr 4:38
mighty warriors, chiefs of the **p**. 1 Chr 7:40
But the **p** of the Ammonites said to 1 Chr 19:3
the king and the **p** and Zadok the 1 Chr 24:6
to Rehoboam and to the **p** of Judah, 2 Chr 12:5
Then the **p** of Israel and the king 2 Chr 12:6
and also some of the **p** of Israel. 2 Chr 21:4
he met the **p** of Judah and the sons of 2 Chr 22:8
And all the **p** and all the people 2 Chr 24:10
of Jehoiada the **p** of Judah came 2 Chr 24:17
and destroyed all the **p** of the people 2 Chr 24:23
the spoil before the **p** and all the 2 Chr 28:14
the house of the king and of the **p**, 2 Chr 28:21
the king and his **p** and all the 2 Chr 30:2
with letters from the king and his **p**, 2 Chr 30:6
king and the **p** commanded by the 2 Chr 30:12
and the **p** gave the assembly 1,000 2 Chr 30:24
Hezekiah and the **p** came and saw 2 Chr 31:8
of the envoys of the **p** of Babylon, 2 Chr 32:31
treasures of the king and of his **p**, 2 Chr 36:18
come upon us, upon our kings, our **p**, Neh 9:32
Our kings, our **p**, our priests, and our Neh 9:34
document are the names of our **p**, Neh 9:38
show the peoples and the **p** her beauty, Est 1:11
the seven **p** of Persia and Media, Est 1:14
This advice pleased the king and the **p**, Est 1:21
or with **p** who had gold, who filled their Jb 3:15
He pours contempt on **p** and loosens the Jb 12:21
the **p** refrained from talking and laid Jb 29:9
who shows no partiality to **p**, nor Jb 34:19
you will make them **p** in all the earth. Ps 45:16
The **p** of the peoples gather as the people Ps 47:9
the lead, the **p** of Judah in their throng, Ps 68:27
Judah in their throng, the **p** of Zebulun, Ps 68:27
princes of Zebulun, the **p** of Naphtali. Ps 68:27
who cuts off the spirit of **p**, who is to be Ps 76:12
all their **p** like Zebah and Zalmunna, Ps 83:11
to bind his **p** at his pleasure and to Ps 105:22
pours contempt on **p** and makes them Ps 107:40
to make them sit with **p**, with the Ps 113:8
sit with princes, with the **p** of his people. Ps 113:8
refuge in the LORD than to trust in **p**. Ps 118:9
Even though **p** sit plotting against me, Ps 119:23
P persecute me without cause, but Ps 119:161
Put not your trust in **p**, in a son of man, Ps 146:3
peoples, **p** and all rulers of the earth! Ps 148:11
by me **p** rule, and nobles, all who Prv 8:16
much less for a slave to rule over **p**. Prv 19:10
and **p** walking on the ground like Eccl 10:7
and your **p** feast in the morning! Eccl 10:16
and your **p** feast at the proper time, Eccl 10:17
Your **p** are rebels and companions of Is 1:23
And I will make boys their **p**, and infants Is 3:4
with the elders and **p** of his people: Is 3:14
The **p** of Zoan are utterly foolish; the Is 19:11
The **p** of Zoan have become fools, and Is 19:13
fools, and the **p** of Memphis are deluded; Is 19:13
eat, they drink. Arise, O **p**; oil the shield! Is 21:5
of crowns, whose merchants were **p**, Is 23:8
righteousness, and **p** will rule in justice. Is 32:1
kingdom, and all its **p** shall be nothing. Is 34:12
who brings **p** to nothing, and makes the Is 40:23
I will profane the **p** of the sanctuary, Is 43:28
p, and they shall prostrate themselves; Is 49:7
of this city kings and **p** who sit on the Jer 17:25
Her **p** have become like deer that find Lam 1:6
her king and **p** are among the nations; Lam 2:9
Her **p** were purer than snow, whiter Lam 4:7
P are hung up by their hands; no Lam 5:12
the son of Benaiah, **p** of the people. Ezk 11:1
her king and her **p** and brought them Ezk 17:12
up a lamentation for the **p** of Israel, Ezk 19:1
people. It is against all the **p** of Israel. Ezk 21:12
"Behold, the **p** of Israel in you, every one Ezk 22:6
Her **p** in her midst are like wolves Ezk 22:27
Then all the **p** of the sea will step down Ezk 26:16
Arabia and all the **p** of Kedar were Ezk 27:21
is there, her kings and all her **p**, Ezk 32:29
"The **p** of the north are there, all of Ezk 32:30
drink the blood of the **p** of the earth— Ezk 39:18
And my **p** shall no more oppress my Ezk 45:8
the Lord GOD: Enough, O **p** of Israel! Ezk 45:9
even rise up against the Prince of **p**, Dn 8:25
spoke in your name to our kings, our **p**, Dn 9:6
open shame, to our kings, to our **p**, Dn 9:8
days, but Michael, one of the chief **p**, Dn 10:13
but one of his **p** shall be stronger than Dn 11:5
The **p** of Judah have become like those Hos 5:10
king glad, and the **p** by their treachery. Hos 7:3
the **p** became sick with the heat of wine; Hos 7:5
their **p** shall fall by the sword because Hos 7:16
me. They set up **p**, but I knew it not. Hos 8:4
And the king and **p** shall soon writhe Hos 8:10
them no more; all their **p** are rebels. Hos 9:15
you said, "Give me a king and **p**"? Hos 13:10
he and his **p** together," says the LORD. Am 1:15
and will kill all its **p** with him," says the Am 2:3
him seven shepherds and eight **p** of men; Mi 5:5
Your **p** are like grasshoppers, your Na 3:17

PRINCESS (2)
All glorious is the **p** in her chamber, Ps 45:13
She who was a **p** among the provinces Lam 1:1

PRINCESSES (3)
Her wisest **p** answer, indeed, she answers Jgs 5:29
700 wives, **p**, and 300 concubines. 1 Kgs 11:3
the men, the women, the children, the **p**, Jer 43:6

PRINCIPAL (2)
the scribes and the **p** men of the people Lk 19:47
chief priests and the **p** men of the Jews Acts 25:2

PRINCIPLES (3)
enslaved to the elementary **p** of the world. Gal 4:3
and worthless elementary **p** of the world, Gal 4:9
you again the basic **p** of the oracles of Heb 5:12

PRISCA (3)
Greet **P** and Aquila, my fellow workers Rom 16:3
Aquila and **P**, together with the 1 Cor 16:19
Greet **P** and Aquila, and the 2 Tm 4:19

PRISCILLA (3)
come from Italy with his wife **P**, Acts 18:2
for Syria, and with him **P** and Aquila. Acts 18:18
but when **P** and Aquila heard him, Acts 18:26

PRISON (72)
took him and put him into the **p**, Gn 39:20
were confined, and he was there in **p**. Gn 39:20
favor in the sight of the keeper of the **p**. Gn 39:21
the keeper of the **p** put Joseph in charge Gn 39:22
of all the prisoners who were in the **p**. Gn 39:22
The keeper of the **p** paid no attention to Gn 39:23
in the **p** where Joseph was confined. Gn 40:3
were confined in the **p**—each his own Gn 40:5
And he ground at the mill in the **p**. Jgs 16:21
us." So they called Samson out of the **p**, Jgs 16:25
"Put this fellow in **p** and feed him 1 Kgs 22:27
shut him up and bound him in **p**. 2 Kgs 17:4
Jehoiachin king of Judah from **p**. 2 Kgs 25:27
Jehoiachin put off his **p** garments. 2 Kgs 25:29
seer and put him in the stocks in **p**, 2 Chr 16:10
Put this fellow in **p** and feed him 2 Chr 18:26
Bring me out of **p**, that I may give Ps 142:7
For he went from **p** to the throne, Eccl 4:14
they will be shut up in a **p**, and after Is 24:22
from the **p** those who sit in darkness. Is 42:7
and the opening of the **p** to those who are Is 61:1
people, for he had not yet been put in **p**. Jer 37:4
the secretary, for it had been made a **p**. Jer 37:15
this people, that you have put me in **p**? Jer 37:18
and put him in **p** till the day of his Jer 52:11
of Judah and brought him out of **p**. Jer 52:31
So Jehoiachin put off his **p** garments. Jer 52:33
judge to the guard, and you be put in **p**. Mt 5:25
when John heard in **p** about the deeds of Mt 11:2
him and put him in **p** for the sake of Mt 14:3
sent and had John beheaded in the **p**, Mt 14:10
and put him in **p** until he should pay Mt 18:30
me, I was in **p** and you came to me.' Mt 25:36
we see you sick or in **p** and visit you?' Mt 25:39
sick and in **p** and you did not visit me.' Mt 25:43
or a stranger or naked or sick or in **p**, Mt 25:44
and bound him in **p** for the sake of Mk 6:17
He went and beheaded him in the **p** Mk 6:27
And among the rebels in **p**, who had Mk 15:7
to them all, that he locked up John in **p**. Lk 3:20
the officer, and the officer put you in **p**. Lk 12:58
to go with you both to **p** and to death." Lk 22:33
been thrown into **p** for an insurrection Lk 23:19
been thrown into **p** for insurrection Lk 23:25
(for John had not yet been put in **p**). Jn 3:24
apostles and put them in the public **p**. Acts 5:18
Lord opened the **p** doors and brought Acts 5:19
and sent to the **p** to have them Acts 5:21
came, they did not find them in the **p**, Acts 5:22
"We found the **p** securely locked and Acts 5:23
whom you put in **p** are standing in the Acts 5:25
and women and committed them to **p**. Acts 8:3
he had seized him, he put him in **p**, Acts 12:4
So Peter was kept in **p**, but earnest Acts 12:5
before the door were guarding the **p**. Acts 12:6
Lord had brought him out of the **p**. Acts 12:17
upon them, they threw them into **p**, Acts 16:23
into the inner **p** and fastened their Acts 16:24
the foundations of the **p** were shaken. Acts 16:26
and saw that the **p** doors were open, Acts 16:27
citizens, and have thrown us into **p**; Acts 16:37
went out of the **p** and visited Lydia. Acts 16:40
and delivering to **p** both men and Acts 22:4
the Jews a favor, Felix left Paul in **p**. Acts 24:27
the saints in **p** after receiving Acts 26:10
Christ, on account of which I am in **p**— Col 4:3
you had compassion on those in **p**, Heb 10:34
Remember those who are in **p**, as Heb 13:3
in prison, as though in **p** with them, Heb 13:3
went and proclaimed to the spirits in **p**, 1 Pt 3:19
is about to throw some of you into **p**, Rv 2:10
ended, Satan will be released from his **p** Rv 20:7

PRISONER (15)
of Babylon took him **p** in the eighth 2 Kgs 24:12
crowd any one **p** whom they wanted. Mt 27:15
then a notorious **p** called Barabbas. Mt 27:16
release for them one **p** for whom they Mk 15:6
"Paul the **p** called me and asked me Acts 23:18
"There is a man left **p** by Felix, Acts 25:14
to me unreasonable, in sending a **p**, Acts 25:27
delivered as a **p** from Jerusalem into Acts 28:17
a **p** for Christ Jesus on behalf of you Eph 3:1
I therefore, a **p** for the Lord, urge you to Eph 4:1
Aristarchus my fellow **p** greets you, and Col 4:10
about our Lord, nor of me his **p**, 2 Tm 1:8
Paul, a **p** for Christ Jesus, and Phlm 1:1
man and now a **p** also for Christ Jesus Phlm 1:9
my fellow **p** in Christ Jesus, Phlm 1:23

PRISONERS (22)
place where the king's **p** were confined, Gn 39:20
in charge of all the **p** who were in the Gn 39:22
There the **p** are at ease together; they hear Jb 3:18
he leads out the **p** to prosperity, but the Ps 68:6
not despise his own people who are **p**. Ps 69:33
Let the groans of the **p** come before you; Ps 79:11
to hear the groans of the **p**, to set free Ps 102:20
of death, **p** in affliction and in irons, Ps 107:10
to the hungry. The LORD sets the **p** free; Ps 146:7
to crouch among the **p** or fall among the Is 10:4
its cities, who did not let his **p** go home?' Is 14:17
will be gathered together as **p** in a pit; Is 24:22
to bring out the **p** from the dungeon, Is 42:7
saying to the **p**, 'Come out,' to those who Is 49:9
crush underfoot all the **p** of the earth, Lam 3:34
I will set your **p** free from the waterless Zec 9:11
Return to your stronghold, O **p** of hope; Zec 9:12
God, and the **p** were listening to them, Acts 16:25
supposing that the **p** had escaped. Acts 16:27
Paul and some other **p** to a centurion Acts 27:1
The soldiers' plan was to kill the **p**, Acts 27:42
Junia, my kinsmen and my fellow **p**. Rom 16:7

PRISONS (2)
them trapped in holes and hidden in **p**; Is 42:22
you up to the synagogues and **p**, Lk 21:12

PRIVATE (5)
her hand and seizes him by the **p** parts, Dt 25:11
"Speak to David in **p** and say, 1 Sm 18:22
you have whispered in **p** rooms shall be Lk 12:3
he also went up, not publicly but in **p**. Jn 7:10
and called her sister Mary, saying in **p**, Jn 11:28

PRIVATELY (10)
midst of the gate to speak with him **p**, 2 Sm 3:27
the disciples came to Jesus **p** and said, Mt 17:19
of Olives, the disciples came to him **p**, Mt 24:3
but **p** to his own disciples he explained Mk 4:34
taking him aside from the crowd **p**, Mk 7:33
the house, his disciples asked him **p**, Mk 9:28
and John and Andrew asked him **p**, Mk 13:3
Then turning to the disciples he said **p**, Lk 10:23
hand, and going aside asked him **p**, Acts 23:19
before them (though **p** before those who Gal 2:2

PRIZE (7)
P her highly, and she will exalt you; she Prv 4:8
live and shall have his life as a **p** of war. Jer 21:9
He shall have his life as a **p** of war, and Jer 38:2
you shall have your life as a **p** of war, Jer 39:18
you your life as a **p** of war in all places Jer 45:5
compete, but only one receives the **p**? 1 Cor 9:24
the goal for the **p** of the upward call Phil 3:14

PRIZED (1)
the city, all its gains, all its **p** belongings, Jer 20:5

PROBLEMS (2)
and solve **p** were found in this Daniel, Dn 5:12

you can give interpretations and solve **p**. Dn 5:16

PROCEDURE (2)
according to the **p** established for 1 Chr 24:19
this was the king's **p** toward all who Est 1:13

PROCEED (4)
Let Pharaoh **p** to appoint overseers Gn 41:34
answer; twice, but I will **p** no further." Jb 40:5
for they **p** from evil to evil, and they do not Jer 9:3
For whatever does not **p** from faith is Rom 14:23

PROCEEDED (2)
these things, he **p** to tell a parable, Lk 19:11
the Jews, he **p** to arrest Peter also. Acts 12:3

PROCEEDING (1)
as it were an error **p** from the ruler: Eccl 10:5

PROCEEDS (8)
according to all that **p** out of his Nm 30:2
then whatever **p** out of her lips Nm 30:12
out of the mouth **p** from the heart, Mt 15:18
Spirit of truth, who **p** from the Father, Jn 15:26
and distributing the **p** to all, Acts 2:45
them and brought the **p** of what was Acts 4:34
himself some of the **p** and brought only Acts 5:2
for yourself part of the **p** of the land? Acts 5:3

PROCESSION (5)
throng and lead them in **p** to the house of Ps 42:4
Your **p** is seen, O God, the procession of Ps 68:24
is seen, O God, the **p** of my God, Ps 68:24
of the nations, with their kings led in **p**. Is 60:11
always leads us in triumphal **p**, 2 Cor 2:14

PROCHORUS (1)
and of the Holy Spirit, and Philip, and **P**, Acts 6:5

PROCLAIM (65)
before you and will **p** before you my Ex 33:19
that you shall **p** as holy convocations; Lv 23:2
which you shall **p** at the time appointed Lv 23:4
which you shall **p** as times of holy Lv 23:37
and **p** liberty throughout the land to all Lv 25:10
For I will **p** the name of the LORD; ascribe Dt 32:3
Now therefore **p** in the ears of the people, Jgs 7:3
And she wrote in the letters, "**P** a fast, 1 Kgs 21:9
set up prophets to **p** concerning you in Neh 6:7
and that they should **p** it and publish it Neh 8:15
shall come and **p** his righteousness to Ps 22:31
I will **p** and tell of them, yet they are more Ps 40:5
me, and I still **p** your wondrous deeds. Ps 71:17
until I **p** your might to another Ps 71:18
The heavens **p** his righteousness, and all Ps 97:6
against them; they **p** their sin like Sodom; Is 3:9
the peoples, **p** that his name is exalted. Is 12:4
Who is like me? Let him **p** it. Let him Is 44:7
declare this with a shout of joy, **p** it, Is 48:20
to **p** liberty to the captives, Is 61:1
to **p** the year of the LORD'S favor, and the Is 61:2
"Go and **p** in the hearing of Jerusalem, Jer 2:2
Go, and **p** these words toward the north, Jer 3:12
Declare in Judah, and **p** in Jerusalem, and Jer 4:5
this in the house of Jacob; **p** it in Judah: Jer 5:20
of the LORD'S house, and **p** there this word, Jer 7:2
"**P** all these words in the cities of Judah Jer 11:6
and **p** there the words that I tell you. Jer 19:2
p, give praise, and say, 'O LORD, save your Jer 31:7
behold, I **p** to you liberty to the sword, Jer 34:17
"Declare in Egypt, and **p** in Migdol; Jer 46:14
Migdol; **p** in Memphis and Tahpanhes; Jer 46:14
"Declare among the nations and **p**, set Jer 50:2
and proclaim, set up a banner and **p**, Jer 50:2
P this among the nations: Consecrate for Jl 3:9
P to the strongholds in Ashdod and to Am 3:9
is leavened, and **p** freewill offerings, Am 4:5
And **p** as you go, saying, 'The kingdom Mt 10:7
hear whispered, **p** on the housetops. Mt 10:27
and he will **p** justice to the Gentiles. Mt 12:18
away and began to **p** in the Decapolis Mk 5:20
all the world and **p** the gospel to the Mk 16:15
he has anointed me to **p** good news to the Lk 4:18
has sent me to **p** liberty to the captives Lk 4:18
to **p** the year of the Lord's favor." Lk 4:19
he sent them out to **p** the kingdom of God Lk 9:2
for you, go and **p** the kingdom of God." Lk 9:60
had in every city those who **p** him, Acts 15:21
who **p** to you the way of salvation." Acts 16:17
saying, "This Jesus, whom I **p** to you, Acts 17:3
worship as unknown, this I **p** to you. Acts 17:23
he would **p** light both to our people Acts 26:23
(that is, the word of faith that we **p**); Rom 10:8
that those who **p** the gospel should 1 Cor 9:14
you **p** the Lord's death until he 1 Cor 11:26
For what we **p** is not ourselves, but 2 Cor 4:5
the gospel that I **p** among the Gentiles, Gal 2:2
my mouth boldly to **p** the mystery of Eph 6:19
The former **p** Christ out of rivalry, not Phil 1:17
Him we **p**, warning everyone and Col 1:28
that you may **p** the excellencies of him 1 Pt 2:9
and testify to it and **p** to you the eternal 1 Jn 1:2
we have seen and heard we **p** also to you, 1 Jn 1:3
we have heard from him and **p** to you, 1 Jn 1:5
an eternal gospel to **p** to those who dwell Rv 14:6

PROCLAIMED (54)
that my name may be **p** in all the earth. Ex 9:16
him there, and **p** the name of the LORD. Ex 34:5
The LORD passed before him and **p**, "The Ex 34:6
and word was **p** throughout the camp, Ex 36:6
a memorial **p** with blast of trumpets, Lv 23:24
because the LORD'S release has been **p**. Dt 15:2
rock of Rimmon and **p** peace to them. Jgs 21:13
they **p** a fast and set Naboth at the 1 Kgs 21:12
and they blew the trumpet and **p**, 2 Kgs 9:13
assembly for Baal." So they **p** it. 2 Kgs 10:20
And they **p** him king and anointed 2 Kgs 11:12
of the LORD that the man of God **p**, 2 Kgs 23:16
and **p** a fast throughout all Judah. 2 Chr 20:3
the testimony. And they **p** him king, 2 Chr 23:11
Then I **p** a fast there, at the river Ahava, Ezr 8:21
by the king is **p** throughout all his Est 1:20
the king's order and his edict were **p**, Est 2:8
was none who declared it, none who **p**, Is 41:26
I declared and saved and **p**, when there Is 43:12
the LORD has **p** to the end of the earth: Is 62:11
then they would have **p** my words to Jer 23:22
of Judah to Jerusalem **p** a fast before the Jer 36:9
And the herald **p** aloud, "You are Dn 3:4
He **p** aloud and said thus: 'Chop down Dn 4:14
words that the LORD **p** by the former Zec 7:7
kingdom will be **p** throughout the Mt 24:14
wherever this gospel is **p** in the whole Mt 26:13
they went out and **p** that people should Mk 6:12
them, the more zealously they **p** it. Mk 7:36
gospel must first be **p** to all nations. Mk 13:10
wherever the gospel is **p** in the whole Mk 14:9
rooms shall be **p** on the housetops. Lk 12:3
of sins should be **p** in his name to Lk 24:47
So Jesus **p**, as he taught in the temple, Jn 7:28
who came after him, also **p** these days. Acts 3:24
city of Samaria and **p** to them the Acts 8:5
And immediately he **p** Jesus in the Acts 9:20
Galilee after the baptism that John **p**: Acts 10:37
they **p** the word of God in the Acts 13:5
John had **p** a baptism of repentance Acts 13:24
man forgiveness of sins is **p** to you, Acts 13:38
every city where we **p** the word of the Acts 15:36
word of God was **p** by Paul at Berea Acts 17:13
because your faith is **p** in all the world. Rom 1:8
my name might be **p** in all the earth." Rom 9:17
Now if Christ is **p** as raised from the 1 Cor 15:12
Jesus Christ, whom we **p** among you, 2 Cor 1:19
another Jesus than the one we **p**, 2 Cor 11:4
in pretense or in truth, Christ is **p**, Phil 1:18
which has been **p** in all creation under Col 1:23
while we **p** to you the gospel of God. 1 Thes 2:9
seen by angels, **p** among the nations, 1 Tm 3:16
message might be fully **p** and all the 2 Tm 4:17
in which he went and **p** to the spirits in 1 Pt 3:19

PROCLAIMING (18)
the square of the city, **p** before him: Est 6:9
the square of the city, **p** before him, Est 6:11
p thanksgiving aloud, and telling all Ps 26:7
what was right in my eyes by **p** liberty, Jer 34:15
You have not obeyed me by **p** liberty, Jer 34:17
in their synagogues and **p** the gospel of Mt 4:23
in their synagogues and **p** the gospel of Mt 9:35
in the wilderness and **p** a baptism of Mk 1:4
came into Galilee, **p** the gospel of God, Mk 1:14
p a baptism of repentance for the Lk 3:3
p and bringing the good news of the Lk 8:1
p throughout the whole city how much Lk 8:39
teaching the people and **p** in Jesus the Acts 4:2
I have gone about **p** the kingdom will Acts 20:25
p the kingdom of God and teaching Acts 28:31
did not come **p** to you the testimony of 1 Cor 2:1
temple of God, **p** himself to be God. 2 Thes 2:4
I saw a strong angel **p** with a loud voice, Rv 5:2

PROCLAIMS (6)
God, and the sky above **p** his handiwork. Ps 19:1
but the heart of fools **p** folly. Prv 12:23
Many a man **p** his own steadfast love, Prv 20:6
from Dan and **p** trouble from Mount Jer 4:15
you by the Jesus, whom Paul **p**." Acts 19:13
someone comes and **p** another Jesus 2 Cor 11:4

PROCLAMATION (12)
And Aaron made **p** and said, Ex 32:5
And you shall make **p** on the same day. Lv 23:21
King Asa made a **p** to all Judah, 1 Kgs 15:22
And **p** was made throughout Judah 2 Chr 24:9
to make a **p** throughout all Israel, 2 Chr 30:5
that he made a **p** throughout all his 2 Chr 36:22
that he made a **p** throughout all his Ezr 1:1
And a **p** was made throughout Judah Ezr 10:7
in every province by **p** to all the peoples Est 3:14
Jerusalem to make a **p** of liberty to them, Jer 34:8
his neck, and a **p** was made about him, Dn 5:29
And he issued a **p** and published through Jon 3:7

PROCONSUL (4)
He was with the **p**, Sergius Paulus, a Acts 13:7
seeking to turn the **p** away from the Acts 13:8
Then the **p** believed, when he saw Acts 13:12
But when Gallio was **p** of Achaia, the Acts 18:12

PROCONSULS (1)
the courts are open, and there are **p**. Acts 19:38

PROCURED (2)
provisions and **p** wives for 2 Chr 11:23
having **p** a band of soldiers and some Jn 18:3

PRODUCE (36)
and take one-fifth of the **p** of the land of Gn 41:34
tried by their secret arts to **p** gnats, Ex 8:18
you have gathered in the **p** of the land, Lv 23:39
to you. You may eat the **p** of the field. Lv 25:12
so that it will **p** a crop sufficient for Lv 25:21
to the Levites as **p** of the threshing Nm 18:30
floor, and as **p** of the winepress. Nm 18:30
all the tithe of your **p** in the same year Dt 14:28
gathered in the **p** from your threshing Dt 16:13
bless you in all your **p** and in all the Dt 16:15
all the tithe of your **p** in the third year, Dt 26:12
of the land, and he ate the **p** of the field, Dt 32:13
with the finest **p** of the ancient Dt 33:15
very day, they ate of the **p** of the land, Jos 5:11
the day after they ate of the **p** of the land. Jos 5:12
them and devour the **p** of the land, Jgs 6:4
land for him and shall bring in the **p**, 2 Sm 9:10
together with all the **p** of the fields 2 Kgs 8:6
and over the **p** of the vineyards for 1 Chr 27:27
oil, honey, and of all the **p** of the field. 2 Chr 31:5
be full, providing all kinds of **p**; Ps 144:13
and with the firstfruits of all your **p**; Prv 3:9
ground, and bread, the **p** of the ground, Is 30:23
and they take root; they grow and **p** fruit; Jer 12:2
in them; plant gardens and eat their **p**. Jer 29:5
and plant gardens and eat their **p**."'" Jer 29:28
that it might **p** branches and bear fruit Ezk 17:8
bear branches and **p** fruit and Ezk 17:23
Its **p** shall be food for the workers of Ezk 48:18
the **p** of the olive fail and the fields yield Hab 3:17
the dew, and the earth has withheld its **p**. Hg 1:10
its fruit, and the ground shall give its **p**, Zec 8:12
through us will **p** thanksgiving to 2 Cor 9:11
quarrels about words, which **p** envy, 1 Tm 6:4
of man does not **p** the righteousness that Jas 1:20
bear olives, or a grapevine **p** figs? Jas 3:12

PRODUCED (10)
plentiful years the earth **p** abundantly, Gn 41:47
eat nothing that is **p** by the grapevine, Nm 6:4
and put forth buds and **p** blossoms, Nm 17:8
became a vine and **p** branches and put Ezk 17:6
Other seeds fell on good soil and **p** grain, Mt 13:8
other seeds fell into good soil and **p** grain, Mk 4:8
"The land of a rich man **p** plentifully, Lk 12:16
p in me all kinds of covetousness. Rom 7:8
this godly grief has **p** in you, 2 Cor 7:11
no prophecy was ever **p** by the will of 2 Pt 1:21

PRODUCES (14)
For pressing milk **p** curds, pressing Prv 30:33
curds, pressing the nose **p** blood, Prv 30:33
blood, and pressing anger **p** strife. Prv 30:33
the fire of coals and **p** a weapon for its Is 54:16
The earth **p** by itself, first the blade, Mk 4:28
of the good treasure of his heart **p** good, Lk 6:45
evil person out of his evil treasure **p** evil, Lk 6:45
knowing that suffering **p** endurance, Rom 5:3
and endurance **p** character, and Rom 5:4
character, and character **p** hope, Rom 5:4
For godly grief **p** a repentance that 2 Cor 7:10
regret, whereas worldly grief **p** death. 2 Cor 7:10
and **p** a crop useful to those for whose Heb 6:7
the testing of your faith **p** steadfastness. Jas 1:3

PRODUCING (2)
you and given to a people **p** its fruits. Mt 21:43
p death in me through what is good, Rom 7:13

PRODUCTS (1)
struck you and all the **p** of your toil with Hg 2:17

PROFANE (34)
for if you wield your tool on it you **p** it. Ex 20:25
Molech, and so **p** the name of your God: Lv 18:21
falsely, and so **p** the name of your God: Lv 19:12
"Do not **p** your daughter by making Lv 19:29
unclean and to **p** my holy name. Lv 20:3
among his people and so **p** himself. Lv 21:4

to their God and not **p** the name of their Lv 21:6
lest he **p** the sanctuary of his God, Lv 21:12
that he may not **p** his offspring among Lv 21:15
that he may not **p** my sanctuaries, Lv 21:23
me, so that they do not **p** my holy name: Lv 22:2
sin for it and die thereby when they **p** it: Lv 22:9
They shall not **p** the holy things of the Lv 22:15
And you shall not **p** my holy name, Lv 22:32
But you shall not **p** the holy things of Nm 18:32
like **p** mockers at a feast, they gnash at Ps 35:16
be poor and steal and **p** the name of my Prv 30:9
Therefore I will **p** the princes of the Is 43:28
who keeps the Sabbath and does not **p** it, Is 56:6
of the earth for spoil, and they shall **p** it. Ezk 7:21
and they shall **p** my treasured place. Ezk 7:22
place. Robbers shall enter and **p** it. Ezk 7:22
you shall no more **p** with your gifts Ezk 20:39
And you, O **p** wicked one, prince of Ezk 21:25
you on the necks of the **p** wicked, Ezk 21:29
they came into my sanctuary to **p** it. Ezk 23:39
Behold, I will **p** my sanctuary, the Ezk 24:21
cast you as a **p** thing from the Ezk 28:16
him shall appear and **p** the temple and Dn 11:31
men; her priests **p** what is holy; Zep 3:4
But you **p** it when you say that the Mal 1:12
priests in the temple **p** the Sabbath and Mt 12:5
He even tried to **p** the temple, but we Acts 24:6
and sinners, for the unholy and **p**, 1 Tm 1:9

PROFANED (31)
because he has **p** what is holy to the Lv 19:8
they **p** the dwelling place of your name, Ps 74:7
angry with my people; I **p** my heritage; Is 47:6
I do it, for how should my name be **p**? Is 48:11
forsaken me and have **p** this place by Jer 19:4
turned around and **p** my name when Jer 34:16
strong, and their holy places shall be **p**. Ezk 7:24
You have **p** me among my people for Ezk 13:19
that it should not be **p** in the sight of Ezk 20:9
live; and my Sabbaths they greatly **p**. Ezk 20:13
that it should not be **p** in the sight of Ezk 20:14
in my statutes, and **p** my Sabbaths; Ezk 20:16
he shall live; they **p** my Sabbaths. Ezk 20:21
that it should not be **p** in the sight of Ezk 20:22
my statutes and **p** my Sabbaths, Ezk 20:24
my holy things and **p** my Sabbaths. Ezk 22:8
And you shall be **p** by your own doing Ezk 22:16
to my law and have **p** my holy things. Ezk 22:26
Sabbaths, so that I am **p** among them. Ezk 22:26
on the same day and **p** my Sabbaths. Ezk 23:38
over my sanctuary when it was **p**, and Ezk 25:3
of your trade you **p** your sanctuaries; Ezk 28:18
they came, they **p** my holy name, Ezk 36:20
of Israel had **p** among the nations Ezk 36:21
which you have **p** among the nations Ezk 36:22
which has been **p** among the nations, Ezk 36:23
and which you have **p** among them. Ezk 36:23
not let my holy name be **p** anymore. Ezk 39:7
the same girl, so that my holy name is **p**; Am 2:7
For Judah has **p** the sanctuary of the Mal 2:11
and has **p** the blood of the covenant Heb 10:29

PROFANES (3)
Everyone who **p** it shall be put to death. Ex 31:14
of any priest, if she **p** herself by whoring, Lv 21:9
herself by whoring, **p** her father; Lv 21:9

PROFANING (6)
you are doing, **p** the Sabbath day? Neh 13:17
wrath on Israel by **p** the Sabbath." Neh 13:18
it fast, who keeps the Sabbath, not **p** it, Is 56:2
to be in my sanctuary, **p** my temple, Ezk 44:7
another, **p** the covenant of our fathers? Mal 2:10
will be guilty of **p** the body and 1 Cor 11:27

PROFESS (2)
for women who **p** godliness—with 1 Tm 2:10
They **p** to know God, but they deny him Ti 1:16

PROFESSING (1)
for by **p** it some have swerved from 1 Tm 6:21

PROFIT (34)
"What **p** is it if we kill our brother and Gn 37:26
Take no interest from him or **p**, but Lv 25:36
at interest, nor give him your food for **p**. Lv 25:37
things that cannot **p** or deliver, 1 Sm 12:21
it is not to the king's **p** to tolerate them. Est 3:8
from the **p** of his trading he will get no Jb 20:18
And what **p** do we get if we pray to him?' Jb 21:15
"What **p** is there in my death, if I go Ps 30:9
from silver and her **p** better than gold. Prv 3:14
gained by wickedness do not **p**, Prv 10:2
Riches do not **p** in the day of wrath, but Prv 11:4
In all toil there is **p**, but mere talk Prv 14:23
wealth by interest and **p** gathers it for Prv 28:8
through a people that cannot **p** them, Is 30:5
them, that brings neither help nor **p**, Is 30:5
of camels, to a people that cannot **p** them. Is 30:6
and the things they delight in do not **p**. Is 44:9
the LORD your God, who teaches you to **p**, Is 48:17
and your deeds, but they will not **p** you. Is 57:12
Baal and went after things that do not **p**. Jer 2:8
their glory for that which does not **p**. Jer 2:11
tired themselves out but **p** nothing. Jer 12:13
worthless things in which there is no **p**. Jer 16:19
them. So they do not **p** this people at all, Jer 23:32
does not lend at interest or take any **p**, Ezk 18:8
lends at interest, and takes **p**; shall he Ezk 18:13
from iniquity, takes no interest or **p**, Ezk 18:17
you take interest and **p** and make gain Ezk 22:12
"What **p** is an idol when its maker has Hab 2:18
What is the **p** of our keeping his Mal 3:14
For what will it **p** a man if he gains the Mt 16:26
For what does it **p** a man to gain the Mk 8:36
For what does it **p** a man if he gains the Lk 9:25
a year there and trade and make a **p**"— Jas 4:13

PROFITABLE (7)
"Can a man be **p** to God? Surely he who Jb 22:2
Surely he who is wise is **p** to himself. Jb 22:2
perceives that her merchandise is **p**. Prv 31:18
or casts an idol that is **p** for nothing? Is 44:10
declaring to you anything that was **p**, Acts 20:20
out by God and **p** for teaching, 2 Tm 3:16
things are excellent and **p** for people. Ti 3:8

PROFITS (1)
'It **p** a man nothing that he should take Jb 34:9

PROFOUND (1)
This mystery is **p**, and I am saying that Eph 5:32

PROFUSE (1)
of a friend; **p** are the kisses of an enemy. Prv 27:6

PROGENY (1)
has no posterity or **p** among his people, Jb 18:19

PROGRESS (2)
you all, for your **p** and joy in the faith, Phil 1:25
to them, so that all may see your **p**. 1 Tm 4:15

PROJECTED (1)
a crown that **p** upward one cubit. 1 Kgs 7:31

PROJECTING (4)
and the tower **p** from the upper Neh 3:25
Water Gate on the east and the **p** tower. Neh 3:26
section opposite the great **p** tower as far Neh 3:27
and from the altar hearth **p** upward, Ezk 43:15

PROJECTION (1)
above the rounded **p** which was 1 Kgs 7:20

PROLONG (6)
and that you may **p** your days in the Dt 4:40
P the life of the king; may his years Ps 61:6
Will you **p** your anger to all Ps 85:5
who hates unjust gain will **p** his days. Prv 28:16
neither will he **p** his days like a Eccl 8:13
see his offspring; he shall **p** his days; Is 53:10

PROLONGED (3)
close at hand and its days will not be **p**. Is 13:22
but their lives were **p** for a season and a Dn 7:12
and he **p** his speech until midnight. Acts 20:7

PROLONGS (4)
Yet God **p** the life of the mighty by his Jb 24:22
The fear of the LORD **p** life, but the Prv 10:27
is a wicked man who **p** his life in his Eccl 7:15
evil a hundred times and **p** his life, Eccl 8:12

PROMINENT (1)
tribunes and the **p** men of the Acts 25:23

PROMISE (66)
under my thigh and **p** to deal kindly Gn 47:29
and I **p** that I will bring you up out of the Ex 3:17
Because of your **p**, and according to 2 Sm 7:21
LORD has fulfilled his **p** that he made. 1 Kgs 8:20
one word has failed of all his good **p**, 1 Kgs 8:56
(This was the **p** of the LORD that he 2 Kgs 15:12
Abraham, his sworn **p** to Isaac, 1 Chr 16:16
according to the **p** of God to exalt 1 Chr 25:5
LORD has fulfilled his **p** that he made. 2 Chr 6:10
his labor who does not keep this **p**. Neh 5:13
And you have kept your **p**, for you are Neh 9:8
with Abraham, his sworn **p** to Isaac, Ps 105:9
For he remembered his holy **p**, and Ps 105:42
pleasant land, having no faith in his **p**. Ps 106:24
Confirm to your servant your **p**, that Ps 119:38
your salvation according to your **p**; Ps 119:41
my affliction, that your **p** gives me life. Ps 119:50
is my portion; I **p** to keep your words. Ps 119:57
be gracious to me according to your **p**. Ps 119:58
according to your **p** to your servant. Ps 119:76
My eyes long for your **p**; I ask, "When Ps 119:82
Uphold me according to your **p**, that Ps 119:116
the fulfillment of your righteous **p**. Ps 119:123
steady my steps according to your **p**, Ps 119:133
Your **p** is well tried, and your servant Ps 119:140
night, that I may meditate on your **p**. Ps 119:148
me; give me life according to your **p**! Ps 119:154
fulfill to you my **p** and bring you back Jer 29:10
upon them all the good that I **p** them. Jer 32:42
when I will fulfill the **p** I made to the Jer 33:14
I am sending the **p** of my Father upon Lk 24:49
but to wait for the **p** of the Father, Acts 1:4
from the Father the **p** of the Holy Acts 2:33
For the **p** is for you and for your Acts 2:39
"But as the time of the **p** drew near, Acts 7:17
of my hope in the **p** made by God to Acts 26:6
For the **p** to Abraham and his Rom 4:13
the heirs, faith is null and the **p** is void. Rom 4:14
in order that the **p** may rest on grace Rom 4:16
him waver concerning the **p** of God, Rom 4:20
the children of the **p** are counted as Rom 9:8
For this is what the **p** said: "About this Rom 9:9
by God, so as to make the **p** void. Gal 3:17
by the law, it no longer comes by **p**; Gal 3:18
but God gave it to Abraham by a **p**. Gal 3:18
come to whom the **p** had been made, Gal 3:19
so that the **p** by faith in Jesus Christ Gal 3:22
offspring, heirs according to **p**. Gal 3:29
of the free woman was born through **p**. Gal 4:23
brothers, like Isaac, are children of **p**. Gal 4:28
and strangers to the covenants of **p**, Eph 2:12
and partakers of the **p** in Christ Jesus Eph 3:6
is the first commandment with a **p**), Eph 6:2
as it holds **p** for the present life and 1 Tm 4:8
God according to the **p** of the life that 2 Tm 1:1
while the **p** of entering his rest still Heb 4:1
For when God made a **p** to Abraham, Heb 6:13
having patiently waited, obtained the **p**. Heb 6:15
heirs of the **p** the unchangeable Heb 6:17
By faith he went to live in the land of **p**, Heb 11:9
Jacob, heirs with him of the same **p**. Heb 11:9
They **p** them freedom, but they 2 Pt 2:19
will say, "Where is the **p** of his coming? 2 Pt 3:4
slow to fulfill his **p** as some count 2 Pt 3:9
But according to his **p** we are waiting 2 Pt 3:13
And this is the **p** that he made to us— 1 Jn 2:25

PROMISED (78)
to Abraham what he has **p** him." Gn 18:19
and the LORD did to Sarah as he had **p**. Gn 21:1
until I have done what I have **p** you." Gn 28:15
that the LORD will give you, as he has **p**, Ex 12:25
this land that I have **p** I will give to your Ex 32:13
you, for the LORD has **p** good to Israel." Nm 10:29
of the Lord be great as you have **p**, Nm 14:17
go up to the place that the LORD has **p**, Nm 14:40
your sheep, and do what you have **p**." Nm 32:24
you are and bless you, as he has **p** you! Dt 1:11
LORD, the God of your fathers, has **p** you, Dt 6:3
from before you, as the LORD has **p**. Dt 6:19
perish quickly, as the LORD has **p** you. Dt 9:3
bring them into the land that he **p** them, Dt 9:28
land that you shall tread, as he **p** you. Dt 11:25
enlarges your territory, as he has **p** you, Dt 12:20
your God will bless you, as he **p** you, Dt 15:6
LORD is their inheritance, as he **p** them. Dt 18:2
all the land that he **p** to give to your Dt 19:8
God what you have **p** with your mouth. Dt 23:23
treasured possession, as he has **p** you, Dt 26:18
holy to the LORD your God, as he **p**." Dt 26:19
LORD, the God of your fathers, has **p** you. Dt 27:3
a journey that I **p** that you should never Dt 28:68
that he may be your God, as he **p** you, Dt 29:13
I have given to you, just as I **p** to Moses. Jos 1:3
given rest to your brothers, as he **p** them. Jos 22:4
land, just as the LORD your God **p** you. Jos 23:5
who fights for you, just as he **p** you. Jos 23:10
the LORD your God **p** concerning you. Jos 23:14
LORD your God **p** concerning you have Jos 23:15
'I **p** that your house and the house of 1 Sm 2:30
it about, for the LORD has **p** David, 2 Sm 3:18
and you have **p** this good thing to 2 Sm 7:28
who has made me a house, as he **p**, 1 Kgs 2:24
gave Solomon wisdom, as he **p** him. 1 Kgs 5:12
fulfilled what he **p** with his mouth 1 Kgs 8:15
on the throne of Israel, as the LORD **p**, 1 Kgs 8:20
my father what you have **p** him, 1 Kgs 8:25
Israel, according to all that he **p**. 1 Kgs 8:56
Israel forever, as I **p** David your father, 1 Kgs 9:5
since he **p** to give a lamp to him and 2 Kgs 8:19
LORD will do the thing that he has **p**: 2 Kgs 20:9
and you have **p** this good thing to 1 Chr 17:26
for the LORD had **p** to make Israel as 1 Chr 27:23
has fulfilled what he **p** with his mouth 2 Chr 6:4
on the throne of Israel, as the LORD **p**, 2 Chr 6:10
my father what you have **p** him, 2 Chr 6:16
place where you have **p** to set your 2 Chr 6:20
and since he had **p** to give a lamp to 2 Chr 21:7
made them swear to do as they had **p**. Neh 5:12

LORD. And the people did as they had **p**. Neh 5:13
money that Haman had **p** to pay into the Est 4:7
uttered and my mouth **p** when I was in Ps 66:14
God has **p** in his holiness: "With Ps 108:7
the LORD will do this thing that he has **p**: Is 38:7
so that he **p** with an oath to give her Mt 14:7
they were glad and **p** to give him Mk 14:11
to show the mercy **p** to our fathers and Lk 1:72
but **p** to give it to him as a possession Acts 7:5
to Israel a Savior, Jesus, as he **p**. Acts 13:23
news that what God **p** to the fathers, Acts 13:32
which he **p** beforehand through his Rom 1:2
that God was able to do what he had **p**. Rom 4:21
very commandment that **p** life proved Rom 7:10
in advance for the gift you have **p**, 2 Cor 9:5
might receive the **p** Spirit through faith. Gal 3:14
him, were sealed with the **p** Holy Spirit, Eph 1:13
who never lies, **p** before the ages began Ti 1:2
may receive the **p** eternal inheritance, Heb 9:15
wavering, for he who **p** is faithful. Heb 10:23
will of God you may receive what is **p**. Heb 10:36
considered him faithful who had **p**. Heb 11:11
not having received the things **p**, Heb 11:13
their faith, did not receive what was **p**, Heb 11:39
shook the earth, but now he has **p**, Heb 12:26
which God has **p** to those who love him. Jas 1:12
which he has **p** to those who love him? Jas 2:5

PROMISES (14)
word of all the good **p** that the LORD had Jos 21:45
ceased? Are his **p** at an end for all time? Ps 77:8
of the law, the worship, and the **p**. Rom 9:4
order to confirm the **p** given to the Rom 15:8
For all the **p** of God find their Yes in 2 Cor 1:20
Since we have these **p**, beloved, let us 2 Cor 7:1
Now the **p** were made to Abraham and Gal 3:16
Is the law then contrary to the **p** of God? Gal 3:21
faith and patience inherit the **p**. Heb 6:12
and blessed him who had the **p**. Heb 7:6
is better, since it is enacted on better **p**. Heb 8:6
who had received the **p** was in the act Heb 11:17
enforced justice, obtained **p**, Heb 11:33
to us his precious and very great **p**, 2 Pt 1:4

PROMISING (2)
deceive you by **p** that Jerusalem will 2 Kgs 19:10
deceive you by **p** that Jerusalem will Is 37:10

PROMOTE (3)
break up my path; they **p** my calamity; Jb 30:13
but to **p** good order and to secure 1 Cor 7:35
which **p** speculations rather than the 1 Tm 1:4

PROMOTED (2)
things King Ahasuerus **p** Haman the Est 3:1
Then the king **p** Shadrach, Meshach, Dn 3:30

PROMOTING (1)
of wisdom in **p** self-made religion and Col 2:23

PROMOTIONS (1)
all the **p** with which the king had Est 5:11

PROMPTED (2)
P by her mother, she said, "Give me the Mt 14:8
Some of the crowd **p** Alexander, Acts 19:33

PROMPTS (1)
that a man's heart **p** him to bring 2 Kgs 12:4

PRONOUNCE (28)
saying, "By you Israel will **p** blessings, Gn 48:20
examined him, he shall **p** him unclean. Lv 13:3
skin, then the priest shall **p** him clean; Lv 13:6
then the priest shall **p** him unclean; Lv 13:8
and the priest shall **p** him unclean. Lv 13:11
he shall **p** him clean of the disease; Lv 13:13
the raw flesh and **p** him unclean. Lv 13:15
the priest shall **p** the diseased person Lv 13:17
then the priest shall **p** him unclean. Lv 13:20
then the priest shall **p** him unclean; Lv 13:22
boil, and the priest shall **p** him clean. Lv 13:23
and the priest shall **p** him unclean; Lv 13:25
then the priest shall **p** him unclean; Lv 13:27
burn, and the priest shall **p** him clean, Lv 13:28
then the priest shall **p** him unclean. Lv 13:30
skin, then the priest shall **p** him clean. Lv 13:34
clean, and the priest shall **p** him clean. Lv 13:37
The priest must **p** him unclean; his Lv 13:44
Then he shall **p** him clean and shall let Lv 14:7
then the priest shall **p** the house clean, Lv 14:48
to the decision which they **p** to you, Dt 17:11
"Sibboleth," for he could not **p** it right. Jgs 12:6
Throne where he was to **p** judgment, 1 Kgs 7:7
to him and **p** blessings in his 1 Chr 23:13
with the judgment you **p** you will be Mt 7:2
Therefore do not **p** judgment before 1 Cor 4:5
do not **p** a blasphemous judgment 2 Pt 2:11
not presume to **p** a blasphemous Jude 1:9

PRONOUNCED (10)
but he had **p** the prophecy against me Neh 6:12
'Why has the LORD **p** all this great evil Jer 16:10
all the disaster that I have **p** against it, Jer 19:15
the disaster that he has **p** against you. Jer 26:13
the disaster that he had **p** against them? Jer 26:19
the disaster that I have **p** against them, Jer 35:17
that the LORD has **p** against this people." Jer 36:7
the disaster that I have **p** against them, Jer 36:31
LORD your God **p** this disaster against Jer 40:2
I have already **p** judgment on the one 1 Cor 5:3

PRONOUNCEMENT (1)
the LORD made this **p** against him: 2 Kgs 9:25

PROOF (6)
put me to the test and put me to the **p**, Ps 95:9
that Moses commanded, for a **p** to them." Mt 8:4
Moses commanded, for a **p** to them." Mk 1:44
as Moses commanded, for a **p** to them." Lk 5:14
So give **p** before the churches of your 2 Cor 8:24
since you seek **p** that Christ is 2 Cor 13:3

PROOFS (2)
bring your **p**, says the King of Jacob. Is 41:21
alive after his suffering by many **p**, Acts 1:3

PROPER (15)
and drink offerings, each on its **p** day, Lv 23:37
God to its **p** condition and 2 Chr 24:13
heart will know the **p** time and the just Eccl 8:5
and your princes feast at the **p** time, Eccl 10:17
wheat in rows and barley in its **p** place, Is 28:25
to give them their food at the **p** time? Mt 24:45
their portion of food at the **p** time? Lk 12:42
is it **p** for a wife to pray to God with 1 Cor 11:13
among you, as is **p** among saints. Eph 5:3
is the testimony given at the **p** time. 1 Tm 2:6
but with what is **p** for women who 1 Tm 2:10
he will display at the **p** time—he who 1 Tm 6:15
and at the **p** time manifested in his word Ti 1:3
God so that at the **p** time he may exalt 1 Pt 5:6
of authority, but left their **p** dwelling, Jude 1:6

PROPERLY (5)
him, 'Prepare supper for me, and dress **p**, Lk 17:8
Let us walk **p** as in the daytime, not Rom 13:13
is not behaving **p** toward his 1 Cor 7:36
equipped, when each part is working **p**, Eph 4:16
you may live **p** before outsiders and 1 Thes 4:12

PROPERTY (41)
give me **p** among you for a burying Gn 23:4
in your presence as **p** for a burying Gn 23:9
over to Abraham as **p** for a burying Gn 23:20
livestock, all his **p** that he had gained, Gn 31:18
Dwell and trade in it, and get **p** in it." Gn 34:10
their **p** and all their beasts be ours? Gn 34:23
and all his **p** that he had acquired in the Gn 36:6
he has put his hand to his neighbor's **p**. Ex 22:8
he has put his hand to his neighbor's **p**. Ex 22:11
a priest buys a slave as his **p** for money, Lv 22:11
shall return to his **p** and each of you Lv 25:10
each of you shall return to his **p**. Lv 25:13
becomes poor and sells part of his **p**, Lv 25:25
he sold it, and then return to his **p**. Lv 25:27
be released, and he shall return to his **p**. Lv 25:28
in your land, and they may be your **p**. Lv 25:45
met him at the **p** of Naboth the 2 Kgs 9:21
were stewards of King David's **p**. 1 Chr 27:31
stewards of all the **p** and livestock of 1 Chr 28:1
the elders all his **p** should be forfeited, Ezr 10:8
everyone lived on his **p** in their towns: Neh 11:3
to get a share of their **p**—the eyes of his Jb 17:5
you shall assign for the **p** of the city an Ezk 45:6
of the holy district and the **p** of the city, Ezk 45:7
the holy district and the **p** of the city, Ezk 45:7
of the land. It is to be his **p** in Israel. Ezk 45:8
to his sons. It is their **p** by inheritance. Ezk 46:16
people, thrusting them out of their **p**. Ezk 46:18
their inheritance out of his own **p**, Ezk 46:18
people shall be scattered from his **p**." Ezk 46:18
portion together with the **p** of the city. Ezk 48:20
portion and of the **p** of the city shall Ezk 48:21
be separate from the **p** of the Levites Ezk 48:22
of the Levites and the **p** of the city, Ezk 48:22
servants and entrusted to them his **p**. Mt 25:14
give me the share of **p** that is coming to Lk 15:12
And he divided his **p** between them. Lk 15:12
he squandered his **p** in reckless living. Lk 15:13
has devoured your **p** with prostitutes, Lk 15:30
with his wife Sapphira, sold a piece of **p**, Acts 5:1
accepted the plundering of your **p**, Heb 10:34

PROPHECIES (3)
As for **p**, they will pass away; as for 1 Cor 13:8
Do not despise **p**, 1 Thes 5:20
with the **p** previously made 1 Tm 1:18

PROPHECY (17)
and in the **p** of Ahijah the Shilonite, 2 Chr 9:29
the **p** of Azariah the son of Oded, 2 Chr 15:8
had pronounced the **p** against me Neh 6:12
in their case the **p** of Isaiah is fulfilled Mt 13:14
grace given to us, let us use them: if **p**, Rom 12:6
working of miracles, to another **p**, 1 Cor 12:10
or knowledge or **p** or teaching? 1 Cor 14:6
while **p** is a sign not for unbelievers 1 Cor 14:22
was given you by **p** when the council 1 Tm 4:14
that no **p** of Scripture comes from 2 Pt 1:20
For no **p** was ever produced by the will 2 Pt 1:21
one who reads aloud the words of this **p**, Rv 1:3
the testimony of Jesus is the spirit of **p**. Rv 19:10
keeps the words of the **p** of this book." Rv 22:7
seal up the words of the **p** of this book, Rv 22:10
hears the words of the **p** of this book: Rv 22:18
from the words of the book of this **p**, Rv 22:19

PROPHESIED (41)
as the Spirit rested on them, they **p**. Nm 11:25
to the tent, and so they **p** in the camp. Nm 11:26
upon him, and he **p** among them. 1 Sm 10:10
saw how he **p** with the prophets, 1 Sm 10:11
messengers of Saul, and they also **p**. 1 Sm 19:20
other messengers, and they also **p**. 1 Sm 19:21
again the third time, and they also **p**. 1 Sm 19:21
and as he went he **p** until he came to 1 Sm 19:23
and he too **p** before Samuel and lay 1 Sm 19:24
And all the prophets **p** so and said, 1 Kgs 22:12
and of Jeduthun, who **p** with lyres, 1 Chr 25:1
who **p** under the direction of the 1 Chr 25:2
who **p** with the lyre in thanksgiving 1 Chr 25:3
And all the prophets **p** so and said, 2 Chr 18:11
of Mareshah **p** against Jehoshaphat, 2 Chr 20:37
p to the Jews who were in Judah and Ezr 5:1
the prophets **p** by Baal and went after Jer 2:8
friends, to whom you have **p** falsely." Jer 20:6
they **p** by Baal and led my people Israel Jer 23:13
ran; I did not speak to them, yet they **p**. Jer 23:21
which Jeremiah **p** against all the Jer 25:13
Why have you **p** in the name of the Jer 26:9
because he has **p** against this city, Jer 26:11
"Micah of Moresheth **p** in the days of Jer 26:18
was another man who **p** in the name of Jer 26:20
He **p** against this city and against this Jer 26:20
the words that you have **p** come true, Jer 28:6
you and me from ancient times **p** war, Jer 28:8
Because Shemaiah had **p** to you when I Jer 29:31
Where are your prophets who **p** to you, Jer 37:19
of Israel who **p** concerning Jerusalem Ezk 13:16
So I **p** as I was commanded. And as I Ezk 37:7
And as I **p**, there was a sound, and Ezk 37:7
So I **p** as he commanded me, and the Ezk 37:10
who in those days **p** for years that I Ezk 38:17
the Prophets and the Law **p** until John, Mt 11:13
was filled with the Holy Spirit and **p**, Lk 1:67
priest that year he **p** that Jesus would die Jn 11:51
had four unmarried daughters, who **p**. Acts 21:9
the prophets who **p** about the grace 1 Pt 1:10
the seventh from Adam, **p**, saying, Jude 1:14

PROPHESIES (13)
for he never **p** good concerning me, 1 Kgs 22:8
for he never **p** good concerning me, 2 Chr 18:7
As for the prophet who **p** peace, when the Jer 28:9
of the LORD over every madman who **p**, Jer 29:26
from now, and he **p** of times far off.' Ezk 12:27
And if anyone again **p**, his father and Zec 13:3
shall pierce him through when he **p**. Zec 13:3
be ashamed of his vision when he **p**. Zec 13:4
man who prays or **p** with his head 1 Cor 11:4
wife who prays or **p** with her head 1 Cor 11:5
the one who **p** speaks to people for 1 Cor 14:3
but the one who **p** builds up the 1 Cor 14:4
The one who **p** is greater than the one 1 Cor 14:5

PROPHESY (71)
and you will **p** with them and be 1 Sm 10:6
he would not **p** good concerning me, 1 Kgs 22:18
he would not **p** good concerning 2 Chr 18:17
prophets, "Do not **p** to us what is right; Is 30:10
speak to us smooth things, **p** illusions, Is 30:10
the prophets **p** falsely, and the priests Jer 5:31
say, "Do not **p** in the name of the LORD, Jer 11:21
the prophets who **p** in my name Jer 14:15
people to whom they **p** shall be cast out Jer 14:16
where the LORD had sent him to **p**, Jer 19:14
the words of the prophets who **p** to you, Jer 23:16
prophets have said who **p** lies in my Jer 23:25
in the heart of the prophets who **p** lies, Jer 23:26
and who **p** the deceit of their own heart, Jer 23:26
I am against those who **p** lying dreams, Jer 23:32
shall **p** against them all these words, Jer 25:30
LORD sent me to **p** against this house Jer 26:12
him, saying, "Why do you **p** and say, Jer 32:3
bared, and you shall **p** against the city. Ezk 4:7

mountains of Israel, and **p** against them, Ezk 6:2
Therefore **p** against them, prophesy, O Ezk 11:4
against them, **p**, O son of man." Ezk 11:4
of man, **p** against the prophets of Israel, Ezk 13:2
say to those who **p** from their own Ezk 13:2
people, who **p** out of their own minds. Ezk 13:17
of their own minds. **P** against them Ezk 13:17
and **p** against the forest land in the Ezk 20:46
sanctuaries. **P** against the land of Israel Ezk 21:2
"Son of man, **p** and say, Thus says the Ezk 21:9
"As for you, son of man, **p**. Clap your Ezk 21:14
"And you, son of man, **p**, and say, Ezk 21:28
the Ammonites and **p** against them. Ezk 25:2
face toward Sidon, and **p** against her Ezk 28:21
and **p** against him and against all Ezk 29:2
"Son of man, **p**, and say, Thus says the Ezk 30:2
man, **p** against the shepherds of Israel; Ezk 34:2
p, and say to them, even to the Ezk 34:2
against Mount Seir, and **p** against it, Ezk 35:2
of man, **p** to the mountains of Israel, Ezk 36:1
therefore **p**, and say, Thus says the Lord Ezk 36:3
Therefore **p** concerning the land of Ezk 36:6
he said to me, "**P** over these bones, Ezk 37:4
Then he said to me, "**P** to the breath; Ezk 37:9
p, son of man, and say to the breath, Ezk 37:9
Therefore **p**, and say to them, Thus Ezk 37:12
and Tubal, and **p** against him Ezk 38:2
son of man, **p**, and say to Gog, Ezk 38:14
you, son of man, **p** against Gog and say, Ezk 39:1
your sons and your daughters shall **p**, Jl 2:28
the prophets, saying, 'You shall not **p**.' Am 2:12
Lord GOD has spoken; who can but **p**?" Am 3:8
Judah, and eat bread there, and **p** there, Am 7:12
but never again **p** at Bethel, for it is the Am 7:13
said to me, 'Go, **p** to my people Israel.' Am 7:15
"You say, 'Do not **p** against Israel, and Am 7:16
'Lord, Lord, did we not **p** in your name, Mt 7:22
Well did Isaiah **p** of you, when he said: Mt 15:7
saying, "**P** to us, you Christ! Who is it Mt 26:68
"Well did Isaiah **p** of you hypocrites, Mk 7:6
"**P**!" And the guards received him with Mk 14:65
him, "**P**! Who is it that struck you?" Lk 22:64
your sons and your daughters shall **p**, Acts 2:17
pour out my Spirit, and they shall **p**. Acts 2:18
For we know in part and we **p** in part, 1 Cor 13:9
gifts, especially that you may **p**. 1 Cor 14:1
speak in tongues, but even more to **p**. 1 Cor 14:5
But if all **p**, and an unbeliever or 1 Cor 14:24
For you can all **p** one by one, so that 1 Cor 14:31
my brothers, earnestly desire to **p**, 1 Cor 14:39
"You must again **p** about many Rv 10:11
witnesses, and they will **p** for 1,260 days, Rv 11:3

PROPHESYING (23)

"Eldad and Medad are **p** in the camp." Nm 11:27
flute, and lyre before them, **p**. 1 Sm 10:5
When he had finished **p**, he came to 1 Sm 10:13
saw the company of the prophets **p**, 1 Sm 19:20
all the prophets were **p** before them. 1 Kgs 22:10
all the prophets were **p** before them. 2 Chr 18:9
prospered through the **p** of Haggai the Ezr 6:14
"The prophets are **p** lies in my name. Jer 14:14
They are **p** to you a lying vision, Jer 14:14
the LORD, heard Jeremiah **p** these things. Jer 20:1
For it is a lie that they are **p** to you, with Jer 27:10
for it is a lie that they are **p** to you. Jer 27:14
but they are **p** falsely in my name, Jer 27:15
you and the prophets who are **p** to you." Jer 27:15
of your prophets who are **p** to you, Jer 27:16
for it is a lie that they are **p** to you. Jer 27:16
a lie that they are **p** to you in my name; Jer 29:9
who are **p** a lie to you in my name: Jer 29:21
Jeremiah of Anathoth who is **p** to you? Jer 29:27
And it came to pass, while I was **p**, that Ezk 11:13
the prophets of Israel, who are **p**, Ezk 13:2
they began speaking in tongues and **p**. Acts 19:6
rain may fall during the days of their **p**, Rv 11:6

PROPHET (233)

then, return the man's wife, for he is a **p**, Gn 20:7
and your brother Aaron shall be your **p**. Ex 7:1
If there is a **p** among you, I the LORD Nm 12:6
"If a **p** or a dreamer of dreams arises Dt 13:1
to the words of that **p** or that dreamer of Dt 13:3
But that **p** or that dreamer of dreams Dt 13:5
up for you a **p** like me from among Dt 18:15
up for them a **p** like you from among Dt 18:18
But the **p** who presumes to speak a word Dt 18:20
of other gods, that same **p** shall die.' Dt 18:20
when a **p** speaks in the name of the Dt 18:22
the **p** has spoken it presumptuously. Dt 18:22
has not arisen a **p** since in Israel like Dt 34:10
the LORD sent a **p** to the people of Israel. Jgs 6:8
was established as a **p** of the LORD. 1 Sm 3:20
seer," for today's "**p**" was formerly 1 Sm 9:9
Then the **p** Gad said to David, "Do not 1 Sm 22:5
the king said to Nathan the **p**, "See 2 Sm 7:2
and sent a message by Nathan the **p**. 2 Sm 12:25
word of the LORD came to the **p** Gad, 2 Sm 24:11
and Nathan the **p** and Shimei and 1 Kgs 1:8
not invite Nathan the **p** or Benaiah or 1 Kgs 1:10
with the king, Nathan the **p** came in. 1 Kgs 1:22
"Here is Nathan the **p**." And when he 1 Kgs 1:23
to me Zadok the priest, Nathan the **p**, 1 Kgs 1:32
and Nathan the **p** there anoint him 1 Kgs 1:34
So Zadok the priest, Nathan the **p**, 1 Kgs 1:38
him Zadok the priest, Nathan the **p**, 1 Kgs 1:44
and Nathan the **p** have anointed him 1 Kgs 1:45
the **p** Ahijah the Shilonite found 1 Kgs 11:29
Now an old **p** lived in Bethel. And 1 Kgs 13:11
to him, "I also am a **p** as you are, 1 Kgs 13:18
came to the **p** who had brought 1 Kgs 13:20
the donkey for the **p** whom he had 1 Kgs 13:23
it in the city where the old **p** lived. 1 Kgs 13:25
And when the **p** who had brought 1 Kgs 13:26
And the **p** took up the body of the 1 Kgs 13:29
Behold, Ahijah the **p** is there, who 1 Kgs 14:2
spoke by his servant Ahijah the **p**. 1 Kgs 14:18
LORD came by the **p** Jehu the son of 1 Kgs 16:7
spoke against Baasha by Jehu the **p**, 1 Kgs 16:12
even I only, am left a **p** of the LORD, 1 Kgs 18:22
Elijah the **p** came near and said, 1 Kgs 18:36
shall anoint to be **p** in your place. 1 Kgs 19:16
a **p** came near to Ahab king of Israel 1 Kgs 20:13
Then the **p** came near to the king of 1 Kgs 20:22
So the **p** departed and waited for the 1 Kgs 20:38
there not here another **p** of the LORD of 1 Kgs 22:7
said, "Is there no **p** of the LORD here, 2 Kgs 3:11
lord were with the **p** who is in 2 Kgs 5:3
may know that there is a **p** in Israel." 2 Kgs 5:8
a great word the **p** has spoken to you; 2 Kgs 5:13
but Elisha, the **p** who is in Israel, tells 2 Kgs 6:12
Then Elisha the **p** called one of the 2 Kgs 9:1
So the young man, the servant of the **p**, 2 Kgs 9:4
Jonah the son of Amittai, the **p**, 2 Kgs 14:25
and Judah by every **p** and every seer, 2 Kgs 17:13
to the **p** Isaiah the son of Amoz. 2 Kgs 19:2
And Isaiah the **p** the son of Amoz 2 Kgs 20:1
And Isaiah the **p** called to the LORD, 2 Kgs 20:11
Then Isaiah the **p** came to King 2 Kgs 20:14
the bones of the **p** who came out of 2 Kgs 23:18
house, David said to Nathan the **p**, 1 Chr 17:1
in the Chronicles of Nathan the **p**, 1 Chr 29:29
in the history of Nathan the **p**, 2 Chr 9:29
Then Shemaiah the **p** came to 2 Chr 12:5
of Shemaiah the **p** and of Iddo 2 Chr 12:15
are written in the story of the **p** Iddo. 2 Chr 13:22
there not here another **p** of the LORD 2 Chr 18:6
came to him from Elijah the **p**, 2 Chr 21:12
with Amaziah and sent to him a **p**, 2 Chr 25:15
be struck down?" So the **p** stopped, 2 Chr 25:16
Isaiah the **p** the son of Amoz wrote. 2 Chr 26:22
But a **p** of the LORD was there, whose 2 Chr 28:9
the king's seer and of Nathan the **p**, 2 Chr 29:25
Hezekiah the king and Isaiah the **p**, 2 Chr 32:20
vision of Isaiah the **p** the son of 2 Chr 32:32
since the days of Samuel the **p**. 2 Chr 35:18
himself before Jeremiah the **p**, 2 Chr 36:12
of Haggai the **p** and Zechariah the Ezr 6:14
David, when Nathan the **p** went to him, Ps 51:T
there is no longer any **p**, and there is Ps 74:9
man and the soldier, the judge and the **p**, Is 3:2
head, and the **p** who teaches lies is the tail; Is 9:15
the priest and the **p** reel with strong drink, Is 28:7
to the **p** Isaiah the son of Amoz. Is 37:2
And Isaiah the **p** the son of Amoz came to Is 38:1
Then Isaiah the **p** came to King Is 39:3
you; I appointed you a **p** to the nations." Jer 1:5
for unjust gain; and from **p** to priest, Jer 6:13
from **p** to priest, everyone deals falsely. Jer 8:10
For both **p** and priest ply their trade Jer 14:18
from the wise, nor the word from the **p**. Jer 18:18
Then Pashhur beat Jeremiah the **p**, and Jer 20:2
"Both **p** and priest are ungodly; even in Jer 23:11
Let the **p** who has a dream tell the Jer 23:28
this people, or a **p** or a priest asks you, Jer 23:33
And as for the **p**, priest, or one of the Jer 23:34
Thus you shall say to the **p**, 'What has Jer 23:37
which Jeremiah the **p** spoke to all the Jer 25:2
the son of Azzur, the **p** from Gibeon, Jer 28:1
Then the **p** Jeremiah spoke to Hananiah Jer 28:5
spoke to Hananiah the **p** in the presence Jer 28:5
and the **p** Jeremiah said, "Amen! May Jer 28:6
As for the **p** who prophesies peace, when Jer 28:9
when the word of that **p** comes to pass, Jer 28:9
that the LORD has truly sent the **p**." Jer 28:9
Then the **p** Hananiah took the Jer 28:10
neck of Jeremiah the **p** and broke them. Jer 28:10
But Jeremiah the **p** went his way. Jer 28:11
Sometime after the **p** Hananiah had Jer 28:12
from off the neck of Jeremiah the **p**, Jer 28:12
And Jeremiah the **p** said to the prophet Jer 28:15
the prophet said to the **p** Hananiah, Jer 28:15
seventh month, the **p** Hananiah died. Jer 28:17
that Jeremiah the **p** sent from Jerusalem Jer 29:1
letter in the hearing of Jeremiah the **p**. Jer 29:29
and Jeremiah the **p** was shut up in the Jer 32:2
Then Jeremiah the **p** spoke all these Jer 34:6
that Jeremiah the **p** ordered him about Jer 36:8
the secretary and Jeremiah the **p**, Jer 36:26
that he spoke through Jeremiah the **p**. Jer 37:2
the son of Maaseiah, to Jeremiah the **p**, Jer 37:3
word of the LORD came to Jeremiah the **p**: Jer 37:6
son of Hananiah, seized Jeremiah the **p**, Jer 37:13
did to Jeremiah the **p** by casting him Jer 38:9
and lift Jeremiah the **p** out of the cistern Jer 38:10
for Jeremiah the **p** and received him Jer 38:14
and said to Jeremiah the **p**, "Let our plea Jer 42:2
Jeremiah the **p** said to them, "I have Jer 42:4
also Jeremiah the **p** and Baruch the son Jer 43:6
that Jeremiah the **p** spoke to Baruch Jer 45:1
to Jeremiah the **p** concerning the Jer 46:1
to Jeremiah the **p** about the coming Jer 46:13
to Jeremiah the **p** concerning the Jer 47:1
to Jeremiah the **p** concerning Elam, Jer 49:34
of the Chaldeans, by Jeremiah the **p**: Jer 50:1
Jeremiah the **p** commanded Seraiah Jer 51:59
Should priest and **p** be killed in the Lam 2:20
will know that a **p** has been among Ezk 2:5
They seek a vision from the **p**, while the Ezk 7:26
before his face, and yet comes to the **p**, Ezk 14:4
yet comes to a **p** to consult me through Ezk 14:7
And if the **p** is deceived and speaks a Ezk 14:9
a word, I, the LORD, have deceived that **p**, Ezk 14:9
punishment of the **p** and the Ezk 14:10
will know that a **p** has been among Ezk 33:33
to the word of the LORD to Jeremiah the **p**, Dn 9:2
righteousness, to seal both vision and **p**, Dn 9:24
the **p** also shall stumble with you by Hos 4:5
The **p** is a fool; the man of the spirit is Hos 9:7
The **p** is the watchman of Ephraim with Hos 9:8
By a **p** the LORD brought Israel up Hos 12:13
Egypt, and by a **p** he was guarded. Hos 12:13
and said to Amaziah, "I was no **p**, Am 7:14
The oracle that Habakkuk the **p** saw. Hab 1:1
A prayer of Habakkuk the **p**, according Hab 3:1
hand of Haggai the **p** to Zerubbabel the Hg 1:1
LORD came by the hand of Haggai the **p**, Hg 1:3
their God, and the words of Haggai the **p**, Hg 1:12
LORD came by the hand of Haggai the **p**, Hg 2:1
word of the LORD came by Haggai the **p**, Hg 2:10
of the LORD came to the **p** Zechariah, Zec 1:1
of the LORD came to the **p** Zechariah, Zec 1:7
"On that day every **p** will be ashamed of Zec 13:4
but he will say, 'I am no **p**, I am a Zec 13:5
send you Elijah the **p** before the great Mal 4:5
what the Lord had spoken by the **p**: Mt 1:22
of Judea, for so it is written by the **p**: Mt 2:5
what the Lord had spoken by the **p**, Mt 2:15
what was spoken by the **p** Jeremiah: Mt 2:17
spoken of by the **p** Isaiah when he said, Mt 3:3
was spoken by the **p** Isaiah might be Mt 4:14
fulfill what was spoken by the **p** Isaiah: Mt 8:17
one who receives a **p** because he is a Mt 10:41
because he is a **p** will receive a Mt 10:41
What then did you go out to see? A **p**? Mt 11:9
Yes, I tell you, and more than a **p**. Mt 11:9
fulfill what was spoken by the **p** Isaiah: Mt 12:17
to it except the sign of the **p** Jonah. Mt 12:39
was to fulfill what was spoken by the **p**: Mt 13:35
"A **p** is not without honor except in his Mt 13:57
people, because they held him to be a **p**. Mt 14:5
place to fulfill what was spoken by the **p**, Mt 21:4
the crowds said, "This is the **p** Jesus, Mt 21:11
for they all hold that John was a **p**." Mt 21:26
because they held him to be a **p**. Mt 21:46
of desolation spoken of by the **p** Daniel, Mt 24:15
had been spoken by the **p** Jeremiah, Mt 27:9
As it is written in Isaiah the **p**, "Behold, I Mk 1:2
said to them, "A **p** is not without honor, Mk 6:4
is Elijah." And others said, "He is a **p**, Mk 6:15
they all held that John really was a **p**. Mk 11:32
will be called the **p** of the Most High; Lk 1:76
in the book of the words of Isaiah the **p**, Lk 3:4
the scroll of the **p** Isaiah was given to Lk 4:17
no **p** is acceptable in his hometown. Lk 4:24
in Israel in the time of the **p** Elisha, Lk 4:27
"A great **p** has arisen among us!" and Lk 7:16
What then did you go out to see? A **p**? Lk 7:26
Yes, I tell you, and more than a **p**. Lk 7:26
he said to himself, "If this man were a **p**, Lk 7:39
cannot be that a **p** should perish away Lk 13:33
they are convinced that John was a **p**." Lk 20:6
a man who was a **p** mighty in deed and Lk 24:19
not." "Are you the **P**?" And he answered, Jn 1:21
the way of the Lord,' as the **p** Isaiah said." Jn 1:23

neither the Christ, nor Elijah, nor the **P**?" Jn 1:25
to him, "Sir, I perceive that you are a **p**. Jn 4:19
had testified that a **p** has no honor in Jn 4:44
"This is indeed the **P** who is to come into Jn 6:14
of the people said, "This really is the **P**." Jn 7:40
and see that no **p** arises from Galilee." Jn 7:52
opened your eyes?" He said, "He is a **p**." Jn 9:17
word spoken by the **p** Isaiah might be Jn 12:38
is what was uttered through the **p** Joel: Acts 2:16
Being therefore a **p**, and knowing that Acts 2:30
raise up for you a **p** like me from your Acts 3:22
not listen to that **p** shall be destroyed Acts 3:23
raise up for you a **p** like me from your Acts 7:37
houses made by hands, as the **p** says, Acts 7:48
and he was reading the **p** Isaiah. Acts 8:28
him reading Isaiah the **p** and asked, Acts 8:30
whom, I ask you, does the **p** say this, Acts 8:34
a Jewish false **p** named Bar-Jesus. Acts 13:6
gave them judges until Samuel the **p**. Acts 13:20
a **p** named Agabus came down from Acts 21:10
to your fathers through Isaiah the **p**: Acts 28:25
If anyone thinks that he is a **p**, or 1 Cor 14:37
One of the Cretans, a **p** of their own, said, Ti 1:12
and out of the mouth of the false **p**, Rv 16:13
with it the false **p** who in its presence Rv 19:20
where the beast and the false **p** were, Rv 20:10

PROPHET'S (3)
"I was no prophet, nor a **p** son, Am 7:14
he is a prophet will receive a **p** reward, Mt 10:41
voice and restrained the **p** madness. 2 Pt 2:16

PROPHETESS (8)
Then Miriam the **p**, the sister of Aaron, Ex 15:20
Now Deborah, a **p**, the wife of Lappidoth, Jgs 4:4
and Asaiah went to Huldah the **p**, 2 Kgs 22:14
king had sent went to Huldah the **p**, 2 Chr 34:22
and also the **p** Noadiah and the rest of Neh 6:14
And I went to the **p**, and she conceived and Is 8:3
And there was a **p**, Anna, the daughter of Lk 2:36
who calls herself a **p** and is teaching and Rv 2:20

PROPHETIC (4)
Where there is no **p** vision the people Prv 29:18
and through the **p** writings has been Rom 16:26
And if I have **p** powers, and 1 Cor 13:2
have something more sure, the **p** word, 2 Pt 1:19

PROPHETS (235)
that all the LORD'S people were **p**, Nm 11:29
meet a group of **p** coming down from 1 Sm 10:5
behold, a group of **p** met him, 1 Sm 10:10
saw how he prophesied with the **p**, 1 Sm 10:11
of Kish? Is Saul also among the **p**?" 1 Sm 10:11
proverb, "Is Saul also among the **p**?" 1 Sm 10:12
the company of the **p** prophesying, 1 Sm 19:20
it is said, "Is Saul also among the **p**?" 1 Sm 19:24
either by dreams, or by Urim, or by **p**. 1 Sm 28:6
no more, either by **p** or by dreams. 1 Sm 28:15
when Jezebel cut off the **p** of the LORD, 1 Kgs 18:4
took a hundred **p** and hid them 1 Kgs 18:4
when Jezebel killed the **p** of the LORD, 1 Kgs 18:13
men of the LORD'S **p** by fifties in a 1 Kgs 18:13
and the 450 **p** of Baal and the 400 1 Kgs 18:19
of Baal and the 400 **p** of Asherah, 1 Kgs 18:19
and gathered the **p** together at 1 Kgs 18:20
the LORD, but Baal's **p** are 450 men. 1 Kgs 18:22
Then Elijah said to the **p** of Baal, 1 Kgs 18:25
said to them, "Seize the **p** of Baal; 1 Kgs 18:40
he had killed all the **p** with the sword. 1 Kgs 19:1
and killed your **p** with the sword, 1 Kgs 19:10
and killed your **p** with the sword, 1 Kgs 19:14
of the sons of the **p** said to his fellow 1 Kgs 20:35
recognized him as one of the **p**. 1 Kgs 20:41
king of Israel gathered the **p** together, 1 Kgs 22:6
and all the **p** were prophesying 1 Kgs 22:10
And all the **p** prophesied so and said, 1 Kgs 22:12
the words of the **p** with one accord 1 Kgs 22:13
spirit in the mouth of all his **p**.' 1 Kgs 22:22
in the mouth of all these your **p**; 1 Kgs 22:23
the sons of the **p** who were in Bethel 2 Kgs 2:3
The sons of the **p** who were at Jericho 2 Kgs 2:5
of the sons of the **p** also went and stood 2 Kgs 2:7
the sons of the **p** who were at Jericho 2 Kgs 2:15
Go to the **p** of your father and to the 2 Kgs 3:13
father and to the **p** of your mother." 2 Kgs 3:13
one of the sons of the **p** cried to Elisha, 2 Kgs 4:1
the sons of the **p** were sitting before 2 Kgs 4:38
and boil stew for the sons of the **p**." 2 Kgs 4:38
two young men of the sons of the **p**. 2 Kgs 5:22
Now the sons of the **p** said to Elisha, 2 Kgs 6:1
of the sons of the **p** and said to him, 2 Kgs 9:1
Jezebel the blood of my servants the **p**, 2 Kgs 9:7
therefore call to me all the **p** of Baal, 2 Kgs 10:19
I sent to you by my servants the **p**." 2 Kgs 17:13
had spoken by all his servants the **p**. 2 Kgs 17:23
the LORD said by his servants the **p**, 2 Kgs 21:10
of Jerusalem and the priests and the **p**, 2 Kgs 23:2
that he spoke by his servants the **p**. 2 Kgs 24:2
anointed ones, do my **p** no harm!" 1 Chr 16:22
king of Israel gathered the **p** together, 2 Chr 18:5
and all the **p** were prophesying before 2 Chr 18:9
And all the **p** prophesied so and said, 2 Chr 18:11
the words of the **p** with one accord 2 Chr 18:12
spirit in the mouth of all his **p**.' 2 Chr 18:21
spirit in the mouth of these your **p**. 2 Chr 18:22
believe his **p**, and you will succeed." 2 Chr 20:20
Yet he sent **p** among them to bring 2 Chr 24:19
was from the LORD through his **p**. 2 Chr 29:25
his words and scoffing at his **p**, 2 Chr 36:16
Now the **p**, Haggai and Zechariah the Ezr 5:1
and the **p** of God were with them, Ezr 5:2
commanded by your servants the **p**, Ezr 9:11
also set up **p** to proclaim concerning Neh 6:7
the rest of the **p** who wanted to make Neh 6:14
behind their back and killed your **p**, Neh 9:26
them by your Spirit through your **p**. Neh 9:30
kings, our princes, our priests, our **p**, Neh 9:32
my anointed ones, do my **p** no harm!" Ps 105:15
sleep, and has closed your eyes (the **p**), Is 29:10
to the seers, "Do not see," and to the **p**, Is 30:10
the **p** prophesied by Baal and went after Jer 2:8
their officials, their priests, and their **p**, Jer 2:26
sword devoured your **p** like a ravening Jer 2:30
shall be appalled and the **p** astounded." Jer 4:9
The **p** will become wind; the word is not Jer 5:13
the **p** prophesy falsely, and the priests Jer 5:31
sent all my servants the **p** to them, Jer 7:25
the bones of the priests, the bones of the **p**, Jer 8:1
sit on David's throne, the priests, the **p**, Jer 13:13
Lord GOD, behold, the **p** say to them, Jer 14:13
"The **p** are prophesying lies in my Jer 14:14
LORD concerning the **p** who prophesy in Jer 14:15
and famine those **p** shall be consumed. Jer 14:15
Concerning the **p**: My heart is broken Jer 23:9
In the **p** of Samaria I saw an unsavory Jer 23:13
But in the **p** of Jerusalem I have seen a Jer 23:14
says the LORD of hosts concerning the **p**: Jer 23:15
for from the **p** of Jerusalem ungodliness Jer 23:15
the words of the **p** who prophesy to you, Jer 23:16
"I did not send the **p**, yet they ran; I did Jer 23:21
have heard what the **p** have said who Jer 23:25
in the heart of the **p** who prophesy lies, Jer 23:26
Therefore, behold, I am against the **p**, Jer 23:30
Behold, I am against the **p**, declares the Jer 23:31
sent to you all his servants the **p**, Jer 25:4
of my servants the **p** whom I send to Jer 26:5
The priests and the **p** and all the people Jer 26:7
the priests and the **p** and all the people Jer 26:8
the priests and the **p** said to the officials Jer 26:11
the people said to the priests and the **p**, Jer 26:16
So do not listen to your **p**, your diviners, Jer 27:9
to the words of the **p** who are saying to Jer 27:14
you and the **p** who are prophesying to Jer 27:15
words of your **p** who are prophesying Jer 27:16
If they are **p**, and if the word of the LORD Jer 27:18
The **p** who preceded you and me from Jer 28:8
of the exiles, and to the priests, the **p**, Jer 29:1
Do not let your **p** and your diviners who Jer 29:8
LORD has raised up **p** for us in Babylon,' Jer 29:15
sent to you by my servants the **p**, Jer 29:19
their officials, their priests and their **p**, Jer 32:32
I have sent to you all my servants the **p**, Jer 35:15
Where are your **p** who prophesied to Jer 37:19
sent to you all my servants the **p**, Jer 44:4
and her **p** find no vision from the LORD. Lam 2:9
Your **p** have seen for you false and Lam 2:14
the sins of her **p** and the iniquities of Lam 4:13
of man, prophesy against the **p** of Israel, Ezk 13:2
Woe to the foolish **p** who follow their Ezk 13:3
Your **p** have been like jackals among Ezk 13:4
will be against the **p** who see false Ezk 13:9
wall, these **p** smear it with whitewash, Ezk 13:10
the **p** of Israel who prophesied Ezk 13:16
The conspiracy of her **p** in her midst Ezk 22:25
And her **p** have smeared whitewash Ezk 22:28
days by my servants the **p** of Israel, Ezk 38:17
have not listened to your servants the **p**, Dn 9:6
he set before us by his servants the **p**. Dn 9:10
Therefore I have hewn them by the **p**; I Hos 6:5
I spoke to the **p**; it was I who Hos 12:10
and through the **p** gave parables. Hos 12:10
And I raised up some of your sons for **p**, Am 2:11
drink wine, and commanded the **p**, Am 2:12
revealing his secret to his servants the **p**. Am 3:7
the LORD concerning the **p** who lead my Mi 3:5
The sun shall go down on the **p**, and the Mi 3:6
its **p** practice divination for money; Mi 3:11
Her **p** are fickle, treacherous men; her Zep 3:4
fathers, to whom the former **p** cried out, Zec 1:4
are they? And the **p**, do they live forever? Zec 1:5
which I commanded my servants the **p**, Zec 1:6
the house of the LORD of hosts and the **p**, Zec 7:3
the LORD proclaimed by the former **p**, Zec 7:7
sent by his Spirit through the former **p**. Zec 7:12
the mouth of the **p** who were present on Zec 8:9
from the land the **p** and the spirit of Zec 13:2
was spoken by the **p** might be fulfilled: Mt 2:23
so they persecuted the **p** who were before Mt 5:12
I have come to abolish the Law or the **P**; Mt 5:17
to them, for this is the Law and the **P**. Mt 7:12
"Beware of false **p**, who come to you in Mt 7:15
For all the **P** and the Law prophesied Mt 11:13
many **p** and righteous people longed to Mt 13:17
and others Jeremiah or one of the **p**." Mt 16:14
depend all the Law and the **P**." Mt 22:40
the tombs of the **p** and decorate the Mt 23:29
them in shedding the blood of the **p**.' Mt 23:30
are sons of those who murdered the **p**. Mt 23:31
Therefore I send you **p** and wise men Mt 23:34
city that kills the **p** and stones those Mt 23:37
And many false **p** will arise and lead Mt 24:11
false christs and false **p** will arise and Mt 24:24
Scriptures of the **p** might be fulfilled." Mt 26:56
"He is a prophet, like one of the **p** of old." Mk 6:15
say, Elijah; and others, one of the **p**." Mk 8:28
False christs and false **p** will arise and Mk 13:22
by the mouth of his holy **p** from of old, Lk 1:70
heaven; for so their fathers did to the **p**. Lk 6:23
you, for so their fathers did to the false **p**. Lk 6:26
others that one of the **p** of old had risen. Lk 9:8
others, that one of the **p** of old has risen." Lk 9:19
tell you that many **p** and kings desired Lk 10:24
the tombs of the **p** whom your fathers Lk 11:47
said, 'I will send them **p** and apostles, Lk 11:49
so that the blood of all the **p**, shed from Lk 11:50
Jacob and all the **p** in the kingdom of Lk 13:28
city that kills the **p** and stones those Lk 13:34
"The Law and the **P** were until John; Lk 16:16
said, 'They have Moses and the **P**; Lk 16:29
'If they do not hear Moses and the **P**, Lk 16:31
of Man by the **p** will be accomplished. Lk 18:31
to believe all that the **p** have spoken! Lk 24:25
beginning with Moses and all the **P**, Lk 24:27
of Moses and the **P** and the Psalms Lk 24:44
Moses in the Law and also the **p** wrote, Jn 1:45
It is written in the **P**, 'And they will all be Jn 6:45
Abraham died, as did the **p**, yet you say, Jn 8:52
Abraham, who died? And the **p** died! Jn 8:53
God foretold by the mouth of all the **p**, Acts 3:18
by the mouth of his holy **p** long ago. Acts 3:21
And all the **p** who have spoken, from Acts 3:24
the sons of the **p** and of the covenant Acts 3:25
as it is written in the book of the **p**: Acts 7:42
Which of the **p** did not your fathers Acts 7:52
To him all the **p** bear witness that Acts 10:43
Now in these days **p** came down from Acts 11:27
the church at Antioch **p** and teachers, Acts 13:1
the reading from the Law and the **P**, Acts 13:15
understand the utterances of the **p**, Acts 13:27
is said in the **P** should come about: Acts 13:40
with this the words of the **p** agree, Acts 15:15
and Silas, who were themselves **p**, Acts 15:32
by the Law and written in the **P**, Acts 24:14
but what the **p** and Moses said Acts 26:22
King Agrippa, do you believe the **p**? Acts 26:27
the Law of Moses and from the **P**. Acts 28:23
beforehand through his **p** in the holy Rom 1:2
the Law and the **P** bear witness to it Rom 3:21
"Lord, they have killed your **p**, they Rom 11:3
the church first apostles, second **p**, 1 Cor 12:28
Are all apostles? Are all **p**? Are all 1 Cor 12:29
Let two or three **p** speak, and let the 1 Cor 14:29
and the spirits of **p** are subject to 1 Cor 14:32
spirits of prophets are subject to **p**. 1 Cor 14:32
on the foundation of the apostles and **p**, Eph 2:20
to his holy apostles and **p** by the Spirit. Eph 3:5
And he gave the apostles, the **p**, the Eph 4:11
killed both the Lord Jesus and the **p**, 1 Thes 2:15
ways, God spoke to our fathers by the **p**, Heb 1:1
of David and Samuel and the **p**— Heb 11:32
take the **p** who spoke in the name of the Jas 5:10
the **p** who prophesied about the grace 1 Pt 1:10
But false **p** also arose among the people, 2 Pt 2:1
of the holy **p** and the commandment 2 Pt 3:2
for many false **p** have gone out into the 1 Jn 4:1
as he announced to his servants the **p**. Rv 10:7
because these two **p** had been a torment Rv 11:10
your servants, the **p** and saints, Rv 11:18
they have shed the blood of saints and **p**, Rv 16:6
and you saints and apostles and **p**, Rv 18:20
was found the blood of **p** and of saints, Rv 18:24
the Lord, the God of the spirits of the **p**, Rv 22:6
with you and your brothers the **p**, Rv 22:9

PROPITIATION (4)
God put forward as a **p** by his blood, Rom 3:25
to make **p** for the sins of the people. Heb 2:17

He is the **p** for our sins, and not for ours 1 Jn 2:2
sent his Son to be the **p** for our sins. 1 Jn 4:10

PROPORTION (6)
for his redemption in **p** to his years of Lv 25:52
the valuation shall be in **p** to its seed. Lv 27:16
be given its inheritance in **p** to its list. Nm 26:54
in **p** to the inheritance that it inherits, Nm 35:8
a number of stripes in **p** to his offense. Dt 25:2
use them: if prophecy, in **p** to our faith; Rom 12:6

PROPORTIONATELY (1)
he shall pay **p** for his redemption some Lv 25:51

PROPOSAL (1)
This **p** pleased Pharaoh and all his Gn 41:37

PROPOSE (2)
And nothing that they **p** to do will now Gn 11:6
for you **p** to bring upon us guilt 2 Chr 28:13

PROPOSED (1)
and the king did as Memucan **p**. Est 1:21

PROPOUND (1)
"Son of man, **p** a riddle, and speak a Ezk 17:2

PROPPED (2)
and the king was **p** up in his chariot 1 Kgs 22:35
king of Israel was **p** up in his 2 Chr 18:34

PROSELYTE (3)
across sea and land to make a single **p**, Mt 23:15
proselyte, and when he becomes a **p**, Mt 23:15
and Nicolaus, a **p** of Antioch. Acts 6:5

PROSELYTES (1)
both Jews and **p**, Cretans and Acts 2:11

PROSPER (24)
his angel with you and **p** your way. Gn 24:40
and you shall not **p** in your ways. Dt 28:29
them, that you may **p** in all that you do. Dt 29:9
"Now I know that the LORD will **p** me, Jgs 17:13
will he not cause to **p** all my help and 2 Sm 23:5
that you may **p** in all that you do and 1 Kgs 2:3
Then you will **p** if you are careful to 1 Chr 22:13
of the LORD, so that you cannot **p**? 2 Chr 24:20
he sought the LORD, God made him **p**. 2 Chr 26:5
"The God of heaven will make us **p**, Neh 2:20
His ways **p** at all times; your judgments Ps 10:5
conceals his transgressions will not **p**, Prv 28:13
for you do not know which will **p**, Eccl 11:6
brought him, and he will **p** in his way. Is 48:15
the will of the LORD shall **p** in his hand. Is 53:10
you trust, and you will not **p** by them. Jer 2:37
the cause of the fatherless, to make it **p**, Jer 5:28
you. Why does the way of the wicked **p**? Jer 12:1
her enemies **p**, because the LORD has Lam 1:5
to the ground, and it will act and **p**. Dn 8:12
he shall make deceit **p** under his hand, Dn 8:25
He shall **p** till the indignation is Dn 11:36
Evildoers not only **p** but they put God Mal 3:15
aside and store it up, as he may **p**, 1 Cor 16:2

PROSPERED (12)
whether the LORD had **p** his journey or Gn 24:21
delay me, since the LORD has **p** my way. Gn 24:56
with him; wherever he went out, he **p**. 2 Kgs 18:7
And he **p**, and all Israel obeyed him. 1 Chr 29:23
on every side." So they built and **p**. 2 Chr 14:7
God, he did with all his heart, and **p**. 2 Chr 31:21
And Hezekiah **p** in all his works. 2 Chr 32:30
Jews built and **p** through the Ezr 6:14
therefore they have not **p**, and all their Jer 10:21
For then we had plenty of food, and **p**, Jer 44:17
So this Daniel **p** during the reign of Dn 6:28
For you say, I am rich, I have **p**, and I Rv 3:17

PROSPERING (3)
if now you are **p** the way that I go, Gn 24:42
the LORD will again take delight in **p** you, Dt 30:9
at ease in my house and **p** in my palace. Dn 4:4

PROSPERITY (25)
their peace or their **p** all your days Dt 23:6
the LORD will make you abound in **p**, Dt 28:11
eye on all the **p** that shall be bestowed 1 Sm 2:32
Your wisdom and **p** surpass the 1 Kgs 10:7
of heart for the **p** that the LORD had 2 Chr 7:10
sons, and never seek their peace or **p**, Ezr 9:12
in **p** the destroyer will come upon him. Jb 15:21
eaten; therefore his **p** will not endure. Jb 20:21
They spend their days in **p**, and in peace Jb 21:13
Behold, is not their **p** in their hand? The Jb 21:16
of soul, never having tasted of **p**. Jb 21:25
and my **p** has passed away like a cloud. Jb 30:15
serve him, they complete their days in **p**, Jb 36:11
As for me, I said in my **p**, "I shall never Ps 30:6
he leads out the prisoners to **p**, but the Ps 68:6
Let the mountains bear **p** for the people, Ps 72:3
arrogant when I saw the **p** of the wicked. Ps 73:3
may look upon the **p** of your chosen Ps 106:5
May you see the **p** of Jerusalem all the Ps 128:5
In the day of **p** be joyful, and in the day Eccl 7:14
I spoke to you in your **p**, but you said, 'I Jer 22:21
to them abundance of **p** and security. Jer 33:6
all the good and all the **p** I provide for it. Jer 33:9
perhaps be a lengthening of your **p**." Dn 4:27
My cities shall again overflow with **p**, Zec 1:17

PROSPEROUS (7)
then himself becomes **p** and finds Lv 25:26
make you more **p** and numerous than Dt 30:5
will make you abundantly **p** in all the Dt 30:9
For then you will make your way **p**, and Jos 1:8
All the **p** of the earth eat and worship; Ps 22:29
had pride, excess of food, and **p** ease, Ezk 16:49
when Jerusalem was inhabited and **p**, Zec 7:7

PROSPERS (4)
goes on diligently and **p** in their hands. Ezr 5:8
does not wither. In all that he does, he **p**. Ps 1:3
yourself over the one who **p** in his way, Ps 37:7
who gives it; wherever he turns he **p**. Prv 17:8

PROSTITUTE (39)
"Should he treat our sister like a **p**?" Gn 34:31
Judah saw her, he thought she was a **p**, Gn 38:15
"Where is the cult **p** who was at Enaim Gn 38:21
they said, "No cult **p** has been here." Gn 38:21
place said, 'No cult **p** has been here.'" Gn 38:22
your daughter by making her a **p**, Lv 19:29
shall not marry a **p** or a woman who Lv 21:7
a woman who has been defiled, or a **p**, Lv 21:14
the daughters of Israel shall be a cult **p**, Dt 23:17
of the sons of Israel shall be a cult **p**. Dt 23:17
not bring the fee of a **p** or the wages of a Dt 23:18
the house of a **p** whose name was Rahab Jos 2:1
Only Rahab the **p** and all who are with Jos 6:17
But Rahab the **p** and her father's Jos 6:25
warrior, but he was the son of a **p**. Jgs 11:1
went to Gaza, and there he saw a **p**, Jgs 16:1
for the price of a **p** is only a loaf of Prv 6:26
the woman meets him, dressed as a **p**, Prv 7:10
For a **p** is a deep pit; an adulteress is a Prv 23:27
happen to Tyre as in the song of the **p**: Is 23:15
a harp; go about the city, O forgotten **p**! Is 23:16
her wages and will **p** herself with all the Is 23:17
these things, the deeds of a brazen **p**, Ezk 16:30
Yet you were not like a **p**, because you Ezk 16:31
"Therefore, O **p**, hear the word of the Ezk 16:35
gone in to her, as men go in to a **p**. Ezk 23:44
my people, and have traded a boy for a **p**, Jl 3:3
"'Your wife shall be a **p** in the city, and Am 7:17
for from the fee of a **p** she gathered them, Mi 1:7
and to the fee of a **p** they shall return. Mi 1:7
all for the countless whorings of the **p**, Na 3:4
and make them members of a **p**? 1 Cor 6:15
is joined to a **p** becomes one body 1 Cor 6:16
By faith Rahab the **p** did not perish Heb 11:31
not also Rahab the **p** justified by works Jas 2:25
judgment of the great **p** who is seated on Rv 17:1
that you saw, where the **p** is seated, Rv 17:15
saw, they and the beast will hate the **p**. Rv 17:16
has judged the great **p** who corrupted the Rv 19:2

PROSTITUTE'S (2)
"Go into the **p** house and bring out from Jos 6:22
You have loved a **p** wages on all Hos 9:1

PROSTITUTES (15)
Then two **p** came to the king and 1 Kgs 3:16
were also male cult **p** in the land. 1 Kgs 14:24
away the male cult **p** out of the land 1 Kgs 15:12
and the **p** washed themselves in it, 1 Kgs 22:38
of the male cult **p** who remained in 1 Kgs 22:46
of the male cult **p** who were in the 2 Kgs 23:7
and their life ends among the cult **p**. Jb 36:14
a companion of **p** squanders his wealth. Prv 29:3
Men give gifts to all **p**, but you gave Ezk 16:33
go aside with **p** and sacrifice with Hos 4:14
prostitutes and sacrifice with cult **p**, Hos 4:14
tax collectors and the **p** go into the Mt 21:31
tax collectors and the **p** believed him. Mt 21:32
has devoured your property with **p**, Lk 15:30
mother of **p** and of earth's Rv 17:5

PROSTITUTION (1)
the land fall into **p** and the land Lv 19:29

PROSTRATE (4)
Then I lay **p** before the LORD as before, Dt 9:18
"So I lay **p** before the LORD for these forty Dt 9:25
I am utterly bowed down and **p**; all the Ps 38:6
princes, and they shall **p** themselves; Is 49:7

PROSTRATED (1)
bowed their heads and **p** themselves. Gn 43:28

PROTECT (10)
itself, to **p** the people of Israel. Nm 3:38
'For my sake **p** the young man 2 Sm 18:12
and horsemen to **p** us against the Ezr 8:22
May the name of the God of Jacob **p** you! Ps 20:1
p me from those who rise up against me; Ps 59:1
I will **p** him, because he knows my Ps 91:14
so the LORD of hosts will **p** Jerusalem; Is 31:5
protect Jerusalem; he will **p** and deliver it; Is 31:5
The LORD of hosts will **p** them, and they Zec 9:15
day the LORD will **p** the inhabitants of Zec 12:8

PROTECTION (10)
Their **p** is removed from them, and the Nm 14:9
up and help you; let them be your **p**! Dt 32:38
and to give us **p** in Judea and Jerusalem. Ezr 9:9
set a guard as a **p** against them day and Neh 4:9
for joy, and spread your **p** over them, Ps 5:11
For the **p** of wisdom is like the Eccl 7:12
of wisdom is like the **p** of money, Eccl 7:12
Or let them lay hold of my **p**, let them Is 27:5
to take refuge in the **p** of Pharaoh and to Is 30:2
Therefore shall the **p** of Pharaoh turn to Is 30:3

PROTECTOR (1)
of the fatherless and **p** of widows is God Ps 68:5

PROTECTS (2)
the LORD **p** him and keeps him alive; he is Ps 41:2
but he who was born of God **p** him, 1 Jn 5:18

PROTEST (1)
I **p**, brothers, by my pride in you, 1 Cor 15:31

PROUD (35)
But when he was strong, he grew **p**, 2 Chr 26:16
done to him, for his heart was **p**. 2 Chr 32:25
The **p** beasts have not trodden it; the lion Jb 28:8
and here shall your **p** waves be stayed'? Jb 38:11
on everyone who is **p** and abase him. Jb 40:11
on everyone who is **p** and bring him Jb 40:12
LORD his trust, who does not turn to the **p**, Ps 40:4
earth; repay to the **p** what they deserve! Ps 94:2
who are at ease, of the contempt of the **p**. Ps 123:4
the house of the **p** but maintains the Prv 15:25
poor than to divide the spoil with the **p**. Prv 16:19
Haughty eyes and a **p** heart, the lamp of Prv 21:4
in spirit is better than the **p** in spirit. Eccl 7:8
has a day against all that is **p** and lofty, Is 2:12
heard of the pride of Moab—how **p** he is! Is 16:6
the **p** crown of the drunkards of Ephraim, Is 28:1
The **p** crown of the drunkards of Is 28:3
ear; be not **p**, for the LORD has spoken. Jer 13:15
of Moab—he is very **p**—of his loftiness, Jer 48:29
"Behold, I am against you, O **p** one, Jer 50:31
The **p** one shall stumble and fall, with Jer 50:32
"Because your heart is **p**, and you have Ezk 28:2
heart has become **p** in your wealth Ezk 28:5
Your heart was **p** because of your Ezk 28:17
fall, and her **p** might shall come down; Ezk 30:6
and her **p** might shall come to an end Ezk 30:18
and its heart was **p** of its height, Ezk 31:10
and her **p** might shall come to an end, Ezk 33:28
he has scattered the **p** in the thoughts of Lk 1:51
So do not become **p**, but stand in awe. Rom 11:20
I have reason to be **p** of my work for Rom 15:17
of Christ I may be **p** that I did not run Phil 2:16
of self, lovers of money, **p**, arrogant, 2 Tm 3:2
Therefore it says, "God opposes the **p**, but Jas 4:6
for "God opposes the **p** but gives grace to 1 Pt 5:5

PROUDLY (8)
Talk no more so very **p**, let not 1 Sm 2:3
"The wings of the ostrich wave **p**, but Jb 39:13
me all day long, for many attack me **p**. Ps 56:2
to execute my anger, my **p** exulting ones. Is 13:3
has done. For she has **p** defied the LORD, Jer 50:29
spirit was hardened so that he dealt **p**, Dn 5:20
wolves; their horsemen press **p** on. Hab 1:8
from your midst your **p** exultant ones, Zep 3:11

PROVE (14)
you, '**P** yourselves by working a miracle,' Ex 7:9
they could not **p** their fathers' houses Ezr 2:59
they could not **p** their fathers' houses Neh 7:61
I am blameless, he would **p** me perverse. Jb 9:20
who will **p** me a liar and show that there Jb 24:25
P me, O LORD, and try me; test my heart Ps 26:2
bring their witnesses to **p** them right, Is 43:9
much fruit and so **p** to be my disciples. Jn 15:8
Neither can they **p** to you what they Acts 24:13
against him that they could not **p**. Acts 25:7
but to **p** by the earnestness of others 2 Cor 8:8
about you may not **p** vain in this 2 Cor 9:3
down, I **p** myself to be a transgressor. Gal 2:18
if they **p** themselves blameless. 1 Tm 3:10

PROVED (7)
forth your case, that you may be **p** right. Is 43:26
p to be a neighbor to the man who fell Lk 10:36
that promised life **p** to be death Rom 7:10
point you have **p** yourselves innocent 2 Cor 7:11

our boasting before Titus has **p** true. 2 Cor 7:14
kind of men we **p** to be among you 1 Thes 1:5
declared by angels **p** to be reliable Heb 2:2

PROVEN (1)
But you know Timothy's **p** worth, how Phil 2:22

PROVERB (17)
And you shall become a horror, a **p**, Dt 28:37
father?" Therefore it became a **p**, 1 Sm 10:12
As the **p** of the ancients says, 'Out of 1 Sm 24:13
Israel will become a **p** and a byword 1 Kgs 9:7
will make it a **p** and a byword among 2 Chr 7:20
I will incline my ear to a **p**; I will solve Ps 49:4
to understand a **p** and a saying, the Prv 1:6
useless, is a **p** in the mouth of fools. Prv 26:7
of a drunkard is a **p** in the mouth of Prv 26:9
what is this **p** that you have about the Ezk 12:22
I will put an end to this **p**, and they Ezk 12:23
shall no more use it as a **p** in Israel.' Ezk 12:23
proverbs will use this **p** about you: Ezk 16:44
by repeating this **p** concerning the land Ezk 18:2
this **p** shall no more be used by you in Ezk 18:3
"Doubtless you will quote to me this **p**, Lk 4:23
What the true **p** says has happened to 2 Pt 2:22

PROVERBS (7)
He also spoke 3,000 **p**, and his songs 1 Kgs 4:32
Your maxims are **p** of ashes; your Jb 13:12
The **p** of Solomon, son of David, king of Prv 1:1
The **p** of Solomon. A wise son makes a Prv 10:1
These also are **p** of Solomon which the Prv 25:1
and arranging many **p** with great care. Eccl 12:9
everyone who uses **p** will use this Ezk 16:44

PROVES (5)
is perfect; the word of the LORD **p** true; 2 Sm 22:31
is perfect; the word of the LORD **p** true; Ps 18:30
Every word of God **p** true; he is a shield Prv 30:5
choke the word, and it **p** unfruitful. Mt 13:22
and choke the word, and it **p** unfruitful. Mk 4:19

PROVIDE (31)
"God will **p** for himself the lamb for a Gn 22:8
name of that place, "The LORD will **p**"; Gn 22:14
now when shall I **p** for my own Gn 30:30
There I will **p** for you, for there are yet Gn 45:11
I will **p** for you and your little ones." Gn 50:21
Sabbath of the land shall **p** food for you, Lv 25:6
P three men from each tribe, and I will Jos 18:4
"**P** for me a man who can play well 1 Sm 16:17
and I will **p** for you with me in 2 Sm 19:33
of your God, which it falls to you to **p**, Ezr 7:20
you may **p** it out of the king's treasury. Ezr 7:20
you **p** their grain, for so you have Ps 65:9
also give bread or **p** meat for his Ps 78:20
the lambs will **p** your clothing, and Prv 27:26
yet they **p** their food in the summer; Prv 30:25
the good and all the prosperity I **p** for it. Jer 33:9
And I will **p** for them renowned Ezk 34:29
seven days you shall **p** daily a male Ezk 43:25
he shall **p** the sin offerings, grain Ezk 45:17
day the prince shall **p** for himself and Ezk 45:22
the festival he shall **p** as a burnt Ezk 45:23
And he shall **p** as a grain offering an Ezk 45:24
grain offering he shall **p** an ephah with Ezk 46:7
"You shall **p** a lamb a year old Ezk 46:13
morning by morning you shall **p** it. Ezk 46:13
And you shall **p** a grain offering with Ezk 46:14
house, eating and drinking what they **p**, Lk 10:7
P yourselves with moneybags that do Lk 12:33
Also **p** mounts for Paul to ride and Acts 23:24
temptation he will also **p** the way of 1 Cor 10:13
if anyone does not **p** for his relatives, 1 Tm 5:8

PROVIDED (30)
the mount of the LORD it shall be **p**." Gn 22:14
And Joseph **p** his father, his brothers, Gn 47:12
So there were **p**, out of the thousands of Nm 31:5
p you are careful to keep all this Dt 19:9
for I have **p** for myself a king among 1 Sm 16:1
He had **p** the king with food while he 2 Sm 19:32
a house under guard and **p** for them, 2 Sm 20:3
who **p** food for the king and his 1 Kgs 4:7
And there I have **p** a place for the ark, 1 Kgs 8:21
David also **p** great quantities of iron 1 Chr 22:3
for it." So David **p** materials in great 1 Chr 22:5
great pains I have **p** for the house of 1 Chr 22:14
of it; timber and stone, too, I have **p**. 1 Chr 22:14
So I have **p** for the house of my God, 1 Chr 29:2
to all that I have **p** for the holy house, 1 Chr 29:3
that we have **p** for building you 1 Chr 29:16
Jerusalem, whom David my father **p**. 2 Chr 2:7
p them with food and drink, 2 Chr 28:15
and he **p** for them on every side. 2 Chr 32:22
He likewise **p** cities for himself, and 2 Chr 32:29
and I **p** for the wood offering at Neh 13:31
And he quickly **p** her with her cosmetics Est 2:9
goodness, O God, you **p** for the needy. Ps 68:10
the flock, without blemish, shall be **p**. Ezk 43:25
meal offering and the oil shall be **p**, Ezk 46:15
others, who **p** for them out of their means. Lk 8:3
p we suffer with him in order that we Rom 8:17
you, **p** you continue in his kindness. Rom 11:22
since God had **p** something better for Heb 11:40
there will be richly **p** for you an 2 Pt 1:11

PROVIDES (5)
Who **p** for the raven its prey, when its Jb 38:41
He **p** food for those who fear him; he Ps 111:5
is yet night and **p** food for her Prv 31:15
When the prince **p** a freewill offering, Ezk 46:12
who richly **p** us with everything to 1 Tm 6:17

PROVIDING (3)
'The LORD your God is **p** you a place of Jos 1:13
meet my wishes by **p** food for my 1 Kgs 5:9
be full, **p** all kinds of produce; Ps 144:13

PROVINCE (44)
were the people of the **p** who came up out Ezr 2:1
and in the rest of the **p** Beyond the River. Ezr 4:10
the men of the **p** Beyond the River, Ezr 4:11
possession in the **p** Beyond the River." Ezr 4:16
and in the rest of the **p** Beyond the River, Ezr 4:17
ruled over the whole **p** Beyond the River, Ezr 4:20
the governor of the **p** Beyond the River Ezr 5:3
the governor of the **p** Beyond the River Ezr 5:6
who were in the **p** Beyond the River sent Ezr 5:6
to the king that we went to the **p** of Judah, Ezr 5:8
the capital that is in the **p** of Media, Ezr 6:2
governor of the **p** Beyond the River, Ezr 6:6
who are in the **p** Beyond the River, Ezr 6:6
the tribute of the **p** from Beyond the Ezr 6:8
the governor of the **p** Beyond the River, Ezr 6:13
shall find in the whole **p** of Babylonia, Ezr 7:16
the treasurers in the **p** Beyond the River: Ezr 7:21
all the people in the **p** Beyond the River, Ezr 7:25
the governors of the **p** Beyond the River, Ezr 8:36
there in the **p** who had survived Neh 1:3
the governors of the **p** Beyond the River, Neh 2:7
the governors of the **p** Beyond the River Neh 2:9
the governor of the **p** Beyond the River. Neh 3:7
the people of the **p** who came up out Neh 7:6
the chiefs of the **p** who lived in Neh 11:3
to every **p** in its own script and to every Est 1:22
to every **p** in its own script and every Est 3:12
a decree in every **p** by proclamation to Est 3:14
And in every **p**, wherever the king's Est 4:3
to each **p** in its own script and to each Est 8:9
of any people or **p** that might attack Est 8:11
was to be issued as a decree in every **p**, Est 8:13
And in every **p** and in every city, Est 8:17
generation, in every clan, **p**, and city, Est 9:28
If you see in a **p** the oppression of the Eccl 5:8
ruler over the whole **p** of Babylon and Dn 2:48
over the affairs of the **p** of Babylon. Dn 2:49
on the plain of Dura, in the **p** of Babylon. Dn 3:1
over the affairs of the **p** of Babylon: Dn 3:12
and Abednego in the **p** of Babylon. Dn 3:30
the capital, which is in the **p** of Elam. Dn 8:2
come into the richest parts of the **p**, Dn 11:24
letter, he asked what **p** he was from. Acts 23:34
days after Festus had arrived in the **p**, Acts 25:1

PROVINCES (27)
a rebellious city, hurtful to kings and **p**, Ezr 4:15
reigned from India to Ethiopia over 127 **p**, Est 1:1
and governors of the **p** were before him, Est 1:3
who are in all the **p** of King Ahasuerus. Est 1:16
He sent letters to all the royal **p**, to every Est 1:22
officers in all the **p** of his kingdom to Est 2:3
of taxes to the **p** and gave gifts with Est 2:18
the peoples in all the **p** of your kingdom. Est 3:8
governors over all the **p** and to the Est 3:12
to all the king's **p** with instruction to Est 3:13
people of the king's **p** know that if any Est 4:11
the Jews who are in all the **p** of the king. Est 8:5
the officials of the **p** from India to Est 8:9
provinces from India to Ethiopia, 127 **p**, Est 8:9
throughout all the **p** of King Ahasuerus, Est 8:12
throughout all the **p** of King Ahasuerus Est 9:2
the officials of the **p** and the satraps and Est 9:3
and his fame spread throughout all the **p**, Est 9:4
they done in the rest of the king's **p**! Est 9:12
were in the king's **p** also gathered to Est 9:16
were in all the **p** of King Ahasuerus, Est 9:20
to the 127 **p** of the kingdom of Est 9:30
gold and the treasure of kings and **p**. Eccl 2:8
a princess among the **p** has become a Lam 1:1
set against him from **p** on every side; Ezk 19:8
all the officials of the **p** to come to the Dn 3:2
the officials of the **p** gathered for the Dn 3:3

PROVING (2)
lived in Damascus by **p** that Jesus was Acts 9:22
explaining and **p** that it was necessary Acts 17:3

PROVISION (9)
and **p** for his father on the journey. Gn 45:23
"This is the **p** for the manslayer, who by Dt 19:4
man had to make **p** for one month in 1 Kgs 4:7
Solomon's **p** for one day was thirty 1 Kgs 4:22
the palace for which I have made **p**." 1 Chr 29:19
them, and a fixed **p** for the singers, Neh 11:23
make the same **p** for sin offerings, Ezk 45:25
Christ, and make no **p** for the flesh, Rom 13:14
these things to secure any such **p**. 1 Cor 9:15

PROVISIONED (1)
mustered and were **p** and went 1 Kgs 20:27

PROVISIONS (18)
Sodom and Gomorrah, and all their **p**, Gn 14:11
and to give them **p** for the journey. Gn 42:25
and gave them **p** for the journey. Gn 45:21
had they prepared any **p** for themselves. Ex 12:39
command the people, 'Prepare your **p**, Jos 1:11
and made ready **p** and took worn-out Jos 9:4
And all their **p** were dry and crumbly. Jos 9:5
'Take **p** in your hand for the journey Jos 9:11
So the men took some of their **p**, but did Jos 9:14
So the people took **p** in their hands, and Jgs 7:8
ten thousand, to bring **p** for the people, Jgs 20:10
a keeper and took the **p** and went, 1 Sm 17:20
him and gave him **p** and gave him 1 Sm 22:10
those officers supplied **p** for King 1 Kgs 4:27
and on oxen, abundant **p** of flour, 1 Chr 12:40
them abundant **p** and procured 2 Chr 11:23
I will abundantly bless her **p**; I will Ps 132:15
countryside to find lodging and get **p**, Lk 9:12

PROVOCATION (6)
because of the **p** of his sons and his Dt 32:19
had I not feared **p** by the enemy, lest Dt 32:27
about me, and my eye dwells on their **p**. Jb 17:2
but a fool's **p** is heavier than both. Prv 27:3
they presented the **p** of their offering; Ezk 20:28
Ephraim has given bitter **p**; so his Hos 12:14

PROVOCATIONS (1)
of all the **p** with which Manasseh 2 Kgs 23:26

PROVOKE (26)
LORD your God, so as to **p** him to anger, Dt 4:25
in the sight of the LORD to **p** him to anger. Dt 9:18
I will **p** them to anger with a foolish Dt 32:21
her rival used to **p** her grievously to 1 Sm 1:6
the house of the LORD, she used to **p** her. 1 Sm 1:7
Ahab did more to **p** the LORD, the 1 Kgs 16:33
for why should you **p** trouble so that 2 Kgs 14:10
that they might **p** me to anger with 2 Kgs 22:17
Why should you **p** trouble so that 2 Chr 25:19
that they might **p** me to anger with 2 Chr 34:25
at peace, and those who **p** God are secure, Jb 12:6
a people who **p** me to my face Is 65:3
offerings to other gods, to **p** me to anger. Jer 7:18
Is it I whom they **p**? declares the LORD. Is Jer 7:19
or **p** me to anger with the work of your Jer 25:6
that you might **p** me to anger with the Jer 25:7
out to other gods, to **p** me to anger. Jer 32:29
have done nothing but **p** me to anger Jer 32:30
Judah that they did to **p** me to anger— Jer 32:32
Why do you **p** me to anger with the Jer 44:8
with violence and **p** me still further Ezk 8:17
your whoring, to **p** me to anger. Ezk 16:26
him hard and to **p** him to speak about Lk 11:53
Shall we **p** the Lord to jealousy? Are 1 Cor 10:22
Fathers, do not **p** your children to anger, Eph 6:4
Fathers, do not **p** your children, lest Col 3:21

PROVOKED (21)
do not forget how you **p** the LORD your God Dt 9:7
Even at Horeb you **p** the LORD to wrath, Dt 9:8
at Kibroth-hattaavah you **p** the LORD to Dt 9:22
with abominations they **p** him to Dt 32:16
they have **p** me to anger with their idols. Dt 32:21
to them. And they **p** the LORD to anger. Jgs 2:12
and they **p** him to jealousy with 1 Kgs 14:22
of the anger to which he **p** the LORD, 1 Kgs 15:30
the anger to which you have **p** me, 1 Kgs 21:22
and worshiped him and **p** the LORD, 1 Kgs 22:53
in my sight and have **p** me to anger, 2 Kgs 21:15
with which Manasseh had **p** him. 2 Kgs 23:26
for they have **p** you to anger in the Neh 4:5
again and again and **p** the Holy One of Ps 78:41
For they **p** him to anger with their high Ps 78:58
they **p** the LORD to anger with their Ps 106:29
her?" "Why have they **p** me to anger Jer 8:19
to you when your fathers **p** me to wrath, Zec 8:14
his spirit was **p** within him as he saw Acts 17:16
Therefore I was **p** with that generation, Heb 3:10
with whom was he **p** for forty years? Heb 3:17

PROVOKES (3)
an end? Or what **p** you that you answer? Jb 16:3

whoever **p** him to anger forfeits his life. Prv 20:2
image of jealousy, which **p** to jealousy. Ezk 8:3

PROVOKING (16)
p him to anger through the work of Dt 31:29
and metal images, **p** me to anger, 1 Kgs 14:9
their Asherim, **p** the LORD to anger. 1 Kgs 14:15
to sin, **p** me to anger with their sins, 1 Kgs 16:2
p him to anger with the work of his 1 Kgs 16:7
p the LORD God of Israel to anger 1 Kgs 16:13
he made Israel to sin, **p** the LORD, 1 Kgs 16:26
wicked things, **p** the LORD to anger, 2 Kgs 17:11
the sight of the LORD, **p** him to anger. 2 Kgs 17:17
the sight of the LORD, **p** him to anger. 2 Kgs 21:6
Israel had made, **p** the LORD to anger. 2 Kgs 23:19
to other gods, **p** to anger the LORD, 2 Chr 28:25
the sight of the LORD, **p** him to anger. 2 Chr 33:6
p me to anger by making offerings to Jer 11:17
evil that they committed, **p** me to anger, Jer 44:3
not become conceited, **p** one another, Gal 5:26

PROWL (2)
On every side the wicked **p**, as vileness is Ps 12:8
which lies desolate; jackals **p** over it. Lam 5:18

PROWLED (1)
He **p** among the lions; he became a Ezk 19:6

PROWLING (2)
howling like dogs and **p** about the city. Ps 59:6
howling like dogs and **p** about the city. Ps 59:14

PROWLS (1)
Your adversary the devil **p** around like a 1 Pt 5:8

PRUDENCE (5)
to give **p** to the simple, knowledge and Prv 1:4
O simple ones, learn **p**; O fools, learn Prv 8:5
"I, wisdom, dwell with **p**, and I find Prv 8:12
a scoffer, and the simple will learn **p**; Prv 19:25
Daniel replied with **p** and discretion to Dn 2:14

PRUDENT (16)
of valor, a man of war, **p** in speech, 1 Sm 16:18
He who gathers in summer is a **p** son, Prv 10:5
but whoever restrains his lips is **p**. Prv 10:19
at once, but the **p** ignores an insult. Prv 12:16
A **p** man conceals knowledge, but the Prv 12:23
In everything the **p** acts with Prv 13:16
The wisdom of the **p** is to discern his Prv 14:8
but the **p** gives thought to his steps. Prv 14:15
but the **p** are crowned with knowledge. Prv 14:18
but whoever heeds reproof is **p**. Prv 15:5
The path of life leads upward for the **p**, Prv 15:24
fathers, but a **p** wife is from the LORD. Prv 19:14
The **p** sees danger and hides himself, Prv 22:3
The **p** sees danger and hides himself, Prv 27:12
Has counsel perished from the **p**? Jer 49:7
Therefore he who is **p** will keep silent in Am 5:13

PRUNE (2)
six years you shall **p** your vineyard and Lv 25:3
not sow your field or **p** your vineyard. Lv 25:4

PRUNED (1)
it shall not be **p** or hoed, and briers and Is 5:6

PRUNES (1)
every branch that does bear fruit he **p**, Jn 15:2

PRUNING (4)
plowshares, and their spears into **p** hooks; Is 2:4
grape, he cuts off the shoots with **p** hooks, Is 18:5
into swords, and your **p** hooks into spears; Jl 3:10
plowshares, and their spears into **p** hooks; Mi 4:3

PSALM (61)
A **P** of David, when he fled from Absalom Ps 3:T
with stringed instruments. A **P** of David. Ps 4:T
choirmaster: for the flutes. A **P** of David. Ps 5:T
to The Sheminith. A **P** of David. Ps 6:T
according to The Gittith. A **P** of David. Ps 8:T
according to Muth-labben. A **P** of David. Ps 9:T
to The Sheminith. A **P** of David. Ps 12:T
To the choirmaster. A **P** of David. Ps 13:T
A **P** of David. Ps 15:T
A **P** of David, the servant of the LORD, Ps 18:T
To the choirmaster. A **P** of David. Ps 19:T
To the choirmaster. A **P** of David. Ps 20:T
To the choirmaster. A **P** of David. Ps 21:T
to The Doe of the Dawn. A **P** of David. Ps 22:T
A **P** of David. Ps 23:T
A **P** of David. Ps 24:T
A **P** of David. Ps 29:T
A **P** of David. A song at the dedication of Ps 30:T
To the choirmaster. A **P** of David. Ps 31:T
A **P** of David, for the memorial offering. Ps 38:T
choirmaster: to Jeduthun. A **P** of David. Ps 39:T
To the choirmaster. A **P** of David. Ps 40:T
To the choirmaster. A **P** of David. Ps 41:T
choirmaster. A **P** of the Sons of Korah. Ps 47:T
of all the earth; sing praises with a **p**! Ps 47:7
A Song. A **P** of the Sons of Korah. Ps 48:T
choirmaster. A **P** of the Sons of Korah. Ps 49:T
A **P** of Asaph. Ps 50:T
A **P** of David, when Nathan the prophet Ps 51:T
according to Jeduthun. A **P** of David. Ps 62:T
A **P** of David, when he was in the Ps 63:T
To the choirmaster. A **P** of David. Ps 64:T
To the choirmaster. A **P** of David. A Ps 65:T
To the choirmaster. A Song. A **P**. Ps 66:T
with stringed instruments. A **P**. Ps 67:T
To the choirmaster. A **P** of David. A Ps 68:T
A **P** of Asaph. Ps 73:T
to Do Not Destroy. A **P** of Asaph. Ps 75:T
stringed instruments. A **P** of Asaph. Ps 76:T
according to Jeduthun. A **P** of Asaph. Ps 77:T
A **P** of Asaph. Ps 79:T
to Lilies. A Testimony. Of Asaph, a **P**. Ps 80:T
A **P** of Asaph. Ps 82:T
A Song. A **P** of Asaph. Ps 83:T
to The Gittith. A **P** of the Sons of Korah. Ps 84:T
choirmaster. A **P** of the Sons of Korah. Ps 85:T
A **P** of the Sons of Korah. A Song. Ps 87:T
A Song. A **P** of the Sons of Korah. To the Ps 88:T
A **P**. A Song for the Sabbath. Ps 92:T
A **P**. Ps 98:T
A **P** for giving thanks. Ps 100:T
A **P** of David. Ps 101:T
A Song. A **P** of David. Ps 108:T
To the choirmaster. A **P** of David. Ps 109:T
A **P** of David. Ps 110:T
To the choirmaster. A **P** of David. Ps 139:T
To the choirmaster. A **P** of David. Ps 140:T
A **P** of David. Ps 141:T
A **P** of David. Ps 143:T
as also it is written in the second **P**, Acts 13:33
Therefore he says also in another **p**, Acts 13:35

PSALMIST (1)
the God of Jacob, the sweet **p** of Israel: 2 Sm 23:1

PSALMS (5)
David himself says in the Book of **P**, Lk 20:42
Prophets and the **P** must be fulfilled." Lk 24:44
"For it is written in the Book of **P**, Acts 1:20
one another in **p** and hymns and Eph 5:19
singing **p** and hymns and spiritual Col 3:16

PTOLEMAIS (1)
the voyage from Tyre, we arrived at **P**, Acts 21:7

PUAH (3)
was named Shiphrah and the other **P**, Ex 1:15
arose to save Israel Tola the son of **P**, Jgs 10:1
Tola, **P**, Jashub, and Shimron, four. 1 Chr 7:1

PUBLIC (9)
in that he hears a **p** adjuration to testify, Lv 5:1
army or be liable for any other **p** duty. Dt 24:5
them from the **p** square of 2 Sm 21:12
for truth has stumbled in the **p** squares, Is 59:14
the day of his **p** appearance to Israel. Lk 1:80
apostles and put them in the **p** prison. Acts 5:18
he powerfully refuted the Jews in **p**, Acts 18:28
teaching you in **p** and from house Acts 20:20
yourself to the **p** reading of Scripture, 1 Tm 4:13

PUBLICLY (5)
being **p** displayed to all peoples, Est 8:13
then he also went up, not **p** but in private. Jn 7:10
said to them, "They have beaten us **p**, Acts 16:37
Jesus Christ was **p** portrayed as crucified. Gal 3:1
sometimes being **p** exposed to Heb 10:33

PUBLISH (3)
p it not in the streets of Ashkelon, 2 Sm 1:20
should proclaim it and **p** it in all their Neh 8:15
and proclaim freewill offerings, **p** them; Am 4:5

PUBLISHED (1)
a proclamation and **p** through Nineveh, Jon 3:7

PUBLISHES (3)
him who brings good news, who **p** peace, Is 52:7
good news of happiness, who **p** salvation, Is 52:7
who brings good news, who **p** peace! Na 1:15

PUBLIUS (2)
the chief man of the island, named **P**, Acts 28:7
that the father of **P** lay sick with fever Acts 28:8

PUDENS (1)
as do **P** and Linus and Claudia and 2 Tm 4:21

PUFFED (5)
"Behold, his soul is **p** up; it is not Hab 2:4
none of you may be **p** up in favor of 1 Cor 4:6
p up without reason by his sensuous Col 2:18
or he may become **p** up with conceit 1 Tm 3:6
he is **p** up with conceit and 1 Tm 6:4

PUFFS (2)
his sight; as for all his foes, he **p** at them. Ps 10:5
knowledge." This "knowledge" **p** up, 1 Cor 8:1

PUL (4)
P the king of Assyria came against 2 Kgs 15:19
and Menahem gave **P** a thousand 2 Kgs 15:19
up the spirit of **P** king of Assyria, 1 Chr 5:26
to the nations, to Tarshish, **P**, and Lud, Is 66:19

PULL (10)
of the elders and **p** his sandal off his Dt 25:9
for he did not **p** the sword out of his Jgs 3:22
and **p** down the altar of Baal that your Jgs 6:25
And also **p** out some from the bundles Ru 2:16
my cheeks to those who **p** out the beard; Is 50:6
P them out like sheep for the slaughter, Jer 12:3
I will build you up and not **p** you down; Jer 42:10
Will he not **p** up its roots and cut off its Ezk 17:9
or many people to **p** it from its roots. Ezk 17:9
day, will not immediately **p** him out?" Lk 14:5

PULLED (11)
worked and that has not **p** in a yoke. Dt 21:3
house of him who had his sandal **p** off.' Dt 25:10
city and the two posts, and **p** them up, Jgs 16:3
from his sleep and **p** away the pin, Jgs 16:14
he **p** down and broke in pieces and 2 Kgs 23:12
high place he **p** down and burned, 2 Kgs 23:15
a beam shall be **p** out of his house, Ezr 6:11
and my cloak and **p** hair from my head Ezr 9:3
some of them and **p** out their hair. Neh 13:25
and my hope has he **p** up like a tree. Jb 19:10
and you will be **p** down from your Is 22:19

PUNISH (56)
do not **p** us because we have done Nm 12:11
that I am about to **p** his house forever, 1 Sm 3:13
And now, because his anger does not **p**, Jb 35:15
Israel. Rouse yourself to **p** all the nations; Ps 59:5
then I will **p** their transgression with Ps 89:32
he will **p** the speech of the arrogant heart Is 10:12
I will **p** the world for its evil, and the Is 13:11
day the LORD will **p** the host of heaven, Is 24:21
from his place to **p** the inhabitants of Is 26:21
strong sword will **p** Leviathan the fleeing Is 27:1
it. Lest anyone **p** it, I keep it night and day; Is 27:3
Shall I not **p** them for these things? Jer 5:9
Shall I not **p** them for these things? Jer 5:29
at the time that I **p** them, they shall be Jer 6:15
when I **p** them, they shall be overthrown, Jer 8:12
Shall I not **p** them for these things? Jer 9:9
when I will **p** all those who are Jer 9:25
the LORD of hosts: "Behold, I will **p** them. Jer 11:22
their iniquity and **p** their sins." Jer 14:10
I will **p** you according to the fruit of Jer 21:14
I will **p** that man and his household. Jer 23:34
I will **p** the king of Babylon and that Jer 25:12
I will **p** that nation with the sword, Jer 27:8
I will **p** Shemaiah of Nehelam and his Jer 29:32
me, and I will **p** all who oppress them. Jer 30:20
And I will **p** him and his offspring and Jer 36:31
I will **p** those who dwell in the land of Jer 44:13
the LORD, that I will **p** you in this place, Jer 44:29
Esau upon him, the time when I **p** him. Jer 49:8
has come, the time when I will **p** you. Jer 50:31
And I will **p** Bel in Babylon, and take Jer 51:44
coming when I will **p** the images of Jer 51:47
O daughter of Edom, he will **p**; Lam 4:22
and I will **p** you for all your Ezk 7:3
have pity, but I will **p** you for your ways, Ezk 7:4
and I will **p** you for all your Ezk 7:8
I will **p** you according to your ways, Ezk 7:9
a little while I will **p** the house of Jehu for Hos 1:4
And I will **p** her for the feast days of the Hos 2:13
I will **p** them for their ways and repay Hos 4:9
I will not **p** your daughters when they Hos 4:14
their iniquity and **p** their sins; Hos 8:13
their iniquity; he will **p** their sins. Hos 9:9
Judah and will **p** Jacob according to Hos 12:2
therefore I will **p** you for all your Am 3:2
on the day I **p** Israel for his Am 3:14
I will **p** the altars of Bethel, Am 3:14
sacrifice—"I will **p** the officials and the Zep 1:8
that day I will **p** everyone who leaps over Zep 1:9
and I will **p** the men who are Zep 1:12
the shepherds, and I will **p** the leaders; Zec 10:3
I will therefore **p** and release him." Lk 23:16
I will therefore **p** and release him." Lk 23:22
let them go, finding no way to **p** them, Acts 4:21
being ready to **p** every disobedience, 2 Cor 10:6
as sent by him to **p** those who do evil 1 Pt 2:14

PUNISHABLE (2)
has committed a crime **p** by death and Dt 21:22
has committed no offense **p** by death. Dt 22:26

PUNISHED (12)
became unclean, so that I **p** its iniquity, Lv 18:25
have **p** us less than our iniquities Ezr 9:13

be an iniquity to be **p** by the judges; Jb 31:11
be an iniquity to be **p** by the judges, Jb 31:28
When a scoffer is **p**, the simple Prv 21:11
and after many days they will be **p**. Is 24:22
This is the city that must be **p**; there is Jer 6:6
the land of Egypt, as I have **p** Jerusalem, Jer 44:13
and his land, as I **p** the king of Assyria. Jer 50:18
them in bonds to Jerusalem to be **p**. Acts 22:5
And I **p** them often in all the Acts 26:11
as dying, and behold, we live; as **p**, and 2 Cor 6:9

PUNISHMENT (58)
LORD, "My **p** is greater than I can bear. Gn 4:13
you be swept away in the **p** of the city." Gn 19:15
no **p** shall come upon you for this 1 Sm 28:10
the morning light, **p** will overtake us. 2 Kgs 7:9
for wrath brings the **p** of the sword, Jb 19:29
has anyone said to God, 'I have borne **p**; Jb 34:31
Add to them **p** upon punishment; may Ps 69:27
Add to them punishment upon **p**; may Ps 69:27
What will you do on the day of **p**, in the Is 10:3
at the time of their **p** they shall perish. Jer 10:15
men of Anathoth, the year of their **p**." Jer 11:23
upon them in the year of their **p**, Jer 23:12
of an enemy, the **p** of a merciless foe, Jer 30:14
come upon them, the time of their **p**. Jer 46:21
I am bringing **p** upon Amon of Thebes, Jer 46:25
things upon Moab, the year of their **p**, Jer 48:44
I am bringing **p** on the king of Babylon Jer 50:18
their day has come, the time of their **p**. Jer 50:27
Be not cut off in her **p**, for this is the time Jer 51:6
at the time of their **p** they shall perish. Jer 51:18
a man, about the **p** of his sins? Lam 3:39
has been greater than the **p** of Sodom, Lam 4:6
The **p** of your iniquity, O daughter of Lam 4:22
and place the **p** of the house of Israel Ezk 4:4
that you lie on it, you shall bear their **p**. Ezk 4:4
to the number of the years of their **p**. Ezk 4:5
long shall you bear the **p** of the house of Ezk 4:5
and bear the **p** of the house of Judah. Ezk 4:6
and rot away because of their **p**. Ezk 4:17
shall bear their **p**—the punishment Ezk 14:10
punishment—the **p** of the prophet Ezk 14:10
the prophet and the **p** of the inquirer Ezk 14:10
day has come, the time of your final **p**, Ezk 21:25
day has come, the time of their final **p**. Ezk 21:29
calamity, at the time of their final **p**, Ezk 35:5
Israel went astray, shall bear their **p**. Ezk 44:10
Lord GOD, and they shall bear their **p**. Ezk 44:12
become a desolation in the day of **p**; Hos 5:9
The days of **p** have come; the days of Hos 9:7
and for four, I will not revoke the **p**, Am 1:3
and for four, I will not revoke the **p**, Am 1:6
Tyre, and for four, I will not revoke the **p**, Am 1:9
and for four, I will not revoke the **p**, Am 1:11
and for four, I will not revoke the **p**, Am 1:13
and for four, I will not revoke the **p**, Am 2:1
and for four, I will not revoke the **p**, Am 2:4
and for four, I will not revoke the **p**, Am 2:6
The day of your watchmen, of your **p**, has Mi 7:4
This shall be the **p** to Egypt and the Zec 14:19
to Egypt and the **p** to all the nations Zec 14:19
And these will go away into eternal **p**, Mt 25:46
a one, this **p** by the majority is enough, 2 Cor 2:6
fear, what longing, what zeal, what **p**! 2 Cor 7:11
will suffer the **p** of eternal 2 Thes 1:9
How much worse **p**, do you think, will Heb 10:29
the unrighteous under **p** until the day 2 Pt 2:9
For fear has to do with **p**, and whoever 1 Jn 4:18
by undergoing a **p** of eternal fire. Jude 1:7

PUNISHMENTS (1)
on the nations and **p** on the peoples, Ps 149:7

PUNITES (1)
Tolaites; of Puvah, the clan of the **P**; Nm 26:23

PUNON (2)
out from Zalmonah and camped at **P**. Nm 33:42
they set out from **P** and camped at Nm 33:43

PUPIL (1)
small and great, teacher and **p** alike. 1 Chr 25:8

PUR (3)
of King Ahasuerus, they cast **P** (that is, Est 3:7
to destroy them, and had cast **P** (that is, Est 9:24
these days Purim, after the term **P**. Est 9:26

PURAH (2)
down to the camp with **P** your servant. Jgs 7:10
he went down with **P** his servant to the Jgs 7:11

PURCHASE (7)
You shall **p** food from them for money, Dt 2:6
for the right of redemption by **p** is yours.' Jer 32:7
Then I took the sealed deed of **p**, Jer 32:11
I gave the deed of **p** to Baruch the son of Jer 32:12
the witnesses who signed the deed of **p**, Jer 32:12
this sealed deed of **p** and this open deed, Jer 32:14
given the deed of **p** to Baruch the son Jer 32:16

PURCHASED (3)
field that Abraham **p** from the Hittites. Gn 25:10
the people pass by whom you have **p**. Ex 15:16
congregation, which you have **p** of old, Ps 74:2

PURE (100)
You shall overlay it with **p** gold, inside Ex 25:11
"You shall make a mercy seat of **p** gold. Ex 25:17
shall overlay it with **p** gold and make a Ex 25:24
you shall make them of **p** gold. Ex 25:29
"You shall make a lampstand of **p** gold. Ex 25:31
piece of hammered work of **p** gold. Ex 25:36
tongs and their trays shall be of **p** gold. Ex 25:38
these utensils, out of a talent of **p** gold. Ex 25:39
they bring to you **p** beaten olive oil for Ex 27:20
and two chains of **p** gold, twisted like Ex 28:14
twisted chains like cords, of **p** gold. Ex 28:22
make a plate of **p** gold and engrave on Ex 28:36
You shall overlay it with **p** gold, its top Ex 30:3
sweet spices with **p** frankincense (of Ex 30:34
seasoned with salt, **p** and holy. Ex 30:35
and the **p** lampstand with all its utensils, Ex 31:8
he overlaid it with **p** gold inside and Ex 37:2
And he made a mercy seat of **p** gold. Two Ex 37:6
And he overlaid it with **p** gold, and Ex 37:11
made the vessels of **p** gold that were to Ex 37:16
He also made the lampstand of **p** gold. Ex 37:17
piece of hammered work of **p** gold. Ex 37:22
and its tongs and its trays of **p** gold. Ex 37:23
all its utensils out of a talent of **p** gold. Ex 37:24
He overlaid it with **p** gold, its top and Ex 37:26
oil also, and the **p** fragrant incense, Ex 37:29
twisted chains like cords, of **p** gold. Ex 39:15
They also made bells of **p** gold, and put Ex 39:25
the plate of the holy crown of **p** gold, Ex 39:30
the lampstand of **p** gold and its lamps Ex 39:37
Israel to bring you **p** oil from beaten Lv 24:2
on the lampstand of **p** gold before the Lv 24:4
on the table of **p** gold before the LORD. Lv 24:6
you shall put **p** frankincense on each Lv 24:7
high, and he overlaid it with **p** gold. 1 Kgs 6:20
the inside of the house with **p** gold, 1 Kgs 6:21
the lampstands of **p** gold, five on the 1 Kgs 7:49
for incense, and fire pans, of **p** gold; 1 Kgs 7:50
the Forest of Lebanon were of **p** gold. 1 Kgs 10:21
and **p** gold for the forks, the basins 1 Chr 28:17
He overlaid it on the inside with **p** gold. 2 Chr 3:4
and their lamps of **p** gold to burn 2 Chr 4:20
for incense, and fire pans, of **p** gold, 2 Chr 4:22
throne and overlaid it with **p** gold. 2 Chr 9:17
the Forest of Lebanon were of **p** gold. 2 Chr 9:20
showbread on the table of **p** gold, 2 Chr 13:11
God? Can a man be **p** before his Maker? Jb 4:17
if you are **p** and upright, surely then he Jb 8:6
For you say, 'My doctrine is **p**, and I am Jb 11:4
What is man, that he can be **p**? Or he Jb 15:14
and the heavens are not **p** in his sight; Jb 15:15
in my hands, and my prayer is **p**. Jb 16:17
How can he who is born of woman be **p**? Jb 25:4
bright, and the stars are not **p** in his eyes; Jb 25:5
equal it, nor can it be valued in **p** gold. Jb 28:19
You say, 'I am **p**, without transgression; I Jb 33:9
The words of the LORD are **p** words, like Ps 12:6
with the purified you show yourself **p**; Ps 18:26
the commandment of the LORD is **p**, Ps 19:8
He who has clean hands and a **p** heart, Ps 24:4
good to Israel, to those who are **p** in heart. Ps 73:1
How can a young man keep his way **p**? Ps 119:9
to the LORD, but gracious words are **p**. Prv 15:26
the ways of a man are **p** in his own eyes, Prv 16:2
Who can say, "I have made my heart **p**; Prv 20:9
whether his conduct is **p** and upright. Prv 20:11
but the conduct of the **p** is upright. Prv 21:8
one of her mother, **p** to her who bore her. Sg 6:9
you a choice vine, wholly of **p** seed. Jer 2:21
grown dim, how the **p** gold is changed! Lam 4:1
and the hair of his head like **p** wool; Dn 7:9
the speech of the peoples to a **p** speech, Zep 3:9
and I will clothe you with **p** vestments." Zec 3:4
be offered to my name, and a **p** offering. Mal 1:11
"Blessed are the **p** in heart, for they shall Mt 5:8
alabaster flask of ointment of **p** nard, Mk 14:3
of expensive ointment made from **p** nard, Jn 12:3
to present you as a **p** virgin to Christ. 2 Cor 11:2
a sincere and **p** devotion to Christ. 2 Cor 11:3
and so be **p** and blameless for the day Phil 1:10
whatever is just, whatever is **p**, Phil 4:8
that issues from a **p** heart and a good 1 Tm 1:5
in the sins of others; keep yourself **p**. 1 Tm 5:22
who call on the Lord from a **p** heart. 2 Tm 2:22
To the **p**, all things are pure, but to the Ti 1:15
To the pure, all things are **p**, but to the Ti 1:15
the defiled and unbelieving, nothing is **p**; Ti 1:15
to be self-controlled, **p**, working at home, Ti 2:5
and our bodies washed with **p** water. Heb 10:22
Religion that is **p** and undefiled before Jas 1:27
But the wisdom from above is first **p**, Jas 3:17
one another earnestly from a **p** heart, 1 Pt 1:22
infants, long for the **p** spiritual milk, 1 Pt 2:2
they see your respectful and **p** conduct. 1 Pt 3:2
hopes in him purifies himself as he is **p**. 1 Jn 3:3
with the seven plagues, clothed in **p**, Rv 15:6
bright and **p**"—for the fine linen is the Rv 19:8
arrayed in fine linen, white and **p**, Rv 19:14
of jasper, while the city was **p** gold, Rv 21:18
and the street of the city was **p** gold, Rv 21:21

PURELY (1)
with the purified you deal **p**, and 2 Sm 22:27

PURER (2)
Her princes were **p** than snow, whiter Lam 4:7
You who are of **p** eyes than to see evil Hab 1:13

PUREST (1)
the lamps, and the tongs, of **p** gold; 2 Chr 4:21

PURGE (16)
So you shall **p** the evil from your midst. Dt 13:5
So you shall **p** the evil from your midst. Dt 17:7
die. So you shall **p** the evil from Israel. Dt 17:12
but you shall **p** the guilt of innocent Dt 19:13
So you shall **p** the evil from your midst. Dt 19:19
So you shall **p** the guilt of innocent Dt 21:9
So you shall **p** the evil from your midst, Dt 21:21
So you shall **p** the evil from your midst. Dt 22:21
So you shall **p** the evil from Israel. Dt 22:22
So you shall **p** the evil from your midst. Dt 22:24
So you shall **p** the evil from your midst. Dt 24:7
them to death and **p** evil from Israel." Jgs 20:13
he began to **p** Judah and Jerusalem 2 Chr 34:3
P me with hyssop, and I shall be clean; Ps 51:7
I will **p** out the rebels from among Ezk 20:38
"**P** the evil person from among you." 1 Cor 5:13

PURIFICATION (8)
sprinkle the water of **p** upon them, and Nm 8:7
of their God and the service of **p**, Neh 12:45
time came for their **p** according to the Lk 2:22
water jars there for the Jewish rites of **p**, Jn 2:6
some of John's disciples and a Jew over **p**. Jn 3:25
when the days of **p** would be fulfilled Acts 21:26
of his power. After making **p** for sins, Heb 1:3
a heifer sanctifies for the **p** of the flesh, Heb 9:13

PURIFIED (17)
altar around it and **p** the altar and Lv 8:15
And the Levites **p** themselves from sin Nm 8:21
it shall also be **p** with the water for Nm 31:23
with the **p** you deal purely, and with 2 Sm 22:27
the Levites had **p** themselves together; Ezr 6:20
priests and the Levites **p** themselves, Neh 12:30
and they **p** the people and the gates Neh 12:30
a furnace on the ground, **p** seven times. Ps 12:6
with the **p** you show yourself pure; and Ps 18:26
and the altar shall be **p**, as it was Ezk 43:22
be purified, as it was **p** with the bull. Ezk 43:22
may be refined, **p**, and made white, Dn 11:35
the next day he **p** himself along with Acts 21:26
this, they found me **p** in the temple, Acts 24:18
law almost everything is **p** with blood, Heb 9:22
heavenly things to be **p** with these rites, Heb 9:23
Having **p** your souls by your obedience 1 Pt 1:22

PURIFIER (1)
He will sit as a refiner and **p** of silver, Mal 3:3

PURIFIES (1)
thus hopes in him **p** himself as he is 1 Jn 3:3

PURIFY (16)
among you and **p** yourselves and Gn 35:2
Also you shall **p** the altar, when you Ex 29:36
p yourselves and your captives on the Nm 31:19
You shall **p** every garment, every Nm 31:20
that they should **p** themselves and Neh 13:22
p yourselves, you who bear the vessels of Is 52:11
who sanctify and **p** themselves to go Is 66:17
Thus you shall **p** the altar and make Ezk 43:20
without blemish, and **p** the sanctuary. Ezk 45:18
Many shall **p** themselves and make Dn 12:10
and he will **p** the sons of Levi and refine Mal 3:3
before the Passover to **p** themselves. Jn 11:55
these men and **p** yourself along with Acts 21:24
all lawlessness and to **p** for himself a Ti 2:14
p our conscience from dead works to Heb 9:14
hands, you sinners, and **p** your hearts, Jas 4:8

PURIFYING (6)
thirty-three days in the blood of her **p**. Lv 12:4
until the days of her **p** are completed. Lv 12:4
in the blood of her **p** for sixty-six days. Lv 12:5
when the days of her **p** are completed, Lv 12:6
(Now she had been **p** herself from her 2 Sm 11:4
When you have finished **p** it, you Ezk 43:23

PURIM (5)
Therefore they called these days **P**, after Est 9:26
that these days of **P** should never fall Est 9:28
confirming this second letter about **P**. Est 9:29
that these days of **P** should be observed Est 9:31
Esther confirmed these practices of **P**, Est 9:32

PURITY (4)
He who loves **p** of heart, and whose Prv 22:11
by **p**, knowledge, patience, kindness, 2 Cor 6:6
in conduct, in love, in faith, in **p**. 1 Tm 4:12
younger women like sisters, in all **p**. 1 Tm 5:2

PURPLE (53)
blue and **p** and scarlet yarns and fine Ex 25:4
linen and blue and **p** and scarlet yarns; Ex 26:1
veil of blue and **p** and scarlet yarns and Ex 26:31
of blue and **p** and scarlet yarns and fine Ex 26:36
of blue and **p** and scarlet yarns and fine Ex 27:16
gold, blue and **p** and scarlet yarns, Ex 28:5
of gold, of blue and **p** and scarlet yarns, Ex 28:6
it, of gold, blue and **p** and scarlet yarns, Ex 28:8
—of gold, blue and **p** and scarlet yarns, Ex 28:15
of blue and **p** and scarlet yarns, Ex 28:33
blue and **p** and scarlet yarns and fine Ex 35:6
possessed blue or **p** or scarlet yarns Ex 35:23
spun in blue and **p** and scarlet yarns Ex 35:25
in blue and **p** and scarlet yarns Ex 35:35
linen and blue and **p** and scarlet yarns, Ex 36:8
veil of blue and **p** and scarlet yarns and Ex 36:35
of blue and **p** and scarlet yarns and fine Ex 36:37
in blue and **p** and scarlet yarns Ex 38:18
in blue and **p** and scarlet yarns Ex 38:23
From the blue and **p** and scarlet yarns Ex 39:1
of gold, blue and **p** and scarlet yarns, Ex 39:2
into the blue and **p** and the scarlet yarns, Ex 39:3
it, of gold, blue and **p** and scarlet yarns, Ex 39:5
it, of gold, blue and **p** and scarlet yarns, Ex 39:8
of blue and **p** and scarlet yarns Ex 39:24
and of blue and **p** and scarlet yarns, Ex 39:29
the altar and spread a **p** cloth over it. Nm 4:13
pendants and the **p** garments worn by Jgs 8:26
gold, silver, bronze, and iron, and in **p**, 2 Chr 2:7
iron, stone, and wood, and in **p**, 2 Chr 2:14
of blue and **p** and crimson fabrics 2 Chr 3:14
of fine linen and **p** to silver rods and Est 1:6
crown and a robe of fine linen and **p**, Est 8:15
her clothing is fine linen and **p**. Prv 31:22
of silver, its back of gold, its seat of **p**; Sg 3:10
Carmel, and your flowing locks are like **p**; Sg 7:5
goldsmith; their clothing is violet and **p**; Jer 10:9
brought up in **p** embrace ash heaps. Lam 4:5
clothed in **p**, governors and Ezk 23:6
blue and **p** from the coasts of Elishah Ezk 27:7
wares emeralds, **p**, embroidered work, Ezk 27:16
shall be clothed with **p** and have a chain Dn 5:7
shall be clothed with **p** and have a Dn 5:16
and Daniel was clothed with **p**, Dn 5:29
And they clothed him in a **p** cloak, Mk 15:17
stripped him of the **p** cloak and put his Mk 15:20
who was clothed in **p** and fine linen Lk 16:19
on his head and arrayed him in a **p** robe. Jn 19:2
the crown of thorns and the **p** robe. Jn 19:5
city of Thyatira, a seller of **p** goods, Acts 16:14
woman was arrayed in **p** and scarlet, Rv 17:4
silver, jewels, pearls, fine linen, **p** cloth, Rv 18:12
clothed in fine linen, in **p** and scarlet, Rv 18:16

PURPOSE (54)
But for this **p** I have raised you up, to Ex 9:16
Look, you have some evil **p** in mind. Ex 10:10
sack, any article that is used for any **p**. Lv 11:32
to help David with singleness of **p**. 1 Chr 12:33
against them to frustrate their **p**, Ezr 4:5
For this **p** he was hired, that I should Neh 6:13
platform that they had made for the **p**. Neh 8:4
your heart; I know that this was your **p**. Jb 10:13
and that no **p** of yours can be thwarted. Jb 42:2
High, to God who fulfills his **p** for me. Ps 57:2
They hold fast to their evil **p**; they talk of Ps 64:5
near who persecute me with evil **p**; Ps 119:150
The LORD will fulfill his **p** for me; your Ps 138:8
The LORD has made everything for its **p**, Prv 16:4
but it is the **p** of the LORD that will Prv 19:21
The **p** in a man's heart is like deep Prv 20:5
This is the **p** that is purposed Is 14:26
will fear because of the **p** that the LORD of Is 19:17
shepherd, and he shall fulfill all my **p**'; Is 44:28
stand, and I will accomplish all my **p**,' Is 46:10
he shall perform his **p** on Babylon, and Is 48:14
of coals and produces a weapon for its **p**. Is 54:16
but it shall accomplish that which I **p**, Is 55:11
you and formed a **p** against you. Jer 49:30
because his **p** concerning Babylon is to Jer 51:11
towns as well; for I was sent for this **p**." Lk 4:43
the lawyers rejected the **p** of God for Lk 7:30
but for this **p** I came baptizing with Jn 1:31
But for this **p** I have come to this hour. Jn 12:27
For this **p** I was born and for this Jn 18:37
born and for this **p** I have come into Jn 18:37
And has he not come here for this **p**, to Acts 9:21
faithful to the Lord with steadfast **p**, Acts 11:23
after he had served the **p** of God in his Acts 13:36
for I have appeared to you for this **p**, Acts 26:16
that they had obtained their **p**, Acts 27:13
The **p** was to make him the father of Rom 4:11
who are called according to his **p**. Rom 8:28
in order that God's **p** of election might Rom 9:11
"For this very **p** I have raised you up, Rom 9:17
the law, then Christ died for no **p**. Gal 2:21
make much of you, but for no good **p**. Gal 4:17
good to be made much of for a good **p**, Gal 4:18
Christ, according to the **p** of his will, Eph 1:5
mystery of his will, according to his **p**, Eph 1:9
according to the **p** of him who Eph 1:11
according to the eternal **p** that he has Eph 3:11
I have sent him to you for this very **p**, Eph 6:22
I have sent him to you for this very **p**, Col 4:8
but because of his own **p** and grace, 2 Tm 1:9
the unchangeable character of his **p**, Heb 6:17
it is to no **p** that the Scripture says, Jas 4:5
Job, and you have seen the **p** of the Lord, Jas 5:11
to carry out his **p** by being of one Rv 17:17

PURPOSED (15)
Now Solomon **p** to build a temple for 2 Chr 2:1
I have **p** that my mouth will not Ps 17:3
planned, so shall it be, and as I have **p**, Is 14:24
purpose that is **p** concerning the whole Is 14:26
For the LORD of hosts has **p**, and who will Is 14:27
the LORD of hosts has **p** against Egypt. Is 19:12
the LORD of hosts has **p** against them. Is 19:17
Who has **p** this against Tyre, the Is 23:8
The LORD of hosts has **p** it, to defile the Is 23:9
bring it to pass; I have **p**, and I will do it. Is 46:11
be dark; for I have spoken; I have **p**; Jer 4:28
The LORD has done what he **p**; he has Lam 2:17
As the LORD of hosts **p** to deal with us for Zec 1:6
"As I **p** to bring disaster to you when Zec 8:14
so again have I **p** in these days to bring Zec 8:15

PURPOSES (6)
keep forever such **p** and thoughts in 1 Chr 29:18
rebellious in their **p** and were brought Ps 106:43
against Edom and the **p** that he has Jer 49:20
and the **p** that he has formed against Jer 50:45
for the LORD'S **p** against Babylon stand, Jer 51:29
and will disclose the **p** of the heart. 1 Cor 4:5

PURSE (2)
lot among us; we will all have one **p**"— Prv 1:14
Those who lavish gold from the **p**, and Is 46:6

PURSES (1)
he who **p** his lips brings evil to pass. Prv 16:30

PURSUE (43)
so that they did not **p** the sons of Jacob. Gn 35:5
Pharaoh's heart, and he will **p** them, Ex 14:4
The enemy said, 'I will **p**, I will overtake, Ex 15:9
blood in hot anger **p** the manslayer and Dt 19:6
They shall **p** you until you perish. Dt 28:22
come upon you and **p** you and overtake Dt 28:45
P them quickly, for you will overtake Jos 2:5
the city were called together to **p** them, Jos 8:16
P your enemies; attack their rear Jos 10:19
come out? After whom do you **p**? 1 Sm 24:14
If men rise up to **p** you and to seek 1 Sm 25:29
does my lord **p** after his servant? 1 Sm 26:18
of the LORD, "Shall I **p** after this band? 1 Sm 30:8
"**P**, for you shall surely overtake and 1 Sm 30:8
and I will arise and **p** David tonight. 2 Sm 17:1
Take your lord's servants and **p** him, 2 Sm 20:6
out from Jerusalem to **p** Sheba the son 2 Sm 20:7
on after Joab to **p** Sheba the son of 2 Sm 20:13
before your foes while they **p** you? 2 Sm 24:13
frighten a driven leaf and **p** dry chaff? Jb 13:25
Why do you, like God, **p** me? Why are Jb 19:22
If you say, 'How we will **p** him!' and, Jb 19:28
let the enemy **p** my soul and overtake it, Ps 7:5
In arrogance the wicked hotly **p** the poor; Ps 10:2
evil and do good; seek peace and **p** it. Ps 34:14
p and seize him, for there is none to Ps 71:11
so may you **p** them with your tempest Ps 83:15
"Listen to me, you who **p** righteousness, Is 51:1
I will **p** them with sword, famine, and Jer 29:18
to silence; the sword shall **p** you. Jer 48:2
You will **p** them in anger and destroy Lam 3:66
you for blood, and blood shall **p** you; Ezk 35:6
bloodshed, therefore blood shall **p** you. Ezk 35:6
She shall **p** her lovers but not overtake Hos 2:7
the good; the enemy shall **p** him. Hos 8:3
and will **p** his enemies into darkness. Na 1:8
who did not **p** righteousness have Rom 9:30
Because they did not **p** it by faith, but Rom 9:32
So then let us **p** what makes for peace Rom 14:19
P love, and earnestly desire the 1 Cor 14:1
P righteousness, godliness, faith, love, 1 Tm 6:11
passions and **p** righteousness, 2 Tm 2:22
do good; let him seek peace and **p** it. 1 Pt 3:11

PURSUED (45)
defeated them and **p** them to Hobah, Gn 14:15
with him and **p** him for seven Gn 31:23
is my sin, that you have hotly **p** me? Gn 31:36
and he **p** the people of Israel while the Ex 14:8
The Egyptians **p** them, all Pharaoh's Ex 14:9
The Egyptians **p** and went in after them Ex 14:23
down and defeated them and **p** them, Nm 14:45
Sea flow over them as they **p** after you, Dt 11:4
So the men **p** after them on the way to the Jos 2:7
and as they **p** Joshua they were drawn Jos 8:16
They left the city open and **p** Israel. Jos 8:17
the open wilderness where they **p** them, Jos 8:24
And the Egyptians **p** your fathers with Jos 24:6
but they **p** him and caught him and cut Jgs 1:6
And Barak **p** the chariots and the army Jgs 4:16
all Manasseh, and they **p** after Midian. Jgs 7:23
Then they **p** Midian, and they brought Jgs 7:25
and he **p** them and captured the two Jgs 8:12
they **p** them and trod them down from Jgs 20:43
And they were **p** hard to Gidom, Jgs 20:45
from Mizpah and **p** the Philistines 1 Sm 7:11
with a shout and **p** the Philistines as 1 Sm 17:52
he **p** after David in the wilderness of 1 Sm 23:25
But David **p**, he and four hundred 1 Sm 30:10
And Asahel **p** Abner, and as he went, 2 Sm 2:19
But Joab and Abishai **p** Abner. And 2 Sm 2:24
the men stopped and **p** Israel no more, 2 Sm 2:28
Abishai his brother **p** Sheba the son 2 Sm 20:10
I **p** my enemies and destroyed them, 2 Sm 22:38
The Syrians fled, and Israel **p** them, 1 Kgs 20:20
And Jehu **p** him and said, "Shoot him 2 Kgs 9:27
of the Chaldeans **p** the king and 2 Kgs 25:5
And Abijah **p** Jeroboam and took 2 Chr 13:19
who were with him **p** them as far as 2 Chr 14:13
my honor is **p** as by the wind, and my Jb 30:15
I **p** my enemies and overtook them, and Ps 18:37
but **p** the poor and needy and the Ps 109:16
For the enemy has **p** my soul; he has Ps 143:3
of the Chaldeans **p** them and overtook Jer 39:5
army of the Chaldeans **p** the king and Jer 52:8
wrapped yourself with anger and **p** us, Lam 3:43
because he **p** his brother with the Am 1:11
but that Israel who **p** a law that would Rom 9:31
immorality and **p** unnatural desire, Jude 1:7
he **p** the woman who had given birth to Rv 12:13

PURSUER (1)
they fled without strength before the **p**. Lam 1:6

PURSUERS (13)
was shut as soon as the **p** had gone out. Jos 2:7
the hills, or the **p** will encounter you, Jos 2:16
three days until the **p** have returned. Jos 2:16
there three days until the **p** returned, Jos 2:22
and the **p** searched all along the way and Jos 2:22
wilderness turned back against the **p**. Jos 8:20
and you cast their **p** into the depths, Neh 9:11
save me from all my **p** and deliver me, Ps 7:1
Draw the spear and javelin against my **p**! Ps 35:3
steeds"; therefore your **p** shall be swift. Is 30:16
her **p** have all overtaken her in the Lam 1:3
Our **p** were swifter than the eagles in Lam 4:19
Our **p** are at our necks; we are weary; we Lam 5:5

PURSUES (12)
and you shall flee when none **p** you. Lv 26:17
sword, and they shall fall when none **p**. Lv 26:36
as if to escape a sword, though none **p**. Lv 26:37
And if the avenger of blood **p** him, they Jos 20:5
will live, but he who **p** evil will die. Prv 11:19
Disaster **p** sinners, but the righteous Prv 13:21
but he loves him who **p** righteousness. Prv 15:9
He **p** them with words, but does not Prv 19:7
Whoever **p** righteousness and Prv 21:21
The wicked flee when no one **p**, but the Prv 28:1
He **p** them and passes on safely, by paths Is 41:3
on the wind and **p** the east wind all Hos 12:1

PURSUING (9)
And behold, as Barak was **p** Sisera, Jael Jgs 4:22
men who were with him, exhausted yet **p**. Jgs 8:4
and I am **p** after Zebah and Zalmunna, Jgs 8:5
Saul went up from **p** the Philistines, 1 Sm 14:46
Saul returned from **p** after David and 1 Sm 23:28
the troops came back from **p** Israel, 2 Sm 18:16
Israel, they turned back from **p** him. 1 Kgs 22:33
they turned back from **p** him. 2 Chr 18:32
with the angel of the LORD **p** them! Ps 35:6

PURSUIT (4)
of them, and went in **p** as far as Dan. Gn 14:14

all your tribes to **p** his name and make Dt 12:5
God will choose to **p** his name there is Dt 12:21
dreamer of dreams shall be **p** to death, Dt 13:5
be first against him to **p** him to death, Dt 13:9
you shall surely **p** the inhabitants of Dt 13:15
and **p** it through his ear into the door, Dt 15:17
the sickle is first **p** to the standing grain. Dt 16:9
the one who is to die shall be **p** to death; Dt 17:6
a person shall not be **p** to death on the Dt 17:6
be first against him to **p** him to death, Dt 17:7
You may not **p** a foreigner over you, Dt 17:15
And I will **p** my words in his mouth, Dt 18:18
you shall **p** all its males to the sword, Dt 20:13
by death and he is **p** to death, Dt 21:22
nor shall a man **p** on a woman's cloak, Dt 22:5
but you shall not **p** any in your bag. Dt 23:24
but you shall not **p** a sickle to your Dt 23:25
"Fathers shall not be **p** to death because Dt 24:16
shall children be **p** to death because Dt 24:16
Each one shall be **p** to death for his own Dt 24:16
you, and you shall **p** it in a basket, Dt 26:2
And he will **p** a yoke of iron on your Dt 28:48
LORD your God will **p** all these curses on Dt 30:7
and you shall **p** them in possession of it. Dt 31:7
P it in their mouths, that this song may Dt 31:19
Book of the Law and **p** it by the side of Dt 31:26
and two have **p** ten thousand to flight, Dt 32:30
they shall **p** incense before you and Dt 33:10
you command him, shall be **p** to death. Jos 1:18
all her relatives and **p** them outside the Jos 6:23
they **p** into the treasury of the house of Jos 6:24
of Israel. And they **p** dust on their heads. Jos 7:6
stolen and lied and **p** them among their Jos 7:11
p your feet on the necks of these kings." Jos 10:24
they came near and **p** their feet on their Jos 10:24
struck them and **p** them to death, Jos 10:26
and struck them and **p** them to death. Jos 11:17
they **p** the Canaanites to forced labor, Jos 17:13
"How long will you **p** off going in to take Jos 18:3
he **p** darkness between you and the Jos 24:7
P away the gods that your fathers Jos 24:14
"Then **p** away the foreign gods that are Jos 24:23
and **p** in place statutes and rules for Jos 24:25
they **p** the Canaanites to forced labor, Jgs 1:28
of flour. The meat he **p** in a basket, Jgs 6:19
in a basket, and the broth he **p** in a pot, Jgs 6:19
cakes, and **p** them on this rock, Jgs 6:20
for him shall be **p** to death by morning. Jgs 6:31
three companies and **p** trumpets into the Jgs 7:16
made an ephod of it and **p** it in his city, Jgs 8:27
leaders of Shechem **p** men in ambush Jgs 9:25
leaders of Shechem **p** confidence in him. Jgs 9:26
and following Abimelech **p** it against Jgs 9:49
So they **p** away the foreign gods from Jgs 10:16
to them, "Let me now **p** a riddle to you. Jgs 14:12
And they said to him, "**P** your riddle, Jgs 14:13
You have **p** a riddle to my people, and Jgs 14:16
tail to tail and **p** a torch between each Jgs 15:4
donkey, and **p** out his hand and took it, Jgs 15:15
and **p** them on his shoulders and carried Jgs 16:3
p your hand on your mouth and come Jgs 18:19
Then he **p** her on the donkey, and the Jgs 19:28
that we may **p** them to death and purge Jgs 20:13
saying, "He shall surely be **p** to death." Jgs 21:5
and **p** on your cloak and go down to the Ru 3:3
six measures of barley and **p** it on her. Ru 3:15
drunk? **P** away your wine from you." 1 Sm 1:14
the will of the LORD to **p** them to death. 1 Sm 2:25
"Please **p** me in one of the priests' 1 Sm 2:36
they took Dagon and **p** him back in 1 Sm 5:3
place it on the cart and **p** in a box at its 1 Sm 6:8
And they **p** the ark of the LORD on the 1 Sm 6:11
then **p** away the foreign gods and the 1 Sm 7:3
the people of Israel **p** away the Baals 1 Sm 7:4
donkeys, and **p** them to his work. 1 Sm 8:16
of which I said to you, '**P** it aside.'" 1 Sm 9:23
the next day Saul **p** the people in 1 Sm 11:11
men, that we may **p** them to death." 1 Sm 11:12
a man shall be **p** to death this day, 1 Sm 11:13
but no one **p** his hand to his mouth, 1 Sm 14:26
so he **p** out the tip of the staff that 1 Sm 14:27
in the honeycomb and **p** his hand to 1 Sm 14:27
He **p** a helmet of bronze on his head 1 Sm 17:38
tested them." So David **p** them off. 1 Sm 17:39
from the brook and **p** them in his 1 Sm 17:40
And David **p** his hand in his bag and 1 Sm 17:49
but he **p** his armor in his tent. 1 Sm 17:54
LORD lives, he shall not be **p** to death." 1 Sm 19:6
it on the bed and **p** a pillow of goats' 1 Sm 19:13
"Why should he be **p** to death? 1 Sm 20:32
was determined to **p** David to death. 1 Sm 20:33
the king would not **p** out their hand 1 Sm 22:17
city of the priests, he **p** to the sword; 1 Sm 22:19
donkey and sheep, he **p** to the sword. 1 Sm 22:19
to **p** out my hand against him, 1 Sm 24:6

'I will not **p** out my hand against my 1 Sm 24:10
me when the LORD **p** me into your 1 Sm 24:18
for who can **p** out his hand against 1 Sm 26:9
forbid that I should **p** out my hand 1 Sm 26:11
and I would not **p** out my hand 1 Sm 26:23
And Saul had **p** the mediums and the 1 Sm 28:3
disguised himself and **p** on other 1 Sm 28:8
and she **p** it before Saul and his 1 Sm 28:25
They **p** his armor in the temple of 1 Sm 31:10
were not afraid to **p** out your hand to 2 Sm 1:14
who **p** ornaments of gold on your 2 Sm 1:24
because he had **p** their brother Asahel 2 Sm 3:30
your clothes and **p** on sackcloth and 2 Sm 3:31
the king's will to **p** to death Abner the 2 Sm 3:37
they struck him and **p** him to death 2 Sm 4:7
Uzzah **p** out his hand to the ark of God 2 Sm 6:6
Saul, whom I **p** away from before you. 2 Sm 7:15
Two lines he measured to be **p** to death, 2 Sm 8:2
Then David **p** garrisons in Aram of 2 Sm 8:6
Then he **p** garrisons in Edom; 2 Sm 8:14
throughout all Edom he **p** garrisons, 2 Sm 8:14
rest of his men he **p** in the charge of 2 Sm 10:10
"The LORD also has **p** away your sin; 2 Sm 12:13
"**P** this woman out of my presence 2 Sm 13:17
So his servant **p** her out and bolted 2 Sm 13:18
And Tamar **p** ashes on her head and 2 Sm 13:19
a mourner and **p** on mourning 2 Sm 14:2
to him." So Joab **p** the words in her 2 Sm 14:3
that we may **p** him to death for the life 2 Sm 14:7
it was he who **p** all these words in the 2 Sm 14:19
guilt in me, let him **p** me to death.'" 2 Sm 14:32
he would **p** out his hand and take 2 Sm 15:5
"Shall not Shimei be **p** to death for 2 Sm 19:21
Shall anyone be **p** to death in Israel 2 Sm 19:22
for the house and **p** them in a house 2 Sm 20:3
because he **p** the Gibeonites to death." 2 Sm 21:1
is it for us to **p** any man to death in 2 Sm 21:4
They were **p** to death in the first days 2 Sm 21:9
that he will not **p** his servant to death 1 Kgs 1:51
'I will not **p** you to death with the 1 Kgs 2:8
Adonijah shall be **p** to death this 1 Kgs 2:24
I will not at this time **p** you to death, 1 Kgs 2:26
struck him down and **p** him to death. 1 Kgs 2:34
The king **p** Benaiah the son of 1 Kgs 2:35
and the king **p** Zadok the priest in the 1 Kgs 2:35
and by no means **p** him to death." 1 Kgs 3:26
and by no means **p** him to death; 1 Kgs 3:27
until the LORD **p** them under the soles 1 Kgs 5:3
He **p** the cherubim in the innermost 1 Kgs 6:27
of stone that Moses **p** there at Horeb, 1 Kgs 8:9
And the king **p** them in the House of 1 Kgs 10:17
which God had **p** into his mind. 1 Kgs 10:24
where I have chosen to **p** my name. 1 Kgs 11:36
the yoke that your father **p** on us'?" 1 Kgs 12:9
in Bethel, and the other he **p** in Dan. 1 Kgs 12:29
tribes of Israel, to **p** his name there. 1 Kgs 14:21
He **p** away the male cult prostitutes 1 Kgs 15:12
lay it on the wood, but **p** no fire to it. 1 Kgs 18:23
lay it on the wood and **p** no fire to it. 1 Kgs 18:23
of your god, but **p** no fire to it." 1 Kgs 18:25
And he **p** the wood in order and cut 1 Kgs 18:33
on the earth and **p** his face between 1 Kgs 18:42
of Hazael shall Jehu **p** to death, 1 Kgs 19:17
of Jehu shall Elisha **p** to death. 1 Kgs 19:17
and **p** commanders in their places, 1 Kgs 20:24
Let us **p** sackcloth around our 1 Kgs 20:31
their waists and **p** ropes on their 1 Kgs 20:32
his clothes and **p** sackcloth on his 1 Kgs 21:27
the LORD has **p** a lying spirit in the 1 Kgs 22:23
"**P** this fellow in prison and feed him 1 Kgs 22:27
and **p** salt in it." So they brought it to 2 Kgs 2:20
for he **p** away the pillar of Baal that his 2 Kgs 3:2
all who were able to **p** on armor, 2 Kgs 3:21
roof with walls and **p** there for him a 2 Kgs 4:10
from their hand and **p** them in the 2 Kgs 5:24
took his garment and **p** it under him 2 Kgs 9:13
and **p** their heads in baskets and sent 2 Kgs 10:7
escape." So when they **p** them to the 2 Kgs 10:25
sons who were being **p** to death, 2 Kgs 11:2
and she **p** him and his nurse in a 2 Kgs 11:2
so that he was not **p** to death. 2 Kgs 11:2
with them and **p** them under oath 2 Kgs 11:4
the ranks is to be **p** to death. 2 Kgs 11:8
the king's son and **p** the crown on 2 Kgs 11:12
and **p** to death with the sword 2 Kgs 11:15
"Let her not be **p** to death in the 2 Kgs 11:15
house, and there she was **p** to death. 2 Kgs 11:16
Athaliah had been **p** to death with 2 Kgs 11:20
who guarded the threshold **p** in it all 2 Kgs 12:9
But he did not **p** to death the children 2 Kgs 14:6
shall not be **p** to death because 2 Kgs 14:6
shall children be **p** to death because 2 Kgs 14:6
him to Lachish and **p** him to death 2 Kgs 14:19
down at Ibleam and **p** him to death 2 Kgs 15:10
in Samaria and **p** him to death 2 Kgs 15:14

he **p** him to death and reigned in his 2 Kgs 15:25
him down and **p** him to death 2 Kgs 15:30
and **p** it on the north side of his 2 Kgs 16:14
that were under it and **p** it on a stone 2 Kgs 16:17
of its own and **p** them in the shrines 2 Kgs 17:29
to Assyria and **p** them in Halah, 2 Kgs 18:11
Behold, I will **p** a spirit in him, so that 2 Kgs 19:7
I will **p** my hook in your nose and 2 Kgs 19:28
said, "In Jerusalem will I **p** my name." 2 Kgs 21:4
of Israel, I will **p** my name forever. 2 Kgs 21:7
against him and **p** the king to 2 Kgs 21:23
Josiah **p** away the mediums and the 2 Kgs 23:24
And Pharaoh Neco **p** him in bonds 2 Kgs 23:33
and **p** out the eyes of Zedekiah and 2 Kgs 25:7
them down and **p** them to death 2 Kgs 25:21
down Gedaliah and **p** him to death 2 Kgs 25:25
So Jehoiachin **p** off his prison 2 Kgs 25:29
of Ham: Cush, Egypt, **P**, and Canaan. 1 Chr 1:8
of the LORD, and he **p** him to death. 1 Chr 2:3
the men whom David **p** in charge of 1 Chr 6:31
And they **p** his armor in the temple 1 Chr 10:10
Therefore the LORD **p** him to death 1 Chr 10:14
and **p** to flight all those in the 1 Chr 12:15
Uzzah **p** out his hand to take hold of 1 Chr 13:9
down because he **p** out his hand 1 Chr 13:10
Then David **p** garrisons in Syria of 1 Chr 18:6
Then he **p** garrisons in Edom, and 1 Chr 18:13
rest of his men he **p** in the charge of 1 Chr 19:11
and **p** to death also Shophach the 1 Chr 19:18
and he **p** his sword back into its 1 Chr 21:27
like a necklace and **p** them on the 2 Chr 3:16
pomegranates and **p** them on 2 Chr 3:16
tablets that Moses **p** there at Horeb, 2 Chr 5:10
and the king **p** them in the House of 2 Chr 9:16
which God had **p** into his mind. 2 Chr 9:23
the yoke that your father **p** on us'?" 2 Chr 10:9
strong, and **p** commanders in them, 2 Chr 11:11
And he **p** shields and spears in all 2 Chr 11:12
tribes of Israel to **p** his name there. 2 Chr 12:13
took courage and **p** away the 2 Chr 15:8
God of Israel, should be **p** to death, 2 Chr 15:13
with the seer and **p** him in the 2 Chr 16:10
the LORD has **p** a lying spirit in the 2 Chr 18:22
P this fellow in prison and feed him 2 Chr 18:26
was brought to Jehu and **p** to death. 2 Chr 22:9
who were about to be **p** to death, 2 Chr 22:11
and she **p** him and his nurse in a 2 Chr 22:11
so that she did not **p** him to death. 2 Chr 22:11
enters the house shall be **p** to death. 2 Chr 23:7
the king's son and **p** the crown on 2 Chr 23:11
her is to be **p** to death with the 2 Chr 23:14
"Do not **p** her to death in the house 2 Chr 23:14
house, and they **p** her to death there. 2 Chr 23:15
Athaliah had been **p** to death with 2 Chr 23:21
But he did not **p** their children to 2 Chr 25:4
him to Lachish and **p** him to death 2 Chr 25:27
of the vestibule and **p** out the lamps 2 Chr 29:7
of Israel, I will **p** my name forever, 2 Chr 33:7
He also **p** commanders of the army 2 Chr 33:14
against him and **p** him to death 2 Chr 33:24
"**P** the holy ark in the house that 2 Chr 35:3
LORD to Babylon and **p** them in his 2 Chr 36:7
kingdom and also **p** it in writing: 2 Chr 36:22
all his kingdom and also **p** it in writing: Ezr 1:1
go and **p** them in the temple that is in Ezr 5:15
You shall **p** them in the house of God. Ezr 6:5
king or people who shall **p** out a hand to Ezr 6:12
who **p** such a thing as this into the Ezr 7:27
with our God to **p** away all these wives Ezr 10:3
pledged themselves to **p** away their Ezr 10:19
what my God had **p** into my heart to Neh 2:12
Then my God **p** it into my heart to Neh 7:5
they had previously **p** the grain Neh 13:5
the king's palace and **p** in custody of Est 2:8
that they may **p** it into the king's Est 3:9
tore his clothes and **p** on sackcloth and Est 4:1
there is but one law—to be **p** to death, Est 4:11
the third day Esther **p** on her royal robes Est 5:1
Have you not **p** a hedge around him and Jb 1:10
my complaint, I will **p** off my sad face, Jb 9:27
If iniquity is in your hand, **p** it far away, Jb 11:14
flesh in my teeth and **p** my life in my Jb 13:14
You **p** my feet in the stocks and watch Jb 13:27
it will bud and **p** out branches like a Jb 14:9
is there who will **p** up security for me? Jb 17:3
"Indeed, the light of the wicked is **p** out, Jb 18:5
his tent, and his lamp above him is **p** out. Jb 18:6
then that God has **p** me in the wrong Jb 19:6
"He has **p** my brothers far from me, and Jb 19:13
is it that the lamp of the wicked is **p** out? Jb 21:17
I die I will not **p** away my integrity from Jb 27:5
I **p** on righteousness, and it clothed me; Jb 29:14
Who has **p** wisdom in the inward parts Jb 38:36
Will you even **p** me in the wrong? Will Jb 40:8
Can you **p** a rope in his nose or pierce his Jb 41:2

or will you **p** him on a leash for your Jb 41:5
sacrifices, and **p** your trust in the LORD. Ps 4:5
You have **p** more joy in my heart than Ps 4:7
shall turn back and be **p** to shame in a Ps 6:10
you have **p** all things under his feet, Ps 8:6
who know your name **p** their trust in Ps 9:10
P them in fear, O LORD! Let the nations Ps 9:20
who does not **p** out his money at interest Ps 15:5
his statutes I did not **p** away from me. Ps 18:22
For you will **p** them to flight; you will Ps 21:12
they trusted and were not **p** to shame. Ps 22:5
in you I trust; let me not be **p** to shame; Ps 25:2
who wait for you shall be **p** to shame; Ps 25:3
Let me not be **p** to shame, for I take Ps 25:20
I take refuge; let me never be **p** to shame; Ps 31:1
O LORD, let me not be **p** to shame, for I Ps 31:17
upon you; let the wicked be **p** to shame; Ps 31:17
Let them be **p** to shame and dishonor Ps 35:4
Let them be **p** to shame and Ps 35:26
they are not **p** to shame in evil times; in Ps 37:19
righteous and seeks to **p** him to death. Ps 37:32
He **p** a new song in my mouth, a song of Ps 40:3
see and fear, and **p** their trust in the LORD. Ps 40:3
Let those be **p** to shame and Ps 40:14
our foes and have **p** to shame those who Ps 44:7
you **p** them to shame, for God has Ps 53:5
in your faithfulness **p** an end to them. Ps 54:5
When I am afraid, I **p** my trust in you. Ps 56:3
of my tossings; **p** my tears in your bottle. Ps 56:8
he will **p** to shame him who tramples on Ps 57:3
P no trust in extortion; set no vain Ps 62:10
hope in you be **p** to shame through me, Ps 69:6
Let them be **p** to shame and confusion Ps 70:2
I take refuge; let me never be **p** to shame! Ps 71:1
May my accusers be **p** to shame and Ps 71:13
for they have been **p** to shame and Ps 71:24
you **p** an end to everyone who is Ps 73:27
of wrath you will **p** on like a belt. Ps 76:10
And he **p** his adversaries to rout; he put Ps 78:66
to rout; he **p** them to everlasting shame. Ps 78:66
Let them be **p** to shame and dismayed Ps 83:17
and **p** away your indignation toward us! Ps 85:4
may see and be **p** to shame because Ps 86:17
You have **p** me in the depths of the pit, in Ps 88:6
is robed; he has **p** on strength as his belt. Ps 93:1
when your fathers **p** me to the test and Ps 95:9
put me to the test and **p** me to the proof, Ps 95:9
All worshipers of images are **p** to shame, Ps 97:7
his neck was **p** in a collar of iron; Ps 105:18
and **p** God to the test in the desert; Ps 106:14
the brokenhearted, to **p** them to death. Ps 109:16
They arise and are **p** to shame, but Ps 109:28
Then I shall not be **p** to shame, having Ps 119:6
P false ways far from me and Ps 119:29
O LORD; let me not be **p** to shame! Ps 119:31
kings and shall not be **p** to shame, Ps 119:46
Let the insolent be **p** to shame, Ps 119:78
statutes, that I may not be **p** to shame! Ps 119:80
and let me not be **p** to shame in my Ps 119:116
He shall not be **p** to shame when he Ps 127:5
who hate Zion be **p** to shame and Ps 129:5
P not your trust in princes, in a son of Ps 146:3
P away from you crooked speech, and Prv 4:24
speech, and **p** devious talk far from you. Prv 4:24
if you have **p** up security for your Prv 6:1
the slothful will be **p** to forced labor. Prv 12:24
the lamp of the wicked will be **p** out. Prv 13:9
garment when he has **p** up security for Prv 20:16
his lamp will be **p** out in utter Prv 20:20
pledges, who **p** up security for debts. Prv 22:26
and **p** a knife to your throat if you are Prv 23:2
the lamp of the wicked will be **p** out. Prv 24:20
Do not **p** yourself forward in the king's Prv 25:6
here," than to be **p** lower in the presence Prv 25:7
garment when he has **p** up security for Prv 27:13
evil, **p** your hand on your mouth. Prv 30:32
he has **p** eternity into man's heart, Eccl 3:11
and **p** away pain from your body, Eccl 11:10
I had **p** off my garment; how could I put it Sg 5:3
put off my garment; how could I **p** it on? Sg 5:3
My beloved **p** his hand to the latch, and Sg 5:4
who **p** darkness for light and light for Is 5:20
who **p** bitter for sweet and sweet for bitter! Is 5:20
ask, and I will not **p** the LORD to the test." Is 7:12
down, but we will **p** cedars in their place." Is 9:10
the weaned child shall **p** his hand on the Is 11:8
They shall **p** out their hand against Is 11:14
I will **p** an end to the pomp of the Is 13:11
presses; I have **p** an end to the shouting. Is 16:10
so the song of the ruthless is **p** down. Is 25:5
shall blossom and **p** forth shoots and Is 27:6
and **p** in wheat in rows and barley in its Is 28:25
his young men shall be **p** to forced labor. Is 31:8
Behold, I will **p** a spirit in him, so that he Is 37:7
I will **p** my hook in your nose and my Is 37:29

against you shall be **p** to shame and Is 41:11
I will **p** in the wilderness the cedar, the Is 41:19
delights; I have **p** my Spirit upon him; Is 42:1
are turned back and utterly **p** to shame, Is 42:17
P me in remembrance; let us argue Is 43:26
nor know, that they may be **p** to shame. Is 44:9
all his companions shall be **p** to shame, Is 44:11
they shall be **p** to shame together. Is 44:11
All of them are **p** to shame and Is 45:16
you shall not be **p** to shame or Is 45:17
I will **p** salvation in Zion, for Israel my Is 46:13
millstones and grind flour, **p** off your veil, Is 47:2
you shall **p** them all on as an ornament; Is 49:18
bereaved and barren, exiled and **p** away, Is 49:21
wait for me shall not be **p** to shame." Is 49:23
and I know that I shall not be **p** to shame. Is 50:7
Awake, awake, **p** on strength, O arm of Is 51:9
And I have **p** my words in your mouth Is 51:16
and I will **p** it into the hand of your Is 51:23
Awake, awake, **p** on your strength, O Is 52:1
p on your beautiful garments, O Is 52:1
LORD to crush him; he has **p** him to grief; Is 53:10
He **p** on righteousness as a breastplate, Is 59:17
he **p** on garments of vengeance for Is 59:17
my words that I have **p** in your mouth, Is 59:21
You who **p** the LORD in remembrance, Is 62:6
Where is he who **p** in the midst of them Is 63:11
rejoice, but you shall be **p** to shame; Is 65:13
and the Lord GOD will **p** you to death, Is 65:15
but it is they who shall be **p** to shame. Is 66:5
Then the LORD **p** out his hand and Jer 1:9
I have **p** my words in your mouth. Jer 1:9
You shall be **p** to shame by Egypt as you Jer 2:36
Egypt as you were **p** to shame by Jer 2:36
For this **p** on sackcloth, lament, and wail, Jer 4:8
O daughter of my people, **p** on sackcloth, Jer 6:26
The wise men shall be **p** to shame; they Jer 8:9
neighbor, and **p** no trust in any brother, Jer 9:4
every goldsmith is **p** to shame by his Jer 10:14
a linen loincloth and **p** it around your Jer 13:1
of the LORD, and **p** it around my waist. Jer 13:2
who forsake you shall be **p** to shame; Jer 17:13
Let those be **p** to shame who persecute Jer 17:18
me, but let me not be **p** to shame; Jer 17:18
and **p** him in the stocks that were in the Jer 20:2
and the wicked he will **p** to the sword, Jer 25:31
for certain that if you **p** me to death, Jer 26:15
of Judah and all Judah **p** him to death? Jer 26:19
the king sought to **p** him to death. Jer 26:21
given over to the people to be **p** to death. Jer 26:24
yoke-bars, and **p** them on your neck. Jer 27:2
and **p** its neck under the yoke of the king Jer 27:8
I have **p** upon the neck of all these Jer 28:14
to **p** him in the stocks and neck irons. Jer 29:26
I will **p** my law within them, and I will Jer 31:33
and **p** them in an earthenware vessel, Jer 32:14
And I will **p** the fear of me in their Jer 32:40
having **p** the scroll in the chamber of Jer 36:20
for he had not yet been **p** in prison. Jer 37:4
people, that you have **p** me in prison? Jer 37:18
to the king, "Let this man be **p** to death, Jer 38:4
heard that they had **p** Jeremiah into the Jer 38:7
"**P** the rags and clothes between your Jer 38:12
you, will you not surely **p** me to death? Jer 38:15
I will not **p** you to death or deliver you Jer 38:16
from us and we will not **p** you to death,' Jer 38:25
He **p** out the eyes of Zedekiah and bound Jer 39:7
because you have **p** your trust in me, Jer 39:18
said to Ishmael, "Do not **p** us to death, Jer 41:8
refrained and did not **p** them to death Jer 41:8
polish your spears, **p** on your armor! Jer 46:4
men of Cush and **P** who handle the Jer 46:9
daughter of Egypt shall be **p** to shame; Jer 46:24
P yourself into your scabbard; rest and Jer 47:6
it is laid waste! Kiriathaim is **p** to shame, Jer 48:1
the fortress is **p** to shame and broken Jer 48:1
Moab is **p** to shame, for it is broken; Jer 48:20
p on sackcloth, lament, and run to and Jer 49:3
'Babylon is taken, Bel is **p** to shame, Jer 50:2
Her images are **p** to shame, her idols are Jer 50:2
every goldsmith is **p** to shame by his Jer 51:17
her whole land shall be **p** to shame, and Jer 51:47
'We are **p** to shame, for we have heard Jer 51:51
He **p** out the eyes of Zedekiah, and Jer 52:11
and **p** him in prison till the day of his Jer 52:11
and **p** them to death at Riblah in the Jer 52:27
So Jehoiachin **p** off his prison Jer 52:33
on their heads and **p** on sackcloth; Lam 2:10
let him **p** his mouth in the dust—there Lam 3:29
And **p** siegeworks against it, and build a Ezk 4:2
and **p** them into a single vessel and Ezk 4:9
They **p** on sackcloth, and horror Ezk 7:18
I will **p** an end to the pride of the strong, Ezk 7:24
He **p** out the form of a hand and took me Ezk 8:3
Behold, they **p** the branch to their nose. Ezk 8:17

and **p** a mark on the foreheads of the Ezk 9:4
took some of it and **p** it into the hands Ezk 10:7
and a new spirit I will **p** within them. Ezk 11:19
I will **p** an end to this proverb, and Ezk 12:23
with ornaments and **p** bracelets on Ezk 16:11
And I **p** a ring on your nose and Ezk 16:12
produced branches and **p** out boughs. Ezk 17:6
With hooks they **p** him in a cage and Ezk 19:9
and I will **p** you in and melt you. Ezk 22:20
Thus I will **p** an end to your lewdness Ezk 23:27
and they **p** bracelets on the hands of Ezk 23:42
Thus will I **p** an end to lewdness in the Ezk 23:48
p in it the pieces of meat, all the good Ezk 24:4
in her midst; she **p** it on the bare rock; Ezk 24:7
turban, and **p** your shoes on your feet; Ezk 24:17
"Persia and Lud and **P** were in your Ezk 27:10
bald for you and **p** sackcloth on their Ezk 27:31
I will **p** hooks in your jaws, and make Ezk 29:4
Cush, and **P**, and Lud, and all Arabia, Ezk 30:5
"I will **p** an end to the wealth of Egypt, Ezk 30:10
destroy the idols and **p** an end to the Ezk 30:13
so I will **p** fear in the land of Egypt. Ezk 30:13
king of Babylon and **p** my sword in Ezk 30:24
when I **p** my sword into the hand of Ezk 30:25
over you, and **p** darkness on your land, Ezk 32:8
at their hand and **p** a stop to their Ezk 34:10
and a new spirit I will **p** within you. Ezk 36:26
And I will **p** my Spirit within you, and Ezk 36:27
you with skin, and **p** breath in you, Ezk 37:6
And I will **p** my Spirit within you, and Ezk 37:14
turn you about and **p** hooks into your Ezk 38:4
Persia, Cush, and **P** are with them, all Ezk 38:5
There they shall **p** the most holy Ezk 42:13
They shall **p** on other garments before Ezk 42:14
Now let them **p** away their whoring Ezk 43:9
some of its blood and **p** it on the four Ezk 43:20
they shall **p** off the garments in which Ezk 44:19
And they shall **p** on other garments, Ezk 44:19
P away violence and oppression, and Ezk 45:9
the sin offering and **p** it on the Ezk 45:19
a chain of gold was **p** around his neck, Dn 5:29
ones, and shall **p** down three kings. Dn 7:24
the transgression, to **p** an end to sin, Dn 9:24
of the week he shall **p** an end to sacrifice Dn 9:27
but a commander shall **p** an end to his Dn 11:18
and I will **p** an end to the kingdom of the Hos 1:4
husband—that she **p** away her whoring Hos 2:2
And I will **p** an end to all her mirth, her Hos 2:11
I will **p** their beloved children to death. Hos 9:16
Ephraim shall be **p** to shame, and Hos 10:6
neck; but I will **p** Ephraim to the yoke; Hos 10:11
P on sackcloth and lament, O priests; Jl 1:13
people shall never again be **p** to shame. Jl 2:26
people shall never again be **p** to shame. Jl 2:27
P in the sickle, for the harvest is ripe. Go Jl 3:13
O you who **p** far away the day of disaster Am 6:3
They called for a fast and **p** on sackcloth, Jon 3:5
be disgraced, and the diviners **p** to shame; Mi 3:7
you shall **p** away, but not preserve, and Mi 6:14
P no trust in a neighbor; have no Mi 7:5
limit; **P** and the Libyans were her helpers. Na 3:9
you shall not be **p** to shame because of Zep 3:11
earns wages does so to **p** them into a bag Hg 1:6
"Let them **p** a clean turban on his head." Zec 3:5
on his head." So they **p** a clean turban on Zec 3:5
and they shall **p** to shame the riders on Zec 10:5
He will not **p** on a hairy cloak in order Zec 13:4
And I will **p** this third into the fire, and Zec 13:9
And thereby **p** me to the test, says the Mal 3:10
only prosper but they **p** God to the test Mal 3:15
man and unwilling to **p** her to shame, Mt 1:19
'You shall not **p** the Lord your God to the Mt 4:7
light a lamp and **p** it under a basket, Mt 5:15
to the guard, and you be **p** in prison. Mt 5:25
about your body, what you will **p** on. Mt 6:25
is new wine **p** into old wineskins. Mt 9:17
But new wine is **p** into fresh wineskins, Mt 9:17
But when the crowd had been **p** outside, Mt 9:25
parents and have them **p** to death, Mt 10:21
I will **p** my Spirit upon him, and he will Mt 12:18
the house empty, swept, and **p** in order. Mt 12:44
He **p** another parable before them, Mt 13:24
He **p** another parable before them, Mt 13:31
and bound him and **p** him in prison for Mt 14:3
though he wanted to **p** him to death, Mt 14:5
others, and they **p** them at his feet, Mt 15:30
a child, he **p** him in the midst of them Mt 18:2
refused and went and **p** him in prison Mt 18:30
and the colt and **p** on them their cloaks, Mt 21:7
a vineyard and **p** a fence around Mt 21:33
"He will **p** those wretches to a Mt 21:41
malice, said, "Why **p** me to the test, Mt 22:18
until I **p** your enemies under your feet'? Mt 22:44
you up to tribulation and **p** you to death, Mt 24:9
him in pieces and **p** him with the Mt 24:51

him, "**P** your sword back into its place. Mt 26:52
Jesus that they might **p** him to death, Mt 26:59
counsel against Jesus to **p** him to death. Mt 27:1
is not lawful to **p** them into the treasury, Mt 27:6
they stripped him and **p** a scarlet robe Mt 27:28
they **p** it on his head and put a reed in Mt 27:29
it on his head and **p** a reed in his right Mt 27:29
of the robe and **p** his own clothes on Mt 27:31
over his head they **p** the charge against Mt 27:37
and **p** it on a reed and gave it to him to Mt 27:48
lamp brought in to be **p** under a basket, Mk 4:21
But he **p** them all outside and took the Mk 5:40
to wear sandals and not **p** on two tunics. Mk 6:9
him and wanted to **p** him to death. Mk 6:19
privately, he **p** his fingers into his ears, Mk 7:33
he took a child and **p** him in the midst Mk 9:36
a vineyard and **p** a fence around Mk 12:1
he said to them, "Why **p** me to the test? Mk 12:15
until I **p** your enemies under your feet.' Mk 12:36
Many rich people **p** in large sums. Mk 12:41
poor widow came and **p** in two small Mk 12:42
this poor widow has **p** in more than all Mk 12:43
of her poverty has **p** in everything she Mk 12:44
parents and have them **p** to death. Mk 13:12
against Jesus to **p** him to death, Mk 14:55
a crown of thorns, they **p** it on him. Mk 15:17
the purple cloak and **p** his own clothes Mk 15:20
p it on a reed and gave it to him to Mk 15:36
'You shall not **p** the Lord your God to Lk 4:12
he asked him to **p** out a little from the Lk 5:3
"**P** out into the deep and let down your Lk 5:4
wine must be **p** into fresh wineskins. Lk 5:38
running over, will be **p** into your lap. Lk 6:38
took a child and **p** him by his side Lk 9:47
a lawyer stood up to **p** him to the test, Lk 10:25
it finds the house swept and **p** in order. Lk 11:25
about your body, what you will **p** on. Lk 12:22
him in pieces and **p** him with the Lk 12:46
officer, and the officer **p** you in prison. Lk 12:58
until I dig around it and **p** on manure. Lk 13:8
all his adversaries were **p** to shame, Lk 13:17
quickly the best robe, and **p** it on him, Lk 15:22
put it on him, and **p** a ring on his hand, Lk 15:22
then did you not **p** my money in the Lk 19:23
saw a poor widow **p** in two small copper Lk 21:2
this poor widow has **p** in more than all Lk 21:3
she out of her poverty **p** in all she had to Lk 21:4
and some of you they will **p** to death. Lk 21:16
were seeking how to **p** him to death, Lk 22:2
led away to be **p** to death with him. Lk 23:32
(for John had not yet been **p** in prison). Jn 3:24
I have no one to **p** me into the pool when Jn 5:7
he said to them, "He **p** mud on my eyes, Jn 9:15
he was to be **p** out of the synagogue.) Jn 9:22
on they made plans to **p** him to death. Jn 11:53
used to help himself to what was **p** into it. Jn 12:6
priests made plans to **p** Lazarus to death Jn 12:10
they would not be **p** out of the Jn 12:42
the devil had already **p** it into the heart Jn 13:2
washed their feet and **p** on his outer Jn 13:12
They will **p** you out of the synagogues. Jn 16:2
to Peter, "**P** your sword into its sheath; Jn 18:11
not lawful for us to **p** anyone to death." Jn 18:31
a crown of thorns and **p** it on his head Jn 19:2
wrote an inscription and **p** it on the Jn 19:19
so they **p** a sponge full of the sour wine Jn 19:29
he said to Thomas, "**P** your finger here, Jn 20:27
and **p** out your hand, and place it in my Jn 20:27
was the Lord, he **p** on his outer garment, Jn 21:7
And they **p** forward two, Joseph called Acts 1:23
arrested them and **p** them in custody Acts 4:3
arrested the apostles and **p** them in the Acts 5:18
The men whom you **p** in prison are Acts 5:25
and gave orders to **p** the men outside Acts 5:34
But Peter **p** them all outside, and knelt Acts 9:40
They **p** him to death by hanging him Acts 10:39
he had seized him, he **p** him in prison, Acts 12:4
"Dress yourself and **p** on your Acts 12:8
that they should be **p** to death. Acts 12:19
appointed day Herod **p** on his royal Acts 12:21
about forty years he **p** up with them Acts 13:18
he **p** them into the inner prison and Acts 16:24
whom the Jews had **p** forward. Acts 19:33
knowledge of the Way, **p** them off, Acts 24:22
but when they were **p** to death I cast Acts 26:10
along the coast of Asia, we **p** to sea, Acts 27:2
The next day we **p** in at Sidon. And Acts 27:3
sailing for Italy and **p** us on board. Acts 27:6
the majority decided to **p** out to sea Acts 27:12
bundle of sticks and **p** them on the Acts 28:3
they **p** on board whatever we needed. Acts 28:10
whom God **p** forward as a propitiation Rom 3:25
and hope does not **p** us to shame, Rom 5:5
if by the Spirit you **p** to death the deeds Rom 8:13
in him will not be **p** to shame." Rom 9:33
in him will not be **p** to shame." Rom 10:11
of darkness and **p** on the armor Rom 13:12
But **p** on the Lord Jesus Christ, and Rom 13:14
decide never to **p** a stumbling block Rom 14:13
anything rather than **p** an obstacle 1 Cor 9:12
We must not **p** Christ to the test, as 1 Cor 10:9
reign until he has **p** all his enemies 1 Cor 15:25
For "God has **p** all things in 1 Cor 15:27
"all things are **p** in subjection," it is 1 Cor 15:27
he is excepted who **p** all things in 1 Cor 15:27
subjected to him who **p** all things in 1 Cor 15:28
perishable body must **p** on the 1 Cor 15:53
body must **p** on immortality. 1 Cor 15:53
of you is to **p** something aside and 1 Cor 16:2
see that you **p** him at ease among 1 Cor 16:10
and who has also **p** his seal on us and 2 Cor 1:22
measure—not to **p** it too severely— 2 Cor 2:5
who would **p** a veil over his face so 2 Cor 3:13
longing to **p** on our heavenly dwelling, 2 Cor 5:2
We **p** no obstacle in anyone's way, so 2 Cor 6:3
him about you, I was not **p** to shame. 2 Cor 7:14
who **p** into the heart of Titus the 2 Cor 8:16
you **p** up with it readily enough. 2 Cor 11:4
and it was **p** in place through angels by Gal 3:19
baptized into Christ have **p** on Christ. Gal 3:27
And he **p** all things under his feet and Eph 1:22
to **p** off your old self, which belongs to Eph 4:22
and to **p** on the new self, created after Eph 4:24
Therefore, having **p** away falsehood, let Eph 4:25
and slander be **p** away from you, Eph 4:31
P on the whole armor of God, that you Eph 6:11
and having **p** on the breastplate of Eph 6:14
having **p** on the readiness given by the Eph 6:15
knowing that I am **p** here for the Phil 1:16
in Christ Jesus and **p** no confidence in Phil 3:3
and authorities and **p** them to open Col 2:15
P to death therefore what is earthly in Col 3:5
But now you must **p** them all away: Col 3:8
seeing that you have **p** off the old self Col 3:9
and have **p** on the new self, which is Col 3:10
P on then, as God's chosen ones, holy Col 3:12
And above all these **p** on love, which Col 3:14
having **p** on the breastplate of faith 1 Thes 5:8
I **p** you under oath before the Lord to 1 Thes 5:27
If you **p** these things before the 1 Tm 4:6
so that you might **p** what remained into Ti 1:5
so that an opponent may be **p** to shame, Ti 2:8
"I will **p** my trust in him." And again, Heb 2:13
where your fathers **p** me to the test and Heb 3:9
I will **p** my laws into their minds, and Heb 8:10
end of the ages to **p** away sin by the Heb 9:26
I will **p** my laws on their hearts, and Heb 10:16
in war, **p** foreign armies to flight. Heb 11:34
is lame may not be **p** out of joint but Heb 12:13
Therefore **p** away all filthiness and Jas 1:21
If we **p** bits into the mouths of horses so Jas 3:3
So **p** away all malice and all deceit and 1 Pt 2:1
believes in him will not be **p** to shame." 1 Pt 2:6
doing good you should **p** to silence the 1 Pt 2:15
behavior in Christ may be **p** to shame. 1 Pt 3:16
being **p** to death in the flesh but made 1 Pt 3:18
Diotrephes, who likes to **p** himself first, 3 Jn 1:9
taught Balak to **p** a stumbling block Rv 2:14
who sat on the cloud, "**P** in your sickle, Rv 14:15
"**P** in your sickle and gather the Rv 14:18
for God has **p** it into their hearts to Rv 17:17

PUTEOLI (1)
and on the second day we came to **P**. Acts 28:13

PUTHITES (1)
the Ithrites, the **P**, the Shumathites, 1 Chr 2:53

PUTIEL (1)
as his wife one of the daughters of **P**, Ex 6:25

PUTS (40)
any like it or whoever **p** any of it on an Ex 30:33
The word that God **p** in my mouth, Nm 22:38
speak what the LORD **p** in my mouth?" Nm 23:12
certificate of divorce and **p** it in her hand Dt 24:1
certificate of divorce and **p** it in her hand Dt 24:3
is beating him and **p** out her hand and Dt 25:11
One man of you **p** to flight a thousand, Jos 23:10
Even in his servants he **p** no trust, and Jb 4:18
Behold, God **p** no trust in his holy ones, Jb 15:15
Man **p** an end to darkness and searches Jb 28:3
"Man **p** his hand to the flinty rock and Jb 28:9
he **p** my feet in the stocks and watches Jb 33:11
as a heap; he **p** the deeps in storehouses. Ps 33:7
him, like a belt that he **p** on every day! Ps 109:19
Whoever **p** up security for a stranger Prv 11:15
gives a pledge and **p** up security in the Prv 17:18
The lot **p** an end to quarrels and Prv 18:18
in pledge when he **p** up security for Prv 20:16
A wicked man **p** on a bold face, but Prv 21:29
when your neighbor **p** you to shame? Prv 25:8
in pledge when he **p** up security for an Prv 27:13
She **p** her hands to the distaff, and her Prv 31:19
war against him who **p** nothing into their Mi 3:5
No one **p** a piece of unshrunk cloth on Mt 9:16
becomes tender and **p** out its leaves, Mt 24:32
And no one **p** new wine into old Mk 2:22
grain is ripe, at once he **p** in the sickle, Mk 4:29
garden plants and **p** out large branches, Mk 4:32
becomes tender and **p** out its leaves, Mk 13:28
he leaves home and **p** his servants in Mk 13:34
from a new garment and **p** it on an old Lk 5:36
And no one **p** new wine into old Lk 5:37
covers it with a jar or **p** it under a bed, Lk 8:16
puts it under a bed, but **p** it on a stand, Lk 8:16
"No one who **p** his hand to the plow and Lk 9:62
one after lighting a lamp **p** it in a cellar Lk 11:33
When the perishable **p** on the 1 Cor 15:54
and the mortal **p** on immortality, 1 Cor 15:54
takes advantage of you, or **p** on airs, 2 Cor 11:20
who want to and **p** them out of the 3 Jn 1:10

PUTTING (24)
gave it to Hagar, **p** it on her shoulder, Gn 21:14
and female, **p** them outside the camp, Nm 5:3
lapped, **p** their hands to their mouths, Jgs 7:6
p the little ones and the livestock and Jgs 18:21
and **p** the blood of war on the belt 1 Kgs 2:5
built, by **p** my name there forever. 1 Kgs 9:3
the child, **p** his mouth on his mouth, 2 Kgs 4:34
p down one and lifting up another. Ps 75:7
not set your heart on **p** him to death. Prv 19:18
p to death souls who should not die Ezk 13:19
his heart and **p** the stumbling block Ezk 14:7
p him under oath (the chief men of Ezk 17:13
watched the people **p** money into the Mk 12:41
up and saw the rich **p** their gifts into the Lk 21:1
why are you **p** God to the test by Acts 15:10
And **p** out to sea from there we sailed Acts 27:4
and **p** his hands on him healed him. Acts 28:8
P in at Syracuse, we stayed there for Acts 28:12
if indeed by **p** it on we may not be 2 Cor 5:3
hands, by **p** off the body of the flesh, Col 2:11
p everything in subjection under his Heb 2:8
feet." Now in **p** everything in subjection Heb 2:8
wearing of gold, or the **p** on of clothing— 1 Pt 3:3
since I know that the **p** off of my body 2 Pt 1:14

PUVAH (2)
Issachar: Tola, **P**, Yob, and Shimron. Gn 46:13
of Tola, the clan of the Tolaites; of **P**, Nm 26:23

PYRE (1)
is made ready, its **p** made deep and wide, Is 30:33

PYRRHUS (1)
of Berea, the son of **P** from Berea, Acts 20:4

Q

QUAIL (4)
In the evening **q** came up and covered Ex 16:13
and it brought **q** from the sea and let Nm 11:31
all the next day, and gathered the **q**. Nm 11:32
They asked, and he brought **q**, and Ps 105:40

QUAKE (7)
You have made the land to **q**; you have Ps 60:2
upon the cherubim; let the earth **q**! Ps 99:1
the mountains might **q** at your presence Is 64:1
I made the nations **q** at the sound of its Ezk 31:16
of the earth, shall **q** at my presence. Ezk 38:20
and the heavens and the earth **q**. Jl 3:16
The mountains **q** before him; the hills Na 1:5

QUAKED (7)
The mountains **q** before the LORD, even Jgs 5:5
the raiders trembled, the earth **q**, 1 Sm 14:15
of the heavens trembled and **q**, 2 Sm 22:8
also of the mountains trembled and **q**, Ps 18:7
the earth **q**, the heavens poured down Ps 68:8
and struck them, and the mountains **q**; Is 5:25
down, the mountains **q** at your presence. Is 64:3

QUAKES (3)
of their stallions the whole land **q**. Jer 8:16
At his wrath the earth **q**, and the Jer 10:10
The earth **q** before them; the heavens Jl 2:10

QUAKING (2)
the mountains, and behold, they were **q**, Jer 4:24
"Son of man, eat your bread with **q**, Ezk 12:18

QUALIFIED (2)
brothers, able men **q** for the service; 1 Chr 26:8
who has **q** you to share in the Col 1:12

QUALITIES (4)
For if these **q** are yours and are 2 Pt 1:8

whoever lacks these **q** is so nearsighted 2 Pt 1:9
if you practice these **q** you will never 2 Pt 1:10
intend always to remind you of these **q**, 2 Pt 1:12

QUANTITIES (12)
and for the lambs, in the prescribed **q**; Nm 29:18
and for the lambs, in the prescribed **q**; Nm 29:21
and for the lambs, in the prescribed **q**; Nm 29:24
and for the lambs, in the prescribed **q**; Nm 29:27
and for the lambs, in the prescribed **q**; Nm 29:30
and for the lambs, in the prescribed **q**; Nm 29:33
and for the lambs, in the prescribed **q**; Nm 29:37
also provided great **q** of iron for 1 Chr 22:3
well as bronze in **q** beyond weighing, 1 Chr 22:3
Tyrians brought great **q** of cedar to 1 Chr 22:4
besides great **q** of onyx and stones for 1 Chr 29:2
made all these things in great **q**, 2 Chr 4:18

QUANTITY (6)
in measures of length or weight or **q**. Lv 19:35
and a very great **q** of spices and 1 Kgs 10:10
materials in great **q** before his death. 1 Chr 22:5
oil, and all measures of **q** or size. 1 Chr 23:29
of gold, and a very great **q** of spices, 2 Chr 9:9
able to haul it in, because of the **q** of fish. Jn 21:6

QUARREL (12)
another well, and they did not **q** over it. Gn 26:22
he said to them, "Do not **q** on the way." Gn 45:24
said to them, "Why do you **q** with me? Ex 17:2
"When men **q** and one strikes the other Ex 21:18
and see how he is seeking a **q** with me." 2 Kgs 5:7
water, so quit before the **q** breaks out. Prv 17:14
Whoever meddles in a **q** not his own is Prv 26:17
you fast only to **q** and to fight and to hit Is 58:4
He will not **q** or cry aloud, nor will Mt 12:19
him, but not to **q** over opinions. Rom 14:1
before God not to **q** about words, 2 Tm 2:14
and cannot obtain, so you fight and **q**. Jas 4:2

QUARRELED (8)
herdsmen of Gerar **q** with Isaac's Gn 26:20
another well, and they **q** over that also, Gn 26:21
Therefore the people **q** with Moses and Ex 17:2
And the people **q** with Moses and said, Nm 20:3
the people of Israel **q** with the LORD, Nm 20:13
of Zin when the congregation **q**, Nm 27:14
with whom you **q** at the waters of Dt 33:8
and they **q** with one another in the 2 Sm 14:6

QUARRELING (12)
because of the **q** of the people of Israel, Ex 17:7
city, and **q** is like the bars of a castle. Prv 18:19
and a wife's **q** is a continual dripping Prv 19:13
from strife, but every fool will be **q**. Prv 20:3
will go out, and **q** and abuse will cease. Prv 22:10
where there is no whisperer, **q** ceases. Prv 26:20
them as they were **q** and tried to Acts 7:26
and sensuality, not in **q** and jealousy. Rom 13:13
people that there is **q** among you, 1 Cor 1:11
wish—that perhaps there may be **q**, 2 Cor 12:20
lifting holy hands without anger or **q**; 1 Tm 2:8
to speak evil of no one, to avoid **q**, to be Ti 3:2

QUARRELS (5)
puts an end to **q** and decides between Prv 18:18
for controversy and for **q** about words, 1 Tm 6:4
you know that they breed **q**. 2 Tm 2:23
dissensions, and **q** about the law, Ti 3:9
What causes **q** and what causes fights Jas 4:1

QUARRELSOME (7)
than in a house shared with a **q** wife. Prv 21:9
land than with a **q** and fretful woman. Prv 21:19
than in a house shared with a **q** wife. Prv 25:24
to fire, so is a **q** man for kindling strife. Prv 26:21
on a rainy day and a **q** wife are alike; Prv 27:15
drunkard, not violent but gentle, not **q**, 1 Tm 3:3
servant must not be **q** but kind to 2 Tm 2:24

QUARRIED (4)
the king's command they **q** out great, 1 Kgs 5:17
buy timber and **q** stone for making 2 Kgs 12:12
buying timber and **q** stone to repair 2 Kgs 22:6
and the builders to buy **q** stone, 2 Chr 34:11

QUARRIES (1)
He who **q** stones is hurt by them, and Eccl 10:9

QUARRY (4)
it was with stone prepared at the **q**, 1 Kgs 6:7
burdens and 80,000 to **q** in the hill 2 Chr 2:2
80,000 to **q** in the hill country, 2 Chr 2:18
and to the **q** from which you were dug. Is 51:1

QUART (1)
saying, "A **q** of wheat for a denarius, Rv 6:6

QUARTER (13)
fine flour, mixed with a **q** of a hin of oil; Nm 15:4
a **q** of a hin of wine for the drink Nm 15:5
mixed with a **q** of a hin of beaten oil. Nm 28:5
drink offering shall be a **q** of a hin for Nm 28:7
for a ram, and a **q** of a hin for a lamb. Nm 28:14
I have with me a **q** of a shekel of silver, 1 Sm 9:8
lived in Jerusalem in the Second **Q**), 2 Kgs 22:14
in the Second **Q**) and spoke to 2 Chr 34:22
of the LORD their God for a **q** of the day; Neh 9:3
for another **q** of it they made confession Neh 9:3
Come against her from every **q**; open Jer 50:26
the Fish Gate, a wail from the Second **Q**, Zep 1:10
were coming to him from every **q**. Mk 1:45

QUARTERMASTER (1)
year of his reign. Seraiah was the **q**. Jer 51:59

QUARTERS (2)
the king's palace, in front of the king's **q**, Est 5:1
four winds from the four **q** of heaven. Jer 49:36

QUARTS (1)
and three **q** of barley for a denarius, Rv 6:6

QUARTUS (1)
the city treasurer, and our brother **Q**, Rom 16:23

QUEEN (53)
Now when the **q** of Sheba heard of the 1 Kgs 10:1
And when the **q** of Sheba had seen all 1 Kgs 10:4
as these that the **q** of Sheba gave to 1 Kgs 10:10
Solomon gave to the **q** of Sheba all 1 Kgs 10:13
wife, the sister of Tahpenes the **q**. 1 Kgs 11:19
from being **q** mother because 1 Kgs 15:13
and the sons of the **q** mother." 2 Kgs 10:13
Now when the **q** of Sheba heard of the 2 Chr 9:1
And when the **q** of Sheba had seen the 2 Chr 9:3
as those that the **q** of Sheba gave to 2 Chr 9:9
Solomon gave to the **q** of Sheba all 2 Chr 9:12
from being **q** mother because 2 Chr 15:16
said to me (the **q** sitting beside him), Neh 2:6
Q Vashti also gave a feast for the women Est 1:9
to bring **Q** Vashti before the king with Est 1:11
But **Q** Vashti refused to come at the Est 1:12
the law, what is to be done to **Q** Vashti, Est 1:15
the king has **Q** Vashti done wrong, Est 1:16
Ahasuerus commanded **Q** Vashti to Est 1:17
pleases the king be **q** instead of Vashti." Est 2:4
head and made her **q** instead of Vashti. Est 2:17
of Mordecai, and he told it to **Q** Esther, Est 2:22
and told her, the **q** was deeply distressed. Est 4:4
when the king saw **Q** Esther standing in Est 5:2
king said to her, "What is it, **Q** Esther? Est 5:3
"Even **Q** Esther let no one but me come Est 5:12
Haman went in to feast with **Q** Esther. Est 7:1
to Esther, "What is your wish, **Q** Esther? Est 7:2
Then **Q** Esther answered, "If I have found Est 7:3
Then King Ahasuerus said to **Q** Esther, Est 7:5
was terrified before the king and the **q**. Est 7:6
stayed to beg for his life from **Q** Esther, Est 7:7
he even assault the **q** in my presence, Est 7:8
Ahasuerus gave to **Q** Esther the house Est 8:1
King Ahasuerus said to **Q** Esther and to Est 8:7
And the king said to **Q** Esther, "In Susa Est 9:12
Then **Q** Esther, the daughter of Abihail, Est 9:29
the Jew and **Q** Esther obligated them, Est 9:31
The command of **Q** Esther confirmed Est 9:32
right hand stands the **q** in gold of Ophir. Ps 45:9
to make cakes for the **q** of heaven. Jer 7:18
Say to the king and the **q** mother: Jer 13:18
after King Jeconiah and the **q** mother, Jer 29:2
make offerings to the **q** of heaven and Jer 44:17
offerings to the **q** of heaven and Jer 44:18
made offerings to the **q** of heaven and Jer 44:19
make offerings to the **q** of heaven and Jer 44:25
The **q**, because of the words of the king Dn 5:10
the banqueting hall, and the **q** declared, Dn 5:10
The **q** of the South will rise up at the Mt 12:42
The **q** of the South will rise up at the Lk 11:31
of Candace, **q** of the Ethiopians, Acts 8:27
since in her heart she says, 'I sit as a **q**, Rv 18:7

QUEEN'S (2)
For the **q** behavior will be made known Est 1:17
have heard of the **q** behavior will say the Est 1:18

QUEENS (3)
There are sixty **q** and eighty concubines, Sg 6:8
the **q** and concubines also, and they Sg 6:9
and their **q** your nursing mothers. Is 49:23

QUENCH (11)
Thus they would **q** my coal that is left 2 Sm 14:7
battle, lest you **q** the lamp of Israel." 2 Sm 21:17
field; the wild donkeys **q** their thirst. Ps 104:11
Many waters cannot **q** love, neither can Sg 8:7
shall burn together, with none to **q** them. Is 1:31
and a faintly burning wick he will not **q**; Is 42:3
forth like fire, and burn with none to **q** it, Jer 4:4
like fire, and burn with none to **q** it, Jer 21:12
it devour, with none to **q** it for Bethel, Am 5:6
and a smoldering wick he will not **q**, Mt 12:20
Do not **q** the Spirit. 1 Thes 5:19

QUENCHED (12)
this place, and it will not be **q**. 2 Kgs 22:17
out on this place and will not be **q**. 2 Chr 34:25
and awakes faint, with his thirst not **q**, Is 29:8
Night and day it shall not be **q**; its Is 34:10
rise, they are extinguished, **q** like a wick: Is 43:17
shall not die, their fire shall not be **q**, Is 66:24
of the ground; it will burn and not be **q**." Jer 7:20
of Jerusalem and shall not be **q**.'" Jer 17:27
The blazing flame shall not be **q**, and Ezk 20:47
LORD have kindled it; it shall not be **q**." Ezk 20:48
worm does not die and the fire is not **q**.' Mk 9:48
q the power of fire, escaped the edge of Heb 11:34

QUESTION (21)
I will **q** you, and you make it known to Jb 38:3
I will **q** you, and you make it known to Jb 40:7
I will **q** you, and you make it known to Jb 42:4
said to Jeremiah, "I will ask you a **q**; Jer 38:14
them, "I also will ask you one **q**, Mt 21:24
resurrection, and they asked him a **q**, Mt 22:23
a lawyer, asked him a **q** to test him. Mt 22:35
gathered together, Jesus asked them a **q**, Mt 22:41
"Why do you **q** these things in your Mk 2:8
said to them, "I will ask you one **q**; Mk 11:29
And they asked him a **q**, saying, Mk 12:18
the scribes and the Pharisees began to **q**, Lk 5:21
them, "Why do you **q** in your hearts? Lk 5:22
answered them, "I also will ask you a **q**. Lk 20:3
and they asked him a **q**, saying, Lk 20:28
they no longer dared to ask him any **q**. Lk 20:40
And they began to **q** one another, Lk 22:23
things and do not need anyone to **q** you; Jn 16:30
the apostles and the elders about this **q**. Acts 15:2
without raising any **q** on the ground 1 Cor 10:25
without raising any **q** on the ground 1 Cor 10:27

QUESTIONED (9)
"The man **q** us carefully about Gn 43:7
a young man of Succoth and **q** him. Jgs 8:14
And Hezekiah **q** the priests and the 2 Chr 31:9
The king **q** him secretly in his house Jer 37:17
so that they **q** among themselves, Mk 1:27
spirit that they thus **q** within themselves, Mk 2:8
So he **q** him at some length, but he made Lk 23:9
The high priest then **q** Jesus about his Jn 18:19
council. And the high priest **q** them, Acts 5:27

QUESTIONING (4)
were sitting there, **q** in their hearts, Mk 2:6
q what this rising from the dead might Mk 9:10
and all were **q** in their hearts Lk 3:15
Do all things without grumbling or **q**, Phil 2:14

QUESTIONS (12)
we told him was in answer to these **q**. Gn 43:7
she came to test him with hard **q**. 1 Kgs 10:1
And Solomon answered all her **q**; 1 Kgs 10:3
to Jerusalem to test him with hard **q**, 2 Chr 9:1
And Solomon answered all her **q**; 2 Chr 9:2
anyone dare to ask him any more **q**. Mt 22:46
no one dared to ask him any more **q**. Mk 12:34
listening to them and asking them **q**. Lk 2:46
is a matter of **q** about words and Acts 18:15
being accused about **q** of their law, Acts 23:29
at a loss how to investigate these **q**, Acts 25:20
judgment on you in **q** of food and Col 2:16

QUICK (7)
and said, "**Q**! Three seahs of fine flour! Gn 18:6
called after the boy, "Hurry! Be **q**! 1 Sm 20:38
of the wily are brought to a **q** end. Jb 5:13
A man of **q** temper acts foolishly, and Prv 14:17
Be not **q** in your spirit to become angry, Eccl 7:9
"Let him be **q**, let him speed his work that Is 5:19
let every person be **q** to hear, slow to Jas 1:19

QUICK-TEMPERED (1)
not be arrogant or **q** or a drunkard or Ti 1:7

QUICKLY (65)
And Abraham went **q** into the tent to Gn 18:6
it to a young man, who prepared it **q**. Gn 18:7
Escape there **q**, for I can do nothing till Gn 19:22
my lord." And she **q** let down her jar Gn 24:18
So she **q** emptied her jar into the Gn 24:20
She **q** let down her jar from her Gn 24:46
"How is it that you have found it so **q**, Gn 27:20
and they **q** brought him out of the pit. Gn 41:14
Then each man **q** lowered his sack to Gn 44:11
They have turned aside **q** out of the way Ex 32:8
And Moses **q** bowed his head toward the Ex 34:8
it and carry it **q** to the congregation Nm 16:46
against you, and he would destroy you **q**. Dt 7:4
drive them out and make them perish **q**, Dt 9:3
said to me, 'Arise, go down **q** from here, Dt 9:12
They have turned aside **q** out of the way Dt 9:12
You had turned aside **q** from the way Dt 9:16
and you will perish **q** off the good land Dt 11:17

destroyed and perish **q** on account of Dt 28:20
Pursue them **q**, for you will overtake Jos 2:5
in the ambush rose **q** out of their place, Jos 8:19
Come up to us **q** and save us and help Jos 10:6
and you shall perish **q** from off the Jos 23:16
those nations, not driving them out **q**, Jgs 2:23
Then he called **q** to the young man his Jgs 9:54
So the woman ran **q** and told her Jgs 13:10
and carry them **q** to the camp to 1 Sm 17:17
David ran **q** toward the battle line to 1 Sm 17:48
third day go down **q** to the place 1 Sm 20:19
calf in the house, and she **q** killed it, 1 Sm 28:24
escape for us from Absalom. Go **q**, 2 Sm 15:14
lest he overtake us **q** and bring down 2 Sm 15:14
Now therefore send **q** and tell David, 2 Sm 17:16
of them went away **q** and came to the 2 Sm 17:18
"Arise, and go **q** over the water, 2 Sm 17:21
and they **q** took it up from him and 1 Kgs 20:33
"Bring **q** Micaiah the son of Imlah." 1 Kgs 22:9
is the king's order, 'Come down **q**!'" 2 Kgs 1:11
that I may **q** go to the man of God and 2 Kgs 4:22
King Rehoboam **q** mounted his 2 Chr 10:18
"Bring **q** Micaiah the son of Imlah." 2 Chr 18:8
see that you act **q**." But the Levites did 2 Chr 24:5
But the Levites did not act **q**. 2 Chr 24:5
And they rushed him out **q**, and he 2 Chr 26:20
and carried them **q** to all the lay 2 Chr 35:13
And he **q** provided her with her cosmetics Est 2:9
Then the king said, "Bring Haman **q**, so Est 5:5
in the way, for his wrath is **q** kindled. Ps 2:12
off! O you my help, come **q** to my aid! Ps 22:19
Answer me **q**, O LORD! My spirit fails! Ps 143:7
him—a threefold cord is not **q** broken. Eccl 4:12
earth; and behold, **q**, speedily they come! Is 5:26
Come to terms **q** with your accuser Mt 5:25
Then go **q** and tell his disciples that he Mt 28:7
So they departed **q** from the tomb with Mt 28:8
'Go out **q** to the streets and lanes of the Lk 14:21
to his servants, 'Bring **q** the best robe, Lk 15:22
your bill, and sit down **q** and write fifty.' Lk 16:6
she heard it, she rose **q** and went to him. Jn 11:29
her, saw Mary rise **q** and go out, Jn 11:31
him, "What you are going to do, do **q**." Jn 13:27
"Get up **q**." And the chains fell off his Acts 12:7
haste and get out of Jerusalem **q**, Acts 22:18
that you are so **q** deserting him who Gal 1:6
not to be **q** shaken in mind or 2 Thes 2:2

QUIET (41)
of the field, while Jacob was a **q** man, Gn 25:27
the gate of the city. They kept **q** all night, Jgs 16:2
of the Sidonians, **q** and unsuspecting, Jgs 18:7
And they said to him, "Keep **q**; put your Jgs 18:19
Laish, to a people **q** and unsuspecting, Jgs 18:27
and we keep **q** and do not take it out 1 Kgs 22:3
And he said, "Yes, I know it; keep **q**." 2 Kgs 2:3
he answered, "Yes, I know it; keep **q**." 2 Kgs 2:5
the city was **q** after Athaliah had 2 Kgs 11:20
land was very broad, **q**, and peaceful, 1 Chr 4:40
I will give peace and **q** to Israel in his 1 Chr 22:9
So the realm of Jehoshaphat was **q**, 2 Chr 20:30
the city was **q** after Athaliah had 2 Chr 23:21
calmed all the people, saying, "Be **q**, Neh 8:11
then I would have lain down and been **q**; Jb 3:13
I am not at ease, nor am I **q**; I have no Jb 3:26
When he is **q**, who can condemn? Jb 34:29
against those who are **q** in the land they Ps 35:20
they were glad that the waters were **q**, Ps 107:30
is a dry morsel with **q** than a house full Prv 17:1
rages and laughs, and there is no **q**. Prv 29:9
the wise heard in **q** are better than the Eccl 9:17
And say to him, 'Be careful, be **q**, do not Is 7:4
The whole earth is at rest and **q**; they Is 14:7
secure dwellings, and in **q** resting places. Is 32:18
for it cannot be **q**, and its waters toss up Is 57:20
and for Jerusalem's sake I will not be **q**, Is 62:1
Jacob shall return and have **q** and ease, Jer 30:10
Jacob shall return and have **q** and ease, Jer 46:27
of the LORD! How long till you are **q**? Jer 47:6
How can it be **q** when the LORD has given Jer 47:7
troubled like the sea that cannot be **q**. Jer 49:23
will fall upon the **q** people who dwell Ezk 38:11
that the sea may **q** down for us?" For the Jon 1:11
then the sea will **q** down for you, for I Jon 1:12
with gladness; he will **q** you by his love; Zep 3:17
you ought to be **q** and do nothing Acts 19:36
language, they became even more **q**. Acts 22:2
that we may lead a peaceful and **q** life, 1 Tm 2:2
over a man; rather, she is to remain **q**. 1 Tm 2:12
beauty of a gentle and **q** spirit, 1 Pt 3:4

QUIETED (3)
But Caleb **q** the people before Moses Nm 13:30
But I have calmed and **q** my soul, like a Ps 131:2
when the town clerk had **q** the crowd, Acts 19:35

QUIETLY (8)
spirit, but a wise man **q** holds it back. Prv 29:11
"I will **q** look from my dwelling like clear Is 18:4
one should wait **q** for the salvation Lam 3:26
Yet I will **q** wait for the day of trouble Hab 3:16
her to shame, resolved to divorce her **q**. Mt 1:19
and to aspire to live **q**, and to mind 1 Thes 4:11
to do their work **q** and to earn their 2 Thes 3:12
a woman learn **q** with all 1 Tm 2:11

QUIETNESS (3)
is a handful of **q** than two hands full Eccl 4:6
in **q** and in trust shall be your strength." Is 30:15
of righteousness, **q** and trust forever. Is 32:17

QUIETS (1)
he who is slow to anger **q** contention. Prv 15:18

QUIRINIUS (1)
first registration when **Q** was governor of Lk 2:2

QUIT (2)
avenged on you, and after that I will **q**." Jgs 15:7
so **q** before the quarrel breaks out. Prv 17:14

QUITE (1)
but of the living. You are **q** wrong." Mk 12:27

QUIVER (8)
your weapons, your **q** and your bow, Gn 27:3
Upon him rattle the **q**, the flashing Jb 39:23
is the man who fills his **q** with them! Ps 127:5
And Elam bore the **q** with chariots and Is 22:6
a polished arrow; in his **q** he hid me away. Is 49:2
Their **q** is like an open tomb; they are all Jer 5:16
into my kidneys the arrows of his **q**; Lam 3:13
body trembles; my lips **q** at the sound; Hab 3:16

QUOTE (1)
"Doubtless you will **q** to me this Lk 4:23

QUOTED (1)
long afterward, in the words already **q**, Heb 4:7

R

RAAMA (1)
Seba, Havilah, Sabta, **R**, and Sabteca. 1 Chr 1:9

RAAMAH (4)
Seba, Havilah, Sabtah, **R**, and Sabteca. Gn 10:7
The sons of **R**: Sheba and Dedan. Gn 10:7
The sons of **R**: Sheba and Dedan. 1 Chr 1:9
of Sheba and **R** traded with you; Ezk 27:22

RAAMIAH (1)
Nehemiah, Azariah, **R**, Nahamani, Neh 7:7

RAAMSES (1)
for Pharaoh store cities, Pithom and **R**. Ex 1:11

RAB-MAG (2)
the Rab-saris, Nergal-sar-ezer the **R**, Jer 39:3
the Rab-saris, Nergal-sar-ezer the **R**, Jer 39:13

RAB-SARIS (3)
of Assyria sent the Tartan, the **R**, 2 Kgs 18:17
Samgar-nebu, Sar-sekim the **R**, Jer 39:3
of the guard, Nebushazban the **R**, Jer 39:13

RABBAH (15)
of iron. Is it not in **R** of the Ammonites? Dt 3:11
to Aroer, which is east of **R**, Jos 13:25
(that is, Kiriath-jearim), and **R**: Jos 15:60
the Ammonites and besieged **R**. 2 Sm 11:1
Joab fought against **R** of the 2 Sm 12:26
and said, "I have fought against **R**; 2 Sm 12:27
and went to **R** and fought against 2 Sm 12:29
of Nahash from **R** of the 2 Sm 17:27
and came and besieged **R**. 1 Chr 20:1
Joab struck down **R** and overthrew it. 1 Chr 20:1
to be heard against **R** of the Ammonites; Jer 49:2
is laid waste! Cry out, O daughters of **R**! Jer 49:3
sword to come to **R** of the Ammonites Ezk 21:20
I will make **R** a pasture for camels and Ezk 25:5
So I will kindle a fire in the wall of **R**, Am 1:14

RABBI (16)
and being called **r** by others. Mt 23:7
But you are not to be called **r**, for you Mt 23:8
answered, "Is it I, **R**?" He said to him, Mt 26:25
"Greetings, **R**!" And he kissed him. Mt 26:49
to Jesus, "**R**, it is good that we are here. Mk 9:5
to him, "**R**, let me recover my sight." Mk 10:51
remembered and said to him, "**R**, look! Mk 11:21
once and said, "**R**!" And he kissed him. Mk 14:45
said to him, "**R**" (which means Teacher), Jn 1:38
him, "**R**, you are the Son of God! Jn 1:49
"**R**, we know that you are a teacher come Jn 3:2
"**R**, he who was with you across the Jn 3:26
were urging him, saying, "**R**, eat." Jn 4:31
to him, "**R**, when did you come here?" Jn 6:25
his disciples asked him, "**R**, who sinned, Jn 9:2
"**R**, the Jews were just now seeking to Jn 11:8

RABBITH (1)
R, Kishion, Ebez, Jos 19:20

RABBLE (3)
Now the **r** that was among them had a Nm 11:4
On my right hand the **r** rise; they push Jb 30:12
and taking some wicked men of the **r**, Acts 17:5

RABBONI (1)
Aramaic, "**R**!" (which means Teacher). Jn 20:16

RABSHAKEH (16)
and the **R** with a great army from 2 Kgs 18:17
And the **R** said to them, "Say to 2 Kgs 18:19
Shebnah, and Joah, said to the **R**, 2 Kgs 18:26
But the **R** said to them, "Has my 2 Kgs 18:27
Then the **R** stood and called out in a 2 Kgs 18:28
torn and told him the words of the **R**. 2 Kgs 18:37
your God heard all the words of the **R**, 2 Kgs 19:4
The **R** returned, and found the king 2 Kgs 19:8
of Assyria sent the **R** from Lachish to Is 36:2
And the **R** said to them, "Say to Hezekiah, Is 36:4
Eliakim, Shebna, and Joah said to the **R**, Is 36:11
But the **R** said, "Has my master sent me Is 36:12
Then the **R** stood and called out in a Is 36:13
torn, and told him the words of the **R**. Is 36:22
your God will hear the words of the **R**, Is 37:4
The **R** returned, and found the king of Is 37:8

RACAL (1)
in **R**, in the cities of the 1 Sm 30:29

RACE (9)
so that the holy **r** has mixed itself with Ezr 9:2
that under the sun the **r** is not to the Eccl 9:11
The chariots **r** madly through the streets; Na 2:4
shrewdly with our **r** and forced our Acts 7:19
belong the patriarchs, and from their **r**, Rom 9:5
know that in a **r** all the runners 1 Cor 9:24
the good fight, I have finished the **r**, 2 Tm 4:7
run with endurance the **r** that is set Heb 12:1
But you are a chosen **r**, a royal 1 Pt 2:9

RACED (1)
"If you have **r** with men on foot, and they Jer 12:5

RACHEL (42)
R his daughter is coming with the Gn 29:6
them, **R** came with her father's sheep, Gn 29:9
soon as Jacob saw **R** the daughter of Gn 29:10
Then Jacob kissed **R** and wept aloud. Gn 29:11
And Jacob told **R** that he was her Gn 29:12
and the name of the younger was **R**. Gn 29:16
but **R** was beautiful in form and Gn 29:17
Jacob loved **R**. And he said, "I will serve Gn 29:18
years for your younger daughter **R**." Gn 29:18
So Jacob served seven years for **R**, and Gn 29:20
to me? Did I not serve with you for **R**? Gn 29:25
gave him his daughter **R** to be his wife. Gn 29:28
Bilhah to his daughter **R** to be her Gn 29:29
So Jacob went in to **R** also, and he loved Gn 29:30
also, and he loved **R** more than Leah, Gn 29:30
opened her womb, but **R** was barren. Gn 29:31
When **R** saw that she bore Jacob no Gn 30:1
Jacob's anger was kindled against **R**, Gn 30:2
Then **R** said, "God has judged me, and Gn 30:6
Then **R** said, "With mighty wrestlings I Gn 30:8
Then **R** said to Leah, "Please give me Gn 30:14
my son's mandrakes also?" **R** said, Gn 30:15
Then God remembered **R**, and God Gn 30:22
As soon as **R** had borne Joseph, Jacob Gn 30:25
Jacob sent and called **R** and Leah into Gn 31:4
Then **R** and Leah answered and said to Gn 31:14
and **R** stole her father's household Gn 31:19
did not know that **R** had stolen them. Gn 31:32
Now **R** had taken the household gods Gn 31:34
children among Leah and **R** and the two Gn 33:1
children, and **R** and Joseph last of all. Gn 33:2
And last Joseph and **R** drew near, and Gn 33:7
from Ephrath, **R** went into labor, Gn 35:16
So **R** died, and she was buried on the Gn 35:19
The sons of **R**: Joseph and Benjamin. Gn 35:24
The sons of **R**, Jacob's wife: Joseph and Gn 46:19
These are the sons of **R**, who were born Gn 46:22
whom Laban gave to **R** his daughter, Gn 46:25
to my sorrow **R** died in the land of Gn 48:7
into your house, like **R** and Leah, Ru 4:11
R is weeping for her children; she Jer 31:15
lamentation, **R** weeping for her children; Mt 2:18

RACHEL'S (5)
R servant Bilhah conceived again and Gn 30:7
went out of Leah's tent and entered **R**. Gn 31:33
It is the pillar of **R** tomb, which is there Gn 35:20
The sons of Bilhah, **R** servant: Dan and Gn 35:25
meet two men by **R** tomb in the 1 Sm 10:2

RACKS (1)
The night **r** my bones, and the pain that Jb 30:17

RADDAI (1)
Nethanel the fourth, **R** the fifth, 1 Chr 2:14

RADIANCE (2)
He is the **r** of the glory of God and the Heb 1:3
glory of God, its **r** like a most rare jewel, Rv 21:11

RADIANT (6)
Those who look to him are **r**, and their Ps 34:5
My beloved is **r** and ruddy, distinguished Sg 5:10
Then you shall see and be **r**; your heart Is 60:5
and they shall be **r** over the goodness of Jer 31:12
My **r** appearance was fearfully changed, Dn 10:8
and his clothes became **r**, intensely Mk 9:3

RAFTERS (2)
was finished with cedar from floor to **r**. 1 Kgs 7:7
of our house are cedar; our **r** are pine. Sg 1:17

RAFTS (2)
and I will make it into **r** to go by sea to 1 Kgs 5:9
bring it to you in **r** by sea to Joppa, 2 Chr 2:16

RAGE (11)
So he turned and went away in a **r**. 2 Kgs 5:12
he was in a **r** with him because of 2 Chr 16:10
killed them in a **r** that has reached 2 Chr 28:9
With fierceness and **r** he swallows the Jb 39:24
Why do the nations **r** and the peoples plot Ps 2:1
The nations **r**, the kingdoms totter; he Ps 46:6
Advance, O horses, and **r**, O chariots! Let Jer 46:9
in furious **r** commanded that Dn 3:13
the king of the south, moved with **r**, Dn 11:11
The sword shall **r** against their cities, Hos 11:6
Holy Spirit, "'Why did the Gentiles **r**, Acts 4:25

RAGED (3)
Because you have **r** against me and 2 Kgs 19:28
Because you have **r** against me and your Is 37:29
The nations **r**, but your wrath came, Rv 11:18

RAGES (2)
to ruin, his heart **r** against the LORD. Prv 19:3
with a fool, the fool only **r** and laughs, Prv 29:9

RAGING (9)
coming in, and your **r** against me. 2 Kgs 19:27
a shelter from the **r** wind and tempest." Ps 55:8
You rule the **r** of the sea; when its waves Ps 89:9
over us would have gone the **r** waters. Ps 124:5
and coming in, and your **r** against me. Is 37:28
the sea, and the sea ceased from its **r**. Jon 1:15
you and writhed; the **r** waters swept on; Hab 3:10
and rebuked the wind and the **r** waves, Lk 8:24
and in **r** fury against them I Acts 26:11

RAGS (3)
and slumber will clothe them with **r**. Prv 23:21
from there old **r** and worn-out clothes, Jer 38:11
"Put the **r** and clothes between your Jer 38:12

RAHAB (14)
whose name was **R** and lodged there. Jos 2:1
Then the king of Jericho sent to **R**, saying, Jos 2:3
Only **R** the prostitute and all who are Jos 6:17
in and brought out **R** and her father and Jos 6:23
But **R** the prostitute and her father's Jos 6:25
beneath him bowed the helpers of **R**. Jb 9:13
by his understanding he shattered **R**. Jb 26:12
who know me I mention **R** and Babylon; Ps 87:4
You crushed **R** like a carcass; you Ps 89:10
I have called her "**R** who sits still." Is 30:7
Was it not you who cut **R** in pieces, that Is 51:9
and Salmon the father of Boaz by **R**, and Mt 1:5
By faith **R** the prostitute did not perish Heb 11:31
was not also **R** the prostitute justified Jas 2:25

RAHAM (1)
Shema fathered **R**, the father of 1 Chr 2:44

RAID (13)
"Raiders shall **r** Gad, but he shall raid Gn 49:19
raid Gad, but he shall **r** at their heels. Gn 49:19
in Judah and made a **r** on Lehi. Jgs 15:9
have made a **r** against the land." 1 Sm 23:27
you made a **r** today?" David would 1 Sm 27:10
had made a **r** against the Negeb 1 Sm 30:1
We had made a **r** against the Negeb 1 Sm 30:14
of David arrived with Joab from a **r**, 2 Sm 3:22
they came down to **r** their livestock. 1 Chr 7:21
come and made a **r** in the Valley of 1 Chr 14:9
yet again made a **r** in the valley. 1 Chr 14:13
groups and made a **r** on the camels and Jb 1:17
breaks in, and the bandits **r** outside. Hos 7:1

RAIDED (1)
him to battle, **r** the cities of Judah, 2 Chr 25:13

RAIDERS (4)
"**R** shall raid Gad, but he shall raid at Gn 49:19
And **r** came out of the camp of the 1 Sm 13:17
garrison and even the **r** trembled, 1 Sm 14:15
helped David against the band of **r**, 1 Chr 12:21

RAIDING (1)
two men who were captains of **r** bands; 2 Sm 4:2

RAIDS (4)
up and made **r** against the Geshurites, 1 Sm 27:8
on one of their **r** had carried off a 2 Kgs 5:2
not come again on **r** into the land of 2 Kgs 6:23
Philistines had made **r** on the cities 2 Chr 28:18

RAIL (1)
All your enemies **r** against you; they Lam 2:16

RAILED (2)
to greet our master, and he **r** at them. 1 Sm 25:14
criminals who were hanged **r** at him, Lk 23:39

RAIN (105)
God had not caused it to **r** on the land, Gn 2:5
seven days I will send **r** on the earth forty Gn 7:4
And **r** fell upon the earth forty days and Gn 7:12
the **r** from the heavens was restrained, Gn 8:2
and the **r** no longer poured upon the Ex 9:33
Pharaoh saw that the **r** and the hail and Ex 9:34
I am about to **r** bread from heaven for Ex 16:4
drinks water by the **r** from heaven, Dt 11:11
he will give the **r** for your land in its Dt 11:14
its season, the early **r** and the later rain, Dt 11:14
its season, the early rain and the later **r**, Dt 11:14
the heavens, so that there will be no **r**, Dt 11:17
to give the **r** to your land in its season Dt 28:12
LORD will make the **r** of your land Dt 28:24
May my teaching drop as the **r**, my Dt 32:2
dew, like gentle **r** upon the tender grass, Dt 32:2
that he may send thunder and **r**. 1 Sm 12:17
the LORD sent thunder and **r** that day, 1 Sm 12:18
let there be no dew or **r** upon you, 2 Sm 1:21
of harvest until **r** fell upon them 2 Sm 21:10
like **r** that makes grass to sprout from 2 Sm 23:4
and there is no **r** because they have 1 Kgs 8:35
walk, and grant **r** upon your land, 1 Kgs 8:36
shall be neither dew nor **r** these years, 1 Kgs 17:1
because there was no **r** in the land. 1 Kgs 17:7
the LORD sends **r** upon the earth.'" 1 Kgs 17:14
and I will send **r** upon the earth." 1 Kgs 18:1
there is a sound of the rushing of **r**." 1 Kgs 18:41
and go down, lest the **r** stop you.'" 1 Kgs 18:44
and wind, and there was a great **r**. 1 Kgs 18:45
the LORD, 'You shall not see wind or **r**, 2 Kgs 3:17
and there is no **r** because they have 2 Chr 6:26
walk, and grant **r** upon your land, 2 Chr 6:27
up the heavens so that there is no **r**, 2 Chr 7:13
this matter and because of the heavy **r**. Ezr 10:9
are many, and it is a time of heavy **r**; Ezr 10:13
he gives **r** on the earth and sends waters Jb 5:10
anger against him and **r** it upon him Jb 20:23
are wet with the **r** of the mountains and Jb 24:8
made a decree for the **r** and a way for the Jb 28:26
They waited for me as for the **r**, and they Jb 29:23
opened their mouths as for the spring **r**. Jb 29:23
drops of water; they distill his mist in **r**, Jb 36:27
for the torrents of **r** and a way for Jb 38:25
to bring **r** on a land where no man is, Jb 38:26
"Has the **r** a father, or who has begotten Jb 38:28
Let him **r** coals on the wicked; fire and Ps 11:6
quaked, the heavens poured down **r**, Ps 68:8
R in abundance, O God, you shed Ps 68:9
May he be like **r** that falls on the mown Ps 72:6
the early **r** also covers it with pools. Ps 84:6
He gave them hail for **r**, and fiery Ps 105:32
lightnings for the **r** and brings forth Ps 135:7
with clouds; he prepares **r** for the earth; Ps 147:8
like the clouds that bring the spring **r**. Prv 16:15
is a continual dripping of **r**. Prv 19:13
clouds and wind without **r** is a man Prv 25:14
The north wind brings forth **r**, and a Prv 25:23
Like snow in summer or **r** in harvest, Prv 26:1
poor is a beating **r** that leaves no food. Prv 28:3
If the clouds are full of **r**, they empty Eccl 11:3
and the clouds return after the **r**, Eccl 12:2
the winter is past; the **r** is over and gone. Sg 2:11
refuge and a shelter from the storm and **r**. Is 4:6
the clouds that they **r** no rain upon it. Is 5:6
the clouds that they rain no **r** upon it. Is 5:6
And he will give **r** for the seed with Is 30:23
He plants a cedar and the **r** nourishes it. Is 44:14
and let the clouds **r** down righteousness; Is 45:8
"For as the **r** and the snow come down Is 55:10
withheld, and the spring **r** has not come; Jer 3:3
our God, who gives the **r** in its season, Jer 5:24
the autumn **r** and the spring rain, Jer 5:24
the autumn rain and the spring **r**, Jer 5:24
He makes lightning for the **r**, and he Jer 10:13
dismayed, since there is no **r** on the land, Jer 14:4
gods of the nations that can bring **r**? Jer 14:22
He makes lightning for the **r**, and he Jer 51:16
bow that is in the cloud on the day of **r**, Ezk 1:28
There will be a deluge of **r**, and you, O Ezk 13:11
shall be a deluge of **r** in my anger, Ezk 13:13
and I will **r** upon him and his hordes Ezk 38:22
may come and **r** righteousness upon Hos 10:12
has given the early **r** for your vindication; Jl 2:23
he has poured down for you abundant **r**, Jl 2:23
abundant rain, the early and the latter **r**, Jl 2:23
"I also withheld the **r** from you when Am 4:7
to the harvest; I would send **r** on one city, Am 4:7
one city, and send no **r** on another city; Am 4:7
one field would have **r**, and the field on Am 4:7
field on which it did not **r** would wither; Am 4:7
Ask **r** from the LORD in the season of the Zec 10:1
the LORD in the season of the spring **r**, Zec 10:1
and he will give them showers of **r**, Zec 10:1
of hosts, there will be no **r** on them. Zec 14:17
then on them there shall be no **r**; Zec 14:18
and sends **r** on the just and on the Mt 5:45
And the **r** fell, and the floods came, and Mt 7:25
And the **r** fell, and the floods came, and Mt 7:27
it had begun to **r** and was cold. Acts 28:2
that has drunk the **r** that often falls on Heb 6:7
he prayed fervently that it might not **r**, Jas 5:17
and six months it did not **r** on the earth. Jas 5:17
he prayed again, and heaven gave **r**, Jas 5:18
that no **r** may fall during the days of Rv 11:6

RAINBOW (2)
the throne was a **r** that had the Rv 4:3
in a cloud, with a **r** over his head, Rv 10:1

RAINED (6)
Then the LORD **r** on Sodom and Gn 19:24
And the LORD **r** hail upon the land of Ex 9:23
and he **r** down on them manna to eat Ps 78:24
he **r** meat on them like dust, winged Ps 78:27
is not cleansed or **r** upon in the day Ezk 22:24
fire and sulfur **r** from heaven and Lk 17:29

RAINS (5)
I will give you your **r** in their season, Lv 26:4
with him torrential **r** and hailstones, Ezk 38:22
as the spring **r** that water the earth." Hos 6:3
by giving you **r** from heaven and Acts 14:17
it, until it receives the early and the late **r**. Jas 5:7

RAINY (1)
continual dripping on a **r** day and a Prv 27:15

RAISE (74)
and **r** up offspring for your brother." Gn 38:8
And beware lest you **r** your eyes to Dt 4:19
"The LORD your God will **r** up for you a Dt 18:15
I will **r** up for them a prophet like you Dt 18:18
And I will **r** up for myself a faithful 1 Sm 2:35
I will **r** up your offspring after you, 2 Sm 7:12
I will **r** up evil against you out of 2 Sm 12:11
him, to **r** him from the ground, 2 Sm 12:17
r an altar to the LORD on the 2 Sm 24:18
the LORD will **r** up for himself a king 1 Kgs 14:14
and cymbals, to **r** sounds of joy. 1 Chr 15:16
I will **r** up your offspring after you, 1 Chr 17:11
should go up and **r** an altar to the 1 Chr 21:18
O LORD, be gracious to me, and **r** me up, Ps 41:10
R a song; sound the tambourine, the Ps 81:2
out for insight and **r** your voice for Prv 2:3
Does not understanding **r** her voice? Prv 8:1
He will **r** a signal for nations afar off, and Is 5:26
He will **r** a signal for the nations and Is 11:12
On a bare hill **r** a signal; cry aloud to Is 13:2
road to Horonaim they **r** a cry of Is 15:5
and I will **r** siegeworks against you. Is 29:3
be built, and I will **r** up their ruins'; Is 44:26
should be my servant to **r** up the tribes of Is 49:6
nations, and **r** my signal to the peoples; Is 49:22
you shall **r** up the foundations of many Is 58:12
they shall **r** up the former devastations; Is 61:4
R a standard toward Zion, flee for safety, Jer 4:6
and **r** a signal on Beth-haccherem, Jer 6:1
r a lamentation on the bare heights, for Jer 7:29
them make haste and **r** a wailing over Jer 9:18
when I will **r** up for David a righteous Jer 23:5
their king, whom I will **r** up for them. Jer 30:9
and **r** shouts for the chief of the nations; Jer 31:7
R a shout against her all around; she Jer 50:15
and fall, with none to **r** him up, Jer 50:32
and they shall **r** the shout of victory Jer 51:14
you, and **r** a roof of shields against you. Ezk 26:8
And they will **r** a lamentation over Ezk 26:17
son of man, **r** a lamentation over Tyre, Ezk 27:2
their wailing they **r** a lamentation for Ezk 27:32
r a lamentation over the king of Tyre, Ezk 28:12
r a lamentation over Pharaoh king of Ezk 32:2
open your graves and **r** you from your Ezk 37:12
graves, and **r** you from your graves, Ezk 37:13
And he shall **r** a great multitude, Dn 11:11
of the north shall again **r** a multitude, Dn 11:13

on the third day he will **r** us up, that we Hos 6:2
High, he shall not **r** them up at all. Hos 11:7
on her land, with none to **r** her up." Am 5:2
behold, I will **r** up against you a nation, Am 6:14
"In that day I will **r** up the booth of Am 9:11
and **r** up its ruins and rebuild it as in Am 9:11
then we will **r** against him seven Mi 5:5
from these stones to **r** up children for Mt 3:9
Heal the sick, **r** the dead, cleanse lepers, Mt 10:8
marry the widow and **r** up children for Mt 22:24
take the widow and **r** up offspring for Mk 12:19
from these stones to **r** up children for Lk 3:8
take the widow and **r** up offspring for Lk 20:28
place, straighten up and **r** your heads, Lk 21:28
temple, and in three days I will **r** it up." Jn 2:19
and will you **r** it up in three days?" Jn 2:20
has given me, but **r** it up on the last day. Jn 6:39
life, and I will **r** him up on the last day." Jn 6:40
him. And I will **r** him up on the last day. Jn 6:44
life, and I will **r** him up on the last day. Jn 6:54
'The Lord God will **r** up for you a Acts 3:22
'God will **r** up for you a prophet like Acts 7:37
the Lord and will also **r** us up by his 1 Cor 6:14
whom he did not **r** if it is true that 1 Cor 15:15
the Lord Jesus will **r** us also with 2 Cor 4:14
was able even to **r** him from the dead, Heb 11:19
who is sick, and the Lord will **r** him up. Jas 5:15

RAISED (123)
But for this purpose I have **r** you up, to Ex 9:16
and put in its poles, and **r** up its pillars. Ex 40:18
Then all the congregation **r** a loud cry, Nm 14:1
children, whom he **r** up in their place, Jos 5:7
And they **r** over him a great heap of Jos 7:26
gate of the city and **r** over it a great heap Jos 8:29
Then the LORD **r** up judges, who saved Jgs 2:16
Whenever the LORD **r** up judges for Jgs 2:18
the LORD **r** up a deliverer for the people of Jgs 3:9
and the LORD **r** up for them a deliverer, Jgs 3:15
of Israel, and they **r** their heads no more. Jgs 8:28
who were with him **r** their voices and 1 Sm 30:4
pit in the forest and **r** over him a very 2 Sm 18:17
up the men who **r** their hand against 2 Sm 18:28
oracle of the man who was **r** on high, 2 Sm 23:1
And the LORD **r** up an adversary 1 Kgs 11:14
God also **r** up as an adversary to 1 Kgs 11:23
whom have you **r** your voice and 2 Kgs 19:22
the LORD), and when the song was **r**, 2 Chr 5:13
the men of Judah **r** the battle shout. 2 Chr 13:15
broken down and **r** towers upon it, 2 Chr 32:5
Ophel, and **r** it to a very great height. 2 Chr 33:14
And they **r** their voices and wept, and Jb 2:12
if I have **r** my hand against the Jb 31:21
those who hate you have **r** their heads. Ps 83:2
Therefore he **r** his hand and swore to Ps 106:26
he commanded and **r** the stormy Ps 107:25
not lifted up; my eyes are not **r** too high; Ps 131:1
He has **r** up a horn for his people, Ps 148:14
no songs are sung, no cheers are **r**; Is 16:10
when a signal is **r** on the mountains, Is 18:3
whom have you **r** your voice and Is 37:23
a road, and my highways shall be **r** up. Is 49:11
'The LORD has **r** up prophets for us in Jer 29:15
waters; the noise of their voice is **r**, Jer 51:55
they **r** a clamor in the house of the LORD Lam 2:7
I held and **r** my enemy destroyed. Lam 2:22
the temple had a **r** platform all around; Ezk 41:8
whom he would, he **r** up, and whom he Dn 5:19
one, like a bear. It was **r** up on one side. Dn 7:5
I **r** my eyes and saw, and behold, a ram Dn 8:3
he **r** his right hand and his left hand Dn 12:7
And I **r** up some of your sons for Am 2:11
Judah, so that no one **r** his head. Zec 1:21
of the one will be **r** against the hand of Zec 14:13
and the deaf hear, and the dead are **r** up, Mt 11:5
the Baptist. He has been **r** from the dead; Mt 14:2
and be killed, and on the third day be **r**. Mt 16:21
until the Son of Man is **r** from the dead." Mt 17:9
and he will be **r** on the third day." And Mt 17:23
and he will be **r** on the third day." Mt 20:19
But after I am **r** up, I will go before you Mt 26:32
the saints who had fallen asleep were **r**, Mt 27:52
the Baptist has been **r** from the dead. Mk 6:14
"John, whom I beheaded, has been **r**." Mk 6:16
And as for the dead being **r**, have you Mk 12:26
But after I am **r** up, I will go before you Mk 14:28
and has **r** up a horn of salvation for us Lk 1:69
and the deaf hear, the dead are **r** up, Lk 7:22
some that John had been **r** from the dead, Lk 9:7
and be killed, and on the third day be **r**." Lk 9:22
woman in the crowd **r** her voice and Lk 11:27
But that the dead are **r**, even Moses Lk 20:37
When therefore he was **r** from the dead, Jn 2:22
was, whom Jesus had **r** from the dead. Jn 12:1
Lazarus, whom he had **r** from the dead. Jn 12:9
of the tomb and **r** him from the dead Jn 12:17
disciples after he was **r** from the dead. Jn 21:14
God **r** him up, loosing the pangs of Acts 2:24
This Jesus God **r** up, and of that we all Acts 2:32
him by the right hand and **r** him up, Acts 3:7
of life, whom God **r** from the dead. Acts 3:15
God, having **r** up his servant, sent him Acts 3:26
whom God **r** from the dead—by him Acts 4:10
The God of our fathers **r** Jesus, whom Acts 5:30
And he gave her his hand and **r** her up. Acts 9:41
but God **r** him on the third day and Acts 10:40
him, he **r** up David to be their king, Acts 13:22
But God **r** him from the dead, Acts 13:30
the fact that he **r** him from the dead, Acts 13:34
but he whom God **r** up did not see Acts 13:37
Then they **r** their voices and said, Acts 22:22
believe in him who **r** from the dead Rom 4:24
our trespasses and **r** for our Rom 4:25
just as Christ was **r** from the dead by Rom 6:4
know that Christ being **r** from the dead Rom 6:9
to him who has been **r** from the dead, Rom 7:4
Spirit of him who **r** Jesus from the Rom 8:11
he who **r** Christ Jesus from the dead Rom 8:11
who was **r**—who is at the right hand Rom 8:34
"For this very purpose I have **r** you up, Rom 9:17
your heart that God **r** him from the Rom 10:9
And God **r** the Lord and will also 1 Cor 6:14
that he was **r** on the third day in 1 Cor 15:4
is proclaimed as **r** from the dead, 1 Cor 15:12
then not even Christ has been **r**. 1 Cor 15:13
And if Christ has not been **r**, then 1 Cor 15:14
testified about God that he **r** Christ, 1 Cor 15:15
if it is true that the dead are not **r**. 1 Cor 15:15
For if the dead are not **r**, not even 1 Cor 15:16
raised, not even Christ has been **r**. 1 Cor 15:16
And if Christ has not been **r**, your 1 Cor 15:17
fact Christ has been **r** from the dead, 1 Cor 15:20
If the dead are not **r** at all, why are 1 Cor 15:29
If the dead are not **r**, "Let us eat and 1 Cor 15:32
will ask, "How are the dead **r**? 1 Cor 15:35
what is **r** is imperishable. 1 Cor 15:42
is sown in dishonor; it is **r** in glory. 1 Cor 15:43
is sown in weakness; it is **r** in power. 1 Cor 15:43
natural body; it is **r** a spiritual body. 1 Cor 15:44
and the dead will be **r** imperishable, 1 Cor 15:52
knowing that he who **r** the Lord Jesus 2 Cor 4:14
who for their sake died and was **r**. 2 Cor 5:15
every lofty opinion **r** against the 2 Cor 10:5
the Father, who **r** him from the dead— Gal 1:1
in Christ when he **r** him from the dead Eph 1:20
and **r** us up with him and seated us with Eph 2:6
you were also **r** with him through Col 2:12
of God, who **r** him from the dead. Col 2:12
If then you have been **r** with Christ, seek Col 3:1
heaven, whom he **r** from the dead, 1 Thes 1:10
who **r** him from the dead and gave him 1 Pt 1:21
sea and on the land **r** his right hand to Rv 10:5

RAISES (12)
life; he brings down to Sheol and **r** up. 1 Sm 2:6
He **r** up the poor from the dust; he lifts 1 Sm 2:8
When he **r** himself up the mighty are Jb 41:25
but he **r** up the needy out of affliction Ps 107:41
He **r** the poor from the dust and lifts the Ps 113:7
who are falling and **r** up all who are Ps 145:14
street, in the markets she **r** her voice; Prv 1:20
But the LORD **r** the adversaries of Rezin Is 9:11
it **r** from their thrones all who were kings Is 14:9
For as the Father **r** the dead and gives Jn 5:21
by any of you that God **r** the dead? Acts 26:8
ourselves but on God who **r** the dead. 2 Cor 1:9

RAISIN (1)
stricken, for the **r** cakes of Kir-hareseth. Is 16:7

RAISING (6)
For behold, I am **r** up the Chaldeans, Hab 1:6
I am **r** up in the land a shepherd who Zec 11:16
to us their children by **r** Jesus, Acts 13:33
assurance to all by **r** him from the Acts 17:31
meat market without **r** any question 1 Cor 10:25
before you without **r** any question 1 Cor 10:27

RAISINS (8)
hundred clusters of **r** and two 1 Sm 25:18
of a cake of figs and two clusters of **r**. 1 Sm 30:12
of meat, and a cake of **r** to each one. 2 Sm 6:19
of bread, a hundred bunches of **r**, 2 Sm 16:1
of flour, cakes of figs, clusters of **r**, 1 Chr 12:40
a portion of meat, and a cake of **r**. 1 Chr 16:3
Sustain me with **r**; refresh me with apples, Sg 2:5
turn to other gods and love cakes of **r**." Hos 3:1

RAKEM (1)
and his sons were Ulam and **R**. 1 Chr 7:16

RAKKATH (1)
Ziddim, Zer, Hammath, **R**, Chinnereth, Jos 19:35

RAKKON (1)
and Me-jarkon and **R** with the territory Jos 19:46

RALLIED (1)
who were with him **r** and went into 1 Sm 14:20

RALLY (1)
the sound of the trumpet, **r** to us there. Neh 4:20

RAM (97)
goat three years old, a **r** three years old, Gn 15:9
and behold, behind him was a **r**, Gn 22:13
went and took the **r** and offered it up Gn 22:13
lay their hands on the head of the **r**, Ex 29:15
you shall kill the **r** and shall take its Ex 29:16
Then you shall cut the **r** into pieces, Ex 29:17
and burn the whole **r** on the altar. It is a Ex 29:18
"You shall take the other **r**, and Aaron Ex 29:19
lay their hands on the head of the **r**, Ex 29:19
and you shall kill the **r** and take part of Ex 29:20
take the fat from the **r** and the fat tail Ex 29:22
right thigh (for it is a **r** of ordination), Ex 29:22
the breast of the **r** of Aaron's ordination Ex 29:26
is contributed from the **r** of ordination, Ex 29:27
"You shall take the **r** of ordination and Ex 29:31
eat the flesh of the **r** and the bread that Ex 29:32
a **r** without blemish out of the flock, Lv 5:15
for him with the **r** of the guilt offering, Lv 5:16
to the priest a **r** without blemish out of Lv 5:18
to the LORD a **r** without blemish out of Lv 6:6
Then he presented the **r** of the burnt Lv 8:18
laid their hands on the head of the **r**. Lv 8:18
He cut the **r** into pieces, and Moses Lv 8:20
Moses burned the whole **r** on the altar. Lv 8:21
Then he presented the other **r**, the ram of Lv 8:22
the other ram, the **r** of ordination, Lv 8:22
laid their hands on the head of the **r**. Lv 8:22
was Moses' portion of the **r** of ordination, Lv 8:29
a sin offering and a **r** for a burnt offering, Lv 9:2
and an ox and a **r** for peace offerings, to Lv 9:4
Then he killed the ox and the **r**, the Lv 9:18
But the fat pieces of the ox and of the **r**, Lv 9:19
sin offering and a **r** for a burnt offering. Lv 16:3
offering, and one **r** for a burnt offering. Lv 16:5
tent of meeting, a **r** for a guilt offering. Lv 19:21
for him with the **r** of the guilt offering Lv 19:22
in addition to the **r** of atonement with Nm 5:8
and one **r** without blemish as a peace Nm 6:14
and he shall offer the **r** as a sacrifice of Nm 6:17
priest shall take the shoulder of the **r**, Nm 6:19
one bull from the herd, one **r**, one male Nm 7:15
one bull from the herd, one **r**, one male Nm 7:21
one bull from the herd, one **r**, one male Nm 7:27
one bull from the herd, one **r**, one male Nm 7:33
one bull from the herd, one **r**, one male Nm 7:39
one bull from the herd, one **r**, one male Nm 7:45
one bull from the herd, one **r**, one male Nm 7:51
one bull from the herd, one **r**, one male Nm 7:57
one bull from the herd, one **r**, one male Nm 7:63
one bull from the herd, one **r**, one male Nm 7:69
one bull from the herd, one **r**, one male Nm 7:75
one bull from the herd, one **r**, one male Nm 7:81
Or for a **r**, you shall offer for a grain Nm 15:6
it shall be done for each bull or **r**, Nm 15:11
offered on each altar a bull and a **r**. Nm 23:2
offered on each altar a bull and a **r**." Nm 23:4
offered a bull and a **r** on each altar. Nm 23:14
offered a bull and a **r** on each altar. Nm 23:30
two bulls from the herd, one **r**, seven Nm 28:11
offering, mixed with oil, for the one **r**; Nm 28:12
wine for a bull, a third of a hin for a **r**, Nm 28:14
two bulls from the herd, one **r**, and Nm 28:19
offer for a bull, and two tenths for a **r**; Nm 28:20
two bulls from the herd, one **r**, seven Nm 28:27
for each bull, two tenths for one **r**, Nm 28:28
one bull from the herd, one **r**, seven Nm 29:2
ephah for the bull, two tenths for the **r**, Nm 29:3
one bull from the herd, one **r**, seven Nm 29:8
for the bull, two tenths for the one **r**, Nm 29:9
one bull, one **r**, seven male lambs a Nm 29:36
drink offerings for the bull, for the **r**, Nm 29:37
Hezron fathered **R**, Ram fathered Ru 4:19
fathered Ram, **R** fathered Amminadab, Ru 4:19
to him: Jerahmeel, **R**, and Chelubai. 1 Chr 2:9
R fathered Amminadab, and 1 Chr 2:10
R, his firstborn, Bunah, Oren, Ozem, 1 Chr 2:25
The sons of **R**, the firstborn of 1 Chr 2:27
guilt offering was a **r** of the flock for Ezr 10:19
of Barachel the Buzite, of the family of **R**, Jb 32:2
blemish and a **r** from the flock Ezk 43:23
from the herd and a **r** from the flock, Ezk 43:25
for each bull, an ephah for each **r**, Ezk 45:24
blemish and a **r** without blemish. Ezk 46:4
grain offering with the **r** shall be an Ezk 46:5
blemish, and six lambs and a **r**, Ezk 46:6
with the bull and an ephah with the **r**, Ezk 46:7
be an ephah, and with a **r** an ephah, Ezk 46:11

a **r** standing on the bank of the canal. Dn 8:3
I saw the **r** charging westward and Dn 8:4
He came to the **r** with the two horns, Dn 8:6
I saw him come close to the **r**, and he was Dn 8:7
him and struck the **r** and broke his two Dn 8:7
And the **r** had no power to stand before Dn 8:7
who could rescue the **r** from his power. Dn 8:7
As for the **r** that you saw with the two Dn 8:20
of Hezron, and Hezron the father of **R**, Mt 1:3
and **R** the father of Amminadab, and Mt 1:4

RAM'S (1)
they make a long blast with the **r** horn, Jos 6:5

RAMAH (37)
Gibeon, **R**, Beeroth, Jos 18:25
as far as Baalath-beer, **R** of the Negeb. Jos 19:8
Then the boundary turns to **R**, Jos 19:29
Adamah, **R**, Hazor, Jos 19:36
palm of Deborah between **R** and Bethel in Jgs 4:5
and spend the night at Gibeah or at **R**." Jgs 19:13
they went back to their house at **R**. 1 Sm 1:19
Then Elkanah went home to **R**. And 1 Sm 2:11
Then he would return to **R**, for his 1 Sm 7:17
together and came to Samuel at **R** 1 Sm 8:4
Then Samuel went to **R**, and Saul 1 Sm 15:34
And Samuel rose up and went to **R**. 1 Sm 16:13
came to Samuel at **R** and told him 1 Sm 19:18
"Behold, David is at Naioth in **R**." 1 Sm 19:19
he himself went to **R** and came to the 1 Sm 19:22
"Behold, they are at Naioth in **R**." 1 Sm 19:22
And he went there to Naioth in **R**. 1 Sm 19:23
until he came to Naioth in **R**. 1 Sm 19:23
fled from Naioth in **R** and came and 1 Sm 20:1
they buried him in his house at **R**. 1 Sm 25:1
for him and buried him in **R**, 1 Sm 28:3
went up against Judah and built **R**, 1 Kgs 15:17
heard of it, he stopped building **R**, 1 Kgs 15:21
away the stones of **R** and its timber, 1 Kgs 15:22
that the Syrians had given him at **R**, 2 Kgs 8:29
went up against Judah and built **R**, 2 Chr 16:1
he stopped building **R** and let his 2 Chr 16:5
away the stones of **R** and its timber, 2 Chr 16:6
the wounds that he had received at **R**, 2 Chr 22:6
The sons of **R** and Geba, 621. Ezr 2:26
The men of **R** and Geba, 621. Neh 7:30
Hazor, **R**, Gittaim, Neh 11:33
they lodge for the night; **R** trembles; Is 10:29
"A voice is heard in **R**, lamentation and Jer 31:15
of the guard had let him go from **R**, Jer 40:1
the horn in Gibeah, the trumpet in **R**. Hos 5:8
"A voice was heard in **R**, weeping and Mt 2:18

RAMATH-LEHI (1)
his hand. And that place was called **R**. Jgs 15:17

RAMATH-MIZPEH (1)
and from Heshbon to **R** and Betonim, Jos 13:26

RAMATHAIM-ZOPHIM (1)
a certain man of **R** of the hill country 1 Sm 1:1

RAMATHITE (1)
the vineyards was Shimei the **R**; 1 Chr 27:27

RAMESES (4)
in the best of the land, in the land of **R**, Gn 47:11
of Israel journeyed from **R** to Succoth, Ex 12:37
They set out from **R** in the first month, Nm 33:3
Israel set out from **R** and camped at Nm 33:5

RAMIAH (1)
R, Izziah, Malchijah, Mijamin, Ezr 10:25

RAMOTH (6)
Reubenites, **R** in Gilead for the Gadites, Dt 4:43
the tribe of Reuben, and **R** in Gilead, Jos 20:8
Gad, **R** in Gilead with its pasturelands, Jos 21:38
for those in Bethel, in **R** of the Negeb, 1 Sm 30:27
R with its pasturelands, and Anem 1 Chr 6:73
R in Gilead with its pasturelands, 1 Chr 6:80

RAMOTH-GILEAD (20)
in **R** (he had the villages of Jair the 1 Kgs 4:13
"Do you know that **R** belongs to us, 1 Kgs 22:3
to battle at **R**?" And Jehoshaphat said 1 Kgs 22:4
them, "Shall I go to battle against **R**, 1 Kgs 22:6
and said, "Go up to **R** and triumph; 1 Kgs 22:12
"Micaiah, shall we go to **R** to battle, 1 Kgs 22:15
that he may go up and fall at **R**?' 1 Kgs 22:20
the king of Judah went up to **R**. 1 Kgs 22:29
war against Hazael king of Syria at **R**, 2 Kgs 8:28
flask of oil in your hand, and go to **R**. 2 Kgs 9:1
the servant of the prophet, went to **R**. 2 Kgs 9:4
on guard at **R** against Hazael king 2 Kgs 9:14
and induced him to go up against **R**. 2 Chr 18:2
go with me to **R**?" He answered him, 2 Chr 18:3
"Shall we go to battle against **R**, 2 Chr 18:5
and said, "Go up to **R** and triumph. 2 Chr 18:11
"Micaiah, shall we go to **R** to battle, 2 Chr 18:14
that he may go up and fall at **R**?' 2 Chr 18:19
the king of Judah went up to **R**. 2 Chr 18:28
war against Hazael king of Syria at **R**. 2 Chr 22:5

RAMP (1)
cast up their siege **r** against me and Jb 19:12

RAMPANT (1)
all filthiness and **r** wickedness and Jas 1:21

RAMPART (4)
the city, and it stood against the **r**, 2 Sm 20:15
he caused **r** and wall to lament; Lam 2:8
Nile, with water around her, her **r** a sea, Na 3:8
has built herself a **r** and heaped up silver Zec 9:3

RAMPARTS (2)
consider well her **r**, go through her Ps 48:13
Man the **r**; watch the road; dress for Na 2:1

RAMS (68)
I have not eaten the **r** of your flocks. Gn 31:38
goats, two hundred ewes and twenty **r**, Gn 32:14
of the herd and two **r** without blemish, Ex 29:1
basket, and bring the bull and the two **r**. Ex 29:3
"Then you shall take one of the **r**, and Ex 29:15
offering and the two **r** and the basket of Lv 8:2
and one bull from the herd and two **r**. Lv 23:18
of peace offerings, two oxen, five **r**, Nm 7:17
of peace offerings, two oxen, five **r**, Nm 7:23
of peace offerings, two oxen, five **r**, Nm 7:29
of peace offerings, two oxen, five **r**, Nm 7:35
of peace offerings, two oxen, five **r**, Nm 7:41
of peace offerings, two oxen, five **r**, Nm 7:47
of peace offerings, two oxen, five **r**, Nm 7:53
of peace offerings, two oxen, five **r**, Nm 7:59
of peace offerings, two oxen, five **r**, Nm 7:65
of peace offerings, two oxen, five **r**, Nm 7:71
of peace offerings, two oxen, five **r**, Nm 7:77
of peace offerings, two oxen, five **r**, Nm 7:83
burnt offering twelve bulls, twelve **r**, Nm 7:87
offerings twenty-four bulls, the **r** sixty, Nm 7:88
for me here seven bulls and seven **r**." Nm 23:1
for me here seven bulls and seven **r**." Nm 23:29
thirteen bulls from the herd, two **r**, Nm 29:13
bulls, two tenths for each of the two **r**, Nm 29:14
day twelve bulls from the herd, two **r**, Nm 29:17
drink offerings for the bulls, for the **r**, Nm 29:18
"On the third day eleven bulls, two **r**, Nm 29:20
drink offerings for the bulls, for the **r**, Nm 29:21
"On the fourth day ten bulls, two **r**, Nm 29:23
drink offerings for the bulls, for the **r**, Nm 29:24
"On the fifth day nine bulls, two **r**, Nm 29:26
drink offerings for the bulls, for the **r**, Nm 29:27
"On the sixth day eight bulls, two **r**, Nm 29:29
drink offerings for the bulls, for the **r**, Nm 29:30
the seventh day seven bulls, two **r**, Nm 29:32
drink offerings for the bulls, for the **r**, Nm 29:33
fat of lambs, **r** of Bashan and goats, Dt 32:14
and to listen than the fat of **r**. 1 Sm 15:22
lambs and the wool of 100,000 **r**. 2 Kgs 3:4
sacrificed seven bulls and seven **r**. 1 Chr 15:26
to the LORD, 1,000 bulls, 1,000 **r**, 1 Chr 29:21
bull or seven **r** becomes a priest 2 Chr 13:9
brought him 7,700 **r** and 7,700 2 Chr 17:11
they brought seven bulls, seven **r**, 2 Chr 29:21
they slaughtered the **r** and their 2 Chr 29:22
brought was 70 bulls, 100 **r**, 2 Chr 29:32
r, or sheep for burnt offerings to the God Ezr 6:9
of this house of God 100 bulls, 200 **r**, Ezr 6:17
all diligence buy bulls, **r**, and lambs, Ezr 7:17
twelve bulls for all Israel, ninety-six **r**, Ezr 8:35
seven bulls and seven **r** and go to my Jb 42:8
with the smoke of the sacrifice of **r**; Ps 66:15
The mountains skipped like **r**, the hills Ps 114:4
O mountains, that you skip like **r**? O Ps 114:6
of burnt offerings of **r** and the fat of Is 1:11
and goats, with the fat of the kidneys of **r**. Is 34:6
the **r** of Nebaioth shall minister to you; Is 60:7
to the slaughter, like **r** and male goats. Jer 51:40
and plant battering **r** against it all Ezk 4:2
for Jerusalem, to set battering **r**, Ezk 21:22
to set battering **r** against the gates, Ezk 21:22
of his battering **r** against your walls, Ezk 26:9
favored dealers in lambs, **r**, and goats; Ezk 27:21
and sheep, between **r** and male goats. Ezk 34:17
blood of the princes of the earth—of **r**, Ezk 39:18
bulls and seven **r** without blemish, Ezk 45:23
the LORD be pleased with thousands of **r**, Mi 6:7

RAMS' (10)
tanned **r** skins, goatskins, acacia wood, Ex 25:5
a covering of tanned **r** skins and a Ex 26:14
tanned **r** skins, and goatskins; acacia Ex 35:7
hair or tanned **r** skins or goatskins Ex 35:23
covering of tanned **r** skins and Ex 36:19
covering of tanned **r** skins and Ex 39:34
bear seven trumpets of **r** horns before the Jos 6:4
bear seven trumpets of **r** horns before the Jos 6:6
the seven trumpets of **r** horns before the Jos 6:8
the seven trumpets of **r** horns before the Jos 6:13

RAN (59)
he **r** from the tent door to meet them and Gn 18:2
And Abraham **r** to the herd and took a Gn 18:7
Then the servant **r** to meet her and Gn 24:17
into the trough and **r** again to the well Gn 24:20
Then the young woman **r** and told her Gn 24:28
Laban **r** out toward the man, to the Gn 24:29
son, and she **r** and told her father. Gn 29:12
he **r** to meet him and embraced him Gn 29:13
But Esau **r** to meet him and embraced Gn 33:4
it became a serpent, and Moses **r** from it. Ex 4:3
and hail, and fire **r** down to the earth. Ex 9:23
And a young man **r** and told Moses, Nm 11:27
it as Moses said and **r** into the midst of Nm 16:47
into the brook that **r** down from the Dt 9:21
sent messengers, and they **r** to the tent; Jos 7:22
they **r** and entered the city and captured Jos 8:19
their south boundary **r** from the end Jos 15:2
And their boundary **r** from Heleph, Jos 19:33
border of the Amorites **r** from the ascent Jgs 1:36
around the camp, and all the army **r**. Jgs 7:21
And Jotham **r** away and fled and went to Jgs 9:21
So the woman **r** quickly and told her Jgs 13:10
and **r** to Eli and said, "Here I am, for 1 Sm 3:5
A man of Benjamin **r** from the battle 1 Sm 4:12
Then they **r** and took him from 1 Sm 10:23
of the baggage and **r** to the ranks 1 Sm 17:22
David **r** quickly toward the battle 1 Sm 17:48
Then David **r** and stood over the 1 Sm 17:51
the arrows that I shoot." As the boy **r**, 1 Sm 20:36
Cushite bowed before Joab, and **r**. 2 Sm 18:21
"Run." Then Ahimaaz **r** by the way 2 Sm 18:23
of Shimei's servants **r** away to 1 Kgs 2:39
And the water **r** around the altar 1 Kgs 18:35
his garment and **r** before Ahab to 1 Kgs 18:46
and he arose and **r** for his life and 1 Kgs 19:3
left the oxen and **r** after Elijah and 1 Kgs 19:20
"I did not send the prophets, yet they **r**; I Jer 23:21
And the pavement **r** along the side of Ezk 40:18
and he **r** at him in his powerful wrath. Dn 8:6
of them at once **r** and took a sponge, Mt 27:48
and great joy, and **r** to tell his disciples. Mt 28:8
from afar, he **r** and fell down before him. Mk 5:6
and they **r** there on foot from all the Mk 6:33
and **r** about the whole region and Mk 6:55
were greatly amazed and **r** up to him Mk 9:15
a man **r** up and knelt before him and Mk 10:17
left the linen cloth and **r** away naked. Mk 14:52
And someone **r** and filled a sponge Mk 15:36
and **r** and embraced him and kissed Lk 15:20
So he **r** on ahead and climbed up into a Lk 19:4
But Peter rose and **r** to the tomb; Lk 24:12
When the wine **r** out, the mother of Jesus Jn 2:3
So she **r** and went to Simon Peter and the Jn 20:2
all the people **r** together to them in the Acts 3:11
So Philip **r** to him and heard him Acts 8:30
open the gate but **r** in and reported Acts 12:14
stirred up, and the people **r** together. Acts 21:30
and centurions and **r** down to them. Acts 21:32
a reef, they **r** the vessel aground. Acts 27:41

RANDOM (2)
drew his bow at **r** and struck the 1 Kgs 22:34
drew his bow at **r** and struck the 2 Chr 18:33

RANGE (2)
the feet of the ox and the donkey **r** free. Is 32:20
which **r** through the whole earth." Zec 4:10

RANGES (1)
He **r** the mountains as his pasture, and Jb 39:8

RANK (3)
Jew was second in **r** to King Ahasuerus, Est 10:3
no king, yet all of them march in **r**; Prv 30:27
the captain of fifty and the man of **r**, the Is 3:3

RANKS (10)
He stood and shouted to the **r** of Israel, 1 Sm 17:8
said, "I defy the **r** of Israel this day. 1 Sm 17:10
and ran to the **r** and went and greeted 1 Sm 17:22
up out of the **r** of the Philistines and 1 Sm 17:23
whoever approaches the **r** is to be 2 Kgs 11:8
army, "Bring her out between the **r**, 2 Kgs 11:15
them, "Bring her out between the **r**, 2 Chr 23:14
north, and there is no straggler in his **r**. Is 14:31
said, 'He who comes after me **r** before me, Jn 1:15
'After me comes a man who **r** before me, Jn 1:30

RANSOM (17)
If a **r** is imposed on him, then he shall Ex 21:30
then each shall give a **r** for his life to Ex 30:12
you shall accept no **r** for the life of a Nm 35:31
you shall accept no **r** for him who has Nm 35:32
down into the pit; I have found a **r**; Jb 33:24
not the greatness of the **r** turn you aside. Jb 36:18

bountifully will also **r** bountifully. 2 Cor 9:6
for whatever one sows, that will he also **r**. Gal 6:7
flesh will from the flesh **r** corruption, Gal 6:8
Spirit will from the Spirit **r** eternal life. Gal 6:8
of doing good, for in due season we will **r**, Gal 6:9
on the cloud, "Put in your sickle, and **r**, Rv 14:15
and reap, for the hour to **r** has come, Rv 14:15

REAPED (4)
in that land and **r** in the same year Gn 26:12
have sown wheat and have **r** thorns; Jer 12:13
plowed iniquity; you have **r** injustice; Hos 10:13
across the earth, and the earth was **r**. Rv 14:16

REAPER (5)
with which the **r** does not fill his hand Ps 129:7
be as when the **r** gathers standing grain Is 17:5
the open field, like sheaves after the **r**, Jer 9:22
shall overtake the **r** and the treader Am 9:13
so that sower and **r** may rejoice together. Jn 4:36

REAPERS (9)
went and gleaned in the field after the **r**, Ru 2:3
And he said to the **r**, "The LORD be with Ru 2:4
young man who was in charge of the **r**, Ru 2:5
who was in charge of the **r** answered, Ru 2:6
and gather among the sheaves after the **r**.' Ru 2:7
in the wine." So she sat beside the **r**, Ru 2:14
out one day to his father among the **r**. 2 Kgs 4:18
and at harvest time I will tell the **r**, Mt 13:30
close of the age, and the **r** are angels. Mt 13:39

REAPING (4)
your eyes be on the field that they are **r**, Ru 2:9
of Beth-shemesh were **r** their wheat 1 Sm 6:13
a hard man, **r** where you did not sow, Mt 25:24
I did not deposit and **r** what I did not Lk 19:22

REAPS (2)
Already the one who **r** is receiving wages Jn 4:36
holds true, 'One sows and another **r**.' Jn 4:37

REAR (21)
And for the **r** of the tabernacle Ex 26:22
for corners of the tabernacle in the **r**; Ex 26:23
side of the tabernacle at the **r** westward. Ex 26:27
For the **r** of the tabernacle westward he Ex 36:27
for corners of the tabernacle in the **r**. Ex 36:28
of the tabernacle at the **r** westward. Ex 36:32
acting as the **r** guard of all the camps, Nm 10:25
and the **r** guard was walking after the Jos 6:9
and the **r** guard was walking after the Jos 6:13
of the city and its **r** guard west of the Jos 8:13
your enemies; attack their **r** guard. Jos 10:19
were passing on in the **r** with Achish, 1 Sm 29:2
go around to their **r**, and come 2 Sm 5:23
him both in front and in the **r**, 2 Sm 10:9
twenty cubits of the **r** of the house 1 Kgs 6:16
and all their **r** parts were inward. 1 Kgs 7:25
him both in front and in the **r**, 1 Chr 19:10
and all their **r** parts were inward. 2 Chr 4:4
the God of Israel will be your **r** guard. Is 52:12
glory of the LORD shall be your **r** guard. Is 58:8
sea, and his **r** guard into the western sea; Jl 2:20

REARED (3)
"Children have I **r** and brought up, Is 1:2
I have neither **r** young men nor brought Is 23:4
the midst of young lions she **r** her cubs. Ezk 19:2

REASON (52)
in the land by **r** of the famine that Gn 41:31
Canaan languished by **r** of the famine. Gn 47:13
but you shall **r** frankly with your Lv 19:17
because he sinned by **r** of the dead Nm 6:11
And you shall bear no sin by **r** of it, Nm 18:32
And this is the **r** why Joshua circumcised Jos 5:4
For this **r** he has not come to the 1 Sm 20:29
And this was the **r** why he lifted up 1 Kgs 11:27
LORD and said, "Does Job fear God for no **r**? Jb 1:9
me against him to destroy him without **r**." Jb 2:3
seventy, or even by **r** of strength eighty; Ps 90:10
let us ambush the innocent without **r**; Prv 1:11
Do not contend with a man for no **r**, Prv 3:30
"Come now, let us **r** together, says the Is 1:18
of branches by **r** of abundant water. Ezk 19:10
eyes to heaven, and my **r** returned to me, Dn 4:34
At the same time my **r** returned to me, Dn 4:36
by **r** of the vision pains have come Dn 10:16
them, "Is this not the **r** you are wrong, Mk 12:24
so that they might find a **r** to accuse him. Lk 6:7
The **r** why you do not hear them is that Jn 8:47
For this **r** the Father loves me, because I Jn 10:17
The **r** why the crowd went to meet him Jn 12:18
for. What is the **r** for your coming?" Acts 10:21
I would have **r** to accept your Acts 18:14
to know the real **r** why he was being Acts 22:30
For this **r** the Jews seized me in the Acts 26:21
because there was no **r** for the death Acts 28:18
For this **r**, therefore, I have asked to Acts 28:20
For this **r** God gave them up to Rom 1:26
For the same **r** you also pay taxes, for Rom 13:6
one who has no **r** to pass judgment Rom 14:22
I have **r** to be proud of my work for Rom 15:17
This is the **r** why I have so often been Rom 15:22
For this **r** I write these things while I 2 Cor 13:10
and then his **r** to boast will be in himself Gal 6:4
For this **r**, because I have heard of your Eph 1:15
For this **r** I, Paul, a prisoner for Christ Eph 3:1
For this **r** I bow my knees before the Eph 3:14
though I myself have **r** for confidence in Phil 3:4
else thinks he has **r** for confidence in Phil 3:4
puffed up without **r** by his sensuous Col 2:18
For this **r**, when I could bear it no 1 Thes 3:5
for this **r**, brothers, in all our distress 1 Thes 3:7
But I received mercy for this **r**, that in 1 Tm 1:16
For this **r** I remind you to fan into 2 Tm 1:6
pure, then peaceable, gentle, open to **r**, Jas 3:17
who asks you for a **r** for the hope that is 1 Pt 3:15
For this very **r**, make every effort to 2 Pt 1:5
The **r** why the world does not know us is 1 Jn 3:1
The **r** the Son of God appeared was to 1 Jn 3:8
For this **r** her plagues will come in a Rv 18:8

REASONABLENESS (1)
Let your **r** be known to everyone. The Phil 4:5

REASONED (6)
Sabbath days he **r** with them from Acts 17:2
So he **r** in the synagogue with the Acts 17:17
And he **r** in the synagogue every Acts 18:4
the synagogue and **r** with the Jews. Acts 18:19
And as he **r** about righteousness and Acts 24:25
thought like a child, I **r** like a child. 1 Cor 13:11

REASONING (3)
But Jesus, knowing the **r** of their hearts, Lk 9:47
r and persuading them about the Acts 19:8
him, **r** daily in the hall of Tyrannus. Acts 19:9

REASSURE (1)
of the truth and **r** our heart before him; 1 Jn 3:19

REBA (2)
slain, Evi, Rekem, Zur, Hur, and **R**, Nm 31:8
and Rekem and Zur and Hur and **R**, Jos 13:21

REBECCA (1)
but also when **R** had conceived Rom 9:10

REBEKAH (28)
(Bethuel fathered **R**.) These eight Gn 22:23
R, who was born to Bethuel the son of Gn 24:15
R had a brother whose name was Gn 24:29
and heard the words of **R** his sister, Gn 24:30
R came out with her water jar on her Gn 24:45
Behold, **R** is before you; take her and Gn 24:51
and garments, and gave them to **R**. Gn 24:53
And they called **R** and said to her, Gn 24:58
So they sent away **R** their sister and her Gn 24:59
And they blessed **R** and said to her, Gn 24:60
Then **R** and her young women arose Gn 24:61
Thus the servant took **R** and went his Gn 24:61
And **R** lifted up her eyes, and when she Gn 24:64
tent of Sarah his mother and took **R**, Gn 24:67
years old when he took **R** to be his wife, Gn 25:20
his prayer, and **R** his wife conceived. Gn 25:21
he ate of his game, but **R** loved Jacob. Gn 25:28
kill me because of **R**," because she was Gn 26:7
and saw Isaac laughing with **R** his wife. Gn 26:8
they made life bitter for Isaac and **R**. Gn 26:35
Now **R** was listening when Isaac spoke Gn 27:5
R said to her son Jacob, "I heard your Gn 27:6
But Jacob said to **R** his mother, Gn 27:11
Then **R** took the best garments of Esau Gn 27:15
of Esau her older son were told to **R**. Gn 27:42
Then **R** said to Isaac, "I loathe my life Gn 27:46
Bethuel the Aramean, the brother of **R**, Gn 28:5
There they buried Isaac and **R** his wife, Gn 49:31

REBEKAH'S (2)
kinsman, and that he was **R** son, Gn 29:12
And Deborah, **R** nurse, died, and she Gn 35:8

REBEL (14)
obey his voice; do not **r** against him, Ex 23:21
Only do not **r** against the LORD. And do Nm 14:9
And if you too **r** against the LORD today Jos 22:18
Only do not **r** against the LORD or make Jos 22:19
us that we should **r** against the LORD Jos 22:29
voice and not **r** against the 1 Sm 12:14
but **r** against the commandment of 1 Sm 12:15
says it, that you and the Jews intend to **r**; Neh 6:6
"There are those who **r** against the light, Jb 24:13
dark; they did not **r** against his words. Ps 105:28
struck down? Why will you continue to **r**? Is 1:5
but if you refuse and **r**, you shall be eaten Is 1:20
that from before birth you were called a **r**. Is 48:8
gash themselves; they **r** against me. Hos 7:14

REBELLED (43)
but in the thirteenth year they **r**. Gn 14:4
because you **r** against my command Nm 20:24
because you **r** against my word in the Nm 27:14
but **r** against the command of the LORD Dt 1:26
but you **r** against the command of the Dt 1:43
then you **r** against the commandment of Dt 9:23
death of Ahab, Moab **r** against Israel. 2 Kgs 1:1
the king of Moab **r** against the king of 2 Kgs 3:5
"The king of Moab has **r** against me. 2 Kgs 3:7
He **r** against the king of Assyria and 2 Kgs 18:7
trust, that you have **r** against me? 2 Kgs 18:20
Then he turned and **r** against him. 2 Kgs 24:1
And Zedekiah **r** against the king of 2 Kgs 24:20
David, rose up and **r** against his lord, 2 Chr 13:6
He also **r** against King 2 Chr 36:13
were disobedient and **r** against you and Neh 9:26
them out, for they have **r** against you. Ps 5:10
How often they **r** against him in the Ps 78:40
Yet they tested and **r** against the Most Ps 78:56
of your steadfast love, but **r** by the Sea, Ps 106:7
for they had **r** against the words of Ps 107:11
brought up, but they have **r** against me. Is 1:2
now trust, that you have **r** against me? Is 36:5
But they **r** and grieved his Holy Spirit; Is 63:10
of the men who have **r** against me. Is 66:24
that you **r** against the LORD your God Jer 3:13
around, because she has **r** against me, Jer 4:17
And Zedekiah **r** against the king of Jer 52:3
the right, for I have **r** against his word; Lam 1:18
"We have transgressed and **r**, and you Lam 3:42
nations of rebels, who have **r** against me. Ezk 2:3
And she has **r** against my rules by doing Ezk 5:6
But he **r** against him by sending his Ezk 17:15
But they **r** against me and were not Ezk 20:8
the house of Israel **r** against me in the Ezk 20:13
But the children **r** against me. They Ezk 20:21
done wrong and acted wickedly and **r**, Dn 9:5
forgiveness, for we have **r** against him Dn 9:9
to them, for they have **r** against me! Hos 7:13
my covenant and **r** against my law. Hos 8:1
because she has **r** against her God; Hos 13:16
deeds by which you have **r** against me; Zep 3:11
who were those who heard and yet **r**? Heb 3:16

REBELLING (2)
are doing? Are you **r** against the king?" Neh 2:19
r against the Most High in the desert. Ps 78:17

REBELLION (16)
because he has taught **r** against the LORD Dt 13:5
an altar this day in **r** against the LORD? Jos 22:16
If it was in **r** or in breach of faith Jos 22:22
For **r** is as the sin of divination, and 1 Sm 15:23
has been in **r** against the house 1 Kgs 12:19
has been in **r** against the house 2 Chr 10:19
and that **r** and sedition have been made Ezr 4:19
For he adds **r** to his sin; he claps his Jb 34:37
An evil man seeks only **r**, and a cruel Prv 17:11
you have uttered **r** against the LORD.'" Jer 28:16
for he has spoken **r** against the LORD.'" Jer 29:32
all the guilt of their sin and **r** against me. Jer 33:8
not come, unless the **r** comes first, 2 Thes 2:3
do not harden your hearts as in the **r**, on Heb 3:8
do not harden your hearts as in the **r**." Heb 3:15
error and perished in Korah's **r**. Jude 1:11

REBELLIOUS (37)
place, you have been **r** against the LORD. Dt 9:7
You have been **r** against the LORD from Dt 9:24
has a stubborn and **r** son who will not Dt 21:18
city, 'This our son is stubborn and **r**; Dt 21:20
For I know how **r** and stubborn you Dt 31:27
you, you have been **r** against the LORD. Dt 31:27
"You son of a perverse, **r** woman, 1 Sm 20:30
are rebuilding that **r** and wicked city. Ezr 4:12
and learn that this city is a **r** city, Ezr 4:15
nations—let not the **r** exalt themselves. Ps 66:7
but the **r** dwell in a parched land. Ps 68:6
gifts among men, even among the **r**, Ps 68:18
fathers, a stubborn and **r** generation, Ps 78:8
but they were **r** in their purposes and Ps 106:43
For they are a **r** people, lying children, Is 30:9
GOD has opened my ear, and I was not **r**; Is 50:5
out my hands all the day to a **r** people, Is 65:2
this people has a stubborn and **r** heart; Jer 5:23
They are all stubbornly **r**, going about Jer 6:28
within me, because I have been very **r**. Lam 1:20
(for they are a **r** house) they will know Ezk 2:5
at their looks, for they are a **r** house. Ezk 2:6
or refuse to hear, for they are a **r** house. Ezk 2:7
Be not **r** like that rebellious house; open Ezk 2:8
Be not rebellious like that **r** house; open Ezk 2:8
at their looks, for they are a **r** house." Ezk 3:9
to reprove them, for they are a **r** house. Ezk 3:26
let him refuse, for they are a **r** house. Ezk 3:27
you dwell in the midst of a **r** house, Ezk 12:2

but hear not, for they are a **r** house. Ezk 12:2
understand, though they are a **r** house. Ezk 12:3
has not the house of Israel, the **r** house, Ezk 12:9
delayed, but in your days, O **r** house, Ezk 12:25
"Say now to the **r** house, Do you not Ezk 17:12
utter a parable to the **r** house and say to Ezk 24:3
And say to the **r** house, to the house of Ezk 44:6
Woe to her who is **r** and defiled, the Zep 3:1

REBELS (10)
to be kept as a sign for the **r**, Nm 17:10
and he said to them, "Hear now, you **r**: Nm 20:10
Whoever **r** against your commandment Jos 1:18
or make us as **r** by building for Jos 22:19
Your princes are **r** and companions of Is 1:23
But **r** and sinners shall be broken Is 1:28
you to the people of Israel, to nations of **r**, Ezk 2:3
I will purge out the **r** from among you, Ezk 20:38
them no more; all their princes are **r**. Hos 9:15
And among the **r** in prison, who had Mk 15:7

REBUILD (18)
is in Judah, and **r** the house of the LORD, Ezr 1:3
stirred to go up to **r** the house of the LORD Ezr 1:5
arose and began to **r** the house of God Ezr 5:2
the elders of the Jews **r** this house of God Ezr 6:7
of my fathers' graves, that I may **r** it." Neh 2:5
we will not be able to **r** the wall." Neh 4:10
If he tears down, none can **r**; if he shuts Jb 12:14
of Israel, and **r** them as they were at first. Jer 33:7
raise up its ruins and **r** it as in the days Am 9:11
and they shall **r** the ruined cities and Am 9:14
has not yet come to **r** the house of the Hg 1:2
shattered but we will **r** the ruins," the Mal 1:4
of God, and to **r** it in three days.'" Mt 26:61
destroy the temple and **r** it in three Mt 27:40
destroy the temple and **r** it in three Mk 15:29
and I will **r** the tent of David that has Acts 15:16
that has fallen; I will **r** its ruins, Acts 15:16
For if I **r** what I tore down, I prove Gal 2:18

REBUILDING (5)
him and of the **r** of the house of 2 Chr 24:27
They are **r** that rebellious and wicked Ezr 4:12
and we are **r** the house that was built Ezr 5:11
Cyrus the king for the **r** of this house of Ezr 5:17
of the Jews for the **r** of this house of God. Ezr 6:8

REBUILDS (1)
be the man who rises up and **r** this city, Jos 6:26

REBUILT (26)
And he **r** the city and settled in it. Jos 19:50
Then they **r** the city and lived in it. Jgs 18:28
their inheritance and **r** the towns and Jgs 21:23
so Solomon **r** Gezer) and Lower 1 Kgs 9:17
For he **r** the high places that 2 Kgs 21:3
Solomon **r** the cities that Hiram had 2 Chr 8:2
For he **r** the high places that his 2 Chr 33:3
if this city is **r** and the walls finished, Ezr 4:13
if this city is **r** and its walls finished, Ezr 4:16
to cease, and that this city be not **r**, Ezr 4:21
that this house of God should be **r**. Ezr 5:13
and let the house of God be **r** on its site." Ezr 5:15
of God at Jerusalem, let the house be **r**, Ezr 6:3
They **r** it and set its doors, its bolts, and Neh 3:13
He **r** it and set its doors, its bolts, and its Neh 3:14
He **r** it and covered it and set its doors, Neh 3:15
it were few, and no houses had been **r**. Neh 7:4
of the earth who **r** ruins for themselves, Jb 3:14
palace is a city no more; it will never be **r**. Is 25:2
And your ancient ruins shall be **r**; you Is 58:12
the city shall be **r** on its mound, and Jer 30:18
the city shall be **r** for the LORD from Jer 31:38
You shall never be **r**, for I am the Ezk 26:14
be inhabited and the waste places **r**. Ezk 36:10
and the waste places shall be **r**. Ezk 36:33
I have **r** the ruined places and Ezk 36:36

REBUKE (47)
it for her to glean, and do not **r** her." Ru 2:16
were laid bare, at the **r** of the LORD, 2 Sm 22:16
This day is a day of distress, of **r**, 2 Kgs 19:3
and will **r** the words that the LORD 2 Kgs 19:4
God of our fathers see and **r** you." 1 Chr 12:17
He will surely **r** you if in secret you Jb 13:10
tremble and are astounded at his **r**. Jb 26:11
O LORD, **r** me not in your anger, nor Ps 6:1
of the world were laid bare at your **r**, Ps 18:15
O LORD, **r** me not in your anger, nor Ps 38:1
Not for your sacrifices do I **r** you; your Ps 50:8
But now I **r** you and lay the charge Ps 50:21
R the beasts that dwell among the reeds, Ps 68:30
At your **r**, O God of Jacob, both rider and Ps 76:6
may they perish at the **r** of your face! Ps 80:16
disciplines the nations, does he not **r**? Ps 94:10
At your **r** they fled; at the sound of your Ps 104:7
You **r** the insolent, accursed ones, who Ps 119:21
let him **r** me—it is oil for my head; Ps 141:5
but a scoffer does not listen to **r**. Prv 13:1
A **r** goes deeper into a man of Prv 17:10
but those who **r** the wicked will have Prv 24:25
Better is open **r** than hidden love. Prv 27:5
lest he **r** you and you be found a liar. Prv 30:6
a man to hear the **r** of the wise than to Eccl 7:5
of many waters, but he will **r** them, Is 17:13
'This day is a day of distress, of **r**, Is 37:3
and will **r** the words that the LORD your Is 37:4
Behold, by my **r** I dry up the sea, I make Is 50:2
the wrath of the LORD, the **r** of your God. Is 51:20
not be angry with you, and will not **r** you. Is 54:9
in fury, and his **r** with flames of fire. Is 66:15
the LORD said to Satan, "The LORD **r** you, Zec 3:2
LORD who has chosen Jerusalem **r** you! Zec 3:2
Behold, I will **r** your offspring, and Mal 2:3
I will **r** the devourer for you, so that it Mal 3:11
took him aside and began to **r** him, Mt 16:22
took him aside and began to **r** him. Mk 8:32
If your brother sins, **r** him, and if he Lk 17:3
to him, "Teacher, **r** your disciples." Lk 19:39
Do not **r** an older man but encourage 1 Tm 5:1
in sin, **r** them in the presence of all, 1 Tm 5:20
reprove, **r**, and exhort, with complete 2 Tm 4:2
and also to **r** those who contradict Ti 1:9
Therefore **r** them sharply, that they may Ti 1:13
things; exhort and **r** with all authority. Ti 2:15
judgment, but said, "The Lord **r** you." Jude 1:9

REBUKED (30)
of my hands and **r** you last night." Gn 31:42
his father **r** him and said to him, Gn 37:10
them; he **r** kings on their account, 1 Chr 16:21
"Man is also **r** with pain on his bed and Jb 33:19
You have **r** the nations; you have made Ps 9:5
been stricken and **r** every morning. Ps 73:14
them; he **r** kings on their account, Ps 105:14
He **r** the Red Sea, and it became dry, and Ps 106:9
have you not **r** Jeremiah of Anathoth Jer 29:27
Then he rose and **r** the winds and the Mt 8:26
And Jesus **r** him, and the demon came Mt 17:18
and pray. The disciples **r** the people, Mt 19:13
The crowd **r** them, telling them to be Mt 20:31
But Jesus **r** him, saying, "Be silent, and Mk 1:25
And he awoke and **r** the wind and said Mk 4:39
seeing his disciples, he **r** Peter and said, Mk 8:33
together, he **r** the unclean spirit, Mk 9:25
touch them, and the disciples **r** them. Mk 10:13
And many **r** him, telling him to be Mk 10:48
and he **r** them for their unbelief and Mk 16:14
But Jesus **r** him, saying, "Be silent and Lk 4:35
And he stood over her and **r** the fever, Lk 4:39
of God!" But he **r** them and would not Lk 4:41
And he awoke and **r** the wind and the Lk 8:24
But Jesus **r** the unclean spirit and healed Lk 9:42
But he turned and **r** them. Lk 9:55
when the disciples saw it, they **r** them. Lk 18:15
And those who were in front **r** him, Lk 18:39
But the other **r** him, saying, "Do you Lk 23:40
but was **r** for his own transgression; a 2 Pt 2:16

REBUKES (6)
not hear, and in whose mouth are no **r**. Ps 38:14
you discipline a man with **r** for sin, Ps 39:11
Whoever **r** a man will afterward find Prv 28:23
and with furious **r**—I am the LORD, Ezk 5:15
vengeance on them with wrathful **r**. Ezk 25:17
He **r** the sea and makes it dry; he dries up Na 1:4

RECAH (1)
of Ir-nahash. These are the men of **R**. 1 Chr 4:12

RECALL (3)
this and stand firm, **r** it to mind, Is 46:8
But **r** the former days when, after you Heb 10:32
be able at any time to **r** these things. 2 Pt 1:15

RECALLING (1)
of the house of Israel, **r** their iniquity, Ezk 29:16

RECEDED (1)
and the waters **r** from the earth Gn 8:3

RECEIVE (130)
its mouth to **r** your brother's blood Gn 4:11
him you shall **r** the contribution for Ex 25:2
that you shall **r** from them: Ex 25:3
You shall make pots for it to **r** its ashes, Ex 27:3
They shall **r** gold, blue and purple and Ex 28:5
which you **r** from the people of Israel. Nm 18:28
up the mountain to **r** the tablets of stone, Dt 9:9
destruction and should **r** no mercy but Jos 11:20
broken up there, and you shall **r** it. 1 Kgs 5:9
was too small to **r** the burnt offering 1 Kgs 8:64
I will **r** none." And he urged him to 2 Kgs 5:16
Levites when the Levites **r** the tithes. Neh 10:38
Shall we **r** good from God, and shall we Jb 2:10
and shall we not **r** evil?" In all this Job Jb 2:10
Why did the knees **r** me? Or why the Jb 3:12
R instruction from his mouth, and lay Jb 22:22
heritage that oppressors **r** from the Jb 27:13
him? Or what does he **r** from your hand? Jb 35:7
He will **r** blessing from the LORD and Ps 24:5
the power of Sheol, for he will **r** me. Ps 49:15
and afterward you will **r** me to glory. Ps 73:24
to **r** instruction in wise dealing, in Prv 1:3
if you **r** my words and treasure up my Prv 2:1
wise of heart will **r** commandments, Prv 10:8
and let your ear **r** the word of his mouth; Jer 9:20
they might not hear and **r** instruction. Jer 17:23
they have not listened to **r** instruction. Jer 32:33
Will you not **r** instruction and listen to Jer 35:13
land of Benjamin to **r** his portion there Jer 37:12
that I shall speak to you **r** in your heart, Ezk 3:10
you shall **r** from me gifts and rewards Dn 2:6
the Most High shall **r** the kingdom and Dn 7:18
they stumble, they shall **r** a little help. Dn 11:34
are the merciful, for they shall **r** mercy. Mt 5:7
And if anyone will not **r** you or listen to Mt 10:14
is a prophet will **r** a prophet's reward, Mt 10:41
righteous person will **r** a righteous Mt 10:41
the blind **r** their sight and the lame Mt 11:5
them, "Not everyone can **r** this saying, Mt 19:11
the one who is able to **r** this receive it." Mt 19:12
the one who is able to receive this **r** it." Mt 19:12
will **r** a hundredfold and will inherit Mt 19:29
came, they thought they would **r** more, Mt 20:10
whatever you ask in prayer, you will **r**, Mt 21:22
the word, immediately **r** it with joy. Mk 4:16
if any place will not **r** you and they will Mk 6:11
whoever does not **r** the kingdom of Mk 10:15
who will not **r** a hundredfold now in Mk 10:30
They will **r** the greater Mk 12:40
lend to those from whom you expect to **r**, Lk 6:34
seen and heard: the blind **r** their sight, Lk 7:22
when they hear the word, **r** it with joy. Lk 8:13
And wherever they do not **r** you, when Lk 9:5
But the people did not **r** him, because his Lk 9:53
you enter a town and they **r** you, Lk 10:8
you enter a town and they do not **r** you, Lk 10:10
to his will, will **r** a severe beating. Lk 12:47
a beating, will **r** a light beating. Lk 12:48
people may **r** me into their houses.' Lk 16:4
it fails they may **r** you into the eternal Lk 16:9
whoever does not **r** the kingdom of God Lk 18:17
who will not **r** many times more in this Lk 18:30
a far country to **r** for himself a Lk 19:12
They will **r** the greater condemnation." Lk 20:47
own, and his own people did not **r** him. Jn 1:11
But to all who did **r** him, who believed in Jn 1:12
seen, but you do not **r** our testimony. Jn 3:11
"A person cannot **r** even one thing unless Jn 3:27
that the testimony that I **r** is from man, Jn 5:34
I do not **r** glory from people. Jn 5:41
my Father's name, and you do not **r** me. Jn 5:43
comes in his own name, you will **r** him. Jn 5:43
when you **r** glory from one another and Jn 5:44
those who believed in him were to **r**, Jn 7:39
me and does not **r** my words has a Jn 12:48
of truth, whom the world cannot **r**, Jn 14:17
Ask, and you will **r**, that your joy may Jn 16:24
and said to them, "**R** the Holy Spirit. Jn 20:22
But you will **r** power when the Holy Acts 1:8
and you will **r** the gift of the Holy Acts 2:38
to go into the temple, he asked to **r** alms. Acts 3:3
expecting to **r** something from them. Acts 3:5
whom heaven must **r** until the time Acts 3:21
he called out, "Lord Jesus, **r** my spirit." Acts 7:59
them that they might **r** the Holy Spirit, Acts 8:15
I lay my hands may **r** the Holy Spirit." Acts 8:19
"Did you **r** the Holy Spirit when you Acts 19:2
'It is more blessed to give than to **r**.'" Acts 20:35
to me, 'Brother Saul, **r** your sight.' Acts 22:13
that they may **r** forgiveness of sins Acts 26:18
will those who **r** the abundance of Rom 5:17
For you did not **r** the spirit of slavery Rom 8:15
to you they also may now **r** mercy. Rom 11:31
is good, and you will **r** his approval, Rom 13:3
and each will **r** his wages according to 1 Cor 3:8
survives, he will **r** a reward. 1 Cor 3:14
each one will **r** his commendation 1 Cor 4:5
What do you have that you did not **r**? 1 Cor 4:7
why do you boast as if you did not **r** it? 1 Cor 4:7
They do it to **r** a perishable wreath, 1 Cor 9:25
that each one may **r** what is due for 2 Cor 5:10
appeal to you not to **r** the grace of God 2 Cor 6:1
or if you **r** a different spirit from the 2 Cor 11:4
For I did not **r** it from any man, nor was Gal 1:12
Did you **r** the Spirit by works of the law Gal 3:2
so that we might **r** the promised Spirit Gal 3:14
law, so that we might **r** adoption as sons. Gal 4:5
does, this he will **r** back from the Lord, Eph 6:8
So **r** him in the Lord with all joy, and Phil 2:29

the Lord you will **r** the inheritance as Col 3:24
r him as you would receive me. Phlm 1:17
receive him as you would **r** me. Phlm 1:17
that we may **r** mercy and find grace to Heb 4:16
of Levi who **r** the priestly office Heb 7:5
are called may **r** the promised eternal Heb 9:15
of God you may **r** what is promised. Heb 10:36
that he was to **r** as an inheritance. Heb 11:8
speaking, he did **r** him back. Heb 11:19
faith, did not **r** what was promised, Heb 11:39
suppose that he will **r** anything from the Jas 1:7
stood the test he will **r** the crown of life, Jas 1:12
wickedness and **r** with meekness Jas 1:21
You ask and do not **r**, because you ask Jas 4:3
you will **r** the unfading crown of glory. 1 Pt 5:4
and whatever we ask we **r** from him, 1 Jn 3:22
If we **r** the testimony of men, the 1 Jn 5:9
do not **r** him into your house or give 2 Jn 1:10
God, to **r** glory and honor and power, Rv 4:11
to **r** power and wealth and wisdom and Rv 5:12
but they are to **r** authority as kings for Rv 17:12

RECEIVED (133)
I **r** your money." Then he brought Gn 43:23
And he **r** the gold from their hand and Ex 32:4
And they **r** from Moses all the Ex 36:3
Behold, I **r** a command to bless: he Nm 23:20
and Eleazar the priest **r** from them the Nm 31:51
and Eleazar the priest **r** the gold from Nm 31:54
houses have **r** their inheritance, Nm 34:14
the half-tribe have **r** their inheritance Nm 34:15
and the Gadites **r** their inheritance, Jos 13:8
that the people of Israel **r** in the land of Jos 14:1
and Ephraim, **r** their inheritance. Jos 16:4
daughters of Manasseh **r** an inheritance Jos 17:6
of Manasseh have **r** their inheritance Jos 18:7
of Aaron the priest **r** by lot from the Jos 21:4
rest of the Kohathites **r** by lot from the Jos 21:5
The Gershonites **r** by lot from the clans Jos 21:6
according to their clans **r** from the tribe Jos 21:7
Then David **r** from her hand what 1 Sm 25:35
avenged the insult I **r** at the hand of 1 Sm 25:39
the king's traders **r** them from Kue 1 Kgs 10:28
Hezekiah **r** the letter from the hand 2 Kgs 19:14
you." Then David **r** them and made 1 Chr 12:18
the wounds that he had **r** at Ramah, 2 Chr 22:6
and the priests **r** the blood and 2 Chr 29:22
the blood that they **r** from the hand 2 Chr 30:16
blood that they **r** from them while 2 Chr 35:11
me stealthily; my ear **r** the whisper of it. Jb 4:12
it; I looked and **r** instruction. Prv 24:32
Hezekiah **r** the letter from the hand of Is 37:14
that she has **r** from the LORD'S hand Is 40:2
King Zedekiah sent for him and **r** him. Jer 37:17
Jeremiah the prophet and **r** him at the Jer 38:14
And Darius the Mede **r** the kingdom, Dn 5:31
and to your sisters, "You have **r** mercy." Hos 2:1
'The wounds I **r** in the house of my Zec 13:6
I say to you, they have **r** their reward. Mt 6:2
I say to you, they have **r** their reward. Mt 6:5
I say to you, they have **r** their reward. Mt 6:16
You **r** without paying; give without pay. Mt 10:8
hour came, each of them **r** a denarius. Mt 20:9
but each of them also **r** a denarius. Mt 20:10
He who had **r** the five talents went at Mt 25:16
But he who had **r** the one talent went Mt 25:18
And he who had **r** the five talents came Mt 25:20
He also who had **r** the one talent came Mt 25:24
coming I should have **r** what was my Mt 25:27
in prayer, believe that you have **r** it, Mk 11:24
And the guards **r** him with blows. Mk 14:65
rich, for you have **r** your consolation. Lk 6:24
because he has **r** him back safe and Lk 15:27
in your lifetime **r** your good things, Lk 16:25
and came down and **r** him joyfully. Lk 19:6
he returned, having **r** the kingdom, Lk 19:15
And from his fullness we have all **r**, Jn 1:16
So I went and washed and **r** my sight." Jn 9:11
again asked him how he had **r** his sight. Jn 9:15
he had been blind and had **r** his sight, Jn 9:18
parents of the man who had **r** his sight Jn 9:18
This charge I have **r** from my Father." Jn 10:18
and they have **r** them and have come to Jn 17:8
When Jesus had **r** the sour wine, he Jn 19:30
and having **r** from the Father the Acts 2:33
So those who **r** his word were baptized, Acts 2:41
they **r** their food with glad and Acts 2:46
He **r** living oracles to give to us. Acts 7:38
you who **r** the law as delivered by Acts 7:53
heard that Samaria had **r** the word of Acts 8:14
on them and they **r** the Holy Spirit. Acts 8:17
who have **r** the Holy Spirit just as we Acts 10:47
the Gentiles also had **r** the word of God. Acts 11:1
Having **r** this order, he put them into Acts 16:24
and Jason has **r** them, and they are all Acts 17:7
they **r** the word with all eagerness, Acts 17:11
the ministry that I **r** from the Lord Acts 20:24
to Jerusalem, the brothers **r** us gladly. Acts 21:17
From them I **r** letters to the brothers, Acts 22:5
at that very hour I **r** my sight and saw Acts 22:13
who **r** us and entertained us Acts 28:7
"We have **r** no letters from Judea Acts 28:21
whom we have **r** grace and apostleship Rom 1:5
by his blood, to be **r** by faith. Rom 3:25
He **r** the sign of circumcision as a seal Rom 4:11
whom we have now **r** reconciliation. Rom 5:11
but you have **r** the Spirit of adoption Rom 8:15
but now have **r** mercy because of Rom 11:30
Now we have **r** not the spirit of the 1 Cor 2:12
If then you **r** it, why do you boast as if 1 Cor 4:7
For I **r** from the Lord what I also 1 Cor 11:23
gospel I preached to you, which you **r**, 1 Cor 15:1
as of first importance what I also **r**: 1 Cor 15:3
felt that we had **r** the sentence of death. 2 Cor 1:9
how you **r** him with fear and 2 Cor 7:15
a different spirit from the one you **r**, 2 Cor 11:4
Five times I **r** at the hands of the 2 Cor 11:24
to you a gospel contrary to the one you **r**, Gal 1:9
but I **r** it through a revelation of Jesus Gal 1:12
despise me, but **r** me as an angel of God, Gal 4:14
you have learned and **r** and heard and Phil 4:9
I have **r** full payment, and more. I am Phil 4:18
having **r** from Epaphroditus the gifts Phil 4:18
Therefore, as you **r** Christ Jesus the Lord, Col 2:6
whom you have **r** instructions—if Col 4:10
ministry that you have **r** in the Lord." Col 4:17
for you **r** the word in much affliction, 1 Thes 1:6
that when you **r** the word of God, 1 Thes 2:13
that as you **r** from us how you ought 1 Thes 4:1
with the tradition that you **r** from us. 2 Thes 3:6
But I **r** mercy because I had acted 1 Tm 1:13
But I **r** mercy for this reason, that in 1 Tm 1:16
created to be **r** with thanksgiving by 1 Tm 4:3
be rejected if it is **r** with thanksgiving, 1 Tm 4:4
transgression or disobedience **r** a just Heb 2:2
and those who formerly **r** the good news Heb 4:6
descent from them **r** tithes from Heb 7:6
the one case tithes are **r** by mortal men, Heb 7:8
(for under it the people **r** the law), Heb 7:11
the people of old **r** their commendation. Heb 11:2
faith Sarah herself **r** power to Heb 11:11
not having **r** the things promised, Heb 11:13
and he who had **r** the promises was in Heb 11:17
Women **r** back their dead by Heb 11:35
works when she **r** the messengers and Jas 2:25
once you had not **r** mercy, but now 1 Pt 2:10
mercy, but now you have **r** mercy. 1 Pt 2:10
As each has **r** a gift, use it to serve one 1 Pt 4:10
For when he **r** honor and glory from 2 Pt 1:17
anointing that you **r** from him abides 1 Jn 2:27
Demetrius has **r** a good testimony from 3 Jn 1:12
as I myself have **r** authority from my Rv 2:27
Remember, then, what you **r** and heard. Rv 3:3
kings who have not yet **r** royal power, Rv 17:12
deceived those who had **r** the mark of Rv 19:20
its image and had not **r** its mark on their Rv 20:4

RECEIVES (38)
besides what he **r** from the sale of his Dt 18:8
who **r** strangers instead of her Ezk 16:32
For everyone who asks **r**, and the one who Mt 7:8
"Whoever **r** you receives me, and Mt 10:40
"Whoever receives you **r** me, and Mt 10:40
and whoever **r** me receives him who Mt 10:40
whoever receives me **r** him who sent Mt 10:40
The one who **r** a prophet because he is Mt 10:41
and the one who **r** a righteous person Mt 10:41
the word and immediately **r** it with joy, Mt 13:20
"Whoever **r** one such child in my name Mt 18:5
one such child in my name **r** me, Mt 18:5
"Whoever **r** one such child in my Mk 9:37
one such child in my name **r** me, Mk 9:37
name receives me, and whoever **r** me, Mk 9:37
me, **r** not me but him who sent me." Mk 9:37
"Whoever **r** this child in my name Lk 9:48
receives this child in my name **r** me, Lk 9:48
and whoever **r** me receives him who sent Lk 9:48
and whoever receives me **r** him who sent Lk 9:48
For everyone who asks **r**, and the one Lk 11:10
"This man **r** sinners and eats with Lk 15:2
and heard, yet no one **r** his testimony. Jn 3:32
Whoever **r** his testimony sets his seal to Jn 3:33
If on the Sabbath a man **r** circumcision, Jn 7:23
whoever **r** the one I send receives me, Jn 13:20
whoever receives the one I send **r** me, Jn 13:20
and whoever **r** me receives the one who Jn 13:20
and whoever receives me **r** the one who Jn 13:20
believes in him **r** forgiveness of sins Acts 10:43
compete, but only one **r** the prize? 1 Cor 9:24
it is cultivated, **r** a blessing from God. Heb 6:7
even say that Levi himself, who **r** tithes, Heb 7:9
and chastises every son whom he **r**." Heb 12:6
it, until it **r** the early and the late rains. Jas 5:7
no one knows except the one who **r** it.' Rv 2:17
beast and its image and **r** a mark on his Rv 14:9
and whoever **r** the mark of its name." Rv 14:11

RECEIVING (12)
in your steps, **r** direction from you, Dt 33:3
in your train and **r** gifts among men, Ps 68:18
And on **r** it they grumbled at the Mt 20:11
for we are **r** the due reward of our deeds; Lk 23:41
one who reaps is **r** wages and gathering Jn 4:36
So, after **r** the morsel of bread, he Jn 13:30
and after **r** a command for Silas and Acts 17:15
in prison after **r** authority from the Acts 26:10
acts with men and **r** in themselves the Rom 1:27
partnership with me in giving and **r**, Phil 4:15
deliberately after **r** the knowledge Heb 10:26
us be grateful for **r** a kingdom that Heb 12:28

RECENT (1)
He must not be a **r** convert, or he may 1 Tm 3:6

RECENTLY (4)
known, to new gods that had come **r**, Dt 32:17
You **r** repented and did what was right Jer 34:15
r come from Italy with his wife Acts 18:2
who **r** stirred up a revolt and led the Acts 21:38

RECEPTION (1)
us the kind of **r** we had among you, 1 Thes 1:9

RECESSED (1)
for the house windows with **r** frames. 1 Kgs 6:4

RECESSES (3)
mountains, to the far **r** of Lebanon; 2 Kgs 19:23
of the sea, or walked in the **r** of the deep? Jb 38:16
the mountains, to the far **r** of Lebanon, Is 37:24

RECHAB (13)
Baanah, and the name of the other **R**, 2 Sm 4:2
Rimmon the Beerothite, **R** and Baanah, 2 Sm 4:5
Then **R** and Baanah his brother 2 Sm 4:6
But David answered **R** and Baanah his 2 Sm 4:9
the son of **R** coming to meet 2 Kgs 10:15
of Baal with Jehonadab the son of **R**, 2 Kgs 10:23
the father of the house of **R**. 1 Chr 2:55
Malchijah the son of **R**, ruler of the Neh 3:14
drink no wine, for Jonadab the son of **R**, Jer 35:6
obeyed the voice of Jonadab the son of **R**, Jer 35:8
Jonadab the son of **R** gave to his sons, Jer 35:14
Jonadab the son of **R** have kept the Jer 35:16
Jonadab the son of **R** shall never lack a Jer 35:19

RECHABITES (4)
the house of the **R** and speak with them Jer 35:2
all his sons and the whole house of the **R**. Jer 35:3
I set before the **R** pitchers full of wine, Jer 35:5
But to the house of the **R** Jeremiah said, Jer 35:18

RECITE (2)
memorial in a book and **r** it in the ears Ex 17:14
right have you to **r** my statutes or take Ps 50:16

RECITED (1)
Moses came and **r** all the words of this Dt 32:44

RECKLESS (4)
Abimelech hired worthless and **r** fellows, Jgs 9:4
from evil, but a fool is **r** and careless. Prv 14:16
he squandered his property in **r** living. Lk 15:13
treacherous, **r**, swollen with conceit, 2 Tm 3:4

RECKLESSNESS (1)
people astray by their lies and their **r**, Jer 23:32

RECKONING (3)
And for your lifeblood I will require a **r**: Gn 9:5
man I will require a **r** for the life of man. Gn 9:5
So now there comes a **r** for his blood." Gn 42:22

RECLINE (4)
east and west and **r** at table with Mt 8:11
for service and have them **r** at table, Lk 12:37
and **r** at table in the kingdom of God. Lk 13:29
the field, 'Come at once and **r** at table'? Lk 17:7

RECLINED (7)
And as Jesus **r** at table in the house, Mt 9:10
she poured it on his head as he **r** at table. Mt 26:7
evening, he **r** at table with the twelve. Mt 26:20
And as he **r** at table in his house, many Mk 2:15
with him, so he went in and **r** at table. Lk 11:37
one of those who **r** at table with him Lk 14:15
And when the hour came, he **r** at table, Lk 22:14

RECLINES (2)
one who **r** at table or one who serves? Lk 22:27
serves? Is it not the one who **r** at table? Lk 22:27

RECLINING (10)
sinners came and were **r** with Jesus and Mt 9:10
and sinners were **r** with Jesus and Mk 2:15
of Simon the leper, as he was **r** at table, Mk 14:3
And as they were **r** at table and eating, Mk 14:18

themselves as they were **r** at table, Mk 16:14
tax collectors and others **r** at table with Lk 5:29
she learned that he was **r** at table in the Lk 7:37
was one of those **r** with him at the Jn 12:2
Jesus loved, was **r** at table close to Jesus, Jn 13:23
the one who had been **r** at table close to Jn 21:20

RECOGNITION (1)
as well as yours. Give **r** to such men. 1 Cor 16:18

RECOGNIZE (11)
And he did not **r** him, because his Gn 27:23
his brothers, but they did not **r** him. Gn 42:8
but arose before one could **r** another. Ru 3:14
him from a distance, they did not **r** him. Jb 2:12
You will **r** them by their fruits. Are Mt 7:16
Thus you will **r** them by their fruits. Mt 7:20
already come, and they did not **r** him, Mt 17:12
they did not **r** him nor understand Acts 13:27
them, "Jesus I know, and Paul I **r**, Acts 19:15
it was day, they did not **r** the land, Acts 27:39
If anyone does not **r** this, he is not 1 Cor 14:38

RECOGNIZED (16)
Joseph saw his brothers and **r** them, but Gn 42:7
And Joseph **r** his brothers, but they did Gn 42:8
they **r** the voice of the young Levite. Jgs 18:3
Saul **r** David's voice and said, "Is this 1 Sm 26:17
And Obadiah **r** him and fell on his 1 Kgs 18:7
the king of Israel **r** him as one of 1 Kgs 20:41
than soot; they are not **r** in the streets; Lam 4:8
And when the men of that place **r** him, Mt 14:35
Now many saw them going and **r** them, Mk 6:33
the boat, the people immediately **r** him Mk 6:54
their eyes were opened, and they **r** him. Lk 24:31
and **r** him as the one who sat at the Acts 3:10
And they **r** that they had been with Acts 4:13
But when they **r** that he was a Jew, for Acts 19:34
are genuine among you may be **r**. 1 Cor 11:19
does not recognize this, he is not **r**. 1 Cor 14:38

RECOGNIZING (2)
But their eyes were kept from **r** him. Lk 24:16
R Peter's voice, in her joy she did not Acts 12:14

RECOILS (1)
like Zeboiim? My heart **r** within me; Hos 11:8

RECOMMENDATION (2)
we need, as some do, letters of **r** to you, 2 Cor 3:1
You yourselves are our letter of **r**, 2 Cor 3:2

RECOMPENSE (13)
Vengeance is mine, and **r**, for the time Dt 32:35
your eyes and see the **r** of the wicked. Ps 91:8
a year of **r** for the cause of Zion. Is 34:8
come with vengeance, with the **r** of God. Is 35:4
is with him, and his **r** before him. Is 40:10
is with the LORD, and my **r** with my God." Is 49:4
I will faithfully give them their **r**, and I Is 61:8
is with him, and his **r** before him." Is 62:11
of the LORD, rendering **r** to his enemies! Is 66:6
and I will **r** them according to their Jer 25:14
in pieces, for the LORD is a God of **r**; Jer 51:56
have come; the days of **r** have come; Hos 9:7
coming soon, bringing my **r** with me, Rv 22:12

RECONCILE (4)
how could this fellow **r** himself to his 1 Sm 29:4
were quarreling and tried to **r** them, Acts 7:26
and might **r** us both to God in one Eph 2:16
and through him to **r** to himself all Col 1:20

RECONCILED (7)
First be **r** to your brother, and then Mt 5:24
were enemies we were **r** to God by the Rom 5:10
Son, much more, now that we are **r**, Rom 5:10
or else be **r** to her husband), 1 Cor 7:11
who through Christ **r** us to himself 2 Cor 5:18
you on behalf of Christ, be **r** to God. 2 Cor 5:20
he has now **r** in his body of flesh by his Col 1:22

RECONCILIATION (4)
whom we have now received **r**. Rom 5:11
rejection means the **r** of the world, Rom 11:15
himself and gave us the ministry of **r**; 2 Cor 5:18
and entrusting to us the message of **r**. 2 Cor 5:19

RECONCILING (1)
in Christ God was **r** the world to 2 Cor 5:19

RECORD (3)
and they kept a genealogical **r**. 1 Chr 4:33
found on which this was written: "A **r**. Ezr 6:2
by canceling the **r** of debt that stood Col 2:14

RECORDED (15)
as they were **r** at the commandment of Ex 38:21
congregation who were **r** was a Ex 38:25
affliction that is not **r** in the book of Dt 28:61
genealogy of their generations was **r**: 1 Chr 5:7
All of these were **r** in genealogies in 1 Chr 5:17
So all Israel was **r** in genealogies, and 1 Chr 9:1
r them in the presence of the king 1 Chr 24:6
which are **r** in the Book of the Kings 2 Chr 20:34
and the weight of everything was **r**. Ezr 8:34
the Levites were **r** as heads of fathers' Neh 12:22
And it was **r** in the book of the Est 2:23
And Mordecai **r** these things and sent Est 9:20
of Purim, and it was **r** in writing. Est 9:32
Let this be **r** for a generation to come, Ps 102:18
everyone who has been **r** for life in Is 4:3

RECORDER (9)
Jehoshaphat the son of Ahilud was **r**, 2 Sm 8:16
the son of Ahilud was the **r**; 2 Sm 20:24
Jehoshaphat the son of Ahilud was **r**; 1 Kgs 4:3
and Joah the son of Asaph, the **r**. 2 Kgs 18:18
and Joah the son of Asaph, the **r**, 2 Kgs 18:37
the son of Ahilud was **r**; 1 Chr 18:15
city, and Joah the son of Joahaz, the **r**, 2 Chr 34:8
and Joah the son of Asaph, the **r**. Is 36:3
and Joah the son of Asaph, the **r**, Is 36:22

RECORDS (6)
These are the **r** of the tabernacle, the Ex 38:21
for everyone who was listed in the **r**, Ex 38:26
to Lehem (now the **r** are ancient). 1 Chr 4:22
in the book of the **r** of your fathers. Ezr 4:15
in the book of the **r** and learn that this Ezr 4:15
The LORD **r** as he registers the peoples, Ps 87:6

RECOUNT (7)
heart; I will **r** all of your wonderful deeds. Ps 9:1
that I may **r** all your praises, that in the Ps 9:14
and they **r** the pain of those you have Ps 69:26
is near. We **r** your wondrous deeds. Ps 75:1
to generation we will **r** your praise. Ps 79:13
I shall live, and **r** the deeds of the LORD. Ps 118:17
I will **r** the steadfast love of the LORD, the Is 63:7

RECOUNTED (2)
wonderful deeds that our fathers **r** to us, Jgs 6:13
And Haman **r** to them the splendor of Est 5:11

RECOVER (17)
if he has not sufficient means to **r** it, Lv 25:28
whether I shall **r** from this sickness." 2 Kgs 1:2
saying, 'Shall I **r** from this sickness?'" 2 Kgs 8:8
saying, 'Shall I **r** from this sickness?'" 2 Kgs 8:9
say to him, 'You shall certainly **r**,' 2 Kgs 8:10
told me that you would certainly **r**." 2 Kgs 8:14
for you shall die; you shall not **r**.'" 2 Kgs 20:1
and lay it on the boil, that he may **r**." 2 Kgs 20:7
Jeroboam did not **r** his power in the 2 Chr 13:20
a second time to **r** the remnant that Is 11:11
order, for you shall die, you shall not **r**." Is 38:1
and apply it to the boil, that he may **r**." Is 38:21
to him, "Rabbi, let me **r** my sight." Mk 10:51
hands on the sick, and they will **r**." Mk 16:18
He said, "Lord, let me **r** my sight." Lk 18:41
And Jesus said to him, "**R** your sight; Lk 18:42
"Lord, if he has fallen asleep, he will **r**." Jn 11:12

RECOVERED (10)
David **r** all that the Amalekites had 1 Sm 30:18
them any of the spoil that we have **r**, 1 Sm 30:22
Joash defeated him and **r** the cities of 2 Kgs 13:25
the king of Syria **r** Elath for Syria and 2 Kgs 16:6
been sick and had **r** from his sickness: Is 38:9
he heard that he had been sick and had **r**. Is 39:1
whom he had **r** from Ishmael the Jer 41:16
and immediately they **r** their sight and Mt 20:34
And immediately he **r** his sight and Mk 10:52
And immediately he **r** his sight and Lk 18:43

RECOVERING (2)
to the captives and **r** of sight to the Lk 4:18
met him and told him that his son was **r**. Jn 4:51

RECOVERS (1)
if the raw flesh **r** and turns white again, Lv 13:16

RED (42)
The first came out **r**, all his body like a Gn 25:25
Jacob, "Let me eat some of that **r** stew, Gn 25:30
locusts and drove them into the **R** Sea. Ex 10:19
way of the wilderness toward the **R** Sea. Ex 13:18
chosen officers were sunk in the **R** Sea. Ex 15:4
made Israel set out from the **R** Sea, Ex 15:22
your border from the **R** Sea to the Sea Ex 23:31
wilderness by the way to the **R** Sea." Nm 14:25
to bring you a **r** heifer without defect, Nm 19:2
Hor they set out by the way to the **R** Sea, Nm 21:4
from Elim and camped by the **R** Sea. Nm 33:10
set out from the **R** Sea and camped in Nm 33:11
wilderness in the direction of the **R** Sea.' Dt 1:40
wilderness in the direction of the **R** Sea, Dt 2:1
the water of the **R** Sea flow over them Dt 11:4
the water of the **R** Sea before you when Jos 2:10
as the LORD your God did to the **R** Sea, Jos 4:23
chariots and horsemen to the **R** Sea. Jos 24:6
the wilderness to the **R** Sea and came to Jgs 11:16
near Eloth on the shore of the **R** Sea, 1 Kgs 9:26
the water opposite them as **r** as blood. 2 Kgs 3:22
Egypt and heard their cry at the **R** Sea, Neh 9:9
My face is **r** with weeping, and on my Jb 16:16
but rebelled by the Sea, at the **R** Sea. Ps 106:7
He rebuked the **R** Sea, and it became Ps 106:9
Ham, and awesome deeds by the **R** Sea. Ps 106:22
to him who divided the **R** Sea in two, Ps 136:13
Pharaoh and his host in the **R** Sea, Ps 136:15
Do not look at wine when it is **r**, when Prv 23:31
though they are **r** like crimson, they shall Is 1:18
Why is your apparel **r**, and your Is 63:2
of their cry shall be heard at the **R** Sea. Jer 49:21
The shield of his mighty men is **r**; his Na 2:3
and behold, a man riding on a **r** horse! Zec 1:8
trees in the glen, and behind him were **r**, Zec 1:8
The first chariot had **r** horses, the second Zec 6:2
'It will be fair weather, for the sky is **r**.' Mt 16:2
today, for the sky is **r** and threatening.' Mt 16:3
in Egypt and at the **R** Sea and in the Acts 7:36
the people crossed the **R** Sea as if on Heb 11:29
And out came another horse, bright **r**. Its Rv 6:4
behold, a great **r** dragon, with seven Rv 12:3

REDDISH (2)
disease is greenish or **r** in the garment, Lv 13:49
of the house with greenish or **r** spots, Lv 14:37

REDDISH-WHITE (4)
there comes a white swelling or a **r** spot, Lv 13:19
of the burn becomes a spot, **r** or white, Lv 13:24
or the bald forehead a **r** diseased area, Lv 13:42
the diseased swelling is **r** on his bald Lv 13:43

REDEEM (54)
and I will **r** you with an outstretched arm Ex 6:6
of a donkey you shall **r** with a lamb, Ex 13:13
or if you will not **r** it you shall break its Ex 13:13
of man among your sons you shall **r**. Ex 13:13
but all the firstborn of my sons I **r**.' Ex 13:15
of a donkey you shall **r** with a lamb, Ex 34:20
or if you will not **r** it you shall break its Ex 34:20
the firstborn of your sons you shall **r**. Ex 34:20
shall come and **r** what his brother Lv 25:25
man has no one to **r** it and then himself Lv 25:26
and finds sufficient means to **r** it, Lv 25:26
city, he may **r** it within a year of its sale. Lv 25:29
the Levites may **r** at any time the Lv 25:32
One of his brothers may **r** him, Lv 25:48
or his uncle or his cousin may **r** him, Lv 25:49
close relative from his clan may **r** him. Lv 25:49
Or if he grows rich he may **r** himself. Lv 25:49
But if he wishes to **r** it, he shall add a Lv 27:13
And if the donor wishes to **r** his house, Lv 27:15
he who dedicates the field wishes to **r** it, Lv 27:19
But if he does not wish to **r** the field, or Lv 27:20
If a man wishes to **r** some of his tithe, Lv 27:31
the firstborn of man you shall **r**, Nm 18:15
of unclean animals you shall **r**. Nm 18:15
old you shall **r** them) you shall Nm 18:16
the firstborn of a goat, you shall not **r**; Nm 18:17
and in the morning, if he will **r** you, Ru 3:13
But if he is not willing to **r** you, then, as Ru 3:13
you, then, as the LORD lives, I will **r** you. Ru 3:13
of my people.' If you will **r** it, redeem it. Ru 4:4
of my people.' If you will redeem it, **r** it. Ru 4:4
for there is no one besides you to **r** it, Ru 4:4
I come after you." And he said, "I will **r** it." Ru 4:4
redeemer said, "I cannot **r** it for myself, Ru 4:6
of redemption yourself, for I cannot **r** it." Ru 4:6
whom God went to **r** to be his people, 2 Sm 7:23
whom God went to **r** to be his 1 Chr 17:21
In famine he will **r** you from death, and Jb 5:20
Or, '**R** me from the hand of the ruthless'? Jb 6:23
R Israel, O God, out of all his troubles. Ps 25:22
integrity; **r** me, and be gracious to me. Ps 26:11
R us for the sake of your steadfast love! Ps 44:26
Draw near to my soul, **r** me; ransom me Ps 69:18
R me from man's oppression, that I Ps 119:134
Plead my cause and **r** me; give me life Ps 119:154
And he will **r** Israel from all his Ps 130:8
Is my hand shortened, that it cannot **r**? Is 50:2
and **r** you from the grasp of the Jer 15:21
I would **r** them, but they speak lies Hos 7:13
of Sheol? Shall I **r** them from Death? Hos 13:14
there the LORD will **r** you from the hand Mi 4:10
hoped that he was the one to **r** Israel. Lk 24:21
to **r** those who were under the law, so that Gal 4:5
himself for us to **r** us from all Ti 2:14

REDEEMED (52)
the angel who has **r** me from all evil, Gn 48:16
love the people whom you have **r**; Ex 15:13
her for himself, then he shall let her be **r**. Ex 21:8
If it is not **r** within a full year, then the Lv 25:30
They may be **r**, and they shall be Lv 25:31

then after he is sold he may be **r**. One of Lv 25:48
And if he is not **r** by these means, then Lv 25:54
another man, it shall not be **r** anymore. Lv 27:20
or, if it is not **r**, it shall be sold at the Lv 27:27
of his inherited field, shall be sold or **r**; Lv 27:28
shall be holy; it shall not be **r**." Lv 27:33
over and above those **r** by the Levites. Nm 3:49
a mighty hand and **r** you from the house Dt 7:8
whom you have **r** through your Dt 9:26
the land of Egypt and **r** you out of the Dt 13:5
of Egypt, and the LORD your God **r** you; Dt 15:15
for your people Israel, whom you have **r**, Dt 21:8
the LORD your God **r** you from there; Dt 24:18
who has **r** my life out of every 2 Sm 4:9
whom you **r** for yourself from Egypt, 2 Sm 7:23
who has **r** my soul out of every 1 Kgs 1:29
people whom you **r** from Egypt? 1 Chr 17:21
whom you have **r** by your great power Neh 1:10
He has **r** my soul from going down into Jb 33:28
you have **r** me, O LORD, faithful God. Ps 31:5
to you; my soul also, which you have **r**. Ps 71:23
which you have **r** to be the tribe of your Ps 74:2
You with your arm **r** your people, the Ps 77:15
or the day when he **r** them from the foe, Ps 78:42
of the foe and **r** them from the power Ps 106:10
Let the **r** of the LORD say so, whom he Ps 107:2
say so, whom he has **r** from trouble Ps 107:2
Zion shall be **r** by justice, and those in Is 1:27
thus says the LORD, who **r** Abraham, Is 29:22
be found there, but the **r** shall walk there. Is 35:9
you, O Israel: "Fear not, for I have **r** you; Is 43:1
like mist; return to me, for I have **r** you. Is 44:22
For the LORD has **r** Jacob, and will be Is 44:23
say, "The LORD has **r** his servant Jacob!" Is 48:20
of the sea a way for the **r** to pass over? Is 51:10
and you shall be **r** without money." Is 52:3
comforted his people; he has **r** Jerusalem. Is 52:9
The Holy People, The **R** of the LORD; Is 62:12
in his love and in his pity he **r** them; Is 63:9
Jacob and has **r** him from hands Jer 31:11
my cause, O Lord; you have **r** my life. Lam 3:58
land of Egypt and **r** you from the house Mi 6:4
and gather them in, for I have **r** them, Zec 10:8
Israel, for he has visited and **r** his people Lk 1:68
Christ **r** us from the curse of the law by Gal 3:13
144,000 who had been **r** from the earth. Rv 14:3
These have been **r** from mankind as Rv 14:4

REDEEMER (28)
then his nearest **r** shall come and Lv 25:25
wings over your servant, for you are a **r**." Ru 3:9
And now it is true that I am a **r**. Yet there Ru 3:12
a redeemer. Yet there is a **r** nearer than I. Ru 3:12
And behold, the **r**, of whom Boaz had Ru 4:1
Then he said to the **r**, "Naomi, who has Ru 4:3
Then the **r** said, "I cannot redeem it for Ru 4:6
So when the **r** said to Boaz, "Buy it for Ru 4:8
has not left you this day without a **r**, Ru 4:14
For I know that my **R** lives, and at the Jb 19:25
your sight, O LORD, my rock and my **r**. Ps 19:14
their rock, the Most High God their **r**. Ps 78:35
for their **R** is strong; he will plead their Prv 23:11
LORD; your **R** is the Holy One of Israel. Is 41:14
Thus says the LORD, your **R**, the Holy Is 43:14
says the LORD, the King of Israel and his **R**, Is 44:6
Thus says the LORD, your **R**, who formed Is 44:24
Our **R**—the LORD of hosts is his name— Is 47:4
Thus says the LORD, your **R**, the Holy Is 48:17
the LORD, the **R** of Israel and his Holy One, Is 49:7
I am the LORD your Savior, and your **R**, Is 49:26
and the Holy One of Israel is your **R**, the Is 54:5
on you," says the LORD, your **R**. Is 54:8
"And a **R** will come to Zion, to those in Is 59:20
I, the LORD, am your Savior and your **R**, Is 60:16
Father, our **R** from of old is your name. Is 63:16
Their **R** is strong; the LORD of hosts is Jer 50:34
sent as both ruler and **r** by the hand of Acts 7:35

REDEEMERS (1)
is a close relative of ours, one of our **r**." Ru 2:20

REDEEMING (1)
in Israel concerning **r** and exchanging: Ru 4:7

REDEEMS (5)
The LORD **r** the life of his servants; none Ps 34:22
He **r** my soul in safety from the battle Ps 55:18
oppression and violence he **r** their life, Ps 72:14
who **r** your life from the pit, who Ps 103:4
has occurred that **r** them from the Heb 9:15

REDEMPTION (26)
shall give for the **r** of his life whatever Ex 21:30
possess, you shall allow a **r** of the land. Lv 25:24
a full year he shall have the right of **r**. Lv 25:29
of the Levites exercises his right of **r**, Lv 25:33
proportionately for his **r** some of his Lv 25:51
and pay for his **r** in proportion to his Lv 25:52
And as the **r** price for the 273 of the Nm 3:46
his sons as the **r** price for those who Nm 3:48
So Moses took the **r** money from those Nm 3:49
And Moses gave the **r** money to Aaron Nm 3:51
And their **r** price (at a month old you Nm 18:16
Take my right of **r** yourself, for I cannot Ru 4:6
He sent **r** to his people; he has Ps 111:9
love, and with him is plentiful **r**. Ps 130:7
in my heart, and my year of **r** had come. Is 63:4
for the right of **r** by purchase is yours.' Jer 32:7
for the right of possession and **r** is yours; Jer 32:8
who were waiting for the **r** of Jerusalem. Lk 2:38
heads, because your **r** is drawing near." Lk 21:28
through the **r** that is in Christ Jesus, Rom 3:24
adoption as sons, the **r** of our bodies. Rom 8:23
and sanctification and **r**. 1 Cor 1:30
In him we have **r** through his blood, the Eph 1:7
whom you were sealed for the day of **r**. Eph 4:30
in whom we have **r**, the forgiveness of Col 1:14
own blood, thus securing an eternal **r**. Heb 9:12

REDNESS (1)
without cause? Who has **r** of eyes? Prv 23:29

REDUCE (3)
on them, you shall by no means **r** it, Ex 5:8
shall by no means **r** your number of Ex 5:19
the years are few, you shall **r** the price, Lv 25:16

REDUCED (2)
but your work will not be **r** in the least.'" Ex 5:11
which the fire has **r** the burnt offering Lv 6:10

REDUCING (1)
pulled down and burned, **r** it to dust. 2 Kgs 23:15

REED (34)
and plump, and they fed in the **r** grass. Gn 41:2
up out of the Nile and fed in the **r** grass. Gn 41:18
strike Israel as a **r** is shaken in the 1 Kgs 14:15
in Egypt, that broken **r** of a staff, 2 Kgs 18:21
They go by like skiffs of **r**, like an eagle Jb 9:26
and tail, palm branch and **r** in one day— Is 9:14
that head or tail, palm branch or **r**, Is 19:15
trusting in Egypt, that broken **r** of a staff, Is 36:6
a bruised **r** he will not break, and a Is 42:3
Is it to bow down his head like a **r**, and to Is 58:5
have been a staff of **r** to the house of Ezk 29:6
cord and a measuring **r** in his hand. Ezk 40:3
length of the measuring **r** in the man's Ezk 40:5
the thickness of the wall, one **r**; Ezk 40:5
the wall, one reed; and the height, one **r**. Ezk 40:5
the threshold of the gate, one **r** deep. Ezk 40:6
rooms, one **r** long and one reed broad; Ezk 40:7
rooms, one reed long and one **r** broad; Ezk 40:7
of the gate at the inner end, one **r**. Ezk 40:7
of the gateway, on the inside, one **r**. Ezk 40:8
chambers measured a full **r** of six long Ezk 41:8
the east side with the measuring **r**, Ezk 42:16
cubits by the measuring **r** all around. Ezk 42:16
cubits by the measuring **r** all around. Ezk 42:17
side, 500 cubits by the measuring **r**. Ezk 42:18
500 cubits by the measuring **r**. Ezk 42:19
to see? A **r** shaken by the wind? Mt 11:7
a bruised **r** he will not break, and a Mt 12:20
his head and put a **r** in his right hand. Mt 27:29
him and took the **r** and struck him on Mt 27:30
and put it on a **r** and gave it to him to Mt 27:48
his head with a **r** and spitting on him Mk 15:19
put it on a **r** and gave it to him to Mk 15:36
to see? A **r** shaken by the wind? Lk 7:24

REEDS (7)
placed it among the **r** by the river bank. Ex 2:3
the basket among the **r** and sent her Ex 2:5
Can **r** flourish where there is no water? Jb 8:11
in the shelter of the **r** and in the marsh. Jb 40:21
the beasts that dwell among the **r**, Ps 68:30
and dry up, **r** and rushes will rot away. Is 19:6
the grass shall become **r** and rushes. Is 35:7

REEF (1)
But striking a **r**, they ran the vessel Acts 27:41

REEL (3)
These also **r** with wine and stagger with Is 28:7
and the prophet **r** with strong drink, Is 28:7
with strong drink, they **r** in vision, Is 28:7

REELAIAH (1)
Jeshua, Nehemiah, Seraiah, **R**, Mordecai, Ezr 2:2

REELED (3)
"Then the earth **r** and rocked; the 2 Sm 22:8
Then the earth **r** and rocked; the Ps 18:7
they **r** and staggered like drunken Ps 107:27

REFERRING (3)
not say, "And to offsprings," **r** to many, Gal 3:16
referring to many, but **r** to one, Gal 3:16
(**r** to things that all perish as they are Col 2:22

REFERS (3)
for it **r** to the appointed time of the end. Dn 8:19
vision, for it **r** to many days from now." Dn 8:26
I am saying that it **r** to Christ and the Eph 5:32

REFINE (4)
for silver, and a place for gold that they **r**. Jb 28:1
"Behold, I will **r** them and test them, for Jer 9:7
the fire, and **r** them as one refines silver, Zec 13:9
the sons of Levi and **r** them like gold and Mal 3:3

REFINED (11)
the most tender and **r** among you will Dt 28:54
most tender and **r** woman among you, Dt 28:56
the altar of incense made of **r** gold, 1 Chr 28:18
of Ophir, and 7,000 talents of **r** silver, 1 Chr 29:4
like silver **r** in a furnace on the ground, Ps 12:6
food full of marrow, of aged wine well **r**. Is 25:6
Behold, I have **r** you, but not as silver; I Is 48:10
shall stumble, so that they may be **r**, Dn 11:35
and make themselves white and be **r**, Dn 12:10
like burnished bronze, **r** in a furnace, Rv 1:15
you to buy from me gold **r** by fire, Rv 3:18

REFINER (1)
He will sit as a **r** and purifier of silver, Mal 3:3

REFINER'S (1)
For he is like a **r** fire and like fullers' Mal 3:2

REFINES (1)
the fire, and refine them as one **r** silver, Zec 13:9

REFINING (1)
in vain the **r** goes on, for the wicked are Jer 6:29

REFLECT (1)
is holy," and to **r** only after making Prv 20:25

REFLECTS (2)
As in water face **r** face, so the heart of Prv 27:19
face, so the heart of man **r** the man. Prv 27:19

REFORMATION (1)
the body imposed until the time of **r**. Heb 9:10

REFORMS (1)
Felix, **r** are being made for this nation, Acts 24:2

REFRAIN (13)
you shall **r** from leaving him with it; Ex 23:5
But if you **r** from vowing, you will not Dt 23:22
Would you therefore **r** from marrying? Ru 1:13
or shall I **r**?" And they said, 1 Kgs 22:6
or shall we **r**?" And he answered 1 Kgs 22:15
or shall I **r**?" And they said, 2 Chr 18:5
or shall I **r**?" And he answered, 2 Chr 18:14
R from anger, and forsake wrath! Fret Ps 37:8
and a time to **r** from embracing; Eccl 3:5
years he shall **r** from attacking the Dn 11:8
have no right to **r** from working for a 1 Cor 9:6
refrained and will **r** from burdening 2 Cor 11:9
be speaking the truth. But I **r** from it, 2 Cor 12:6

REFRAINED (4)
the princes **r** from talking and laid their Jb 29:9
in the fields." So he **r** and did not put Jer 41:8
spare you that I **r** from coming again 2 Cor 1:23
So I **r** and will refrain from 2 Cor 11:9

REFRAINS (1)
and he who **r** from marriage will do 1 Cor 7:38

REFRESH (4)
of bread, that you may **r** yourselves, Gn 18:5
"Come home with me, and **r** yourself, 1 Kgs 13:7
r me with apples, for I am sick with love. Sg 2:5
you in the Lord. **R** my heart in Christ. Phlm 1:20

REFRESHED (9)
woman, and the alien, may be **r**. Ex 23:12
the seventh day he rested and was **r**.'" Ex 31:17
his hand. So Saul was **r** and was well, 1 Sm 16:23
at the Jordan. And there he **r** himself. 2 Sm 16:14
with joy and be **r** in your company. Rom 15:32
for they **r** my spirit as well as yours. 1 Cor 16:18
his spirit has been **r** by you all. 2 Cor 7:13
for he often **r** me and was not 2 Tm 1:16
of the saints have been **r** through you. Phlm 1:7

REFRESHES (2)
the heart, and good news **r** the bones. Prv 15:30
send him; he **r** the soul of his masters. Prv 25:13

REFRESHING (1)
that times of **r** may come from the Acts 3:20

REFRESHMENT (1)
to your flesh and **r** to your bones. Prv 3:8

REFUGE (92)
to the Levites shall be the six cities of **r**, Nm 35:6
select cities to be cities of **r** for you, Nm 35:11
shall be for you a **r** from the avenger, Nm 35:12
you give shall be your six cities of **r**. Nm 35:13
in the land of Canaan, to be cities of **r**. Nm 35:14

six cities shall be for **r** for the people of Nm 35:15
him to his city of **r** to which he had Nm 35:25
of his city of **r** to which he fled, Nm 35:26
outside the boundaries of his city of **r**, Nm 35:27
in his city of **r** until the death of Nm 35:28
for him who has fled to his city of **r**, Nm 35:32
gods, the rock in which they took **r**, Dt 32:37
people of Israel, 'Appoint the cities of **r**, Jos 20:2
shall be for you a **r** from the avenger of Jos 20:3
Hebron, the city of **r** for the manslayer, Jos 21:13
the city of **r** for the manslayer, Jos 21:21
the city of **r** for the manslayer, Jos 21:27
the city of **r** for the manslayer, Jos 21:32
the city of **r** for the manslayer, Jos 21:38
you, then come and take **r** in my shade, Jgs 9:15
whose wings you have come to take **r**!" Ru 2:12
my God, my rock, in whom I take **r**, 2 Sm 22:3
salvation, my stronghold and my **r**, 2 Sm 22:3
for all those who take **r** in him. 2 Sm 22:31
God is my strong **r** and has made my 2 Sm 22:33
of Aaron they gave the cities of **r**: 1 Chr 6:57
They were given the cities of **r**: 1 Chr 6:67
Blessed are all who take **r** in him. Ps 2:12
But let all who take **r** in you rejoice; let Ps 5:11
O LORD my God, in you do I take **r**; save me Ps 7:1
In the LORD I take **r**; how can you say to Ps 11:1
plans of the poor, but the LORD is his **r**. Ps 14:6
Preserve me, O God, for in you I take **r**. Ps 16:1
those who seek **r** from their adversaries Ps 17:7
my God, my rock, in whom I take **r**, Ps 18:2
a shield for all those who take **r** in him. Ps 18:30
not be put to shame, for I take **r** in you. Ps 25:20
people; he is the saving **r** of his anointed. Ps 28:8
In you, O LORD, do I take **r**; let me never Ps 31:1
Be a rock of **r** for me, a strong fortress to Ps 31:2
have hidden for me, for you are my **r**. Ps 31:4
and worked for those who take **r** in you, Ps 31:19
Blessed is the man who takes **r** in him! Ps 34:8
none of those who take **r** in him will be Ps 34:22
of mankind take **r** in the shadow Ps 36:7
saves them, because they take **r** in him. Ps 37:40
For you are the God in whom I take **r**; Ps 43:2
God is our **r** and strength, a very present Ps 46:1
the man who would not make God his **r**, Ps 52:7
his riches and sought **r** in his own Ps 52:7
to me, for in you my soul takes **r**; Ps 57:1
in the shadow of your wings I will take **r**, Ps 57:1
to me a fortress and a **r** in the day of my Ps 59:16
for you have been my **r**, a strong tower Ps 61:3
Let me take **r** under the shelter of your Ps 61:4
my glory; my mighty rock, my **r** is God. Ps 62:7
your heart before him; God is a **r** for us. Ps 62:8
rejoice in the LORD and take **r** in him! Ps 64:10
In you, O LORD, do I take **r**; let me never Ps 71:1
Be to me a rock of **r**, to which I may Ps 71:3
to many, but you are my strong **r**. Ps 71:7
I have made the Lord GOD my **r**, that I Ps 73:28
say to the LORD, "My **r** and my fortress, Ps 91:2
and under his wings you will find **r**; Ps 91:4
place—the Most High, who is my **r**— Ps 91:9
and my God the rock of my **r**. Ps 94:22
the rocks are a **r** for the rock badgers. Ps 104:18
It is better to take **r** in the LORD than to Ps 118:8
It is better to take **r** in the LORD than to Ps 118:9
you, O GOD, my Lord; in you I seek **r**; Ps 141:8
takes notice of me; no **r** remains to me; Ps 142:4
I say, "You are my **r**, my portion in the Ps 142:5
enemies, O LORD! I have fled to you for **r**! Ps 143:9
my shield and he in whom I take **r**, Ps 144:2
and his children will have a **r**. Prv 14:26
but the righteous finds **r** in his death. Prv 14:32
is a shield to those who take **r** in him. Prv 30:5
and for a **r** and a shelter from the storm Is 4:6
in her the afflicted of his people find **r**." Is 14:32
not remembered the Rock of your **r**; Is 17:10
come to us, for we have made lies our **r**, Is 28:15
and hail will sweep away the **r** of lies, Is 28:17
to take **r** in the protection of Pharaoh and Is 30:2
But he who takes **r** in me shall possess Is 57:13
stronghold, my **r** in the day of trouble, Jer 16:19
me; you are my **r** in the day of disaster. Jer 17:17
No **r** will remain for the shepherds, nor Jer 25:35
But the LORD is a **r** to his people, a Jl 3:16
he knows those who take **r** in him. Na 1:7
you will seek a **r** from the enemy. Na 3:11
They shall seek **r** in the name of the Zep 3:12
who have fled for **r** might have strong Heb 6:18

REFUSE (39)
he may serve me." If you **r** to let him go, Ex 4:23
But if you **r** to let them go, behold, I will Ex 8:2
For if you **r** to let them go and still hold Ex 9:2
'How long will you **r** to humble yourself Ex 10:3
For if you **r** to let my people go, behold, Ex 10:4
"How long will you **r** to keep my Ex 16:28
do not **r** me." She said to him, 1 Kgs 2:16
Solomon—he will not **r** you—to give 1 Kgs 2:17
do not **r** me." And the king said to 1 Kgs 2:20
my mother, for I will not **r** you." 1 Kgs 2:20
and my gold, and I did not **r** him." 1 Kgs 20:7
it is oil for my head; let my head not **r** it. Ps 141:5
he will **r** though you multiply gifts. Prv 6:35
away, because they **r** to do what is just. Prv 21:7
kills him, for his hands **r** to labor. Prv 21:25
but if you **r** and rebel, you shall be eaten Is 1:20
and their corpses were as **r** in the midst of Is 5:25
he knows how to **r** the evil and choose Is 7:15
boy knows how to **r** the evil and choose Is 7:16
forehead of a whore; you **r** to be ashamed. Jer 3:3
They hold fast to deceit; they **r** to return. Jer 8:5
and deceit upon deceit, they **r** to know me, Jer 9:6
evil people, who **r** to hear my words, Jer 13:10
"And if they **r** to accept the cup from Jer 25:28
But if you **r** to surrender, this is the Jer 38:21
held them fast; they **r** to let them go. Jer 50:33
whether they hear or **r** to hear (for they Ezk 2:5
to them, whether they hear or **r** to hear, Ezk 2:7
GOD,' whether they hear or **r** to hear." Ezk 3:11
and he who will **r** to hear, let him Ezk 3:27
he who will refuse to hear, let him **r**, Ezk 3:27
and do not **r** the one who would borrow Mt 5:42
yet you **r** to come to me that you may Jn 5:40
I **r** to be a judge of these things." Acts 18:15
scum of the world, the **r** of all things. 1 Cor 4:13
We **r** to practice cunning or to tamper 2 Cor 4:2
But **r** to enroll younger widows, for 1 Tm 5:11
that you do not **r** him who is Heb 12:25
at their dead bodies and **r** to let them be Rv 11:9

REFUSED (31)
him, but he **r** to be comforted and said, Gn 37:35
But he **r** and said to his master's wife, Gn 39:8
But his father **r** and said, "I know, my Gn 48:19
when Pharaoh stubbornly **r** to let us Ex 13:15
Thus Edom **r** to give Israel passage Nm 20:21
for the LORD has **r** to let me go with Nm 22:13
But the people **r** to obey the voice of 1 Sm 8:19
He **r** and said, "I will not eat." But his 1 Sm 28:23
But he **r** to turn aside. Therefore 2 Sm 2:23
it out before him, but he **r** to eat. 2 Sm 13:9
please." But the man **r** to strike him. 1 Kgs 20:35
which he **r** to give you for money, 1 Kgs 21:15
And he urged him to take it, but he **r**. 2 Kgs 5:16
They **r** to obey and were not mindful of Neh 9:17
But Queen Vashti **r** to come at the Est 1:12
but **r** to walk according to his law. Ps 78:10
I have called and you **r** to listen, Prv 1:24
"Because this people have **r** the waters of Is 8:6
them, but they **r** to take correction. Jer 5:3
harder than rock; they have **r** to repent. Jer 5:3
forefathers, who **r** to hear my words. Jer 11:10
because they have **r** to return to me. Hos 11:5
But they **r** to pay attention and turned a Zec 7:11
she **r** to be comforted, because they are Mt 2:18
He **r** and went and put him in prison Mt 18:30
But he was angry and **r** to go in. His Lk 15:28
For a while he **r**, but afterward he said to Lk 18:4
Our fathers **r** to obey him, but thrust Acts 7:39
because they **r** to love the truth and 2 Thes 2:10
r to be called the son of Pharaoh's Heb 11:24
escape when they **r** him who warned Heb 12:25

REFUSES (11)
is hardened; he **r** to let the people go. Ex 7:14
If her father utterly **r** to give her to him, Ex 22:17
and said, "Balaam **r** to come with us." Nm 22:14
'My husband's brother **r** to perpetuate Dt 25:7
My appetite **r** to touch them; they are as Jb 6:7
wearying; my soul **r** to be comforted. Ps 77:2
she **r** to be comforted for her children, Jer 31:15
If he **r** to listen to them, tell it to the Mt 18:17
And if he **r** to listen even to the church, Mt 18:17
with that, he **r** to welcome the brothers, 3 Jn 1:10
but she **r** to repent of her sexual Rv 2:21

REFUSING (5)
my wound incurable, **r** to be healed? Jer 15:18
his stubborn, evil will, **r** to listen to me. Jer 16:12
their neck, **r** to hear my words." Jer 19:15
and turned aside, **r** to obey your voice. Dn 9:11
were tortured, **r** to accept release, Heb 11:35

REFUTED (2)
none among you who **r** Job or who Jb 32:12
for he powerfully **r** the Jews in public, Acts 18:28

REGAIN (3)
back, nor do they **r** the paths of life. Prv 2:19
on him so that he might **r** his sight." Acts 9:12
so that you may **r** your sight and be Acts 9:17

REGAINED (1)
fell from his eyes, and he **r** his sight. Acts 9:18

REGARD (56)
And the LORD had **r** for Abel and his Gn 4:4
but for Cain and his offering he had no **r**. Gn 4:5
that Laban did not **r** him with favor as Gn 31:2
your father does not **r** me with favor as Gn 31:5
labor at it and pay no **r** to lying words." Ex 5:9
You shall **r** them as detestable; you Lv 11:11
then you shall **r** its fruit as forbidden. Lv 19:23
all that needs to be done with **r** to them. Nm 4:26
Do not **r** the stubbornness of this people, Dt 9:27
of his father and mother, 'I **r** them not'; Dt 33:9
Israel broke faith in **r** to the devoted Jos 7:1
shall be innocent in **r** to the Philistines, Jgs 15:3
Do not **r** your servant as a worthless 1 Sm 1:16
not my lord **r** this worthless fellow, 1 Sm 25:25
that you should show **r** for a dead dog 2 Sm 9:8
Yet have **r** to the prayer of your 1 Kgs 8:28
not that I have **r** for Jehoshaphat the 2 Kgs 3:14
without **r** to their divisions, 2 Chr 5:11
Yet have **r** to the prayer of your 2 Chr 6:19
may write as you please with **r** to the Jews, Est 8:8
with **r** to their fasts and their lamenting. Est 9:31
I am blameless; I **r** not myself; I loathe Jb 9:21
him and had no **r** for any of his Jb 34:27
empty cry, nor does the Almighty **r** it. Jb 35:13
he does not **r** any who are wise in their Jb 37:24
With **r** to the works of man, by the word Ps 17:4
all your offerings and **r** with favor your Ps 20:3
Because they do not **r** the works of the Ps 28:5
I hate those who pay **r** to worthless idols, Ps 31:6
Have **r** for the covenant, for the dark Ps 74:20
heaven, and see; have **r** for this vine, Ps 80:14
be safe and have **r** for your statutes Ps 119:117
O LORD, what is man that you **r** him, or Ps 144:3
Whoever is righteous has **r** for the life Prv 12:10
in my heart with **r** to the children of Eccl 3:18
but they do not **r** the deeds of the LORD, Is 5:12
the LORD of hosts, him you shall **r** as holy. Is 8:13
who have no **r** for silver and do not Is 13:17
cities are despised; there is no **r** for man. Is 33:8
so I will **r** as good the exiles from Judah, Jer 24:5
them; he will **r** them no more; Lam 4:16
against Daniel with **r** to the kingdom, Dn 6:4
Those who pay **r** to vain idols forsake Jon 2:8
for with **r** to this sect we know that Acts 28:22
sin, you were free in **r** to righteousness. Rom 6:20
not let what you **r** as good be spoken Rom 14:16
This is how one should **r** us, as 1 Cor 4:1
we **r** no one according to the flesh. 2 Cor 5:16
to the flesh, we **r** him thus no longer. 2 Cor 5:16
will boast only with **r** to the area of 2 Cor 10:13
or with **r** to a festival or a new moon or Col 2:16
Do not **r** him as an enemy, but warn 2 Thes 3:15
a yoke as slaves **r** their own masters as 1 Tm 6:1
do not **r** lightly the discipline of the Heb 12:5
but in your hearts **r** Christ the Lord as 1 Pt 3:15
Silvanus, a faithful brother as I **r** him, 1 Pt 5:12

REGARDED (10)
Are we not **r** by him as foreigners? For Gn 31:15
we are **r** as sheep to be slaughtered. Ps 44:22
Shall the potter be **r** as the clay, that the Is 29:16
the fruitful field shall be **r** as a forest? Is 29:17
fine gold, how they are **r** as earthen pots, Lam 4:2
they would be **r** as a strange thing. Hos 8:12
of them was to be **r** as the greatest. Lk 22:24
uncircumcision be **r** as Rom 2:26
we are **r** as sheep to be slaughtered." Rom 8:36
though we once **r** Christ according to 2 Cor 5:16

REGARDING (7)
R the words that you have heard, 2 Kgs 22:18
R the words that you have heard, 2 Chr 34:26
I make a decree **r** what you shall do for Ezr 6:8
they perish forever without anyone **r** it. Jb 4:20
Stop **r** man in whose nostrils is breath, Is 2:22
Jerusalem and be tried there **r** them. Acts 25:20
in mind and disqualified **r** the faith. 2 Tm 3:8

REGARDS (8)
Only as **r** the throne will I be greater Gn 41:40
nor **r** the rich more than the poor, Jb 34:19
he **r** the prayer of the destitute and does Ps 102:17
though the LORD is high, he **r** the lowly, Ps 138:6
and he who **r** the clouds will not reap. Eccl 11:4
because he no longer **r** the offering or Mal 2:13
As **r** the gospel, they are enemies of Rom 11:28
But as **r** election, they are beloved for Rom 11:28

REGEM (1)
R, Jotham, Geshan, Pelet, Ephah, and 1 Chr 2:47

REGEM-MELECH (1)
had sent Sharezer and **R** and their men to Zec 7:2

REGENERATION (1)
by the washing of **r** and renewal of the Ti 3:5

REGION (39)
valley lying in the **r** of Moab by the Nm 21:20
them—sixty cities, the whole **r** of Argob, Dt 3:4
kingdom of Og, that is, all the **r** of Argob, Dt 3:13
the Manassite took all the **r** of Argob, Dt 3:14
and the **r** of the Geshurites and Jos 13:11
Their **r** extended from Mahanaim, Jos 13:30
they came to the **r** of the Jordan that Jos 22:10
of Canaan, in the **r** about the Jordan, Jos 22:11
fathers served in the **r** beyond the River, Jos 24:15
when you marched from the **r** of Edom, Jgs 5:4
in Gilead, and he had the **r** of Argob, 1 Kgs 4:13
dominion over all the **r** west of the 1 Kgs 4:24
throughout all the **r** east of Gilead. 1 Chr 5:10
and from the **r** of Geba and Neh 12:29
toward the eastern **r** and goes down Ezk 47:8
and in all that **r** who were two years Mt 2:16
Judea and all the **r** about the Jordan were Mt 3:5
those dwelling in the **r** and shadow of Mt 4:16
him, they begged him to leave their **r**. Mt 8:34
around to all that **r** and brought to Mt 14:35
woman from that **r** came out and Mt 15:22
the boat and went to the **r** of Magadan. Mt 15:39
Galilee and entered the **r** of Judea beyond Mt 19:1
all the surrounding **r** of Galilee. Mk 1:28
to beg Jesus to depart from their **r**. Mk 5:17
ran about the whole **r** and began to Mk 6:55
went away to the **r** of Tyre and Sidon. Mk 7:24
he returned from the **r** of Tyre and went Mk 7:31
Sea of Galilee, in the **r** of the Decapolis. Mk 7:31
and went to the **r** of Judea and beyond Mk 10:1
And in the same **r** there were shepherds Lk 2:8
Philip tetrarch of the **r** of Ituraea and Lk 3:1
he went into all the **r** around the Jordan, Lk 3:3
into every place in the surrounding **r**. Lk 4:37
from there to the **r** near the wilderness, Jn 11:54
spreading throughout the whole **r**. Acts 13:49
went through the **r** of Phrygia and Acts 16:6
the next through the **r** of Galatia and Acts 18:23
and throughout all the **r** of Judea, Acts 26:20

REGIONS (8)
all the **r** of the Philistines, and all those Jos 13:2
depths of the pit, in the **r** dark and deep. Ps 88:6
O Tyre and Sidon, and all the **r** of Philistia? Jl 3:4
scattered throughout the **r** of Judea and Acts 8:1
gone through those **r** and had given Acts 20:2
have any room for work in these **r**, Rom 15:23
not be silenced in the **r** of Achaia. 2 Cor 11:10
I went into the **r** of Syria and Cilicia. Gal 1:21

REGISTER (1)
nor be enrolled in the **r** of the house of Ezk 13:9

REGISTERED (7)
together, who **r** themselves by clans, Nm 1:18
They were among those **r**, but they Nm 11:26
These, **r** by name, came in the days 1 Chr 4:41
Zechariah, with whom were **r** 150 men. Ezr 8:3
Augustus that all the world should be **r**. Lk 2:1
And all went to be **r**, each to his own Lk 2:3
to be **r** with Mary, his betrothed, who was Lk 2:5

REGISTERS (1)
The LORD records as he **r** the peoples, Ps 87:6

REGISTRATION (3)
These sought their **r** among those Ezr 2:62
These sought their **r** among those Neh 7:64
This was the first **r** when Quirinius was Lk 2:2

REGRET (7)
"I **r** that I have made Saul king, for 1 Sm 15:11
Glory of Israel will not lie or have **r**, 1 Sm 15:29
is not a man, that he should have **r**." 1 Sm 15:29
And he departed with no one's **r**. 2 Chr 21:20
I do not **r** it—though I did regret it, 2 Cor 7:8
I do not regret it—though I did **r** it, 2 Cor 7:8
that leads to salvation without **r**, 2 Cor 7:10

REGRETTED (1)
And the LORD **r** that he had made 1 Sm 15:35

REGULAR (37)
bring them to **r** remembrance before Ex 28:29
shall be a **r** burnt offering throughout Ex 29:42
a **r** incense offering before the LORD Ex 30:8
ephah of fine flour as a **r** grain offering, Lv 6:20
the **r** show bread also shall be on it. Nm 4:7
fragrant incense, the **r** grain offering, Nm 4:16
blemish, day by day, as a **r** offering. Nm 28:3
It is a **r** burnt offering, which was Nm 28:6
besides the **r** burnt offering and its Nm 28:10
offered besides the **r** burnt offering Nm 28:15
which is for a **r** burnt offering. Nm 28:23
offered besides the **r** burnt offering Nm 28:24
Besides the **r** burnt offering and its Nm 28:31
and the **r** burnt offering and its grain Nm 29:6
and the **r** burnt offering and its grain Nm 29:11
offering, besides the **r** burnt offering, Nm 29:16
besides the **r** burnt offering and its Nm 29:19
besides the **r** burnt offering and its Nm 29:22
offering, besides the **r** burnt offering, Nm 29:25
besides the **r** burnt offering and its Nm 29:28
offering; besides the **r** burnt offering, Nm 29:31
offering; besides the **r** burnt offering, Nm 29:34
besides the **r** burnt offering and its Nm 29:38
a **r** allowance was given him by the 2 Kgs 25:30
and for the **r** arrangement of the 2 Chr 2:4
and after that the **r** burnt offerings, the Ezr 3:5
the showbread, the **r** grain offering, Neh 10:33
grain offering, the **r** burnt offering, Neh 10:33
since this was the **r** period of their Est 2:12
a **r** allowance was given him by the Jer 52:34
by morning, for a **r** burnt offering. Ezk 46:15
And the **r** burnt offering was taken Dn 8:11
together with the **r** burnt offering Dn 8:12
vision concerning the **r** burnt offering, Dn 8:13
shall take away the **r** burnt offering. Dn 11:31
the time that the **r** burnt offering is Dn 12:11
it shall be settled in the **r** assembly. Acts 19:39

REGULARLY (19)
of the Presence on the table before me **r**. Ex 25:30
that a lamp may **r** be set up to burn. Ex 27:20
of Israel on his heart before the LORD **r**. Ex 28:30
It shall **r** be on his forehead, that they Ex 28:38
two lambs a year old day by day **r**. Ex 29:38
that a light may be kept burning **r**. Lv 24:2
evening to morning before the LORD **r**. Lv 24:3
lampstand of pure gold before the LORD **r**. Lv 24:4
Aaron shall arrange it before the LORD **r**; Lv 24:8
his life he dined **r** at the king's table, 2 Kgs 25:29
to blow trumpets **r** before the ark 1 Chr 16:6
the LORD to minister **r** before the ark 1 Chr 16:37
of burnt offering **r** morning and 1 Chr 16:40
required of them, **r** before the LORD. 1 Chr 23:31
house of the LORD **r** all the days of 2 Chr 24:14
of his life he dined **r** at the king's table, Jer 52:33
through the land **r** and bury those Ezk 39:14
and wonders were **r** done among the Acts 5:12
the priests go **r** into the first section, Heb 9:6

REGULATIONS (4)
months under the **r** for the women, Est 2:12
alive in the world, do you submit to **r**— Col 2:20
the first covenant had **r** for worship and Heb 9:1
r for the body imposed until the time of Heb 9:10

REHABIAH (5)
The sons of Eliezer: **R** the chief. 1 Chr 23:17
but the sons of **R** were very many. 1 Chr 23:17
Of **R**: of the sons of Rehabiah, 1 Chr 24:21
of the sons of **R**, Isshiah the chief. 1 Chr 24:21
from Eliezer were his son **R**, and his 1 Chr 26:25

REHOB (10)
land from the wilderness of Zin to **R**, Nm 13:21
Ebron, **R**, Hammon, Kanah, as far as Jos 19:28
Aphek and **R**—twenty-two cities with Jos 19:30
and **R** with its pasturelands—four Jos 21:31
Achzib or of Helbah or of Aphik or of **R**, Jgs 1:31
also defeated Hadadezer the son of **R**, 2 Sm 8:3
the spoil of Hadadezer the son of **R**, 2 Sm 8:12
of Zobah and of **R** and the men of 2 Sm 10:8
and **R** with its pasturelands; 1 Chr 6:75
Mica, **R**, Hashabiah, Neh 10:11

REHOBOAM (52)
And **R** his son reigned in his place. 1 Kgs 11:43
R went to Shechem, for all Israel had 1 Kgs 12:1
of Israel came and said to **R**, 1 Kgs 12:3
Then King **R** took counsel with the 1 Kgs 12:6
the people came to **R** the third day, 1 Kgs 12:12
But **R** reigned over the people of 1 Kgs 12:17
Then King **R** sent Adoram, who was 1 Kgs 12:18
And King **R** hurried to mount his 1 Kgs 12:18
When **R** came to Jerusalem, he 1 Kgs 12:21
restore the kingdom to **R** the son of 1 Kgs 12:21
"Say to **R** the son of Solomon, king 1 Kgs 12:23
to their lord, to **R** king of Judah, 1 Kgs 12:27
me and return to **R** king of Judah." 1 Kgs 12:27
Now **R** the son of Solomon reigned 1 Kgs 14:21
R was forty-one years old when he 1 Kgs 14:21
In the fifth year of King **R**, Shishak 1 Kgs 14:25
and King **R** made in their place 1 Kgs 14:27
rest of the acts of **R** and all that he 1 Kgs 14:29
was war between **R** and Jeroboam 1 Kgs 14:30
And **R** slept with his fathers and was 1 Kgs 14:31
was war between **R** and Jeroboam all 1 Kgs 15:6
The son of Solomon was **R**, Abijah 1 Chr 3:10
and **R** his son reigned in his place. 2 Chr 9:31
R went to Shechem, for all Israel had 2 Chr 10:1
and all Israel came and said to **R**, 2 Chr 10:3
Then King **R** took counsel with the 2 Chr 10:6
the people came to **R** the third day, 2 Chr 10:12
King **R** spoke to them according to 2 Chr 10:14
But **R** reigned over the people of 2 Chr 10:17
Then King **R** sent Hadoram, who 2 Chr 10:18
And King **R** quickly mounted his 2 Chr 10:18
When **R** came to Jerusalem, he 2 Chr 11:1
Israel, to restore the kingdom to **R**. 2 Chr 11:1
"Say to **R** the son of Solomon, king of 2 Chr 11:3
R lived in Jerusalem, and he built 2 Chr 11:5
three years they made **R** the son of 2 Chr 11:17
R took as wife Mahalath the 2 Chr 11:18
R loved Maacah the daughter of 2 Chr 11:21
And **R** appointed Abijah the son of 2 Chr 11:22
the rule of **R** was established and 2 Chr 12:1
In the fifth year of King **R**, because 2 Chr 12:2
the prophet came to **R** and to the 2 Chr 12:5
and King **R** made in their place 2 Chr 12:10
So King **R** grew strong in Jerusalem 2 Chr 12:13
R was forty-one years old when he 2 Chr 12:13
Now the acts of **R**, from first to last, 2 Chr 12:15
wars between **R** and Jeroboam. 2 Chr 12:15
And **R** slept with his fathers and was 2 Chr 12:16
about him and defied **R** the son of 2 Chr 13:7
when **R** was young and irresolute 2 Chr 13:7
and Solomon the father of **R**, and Mt 1:7
of Rehoboam, and **R** the father of Abijah, Mt 1:7

REHOBOTH (3)
So he called its name **R**, saying, "For Gn 26:22
and Shaul of **R** on the Euphrates Gn 36:37
and Shaul of **R** on the Euphrates 1 Chr 1:48

REHOBOTH-IR (1)
Assyria and built Nineveh, **R**, Calah, Gn 10:11

REHUM (8)
Bilshan, Mispar, Bigvai, **R**, and Baanah. Ezr 2:2
R the commander and Shimshai the Ezr 4:8
R the commander, Shimshai the scribe, Ezr 4:9
"To **R** the commander and Shimshai Ezr 4:17
was read before **R** and Shimshai the Ezr 4:23
the Levites repaired: **R** the son of Bani. Neh 3:17
R, Hashabnah, Maaseiah, Neh 10:25
Shecaniah, **R**, Meremoth, Neh 12:3

REI (1)
and Shimei and **R** and David's mighty 1 Kgs 1:8

REIGN (146)
to him, "Are you indeed to **r** over us? Gn 37:8
The LORD will **r** forever and ever." Ex 15:18
and they said to the olive tree, '**R** over us.' Jgs 9:8
to the fig tree, 'You come and **r** over us.' Jgs 9:10
to the vine, 'You come and **r** over us.' Jgs 9:12
the bramble, 'You come and **r** over us.' Jgs 9:14
of the king who shall **r** over them." 1 Sm 8:9
ways of the king who will **r** over you: 1 Sm 8:11
And you shall **r** over the people of the 1 Sm 10:1
is it that said, 'Shall Saul **r** over us?' 1 Sm 11:12
me, 'No, but a king shall **r** over us,' 1 Sm 12:12
was … years old when he began to **r**, 1 Sm 13:1
old when he began to **r** over Israel, 2 Sm 2:10
and that you may **r** over all that your 2 Sm 3:21
thirty years old when he began to **r**, 2 Sm 5:4
"Solomon your son shall **r** after me, 1 Kgs 1:13
'Solomon your son shall **r** after me, 1 Kgs 1:17
you said, 'Adonijah shall **r** after me, 1 Kgs 1:24
'Solomon your son shall **r** after me, 1 Kgs 1:30
that all Israel fully expected me to **r**. 1 Kgs 2:15
fourth year of Solomon's **r** over Israel, 1 Kgs 6:1
and you shall **r** over all that your 1 Kgs 11:37
years old when he began to **r**, 1 Kgs 14:21
Nebat, Abijam began to **r** over Judah. 1 Kgs 15:1
of Israel, Asa began to **r** over Judah, 1 Kgs 15:9
of Jeroboam began to **r** over Israel in 1 Kgs 15:25
of Ahijah began to **r** over all Israel 1 Kgs 15:33
of Baasha began to **r** over Israel in 1 Kgs 16:8
When he began to **r**, as soon as he 1 Kgs 16:11
Judah, Omri began to **r** over Israel, 1 Kgs 16:23
son of Omri began to **r** over Israel, 1 Kgs 16:29
of Asa began to **r** over Judah in the 1 Kgs 22:41
years old when he began to **r**, 1 Kgs 22:42
of Ahab began to **r** over Israel in 1 Kgs 22:51
son who was to **r** in his place and 2 Kgs 3:27
king of Judah, began to **r**. 2 Kgs 8:16
of Jehoram, king of Judah, began to **r**. 2 Kgs 8:25
years old when he began to **r**, 2 Kgs 8:26
Ahaziah began to **r** over Judah. 2 Kgs 9:29
seven years old when he began to **r**. 2 Kgs 11:21
year of Jehu, Jehoash began to **r**, 2 Kgs 12:1
of Jehu began to **r** over Israel in 2 Kgs 13:1
of Jehoahaz began to **r** over Israel in 2 Kgs 13:10
of Joash, king of Judah, began to **r**. 2 Kgs 14:1
years old when he began to **r**, 2 Kgs 14:2
of Israel, began to **r** in Samaria, 2 Kgs 14:23
Amaziah, king of Judah, began to **r**. 2 Kgs 15:1
sixteen years old when he began to **r**, 2 Kgs 15:2
Jabesh began to **r** in the thirty-ninth 2 Kgs 15:13
son of Gadi began to **r** over Israel, 2 Kgs 15:17
Menahem began to **r** over Israel in 2 Kgs 15:23
of Remaliah began to **r** over Israel in 2 Kgs 15:27

of Uzziah, king of Judah, began to **r**. 2 Kgs 15:32
years old when he began to **r**, 2 Kgs 15:33
of Jotham, king of Judah, began to **r**. 2 Kgs 16:1
twenty years old when he began to **r**, 2 Kgs 16:2
of Elah began to **r** in Samaria over 2 Kgs 17:1
of Ahaz, king of Judah, began to **r**. 2 Kgs 18:1
years old when he began to **r**, 2 Kgs 18:2
twelve years old when he began to **r**, 2 Kgs 21:1
years old when he began to **r**, 2 Kgs 21:19
eight years old when he began to **r**, 2 Kgs 22:1
years old when he began to **r**, 2 Kgs 23:31
that he might not **r** in Jerusalem, 2 Kgs 23:33
years old when he began to **r**, 2 Kgs 23:36
prisoner in the eighth year of his **r** 2 Kgs 24:12
And in the ninth year of his **r**, in the 2 Kgs 25:1
in the year that he began to **r**, 2 Kgs 25:27
year of David's **r** search was made 1 Chr 26:31
month of the fourth year of his **r**. 2 Chr 3:2
years old when he began to **r**, 2 Chr 12:13
Abijah began to **r** over Judah. 2 Chr 13:1
of the fifteenth year of the **r** of Asa. 2 Chr 15:10
the thirty-fifth year of the **r** of Asa. 2 Chr 15:19
In the thirty-sixth year of the **r** of Asa, 2 Chr 16:1
year of his **r** Asa was diseased 2 Chr 16:12
dying in the forty-first year of his **r**. 2 Chr 16:13
third year of his **r** he sent his 2 Chr 17:7
years old when he began to **r**, 2 Chr 20:31
years old when he began to **r**, 2 Chr 21:20
years old when he began to **r**, 2 Chr 22:2
Let him **r**, as the LORD spoke 2 Chr 23:3
seven years old when he began to **r**, 2 Chr 24:1
years old when he began to **r**, 2 Chr 25:1
sixteen years old when he began to **r**, 2 Chr 26:3
years old when he began to **r**, 2 Chr 27:1
years old when he began to **r**, 2 Chr 27:8
twenty years old when he began to **r**, 2 Chr 28:1
Hezekiah began to **r** when he was 2 Chr 29:1
In the first year of his **r**, in the first 2 Chr 29:3
discarded in his **r** when he was 2 Chr 29:19
twelve years old when he began to **r**, 2 Chr 33:1
years old when he began to **r**, 2 Chr 33:21
eight years old when he began to **r**, 2 Chr 34:1
For in the eighth year of his **r**, while 2 Chr 34:3
Now in the eighteenth year of his **r**, 2 Chr 34:8
year of the **r** of Josiah this 2 Chr 35:19
years old when he began to **r**, 2 Chr 36:2
years old when he began to **r**, 2 Chr 36:5
years old when he began to **r**, 2 Chr 36:11
even until the **r** of Darius king of Persia. Ezr 4:5
And in the **r** of Ahasuerus, in the Ezr 4:6
of Ahasuerus, in the beginning of his **r**, Ezr 4:6
second year of the **r** of Darius king of Ezr 4:24
sixth year of the **r** of Darius the king. Ezr 6:15
this, in the **r** of Artaxerxes king of Persia, Ezr 7:1
in the **r** of Artaxerxes the king: Ezr 8:1
the priests in the **r** of Darius the Neh 12:22
the third year of his **r** he gave a feast for Est 1:3
of Tebeth, in the seventh year of his **r**, Est 2:16
that a godless man should not **r**, that he Jb 34:30
The LORD will **r** forever, your God, O Ps 146:10
By me kings **r**, and rulers decree what is Prv 8:15
Behold, a king will **r** in righteousness, Is 32:1
of Judah, in the thirteenth year of his **r**. Jer 1:2
and he shall **r** as king and deal wisely, Jer 23:5
the beginning of the **r** of Jehoiakim the Jer 26:1
the beginning of the **r** of Zedekiah the Jer 27:1
the beginning of the **r** of Zedekiah king Jer 28:1
shall not have a son to **r** on his throne, Jer 33:21
the beginning of the **r** of Zedekiah king Jer 49:34
to Babylon, in the fourth year of his **r**. Jer 51:59
And in the ninth year of his **r**, in the Jer 52:4
But you, O LORD, **r** forever; your throne Lam 5:19
third year of the **r** of Jehoiakim king of Dn 1:1
second year of the **r** of Nebuchadnezzar, Dn 2:1
prospered during the **r** of Darius and Dn 6:28
of Darius and the **r** of Cyrus the Persian Dn 6:28
third year of the **r** of King Belshazzar a Dn 8:1
in the first year of his **r**, I, Daniel, Dn 9:2
and the LORD will **r** over them in Mount Mi 4:7
and he will **r** over the house of Jacob Lk 1:33
fifteenth year of the **r** of Tiberius Caesar, Lk 3:1
'We do not want this man to **r** over us.' Lk 19:14
who did not want me to **r** over them, Lk 19:27
gift of righteousness **r** in life through Rom 5:17
also might **r** through righteousness Rom 5:21
Let not sin therefore **r** in your mortal Rom 6:12
And would that you did **r**, so that we 1 Cor 4:8
For he must **r** until he has put all 1 Cor 15:25
if we endure, we will also **r** with him; 2 Tm 2:12
our God, and they shall **r** on the earth." Rv 5:10
Christ, and he shall **r** forever and ever." Rv 11:15
taken your great power and begun to **r**. Rv 11:17
and they will **r** with him for a thousand Rv 20:6
light, and they will **r** forever and ever. Rv 22:5

REIGNED (165)
are the kings who **r** in the land of Gn 36:31
before any king **r** over the Israelites. Gn 36:31
Bela the son of Beor **r** in Edom, the Gn 36:32
son of Zerah of Bozrah **r** in his place. Gn 36:33
land of the Temanites **r** in his place. Gn 36:34
in the country of Moab, **r** in his place, Gn 36:35
Samlah of Masrekah **r** in his place. Gn 36:36
on the Euphrates **r** in his place. Gn 36:37
the son of Achbor **r** in his place. Gn 36:38
Achbor died, and Hadar **r** in his place, Gn 36:39
of the Amorites, who **r** in Heshbon, Jos 13:10
who **r** in Ashtaroth and in Edrei (he Jos 13:12
of the Amorites, who **r** in Heshbon, Jos 13:21
of Jabin king of Canaan, who **r** in Hazor. Jgs 4:2
and he **r** … and two years over Israel. 1 Sm 13:1
to reign over Israel, and he **r** two years. 2 Sm 2:10
he began to reign, and he **r** forty years. 2 Sm 5:4
At Hebron he **r** over Judah seven years 2 Sm 5:5
and at Jerusalem he **r** over all Israel 2 Sm 5:5
So David **r** over all Israel. And David 2 Sm 8:15
and Hanun his son **r** in his place. 2 Sm 10:1
of Saul, in whose place you have **r**, 2 Sm 16:8
the time that David **r** over Israel was 1 Kgs 2:11
He **r** seven years in Hebron and 1 Kgs 2:11
he loathed Israel and **r** over Syria. 1 Kgs 11:25
time that Solomon **r** in Jerusalem 1 Kgs 11:42
Rehoboam his son **r** in his place. 1 Kgs 11:43
But Rehoboam **r** over the people of 1 Kgs 12:17
how he warred and how he **r**, 1 Kgs 14:19
that Jeroboam **r** was twenty-two 1 Kgs 14:20
and Nadab his son **r** in his place. 1 Kgs 14:20
the son of Solomon **r** in Judah. 1 Kgs 14:21
and he **r** seventeen years in 1 Kgs 14:21
And Abijam his son **r** in his place. 1 Kgs 14:31
He **r** for three years in Jerusalem. His 1 Kgs 15:2
David. And Asa his son **r** in his place. 1 Kgs 15:8
and he **r** forty-one years in 1 Kgs 15:10
Jehoshaphat his son **r** in his place. 1 Kgs 15:24
Judah, and he **r** over Israel two years. 1 Kgs 15:25
Asa king of Judah and **r** in his place. 1 Kgs 15:28
Tirzah, and he **r** twenty-four years. 1 Kgs 15:33
and Elah his son **r** in his place. 1 Kgs 16:6
Israel in Tirzah, and he **r** two years. 1 Kgs 16:8
king of Judah, and **r** in his place. 1 Kgs 16:10
Judah, Zimri **r** seven days in Tirzah. 1 Kgs 16:15
over Israel, and he **r** for twelve years; 1 Kgs 16:23
years; six years he **r** in Tirzah. 1 Kgs 16:23
and Ahab his son **r** in his place. 1 Kgs 16:28
the son of Omri **r** over Israel in 1 Kgs 16:29
and Ahaziah his son **r** in his place. 1 Kgs 22:40
and he **r** twenty-five years in 1 Kgs 22:42
and Jehoram his son **r** in his place. 1 Kgs 22:50
Judah, and he **r** two years over Israel. 1 Kgs 22:51
in Samaria, and he **r** twelve years. 2 Kgs 3:1
and he **r** eight years in Jerusalem. 2 Kgs 8:17
and Ahaziah his son **r** in his place. 2 Kgs 8:24
reign, and he **r** one year in Jerusalem. 2 Kgs 8:26
And Jehoahaz his son **r** in his place. 2 Kgs 10:35
The time that Jehu **r** over Israel in 2 Kgs 10:36
LORD, while Athaliah **r** over the land. 2 Kgs 11:3
and he **r** forty years in Jerusalem. 2 Kgs 12:1
and Amaziah his son **r** in his place. 2 Kgs 12:21
in Samaria, and he **r** seventeen years. 2 Kgs 13:1
and Joash his son **r** in his place. 2 Kgs 13:9
in Samaria, and he **r** sixteen years. 2 Kgs 13:10
and he **r** twenty-nine years in 2 Kgs 14:2
and Jeroboam his son **r** in his place. 2 Kgs 14:16
in Samaria, and he **r** forty-one years. 2 Kgs 14:23
Zechariah his son **r** in his place. 2 Kgs 14:29
and he **r** fifty-two years in Jerusalem. 2 Kgs 15:2
and Jotham his son **r** in his place. 2 Kgs 15:7
the son of Jeroboam **r** over Israel in 2 Kgs 15:8
put him to death and **r** in his place. 2 Kgs 15:10
and he **r** one month in Samaria. 2 Kgs 15:13
put him to death and **r** in his place. 2 Kgs 15:14
Israel, and he **r** ten years in Samaria. 2 Kgs 15:17
and Pekahiah his son **r** in his place. 2 Kgs 15:22
in Samaria, and he **r** two years. 2 Kgs 15:23
put him to death and **r** in his place. 2 Kgs 15:25
in Samaria, and he **r** twenty years. 2 Kgs 15:27
put him to death and **r** in his place, 2 Kgs 15:30
and he **r** sixteen years in Jerusalem. 2 Kgs 15:33
and Ahaz his son **r** in his place. 2 Kgs 15:38
and he **r** sixteen years in Jerusalem. 2 Kgs 16:2
and Hezekiah his son **r** in his place. 2 Kgs 16:20
over Israel, and he **r** nine years. 2 Kgs 17:1
and he **r** twenty-nine years in 2 Kgs 18:2
Esarhaddon his son **r** in his place. 2 Kgs 19:37
and Manasseh his son **r** in his place. 2 Kgs 20:21
and he **r** fifty-five years in Jerusalem. 2 Kgs 21:1
and Amon his son **r** in his place. 2 Kgs 21:18
and he **r** two years in Jerusalem. 2 Kgs 21:19
and Josiah his son **r** in his place. 2 Kgs 21:26
and he **r** thirty-one years in 2 Kgs 22:1
and he **r** three months in Jerusalem. 2 Kgs 23:31
and he **r** eleven years in Jerusalem. 2 Kgs 23:36
and Jehoiachin his son **r** in his place. 2 Kgs 24:6
and he **r** three months in Jerusalem. 2 Kgs 24:8
and he **r** eleven years in Jerusalem. 2 Kgs 24:18
are the kings who **r** in the land of 1 Chr 1:43
before any king **r** over the people 1 Chr 1:43
son of Zerah of Bozrah **r** in his place. 1 Chr 1:44
land of the Temanites **r** in his place. 1 Chr 1:45
the country of Moab, **r** in his place, 1 Chr 1:46
Samlah of Masrekah **r** in his place. 1 Chr 1:47
on the Euphrates **r** in his place. 1 Chr 1:48
the son of Achbor, **r** in his place. 1 Chr 1:49
died, and Hadad **r** in his place, 1 Chr 1:50
where he **r** for seven years and six 1 Chr 3:4
And he **r** thirty-three years in 1 Chr 3:4
These were their cities until David **r**. 1 Chr 4:31
So David **r** over all Israel, and he 1 Chr 18:14
died, and his son **r** in his place. 1 Chr 19:1
the son of Jesse **r** over all Israel. 1 Chr 29:26
The time that he **r** over Israel was 1 Chr 29:27
He **r** seven years in Hebron and 1 Chr 29:27
And Solomon his son **r** in his place. 1 Chr 29:28
to Jerusalem. And he **r** over Israel. 2 Chr 1:13
Solomon **r** in Jerusalem over all 2 Chr 9:30
and Rehoboam his son **r** in his place. 2 Chr 9:31
But Rehoboam **r** over the people of 2 Chr 10:17
grew strong in Jerusalem and **r**. 2 Chr 12:13
and he **r** seventeen years in 2 Chr 12:13
and Abijah his son **r** in his place. 2 Chr 12:16
He **r** for three years in Jerusalem. His 2 Chr 13:2
David. And Asa his son **r** in his place. 2 Chr 14:1
Jehoshaphat his son **r** in his place 2 Chr 17:1
Thus Jehoshaphat **r** over Judah. He 2 Chr 20:31
and he **r** twenty-five years in 2 Chr 20:31
and Jehoram his son **r** in his place. 2 Chr 21:1
and he **r** eight years in Jerusalem. 2 Chr 21:5
and he **r** eight years in Jerusalem. 2 Chr 21:20
the son of Jehoram king of Judah **r**. 2 Chr 22:1
reign, and he **r** one year in Jerusalem. 2 Chr 22:2
God, while Athaliah **r** over the land. 2 Chr 22:12
and he **r** forty years in Jerusalem. 2 Chr 24:1
And Amaziah his son **r** in his place. 2 Chr 24:27
and he **r** twenty-nine years in 2 Chr 25:1
and he **r** fifty-two years in Jerusalem. 2 Chr 26:3
And Jotham his son **r** in his place. 2 Chr 26:23
and he **r** sixteen years in Jerusalem. 2 Chr 27:1
and he **r** sixteen years in Jerusalem. 2 Chr 27:8
and Ahaz his son **r** in his place. 2 Chr 27:9
and he **r** sixteen years in Jerusalem. 2 Chr 28:1
And Hezekiah his son **r** in his place. 2 Chr 28:27
and he **r** twenty-nine years in 2 Chr 29:1
Manasseh his son **r** in his place. 2 Chr 32:33
and he **r** fifty-five years in Jerusalem. 2 Chr 33:1
and Amon his son **r** in his place. 2 Chr 33:20
and he **r** two years in Jerusalem. 2 Chr 33:21
and he **r** thirty-one years in 2 Chr 34:1
and he **r** three months in Jerusalem. 2 Chr 36:2
and he **r** eleven years in Jerusalem. 2 Chr 36:5
Jehoiachin his son **r** in his place. 2 Chr 36:8
and he **r** three months and ten days 2 Chr 36:9
and he **r** eleven years in Jerusalem. 2 Chr 36:11
the Ahasuerus who **r** from India to Est 1:1
Esarhaddon his son **r** in his place. Is 37:38
who **r** instead of Josiah his father, Jer 22:11
r instead of Coniah the son of Jer 37:1
king; and he **r** eleven years in Jerusalem. Jer 52:1
Yet death **r** from Adam to Moses, even Rom 5:14
death **r** through that one man, Rom 5:17
so that, as sin **r** in death, grace also Rom 5:21
They came to life and **r** with Christ for a Rv 20:4

REIGNING (1)
that Archelaus was **r** over Judea in Mt 2:22

REIGNS (10)
and the king who **r** over you will 1 Sm 12:14
among the nations, "The LORD **r**!" 1 Chr 16:31
God **r** over the nations; God sits on his Ps 47:8
The LORD **r**; he is robed in majesty; the Ps 93:1
Say among the nations, "The LORD **r**! Ps 96:10
The LORD **r**, let the earth rejoice; let the Ps 97:1
The LORD **r**; let the peoples tremble! He Ps 99:1
the LORD of hosts **r** on Mount Zion and Is 24:23
who says to Zion, "Your God **r**." Is 52:7
For the Lord our God the Almighty **r**. Rv 19:6

REIN (1)
"You give your mouth free **r** for evil, Ps 50:19

REINED (1)
Then Joram **r** about and fled, saying 2 Kgs 9:23

REJECT (9)
"Behold, God will not **r** a blameless man, Jb 8:20
repayment to suit you, because you **r** it? Jb 34:33
a way that is not good; he does not **r** evil. Ps 36:4
Rouse yourself! Do not **r** us forever! Ps 44:23

then I will **r** the offspring of Jacob and Jer 33:26
I **r** you from being a priest to me. Hos 4:6
My God will **r** them because they have Hos 9:17
we escape if we **r** him who warns from Heb 12:25
dreams, defile the flesh, **r** authority, Jude 1:8

REJECTED (60)
because you have **r** the LORD who is Nm 11:20
shall know the land that you have **r**. Nm 14:31
they say to you, for they have not **r** you, 1 Sm 8:7
but they have **r** me from being king 1 Sm 8:7
But today you have **r** your God, who 1 Sm 10:19
Because you have **r** the word of the 1 Sm 15:23
he has also **r** you from being king." 1 Sm 15:23
For you have **r** the word of the LORD, 1 Sm 15:26
and the LORD has **r** you from being 1 Sm 15:26
since I have **r** him from being king 1 Sm 16:1
of his stature, because I have **r** him. 1 Sm 16:7
And the LORD **r** all the descendants 2 Kgs 17:20
"If I have **r** the cause of my manservant Jb 31:13
whom I take refuge; why have you **r** me? Ps 43:2
But you have **r** us and disgraced us and Ps 44:9
put them to shame, for God has **r** them. Ps 53:5
O God, you have **r** us, broken our Ps 60:1
Have you not **r** us, O God? You do not Ps 60:10
because he has not **r** my prayer or Ps 66:20
was full of wrath, and he utterly **r** Israel. Ps 78:59
He **r** the tent of Joseph; he did not choose Ps 78:67
But now you have cast off and **r**; you Ps 89:38
Have you not **r** us, O God? You do not Ps 108:11
that the builders **r** has become the Ps 118:22
For you have **r** your people, the house of Is 2:6
for they have **r** the law of the LORD of Is 5:24
He was despised and **r** by men; a man of Is 53:3
for the LORD has **r** those in whom you Jer 2:37
words; and as for my law, they have **r** it. Jer 6:19
R silver they are called, for the LORD has Jer 6:30
they are called, for the LORD has **r** them." Jer 6:30
for the LORD has **r** and forsaken the Jer 7:29
behold, they have **r** the word of the LORD, Jer 8:9
Have you utterly **r** Judah? Does your Jer 14:19
You have **r** me, declares the LORD; you Jer 15:6
'The LORD has **r** the two clans that he Jer 33:24
"The Lord **r** all my mighty men in my Lam 1:15
unless you have utterly **r** us, and you Lam 5:22
for they have **r** my rules and have not Ezk 5:6
walk in my statutes but **r** my rules, Ezk 20:13
because they **r** my rules and did not Ezk 20:16
but had **r** my statutes and profaned Ezk 20:24
because you have **r** knowledge, I reject Hos 4:6
because they have **r** the law of the LORD, Am 2:4
shall be as though I had not **r** them, Zec 10:6
that the builders **r** has become the Mt 21:42
many things and be **r** by the elders and Mk 8:31
that the builders **r** has become the Mk 12:10
and the lawyers **r** the purpose of Lk 7:30
many things and be **r** by the elders and Lk 9:22
things and be **r** by this generation. Lk 17:25
that the builders **r** has become the Lk 20:17
Jesus is the stone that was **r** by you, Acts 4:11
"This Moses, whom they **r**, saying, Acts 7:35
I ask, then, has God **r** his people? By no Rom 11:1
God has not **r** his people whom he Rom 11:2
and nothing is to be **r** if it is received 1 Tm 4:4
to inherit the blessing, he was **r**, Heb 12:17
a living stone **r** by men but in the sight 1 Pt 2:4
stone that the builders **r** has become the 1 Pt 2:7

REJECTING (2)
a fine way of **r** the commandment of God Mk 7:9
and a good conscience. By **r** this, 1 Tm 1:19

REJECTION (1)
For if their **r** means the Rom 11:15

REJECTS (6)
but he who **r** reproof leads others Prv 10:17
me, and the one who **r** you rejects me, Lk 10:16
me, and the one who rejects you **r** me, Lk 10:16
and the one who **r** me rejects him who Lk 10:16
one who rejects me **r** him who sent Lk 10:16
The one who **r** me and does not receive Jn 12:48

REJOICE (161)
and you shall **r** before the LORD your Lv 23:40
the LORD your God, and you shall **r**, Dt 12:7
And you shall **r** before the LORD your Dt 12:12
And you shall **r** before the LORD your Dt 12:18
there before the LORD your God and **r**, Dt 14:26
And you shall **r** before the LORD your Dt 16:11
You shall **r** in your feast, you and your Dt 16:14
And you shall **r** in all the good that the Dt 26:11
and you shall **r** before the LORD your Dt 27:7
"**R** with him, O heavens; bow down to Dt 32:43
And of Zebulun he saids, "**R**, Zebulun, Dt 33:18
his house this day, then **r** in Abimelech, Jgs 9:19
in Abimelech, and let him also **r** in you. Jgs 9:19
sacrifice to Dagon their god and to **r**, Jgs 16:23
enemies, because I **r** in your salvation. 1 Sm 2:1
lest the daughters of the Philistines **r**, 2 Sm 1:20
hearts of those who seek the LORD **r**! 1 Chr 16:10
heavens be glad, and let the earth **r**, 1 Chr 16:31
let your saints **r** in your goodness. 2 Chr 6:41
had made them **r** over their 2 Chr 20:27
God had made them **r** with great joy; Neh 12:43
Let it not **r** among the days of the year; let Jb 3:6
who **r** exceedingly and are glad when Jb 3:22
and the lyre and **r** to the sound of Jb 21:12
the LORD with fear, and **r** with trembling. Ps 2:11
But let all who take refuge in you **r**; let Ps 5:11
of Zion I may **r** in your salvation. Ps 9:14
him," lest my foes **r** because I am Ps 13:4
love; my heart shall **r** in your salvation. Ps 13:5
the fortunes of his people, let Jacob **r**, Ps 14:7
up and have not let my foes **r** over me. Ps 30:1
I will **r** and be glad in your steadfast love, Ps 31:7
Be glad in the LORD, and **r**, O righteous, Ps 32:11
Then my soul will **r** in the LORD, exulting Ps 35:9
Let not those **r** over me who are Ps 35:19
and let them not **r** over me! Ps 35:24
disappointed altogether who **r** at my Ps 35:26
For I said, "Only let them not **r** over me, Ps 38:16
may all who seek you **r** and be glad in Ps 40:16
daughters of Judah **r** because of your Ps 48:11
let the bones that you have broken **r**. Ps 51:8
the fortunes of his people, Let Jacob **r**, Ps 53:6
The righteous will **r** when he sees the Ps 58:10
But the king shall **r** in God; all who Ps 63:11
Let the righteous one **r** in the LORD and Ps 64:10
the river on foot. There did we **r** in him, Ps 66:6
May all who seek you **r** and be glad in Ps 70:4
us again, that your people may **r** in you? Ps 85:6
foes; you have made all his enemies **r**. Ps 89:42
that we may **r** and be glad all our days. Ps 90:14
the heavens be glad, and let the earth **r**; Ps 96:11
The LORD reigns, let the earth **r**; let the Ps 97:1
and is glad, and the daughters of Judah **r**, Ps 97:8
R in the LORD, O you righteous, and give Ps 97:12
forever; may the LORD **r** in his works, Ps 104:31
be pleasing to him, for I **r** in the LORD. Ps 104:34
the hearts of those who seek the LORD **r**! Ps 105:3
that I may **r** in the gladness of your Ps 106:5
has made; let us **r** and be glad in it. Ps 118:24
Those who fear you shall see me and **r**, Ps 119:74
I **r** at your word like one who finds Ps 119:162
let the children of Zion **r** in their King! Ps 149:2
who **r** in doing evil and delight in the Prv 2:14
blessed, and **r** in the wife of your youth, Prv 5:18
father of the righteous will greatly **r**; Prv 23:24
mother be glad; let her who bore you **r**. Prv 23:25
Do not **r** when your enemy falls, and Prv 24:17
the righteous increase, the people **r**, Prv 29:2
than that a man should **r** in his work, Eccl 3:22
those who come later will not **r** in him. Eccl 4:16
to accept his lot and **r** in his toil—this Eccl 5:19
lives many years, let him **r** in them all; Eccl 11:8
R, O young man, in your youth, and Eccl 11:9
We will exult and **r** in you; we will extol Sg 1:4
and **r** over Rezin and the son of Remaliah, Is 8:6
they **r** before you as with joy at the harvest, Is 9:3
the Lord does not **r** over their young men, Is 9:17
The cypresses **r** at you, the cedars of Is 14:8
R not, O Philistia, all of you, that the rod Is 14:29
him; let us be glad and **r** in his salvation." Is 25:9
the desert shall **r** and blossom like the Is 35:1
blossom abundantly and **r** with joy and Is 35:2
them. And you shall **r** in the LORD; Is 41:16
Chaldeans, in the ships in which they **r**. Is 43:14
of dishonor they shall **r** in their lot; Is 61:7
I will greatly **r** in the LORD; my soul shall Is 61:10
the bride, so shall your God **r** over you. Is 62:5
behold, my servants shall **r**, but you Is 65:13
But be glad and **r** forever in that which I Is 65:18
I will **r** in Jerusalem and be glad in my Is 65:19
"**R** with Jerusalem, and be glad for her, Is 66:10
r with her in joy, all you who mourn Is 66:10
You shall see, and your heart shall **r**; Is 66:14
in the company of revelers, nor did I **r**; Jer 15:17
shall the young women **r** in the dance, Jer 31:13
I will **r** in doing them good, and I will Jer 32:41
"Though you **r**, though you exult, O Jer 50:11
has made the enemy **r** over you and Lam 2:17
R and be glad, O daughter of Edom, Lam 4:21
Let not the buyer **r**, nor the seller Ezk 7:12
to flash like lightning! (Or shall we **r**? Ezk 21:10
R not, O Israel! Exult not like the peoples; Hos 9:1
be glad and **r**, for the LORD has done great Jl 2:21
of Zion, and **r** in the LORD your God, Jl 2:23
you who **r** in Lo-debar, who say, "Have Am 6:13
do not **r** over the people of Judah in the Ob 1:12
R not over me, O my enemy; when I fall, I Mi 7:8
yet I will **r** in the LORD; I will take joy in Hab 3:18
R and exult with all your heart, O Zep 3:14
save; he will **r** over you with gladness; Zep 3:17
Sing and **r**, O daughter of Zion, for Zec 2:10
despised the day of small things shall **r**, Zec 4:10
R greatly, O daughter of Zion! Shout Zec 9:9
be glad; their hearts shall **r** in the LORD. Zec 10:7
R and be glad, for your reward is great in Mt 5:12
gladness, and many will **r** at his birth, Lk 1:14
R in that day, and leap for joy, for Lk 6:23
Nevertheless, do not **r** in this, that the Lk 10:20
but **r** that your names are written in Lk 10:20
neighbors, saying to them, '**R** with me, Lk 15:6
and neighbors, saying, '**R** with me, Lk 15:9
his disciples began to **r** and praise God Lk 19:37
so that sower and reaper may **r** together. Jn 4:36
and you were willing to **r** for a while in Jn 5:35
weep and lament, but the world will **r**. Jn 16:20
see you again and your hearts will **r**, Jn 16:22
and we **r** in hope of the glory of God. Rom 5:2
More than that, we **r** in our sufferings, Rom 5:3
we also **r** in God through our Lord Rom 5:11
R in hope, be patient in tribulation, Rom 12:12
R with those who rejoice, weep with Rom 12:15
Rejoice with those who **r**, weep with Rom 12:15
And again it is said, "**R**, O Gentiles, Rom 15:10
is known to all, so that I **r** over you, Rom 16:19
and those who **r** as though they were 1 Cor 7:30
member is honored, all **r** together. 1 Cor 12:26
it does not **r** at wrongdoing, but 1 Cor 13:6
I **r** at the coming of Stephanas and 1 Cor 16:17
those who should have made me **r**, 2 Cor 2:3
As it is, I **r**, not because you were 2 Cor 7:9
I **r**, because I have perfect confidence 2 Cor 7:16
brothers, **r**. Aim for restoration, 2 Cor 13:11
"**R**, O barren one who does not bear; Gal 4:27
Christ is proclaimed, and in that I **r**. Phil 1:18
and in that I rejoice. Yes, and I will **r**, Phil 1:18
faith, I am glad and **r** with you all. Phil 2:17
you also should be glad and **r** with me. Phil 2:18
that you may **r** at seeing him again, Phil 2:28
Finally, my brothers, **r** in the Lord. To Phil 3:1
R in the Lord always; again I will say, Phil 4:4
in the Lord always; again I will say, **R**. Phil 4:4
Now I **r** in my sufferings for your sake, Col 1:24
R always, 1 Thes 5:16
In this you **r**, though now for a little 1 Pt 1:6
you believe in him and **r** with joy that is 1 Pt 1:8
But **r** insofar as you share Christ's 1 Pt 4:13
that you may also **r** and be glad when 1 Pt 4:13
on the earth will **r** over them and make Rv 11:10
r, O heavens and you who dwell in Rv 12:12
R over her, O heaven, and you saints Rv 18:20
Let us **r** and exult and give him the Rv 19:7

REJOICED (38)
And Jethro **r** for all the good that the Ex 18:9
eyes and saw the ark, they **r** to see it. 1 Sm 6:13
and all the men of Israel **r** greatly. 1 Sm 11:15
for all Israel. You saw it, and **r**. 1 Sm 19:5
of Solomon, he **r** greatly and said, 1 Kgs 5:7
So all the people of the land **r**, and 2 Kgs 11:20
Then the people **r** because they had 1 Chr 29:9
LORD. David the king also **r** greatly. 1 Chr 29:9
And all Judah **r** over the oath, for 2 Chr 15:15
So all the people of the land **r**, and 2 Chr 23:21
all the people **r** and brought their 2 Chr 24:10
all the people **r** because God had 2 Chr 29:36
the sojourners who lived in Judah, **r**. 2 Chr 30:25
offered great sacrifices that day and **r**, Neh 12:43
joy; the women and children also **r**. Neh 12:43
for Judah **r** over the priests and the Neh 12:44
and the city of Susa shouted and **r**. Est 8:15
if I have **r** because my wealth was Jb 31:25
"If I have **r** at the ruin of him who hated Jb 31:29
at my stumbling they **r** and gathered; Ps 35:15
leaders of the forces with him, they **r**. Jer 41:13
stamped your feet and **r** with all the Ezk 25:6
As you **r** over the inheritance of the Ezk 35:15
priests—those who **r** over it and over Hos 10:5
star, they **r** exceedingly with great joy. Mt 2:10
great mercy to her, and they **r** with her. Lk 1:58
that same hour he **r** in the Holy Spirit Lk 10:21
and all the people **r** at all the glorious Lk 13:17
Your father Abraham **r** that he would Jn 8:56
If you loved me, you would have **r**, Jn 14:28
my heart was glad, and my tongue **r**; Acts 2:26
they **r** because of its encouragement. Acts 15:31
And he **r** along with his entire Acts 16:34
your zeal for me, so that I **r** still more. 2 Cor 7:7
we **r** still more at the joy of Titus, 2 Cor 7:13
I **r** in the Lord greatly that now at Phil 4:10
I **r** greatly to find some of your children 2 Jn 1:4
For I **r** greatly when the brothers came 3 Jn 1:3

REJOICES (13)
my heart is glad, and my whole being **r**; Ps 16:9
O LORD, in your strength the king **r**, and Ps 21:1

goes well with the righteous, the city **r**, Prv 11:10
The light of the righteous **r**, but the Prv 13:9
The light of the eyes **r** the heart, and Prv 15:30
but a righteous man sings and **r**. Prv 29:6
and as the bridegroom **r** over the bride, Is 62:5
While the whole earth **r**, I will make Ezk 35:14
them in his dragnet; so he **r** and is glad. Hab 1:15
he **r** over it more than over the Mt 18:13
and my spirit **r** in God my Savior, Lk 1:47
him, **r** greatly at the bridegroom's voice. Jn 3:29
at wrongdoing, but **r** with the truth. 1 Cor 13:6

REJOICING (23)
Obed-edom to the city of David with **r**. 2 Sm 6:12
playing on pipes, and **r** with great joy, 1 Kgs 1:40
and they have gone up from there **r**, 1 Kgs 1:45
of the land **r** and blowing trumpets. 2 Kgs 11:14
and all Israel were **r** before God with 1 Chr 13:8
the house of Obed-edom with **r**. 1 Chr 15:25
and saw King David dancing and **r**, 1 Chr 15:29
of the land **r** and blowing trumpets, 2 Chr 23:13
of Moses, with **r** and with singing, 2 Chr 23:18
to send portions and to make great **r**, Neh 8:12
not done so. And there was very great **r**. Neh 8:17
precepts of the LORD are right, **r** the heart; Ps 19:8
daily his delight, **r** before him always, Prv 8:30
r in his inhabited world and delighting Prv 8:31
me, **r** as if to devour the poor in secret. Hab 3:14
found it, he lays it on his shoulders, **r**. Lk 15:5
r that they were counted worthy to Acts 5:41
to the idol and were **r** in the works of Acts 7:41
him no more, and went on his way **r**. Acts 8:39
they began **r** and glorifying the word Acts 13:48
rejoice as though they were not **r**, 1 Cor 7:30
as sorrowful, yet always **r**; as poor, yet 2 Cor 6:10
r to see your good order and the firmness Col 2:5

REKEM (5)
with the rest of their slain, Evi, **R**, Zur, Nm 31:8
Evi and **R** and Zur and Hur and Reba, Jos 13:21
R, Irpeel, Taralah, Jos 18:27
Korah, Tappuah, **R** and Shema. 1 Chr 2:43
Jorkeam; and **R** fathered Shammai. 1 Chr 2:44

RELATED (5)
of our God, and who was **r** to Tobiah, Neh 13:4
and having **r** everything to them, he Acts 10:8
and Paul as they **r** what signs and Acts 15:12
Simeon has **r** how God first visited Acts 15:14
he **r** one by one the things that God Acts 21:19

RELATION (1)
to act on behalf of men in **r** to God, Heb 5:1

RELATIONS (3)
women exchanged natural **r** for those Rom 1:26
gave up natural **r** with women and Rom 1:27
not to have sexual **r** with a woman." 1 Cor 7:1

RELATIVE (13)
father's sister; she is your father's **r**. Lv 18:12
sister, for she is your mother's **r**. Lv 18:13
sister, for that is to make naked one's **r**; Lv 20:19
or a close **r** from his clan may redeem Lv 25:49
of Shechem, because he is your **r**— Jgs 9:18
Now Naomi had a **r** of her husband's, a Ru 2:1
said to her, "The man is a close **r** of ours, Ru 2:20
Is not Boaz our **r**, with whose young Ru 3:2
of land that belonged to our **r** Elimelech. Ru 4:3
"Because the king is our close **r**. 2 Sm 19:42
And when one's **r**, the one who anoints Am 6:10
your **r** Elizabeth in her old age has also Lk 1:36
a **r** of the man whose ear Peter had cut Jn 18:26

RELATIVES (30)
one of his close **r** to uncover nakedness. Lv 18:6
to uncover her nakedness; they are **r**; Lv 18:17
except for his closest **r**, his mother, his Lv 21:2
they brought all her **r** and put them Jos 6:23
Shechem to his mother's **r** and said to Jgs 9:1
And his mother's **r** spoke all these words Jgs 9:3
of Ebed moved into Shechem with his **r**, Jgs 9:26
of Ebed and his **r** have come to Jgs 9:31
and Zebul drove out Gaal and his **r**, Jgs 9:41
woman among the daughters of your **r**, Jgs 14:3
Saul, "Who am I, and who are my **r**, 1 Sm 18:18
or fight against your **r** the people of 1 Kgs 12:24
a single male of his **r** or his friends. 1 Kgs 16:11
Jehu met the **r** of Ahaziah king of 2 Kgs 10:13
answered, "We are the **r** of Ahaziah, 2 Kgs 10:13
And also their **r**, from as far as 1 Chr 12:40
not go up or fight against your **r**. 2 Chr 11:4
Israel took captive 200,000 of their **r**, 2 Chr 28:8
captives from your **r** whom you 2 Chr 28:11
and his **r**, Shemaiah, Azarel, Milalai, Neh 12:36
My **r** have failed me, my close friends Jb 19:14
hometown and among his **r** and in his Mk 6:4
And her neighbors and **r** heard that the Lk 1:58
"None of your **r** is called by this name." Lk 1:61
him among their **r** and acquaintances, Lk 2:44
brothers or your **r** or rich neighbors, Lk 14:12
parents and brothers and **r** and friends, Lk 21:16
called together his **r** and close friends. Acts 10:24
if anyone does not provide for his **r**, 1 Tm 5:8
believing woman has **r** who are 1 Tm 5:16

RELAX (2)
"Do not **r** your hand from your servants. Jos 10:6
for many years; **r**, eat, drink, be merry.' Lk 12:19

RELAXES (1)
Therefore whoever **r** one of the least of Mt 5:19

RELEASE (26)
of every seven years you shall grant a **r**. Dt 15:1
And this is the manner of the **r**: every Dt 15:2
every creditor shall **r** what he has lent to Dt 15:2
because the LORD'S **r** has been Dt 15:2
is with your brother your hand shall **r**. Dt 15:3
'The seventh year, the year of **r** is near,' Dt 15:9
years, at the set time in the year of **r**, Dt 31:10
I **r** you today from the chains on your Jer 40:4
was accustomed to **r** for the crowd Mt 27:15
"Whom do you want me to **r** for you: Mt 27:17
do you want me to **r** for you?" And they Mt 27:21
feast he used to **r** for them one prisoner Mk 15:6
"Do you want me to **r** for you the King Mk 15:9
to have him **r** for them Barabbas Mk 15:11
I will therefore punish and **r** him." Lk 23:16
with this man, and **r** to us Barabbas"— Lk 23:18
them once more, desiring to **r** Jesus, Lk 23:20
I will therefore punish and **r** him." Lk 23:22
custom that I should **r** one man for you Jn 18:39
do you want me to **r** to you the King of Jn 18:39
I have authority to **r** you and authority Jn 19:10
From then on Pilate sought to **r** him, Jn 19:12
the Jews cried out, "If you **r** this man, Jn 19:12
Pilate, when he had decided to **r** him. Acts 3:13
were tortured, refusing to accept **r**, Heb 11:35
"**R** the four angels who are bound at the Rv 9:14

RELEASED (21)
In the jubilee it shall be **r**, and he shall Lv 25:28
it shall not be **r** in the jubilee. Lv 25:30
and they shall be **r** in the jubilee. Lv 25:31
they possess shall be **r** in the jubilee. Lv 25:33
with him shall be **r** in the year of Lv 25:54
But the field, when it is **r** in the jubilee, Lv 27:21
The king sent and **r** him; the ruler of Ps 105:20
who is bowed down shall speedily be **r**; Is 51:14
when Pashhur **r** Jeremiah from the Jer 20:3
of that servant **r** him and forgave Mt 18:27
Then he **r** for them Barabbas, and Mt 27:26
his ears were opened, his tongue was **r**, Mk 7:35
the crowd, **r** for them Barabbas, Mk 15:15
He **r** the man who had been thrown Lk 23:25
When they were **r**, they went to their Acts 4:23
husband dies she is **r** from the law of Rom 7:2
But now we are **r** from the law, having Rom 7:6
that our brother Timothy has been **r**, Heb 13:23
year, were **r** to kill a third of mankind. Rv 9:15
After that he must be **r** for a little while. Rv 20:3
ended, Satan will be **r** from his prison Rv 20:7

RELENT (12)
burning anger and **r** from this disaster Ex 32:12
a grain offering. Shall I **r** for these things? Is 57:6
I will **r** of the disaster that I intended to Jer 18:8
then I will **r** of the good that I had Jer 18:10
that I may **r** of the disaster that I intend Jer 26:3
and the LORD will **r** of the disaster that Jer 26:13
did not the LORD **r** of the disaster that Jer 26:19
for I **r** of the disaster that I did to you. Jer 42:10
go back; I will not spare; I will not **r**; Ezk 24:14
knows whether he will not turn and **r**, Jl 2:14
God may turn and **r** and turn from his Jon 3:9
provoked me to wrath, and I did not **r**, Zec 8:14

RELENTED (9)
And the LORD **r** from the disaster that he Ex 32:14
the LORD **r** from the calamity and 2 Sm 24:16
saw, and he **r** from the calamity. 1 Chr 21:15
and **r** according to the abundance of Ps 106:45
I have not **r**, nor will I turn back." Jer 4:28
For after I had turned away, I **r**, and Jer 31:19
The LORD **r** concerning this; "It shall not Am 7:3
The LORD **r** concerning this; "This also Am 7:6
God **r** of the disaster that he had said he Jon 3:10

RELENTING (2)
you and destroyed you—I am weary of **r**. Jer 15:6
in steadfast love, and **r** from disaster. Jon 4:2

RELENTS (2)
no man **r** of his evil, saying, 'What have I Jer 8:6
in steadfast love; and he **r** over disaster. Jl 2:13

RELIABLE (3)
Mattaniah, for they were considered **r**, Neh 13:13
And I will get **r** witnesses, Uriah the priest Is 8:2
proved to be **r** and every transgression Heb 2:2

RELIANCE (1)
never again be the **r** of the house of Ezk 29:16

RELIED (3)
because they **r** on the LORD, 2 Chr 13:18
"Because you **r** on the king of Syria, 2 Chr 16:7
Yet because you **r** on the LORD, 2 Chr 16:8

RELIEF (10)
one shall bring us **r** from our work and Gn 5:29
r and deliverance will rise for the Jews Est 4:14
and got **r** from their enemies and killed Est 9:16
which the Jews got **r** from their enemies, Est 9:22
I must speak, that I may find **r**; I must Jb 32:20
You have given me **r** when I was in Ps 4:1
I will get **r** from my enemies and avenge Is 1:24
to send **r** to the brothers living in Acts 11:29
of taking part in the **r** of the saints— 2 Cor 8:4
and to grant **r** to you who are afflicted 2 Thes 1:7

RELIEVE (1)
a cave, and Saul went in to **r** himself. 1 Sm 24:3

RELIEVED (1)
"I **r** your shoulder of the burden; your Ps 81:6

RELIEVING (2)
"Surely he is **r** himself in the closet of Jgs 3:24
he is musing, or he is **r** himself, 1 Kgs 18:27

RELIGION (5)
him about their own **r** and about a Acts 25:19
strictest party of our **r** I have lived as Acts 26:5
promoting self-made **r** and asceticism Col 2:23
his heart, this person's **r** is worthless. Jas 1:26
R that is pure and undefiled before God, Jas 1:27

RELIGIOUS (2)
that in every way you are very **r**. Acts 17:22
anyone thinks he is **r** and does not Jas 1:26

RELUCTANTLY (1)
his mind, not **r** or under compulsion, 2 Cor 9:7

RELY (10)
us, O LORD our God, for we **r** on you, 2 Chr 14:11
and did not **r** on the LORD your God, 2 Chr 16:7
and perverseness and **r** on them, Is 30:12
go down to Egypt for help and **r** on horses, Is 31:1
the name of the LORD and **r** on his God. Is 50:10
they **r** on empty pleas, they speak lies, Is 59:4
You **r** on the sword, you commit Ezk 33:26
yourself a Jew and **r** on the law and Rom 2:17
was to make us **r** not on ourselves but 2 Cor 1:9
For all who **r** on works of the law are Gal 3:10

RELYING (1)
these people also, **r** on their dreams, Jude 1:8

REMAIN (103)
"Let the young woman **r** with us a Gn 24:55
"**R** a widow in your father's house, Gn 38:11
your brother, while you **r** confined, Gn 42:16
of your brothers **r** confined where you Gn 42:19
please let your servant **r** instead of the Gn 44:33
your flocks and your herds **r** behind." Ex 10:24
shall let none of it **r** until the morning; Ex 12:10
R each of you in his place; let no one go Ex 16:29
the fat of my feast **r** until the morning. Ex 23:18
The poles shall **r** in the rings of the ark; Ex 25:15
or of the bread **r** until the morning, Ex 29:34
of the Passover **r** until the morning. Ex 34:25
of meeting you shall **r** day and night for Lv 8:35
unclean and shall **r** unclean for you. Lv 11:35
He shall **r** unclean as long as he has the Lv 13:46
hired servant shall not **r** with you all Lv 19:13
it shall **r** seven days with its mother, Lv 22:27
then what he sold shall **r** in the hand of Lv 25:28
If there **r** but a few years until the year Lv 25:52
to the years that **r** until the year of Lv 27:18
to its valuation price, and it shall **r** his. Lv 27:19
shall **r** there in the cities of Gilead, Nm 32:26
our inheritance shall **r** with us Nm 32:32
them whom you let **r** shall be as Nm 33:55
For he must **r** in his city of refuge Nm 35:28
much livestock) shall **r** in the cities Dt 3:19
of the first day **r** all night until morning. Dt 16:4
was captured and shall **r** in your house Dt 21:13
his body shall not **r** all night on the Dt 21:23
and your livestock shall **r** in the land Jos 1:14
far from the city, but all of you **r** ready. Jos 8:4
of the cave, which **r** to this very day. Jos 10:27
in Gath, and in Ashdod did some **r**. Jos 11:22
him a place, and he shall **r** with them. Jos 20:4
And he shall **r** in that city until he has Jos 20:6
for your tribes those nations that **r**, Jos 23:4
R tonight, and in the morning, if he will Ru 3:13
of the God of Israel must not **r** with us, 1 Sm 5:7
saying, "Let David **r** in my service, 1 Sm 16:22

in hand, and **r** beside the stone heap. 1 Sm 20:19
to David, "Do not **r** in the stronghold; 1 Sm 22:5
"**R** at Jericho until your beards have 2 Sm 10:5
said to Uriah, "**R** here today also, 2 Sm 11:12
banished one will not **r** an outcast. 2 Sm 14:14
his I will be, and with him I will **r**. 2 Sm 16:18
to our brothers who **r** in all the lands 1 Chr 13:2
"**R** at Jericho until your beards have 1 Chr 19:5
go into their lairs, and **r** in their dens. Jb 37:8
and their heritage will **r** forever; Ps 37:18
Man in his pomp will not **r**; he is like Ps 49:12
They will perish, but you will **r**; they Ps 102:26
and those with integrity will **r** in it, Prv 2:21
And though a tenth **r** in it, it will be Is 6:13
and those who **r** will be very few and Is 16:14
Asherim or incense altars will **r** standing. Is 27:9
new earth that I make shall **r** before me, Is 66:22
so shall your offspring and your name **r**. Is 66:22
when heat comes, for its leaves **r** green, Jer 17:8
remnant of Jerusalem who **r** in this land, Jer 24:8
No refuge will **r** for the shepherds, nor Jer 25:35
carried to Babylon and **r** there until the Jer 27:22
and there he shall **r** until I visit him, Jer 32:5
If you **r**, then return to Gedaliah the son Jer 40:5
If you will **r** in this land, then I will Jer 42:10
on you and let you **r** in your own land. Jer 42:12
if you say, 'We will not **r** in this land,' Jer 42:13
of the LORD, to **r** in the land of Judah. Jer 43:4
fighting; they **r** in their strongholds; Jer 51:30
and you **r** exceedingly angry with us. Lam 5:22
None of them shall **r**, nor their Ezk 7:11
crown. Things shall not **r** as they are. Ezk 21:26
LORD said to me, "This gate shall **r** shut; Ezk 44:2
entered by it. Therefore it shall **r** shut. Ezk 44:2
They shall not **r** in the land of the LORD, Hos 9:3
And if ten men **r** in one house, they shall Am 6:9
And it shall **r** in his house and consume Zec 5:4
But Jerusalem shall **r** aloft on its site Zec 14:10
flee to Egypt, and **r** there until I tell you, Mt 2:13
to death; **r** here, and watch with me." Mt 26:38
even to death. **R** here and watch." Mk 14:34
And **r** in the same house, eating and Lk 10:7
whom you see the Spirit descend and **r**, Jn 1:33
The slave does not **r** in the house forever; Jn 8:35
believes in me may not **r** in darkness. Jn 12:46
the bodies would not **r** on the cross on Jn 19:31
"If it is my will that he **r** until I come, Jn 21:22
"If it is my will that he **r** until I come, Jn 21:23
remained unsold, did it not **r** your own? Acts 5:4
they asked him to **r** for some days. Acts 10:48
exhorted them all to **r** faithful to the Acts 11:23
it is good for them to **r** single as I am. 1 Cor 7:8
she should **r** unmarried or else be 1 Cor 7:11
Each one should **r** in the condition in 1 Cor 7:20
was called, there let him **r** with God. 1 Cor 7:24
it is good for a person to **r** as he is. 1 Cor 7:26
But to **r** in the flesh is more necessary Phil 1:24
know that I will **r** and continue with Phil 1:25
r at Ephesus that you may charge 1 Tm 1:3
over a man; rather, she is to **r** quiet. 1 Tm 2:12
those that are not cannot **r** hidden. 1 Tm 5:25
they will perish, but you **r**; they will all Heb 1:11
things that cannot be shaken may **r**. Heb 12:27
does come he must **r** only a little while. Rv 17:10

REMAINDER (6)
then you shall burn the **r** with fire. Ex 29:34
And the **r** shall be for the priest, as in the Lv 5:13
that is, the **r** of the clans of the Levites, Jos 21:40
And the **r** of the archers of the mighty Is 21:17
"The **r**, 5,000 cubits in breadth and Ezk 48:15
The **r** of the length alongside the holy Ezk 48:18

REMAINED (87)
So Tamar went and **r** in her father's Gn 38:11
yet his bow **r** unmoved; his arms were Gn 49:24
So Joseph **r** in Egypt, he and his father's Gn 50:22
So Pharaoh's heart **r** hardened, and he Ex 7:22
servants, and from his people; not one **r**. Ex 8:31
Not a green thing **r**, neither tree nor Ex 10:15
them into the sea, not one of them **r**. Ex 14:28
over the tabernacle, they **r** in camp. Nm 9:18
command of the LORD they **r** in camp; Nm 9:20
sometimes the cloud **r** from evening Nm 9:21
the people of Israel **r** in camp and did Nm 9:22
Now two men **r** in the camp, one Nm 11:26
to Hazeroth, and they **r** at Hazeroth. Nm 11:35
Caleb the son of Jephunneh **r** alive. Nm 14:38
and their inheritance **r** in the tribe of Nm 36:12
So you **r** at Kadesh many days, the days Dt 1:46
many days, the days that you **r** there. Dt 1:46
So we **r** in the valley opposite Beth-peor. Dt 3:29
I **r** on the mountain forty days and forty Dt 9:9
into the hills and **r** there three days until Jos 2:22
they **r** in their places in the camp until Jos 5:8
when the remnant that **r** of them had Jos 10:20
There **r** among the people of Israel seven Jos 18:2
of the people returned, and 10,000 **r**. Jgs 7:3
not consent. So Israel **r** at Kadesh. Jgs 11:17
him stay, and he **r** with him three days. Jgs 19:4
rock of Rimmon and **r** at the rock of Jgs 20:47
into the country of Moab and **r** there. Ru 1:2
So the woman **r** and nursed her 1 Sm 1:23
And David **r** in the strongholds in 1 Sm 23:14
David **r** at Horesh, and Jonathan 1 Sm 23:18
while two hundred **r** with the 1 Sm 25:13
But David **r** in the wilderness. 1 Sm 26:3
David **r** two days in Ziklag. 2 Sm 1:1
the ark of the LORD **r** in the house of 2 Sm 6:11
Rabbah. But David **r** at Jerusalem. 2 Sm 11:1
back." So Uriah **r** in Jerusalem that 2 Sm 11:12
back to Jerusalem, and they **r** there. 2 Sm 15:29
and all Israel **r** there six months, 1 Kgs 11:16
cult prostitutes who **r** in the days 1 Kgs 22:46
struck down all who **r** of the house 2 Kgs 10:11
struck down all who **r** to Ahab in 2 Kgs 10:17
And he **r** with her six years, hidden in 2 Kgs 11:3
and the Asherah also **r** in Samaria.) 2 Kgs 13:6
craftsmen and the smiths. None **r**, 2 Kgs 24:14
over the people who **r** in the land of 2 Kgs 25:22
the ark of God **r** with the household 1 Chr 13:14
Rabbah. But David **r** at Jerusalem. 1 Chr 20:1
Ethiopians fell until none **r** alive, 2 Chr 14:13
And he **r** with them six years, 2 Chr 22:12
to Jerusalem, and there we **r** three days. Ezr 8:32
Law, while the people **r** in their places. Neh 8:7
nine out of ten **r** in the other towns. Neh 11:1
Jerusalem. Also my wisdom **r** with me. Eccl 2:9
the only fortified cities of Judah that **r**. Jer 34:7
and there **r** of them only wounded men, Jer 37:10
dungeon cells and **r** there many days, Jer 37:16
So Jeremiah **r** in the court of the guard. Jer 37:21
And Jeremiah **r** in the court of the Jer 38:13
And Jeremiah **r** in the court of the Jer 38:28
deserted to him, and the people who **r**. Jer 39:9
him, and its roots **r** where it stood. Ezk 17:6
But Daniel **r** at the king's court. Dn 2:49
and **r** there until the death of Herod. Mt 2:15
Sodom, it would have **r** until this day. Mt 11:23
But Jesus **r** silent. And the high priest Mt 26:63
But he **r** silent and made no answer. Mk 14:61
kept making signs to them and **r** mute. Lk 1:22
And Mary **r** with her about three Lk 1:56
But they **r** silent. Then he took him and Lk 14:4
from heaven like a dove, and it **r** on him. Jn 1:32
and he **r** there with them and was Jn 3:22
day the crowd that **r** on the other side Jn 6:22
After saying this, he **r** in Galilee. Jn 7:9
been baptizing at first, and there he **r**. Jn 10:40
him, but Mary **r** seated in the house. Jn 11:20
While it **r** unsold, did it not remain Acts 5:4
So they **r** for a long time, speaking Acts 14:3
And they **r** no little time with the Acts 14:28
But Paul and Barnabas **r** in Antioch, Acts 15:35
colony. We **r** in this city some days. Acts 16:12
sea, but Silas and Timothy **r** there. Acts 17:14
The bow stuck and **r** immovable, Acts 27:41
to visit Cephas and **r** with him fifteen Gal 1:18
Erastus **r** at Corinth, and I left 2 Tm 4:20
so that you might put what **r** into order, Ti 1:5
consider those blessed who **r** steadfast. Jas 5:11

REMAINING (16)
and the names of the **r** six on the other Ex 28:10
Now the plunder **r** of the spoil that the Nm 31:32
their power is gone and there is none **r**, Dt 32:36
every person in it; he left none **r**. Jos 10:28
every person in it; he left none **r** in it. Jos 10:30
him and his people, until he left none **r**. Jos 10:33
He left none **r**, as he had done to Eglon, Jos 10:37
every person in it; he left none **r**. Jos 10:39
He left none **r**, but devoted to Jos 10:40
they struck them until he left none **r**. Jos 11:8
mix with these nations **r** among you or Jos 23:7
of these nations **r** among you and Jos 23:12
some men take five of the **r** horses, 2 Kgs 7:13
his priests, until he left him none **r**. 2 Kgs 10:11
and bury those travelers **r** on the face Ezk 39:14
none of them **r** among the nations Ezk 39:28

REMAINS (48)
While the earth **r**, seedtime and harvest, Gn 8:22
anything that **r** until the morning you Ex 12:10
And the part that **r** of the curtains of Ex 26:12
of the tent, the half curtain that **r**, Ex 26:12
And the extra that **r** in the length of the Ex 26:13
on the next day what **r** of it shall be Lv 7:16
But what **r** of the flesh of the sacrifice on Lv 7:17
And what **r** of the flesh and the bread Lv 8:32
But if the spot **r** in one place and does Lv 13:23
But if the spot **r** in one place and does Lv 13:28
some of the oil that **r** in his hand the Lv 14:17
a great heap of stones that **r** to this day. Jos 7:26
and there **r** yet very much land to Jos 13:1
This is the land that yet **r**: all the regions Jos 13:2
he said, "There **r** yet the youngest, 1 Sm 16:11
the king, "Behold, he **r** in Jerusalem, 2 Sm 16:3
the son of Shaphat **r** on his shoulders 2 Kgs 6:31
that I have erred, my error **r** with myself. Jb 19:4
takes notice of me; no refuge **r** to me; Ps 142:4
but a man of understanding **r** silent. Prv 11:12
comes, but the earth **r** forever. Eccl 1:4
is left in Zion and **r** in Jerusalem will be Is 4:3
whose stump **r** when it is felled." The holy Is 6:13
Nothing **r** but to crouch among the Is 10:4
recover the remnant that **r** of his people, Is 11:11
for the remnant that **r** of his people, Is 11:16
all the remnant that **r** of this evil family Jer 8:3
from Tyre and Sidon every helper that **r**. Jer 47:4
so his taste **r** in him, and his scent is Jer 48:11
so that there **r** in it no strong stem, Ezk 19:14
"What **r** on both sides of the holy Ezk 48:21
For now no strength **r** in me, and no Dn 10:17
out of Egypt. My Spirit **r** in your midst. Hg 2:5
earth, and behold, all the earth **r** at rest.' Zec 1:11
see life, but the wrath of God **r** on him. Jn 3:36
in the house forever; the son **r** forever. Jn 8:35
now that you say, 'We see,' your guilt **r**. Jn 9:41
falls into the earth and dies, it **r** alone; Jn 12:24
from the Law that the Christ **r** forever. Jn 12:34
she is happier if she **r** as she is. 1 Cor 7:40
covenant, that same veil **r** unlifted, 2 Cor 3:14
he **r** faithful—for he cannot deny 2 Tm 2:13
Since therefore it **r** for some to enter it, Heb 4:6
there **r** a Sabbath rest for the people of Heb 4:9
there no longer **r** a sacrifice for sins, Heb 10:26
is the man who **r** steadfast under trial, Jas 1:12
word of the Lord **r** forever." And this 1 Pt 1:25
and strengthen what **r** and is about to die, Rv 3:2

REMALIAH (13)
And Pekah the son of **R**, his captain, 2 Kgs 15:25
Pekah the son of **R** began to reign 2 Kgs 15:27
Pekah the son of **R** and struck him 2 Kgs 15:30
second year of Pekah the son of **R**, 2 Kgs 15:32
Pekah the son of **R** against Judah. 2 Kgs 15:37
year of Pekah the son of **R**, 2 Kgs 16:1
king of Syria and Pekah the son of **R**, 2 Kgs 16:5
the son of **R** killed 120,000 from 2 Chr 28:6
and Pekah the son of **R** the king of Israel Is 7:1
anger of Rezin and Syria and the son of **R**. Is 7:4
Syria, with Ephraim and the son of **R**, Is 7:5
and the head of Samaria is the son of **R**. Is 7:9
and rejoice over Rezin and the son of **R**, Is 8:6

REMEDY (1)
his people, until there was no **r**. 2 Chr 36:16

REMEMBER (166)
I will **r** my covenant that is between me Gn 9:15
will see it and **r** the everlasting covenant Gn 9:16
Only **r** me, when it is well with you, Gn 40:14
the chief cupbearer did not **r** Joseph, Gn 40:23
said to Pharaoh, "I **r** my offenses today. Gn 41:9
"**R** this day in which you came out from Ex 13:3
"**R** the Sabbath day, to keep it holy. Ex 20:8
R Abraham, Isaac, and Israel, your Ex 32:13
then I will **r** my covenant with Jacob, Lv 26:42
and I will **r** my covenant with Isaac Lv 26:42
with Abraham, and I will **r** the land. Lv 26:42
will for their sake **r** the covenant with Lv 26:45
We **r** the fish we ate in Egypt that cost Nm 11:5
look at and **r** all the commandments Nm 15:39
So you shall **r** and do all my Nm 15:40
You shall **r** that you were a slave in the Dt 5:15
them but you shall **r** what the LORD your Dt 7:18
And you shall **r** the whole way that the Dt 8:2
You shall **r** the LORD your God, for it is he Dt 8:18
R and do not forget how you provoked the Dt 9:7
R your servants, Abraham, Isaac, and Dt 9:27
You shall **r** that you were a slave in the Dt 15:15
of your life you may **r** the day when you Dt 16:3
You shall **r** that you were a slave in Dt 16:12
R what the LORD your God did to Miriam Dt 24:9
but you shall **r** that you were a slave in Dt 24:18
You shall **r** that you were a slave in the Dt 24:22
"**R** what Amalek did to you on the way Dt 25:17
R the days of old; consider the years of Dt 32:7
"**R** the word that Moses the servant of the Jos 1:13
of Israel did not **r** the LORD their God, Jgs 8:34
R also that I am your bone and your Jgs 9:2
please **r** me and please strengthen me Jgs 16:28
of your servant and **r** me and not 1 Sm 1:11
with my lord, then **r** your servant." 1 Sm 25:31
hold me guilty or **r** how your servant 2 Sm 19:19
to Naboth the Jezreelite. For **r**, 2 Kgs 9:25
please **r** how I have walked before you 2 Kgs 20:3
R the wondrous works that he has 1 Chr 16:12
R his covenant forever, the word 1 Chr 16:15

R your steadfast love for David your 2 Chr 6:42
the king did not **r** the kindness that 2 Chr 24:22
R the word that you commanded your Neh 1:8
R the Lord, who is great and awesome, Neh 4:14
R for my good, O my God, all that I Neh 5:19
R Tobiah and Sanballat, O my God, Neh 6:14
R me, O my God, concerning this, Neh 13:14
R this also in my favor, O my God, Neh 13:22
R them, O my God, because they have Neh 13:29
firstfruits. **R** me, O my God, for good. Neh 13:31
"**R**: who that was innocent ever perished? Jb 4:7
"**R** that my life is a breath; my eye will Jb 7:7
R that you have made me like clay; and Jb 10:9
you will **r** it as waters that have passed Jb 11:16
would appoint me a set time, and **r** me! Jb 14:13
When I **r** I am dismayed, and shuddering Jb 21:6
"**R** to extol his work, of which men have Jb 36:24
r the battle—you will not do it again! Jb 41:8
May he **r** all your offerings and regard Ps 20:3
ends of the earth shall **r** and turn to the Ps 22:27
R your mercy, O LORD, and your steadfast Ps 25:6
R not the sins of my youth or my Ps 25:7
according to your steadfast love **r** me, for Ps 25:7
These things I **r**, as I pour out my soul: Ps 42:4
therefore I **r** you from the land of Jordan Ps 42:6
when I **r** you upon my bed, and meditate Ps 63:6
R your congregation, which you have Ps 74:2
R Mount Zion, where you have dwelt. Ps 74:2
R this, O LORD, how the enemy scoffs, Ps 74:18
r how the foolish scoff at you all the Ps 74:22
When I **r** God, I moan; when I meditate, Ps 77:3
I said, "Let me **r** my song in the night; let Ps 77:6
I will **r** the deeds of the LORD; yes, I will Ps 77:11
LORD; yes, I will **r** your wonders of old. Ps 77:11
They did not **r** his power or the day Ps 78:42
Do not **r** against us our former Ps 79:8
grave, like those whom you **r** no more, Ps 88:5
R how short my time is! For what Ps 89:47
R, O Lord, how your servants are Ps 89:50
keep his covenant and **r** to do his Ps 103:18
R the wondrous works that he has done, Ps 105:5
R me, O LORD, when you show favor to Ps 106:4
they did not **r** the abundance of your Ps 106:7
For he did not **r** to show kindness, but Ps 109:16
R your word to your servant, in which Ps 119:49
I **r** your name in the night, O LORD, Ps 119:55
R, O LORD, in David's favor, all the Ps 132:1
the roof of my mouth, if I do not **r** you, Ps 137:6
R, O LORD, against the Edomites the day Ps 137:7
I **r** the days of old; I meditate on all that Ps 143:5
their poverty and **r** their misery no Prv 31:7
For he will not much **r** the days of his Eccl 5:20
but let him **r** that the days of darkness Eccl 11:8
R also your Creator in the days of your Eccl 12:1
r how I have walked before you in Is 38:3
"**R** not the former things, nor consider Is 43:18
my own sake, and I will not **r** your sins. Is 43:25
R these things, O Jacob, and Israel, for Is 44:21
"**R** this and stand firm, recall it to mind, Is 46:8
r the former things of old; for I am God, Is 46:9
not lay these things to heart or **r** their end. Is 47:7
of your widowhood you will **r** no more. Is 54:4
fear, so that you lied, and did not **r** me, Is 57:11
those who **r** you in your ways. Is 64:5
angry, O LORD, and **r** not iniquity forever. Is 64:9
the LORD, "I **r** the devotion of your youth, Jer 2:2
now he will **r** their iniquity and punish Jer 14:10
r and do not break your covenant with Jer 14:21
r me and visit me, and take vengeance Jer 15:15
while their children **r** their altars and Jer 17:2
R how I stood before you to speak good Jer 18:20
as I speak against him, I do **r** him still. Jer 31:20
iniquity, and I will **r** their sin no more." Jer 31:34
of the land, did not the LORD **r** them? Jer 44:21
R the LORD from far away, and let Jer 51:50
R my affliction and my wanderings, Lam 3:19
R, O LORD, what has befallen us; look, Lam 5:1
you who escape will **r** me among the Ezk 6:9
whorings you did not **r** the days of Ezk 16:22
yet I will **r** my covenant with you in Ezk 16:60
Then you will **r** your ways and be Ezk 16:61
that you may **r** and be confounded, Ezk 16:63
And there you shall **r** your ways and Ezk 20:43
your eyes to them or **r** Egypt anymore. Ezk 23:27
Then you will **r** your evil ways, and Ezk 36:31
they do not consider that I **r** all their evil. Hos 7:2
Now he will **r** their iniquity and punish Hos 8:13
days of Gibeah: he will **r** their iniquity; Hos 9:9
and did not **r** the covenant of Am 1:9
r what Balak king of Moab devised, Mi 6:5
years make it known; in wrath **r** mercy. Hab 3:2
yet in far countries they shall **r** me, Zec 10:9
"**R** the law of my servant Moses, the Mal 4:4
the altar and there **r** that your brother Mt 5:23
Do you not **r** the five loaves for the five Mt 16:9
said, "Sir, we **r** how that impostor said, Mt 27:63
ears do you not hear? And do you not **r**? Mk 8:18
our fathers and to **r** his holy covenant, Lk 1:72
r that you in your lifetime received Lk 16:25
R Lot's wife. Lk 17:32
r me when you come into your Lk 23:42
R how he told you, while he was still in Lk 24:6
R the word that I said to you: 'A servant Jn 15:20
hour comes you may **r** that I told them Jn 16:4
help the weak and **r** the words of the Acts 20:35
r it is not you who support the root, Rom 11:18
you because you **r** me in everything 1 Cor 11:2
Only, they asked us to **r** the poor, the Gal 2:10
Therefore **r** that at one time you Eph 2:11
r that you were at that time separated Eph 2:12
with my own hand. **R** my chains. Col 4:18
For you **r**, brothers, our labor and 1 Thes 2:9
that you always **r** us kindly and 1 Thes 3:6
Do you not **r** that when I was still 2 Thes 2:5
as I **r** you constantly in my prayers 2 Tm 1:3
As I **r** your tears, I long to see you, that 2 Tm 1:4
R Jesus Christ, risen from the dead, the 2 Tm 2:8
God always when I **r** you in my Phlm 1:4
and I will **r** their sins no more." Heb 8:12
"I will **r** their sins and their lawless Heb 10:17
R those who are in prison, as though in Heb 13:3
R your leaders, those who spoke to you Heb 13:7
that you should **r** the predictions of the 2 Pt 3:2
But you must **r**, beloved, the Jude 1:17
R therefore from where you have fallen; Rv 2:5
R, then, what you received and heard. Rv 3:3

REMEMBERED (59)
But God **r** Noah and all the beasts and all Gn 8:1
God **r** Abraham and sent Lot out of the Gn 19:29
Then God **r** Rachel, and God listened to Gn 30:22
And Joseph **r** the dreams that he had Gn 42:9
and God **r** his covenant with Abraham, Ex 2:24
I am to be **r** throughout all generations. Ex 3:15
hold as slaves, and I have **r** my covenant. Ex 6:5
cause my name to be **r** I will come to Ex 20:24
that you may be **r** before the LORD your Nm 10:9
Hannah his wife, and the LORD **r** her. 1 Sm 1:19
he **r** Vashti and what she had done and Est 2:1
days should be **r** and kept throughout Est 9:28
they are no longer **r**, so wickedness is Jb 24:20
your name to be **r** in all generations; Ps 45:17
They **r** that God was their rock, the Ps 78:35
He **r** that they were but flesh, a wind Ps 78:39
let the name of Israel be **r** no more!" Ps 83:4
He has **r** his steadfast love and Ps 98:3
you are **r** throughout all generations. Ps 102:12
For he **r** his holy promise, and Ps 105:42
For their sake he **r** his covenant, and Ps 106:45
of his fathers be **r** before the LORD, Ps 109:14
has caused his wondrous works to be **r**; Ps 111:4
never be moved; he will be **r** forever. Ps 112:6
The LORD has **r** us; he will bless us; he Ps 115:12
It is he who **r** us in our low estate, for Ps 136:23
we sat down and wept, when we **r** Zion. Ps 137:1
the city. Yet no one **r** that poor man. Eccl 9:15
salvation and have not **r** the Rock of Is 17:10
sing many songs, that you may be **r**." Is 23:16
Then he **r** the days of old, of Moses and Is 63:11
things shall not be **r** or come into mind. Is 65:17
not come to mind or be **r** or missed; Jer 3:16
the living, that his name be **r** no more." Jer 11:19
he has not **r** his footstool in the day of Lam 2:1
deeds that he has done shall not be **r**, Ezk 3:20
Because you have not **r** the days of Ezk 16:43
has committed shall be **r** against him; Ezk 18:22
deeds that he has done shall be **r**; Ezk 18:24
you have made your guilt to be **r**, Ezk 21:24
You shall be no more **r**, for I the LORD Ezk 21:32
Ammonites may be **r** no more among Ezk 25:10
none of his righteous deeds shall be **r**, Ezk 33:13
has committed shall be **r** against him. Ezk 33:16
and they shall be **r** by name no more. Hos 2:17
my life was fainting away, I **r** the LORD, Jon 2:7
land, so that they shall be **r** no more. Zec 13:2
And Peter **r** the saying of Jesus, "Before Mt 26:75
And Peter **r** and said to him, "Rabbi, Mk 11:21
And Peter **r** how Jesus had said to him, Mk 14:72
And Peter **r** the saying of the Lord, how Lk 22:61
And they **r** his words, Lk 24:8
His disciples **r** that it was written, "Zeal Jn 2:17
dead, his disciples **r** that he had said this, Jn 2:22
then they **r** that these things had been Jn 12:16
your alms have been **r** before God. Acts 10:31
And I **r** the word of the Lord, how he Acts 11:16
fell, and God **r** Babylon the great, Rv 16:19
as heaven, and God has **r** her iniquities. Rv 18:5

REMEMBERING (4)
her whoring, **r** the days of her youth, Ezk 23:19
r that for three years I did not cease Acts 20:31
thanks for you, **r** you in my prayers, Eph 1:16
r before our God and Father your 1 Thes 1:3

REMEMBERS (8)
our frame; he **r** that we are dust. Ps 103:14
He **r** his covenant forever, the word that Ps 105:8
who fear him; he **r** his covenant forever. Ps 111:5
Jerusalem **r** in the days of her affliction Lam 1:7
My soul continually **r** it and is bowed Lam 3:20
He **r** his officers; they stumble as they go, Na 2:5
the baby, she no longer **r** the anguish, Jn 16:21
as he **r** the obedience of you all, 2 Cor 7:15

REMEMBRANCE (28)
as stones of **r** for the sons of Israel. Ex 28:12
the LORD on his two shoulders for **r**. Ex 28:12
bring them to regular **r** before the LORD. Ex 28:29
the people of Israel to **r** before the LORD, Ex 30:16
ephod to be stones of **r** for the sons of Ex 39:7
of jealousy, a grain offering of **r**, Nm 5:15
remembrance, bringing iniquity to **r**. Nm 5:15
in her hands the grain offering of **r**, Nm 5:18
keep my name in **r**." He called the 2 Sm 18:18
to bring my sin to **r** and to cause the 1 Kgs 17:18
For in death there is no **r** of you; in Sheol Ps 6:5
There is no **r** of former things, nor will Eccl 1:11
will there be any **r** of later things yet Eccl 1:11
as of the fool there is no enduring **r**, Eccl 2:16
your name and **r** are the desire of our Is 26:8
us, but your name alone we bring to **r**. Is 26:13
destruction and wiped out all **r** of them. Is 26:14
Put me in **r**; let us argue together; set Is 43:26
You who put the LORD in **r**, take no rest, Is 62:6
oaths, but he brings their guilt to **r**, Ezk 21:23
appear—because you have come to **r**, Ezk 21:24
and a book of **r** was written before him Mal 3:16
his servant Israel, in **r** of his mercy, Lk 1:54
is given for you. Do this in **r** of me." Lk 22:19
and bring to your **r** all that I have Jn 14:26
which is for you. Do this in **r** of me." 1 Cor 11:24
as often as you drink it, in **r** of me." 1 Cor 11:25
I thank my God in all my **r** of you, Phil 1:3

REMETH (1)
R, En-gannim, En-haddah, Jos 19:21

REMIND (9)
I will **r** them of your righteousness, Ps 71:16
Lord, to **r** you of my ways in Christ, 1 Cor 4:17
Now I would **r** you, brothers, of the 1 Cor 15:1
let him **r** himself that just as he is 2 Cor 10:7
For this reason I **r** you to fan into 2 Tm 1:6
R them of these things, and charge 2 Tm 2:14
R them to be submissive to rulers and Ti 3:1
I intend always to **r** you of these 2 Pt 1:12
Now I want to **r** you, although you once Jude 1:5

REMINDED (1)
I am **r** of your sincere faith, a faith that 2 Tm 1:5

REMINDER (7)
They shall be a **r** of you before your Nm 10:10
to be a **r** to the people of Israel, so that Nm 16:40
the temple of the LORD as a **r** to Helem, Zec 6:14
to you very boldly by way of **r**, Rom 15:15
sacrifices there is a **r** of sin every year. Heb 10:3
in this body, to stir you up by way of **r**, 2 Pt 1:13
up your sincere mind by way of **r**, 2 Pt 3:1

REMISSION (1)
He also granted a **r** of taxes to the Est 2:18

REMNANT (83)
you to preserve for you a **r** on earth, Gn 45:7
Bashan was left of the **r** of the Rephaim. Dt 3:11
and when the **r** that remained of them Jos 10:20
of Bashan, one of the **r** of the Rephaim, Jos 12:4
alone was left of the **r** of the Rephaim); Jos 13:12
and cling to the **r** of these nations Jos 23:12
Then down marched the **r** of the noble; Jgs 5:13
neither name nor **r** on the face 2 Sm 14:7
of Israel but of the **r** of the Amorites. 2 Sm 21:2
he exterminated the **r** of the male 1 Kgs 22:46
up your prayer for the **r** that is left." 2 Kgs 19:4
And the surviving **r** of the house of 2 Kgs 19:30
For out of Jerusalem shall go a **r**, 2 Kgs 19:31
I will forsake the **r** of my heritage 2 Kgs 21:14
they defeated the **r** of the Amalekites 1 Chr 4:43
turn again to the **r** of you who have 2 Chr 30:6
and from all the **r** of Israel and from 2 Chr 34:9
to leave us a **r** and to give us a secure Ezr 9:8
and have given us such a **r** as this, Ezr 9:13
us, so that there should be no **r**, Ezr 9:14
just, for we are left a **r** that has escaped, Ezr 9:15
"The **r** there in the province who had Neh 1:3
the **r** of wrath you will put on like a Ps 76:10
The **r** of the trees of his forest will be so Is 10:19
In that day the **r** of Israel and the Is 10:20
A **r** will return, the remnant of Jacob, to Is 10:21
A remnant will return, the **r** of Jacob, to Is 10:21

of the sea, only a **r** of them will return. Is 10:22
time to recover the **r** that remains of his Is 11:11
from Assyria for the **r** that remains of Is 11:16
will cut off from Babylon name and **r**, Is 14:22
root with famine, and your **r** it will slay. Is 14:30
of Moab who escape, for the **r** of the land. Is 15:9
and the **r** of Syria will be like the glory of Is 17:3
a diadem of beauty, to the **r** of his people, Is 28:5
lift up your prayer for the **r** that is left.'" Is 37:4
And the surviving **r** of the house of Is 37:31
For out of Jerusalem shall go a **r**, and Is 37:32
of Jacob, all the **r** of the house of Israel, Is 46:3
glean thoroughly as a vine the **r** of Israel; Jer 6:9
to life by all the **r** that remains of this evil Jer 8:3
Then I will gather the **r** of my flock out Jer 23:3
the **r** of Jerusalem who remain in this Jer 24:8
Gaza, Ekron, and the **r** of Ashdod); Jer 25:20
'O LORD, save your people, the **r** of Israel.' Jer 31:7
Babylon had left a **r** in Judah and had Jer 40:11
and the **r** of Judah would perish?" Jer 40:15
for all this **r**—because we are left with Jer 42:2
hear the word of the LORD, O **r** of Judah. Jer 42:15
They shall have no **r** or survivor from Jer 42:17
The LORD has said to you, O **r** of Judah, Jer 42:19
forces took all the **r** of Judah who had Jer 43:5
the midst of Judah, leaving you no **r**? Jer 44:7
I will take the **r** of Judah who have set Jer 44:12
so that none of the **r** of Judah who have Jer 44:14
and all the **r** of Judah, who came to the Jer 44:28
the **r** of the coastland of Caphtor. Jer 47:4
O **r** of their valley, how long will you Jer 47:5
I will pardon those whom I leave as a **r**. Jer 50:20
Will you destroy all the **r** of Israel in the Ezk 9:8
you make a full end of the **r** of Israel?" Ezk 11:13
and the **r** of the Philistines shall perish," Am 1:8
will be gracious to the **r** of Joseph. Am 5:15
they may possess the **r** of Edom and all Am 9:12
you, O Jacob; I will gather the **r** of Israel; Mi 2:12
and the lame I will make the **r**, and those Mi 4:7
Then the **r** of Jacob shall be in the midst Mi 5:7
And the **r** of Jacob shall be among the Mi 5:8
transgression for the **r** of his Mi 7:18
all the **r** of the peoples shall plunder you, Hab 2:8
off from this place the **r** of Baal and the Zep 1:4
the possession of the **r** of the house of Zep 2:7
The **r** of my people shall plunder them, Zep 2:9
high priest, with all the **r** of the people, Hg 1:12
and the spirit of all the **r** of the people. Hg 1:14
high priest, and to all the **r** of the people, Hg 2:2
in the sight of the **r** of this people in those Zec 8:6
will not deal with the **r** of this people as Zec 8:11
And I will cause the **r** of this people to Zec 8:12
its teeth; it too shall be a **r** for our God; Zec 9:7
that the **r** of mankind may seek the Acts 15:17
the sea, only a **r** of them will be saved, Rom 9:27
So too at the present time there is a **r**, Rom 11:5

REMOTE (3)
all their iniquities on itself to a **r** area, Lv 16:22
was sojourning in the **r** parts of the hill Jgs 19:1
in Judah to the **r** parts of the hill Jgs 19:18

REMOTEST (1)
cypresses, to come to its **r** height, Is 37:24

REMOVAL (3)
this will be the full fruit of the **r** of his sin: Is 27:9
more," indicates the **r** of things that Heb 12:27
not as a **r** of dirt from the body but as 1 Pt 3:21

REMOVE (52)
your God only to **r** this death from me." Ex 10:17
first day you shall **r** leaven out of your Ex 12:15
to speak with him, he would **r** the veil, Ex 34:34
He shall **r** its crop with its contents and Lv 1:16
the liver that he shall **r** with the kidneys. Lv 3:4
he shall **r** the whole fat tail, cut off close to Lv 3:9
the liver that he shall **r** with the kidneys. Lv 3:10
the liver that he shall **r** with the kidneys. Lv 3:15
bull of the sin offering he shall **r** from it, Lv 4:8
the liver that he shall **r** with the kidneys Lv 4:9
And all its fat he shall **r**, as the fat is Lv 4:31
And all its fat he shall **r** as the fat of the Lv 4:35
the liver that he shall **r** with the kidneys. Lv 7:4
And I will **r** harmful beasts from the Lv 26:6
my hand! Then I would **r** Abimelech. Jgs 9:29
r the kings, each from his post, and 1 Kgs 20:24
"I will **r** Judah also out of my sight, 2 Kgs 23:27
of the LORD, to **r** them out of his sight, 2 Kgs 24:3
and I will no more **r** the foot of Israel 2 Chr 33:8
if you **r** injustice far from your tents, Jb 22:23
R your stroke from me; I am spent by Ps 39:10
but I will not **r** from him my steadfast Ps 89:33
far does he **r** our transgressions from Ps 103:12
R far from me falsehood and lying; give Prv 30:8
R vexation from your heart, and put Eccl 11:10
r the evil of your deeds from before my Is 1:16
dross as with lye and **r** all your alloy. Is 1:25
I will do to my vineyard. I will **r** its hedge, Is 5:5
I **r** the boundaries of peoples, and Is 10:13
r every obstruction from my people's Is 57:14
If you **r** your detestable things from my Jer 4:1
r the foreskin of your hearts, O men of Jer 4:4
I will **r** you from the face of the earth. Jer 28:16
this day, so that I will **r** it from my sight Jer 32:31
they will **r** from it all its detestable Ezk 11:18
I will **r** the heart of stone from their Ezk 11:19
R the turban and take off the crown. Ezk 21:26
their thrones and **r** their robes and Ezk 26:16
And I will **r** the heart of stone from Ezk 36:26
For I will **r** the names of the Baals from Hos 2:17
"I will **r** the northerner far from you, and Jl 2:20
the Greeks in order to **r** them far from their Jl 3:6
from which you cannot **r** your necks, Mi 2:3
for then I will **r** from your midst your Zep 3:11
"**R** the filthy garments from him." And Zec 3:4
and I will **r** the iniquity of this land in a Zec 3:9
And also I will **r** from the land the Zec 13:2
possible for you. **R** this cup from me. Mk 14:36
if you are willing, **r** this cup from me. Lk 22:42
him not seek to **r** the marks of 1 Cor 7:18
I have all faith, so as to **r** mountains, 1 Cor 13:2
come to you and **r** your lampstand from Rv 2:5

REMOVED (49)
And Noah **r** the covering of the ark and Gn 8:13
But that day Laban **r** the male goats Gn 30:35
Then Joseph **r** them from his knees, Gn 48:12
and **r** the swarms of flies from Pharaoh, Ex 8:31
as the fat is **r** from the peace offerings, Lv 4:31
fat of the lamb is **r** from the sacrifice of Lv 4:35
When the cloud **r** from over the tent, Nm 12:10
Their protection is **r** from them, and Nm 14:9
'I have **r** the sacred portion out of my Dt 26:13
or **r** any of it while I was unclean, Dt 26:14
So Saul **r** him from his presence and 1 Sm 18:13
which is **r** from before the LORD, 1 Sm 21:6
of the land and **r** all the idols that 1 Kgs 15:12
He also **r** Maacah his mother from 1 Kgs 15:13
But the high places were not **r**; the 2 Kgs 14:4
the high places were not **r**. 2 Kgs 15:35
before the LORD he **r** from the front 2 Kgs 16:14
of the stands and **r** the basin from 2 Kgs 16:17
angry with Israel and **r** them out of 2 Kgs 17:18
until the LORD **r** Israel out of his 2 Kgs 17:23
He **r** the high places and broke the 2 Kgs 18:4
places and altars Hezekiah has **r**, 2 Kgs 18:22
And he **r** the horses that the kings of 2 Kgs 23:11
And Josiah **r** all the shrines also of 2 Kgs 23:19
out of my sight, as I have **r** Israel, 2 Kgs 23:27
King Asa **r** from being queen 2 Chr 15:16
set to work and **r** the altars that were 2 Chr 30:14
away, and the rock is **r** from its place; Jb 14:18
for you, or the rock be **r** out of its place? Jb 18:4
my prayer or **r** his steadfast love Ps 66:20
The righteous will never be **r**, but the Prv 10:30
he **r** them with his fierce breath in the Is 27:8
high places and altars Hezekiah has **r**, Is 36:7
is plucked up and **r** from me like a Is 38:12
may depart and the hills be **r**, Is 54:10
of peace shall not be **r**," says the LORD, Is 54:10
refining goes on, for the wicked are not **r**. Jer 6:29
that you will be **r** far from your land, Jer 27:10
Though I **r** them far off among the Ezk 11:16
before me. So I **r** them, when I saw it. Ezk 16:50
and he arose from his throne, **r** his robe, Jon 3:6
of the crowd, they **r** the roof above him, Mk 2:4
so that when I am **r** from management, Lk 16:4
God **r** him from there into this land in Acts 7:4
And when he had **r** him, he raised up Acts 13:22
has done this be **r** from among you. 1 Cor 5:2
one turns to the Lord, the veil is **r**. 2 Cor 3:16
case the offense of the cross has been **r**. Gal 5:11
and island was **r** from its place. Rv 6:14

REMOVES (4)
he who **r** mountains, and they know it Jb 9:5
and the LORD **r** people far away, and the Is 6:12
seasons; he **r** kings and sets up kings; Dn 2:21
of my people; how he **r** it from me! Mi 2:4

REMOVING (1)
r from it every speckled and spotted Gn 30:32

REND (2)
Oh that you would **r** the heavens and Is 64:1
and **r** your hearts and not your Jl 2:13

RENDER (17)
offering of theirs, which they **r** to me, Nm 18:9
forgive and act and **r** to each whose 1 Kgs 8:39
place and forgive and **r** to each whose 2 Chr 6:30
of their hands; **r** them their due reward. Ps 28:4
Those who **r** me evil for good accuse Ps 38:20
O God; I will **r** thank offerings to you. Ps 56:12
For you will **r** to a man according to Ps 62:12
and of the coastlands **r** him tribute; Ps 72:10
What shall I **r** to the LORD for all his Ps 116:12
to the coastlands he will **r** repayment. Is 59:18
the whirlwind, to **r** his anger in fury, Is 66:15
says the LORD of hosts, **R** true judgments, Zec 7:9
r in your gates judgments that are true Zec 8:16
"Therefore **r** to Caesar the things that Mt 22:21
"**R** to Caesar the things that are Mk 12:17
"Then **r** to Caesar the things that are Lk 20:25
He will **r** to each one according to his Rom 2:6

RENDERED (2)
of the judgment that the king had **r**, 1 Kgs 3:28
know all the service he **r** at Ephesus. 2 Tm 1:18

RENDERING (3)
of the LORD, **r** recompense to his enemies! Is 66:6
vengeance, the repayment he is **r** her. Jer 51:6
r service with a good will as to the Lord Eph 6:7

RENDING (1)
lion they tear my soul apart, **r** it in pieces, Ps 7:2

RENEW (7)
to Gilgal and there **r** the kingdom." 1 Sm 11:14
You **r** your witnesses against me and Jb 10:17
O God, and **r** a right spirit within me. Ps 51:10
and you **r** the face of the ground. Ps 104:30
wait for the LORD shall **r** their strength; Is 40:31
coastlands; let the peoples **r** their strength; Is 41:1
may be restored! **R** our days as of old— Lam 5:21

RENEWAL (3)
I would wait, till my **r** should come. Jb 14:14
be transformed by the **r** of your mind, Rom 12:2
washing of regeneration and **r** of the Holy Ti 3:5

RENEWED (6)
like grass that is **r** in the morning: Ps 90:5
in the morning it flourishes and is **r**; in Ps 90:6
so that your youth is **r** like the eagle's. Ps 103:5
inner nature is being **r** day by day. 2 Cor 4:16
and to be **r** in the spirit of your minds, Eph 4:23
which is being **r** in knowledge after the Col 3:10

RENOUNCE (3)
Why does the wicked **r** God and say in Ps 10:13
of you who does not **r** all that he has Lk 14:33
training us to **r** ungodliness and worldly Ti 2:12

RENOUNCED (2)
You have **r** the covenant with your Ps 89:39
But we have **r** disgraceful, 2 Cor 4:2

RENOUNCES (1)
greedy for gain curses and **r** the LORD. Ps 10:3

RENOWN (8)
men who were of old, the men of **r**. Gn 6:4
name, O LORD, endures forever, your **r**, Ps 135:13
the **r** of Moab is no more. In Heshbon Jer 48:2
And your **r** went forth among the Ezk 16:14
because of your **r** and lavished your Ezk 16:15
all of them, officers and men of **r**, Ezk 23:23
it will bring them **r** on the day that Ezk 39:13
shame into praise and **r** in all the earth. Zep 3:19

RENOWNED (9)
in Ephrathah and be **r** in Bethlehem, Ru 4:11
and may his name be **r** in Israel! Ru 4:14
He was the most **r** of the thirty and 2 Sm 23:19
He was **r** among the thirty, but he 2 Sm 23:23
He was the most **r** of the thirty and 1 Chr 11:21
He was **r** among the thirty, but he 1 Chr 11:25
were inhabited from the seas, O city **r**, Ezk 26:17
provide for them **r** plantations so that Ezk 34:29
I will make you **r** and praised among Zep 3:20

REPAID (11)
to them, 'Why have you **r** evil for good? Gn 44:4
so God has **r** me." And they brought him Jgs 1:7
than I, for you have **r** me good, 1 Sm 24:17
me good, whereas I have **r** you evil. 1 Sm 24:17
what was right, and it was not **r** to me. Jb 33:27
if I have **r** my friend with evil or plundered Ps 7:4
If the righteous is **r** on earth, how Prv 11:31
Should good be **r** with evil? Yet they Jer 18:20
also invite you in return and you be **r**. Lk 14:12
You will be **r** at the resurrection of the Lk 14:14
a gift to him that he might be **r**?" Rom 11:35

REPAIR (11)
and let them **r** the house wherever 2 Kgs 12:5
hand it over for the **r** of the house." 2 Kgs 12:7
and that they should not **r** the house. 2 Kgs 12:8
and quarried stone to **r** the house. 2 Kgs 22:6
all Israel money to **r** the house of 2 Chr 24:5
iron and bronze to **r** the house of the 2 Chr 24:12
to **r** the house of the LORD his God. 2 Chr 34:8
set up the house of our God, to **r** its ruins, Ezr 9:9
torn it open; **r** its breaches, for it totters. Ps 60:2

they shall **r** the ruined cities, the Is 61:4
David that is fallen and **r** its breaches, Am 9:11

REPAIRED (42)
And he **r** the altar of the LORD that 1 Kgs 18:30
circuit, and Joab **r** the rest of the city. 1 Chr 11:8
and he **r** the altar of the LORD that was 2 Chr 15:8
of the house of the LORD and **r** them. 2 Chr 29:3
the son of Uriah, son of Hakkoz **r**. Neh 3:4
son of Berechiah, son of Meshezabel **r**. Neh 3:4
next to them Zadok the son of Baana **r**. Neh 3:4
And next to them the Tekoites **r**, but Neh 3:5
the son of Besodeiah **r** the Gate of Neh 3:6
next to them **r** Melatiah the Gibeonite Neh 3:7
goldsmiths, **r**. Next to him Hananiah, Neh 3:8
r, and they restored Jerusalem as far as Neh 3:8
ruler of half the district of Jerusalem, **r**. Neh 3:9
son of Harumaph **r** opposite his house. Neh 3:10
Hattush the son of Hashabneiah **r**. Neh 3:10
son of Pahath-moab **r** another section Neh 3:11
of Jerusalem, **r**, he and his daughters. Neh 3:12
inhabitants of Zanoah **r** the Valley Neh 3:13
and **r** a thousand cubits of the wall, Neh 3:13
of Beth-haccherem, **r** the Dung Gate. Neh 3:14
district of Mizpah, **r** the Fountain Gate. Neh 3:15
r to a point opposite the tombs of Neh 3:16
After him the Levites **r**: Rehum the son Neh 3:17
the district of Keilah, **r** for his district. Neh 3:17
After him their brothers **r**: Bavvai the Neh 3:18
r another section opposite the ascent to Neh 3:19
son of Zabbai **r** another section from Neh 3:20
son of Hakkoz **r** another section from Neh 3:21
the men of the surrounding area, **r**. Neh 3:22
and Hasshub **r** opposite their Neh 3:23
son of Ananiah **r** beside his own Neh 3:23
the son of Henadad **r** another section, Neh 3:24
the son of Uzai **r** opposite the buttress Neh 3:25
servants living on Ophel **r** to a point Neh 3:26
him the Tekoites **r** another section Neh 3:27
Above the Horse Gate the priests **r**, Neh 3:28
the son of Immer **r** opposite his own Neh 3:29
the keeper of the East Gate, **r**. Neh 3:29
sixth son of Zalaph **r** another section. Neh 3:30
son of Berechiah **r** opposite his Neh 3:30
r as far as the house of the temple Neh 3:31
the goldsmiths and the merchants **r**. Neh 3:32

REPAIRER (1)
you shall be called the **r** of the breach, Is 58:12

REPAIRING (7)
them, "Why are you not **r** the house? 2 Kgs 12:7
workmen who were **r** the house of 2 Kgs 12:14
at the house of the LORD, **r** the house 2 Kgs 22:5
and the **r** went forward in their 2 Chr 24:13
LORD gave it for **r** and restoring the 2 Chr 34:10
the walls and **r** the foundations. Ezr 4:12
Ashdodites heard that the **r** of the walls Neh 4:7

REPAIRS (4)
wherever any need of **r** is discovered." 2 Kgs 12:5
priests had made no **r** on the house. 2 Kgs 12:6
stone for making **r** on the house 2 Kgs 12:12
for any outlay for the **r** of the house. 2 Kgs 12:12

REPAY (44)
has not kept it in, he shall **r** ox for ox, Ex 21:36
it or sells it, he shall **r** five oxen for an ox, Ex 22:1
who hates him. He will **r** him to his face. Dt 7:10
Do you thus **r** the LORD, you foolish and Dt 32:6
adversaries and will **r** those who hate Dt 32:41
come they may **r** Gibeah of Benjamin, Jgs 20:10
The LORD **r** you for what you have done, Ru 2:12
The LORD **r** the evildoer according to 2 Sm 3:39
that the LORD will **r** me with good for 2 Sm 16:12
should the king **r** me with such 2 Sm 19:36
the LORD—I will **r** you on this plot of 2 Kgs 9:26
to the work of a man he will **r** him, Jb 34:11
first given to me, that I should **r** him? Jb 41:11
They **r** me evil for good; my soul is Ps 35:12
me, and raise me up, that I may **r** them! Ps 41:10
earth; **r** to the proud what they deserve! Ps 94:2
nor **r** us according to our iniquities. Ps 103:10
LORD, and he will **r** him for his deed. Prv 19:17
Do not say, "I will **r** evil"; wait for the Prv 20:22
and will he not **r** man according to his Prv 24:12
According to their deeds, so will he **r**, Is 59:18
me: "I will not keep silent, but I will **r**; Is 65:6
will repay; I will indeed **r** into their bosom Is 65:6
first I will doubly **r** their iniquity and Jer 16:18
but you **r** the guilt of fathers to their Jer 32:18
R her according to her deeds; do to her Jer 50:29
"I will **r** Babylon and all the Jer 51:24
is a God of recompense; he will surely **r**. Jer 51:56
"You will **r** them, O LORD, according to Lam 3:64
for their ways and **r** them for their deeds. Hos 4:9
he will **r** him according to his deeds. Hos 12:2
on him and will **r** him for his Hos 12:14
then he will **r** each person according Mt 16:27
spend, I will **r** you when I come back.' Lk 10:35
be blessed, because they cannot **r** you. Lk 14:14
R no one evil for evil, but give Rom 12:17
written, "Vengeance is mine, I will **r**, Rom 12:19
it just to **r** with affliction those 2 Thes 1:6
the Lord will **r** him according to his 2 Tm 4:14
I will **r** it—to say nothing of your Phlm 1:19
is mine; I will **r**." And again, Heb 10:30
Do not **r** evil for evil or reviling for 1 Pt 3:9
others, and **r** her double for her deeds; Rv 18:6
me, to **r** everyone for what he has done. Rv 22:12

REPAYING (1)
r the guilty by bringing his conduct 2 Chr 6:23

REPAYMENT (4)
Will he then make **r** to suit you, Jb 34:33
to his adversaries, **r** to his enemies; Is 59:18
to the coastlands he will render **r**. Is 59:18
vengeance, the **r** he is rendering her. Jer 51:6

REPAYS (6)
and **r** to their face those who hate him, Dt 7:10
He **r** those who hate him and cleanses Dt 32:43
and who **r** him for what he has done? Jb 21:31
faithful but abundantly **r** the one who Ps 31:23
shall he be who **r** you with what you Ps 137:8
See that no one **r** anyone evil for evil, 1 Thes 5:15

REPEALED (1)
and the Medes so that it may not be **r**, Est 1:19

REPEAT (2)
there they **r** the righteous triumphs of Jgs 5:11
I **r**, let no one think me foolish. But 2 Cor 11:16

REPEATED (3)
he **r** them in the ears of the LORD. 1 Sm 8:21
were heard, they **r** them before Saul, 1 Sm 17:31
this before a hundred men?" So he **r**, 2 Kgs 4:43

REPEATEDLY (4)
which my soul has sought **r**, but I Eccl 7:28
Nor was it to offer himself **r**, as the Heb 9:25
had to suffer **r** since the foundation Heb 9:26
service, offering **r** the same sacrifices, Heb 10:11

REPEATING (1)
you mean by **r** this proverb Ezk 18:2

REPEATS (2)
but he who **r** a matter separates close Prv 17:9
to his vomit is a fool who **r** his folly. Prv 26:11

REPENT (37)
and **r** and plead with you in the land 1 Kgs 8:47
if they **r** with all their mind and with 1 Kgs 8:48
and **r** and plead with you in the land 2 Chr 6:37
if they **r** with all their mind and with 2 Chr 6:38
I despise myself, and **r** in dust and ashes." Jb 42:6
If a man does not **r**, God will whet his Ps 7:12
by justice, and those in her who **r**, Is 1:27
harder than rock; they have refused to **r**. Jer 5:3
R and turn away from your idols, and Ezk 14:6
R and turn from all your Ezk 18:30
"**R**, for the kingdom of heaven is at hand." Mt 3:2
"**R**, for the kingdom of heaven is at Mt 4:17
had been done, because they did not **r**. Mt 11:20
is at hand; **r** and believe in the gospel." Mk 1:15
and proclaimed that people should **r**. Mk 6:12
but unless you **r**, you will all likewise Lk 13:3
but unless you **r**, you will all likewise Lk 13:5
goes to them from the dead, they will **r**.' Lk 16:30
turns to you seven times, saying, 'I **r**,' Lk 17:4
"**R** and be baptized every one of you in Acts 2:38
R therefore, and turn again, that your Acts 3:19
R, therefore, of this wickedness of Acts 8:22
commands all people everywhere to **r**, Acts 17:30
that they should **r** and turn to God, Acts 26:20
rejected, for he found no chance to **r**, Heb 12:17
fallen; **r**, and do the works you did at first. Rv 2:5
lampstand from its place, unless you **r**. Rv 2:5
Therefore **r**. If not, I will come to you Rv 2:16
I gave her time to **r**, but she refuses to Rv 2:21
but she refuses to **r** of her sexual Rv 2:21
tribulation, unless they **r** of her works, Rv 2:22
you received and heard. Keep it, and **r**. Rv 3:3
and discipline, so be zealous and **r**. Rv 3:19
did not **r** of the works of their hands nor Rv 9:20
nor did they **r** of their murders or their Rv 9:21
They did not **r** and give him glory. Rv 16:9
and sores. They did not **r** of their deeds. Rv 16:11

REPENTANCE (20)
Bear fruit in keeping with **r**. Mt 3:8
"I baptize you with water for **r**, but he Mt 3:11
a baptism of **r** for the forgiveness Mk 1:4
a baptism of **r** for the forgiveness Lk 3:3
Bear fruits in keeping with **r**. And do not Lk 3:8
to call the righteous but sinners to **r**." Lk 5:32
righteous persons who need no **r**. Lk 15:7
and that **r** and forgiveness of sins Lk 24:47
to give **r** to Israel and forgiveness of Acts 5:31
also God has granted **r** that leads to Acts 11:18
proclaimed a baptism of **r** to all the Acts 13:24
"John baptized with the baptism of **r**, Acts 19:4
and to Greeks of **r** toward God and of Acts 20:21
deeds in keeping with their **r**. Acts 26:20
kindness is meant to lead you to **r**? Rom 2:4
godly grief produces a **r** that leads to 2 Cor 7:10
perhaps grant them **r** leading to a 2 Tm 2:25
again a foundation of **r** from dead works Heb 6:1
to restore again to **r** those who have once Heb 6:4
perish, but that all should reach **r**. 2 Pt 3:9

REPENTED (8)
him; they **r** and sought God earnestly. Ps 78:34
You recently **r** and did what was right Jer 34:15
overtake your fathers? So they **r** and said, Zec 1:6
they would have **r** long ago in Mt 11:21
it, for they **r** at the preaching of Jonah, Mt 12:41
and Sidon, they would have **r** long ago, Lk 10:13
it, for they **r** at the preaching of Jonah, Lk 11:32
and have not **r** of the impurity, 2 Cor 12:21

REPENTING (1)
but because you were grieved into **r**. 2 Cor 7:9

REPENTS (3)
one sinner who **r** than over ninety-nine Lk 15:7
angels of God over one sinner who **r**." Lk 15:10
brother sins, rebuke him, and if he **r**, Lk 17:3

REPHAEL (1)
Othni, **R**, Obed and Elzabad, whose 1 Chr 26:7

REPHAH (1)
R was his son, Resheph his son, 1 Chr 7:25

REPHAIAH (5)
Pelatiah and Jeshaiah, his son **R**, his 1 Chr 3:21
Pelatiah, Neariah, **R**, and Uzziel, 1 Chr 4:42
Uzzi, **R**, Jeriel, Jahmai, Ibsam, and 1 Chr 7:2
fathered Binea, and **R** was his son, 1 Chr 9:43
Next to them **R** the son of Hur, ruler of Neh 3:9

REPHAIM (18)
defeated the **R** in Ashteroth-karnaim, Gn 14:5
the Hittites, the Perizzites, the **R**, Gn 15:20
the Anakim they are also counted as **R**, Dt 2:11
(It is also counted as a land of **R**. Dt 2:20
R formerly lived there—but the Dt 2:20
Bashan was left of the remnant of the **R**. Dt 3:11
portion of Bashan is called the land of **R**. Dt 3:13
of Bashan, one of the remnant of the **R**, Jos 12:4
alone was left of the remnant of the **R**); Jos 13:12
at the northern end of the Valley of **R**. Jos 15:8
in the land of the Perizzites and the **R**, Jos 17:15
is at the north end of the Valley of **R**. Jos 18:16
and spread out in the Valley of **R**. 2 Sm 5:18
and spread out in the Valley of **R**. 2 Sm 5:22
was encamped in the Valley of **R**. 2 Sm 23:13
was encamped in the Valley of **R**. 1 Chr 11:15
and made a raid in the Valley of **R**. 1 Chr 14:9
gleans the ears of grain in the Valley of **R**. Is 17:5

REPHAN (1)
of Moloch and the star of your god **R**, Acts 7:43

REPHIDIM (5)
of the LORD, and camped at **R**, Ex 17:1
came and fought with Israel at **R**. Ex 17:8
They set out from **R** and came into the Ex 19:2
set out from Alush and camped at **R**, Nm 33:14
they set out from **R** and camped in the Nm 33:15

REPLACE (1)
and to **r** every man's money in his Gn 42:25

REPLACED (2)
which was **r** in our sacks the first time, Gn 43:18
to be **r** by hot bread on the day it is 1 Sm 21:6

REPLANTED (1)
ruined places and **r** that which was Ezk 36:36

REPLENISH (1)
and every languishing soul I will **r**." Jer 31:25

REPLENISHED (1)
I shall be **r**, now that she is laid waste,' Ezk 26:2

REPLIED (20)
"What pledge shall I give you?" She **r**, Gn 38:18
And Judah **r**, "Let her keep the things Gn 38:23
They **r**, "The man questioned us Gn 43:7
He **r**, "Peace to you, do not be afraid. Gn 43:23
And she **r**, "All that you say I will do." Ru 3:5
She **r**, "Wait, my daughter, until you Ru 3:18
The king **r** to him, "Do as he has said, 1 Kgs 2:31
Then I **r** to them, "The God of heaven Neh 2:20
Then Daniel **r** with prudence and Dn 2:14
But the centurion **r**, "Lord, I am not Mt 8:8
But he **r** to the man who told him, Mt 12:48

Simon Peter **r**, "You are the Christ, the Mt 16:16
But he **r** to one of them, 'Friend, I am Mt 20:13
asked him, "What is your name?" He **r**, Mk 5:9
Jesus **r**, "A man was going down from Lk 10:30
They **r**, "Are you from Galilee too? Jn 7:52
After they finished speaking, James **r**, Acts 15:13
Paul **r**, "I am a Jew, from Tarsus in Acts 21:39
had nodded to him to speak, Paul **r**: Acts 24:10
Festus **r** that Paul was being kept at Acts 25:4

REPLY (8)
and if anyone greets you, do not **r**. 2 Kgs 4:29
And this was their **r** to us: 'We are the Ezr 5:11
Then Mordecai told them to **r** to Esther, Est 4:13
Then Esther told them to **r** to Mordecai, Est 4:15
or let me speak, and you **r** to me. Jb 13:22
Then Peter said in **r**, "See, we have left Mt 19:27
And they could not **r** to these things. Lk 14:6
But what is God's **r** to him? "I have Rom 11:4

REPORT (36)
Joseph brought a bad **r** of them to their Gn 37:2
When the **r** was heard in Pharaoh's Gn 45:16
"You shall not spread a false **r**. You shall Ex 23:1
people of Israel a bad **r** of the land that Nm 13:32
bringing up a bad **r** about the land— Nm 14:36
who brought up a bad **r** of the land— Nm 14:37
who shall hear the **r** of you and shall Dt 2:25
For we have heard a **r** of him, and all that Jos 9:9
And the **r** was good in the eyes of the Jos 22:33
brothers said to them, "What do you **r**?" Jgs 18:8
it is no good **r** that I hear the people of 1 Sm 2:24
"The **r** was true that I heard in my 1 Kgs 10:6
prosperity surpass the **r** that I heard. 1 Kgs 10:7
Beersheba to Dan, and bring me a **r**, 1 Chr 21:2
"The **r** was true that I heard in my 2 Chr 9:5
told me; you surpass the **r** that I heard. 2 Chr 9:6
them until the **r** should reach Darius Ezr 5:5
They sent him a **r**, in which was written Ezr 5:7
When the **r** comes to Egypt, they will be Is 23:5
will be in anguish over the **r** about Tyre. Is 23:5
We have heard the **r** of it; our hands fall Jer 6:24
"We must **r** all these words to the Jer 36:16
king of Babylon heard the **r** of them, Jer 50:43
be not fearful at the **r** heard in the land, Jer 51:46
when a **r** comes in one year and Jer 51:46
year and afterward a **r** in another year, Jer 51:46
will come to you to **r** to you the news. Ezk 24:26
them according to the **r** made to their Hos 7:12
We have heard a **r** from the LORD, and a Ob 1:1
O LORD, I have heard the **r** of you, and Hab 3:2
And the **r** of this went through all that Mt 9:26
and a **r** about him went out through all Lk 4:14
now even more the **r** about him went Lk 5:15
And this **r** about him spread through Lk 7:17
The **r** of this came to the ears of the Acts 11:22
For they themselves **r** concerning us 1 Thes 1:9

REPORTED (25)
we will do." And Moses **r** the words of the Ex 19:8
they **r** the matter in the ears of the 1 Sm 11:4
and Jonathan **r** to him all these 1 Sm 19:7
sent out scouts, and they **r** to him, 1 Kgs 20:17
behind me." And the watchman **r**, 2 Kgs 9:18
Again the watchman **r**, "He reached 2 Kgs 9:20
came to the king, and **r** to the king, 2 Kgs 22:9
the king, and further **r** to the king, 2 Chr 34:16
was written, "It is **r** among the nations, Neh 6:6
in my presence and **r** my words to him. Neh 6:19
in Susa the citadel was **r** to the king. Est 9:11
and they **r** all the words to the king. Jer 36:20
and they went and **r** to their master all Mt 18:31
some days, it was **r** that he was at home. Mk 2:1
The disciples of John **r** all these things to Lk 7:18
the servant came and **r** these things to Lk 14:21
to their friends and **r** what the chief Acts 4:23
in the prison, so they returned and **r**, Acts 5:22
but ran in and **r** that Peter was Acts 12:14
And the jailer **r** these words to Paul, Acts 16:36
The police **r** these words to the Acts 16:38
coming here has **r** or spoken any Acts 28:21
For it has been **r** to me by Chloe's 1 Cor 1:11
It is actually **r** that there is sexual 1 Cor 5:1
faith and love and **r** that you always 1 Thes 3:6

REPORTS (6)
did not believe the **r** until I came and 1 Kgs 10:7
I did not believe the **r** until I came and 2 Chr 9:6
And according to these **r** you wish to Neh 6:6
And now the king will hear of these **r**. Neh 6:7
She had heard the **r** about Jesus and Mk 5:27
And **r** about him went out into every Lk 4:37

REPOSE (1)
rest; give rest to the weary; and this is **r**"; Is 28:12

REPRESENT (2)
You shall **r** the people before God and Ex 18:19
to **r** you before the Chaldeans who will Jer 40:10

REPRESENTING (1)
twelve men, each **r** his fathers' house. Nm 1:44

REPROACH (48)
and said, "God has taken away my **r**." Gn 30:23
have rolled away the **r** of Egypt from Jos 5:9
among the sheaves, and do not **r** her. Ru 2:15
and takes away the **r** from Israel? 1 Sm 17:26
These ten times you have cast **r** upon me; Jb 19:3
my heart does not **r** me for any of my Jb 27:6
nor takes up a **r** against his friend; Ps 15:3
of all my adversaries I have become a **r**, Ps 31:11
For it is for your sake that I have borne **r**, Ps 69:7
of those who **r** you have fallen Ps 69:9
my soul with fasting, it became my **r**. Ps 69:10
You know my **r**, and my shame and Ps 69:19
Turn away the **r** that I dread, for your Ps 119:39
a nation, but sin is a **r** to any people. Prv 14:34
is a son who brings shame and **r**. Prv 19:26
be called by your name; take away our **r**." Is 4:1
and the **r** of his people he will take away Is 25:8
fear not the **r** of man, nor be dismayed at Is 51:7
and the **r** of your widowhood you will Is 54:4
away; know that for your sake I bear **r**. Jer 15:15
become for me a **r** and derision all day Jer 20:8
upon you everlasting **r** and perpetual Jer 23:40
to all the kingdoms of the earth, to be a **r**, Jer 24:9
and a **r** among all the nations where I Jer 29:18
are put to shame, for we have heard **r**; Jer 51:51
and an object of **r** among the nations Ezk 5:14
You shall be a **r** and a taunt, a warning Ezk 5:15
an object of **r** for the daughters Ezk 16:57
Ammonites and concerning their **r**; Ezk 21:28
I have made you a **r** to the nations, Ezk 22:4
no longer suffer the **r** of the nations. Ezk 34:29
you have suffered the **r** of the nations. Ezk 36:6
around you shall themselves suffer **r**. Ezk 36:7
you hear anymore the **r** of the nations, Ezk 36:15
O LORD, and make not your heritage a **r**, Jl 2:17
more make you a **r** among the nations. Jl 2:19
so that you will no longer suffer **r**. Zep 3:18
me, to take away my **r** among people." Lk 1:25
and blameless and above **r** before him, Col 1:22
Therefore an overseer must be above **r**, 1 Tm 3:2
as well, so that they may be without **r**. 1 Tm 5:7
and free from **r** until the appearing 1 Tm 6:14
if anyone is above **r**, the husband of one Ti 1:6
as God's steward, must be above **r**. Ti 1:7
publicly exposed to **r** and affliction, Heb 10:33
He considered the **r** of Christ greater Heb 11:26
the camp and bear the **r** he endured. Heb 13:13
who gives generously to all without **r**, Jas 1:5

REPROACHED (1)
reproaches of those who **r** you fell on Rom 15:3

REPROACHES (4)
and the **r** of those who reproach you Ps 69:9
R have broken my heart, so that I am in Ps 69:20
glad, that I may answer him who **r** me. Prv 27:11
"The **r** of those who reproached you Rom 15:3

REPROOF (16)
But what does **r** from you reprove? Jb 6:25
If you turn at my **r**, behold, I will pour Prv 1:23
counsel and would have none of my **r**, Prv 1:25
of my counsel and despised all my **r**, Prv 1:30
LORD'S discipline or be weary of his **r**, Prv 3:11
discipline, and my heart despised **r**! Prv 5:12
he who rejects **r** leads others astray. Prv 10:17
knowledge, but he who hates **r** is stupid. Prv 12:1
but whoever heeds **r** is honored. Prv 13:18
but whoever heeds **r** is prudent. Prv 15:5
the way; whoever hates **r** will die. Prv 15:10
listens to life-giving **r** will dwell Prv 15:31
he who listens to **r** gains intelligence. Prv 15:32
The rod and **r** give wisdom, but a Prv 29:15
O Rock, have established them for **r**. Hab 1:12
God and profitable for teaching, for **r**, 2 Tm 3:16

REPROOFS (1)
and the **r** of discipline are the way of Prv 6:23

REPROVE (9)
words! But what does reproof from you **r**? Jb 6:25
Do you think that you can **r** words, when Jb 6:26
Do not **r** a scoffer, or he will hate you; Prv 9:8
you; **r** a wise man, and he will love you. Prv 9:8
r a man of understanding, and he will Prv 19:25
you, and your apostasy will **r** you. Jer 2:19
shall be mute and unable to **r** them, Ezk 3:26
r, rebuke, and exhort, with complete 2 Tm 4:2
Those whom I love, I **r** and discipline, so Rv 3:19

REPROVED (5)
When Abraham **r** Abimelech about a Gn 21:25
A scoffer does not like to be **r**; he will Prv 15:12
He who is often **r**, yet stiffens his neck, Prv 29:1
who had been **r** by him for Herodias, Lk 3:19
the Lord, nor be weary when **r** by him. Heb 12:5

REPROVER (1)
of gold is a wise **r** to a listening ear. Prv 25:12

REPROVES (6)
"Behold, blessed is the one whom God **r**; Jb 5:17
fear of him that he **r** you and enters into Jb 22:4
for the LORD **r** him whom he loves, as a Prv 3:12
and he who **r** a wicked man incurs Prv 9:7
lay a snare for him who **r** in the gate, Is 29:21
They hate him who **r** in the gate, and Am 5:10

REPTILE (1)
of beast and bird, of **r** and sea creature, Jas 3:7

REPTILES (4)
also of beasts, and of birds, and of **r**, 1 Kgs 4:33
kinds of animals and **r** and birds of Acts 10:12
beasts of prey and **r** and birds of the Acts 11:6
man and birds and animals and **r**. Rom 1:23

REPULSE (2)
How then can you **r** a single captain 2 Kgs 18:24
How then can you **r** a single captain Is 36:9

REPUTATION (3)
I am a poor man and have no **r**?" 1 Sm 18:23
and having a **r** for good works: if she 1 Tm 5:10
your works. You have the **r** of being alive, Rv 3:1

REPUTE (2)
upon you, and your ill **r** have no end. Prv 25:10
from among you seven men of good **r**, Acts 6:3

REQUEST (17)
said to them, "Let me make a **r** of you: Jgs 8:24
will perform the **r** of his servant. 2 Sm 14:15
has granted the **r** of his servant." 2 Sm 14:22
And now I have one **r** to make of you; 1 Kgs 2:16
"I have one small **r** to make of you; 1 Kgs 2:20
the king said to her, "Make your **r**, 1 Kgs 2:20
is it, Queen Esther? What is your **r**? Est 5:3
shall be granted you. And what is your **r**? Est 5:6
Esther answered, "My wish and my **r** is: Est 5:7
king to grant my wish and fulfill my **r**, Est 5:8
shall be granted you. And what is your **r**? Est 7:2
me for my wish, and my people for my **r**. Est 7:3
you. And what further is your **r**? Est 9:12
"Oh that I might have my **r**, and that God Jb 6:8
and have not withheld the **r** of his lips. Ps 21:2
the LORD your God according to your **r**, Jer 42:4
Daniel made a **r** of the king, and he Dn 2:49

REQUESTED (2)
earrings that he **r** was 1,700 shekels Jgs 8:26
Daniel went in and **r** the king to appoint Dn 2:16

REQUESTING (1)
"What are you **r**?" So I prayed to the God Neh 2:4

REQUESTS (2)
thanksgiving let your **r** be made known Phil 4:6
that we have the **r** that we have asked 1 Jn 5:15

REQUIRE (21)
for your lifeblood I will **r** a reckoning: Gn 9:5
from every beast I will **r** it and from man. Gn 9:5
fellow man I will **r** a reckoning for the Gn 9:5
safety. From my hand you shall **r** him. Gn 43:9
what does the LORD your God **r** of you, Dt 10:12
in my name, I myself will **r** it of him. Dt 18:19
LORD your God will surely **r** it of you, Dt 23:21
But one thing I **r** of you; that is, you 2 Sm 3:13
shall I not now **r** his blood at your 2 Sm 4:11
Why then should my lord **r** this? 1 Chr 21:3
as the priests at Jerusalem **r**—let that be Ezr 6:9
restore these and **r** nothing from them. Neh 5:12
but his blood I will **r** at your hand. Ezk 3:18
but his blood I will **r** at your hand. Ezk 3:20
there I will **r** your contributions and Ezk 20:40
his blood I will **r** at the watchman's Ezk 33:6
but his blood I will **r** at your hand. Ezk 33:8
and I will **r** my sheep at their hand Ezk 34:10
and what does the LORD **r** of you but to do Mi 6:8
our more presentable parts do not **r**. 1 Cor 12:24
marriage and **r** abstinence from 1 Tm 4:3

REQUIRED (27)
From my hand you **r** it, whether stolen Gn 31:39
Forty days were **r** for it, for that is how Gn 50:3
that is how many are **r** for embalming. Gn 50:3
the objects that they are **r** to carry. Nm 4:32
priest and bring the offering **r** of her, Nm 5:15
because the king's business **r** haste." 1 Sm 21:8
brought to the place where it was **r**, 1 Kgs 4:28
king of Assyria **r** of Hezekiah king 2 Kgs 18:14
for they were **r** to count them when 1 Chr 9:28
before the ark as each day **r**, 1 Chr 16:37
according to the number **r** of them, 1 Chr 23:31
as the duty of each day **r**, offering 2 Chr 8:13

the priests as the duty of each day **r**, 2 Chr 8:14
"Why have you not **r** the Levites to 2 Chr 24:6
duty of each day **r**—for their service 2 Chr 31:16
according to the rule, as each day **r**, Ezr 3:4
And whatever else is **r** for the house of Ezr 7:20
for the singers, as every day **r**. Neh 11:23
into them the portions **r** by the Law Neh 12:44
offering and sin offering you have not **r**. Ps 40:6
For there our captors **r** of us songs, and Ps 137:3
who has **r** of you this trampling of my Is 1:12
I tell you, it will be **r** of this generation. Lk 11:51
This night your soul is **r** of you, and Lk 12:20
was given, of him much will be **r**, Lk 12:48
it is **r** of stewards that they be found 1 Cor 4:2
to command you to do what is **r**, Phlm 1:8

REQUIREMENT (2)
order that the righteous **r** of the law Rom 8:4
of a legal **r** concerning bodily descent, Heb 7:16

REQUIREMENTS (1)
you no greater burden than these **r**: Acts 15:28

REQUIRES (4)
of his people Israel, as each day **r**, 1 Kgs 8:59
the Law of the God of heaven, **r** of you, Ezr 7:21
the law, by nature do what the law **r**, Rom 2:14
produce the righteousness that God **r**. Jas 1:20

REQUIRING (1)
"If any case arises **r** decision between one Dt 17:8

RESCUE (34)
—that he might **r** him out of their Gn 37:22
Their cry for **r** from slavery came up to Ex 2:23
him with it; you shall **r** it with him. Ex 23:5
congregation shall **r** the manslayer Nm 35:25
cried for help there was no one to **r** her. Dt 22:27
one draws near to **r** her husband from Dt 25:11
surely overtake and shall surely **r**." 1 Sm 30:8
Come up and **r** me from the hand of 2 Kgs 16:7
let him **r** him, for he delights in him!" Ps 22:8
Incline your ear to me; **r** me speedily! Be Ps 31:2
r me from the hand of my enemies and Ps 31:15
and by its great might it cannot **r**. Ps 33:17
R me from their destruction, my Ps 35:17
your righteousness deliver me and **r** me; Ps 71:2
R me, O my God, from the hand of the Ps 71:4
R the weak and the needy; deliver them Ps 82:4
in trouble; I will **r** him and honor him. Ps 91:15
r me and deliver me from the many Ps 144:7
R me and deliver me from the hand of Ps 144:11
R those who are being taken away to Prv 24:11
prey; they carry it off, and none can **r**. Is 5:29
and deliver it; he will spare and **r** it." Is 31:5
have become plunder with none to **r**, Is 42:22
I will **r** my sheep from their mouths, Ezk 34:10
and I will **r** them from all places Ezk 34:12
I will **r** my flock; they shall no longer Ezk 34:22
other god who is able to **r** in this way." Dn 3:29
labored till the sun went down to **r** him. Dn 6:14
was no one who could **r** from his power. Dn 8:4
was no one who could **r** the ram from his Dn 8:7
and no one shall **r** her out of my hand. Hos 2:10
I will carry off, and no one shall **r**. Hos 5:14
The Lord will **r** me from every evil 2 Tm 4:18
Lord knows how to **r** the godly from 2 Pt 2:9

RESCUED (22)
heard it, he **r** him out of their hands, Gn 37:21
taken, and David **r** his two wives. 1 Sm 30:18
He **r** me from my strong enemy, 2 Sm 22:18
me out into a broad place; he **r** me, 2 Sm 22:20
that he is **r** in the day of wrath? Jb 21:30
day when the LORD **r** him from the hand Ps 18:T
He **r** me from my strong enemy and Ps 18:17
me out into a broad place; he **r** me, Ps 18:19
me; you **r** me from the man of violence. Ps 18:48
To you they cried and were **r**; in you they Ps 22:5
You have **r** me from the horns of the Ps 22:21
and **r** us from our foes, for his Ps 136:24
mighty, or the captives of a tyrant be **r**? Is 49:24
be taken, and the prey of the tyrant be **r**, Is 49:25
of Israel who dwell in Samaria be **r**, Am 3:12
There you shall be **r**; there the LORD will Mi 4:10
and **r** him out of all his afflictions and Acts 7:10
sent his angel and **r** me from the Acts 12:11
them with the soldiers and **r** him, Acts 23:27
yet from them all the Lord **r** me. 2 Tm 3:11
it. So I was **r** from the lion's mouth. 2 Tm 4:17
and if he **r** righteous Lot, greatly 2 Pt 2:7

RESCUES (3)
who **r** David his servant from the Ps 144:10
He delivers and **r**; he works signs and Dn 6:27
"As the shepherd **r** from the mouth of Am 3:12

RESEMBLED (1)
Every one of them **r** the son of a king." Jgs 8:18

RESEMBLING (3)
of the Holy Place was something **r** Ezk 41:21
God for images **r** mortal man and Rom 1:23
but **r** the Son of God he continues a Heb 7:3

RESEN (1)
R between Nineveh and Calah; that is Gn 10:12

RESENTFUL (1)
on its own way; it is not irritable or **r**; 1 Cor 13:5

RESERVE (1)
food shall be a **r** for the land against Gn 41:36

RESERVED (7)
"Have you not **r** a blessing for me?" Gn 27:36
of the most holy things, **r** from the fire: Nm 18:9
for there a commander's portion was **r**; Dt 33:21
apportion the contribution **r** for the 2 Chr 31:14
which I have **r** for the time of trouble, Jb 38:23
the gloom of utter darkness has been **r**. 2 Pt 2:17
of utter darkness has been **r** forever. Jude 1:13

RESERVOIR (1)
You made a **r** between the two walls for Is 22:11

RESHEPH (1)
Rephah was his son, **R** his son, Telah 1 Chr 7:25

RESIDE (1)
the sojourners who **r** among you and Ezk 47:22

RESIDENCE (1)
power as a royal **r** and for the glory Dn 4:30

RESIDENT (3)
gather together the **r** aliens who were 1 Chr 22:2
counted all the **r** aliens who were 2 Chr 2:17
do no wrong or violence to the **r** alien, Jer 22:3

RESIDENTS (4)
and Elamites and **r** of Mesopotamia, Acts 2:9
And all the **r** of Lydda and Sharon saw Acts 9:35
so that all the **r** of Asia heard the Acts 19:10
known to all the **r** of Ephesus, Acts 19:17

RESIDES (1)
In whatever tribe the sojourner **r**, Ezk 47:23

RESIDING (1)
and Simeon who were **r** with them, 2 Chr 15:9

RESIST (7)
I say to you, Do not **r** the one who is evil. Mt 5:39
and ears, you always **r** the Holy Spirit. Acts 7:51
find fault? For who can **r** his will?" Rom 9:19
and those who **r** will incur judgment. Rom 13:2
God. **R** the devil, and he will flee from you. Jas 4:7
the righteous person. He does not **r** you. Jas 5:6
R him, firm in your faith, knowing that 1 Pt 5:9

RESISTED (1)
sin you have not yet **r** to the point of Heb 12:4

RESISTS (2)
Therefore whoever **r** the authorities Rom 13:2
resists the authorities **r** what God has Rom 13:2

RESOLUTELY (1)
He set to work **r** and built up all the 2 Chr 32:5

RESOLVE (1)
and may fulfill every **r** for good and 2 Thes 1:11

RESOLVED (3)
But Daniel **r** that he would not defile Dn 1:8
her to shame, **r** to divorce her quietly. Mt 1:19
after these events Paul **r** in the Spirit Acts 19:21

RESORTED (1)
And Solomon and the assembly **r** to it. 2 Chr 1:5

RESOUND (1)
The clamor will **r** to the ends of the Jer 25:31

RESOUNDED (1)
a mighty shout, so that the earth **r**. 1 Sm 4:5

RESOURCE (1)
help in me, when **r** is driven from me? Jb 6:13

RESPECT (19)
to the LORD, "Do not **r** their offering. Nm 16:15
nation who shall not **r** the old or show Dt 28:50
will be guiltless with **r** to this oath of Jos 2:17
shall be guiltless with **r** to your oath Jos 2:20
hands; no **r** is shown to the elders. Lam 5:12
to them, saying, 'They will **r** my son.' Mt 21:37
to them, saying, 'They will **r** my son.' Mk 12:6
'Though I neither fear God nor **r** man, Lk 18:4
beloved son; perhaps they will **r** him.' Lk 20:13
It is with **r** to the hope and the Acts 23:6
'It is with **r** to the resurrection of the Acts 24:21
is owed, **r** to whom respect is owed, Rom 13:7
is owed, respect to whom **r** is owed, Rom 13:7
to **r** those who labor among you and 1 Thes 5:12
to be made like his brothers in every **r**, Heb 2:17
one who in every **r** has been tempted as Heb 4:15
be subject to your masters with all **r**, 1 Pt 2:18
yet do it with gentleness and **r**, having a 1 Pt 3:16
With **r** to this they are surprised when 1 Pt 4:4

RESPECTABLE (2)
should adorn themselves in **r** apparel, 1 Tm 2:9
self-controlled, **r**, hospitable, 1 Tm 3:2

RESPECTED (3)
a **r** member of the Council, Mk 15:43
judge who neither feared God nor **r** man. Lk 18:2
who disciplined us and we **r** them. Heb 12:9

RESPECTFUL (1)
when they see your **r** and pure conduct. 1 Pt 3:2

RESPECTS (2)
let the wife see that she **r** her husband. Eph 5:33
Show yourself in all **r** to be a model of Ti 2:7

RESPITE (5)
when Pharaoh saw that there was a **r**, Ex 8:15
these nations you shall find no **r**, Dt 28:65
"Give us seven days **r** that we may 1 Sm 11:3
Give yourself no rest, your eyes no **r**! Lam 2:18
will flow without ceasing, without **r**, Lam 3:49

RESPOND (2)
though he understands, he will not **r**. Prv 29:19
and the beam from the woodwork **r**. Hab 2:11

RESPONDED (3)
And after that God **r** to the plea for 2 Sm 21:14
So the LORD **r** to the plea for the land, 2 Sm 24:25
And Jesus **r** to the lawyers and Pharisees, Lk 14:3

RESPONDS (1)
And if it **r** to you peaceably and it opens Dt 20:11

RESPONSE (1)
"And you shall make **r** before the LORD Dt 26:5

RESPONSIBILITY (1)
the **r** of the Levites under the direction Ex 38:21

RESPONSIVELY (1)
And they sang **r**, praising and giving Ezr 3:11

REST (308)
the ark came to **r** on the mountains of Gn 8:4
them, and the **r** fled to the hill country. Gn 14:10
feet, and **r** yourselves under the tree, Gn 18:4
Jacob pastured the **r** of Laban's flock. Gn 30:36
and let the **r** go and carry grain for the Gn 42:19
and the **r** of you shall be innocent." Gn 44:10
it was restored like the **r** of his flesh. Ex 4:7
you make them **r** from their burdens!" Ex 5:5
'Tomorrow is a day of solemn **r**, a holy Ex 16:23
year you shall let it **r** and lie fallow, Ex 23:11
but on the seventh day you shall **r**; Ex 23:12
your ox and your donkey may have **r**, Ex 23:12
and the **r** of the blood you shall pour Ex 29:12
and throw the **r** of the blood against the Ex 29:20
seventh day is a Sabbath of solemn **r**, Ex 31:15
will go with you, and I will give you **r**." Ex 33:14
but on the seventh day you shall **r**. Ex 34:21
time and in harvest you shall **r**. Ex 34:21
you shall have a Sabbath of solemn **r**, Ex 35:2
But the **r** of the grain offering shall be for Lv 2:3
But the **r** of the grain offering shall be Lv 2:10
and all the **r** of the blood of the bull he Lv 4:7
all the **r** of the bull—he shall carry Lv 4:12
and the **r** of the blood he shall pour out Lv 4:18
offering and pour out the **r** of its blood at Lv 4:25
and pour out all the **r** of its blood at the Lv 4:30
and pour out all the **r** of its blood at the Lv 4:34
while the **r** of the blood shall be drained Lv 5:9
And the **r** of it Aaron and his sons shall Lv 6:16
And the **r** of the oil that is in the priest's Lv 14:18
And the **r** of the oil that is in the priest's Lv 14:29
It is a Sabbath of solemn **r** to you, and Lv 16:31
the seventh day is a Sabbath of solemn **r**, Lv 23:3
you shall observe a day of solemn **r**, Lv 23:24
shall be to you a Sabbath of solemn **r**, Lv 23:32
On the first day shall be a solemn **r**, Lv 23:39
on the eighth day shall be a solemn **r**. Lv 23:39
be a Sabbath of solemn **r** for the land, Lv 25:4
It shall be a year of solemn **r** for the land. Lv 25:5
then the land shall **r**, and enjoy its Lv 26:34
As long as it lies desolate it shall have **r**, Lv 26:35
the **r** that it did not have on your Lv 26:35
then the **r** shall be counted to the Nm 18:30
of Midian with the **r** of their slain, Nm 31:8
The **r** of Gilead, and all Bashan, the Dt 3:13
until the LORD gives **r** to your brothers, as Dt 3:20
your female servant may **r** as well as Dt 5:14
yet come to the **r** and to the inheritance Dt 12:9
when he gives you **r** from all your Dt 12:10
And the **r** shall hear and fear, and shall Dt 19:20
God has given you **r** from all your Dt 25:19
May these **r** on the head of Joseph, on Dt 33:16
you a place of **r** and will give you Jos 1:13

until the LORD gives **r** to your brothers as Jos 1:15
earth, shall **r** in the waters of the Jordan, Jos 3:13
And the land had **r** from war. Jos 11:23
of Israel among the **r** of their slain. Jos 13:22
the **r** of the kingdom of Sihon king of Jos 13:27
And the land had **r** from war. Jos 14:15
were made to the **r** of the people of Jos 17:2
was allotted to the **r** of the people of Jos 17:6
And the **r** of the Kohathites received by Jos 21:5
As to the **r** of the Kohathites belonging Jos 21:20
the clans of the **r** of the Kohathites were Jos 21:26
And to the **r** of the Levites, the Merarite Jos 21:34
the LORD gave them **r** on every side just Jos 21:44
your God has given **r** to your brothers, Jos 22:4
the LORD had given **r** to Israel from all Jos 23:1
So the land had **r** forty years. Then Jgs 3:11
And the land had **r** for eighty years. Jgs 3:30
And the land had **r** for forty years. Jgs 5:31
but all the **r** of the people knelt down to Jgs 7:6
And he sent all the **r** of Israel every man Jgs 7:8
And the land had **r** forty years in the Jgs 8:28
The LORD grant that you may find **r**, each Ru 1:9
morning until now, except for a short **r**." Ru 2:7
"My daughter, should I not seek **r** for you, Ru 3:1
for the man will not **r** but will settle the Ru 3:18
The **r** of the people he sent home, 1 Sm 13:2
The **r** of the people went up after Saul 1 Sm 13:15
and the **r** we have devoted to 1 Sm 15:15
as he was taking his noonday **r**. 2 Sm 4:5
LORD had given him **r** from all his 2 Sm 7:1
I will give you **r** from all your 2 Sm 7:11
The **r** of his men he put in the 2 Sm 10:10
Now then gather the **r** of the people 2 Sm 12:28
of my lord the king will set me at **r**,' 2 Sm 14:17
my God has given me **r** on every side. 1 Kgs 5:4
LORD who has given **r** to his people 1 Kgs 8:56
Now the **r** of the acts of Solomon, 1 Kgs 11:41
Benjamin, and to the **r** of the people, 1 Kgs 12:23
Now the **r** of the acts of Jeroboam, 1 Kgs 14:19
Now the **r** of the acts of Rehoboam 1 Kgs 14:29
The **r** of the acts of Abijam and all 1 Kgs 15:7
Now the **r** of all the acts of Asa, all 1 Kgs 15:23
Now the **r** of the acts of Nadab and 1 Kgs 15:31
Now the **r** of the acts of Baasha and 1 Kgs 16:5
Now the **r** of the acts of Elah and all 1 Kgs 16:14
Now the **r** of the acts of Zimri, and 1 Kgs 16:20
Now the **r** of the acts of Omri that he 1 Kgs 16:27
And the **r** fled into the city of Aphek, 1 Kgs 20:30
Now the **r** of the acts of Ahab and 1 Kgs 22:39
Now the **r** of the acts of Jehoshaphat, 1 Kgs 22:45
Now the **r** of the acts of Ahaziah that 2 Kgs 1:18
you and your sons can live on the **r**." 2 Kgs 4:7
Now the **r** of the acts of Joram, and all 2 Kgs 8:23
Now the **r** of the acts of Jehu and all 2 Kgs 10:34
Now the **r** of the acts of Joash and all 2 Kgs 12:19
Now the **r** of the acts of Jehoahaz and 2 Kgs 13:8
Now the **r** of the acts of Joash and all 2 Kgs 13:12
Now the **r** of the acts of Jehoash that 2 Kgs 14:15
Now the **r** of the deeds of Amaziah, 2 Kgs 14:18
Now the **r** of the acts of Jeroboam 2 Kgs 14:28
Now the **r** of the acts of Azariah, and 2 Kgs 15:6
Now the **r** of the deeds of Zechariah, 2 Kgs 15:11
Now the **r** of the deeds of Shallum, 2 Kgs 15:15
Now the **r** of the deeds of Menahem 2 Kgs 15:21
Now the **r** of the deeds of Pekahiah 2 Kgs 15:26
Now the **r** of the acts of Pekah and 2 Kgs 15:31
Now the **r** of the acts of Jotham and 2 Kgs 15:36
Now the **r** of the acts of Ahaz that he 2 Kgs 16:19
On what do you **r** this trust of 2 Kgs 18:19
The **r** of the deeds of Hezekiah and 2 Kgs 20:20
Now the **r** of the acts of Manasseh 2 Kgs 21:17
Now the **r** of the acts of Amon that 2 Kgs 21:25
Now the **r** of the acts of Josiah and 2 Kgs 23:28
Now the **r** of the deeds of Jehoiakim 2 Kgs 24:5
And the **r** of the people who were left 2 Kgs 25:11
together with the **r** of the multitude, 2 Kgs 25:11
To the **r** of the Kohathites were given 1 Chr 6:61
for the **r** of the clans of the 1 Chr 6:70
To the **r** of the Merarites were allotted 1 Chr 6:77
and Joab repaired the **r** of the city. 1 Chr 11:8
all the **r** of Israel were of a single 1 Chr 12:38
Jeduthun and the **r** of those chosen 1 Chr 16:41
The **r** of his men he put in the 1 Chr 19:11
born to you who shall be a man of **r**. 1 Chr 22:9
I will give him **r** from all his 1 Chr 22:9
of Israel, has given **r** to his people, 1 Chr 23:25
And of the **r** of the sons of Levi: of 1 Chr 24:20
to build a house of **r** for the ark of the 1 Chr 28:2
Now the **r** of the acts of Solomon, 2 Chr 9:29
The **r** of the acts of Abijah, his ways 2 Chr 13:22
his days the land had **r** for ten years. 2 Chr 14:1
And the kingdom had **r** under him. 2 Chr 14:5
cities in Judah, for the land had **r**. 2 Chr 14:6
the LORD gave them **r** all around. 2 Chr 15:15
for his God gave him **r** all around. 2 Chr 20:30
Now the **r** of the acts of 2 Chr 20:34
they brought the **r** of the money 2 Chr 24:14
Now the **r** of the deeds of Amaziah, 2 Chr 25:26
Now the **r** of the acts of Uzziah, 2 Chr 26:22
Now the **r** of the acts of Jotham, and 2 Chr 27:7
Now the **r** of his acts and all his 2 Chr 28:26
Now the **r** of the acts of Hezekiah 2 Chr 32:32
Now the **r** of the acts of Manasseh, 2 Chr 33:18
Now the **r** of the acts of Josiah, and 2 Chr 35:26
Now the **r** of the acts of Jehoiakim, 2 Chr 36:8
and all the **r** of Israel in their towns. Ezr 2:70
together with the **r** of their kinsmen, Ezr 3:8
and the **r** of the heads of fathers' houses Ezr 4:3
and Tabeel and the **r** of their associates Ezr 4:7
the scribe, and the **r** of their associates, Ezr 4:9
and the **r** of the nations whom the great Ezr 4:10
Samaria and in the **r** of the province Ezr 4:10
the scribe and the **r** of their associates Ezr 4:17
Samaria and in the **r** of the province Ezr 4:17
Levites, and the **r** of the returned exiles, Ezr 6:16
to do with the **r** of the silver and Ezr 7:18
and the **r** who were to do the work. Neh 2:16
the officials and to the **r** of the people, Neh 4:14
the officials and to the **r** of the people, Neh 4:19
the Arab and the **r** of our enemies heard Neh 6:1
Noadiah and the **r** of the prophets Neh 6:14
And what the **r** of the people gave was Neh 7:72
But after they had **r** they did evil again Neh 9:28
The **r** of the people, the priests, the Neh 10:28
And the **r** of the people cast lots to Neh 11:1
And the **r** of Israel, and of the priests Neh 11:20
they done in the **r** of the king's Est 9:12
Now the **r** of the Jews who were in the Est 9:16
have slept; then I would have been at **r**, Jb 3:13
troubling, and there the weary are at **r**. Jb 3:17
I quiet; I have no **r**, but trouble comes." Jb 3:26
around and take your **r** in security. Jb 11:18
and the pain that gnaws me takes no **r**. Jb 30:17
not answer, and by night, but I find no **r**. Ps 22:2
like a dove! I would fly away and be at **r**; Ps 55:6
are not stricken like the **r** of mankind. Ps 73:5
to give him **r** from days of trouble, until Ps 94:13
my wrath, "They shall not enter my **r**." Ps 95:11
Return, O my soul, to your **r**; for the Ps 116:7
of wickedness shall not **r** on the land Ps 125:3
that you rise up early and go late to **r**, Ps 127:2
a little folding of the hands to **r**, Prv 6:10
of good sense will **r** in the assembly of Prv 21:16
a little folding of the hands to **r**, Prv 24:33
your son, and he will give you **r**; Prv 29:17
Even in the night his heart does not **r**. Eccl 2:23
anything, yet it finds **r** rather than he. Eccl 6:5
calmness will lay great offenses to **r**. Eccl 10:4
the Spirit of the LORD shall **r** upon him, Is 11:2
LORD has given you **r** from your pain and Is 14:3
The whole earth is at **r** and quiet; they Is 14:7
Cyprus, even there you will have no **r**." Is 23:12
of the LORD will **r** on this mountain, Is 25:10
to whom he has said, "This is **r**; give rest Is 28:12
said, "This is rest; give **r** to the weary; Is 28:12
"In returning and **r** you shall be saved; Is 30:15
On what do you **r** this trust of yours? Is 36:4
to the gates of Sheol for the **r** of my years. Is 38:10
And the **r** of it he makes into a god, his Is 44:17
shall I make the **r** of it an abomination? Is 44:19
they **r** in their beds who walk in their Is 57:2
put the LORD in remembrance, take no **r**, Is 62:6
and give him no **r** until he establishes Is 62:7
valley, the Spirit of the LORD gave them **r**. Is 63:14
for me, and what is the place of my **r**? Is 66:1
and walk in it, and find **r** for your souls. Jer 6:16
And the **r** of them I will give to the sword Jer 15:9
and the **r** of the vessels that are left in Jer 27:19
the wilderness; when Israel sought for **r**, Jer 31:2
with all the **r** of the officers of the king of Jer 39:3
exile to Babylon the **r** of the people who Jer 39:9
took captive all the **r** of the people who Jer 41:10
from Mizpah all the **r** of the people Jer 41:16
with my groaning, and I find no **r**.' Jer 45:3
into your scabbard; **r** and be still! Jer 47:6
cause, that he may give **r** to the earth, Jer 50:34
of the people and the **r** of the people who Jer 52:15
together with the **r** of the artisans. Jer 52:15
Give yourself no **r**, your eyes no Lam 2:18
necks; we are weary; we are given no **r**. Lam 5:5
and destroy the **r** of the seacoast. Ezk 25:16
be laid to **r** with the uncircumcised.' Ezk 32:19
be laid to **r** among the Ezk 32:32
with your feet the **r** of your pasture; Ezk 34:18
you must muddy the **r** of the water Ezk 34:18
the possession of the **r** of the nations, Ezk 36:3
and derision to the **r** of the nations all Ezk 36:4
hot jealousy against the **r** of the nations Ezk 36:5
that a blessing may **r** on your house. Ezk 44:30
"As for the **r** of the tribes: from the east Ezk 48:23
be destroyed with the **r** of the wise men Dn 2:18
As for the **r** of the beasts, their dominion Dn 7:12
beast, which was different from all the **r**, Dn 7:19
And you shall **r** and shall stand in Dn 12:13
Arise and go, for this is no place to **r**, Mi 2:10
then the **r** of his brothers shall return to Mi 5:3
an arrogant man who is never at **r**. Hab 2:5
and behold, all the earth remains at **r**.' Zec 1:11
set my Spirit at **r** in the north country." Zec 6:8
but the **r** of the people shall not be cut Zec 14:2
until it came to **r** over the place where Mt 2:9
like a dove and coming to **r** on him; Mt 3:16
are heavy laden, and I will give you **r**. Mt 11:28
and you will find **r** for your souls. Mt 11:29
through waterless places seeking **r**, Mt 12:43
while the **r** seized his servants, treated Mt 22:6
to them, "Sleep and take your **r** later on. Mt 26:45
a desolate place and **r** a while." For Mk 6:31
you still sleeping and taking your **r**? Mk 14:41
And they went back and told the **r**, but Mk 16:13
is there, your peace will **r** upon him. Lk 10:6
through waterless places seeking **r**, Lk 11:24
that, why are you anxious about the **r**? Lk 12:26
these things to the eleven and to all the **r**. Lk 24:9
thought that he meant taking **r** in sleep. Jn 11:13
said to Peter and the **r** of the apostles, Acts 2:37
None of the **r** dared join them, but the Acts 5:13
the Lord, or what is the place of my **r**? Acts 7:49
as security from Jason and the **r**, Acts 17:9
and the **r** on planks or on pieces of Acts 27:44
the **r** of the people on the island who Acts 28:9
as well as among the **r** of the Gentiles. Rom 1:13
that the promise may **r** on grace and Rom 4:16
obtained it, but the **r** were hardened, Rom 11:7
your faith might not **r** in the wisdom 1 Cor 2:5
To the **r** I say (I, not the Lord) that if 1 Cor 7:12
spirit was not at **r** because I did not 2 Cor 2:13
into Macedonia, our bodies had no **r**, 2 Cor 7:5
the power of Christ may **r** upon me. 2 Cor 12:9
favored than the **r** of the churches, 2 Cor 12:13
And the **r** of the Jews acted Gal 2:13
children of wrath, like the **r** of mankind. Eph 2:3
and to all the **r** that my imprisonment Phil 1:13
with Clement and the **r** of my fellow Phil 4:3
of all, so that the **r** may stand in fear. 1 Tm 5:20
my wrath, 'They shall not enter my **r**.'" Heb 3:11
swear that they would not enter his **r**, Heb 3:18
the promise of entering his **r** still stands, Heb 4:1
For we who have believed enter that **r**, as Heb 4:3
not enter my **r**,'" although his works Heb 4:3
he said, "They shall not enter my **r**." Heb 4:5
For if Joshua had given them **r**, God Heb 4:8
there remains a Sabbath **r** for the people Heb 4:9
has entered God's **r** has also rested Heb 4:10
Let us therefore strive to enter that **r**, so Heb 4:11
so as to live for the **r** of the time in the 1 Pt 4:2
But to the **r** of you in Thyatira, who do Rv 2:24
a white robe and told to **r** a little longer, Rv 6:11
The **r** of mankind, who were not killed Rv 9:20
and the **r** were terrified and gave glory Rv 11:13
to make war on the **r** of her offspring, Rv 12:17
up forever and ever, and they have no **r**, Rv 14:11
"that they may **r** from their labors, Rv 14:13
And the **r** were slain by the sword that Rv 19:21
The **r** of the dead did not come to life Rv 20:5

RESTED (20)

and he **r** on the seventh day from all his Gn 2:2
because on it God **r** from all his work Gn 2:3
So the people **r** on the seventh day. Ex 16:30
that is in them, and **r** the seventh day. Ex 20:11
seventh day he **r** and was refreshed.'" Ex 31:17
long as the cloud **r** over the tabernacle, Nm 9:18
And when it **r**, he said, "Return, O Nm 10:36
And as soon as the Spirit **r** on them, Nm 11:25
Medad, and the Spirit **r** on them. Nm 11:26
of the house of Joseph **r** heavily on them, Jgs 1:35
middle pillars on which the house **r**, Jgs 16:29
turned into the chamber and **r** there. 2 Kgs 4:11
of the LORD after the ark **r** there. 1 Chr 6:31
the fourteenth day they **r** and made that Est 9:17
fourteenth, and **r** on the fifteenth day, Est 9:18
cherub on which it **r** to the threshold of Ezk 9:3
On the Sabbath they **r** according to the Lk 23:56
appeared to them and **r** on each one of Acts 2:3
"And God **r** on the seventh day from all Heb 4:4
God's rest has also **r** from his works as Heb 4:10

RESTING (13)

He saw that a **r** place was good, and Gn 49:15
journey, to seek out a **r** place for them. Nm 10:33
and there shall be no **r** place for the sole Dt 28:65
O LORD God, and go to your **r** place, 2 Chr 6:41
blood, and let my cry find no **r** place. Jb 16:18
Arise, O LORD, and go to your **r** place, Ps 132:8
"This is my **r** place forever; here I will Ps 132:14

and his **r** place shall be glorious. Is 11:10
secure dwellings, and in quiet **r** places. Is 32:18
settles and finds for herself a **r** place. Is 34:14
habitations of shepherds **r** their flocks. Jer 33:12
the nations, but finds no **r** place; Lam 1:3
of Hadrach and Damascus is its **r** place. Zec 9:1

RESTITUTION (11)
he shall make **r** from the best in his own Ex 22:5
he who started the fire shall make full **r**. Ex 22:6
the oath, and he shall not make **r**. Ex 22:11
from him, he shall make **r** to its owner. Ex 22:12
He shall not make **r** for what has been Ex 22:13
not being with it, he shall make full **r**. Ex 22:14
owner was with it, he shall not make **r**; Ex 22:15
He shall also make **r** for what he has Lv 5:16
And he shall make full **r** for his wrong, Nm 5:7
next of kin to whom **r** may be made for Nm 5:8
the **r** for wrong shall go to the LORD for Nm 5:8

RESTLESS (4)
but when you grow **r** you shall break Gn 27:40
me; I am **r** in my complaint and I moan, Ps 55:2
have done—a **r** young camel running Jer 2:23
tongue. It is a **r** evil, full of deadly poison. Jas 3:8

RESTORATION (3)
the owner of the pit shall make **r**. He Ex 21:34
are strong. Your **r** is what we pray for. 2 Cor 13:9
Aim for **r**, comfort one another, 2 Cor 13:11

RESTORE (74)
out of their hand to **r** him to his father. Gn 37:22
up your head and **r** you to your office, Gn 40:13
his guilt and will **r** what he took by Lv 6:4
he shall **r** it in full and shall add a fifth to Lv 6:5
the congregation shall **r** him to his Nm 35:25
seeks it. Then you shall **r** it to him. Dt 22:2
You shall **r** to him the pledge as the sun Dt 24:13
LORD your God will **r** your fortunes and Dt 30:3
Jordan; now therefore **r** it peaceably." Jgs 11:13
image. Now therefore I will **r** it to you." Jgs 17:3
against me and I will **r** it to you." 1 Sm 12:3
as he went to **r** his power at the river 2 Sm 8:3
and I will **r** to you all the land of Saul 2 Sm 9:7
and he shall **r** the lamb fourfold, 2 Sm 12:6
to **r** the kingdom to Rehoboam the 1 Kgs 12:21
father took from your father I will **r**, 1 Kgs 20:34
for her, saying, "**R** all that was hers, 2 Kgs 8:6
to **r** the kingdom to Rehoboam. 2 Chr 11:1
this Joash decided to **r** the house of 2 Chr 24:4
and carpenters to **r** the house of 2 Chr 24:12
doing? Will they **r** it for themselves? Neh 4:2
"We will **r** these and require nothing Neh 5:12
for you and **r** your rightful habitation. Jb 8:6
in his illness you **r** him to full health. Ps 41:3
R to me the joy of your salvation, and Ps 51:12
defenses; you have been angry; oh, **r** us. Ps 60:1
lies. What I did not steal must I now **r**? Ps 69:4
R us, O God; let your face shine, that we Ps 80:3
R us, O God of hosts; let your face shine, Ps 80:7
R us, O LORD God of hosts! let your face Ps 80:19
R us again, O God of our salvation, and Ps 85:4
R our fortunes, O LORD, like streams in Ps 126:4
And I will **r** your judges as at the first, and Is 1:26
Oh **r** me to health and make me live! Is 38:16
to rescue, spoil with none to say, "**R**!" Is 42:22
I will lead him and **r** comfort to him and Is 57:18
"If you return, I will **r** you, and you Jer 15:19
bring them back and **r** them to this Jer 27:22
and I will **r** your fortunes and gather Jer 29:14
when I will **r** the fortunes of my people, Jer 30:3
For I will **r** health to you, and your Jer 30:17
I will **r** the fortunes of the tents of Jacob Jer 30:18
and in its cities, when I **r** their fortunes: Jer 31:23
for I will **r** their fortunes, declares the Jer 32:44
I will **r** the fortunes of Judah and the Jer 33:7
For I will **r** the fortunes of the land as at Jer 33:11
For I will **r** their fortunes and will have Jer 33:26
Yet I will **r** the fortunes of Moab in the Jer 48:47
"But afterward I will **r** the fortunes of the Jer 49:6
latter days I will **r** the fortunes of Elam, Jer 49:39
I will **r** Israel to his pasture, and he Jer 50:19
your iniquity to **r** your fortunes, Lam 2:14
R us to yourself, O LORD, that we may Lam 5:21
"I will **r** their fortunes, both the Ezk 16:53
and I will **r** your own fortunes in their Ezk 16:53
robbery, does not **r** the pledge, Ezk 18:12
and I will **r** the fortunes of Egypt and Ezk 29:14
Now I will **r** the fortunes of Jacob and Ezk 39:25
of the word to **r** and build Jerusalem to Dn 9:25
when I **r** the fortunes of my people. Hos 6:11
I will **r** to you the years that the swarming Jl 2:25
when I **r** the fortunes of Judah and Jl 3:1
I will **r** the fortunes of my people Israel, Am 9:14
be mindful of them and **r** their fortunes. Zep 2:7
when I **r** your fortunes before your Zep 3:20
I declare that I will **r** to you double. Zec 9:12
does come, and he will **r** all things. Mt 17:11
"Elijah does come first to **r** all things. Mk 9:12
anyone of anything, I **r** it fourfold." Lk 19:8
you at this time **r** the kingdom to Acts 1:6
I will rebuild its ruins, and I will **r** it, Acts 15:16
who are spiritual should **r** him in a spirit Gal 6:1
it is impossible to **r** again to repentance Heb 6:4
eternal glory in Christ, will himself **r**, 1 Pt 5:10

RESTORED (41)
He **r** the chief cupbearer to his Gn 40:21
I was **r** to my office, and the baker was Gn 41:13
behold, it was **r** like the rest of his flesh. Ex 4:7
your face, but shall not be **r** to you. Dt 28:31
And he **r** the 1,100 pieces of silver to his Jgs 17:3
So when he **r** the money to his mother, Jgs 17:4
had taken from Israel were **r** to Israel, 1 Sm 7:14
my hand may be **r** to me." And the 1 Kgs 13:6
the king's hand was **r** to him and 1 Kgs 13:6
seven times, and your flesh shall be **r**, 2 Kgs 5:10
and his flesh was **r** like the flesh of a 2 Kgs 5:14
the woman whose son he had **r** to life, 2 Kgs 8:1
king how Elisha had **r** the dead to life, 2 Kgs 8:5
whose son he had **r** to life appealed to 2 Kgs 8:5
here is her son whom Elisha **r** to life." 2 Kgs 8:5
He built Elath and **r** it to Judah, after 2 Kgs 14:22
He **r** the border of Israel from 2 Kgs 14:25
and how he **r** Damascus and 2 Kgs 14:28
and they **r** the house of God to its 2 Chr 24:13
He built Eloth and **r** it to Judah, after 2 Chr 26:2
of the house of the LORD was **r**. 2 Chr 29:35
He also **r** the altar of the LORD and 2 Chr 33:16
be **r** and brought back to the temple that Ezr 6:5
and they **r** Jerusalem as far as the Broad Neh 3:8
And the LORD **r** the fortunes of Job, when Jb 42:10
you **r** me to life from among those who Ps 30:3
you **r** your inheritance as it languished; Ps 68:9
to your land; you **r** the fortunes of Jacob. Ps 85:1
When the LORD **r** the fortunes of Zion, Ps 126:1
of the daughter of my people not been **r**? Jer 8:22
bring me back that I may be **r**, for you Jer 31:18
to yourself, O LORD, that we may be **r**! Lam 5:21
go against the land that is **r** from war, Ezk 38:8
the sanctuary shall be **r** to its rightful Dn 8:14
lost its taste, how shall its saltiness be **r**? Mt 5:13
the man stretched it out, and it was **r**, Mt 12:13
He stretched it out, and his hand was **r**. Mk 3:5
and he opened his eyes, his sight was **r**, Mk 8:25
And he did so, and his hand was **r**. Lk 6:10
its taste, how shall its saltiness be **r**? Lk 14:34
that I may be **r** to you the sooner. Heb 13:19

RESTORER (2)
shall be to you a **r** of life and a nourisher Ru 4:15
of the breach, the **r** of streets to dwell in. Is 58:12

RESTORES (6)
joy, and he **r** to man his righteousness. Jb 33:26
When the LORD **r** the fortunes of his Ps 14:7
He **r** my soul. He leads me in paths of Ps 23:3
When God **r** the fortunes of his people, Ps 53:6
anyone, but **r** to the debtor his pledge, Ezk 18:7
if the wicked **r** the pledge, gives back Ezk 33:15

RESTORING (3)
gave it for repairing and **r** the house. 2 Chr 34:10
For the LORD is **r** the majesty of Jacob as Na 2:2
until the time for **r** all the things about Acts 3:21

RESTRAIN (11)
God, and he did not **r** them. 1 Sm 3:13
to you! He it is who shall **r** my people." 1 Sm 9:17
"Therefore I will not **r** my mouth; I will Jb 7:11
and he does not **r** the lightnings when his Jb 37:4
you will not **r** your mercy from me; Ps 40:11
to **r** her is to restrain the wind or to Prv 27:16
to restrain her is to **r** the wind or to Prv 27:16
for the sake of my praise I **r** it for you, Is 48:9
Will you **r** yourself at these things, O Is 64:12
sniffing the wind! Who can **r** her lust? Jer 2:24
he did not **r** his hand from destroying; Lam 2:8

RESTRAINED (13)
closed, the rain from the heavens was **r**, Gn 8:2
So the people were **r** from bringing, Ex 36:6
the LORD has **r** you from bloodguilt 1 Sm 25:26
who has **r** me from hurting you, 1 Sm 25:34
pursuing Israel, for Joab **r** them. 2 Sm 18:16
Haman **r** himself and went home, Est 5:10
behold, I have not **r** my lips, as you Ps 40:9
he **r** his anger often and did not stir up Ps 78:38
my peace; I have kept still and **r** myself; Is 42:14
wander thus; they have not **r** their feet; Jer 14:10
closed the deep over it, and **r** its rivers, Ezk 31:15
words they scarcely **r** the people from Acts 14:18
human voice and **r** the prophet's 2 Pt 2:16

RESTRAINING (1)
you know what is **r** him now so that 2 Thes 2:6

RESTRAINS (3)
but whoever **r** his lips is prudent. Prv 10:19
Whoever **r** his words has knowledge, Prv 17:27
Only he who now **r** it will do so until 2 Thes 2:7

RESTRAINT (4)
me, they have cast off **r** in my presence. Jb 30:11
prophetic vision the people cast off **r**, Prv 29:18
of Tarshish; there is no **r** anymore. Is 23:10
benefit, not to lay any **r** upon you, 1 Cor 7:35

RESTRICTED (2)
You are not **r** by us, but you are 2 Cor 6:12
but you are **r** in your own affections. 2 Cor 6:12

RESTS (8)
feel the pillars on which the house **r**, Jgs 16:26
spirit of Elijah **r** on Elisha." And 2 Kgs 2:15
the seat were arm **r** and two lions 2 Chr 9:18
two lions standing beside the arm **r**, 2 Chr 9:18
On God **r** my salvation and my glory; Ps 62:7
Wisdom **r** in the heart of a man of Prv 14:33
to life, and whoever has it **r** satisfied; Prv 19:23
Spirit of glory and of God **r** upon you. 1 Pt 4:14

RESULT (6)
will be peace, and the **r** of righteousness, Is 32:17
with the **r** that you will be removed far Jer 27:10
with the **r** that I will drive you out and Jer 27:15
gift is not like the **r** of that one man's Rom 5:16
not a **r** of works, so that no one may Eph 2:9
—may be found to **r** in praise and glory 1 Pt 1:7

RESUMED (1)
on his outer garments and **r** his place, Jn 13:12

RESURRECTION (41)
came to him, who say that there is no **r**, Mt 22:23
In the **r**, therefore, of the seven, whose Mt 22:28
For in the **r** they neither marry nor are Mt 22:30
And as for the **r** of the dead, have you Mt 22:31
the tombs after his **r** they went into the Mt 27:53
to him, who say that there is no **r**. Mk 12:18
In the **r**, when they rise again, whose Mk 12:23
You will be repaid at the **r** of the just." Lk 14:14
those who deny that there is a **r**, Lk 20:27
In the **r**, therefore, whose wife will the Lk 20:33
age and to the **r** from the dead neither Lk 20:35
and are sons of God, being sons of the **r**. Lk 20:36
those who have done good to the **r** of life, Jn 5:29
who have done evil to the **r** of judgment. Jn 5:29
will rise again in the **r** on the last day." Jn 11:24
Jesus said to her, "I am the **r** and the life. Jn 11:25
become with us a witness to his **r**." Acts 1:22
and spoke about the **r** of the Christ, Acts 2:31
in Jesus the **r** from the dead. Acts 4:2
their testimony to the **r** of the Lord Acts 4:33
he was preaching Jesus and the **r**. Acts 17:18
when they heard of the **r** of the dead, Acts 17:32
to the hope and the **r** of the dead that I Acts 23:6
the Sadducees say that there is no **r**, Acts 23:8
that there will be a **r** of both the just Acts 24:15
is with respect to the **r** of the dead that Acts 24:21
Spirit of holiness by his **r** from the dead, Rom 1:4
be united with him in a **r** like his. Rom 6:5
say that there is no **r** of the dead? 1 Cor 15:12
But if there is no **r** of the dead, then 1 Cor 15:13
man has come also the **r** of the dead. 1 Cor 15:21
So is it with the **r** of the dead. What 1 Cor 15:42
may know him and the power of his **r**, Phil 3:10
I may attain the **r** from the dead. Phil 3:11
saying that the **r** has already 2 Tm 2:18
the laying on of hands, the **r** of the dead, Heb 6:2
received back their dead by **r**. Heb 11:35
living hope through the **r** of Jesus Christ 1 Pt 1:3
through the **r** of Jesus Christ, 1 Pt 3:21
years were ended. This is the first **r**. Rv 20:5
holy is the one who shares in the first **r**! Rv 20:6

RETAIN (5)
No man has power to **r** the spirit, or Eccl 8:8
come upon me, and I **r** no strength. Dn 10:16
But she shall not **r** the strength of her Dn 11:6
and the strong shall not **r** his strength, Am 2:14
He does not **r** his anger forever, Mi 7:18

RETAINED (3)
every man to his tent, but **r** the 300 men. Jgs 7:8
were offered, and let its foundations be **r**. Ezr 6:3
fearfully changed, and I **r** no strength. Dn 10:8

RETINUE (2)
came to Jerusalem with a very great **r**, 1 Kgs 10:2
a very great **r** and camels bearing 2 Chr 9:1

RETORT (1)
At this **r** Moses fled and became an Acts 7:29

RETRIBUTION (2)

a stumbling block and a **r** for them; Rom 11:9
or disobedience received a just **r**, Heb 2:2

RETURN (257)

shall eat bread, till you **r** to the ground, Gn 3:19
you are dust, and to dust you shall **r**." Gn 3:19
dove, and she did not **r** to him anymore. Gn 8:12
After his **r** from the defeat of Gn 14:17
"**R** to your mistress and submit to her." Gn 16:9
"I will surely **r** to you about this time Gn 18:10
appointed time I will **r** to you about Gn 18:14
Now then, **r** the man's wife, for he is a Gn 20:7
But if you do not **r** her, know that you Gn 20:7
the other also in **r** for serving me Gn 29:27
"**R** to the land of your fathers and to Gn 31:3
out from this land and **r** to the land of Gn 31:13
'**R** to your country and to your kindred, Gn 32:9
up and bury my father. Then I will **r**." Gn 50:5
when they see war and **r** to Egypt." Ex 13:17
you shall **r** it to him before the sun goes Ex 22:26
"Wait here for us until we **r** to you. Ex 24:14
each of you shall **r** to his property and Lv 25:10
and each of you shall **r** to his clan. Lv 25:10
each of you shall **r** to his property. Lv 25:13
he sold it, and then **r** to his property. Lv 25:27
released, and he shall **r** to his property. Lv 25:28
his own clan and **r** to the possession of Lv 25:41
jubilee the field shall **r** to him from Lv 27:24
when it rested, he said, "**R**, O LORD, Nm 10:36
in **r** for their service that they do, Nm 18:21
is your reward in **r** for your service in Nm 18:31
Balaam's mouth and said, "**R** to Balak, Nm 23:5
in his mouth and said, "**R** to Balak, Nm 23:16
We will not **r** to our homes until each Nm 32:18
after that you shall **r** and be free of Nm 32:22
priest the manslayer may **r** to the land Nm 35:28
that he may **r** to dwell in the land Nm 35:32
each of you may **r** to his possession Dt 3:20
you will **r** to the LORD your God and obey Dt 4:30
Go and say to them, "**R** to your tents." Dt 5:30
or cause the people to **r** to Egypt in order Dt 17:16
you, 'You shall never **r** that way again.' Dt 17:16
and **r** to the LORD your God, you and your Dt 30:2
Then you shall **r** to the land of your Jos 1:15
land and write a description and **r** to me. Jos 18:8
Then the manslayer may **r** to his own Jos 20:6
you." And he said, "I will stay till you **r**." Jgs 6:18
let him **r** home and hurry away from Jgs 7:3
Gideon) in **r** for all the good that he had Jgs 8:35
of the men of Shechem **r** on their heads, Jgs 9:57
to meet me when I **r** in peace from the Jgs 11:31
tent, and none of us will **r** to his house. Jgs 20:8
her daughters-in-law to **r** from the Ru 1:6
went on the way to **r** to the land of Judah. Ru 1:7
"Go, **r** each of you to her mother's house. Ru 1:8
"No, we will **r** with you to your people." Ru 1:10
to her gods; **r** after your sister-in-law." Ru 1:15
to leave you or to **r** from following you. Ru 1:16
So then they would **r** to their home. 1 Sm 2:20
of Israel, and let it **r** to its own place, 1 Sm 5:11
but by all means **r** him a guilt offering. 1 Sm 6:3
offering that we shall **r** to him?" They 1 Sm 6:4
Then he would **r** to Ramah, for his 1 Sm 7:17
pardon my sin and **r** with me that I 1 Sm 15:25
said to Saul, "I will not **r** with you. 1 Sm 15:26
and before Israel, and **r** with me, 1 Sm 15:30
would not let him **r** to his father's 1 Sm 18:2
R, my son David, for I will no more 1 Sm 26:21
that he may **r** to the place to which 1 Sm 29:4
in the morning to **r** to the land of 1 Sm 29:11
said to him, "Go, **r**." And he returned. 2 Sm 3:16
your beards have grown and then **r**." 2 Sm 10:5
go to him, but he will not **r** to me." 2 Sm 12:23
But if you **r** to the city and say to 2 Sm 15:34
"**R**, both you and all your servants." 2 Sm 19:14
Please let your servant **r**, that I may 2 Sm 19:37
what answer I shall **r** to him who 2 Sm 24:13
Every man **r** to his home, for this 1 Kgs 12:24
kill me and **r** to Rehoboam king 1 Kgs 12:27
nor drink water nor **r** by the way that 1 Kgs 13:9
way and did not **r** by the way that 1 Kgs 13:10
And he said, "I may not **r** with you, 1 Kgs 13:16
nor **r** by the way that you came.'" 1 Kgs 13:17
r on your way to the wilderness of 1 Kgs 19:15
let each **r** to his home in peace.'" 1 Kgs 22:17
And Micaiah said, "If you **r** in peace, 1 Kgs 22:28
hear a rumor and **r** to his own land, 2 Kgs 19:7
that he came, by the same he shall **r**, 2 Kgs 19:33
your beards have grown and then **r**." 1 Chr 19:5
what answer I shall **r** to him who 1 Chr 21:12
R every man to his home, for this 2 Chr 11:4
let each **r** to his home in peace.'" 2 Chr 18:16
bread and water until I **r** in peace.'" 2 Chr 18:26
Micaiah said, "If you **r** in peace, 2 Chr 18:27
chest and take it and **r** it to its place. 2 Chr 24:11
"O people of Israel, **r** to the LORD, 2 Chr 30:6
For if you **r** to the LORD, your 2 Chr 30:9
with their captors and **r** to this land. 2 Chr 30:9
his face from you, if you **r** to him." 2 Chr 30:9
did not make **r** according to the 2 Chr 32:25
but if you **r** to me and keep my Neh 1:9
and when will you **r**?" So it pleased the Neh 2:6
to us ten times, "You must **r** to us." Neh 4:12
R to them this very day their fields, Neh 5:11
appointed a leader to **r** to their slavery Neh 9:17
the morning she would **r** to the second Est 2:14
against the Jews should **r** on his own Est 9:25
my mother's womb, and naked shall I **r**. Jb 1:21
like clay; and will you **r** me to the dust? Jb 10:9
go—and I shall not **r**—to the land of Jb 10:21
believe that he will **r** out of darkness, Jb 15:22
go the way from which I shall not **r**. Jb 16:22
If you **r** to the Almighty you will be Jb 22:23
let him **r** to the days of his youthful Jb 33:25
together, and man would **r** to dust. Jb 34:15
commands that they **r** from iniquity. Jb 36:10
open; they go out and do not **r** to them. Jb 39:4
him that he will **r** your grain and Jb 39:12
be gathered about you; over it **r** on high. Ps 7:7
The wicked shall **r** to Sheol, all the Ps 9:17
your ways, and sinners will **r** to you. Ps 51:13
He will **r** the evil to my enemies; in your Ps 54:5
when Joab on his **r** struck down twelve Ps 60:T
R sevenfold into the lap of our Ps 79:12
You **r** man to dust and say, "Return, O Ps 90:3
to dust and say, "**R**, O children of man!" Ps 90:3
R, O LORD! How long? Have pity on your Ps 90:13
for justice will **r** to the righteous, and Ps 94:15
breath, they die and **r** to their dust. Ps 104:29
In **r** for my love they accuse me, but I Ps 109:4
R, O my soul, to your rest; for the LORD Ps 116:7
All are from the dust, and to dust all **r**. Eccl 3:20
and the clouds **r** after the rain, Eccl 12:2
R, return, O Shulammite, return, return, Sg 6:13
Return, **r**, O Shulammite, return, return, Sg 6:13
Return, return, O Shulammite, **r**, return, Sg 6:13
return, **r**, that we may look upon you. Sg 6:13
A remnant will **r**, the remnant of Jacob, Is 10:21
of the sea, only a remnant of them will **r**. Is 10:22
and healing, and they will **r** to the LORD, Is 19:22
and she will **r** to her wages and will Is 23:17
of the LORD shall **r** and come to Zion Is 35:10
shall hear a rumor and **r** to his own land, Is 37:7
that he came, by the same he shall **r**, Is 37:34
and I love you, I give men in **r** for you, Is 43:4
mist; **r** to me, for I have redeemed you. Is 44:22
in righteousness a word that shall not **r**: Is 45:23
of the LORD shall **r** and come to Zion Is 51:11
to eye they see the **r** of the LORD to Zion. Is 52:8
let him **r** to the LORD, that he may have Is 55:7
heaven and do not **r** there but water the Is 55:10
my mouth; it shall not **r** to me empty, Is 55:11
R for the sake of your servants, the tribes Is 63:17
another man's wife, will he **r** to her? Jer 3:1
with many lovers; and would you **r** to me? Jer 3:1
she has done all this she will **r** to me,' Jer 3:7
she will return to me,' but she did not **r**, Jer 3:7
sister Judah did not **r** to me with her Jer 3:10
the north, and say, "'**R**, faithless Israel, Jer 3:12
R, O faithless children, declares the LORD; Jer 3:14
"**R**, O faithless sons; I will heal your Jer 3:22
"If you **r**, O Israel, declares the LORD, to me Jer 4:1
declares the LORD, to me you should **r**. Jer 4:1
again? If one turns away, does he not **r**? Jer 8:4
They hold fast to deceit; they refuse to **r**. Jer 8:5
no water; they **r** with their vessels empty; Jer 14:3
"If you **r**, I will restore you, and you Jer 15:19
R, every one from his evil way, and Jer 18:11
for he shall **r** no more to see his native Jer 22:10
this place: "He shall **r** here no more, Jer 22:11
to the land to which they will long to **r**, Jer 22:27
long to return, there they shall not **r**." Jer 22:27
for they shall **r** to me with their whole Jer 24:7
Jacob shall **r** and have quiet and ease, Jer 30:10
a great company, they shall **r** here. Jer 31:8
R, O virgin Israel, return to these your Jer 31:21
O virgin Israel, **r** to these your cities. Jer 31:21
came to help you is about to **r** to Egypt, Jer 37:7
then **r** to Gedaliah the son of Ahikam, Jer 40:5
escape or survive or **r** to the land of Jer 44:14
to which they desire to **r** to dwell there. Jer 44:14
For they shall not **r**, except some Jer 44:14
escape the sword shall **r** from the land Jer 44:28
Jacob shall **r** and have quiet and ease, Jer 46:27
warrior who does not **r** empty-handed. Jer 50:9
examine our ways, and **r** to the LORD! Lam 3:40
For the seller shall not **r** to what he has Ezk 7:13
her daughters shall **r** to their former Ezk 16:55
her daughters shall **r** to their former Ezk 16:55
your daughters shall **r** to your former Ezk 16:55
that he broke. I will **r** it upon his head. Ezk 17:19
R it to its sheath. In the place where Ezk 21:30
And they shall **r** your lewdness upon Ezk 23:49
no one shall **r** by way of the gate by Ezk 46:9
But now I will **r** to fight against the Dn 10:20
of the south but shall **r** to his own land. Dn 11:9
And he shall **r** to his land with great Dn 11:28
work his will and **r** to his own land. Dn 11:28
appointed he shall **r** and come into Dn 11:29
say, 'I will go and **r** to my first husband, Hos 2:7
children of Israel shall **r** and seek the Hos 3:5
do not permit them to **r** to their God. Hos 5:4
I will **r** again to my place, until they Hos 5:15
"Come, let us **r** to the LORD; for he has Hos 6:1
yet they do not **r** to the LORD their God, Hos 7:10
They **r**, but not upward; they are like a Hos 7:16
punish their sins; they shall **r** to Egypt. Hos 8:13
the LORD, but Ephraim shall **r** to Egypt, Hos 9:3
They shall not **r** to the land of Egypt, Hos 11:5
because they have refused to **r** to me. Hos 11:5
and I will **r** them to their homes, Hos 11:11
God, **r**, hold fast to love and justice, Hos 12:6
R, O Israel, to the LORD your God, for Hos 14:1
Take with you words and **r** to the LORD; Hos 14:2
They shall **r** and dwell beneath my Hos 14:7
the LORD, "**r** to me with all your heart, Jl 2:12
and not your garments." **R** to the LORD, Jl 2:13
I will **r** your payment on your own head Jl 3:4
and I will **r** your payment on your own Jl 3:7
yet you did not **r** to me," declares the Am 4:6
yet you did not **r** to me," declares the Am 4:8
yet you did not **r** to me," declares the Am 4:9
yet you did not **r** to me," declares the Am 4:10
yet you did not **r** to me," declares the Am 4:11
your deeds shall **r** on your own head. Ob 1:15
and to the fee of a prostitute they shall **r**. Mi 1:7
rest of his brothers shall **r** to the people of Mi 5:3
shall be their lot in **r** for their pride, Zep 2:10
R to me, says the LORD of hosts, and I will Zec 1:3
says the LORD of hosts, and I will **r** to you, Zec 1:3
R from your evil ways and from your Zec 1:4
R to your stronghold, O prisoners of Zec 9:12
with their children they shall live and **r**. Zec 10:9
R to me, and I will return to you, says the Mal 3:7
Return to me, and I will **r** to you, says the Mal 3:7
of hosts. But you say, 'How shall we **r**?' Mal 3:7
warned in a dream not to **r** to Herod, Mt 2:12
it is not worthy, let your peace **r** to you. Mt 10:13
'I will **r** to my house from which I Mt 12:44
what shall a man give in **r** for his life? Mt 16:26
what can a man give in **r** for his life? Mk 8:37
good, and lend, expecting nothing in **r**, Lk 6:35
"**R** to your home, and declare how much Lk 8:39
On their **r** the apostles told him all that Lk 9:10
rest upon him. But if not, it will **r** to you. Lk 10:6
'I will **r** to my house from which I Lk 11:24
also invite you in **r** and you be repaid. Lk 14:12
no one found to **r** and give praise to Lk 17:18
for himself a kingdom and then **r**. Lk 19:12
the dead, no more to **r** to corruption, Acts 13:34
"'After this I will **r**, and I will rebuild Acts 15:16
"Let us **r** and visit the brothers in Acts 15:36
"I will **r** to you if God wills," and he Acts 18:21
he decided to **r** through Macedonia. Acts 20:3
next year I will **r** and Sarah shall have Rom 9:9
way in peace, that he may **r** to me, 1 Cor 16:11
In **r** (I speak as to children) widen 2 Cor 6:13
thanksgiving can we **r** to God for 1 Thes 3:9
and to make some **r** to their parents, 1 Tm 5:4
they would have had opportunity to **r**. Heb 11:15
he was reviled, he did not revile in **r**; 1 Pt 2:23

RETURNED (163)

to set her foot, and she **r** to him to the ark, Gn 8:9
and Abraham **r** to his place. Gn 18:33
Abraham, and **r** Sarah his wife to him. Gn 20:14
his army rose up and **r** to the land of Gn 21:32
So Abraham **r** to his young men, and Gn 22:19
Now Isaac had **r** from Beer-lahai-roi Gn 24:62
Then Laban departed and **r** home. Gn 31:55
And the messengers **r** to Jacob, saying, Gn 32:6
So Esau **r** that day on his way to Seir. Gn 33:16
When Reuben **r** to the pit and saw that Gn 37:29
and **r** to his brothers and said, "The Gn 37:30
So he **r** to Judah and said, "I have not Gn 38:22
And he **r** to them and spoke to them. Gn 42:24
delayed, we would now have **r** twice." Gn 43:10
the money that was **r** in the mouth of Gn 43:12
his donkey, and they **r** to the city. Gn 44:13
Joseph **r** to Egypt with his brothers and Gn 50:14
and the sea **r** to its normal course when Ex 14:27
The waters **r** and covered the chariots Ex 14:28
So Moses **r** to the LORD and said, "Alas, Ex 32:31
leaders of the congregation **r** to him, Ex 34:31
and the elders of Israel **r** to the camp. Nm 11:30
of forty days they **r** from spying out Nm 13:25

who **r** and made all the congregation Nm 14:36
And Aaron **r** to Moses at the entrance Nm 16:50
And he **r** to him, and behold, he and all Nm 23:6
And you **r** and wept before the LORD, but Dt 1:45
three days until the pursuers have **r**. Jos 2:16
there three days until the pursuers **r**, Jos 2:22
Then the two men **r**. They came down Jos 2:23
waters of the Jordan **r** to their place and Jos 4:18
the city once, and **r** into the camp. Jos 6:14
And they **r** to Joshua and said to him, "Do Jos 7:3
all Israel **r** to Ai and struck it down with Jos 8:24
So Joshua **r**, and all Israel with him, to Jos 10:15
then all the people **r** safe to Joshua in Jos 10:21
Then Joshua **r**, and all Israel with him, Jos 10:43
and the half-tribe of Manasseh **r** home, Jos 22:9
r from the people of Reuben and the Jos 22:32
Gilead.'" Then 22,000 of the people **r**, Jgs 7:3
And he **r** to the camp of Israel and said, Jgs 7:15
the son of Joash **r** from the battle by Jgs 8:13
Thus God **r** the evil of Abimelech, Jgs 9:56
end of two months, she **r** to her father, Jgs 11:39
After some days he **r** to take her. And he Jgs 14:8
And when he drank, his spirit **r**, and he Jgs 15:19
And Benjamin **r** at that time. And they Jgs 21:14
they went and **r** to their inheritance Jgs 21:23
So Naomi **r**, and Ruth the Moabite her Ru 1:22
her, who **r** from the country of Moab. Ru 1:22
saw it, they **r** that day to Ekron. 1 Sm 6:16
tumors that the Philistines **r** as a guilt 1 Sm 6:17
"The Philistines have **r** the ark of the 1 Sm 6:21
as soon as David **r** from the striking 1 Sm 17:57
when David **r** from striking down the 1 Sm 18:6
So Saul **r** from pursuing after David 1 Sm 23:28
When Saul **r** from following the 1 Sm 24:1
to him, and he has **r** me evil for good. 1 Sm 25:21
The LORD has **r** the evil of Nabal on 1 Sm 25:39
went his way, and Saul **r** to his place. 1 Sm 26:25
when David had **r** from striking down 2 Sm 1:1
and the sword of Saul **r** not empty. 2 Sm 1:22
Joab **r** from the pursuit of Abner. And 2 Sm 2:30
said to him, "Go, return." And he **r**. 2 Sm 3:16
And when Abner **r** to Hebron, Joab 2 Sm 3:27
And David **r** to bless his household. 2 Sm 6:20
himself when he **r** from striking 2 Sm 8:13
Then Joab **r** from fighting against 2 Sm 10:14
Then she **r** to her house. 2 Sm 11:4
and all the people **r** to Jerusalem. 2 Sm 12:31
not find them, they **r** to Jerusalem. 2 Sm 17:20
him, and he **r** to his own home. 2 Sm 19:39
And Joab **r** to Jerusalem to the king. 2 Sm 20:22
and the men **r** after him only to strip 2 Sm 23:10
gone from Jerusalem to Gath and **r**, 1 Kgs 2:41
then Jeroboam **r** from Egypt. 1 Kgs 12:2
all Israel heard that Jeroboam had **r**, 1 Kgs 12:20
And he **r** from following him and 1 Kgs 19:21
The messengers **r** to the king, and he 2 Kgs 1:5
he said to them, "Why have you **r**?" 2 Kgs 1:5
and from there he **r** to Samaria. 2 Kgs 2:25
from him and **r** to their own 2 Kgs 3:27
Therefore he **r** to meet him and told 2 Kgs 4:31
Then he **r** to the man of God, he and 2 Kgs 5:15
And the messengers **r** and told the 2 Kgs 7:15
when the woman **r** from the land of 2 Kgs 8:3
And King Joram **r** to be healed in 2 Kgs 8:29
but King Joram had **r** to be healed in 2 Kgs 9:15
also hostages, and he **r** to Samaria. 2 Kgs 14:14
The Rabshakeh **r**, and found the 2 Kgs 19:8
on them. Then he **r** to Jerusalem. 2 Kgs 23:20
ruled in Moab and **r** to Lehem (now 1 Chr 4:22
and all the people **r** to Jerusalem. 1 Chr 20:3
then Jeroboam **r** from Egypt. 2 Chr 10:2
word of the LORD and **r** and did not go 2 Chr 11:4
camels. Then they **r** to Jerusalem. 2 Chr 14:15
the king of Judah **r** in safety to his 2 Chr 19:1
Then they **r**, every man of Judah 2 Chr 20:27
and he **r** to be healed in Jezreel of the 2 Chr 22:6
with Judah and **r** home in fierce 2 Chr 25:10
also hostages, and he **r** to Samaria. 2 Chr 25:24
palm trees. Then they **r** to Samaria. 2 Chr 28:15
all the people of Israel **r** to their cities, 2 Chr 31:1
So he **r** with shame of face to his 2 Chr 32:21
land of Israel. Then he **r** to Jerusalem. 2 Chr 34:7
They **r** to Jerusalem and Judah, each to Ezr 2:1
heard that the **r** exiles were building Ezr 4:1
then an answer be **r** by letter concerning Ezr 5:5
the Levites, and the rest of the **r** exiles, Ezr 6:16
month, the **r** exiles kept the Passover. Ezr 6:19
the Passover lamb for all the **r** exiles, Ezr 6:20
the people of Israel who had **r** from exile, Ezr 6:21
had come from captivity, the **r** exiles, Ezr 8:35
of the faithlessness of the **r** exiles, Ezr 9:4
Jerusalem to all the **r** exiles that they Ezr 10:7
Then the **r** exiles did so. Ezra the priest Ezr 10:16
entered by the Valley Gate, and so **r**. Neh 2:15
their plan, we all **r** to the wall, Neh 4:15
They **r** to Jerusalem and Judah, each to Neh 7:6
of those who had **r** from the captivity Neh 8:17
Then Mordecai **r** to the king's gate. But Est 6:12
And the king **r** from the palace garden to Est 7:8
The Rabshakeh **r**, and found the king of Is 37:8
Assyria departed and **r** home and lived Is 37:37
then all the Judeans **r** from all the Jer 40:12
of Judah who had **r** to live in the Jer 43:5
I have **r** your deeds upon your head, Ezk 16:43
I have **r** their way upon their heads, Ezk 22:31
eyes to heaven, and my reason **r** to me, Dn 4:34
At the same time my reason **r** to me, and Dn 4:36
my majesty and splendor **r** to me. Dn 4:36
LORD, I have **r** to Jerusalem with mercy; Zec 1:16
I have **r** to Zion and will dwell in the Zec 8:3
And when he **r** to Capernaum after some Mk 2:1
The apostles **r** to Jesus and told him all Mk 6:30
Then he **r** from the region of Tyre and Mk 7:31
about three months and **r** to her home. Lk 1:56
And the shepherds **r**, glorifying and Lk 2:20
the Law of the Lord, they **r** into Galilee, Lk 2:39
did not find him, they **r** to Jerusalem, Lk 2:45
r from the Jordan and was led by the Lk 4:1
And Jesus **r** in the power of the Spirit to Lk 4:14
those who had been sent **r** to the house, Lk 7:10
great fear. So he got into the boat and **r**. Lk 8:37
Now when Jesus **r**, the crowd welcomed Lk 8:40
And her spirit **r**, and she got up at once. Lk 8:55
The seventy-two **r** with joy, saying, Lk 10:17
When he **r**, having received the Lk 19:15
place, **r** home beating their breasts. Lk 23:48
Then they **r** and prepared spices and Lk 23:56
rose that same hour and **r** to Jerusalem. Lk 24:33
worshiped him and **r** to Jerusalem with Lk 24:52
Then they **r** to Jerusalem from the Acts 1:12
in the prison, so they **r** and reported, Acts 5:22
word of the Lord, they **r** to Jerusalem, Acts 8:25
Barnabas and Saul **r** from Jerusalem Acts 12:25
John left them and **r** to Jerusalem, Acts 13:13
they **r** to Lystra and to Iconium and Acts 14:21
on board the ship, and they **r** home. Acts 21:6
"When I had **r** to Jerusalem and was Acts 22:17
the next day they **r** to the barracks, Acts 23:32
into Arabia, and **r** again to Damascus. Gal 1:17
but have now **r** to the Shepherd and 1 Pt 2:25

RETURNING (9)
which you are **r** to him as a guilt 1 Sm 6:8
"If you are **r** to the LORD with all your 1 Sm 7:3
their head, **r** to Jerusalem with joy, 2 Chr 20:27
Israel, "In **r** and rest you shall be saved; Is 30:15
In the morning, as he was **r** to the city, Mt 21:18
when the feast was ended, as they were **r**, Lk 2:43
and **r** from the tomb they told all these Lk 24:9
and was **r**, seated in his chariot, and he Acts 8:28
met Abraham **r** from the slaughter of Heb 7:1

RETURNS (11)
has no child and **r** to her father's house, Lv 22:13
he **r** no more to his house, nor does his Jb 7:10
His mischief **r** upon his own head, and Ps 7:16
his breath departs he **r** to the earth; Ps 146:4
If anyone **r** evil for good, evil will not Prv 17:13
Like a dog that **r** to his vomit is a fool Prv 26:11
the wind, and on its circuits the wind **r**. Eccl 1:6
and the dust **r** to the earth as it was, Eccl 12:7
was, and the spirit **r** to God who gave it. Eccl 12:7
"The dog **r** to its own vomit, and the 2 Pt 2:22
herself, **r** to wallow in the mire." 2 Pt 2:22

REU (6)
Peleg had lived 30 years, he fathered **R**. Gn 11:18
lived after he fathered **R** 209 years and Gn 11:19
When **R** had lived 32 years, he fathered Gn 11:20
And **R** lived after he fathered Serug 207 Gn 11:21
Eber, Peleg, **R**; 1 Chr 1:25
the son of Serug, the son of **R**, the son of Lk 3:35

REUBEN (73)
bore a son, and she called his name **R**, Gn 29:32
of wheat harvest **R** went and found Gn 30:14
R went and lay with Bilhah his father's Gn 35:22
R (Jacob's firstborn), Simeon, Levi, Gn 35:23
But when **R** heard it, he rescued him Gn 37:21
And **R** said to them, "Shed no blood; Gn 37:22
When **R** returned to the pit and saw Gn 37:29
And **R** answered them, "Did I not tell Gn 42:22
Then **R** said to his father, "Kill my two Gn 42:37
Jacob and his sons. **R**, Jacob's firstborn, Gn 46:8
and the sons of **R**: Hanoch, Pallu, Gn 46:9
shall be mine, as **R** and Simeon are. Gn 48:5
"**R**, you are my firstborn, my might, and Gn 49:3
R, Simeon, Levi, and Judah, Ex 1:2
the sons of **R**, the firstborn of Israel: Ex 6:14
and Carmi; these are the clans of **R**. Ex 6:14
of the men who shall assist you. From **R**, Nm 1:5
The people of **R**, Israel's firstborn, their Nm 1:20
those listed of the tribe of **R** were 46,500. Nm 1:21
of the camp of **R** by their companies, Nm 2:10
of the people of **R** being Elizur the son Nm 2:10
All those listed of the camp of **R**, by Nm 2:16
of Shedeur, the chief of the people of **R**: Nm 7:30
of the camp of **R** set out by their Nm 10:18
From the tribe of **R**, Shammua the son Nm 13:4
and On the son of Peleth, sons of **R**, Nm 16:1
R, the firstborn of Israel; the sons of Nm 26:5
the firstborn of Israel; the sons of **R**: Nm 26:5
Now the people of **R** and the people of Nm 32:1
and the people of **R** came and said to Nm 32:2
the people of Gad and to the people of **R**, Nm 32:6
Gad and the people of **R** said to Moses, Nm 32:25
the people of Gad and the people of **R**, Nm 32:29
of Gad and the people of **R** answered, Nm 32:31
to the people of **R** and to the half-tribe Nm 32:33
And the people of **R** built Heshbon, Nm 32:37
of the people of **R** by fathers' houses Nm 34:14
and Abiram the sons of Eliab, son of **R**, Dt 11:6
R, Gad, Asher, Zebulun, Dan, and Dt 27:13
"Let **R** live, and not die, but let his men Dt 33:6
The sons of **R** and the sons of Gad and Jos 4:12
of the people of **R** according to their Jos 13:15
of the people of **R** was the Jordan as Jos 13:23
was the inheritance of the people of **R**, Jos 13:23
up to the stone of Bohan the son of **R**. Jos 15:6
And Gad and **R** and half the tribe of Jos 18:7
to the stone of Bohan the son of **R**, Jos 18:17
on the tableland, from the tribe of **R**, Jos 20:8
their clans received from the tribe of **R**, Jos 21:7
and out of the tribe of **R**, Bezer with its Jos 21:36
So the people of **R** and the people of Gad Jos 22:9
the people of **R** and the people of Gad Jos 22:10
the people of **R** and the people of Gad Jos 22:11
sent to the people of **R** and the people of Jos 22:13
And they came to the people of **R**, the Jos 22:15
Then the people of **R**, the people of Gad, Jos 22:21
you, you people of **R** and people of Gad. Jos 22:25
that the people of **R** and the people of Jos 22:30
said to the people of **R** and the people of Jos 22:31
from the people of **R** and the people of Jos 22:32
where the people of **R** and the people of Jos 22:33
The people of **R** and the people of Gad Jos 22:34
Among the clans of **R** there were great Jgs 5:15
Among the clans of **R** there were great Jgs 5:16
R, Simeon, Levi, Judah, Issachar, 1 Chr 2:1
The sons of **R** the firstborn of Israel 1 Chr 5:1
the sons of **R**, the firstborn of Israel: 1 Chr 5:3
twelve cities out of the tribes of **R**, 1 Chr 6:63
of the Jordan, out of the tribe of **R**: 1 Chr 6:78
the east side to the west, **R**, one portion. Ezk 48:6
Adjoining the territory of **R**, from the Ezk 48:7
three gates, the gate of **R**, the gate of Ezk 48:31
were sealed, 12,000 from the tribe of **R**, Rv 7:5

REUBENITE (1)
Adina the son of Shiza the **R**, a 1 Chr 11:42

REUBENITES (17)
These are the clans of the **R**, and those Nm 26:7
I gave to the **R** and the Gadites the Dt 3:12
and to the **R** and the Gadites I gave the Dt 3:16
the wilderness on the tableland for the **R**, Dt 4:43
and gave it for an inheritance to the **R**, Dt 29:8
And to the **R**, the Gadites, and the Jos 1:12
a possession to the **R** and the Gadites and Jos 12:6
tribe of Manasseh the **R** and the Gadites Jos 13:8
Joshua summoned the **R** and the Gadites Jos 22:1
of Gilead, the Gadites, and the **R**, 2 Kgs 10:33
away into exile; he was a chief of the **R**. 1 Chr 5:6
The **R**, the Gadites, and the half-tribe 1 Chr 5:18
took them into exile, namely, the **R**, 1 Chr 5:26
the Reubenite, a leader of the **R**, 1 Chr 11:42
Of the **R** and Gadites and the 1 Chr 12:37
to have the oversight of the **R**, 1 Chr 26:32
Over the tribes of Israel, for the **R**, 1 Chr 27:16

REUEL (11)
bore to Esau, Eliphaz; Basemath bore **R**; Gn 36:4
R the son of Basemath the wife of Esau. Gn 36:10
These are the sons of **R**: Nahath, Zerah, Gn 36:13
These are the sons of **R**, Esau's son: the Gn 36:17
these are the chiefs of **R** in the land of Gn 36:17
When they came home to their father **R**, Ex 2:18
of Gad being Eliasaph the son of **R**, Nm 2:14
to Hobab the son of **R** the Midianite, Nm 10:29
Eliphaz, **R**, Jeush, Jalam, and Korah. 1 Chr 1:35
The sons of **R**: Nahath, Zerah, 1 Chr 1:37
the son of Shephatiah, son of **R**, 1 Chr 9:8

REUMAH (1)
his concubine, whose name was **R**, Gn 22:24

REVEAL (10)
'Did I indeed **r** myself to the house of 1 Sm 2:27
The heavens will **r** his iniquity, and the Jb 20:27
himself, and do not **r** another's secret, Prv 25:9

shelter the outcasts; do not **r** the fugitive; Is 16:3
will heal them and **r** to them abundance Jer 33:6
you have been able to **r** this mystery." Dn 2:47
to whom the Son chooses to **r** him. Mt 11:27
to whom the Son chooses to **r** him." Lk 10:22
was pleased to **r** his Son to me, in order Gal 1:16
otherwise, God will **r** that also to you. Phil 3:15

REVEALED (50)
because there God had **r** himself to him Gn 35:7
God has **r** to Pharaoh what he is about Gn 41:25
the things that are **r** belong to us and Dt 29:29
of the LORD had not yet been **r** to him. 1 Sm 3:7
for the LORD **r** himself to Samuel at 1 Sm 3:21
Saul came, the LORD had **r** to Samuel: 1 Sm 9:15
have **r** to your servant that you will 1 Chr 17:25
Have the gates of death been **r** to you, or Jb 38:17
he has **r** his righteousness in the sight of Ps 98:2
LORD of hosts has **r** himself in my ears: Is 22:14
From the land of Cyprus it is **r** to them. Is 23:1
And the glory of the LORD shall be **r**, and Is 40:5
to whom has the arm of the LORD been **r**? Is 53:1
will come, and my deliverance be **r**. Is 56:1
Then the mystery was **r** to Daniel in a Dn 2:19
as for me, this mystery has been **r** to me, Dn 2:30
king of Persia a word was **r** to Daniel, Dn 10:1
heal Israel, the iniquity of Ephraim is **r**, Hos 7:1
nothing is covered that will not be **r**, Mt 10:26
and understanding and **r** them to little Mt 11:25
flesh and blood has not **r** this to you, Mt 16:17
And it had been **r** to him by the Holy Lk 2:26
thoughts from many hearts may be **r**." Lk 2:35
and understanding and **r** them to little Lk 10:21
Nothing is covered up that will not be **r**, Lk 12:2
be on the day when the Son of Man is **r**. Lk 17:30
with water, that he might be **r** to Israel." Jn 1:31
whom has the arm of the Lord been **r**?" Jn 12:38
After this Jesus **r** himself again to the Jn 21:1
of Tiberias, and he **r** himself in this way. Jn 21:1
time that Jesus was **r** to the disciples Jn 21:14
of God is **r** from faith for Rom 1:17
wrath of God is **r** from heaven against Rom 1:18
God's righteous judgment will be **r**. Rom 2:5
with the glory that is to be **r** to us. Rom 8:18
these things God has **r** to us through 1 Cor 2:10
disclose it, because it will be **r** by fire, 1 Cor 3:13
for us might be **r** to you in the 2 Cor 7:12
until the coming faith would be **r**. Gal 3:23
as it has now been **r** to his holy apostles Eph 3:5
and generations but now **r** to his saints. Col 1:26
the Lord Jesus is **r** from heaven with 2 Thes 1:7
first, and the man of lawlessness is **r**, 2 Thes 2:3
now so that he may be **r** in his time. 2 Thes 2:6
And then the lawless one will be **r**, 2 Thes 2:8
a salvation ready to be **r** in the last time. 1 Pt 1:5
It was **r** to them that they were serving 1 Pt 1:12
rejoice and be glad when his glory is **r**. 1 Pt 4:13
in the glory that is going to be **r**: 1 Pt 5:1
for your righteous acts have been **r**." Rv 15:4

REVEALER (1)
and Lord of kings, and a **r** of mysteries, Dn 2:47

REVEALING (3)
GOD does nothing without **r** his secret to Am 3:7
eager longing for the **r** of the sons of Rom 8:19
as you wait for the **r** of our Lord Jesus 1 Cor 1:7

REVEALS (6)
speech, and night to night **r** knowledge. Ps 19:2
goes about slandering **r** secrets, Prv 11:13
goes about slandering **r** secrets; Prv 20:19
he **r** deep and hidden things; he knows Dn 2:22
is a God in heaven who **r** mysteries, Dn 2:28
and he who **r** mysteries made known to Dn 2:29

REVEL (1)
count it pleasure to **r** in the daytime. 2 Pt 2:13

REVELATION (13)
have made this **r** to your servant, 2 Sm 7:27
a light for **r** to the Gentiles, and for glory Lk 2:32
according to the **r** of the mystery that Rom 16:25
I bring you some **r** or knowledge or 1 Cor 14:6
each one has a hymn, a lesson, a **r**, 1 Cor 14:26
If a **r** is made to another sitting 1 Cor 14:30
I received it through a **r** of Jesus Christ. Gal 1:12
up because of a **r** and set before them Gal 2:2
of wisdom and of **r** in the knowledge of Eph 1:17
mystery was made known to me by **r**, Eph 3:3
glory and honor at the **r** of Jesus Christ. 1 Pt 1:7
brought to you at the **r** of Jesus Christ. 1 Pt 1:13
The **r** of Jesus Christ, which God gave Rv 1:1

REVELATIONS (2)
will go on to visions and **r** of the Lord. 2 Cor 12:1
by the surpassing greatness of the **r**, 2 Cor 12:7

REVELERS (2)
go down, her **r** and he who exults in her. Is 5:14
I did not sit in the company of **r**, nor did Jer 15:17

REVELING (1)
and blemishes, **r** in their deceptions, 2 Pt 2:13

REVELRY (1)
and the **r** of those who stretch Am 6:7

REVENGE (3)
If Cain's **r** is sevenfold, then Lamech's is Gn 4:24
and he will not spare when he takes **r**. Prv 6:34
overcome him and take our **r** on him." Jer 20:10

REVENGEFULLY (2)
Because Edom acted **r** against the Ezk 25:12
the Philistines acted **r** and took Ezk 25:15

REVENUE (5)
or toll, and the royal **r** will be impaired. Ezr 4:13
full and without delay from the royal **r**, Ezr 6:8
on many waters your **r** was the grain of Is 23:3
are owed, **r** to whom revenue is owed, Rom 13:7
are owed, revenue to whom **r** is owed, Rom 13:7

REVENUES (1)
than great **r** with injustice. Prv 16:8

REVERE (1)
one of you shall **r** his mother and his Lv 19:3

REVERENCE (5)
keep my Sabbaths and **r** my sanctuary: Lv 19:30
keep my Sabbaths and **r** my sanctuary: Lv 26:2
to one another out of **r** for Christ. Eph 5:21
death, and he was heard because of his **r**. Heb 5:7
acceptable worship, with **r** and awe, Heb 12:28

REVERENT (2)
women likewise are to be **r** in behavior, Ti 2:3
in **r** fear constructed an ark for the Heb 11:7

REVERES (1)
but he who **r** the commandment will Prv 13:13

REVERSE (1)
the mastery over them, the **r** occurred: Est 9:1

REVERT (1)
of liberty. Then it shall **r** to the prince; Ezk 46:17

REVIEWED (1)
As I **r** the people and the priests, I found Ezr 8:15

REVILE (7)
"You shall not **r** God, nor curse a ruler Ex 22:28
Is the enemy to **r** your name forever? Ps 74:10
are you when others **r** you and persecute Mt 5:11
they exclude you and **r** you and spurn Lk 6:22
said, "Would you **r** God's high priest?" Acts 23:4
he was reviled, he did not **r** in return; 1 Pt 2:23
those who **r** your good behavior in 1 Pt 3:16

REVILED (13)
god and ate and drank and **r** Abimelech. Jgs 9:27
of the king of Assyria have **r** me. 2 Kgs 19:6
"Whom have you mocked and **r**? 2 Kgs 19:22
men of the king of Assyria have **r** me. Is 37:6
"Whom have you mocked and **r**? Is 37:23
crucified with him also **r** him in the Mt 27:44
were crucified with him also **r** him. Mk 15:32
And they **r** him, saying, "You are his Jn 9:28
And when they opposed and **r** him, he Acts 18:6
with our own hands. When **r**, 1 Cor 4:12
of God and the teaching may not be **r**. 1 Tm 6:1
that the word of God may not be **r**. Ti 2:5
When he was **r**, he did not revile in 1 Pt 2:23

REVILER (2)
at the sound of the taunter and **r**, at the Ps 44:16
greed, or is an idolater, **r**, drunkard, 1 Cor 5:11

REVILERS (1)
nor the greedy, nor drunkards, nor **r**, 1 Cor 6:10

REVILES (4)
he is native or a sojourner, **r** the LORD, Nm 15:30
and a foolish people **r** your name. Ps 74:18
'Whoever **r** father or mother must Mt 15:4
'Whoever **r** father or mother must Mk 7:10

REVILING (4)
Jacob to utter destruction and Israel to **r**. Is 43:28
what was spoken by Paul, **r** him. Acts 13:45
not repay evil for evil or **r** for reviling, 1 Pt 3:9
not repay evil for evil or reviling for **r**, 1 Pt 3:9

REVILINGS (3)
of man, nor be dismayed at their **r**. Is 51:7
have heard all the **r** that you uttered Ezk 35:12
of Moab and the **r** of the Ammonites, Zep 2:8

REVIVE (11)
Will they **r** the stones out of the heaps of Neh 4:2
you who seek God, let your hearts **r**. Ps 69:32
and calamities will **r** me again; Ps 71:20
Will you not **r** us again, that your people Ps 85:6
lowly spirit, to **r** the spirit of the lowly, Is 57:15
lowly, and to **r** the heart of the contrite. Is 57:15
treasures for food to **r** their strength. Lam 1:11
is far from me, one to **r** my spirit; Lam 1:16
they sought food to **r** their strength. Lam 1:19
After two days he will **r** us; on the third Hos 6:2
In the midst of the years **r** it; in the midst Hab 3:2

REVIVED (6)
him, the spirit of their father Jacob **r**. Gn 45:27
he drank, his spirit returned, and he **r**. Jgs 15:19
And when he had eaten, his spirit **r**, 1 Sm 30:12
came into him again, and he **r**. 1 Kgs 17:22
of Elisha, he **r** and stood on his feet. 2 Kgs 13:21
at length you have **r** your concern for Phil 4:10

REVIVING (3)
eyes and grant us a little **r** in our slavery. Ezr 9:8
to grant us some **r** to set up the house of Ezr 9:9
The law of the LORD is perfect, **r** the soul; Ps 19:7

REVOKE (10)
bless: he has blessed, and I cannot **r** it. Nm 23:20
order be written to **r** the letters devised by Est 8:5
and for four, I will not **r** the punishment, Am 1:3
and for four, I will not **r** the punishment, Am 1:6
and for four, I will not **r** the punishment, Am 1:9
for four, I will not **r** the punishment, Am 1:11
for four, I will not **r** the punishment, Am 1:13
and for four, I will not **r** the punishment, Am 2:1
and for four, I will not **r** the punishment, Am 2:4
and for four, I will not **r** the punishment, Am 2:6

REVOKED (3)
sealed with the king's ring cannot be **r**." Est 8:8
and the Persians, which cannot be **r**." Dn 6:8
and Persians, which cannot be **r**." Dn 6:12

REVOLT (2)
our God, speaking oppression and **r**, Is 59:13
recently stirred up a **r** and led the four Acts 21:38

REVOLTED (7)
In his days Edom **r** from the rule of 2 Kgs 8:20
So Edom **r** from the rule of Judah to 2 Kgs 8:22
day. Then Libnah **r** at the same time. 2 Kgs 8:22
In his days Edom **r** from the rule of 2 Chr 21:8
So Edom **r** from the rule of Judah to 2 Chr 21:10
time Libnah also **r** from his rule, 2 Chr 21:10
to him from whom people have deeply **r**, Is 31:6

REVOLTERS (1)
And the **r** have gone deep into slaughter, Hos 5:2

REWARD (49)
your shield; your **r** shall be very great." Gn 15:1
for it is your **r** in return for your Nm 18:31
and a full **r** be given you by the LORD, Ru 2:12
So may the LORD **r** you with good for 1 Sm 24:19
which was the **r** I gave him for his 2 Sm 4:10
you will have no **r** for the news?" 2 Sm 18:22
the king repay me with such a **r**? 2 Sm 19:36
yourself, and I will give you a **r**." 1 Kgs 13:7
they **r** us by coming to drive us out 2 Chr 20:11
in keeping them there is great **r**. Ps 19:11
of their hands; render them their due **r**. Ps 28:4
"Surely there is a **r** for the righteous; Ps 58:11
So they **r** me evil for good, and hatred Ps 109:5
May this be the **r** of my accusers from Ps 109:20
from the LORD, the fruit of the womb a **r**. Ps 127:3
who sows righteousness gets a sure **r**. Prv 11:18
The **r** for humility and fear of the LORD Prv 22:4
on his head, and the LORD will **r** you. Prv 25:22
toil, and this was my **r** for all my toil. Eccl 2:10
because they have a good **r** for their toil. Eccl 4:9
nothing, and they have no more **r**, Eccl 9:5
behold, his **r** is with him, and his Is 40:10
not for price or **r**," says the LORD of hosts. Is 45:13
behold, his **r** is with him, and his Is 62:11
tears, for there is a **r** for your work, Jer 31:16
be glad, for your **r** is great in heaven, Mt 5:12
those who love you, what **r** do you have? Mt 5:46
you will have no **r** from your Father who Mt 6:1
I say to you, they have received their **r**. Mt 6:2
your Father who sees in secret will **r** you. Mt 6:4
I say to you, they have received their **r**. Mt 6:5
your Father who sees in secret will **r** you. Mt 6:6
I say to you, they have received their **r**. Mt 6:16
Father who sees in secret will **r** you. Mt 6:18
is a prophet will receive a prophet's **r**, Mt 10:41
will receive a righteous person's **r**. Mt 10:41
to you, he will by no means lose his **r**." Mt 10:42
to Christ will by no means lose his **r**. Mk 9:41
joy, for behold, your **r** is great in heaven; Lk 6:23
in return, and your **r** will be great, Lk 6:35
we are receiving the due **r** of our deeds; Lk 23:41
a field with the **r** of his wickedness, Acts 1:18
survives, he will receive a **r**. 1 Cor 3:14
if I do this of my own will, I have a **r**, 1 Cor 9:17
What then is my **r**? That in my 1 Cor 9:18
will receive the inheritance as your **r**. Col 3:24

your confidence, which has a great **r**. Heb 10:35
of Egypt, for he was looking to the **r**. Heb 11:26
have worked for, but may win a full **r**. 2 Jn 1:8

REWARDED (7)
the cleanness of my hands he **r** me. 2 Sm 22:21
And the LORD has **r** me according to 2 Sm 22:25
be weak, for your work shall be **r**." 2 Chr 15:7
to the cleanness of my hands he **r** me. Ps 18:20
So the LORD has **r** me according to my Ps 18:24
reveres the commandment will be **r**. Prv 13:13
but the righteous are **r** with good. Prv 13:21

REWARDING (4)
the righteous by **r** him according to 1 Kgs 8:32
the righteous by **r** him according to 2 Chr 6:23
r each one according to his ways and Jer 32:19
to be judged, and for **r** your servants, Rv 11:18

REWARDS (4)
The LORD **r** every man for his 1 Sm 26:23
from me gifts and **r** and great honor. Dn 2:6
for yourself, and give your **r** to another. Dn 5:17
exists and that he **r** those who seek Heb 11:6

REWORKED (1)
hand, and he **r** it into another vessel, Jer 18:4

REZEPH (2)
R, and the people of Eden who were 2 Kgs 19:12
R, and the people of Eden who were in Is 37:12

REZIN (11)
LORD began to send **R** the king of 2 Kgs 15:37
Then **R** king of Syria and Pekah the 2 Kgs 16:5
At that time **R** the king of Syria 2 Kgs 16:6
people captive to Kir, and he killed **R**. 2 Kgs 16:9
the sons of **R**, the sons of Nekoda, the Ezr 2:48
the sons of Reaiah, the sons of **R**, the Neh 7:50
R the king of Syria and Pekah the son of Is 7:1
at the fierce anger of **R** and Syria and the Is 7:4
Damascus, and the head of Damascus is **R**. Is 7:8
and rejoice over **R** and the son of Is 8:6
raises the adversaries of **R** against him, Is 9:11

REZON (1)
to him, **R** the son of Eliada, 1 Kgs 11:23

RHEGIUM (1)
we made a circuit and arrived at **R**. Acts 28:13

RHESA (1)
the son of Joanan, the son of **R**, the son of Lk 3:27

RHODA (1)
servant girl named **R** came to answer. Acts 12:13

RHODES (1)
course to Cos, and the next day to **R**, Acts 21:1

RIB (1)
And the **r** that the LORD God had taken Gn 2:22

RIBAI (2)
Ittai the son of **R** of Gibeah of the 2 Sm 23:29
Ithai the son of **R** of Gibeah of the 1 Chr 11:31

RIBLAH (12)
down from Shepham to **R** on the east Nm 34:11
put him in bonds at **R** in the land of 2 Kgs 23:33
him up to the king of Babylon at **R**, 2 Kgs 25:6
them to the king of Babylon at **R**. 2 Kgs 25:20
put them to death at **R** in the land of 2 Kgs 25:21
Nebuchadnezzar king of Babylon, at **R**, Jer 39:5
the sons of Zedekiah at **R** before his eyes, Jer 39:6
the king of Babylon at **R** in the land of Jer 52:9
all the officials of Judah at **R**. Jer 52:10
them to the king of Babylon at **R**. Jer 52:26
put them to death at **R** in the land of Jer 52:27
places, from the wilderness to **R**. Ezk 6:14

RIBS (2)
slept took one of his **r** and closed up its Gn 2:21
It had three **r** in its mouth between its Dn 7:5

RICH (102)
Now Abram was very **r** in livestock, in Gn 13:2
you should say, 'I have made Abram **r**.' Gn 14:23
and the man became **r**, and gained Gn 26:13
"Asher's food shall be **r**, and he shall Gn 49:20
The **r** shall not give more, and the poor Ex 30:15
or sojourner with you becomes **r**, Lv 25:47
Or if he grows **r** he may redeem Lv 25:49
and whether the land is **r** or poor, and Nm 13:20
of the sun and the **r** yield of the months, Dt 33:14
you who sit on **r** carpets and you who Jgs 5:10
after young men, whether poor or **r**. Ru 3:10
The LORD makes poor and makes **r**; he 1 Sm 2:7
The man was very **r**; he had three 1 Sm 25:2
city, the one **r** and the other poor. 2 Sm 12:1
The **r** man had very many flocks and 2 Sm 12:2
there came a traveler to the **r** man, 2 Sm 12:4
where they found **r**, good pasture, and 1 Chr 4:40
captured fortified cities and a **r** land, Neh 9:25
and in the large and **r** land that you set Neh 9:35
And its **r** yield goes to the kings whom Neh 9:37
he will not be **r**, and his wealth will not Jb 15:29
He goes to bed **r**, but will do so no more; Jb 27:19
nor regards the **r** more than the poor, Jb 34:19
For you meet him with **r** blessings; you Ps 21:3
both low and high, **r** and poor together! Ps 49:2
Be not afraid when a man becomes **r**, Ps 49:16
will be satisfied as with fat and **r** food, Ps 63:5
but the hand of the diligent makes **r**. Prv 10:4
A **r** man's wealth is his strong city; the Prv 10:15
The blessing of the LORD makes **r**, and Prv 10:22
One pretends to be **r**, yet has nothing; Prv 13:7
neighbor, but the **r** has many friends. Prv 14:20
A **r** man's wealth is his strong city, Prv 18:11
entreaties, but the **r** answer roughly. Prv 18:23
he who loves wine and oil will not be **r**. Prv 21:17
The **r** and the poor meet together; the Prv 22:2
The **r** rules over the poor, and the Prv 22:7
his own wealth, or gives to the **r**, Prv 22:16
his integrity than a **r** man who is Prv 28:6
A **r** man is wise in his own eyes, but a Prv 28:11
whoever hastens to be **r** will not go Prv 28:20
full stomach of the **r** will not let him Eccl 5:12
places, and the **r** sit in a low place. Eccl 10:6
nor in your bedroom curse the **r**, Eccl 10:20
and instead of a **r** robe, a skirt of Is 3:24
shall eat among the ruins of the **r**. Is 5:17
will make for all peoples a feast of **r** food, Is 25:6
well-aged wine, of **r** food full of marrow, Is 25:6
the head of the **r** valley of those overcome Is 28:1
which is on the head of the **r** valley, Is 28:4
ground, which will be **r** and plenteous. Is 30:23
the wicked and with a **r** man in his death, Is 53:9
is good, and delight yourselves in **r** food. Is 55:2
therefore they have become great and **r**; Jer 5:27
let not the **r** man boast in his riches, Jer 9:23
dwell by many waters, **r** in treasures, Jer 51:13
pinions, **r** in plumage of many colors, Ezk 17:3
and on **r** pasture they shall feed on the Ezk 34:14
Ephraim has said, "Ah, but I am **r**; I Hos 12:8
and have carried my **r** treasures into your Jl 3:5
you strip the **r** robe from those who pass Mi 2:8
Your **r** men are full of violence; your Mi 6:12
he lives in luxury, and his food is **r**. Hab 1:16
'Blessed be the LORD, I have become **r**,' Zec 11:5
with difficulty will a **r** person enter the Mt 19:23
a needle than for a **r** person to enter the Mt 19:24
there came a **r** man from Arimathea, Mt 27:57
a needle than for a **r** person to enter the Mk 10:25
box. Many **r** people put in large sums. Mk 12:41
and the **r** he has sent empty away. Lk 1:53
"But woe to you who are **r**, for you have Lk 6:24
land of a **r** man produced plentifully, Lk 12:16
for himself and is not **r** toward God." Lk 12:21
or your relatives or **r** neighbors, Lk 14:12
"There was a **r** man who had a Lk 16:1
"There was a **r** man who was clothed Lk 16:19
with what fell from the **r** man's table. Lk 16:21
The **r** man also died and was buried, Lk 16:22
very sad, for he was extremely **r**. Lk 18:23
a needle than for a **r** person to enter the Lk 18:25
He was a chief tax collector and was **r**. Lk 19:2
up and saw the **r** putting their gifts into Lk 21:1
you want! Already you have become **r**! 1 Cor 4:8
as poor, yet making many **r**; 2 Cor 6:10
Jesus Christ, that though he was **r**, 2 Cor 8:9
you by his poverty might become **r**. 2 Cor 8:9
But God, being **r** in mercy, because of Eph 2:4
who desire to be **r** fall into temptation, 1 Tm 6:9
As for the **r** in this present age, charge 1 Tm 6:17
are to do good, to be **r** in good works, 1 Tm 6:18
and the **r** in his humiliation, because Jas 1:10
So also will the **r** man fade away in the Jas 1:11
in the world to be **r** in faith and heirs of Jas 2:5
Are not the **r** the ones who oppress you, Jas 2:6
Come now, you **r**, weep and howl for the Jas 5:1
poverty (but you are **r**) and the slander of Rv 2:9
For you say, I am **r**, I have prospered, and Rv 3:17
gold refined by fire, so that you may be **r**, Rv 3:18
the generals and the **r** and the powerful, Rv 6:15
both small and great, both **r** and poor, Rv 13:16
the earth have grown **r** from the power of Rv 18:3
had ships at sea grew **r** by her wealth! Rv 18:19

RICHER (2)
One gives freely, yet grows all the **r**; Prv 11:24
a fourth shall be far **r** than all of them. Dn 11:2

RICHES (61)
kills him with great **r** and will give 1 Sm 17:25
for yourself long life or **r** or the life of 1 Kgs 3:11
have not asked, both **r** and honor, 1 Kgs 3:13
of the earth in **r** and in wisdom. 1 Kgs 10:23
Both **r** and honor come from you, 1 Chr 29:12
good age, full of days, **r**, and honor. 1 Chr 29:28
I will also give you **r**, possessions, and 2 Chr 1:12
of the earth in **r** and in wisdom. 2 Chr 9:22
and he had great **r** and honor. 2 Chr 17:5
Jehoshaphat had great **r** and honor, 2 Chr 18:1
had very great **r** and honor, 2 Chr 32:27
while he showed the **r** of his royal glory Est 1:4
recounted to them the splendor of his **r**, Est 5:11
He swallows down **r** and vomits them Jb 20:15
and boast of the abundance of their **r**? Ps 49:6
abundance of his **r** and sought refuge Ps 52:7
no vain hopes on robbery; if **r** increase, Ps 62:10
always at ease, they increase in **r**. Ps 73:12
Wealth and **r** are in his house, and his Ps 112:3
I delight as much as in all **r**. Ps 119:14
hand; in her left hand are **r** and honor. Prv 3:16
R and honor are with me, enduring Prv 8:18
R do not profit in the day of wrath, but Prv 11:4
gets honor, and violent men get **r**. Prv 11:16
Whoever trusts in his **r** will fall, but Prv 11:28
is to be chosen rather than great **r**, Prv 22:1
fear of the LORD is **r** and honor and life. Prv 22:4
filled with all precious and pleasant **r**. Prv 24:4
for **r** do not last forever; and does a Prv 27:24
lying; give me neither poverty nor **r**; Prv 30:8
and his eyes are never satisfied with **r**, Eccl 4:8
r were kept by their owner to his hurt, Eccl 5:13
and those **r** were lost in a bad venture. Eccl 5:14
to the wise, nor **r** to the intelligent, Eccl 9:11
they carry their **r** on the backs of Is 30:6
let not the rich man boast in his **r**, Jer 9:23
so is he who gets **r** but not by justice; Jer 17:11
Therefore the **r** they gained have Jer 48:36
will plunder your **r** and loot your Ezk 26:12
Your **r**, your wares, your Ezk 27:27
he has become strong through his **r**, Dn 11:2
the deceitfulness of **r** choke the word, Mt 13:22
the deceitfulness of **r** and the desires Mk 4:19
by the cares and **r** and pleasures of life, Lk 8:14
who will entrust to you the true **r**? Lk 16:11
you presume on the **r** of his kindness Rom 2:4
to make known the **r** of his glory for Rom 9:23
bestowing his **r** on all who call on Rom 10:12
their trespass means **r** for the world, Rom 11:12
their failure means **r** for the Gentiles, Rom 11:12
the depth of the **r** and wisdom and Rom 11:33
according to the **r** of his grace, Eph 1:7
what are the **r** of his glorious Eph 1:18
show the immeasurable **r** of his grace Eph 2:7
Gentiles the unsearchable **r** of Christ, Eph 3:8
that according to the **r** of his glory he Eph 3:16
yours according to his **r** in glory in Phil 4:19
the Gentiles are the **r** of the glory of Col 1:27
to reach all the **r** of full assurance of Col 2:2
their hopes on the uncertainty of **r**, 1 Tm 6:17
Your **r** have rotted and your garments are Jas 5:2

RICHEST (2)
your favor with gifts, the **r** of the people. Ps 45:12
shall come into the **r** parts of the Dn 11:24

RICHLY (5)
the soul of the diligent is **r** supplied. Prv 13:4
Let the word of Christ dwell in you **r**, Col 3:16
who **r** provides us with everything to 1 Tm 6:17
poured out on us **r** through Jesus Christ Ti 3:6
way there will be **r** provided for you an 2 Pt 1:11

RIDDEN (2)
on which you have **r** all your life long Nm 22:30
worn, and the horse that the king has **r**, Est 6:8

RIDDLE (10)
to them, "Let me now put a **r** to you. Jgs 14:12
And they said to him, "Put your **r**, Jgs 14:13
in three days they could not solve the **r**. Jgs 14:14
your husband to tell us what the **r** is, Jgs 14:15
You have put a **r** to my people, and you Jgs 14:16
hard. Then she told the **r** to her people. Jgs 14:17
you would not have found out my **r**." Jgs 14:18
garments to those who had told the **r**. Jgs 14:19
I will solve my **r** to the music of the lyre. Ps 49:4
"Son of man, propound a **r**, and speak a Ezk 17:2

RIDDLES (5)
mouth to mouth, clearly, and not in **r**, Nm 12:8
saying, the words of the wise and their **r**. Prv 1:6
to interpret dreams, explain **r**, Dn 5:12
of bold face, one who understands **r**, Dn 8:23
him, with scoffing and **r** for him, Hab 2:6

RIDE (21)
And he made him **r** in his second Gn 41:43
his sons and had them **r** on a donkey, Ex 4:20
He made him **r** on the high places of the Dt 32:13
"Tell of it, you who **r** on white donkeys, Jgs 5:10
are for the king's household to **r** on, 2 Sm 16:2
that I may **r** on it and go with the 2 Sm 19:26
have Solomon my son **r** on my own 1 Kgs 1:33

and had Solomon **r** on King David's 1 Kgs 1:38
And they had him **r** on the king's 1 Kgs 1:44
Turn around and **r** behind me." And 2 Kgs 9:18
Turn around and **r** behind me." 2 Kgs 9:19
So he had him **r** in his chariot. 2 Kgs 10:16
you make me **r** on it, and you toss me Jb 30:22
In your majesty **r** out victoriously for the Ps 45:4
you let men **r** over our heads; we went Ps 66:12
away; and, "We will **r** upon swift steeds"; Is 30:16
and I will make you **r** on the heights of Is 58:14
they **r** on horses, set in array as a man Jer 6:23
they **r** on horses, arrayed as a man for Jer 50:42
not save us; we will not **r** on horses; Hos 14:3
mounts for Paul to **r** and bring him Acts 23:24

RIDER (10)
heels so that his **r** falls backward. Gn 49:17
the horse and his **r** he has thrown into Ex 15:1
the horse and his **r** he has thrown into Ex 15:21
to flee, she laughs at the horse and his **r**. Jb 39:18
of Jacob, both **r** and horse lay stunned. Ps 76:6
I break in pieces the horse and his **r**; Jer 51:21
with panic, and its **r** with madness. Zec 12:4
And its **r** had a bow, and a crown was Rv 6:2
Its **r** was permitted to take peace from the Rv 6:4
And its **r** had a pair of scales in his hand. Rv 6:5

RIDER'S (1)
And its **r** name was Death, and Hades Rv 6:8

RIDERS (10)
able on your part to set **r** on them. 2 Kgs 18:23
When he sees **r**, horsemen in pairs, riders Is 21:7
riders, horsemen in pairs, **r** on donkeys, Is 21:7
in pairs, riders on donkeys, **r** on camels, Is 21:7
And behold, here come **r**, horsemen in Is 21:9
you are able on your part to set **r** on them. Is 36:8
and overthrow the chariots and their **r**. Hg 2:22
the horses and their **r** shall go down, Hg 2:22
they shall put to shame the **r** on horses. Zec 10:5
men, the flesh of horses and their **r**, Rv 19:18

RIDES (6)
with the discharge **r** shall be unclean. Lv 15:9
who **r** through the heavens to your Dt 33:26
a song to him who **r** through the deserts; Ps 68:4
to him who **r** in the heavens, the Ps 68:33
chariot; he **r** on the wings of the wind; Ps 104:3
nor shall he who **r** the horse save his Am 2:15

RIDGES (1)
its furrows abundantly, settling its **r**, Ps 65:10

RIDICULED (1)
heard all these things, and they **r** him. Lk 16:14

RIDING (12)
Now he was **r** on the donkey, Nm 22:22
Absalom was **r** on his mule, and the 2 Sm 18:9
by mounted couriers **r** on swift horses Est 8:10
the LORD is **r** on a swift cloud and comes Is 19:1
of David, **r** in chariots and on horses, Jer 17:25
of David, **r** in chariots and on horses, Jer 22:4
young men, horsemen **r** on horses. Ezk 23:6
in full armor, horsemen **r** on horses, Ezk 23:12
of renown, all of them **r** on horses. Ezk 23:23
traded with you in saddlecloths for **r**. Ezk 27:20
with you, all of them **r** on horses, Ezk 38:15
and behold, a man **r** on a red horse! Zec 1:8

RIGHT (404)
take the left hand, then I will go to the **r**, Gn 13:9
go to the right, or if you take the **r** hand, Gn 13:9
had led me by the **r** way to take the Gn 24:48
I may turn to the **r** hand or to the left." Gn 24:49
Ephraim in his **r** hand toward Israel's Gn 48:13
in his left hand toward Israel's **r** hand, Gn 48:13
Israel stretched out his **r** hand and laid Gn 48:14
his father laid his **r** hand on the head Gn 48:17
put your **r** hand on his head." Gn 48:18
Moses said, "It would not be **r** to do so, Ex 8:26
the LORD is in the **r**, and I and my people Ex 9:27
to them on their **r** hand and on their Ex 14:22
to them on their **r** hand and on their Ex 14:29
Your **r** hand, O LORD, glorious in power, Ex 15:6
O LORD, glorious in power, your **r** hand, Ex 15:6
You stretched out your **r** hand; the Ex 15:12
God, and do that which is **r** in his eyes, Ex 15:26
He shall have no **r** to sell her to a foreign Ex 21:8
the cause of those who are in the **r**. Ex 23:8
it on the tip of the **r** ear of Aaron and on Ex 29:20
and on the tips of the **r** ears of his sons, Ex 29:20
the thumbs of their **r** hands and on the Ex 29:20
and on the great toes of their **r** feet, Ex 29:20
and the **r** thigh (for it is a ram of Ex 29:22
And the **r** thigh you shall give to the Lv 7:32
fat shall have the **r** thigh for a portion. Lv 7:33
on the lobe of Aaron's **r** ear and on the Lv 8:23
on the thumb of his **r** hand and on the Lv 8:23
hand and on the big toe of his **r** foot. Lv 8:23
on the lobes of their **r** ears and on the Lv 8:24
the thumbs of their **r** hands and on the Lv 8:24
hands and on the big toes of their **r** feet. Lv 8:24
kidneys with their fat and the **r** thigh, Lv 8:25
on the pieces of fat and on the **r** thigh. Lv 8:26
the breasts and the **r** thigh Aaron waved Lv 9:21
it on the lobe of the **r** ear of him who is Lv 14:14
on the thumb of his **r** hand and on the Lv 14:14
hand and on the big toe of his **r** foot. Lv 14:14
and dip his **r** finger in the oil that is in Lv 14:16
on the lobe of the **r** ear of him who is Lv 14:17
on the thumb of his **r** hand and on the Lv 14:17
hand and on the big toe of his **r** foot, Lv 14:17
it on the lobe of the **r** ear of him who is Lv 14:25
on the thumb of his **r** hand and on the Lv 14:25
hand and on the big toe of his **r** foot. Lv 14:25
shall sprinkle with his **r** finger some of Lv 14:27
on the lobe of the **r** ear of him who is Lv 14:28
on the thumb of his **r** hand and on the Lv 14:28
hand and on the big toe of his **r** foot, Lv 14:28
shall not reap your field **r** up to its edge, Lv 19:9
shall not reap your field **r** up to its edge, Lv 23:22
year he shall have the **r** of redemption. Lv 25:29
Levites exercises his **r** of redemption, Lv 25:33
is waved and as the **r** thigh are yours. Nm 18:18
not turn aside to the **r** hand or to the Nm 20:17
way to turn either to the **r** or to the left. Nm 22:26
"The daughters of Zelophehad are **r**. Nm 27:7
"The tribe of the people of Joseph is **r**. Nm 36:5
turn aside neither to the **r** nor to the left. Dt 2:27
They are **r** in all that they have spoken. Dt 5:28
not turn aside to the **r** hand or to the left. Dt 5:32
you shall do what is **r** and good in the Dt 6:18
everyone doing whatever is **r** in his own Dt 12:8
when you do what is **r** in the sight of the Dt 12:25
do what is good and **r** in the sight of the Dt 12:28
and doing what is **r** in the sight of the Dt 13:18
another, one kind of legal **r** and another, Dt 17:8
to you, either to the **r** hand or to the left. Dt 17:11
either to the **r** hand or to the left, Dt 17:20
'They are **r** in what they have spoken. Dt 18:17
when you do what is **r** in the sight of the Dt 21:9
strength. The **r** of the firstborn is his. Dt 21:17
you today, to the **r** hand or to the left, Dt 28:14
ones, with flaming fire at his **r** hand. Dt 33:2
mountain; there they offer **r** sacrifices; Dt 33:19
turn from it to the **r** hand or to the left, Jos 1:7
seems good and **r** in your sight Jos 9:25
from it neither to the **r** hand nor to the Jos 23:6
bound it on his **r** thigh under his Jgs 3:16
hand, took the sword from his **r** thigh, Jgs 3:21
tent peg and her **r** hand to the Jgs 5:26
and in their **r** hands the trumpets to Jgs 7:20
for he could not pronounce it **r**. Jgs 12:6
"Get her for me, for she is **r** in my eyes." Jgs 14:3
woman, and she was **r** in Samson's eyes. Jgs 14:7
his **r** hand on the one and his left hand Jgs 16:29
Everyone did what was **r** in his own eyes. Jgs 17:6
Everyone did what was **r** in his own Jgs 21:25
Take my **r** of redemption yourself, for I Ru 4:6
turned neither to the **r** nor to the left, 1 Sm 6:12
you, that I gouge out all your **r** eyes, 1 Sm 11:2
you in the good and the **r** way. 1 Sm 12:23
to me it seems **r** that you should 1 Sm 29:6
turned neither to the **r** hand nor to the 2 Sm 2:19
"Turn aside to your **r** hand or to your 2 Sm 2:21
cannot turn to the **r** hand or to the 2 Sm 14:19
him, "See, your claims are good and **r**, 2 Sm 15:3
men were on his **r** hand and on his 2 Sm 16:6
And the advice seemed **r** in the eyes of 2 Sm 17:4
at your table. What further **r** have I, 2 Sm 19:28
the beard with his **r** hand to kiss him. 2 Sm 20:9
king's mother, and she sat on his **r**. 1 Kgs 2:19
understanding to discern what is **r**, 1 Kgs 3:11
doing what is **r** in my sight and 1 Kgs 11:33
and do what is **r** in my eyes by 1 Kgs 11:38
only that which was **r** in my eyes, 1 Kgs 14:8
David did what was **r** in the eyes of 1 Kgs 15:5
Asa did what was **r** in the eyes of 1 Kgs 15:11
beside him on his **r** hand and on his 1 Kgs 22:19
doing what was **r** in the sight of the 1 Kgs 22:43
to one another, "We are not doing **r**. 2 Kgs 7:9
in carrying out what is **r** in my eyes, 2 Kgs 10:30
Jehoash did what was **r** in the eyes of 2 Kgs 12:2
the altar on the **r** side as one entered 2 Kgs 12:9
And he did what was **r** in the eyes of 2 Kgs 14:3
And he did what was **r** in the eyes of 2 Kgs 15:3
And he did what was **r** in the eyes of 2 Kgs 15:34
did not do what was **r** in the eyes of 2 Kgs 16:2
LORD their God things that were not **r**. 2 Kgs 17:9
And he did what was **r** in the eyes of 2 Kgs 18:3
And he did what was **r** in the eyes of 2 Kgs 22:2
not turn aside to the **r** or to the left. 2 Kgs 22:2
Asaph, who stood on his **r** hand, 1 Chr 6:39
stones with either the **r** or the left 1 Chr 12:2
for the thing was **r** in the eyes of all 1 Chr 13:4
did what was good and **r** in the eyes of 2 Chr 14:2
standing on his **r** hand and on 2 Chr 18:18
doing what was **r** in the sight of the 2 Chr 20:32
Joash did what was **r** in the eyes of 2 Chr 24:2
And he did what was **r** in the eyes of 2 Chr 25:2
And he did what was **r** in the eyes of 2 Chr 26:4
And he did what was **r** in the eyes of 2 Chr 27:2
did not do what was **r** in the eyes of 2 Chr 28:1
And he did what was **r** in the eyes of 2 Chr 29:2
and the plan seemed **r** to the king and 2 Chr 30:4
was good and **r** and faithful before 2 Chr 31:20
And he did what was **r** in the eyes of 2 Chr 34:2
not turn aside to the **r** hand or to the 2 Chr 34:2
have no portion or **r** or claim in Neh 2:20
each kept his weapon at his **r** hand. Neh 4:23
Hilkiah, and Maaseiah on his **r** hand, Neh 8:4
heaven and gave them **r** rules and true Neh 9:13
and if the thing seems **r** before the king, Est 8:5
'Can mortal man be in the **r** before God? Jb 4:17
Or does the Almighty pervert the **r**? Jb 8:3
how can a man be in the **r** before God? Jb 9:2
Though I am in the **r**, I cannot answer Jb 9:15
Though I am in the **r**, my own mouth Jb 9:20
If I am in the **r**, I cannot lift up my head, Jb 10:15
and a man full of talk be judged **r**? Jb 11:2
my case; I know that I shall be in the **r**. Jb 13:18
to the Almighty if you are in the **r**, Jb 22:3
he turns to the **r** hand, but I do not see Jb 23:9
then can man be in the **r** before God? Jb 25:4
"As God lives, who has taken away my **r**, Jb 27:2
Far be it from me to say that you are **r**; Jb 27:5
On my **r** hand the rabble rise; they push Jb 30:12
nor the aged who understand what is **r**. Jb 32:9
"Behold, in this you are not **r**. I will Jb 33:12
to declare to man what is **r** for him, Jb 33:23
'I sinned and perverted what was **r**, and Jb 33:27
Let us choose what is **r**; let us know Jb 34:4
For Job has said, 'I am in the **r**, and God Jb 34:5
the right, and God has taken away my **r**; Jb 34:5
in spite of my **r** I am counted a liar; my Jb 34:6
just? Do you say, 'It is my **r** before God,' Jb 35:2
alive, but gives the afflicted their **r**. Jb 36:6
condemn me that you may be in the **r**? Jb 40:8
you that your own **r** hand can save you. Jb 40:14
for you have not spoken of me what is **r**, Jb 42:7
For you have not spoken of me what is **r**, Jb 42:8
Offer **r** sacrifices, and put your trust in the Ps 4:5
and does what is **r** and speaks truth in Ps 15:2
because he is at my **r** hand, I shall not be Ps 16:8
at your **r** hand are pleasures Ps 16:11
come! Let your eyes behold the **r**! Ps 17:2
from their adversaries at your **r** hand. Ps 17:7
and your **r** hand supported me, Ps 18:35
the precepts of the LORD are **r**, rejoicing Ps 19:8
with the saving might of his **r** hand. Ps 20:6
your **r** hand will find out those who hate Ps 21:8
He leads the humble in what is **r**, and Ps 25:9
and whose **r** hands are full of bribes. Ps 26:10
them, but your **r** hand and your arm, Ps 44:3
let your **r** hand teach you awesome Ps 45:4
at your **r** hand stands the queen in gold Ps 45:9
Your **r** hand is filled with Ps 48:10
"What **r** have you to recite my statutes Ps 50:16
O God, and renew a **r** spirit within me. Ps 51:10
then will you delight in **r** sacrifices, in Ps 51:19
and lying more than speaking what is **r**. Ps 52:3
Do you indeed decree what is **r**, you gods? Ps 58:1
salvation by your **r** hand and answer Ps 60:5
clings to you; your **r** hand upholds me. Ps 63:8
with you; you hold my **r** hand. Ps 73:23
you hold back your hand, your **r** hand? Ps 74:11
to the years of the **r** hand of the Most Ps 77:10
mountain which his **r** hand had won. Ps 78:54
the stock that your **r** hand planted, and Ps 80:15
hand be on the man of your **r** hand, Ps 80:17
maintain the **r** of the afflicted and the Ps 82:3
strong is your hand, high your **r** hand. Ps 89:13
on the sea and his **r** hand on the rivers. Ps 89:25
You have exalted the **r** hand of his foes; Ps 89:42
your side, ten thousand at your **r** hand, Ps 91:7
His **r** hand and his holy arm have Ps 98:1
salvation by your **r** hand and answer Ps 108:6
him; let an accuser stand at his **r** hand. Ps 109:6
he stands at the **r** hand of the needy, Ps 109:31
"Sit at my **r** hand, until I make your Ps 110:1
The Lord is at your **r** hand; he will Ps 110:5
"The **r** hand of the LORD does valiantly, Ps 118:15
the **r** hand of the LORD exalts, the right Ps 118:16
the **r** hand of the LORD does valiantly!" Ps 118:16
I have done what is just and **r**; do not Ps 119:121
I consider all your precepts to be **r**; Ps 119:128
are you, O LORD, and **r** are your rules. Ps 119:137
for all your commandments are **r**. Ps 119:172
the LORD is your shade on your **r** hand. Ps 121:5

Jerusalem, let my **r** hand forget its skill! Ps 137:5
enemies, and your **r** hand delivers me. Ps 138:7
me, and your **r** hand shall hold me. Ps 139:10
Look to the **r** and see: there is none who Ps 142:4
speak lies and whose **r** hand is a right Ps 144:8
right hand is a **r** hand of falsehood. Ps 144:8
speak lies and whose **r** hand is a right Ps 144:11
right hand is a **r** hand of falsehood. Ps 144:11
Long life is in her **r** hand; in her left Prv 3:16
Do not swerve to the **r** or to the left; turn Prv 4:27
and from my lips will come what is **r**, Prv 8:6
and **r** to those who find knowledge. Prv 8:9
The way of a fool is **r** in his own eyes, Prv 12:15
There is a way that seems **r** to a man, Prv 14:12
he loves him who speaks what is **r**. Prv 16:13
There is a way that seems **r** to a man, Prv 16:25
one who states his case first seems **r**, Prv 18:17
Every way of a man is **r** in his own eyes, Prv 21:2
to make you know what is **r** and true, Prv 22:21
exult when your lips speak what is **r**. Prv 23:16
"You are in the **r**," will be cursed by Prv 24:24
wind or to grasp oil in one's **r** hand. Prv 27:16
wise man's heart inclines him to the **r**, Eccl 10:2
my head, and his **r** hand embraces me! Sg 2:6
my head, and his **r** hand embraces me! Sg 8:3
a bribe, and deprive the innocent of his **r**! Is 5:23
They slice meat on the **r**, but are still Is 9:20
and to rob the poor of my people of their **r**, Is 10:2
insolence; in his idle boasting he is not **r**. Is 16:6
plea turn aside him who is in the **r**. Is 29:21
"Do not prophesy to us what is **r**; Is 30:10
when you turn to the **r** or when you turn Is 30:21
even when the plea of the needy is **r**. Is 32:7
and my **r** is disregarded by my God"? Is 40:27
uphold you with my righteous **r** hand. Is 41:10
I, the LORD your God, hold your **r** hand; Is 41:13
beforehand, that we might say, "He is **r**"? Is 41:26
bring their witnesses to prove them **r**, Is 43:9
your case, that you may be proved **r**. Is 43:26
or say, "Is there not a lie in my **r** hand?" Is 44:20
to Cyrus, whose **r** hand I have grasped, Is 45:1
LORD speak the truth; I declare what is **r**. Is 45:19
the God of Israel, but not in truth or **r**. Is 48:1
and my **r** hand spread out the heavens; Is 48:13
yet surely my **r** is with the LORD, and my Is 49:4
will spread abroad to the **r** and to the left, Is 54:3
LORD has sworn by his **r** hand and by his Is 62:8
arm to go at the **r** hand of Moses, Is 63:12
What **r** has my beloved in my house, Jer 11:15
were the signet ring on my **r** hand, Jer 22:24
course is evil, and their might is not **r**. Jer 23:10
Do with me as seems good and **r** to you. Jer 26:14
I give it to whomever it seems **r** to me. Jer 27:5
for the **r** of redemption by purchase is Jer 32:7
for the **r** of possession and redemption is Jer 32:8
and did what was **r** in my eyes by Jer 34:15
wherever you think it good and **r** to go. Jer 40:4
go wherever you think it **r** to go." So the Jer 40:5
"The LORD is in the **r**, for I have Lam 1:18
withdrawn from them his **r** hand in the Lam 2:3
an enemy, with his **r** hand set like a foe; Lam 2:4
four had the face of a lion on the **r** side, Ezk 1:10
down a second time, but on your **r** side, Ezk 4:6
they, they are more in the **r** than you. Ezk 16:52
righteous and does what is just and **r**— Ezk 18:5
the son has done what is just and **r**, Ezk 18:19
statutes and does what is just and **r**, Ezk 18:21
and does what is just and **r**, Ezk 18:27
Cut sharply to the **r**; set yourself to the Ezk 21:16
Into his **r** hand comes the divination Ezk 21:22
his sin and does what is just and **r**, Ezk 33:14
He has done what is just and **r**; he Ezk 33:16
and does what is just and **r**, Ezk 33:19
your arrows drop out of your **r** hand. Ezk 39:3
for all his works are **r** and his ways are Dn 4:37
he raised his **r** hand and his left hand Dn 12:7
for at the **r** time he does not present Hos 13:13
for the ways of the LORD are **r**, and the Hos 14:9
know how to do **r**," declares the LORD, Am 3:10
do not know their **r** hand from their left, Jon 4:11
cup in the LORD'S **r** hand will come Hab 2:16
Satan standing at his **r** hand to accuse Zec 3:1
will give you the **r** of access among those Zec 3:7
one on the **r** of the bowl and the other on Zec 4:3
two olive trees on the **r** and the left of the Zec 4:11
the sword strike his arm and his **r** eye! Zec 11:17
withered, his **r** eye utterly blinded!" Zec 11:17
they shall devour to the **r** and to the left Zec 12:6
If your **r** eye causes you to sin, tear it out Mt 5:29
And if your **r** hand causes you to sin, Mt 5:30
But if anyone slaps you on the **r** cheek, Mt 5:39
hand know what your **r** hand is doing, Mt 6:3
"It is not **r** to take the children's bread Mt 15:26
too, and whatever is **r** I will give you.' Mt 20:4
one at your **r** hand and one at your left, Mt 20:21
but to sit at my **r** hand and at my left is Mt 20:23
Lord said to my Lord, Sit at my **r** hand, Mt 22:44
And he will place the sheep on his **r**, Mt 25:33
the King will say to those on his **r**, Mt 25:34
Man seated at the **r** hand of Power and Mt 26:64
his head and put a reed in his **r** hand. Mt 27:29
him, one on the **r** and one on the left. Mt 27:38
sitting there, clothed and in his **r** mind, Mk 5:15
for it is not **r** to take the children's Mk 7:27
one at your **r** hand and one at your Mk 10:37
but to sit at my **r** hand or at my left is Mk 10:40
And the scribe said to him, "You are **r**, Mk 12:32
Lord said to my Lord, Sit at my **r** hand, Mk 12:36
r into the courtyard of the high priest. Mk 14:54
of Man seated at the **r** hand of Power, Mk 14:62
one on his **r** and one on his left. Mk 15:27
saw a young man sitting on the **r** side, Mk 16:5
and sat down at the **r** hand of God. Mk 16:19
Lord standing on the **r** side of the altar Lk 1:11
was there whose **r** hand was withered. Lk 6:6
feet of Jesus, clothed and in his **r** mind, Lk 8:35
you not judge for yourselves what is **r**? Lk 12:57
Lord said to my Lord, Sit at my **r** hand, Lk 20:42
of the high priest and cut off his **r** ear. Lk 22:50
be seated at the **r** hand of the power Lk 22:69
one on his **r** and one on his left. Lk 23:33
he gave the **r** to become children of God, Jn 1:12
Jesus said to her, "You are **r** in saying, Jn 4:17
but judge with **r** judgment." Jn 7:24
"Are we not **r** in saying that you are a Jn 8:48
me Teacher and Lord, and you are **r**, Jn 13:13
priest's servant and cut off his **r** ear. Jn 18:10
but if what I said is **r**, why do you strike Jn 18:23
"Cast the net on the **r** side of the boat, Jn 21:6
for he is at my **r** hand that I may not Acts 2:25
therefore exalted at the **r** hand of God, Acts 2:33
Lord said to my Lord, Sit at my **r** hand, Acts 2:34
took him by the **r** hand and raised him Acts 3:7
"Whether it is **r** in the sight of God to Acts 4:19
exalted him at his **r** hand as Leader Acts 5:31
"It is not **r** that we should give up Acts 6:2
Jesus standing at the **r** hand of God. Acts 7:55
of Man standing at the **r** hand of God." Acts 7:56
for your heart is not **r** before God. Acts 8:21
and does what is **r** is acceptable to Acts 10:35
"The Holy Spirit was **r** in saying to Acts 28:25
at the **r** time Christ died for the Rom 5:6
For I have the desire to do what is **r**, Rom 7:18
it to be a law that when I want to do **r**, Rom 7:21
raised—who is at the **r** hand of God, Rom 8:34
Has the potter no **r** over the clay, to Rom 9:21
take care that this **r** of yours does not 1 Cor 8:9
Do we not have the **r** to eat and drink? 1 Cor 9:4
Do we not have the **r** to take along a 1 Cor 9:5
I who have no **r** to refrain from 1 Cor 9:6
we have not made use of this **r**, 1 Cor 9:12
to make full use of my **r** in the gospel. 1 Cor 9:18
from your drunken stupor, as is **r**, 1 Cor 15:34
if we are in our **r** mind, it is for you. 2 Cor 5:13
of righteousness for the **r** hand and for 2 Cor 6:7
test, but that you may do what is **r**, 2 Cor 13:7
they gave the **r** hand of fellowship to Gal 2:9
seated him at his **r** hand in the Eph 1:20
found in all that is good and **r** and true), Eph 5:9
your parents in the Lord, for this is **r**. Eph 6:1
It is **r** for me to feel this way about you Phil 1:7
Christ is, seated at the **r** hand of God. Col 3:1
to God for you, brothers, as is **r**, 2 Thes 1:3
not because we do not have that **r**, 2 Thes 3:9
he sat down at the **r** hand of the Majesty Heb 1:3
"Sit at my **r** hand until I make your Heb 1:13
who is seated at the **r** hand of the throne Heb 8:1
sins, he sat down at the **r** hand of God, Heb 10:12
and is seated at the **r** hand of the throne Heb 12:2
who serve the tent have no **r** to eat. Heb 13:10
So whoever knows the **r** thing to do and Jas 4:17
into heaven and is at the **r** hand of God, 1 Pt 3:22
I think it **r**, as long as I am in this body, 2 Pt 1:13
Forsaking the **r** way, they have gone 2 Pt 2:15
In his **r** hand he held seven stars, from Rv 1:16
But he laid his **r** hand on me, saying, Rv 1:17
seven stars that you saw in my **r** hand, Rv 1:20
who holds the seven stars in his **r** hand, Rv 2:1
Then I saw in the **r** hand of him who was Rv 5:1
the scroll from the **r** hand of him who Rv 5:7
his hand. And he set his **r** foot on the sea, Rv 10:2
on the land raised his **r** hand to heaven Rv 10:5
be marked on the **r** hand or the Rv 13:16
be filthy, and the righteous still do **r**, Rv 22:11
that they may have the **r** to the tree of Rv 22:14

RIGHTEOUS (283)

Noah was a **r** man, blameless in his Gn 6:9
have seen that you are **r** before me in this Gn 7:1
sweep away the **r** with the wicked? Gn 18:23
Suppose there are fifty **r** within the city. Gn 18:24
not spare it for the fifty **r** who are in it? Gn 18:24
to put the **r** to death with the wicked, Gn 18:25
wicked, so that the **r** fare as the wicked! Gn 18:25
"If I find at Sodom fifty **r** in the city, Gn 18:26
Suppose five of the fifty **r** are lacking. Gn 18:28
them and said, "She is more **r** than I, Gn 38:26
and do not kill the innocent and **r**, Ex 23:7
has statutes and rules so **r** as all this law Dt 4:8
shall judge the people with **r** judgment. Dt 16:18
the wise and subverts the cause of the **r**. Dt 16:19
there they repeat the **r** triumphs of the Jgs 5:11
the **r** triumphs of his villagers in Israel. Jgs 5:11
LORD concerning all the **r** deeds of the 1 Sm 12:7
to David, "You are more **r** than I, 1 Sm 24:17
men have killed a **r** man in his own 2 Sm 4:11
two men more **r** and better than 1 Kgs 2:32
and vindicating the **r** by rewarding 1 Kgs 8:32
and vindicating the **r** by rewarding 2 Chr 6:23
themselves and said, "The LORD is **r**." 2 Chr 12:6
have kept your promise, for you are **r**. Neh 9:8
Yet you have been **r** in all that has Neh 9:33
is born of a woman, that he can be **r**? Jb 15:14
Yet the **r** holds to his way, and he who Jb 17:9
The **r** see it and are glad; the innocent Jb 22:19
he may pile it up, but the **r** will wear it, Jb 27:17
Job, because he was **r** in his own eyes. Jb 32:1
you condemn him who is **r** and mighty, Jb 34:17
If you are **r**, what do you give to him? Or Jb 35:7
He does not withdraw his eyes from the **r**, Jb 36:7
nor sinners in the congregation of the **r**; Ps 1:5
for the LORD knows the way of the **r**, but Ps 1:6
For you bless the **r**, O LORD; you cover Ps 5:12
may you establish the **r**—you who test Ps 7:9
who test the minds and hearts, O **r** God! Ps 7:9
God is a **r** judge, and a God who feels Ps 7:11
have sat on the throne, giving **r** judgment. Ps 9:4
are destroyed, what can the **r** do?" Ps 11:3
The LORD tests the **r**, but his soul hates Ps 11:5
For the LORD is **r**; he loves righteous Ps 11:7
the LORD is righteous; he loves **r** deeds; Ps 11:7
for God is with the generation of the **r**. Ps 14:5
of the LORD are true, and **r** altogether. Ps 19:9
insolently against the **r** in pride and Ps 31:18
Be glad in the LORD, and rejoice, O **r**, and Ps 32:11
Shout for joy in the LORD, O you **r**! Praise Ps 33:1
LORD are toward the **r** and his ears Ps 34:15
When the **r** cry for help, the LORD hears Ps 34:17
Many are the afflictions of the **r**, but the Ps 34:19
who hate the **r** will be condemned. Ps 34:21
plots against the **r** and gnashes his Ps 37:12
the little that the **r** has than the Ps 37:16
be broken, but the LORD upholds the **r**. Ps 37:17
back, but the **r** is generous and gives; Ps 37:21
have not seen the **r** forsaken or his Ps 37:25
The **r** shall inherit the land and dwell Ps 37:29
The mouth of the **r** utters wisdom, and Ps 37:30
wicked watches for the **r** and seeks to Ps 37:32
The salvation of the **r** is from the LORD; Ps 37:39
The **r** shall see and fear, and shall laugh Ps 52:6
he will never permit the **r** to be moved. Ps 55:22
The **r** will rejoice when he sees the Ps 58:10
say, "Surely there is a reward for the **r**; Ps 58:11
Let the **r** one rejoice in the LORD and Ps 64:10
But the **r** shall be glad; they shall exult Ps 68:3
let them not be enrolled among the **r**. Ps 69:28
My mouth will tell of your **r** acts, of Ps 71:15
will talk of your **r** help all the day Ps 71:24
In his days may the **r** flourish, and peace Ps 72:7
but the horns of the **r** shall be lifted up. Ps 75:10
The **r** flourish like the palm tree and Ps 92:12
for justice will return to the **r**, and all Ps 94:15
the life of the **r** and condemn the Ps 94:21
Light is sown for the **r**, and joy for the Ps 97:11
Rejoice in the LORD, O you **r**, and give Ps 97:12
upright; he is gracious, merciful, and **r**. Ps 112:4
For the **r** will never be moved; he will be Ps 112:6
Gracious is the LORD, and **r**; our God is Ps 116:5
of salvation are in the tents of the **r**: Ps 118:15
the LORD; the **r** shall enter through it. Ps 118:20
upright heart, when I learn your **r** rules. Ps 119:7
to praise you, because of your **r** rules. Ps 119:62
I know, O LORD, that your rules are **r**, Ps 119:75
confirmed it, to keep your **r** rules. Ps 119:106
for the fulfillment of your **r** promise. Ps 119:123
R are you, O LORD, and right are your Ps 119:137
Your righteousness is **r** forever, and Ps 119:142
Your testimonies are **r** forever; give Ps 119:144
one of your **r** rules endures forever. Ps 119:160
a day I praise you for your **r** rules. Ps 119:164
not rest on the land allotted to the **r**, Ps 125:3
lest the **r** stretch out their hands to do Ps 125:3
The LORD is **r**; he has cut the cords of Ps 129:4
Surely the **r** shall give thanks to your Ps 140:13
Let a **r** man strike me—it is a kindness; Ps 141:5
The **r** will surround me, for you will Ps 142:7

for no one living is **r** before you. Ps 143:2
The LORD is **r** in all his ways and kind Ps 145:17
are bowed down; the LORD loves the **r**. Ps 146:8
the good and keep to the paths of the **r**. Prv 2:20
but he blesses the dwelling of the **r**. Prv 3:33
But the path of the **r** is like the light of Prv 4:18
All the words of my mouth are **r**; there is Prv 8:8
teach a **r** man, and he will increase in Prv 9:9
The LORD does not let the **r** go hungry, Prv 10:3
Blessings are on the head of the **r**, but Prv 10:6
The memory of the **r** is a blessing, but Prv 10:7
The mouth of the **r** is a fountain of Prv 10:11
The wage of the **r** leads to life, the gain Prv 10:16
The tongue of the **r** is choice silver; the Prv 10:20
The lips of the **r** feed many, but fools Prv 10:21
but the desire of the **r** will be granted. Prv 10:24
more, but the **r** is established forever. Prv 10:25
The hope of the **r** brings joy, but the Prv 10:28
The **r** will never be removed, but the Prv 10:30
mouth of the **r** brings forth wisdom, Prv 10:31
The lips of the **r** know what is Prv 10:32
The **r** is delivered from trouble, and the Prv 11:8
but by knowledge the **r** are delivered. Prv 11:9
When it goes well with the **r**, the city Prv 11:10
the offspring of the **r** will be delivered. Prv 11:21
The desire of the **r** ends only in good; Prv 11:23
but the **r** will flourish like a green leaf. Prv 11:28
The fruit of the **r** is a tree of life, and Prv 11:30
If the **r** is repaid on earth, how much Prv 11:31
the root of the **r** will never be moved. Prv 12:3
The thoughts of the **r** are just; the Prv 12:5
more, but the house of the **r** will stand. Prv 12:7
Whoever is **r** has regard for the life of Prv 12:10
but the root of the **r** bears fruit. Prv 12:12
lips, but the **r** escapes from trouble. Prv 12:13
No ill befalls the **r**, but the wicked are Prv 12:21
One who is **r** is a guide to his Prv 12:26
The **r** hates falsehood, but the wicked Prv 13:5
The light of the **r** rejoices, but the lamp Prv 13:9
but the **r** are rewarded with good. Prv 13:21
the sinner's wealth is laid up for the **r**. Prv 13:22
The **r** has enough to satisfy his Prv 13:25
good, the wicked at the gates of the **r**. Prv 14:19
but the **r** finds refuge in his death. Prv 14:32
the house of the **r** there is much Prv 15:6
The heart of the **r** ponders how to Prv 15:28
but he hears the prayer of the **r**. Prv 15:29
R lips are the delight of a king, and he Prv 16:13
a crown of glory; it is gained in a **r** life. Prv 16:31
he who condemns the **r** are both alike Prv 17:15
impose a fine on a **r** man is not good, Prv 17:26
the wicked or to deprive the **r** of justice. Prv 18:5
the **r** man runs into it and is safe. Prv 18:10
The **r** who walks in his integrity— Prv 20:7
The **R** One observes the house of the Prv 21:12
is a joy to the **r** but terror to evildoers. Prv 21:15
The wicked is a ransom for the **r**, and Prv 21:18
but the **r** gives and does not hold back. Prv 21:26
The father of the **r** will greatly rejoice; Prv 23:24
man against the dwelling of the **r**; Prv 24:15
for the **r** falls seven times and rises Prv 24:16
polluted fountain is a **r** man who gives Prv 25:26
one pursues, but the **r** are bold as a lion. Prv 28:1
When the **r** triumph, there is great Prv 28:12
but when they perish, the **r** increase. Prv 28:28
When the **r** increase, the people rejoice, Prv 29:2
but a **r** man sings and rejoices. Prv 29:6
A **r** man knows the rights of the poor; a Prv 29:7
but the **r** will look upon their Prv 29:16
man is an abomination to the **r**, Prv 29:27
God will judge the **r** and the wicked, Eccl 3:17
There is a **r** man who perishes in his Eccl 7:15
Be not overly **r**, and do not make Eccl 7:16
there is not a **r** man on earth who Eccl 7:20
that there are **r** people to whom it Eccl 8:14
according to the deeds of the **r**. Eccl 8:14
how the **r** and the wise and their deeds Eccl 9:1
event happens to the **r** and the wicked, Eccl 9:2
Tell the **r** that it shall be well with them, Is 3:10
songs of praise, of glory to the **R** One. Is 24:16
that the **r** nation that keeps faith may Is 26:2
The path of the **r** is level; you make level Is 26:7
is level; you make level the way of the **r**. Is 26:7
I will uphold you with my **r** right hand. Is 41:10
god besides me, a **r** God and a Savior; Is 45:21
by his knowledge shall the **r** one, my Is 53:11
servant, make many to be accounted **r**, Is 53:11
The **r** man perishes, and no one lays it to Is 57:1
For the **r** man is taken away from Is 57:1
of their God; they ask of me **r** judgments; Is 58:2
Your people shall all be **r**; they shall Is 60:21
and all our **r** deeds are like a polluted Is 64:6
shown herself more **r** than treacherous Jer 3:11
R are you, O LORD, when I complain to Jer 12:1
O LORD of hosts, who tests the **r**, who Jer 20:12
I will raise up for David a **r** Branch, Jer 23:5
I will cause a **r** Branch to spring up Jer 33:15
in the midst of her the blood of the **r**. Lam 4:13
if a **r** person turns from his Ezk 3:20
and his **r** deeds that he has done shall Ezk 3:20
But if you warn the **r** person not to sin, Ezk 3:21
you have disheartened the **r** falsely, Ezk 13:22
made your sisters appear **r** by all the Ezk 16:51
you have made your sisters appear **r**. Ezk 16:52
"If a man is **r** and does what is just and Ezk 18:5
my rules by acting faithfully—he is **r**; Ezk 18:9
righteousness of the **r** shall be upon Ezk 18:20
But when a **r** person turns away from Ezk 18:24
None of the **r** deeds that he has done Ezk 18:24
When a **r** person turns away from his Ezk 18:26
cut off from you both **r** and wicked. Ezk 21:3
cut off from you both **r** and wicked, Ezk 21:4
But **r** men shall pass judgment on Ezk 23:45
righteousness of the **r** shall not deliver Ezk 33:12
and the **r** shall not be able to live by Ezk 33:12
I say to the **r** that he shall surely Ezk 33:13
none of his **r** deeds shall be Ezk 33:13
When the **r** turns from his Ezk 33:18
the LORD our God is **r** in all the works Dn 9:14
"O Lord, according to all your **r** acts, let Dn 9:16
because they sell the **r** for silver, Am 2:6
are your sins—you who afflict the **r**, Am 5:12
For the wicked surround the **r**; so Hab 1:4
swallows up the man more **r** than he? Hab 1:13
him, but the **r** shall live by his faith. Hab 2:4
The LORD within her is **r**; he does no Zep 3:5
r and having salvation is he, humble Zec 9:9
distinction between the **r** and the Mal 3:18
For I came not to call the **r**, but sinners." Mt 9:13
one who receives a **r** person because he Mt 10:41
because he is a **r** person will receive a Mt 10:41
person will receive a **r** person's reward. Mt 10:41
many prophets and **r** people longed to Mt 13:17
Then the **r** will shine like the sun in Mt 13:43
out and separate the evil from the **r** Mt 13:49
you also outwardly appear **r** to others, Mt 23:28
and decorate the monuments of the **r**, Mt 23:29
may come all the **r** blood shed on Mt 23:35
Then the **r** will answer him, saying, Mt 25:37
punishment, but the **r** into eternal life." Mt 25:46
"Have nothing to do with that **r** man, Mt 27:19
I came not to call the **r**, but sinners." Mk 2:17
knowing that he was a **r** and holy man, Mk 6:20
And they were both **r** before God, walking Lk 1:6
Simeon, and this man was **r** and devout, Lk 2:25
come to call the **r** but sinners to Lk 5:32
than over ninety-nine **r** persons who Lk 15:7
trusted in themselves that they were **r**, Lk 18:9
of the council, a good and **r** man, Lk 23:50
O **r** Father, even though the world does Jn 17:25
But you denied the Holy and **R** One, Acts 3:14
beforehand the coming of the **R** One, Acts 7:52
to see the **R** One and to hear a voice Acts 22:14
it is written, "The **r** shall live by faith." Rom 1:17
of wrath when God's **r** judgment will be Rom 2:5
of the law who are **r** before God, Rom 2:13
as it is written: "None is **r**, no, not one; Rom 3:10
scarcely die for a **r** person—though Rom 5:7
obedience the many will be made **r**. Rom 5:19
is holy and **r** and good. Rom 7:12
in order that the **r** requirement of the Rom 8:4
the law, for "The **r** shall live by faith." Gal 3:11
how holy and **r** and blameless was 1 Thes 2:10
is evidence of the **r** judgment of God, 2 Thes 1:5
which the Lord, the **r** judge, 2 Tm 4:8
but my **r** one shall live by faith, and if Heb 10:38
which he was commended as **r**, Heb 11:4
and to the spirits of the **r** made perfect, Heb 12:23
you have murdered the **r** person. Jas 5:6
The prayer of a **r** person has great power Jas 5:16
For the eyes of the Lord are on the **r**, 1 Pt 3:12
once for sins, the **r** for the unrighteous, 1 Pt 3:18
And "If the **r** is scarcely saved, what 1 Pt 4:18
and if he rescued **r** Lot, greatly distressed 2 Pt 2:7
(for as that **r** man lived among them 2 Pt 2:8
he was tormenting his **r** soul over their 2 Pt 2:8
with the Father, Jesus Christ the **r**. 1 Jn 2:1
If you know that he is **r**, you may be 1 Jn 2:29
Whoever practices righteousness is **r**, as 1 Jn 3:7
righteousness is righteous, as he is **r**. 1 Jn 3:7
own deeds were evil and his brother's **r**. 1 Jn 3:12
you, for your **r** acts have been revealed." Rv 15:4
the fine linen is the **r** deeds of the saints. Rv 19:8
still be filthy, and the **r** still do right, Rv 22:11

RIGHTEOUSLY (4)
and judge **r** between a man and his Dt 1:16
Open your mouth, judge **r**, defend the Prv 31:9
He who walks **r** and speaks uprightly, Is 33:15
But, O LORD of hosts, who judges **r**, who Jer 11:20

RIGHTEOUSNESS (272)
the LORD, and he counted it to him as **r**. Gn 15:6
way of the LORD by doing **r** and justice, Gn 18:19
but in **r** shall you judge your neighbor. Lv 19:15
And it will be **r** for us, if we are careful to Dt 6:25
'It is because of my **r** that the LORD has Dt 9:4
Not because of your **r** or the uprightness Dt 9:5
good land to possess because of your **r**, Dt 9:6
And it shall be **r** for you before the LORD Dt 24:13
man for his **r** and his faithfulness, 1 Sm 26:23
dealt with me according to my **r**; 2 Sm 22:21
has rewarded me according to my **r**, 2 Sm 22:25
walked before you in faithfulness, in **r**, 1 Kgs 3:6
by rewarding him according to his **r**. 1 Kgs 8:32
that you may execute justice and **r**." 1 Kgs 10:9
by rewarding him according to his **r**. 2 Chr 6:23
that you may execute justice and **r**." 2 Chr 9:8
I hold fast my **r** and will not let it go; my Jb 27:6
I put on **r**, and it clothed me; my justice Jb 29:14
of joy, and he restores to man his **r**. Jb 33:26
like yourself, and your **r** a son of man. Jb 35:8
from afar and ascribe **r** to my Maker. Jb 36:3
justice and abundant **r** he will not Jb 37:23
Answer me when I call, O God of my **r**! Ps 4:1
O LORD, in your **r** because of my enemies; Ps 5:8
according to my **r** and according to the Ps 7:8
give to the LORD the thanks due to his **r**, Ps 7:17
and he judges the world with **r**; he judges Ps 9:8
As for me, I shall behold your face in **r**; Ps 17:15
LORD dealt with me according to my **r**; Ps 18:20
has rewarded me according to my **r**, Ps 18:24
come and proclaim his **r** to a people yet Ps 22:31
me in paths of **r** for his name's sake. Ps 23:3
from the LORD and **r** from the God of Ps 24:5
be put to shame; in your **r** deliver me! Ps 31:1
He loves **r** and justice; the earth is full of Ps 33:5
O LORD, my God, according to your **r**, Ps 35:24
who delight in my **r** shout for joy and Ps 35:27
shall tell of your **r** and of your praise Ps 35:28
Your **r** is like the mountains of God; Ps 36:6
you, and your **r** to the upright of heart! Ps 36:10
He will bring forth your **r** as the light, Ps 37:6
the cause of truth and meekness and **r**; Ps 45:4
you have loved **r** and hated wickedness. Ps 45:7
earth. Your right hand is filled with **r**. Ps 48:10
The heavens declare his **r**, for God Ps 50:6
my tongue will sing aloud of your **r**. Ps 51:14
By awesome deeds you answer us with **r**, Ps 65:5
In your **r** deliver me and rescue me; Ps 71:2
I will remind them of your **r**, yours Ps 71:16
Your **r**, O God, reaches the high Ps 71:19
O God, and your **r** to the royal son! Ps 72:1
May he judge your people with **r**, and Ps 72:2
for the people, and the hills, in **r**! Ps 72:3
meet; **r** and peace kiss each other. Ps 85:10
ground, and **r** looks down from the sky. Ps 85:11
R will go before him and make his Ps 85:13
or your **r** in the land of forgetfulness? Ps 88:12
R and justice are the foundation of your Ps 89:14
all the day and in your **r** are exalted. Ps 89:16
He will judge the world in **r**, and the Ps 96:13
r and justice are the foundation of his Ps 97:2
The heavens proclaim his **r**, and all the Ps 97:6
he has revealed his **r** in the sight of the Ps 98:2
He will judge the world with **r**, and the Ps 98:9
you have executed justice and **r** in Jacob. Ps 99:4
The LORD works **r** and justice for all Ps 103:6
him, and his **r** to children's children, Ps 103:17
observe justice, who do **r** at all times! Ps 106:3
to him as **r** from generation to Ps 106:31
is his work, and his **r** endures forever. Ps 111:3
in his house, and his **r** endures forever. Ps 112:3
given to the poor; his **r** endures forever; Ps 112:9
Open to me the gates of **r**, that I may Ps 118:19
your precepts; in your **r** give me life! Ps 119:40
your testimonies in **r** and in all Ps 119:138
Your **r** is righteous forever, and your Ps 119:142
Let your priests be clothed with **r**, and Ps 132:9
your faithfulness answer me, in your **r**! Ps 143:1
In your **r** bring my soul out of Ps 143:11
goodness and shall sing aloud of your **r**. Ps 145:7
receive instruction in wise dealing, in **r**, Prv 1:3
you will understand **r** and justice and Prv 2:9
are with me, enduring wealth and **r**. Prv 8:18
I walk in the way of **r**, in the paths of Prv 8:20
do not profit, but **r** delivers from death. Prv 10:2
day of wrath, but **r** delivers from death. Prv 11:4
The **r** of the blameless keeps his way Prv 11:5
The **r** of the upright delivers them, but Prv 11:6
but one who sows **r** gets a sure reward. Prv 11:18
Whoever is steadfast in **r** will live, but Prv 11:19
In the path of **r** is life, and in its Prv 12:28
R guards him whose way is blameless, Prv 13:6
R exalts a nation, but sin is a reproach Prv 14:34
LORD, but he loves him who pursues **r**. Prv 15:9

is a little with **r** than great revenues Prv 16:8
evil, for the throne is established by **r**. Prv 16:12
To do **r** and justice is more acceptable Prv 21:3
Whoever pursues **r** and kindness will Prv 21:21
kindness will find life, **r**, and honor. Prv 21:21
and his throne will be established in **r**. Prv 25:5
was wickedness, and in the place of **r**, Eccl 3:16
poor and the violation of justice and **r**, Eccl 5:8
a righteous man who perishes in his **r**, Eccl 7:15
R lodged in her, but now murderers. Is 1:21
Afterward you shall be called the city of **r**, Is 1:26
justice, and those in her who repent, by **r**. Is 1:27
for justice, but behold, bloodshed; for **r**, Is 5:7
the Holy God shows himself holy in **r**. Is 5:16
with justice and with **r** from this time Is 9:7
is decreed, overflowing with **r**. Is 10:22
but with **r** he shall judge the poor, and Is 11:4
R shall be the belt of his waist, and Is 11:5
and seeks justice and is swift to do **r**." Is 16:5
the inhabitants of the world learn **r**. Is 26:9
shown to the wicked, he does not learn **r**; Is 26:10
justice the line, and **r** the plumb line; Is 28:17
Behold, a king will reign in **r**, and princes Is 32:1
and **r** abide in the fruitful field. Is 32:16
And the effect of **r** will be peace, and the Is 32:17
will be peace, and the result of **r**, Is 32:17
high; he will fill Zion with justice and **r**, Is 33:5
"I am the LORD; I have called you in **r**; I Is 42:6
above, and let the clouds rain down **r**; Is 45:8
open, that salvation and **r** may bear fruit; Is 45:8
I have stirred him up in **r**, and I will Is 45:13
has gone out in **r** a word that shall Is 45:23
it shall be said of me, are **r** and strength; Is 45:24
of heart, you who are far from **r**: Is 46:12
I bring near my **r**; it is not far off, and Is 46:13
and your **r** like the waves of the sea; Is 48:18
"Listen to me, you who pursue **r**, you who Is 51:1
My **r** draws near, my salvation has gone Is 51:5
forever, and my **r** will never be dismayed. Is 51:6
"Listen to me, you who know **r**, the people Is 51:7
but my **r** will be forever, and my Is 51:8
In **r** you shall be established; you shall Is 54:14
"Keep justice, and do **r**, for soon my Is 56:1
I will declare your **r** and your deeds, but Is 57:12
a nation that did **r** and did not forsake Is 58:2
up speedily; your **r** shall go before you; Is 58:8
is far from us, and **r** does not overtake us; Is 59:9
is turned back, and **r** stands afar off; Is 59:14
him salvation, and his **r** upheld him. Is 59:16
He put on **r** as a breastplate, and a Is 59:17
overseers peace and your taskmasters **r**. Is 60:17
that they may be called oaks of **r**, the Is 61:3
he has covered me with the robe of **r**, as Is 61:10
Lord GOD will cause **r** and praise to Is 61:11
quiet, until her **r** goes forth as brightness, Is 62:1
The nations shall see your **r**, and all the Is 62:2
"It is I, speaking in **r**, mighty to save." Is 63:1
You meet him who joyfully works **r**, Is 64:5
LORD lives,' in truth, in justice, and in **r**, Jer 4:2
steadfast love, justice, and **r** in the earth. Jer 9:24
Do justice and **r**, and deliver from the Jer 22:3
eat and drink and do justice and **r**? Jer 22:15
shall execute justice and **r** in the land. Jer 23:5
he will be called: 'The LORD is our **r**.' Jer 23:6
"'The LORD bless you, O habitation of **r**, Jer 31:23
shall execute justice and **r** in the land. Jer 33:15
it will be called: 'The LORD is our **r**.' Jer 33:16
against the LORD, their habitation of **r**, Jer 50:7
turns from his **r** and commits Ezk 3:20
deliver but their own lives by their **r**, Ezk 14:14
deliver but their own lives by their **r**. Ezk 14:20
The **r** of the righteous shall be upon Ezk 18:20
for the **r** that he has done he shall live. Ezk 18:22
away from his **r** and does injustice Ezk 18:24
away from his **r** and does injustice, Ezk 18:26
The **r** of the righteous shall not deliver Ezk 33:12
be able to live by his **r** when he sins. Ezk 33:12
if he trusts in his **r** and does injustice, Ezk 33:13
turns from his **r** and does injustice, Ezk 33:18
oppression, and execute justice and **r**. Ezk 45:9
break off your sins by practicing **r**, and Dn 4:27
To you, O Lord, belongs **r**, but to us open Dn 9:7
our pleas before you because of our **r**, Dn 9:18
for iniquity, to bring in everlasting **r**, Dn 9:24
and those who turn many to **r**, like the Dn 12:3
betroth you to me in **r** and in justice, Hos 2:19
Sow for yourselves **r**; reap steadfast Hos 10:12
he may come and rain **r** upon you. Hos 10:12
wormwood and cast down **r** to the earth! Am 5:7
and **r** like an ever-flowing stream. Am 5:24
and the fruit of **r** into wormwood— Am 6:12
land, who do his just commands; seek **r**; Zep 2:3
be their God, in faithfulness and in **r**." Zec 8:8
they will bring offerings in **r** to the LORD. Mal 3:3
the sun of **r** shall rise with healing in its Mal 4:2
for us to fulfill all **r**." Then he consented. Mt 3:15
are those who hunger and thirst for **r**, Mt 5:6
unless your **r** exceeds that of the scribes Mt 5:20
of practicing your **r** before other people Mt 6:1
seek first the kingdom of God and his **r**, Mt 6:33
For John came to you in the way of **r**, Mt 21:32
in holiness and **r** before him all our Lk 1:75
concerning sin and **r** and judgment: Jn 16:8
concerning **r**, because I go to the Jn 16:10
son of the devil, you enemy of all **r**, Acts 13:10
judge the world in **r** by a man whom Acts 17:31
he reasoned about **r** and self-control Acts 24:25
For in it the **r** of God is revealed from Rom 1:17
serves to show the **r** of God, Rom 3:5
But now the **r** of God has been Rom 3:21
the **r** of God through faith in Jesus Rom 3:22
This was to show God's **r**, because in Rom 3:25
It was to show his **r** at the present time, Rom 3:26
God, and it was counted to him as **r**." Rom 4:3
the ungodly, his faith is counted as **r**, Rom 4:5
whom God counts **r** apart from works: Rom 4:6
faith was counted to Abraham as **r**. Rom 4:9
as a seal of the **r** that he had by faith Rom 4:11
so that **r** would be counted to them as Rom 4:11
the law but through the **r** of faith. Rom 4:13
his faith was "counted to him as **r**." Rom 4:22
the free gift of **r** reign in life through Rom 5:17
so one act of **r** leads to justification Rom 5:18
might reign through **r** leading to Rom 5:21
members to God as instruments for **r**. Rom 6:13
or of obedience, which leads to **r**? Rom 6:16
free from sin, have become slaves of **r**. Rom 6:18
as slaves to **r** leading to sanctification. Rom 6:19
of sin, you were free in regard to **r**. Rom 6:20
of sin, the Spirit is life because of **r**. Rom 8:10
who did not pursue **r** have attained it, Rom 9:30
attained it, that is, a **r** that is by faith; Rom 9:30
that would lead to **r** did not succeed in Rom 9:31
ignorant of the **r** that comes from Rom 10:3
own, they did not submit to God's **r**. Rom 10:3
of the law for **r** to everyone who Rom 10:4
Moses writes about the **r** that is based Rom 10:5
But the **r** based on faith says, "Do not Rom 10:6
and drinking but of **r** and peace and Rom 14:17
wisdom and our **r** and sanctification 1 Cor 1:30
the ministry of **r** must far exceed it in 2 Cor 3:9
him we might become the **r** of God. 2 Cor 5:21
with the weapons of **r** for the right 2 Cor 6:7
partnership has **r** with lawlessness? 2 Cor 6:14
to the poor; his **r** endures forever." 2 Cor 9:9
and increase the harvest of your **r**. 2 Cor 9:10
disguise themselves as servants of **r**. 2 Cor 11:15
God, and it was counted to him as **r**"? Gal 3:6
life, then **r** would indeed be by the law. Gal 3:21
ourselves eagerly wait for the hope of **r**. Gal 5:5
likeness of God in true **r** and holiness. Eph 4:24
and having put on the breastplate of **r**, Eph 6:14
with the fruit of **r** that comes through Phil 1:11
as to **r**, under the law blameless. Phil 3:6
not having a **r** of my own that comes Phil 3:9
the **r** from God that depends on faith— Phil 3:9
of God, flee these things. Pursue **r**, 1 Tm 6:11
flee youthful passions and pursue **r**, 2 Tm 2:22
for correction, and for training in **r**, 2 Tm 3:16
there is laid up for me the crown of **r**, 2 Tm 4:8
us, not because of works done by us in **r**, Ti 3:5
You have loved **r** and hated wickedness; Heb 1:9
on milk is unskilled in the word of **r**, Heb 5:13
by translation of his name, king of **r**, Heb 7:2
an heir of the **r** that comes by faith. Heb 11:7
the peaceful fruit of **r** to those who Heb 12:11
does not produce the **r** that God requires. Jas 1:20
was counted to him as **r**"—and he was Jas 2:23
And a harvest of **r** is sown in peace by Jas 3:18
that we might die to sin and live to **r**. 1 Pt 2:24
with ours by the **r** of our God and 2 Pt 1:1
world, but preserved Noah, a herald of **r**, 2 Pt 2:5
known the way of **r** than after knowing 2 Pt 2:21
and a new earth in which **r** dwells. 2 Pt 3:13
everyone who practices **r** has been 1 Jn 2:29
you. Whoever practices **r** is righteous, 1 Jn 3:7
whoever does not practice **r** is not of 1 Jn 3:10
and in **r** he judges and makes war. Rv 19:11

RIGHTEOUSNESS' (3)
The LORD was pleased, for his **r** sake, to Is 42:21
are those who are persecuted for **r** sake, Mt 5:10
even if you should suffer for **r** sake, 1 Pt 3:14

RIGHTFUL (3)
for you and restore your **r** habitation. Jb 8:6
shall be restored to its **r** state." Dn 8:14
If others share this **r** claim on you, do 1 Cor 9:12

RIGHTLY (9)
Esau said, "Is he not **r** named Jacob? Gn 27:36
one who orders his way **r** I will show the Ps 50:23
love more than wine; **r** do they love you. Sg 1:4
For he is **r** instructed; his God teaches Is 28:26
and listened, but they have not spoken **r**; Jer 8:6
he said to him, "You have judged **r**." Lk 7:43
we know that you speak and teach **r**, Lk 20:21
the judgment of God **r** falls on those Rom 2:2
r handling the word of truth. 2 Tm 2:15

RIGHTS (9)
her food, her clothing, or her marital **r**. Ex 21:10
told the people the **r** and duties of the 1 Sm 10:25
righteous man knows the **r** of the poor; Prv 29:7
decreed and pervert the **r** of all the Prv 31:5
mute, for the **r** of all who are destitute. Prv 31:8
defend the **r** of the poor and needy. Prv 31:9
and they do not defend the **r** of the needy. Jer 5:28
should give to his wife her conjugal **r**, 1 Cor 7:3
I have made no use of any of these **r**, 1 Cor 9:15

RIGID (1)
and grinds his teeth and becomes **r**. Mk 9:18

RIM (7)
you shall make a **r** around it a Ex 25:25
and a molding of gold around the **r**. Ex 25:25
And he made a **r** around it a Ex 37:12
made a molding of gold around the **r**. Ex 37:12
with a **r** of one span around its edge. Ezk 43:13
with a **r** around it half a cubit broad, Ezk 43:17
of the ledge and upon the **r** all around. Ezk 43:20

RIMMON (15)
Lebaoth, Shilhim, Ain, and **R**: in all, Jos 15:32
Ain, **R**, Ether, and Ashan—four cities Jos 19:7
and going on to **R** it bends toward Jos 19:13
toward the wilderness to the rock of **R**. Jgs 20:45
to the rock of **R** and remained at the Jgs 20:47
remained at the rock of **R** four months. Jgs 20:47
at the rock of **R** and proclaimed peace Jgs 21:13
sons of **R** a man of Benjamin from 2 Sm 4:2
Now the sons of **R** the Beerothite, 2 Sm 4:5
brother, the sons of **R** the Beerothite, 2 Sm 4:9
into the house of **R** to worship there, 2 Kgs 5:18
and I bow myself in the house of **R**, 2 Kgs 5:18
when I bow myself in the house of **R**, 2 Kgs 5:18
villages were Etam, Ain, **R**, Tochen, 1 Chr 4:32
from Geba to **R** south of Jerusalem. Zec 14:10

RIMMON-PEREZ (2)
out from Rithmah and camped at **R**. Nm 33:19
they set out from **R** and camped at Nm 33:20

RIMMONO (1)
R with its pasturelands, Tabor with 1 Chr 6:77

RIMS (4)
their axles, their **r**, their spokes, and 1 Kgs 7:33
And their **r** were tall and awesome, and Ezk 1:18
and the **r** of all four were full of eyes all Ezk 1:18
And their whole body, their **r**, and Ezk 10:12

RING (21)
man took a gold **r** weighing a half Gn 24:22
as he saw the **r** and the bracelets on Gn 24:30
So I put the **r** on her nose and the Gn 24:47
took his signet **r** from his hand Gn 41:42
but joined at the top, at the first **r**. Ex 26:24
but joined at the top, at the first **r**. Ex 36:29
king took his signet **r** from his hand Est 3:10
and sealed with the king's signet **r**. Est 3:12
And the king took off his signet **r**, which Est 8:2
of the king, and seal it with the king's **r**, Est 8:8
with the king's **r** cannot be revoked." Est 8:8
and sealed it with the king's signet **r**. Est 8:10
him a piece of money and a **r** of gold. Jb 42:11
Like a gold **r** in a pig's snout is a Prv 11:22
Like a gold **r** or an ornament of gold is Prv 25:12
were the signet **r** on my right hand, Jer 22:24
And I put a **r** on your nose and Ezk 16:12
adorned herself with her **r** and jewelry, Hos 2:13
the LORD, and make you like a signet **r**, Hg 2:23
put it on him, and put a **r** on his hand, Lk 15:22
man wearing a gold **r** and fine clothing Jas 2:2

RINGLEADER (1)
the world and is a **r** of the sect of the Acts 24:5

RINGS (44)
had, and the **r** that were in their ears. Gn 35:4
You shall cast four **r** of gold for it and Ex 25:12
its four feet, two **r** on the one side of it, Ex 25:12
of it, and two **r** on the other side of it. Ex 25:12
put the poles into the **r** on the sides of Ex 25:14
poles shall remain in the **r** of the ark; Ex 25:15
you shall make for it four **r** of gold, Ex 25:26
and fasten the **r** to the four corners at Ex 25:26
Close to the frame the **r** shall lie, as Ex 25:27
and shall make their **r** of gold for Ex 26:29
shall make four bronze **r** at its four Ex 27:4
And the poles shall be put through the **r**, Ex 27:7
make for the breastpiece two **r** of gold, Ex 28:23

and put the two **r** on the two edges of the Ex 28:23
of gold in the two **r** at the edges of the Ex 28:24
You shall make two **r** of gold, and put Ex 28:26
And you shall make two **r** of gold, and Ex 28:27
the breastpiece by its **r** to the rings of Ex 28:28
by its rings to the **r** of the ephod with a Ex 28:28
And you shall make two golden **r** for it. Ex 30:4
"Take off the **r** of gold that are in the ears Ex 32:2
the people took off the **r** of gold that were Ex 32:3
and earrings and signet **r** and armlets, Ex 35:22
and made their **r** of gold for holders for Ex 36:34
he cast for it four **r** of gold for its four Ex 37:3
two **r** on its one side and two rings on its Ex 37:3
on its one side and two **r** on its other side. Ex 37:3
put the poles into the **r** on the sides of the Ex 37:5
He cast for it four **r** of gold and fastened Ex 37:13
gold and fastened the **r** to the four Ex 37:13
Close to the frame were the **r**, as holders Ex 37:14
and made two **r** of gold on it under its Ex 37:27
He cast four **r** on the four corners of the Ex 38:5
the poles through the **r** on the sides of Ex 38:7
settings of gold filigree and two gold **r**, Ex 39:16
and put the two **r** on the two edges of the Ex 39:16
of gold in the two **r** at the edges of the Ex 39:17
Then they made two **r** of gold, and put Ex 39:19
And they made two **r** of gold, and Ex 39:20
the breastpiece by its **r** to the rings of Ex 39:21
by its rings to the **r** of the ephod with a Ex 39:21
gold, armlets and bracelets, signet **r**, Nm 31:50
the signet **r** and nose rings; Is 3:21
the signet rings and nose **r**; Is 3:21

RINNAH (1)
Amnon, **R**, Ben-hanan, and Tilon. 1 Chr 4:20

RINSE (1)
these they were to **r** off what was used 2 Chr 4:6

RINSED (4)
that shall be scoured and **r** in water. Lv 6:28
touches without having **r** his hands in Lv 15:11
every vessel of wood shall be **r** in water. Lv 15:12
with my delicacies; he has **r** me out. Jer 51:34

RIOT (1)
but rather that a **r** was beginning, Mt 27:24

RIOTING (1)
danger of being charged with **r** today, Acts 19:40

RIOTS (2)
one who stirs up **r** among all the Jews Acts 24:5
beatings, imprisonments, **r**, labors, 2 Cor 6:5

RIP (2)
little ones and **r** open their pregnant 2 Kgs 8:12
lion, as a wild beast would **r** them open. Hos 13:8

RIPE (8)
was the season of the first **r** grapes. Nm 13:20
blossoms, and it bore **r** almonds. Nm 17:8
The first **r** fruits of all that is in their Nm 18:13
shall come to your grave in **r** old age, Jb 5:26
Put in the sickle, for the harvest is **r**. Go Jl 3:13
But when the grain is **r**, at once he puts Mk 4:29
for the harvest of the earth is fully **r**." Rv 14:15
vine of the earth, for its grapes are **r**." Rv 14:18

RIPENED (1)
forth, and the clusters **r** into grapes. Gn 40:10

RIPENING (1)
is over, and the flower becomes a **r** grape, Is 18:5

RIPENS (1)
The fig tree **r** its figs, and the vines are in Sg 2:13

RIPHATH (2)
of Gomer: Ashkenaz, **R**, and Togarmah. Gn 10:3
Gomer: Ashkenaz, **R**, and Togarmah. 1 Chr 1:6

RIPPED (3)
and he **r** open all the women in it 2 Kgs 15:16
and their pregnant women **r** open. Hos 13:16
because they have **r** open pregnant Am 1:13

RISE (157)
Then you may **r** up early and go on Gn 19:2
be angry that I cannot **r** before you, Gn 31:35
"**R** up early in the morning and present Ex 8:20
"**R** up early in the morning and present Ex 9:13
nor did anyone **r** from his place for Ex 10:23
out to the tent, all the people would **r** up, Ex 33:8
all the people would **r** up and worship, Ex 33:10
come to call you, **r**, go with them; Nm 22:20
up his discourse and said, "**R**, Balak, Nm 23:18
and a scepter shall **r** out of Israel; Nm 24:17
'Now **r** up and go over the brook Zered.' Dt 2:13
'**R** up, set out on your journey and go Dt 2:24
and when you lie down, and when you **r**. Dt 6:7
when you lie down, and when you **r**. Dt 11:19
cause your enemies who **r** against you to Dt 28:7
is among you shall **r** higher and higher Dt 28:43
your children who **r** up after you, Dt 29:22
Then this people will **r** and whore after Dt 31:16
Let them **r** up and help you; let them be Dt 32:38
who hate him, that they **r** not again." Dt 33:11
Then you shall **r** up from the ambush Jos 8:7
"**R** and kill them!" But the young man Jgs 8:20
said, "**R** yourself and fall upon us, Jgs 8:21
sun is up, **r** early and rush upon the city. Jgs 9:33
a great cloud of smoke **r** up out of the Jgs 20:38
the signal began to **r** out of the city Jgs 20:40
If men **r** up to pursue you and to seek 1 Sm 25:29
Now then **r** early in the morning 1 Sm 29:10
Absalom used to **r** early and stand 2 Sm 15:2
king and all who **r** up against you 2 Sm 18:32
them through, so that they did not **r**; 2 Sm 22:39
made those who **r** against me sink 2 Sm 22:40
in and have him **r** from among his 2 Kgs 9:2
"Let us **r** up and build." So they Neh 2:18
relief and deliverance will **r** for the Jews Est 4:14
and he would **r** early in the morning and Jb 1:5
who commands the sun, and it does not **r**; Jb 9:7
me; when I **r** they talk against me. Jb 19:18
and the earth will **r** up against him. Jb 20:27
they **r** up when they despair of life. Jb 24:22
On my right hand the rabble **r**; they Jb 30:12
through, so that they were not able to **r**; Ps 18:38
you made those who **r** against me sink Ps 18:39
and fall, but we **r** and stand upright. Ps 20:8
of shield and buckler and **r** for my help! Ps 35:2
Malicious witnesses **r** up; they ask me Ps 35:11
they are thrust down, unable to **r**. Ps 36:12
he will not **r** again from where he lies." Ps 41:8
we tread down those who **r** up against us. Ps 44:5
R up; come to our help! Redeem us for Ps 44:26
me from those who **r** up against me; Ps 59:1
the uproar of those who **r** against you, Ps 74:23
Do the departed **r** up to praise you? Ps 88:10
the sea; when its waves **r**, you still them. Ps 89:9
R up, O judge of the earth; repay to the Ps 94:2
At midnight I **r** to praise you, because Ps 119:62
I **r** before dawn and cry for help; I Ps 119:147
is in vain that you **r** up early and go late Ps 127:2
is who makes the clouds **r** at the end of Ps 135:7
know when I sit down and when I **r** up; Ps 139:2
not loathe those who **r** up against you? Ps 139:21
into fire, into miry pits, no more to **r**! Ps 140:10
for disaster from them will **r** suddenly, Prv 24:22
is great glory, but when the wicked **r**, Prv 28:12
When the wicked **r**, people hide Prv 28:28
Her children **r** up and call her blessed; Prv 31:28
I will **r** now and go about the city, in the Sg 3:2
Woe to those who **r** early in the morning, Is 5:11
And it will **r** over all its channels and go Is 8:7
fathers, lest they **r** and possess the earth, Is 14:21
"I will **r** up against them," declares the Is 14:22
upon it, and it falls, and will not **r** again. Is 24:20
Your dead shall live; their bodies shall **r**. Is 26:19
For the LORD will **r** up as on Mount Is 28:21
R up, you women who are at ease, hear Is 32:9
and the stench of their corpses shall **r**; Is 34:3
they lie down, they cannot **r**, they are Is 43:17
then shall your light **r** in the darkness Is 58:10
LORD: When men fall, do they not **r** again? Jer 8:4
he makes the mist **r** from the ends of Jer 10:13
drunk and vomit, fall and **r** no more, Jer 25:27
they would **r** up and burn this city with Jer 37:10
He said, 'I will **r**, I will cover the earth, I Jer 46:8
come against her, and **r** up for battle! Jer 49:14
the LORD: "**R** up, advance against Kedar! Jer 49:28
"**R** up, advance against a nation at ease, Jer 49:31
he makes the mist **r** from the ends of Jer 51:16
'Thus shall Babylon sink, to **r** no more, Jer 51:64
And he shall even **r** up against the Dn 8:25
times many shall **r** against the king Dn 11:14
the stench and foul smell of him will **r**, Jl 2:20
"Fallen, no more to **r**, is the virgin Israel; Am 5:2
and I will **r** against the house of Am 7:9
dwells in it, and all of it **r** like the Nile, Am 8:8
they shall fall, and never **r** again." Am 8:14
has been sent among the nations: "**R** up! Ob 1:1
"Rise up! Let us **r** against her for battle!" Ob 1:1
me, O my enemy; when I fall, I shall **r**; Mi 7:8
end; trouble will not **r** up a second time. Na 1:9
"for the day when I **r** up to seize the prey. Zep 3:8
of righteousness shall **r** with healing in Mal 4:2
said, "**R**, take the child and his mother, Mt 2:13
"**R**, take the child and his mother and go Mt 2:20
For he makes his sun **r** on the evil and Mt 5:45
sins are forgiven,' or to say, '**R** and walk'? Mt 9:5
sins"—he then said to the paralytic—"**R**, Mt 9:6
and children will **r** against parents and Mt 10:21
men of Nineveh will **r** up at the Mt 12:41
of the South will **r** up at the judgment Mt 12:42
them, saying, "**R**, and have no fear." Mt 17:7
For nation will **r** against nation, and Mt 24:7
R, let us be going; see, my betrayer is at Mt 26:46
was still alive, 'After three days I will **r**.' Mt 27:63
or to say, '**R**, take up your bed and walk'? Mk 2:9
"I say to you, **r**, pick up your bed, and Mk 2:11
be killed, and after three days **r** again. Mk 8:31
he is killed, after three days he will **r**." Mk 9:31
him. And after three days he will **r**." Mk 10:34
In the resurrection, when they **r** again, Mk 12:23
For when they **r** from the dead, they Mk 12:25
For nation will **r** against nation, and Mk 13:8
and children will **r** against parents Mk 13:12
R, let us be going; see, my betrayer is at Mk 14:42
are forgiven you,' or to say, '**R** and walk'? Lk 5:23
you, **r**, pick up your bed and go home." Lk 5:24
his impudence he will **r** and give him Lk 11:8
of the South will **r** up at the judgment Lk 11:31
men of Nineveh will **r** up at the Lk 11:32
if someone should **r** from the dead.'" Lk 16:31
he said to him, "**R** and go your way; Lk 17:19
him, and on the third day he will **r**." Lk 18:33
to them, "Nation will **r** against nation, Lk 21:10
R and pray that you may not enter into Lk 22:46
and be crucified and on the third day **r**." Lk 24:7
and on the third day **r** from the dead, Lk 24:46
said to her, "Your brother will **r** again." Jn 11:23
know that he will **r** again in the Jn 11:24
her, saw Mary **r** quickly and go out, Jn 11:31
I love the Father. **R**, let us go from here. Jn 14:31
Scripture, that he must **r** from the dead. Jn 20:9
Christ of Nazareth, **r** up and walk!" Acts 3:6
"**R** and go toward the south to the road Acts 8:26
But **r** and enter the city, and you will be Acts 9:6
"**R** and go to the street called Straight, Acts 9:11
r and make your bed." And Acts 9:34
there came a voice to him: "**R**, Peter; Acts 10:13
R and go down and accompany them Acts 10:20
I heard a voice saying to me, '**R**, Peter; Acts 11:7
Christ to suffer and to **r** from the dead, Acts 17:3
said to me, '**R**, and go into Damascus, Acts 22:10
R and be baptized and wash away Acts 22:16
But **r** and stand upon your feet, for I Acts 26:16
by being the first to **r** from the dead, Acts 26:23
And the dead in Christ will **r** first. 1 Thes 4:16
so that they might **r** again to a better Heb 11:35
"**R** and measure the temple of God and Rv 11:1
and is about to **r** from the bottomless pit Rv 17:8

RISEN (31)
The sun had **r** on the earth when Lot Gn 19:23
but if the sun has **r** on him, there shall Ex 22:3
you have **r** in your fathers' place, Nm 32:14
and you have **r** up against my father's Jgs 9:18
for him, so that he has **r** against me, 1 Sm 22:13
whole clan has **r** against your 2 Sm 14:7
For I have **r** in the place of David my 1 Kgs 8:20
For I have **r** in the place of David my 2 Chr 6:10
this city from of old has **r** against kings, Ezr 4:19
for our iniquities have **r** higher than our Ezr 9:6
and my leanness has **r** up against me; Jb 16:8
for false witnesses have **r** against me, Ps 27:12
For strangers have **r** against me; ruthless Ps 54:3
insolent men have **r** up against me; Ps 86:14
and the glory of the LORD has **r** upon you. Is 60:1
not pass through, for the water had **r**. Ezk 47:5
lately my people have **r** up as an enemy; Mi 2:8
tell the people, 'He has **r** from the dead,' Mt 27:64
He is not here, for he has **r**, as he said. Mt 28:6
his disciples that he has **r** from the dead, Mt 28:7
And if Satan has **r** up against himself Mk 3:26
the Son of Man had **r** from the dead. Mk 9:9
day of the week, when the sun had **r**, Mk 16:2
was crucified. He has **r**; he is not here. Mk 16:6
those who saw him after he had **r**. Mk 16:14
that one of the prophets of old had **r**. Lk 9:8
that one of the prophets of old has **r**." Lk 9:19
of the house has **r** and shut the door, Lk 13:25
He is not here, but has **r**. Remember how Lk 24:6
saying, "The Lord has **r** indeed, and Lk 24:34
Jesus Christ, **r** from the dead, 2 Tm 2:8

RISES (31)
then if the man **r** again and walks Ex 21:19
As a lioness it **r** up and as a lion it lifts Nm 23:24
be the man who **r** up and rebuilds this Jos 6:26
Mount Halak, which **r** toward Seir, Jos 11:17
that **r** toward Seir (and Joshua gave their Jos 12:7
like the sun as he **r** in his might." And Jgs 5:31
then, if the king's anger **r**, and if he 2 Sm 11:20
so a man lies down and **r** not again; till Jb 14:12
The murderer **r** before it is light, that he Jb 24:14
and let him who **r** up against me be as Jb 27:7
what then shall I do when God **r** up? Jb 31:14
the cattle also declare that he **r**. Jb 36:33
Who **r** up for me against the wicked? Ps 94:16
When the sun **r**, they steal away and Ps 104:22
falls seven times and **r** again, Prv 24:16

She **r** while it is yet night and provides Prv 31:15
The sun **r**, and the sun goes down, and Eccl 1:5
and hastens to the place where it **r**. Eccl 1:5
If the anger of the ruler **r** against you, Eccl 10:4
and one **r** up at the sound of a bird, Eccl 12:4
his majesty, when he **r** to terrify the earth. Is 2:19
his majesty, when he **r** to terrify the earth. Is 2:21
every tongue that **r** against you in Is 54:17
Egypt **r** like the Nile, like rivers whose Jer 46:8
in it mourn, and all of it **r** like the Nile, Am 9:5
the daughter **r** up against her mother, Mi 7:6
fences in a day of cold—when the sun **r**, Na 3:17
He sleeps and **r** night and day, and the Mk 4:27
For the sun **r** with its scorching heat Jas 1:11
and the morning star **r** in your hearts, 2 Pt 1:19
the beast that **r** from the bottomless pit Rv 11:7

RISING (24)
a man's hand is **r** from the sea." And 1 Kgs 18:44
many are my foes! Many are **r** against me; Ps 3:1
Its **r** is from the end of the heavens, and Ps 19:6
the earth from the **r** of the sun to Ps 50:1
From the **r** of the sun to its setting, the Ps 113:3
a loud voice, **r** early in the morning, Prv 27:14
the sun will be dark at its **r**, and the Is 13:10
with his anger, and in thick **r** smoke; Is 30:27
and he has come, from the **r** of the sun, Is 41:25
from the **r** of the sun and from the west, Is 45:6
west, and his glory from the **r** of the sun; Is 59:19
and kings to the brightness of your **r**. Is 60:3
"Who is this, **r** like the Nile, like rivers Jer 46:7
Behold, waters are **r** out of the north, and Jer 47:2
Behold their sitting and their **r**; I am Lam 3:63
shall come, **r** from the wilderness, Hos 13:15
For from the **r** of the sun to its setting Mal 1:11
And **r** very early in the morning, while Mk 1:35
questioning what this **r** from the dead Mk 9:10
for the fall and **r** of many in Israel, Lk 2:34
"When you see a cloud **r** in the west, Lk 12:54
angel ascending from the **r** of the sun, Rv 7:2
And I saw a beast **r** out of the sea, with Rv 13:1
I saw another beast **r** out of the earth. Rv 13:11

RISK (2)
who went at the **r** of their lives?" 2 Sm 23:17
For at the **r** of their lives they 1 Chr 11:19

RISKED (4)
is a people who **r** their lives to the Jgs 5:18
fought for you and **r** his life and Jgs 9:17
men who have **r** their lives for the Acts 15:26
who **r** their necks for my life, to whom Rom 16:4

RISKING (1)
r his life to complete what was lacking Phil 2:30

RISSAH (2)
set out from Libnah and camped at **R**. Nm 33:21
they set out from **R** and camped at Nm 33:22

RITE (1)
You shall observe this **r** as a statute for Ex 12:24

RITES (2)
jars there for the Jewish **r** of purification, Jn 2:6
things to be purified with these **r**, Heb 9:23

RITHMAH (2)
out from Hazeroth and camped at **R**. Nm 33:18
they set out from **R** and camped at Nm 33:19

RITUAL (1)
first section, performing their **r** duties, Heb 9:6

RIVAL (3)
take a woman as a **r** wife to her sister, Lv 18:18
And her **r** used to provoke her 1 Sm 1:6
in the garden of God could not **r** it, Ezk 31:8

RIVALRIES (1)
jealousy, fits of anger, **r**, dissensions, Gal 5:20

RIVALRY (3)
indeed preach Christ from envy and **r**, Phil 1:15
The former proclaim Christ out of **r**, Phil 1:17
Do nothing from **r** or conceit, but in Phil 2:3

RIVER (93)
A **r** flowed out of Eden to water the Gn 2:10
The name of the second **r** is the Gihon. Gn 2:13
And the name of the third **r** is the Tigris, Gn 2:14
And the fourth **r** is the Euphrates. Gn 2:14
from the **r** of Egypt to the great river, Gn 15:18
from the river of Egypt to the great **r**, Gn 15:18
to the great river, the **r** Euphrates, Gn 15:18
placed it among the reeds by the **r** bank. Ex 2:3
of Pharaoh came down to bathe at the **r**, Ex 2:5
her young women walked beside the **r**. Ex 2:5
which is near the **R** in the land of the Nm 22:5
stretch afar, like gardens beside a **r**, Nm 24:6
and Lebanon, as far as the great **r**, Dt 1:7
as far as the great river, the **r** Euphrates. Dt 1:7
the banks of the **r** Jabbok and the cities Dt 2:37
as a border, as far over as the **r** Jabbok, Dt 3:16
to the Lebanon and from the **R**, Dt 11:24
and from the River, the **r** Euphrates, Dt 11:24
and this Lebanon as far as the great **r**, Jos 1:4
as far as the great river, the **r** Euphrates, Jos 1:4
of the valley as far as the **r** Jabbok, Jos 12:2
from beyond the **R** and led him Jos 24:3
served beyond the **R** and in Egypt, Jos 24:14
served in the region beyond the **R**, Jos 24:15
meet you by the **r** Kishon with his Jgs 4:7
Harosheth-hagoyim to the **r** Kishon. Jgs 4:13
to restore his power at the **r** Euphrates. 2 Sm 8:3
and on the Habor, the **r** of Gozan, 2 Kgs 17:6
and on the Habor, the **r** of Gozan, 2 Kgs 18:11
king of Assyria to the **r** Euphrates. 2 Kgs 23:29
the Brook of Egypt to the **r** Euphrates. 2 Kgs 24:7
Halah, Habor, Hara, and the **r** Gozan, 1 Chr 5:26
up his monument at the **r** Euphrates. 1 Chr 18:3
in the rest of the province Beyond the **R**. Ezr 4:10
the men of the province Beyond the **R**, Ezr 4:11
in the province Beyond the **R**." Ezr 4:16
in the rest of the province Beyond the **R**, Ezr 4:17
over the whole province Beyond the **R**, Ezr 4:20
Beyond the **R** and Shethar-bozenai Ezr 5:3
Beyond the **R** and Shethar-bozenai Ezr 5:6
the province Beyond the **R** sent to Darius Ezr 5:6
governor of the province Beyond the **R**, Ezr 6:6
who are in the province Beyond the **R**, Ezr 6:6
of the province from Beyond the **R**. Ezr 6:8
governor of the province Beyond the **R**, Ezr 6:13
treasurers in the province Beyond the **R**: Ezr 7:21
the people in the province Beyond the **R**, Ezr 7:25
gathered them to the **r** that runs to Ezr 8:15
I proclaimed a fast there, at the **r** Ahava, Ezr 8:21
we departed from the **r** Ahava on the Ezr 8:31
governors of the province Beyond the **R**, Ezr 8:36
governors of the province Beyond the **R**, Neh 2:7
province Beyond the **R** and gave them Neh 2:9
governor of the province Beyond the **R**. Neh 3:7
a lake and a **r** wastes away and dries Jb 14:11
if the **r** is turbulent he is not frightened; Jb 40:23
them drink from the **r** of your delights. Ps 36:8
There is a **r** whose streams make glad Ps 46:4
enrich it; the **r** of God is full of water; Ps 65:9
land; they passed through the **r** on foot. Ps 66:6
and from the **R** to the ends of the earth! Ps 72:8
to the sea and its shoots to the **R**. Ps 80:11
as to Sisera and Jabin at the **r** Kishon, Ps 83:9
it flowed through the desert like a **r**. Ps 105:41
that is hired beyond the **R**—with the king Is 7:20
up against them the waters of the **R**, Is 8:7
his hand over the **R** with his scorching Is 11:15
up, and the **r** will be dry and parched, Is 19:5
that day from the **r** Euphrates to the Is 27:12
your peace would have been like a **r**, Is 48:18
I will extend peace to her like a **r**, Is 66:12
was by the **r** Euphrates at Carchemish Jer 46:2
the north by the **r** Euphrates they have Jer 46:6
the north country by the **r** Euphrates. Jer 46:10
and it was a **r** that I could not pass Ezk 47:5
a **r** that could not be passed through. Ezk 47:5
he led me back to the bank of the **r**. Ezk 47:6
on the bank of the **r** very many trees on Ezk 47:7
And wherever the **r** goes, every living Ezk 47:9
so everything will live where the **r** goes. Ezk 47:9
on the banks, on both sides of the **r**, Ezk 47:12
on the bank of the great **r** (that is, Dn 10:4
cities of Egypt, and from Egypt to the **R**, Mi 7:12
The **r** gates are opened; the palace melts Na 2:6
and from the **R** to the ends of the earth. Zec 9:10
they were baptized by him in the **r** Jordan, Mt 3:6
being baptized by him in the **r** Jordan, Mk 1:5
who are bound at the great **r** Euphrates." Rv 9:14
poured water like a **r** out of his mouth Rv 12:15
and swallowed the **r** that the dragon Rv 12:16
out his bowl on the great **r** Euphrates, Rv 16:12
the angel showed me the **r** of the water of Rv 22:1
also, on either side of the **r**, the tree of life Rv 22:2

RIVERS (43)
and there it divided and became four **r**. Gn 2:10
over the waters of Egypt, over their **r**, Ex 7:19
out your hand with your staff over the **r**, Ex 8:5
scales, whether in the seas or in the **r**, Lv 11:9
in the seas or the **r** that has not fins and Lv 11:10
and Pharpar, the **r** of Damascus, 2 Kgs 5:12
He will not look upon the **r**, the streams Jb 20:17
the seas and established it upon the **r**. Ps 24:2
and caused waters to flow down like **r**. Ps 78:16
He turned their **r** to blood, so that they Ps 78:44
on the sea and his right hand on the **r**. Ps 89:25
Let the **r** clap their hands; let the hills Ps 98:8
He turns **r** into a desert, springs of Ps 107:33
wings that is beyond the **r** of Cush, Is 18:1
and conquering, whose land the **r** divide. Is 18:2
and conquering, whose land the **r** divide, Is 18:7
be for us a place of broad **r** and streams, Is 33:21
I will open **r** on the bare heights, and Is 41:18
I will turn the **r** into islands, and dry up Is 42:15
and through the **r**, they shall not Is 43:2
way in the wilderness and **r** in the desert. Is 43:19
water in the wilderness, **r** in the desert, Is 43:20
to the deep, 'Be dry; I will dry up your **r**'; Is 44:27
uncover your legs, pass through the **r**. Is 47:2
I dry up the sea, I make the **r** a desert; Is 50:2
like the Nile, like **r** whose waters surge? Jer 46:7
like the Nile, like **r** whose waters surge. Jer 46:8
my eyes flow with **r** of tears because of Lam 3:48
making its **r** flow around the place of Ezk 31:4
the deep over it, and restrained its **r**, Ezk 31:15
you burst forth in your **r**, trouble the Ezk 32:2
waters with your feet, and foul their **r**. Ezk 32:2
clear, and cause their **r** to run like oil, Ezk 32:14
of rams, with ten thousands of **r** of oil? Mi 6:7
sea and makes it dry; he dries up all the **r**; Na 1:4
Was your wrath against the **r**, O LORD? Hab 3:8
Was your anger against the **r**, or your Hab 3:8
arrows. Selah You split the earth with **r**. Hab 3:9
From beyond the **r** of Cush my Zep 3:10
of his heart will flow **r** of living water.'" Jn 7:38
frequent journeys, in danger from **r**, 2 Cor 11:26
on a third of the **r** and on the springs of Rv 8:10
out his bowl into the **r** and the springs of Rv 16:4

RIVERSIDE (1)
day we went outside the gate to the **r**, Acts 16:13

RIZIA (1)
sons of Ulla: Arah, Hanniel, and **R**. 1 Chr 7:39

RIZPAH (4)
had a concubine whose name was **R**, 2 Sm 3:7
the two sons of **R** the daughter of 2 Sm 21:8
Then **R** the daughter of Aiah took 2 Sm 21:10
was told what **R** the daughter of 2 Sm 21:11

ROAD (45)
Enaim, which is on the **r** to Timnah. Gn 38:14
the angel of the LORD standing in the **r**, Nm 22:23
aside out of the **r** and went into the Nm 22:23
the donkey, to turn her into the **r**. Nm 22:23
that you stood in the **r** against me. Nm 22:34
away from the Arabah **r** from Elath and Dt 2:8
I will go only by the **r**; I will turn aside Dt 2:27
not beyond the Jordan, west of the **r**, Dt 11:30
who misleads a blind man on the **r**.' Dt 27:18
the **r** on which you are going will not lead Jgs 4:9
sitting on his seat by the **r** watching, 1 Sm 4:13
which is beside the **r** on the east of 1 Sm 26:3
coming from the **r** behind him by 2 Sm 13:34
So David and his men went on the **r**, 2 Sm 16:13
the Shilonite found him on the **r**. 1 Kgs 11:29
met him on the **r** and killed him. 1 Kgs 13:24
And his body was thrown in the **r**, 1 Kgs 13:24
body thrown in the **r** and the lion 1 Kgs 13:25
and found his body thrown in the **r**, 1 Kgs 13:28
of Shallecheth on the **r** that goes up. 1 Chr 26:16
were four at the **r** and two at the 1 Chr 26:18
They thrust the poor off the **r**; the poor of Jb 24:4
her corner, taking the **r** to her house Prv 7:8
sluggard says, "There is a lion in the **r**! Prv 26:13
Even when the fool walks on the **r**, he Eccl 10:3
on the **r** to Horonaim they raise a cry of Is 15:5
And I will make all my mountains a **r**, Is 49:11
not out into the field, nor walk on the **r**, Jer 6:25
"Set up **r** markers for yourself; make Jer 31:21
the highway, the **r** by which you went. Jer 31:21
Man the ramparts; watch the **r**; dress for Na 2:1
of the crowd spread their cloaks on the **r**, Mt 21:8
from the trees and spread them on the **r**. Mt 21:8
And they were on the **r**, going up to Mk 10:32
And many spread their cloaks on the **r**, Mk 11:8
As they were going along the **r**, someone Lk 9:57
no sandals, and greet no one on the **r**. Lk 10:4
chance a priest was going down that **r**, Lk 10:31
along, they spread their cloaks on the **r**. Lk 19:36
within us while he talked to us on the **r**, Lk 24:32
they told what had happened on the **r**, Lk 24:35
the south to the **r** that goes down from Acts 8:26
were going along the **r** they came to Acts 8:36
to you on the **r** by which you came Acts 9:17
to them how on the **r** he had seen the Acts 9:27

ROADS (9)
so that your **r** shall be deserted. Lv 26:22
you not asked those who travel the **r**, Jb 21:29
paths; they have made their **r** crooked; Is 59:8
"Stand by the **r**, and look, and ask for the Jer 6:16
stumble in their ways, in the ancient **r**, Jer 18:15
ancient roads, and to walk into side **r**, Jer 18:15
The **r** to Zion mourn, for none come to Lam 1:4
therefore to the main **r** and invite to the Mt 22:9
went out into the **r** and gathered all Mt 22:10

ROADSIDE (5)
He turned to her at the **r** and said, Gn 38:16
was at Enaim at the **r**?" And they said, Gn 38:21
were two blind men sitting by the **r**, Mt 20:30
son of Timaeus, was sitting by the **r**. Mk 10:46
man was sitting by the **r** begging. Lk 18:35

ROAMED (1)
where David and his men had **r**. 1 Sm 30:31

ROAR (28)
Let the sea **r**, and all that fills it; let 1 Chr 16:32
The **r** of the lion, the voice of the fierce Jb 4:10
you toss me about in the **r** of the storm. Jb 30:22
calls to deep at the **r** of your waterfalls; Ps 42:7
though its waters **r** and foam, though the Ps 46:3
rejoice; let the sea **r**, and all that fills it; Ps 96:11
Let the sea **r**, and all that fills it; the world Ps 98:7
The young lions **r** for their prey, Ps 104:21
is like a lion, like young lions they **r**; Is 5:29
Ah, the **r** of nations; they roar like the Is 17:12
they **r** like the roaring of mighty waters! Is 17:12
The nations **r** like the roaring of many Is 17:13
sea so that its waves **r**—the LORD of hosts Is 51:15
though they **r**, they cannot pass over it. Jer 5:22
But with the **r** of a great tempest he will Jer 11:16
them: "'The LORD will **r** from on high, Jer 25:30
he will **r** mightily against his fold, and Jer 25:30
sea so that its waves **r**—the LORD of Jer 31:35
"They shall **r** together like lions; they Jer 51:38
Their waves **r** like many waters; the Jer 51:55
go after the LORD; he will **r** like a lion; Hos 11:10
Does a lion **r** in the forest, when he has Am 3:4
they shall drink and **r** as if drunk with Zec 9:15
The sound of the **r** of the lions, for the Zec 11:3
the heavens will pass away with a **r**, 2 Pt 3:10
his voice was like the **r** of many waters. Rv 1:15
from heaven like the **r** of many waters Rv 14:2
like the **r** of many waters and like the Rv 19:6

ROARED (4)
Your foes have **r** in the midst of your Ps 74:4
The lions have **r** against him; they have Jer 2:15
roared against him; they have **r** loudly. Jer 2:15
The lion has **r**; who will not fear? The Am 3:8

ROARING (17)
a young lion came toward him **r**. Jgs 14:5
at me, like a ravening and **r** lion. Ps 22:13
who stills the **r** of the seas, the roaring of Ps 65:7
roaring of the seas, the **r** of their waves, Ps 65:7
up their voice; the floods lift up their **r**. Ps 93:3
Like a **r** lion or a charging bear is a Prv 28:15
Their **r** is like a lion, like young lions Is 5:29
they roar like the **r** of mighty waters! Is 17:12
nations roar like the **r** of many waters, Is 17:13
the sound of them is like the **r** sea; Jer 6:23
sound of them is like the **r** of the sea; Jer 50:42
all who were in it at the sound of his **r**. Ezk 19:7
midst is like a **r** lion tearing the prey; Ezk 22:25
Her officials within her are **r** lions; her Zep 3:3
perplexity because of the **r** of the sea Lk 21:25
the devil prowls around like a **r** lion, 1 Pt 5:8
called out with a loud voice, like a lion **r**. Rv 10:3

ROARS (4)
After it his voice **r**; he thunders with his Jb 37:4
when he **r**, his children shall come Hos 11:10
The LORD **r** from Zion, and utters his Jl 3:16
"The LORD **r** from Zion and utters his Am 1:2

ROAST (2)
"Give meat for the priest to **r**, 1 Sm 2:15
is slothful will not **r** his game, Prv 12:27

ROASTED (7)
eat the flesh that night, **r** on the fire; Ex 12:8
eat any of it raw or boiled in water, but **r**, Ex 12:9
of your firstfruits fresh ears, **r** with fire, Lv 2:14
the reapers, and he passed to her **r** grain. Ru 2:14
And they **r** the Passover lamb with 2 Chr 35:13
on its coals; I **r** meat and have eaten. Is 44:19
the king of Babylon **r** in the fire," Jer 29:22

ROASTS (1)
half he eats meat; he **r** it and is satisfied. Is 44:16

ROB (8)
not oppress your neighbor or **r** him. Lv 19:13
Do not **r** the poor, because he is poor, Prv 22:22
plead their cause and **r** of life those Prv 22:23
cause and rob of life those who **r** them. Prv 22:23
needy from justice and to **r** the poor of my Is 10:2
and they will **r** you of your children. Ezk 5:17
Will man **r** God? Yet you are robbing Mal 3:8
who abhor idols, do you **r** temples? Rom 2:22

ROBBED (11)
be only oppressed and **r** continually, Dt 28:29
and they **r** all who passed by them along Jgs 9:25
like a bear **r** of her cubs in the field. 2 Sm 17:8
they are **r** of sleep unless they have Prv 4:16
man meet a she-bear **r** of her cubs Prv 17:12
of the oppressor him who has been **r**, Jer 21:12
of the oppressor him who has been **r**. Jer 22:3
he practiced extortion, **r** his brother, Ezk 18:18
upon them like a bear **r** of her cubs; Hos 13:8
me. But you say, 'How have we **r** you?' Mal 3:8
I **r** other churches by accepting 2 Cor 11:8

ROBBER (8)
poverty will come upon you like a **r**, Prv 6:11
in wait like a **r** and increases the Prv 23:28
poverty will come upon you like a **r**, Prv 24:34
"Have you come out as against a **r**, Mt 26:55
"Have you come out as against a **r**, Mk 14:48
"Have you come out as against a **r**, Lk 22:52
another way, that man is a thief and a **r**. Jn 10:1
but Barabbas!" Now Barabbas was a **r**. Jn 18:40

ROBBERS (14)
The tents of **r** are at peace, and those who Jb 12:6
name, become a den of **r** in your eyes? Jer 7:11
place. **R** shall enter and profane it. Ezk 7:22
As **r** lie in wait for a man, so the priests Hos 6:9
of prayer,' but you make it a den of **r**." Mt 21:13
Then two **r** were crucified with him, Mt 27:38
And the **r** who were crucified with him Mt 27:44
But you have made it a den of **r**." Mk 11:17
And with him they crucified two **r**, Mk 15:27
to Jericho, and he fell among **r**, Lk 10:30
to the man who fell among the **r**?" Lk 10:36
but you have made it a den of **r**." Lk 19:46
who came before me are thieves and **r**, Jn 10:8
danger from rivers, danger from **r**, 2 Cor 11:26

ROBBERY (10)
matter of deposit or security, or through **r**, Lv 6:2
restore what he took by **r** or what he got Lv 6:4
in extortion; set no vain hopes on **r**; Ps 62:10
I the LORD love justice; I hate **r** and wrong; Is 61:8
to the debtor his pledge, commits no **r**, Ezk 18:7
the poor and needy, commits **r**, Ezk 18:12
exacts no pledge, commits no **r**, Ezk 18:16
practiced extortion and committed **r**. Ezk 22:29
gives back what he has taken by **r**, Ezk 33:15
up violence and **r** in their strongholds." Am 3:10

ROBBING (3)
Keilah and are **r** the threshing floors." 1 Sm 23:1
Will man rob God? Yet you are **r** me. Mal 3:8
are cursed with a curse, for you are **r** me, Mal 3:9

ROBE (53)
And he made him a **r** of many colors. Gn 37:3
his brothers, they stripped him of his **r**, Gn 37:23
robe, the **r** of many colors that he wore. Gn 37:23
they took Joseph's **r** and slaughtered a Gn 37:31
a goat and dipped the **r** in the blood. Gn 37:31
And they sent the **r** of many colors and Gn 37:32
whether it is your son's **r** or not." Gn 37:32
identified it and said, "It is my son's **r**. Gn 37:33
a breastpiece, an ephod, a **r**, a coat of Ex 28:4
"You shall make the **r** of the ephod all Ex 28:31
pomegranate, around the hem of the **r**. Ex 28:34
on Aaron the coat and the **r** of the ephod, Ex 29:5
He also made the **r** of the ephod woven Ex 39:22
and the opening of the **r** in it was like Ex 39:23
hem of the **r** they made pomegranates Ex 39:24
all around the hem of the **r**, Ex 39:25
the hem of the **r** for ministering, Ex 39:26
clothed him with the **r** and put the ephod Lv 8:7
make for him a little **r** and take it to 1 Sm 2:19
go away, Saul seized the skirt of his **r**, 1 Sm 15:27
stripped himself of the **r** that was on 1 Sm 18:4
stealthily cut off a corner of Saul's **r**. 1 Sm 24:4
he had cut off a corner of Saul's **r**. 1 Sm 24:5
see the corner of your **r** in my hand. 1 Sm 24:11
the corner of your **r** and did not kill 1 Sm 24:11
is wrapped in a **r**." And Saul knew 1 Sm 28:14
was wearing a long **r** with sleeves, 2 Sm 13:18
and tore the long **r** that she wore. 2 Sm 13:19
was clothed with a **r** of fine linen, 1 Chr 15:27
golden crown and a **r** of fine linen and Est 8:15
arose and tore his **r** and shaved his head Jb 1:20
my justice was like a **r** and a turban. Jb 29:14
You will change them like a **r**, and Ps 102:26
and instead of a rich **r**, a skirt of Is 3:24
up; and the train of his **r** filled the temple. Is 6:1
and I will clothe him with your **r**, and Is 22:21
flour, put off your veil, strip off your **r**, Is 47:2
covered me with the **r** of righteousness, Is 61:10
and bind them in the skirts of your **r**. Ezk 5:3
he arose from his throne, removed his **r**, Jon 3:6
you strip the rich **r** from those who pass Mi 2:8
tongue shall take hold of the **r** of a Jew, Zec 8:23
him and put a scarlet **r** on him, Mt 27:28
stripped him of the **r** and put his own Mt 27:31
on the right side, dressed in a white **r**, Mk 16:5
his servants, 'Bring quickly the best **r**, Lk 15:22
his head and arrayed him in a purple **r**. Jn 19:2
the crown of thorns and the purple **r**. Jn 19:5
like a **r** you will roll them up, like a Heb 1:12
clothed with a long **r** and with a golden Rv 1:13
were each given a white **r** and told to rest Rv 6:11
He is clothed in a **r** dipped in blood, and Rv 19:13
On his **r** and on his thigh he has a Rv 19:16

ROBED (2)
The LORD reigns; he is **r** in majesty; the Ps 93:1
he is robed in majesty; the LORD is **r**; Ps 93:1

ROBES (26)
on their thrones, arrayed in their **r**, 1 Kgs 22:10
but you wear your **r**." And the king 1 Kgs 22:30
on their thrones, arrayed in their **r**. 2 Chr 18:9
but you wear your **r**." And the king 2 Chr 18:29
Esther put on her royal **r** and stood in the Est 5:1
let royal **r** be brought, which the king Est 6:8
And let the **r** and the horse be handed Est 6:9
take the **r** and the horse, as you have Est 6:10
So Haman took the **r** and the horse, and Est 6:11
of the king in royal **r** of blue and white, Est 8:15
and they tore their **r** and sprinkled dust Jb 2:12
your **r** are all fragrant with myrrh and Ps 45:8
chamber, with **r** interwoven with gold. Ps 45:13
In many-colored **r** she is led to the king, Ps 45:14
running down on the collar of his **r**! Ps 133:2
the festal **r**, the mantles, the cloaks, and Is 3:22
and remove their **r** and strip off Ezk 26:16
Then the high priest tore his **r** and said, Mt 26:65
around in long **r** and like greetings Mk 12:38
who like to walk around in long **r**, Lk 20:46
two men stood by them in white **r**, Acts 1:10
day Herod put on his royal **r**, Acts 12:21
and before the Lamb, clothed in white **r**, Rv 7:9
"Who are these, clothed in white **r**, Rv 7:13
have washed their **r** and made them Rv 7:14
Blessed are those who wash their **r**, so Rv 22:14

ROBS (2)
poor and needy from him who **r** him?" Ps 35:10
Whoever **r** his father or his mother Prv 28:24

ROCK (124)
stand before you there on the **r** at Horeb, Ex 17:6
rock at Horeb, and you shall strike the **r**, Ex 17:6
by me where you shall stand on the **r**, Ex 33:21
by I will put you in a cleft of the **r**, Ex 33:22
And the **r** badger, because it chews the Lv 11:5
and tell the **r** before their eyes to yield Nm 20:8
water out of the **r** for them and give Nm 20:8
the assembly together before the **r**, Nm 20:10
we bring water for you out of this **r**?" Nm 20:10
hand and struck the **r** with his staff Nm 20:11
place, and your nest is set in the **r**. Nm 24:21
brought you water out of the flinty **r**, Dt 8:15
the camel, the hare, and the **r** badger, Dt 14:7
"The **R**, his work is perfect, for all his Dt 32:4
he suckled him with honey out of the **r**, Dt 32:13
of the rock, and oil out of the flinty **r**. Dt 32:13
and scoffed at the **R** of his salvation. Dt 32:15
were unmindful of the **R** that bore you, Dt 32:18
to flight, unless their **R** had sold them, Dt 32:30
For their **r** is not as our Rock; our Dt 32:31
For their rock is not as our **R**; our Dt 32:31
gods, the **r** in which they took refuge, Dt 32:37
cakes, and put them on this **r**, Jgs 6:20
sprang up from the **r** and consumed the Jgs 6:21
They killed Oreb at the **r** of Oreb, and Jgs 7:25
and offered it on the **r** to the LORD, Jgs 13:19
and stayed in the cleft of the **r** of Etam. Jgs 15:8
went down to the cleft of the **r** of Etam, Jgs 15:11
ropes and brought him up from the **r**. Jgs 15:13
the wilderness to the **r** of Rimmon. Jgs 20:45
the wilderness to the **r** of Rimmon and Jgs 20:47
and remained at the **r** of Rimmon four Jgs 20:47
who were at the **r** of Rimmon and Jgs 21:13
besides you; there is no **r** like our God. 1 Sm 2:2
went down to the **r** and lived in the 1 Sm 23:25
that place was called the **R** of Escape. 1 Sm 23:28
and spread it for herself on the **r**, 2 Sm 21:10
"The LORD is my **r** and my fortress 2 Sm 22:2
my God, my **r**, in whom I take refuge, 2 Sm 22:3
And who is a **r**, except our God? 2 Sm 22:32
"The LORD lives, and blessed be my **r**, 2 Sm 22:47
be my God, the **r** of my salvation, 2 Sm 22:47
spoken; the **R** of Israel has said to me: 2 Sm 23:3
went down to the **r** to David at the 1 Chr 11:15
the top of a **r** and threw them down 2 Chr 25:12
them down from the top of the **r**, 2 Chr 25:12
for them out of the **r** for their thirst, Neh 9:15
and the **r** is removed from its place; Jb 14:18
you, or the **r** be removed out of its place? Jb 18:4
lead they were engraved in the **r** forever! Jb 19:24
and cling to the **r** for lack of shelter. Jb 24:8

to the flinty **r** and overturns mountains Jb 28:9
and the **r** poured out for me streams of Jb 29:6
On the **r** he dwells and makes his home, Jb 39:28
The LORD is my **r** and my fortress and Ps 18:2
fortress and my deliverer, my God, my **r**, Ps 18:2
LORD? And who is a **r**, except our God? Ps 18:31
The LORD lives, and blessed be my **r**, Ps 18:46
sight, O LORD, my **r** and my redeemer. Ps 19:14
of his tent; he will lift me high upon a **r**. Ps 27:5
To you, O LORD, I call; my **r**, be not deaf Ps 28:1
Be a **r** of refuge for me, a strong fortress Ps 31:2
For you are my **r** and my fortress; and Ps 31:3
of the miry bog, and set my feet upon a **r**, Ps 40:2
I say to God, my **r**: "Why have you Ps 42:9
Lead me to the **r** that is higher than I, Ps 61:2
He only is my **r** and my salvation, my Ps 62:2
He only is my **r** and my salvation, my Ps 62:6
glory; my mighty **r**, my refuge is God. Ps 62:7
Be to me a **r** of refuge, to which I may Ps 71:3
me, for you are my **r** and my fortress. Ps 71:3
come out of the **r** and caused waters to Ps 78:16
He struck the **r** so that water gushed out Ps 78:20
They remembered that God was their **r**, Ps 78:35
with honey from the **r** I would satisfy Ps 81:16
my God, and the **R** of my salvation.' Ps 89:26
he is my **r**, and there is no Ps 92:15
and my God the **r** of my refuge. Ps 94:22
a joyful noise to the **r** of our salvation! Ps 95:1
rocks are a refuge for the **r** badgers. Ps 104:18
He opened the **r**, and water gushed out; Ps 105:41
who turns the **r** into a pool of water, the Ps 114:8
ones and dashes them against the **r**! Ps 137:9
Blessed be the LORD, my **r**, who trains Ps 144:1
in the sky, the way of a serpent on a **r**, Prv 30:19
the **r** badgers are a people not mighty, Prv 30:26
O my dove, in the clefts of the **r**, in the Sg 2:14
Enter into the **r** and hide in the dust from Is 2:10
of offense and a **r** of stumbling to both Is 8:14
when he struck Midian at the **r** of Oreb. Is 10:26
not remembered the **R** of your refuge; Is 17:10
carve a dwelling for yourself in the **r**? Is 22:16
for the LORD GOD is an everlasting **r**. Is 26:4
mountain of the LORD, to the **R** of Israel. Is 30:29
His **r** shall pass away in terror, and his Is 31:9
like the shade of a great **r** in a weary land. Is 32:2
me? There is no **R**; I know not any." Is 44:8
he made water flow for them from the **r**; Is 48:21
he split the **r** and the water gushed out. Is 48:21
look to the **r** from which you were hewn, Is 51:1
They have made their faces harder than **r**; Jer 5:3
and hide it there in a cleft of the **r**." Jer 13:4
of the valley, O **r** of the plain, Jer 21:13
a hammer that breaks the **r** in pieces? Jer 23:29
"Leave the cities, and dwell in the **r**, O Jer 48:28
heart, you who live in the clefts of the **r**, Jer 49:16
is in her midst; she put it on the bare **r**; Ezk 24:7
have set on the bare **r** the blood she has Ezk 24:8
soil from her and make her a bare **r**. Ezk 26:4
I will make you a bare **r**. You shall be Ezk 26:14
you, you who live in the clefts of the **r**, Ob 1:3
them as a judgment, and you, O **R**, Hab 1:12
a wise man who built his house on the **r**. Mt 7:24
because it had been founded on the **r**. Mt 7:25
and on this **r** I will build my church, Mt 16:18
new tomb, which he had cut in the **r**. Mt 27:60
a tomb that had been cut out of the **r**. Mk 15:46
deep and laid the foundation on the **r**. Lk 6:48
And some fell on the **r**, and as it grew up, Lk 8:6
And the ones on the **r** are those who, Lk 8:13
stone of stumbling, and a **r** of offense; Rom 9:33
from the spiritual **R** that followed 1 Cor 10:4
followed them, and the **R** was Christ. 1 Cor 10:4
and a **r** of offense." They stumble 1 Pt 2:8

ROCKED (2)
"Then the earth reeled and **r**; the 2 Sm 22:8
Then the earth reeled and **r**; the Ps 18:7

ROCKS (20)
in holes and in **r** and in tombs and 1 Sm 13:6
his men in front of the Wildgoats' **R**. 1 Sm 24:2
broke in pieces the **r** before the LORD, 1 Kgs 19:11
He cuts out channels in the **r**, and his Jb 28:10
dwell, in holes of the earth and of the **r**. Jb 30:6
He split **r** in the wilderness and gave Ps 78:15
the **r** are a refuge for the rock badgers. Ps 104:18
enter the caves of the **r** and the holes of Is 2:19
enter the caverns of the **r** and the clefts of Is 2:21
the steep ravines, and in the clefts of the **r**, Is 7:19
place of defense will be the fortresses of **r**; Is 33:16
in the valleys, under the clefts of the **r**? Is 57:5
they enter thickets; they climb among **r**; Jer 4:29
every hill, and out of the clefts of the **r**. Jer 16:16
Do horses run on **r**? Does one plow Am 6:12
and the **r** are broken into pieces by him. Na 1:6
the earth shook, and the **r** were split. Mt 27:51
fearing that we might run on the **r**, Acts 27:29
and among the **r** of the mountains, Rv 6:15
calling to the mountains and **r**, "Fall on Rv 6:16

ROCKY (7)
there was a **r** crag on the one side and 1 Sm 14:4
the one side and a **r** crag on the other 1 Sm 14:4
his home, on the **r** crag and stronghold. Jb 39:28
Other seeds fell on **r** ground, where they Mt 13:5
As for what was sown on **r** ground, this Mt 13:20
Other seed fell on **r** ground, where it did Mk 4:5
these are the ones sown on **r** ground: Mk 4:16

ROD (39)
with a **r** and the slave dies under his Ex 21:20
will discipline him with the **r** of men, 2 Sm 7:14
Let him take his **r** away from me, and let Jb 9:34
from fear, and no **r** of God is upon them. Jb 21:9
break them with a **r** of iron and dash Ps 2:9
your **r** and your staff, they comfort me. Ps 23:4
transgression with the **r** and their Ps 89:32
but a **r** is for the back of him who Prv 10:13
Whoever spares the **r** hates his son, Prv 13:24
mouth of a fool comes a **r** for his back, Prv 14:3
calamity, and the **r** of his fury will fail. Prv 22:8
but the **r** of discipline drives it far Prv 22:15
if you strike him with a **r**, he will not Prv 23:13
If you strike him with the **r**, you will Prv 23:14
donkey, and a **r** for the back of fools. Prv 26:3
The **r** and reproof give wisdom, but a Prv 29:15
staff for his shoulder, the **r** of his oppressor, Is 9:4
Ah, Assyria, the **r** of my anger; the staff in Is 10:5
As if a **r** should wield him who lifts it, or Is 10:15
they strike with the **r** and lift up their Is 10:24
strike the earth with the **r** of his mouth, Is 11:4
that the **r** that struck you is broken, Is 14:29
out with a stick, and cumin with a **r**. Is 28:27
of the LORD, when he strikes with his **r**. Is 30:31
seen affliction under the **r** of his wrath; Lam 3:1
doom has come; the **r** has blossomed; Ezk 7:10
has grown up into a **r** of wickedness. Ezk 7:11
I will make you pass under the **r**, and I Ezk 20:37
You have despised the **r**, my son, with Ezk 21:10
if you despise the **r**?" declares the Lord Ezk 21:13
with a **r** they strike the judge of Israel on Mi 5:1
"Hear of the **r** and of him who appointed Mi 6:9
Shall I come to you with a **r**, or with 1 Cor 4:21
and he will rule them with a **r** of iron, as Rv 2:27
I was given a measuring **r** like a staff, Rv 11:1
is to rule all the nations with a **r** of iron, Rv 12:5
and he will rule them with a **r** of iron. Rv 19:15
me had a measuring **r** of gold to Rv 21:15
And he measured the city with his **r**, Rv 21:16

RODANIM (1)
Elishah, Tarshish, Kittim, and **R**. 1 Chr 1:7

RODE (13)
women arose and **r** on the camels Gn 24:61
had thirty sons who **r** on thirty donkeys, Jgs 10:4
grandsons, who **r** on seventy donkeys, Jgs 12:14
And as she **r** on the donkey and 1 Sm 25:20
He **r** on a cherub and flew; he was 2 Sm 22:11
And Ahab **r** and went to Jezreel. 1 Kgs 18:45
when you and I **r** side by side behind 2 Kgs 9:25
with me but the one on which I **r**. Neh 2:12
in the king's service, **r** out hurriedly, Est 8:14
He **r** on a cherub and flew; he came Ps 18:10
the sea, when you **r** on your horses, Hab 3:8
And as he **r** along, they spread their Lk 19:36
in my vision and those who **r** them: Rv 9:17

RODS (4)
and purple to silver **r** and marble pillars, Est 1:6
His arms are **r** of gold, set with jewels. His Sg 5:14
and gave orders to beat them with **r**. Acts 16:22
Three times I was beaten with **r**. 2 Cor 11:25

ROEBUCK (1)
the deer, the gazelle, the **r**, the wild goat, Dt 14:5

ROEBUCKS (1)
deer, gazelles, **r**, and fattened fowl. 1 Kgs 4:23

ROGELIM (2)
and Barzillai the Gileadite from **R**, 2 Sm 17:27
the Gileadite had come down from **R**, 2 Sm 19:31

ROHGAH (1)
his brother: **R**, Jehubbah, and Aram. 1 Chr 7:34

ROLL (13)
the shepherds would **r** the stone from Gn 29:3
"**R** large stones against the mouth of Jos 10:18
r a great stone to me here." 1 Sm 14:33
they come; amid the crash they **r** on. Jb 30:14
and they **r** upward in a column of smoke. Is 9:18
rot away, and the skies **r** up like a scroll. Is 34:4
people, put on sackcloth, and **r** in ashes; Jer 6:26
shepherds, and cry out, and **r** in ashes, Jer 25:34
you, and **r** you down from the crags, Jer 51:25
But let justice **r** down like waters, and Am 5:24
in Beth-le-aphrah **r** yourselves in the Mi 1:10
"Who will **r** away the stone for us from Mk 16:3
like a robe you will **r** them up, like a Heb 1:12

ROLLED (15)
and the stone is **r** from the mouth of Gn 29:8
Jacob came near and **r** the stone from Gn 29:10
"Today I have **r** away the reproach of Jos 5:9
took his cloak and **r** it up and struck 2 Kgs 2:8
tumult and every garment **r** in blood will Is 9:5
sledge, nor is a cart wheel **r** over cumin, Is 28:27
tent; like a weaver I have **r** up my life; Is 38:12
And he **r** a great stone to the entrance Mt 27:60
heaven and came and **r** back the stone Mt 28:2
and he fell on the ground and **r** about, Mk 9:20
And he **r** a stone against the entrance Mk 15:46
that the stone had been **r** back—it was Mk 16:4
And he **r** up the scroll and gave it back Lk 4:20
they found the stone **r** away from the Lk 24:2
vanished like a scroll that is being **r** up, Rv 6:14

ROLLING (1)
will come back on him who starts it **r**. Prv 26:27

ROMAMTI-EZER (2)
Hanani, Eliathah, Giddalti, and **R**, 1 Chr 25:4
to the twenty-fourth, to **R**, his sons 1 Chr 25:31

ROMAN (8)
district of Macedonia and a **R** colony. Acts 16:12
men who are **R** citizens, Acts 16:37
they heard that they were **R** citizens. Acts 16:38
who is a **R** citizen and Acts 22:25
to do? For this man is a **R** citizen." Acts 22:26
me, are you a **R** citizen?" And he said, Acts 22:27
that Paul was a **R** citizen and that he Acts 22:29
learned that he was a **R** citizen. Acts 23:27

ROMANS (4)
and the **R** will come and take away both Jn 11:48
lawful for us as **R** to accept or Acts 16:21
the custom of the **R** to give up anyone Acts 25:16
Jerusalem into the hands of the **R**. Acts 28:17

ROME (9)
to Cyrene, and visitors from **R**, Acts 2:10
commanded all the Jews to leave **R**. Acts 18:2
I have been there, I must also see **R**." Acts 19:21
so you must testify also in **R**." Acts 23:11
for seven days. And so we came to **R**. Acts 28:14
And when we came into **R**, Paul was Acts 28:16
To all those in **R** who are loved by God Rom 1:7
the gospel to you also who are in **R**. Rom 1:15
when he arrived in **R** he searched for 2 Tm 1:17

ROOF (32)
Make a **r** for the ark, and finish it to a Gn 6:16
have come under the shelter of my **r**." Gn 19:8
you shall make a parapet for your **r**, Dt 22:8
them up to the **r** and hid them with Jos 2:6
of flax that she had laid in order on the **r**. Jos 2:6
lay down, she came up to them on the **r** Jos 2:8
was sitting alone in his cool **r** chamber. Jgs 3:20
the doors of the **r** chamber behind him Jgs 3:23
the doors of the **r** chamber were locked, Jgs 3:24
did not open the doors of the **r** chamber, Jgs 3:25
in, and they went up to the **r** of the tower. Jgs 9:51
and on the **r** there were about 3,000 Jgs 16:27
a bed was spread for Saul on the **r**, 1 Sm 9:25
dawn Samuel called to Saul on the **r**, 1 Sm 9:26
was walking on the **r** of the king's 2 Sm 11:2
he saw from the **r** a woman bathing; 2 Sm 11:2
pitched a tent for Absalom on the **r**. 2 Sm 16:22
went up to the **r** of the gate by 2 Sm 18:24
small room on the **r** with walls and 2 Kgs 4:10
the altars on the **r** of the upper 2 Kgs 23:12
booths for themselves, each on his **r**, Neh 8:16
tongue stuck to the **r** of their mouth. Jb 29:10
my tongue stick to the **r** of my mouth, Ps 137:6
Through sloth the **r** sinks in, and Eccl 10:18
infant sticks to the **r** of its mouth for Lam 4:4
tongue cling to the **r** of your mouth, Ezk 3:26
and raise a **r** of shields against you. Ezk 26:8
was walking on the **r** of the royal palace Dn 4:29
not worthy to have you come under my **r**, Mt 8:8
crowd, they removed the **r** above him, Mk 2:4
they went up on the **r** and let him down Lk 5:19
not worthy to have you come under my **r**. Lk 7:6

ROOFED (1)
Bethesda, which has five **r** colonnades. Jn 5:2

ROOFS (3)
houses on whose **r** offerings have been Jer 19:13
houses on whose **r** offerings have been Jer 32:29
who bow down on the **r** to the host of the Zep 1:5

ROOM (33)
Is there **r** in your father's house for us Gn 24:23
and fodder, and **r** to spend the night." Gn 24:25

"For now the LORD has made **r** for us, Gn 26:22
us make a small **r** on the roof with 2 Kgs 4:10
went into the inner **r** of the house of 2 Kgs 10:25
and of the **r** for the mercy seat; 1 Chr 28:11
but there was no **r** for the animal that Neh 2:14
inside the throne **r** opposite the entrance Est 5:1
A man's gift makes **r** for him and Prv 18:16
add field to field, until there is no more **r**, Is 5:8
for me; make **r** for me to dwell in.' Is 49:20
Topheth, because there is no **r** elsewhere. Jer 7:32
in the dark, each in his **r** of pictures? Ezk 8:12
of the one side **r** to the ceiling of Ezk 40:13
went into the inner **r** and measured the Ezk 41:3
And he measured the length of the **r**, Ezk 41:4
above the door, even to the inner **r**, Ezk 41:17
Let the bridegroom leave his **r**, and the Jl 2:16
to Lebanon, till there is no **r** for them. Zec 10:10
go into your **r** and shut the door and pray Mt 6:6
together, so that there was no more **r**, Mk 2:2
Teacher says, Where is my guest **r**, Mk 14:14
a large upper **r** furnished and ready; Mk 14:15
has been done, and still there is **r**.' Lk 14:22
says to you, Where is the guest **r**, Lk 22:11
show you a large upper **r** furnished; Lk 22:12
entered, they went up to the upper **r**, Acts 1:13
washed her, they laid her in an upper **r**. Acts 9:37
arrived, they took him to the upper **r**. Acts 9:39
lamps in the upper **r** where we were Acts 20:8
no longer have any **r** for work in Rom 15:23
Make **r** in your hearts for us. We have 2 Cor 7:2
same time, prepare a guest **r** for me, Phlm 1:22

ROOMS (20)
Make **r** in the ark, and cover it inside Gn 6:14
open flowers, in the inner and outer **r**. 1 Kgs 6:29
with gold in the inner and outer **r**. 1 Kgs 6:30
its houses, its treasuries, its upper **r**, 1 Chr 28:11
by knowledge the **r** are filled with all Prv 24:4
and his upper **r** by injustice, Jer 22:13
a great house with spacious upper **r**,' Jer 22:14
And the side **r**, one reed long and one Ezk 40:7
and the space between the side **r**, five Ezk 40:7
there were three side **r** on either side of Ezk 40:10
There was a barrier before the side **r**, Ezk 40:12
And the side **r** were six cubits on Ezk 40:12
toward the side **r** and toward their Ezk 40:16
Its side **r**, three on either side, and its Ezk 40:21
Its side **r**, its jambs, and its vestibule Ezk 40:29
Its side **r**, its jambs, and its vestibule Ezk 40:33
Its side **r**, its jambs, and its vestibule Ezk 40:36
If they say, 'Look, he is in the inner **r**,' Mt 24:26
whispered in private **r** shall be Lk 12:3
In my Father's house are many **r**. If it Jn 14:2

ROOSTER (13)
the strutting **r**, the he-goat, and a king Prv 30:31
you, this very night, before the **r** crows, Mt 26:34
man." And immediately the **r** crowed. Mt 26:74
the saying of Jesus, "Before the **r** crows, Mt 26:75
very night, before the **r** crows twice, Mk 14:30
out into the gateway and the **r** crowed. Mk 14:68
And immediately the **r** crowed a Mk 14:72
said to him, "Before the **r** crows twice, Mk 14:72
you, Peter, the **r** will not crow this day, Lk 22:34
he was still speaking, the **r** crowed. Lk 22:60
said to him, "Before the **r** crows today, Lk 22:61
the **r** will not crow till you have denied Jn 13:38
again denied it, and at once a **r** crowed. Jn 18:27

ROOT (41)
among you a **r** bearing poisonous and Dt 29:18
From Ephraim their **r** they marched Jgs 5:14
and **r** up Israel out of this good land 1 Kgs 14:15
shall again take **r** downward and 2 Kgs 19:30
I have seen the fool taking **r**, but suddenly Jb 5:3
Though its **r** grow old in the earth, and Jb 14:8
'The **r** of the matter is found in him,' Jb 19:28
it would burn to the **r** all my increase. Jb 31:12
for it; it took deep **r** and filled the land. Ps 80:9
but the **r** of the righteous will never be Prv 12:3
but the **r** of the righteous bears fruit. Prv 12:12
the flame, so their **r** will be as rottenness, Is 5:24
In that day the **r** of Jesse, who shall stand Is 11:10
for from the serpent's **r** will come forth Is 14:29
but I will kill your **r** with famine, and Is 14:30
In days to come Jacob shall take **r**, Israel Is 27:6
shall again take **r** downward and bear Is 37:31
has their stem taken **r** in the earth, Is 40:24
plant, and like a **r** out of dry ground; Is 53:2
You plant them, and they take **r**; they Jer 12:2
Ephraim is stricken; their **r** is dried up; Hos 9:16
he shall take **r** like the trees of Hos 14:5
and I will **r** out your Asherah images Mi 5:14
it will leave them neither **r** nor branch. Mal 4:1
now the axe is laid to the **r** of the trees. Mt 3:10
And since they had no **r**, they withered Mt 13:6
yet he has no **r** in himself, but endures Mt 13:21
gathering the weeds you **r** up the wheat Mt 13:29
it was scorched, and since it had no **r**, Mk 4:6
And they have no **r** in themselves, but Mk 4:17
now the axe is laid to the **r** of the trees. Lk 3:9
But these have no **r**; they believe for a Lk 8:13
is the whole lump, and if the **r** is holy, Rom 11:16
share in the nourishing **r** of the olive Rom 11:17
it is not you who support the **r**, Rom 11:18
the root, but the **r** that supports you. Rom 11:18
Isaiah says, "The **r** of Jesse will come, Rom 15:12
love of money is a **r** of all kinds of 1 Tm 6:10
that no "**r** of bitterness" springs up Heb 12:15
Lion of the tribe of Judah, the **R** of David, Rv 5:5
I am the **r** and the descendant of David, Rv 22:16

ROOTED (6)
eat, and let what grows for me be **r** out. Jb 31:8
in everlasting ruins; their cities you **r** out; Ps 9:6
and the treacherous will be **r** out of it. Prv 2:22
Father has not planted will be **r** up. Mt 15:13
that you, being **r** and grounded in love, Eph 3:17
r and built up in him and established in Col 2:7

ROOTS (21)
His **r** entwine the stone heap; he looks Jb 8:17
His **r** dry up beneath, and his branches Jb 18:16
rock and overturns mountains by the **r**. Jb 28:9
my **r** spread out to the waters, with the Jb 29:19
and the **r** of the broom tree for their food. Jb 30:4
about him and covers the **r** of the sea. Jb 36:30
and a branch from his **r** shall bear fruit. Is 11:1
water, that sends out its **r** by the stream, Jer 17:8
him, and its **r** remained where it stood. Ezk 17:6
this vine bent its **r** toward him and shot Ezk 17:7
he not pull up its **r** and cut off its fruit, Ezk 17:9
arm or many people to pull it from its **r**. Ezk 17:9
for its **r** went down to abundant waters. Ezk 31:7
But leave the stump of its **r** in the earth, Dn 4:15
but leave the stump of its **r** in the earth, Dn 4:23
to leave the stump of the **r** of the tree, Dn 4:26
the first horns were plucked up by the **r**. Dn 7:8
a branch from her **r** one shall arise in Dn 11:7
his fruit above and his **r** beneath. Am 2:9
at the **r** of the mountains. I went down to Jon 2:6
saw the fig tree withered away to its **r**. Mk 11:20

ROPE (4)
them down by a **r** through the window, Jos 2:15
A **r** is hidden for him in the ground, a Jb 18:10
Can you put a **r** in his nose or pierce his Jb 41:2
be rottenness; and instead of a belt, a **r**; Is 3:24

ROPES (16)
him with two new **r** and brought him Jgs 15:13
and the **r** that were on his arms Jgs 15:14
bind me with new **r** that have not been Jgs 16:11
So Delilah took new **r** and bound him Jgs 16:12
But he snapped the **r** off his arms like a Jgs 16:12
all Israel will bring **r** to that city, 2 Sm 17:13
our waists and **r** on our heads 1 Kgs 20:31
their waists and put **r** on their heads 1 Kgs 20:32
Can you bind him in the furrow with **r**, Jb 39:10
of falsehood, who draw sin as with cart **r**, Is 5:18
of the guard, letting Jeremiah down by **r**. Jer 38:6
let down to Jeremiah in the cistern by **r**. Jer 38:11
armpits and the **r**." Jeremiah did so. Jer 38:12
drew Jeremiah up with **r** and lifted him Jer 38:13
soldiers cut away the **r** of the ship's Acts 27:32
time loosening the **r** that tied the Acts 27:40

ROSE (155)
Cain **r** up against his brother Abel and Gn 4:8
up the ark, and it **r** high above the earth. Gn 7:17
he **r** to meet them and bowed himself Gn 19:1
So Abimelech **r** early in the morning Gn 20:8
So Abraham **r** early in the morning Gn 21:14
of his army **r** up and returned Gn 21:32
So Abraham **r** early in the morning, Gn 22:3
And Abraham **r** up from before his Gn 23:3
Abraham **r** and bowed to the Hittites, Gn 23:7
ate and drank and **r** and went his way. Gn 25:34
the morning they **r** early and Gn 26:31
The sun **r** upon him as he passed Gn 32:31
and all his daughters **r** up to comfort Gn 37:35
And Pharaoh **r** up in the night, he and Ex 12:30
He **r** early in the morning and built an Ex 24:4
So Moses **r** with his assistant Joshua, Ex 24:13
And they **r** up early the next day and Ex 32:6
down to eat and drink and **r** up to play. Ex 32:6
And he **r** early in the morning and went Ex 34:4
And the people **r** all that day and all Nm 11:32
And they **r** early in the morning and Nm 14:40
And they **r** up before Moses, with a Nm 16:2
Then Moses **r** and went to Dathan Nm 16:25
So Balaam **r** in the morning and said Nm 22:13
the princes of Moab **r** and went to Nm 22:14
So Balaam **r** in the morning and Nm 22:21
Then Balaam **r** and went back to his Nm 24:25
he **r** and left the congregation and took Nm 25:7
Then Joshua **r** early in the morning and Jos 3:1
from above stood and **r** up in a heap Jos 3:16
Then Joshua **r** early in the morning, Jos 6:12
On the seventh day they **r** early, at the Jos 6:15
So Joshua **r** early in the morning and Jos 7:16
men in the ambush **r** quickly out of Jos 8:19
men of the town **r** early in the morning, Jgs 6:28
When he **r** early next morning and Jgs 6:38
who were with him **r** early and encamped Jgs 7:1
who were with him **r** up by night and Jgs 9:34
who were with him **r** from the ambush. Jgs 9:35
So he **r** against them and killed them. Jgs 9:43
And when the man **r** up to go, his Jgs 19:7
and his servant **r** up to depart, Jgs 19:9
He **r** up and departed and arrived Jgs 19:10
And her master **r** up in the morning, Jgs 19:27
and the man **r** up and went away to his Jgs 19:28
the leaders of Gibeah **r** against me and Jgs 20:5
the people of Israel **r** in the morning Jgs 20:19
all the men of Israel **r** up out of their Jgs 20:33
next day the people **r** early and built Jgs 21:4
When she **r** to glean, Boaz instructed his Ru 2:15
eaten and drunk in Shiloh, Hannah **r**. 1 Sm 1:9
They **r** early in the morning and 1 Sm 1:19
the people of Ashdod **r** early the next 1 Sm 5:3
But when they **r** early on the next 1 Sm 5:4
The one crag **r** on the north in front 1 Sm 14:5
And Samuel **r** early to meet Saul in 1 Sm 15:12
And Samuel **r** up and went to 1 Sm 16:13
And David **r** early in the morning 1 Sm 17:20
of Israel and Judah **r** with a shout 1 Sm 17:52
And Jonathan **r** from the table in 1 Sm 20:34
David **r** from beside the stone heap 1 Sm 20:41
forever.'" And he **r** and departed, 1 Sm 20:42
And David **r** and fled that day from 1 Sm 21:10
son, **r** and went to David at Horesh, 1 Sm 23:16
And Saul **r** up and left the cave and 1 Sm 24:7
Then David **r** and went down to the 1 Sm 25:1
And she **r** and bowed with her face to 1 Sm 25:41
Abigail hurried and **r** and mounted 1 Sm 25:42
Then David **r** and came to the place 1 Sm 26:5
Then they **r** and went away that 1 Sm 28:25
hand of all who **r** up against you." 2 Sm 18:31
me above those who **r** against me; 2 Sm 22:49
He **r** and struck down the Philistines 2 Sm 23:10
guests of Adonijah trembled and **r**, 1 Kgs 1:49
And the king **r** to meet her and bowed 1 Kgs 2:19
When I **r** in the morning to nurse my 1 Kgs 3:21
And when they **r** early in the 2 Kgs 3:22
the Israelites **r** and struck the 2 Kgs 3:24
the man of God **r** early in the 2 Kgs 6:15
And the king **r** in the night and said 2 Kgs 7:12
with all his chariots and **r** by night, 2 Kgs 8:21
Then King David **r** to his feet and 1 Chr 28:2
r up and rebelled against his lord, 2 Chr 13:6
And they **r** early in the morning 2 Chr 20:20
Ammon and Moab **r** against the 2 Chr 20:23
and he **r** by night and struck the 2 Chr 21:9
mentioned by name **r** and took the 2 Chr 28:15
Hezekiah the king **r** early and 2 Chr 29:20
of the LORD **r** against his people, 2 Chr 36:16
Then **r** up the heads of the fathers' Ezr 1:5
the evening sacrifice I **r** from my fasting, Ezr 9:5
Eliashib the high priest **r** up with his Neh 3:1
that he neither **r** nor trembled before Est 5:9
Esther **r** and stood before the king. And Est 8:5
and withdrew, and the aged **r** and stood; Jb 29:8
me above those who **r** against me; Ps 18:48
Jacob; his anger **r** against Israel, Ps 78:21
the anger of God **r** against them, and he Ps 78:31
The mountains **r**, the valleys sank Ps 104:8
on our side when people **r** up against us, Ps 124:2
I am a **r** of Sharon, a lily of the valleys. Sg 2:1
ten men with him **r** up and struck down Jer 41:2
the living creatures **r** from the earth, Ezk 1:19
rose from the earth, the wheels **r**. Ezk 1:19
went, and the wheels **r** along with them, Ezk 1:20
stood; and when those **r** from the earth, Ezk 1:21
the earth, the wheels **r** along with them, Ezk 1:21
was astonished and **r** up in haste. Dn 3:24
Then I **r** and went about the king's Dn 8:27
But Jonah **r** to flee to Tarshish from the Jon 1:3
When the sun **r**, God appointed a Jon 4:8
saw his star when it **r** and have come to Mt 2:2
had seen when it **r** went before them until Mt 2:9
And he **r** and took the child and his Mt 2:14
And he **r** and took the child and his Mt 2:21
her, and she **r** and began to serve him. Mt 8:15
little faith?" Then he **r** and rebuked the Mt 8:26
And he **r** and went home. Mt 9:7
"Follow me." And he **r** and followed him. Mt 9:9
And Jesus **r** and followed him, with his Mt 9:19
but when the sun **r** they were scorched. Mt 13:6
all those virgins **r** and trimmed their Mt 25:7

And he **r** and immediately picked up Mk 2:12
me." And he **r** and followed him. Mk 2:14
And when the sun **r** it was scorched, and Mk 4:6
[[Now when he **r** early on the first day Mk 16:9
And they **r** up and drove him out of the Lk 4:29
and immediately she **r** and began to Lk 4:39
And immediately he **r** up before them Lk 5:25
everything, he **r** and followed him. Lk 5:28
and stand here." And he **r** and stood there. Lk 6:8
And when he **r** from prayer, he came to Lk 22:45
But Peter **r** and ran to the tomb; Lk 24:12
And they **r** that same hour and Lk 24:33
heard it, she **r** quickly and went to him. Jn 11:29
r from supper. He laid aside his outer Jn 13:4
The young men **r** and wrapped him up Acts 5:6
But the high priest **r** up, and all who Acts 5:17
For before these days Theudas **r** up, Acts 5:36
him Judas the Galilean **r** up in the Acts 5:37
Asia, **r** up and disputed with Stephen. Acts 6:9
And he **r** and went. And there was an Acts 8:27
Saul **r** from the ground, and although Acts 9:8
his sight. Then he **r** and was baptized; Acts 9:18
your bed." And immediately he **r**. Acts 9:34
So Peter **r** and went with them. And Acts 9:39
The next day he **r** and went away Acts 10:23
with him after he **r** from the dead. Acts 10:41
him, he **r** up and entered the city, Acts 14:20
party of the Pharisees **r** up and said, Acts 15:5
Then the king **r**, and the governor Acts 26:30
to eat and drink and **r** up to play." 1 Cor 10:7
believe that Jesus died and **r** again, 1 Thes 4:14
r before God from the hand of the angel. Rv 8:4
and from the shaft **r** smoke like the Rv 9:2

ROSH (1)
Gera, Naaman, Ehi, **R**, Muppim, Gn 46:21

ROT (15)
whether the **r** is on the back or on the Lv 13:55
who are left shall **r** away in your Lv 26:39
fathers they shall **r** away like them. Lv 26:39
but the name of the wicked will **r**. Prv 10:7
the flesh, but envy makes the bones **r**. Prv 14:30
and dry up, reeds and rushes will **r** away. Is 19:6
All the host of heaven shall **r** away, and Is 34:4
an offering chooses wood that will not **r**; Is 40:20
and **r** away because of their Ezk 4:17
but you shall **r** away in your Ezk 24:23
us, and we **r** away because of them. Ezk 33:10
and like dry **r** to the house of Judah. Hos 5:12
their flesh will **r** while they are still Zec 14:12
feet, their eyes will **r** in their sockets, Zec 14:12
their tongues will **r** in their mouths. Zec 14:12

ROTTED (1)
Your riches have **r** and your garments Jas 5:2

ROTTEN (3)
Man wastes away like a **r** thing, like a Jb 13:28
iron as straw, and bronze as **r** wood. Jb 41:27
figs that are so **r** they cannot be eaten. Jer 29:17

ROTTENNESS (4)
brings shame is like **r** in his bones. Prv 12:4
Instead of perfume there will be **r**; and Is 3:24
in the flame, so their root will be as **r**, Is 5:24
at the sound; **r** enters into my bones; Hab 3:16

ROUGH (4)
become level, and the **r** places a plain. Is 40:4
into light, the **r** places into level ground. Is 42:16
and the **r** places shall become level ways, Lk 3:5
The sea became **r** because a strong wind Jn 6:18

ROUGHLY (4)
them like strangers and spoke **r** to them. Gn 42:7
spoke **r** to us and took us to be spies of Gn 42:30
tell me if your father answers you **r**?" 1 Sm 20:10
use entreaties, but the rich answer **r**. Prv 18:23

ROUND (7)
You shall not **r** off the hair on your Lv 19:27
It was **r**, ten cubits from brim to 1 Kgs 7:23
Its opening was **r**, as a pedestal is 1 Kgs 7:31
and its panels were square, not **r**. 1 Kgs 7:31
stand there was a **r** band half a cubit 1 Kgs 7:35
It was **r**, ten cubits from brim to brim, 2 Chr 4:2
Add year to year; let the feasts run their **r**. Is 29:1

ROUNDED (3)
also above the **r** projection which 1 Kgs 7:20
Your **r** thighs are like jewels, the work of a Sg 7:1
Your navel is a **r** bowl that never lacks Sg 7:2

ROUSE (10)
a lion and as a lioness; who dares **r** him? Gn 49:9
and like a lioness; who will **r** him up? Nm 24:9
of the balsam trees, then **r** yourself, 2 Sm 5:24
the day, who are ready to **r** up Leviathan. Jb 3:8
surely then he will **r** himself for you and Jb 8:6
Awake and **r** yourself for my Ps 35:23
are you sleeping, O Lord? **R** yourself! Ps 44:23
R yourself to punish all the nations; Ps 59:5
awakes, O Lord, when you **r** yourself, Ps 73:20
To **r** my wrath, to take vengeance, I Ezk 24:8

ROUSED (5)
will not awake or be **r** out of his sleep. Jb 14:12
before you when once your anger is **r**? Ps 76:7
as in the Valley of Gibeon he will be **r**; Is 28:21
GOD, my wrath will be **r** in my anger. Ezk 38:18
for he has **r** himself from his holy Zec 2:13

ROUSES (3)
When she **r** herself to flee, she laughs at Jb 39:18
it **r** the shades to greet you, all who were Is 14:9
name, who **r** himself to take hold of you; Is 64:7

ROUT (2)
And he put his adversaries to **r**; he put Ps 78:66
them; send out your arrows and **r** them! Ps 144:6

ROUTED (7)
And the LORD **r** Sisera and all his Jgs 4:15
Benjamin said, "They are **r** before us, Jgs 20:32
and they were **r** before Israel. 1 Sm 7:10
Wherever he turned he **r** them. 1 Sm 14:47
them; lightning, and **r** them. 2 Sm 22:15
against Judah, so that they were **r**. 2 Chr 20:22
he flashed forth lightnings and **r** them. Ps 18:14

ROW (13)
A **r** of sardius, topaz, and carbuncle Ex 28:17
and carbuncle shall be the first **r**; Ex 28:17
and the second **r** an emerald, a Ex 28:18
and the third **r** a jacinth, an agate, and Ex 28:19
and the fourth **r** a beryl, an onyx, and a Ex 28:20
A **r** of sardius, topaz, and carbuncle Ex 39:10
topaz, and carbuncle was the first **r**; Ex 39:10
and the second **r**, an emerald, a Ex 39:11
and the third **r**, a jacinth, an agate, and Ex 39:12
and the fourth **r**, a beryl, an onyx, and a Ex 39:13
the forty-five pillars, fifteen in each **r**. 1 Kgs 7:3
to the north **r** of the holy chambers Ezk 46:19
of the four courts was a **r** of masonry, Ezk 46:23

ROWED (2)
the men **r** hard to get back to dry land, Jon 1:13
When they had **r** about three or four Jn 6:19

ROWERS (2)
of Sidon and Arvad were your **r**; Ezk 27:8
"Your **r** have brought you out into the Ezk 27:26

ROWS (16)
You shall set in it four **r** of stones. A Ex 28:17
And they set in it four **r** of stones. A row Ex 39:10
it was built on four **r** of cedar pillars, 1 Kgs 7:2
There were window frames in three **r**, 1 Kgs 7:4
pomegranates in two **r** around the 1 Kgs 7:18
pomegranates in two **r** all around, 1 Kgs 7:20
The gourds were in two **r**, cast with it 1 Kgs 7:24
two **r** of pomegranates for each 1 Kgs 7:42
The gourds were in two **r**, cast with it 2 Chr 4:3
two **r** of pomegranates for each 2 Chr 4:13
among the olive **r** of the wicked they Jb 24:11
His back is made of **r** of shields, shut up Jb 41:15
like the tower of David, built in **r** of stone; Sg 4:4
and put in wheat in **r** and barley in its Is 28:25
"Go up through her vine **r** and destroy, Jer 5:10
at the bottom of the **r** all around. Ezk 46:23

ROYAL (59)
be rich, and he shall yield **r** delicacies. Gn 49:20
was a great city, like one of the **r** cities, Jos 10:2
servant dwell in the **r** city with you?" 1 Sm 27:5
the Ammonites and took the **r** city. 2 Sm 12:26
sons, and all the **r** officials of Judah, 1 Kgs 1:9
Solomon sits on the **r** throne. 1 Kgs 1:46
will establish your **r** throne over Israel 1 Kgs 9:5
He was of the **r** house in Edom. 1 Kgs 11:14
down to visit the **r** princes and the 2 Kgs 10:13
arose and destroyed all the **r** family. 2 Kgs 11:1
as soon as the **r** power was firmly in 2 Kgs 14:5
to confirm his hold on the **r** power. 2 Kgs 15:19
son of Elishama, of the **r** family, 2 Kgs 25:25
I will establish his **r** throne in Israel 1 Chr 22:10
on him such **r** majesty as had 1 Chr 29:25
of the LORD, and a **r** palace for himself. 2 Chr 2:1
the LORD and a **r** palace for himself. 2 Chr 2:12
then I will establish your **r** throne, as 2 Chr 7:18
and destroyed all the **r** family of the 2 Chr 22:10
they set the king on the **r** throne. 2 Chr 23:20
as soon as the **r** power was firmly his, 2 Chr 25:3
"Have we made you a **r** counselor? 2 Chr 25:16
toll, and the **r** revenue will be impaired. Ezr 4:13
be made in the **r** archives there in Ezr 5:17
Let the cost be paid from the **r** treasury. Ezr 6:4
and without delay from the **r** revenue, Ezr 6:8
Ahasuerus sat on his **r** throne in Susa, Est 1:2
the riches of his **r** glory and the splendor Est 1:4
and the **r** wine was lavished according to Est 1:7
Vashti before the king with her **r** crown, Est 1:11
the king, let a **r** order go out from him, Est 1:19
the king give her **r** position to another Est 1:19
He sent letters to all the **r** provinces, to Est 1:22
King Ahasuerus into his **r** palace in the Est 2:16
so that he set the **r** crown on her head Est 2:17
and gave gifts with **r** generosity. Est 2:18
Esther put on her **r** robes and stood in Est 5:1
was sitting on his **r** throne inside the Est 5:1
let **r** robes be brought, which the king Est 6:8
and on whose head a **r** crown is set. Est 6:8
the king's service, bred from the **r** stud, Est 8:10
of the king in **r** robes of blue and Est 8:15
governors and the **r** agents also helped Est 9:3
God, and your righteousness to the **r** son! Ps 72:1
and a **r** diadem in the hand of your God. Is 62:3
son of Elishama, of the **r** family, Jer 41:1
he will spread his **r** canopy over them. Jer 43:10
took one of the **r** offspring and made a Ezk 17:13
both of the **r** family and of the nobility, Dn 1:3
on the roof of the **r** palace of Babylon, Dn 4:29
mighty power as a **r** residence and for Dn 4:30
that in all my **r** dominion people are to Dn 6:26
person to whom **r** majesty has not Dn 11:21
of the LORD and shall bear **r** honor, Zec 6:13
day Herod put on his **r** robes, Acts 12:21
you really fulfill the **r** law according to Jas 2:8
you are a chosen race, a **r** priesthood, 1 Pt 2:9
who have not yet received **r** power, Rv 17:12
and handing over their **r** power to the Rv 17:17

ROYALTY (1)
beautiful and advanced to **r**. Ezk 16:13

RUBBED (2)
water to cleanse you, nor **r** with salt, Ezk 16:4
bald, and every shoulder was **r** bare, Ezk 29:18

RUBBING (1)
heads of grain, **r** them in their hands. Lk 6:1

RUBBISH (2)
revive the stones out of the heaps of **r**, Neh 4:2
loss of all things and count them as **r**, Phil 3:8

RUBBLE (2)
is failing. There is too much **r**. Neh 4:10
fish of the sea, and the **r** with the wicked. Zep 1:3

RUBY (1)
work, fine linen, coral, and **r**. Ezk 27:16

RUDDER (1)
by a very small **r** wherever the will of Jas 3:4

RUDDERS (1)
loosening the ropes that tied the **r**. Acts 27:40

RUDDY (4)
Now he was **r** and had beautiful eyes 1 Sm 16:12
r and handsome in appearance. 1 Sm 17:42
My beloved is radiant and **r**, Sg 5:10
their bodies were more **r** than coral, the Lam 4:7

RUDE (1)
or **r**. It does not insist on its own way; 1 Cor 13:5

RUE (1)
you tithe mint and **r** and every herb, Lk 11:42

RUFUS (2)
the father of Alexander and **R**, Mk 15:21
Greet **R**, chosen in the Lord; also his Rom 16:13

RUG (1)
the tent, and she covered him with a **r**. Jgs 4:18

RUGS (1)
They prepare the table, they spread the **r**, Is 21:5

RUIN (47)
delight in bringing **r** upon you and Dt 28:63
quickly and bring down **r** on us and 2 Sm 15:14
of water and **r** every good piece 2 Kgs 3:19
But they were the **r** of him and of 2 Chr 28:23
the kings of Judah had let go to **r**. 2 Chr 34:11
I have rejoiced at the **r** of him who hated Jb 31:29
hurt speak of **r** and meditate treachery Ps 38:12
r is in its midst; oppression and fraud Ps 55:11
They are brought to **r**, with their own Ps 64:8
slippery places; you make them fall to **r**. Ps 73:18
the way of the wicked he brings to **r**. Ps 146:9
sudden terror or of the **r** of the wicked, Prv 3:25
the brink of utter **r** in the assembled Prv 5:14
but a babbling fool will come to **r**. Prv 10:8
but a babbling fool will come to **r**. Prv 10:10
but the mouth of a fool brings **r** near. Prv 10:14
city; the poverty of the poor is their **r**. Prv 10:15
he who opens wide his lips comes to **r**. Prv 13:3
the way of the treacherous is their **r**. Prv 13:15
A fool's mouth is his **r**, and his lips are Prv 18:7
of many companions may come to **r**, Prv 18:24
When a man's folly brings his way to **r**, Prv 19:3

A foolish son is **r** to his father, and a Prv 19:13
he throws the wicked down to **r**. Prv 21:12
and who knows the **r** that will come Prv 24:22
and a flattering mouth works **r**. Prv 26:28
in the **r** that will come from afar? Is 10:3
her palaces bare, they made her a **r**. Is 23:13
made the city a heap, the fortified city a **r**; Is 25:2
plans wicked schemes to **r** the poor with Is 32:7
and **r** shall come upon you suddenly, of Is 47:11
land shall become a **r** and a waste, Jer 25:11
For Memphis shall become a waste, a **r**, Jer 46:19
For your **r** is vast as the sea; who can Lam 2:13
transgressions, lest iniquity be your **r**. Ezk 18:30
A **r**, ruin, ruin I will make it. This also Ezk 21:27
A ruin, **r**, ruin I will make it. This also Ezk 21:27
A ruin, ruin, **r** I will make it. This also Ezk 21:27
"They shall bring to **r** the pride of Ezk 32:12
without understanding shall come to **r**. Hos 4:14
but are not grieved over the **r** of Joseph! Am 6:6
the people of Judah in the day of their **r**; Ob 1:12
Desolate! Desolation and **r**! Hearts melt Na 2:10
and anguish, a day of **r** and devastation, Zep 1:15
it fell, and the **r** of that house was great." Lk 6:49
in their paths are **r** and misery, Rom 3:16
plunge people into **r** and destruction. 1 Tm 6:9

RUINED (18)
of Egypt the land was **r** by the swarms of Ex 8:24
you not yet understand that Egypt is **r**?" Ex 10:7
king, but without people a prince is **r**. Prv 14:28
they shall repair the **r** cities, the Is 61:4
than eagles—woe to us, for we are **r**! Jer 4:13
Why is the land **r** and laid waste like a Jer 9:12
is heard from Zion: 'How we are **r**! Jer 9:19
ground; he has **r** and broken her bars; Lam 2:9
shall be waste and the high places **r**, Ezk 6:6
so that your altars will be waste and **r**, Ezk 6:6
waste and desolate and **r** cities are now Ezk 36:35
have rebuilt the **r** places and replanted Ezk 36:36
shall rebuild the **r** cities and inhabit Am 9:14
moan bitterly, and say, "We are utterly **r**; Mi 2:4
plundered them and **r** their branches. Na 2:2
has fallen, for the glorious trees are **r**! Zec 11:2
of the shepherds, for their glory is **r**! Zec 11:3
lions, for the thicket of the Jordan is **r**! Zec 11:3

RUINS (46)
Ai and made it forever a heap of **r**, Jos 8:28
this house will become a heap of **r**. 1 Kgs 9:8
turn fortified cities into heaps of **r**, 2 Kgs 19:25
far as Naphtali, in their **r** all around, 2 Chr 34:6
set up the house of our God, to repair its **r**, Ezr 9:9
the place of my fathers' graves, lies in **r**, Neh 2:3
how Jerusalem lies in **r** with its gates Neh 2:17
of the earth who rebuilt **r** for themselves, Jb 3:14
which were ready to become heaps of **r**; Jb 15:28
one in a heap of **r** stretch out his hand, Jb 30:24
enemy came to an end in everlasting **r**; Ps 9:6
Direct your steps to the perpetual **r**; the Ps 74:3
temple; they have laid Jerusalem in **r**. Ps 79:1
you have laid his strongholds in **r**. Ps 89:40
food far from the **r** they inhabit! Ps 109:10
and this heap of **r** shall be under your Is 3:6
nomads shall eat among the **r** of the rich. Is 5:17
to be a city and will become a heap of **r**. Is 17:1
in the city; the gates are battered into **r**. Is 24:12
fortified cities crash into heaps of **r**, Is 37:26
shall be built, and I will raise up their **r**'; Is 44:26
And your ancient **r** shall be rebuilt; you Is 58:12
They shall build up the ancient **r**; they Is 61:4
all our pleasant places have become **r**. Is 64:11
his cities are in **r**, without inhabitant. Jer 2:15
your cities will be **r** without inhabitant. Jer 4:7
its cities were laid in **r** before the LORD, Jer 4:26
I will make Jerusalem a heap of **r**, a lair Jer 9:11
Jerusalem shall become a heap of **r**, Jer 26:18
and Babylon shall become a heap of **r**, Jer 51:37
he has laid in **r** its strongholds, and he Lam 2:5
a garden, laid in **r** his meeting place; Lam 2:6
determined to lay in **r** the wall of the Lam 2:8
have been like jackals among **r**, Ezk 13:4
the world below, among **r** from of old, Ezk 26:20
limb, and your houses shall be laid in **r**. Dn 2:5
from limb, and their houses laid in **r**, Dn 3:29
and raise up its **r** and rebuild it as in Am 9:11
Jerusalem shall become a heap of **r**, and Mi 3:12
off nations; their battlements are in **r**; Zep 3:6
paneled houses, while this house lies in **r**? Hg 1:4
Because of my house that lies in **r**, while Hg 1:9
we will rebuild the **r**," the LORD of hosts Mal 1:4
I will rebuild its **r**, and I will restore it, Acts 15:16
"Bad company **r** good morals." 1 Cor 15:33
does no good, but only **r** the hearers. 2 Tm 2:14

RULE (90)
—the greater light to **r** the day and the Gn 1:16
and the lesser light to **r** the night—and Gn 1:16
to **r** over the day and over the night, and Gn 1:18
your husband, and he shall **r** over you." Gn 3:16
desire is for you, but you must **r** over it." Gn 4:7
Or are you indeed to **r** over us?" So they Gn 37:8
LORD made for them a statute and a **r**, Ex 15:25
be dealt with according to this same **r**. Ex 21:31
for a burnt offering according to the **r**. Lv 5:10
offering and offered it according to the **r**. Lv 9:16
shall have the same **r** for the sojourner Lv 24:22
You shall not **r** over him ruthlessly but Lv 25:43
the people of Israel you shall not **r**, Lv 25:46
He shall not **r** ruthlessly over him in Lv 25:53
Those who hate you shall **r** over you, Lv 26:17
of the Passover and according to its **r**, Nm 9:14
One law and one **r** shall be for you Nm 15:16
its drink offering, according to the **r**, Nm 15:24
for the people of Israel a statute and **r**, Nm 27:11
offering, according to the **r** for them, Nm 29:6
for a statute and **r** for you throughout Nm 35:29
and you shall **r** over many nations, Dt 15:6
nations, but they shall not **r** over you. Dt 15:6
men of Israel said to Gideon, "**R** over us, Jgs 8:22
said to them, "I will not **r** over you, Jgs 8:23
you, and my son will not **r** over you; Jgs 8:23
rule over you; the LORD will **r** over you." Jgs 8:23
of the sons of Jerubbaal **r** over you, Jgs 9:2
rule over you, or that one **r** over you?' Jgs 9:2
a statute and a **r** for Israel from that 1 Sm 30:25
revolted from the **r** of Judah and 2 Kgs 8:20
Edom revolted from the **r** of Judah to 2 Kgs 8:22
not seek him according to the **r**." 1 Chr 15:13
come from you, and you **r** over all. 1 Chr 29:12
accounts of all his **r** and his might 1 Chr 29:30
'You shall not lack a man to **r** Israel.' 2 Chr 7:18
When the **r** of Rehoboam was 2 Chr 12:1
You **r** over all the kingdoms of the 2 Chr 20:6
revolted from the **r** of Judah and 2 Chr 21:8
revolted from the **r** of Judah to 2 Chr 21:10
Libnah also revolted from his **r**, 2 Chr 21:10
had no one able to **r** the kingdom. 2 Chr 22:9
lamb with fire according to the **r**; 2 Chr 35:13
They made these a **r** in Israel; 2 Chr 35:25
offerings by number according to the **r**, Ezr 3:4
a solemn assembly, according to the **r**. Neh 8:18
They **r** over our bodies and over our Neh 9:37
Can you establish their **r** on the earth? Jb 38:33
and the upright shall **r** over them in the Ps 49:14
statute for Israel, a **r** of the God of Jacob. Ps 81:4
You **r** the raging of the sea; when its Ps 89:9
scepter. **R** in the midst of your enemies! Ps 110:2
the sun to **r** over the day, for his Ps 136:8
the moon and stars to **r** over the night, Ps 136:9
by me princes **r**, and nobles, all who Prv 8:16
The hand of the diligent will **r**, while Prv 12:24
who deals wisely will **r** over a son who Prv 17:2
much less for a slave to **r** over princes. Prv 19:10
people rejoice, but when the wicked **r**, Prv 29:2
princes, and infants shall **r** over them. Is 3:4
this heap of ruins shall be under your **r**"; Is 3:6
their oppressors, and women **r** over them. Is 3:12
and **r** over those who oppressed them. Is 14:2
master, and a fierce king will **r** over them, Is 19:4
scoffers, who **r** this people in Jerusalem! Is 28:14
and princes will **r** in justice. Is 32:1
and the priests **r** at their direction; Jer 5:31
of his offspring to **r** over the offspring of Jer 33:26
Slaves **r** over us; there is none to deliver Lam 5:8
will never again **r** over the nations. Ezk 29:15
making you **r** over them all—you are Dn 2:38
bronze, which shall **r** over all the earth. Dn 2:39
who shall **r** with great dominion and do Dn 11:3
shall be stronger than he and shall **r**, Dn 11:5
go up to Mount Zion to **r** Mount Esau, Ob 1:21
then you shall **r** my house and have Zec 3:7
honor, and shall sit and **r** on his throne. Zec 6:13
his **r** shall be from sea to sea, and from Zec 9:10
even he who arises to **r** the Gentiles; Rom 15:12
so that we might share the **r** with you! 1 Cor 4:8
him. This is my **r** in all the churches. 1 Cor 7:17
after destroying every **r** and every 1 Cor 15:24
And as for all who walk by this **r**, peace Gal 6:16
far above all **r** and authority and power Eph 1:21
who is the head of all **r** and authority. Col 2:10
let the peace of Christ **r** in your hearts, Col 3:15
the elders who **r** well be considered 1 Tm 5:17
and he will **r** them with a rod of iron, as Rv 2:27
one who is to **r** all the nations with a rod Rv 12:5
and he will **r** them with a rod of iron. Rv 19:15

RULED (16)
who lived at Heshbon and **r** from Aroer, Jos 12:2
and **r** over Mount Hermon and Salecah Jos 12:5
Abimelech **r** over Israel three years. Jgs 9:22
At that time the Philistines **r** over Israel. Jgs 14:4
days when the judges **r** there was a Ru 1:1
Solomon **r** over all the kingdoms 1 Kgs 4:21
who **r** in Moab and returned to 1 Chr 4:22
And he **r** over all the kings from the 2 Chr 9:26
who **r** over the whole province Beyond Ezr 4:20
those who hated them **r** over them. Ps 106:41
that **r** the nations in anger with Is 14:6
other lords besides you have **r** over us, Is 26:13
like those over whom you have never **r**, Is 63:19
force and harshness you have **r** them. Ezk 34:4
us and against our rulers who **r** us, Dn 9:12
to the authority with which he **r**, Dn 11:4

RULER (60)
of all his house and **r** over all the land of Gn 45:8
and he is **r** over all the land of Egypt." Gn 45:26
revile God, nor curse a **r** of your people. Ex 22:28
When Zebul the **r** of the city heard the Jgs 9:30
appointed him to be **r** over Israel and 1 Kgs 1:35
but I will make him **r** all the days of 1 Kgs 11:34
of Hur, **r** of half the district of Jerusalem, Neh 3:9
r of half the district of Jerusalem, Neh 3:12
r of the district of Beth-haccherem, Neh 3:14
Col-hozeh, **r** of the district of Mizpah, Neh 3:15
r of half the district of Beth-zur, Neh 3:16
r of half the district of Keilah, Neh 3:17
r of half the district of Keilah. Neh 3:18
Ezer the son of Jeshua, **r** of Mizpah, Neh 3:19
son of Ahitub, **r** of the house of God, Neh 11:11
him; the **r** of the peoples set him free; Ps 105:20
of his house and **r** of all his Ps 105:21
Without having any chief, officer, or **r**, Prv 6:7
When you sit down to eat with a **r**, Prv 23:1
With patience a **r** may be persuaded, Prv 25:15
bear is a wicked **r** over a poor people. Prv 28:15
A **r** who lacks understanding is a Prv 28:16
If a **r** listens to falsehood, all his Prv 29:12
Many seek the face of a **r**, but it is Prv 29:26
than the shouting of a **r** among fools. Eccl 9:17
If the anger of the **r** rises against you, Eccl 10:4
it were an error proceeding from the **r**: Eccl 10:5
Send the lamb to the **r** of the land, from Is 16:1
their **r** shall come out from their midst; Jer 30:21
is in the land, and **r** is against ruler. Jer 51:46
is in the land, and ruler is against **r**. Jer 51:46
and made him **r** over the whole Dn 2:48
and shall be the third **r** in the kingdom." Dn 5:7
shall be the third **r** in the kingdom." Dn 5:16
he should be the third **r** in the kingdom. Dn 5:29
He shall become **r** of the treasures of Dn 11:43
I will cut off the **r** from its midst, and Am 2:3
forth for me one who is to be **r** in Israel, Mi 5:2
like crawling things that have no **r**. Hab 1:14
from him every **r**—all of them together. Zec 10:4
you shall come a **r** who will shepherd my Mt 2:6
a **r** came in and knelt before him, Mt 9:18
Jesus said to the **r** of the synagogue, Mk 5:36
to the house of the **r** of the synagogue, Mk 5:38
Jairus, who was a **r** of the synagogue. Lk 8:41
But the **r** of the synagogue, indignant Lk 13:14
dine at the house of a **r** of the Pharisees, Lk 14:1
And a **r** asked him, "Good Teacher, Lk 18:18
named Nicodemus, a **r** of the Jews. Jn 3:1
now will the **r** of this world be cast out. Jn 12:31
you, for the **r** of this world is coming. Jn 14:30
because the **r** of this world is judged. Jn 16:11
who made him **r** over Egypt and over Acts 7:10
'Who made you a **r** and a judge over Acts 7:27
'Who made you a **r** and a judge?' Acts 7:35
God sent as both **r** and redeemer by the Acts 7:35
Crispus, the **r** of the synagogue, Acts 18:8
Sosthenes, the **r** of the synagogue, Acts 18:17
not speak evil of a **r** of your people.'" Acts 23:5
of the dead, and the **r** of kings on earth. Rv 1:5

RULER'S (4)
nor the **r** staff from between his feet, Gn 49:10
Jesus came to the **r** house and saw the Mt 9:23
there came from the **r** house some who Mk 5:35
someone from the **r** house came and Lk 8:49

RULERS (53)
there are five **r** of the Philistines, Jos 13:3
know that the Philistines are **r** over us? Jgs 15:11
them to Samaria, to the **r** of the city, 2 Kgs 10:1
for the **r** of the Philistines took 1 Chr 12:19
sons born who were **r** in their fathers' 1 Chr 26:6
and the **r** take counsel together, Ps 2:2
be wise; be warned, O **r** of the earth. Ps 2:10
Can wicked **r** be allied with you, those Ps 94:20
peoples, princes and all **r** of the earth! Ps 148:11
kings reign, and **r** decree what is just; Prv 8:15
a land transgresses, it has many **r**, Prv 28:2
wine, or for **r** to take strong drink, Prv 31:4
wise man more than ten **r** who are in a Eccl 7:19
the word of the LORD, you **r** of Sodom! Is 1:10
the staff of the wicked, the scepter of **r**, Is 14:5
and makes the **r** of the earth as Is 40:23
he shall trample on **r** as on mortar, as Is 41:25

abhorred by the nation, the servant of **r**: Is 49:7
Their **r** wail," declares the LORD, "and Is 52:5
in dishonor the kingdom and its **r**. Lam 2:2
us and against our **r** who ruled us, Dn 9:12
He shall make them **r** over many and Dn 11:39
to whoring; their **r** dearly love shame. Hos 4:18
hot as an oven, and they devour their **r**. Hos 7:7
Where are all your **r**—those of whom Hos 13:10
you heads of Jacob and **r** of the house of Mi 3:1
the house of Jacob and **r** of the house of Mi 3:9
kings they scoff, and at **r** they laugh. Hab 1:10
by no means least among the **r** of Judah; Mt 2:6
"You know that the **r** of the Gentiles Mt 20:25
came one of the **r** of the synagogue, Mk 5:22
who are considered **r** of the Gentiles Mk 10:42
synagogues and the **r** and the Lk 12:11
chief priests and the **r** and the people, Lk 23:13
by, watching, but the **r** scoffed at him, Lk 23:35
our chief priests and **r** delivered him up Lk 24:20
acted in ignorance, as did also your **r**. Acts 3:17
the next day their **r** and elders and Acts 4:5
said to them, "**R** of the people and elders, Acts 4:8
and the **r** were gathered together, Acts 4:26
the **r** of the synagogue sent a message Acts 13:15
who live in Jerusalem and their **r**, Acts 13:27
by both Gentiles and Jews, with their **r**, Acts 14:5
into the marketplace before the **r**. Acts 16:19
neither death nor life, nor angels nor **r**, Rom 8:38
For **r** are not a terror to good conduct, Rom 13:3
of this age or of the **r** of this age, 1 Cor 2:6
None of the **r** of this age understood 1 Cor 2:8
made known to the **r** and authorities in Eph 3:10
flesh and blood, but against the **r**, Eph 6:12
or dominions or **r** or authorities— Col 1:16
He disarmed the **r** and authorities and Col 2:15
to be submissive to **r** and authorities, Ti 3:1

RULERS' (1)
Its strong stems became **r** scepters; Ezk 19:11

RULES (112)
"Now these are the **r** that you shall set Ex 21:1
all the words of the LORD and all the **r**. Ex 24:3
You shall follow my **r** and keep my Lv 18:4
therefore keep my statutes and my **r**; Lv 18:5
my statutes and my **r** and do none of Lv 18:26
observe all my statutes and all my **r**, Lv 19:37
my statutes and all my **r** and do them, Lv 20:22
and keep my **r** and perform them, Lv 25:18
statutes, and if your soul abhors my **r**, Lv 26:15
they spurned my **r** and their soul Lv 26:43
are the statutes and **r** and laws that the Lv 26:46
statutes and all its **r** you shall keep it." Nm 9:3
of blood, in accordance with these **r**. Nm 35:24
commandments and the **r** that the Nm 36:13
to the statutes and the **r** that I am teaching Dt 4:1
See, I have taught you statutes and **r**, as Dt 4:5
that has statutes and **r** so righteous as all Dt 4:8
at that time to teach you statutes and **r**, Dt 4:14
the testimonies, the statutes, and the **r**, Dt 4:45
the statutes and the **r** that I speak in your Dt 5:1
the statutes and the **r** that you shall Dt 5:31
the statutes and the **r** that the LORD your Dt 6:1
the statutes and the **r** that the LORD our Dt 6:20
the statutes and the **r** that I command Dt 7:11
you listen to these **r** and keep and do Dt 7:12
commandments and his **r** and his Dt 8:11
and keep his charge, his statutes, his **r**, Dt 11:1
the statutes and the **r** that I am setting Dt 11:32
are the statutes and **r** that you shall be Dt 12:1
you to do these statutes and **r**. Dt 26:16
and his commandments and his **r**, Dt 26:17
and his statutes and his **r**, Dt 30:16
shall teach Jacob your **r** and Israel your Dt 33:10
in place statutes and **r** for them at Jos 24:25
For all his **r** were before me, and 2 Sm 22:23
When one **r** justly over men, ruling 2 Sm 23:3
his statutes, his commandments, his **r**, 1 Kgs 2:3
statutes and obey my **r** and keep all 1 Kgs 6:12
his statutes, and his **r**, 1 Kgs 8:58
and keeping my statutes and my **r**, 1 Kgs 9:4
and keeping my statutes and my **r**, 1 Kgs 11:33
the statutes or the **r** or the law or 2 Kgs 17:34
the statutes and the **r** and the law 2 Kgs 17:37
the statutes and the **r** that the LORD 1 Chr 22:13
my commandments and my **r**, 1 Chr 28:7
and keeping my statutes and my **r**, 2 Chr 7:17
law or commandment, statutes or **r**, 2 Chr 19:10
to the sanctuary's **r** of cleanness." 2 Chr 30:19
and the **r** given through Moses." 2 Chr 33:8
and to teach his statutes and **r** in Israel. Ezr 7:10
and the **r** that you commanded your Neh 1:7
and gave them right **r** and true laws, Neh 9:13
but sinned against your **r**, Neh 9:29
our Lord and his **r** and his statutes. Neh 10:29
For all his **r** were before me, and his Ps 18:22
the **r** of the LORD are true, and righteous Ps 19:9
to the LORD, and he **r** over the nations. Ps 22:28
may know that God **r** over Jacob to the Ps 59:13
who **r** by his might forever, whose eyes Ps 66:7
law and do not walk according to my **r**, Ps 89:30
heavens, and his kingdom **r** over all. Ps 103:19
heart, when I learn your righteous **r**. Ps 119:7
lips I declare all the **r** of your mouth. Ps 119:13
with longing for your **r** at all times. Ps 119:20
of faithfulness; I set your **r** before me. Ps 119:30
that I dread, for your **r** are good. Ps 119:39
of my mouth, for my hope is in your **r**. Ps 119:43
When I think of your **r** from of old, I Ps 119:52
you, because of your righteous **r**. Ps 119:62
O LORD, that your **r** are righteous, Ps 119:75
I do not turn aside from your **r**, for Ps 119:102
it, to keep your righteous **r**. Ps 119:106
praise, O LORD, and teach me your **r**. Ps 119:108
are you, O LORD, and right are your **r**. Ps 119:137
give me life according to your **r**. Ps 119:156
of your righteous **r** endures forever. Ps 119:160
day I praise you for your righteous **r**. Ps 119:164
praise you, and let your **r** help me. Ps 119:175
to Jacob, his statutes and **r** to Israel. Ps 147:19
other nation; they do not know his **r**. Ps 147:20
and he who **r** his spirit than he who Prv 16:32
The rich **r** over the poor, and the Prv 22:7
with might, and his arm **r** for him; Is 40:10
but my people know not the **r** of the LORD. Jer 8:7
rebelled against my **r** by doing Ezk 5:6
they have rejected my **r** and have not Ezk 5:6
walked in my statutes or obeyed my **r**, Ezk 5:7
acted according to the **r** of the nations Ezk 5:7
in my statutes, nor obeyed my **r**, Ezk 11:12
acted according to the **r** of the nations Ezk 11:12
statutes and keep my **r** and obey them. Ezk 11:20
and keeps my **r** by acting faithfully— Ezk 18:9
takes no interest or profit, obeys my **r**, Ezk 18:17
and made known to them my **r**, Ezk 20:11
walk in my statutes but rejected my **r**, Ezk 20:13
because they rejected my **r** and did not Ezk 20:16
of your fathers, nor keep their **r**, Ezk 20:18
statutes, and be careful to obey my **r**, Ezk 20:19
and were not careful to obey my **r**, Ezk 20:21
because they had not obeyed my **r**, Ezk 20:24
were not good and **r** by which they Ezk 20:25
statutes and be careful to obey my **r**. Ezk 36:27
shall walk in my **r** and be careful to Ezk 37:24
that the Most High **r** the kingdom of Dn 4:17
that the Most High **r** the kingdom of Dn 4:25
the time that you know that Heaven **r**. Dn 4:26
that the Most High **r** the kingdom of Dn 4:32
the Most High God **r** the kingdom of Dn 5:21
aside from your commandments and **r**. Dn 9:5
the statutes and **r** that I commanded Mal 4:4
to keep these **r** without prejudging, 1 Tm 5:21
unless he competes according to the **r**. 2 Tm 2:5

RULING (4)
justly over men, **r** in the fear of God, 2 Sm 23:3
According to the **r** of David his 2 Chr 8:14
throne of David and **r** again in Judah." Jer 22:30
in it no strong stem, no scepter for **r**. Ezk 19:14

RUMAH (1)
the daughter of Pedaiah of **R**. 2 Kgs 23:36

RUMBLE (1)
The crack of the whip, and **r** of the wheel, Na 3:2

RUMBLING (3)
his voice and the **r** that comes from his Jb 37:2
of his chariots, at the **r** of their wheels, Jer 47:3
As with the **r** of chariots, they leap on the Jl 2:5

RUMBLINGS (4)
of lightning, and **r** and peals of thunder, Rv 4:5
peals of thunder, **r**, flashes of lightning, Rv 8:5
flashes of lightning, **r**, peals of thunder, Rv 11:19
flashes of lightning, **r**, peals of thunder, Rv 16:18

RUMOR (6)
he shall hear a **r** and return to his 2 Kgs 19:7
'We have heard a **r** of it with our ears.' Jb 28:22
that he shall hear a **r** and return to his Is 37:7
A voice, a **r**! Behold, it comes!—a great Jer 10:22
comes upon disaster; **r** follows rumor. Ezk 7:26
comes upon disaster; rumor follows **r**. Ezk 7:26

RUMORS (2)
And you will hear of wars and **r** of wars. Mt 24:6
when you hear of wars and **r** of wars, Mk 13:7

RUN (67)
a spring; his branches **r** over the wall. Gn 49:22
up the frames, shall **r** from end to end. Ex 26:28
the middle bar to **r** from end to end Ex 36:33
southern border shall **r** from the end Nm 34:3
horsemen and to **r** before his chariots. 1 Sm 8:11
leave of me to **r** to Bethlehem his city, 1 Sm 20:6
"**R** and find the arrows that I shoot." 1 Sm 20:36
and let his spittle **r** down his beard. 1 Sm 21:13
horses, and fifty men to **r** before him. 2 Sm 15:1
"Let me **r** and carry news to the king 2 Sm 18:19
let me also **r** after the Cushite." And 2 Sm 18:22
And Joab said, "Why will you **r**, 2 Sm 18:22
he said, "I will **r**." So he said to him, 2 Sm 18:23
"**R**." Then Ahimaaz ran by the way 2 Sm 18:23
For by you I can **r** against a troop, 2 Sm 22:30
and fifty men to **r** before him. 1 Kgs 1:5
R at once to meet her and say to her, 2 Kgs 4:26
I will **r** after him and get something 2 Kgs 5:20
eyes of the LORD **r** to and fro 2 Chr 16:9
I said, "Should such a man as I **r** away? Neh 6:11
the days of the feast had **r** their course, Jb 1:5
sorrows of those who **r** after another god Ps 16:4
For by you I can **r** against a troop, and Ps 18:29
no fault of mine, they **r** and make ready. Ps 59:4
I will **r** in the way of your Ps 119:32
for their feet **r** to evil, and they make Prv 1:16
step will not be hampered, and if you **r**, Prv 4:12
plans, feet that make haste to **r** to evil, Prv 6:18
All streams **r** to the sea, but the sea is Eccl 1:7
Draw me after you; let us **r**. The king has Sg 1:4
that they may **r** after strong drink, Is 5:11
year to year; let the feasts **r** their round. Is 29:1
eagles; they shall **r** and not be weary; Is 40:31
that did not know you shall **r** to you, Is 55:5
Their feet **r** to evil, and they are swift to Is 59:7
R to and fro through the streets of Jer 5:1
that our eyes may **r** down with tears and Jer 9:18
weep bitterly and **r** down with tears, Jer 13:17
'Let my eyes **r** down with tears night Jer 14:17
I have not **r** away from being your Jer 17:16
Do the mountain waters **r** dry, the cold Jer 18:14
and **r** to and fro among the hedges! Jer 49:3
suddenly make him **r** away from her. Jer 49:19
suddenly make them **r** away from her, Jer 50:44
or weep, nor shall your tears **r** down. Ezk 24:16
and cause their rivers to **r** like oil, Ezk 32:14
So the boundary shall **r** from the sea Ezk 47:17
the boundary shall **r** between Hauran Ezk 47:18
it shall **r** from Tamar as far as the Ezk 47:19
the boundary shall **r** from Tamar to Ezk 48:28
Many shall **r** to and fro, and knowledge Dn 12:4
of horses, and like war horses they **r**. Jl 2:4
leap upon the city, they **r** upon the walls, Jl 2:9
Do horses **r** on rocks? Does one plow Am 6:12
they shall **r** to and fro, to seek the word Am 8:12
is like a pool whose waters **r** away. Na 2:8
on tablets, so he may **r** who reads it. Hab 2:2
said to him, "**R**, say to that young man, Zec 2:4
that they would **r** aground on the Acts 27:17
But we must **r** aground on some Acts 27:26
fearing that we might **r** on the rocks, Acts 27:29
if possible to **r** the ship ashore. Acts 27:39
the prize? So **r** that you may obtain it. 1 Cor 9:24
So I do not **r** aimlessly; I do not box as 1 Cor 9:26
I was not running or had not **r** in vain. Gal 2:2
proud that I did not **r** in vain or labor Phil 2:16
and let us **r** with endurance the race Heb 12:1

RUNNER (2)
"My days are swifter than a **r**; they flee Jb 9:25
One **r** runs to meet another, and one Jer 51:31

RUNNERS (1)
know that in a race all the **r** compete, 1 Cor 9:24

RUNNING (20)
the heifer down to a valley with **r** water, Dt 21:4
and looked, he saw a man **r** alone. 2 Sm 18:24
The watchman saw another man **r**. 2 Sm 18:26
another man **r** alone!" The king 2 Sm 18:26
"I think the **r** of the first is like the 2 Sm 18:27
first is like the **r** of Ahimaaz the son 2 Sm 18:27
house, **r** around the walls of the house, 1 Kgs 6:5
Naaman saw someone **r** after him, 2 Kgs 5:21
of the people **r** and praising the 2 Chr 23:12
r stubbornly against him with a Jb 15:26
oil on the head, **r** down on the beard, Ps 133:2
r down on the collar of his robes! Ps 133:2
hill there will be brooks **r** with water, Is 30:25
a restless young camel **r** here and there, Jer 2:23
Jesus saw that a crowd came **r** together, Mk 9:25
pressed down, shaken together, **r** over, Lk 6:38
Both of them were **r** together, but the Jn 20:4
R under the lee of a small island Acts 27:16
make sure I was not **r** or had not run in Gal 2:2
You were **r** well. Who hindered you from Gal 5:7

RUNS (11)
whether his body **r** with his discharge, Lv 15:3
on the north side **r** from the bay of Jos 15:5
them to the river that **r** to Ahava, Ezr 8:15
breach; he **r** upon me like a warrior. Jb 16:14
when the dust **r** into a mass and the Jb 38:38

like a strong man, **r** its course with joy. Ps 19:5
Let them vanish like water that **r** away; Ps 58:7
to the earth; his word **r** swiftly. Ps 147:15
the righteous man **r** into it and is safe. Prv 18:10
Everyone loves a bribe and **r** after gifts. Is 1:23
One runner **r** to meet another, and one Jer 51:31

RURAL (1)
of the villages, who live in the **r** towns, Est 9:19

RUSH (5)
sun is up, rise early and **r** upon the city. Jgs 9:33
the Spirit of the LORD will **r** upon you, 1 Sm 10:6
be found; surely in the **r** of great waters, Ps 32:6
of the north shall **r** upon him like a Dn 11:40
they **r** to and fro through the squares; Na 2:4

RUSHED (21)
Barak; into the valley they **r** at his heels. Jgs 5:15
that was with him **r** forward and stood Jgs 9:44
while the two companies **r** upon all who Jgs 9:44
Then the Spirit of the LORD **r** upon him, Jgs 14:6
And the Spirit of the LORD **r** upon him, Jgs 14:19
Then the Spirit of the LORD **r** upon him, Jgs 15:14
who were in ambush **r** out of their Jgs 20:33
ambush hurried and **r** against Gibeah; Jgs 20:37
and the Spirit of God **r** upon him, 1 Sm 10:10
the Spirit of God **r** upon Saul when he 1 Sm 11:6
Spirit of the LORD **r** upon David from 1 Sm 16:13
spirit from God **r** upon Saul, 1 Sm 18:10
r down to the Jordan before the king, 2 Sm 19:17
And they **r** him out quickly, and he 2 Chr 26:20
the whole herd **r** down the steep bank Mt 8:32
r down the steep bank into the sea and Mk 5:13
and the herd **r** down the steep bank into Lk 8:33
their ears and **r** together at him. Acts 7:57
tore their garments and **r** out into the Acts 14:14
the jailer called for lights and **r** in, Acts 16:29
and they **r** together into the theater, Acts 19:29

RUSHES (5)
confident though Jordan **r** against his Jb 40:23
as from a boiling pot and burning **r**. Jb 41:20
pierces its liver; as a bird **r** into a snare; Prv 7:23
and dry up, reeds and **r** will rot away. Is 19:6
down, the grass shall become reeds and **r**. Is 35:7

RUSHING (5)
for there is a sound of the **r** of rain." 1 Kgs 18:41
for he will come like a **r** stream, which Is 59:19
of his stallions, at the **r** of his chariots, Jer 47:3
heaven a sound like a mighty **r** wind, Acts 2:2
many chariots with horses **r** into battle. Rv 9:9

RUST (2)
where moth and **r** destroy and where Mt 6:19
neither moth nor **r** destroys and where Mt 6:20

RUTH (13)
was Orpah and the name of the other **R**. Ru 1:4
her mother-in-law, but **R** clung to her. Ru 1:14
But **R** said, "Do not urge me to leave you Ru 1:16
and **R** the Moabite her daughter-in-law Ru 1:22
And **R** the Moabite said to Naomi, "Let Ru 2:2
Then Boaz said to **R**, "Now, listen, my Ru 2:8
And **R** the Moabite said, "Besides, he said Ru 2:21
And Naomi said to **R**, her Ru 2:22
are you?" And she answered, "I am **R**, Ru 3:9
Naomi, you also acquire **R** the Moabite, Ru 4:5
Also **R** the Moabite, the widow of Ru 4:10
So Boaz took **R**, and she became his wife. Ru 4:13
Rahab, and Boaz the father of Obed by **R**, Mt 1:5

RUTHLESS (17)
Or, 'Redeem me from the hand of the **r**'? Jb 6:23
all the years that are laid up for the **r**. Jb 15:20
I have seen a wicked, **r** man, spreading Ps 37:35
risen against me; **r** men seek my life; Ps 54:3
a band of **r** men seek my life, and they Ps 86:14
and lay low the pompous pride of the **r**. Is 13:11
you; cities of **r** nations will fear you. Is 25:3
for the breath of the **r** is like a storm Is 25:4
a cloud, so the song of the **r** is put down. Is 25:5
the multitude of the **r** like passing chaff. Is 29:5
For the **r** shall come to nothing and the Is 29:20
redeem you from the grasp of the **r**." Jer 15:21
upon you, the most **r** of the nations; Ezk 28:7
people with him, the most **r** of nations, Ezk 30:11
Foreigners, the most **r** of nations, have Ezk 31:12
ones, all of them most **r** of nations. Ezk 32:12
foolish, faithless, heartless, **r**. Rom 1:31

RUTHLESSLY (6)
So they **r** made the people of Israel work Ex 1:13
all their work they **r** made them work as Ex 1:14
not rule over him **r** but shall fear your Lv 25:43
you shall not rule, one over another **r**. Lv 25:46
He shall not rule **r** over him in your Lv 25:53
that is smashed so **r** that among its Is 30:14

S

SABACHTHANI (2)
voice, saying, "Eli, Eli, lema **s**?" that is, Mt 27:46
"Eloi, Eloi, lema **s**?" which means, Mk 15:34

SABBATH (138)
day of solemn rest, a holy **S** to the LORD; Ex 16:23
"Eat it today, for today is a **S** to the LORD; Ex 16:25
it, but on the seventh day, which is a **S**, Ex 16:26
The LORD has given you the **S**; therefore Ex 16:29
"Remember the **S** day, to keep it holy. Ex 20:8
the seventh day is a **S** to the LORD your Ex 20:10
the LORD blessed the **S** day and made it Ex 20:11
You shall keep the **S**, because it is holy Ex 31:14
the seventh day is a **S** of solemn rest, Ex 31:15
does any work on the **S** day shall be put Ex 31:15
the people of Israel shall keep the **S**, Ex 31:16
observing the **S** throughout their Ex 31:16
day you shall have a **S** of solemn rest, Ex 35:2
in all your dwelling places on the **S** day." Ex 35:3
It is a **S** of solemn rest to you, and you Lv 16:31
on the seventh day is a **S** of solemn rest, Lv 23:3
It is a **S** to the LORD in all your dwelling Lv 23:3
the day after the **S** the priest shall wave Lv 23:11
full weeks from the day after the **S**, Lv 23:15
fifty days to the day after the seventh **S**. Lv 23:16
It shall be to you a **S** of solemn rest, and Lv 23:32
to evening shall you keep your **S**." Lv 23:32
Every **S** day Aaron shall arrange it Lv 24:8
you, the land shall keep a **S** to the LORD. Lv 25:2
year there shall be a **S** of solemn rest for Lv 25:4
solemn rest for the land, a **S** to the LORD. Lv 25:4
The **S** of the land shall provide food for Lv 25:6
a man gathering sticks on the **S** day. Nm 15:32
"On the **S** day, two male lambs a year Nm 28:9
this is the burnt offering of every **S**, Nm 28:10
"'Observe the **S** day, to keep it holy, as the Dt 5:12
the seventh day is a **S** to the LORD your Dt 5:14
God commanded you to keep the **S** day. Dt 5:15
is neither new moon nor **S**." She said, 2 Kgs 4:23
off duty on the **S** and guard the king's 2 Kgs 11:5
in force on the **S** and guard the house 2 Kgs 11:7
men who were to go off duty on the **S**, 2 Kgs 11:9
who were to come on duty on the **S**, 2 Kgs 11:9
covered way for the **S** that had been 2 Kgs 16:18
the showbread, to prepare it every **S**. 1 Chr 9:32
Levites who come off duty on the **S**, 2 Chr 23:4
men, who were to go off duty on the **S**, 2 Chr 23:8
who were to come on duty on the **S**, 2 Chr 23:8
the days that it lay desolate it kept **S**, 2 Chr 36:21
them your holy **S** and commanded Neh 9:14
or any grain on the **S** day to sell, Neh 10:31
buy from them on the **S** or on a holy Neh 10:31
people treading winepresses on the **S**, Neh 13:15
brought into Jerusalem on the **S** day. Neh 13:15
and sold them on the **S** to the people of Neh 13:16
you are doing, profaning the **S** day? Neh 13:17
wrath on Israel by profaning the **S**." Neh 13:18
at the gates of Jerusalem before the **S**, Neh 13:19
should not be opened until after the **S**. Neh 13:19
might be brought in on the **S** day. Neh 13:19
time on they did not come on the **S**. Neh 13:21
the gates, to keep the **S** day holy. Neh 13:22
A Psalm. A Song for the **S**. Ps 92:T
New moon and **S** and the calling of Is 1:13
of man who holds it fast, who keeps the **S**, Is 56:2
everyone who keeps the **S** and does not Is 56:6
"If you turn back your foot from the **S**, Is 58:13
and call the **S** a delight and the holy day Is 58:13
to new moon, and from **S** to Sabbath, Is 66:23
to new moon, and from Sabbath to **S**, Is 66:23
bear a burden on the **S** day or bring it Jer 17:21
of your houses on the **S** or do any work, Jer 17:22
do any work, but keep the **S** day holy, Jer 17:22
by the gates of this city on the **S** day, Jer 17:24
but keep the **S** day holy and do no work Jer 17:24
not listen to me, to keep the **S** day holy, Jer 17:27
by the gates of Jerusalem on the **S** day, Jer 17:27
has made Zion forget festival and **S**, Lam 2:6
but on the **S** day it shall be opened, Ezk 46:1
to the LORD on the **S** day shall be six Ezk 46:4
peace offerings as he does on the **S** day. Ezk 46:12
And the **S**, that we may offer wheat for Am 8:5
went through the grainfields on the **S**. Mt 12:1
doing what is not lawful to do on the **S**." Mt 12:2
the Law how on the **S** the priests in the Mt 12:5
temple profane the **S** and are guiltless? Mt 12:5
For the Son of Man is lord of the **S**." Mt 12:8
lawful to heal on the **S**?" — so that they Mt 12:10
has a sheep, if it falls into a pit on the **S**, Mt 12:11
So it is lawful to do good on the **S**." Mt 12:12
flight may not be in winter or on a **S**. Mt 24:20
Now after the **S**, toward the dawn of the Mt 28:1
and immediately on the **S** he entered the Mk 1:21
One **S** he was going through the Mk 2:23
they doing what is not lawful on the **S**?" Mk 2:24
said to them, "The **S** was made for man, Mk 2:27
was made for man, not man for the **S**. Mk 2:27
So the Son of Man is lord even of the **S**." Mk 2:28
see whether he would heal him on the **S**, Mk 3:2
"Is it lawful on the **S** to do good or to do Mk 3:4
And on the **S** he began to teach in the Mk 6:2
that is, the day before the **S**, Mk 15:42
When the **S** was past, Mary Magdalene Mk 16:1
he went to the synagogue on the **S** day, Lk 4:16
And he was teaching them on the **S**, Lk 4:31
On a **S**, while he was going through the Lk 6:1
doing what is not lawful to do on the **S**?" Lk 6:2
to them, "The Son of Man is lord of the **S**." Lk 6:5
On another **S**, he entered the synagogue Lk 6:6
to see whether he would heal on the **S**, Lk 6:7
is it lawful on the **S** to do good or to do Lk 6:9
in one of the synagogues on the **S**. Lk 13:10
because Jesus had healed on the **S**, Lk 13:14
and be healed, and not on the **S** day." Lk 13:14
each of you on the **S** untie his ox or his Lk 13:15
be loosed from this bond on the **S** day?" Lk 13:16
One **S**, when he went to dine at the house Lk 14:1
saying, "Is it lawful to heal on the **S**, Lk 14:3
ox that has fallen into a well on a **S** day, Lk 14:5
Preparation, and the **S** was beginning. Lk 23:54
On the **S** they rested according to the Lk 23:56
bed and walked. Now that day was the **S**. Jn 5:9
the man who had been healed, "It is the **S**, Jn 5:10
he was doing these things on the **S**. Jn 5:16
because not only was he breaking the **S**, Jn 5:18
and you circumcise a man on the **S**. Jn 7:22
If on the **S** a man receives circumcision, Jn 7:23
with me because on the **S** I made a man's Jn 7:23
Now it was a **S** day when Jesus made the Jn 9:14
he does not keep the **S**." But others said, Jn 9:16
the cross on the **S** (for that Sabbath was Jn 19:31
the Sabbath (for that **S** was a high day), Jn 19:31
Jerusalem, a **S** day's journey away. Acts 1:12
And on the **S** day they went into the Acts 13:14
the prophets, which are read every **S**, Acts 13:27
things might be told them the next **S**. Acts 13:42
The next **S** almost the whole city Acts 13:44
he is read every **S** in the synagogues." Acts 15:21
And on the **S** day we went outside the Acts 16:13
and on three **S** days he reasoned with Acts 17:2
he reasoned in the synagogue every **S**, Acts 18:4
to a festival or a new moon or a **S**. Col 2:16
there remains a **S** rest for the people of Heb 4:9

SABBATHS (29)
say, 'Above all you shall keep my **S**, Ex 31:13
and his father, and you shall keep my **S**: Lv 19:3
You shall keep my **S** and reverence my Lv 19:30
besides the LORD'S **S** and besides your Lv 23:38
You shall keep my **S** and reverence my Lv 26:2
the land shall enjoy its **S** as long as it Lv 26:34
then the land shall rest, and enjoy its **S**. Lv 26:34
not have on your **S** when you were Lv 26:35
them and enjoy its **S** while it lies Lv 26:43
were offered to the LORD on **S**, 1 Chr 23:31
on the **S** and the new moons and the 2 Chr 2:4
commandment of Moses for the **S**, 2 Chr 8:13
and the burnt offerings for the **S**, 2 Chr 31:3
until the land had enjoyed its **S**. 2 Chr 36:21
the regular burnt offering, the **S**, Neh 10:33
"To the eunuchs who keep my **S**, who Is 56:4
Moreover, I gave them my **S**, as a sign Ezk 20:12
live; and my **S** they greatly profaned. Ezk 20:13
in my statutes, and profaned my **S**; Ezk 20:16
and keep my **S** holy that they may be Ezk 20:20
he shall live; they profaned my **S**. Ezk 20:21
my statutes and profaned my **S**, Ezk 20:24
my holy things and profaned my **S**. Ezk 22:8
and they have disregarded my **S**, Ezk 22:26
on the same day and profaned my **S**. Ezk 23:38
feasts, and they shall keep my **S** holy. Ezk 44:24
at the feasts, the new moons, and the **S**, Ezk 45:17
before the LORD on the **S** and on the new Ezk 46:3
mirth, her feasts, her new moons, her **S**, Hos 2:11

SABEANS (3)
and the **S** fell upon them and took them Jb 1:15
and the merchandise of Cush, and the **S**, Is 45:14
of Judah, and they will sell them to the **S**, Jl 3:8

SABTA (1)
Seba, Havilah, **S**, Raama, and Sabteca. 1 Chr 1:9

SABTAH (1)
Seba, Havilah, **S**, Raamah, and Sabteca. Gn 10:7

SABTECA (2)
Seba, Havilah, Sabtah, Raamah, and **S**. Gn 10:7
Seba, Havilah, Sabta, Raama, and **S**. 1 Chr 1:9

SACHAR (2)
Ahiam the son of **S** the Hararite, 1 Chr 11:35
second, Joah the third, **S** the fourth, 1 Chr 26:4

SACHET (1)
beloved is to me a **s** of myrrh that lies Sg 1:13

SACHIA (1)
Jeuz, **S**, and Mirmah. These were his 1 Chr 8:10

SACK (13)
to replace every man's money in his **s**, Gn 42:25
of them opened his **s** to give his donkey Gn 42:27
saw his money in the mouth of his **s**. Gn 42:27
the mouth of my **s**!" At this their Gn 42:28
man's bundle of money was in his **s**. Gn 42:35
man's money in the mouth of his **s**, Gn 43:21
man's money in the mouth of his **s**, Gn 44:1
in the mouth of the **s** of the youngest, Gn 44:2
quickly lowered his **s** to the ground, Gn 44:11
ground, and each man opened his **s**. Gn 44:11
the cup was found in Benjamin's **s**. Gn 44:12
of wood or a garment or a skin or a **s**, Lv 11:32
barley and fresh ears of grain in his **s**. 2 Kgs 4:42

SACKCLOTH (48)
his garments and put **s** on his loins Gn 37:34
and put on **s** and mourn before 2 Sm 3:31
daughter of Aiah took **s** and spread it 2 Sm 21:10
Let us put **s** around our waists and 1 Kgs 20:31
So they tied **s** around their waists 1 Kgs 20:32
his clothes and put **s** on his flesh 1 Kgs 21:27
fasted and lay in **s** and went about 1 Kgs 21:27
he had **s** beneath on his body— 2 Kgs 6:30
covered himself with **s** and went into 2 Kgs 19:1
and the senior priests, covered with **s**, 2 Kgs 19:2
David and the elders, clothed in **s**, 1 Chr 21:16
were assembled with fasting and in **s**, Neh 9:1
tore his clothes and put on **s** and ashes, Est 4:1
to enter the king's gate clothed in **s**. Est 4:2
and many of them lay in **s** and ashes. Est 4:3
Mordecai, so that he might take off his **s**, Est 4:4
I have sewed **s** upon my skin and have Jb 16:15
you have loosed my **s** and clothed me Ps 30:11
But I, when they were sick—I wore **s**; I Ps 35:13
When I made **s** my clothing, I became Ps 69:11
and instead of a rich robe, a skirt of **s**; Is 3:24
in the streets they wear **s**; on the Is 15:3
and loose the **s** from your waist and take Is 20:2
mourning, for baldness and wearing **s**; Is 22:12
bare, and tie **s** around your waist. Is 32:11
and covered himself with **s** and went into Is 37:1
and the senior priests, covered with **s**, Is 37:2
blackness and make **s** their covering." Is 50:3
and to spread **s** and ashes under him? Is 58:5
For this put on **s**, lament, and wail, for the Jer 4:8
O daughter of my people, put on **s**, and Jer 6:26
are gashes, and around the waist is **s**. Jer 48:37
put on **s**, lament, and run to and fro Jer 49:3
dust on their heads and put on **s**; Lam 2:10
They put on **s**, and horror covers them. Ezk 7:18
bald for you and put **s** on their waist, Ezk 27:31
for mercy with fasting and **s** and ashes. Dn 9:3
like a virgin wearing **s** for the bridegroom Jl 1:8
Put on **s** and lament, O priests; wail, O Jl 1:13
Go in, pass the night in **s**, O ministers of Jl 1:13
I will bring **s** on every waist and Am 8:10
They called for a fast and put on **s**, from Jon 3:5
removed his robe, covered himself with **s**, Jon 3:6
but let man and beast be covered with **s**, Jon 3:8
have repented long ago in **s** and ashes. Mt 11:21
long ago, sitting in **s** and ashes. Lk 10:13
and the sun became black as **s**, Rv 6:12
prophesy for 1,260 days, clothed in **s**." Rv 11:3

SACKED (2)
that time Menahem **s** Tiphsah and 2 Kgs 15:16
Therefore he **s** it, and he ripped open 2 Kgs 15:16

SACKS (10)
As they emptied their **s**, behold, every Gn 42:35
was returned in the mouth of your **s**. Gn 43:12
was replaced in our **s** the first time, Gn 43:18
to the lodging place we opened our **s**, Gn 43:21
know who put our money in our **s**." Gn 43:22
has put treasure in your **s** for you. Gn 43:23
of his house, "Fill the men's **s** with food, Gn 44:1
the mouths of our **s** we brought back to Gn 44:8
and took worn-out **s** for their donkeys, Jos 9:4
For the bread in our **s** is gone, and 1 Sm 9:7

SACRED (17)
make of these a **s** anointing oil blended Ex 30:25
'I have removed the **s** portion out of my Dt 26:13
of the LORD the **s** gifts of his father 1 Kgs 15:15
gifts of his father and his own **s** gifts, 1 Kgs 15:15
took all the **s** gifts that Jehoshaphat 2 Kgs 12:18
had dedicated, and his own **s** gifts, 2 Kgs 12:18
music and instruments for **s** song. 1 Chr 16:42
for there were **s** officers and officers 1 Chr 24:5
house of God the **s** gifts of his father 2 Chr 15:18
of his father and his own **s** gifts, 2 Chr 15:18
toward the east, shall be **s** to the LORD. Jer 31:40
of your gifts, with all your **s** offerings. Ezk 20:40
to the temple, outside the **s** area. Ezk 43:21
or the temple that has made the gold **s**? Mt 23:17
gift or the altar that makes the gift **s**? Mt 23:19
and of the **s** stone that fell from the Acts 19:35
been acquainted with the **s** writings, 2 Tm 3:15

SACRIFICE (177)
and Jacob offered a **s** in the hill Gn 31:54
that we may **s** to the LORD our God.' Ex 3:18
wilderness that we may **s** to the LORD our Ex 5:3
they cry, 'Let us go and offer **s** to our God.' Ex 5:8
you say, 'Let us go and **s** to the LORD.' Ex 5:17
I will let the people go to **s** to the LORD." Ex 8:8
said, "Go, **s** to your God within the land." Ex 8:25
the offerings we shall **s** to the LORD our Ex 8:26
If we **s** offerings abominable to the Ex 8:26
into the wilderness and **s** to the LORD our Ex 8:27
will let you go to **s** to the LORD your God Ex 8:28
not letting the people go to **s** to the LORD." Ex 8:29
that we may **s** to the LORD our God. Ex 10:25
say, 'It is the **s** of the LORD'S Passover, Ex 12:27
Therefore I **s** to the LORD all the males Ex 13:15
make for me and **s** on it your burnt Ex 20:24
blood of my **s** with anything leavened, Ex 23:18
after their gods and **s** to their gods and Ex 34:15
and you are invited, you eat of his **s**, Ex 34:15
blood of my **s** with anything leavened, Ex 34:25
or let the **s** of the Feast of the Passover Ex 34:25
"If his offering is a **s** of peace offering, if he Lv 3:1
And from the **s** of the peace offering, as a Lv 3:3
"If his offering for a **s** of peace offering to Lv 3:6
Then from the **s** of the peace offering he Lv 3:9
the ox of the **s** of the peace offerings); Lv 4:10
like the fat of the **s** of peace offerings. Lv 4:26
is removed from the **s** of peace offerings, Lv 4:35
is the law of the **s** of peace offerings that Lv 7:11
the thanksgiving **s** unleavened loaves Lv 7:12
With the **s** of his peace offerings for Lv 7:13
the flesh of the **s** of his peace offerings Lv 7:15
But if the **s** of his offering is a vow Lv 7:16
be eaten on the day that he offers his **s**, Lv 7:16
of the flesh of the **s** on the third day shall Lv 7:17
of the flesh of the **s** of his peace offering Lv 7:18
of the flesh of the **s** of the LORD'S peace Lv 7:20
some flesh from the **s** of the LORD'S peace Lv 7:21
Whoever offers the **s** of his peace Lv 7:29
the LORD from the **s** of his peace Lv 7:29
a contribution from the **s** of your peace Lv 7:32
for peace offerings, to **s** before the LORD, Lv 9:4
the **s** of peace offerings for the people. Lv 9:18
their sacrifices that they **s** in the open Lv 17:5
and **s** them as sacrifices of peace Lv 17:5
they shall no more **s** their sacrifices to Lv 17:7
them, who offers a burnt offering or **s** Lv 17:8
"When you offer a **s** of peace offerings to Lv 19:5
anyone offers a **s** of peace offerings Lv 22:21
And when you **s** a sacrifice of Lv 22:29
you sacrifice a **s** of thanksgiving to Lv 22:29
you shall **s** it so that you may be Lv 22:29
a year old as a **s** of peace offerings. Lv 23:19
offer the ram as a **s** of peace offering to Nm 6:17
that is under the **s** of the peace offering. Nm 6:18
and for the **s** of peace offerings, two Nm 7:17
and for the **s** of peace offerings, two Nm 7:23
and for the **s** of peace offerings, two Nm 7:29
and for the **s** of peace offerings, two Nm 7:35
and for the **s** of peace offerings, two Nm 7:41
and for the **s** of peace offerings, two Nm 7:47
and for the **s** of peace offerings, two Nm 7:53
and for the **s** of peace offerings, two Nm 7:59
and for the **s** of peace offerings, two Nm 7:65
and for the **s** of peace offerings, two Nm 7:71
and for the **s** of peace offerings, two Nm 7:77
and for the **s** of peace offerings, two Nm 7:83
the cattle for the **s** of peace offerings Nm 7:88
food offering or a burnt offering or a **s**, Nm 15:3
with the burnt offering, or for the **s**, Nm 15:5
you offer a bull as a burnt offering or **s**, Nm 15:8
you shall not **s** it to the LORD your God. Dt 15:21
shall offer the Passover **s** to the LORD Dt 16:2
of the flesh that you **s** on the evening of Dt 16:4
not offer the Passover **s** within any of Dt 16:5
in it, there you shall offer the Passover **s**, Dt 16:6
"You shall not **s** to the LORD your God an Dt 17:1
from the people, from those offering a **s**, Dt 18:3
and you shall **s** peace offerings and shall Dt 27:7
altar, not for burnt offering, nor for **s**, Jos 22:26
made, not for burnt offerings, nor for **s**, Jos 22:28
for burnt offering, grain offering, or **s**, Jos 22:29
to offer a great **s** to Dagon their god Jgs 16:23
city to worship and to **s** to the LORD of 1 Sm 1:3
to the LORD the yearly **s** and to pay his 1 Sm 1:21
was that when any man offered **s**, 1 Sm 2:13
with her husband to offer the yearly **s**. 1 Sm 2:19
be atoned for by **s** or offering forever." 1 Sm 3:14
the people have a **s** today on the high 1 Sm 9:12
he comes, since he must bless the **s**; 1 Sm 9:13
offerings and to **s** peace offerings. 1 Sm 10:8
and of the oxen to **s** to the LORD your 1 Sm 15:15
to **s** to the LORD your God in Gilgal." 1 Sm 15:21
Behold, to obey is better than **s**, and 1 Sm 15:22
and say, 'I have come to **s** to the LORD.' 1 Sm 16:2
And invite Jesse to the **s**, and I will 1 Sm 16:3
I have come to **s** to the LORD. 1 Sm 16:5
with me to the **s**." And he consecrated 1 Sm 16:5
and his sons and invited them to the **s**. 1 Sm 16:5
for there is a yearly **s** there for all the 1 Sm 20:6
go, for our clan holds a **s** in the city, 1 Sm 20:29
And the king went to Gibeon to **s** there, 1 Kgs 3:4
with him, offered **s** before the LORD. 1 Kgs 8:62
and he shall **s** on you the priests of 1 Kgs 13:2
about the time of offering the **s**, 2 Kgs 3:20
offer burnt offering or **s** to any god 2 Kgs 5:17
for I have a great **s** to offer to Baal. 2 Kgs 10:19
people continued to **s** and make 2 Kgs 12:3
offering and all the blood of the **s**, 2 Kgs 16:15
to them or serve them or **s** to them, 2 Kgs 17:35
to him, and to him you shall **s**. 2 Kgs 17:36
all the people offered **s** before the LORD. 2 Chr 7:4
offered as a **s** 22,000 oxen and 2 Chr 7:5
this place for myself as a house of **s**. 2 Chr 7:12
Israel to Jerusalem to **s** to the LORD, 2 Chr 11:16
I will **s** to them that they may help 2 Chr 28:23
while I sat appalled until the evening **s**. Ezr 9:4
And at the evening **s** I rose from my Ezr 9:5
restore it for themselves? Will they **s**? Neh 4:2
morning I prepare a **s** for you and watch. Ps 5:3
S and offering you have not desired, but Ps 40:6
who made a covenant with me by **s**!" Ps 50:5
Offer to God a **s** of thanksgiving, and Ps 50:14
thanksgiving as his **s** glorifies me; Ps 50:23
For you will not delight in **s**, or I would Ps 51:16
With a freewill offering I will **s** to you; I Ps 54:6
with the smoke of the **s** of rams; Ps 66:15
offer to you the **s** of thanksgiving and Ps 116:17
Bind the festal **s** with cords, up to the Ps 118:27
lifting up of my hands as the evening **s**! Ps 141:2
The **s** of the wicked is an abomination Prv 15:8
is more acceptable to the LORD than **s**. Prv 21:3
The **s** of the wicked is an Prv 21:27
listen is better than to offer the **s** of fools, Eccl 5:1
who sacrifices and him who does not **s**. Eccl 9:2
day and worship with **s** and offering, Is 19:21
For the LORD has a **s** in Bozrah, a great Is 34:6
your bed, and there you went up to offer **s**. Is 57:7
of hosts holds a **s** in the north country Jer 46:10
him who offers **s** in the high place and Jer 48:35
their children in **s** to their idols, Ezk 23:39
burnt offering and the **s** for the people, Ezk 44:11
swift flight at the time of the evening **s**. Dn 9:21
he shall put an end to **s** and offering. Dn 9:27
king or prince, without **s** or pillar, Hos 3:4
They **s** on the tops of the mountains Hos 4:13
with prostitutes and **s** with cult Hos 4:14
For I desire steadfast love and not **s**, the Hos 6:6
offerings, they **s** meat and eat it, Hos 8:13
to nothing: in Gilgal they **s** bulls; Hos 12:11
who offer human **s** kiss calves!" Hos 13:2
offer a **s** of thanksgiving of that which is Am 4:5
and they offered a **s** to the LORD and Jon 1:16
the voice of thanksgiving will **s** to you; Jon 2:9
has prepared a **s** and consecrated his Zep 1:7
the day of the LORD'S **s**—"I will punish Zep 1:8
so that all who **s** may come and take Zec 14:21
and boil the meat of the **s** in them. Zec 14:21
When you offer blind animals in **s**, is Mal 1:8
this means, 'I desire mercy, and not **s**.' Mt 9:13
this means, 'I desire mercy, and not **s**,' Mt 12:7
and to offer a **s** according to what is said Lk 2:24
and offered a **s** to the idol and were Acts 7:41
and wanted to offer **s** with the crowds. Acts 14:13
the people from offering **s** to them. Acts 14:18
to present your bodies as a living **s**, Rom 12:1
that what pagans **s** they offer to 1 Cor 10:20
has been offered in **s**," then do not 1 Cor 10:28
for us, a fragrant offering and **s** to God. Eph 5:2
a **s** acceptable and pleasing to God. Phil 4:18
he is obligated to offer **s** for his own sins Heb 5:3
ages to put away sin by the **s** of himself. Heb 9:26
offered for all time a single **s** for sins, Heb 10:12
there no longer remains a **s** for sins, Heb 10:26
to God a more acceptable **s** than Cain, Heb 11:4
high priest as a **s** for sin are burned Heb 13:11
continually offer up a **s** of praise to Heb 13:15

SACRIFICED (41)
burnt offerings and **s** peace offerings of Ex 24:5

have worshiped it and **s** to it and said, Ex 32:8
And Balak **s** oxen and sheep, and sent Nm 22:40
They **s** to demons that were no gods, to Dt 32:17
to the LORD and **s** peace offerings. Jos 8:31
Bochim. And they **s** there to the LORD. Jgs 2:5
On the day when Elkanah **s**, he would 1 Sm 1:4
burnt offerings and **s** sacrifices on 1 Sm 6:15
There they **s** peace offerings before 1 Sm 11:15
he **s** an ox and a fattened animal. 2 Sm 6:13
Adonijah **s** sheep, oxen, and fattened 1 Kgs 1:9
He has **s** oxen, fattened cattle, and 1 Kgs 1:19
gone down this day and has **s** oxen, 1 Kgs 1:25
only he **s** and made offerings at the 1 Kgs 3:3
made offerings and **s** to their gods. 1 Kgs 11:8
yoke of oxen and **s** them and boiled 1 Kgs 19:21
the people still **s** and made offerings 1 Kgs 22:43
the people still **s** and made offerings 2 Kgs 14:4
The people still **s** and made offerings 2 Kgs 15:4
The people still **s** and made offerings 2 Kgs 15:35
And he **s** and made offerings on the 2 Kgs 16:4
who **s** for them in the shrines of the 2 Kgs 17:32
And he **s** all the priests of the high 2 Kgs 23:20
they **s** seven bulls and seven rams. 1 Chr 15:26
of Ornan the Jebusite, he **s** there. 1 Chr 21:28
They **s** to the LORD on that day from 2 Chr 15:11
And he **s** and made offerings on the 2 Chr 28:4
For he **s** to the gods of Damascus 2 Chr 28:23
the people still **s** at the high places, 2 Chr 33:17
Amon **s** to all the images that 2 Chr 33:22
graves of those who had **s** to them. 2 Chr 34:4
They **s** their sons and their daughters Ps 106:37
whom they **s** to the idols of Canaan, Ps 106:38
and these you **s** to them to be Ezk 16:20
Bread, when they **s** the Passover lamb, Mk 14:12
on which the Passover lamb had to be **s**. Lk 22:7
from what has been **s** to idols, Acts 15:29
from what has been **s** to idols, Acts 21:25
Christ, our Passover lamb, has been **s**. 1 Cor 5:7
they might eat food **s** to idols and Rv 2:14
immorality and to eat food **s** to idols. Rv 2:20

SACRIFICES (82)
and offered **s** to the God of his father Gn 46:1
also let us have **s** and burnt offerings, Ex 10:25
brought a burnt offering and **s** to God; Ex 18:12
"Whoever **s** to any god, other than the Ex 22:20
out of the **s** of their peace offerings, Lv 7:34
sons' due from the **s** of the peace Lv 10:14
may bring their **s** that they sacrifice Lv 17:5
and sacrifice them as **s** of peace offerings Lv 17:5
no more sacrifice their **s** to goat demons, Lv 17:7
grain offerings, **s** and drink offerings, Lv 23:37
offerings and over the **s** of your peace Nm 10:10
invited the people to the **s** of their gods, Nm 25:2
bring your burnt offerings and your **s**, Dt 12:6
your burnt offerings and your **s**, your Dt 12:11
The blood of your **s** shall be poured out Dt 12:27
ate the fat of their **s** and drank the wine Dt 32:38
their mountain; there they offer right **s**; Dt 33:19
burnt offerings and **s** and peace Jos 22:27
do you scorn my **s** and my offerings 1 Sm 2:29
offerings and sacrificed **s** on that day 1 Sm 6:15
delight in burnt offerings and **s**, 1 Sm 15:22
while Absalom was offering the **s**, 2 Sm 15:12
go up to offer **s** in the temple of 1 Kgs 12:27
Judah, and he offered **s** on the altar. 1 Kgs 12:32
in to offer **s** and burnt offerings. 2 Kgs 10:24
And they offered **s** to the LORD, and 1 Chr 29:21
and **s** in abundance for all Israel. 1 Chr 29:21
the burnt offering and the **s**, 2 Chr 7:1
bring **s** and thank offerings to the 2 Chr 29:31
the assembly brought **s** and thank 2 Chr 29:31
and on it you shall burn your **s**"? 2 Chr 32:12
and offered on it **s** of peace offerings 2 Chr 33:16
them while the Levites flayed the **s**. 2 Chr 35:11
be rebuilt, the place where **s** were offered, Ezr 6:3
they may offer pleasing **s** to the God of Ezr 6:10
And they offered great **s** that day and Neh 12:43
Offer right **s**, and put your trust in the Ps 4:5
and regard with favor your burnt **s**! Ps 20:3
I will offer in his tent **s** with shouts of joy; Ps 27:6
Not for your **s** do I rebuke you; your Ps 50:8
The **s** of God are a broken spirit; a Ps 51:17
then will you delight in right **s**, in Ps 51:19
of Peor, and ate **s** offered to the dead; Ps 106:28
And let them offer **s** of thanksgiving, Ps 107:22
"I had to offer **s**, and today I have paid Prv 7:14
to him who **s** and him who does not Eccl 9:2
"What to me is the multitude of your **s**? Is 1:11
offerings, or honored me with your **s**. Is 43:23
or satisfied me with the fat of your **s**. Is 43:24
offerings and their **s** will be accepted Is 56:7
one who kills a man; he who **s** a lamb, Is 66:3
acceptable, nor your **s** pleasing to me. Jer 6:20
"Add your burnt offerings to your **s**, and Jer 7:21
them concerning burnt offerings and **s**. Jer 7:22
Negeb, bringing burnt offerings and **s**, Jer 17:26
grain offerings, and to make **s** forever." Jer 33:18
they offered their **s** and there they Ezk 20:28
Like the flock for **s**, like the flock at Ezk 36:38
offerings and the **s** were slaughtered. Ezk 40:42
temple shall boil the **s** of the people." Ezk 46:24
shall be ashamed because of their **s**. Hos 4:19
LORD, and their **s** shall not please him. Hos 9:4
bring your **s** every morning, Am 4:4
you bring to me **s** and offerings during Am 5:25
Therefore he **s** to his net and makes Hab 1:16
and yet **s** to the Lord what is blemished. Mal 1:14
than all whole burnt offerings and **s**." Mk 12:33
blood Pilate had mingled with their **s**. Lk 13:1
you bring to me slain beasts and **s**, Acts 7:42
who eat the **s** participants in the 1 Cor 10:18
to God, to offer gifts and **s** for sins. Heb 5:1
like those high priests, to offer **s** daily, Heb 7:27
priest is appointed to offer gifts and **s**; Heb 8:3
gifts and **s** are offered that cannot perfect Heb 9:9
themselves with better **s** than these. Heb 9:23
by the same **s** that are continually Heb 10:1
But in these **s** there is a reminder of sin Heb 10:3
"**S** and offerings you have not desired, Heb 10:5
taken pleasure in **s** and offerings and Heb 10:8
service, offering repeatedly the same **s**, Heb 10:11
have, for such **s** are pleasing to God. Heb 13:16
to offer spiritual **s** acceptable to God 1 Pt 2:5

SACRIFICIAL (7)
Can even **s** flesh avert your doom? Jer 11:15
from all around to the **s** feast that I am Ezk 39:17
a great **s** feast on the mountains of Ezk 39:17
at the **s** feast that I am preparing for Ezk 39:19
As for my **s** offerings, they sacrifice Hos 8:13
at the altar share in the **s** offerings? 1 Cor 9:13
offering upon the **s** offering of your Phil 2:17

SACRIFICING (9)
come and say to the man who was **s**, 1 Sm 2:15
The people were **s** at the high places, 1 Kgs 3:2
s so many sheep and oxen that they 1 Kgs 8:5
Bethel, **s** to the calves that he made. 1 Kgs 12:32
s so many sheep and oxen that they 2 Chr 5:6
s peace offerings and giving thanks 2 Chr 30:22
and we have been **s** to him ever since the Ezr 4:2
s in gardens and making offerings on Is 65:3
they kept **s** to the Baals and burning Hos 11:2

SACRILEGIOUS (1)
who are neither **s** nor blasphemers of Acts 19:37

SAD (8)
you not eat? And why is your heart **s**? 1 Sm 1:8
and ate, and her face was no longer **s**. 1 Sm 1:18
Now I had not been **s** in his presence. Neh 2:1
the king said to me, "Why is your face **s**, Neh 2:2
Why should not my face be **s**, when the Neh 2:3
my complaint, I will put off my **s** face, Jb 9:27
heard these things, he became very **s**, Lk 18:23
walk?" And they stood still, looking **s**. Lk 24:17

SADDLE (5)
them in the camel's **s** and sat on them. Gn 31:34
And any **s** on which the one with the Lv 15:9
to him, 'I will **s** a donkey for myself, 2 Sm 19:26
"**S** the donkey for me." So they 1 Kgs 13:13
"**S** the donkey for me." And they 1 Kgs 13:27

SADDLECLOTHS (1)
Dedan traded with you in **s** for riding. Ezk 27:20

SADDLED (10)
rose early in the morning, **s** his donkey, Gn 22:3
in the morning and **s** his donkey and Nm 22:21
He had with him a couple of **s** donkeys, Jgs 19:10
met him, with a couple of donkeys **s**, 2 Sm 16:1
he **s** his donkey and went off home to 2 Sm 17:23
Shimei arose and **s** a donkey and 1 Kgs 2:40
for me." So they **s** the donkey for 1 Kgs 13:13
he **s** the donkey for the prophet 1 Kgs 13:23
the donkey for me." And they **s** it. 1 Kgs 13:27
Then she **s** the donkey, and she said 2 Kgs 4:24

SADDUCEES (14)
the Pharisees and **S** coming for baptism, Mt 3:7
And the Pharisees and **S** came, and to Mt 16:1
of the leaven of the Pharisees and **S**." Mt 16:6
of the leaven of the Pharisees and **S**." Mt 16:11
of the teaching of the Pharisees and **S**. Mt 16:12
The same day **S** came to him, who say Mt 22:23
heard that he had silenced the **S**, Mt 22:34
And **S** came to him, who say that there Mk 12:18
There came to him some **S**, those who Lk 20:27
the temple and the **S** came upon them, Acts 4:1
with him (that is, the party of the **S**), Acts 5:17
that one part were **S** and the other Acts 23:6
arose between the Pharisees and the **S**, Acts 23:7
For the **S** say that there is no Acts 23:8

SADNESS (3)
This is nothing but **s** of the heart." Neh 2:2
for by **s** of face the heart is made glad. Eccl 7:3
Jesus, looking at him with **s**, said, "How Lk 18:24

SAFE (18)
that you have in the field into **s** shelter, Ex 9:19
his neighbor money or goods to keep **s**, Ex 22:7
an ox or a sheep or any beast to keep **s**, Ex 22:10
in his heart, saying, 'I shall be **s**, Dt 29:19
all the people returned **s** to Joshua in Jos 10:21
it is **s** for you and there is no danger. 1 Sm 20:21
his enemy, will he let him go away **s**? 1 Sm 24:19
seek from him a **s** journey for ourselves, Ezr 8:21
Their houses are **s** from fear, and no rod Jb 21:9
that I may be **s** and have regard for Ps 119:117
righteous man runs into it and is **s**. Prv 18:10
but whoever trusts in the LORD is **s**. Prv 29:25
And if in a **s** land you are so trusting, Jer 12:5
on high, to be **s** from the reach of harm! Hab 2:9
and holy man, and he kept him **s**. Mk 6:20
guards his own palace, his goods are **s**; Lk 11:21
he has received him back **s** and sound.' Lk 15:27
you is no trouble to me and is **s** for you. Phil 3:1

SAFEKEEPING (1)
your life. With me you shall be in **s**." 1 Sm 22:23

SAFELY (10)
And Jacob came **s** to the city of Gn 33:18
my lord the king has come **s** home." 2 Sm 19:30
into their own nets, while I pass by **s**. Ps 141:10
He pursues them and passes on **s**, by Is 41:3
ordering the jailer to keep them **s**. Acts 16:23
ride and bring him **s** to Felix the Acts 23:24
it was that all were brought **s** to land. Acts 27:44
After we were brought **s** through, we Acts 28:1
and bring me **s** into his heavenly 2 Tm 4:18
persons, were brought **s** through water. 1 Pt 3:20

SAFETY (25)
I will be a pledge of his **s**. From my hand Gn 43:9
became a pledge of **s** for the boy to Gn 44:32
enemies around, so that you live in **s**, Dt 12:10
"The beloved of the LORD dwells in **s**. Dt 33:12
So Israel lived in **s**, Jacob lived alone, in Dt 33:28
on every side, and you lived in **s**. 1 Sm 12:11
send you away, that you may go in **s**. 1 Sm 20:13
until the day he came back in **s**. 2 Sm 19:24
And Judah and Israel lived in **s**, from 1 Kgs 4:25
of Judah returned in **s** to his house in 2 Chr 19:1
His children are far from **s**; they are Jb 5:4
and those who mourn are lifted to **s**. Jb 5:11
for you alone, O LORD, make me dwell in **s**. Ps 4:8
place him in the **s** for which he longs." Ps 12:5
redeems my soul in **s** from the battle Ps 55:18
He led them in **s**, so that they were not Ps 78:53
an abundance of counselors there is **s**. Prv 11:14
the inhabitants of Gebim flee for **s**. Is 10:31
will graze, and the needy lie down in **s**; Is 14:30
Lord, I am oppressed; be my pledge of **s**! Is 38:14
Raise a standard toward Zion, flee for **s**, Jer 4:6
Flee for **s**, O people of Benjamin, from the Jer 6:1
place, and I will make them dwell in **s**. Jer 32:37
land, and I will make you lie down in **s**. Hos 2:18
neither was there any **s** from the foe for Zec 8:10

SAFFRON (1)
nard and **s**, calamus and cinnamon, Sg 4:14

SAHAR (1)
kind; wine of Helbon and wool of **S** Ezk 27:18

SAIL (17)
firm in its place or keep the **s** spread out. Is 33:23
linen from Egypt was your **s**, Ezk 27:7
his companions set **s** from Paphos Acts 13:13
So, setting **s** from Troas, we made a Acts 16:11
of the brothers and set **s** for Syria, Acts 18:18
God wills," and he set **s** from Ephesus. Acts 18:21
Jews as he was about to set **s** for Syria, Acts 20:3
ahead to the ship, we set **s** for Assos, Acts 20:13
Paul had decided to **s** past Ephesus, Acts 20:16
we had parted from them and set **s**, Acts 21:1
to Phoenicia, we went aboard and set **s**. Acts 21:2
was decided that we should **s** for Italy, Acts 27:1
which was about to **s** to the ports Acts 27:2
and not have set **s** from Crete and Acts 27:21
granted you all those who **s** with you.' Acts 27:24
greatly, and when we were about to **s**, Acts 28:10
three months we set **s** in a ship that Acts 28:11

SAILED (12)
and as they **s** he fell asleep. And a Lk 8:23
Then they **s** to the country of the Lk 8:26
and from there they **s** to Cyprus. Acts 13:4
and from there they **s** to Antioch, Acts 14:26
with him and **s** away to Cyprus, Acts 15:39
but we **s** away from Philippi after the Acts 20:6
it on the left we **s** to Syria and landed at Acts 21:3

to sea from there we **s** under the lee of Acts 27:4
And when we had **s** across the open sea Acts 27:5
We **s** slowly for a number of days and Acts 27:7
we **s** under the lee of Crete off Salmone. Acts 27:7
weighed anchor and **s** along Crete, Acts 27:13

SAILING (2)
And **s** from there we came the Acts 20:15
a ship of Alexandria **s** for Italy and put Acts 27:6

SAILORS (3)
about midnight the **s** suspected that Acts 27:27
And as the **s** were seeking to escape Acts 27:30
men, **s** and all whose trade is on the sea, Rv 18:17

SAINT (1)
Greet every **s** in Christ Jesus. The Phil 4:21

SAINTS (81)
and let your **s** rejoice in your 2 Chr 6:41
As for the **s** in the land, they are the Ps 16:3
Sing praises to the LORD, O you his **s**, and Ps 30:4
Love the LORD, all you his **s**! The LORD Ps 31:23
Oh, fear the LORD, you his **s**, for those Ps 34:9
loves justice; he will not forsake his **s**. Ps 37:28
he will speak peace to his people, to his **s**; Ps 85:8
He preserves the lives of his **s**; he Ps 97:10
sight of the LORD is the death of his **s**. Ps 116:15
and let your **s** shout for joy. Ps 132:9
salvation, and her **s** will shout for joy. Ps 132:16
O LORD, and all your **s** shall bless you! Ps 145:10
horn for his people, praise for all his **s**, Ps 148:14
and watching over the way of his **s**. Prv 2:8
But the **s** of the Most High shall receive Dn 7:18
made war with the **s** and prevailed over Dn 7:21
was given for the **s** of the Most High, Dn 7:22
came when the **s** possessed the Dn 7:22
shall wear out the **s** of the Most High, Dn 7:25
to the people of the **s** of the Most High; Dn 7:27
men and the people who are the **s**. Dn 8:24
many bodies of the **s** who had fallen Mt 27:52
evil he has done to your **s** at Jerusalem. Acts 9:13
down also to the **s** who lived at Lydda. Acts 9:32
Then calling the **s** and widows, he Acts 9:41
up many of the **s** in prison after Acts 26:10
who are loved by God and called to be **s**: Rom 1:7
intercedes for the **s** according to the Rom 8:27
to the needs of the **s** and seek to show Rom 12:13
to Jerusalem bringing aid to the **s**. Rom 15:25
the poor among the **s** at Jerusalem. Rom 15:26
Jerusalem may be acceptable to the **s**, Rom 15:31
in the Lord in a way worthy of the **s**, Rom 16:2
and all the **s** who are with them. Rom 16:15
called to be **s** together with all those 1 Cor 1:2
the unrighteous instead of the **s**? 1 Cor 6:1
not know that the **s** will judge the 1 Cor 6:2
As in all the churches of the **s**, 1 Cor 14:33
concerning the collection for the **s**: 1 Cor 16:1
themselves to the service of the **s**— 1 Cor 16:15
with all the **s** who are in the whole of 2 Cor 1:1
of taking part in the relief of the **s**— 2 Cor 8:4
to you about the ministry for the **s**, 2 Cor 9:1
not only supplying the needs of the **s**, 2 Cor 9:12
All the **s** greet you. 2 Cor 13:13
will of God, To the **s** who are in Ephesus, Eph 1:1
Jesus and your love toward all the **s**, Eph 1:15
of his glorious inheritance in the **s**, Eph 1:18
citizens with the **s** and members of Eph 2:19
though I am the very least of all the **s**, Eph 3:8
comprehend with all the **s** what is the Eph 3:18
to equip the **s** for the work of ministry, Eph 4:12
among you, as is proper among **s**. Eph 5:3
making supplication for all the **s**, Eph 6:18
To all the **s** in Christ Jesus who are at Phil 1:1
All the **s** greet you, especially those of Phil 4:22
To the **s** and faithful brothers in Christ Col 1:2
and of the love that you have for all the **s**, Col 1:4
in the inheritance of the **s** in light. Col 1:12
generations but now revealed to his **s**. Col 1:26
of our Lord Jesus with all his **s**. 1 Thes 3:13
on that day to be glorified in his **s**, 2 Thes 1:10
has washed the feet of the **s**, 1 Tm 5:10
toward the Lord Jesus and all the **s**, Phlm 1:5
the hearts of the **s** have been refreshed Phlm 1:7
showed for his sake in serving the **s**, Heb 6:10
Greet all your leaders and all the **s**. Heb 13:24
that was once for all delivered to the **s**. Jude 1:3
of incense, which are the prayers of the **s**. Rv 5:8
the prayers of all the **s** on the golden altar Rv 8:3
of the incense, with the prayers of the **s**, Rv 8:4
your servants, the prophets and **s**, Rv 11:18
make war on the **s** and to conquer them. Rv 13:7
for the endurance and faith of the **s**. Rv 13:10
Here is a call for the endurance of the **s**, Rv 14:12
have shed the blood of **s** and prophets, Rv 16:6
woman, drunk with the blood of the **s**, Rv 17:6
and you **s** and apostles and prophets, Rv 18:20
found the blood of prophets and of **s**, Rv 18:24
fine linen is the righteous deeds of the **s**. Rv 19:8
the camp of the **s** and the beloved city, Rv 20:9

SAKE (157)
that my life may be spared for your **s**." Gn 12:13
And for her **s** he dealt well with Gn 12:16
I will spare the whole place for their **s**." Gn 18:26
"For the **s** of forty I will not do it." Gn 18:29
"For the **s** of twenty I will not destroy Gn 18:31
"For the **s** of ten I will not destroy it." Gn 18:32
for my servant Abraham's **s**." Gn 26:24
the Egyptian's house for Joseph's **s**; Gn 39:5
and to the Egyptians for Israel's **s**, Ex 18:8
will for their **s** remember the covenant Lv 26:45
to him, "Are you jealous for my **s**? Nm 11:29
has done to all these nations for your **s**, Jos 23:3
bitter to me for your **s** that the hand of Ru 1:13
his people, for his great name's **s**, 1 Sm 12:22
his kingdom for the **s** of his people 2 Sm 5:12
show him kindness for Jonathan's **s**?" 2 Sm 9:1
you kindness for the **s** of your father 2 Sm 9:7
"Deal gently for my **s** with the young 2 Sm 18:5
'For my **s** protect the young man 2 Sm 18:12
from a far country for your name's **s** 1 Kgs 8:41
Yet for the **s** of David your father I 1 Kgs 11:12
for the **s** of David my servant and for 1 Kgs 11:13
and for the **s** of Jerusalem that 1 Kgs 11:13
for the **s** of my servant David and for 1 Kgs 11:32
David and for the **s** of Jerusalem, 1 Kgs 11:32
for the **s** of David my servant whom 1 Kgs 11:34
for David's **s** the LORD his God gave 1 Kgs 15:4
Judah, for the **s** of David his servant, 2 Kgs 8:19
for my own **s** and for the sake of my 2 Kgs 19:34
sake and for the **s** of my servant 2 Kgs 19:34
city for my own **s** and for my servant 2 Kgs 20:6
sake and for my servant David's **s**." 2 Kgs 20:6
highly exalted for the **s** of his people 1 Chr 14:2
For your servant's **s**, O LORD, and 1 Chr 17:19
far country for the **s** of your great 2 Chr 6:32
save me for the **s** of your steadfast love. Ps 6:4
paths of righteousness for his name's **s**. Ps 23:3
remember me, for the **s** of your goodness, Ps 25:7
For your name's **s**, O LORD, pardon my Ps 25:11
and for your name's **s** you lead me and Ps 31:3
Yet for your **s** we are killed all the day Ps 44:22
Redeem us for the **s** of your steadfast Ps 44:26
For it is for your **s** that I have borne Ps 69:7
and atone for our sins, for your name's **s**! Ps 79:9
Yet he saved them for his name's **s**, that Ps 106:8
For their **s** he remembered his Ps 106:45
deal on my behalf for your name's **s**; Ps 109:21
for the **s** of your steadfast love and your Ps 115:1
brothers and companions' **s** I will say, Ps 122:8
For the **s** of the house of the LORD our Ps 122:9
For the **s** of your servant David, do not Ps 132:10
For your name's **s**, O LORD, preserve Ps 143:11
for my own **s** and for the sake of my Is 37:35
sake and for the **s** of my servant David." Is 37:35
was pleased, for his righteousness' **s**, Is 42:21
"For your **s** I send to Babylon and bring Is 43:14
out your transgressions for my own **s**, Is 43:25
For the **s** of my servant Jacob, and Israel Is 45:4
"For my name's **s** I defer my anger, for the Is 48:9
for the **s** of my praise I restrain it for you, Is 48:9
For my own **s**, for my own sake, I do it, Is 48:11
For my own sake, for my own **s**, I do it, Is 48:11
For Zion's **s** I will not keep silent, and for Is 62:1
and for Jerusalem's **s** I will not be quiet, Is 62:1
not? Return for the **s** of your servants, Is 63:17
in it,' so I will do for my servants' **s**, Is 65:8
cast you out for my name's **s** have said, Is 66:5
us, act, O LORD, for your name's **s**; Jer 14:7
Do not spurn us, for your name's **s**; do Jer 14:21
know that for your **s** I bear reproach. Jer 15:15
Take care for the **s** of your lives, and do Jer 17:21
But I acted for the **s** of my name, that it Ezk 20:9
But I acted for the **s** of my name, that Ezk 20:14
hand and acted for the **s** of my name, Ezk 20:22
when I deal with you for my name's **s**, Ezk 20:44
wisdom for the **s** of your splendor. Ezk 28:17
It is not for your **s**, O house of Israel, Ezk 36:22
to act, but for the **s** of my holy name, Ezk 36:22
It is not for your **s** that I will act, Ezk 36:32
his pleas for mercy, and for your own **s**, Dn 9:17
Delay not, for your own **s**, O my God, Dn 9:19
But for the **s** of the house of Judah I will Zec 12:4
who are persecuted for righteousness' **s**, Mt 5:10
before governors and kings for my **s**, Mt 10:18
will be hated by all for my name's **s**. Mt 10:22
loses his life for my **s** will find it. Mt 10:39
put him in prison for the **s** of Herodias, Mt 14:3
of God for the **s** of your tradition? Mt 15:3
So for the **s** of your tradition you have Mt 15:6
loses his life for my **s** will find it. Mt 16:25
eunuchs for the **s** of the kingdom Mt 19:12
or children or lands, for my name's **s**, Mt 19:29
be hated by all nations for my name's **s**. Mt 24:9
But for the **s** of the elect those days will Mt 24:22
him in prison for the **s** of Herodias, Mk 6:17
his life for my **s** and the gospel's will Mk 8:35
or lands, for my **s** and for the gospel, Mk 10:29
before governors and kings for my **s**, Mk 13:9
will be hated by all for my name's **s**. Mk 13:13
be saved. But for the **s** of the elect, Mk 13:20
loses his life for my **s** will save it. Lk 9:24
for the **s** of the kingdom of God, Lk 18:29
kings and governors for my name's **s**. Lk 21:12
will be hated by all for my name's **s**. Lk 21:17
and for your **s** I am glad that I was not Jn 11:15
"This voice has come for your **s**, Jn 12:30
And for their **s** I consecrate myself, that Jn 17:19
he must suffer for the **s** of my name." Acts 9:16
their lives for the **s** of our Lord Jesus Acts 15:26
of faith for the **s** of his name among Rom 1:5
him" were not written for his **s** alone, Rom 4:23
"For your **s** we are being killed all the Rom 8:36
off from Christ for the **s** of my brothers, Rom 9:3
they are enemies of God for your **s**. Rom 11:28
beloved for the **s** of their forefathers. Rom 11:28
wrath but also for the **s** of conscience. Rom 13:5
Do not, for the **s** of food, destroy the Rom 14:20
We are fools for Christ's **s**, but you 1 Cor 4:10
Does he not speak entirely for our **s**? 1 Cor 9:10
It was written for our **s**, because the 1 Cor 9:10
I do it all for the **s** of the gospel, that I 1 Cor 9:23
for the **s** of the one who informed 1 Cor 10:28
you, and for the **s** of conscience— 1 Cor 10:28
has been for your **s** in the presence of 2 Cor 2:10
ourselves as your servants for Jesus' **s**. 2 Cor 4:5
being given over to death for Jesus' **s**, 2 Cor 4:11
For it is all for your **s**, so that as grace 2 Cor 4:15
him who for their **s** died and was 2 Cor 5:15
For our **s** he made him to be sin who 2 Cor 5:21
it was not for the **s** of the one who did 2 Cor 7:12
nor for the **s** of the one who suffered 2 Cor 7:12
rich, yet for your **s** he became poor, 2 Cor 8:9
For the **s** of Christ, then, I am 2 Cor 12:10
you that for the **s** of Christ you should Phil 1:29
believe in him but also suffer for his **s**, Phil 1:29
had, I counted as loss for the **s** of Christ. Phil 3:7
For his **s** I have suffered the loss of all Phil 3:8
I rejoice in my sufferings for your **s**, Col 1:24
Christ's afflictions for the **s** of his body, Col 1:24
proved to be among you for your **s**. 1 Thes 1:5
that we feel for your **s** before our God, 1 Thes 3:9
little wine for the **s** of your stomach 1 Tm 5:23
everything for the **s** of the elect, 2 Tm 2:10
for the **s** of the faith of God's elect and Ti 1:1
thing that is in us for the **s** of Christ. Phlm 1:6
yet for love's **s** I prefer to appeal to you Phlm 1:9
out to serve for the **s** of those who are to Heb 1:14
to those for whose **s** it is cultivated, Heb 6:7
you showed for his **s** in serving the Heb 6:10
manifest in the last times for your **s**, 1 Pt 1:20
subject for the Lord's **s** to every human 1 Pt 2:13
you should suffer for righteousness' **s**, 1 Pt 3:14
sober-minded for the **s** of your prayers. 1 Pt 4:7
your sins are forgiven for his name's **s**. 1 Jn 2:12
they have gone out for the **s** of the name, 3 Jn 1:7
themselves for the **s** of gain to Jude 1:11
patiently and bearing up for my name's **s**, Rv 2:3

SALA (1)
son of Obed, the son of Boaz, the son of **S**, Lk 3:32

SALAMIS (1)
When they arrived at **S**, they Acts 13:5

SALE (9)
that there was grain for **s** in Egypt, Gn 42:1
heard that there is grain for **s** in Egypt. Gn 42:2
if you make a **s** to your neighbor or Lv 25:14
he may redeem it within a year of its **s**. Lv 25:29
the price of his **s** shall vary with the Lv 25:50
for his redemption some of his **s** price. Lv 25:51
he receives from the **s** of his patrimony. Dt 18:8
offer yourselves for **s** to your enemies Dt 28:68
Sabbath, that we may offer wheat for **s**, Am 8:5

SALECAH (4)
and all Bashan, as far as **S** and Edrei, Dt 3:10
Mount Hermon and **S** and all Bashan Jos 12:5
Mount Hermon, and all Bashan to **S**; Jos 13:11
in the land of Bashan as far as **S**: 1 Chr 5:11

SALEM (4)
Melchizedek king of **S** brought out Gn 14:18
His abode has been established in **S**, his Ps 76:2
For this Melchizedek, king of **S**, priest of Heb 7:1
and then he is also king of **S**, Heb 7:2

SALIM (1)
John also was baptizing at Aenon near **S**, Jn 3:23

SALIVA (1)
on the ground and made mud with the **s**. Jn 9:6

SALLAI (1)
of **S**, Kallai; of Amok, Eber; Neh 12:20

SALLU (3)
S the son of Meshullam, son of 1 Chr 9:7
S the son of Meshullam, son of Joed, Neh 11:7
S, Amok, Hilkiah, Jedaiah. These were Neh 12:7

SALMA (2)
S, the father of Bethlehem, and 1 Chr 2:51
The sons of **S**: Bethlehem, the 1 Chr 2:54

SALMON (6)
fathered Nahshon, Nahshon fathered **S**, Ru 4:20
S fathered Boaz, Boaz fathered Obed, Ru 4:21
Nahshon fathered **S**, Salmon 1 Chr 2:11
fathered Salmon, **S** fathered Boaz, 1 Chr 2:11
of Nahshon, and Nahshon the father of **S**, Mt 1:4
and **S** the father of Boaz by Rahab, and Mt 1:5

SALMONE (1)
we sailed under the lee of Crete off **S**. Acts 27:7

SALOME (2)
James the younger and of Joses, and **S**. Mk 15:40
mother of James and **S** bought spices, Mk 16:1

SALT (46)
the Valley of Siddim (that is, the **S** Sea). Gn 14:3
back, and she became a pillar of **s**. Gn 19:26
as by the perfumer, seasoned with **s**, Ex 30:35
season all your grain offerings with **s**. Lv 2:13
shall not let the **s** of the covenant with Lv 2:13
with all your offerings you shall offer **s**. Lv 2:13
is a covenant of **s** forever before the Nm 18:19
from the end of the **S** Sea on the east. Nm 34:3
and its limit shall be at the **S** Sea. Nm 34:12
as far as the Sea of the Arabah, the **S** Sea, Dt 3:17
land burned out with brimstone and **s**, Dt 29:23
toward the Sea of the Arabah, the **S** Sea, Jos 3:16
to the Sea of the Arabah, the **S** Sea, Jos 12:3
boundary ran from the end of the **S** Sea, Jos 15:2
And the east boundary is the **S** Sea, to Jos 15:5
Nibshan, the City of **S**, and Engedi: six Jos 15:62
ends at the northern bay of the **S** Sea, Jos 18:19
and he razed the city and sowed it with **s**. Jgs 9:45
18,000 Edomites in the Valley of **S**. 2 Sm 8:13
and put **s** in it." So they brought it to 2 Kgs 2:20
of water and threw **s** in it and said, 2 Kgs 2:21
in the Valley of **S** and took Sela by 2 Kgs 14:7
18,000 Edomites in the Valley of **S**. 1 Chr 18:12
and his sons by a covenant of **s**? 2 Chr 13:5
to the Valley of **S** and struck down 2 Chr 25:11
because we eat the **s** of the palace and Ezr 4:14
to the God of heaven, wheat, **s**, wine, Ezr 6:9
and **s** without prescribing how much. Ezr 7:22
that which is tasteless be eaten without **s**, Jb 6:6
his home and the **s** land for his dwelling Jb 39:6
thousand of Edom in the Valley of **S**. Ps 60:T
the wilderness, in an uninhabited **s** land. Jer 17:6
to cleanse you, nor rubbed with **s**, Ezk 16:4
priests shall sprinkle **s** on them and Ezk 43:24
become fresh; they are to be left for **s**. Ezk 47:11
a land possessed by nettles and **s** pits, Zep 2:9
"You are the **s** of the earth, but if salt has Mt 5:13
salt of the earth, but if **s** has lost its taste, Mt 5:13
S is good, but if the salt has lost its Mk 9:50
is good, but if the **s** has lost its saltiness, Mk 9:50
Have **s** in yourselves, and be at peace Mk 9:50
"**S** is good, but if salt has lost its taste, Lk 14:34
"Salt is good, but if **s** has lost its taste, Lk 14:34
always be gracious, seasoned with **s**, Col 4:6
same opening both fresh and **s** water? Jas 3:11
Neither can a **s** pond yield fresh water. Jas 3:12

SALTED (1)
For everyone will be **s** with fire. Mk 9:49

SALTINESS (3)
lost its taste, how shall its **s** be restored? Mt 5:13
Salt is good, but if the salt has lost its **s**, Mk 9:50
lost its taste, how shall its **s** be restored? Lk 14:34

SALTWORT (1)
they pick **s** and the leaves of bushes, and Jb 30:4

SALTY (2)
a fruitful land into a **s** waste, because Ps 107:34
saltiness, how will you make it **s** again? Mk 9:50

SALU (1)
woman, was Zimri the son of **S**, Nm 25:14

SALUTE (1)
And they began to **s** him, "Hail, King Mk 15:18

SALVATION (170)
I wait for your **s**, O LORD. Gn 49:18
stand firm, and see the **s** of the LORD, Ex 14:13
and my song, and he has become my **s**; Ex 15:2
him and scoffed at the Rock of his **s**. Dt 32:15
have granted this great **s** by the hand of Jgs 15:18
enemies, because I rejoice in your **s**. 1 Sm 2:1
the LORD has worked **s** in Israel." 1 Sm 11:13
has worked this great **s** in Israel? 1 Sm 14:45
the LORD worked a great **s** for all Israel. 1 Sm 19:5
my shield, and the horn of my **s**, 2 Sm 22:3
have given me the shield of your **s**, 2 Sm 22:36
exalted be my God, the rock of my **s**, 2 Sm 22:47
Great **s** he brings to his king, and 2 Sm 22:51
earth! Tell of his **s** from day to day. 1 Chr 16:23
"Save us, O God of our **s**, and gather 1 Chr 16:35
priests, O LORD God, be clothed with **s**, 2 Chr 6:41
and see the **s** of the LORD on your 2 Chr 20:17
This will be my **s**, that the godless shall Jb 13:16
of my soul, there is no **s** for him in God. Ps 3:2
S belongs to the LORD; your blessing be on Ps 3:8
daughter of Zion I may rejoice in your **s**. Ps 9:14
love; my heart shall rejoice in your **s**. Ps 13:5
that **s** for Israel would come out of Zion! Ps 14:7
refuge, my shield, and the horn of my **s**, Ps 18:2
You have given me the shield of your **s**, Ps 18:35
rock, and exalted be the God of my **s**— Ps 18:46
Great **s** he brings to his king, and Ps 18:50
May we shout for joy over your **s**, and in Ps 20:5
and in your **s** how greatly he exults! Ps 21:1
His glory is great through your **s**; Ps 21:5
and righteousness from the God of his **s**. Ps 24:5
teach me, for you are the God of my **s**; Ps 25:5
The LORD is my light and my **s**; whom Ps 27:1
not off; forsake me not, O God of my **s**! Ps 27:9
The war horse is a false hope for **s**, and Ps 33:17
pursuers! Say to my soul, "I am your **s**!" Ps 35:3
will rejoice in the LORD, exulting in his **s**. Ps 35:9
The **s** of the righteous is from the LORD; Ps 37:39
Make haste to help me, O Lord, my **s**! Ps 38:22
spoken of your faithfulness and your **s**; Ps 40:10
those who love your **s** say continually, Ps 40:16
in God; for I shall again praise him, my **s** Ps 42:5
again praise him, my **s** and my God. Ps 42:11
again praise him, my **s** and my God. Ps 43:5
are my King, O God; ordain **s** for Jacob! Ps 44:4
way rightly I will show the **s** of God!" Ps 50:23
Restore to me the joy of your **s**, and Ps 51:12
bloodguiltiness, O God, O God of my **s**, Ps 51:14
that **s** for Israel would come out of Zion! Ps 53:6
give **s** by your right hand and answer us! Ps 60:5
against the foe, for vain is the **s** of man! Ps 60:11
waits in silence; from him comes my **s**. Ps 62:1
He only is my rock and my **s**, my Ps 62:2
He only is my rock and my **s**, my Ps 62:6
On God rests my **s** and my glory; my Ps 62:7
us with righteousness, O God of our **s**, Ps 65:5
who daily bears us up; God is our **s**. Ps 68:19
Our God is a God of **s**, and to GOD, the Ps 68:20
pain; let your **s**, O God, set me on high! Ps 69:29
May those who love your **s** say evermore, Ps 70:4
acts, of your deeds of **s** all the day, Ps 71:15
old, working **s** in the midst of the earth. Ps 74:12
Help us, O God of our **s**, for the glory of Ps 79:9
Restore us again, O God of our **s**, and put Ps 85:4
love, O LORD, and grant us your **s**. Ps 85:7
Surely his **s** is near to those who fear Ps 85:9
O LORD, God of my **s**; I cry out day and Ps 88:1
Father, my God, and the Rock of my **s**.' Ps 89:26
I will satisfy him and show him my **s**." Ps 91:16
make a joyful noise to the rock of our **s**! Ps 95:1
his name; tell of his **s** from day to day. Ps 96:2
and his holy arm have worked **s** for him. Ps 98:1
The LORD has made known his **s**; he has Ps 98:2
of the earth have seen the **s** of our God. Ps 98:3
give **s** by your right hand and answer Ps 108:6
the foe, for vain is the **s** of man! Ps 108:12
lift up the cup of **s** and call on the Ps 116:13
and my song; he has become my **s**. Ps 118:14
Glad songs of **s** are in the tents of the Ps 118:15
answered me and have become my **s**. Ps 118:21
your **s** according to your promise; Ps 119:41
My soul longs for your **s**; I hope in Ps 119:81
eyes long for your **s** and for the Ps 119:123
S is far from the wicked, for they do Ps 119:155
I hope for your **s**, O LORD, and I do Ps 119:166
I long for your **s**, O LORD, and your Ps 119:174
Her priests I will clothe with **s**, and her Ps 132:16
O LORD, my Lord, the strength of my **s**, Ps 140:7
in a son of man, in whom there is no **s**. Ps 146:3
people; he adorns the humble with **s**. Ps 149:4
"Behold, God is my **s**; I will trust, and will Is 12:2
and my song, and he has become my **s**." Is 12:2
you will draw water from the wells of **s**. Is 12:3
the God of your **s** and have not Is 17:10
him; let us be glad and rejoice in his **s**." Is 25:9
city; he sets up **s** as walls and bulwarks. Is 26:1
morning, our **s** in the time of trouble. Is 33:2
stability of your times, abundance of **s**, Is 33:6
that **s** and righteousness may bear fruit; Is 45:8
is saved by the LORD with everlasting **s**; Is 45:17
it is not far off, and my **s** will not delay; Is 46:13
I will put **s** in Zion, for Israel my glory." Is 46:13
that my **s** may reach to the end of the Is 49:6
you; in a day of **s** I have helped you; Is 49:8
draws near, my **s** has gone out, Is 51:5
but my **s** will be forever, and my Is 51:6
be forever, and my **s** to all generations." Is 51:8
good news of happiness, who publishes **s**, Is 52:7
of the earth shall see the **s** of our God. Is 52:10
righteousness, for soon my **s** will come, Is 56:1
hope for justice, but there is none; for **s**, Is 59:11
then his own arm brought him **s**, and Is 59:16
and a helmet of **s** on his head; Is 59:17
you shall call your walls **S**, and your Is 60:18
has clothed me with the garments of **s**; Is 61:10
brightness, and her **s** as a burning torch. Is 62:1
daughter of Zion, "Behold, your **s** comes; Is 62:11
so my own arm brought me **s**, and my Is 63:5
in the LORD our God is the **s** of Israel. Jer 3:23
wait quietly for the **s** of the LORD. Lam 3:26
vowed I will pay. **S** belongs to the LORD!" Jon 2:9
to the LORD; I will wait for the God of my **s**; Mi 7:7
on your horses, on your chariot of **s**? Hab 3:8
You went out for the **s** of your people, Hab 3:13
your people, for the **s** of your anointed. Hab 3:13
LORD; I will take joy in the God of my **s**. Hab 3:18
righteous and having **s** is he, humble Zec 9:9
"And the LORD will give **s** to the tents of Zec 12:7
raised up a horn of **s** for us in the house Lk 1:69
to give knowledge of **s** to his people in Lk 1:77
for my eyes have seen your **s** Lk 2:30
and all flesh shall see the **s** of God.'" Lk 3:6
to him, "Today **s** has come to this house, Lk 19:9
what we know, for **s** is from the Jews. Jn 4:22
And there is **s** in no one else, for there Acts 4:12
God was giving them **s** by his hand, Acts 7:25
us has been sent the message of this **s**. Acts 13:26
that you may bring **s** to the ends of Acts 13:47
who proclaim to you the way of **s**." Acts 16:17
to you that this **s** of God has been Acts 28:28
power of God for **s** to everyone who Rom 1:16
through their trespass **s** has come to Rom 11:11
For **s** is nearer to us now than when Rom 13:11
afflicted, it is for your comfort and **s**; 2 Cor 1:6
and in a day of **s** I have helped you." 2 Cor 6:2
time; behold, now is the day of **s**. 2 Cor 6:2
that leads to **s** without regret, 2 Cor 7:10
the word of truth, the gospel of your **s**, Eph 1:13
and take the helmet of **s**, and the sword Eph 6:17
of their destruction, but of your **s**, Phil 1:28
work out your own **s** with fear and Phil 2:12
love, and for a helmet the hope of **s**. 1 Thes 5:8
but to obtain **s** through our Lord 1 Thes 5:9
also may obtain the **s** that is in 2 Tm 2:10
make you wise for **s** through faith in 2 Tm 3:15
has appeared, bringing **s** for all people, Ti 2:11
the sake of those who are to inherit **s**? Heb 1:14
we escape if we neglect such a great **s**? Heb 2:3
founder of their **s** perfect through Heb 2:10
the source of eternal **s** to all who obey Heb 5:9
of better things—things that belong to **s**. Heb 6:9
through faith for a **s** ready to be revealed 1 Pt 1:5
of your faith, the **s** of your souls. 1 Pt 1:9
Concerning this **s**, the prophets who 1 Pt 1:10
milk, that by it you may grow up to **s**— 1 Pt 2:2
count the patience of our Lord as **s**, 2 Pt 3:15
to write to you about our common **s**, Jude 1:3
"**S** belongs to our God who sits on the Rv 7:10
"Now the **s** and the power and the Rv 12:10
S and glory and power belong to our Rv 19:1

SALVE (1)
not be seen, and **s** to anoint your eyes, Rv 3:18

SAMARIA (122)
in the cities of **S** shall surely come to 1 Kgs 13:32
bought the hill of **S** from Shemer for 1 Kgs 16:24
the name of the city that he built **S**, 1 Kgs 16:24
with his fathers and was buried in **S**, 1 Kgs 16:28
over Israel in **S** twenty-two years. 1 Kgs 16:29
house of Baal, which he built in **S**. 1 Kgs 16:32
Now the famine was severe in **S**. 1 Kgs 18:2
and closed in on **S** and fought against 1 Kgs 20:1
if the dust of **S** shall suffice for 1 Kgs 20:10
him, "Men are coming out from **S**." 1 Kgs 20:17
my father did in **S**." And Ahab said, 1 Kgs 20:34
vexed and sullen and came to **S**. 1 Kgs 20:43
beside the palace of Ahab king of **S**. 1 Kgs 21:1
Ahab king of Israel, who is in **S**; 1 Kgs 21:18
floor at the entrance of the gate of **S**, 1 Kgs 22:10
the king died, and was brought to **S**. 1 Kgs 22:37
And they buried the king in **S**. 1 Kgs 22:37
washed the chariot by the pool of **S**, 1 Kgs 22:38
over Israel in **S** in the seventeenth 1 Kgs 22:51

the lattice in his upper chamber in **S**, 2 Kgs 1:2
to meet the messengers of the king of **S**, 2 Kgs 1:3
and from there he returned to **S**. 2 Kgs 2:25
of Ahab became king over Israel in **S**, 2 Kgs 3:1
Jehoram marched out of **S** at that time 2 Kgs 3:6
lord were with the prophet who is in **S**! 2 Kgs 5:3
you seek." And he led them to **S**. 2 Kgs 6:19
As soon as they entered **S**, Elisha said, 2 Kgs 6:20
behold, they were in the midst of **S**. 2 Kgs 6:20
army and went up and besieged **S**. 2 Kgs 6:24
And there was a great famine in **S**, as 2 Kgs 6:25
of barley for a shekel, at the gate of **S**." 2 Kgs 7:1
this time tomorrow in the gate of **S**," 2 Kgs 7:18
Now Ahab had seventy sons in **S**. So 2 Kgs 10:1
Jehu wrote letters and sent them to **S**, 2 Kgs 10:1
Then he set out and went to **S**. On 2 Kgs 10:12
And when he came to **S**, he struck 2 Kgs 10:17
all who remained to Ahab in **S**, 2 Kgs 10:17
fathers, and they buried him in **S**. 2 Kgs 10:35
over Israel in **S** was twenty-eight 2 Kgs 10:36
of Jehu began to reign over Israel in **S**, 2 Kgs 13:1
and the Asherah also remained in **S**.) 2 Kgs 13:6
his fathers, and they buried him in **S**, 2 Kgs 13:9
began to reign over Israel in **S**, 2 Kgs 13:10
Joash was buried in **S** with the kings 2 Kgs 13:13
also hostages, and he returned to **S**. 2 Kgs 14:14
and was buried in **S** with the kings 2 Kgs 14:16
king of Israel, began to reign in **S**, 2 Kgs 14:23
reigned over Israel in **S** six months. 2 Kgs 15:8
and he reigned one month in **S**. 2 Kgs 15:13
up from Tirzah and came to **S**, 2 Kgs 15:14
son of Jabesh in **S** and put him to 2 Kgs 15:14
Israel, and he reigned ten years in **S**. 2 Kgs 15:17
began to reign over Israel in **S**, 2 Kgs 15:23
Gilead, and struck him down in **S**, 2 Kgs 15:25
began to reign over Israel in **S**, 2 Kgs 15:27
Elah began to reign in **S** over Israel, 2 Kgs 17:1
invaded all the land and came to **S**, 2 Kgs 17:5
the king of Assyria captured **S**, 2 Kgs 17:6
in the cities of **S** instead of the people 2 Kgs 17:24
took possession of **S** and lived in 2 Kgs 17:24
in the cities of **S** do not know the 2 Kgs 17:26
carried away from **S** came and lived 2 Kgs 17:28
came up against **S** and besieged it, 2 Kgs 18:9
Hoshea king of Israel, **S** was taken. 2 Kgs 18:10
Have they delivered **S** out of my 2 Kgs 18:34
Jerusalem the measuring line of **S**, 2 Kgs 21:13
of the prophet who came out of **S**. 2 Kgs 23:18
places that were in the cities of **S**, 2 Kgs 23:19
years he went down to Ahab in **S**. 2 Chr 18:2
floor at the entrance of the gate of **S**, 2 Chr 18:9
he was captured while hiding in **S**, 2 Chr 22:9
of Judah, from **S** to Beth-horon, 2 Chr 25:13
also hostages, and he returned to **S**. 2 Chr 25:24
them and brought the spoil to **S**. 2 Chr 28:8
army that came to **S** and said to 2 Chr 28:9
palm trees. Then they returned to **S**. 2 Chr 28:15
settled in the cities of **S** and in the rest of Ezr 4:10
associates who live in **S** and in the rest Ezr 4:17
of his brothers and of the army of **S**, Neh 4:2
"'And the head of Ephraim is **S**, and the Is 7:9
and the head of **S** is the son of Remaliah. Is 7:9
and the spoil of **S** will be carried away Is 8:4
know, Ephraim and the inhabitants of **S**, Is 9:9
like Arpad? Is not **S** like Damascus? Is 10:9
greater than those of Jerusalem and **S**, Is 10:10
as I have done to **S** and her images?" Is 10:11
Have they delivered **S** out of my hand? Is 36:19
In the prophets of **S** I saw an unsavory Jer 23:13
plant vineyards on the mountains of **S**; Jer 31:5
arrived from Shechem and Shiloh and **S**, Jer 41:5
And your elder sister is **S**, who lived Ezk 16:46
S has not committed half your sins. Ezk 16:51
the fortunes of **S** and her daughters, Ezk 16:53
and **S** and her daughters shall return Ezk 16:55
As for their names, Oholah is **S**, and Ezk 23:4
desolation, the cup of your sister **S**; Ezk 23:33
is revealed, and the evil deeds of **S**; Hos 7:1
I have spurned your calf, O **S**. My anger Hos 8:5
The calf of **S** shall be broken to pieces. Hos 8:6
The inhabitants of **S** tremble for the Hos 10:5
S shall bear her guilt, because she has Hos 13:16
yourselves on the mountains of **S**, Am 3:9
of Israel who dwell in **S** be rescued, Am 3:12
Bashan, who are on the mountain of **S**, Am 4:1
who feel secure on the mountain of **S**, Am 6:1
Those who swear by the Guilt of **S**, and Am 8:14
the land of Ephraim and the land of **S**, Ob 1:19
he saw concerning **S** and Jerusalem. Mi 1:1
is the transgression of Jacob? Is it not **S**? Mi 1:5
Therefore I will make **S** a heap in the Mi 1:6
passing along between **S** and Galilee. Lk 17:11
And he had to pass through **S**. Jn 4:4
So he came to a town of **S** called Sychar, Jn 4:5
There came a woman of **S** to draw water. Jn 4:7
a woman of **S**?" (For Jews have no Jn 4:9
in Jerusalem and in all Judea and **S**, Acts 1:8
throughout the regions of Judea and **S**, Acts 8:1
to the city of **S** and proclaimed to them Acts 8:5
in the city and amazed the people of **S**, Acts 8:9
Jerusalem heard that **S** had received Acts 8:14
Judea and Galilee and **S** had peace and Acts 9:31
passed through both Phoenicia and **S**, Acts 15:3

SAMARIA'S (1)
S king shall perish like a twig on the Hos 10:7

SAMARITAN (4)
But a **S**, as he journeyed, came to where Lk 10:33
giving him thanks. Now he was a **S**. Lk 17:16
The **S** woman said to him, "How is it that Jn 4:9
that you are a **S** and have a demon?" Jn 8:48

SAMARITANS (7)
the high places that the **S** had made, 2 Kgs 17:29
the Gentiles and enter no town of the **S**, Mt 10:5
who went and entered a village of the **S**, Lk 9:52
(For Jews have no dealings with **S**.) Jn 4:9
Many **S** from that town believed in him Jn 4:39
So when the **S** came to him, they asked Jn 4:40
the gospel to many villages of the **S**. Acts 8:25

SAME (212)
On the very **s** day Noah and his sons, Gn 7:13
earth had one language and the **s** words. Gn 11:1
and reaped in the **s** year a hundredfold. Gn 26:12
appeared to him the **s** night and said, Gn 26:24
That **s** day Isaac's servants came and Gn 26:32
"You shall say the **s** thing to Esau Gn 32:19
The **s** night he arose and took his two Gn 32:22
and she told him the **s** story, saying, Gn 39:17
we dreamed on the **s** night, he and I, Gn 41:11
The **s** day Pharaoh commanded the Ex 5:6
still deliver the **s** number of bricks." Ex 5:18
Egypt, also did the **s** by their secret arts. Ex 7:11
of Egypt did the **s** by their secret arts. Ex 7:22
the magicians did the **s** by their secret Ex 8:7
so this **s** night is a night of watching Ex 12:42
be dealt with according to this **s** rule. Ex 21:31
You shall do the **s** with your oxen and Ex 22:30
all the curtains shall be the **s** size. Ex 26:2
The eleven curtains shall be the **s** size. Ex 26:8
cubits. All the curtains were the **s** size. Ex 36:9
The eleven curtains were the **s** size. Ex 36:15
It shall be eaten the **s** day you offer it or Lv 19:6
It shall be eaten on the **s** day; you shall Lv 22:30
fifteenth day of the **s** month is the Feast Lv 23:6
grain parched or fresh until this **s** day, Lv 23:14
shall make proclamation on the **s** day. Lv 23:21
You shall have the **s** rule for the Lv 24:22
scarlet and cover the **s** with a covering Nm 4:8
he shall consecrate his head that **s** day Nm 6:11
will do to us, the **s** will we do to you." Nm 10:32
In the **s** way you shall offer daily, for Nm 28:24
And I prayed for Aaron also at the **s** time. Dt 9:20
on the tablets, in the **s** writing as before, Dt 10:4
their gods?—that I also may do the **s**.' Dt 12:30
of your produce in the **s** year and lay it Dt 14:28
to your female slave you shall do the **s**. Dt 15:17
of other gods, that **s** prophet shall die.' Dt 18:20
tree, but you shall bury him the **s** day, Dt 21:23
you shall do the **s** with his donkey or Dt 22:3
shall give him his wages on the **s** day, Dt 24:15
wrote this song the **s** day and taught it Dt 31:22
the city in the **s** manner seven times. Jos 6:15
That **s** night the LORD said to him, "Arise, Jgs 7:9
to Penuel, and spoke to them in the **s** way, Jgs 8:8
battle line in the **s** place where they had Jgs 20:22
both of them shall die on the **s** day. 1 Sm 2:34
line and came to Shiloh the **s** day, 1 Sm 4:12
for the **s** plague was on all of you and 1 Sm 6:4
and spoke the **s** words as before. 1 Sm 17:23
people answered him in the **s** way, 1 Sm 17:27
another, and spoke in the **s** way, 1 Sm 17:30
and all his men, on the **s** day together. 1 Sm 31:6
But that **s** night the word of the LORD 2 Sm 7:4
this woman and I live in the **s** house, 1 Kgs 3:17
cherubim had the **s** measure and the 1 Kgs 6:25
the same measure and the **s** form. 1 Kgs 6:25
fingers. The second pillar was the **s**. 1 Kgs 7:15
and he did the **s** with the other 1 Kgs 7:18
of the **s** measure and the same form. 1 Kgs 7:37
of the same measure and the **s** form. 1 Kgs 7:37
The **s** day the king consecrated the 1 Kgs 8:64
And he gave a sign the **s** day, saying, 1 Kgs 13:3
Then Libnah revolted at the **s** time. 2 Kgs 8:22
second year what springs of the **s**. 2 Kgs 19:29
he came, by the **s** he shall return, 2 Kgs 19:33
And the second pillar had the **s**, with 2 Kgs 25:17
But that **s** night the word of the LORD 1 Chr 17:3
some of the people at the **s** time. 2 Chr 16:10
paid him the **s** amount in the 2 Chr 27:5
to the LORD—this **s** King Ahaz. 2 Chr 28:22
Has not this **s** Hezekiah taken away 2 Chr 32:12
This **s** Hezekiah closed the upper 2 Chr 32:30
At the **s** time Tattenai the governor of the Ezr 5:3
and I answered them in the **s** manner. Neh 6:4
In the **s** way Sanballat for the fifth time Neh 6:5
behavior will say the **s** to all the king's Est 1:18
of Adar, on the thirteenth day of the **s**, Est 9:1
Adar and also the fifteenth day of the **s**, Est 9:21
plow iniquity and sow trouble reap the **s**. Jb 4:8
but you are the **s**, and your years have Ps 102:27
I perceived that the **s** event happens to Eccl 2:14
and what happens to the beasts is the **s**; Eccl 3:19
They all have the **s** breath, and man Eccl 3:19
It is the **s** for all, since the same event Eccl 9:2
since the **s** event happens to the Eccl 9:2
the sun, that the **s** event happens to all. Eccl 9:3
that he came, by the **s** he shall return, Is 37:34
In that **s** year, at the beginning of the Jer 28:1
In that **s** year, in the seventh month, the Jer 28:17
them vineyards and fields at the **s** time. Jer 39:10
And the second pillar had the **s**, with Jer 52:22
And the four had the **s** likeness, their Ezk 1:16
the four had the **s** likeness, Ezk 10:10
they were the **s** faces whose Ezk 10:22
and does the **s** abominations that the Ezk 18:24
of them shall come from the **s** land. Ezk 21:19
was defiled; they both took the **s** way. Ezk 23:13
sanctuary on the **s** day and profaned Ezk 23:38
on the **s** day they came into my Ezk 23:39
The three were of the **s** size, and the Ezk 40:10
jambs on either side were of the **s** size. Ezk 40:10
vestibule were of the **s** size as those of Ezk 40:21
palm trees were of the **s** size as those of Ezk 40:22
they had the **s** size as the others. Ezk 40:24
gate. It was of the **s** size as the others. Ezk 40:28
vestibule were of the **s** size as the Ezk 40:29
gate. It was of the **s** size as the others. Ezk 40:32
vestibule were of the **s** size as the Ezk 40:33
it. It had the **s** size as the others. Ezk 40:35
vestibule were of the **s** size as the Ezk 40:36
the north, of the **s** length and breadth, Ezk 42:11
with the **s** exits and arrangements and Ezk 42:11
the gate, and shall go out by the **s** way." Ezk 44:3
and the bath shall be of the **s** measure, Ezk 45:11
You shall do the **s** on the seventh day Ezk 45:20
he shall make the **s** provision for sin Ezk 45:25
gate, and he shall go out by the **s** way. Ezk 46:8
thirty broad; the four were of the **s** size. Ezk 46:22
At the **s** time my reason returned to me, Dn 4:36
They shall speak lies at the **s** table, but Dn 11:27
a man and his father go in to the **s** girl, Am 2:7
and go the **s** day to the house of Josiah, Zec 6:10
In the **s** way, let your light shine before Mt 5:16
others to do the **s** will be called least Mt 5:19
Do not even the tax collectors do the **s**? Mt 5:46
Do not even the Gentiles do the **s**? Mt 5:47
That **s** day Jesus went out of the house Mt 13:1
But when that **s** servant went out, he Mt 18:28
hour and the ninth hour, he did the **s**. Mt 20:5
he went to the other son and said the **s**. Mt 21:30
the first. And they did the **s** to them. Mt 21:36
The **s** day Sadducees came to him, who Mt 22:23
you!" And all the disciples said the **s**. Mt 26:35
third time, saying the **s** words again. Mt 26:44
with him also reviled him in the **s** way. Mt 27:44
not deny you." And they all said the **s**. Mk 14:31
away and prayed, saying the **s** words. Mk 14:39
And in the **s** region there were shepherds Lk 2:8
is that to you? For even sinners do the **s**. Lk 6:33
to sinners, to get back the **s** amount. Lk 6:34
And remain in the **s** house, eating and Lk 10:7
In that **s** hour he rejoiced in the Holy Lk 10:21
are under the **s** sentence of Lk 23:40
And they rose that **s** hour and returned Lk 24:33
will come in the **s** way as you saw him Acts 1:11
If then God gave the **s** gift to them as Acts 11:17
will tell you the **s** things by word of Acts 15:27
he took them the **s** hour of the night Acts 16:33
he was of the **s** trade he stayed with Acts 18:3
At the **s** time he hoped that money Acts 24:26
at the **s** time loosening the ropes that Acts 27:40
the judge, practice the very **s** things. Rom 2:1
make out of the **s** lump one vessel for Rom 9:21
the **s** Lord is Lord of all, bestowing Rom 10:12
do not all have the **s** function, Rom 12:4
For the **s** reason you also pay taxes, for Rom 13:6
be united in the **s** mind and the same 1 Cor 1:10
the same mind and the **s** judgment. 1 Cor 1:10
authority? Does not the Law say the **s**? 1 Cor 9:8
In the **s** way, the Lord commanded 1 Cor 9:14
and all ate the **s** spiritual food, 1 Cor 10:3
and all drank the **s** spiritual drink. 1 Cor 10:4
head—it is the **s** as if her head were 1 Cor 11:5
In the **s** way also he took the cup, 1 Cor 11:25

are varieties of gifts, but the **s** Spirit; 1 Cor 12:4
are varieties of service, but the **s** Lord; 1 Cor 12:5
but it is the **s** God who empowers 1 Cor 12:6
knowledge according to the **s** Spirit, 1 Cor 12:8
to another faith by the **s** Spirit, to 1 Cor 12:9
empowered by one and the **s** Spirit, 1 Cor 12:11
may have the **s** care for one 1 Cor 12:25
For not all flesh is the **s**, but there is 1 Cor 15:39
patiently endure the **s** sufferings that 2 Cor 1:6
"Yes, yes" and "No, no" at the **s** time? 2 Cor 1:17
that **s** veil remains unlifted, 2 Cor 3:14
transformed into the **s** image from 2 Cor 3:18
Since we have the **s** spirit of faith 2 Cor 4:13
heart of Titus the **s** earnest care I 2 Cor 8:16
they work on the **s** terms as we do. 2 Cor 11:12
of you? Did we not act in the **s** spirit? 2 Cor 12:18
spirit? Did we not take the **s** steps? 2 Cor 12:18
In the **s** way we also, when we were Gal 4:3
are fellow heirs, members of the **s** body, Eph 3:6
In the **s** way husbands should love Eph 5:28
Masters, do the **s** to them, and stop your Eph 6:9
engaged in the **s** conflict that you saw I Phil 1:30
complete my joy by being of the **s** mind, Phil 2:2
of the same mind, having the **s** love, Phil 2:2
To write the **s** things to you is no Phil 3:1
At the **s** time, pray also for us, that God Col 4:3
you suffered the **s** things from your 1 Thes 2:14
At the **s** time, prepare a guest room Phlm 1:22
But you are the **s**, and your years will Heb 1:12
likewise partook of the **s** things, Heb 2:14
may fall by the **s** sort of disobedience. Heb 4:11
you to show the **s** earnestness to have Heb 6:11
And in the **s** way he sprinkled with the Heb 9:21
by the **s** sacrifices that are continually Heb 10:1
offering repeatedly the **s** sacrifices, Heb 10:11
Jacob, heirs with him of the **s** promise. Heb 11:9
when they attempted to do the **s**, Heb 11:29
Christ is the **s** yesterday and today Heb 13:8
And in the **s** way was not also Rahab the Jas 2:25
From the **s** mouth come blessing and Jas 3:10
pour forth from the **s** opening both fresh Jas 3:11
yourselves with the **s** way of thinking, 1 Pt 4:1
join them in the **s** flood of debauchery, 1 Pt 4:4
knowing that the **s** kinds of suffering 1 Pt 5:9
But by the **s** word the heavens and earth 2 Pt 3:7
ought to walk in the **s** way in which he 1 Jn 2:6
At the **s** time, it is a new commandment 1 Jn 2:8
foursquare; its length the **s** as its width. Rv 21:16

SAMGAR-NEBU (1)

S, Sar-sekim the Rab-saris, Jer 39:3

SAMLAH (4)

and **S** of Masrekah reigned in his Gn 36:36
S died, and Shaul of Rehoboth on the Gn 36:37
and **S** of Masrekah reigned in his 1 Chr 1:47
S died, and Shaul of Rehoboth on the 1 Chr 1:48

SAMOS (1)

Chios; the next day we touched at **S**; Acts 20:15

SAMOTHRACE (1)

Troas, we made a direct voyage to **S**, Acts 16:11

SAMSON (35)

bore a son and called his name **S**. Jgs 13:24
S went down to Timnah, and at Timnah Jgs 14:1
Philistines?" But **S** said to Jgs 14:3
Then **S** went down with his father and Jgs 14:5
woman, and **S** prepared a feast there, Jgs 14:10
And **S** said to them, "Let me now put a Jgs 14:12
S went to visit his wife with a young Jgs 15:1
And **S** said to them, "This time I shall be Jgs 15:3
So **S** went and caught 300 foxes and took Jgs 15:4
said, "**S**, the son-in-law of the Timnite, Jgs 15:6
And **S** said to them, "If this is what you Jgs 15:7
said, "We have come up to bind **S**, Jgs 15:10
cleft of the rock of Etam, and said to **S**, Jgs 15:11
of the Philistines." And **S** said to them, Jgs 15:12
And **S** said, "With the jawbone of a Jgs 15:16
S went to Gaza, and there he saw a Jgs 16:1
"**S** has come here." And they surrounded Jgs 16:2
But **S** lay till midnight, and at midnight Jgs 16:3
So Delilah said to **S**, "Please tell me Jgs 16:6
S said to her, "If they bind me with seven Jgs 16:7
you, **S**!" But he snapped the bowstrings, Jgs 16:9
Then Delilah said to **S**, "Behold, you Jgs 16:10
S!" And the men lying in ambush were Jgs 16:12
Then Delilah said to **S**, "Until now you Jgs 16:13
S!" But he awoke from his sleep and Jgs 16:14
S!" And he awoke from his sleep and Jgs 16:20
"Our god has given **S** our enemy into Jgs 16:23
hearts were merry, they said, "Call **S**, Jgs 16:25
us." So they called **S** out of the prison, Jgs 16:25
And **S** said to the young man who held Jgs 16:26
who looked on while **S** entertained. Jgs 16:27
Then **S** called to the LORD and said, "O Jgs 16:28
And **S** grasped the two middle pillars Jgs 16:29
And **S** said, "Let me die with the Jgs 16:30
to tell of Gideon, Barak, **S**, Jephthah, Heb 11:32

SAMSON'S (4)

the woman, and she was right in **S** eyes. Jgs 14:7
On the fourth day they said to **S** wife, Jgs 14:15
And **S** wife wept over him and said, Jgs 14:16
And **S** wife was given to his Jgs 14:20

SAMUEL (142)

bore a son, and she called his name **S**, 1 Sm 1:20
S was ministering before the LORD, a 1 Sm 2:18
And the young man **S** grew in the 1 Sm 2:21
the young man **S** continued to grow 1 Sm 2:26
the young man **S** was ministering to 1 Sm 3:1
and **S** was lying down in the temple of 1 Sm 3:3
Then the LORD called **S**, and he said, 1 Sm 3:4
"**S**!" and Samuel arose and went to Eli 1 Sm 3:6
"Samuel!" and **S** arose and went to Eli 1 Sm 3:6
Now **S** did not yet know the LORD, and 1 Sm 3:7
And the LORD called **S** again the third 1 Sm 3:8
Therefore Eli said to **S**, "Go, lie down, 1 Sm 3:9
your servant hears.'" So **S** went and lay 1 Sm 3:9
times, "**S**! Samuel!" And Samuel said, 1 Sm 3:10
S!" And Samuel said, "Speak, for your 1 Sm 3:10
Samuel!" And **S** said, "Speak, for your 1 Sm 3:10
Then the LORD said to **S**, "Behold, I am 1 Sm 3:11
S lay until morning; then he opened 1 Sm 3:15
And **S** was afraid to tell the vision to 1 Sm 3:15
But Eli called **S** and said, "Samuel, my 1 Sm 3:16
and said, "**S**, my son." And he said, 1 Sm 3:16
So **S** told him everything and hid 1 Sm 3:18
And **S** grew, and the LORD was with 1 Sm 3:19
knew that **S** was established 1 Sm 3:20
revealed himself to **S** at Shiloh by 1 Sm 3:21
And the word of **S** came to all Israel. 1 Sm 4:1
And **S** said to all the house of Israel, "If 1 Sm 7:3
Then **S** said, "Gather all Israel at 1 Sm 7:5
the LORD." And **S** judged the people 1 Sm 7:6
And the people of Israel said to **S**, "Do 1 Sm 7:8
So **S** took a nursing lamb and offered it 1 Sm 7:9
And **S** cried out to the LORD for Israel, 1 Sm 7:9
As **S** was offering up the burnt 1 Sm 7:10
Then **S** took a stone and set it up 1 Sm 7:12
the Philistines all the days of **S**. 1 Sm 7:13
S judged Israel all the days of his life. 1 Sm 7:15
When **S** became old, he made his sons 1 Sm 8:1
together and came to **S** at Ramah 1 Sm 8:4
the thing displeased **S** when they said, 1 Sm 8:6
to judge us." And **S** prayed to the LORD. 1 Sm 8:6
And the LORD said to **S**, "Obey the voice 1 Sm 8:7
So **S** told all the words of the LORD to 1 Sm 8:10
people refused to obey the voice of **S**. 1 Sm 8:19
And when **S** had heard all the words 1 Sm 8:21
And the LORD said to **S**, "Obey their 1 Sm 8:22
make them a king." **S** then said to the 1 Sm 8:22
they saw **S** coming out toward them 1 Sm 9:14
Saul came, the LORD had revealed to **S**: 1 Sm 9:15
When **S** saw Saul, the LORD told him, 1 Sm 9:17
Then Saul approached **S** in the gate 1 Sm 9:18
S answered Saul, "I am the seer. Go up 1 Sm 9:19
Then **S** took Saul and his young man 1 Sm 9:22
And **S** said to the cook, "Bring the 1 Sm 9:23
and set them before Saul. And **S** said, 1 Sm 9:24
guests." So Saul ate with **S** that day. 1 Sm 9:24
the break of dawn **S** called to Saul on 1 Sm 9:26
and both he and **S** went out into the 1 Sm 9:26
the outskirts of the city, **S** said to Saul, 1 Sm 9:27
Then **S** took a flask of oil and poured 1 Sm 10:1
When he turned his back to leave **S**, 1 Sm 10:9
were not to be found, we went to **S**." 1 Sm 10:14
"Please tell me what **S** said to you." 1 Sm 10:15
kingdom, of which **S** had spoken, 1 Sm 10:16
Now **S** called the people together to 1 Sm 10:17
Then **S** brought all the tribes of 1 Sm 10:20
And **S** said to all the people, "Do you 1 Sm 10:24
Then **S** told the people the rights and 1 Sm 10:25
Then **S** sent all the people away, each 1 Sm 10:25
does not come out after Saul and **S**, 1 Sm 11:7
Then the people said to **S**, "Who is it 1 Sm 11:12
Then **S** said to the people, "Come, let 1 Sm 11:14
And **S** said to all Israel, "Behold, I have 1 Sm 12:1
And **S** said to the people, "The LORD is 1 Sm 12:6
and Jephthah and **S** and delivered 1 Sm 12:11
So **S** called upon the LORD, and the 1 Sm 12:18
people greatly feared the LORD and **S**. 1 Sm 12:18
And all the people said to **S**, "Pray for 1 Sm 12:19
And **S** said to the people, "Do not be 1 Sm 12:20
seven days, the time appointed by **S**. 1 Sm 13:8
But **S** did not come to Gilgal, and the 1 Sm 13:8
the burnt offering, behold, **S** came. 1 Sm 13:10
S said, "What have you done?" And 1 Sm 13:11
And **S** said to Saul, "You have done 1 Sm 13:13
And **S** arose and went up from 1 Sm 13:15
And **S** said to Saul, "The LORD sent me 1 Sm 15:1
The word of the LORD came to **S**: 1 Sm 15:10
commandments." And **S** was angry, 1 Sm 15:11
And **S** rose early to meet Saul in the 1 Sm 15:12
And it was told **S**, "Saul came to 1 Sm 15:12
And **S** came to Saul, and Saul said to 1 Sm 15:13
And **S** said, "What then is this 1 Sm 15:14
Then **S** said to Saul, "Stop! I will tell 1 Sm 15:16
And **S** said, "Though you are little in 1 Sm 15:17
And Saul said to **S**, "I have obeyed 1 Sm 15:20
And **S** said, "Has the LORD as great 1 Sm 15:22
Saul said to **S**, "I have sinned, for I 1 Sm 15:24
And **S** said to Saul, "I will not return 1 Sm 15:26
As **S** turned to go away, Saul seized 1 Sm 15:27
And **S** said to him, "The LORD has 1 Sm 15:28
So **S** turned back after Saul, and 1 Sm 15:31
Then **S** said, "Bring here to me Agag 1 Sm 15:32
And **S** said, "As your sword has 1 Sm 15:33
among women." And **S** hacked Agag 1 Sm 15:33
Then **S** went to Ramah, and Saul 1 Sm 15:34
And **S** did not see Saul again until 1 Sm 15:35
of his death, but **S** grieved over Saul. 1 Sm 15:35
The LORD said to **S**, "How long will 1 Sm 16:1
And **S** said, "How can I go? If Saul 1 Sm 16:2
S did what the LORD commanded and 1 Sm 16:4
But the LORD said to **S**, "Do not look on 1 Sm 16:7
and made him pass before **S**. 1 Sm 16:8
made seven of his sons pass before **S**. 1 Sm 16:10
And **S** said to Jesse, "The LORD has 1 Sm 16:10
Then **S** said to Jesse, "Are all your 1 Sm 16:11
the sheep." And **S** said to Jesse, 1 Sm 16:11
Then **S** took the horn of oil and 1 Sm 16:13
And **S** rose up and went to Ramah. 1 Sm 16:13
and he came to **S** at Ramah and told 1 Sm 19:18
And he and **S** went and lived at 1 Sm 19:18
and **S** standing as head over them, 1 Sm 19:20
"Where are **S** and David?" And one 1 Sm 19:22
too prophesied before **S** and lay 1 Sm 19:24
Now **S** died. And all Israel assembled 1 Sm 25:1
Now **S** had died, and all Israel had 1 Sm 28:3
you?" He said, "Bring up **S** for me." 1 Sm 28:11
When the woman saw **S**, she cried 1 Sm 28:12
a robe." And Saul knew that it was **S**, 1 Sm 28:14
Then **S** said to Saul, "Why have you 1 Sm 28:15
And **S** said, "Why then do you ask 1 Sm 28:16
with fear because of the words of **S**. 1 Sm 28:20
The sons of **S**: Joel his firstborn, the 1 Chr 6:28
the singer the son of Joel, son of **S**, 1 Chr 6:33
David and **S** the seer established 1 Chr 9:22
to the word of the LORD by **S**. 1 Chr 11:3
Also all that **S** the seer and Saul the 1 Chr 26:28
in the Chronicles of **S** the seer, 1 Chr 29:29
since the days of **S** the prophet. 2 Chr 35:18
S also was among those who called upon Ps 99:6
"Though Moses and **S** stood before me, Jer 15:1
from **S** and those who came after him, Acts 3:24
gave them judges until **S** the prophet. Acts 13:20
of David and **S** and the prophets— Heb 11:32

SANBALLAT (10)

But when **S** the Horonite and Tobiah, Neh 2:10
But when **S** the Horonite and Tobiah Neh 2:19
Now when **S** heard that we were Neh 4:1
But when **S** and Tobiah and the Arabs Neh 4:7
Now when **S** and Tobiah and Geshem Neh 6:1
S and Geshem sent to me, saying, Neh 6:2
In the same way **S** for the fifth time sent Neh 6:5
because Tobiah and **S** had hired him. Neh 6:12
Remember Tobiah and **S**, O my God, Neh 6:14
was the son-in-law of **S** the Horonite. Neh 13:28

SANCTIFICATION (6)

as slaves to righteousness leading to **s**. Rom 6:19
the fruit you get leads to **s** and its end, Rom 6:22
righteousness and **s** and redemption. 1 Cor 1:30
For this is the will of God, your **s**: that 1 Thes 4:3
through **s** by the Spirit and belief in 2 Thes 2:13
of God the Father, in the **s** of the Spirit, 1 Pt 1:2

SANCTIFIED (13)

of Israel, and it shall be **s** by my glory. Ex 29:43
those who are near me I will be **s**, Lv 10:3
that I may be **s** among the people of Lv 22:32
myself, that they also may be **s** in truth. Jn 17:19
among all those who are **s**. Acts 20:32
among those who are **s** by faith in Acts 26:18
be acceptable, **s** by the Holy Spirit. Rom 15:16
is in Corinth, to those **s** in Christ Jesus, 1 Cor 1:2
But you were washed, you were **s**, you 1 Cor 6:11
and those who are **s** all have one origin. Heb 2:11
we have been **s** through the offering Heb 10:10
for all time those who are being **s**. Heb 10:14
of the covenant by which he was **s**, Heb 10:29

SANCTIFIES (10)

and do them; I am the LORD who **s** you. Lv 20:8
people, for I am the LORD who **s** him." Lv 21:15
for I am the LORD who **s** them." Lv 21:23
profane it: I am the LORD who **s** them. Lv 22:9

things: for I am the LORD who **s** them." Lv 22:16
of Israel. I am the LORD who **s** you, Lv 22:32
know that I am the LORD who **s** them. Ezk 20:12
know that I am the LORD who **s** Israel, Ezk 37:28
For he who **s** and those who are Heb 2:11
ashes of a heifer **s** for the purification Heb 9:13

SANCTIFY (11)
you may know that I, the LORD, **s** you. Ex 31:13
You shall **s** him, for he offers the bread Lv 21:8
be holy to you, for I, the LORD, who **s** you, Lv 21:8
"**S** a solemn assembly for Baal." So 2 Kgs 10:20
in his midst, they will **s** my name; Is 29:23
they will **s** the Holy One of Jacob and Is 29:23
"Those who **s** and purify themselves to Is 66:17
S them in the truth; your word is truth. Jn 17:17
that he might **s** her, having cleansed Eph 5:26
of peace himself **s** you completely, 1 Thes 5:23
gate in order to **s** the people through Heb 13:12

SANCTUARIES (5)
blemish, that he may not profane my **s**, Lv 21:23
waste and will make your **s** desolate, Lv 26:31
Jerusalem and preach against the **s**. Ezk 21:2
of your trade you profaned your **s**; Ezk 28:18
and the **s** of Israel shall be laid waste, Am 7:9

SANCTUARY (148)
you have made for your abode, the **s**, Ex 15:17
And let them make me a **s**, that I may Ex 25:8
the shekel of the **s** (the shekel is twenty Ex 30:13
cassia, according to the shekel of the **s**, Ex 30:24
the construction of the **s** shall work in Ex 36:1
had brought for doing the work on the **s**. Ex 36:3
doing every sort of task on the **s** came, Ex 36:4
the contribution for the **s**." So the people Ex 36:6
work, in all the construction of the **s**, Ex 38:24
and 730 shekels, by the shekel of the **s**. Ex 38:24
1,775 shekels, by the shekel of the **s**: Ex 38:25
is, half a shekel, by the shekel of the **s**), Ex 38:26
the bases of the **s** and the bases of Ex 38:27
before the LORD in front of the veil of the **s**. Lv 4:6
shekels, according to the shekel of the **s**, Lv 5:15
from the front of the **s** and out of the Lv 10:4
the sin offering in the place of the **s**, Lv 10:17
not brought into the inner part of the **s**. Lv 10:18
certainly ought to have eaten it in the **s**, Lv 10:18
anything holy, nor come into the **s**, Lv 12:4
the burnt offering, in the place of the **s**. Lv 14:13
shall make atonement for the holy **s**, Lv 16:33
keep my Sabbaths and reverence my **s**: Lv 19:30
to make my **s** unclean and to profane Lv 20:3
He shall not go out of the **s**, lest he Lv 21:12
lest he profane the **s** of his God, Lv 21:12
keep my Sabbaths and reverence my **s**: Lv 26:2
of silver, according to the shekel of the **s**. Lv 27:3
be according to the shekel of the **s**: Lv 27:25
were 8,600, keeping guard over the **s**. Nm 3:28
the vessels of the **s** with which the Nm 3:31
of those who kept guard over the **s**. Nm 3:32
and his sons, guarding the **s** itself, Nm 3:38
the shekel of the **s** (the shekel of twenty Nm 3:47
1,365 shekels, by the shekel of the **s**. Nm 3:50
that are used in the **s** and put them in a Nm 4:12
have finished covering the **s** and all the Nm 4:15
and all the furnishings of the **s**, Nm 4:15
all that is in it, of the **s** and its vessels." Nm 4:16
according to the shekel of the **s**, Nm 7:13
according to the shekel of the **s**, Nm 7:19
according to the shekel of the **s**, Nm 7:25
according to the shekel of the **s**, Nm 7:31
according to the shekel of the **s**, Nm 7:37
according to the shekel of the **s**, Nm 7:43
according to the shekel of the **s**, Nm 7:49
according to the shekel of the **s**, Nm 7:55
according to the shekel of the **s**, Nm 7:61
according to the shekel of the **s**, Nm 7:67
according to the shekel of the **s**, Nm 7:73
according to the shekel of the **s**, Nm 7:79
shekels according to the shekel of the **s**, Nm 7:85
apiece according to the shekel of the **s**, Nm 7:86
the people of Israel come near the **s**." Nm 8:19
bear iniquity connected with the **s**, Nm 18:1
to the vessels of the **s** or to the altar lest Nm 18:3
keep guard over the **s** and over the Nm 18:5
silver, according to the shekel of the **s**, Nm 18:16
since he has defiled the **s** of the LORD. Nm 19:20
the vessels of the **s** and the trumpets for Nm 31:6
terebinth that was by the **s** of the LORD. Jos 24:26
house, both the nave and the inner **s**. 1 Kgs 6:5
and he built this within as an inner **s**, 1 Kgs 6:16
is, the nave in front of the inner **s**, 1 Kgs 6:17
The inner **s** he prepared in the 1 Kgs 6:19
The inner **s** was twenty cubits long, 1 Kgs 6:20
of gold across, in front of the inner **s**, 1 Kgs 6:21
to the inner **s** he overlaid with 1 Kgs 6:22
In the inner **s** he made two cherubim 1 Kgs 6:23
entrance to the inner **s** he made doors 1 Kgs 6:31
five on the north, before the inner **s**; 1 Kgs 7:49
to its place in the inner **s** of the house, 1 Kgs 8:6
from the Holy Place before the inner **s**; 1 Kgs 8:8
Arise and build the **s** of the LORD 1 Chr 22:19
of the tent of meeting and the **s**, 1 Chr 23:32
you to build a house for the **s**; 1 Chr 28:10
pure gold to burn before the inner **s**, 2 Chr 4:20
to its place, in the inner **s** of the house, 2 Chr 5:7
from the Holy Place before the inner **s**, 2 Chr 5:9
built for you in it a **s** for your name, 2 Chr 20:8
Go out of the **s**, for you have done 2 Chr 26:18
and for the **s** and for Judah. 2 Chr 29:21
to the LORD and come to his **s**, 2 Chr 30:8
the house of their **s** and had no 2 Chr 36:17
where the vessels of the **s** are, Neh 10:39
you help from the **s** and give you support Ps 20:2
up my hands toward your most holy **s**. Ps 28:2
So I have looked upon you in the **s**, Ps 63:2
is among them; Sinai is now in the **s**. Ps 68:17
of my God, my King, into the **s**— Ps 68:24
Awesome is God from his **s**; the God of Ps 68:35
until I went into the **s** of God; then I Ps 73:17
enemy has destroyed everything in the **s**! Ps 74:3
They set your **s** on fire; they profaned the Ps 74:7
He built his **s** like the high heavens, Ps 78:69
him; strength and beauty are in his **s**. Ps 96:6
Judah became his **s**, Israel his Ps 114:2
Praise God in his **s**; praise him in his Ps 150:1
And he will become a **s** and a stone of Is 8:14
place, when he comes to his **s** to pray, Is 16:12
I will profane the princes of the **s**, Is 43:28
the pine, to beautify the place of my **s**, Is 60:13
it shall drink it in the courts of my **s**." Is 62:9
adversaries have trampled down your **s**. Is 63:18
the beginning is the place of our **s**. Jer 17:12
she has seen the nations enter her **s**, Lam 1:10
has scorned his altar, disowned his **s**; Lam 2:7
prophet be killed in the **s** of the Lord? Lam 2:20
you have defiled my **s** with all your Ezk 5:11
here, to drive me far from my **s**? Ezk 8:6
And begin at my **s**." So they began with Ezk 9:6
yet I have been a **s** to them for a while Ezk 11:16
they have defiled my **s** on the same Ezk 23:38
day they came into my **s** to profane it. Ezk 23:39
Behold, I will profane my **s**, the pride Ezk 24:21
over my **s** when it was profaned, and Ezk 25:3
and will set my **s** in their midst Ezk 37:26
when my **s** is in their midst Ezk 37:28
me back to the outer gate of the **s**, Ezk 44:1
the temple and all the exits from the **s**. Ezk 44:5
in heart and flesh, to be in my **s**, Ezk 44:7
to keep my charge for you in my **s**. Ezk 44:8
the people of Israel, shall enter my **s**. Ezk 44:9
They shall be ministers in my **s**, Ezk 44:11
the charge of my **s** when the people of Ezk 44:15
They shall enter my **s**, and they shall Ezk 44:16
of 500 by 500 cubits shall be for the **s**, Ezk 45:2
10,000 broad, in which shall be the **s**, Ezk 45:3
who minister in the **s** and approach the Ezk 45:4
their houses and a holy place for the **s**. Ezk 45:4
without blemish, and purify the **s**. Ezk 45:18
the water for them flows from the **s**. Ezk 47:12
to the west, with the **s** in the midst of it. Ezk 48:8
with the **s** of the LORD in the midst of it. Ezk 48:10
holy portion with the **s** of the temple Ezk 48:21
and the place of his **s** was overthrown. Dn 8:11
the giving over of the **s** and host to be Dn 8:13
Then the **s** shall be restored to its Dn 8:14
make your face to shine upon your **s**, Dn 9:17
to come shall destroy the city and the **s**. Dn 9:26
prophesy at Bethel, for it is the king's **s**, Am 7:13
Judah has profaned the **s** of the LORD, Mal 2:11
murdered between the **s** and the altar. Mt 23:35
perished between the altar and the **s**. Lk 11:51
and the **s** of the tent of witness in heaven Rv 15:5
and out of the **s** came the seven angels Rv 15:6
and the **s** was filled with smoke from the Rv 15:8
one could enter the **s** until the seven Rv 15:8

SANCTUARY'S (1)
according to the **s** rules of 2 Chr 30:19

SAND (29)
of heaven and as the **s** that is on the Gn 22:17
make your offspring as the **s** of the sea, Gn 32:12
great abundance, like the **s** of the sea, Gn 41:49
down the Egyptian and hid him in the **s**. Ex 2:12
monitor lizard, the lizard, the **s** lizard, Lv 11:30
seas and the hidden treasures of the **s**." Dt 33:19
in number like the **s** that is on the Jos 11:4
as the **s** that is on the seashore in Jgs 7:12
and troops like the **s** on the seashore 1 Sm 13:5
as the **s** by the sea for multitude, 2 Sm 17:11
were as many as the **s** by the sea. 1 Kgs 4:20
of mind like the **s** on the seashore, 1 Kgs 4:29
it would be heavier than the **s** of the sea; Jb 6:3
and I shall multiply my days as the **s**, Jb 29:18
dust, winged birds like the **s** of the seas; Ps 78:27
count them, they are more than the **s**. Ps 139:18
A stone is heavy, and **s** is weighty, but a Prv 27:3
your people Israel be as the **s** of the sea, Is 10:22
the burning **s** shall become a pool, and Is 35:7
offspring would have been like the **s**, Is 48:19
I placed the **s** as the boundary for the sea, Jer 5:22
more in number than the **s** of the seas; Jer 15:8
of Israel shall be like the **s** of the sea, Hos 1:10
forward. They gather captives like **s**. Hab 1:9
man who built his house on the **s**. Mt 7:26
the sons of Israel be as the **s** of the sea, Rom 9:27
innumerable grains of **s** by the Heb 11:12
Jesus. And he stood on the **s** of the sea. Rv 12:17
their number is like the **s** of the sea. Rv 20:8

SANDAL (7)
a thread or a **s** strap or anything that Gn 14:23
the elders and pull his **s** off his foot and Dt 25:9
house of him who had his **s** pulled off.' Dt 25:10
the one drew off his **s** and gave it to the Ru 4:7
"Buy it for yourself," he drew off his **s**. Ru 4:8
a waistband is loose, not a **s** strap broken; Is 5:27
the strap of whose **s** I am not worthy to Jn 1:27

SANDALS (23)
take your **s** off your feet, for the place on Ex 3:5
your belt fastened, your **s** on your feet, Ex 12:11
and your **s** have not worn off your feet. Dt 29:5
Joshua, "Take off your **s** from your feet, Jos 5:15
with worn-out, patched **s** on their feet, Jos 9:5
And these garments and **s** of ours are Jos 9:13
his waist and on the **s** on his feet. 1 Kgs 2:5
They clothed them, gave them **s**, 2 Chr 28:15
How beautiful are your feet in **s**, O noble Sg 7:1
and he will lead people across in **s**. Is 11:15
and take off your **s** from your feet," and Is 20:2
for silver, and the needy for a pair of **s**— Am 2:6
needy for a pair of **s** and sell the chaff of Am 8:6
than I, whose **s** I am not worthy to carry. Mt 3:11
nor two tunics nor **s** nor a staff, Mt 10:10
the strap of whose **s** I am not worthy to Mk 1:7
but to wear **s** and not put on two tunics. Mk 6:9
the strap of whose **s** I am not worthy to Lk 3:16
Carry no moneybag, no knapsack, no **s**, Lk 10:4
with no moneybag or knapsack or **s**, Lk 22:35
to him, 'Take off the **s** from your feet, Acts 7:33
and put on your **s**." And he did so. Acts 12:8
the **s** of whose feet I am not worthy to Acts 13:25

SANDS (1)
be numbered and the **s** of the sea Jer 33:22

SANG (15)
and the people of Israel **s** this song to the Ex 15:1
And Miriam **s** to them: "Sing to the Ex 15:21
Then Israel **s** this song: "Spring up, O Nm 21:17
Then **s** Deborah and Barak the son of Jgs 5:1
And the women **s** to one another as 1 Sm 18:7
and the singers **s** and the trumpeters 2 Chr 29:28
And they **s** praises with gladness, 2 Chr 29:30
And they **s** responsively, praising and Ezr 3:11
And the singers **s** with Jezrahiah as Neh 12:42
the morning stars **s** together and all Jb 38:7
which he **s** to the LORD concerning the Ps 7:T
believed his words; they **s** his praise. Ps 106:12
we **s** a dirge, and you did not mourn.' Mt 11:17
we **s** a dirge, and you did not weep.' Lk 7:32
And they **s** a new song, saying, "Worthy Rv 5:9

SANK (11)
they **s** like lead in the mighty waters. Ex 15:10
Between her feet he **s**, he fell, he lay still; Jgs 5:27
he lay still; between her feet he **s**, he fell; Jgs 5:27
he fell; where he **s**, there he fell—dead. Jgs 5:27
The stone **s** into his forehead, and he 1 Sm 17:49
his heart, and he **s** in his chariot. 2 Kgs 9:24
stripped of their spoil; they **s** into sleep; Ps 76:5
the valleys **s** down to the place that you Ps 104:8
only mud, and Jeremiah **s** in the mud. Jer 38:6
scattered; the everlasting hills **s** low. Hab 3:6
s into a deep sleep as Paul talked still Acts 20:9

SANSANNAH (1)
Ziklag, Madmannah, **S**, Jos 15:31

SAP (1)
old age; they are ever full of **s** and green, Ps 92:14

SAPH (1)
the Hushathite struck down **S**, 2 Sm 21:18

SAPPHIRA (1)
a man named Ananias, with his wife **S**, Acts 5:1

SAPPHIRE (10)
his feet as it were a pavement of **s** stone, Ex 24:10
and the second row an emerald, a **s**, and Ex 28:18
and the second row, an emerald, a **s**, Ex 39:11

the gold of Ophir, in precious onyx or **s**. Jb 28:16
the beauty of their form was like **s**. Lam 4:7
of a throne, in appearance like **s**; Ezk 1:26
above them something like a **s**, Ezk 10:1
beryl, onyx, and jasper, **s**, emerald, Ezk 28:13
the color of fire and of **s** and of sulfur, Rv 9:17
The first was jasper, the second **s**, the Rv 21:19

SAPPHIRES (3)
Its stones are the place of **s**, and it has Jb 28:6
body is polished ivory, bedecked with **s**. Sg 5:14
and lay your foundations with **s**. Is 54:11

SAR-SEKIM (1)
Samgar-nebu, **S** the Rab-saris, Jer 39:3

SARAH (40)
name Sarai, but **S** shall be her name. Gn 17:15
who is a hundred years old? Shall **S**, Gn 17:17
but **S** your wife shall bear you a son, Gn 17:19
whom **S** shall bear to you at this time Gn 17:21
went quickly into the tent to **S** and said, Gn 18:6
"Where is **S** your wife?" And he said, Gn 18:9
and **S** your wife shall have a son." And Gn 18:10
have a son." And **S** was listening at the Gn 18:10
Now Abraham and **S** were old, Gn 18:11
way of women had ceased to be with **S**. Gn 18:11
So **S** laughed to herself, saying, "After I Gn 18:12
Abraham, "Why did **S** laugh and say, Gn 18:13
time next year, and **S** shall have a son." Gn 18:14
But **S** denied it, saying, "I did not Gn 18:15
And Abraham said of **S** his wife, "She is Gn 20:2
king of Gerar sent and took **S**. Gn 20:2
and returned **S** his wife to him. Gn 20:14
To **S** he said, "Behold, I have given Gn 20:16
the house of Abimelech because of **S**, Gn 20:18
The LORD visited **S** as he had said, and Gn 21:1
the LORD did to **S** as he had promised. Gn 21:1
And **S** conceived and bore Abraham a Gn 21:2
was born to him, whom **S** bore him, Gn 21:3
And **S** said, "God has made laughter for Gn 21:6
to Abraham that **S** would nurse Gn 21:7
But **S** saw the son of Hagar the Egyptian, Gn 21:9
Whatever **S** says to you, do as she tells Gn 21:12
S lived 127 years; these were the years of Gn 23:1
years; these were the years of the life of **S**. Gn 23:1
And **S** died at Kiriath-arba (that is, Gn 23:2
went in to mourn for **S** and to weep for Gn 23:2
Abraham buried **S** his wife in the cave Gn 23:19
And **S** my master's wife bore a son to Gn 24:36
into the tent of **S** his mother and took Gn 24:67
Abraham was buried, with **S** his wife. Gn 25:10
they buried Abraham and **S** his wife. Gn 49:31
your father and to **S** who bore you; Is 51:2
I will return and **S** shall have a son." Rom 9:9
By faith **S** herself received power to Heb 11:11
as **S** obeyed Abraham, calling him lord. 1 Pt 3:6

SARAH'S (2)
whom Hagar the Egyptian, **S** servant, Gn 25:12
considered the barrenness of **S** womb. Rom 4:19

SARAI (17)
The name of Abram's wife was **S**, and Gn 11:29
Now **S** was barren; she had no child. Gn 11:30
grandson, and **S** his daughter-in-law, Gn 11:31
And Abram took **S** his wife, and Lot his Gn 12:5
to enter Egypt, he said to **S** his wife, Gn 12:11
house with great plagues because of **S**, Gn 12:17
Now **S**, Abram's wife, had borne him no Gn 16:1
And **S** said to Abram, "Behold now, the Gn 16:2
And Abram listened to the voice of **S**. Gn 16:2
in the land of Canaan, **S**, Abram's wife, Gn 16:3
And **S** said to Abram, "May the wrong Gn 16:5
But Abram said to **S**, "Behold, your Gn 16:6
you please." Then **S** dealt harshly with Gn 16:6
And he said, "Hagar, servant of **S**, where Gn 16:8
said, "I am fleeing from my mistress **S**." Gn 16:8
said to Abraham, "As for **S** your wife, Gn 17:15
wife, you shall not call her name **S**, Gn 17:15

SARAPH (1)
the men of Cozeba, and Joash, and **S**, 1 Chr 4:22

SARDIS (3)
to Thyatira and to **S** and to Philadelphia Rv 1:11
"And to the angel of the church in **S** write: Rv 3:1
Yet you have still a few names in **S**, people Rv 3:4

SARDIUS (3)
A row of **s**, topaz, and carbuncle shall Ex 28:17
A row of **s**, topaz, and carbuncle was Ex 39:10
stone was your covering, **s**, topaz, Ezk 28:13

SARGON (1)
who was sent by **S** the king of Assyria, Is 20:1

SARID (2)
of their inheritance reached as far as **S**. Jos 19:10
From **S** it goes in the other direction Jos 19:12

SASH (7)
coat of checker work, a turban, and a **s**. Ex 28:4
shall make a **s** embroidered with Ex 28:39
and the **s** of fine twined linen and of Ex 39:29
him and tied the **s** around his waist and Lv 8:7
he shall tie the linen **s** around his waist, Lv 16:4
your robe, and will bind your **s** on him, Is 22:21
and with a golden **s** around his chest. Rv 1:13

SASHES (6)
you shall make coats and **s** and caps. Ex 28:40
and his sons with **s** and bind caps on Ex 29:9
with coats and tied **s** around their waists Lv 8:13
them; she delivers **s** to the merchant. Prv 31:24
the headdresses, the armlets, the **s**, the Is 3:20
linen, with golden **s** around their chests. Rv 15:6

SAT (119)
as he **s** at the door of his tent in the heat Gn 18:1
she went and **s** down opposite him Gn 21:16
the child." And as she **s** opposite him, Gn 21:16
in the camel's saddle and **s** on them. Gn 31:34
Then they **s** down to eat. And looking Gn 37:25
up, and **s** at the entrance to Enaim, Gn 38:14
And they **s** before him, the firstborn Gn 43:33
summoned his strength and **s** up in bed. Gn 48:2
land of Midian. And he **s** down by a well. Ex 2:15
of Pharaoh who **s** on his throne Ex 12:29
when we **s** by the meat pots and ate Ex 16:3
and put it under him, and he **s** on it, Ex 17:12
The next day Moses **s** to judge the Ex 18:13
And the people **s** down to eat and drink Ex 32:6
with the discharge has **s** shall wash his Lv 15:6
Asher **s** still at the coast of the sea, Jgs 5:17
the LORD came and **s** under the terebinth Jgs 6:11
again to the woman as she **s** in the field. Jgs 13:9
So the two of them **s** and ate and drank Jgs 19:6
And he went in and **s** down in the open Jgs 19:15
They **s** there before the LORD and fasted Jgs 20:26
came to Bethel and **s** there till evening Jgs 21:2
in the wine." So she **s** beside the reapers, Ru 2:14
had gone up to the gate and **s** down there. Ru 4:1
here." And he turned aside and **s** down. Ru 4:1
and said, "Sit down here." So they **s** down. Ru 4:2
as he **s** in his house with his spear in 1 Sm 19:9
came, the king **s** down to eat food. 1 Sm 20:24
The king **s** on his seat, as at other 1 Sm 20:25
seat by the wall. Jonathan **s** opposite, 1 Sm 20:25
opposite, and Abner **s** by Saul's side, 1 Sm 20:25
from the earth and **s** on the bed. 1 Sm 28:23
And they **s** down, the one on the one 2 Sm 2:13
David went in and **s** before the LORD 2 Sm 7:18
So Solomon **s** on the throne of David 1 Kgs 2:12
Then he **s** on his throne and had a 1 Kgs 2:19
king's mother, and she **s** on his right. 1 Kgs 2:19
And as they **s** at the table, the word 1 Kgs 13:20
and came and **s** down under a 1 Kgs 19:4
men came in and **s** opposite him. 1 Kgs 21:13
the child **s** on her lap till noon, 2 Kgs 4:20
and Jeroboam **s** on his throne. 2 Kgs 13:13
David went in and **s** before the LORD 1 Chr 17:16
Then Solomon **s** on the throne of 1 Chr 29:23
from my head and beard and **s** appalled. Ezr 9:3
around me while I **s** appalled until the Ezr 9:4
And all the people **s** in the open square Ezr 10:9
tenth month they **s** down to examine Ezr 10:16
heard these words I **s** down and wept and Neh 1:4
when King Ahasuerus **s** on his royal Est 1:2
king's face, and **s** first in the kingdom): Est 1:14
the king and Haman **s** down to drink, Est 3:15
to scrape himself while he **s** in the ashes. Jb 2:8
And they **s** with him on the ground seven Jb 2:13
I chose their way and **s** as chief, and I Jb 29:25
you have **s** on the throne, giving righteous Ps 9:4
Some **s** in darkness and in the shadow Ps 107:10
of Babylon, there we **s** down and wept, Ps 137:1
With great delight I **s** in his shadow, and Sg 2:3
waysides you have **s** awaiting lovers like Jer 3:2
of revelers, nor did I rejoice; I **s** alone, Jer 15:17
of Babylon came and **s** in the middle Jer 39:3
canal, and I **s** where they were dwelling. Ezk 3:15
And I **s** there overwhelmed among Ezk 3:15
day of the month, as I **s** in my house, Ezk 8:1
there **s** women weeping for Tammuz. Ezk 8:14
of Israel came to me and **s** before me. Ezk 14:1
to inquire of the LORD, and **s** before me. Ezk 20:1
You **s** on a stately couch, with a table Ezk 23:41
before him; the court **s** in judgment, Dn 7:10
himself with sackcloth, and **s** in ashes. Jon 3:6
went out of the city and **s** to the east of the Jon 4:5
He **s** under it in the shade, till he should Jon 4:5
you better than Thebes that **s** by the Nile, Na 3:8
on the mountain, and when he **s** down, Mt 5:1
out of the house and **s** beside the sea. Mt 13:1
so that he got into a boat and **s** down. Mt 13:2
drew it ashore and **s** down and sorted Mt 13:48
up on the mountain and **s** down there. Mt 15:29
on them their cloaks, and he **s** on them. Mt 21:7
As he **s** on the Mount of Olives, the Mt 24:3
Day after day I **s** in the temple teaching, Mt 26:55
and going inside he **s** with the guards Mt 26:58
Then they **s** down and kept watch over Mt 27:36
and rolled back the stone and **s** on it. Mt 28:2
about at those who **s** around him, Mk 3:34
he got into a boat and **s** in it on the sea, Mk 4:1
So they **s** down in groups, by hundreds Mk 6:40
And he **s** down and called the twelve. Mk 9:35
a colt tied, on which no one has ever **s**. Mk 11:2
threw their cloaks on it, and he **s** on it. Mk 11:7
And he **s** down opposite the treasury Mk 12:41
And as he **s** on the Mount of Olives Mk 13:3
up into heaven and **s** down at the right Mk 16:19
it back to the attendant and **s** down. Lk 4:20
And he **s** down and taught the people Lk 5:3
And the dead man **s** up and began to Lk 7:15
who **s** at the Lord's feet and listened to Lk 10:39
tied, on which no one has ever yet **s**. Lk 19:30
of the courtyard and **s** down together, Lk 22:55
together, Peter **s** down among them. Lk 22:55
seeing him as he **s** in the light and Lk 22:56
and there he **s** down with his disciples. Jn 6:3
So the men **s** down, about five thousand Jn 6:10
to him, and he **s** down and taught them. Jn 8:2
Jesus found a young donkey and **s** on it, Jn 12:14
brought Jesus out and **s** down on the Jn 19:13
as the one who **s** at the Beautiful Gate Acts 3:10
all who **s** in the council saw that his Acts 6:15
eyes, and when she saw Peter she **s** up. Acts 9:40
went into the synagogue and **s** down. Acts 13:14
and we **s** down and spoke to the Acts 16:13
"The people **s** down to eat and drink 1 Cor 10:7
he **s** down at the right hand of the Heb 1:3
he **s** down at the right hand of God, Heb 10:12
I also conquered and **s** down with my Rv 3:21
And he who **s** there had the appearance of Rv 4:3
a loud voice to him who **s** on the cloud, Rv 14:15
So he who **s** on the cloud swung his Rv 14:16

SATAN (53)
Then **S** stood against Israel and 1 Chr 21:1
the LORD, and **S** also came among them. Jb 1:6
The LORD said to **S**, "From where have you Jb 1:7
have you come?" **S** answered the LORD Jb 1:7
And the LORD said to **S**, "Have you Jb 1:8
Then **S** answered the LORD and said, "Does Jb 1:9
And the LORD said to **S**, "Behold, all that Jb 1:12
out your hand." So **S** went out from the Jb 1:12
and **S** also came among them to present Jb 2:1
And the LORD said to **S**, "From where have Jb 2:2
have you come?" **S** answered the LORD Jb 2:2
And the LORD said to **S**, "Have you Jb 2:3
Then **S** answered the LORD and said, "Skin Jb 2:4
And the LORD said to **S**, "Behold, he is in Jb 2:6
So **S** went out from the presence of the Jb 2:7
and **S** standing at his right hand to Zec 3:1
And the LORD said to **S**, "The LORD rebuke Zec 3:2
to Satan, "The LORD rebuke you, O **S**! Zec 3:2
said to him, "Be gone, **S**! For it is written, Mt 4:10
And if **S** casts out Satan, he is divided Mt 12:26
And if Satan casts out **S**, he is divided Mt 12:26
me, **S**! You are a hindrance to me. Mt 16:23
forty days, being tempted by **S**. Mk 1:13
in parables, "How can **S** cast out Satan? Mk 3:23
in parables, "How can Satan cast out **S**? Mk 3:23
And if **S** has risen up against himself Mk 3:26
S immediately comes and takes away Mk 4:15
S! For you are not setting your mind on Mk 8:33
"I saw **S** fall like lightning from Lk 10:18
And if **S** also is divided against himself, Lk 11:18
of Abraham whom **S** bound for Lk 13:16
Then **S** entered into Judas called Lk 22:3
behold, **S** demanded to have you, Lk 22:31
taken the morsel, **S** entered into him. Jn 13:27
why has **S** filled your heart to lie to the Acts 5:3
light and from the power of **S** to God, Acts 26:18
will soon crush **S** under your feet. Rom 16:20
this man to **S** for the destruction 1 Cor 5:5
so that **S** may not tempt you because 1 Cor 7:5
that we would not be outwitted by **S**; 2 Cor 2:11
for even **S** disguises himself as an 2 Cor 11:14
flesh, a messenger of **S** to harass me, 2 Cor 12:7
and again—but **S** hindered us. 1 Thes 2:18
by the activity of **S** with all power and 2 Thes 2:9
have handed over to **S** that they may 1 Tm 1:20
For some have already strayed after **S**. 1 Tm 5:15
Jews and are not, but are a synagogue of **S**. Rv 2:9
was killed among you, where **S** dwells. Rv 2:13
what some call the deep things of **S**, Rv 2:24
of the synagogue of **S** who say that they Rv 3:9
serpent, who is called the devil and **S**, Rv 12:9
ancient serpent, who is the devil and **S**, Rv 20:2
ended, **S** will be released from his prison Rv 20:7

SATAN'S (1)
where you dwell, where **S** throne is. Rv 2:13

SATED (5)
he said, "O Naphtali, **s** with favor, Dt 33:23
The LORD has a sword; it is **s** with blood; it Is 34:6
shall devour and be **s** and drink its fill Jer 46:10
all who plunder her shall be **s**, declares Jer 50:10
he has **s** me with wormwood. Lam 3:15

SATISFIED (50)
weight, and you shall eat and not be **s**. Lv 26:26
And she ate until she was **s**, and she had Ru 2:14
what food she had left over after being **s**. Ru 2:18
me? Why are you not **s** with my flesh? Jb 19:22
with treasure; they are **s** with children, Ps 17:14
I awake, I shall be **s** with your likeness. Ps 17:15
The afflicted shall eat and be **s**; those Ps 22:26
My soul will be **s** as with fat and rich Ps 63:5
We shall be **s** with the goodness of your Ps 65:4
But before they had **s** their craving, Ps 78:30
the earth is **s** with the fruit of your Ps 104:13
of his mouth a man is **s** with good, Prv 12:14
of a man's mouth his stomach is **s**; Prv 18:20
satisfied; he is **s** by the yield of his lips. Prv 18:20
leads to life, and whoever has it rests **s**; Prv 19:23
Sheol and Abaddon are never **s**, and Prv 27:20
and never **s** are the eyes of man. Prv 27:20
Three things are never **s**; four never Prv 30:15
womb, the land never **s** with water, Prv 30:16
the eye is not **s** with seeing, nor the ear Eccl 1:8
toil, and his eyes are never **s** with riches, Eccl 4:8
loves money will not be **s** with money, Eccl 5:10
his soul is not **s** with life's good things, Eccl 6:3
is for his mouth, yet his appetite is not **s**. Eccl 6:7
and they devour on the left, but are not **s**; Is 9:20
eating and awakes with his hunger not **s**, Is 29:8
or **s** me with the fat of your sacrifices. Is 43:24
half he eats meat; he roasts it and is **s**. Is 44:16
anguish of his soul he shall see and be **s**; Is 53:11
may nurse and be **s** from her consoling Is 66:11
my people shall be **s** with my goodness, Jer 31:14
and his desire shall be **s** on the hills of Jer 50:19
the Assyrians, because you were not **s**; Ezk 16:28
with them, and still you were not **s**. Ezk 16:28
and even with this you were not **s**. Ezk 16:29
anymore till I have **s** my fury upon Ezk 24:13
from the seas, you **s** many peoples; Ezk 27:33
They shall eat, but not be **s**; they shall Hos 4:10
you grain, wine, and oil, and you will be **s**; Jl 2:19
"You shall eat in plenty and be **s**, and Jl 2:26
city to drink water, and would not be **s**; Am 4:8
You shall eat, but not be **s**, and there Mi 6:14
for righteousness, for they shall be **s**. Mt 5:6
And they all ate and were **s**. And they Mt 14:20
And they all ate and were **s**. And they Mt 15:37
And they all ate and were **s**. Mk 6:42
And they ate and were **s**. And they took Mk 8:8
who are hungry now, for you shall be **s**. Lk 6:21
And they all ate and were **s**. And what Lk 9:17
I myself am **s** about you, my Rom 15:14

SATISFIES (2)
who **s** you with good so that your youth Ps 103:5
For he **s** the longing soul, and the Ps 107:9

SATISFY (19)
to **s** the waste and desolate land, and to Jb 38:27
lion, or **s** the appetite of the young lions, Jb 38:39
honey from the rock I would **s** you." Ps 81:16
S us in the morning with your steadfast Ps 90:14
long life I will **s** him and show him Ps 91:16
I will **s** her poor with bread. Ps 132:15
you **s** the desire of every living thing. Ps 145:16
if he steals to **s** his appetite when he Prv 6:30
righteous has enough to **s** his appetite, Prv 13:25
and your labor for that which does not **s**? Is 55:2
out for the hungry and **s** the desire of the Is 58:10
you continually and **s** your desire in Is 58:11
For I will **s** the weary soul, and every Jer 31:25
vent my fury upon them and **s** myself. Ezk 5:13
They cannot **s** their hunger or fill their Ezk 7:19
So will I **s** my wrath on you, and my Ezk 16:42
clap my hands, and I will **s** my fury; Ezk 21:17
we will **s** him and keep you out of Mt 28:14
So Pilate, wishing to **s** the crowd, Mk 15:15

SATISFYING (1)
s your hearts with food and Acts 14:17

SATRAPS (13)
commissions to the king's **s** and to the Ezr 8:36
written to the king's **s** and to the Est 3:12
to the **s** and the governors and the Est 8:9
the provinces and the **s** and the governors Est 9:3
Nebuchadnezzar sent to gather the **s**, Dn 3:2
Then the **s**, the prefects, and the Dn 3:3
And the **s**, the prefects, the governors, Dn 3:27
Darius to set over the kingdom 120 **s**, Dn 6:1
to whom these **s** should give account, Dn 6:2
above all the other presidents and **s**, Dn 6:3
the presidents and the **s** sought to find a Dn 6:4
these presidents and **s** came by Dn 6:6
of the kingdom, the prefects and the **s**, Dn 6:7

SAUL (395)
And he had a son whose name was **S**, a 1 Sm 9:2
So Kish said to **S** his son, "Take one of 1 Sm 9:3
S said to his servant who was with him, 1 Sm 9:5
Then **S** said to his servant, "But if we 1 Sm 9:7
The servant answered **S** again, "Here, I 1 Sm 9:8
And **S** said to his servant, "Well said; 1 Sm 9:10
Now the day before **S** came, the LORD 1 Sm 9:15
When Samuel saw **S**, the LORD told 1 Sm 9:17
Then **S** approached Samuel in the 1 Sm 9:18
Samuel answered **S**, "I am the seer. Go 1 Sm 9:19
S answered, "Am I not a Benjaminite, 1 Sm 9:21
Then Samuel took **S** and his young 1 Sm 9:22
what was on it and set them before **S**. 1 Sm 9:24
with the guests." So **S** ate with Samuel 1 Sm 9:24
a bed was spread for **S** on the roof, 1 Sm 9:25
dawn Samuel called to **S** on the roof, 1 Sm 9:26
send you on your way." So **S** arose, 1 Sm 9:26
outskirts of the city, Samuel said to **S**, 1 Sm 9:27
Kish? Is **S** also among the prophets?" 1 Sm 10:11
"Is **S** also among the prophets?" 1 Sm 10:12
And **S** said to his uncle, "He told us 1 Sm 10:16
and **S** the son of Kish was taken by 1 Sm 10:21
S also went to his home at Gibeah, 1 Sm 10:26
the messengers came to Gibeah of **S**, 1 Sm 11:4
S was coming from the field behind 1 Sm 11:5
the field behind the oxen. And **S** said, 1 Sm 11:5
of God rushed upon **S** when he heard 1 Sm 11:6
does not come out after **S** and Samuel, 1 Sm 11:7
And the next day **S** put the people in 1 Sm 11:11
is it that said, 'Shall **S** reign over us?' 1 Sm 11:12
But **S** said, "Not a man shall be put 1 Sm 11:13
there they made **S** king before the 1 Sm 11:15
and there **S** and all the men of Israel 1 Sm 11:15
S was … years old when he began to 1 Sm 13:1
S chose three thousand men of Israel. 1 Sm 13:2
thousand were with **S** in Michmash 1 Sm 13:2
And **S** blew the trumpet throughout 1 Sm 13:3
heard it said that **S** had defeated the 1 Sm 13:4
were called out to join **S** at Gilgal. 1 Sm 13:4
S was still at Gilgal, and all the people 1 Sm 13:7
So **S** said, "Bring the burnt offering 1 Sm 13:9
And **S** went out to meet him and 1 Sm 13:10
"What have you done?" And **S** said, 1 Sm 13:11
And Samuel said to **S**, "You have 1 Sm 13:13
people went up after **S** to meet the 1 Sm 13:15
And **S** numbered the people who 1 Sm 13:15
And **S** and Jonathan his son and the 1 Sm 13:16
of the people with **S** and Jonathan, 1 Sm 13:22
but **S** and Jonathan his son had 1 Sm 13:22
Jonathan the son of **S** said to the 1 Sm 14:1
S was staying in the outskirts of 1 Sm 14:2
And the watchmen of **S** in Gibeah of 1 Sm 14:16
Then **S** said to the people who were 1 Sm 14:17
So **S** said to Ahijah, "Bring the ark of 1 Sm 14:18
Now while **S** was talking to the 1 Sm 14:19
So **S** said to the priest, "Withdraw 1 Sm 14:19
Then **S** and all the people who were 1 Sm 14:20
who were with **S** and Jonathan. 1 Sm 14:21
so **S** had laid an oath on the people, 1 Sm 14:24
Then they told **S**, "Behold, the people 1 Sm 14:33
And **S** said, "Disperse yourselves 1 Sm 14:34
And **S** built an altar to the LORD; it 1 Sm 14:35
Then **S** said, "Let us go down after 1 Sm 14:36
And **S** inquired of God, "Shall I go 1 Sm 14:37
And **S** said, "Come here, all you 1 Sm 14:38
other side." And the people said to **S**, 1 Sm 14:40
Therefore **S** said, "O LORD God of 1 Sm 14:41
And Jonathan and **S** were taken, 1 Sm 14:41
Then **S** said, "Cast the lot between 1 Sm 14:42
Then **S** said to Jonathan, "Tell me 1 Sm 14:43
And **S** said, "God do so to me and 1 Sm 14:44
Then the people said to **S**, "Shall 1 Sm 14:45
Then **S** went up from pursuing the 1 Sm 14:46
When **S** had taken the kingship over 1 Sm 14:47
Now the sons of **S** were Jonathan, 1 Sm 14:49
Kish was the father of **S**, and Ner the 1 Sm 14:51
the Philistines all the days of **S**. 1 Sm 14:52
And when **S** saw any strong man, or 1 Sm 14:52
And Samuel said to **S**, "The LORD sent 1 Sm 15:1
So **S** summoned the people and 1 Sm 15:4
And **S** came to the city of Amalek and 1 Sm 15:5
Then **S** said to the Kenites, "Go, 1 Sm 15:6
And **S** defeated the Amalekites from 1 Sm 15:7
But **S** and the people spared Agag and 1 Sm 15:9
"I regret that I have made **S** king, for 1 Sm 15:11
rose early to meet **S** in the morning. 1 Sm 15:12
was told Samuel, "**S** came to Carmel, 1 Sm 15:12
And Samuel came to **S**, and Saul 1 Sm 15:13
came to Saul, and **S** said to him, 1 Sm 15:13
S said, "They have brought them 1 Sm 15:15
Then Samuel said to **S**, "Stop! I will 1 Sm 15:16
And **S** said to Samuel, "I have obeyed 1 Sm 15:20
S said to Samuel, "I have sinned, for I 1 Sm 15:24
And Samuel said to **S**, "I will not 1 Sm 15:26
away, **S** seized the skirt of his robe, 1 Sm 15:27
So Samuel turned back after **S**, and 1 Sm 15:31
Saul, and **S** bowed before the LORD. 1 Sm 15:31
and **S** went up to his house in 1 Sm 15:34
went up to his house in Gibeah of **S**. 1 Sm 15:34
Samuel did not see **S** again until the 1 Sm 15:35
his death, but Samuel grieved over **S**. 1 Sm 15:35
that he had made **S** king over Israel. 1 Sm 15:35
"How long will you grieve over **S**, 1 Sm 16:1
If **S** hears it, he will kill me." And the 1 Sm 16:2
Spirit of the LORD departed from **S**, 1 Sm 16:14
So **S** said to his servants, "Provide for 1 Sm 16:17
Therefore **S** sent messengers to Jesse 1 Sm 16:19
and sent them by David his son to **S**. 1 Sm 16:20
And David came to **S** and entered his 1 Sm 16:21
And **S** loved him greatly, and he 1 Sm 16:21
And **S** sent to Jesse, saying, "Let 1 Sm 16:22
the evil spirit from God was upon **S**, 1 Sm 16:23
So **S** was refreshed and was well, and 1 Sm 16:23
And **S** and the men of Israel were 1 Sm 17:2
and are you not servants of **S**? 1 Sm 17:8
When **S** and all Israel heard these 1 Sm 17:11
In the days of **S** the man was already 1 Sm 17:12
of Jesse had followed **S** to the battle. 1 Sm 17:13
youngest. The three eldest followed **S**, 1 Sm 17:14
back and forth from **S** to feed his 1 Sm 17:15
Now **S** and they and all the men of 1 Sm 17:19
heard, they repeated them before **S**, 1 Sm 17:31
And David said to **S**, "Let no man's 1 Sm 17:32
And **S** said to David, "You are not 1 Sm 17:33
But David said to **S**, "Your servant 1 Sm 17:34
this Philistine." And **S** said to David, 1 Sm 17:37
Then **S** clothed David with his 1 Sm 17:38
Then David said to **S**, "I cannot go 1 Sm 17:39
As soon as **S** saw David go out 1 Sm 17:55
brought him before **S** with the head 1 Sm 17:57
And **S** said to him, "Whose son are 1 Sm 17:58
soon as he had finished speaking to **S**, 1 Sm 18:1
And **S** took him that day and would 1 Sm 18:2
was successful wherever **S** sent him, 1 Sm 18:5
so that **S** set him over the men of war. 1 Sm 18:5
singing and dancing, to meet King **S**, 1 Sm 18:6
"**S** has struck down his thousands, 1 Sm 18:7
And **S** was very angry, and this saying 1 Sm 18:8
And **S** eyed David from that day on. 1 Sm 18:9
spirit from God rushed upon **S**, 1 Sm 18:10
by day. **S** had his spear in his hand. 1 Sm 18:10
And **S** hurled the spear, for he 1 Sm 18:11
S was afraid of David because the 1 Sm 18:12
with him but had departed from **S**. 1 Sm 18:12
So **S** removed him from his presence 1 Sm 18:13
And when **S** saw that he had great 1 Sm 18:15
Then **S** said to David, "Here is my 1 Sm 18:17
the LORD'S battles." For **S** thought, 1 Sm 18:17
And David said to **S**, "Who am I, and 1 Sm 18:18
And they told **S**, and the thing 1 Sm 18:20
S thought, "Let me give her to him, 1 Sm 18:21
against him." Therefore **S** said to 1 Sm 18:21
And **S** commanded his servants, 1 Sm 18:22
And the servants of **S** told him, 1 Sm 18:24
Then **S** said, "Thus shall you say to 1 Sm 18:25
king's enemies.'" Now **S** thought to 1 Sm 18:25
And **S** gave him his daughter 1 Sm 18:27
But when **S** saw and knew that the 1 Sm 18:28
S was even more afraid of David. So 1 Sm 18:29
So **S** was David's enemy continually. 1 Sm 18:29
success than all the servants of **S**, 1 Sm 18:30
And **S** spoke to Jonathan his son and 1 Sm 19:1
David, "**S** my father seeks to kill you. 1 Sm 19:2
well of David to **S** his father and said 1 Sm 19:4
And **S** listened to the voice of 1 Sm 19:6
S swore, "As the LORD lives, he shall 1 Sm 19:6
And Jonathan brought David to **S**, 1 Sm 19:7
spirit from the LORD came upon **S**, 1 Sm 19:9
And **S** sought to pin David to the 1 Sm 19:10
wall with the spear, but he eluded **S**, 1 Sm 19:10
S sent messengers to David's house 1 Sm 19:11
And when **S** sent messengers to take 1 Sm 19:14
Then **S** sent the messengers to see 1 Sm 19:15
S said to Michal, "Why have you 1 Sm 19:17
escaped?" And Michal answered **S**, 1 Sm 19:17
told him all that **S** had done to him. 1 Sm 19:18
And it was told **S**, "Behold, David is 1 Sm 19:19
Then **S** sent messengers to take 1 Sm 19:20
God came upon the messengers of **S**, 1 Sm 19:20
When it was told **S**, he sent other 1 Sm 19:21
And **S** sent messengers again the 1 Sm 19:21
said, "Is **S** also among the prophets?" 1 Sm 19:24
Yet **S** did not say anything that day, 1 Sm 20:26

And **S** said to Jonathan his son, 1 Sm 20:27
Jonathan answered **S**, "David 1 Sm 20:28
Jonathan answered **S** his father, 1 Sm 20:32
But **S** hurled his spear at him to 1 Sm 20:33
of the servants of **S** was there that day, 1 Sm 21:7
fled that day from **S** and went to 1 Sm 21:10
'**S** has struck down his thousands, 1 Sm 21:11
Now **S** heard that David was 1 Sm 22:6
S was sitting at Gibeah under the 1 Sm 22:6
And **S** said to his servants who stood 1 Sm 22:7
who stood by the servants of **S**, 1 Sm 22:9
And **S** said, "Hear now, son of 1 Sm 22:12
And **S** said to him, "Why have you 1 Sm 22:13
told David that **S** had killed the 1 Sm 22:21
was there, that he would surely tell **S**. 1 Sm 22:22
Now it was told **S** that David had 1 Sm 23:7
David had come to Keilah. And **S** said, 1 Sm 23:7
And **S** summoned all the people to 1 Sm 23:8
David knew that **S** was plotting harm 1 Sm 23:9
surely heard that **S** seeks to come 1 Sm 23:10
Will **S** come down, as your servant 1 Sm 23:11
into the hand of **S**?" And the LORD 1 Sm 23:12
When **S** was told that David had 1 Sm 23:13
And **S** sought him every day, but 1 Sm 23:14
David saw that **S** had come out to 1 Sm 23:15
for the hand of **S** my father shall not 1 Sm 23:17
to you. **S** my father also knows this." 1 Sm 23:17
the Ziphites went up to **S** at Gibeah, 1 Sm 23:19
And **S** said, "May you be blessed by 1 Sm 23:21
arose and went to Ziph ahead of **S**. 1 Sm 23:24
And **S** and his men went to seek him. 1 Sm 23:25
of Maon. And when **S** heard that, 1 Sm 23:25
S went on one side of the mountain, 1 Sm 23:26
was hurrying to get away from **S**. 1 Sm 23:26
As **S** and his men were closing in on 1 Sm 23:26
a messenger came to **S**, saying, 1 Sm 23:27
So **S** returned from pursuing after 1 Sm 23:28
When **S** returned from following the 1 Sm 24:1
Then **S** took three thousand chosen 1 Sm 24:2
cave, and **S** went in to relieve himself. 1 Sm 24:3
and did not permit them to attack **S**. 1 Sm 24:7
And **S** rose up and left the cave and 1 Sm 24:7
out of the cave, and called after **S**, 1 Sm 24:8
king!" And when **S** looked behind 1 Sm 24:8
And David said to **S**, "Why do you 1 Sm 24:9
finished speaking these words to **S**, 1 Sm 24:16
speaking these words to Saul, **S** said, 1 Sm 24:16
my son David?" And **S** lifted up his 1 Sm 24:16
And David swore this to **S**. Then 1 Sm 24:22
Then **S** went home, but David and 1 Sm 24:22
S had given Michal his daughter, 1 Sm 25:44
the Ziphites came to **S** at Gibeah, 1 Sm 26:1
So **S** arose and went down to the 1 Sm 26:2
And **S** encamped on the hill of 1 Sm 26:3
When he saw that **S** came after him 1 Sm 26:3
out spies and learned that **S** had come. 1 Sm 26:4
to the place where **S** had encamped. 1 Sm 26:5
And David saw the place where **S** lay, 1 Sm 26:5
S was lying within the encampment, 1 Sm 26:5
the camp to **S**?" And Abishai said, 1 Sm 26:6
And there lay **S** sleeping within the 1 Sm 26:7
S recognized David's voice and said, 1 Sm 26:17
Then **S** said, "I have sinned. Return, 1 Sm 26:21
Then **S** said to David, "Blessed be 1 Sm 26:25
his way, and **S** returned to his place. 1 Sm 26:25
shall perish one day by the hand of **S**. 1 Sm 27:1
Then **S** will despair of seeking me any 1 Sm 27:1
when it was told **S** that David had fled 1 Sm 27:4
And **S** had put the mediums and the 1 Sm 28:3
And **S** gathered all Israel, and they 1 Sm 28:4
When **S** saw the army of the 1 Sm 28:5
And when **S** inquired of the LORD, the 1 Sm 28:6
Then **S** said to his servants, "Seek out 1 Sm 28:7
So **S** disguised himself and put on 1 Sm 28:8
"Surely you know what **S** has done, 1 Sm 28:9
But **S** swore to her by the LORD, "As 1 Sm 28:10
And the woman said to **S**, "Why 1 Sm 28:12
have you deceived me? You are **S**." 1 Sm 28:12
you see?" And the woman said to **S**, 1 Sm 28:13
in a robe." And **S** knew that it was 1 Sm 28:14
Then Samuel said to **S**, "Why have 1 Sm 28:15
me by bringing me up?" **S** answered, 1 Sm 28:15
Then **S** fell at once full length on the 1 Sm 28:20
And the woman came to **S**, and 1 Sm 28:21
she put it before **S** and his servants, 1 Sm 28:25
"Is this not David, the servant of **S**, 1 Sm 29:3
'**S** has struck down his thousands, 1 Sm 29:5
the Philistines overtook **S** and his 1 Sm 31:2
and Malchi-shua, the sons of **S**. 1 Sm 31:2
The battle pressed hard against **S**, and 1 Sm 31:3
Then **S** said to his armor-bearer, 1 Sm 31:4
Therefore **S** took his own sword and 1 Sm 31:4
his armor-bearer saw that **S** was dead, 1 Sm 31:5
Thus **S** died, and his three sons, and 1 Sm 31:6
had fled and that **S** and his sons were 1 Sm 31:7
they found **S** and his three sons fallen 1 Sm 31:8
what the Philistines had done to **S**, 1 Sm 31:11
took the body of **S** and the bodies of 1 Sm 31:12
After the death of **S**, when David had 2 Sm 1:1
and **S** and his son Jonathan are also 2 Sm 1:4
do you know that **S** and his son 2 Sm 1:5
and there was **S** leaning on his spear, 2 Sm 1:6
until evening for **S** and for Jonathan 2 Sm 1:12
this lamentation over **S** and Jonathan 2 Sm 1:17
the mighty was defiled, the shield of **S**, 2 Sm 1:21
the sword of **S** returned not empty. 2 Sm 1:22
"**S** and Jonathan, beloved and lovely! 2 Sm 1:23
"You daughters of Israel, weep over **S**, 2 Sm 1:24
men of Jabesh-gilead who buried **S**," 2 Sm 2:4
showed this loyalty to **S** your lord and 2 Sm 2:5
and be valiant, for **S** your lord is dead, 2 Sm 2:7
the son of **S** and brought him 2 Sm 2:8
servants of Ish-bosheth the son of **S**, 2 Sm 2:12
and Ish-bosheth the son of **S**, 2 Sm 2:15
between the house of **S** and the house of 2 Sm 3:1
the house of **S** became weaker and 2 Sm 3:1
between the house of **S** and the house of 2 Sm 3:6
himself strong in the house of **S**. 2 Sm 3:6
Now **S** had a concubine whose name 2 Sm 3:7
love to the house of **S** your father, 2 Sm 3:8
from the house of **S** and set up the 2 Sm 3:10
Jonathan, the son of **S**, had a son who 2 Sm 4:4
the news about **S** and Jonathan came 2 Sm 4:4
is the head of Ish-bosheth, the son of **S**, 2 Sm 4:8
king this day on **S** and on his 2 Sm 4:8
when one told me, 'Behold, **S** is dead,' 2 Sm 4:10
In times past, when **S** was king over us, 2 Sm 5:2
the daughter of **S** looked out of 2 Sm 6:16
Michal the daughter of **S** came out to 2 Sm 6:20
Michal the daughter of **S** had no child 2 Sm 6:23
depart from him, as I took it from **S**, 2 Sm 7:15
there still anyone left of the house of **S**, 2 Sm 9:1
of the house of **S** whose name was Ziba, 2 Sm 9:2
not still someone of the house of **S**, 2 Sm 9:3
the son of Jonathan, son of **S**, 2 Sm 9:6
to you all the land of **S** your father, 2 Sm 9:7
"All that belonged to **S** and to all his 2 Sm 9:9
I delivered you out of the hand of **S**. 2 Sm 12:7
a man of the family of the house of **S**, 2 Sm 16:5
on you all the blood of the house of **S**, 2 Sm 16:8
Ziba the servant of the house of **S**, 2 Sm 19:17
the son of **S** came down to 2 Sm 19:24
"There is bloodguilt on **S** and on his 2 Sm 21:1
S had sought to strike them down in 2 Sm 21:2
or gold between us and **S** or his house; 2 Sm 21:4
them before the LORD at Gibeah of **S**, 2 Sm 21:6
David and Jonathan the son of **S**. 2 Sm 21:7
daughter of Aiah, whom she bore to **S**, 2 Sm 21:8
five sons of Merab the daughter of **S**, 2 Sm 21:8
of Aiah, the concubine of **S**, 2 Sm 21:11
took the bones of **S** and the bones of 2 Sm 21:12
the Philistines killed **S** on Gilboa. 2 Sm 21:12
there the bones of **S** and the bones of 2 Sm 21:13
buried the bones of **S** and his son 2 Sm 21:14
his enemies, and from the hand of **S**. 2 Sm 22:1
in the days of **S** they waged war 1 Chr 5:10
Ner was the father of Kish, Kish of **S**, 1 Chr 8:33
of Kish, Kish of Saul, **S** of Jonathan, 1 Chr 8:33
Ner fathered Kish, Kish fathered **S**, 1 Chr 9:39
fathered Saul, **S** fathered Jonathan, 1 Chr 9:39
the Philistines overtook **S** and his 1 Chr 10:2
and Malchi-shua, the sons of **S**. 1 Chr 10:2
The battle pressed hard against **S**, 1 Chr 10:3
Then **S** said to his armor-bearer, 1 Chr 10:4
Therefore **S** took his own sword and 1 Chr 10:4
armor-bearer saw that **S** was dead, 1 Chr 10:5
Thus **S** died; he and his three sons 1 Chr 10:6
had fled and that **S** and his sons were 1 Chr 10:7
they found **S** and his sons fallen on 1 Chr 10:8
that the Philistines had done to **S**, 1 Chr 10:11
away the body of **S** and the bodies of 1 Chr 10:12
So **S** died for his breach of faith. He 1 Chr 10:13
In times past, even when **S** was king, 1 Chr 11:2
about freely because of **S** the son of 1 Chr 12:1
Philistines for the battle against **S**. 1 Chr 12:19
he will desert to his master **S**.") 1 Chr 12:19
turn the kingdom of **S** over to him, 1 Chr 12:23
the Benjaminites, the kinsmen of **S**, 1 Chr 12:29
their allegiance to the house of **S**. 1 Chr 12:29
for we did not seek it in the days of **S**." 1 Chr 13:3
the daughter of **S** looked out of 1 Chr 15:29
Samuel the seer and **S** the son of 1 Chr 26:28
all his enemies, and from the hand of **S**. Ps 18:T
Doeg, the Edomite, came and told **S**, Ps 52:T
when the Ziphites went and told **S**, Ps 54:T
Miktam of David, when he fled from **S**, Ps 57:T
when **S** sent men to watch his house in Ps 59:T
Ramah trembles; Gibeah of **S** has fled. Is 10:29
at the feet of a young man named **S**. Acts 7:58
And **S** approved of his execution. And Acts 8:1
But **S** was ravaging the church, and Acts 8:3
But **S**, still breathing threats and Acts 9:1
he heard a voice saying to him, "**S**, Saul, Acts 9:4
"Saul, **S**, why are you persecuting me?" Acts 9:4
S rose from the ground, and although Acts 9:8
look for a man of Tarsus named **S**, Acts 9:11
his hands on him he said, "Brother **S**, Acts 9:17
But **S** increased all the more in Acts 9:22
but their plot became known to **S**. Acts 9:24
went to Tarsus to look for **S**, Acts 11:25
elders by the hand of Barnabas and **S**. Acts 11:30
And Barnabas and **S** returned from Acts 12:25
the court of Herod the tetrarch, and **S**. Acts 13:1
for me Barnabas and **S** for the work to Acts 13:2
Barnabas and **S** and sought Acts 13:7
But **S**, who was also called Paul, filled Acts 13:9
and God gave them **S** the son of Kish, Acts 13:21
heard a voice saying to me, '**S**, Saul, Acts 22:7
'Saul, **S**, why are you persecuting me?' Acts 22:7
standing by me said to me, 'Brother **S**, Acts 22:13
me in the Hebrew language, '**S**, Saul, Acts 26:14
'Saul, **S**, why are you persecuting me? Acts 26:14

SAUL'S (29)

Now the donkeys of Kish, **S** father, were 1 Sm 9:3
S uncle said to him and to his 1 Sm 10:14
And **S** uncle said, "Please tell me 1 Sm 10:15
the name of **S** wife was Ahinoam 1 Sm 14:50
was Abner the son of Ner, **S** uncle. 1 Sm 14:50
And **S** servants said to him, "Behold 1 Sm 16:15
and also in the sight of **S** servants. 1 Sm 18:5
at the time when Merab, **S** daughter, 1 Sm 18:19
Now **S** daughter Michal loved David. 1 Sm 18:20
And **S** servants spoke those words in 1 Sm 18:23
David, and that Michal, **S** daughter, 1 Sm 18:28
But Jonathan, **S** son, delighted much 1 Sm 19:1
sat opposite, and Abner sat by **S** side, 1 Sm 20:25
Then **S** anger was kindled against 1 Sm 20:30
the Edomite, the chief of **S** herdsmen. 1 Sm 21:7
And Jonathan, **S** son, rose and went 1 Sm 23:16
stealthily cut off a corner of **S** robe. 1 Sm 24:4
he had cut off a corner of **S** robe. 1 Sm 24:5
and the jar of water from **S** head, 1 Sm 26:12
day, behold, a man came from **S** camp, 2 Sm 1:2
the son of Ner, commander of **S** army, 2 Sm 2:8
Ish-bosheth, **S** son, was forty years old 2 Sm 2:10
you first bring Michal, **S** daughter, 2 Sm 3:13
sent messengers to Ish-bosheth, **S** son, 2 Sm 3:14
When Ish-bosheth, **S** son, heard that 2 Sm 4:1
Now **S** son had two men who were 2 Sm 4:2
Then the king called Ziba, **S** servant, 2 Sm 9:9
the son of **S** son Jonathan, 2 Sm 21:7
they were Benjaminites, **S** kinsmen. 1 Chr 12:2

SAVE (165)

flee to one of these cities and **s** his life: Dt 4:42
who by fleeing there may **s** his life. Dt 19:4
you shall **s** alive nothing that breathes, Dt 20:16
that you will **s** alive my father and Jos 2:13
up to us quickly and **s** us and help us, Jos 10:6
might of yours and **s** Israel from the Jgs 6:14
to him, "Please, Lord, how can I **s** Israel? Jgs 6:15
contend for Baal? Or will you **s** him? Jgs 6:31
to God, "If you will **s** Israel by my hand, Jgs 6:36
know that you will **s** Israel by my hand, Jgs 6:37
men who lapped I will **s** you and give the Jgs 7:7
there arose to **s** Israel Tola the Jgs 10:1
"Did I not **s** you from the Egyptians Jgs 10:11
gods; therefore I will **s** you no more. Jgs 10:13
let them **s** you in the time of your Jgs 10:14
you, you did not **s** me from their hand. Jgs 12:2
when I saw that you would not **s** me, Jgs 12:3
he shall begin to **s** Israel from the hand Jgs 13:5
come among us and **s** us from the 1 Sm 4:3
that he may **s** us from the hand of the 1 Sm 7:8
He shall **s** my people from the hand of 1 Sm 9:16
LORD and you will **s** them from the 1 Sm 10:1
"How can this man **s** us?" And they 1 Sm 10:27
Then, if there is no one to **s** us, we will 1 Sm 11:3
attack the Philistines and **s** Keilah." 1 Sm 23:2
servant David I will **s** my people Israel 2 Sm 3:18
were afraid to **s** the Ammonites 2 Sm 10:19
and paid homage and said, "**S** me, 2 Sm 14:4
my savior; you **s** me from violence. 2 Sm 22:3
You **s** a humble people, but your 2 Sm 22:28
They looked, but there was none to **s**; 2 Sm 22:42
that you may **s** your own life and the 1 Kgs 1:12
may find grass and **s** the horses and 1 Kgs 18:5
So now, O LORD our God, **s** us, please, 2 Kgs 19:19
For I will defend this city to **s** it, for 2 Kgs 19:34
"**S** us, O God of our salvation, and 1 Chr 16:35
not willing to **s** the Ammonites any 1 Chr 19:19
affliction, and you will hear and **s**.' 2 Chr 20:9
that your own right hand can **s** you. Jb 40:14
Arise, O LORD! **S** me, O my God! For you Ps 3:7
s me for the sake of your steadfast love. Ps 6:4

s me from all my pursuers and deliver me, Ps 7:1
S, O LORD, for the godly one is gone; for Ps 12:1
For you **s** a humble people, but the Ps 18:27
cried for help, but there was none to **s**; Ps 18:41
O LORD, **s** the king! May he answer us Ps 20:9
S me from the mouth of the lion! You Ps 22:21
s your people and bless your heritage! Ps 28:9
of refuge for me, a strong fortress to **s** me! Ps 31:2
servant; **s** me in your steadfast love! Ps 31:16
great deep; man and beast you **s**, O LORD. Ps 36:6
the land, nor did their own arm **s** them, Ps 44:3
bow do I trust, nor can my sword **s** me. Ps 44:6
O God, **s** me, by your name, and Ps 54:1
But I call to God, and the LORD will **s** me. Ps 55:16
He will send from heaven and **s** me; he Ps 57:3
evil, and **s** me from bloodthirsty men. Ps 59:2
S me, O God! For the waters have come Ps 69:1
For God will **s** Zion and build up the Ps 69:35
me; incline your ear to me, and **s** me! Ps 71:2
you have given the command to **s** me, Ps 71:3
to **s** all the humble of the earth. Ps 76:9
stir up your might and come to **s** us! Ps 80:2
s your servant, who trusts in you—you Ps 86:2
and **s** the son of your maidservant. Ps 86:16
your people; help me when you **s** them, Ps 106:4
S us, O LORD our God, and gather us Ps 106:47
S me according to your steadfast love! Ps 109:26
to **s** him from those who condemn his Ps 109:31
S us, we pray, O LORD! O LORD, we pray, Ps 118:25
s me, for I have sought your precepts. Ps 119:94
s me, that I may observe your Ps 119:146
then do this, my son, and **s** yourself, for Prv 6:3
s yourself like a gazelle from the hand of Prv 6:5
the rod, you will **s** his soul from Sheol. Prv 23:14
have waited for him, that he might **s** us. Is 25:9
the LORD is our king; he will **s** us. Is 33:22
of God. He will come and **s** you." Is 35:4
O LORD our God, **s** us from his hand, Is 37:20
For I will defend this city to **s** it, for my Is 37:35
The LORD will **s** me, and we will play my Is 38:20
keep on praying to a god that cannot **s**. Is 45:20
down together; they cannot **s** the burden, Is 46:2
and I will bear; I will carry and will **s**. Is 46:4
does not answer or **s** him from his Is 46:7
let them stand forth and **s** you, those Is 47:13
own direction; there is no one to **s** you. Is 47:15
with you, and I will **s** your children. Is 49:25
hand is not shortened, that it cannot **s**, Is 59:1
I, speaking in righteousness, mighty to **s**." Is 63:1
of their trouble they say, 'Arise and **s** us!' Jer 2:27
Let them arise, if they can **s** you, in your Jer 2:28
but they cannot **s** them in the time of Jer 11:12
like a mighty warrior who cannot **s**? Jer 14:9
I am with you to **s** you and deliver you, Jer 15:20
s me, and I shall be saved, for you are Jer 17:14
for behold, I will **s** you from far away, Jer 30:10
For I am with you to **s** you, declares the Jer 30:11
praise, and say, 'O LORD, **s** your people, Jer 31:7
For I will surely **s** you, and you shall Jer 39:18
to **s** you and to deliver you from his Jer 42:11
for behold, I will **s** you from far away, Jer 46:27
Flee! **S** yourselves! You will be like a Jer 48:6
midst of Babylon; let every one **s** his life! Jer 51:6
Let every one **s** his life from the fierce Jer 51:45
for a nation which could not **s**. Lam 4:17
his wicked way, in order to **s** his life, Ezk 3:18
not turn from his evil way to **s** his life, Ezk 13:22
is just and right, he shall **s** his life. Ezk 18:27
But I will **s** them from all the Ezk 37:23
and I will **s** them by the LORD their God. Hos 1:7
I will not **s** them by bow or by sword or Hos 1:7
your king, to **s** you in all your cities? Hos 13:10
Assyria shall not **s** us; we will not ride Hos 14:3
strength, nor shall the mighty **s** his life; Am 2:14
who is swift of foot shall not **s** himself, Am 2:15
shall he who rides the horse **s** his life; Am 2:15
his head, to **s** him from his discomfort. Jon 4:6
to you "Violence!" and you will not **s**? Hab 1:2
in your midst, a mighty one who will **s**; Zep 3:17
And I will **s** the lame and gather the Zep 3:19
I will **s** my people from the east country Zec 8:7
and house of Israel, so will I **s** you, Zec 8:13
that day the LORD their God will **s** them, Zec 9:16
Judah, and I will **s** the house of Joseph. Zec 10:6
for he will **s** his people from their sins." Mt 1:21
they went and woke him, saying, "**S** us, Mt 8:25
to sink he cried out, "Lord, **s** me." Mt 14:30
For whoever would **s** his life will lose it, Mt 16:25
and rebuild it in three days, **s** yourself! Mt 27:40
"He saved others; he cannot **s** himself. Mt 27:42
see whether Elijah will come to **s** him." Mt 27:49
to **s** life or to kill?" But they were silent. Mk 3:4
For whoever would **s** his life will lose it, Mk 8:35
life for my sake and the gospel's will **s** it. Mk 8:35
s yourself, and come down from the Mk 15:30
"He saved others; he cannot **s** himself. Mk 15:31
or to do harm, to **s** life or to destroy it?" Lk 6:9
For whoever would **s** his life will lose it, Lk 9:24
loses his life for my sake will **s** it. Lk 9:24
of Man came to seek and to **s** the lost." Lk 19:10
let him **s** himself, if he is the Christ of Lk 23:35
are the King of the Jews, **s** yourself!" Lk 23:37
you not the Christ? **S** yourself and us!" Lk 23:39
I say? 'Father, **s** me from this hour'? Jn 12:27
to judge the world but to **s** the world. Jn 12:47
"**S** yourselves from this crooked Acts 2:40
But the centurion, wishing to **s** Paul, Acts 27:43
jealous, and thus **s** some of them. Rom 11:14
we preach to **s** those who believe. 1 Cor 1:21
whether you will **s** your husband? 1 Cor 7:16
know whether you will **s** your wife? 1 Cor 7:16
that by all means I might **s** some. 1 Cor 9:22
are not obligated to **s** up for their 2 Cor 12:14
came into the world to **s** sinners, 1 Tm 1:15
so doing you will **s** both yourself and 1 Tm 4:16
him who was able to **s** him from death, Heb 5:7
he is able to **s** to the uttermost those Heb 7:25
with sin but to **s** those who are eagerly Heb 9:28
word, which is able to **s** your souls. Jas 1:21
not have works? Can that faith **s** him? Jas 2:14
judge, he who is able to **s** and to destroy. Jas 4:12
the prayer of faith will **s** the one who is Jas 5:15
from his wandering will **s** his soul from Jas 5:20
s others by snatching them out of the Jude 1:23

SAVED (108)
a little one?—and my life will be **s**!" Gn 19:20
And they said, "You have **s** our lives; Gn 47:25
away, but Moses stood up and **s** them, Ex 2:17
Thus the LORD **s** Israel that day from Ex 14:30
and you shall be **s** from your enemies. Nm 10:9
Who is like you, a people **s** by the LORD, Dt 33:29
all who belonged to her, Joshua **s** alive. Jos 6:25
who **s** them out of the hand of those who Jgs 2:16
and he **s** them from the hand of their Jgs 2:18
for the people of Israel, who **s** them, Jgs 3:9
with an oxgoad, and he also **s** Israel. Jgs 3:31
over me, saying, 'My own hand has **s** me.' Jgs 7:2
the LORD lives, if you had **s** them alive, Jgs 8:19
for you have **s** us from the hand of Jgs 8:22
out to me, and I **s** you out of their hand. Jgs 10:12
women whom they had **s** alive of the Jgs 21:14
So the LORD **s** Israel that day. And the 1 Sm 14:23
So David **s** the inhabitants of Keilah. 1 Sm 23:5
who have this day **s** your life and the 2 Sm 19:5
of our enemies and **s** us from the 2 Sm 19:9
praised, and I am **s** from my enemies. 2 Sm 22:4
so that he **s** himself there more than 2 Kgs 6:10
so he **s** them by the hand of 2 Kgs 14:27
And the LORD **s** them by a great 1 Chr 11:14
So the LORD **s** Hezekiah and the 2 Chr 32:22
them saviors who **s** them from the Neh 9:27
for Mordecai, whose word **s** the king, Est 7:9
How you have **s** the arm that has no Jb 26:2
be praised, and I am **s** from my enemies. Ps 18:3
The king is not **s** by his great army; a Ps 33:16
the LORD heard him and **s** him out of all Ps 34:6
But you have **s** us from our foes and Ps 44:7
let your face shine, that we may be **s**! Ps 80:3
let your face shine, that we may be **s**! Ps 80:7
let your face shine, that we may be **s**! Ps 80:19
Yet he **s** them for his name's sake, that Ps 106:8
So he **s** them from the hand of the foe Ps 106:10
when I was brought low, he **s** me. Ps 116:6
"In returning and rest you shall be **s**; Is 30:15
I declared and **s** and proclaimed, when Is 43:12
But Israel is **s** by the LORD with Is 45:17
"Turn to me and be **s**, all the ends of the Is 45:22
and the angel of his presence **s** them; Is 63:9
have been a long time, and shall we be **s**? Is 64:5
your heart from evil, that you may be **s**. Jer 4:14
the summer is ended, and we are not **s**." Jer 8:20
save me, and I shall be **s**, for you are my Jer 17:14
In his days Judah will be **s**, and Israel Jer 23:6
for Jacob; yet he shall be **s** out of it. Jer 30:7
days Judah will be **s** and Jerusalem will Jer 33:16
taken warning, he would have **s** his life. Ezk 33:5
he who has **s** Daniel from the power of Dn 6:27
calls on the name of the LORD shall be **s**. Jl 2:32
one who endures to the end will be **s**. Mt 10:22
saying, "Who then can be **s**?" Mt 19:25
one who endures to the end will be **s**. Mt 24:13
cut short, no human being would be **s**. Mt 24:22
"He **s** others; he cannot save himself. Mt 27:42
and said to him, "Then who can be **s**?" Mk 10:26
one who endures to the end will be **s**. Mk 13:13
the days, no human being would be **s**. Mk 13:20
to one another, saying, "He **s** others; Mk 15:31
believes and is baptized will be **s**, Mk 16:16
that we should be **s** from our enemies Lk 1:71
to the woman, "Your faith has **s** you; Lk 7:50
so that they may not believe and be **s**. Lk 8:12
will those who are **s** be few?" And he Lk 13:23
heard it said, "Then who can be **s**?" Lk 18:26
scoffed at him, saying, "He **s** others; Lk 23:35
that the world might be **s** through him. Jn 3:17
I say these things so that you may be **s**. Jn 5:34
he will be **s** and will go in and out and Jn 10:9
upon the name of the Lord shall be **s**.' Acts 2:21
day by day those who were being **s**. Acts 2:47
among men by which we must be **s**." Acts 4:12
a message by which you will be **s**, Acts 11:14
the custom of Moses, you cannot be **s**." Acts 15:1
that we will be **s** through the grace of Acts 15:11
said, "Sirs, what must I do to be **s**?" Acts 16:30
in the Lord Jesus, and you will be **s**, Acts 16:31
hope of our being **s** was at last Acts 27:20
stay in the ship, you cannot be **s**." Acts 27:31
more shall we be **s** by him from the Rom 5:9
are reconciled, shall we be **s** by his life. Rom 5:10
For in this hope we were **s**. Now hope Rom 8:24
sea, only a remnant of them will be **s**, Rom 9:27
to God for them is that they may be **s**. Rom 10:1
him from the dead, you will be **s**. Rom 10:9
the mouth one confesses and is **s**. Rom 10:10
on the name of the Lord will be **s**." Rom 10:13
And in this way all Israel will be **s**, as Rom 11:26
to us who are being **s** it is the power of 1 Cor 1:18
loss, though he himself will be **s**, 1 Cor 3:15
that his spirit may be **s** in the day of 1 Cor 5:5
that of many, that they may be **s**. 1 Cor 10:33
and by which you are being **s**, if you 1 Cor 15:2
who are being **s** and among those 2 Cor 2:15
Christ—by grace you have been **s**— Eph 2:5
by grace you have been **s** through faith. Eph 2:8
that they might be **s**—so as always 1 Thes 2:16
refused to love the truth and so be **s**. 2 Thes 2:10
chose you as the firstfruits to be **s**, 2 Thes 2:13
desires all people to be **s** and to come to 1 Tm 2:4
she will be **s** through childbearing— 1 Tm 2:15
who **s** us and called us to a holy 2 Tm 1:9
he **s** us, not because of works done by us Ti 3:5
And "If the righteous is scarcely **s**, 1 Pt 4:18
who **s** a people out of the land of Egypt, Jude 1:5

SAVES (13)
who **s** you from all your calamities 1 Sm 10:19
For as the LORD lives who **s** Israel, 1 Sm 14:39
know that the LORD **s** not with sword 1 Sm 17:47
But he **s** the needy from the sword of their Jb 5:15
is because of pride'; but he **s** the lowly. Jb 22:29
is with God, who **s** the upright in heart. Ps 7:10
Now I know that the LORD **s** his anointed; Ps 20:6
the brokenhearted and **s** the crushed in Ps 34:18
them from the wicked and **s** them, Ps 37:40
the needy, and **s** the lives of the needy. Ps 72:13
he also hears their cry and **s** them. Ps 145:19
A truthful witness **s** lives, but one who Prv 14:25
which corresponds to this, now **s** you, 1 Pt 3:21

SAVING (11)
shown me great kindness in **s** my life. Gn 19:19
hinder the LORD from **s** by many or by 1 Sm 14:6
bloodguilt and from **s** with your 1 Sm 25:26
holy heaven with the **s** might of his right Ps 20:6
Why are you so far from **s** me, from the Ps 22:1
people; he is the **s** refuge of his anointed. Ps 28:8
earth, your **s** power among all nations. Ps 67:2
love answer me in your **s** faithfulness. Ps 69:13
in God and did not trust his **s** power. Ps 78:22
you may know the **s** acts of the LORD." Mi 6:5
an ark for the **s** of his household. Heb 11:7

SAVIOR (38)
my stronghold and my refuge, my **s**; 2 Sm 22:3
(Therefore the LORD gave Israel a **s**, so 2 Kgs 13:5
O **S** of those who seek refuge from their Ps 17:7
They forgot God, their **S**, who had Ps 106:21
he will send them a **s** and defender, Is 19:20
your God, the Holy One of Israel, your **S**. Is 43:3
the LORD, and besides me there is no **s**. Is 43:11
hides yourself, O God of Israel, the **S**. Is 45:15
god besides me, a righteous God and a **S**; Is 45:21
shall know that I am the LORD your **S**, Is 49:26
the LORD, am your **S** and your Redeemer, Is 60:16
not deal falsely." And he became their **S**. Is 63:8
hope of Israel, its **s** in time of trouble, Jer 14:8
but me, and besides me there is no **s**. Hos 13:4
and my spirit rejoices in God my **S**, Lk 1:47
is born this day in the city of David a **S**, Lk 2:11
that this is indeed the **S** of the world." Jn 4:42
him at his right hand as Leader and **S**, Acts 5:31
God has brought to Israel a **S**, Acts 13:23
church, his body, and is himself its **S**. Eph 5:23
is in heaven, and from it we await a **S**, Phil 3:20
command of God our **S** and of Christ 1 Tm 1:1
it is pleasing in the sight of God our **S**, 1 Tm 2:3
living God, who is the **S** of all people, 1 Tm 4:10

the appearing of our **S** Christ Jesus, 2 Tm 1:10
entrusted by the command of God our **S**; Ti 1:3
God the Father and Christ Jesus our **S**. Ti 1:4
may adorn the doctrine of God our **S**. Ti 2:10
glory of our great God and **S** Jesus Christ, Ti 2:13
loving kindness of God our **S** appeared, Ti 3:4
on us richly through Jesus Christ our **S**, Ti 3:6
of our God and **S** Jesus Christ: 2 Pt 1:1
of our Lord and **S** Jesus Christ. 2 Pt 1:11
of our Lord and **S** Jesus Christ, 2 Pt 2:20
of the Lord and **S** through your apostles, 2 Pt 3:2
of our Lord and **S** Jesus Christ. 2 Pt 3:18
sent his Son to be the **S** of the world. 1 Jn 4:14
to the only God, our **S**, through Jesus Jude 1:25

SAVIORS (2)
you gave them **s** who saved them Neh 9:27
S shall go up to Mount Zion to rule Ob 1:21

SAW (599)
And God **s** that the light was good. And Gn 1:4
called Seas. And God **s** that it was good. Gn 1:10
to its kind. And God **s** that it was good. Gn 1:12
darkness. And God **s** that it was good. Gn 1:18
to its kind. And God **s** that it was good. Gn 1:21
to its kind. And God **s** that it was good. Gn 1:25
And God **s** everything that he had made, Gn 1:31
So when the woman **s** that the tree was Gn 3:6
the sons of God **s** that the daughters of Gn 6:2
The LORD **s** that the wickedness of man Gn 6:5
And God **s** the earth, and behold, it was Gn 6:12
s the nakedness of his father and told Gn 9:22
the Egyptians **s** that the woman was Gn 12:14
when the princes of Pharaoh **s** her, Gn 12:15
up his eyes and **s** that the Jordan Valley Gn 13:10
And when she **s** that she had conceived, Gn 16:4
and when she **s** that she had conceived, Gn 16:5
When he **s** them, he ran from the tent Gn 18:2
When Lot **s** them, he rose to meet them Gn 19:1
But Sarah **s** the son of Hagar the Gn 21:9
her eyes, and she **s** a well of water. Gn 21:19
up his eyes and **s** the place from afar. Gn 22:4
As soon as he **s** the ring and the Gn 24:30
And he lifted up his eyes and **s**, and Gn 24:63
lifted up her eyes, and when she **s** Isaac, Gn 24:64
of a window and **s** Isaac laughing with Gn 26:8
Now Esau **s** that Isaac had blessed Gn 28:6
So when Esau **s** that the Canaanite Gn 28:8
As he looked, he **s** a well in the field, and Gn 29:2
as soon as Jacob **s** Rachel the daughter Gn 29:10
When the LORD **s** that Leah was hated, Gn 29:31
When Rachel **s** that she bore Jacob no Gn 30:1
When Leah **s** that she had ceased Gn 30:9
And Jacob **s** that Laban did not regard Gn 31:2
lifted up my eyes and **s** in a dream that Gn 31:10
God **s** my affliction and the labor of Gn 31:42
And when Jacob **s** them he said, "This is Gn 32:2
When the man **s** that he did not Gn 32:25
up his eyes and **s** the women and Gn 33:5
the Hivite, the prince of the land, **s** her, Gn 34:2
But when his brothers **s** that their father Gn 37:4
They **s** him from afar, and before he Gn 37:18
And looking up they **s** a caravan of Gn 37:25
to the pit and **s** that Joseph was not Gn 37:29
There Judah **s** the daughter of a certain Gn 38:2
For she **s** that Shelah was grown up, Gn 38:14
When Judah **s** her, he thought she was Gn 38:15
His master **s** that the LORD was with him Gn 39:3
And as soon as she **s** that he had left Gn 39:13
morning, he **s** that they were troubled. Gn 40:6
the chief baker **s** that the Gn 40:16
I also **s** in my dream seven ears Gn 41:22
Joseph **s** his brothers and recognized Gn 42:7
in that we **s** the distress of his soul, Gn 42:21
he **s** his money in the mouth of his Gn 42:27
they and their father **s** their bundles of Gn 42:35
When Joseph **s** Benjamin with them, Gn 43:16
his eyes and **s** his brother Benjamin, Gn 43:29
and when he **s** the wagons that Joseph Gn 45:27
When Israel **s** Joseph's sons, he said, Gn 48:8
When Joseph **s** that his father laid his Gn 48:17
He **s** that a resting place was good, and Gn 49:15
s the mourning on the threshing floor Gn 50:11
When Joseph's brothers **s** that their Gn 50:15
And Joseph **s** Ephraim's children of the Gn 50:23
and when she **s** that he was a fine child, Ex 2:2
She **s** the basket among the reeds and sent Ex 2:5
When she opened it, she **s** the child, and Ex 2:6
and he **s** an Egyptian beating a Hebrew, Ex 2:11
God **s** the people of Israel—and God Ex 2:25
When the LORD **s** that he turned aside to Ex 3:4
of the people of Israel **s** that they were in Ex 5:19
But when Pharaoh **s** that there was a Ex 8:15
But when Pharaoh **s** that the rain and Ex 9:34
and Israel **s** the Egyptians dead on the Ex 14:30
Israel **s** the great power that the LORD Ex 14:31
When the people of Israel **s** it, they said Ex 16:15
When Moses' father-in-law **s** all that he Ex 18:14
when all the people **s** the thunder and Ex 20:18
and they **s** the God of Israel. There was Ex 24:10
When the people **s** that Moses delayed to Ex 32:1
When Aaron **s** this, he built an altar Ex 32:5
near the camp and **s** the calf and the Ex 32:19
And when Moses **s** that the people had Ex 32:25
when all the people **s** the pillar of cloud Ex 33:10
and all the people of Israel **s** Moses, Ex 34:30
And Moses **s** all the work, and behold, Ex 39:43
on the altar, and when all the people **s** it, Lv 9:24
we **s** the descendants of Anak there. Nm 13:28
all the people that we **s** in it are of Nm 13:32
And there we **s** the Nephilim (the sons Nm 13:33
all the congregation **s** that Aaron had Nm 20:29
the son of Zippor **s** all that Israel had Nm 22:2
And the donkey **s** the angel of the Nm 22:23
And when the donkey **s** the angel of Nm 22:25
When the donkey **s** the angel of the Nm 22:27
and he **s** the angel of the LORD Nm 22:31
The donkey **s** me and turned aside Nm 22:33
and from there he **s** a fraction of the Nm 22:41
When Balaam **s** that it pleased the Nm 24:1
up his eyes and **s** Israel camping tribe Nm 24:2
of Eleazar, son of Aaron the priest, **s** it, Nm 25:7
And they **s** the land of Jazer and the Nm 32:1
to the Valley of Eshcol and **s** the land, Nm 32:9
and terrifying wilderness that you **s**, Dt 1:19
heard the sound of words, but **s** no form; Dt 4:12
Since you **s** no form on the day that the Dt 4:15
the great trials that your eyes **s**, the signs, Dt 7:19
heard our voice and **s** our affliction, Dt 26:7
the great trials that your eyes **s**, the signs, Dt 29:3
"The LORD **s** it and spurned them, Dt 32:19
when I **s** among the spoil a beautiful Jos 7:21
And as soon as the king of Ai **s** this, he Jos 8:14
Joshua and all Israel **s** that the ambush Jos 8:21
and your eyes **s** what I did in Egypt. Jos 24:7
And the spies **s** a man coming out of the Jgs 1:24
and when they **s** that the doors of the Jgs 3:24
And when Gaal **s** the people, he said to Jgs 9:36
And he looked and **s** the people coming Jgs 9:43
the men of Israel **s** that Abimelech was Jgs 9:55
And as soon as he **s** her, he tore his Jgs 11:35
And when I **s** that you would not save Jgs 12:3
and at Timnah he **s** one of the daughters Jgs 14:1
"I **s** one of the daughters of the Jgs 14:2
As soon as the people **s** him, they Jgs 14:11
went to Gaza, and there he **s** a prostitute, Jgs 16:1
When Delilah **s** that he had told her all Jgs 16:18
And when the people **s** him, they Jgs 16:24
came to Laish and **s** the people who were Jgs 18:7
And when Micah **s** that they were too Jgs 18:26
And when the girl's father **s** him, he Jgs 19:3
up his eyes and **s** the traveler in the Jgs 19:17
And all who **s** it said, "Such a thing has Jgs 19:30
the people of Benjamin **s** that they were Jgs 20:36
for they **s** that disaster was close upon Jgs 20:41
And when Naomi **s** that she was Ru 1:18
Her mother-in-law **s** what she had Ru 2:18
the men of Ashdod **s** how things were, 1 Sm 5:7
they lifted up their eyes and **s** the ark, 1 Sm 6:13
the five lords of the Philistines **s** it, 1 Sm 6:16
they **s** Samuel coming out toward 1 Sm 9:14
When Samuel **s** Saul, the LORD told 1 Sm 9:17
knew him previously **s** how he 1 Sm 10:11
And when we **s** they were not to be 1 Sm 10:14
And when you **s** that Nahash the 1 Sm 12:12
the men of Israel **s** that they were in 1 Sm 13:6
"When I **s** that the people were 1 Sm 13:11
And when Saul **s** any strong man, 1 Sm 14:52
men of Israel, when they **s** the man, 1 Sm 17:24
the Philistine looked and **s** David, 1 Sm 17:42
When the Philistines **s** that their 1 Sm 17:51
As soon as Saul **s** David go out 1 Sm 17:55
And when Saul **s** that he had great 1 Sm 18:15
But when Saul **s** and knew that the 1 Sm 18:28
great salvation for all Israel. You **s** it, 1 Sm 19:5
and when they **s** the company of the 1 Sm 19:20
"I **s** the son of Jesse coming to Nob, 1 Sm 22:9
David **s** that Saul had come out to 1 Sm 23:15
When Abigail **s** David, she hurried 1 Sm 25:23
When he **s** that Saul came after him 1 Sm 26:3
And David **s** the place where Saul lay, 1 Sm 26:5
No man **s** it or knew it, nor did any 1 Sm 26:12
When Saul **s** the army of the 1 Sm 28:5
When the woman **s** Samuel, she 1 Sm 28:12
and when she **s** that he was terrified, 1 Sm 28:21
when his armor-bearer **s** that Saul 1 Sm 31:5
beyond the Jordan **s** that the men 1 Sm 31:7
when he looked behind him, he **s** me, 2 Sm 1:7
the window and **s** King David leaping 2 Sm 6:16
When the Ammonites **s** that they had 2 Sm 10:6
When Joab **s** that the battle was set 2 Sm 10:9
when the Ammonites **s** that the 2 Sm 10:14
But when the Syrians **s** that they had 2 Sm 10:15
servants of Hadadezer **s** that they had 2 Sm 10:19
that he **s** from the roof a woman 2 Sm 11:2
But when David **s** that his servants 2 Sm 12:19
But a young man **s** them and told 2 Sm 17:18
When Ahithophel **s** that his counsel 2 Sm 17:23
And a certain man **s** it and told Joab, 2 Sm 18:10
I **s** Absalom hanging in an oak." 2 Sm 18:10
who told him, "What, you **s** him! 2 Sm 18:11
looked, he **s** a man running alone. 2 Sm 18:24
The watchman **s** another man 2 Sm 18:26
your servant, I **s** a great commotion, 2 Sm 18:29
And when the man **s** that all the 2 Sm 20:12
the LORD when he **s** the angel who 2 Sm 24:17
he **s** the king and his servants 2 Sm 24:20
and when Solomon **s** that the young 1 Kgs 11:28
And when all Israel **s** that the king 1 Kgs 12:16
passed by and **s** the body thrown 1 Kgs 13:25
And when Zimri **s** that the city was 1 Kgs 16:18
When Ahab **s** Elijah, Ahab said to 1 Kgs 18:17
And when all the people **s** it, they fell 1 Kgs 18:39
"I **s** all Israel scattered on the 1 Kgs 22:17
I **s** the LORD sitting on his throne, 1 Kgs 22:19
of the chariots **s** Jehoshaphat, 1 Kgs 22:32
captains of the chariots **s** that it was 1 Kgs 22:33
And Elisha **s** it and he cried, "My 2 Kgs 2:12
horsemen!" And he **s** him no more. 2 Kgs 2:12
were at Jericho **s** him opposite them, 2 Kgs 2:15
turned around, and when he **s** them, 2 Kgs 2:24
the Moabites **s** the water opposite 2 Kgs 3:22
the king of Moab **s** that the battle was 2 Kgs 3:26
When the man of God **s** her coming, 2 Kgs 4:25
he **s** the child lying dead on his bed. 2 Kgs 4:32
when Naaman **s** someone running 2 Kgs 5:21
the eyes of the young man, and he **s**, 2 Kgs 6:17
the LORD opened their eyes and they **s**, 2 Kgs 6:20
As soon as the king of Israel **s** them, 2 Kgs 6:21
and he **s** the company of Jehu as he 2 Kgs 9:17
And when Joram **s** Jehu, he said, "Is it 2 Kgs 9:22
'As surely as I **s** yesterday the blood of 2 Kgs 9:26
Ahaziah the king of Judah **s** this, 2 Kgs 9:27
the mother of Ahaziah **s** that her son 2 Kgs 11:1
And whenever they **s** that there was 2 Kgs 12:10
him, for he **s** the oppression of Israel, 2 Kgs 13:4
For the LORD **s** that the affliction of 2 Kgs 14:26
he **s** the altar that was at Damascus. 2 Kgs 16:10
he **s** the tombs there on the mount. 2 Kgs 23:16
at Megiddo, as soon as he **s** him. 2 Kgs 23:29
when his armor-bearer **s** that Saul 1 Chr 10:5
were in the valley **s** that the army had 1 Chr 10:7
the window and **s** King David 1 Chr 15:29
When the Ammonites **s** that they 1 Chr 19:6
When Joab **s** that the battle was set 1 Chr 19:10
when the Ammonites **s** that the 1 Chr 19:15
when the Syrians **s** that they had 1 Chr 19:16
servants of Hadadezer **s** that they 1 Chr 19:19
was about to destroy it, the LORD **s**, 1 Chr 21:15
lifted his eyes and **s** the angel of the 1 Chr 21:16
He turned and **s** the angel, and his 1 Chr 21:20
Ornan looked and **s** David and went 1 Chr 21:21
when David **s** that the LORD had 1 Chr 21:28
the people of Israel **s** the fire come 2 Chr 7:3
And when all Israel **s** that the king 2 Chr 10:16
When the LORD **s** that they humbled 2 Chr 12:7
from Israel when they **s** that the LORD 2 Chr 15:9
"I **s** all Israel scattered on the 2 Chr 18:16
I **s** the LORD sitting on his throne, 2 Chr 18:18
of the chariots **s** Jehoshaphat, 2 Chr 18:31
captains of the chariots **s** that it was 2 Chr 18:32
mother of Ahaziah **s** that her son 2 Chr 22:10
when they **s** that there was much 2 Chr 24:11
the princes came and **s** the heaps, 2 Chr 31:8
when Hezekiah **s** that Sennacherib 2 Chr 32:2
voice when they **s** the foundation of Ezr 3:12
And I understood and **s** that God had Neh 6:12
"And you **s** the affliction of our fathers Neh 9:9
In those days I **s** in Judah people Neh 13:15
In those days also I **s** the Jews who had Neh 13:23
Persia and Media, who **s** the king's face, Est 1:14
favor in the eyes of all who **s** her. Est 2:15
And when Haman **s** that Mordecai did Est 3:5
when the king **s** Queen Esther standing Est 5:2
But when Haman **s** Mordecai in the Est 5:9
for he **s** that harm was determined Est 7:7
And when they **s** him from a distance, Jb 2:12
for they **s** that his suffering was very Jb 2:13
The eye that **s** him will see him no more, Jb 20:9
then he **s** it and declared it; he Jb 28:27
the young men **s** me and withdrew, and Jb 29:8
it called me blessed, and when the eye **s**, Jb 29:11
because I **s** my help in the gate, Jb 31:21
And when Elihu **s** that there was no Jb 32:5
this Job lived 140 years, and **s** his sons, Jb 42:16
As soon as they **s** it, they were astounded; Ps 48:5

the arrogant when I **s** the prosperity of Ps 73:3
When the waters **s** you, O God, when Ps 77:16
saw you, O God, when the waters **s** you, Ps 77:16
they **s** the deeds of the LORD, his Ps 107:24
Your eyes **s** my unformed substance; Ps 139:16
Then I **s** and considered it; I looked Prv 24:32
Then I **s** that there is more gain in Eccl 2:13
This also, I **s**, is from the hand of God, Eccl 2:24
I **s** under the sun that in the place of Eccl 3:16
So I **s** that there is nothing better than Eccl 3:22
Again I **s** all the oppressions that are Eccl 4:1
Then I **s** that all toil and all skill in Eccl 4:4
Again, I **s** vanity under the sun: Eccl 4:7
I **s** all the living who move about Eccl 4:15
Then I **s** the wicked buried. They used Eccl 8:10
then I **s** all the work of God, that man Eccl 8:17
Again I **s** that under the sun the race is Eccl 9:11
The young women **s** her and called her Sg 6:9
which he **s** concerning Judah and Is 1:1
the son of Amoz **s** concerning Judah and Is 2:1
King Uzziah died I **s** the Lord sitting upon Is 6:1
or the **s** magnify itself against him who Is 10:15
Babylon which Isaiah the son of Amoz **s**. Is 13:1
Then he who **s** cried out: "Upon a Is 21:8
and you **s** that the breaches of the city of Is 22:9
The LORD **s** it, and it displeased him that Is 59:15
He **s** that there was no man, and Is 59:16
and her treacherous sister Judah **s** it. Jer 3:7
She **s** that for all the adulteries of that Jer 3:8
of Samaria I **s** an unsavory thing: Jer 23:13
king of Judah and all the soldiers **s** them, Jer 39:4
were with Ishmael **s** Johanan the son Jer 41:13
food, and prospered, and **s** no disaster. Jer 44:17
were opened, and I **s** visions of God. Ezk 1:1
I **s** a wheel on the earth beside the living Ezk 1:15
of his waist I **s** as it were gleaming Ezk 1:27
appearance of his waist I **s** as it were the Ezk 1:27
And when I **s** it, I fell on my face, and I Ezk 1:28
there, like the vision that I **s** in the valley. Ezk 8:4
So I went in and **s**. And there, engraved Ezk 8:10
living creatures that I **s** by the Chebar Ezk 10:15
creatures that I **s** underneath the God Ezk 10:20
And I **s** among them Jaazaniah the son Ezk 11:1
concerning Jerusalem and **s** visions of Ezk 13:16
passed by you and **s** you wallowing in Ezk 16:6
I passed by you again and **s** you, Ezk 16:8
me. So I removed them, when I **s** it. Ezk 16:50
When she **s** that she waited in vain, Ezk 19:5
then wherever they **s** any high hill or Ezk 20:28
"Her sister Oholibah **s** this, and she Ezk 23:11
And I **s** that she was defiled; they both Ezk 23:13
She **s** men portrayed on the wall, the Ezk 23:14
When she **s** them, she lusted after Ezk 23:16
the earth in the sight of all who **s** you. Ezk 28:18
I **s** also that the temple had a raised Ezk 41:8
And the vision I **s** was just like the Ezk 43:3
I **s** on the bank of the river very many Ezk 47:7
"You **s**, O king, and behold, a great Dn 2:31
And as you **s** the feet and toes, partly of Dn 2:41
just as you **s** iron mixed with the soft Dn 2:41
As you **s** the iron mixed with soft clay, Dn 2:43
just as you **s** that a stone was cut from a Dn 2:45
gathered together and **s** that the fire Dn 3:27
I **s** a dream that made me afraid. As I lay Dn 4:5
dream that I **s** and their interpretation. Dn 4:9
of my head as I lay in bed were these: I **s**, Dn 4:10
"I **s** in the visions of my head as I lay in Dn 4:13
I, King Nebuchadnezzar, **s**. And you, Dn 4:18
The tree you **s**, which grew and became Dn 4:20
And because the king **s** a watcher, a Dn 4:23
And the king **s** the hand as it wrote. Dn 5:5
Daniel **s** a dream and visions of his head Dn 7:1
declared, "I **s** in my vision by night, Dn 7:2
After this I **s** in the night visions, and Dn 7:7
I **s** in the night visions, and behold, with Dn 7:13
And I **s** in the vision; and when I saw, I Dn 8:2
and when I **s**, I was in Susa the capital, Dn 8:2
And I **s** in the vision, and I was at the Ulai Dn 8:2
I raised my eyes and **s**, and behold, a ram Dn 8:3
I **s** the ram charging westward and Dn 8:4
I **s** him come close to the ram, and he was Dn 8:7
the ram that you **s** with the two horns, Dn 8:20
And I, Daniel, alone **s** the vision, for the Dn 10:7
I was left alone and **s** this great vision, Dn 10:8
When Ephraim **s** his sickness, and Hos 5:13
tree in its first season, I **s** your fathers. Hos 9:10
which he **s** concerning Israel in the days Am 1:1
I **s** the LORD standing beside the altar, Am 9:1
When God **s** what they did, how they Jon 3:10
which he **s** concerning Samaria and Mi 1:1
oracle that Habakkuk the prophet **s**. Hab 1:1
I **s** the tents of Cushan in affliction; the Hab 3:7
The mountains **s** you and writhed; the Hab 3:10
is left among you who **s** this house in its Hg 2:3
"I **s** in the night, and behold, a man Zec 1:8

And I lifted my eyes and **s**, and behold, Zec 1:18
And I lifted my eyes and **s**, and behold, a Zec 2:1
Again I lifted my eyes and **s**, and behold, Zec 5:1
Then I lifted my eyes and **s**, and behold, Zec 5:9
Again I lifted my eyes and **s**, and behold, Zec 6:1
For we **s** his star when it rose and have Mt 2:2
When they **s** the star, they rejoiced Mt 2:10
into the house they **s** the child with Mt 2:11
when he **s** that he had been tricked by Mt 2:16
But when he **s** many of the Pharisees and Mt 3:7
and he **s** the Spirit of God descending Mt 3:16
by the Sea of Galilee, he **s** two brothers, Mt 4:18
on from there he **s** two other brothers, Mt 4:21
he **s** his mother-in-law lying sick with a Mt 8:14
Now when Jesus **s** a great crowd around Mt 8:18
out to meet Jesus, and when they **s** him, Mt 8:34
And when Jesus **s** their faith, he said to Mt 9:2
When the crowds **s** it, they were afraid, Mt 9:8
he **s** a man called Matthew sitting at the Mt 9:9
And when the Pharisees **s** this, they said Mt 9:11
the ruler's house and **s** the flute players Mt 9:23
When he **s** the crowds, he had Mt 9:36
But when the Pharisees **s** it, they said to Mt 12:2
him, so that the man spoke and **s**. Mt 12:22
he went ashore he **s** a great crowd, Mt 14:14
when the disciples **s** him walking on Mt 14:26
But when he **s** the wind, he was afraid, Mt 14:30
when they **s** the mute speaking, Mt 15:31
their eyes, they **s** no one but Jesus only. Mt 17:8
his fellow servants **s** what had taken Mt 18:31
the third hour he **s** others standing idle Mt 20:3
and the scribes **s** the wonderful things Mt 21:15
When the disciples **s** it, they marveled, Mt 21:20
And even when you **s** it, you did not Mt 21:32
But when the tenants **s** the son, they Mt 21:38
he **s** there a man who had no wedding Mt 22:11
And when the disciples **s** it, they were Mt 26:8
entrance, another servant girl **s** him, Mt 26:71
betrayer, **s** that Jesus was condemned, Mt 27:3
So when Pilate **s** that he was gaining Mt 27:24
s the earthquake and what took place, Mt 27:54
And when they **s** him they worshiped Mt 28:17
immediately he **s** the heavens opening Mk 1:10
he **s** Simon and Andrew the brother of Mk 1:16
he **s** James the son of Zebedee and John Mk 1:19
And when Jesus **s** their faith, he said to Mk 2:5
"We never **s** anything like this!" Mk 2:12
he **s** Levi the son of Alphaeus sitting at Mk 2:14
when they **s** that he was eating with Mk 2:16
whenever the unclean spirits **s** him, Mk 3:11
And when he **s** Jesus from afar, he ran Mk 5:6
to Jesus and **s** the demon-possessed Mk 5:15
synagogue, and Jesus **s** a commotion, Mk 5:38
Now many **s** them going and Mk 6:33
he went ashore he **s** a great crowd, Mk 6:34
And he **s** that they were making Mk 6:48
but when they **s** him walking on the Mk 6:49
for they all **s** him and were terrified. But Mk 6:50
they **s** that some of his disciples ate with Mk 7:2
restored, and he **s** everything clearly. Mk 8:25
they no longer **s** anyone with them but Mk 9:8
they **s** a great crowd around them, Mk 9:14
all the crowd, when they **s** him, Mk 9:15
And when the spirit **s** him, immediately Mk 9:20
And when Jesus **s** that a crowd came Mk 9:25
we **s** someone casting out demons in Mk 9:38
But when Jesus **s** it, he was indignant Mk 10:14
they **s** the fig tree withered away to its Mk 11:20
And when Jesus **s** that he answered Mk 12:34
And the servant girl **s** him and began Mk 14:69
s that in this way he breathed his last, Mk 15:39
the mother of Joses **s** where he was Mk 15:47
they **s** that the stone had been rolled Mk 16:4
they **s** a young man sitting on the right Mk 16:5
not believed those who **s** him after he Mk 16:14
Zechariah was troubled when he **s** him, Lk 1:12
And when they **s** it, they made known Lk 2:17
And when his parents **s** him, they were Lk 2:48
and he **s** two boats by the lake, but the Lk 5:2
But when Simon Peter **s** it, he fell down at Lk 5:8
And when he **s** Jesus, he fell on his face Lk 5:12
And when he **s** their faith, he said, "Man, Lk 5:20
he went out and **s** a tax collector named Lk 5:27
And when the Lord **s** her, he had Lk 7:13
the Pharisee who had invited him **s** this, Lk 7:39
When he **s** Jesus, he cried out and fell Lk 8:28
When the herdsmen **s** what had Lk 8:34
And when the woman **s** that she was not Lk 8:47
became fully awake they **s** his glory and Lk 9:32
we **s** someone casting out demons in Lk 9:49
when his disciples James and John **s** it, Lk 9:54
"I **s** Satan fall like lightning from Lk 10:18
and when he **s** him he passed by on the Lk 10:31
when he came to the place and **s** him, Lk 10:32
to where he was, and when he **s** him, Lk 10:33

When Jesus **s** her, he called her over Lk 13:12
his father **s** him and felt compassion, Lk 15:20
up his eyes and **s** Abraham far off and Lk 16:23
When he **s** them he said to them, "Go Lk 17:14
of them, when he **s** that he was healed, Lk 17:15
And when the disciples **s** it, they Lk 18:15
And all the people, when they **s** it, gave Lk 18:43
And when they **s** it, they all grumbled, Lk 19:7
And when he drew near and **s** the city, Lk 19:41
But when the tenants **s** him, they said Lk 20:14
Jesus looked up and **s** the rich putting Lk 21:1
and he **s** a poor widow put in two small Lk 21:2
were around him **s** what would follow, Lk 22:49
little later someone else **s** him and said, Lk 22:58
When Herod **s** Jesus, he was very glad, Lk 23:8
when the centurion **s** what had taken Lk 23:47
when they **s** what had taken place, Lk 23:48
Galilee followed and **s** the tomb and Lk 23:55
in, he **s** the linen cloths by themselves; Lk 24:12
frightened and thought they **s** a spirit. Lk 24:37
The next day he **s** Jesus coming toward Jn 1:29
"I **s** the Spirit descend from heaven like a Jn 1:32
Jesus turned and **s** them following and Jn 1:38
So they came and **s** where he was staying, Jn 1:39
Jesus **s** Nathanael coming toward him Jn 1:47
when you were under the fig tree, I **s** you." Jn 1:48
I said to you, 'I **s** you under the fig tree,' Jn 1:50
in his name when they **s** the signs that he Jn 2:23
When Jesus **s** him lying there and knew Jn 5:6
because they **s** the signs that he was doing Jn 6:2
When the people **s** the sign that he had Jn 6:14
they **s** Jesus walking on the sea and Jn 6:19
other side of the sea **s** that there had been Jn 6:22
So when the crowd **s** that Jesus was not Jn 6:24
are seeking me, not because you **s** signs, Jn 6:26
would see my day. He **s** it and was glad." Jn 8:56
he passed by, he **s** a man blind from birth. Jn 9:1
her, **s** Mary rise quickly and go out, Jn 11:31
came to where Jesus was and **s** him, Jn 11:32
When Jesus **s** her weeping, and the Jews Jn 11:33
these things because he **s** his glory and Jn 12:41
the chief priests and the officers **s** him, Jn 19:6
When Jesus **s** his mother and the Jn 19:26
came to Jesus and **s** that he was already Jn 19:33
He who **s** it has borne witness—his Jn 19:35
and **s** that the stone had been taken away Jn 20:1
look in, he **s** the linen cloths lying there, Jn 20:5
tomb. He **s** the linen cloths lying there, Jn 20:6
first, also went in, and he **s** and believed; Jn 20:8
And she **s** two angels in white, sitting Jn 20:12
she turned around and **s** Jesus standing, Jn 20:14
were glad when they **s** the Lord. Jn 20:20
on land, they **s** a charcoal fire in place, Jn 21:9
Peter turned and **s** the disciple whom Jn 21:20
When Peter **s** him, he said to Jesus, Jn 21:21
same way as you **s** him go into Acts 1:11
him, "'I **s** the Lord always before me, Acts 2:25
And all the people **s** him walking and Acts 3:9
And when Peter **s** it he addressed the Acts 3:12
Now when they **s** the boldness of Peter Acts 4:13
sat in the council **s** that his face was Acts 6:15
When Moses **s** it, he was amazed at the Acts 7:31
gazed into heaven and **s** the glory of Acts 7:55
they heard him and **s** the signs that he Acts 8:6
Now when Simon **s** that the Spirit was Acts 8:18
away, and the eunuch **s** him no more, Acts 8:39
his eyes were opened, he **s** nothing. Acts 9:8
residents of Lydda and Sharon **s** him, Acts 9:35
eyes, and when she **s** Peter she sat up. Acts 9:40
hour of the day he **s** clearly in a vision Acts 10:3
and **s** the heavens opened and Acts 10:11
praying, and in a trance I **s** a vision, Acts 11:5
When he came and **s** the grace of Acts 11:23
and when he **s** that it pleased the Jews, Acts 12:3
opened, they **s** him and were amazed. Acts 12:16
when he **s** what had occurred, Acts 13:12
with his fathers and **s** corruption, Acts 13:36
But when the Jews **s** the crowds, they Acts 13:45
when the crowds **s** what Paul had Acts 14:11
when her owners **s** that their hope Acts 16:19
the jailer woke and **s** that the prison Acts 16:27
within him as he **s** that the city was Acts 17:16
And when they **s** the tribune and the Acts 21:32
who were with me **s** the light but did Acts 22:9
hour I received my sight and **s** him. Acts 22:13
and **s** him saying to me, 'Make haste Acts 22:18
I **s** on the way a light from heaven, Acts 26:13
the native people **s** the creature Acts 28:4
a long time and **s** no misfortune come Acts 28:6
But I **s** none of the other apostles except Gal 1:19
when they **s** that I had been entrusted Gal 2:7
But when I **s** that their conduct was not Gal 2:14
same conflict that you **s** I had and now Phil 1:30
put me to the test and **s** my works Heb 3:9
because they **s** that the child was Heb 11:23

their lawless deeds that he **s** and heard); 2 Pt 2:8
of Jesus Christ, even to all that he **s**. Rv 1:2
on turning I **s** seven golden lampstands, Rv 1:12
When I **s** him, I fell at his feet as though Rv 1:17
seven stars that you **s** in my right hand, Rv 1:20
Then I **s** in the right hand of him who Rv 5:1
And I **s** a strong angel proclaiming with a Rv 5:2
among the elders I **s** a Lamb standing, Rv 5:6
I **s** under the altar the souls of those who Rv 6:9
After this I **s** four angels standing at the Rv 7:1
Then I **s** another angel ascending from Rv 7:2
Then I **s** the seven angels who stand Rv 8:2
and I **s** a star fallen from heaven to earth, Rv 9:1
And this is how I **s** the horses in my Rv 9:17
Then I **s** another mighty angel coming Rv 10:1
the angel whom I **s** standing on the sea Rv 10:5
and great fear fell on those who **s** them. Rv 11:11
And when the dragon **s** that he had Rv 12:13
And I **s** a beast rising out of the sea, with Rv 13:1
And the beast that I **s** was like a leopard; Rv 13:2
Then I **s** another beast rising out of the Rv 13:11
Then I **s** another angel flying directly Rv 14:6
Then I **s** another sign in heaven, great Rv 15:1
And I **s** what appeared to be a sea of glass Rv 15:2
And I **s**, coming out of the mouth of the Rv 16:13
and I **s** a woman sitting on a scarlet Rv 17:3
And I **s** the woman, drunk with the Rv 17:6
Jesus. When I **s** her, I marveled greatly. Rv 17:6
The beast that you **s** was, and is not, and Rv 17:8
ten horns that you **s** are ten kings who Rv 17:12
said to me, "The waters that you **s**, Rv 17:15
And the ten horns that you **s**, they and Rv 17:16
the woman that you **s** is the great city Rv 17:18
After this I **s** another angel coming Rv 18:1
and cried out as they **s** the smoke of her Rv 18:18
Then I **s** heaven opened, and behold, a Rv 19:11
Then I **s** an angel standing in the sun, Rv 19:17
And I **s** the beast and the kings of the Rv 19:19
Then I **s** an angel coming down from Rv 20:1
Then I **s** thrones, and seated on them Rv 20:4
Also I **s** the souls of those who had been Rv 20:4
Then I **s** a great white throne and him Rv 20:11
And I **s** the dead, great and small, Rv 20:12
Then I **s** a new heaven and a new earth, Rv 21:1
And I **s** the holy city, new Jerusalem, Rv 21:2
And I **s** no temple in the city, for its Rv 21:22
the one who heard and **s** these things. Rv 22:8
And when I heard and **s** them, I fell down Rv 22:8

SAWED (1)
cut according to measure, **s** with saws, 1 Kgs 7:9

SAWN (1)
They were stoned, they were **s** in two, Heb 11:37

SAWS (3)
them to labor with **s** and iron picks 2 Sm 12:31
according to measure, sawed with **s**, 1 Kgs 7:9
them to labor with **s** and iron picks 1 Chr 20:3

SAYINGS (12)
acts of Abijah, his ways and his **s**, 2 Chr 13:22
for your words, I listened for your wise **s**, Jb 32:11
a parable; I will utter dark **s** from of old, Ps 78:2
to my words; incline your ear to my **s**. Prv 4:20
written for you thirty **s** of counsel and Prv 22:20
These also are **s** of the wise. Partiality Prv 24:23
nails firmly fixed are the collected **s**; Eccl 12:11
And when Jesus finished these **s**, the Mt 7:28
Now when Jesus had finished these **s**, he Mt 19:1
When Jesus had finished all these **s**, he Mt 26:1
he had finished all his **s** in the hearing of Lk 7:1
eight days after these **s** he took with him Lk 9:28

SCAB (1)
Lord will strike with a **s** the heads of the Is 3:17

SCABBARD (1)
Put yourself into your **s**; rest and be still! Jer 47:6

SCABS (3)
itching disease or **s** or crushed testicles. Lv 21:20
or an itch or **s** you shall not offer Lv 22:22
Egypt, and with tumors and **s** and itch, Dt 28:27

SCALE (3)
Israel between the **s** armor and the 1 Kgs 22:34
Israel between the **s** armor and the 2 Chr 18:33
they charge; like soldiers they **s** the wall. Jl 2:7

SCALES (17)
in the waters that has fins and **s**, Lv 11:9
or the rivers that has not fins and **s**, Lv 11:10
has not fins and **s** is detestable to you. Lv 11:12
whatever has fins and **s** you may eat. Dt 14:9
not have fins and **s** you shall not eat; Dt 14:10
A just balance and **s** are the LORD'S; all Prv 16:11
to the LORD, and false **s** are not good. Prv 20:23
A wise man **s** the city of the mighty Prv 21:22
the mountains in **s** and the hills Is 40:12
and are accounted as the dust on the **s**; Is 40:15
the purse, and weigh out silver in the **s**, Is 46:6
witnesses, and weighed the money on **s**. Jer 32:10
the fish of your streams stick to your **s**; Ezk 29:4
of your streams that stick to your **s**. Ezk 29:4
the man with wicked **s** and with a bag Mi 6:11
something like **s** fell from Acts 9:18
And its rider had a pair of **s** in his hand. Rv 6:5

SCALP (1)
like a lion; he tears off arm and **s**. Dt 33:20

SCANT (1)
and the **s** measure that is accursed? Mi 6:10

SCAR (2)
does not spread, it is the **s** of the boil, Lv 13:23
him clean, for it is the **s** of the burn. Lv 13:28

SCARCELY (8)
when Jacob had **s** gone out from the Gn 27:30
S had I passed them when I found him Sg 3:4
S are they planted, scarcely sown, Is 40:24
Scarcely are they planted, **s** sown, Is 40:24
s has their stem taken root in the earth, Is 40:24
these words they **s** restrained the Acts 14:18
For one will **s** die for a righteous person Rom 5:7
And "If the righteous is **s** saved, what 1 Pt 4:18

SCARCITY (1)
in which you will eat bread without **s**, Dt 8:9

SCARE (1)
then you **s** me with dreams and terrify Jb 7:14

SCARECROWS (1)
Their idols are like **s** in a cucumber Jer 10:5

SCARLET (49)
took and tied a **s** thread on his hand, Gn 38:28
came out with the **s** thread on his Gn 38:30
blue and purple and **s** yarns and fine Ex 25:4
linen and blue and purple and **s** yarns; Ex 26:1
blue and purple and **s** yarns and fine Ex 26:31
blue and purple and **s** yarns and fine Ex 26:36
blue and purple and **s** yarns and fine Ex 27:16
gold, blue and purple and **s** yarns, Ex 28:5
of gold, of blue and purple and **s** yarns, Ex 28:6
it, of gold, blue and purple and **s** yarns, Ex 28:8
—of gold, blue and purple and **s** yarns, Ex 28:15
of blue and purple and **s** yarns, Ex 28:33
blue and purple and **s** yarns and fine Ex 35:6
blue or purple or **s** yarns or fine linen Ex 35:23
blue and purple and **s** yarns and fine Ex 35:25
blue and purple and **s** yarns and fine Ex 35:35
linen and blue and purple and **s** yarns, Ex 36:8
blue and purple and **s** yarns and fine Ex 36:35
blue and purple and **s** yarns and fine Ex 36:37
blue and purple and **s** yarns and fine Ex 38:18
blue and purple and **s** yarns and fine Ex 38:23
blue and purple and **s** yarns they made Ex 39:1
of gold, blue and purple and **s** yarns, Ex 39:2
into the blue and purple and the **s** yarns, Ex 39:3
it, of gold, blue and purple and **s** yarns, Ex 39:5
of gold, blue and purple and **s** yarns, Ex 39:8
blue and purple and **s** yarns and fine Ex 39:24
and of blue and purple and **s** yarns, Ex 39:29
and cedarwood and **s** yarn and hyssop. Lv 14:4
the cedarwood and the **s** yarn and the Lv 14:6
with cedarwood and **s** yarn and hyssop, Lv 14:49
and the hyssop and the **s** yarn, Lv 14:51
the cedarwood and hyssop and **s** yarn. Lv 14:52
them a cloth of **s** and cover the same Nm 4:8
take cedarwood and hyssop and **s** yarn, Nm 19:6
you shall tie this **s** cord in the window Jos 2:18
And she tied the **s** cord in the window. Jos 2:21
who clothed you luxuriously in **s**, 2 Sm 1:24
for all her household are clothed in **s**. Prv 31:21
Your lips are like a **s** thread, and your Sg 4:3
though your sins are like **s**, they shall be Is 1:18
what do you mean that you dress in **s**, Jer 4:30
men is red; his soldiers are clothed in **s**. Na 2:3
stripped him and put a **s** robe on him, Mt 27:28
with water and **s** wool and hyssop, Heb 9:19
woman sitting on a **s** beast that was full Rv 17:3
The woman was arrayed in purple and **s**, Rv 17:4
fine linen, purple cloth, silk, **s** cloth, Rv 18:12
clothed in fine linen, in purple and **s**, Rv 18:16

SCARVES (1)
the pendants, the bracelets, and the **s**; Is 3:19

SCATTER (36)
them in Jacob and **s** them in Israel. Gn 49:7
And I will **s** you among the nations, Lv 26:33
Then **s** the fire far and wide, for they Nm 16:37
And the LORD will **s** you among the Dt 4:27
"And the LORD will **s** you among all Dt 28:64
their fathers and **s** them beyond the 1 Kgs 14:15
I will **s** you among the peoples, Neh 1:8
moisture; the clouds **s** his lightning. Jb 37:11
s the peoples who delight in war. Ps 68:30
Flash forth the lightning and **s** them; Ps 144:6
will twist its surface and **s** its inhabitants. Is 24:1
has leveled its surface, does he not **s** dill, Is 28:25
You will **s** them as unclean things. Is 30:22
away, and the tempest shall **s** them. Is 41:16
I will **s** them among the nations whom Jer 9:16
I will **s** you like chaff driven by the Jer 13:24
east wind I will **s** them before the Jer 18:17
shepherds who destroy and **s** the sheep of Jer 23:1
I will **s** to every wind those who cut the Jer 49:32
And I will **s** them to all those winds, Jer 49:36
And a third part you shall **s** to the wind, Ezk 5:2
who survive I will **s** to all the winds. Ezk 5:10
a third part I will **s** to all the winds and Ezk 5:12
and I will **s** your bones around your Ezk 6:5
and **s** them over the city." And he went Ezk 10:2
And I will **s** toward every wind all who Ezk 12:14
the nations and **s** them among the Ezk 12:15
that I would **s** them among the Ezk 20:23
I will **s** you among the nations and Ezk 22:15
I will **s** the Egyptians among the Ezk 29:12
I will **s** the Egyptians among the Ezk 30:23
And I will **s** the Egyptians among the Ezk 30:26
strip off its leaves and **s** its fruit. Dn 4:14
who came like a whirlwind to **s** me, Hab 3:14
horns against the land of Judah to **s** it." Zec 1:21
as if a man should **s** seed on the ground. Mk 4:26

SCATTERED (68)
So the people were **s** throughout all the Ex 5:12
it to powder and **s** it on the water Ex 32:20
O LORD, and let your enemies be **s**, Nm 10:35
where the LORD your God has **s** you. Dt 30:3
And those who survived were **s**, so 1 Sm 11:11
the well's mouth and **s** grain on it, 2 Sm 17:19
And he sent out arrows and **s** them; 2 Sm 22:15
"I saw all Israel **s** on the mountains, 1 Kgs 22:17
and all his army was **s** from him. 2 Kgs 25:5
"I saw all Israel **s** on the mountains, 2 Chr 18:16
dust of them and **s** it over the graves 2 Chr 34:4
is a certain people **s** abroad and dispersed Est 3:8
of prey, and the cubs of the lioness are **s**. Jb 4:11
of his; sulfur is **s** over his habitation. Jb 18:15
where the east wind is **s** upon the earth? Jb 38:24
And he sent out his arrows and **s** them; Ps 18:14
for slaughter and have **s** us among the Ps 44:11
God shall arise, his enemies shall be **s**; Ps 68:1
you **s** your enemies with your mighty Ps 89:10
shall perish; all evildoers shall be **s**. Ps 92:9
so shall our bones be **s** at the mouth of Ps 141:7
Should your springs be **s** abroad, Prv 5:16
Like fleeing birds, like a **s** nest, so are the Is 16:2
when you lift yourself up, nations are **s**, Is 33:3
LORD your God and **s** your favors among Jer 3:13
not prospered, and all their flock is **s**. Jer 10:21
"You have **s** my flock and have driven Jer 23:2
of all the nations among whom I **s** you, Jer 30:11
say, 'He who **s** Israel will gather him, Jer 31:10
who are gathered about you would be **s**, Jer 40:15
And all his army was **s** from him. Jer 52:8
The holy stones lie **s** at the head of every Lam 4:1
The LORD himself has **s** them; he will Lam 4:16
when you are **s** through the countries, Ezk 6:8
and though I **s** them among the Ezk 11:16
the countries where you have been **s**, Ezk 11:17
the survivors shall be **s** to every wind, Ezk 17:21
out of the countries where you are **s**, Ezk 20:34
the countries where you have been **s**. Ezk 20:41
the peoples among whom they are **s**, Ezk 28:25
the peoples among whom they were **s**, Ezk 29:13
So they were **s**, because there was no Ezk 34:5
My sheep were **s**; they wandered over all Ezk 34:6
My sheep were **s** over all the face of the Ezk 34:6
is among his sheep that have been **s**, Ezk 34:12
where they have been **s** on a day of Ezk 34:12
horns, till you have **s** them abroad, Ezk 34:21
I **s** them among the nations, and they Ezk 36:19
people shall be **s** from his property." Ezk 46:18
because they have **s** them among the Jl 3:2
Your people are **s** on the mountains Na 3:18
then the eternal mountains were **s**; Hab 3:6
"These are the horns that have **s** Judah, Zec 1:19
said, "These are the horns that **s** Judah, Zec 1:21
"and I **s** them with a whirlwind among Zec 7:14
Though I **s** them among the nations, Zec 10:9
the shepherd, and the sheep will be **s**; Zec 13:7
and gathering where you **s** no seed, Mt 25:24
not sowed and gather where I **s** no seed? Mt 25:26
and the sheep of the flock will be **s**.' Mt 26:31
the shepherd, and the sheep will be **s**.' Mk 14:27
he has **s** the proud in the thoughts of Lk 1:51
the children of God who are **s** abroad. Jn 11:52
indeed it has come, when you will be **s**, Jn 16:32
and all who followed him were **s**. Acts 5:37
they were all **s** throughout the regions Acts 8:1

delivered over to the chief priests and **s**, Mt 20:18
priests and the **s** saw the wonderful Mt 21:15
"The **s** and the Pharisees sit on Moses' Mt 23:2
"But woe to you, **s** and Pharisees, Mt 23:13
Woe to you, **s** and Pharisees, Mt 23:15
"Woe to you, **s** and Pharisees, Mt 23:23
"Woe to you, **s** and Pharisees, Mt 23:25
"Woe to you, **s** and Pharisees, Mt 23:27
"Woe to you, **s** and Pharisees, Mt 23:29
send you prophets and wise men and **s**, Mt 23:34
where the **s** and the elders had gathered. Mt 26:57
the chief priests, with the **s** and elders, Mt 27:41
one who had authority, and not as the **s**. Mk 1:22
Now some of the **s** were sitting there, Mk 2:6
And the **s** of the Pharisees, when they Mk 2:16
And the **s** who came down from Mk 3:22
with some of the **s** who had come from Mk 7:1
And the Pharisees and the **s** asked him, Mk 7:5
the chief priests and the **s** and be killed, Mk 8:31
"Why do the **s** say that first Elijah must Mk 9:11
around them, and **s** arguing with them. Mk 9:14
over to the chief priests and the **s**, Mk 10:33
chief priests and the **s** heard it and Mk 11:18
chief priests and the **s** and the elders Mk 11:27
And one of the **s** came up and heard Mk 12:28
"How can the **s** say that the Christ is Mk 12:35
his teaching he said, "Beware of the **s**, Mk 12:38
chief priests and the **s** were seeking how Mk 14:1
chief priests and the **s** and the elders. Mk 14:43
and the elders and the **s** came together. Mk 14:53
with the elders and **s** and the whole Mk 15:1
chief priests with the **s** mocked him to Mk 15:31
And the **s** and the Pharisees began to Lk 5:21
Pharisees and their **s** grumbled at his Lk 5:30
And the **s** and the Pharisees watched him, Lk 6:7
by the elders and chief priests and **s**, Lk 9:22
the **s** and the Pharisees began to press Lk 11:53
And the Pharisees and the **s** grumbled, Lk 15:2
chief priests and the **s** and the principal Lk 19:47
chief priests and the **s** with the elders Lk 20:1
The **s** and the chief priests sought to Lk 20:19
Then some of the **s** answered, Lk 20:39
"Beware of the **s**, who like to walk Lk 20:46
chief priests and the **s** were seeking how Lk 22:2
together, both chief priests and **s**. Lk 22:66
The chief priests and the **s** stood by, Lk 23:10
The **s** and the Pharisees brought a woman Jn 8:3
and elders and **s** gathered together in Acts 4:5
up the people and the elders and the **s**, Acts 6:12
and some of the **s** of the Pharisees' Acts 23:9

SCRIPT (4)
province in its own **s** and to every people Est 1:22
province in its own **s** and every people in Est 3:12
province in its own **s** and to each people Est 8:9
to the Jews in their **s** and their language. Est 8:9

SCRIPTURE (32)
Have you not read this **S**: "'The stone Mk 12:10
"Today this **S** has been fulfilled in your Lk 4:21
I tell you that this **S** must be fulfilled in Lk 22:37
and they believed the **S** and the word that Jn 2:22
believes in me, as the **S** has said, Jn 7:38
Has not the **S** said that the Christ comes Jn 7:42
God came—and **S** cannot be broken— Jn 10:35
But the **S** will be fulfilled, 'He who ate Jn 13:18
that the **S** might be fulfilled. Jn 17:12
be." This was to fulfill the **S** which says, Jn 19:24
was now finished, said (to fulfill the **S**), Jn 19:28
took place that the **S** might be fulfilled: Jn 19:36
And again another **S** says, "They will Jn 19:37
for as yet they did not understand the **S**, Jn 20:9
"Brothers, the **S** had to be fulfilled, Acts 1:16
the passage of the **S** that he was Acts 8:32
and beginning with this **S** he told him Acts 8:35
For what does the **S** say? "Abraham Rom 4:3
For the **S** says to Pharaoh, "For this Rom 9:17
For the **S** says, "Everyone who Rom 10:11
not know what the **S** says of Elijah, Rom 11:2
And the **S**, foreseeing that God would Gal 3:8
But the **S** imprisoned everything under Gal 3:22
But what does the **S** say? "Cast out the Gal 4:30
yourself to the public reading of **S**, 1 Tm 4:13
For the **S** says, "You shall not muzzle 1 Tm 5:18
All **S** is breathed out by God and 2 Tm 3:16
fulfill the royal law according to the **S**, Jas 2:8
and the **S** was fulfilled that says, Jas 2:23
suppose it is to no purpose that the **S** says, Jas 4:5
For it stands in **S**: "Behold, I am laying 1 Pt 2:6
no prophecy of **S** comes from 2 Pt 1:20

SCRIPTURES (19)
to them, "Have you never read in the **S**: Mt 21:42
you know neither the **S** nor the power Mt 22:29
But how then should the **S** be fulfilled, Mt 26:54
taken place that the **S** of the prophets Mt 26:56
you know neither the **S** nor the power Mk 12:24
not seize me. But let the **S** be fulfilled." Mk 14:49
them in all the **S** the things concerning Lk 24:27
the road, while he opened to us the **S**?" Lk 24:32
their minds to understand the **S**, Lk 24:45
You search the **S** because you think that Jn 5:39
he reasoned with them from the **S**, Acts 17:2
examining the **S** daily to see if these Acts 17:11
an eloquent man, competent in the **S**. Acts 18:24
showing by the **S** that the Christ was Acts 18:28
through his prophets in the holy **S**, Rom 1:2
encouragement of the **S** we might Rom 15:4
for our sins in accordance with the **S**, 1 Cor 15:3
third day in accordance with the **S**, 1 Cor 15:4
own destruction, as they do the other **S**. 2 Pt 3:16

SCROLL (46)
a **s** was found on which this was written: Ezr 6:2
in the **s** of the book it is written of me: Ps 40:7
rot away, and the skies roll up like a **s**. Is 34:4
"Take a **s** and write on it all the words Jer 36:2
Baruch wrote on a **s** at the dictation of Jer 36:4
the LORD from the **s** that you have Jer 36:6
about reading from the **s** the words of Jer 36:8
read the words of Jeremiah from the **s**, Jer 36:10
all the words of the LORD from the **s**, Jer 36:11
when Baruch read the **s** in the hearing Jer 36:13
in your hand the **s** that you read in Jer 36:14
of Neriah took the **s** in his hand and Jer 36:14
while I wrote them with ink on the **s**." Jer 36:18
having put the **s** in the chamber of Jer 36:20
Then the king sent Jehudi to get the **s**, Jer 36:21
until the entire **s** was consumed in the Jer 36:23
urged the king not to burn the **s**, Jer 36:25
king had burned the **s** with the words Jer 36:27
"Take another **s** and write on it all the Jer 36:28
the former words that were in the first **s**, Jer 36:28
says the LORD, You have burned this **s**, Jer 36:29
Jeremiah took another **s** and gave it Jer 36:32
the words of the **s** that Jehoiakim king Jer 36:32
to me, and behold, a **s** of a book was in it. Ezk 2:9
Eat this **s**, and go, speak to the house of Ezk 3:1
my mouth, and he gave me this **s** to eat. Ezk 3:2
feed your belly with this **s** that I give you Ezk 3:3
my eyes and saw, and behold, a flying **s**! Zec 5:1
do you see?" I answered, "I see a flying **s**. Zec 5:2
And the **s** of the prophet Isaiah was Lk 4:17
He unrolled the **s** and found the place Lk 4:17
And he rolled up the **s** and gave it back Lk 4:20
it is written of me in the **s** of the book.'" Heb 10:7
on the throne a **s** written within and on Rv 5:1
worthy to open the **s** and break its seals?" Rv 5:2
was able to open the **s** or to look into it, Rv 5:3
found worthy to open the **s** or to look into Rv 5:4
that he can open the **s** and its seven seals." Rv 5:5
went and took the **s** from the right hand Rv 5:7
And when he had taken the **s**, the four Rv 5:8
are you to take the **s** and to open its seals, Rv 5:9
sky vanished like a **s** that is being rolled Rv 6:14
He had a little **s** open in his hand. And he Rv 10:2
take the **s** that is open in the hand of the Rv 10:8
angel and told him to give me the little **s**. Rv 10:9
And I took the little **s** from the hand of Rv 10:10

SCUM (2)
have made us **s** and garbage among Lam 3:45
and are still, like the **s** of the world, 1 Cor 4:13

SCYTHIAN (1)
uncircumcised, barbarian, **S**, slave, Col 3:11

SEA (392)
created the great **s** creatures and every Gn 1:21
over the fish of the **s** and over the birds Gn 1:26
over the fish of the **s** and over the birds Gn 1:28
on the ground and all the fish of the **s**. Gn 9:2
the Valley of Siddim (that is, the Salt **S**). Gn 14:3
your offspring as the sand of the **s**, Gn 32:12
great abundance, like the sand of the **s**, Gn 41:49
shall dwell at the shore of the **s**; Gn 49:13
locusts and drove them into the Red **S**. Ex 10:19
way of the wilderness toward the Red **S**. Ex 13:18
Pi-hahiroth, between Migdol and the **s**, Ex 14:2
you shall encamp facing it, by the **s**. Ex 14:2
and overtook them encamped at the **s**, Ex 14:9
out your hand over the **s** and divide it, Ex 14:16
may go through the **s** on dry ground. Ex 14:16
Moses stretched out his hand over the **s**, Ex 14:21
the LORD drove the **s** back by a strong Ex 14:21
wind all night and made the **s** dry land, Ex 14:21
into the midst of the **s** on dry ground, Ex 14:22
in after them into the midst of the **s**, Ex 14:23
"Stretch out your hand over the **s**, Ex 14:26
Moses stretched out his hand over the **s**, Ex 14:27
and the **s** returned to its normal course Ex 14:27
the Egyptians into the midst of the **s**. Ex 14:27
that had followed them into the **s**, Ex 14:28
walked on dry ground through the **s**, Ex 14:29
and his rider he has thrown into the **s**. Ex 15:1
chariots and his host he cast into the **s**, Ex 15:4
chosen officers were sunk in the Red **S**. Ex 15:4
the deeps congealed in the heart of the **s**. Ex 15:8
with your wind; the **s** covered them; Ex 15:10
and his horsemen went into the **s**, Ex 15:19
back the waters of the **s** upon them, Ex 15:19
on dry ground in the midst of the **s**. Ex 15:19
and his rider he has thrown into the **s**." Ex 15:21
made Israel set out from the Red **S**, Ex 15:22
the LORD made heaven and earth, the **s**, Ex 20:11
your border from the Red **S** to the Sea of Ex 23:31
the Red Sea to the **S** of the Philistines, Ex 23:31
the ostrich, the nighthawk, the **s** gull, Lv 11:16
the fish of the **s** be gathered together Nm 11:22
brought quail from the **s** and let them Nm 11:31
And the Canaanites dwell by the **s**, Nm 13:29
wilderness by the way to the Red **S**." Nm 14:25
Hor they set out by the way to the Red **S**, Nm 21:4
the midst of the **s** into the wilderness, Nm 33:8
from Elim and camped by the Red **S**. Nm 33:10
out from the Red **S** and camped in the Nm 33:11
from the end of the Salt **S** on the east. Nm 34:3
of Egypt, and its limit shall be at the **s**. Nm 34:5
shall have the Great **S** and its coast. Nm 34:6
from the Great **S** you shall draw a line Nm 34:7
the shoulder of the **S** of Chinnereth on Nm 34:11
and its limit shall be at the Salt **S**. Nm 34:12
wilderness in the direction of the Red **S**.' Dt 1:40
wilderness in the direction of the Red **S**, Dt 2:1
Chinnereth as far as the **S** of the Arabah, Dt 3:17
as far as the Sea of the Arabah, the Salt **S**, Dt 3:17
the Jordan as far as the **S** of the Arabah, Dt 4:49
the water of the Red **S** flow over them as Dt 11:4
the river Euphrates, to the western **s**. Dt 11:24
the ostrich, the nighthawk, the **s** gull, Dt 14:15
Neither is it beyond the **s**, that you Dt 30:13
'Who will go over the **s** for us and bring Dt 30:13
the land of Judah as far as the western **s**, Dt 34:2
Hittites to the Great **S** toward the going Jos 1:4
water of the Red **S** before you when you Jos 2:10
down toward the **S** of the Arabah, Jos 3:16
toward the Sea of the Arabah, the Salt **S**, Jos 3:16
as the LORD your God did to the Red **S**, Jos 4:23
of the Canaanites who were by the **s**, Jos 5:1
the coast of the Great **S** toward Lebanon, Jos 9:1
Arabah to the **S** of Chinneroth eastward, Jos 12:3
Beth-jeshimoth, to the **S** of the Arabah, Jos 12:3
to the Sea of the Arabah, the Salt **S**, Jos 12:3
to the lower end of the **S** of Chinnereth, Jos 13:27
boundary ran from the end of the Salt **S**, Jos 15:2
of Egypt, and comes to its end at the **s**. Jos 15:4
And the east boundary is the Salt **S**, to Jos 15:5
from the bay of the **s** at the mouth of the Jos 15:5
the boundary comes to an end at the **s**. Jos 15:11
was the Great **S** with its coastline. Jos 15:12
from Ekron to the **s**, all that were by Jos 15:46
and the Great **S** with its coastline. Jos 15:47
then to Gezer, and it ends at the **s**. Jos 16:3
the boundary goes from there to the **s**. Jos 16:6
to the brook Kanah and ends at the **s**. Jos 16:8
north side of the brook and ends at the **s**, Jos 17:9
with the **s** forming its boundary. Jos 17:10
ends at the northern bay of the Salt **S**, Jos 18:19
turns to Hosah, and it ends at the **s**; Jos 19:29
the Jordan to the Great **S** in the west. Jos 23:4
out of Egypt, and you came to the **s**. Jos 24:6
chariots and horsemen to the Red **S**. Jos 24:6
and made the **s** come upon them Jos 24:7
Asher sat still at the coast of the **s**, Jgs 5:17
wilderness to the Red **S** and came to Jgs 11:16
as the sand by the **s** for multitude, 2 Sm 17:11
Then the channels of the **s** were seen; 2 Sm 22:16
were as many as the sand by the **s**. 1 Kgs 4:20
bring it down to the **s** from Lebanon, 1 Kgs 5:9
into rafts to go by **s** to the place you 1 Kgs 5:9
Then he made the **s** of cast metal. It 1 Kgs 7:23
cubits, compassing the **s** all around. 1 Kgs 7:24
The **s** was set on them, and all their 1 Kgs 7:25
And he set the **s** at the southeast 1 Kgs 7:39
and the one **s**, and the twelve oxen 1 Kgs 7:44
and the twelve oxen underneath the **s**. 1 Kgs 7:44
near Eloth on the shore of the Red **S**, 1 Kgs 9:26
seamen who were familiar with the **s**, 1 Kgs 9:27
ships of Tarshish at **s** with the fleet 1 Kgs 10:22
look toward the **s**." And he went up 1 Kgs 18:43
is rising from the **s**." And he said, 1 Kgs 18:44
as far as the **S** of the Arabah, 2 Kgs 14:25
he took down the **s** from off the 2 Kgs 16:17
stands and the bronze **s** that were in 2 Kgs 25:13
As for the two pillars, the one **s**, and 2 Kgs 25:16
Let the **s** roar, and all that fills it; let 1 Chr 16:32
made the bronze **s** and the pillars 1 Chr 18:8
bring it to you in rafts by **s** to Joppa, 2 Chr 2:16
Then he made the **s** of cast metal. It 2 Chr 4:2

cubits, compassing the **s** all around. 2 Chr 4:3
The **s** was set on them, and all their 2 Chr 4:4
and the **s** was for the priests to wash in. 2 Chr 4:6
And he set the **s** at the southeast 2 Chr 4:10
and the one **s**, and the twelve oxen 2 Chr 4:15
and Eloth on the shore of the **s**, 2 Chr 8:17
and servants familiar with the **s**, 2 Chr 8:18
you from Edom, from beyond the **s**; 2 Chr 20:2
bring cedar trees from Lebanon to the **s**, Ezr 3:7
Egypt and heard their cry at the Red **S**, Neh 9:9
And you divided the **s** before them, so Neh 9:11
through the midst of the **s** on dry land, Neh 9:11
the land and on the coastlands of the **s**. Est 10:1
it would be heavier than the sand of the **s**; Jb 6:3
Am I the **s**, or a sea monster, that you set Jb 7:12
Am I the sea, or a **s** monster, that you set Jb 7:12
heavens and trampled the waves of the **s**; Jb 9:8
than the earth and broader than the **s**. Jb 11:9
and the fish of the **s** will declare to you. Jb 12:8
By his power he stilled the **s**; by his Jb 26:12
deep says, 'It is not in me,' and the **s** says, Jb 28:14
about him and covers the roots of the **s**. Jb 36:30
"Or who shut in the **s** with doors when it Jb 38:8
you entered into the springs of the **s**, Jb 38:16
he makes the **s** like a pot of ointment. Jb 41:31
birds of the heavens, and the fish of the **s**, Ps 8:8
Then the channels of the **s** were seen, Ps 18:15
He gathers the waters of the **s** as a heap; Ps 33:7
be moved into the heart of the **s**, Ps 46:2
He turned the **s** into dry land; they passed Ps 66:6
them back from the depths of the **s**, Ps 68:22
May he have dominion from **s** to sea, Ps 72:8
May he have dominion from sea to **s**, Ps 72:8
You divided the **s** by your might; you Ps 74:13
the heads of the **s** monsters on the Ps 74:13
Your way was through the **s**, your path Ps 77:19
He divided the **s** and let them pass Ps 78:13
but the **s** overwhelmed their enemies. Ps 78:53
its branches to the **s** and its shoots to Ps 80:11
You rule the raging of the **s**; when its Ps 89:9
set his hand on the **s** and his right hand Ps 89:25
waters, mightier than the waves of the **s**, Ps 93:4
The **s** is his, for he made it, and his Ps 95:5
rejoice; let the **s** roar, and all that fills it; Ps 96:11
Let the **s** roar, and all that fills it; the Ps 98:7
Here is the **s**, great and wide, which Ps 104:25
steadfast love, but rebelled by the **S**, Ps 106:7
but rebelled by the Sea, at the Red **S**. Ps 106:7
He rebuked the Red **S**, and it became Ps 106:9
Ham, and awesome deeds by the Red **S**. Ps 106:22
Some went down to the **s** in ships, Ps 107:23
which lifted up the waves of the **s**. Ps 107:25
and the waves of the **s** were hushed. Ps 107:29
The **s** looked and fled; Jordan turned Ps 114:3
What ails you, O **s**, that you flee? O Ps 114:5
to him who divided the Red **S** in two, Ps 136:13
Pharaoh and his host in the Red **S**, Ps 136:15
and dwell in the uttermost parts of the **s**, Ps 139:9
who made heaven and earth, the **s**, and Ps 146:6
you great **s** creatures and all deeps, Ps 148:7
when he assigned to the **s** its limit, so Prv 8:29
who lies down in the midst of the **s**, Prv 23:34
All streams run to the **s**, but the sea is Eccl 1:7
run to the sea, but the **s** is not full; Eccl 1:7
it on that day, like the growling of the **s**. Is 5:30
time he has made glorious the way of the **s**, Is 9:1
your people Israel be as the sand of the **s**, Is 10:22
And his staff will be over the **s**, and he Is 10:26
of the LORD as the waters cover the **s**. Is 11:9
and from the coastlands of the **s**. Is 11:11
destroy the tongue of the **S** of Egypt, Is 11:15
spread abroad and passed over the **s**. Is 16:8
thunder like the thundering of the **s**! Is 17:12
which sends ambassadors by the **s**, in Is 18:2
And the waters of the **s** will be dried up, Is 19:5
oracle concerning the wilderness of the **s**. Is 21:1
the merchants of Sidon, who cross the **s**, Is 23:2
ashamed, O Sidon, for the **s** has spoken, Is 23:4
sea has spoken, the stronghold of the **s**, Is 23:4
He has stretched out his hand over the **s**; Is 23:11
in the coastlands of the **s**, give glory to Is 24:15
he will slay the dragon that is in the **s**. Is 27:1
of the earth, you who go down to the **s**, Is 42:10
says the LORD, who makes a way in the **s**, Is 43:16
righteousness like the waves of the **s**; Is 48:18
Behold, by my rebuke I dry up the **s**, I Is 50:2
Was it not you who dried up the **s**, the Is 51:10
made the depths of the **s** a way for the Is 51:10
who stirs up the **s** so that its waves roar Is 51:15
But the wicked are like the tossing **s**; for Is 57:20
the abundance of the **s** shall be turned to Is 60:5
up out of the **s** with the shepherds of Is 63:11
the sand as the boundary for the **s**, Jer 5:22
the sound of them is like the roaring **s**; Jer 6:23
the kings of the coastland across the **s**; Jer 25:22
of hosts concerning the pillars, the **s**, Jer 27:19
who stirs up the **s** so that its waves roar Jer 31:35
the sands of the **s** cannot be measured, Jer 33:22
mountains and like Carmel by the **s**, Jer 46:18
Your branches passed over the **s**, Jer 48:32
over the sea, reached to the **S** of Jazer; Jer 48:32
of their cry shall be heard at the Red **S**. Jer 49:21
are troubled like the **s** that cannot be Jer 49:23
of them is like the roaring of the **s**; Jer 50:42
will dry up her **s** and make her Jer 51:36
The **s** has come up on Babylon; she is Jer 51:42
stands and the bronze **s** that were in the Jer 52:17
As for the two pillars, the one **s**, the Jer 52:20
bronze bulls that were under the **s**, Jer 52:20
For your ruin is vast as the **s**; who can Lam 2:13
you, as the **s** brings up its waves. Ezk 26:3
in the midst of the **s** a place for the Ezk 26:5
the princes of the **s** will step down Ezk 26:16
renowned, who was mighty on the **s**; Ezk 26:17
that are on the **s** are dismayed at your Ezk 26:18
who dwells at the entrances to the **s**, Ezk 27:3
the ships of the **s** with their mariners Ezk 27:9
all the pilots of the **s** stand on the land Ezk 27:29
one destroyed in the midst of the **s**? Ezk 27:32
The fish of the **s** and the birds of the Ezk 38:20
Valley of the Travelers, east of the **s**. Ezk 39:11
down into the Arabah, and enters the **s**; Ezk 47:8
when the water flows into the **s**, the Ezk 47:8
the waters of the **s** may become fresh; Ezk 47:9
Fishermen will stand beside the **s**. Ezk 47:10
kinds, like the fish of the Great **S**. Ezk 47:10
from the Great **S** by way of Hethlon to Ezk 47:15
shall run from the **s** to Hazar-enan, Ezk 47:17
to the eastern **s** and as far as Tamar. Ezk 47:18
the Brook of Egypt to the Great **S**. Ezk 47:19
the Great **S** shall be the boundary to a Ezk 47:20
the Brook of Egypt to the Great **S**. Ezk 48:28
of heaven were stirring up the great **s**. Dn 7:2
four great beasts came up out of the **s**, Dn 7:3
tents between the **s** and the glorious Dn 11:45
of Israel shall be like the sand of the **s**, Hos 1:10
and even the fish of the **s** are taken away. Hos 4:3
land, his vanguard into the eastern **s**, Jl 2:20
sea, and his rear guard into the western **s**; Jl 2:20
the waters of the **s** and pours them out Am 5:8
They shall wander from **s** to sea, and Am 8:12
They shall wander from sea to **s**, and Am 8:12
from my sight at the bottom of the **s**, Am 9:3
the waters of the **s** and pours them out Am 9:6
the LORD hurled a great wind upon the **s**, Jon 1:4
and there was a mighty tempest on the **s**, Jon 1:4
in the ship into the **s** to lighten it for Jon 1:5
who made the **s** and the dry land." Jon 1:9
that the **s** may quiet down for us?" For Jon 1:11
for us?" For the **s** grew more and more Jon 1:11
"Pick me up and hurl me into the **s**; Jon 1:12
then the **s** will quiet down for you, for I Jon 1:12
for the **s** grew more and more Jon 1:13
up Jonah and hurled him into the **s**, Jon 1:15
the sea, and the **s** ceased from its raging. Jon 1:15
from **s** to sea and from mountain to Mi 7:12
from sea to **s** and from mountain to Mi 7:12
cast all our sins into the depths of the **s**. Mi 7:19
He rebukes the **s** and makes it dry; he Na 1:4
with water around her, her rampart a **s**, Na 3:8
make mankind like the fish of the **s**, Hab 1:14
of the LORD as the waters cover the **s**. Hab 2:14
rivers, or your indignation against the **s**, Hab 3:8
You trampled the **s** with your horses, Hab 3:15
birds of the heavens and the fish of the **s**, Zep 1:3
and the earth and the **s** and the dry land. Hg 2:6
and strike down her power on the **s**, Zec 9:4
his rule shall be from **s** to sea, and from Zec 9:10
his rule shall be from sea to **s**, and from Zec 9:10
pass through the **s** of troubles and Zec 10:11
and strike down the waves of the **s**, Zec 10:11
them to the eastern **s** and half of them Zec 14:8
sea and half of them to the western **s**. Zec 14:8
went and lived in Capernaum by the **s**, Mt 4:13
the land of Naphtali, the way of the **s**, Mt 4:15
While walking by the **S** of Galilee, he Mt 4:18
his brother, casting a net into the **s**, Mt 4:18
there arose a great storm on the **s**, Mt 8:24
he rose and rebuked the winds and the **s**, Mt 8:26
is this, that even winds and **s** obey him?" Mt 8:27
steep bank into the **s** and drowned in the Mt 8:32
out of the house and sat beside the **s**. Mt 13:1
was thrown into the **s** and gathered fish Mt 13:47
he came to them, walking on the **s**. Mt 14:25
the disciples saw him walking on the **s**, Mt 14:26
and walked beside the **S** of Galilee. Mt 15:29
go to the **s** and cast a hook and take the Mt 17:27
and to be drowned in the depth of the **s**. Mt 18:6
'Be taken up and thrown into the **s**,' Mt 21:21
For you travel across **s** and land to Mt 23:15
Passing alongside the **S** of Galilee, he Mk 1:16
of Simon casting a net into the **s**, Mk 1:16
He went out again beside the **s**, and all Mk 2:13
Jesus withdrew with his disciples to the **s**, Mk 3:7
Again he began to teach beside the **s**. Mk 4:1
he got into a boat and sat in it on the **s**, Mk 4:1
crowd was beside the **s** on the land. Mk 4:1
and rebuked the wind and said to the **s**, Mk 4:39
is this, that even wind and **s** obey him?" Mk 4:41
They came to the other side of the **s**, to Mk 5:1
steep bank into the **s** and were drowned Mk 5:13
into the sea and were drowned in the **s**. Mk 5:13
about him, and he was beside the **s**. Mk 5:21
came, the boat was out on the **s**, Mk 6:47
he came to them, walking on the **s**. Mk 6:48
him walking on the **s** they thought it Mk 6:49
went through Sidon to the **S** of Galilee, Mk 7:31
his neck and he were thrown into the **s**. Mk 9:42
'Be taken up and thrown into the **s**,' Mk 11:23
were cast into the **s** than that he should Lk 17:2
tree, 'Be uprooted and planted in the **s**,' Lk 17:6
of the roaring of the **s** and the waves, Lk 21:25
away to the other side of the **S** of Galilee, Jn 6:1
Sea of Galilee, which is the **S** of Tiberias. Jn 6:1
came, his disciples went down to the **s**, Jn 6:16
and started across the **s** to Capernaum. Jn 6:17
The **s** became rough because a strong Jn 6:18
Jesus walking on the **s** and coming near Jn 6:19
the other side of the **s** saw that there had Jn 6:22
they found him on the other side of the **s**, Jn 6:25
to the disciples by the **S** of Tiberias, Jn 21:1
for work, and threw himself into the **s**. Jn 21:7
the earth and the **s** and everything in Acts 4:24
and at the Red **S** and in the wilderness Acts 7:36
house of Simon, a tanner, by the **s**.' Acts 10:32
and the earth and the **s** and all that is Acts 14:15
sent Paul off on his way to the **s**, Acts 17:14
along the coast of Asia, we put to **s**, Acts 27:2
And putting out to **s** from there we Acts 27:4
sailed across the open **s** along the coast Acts 27:5
decided to put out to **s** from there, Acts 27:12
being driven across the Adriatic **S**, Acts 27:27
boat into the **s** under pretense of Acts 27:30
throwing out the wheat into the **s**. Acts 27:38
off the anchors and left them in the **s**, Acts 27:40
Though he has escaped from the **s**, Acts 28:4
sons of Israel be as the sand of the **s**, Rom 9:27
cloud, and all passed through the **s**, 1 Cor 10:1
into Moses in the cloud and in the **s**, 1 Cor 10:2
a night and a day I was adrift at **s**; 2 Cor 11:25
in the wilderness, danger at **s**, 2 Cor 11:26
people crossed the Red **S** as if on dry Heb 11:29
like a wave of the **s** that is driven and Jas 1:6
of beast and bird, of reptile and **s** creature, Jas 3:7
wild waves of the **s**, casting up the Jude 1:13
the throne there was as it were a **s** of glass, Rv 4:6
earth and under the earth and in the **s**, Rv 5:13
blow on earth or **s** or against any tree. Rv 7:1
been given power to harm earth and **s**, Rv 7:2
not harm the earth or the **s** or the trees, Rv 7:3
burning with fire, was thrown into the **s**, Rv 8:8
the sea, and a third of the **s** became blood. Rv 8:8
third of the living creatures in the **s** died, Rv 8:9
And he set his right foot on the **s**, and his Rv 10:2
I saw standing on the **s** and on the land Rv 10:5
what is in it, and the **s** and what is in it, Rv 10:6
is standing on the **s** and on the land." Rv 10:8
But woe to you, O earth and **s**, for the Rv 12:12
Jesus. And he stood on the sand of the **s**. Rv 12:17
And I saw a beast rising out of the **s**, with Rv 13:1
earth, the **s** and the springs of water." Rv 14:7
appeared to be a **s** of glass mingled with Rv 15:2
standing beside the **s** of glass with harps Rv 15:2
angel poured out his bowl into the **s**, Rv 16:3
every living thing died that was in the **s**. Rv 16:3
sailors and all whose trade is on the **s**, Rv 18:17
all who had ships at **s** grew rich by her Rv 18:19
a great millstone and threw it into the **s**, Rv 18:21
their number is like the sand of the **s**. Rv 20:8
And the **s** gave up the dead who were in Rv 20:13
had passed away, and the **s** was no more. Rv 21:1

SEACOAST (6)
lowland and in the Negeb and by the **s**, Dt 1:7
and destroy the rest of the **s**. Ezk 25:16
Woe to you inhabitants of the **s**, you Zep 2:5
And you, O **s**, shall be pastures, with Zep 2:6
The **s** shall become the possession of the Zep 2:7
and Jerusalem and the **s** of Tyre and Lk 6:17

SEAFARING (1)
waste." And all shipmasters and **s** men, Rv 18:17

SEAH (4)
first lamb a tenth **s** of fine flour Ex 29:40
about this time a **s** of fine flour shall 2 Kgs 7:1
So a **s** of fine flour was sold for a 2 Kgs 7:16

and a **s** of fine flour for a shekel, 2 Kgs 7:18

SEAHS (6)
and said, "Quick! Three **s** of fine flour! Gn 18:6
prepared and five **s** of parched grain 1 Sm 25:18
great as would contain two **s** of seed. 1 Kgs 18:32
shekel, and two **s** of barley for a shekel, 2 Kgs 7:1
and two **s** of barley for a shekel, 2 Kgs 7:16
"Two **s** of barley shall be sold for a 2 Kgs 7:18

SEAL (26)
name and sealed them with his **s**, 1 Kgs 21:8
of the king, and **s** it with the king's ring, Est 8:8
It is changed like clay under the **s**, and Jb 38:14
of shields, shut up closely as with a **s**. Jb 41:15
Set me as a **s** upon your heart, as a seal Sg 8:6
upon your heart, as a **s** upon your arm, Sg 8:6
s the teaching among my disciples. Is 8:16
has been told is true, but **s** up the vision, Dn 8:26
to **s** both vision and prophet, Dn 9:24
shut up the words and **s** the book, Dn 12:4
receives his testimony sets his **s** to this, Jn 3:33
For on him God the Father has set his **s**." Jn 6:27
circumcision as a **s** of the Rom 4:11
for you are the **s** of my apostleship in 1 Cor 9:2
has also put his **s** on us and given 2 Cor 1:22
foundation stands, bearing this **s**: 2 Tm 2:19
When he opened the second **s**, I heard the Rv 6:3
When he opened the third **s**, I heard the Rv 6:5
When he opened the fourth **s**, I heard the Rv 6:7
When he opened the fifth **s**, I saw under Rv 6:9
When he opened the sixth **s**, I looked, Rv 6:12
of the sun, with the **s** of the living God, Rv 7:2
When the Lamb opened the seventh **s**, Rv 8:1
who do not have the **s** of God on their Rv 9:4
"**S** up what the seven thunders have said, Rv 10:4
"Do not **s** up the words of the prophecy Rv 22:10

SEALED (25)
in store with me, **s** up in my treasuries? Dt 32:34
in Ahab's name and **s** them with his 1 Kgs 21:8
on the **s** document are the names of Neh 9:38
of King Ahasuerus and **s** with the king's Est 3:12
of the king and **s** with the king's ring Est 8:8
of King Ahasuerus and **s** it with the Est 8:10
my transgression would be **s** up in a Jb 14:17
my bride, a spring locked, a fountain **s**. Sg 4:12
to you like the words of a book that is **s**. Is 29:11
"Read this," he says, "I cannot, for it is **s**." Is 29:11
I signed the deed, **s** it, got witnesses, and Jer 32:10
Then I took the **s** deed of purchase, Jer 32:11
both this **s** deed of purchase and this Jer 32:14
shall be signed and **s** and witnessed, Jer 32:44
and the king **s** it with his own signet Dn 6:17
words are shut up and **s** until the time of Dn 12:9
were **s** with the promised Holy Spirit, Eph 1:13
by whom you were **s** for the day of Eph 4:30
and on the back, **s** with seven seals. Rv 5:1
until we have **s** the servants of our God on Rv 7:3
And I heard the number of the **s**, 144,000, Rv 7:4
s from every tribe of the sons of Israel: Rv 7:4
12,000 from the tribe of Judah were **s**, Rv 7:5
12,000 from the tribe of Benjamin were **s**. Rv 7:8
into the pit, and shut it and **s** it over him, Rv 20:3

SEALING (1)
the tomb secure by **s** the stone and Mt 27:66

SEALS (8)
On the **s** are the names of Nehemiah Neh 10:1
and it does not rise; who **s** up the stars; Jb 9:7
He **s** up the hand of every man, that all Jb 37:7
and on the back, sealed with seven **s**. Rv 5:1
worthy to open the scroll and break its **s**?" Rv 5:2
he can open the scroll and its seven **s**." Rv 5:5
are you to take the scroll and to open its **s**, Rv 5:9
when the Lamb opened one of the seven **s**, Rv 6:1

SEAM (2)
at its **s** above the skillfully woven band Ex 28:27
at its **s** above the skillfully woven band Ex 39:20

SEAMEN (1)
s who were familiar with the sea, 1 Kgs 9:27

SEAMLESS (1)
But the tunic was **s**, woven in one piece Jn 19:23

SEAMS (1)
men were in you, caulking your **s**; Ezk 27:9

SEARCH (41)
if you **s** after him with all your heart and Dt 4:29
inquire and make **s** and ask diligently. Dt 13:14
have come here tonight to **s** out the land." Jos 2:2
for they have come to **s** out all the land." Jos 2:3
I will **s** him out among all the 1 Sm 23:23
the Philistines went up to **s** for David. 2 Sm 5:17
his servants to you to **s** the city and to 2 Sm 10:3
and they shall **s** your house and the 1 Kgs 20:6
"**S**, and see that there is no servant of 2 Kgs 10:23
the Philistines went up to **s** for David. 1 Chr 14:8
come to you to **s** and to overthrow 1 Chr 19:3
of David's reign **s** was made and 1 Chr 26:31
in order that **s** may be made in the book Ezr 4:15
I made a decree, and **s** has been made, Ezr 4:19
let **s** be made in the royal archives there Ezr 5:17
a decree, and **s** was made in Babylonia, Ezr 6:1
seek out my iniquity and **s** for my sin, Jb 10:6
They **s** out injustice, saying, "We have Ps 64:6
accomplished a diligent **s**." For the Ps 64:6
heart." Then my spirit made a diligent **s**: Ps 77:6
You **s** out my path and my lying down Ps 139:3
S me, O God, and know my heart! Try Ps 139:23
seek it like silver and **s** for it as for Prv 2:4
but the glory of kings is to **s** things out. Prv 25:2
to seek and to **s** out by wisdom all Eccl 1:13
heart to know and to **s** out and to seek Eccl 7:25
S her squares to see if you can find a man, Jer 5:1
"I the LORD **s** the heart and test the Jer 17:10
her people groan as they **s** for bread; Lam 1:11
earth, with none to **s** or seek for them. Ezk 34:6
I myself will **s** for my sheep and will Ezk 34:11
seven months they will make their **s**. Ezk 39:14
from there I will **s** them out and take Am 9:3
that time I will **s** Jerusalem with lamps, Zep 1:12
saying, "Go and **s** diligently for the child, Mt 2:8
you, for Herod is about to **s** for the child, Mt 2:13
is like a merchant in **s** of fine pearls, Mt 13:45
mountains and go in **s** of the one that Mt 18:12
then they began to **s** for him among Lk 2:44
You **s** the Scriptures because you think Jn 5:39
S and see that no prophet arises from Jn 7:52

SEARCHED (18)
is upon me." So he **s** but did not find Gn 31:35
And he **s**, beginning with the eldest Gn 44:12
and the pursuers **s** all along the way and Jos 2:22
And after they had **s** and inquired, Jgs 6:29
He **s** for Ahaziah, and he was 2 Chr 22:9
Behold, this we have **s** out; it is true. Hear, Jb 5:27
and consider what the fathers have **s** out. Jb 8:8
declared it; he established it, and **s** it out. Jb 28:27
and I **s** out the cause of him whom I did Jb 29:16
sayings, while you **s** out what to say. Jb 32:11
O LORD, you have **s** me and known me! Ps 139:1
I **s** with my heart how to cheer my body Eccl 2:3
into a land that I had **s** out for them, Ezk 20:6
my shepherds have not **s** for my sheep, Ezk 34:8
and those who were with him **s** for him, Mk 1:36
And after Herod **s** for him and did not Acts 12:19
arrived in Rome he **s** for me earnestly 2 Tm 1:17
to be yours **s** and inquired carefully, 1 Pt 1:10

SEARCHES (8)
for the LORD **s** all hearts and 1 Chr 28:9
it be well with you when he **s** you out? Jb 13:9
end to darkness and **s** out to the farthest Jb 28:3
pasture, and he **s** after every green thing. Jb 39:8
but evil comes to him who **s** for it. Prv 11:27
And he who **s** hearts knows what is Rom 8:27
For the Spirit **s** everything, even the 1 Cor 2:10
that I am he who **s** mind and heart, Rv 2:23

SEARCHING (4)
who does great things beyond **s** out, and Jb 9:10
of the LORD, **s** all his innermost parts. Prv 20:27
they returned to Jerusalem, **s** for him. Lk 2:45
father and I have been **s** for you in great Lk 2:48

SEARCHINGS (2)
of Reuben there were great **s** of heart. Jgs 5:15
of Reuben there were great **s** of heart. Jgs 5:16

SEARED (1)
of liars whose consciences are **s**, 1 Tm 4:2

SEAS (27)
that were gathered together he called **S**. Gn 1:10
and multiply and fill the waters in the **s**, Gn 1:22
scales, whether in the **s** or in the rivers, Lv 11:9
But anything in the **s** or the rivers that Lv 11:10
the abundance of the **s** and the hidden Dt 33:19
that is on it, the **s** and all that is in them; Neh 9:6
whatever passes along the paths of the **s**. Ps 8:8
founded it upon the **s** and established it Ps 24:2
the ends of the earth and of the farthest **s**; Ps 65:5
who stills the roaring of the **s**, the Ps 65:7
the **s** and everything that moves in Ps 69:34
dust, winged birds like the sand of the **s**; Ps 78:27
and on earth, in the **s** and all deeps. Ps 135:6
a rock, the way of a ship on the high **s**, Prv 30:19
more in number than the sand of the **s**; Jer 15:8
you who were inhabited from the **s**, Ezk 26:17
Your borders are in the heart of the **s**; Ezk 27:4
and heavily laden in the heart of the **s**. Ezk 27:25
have brought you out into the high **s**. Ezk 27:26
has wrecked you in the heart of the **s**. Ezk 27:26
into the heart of the **s** on the day of Ezk 27:27
When your wares came from the **s**, Ezk 27:33
Now you are wrecked by the **s**, in the Ezk 27:34
the seat of the gods, in the heart of the **s**,' Ezk 28:2
death of the slain in the heart of the **s**. Ezk 28:8
but you are like a dragon in the **s**; Ezk 32:2
me into the deep, into the heart of the **s**, Jon 2:3

SEASHORE (8)
heaven and as the sand that is on the **s**. Gn 22:17
Israel saw the Egyptians dead on the **s**. Ex 14:30
in number like the sand that is on the **s**, Jos 11:4
the sand that is on the **s** in abundance. Jgs 7:12
like the sand on the **s** in multitude. 1 Sm 13:5
of mind like the sand on the **s**, 1 Kgs 4:29
and against the **s** he has appointed Jer 47:7
innumerable grains of sand by the **s**. Heb 11:12

SEASIDE (1)
a tanner, whose house is by the **s**." Acts 10:6

SEASON (26)
In the breeding **s** of the flock I lifted up Gn 31:10
You shall **s** all your grain offerings with Lv 2:13
then I will give you your rains in their **s**, Lv 26:4
Now the time was the **s** of the first ripe Nm 13:20
will give the rain for your land in its **s**, Dt 11:14
to your land in its **s** and to bless all the Dt 28:12
And he said, "At this **s**, about this 2 Kgs 4:16
old age, like a sheaf gathered up in its **s**. Jb 5:26
you lead forth the Mazzaroth in their **s**, Jb 38:32
of water that yields its fruit in its **s**, Ps 1:3
to you, to give them their food in due **s**. Ps 104:27
and you give them their food in due **s**. Ps 145:15
is a joy to a man, and a word in **s**, Prv 15:23
For everything there is a **s**, and a time Eccl 3:1
LORD our God, who gives the rain in its **s**, Jer 5:24
I will send down the showers in their **s**; Ezk 34:26
lives were prolonged for a **s** and a time. Dn 7:12
grain in its time, and my wine in its **s**, Hos 2:9
the first fruit on the fig tree in its first **s**, Hos 9:10
the LORD in the **s** of the spring rain, Zec 10:1
When the **s** for fruit drew near, he sent Mt 21:34
but leaves, for it was not the **s** for figs. Mk 11:13
When the **s** came, he sent a servant to Mk 12:2
of doing good, for in due **s** we will reap, Gal 6:9
word; be ready in **s** and out of season; 2 Tm 4:2
word; be ready in season and out of **s**; 2 Tm 4:2

SEASONED (6)
blended as by the perfumer, **s** with salt, Ex 30:35
Of Zebulun 50,000 **s** troops, 1 Chr 12:33
Of Asher 40,000 **s** troops ready for 1 Chr 12:36
mighty men and all the **s** warriors. 1 Chr 28:1
that work the ground will eat **s** fodder, Is 30:24
speech always be gracious, **s** with salt, Col 4:6

SEASONS (10)
And let them be for signs and for **s**, and Gn 1:14
should be observed at their appointed **s**, Est 9:31
He made the moon to mark the **s**; the Ps 104:19
He changes times and **s**; he removes Dn 2:21
the house of Judah **s** of joy and gladness Zec 8:19
who will give him the fruits in their **s**." Mt 21:41
to know times or **s** that the Father has Acts 1:7
you rains from heaven and fruitful **s**, Acts 14:17
days and months and **s** and years! Gal 4:10
Now concerning the times and the **s**, 1 Thes 5:1

SEAT (67)
shall make a mercy **s** of pure gold. Ex 25:17
them, on the two ends of the mercy **s**. Ex 25:18
piece with the mercy **s** shall you make Ex 25:19
overshadowing the mercy **s** with their Ex 25:20
toward the mercy **s** shall the faces of Ex 25:20
you shall put the mercy **s** on the top of Ex 25:21
with you, and from above the mercy **s**, Ex 25:22
You shall put the mercy **s** on the ark of Ex 26:34
in front of the mercy **s** that is above the Ex 30:6
testimony, and the mercy **s** that is on it, Ex 31:7
the ark with its poles, the mercy **s**, and Ex 35:12
And he made a mercy **s** of pure gold. Ex 37:6
work on the two ends of the mercy **s**, Ex 37:7
piece with the mercy **s** he made the Ex 37:8
overshadowing the mercy **s** with their Ex 37:9
toward the mercy **s** were the faces of the Ex 37:9
with its poles and the mercy **s**; Ex 39:35
and set the mercy **s** above on the ark. Ex 40:20
before the mercy **s** that is on the ark, Lv 16:2
appear in the cloud over the mercy **s**. Lv 16:2
may cover the mercy **s** that is over the Lv 16:13
the front of the mercy **s** on the east side, Lv 16:14
front of the mercy **s** he shall sprinkle Lv 16:14
it over the mercy **s** and in front of Lv 16:15
mercy seat and in front of the mercy **s**. Lv 16:15
from above the mercy **s** that was on the Nm 7:89
the valleys that extends to the **s** of Ar, Nm 21:15
God for you." And he arose from his **s**. Jgs 3:20
was sitting on the **s** beside the doorpost 1 Sm 1:9

with princes and inherit a **s** of honor. 1 Sm 2:8
was sitting on his **s** by the road 1 Sm 4:13
over backward from his **s** by the side 1 Sm 4:18
because your **s** will be empty. 1 Sm 20:18
The king sat on his **s**, as at other 1 Sm 20:25
at other times, on the **s** by the wall. 1 Sm 20:25
king arose and took his **s** in the gate. 2 Sm 19:8
throne and had a **s** brought for the 1 Kgs 2:19
each side of the **s** were armrests and 1 Kgs 10:19
And he took his **s** on the throne of 2 Kgs 11:19
and gave him a **s** above the seats of 2 Kgs 25:28
and of the room for the mercy **s**; 1 Chr 28:11
each side of the **s** were arm rests and 2 Chr 9:18
cases. They had their **s** at Jerusalem. 2 Chr 19:8
the **s** of the governor of the province Neh 3:7
find him, that I might come even to his **s**! Jb 23:3
city, when I prepared my **s** in the square, Jb 29:7
way of sinners, nor sits in the **s** of scoffers; Ps 1:1
she takes a **s** on the highest places of the Prv 9:14
of silver, its back of gold, its **s** of purple; Sg 3:10
"Take a lowly **s**, for your beautiful Jer 13:18
the LORD and took their **s** in the entry of Jer 26:10
and gave him a **s** above the seats of the Jer 52:32
where was the **s** of the image of jealousy, Ezk 8:3
'I am a god, I sit in the **s** of the gods, Ezk 28:2
and the Ancient of days took his **s**; Dn 7:9
disaster and bring near the **s** of violence? Am 6:3
scribes and the Pharisees sit on Moses' **s**, Mt 23:2
while he was sitting on the judgment **s**, Mt 27:19
you love the best **s** in the synagogues Lk 11:43
down on the judgment **s** at a place Jn 19:13
robes, took his **s** upon the throne, Acts 12:21
day he took his **s** on the tribunal and Acts 25:6
next day took my **s** on the tribunal Acts 25:17
stand before the judgment **s** of God; Rom 14:10
before the judgment **s** of Christ, 2 Cor 5:10
so that he takes his **s** in the temple of 2 Thes 2:4
of glory overshadowing the mercy **s**. Heb 9:5

SEATED (30)
soon as he had **s** himself on his 1 Kgs 16:11
like the LORD our God, who is **s** on high, Ps 113:5
yourself from the dust and arise; be **s**, Is 52:2
and **s** above the likeness of a throne Ezk 1:26
see the Son of Man **s** at the right hand Mt 26:64
see the Son of Man **s** at the right hand Mk 14:62
Son of Man shall be **s** at the right hand Lk 22:69
he distributed them to those who were **s**. Jn 6:11
him, but Mary remained **s** in the house. Jn 11:20
and was returning, **s** in his chariot, Acts 8:28
from the dead and **s** him at his right Eph 1:20
us up with him and **s** us with him in the Eph 2:6
Christ is, **s** at the right hand of God. Col 3:1
one who is **s** at the right hand of the Heb 8:1
and is **s** at the right hand of the throne Heb 12:2
stood in heaven, with one **s** on the throne. Rv 4:2
and **s** on the thrones were twenty-four Rv 4:4
and thanks to him who is **s** on the throne, Rv 4:9
before him who is **s** on the throne and Rv 4:10
hand of him who was **s** on the throne a Rv 5:1
hand of him who was **s** on the throne. Rv 5:7
the face of him who is **s** on the throne, Rv 6:16
and **s** on the cloud one like a son of Rv 14:14
great prostitute who is **s** on many waters, Rv 17:1
mountains on which the woman is **s**; Rv 17:9
that you saw, where the prostitute is **s**, Rv 17:15
worshiped God who was **s** on the throne, Rv 19:4
and **s** on them were those to whom the Rv 20:4
white throne and him who was **s** on it. Rv 20:11
And he who was **s** on the throne said, Rv 21:5

SEATING (2)
food of his table, the **s** of his officials, 1 Kgs 10:5
food of his table, the **s** of his officials, 2 Chr 9:4

SEATS (7)
a seat above the **s** of the kings who 2 Kgs 25:28
him a seat above the **s** of the kings who Jer 52:32
money-changers and the **s** of those Mt 21:12
at feasts and the best **s** in the synagogues Mt 23:6
money-changers and the **s** of those Mk 11:15
and have the best **s** in the synagogues Mk 12:39
and the best **s** in the synagogues Lk 20:46

SEBA (4)
S, Havilah, Sabtah, Raamah, and Gn 10:7
S, Havilah, Sabta, Raama, and 1 Chr 1:9
the kings of Sheba and **S** bring gifts! Ps 72:10
ransom, Cush and **S** in exchange for you. Is 43:3

SEBAM (1)
Nimrah, Heshbon, Elealeh, **S**, Nebo, Nm 32:3

SECACAH (1)
the wilderness, Beth-arabah, Middin, **S**, Jos 15:61

SECOND (180)
and there was morning, the **s** day. Gn 1:8
The name of the **s** river is the Gihon. It Gn 2:13
Make it with lower, **s**, and third decks. Gn 6:16
year of Noah's life, in the **s** month, Gn 7:11
In the **s** month, on the twenty-seventh Gn 8:14
to Abraham a **s** time from heaven Gn 22:15
conceived again and bore Jacob a **s** son. Gn 30:7
servant Zilpah bore Jacob a **s** son. Gn 30:12
likewise instructed the **s** and the third Gn 32:19
And he fell asleep and dreamed a **s** time. Gn 41:5
And he made him ride in his **s** chariot. Gn 41:43
The name of the **s** he called Ephraim, Gn 41:52
fifteenth day of the **s** month after they Ex 16:1
edge of the outermost curtain in the **s** set. Ex 26:4
the edge of the curtain that is in the **s** set; Ex 26:5
curtain that is outermost in the **s** set. Ex 26:10
and for the **s** side of the tabernacle, on Ex 26:20
and the **s** row an emerald, a sapphire, Ex 28:18
of the outermost curtain of the **s** set. Ex 36:11
edge of the curtain that was in the **s** set. Ex 36:12
For the **s** side of the tabernacle, on the Ex 36:25
and the **s** row, an emerald, a sapphire, Ex 39:11
In the first month in the **s** year, on the Ex 40:17
he shall offer the **s** for a burnt offering Lv 5:10
it, shall then be washed a **s** time, Lv 13:58
meeting, on the first day of the **s** month, Nm 1:1
in the **s** year after they had come out of Nm 1:1
and on the first day of the **s** month, Nm 1:18
were 151,450. They shall set out **s**. Nm 2:16
On the **s** day Nethanel the son of Zuar, Nm 7:18
first month of the **s** year after they had Nm 9:1
In the **s** month on the fourteenth day at Nm 9:11
when you blow an alarm the **s** time, Nm 10:6
In the **s** year, in the second month, on Nm 10:11
In the second year, in the **s** month, on Nm 10:11
"On the **s** day twelve bulls from the Nm 29:17
circumcise the sons of Israel a **s** time." Jos 5:2
And the **s** day they marched around the Jos 6:14
captured it on the **s** day and struck it Jos 10:32
The **s** lot came out for Simeon, for the Jos 19:1
bull, and the **s** bull seven years old, Jgs 6:25
Then take the **s** bull and offer it as a Jgs 6:26
and the **s** bull was offered on the altar Jgs 6:28
the people of Benjamin the **s** day. Jgs 20:24
against them out of Gibeah the **s** day, Jgs 20:25
son was Joel, and the name of his **s**, 1 Sm 8:2
Saul said to David a **s** time, 1 Sm 18:21
But on the **s** day, the day after the 1 Sm 20:27
ate no food the **s** day of the month, 1 Sm 20:34
and his **s**, Chileab, of Abigail the 2 Sm 3:3
And he sent a **s** time, but Joab would 2 Sm 14:29
ground without striking a **s** blow, 2 Sm 20:10
month of Ziv, which is the **s** month, 1 Kgs 6:1
fingers. The **s** pillar was the same. 1 Kgs 7:15
the LORD appeared to Solomon a **s** time, 1 Kgs 9:2
over Israel in the **s** year of Asa king 1 Kgs 15:25
"Do it a **s** time." And they did it a 1 Kgs 18:34
time." And they did it a **s** time. 1 Kgs 18:34
came again a **s** time and touched 1 Kgs 19:7
his place in the **s** year of Jehoram the 2 Kgs 1:17
Then he sent out a **s** horseman, who 2 Kgs 9:19
Then he wrote to them a **s** letter, 2 Kgs 10:6
In the **s** year of Joash the son of 2 Kgs 14:1
In the **s** year of Pekah the son of 2 Kgs 15:32
and in the **s** year what springs of the 2 Kgs 19:29
lived in Jerusalem in the **S** Quarter), 2 Kgs 22:14
the priests of the **s** order and the 2 Kgs 23:4
And the **s** pillar had the same, with 2 Kgs 25:17
and Zephaniah the **s** priest and the 2 Kgs 25:18
Eliab his firstborn, Abinadab the **s**, 1 Chr 2:13
by Ahinoam the Jezreelite; the **s**, 1 Chr 3:1
the firstborn, the **s** Jehoiakim, 1 Chr 3:15
Joel the chief, Shapham the **s**, Janai, 1 Chr 5:12
Joel his firstborn, the **s** Abijah. 1 Chr 6:28
the name of the **s** was Zelophehad, 1 Chr 7:15
Bela his firstborn, Ashbel the **s**, 1 Chr 8:1
Ulam his firstborn, Jeush the **s**, and 1 Chr 8:39
Ezer the chief, Obadiah **s**, Eliab third, 1 Chr 12:9
them their brothers of the **s** order, 1 Chr 15:18
chief, and **s** to him were Zechariah, 1 Chr 16:5
was the chief, and Zizah the **s**; 1 Chr 23:11
Jeriah the chief, Amariah the **s**, 1 Chr 23:19
Micah the chief and Isshiah the **s**. 1 Chr 23:20
lot fell to Jehoiarib, the **s** to Jedaiah, 1 Chr 24:7
Jeriah the chief, Amariah the **s**, 1 Chr 24:23
the **s** to Gedaliah, to him and his 1 Chr 25:9
Zechariah the firstborn, Jediael the **s**, 1 Chr 26:2
the firstborn, Jehozabad the **s**, 1 Chr 26:4
Hilkiah the **s**, Tebaliah the third, 1 Chr 26:11
charge of the division of the **s** month; 1 Chr 27:4
the son of David king the **s** time, 1 Chr 29:22
to build in the **s** month of the fourth 2 Chr 3:2
same amount in the **s** and the third 2 Chr 27:5
to keep the Passover in the **s** month— 2 Chr 30:2
Unleavened Bread in the **s** month, 2 Chr 30:13
the fourteenth day of the **s** month. 2 Chr 30:15
Levite, with Shimei his brother as **s**, 2 Chr 31:12
Jerusalem in the **S** Quarter) and 2 Chr 34:22
him in his **s** chariot and brought 2 Chr 35:24
Now in the **s** year after their coming to Ezr 3:8
of God at Jerusalem, in the **s** month, Ezr 3:8
and it ceased until the **s** year of the reign Ezr 4:24
On the **s** day the heads of fathers' Neh 8:13
son of Hassenuah was **s** over the city. Neh 11:9
the **s** among his brothers; Neh 11:17
would return to the **s** harem in custody Est 2:14
were gathered together the **s** time, Est 2:19
And on the **s** day, as they were drinking Est 7:2
confirming this **s** letter about Purim. Est 9:29
Mordecai the Jew was **s** in rank to King Est 10:3
Jemimah, and the name of the **s** Keziah, Jb 42:14
be blotted out in the **s** generation! Ps 109:13
his hand yet a **s** time to recover the Is 11:11
and in the **s** year what springs from that. Is 37:30
word of the LORD came to me a **s** time, Jer 1:13
the word of the LORD came to me a **s** time, Jer 13:3
of the LORD came to Jeremiah a **s** time, Jer 33:1
And the **s** pillar had the same, with Jer 52:22
chief priest, and Zephaniah the **s** priest, Jer 52:24
these, you shall lie down a **s** time, Ezk 4:6
and the **s** face was a human face, Ezk 10:14
And on the **s** day you shall offer a Ezk 43:22
In the **s** year of the reign of Dn 2:1
They answered a **s** time and said, "Let the Dn 2:7
And behold, another beast, a **s** one, like a Dn 7:5
of the LORD came to Jonah the **s** time, Jon 3:1
end; trouble will not rise up a **s** time. Na 1:9
Fish Gate, a wail from the **S** Quarter, Zep 1:10
In the **s** year of Darius the king, in the Hg 1:1
month, in the **s** year of Darius the king. Hg 1:15
the ninth month, in the **s** year of Darius, Hg 2:10
of the LORD came a **s** time to Haggai on Hg 2:20
the eighth month, in the **s** year of Darius, Zec 1:1
month of Shebat, in the **s** year of Darius, Zec 1:7
And a **s** time I answered and said to Zec 4:12
had red horses, the **s** black horses, Zec 6:2
Then I broke my **s** staff Union, Zec 11:14
And this **s** thing you do. You cover the Mal 2:13
So too the **s** and third, down to the Mt 22:26
And a **s** is like it: You shall love your Mt 22:39
Again, for the **s** time, he went away and Mt 26:42
And the **s** took her, and died, leaving Mk 12:21
The **s** is this: 'You shall love your Mk 12:31
the rooster crowed a **s** time. Mk 14:72
If he comes in the **s** watch, or in the Lk 12:38
And the **s** came, saying, 'Lord, your Lk 19:18
And the **s** Lk 20:30
Can he enter a **s** time into his mother's Jn 3:4
This was now the **s** sign that Jesus did Jn 4:54
So for the **s** time they called the man who Jn 9:24
He said to him a **s** time, "Simon, son of Jn 21:16
And on the **s** visit Joseph made himself Acts 7:13
the voice came to him again a **s** time, Acts 10:15
voice answered a **s** time from heaven, Acts 11:9
had passed the first and the **s** guard, Acts 12:10
as also it is written in the **s** Psalm, Acts 13:33
and on the **s** day we came to Puteoli. Acts 28:13
the church first apostles, **s** prophets, 1 Cor 12:28
of dust; the **s** man is from heaven. 1 Cor 15:47
might have a **s** experience of grace. 2 Cor 1:15
as I did when present on my **s** visit, 2 Cor 13:2
have been no occasion to look for a **s**. Heb 8:7
Behind the **s** curtain was a second Heb 9:3
second curtain was a **s** section called the Heb 9:3
but into the **s** only the high priest goes, Heb 9:7
the sins of many, will appear a **s** time, Heb 9:28
the first in order to establish the **s**. Heb 10:9
This is now the **s** letter that I am writing 2 Pt 3:1
conquers will not be hurt by the **s** death.' Rv 2:11
like a lion, the **s** living creature like an ox, Rv 4:7
When he opened the **s** seal, I heard the Rv 6:3
seal, I heard the **s** living creature say, Rv 6:3
The **s** angel blew his trumpet, and Rv 8:8
The **s** woe has passed; behold, the third Rv 11:14
Another angel, a **s**, followed, saying, Rv 14:8
The **s** angel poured out his bowl into the Rv 16:3
Over such the **s** death has no power, but Rv 20:6
fire. This is the **s** death, the lake of fire. Rv 20:14
fire and sulfur, which is the **s** death." Rv 21:8
The first was jasper, the **s** sapphire, the Rv 21:19

SECRET (47)
Egypt, also did the same by their **s** arts. Ex 7:11
of Egypt did the same by their **s** arts. Ex 7:22
the same by their **s** arts and made frogs Ex 8:7
tried by their **s** arts to produce Ex 8:18
of a craftsman, and sets it up in **s**.' Dt 27:15
who strikes down his neighbor in **s**.' Dt 27:24
"The **s** things belong to the LORD our Dt 29:29
and said, "I have a **s** message for you, Jgs 3:19
So the **s** of his strength was not known. Jgs 16:9
Stay in a **s** place and hide yourself. 1 Sm 19:2
Absalom sent **s** messengers 2 Sm 15:10

rebuke you if in **s** you show partiality. Jb 13:10
and you teach me wisdom in the **s** heart. Ps 51:6
Hide me from the **s** plots of the wicked, Ps 64:2
I answered you in the **s** place of thunder; Ps 81:7
our **s** sins in the light of your presence. Ps 90:8
from you, when I was being made in **s**, Ps 139:15
sweet, and bread eaten in **s** is pleasant." Prv 9:17
accepts a bribe in **s** to pervert the ways Prv 17:23
A gift in **s** averts anger, and a Prv 21:14
himself, and do not reveal another's **s**, Prv 25:9
into judgment, with every **s** thing, Eccl 12:14
and the LORD will lay bare their **s** parts. Is 3:17
of darkness and the hoards in **s** places, Is 45:3
I did not speak in **s**, in a land of Is 45:19
the beginning I have not spoken in **s**, Is 48:16
in tombs, and spend the night in **s** places; Is 65:4
my soul will weep in **s** for your pride; Jer 13:17
a man hide himself in **s** places so that I Jer 23:24
than Daniel; no **s** is hidden from you; Ezk 28:3
without revealing his **s** to his servants Am 3:7
rejoicing as if to devour the poor in **s**. Hab 3:14
so that your giving may be in **s**. And your Mt 6:4
Father who sees in **s** will reward you. Mt 6:4
door and pray to your Father who is in **s**. Mt 6:6
Father who sees in **s** will reward you. Mt 6:6
others but by your Father who is in **s**. Mt 6:18
Father who sees in **s** will reward you. Mt 6:18
has been given the **s** of the kingdom of Mk 4:11
nor is anything **s** except to come to Mk 4:22
nor is anything **s** that will not be known Lk 8:17
For no one works in **s** if he seeks to be Jn 7:4
come together. I have said nothing in **s**. Jn 18:20
mystery that was kept **s** for long ages Rom 16:25
But we impart a **s** and hidden wisdom 1 Cor 2:7
to speak of the things that they do in **s**. Eph 5:12
I have learned the **s** of facing plenty Phil 4:12

SECRETARIES (1)
and Ahijah the sons of Shisha were **s**; 1 Kgs 4:3

SECRETARY (29)
were priests, and Seraiah was **s**, 2 Sm 8:17
and Sheva was **s**; and Zadok and 2 Sm 20:25
the king's **s** and the high priest 2 Kgs 12:10
the household, and Shebnah the **s**, 2 Kgs 18:18
the household, and Shebna the **s**, 2 Kgs 18:37
over the household, and Shebna the **s**, 2 Kgs 19:2
of Azaliah, son of Meshullam, the **s**, 2 Kgs 22:3
the high priest said to Shaphan the **s**, 2 Kgs 22:8
And Shaphan the **s** came to the king, 2 Kgs 22:9
Then Shaphan the **s** told the king, 2 Kgs 22:10
son of Micaiah, and Shaphan the **s**, 2 Kgs 22:12
and the **s** of the commander of the 2 Kgs 25:19
were priests; and Shavsha was **s**; 1 Chr 18:16
the king's **s** and the officer of the 2 Chr 24:11
by Jeiel the **s** and Maaseiah the 2 Chr 26:11
answered and said to Shaphan the **s**, 2 Chr 34:15
Then Shaphan the **s** told the king, 2 Chr 34:18
the son of Micah, Shaphan the **s**, 2 Chr 34:20
over the household, and Shebna the **s**, Is 36:3
over the household, and Shebna the **s**, Is 36:22
over the household, and Shebna the **s**, Is 37:2
of Gemariah the son of Shaphan the **s**, Jer 36:10
Elishama the **s**, Delaiah the son of Jer 36:12
in the chamber of Elishama the **s**, Jer 36:20
it from the chamber of Elishama the **s**. Jer 36:21
to seize Baruch the **s** and Jeremiah the Jer 36:26
him in the house of Jonathan the **s**, Jer 37:15
me back to the house of Jonathan the **s**, Jer 37:20
and the **s** of the commander of the Jer 52:25

SECRETARY'S (1)
to the king's house, into the **s** chamber, Jer 36:12

SECRETLY (19)
Why did you flee **s** and trick me, and Gn 31:27
who is as your own soul entices you **s**, Dt 13:6
lacking everything she will eat them **s**, Dt 28:57
Nun sent two men **s** from Shittim as Jos 2:1
And he sent messengers to Abimelech **s**, Jgs 9:31
For you did it **s**, but I will do this 2 Sm 12:12
people of Israel did **s** against the LORD 2 Kgs 17:9
and my heart has been **s** enticed, and Jb 31:27
they talk of laying snares **s**, thinking, Ps 64:5
slanders his neighbor **s** I will destroy. Ps 101:5
king questioned him **s** in his house Jer 37:17
King Zedekiah swore **s** to Jeremiah, Jer 38:16
son of Kareah spoke **s** to Gedaliah at Jer 40:15
the wise men **s** and ascertained from Mt 2:7
of Jesus, but **s** for fear of the Jews, Jn 19:38
Then they **s** instigated men who said, Acts 6:11
and do they now throw us out **s**? Acts 16:37
because of false brothers **s** brought in— Gal 2:4
who will **s** bring in destructive heresies, 2 Pt 2:1

SECRETS (8)
that he would tell you the **s** of wisdom! Jb 11:6
this? For he knows the **s** of the heart. Ps 44:21
goes about slandering reveals **s**, Prv 11:13
goes about slandering reveals **s**; Prv 20:19
given to know the **s** of the kingdom of Mt 13:11
given to know the **s** of the kingdom of Lk 8:10
God judges the **s** of men by Christ Rom 2:16
the **s** of his heart are disclosed, and 1 Cor 14:25

SECT (3)
a ringleader of the **s** of the Nazarenes. Acts 24:5
to the Way, which they call a **s**, Acts 24:14
with regard to this **s** we know that Acts 28:22

SECTION (13)
repaired another **s** and the Neh 3:11
repaired another **s** opposite the ascent Neh 3:19
Zabbai repaired another **s** from the Neh 3:20
Hakkoz repaired another **s** from the Neh 3:21
the son of Henadad repaired another **s**, Neh 3:24
repaired another **s** opposite the Neh 3:27
sixth son of Zalaph repaired another **s**. Neh 3:30
shall measure off a **s** 25,000 cubits long Ezk 45:3
Another **s**, 25,000 cubits long and Ezk 45:5
For a tent was prepared, the first **s**, in Heb 9:2
curtain was a second **s** called the Most Heb 9:3
the priests go regularly into the first **s**, Heb 9:6
as long as the first **s** is still standing Heb 9:8

SECU (1)
came to the great well that is in **S**. 1 Sm 19:22

SECUNDUS (1)
the Thessalonians, Aristarchus and **S**; Acts 20:4

SECURE (31)
the city while it felt **s** and killed all the Gn 34:25
attacked the army, for the army felt **s**. Jgs 8:11
of a deer and set me **s** on the heights. 2 Sm 22:34
covenant, ordered in all things and **s**. 2 Sm 23:5
Rehoboam the son of Solomon **s**, 2 Chr 11:17
and to give us a **s** hold within his holy Ezr 9:8
blemish; you will be **s** and will not fear. Jb 11:15
And you will feel **s**, because there is Jb 11:18
peace, and those who provoke God are **s**, Jb 12:6
full vigor, being wholly at ease and **s**, Jb 21:23
being rejoices; my flesh also dwells **s**. Ps 16:9
feet of a deer and set me **s** on the heights. Ps 18:33
my feet upon a rock, making my steps **s**. Ps 40:2
children of your servants shall dwell **s**; Ps 102:28
"May they be **s** who love you! Ps 122:6
listens to me will dwell **s** and will be at Prv 1:33
hates striking hands in pledge is **s**. Prv 11:15
I will fasten him like a peg in a **s** place, Is 22:23
was fastened in a **s** place will give way, Is 22:25
in a peaceful habitation, in **s** dwellings, Is 32:18
You felt **s** in your wickedness, you said, Is 47:10
bound with cords and made **s**. Ezk 27:24
and they shall be **s** in their land. Ezk 34:27
to those who feel **s** on the mountain of Am 6:1
And they shall dwell **s**, for now he shall Mi 5:4
tomb to be made **s** until the third day, Mt 27:64
soldiers. Go, make it as **s** as you can." Mt 27:65
and made the tomb **s** by sealing the Mt 27:66
with difficulty to **s** the ship's boat. Acts 27:16
order and to **s** your undivided 1 Cor 7:35
these things to **s** any such provision. 1 Cor 9:15

SECURELY (20)
and then you will dwell in the land **s**. Lv 25:18
you will eat your fill and dwell in it **s**. Lv 25:19
to the full and dwell in your land **s**. Lv 26:5
Then you will walk on your way **s**, and Prv 3:23
Whoever walks in integrity walks **s**, Prv 10:9
hear this, you lover of pleasures, who sit **s**, Is 47:8
will be saved, and Israel will dwell **s**. Jer 23:6
be saved and Jerusalem will dwell **s**. Jer 33:16
against a nation at ease, that dwells **s**, Jer 49:31
And they shall dwell **s** in it, and they Ezk 28:26
They shall dwell **s**, when I execute Ezk 28:26
they may dwell **s** in the wilderness Ezk 34:25
They shall dwell **s**, and none shall Ezk 34:28
out from the peoples and now dwell **s**, Ezk 38:8
fall upon the quiet people who dwell **s**, Ezk 38:11
when my people Israel are dwelling **s**, Ezk 38:14
on those who dwell **s** in the coastlands, Ezk 39:6
when they dwell **s** in their land with Ezk 39:26
This is the exultant city that lived **s**, Zep 2:15
"We found the prison **s** locked and the Acts 5:23

SECURING (1)
blood, thus **s** an eternal redemption. Heb 9:12

SECURITY (20)
his neighbor in a matter of deposit or **s**, Lv 6:2
who were there, how they lived in **s**, Jgs 18:7
will be peace and **s** in my days?" 2 Kgs 20:19
will look around and take your rest in **s**. Jb 11:18
who is there who will put up **s** for me? Jb 17:3
He gives them **s**, and they are supported, Jb 24:23
your walls and **s** within your towers!" Ps 122:7
if you have put up **s** for your neighbor, Prv 6:1
Whoever puts up **s** for a stranger will Prv 11:15
pledge and puts up **s** in the presence of Prv 17:18
when he has put up **s** for a stranger, Prv 20:16
when he puts up **s** for foreigners. Prv 20:16
give pledges, who put up **s** for debts. Prv 22:26
when he has put up **s** for a stranger, Prv 27:13
when he puts up **s** for an adulteress. Prv 27:13
"There will be peace and **s** in my days." Is 39:8
to them abundance of prosperity and **s**. Jer 33:6
destruction. Jerusalem shall dwell in **s**. Zec 14:11
had taken money as **s** from Jason and Acts 17:9
is peace and **s**," then sudden 1 Thes 5:3

SEDITION (2)
and that **s** was stirred up in it from of Ezr 4:15
that rebellion and **s** have been made Ezr 4:19

SEDUCE (2)
came up to her and said to her, "**S** him, Jgs 16:5
He shall **s** with flattery those who Dn 11:32

SEDUCES (1)
"If a man **s** a virgin who is not engaged Ex 22:16

SEDUCING (1)
and is teaching and **s** my servants to Rv 2:20

SEDUCTIVE (2)
With much **s** speech she persuades Prv 7:21
is loud; she is **s** and knows nothing. Prv 9:13

SEE (708)
them to the man to **s** what he would call Gn 2:19
to **s** if the waters had subsided from the Gn 8:8
I will **s** it and remember the everlasting Gn 9:16
they did not **s** their father's nakedness. Gn 9:23
the LORD came down to **s** the city and the Gn 11:5
and when the Egyptians **s** you, they Gn 12:12
all the land that you **s** I will give to you Gn 13:15
will go down to **s** whether they have Gn 18:21
said to Abraham, "What did you **s**, Gn 20:10
"**S** to it that you do not take my son Gn 24:6
"We **s** plainly that the LORD has been Gn 26:28
his eyes were dim so that he could not **s**, Gn 27:1
"**S**, the smell of my son is as the smell Gn 27:27
with him?" They said, "It is well; and **s**, Gn 29:6
"I **s** that your father does not regard me Gn 31:5
And he said, 'Lift up your eyes and **s**, Gn 31:12
my flocks, and all that you **s** is mine. Gn 31:43
s, God is witness between you and me." Gn 31:50
to Jacob, "**S** this heap and the pillar, Gn 31:51
of me, and afterward I shall **s** his face. Gn 32:20
went out to **s** the women of the land. Gn 34:1
s if it is well with your brothers and Gn 37:14
and we will **s** what will become of his Gn 37:20
own, or we shall be laughed at. You **s**, Gn 38:23
"**S**, he has brought among us a Hebrew Gn 39:14
"**S**, I have set you over all the land of Gn 41:41
you have come to **s** the nakedness of the Gn 42:9
of the land that you have come to **s**." Gn 42:12
'You shall not **s** my face unless your Gn 43:3
man said to us, 'You shall not **s** my face, Gn 43:5
you, you shall not **s** my face again.' Gn 44:23
For we cannot **s** the man's face unless Gn 44:26
I fear to **s** the evil that would find my Gn 44:34
And now your eyes **s**, and the eyes of Gn 45:12
and the eyes of my brother Benjamin **s**, Gn 45:12
alive. I will go and **s** him before I die." Gn 45:28
dim with age, so that he could not **s**. Gn 48:10
Joseph, "I never expected to **s** your face; Gn 48:11
God has let me **s** your offspring also." Gn 48:11
the Hebrew women and **s** them on the Ex 1:16
said, "I will turn aside to **s** this great sight, Ex 3:3
the LORD saw that he turned aside to **s**, Ex 3:4
brothers in Egypt to **s** whether they are Ex 4:18
s that you do before Pharaoh all the Ex 4:21
"Now you shall **s** what I will do to Ex 6:1
"**S**, I have made you like God to Pharaoh, Ex 7:1
of the land, so that no one can **s** the land. Ex 10:5
They did not **s** one another, nor did Ex 10:23
take care never to **s** my face again, for Ex 10:28
for on the day you **s** my face you shall Ex 10:28
you say! I will not **s** your face again." Ex 10:29
And when I **s** the blood, I will pass over Ex 12:13
minds when they **s** war and return Ex 13:17
firm, and **s** the salvation of the LORD, Ex 14:13
For the Egyptians whom you **s** today, Ex 14:13
you see today, you shall never **s** again. Ex 14:13
the morning you shall **s** the glory of the Ex 16:7
S! The LORD has given you the Sabbath; Ex 16:29
so that they may **s** the bread with Ex 16:32
between them both to **s** whether or not Ex 22:11
If you **s** the donkey of one who hates you Ex 23:5
And **s** that you make them after the Ex 25:40
"**S**, I have called by name Bezalel the son Ex 31:2
said to the LORD, "**S**, you say to me, Ex 33:12
But," he said, "you cannot **s** my face, Ex 33:20
face, for man shall not **s** me and live." Ex 33:20

my hand, and you shall **s** my back,	Ex 33:23
whom you are shall **s** the work of the	Ex 34:10
people of Israel would **s** the face of	Ex 34:35
"**S**, the LORD has called by name Bezalel	Ex 35:30
head to foot, so far as the priest can **s**,	Lv 13:12
the priest shall go in to **s** the house.	Lv 14:36
that I may not **s** my wretchedness."	Nm 11:15
Now you shall **s** whether my word	Nm 11:23
and **s** what the land is, and whether	Nm 13:18
shall **s** the land that I swore to give to	Nm 14:23
of those who despised me shall **s** it.	Nm 14:23
For from the top of the crags I **s** him,	Nm 23:9
place, from which you may **s** them.	Nm 23:13
You shall **s** only a fraction of them	Nm 23:13
of them and shall not **s** them all.	Nm 23:13
I **s** him, but not now; I behold him,	Nm 24:17
of Abarim and **s** the land that	Nm 27:12
old; **s** that they are without blemish;	Nm 28:19
S that they are without blemish.	Nm 28:31
old: **s** that they are without blemish.	Nm 29:8
from Kadesh-barnea to **s** the land.	Nm 32:8
shall **s** the land that I swore to give to	Nm 32:11
S, I have set the land before you. Go in and	Dt 1:8
S, the LORD your God has set the land	Dt 1:21
this evil generation shall **s** the good land	Dt 1:35
He shall **s** it, and to him and to his	Dt 1:36
me go over and **s** the good land beyond	Dt 3:25
possession of the land that you shall **s**.'	Dt 3:28
S, I have taught you statutes and rules, as	Dt 4:5
and when you **s** the sun and the moon	Dt 4:19
the work of human hands, that neither **s**,	Dt 4:28
And on earth he let you **s** his great fire,	Dt 4:36
"**S**, I am setting before you today a	Dt 11:26
burnt offerings at any place that you **s**,	Dt 12:13
the LORD my God or **s** this great fire any	Dt 18:16
and **s** horses and chariots and an army	Dt 20:1
shed this blood, nor did our eyes **s** it shed.	Dt 21:7
and you **s** among the captives a	Dt 21:11
"You shall not **s** your brother's ox or his	Dt 22:1
You shall not **s** your brother's donkey or	Dt 22:4
he may not **s** anything indecent among	Dt 23:14
of the earth shall **s** that you are called	Dt 28:10
mad by the sights that your eyes **s**.	Dt 28:34
and the sights that your eyes shall **s**.	Dt 28:67
to understand or eyes to **s** or ears to hear.	Dt 29:4
when they **s** the afflictions of that land	Dt 29:22
"**S**, I have set before you today life and	Dt 30:15
I will **s** what their end will be, For they	Dt 32:20
"'**S** now that I, even I, am he, and there is	Dt 32:39
For you shall **s** the land before you, but	Dt 32:52
I have let you **s** it with your eyes,	Dt 34:4
"As soon as you **s** the ark of the covenant	Jos 3:3
he would not let them **s** the land that the	Jos 5:6
"**S**, I have given Jericho into your hand,	Jos 6:2
I coveted them and took them. And **s**,	Jos 7:21
S, I have given into your hand the king of	Jos 8:1
of the Lord. **S**, I have commanded you."	Jos 8:8
he turned aside to **s** the carcass of the	Jgs 14:8
him, and **s** where his great strength lies,	Jgs 16:5
"**S**, your sister-in-law has gone back to	Ru 1:15
S, he is winnowing barley tonight at the	Ru 3:2
to grow dim so that he could not **s**,	1 Sm 3:2
his eyes were set so that he could not **s**.	1 Sm 4:15
and saw the ark, they rejoiced to **s** it.	1 Sm 6:13
"**S**, what was kept is set before you.	1 Sm 9:24
"Do you **s** him whom the LORD has	1 Sm 10:24
stand still and **s** this great thing	1 Sm 12:16
shall know and **s** that your	1 Sm 12:17
"Count and **s** who has gone from	1 Sm 14:17
S how my eyes have become bright	1 Sm 14:29
and know and **s** how this sin has	1 Sm 14:38
Samuel did not **s** Saul again until	1 Sm 15:35
S if your brothers are well, and bring	1 Sm 17:18
you have come down to **s** the battle."	1 Sm 17:28
Saul sent the messengers to **s** David,	1 Sm 19:15
let me get away and **s** my brothers.'	1 Sm 20:29
"Behold, you **s** the man is mad.	1 Sm 21:14
Know and **s** the place where his foot	1 Sm 23:22
S therefore and take note of all the	1 Sm 23:23
S, my father, see the corner of your	1 Sm 24:11
s the corner of your robe in my	1 Sm 24:11
you may know and **s** that there is no	1 Sm 24:11
and **s** to it and plead my cause and	1 Sm 24:15
servant did not **s** the young men	1 Sm 25:25
S, I have obeyed your voice, and I	1 Sm 25:35
And now **s** where the king's spear is	1 Sm 26:16
What do you **s**?" And the woman	1 Sm 28:13
"I **s** a god coming up out of the	1 Sm 28:13
you shall not **s** my face unless you	2 Sm 3:13
when you come to **s** my face."	2 Sm 3:13
said to Nathan the prophet, "**S** now,	2 Sm 7:2
And when your father comes to **s** you,	2 Sm 13:5
that I may **s** it and eat it from her	2 Sm 13:5
And when the king came to **s** him,	2 Sm 13:6
"**S**, Joab's field is next to mine,	2 Sm 14:30
"**S**, your claims are good and right,	2 Sm 15:3
me back and let me **s** both it and his	2 Sm 15:25
S, I will wait at the fords of the	2 Sm 15:28
S, your evil is on you, for you are a	2 Sm 16:8
"**S**, another man running alone!"	2 Sm 18:26
the eyes of my lord the king still **s** it,	2 Sm 24:3
came from Tyre to **s** the cities that	1 Kgs 9:12
Now Ahijah could not **s**, for his eyes	1 Kgs 14:4
And Elijah said, "**S**, your son lives."	1 Kgs 17:23
and **s** how this man is seeking	1 Kgs 20:7
you shall **s** on that day when you go	1 Kgs 22:25
if you **s** me as I am being taken from	2 Kgs 2:10
be so for you, but if you do not **s** me,	2 Kgs 2:10
I would neither look at you nor **s** you.	2 Kgs 3:14
LORD, 'You shall not **s** wind or rain,	2 Kgs 3:17
'**S**, you have taken all this trouble for	2 Kgs 4:13
and **s** how he is seeking a quarrel with	2 Kgs 5:7
"**S**, my master has spared this	2 Kgs 5:20
"**S**, the place where we dwell under	2 Kgs 6:1
And he said, "Go and **s** where he is,	2 Kgs 6:13
eyes that he may **s**." So the LORD	2 Kgs 6:17
that they may **s**." So the LORD opened	2 Kgs 6:20
"Do you **s** how this murderer has sent	2 Kgs 6:32
"You shall **s** it with your own eyes,	2 Kgs 7:2
already perished. Let us send and **s**."	2 Kgs 7:13
of the Syrians, saying, "Go and **s**."	2 Kgs 7:14
"You shall **s** it with your own eyes,	2 Kgs 7:19
Judah went down to **s** Joram the son	2 Kgs 8:29
"I **s** a company." And Joram said,	2 Kgs 9:17
"**S** now to this cursed woman and	2 Kgs 9:34
and **s** my zeal for the LORD." So he	2 Kgs 10:16
and **s** that there is no servant of the	2 Kgs 10:23
hear; open your eyes, O LORD, and **s**;	2 Kgs 19:16
your eyes shall not **s** all the disaster	2 Kgs 22:20
monument that I **s**?" And the men	2 Kgs 23:17
of our fathers **s** and rebuke you."	1 Chr 12:17
S, I give the oxen for burnt offerings	1 Chr 21:23
you shall **s** on that day when you go	2 Chr 18:24
and **s** the salvation of the LORD on	2 Chr 20:17
Judah went down to **s** Joram the son	2 Chr 22:6
and **s** that you act quickly." But the	2 Chr 24:5
said, "May the LORD **s** and avenge!"	2 Chr 24:22
say, '**S**, I have struck down Edom,'	2 Chr 25:19
hissing, as you **s** with your own eyes.	2 Chr 29:8
he made them a desolation, as you **s**.	2 Chr 30:7
your eyes shall not **s** all the disaster	2 Chr 34:28
to **s** whether a decree was issued by	Ezr 5:17
to them, "You **s** the trouble we are in,	Neh 2:17
will not know or **s** till we come among	Neh 4:11
in order to **s** whether Mordecai's words	Est 3:4
so long as I **s** Mordecai the Jew sitting at	Est 5:13
how can I bear to **s** the calamity that is	Est 8:6
how can I bear to **s** the destruction of my	Est 8:6
none, nor **s** the eyelids of the morning,	Jb 3:9
child, as infants who never **s** the light?	Jb 3:16
you **s** my calamity and are afraid.	Jb 6:21
is a breath; my eye will never again **s** good.	Jb 7:7
Behold, he passes by me, and I **s** him not;	Jb 9:11
a runner; they flee away; they **s** no good.	Jb 9:25
you eyes of flesh? Do you **s** as man sees?	Jb 10:4
then is my hope? Who will **s** my hope?	Jb 17:15
destroyed, yet in my flesh I shall **s** God,	Jb 19:26
whom I shall **s** for myself, and my eyes	Jb 19:27
eye that saw him will **s** him no more,	Jb 20:9
Let their own eyes **s** their destruction,	Jb 21:20
or darkness, so that you cannot **s**, and a	Jb 22:11
S the highest stars, how lofty they are!	Jb 22:12
clouds veil him, so that he does not **s**,	Jb 22:14
The righteous **s** it and are glad; the	Jb 22:19
to the right hand, but I do not **s** him.	Jb 23:9
do those who know him never **s** his days?	Jb 24:1
the twilight, saying, 'No eye will **s** me';	Jb 24:15
Does not he **s** my ways and number all	Jb 31:4
their wickedness in a place for all to **s**,	Jb 34:26
teach me what I do not **s**; if I have done	Jb 34:32
Look at the heavens, and **s**; and behold	Jb 35:5
when you say that you do not **s** him,	Jb 35:14
S my affliction from those who hate me,	Ps 9:13
has hidden his face, he will never **s** it."	Ps 10:11
But you do **s**, for you note mischief and	Ps 10:14
his eyes **s**, his eyelids test, the children of	Ps 11:4
to **s** if there are any who understand,	Ps 14:2
Sheol, or let your holy one **s** corruption.	Ps 16:10
All who **s** me mock me; they make	Ps 22:7
those who **s** me in the street flee from	Ps 31:11
Oh, taste and **s** that the LORD is good!	Ps 34:8
loves many days, that he may **s** good?	Ps 34:12
of life; in your light do we **s** light.	Ps 36:9
praise to our God. Many will **s** and fear,	Ps 40:3
have overtaken me, and I cannot **s**;	Ps 40:12
And when one comes to **s** me, he utters	Ps 41:6
should live on forever and never **s** the pit.	Ps 49:9
his fathers, who will never again **s** light.	Ps 49:19
If you **s** a thief, you are pleased with	Ps 50:18
The righteous shall **s** and fear, and shall	Ps 52:6
"**S** the man who would not make God his	Ps 52:7
the children of man to **s** if there are any	Ps 53:2
for I **s** violence and strife in the city.	Ps 55:9
ready. Awake, come to meet me, and **s**!	Ps 59:4
have made your people **s** hard things;	Ps 60:3
secretly, thinking, who can **s** them?	Ps 64:5
all who **s** them will wag their heads.	Ps 64:8
Come and **s** what God has done: he is	Ps 66:5
eyes be darkened, so that they cannot **s**,	Ps 69:23
When the humble **s** it they will be glad;	Ps 69:32
have made me **s** many troubles and	Ps 71:20
We do not **s** our signs; there is no longer	Ps 74:9
Look down from heaven, and **s**; have	Ps 80:14
those who hate me may **s** and be put to	Ps 86:17
What man can live and never **s** death?	Ps 89:48
with your eyes and **s** the recompense of	Ps 91:8
and they say, "The LORD does not **s**; the	Ps 94:7
He who formed the eye, does he not **s**?	Ps 94:9
and all the peoples **s** his glory.	Ps 97:6
The upright **s** it and are glad, and all	Ps 107:42
when they **s** me, they wag their heads.	Ps 109:25
but do not speak; eyes, but do not **s**.	Ps 115:5
who fear you shall **s** me and rejoice,	Ps 119:74
May you **s** the prosperity of Jerusalem	Ps 128:5
May you **s** your children's children!	Ps 128:6
not speak; they have eyes, but do not **s**;	Ps 135:16
And **s** if there be any grievous way in	Ps 139:24
Look to the right and **s**: there is none	Ps 142:4
Do you **s** a man skillful in his work?	Prv 22:29
Your eyes will **s** strange things, and	Prv 23:33
lest the LORD **s** it and be displeased, and	Prv 24:18
Do you **s** a man who is wise in his own	Prv 26:12
Do you **s** a man who is hasty in his	Prv 29:20
of which it is said, "**S**, this is new"?	Eccl 1:10
till I might **s** what was good for the	Eccl 2:3
that they may **s** that they themselves	Eccl 3:18
can bring him to **s** what will be after	Eccl 3:22
If you **s** in a province the oppression of	Eccl 5:8
their owner but to **s** them with his	Eccl 5:11
an advantage to those who **s** the sun.	Eccl 7:11
S, this alone I found, that God made	Eccl 7:29
and to **s** the business that is done on	Eccl 8:16
day nor night do one's eyes **s** sleep,	Eccl 8:16
it is pleasant for the eyes to **s** the sun.	Eccl 11:7
crannies of the cliff, let me **s** your face,	Sg 2:14
to **s** whether the vines had budded,	Sg 6:11
to the vineyards and **s** whether the vines	Sg 7:12
of the LORD, or **s** the work of his hands.	Is 5:12
let him speed his work that we may **s** it;	Is 5:19
lest they **s** with their eyes, and hear with	Is 6:10
He shall not judge by what his eyes **s**, or	Is 11:3
Those who **s** you will stare at you and	Is 14:16
hear; I am dismayed so that I cannot **s**.	Is 21:3
did it, or **s** him who planned it long ago.	Is 22:11
corruptly and does not **s** the majesty of	Is 26:10
hand is lifted up, but they do not **s** it.	Is 26:11
Let them **s** your zeal for your people, and	Is 26:11
darkness the eyes of the blind shall **s**.	Is 29:18
the seers, "Do not **s**," and to the prophets,	Is 30:10
but your eyes shall **s** your Teacher.	Is 30:20
the eyes of those who **s** will not be closed,	Is 32:3
they will **s** a land that stretches afar.	Is 33:17
You will **s** no more the insolent people,	Is 33:19
Your eyes will **s** Jerusalem, an	Is 33:20
They shall **s** the glory of the LORD, the	Is 35:2
and hear; open your eyes, O LORD, and **s**;	Is 37:17
I said, I shall not **s** the LORD, the LORD in	Is 38:11
revealed, and all flesh shall **s** it together,	Is 40:5
Lift up your eyes on high and **s**: who	Is 40:26
that they may **s** and know, may	Is 41:20
and look, you blind, that you may **s**!	Is 42:18
Their witnesses neither **s** nor know, that	Is 44:9
shut their eyes, so that they cannot **s**,	Is 44:18
"You have heard; now **s** all this; and will	Is 48:6
servant of rulers: "Kings shall **s** and arise;	Is 49:7
Lift up your eyes around and **s**; they all	Is 49:18
for eye to eye they **s** the return of the LORD	Is 52:8
of the earth shall **s** the salvation of our	Is 52:10
which has not been told them they **s**,	Is 52:15
offering for sin, he shall **s** his offspring;	Is 53:10
of his soul he shall **s** and be satisfied;	Is 53:11
'Why have we fasted, and you **s** it not?	Is 58:3
into your house; when you **s** the naked,	Is 58:7
Lift up your eyes all around, and **s**; they	Is 60:4
Then you shall **s** and be radiant; your	Is 60:5
all who **s** them shall acknowledge them,	Is 61:9
The nations shall **s** your righteousness,	Is 62:2
Look down from heaven and **s**, from	Is 63:15
LORD be glorified, that we may **s** your joy';	Is 66:5
You shall **s**, and your heart shall rejoice;	Is 66:14
they shall come and shall **s** my glory,	Is 66:18
S, I have set you this day over nations	Jer 1:10
"Jeremiah, what do you **s**?" And I said,	Jer 1:11
see?" And I said, "I **s** an almond branch."	Jer 1:11
saying, "What do you **s**?" And I said,	Jer 1:13

do you see?" And I said, "I **s** a boiling pot, Jer 1:13
For cross to the coasts of Cyprus and **s**, Jer 2:10
care; **s** if there has been such a thing. Jer 2:10
Know and **s** that it is evil and bitter for Jer 2:19
up your eyes to the bare heights, and **s**! Jer 3:2
How long must I **s** the standard and hear Jer 4:21
Search her squares to **s** if you can find a Jer 5:1
upon us, nor shall we **s** sword or famine. Jer 5:12
people, who have eyes, but **s** not, Jer 5:21
and **s** what I did to it because of the evil Jer 7:12
Do you not **s** what they are doing in the Jer 7:17
let me **s** your vengeance upon them, Jer 11:20
But you, O LORD, know me; you **s** me, Jer 12:3
they said, "He will not **s** our latter end." Jer 12:4
up your eyes and **s** those who come Jer 13:20
say to them, 'You shall not **s** the sword, Jer 14:13
desert, and shall not **s** any good come. Jer 17:6
let me **s** your vengeance upon them, Jer 20:12
out from the womb to **s** toil and sorrow, Jer 20:18
return no more to **s** his native land. Jer 22:10
and he shall never **s** this land again." Jer 22:12
council of the LORD to **s** and to hear his Jer 23:18
in secret places so that I cannot **s** him? Jer 23:24
the LORD said to me, "What do you **s**, Jer 24:3
and he shall not **s** the good that I will do Jer 29:32
Ask now, and **s**, can a man bear a child? Jer 30:6
Why then do I **s** every man with his Jer 30:6
him face to face and **s** him eye to eye. Jer 32:4
has come to pass, and behold, you **s** it. Jer 32:24
You shall **s** the king of Babylon eye to Jer 34:3
S, the whole land is before you; go Jer 40:4
are left with but a few, as your eyes **s** us— Jer 42:2
where we shall not **s** war or hear the Jer 42:14
a taunt. You shall **s** this place no more. Jer 42:18
s that you read all these words, Jer 51:61
"Look, O LORD, and **s**, for I am Lam 1:11
Look and **s** if there is any sorrow like Lam 1:12
all you peoples, and **s** my suffering; Lam 1:18
we longed for; now we have it; we **s** it!" Lam 2:16
Look, O LORD, and **s**! With whom have Lam 2:20
befallen us; look, and **s** our disgrace! Lam 5:1
"**S**, I assign to you cow's dung instead of Ezk 4:15
of man, do you **s** what they are doing, Ezk 8:6
But you will **s** still greater Ezk 8:6
and **s** the vile abominations that they Ezk 8:9
For they say, 'The LORD does not **s** us, Ezk 8:12
"You will **s** still greater abominations Ezk 8:13
You will **s** still greater abominations Ezk 8:15
the land, and the LORD does not **s**.' Ezk 9:9
a rebellious house, who have eyes to **s**, Ezk 12:2
house, who have eyes to see, but **s** not, Ezk 12:2
your face that you may not **s** the land, Ezk 12:6
that he may not **s** the land with his Ezk 12:12
of the Chaldeans, yet he shall not **s** it, Ezk 12:13
the prophets who **s** false visions and Ezk 13:9
you shall no more **s** false visions nor Ezk 13:23
And you **s** their ways and their deeds, Ezk 14:22
when you **s** their ways and their deeds, Ezk 14:23
that they may **s** all your nakedness. Ezk 16:37
All flesh shall **s** that I the LORD have Ezk 20:48
while they **s** for you false visions, Ezk 21:29
the nations shall **s** my judgment that Ezk 39:21
Declare all that you **s** to the house of Ezk 40:4
of man, mark well, **s** with your eyes, Ezk 44:5
for why should he **s** that you were in Dn 1:10
your servants according to what you **s**." Dn 1:13
because you **s** that the word from me is Dn 2:8
and said, "But I **s** four men unbound, Dn 3:25
stone, which do not **s** or hear or know, Dn 5:23
Open your eyes and **s** our desolations, Dn 9:18
who were with me did not **s** the vision, Dn 10:7
and your young men shall **s** visions. Jl 2:28
and **s** the great tumults within her, Am 3:9
Pass over to Calneh, and **s**, and from Am 6:2
me, "Amos, what do you **s**?" And I said, Am 7:8
said, "Amos, what do you **s**?" And I said, Am 8:2
till he should **s** what would become of Jon 4:5
Then my enemy will **s**, and shame will Mi 7:10
The nations shall **s** and be ashamed of Mi 7:16
Why do you make me **s** iniquity, and Hab 1:3
"Look among the nations, and **s**; Hab 1:5
purer eyes than to **s** evil and cannot Hab 1:13
and look out to **s** what he will say to me, Hab 2:1
in its former glory? How do you **s** it now? Hg 2:3
to **s** what is its width and what is its Zec 2:2
he said to me, "What do you **s**?" I said, Zec 4:2
said to me, "What do you see?" I said, "I **s**, Zec 4:2
and shall **s** the plumb line in the hand Zec 4:10
said to me, "What do you **s**?" I answered, Zec 5:2
you see?" I answered, "I **s** a flying scroll. Zec 5:2
"Lift your eyes and **s** what this is that is Zec 5:5
Ashkelon shall **s** it, and be afraid; Gaza Zec 9:5
over them, for now I **s** with my own eyes. Zec 9:8
utter nonsense, and the diviners **s** lies; Zec 10:2
Their children shall **s** it and be glad; Zec 10:7

Your own eyes shall **s** this, and you Mal 1:5
more you shall **s** the distinction Mal 3:18
are the pure in heart, for they shall **s** God. Mt 5:8
so that they may **s** your good works and Mt 5:16
Why do you **s** the speck that is in your Mt 7:3
and then you will **s** clearly to take the Mt 7:5
him, "**S** that you say nothing to anyone, Mt 8:4
them, "**S** that no one knows about it." Mt 9:30
"Go and tell John what you hear and **s**: Mt 11:4
did you go out into the wilderness to **s**? Mt 11:7
What then did you go out to **s**? A man Mt 11:8
What then did you go out to **s**? A Mt 11:9
we wish to **s** a sign from you." Mt 12:38
parables, because seeing they do not **s**, Mt 13:13
you will indeed **s** but never perceive. Mt 13:14
lest they should **s** with their eyes and Mt 13:15
But blessed are your eyes, for they **s**, Mt 13:16
people longed to **s** what you see, Mt 13:17
people longed to see what you **s**, Mt 13:17
to see what you see, and did not **s** it, Mt 13:17
Do you not **s** that whatever goes into Mt 15:17
taste death until they **s** the Son of Man Mt 16:28
"**S** that you do not despise one of these Mt 18:10
heaven their angels always **s** the face of Mt 18:10
"**S**, we have left everything and followed Mt 19:27
"**S**, we are going up to Jerusalem. And Mt 20:18
are invited, **S**, I have prepared my dinner, Mt 22:4
S, your house is left to you desolate. Mt 23:38
For I tell you, you will not **s** me again, Mt 23:39
But he answered them, "You **s** all these, Mt 24:2
them, "**S** that no one leads you astray. Mt 24:4
S that you are not alarmed, for this must Mt 24:6
"So when you **s** the abomination of Mt 24:15
S, I have told you beforehand. Mt 24:25
and they will **s** the Son of Man coming Mt 24:30
So also, when you **s** all these things, Mt 24:33
when did we **s** you hungry and feed Mt 25:37
And when did we **s** you a stranger and Mt 25:38
And when did we **s** you sick or in Mt 25:39
when did we **s** you hungry or thirsty or Mt 25:44
S, the hour is at hand, and the Son of Mt 26:45
us be going; **s**, my betrayer is at hand." Mt 26:46
he sat with the guards to **s** the end. Mt 26:58
from now on you will **s** the Son of Man Mt 26:64
"What is that to us? **S** to it yourself." Mt 27:4
of this man's blood; **s** to it yourselves." Mt 27:24
let us **s** whether Elijah will come to Mt 27:49
and the other Mary went to **s** the tomb. Mt 28:1
he said. Come, **s** the place where he lay. Mt 28:6
you to Galilee; there you will **s** him. Mt 28:7
you will see him. **S**, I have told you." Mt 28:7
go to Galilee, and there they will **s** me." Mt 28:10
him, "**S** that you say nothing to anyone, Mk 1:44
to **s** whether he would heal him on the Mk 3:2
"they may indeed **s** but not perceive, Mk 4:12
And people came to **s** what it was that Mk 5:14
"You **s** the crowd pressing around you, Mk 5:31
he looked around to **s** who had done it. Mk 5:32
Go and **s**." And when they had found Mk 6:38
Do you not **s** that whatever goes into a Mk 7:18
Having eyes do you not **s**, and having Mk 8:18
he asked him, "Do you **s** anything?" Mk 8:23
And he looked up and said, "I **s** men, Mk 8:24
taste death until they **s** the kingdom of Mk 9:1
"**S**, we have left everything and Mk 10:28
"**S**, we are going up to Jerusalem, Mk 10:33
he went to **s** if he could find anything Mk 11:13
to him, "Do you **s** these great buildings? Mk 13:2
to them, "**S** that no one leads you astray. Mk 13:5
"But when you **s** the abomination of Mk 13:14
And then they will **s** the Son of Man Mk 13:26
when you **s** these things taking place, Mk 13:29
us be going; **s**, my betrayer is at hand." Mk 14:42
and you will **s** the Son of Man seated at Mk 14:62
S how many charges they bring Mk 15:4
that we may **s** and believe." Those Mk 15:32
let us **s** whether Elijah will come to Mk 15:36
here. **S** the place where they laid him. Mk 16:6
There you will **s** him, just as he told Mk 16:7
over to Bethlehem and **s** this thing that Lk 2:15
that he would not **s** death before he had Lk 2:26
and all flesh shall **s** the salvation of God.'" Lk 3:6
to **s** whether he would heal on the Lk 6:7
Why do you **s** the speck that is in your Lk 6:41
you yourself do not **s** the log that is Lk 6:42
and then you will **s** clearly to take out Lk 6:42
did you go out into the wilderness to **s**? Lk 7:24
What then did you go out to **s**? A man Lk 7:25
What then did you go out to **s**? A Lk 7:26
said to Simon, "Do you **s** this woman? Lk 7:44
parables, so that 'seeing they may not **s**, Lk 8:10
so that those who enter may **s** the light. Lk 8:16
are standing outside, desiring to **s** you." Lk 8:20
people went out to **s** what had happened, Lk 8:35
such things?" And he sought to **s** him. Lk 9:9

taste death until they **s** the kingdom of Lk 9:27
are the eyes that **s** what you see! Lk 10:23
are the eyes that see what you **s**! Lk 10:23
and kings desired to **s** what you see, Lk 10:24
and kings desired to see what you **s**, Lk 10:24
to see what you see, and did not **s** it, Lk 10:24
so that those who enter may **s** the light. Lk 11:33
Pharisee was astonished to **s** that he did Lk 11:38
"When you **s** a cloud rising in the west, Lk 12:54
And when you **s** the south wind Lk 12:55
when you **s** Abraham and Isaac and Lk 13:28
you, you will not **s** me until you say, Lk 13:35
a field, and I must go out and **s** it. Lk 14:18
finish, all who **s** it begin to mock him, Lk 14:29
you will desire to **s** one of the days Lk 17:22
of the Son of Man, and you will not **s** it. Lk 17:22
"**S**, we have left our homes and followed Lk 18:28
them, "**S**, we are going up to Jerusalem, Lk 18:31
And he was seeking to **s** who Jesus was, Lk 19:3
up into a sycamore tree to **s** him, Lk 19:4
"As for these things that you **s**, the days Lk 21:6
he said, "**S** that you are not led astray. Lk 21:8
"But when you **s** Jerusalem surrounded Lk 21:20
And then they will **s** the Son of Man Lk 21:27
you **s** for yourselves and know that the Lk 21:30
when you **s** these things taking place, Lk 21:31
glad, for he had long desired to **s** him, Lk 23:8
he was hoping to **s** some sign done by Lk 23:8
had said, but him they did not **s**." Lk 24:24
S my hands and my feet, that it is I Lk 24:39
feet, that it is I myself. Touch me, and **s**. Lk 24:39
flesh and bones as you **s** that I have." Lk 24:39
'He on whom you **s** the Spirit descend Jn 1:33
"Come and you will **s**." So they came and Jn 1:39
Philip said to him, "Come and **s**." Jn 1:46
You will **s** greater things than these." Jn 1:50
I say to you, you will **s** heaven opened, Jn 1:51
born again he cannot **s** the kingdom of Jn 3:3
does not obey the Son shall not **s** life, Jn 3:36
s a man who told me all that I ever did. Jn 4:29
and **s** that the fields are white for harvest. Jn 4:35
"Unless you **s** signs and wonders you Jn 4:48
temple and said to him, "**S**, you are well! Jn 5:14
you do, that we may **s** and believe you? Jn 6:30
what if you were to **s** the Son of Man Jn 6:62
your disciples also may **s** the works you Jn 7:3
Search and **s** that no prophet arises from Jn 7:52
keeps my word, he will never **s** death." Jn 8:51
rejoiced that he would **s** my day. Jn 8:56
mud on my eyes, and I washed, and I **s**." Jn 9:15
born blind? How then does he now **s**?" Jn 9:19
know, that though I was blind, now I **s**." Jn 9:25
world, that those who do not **s** may see, Jn 9:39
world, that those who do not see may **s**, Jn 9:39
see, and those who **s** may become blind." Jn 9:39
but now that you say, 'We **s**,' your guilt Jn 9:41
They said to him, "Lord, come and **s**." Jn 11:34
So the Jews said, "**S** how he loved him!" Jn 11:36
you believed you would **s** the glory of Jn 11:40
on account of him but also to **s** Lazarus, Jn 12:9
"You **s** that you are gaining nothing. Jn 12:19
and asked him, "Sir, we wish to **s** Jesus." Jn 12:21
their heart, lest they **s** with their eyes, Jn 12:40
while and the world will **s** me no more, Jn 14:19
will see me no more, but you will **s** me. Jn 14:19
the Father, and you will **s** me no longer; Jn 16:10
little while, and you will **s** me no longer; Jn 16:16
again a little while, and you will **s** me." Jn 16:16
us, 'A little while, and you will not **s** me, Jn 16:17
again a little while, and you will **s** me'; Jn 16:17
'A little while and you will not **s** me, Jn 16:19
again a little while and you will **s** me'? Jn 16:19
but I will **s** you again and your hearts Jn 16:22
to **s** my glory that you have given me Jn 17:24
"Did I not **s** you in the garden with Jn 18:26
"**S**, I am bringing him out to you that Jn 19:4
cast lots for it to **s** whose it shall be." Jn 19:24
"Unless I **s** in his hands the mark of the Jn 20:25
"Put your finger here, and **s** my hands; Jn 20:27
and your young men shall **s** visions, Acts 2:17
or let your Holy One **s** corruption. Acts 2:27
Hades, nor did his flesh **s** corruption. Acts 2:31
man strong whom you **s** and know, Acts 3:16
said, "Behold, I **s** the heavens opened, Acts 7:56
For I **s** that you are in the gall of Acts 8:23
and the eunuch said, "**S**, here is water! Acts 8:36
be blind and unable to **s** the sun for a Acts 13:11
not let your Holy One **s** corruption.' Acts 13:35
God raised up did not **s** corruption. Acts 13:37
word of the Lord, and **s** how they are." Acts 15:36
Scriptures daily to **s** if these things Acts 17:11
to leave Rome. And he went to **s** them, Acts 18:2
and your own law, **s** to it yourselves. Acts 18:15
have been there, I must also **s** Rome." Acts 19:21
And you **s** and hear that not only in Acts 19:26

the kingdom will **s** my face again. Acts 20:25
that they would not **s** his face again. Acts 20:38
And they said to him, "You **s**, Acts 21:20
since I could not **s** because of the Acts 22:11
to **s** the Righteous One and to hear a Acts 22:14
you **s** this man about whom the Acts 25:24
I have asked to **s** you and speak with Acts 28:20
you will indeed **s** but never perceive. Acts 28:26
lest they should **s** with their eyes and Acts 28:27
For I long to **s** you, that I may impart Rom 1:11
since they did not **s** fit to acknowledge Rom 1:28
but I **s** in my members another law Rom 7:23
But if we hope for what we do not **s**, we Rom 8:25
eyes that would not **s** and ears that Rom 11:8
be darkened so that they cannot **s**, Rom 11:10
have never been told of him will **s**, Rom 15:21
I hope to **s** you in passing as I go to Rom 15:24
For now we **s** in a mirror dimly, but 1 Cor 13:12
I do not want to **s** you now just in 1 Cor 16:7
s that you put him at ease among 1 Cor 16:10
it, for I **s** that that letter grieved you, 2 Cor 7:8
For **s** what earnestness this godly 2 Cor 7:11
our love for you—**s** that you excel in 2 Cor 8:7
to **s** whether you are in the faith. 2 Cor 13:5
S with what large letters I am writing to Gal 6:11
and let the wife **s** that she respects her Eph 5:33
whether I come and **s** you or am Phil 1:27
just as soon as I **s** how it will go with Phil 2:23
rejoicing to **s** your good order and the Col 2:5
S to it that no one takes you captive by Col 2:8
and **s** that you also read the letter from Col 4:16
"**S** that you fulfill the ministry that you Col 4:17
with great desire to **s** you face to 1 Thes 2:17
remember us kindly and long to **s** us, 1 Thes 3:6
long to see us, as we long to **s** you— 1 Thes 3:6
day that we may **s** you face to face 1 Thes 3:10
S that no one repays anyone evil for 1 Thes 5:15
them, so that all may **s** your progress. 1 Tm 4:15
whom no one has ever seen or can **s**. 1 Tm 6:16
I remember your tears, I long to **s** you, 2 Tm 1:4
on their way; **s** that they lack nothing. Ti 3:13
we do not yet **s** everything in subjection Heb 2:8
But we **s** him who for a little while was Heb 2:9
So we **s** that they were unable to enter Heb 3:19
S how great this man was to whom Heb 7:4
"**S** that you make everything according Heb 8:5
the more as you **s** the Day drawing Heb 10:25
taken up so that he should not **s** death, Heb 11:5
without which no one will **s** the Lord. Heb 12:14
S to it that no one fails to obtain the Heb 12:15
S that you do not refuse him who is Heb 12:25
with whom I shall **s** you if he comes Heb 13:23
You **s** that faith was active along with Jas 2:22
You **s** that a person is justified by works Jas 2:24
S how the farmer waits for the precious Jas 5:7
Though you do not now **s** him, you 1 Pt 1:8
they may **s** your good deeds and glorify 1 Pt 2:12
when they **s** your respectful and pure 1 Pt 3:2
desires to love life and **s** good days, 1 Pt 3:10
S what kind of love the Father has given 1 Jn 3:1
him, because we shall **s** him as he is. 1 Jn 3:2
test the spirits to **s** whether they are from 1 Jn 4:1
I hope to **s** you soon, and we will talk 3 Jn 1:14
with the clouds, and every eye will **s** him, Rv 1:7
"Write what you **s** in a book and send it Rv 1:11
Then I turned to **s** the voice that was Rv 1:12
to anoint your eyes, so that you may **s**. Rv 3:18
wood, which cannot **s** or hear or walk, Rv 9:20
of the world will marvel to **s** the beast, Rv 17:8
no widow, and mourning I shall never **s**.' Rv 18:7
over her when they **s** the smoke of her Rv 18:9
They will **s** his face, and his name will Rv 22:4

SEED (62)
sprout vegetation, plants yielding **s**, Gn 1:11
trees bearing fruit in which is their **s**, Gn 1:11
plants yielding **s** according to their own Gn 1:12
trees bearing fruit in which is their **s**, Gn 1:12
you every plant yielding **s** that is on the Gn 1:29
earth, and every tree with **s** in its fruit. Gn 1:29
And give us **s** that we may live and not Gn 47:19
Now here is **s** for you, and you shall Gn 47:23
as **s** for the field and as food for Gn 47:24
It was like coriander **s**, white, and the Ex 16:31
carcass falls upon any **s** grain that is to Lv 11:37
water is put on the **s** and any part of Lv 11:38
not sow your field with two kinds of **s**, Lv 19:19
And you shall sow your **s** in vain, for Lv 26:16
valuation shall be in proportion to its **s**. Lv 27:16
A homer of barley **s** shall be valued at Lv 27:16
whether of the **s** of the land or of the Lv 27:30
Now the manna was like coriander **s**, Nm 11:7
and his **s** shall be in many waters; Nm 24:7
where you sowed your **s** and irrigated it, Dt 11:10
the yield of your **s** that comes from the Dt 14:22
sow your vineyard with two kinds of **s**, Dt 22:9
You shall carry much **s** into the field Dt 28:38
as would contain two seahs of **s**. 1 Kgs 18:32
out weeping, bearing the **s** for sowing, Ps 126:6
In the morning sow your **s**, and at Eccl 11:6
and a homer of **s** shall yield but an Is 5:10
when it is felled." The holy **s** is its stump. Is 6:13
give rain for the **s** with which you sow Is 30:23
giving **s** to the sower and bread to the Is 55:10
you a choice vine, wholly of pure **s**. Jer 2:21
of Judah with the **s** of man and the Jer 31:27
with the seed of man and the **s** of beast. Jer 31:27
not build a house; you shall not sow **s**; Jer 35:7
in. We have no vineyard or field or **s**, Jer 35:9
Then he took of the **s** of the land and Ezk 17:5
The **s** shrivels under the clods; the Jl 1:17
treader of grapes him who sows the **s**; Am 9:13
Is the **s** yet in the barn? Indeed, the vine, Hg 2:19
to a man who sowed good **s** in his field, Mt 13:24
did you not sow good **s** in your field? Mt 13:27
a grain of mustard **s** that a man took Mt 13:31
one who sows the good **s** is the Son of Mt 13:37
and the good **s** is the children of the Mt 13:38
have faith like a grain of mustard **s**, Mt 17:20
gathering where you scattered no **s**, Mt 25:24
and gather where I scattered no **s**? Mt 25:26
as he sowed, some **s** fell along the path, Mk 4:4
Other **s** fell on rocky ground, where it did Mk 4:5
Other **s** fell among thorns, and the Mk 4:7
if a man should scatter **s** on the ground. Mk 4:26
and day, and the **s** sprouts and grows; Mk 4:27
It is like a grain of mustard **s**, which, Mk 4:31
"A sower went out to sow his **s**. And as he Lk 8:5
parable is this: The **s** is the word of God. Lk 8:11
a grain of mustard **s** that a man took Lk 13:19
you had faith like a grain of mustard **s**, Lk 17:6
and to each kind of **s** its own body. 1 Cor 15:38
He who supplies **s** to the sower and 2 Cor 9:10
and multiply your **s** for sowing and 2 Cor 9:10
not of perishable **s** but of imperishable, 1 Pt 1:23
of sinning, for God's **s** abides in him, 1 Jn 3:9

SEEDS (8)
grapevine, not even the **s** or the skins. Nm 6:4
as he sowed, some **s** fell along the path, Mt 13:4
Other **s** fell on rocky ground, where they Mt 13:5
Other **s** fell among thorns, and the Mt 13:7
Other **s** fell on good soil and produced Mt 13:8
It is the smallest of all **s**, but when it Mt 13:32
And other **s** fell into good soil and Mk 4:8
is the smallest of all the **s** on earth, Mk 4:31

SEEDTIME (1)
While the earth remains, **s** and harvest, Gn 8:22

SEEING (55)
her, "You are a God of **s**," for she said, Gn 16:13
s that Abraham shall surely become a Gn 18:18
God, **s** you have not withheld your son, Gn 22:12
s that you hate me and have sent me Gn 26:27
face, which is like **s** the face of God, Gn 33:10
looked this way and that, and **s** no one, Ex 2:12
Who makes him mute, or deaf, or **s**, or Ex 4:11
or is driven away, without anyone **s** it, Ex 22:10
and without **s** him dropped it on him, Nm 35:23
you ask my name, **s** it is wonderful?" Jgs 13:18
him, **s** he is the LORD'S anointed." 1 Sm 24:6
s that you will have no reward for 2 Sm 18:22
And anyone who came by, **s** him, 2 Sm 20:12
throne this day, my own eyes **s** it.'" 1 Kgs 1:48
s that those who are left here will fare 2 Kgs 7:13
s your master's sons are with you, 2 Kgs 10:2
deeds and for our great guilt, **s** that you, Ezr 9:13
is your face sad, **s** you are not sick? Neh 2:2
s that he judges those who are on high? Jb 21:22
The hearing ear and the **s** eye, the LORD Prv 20:12
the eye is not satisfied with **s**, nor the ear Eccl 1:8
s that in the days to come all will have Eccl 2:16
s that I must leave it to the man who Eccl 2:18
understand; keep on **s**, but do not perceive.' Is 6:9
"**s** that my people are taken away for Is 52:5
s false visions and divining lies for Ezk 22:28
S the crowds, he went up on the Mt 5:1
Jesus turned, and **s** her he said, "Take Mt 9:22
in parables, because **s** they do not see, Mt 13:13
the lame walking, and the blind **s**. Mt 15:31
And **s** a fig tree by the wayside, he went Mt 21:19
synagogue, Jairus by name, and **s** him, Mk 5:22
But turning and **s** his disciples, he Mk 8:33
And **s** in the distance a fig tree in leaf, Mk 11:13
and **s** that he answered them well, Mk 12:28
and **s** Peter warming himself, she Mk 14:67
in parables, so that 's they may not see, Lk 8:10
s him as he sat in the light and looking Lk 22:56
and **s** that a large crowd was coming Jn 6:5
So he went and washed and came back **s**. Jn 9:7
that you yourselves are **s** and hearing. Acts 2:33
S Peter and John about to go into the Acts 3:3
But **s** the man who was healed Acts 4:14
And **s** one of them being wronged, he Acts 7:24
And **s** signs and great miracles Acts 8:13
hearing the voice but **s** no one. Acts 9:7
real, but thought he was **s** a vision. Acts 12:9
intently at him and **s** that he had faith Acts 14:9
S then that these things cannot be Acts 19:36
Jews from Asia, **s** him in the temple, Acts 21:27
Three Taverns to meet us. On **s** them, Acts 28:15
to keep them from **s** the light of the 2 Cor 4:4
that you may rejoice at **s** him again, Phil 2:28
s that you have put off the old self with Col 3:9
for he endured as **s** him who is Heb 11:27

SEEK (238)
the priest need not **s** for the yellow hair; Lv 13:36
mediums or wizards; do not **s** them out, Lv 19:31
to **s** out a resting place for them. Nm 10:33
And would you **s** the priesthood also? Nm 16:10
not his enemy and did not **s** his harm, Nm 35:23
you in the way to **s** you out a place to Dt 1:33
from there you will **s** the LORD your God Dt 4:29
But you shall **s** the place that the LORD Dt 12:5
You shall not **s** their peace or their Dt 23:6
"My daughter, should I not **s** rest for you, Ru 3:1
donkeys that you went to **s** are found, 1 Sm 10:2
go?" And he said, "To **s** the donkeys. 1 Sm 10:14
are before you to **s** out a man who 1 Sm 16:16
that Saul had come out to **s** his life. 1 Sm 23:15
And Saul and his men went to **s** him. 1 Sm 23:25
Israel and went to **s** David and his 1 Sm 24:2
enemies and those who **s** to do evil to 1 Sm 25:26
up to pursue you and to **s** your life, 1 Sm 25:29
men of Israel to **s** David in the 1 Sm 26:2
has come out to **s** a single flea like 1 Sm 26:20
"**S** out for me a woman who is a 1 Sm 28:7
You **s** the life of only one man, and all 2 Sm 17:3
You **s** to destroy a city that is a 2 Sm 20:19
to Gath to Achish to **s** his servants. 1 Kgs 2:40
where my lord has not sent to **s** you. 1 Kgs 18:10
I only, am left, and they **s** my life, 1 Kgs 19:10
I only, am left, and they **s** my life, 1 Kgs 19:14
Please let them go and **s** your master. 2 Kgs 2:16
the man whom you **s**." And he led 2 Kgs 6:19
valley, to **s** pasture for their flocks, 1 Chr 4:39
He did not **s** guidance from the 1 Chr 10:14
for we did not **s** it in the days of Saul." 1 Chr 13:3
we did not **s** him according to 1 Chr 15:13
of those who **s** the LORD rejoice! 1 Chr 16:10
S the LORD and his strength; seek his 1 Chr 16:11
s his presence continually! 1 Chr 16:11
mind and heart to **s** the LORD your 1 Chr 22:19
observe and **s** out all the 1 Chr 28:8
If you **s** him, he will be found by you, 1 Chr 28:9
and pray and **s** my face and turn 2 Chr 7:14
set their hearts to **s** the LORD God of 2 Chr 11:16
he did not set his heart to **s** the LORD. 2 Chr 12:14
and commanded Judah to **s** the LORD, 2 Chr 14:4
If you **s** him, he will be found by you, 2 Chr 15:2
into a covenant to **s** the LORD, 2 Chr 15:12
that whoever would not **s** the LORD, 2 Chr 15:13
in his disease he did not **s** the LORD, 2 Chr 16:12
father David. He did not **s** the Baals, 2 Chr 17:3
and have set your heart to **s** God." 2 Chr 19:3
afraid and set his face to **s** the LORD, 2 Chr 20:3
Judah assembled to **s** help from the 2 Chr 20:4
of Judah they came to **s** the LORD. 2 Chr 20:4
He set himself to **s** God in the days of 2 Chr 26:5
who sets his heart to **s** God, the LORD, 2 Chr 30:19
he began to **s** the God of David his 2 Chr 34:3
to **s** from him a safe journey for Ezr 8:21
of our God is for good on all who **s** him, Ezr 8:22
and never **s** their peace or prosperity, Ezr 9:12
someone had come to **s** the welfare of Neh 2:10
May God above not **s** it, nor light shine Jb 3:4
"As for me, I would **s** God, and to God Jb 5:8
earth; you will **s** me, but I shall not be." Jb 7:21
If you will **s** God and plead with the Jb 8:5
that you **s** out my iniquity and search for Jb 10:6
His children will **s** the favor of the poor, Jb 20:10
will you love vain words and **s** after lies? Ps 4:2
LORD, have not forsaken those who **s** you. Ps 9:10
of his face the wicked does not **s** him; Ps 10:4
any who understand, who **s** after God. Ps 14:2
Savior of those who **s** refuge from their Ps 17:7
those who **s** him shall praise the LORD! Ps 22:26
is the generation of those who **s** him, Ps 24:6
him, who **s** the face of the God of Jacob. Ps 24:6
I asked of the LORD, that will I **s** after: Ps 27:4
said, "**S** my face." My heart says to you, Ps 27:8
says to you, "Your face, LORD, do I **s**." Ps 27:8
but those who **s** the LORD lack no good Ps 34:10
evil and do good; **s** peace and pursue it. Ps 34:14
shame and dishonor who **s** after my life! Ps 35:4
Those who **s** my life lay their snares; Ps 38:12
those who **s** my hurt speak of ruin and Ps 38:12

disappointed altogether who **s** to snatch Ps 40:14
But may all who **s** you rejoice and be Ps 40:16
people of Tyre will **s** your favor with Ps 45:12
any who understand, who **s** after God. Ps 53:2
risen against me; ruthless men **s** my life; Ps 54:3
O God, you are my God; earnestly I **s** you; Ps 63:1
But those who **s** to destroy my life shall Ps 63:9
let not those who **s** you be brought to Ps 69:6
you who **s** God, let your hearts revive. Ps 69:32
to shame and confusion who **s** my life! Ps 70:2
May all who **s** you rejoice and be glad in Ps 70:4
may they be covered who **s** my hurt. Ps 71:13
In the day of my trouble I **s** the Lord; in Ps 77:2
shame, that they may **s** your name, Ps 83:16
a band of ruthless men **s** my life, and Ps 86:14
hearts of those who **s** the LORD rejoice! Ps 105:3
S the LORD and his strength; seek his Ps 105:4
strength; **s** his presence continually! Ps 105:4
who **s** him with their whole heart, Ps 119:2
With my whole heart I **s** you; let me Ps 119:10
for they do not **s** your statutes. Ps 119:155
s your servant, for I do not forget Ps 119:176
of the LORD our God, I will **s** your good. Ps 122:9
you, O GOD, my Lord; in you I **s** refuge; Ps 141:8
they will **s** me diligently but will not Prv 1:28
if you **s** it like silver and search for it as Prv 2:4
come out to meet you, to **s** you eagerly, Prv 7:15
and those who **s** me diligently find me. Prv 8:17
Many **s** the favor of a generous man, Prv 19:6
he will **s** at harvest and have nothing. Prv 20:4
nor is it glorious to **s** one's own glory. Prv 25:27
but those who **s** the LORD understand it Prv 28:5
who is blameless and **s** the life of the Prv 29:10
Many **s** the face of a ruler, but it is Prv 29:26
applied my heart to **s** and to search out Eccl 1:13
a time to **s**, and a time to lose; a time to Eccl 3:6
search out and to **s** wisdom and the Eccl 7:25
squares; I will **s** him whom my soul loves. Sg 3:2
turned, that we may **s** him with you? Sg 6:1
to do good; **s** justice, correct oppression; Is 1:17
of Pharaoh and to **s** shelter in the shadow Is 30:2
S and read from the book of the LORD: Is 34:16
You shall **s** those who contend with you, Is 41:12
When the poor and needy **s** water, and Is 41:17
to the offspring of Jacob, '**S** me in vain.' Is 45:19
righteousness, you who **s** the LORD: Is 51:1
"**S** the LORD while he may be found; call Is 55:6
Yet they **s** me daily and delight to know Is 58:2
day of your fast you **s** your own pleasure, Is 58:3
to be found by those who did not **s** me. Is 65:1
None who **s** her need weary themselves; Jer 2:24
well you direct your course to **s** love! Jer 2:33
Your lovers despise you; they **s** your life. Jer 4:30
the men of Anathoth, who **s** your life, Jer 11:21
and by the hand of those who **s** their life. Jer 19:7
enemies and those who **s** their life afflict Jer 19:9
into the hand of those who **s** their lives. Jer 21:7
into the hand of those who **s** your life, Jer 22:25
But **s** the welfare of the city where I have Jer 29:7
You will **s** me and find me. When you Jer 29:13
When you **s** me with all your heart, Jer 29:13
into the hand of those who **s** their lives. Jer 34:20
into the hand of those who **s** their lives, Jer 34:21
the hand of these men who **s** your life." Jer 38:16
into the hand of those who **s** his life, Jer 44:30
And do you **s** great things for yourself? Jer 45:5
S them not, for behold, I am bringing Jer 45:5
into the hand of those who **s** their life, Jer 46:26
and before those who **s** their life. Jer 49:37
and they shall **s** the LORD their God. Jer 50:4
anguish comes, they will **s** peace, Ezk 7:25
They **s** a vision from the prophet, while Ezk 7:26
with none to search or **s** for them. Ezk 34:6
for my sheep and will **s** them out. Ezk 34:11
scattered, so will I **s** out my sheep, Ezk 34:12
I will **s** the lost, and I will bring back Ezk 34:16
and told them to **s** mercy from the God Dn 2:18
and she shall **s** them but shall not find Hos 2:7
Israel shall return and **s** the LORD their Hos 3:5
and herds they shall go to **s** the LORD, Hos 5:6
acknowledge their guilt and **s** my face, Hos 5:15
and in their distress earnestly **s** me. Hos 5:15
return to the LORD their God, nor **s** him, Hos 7:10
ground, for it is the time to **s** the LORD, Hos 10:12
to the house of Israel: "**S** me and live; Am 5:4
but do not **s** Bethel, and do not enter into Am 5:5
S the LORD and live, lest he break out like Am 5:6
S good, and not evil, that you may live; Am 5:14
run to and fro, to **s** the word of the LORD, Am 8:12
her? Where shall I **s** comforters for you? Na 3:7
you will **s** a refuge from the enemy. Na 3:11
who do not **s** the LORD or inquire of him." Zep 1:6
S the LORD, all you humble of the land, Zep 2:3
do his just commands; **s** righteousness; Zep 2:3
seek righteousness; **s** humility; Zep 2:3
They shall **s** refuge in the name of the Zep 3:12
of the LORD and to **s** the LORD of hosts; Zec 8:21
nations shall come to **s** the LORD of Zec 8:22
or **s** the young or heal the maimed or Zec 11:16
on that day I will **s** to destroy all the Zec 12:9
and people should **s** instruction from Mal 2:7
Lord whom you **s** will suddenly come Mal 3:1
For the Gentiles **s** after all these things, Mt 6:32
But **s** first the kingdom of God and his Mt 6:33
will be given to you; **s**, and you will find; Mt 7:7
I know that you **s** Jesus who was Mt 28:5
"Why does this generation **s** a sign? Mk 8:12
You **s** Jesus of Nazareth, who was Mk 16:6
will be given to you; **s**, and you will find; Lk 11:9
And do not **s** what you are to eat and Lk 12:29
of the world **s** after these things, Lk 12:30
Instead, **s** his kingdom, and these Lk 12:31
you, will **s** to enter and will not be able. Lk 13:24
the house and **s** diligently until she Lk 15:8
Son of Man came to **s** and to save the Lk 19:10
"Why do you **s** the living among the Lk 24:5
but no one said, "What do you **s**?" or, Jn 4:27
because I **s** not my own will but the will Jn 5:30
another and do not **s** the glory that Jn 5:44
keeps the law. Why do you **s** to kill me?" Jn 7:19
"Is not this the man whom they **s** to kill? Jn 7:25
You will **s** me and you will not find me. Jn 7:34
'You will **s** me and you will not find me,' Jn 7:36
"I am going away, and you will **s** me, Jn 8:21
yet you **s** to kill me because my word Jn 8:37
but now you **s** to kill me, a man who has Jn 8:40
Yet I do not **s** my own glory; there is One Jn 8:50
You will **s** me, and just as I said to the Jn 13:33
and said to them, "Whom do you **s**?" Jn 18:4
again, "Whom do you **s**?" And they said, Jn 18:7
I am he. So, if you **s** me, let these men go." Jn 18:8
remnant of mankind may **s** the Lord, Acts 15:17
that they should **s** God, in the hope Acts 17:27
But if you **s** anything further, it shall Acts 19:39
to die, I do not **s** to escape death. Acts 25:11
patience in well-doing **s** for glory and Rom 2:7
found by those who did not **s** me; Rom 10:20
and I alone am left, and they **s** my life." Rom 11:3
the saints and **s** to show hospitality. Rom 12:13
demand signs and Greeks **s** wisdom, 1 Cor 1:22
Let him not **s** to remove the marks of 1 Cor 7:18
Let him not **s** circumcision. 1 Cor 7:18
bound to a wife? Do not **s** to be free. 1 Cor 7:27
you free from a wife? Do not **s** a wife. 1 Cor 7:27
Let no one **s** his own good, but the 1 Cor 10:24
for I **s** not what is yours but you. 2 Cor 12:14
since you **s** proof that Christ is 2 Cor 13:3
They all **s** their own interests, not those Phil 2:21
Not that I **s** the gift, but I seek the fruit Phil 4:17
but I **s** the fruit that increases to your Phil 4:17
with Christ, **s** the things that are above, Col 3:1
Nor did we **s** glory from people, 1 Thes 2:6
but always **s** to do good to one 1 Thes 5:15
and that he rewards those who **s** him. Heb 11:6
city, but we **s** the city that is to come. Heb 13:14
do good; let him **s** peace and pursue it. 1 Pt 3:11
those days people will **s** death and will not Rv 9:6

SEEKING (60)

the man asked him, "What are you **s**?" Gn 37:15
"I am **s** my brothers," he said. "Tell me, Gn 37:16
the men who were **s** your life are dead." Ex 4:19
the man whom you are **s**." So he went in Jgs 4:22
for he was **s** an opportunity against the Jgs 14:4
people of Dan was **s** for itself an Jgs 18:1
Saul will despair of **s** me any longer 1 Sm 27:1
past you have been **s** David as king 2 Sm 3:17
me that you are now **s** to go to your 1 Kgs 11:22
and see how this man is **s** trouble, 1 Kgs 20:7
and see how he is **s** a quarrel with me." 2 Kgs 5:7
consulted a medium, **s** guidance. 1 Chr 10:13
and the commandments, **s** his God, 2 Chr 31:21
desert the poor go out to their toil, **s** game; Jb 24:5
for their prey, **s** their food from God. Ps 104:21
s food far from the ruins they inhabit! Ps 109:10
However much man may toil in **s**, he Eccl 8:17
your own ways, or **s** your own pleasure, Is 58:13
For this man is not **s** the welfare of this Jer 38:4
s him by prayer and pleas for mercy with Dn 9:3
union? And what was the one God **s**? Mal 2:15
passes through waterless places **s** rest, Mt 12:43
although they were **s** to arrest him, Mt 21:46
whole Council were **s** false testimony Mt 26:59
and your brothers are outside, **s** you." Mk 3:32
s from him a sign from heaven to test Mk 8:11
heard it and were **s** a way to destroy Mk 11:18
And they were **s** to arrest him but Mk 12:12
and the scribes were **s** how to arrest Mk 14:1
Council were **s** testimony against Mk 14:55
and they were **s** to bring him in and lay Lk 5:18
kept **s** from him a sign from heaven. Lk 11:16
passes through waterless places **s** rest, Lk 11:24
and he came **s** fruit on it and found Lk 13:6
years now I have come **s** fruit on this fig Lk 13:7
And he was **s** to see who Jesus was, but Lk 19:3
men of the people were **s** to destroy him, Lk 19:47
and the scribes were **s** how to put him Lk 22:2
"What are you **s**?" And they said to him, Jn 1:38
for the Father is **s** such people to worship Jn 4:23
was why the Jews were **s** all the more to Jn 5:18
boats and went to Capernaum, **s** Jesus. Jn 6:24
"Truly, truly, I say to you, you are **s** me, Jn 6:26
Judea, because the Jews were **s** to kill him. Jn 7:1
have a demon! Who is **s** to kill you?" Jn 7:20
So they were **s** to arrest him, but no one Jn 7:30
the Jews were just now **s** to stone you, Jn 11:8
Whom are you **s**?" Supposing him to be Jn 20:15
Hellenists. But they were **s** to kill him. Acts 9:29
s to turn the proconsul away from the Acts 13:8
and he went about **s** people to lead Acts 13:11
s to bring them out to the crowd. Acts 17:5
And as they were **s** to kill him, word Acts 21:31
as the sailors were **s** to escape from Acts 27:30
from God, and **s** to establish their own, Rom 10:3
Israel failed to obtain what it was **s**. Rom 11:7
I do, not **s** my own advantage, 1 Cor 10:33
For am I now **s** the approval of man, or Gal 1:10
it clear that they are **s** a homeland. Heb 11:14
like a roaring lion, **s** someone to devour. 1 Pt 5:8

SEEKS (37)

stay with you until your brother **s** it. Dt 22:2
David, "Saul my father **s** to kill you. 1 Sm 19:2
before your father, that he **s** my life?" 1 Sm 20:1
for he who **s** my life seeks your life. 1 Sm 22:23
for he who seeks my life **s** your life. 1 Sm 22:23
surely heard that Saul **s** to come to 1 Sm 23:10
who say, 'Behold, David **s** your harm'? 1 Sm 24:9
"Behold, my own son **s** my life; 2 Sm 16:11
for the righteous and **s** to put him to Ps 37:32
Whoever diligently **s** good seeks favor, Prv 11:27
Whoever diligently seeks good **s** favor, Prv 11:27
A scoffer **s** wisdom in vain, but Prv 14:6
who has understanding **s** knowledge, Prv 15:14
Whoever covers an offense **s** love, but Prv 17:9
An evil man **s** only rebellion, and a Prv 17:11
makes his door high **s** destruction. Prv 17:19
Whoever isolates himself **s** his own Prv 18:1
and the ear of the wise **s** knowledge. Prv 18:15
She **s** wool and flax, and works with Prv 31:13
and God **s** what has been driven away. Eccl 3:15
one who judges and **s** justice and is swift Is 16:5
my spirit within me earnestly **s** you. Is 26:9
he **s** out a skillful craftsman to set up an Is 40:20
a man, one who does justice and **s** truth, Jer 5:1
wait for him, to the soul who **s** him. Lam 3:25
As a shepherd **s** out his flock when he Ezk 34:12
asks receives, and the one who **s** finds, Mt 7:8
and adulterous generation **s** for a sign, Mt 12:39
and adulterous generation **s** for a sign, Mt 16:4
asks receives, and the one who **s** finds, Lk 11:10
It **s** for a sign, but no sign will be given Lk 11:29
Whoever **s** to preserve his life will lose Lk 17:33
works in secret if he **s** to be known openly. Jn 7:4
on his own authority **s** his own glory, Jn 7:18
but the one who **s** the glory of him who Jn 7:18
there is One who **s** it, and he is the judge. Jn 8:50
no one understands; no one **s** for God. Rom 3:11

SEEM (13)

and I shall **s** to be mocking him and Gn 27:12
It shall not **s** hard to you when you let Dt 15:18
"Does it **s** to you a little thing to 1 Sm 18:23
him as it shall **s** good to you." Then 1 Sm 24:4
you make yourself **s** tortuous. 2 Sm 22:27
not all the hardship **s** little to you that Neh 9:32
Does it **s** good to you to oppress, to despise Jb 10:3
crooked you make yourself **s** tortuous. Ps 18:26
bows bent, their horses' hoofs **s** like flint, Is 5:28
to them it will **s** like a false divination. Ezk 21:23
of the body that **s** to be weaker are 1 Cor 12:22
right, though we may **s** to have failed. 2 Cor 13:7
lest any of you should **s** to have failed to Heb 4:1

SEEMED (27)

the city." But he **s** to his sons-in-law to Gn 19:14
and they **s** to him but a few days Gn 29:20
and we **s** to ourselves like Nm 13:33
grasshoppers, and so we **s** to them." Nm 13:33
The thing **s** good to me, and I took twelve Dt 1:23
and it **s** impossible to Amnon to do 2 Sm 13:2
And the advice **s** right in the eyes of 2 Sm 17:4
and the plan **s** right to the king and 2 Chr 30:4
this, it **s** to me a wearisome task, Ps 73:16
under the sun, and it **s** great to me. Eccl 9:13
vessel, as it **s** good to the potter to do. Jer 18:4
It has **s** good to me to show the signs and Dn 4:2
and that **s** greater than its companions. Dn 7:20

it **s** good to me also, having followed all Lk 1:3
but these words **s** to them an idle tale, Lk 24:11
Then it **s** good to the apostles and the Acts 15:22
it has **s** good to us, having come to Acts 15:25
For it has **s** good to the Holy Spirit Acts 15:28
before those who **s** influential) the gospel Gal 2:2
And from those who **s** to be influential Gal 2:6
who **s** influential added nothing to me. Gal 2:6
and Cephas and John, who **s** to be pillars, Gal 2:9
us for a short time as it **s** best to them, Heb 12:10
And I heard what **s** to be a voice in the Rv 6:6
One of its heads **s** to have a mortal Rv 13:3
After this I heard what **s** to be the loud Rv 19:1
Then I heard what **s** to be the voice of a Rv 19:6

SEEMING (1)
word, or a letter **s** to be from us, 2 Thes 2:2

SEEMS (38)
'There **s** to me to be some case of Lv 14:35
Whatever **s** good and right in your sight Jos 9:25
sinned; do to us whatever **s** good to you. Jgs 10:15
and do with them what **s** good to you, Jgs 19:24
said to her, "Do what **s** best to you; 1 Sm 1:23
LORD. Let him do what **s** good to him." 1 Sm 3:18
do to us whatever **s** good to you." 1 Sm 11:10
"Do whatever **s** good to you." But the 1 Sm 14:36
said to Saul, "Do what **s** good to you." 1 Sm 14:40
and to me it **s** right that you should 1 Sm 29:6
the LORD do what **s** good to him." 2 Sm 10:12
him do to me what **s** good to him." 2 Sm 15:26
"Whatever **s** best to you I will do." So 2 Sm 18:4
God; do therefore what **s** good to you. 2 Sm 19:27
do for him whatever **s** good to you." 2 Sm 19:37
do for him whatever **s** good to you, 2 Sm 19:38
take and offer up what **s** good to him. 2 Sm 24:22
or, if it **s** good to you, I will give you 1 Kgs 21:2
"If it **s** good to you and from the LORD 1 Chr 13:2
the LORD do what **s** good to him." 1 Chr 19:13
lord the king do what **s** good to him. 1 Chr 21:23
Therefore, if it **s** good to the king, let Ezr 5:17
Whatever **s** good to you and your Ezr 7:18
also, to do with them as it **s** good to you." Est 3:11
and if the thing **s** right before the king, Est 8:5
There is a way that **s** right to a man, Prv 14:12
There is a way that **s** right to a man, Prv 16:25
one who states his case first **s** right, Prv 18:17
Do with me as **s** good and right to you. Jer 26:14
and I give it to whomever it **s** right to me. Jer 27:5
If it **s** good to you to come with me to Jer 40:4
but if it **s** wrong to you to come with me Jer 40:4
If it **s** slow, wait for it; it will surely Hab 2:3
I said to them, "If it **s** good to you, Zec 11:12
"He **s** to be a preacher of foreign Acts 17:18
For it **s** to me unreasonable, in Acts 25:27
If it **s** advisable that I should go also, 1 Cor 16:4
all discipline **s** painful rather Heb 12:11

SEEN (253)
for I have **s** that you are righteous before Gn 7:1
month, the tops of the mountains were **s**. Gn 8:5
the earth and the bow is **s** in the clouds, Gn 9:14
"Truly here I have **s** him who looks Gn 16:13
for I have **s** all that Laban is doing to Gn 31:12
saying, "For I have **s** God face to face, Gn 32:30
For I have **s** your face, which is like Gn 33:10
such as I had never **s** in all the land of Gn 41:19
to pieces, and I have never **s** him since. Gn 44:28
in Egypt, and of all that you have **s**. Gn 45:13
since I have **s** your face and know that Gn 46:30
"I have surely **s** the affliction of my people Ex 3:7
and I have also **s** the oppression with Ex 3:9
Israel and that he had **s** their affliction, Ex 4:31
fathers nor your grandfathers have **s**, Ex 10:6
no leavened bread shall be **s** with you, Ex 13:7
and no leaven shall be **s** with you in all Ex 13:7
You yourselves have **s** what I did to the Ex 19:4
'You have **s** for yourselves that I have Ex 20:22
LORD said to Moses, "I have **s** this people, Ex 32:9
my back, but my face shall not be **s**." Ex 33:23
let no one be **s** throughout all the Ex 34:3
whether he has **s** or come to know the Lv 5:1
For you, O LORD, are **s** face to face, and Nm 14:14
the men who have **s** my glory and my Nm 14:22
Jacob, nor has he **s** trouble in Israel. Nm 23:21
When you have **s** it, you also shall be Nm 27:13
we have **s** the sons of the Anakim there."' Dt 1:28
where you have **s** how the LORD your God Dt 1:31
'Your eyes have **s** all that the LORD your Dt 3:21
Your eyes have **s** what the LORD did at Dt 4:3
forget the things that your eyes have **s**, Dt 4:9
This day we have **s** God speak with man Dt 5:24
the LORD said to me, 'I have **s** this people, Dt 9:13
terrifying things that your eyes have **s**. Dt 10:21
children who have not known or **s** it), Dt 11:2
For your eyes have **s** all the great work of Dt 11:7
No leaven shall be **s** with you in all your Dt 16:4
"You have **s** all that the LORD did before Dt 29:2
And you have **s** their detestable things, Dt 29:17
And you have **s** all that the LORD your Jos 23:3
who had **s** all the great work that the LORD Jgs 2:7
or spear to be **s** among forty thousand in Jgs 5:8
For now I have **s** the angel of the LORD Jgs 6:22
were with him, "What you have **s** me do, Jgs 9:48
shall surely die, for we have **s** God." Jgs 13:22
up against them, for we have **s** the land, Jgs 18:9
never happened or been **s** from the day Jgs 19:30
For I have **s** my people, because their 1 Sm 9:16
I have **s** a son of Jesse the 1 Sm 16:18
"Have you **s** this man who has come 1 Sm 17:25
his foot is, and who has **s** him there, 1 Sm 23:22
day your eyes have **s** how the LORD 1 Sm 24:10
were not to be **s** entering the city. 2 Sm 17:17
what you have **s**." The Cushite 2 Sm 18:21
he was **s** on the wings of the wind. 2 Sm 22:11
Then the channels of the sea were **s**; 2 Sm 22:16
flowers. All was cedar; no stone was **s**. 1 Kgs 6:18
of the poles were **s** from the Holy Place 1 Kgs 8:8
but they could not be **s** from outside. 1 Kgs 8:8
queen of Sheba had **s** all the wisdom 1 Kgs 10:4
I came and my own eyes had **s** it. 1 Kgs 10:7
wood has come or been **s** to this day. 1 Kgs 10:12
Have you **s** all this great multitude? 1 Kgs 20:13
"Have you **s** how Ahab has 1 Kgs 21:29
was no one to be **s** or heard there, 2 Kgs 7:10
marauding band was **s** and the man 2 Kgs 13:21
heard your prayer; I have **s** your tears. 2 Kgs 20:5
"What have they **s** in your house?" 2 Kgs 20:15
"They have **s** all that is in my house; 2 Kgs 20:15
abominations that were **s** in the 2 Kgs 23:24
and now I have **s** your people, 1 Chr 29:17
of the poles were **s** from the Holy Place 2 Chr 5:9
but they could not be **s** from outside. 2 Chr 5:9
queen of Sheba had **s** the wisdom of 2 Chr 9:3
until I came and my own eyes had **s** it. 2 Chr 9:6
There never was **s** the like of them 2 Chr 9:11
old men who had **s** the first house, Ezr 3:12
As I have **s**, those who plow iniquity and Jb 4:8
I have **s** the fool taking root, but suddenly Jb 5:3
deny him, saying, 'I have never **s** you.' Jb 8:18
that I had died before any eye had **s** me Jb 10:18
"Behold, my eye has **s** all this, my ear has Jb 13:1
hear me, and what I have **s** I will declare Jb 15:17
dung; those who have **s** him will say, Jb 20:7
Behold, all of you have **s** it yourselves; Jb 27:12
knows, and the falcon's eye has not **s** it. Jb 28:7
if I have **s** anyone perish for lack of Jb 31:19
is so wasted away that it cannot be **s**, Jb 33:21
and his bones that were not **s** stick out. Jb 33:21
or have you **s** the gates of deep Jb 38:17
or have you **s** the storehouses of the Jb 38:22
Then the channels of the sea were **s**, Ps 18:15
love, because you have **s** my affliction; Ps 31:7
they say, "Aha, Aha! our eyes have **s** it!" Ps 35:21
You have **s**, O LORD; be not silent! O Ps 35:22
yet I have not **s** the righteous forsaken Ps 37:25
I have **s** a wicked, ruthless man, Ps 37:35
so have we **s** in the city of the LORD of Ps 48:8
Your procession is **s**, O God, the Ps 68:24
and for as many years as we have **s** evil. Ps 90:15
My eyes have **s** the downfall of my Ps 92:11
to the proof, though they had **s** my work. Ps 95:9
of the earth have **s** the salvation of our Ps 98:3
I have **s** a limit to all perfection, but Ps 119:96
and I have **s** among the simple, I have Prv 7:7
of a noble. What your eyes have **s** Prv 25:7
I have **s** everything that is done under Eccl 1:14
I have **s** the business that God has Eccl 3:10
yet been and has not **s** the evil deeds that Eccl 4:3
evil that I have **s** under the sun: Eccl 5:13
what I have **s** to be good and fitting is Eccl 5:18
is an evil that I have **s** under the sun, Eccl 6:1
it has not **s** the sun or known anything, Eccl 6:5
In my vain life I have **s** everything. Eccl 7:15
I have also **s** this example of wisdom Eccl 9:13
is an evil that I have **s** under the sun, Eccl 10:5
I have **s** slaves on horses, and princes Eccl 10:7
"Have you **s** him whom my soul loves?" Sg 3:3
for my eyes have **s** the King, the LORD of Is 6:5
walked in darkness have **s** a great light; Is 9:2
the descending blow of his arm to be **s**, Is 30:30
heard your prayer; I have **s** your tears. Is 38:5
"What have they **s** in your house?" Is 39:4
"They have **s** all that is in my house. Is 39:4
The coastlands have **s** and are afraid; the Is 41:5
says, "Aha, I am warm, I have **s** the fire!" Is 44:16
uncovered, and your disgrace shall be **s**. Is 47:3
I have **s** his ways, but I will heal him; I Is 57:18
you, and his glory will be **s** upon you. Is 60:2
by the ear, no eye has **s** a God besides you, Is 64:4
such a thing? Who has **s** such things? Is 66:8
have not heard my fame or **s** my glory. Is 66:19
the LORD said to me, "You have **s** well, Jer 1:12
"Have you **s** what she did, that faithless Jer 3:6
Behold, I myself have **s** it, declares the Jer 7:11
your face, and your shame will be **s**. Jer 13:26
I have **s** your abominations, your Jer 13:27
of Jerusalem I have **s** a horrible thing: Jer 23:14
You have **s** all the disaster that I brought Jer 44:2
Why have I **s** it? They are dismayed and Jer 46:5
her, for they have **s** her nakedness; Lam 1:8
for she has **s** the nations enter her Lam 1:10
Your prophets have **s** for you false and Lam 2:14
but have **s** for you oracles that are Lam 2:14
the man who has **s** affliction under the Lam 3:1
You have **s** the wrong done to me, O Lam 3:59
You have **s** all their vengeance, all Lam 3:60
glory that I had **s** by the Chebar canal, Ezk 3:23
have you **s** what the elders of the house Ezk 8:12
Then he said to me, "Have you **s** this, O Ezk 8:15
Then he said to me, "Have you **s** this, O Ezk 8:17
appearance I had **s** by the Chebar Ezk 10:22
vision that I had **s** went up from me. Ezk 11:24
their own spirit, and have **s** nothing! Ezk 13:3
They have **s** false visions and lying Ezk 13:6
Have you not **s** a false vision and Ezk 13:7
uttered falsehood and **s** lying visions, Ezk 13:8
it was **s** in its height with the mass of Ezk 19:11
the vision that I had **s** when he came to Ezk 43:3
vision that I had **s** by the Chebar canal. Ezk 43:3
have you **s** this?" Then he led me back Ezk 47:6
of ten days it was **s** that they were better Dn 1:15
that I have **s** and its interpretation?" Dn 2:26
which I had **s** standing on the bank of Dn 8:6
When I, Daniel, had **s** the vision, I Dn 8:15
whom I had **s** in the vision at the first, Dn 9:21
house of Israel I have **s** a horrible thing; Hos 6:10
Ephraim, as I have **s**, was like a young Hos 9:13
the star that they had **s** when it rose went Mt 2:9
in darkness have **s** a great light, Mt 4:16
other people in order to be **s** by them, Mt 6:1
corners, that they may be **s** by others. Mt 6:5
that their fasting may be **s** by others. Mt 6:16
fasting may not be **s** by others but by Mt 6:18
was anything like this **s** in Israel." Mt 9:33
They do all their deeds to be **s** by others. Mt 23:5
And those who had **s** it described to Mk 5:16
them to tell no one what they had **s**, Mk 9:9
he was alive and had been **s** by her, Mk 16:11
they realized that he had **s** a vision in the Lk 1:22
God for all they had heard and **s**, Lk 2:20
death before he had **s** the Lord's Christ. Lk 2:26
for my eyes have **s** your salvation Lk 2:30
"We have **s** extraordinary things today." Lk 5:26
and tell John what you have **s** and heard: Lk 7:22
And those who had **s** it told them how Lk 8:36
those days anything of what they had **s**. Lk 9:36
all the mighty works that they had **s**, Lk 19:37
that they had even **s** a vision of angels, Lk 24:23
dwelt among us, and we have **s** his glory, Jn 1:14
No one has ever **s** God; the only God, who Jn 1:18
And I have **s** and have borne witness that Jn 1:34
and bear witness to what we have **s**, Jn 3:11
it may be clearly **s** that his deeds have Jn 3:21
bears witness to what he has **s** and heard, Jn 3:32
having **s** all that he had done in Jn 4:45
never heard, his form you have never **s**, Jn 5:37
to you that you have **s** me and yet do not Jn 6:36
not that anyone has **s** the Father except Jn 6:46
he who is from God; he has **s** the Father. Jn 6:46
I speak of what I have **s** with my Father, Jn 8:38
years old, and have you **s** Abraham?" Jn 8:57
and those who had **s** him before as a Jn 9:8
Jesus said to him, "You have **s** him, and Jn 9:37
come with Mary and had **s** what he did, Jn 11:45
on you do know him and have **s** him." Jn 14:7
Whoever has **s** me has seen the Father. Jn 14:9
Whoever has seen me has **s** the Father. Jn 14:9
but now they have **s** and hated both me Jn 15:24
"I have **s** the Lord"—and that he had Jn 20:18
"We have **s** the Lord." But he said to Jn 20:25
you believed because you have **s** me? Jn 20:29
those who have not **s** and yet have Jn 20:29
speak of what we have **s** and heard." Acts 4:20
I have surely **s** the affliction of my Acts 7:34
according to the pattern that he had **s**. Acts 7:44
and he has **s** in a vision a man named Acts 9:12
how on the road he had **s** the Lord, Acts 9:27
the vision that he had **s** might mean, Acts 10:17
us how he had **s** the angel stand in Acts 11:13
And when Paul had **s** the vision, Acts 16:10
And when they had **s** the brothers, Acts 16:40
they had previously **s** Trophimus the Acts 21:29
of what you have **s** and heard. Acts 22:15
in which you have **s** me and to those Acts 26:16
saved. Now hope that is **s** is not hope. Rom 8:24
as it is written, "What no eye has **s**, 1 Cor 2:9

apostle? Have I not **s** Jesus our Lord? 1 Cor 9:1
the things that are **s** but to the things 2 Cor 4:18
For the things that are **s** are transient, 2 Cor 4:18
received and heard and **s** in me— Phil 4:9
for all who have not **s** me face to face, Col 2:1
vindicated by the Spirit, **s** by angels, 1 Tm 3:16
whom no one has ever **s** or can see. 1 Tm 6:16
for, the conviction of things not **s**. Heb 11:1
so that what is **s** was not made out of Heb 11:3
but having **s** them and greeted them Heb 11:13
and you have **s** the purpose of the Lord, Jas 5:11
Though you have not **s** him, you love 1 Pt 1:8
heard, which we have **s** with our eyes, 1 Jn 1:1
life was made manifest, and we have **s** it, 1 Jn 1:2
that which we have **s** and heard we 1 Jn 1:3
on sinning has either **s** him or known 1 Jn 3:6
No one has ever **s** God; if we love one 1 Jn 4:12
And we have **s** and testify that the 1 Jn 4:14
whom he has **s** cannot love God 1 Jn 4:20
cannot love God whom he has not **s**. 1 Jn 4:20
God; whoever does evil has not **s** God. 3 Jn 1:11
therefore the things that you have **s**, Rv 1:19
shame of your nakedness may not be **s**, Rv 3:18
his covenant was **s** within his temple. Rv 11:19
not go about naked and be **s** exposed!") Rv 16:15

SEER (23)
us go to the **s**," for today's "prophet" 1 Sm 9:9
"prophet" was formerly called a **s**.) 1 Sm 9:9
water and said to them, "Is the **s** here?" 1 Sm 9:11
"Tell me where is the house of the **s**?" 1 Sm 9:18
Samuel answered Saul, "I am the **s**. Go 1 Sm 9:19
to Zadok the priest, "Are you not a **s**? 2 Sm 15:27
came to the prophet Gad, David's **s**, 2 Sm 24:11
Judah by every prophet and every **s**, 2 Kgs 17:13
and Samuel the **s** established them in 1 Chr 9:22
And the LORD spoke to Gad, David's **s**, 1 Chr 21:9
were the sons of Heman the king's **s**, 1 Chr 25:5
all that Samuel the **s** and Saul the 1 Chr 26:28
in the Chronicles of Samuel the **s**, 1 Chr 29:29
and in the Chronicles of Gad the **s**, 1 Chr 29:29
of Iddo the **s** concerning Jeroboam 2 Chr 9:29
the prophet and of Iddo the **s**? 2 Chr 12:15
that time Hanani the **s** came to Asa 2 Chr 16:7
was angry with the **s** and put him in 2 Chr 16:10
son of Hanani the **s** went out to meet 2 Chr 19:2
of Gad the king's **s** and of Nathan 2 Chr 29:25
words of David and of Asaph the **s**. 2 Chr 29:30
Heman, and Jeduthun the king's **s**; 2 Chr 35:15
And Amaziah said to Amos, "O **s**, go, Am 7:12

SEERS (5)
the words of the **s** who spoke to him 2 Chr 33:18
written in the Chronicles of the **S**. 2 Chr 33:19
and covered your heads (the **s**). Is 29:10
who say to the **s**, "Do not see," and to the Is 30:10
the **s** shall be disgraced, and the diviners Mi 3:7

SEES (62)
as soon as he **s** that the boy is not with Gn 44:31
out to meet you, and when he **s** you, Ex 4:14
and when he **s** the blood on the lintel Ex 12:23
of his mother, and **s** her nakedness, Lv 20:17
nakedness, and she **s** his nakedness, Lv 20:17
everyone who is bitten, when he **s** it, Nm 21:8
God, who **s** the vision of the Almighty, Nm 24:4
who **s** the vision of the Almighty, Nm 24:16
when he **s** that their power is gone and Dt 32:36
For the LORD **s** not as man sees: man 1 Sm 16:7
For the LORD sees not as man **s**: man 1 Sm 16:7
of this city is pleasant, as my lord **s**, 2 Kgs 2:19
The eye of him who **s** me will behold me Jb 7:8
you eyes of flesh? Do you see as man **s**? Jb 10:4
when he **s** iniquity, will he not consider Jb 11:11
and his eye **s** every precious thing. Jb 28:10
of the earth and **s** everything under the Jb 28:24
he **s** his face with a shout of joy, and he Jb 33:26
the ways of a man, and he **s** all his steps. Jb 34:21
He **s** everything that is high; he is king Jb 41:34
hearing of the ear, but now my eye **s** you; Jb 42:5
heaven; he **s** all the children of man; Ps 33:13
wicked, for he **s** that his day is coming. Ps 37:13
For he **s** that even the wise die; the fool Ps 49:10
the stillborn child who never **s** the sun. Ps 58:8
will rejoice when he **s** the vengeance; Ps 58:10
up the world; the earth **s** and trembles. Ps 97:4
The wicked man **s** it and is angry; he Ps 112:10
The prudent **s** danger and hides Prv 22:3
The prudent **s** danger and hides Prv 27:12
watchman; let him announce what he **s**. Is 21:6
When he **s** riders, horsemen in pairs, Is 21:7
when someone **s** it, he swallows it as soon Is 28:4
in the dark, and who say, "Who **s** us? Is 29:15
For when he **s** his children, the work of Is 29:23
He **s** many things, but does not observe Is 42:20
wickedness, you said, "No one **s** me"; Is 47:10
who **s** the heart and the mind, Jer 20:12
LORD from heaven looks down and **s**; Lam 3:50
'The vision that he **s** is for many days Ezk 12:27
fathers a son who **s** all the sins that Ezk 18:14
the sins that his father has done; he **s**, Ezk 18:14
"When Pharaoh **s** them, he will be Ezk 32:31
and if he **s** the sword coming upon the Ezk 33:3
if the watchman **s** the sword coming Ezk 33:6
the land and anyone **s** a human bone, Ezk 39:15
And your Father who **s** in secret will Mt 6:4
And your Father who **s** in secret will Mt 6:6
And your Father who **s** in secret will Mt 6:18
but only what he **s** the Father doing. Jn 5:19
But how he now **s** we do not know, nor do Jn 9:21
s the wolf coming and leaves the sheep Jn 10:12
because he **s** the light of this world. Jn 11:9
And whoever **s** me sees him who sent Jn 12:45
And whoever sees me **s** him who sent Jn 12:45
because it neither **s** him nor knows Jn 14:17
not hope. For who hopes for what he **s**? Rom 8:24
For who **s** anything different in you? 1 Cor 4:7
For if anyone **s** you who have 1 Cor 8:10
more of me than he **s** in me or hears 2 Cor 12:6
the world's goods and **s** his brother in 1 Jn 3:17
If anyone **s** his brother committing a 1 Jn 5:16

SEETHE (1)
it; boil it well; **s** also its bones in it. Ezk 24:5

SEGUB (3)
at the cost of his youngest son **S**, 1 Kgs 16:34
sixty years old, and she bore him **S**. 1 Chr 2:21
And **S** fathered Jair, who had 1 Chr 2:22

SEIR (39)
their hill country of **S** as far as El-paran Gn 14:6
him to Esau his brother in the land of **S**, Gn 32:3
children, until I come to my lord in **S**." Gn 33:14
Esau returned that day on his way to **S**. Gn 33:16
So Esau settled in the hill country of **S**. Gn 36:8
of the Edomites in the hill country of **S**. Gn 36:9
These are the sons of **S** the Horite, the Gn 36:20
the sons of **S** in the land of Edom. Gn 36:21
Horites, chief by chief in the land of **S**. Gn 36:30
S also, his enemies, shall be Nm 24:18
by the way of Mount **S** to Kadesh-barnea. Dt 1:2
beat you down in **S** as far as Hormah. Dt 1:44
many days we traveled around Mount **S**. Dt 2:1
brothers, the people of Esau, who live in **S**; Dt 2:4
because I have given Mount **S** to Esau as a Dt 2:5
brothers, the people of Esau, who live in **S**, Dt 2:8
The Horites also lived in **S** formerly, but Dt 2:12
did for the people of Esau, who live in **S**, Dt 2:22
Esau who live in **S** and the Moabites who Dt 2:29
from Sinai and dawned from **S** upon us; Dt 33:2
Mount Halak, which rises toward **S**, Jos 11:17
that rises toward **S** (and Joshua gave Jos 12:7
circles west of Baalah to Mount **S**, Jos 15:10
Esau the hill country of **S** to possess, Jos 24:4
"LORD, when you went out from **S**, when Jgs 5:4
The sons of **S**: Lotan, Shobal, Zibeon, 1 Chr 1:38
of the Simeonites, went to Mount **S**, 1 Chr 4:42
of Ammon and Moab and Mount **S**, 2 Chr 20:10
of Ammon, Moab, and Mount **S**, 2 Chr 20:22
against the inhabitants of Mount **S**, 2 Chr 20:23
made an end of the inhabitants of **S**, 2 Chr 20:23
and struck down 10,000 men of **S**. 2 Chr 25:11
gods of the men of **S** and set them up 2 Chr 25:14
One is calling to me from **S**, Is 21:11
Because Moab and **S** said, 'Behold, the Ezk 25:8
of man, set your face against Mount **S**, Ezk 35:2
Behold, I am against you, Mount **S**, and Ezk 35:3
I will make Mount **S** a waste and a Ezk 35:7
you shall be desolate, Mount **S**, and all Ezk 35:15

SEIRAH (1)
passed beyond the idols and escaped to **S**. Jgs 3:26

SEIZE (36)
make us servants and **s** our donkeys." Gn 43:18
rise up from the ambush and **s** the city, Jos 8:7
and **s** one of the young men and take 2 Sm 2:21
altar, saying, "**S** him." And his hand, 1 Kgs 13:4
said to them, "**S** the prophets of Baal; 1 Kgs 18:40
the king of Israel said, "**S** Micaiah, 1 Kgs 22:26
I may send and **s** him." It was told 2 Kgs 6:13
"**S** Micaiah and take him back to 2 Chr 18:25
That night—let thick darkness **s** it! Let it Jb 3:6
they **s** flocks and pasture them. Jb 24:2
the wicked; judgment and justice **s** you. Jb 36:17
thicket; he lurks that he may **s** the poor; Ps 10:9
pursue and **s** him, for there is none to Ps 71:11
May the creditor **s** all that he has; may Ps 109:11
they roar; they growl and **s** their prey; Is 5:29
him, to take spoil and **s** plunder, Is 10:6
dismayed: pangs and agony will **s** them; Is 13:8
strong man. He will **s** firm hold on you Is 22:17
plunder them and **s** them and carry Jer 20:5
son of Abdeel to **s** Baruch the secretary Jer 36:26
They shall **s** your sons and your Ezk 23:25
to **s** spoil and carry off plunder, to Ezk 38:12
say to you, 'Have you come to **s** spoil? Ezk 38:13
livestock and goods, to **s** great spoil?' Ezk 38:13
They will **s** the spoil of those who Ezk 39:10
They covet fields and **s** them, and houses, Mi 2:2
of the earth, to **s** dwellings not their own. Hab 1:6
"for the day when I rise up to **s** the prey. Zep 3:8
so that each will **s** the hand of another, Zec 14:13
"The one I will kiss is the man; **s** him." Mt 26:48
temple teaching, and you did not **s** me. Mt 26:55
family heard it, they went out to **s** him, Mk 3:21
S him and lead him away under Mk 14:44
temple teaching, and you did not **s** me. Mk 14:49
city of Damascus in order to **s** me, 2 Cor 11:32
have, so that no one may **s** your crown. Rv 3:11

SEIZED (55)
So the men **s** him and his wife and his Gn 19:16
water that Abimelech's servants had **s**, Gn 21:25
he **s** her and lay with her and Gn 34:2
pangs have **s** the inhabitants of Ex 15:14
donkey shall be **s** before your face, Dt 28:31
down after him and **s** the fords of the Jgs 3:28
Then they **s** him and slaughtered him at Jgs 12:6
And the Philistines **s** him and gouged Jgs 16:21
So the man **s** his concubine and made Jgs 19:25
go away, Saul **s** the skirt of his robe, 1 Sm 15:27
me and kill me, for anguish has **s** me, 2 Sm 1:9
I **s** him and killed him at Ziklag, 2 Sm 4:10
of them escape." And they **s** them. 1 Kgs 18:40
And he **s** all the gold and silver, and 2 Kgs 14:14
And he **s** all the gold and silver, and 2 Chr 25:24
He **s** also the treasuries of the king's 2 Chr 25:24
he **s** me by the neck and dashed me to Jb 16:12
he has **s** a house that he did not build. Jb 20:19
when the Philistines **s** him in Gath. Ps 56:T
pangs have **s** me, like the pangs of a Is 21:3
are afraid; trembling has **s** the godless: Is 33:14
of Hananiah, **s** Jeremiah the prophet, Jer 37:13
and **s** Jeremiah and brought him to the Jer 37:14
but shall be **s** by the king of Babylon, Jer 38:23
shall be taken and the strongholds **s**. Jer 48:41
she turned to flee, and panic **s** her; Jer 49:24
his hands fell helpless; anguish **s** him, Jer 50:43
the fords have been **s**, the marshes are Jer 51:32
is taken, the praise of the whole earth **s**! Jer 51:41
and **s** their widows. He laid waste their Ezk 19:7
they **s** her sons and her daughters; Ezk 23:10
that pain **s** you like a woman in labor? Mi 4:9
For Herod had **s** John and bound him Mt 14:3
while the rest **s** his servants, treated Mt 22:6
up and laid hands on Jesus and **s** him. Mt 26:50
Then those who had **s** Jesus led him to Mt 26:57
who had sent and **s** John and bound Mk 6:17
they laid hands on him and **s** him. Mk 14:46
cloth about his body. And they **s** him, Mk 14:51
and astonishment had **s** them, Mk 16:8
And amazement **s** them all, and they Lk 5:26
Fear **s** them all, and they glorified God, Lk 7:16
the man. (For many a time it had **s** him. Lk 8:29
them, for they were **s** with great fear. Lk 8:37
Then they **s** him and led him away, Lk 22:54
him away, they **s** one Simon of Cyrene, Lk 23:26
upon him and **s** him and brought Acts 6:12
And when he had **s** him, he put him in Acts 12:4
they **s** Paul and Silas and dragged Acts 16:19
And they all **s** Sosthenes, the ruler of Acts 18:17
They **s** Paul and dragged him out of Acts 21:30
This man was **s** by the Jews and was Acts 23:27
to profane the temple, but we **s** him. Acts 24:6
this reason the Jews **s** me in the Acts 26:21
And he **s** the dragon, that ancient Rv 20:2

SEIZES (12)
trembling **s** the leaders of Moab; Ex 15:15
and the man **s** her and lies with her, Dt 22:25
betrothed, and **s** her and lies with her, Dt 22:28
out her hand and **s** him by the private Dt 25:11
A trap **s** him by the heel; a snare lays Jb 18:9
at his day, and horror **s** them of the east. Jb 18:20
dismayed, and shuddering **s** my flesh. Jb 21:6
he **s** the poor when he draws him into his Ps 10:9
Hot indignation **s** me because of the Ps 119:53
She **s** him and kisses him, and with Prv 7:13
And whenever it **s** him, it throws him Mk 9:18
And behold, a spirit **s** him, and he Lk 9:39

SEIZING (3)
him a hundred denarii, and **s** him, Mt 18:28
s an opportunity through the Rom 7:8
s an opportunity through the Rom 7:11

SELA (4)
of Akrabbim, from **S** and upward. Jgs 1:36
Valley of Salt and took **S** by storm, 2 Kgs 14:7
the lamb to the ruler of the land, from **S**, Is 16:1

let the habitants of **S** sing for joy, let Is 42:11

SELAH (74)
there is no salvation for him in God. **S** Ps 3:2
and he answered me from his holy hill. **S** Ps 3:4
LORD; your blessing be on your people! **S** Ps 3:8
you love vain words and seek after lies? **S** Ps 4:2
own hearts on your beds, and be silent. **S** Ps 4:4
the ground and lay my glory in the dust. **S** Ps 7:5
the work of their own hands. Higgaion. **S** Ps 9:16
nations know that they are but men! **S** Ps 9:20
with favor your burnt sacrifices! **S** Ps 20:3
not withheld the request of his lips. **S** Ps 21:2
who seek the face of the God of Jacob. **S** Ps 24:6
LORD of hosts, he is the King of glory! **S** Ps 24:10
was dried up as by the heat of summer. **S** Ps 32:4
and you forgave the iniquity of my sin. **S** Ps 32:5
me with shouts of deliverance. **S** Ps 32:7
all mankind stands as a mere breath! **S** Ps 39:5
surely all mankind is a mere breath! **S** Ps 39:11
will give thanks to your name forever. **S** Ps 44:8
the mountains tremble at its swelling. **S** Ps 46:3
us; the God of Jacob is our fortress. **S** Ps 46:7
us; the God of Jacob is our fortress. **S** Ps 46:11
us, the pride of Jacob whom he loves. **S** Ps 47:4
God, which God will establish forever. **S** Ps 48:8
them people approve of their boasts. **S** Ps 49:13
power of Sheol, for he will receive me. **S** Ps 49:15
for God himself is judge! **S** Ps 50:6
more than speaking what is right. **S** Ps 52:3
uproot you from the land of the living. **S** Ps 52:5
they do not set God before themselves. **S** Ps 54:3
away; I would lodge in the wilderness; **S** Ps 55:7
S because they do not change and do Ps 55:19
S God will send out his steadfast love and Ps 57:3
but they have fallen into it themselves. **S** Ps 57:6
of those who treacherously plot evil. **S** Ps 59:5
over Jacob to the ends of the earth. **S** Ps 59:13
that they may flee to it from the bow. **S** Ps 60:4
refuge under the shelter of your wings! **S** Ps 61:4
their mouths, but inwardly they curse. **S** Ps 62:4
heart before him; God is a refuge for us. **S** Ps 62:8
to you; they sing praises to your name." **S** Ps 66:4
let not the rebellious exalt themselves. **S** Ps 66:7
make an offering of bulls and goats. **S** Ps 66:15
us and make his face to shine upon us, **S** Ps 67:1
and guide the nations upon earth. **S** Ps 67:4
you marched through the wilderness, **S** Ps 68:7
bears us up; God is our salvation. **S** Ps 68:19
sing to God; sing praises to the Lord, **S** Ps 68:32
it is I who keep steady its pillars. **S** Ps 75:3
the sword, and the weapons of war. **S** Ps 76:3
to save all the humble of the earth. **S** Ps 76:9
when I meditate, my spirit faints. **S** Ps 77:3
he in anger shut up his compassion?" **S** Ps 77:9
the children of Jacob and Joseph. **S** Ps 77:15
I tested you at the waters of Meribah. **S** Ps 81:7
and show partiality to the wicked? **S** Ps 82:2
the strong arm of the children of Lot. **S** Ps 83:8
your house, ever singing your praise! **S** Ps 84:4
my prayer; give ear, O God of Jacob! **S** Ps 84:8
your people; you covered all their sin. **S** Ps 85:2
things of you are spoken, O city of God. **S** Ps 87:3
the peoples, "This one was born there." **S** Ps 87:6
overwhelm me with all your waves. **S** Ps 88:7
Do the departed rise up to praise you? **S** Ps 88:10
build your throne for all generations.'" **S** Ps 89:4
a faithful witness in the skies." **S** Ps 89:37
you have covered him with shame. **S** Ps 89:45
his soul from the power of Sheol? **S** Ps 89:48
under their lips is the venom of asps. **S** Ps 140:3
the way they have set snares for me. **S** Ps 140:5
their evil plot or they will be exalted! **S** Ps 140:8
thirsts for you like a parched land. **S** Ps 143:6
and the earth was full of his praise. **S** Hab 3:3
arrows. **S** You split the earth with rivers. Hab 3:9
laying him bare from thigh to neck. **S** Hab 3:13

SELDOM (1)
Let your foot be **s** in your neighbor's Prv 25:17

SELECT (4)
therefore let Pharaoh **s** a discerning Gn 41:33
"Go and **s** lambs for yourselves Ex 12:21
then you shall **s** cities to be cities of Nm 35:11
s the best and fittest of your master's 2 Kgs 10:3

SELECTED (1)
Ezra the priest **s** men, heads of fathers' Ezr 10:16

SELED (2)
The sons of Nadab: **S** and Appaim; 1 Chr 2:30
and Appaim; and **S** died childless. 1 Chr 2:30

SELEUCIA (1)
by the Holy Spirit, they went down to **S**, Acts 13:4

SELF (10)
to whom you swore by your own **s**, Ex 32:13
their mouth; their inmost **s** is destruction; Ps 5:9
and my inmost **s** for Kir-hareseth. Is 16:11
know that our old **s** was crucified with Rom 6:6
to put off your old **s**, which belongs to Eph 4:22
and to put on the new **s**, created after Eph 4:24
have put off the old **s** with its practices Col 3:9
and have put on the new **s**, which is Col 3:10
For people will be lovers of **s**, lovers of 2 Tm 3:2
of your owing me even your own **s**. Phlm 1:19

SELF-CONDEMNED (1)
a person is warped and sinful; he is **s**. Ti 3:11

SELF-CONTROL (12)
A man without **s** is like a city broken Prv 25:28
about righteousness and **s** and the Acts 24:25
tempt you because of your lack of **s**. 1 Cor 7:5
But if they cannot exercise **s**, they 1 Cor 7:9
Every athlete exercises **s** in all things. 1 Cor 9:25
s; against such things there is no law. Gal 5:23
apparel, with modesty and **s**, 1 Tm 2:9
in faith and love and holiness, with **s**. 1 Tm 2:15
not of fear but of power and love and **s**. 2 Tm 1:7
unappeasable, slanderous, without **s**, 2 Tm 3:3
and knowledge with **s**, and self-control 2 Pt 1:6
self-control, and **s** with steadfastness, 2 Pt 1:6

SELF-CONTROLLED (7)
one wife, sober-minded, **s**, respectable, 1 Tm 3:2
but hospitable, a lover of good, **s**, upright, Ti 1:8
sober-minded, dignified, **s**, sound in faith, Ti 2:2
to be **s**, pure, working at home, kind, and Ti 2:5
Likewise, urge the younger men to be **s**. Ti 2:6
and worldly passions, and to live **s**, Ti 2:12
therefore be **s** and sober-minded for the 1 Pt 4:7

SELF-INDULGENCE (2)
but inside they are full of greed and **s**. Mt 23:25
have lived on the earth in luxury and in **s**. Jas 5:5

SELF-INDULGENT (1)
but she who is **s** is dead even while she 1 Tm 5:6

SELF-MADE (1)
wisdom in promoting **s** religion and Col 2:23

SELF-SEEKING (1)
but for those who are **s** and do not obey Rom 2:8

SELFISH (3)
to your testimonies, and not to **s** gain! Ps 119:36
bitter jealousy and **s** ambition in your Jas 3:14
For where jealousy and **s** ambition exist, Jas 3:16

SELL (28)
said, "**S** me your birthright now." Gn 25:31
Come, let us **s** him to the Ishmaelites, Gn 37:27
therefore they did not **s** their land. Gn 47:22
shall have no right to **s** her to a foreign Ex 21:8
then they shall **s** the live ox and share Ex 21:35
and he shall **s** to you according to the Lv 25:15
You shall **s** me food for money, that I Dt 2:28
eat it, or you may **s** it to a foreigner. Dt 14:21
But you shall not **s** her for money, nor Dt 21:14
for the LORD will **s** Sisera into the hand of Jgs 4:9
said, "Go, **s** the oil and pay your debts, 2 Kgs 4:7
but you even **s** your brothers that they Neh 5:8
or any grain on the Sabbath day to **s**, Neh 10:31
Buy truth, and do not **s** it; buy Prv 23:23
up the Nile and will **s** the land into the Ezk 30:12
They shall not **s** or exchange any of it. Ezk 48:14
I will **s** your sons and your daughters into Jl 3:8
Judah, and they will **s** them to the Sabeans, Jl 3:8
because they **s** the righteous for silver, Am 2:6
new moon be over, that we may **s** grain? Am 8:5
a pair of sandals and **s** the chaff of the Am 8:6
unpunished, and those who **s** them say, Zec 11:5
s what you possess and give to the poor, Mt 19:21
s all that you have and give to the Mk 10:21
S your possessions, and give to the Lk 12:33
S all that you have and distribute to the Lk 18:22
who has no sword **s** his cloak and buy Lk 22:36
no one can buy or **s** unless he has the Rv 13:17

SELLER (4)
mistress; as with the buyer, so with the **s**; Is 24:2
not the buyer rejoice, nor the **s** mourn, Ezk 7:12
For the **s** shall not return to what he Ezk 7:13
city of Thyatira, a **s** of purple goods, Acts 16:14

SELLERS (1)
the merchants and **s** of all kinds Neh 13:20

SELLING (5)
number of the crops that he is **s** to you. Lv 25:16
is **s** the parcel of land that belonged to our Ru 4:3
eating and drinking, buying and **s**, Lk 17:28
found those who were **s** oxen and sheep Jn 2:14
And they were **s** their possessions and Acts 2:45

SELLS (11)
"When a man **s** his daughter as a slave, Ex 21:7
"Whoever steals a man and **s** him, and Ex 21:16
steals an ox or a sheep, and kills it or **s** it, Ex 22:1
brother becomes poor and **s** part of his Lv 25:25
"If a man **s** a dwelling house in a walled Lv 25:29
poor beside you and **s** himself to you, Lv 25:39
him becomes poor and **s** himself to the Lv 25:47
and if he treats him as a slave or **s** him, Dt 24:7
blessing is on the head of him who **s** it. Prv 11:26
makes linen garments and **s** them; Prv 31:24
his joy he goes and **s** all that he has and Mt 13:44

SELVES (2)
among your own **s** will arise men Acts 20:30
the gospel of God but also our own **s**, 1 Thes 2:8

SEMACHIAH (1)
brothers were able men, Elihu and **S**. 1 Chr 26:7

SEMBLANCE (1)
was so marred, beyond human **s**, Is 52:14

SEMEIN (1)
the son of Mattathias, the son of **S**, Lk 3:26

SEMEN (6)
wife he would waste the **s** on the ground, Gn 38:9
"If a man has an emission of **s**, he shall Lv 15:16
skin on which the **s** comes shall be Lv 15:17
a woman and has an emission of **s**, Lv 15:18
and for him who has an emission of **s**, Lv 15:32
or a man who has had an emission of **s**, Lv 22:4

SENAAH (2)
The sons of **S**, 3,630. Ezr 2:35
The sons of **S**, 3,930. Neh 7:38

SENATE (1)
council and all the **s** of Israel and sent Acts 5:21

SEND (243)
in seven days I will **s** rain on the earth Gn 7:4
this land,' he will **s** his angel before you, Gn 24:7
will **s** his angel with you and prosper Gn 24:40
he said, "**S** me away to my master." Gn 24:54
S me away that I may go to my Gn 24:56
Then I will **s** and bring you from there. Gn 27:45
Jacob said to Laban, "**S** me away, Gn 30:25
I will **s** you to them." And he said to Gn 37:13
"I will **s** you a young goat from the Gn 38:17
you give me a pledge, until you **s** it—" Gn 38:17
But Jacob did not **s** Benjamin, Joseph's Gn 42:4
S one of you, and let him bring your Gn 42:16
If you will **s** our brother with us, we will Gn 43:4
But if you will not **s** him, we will not go Gn 43:5
to Israel his father, "**S** the boy with me, Gn 43:8
and may he **s** back your other brother Gn 43:14
I will **s** you to Pharaoh that you may Ex 3:10
"Oh, my Lord, please **s** someone else." Ex 4:13
to this people? Why did you ever **s** me? Ex 5:22
for with a strong hand he will **s** them out, Ex 6:1
I will **s** swarms of flies on you and your Ex 8:21
For this time I will **s** all my plagues on Ex 9:14
Now therefore **s**, get your livestock and Ex 9:19
with the people to **s** them out of the Ex 12:33
your adversaries; you **s** out your fury; Ex 15:7
I **s** an angel before you to guard you on Ex 23:20
I will **s** my terror before you and will Ex 23:27
And I will **s** hornets before you, which Ex 23:28
I will **s** an angel before you, and I will Ex 33:2
let me know whom you will **s** with me. Ex 33:12
head of the goat and **s** it away into the Lv 16:21
cities, I will **s** pestilence among you, Lv 26:25
I will **s** faintness into their hearts in the Lv 26:36
"**S** men to spy out the land of Canaan, Nm 13:2
tribe of their fathers you shall **s** a man, Nm 13:2
"Did I not **s** to you to call you? Nm 22:37
You shall **s** a thousand from each of Nm 31:4
me and said, 'Let us **s** men before us, Dt 1:22
your God will **s** hornets among them, Dt 7:20
of his city shall **s** and take him from Dt 19:12
"The LORD will **s** on you curses, Dt 28:20
whom the LORD will **s** against you, Dt 28:48
I will **s** the teeth of beasts against them, Dt 32:24
do, and wherever you **s** us we will go. Jos 1:16
and I will **s** them out that they may set Jos 18:4
the hand of Midian; do not I **s** you?" Jgs 6:14
"**S** away the ark of the God of Israel, 1 Sm 5:11
us with what we shall **s** it to its place." 1 Sm 6:2
"If you **s** away the ark of the God of 1 Sm 6:3
of the God of Israel, do not **s** it empty, 1 Sm 6:3
them, did they not **s** the people away, 1 Sm 6:6
Then **s** it off and let it go its way 1 Sm 6:8
about this time I will **s** to you a man 1 Sm 9:16
that I may **s** you on your way." So 1 Sm 9:26
that we may **s** messengers through all 1 Sm 11:3
that he may **s** thunder and rain. 1 Sm 12:17
I will **s** you to Jesse the Bethlehemite, 1 Sm 16:1
Samuel said to Jesse, "**S** and get him, 1 Sm 16:11
Jesse and said, "**S** me David your son, 1 Sm 16:19
shall I not then **s** and disclose it to 1 Sm 20:12

not disclose it to you and **s** you away, 1 Sm 20:13
And behold, I will **s** the young man, 1 Sm 20:21
Therefore **s** and bring him to me, for 1 Sm 20:31
of the matter about which I **s** you, 1 Sm 21:2
said to him, "**S** the man back, 1 Sm 29:4
"**S** me Uriah the Hittite." And Joab 2 Sm 11:6
and tomorrow I will **s** you back." So 2 Sm 11:12
"**S** out everyone from me." So 2 Sm 13:9
sent for Joab, to **s** him to the king, 2 Sm 14:29
here, that I may **s** you to the king, 2 Sm 14:32
them you shall **s** to me everything 2 Sm 15:36
Now therefore **s** quickly and tell 2 Sm 17:16
it is better that you **s** us help from the 2 Sm 18:3
by whatever way you shall **s** them, 1 Kgs 8:44
and I will **s** rain upon the earth." 1 Kgs 18:1
Now therefore **s** and gather all Israel 1 Kgs 18:19
Nevertheless I will **s** my servants to 1 Kgs 20:6
And he said, "You shall not **s**." 2 Kgs 2:16
"**S**." They sent therefore fifty men. 2 Kgs 2:17
"**S** me one of the servants and one of 2 Kgs 4:22
and I will **s** a letter to the king of 2 Kgs 5:5
that I may **s** and seize him." It was 2 Kgs 6:13
already perished. Let us **s** and see." 2 Kgs 7:13
a horseman and **s** to meet them, 2 Kgs 9:17
the LORD began to **s** Rezin the king of 2 Kgs 15:37
"**S** there one of the priests whom you 2 Kgs 17:27
let us **s** abroad to our brothers who 1 Chr 13:2
So now **s** me a man skilled to work in 2 Chr 2:7
S me also cedar, cypress, and algum 2 Chr 2:8
has spoken, let him **s** to his servants. 2 Chr 2:15
by whatever way you shall **s** them, 2 Chr 6:34
or **s** pestilence among my people, 2 Chr 7:13
and **s** back the captives from your 2 Chr 28:11
province Beyond the River, **s** greeting. Ezr 4:11
therefore we **s** and inform the king, Ezr 4:14
And let the king **s** us his pleasure in this Ezr 5:17
to **s** us ministers for the house of our Ezr 8:17
in your sight, that you **s** me to Judah, Neh 2:5
it pleased the king to **s** me when I had Neh 2:6
sweet wine and **s** portions to anyone Neh 8:10
and drink and to **s** portions and to Neh 8:12
a day on which they **s** gifts of food to one Est 9:19
and they would **s** and invite their three Jb 1:4
course, Job would **s** and consecrate them, Jb 1:5
his countenance, and **s** him away. Jb 14:20
the full God will **s** his burning anger Jb 20:23
They **s** out their little boys like a flock, Jb 21:11
Can you **s** forth lightnings, that they Jb 38:35
May he **s** you help from the sanctuary Ps 20:2
S out your light and your truth; let them Ps 43:3
He will **s** from heaven and save me; he Ps 57:3
Selah God will **s** out his steadfast love Ps 57:3
When you **s** forth your Spirit, they are Ps 104:30
them; **s** out your arrows and rout them! Ps 144:6
so is the sluggard to those who **s** him. Prv 10:26
faithful messenger to those who **s** him; Prv 25:13
voice of the Lord saying, "Whom shall I **s**, Is 6:8
go for us?" Then I said, "Here am I! **S** me." Is 6:8
Against a godless nation I **s** him, and Is 10:6
of hosts will **s** wasting sickness among Is 10:16
S the lamb to the ruler of the land, from Is 16:1
he will **s** them a savior and defender, Is 19:20
or deaf as my messenger whom I **s**? Is 42:19
"For your sake I **s** to Babylon and bring Is 43:14
it, **s** it out to the end of the earth; Is 48:20
from them I will **s** survivors to the Is 66:19
for to all to whom I **s** you, you shall go, Jer 1:7
see, or **s** to Kedar and examine with care; Jer 2:10
known, and I will **s** the sword after them, Jer 9:16
come; **s** for the skillful women to come; Jer 9:17
Her nobles **s** their servants for water; Jer 14:3
I did not **s** them, nor did I command Jer 14:14
in my name although I did not **s** them, Jer 14:15
S them out of my sight, and let them go! Jer 15:1
afterward I will **s** for many hunters, Jer 16:16
"I did not **s** the prophets, yet they ran; I Jer 23:21
when I did not **s** them or charge them. Jer 23:32
And I will **s** sword, famine, and Jer 24:10
I will **s** for all the tribes of the north, Jer 25:9
all the nations to whom I **s** you drink it. Jer 25:15
the prophets whom I **s** to you urgently, Jer 26:5
S word to the king of Edom, the king of Jer 27:3
name; I did not **s** them, declares the LORD. Jer 29:9
"**S** to all the exiles, saying, 'Thus says Jer 29:31
prophesied to you when I did not **s** him, Jer 29:31
before you and do not **s** me back to the Jer 37:20
that he would not **s** me back to the Jer 38:26
The LORD our God did not **s** you to say, Jer 43:2
I will **s** and take Nebuchadnezzar the Jer 43:10
when I shall **s** to him pourers who will Jer 48:12
I will **s** the sword after them, until I Jer 49:37
and I will **s** to Babylon winnowers, and Jer 51:2
of man, I **s** you to the people of Israel, Ezk 2:3
I **s** you to them, and you shall say to Ezk 2:4
when I **s** against you the deadly arrows Ezk 5:16
which I will **s** to destroy you, Ezk 5:16
I will **s** famine and wild beasts against Ezk 5:17
you, and I will **s** my anger upon you; Ezk 7:3
supply of bread and **s** famine upon it, Ezk 14:13
"Or if I **s** a pestilence into that land Ezk 14:19
more when I **s** upon Jerusalem my Ezk 14:21
for I will **s** pestilence into her, and Ezk 28:23
multitude of Egypt, and **s** them down, Ezk 32:18
and I will **s** down the showers in their Ezk 34:26
I will **s** fire on Magog and on those who Ezk 39:6
place one who shall **s** an exactor of Dn 11:20
so I will **s** a fire upon his cities, and it Hos 8:14
So I will **s** a fire upon the house of Am 1:4
So I will **s** a fire upon the wall of Gaza, Am 1:7
So I will **s** a fire upon the wall of Tyre, Am 1:10
So I will **s** a fire upon Teman, and it Am 1:12
So I will **s** a fire upon Moab, and it shall Am 2:2
So I will **s** a fire upon Judah, and it shall Am 2:5
I would **s** rain on one city, and send no Am 4:7
one city, and **s** no rain on another city; Am 4:7
and I will **s** you into exile beyond Am 5:27
"when I will **s** a famine on the land— Am 8:11
I will **s** it out, declares the LORD of hosts, Zec 5:4
then I will **s** the curse upon you and I Mal 2:2
I **s** my messenger and he will prepare the Mal 3:1
I will **s** you Elijah the prophet before the Mal 4:5
us out, **s** us away into the herd of pigs." Mt 8:31
of the harvest to **s** out laborers into his Mt 9:38
I **s** my messenger before your face, Mt 11:10
The Son of Man will **s** his angels, and Mt 13:41
s the crowds away to go into the Mt 14:15
and begged him, saying, "**S** her away, Mt 15:23
I am unwilling to **s** them away hungry, Mt 15:32
certificate of divorce and to **s** her away?" Mt 19:7
needs them,' and he will **s** them at once." Mt 21:3
Therefore I **s** you prophets and wise Mt 23:34
And he will **s** out his angels with a loud Mt 24:31
he will at once **s** me more than twelve Mt 26:53
I **s** my messenger before your face, Mk 1:2
him and he might **s** them out to preach Mk 3:14
him earnestly not to **s** them out of the Mk 5:10
begged him, saying, "**S** us to the pigs; Mk 5:12
twelve and began to **s** them out two by Mk 6:7
S them away to go into the surrounding Mk 6:36
And if I **s** them away hungry to their Mk 8:3
certificate of divorce and to **s** her away." Mk 10:4
of it and will **s** it back here Mk 11:3
And then he will **s** out the angels and Mk 13:27
I **s** my messenger before your face, Lk 7:27
"**S** the crowd away to go into the Lk 9:12
of the harvest to **s** out laborers into his Lk 10:2
'I will **s** them prophets and apostles, Lk 11:49
and **s** Lazarus to dip the end of his Lk 16:24
father, to **s** him to my father's house— Lk 16:27
I will **s** my beloved son; perhaps they Lk 20:13
For God did not **s** his Son into the world Jn 3:17
whoever receives the one I **s** receives me, Jn 13:20
whom the Father will **s** in my name, Jn 14:26
whom I will **s** to you from the Father, Jn 15:26
to you. But if I go, I will **s** him to you. Jn 16:7
and that he may **s** the Christ appointed Acts 3:20
And now come, I will **s** you to Egypt.' Acts 7:34
and I will **s** you into exile beyond Acts 7:43
And now **s** men to Joppa and bring one Acts 10:5
by a holy angel to **s** for you to come Acts 10:22
S therefore to Joppa and ask for Acts 10:32
'**S** to Joppa and bring Simon who is Acts 11:13
to **s** relief to the brothers living in Acts 11:29
among them and **s** them to Antioch Acts 15:22
to choose men and **s** them to you Acts 15:25
for I will **s** you far away to the Acts 22:21
held until I could **s** him to Caesar." Acts 25:21
I decided to go ahead and **s** him. Acts 25:25
For Christ did not **s** me to baptize but 1 Cor 1:17
I will **s** those whom you accredit by 1 Cor 16:3
churches of Asia **s** you greetings. 1 Cor 16:19
s you hearty greetings in the Lord. 1 Cor 16:19
All the brothers **s** you greetings. 1 Cor 16:20
Macedonia and have you **s** me on my 2 Cor 1:16
the Lord Jesus to **s** Timothy to you Phil 2:19
I hope therefore to **s** him just as soon as Phil 2:23
it necessary to **s** to you Epaphroditus Phil 2:25
I am the more eager to **s** him, therefore, Phil 2:28
When I **s** Artemas or Tychicus to you, Ti 3:12
All who are with me **s** greetings to you. Ti 3:15
who come from Italy **s** you greetings. Heb 13:24
will do well to **s** them on their journey 3 Jn 1:6
see in a book and **s** it to the seven Rv 1:11

SENDING (30)

for this wrong in **s** me away is 2 Sm 13:16
I am **s** to you a present of silver and 1 Kgs 15:19
Israel that you are **s** to inquire of 2 Kgs 1:6
Behold, I am **s** to you silver and gold. 2 Chr 16:3
days for **s** gifts of food to one another Est 9:22
For behold, I am **s** among you serpents, Jer 8:17
"Behold, I am **s** for many fishers, Jer 16:16
of the sword that I am **s** among them." Jer 25:16
of the sword that I am **s** among you.' Jer 25:27
of hosts, behold, I am **s** on them sword, Jer 29:17
the prophets, **s** them persistently, Jer 35:15
the LORD our God to whom we are **s** you, Jer 42:6
against him by **s** his ambassadors to Ezk 17:15
s forth its streams to all the trees of the Ezk 31:4
to his people, "Behold, I am **s** to you grain, Jl 2:19
I am **s** you out as sheep in the midst of Mt 10:16
And after **s** away the crowds, he got Mt 15:39
I am **s** you out as lambs in the midst of Lk 10:3
I am **s** the promise of my Father upon Lk 24:49
Father has sent me, even so I am **s** you." Jn 20:21
s it to the elders by the hand of Acts 11:30
to me unreasonable, in **s** a prisoner, Acts 25:27
the Gentiles—to whom I am **s** you Acts 26:17
By **s** his own Son in the likeness of Rom 8:3
With him we are **s** the brother who is 2 Cor 8:18
them we are **s** our brother whom 2 Cor 8:22
But I am **s** the brothers so that our 2 Cor 9:3
I am **s** him back to you, sending my Phlm 1:12
him back to you, **s** my very heart. Phlm 1:12
He made it known by **s** his angel to his Rv 1:1

SENDS (20)

it in her hand and **s** her out of his house, Dt 24:1
it in her hand and **s** her out of his house, Dt 24:3
day that the LORD **s** rain upon the 1 Kgs 17:14
that this man **s** word to me to cure a 2 Kgs 5:7
on the earth and **s** waters on the fields; Jb 5:10
the waters, they dry up; if he **s** them out, Jb 12:15
behold, he **s** out his voice, his mighty Ps 68:33
The LORD **s** forth from Zion your Ps 110:2
He **s** out his command to the earth; his Ps 147:15
He **s** out his word, and melts them; he Ps 147:18
Whoever **s** a message by the hand of a Prv 26:6
which **s** ambassadors by the sea, in Is 18:2
water, that **s** out its roots by the stream, Jer 17:8
which the LORD your God **s** you to us. Jer 42:5
and **s** rain on the just and on the unjust. Mt 5:45
he **s** a delegation and asks for terms of Lk 14:32
Therefore God **s** them a strong 2 Thes 2:11
Eubulus **s** greetings to you, as do 2 Tm 4:21
in Christ Jesus, **s** greetings to you, Phlm 1:23
who is likewise chosen, **s** you greetings, 1 Pt 5:13

SENEH (1)

Bozez, and the name of the other **S**. 1 Sm 14:4

SENIOR (2)

the secretary, and the **s** priests, 2 Kgs 19:2
Shebna the secretary, and the **s** priests, Is 37:2

SENIR (4)

Sirion, while the Amorites call it **S**), Dt 3:9
Baal-hermon, **S**, and Mount Hermon. 1 Chr 5:23
Amana, from the peak of **S** and Hermon, Sg 4:8
made all your planks of fir trees from **S**; Ezk 27:5

SENNACHERIB (13)

S king of Assyria came up against 2 Kgs 18:13
and hear the words of **S**, which he 2 Kgs 19:16
to me about **S** king of Assyria 2 Kgs 19:20
Then **S** king of Assyria departed and 2 Kgs 19:36
S king of Assyria came and invaded 2 Chr 32:1
Hezekiah saw that **S** had come and 2 Chr 32:2
After this, **S**, king of Assyria, who 2 Chr 32:9
"Thus says **S** king of Assyria, 'On 2 Chr 32:10
from the hand of **S** king of Assyria 2 Chr 32:22
S king of Assyria came up against all the Is 36:1
and hear all the words of **S**, which he Is 37:17
to me concerning **S** king of Assyria, Is 37:21
Then **S** king of Assyria departed and Is 37:37

SENSE (26)

Law of God, clearly, and they gave the **s**, Neh 8:8
He who commits adultery lacks **s**; he Prv 6:32
the youths, a young man lacking **s**, Prv 7:7
ones, learn prudence; O fools, learn **s**. Prv 8:5
in here!" To him who lacks **s** she says, Prv 9:4
here!" And to him who lacks **s** she says, Prv 9:16
rod is for the back of him who lacks **s**. Prv 10:13
feed many, but fools die for lack of **s**. Prv 10:21
belittles his neighbor lacks **s**, Prv 11:12
is commended according to his good **s**, Prv 12:8
follows worthless pursuits lacks **s**. Prv 12:11
Good **s** wins favor, but the way of the Prv 13:15
Folly is a joy to him who lacks **s**, but a Prv 15:21
Good **s** is a fountain of life to him who Prv 16:22
to buy wisdom when he has no **s**? Prv 17:16
One who lacks **s** gives a pledge and Prv 17:18
Whoever gets **s** loves his own soul; he Prv 19:8
Good **s** makes one slow to anger, and it Prv 19:11
from the way of good **s** will rest in the Prv 21:16
he will despise the good **s** of your words. Prv 23:9
by the vineyard of a man lacking **s**, Prv 24:30
the fool walks on the road, he lacks **s**, Eccl 10:3

"These are only the poor; they have no **s**; Jer 5:4
is like a dove, silly and without **s**, Hos 7:11
where would be the **s** of hearing? 1 Cor 12:17
ear, where would be the **s** of smell? 1 Cor 12:17

SENSELESS (4)
repay the LORD, you foolish and **s** people? Dt 32:6
A **s**, a nameless brood, they have been Jb 30:8
"Hear this, O foolish and **s** people, who Jer 5:21
into many **s** and harmful desires that 1 Tm 6:9

SENSIBLE (1)
I speak as to **s** people; judge for 1 Cor 10:15

SENSIBLY (1)
than seven men who can answer **s**. Prv 26:16

SENSUAL (2)
greatly distressed by the **s** conduct of the 2 Pt 2:7
they entice by **s** passions of the flesh 2 Pt 2:18

SENSUALITY (8)
coveting, wickedness, deceit, **s**, envy, Mk 7:22
not in sexual immorality and **s**, Rom 13:13
and **s** that they have practiced. 2 Cor 12:21
evident: sexual immorality, impurity, **s**, Gal 5:19
and have given themselves up to **s**, Eph 4:19
what the Gentiles want to do, living in **s**, 1 Pt 4:3
And many will follow their **s**, and 2 Pt 2:2
of our God into **s** and deny our only Jude 1:4

SENSUOUS (1)
puffed up without reason by his **s** mind, Col 2:18

SENT (669)
therefore the LORD God **s** him out from Gn 3:23
and **s** forth a raven. It went to and fro Gn 8:7
Then he **s** forth a dove from him, to see if Gn 8:8
and again he **s** forth the dove out of the Gn 8:10
another seven days and **s** forth the dove, Gn 8:12
and they **s** him away with his wife and Gn 12:20
and the LORD has **s** us to destroy it." Gn 19:13
remembered Abraham and **s** Lot out Gn 19:29
king of Gerar **s** and took Sarah. Gn 20:2
along with the child, and **s** her away. Gn 21:14
So they **s** away Rebekah their sister Gn 24:59
was still living he **s** them away from his Gn 25:6
hate me and have **s** me away from Gn 26:27
but good and have **s** you away in Gn 26:29
And Isaac **s** them on their way, and Gn 26:31
So she **s** and called Jacob her younger Gn 27:42
Thus Isaac **s** Jacob away. And he went Gn 28:5
had blessed Jacob and **s** him away to Gn 28:6
So Jacob **s** and called Rachel and Leah Gn 31:4
that I might have **s** you away with Gn 31:27
you would have **s** me away Gn 31:42
And Jacob **s** messengers before him to Gn 32:3
I have **s** to tell my lord, in order that I Gn 32:5
They are a present **s** to my lord Esau. Gn 32:18
He took them and **s** them across the Gn 32:23
me word." So he **s** him from the Valley Gn 37:14
And they **s** the robe of many colors Gn 37:32
When Judah **s** the young goat by his Gn 38:20
You see, I **s** this young goat, and you Gn 38:23
out, she **s** word to her father-in-law, Gn 38:25
and he **s** and called for all the Gn 41:8
Then Pharaoh **s** and called Joseph, and Gn 41:14
the men were **s** away with their donkeys. Gn 44:3
for God **s** me before you to preserve life. Gn 45:5
And God **s** me before you to preserve for Gn 45:7
So it was not you who **s** me here, but Gn 45:8
To his father he **s** as follows: ten Gn 45:23
Then he **s** his brothers away, and as Gn 45:24
wagons that Joseph had **s** to carry him, Gn 45:27
that Pharaoh had **s** to carry him. Gn 46:5
He had **s** Judah ahead of him to Joseph Gn 46:28
So they **s** a message to Joseph, saying, Gn 50:16
the reeds and **s** her servant woman, Ex 2:5
be the sign for you, that I have **s** you: Ex 3:12
God of your fathers has **s** me to you,' Ex 3:13
people of Israel, 'I AM has **s** me to you.'" Ex 3:14
and the God of Jacob, has **s** me to you.' Ex 3:15
LORD with which he had **s** him to speak, Ex 4:28
the God of the Hebrews, **s** me to you, Ex 7:16
And Pharaoh **s**, and behold, not one of the Ex 9:7
heaven, and the LORD **s** thunder and hail, Ex 9:23
Then Pharaoh **s** and called Moses and Ex 9:27
Moses' wife, after he had **s** her home, Ex 18:2
And when he **s** word to Moses, "I, your Ex 18:6
And he **s** young men of the people of Ex 24:5
Then the LORD **s** a plague on the people, Ex 32:35
that it may be **s** away into the Lv 16:10
So Moses **s** them from the wilderness of Nm 13:3
the men whom Moses **s** to spy out the Nm 13:16
Moses **s** them to spy out the land of Nm 13:17
came to the land to which you **s** us. Nm 13:27
the men whom Moses **s** to spy out the Nm 14:36
And Moses **s** to call Dathan and Nm 16:12
know that the LORD has **s** me to do all Nm 16:28
mankind, then the LORD has not **s** me. Nm 16:29
Moses **s** messengers from Kadesh to Nm 20:14
heard our voice and **s** an angel and Nm 20:16
Then the LORD **s** fiery serpents among Nm 21:6
Then Israel **s** messengers to Sihon Nm 21:21
And Moses **s** to spy out Jazer, and they Nm 21:32
s messengers to Balaam the son of Beor Nm 22:5
of Zippor, king of Moab, has **s** to me, Nm 22:10
Once again Balak **s** princes, more in Nm 22:15
and **s** for Balaam and for the princes Nm 22:40
your messengers whom you **s** to me, Nm 24:12
And Moses **s** them to the war, a Nm 31:6
when I **s** them from Kadesh-barnea to Nm 32:8
"So I **s** messengers from the wilderness of Dt 2:26
when the LORD **s** you from Dt 9:23
her former husband, who **s** her away, Dt 24:4
the wonders that the LORD **s** him to do in Dt 34:11
the son of Nun **s** two men secretly from Jos 2:1
Then the king of Jericho **s** to Rahab, Jos 2:3
words, so be it." Then she **s** them away, Jos 2:21
she hid the messengers whom we **s**. Jos 6:17
messengers whom Joshua **s** to spy out Jos 6:25
Joshua **s** men from Jericho to Ai, which is Jos 7:2
So Joshua **s** messengers, and they ran to Jos 7:22
men of valor and **s** them out by night. Jos 8:3
So Joshua **s** them out. And they went to Jos 8:9
king of Jerusalem **s** to Hoham king Jos 10:3
the men of Gibeon **s** to Joshua at the Jos 10:6
of this, he **s** to Jobab king of Madon, Jos 11:1
of the LORD **s** me from Kadesh-barnea Jos 14:7
as I was in the day that Moses **s** me; Jos 14:11
Joshua blessed them and **s** them away, Jos 22:6
And when Joshua **s** them away to their Jos 22:7
the people of Israel **s** to the people of Jos 22:13
And I **s** Moses and Aaron, and I plagued Jos 24:5
And he **s** and invited Balaam the son of Jos 24:9
And I **s** the hornet before you, which Jos 24:12
So Joshua **s** the people away, every man Jos 24:28
The people of Israel **s** tribute by him to Jgs 3:15
he **s** away the people who carried the Jgs 3:18
She **s** and summoned Barak the son of Jgs 4:6
She **s** her hand to the tent peg and her Jgs 5:26
the LORD **s** a prophet to the people of Israel. Jgs 6:8
And he **s** messengers throughout all Jgs 6:35
And he **s** messengers to Asher, Zebulun, Jgs 6:35
And he **s** all the rest of Israel every man to Jgs 7:8
Gideon **s** messengers throughout all the Jgs 7:24
And God **s** an evil spirit between Jgs 9:23
And he **s** messengers to Abimelech Jgs 9:31
Then Jephthah **s** messengers to the Jgs 11:12
Jephthah again **s** messengers to the Jgs 11:14
Israel then **s** messengers to the king of Jgs 11:17
And they **s** also to the king of Moab, Jgs 11:17
Israel then **s** messengers to Sihon king Jgs 11:19
the words of Jephthah that he **s** to him. Jgs 11:28
"Go." Then he **s** her away for two Jgs 11:38
of God whom you **s** come again to us Jgs 13:8
she **s** and called the lords of the Jgs 16:18
the people of Dan **s** five able men from Jgs 18:2
and **s** her throughout all the territory Jgs 19:29
her in pieces and **s** her throughout all Jgs 20:6
the tribes of Israel **s** men through all Jgs 20:12
So the congregation **s** 12,000 of their Jgs 21:10
the whole congregation **s** word to the Jgs 21:13
So the people **s** to Shiloh and brought 1 Sm 4:4
So they **s** and gathered together all the 1 Sm 5:8
So they **s** the ark of God to Ekron. But 1 Sm 5:10
They **s** therefore and gathered 1 Sm 5:11
So they **s** messengers to the 1 Sm 6:21
Then Samuel **s** all the people away, 1 Sm 10:25
in pieces and **s** them throughout all 1 Sm 11:7
LORD and the LORD **s** Moses and Aaron, 1 Sm 12:8
And the LORD **s** Jerubbaal and Barak 1 Sm 12:11
and the LORD **s** thunder and rain that 1 Sm 12:18
The rest of the people he **s** home, every 1 Sm 13:2
"The LORD **s** me to anoint you king 1 Sm 15:1
And the LORD **s** you on a mission and 1 Sm 15:18
the mission on which the LORD **s** me. 1 Sm 15:20
And he **s** and brought him in. Now 1 Sm 16:12
Therefore Saul **s** messengers to Jesse 1 Sm 16:19
a young goat and **s** them by David 1 Sm 16:20
And Saul **s** to Jesse, saying, "Let 1 Sm 16:22
them before Saul, and he **s** for him. 1 Sm 17:31
was successful wherever Saul **s** him, 1 Sm 18:5
Saul **s** messengers to David's house 1 Sm 19:11
And when Saul **s** messengers to take 1 Sm 19:14
Then Saul **s** the messengers to see 1 Sm 19:15
Then Saul **s** messengers to take 1 Sm 19:20
was told Saul, he **s** other messengers, 1 Sm 19:21
And Saul **s** messengers again the 1 Sm 19:21
then go, for the LORD has **s** you away. 1 Sm 20:22
Then the king **s** to summon 1 Sm 22:11
So David **s** ten young men. And David 1 Sm 25:5
David **s** messengers out of the 1 Sm 25:14
young men of my lord, whom you **s**. 1 Sm 25:25
who **s** you this day to meet me! 1 Sm 25:32
head." Then David **s** and spoke to 1 Sm 25:39
"David has **s** us to you to take you to 1 Sm 25:40
David **s** out spies and learned that 1 Sm 26:4
he **s** part of the spoil to his friends, 1 Sm 30:26
armor and **s** messengers throughout 1 Sm 31:9
David **s** messengers to the men of 2 Sm 2:5
And Abner **s** messengers to David on 2 Sm 3:12
Then David **s** messengers to 2 Sm 3:14
And Ish-bosheth **s** and took her from 2 Sm 3:15
heart desires." So David **s** Abner away, 2 Sm 3:21
at Hebron, for he had **s** him away, 2 Sm 3:22
Why is it that you have **s** him away, 2 Sm 3:24
presence, he **s** messengers after Abner, 2 Sm 3:26
king of Tyre **s** messengers to David, 2 Sm 5:11
Toi **s** his son Joram to King David, to 2 Sm 8:10
Then King David **s** and brought him 2 Sm 9:5
with me." So David **s** by his servants 2 Sm 10:2
because David has **s** comforters to 2 Sm 10:3
Has not David **s** his servants to you to 2 Sm 10:3
at their hips, and **s** them away. 2 Sm 10:4
it was told David, he **s** to meet them, 2 Sm 10:5
the Ammonites **s** and hired the 2 Sm 10:6
he **s** Joab and all the host of the 2 Sm 10:7
And Hadadezer **s** and brought out 2 Sm 10:16
kings go out to battle, David **s** Joab, 2 Sm 11:1
And David **s** and inquired about the 2 Sm 11:3
So David **s** messengers and took her, 2 Sm 11:4
conceived, and she **s** and told David, 2 Sm 11:5
So David **s** word to Joab, "Send me 2 Sm 11:6
Hittite." And Joab **s** Uriah to David. 2 Sm 11:6
a letter to Joab and **s** it by the hand of 2 Sm 11:14
Then Joab **s** and told David all the 2 Sm 11:18
David all that Joab had **s** him to tell. 2 Sm 11:22
David **s** and brought her to his 2 Sm 11:27
And the LORD **s** Nathan to David. He 2 Sm 12:1
and **s** a message by Nathan the 2 Sm 12:25
And Joab **s** messengers to David and 2 Sm 12:27
Then David **s** home to Tamar, saying, 2 Sm 13:7
And Joab **s** to Tekoa and brought 2 Sm 14:2
Then Absalom **s** for Joab, to send 2 Sm 14:29
And he **s** a second time, but Joab 2 Sm 14:29
Joab, "Behold, I **s** word to you, 2 Sm 14:32
But Absalom **s** secret messengers 2 Sm 15:10
he **s** for Ahithophel the Gilonite, 2 Sm 15:12
And David **s** out the army, one third 2 Sm 18:2
"When Joab **s** the king's servant, 2 Sm 18:29
And King David **s** this message to 2 Sm 19:11
man, so that they **s** word to the king, 2 Sm 19:14
And he **s** out arrows and scattered 2 Sm 22:15
"He **s** from on high, he took me; he 2 Sm 22:17
I shall return to him who **s** me." 2 Sm 24:13
So the LORD **s** a pestilence on Israel 2 Sm 24:15
and the king has **s** with him Zadok 1 Kgs 1:44
So King Solomon **s**, and they brought 1 Kgs 1:53
So King Solomon **s** Benaiah the son 1 Kgs 2:25
the altar," Solomon **s** Benaiah the son 1 Kgs 2:29
Then the king **s** and summoned 1 Kgs 2:36
the king **s** and summoned Shimei 1 Kgs 2:42
Hiram king of Tyre **s** his servants to 1 Kgs 5:1
And Solomon **s** word to Hiram, 1 Kgs 5:2
And Hiram **s** to Solomon, saying, "I 1 Kgs 5:8
the message that you have **s** to me. 1 Kgs 5:8
And he **s** them to Lebanon, 10,000 a 1 Kgs 5:14
And King Solomon **s** and brought 1 Kgs 7:13
the eighth day he **s** the people away, 1 Kgs 8:66
Hiram had **s** to the king 120 talents of 1 Kgs 9:14
And Hiram **s** with the fleet his 1 Kgs 9:27
And they **s** and called him, and 1 Kgs 12:3
Then King Rehoboam **s** Adoram, 1 Kgs 12:18
they **s** and called him to the 1 Kgs 12:20
And King Asa **s** them to Ben-hadad 1 Kgs 15:18
King Asa and **s** the commanders of 1 Kgs 15:20
where my lord has not **s** to seek you. 1 Kgs 18:10
So Ahab **s** to all the people of Israel 1 Kgs 18:20
Then Jezebel **s** a messenger to Elijah, 1 Kgs 19:2
And he **s** messengers into the city to 1 Kgs 20:2
'I **s** to you, saying, "Deliver to me your 1 Kgs 20:5
for he **s** to me for my wives and my 1 Kgs 20:7
Ben-hadad **s** to him and said, "The 1 Kgs 20:10
first. And Ben-hadad **s** out scouts, 1 Kgs 20:17
and she **s** the letters to the elders and 1 Kgs 21:8
did as Jezebel had **s** word to them. 1 Kgs 21:11
in the letters that she had **s** to them, 1 Kgs 21:11
Then they **s** to Jezebel, saying, 1 Kgs 21:14
so he **s** messengers, telling them, "Go, 2 Kgs 1:2
to us, 'Go back to the king who **s** you, 2 Kgs 1:6
Then the king **s** to him a captain of 2 Kgs 1:9
Again the king **s** to him another 2 Kgs 1:11
Again the king **s** the captain of a 2 Kgs 1:13
'Because you have **s** messengers to 2 Kgs 1:16
for the LORD has **s** me as far as Bethel." 2 Kgs 2:2
for the LORD has **s** me to Jericho." But 2 Kgs 2:4
for the LORD has **s** me to the Jordan." 2 Kgs 2:6
"Send." They **s** therefore fifty men. 2 Kgs 2:17

he went and **s** word to Jehoshaphat 2 Kgs 3:7
know that I have **s** to you Naaman my 2 Kgs 5:6
had torn his clothes, he **s** to the king, 2 Kgs 5:8
And Elisha **s** a messenger to him, 2 Kgs 5:10
is well. My master has **s** me to say, 2 Kgs 5:22
in the house, and he **s** the men away, 2 Kgs 5:24
But the man of God **s** word to the king 2 Kgs 6:9
the king of Israel **s** to the place about 2 Kgs 6:10
So he **s** there horses and chariots and 2 Kgs 6:14
eaten and drunk, he **s** them away, 2 Kgs 6:23
how this murderer has **s** to take off 2 Kgs 6:32
and the king **s** them after the army of 2 Kgs 7:14
king of Syria has **s** me to you, 2 Kgs 8:9
Then he **s** out a second horseman, 2 Kgs 9:19
wrote letters and **s** them to Samaria, 2 Kgs 10:1
elders and the guardians, **s** to Jehu, 2 Kgs 10:5
heads in baskets and **s** them to him 2 Kgs 10:7
And Jehu **s** throughout all Israel, 2 Kgs 10:21
seventh year Jehoiada **s** and brought 2 Kgs 11:4
and **s** these to Hazael king of Syria. 2 Kgs 12:18
Then Amaziah **s** messengers to 2 Kgs 14:8
king of Israel **s** word to Amaziah 2 Kgs 14:9
"A thistle on Lebanon **s** to a cedar on 2 Kgs 14:9
But they **s** after him to Lachish and 2 Kgs 14:19
So Ahaz **s** messengers to 2 Kgs 16:7
the king's house and **s** a present to the 2 Kgs 16:8
And King Ahaz **s** to Uriah the priest 2 Kgs 16:10
King Ahaz had **s** from Damascus, 2 Kgs 16:11
for he had **s** messengers to So, 2 Kgs 17:4
and that I **s** to you by my servants 2 Kgs 17:13
Therefore the LORD **s** lions among 2 Kgs 17:25
Therefore he has **s** lions among 2 Kgs 17:26
Hezekiah king of Judah **s** to the king 2 Kgs 18:14
the king of Assyria **s** the Tartan, 2 Kgs 18:17
"Has my master **s** me to speak these 2 Kgs 18:27
And he **s** Eliakim, who was over the 2 Kgs 19:2
king of Assyria has **s** to mock the 2 Kgs 19:4
you." So he **s** messengers again to 2 Kgs 19:9
which he has **s** to mock the living 2 Kgs 19:16
the son of Amoz **s** to Hezekiah, 2 Kgs 19:20
s envoys with letters and a present to 2 Kgs 20:12
the king **s** Shaphan the son of 2 Kgs 22:3
'Tell the man who **s** you to me, 2 Kgs 22:15
who **s** you to inquire of the LORD, 2 Kgs 22:18
Then the king **s**, and all the elders of 2 Kgs 23:1
And he **s** and took the bones out of 2 Kgs 23:16
And the LORD **s** against him bands of 2 Kgs 24:2
and **s** them against Judah to destroy 2 Kgs 24:2
when the LORD **s** Judah and Jerusalem 1 Chr 6:15
after he had **s** away Hushim and 1 Chr 8:8
and **s** messengers throughout the 1 Chr 10:9
took counsel and **s** him away, 1 Chr 12:19
king of Tyre **s** messengers to David, 1 Chr 14:1
he **s** his son Hadoram to King 1 Chr 18:10
And he **s** all sorts of articles of gold, 1 Chr 18:10
me." So David **s** messengers to 1 Chr 19:2
because David has **s** comforters to 1 Chr 19:3
at their hips, and **s** them away; 1 Chr 19:4
men, he **s** messengers to meet them, 1 Chr 19:5
and the Ammonites **s** 1,000 talents of 1 Chr 19:6
he **s** Joab and all the army of the 1 Chr 19:8
they **s** messengers and brought out 1 Chr 19:16
I shall return to him who **s** me." 1 Chr 21:12
So the LORD **s** a pestilence on Israel, 1 Chr 21:14
And God **s** the angel to Jerusalem to 1 Chr 21:15
And Solomon **s** word to Hiram the 2 Chr 2:3
David my father and **s** him cedar to 2 Chr 2:3
in a letter that he **s** to Solomon, 2 Chr 2:11
"Now I have **s** a skilled man, who has 2 Chr 2:13
seventh month he **s** the people away 2 Chr 7:10
And Hiram **s** to him by the hand of 2 Chr 8:18
And they **s** and called him. And 2 Chr 10:3
Then King Rehoboam **s** Hadoram, 2 Chr 10:18
Jeroboam had **s** an ambush around 2 Chr 13:13
king's house and **s** them to 2 Chr 16:2
King Asa and **s** the commanders of 2 Chr 16:4
year of his reign he **s** his officials, 2 Chr 17:7
Yet he **s** prophets among them to 2 Chr 24:19
the people and **s** all their spoil 2 Chr 24:23
of the army whom Amaziah **s** back, 2 Chr 25:13
angry with Amaziah and **s** to him a 2 Chr 25:15
took counsel and **s** to Joash the 2 Chr 25:17
the king of Israel **s** word to Amaziah 2 Chr 25:18
"A thistle on Lebanon **s** to a cedar 2 Chr 25:18
But they **s** after him to Lachish and 2 Chr 25:27
that time King Ahaz **s** to the king of 2 Chr 28:16
Hezekiah **s** to all Israel and Judah, 2 Chr 30:1
s his servants to Jerusalem to 2 Chr 32:9
And the LORD **s** an angel, who cut off 2 Chr 32:21
who had been **s** to him to inquire 2 Chr 32:31
he **s** Shaphan the son of Azaliah, 2 Chr 34:8
the king had **s** went to Huldah 2 Chr 34:22
'Tell the man who **s** you to me, 2 Chr 34:23
who **s** you to inquire of the LORD, 2 Chr 34:26
Then the king **s** and gathered 2 Chr 34:29
But he **s** envoys to him, saying, 2 Chr 35:21
King Nebuchadnezzar **s** and 2 Chr 36:10
s persistently to them by his 2 Chr 36:15
(This is a copy of the letter that they **s**.) Ezr 4:11
The king **s** an answer: "To Rehum the Ezr 4:17
the letter that you **s** to us has been Ezr 4:18
province Beyond the River **s** to Darius the Ezr 5:6
They **s** him a report, in which was Ezr 5:7
according to the word **s** by Darius the Ezr 6:13
For you are **s** by the king and his seven Ezr 7:14
Then I **s** for Eliezer, Ariel, Shemaiah, Ezr 8:16
and **s** them to Iddo, the leading man at Ezr 8:17
Now the king had **s** with me officers of Neh 2:9
Sanballat and Geshem **s** to me, saying, Neh 6:2
And I **s** messengers to them, saying, "I Neh 6:3
And they **s** to me four times in this way, Neh 6:4
for the fifth time **s** his servant to me Neh 6:5
Then I **s** to him, saying, "No such Neh 6:8
and saw that God had not **s** him, Neh 6:12
the nobles of Judah **s** many letters to Neh 6:17
And Tobiah **s** letters to make me Neh 6:19
He **s** letters to all the royal provinces, to Est 1:22
Letters were **s** by couriers to all the Est 3:13
She **s** garments to clothe Mordecai, so Est 4:4
and he **s** and brought his friends and Est 5:10
Then he **s** the letters by mounted Est 8:10
recorded these things and **s** letters to all Est 9:20
Letters were **s** to all the Jews, to the 127 Est 9:30
You have **s** widows away empty, and the Jb 22:9
And he **s** out his arrows and scattered Ps 18:14
He **s** from on high, he took me; he drew Ps 18:16
when Saul **s** men to watch his house in Ps 59:T
angels; he **s** them food in abundance. Ps 78:25
He **s** among them swarms of flies, Ps 78:45
It **s** out its branches to the sea and its Ps 80:11
he had **s** a man ahead of them, Joseph, Ps 105:17
The king **s** and released him; the ruler Ps 105:20
He **s** Moses, his servant, and Aaron, Ps 105:26
He **s** darkness, and made the land Ps 105:28
but **s** a wasting disease among them. Ps 106:15
He **s** out his word and healed them, Ps 107:20
He **s** redemption to his people; he has Ps 111:9
s signs and wonders against Pharaoh Ps 135:9
She has **s** out her young women to call Prv 9:3
cruel messenger will be **s** against him. Prv 17:11
give a true answer to those who **s** you? Prv 22:21
The Lord has **s** a word against Jacob, and Is 9:8
who was **s** by Sargon the king of Assyria, Is 20:1
the king of Assyria **s** the Rabshakeh from Is 36:2
"Has my master **s** me to speak these Is 36:12
And he **s** Eliakim, who was over the Is 37:2
king of Assyria has **s** to mock the living Is 37:4
he heard it, he **s** messengers to Hezekiah, Is 37:9
which he has **s** to mock the living God. Is 37:17
Isaiah the son of Amoz **s** to Hezekiah, Is 37:21
s envoys with letters and a present to Is 39:1
there." And now the Lord GOD has **s** me, Is 48:16
of divorce, with which I **s** her away? Is 50:1
transgressions your mother was **s** away. Is 50:1
succeed in the thing for which I **s** it. Is 55:11
you **s** your envoys far off, and sent down Is 57:9
envoys far off, and **s** down even to Sheol. Is 57:9
he has **s** me to bind up the Is 61:1
I had **s** her away with a decree of divorce. Jer 3:8
I have persistently **s** all my servants the Jer 7:25
where the LORD had **s** him to prophesy, Jer 19:14
when King Zedekiah **s** to him Pashhur Jer 21:1
burden of the LORD," when I **s** to you, Jer 23:38
whom I have **s** away from this place to Jer 24:5
the LORD persistently **s** to you all Jer 25:4
to whom the LORD **s** me drink it: Jer 25:17
"The LORD **s** me to prophesy against Jer 26:12
for in truth the LORD **s** me to you to Jer 26:15
Then King Jehoiakim **s** to Egypt Jer 26:22
I have not **s** them, declares the LORD, Jer 27:15
that the LORD has truly **s** the prophet." Jer 28:9
Hananiah, the LORD has not **s** you, Jer 28:15
Jeremiah the prophet **s** from Jerusalem Jer 29:1
The letter was **s** by the hand of Elasah Jer 29:3
Zedekiah king of Judah **s** to Babylon to Jer 29:3
exiles whom I have **s** into exile from Jer 29:4
of the city where I have **s** you into exile, Jer 29:7
the place from which I **s** you into exile. Jer 29:14
that I persistently **s** to you by my Jer 29:19
exiles whom I **s** away from Jerusalem Jer 29:20
You have **s** letters in your name to all Jer 29:25
For he has **s** to us in Babylon, saying, Jer 29:28
I have **s** to you all my servants the Jer 35:15
Then all the officials **s** Jehudi the son of Jer 36:14
Then the king **s** Jehudi to get the scroll, Jer 36:21
King Zedekiah **s** Jehucal the son of Jer 37:3
the king of Judah who **s** you to me to Jer 37:7
King Zedekiah **s** for him and received Jer 37:17
King Zedekiah **s** for Jeremiah the Jer 38:14
s and took Jeremiah from the court of Jer 39:14
the Ammonites has **s** Ishmael the son Jer 40:14
to whom you **s** me to present your plea Jer 42:9
For you **s** me to the LORD your God, Jer 42:20
in anything that he **s** me to tell you. Jer 42:21
the LORD their God had **s** him to them, Jer 43:1
Yet I persistently **s** to you all my servants Jer 44:4
envoy has been **s** among the nations: Jer 49:14
"From on high he **s** fire; into my Lam 1:13
For you are not **s** to a people of foreign Ezk 3:5
Surely, if I **s** you to such, they would Ezk 3:6
LORD,' when the LORD has not **s** them, Ezk 13:6
there they **s** up their pleasing aromas, Ezk 20:28
after them and **s** messengers to them Ezk 23:16
They even **s** for men to come from Ezk 23:40
afar, to whom a messenger was **s**; Ezk 23:40
because I **s** them into exile among the Ezk 39:28
Then King Nebuchadnezzar **s** to gather Dn 3:2
who has **s** his angel and delivered his Dn 3:28
from his presence the hand was **s**, Dn 5:24
My God **s** his angel and shut the lions' Dn 6:22
now I have been **s** to you." And when Dn 10:11
went to Assyria, and **s** to the great king. Hos 5:13
my great army, which I **s** among you. Jl 2:25
"I **s** among you a pestilence after the Am 4:10
the priest of Bethel **s** to Jeroboam king Am 7:10
messenger has been **s** among the nations: Ob 1:1
of slavery, and I **s** before you Moses, Mi 6:4
as the LORD their God had **s** him. Hg 1:12
whom the LORD has **s** to patrol the Zec 1:10
after his glory **s** me to the nations who Zec 2:8
know that the LORD of hosts has **s** me. Zec 2:9
that the LORD of hosts has **s** me to you. Zec 2:11
that the LORD of hosts has **s** me to you. Zec 4:9
that the LORD of hosts has **s** me to you. Zec 6:15
of Bethel had **s** Sharezer and Zec 7:2
LORD of hosts had **s** by his Spirit Zec 7:12
know that I have **s** this command to Mal 2:4
And he **s** them to Bethlehem, saying, "Go Mt 2:8
and he **s** and killed all the male children Mt 2:16
These twelve Jesus **s** out, instructing Mt 10:5
receives me receives him who **s** me. Mt 10:40
of the Christ, he **s** word by his disciples Mt 11:2
He **s** and had John beheaded in the Mt 14:10
they **s** around to all that region and Mt 14:35
"I was **s** only to the lost sheep of the Mt 15:24
a day, he **s** them into his vineyard. Mt 20:2
of Olives, then Jesus **s** two disciples, Mt 21:1
he **s** his servants to the tenants to get Mt 21:34
Again he **s** other servants, more than Mt 21:36
Finally he **s** his son to them, saying, Mt 21:37
and **s** his servants to call those who were Mt 22:3
Again he **s** other servants, saying, 'Tell Mt 22:4
and he **s** his troops and destroyed those Mt 22:7
And they **s** their disciples to him, along Mt 22:16
and stones those who are **s** to it! Mt 23:37
judgment seat, his wife **s** word to him, Mt 27:19
sternly charged him and **s** him away at Mk 1:43
and standing outside they **s** to him and Mk 3:31
was Herod who had **s** and seized John Mk 6:17
immediately the king **s** an executioner Mk 6:27
thousand people. And he **s** them away. Mk 8:9
And he **s** him to his home, saying, "Do Mk 8:26
me, receives not me but him who **s** me." Mk 9:37
of Olives, Jesus **s** two of his disciples Mk 11:1
he **s** a servant to the tenants to get from Mk 12:2
beat him and **s** him away Mk 12:3
Again he **s** to them another servant, Mk 12:4
And he **s** another, and him they killed. Mk 12:5
Finally he **s** him to them, saying, 'They Mk 12:6
And they **s** to him some of the Mk 12:13
And he **s** two of his disciples and said Mk 14:13
and I was **s** to speak to you and to bring Lk 1:19
the angel Gabriel was **s** from God to a Lk 1:26
and the rich he has **s** empty away. Lk 1:53
He has **s** me to proclaim liberty to the Lk 4:18
and Elijah was **s** to none of them but Lk 4:26
as well; for I was **s** for this purpose." Lk 4:43
about Jesus, he **s** to him elders of the Jews, Lk 7:3
from the house, the centurion **s** friends, Lk 7:6
those who had been **s** returned to the Lk 7:10
his disciples to him, **s** them to the Lord, Lk 7:19
said, "John the Baptist has **s** us to you, Lk 7:20
be with him, but Jesus **s** him away, Lk 8:38
and he **s** them out to proclaim the Lk 9:2
receives me receives him who **s** me. Lk 9:48
And he **s** messengers ahead of him, who Lk 9:52
seventy-two others and **s** them on ahead Lk 10:1
who rejects me rejects him who **s** me." Lk 10:16
and stones those who are **s** to it! Lk 13:34
him and healed him and **s** him away. Lk 14:4
for the banquet he **s** his servant to say Lk 14:17
who **s** him into his fields to feed pigs. Lk 15:15
hated him and **s** a delegation after Lk 19:14
is called Olivet, he **s** two of the disciples, Lk 19:29
So those who were **s** went away and Lk 19:32

came, he **s** a servant to the tenants, Lk 20:10
beat him and **s** him away Lk 20:10
And he **s** another servant. But they also Lk 20:11
and **s** him away empty-handed. Lk 20:11
And he **s** yet a third. This one also they Lk 20:12
So they watched him and **s** spies, who Lk 20:20
So Jesus **s** Peter and John, saying, "Go Lk 22:8
"When I **s** you out with no moneybag Lk 22:35
jurisdiction, he **s** him over to Herod, Lk 23:7
clothing, he **s** him back to Pilate. Lk 23:11
did Herod, for he **s** him back to us. Lk 23:15
There was a man **s** from God, whose name Jn 1:6
when the Jews **s** priests and Levites from Jn 1:19
need to give an answer to those who **s** us. Jn 1:22
they had been **s** from the Pharisees.) Jn 1:24
but he who **s** me to baptize with water Jn 1:33
the Christ, but I have been **s** before him.' Jn 3:28
he whom God has **s** utters the words of Jn 3:34
will of him who **s** me and to accomplish Jn 4:34
I **s** you to reap that for which you did not Jn 4:38
does not honor the Father who **s** him. Jn 5:23
and believes him who **s** me has eternal Jn 5:24
own will but the will of him who **s** me. Jn 5:30
You **s** to John, and he has borne witness Jn 5:33
about me that the Father has **s** me. Jn 5:36
And the Father who **s** me has himself Jn 5:37
do not believe the one whom he has **s**. Jn 5:38
that you believe in him whom he has **s**." Jn 6:29
own will but the will of him who **s** me. Jn 6:38
And this is the will of him who **s** me, that Jn 6:39
unless the Father who **s** me draws him. Jn 6:44
As the living Father **s** me, and I live Jn 6:57
teaching is not mine, but his who **s** me. Jn 7:16
seeks the glory of him who **s** him is true, Jn 7:18
He who **s** me is true, and him you do not Jn 7:28
him, for I come from him, and he **s** me." Jn 7:29
priests and Pharisees **s** officers to arrest Jn 7:32
and then I am going to him who **s** me. Jn 7:33
judge, but I and the Father who **s** me. Jn 8:16
and the Father who **s** me bears witness Jn 8:18
much to judge, but he who **s** me is true, Jn 8:26
And he who **s** me is with me. He has not Jn 8:29
came not of my own accord, but he **s** me. Jn 8:42
the works of him who **s** me while it is day; Jn 9:4
in the pool of Siloam" (which means **S**). Jn 9:7
Father consecrated and **s** into the world, Jn 10:36
So the sisters **s** to him, saying, "Lord, he Jn 11:3
that they may believe that you **s** me." Jn 11:42
believes not in me but in him who **s** me. Jn 12:44
whoever sees me sees him who **s** me. Jn 12:45
but the Father who **s** me has himself Jn 12:49
greater than the one who **s** him. Jn 13:16
receives me receives the one who **s** me." Jn 13:20
is not mine but the Father's who **s** me. Jn 14:24
they do not know him who **s** me. Jn 15:21
But now I am going to him who **s** me, Jn 16:5
God, and Jesus Christ whom you have **s**. Jn 17:3
and they have believed that you **s** me. Jn 17:8
As you **s** me into the world, so I have Jn 17:18
world, so I have **s** them into the world. Jn 17:18
world may believe that you have **s** me. Jn 17:21
may know that you **s** me and loved Jn 17:23
and these know that you have **s** me. Jn 17:25
Annas then **s** him bound to Caiaphas Jn 18:24
As the Father has **s** me, even so I am Jn 20:21
up his servant, **s** him to you first, Acts 3:26
senate of Israel and **s** to the prison to Acts 5:21
he **s** out our fathers on their first visit. Acts 7:12
And Joseph **s** and summoned Jacob Acts 7:14
—this man God **s** as both ruler and Acts 7:35
of God, they **s** to them Peter and John, Acts 8:14
which you came has **s** me so that you Acts 9:17
down to Caesarea and **s** him off to Acts 9:30
that Peter was there, **s** two men to him, Acts 9:38
everything to them, he **s** them to Joppa. Acts 10:8
the men who were **s** by Cornelius, Acts 10:17
without hesitation, for I have **s** them." Acts 10:20
So when I was **s** for, I came without Acts 10:29
I ask then why you **s** for me." Acts 10:29
So I **s** for you at once, and you have Acts 10:33
As for the word that he **s** to Israel, Acts 10:36
we were, **s** to me from Caesarea. Acts 11:11
and they **s** Barnabas to Antioch. Acts 11:22
that the Lord has **s** his angel and Acts 12:11
their hands on them and **s** them off. Acts 13:3
So, being **s** out by the Holy Spirit, they Acts 13:4
of the synagogue **s** a message to Acts 13:15
to us has been **s** the message of this Acts 13:26
being **s** on their way by the church, Acts 15:3
They **s** Judas called Barsabbas, and Acts 15:22
We have therefore **s** Judas and Silas, Acts 15:27
So when they were **s** off, they went Acts 15:30
they were **s** off in peace by the Acts 15:33
the brothers to those who had **s** them. Acts 15:33
was day, the magistrates **s** the police, Acts 16:35
"The magistrates have **s** to let you go. Acts 16:36
The brothers immediately **s** Paul and Acts 17:10
the brothers immediately **s** Paul off Acts 17:14
And having **s** into Macedonia two of Acts 19:22
s to him and were urging him not to Acts 19:31
uproar ceased, Paul **s** for the disciples, Acts 20:1
from Miletus he **s** to Ephesus and Acts 20:17
we have **s** a letter with our judgment Acts 21:25
the man, I **s** him to you at once, Acts 23:30
and he **s** for Paul and heard him Acts 24:24
So he **s** for him often and conversed Acts 24:26
of God has been **s** to the Gentiles; Acts 28:28
are they to preach unless they are **s**? Rom 10:15
That is why I **s** you Timothy, my 1 Cor 4:17
any of those whom I **s** to you? 2 Cor 12:17
to go, and **s** the brother with him. 2 Cor 12:18
of time had come, God **s** forth his Son, Gal 4:4
God has **s** the Spirit of his Son into our Gal 4:6
I have **s** him to you for this very Eph 6:22
in Thessalonica you **s** me help for Phil 4:16
from Epaphroditus the gifts you **s**, Phil 4:18
I have **s** him to you for this very purpose, Col 4:8
and we **s** Timothy, our brother and 1 Thes 3:2
longer, I **s** to learn about your faith, 1 Thes 3:5
Tychicus I have **s** to Ephesus. 2 Tm 4:12
not all ministering spirits **s** out to serve Heb 1:14
the messengers and **s** them out by Jas 2:25
you by the Holy Spirit **s** from heaven, 1 Pt 1:12
or to governors as **s** by him to punish 1 Pt 2:14
that God **s** his only Son into the world, 1 Jn 4:9
that he loved us and **s** his Son to be the 1 Jn 4:10
that the Father has **s** his Son to be 1 Jn 4:14
the seven spirits of God **s** out into all the Rv 5:6
has **s** his angel to show his servants Rv 22:6
have **s** my angel to testify to you about Rv 22:16

SENTENCE (15)
be judge and give **s** between me and 1 Sm 24:15
at Riblah, and they passed **s** on him. 2 Kgs 25:6
Because the **s** against an evil deed is Eccl 8:11
"This man deserves the **s** of death, Jer 26:11
man does not deserve the **s** of death, Jer 26:16
land of Hamath; and he passed **s** on him. Jer 39:5
land of Hamath, and he passed **s** on him. Jer 52:9
on them with the **s** of adulteresses, Ezk 23:45
and with the **s** of women who shed Ezk 23:45
known to me, there is but one **s** for you. Dn 2:9
The **s** is by the decree of the watchers, Dn 4:17
are under the same **s** of condemnation? Lk 23:40
asking for a **s** of condemnation Acts 25:15
will carry out his **s** upon the earth Rom 9:28
felt that we had received the **s** of death. 2 Cor 1:9

SENTENCED (2)
how are you to escape being **s** to hell? Mt 23:33
as last of all, like men **s** to death, 1 Cor 4:9

SENTRIES (2)
and **s** before the door were guarding Acts 12:6
he examined the **s** and ordered that Acts 12:19

SENTRY (1)
a **s** there named Irijah the son of Jer 37:13

SEORIM (1)
the third to Harim, the fourth to **S**, 1 Chr 24:8

SEPARATE (30)
and let it **s** the waters from the waters." Gn 1:6
of the heavens to **s** the day from the Gn 1:14
and to **s** the light from the darkness. Gn 1:18
land before you? **S** yourself from me. Gn 13:9
they shall be **s** beneath, but joined at Ex 26:24
And the veil shall **s** for you the Holy Ex 26:33
And they were **s** beneath but joined at Ex 36:29
people of Israel **s** from their Lv 15:31
You shall therefore **s** the clean beast Lv 20:25
of a Nazirite, to **s** himself to the LORD, Nm 6:2
he shall **s** himself from wine and strong Nm 6:3
and **s** himself to the LORD for the days of Nm 6:12
"Thus you shall **s** the Levites from Nm 8:14
"**S** yourselves from among this Nm 16:21
There was no one to **s** them, and one 2 Sm 14:6
of his death, and he lived in a **s** house. 2 Kgs 15:5
and being a leper lived in a **s** house, 2 Chr 26:21
S yourselves from the peoples of the Ezr 10:11
"The LORD will surely **s** me from his Is 56:3
that was facing the **s** yard on the west Ezk 41:12
were opposite the **s** yard and opposite Ezk 42:1
It shall be **s** from the property of the Ezk 48:22
will come out and **s** the evil from the Mt 13:49
God has joined together, let not man **s**." Mt 19:6
and he will **s** people one from another Mt 25:32
God has joined together, let not man **s**." Mk 10:9
Who shall **s** us from the love of Rom 8:35
will be able to **s** us from the love of Rom 8:39
wife should not **s** from her husband 1 Cor 7:10
from their midst, and be **s** from them, 2 Cor 6:17

SEPARATED (23)
And God **s** the light from the darkness. Gn 1:4
made the expanse and **s** the waters that Gn 1:7
east. Thus they **s** from each other. Gn 13:11
to Abram, after Lot had **s** from him, Gn 13:14
And Jacob **s** the lambs and set the Gn 30:40
God, who have **s** you from the peoples. Lv 20:24
am holy and have **s** you from the Lv 20:26
God of Israel has **s** you from the Nm 16:9
which Moses **s** from that of the men Nm 31:42
Heber the Kenite had **s** from the Kenites, Jgs 4:11
For you **s** them from among all the 1 Kgs 8:53
and horses of fire **s** the two of them. 2 Kgs 2:11
had joined them and **s** himself from the Ezr 6:21
Levites have not **s** themselves from the Ezr 9:1
widely spread, and we are **s** on the wall, Neh 4:19
And the Israelites **s** themselves from all Neh 9:2
all who have **s** themselves from the Neh 10:28
they **s** from Israel all those of foreign Neh 13:3
they clasp each other and cannot be **s**. Jb 41:17
so that they **s** from each other. Acts 15:39
they came he drew back and **s** himself, Gal 2:12
you were at that time **s** from Christ, Eph 2:12
innocent, unstained, **s** from sinners, Heb 7:26

SEPARATES (7)
completed for which he **s** himself to the Nm 6:5
the days that he **s** himself to the LORD Nm 6:6
strife, and a whisperer **s** close friends. Prv 16:28
he who repeats a matter **s** close friends. Prv 17:9
in Israel, who **s** himself from me, Ezk 14:7
another as a shepherd **s** the sheep from Mt 25:32
But if the unbelieving partner **s**, let it 1 Cor 7:15

SEPARATION (9)
All the days of his **s** he shall eat nothing Nm 6:4
"All the days of his vow of **s**, no razor Nm 6:5
because his **s** to God is on his head. Nm 6:7
All the days of his **s** he is holy to the Nm 6:8
for the days of his **s** and bring a male Nm 6:12
shall be void, because his **s** was defiled. Nm 6:12
the time of his **s** has been completed: Nm 6:13
iniquities have made a **s** between you and Is 59:2
to make a **s** between the holy and the Ezk 42:20

SEPHAR (1)
in the direction of **S** to the hill country Gn 10:30

SEPHARAD (1)
Jerusalem who are in **S** shall possess the Ob 1:20

SEPHARVAIM (6)
Cuthah, Avva, Hamath, and **S**, 2 Kgs 17:24
and Anammelech, the gods of **S**. 2 Kgs 17:31
Where are the gods of **S**, Hena, and 2 Kgs 18:34
of Arpad, the king of the city of **S**, 2 Kgs 19:13
and Arpad? Where are the gods of **S**? Is 36:19
king of Arpad, the king of the city of **S**, Is 37:13

SEPHARVITES (1)
and the **S** burned their children in 2 Kgs 17:31

SERAH (3)
Ishvi, Beriah, with **S** their sister. Gn 46:17
name of the daughter of Asher was **S**. Nm 26:46
Ishvi, Beriah, and their sister **S**. 1 Chr 7:30

SERAIAH (20)
were priests, and **S** was secretary, 2 Sm 8:17
of the guard took **S** the chief priest 2 Kgs 25:18
and **S** the son of Tanhumeth the 2 Kgs 25:23
The sons of Kenaz: Othniel and **S**; 1 Chr 4:13
and **S** fathered Joab, the father of 1 Chr 4:14
Jehu the son of Joshibiah, son of **S**, 1 Chr 4:35
Azariah fathered **S**, Seraiah fathered 1 Chr 6:14
Seraiah, **S** fathered Jehozadak; 1 Chr 6:14
Jeshua, Nehemiah, **S**, Reelaiah, Ezr 2:2
king of Persia, Ezra the son of **S**, Ezr 7:1
S, Azariah, Jeremiah, Neh 10:2
S the son of Hilkiah, son of Neh 11:11
Shealtiel, and Jeshua: **S**, Jeremiah, Ezra, Neh 12:1
priests, heads of fathers' houses: of **S**, Neh 12:12
the king's son and **S** the son of Azriel Jer 36:26
son of Kareah, **S** the son of Tanhumeth, Jer 40:8
the prophet commanded **S** the son of Jer 51:59
of his reign. **S** was the quartermaster. Jer 51:59
And Jeremiah said to **S**: "When you Jer 51:61
of the guard took **S** the chief priest, Jer 52:24

SERAPHIM (2)
Above him stood the **s**. Each had six Is 6:2
Then one of the **s** flew to me, having in his Is 6:6

SERED (2)
sons of Zebulun: **S**, Elon, and Jahleel. Gn 46:14
according to their clans: of **S**, Nm 26:26

SEREDITES (1)
their clans: of Sered, the clan of the **S**; Nm 26:26

SERGIUS (1)
He was with the proconsul, **S** Paulus, a Acts 13:7

SERIOUS (2)
or blind or has any **s** blemish whatever, Dt 15:21
bringing many and **s** charges against Acts 25:7

SERPENT (38)
Now the **s** was more crafty than any Gn 3:1
And the woman said to the **s**, "We may Gn 3:2
But the **s** said to the woman, "You will Gn 3:4
The woman said, "The **s** deceived me, Gn 3:13
The LORD God said to the **s**, "Because Gn 3:14
Dan shall be a **s** in the way, a viper by Gn 49:17
threw it on the ground, and it became a **s**, Ex 4:3
before Pharaoh, that it may become a **s**.'" Ex 7:9
and his servants, and it became a **s**. Ex 7:10
your hand the staff that turned into a **s**. Ex 7:15
"Make a fiery **s** and set it on a pole, Nm 21:8
So Moses made a bronze **s** and set it on Nm 21:9
And if a **s** bit anyone, he would look at Nm 21:9
he would look at the bronze **s** and live. Nm 21:9
in pieces the bronze **s** that Moses had 2 Kgs 18:4
made fair; his hand pierced the fleeing **s**. Jb 26:13
They have venom like the venom of a **s**, Ps 58:4
young lion and the **s** you will trample Ps 91:13
end it bites like a **s** and stings like an Prv 23:32
in the sky, the way of a **s** on a rock, Prv 30:19
and a **s** will bite him who breaks Eccl 10:8
If the **s** bites before it is charmed, Eccl 10:11
and its fruit will be a flying fiery **s**. Is 14:29
sword will punish Leviathan the fleeing **s**, Is 27:1
fleeing serpent, Leviathan the twisting **s**, Is 27:1
the lion, the adder and the flying fiery **s**, Is 30:6
makes a sound like a **s** gliding away; Jer 46:22
hand against the wall, and a **s** bit him. Am 5:19
of the sea, there I will command the **s**, Am 9:3
they shall lick the dust like a **s**, like the Mi 7:17
Or if he asks for a fish, will give him a **s**? Mt 7:10
fish, will instead of a fish give him a **s**; Lk 11:11
as Moses lifted up the **s** in the wilderness, Jn 3:14
afraid that as the **s** deceived Eve by 2 Cor 11:3
dragon was thrown down, that ancient **s**, Rv 12:9
fly from the **s** into the wilderness, Rv 12:14
The **s** poured water like a river out of Rv 12:15
And he seized the dragon, that ancient **s**, Rv 20:2

SERPENT'S (4)
and fattened cattle by the **S** Stone, 1 Kgs 1:9
They make their tongue sharp as a **s**, Ps 140:3
for from the **s** root will come forth an Is 14:29
like the ox, and dust shall be the **s** food. Is 65:25

SERPENTS (12)
cast down his staff, and they became **s**. Ex 7:12
the LORD sent fiery **s** among the people, Nm 21:6
he take away the **s** from us." So Moses Nm 21:7
with its fiery **s** and scorpions and thirsty Dt 8:15
is the poison of **s** and the cruel venom Dt 32:33
For behold, I am sending among you **s**, Jer 8:17
so be wise as **s** and innocent as doves. Mt 10:16
You **s**, you brood of vipers, how are you Mt 23:33
they will pick up **s** with their hands; Mk 16:18
authority to tread on **s** and scorpions, Lk 10:19
of them did and were destroyed by **s**, 1 Cor 10:9
tails, for their tails are like **s** with heads, Rv 9:19

SERUG (6)
Reu had lived 32 years, he fathered **S**. Gn 11:20
lived after he fathered **S** 207 years and Gn 11:21
When **S** had lived 30 years, he fathered Gn 11:22
And **S** lived after he fathered Nahor Gn 11:23
S, Nahor, Terah; 1 Chr 1:26
the son of **S**, the son of Reu, the son of Lk 3:35

SERVANT (564)
a **s** of servants shall he be to his Gn 9:25
God of Shem; and let Canaan be his **s**. Gn 9:26
tents of Shem, and let Canaan be his **s**." Gn 9:27
a female Egyptian **s** whose name was Gn 16:1
Go in to my **s**; it may be that I shall Gn 16:2
wife, took Hagar the Egyptian, her **s**, Gn 16:3
be on you! I gave my **s** to your embrace, Gn 16:5
Sarai, "Behold, your **s** is in your power; Gn 16:6
And he said, "Hagar, **s** of Sarai, where Gn 16:8
in your sight, do not pass by your **s**. Gn 18:3
you have come to your **s**." So they said, Gn 18:5
your **s** has found favor in your sight, Gn 19:19
And Abraham said to his **s**, the oldest of Gn 24:2
The **s** said to him, "Perhaps the woman Gn 24:5
So the **s** put his hand under the thigh of Gn 24:9
Then the **s** took ten of his master's Gn 24:10
you have appointed for your **s** Isaac. Gn 24:14
Then the **s** ran to meet her and said, Gn 24:17
So he said, "I am Abraham's **s**. Gn 24:34
When Abraham's **s** heard their words, Gn 24:52
And the **s** brought out jewelry of silver Gn 24:53
nurse, and Abraham's **s** and his men. Gn 24:59
Thus the **s** took Rebekah and went his Gn 24:61
and said to the **s**, "Who is that man, Gn 24:65
in the field to meet us?" The **s** said, Gn 24:65
And the **s** told Isaac all the things that Gn 24:66
whom Hagar the Egyptian, Sarah's **s**, Gn 25:12
offspring for my **s** Abraham's sake." Gn 26:24
(Laban gave his female **s** Zilpah to his Gn 29:24
to his daughter Leah to be her **s**.) Gn 29:24
(Laban gave his female **s** Bilhah to his Gn 29:29
to his daughter Rachel to be her **s**.) Gn 29:29
Then she said, "Here is my **s** Bilhah; go Gn 30:3
So she gave him her **s** Bilhah as a wife, Gn 30:4
Rachel's **s** Bilhah conceived again and Gn 30:7
she took her **s** Zilpah and gave her to Gn 30:9
Then Leah's **s** Zilpah bore Jacob a son. Gn 30:10
Leah's **s** Zilpah bore Jacob a second Gn 30:12
because I gave my **s** to my husband." Gn 30:18
Thus says your **s** Jacob, 'I have Gn 32:4
that you have shown to your **s**, Gn 32:10
shall say, 'They belong to your **s** Jacob. Gn 32:18
your **s** Jacob is behind us.'" For he Gn 32:20
God has graciously given your **s**." Gn 33:5
Let my lord pass on ahead of his **s**, and Gn 33:14
The sons of Bilhah, Rachel's **s**: Dan Gn 35:25
The sons of Zilpah, Leah's **s**: Gad and Gn 35:26
the same story, saying, "The Hebrew **s**, Gn 39:17
is the way your **s** treated me," his anger Gn 39:19
with us, a **s** of the captain of the guard. Gn 41:12
They said, "Your **s** our father is well; Gn 43:28
he who is found with it shall be my **s**, Gn 44:10
hand the cup was found shall be my **s**. Gn 44:17
please let your **s** speak a word in my Gn 44:18
let not your anger burn against your **s**, Gn 44:18
we went back to your **s** my father, Gn 44:24
Then your **s** my father said to us, 'You Gn 44:27
as soon as I come to your **s** my father, Gn 44:30
gray hairs of your **s** our father with Gn 44:31
For your **s** became a pledge of safety Gn 44:32
please let your **s** remain instead of the Gn 44:33
instead of the boy as a **s** to my lord, Gn 44:33
to bear, and became a **s** at forced labor. Gn 49:15
among the reeds and sent her **s** woman, Ex 2:5
past or since you have spoken to your **s**, Ex 4:10
No foreigner or hired **s** may eat of it. Ex 12:45
believed in the LORD and in his **s** Moses. Ex 14:31
son, or your daughter, your male **s**, Ex 20:10
your male servant, or your female **s**, Ex 20:10
your neighbor's wife, or his male **s**, Ex 20:17
or his male servant, or his female **s**, Ex 20:17
have rest, and the son of your **s** woman, Ex 23:12
wages of a hired **s** shall not remain Lv 19:13
of the priest or hired **s** shall eat of a holy Lv 22:10
and for your hired **s** and the sojourner Lv 25:6
you as a hired **s** and as a sojourner. Lv 25:40
shall be rated as the time of a hired **s**. Lv 25:50
treat him as a **s** hired year by year. Lv 25:53
"Why have you dealt ill with your **s**? Nm 11:11
Not so with my **s** Moses. He is faithful Nm 12:7
afraid to speak against my **s** Moses?" Nm 12:8
But my **s** Caleb, because he has a Nm 14:24
begun to show your **s** your greatness and Dt 3:24
daughter or your male **s** or your female Dt 5:14
or your male servant or your female **s**, Dt 5:14
that your male **s** and your female Dt 5:14
servant and your female **s** may rest as Dt 5:14
neighbor's house, his field, or his male **s**, Dt 5:21
field, or his male servant, or his female **s**, Dt 5:21
your male **s** and your female servant, Dt 12:18
your male servant and your female **s**, Dt 12:18
the cost of a hired **s** he has served you Dt 15:18
your male **s** and your female servant, Dt 16:11
your male servant and your female **s**, Dt 16:11
your male **s** and your female servant, Dt 16:14
your male servant and your female **s**, Dt 16:14
not oppress a hired **s** who is poor and Dt 24:14
So Moses the **s** of the LORD died there in Dt 34:5
After the death of Moses the **s** of the LORD, Jos 1:1
"Moses my **s** is dead. Now therefore arise, Jos 1:2
law that Moses my **s** commanded you. Jos 1:7
word that Moses the **s** of the LORD Jos 1:13
land that Moses the **s** of the LORD gave Jos 1:15
him, "What does my lord say to his **s**?" Jos 5:14
just as Moses the **s** of the LORD had Jos 8:31
just as Moses the **s** of the LORD had Jos 8:33
God had commanded his **s** Moses to give Jos 9:24
just as Moses the **s** of the LORD had Jos 11:12
the LORD had commanded Moses his **s**, Jos 11:15
Moses, the **s** of the LORD, and the people Jos 12:6
And Moses the **s** of the LORD gave their Jos 12:6
as Moses the **s** of the LORD gave them: Jos 13:8
old when Moses the **s** of the LORD sent Jos 14:7
which Moses the **s** of the LORD gave Jos 18:7
all that Moses the **s** of the LORD Jos 22:2
which Moses the **s** of the LORD gave you Jos 22:4
law that Moses the **s** of the LORD Jos 22:5
the son of Nun, the **s** of the LORD, Jos 24:29
Joshua the son of Nun, the **s** of the LORD, Jgs 2:8
go down to the camp with Purah your **s**. Jgs 7:10
down with Purah his **s** to the outposts of Jgs 7:11
Abimelech, the son of his female **s**, Jgs 9:18
great salvation by the hand of your **s**, Jgs 15:18
He had with him his **s** and a couple of Jgs 19:3
his concubine and his **s** rose up to Jgs 19:9
over, and the **s** said to his master, Jgs 19:11
me and your female **s** and the young Jgs 19:19
And the **s** who was in charge of the Ru 2:6
me and spoken kindly to your **s**, Ru 2:13
And she answered, "I am Ruth, your **s**. Ru 3:9
Spread your wings over your **s**, for you Ru 3:9
affliction of your **s** and remember me 1 Sm 1:11
remember me and not forget your **s**, 1 Sm 1:11
servant, but will give to your **s** a son, 1 Sm 1:11
Do not regard your **s** as a worthless 1 Sm 1:16
"Let your **s** find favor in your eyes." 1 Sm 1:18
sacrifice, the priest's **s** would come, 1 Sm 2:13
the priest's **s** would come and say to 1 Sm 2:15
for your **s** hears.'" So Samuel went and 1 Sm 3:9
said, "Speak, for your **s** hears." 1 Sm 3:10
Saul said to his **s** who was with him, 1 Sm 9:5
Then Saul said to his **s**, "But if we go, 1 Sm 9:7
The **s** answered Saul again, "Here, I 1 Sm 9:8
And Saul said to his **s**, "Well said; 1 Sm 9:10
Saul, "Tell the **s** to pass on before us, 1 Sm 9:27
Saul's uncle said to him and to his **s**, 1 Sm 10:14
you not answered your **s** this day? 1 Sm 14:41
Your **s** will go and fight with this 1 Sm 17:32
"Your **s** used to keep sheep for his 1 Sm 17:34
Your **s** has struck down both lions 1 Sm 17:36
son of your **s** Jesse the Bethlehemite." 1 Sm 17:58
not the king sin against his **s** David, 1 Sm 19:4
it will be well with your **s**, but if he is 1 Sm 20:7
Therefore deal kindly with your **s**, for 1 Sm 20:8
have brought your **s** into a covenant 1 Sm 20:8
son has stirred up my **s** against me, 1 Sm 22:8
impute anything to his **s** or to all the 1 Sm 22:15
for your **s** has known nothing of all 1 Sm 22:15
your **s** has surely heard that Saul 1 Sm 23:10
come down, as your **s** has heard? 1 Sm 23:11
please tell your **s**." And the LORD said, 1 Sm 23:11
Please let your **s** speak in your ears, 1 Sm 25:24
ears, and hear the words of your **s**. 1 Sm 25:24
But I your **s** did not see the young 1 Sm 25:25
present that your **s** has brought to 1 Sm 25:27
Please forgive the trespass of your **s**. 1 Sm 25:28
my lord, then remember your **s**." 1 Sm 25:31
kept back his **s** from wrongdoing. 1 Sm 25:39
your handmaid is a **s** to wash the feet 1 Sm 25:41
does my lord pursue after his **s**? 1 Sm 26:18
lord the king hear the words of his **s**. 1 Sm 26:19
For why should your **s** dwell in the 1 Sm 27:5
therefore he shall always be my **s**." 1 Sm 27:12
shall know what your **s** can do." And 1 Sm 28:2
him, "Behold, your **s** has obeyed you. 1 Sm 28:21
Now therefore, you also obey your **s**. 1 Sm 28:22
"Is this not David, the **s** of Saul, 1 Sm 29:3
you found in your **s** from the day I 1 Sm 29:8
man of Egypt, **s** to an Amalekite, 1 Sm 30:13
'By the hand of my **s** David I will save 2 Sm 3:18
"Go and tell my **s** David, 'Thus says the 2 Sm 7:5
thus you shall say to my **s** David, 2 Sm 7:8
For you know your **s**, O Lord GOD! 2 Sm 7:20
greatness, to make your **s** know it. 2 Sm 7:21
concerning your **s** and concerning 2 Sm 7:25
the house of your **s** David will be 2 Sm 7:26
have made this revelation to your **s**, 2 Sm 7:27
Therefore your **s** has found courage 2 Sm 7:27
promised this good thing to your **s**. 2 Sm 7:28
please you to bless the house of your **s**, 2 Sm 7:29
house of your **s** be blessed forever." 2 Sm 7:29
Now there was a **s** of the house of Saul 2 Sm 9:2
you Ziba?" And he said, "I am your **s**." 2 Sm 9:2
he answered, "Behold, I am your **s**." 2 Sm 9:6
paid homage and said, "What is your **s**, 2 Sm 9:8
Then the king called Ziba, Saul's **s**, 2 Sm 9:9
my lord the king commands his **s**, 2 Sm 9:11
so will your **s** do." So Mephibosheth 2 Sm 9:11
'Your **s** Uriah the Hittite is dead 2 Sm 11:21
and your **s** Uriah the Hittite is dead 2 Sm 11:24
So his **s** put her out and bolted the 2 Sm 13:18
"Behold, your **s** has sheepshearers. 2 Sm 13:24
and his servants go with your **s**." 2 Sm 13:24
as your **s** said, so it has come about." 2 Sm 13:35
And your **s** had two sons, and they 2 Sm 14:6
whole clan has risen against your **s**, 2 Sm 14:7
"Please let your **s** speak a word to my 2 Sm 14:12
made me afraid, and your **s** thought, 2 Sm 14:15
will perform the request of his **s**. 2 Sm 14:15
hear and deliver his **s** from the hand 2 Sm 14:16
And your **s** thought, 'The word of 2 Sm 14:17
It was your **s** Joab who commanded 2 Sm 14:19
these words in the mouth of your **s**. 2 Sm 14:19
course of things your **s** Joab did this. 2 Sm 14:20
"Today your **s** knows that I have 2 Sm 14:22

has granted the request of his **s**." 2 Sm 14:22
"Your **s** is of such and such a tribe in 2 Sm 15:2
For your **s** vowed a vow while I lived 2 Sm 15:8
or for life, there also will your **s** be." 2 Sm 15:21
and say to Absalom, 'I will be your **s**, 2 Sm 15:34
been your father's **s** in time past, 2 Sm 15:34
in time past, so now I will be your **s**,' 2 Sm 15:34
Ziba the **s** of Mephibosheth met him, 2 Sm 16:1
A female **s** was to go and tell them, 2 Sm 17:17
"When Joab sent the king's **s**, 2 Sm 18:29
Joab sent the king's servant, your **s**, 2 Sm 18:29
And Ziba the **s** of the house of Saul, 2 Sm 19:17
remember how your **s** did wrong on 2 Sm 19:19
For your **s** knows that I have sinned. 2 Sm 19:20
"My lord, O king, my **s** deceived me, 2 Sm 19:26
deceived me, for your **s** said to him, 2 Sm 19:26
go with the king.' For your **s** is lame. 2 Sm 19:26
He has slandered your **s** to my lord 2 Sm 19:27
but you set your **s** among those who 2 Sm 19:28
Can your **s** taste what he eats or 2 Sm 19:35
Why then should your **s** be an added 2 Sm 19:35
Your **s** will go a little way over the 2 Sm 19:36
Please let your **s** return, that I may 2 Sm 19:37
But here is your **s** Chimham. 2 Sm 19:37
words of your **s**." And he answered, 2 Sm 20:17
take away the iniquity of your **s**, 2 Sm 24:10
the king come to his **s**?" David said, 2 Sm 24:21
not, my lord the king, swear to your **s**, 1 Kgs 1:13
you swore to your **s** by the LORD your 1 Kgs 1:17
but Solomon your **s** he has not 1 Kgs 1:19
But me, your **s**, and Zadok the priest, 1 Kgs 1:26
and your **s** Solomon he has not 1 Kgs 1:26
he will not put his **s** to death with the 1 Kgs 1:51
so will your **s** do." So Shimei lived in 1 Kgs 2:38
love to your **s** David my father, 1 Kgs 3:6
you have made your **s** king in place of 1 Kgs 3:7
And your **s** is in the midst of your 1 Kgs 3:8
Give your **s** therefore an 1 Kgs 3:9
from beside me, while your **s** slept, 1 Kgs 3:20
kept with your **s** David my father 1 Kgs 8:24
keep for your **s** David my father what 1 Kgs 8:25
spoken to your **s** David my father. 1 Kgs 8:26
to the prayer of your **s** and to his plea, 1 Kgs 8:28
prayer that your **s** prays before you 1 Kgs 8:28
prayer that your **s** offers toward this 1 Kgs 8:29
the plea of your **s** and of your people 1 Kgs 8:30
to the plea of your **s** and to the plea of 1 Kgs 8:52
you declared through Moses your **s**, 1 Kgs 8:53
which he spoke by Moses his **s**. 1 Kgs 8:56
the cause of his **s** and the cause of 1 Kgs 8:59
shown to David his **s** and to Israel his 1 Kgs 8:66
from you and will give it to your **s**. 1 Kgs 11:11
sake of David my **s** and for the sake 1 Kgs 11:13
of Zeredah, a **s** of Solomon, 1 Kgs 11:26
the sake of my **s** David and for the 1 Kgs 11:32
sake of David my **s** whom I chose, 1 Kgs 11:34
that David my **s** may always have a 1 Kgs 11:36
commandments, as David my **s** did, 1 Kgs 11:38
"If you will be a **s** to this people today 1 Kgs 12:7
you have not been like my **s** David, 1 Kgs 14:8
spoke by his **s** Ahijah the prophet. 1 Kgs 14:18
spoke by his **s** Ahijah the Shilonite. 1 Kgs 15:29
But his **s** Zimri, commander of half 1 Kgs 16:9
you would give your **s** into the hand 1 Kgs 18:9
although I your **s** have feared the 1 Kgs 18:12
God in Israel, and that I am your **s**, 1 Kgs 18:36
And he said to his **s**, "Go up now, 1 Kgs 18:43
belongs to Judah, and left his **s** there. 1 Kgs 19:3
you first demanded of your **s** I will do, 1 Kgs 20:9
and said, "Your **s** Ben-hadad says, 1 Kgs 20:32
"Your **s** went out into the midst of 1 Kgs 20:39
And as your **s** was busy here and 1 Kgs 20:40
to Elisha, "Your **s** my husband is dead, 2 Kgs 4:1
you know that your **s** feared the LORD, 2 Kgs 4:1
"Your **s** has nothing in the house 2 Kgs 4:2
And he said to Gehazi his **s**, "Call this 2 Kgs 4:12
O man of God; do not lie to your **s**." 2 Kgs 4:16
my head!" The father said to his **s**, 2 Kgs 4:19
the donkey, and she said to her **s**, 2 Kgs 4:24
her coming, he said to Gehazi his **s**, 2 Kgs 4:25
sitting before him, he said to his **s**, 2 Kgs 4:38
But his **s** said, "How can I set this 2 Kgs 4:43
that I have sent to you Naaman my **s**, 2 Kgs 5:6
so accept now a present from your **s**." 2 Kgs 5:15
be given to your **s** two mules' load of 2 Kgs 5:17
from now on your **s** will not offer 2 Kgs 5:17
matter may the LORD pardon your **s**: 2 Kgs 5:18
LORD pardon your **s** in this matter." 2 Kgs 5:18
the **s** of Elisha the man of God, 2 Kgs 5:20
And he said, "Your **s** went nowhere." 2 Kgs 5:25
When the **s** of the man of God rose 2 Kgs 6:15
And the **s** said, "Alas, my master! 2 Kgs 6:15
talking with Gehazi the **s** of the man of 2 Kgs 8:4
And Hazael said, "What is your **s**, 2 Kgs 8:13
Judah, for the sake of David his **s**, 2 Kgs 8:19

So the young man, the **s** of the prophet, 2 Kgs 9:4
he spoke by his **s** Elijah the Tishbite, 2 Kgs 9:36
done what he said by his **s** Elijah." 2 Kgs 10:10
see that there is no **s** of the LORD here 2 Kgs 10:23
he spoke by his **s** Jonah the son of 2 Kgs 14:25
saying, "I am your **s** and your son. 2 Kgs 16:7
all that Moses the **s** of the LORD 2 Kgs 18:12
and for the sake of my **s** David." 2 Kgs 19:34
own sake and for my **s** David's sake." 2 Kgs 20:6
Law that my **s** Moses commanded 2 Kgs 21:8
secretary, and Asaiah the king's **s**, 2 Kgs 22:12
Jehoiakim became his **s** three years. 2 Kgs 24:1
a **s** of the king of Babylon, 2 Kgs 25:8
all that Moses the **s** of God had 1 Chr 6:49
O offspring of Israel his **s**, sons of 1 Chr 16:13
"Go and tell my **s** David, 'Thus says 1 Chr 17:4
thus shall you say to my **s** David, 1 Chr 17:7
say to you for honoring your **s**? 1 Chr 17:18
your servant? For you know your **s**. 1 Chr 17:18
concerning your **s** and concerning 1 Chr 17:23
the house of your **s** David will be 1 Chr 17:24
have revealed to your **s** that you will 1 Chr 17:25
Therefore your **s** has found courage 1 Chr 17:25
promised this good thing to your **s**. 1 Chr 17:26
pleased to bless the house of your **s**, 1 Chr 17:27
take away the iniquity of your **s**, 1 Chr 21:8
which Moses the **s** of the LORD had 2 Chr 1:3
kept with your **s** David my father 2 Chr 6:15
keep for your **s** David my father what 2 Chr 6:16
you have spoken to your **s** David. 2 Chr 6:17
to the prayer of your **s** and to his plea, 2 Chr 6:19
prayer that your **s** prays before you, 2 Chr 6:19
prayer that your **s** offers toward this 2 Chr 6:20
the pleas of your **s** and of your people 2 Chr 6:21
your steadfast love for David your **s**." 2 Chr 6:42
a **s** of Solomon the son of David, 2 Chr 13:6
tax levied by Moses, the **s** of the LORD, 2 Chr 24:6
tax that Moses the **s** of God laid on 2 Chr 24:9
GOD and against his **s** Hezekiah. 2 Chr 32:16
secretary, and Asaiah the king's **s**, 2 Chr 34:20
hear the prayer of your **s** that I now pray Neh 1:6
that you commanded your **s** Moses. Neh 1:7
that you commanded your **s** Moses, Neh 1:8
ear be attentive to the prayer of your **s**, Neh 1:11
name, and give success to your **s** today, Neh 1:11
and if your **s** has found favor in your Neh 2:5
Horonite and Tobiah, the Ammonite **s**, Neh 2:10
Tobiah the Ammonite **s** and Geshem Neh 2:19
every man and his **s** pass the night Neh 4:22
the fifth time sent his **s** to me with an Neh 6:5
statutes and a law by Moses your **s**. Neh 9:14
that was given by Moses the **s** of God, Neh 10:29
to Satan, "Have you considered my **s** Job, Jb 1:8
to Satan, "Have you considered my **s** Job, Jb 2:3
I call to my **s**, but he gives me no Jb 19:16
with you to take him for your **s** forever? Jb 41:4
of me what is right, as my **s** Job has. Jb 42:7
rams and go to my **s** Job and offer up a Jb 42:8
And my **s** Job shall pray for you, for I will Jb 42:8
of me what is right, as my **s** Job has." Jb 42:8
A Psalm of David, the **s** of the LORD, who Ps 18:T
Moreover, by them is your **s** warned; in Ps 19:11
Keep back your **s** also from Ps 19:13
from me. Turn not your **s** away in anger, Ps 27:9
Make your face shine on your **s**; save Ps 31:16
who delights in the welfare of his **s**!" Ps 35:27
choirmaster. Of David, the **s** of the Lord. Ps 36:T
Hide not your face from your **s**; for I am Ps 69:17
He chose David his **s** and took him Ps 78:70
save your **s**, who trusts in you—you are Ps 86:2
Gladden the soul of your **s**, for to you, O Ps 86:4
give your strength to your **s**, and save Ps 86:16
chosen one; I have sworn to David my **s**: Ps 89:3
I have found David, my **s**; with my holy Ps 89:20
renounced the covenant with your **s**; Ps 89:39
O offspring of Abraham, his **s**, children Ps 105:6
He sent Moses, his **s**, and Aaron, Ps 105:26
his holy promise, and Abraham, his **s**. Ps 105:42
put to shame, but your **s** will be glad! Ps 109:28
O LORD, I am your **s**; I am your servant, Ps 116:16
I am your **s**, the son of your Ps 116:16
Deal bountifully with your **s**, that I Ps 119:17
your **s** will meditate on your statutes. Ps 119:23
Confirm to your **s** your promise, that Ps 119:38
Remember your word to your **s**, in Ps 119:49
You have dealt well with your **s**, O Ps 119:65
according to your promise to your **s**. Ps 119:76
How long must your **s** endure? When Ps 119:84
Give your **s** a pledge of good; let not Ps 119:122
Deal with your **s** according to your Ps 119:124
I am your **s**; give me understanding, Ps 119:125
Make your face shine upon your **s**, Ps 119:135
is well tried, and your **s** loves it. Ps 119:140
seek your **s**, for I do not forget your Ps 119:176
For the sake of your **s** David, do not Ps 132:10

a heritage to Israel his **s**, for his Ps 136:22
Enter not into judgment with your **s**, Ps 143:2
adversaries of my soul, for I am your **s**. Ps 143:12
rescues David his **s** from the cruel Ps 144:10
and the fool will be **s** to the wise of Prv 11:29
be lowly and have a **s** than to play the Prv 12:9
A **s** who deals wisely has the king's Prv 14:35
A **s** who deals wisely will rule over a son Prv 17:2
By mere words a **s** is not disciplined, Prv 29:19
pampers his **s** from childhood Prv 29:21
Do not slander a **s** to his master, lest he Prv 30:10
say, lest you hear your **s** cursing you. Eccl 7:21
"As my **s** Isaiah has walked naked and Is 20:3
day I will call my **s** Eliakim the son of Is 22:20
sake and for the sake of my **s** David." Is 37:35
But you, Israel, my **s**, Jacob, whom I have Is 41:8
corners, saying to you, "You are my **s**, Is 41:9
Behold my **s**, whom I uphold, my chosen, Is 42:1
Who is blind but my **s**, or deaf as my Is 42:19
one, or blind as the **s** of the LORD? Is 42:19
LORD, "and my **s** whom I have chosen, Is 43:10
"But now hear, O Jacob my **s**, Israel Is 44:1
Fear not, O Jacob my **s**, Jeshurun whom I Is 44:2
O Jacob, and Israel, for you are my **s**; Is 44:21
my servant; I formed you; you are my **s**; Is 44:21
the word of his **s** and fulfills the counsel Is 44:26
For the sake of my **s** Jacob, and Israel my Is 45:4
"The LORD has redeemed his **s** Jacob!" Is 48:20
And he said to me, "You are my **s**, Israel, Is 49:3
formed me from the womb to be his **s**, Is 49:5
that you should be my **s** to raise up the Is 49:6
abhorred by the nation, the **s** of rulers: Is 49:7
the LORD and obeys the voice of his **s**? Is 50:10
Behold, my **s** shall act wisely; he shall be Is 52:13
knowledge shall the righteous one, my **s**, Is 53:11
"Is Israel a slave? Is he a homeborn **s**? Jer 2:14
the king of Babylon, my **s**, Jer 25:9
the king of Babylon, my **s**, Jer 27:6
shall no more make a **s** of him. Jer 30:8
"Then fear not, O Jacob my **s**, declares Jer 30:10
with David my **s** may be broken, Jer 33:21
multiply the offspring of David my **s**, Jer 33:22
Jacob and David my **s** and will not Jer 33:26
the king of Babylon, my **s**, Jer 43:10
"But fear not, O Jacob my **s**, nor be Jer 46:27
Fear not, O Jacob my **s**, declares the Jer 46:28
own land that I gave to my **s** Jacob. Ezk 28:25
over them one shepherd, my **s** David, Ezk 34:23
and my **s** David shall be prince Ezk 34:24
"My **s** David shall be king over them, Ezk 37:24
in the land that I gave to my **s** Jacob, Ezk 37:25
and David my **s** shall be their prince Ezk 37:25
to Daniel, "O Daniel, **s** of the living God, Dn 6:20
the Law of Moses the **s** of God have been Dn 9:11
to the prayer of your **s** and to his pleas Dn 9:17
How can my lord's **s** talk with my Dn 10:17
I will take you, O Zerubbabel my **s**, Hg 2:23
behold, I will bring my **s** the Branch. Zec 3:8
honors his father, and a **s** his master. Mal 1:6
"Remember the law of my **s** Moses, the Mal 4:4
"Lord, my **s** is lying paralyzed at home, Mt 8:6
say the word, and my **s** will be healed. Mt 8:8
'Come,' and he comes, and to my **s**, Mt 8:9
have believed." And the **s** was healed at Mt 8:13
his teacher, nor a **s** above his master. Mt 10:24
his teacher, and the **s** like his master. Mt 10:25
"Behold, my **s** whom I have chosen, my Mt 12:18
So the **s** fell on his knees, imploring Mt 18:26
the master of that **s** released him and Mt 18:27
But when that same **s** went out, he Mt 18:28
So his fellow **s** fell down and pleaded Mt 18:29
him and said to him, 'You wicked **s**! Mt 18:32
you have had mercy on your fellow **s**, Mt 18:33
be great among you must be your **s**, Mt 20:26
greatest among you shall be your **s**. Mt 23:11
"Who then is the faithful and wise **s**, Mt 24:45
Blessed is that **s** whom his master will Mt 24:46
But if that wicked **s** says to himself, Mt 24:48
the master of that **s** will come on a day Mt 24:50
to him, 'Well done, good and faithful **s**. Mt 25:21
to him, 'Well done, good and faithful **s**. Mt 25:23
him, 'You wicked and slothful **s**! Mt 25:26
And cast the worthless **s** into the outer Mt 25:30
sword and struck the **s** of the high Mt 26:51
And a **s** girl came up to him and said, Mt 26:69
to the entrance, another **s** girl saw him, Mt 26:71
first, he must be last of all and **s** of all." Mk 9:35
be great among you must be your **s**, Mk 10:43
he sent a **s** to the tenants to get from Mk 12:2
Again he sent to them another **s**, and Mk 12:4
sword and struck the **s** of the high Mk 14:47
one of the **s** girls of the high priest Mk 14:66
And the **s** girl saw him and began Mk 14:69
said, "Behold, I am the **s** of the Lord; Lk 1:38
has looked on the humble estate of his **s**. Lk 1:48

He has helped his **s** Israel, in Lk 1:54
for us in the house of his **s** David, Lk 1:69
you are letting your **s** depart in peace, Lk 2:29
a centurion had a **s** who was sick and Lk 7:2
Jews, asking him to come and heal his **s**. Lk 7:3
But say the word, and let my **s** be healed. Lk 7:7
and to my **s**, 'Do this,' and he does it." Lk 7:8
to the house, they found the **s** well. Lk 7:10
Blessed is that **s** whom his master will Lk 12:43
But if that **s** says to himself, 'My master Lk 12:45
the master of that **s** will come on a day Lk 12:46
And that **s** who knew his master's will Lk 12:47
the banquet he sent his **s** to say to those Lk 14:17
So the **s** came and reported these things Lk 14:21
house became angry and said to his **s**, Lk 14:21
And the **s** said, 'Sir, what you Lk 14:22
And the master said to the **s**, 'Go out to Lk 14:23
No **s** can serve two masters, for either Lk 16:13
you who has a **s** plowing or keeping Lk 17:7
Does he thank the **s** because he did what Lk 17:9
And he said to him, 'Well done, good **s**! Lk 19:17
with your own words, you wicked **s**! Lk 19:22
time came, he sent a **s** to the tenants, Lk 20:10
And he sent another **s**. But they also Lk 20:11
of them struck the **s** of the high priest Lk 22:50
Then a **s** girl, seeing him as he sat in Lk 22:56
and where I am, there will my **s** be also. Jn 12:26
you, a **s** is not greater than his master, Jn 13:16
for the **s** does not know what his master Jn 15:15
you: 'A **s** is not greater than his master.' Jn 15:20
struck the high priest's **s** and cut off his Jn 18:10
and spoke to the **s** girl who kept watch Jn 18:16
The **s** girl at the door said to Peter, "You Jn 18:17
God of our fathers, glorified his **s** Jesus, Acts 3:13
God, having raised up his **s**, sent him Acts 3:26
the mouth of our father David, your **s**, Acts 4:25
together against your holy **s** Jesus, Acts 4:27
the name of your holy **s** Jesus." Acts 4:30
a **s** girl named Rhoda came to Acts 12:13
appoint you as a **s** and witness to the Acts 26:16
Paul, a **s** of Christ Jesus, called to be an Rom 1:1
for he is God's **s** for your good. But if Rom 13:4
For he is the **s** of God, an avenger who Rom 13:4
to pass judgment on the **s** of another? Rom 14:4
Christ became a **s** to the circumcised Rom 15:8
a **s** of the church at Cenchreae, Rom 16:1
from all, I have made myself a **s** to all, 1 Cor 9:19
please man, I would not be a **s** of Christ. Gal 1:10
to be sinners, is Christ then a **s** of sin? Gal 2:17
himself nothing, taking the form of a **s**, Phil 2:7
it from Epaphras our beloved fellow **s**. Col 1:7
minister and fellow **s** in the Lord. Col 4:7
who is one of you, a **s** of Christ Jesus, Col 4:12
you will be a good **s** of Christ Jesus, 1 Tm 4:6
And the Lord's **s** must not be 2 Tm 2:24
a **s** of God and an apostle of Jesus Christ, Ti 1:1
was faithful in all God's house as a **s**, Heb 3:5
a **s** of God and of the Lord Jesus Christ, Jas 1:1
Peter, a **s** and apostle of Jesus Christ, 2 Pt 1:1
a **s** of Jesus Christ and brother of James, Jude 1:1
known by sending his angel to his **s** John, Rv 1:1
they sing the song of Moses, the **s** of God, Rv 15:3
I am a fellow **s** with you and your Rv 19:10
I am a fellow **s** with you and your Rv 22:9

SERVANT'S (5)
turn aside to your **s** house and spend the Gn 19:2
spoken also of your **s** house for a great 2 Sm 7:19
also spoken of your **s** house for a 1 Chr 17:17
For your **s** sake, O LORD, and 1 Chr 17:19
right ear. (The **s** name was Malchus.) Jn 18:10

SERVANTS (487)
a servant of **s** shall he be to his Gn 9:25
had sheep, oxen, male donkeys, male **s**, Gn 12:16
male donkeys, male servants, female **s**, Gn 12:16
against them by night, he and his **s**, Gn 14:15
that is not theirs and will be **s** there, Gn 15:13
and called all his **s** and told them all Gn 20:8
oxen, and male **s** and female servants, Gn 20:14
oxen, and male servants and female **s**, Gn 20:14
of water that Abimelech's **s** had seized, Gn 21:25
and gold, male **s** and female servants, Gn 24:35
and gold, male servants and female **s**, Gn 24:35
of flocks and herds and many **s**, Gn 26:14
wells that his father's **s** had dug in the Gn 26:15
But when Isaac's **s** dug in the valley Gn 26:19
there. And there Isaac's **s** dug a well. Gn 26:25
That same day Isaac's **s** came and told Gn 26:32
his brothers I have given to him for **s**, Gn 27:37
flocks, female **s** and male servants, Gn 30:43
flocks, female servants and male **s**, Gn 30:43
and into the tent of the two female **s**, Gn 31:33
I have oxen, donkeys, flocks, male **s**, and Gn 32:5
flocks, male servants, and female **s**. Gn 32:5
These he handed over to his **s**, every Gn 32:16
every drove by itself, and said to his **s**, Gn 32:16
took his two wives, his two female **s**, Gn 32:22
Leah and Rachel and the two female **s**. Gn 33:1
And he put the **s** with their children in Gn 33:2
Then the **s** drew near, they and their Gn 33:6
a feast for all his **s** and lifted up the Gn 40:20
head of the chief baker among his **s**. Gn 40:20
was angry with his **s** and put me and Gn 41:10
proposal pleased Pharaoh and all his **s**. Gn 41:37
And Pharaoh said to his **s**, "Can we Gn 41:38
my lord, your **s** have come to buy food. Gn 42:10
men. Your **s** have never been spies." Gn 42:11
And they said, "We, your **s**, are twelve Gn 42:13
us to make us **s** and seize our Gn 43:18
Far be it from your **s** to do such a thing! Gn 44:7
Whichever of your **s** is found with it Gn 44:9
die, and we also will be my lord's **s**." Gn 44:9
God has found out the guilt of your **s**; Gn 44:16
behold, we are my lord's **s**, both we and Gn 44:16
My lord asked his **s**, saying, 'Have you Gn 44:19
Then you said to your **s**, 'Bring him Gn 44:21
Then you said to your **s**, 'Unless your Gn 44:23
and your **s** will bring down the gray Gn 44:31
come," it pleased Pharaoh and his **s**. Gn 45:16
'Your **s** have been keepers of livestock Gn 46:34
said to Pharaoh, "Your **s** are shepherds, Gn 47:3
please let your **s** dwell in the land of Gn 47:4
we with our land will be **s** to Pharaoh. Gn 47:19
he made **s** of them from one end of Gn 47:21
my lord, we will be **s** to Pharaoh." Gn 47:25
Joseph commanded his **s** the physicians Gn 50:2
With him went up all the **s** of Pharaoh, Gn 50:7
the transgression of the **s** of the God of Gn 50:17
him and said, "Behold, we are your **s**." Gn 50:18
"Why do you treat your **s** like this? Ex 5:15
No straw is given to your **s**, yet they say Ex 5:16
And behold, your **s** are beaten; but the Ex 5:16
stink in the sight of Pharaoh and his **s**, Ex 5:21
down his staff before Pharaoh and his **s**, Ex 7:10
in the sight of his **s** he lifted up the staff Ex 7:20
into the houses of your **s** and your people, Ex 8:3
and on your people and on all your **s**."'" Ex 8:4
for you and for your **s** and for your people, Ex 8:9
your houses and your **s** and your people. Ex 8:11
flies on you and your **s** and your people, Ex 8:21
may depart from Pharaoh, from his **s**, Ex 8:29
of flies from Pharaoh, from his **s**, Ex 8:31
yourself, and on your **s** and your people, Ex 9:14
LORD among the **s** of Pharaoh hurried Ex 9:20
But as for you and your **s**, I know that Ex 9:30
and hardened his heart, he and his **s**. Ex 9:34
hardened his heart and the heart of his **s**, Ex 10:1
the houses of all your **s** and of all the Ex 10:6
Then Pharaoh's **s** said to him, "How Ex 10:7
the sight of Pharaoh's **s** and in the sight Ex 11:3
And all these your **s** shall come down to Ex 11:8
he and all his **s** and all the Egyptians. Ex 12:30
Pharaoh and his **s** was changed toward Ex 14:5
Abraham, Isaac, and Israel, your **s**, Ex 32:13
For they are my **s**, whom I brought out Lv 25:42
it is to me that the people of Israel are **s**. Lv 25:55
They are my **s** whom I brought out of Lv 25:55
answered and said to the **s** of Balak, Nm 22:18
donkey, and his two **s** were with him. Nm 22:22
"Your **s** have counted the men of war Nm 31:49
livestock, and your **s** have livestock." Nm 32:4
land be given to your **s** for a possession. Nm 32:5
"Your **s** will do as my lord Nm 32:25
but your **s** will pass over, every man Nm 32:27
"What the LORD has said to your **s**, Nm 32:31
Remember your **s**, Abraham, Isaac, and Dt 9:27
your male **s** and your female servants, Dt 12:12
your male servants and your female **s**, Dt 12:12
Pharaoh and to all his **s** and to all his Dt 29:2
people and have compassion on his **s**, Dt 32:36
Pharaoh and to all his **s** and to all his Dt 34:11
"We are your **s**." And Joshua said to Jos 9:8
a very distant country your **s** have come, Jos 9:9
them and say to them, "We are your **s**. Jos 9:11
of you shall never be anything but **s**, Jos 9:23
it was told to your **s** for a certainty that Jos 9:24
"Do not relax your hand from your **s**. Jos 10:6
When he had gone, the **s** came, and Jgs 3:24
took ten men of his **s** and did as the LORD Jgs 6:27
and the young man with your **s**. Jgs 19:19
servant, though I am not one of your **s**." Ru 2:13
olive orchards and give them to his **s**. 1 Sm 8:14
and give it to his officers and to his **s**. 1 Sm 8:15
take your male **s** and female servants 1 Sm 8:16
servants and female **s** and the best 1 Sm 8:16
"Pray for your **s** to the LORD your 1 Sm 12:19
And Saul's **s** said to him, "Behold 1 Sm 16:15
now command your **s** who are 1 Sm 16:16
So Saul said to his **s**, "Provide for me 1 Sm 16:17
a Philistine, and are you not **s** of Saul? 1 Sm 17:8
and kill me, then we will be your **s**. 1 Sm 17:9
then you shall be our **s** and serve us." 1 Sm 17:9
people and also in the sight of Saul's **s**. 1 Sm 18:5
And Saul commanded his **s**, "Speak 1 Sm 18:22
delight in you, and all his **s** love you. 1 Sm 18:22
And Saul's **s** spoke those words in 1 Sm 18:23
And the **s** of Saul told him, "Thus 1 Sm 18:24
And when his **s** told David these 1 Sm 18:26
more success than all the **s** of Saul, 1 Sm 18:30
to Jonathan his son and to all his **s**, 1 Sm 19:1
certain man of the **s** of Saul was there 1 Sm 21:7
And the **s** of Achish said to him, "Is 1 Sm 21:11
Then Achish said to his **s**, "Behold, 1 Sm 21:14
and all his **s** were standing about 1 Sm 22:6
Saul said to his **s** who stood about 1 Sm 22:7
Edomite, who stood by the **s** of Saul, 1 Sm 22:9
who among all your **s** is so faithful 1 Sm 22:14
it to me." But the **s** of the king would 1 Sm 22:17
at hand to your **s** and to your son 1 Sm 25:8
And Nabal answered David's **s**, 1 Sm 25:10
There are many **s** these days who are 1 Sm 25:10
When the **s** of David came to 1 Sm 25:40
to wash the feet of the **s** of my lord." 1 Sm 25:41
Then Saul said to his **s**, "Seek out for 1 Sm 28:7
inquire of her." And his **s** said to him, 1 Sm 28:7
and said, "I will not eat." But his **s**, 1 Sm 28:23
and she put it before Saul and his **s**, 1 Sm 28:25
the morning with the **s** of your lord 1 Sm 29:10
and the **s** of Ish-bosheth the son of 2 Sm 2:12
of Zeruiah and the **s** of David went out 2 Sm 2:13
of Saul, and twelve of the **s** of David. 2 Sm 2:15
were beaten before the **s** of David. 2 Sm 2:17
missing from David's **s** nineteen men 2 Sm 2:30
But the **s** of David had struck down of 2 Sm 2:31
Just then the **s** of David arrived with 2 Sm 3:22
And the king said to his **s**, "Do you 2 Sm 3:38
the eyes of his servants' female **s**, 2 Sm 6:20
But by the female **s** of whom you have 2 Sm 6:22
the Moabites became **s** to David and 2 Sm 8:2
and the Syrians became **s** to David and 2 Sm 8:6
were carried by the **s** of Hadadezer and 2 Sm 8:7
all the Edomites became David's **s**. 2 Sm 8:14
your sons and your **s** shall till the 2 Sm 9:10
Ziba had fifteen sons and twenty **s**. 2 Sm 9:10
house became Mephibosheth's **s**. 2 Sm 9:12
David sent by his **s** to console him 2 Sm 10:2
And David's **s** came into the land of 2 Sm 10:2
not David sent his **s** to you to search 2 Sm 10:3
Hanun took David's **s** and shaved off 2 Sm 10:4
kings who were **s** of Hadadezer saw 2 Sm 10:19
David sent Joab, and his **s** with him, 2 Sm 11:1
king's house with all the **s** of his lord, 2 Sm 11:9
my lord Joab and the **s** of my lord are 2 Sm 11:11
on his couch with the **s** of his lord, 2 Sm 11:13
and some of the **s** of David among 2 Sm 11:17
archers shot at your **s** from the wall. 2 Sm 11:24
Some of the king's **s** are dead, and 2 Sm 11:24
And the **s** of David were afraid to tell 2 Sm 12:18
saw that his **s** were whispering 2 Sm 12:19
And David said to his **s**, "Is the child 2 Sm 12:19
Then his **s** said to him, "What is this 2 Sm 12:21
the king and his **s** go with your 2 Sm 13:24
Then Absalom commanded his **s**, 2 Sm 13:28
So the **s** of Absalom did to Amnon as 2 Sm 13:29
And all his **s** who were standing by 2 Sm 13:31
also and all his **s** wept very bitterly. 2 Sm 13:36
Then he said to his **s**, "See, Joab's 2 Sm 14:30
on fire." So Absalom's **s** set the field 2 Sm 14:30
"Why have your **s** set my field on 2 Sm 14:31
said to all his **s** who were with him 2 Sm 15:14
And the king's **s** said to the king, 2 Sm 15:15
your **s** are ready to do whatever my 2 Sm 15:15
And all his **s** passed by him, and all 2 Sm 15:18
David and at all the **s** of King David, 2 Sm 16:6
said to Abishai and to all his **s**, 2 Sm 16:11
When Absalom's **s** came to the 2 Sm 17:20
were defeated there by the **s** of David, 2 Sm 18:7
happened to meet the **s** of David. 2 Sm 18:9
with shame the faces of all your **s**, 2 Sm 19:5
that commanders and **s** are nothing 2 Sm 19:6
go out and speak kindly to your **s**, 2 Sm 19:7
"Return, both you and all your **s**." 2 Sm 19:14
his fifteen sons and his twenty **s**, 2 Sm 19:17
Take your lord's **s** and pursue him, 2 Sm 20:6
David went down together with his **s**, 2 Sm 21:15
of David and by the hand of his **s**. 2 Sm 21:22
the king and his **s** coming on toward 2 Sm 24:20
Therefore his **s** said to him, "Let a 1 Kgs 1:2
have not told your **s** who should sit 1 Kgs 1:27
"Take with you the **s** of your lord and 1 Kgs 1:33
the king's **s** came to congratulate our 1 Kgs 1:47
that two of Shimei's **s** ran away to 1 Kgs 2:39
Shimei, "Behold, your **s** are in Gath," 1 Kgs 2:39
went to Gath to Achish to seek his **s**. 1 Kgs 2:40
went and brought his **s** from Gath. 1 Kgs 2:40

and made a feast for all his **s**. 1 Kgs 3:15
of Tyre sent his **s** to Solomon when he 1 Kgs 5:1
And my **s** will join your servants, and I 1 Kgs 5:6
And my servants will join your **s**, and I 1 Kgs 5:6
pay you for your **s** such wages as you 1 Kgs 5:6
My **s** shall bring it down to the sea 1 Kgs 5:9
love to your **s** who walk before 1 Kgs 8:23
in heaven and act and judge your **s**, 1 Kgs 8:32
heaven and forgive the sin of your **s**, 1 Kgs 8:36
And Hiram sent with the fleet his **s**, 1 Kgs 9:27
sea, together with the **s** of Solomon. 1 Kgs 9:27
officials, and the attendance of his **s**, 1 Kgs 10:5
Happy are your **s**, who continually 1 Kgs 10:8
back to her own land with her **s**. 1 Kgs 10:13
certain Edomites of his father's **s**, 1 Kgs 11:17
then they will be your **s** forever." 1 Kgs 12:7
gave them into the hands of his **s**. 1 Kgs 15:18
I will send my **s** to you tomorrow 1 Kgs 20:6
the houses of your **s** and lay hands on 1 Kgs 20:6
By the **s** of the governors of the 1 Kgs 20:14
he mustered the **s** of the governors 1 Kgs 20:15
The **s** of the governors of the 1 Kgs 20:17
the **s** of the governors of the districts 1 Kgs 20:19
And the **s** of the king of Syria said to 1 Kgs 20:23
And his **s** said to him, "Behold now, 1 Kgs 20:31
And the king of Israel said to his **s**, 1 Kgs 22:3
"Let my **s** go with your servants in 1 Kgs 22:49
go with your **s** in the ships," 1 Kgs 22:49
and the life of these fifty **s** of yours, 2 Kgs 1:13
there are with your **s** fifty strong men. 2 Kgs 2:16
one of the king of Israel's **s** answered, 2 Kgs 3:11
"Send me one of the **s** and one of the 2 Kgs 4:22
But his **s** came near and said to him, 2 Kgs 5:13
and laid them on two of his **s**. 2 Kgs 5:23
oxen, male **s** and female servants? 2 Kgs 5:26
oxen, male servants and female **s**? 2 Kgs 5:26
to go with your **s**." And he answered, 2 Kgs 6:3
Israel, he took counsel with his **s**, 2 Kgs 6:8
and he called his **s** and said to them, 2 Kgs 6:11
And one of his **s** said, "None, my lord, 2 Kgs 6:12
rose in the night and said to his **s**, 2 Kgs 7:12
And one of his **s** said, "Let some men 2 Kgs 7:13
Jezebel the blood of my **s** the prophets, 2 Kgs 9:7
and the blood of all the **s** of the LORD. 2 Kgs 9:7
Jehu came out to the **s** of his master, 2 Kgs 9:11
His **s** carried him in a chariot to 2 Kgs 9:28
sent to Jehu, saying, "We are your **s**, 2 Kgs 10:5
His **s** arose and made a conspiracy 2 Kgs 12:20
Jehozabad the son of Shomer, his **s**, 2 Kgs 12:21
he struck down his **s** who had struck 2 Kgs 14:5
I sent to you by my **s** the prophets." 2 Kgs 17:13
had spoken by all his **s** the prophets. 2 Kgs 17:23
among the least of my master's **s**, 2 Kgs 18:24
"Please speak to your **s** in Aramaic, 2 Kgs 18:26
When the **s** of King Hezekiah came 2 Kgs 19:5
with which the **s** of the king of 2 Kgs 19:6
the LORD said by his **s** the prophets, 2 Kgs 21:10
And the **s** of Amon conspired 2 Kgs 21:23
"Your **s** have emptied out the money 2 Kgs 22:9
And his **s** carried him dead in a 2 Kgs 23:30
that he spoke by his **s** the prophets. 2 Kgs 24:2
that time the **s** of Nebuchadnezzar 2 Kgs 24:10
the city while his **s** were besieging it, 2 Kgs 24:11
mother and his **s** and his officials 2 Kgs 24:12
priests, the Levites, and the temple **s**. 1 Chr 9:2
the Moabites became **s** to David and 1 Chr 18:2
the Syrians became **s** to David and 1 Chr 18:6
carried by the **s** of Hadadezer and 1 Chr 18:7
all the Edomites became David's **s**. 1 Chr 18:13
And David's **s** came to the land of the 1 Chr 19:2
Have not his **s** come to you to search 1 Chr 19:3
Hanun took David's **s** and shaved 1 Chr 19:4
And when the **s** of Hadadezer saw 1 Chr 19:19
of David and by the hand of his **s**. 1 Chr 20:8
lord the king, all of them my lord's **s**? 1 Chr 21:3
I know that your **s** know how to cut 2 Chr 2:8
And my **s** will be with your servants, 2 Chr 2:8
And my servants will be with your **s**, 2 Chr 2:8
I will give for your **s**, the woodsmen 2 Chr 2:10
lord has spoken, let him send to his **s**. 2 Chr 2:15
love to your **s** who walk before 2 Chr 6:14
heaven and act and judge your **s**, 2 Chr 6:23
heaven and forgive the sin of your **s**, 2 Chr 6:27
the hand of his **s** ships and servants 2 Chr 8:18
servants ships and **s** familiar with 2 Chr 8:18
together with the **s** of Solomon and 2 Chr 8:18
officials, and the attendance of his **s**, 2 Chr 9:4
Happy are these your **s**, who 2 Chr 9:7
the **s** of Hiram and the servants of 2 Chr 9:10
of Hiram and the **s** of Solomon, 2 Chr 9:10
back to her own land with her **s**. 2 Chr 9:12
went to Tarshish with the **s** of Hiram. 2 Chr 9:21
then they will be your **s** forever." 2 Chr 10:7
Nevertheless, they shall be **s** to him, 2 Chr 12:8
his **s** conspired against him 2 Chr 24:25
he killed his **s** who had struck down 2 Chr 25:3
sent his **s** to Jerusalem to Hezekiah 2 Chr 32:9
And his **s** said still more against the 2 Chr 32:16
And his **s** conspired against him 2 Chr 33:24
committed to your **s** they are doing. 2 Chr 34:16
And the king said to his **s**, "Take me 2 Chr 35:23
So his **s** took him out of the chariot 2 Chr 35:24
and they became **s** to him and to his 2 Chr 36:20
The temple **s**: the sons of Ziha, the sons Ezr 2:43
The sons of Solomon's **s**: the sons of Ezr 2:55
All the temple **s** and the sons of Ezr 2:58
and the sons of Solomon's **s** were 392. Ezr 2:58
besides their male and female **s**, of Ezr 2:65
and the temple **s** lived in their towns, Ezr 2:70
"To Artaxerxes the king: Your **s**, the Ezr 4:11
'We are the **s** of the God of heaven and Ezr 5:11
singers and gatekeepers, and the temple **s**. Ezr 7:7
singers, the doorkeepers, the temple **s**, Ezr 7:24
servants, or other **s** of this house of God. Ezr 7:24
brothers and the temple **s** at the place Ezr 8:17
besides 220 of the temple **s**, whom David Ezr 8:20
commanded by your **s** the prophets, Ezr 9:11
and night for the people of Israel your **s**, Neh 1:6
They are your **s** and your people, Neh 1:10
the prayer of your **s** who delight to fear Neh 1:11
and we his **s** will arise and build, Neh 2:20
and the temple **s** living on Ophel Neh 3:26
house of the temple **s** and of the Neh 3:31
half of my **s** worked on construction, Neh 4:16
my brothers nor my **s** nor the men of Neh 4:23
brothers and my **s** are lending them Neh 5:10
Even their **s** lorded it over the people. Neh 5:15
and all my **s** were gathered there for the Neh 5:16
The temple **s**: the sons of Ziha, the sons Neh 7:46
The sons of Solomon's **s**: the sons of Neh 7:57
All the temple **s** and the sons of Neh 7:60
and the sons of Solomon's **s** were 392. Neh 7:60
besides their male and female **s**, of Neh 7:67
some of the people, the temple **s**, Neh 7:73
Pharaoh and all his **s** and all the Neh 9:10
gatekeepers, the singers, the temple **s**, Neh 10:28
the priests, the Levites, the temple **s**, Neh 11:3
and the descendants of Solomon's **s**. Neh 11:3
But the temple **s** lived on Ophel; and Neh 11:21
and Gishpa were over the temple **s**. Neh 11:21
I stationed some of my **s** at the gates, Neh 13:19
he gave a feast for all his officials and **s**. Est 1:3
a great feast for all his officials and **s**; Est 2:18
And all the king's **s** who were at the Est 3:2
Then the king's **s** who were at the king's Est 3:3
"All the king's **s** and the people of the Est 4:11
above the officials and the **s** of the king. Est 5:11
and 500 female donkeys, and very many **s**, Jb 1:3
and struck down the **s** with the edge of Jb 1:15
the sheep and the **s** and consumed them, Jb 1:16
and struck down the **s** with the edge of Jb 1:17
Even in his **s** he puts no trust, and his Jb 4:18
The LORD redeems the life of his **s**; none Ps 34:22
the offspring of his **s** shall inherit it, Ps 69:36
given the bodies of your **s** to the birds of Ps 79:2
blood of your **s** be known among Ps 79:10
O Lord, how your **s** are mocked, Ps 89:50
O LORD! How long? Have pity on your **s**! Ps 90:13
Let your work be shown to your **s**, and Ps 90:16
For your **s** hold her stones dear and Ps 102:14
children of your **s** shall dwell secure; Ps 102:28
his people, to deal craftily with his **s**. Ps 105:25
Praise, O **s** of the LORD, praise the name Ps 113:1
this day, for all things are your **s**. Ps 119:91
as the eyes of **s** look to the hand of their Ps 123:2
bless the LORD, all you **s** of the LORD, Ps 134:1
of the LORD, give praise, O **s** of the LORD, Ps 135:1
wonders against Pharaoh and all his **s**; Ps 135:9
people and have compassion on his **s**. Ps 135:14
captain among the least of my master's **s**, Is 36:9
"Please speak to your **s** in Aramaic, Is 36:11
When the **s** of King Hezekiah came to Is 37:5
By your **s** you have mocked the Lord, Is 37:24
is the heritage of the **s** of the LORD and Is 54:17
love the name of the LORD, and to be his **s**, Is 56:6
Return for the sake of your **s**, the tribes Is 63:17
possess it, and my **s** shall dwell there. Is 65:9
"Behold, my **s** shall eat, but you shall be Is 65:13
behold, my **s** shall drink, but you shall Is 65:13
behold, my **s** shall rejoice, but you shall Is 65:13
my **s** shall sing for gladness of heart, Is 65:14
but his **s** he will call by another name. Is 65:15
of the LORD shall be known to his **s**, Is 66:14
persistently sent all my **s** the prophets to Jer 7:25
Her nobles send their **s** for water; they Jer 14:3
king of Judah and his **s** and the people in Jer 21:7
on the throne of David, you, and your **s**, Jer 22:2
horses, they and their **s** and their people. Jer 22:4
sent to you all his **s** the prophets, Jer 25:4
Pharaoh king of Egypt, his **s**, his Jer 25:19
to the words of my **s** the prophets whom I Jer 26:5
sent to you by my **s** the prophets, Jer 29:19
I have sent to you all my **s** the prophets, Jer 35:15
nor any of his **s** who heard all these Jer 36:24
offspring and his **s** for their iniquity. Jer 36:31
But neither he nor his **s** nor the people of Jer 37:2
I done to you or your **s** or this people, Jer 37:18
sent to you all my **s** the prophets, Jer 44:4
former days by my **s** the prophets of Ezk 38:17
out of his inheritance to one of his **s**, Ezk 46:17
"Test your **s** for ten days; let us be given Dn 1:12
and deal with your **s** according to what Dn 1:13
king, live forever! Tell your **s** the dream, Dn 2:4
said, "Let the king tell his **s** the dream, Dn 2:7
and Abednego, **s** of the Most High God, Dn 3:26
has sent his angel and delivered his **s**, Dn 3:28
have not listened to your **s** the prophets, Dn 9:6
he set before us by his **s** the prophets. Dn 9:10
on the male and female **s** in those days I Jl 2:29
revealing his secret to his **s** the prophets. Am 3:7
which I commanded my **s** the prophets, Zec 1:6
And the **s** of the master of the house Mt 13:27
So the **s** said to him, 'Then do you want Mt 13:28
and he said to his **s**, "This is John the Mt 14:2
wished to settle accounts with his **s**. Mt 18:23
one of his fellow **s** who owed him a Mt 18:28
When his fellow **s** saw what had taken Mt 18:31
he sent his **s** to the tenants to get his Mt 21:34
the tenants took his **s** and beat one, Mt 21:35
Again he sent other **s**, more than the Mt 21:36
and sent his **s** to call those who were Mt 22:3
Again he sent other **s**, saying, 'Tell those Mt 22:4
while the rest seized his **s**, treated them Mt 22:6
Then he said to his **s**, 'The wedding feast Mt 22:8
And those **s** went out into the roads and Mt 22:10
to beat his fellow **s** and eats and drinks Mt 24:49
who called his **s** and entrusted to them Mt 25:14
the master of those **s** came and settled Mt 25:19
boat with the hired **s** and followed him. Mk 1:20
leaves home and puts his **s** in charge, Mk 13:34
Blessed are those **s** whom the master Lk 12:37
finds them awake, blessed are those **s**! Lk 12:38
begins to beat the male and female **s**, Lk 12:45
of my father's hired **s** have more than Lk 15:17
son. Treat me as one of your hired **s**."' Lk 15:19
But the father said to his **s**, 'Bring Lk 15:22
called one of the **s** and asked what these Lk 15:26
commanded, say, 'We are unworthy **s**; Lk 17:10
Calling ten of his **s**, he gave them ten Lk 19:13
he ordered these **s** to whom he had Lk 19:15
His mother said to the **s**, "Do whatever he Jn 2:5
Jesus said to the **s**, "Fill the jars with Jn 2:7
came from (though the **s** who had drawn Jn 2:9
his **s** met him and told him that his son Jn 4:51
No longer do I call you **s**, for the servant Jn 15:15
Now the **s** and officers had made a Jn 18:18
One of the **s** of the high priest, a relative Jn 18:26
world, my **s** would have been fighting, Jn 18:36
on my male **s** and female servants Acts 2:18
servants and female **s** in those days Acts 2:18
and grant to your **s** to continue to Acts 4:29
called two of his **s** and a devout soldier Acts 10:7
"These men are **s** of the Most High Acts 16:17
S through whom you believed, as the 1 Cor 3:5
as **s** of Christ and stewards of the 1 Cor 4:1
with ourselves as your **s** for Jesus' sake. 2 Cor 4:5
but as **s** of God we commend ourselves 2 Cor 6:4
So it is no surprise if his **s**, also, 2 Cor 11:15
themselves as **s** of righteousness. 2 Cor 11:15
Are they **s** of Christ? I am a better 2 Cor 11:23
as people-pleasers, but as **s** of Christ, Eph 6:6
Paul and Timothy, **s** of Christ Jesus, To Phil 1:1
cover-up for evil, but living as **s** of God. 1 Pt 2:16
S, be subject to your masters with all 1 Pt 2:18
him to show to his **s** the things that must Rv 1:1
and seducing my **s** to practice sexual Rv 2:20
of their fellow **s** and their brothers Rv 6:11
until we have sealed the **s** of our God on Rv 7:3
as he announced to his **s** the prophets. Rv 10:7
to be judged, and for rewarding your **s**, Rv 11:18
has avenged on her the blood of his **s**." Rv 19:2
saying, "Praise our God, all you his **s**, Rv 19:5
will be in it, and his **s** will worship him. Rv 22:3
angel to show his **s** what must soon take Rv 22:6

SERVANTS' (4)
for there is no pasture for your **s** flocks, Gn 47:4
house of Pharaoh and into his **s** houses. Ex 8:24
the eyes of his **s** female servants, 2 Sm 6:20
a blessing in it,' so I will do for my **s** sake, Is 65:8

SERVE (213)
It shall **s** as food for you and for them." Gn 6:21
judgment on the nation that they **s**, Gn 15:14
other, the older shall **s** the younger." Gn 25:23
Let peoples **s** you, and nations bow Gn 27:29

live, and you shall **s** your brother; Gn 27:40
should you therefore **s** me for nothing? Gn 29:15
"I will **s** you seven years for your Gn 29:18
to me? Did I not **s** with you for Rachel? Gn 29:25
himself he said, "**S** the food." Gn 43:31
"When you **s** as midwife to the Hebrew Ex 1:16
you shall **s** God on this mountain." Ex 3:12
son go that he may **s** me." If you refuse to Ex 4:23
go, that they may **s** me in the wilderness. Ex 7:16
"Let my people go, that they may **s** me. Ex 8:1
"Let my people go, that they may **s** me. Ex 8:20
"Let my people go, that they may **s** me. Ex 9:1
"Let my people go, that they may **s** me. Ex 9:13
Let my people go, that they may **s** me. Ex 10:3
go, that they may **s** the LORD their God. Ex 10:7
said to them, "Go, **s** the LORD your God. Ex 10:8
the men among you, and **s** the LORD, Ex 10:11
called Moses and said, "Go, **s** the LORD; Ex 10:24
take of them to **s** the LORD our God, Ex 10:26
with what we must **s** the LORD until we Ex 10:26
and go, **s** the LORD, as you have said. Ex 12:31
us alone that we may **s** the Egyptians'? Ex 14:12
better for us to **s** the Egyptians than to Ex 14:12
shall not bow down to them or **s** them, Ex 20:5
buy a Hebrew slave, he shall **s** six years, Ex 21:2
not bow down to their gods nor **s** them, Ex 23:24
You shall **s** the LORD your God, and he Ex 23:25
for if you **s** their gods, it will surely be a Ex 23:33
to **s** me as priests—Aaron and Aaron's Ex 28:1
brother and his sons to **s** me as priests. Ex 28:4
them, that they may **s** me as priests. Ex 28:41
them, that they may **s** me as priests. Ex 29:1
sons I will consecrate to **s** me as priests. Ex 29:44
them, that they may **s** me as priests. Ex 30:30
him, that he may **s** me as priest. Ex 40:13
father, that they may **s** me as priests. Ex 40:15
they were presented to **s** as priests of the Lv 7:35
you shall not make him **s** as a slave: Lv 25:39
He shall **s** with you until the year of the Lv 25:40
priests, whom he ordained to **s** as priests. Nm 3:3
Levites shall go in to **s** at the tent of Nm 8:15
the duty of the service and **s** no more. Nm 8:25
and you will **s** as eyes for us. Nm 10:31
that is within the veil; and you shall **s**. Nm 18:7
away and bow down to them and **s** them, Dt 4:19
And there you will **s** gods of wood and Dt 4:28
shall not bow down to them or **s** them; Dt 5:9
Him you shall **s** and by his name you Dt 6:13
sons from following me, to **s** other gods. Dt 7:4
pity them, neither shall you **s** their gods, Dt 7:16
after other gods and **s** them and worship Dt 8:19
to **s** the LORD your God with all your Dt 10:12
You shall **s** him and hold fast to him, Dt 10:20
and to **s** him with all your heart and Dt 11:13
you turn aside and **s** other gods and Dt 11:16
'How did these nations **s** their gods? Dt 12:30
you have not known, 'and let us **s** them,' Dt 13:2
and you shall **s** him and hold fast to Dt 13:4
saying, 'Let us go and **s** other gods,' Dt 13:6
city, saying, 'Let us go and **s** other gods,' Dt 13:13
is sold to you, he shall **s** you six years, Dt 15:12
do forced labor for you and shall **s** you. Dt 20:11
the left, to go after other gods to **s** them. Dt 28:14
And there you shall **s** other gods of Dt 28:36
Because you did not **s** the LORD your Dt 28:47
therefore you shall **s** your enemies Dt 28:48
and there you shall **s** other gods of wood Dt 28:64
our God to go and **s** the gods of those Dt 29:18
away to worship other gods and **s** them, Dt 30:17
they will turn to other gods and **s** them, Dt 31:20
cling to him and to **s** him with all your Jos 22:5
swear by them or **s** them or bow down Jos 23:7
and go and **s** other gods and bow down Jos 23:16
fear the LORD and **s** him in sincerity Jos 24:14
the River and in Egypt, and **s** the LORD. Jos 24:14
if it is evil in your eyes to **s** the LORD, Jos 24:15
LORD, choose this day whom you will **s**, Jos 24:15
me and my house, we will **s** the LORD." Jos 24:15
should forsake the LORD to **s** other gods, Jos 24:16
Therefore we also will **s** the LORD, for he Jos 24:18
people, "You are not able to **s** the LORD, Jos 24:19
forsake the LORD and **s** foreign gods, Jos 24:20
to Joshua, "No, but we will **s** the LORD." Jos 24:21
the LORD, to **s** him." And they said, Jos 24:22
to Joshua, "The LORD our God we will **s**, Jos 24:24
we of Shechem, that we should **s** him? Jgs 9:28
S the men of Hamor the father of Jgs 9:28
of Shechem; but why should we **s** him? Jgs 9:28
is Abimelech, that we should **s** him?' Jgs 9:38
they forsook the LORD and did not **s** him. Jgs 10:6
your heart to the LORD and **s** him only, 1 Sm 7:3
a treaty with us, and we will **s** you." 1 Sm 11:1
of our enemies, that we may **s** you.' 1 Sm 12:10
fear the LORD and **s** him and obey his 1 Sm 12:14
but **s** the LORD with all your heart. 1 Sm 12:20
the LORD and **s** him faithfully with 1 Sm 12:24
you shall be our servants and **s** us." 1 Sm 17:9
of the LORD, saying, 'Go, **s** other gods.' 1 Sm 26:19
And again, whom should I **s**? Should 2 Sm 16:19
served your father, so I will **s** you." 2 Sm 16:19
but go and **s** other gods and worship 1 Kgs 9:6
heavy yoke on us, and we will **s** you." 1 Kgs 12:4
to this people today and **s** them, 1 Kgs 12:7
a little, but Jehu will **s** him much. 2 Kgs 10:18
to them or **s** them or sacrifice 2 Kgs 17:35
king of Assyria and would not **s** him. 2 Kgs 18:7
in the land and **s** the king of 2 Kgs 25:24
of your father and **s** him with a 1 Chr 28:9
and go and **s** other gods and worship 2 Chr 7:19
heavy yoke on us, and we will **s** you." 2 Chr 10:4
and the Levites will **s** you as officers. 2 Chr 19:11
forever, and **s** the LORD your God, 2 Chr 30:8
he commanded Judah to **s** the LORD, 2 Chr 33:16
present in Israel **s** the LORD their 2 Chr 34:33
Now **s** the LORD your God and his 2 Chr 35:3
nobles would not stoop to **s** their Lord. Neh 3:5
they did not **s** you or turn from their Neh 9:35
is the Almighty, that we should **s** him? Jb 21:15
If they listen and **s** him, they complete Jb 36:11
"Is the wild ox willing to **s** you? Will he Jb 39:9
S the LORD with fear, and rejoice with Ps 2:11
Posterity shall **s** him; it shall be told of Ps 22:30
fall down before him, all nations **s** him! Ps 72:11
S the LORD with gladness! Come into his Ps 100:2
service with which you were made to **s**, Is 14:3
Their webs will not **s** as clothing; men Is 59:6
that will not **s** you shall perish; Is 60:12
your bonds; but you said, 'I will not **s**.' Jer 2:20
so you shall **s** foreigners in a land that is Jer 5:19
have gone after other gods to **s** them. Jer 11:10
after other gods to **s** them and worship Jer 13:10
I will make you **s** your enemies in a Jer 15:14
and there you shall **s** other gods day Jer 16:13
and I will make you **s** your enemies in a Jer 17:4
makes his neighbor **s** him for nothing Jer 22:13
after other gods to **s** and worship them, Jer 25:6
and these nations shall **s** the king of Jer 25:11
him also the beasts of the field to **s** him. Jer 27:6
All the nations shall **s** him and his son Jer 27:7
will not **s** this Nebuchadnezzar Jer 27:8
'You shall not **s** the king of Babylon.' Jer 27:9
yoke of the king of Babylon and **s** him, Jer 27:11
and **s** him and his people and live. Jer 27:12
nation that will not **s** the king of Jer 27:13
'You shall not **s** the king of Babylon,' Jer 27:14
to them; **s** the king of Babylon and live. Jer 27:17
iron yoke to **s** Nebuchadnezzar king of Jer 28:14
king of Babylon, and they shall **s** him, Jer 28:14
But they shall **s** the LORD their God and Jer 30:9
and do not go after other gods to **s** them, Jer 35:15
"Do not be afraid to **s** the Chaldeans. Jer 40:9
in the land and **s** the king of Babylon, Jer 40:9
to make offerings and **s** other gods that Jer 44:3
Go **s** every one of you his idols, now Ezk 20:39
all of them, shall **s** me in the land. Ezk 20:40
of the temple to **s** as supports for the Ezk 41:6
not come near to me, to **s** me as priest, Ezk 44:13
they do not **s** your gods or worship the Dn 3:12
that you do not **s** my gods or worship Dn 3:14
our God whom we **s** is able to deliver us Dn 3:17
that we will not **s** your gods or worship Dn 3:18
bodies rather than **s** and worship any Dn 3:28
your God, whom you **s** continually, Dn 6:16
has your God, whom you **s** continually, Dn 6:20
nations, and languages should **s** him; Dn 7:14
all dominions shall **s** and obey them.' Dn 7:27
of the LORD and **s** him with one accord. Zep 3:9
You have said, 'It is vain to **s** God. Mal 3:14
serves God and one who does not **s** him. Mal 3:18
your God and him only shall you **s**.'" Mt 4:10
"No one can **s** two masters, for either he Mt 6:24
the other. You cannot **s** God and money. Mt 6:24
left her, and she rose and began to **s** him. Mt 8:15
of Man came not to be served but to **s**, Mt 20:28
fever left her, and she began to **s** them. Mk 1:31
of Man came not to be served but to **s**, Mk 10:45
our enemies, might **s** him without fear, Lk 1:74
your God, and him only shall you **s**.'" Lk 4:8
she rose and began to **s** them. Lk 4:39
that my sister has left me to **s** alone? Lk 10:40
at table, and he will come and **s** them. Lk 12:37
No servant can **s** two masters, for Lk 16:13
other. You cannot **s** God and money." Lk 16:13
properly, and **s** me while I eat and drink, Lk 17:8
preaching the word of God to **s** tables. Acts 6:2
'But I will judge the nation that they **s**,' Acts 7:7
whom I **s** with my spirit in the gospel of Rom 1:9
so that we **s** not under the old written Rom 7:6
I myself **s** the law of God with my Rom 7:25
but with my flesh I **s** the law of sin. Rom 7:25
told, "The older will **s** the younger." Rom 9:12
in zeal, be fervent in spirit, **s** the Lord. Rom 12:11
persons do not **s** our Lord Christ, Rom 16:18
and those who **s** at the altar share in 1 Cor 9:13
support from them in order to **s** you. 2 Cor 11:8
flesh, but through love **s** one another. Gal 5:13
God from idols to **s** the living and 1 Thes 1:9
then let them **s** as deacons if they 1 Tm 3:10
For those who **s** well as deacons gain 1 Tm 3:13
rather they must **s** all the better since 1 Tm 6:2
I thank God whom I **s**, as did my 2 Tm 1:3
order that he might **s** me on your Phlm 1:13
spirits sent out to **s** for the sake of Heb 1:14
They **s** a copy and shadow of the Heb 8:5
from dead works to **s** the living God. Heb 9:14
from which those who **s** the tent have Heb 13:10
received a gift, use it to **s** one another, 1 Pt 4:10
s as an example by undergoing a Jude 1:7
and **s** him day and night in his temple; Rv 7:15

SERVED (80)

Twelve years they had **s** Chedorlaomer, Gn 14:4
So Jacob **s** seven years for Rachel, and Gn 29:20
and **s** Laban for another seven years. Gn 29:30
my children for whom I have **s** you, Gn 30:26
"You yourself know how I have **s** you, Gn 30:29
know that I have **s** your father with all Gn 31:6
I **s** you fourteen years for your two Gn 31:41
They **s** him by himself, and them by Gn 43:32
So Eleazar and Ithamar **s** as priests in Nm 3:4
all who **s** in the tent of meeting, Nm 4:37
all who **s** in the tent of meeting, Nm 4:41
of the men who had **s** in the army— Nm 31:42
whom you shall dispossess **s** their gods, Dt 12:2
of a hired servant he has **s** you six years. Dt 15:18
and has gone and **s** other gods and Dt 17:3
and went and **s** other gods and Dt 29:26
and of Nahor; and they **s** other gods. Jos 24:2
that your fathers **s** beyond the River Jos 24:14
the gods your fathers **s** in the region Jos 24:15
Israel **s** the LORD all the days of Joshua, Jos 24:31
And the people **s** the LORD all the days of Jgs 2:7
in the sight of the LORD and **s** the Baals. Jgs 2:11
abandoned the LORD and **s** the Baals and Jgs 2:13
gave to their sons, and they **s** their gods. Jgs 3:6
the LORD their God and **s** the Baals and the Jgs 3:7
of Israel **s** Cushan-rishathaim eight Jgs 3:8
the people of Israel **s** Eglon the king of Jgs 3:14
sight of the LORD and **s** the Baals and the Jgs 10:6
our God and have **s** the Baals." Jgs 10:10
you have forsaken me and **s** other gods; Jgs 10:13
gods from among them and **s** the LORD, Jgs 10:16
Ashtaroth, and they **s** the LORD only. 1 Sm 7:4
the LORD and have **s** the Baals and 1 Sm 12:10
the young man who **s** him and said, 2 Sm 13:17
As I have **s** your father, so I will serve 2 Sm 16:19
people whom I had not known **s** me. 2 Sm 22:44
brought tribute and **s** Solomon all 1 Kgs 4:21
gods and worshiped them and **s** them. 1 Kgs 9:9
and went and **s** Baal and worshiped 1 Kgs 16:31
He **s** Baal and worshiped him and 1 Kgs 22:53
said to them, "Ahab **s** Baal a little, 2 Kgs 10:18
and they **s** idols, of which the LORD 2 Kgs 17:12
all the host of heaven and **s** Baal. 2 Kgs 17:16
the LORD but also **s** their own gods, 2 Kgs 17:33
LORD and also **s** their carved images. 2 Kgs 17:41
all the host of heaven and **s** them. 2 Kgs 21:3
father walked and **s** the idols that 2 Kgs 21:21
that his father **s** and worshiped 2 Kgs 21:21
(it was he who **s** as priest in the 1 Chr 6:10
are the men who **s** and their sons. 1 Chr 6:33
and their officers who **s** the king in 1 Chr 27:1
He **s** for the first month. 1 Chr 27:3
of the divisions that **s** the king, 1 Chr 28:1
and worshiped them and **s** them. 2 Chr 7:22
and **s** the Asherim and the idols. 2 Chr 24:18
all the host of heaven and **s** them. 2 Chr 33:3
his father had made, and **s** them. 2 Chr 33:22
Drinks were **s** in golden vessels, vessels Est 1:7
the seven eunuchs who **s** in the presence Est 1:10
people whom I had not known **s** me. Ps 18:43
They **s** their idols, which became a Ps 106:36
have forsaken me and **s** foreign gods in Jer 5:19
of heaven, which they have loved and **s**, Jer 8:2
gods and have **s** and worshiped them, Jer 16:11
and worshiped other gods and **s** them.'"" Jer 22:9
sold to you and has **s** you six years; Jer 34:14
bodyguard, who **s** the king of Babylon, Jer 52:12
a thousand thousands **s** him, and ten Dn 7:10
there Israel **s** for a wife, and for a wife Hos 12:12
become plunder for those who **s** them. Zec 2:9
of Man came not to be **s** but to serve, Mt 20:28
of Man came not to be **s** but to serve, Mk 10:45
'Look, these many years I have **s** you, Lk 15:29
gave a dinner for him there. Martha **s**, Jn 12:2
after he had **s** the purpose of God in Acts 13:36

nor is he **s** by human hands, as Acts 17:25
and worshiped and **s** the creature Rom 1:25
to me has really **s** to advance the Phil 1:12
with a father he has **s** with me in the Phil 2:22
which no one has ever **s** at the altar. Heb 7:13

SERVES (13)
as a man spares his son who **s** him. Mal 3:17
between one who **s** God and one who Mal 3:18
youngest, and the leader as one who **s**. Lk 22:26
one who reclines at table or one who **s**? Lk 22:27
But I am among you as the one who **s**. Lk 22:27
to him, "Everyone **s** the good wine first, Jn 2:10
If anyone **s** me, he must follow me; and Jn 12:26
If anyone **s** me, the Father will honor Jn 12:26
if our unrighteousness **s** to show the Rom 3:5
Whoever thus **s** Christ is acceptable Rom 14:18
Who **s** as a soldier at his own expense? 1 Cor 9:7
who speaks oracles of God; whoever **s**, 1 Pt 4:11
as one who **s** by the strength that God 1 Pt 4:11

SERVICE (148)
for you know the **s** that I have given Gn 30:26
when he entered the **s** of Pharaoh king Gn 41:46
and made their lives bitter with hard **s**, Ex 1:14
he has promised, you shall keep this **s**. Ex 12:25
to you, 'What do you mean by this **s**?' Ex 12:26
you shall keep this **s** in this month. Ex 13:5
shall give it for the **s** of the tent of Ex 30:16
of his sons, for their **s** as priests, Ex 31:10
been ordained for the **s** of the LORD, Ex 32:29
of his sons, for their **s** as priests." Ex 35:19
for the tent of meeting, and for all its **s**, Ex 35:21
the utensils for the **s** of the tabernacle, Ex 39:40
of his sons for their **s** as priests. Ex 39:41
in proportion to his years of **s**. Lv 25:52
cords—all the **s** connected with these. Nm 3:26
screen; all the **s** connected with these. Nm 3:31
all the **s** connected with these; Nm 3:36
This is the **s** of the sons of Kohath in the Nm 4:4
all the vessels of the **s** that are used in Nm 4:12
the altar, which are used for the **s** there, Nm 4:14
to do duty, to do **s** in the tent of meeting. Nm 4:23
This is the **s** of the clans of the Nm 4:24
cords and all the equipment for their **s**. Nm 4:26
All the **s** of the sons of the Gershonites Nm 4:27
This is the **s** of the clans of the sons of Nm 4:28
duty, to do the **s** of the tent of meeting. Nm 4:30
as the whole of their **s** in the tent of Nm 4:31
This is the **s** of the clans of the sons of Nm 4:33
the whole of their **s** in the tent of Nm 4:33
on duty, for **s** in the tent of meeting; Nm 4:35
could come on duty for **s** in the tent of Nm 4:39
on duty, for **s** in the tent of meeting— Nm 4:43
come to do the **s** of ministry and the Nm 4:47
ministry and the **s** of bearing burdens Nm 4:47
may be used in the **s** of the tent of Nm 7:5
Levites, to each man according to his **s**." Nm 7:5
sons of Gershon, according to their **s**. Nm 7:7
the sons of Merari, according to their **s**, Nm 7:8
were charged with the **s** of the holy Nm 7:9
that they may do the **s** of the LORD. Nm 8:11
to do the **s** for the people of Israel at the Nm 8:19
went in to do their **s** in the tent of Nm 8:22
to do duty in the **s** of the tent of Nm 8:24
the duty of the **s** and serve no more. Nm 8:25
keeping guard, but they shall do no **s**. Nm 8:26
to do **s** in the tabernacle of the LORD Nm 16:9
tent of meeting for all the **s** of the tent, Nm 18:4
LORD, to do the **s** of the tent of meeting. Nm 18:6
in return for their **s** that they do, Nm 18:21
they do, their **s** in the tent of meeting, Nm 18:21
the Levites shall do the **s** of the tent of Nm 18:23
in return for your **s** in the tent of Nm 18:31
who had come from **s** in the war. Nm 31:14
that we do perform the **s** of the LORD in Jos 22:27
came to Saul and entered his **s**. 1 Sm 16:21
saying, "Let David remain in my **s**, 1 Sm 16:22
the day I entered your **s** until now, 1 Sm 29:8
let her wait on the king and be in his **s**. 1 Kgs 1:2
and she was of **s** to the king and 1 Kgs 1:4
lighten the hard **s** of your father 1 Kgs 12:4
she worked in the **s** of Naaman's wife. 2 Kgs 5:2
of bronze used in the temple **s**, 2 Kgs 25:14
They lived there in the king's **s**. 1 Chr 4:23
put in charge of the **s** of song in the 1 Chr 6:31
they performed their **s** according to 1 Chr 6:32
for all the **s** of the tabernacle 1 Chr 6:48
enrolled by genealogies, for **s** in war, 1 Chr 7:40
for the work of the **s** of the house of 1 Chr 9:13
were in charge of the work of the **s**, 1 Chr 9:19
them had charge of the utensils of **s**, 1 Chr 9:28
of the temple free from other **s**, 1 Chr 9:33
chief officials in the **s** of the king. 1 Chr 18:17
do the work for the **s** of the house of 1 Chr 23:24
or any of the things for its **s**." 1 Chr 23:26
of Aaron for the **s** of the house of 1 Chr 23:28
any work for the **s** of the house of 1 Chr 23:28
for the **s** of the house of the LORD. 1 Chr 23:32
to the appointed duties in their **s**. 1 Chr 24:3
duty in their **s** to come into 1 Chr 24:19
the chiefs of the **s** also set apart for 1 Chr 25:1
set apart for the **s** the sons of Asaph, 1 Chr 25:1
and lyres for the **s** of the house of 1 Chr 25:6
brothers, able men qualified for the **s**; 1 Chr 26:8
of the LORD and for the **s** of the king. 1 Chr 26:30
all the work of the **s** in the house of 1 Chr 28:13
the vessels for the **s** in the house of 1 Chr 28:13
gold for all golden vessels for each **s**, 1 Chr 28:14
weight of silver vessels for each **s**, 1 Chr 28:14
the use of each lampstand in the **s**, 1 Chr 28:15
all the work for the **s** of the house of 1 Chr 28:20
Levites for all the **s** of the house of 1 Chr 28:21
man who has skill for any kind of **s**; 1 Chr 28:21
They gave for the **s** of the house of 1 Chr 29:7
the divisions of the priests for their **s**, 2 Chr 8:14
lighten the hard **s** of your father 2 Chr 10:4
they may know my **s** and the service 2 Chr 12:8
my service and the **s** of the kingdoms 2 Chr 12:8
of Aaron, and Levites for their **s**. 2 Chr 13:10
a volunteer for the **s** of the LORD, 2 Chr 17:16
These were in the **s** of the king, 2 Chr 17:19
both for the **s** and for the burnt 2 Chr 24:14
Thus the **s** of the house of the LORD 2 Chr 29:35
good skill in the **s** of the LORD. 2 Chr 30:22
by division, each according to his **s**, 2 Chr 31:2
—for their **s** according to their 2 Chr 31:16
he undertook in the **s** of the house of 2 Chr 31:21
all who did work in every kind of **s**, 2 Chr 34:13
them in the **s** of the house 2 Chr 35:2
When the **s** had been prepared for, 2 Chr 35:10
did not need to depart from their **s**, 2 Chr 35:15
So all the **s** of the LORD was prepared 2 Chr 35:16
divisions, for the **s** of God at Jerusalem, Ezr 6:18
been given you for the **s** of the house of Ezr 7:19
because the **s** was too heavy on this Neh 5:18
of a shekel for the **s** of the house of Neh 10:32
brothers stood opposite them in the **s**. Neh 12:9
And they performed the **s** of their God Neh 12:45
of their God and the **s** of purification, Neh 12:45
for the house of my God and for his **s**. Neh 13:14
horses that were used in the king's **s**, Est 8:10
horses that were used in the king's **s**, Est 8:14
"Has not man a hard **s** on earth, and are Jb 7:1
All the days of my **s** I would wait, till my Jb 14:14
turmoil and the hard **s** with which you Is 14:3
you must set him free from your **s**.' Jer 34:14
vessels of bronze used in the temple **s**; Jer 52:18
to do all its **s** and all that is to be done Ezk 44:14
And when his time of **s** was ended, he Lk 1:23
will dress himself for **s** and have them Lk 12:37
you will think he is offering **s** to God. Jn 16:2
when they had completed their **s**, Acts 12:25
if **s**, in our serving; the one who Rom 12:7
Gentiles in the priestly **s** of the gospel Rom 15:16
also to be of **s** to them in material Rom 15:27
and that my **s** for Jerusalem may be Rom 15:31
in the temple **s** get their food 1 Cor 9:13
and there are varieties of **s**, but the 1 Cor 12:5
themselves to the **s** of the saints 1 Cor 16:15
the ministry of this **s** is not only 2 Cor 9:12
By their approval of this **s**, they will 2 Cor 9:13
rendering **s** with a good will as to the Eph 6:7
what was lacking in your **s** to me. Phil 2:30
me faithful, appointing me to his **s**, 1 Tm 1:12
by their good **s** are believers and 1 Tm 6:2
well know all the **s** he rendered at 2 Tm 1:18
and faithful high priest in the **s** of God, Heb 2:17
And every priest stands daily at his **s**, Heb 10:11
and faith and **s** and patient endurance, Rv 2:19

SERVING (16)
also in return for **s** me another seven Gn 29:27
that we have let Israel go from **s** us?" Ex 14:5
Gershonites, in **s** and bearing burdens: Nm 4:24
each one with his task of **s** or carrying. Nm 4:49
gods, **s** them and bowing down to them. Jgs 2:19
the women who were **s** at the entrance 1 Sm 2:22
day, forsaking me and **s** other gods, 1 Sm 8:8
cast them out from **s** as priests of 2 Chr 11:14
Egypt was your sail, **s** as your banner; Ezk 27:7
Now while he was **s** as priest before God Lk 1:8
Martha was distracted with much **s**. Lk 10:40
s the Lord with all humility and with Acts 20:19
if service, in our **s**; the one who Rom 12:7
your reward. You are **s** the Lord Christ. Col 3:24
you showed for his sake in **s** the saints, Heb 6:10
that they were **s** not themselves but 1 Pt 1:12

SERVITUDE (1)
exile because of affliction and hard **s**; Lam 1:3

SET (743)
And God **s** them in the expanse of the Gn 1:17
and **s** the door of the ark in its side. Gn 6:16
But the dove found no place to **s** her foot, Gn 8:9
I have **s** my bow in the cloud, and it Gn 9:13
and they **s** out to go to the land of Gn 12:5
he had prepared, and **s** it before them. Gn 18:8
Then the men **s** out from there, and Gn 18:16
went with them to **s** them on their way. Gn 18:16
brought him out and **s** him outside the Gn 19:16
Abraham **s** seven ewe lambs of the Gn 21:28
ewe lambs that you have **s** apart?" Gn 21:29
Then food was **s** before him to eat. But Gn 24:33
there that night, because the sun had **s**. Gn 28:11
there was a ladder **s** up on the earth, Gn 28:12
put under his head and **s** it up for a Gn 28:18
stone, which I have **s** up for a pillar, Gn 28:22
And he **s** a distance of three days' Gn 30:36
He **s** the sticks that he had peeled in Gn 30:38
separated the lambs and **s** the faces of Gn 30:40
So Jacob arose and **s** his sons and his Gn 31:17
and **s** his face toward the hill country Gn 31:21
S it here before my kinsmen and your Gn 31:37
Jacob took a stone and **s** it up as a Gn 31:45
which I have **s** between you and me. Gn 31:51
And Jacob **s** up a pillar in the place Gn 35:14
and Jacob **s** up a pillar over her tomb. Gn 35:20
man, and **s** him over the land of Egypt. Gn 41:33
I have **s** you over all the land of Egypt." Gn 41:41
the knee!" Thus he **s** him over all the Gn 41:43
him back to you and **s** him before you, Gn 43:9
to me, that I may **s** my eyes on him.' Gn 44:21
Then Jacob **s** out from Beersheba. The Gn 46:5
of him who was **s** apart from his Gn 49:26
Therefore they **s** taskmasters over them Ex 1:11
Pharaoh's taskmasters had **s** over them, Ex 5:14
on that day I will **s** apart the land of Ex 8:22
And the LORD **s** a time, saying, Ex 9:5
you shall **s** apart to the LORD all that Ex 13:12
Then Moses made Israel **s** out from the Ex 15:22
They **s** out from Elim, and all the Ex 16:1
They **s** out from Rephidim and came Ex 19:2
of the people and **s** before them all these Ex 19:7
And you shall **s** limits for the people all Ex 19:12
'**S** limits around the mountain and Ex 19:23
the rules that you shall **s** before them. Ex 21:1
And I will **s** your border from the Red Ex 23:31
And you shall **s** the bread of the Ex 25:30
And the lamps shall be **s** up so as to Ex 25:37
of the outermost curtain in the first **s**. Ex 26:4
of the outermost curtain in the second **s**. Ex 26:4
of the curtain that is in the second **s**; Ex 26:5
the curtain that is outermost in one **s**, Ex 26:10
that is outermost in the second **s**. Ex 26:10
And you shall **s** the table outside the Ex 26:35
And you shall **s** it under the ledge of the Ex 27:5
a lamp may regularly be **s** up to burn. Ex 27:20
And you shall **s** the two stones on the Ex 28:12
You shall **s** in it four rows of stones. A Ex 28:17
a jasper. They shall be **s** in gold filigree. Ex 28:20
And you shall **s** the turban on his head Ex 29:6
know the people, that they are **s** on evil. Ex 32:22
brought onyx stones and stones to be **s**, Ex 35:27
of the outermost curtain of the first **s**. Ex 36:11
the outermost curtain of the second **s**. Ex 36:11
of the curtain that was in the second **s**. Ex 36:12
of the outermost curtain of the one **s**, Ex 36:17
And he **s** them on the shoulder pieces of Ex 39:7
And they **s** in it four rows of stones. A Ex 39:10
lamps with the lamps **s** and all its Ex 39:37
in the lampstand and **s** up its lamps. Ex 40:4
and **s** up the screen for the door of the Ex 40:5
You shall **s** the altar of burnt offering Ex 40:6
And you shall **s** up the court all around, Ex 40:8
He laid its bases, and **s** up its frames, Ex 40:18
on the ark and **s** the mercy seat above Ex 40:20
into the tabernacle and **s** up the veil of Ex 40:21
and **s** up the lamps before the LORD, as Ex 40:25
And he **s** the altar of burnt offering at Ex 40:29
He **s** the basin between the tent of Ex 40:30
and **s** up the screen of the gate of the Ex 40:33
the people of Israel would **s** out. Ex 40:36
then they did not **s** out till the day that Ex 40:37
And he **s** the turban on his head, and on Lv 8:9
the turban, in front, he **s** the golden plate, Lv 8:9
who cleanses him shall **s** the man who Lv 14:11
the two goats and **s** them before the LORD Lv 16:7
I will **s** my face against that person who Lv 17:10
I myself will **s** my face against that man Lv 20:3
then I will **s** my face against that man Lv 20:5
I will **s** my face against that person and Lv 20:6
which I have **s** apart for you to hold Lv 20:25
And you shall **s** them in two piles, six in Lv 24:6
and you shall not **s** up a figured stone in Lv 26:1
I will **s** my face against you, and you Lv 26:17

When the tabernacle is to **s** out, the Nm 1:51
is to be pitched, the Levites shall **s** it up. Nm 1:51
They shall **s** out first on the march. Nm 2:9
were 151,450. They shall **s** out second. Nm 2:16
"Then the tent of meeting shall **s** out, Nm 2:17
as they camp, so shall they **s** out, each Nm 2:17
They shall **s** out third on the march. Nm 2:24
Dan were 157,600. They shall **s** out last, Nm 2:31
by their standards, and so they **s** out, Nm 2:34
near, and **s** them before Aaron the priest, Nm 3:6
When the camp is to **s** out, Aaron and Nm 4:5
bring her near and **s** her before the Nm 5:16
the priest shall **s** the woman before Nm 5:18
Then he shall **s** the woman before the Nm 5:30
say to him, When you **s** up the lamps, Nm 8:2
he **s** up its lamps in front of the Nm 8:3
And you shall **s** the Levites before Nm 8:13
the day that the tabernacle was **s** up, Nm 9:15
tent, after that the people of Israel **s** out, Nm 9:17
of the LORD the people of Israel **s** out, Nm 9:18
charge of the LORD and did not **s** out. Nm 9:19
to the command of the LORD they **s** out. Nm 9:20
cloud lifted in the morning, they **s** out, Nm 9:21
night, when the cloud lifted they **s** out. Nm 9:21
remained in camp and did not **s** out, Nm 9:22
not set out, but when it lifted they **s** out. Nm 9:22
at the command of the LORD they **s** out. Nm 9:23
that are on the east side shall **s** out. Nm 10:5
that are on the south side shall **s** out. Nm 10:6
to be blown whenever they are to **s** out. Nm 10:6
the people of Israel **s** out by stages Nm 10:12
They **s** out for the first time at the Nm 10:13
the people of Judah **s** out first by their Nm 10:14
who carried the tabernacle, **s** out. Nm 10:17
the camp of Reuben **s** out by their Nm 10:18
Then the Kohathites **s** out, carrying Nm 10:21
the tabernacle was **s** up before their Nm 10:21
the people of Ephraim **s** out by their Nm 10:22
the camps, **s** out by their companies, Nm 10:25
by their companies, when they **s** out. Nm 10:28
So they **s** out from the mount of the Nm 10:33
whenever they **s** out from the camp. Nm 10:34
And whenever the ark **s** out, Moses Nm 10:35
the people did not **s** out on the march Nm 12:15
that the people **s** out from Hazeroth, Nm 12:16
turn tomorrow and **s** out for the Nm 14:25
From Mount Hor they **s** out by the way Nm 21:4
"Make a fiery serpent and **s** it on a pole, Nm 21:8
a bronze serpent and **s** it on a pole. Nm 21:9
the people of Israel **s** out and camped Nm 21:10
And they **s** out from Oboth and Nm 21:11
From there they **s** out and camped in Nm 21:12
From there they **s** out and camped on Nm 21:13
the people of Israel **s** out and camped in Nm 22:1
but **s** his face toward the wilderness. Nm 24:1
place, and your nest is **s** in the rock. Nm 24:21
They **s** out from Rameses in the first Nm 33:3
the people of Israel **s** out from Rameses Nm 33:5
And they **s** out from Succoth and Nm 33:6
And they **s** out from Etham and turned Nm 33:7
And they **s** out from before Hahiroth Nm 33:8
And they **s** out from Marah and came Nm 33:9
And they **s** out from Elim and Nm 33:10
And they **s** out from the Red Sea and Nm 33:11
And they **s** out from the wilderness of Nm 33:12
And they **s** out from Dophkah and Nm 33:13
And they **s** out from Alush and Nm 33:14
And they **s** out from Rephidim and Nm 33:15
And they **s** out from the wilderness of Nm 33:16
And they **s** out from Kibroth-hattaavah Nm 33:17
And they **s** out from Hazeroth and Nm 33:18
And they **s** out from Rithmah and Nm 33:19
And they **s** out from Rimmon-perez Nm 33:20
And they **s** out from Libnah and Nm 33:21
And they **s** out from Rissah and Nm 33:22
And they **s** out from Kehelathah and Nm 33:23
And they **s** out from Mount Shepher Nm 33:24
And they **s** out from Haradah and Nm 33:25
And they **s** out from Makheloth and Nm 33:26
And they **s** out from Tahath and Nm 33:27
And they **s** out from Terah and Nm 33:28
And they **s** out from Mithkah and Nm 33:29
And they **s** out from Hashmonah and Nm 33:30
And they **s** out from Moseroth and Nm 33:31
And they **s** out from Bene-jaakan and Nm 33:32
And they **s** out from Hor-haggidgad Nm 33:33
And they **s** out from Jotbathah and Nm 33:34
And they **s** out from Abronah and Nm 33:35
And they **s** out from Ezion-geber and Nm 33:36
And they **s** out from Kadesh and Nm 33:37
And they **s** out from Mount Hor and Nm 33:41
And they **s** out from Zalmonah and Nm 33:42
And they **s** out from Punon and Nm 33:43
And they **s** out from Oboth and Nm 33:44
And they **s** out from Iyim and camped Nm 33:45
And they **s** out from Dibon-gad and Nm 33:46
And they **s** out from Almon-diblathaim Nm 33:47
And they **s** out from the mountains of Nm 33:48
See, I have **s** the land before you. Go in Dt 1:8
men, and **s** them as heads over you, Dt 1:15
"Then we **s** out from Horeb and went Dt 1:19
LORD your God has **s** the land before you. Dt 1:21
s out on your journey and go over the Dt 2:24
as all this law that I **s** before you today? Dt 4:8
Then Moses **s** apart three cities in the Dt 4:41
the law that Moses **s** before the people of Dt 4:44
people that the LORD **s** his love on you Dt 7:7
At that time the LORD **s** apart the tribe of Dt 10:8
Yet the LORD **s** his heart in love on your Dt 10:15
you shall **s** the blessing on Mount Dt 11:29
your God chooses, to **s** his name there, Dt 14:24
And you shall not **s** up a pillar, which Dt 16:22
it and then say, 'I will **s** a king over me, Dt 17:14
you may indeed **s** a king over you Dt 17:15
your brothers you shall **s** as king over Dt 17:15
you shall **s** apart three cities for Dt 19:2
you, You shall **s** apart three cities. Dt 19:7
landmark, which the men of old have **s**, Dt 19:14
and do not **s** the guilt of innocent blood Dt 21:8
from your hand and **s** it down before the Dt 26:4
And you shall **s** it down before the LORD Dt 26:10
and that he will **s** you in praise and in Dt 26:19
you shall **s** up large stones and plaster Dt 27:2
the Jordan, you shall **s** up these stones, Dt 27:4
LORD your God will **s** you high above all Dt 28:1
your king whom you **s** over you to a Dt 28:36
would not venture to **s** the sole of her Dt 28:56
and the curse, which I have **s** before you, Dt 30:1
I have **s** before you today life and good, Dt 30:15
that I have **s** before you life and death, Dt 30:19
years, at the **s** time in the year of release, Dt 31:10
the morning and they **s** out from Shittim. Jos 3:1
then you shall **s** out from your place and Jos 3:3
So when the people **s** out from their tents Jos 3:14
And Joshua **s** up twelve stones in the Jos 4:9
out of the Jordan, Joshua **s** up at Gilgal. Jos 4:20
his youngest son shall he **s** up its gates." Jos 6:26
taken the city, you shall **s** the city on fire. Jos 8:8
about 5,000 men and **s** them in ambush Jos 8:12
it. And they hurried to **s** the city on fire. Jos 8:19
journey on the day we **s** out to come to Jos 9:12
the people of Israel **s** out and reached Jos 9:17
did not hurry to **s** for about a whole Jos 10:13
mouth of the cave and **s** men by it to Jos 10:18
and they **s** large stones against the Jos 10:27
the towns that were **s** apart for the people Jos 16:9
assembled at Shiloh and **s** up the tent of Jos 18:1
them out that they may **s** out and go up Jos 18:4
So they **s** apart Kedesh in Galilee in the Jos 20:7
a large stone and **s** it up there under Jos 24:26
the edge of the sword and **s** the city on fire. Jgs 1:8
Since you have **s** me in the land of the Jgs 1:15
out my present and **s** it before you." And Jgs 6:18
as a dog laps, you shall **s** by himself. Jgs 7:5
watch, when they had just **s** the watch. Jgs 7:19
the LORD **s** every man's sword against his Jgs 7:22
with you, and **s** an ambush in the field. Jgs 9:32
up by night and **s** an ambush against Jgs 9:34
three companies and **s** an ambush in Jgs 9:43
and they **s** the stronghold on fire over Jgs 9:49
And when he had **s** fire to the torches, he Jgs 15:5
of the Philistines and **s** fire to the Jgs 15:5
the place and **s** an ambush for Jgs 16:2
of war, **s** out from Zorah and Eshtaol, Jgs 18:11
the people of Dan **s** up the carved image Jgs 18:30
So they **s** up Micah's carved image that Jgs 18:31
So Israel **s** men in ambush around Jgs 20:29
the third day and **s** themselves in array Jgs 20:30
of their place and **s** themselves in array Jgs 20:33
whom they had **s** against Gibeah. Jgs 20:36
the towns that they found they **s** on fire. Jgs 20:48
So she **s** out from the place where she was Ru 1:7
So she **s** out and went and gleaned in the Ru 2:3
LORD'S, and on them he has **s** the world. 1 Sm 2:8
and his eyes were **s** so that he could 1 Sm 4:15
house of Dagon and **s** it up beside 1 Sm 5:2
and **s** them upon the great stone. 1 Sm 6:15
beside which they **s** down the ark 1 Sm 6:18
took a stone and **s** it up between 1 Sm 7:12
days ago, do not **s** your mind on them, 1 Sm 9:20
was on it and **s** them before Saul. 1 Sm 9:24
"See, what was kept is **s** before you. 1 Sm 9:24
have said to him, '**S** a king over us.' 1 Sm 10:19
the LORD has **s** a king over you. 1 Sm 12:13
he **s** up a monument for himself and 1 Sm 15:12
so that Saul **s** him over the men of 1 Sm 18:5
Let me **s** a morsel of bread before 1 Sm 28:22
So David **s** out with his men early in 1 Sm 29:11
So David **s** out, and the six hundred 1 Sm 30:9
house of Saul and **s** up the throne of 2 Sm 3:10
Beerothite, Rechab and Baanah, **s** out, 2 Sm 4:5
the ark of the LORD and **s** it in its place, 2 Sm 6:17
that the battle was **s** against him both 2 Sm 10:9
"**S** Uriah in the forefront of the 2 Sm 11:15
he asked, they **s** food before him, 2 Sm 12:20
were in it and **s** them to labor with 2 Sm 12:31
of my lord the king will **s** me at rest,' 2 Sm 14:17
go and **s** it on fire." So Absalom's 2 Sm 14:30
So Absalom's servants **s** the field on 2 Sm 14:30
have your servants **s** my field on 2 Sm 14:31
And they **s** down the ark of God until 2 Sm 15:24
He **s** his house in order and hanged 2 Sm 17:23
Now Absalom had **s** Amasa over the 2 Sm 17:25
with him and **s** over them 2 Sm 18:1
had taken and **s** up for himself 2 Sm 18:18
but you **s** your servant among those 2 Sm 19:28
he delayed beyond the **s** time that had 2 Sm 20:5
feet of a deer and **s** me secure on the 2 Sm 22:34
And David **s** him over his 2 Sm 23:23
whom I will **s** on your throne in your 1 Kgs 5:5
for your servants such wages as you **s**, 1 Kgs 5:6
to **s** there the ark of the covenant of 1 Kgs 6:19
of cast bronze to **s** on the tops of 1 Kgs 7:16
He **s** up the pillars at the vestibule of 1 Kgs 7:21
He **s** up the pillar on the south and 1 Kgs 7:21
and he **s** up the pillar on the north 1 Kgs 7:21
The sea was **s** on them, and all their 1 Kgs 7:25
and the panels were **s** in the frames, 1 Kgs 7:28
the panels that were **s** in the frames 1 Kgs 7:29
And he **s** the stands, five on the south 1 Kgs 7:39
And he **s** the sea at the southeast 1 Kgs 7:39
my statutes that I have **s** before you, 1 Kgs 9:6
delighted in you and **s** you on the 1 Kgs 10:9
They **s** out from Midian and came 1 Kgs 11:18
And he **s** one in Bethel, and the other 1 Kgs 12:29
and **s** up its gates at the cost of his 1 Kgs 16:34
and **s** Naboth at the head of the 1 Kgs 21:9
And **s** two worthless men opposite 1 Kgs 21:10
a fast and **s** Naboth at the 1 Kgs 21:12
And when one is full, **s** it aside." 2 Kgs 4:4
So she **s** out and came to the man of 2 Kgs 4:25
said to his servant, "**S** on the large pot, 2 Kgs 4:38
"How can I **s** this before a hundred 2 Kgs 4:43
So he **s** it before them. And they ate 2 Kgs 4:44
S bread and water before them, that 2 Kgs 6:22
You will **s** on fire their fortresses, and 2 Kgs 8:12
the rule of Judah and **s** up a king of 2 Kgs 8:20
and Ahaziah king of Judah **s** out, 2 Kgs 9:21
your master's sons and **s** him on his 2 Kgs 10:3
Then he **s** out and went to Samaria. 2 Kgs 10:12
captains who were **s** over the army, 2 Kgs 11:15
the lid of it and **s** it beside the altar on 2 Kgs 12:9
But when Hazael **s** his face to go up 2 Kgs 12:17
They **s** up for themselves pillars and 2 Kgs 17:10
on your part to **s** riders on them. 2 Kgs 18:23
he has **s** out to fight against you." So 2 Kgs 19:9
says the LORD, '**S** your house in order, 2 Kgs 20:1
that he had made he **s** in the house of 2 Kgs 21:7
And David **s** him over his 1 Chr 11:25
the ark of God and **s** it inside the tent 1 Chr 16:1
as he went to **s** up his monument at 1 Chr 18:3
the battle was **s** against him both 1 Chr 19:10
And when David **s** the battle in 1 Chr 19:17
were in it and **s** them to labor with 1 Chr 20:3
and he **s** stonecutters to prepare 1 Chr 22:2
Now **s** your mind and heart to seek 1 Chr 22:19
Aaron was **s** apart to dedicate the 1 Chr 23:13
of the service also **s** apart for the 1 Chr 25:1
He **s** up the pillars in front of the 2 Chr 3:17
The sea was **s** on them, and all their 2 Chr 4:4
to wash, and **s** five on the south side, 2 Chr 4:6
prescribed, and **s** them in the temple, 2 Chr 4:7
And he **s** the sea at the southeast 2 Chr 4:10
And there I have **s** the ark, in which 2 Chr 6:11
cubits high, and had **s** it in the court, 2 Chr 6:13
you have promised to **s** your name, 2 Chr 6:20
that I have **s** before you, 2 Chr 7:19
delighted in you and **s** you on his 2 Chr 9:8
And those who had **s** their hearts to 2 Chr 11:16
for he did not **s** his heart to seek the 2 Chr 12:14
s out the showbread on the table of 2 Chr 13:11
cities of Judah and **s** garrisons in the 2 Chr 17:2
and have **s** your heart to seek God." 2 Chr 19:3
was afraid and **s** his face to 2 Chr 20:3
the LORD **s** an ambush against the 2 Chr 20:22
had not yet **s** their hearts upon 2 Chr 20:33
the rule of Judah and **s** up a king of 2 Chr 21:8
And he **s** all the people as a guard 2 Chr 23:10
captains who were **s** over the army, 2 Chr 23:14
And they **s** the king on the royal 2 Chr 23:20
made a chest and **s** it outside the gate 2 Chr 24:8
men of Judah and **s** them by fathers' 2 Chr 25:5
the men of Seir and **s** them up as his 2 Chr 25:14
He **s** himself to seek God in the days 2 Chr 26:5
They **s** to work and removed the 2 Chr 30:14

He **s** to work resolutely and built up 2 Chr 32:5
And he **s** combat commanders over 2 Chr 32:6
that he had made he **s** in the house of 2 Chr 33:7
high places and **s** up the Asherim 2 Chr 33:19
Over them were **s** Jahath and 2 Chr 34:12
And they **s** aside the burnt offerings 2 Chr 35:12
They **s** the altar in its place, for fear was Ezr 3:3
And they **s** the priests in their divisions Ezr 6:18
For Ezra had **s** his heart to study the Ezr 7:10
and his officials had **s** apart to attend Ezr 8:20
Then I **s** apart twelve of the leading Ezr 8:24
us some reviving to **s** up the house of Ezr 9:9
They consecrated it and **s** its doors. Neh 3:1
They laid its beams and **s** its doors, its Neh 3:3
They laid its beams and **s** its doors, its Neh 3:6
They rebuilt it and **s** its doors, its bolts, Neh 3:13
He rebuilt it and **s** its doors, its bolts, Neh 3:14
rebuilt it and covered it and **s** its doors, Neh 3:15
prayed to our God and **s** a guard as a Neh 4:9
that time I had not **s** up the doors in the Neh 6:1
And you have also **s** up prophets to Neh 6:7
had been built and I had **s** up the doors, Neh 7:1
and rich land that you **s** before them, Neh 9:35
whom you have **s** over us because Neh 9:37
and they **s** apart that which was for Neh 12:47
and the Levites **s** apart that which Neh 12:47
them together and **s** them in their Neh 13:11
so that he **s** the royal crown on her head Est 2:17
advanced him and **s** his throne above Est 3:1
and on whose head a royal crown is **s**. Est 6:8
And Esther **s** Mordecai over the house of Est 8:2
sea monster, that you **s** a guard over me? Jb 7:12
him, and that you **s** your heart on him, Jb 7:17
you **s** a limit for the soles of my feet. Jb 13:27
that you would appoint me a **s** time, Jb 14:13
me to pieces; he **s** me up as his target; Jb 16:12
and he has **s** darkness upon my paths. Jb 19:8
would have disdained to **s** with the dogs Jb 30:1
you can; **s** your words in order before me; Jb 33:5
If he should **s** his heart to it and gather Jb 34:14
and what was **s** on your table was full of Jb 36:16
limits for it and **s** bars and doors, Jb 38:10
The kings of the earth **s** themselves, and Ps 2:2
"As for me, I have **s** my King on Zion, my Ps 2:6
people who have **s** themselves against me Ps 3:6
that the LORD has **s** apart the godly for Ps 4:3
You have **s** your glory above the heavens. Ps 8:1
and the stars, which you have **s** in place, Ps 8:3
I have **s** the LORD always before me; Ps 16:8
they **s** their eyes to cast us to the Ps 17:11
feet of a deer and **s** me secure on the Ps 18:33
world. In them he has **s** a tent for the sun, Ps 19:4
the name of our God **s** up our banners! Ps 20:5
you **s** a crown of fine gold upon his head. Ps 21:3
you have **s** my feet in a broad place. Ps 31:8
the miry bog, and **s** my feet upon a rock, Ps 40:2
and **s** me in your presence forever. Ps 41:12
afflicted the peoples, but them you **s** free; Ps 44:2
life; they do not **s** God before themselves. Ps 54:3
They **s** a net for my steps; my soul was Ps 57:6
You have **s** up a banner for those who Ps 60:4
extortion; **s** no vain hopes on robbery; Ps 62:10
increase, **s** not your heart on them. Ps 62:10
let your salvation, O God, **s** me on high! Ps 69:29
They **s** their mouths against the Ps 73:9
Truly you **s** them in slippery places; Ps 73:18
place; they **s** up their own signs for signs. Ps 74:4
They **s** your sanctuary on fire; they Ps 74:7
"At the **s** time that I appoint I will judge Ps 75:2
so that they should **s** their hope in God Ps 78:7
life, and they do not **s** you before them. Ps 86:14
like one **s** loose among the dead, like the Ps 88:5
I will **s** his hand on the sea and his right Ps 89:25
You have **s** our iniquities before you, our Ps 90:8
I will not **s** before my eyes anything Ps 101:3
to **s** free those who were doomed to die, Ps 102:20
He **s** the earth on its foundations, so Ps 104:5
You **s** a boundary that they may not Ps 104:9
him; the ruler of the peoples **s** him free; Ps 105:20
the LORD answered me and **s** me free. Ps 118:5
faithfulness; I **s** your rules before me. Ps 119:30
There thrones for judgment were **s**, the Ps 122:5
of your body I will **s** on your throne. Ps 132:11
if I do not **s** Jerusalem above my highest Ps 137:6
the way they have **s** snares for me. Ps 140:5
S a guard, O LORD, over my mouth; keep Ps 141:3
they **s** an ambush for their own lives. Prv 1:18
Ages ago I was **s** up, at the first, before Prv 8:23
mixed her wine; she has also **s** her table. Prv 9:2
do not **s** your heart on putting him to Prv 19:18
landmark that your fathers have **s**. Prv 22:28
Scoffers **s** a city aflame, but the wise Prv 29:8
the children of man is fully **s** to do evil. Eccl 8:11
folly is **s** in many high places, and the Eccl 10:6
His arms are rods of gold, **s** with jewels. Sg 5:14

alabaster columns, **s** on bases of gold. Sg 5:15
my desire **s** me among the chariots of Sg 6:12
S me as a seal upon your heart, as a seal Sg 8:6
and **s** up the son of Tabeel as king in the Is 7:6
Israel, and will **s** them in their own land, Is 14:1
stars of God I will **s** my throne on high; Is 14:13
the Lord said to me: "Go, **s** a watchman; Is 21:6
who **s** out to go down to Egypt, without Is 30:2
are able on your part to **s** riders on them. Is 36:8
"He has **s** out to fight against you." And Is 37:9
S your house in order, for you shall die, Is 38:1
a skillful craftsman to **s** up an idol that Is 40:20
I will **s** in the desert the cypress, the Is 41:19
S forth your case, says the LORD; bring Is 41:21
it **s** him on fire all around, but he did Is 42:25
s forth your case, that you may be Is 43:26
Let him declare and **s** it before me, since I Is 44:7
shall build my city and **s** my exiles free, Is 45:13
they carry it, they **s** it in its place, Is 46:7
therefore I have **s** my face like a flint, and Is 50:7
and I will **s** my justice for a light to the Is 51:4
behold, I will **s** your stones in antimony, Is 54:11
and lofty mountain you have **s** your bed, Is 57:7
doorpost you have **s** up your memorial; Is 57:8
walls, O Jerusalem, I have **s** watchmen; Is 62:6
who **s** a table for Fortune and fill cups of Is 65:11
and I will **s** a sign among them. And Is 66:19
I have **s** you this day over nations and Jer 1:10
and every one shall **s** his throne at the Jer 1:15
said How I would **s** you among my sons, Jer 3:19
thicket, a destroyer of nations has **s** out; Jer 4:7
in wait. They **s** a trap; they catch men. Jer 5:26
I **s** watchmen over you, saying, 'Pay Jer 6:17
on horses, **s** in array as a man for battle, Jer 6:23
They have **s** their detestable things in Jer 7:30
forsaken my law that I **s** before them, Jer 9:13
my tent again and to **s** up my curtains. Jer 10:20
are the altars you have **s** up to shame, Jer 11:13
roar of a great tempest he will **s** fire to it, Jer 11:16
and **s** them apart for the day of Jer 12:3
you say when they **s** as head over you Jer 13:21
We **s** our hope on you, for you do all Jer 14:22
"Have I not **s** you free for their good? Jer 15:11
A glorious throne **s** on high from the Jer 17:12
I **s** before you the way of life and the way Jer 21:8
For I have **s** my face against this city Jer 21:10
I will **s** shepherds over them who will Jer 23:4
I will **s** my eyes on them for good, and I Jer 24:6
walk in my law that I have **s** before you, Jer 26:4
"**S** up road markers for yourself; make Jer 31:21
and the children's teeth are **s** on edge.' Jer 31:29
sour grapes, his teeth shall be **s** on edge. Jer 31:30
city shall come and **s** this city on fire Jer 32:29
They **s** up their abominations in the Jer 32:34
that everyone should **s** free his Hebrew Jer 34:9
that everyone would **s** free his slave, Jer 34:10
again. They obeyed and **s** them free. Jer 34:10
male and female slaves they had **s** free, Jer 34:11
each of you must **s** free the fellow Jer 34:14
you must **s** him free from your service.' Jer 34:14
whom you had **s** free according to their Jer 34:16
Then I **s** before the Rechabites pitchers Jer 35:5
Jeremiah **s** out from Jerusalem to go to Jer 37:12
took them captive and **s** out to cross Jer 41:10
If you **s** your faces to enter Egypt and go Jer 42:15
All the men who **s** their faces to go to Jer 42:17
the son of Neriah has **s** you against us, Jer 43:3
and I will **s** his throne above these Jer 43:10
my statutes that I **s** before you and Jer 44:10
I will **s** my face against you for harm, Jer 44:11
of Judah who have **s** their faces to come Jer 44:12
and I will **s** my throne in Elam and Jer 49:38
proclaim, **s** up a banner and proclaim, Jer 50:2
S yourselves in array against Babylon Jer 50:14
I **s** a snare for you and you were taken, Jer 50:24
"**S** up a standard against the walls of Jer 51:12
the watch strong; **s** up watchmen; Jer 51:12
"**S** up a standard on the earth; blow the Jer 51:27
together; they were **s** upon my neck; Lam 1:14
in his anger has **s** the daughter of Zion Lam 2:1
enemy, with his right hand **s** like a foe; Lam 2:4
he bent his bow and **s** me as a target Lam 3:12
entered into me and **s** me on my feet, Ezk 2:2
entered into me and **s** me on my feet, Ezk 3:24
S camps also against it, and plant Ezk 4:2
and **s** your face toward it, and let it be in Ezk 4:3
And you shall **s** your face toward the Ezk 4:7
I have **s** her in the center of the nations, Ezk 5:5
s your face toward the mountains of Ezk 6:2
s your face against the daughters of Ezk 13:17
and **s** the stumbling block of their Ezk 14:3
And I will **s** my face against that man; I Ezk 14:8
And I will **s** my face against them. Ezk 15:7
LORD, when I **s** my face against them. Ezk 15:7
and **s** my oil and my incense before Ezk 16:18

and honey—you **s** before them for a Ezk 16:19
to a land of trade and **s** it in a city of Ezk 17:4
waters. He **s** it like a willow twig, Ezk 17:5
lofty top of the cedar and will **s** it out. Ezk 17:22
and the children's teeth are **s** on edge'? Ezk 18:2
Then the nations **s** against him from Ezk 19:8
and their eyes were **s** on their fathers' Ezk 20:24
s your face toward the southland; Ezk 20:46
s your face toward Jerusalem and Ezk 21:2
s yourself to the left, wherever your Ezk 21:16
for Jerusalem, to **s** battering rams, Ezk 21:22
to **s** battering rams against the gates, Ezk 21:22
They shall **s** themselves against you Ezk 23:24
the Lord GOD: "**S** on the pot, set it on; Ezk 24:3
the Lord GOD: "Set on the pot, **s** it on; Ezk 24:3
I have **s** on the bare rock the blood she Ezk 24:8
Then **s** it empty upon the coals, that it Ezk 24:11
s your face toward the Ammonites and Ezk 25:2
and they shall **s** their encampments Ezk 25:4
He will **s** up a siege wall against you Ezk 26:8
but I will **s** beauty in the land of the Ezk 26:20
of man, **s** your face toward Sidon, Ezk 28:21
s your face against Pharaoh king of Ezk 29:2
the LORD, when I have **s** fire to Egypt, Ezk 30:8
a desolation and will **s** fire to Zoan Ezk 30:14
And I will **s** fire to Egypt; Pelusium Ezk 30:16
it towered high and **s** its top among Ezk 31:10
towering height or **s** their tops among Ezk 31:14
whose graves are **s** in the uttermost Ezk 32:23
they act; their heart is **s** on their gain. Ezk 33:31
And I will **s** up over them one Ezk 34:23
of man, **s** your face against Mount Seir, Ezk 35:2
Spirit of the LORD and **s** me down in the Ezk 37:1
And I will **s** them in their land and Ezk 37:26
and will **s** my sanctuary in their Ezk 37:26
"Son of man, **s** your face toward Gog, of Ezk 38:2
They will **s** apart men to travel Ezk 39:14
bone, then he shall **s** up a sign by it, Ezk 39:15
"And I will **s** my glory among the Ezk 39:21
and **s** me down on a very high Ezk 40:2
and **s** your heart upon all that I shall Ezk 40:4
upper chambers were **s** back from the Ezk 42:6
but you have **s** others to keep my Ezk 44:8
you shall **s** apart for the LORD a portion Ezk 45:1
"Alongside the portion **s** apart as the Ezk 45:6
be the portion which you shall **s** apart, Ezk 48:8
portion that you shall **s** apart for the Ezk 48:9
portion that you shall **s** apart shall be Ezk 48:20
God of heaven will **s** up a kingdom that Dn 2:44
He **s** it up on the plain of Dura, in the Dn 3:1
that King Nebuchadnezzar had **s** up. Dn 3:2
that King Nebuchadnezzar had **s** up. Dn 3:3
image that Nebuchadnezzar had **s** up. Dn 3:3
that King Nebuchadnezzar has **s** up. Dn 3:5
that King Nebuchadnezzar had **s** up. Dn 3:7
the golden image that you have **s** up." Dn 3:12
the golden image that I have **s** up? Dn 3:14
the golden image that you have **s** up." Dn 3:18
him, and **s** aside the king's command, Dn 3:28
It pleased Darius to **s** over the kingdom Dn 6:1
the king planned to **s** him over the whole Dn 6:3
was much distressed and **s** his mind to Dn 6:14
which he **s** before us by his servants the Dn 9:10
touched me and **s** me trembling on Dn 10:10
first day that you **s** your heart to Dn 10:12
He shall **s** his face to come with the Dn 11:17
his heart shall be **s** against the holy Dn 11:28
And they shall **s** up the abomination Dn 11:31
that makes desolate is **s** up, Dn 12:11
S the trumpet to your lips! One like a Hos 8:1
me. They **s** up princes, but I knew it not. Hos 8:4
though your nest is **s** among the stars, Ob 1:4
eat your bread have **s** a trap beneath you Ob 1:7
I will **s** them together like sheep in a fold, Mi 2:12
hasten to the wall; the siege tower is **s** up. Na 2:5
gain for his house, to **s** his nest on high, Hab 2:9
on the stone that I have **s** before Joshua, Zec 3:9
they will **s** the basket down there on its Zec 5:11
the north country have **s** my Spirit at Zec 6:8
a crown, and **s** it on the head of Joshua, Zec 6:11
for I **s** every man against his neighbor. Zec 8:10
I will **s** your prisoners free from the Zec 9:11
day that is coming shall **s** them ablaze, Mal 4:1
to the holy city and **s** him on the pinnacle Mt 4:5
A city **s** on a hill cannot be hidden. Mt 5:14
For I have come to **s** a man against his Mt 10:35
his master has **s** over his household, Mt 24:45
he will **s** him over all his possessions. Mt 24:47
over a little; I will **s** you over much. Mt 25:21
over a little; I will **s** you over much. Mt 25:23
whom a price had been **s** by some of the Mt 27:9
to the disciples to **s** before the people. Mk 6:41
to his disciples to **s** before the people; Mk 8:6
people; and they **s** them before the crowd. Mk 8:6
that these also should be **s** before them. Mk 8:7

And the disciples **s** out and went to the Mk 14:16
him to Jerusalem and **s** him on the Lk 4:9
to **s** at liberty those who are oppressed, Lk 4:18
For I too am a man **s** under authority, Lk 7:8
the other side of the lake." So they **s** out, Lk 8:22
to the disciples to **s** before the crowd. Lk 9:16
up, he **s** his face to go to Jerusalem. Lk 9:51
his face was **s** toward Jerusalem. Lk 9:53
receive you, eat what is **s** before you. Lk 10:8
Then he **s** him on his own animal and Lk 10:34
and I have nothing to **s** before him'; Lk 11:6
his master will **s** over his household, Lk 12:42
he will **s** him over all his possessions. Lk 12:44
cloaks on the colt, they **s** Jesus on it. Lk 19:35
your enemies will **s** up a barricade Lk 19:43
Moses, on whom you have **s** your hope. Jn 5:45
on him God the Father has **s** his seal." Jn 6:27
the truth, and the truth will **s** you free." Jn 8:32
him that he would **s** one of his Acts 2:30
And when they had **s** them in the midst, Acts 4:7
The kings of the earth **s** themselves, Acts 4:26
them, they **s** them before the council. Acts 5:27
These they **s** before the apostles, and Acts 6:6
and they **s** up false witnesses who said, Acts 6:13
"**S** apart for me Barnabas and Saul for Acts 13:2
and his companions **s** sail from Acts 13:13
his house and **s** food before them. Acts 16:34
formed a mob, **s** the city in an uproar, Acts 17:5
of the brothers and **s** sail for Syria, Acts 18:18
wills," and he **s** sail from Ephesus. Acts 18:21
Jews as he was about to **s** sail for Syria, Acts 20:3
ahead to the ship, we **s** sail for Assos, Acts 20:13
from the first day that I **s** foot in Asia, Acts 20:18
we had parted from them and **s** sail, Acts 21:1
Phoenicia, we went aboard and **s** sail. Acts 21:2
Paul down and **s** him before them. Acts 22:30
man could have been **s** free if he had Acts 26:32
me and not have **s** sail from Crete Acts 27:21
After three months we **s** sail in a ship Acts 28:11
me, they wished to **s** me at liberty, Acts 28:18
an apostle, **s** apart for the gospel of God, Rom 1:1
who has died has been **s** free from sin. Rom 6:7
and, having been **s** free from sin, have Rom 6:18
that you have been **s** free from sin and Rom 6:22
the Spirit of life has **s** you free in Christ Rom 8:2
according to the flesh **s** their minds on Rom 8:5
according to the Spirit **s** their minds on Rom 8:5
To **s** the mind on the flesh is death, but Rom 8:6
but to **s** the mind on the Spirit is life Rom 8:6
For the mind that is **s** on the flesh is Rom 8:7
creation itself will be **s** free from its Rom 8:21
eat whatever is **s** before you without 1 Cor 10:27
On him we have **s** our hope that he 2 Cor 1:10
when he who had **s** me apart before I Gal 1:15
a revelation and **s** before them (though Gal 2:2
managers until the date **s** by his father. Gal 4:2
For freedom Christ has **s** us free; stand Gal 5:1
his purpose, which he **s** forth in Christ Eph 1:9
shame, with minds **s** on earthly things. Phil 3:19
This he **s** aside, nailing it to the cross. Col 2:14
S your minds on things that are above, Col 3:2
we have our hope **s** on the living God, 1 Tm 4:10
but **s** the believers an example in 1 Tm 4:12
has **s** her hope on God and continues 1 Tm 5:5
nor to **s** their hopes on the 1 Tm 6:17
for honorable use, **s** apart as holy, 2 Tm 2:21
to hold fast to the hope **s** before us. Heb 6:18
commandment is **s** aside because Heb 7:18
places, in the true tent that the Lord **s** up, Heb 8:2
Anyone who has **s** aside the law of Heb 10:28
endurance the race that is **s** before us, Heb 12:1
the joy that was **s** before him endured Heb 12:2
How great a forest is **s** ablaze by such a Jas 3:5
The tongue is **s** among our members, Jas 3:6
entire course of life, and **s** on fire by hell. Jas 3:6
s your hope fully on the grace that will 1 Pt 1:13
the heavens will be **s** on fire and 2 Pt 3:12
Behold, I have **s** before you an open door, Rv 3:8
And he **s** his right foot on the sea, and Rv 10:2

SETH (9)
she bore a son and called his name **S**, Gn 4:25
To **S** also a son was born, and he called Gn 4:26
after his image, and named him **S**. Gn 5:3
Adam after he fathered **S** were 800 years; Gn 5:4
When **S** had lived 105 years, he fathered Gn 5:6
S lived after he fathered Enosh 807 years Gn 5:7
Thus all the days of **S** were 912 years, and Gn 5:8
Adam, **S**, Enosh; 1 Chr 1:1
the son of Enos, the son of **S**, the son of Lk 3:38

SETHUR (1)
tribe of Asher, **S** the son of Michael; Nm 13:13

SETS (24)
and when Aaron **s** up the lamps at Ex 30:8
of the sanctuary, as the camp **s** out, Nm 4:15
himself in water, and as the sun **s**, Dt 23:11
restore to him the pledge as the sun **s**, Dt 24:13
before the sun **s** (for he is poor and Dt 24:15
of a craftsman, and **s** it up in secret.' Dt 27:15
and **s** on fire the foundations of the Dt 32:22
who **s** his heart to seek God, the 2 Chr 30:19
he **s** on high those who are lowly, and Jb 5:11
without investigation and **s** others in Jb 34:24
kings on the throne he **s** them forever, Jb 36:7
he **s** himself in a way that is not good; Ps 36:4
as the flame **s** the mountains ablaze, Ps 83:14
hungry. The LORD **s** the prisoners free; Ps 146:7
The discerning **s** his face toward Prv 17:24
he **s** up salvation as walls and bulwarks. Is 26:1
as when one **s** out to the sound of the Is 30:29
oppressor, when he **s** himself to destroy? Is 51:13
his heart and **s** the stumbling block Ezk 14:4
he removes kings and **s** up kings; Dn 2:21
whom he will and **s** over it the lowliest Dn 4:17
of mankind and **s** over it whom Dn 5:21
receives his testimony **s** his seal to Jn 3:33
So if the Son **s** you free, you will be free Jn 8:36

SETTING (26)
onyx stones, and stones for **s**, for the Ex 25:7
in cutting stones for **s**, and in carving Ex 31:5
and onyx stones and stones for **s**, for the Ex 35:9
in cutting stones for **s**, and in carving Ex 35:33
Moses had finished **s** up the tabernacle Nm 7:1
"We are **s** out for the place of which Nm 10:29
I am **s** before you today a blessing and a Dt 11:26
the rules that I am **s** before you today. Dt 11:32
on which we are **s** out will succeed." Jgs 18:5
the axes and for **s** the goads. 1 Sm 13:21
in Jerusalem, **s** up his son after him, 1 Kgs 15:4
quantities of onyx and stones for **s**, 1 Chr 29:2
earth from the rising of the sun to its **s**. Ps 50:1
seasons; the sun knows its time for **s**. Ps 104:19
From the rising of the sun to its **s**, the Ps 113:3
is like apples of gold in a **s** of silver. Prv 25:11
by **s** their threshold by my threshold Ezk 43:8
I am **s** a plumb line in the midst of my Am 7:8
of the sun to its **s** my name will be Mal 1:11
For you are not **s** your mind on the Mt 16:23
by sealing the stone and **s** a guard. Mt 27:66
For you are not **s** your mind on the Mk 8:33
And as he was **s** out on his journey, a Mk 10:17
Now when the sun was **s**, all those who Lk 4:40
So, **s** sail from Troas, we made a Acts 16:11
body, **s** on fire the entire course of life, Jas 3:6

SETTINGS (10)
shall enclose them in **s** of gold filigree. Ex 28:11
You shall make **s** of gold filigree, Ex 28:13
shall attach the corded chains to the **s**. Ex 28:14
you shall attach to the two **s** of filigree, Ex 28:25
onyx stones, enclosed in **s** of gold filigree, Ex 39:6
They were enclosed in **s** of gold filigree. Ex 39:13
And they made two **s** of gold filigree Ex 39:16
of the two cords to the two **s** of filigree. Ex 39:18
the house with **s** of precious stones. 2 Chr 3:6
gold were your **s** and your engravings. Ezk 28:13

SETTLE (14)
S your father and your brothers in the Gn 47:6
Let them **s** in the land of Goshen, and if Gn 47:6
that your enemies who **s** in it shall be Lv 26:32
take possession of the land and **s** in it, Nm 33:53
written in this book will **s** upon him, Dt 29:20
will not rest but will **s** the matter today." Ru 3:18
will all come and **s** in the steep ravines, Is 7:19
old, whose feet carried her to **s** far away? Is 23:7
all the birds of the heavens to **s** on you, Ezk 32:4
who wished to **s** accounts with his Mt 18:23
When he began to **s**, one was brought Mt 18:24
make an effort to **s** with him on the Lk 12:58
S it therefore in your minds not to Lk 21:14
you wise enough to **s** a dispute between 1 Cor 6:5

SETTLED (40)
presence of the LORD and **s** in the land of Gn 4:16
a plain in the land of Shinar and **s** there. Gn 11:2
when they came to Haran, they **s** there. Gn 11:31
Abram **s** in the land of Canaan, while Gn 13:12
while Lot **s** among the cities of the Gn 13:12
his tent and came and **s** by the oaks of Gn 13:18
his son. And Isaac **s** at Beer-lahai-roi. Gn 25:11
They **s** from Havilah to Shur, which is Gn 25:18
He **s** over against all his kinsmen. Gn 25:18
So Isaac **s** in Gerar. Gn 26:6
in the valley of Gerar and **s** there. Gn 26:17
So Esau **s** in the hill country of Seir. Gn 36:8
Then Joseph **s** his father and his Gn 47:11
Thus Israel **s** in the land of Egypt, in Gn 47:27
land of Egypt and **s** on the whole Ex 10:14
of meeting because the cloud **s** on it, Ex 40:35
in the place where the cloud **s** down, Nm 9:17
And the cloud **s** down in the Nm 10:12
and Israel **s** in all the cities of the Nm 21:25
the son of Manasseh, and he **s** in it. Nm 32:40
from before them and **s** in their place, Dt 2:12
dispossessed them and **s** in their place, Dt 2:21
dispossessed them and **s** in their place Dt 2:22
destroyed them and **s** in their place.) Dt 2:23
dispute and every assault shall be **s**. Dt 21:5
they took possession of it and **s** in it, Jos 19:47
And he rebuilt the city and **s** in it. Jos 19:50
took possession of it, and they **s** there. Jos 21:43
of Reuben and the people of Gad were **s**. Jos 22:33
and they went and **s** with the people. Jgs 1:16
at Abel,' and so they **s** a matter. 2 Sm 20:18
to this day, and **s** in their place, 1 Chr 4:41
him, and **s** the people of Israel in them. 2 Chr 8:2
with its villages. And they **s** there. 2 Chr 28:18
Osnappar deported and **s** in the cities Ezr 4:10
for a possession and **s** the tribes of Israel Ps 78:55
from his youth and has **s** on his dregs; Jer 48:11
Gad, and his people **s** in its cities? Jer 49:1
servants came and **s** accounts with Mt 25:19
it shall be **s** in the regular assembly. Acts 19:39

SETTLEMENTS (3)
These were their **s**, and they kept a 1 Chr 4:33
according to their **s** within their 1 Chr 6:54
Their possessions and **s** were Bethel 1 Chr 7:28

SETTLES (2)
God **s** the solitary in a home; he leads out Ps 68:6
there the night bird **s** and finds for Is 34:14

SETTLING (2)
its furrows abundantly, **s** its ridges, Ps 65:10
like clouds of locusts **s** on the fences in Na 3:17

SEVEN (370)
Take with you **s** pairs of all clean Gn 7:2
and **s** pairs of the birds of the heavens Gn 7:3
For in **s** days I will send rain on the earth Gn 7:4
And after **s** days the waters of the flood Gn 7:10
He waited another **s** days, and again he Gn 8:10
Then he waited another **s** days and sent Gn 8:12
Abraham set **s** ewe lambs of the flock Gn 21:28
the meaning of these **s** ewe lambs that Gn 21:29
"These **s** ewe lambs you will take from Gn 21:30
"I will serve you **s** years for your Gn 29:18
So Jacob served **s** years for Rachel, and Gn 29:20
return for serving me another **s** years." Gn 29:27
and served Laban for another **s** years. Gn 29:30
pursued him for **s** days and followed Gn 31:23
bowing himself to the ground **s** times, Gn 33:3
out of the Nile **s** cows attractive and Gn 41:2
And behold, **s** other cows, ugly and thin, Gn 41:3
ugly, thin cows ate up the **s** attractive, Gn 41:4
And behold, **s** ears of grain, plump and Gn 41:5
And behold, after them sprouted **s** ears, Gn 41:6
the thin ears swallowed up the **s** plump, Gn 41:7
S cows, plump and attractive, came up Gn 41:18
S other cows came up after them, poor Gn 41:19
cows ate up the first **s** plump cows, Gn 41:20
saw in my dream **s** ears growing on Gn 41:22
S ears, withered, thin, and blighted by Gn 41:23
thin ears swallowed up the **s** good ears. Gn 41:24
The **s** good cows are seven years, and Gn 41:26
The seven good cows are **s** years, and Gn 41:26
and the **s** good ears are seven years; Gn 41:26
and the seven good ears are **s** years; Gn 41:26
The **s** lean and ugly cows that came up Gn 41:27
that came up after them are **s** years, Gn 41:27
and the **s** empty ears blighted by the Gn 41:27
the east wind are also **s** years of famine. Gn 41:27
There will come **s** years of great plenty Gn 41:29
them there will arise **s** years of famine, Gn 41:30
of Egypt during the **s** plentiful years. Gn 41:34
the land against the **s** years of famine Gn 41:36
During the **s** plentiful years the earth Gn 41:47
gathered up all the food of these **s** years, Gn 41:48
The **s** years of plenty that occurred in Gn 41:53
and the **s** years of famine began to Gn 41:54
she bore to Jacob—**s** persons in all. Gn 46:25
made a mourning for his father **s** days. Gn 50:10
the priest of Midian had **s** daughters, Ex 2:16
S full days passed after the LORD had Ex 7:25
S days you shall eat unleavened bread. Ex 12:15
For **s** days no leaven is to be found in Ex 12:19
S days you shall eat unleavened bread, Ex 13:6
bread shall be eaten for **s** days; Ex 13:7
sheep: **s** days it shall be with its mother; Ex 22:30
eat unleavened bread for **s** days at the Ex 23:15
You shall make **s** lamps for it. And the Ex 25:37
the Holy Place, shall wear them **s** days. Ex 29:30
Through **s** days shall you ordain them, Ex 29:35
S days you shall make atonement for Ex 29:37
S days you shall eat unleavened bread, Ex 34:18
And he made its **s** lamps and its tongs Ex 37:23

part of the blood **s** times before the LORD Lv 4:6
blood and sprinkle it **s** times before the Lv 4:17
sprinkled some of it on the altar **s** times, Lv 8:11
entrance of the tent of meeting for **s** days, Lv 8:33
for it will take **s** days to ordain you. Lv 8:33
shall remain day and night for **s** days, Lv 8:35
child, then she shall be unclean **s** days. Lv 12:2
shut up the diseased person for **s** days. Lv 13:4
shall shut him up for another **s** days. Lv 13:5
the priest shall shut him up **s** days. Lv 13:21
the priest shall shut him up **s** days, Lv 13:26
with the itching disease for **s** days, Lv 13:31
the itching disease for another **s** days. Lv 13:33
that which has the disease for **s** days. Lv 13:50
he shall shut it up for another **s** days. Lv 13:54
he shall sprinkle it **s** times on him who Lv 14:7
the camp, but live outside his tent **s** days. Lv 14:8
oil with his finger **s** times before the Lv 14:16
in his left hand **s** times before the LORD. Lv 14:27
the house and shut up the house **s** days. Lv 14:38
water and sprinkle the house **s** times. Lv 14:51
shall count for himself **s** days for his Lv 15:13
in her menstrual impurity for **s** days, Lv 15:19
upon him, he shall be unclean **s** days, Lv 15:24
she shall count for herself **s** days, Lv 15:28
of the blood with his finger **s** times. Lv 16:14
the blood on it with his finger **s** times, Lv 16:19
it shall remain **s** days with its mother, Lv 22:27
for **s** days you shall eat unleavened Lv 23:6
a food offering to the LORD for **s** days. Lv 23:8
"You shall count **s** full weeks from the Lv 23:15
present with the bread **s** lambs a year Lv 23:18
seventh month and for **s** days is the Lv 23:34
For **s** days you shall present food Lv 23:36
celebrate the feast of the LORD **s** days. Lv 23:39
rejoice before the LORD your God **s** days. Lv 23:40
a feast to the LORD for **s** days in the year. Lv 23:41
You shall dwell in booths for **s** days. Lv 23:42
"You shall count **s** weeks of years, seven Lv 25:8
seven weeks of years, **s** times seven years, Lv 25:8
seven weeks of years, seven times **s** years, Lv 25:8
that the time of the **s** weeks of years shall Lv 25:8
the **s** lamps shall give light in front of Nm 8:2
should she not be shamed **s** days? Nm 12:14
her be shut outside the camp **s** days, Nm 12:14
was shut outside the camp **s** days, Nm 12:15
(Hebron was built **s** years before Nm 13:22
the front of the tent of meeting **s** times. Nm 19:4
of any person shall be unclean **s** days. Nm 19:11
is in the tent shall be unclean **s** days. Nm 19:14
or a grave, shall be unclean **s** days. Nm 19:16
to Balak, "Build for me here **s** altars, Nm 23:1
prepare for me here **s** bulls and seven Nm 23:1
for me here seven bulls and **s** rams." Nm 23:1
"I have arranged the **s** altars and I have Nm 23:4
and built **s** altars and offered a bull Nm 23:14
for me here **s** altars and prepare Nm 23:29
prepare for me here **s** bulls and seven Nm 23:29
for me here seven bulls and **s** rams." Nm 23:29
s male lambs a year old without Nm 28:11
S days shall unleavened bread be Nm 28:17
one ram, and **s** male lambs a year old; Nm 28:19
shall you offer for each of the **s** lambs; Nm 28:21
way you shall offer daily, for **s** days, Nm 28:24
one ram, **s** male lambs a year old; Nm 28:27
a tenth for each of the **s** lambs; Nm 28:29
s male lambs a year old without Nm 29:2
and one tenth for each of the **s** lambs; Nm 29:4
herd, one ram, **s** male lambs a year old: Nm 29:8
a tenth for each of the **s** lambs: Nm 29:10
shall keep a feast to the LORD **s** days. Nm 29:12
"On the seventh day **s** bulls, two rams, Nm 29:32
s male lambs a year old without Nm 29:36
Encamp outside the camp **s** days. Nm 31:19
s nations more numerous and mightier Dt 7:1
the end of every **s** years you shall grant Dt 15:1
S days you shall eat it with unleavened Dt 16:3
with you in all your territory for **s** days, Dt 16:4
"You shall count **s** weeks. Begin to count Dt 16:9
Begin to count the **s** weeks from the time Dt 16:9
shall keep the Feast of Booths **s** days, Dt 16:13
For **s** days you shall keep the feast to the Dt 16:15
you one way and flee before you **s** ways. Dt 28:7
them and flee **s** ways before them. Dt 28:25
them, "At the end of every **s** years, Dt 31:10
S priests shall bear seven trumpets of Jos 6:4
priests shall bear **s** trumpets of rams' Jos 6:4
you shall march around the city **s** times, Jos 6:4
the covenant and let **s** priests bear seven Jos 6:6
let seven priests bear **s** trumpets of rams' Jos 6:6
the **s** priests bearing the seven trumpets of Jos 6:8
priests bearing the **s** trumpets of rams' Jos 6:8
And the **s** priests bearing the seven Jos 6:13
priests bearing the **s** trumpets of rams' Jos 6:13
the city in the same manner **s** times. Jos 6:15
they marched around the city **s** times. Jos 6:15
people of Israel **s** tribes whose Jos 18:2
They shall divide it into **s** portions. Jos 18:5
the land in **s** divisions and bring Jos 18:6
description of it by towns in **s** divisions. Jos 18:9
them into the hand of Midian **s** years. Jgs 6:1
bull, and the second bull **s** years old, Jgs 6:25
his sons. And he judged Israel **s** years. Jgs 12:9
what it is, within the **s** days of the feast, Jgs 14:12
wept before him the **s** days that their Jgs 14:17
bind me with **s** fresh bowstrings that Jgs 16:7
up to her **s** fresh bowstrings that Jgs 16:8
"If you weave the **s** locks of my head Jgs 16:13
Delilah took the **s** locks of his head and Jgs 16:14
him shave off the **s** locks of his head. Jgs 16:19
you, who is more to you than **s** sons, Ru 4:15
The barren has borne **s**, but she who 1 Sm 2:5
country of the Philistines **s** months. 1 Sm 6:1
S days you shall wait, until I come to 1 Sm 10:8
"Give us **s** days respite that we may 1 Sm 11:3
He waited **s** days, the time appointed 1 Sm 13:8
And Jesse made **s** of his sons pass 1 Sm 16:10
tree in Jabesh and fasted **s** days. 1 Sm 31:13
house of Judah was **s** years and six 2 Sm 2:11
he reigned over Judah **s** years and six 2 Sm 5:5
let **s** of his sons be given to us, so that 2 Sm 21:6
and the **s** of them perished together. 2 Sm 21:9
He reigned **s** years in Hebron and 1 Kgs 2:11
and the third was **s** cubits broad. 1 Kgs 6:6
He was **s** years in building it. 1 Kgs 6:38
before the LORD our God, **s** days. 1 Kgs 8:65
Zimri reigned **s** days in Tirzah. 1 Kgs 16:15
And he said, "Go again," **s** times. 1 Kgs 18:43
Yet I will leave **s** thousand in Israel, 1 Kgs 19:18
all the people of Israel, **s** thousand. 1 Kgs 20:15
opposite one another **s** days. 1 Kgs 20:29
made a circuitous march of **s** days, 2 Kgs 3:9
The child sneezed **s** times, and the 2 Kgs 4:35
"Go and wash in the Jordan **s** times, 2 Kgs 5:10
and dipped himself **s** times in the 2 Kgs 5:14
it will come upon the land for **s** years." 2 Kgs 8:1
in the land of the Philistines **s** years. 2 Kgs 8:2
And at the end of the **s** years, when the 2 Kgs 8:3
Jehoash was **s** years old when he 2 Kgs 11:21
where he reigned for **s** years and six 1 Chr 3:4
Johanan, Delaiah, and Anani, **s**. 1 Chr 3:24
Sheba, Jorai, Jacan, Zia and Eber, **s**. 1 Chr 5:13
obligated to come in every **s** days, 1 Chr 9:25
the oak in Jabesh and fasted **s** days. 1 Chr 10:12
they sacrificed **s** bulls and seven 1 Chr 15:26
sacrificed seven bulls and **s** rams. 1 Chr 15:26
He reigned **s** years in Hebron and 1 Chr 29:27
time Solomon held the feast for **s** days, 2 Chr 7:8
dedication of the altar **s** days and the 2 Chr 7:9
altar seven days and the feast **s** days. 2 Chr 7:9
a young bull or **s** rams becomes a 2 Chr 13:9
Joash was **s** years old when he began 2 Chr 24:1
And they brought **s** bulls, seven 2 Chr 29:21
they brought seven bulls, **s** rams, 2 Chr 29:21
seven bulls, seven rams, **s** lambs, 2 Chr 29:21
and **s** male goats for a sin offering 2 Chr 29:21
of Unleavened Bread **s** days with 2 Chr 30:21
ate the food of the festival for **s** days, 2 Chr 30:22
to keep the feast for another **s** days. 2 Chr 30:23
it for another **s** days with gladness. 2 Chr 30:23
Feast of Unleavened Bread **s** days. 2 Chr 35:17
of Unleavened Bread **s** days with joy, Ezr 6:22
the king and his **s** counselors to make Ezr 7:14
They kept the feast **s** days, and on the Neh 8:18
a feast lasting for **s** days in the court of Est 1:5
the **s** eunuchs who served in the Est 1:10
the **s** princes of Persia and Media, Est 1:14
and with **s** chosen young women from Est 2:9
were born to him **s** sons and three Jb 1:2
him on the ground **s** days and seven Jb 2:13
on the ground seven days and **s** nights, Jb 2:13
six troubles; in **s** no evil shall touch you. Jb 5:19
Now therefore take **s** bulls and seven Jb 42:8
take seven bulls and **s** rams and go to Jb 42:8
He had also **s** sons and three daughters. Jb 42:13
furnace on the ground, purified **s** times. Ps 12:6
S times a day I praise you for your Ps 119:164
s that are an abomination to him: Prv 6:16
her house; she has hewn her **s** pillars. Prv 9:1
for the righteous falls **s** times and rises Prv 24:16
his own eyes than **s** men who can Prv 26:16
for there are **s** abominations in his Prv 26:25
Give a portion to **s**, or even to eight, for Eccl 11:2
And **s** women shall take hold of one man Is 4:1
breath, and strike it into **s** channels, Is 11:15
will be sevenfold, as the light of **s** days, Is 30:26
She who bore **s** has grown feeble; she has Jer 15:9
'At the end of **s** years each of you must Jer 34:14
of war, and **s** men of the king's council, Jer 52:25
there overwhelmed among them **s** days. Ezk 3:15
And at the end of **s** days, the word of the Ezk 3:16
they will make fires of them for **s** years, Ezk 39:9
For **s** months the house of Israel will Ezk 39:12
At the end of **s** months they will make Ezk 39:14
And by **s** steps people would go up to Ezk 40:22
And there were **s** steps leading up to it, Ezk 40:26
on either side of the entrance, **s** cubits. Ezk 41:3
For **s** days you shall provide daily a Ezk 43:25
S days shall they make atonement for Ezk 43:26
clean, they shall count **s** days for him. Ezk 44:26
and for **s** days unleavened bread shall Ezk 45:21
And on the **s** days of the festival he Ezk 45:23
offering to the LORD **s** young bulls and Ezk 45:23
young bulls and **s** rams without Ezk 45:23
blemish, on each of the **s** days; Ezk 45:23
month and for the **s** days of the feast, Ezk 45:25
the furnace heated **s** times more than Dn 3:19
and let **s** periods of time pass over him. Dn 4:16
field, till **s** periods of time pass over him,' Dn 4:23
and **s** periods of time shall pass over Dn 4:25
and **s** periods of time shall pass over Dn 4:32
one, a prince, there shall be **s** weeks. Dn 9:25
raise against him **s** shepherds and eight Mi 5:5
Joshua, on a single stone with **s** eyes, Zec 3:9
a bowl on the top of it, and **s** lamps on it, Zec 4:2
with **s** lips on each of the lamps that are Zec 4:2
"These **s** are the eyes of the LORD, which Zec 4:10
and brings with it **s** other spirits more Mt 12:45
They said, "**S**, and a few small fish." Mt 15:34
he took the **s** loaves and the fish, and Mt 15:36
And they took up **s** baskets full of the Mt 15:37
Or the **s** loaves for the four thousand, Mt 16:10
I forgive him? As many as **s** times?" Mt 18:21
said to him, "I do not say to you **s** times, Mt 18:22
to you seven times, but seventy times **s**. Mt 18:22
Now there were **s** brothers among us. Mt 22:25
In the resurrection, therefore, of the **s**, Mt 22:28
loaves do you have?" They said, "**S**." Mk 8:5
And he took the **s** loaves, and having Mk 8:6
the broken pieces left over, **s** baskets full. Mk 8:8
"And the **s** for the four thousand, how Mk 8:20
you take up?" And they said to him, "**S**." Mk 8:20
There were **s** brothers; the first took a Mk 12:20
And the **s** left no offspring. Last of all Mk 12:22
will she be? For the **s** had her as wife." Mk 12:23
from whom he had cast out **s** demons. Mk 16:9
with her husband **s** years from when Lk 2:36
from whom **s** demons had gone out, Lk 8:2
it goes and brings **s** other spirits more Lk 11:26
if he sins against you **s** times in the day, Lk 17:4
in the day, and turns to you **s** times, Lk 17:4
Now there were **s** brothers. The first Lk 20:29
and likewise all **s** left no children and Lk 20:31
woman be? For the **s** had her as wife." Lk 20:33
about **s** miles from Jerusalem, Lk 24:13
out from among you **s** men of good Acts 6:3
And after destroying **s** nations in the Acts 13:19
S sons of a Jewish high priest named Acts 19:14
at Troas, where we stayed for **s** days. Acts 20:6
the disciples, we stayed there for **s** days. Acts 21:4
the evangelist, who was one of the **s**, Acts 21:8
When the **s** days were almost Acts 21:27
invited to stay with them for **s** days. Acts 28:14
kept for myself **s** thousand men who Rom 11:4
they had been encircled for **s** days. Heb 11:30
a herald of righteousness, with **s** others, 2 Pt 2:5
John to the **s** churches that are in Asia: Rv 1:4
and from the **s** spirits who are before his Rv 1:4
in a book and send it to the **s** churches, Rv 1:11
on turning I saw **s** golden lampstands, Rv 1:12
In his right hand he held **s** stars, from Rv 1:16
the mystery of the **s** stars that you saw Rv 1:20
right hand, and the **s** golden lampstands, Rv 1:20
the **s** stars are the angels of the seven Rv 1:20
stars are the angels of the **s** churches, Rv 1:20
and the **s** lampstands are the seven Rv 1:20
the seven lampstands are the **s** churches. Rv 1:20
of him who holds the **s** stars in his right Rv 2:1
walks among the **s** golden lampstands. Rv 2:1
of him who has the **s** spirits of God and Rv 3:1
the seven spirits of God and the **s** stars. Rv 3:1
the throne were burning **s** torches of fire, Rv 4:5
of fire, which are the **s** spirits of God, Rv 4:5
and on the back, sealed with **s** seals. Rv 5:1
that he can open the scroll and its **s** seals." Rv 5:5
slain, with **s** horns and with seven eyes, Rv 5:6
slain, with seven horns and with **s** eyes, Rv 5:6
which are the **s** spirits of God sent out into Rv 5:6
when the Lamb opened one of the **s** seals, Rv 6:1
Then I saw the **s** angels who stand before Rv 8:2
God, and **s** trumpets were given to them. Rv 8:2
Now the **s** angels who had the seven Rv 8:6
angels who had the **s** trumpets prepared to Rv 8:6
he called out, the **s** thunders sounded. Rv 10:3
And when the **s** thunders had sounded, I Rv 10:4

“Seal up what the **s** thunders have said, Rv 10:4
S thousand people were killed in the Rv 11:13
red dragon, with **s** heads and ten horns, Rv 12:3
ten horns, and on his heads **s** diadems. Rv 12:3
of the sea, with ten horns and **s** heads, Rv 13:1
amazing, **s** angels with seven plagues, Rv 15:1
amazing, seven angels with **s** plagues, Rv 15:1
the sanctuary came the **s** angels with the Rv 15:6
the seven angels with the **s** plagues, Rv 15:6
gave to the **s** angels seven golden Rv 15:7
to the seven angels **s** golden bowls full of Rv 15:7
the sanctuary until the **s** plagues of the Rv 15:8
plagues of the **s** angels were finished. Rv 15:8
from the temple telling the **s** angels, Rv 16:1
out on the earth the **s** bowls of the wrath Rv 16:1
Then one of the **s** angels who had the Rv 17:1
angels who had the **s** bowls came and Rv 17:1
names, and it had **s** heads and ten horns. Rv 17:3
of the beast with **s** heads and ten horns Rv 17:7
the **s** heads are seven mountains on Rv 17:9
seven heads are **s** mountains on which Rv 17:9
they are also **s** kings, five of whom have Rv 17:10
it is an eighth but it belongs to the **s**, Rv 17:11
came one of the **s** angels who had the Rv 21:9
angels who had the **s** bowls full of the Rv 21:9
bowls full of the **s** last plagues and spoke Rv 21:9

SEVENFOLD (9)
be taken on him **s**.” And the LORD put Gn 4:15
If Cain's revenge is **s**, then Lamech's is Gn 4:24
discipline you again **s** for your sins, Lv 26:18
continue striking you, **s** for your sins. Lv 26:21
I myself will strike you **s** for your sins. Lv 26:24
will discipline you **s** for your sins. Lv 26:28
Return **s** into the lap of our neighbors Ps 79:12
but if he is caught, he will pay **s**; he will Prv 6:31
sun, and the light of the sun will be **s**, Is 30:26

SEVENTEEN (6)
Joseph, being **s** years old, was pasturing Gn 37:2
Jacob lived in the land of Egypt **s** years. Gn 47:28
and he reigned **s** years in Jerusalem, 1 Kgs 14:21
in Samaria, and he reigned **s** years. 2 Kgs 13:1
and he reigned **s** years in Jerusalem, 2 Chr 12:13
out the money to him, **s** shekels of silver. Jer 32:9

SEVENTEENTH (6)
month, on the **s** day of the month, Gn 7:11
month, on the **s** day of the month, Gn 8:4
Samaria in the **s** year of 1 Kgs 22:51
In the **s** year of Pekah the son of 2 Kgs 16:1
the **s** to Hezir, the eighteenth to 1 Chr 24:15
to the **s**, to Joshbekashah, his sons 1 Chr 25:24

SEVENTH (115)
And on the **s** day God finished his work Gn 2:2
and he rested on the **s** day from all his Gn 2:2
So God blessed the **s** day and made it Gn 2:3
and in the **s** month, on the seventeenth Gn 8:4
from the first day until the **s** day, Ex 12:15
and on the **s** day a holy assembly. Ex 12:16
and on the **s** day there shall be a feast to Ex 13:6
you shall gather it, but on the **s** day, Ex 16:26
On the **s** day some of the people went Ex 16:27
no one go out of his place on the **s** day.” Ex 16:29
So the people rested on the **s** day. Ex 16:30
but the **s** day is a Sabbath to the LORD Ex 20:10
all that is in them, and rested the **s** day. Ex 20:11
years, and in the **s** he shall go out free, Ex 21:2
but the **s** year you shall let it rest and lie Ex 23:11
work, but on the **s** day you shall rest; Ex 23:12
And on the **s** day he called to Moses out Ex 24:16
but the **s** day is a Sabbath of solemn Ex 31:15
and on the **s** day he rested and was Ex 31:17
work, but on the **s** day you shall rest. Ex 34:21
but on the **s** day you shall have a Ex 35:2
priest shall examine him on the **s** day, Lv 13:5
shall examine him again on the **s** day, Lv 13:6
the priest shall examine him the **s** day. Lv 13:27
and on the **s** day the priest shall Lv 13:32
And on the **s** day the priest shall Lv 13:34
shall examine the disease on the **s** day. Lv 13:51
And on the **s** day he shall shave off all Lv 14:9
priest shall come again on the **s** day, Lv 14:39
to you forever that in the **s** month, Lv 16:29
but on the **s** day is a Sabbath of solemn Lv 23:3
On the **s** day is a holy convocation; you Lv 23:8
fifty days to the day after the **s** Sabbath. Lv 23:16
people of Israel, saying, In the **s** month, Lv 23:24
the tenth day of this **s** month is the Day Lv 23:27
fifteenth day of this **s** month and for Lv 23:34
“On the fifteenth day of the **s** month, Lv 23:39
you shall celebrate it in the **s** month. Lv 23:41
but in the **s** year there shall be a Lv 25:4
trumpet on the tenth day of the **s** month. Lv 25:9
say, ‘What shall we eat in the **s** year, Lv 25:20
cleansing; on the **s** day he shall shave it. Nm 6:9
On the **s** day Elishama the son of Nm 7:48
on the third day and on the **s** day, Nm 19:12
on the third day and on the **s** day, Nm 19:12
on the third day and on the **s** day. Nm 19:19
Thus on the **s** day he shall cleanse Nm 19:19
And on the **s** day you shall have a Nm 28:25
first day of the **s** month you shall have Nm 29:1
tenth day of this **s** month you shall Nm 29:7
fifteenth day of the **s** month you shall Nm 29:12
“On the **s** day seven bulls, two rams, Nm 29:32
on the third day and on the **s** day. Nm 31:19
must wash your clothes on the **s** day, Nm 31:24
but the **s** day is a Sabbath to the LORD Dt 5:14
in your heart and you say, ‘The **s** year, Dt 15:9
and in the **s** year you shall let him go Dt 15:12
and on the **s** day there shall be a solemn Dt 16:8
On the **s** day you shall march around the Jos 6:4
On the **s** day they rose early, at the dawn Jos 6:15
And at the **s** time, when the priests had Jos 6:16
The **s** lot came out for the tribe of the Jos 19:40
lasted, and on the **s** day he told her, Jgs 14:17
said to him on the **s** day before the sun Jgs 14:18
On the **s** day the child died. And the 2 Sm 12:18
Ethanim, which is the **s** month. 1 Kgs 8:2
And at the **s** time he said, “Behold, a 1 Kgs 18:44
Then on the **s** day the battle was 1 Kgs 20:29
But in the **s** year Jehoiada sent and 2 Kgs 11:4
In the **s** year of Jehu, Jehoash began to 2 Kgs 12:1
which was the **s** year of Hoshea son of 2 Kgs 18:9
on the **s** day of the month—that was 2 Kgs 25:8
But in the **s** month, Ishmael the son 2 Kgs 25:25
Ozem the sixth, David the **s**. 1 Chr 2:15
Attai sixth, Eliel **s**, 1 Chr 12:11
the **s** to Hakkoz, the eighth to 1 Chr 24:10
the **s** to Jesharelah, his sons and his 1 Chr 25:14
the sixth, Eliehoenai the **s**. 1 Chr 26:3
Ammiel the sixth, Issachar the **s**, 1 Chr 26:5
S, for the seventh month, was Helez 1 Chr 27:10
Seventh, for the **s** month, was Helez 1 Chr 27:10
king at the feast that is in the **s** month. 2 Chr 5:3
day of the **s** month he sent 2 Chr 7:10
But in the **s** year Jehoiada took 2 Chr 23:1
and finished them in the **s** month. 2 Chr 31:7
When the **s** month came, and the Ezr 3:1
the first day of the **s** month they began to Ezr 3:6
in the **s** year of Artaxerxes the king, Ezr 7:7
which was in the **s** year of the king. Ezr 7:8
And when the **s** month had come, Neh 7:73
heard, on the first day of the **s** month. Neh 8:2
booths during the feast of the **s** month, Neh 8:14
the crops of the **s** year and the Neh 10:31
On the **s** day, when the heart of the king Est 1:10
of Tebeth, in the **s** year of his reign, Est 2:16
In that same year, in the **s** month, the Jer 28:17
In the **s** month, Ishmael the son of Jer 41:1
captive: in the **s** year, 3,023 Judeans; Jer 52:28
In the **s** year, in the fifth month, on the Ezk 20:1
first month, on the **s** day of the month, Ezk 30:20
do the same on the **s** day of the month Ezk 45:20
In the **s** month, on the fifteenth day of Ezk 45:25
In the **s** month, on the twenty-first day of Hg 2:1
mourned in the fifth month and in the **s**, Zec 7:5
and the fast of the **s** and the fast of the Zec 8:19
too the second and third, down to the **s**. Mt 22:26
“Yesterday at the **s** hour the fever left Jn 4:52
somewhere spoken of the **s** day in this Heb 4:4
God rested on the **s** day from all his Heb 4:4
these that Enoch, the **s** from Adam, Jude 1:14
When the Lamb opened the **s** seal, there Rv 8:1
call to be sounded by the **s** angel, Rv 10:7
Then the **s** angel blew his trumpet, and Rv 11:15
The **s** angel poured out his bowl into Rv 16:17
the sixth carnelian, the **s** chrysolite, Rv 21:20

SEVENTY (42)
of Jacob who came into Egypt were **s**. Gn 46:27
And the Egyptians wept for him **s** days. Gn 50:3
the descendants of Jacob were **s** persons; Ex 1:5
springs of water and **s** palm trees, Ex 15:27
and Abihu, and **s** of the elders of Israel, Ex 24:1
and **s** of the elders of Israel went up, Ex 24:9
that was offered was **s** talents and 2,400 Ex 38:29
“Gather for me **s** men of the elders of Nm 11:16
And he gathered **s** men of the elders of Nm 11:24
was on him and put it on the **s** elders. Nm 11:25
springs of water and **s** palm trees, Nm 33:9
fathers went down to Egypt **s** persons, Dt 10:22
“**S** kings with their thumbs and their big Jgs 1:7
Now Gideon had **s** sons, his own Jgs 8:30
that all **s** of the sons of Jerubbaal rule Jgs 9:2
And they gave him **s** pieces of silver out of Jgs 9:4
his brothers the sons of Jerubbaal, **s** men, Jgs 9:5
have killed his sons, **s** men on one stone, Jgs 9:18
violence done to the **s** sons of Jerubbaal Jgs 9:24
his father in killing his **s** brothers. Jgs 9:56
grandsons, who rode on **s** donkeys, Jgs 12:14
He struck **s** men of them, and the 1 Sm 6:19
Now Ahab had **s** sons in Samaria. So 2 Kgs 10:1
time.” Now the king's sons, **s** persons, 2 Kgs 10:6
sons and slaughtered them, **s** persons, 2 Kgs 10:7
S thousand of them he assigned to 2 Chr 2:18
it kept Sabbath, to fulfill **s** years. 2 Chr 36:21
The years of our life are **s**, or even by Ps 90:10
day Tyre will be forgotten for **s** years, Is 23:15
At the end of **s** years, it will happen to Is 23:15
At the end of **s** years, the LORD will visit Is 23:17
shall serve the king of Babylon **s** years. Jer 25:11
Then after **s** years are completed, I will Jer 25:12
When **s** years are completed for Jer 29:10
And before them stood **s** men of the Ezk 8:11
on the west side was **s** cubits broad, Ezk 41:12
desolations of Jerusalem, namely, **s** years. Dn 9:2
“**S** weeks are decreed about your people Dn 9:24
you have been angry these **s** years?’ Zec 1:12
and in the seventh, for these **s** years, Zec 7:5
to you seven times, but **s** times seven. Mt 18:22
with **s** horsemen and two hundred Acts 23:23

SEVENTY-FIVE (3)
Abram was **s** years old when he Gn 12:4
and aloes, about **s** pounds in weight. Jn 19:39
and all his kindred, **s** persons in all. Acts 7:14

SEVENTY-SEVEN (2)
officials and elders of Succoth, **s** men. Jgs 8:14
for all Israel, ninety-six rams, **s** lambs, Ezr 8:35

SEVENTY-SEVENFOLD (1)
is sevenfold, then Lamech's is **s**.” Gn 4:24

SEVENTY-TWO (2)
this the Lord appointed **s** others and sent Lk 10:1
The **s** returned with joy, saying, “Lord, Lk 10:17

SEVER (2)
its wings, but shall not **s** it completely. Lv 1:17
its neck but shall not **s** it completely, Lv 5:8

SEVERAL (5)
finished distributing the **s** territories of Jos 19:49
The cities of the **s** clans of the Jos 21:33
As for the cities of the **s** Merarite clans, Jos 21:40
were men in the **s** cities who were 2 Chr 31:19
Now after **s** years I came to bring Acts 24:17

SEVERE (25)
there, for the famine was **s** in the land. Gn 12:10
that will follow, for it will be very **s**. Gn 41:31
for the famine was **s** in the land of Gn 41:56
because the famine was **s** over all the Gn 41:57
Now the famine was **s** in the land. Gn 43:1
for the famine is **s** in the land of Gn 47:4
all the land, for the famine was very **s**, Gn 47:13
because the famine was **s** on them. Gn 47:20
fall with a very **s** plague upon your Ex 9:3
afflictions, afflictions **s** and lasting, Dt 28:59
the sons of Zeruiah, are more **s** than I. 2 Sm 3:39
his illness was so **s** that there was no 1 Kgs 17:17
Now the famine was **s** in Samaria. 1 Kgs 18:2
the famine was so **s** in the city that 2 Kgs 25:3
in his feet, and his disease became **s**. 2 Chr 16:12
will have a **s** sickness with a 2 Chr 21:15
There is **s** discipline for him who Prv 15:10
the famine was so **s** in the city that Jer 52:6
to his will, will receive a **s** beating. Lk 12:47
a **s** famine arose in that country, Lk 15:14
afraid of you, because you are a **s** man. Lk 19:21
You knew that I was a **s** man, taking Lk 19:22
for in a **s** test of affliction, their 2 Cor 8:2
may not have to be **s** in my use of 2 Cor 13:10
of the hail, because the plague was so **s**. Rv 16:21

SEVERED (2)
His confidence is **s**, and his trust is a Jb 8:14
You are **s** from Christ, you who would Gal 5:4

SEVERELY (8)
him, shot at him, and harassed him **s**, Gn 49:23
Ephraim, so that Israel was **s** distressed. Jgs 10:9
After he had dealt **s** with them, did they 1 Sm 6:6
from him, leaving him **s** wounded, 2 Chr 24:25
The LORD has disciplined me **s**, but he Ps 118:18
I am **s** afflicted; give me life, O LORD, Ps 119:107
my daughter is **s** oppressed by a Mt 15:22
—not to put it too **s**—to all of you. 2 Cor 2:5

SEVERITY (3)
then the kindness and the **s** of God: Rom 11:22
s toward those who have fallen, but Rom 11:22
and asceticism and **s** to the body, Col 2:23

SEW (2)
a time to tear, and a time to **s**; a time to Eccl 3:7
the women who **s** magic bands upon Ezk 13:18

SEWED (2)
And they **s** fig leaves together and made Gn 3:7
I have **s** sackcloth upon my skin and Jb 16:15

SEWS (1)
No one **s** a piece of unshrunk cloth on Mk 2:21

SEXUAL (32)
except on the ground of **s** immorality, Mt 5:32
murder, adultery, **s** immorality, Mt 15:19
his wife, except for **s** immorality, Mt 19:9
man, come evil thoughts, **s** immorality, Mk 7:21
him, "We were not born of **s** immorality. Jn 8:41
by idols, and from **s** immorality, Acts 15:20
strangled, and from **s** immorality. Acts 15:29
strangled, and from **s** immorality." Acts 21:25
not in **s** immorality and sensuality, Rom 13:13
that there is **s** immorality among you, 1 Cor 5:1
he is guilty of **s** immorality or greed, 1 Cor 5:11
body is not meant for **s** immorality, 1 Cor 6:13
Flee from **s** immorality. Every other 1 Cor 6:18
man not to have **s** relations with a 1 Cor 7:1
of the temptation to **s** immorality, 1 Cor 7:2
not indulge in **s** immorality as some 1 Cor 10:8
of the impurity, **s** immorality, 2 Cor 12:21
s immorality, impurity, sensuality, Gal 5:19
But **s** immorality and all impurity or Eph 5:3
s immorality, impurity, passion, evil Col 3:5
that you abstain from **s** immorality; 1 Thes 4:3
likewise indulged in **s** immorality and Jude 1:7
to idols and practice **s** immorality. Rv 2:14
servants to practice **s** immorality and to Rv 2:20
she refuses to repent of her **s** immorality. Rv 2:21
sorceries or their **s** immorality or their Rv 9:21
wine of the passion of her **s** immorality." Rv 14:8
the earth have committed **s** immorality, Rv 17:2
wine of whose **s** immorality the dwellers Rv 17:2
and the impurities of her **s** immorality. Rv 17:4
wine of the passion of her **s** immorality, Rv 18:3
who committed **s** immorality and lived Rv 18:9

SEXUALLY (13)
you shall not lie **s** with your neighbor's Lv 18:20
"If a man lies **s** with a woman who is a Lv 19:20
if a man lies with her **s**, and it is hidden Nm 5:13
to associate with **s** immoral people— 1 Cor 5:9
at all meaning the **s** immoral of this 1 Cor 5:10
neither the **s** immoral, nor idolaters, 1 Cor 6:9
but the **s** immoral person sins 1 Cor 6:18
everyone who is **s** immoral or impure, Eph 5:5
the **s** immoral, men who practice 1 Tm 1:10
that no one is **s** immoral or unholy Heb 12:16
will judge the **s** immoral and Heb 13:4
as for murderers, the **s** immoral, Rv 21:8
sorcerers and the **s** immoral and Rv 22:15

SHAALABBIN (1)
S, Aijalon, Ithlah, Jos 19:42

SHAALBIM (2)
in Mount Heres, in Aijalon, and in **S**, Jgs 1:35
Ben-deker, in Makaz, **S**, Beth-shemesh, 1 Kgs 4:9

SHAALBONITE (2)
Eliahba the **S**, the sons of Jashen, 2 Sm 23:32
of Baharum, Eliahba the **S**, 1 Chr 11:33

SHAALIM (1)
And they passed through the land of **S**, 1 Sm 9:4

SHAAPH (2)
Jotham, Geshan, Pelet, Ephah, and **S**. 1 Chr 2:47
She also bore **S** the father of 1 Chr 2:49

SHAARAIM (3)
S, Adithaim, Gederah, Gederothaim: Jos 15:36
fell on the way from **S** as far as Gath 1 Sm 17:52
Hazar-susim, Beth-biri, and **S**. 1 Chr 4:31

SHAASHGAZ (1)
to the second harem in custody of **S**, Est 2:14

SHABBETHAI (3)
and Meshullam and **S** the Levite Ezr 10:15
Sherebiah, Jamin, Akkub, **S**, Hodiah, Neh 8:7
and **S** and Jozabad, of the chiefs of the Neh 11:16

SHABBY (1)
a poor man in **s** clothing also comes in, Jas 2:2

SHACKLES (4)
to Gaza and bound him with bronze **s**. Jgs 16:21
had often been bound with **s** and chains, Mk 5:4
apart, and he broke the **s** in pieces. Mk 5:4
guard and bound with chains and **s**, Lk 8:29

SHADE (17)
you, then come and take refuge in my **s**, Jgs 9:15
For his **s** the lotus trees cover him; the Jb 40:22
The mountains were covered with its **s**, Ps 80:10
the LORD is your **s** on your right hand. Ps 121:5
will be a booth for **s** by day from the heat, Is 4:6
make your **s** like night at the height of Is 16:3
from the storm and a **s** from the heat; Is 25:4
as heat by the **s** of a cloud, so the song of Is 25:5
like the **s** of a great rock in a weary land. Is 32:2
in the **s** of its branches birds of every Ezk 17:23
with beautiful branches and forest **s**, Ezk 31:3
The beasts of the field found **s** under it, Dn 4:12
under which beasts of the field found **s**, Dn 4:21
and terebinth, because their **s** is good. Hos 4:13
He sat under it in the **s**, till he should see Jon 4:5
Jonah, that it might be a **s** over his head, Jon 4:6
birds of the air can make nests in its **s**." Mk 4:32

SHADES (2)
you come; it rouses the **s** to greet you, Is 14:9
not live; they are **s**, they will not arise; Is 26:14

SHADOW (47)
"You mistake the **s** of the mountains for Jgs 9:36
shall the **s** go forward ten steps, or go 2 Kgs 20:9
easy thing for the **s** to lengthen ten 2 Kgs 20:10
Rather let the **s** go back ten steps." 2 Kgs 20:10
and he brought the **s** back ten steps, 2 Kgs 20:11
Our days on the earth are like a **s**, 1 Chr 29:15
Like a slave who longs for the **s**, and like a Jb 7:2
nothing, for our days on earth are a **s**. Jb 8:9
to the land of darkness and deep **s**, Jb 10:21
darkness, like deep **s** without any order, Jb 10:22
he flees like a **s** and continues not. Jb 14:2
and all my members are like a **s**. Jb 17:7
your eye; hide me in the **s** of your wings, Ps 17:8
walk through the valley of the **s** of death, Ps 23:4
take refuge in the **s** of your wings. Ps 36:7
Surely a man goes about as a **s**! Surely Ps 39:6
and covered us with the **s** of death. Ps 44:19
in the **s** of your wings I will take refuge, Ps 57:1
and in the **s** of your wings I will sing for Ps 63:7
High will abide in the **s** of the Almighty. Ps 91:1
My days are like an evening **s**; I wither Ps 102:11
sat in darkness and in the **s** of death, Ps 107:10
out of darkness and the **s** of death, Ps 107:14
I am gone like a **s** at evening; I am Ps 109:23
a breath; his days are like a passing **s**. Ps 144:4
his vain life, which he passes like a **s**? Eccl 6:12
will he prolong his days like a **s**, Eccl 8:13
With great delight I sat in his **s**, and his Sg 2:3
and to seek shelter in the **s** of Egypt! Is 30:2
and the shelter in the **s** of Egypt to your Is 30:3
hatches and gathers her young in her **s**; Is 34:15
I will make the **s** cast by the declining Is 38:8
sword; in the **s** of his hand he hid me; Is 49:2
and covered you in the **s** of my hand, Is 51:16
"In the **s** of Heshbon fugitives stop Jer 48:45
"Under his **s** we shall live among the Lam 4:20
and under its **s** lived all great nations. Ezk 31:6
have gone away from its **s** and left it. Ezk 31:12
lived under its **s** among the nations. Ezk 31:17
shall return and dwell beneath my **s**; Hos 14:7
dwelling in the region and **s** of death, Mt 4:16
who sit in darkness and in the **s** of death, Lk 1:79
by at least his **s** might fall on some Acts 5:15
These are a **s** of the things to come, but Col 2:17
serve a copy and **s** of the heavenly Heb 8:5
the law has but a **s** of the good things to Heb 10:1
there is no variation or **s** due to change. Jas 1:17

SHADOWS (3)
Until the day breathes and the **s** flee, Sg 2:17
Until the day breathes and the **s** flee, I will Sg 4:6
declines, for the **s** of evening lengthen! Jer 6:4

SHADRACH (15)
Belteshazzar, Hananiah he called **S**, Dn 1:7
request of the king, and he appointed **S**, Dn 2:49
of Babylon: **S**, Meshach, and Abednego. Dn 3:12
in furious rage commanded that **S**, Dn 3:13
and said to them, "Is it true, O **S**, Dn 3:14
S, Meshach, and Abednego answered Dn 3:16
of his face was changed against **S**, Dn 3:19
the mighty men of his army to bind **S**, Dn 3:20
the fire killed those men who took up **S**, Dn 3:22
And these three men, **S**, Meshach, and Dn 3:23
he declared, "**S**, Meshach, and Dn 3:26
God, come out, and come here!" Then **S**, Dn 3:26
and said, "Blessed be the God of **S**, Dn 3:28
speaks anything against the God of **S**, Dn 3:29
Then the king promoted **S**, Meshach, Dn 3:30

SHAFT (9)
The **s** of his spear was like a weaver's 1 Sm 17:7
get up the water **s** to attack 'the lame 2 Sm 5:8
the **s** of whose spear was like a 2 Sm 21:19
himself with iron and the **s** of a spear, 2 Sm 23:7
the **s** of whose spear was like a 1 Chr 20:5
given the key to the **s** of the bottomless pit. Rv 9:1
He opened the **s** of the bottomless pit, and Rv 9:2
and from the **s** rose smoke like the smoke Rv 9:2
were darkened with the smoke from the **s**. Rv 9:2

SHAFTS (2)
He opens **s** in a valley away from where Jb 28:4
weapons, making his arrows fiery **s**. Ps 7:13

SHAGEE (1)
Jonathan the son of **S** the Hararite, 1 Chr 11:34

SHAHARAIM (1)
And **S** fathered sons in the country of 1 Chr 8:8

SHAHAZUMAH (1)
touches Tabor, **S**, and Beth-shemesh, Jos 19:22

SHAKE (24)
at other times and **s** myself free." But he Jgs 16:20
"So may God **s** out every man from his Neh 5:13
trembling, which made all my bones **s**. Jb 4:14
He will **s** off his unripe grape like the Jb 15:33
together against you and **s** my head at Jb 16:4
as the trees of the forest **s** before the wind. Is 7:2
he will **s** his fist at the mount of the Is 10:32
and Bashan and Carmel **s** off their leaves. Is 33:9
S yourself from the dust and arise; be Is 52:2
is broken within me; all my bones **s**; Jer 23:9
Your walls will **s** at the noise of the Ezk 26:10
Will not the coastlands **s** at the sound Ezk 26:15
you broke and made all their loins to **s**. Ezk 29:7
the capitals until the thresholds **s**, Am 9:1
and **s** the house of Israel among all the Am 9:9
I will **s** the heavens and the earth and the Hg 2:6
And I will **s** all nations, so that the Hg 2:7
I am about to **s** the heavens and the Hg 2:21
"Behold, I will **s** my hand over them, and Zec 2:9
s off the dust from your feet when you Mt 10:14
s off the dust that is on your feet as a Mk 6:11
against that house and could not **s** it, Lk 6:48
you leave that town **s** off the dust from Lk 9:5
once more I will **s** not only the earth Heb 12:26

SHAKEN (28)
Israel as a reed is **s** in the water, 1 Kgs 14:15
So may he be **s** out and emptied." And Neh 5:13
the people are **s** and pass away, Jb 34:20
the earth, and the wicked be **s** out of it? Jb 38:13
him," lest my foes rejoice because I am **s**. Ps 13:4
he is at my right hand, I shall not be **s**. Ps 16:8
my fortress; I shall not be greatly **s**. Ps 62:2
salvation, my fortress; I shall not be **s**. Ps 62:6
all the foundations of the earth are **s**. Ps 82:5
at evening; I am **s** off like a locust. Ps 109:23
and the earth will be **s** out of its place, Is 13:13
over the sea; he has **s** the kingdoms; Is 23:11
is split apart, the earth is violently **s**. Is 24:19
with first-ripe figs—if **s** they fall into the Na 3:12
wilderness to see? A reed **s** by the wind? Mt 11:7
and the powers of the heavens will be **s**. Mt 24:29
the powers in the heavens will be **s**. Mk 13:25
Good measure, pressed down, **s** together, Lk 6:38
wilderness to see? A reed **s** by the wind? Lk 7:24
For the powers of the heavens will be **s**. Lk 21:26
is at my right hand that I may not be **s**; Acts 2:25
they were gathered together was **s**, Acts 4:31
the foundations of the prison were **s**. Acts 16:26
not to be quickly **s** in mind or 2 Thes 2:2
removal of things that are **s**—that is, Heb 12:27
things that cannot be **s** may remain. Heb 12:27
receiving a kingdom that cannot be **s**, Heb 12:28
sheds its winter fruit when **s** by a gale. Rv 6:13

SHAKES (10)
who **s** the earth out of its place, and its Jb 9:6
The voice of the LORD **s** the wilderness; Ps 29:8
the LORD **s** the wilderness of Kadesh. Ps 29:8
hand that the LORD of hosts **s** over them. Is 19:16
the gain of oppressions, who **s** his hands, Is 33:15
passes by it is horrified and **s** his head. Jer 18:16
He **s** the arrows; he consults the Ezk 21:21
cry of your pilots the countryside **s**, Ezk 27:28
all the nations as one **s** with a sieve, Am 9:9
who passes by her hisses and **s** his fist. Zep 2:15

SHALISHAH (1)
and passed through the land of **S**, 1 Sm 9:4

SHALLECHETH (1)
at the gate of **S** on the road that goes 1 Chr 26:16

SHALLUM (28)
S the son of Jabesh conspired 2 Kgs 15:10
S the son of Jabesh began to reign in 2 Kgs 15:13
and he struck down **S** the son of 2 Kgs 15:14
Now the rest of the deeds of **S**, and 2 Kgs 15:15
the wife of **S** the son of Tikvah, 2 Kgs 22:14
Sismai, and Sismai fathered **S**. 1 Chr 2:40
S fathered Jekamiah, and Jekamiah 1 Chr 2:41
the third Zedekiah, the fourth **S**. 1 Chr 3:15
S was his son, Mibsam his son, 1 Chr 4:25
fathered Zadok, Zadok fathered **S**, 1 Chr 6:12
S fathered Hilkiah, Hilkiah fathered 1 Chr 6:13
Jahziel, Guni, Jezer and **S**, the 1 Chr 7:13
The gatekeepers were **S**, Akkub, 1 Chr 9:17
and their kinsmen (**S** was the chief); 1 Chr 9:17
S the son of Kore, son of Ebiasaph, 1 Chr 9:19
the firstborn of **S** the Korahite, 1 Chr 9:31

Jehizkiah the son of **S**, 2 Chr 28:12
the wife of **S** the son of Tokhath, 2 Chr 34:22
the sons of **S**, the sons of Ater, the sons Ezr 2:42
son of **S**, son of Zadok, son of Ahitub, Ezr 7:2
Of the gatekeepers: **S**, Telem, and Uri. Ezr 10:24
S, Amariah, and Joseph. Ezr 10:42
Next to him **S** the son of Hallohesh, Neh 3:12
And **S** the son of Col-hozeh, ruler of the Neh 3:15
the sons of **S**, the sons of Ater, the sons Neh 7:45
says the LORD concerning **S** the son of Jer 22:11
Hanamel the son of **S** your uncle will Jer 32:7
the chamber of Maaseiah the son of **S**, Jer 35:4

SHALMAI (1)
the sons of Hagaba, the sons of **S**, Neh 7:48

SHALMAN (1)
as **S** destroyed Beth-arbel on the day of Hos 10:14

SHALMANESER (2)
him came up **S** king of Assyria. 2 Kgs 17:3
S king of Assyria came up against 2 Kgs 18:9

SHAMA (1)
S and Jeiel the sons of Hotham the 1 Chr 11:44

SHAME (153)
chosen the son of Jesse to your own **s**, 1 Sm 20:30
and to the **s** of your mother's 1 Sm 20:30
As for me, where could I carry my **s**? 2 Sm 13:13
have today covered with **s** the faces of 2 Sm 19:5
So he returned with **s** of face to his 2 Chr 32:21
to captivity, to plundering, and to utter **s**, Ezr 9:7
the exile is in great trouble and **s**. Neh 1:3
who hate you will be clothed with **s**, Jb 8:22
and when you mock, shall no one **s** you? Jb 11:3
long shall my honor be turned into **s**? Ps 4:2
turn back and be put to **s** in a moment. Ps 6:10
You would **s** the plans of the poor, but Ps 14:6
in you they trusted and were not put to **s**. Ps 22:5
God, in you I trust; let me not be put to **s**; Ps 25:2
none who wait for you shall be put to **s**; Ps 25:3
Let me not be put to **s**, for I take refuge Ps 25:20
do I take refuge; let me never be put to **s**; Ps 31:1
O LORD, let me not be put to **s**, for I call Ps 31:17
call upon you; let the wicked be put to **s**; Ps 31:17
them be put to **s** and dishonor who seek Ps 35:4
be put to **s** and disappointed altogether Ps 35:26
be clothed with **s** and dishonor who Ps 35:26
they are not put to **s** in evil times; in the Ps 37:19
be put to **s** and disappointed altogether Ps 40:14
appalled because of their **s** who say to Ps 40:15
foes and have put to **s** those who hate us. Ps 44:7
is before me, and **s** has covered my face Ps 44:15
you put them to **s**, for God has rejected Ps 53:5
he will put to **s** him who tramples on me. Ps 57:3
who hope in you be put to **s** through me, Ps 69:6
reproach, and my **s** and my dishonor; Ps 69:19
them be put to **s** and confusion who seek Ps 70:2
turn back because of their **s** who say, Ps 70:3
do I take refuge; let me never be put to **s**! Ps 71:1
my accusers be put to **s** and consumed; Ps 71:13
been put to **s** and disappointed who Ps 71:24
Let not the downtrodden turn back in **s**; Ps 74:21
to rout; he put them to everlasting **s**. Ps 78:66
Fill their faces with **s**, that they may Ps 83:16
them be put to **s** and dismayed forever; Ps 83:17
may see and be put to **s** because you, Ps 86:17
his youth; you have covered him with **s**. Ps 89:45
All worshipers of images are put to **s**, Ps 97:7
They arise and are put to **s**, but your Ps 109:28
wrapped in their own **s** as in a cloak! Ps 109:29
Then I shall not be put to **s**, having my Ps 119:6
O LORD; let me not be put to **s**! Ps 119:31
before kings and shall not be put to **s**, Ps 119:46
Let the insolent be put to **s**, because Ps 119:78
statutes, that I may not be put to **s**! Ps 119:80
and let me not be put to **s** in my hope! Ps 119:116
not be put to **s** when he speaks with Ps 127:5
Zion be put to **s** and turned backward! Ps 129:5
His enemies I will clothe with **s**, but on Ps 132:18
sleeps in harvest is a son who brings **s**. Prv 10:5
but she who brings **s** is like rottenness Prv 12:4
but the wicked brings **s** and disgrace. Prv 13:5
before he hears, it is his folly and **s**. Prv 18:13
is a son who brings **s** and reproach. Prv 19:26
end, when your neighbor puts you to **s**? Prv 25:8
he who hears you bring **s** upon you, Prv 25:10
left to himself brings **s** to his mother. Prv 29:15
chariots, you **s** of your master's house. Is 22:18
the protection of Pharaoh turn to your **s**, Is 30:3
everyone comes to **s** through a people that Is 30:5
help nor profit, but **s** and disgrace." Is 30:5
you shall be put to **s** and confounded; Is 41:11
are turned back and utterly put to **s**, Is 42:17
see nor know, that they may be put to **s**. Is 44:9
all his companions shall be put to **s**, Is 44:11
terrified; they shall be put to **s** together. Is 44:11
All of them are put to **s** and confounded; Is 45:16
shall not be put to **s** or confounded to all Is 45:17
who wait for me shall not be put to **s**." Is 49:23
and I know that I shall not be put to **s**. Is 50:7
for you will forget the **s** of your youth, Is 54:4
Instead of your **s** there shall be a double Is 61:7
shall rejoice, but you shall be put to **s**; Is 65:13
joy'; but it is they who shall be put to **s**. Is 66:5
You shall be put to **s** by Egypt as you Jer 2:36
by Egypt as you were put to **s** by Assyria. Jer 2:36
Let us lie down in our **s**, and let our Jer 3:25
LORD. Is it not themselves, to their own **s**? Jer 7:19
The wise men shall be put to **s**; they shall Jer 8:9
every goldsmith is put to **s** by his idols, Jer 10:14
are the altars you have set up to **s**, Jer 11:13
over your face, and your **s** will be seen. Jer 13:26
all who forsake you shall be put to **s**; Jer 17:13
Let those be put to **s** who persecute me, Jer 17:18
persecute me, but let me not be put to **s**; Jer 17:18
and sorrow, and spend my days in **s**? Jer 20:18
everlasting reproach and perpetual **s**, Jer 23:40
The nations have heard of your **s**, and Jer 46:12
The daughter of Egypt shall be put to **s**; Jer 46:24
Kiriathaim is put to **s**, it is taken; the Jer 48:1
the fortress is put to **s** and broken down; Jer 48:1
Moab is put to **s**, for it is broken; wail Jer 48:20
How Moab has turned his back in **s**! Jer 48:39
'Babylon is taken, Bel is put to **s**, Jer 50:2
Her images are put to **s**, her idols are Jer 50:2
every goldsmith is put to **s** by his idols, Jer 51:17
her whole land shall be put to **s**, and all Jer 51:47
'We are put to **s**, for we have heard Jer 51:51
S is on all faces, and baldness on all Ezk 7:18
your mouth again because of your **s**, Ezk 16:63
and they bear their **s** with those who Ezk 32:24
and they bear their **s** with those who Ezk 32:25
have gone down in **s** with the slain, Ezk 32:30
and bear their **s** with those who go Ezk 32:30
They shall forget their **s** and all the Ezk 39:26
shall bear their **s** and the Ezk 44:13
belongs righteousness, but to us open **s**, Dn 9:7
To us, O Lord, belongs open **s**, to our Dn 9:8
and some to **s** and everlasting contempt. Dn 12:2
me; I will change their glory into **s**. Hos 4:7
to whoring; their rulers dearly love **s**. Hos 4:18
themselves to the thing of **s**, Hos 9:10
Ephraim shall be put to **s**, and Israel Hos 10:6
my people shall never again be put to **s**. Jl 2:26
my people shall never again be put to **s**. Jl 2:27
to your brother Jacob, **s** shall cover you, Ob 1:10
of Shaphir, in nakedness and **s**; Mi 1:11
be disgraced, and the diviners put to **s**; Mi 3:7
see, and **s** will cover her who said to me, Mi 7:10
your nakedness and kingdoms at your **s**. Na 3:5
You have devised **s** for your house by Hab 2:10
will have your fill of **s** instead of glory. Hab 2:16
and utter **s** will come upon your glory! Hab 2:16
does not fail; but the unjust knows no **s**. Zep 3:5
not be put to **s** because of the deeds Zep 3:11
I will change their **s** into praise and Zep 3:19
they shall put to **s** the riders on horses. Zec 10:5
a just man and unwilling to put her to **s**, Mt 1:19
things, all his adversaries were put to **s**, Lk 13:17
you will begin with **s** to take the lowest Lk 14:9
and hope does not put us to **s**, because Rom 5:5
believes in him will not be put to **s**." Rom 9:33
believes in him will not be put to **s**." Rom 10:11
is foolish in the world to **s** the wise; 1 Cor 1:27
is weak in the world to **s** the strong; 1 Cor 1:27
I say this to your **s**. Can it be that there 1 Cor 6:5
of God. I say this to your **s**. 1 Cor 15:34
to him about you, I was not put to **s**. 2 Cor 7:14
To my **s**, I must say, we were too 2 Cor 11:21
is their belly, and they glory in their **s**, Phil 3:19
and authorities and put them to open **s**, Col 2:15
so that an opponent may be put to **s**, Ti 2:8
him endured the cross, despising the **s**, Heb 12:2
believes in him will not be put to **s**." 1 Pt 2:6
behavior in Christ may be put to **s**. 1 Pt 3:16
shrink from him in **s** at his coming. 1 Jn 2:28
sea, casting up the foam of their own **s**; Jude 1:13
yourself and the **s** of your nakedness Rv 3:18

SHAMED (7)
face, should she not be **s** seven days? Nm 12:14
"As a thief is **s** when caught, so the Jer 2:26
caught, so the house of Israel shall be **s**: Jer 2:26
We are utterly **s**, because we have left the Jer 9:19
yet day; she has been **s** and disgraced. Jer 15:9
They will be greatly **s**, for they will not Jer 20:11
your mother shall be utterly **s**, and she Jer 50:12

SHAMEFUL (5)
from our youth the **s** thing has devoured Jer 3:24
For it is **s** for a woman to speak in 1 Cor 14:35
For it is **s** even to speak of the things Eph 5:12
families by teaching for **s** gain what they Ti 1:11
have you; not for **s** gain, but eagerly; 1 Pt 5:2

SHAMEFULLY (8)
but his wrath falls on one who acts **s**. Prv 14:35
over a son who acts **s** and will share the Prv 17:2
she who conceived them has acted **s**. Hos 2:5
rest seized his servants, treated them **s**, Mt 22:6
him on the head and treated him **s**. Mk 12:4
will be mocked and **s** treated and spit Lk 18:32
But they also beat and treated him **s**, Lk 20:11
suffered and been **s** treated at 1 Thes 2:2

SHAMELESS (2)
Gather together, yes, gather, O **s** nation, Zep 2:1
men committing **s** acts with men and Rom 1:27

SHAMELESSLY (1)
vulgar fellows **s** uncovers himself!" 2 Sm 6:20

SHAMES (1)
a companion of gluttons **s** his father. Prv 28:7

SHAMGAR (2)
After him was **S** the son of Anath, who Jgs 3:31
"In the days of **S**, son of Anath, in the days Jgs 5:6

SHAMHUTH (1)
the fifth month, was **S** the Izrahite; 1 Chr 27:8

SHAMIR (4)
And in the hill country, **S**, Jattir, Socoh, Jos 15:48
and he lived at **S** in the hill country of Jgs 10:1
years. Then he died and was buried at **S**. Jgs 10:2
Micah; of the sons of Micah, **S**. 1 Chr 24:24

SHAMLAI (1)
the sons of Hagab, the sons of **S**, the Ezr 2:46

SHAMMA (1)
Bezer, Hod, **S**, Shilshah, Ithran, and 1 Chr 7:37

SHAMMAH (8)
Reuel: Nahath, Zerah, **S**, and Mizzah. Gn 36:13
chiefs Nahath, Zerah, **S**, and Mizzah; Gn 36:17
Then Jesse made **S** pass by. And he 1 Sm 16:9
to him Abinadab, and the third **S**. 1 Sm 17:13
And next to him was **S**, the son of 2 Sm 23:11
S of Harod, Elika of Harod, 2 Sm 23:25
S the Hararite, Ahiam the son of 2 Sm 23:33
Reuel: Nahath, Zerah, **S**, and Mizzah. 1 Chr 1:37

SHAMMAI (5)
The sons of Onam: **S** and Jada. The 1 Chr 2:28
The sons of **S**: Nadab and Abishur. 1 Chr 2:28
of Jorkeam; and Rekem fathered **S**. 1 Chr 2:44
The son of **S**: Maon; and Maon 1 Chr 2:45
and bore Miriam, **S**, and Ishbah, 1 Chr 4:17

SHAMMAI'S (1)
The sons of Jada, **S** brother: Jether 1 Chr 2:32

SHAMMOTH (1)
S of Harod, Helez the Pelonite, 1 Chr 11:27

SHAMMUA (5)
tribe of Reuben, **S** the son of Zaccur; Nm 13:4
S, Shobab, Nathan, Solomon, 2 Sm 5:14
S, Shobab, Nathan, Solomon, 1 Chr 14:4
and Abda the son of **S**, son of Galal, Neh 11:17
of Bilgah, **S**; of Shemaiah, Neh 12:18

SHAMSHERAI (1)
S, Shehariah, Athaliah, 1 Chr 8:26

SHAPED (2)
Before the mountains had been **s**, Prv 8:25
is an idol when its maker has **s** it, Hab 2:18

SHAPES (2)
He **s** it with planes and marks it with a Is 44:13
He **s** it into the figure of a man, with the Is 44:13

SHAPHAM (1)
Joel the chief, **S** the second, Janai, and 1 Chr 5:12

SHAPHAN (30)
the king sent **S** the son of Azaliah, 2 Kgs 22:3
the high priest said to **S** the secretary, 2 Kgs 22:8
And Hilkiah gave the book to **S**, 2 Kgs 22:8
And **S** the secretary came to the king, 2 Kgs 22:9
Then **S** the secretary told the king, 2 Kgs 22:10
me a book." And **S** read it before the 2 Kgs 22:10
the priest, and Ahikam the son of **S**, 2 Kgs 22:12
son of Micaiah, and **S** the secretary, 2 Kgs 22:12
and Ahikam, and Achbor, and **S**, 2 Kgs 22:14
the son of Ahikam, son of **S**, 2 Kgs 25:22
house, he sent **S** the son of Azaliah, 2 Chr 34:8
answered and said to **S** the secretary, 2 Chr 34:15
And Hilkiah gave the book to **S**. 2 Chr 34:15
S brought the book to the king, and 2 Chr 34:16
Then **S** the secretary told the king, 2 Chr 34:18
me a book." And **S** read from it 2 Chr 34:18
Hilkiah, Ahikam the son of **S**, 2 Chr 34:20
the son of Micah, **S** the secretary, 2 Chr 34:20
Ahikam the son of **S** was with Jeremiah Jer 26:24

Elasah the son of **S** and Gemariah the Jer 29:3
of Gemariah the son of **S** the secretary, Jer 36:10
Micaiah the son of Gemariah, son of **S**, Jer 36:11
son of Achbor, Gemariah the son of **S**, Jer 36:12
Gedaliah the son of Ahikam, son of **S**, Jer 39:14
to Gedaliah the son of Ahikam, son of **S**, Jer 40:5
Gedaliah the son of Ahikam, son of **S**, Jer 40:9
Gedaliah the son of Ahikam, son of **S**, Jer 40:11
Gedaliah the son of Ahikam, son of **S**, Jer 41:2
Gedaliah the son of Ahikam, son of **S**; Jer 43:6
the son of **S** standing among them. Ezk 8:11

SHAPHAT (8)
the tribe of Simeon, **S** the son of Hori; Nm 13:5
the son of **S** of Abel-meholah you 1 Kgs 19:16
there and found Elisha the son of **S**, 1 Kgs 19:19
answered, "Elisha the son of **S** is here, 2 Kgs 3:11
Elisha the son of **S** remains on his 2 Kgs 6:31
Hattush, Igal, Bariah, Neariah, and **S**, 1 Chr 3:22
the second, Janai, and **S** in Bashan. 1 Chr 5:12
in the valleys was **S** the son of Adlai. 1 Chr 27:29

SHAPHIR (1)
Pass on your way, inhabitants of **S**, in Mi 1:11

SHAPING (1)
I am **s** disaster against you and Jer 18:11

SHARAI (1)
Machnadebai, Shashai, **S**, Ezr 10:40

SHARAR (1)
Ahiam the son of **S** the Hararite, 2 Sm 23:33

SHARD (1)
its fragments not a **s** is found with Is 30:14

SHARDS (1)
it and drain it out, and gnaw its **s**, Ezk 23:34

SHARE (47)
and the **s** of the men who went with Gn 14:24
Aner, Eshcol, and Mamre take their **s**." Gn 14:24
they shall sell the live ox and **s** its price, Ex 21:35
and the dead beast also they shall **s**. Ex 21:35
I should have no **s** in the heritage of 1 Sm 26:19
For as his **s** is who goes down into 1 Sm 30:24
so shall his **s** be who stays by the 1 Sm 30:24
by the baggage. They shall **s** alike." 1 Sm 30:24
his friends to get a **s** of their property— Jb 17:5
I also will answer with my **s**; I also will Jb 32:17
and given her no **s** in understanding. Jb 39:17
shamefully and will **s** the inheritance Prv 17:2
forever they have no more **s** in all that is Eccl 9:6
Is it not to **s** your bread with the hungry Is 58:7
has two tunics is to **s** with him who has Lk 3:11
give me the **s** of property that is coming Lk 15:12
do not wash you, you have no **s** with me." Jn 13:8
was allotted his **s** in this ministry." Acts 1:17
others and now **s** in the nourishing Rom 11:17
have come to **s** in their spiritual Rom 15:27
so that we might **s** the rule with you! 1 Cor 4:8
If others **s** this rightful claim on you, 1 Cor 9:12
serve at the altar **s** in the sacrificial 1 Cor 9:13
that I may **s** with them in its 1 Cor 9:23
For as we **s** abundantly in Christ's 2 Cor 1:5
through Christ we **s** abundantly in 2 Cor 1:5
know that as you **s** in our sufferings, 2 Cor 1:7
you will also **s** in our comfort. 2 Cor 1:7
does a believer **s** with an unbeliever? 2 Cor 6:15
taught the word must **s** all good things Gal 6:6
have something to **s** with anyone in Eph 4:28
resurrection, and may **s** his sufferings, Phil 3:10
Yet it was kind of you to **s** my trouble. Phil 4:14
has qualified you to **s** in the inheritance Col 1:12
we were ready to **s** with you not only 1 Thes 2:8
works, to be generous and ready to **s**, 1 Tm 6:18
but **s** in suffering for the gospel by the 2 Tm 1:8
S in suffering as a good soldier of 2 Tm 2:3
ought to have the first **s** of the crops. 2 Tm 2:6
therefore the children **s** in flesh and Heb 2:14
you who **s** in a heavenly calling, Heb 3:1
For we **s** in Christ, if indeed we hold Heb 3:14
our good, that we may **s** his holiness. Heb 12:10
to do good and to **s** what you have, Heb 13:16
insofar as you **s** Christ's sufferings, 1 Pt 4:13
part in her sins, lest you **s** in her plagues; Rv 18:4
God will take away his **s** in the tree of Rv 22:19

SHARED (5)
shall be **s** equally among all the sons of Lv 7:10
and because you **s** in all my father's 1 Kgs 2:26
than in a house **s** with a quarrelsome Prv 21:9
than in a house **s** with a quarrelsome Prv 25:24
gift, and have **s** in the Holy Spirit, Heb 6:4

SHARES (5)
of Judah, "We have ten **s** in the king, 2 Sm 19:43
bitterness, and no stranger **s** its joy. Prv 14:10
blessed, for he **s** his bread with the poor. Prv 22:9
to the one who **s** the faith of Abraham, Rom 4:16
is the one who **s** in the first resurrection! Rv 20:6

SHAREZER (3)
his god, Adrammelech and **S**, 2 Kgs 19:37
Nisroch his god, Adrammelech and **S**, Is 37:38
Bethel had sent **S** and Regem-melech and Zec 7:2

SHARING (2)
thresh in hope of **s** in the crop. 1 Cor 9:10
and I pray that the **s** of your faith may Phlm 1:6

SHARON (7)
the pasturelands of **S** to their limits. 1 Chr 5:16
that pastured in **S** was Shitrai the 1 Chr 27:29
I am a rose of **S**, a lily of the valleys. Sg 2:1
S is like a desert, and Bashan and Carmel Is 33:9
given to it, the majesty of Carmel and **S**. Is 35:2
S shall become a pasture for flocks, and Is 65:10
the residents of Lydda and **S** saw him, Acts 9:35

SHARONITE (1)
in Sharon was Shitrai the **S**; 1 Chr 27:29

SHARP (19)
His underparts are like **s** potsherds; he Jb 41:30
Your arrows are **s** in the heart of the Ps 45:5
tongue plots destruction, like a **s** razor, Ps 52:2
and arrows, whose tongues are **s** swords. Ps 57:4
A warrior's **s** arrows, with glowing Ps 120:4
They make their tongue **s** as a serpent's, Ps 140:3
as wormwood, **s** as a two-edged sword. Prv 5:4
a war club, or a sword, or a **s** arrow. Prv 25:18
their arrows are **s**, all their bows bent, Is 5:28
sledge, new, **s**, and having teeth; Is 41:15
He made my mouth like a **s** sword; in the Is 49:2
"And you, O son of man, take a **s** sword. Ezk 5:1
And there arose a **s** disagreement, so Acts 15:39
his mouth came a **s** two-edged sword, Rv 1:16
of him who has the **s** two-edged sword. Rv 2:12
on his head, and a **s** sickle in his hand. Rv 14:14
in heaven, and he too had a **s** sickle. Rv 14:17
voice to the one who had the **s** sickle, Rv 14:18
his mouth comes a **s** sword with which Rv 19:15

SHARPEN (4)
if I **s** my flashing sword and my hand Dt 32:41
to the Philistines to **s** his plowshare, 1 Sm 13:20
is blunt, and one does not **s** the edge, Eccl 10:10
"**S** the arrows! Take up the shields! The Jer 51:11

SHARPENED (3)
sword, a sword is **s** and also polished, Ezk 21:9
s for slaughter, polished to flash like Ezk 21:10
It is **s** and polished to be given into the Ezk 21:11

SHARPENING (1)
of a shekel for **s** the axes and for 1 Sm 13:21

SHARPENS (3)
me; my adversary **s** his eyes against me. Jb 16:9
Iron **s** iron, and one man sharpens Prv 27:17
sharpens iron, and one man **s** another. Prv 27:17

SHARPER (1)
and active, **s** than any two-edged sword, Heb 4:12

SHARPLY (3)
Cut **s** to the right; set yourself to the Ezk 21:16
party stood up and contended **s**, Acts 23:9
Therefore rebuke them **s**, that they may Ti 1:13

SHARUHEN (1)
and **S**—thirteen cities with their Jos 19:6

SHASHAI (1)
Machnadebai, **S**, Sharai, Ezr 10:40

SHASHAK (2)
and Ahio, **S**, and Jeremoth. 1 Chr 8:14
and Penuel were the sons of **S**. 1 Chr 8:25

SHATTER (3)
he will **s** kings on the day of his wrath. Ps 110:5
he will **s** chiefs over the wide earth. Ps 110:6
and **s** them on the heads of all the people; Am 9:1

SHATTERED (11)
his head; she **s** and pierced his temple. Jgs 5:26
sea; by his understanding he **s** Rahab. Jb 26:12
the east wind you **s** the ships of Tarshish. Ps 48:7
trees, and **s** the trees of their country. Ps 105:33
or the pitcher is **s** at the fountain, Eccl 12:6
Be broken, you peoples, and be **s**; give ear, Is 8:9
countries; strap on your armor and be **s**; Is 8:9
be shattered; strap on your armor and be **s**. Is 8:9
of her gods he has **s** to the ground." Is 21:9
of my people is **s** with a great wound, Jer 14:17
"We are **s** but we will rebuild the ruins," Mal 1:4

SHATTERING (1)
and that when the **s** of the power of the Dn 12:7

SHATTERS (7)
your right hand, O LORD, **s** the enemy. Ex 15:6
For he wounds, but he binds up; he **s**, but Jb 5:18
He **s** the mighty without investigation Jb 34:24
earth; he breaks the bow and **s** the spear; Ps 46:9
For he **s** the doors of bronze and cuts Ps 107:16
iron breaks to pieces and **s** all things. Dn 2:40
that he foams at the mouth; and **s** him, Lk 9:39

SHAUL (9)
and **S** of Rehoboth on the Euphrates Gn 36:37
S died, and Baal-hanan the son of Gn 36:38
Jamin, Ohad, Jachin, Zohar, and **S**, Gn 46:10
Jamin, Ohad, Jachin, Zohar, and **S**, Ex 6:15
Zerah, the clan of the Zerahites; of **S**, Nm 26:13
and **S** of Rehoboth on the Euphrates 1 Chr 1:48
S died, and Baal-hanan, the son of 1 Chr 1:49
Nemuel, Jamin, Jarib, Zerah, **S**; 1 Chr 4:24
son, Uzziah his son, and **S** his son. 1 Chr 6:24

SHAULITES (1)
Zerahites; of Shaul, the clan of the **S**. Nm 26:13

SHAVE (15)
then he shall **s** himself, but the itch he Lv 13:33
himself, but the itch he shall not **s**; Lv 13:33
wash his clothes and **s** off all his hair Lv 14:8
the seventh day he shall **s** off all his hair Lv 14:9
He shall **s** off all his hair, and then he Lv 14:9
heads, nor **s** off the edges of their beards, Lv 21:5
then he shall **s** his head on the day of his Nm 6:9
on the seventh day he shall **s** it. Nm 6:9
the Nazirite shall **s** his consecrated Nm 6:18
she shall **s** her head and pare her nails. Dt 21:12
man and had him **s** off the seven locks Jgs 16:19
that day the Lord will **s** with a razor that Is 7:20
They shall not **s** their heads or let Ezk 44:20
so that they may **s** their heads. Acts 21:24
a wife to cut off her hair or **s** her head, 1 Cor 11:6

SHAVED (10)
when he had **s** himself and changed Gn 41:14
after he has **s** the hair of his Nm 6:19
If my head is **s**, then my strength will Jgs 16:17
began to grow again after it had been **s**. Jgs 16:22
David's servants and **s** off half the 2 Sm 10:4
David's servants and **s** them and cut 1 Chr 19:4
and tore his robe and **s** his head and fell Jb 1:20
and Tahpanhes have **s** the crown of Jer 2:16
with their beards **s** and their clothes Jer 41:5
"For every head is **s** and every beard cut Jer 48:37

SHAVEH (1)
to meet him at the Valley of **S** (that is, Gn 14:17

SHAVEH-KIRIATHAIM (1)
the Zuzim in Ham, the Emim in **S**, Gn 14:5

SHAVEN (1)
—it is the same as if her head were **s**. 1 Cor 11:5

SHAVSHA (1)
were priests; and **S** was secretary; 1 Chr 18:16

SHE-BEAR (1)
Let a man meet a **s** robbed of her cubs Prv 17:12

SHE-BEARS (1)
And two **s** came out of the woods and 2 Kgs 2:24

SHEAF (8)
behold, my **s** arose and stood upright. Gn 37:7
around it and bowed down to my **s**." Gn 37:7
you shall bring the **s** of the firstfruits of Lv 23:10
and he shall wave the **s** before the LORD, Lv 23:11
And on the day when you wave the **s**, Lv 23:12
that you brought the **s** of the wave Lv 23:15
in your field and forget a **s** in the field, Dt 24:19
old age, like a **s** gathered up in its season. Jb 5:26

SHEAL (1)
Adaiah, Jashub, **S**, and Jeremoth. Ezr 10:29

SHEALTIEL (13)
of Jeconiah, the captive: **S** his son, 1 Chr 3:17
the son of **S** with his kinsmen, Ezr 3:2
Zerubbabel the son of **S** and Jeshua the Ezr 3:8
Zerubbabel the son of **S** and Jeshua the Ezr 5:2
came up with Zerubbabel the son of **S**, Neh 12:1
the prophet to Zerubbabel the son of **S**, Hg 1:1
Then Zerubbabel the son of **S**, and Hg 1:12
up the spirit of Zerubbabel the son of **S**, Hg 1:14
"Speak now to Zerubbabel the son of **S**, Hg 2:2
O Zerubbabel my servant, the son of **S**, Hg 2:23
Jechoniah was the father of **S**, and Mt 1:12
and **S** the father of Zerubbabel, Mt 1:12
the son of Zerubbabel, the son of **S**, Lk 3:27

SHEAR (3)
Laban had gone to **s** his sheep, and Gn 31:19
is going up to Timnah to **s** his sheep," Gn 38:13
herd, nor **s** the firstborn of your flock. Dt 15:19

SHEAR-JASHUB (1)
"Go out to meet Ahaz, you and **S** your son, Is 7:3

SHEARER (1)
and like a lamb before its **s** is silent, Acts 8:32

SHEARERS (3)
I hear that you have **s**. Now your 1 Sm 25:7
I have killed for my **s** and give it to 1 Sm 25:11
and like a sheep that before its **s** is silent, Is 53:7

SHEARIAH (2)
Bocheru, Ishmael, **S**, Obadiah, 1 Chr 8:38
Bocheru, Ishmael, **S**, Obadiah, 1 Chr 9:44

SHEARING (2)
goats. He was **s** his sheep in Carmel. 1 Sm 25:2
wilderness that Nabal was **s** his sheep. 1 Sm 25:4

SHEATH (9)
it out of its **s** and killed him and 1 Sm 17:51
a sword in its **s** fastened on his thigh, 2 Sm 20:8
and he put his sword back into its **s**. 1 Chr 21:27
my sword from its **s** and will cut off Ezk 21:3
be drawn from its **s** against all flesh Ezk 21:4
I have drawn my sword from its **s**; it Ezk 21:5
Return it to its **s**. In the place where Ezk 21:30
You stripped the **s** from your bow, Hab 3:9
said to Peter, "Put your sword into its **s**; Jn 18:11

SHEATHED (1)
from its sheath; it shall not be **s** again. Ezk 21:5

SHEAVES (11)
Behold, we were binding **s** in the field, Gn 37:7
your **s** gathered around it and bowed Gn 37:7
and gather among the **s** after the reapers.' Ru 2:7
saying, "Let her glean even among the **s**, Ru 2:15
clothing; hungry, they carry the **s**; Jb 24:10
shouts of joy, bringing his **s** with him. Ps 126:6
his hand nor the binder of **s** his arms, Ps 129:7
the open field, like **s** after the reaper, Jer 9:22
place, as a cart full of **s** presses down. Am 2:13
has gathered them as **s** to the threshing Mi 4:12
of wood, like a flaming torch among **s**. Zec 12:6

SHEBA (33)
The sons of Raamah: **S** and Dedan. Gn 10:7
Obal, Abimael, **S**, Gn 10:28
Jokshan fathered **S** and Dedan. The sons Gn 25:3
inheritance Beersheba, **S**, Moladah, Jos 19:2
a worthless man, whose name was **S**, 2 Sm 20:1
from David and followed **S** the son of 2 Sm 20:2
"Now **S** the son of Bichri will do us 2 Sm 20:6
from Jerusalem to pursue **S** the son of 2 Sm 20:7
his brother pursued **S** the son of 2 Sm 20:10
after Joab to pursue **S** the son of 2 Sm 20:13
And **S** passed through all the tribes 2 Sm 20:14
Ephraim, called **S** the son of Bichri, 2 Sm 20:21
cut off the head of **S** the son of Bichri 2 Sm 20:22
when the queen of **S** heard of the fame 1 Kgs 10:1
when the queen of **S** had seen all the 1 Kgs 10:4
that the queen of **S** gave to King 1 Kgs 10:10
to the queen of **S** all that she desired, 1 Kgs 10:13
The sons of Raamah: **S** and Dedan. 1 Chr 1:9
Obal, Abimael, **S**, 1 Chr 1:22
The sons of Jokshan: **S** and Dedan. 1 Chr 1:32
Michael, Meshullam, **S**, Jorai, Jacan, 1 Chr 5:13
when the queen of **S** heard of the fame 2 Chr 9:1
when the queen of **S** had seen the 2 Chr 9:3
that the queen of **S** gave to King 2 Chr 9:9
to the queen of **S** all that she desired, 2 Chr 9:12
of Tema look, the travelers of **S** hope. Jb 6:19
may the kings of **S** and Seba bring Ps 72:10
he live; may gold of **S** be given to him! Ps 72:15
and Ephah; all those from **S** shall come. Is 60:6
me is frankincense that comes from **S**, Jer 6:20
The traders of **S** and Raamah traded Ezk 27:22
Haran, Canneh, Eden, traders of **S**, Ezk 27:23
S and Dedan and the merchants of Ezk 38:13

SHEBANIAH (7)
S, Joshaphat, Nethanel, Amasai, 1 Chr 15:24
stood Jeshua, Bani, Kadmiel, **S**, Bunni, Neh 9:4
Sherebiah, Hodiah, **S**, and Pethahiah, Neh 9:5
Hattush, **S**, Malluch, Neh 10:4
and their brothers, **S**, Hodiah, Kelita, Neh 10:10
Zaccur, Sherebiah, **S**, Neh 10:12
of Malluchi, Jonathan; of **S**, Joseph; Neh 12:14

SHEBARIM (1)
the gate as far as **S** and struck them at the Jos 7:5

SHEBAT (1)
month, which is the month of **S**, Zec 1:7

SHEBER (1)
concubine, bore **S** and Tirhanah. 1 Chr 2:48

SHEBNA (7)
the household, and **S** the secretary, 2 Kgs 18:37
the household, and **S** the secretary, 2 Kgs 19:2
of hosts, "Come, go to this steward, to **S**, Is 22:15
over the household, and **S** the secretary, Is 36:3
S, and Joah said to the Rabshakeh, Is 36:11
over the household, and **S** the secretary, Is 36:22
over the household, and **S** the secretary, Is 37:2

SHEBNAH (2)
the household, and **S** the secretary, 2 Kgs 18:18
Eliakim the son of Hilkiah, and **S**, 2 Kgs 18:26

SHEBUEL (3)
The sons of Gershom: **S** the chief. 1 Chr 23:16
Mattaniah, Uzziel, **S** and Jerimoth, 1 Chr 25:4
and **S** the son of Gershom, son of 1 Chr 26:24

SHECANIAH (10)
Arnan, his son Obadiah, his son **S**. 1 Chr 3:21
The son of **S**: Shemaiah. And the 1 Chr 3:22
the ninth to Jeshua, the tenth to **S**, 1 Chr 24:11
and **S** were faithfully assisting him 2 Chr 31:15
Of the sons of **S**, who was of the sons of Ezr 8:3
Of the sons of Zattu, **S** the son of Jahaziel, Ezr 8:5
And **S** the son of Jehiel, of the sons of Ezr 10:2
After him Shemaiah the son of **S**, the Neh 3:29
was the son-in-law of **S** the son of Neh 6:18
S, Rehum, Meremoth, Neh 12:3

SHECHEM (66)
through the land to the place at **S**, Gn 12:6
And Jacob came safely to the city of **S**, Gn 33:18
And when **S** the son of Hamor the Gn 34:2
So **S** spoke to his father Hamor, saying, Gn 34:4
Hamor the father of **S** went out to Jacob Gn 34:6
soul of my son **S** longs for your Gn 34:8
S also said to her father and to her Gn 34:11
of Jacob answered **S** and his father Gn 34:13
pleased Hamor and Hamor's son **S**. Gn 34:18
Hamor and his son **S** came to the gate Gn 34:20
city listened to Hamor and his son **S**, Gn 34:24
Hamor and his son **S** with the sword Gn 34:26
under the terebinth tree that was near **S**. Gn 35:4
to pasture their father's flock near **S**. Gn 37:12
your brothers pasturing the flock at **S**? Gn 37:13
the Valley of Hebron, and he came to **S**. Gn 37:14
and of **S**, the clan of the Shechemites; Nm 26:31
clans, Abiezer, Helek, Asriel, **S**, Hepher, Jos 17:2
to Michmethath, which is east of **S**, Jos 17:7
and **S** in the hill country of Ephraim, Jos 20:7
To them were given **S**, the city of refuge Jos 21:21
tribes of Israel to **S** and summoned the Jos 24:1
place statutes and rules for them at **S**. Jos 24:25
up from Egypt, they buried them at **S**, Jos 24:32
Hamor the father of **S** for a hundred Jos 24:32
concubine who was in **S** also bore him Jgs 8:31
of Jerubbaal went to **S** to his mother's Jgs 9:1
"Say in the ears of all the leaders of **S**, Jgs 9:2
behalf in the ears of all the leaders of **S**, Jgs 9:3
And all the leaders of **S** came together, Jgs 9:6
king, by the oak of the pillar at **S**. Jgs 9:6
to them, "Listen to me, you leaders of **S**, Jgs 9:7
servant, king over the leaders of **S**, Jgs 9:18
devour the leaders of **S** and Beth-millo; Jgs 9:20
the leaders of **S** and from Beth-millo Jgs 9:20
between Abimelech and the leaders of **S**, Jgs 9:23
the leaders of **S** dealt treacherously with Jgs 9:23
who killed them, and on the men of **S**, Jgs 9:24
And the leaders of **S** put men in ambush Jgs 9:25
of Ebed moved into **S** with his relatives, Jgs 9:26
and the leaders of **S** put confidence in Jgs 9:26
is Abimelech, and who are we of **S**, Jgs 9:28
Serve the men of Hamor the father of **S**; Jgs 9:28
of Ebed and his relatives have come to **S**, Jgs 9:31
an ambush against **S** in four Jgs 9:34
of the leaders of **S** and fought with Jgs 9:39
so that they could not dwell at **S**. Jgs 9:41
the leaders of the Tower of **S** heard of it, Jgs 9:46
of the Tower of **S** were gathered together. Jgs 9:47
all the people of the Tower of **S** also died, Jgs 9:49
of the men of **S** return on their heads, Jgs 9:57
highway that goes up from Bethel to **S**, Jgs 21:19
Rehoboam went to **S**, for all Israel 1 Kgs 12:1
Israel had come to **S** to make him 1 Kgs 12:1
Then Jeroboam built **S** in the hill 1 Kgs 12:25
S with its pasturelands in the hill 1 Chr 6:67
of Shemida were Ahian, **S**, Likhi, 1 Chr 7:19
Gezer and its towns, **S** and its towns, 1 Chr 7:28
Rehoboam went to **S**, for all Israel 2 Chr 10:1
Israel had come to **S** to make him 2 Chr 10:1
I will divide up **S** and portion out the Ps 60:6
I will divide up **S** and portion out the Ps 108:7
men arrived from **S** and Shiloh and Jer 41:5
together; they murder on the way to **S**; Hos 6:9
were carried back to **S** and laid in the Acts 7:16
of silver from the sons of Hamor in **S**. Acts 7:16

SHECHEM'S (2)
And from the sons of Hamor, **S** father, Gn 33:19
took Dinah out of **S** house and went Gn 34:26

SHECHEMITES (1)
and of Shechem, the clan of the **S**; Nm 26:31

SHED (42)
of man, by man shall his blood be **s**, Gn 9:6
And Reuben said to them, "**S** no blood; Gn 37:22
He has **s** blood, and that man shall be Lv 17:4
for the land for the blood that is **s** in it, Nm 35:33
except by the blood of the one who **s** it. Nm 35:33
lest innocent blood be **s** in your land Dt 19:10
testify, 'Our hands did not **s** this blood, Dt 21:7
shed this blood, nor did our eyes see it **s**. Dt 21:7
who takes a bribe to **s** innocent blood.' Dt 27:25
for having **s** blood without 1 Sm 25:31
peace for blood that had been **s** in war, 1 Kgs 2:5
the blood that Joab **s** without cause. 1 Kgs 2:31
Manasseh **s** very much innocent 2 Kgs 21:16
for the innocent blood that he had **s**. 2 Kgs 24:4
'You have **s** much blood and have 1 Chr 22:8
because you have **s** so much blood 1 Chr 22:8
are a man of war and have **s** blood.' 1 Chr 28:3
in abundance, O God, you **s** abroad; Ps 68:9
My eyes **s** streams of tears, because Ps 119:136
to evil, and they make haste to **s** blood. Prv 1:16
and hands that **s** innocent blood, Prv 6:17
rising, and the moon will not **s** its light. Is 13:10
the earth will disclose the blood **s** on it, Is 26:21
and they are swift to **s** innocent blood; Is 59:7
widow, or **s** innocent blood in this place, Jer 7:6
nor **s** innocent blood in this place. Jer 22:3
who **s** in the midst of her the blood of Lam 4:13
commit adultery and **s** blood are Ezk 16:38
guilty by the blood that you have **s**, Ezk 22:4
are men in you who slander to **s** blood, Ezk 22:9
In you they take bribes to **s** blood; you Ezk 22:12
the sentence of women who **s** blood, Ezk 23:45
For the blood she has **s** is in her midst; Ezk 24:7
set on the bare rock the blood she has **s**, Ezk 24:8
up your eyes to your idols and **s** blood; Ezk 33:25
the blood that they had **s** in the land, Ezk 36:18
because they have **s** innocent blood in Jl 3:19
all the righteous blood **s** on earth, Mt 23:35
s from the foundation of the world, Lk 11:50
of Stephen your witness was being **s**, Acts 22:20
"Their feet are swift to **s** blood; Rom 3:15
For they have **s** the blood of saints and Rv 16:6

SHEDDER (1)
a son who is violent, a **s** of blood, Ezk 18:10

SHEDDING (6)
dishonest gain, for **s** innocent blood, Jer 22:17
to his power, have been bent on **s** blood. Ezk 22:6
like wolves tearing the prey, **s** blood, Ezk 22:27
part with them in **s** the blood of the Mt 23:30
and without the **s** of blood there is no Heb 9:22
yet resisted to the point of **s** your blood. Heb 12:4

SHEDEUR (5)
you. From Reuben, Elizur the son of **S**; Nm 1:5
of Reuben being Elizur the son of **S**, Nm 2:10
On the fourth day Elizur the son of **S**, Nm 7:30
was the offering of Elizur the son of **S**. Nm 7:35
company was Elizur the son of **S**. Nm 10:18

SHEDS (3)
"Whoever **s** the blood of man, by man Gn 9:6
A city that **s** blood in her midst, so that Ezk 22:3
as the fig tree **s** its winter fruit when Rv 6:13

SHEEP (200)
Now Abel was a keeper of **s**, and Cain a Gn 4:2
and he had **s**, oxen, male donkeys, Gn 12:16
Then Abimelech took **s** and oxen, and Gn 20:14
So Abraham took **s** and oxen and gave Gn 21:27
behold, three flocks of **s** lying beside it, Gn 29:2
the mouth of the well and water the **s**, Gn 29:3
his daughter is coming with the **s**!" Gn 29:6
gathered together. Water the **s** and go, Gn 29:7
mouth of the well; then we water the **s**." Gn 29:8
them, Rachel came with her father's **s**, Gn 29:9
and the **s** of Laban his mother's Gn 29:10
speckled and spotted **s** and every black Gn 30:32
Laban had gone to shear his **s**, and Gn 31:19
is going up to Timnah to shear his **s**," Gn 38:13
may take it from the **s** or from the goats, Ex 12:5
peace offerings, your **s** and your oxen. Ex 20:24
"If a man steals an ox or a **s**, and kills it Ex 22:1
oxen for an ox, and four **s** for a sheep. Ex 22:1
oxen for an ox, and four sheep for a **s**. Ex 22:1
whether it is an ox or a donkey or a **s**, Ex 22:4
it is for an ox, for a donkey, for a **s**, Ex 22:9
or an ox or a **s** or any beast to keep Ex 22:10
same with your oxen and with your **s**: Ex 22:30
livestock, the firstborn of cow and **s**. Ex 34:19
is from the flock, from the **s** or goats, Lv 1:10
You shall eat no fat, of ox or **s** or goat. Lv 7:23
of the bulls or the **s** or the goats. Lv 22:19
"When an ox or **s** or goat is born, it Lv 22:27
kill an ox or a **s** and her young in one Lv 22:28
whether ox or **s**, it is the LORD'S. Lv 27:26

of a cow, or the firstborn of a **s**, Nm 18:17
And Balak sacrificed oxen and **s**, and Nm 22:40
may not be as **s** that have no Nm 27:17
that the army took was 675,000 **s**, Nm 31:32
out in the army, numbered 337,500 **s**, Nm 31:36
and the LORD'S tribute of **s** was 675. Nm 31:37
the congregation's half was 337,500 **s**, Nm 31:43
your little ones and folds for your **s**, Nm 32:24
fortified cities, and folds for **s**. Nm 32:36
you may eat: the ox, the **s**, the goat, Dt 14:4
ibex, the antelope, and the mountain **s**. Dt 14:5
you desire—oxen or **s** or wine or strong Dt 14:26
God an ox or a **s** in which is a blemish, Dt 17:1
offering a sacrifice, whether an ox or a **s**: Dt 18:3
of your oil, and the first fleece of your **s**, Dt 18:4
brother's ox or his **s** going astray and Dt 22:1
Your **s** shall be given to your enemies, Dt 28:31
young and old, oxen, **s**, and donkeys, Jos 6:21
oxen and donkeys and **s** and his tent and Jos 7:24
in Israel and no **s** or ox or donkey. Jgs 6:4
the spoil and took **s** and oxen and 1 Sm 14:32
his ox or his **s** and slaughter them 1 Sm 14:34
woman, child and infant, ox and **s**, 1 Sm 15:3
and the best of the **s** and of the oxen 1 Sm 15:9
this bleating of the **s** in my ears and 1 Sm 15:14
the best of the **s** and of the oxen 1 Sm 15:15
people took of the spoil, **s** and oxen, 1 Sm 15:21
is keeping the **s**." And Samuel said 1 Sm 16:11
David your son, who is with the **s**." 1 Sm 16:19
to feed his father's **s** at Bethlehem. 1 Sm 17:15
morning and left the **s** with a keeper 1 Sm 17:20
you left those few **s** in the wilderness? 1 Sm 17:28
servant used to keep **s** for his father. 1 Sm 17:34
child and infant, ox, donkey and **s**, 1 Sm 22:19
had three thousand **s** and a thousand 1 Sm 25:2
He was shearing his **s** in Carmel. 1 Sm 25:2
that Nabal was shearing his **s**. 1 Sm 25:4
we were with them keeping the **s**. 1 Sm 25:16
wine and five **s** already prepared and 1 Sm 25:18
alive, but would take away the **s**, 1 Sm 27:9
from the pasture, from following the **s**, 2 Sm 7:8
and curds and **s** and cheese from 2 Sm 17:29
But these **s**, what have they done? 2 Sm 24:17
Adonijah sacrificed **s**, oxen, and 1 Kgs 1:9
fattened cattle, and **s** in abundance, 1 Kgs 1:19
fattened cattle, and **s** in abundance, 1 Kgs 1:25
twenty pasture-fed cattle, a hundred **s**, 1 Kgs 4:23
sacrificing so many **s** and oxen that 1 Kgs 8:5
to the LORD 22,000 oxen and 120,000 **s**. 1 Kgs 8:63
as **s** that have no shepherd. 1 Kgs 22:17
Mesha king of Moab was a **s** breeder, 2 Kgs 3:4
orchards and vineyards, **s** and oxen, 2 Kgs 5:26
50,000 of their camels, 250,000 **s**, 1 Chr 5:21
and wine and oil, oxen and **s**, 1 Chr 12:40
the pasture, from following the **s**, 1 Chr 17:7
But these **s**, what have they done? 1 Chr 21:17
sacrificing so many **s** and oxen that 2 Chr 5:6
a sacrifice 22,000 oxen and 120,000 **s**. 2 Chr 7:5
and carried away **s** in abundance 2 Chr 14:15
had brought 700 oxen and 7,000 **s**. 2 Chr 15:11
an abundance of **s** and oxen for 2 Chr 18:2
as **s** that have no shepherd. 2 Chr 18:16
offerings were 600 bulls and 3,000 **s**. 2 Chr 29:33
1,000 bulls and 7,000 **s** for offerings, 2 Chr 30:24
assembly 1,000 bulls and 10,000 **s**. 2 Chr 30:24
brought in the tithe of cattle and **s**, 2 Chr 31:6
or **s** for burnt offerings to the God of Ezr 6:9
the priests, and they built the **S** Gate. Neh 3:1
corner and the **S** Gate the goldsmiths Neh 3:32
was one ox and six choice **s** and birds, Neh 5:18
Tower of the Hundred, to the **S** Gate; Neh 12:39
He possessed 7,000 **s**, 3,000 camels, 500 Jb 1:3
and burned up the **s** and the servants and Jb 1:16
was not warmed with the fleece of my **s**, Jb 31:20
And he had 14,000 **s**, 6,000 camels, Jb 42:12
all **s** and oxen, and also the beasts of the Ps 8:7
have made us like **s** for slaughter and Ps 44:11
we are regarded as **s** to be slaughtered. Ps 44:22
Like **s** they are appointed for Sheol; Ps 49:14
smoke against the **s** of your pasture? Ps 74:1
out his people like **s** and guided them in Ps 78:52
we your people, the **s** of your pasture, Ps 79:13
of his pasture, and the **s** of his hand. Ps 95:7
are his people, and the **s** of his pasture. Ps 100:3
I have gone astray like a lost **s**; seek Ps 119:176
may our **s** bring forth thousands and Ps 144:13
will keep alive a young cow and two **s**, Is 7:21
cattle are let loose and where **s** tread. Is 7:25
or like **s** with none to gather them, Is 13:14
killing oxen and slaughtering **s**, Is 22:13
brought me your **s** for burnt offerings, Is 43:23
All we like **s** have gone astray; we have Is 53:6
and like a **s** that before its shearers is Is 53:7
Pull them out like **s** for the slaughter, Jer 12:3
destroy and scatter the **s** of my pasture!" Jer 23:1
"My people have been lost **s**. Their Jer 50:6
"Israel is a hunted **s** driven away by Jer 50:17
Should not shepherds feed the **s**? Ezk 34:2
the fat ones, but you do not feed the **s**. Ezk 34:3
My **s** were scattered; they wandered over Ezk 34:6
My **s** were scattered over all the face of Ezk 34:6
surely because my **s** have become a Ezk 34:8
and my **s** have become food for all the Ezk 34:8
shepherds have not searched for my **s**, Ezk 34:8
fed themselves, and have not fed my **s**, Ezk 34:8
I will require my **s** at their hand and Ezk 34:10
and put a stop to their feeding the **s**. Ezk 34:10
I will rescue my **s** from their mouths, Ezk 34:10
will search for my **s** and will seek Ezk 34:11
he is among his **s** that have been Ezk 34:12
been scattered, so will I seek out my **s**, Ezk 34:12
I myself will be the shepherd of my **s**, Ezk 34:15
Behold, I judge between **s** and sheep, Ezk 34:17
Behold, I judge between sheep and **s**, Ezk 34:17
And must my **s** eat what you have Ezk 34:19
judge between the fat **s** and the lean Ezk 34:20
between the fat sheep and the lean **s**. Ezk 34:20
And I will judge between **s** and sheep. Ezk 34:22
And I will judge between sheep and **s**. Ezk 34:22
And you are my **s**, human sheep of Ezk 34:31
are my sheep, human **s** of my pasture, Ezk 34:31
And one **s** from every flock of two Ezk 45:15
for a wife, and for a wife he guarded **s**. Hos 12:12
for them; even the flocks of **s** suffer. Jl 1:18
I will set them together like **s** in a fold, Mi 2:12
like a young lion among the flocks of **s**, Mi 5:8
Therefore the people wander like **s**; they Zec 10:2
to be slaughtered by the **s** traders. Zec 11:7
I named Union. And I tended the **s**. Zec 11:7
on that day, and the **s** traders, Zec 11:11
the shepherd, and the **s** will be scattered; Zec 13:7
and helpless, like **s** without a shepherd. Mt 9:36
go rather to the lost **s** of the house of Mt 10:6
am sending you out as **s** in the midst of Mt 10:16
them, "Which one of you who has a **s**, Mt 12:11
much more value is a man than a **s**! Mt 12:12
sent only to the lost **s** of the house of Mt 15:24
man has a hundred **s** and one of them Mt 18:12
shepherd separates the **s** from the goats. Mt 25:32
And he will place the **s** on his right, but Mt 25:33
and the **s** of the flock will be scattered.' Mt 26:31
they were like **s** without a shepherd. Mk 6:34
shepherd, and the **s** will be scattered.' Mk 14:27
"What man of you, having a hundred **s**, Lk 15:4
me, for I have found my **s** that was lost.' Lk 15:6
servant plowing or keeping **s** say to him Lk 17:7
who were selling oxen and **s** and pigeons, Jn 2:14
all out of the temple, with the **s** and oxen. Jn 2:15
there is in Jerusalem by the **S** Gate a pool, Jn 5:2
enters by the door is the shepherd of the **s**. Jn 10:2
The **s** hear his voice, and he calls his Jn 10:3
and he calls his own **s** by name and leads Jn 10:3
goes before them, and the **s** follow him, Jn 10:4
truly, I say to you, I am the door of the **s**. Jn 10:7
robbers, but the **s** did not listen to them. Jn 10:8
shepherd lays down his life for the **s**. Jn 10:11
not a shepherd, who does not own the **s**, Jn 10:12
wolf coming and leaves the **s** and flees, Jn 10:12
hired hand and cares nothing for the **s**. Jn 10:13
Father; and I lay down my life for the **s**. Jn 10:15
And I have other **s** that are not of this Jn 10:16
My **s** hear my voice, and I know them, Jn 10:27
I love you." He said to him, "Tend my **s**." Jn 21:16
love you." Jesus said to him, "Feed my **s**. Jn 21:17
"Like a **s** he was led to the slaughter Acts 8:32
we are regarded as **s** to be slaughtered." Rom 8:36
went about in skins of **s** and goats, Heb 11:37
Lord Jesus, the great shepherd of the **s**, Heb 13:20
For you were straying like **s**, but have 1 Pt 2:25
wine, oil, fine flour, wheat, cattle and **s**, Rv 18:13

SHEEP'S (1)
come to you in **s** clothing but inwardly Mt 7:15

SHEEPFOLD (1)
who does not enter the **s** by the door but Jn 10:1

SHEEPFOLDS (7)
donkey, crouching between the **s**. Gn 49:14
"We will build **s** here for our Nm 32:16
Why did you sit still among the **s**, to Jgs 5:16
And he came to the **s** by the way, 1 Sm 24:3
stalls for all kinds of cattle, and **s**. 2 Chr 32:28
you men lie among the **s**—the wings of Ps 68:13
his servant and took him from the **s**; Ps 78:70

SHEEPSHEARERS (3)
he went up to Timnah to his **s**, Gn 38:12
years Absalom had **s** at Baal-hazor, 2 Sm 13:23
said, "Behold, your servant has **s**. 2 Sm 13:24

SHEER (1)
and it will be **s** terror to understand the Is 28:19

SHEERAH (1)
His daughter was **S**, who built both 1 Chr 7:24

SHEET (2)
something like a great **s** descending, Acts 10:11
something like a great **s** descending, Acts 11:5

SHEHARIAH (1)
Shamsherai, **S**, Athaliah, 1 Chr 8:26

SHEKEL (46)
took a gold ring weighing a half **s**, Gn 24:22
half a **s** according to the shekel of the Ex 30:13
according to the **s** of the sanctuary Ex 30:13
the sanctuary (the **s** is twenty gerahs), Ex 30:13
half a **s** as an offering to the LORD. Ex 30:13
poor shall not give less, than the half **s**, Ex 30:15
according to the **s** of the sanctuary, Ex 30:24
730 shekels, by the **s** of the sanctuary. Ex 38:24
1,775 shekels, by the **s** of the sanctuary: Ex 38:25
a beka a head (that is, half a **s**, by the Ex 38:26
a shekel, by the **s** of the sanctuary), Ex 38:26
according to the **s** of the sanctuary, Lv 5:15
according to the **s** of the sanctuary. Lv 27:3
be according to the **s** of the sanctuary: Lv 27:25
twenty gerahs shall make a **s**. Lv 27:25
according to the **s** of the sanctuary Nm 3:47
the sanctuary (the **s** of twenty gerahs), Nm 3:47
1,365 shekels, by the **s** of the sanctuary. Nm 3:50
according to the **s** of the sanctuary, Nm 7:13
according to the **s** of the sanctuary, Nm 7:19
according to the **s** of the sanctuary, Nm 7:25
according to the **s** of the sanctuary, Nm 7:31
according to the **s** of the sanctuary, Nm 7:37
according to the **s** of the sanctuary, Nm 7:43
according to the **s** of the sanctuary, Nm 7:49
according to the **s** of the sanctuary, Nm 7:55
according to the **s** of the sanctuary, Nm 7:61
according to the **s** of the sanctuary, Nm 7:67
according to the **s** of the sanctuary, Nm 7:73
according to the **s** of the sanctuary, Nm 7:79
according to the **s** of the sanctuary, Nm 7:85
according to the **s** of the sanctuary, Nm 7:86
according to the **s** of the sanctuary, Nm 18:16
I have with me a quarter of a **s** of silver, 1 Sm 9:8
two-thirds of a **s** for the plowshares 1 Sm 13:21
a third of a **s** for sharpening the axes 1 Sm 13:21
a seah of fine flour shall be sold for a **s**, 2 Kgs 7:1
shekel, and two seahs of barley for a **s**, 2 Kgs 7:1
So a seah of fine flour was sold for a **s**, 2 Kgs 7:16
and two seahs of barley for a **s**, 2 Kgs 7:16
seahs of barley shall be sold for a **s**, 2 Kgs 7:18
shekel, and a seah of fine flour for a **s**, 2 Kgs 7:18
a third part of a **s** for the service of the Neh 10:32
The **s** shall be twenty gerahs; twenty Ezk 45:12
ephah small and the **s** great and deal Am 8:5
you open its mouth you will find a **s**. Mt 17:27

SHEKELS (94)
of land worth four hundred **s** of silver, Gn 23:15
of the Hittites, four hundred **s** of silver, Gn 23:16
for her arms weighing ten gold **s**, Gn 24:22
to the Ishmaelites for twenty **s** of silver. Gn 37:28
he gave three hundred **s** of silver and Gn 45:22
give to their master thirty **s** of silver, Ex 21:32
of liquid myrrh 500 **s**, and of Ex 30:23
was twenty-nine talents and 730 **s**, Ex 38:24
was a hundred talents and 1,775 **s**, Ex 38:25
And of the 1,775 **s** he made hooks for Ex 38:28
offered was seventy talents and 2,400 **s**; Ex 38:29
out of the flock, valued in silver **s**, Lv 5:15
to sixty years old shall be fifty **s** of silver, Lv 27:3
a female, the valuation shall be thirty **s**. Lv 27:4
valuation shall be for a male twenty **s**, Lv 27:5
twenty shekels, and for a female ten **s**. Lv 27:5
shall be for a male five **s** of silver, Lv 27:6
the valuation shall be three **s** of silver. Lv 27:6
valuation for a male shall be fifteen **s**, Lv 27:7
be fifteen shekels, and for a female ten **s**. Lv 27:7
seed shall be valued at fifty **s** of silver. Lv 27:16
you shall take five **s** per head; you shall Nm 3:47
of Israel he took the money, 1,365 **s**, Nm 3:50
one silver plate whose weight was 130 **s**, Nm 7:13
130 shekels, one silver basin of 70 **s**, Nm 7:13
one golden dish of 10 **s**, full of incense; Nm 7:14
one silver plate whose weight was 130 **s**, Nm 7:19
130 shekels, one silver basin of 70 **s**, Nm 7:19
one golden dish of 10 **s**, full of incense; Nm 7:20
one silver plate whose weight was 130 **s**, Nm 7:25
130 shekels, one silver basin of 70 **s**, Nm 7:25
one golden dish of 10 **s**, full of incense; Nm 7:26
one silver plate whose weight was 130 **s**, Nm 7:31
130 shekels, one silver basin of 70 **s**, Nm 7:31
one golden dish of 10 **s**, full of incense; Nm 7:32
one silver plate whose weight was 130 **s**, Nm 7:37
130 shekels, one silver basin of 70 **s**, Nm 7:37
one golden dish of 10 **s**, full of incense; Nm 7:38

one silver plate whose weight was 130 **s**, Nm 7:43
130 shekels, one silver basin of 70 **s**, Nm 7:43
one golden dish of 10 **s**, full of incense; Nm 7:44
one silver plate whose weight was 130 **s**, Nm 7:49
130 shekels, one silver basin of 70 **s**, Nm 7:49
one golden dish of 10 **s**, full of incense; Nm 7:50
one silver plate whose weight was 130 **s**, Nm 7:55
130 shekels, one silver basin of 70 **s**, Nm 7:55
one golden dish of 10 **s**, full of incense; Nm 7:56
one silver plate whose weight was 130 **s**, Nm 7:61
130 shekels, one silver basin of 70 **s**, Nm 7:61
one golden dish of 10 **s**, full of incense; Nm 7:62
one silver plate whose weight was 130 **s**, Nm 7:67
130 shekels, one silver basin of 70 **s**, Nm 7:67
one golden dish of 10 **s**, full of incense; Nm 7:68
one silver plate whose weight was 130 **s**, Nm 7:73
130 shekels, one silver basin of 70 **s**, Nm 7:73
one golden dish of 10 **s**, full of incense; Nm 7:74
one silver plate whose weight was 130 **s**, Nm 7:79
130 shekels, one silver basin of 70 **s**, Nm 7:79
one golden dish of 10 **s**, full of incense; Nm 7:80
plate weighing 130 **s** and each basin Nm 7:85
of the vessels 2,400 **s** according to the Nm 7:85
weighing 10 **s** apiece according to the Nm 7:86
all the gold of the dishes being 120 **s**; Nm 7:86
them) you shall fix at five **s** in silver, Nm 18:16
of hundreds, was 16,750 **s**. Nm 31:52
fine him a hundred **s** of silver and give Dt 22:19
of the young woman fifty **s** of silver, Dt 22:29
cloak from Shinar, and 200 **s** of silver, Jos 7:21
of silver, and a bar of gold weighing 50 **s**, Jos 7:21
that he requested was 1,700 **s** of gold, Jgs 8:26
coat was five thousand **s** of bronze. 1 Sm 17:5
head weighed six hundred **s** of iron. 1 Sm 17:7
two hundred **s** by the king's weight. 2 Sm 14:26
weighed three hundred **s** of bronze, 2 Sm 21:16
floor and the oxen for fifty **s** of silver. 2 Sm 24:24
600 **s** of gold went into each shield. 1 Kgs 10:16
from Egypt for 600 **s** of silver and a 1 Kgs 10:29
talents of silver, six thousand **s** of gold, 2 Kgs 5:5
head was sold for eighty **s** of silver, 2 Kgs 6:25
kab of dove's dung for five **s** of silver. 2 Kgs 6:25
fifty **s** of silver from every man, 2 Kgs 15:20
David paid Ornan 600 **s** of gold by 1 Chr 21:25
chariot from Egypt for 600 **s** of silver, 2 Chr 1:17
weight of gold for the nails was fifty **s**. 2 Chr 3:9
600 **s** of beaten gold went into each 2 Chr 9:15
300 **s** of gold went into each shield; 2 Chr 9:16
for their daily ration forty **s** of silver. Neh 5:15
vines, worth a thousand **s** of silver, Is 7:23
the money to him, seventeen **s** of silver. Jer 32:9
eat shall be by weight, twenty **s** a day; Ezk 4:10
twenty **s** plus twenty-five shekels plus Ezk 45:12
shekels plus twenty-five **s** plus fifteen Ezk 45:12
shekels plus fifteen **s** shall be your Ezk 45:12
I bought her for fifteen **s** of silver and a Hos 3:2

SHELAH (19)
Arpachshad fathered **S**; and Shelah Gn 10:24
fathered Shelah; and **S** fathered Eber. Gn 10:24
had lived 35 years, he fathered **S**. Gn 11:12
lived after he fathered **S** 403 years and Gn 11:13
When **S** had lived 30 years, he fathered Gn 11:14
And **S** lived after he fathered Eber 403 Gn 11:15
bore a son, and she called his name **S**. Gn 38:5
till **S** my son grows up"—for he feared Gn 38:11
For she saw that **S** was grown up, and Gn 38:14
give her to my son **S**." And he did not Gn 38:26
Er, Onan, **S**, Perez, and Zerah (but Er Gn 46:12
according to their clans were: of **S**, Nm 26:20
Arpachshad fathered **S**, and Shelah 1 Chr 1:18
fathered Shelah, and **S** fathered Eber. 1 Chr 1:18
Shem, Arpachshad, **S**; 1 Chr 1:24
The sons of Judah: Er, Onan and **S**; 1 Chr 2:3
The sons of **S** the son of Judah: Er the 1 Chr 4:21
of the Pool of **S** of the king's garden, Neh 3:15
son of Peleg, the son of Eber, the son of **S**, Lk 3:35

SHELANITES (1)
were: of Shelah, the clan of the **S**; Nm 26:20

SHELEMIAH (10)
The lot for the east fell to **S**. They 1 Chr 26:14
S, Nathan, Adaiah, Ezr 10:39
Azarel, **S**, Shemariah, Ezr 10:41
Hananiah the son of **S** and Hanun the Neh 3:30
over the storehouses **S** the priest, Neh 13:13
Jehudi the son of Nethaniah, son of **S**, Jer 36:14
son of Azriel and **S** the son of Abdeel Jer 36:26
King Zedekiah sent Jehucal the son of **S**, Jer 37:3
a sentry there named Irijah the son of **S**, Jer 37:13
the son of Pashhur, Jucal the son of **S**, Jer 38:1

SHELEPH (2)
fathered Almodad, **S**, Hazarmaveth, Gn 10:26
fathered Almodad, **S**, Hazarmaveth, 1 Chr 1:20

SHELESH (1)
brother: Zophah, Imna, **S**, and Amal. 1 Chr 7:35

SHELOMI (1)
of Asher a chief, Ahihud the son of **S**. Nm 34:27

SHELOMITH (5)
His mother's name was **S**, the daughter Lv 24:11
and Hananiah, and **S** was their sister; 1 Chr 3:19
The sons of Izhar: **S** the chief. 1 Chr 23:18
bore him Abijah, Attai, Ziza, and **S**. 2 Chr 11:20
the sons of Bani, **S** the son of Josiphiah, Ezr 8:10

SHELOMOTH (6)
of Shimei: **S**, Haziel, and Haran, three. 1 Chr 23:9
S; of the sons of Shelomoth, 1 Chr 24:22
Shelomoth; of the sons of **S**, Jahath. 1 Chr 24:22
and his son Zichri, and his son **S**. 1 Chr 26:25
This **S** and his brothers were in 1 Chr 26:26
in the care of **S** and his brothers. 1 Chr 26:28

SHELTER (19)
they have come under the **s** of my roof." Gn 19:8
all that you have in the field into safe **s**, Ex 9:19
and cling to the rock for lack of **s**. Jb 24:8
in the **s** of the reeds and in the marsh. Jb 40:21
will hide me in his **s** in the day of Ps 27:5
store them in your **s** from the strife of Ps 31:20
hurry to find a **s** from the raging wind Ps 55:8
take refuge under the **s** of your wings! Ps 61:4
He who dwells in the **s** of the Most High Ps 91:1
for a refuge and a **s** from the storm and Is 4:6
night at the height of noon; **s** the outcasts; Is 16:3
you; be a **s** to them from the destroyer. Is 16:4
a **s** from the storm and a shade from the Is 25:4
and in falsehood we have taken **s**"; Is 28:15
of lies, and waters will overwhelm the **s**." Is 28:17
of Pharaoh and to seek **s** in the shadow of Is 30:2
and the **s** in the shadow of Egypt to your Is 30:3
place from the wind, a **s** from the storm, Is 32:2
on the throne will **s** them with his Rv 7:15

SHELUMIEL (5)
from Simeon, **S** the son of Zurishaddai; Nm 1:6
people of Simeon being **S** the son of Nm 2:12
On the fifth day **S** the son of Nm 7:36
was the offering of **S** the son of Nm 7:41
people of Simeon was **S** the son of Nm 10:19

SHEM (18)
was 500 years old, Noah fathered **S**, Gn 5:32
And Noah had three sons, **S**, Ham, and Gn 6:10
and his sons, **S** and Ham and Japheth, Gn 7:13
who went forth from the ark were **S**, Gn 9:18
Then **S** and Japheth took a garment, Gn 9:23
said, "Blessed be the LORD, the God of **S**; Gn 9:26
and let him dwell in the tents of **S**, Gn 9:27
generations of the sons of Noah, **S**, Ham, Gn 10:1
To **S** also, the father of all the children Gn 10:21
The sons of **S**: Elam, Asshur, Gn 10:22
These are the sons of **S**, by their clans, Gn 10:31
These are the generations of **S**. When Gn 11:10
When **S** was 100 years old, he fathered Gn 11:10
And **S** lived after he fathered Gn 11:11
Noah, **S**, Ham, and Japheth. 1 Chr 1:4
The sons of **S**: Elam, Asshur, 1 Chr 1:17
S, Arpachshad, Shelah; 1 Chr 1:24
the son of Arphaxad, the son of **S**, Lk 3:36

SHEMA (6)
Amam, **S**, Moladah, Jos 15:26
Korah, Tappuah, Rekem and **S**. 1 Chr 2:43
S fathered Raham, the father of 1 Chr 2:44
and Bela the son of Azaz, son of **S**, son 1 Chr 5:8
and Beriah and **S** (they were heads of 1 Chr 8:13
beside him stood Mattithiah, **S**, Anaiah, Neh 8:4

SHEMAAH (1)
then Joash, both sons of **S** of Gibeah; 1 Chr 12:3

SHEMAIAH (41)
of God came to **S** the man of God: 1 Kgs 12:22
S. And the sons of Shemaiah: 1 Chr 3:22
And the sons of **S**: Hattush, Igal, 1 Chr 3:22
of Jedaiah, son of Shimri, son of **S**— 1 Chr 4:37
S his son, Gog his son, Shimei his son, 1 Chr 5:4
S the son of Hasshub, son of 1 Chr 9:14
and Obadiah the son of **S**, son of 1 Chr 9:16
of the sons of Elizaphan, **S** the chief, 1 Chr 15:8
Levites Uriel, Asaiah, Joel, **S**, Eliel, 1 Chr 15:11
And the scribe **S**, the son of Nethanel, 1 Chr 24:6
S the firstborn, Jehozabad the second, 1 Chr 26:4
Also to his son **S** were sons born who 1 Chr 26:6
The sons of **S**: Othni, Rephael, Obed 1 Chr 26:7
of the LORD came to **S** the man of God: 2 Chr 11:2
Then **S** the prophet came to 2 Chr 12:5
the word of the LORD came to **S**: 2 Chr 12:7
the chronicles of **S** the prophet and 2 Chr 12:15
with them the Levites, **S**, Nethaniah, 2 Chr 17:8
the sons of Jeduthun, **S** and Uzziel. 2 Chr 29:14
Miniamin, Jeshua, **S**, Amariah, 2 Chr 31:15
and **S** and Nethanel his brothers, 2 Chr 35:9
names being Eliphelet, Jeuel, and **S**, Ezr 8:13
I sent for Eliezer, Ariel, **S**, Elnathan, Ezr 8:16
Maaseiah, Elijah, **S**, Jehiel, and Uzziah. Ezr 10:21
Isshijah, Malchijah, **S**, Shimeon, Ezr 10:31
After him **S** the son of Shecaniah, the Neh 3:29
into the house of **S** the son of Delaiah, Neh 6:10
Maaziah, Bilgai, **S**; these are the priests. Neh 10:8
S the son of Hasshub, son of Neh 11:15
S, Joiarib, Jedaiah, Neh 12:6
of Bilgah, Shammua; of **S**, Neh 12:18
Judah, Benjamin, **S**, and Jeremiah, Neh 12:34
the son of Jonathan, son of **S**, Neh 12:35
and his relatives, **S**, Azarel, Milalai, Neh 12:36
and Maaseiah, **S**, Eleazar, Uzzi, Neh 12:42
Uriah the son of **S** from Kiriath-jearim. Jer 26:20
To **S** of Nehelam you shall say: Jer 29:24
the LORD concerning **S** of Nehelam: Jer 29:31
Because **S** had prophesied to you when I Jer 29:31
I will punish **S** of Nehelam and his Jer 29:32
the secretary, Delaiah the son of **S**, Jer 36:12

SHEMARIAH (4)
Bealiah, **S**, Shephatiah the Haruphite; 1 Chr 12:5
him sons, Jeush, **S**, and Zaham. 2 Chr 11:19
Benjamin, Malluch, and **S**. Ezr 10:32
Azarel, Shelemiah, **S**, Ezr 10:41

SHEMEBER (1)
king of Admah, **S** king of Zeboiim, Gn 14:2

SHEMED (1)
Eber, Misham, and **S**, who built Ono 1 Chr 8:12

SHEMER (4)
of Samaria from **S** for two talents 1 Kgs 16:24
built Samaria, after the name of **S**, 1 Kgs 16:24
son of Amzi, son of Bani, son of **S**, 1 Chr 6:46
The sons of **S** his brother: Rohgah, 1 Chr 7:34

SHEMIDA (3)
and of **S**, the clan of the Shemidaites; Nm 26:32
Helek, Asriel, Shechem, Hepher, and **S**. Jos 17:2
The sons of **S** were Ahian, Shechem, 1 Chr 7:19

SHEMIDAITES (1)
and of Shemida, the clan of the **S**; and Nm 26:32

SHEMINITH (3)
to lead with lyres according to the **S**. 1 Chr 15:21
stringed instruments; according to The **S**. Ps 6:T
To the choirmaster: according to The **S**. Ps 12:T

SHEMIRAMOTH (4)
order, Zechariah, Jaaziel, **S**, Jehiel, 1 Chr 15:18
Zechariah, Aziel, **S**, Jehiel, Unni, 1 Chr 15:20
to him were Zechariah, Jeiel, **S**, Jehiel, 1 Chr 16:5
Zebadiah, Asahel, **S**, Jehonathan, 2 Chr 17:8

SHEMUEL (2)
of Simeon, **S** the son of Ammihud. Nm 34:20
Rephaiah, Jeriel, Jahmai, Ibsam, and **S**, 1 Chr 7:2

SHEN (1)
between Mizpah and **S** and called its 1 Sm 7:12

SHENAZZAR (1)
Malchiram, Pedaiah, **S**, Jekamiah, 1 Chr 3:18

SHEOL (65)
"No, I shall go down to **S** to my son, Gn 37:35
down my gray hairs with sorrow to **S**." Gn 42:38
bring down my gray hairs in evil to **S**.' Gn 44:29
servant our father with sorrow to **S**. Gn 44:31
them, and they go down alive into **S**, Nm 16:30
to them went down alive into **S**, Nm 16:33
anger, and it burns to the depths of **S**, Dt 32:22
life; he brings down to **S** and raises up. 1 Sm 2:6
the cords of **S** entangled me; the 2 Sm 22:6
let his gray head go down to **S** in peace. 1 Kgs 2:6
his gray head down with blood to **S**." 1 Kgs 2:9
he who goes down to **S** does not come up; Jb 7:9
do? Deeper than **S**—what can you know? Jb 11:8
Oh that you would hide me in **S**, that Jb 14:13
If I hope for **S** as my house, if I make my Jb 17:13
Will it go down to the bars of **S**? Shall Jb 17:16
and in peace they go down to **S**. Jb 21:13
waters; so does **S** those who have sinned. Jb 24:19
S is naked before God, and Abaddon has Jb 26:6
of you; in **S** who will give you praise? Ps 6:5
The wicked shall return to **S**, all the Ps 9:17
For you will not abandon my soul to **S**, Ps 16:10
the cords of **S** entangled me; the snares of Ps 18:5
you have brought up my soul from **S**; Ps 30:3
put to shame; let them go silently to **S**. Ps 31:17
Like sheep they are appointed for **S**; Ps 49:14
Their form shall be consumed in **S**, Ps 49:14
ransom my soul from the power of **S**, Ps 49:15
over them; let them go down to **S** alive; Ps 55:15
delivered my soul from the depths of **S**. Ps 86:13
of troubles, and my life draws near to **S**. Ps 88:3

deliver his soul from the power of **S**? Ps 89:48
me; the pangs of **S** laid hold on me; Ps 116:3
If I make my bed in **S**, you are there! Ps 139:8
bones be scattered at the mouth of **S**. Ps 141:7
like **S** let us swallow them alive, and Prv 1:12
to death; her steps follow the path to **S**; Prv 5:5
Her house is the way to **S**, going down to Prv 7:27
that her guests are in the depths of **S**. Prv 9:18
S and Abaddon lie open before the Prv 15:11
he may turn away from **S** beneath. Prv 15:24
the rod, you will save his soul from **S**. Prv 23:14
S and Abaddon are never satisfied, and Prv 27:20
S, the barren womb, the land never Prv 30:16
thought or knowledge or wisdom in **S**, Eccl 9:10
Therefore **S** has enlarged its appetite and Is 5:14
God; let it be deep as **S** or high as heaven." Is 7:11
S beneath is stirred up to meet you when Is 14:9
Your pomp is brought down to **S**, the Is 14:11
But you are brought down to **S**, to the far Is 14:15
death, and with **S** we have an agreement, Is 28:15
your agreement with **S** will not stand; Is 28:18
consigned to the gates of **S** for the rest of Is 38:10
For **S** does not thank you; death does not Is 38:18
envoys far off, and sent down even to **S**. Is 57:9
went down to **S** I caused mourning; Ezk 31:15
I cast it down to **S** with those who go Ezk 31:16
They also went down to **S** with it, to Ezk 31:17
their helpers, out of the midst of **S**: Ezk 32:21
went down to **S** with their weapons Ezk 32:27
I ransom them from the power of **S**? Hos 13:14
O Death, where are your plagues? O **S**, Hos 13:14
"If they dig into **S**, from there shall my Am 9:2
out of the belly of **S** I cried, and you heard Jon 2:2
His greed is as wide as **S**; like death he Hab 2:5

SHEPHAM (2)
eastern border from Hazar-enan to **S**. Nm 34:10
shall go down from **S** to Riblah on the Nm 34:11

SHEPHATIAH (13)
and the fifth, **S** the son of Abital; 2 Sm 3:4
the fifth, **S**, by Abital; the sixth, 1 Chr 3:3
Michri, and Meshullam the son of **S**, 1 Chr 9:8
Bealiah, Shemariah, **S** the Haruphite; 1 Chr 12:5
Simeonites, **S** the son of Maacah; 1 Chr 27:16
Zechariah, Azariah, Michael, and **S**; 2 Chr 21:2
The sons of **S**, 372. Ezr 2:4
the sons of **S**, the sons of Hattil, the sons Ezr 2:57
Of the sons of **S**, Zebadiah the son of Ezr 8:8
The sons of **S**, 372. Neh 7:9
the sons of **S**, the sons of Hattil, the Neh 7:59
of Zechariah, son of Amariah, son of **S**, Neh 11:4
Now **S** the son of Mattan, Gedaliah the Jer 38:1

SHEPHELAH (10)
as plentiful as the sycamore of the **S**. 1 Kgs 10:27
trees in the **S** was Baal-hanan the 1 Chr 27:28
as plentiful as the sycamore of the **S**. 2 Chr 1:15
as plentiful as the sycamore of the **S**. 2 Chr 9:27
herds, both in the **S** and in the plain, 2 Chr 26:10
the cities in the **S** and the Negeb of 2 Chr 28:18
from the land of Benjamin, from the **S**, Jer 17:26
of the hill country, in the cities of the **S**, Jer 32:44
of the hill country, in the cities of the **S**, Jer 33:13
and those of the **S** shall possess the land Ob 1:19

SHEPHER (2)
Kehelathah and camped at Mount **S**. Nm 33:23
set out from Mount **S** and camped at Nm 33:24

SHEPHERD (62)
for every **s** is an abomination to the Gn 46:34
who has been my **s** all my life long Gn 48:15
One of Jacob (from there is the **S**, Gn 49:24
may not be as sheep that have no **s**." Nm 27:17
you, 'You shall be **s** of my people Israel, 2 Sm 5:2
I commanded to **s** my people Israel, 2 Sm 7:7
mountains, as sheep that have no **s**. 1 Kgs 22:17
'You shall be **s** of my people Israel, 1 Chr 11:2
whom I commanded to **s** my people, 1 Chr 17:6
mountains, as sheep that have no **s**. 2 Chr 18:16
The LORD is my **s**; I shall not want. Ps 23:1
Be their **s** and carry them forever. Ps 28:9
Death shall be their **s**, and the upright Ps 49:14
he brought him to **s** Jacob his people, Ps 78:71
Give ear, O **S** of Israel, you who lead Ps 80:1
sayings; they are given by one **S**. Eccl 12:11
He will tend his flock like a **s**; he will Is 40:11
who says of Cyrus, 'He is my **s**, and he Is 44:28
I have not run away from being your **s**, Jer 17:16
The wind shall **s** all your shepherds, Jer 22:22
will keep him as a **s** keeps his flock.' Jer 31:10
land of Egypt as a **s** cleans his cloak of Jer 43:12
me? What **s** can stand before me? Jer 49:19
me? What **s** can stand before me? Jer 50:44
I break in pieces the **s** and his flock; Jer 51:23
were scattered, because there was no **s**, Ezk 34:5
all the wild beasts, since there was no **s**, Ezk 34:8
As a **s** seeks out his flock when he is Ezk 34:12
I myself will be the **s** of my sheep, and Ezk 34:15
And I will set up over them one **s**, my Ezk 34:23
he shall feed them and be their **s**. Ezk 34:23
them, and they shall all have one **s**. Ezk 37:24
"As the **s** rescues from the mouth of the Am 3:12
And he shall stand and **s** his flock in the Mi 5:4
they shall **s** the land of Assyria with the Mi 5:6
S your people with your staff, the flock Mi 7:14
sheep; they are afflicted for lack of a **s**. Zec 10:2
"Become **s** of the flock doomed to Zec 11:4
So I became the **s** of the flock doomed to Zec 11:7
So I said, "I will not be your **s**. What is Zec 11:9
more the equipment of a foolish **s**. Zec 11:15
up in the land a **s** who does not care Zec 11:16
"Woe to my worthless **s**, who deserts Zec 11:17
"Awake, O sword, against my **s**, against Zec 13:7
"Strike the **s**, and the sheep will be Zec 13:7
a ruler who will **s** my people Israel.'" Mt 2:6
and helpless, like sheep without a **s**. Mt 9:36
from another as a **s** separates the sheep Mt 25:32
For it is written, 'I will strike the **s**, and Mt 26:31
they were like sheep without a **s**. Mk 6:34
for it is written, 'I will strike the **s**, Mk 14:27
enters by the door is the **s** of the sheep. Jn 10:2
I am the good **s**. The good shepherd lays Jn 10:11
The good **s** lays down his life for the Jn 10:11
He who is a hired hand and not a **s**, who Jn 10:12
I am the good **s**. I know my own and my Jn 10:14
voice. So there will be one flock, one **s**. Jn 10:16
our Lord Jesus, the great **s** of the sheep, Heb 13:20
now returned to the **S** and Overseer of 1 Pt 2:25
s the flock of God that is among you, 1 Pt 5:2
And when the chief **S** appears, you will 1 Pt 5:4
in the midst of the throne will be their **s**, Rv 7:17

SHEPHERD'S (2)
brook and put them in his **s** pouch. 1 Sm 17:40
up and removed from me like a **s** tent; Is 38:12

SHEPHERDED (1)
upright heart he **s** them and guided Ps 78:72

SHEPHERDESS (1)
with her father's sheep, for she was a **s**. Gn 29:9

SHEPHERDS (49)
the **s** would roll the stone from the Gn 29:3
And the men are **s**, for they have been Gn 46:32
said to Pharaoh, "Your servants are **s**, Gn 47:3
The **s** came and drove them away, but Ex 2:17
of the hand of the **s** and even drew water Ex 2:19
children shall be **s** in the wilderness Nm 14:33
Now your **s** have been with us, and we 1 Sm 25:7
when he was at Beth-eked of the **S**, 2 Kgs 10:12
no **s** will make their flocks lie down Is 13:20
and when a band of **s** is called out against Is 31:4
But they are **s** who have no Is 56:11
up out of the sea with the **s** of his flock? Is 63:11
know me; the **s** transgressed against me; Jer 2:8
I will give you **s** after my own heart, Jer 3:15
S with their flocks shall come against Jer 6:3
For the **s** are stupid and do not inquire Jer 10:21
Many **s** have destroyed my vineyard; Jer 12:10
The wind shall shepherd all your **s**, and Jer 22:22
"Woe to the **s** who destroy and scatter Jer 23:1
concerning the **s** who care for my Jer 23:2
I will set **s** over them who will care for Jer 23:4
"Wail, you **s**, and cry out, and roll in Jer 25:34
No refuge will remain for the **s**, nor Jer 25:35
A voice—the cry of the **s**, and the wail Jer 25:36
be habitations of **s** resting their flocks. Jer 33:12
Their **s** have led them astray, turning Jer 50:6
of man, prophesy against the **s** of Israel; Ezk 34:2
prophesy, and say to them, even to the **s**, Ezk 34:2
s of Israel who have been feeding Ezk 34:2
yourselves! Should not **s** feed the sheep? Ezk 34:2
"Therefore, you **s**, hear the word of the Ezk 34:7
and because my **s** have not searched Ezk 34:8
sheep, but the **s** have fed themselves, Ezk 34:8
therefore, you **s**, hear the word of the Ezk 34:9
Lord GOD, Behold, I am against the **s**, Ezk 34:10
No longer shall the **s** feed themselves. Ezk 34:10
of Amos, who was among the **s** of Tekoa, Am 1:1
the pastures of the **s** mourn, and the top Am 1:2
against him seven **s** and eight princes Mi 5:5
Your **s** are asleep, O king of Assyria; Na 3:18
with meadows for **s** and folds for flocks. Zep 2:6
"My anger is hot against the **s**, and I Zec 10:3
The sound of the wail of the **s**, for their Zec 11:3
and their own **s** have no pity on them. Zec 11:5
In one month I destroyed the three **s**. Zec 11:8
same region there were **s** out in the field, Lk 2:8
into heaven, the **s** said to one another, Lk 2:15
it wondered at what the **s** told them. Lk 2:18
And the **s** returned, glorifying and Lk 2:20

SHEPHERDS' (1)
your young goats beside the **s** tents. Sg 1:8

SHEPHO (2)
Alvan, Manahath, Ebal, **S**, and Onam. Gn 36:23
Manahath, Ebal, **S**, and Onam. 1 Chr 1:40

SHEPHUPHAM (1)
of **S**, the clan of the Shuphamites; of Nm 26:39

SHEPHUPHAN (1)
Gera, **S**, and Huram. 1 Chr 8:5

SHEREBIAH (8)
namely **S** with his sons and kinsmen, Ezr 8:18
S, Hashabiah, and ten of their kinsmen Ezr 8:24
Also Jeshua, Bani, **S**, Jamin, Akkub, Neh 8:7
Kadmiel, Shebaniah, Bunni, **S**, Bani, Neh 9:4
Kadmiel, Bani, Hashabneiah, **S**, Hodiah, Neh 9:5
Zaccur, **S**, Shebaniah, Neh 10:12
Jeshua, Binnui, Kadmiel, **S**, Judah, and Neh 12:8
S, and Jeshua the son of Kadmiel, Neh 12:24

SHERESH (1)
and the name of his brother was **S**; 1 Chr 7:16

SHESHAI (3)
Ahiman, **S**, and Talmai, the Nm 13:22
of Anak, **S** and Ahiman and Talmai, Jos 15:14
and they defeated **S** and Ahiman and Jgs 1:10

SHESHAN (5)
son of Ishi: **S**. The son of Sheshan: 1 Chr 2:31
of Ishi: Sheshan. The son of **S**: Ahlai. 1 Chr 2:31
Now **S** had no sons, only daughters, 1 Chr 2:34
but **S** had an Egyptian slave whose 1 Chr 2:34
So **S** gave his daughter in marriage to 1 Chr 2:35

SHESHBAZZAR (4)
counted them out to **S** the prince of Ezr 1:8
All these did **S** bring up, when the exiles Ezr 1:11
were delivered to one whose name was **S**, Ezr 5:14
Then this **S** came and laid the Ezr 5:16

SHETH (1)
and break down all the sons of **S**. Nm 24:17

SHETHAR (1)
to him being Carshena, **S**, Admatha, Est 1:14

SHETHAR-BOZENAI (4)
the River and **S** and their associates Ezr 5:3
the River and **S** and his associates Ezr 5:6
S, and your associates the governors who Ezr 6:6
S, and their associates did with all Ezr 6:13

SHEVA (2)
and **S** was secretary; and Zadok and 2 Sm 20:25
S the father of Machbenah and the 1 Chr 2:49

SHIBAH (1)
He called it **S**; therefore the name of the Gn 26:33

SHIBBOLETH (1)
said to him, "Then say **S**," and he said, Jgs 12:6

SHIELD (53)
a vision: "Fear not, Abram, I am your **s**; Gn 15:1
saved by the LORD, the **s** of your help, Dt 33:29
Was **s** or spear to be seen among forty Jgs 5:8
For there the **s** of the mighty was 2 Sm 1:21
the mighty was defiled, the **s** of Saul, 2 Sm 1:21
my rock, in whom I take refuge, my **s**, 2 Sm 22:3
he is a **s** for all those who take refuge 2 Sm 22:31
given me the **s** of your salvation, 2 Sm 22:36
600 shekels of gold went into each **s**. 1 Kgs 10:16
three minas of gold went into each **s**. 1 Kgs 10:17
come before it with a **s** or cast up a 2 Kgs 19:32
men who carried **s** and sword, 1 Chr 5:18
warriors, expert with **s** and spear, 1 Chr 12:8
of Judah bearing **s** and spear were 1 Chr 12:24
37,000 men armed with **s** and spear. 1 Chr 12:34
of beaten gold went into each **s**. 2 Chr 9:15
300 shekels of gold went into each **s**; 2 Chr 9:16
200,000 men armed with bow and **s**; 2 Chr 17:17
fit for war, able to handle spear and **s**. 2 Chr 25:5
against him with a thickly bossed **s**; Jb 15:26
But you, O LORD, are a **s** about me, my Ps 3:3
you cover him with favor as with a **s**. Ps 5:12
My **s** is with God, who saves the upright Ps 7:10
my rock, in whom I take refuge, my **s**, Ps 18:2
he is a **s** for all those who take refuge in Ps 18:30
have given me the **s** of your salvation, Ps 18:35
The LORD is my strength and my **s**; in Ps 28:7
for the LORD; he is our help and our **s**. Ps 33:20
Take hold of **s** and buckler and rise for Ps 35:2
and bring them down, O Lord, our **s**! Ps 59:11
he broke the flashing arrows, the **s**, Ps 76:3
Behold our **s**, O God; look on the face of Ps 84:9
For the LORD God is a sun and **s**; the Ps 84:11
For our **s** belongs to the LORD, our king Ps 89:18
his faithfulness is a **s** and buckler. Ps 91:4
in the LORD! He is their help and their **s**. Ps 115:9
the LORD! He is their help and their **s**. Ps 115:10

the LORD! He is their help and their **s**. Ps 115:11
You are my hiding place and my **s**; I Ps 119:114
my **s** and he in whom I take refuge, Ps 144:2
he is a **s** to those who walk in integrity, Prv 2:7
he is a **s** to those who take refuge in Prv 30:5
eat, they drink. Arise, O princes; oil the **s**! Is 21:5
and horsemen, and Kir uncovered the **s**. Is 22:6
come before it with a **s** or cast up a siege Is 37:33
"Prepare buckler and **s**, and advance for Jer 46:3
men of Cush and Put who handle the **s**, Jer 46:9
every side with buckler, **s**, and helmet; Ezk 23:24
They hung the **s** and helmet in you; Ezk 27:10
host, all of them with buckler and **s**, Ezk 38:4
them, all of them with **s** and helmet; Ezk 38:5
The **s** of his mighty men is red; his Na 2:3
circumstances take up the **s** of faith, Eph 6:16

SHIELD-BEARER (2)
of iron. And his **s** went before him. 1 Sm 17:7
to David, with his **s** in front of him. 1 Sm 17:41

SHIELDS (27)
And David took the **s** of gold that were 2 Sm 8:7
made 200 large **s** of beaten gold; 1 Kgs 10:16
And he made 300 **s** of beaten gold; 1 Kgs 10:17
took away all the **s** of gold that 1 Kgs 14:26
made in their place **s** of bronze, 1 Kgs 14:27
the spears and **s** that had been 2 Kgs 11:10
And David took the **s** of gold that 1 Chr 18:7
made 200 large **s** of beaten gold; 2 Chr 9:15
And he made 300 **s** of beaten gold; 2 Chr 9:16
And he put **s** and spears in all the 2 Chr 11:12
also took away the **s** of gold that 2 Chr 12:9
made in their place **s** of bronze and 2 Chr 12:10
Judah, armed with large **s** and spears, 2 Chr 14:8
Benjamin that carried **s** and drew 2 Chr 14:8
the large and small **s** that had been 2 Chr 23:9
Uzziah prepared for all the army **s**, 2 Chr 26:14
made weapons and **s** in abundance. 2 Chr 32:5
for precious stones, for spices, for **s**, 2 Chr 32:27
and half held the spears, **s**, bows, Neh 4:16
His back is made of rows of **s**, shut up Jb 41:15
For the **s** of the earth belong to God; he is Ps 47:9
on it hang a thousand **s**, all of them Sg 4:4
shields, all of them **s** of warriors. Sg 4:4
"Sharpen the arrows! Take up the **s**! Jer 51:11
you, and raise a roof of **s** against you. Ezk 26:8
They hung their **s** on your walls all Ezk 27:11
and burn them, **s** and bucklers, Ezk 39:9

SHIFTING (1)
not **s** from the hope of the gospel that Col 1:23

SHIFTS (1)
to Lebanon, 10,000 a month in **s**. 1 Kgs 5:14

SHIGGAION (1)
A **S** of David, which he sang to the LORD Ps 7:T

SHIGIONOTH (1)
Habakkuk the prophet, according to **S**. Hab 3:1

SHIHOR (2)
(from the **S**, which is east of Egypt, Jos 13:3
waters your revenue was the grain of **S**, Is 23:3

SHIHOR-LIBNATH (1)
On the west it touches Carmel and **S**, Jos 19:26

SHIKKERON (1)
bends around to **S** and passes along Jos 15:11

SHILHI (2)
was Azubah the daughter of **S**. 1 Kgs 22:42
was Azubah the daughter of **S**. 2 Chr 20:31

SHILHIM (1)
Lebaoth, **S**, Ain, and Rimmon: in all, Jos 15:32

SHILLEM (2)
of Naphtali: Jahzeel, Guni, Jezer, and **S**. Gn 46:24
of Jezer, the clan of the Jezerites; of **S**, Nm 26:49

SHILLEMITES (1)
Jezerites; of Shillem, the clan of the **S**. Nm 26:49

SHILOAH (1)
refused the waters of **S** that flow gently, Is 8:6

SHILOH (32)
of Israel assembled at **S** and set up the Jos 18:1
lots for you here before the LORD in **S**." Jos 18:8
they came to Joshua to the camp at **S**, Jos 18:9
cast lots for them in **S** before the LORD. Jos 18:10
distributed by lot at **S** before the LORD, Jos 19:51
they said to them at **S** in the land of Jos 21:2
parting from the people of Israel at **S**, Jos 22:9
of Israel gathered at **S** to make war Jos 22:12
as long as the house of God was at **S**. Jgs 18:31
they brought them to the camp at **S**, Jgs 21:12
there is the yearly feast of the LORD at **S**, Jgs 21:19
If the daughters of **S** come out to dance Jgs 21:21
man his wife from the daughters of **S**, Jgs 21:21
to sacrifice to the LORD of hosts at **S**, 1 Sm 1:3
After they had eaten and drunk in **S**, 1 Sm 1:9
him to the house of the LORD at **S**. 1 Sm 1:24
what they did at **S** to all the Israelites 1 Sm 2:14
And the LORD appeared again at **S**, for 1 Sm 3:21
himself to Samuel at **S** by the word of 1 Sm 3:21
of the covenant of the LORD here from **S**, 1 Sm 4:3
the people sent to **S** and brought from 1 Sm 4:4
line and came to **S** the same day, 1 Sm 4:12
son of Eli, the priest of the LORD in **S**, 1 Sm 14:3
concerning the house of Eli in **S**. 1 Kgs 2:27
are the wife of Jeroboam, and go to **S**. 1 Kgs 14:2
arose and went to **S** and came to the 1 Kgs 14:4
He forsook his dwelling at **S**, the tent Ps 78:60
Go now to my place that was in **S**, where Jer 7:12
to you and to your fathers, as I did to **S**. Jer 7:14
then I will make this house like **S**, and I Jer 26:6
LORD, saying, 'This house shall be like **S**, Jer 26:9
from Shechem and **S** and Samaria, Jer 41:5

SHILONITE (6)
prophet Ahijah the **S** found him on 1 Kgs 11:29
by Ahijah the **S** to Jeroboam the 1 Kgs 12:15
spoke by his servant Ahijah the **S**. 1 Kgs 15:29
and in the prophecy of Ahijah the **S**, 2 Chr 9:29
by Ahijah the **S** to Jeroboam the 2 Chr 10:15
Joiarib, son of Zechariah, son of the **S**. Neh 11:5

SHILONITES (1)
And of the **S**: Asaiah the firstborn, and 1 Chr 9:5

SHILSHAH (1)
Bezer, Hod, Shamma, **S**, Ithran, and 1 Chr 7:37

SHIMEA (5)
Abinadab the second, **S** the third, 1 Chr 2:13
S, Shobab, Nathan and Solomon, four 1 Chr 3:5
S his son, Haggiah his son, and 1 Chr 6:30
Asaph the son of Berechiah, son of **S**, 1 Chr 6:39
taunted Israel, Jonathan the son of **S**, 1 Chr 20:7

SHIMEAH (3)
name was Jonadab, the son of **S**, 2 Sm 13:3
But Jonadab the son of **S**, David's 2 Sm 13:32
and Mikloth (he fathered **S**). Now 1 Chr 8:32

SHIMEAM (1)
and Mikloth was the father of **S**; and 1 Chr 9:38

SHIMEATH (2)
the son of **S** and Jehozabad the 2 Kgs 12:21
Zabad the son of **S** the Ammonite, 2 Chr 24:26

SHIMEATHITES (1)
Tirathites, the **S** and the Sucathites. 1 Chr 2:55

SHIMEI (44)
of Gershon: Libni and **S**, by their clans. Ex 6:17
of Gershon by their clans: Libni and **S**. Nm 3:18
the house of Saul, whose name was **S**, 2 Sm 16:5
And **S** said as he cursed, "Get out, get 2 Sm 16:7
while **S** went along on the hillside 2 Sm 16:13
And **S** the son of Gera, the 2 Sm 19:16
And **S** the son of Gera fell down 2 Sm 19:18
"Shall not **S** be put to death for this, 2 Sm 19:21
And the king said to **S**, "You shall 2 Sm 19:23
taunted Israel, Jonathan the son of **S**, 2 Sm 21:21
Nathan the prophet and **S** and Rei and 1 Kgs 1:8
there is also with you **S** the son of Gera, 1 Kgs 2:8
sent and summoned **S** and said to 1 Kgs 2:36
And **S** said to the king, "What you 1 Kgs 2:38
servant do." So **S** lived in Jerusalem 1 Kgs 2:38
And when it was told **S**, "Behold, your 1 Kgs 2:39
S arose and saddled a donkey and 1 Kgs 2:40
S went and brought his servants 1 Kgs 2:40
was told that **S** had gone from 1 Kgs 2:41
sent and summoned **S** and said to 1 Kgs 2:42
The king also said to **S**, "You know 1 Kgs 2:44
S the son of Ela, in Benjamin; 1 Kgs 4:18
sons of Pedaiah: Zerubbabel and **S**; 1 Chr 3:19
his son, Zaccur his son, **S** his son. 1 Chr 4:26
S had sixteen sons and six daughters; 1 Chr 4:27
his son, Gog his son, **S** his son, 1 Chr 5:4
of the sons of Gershom: Libni and **S**. 1 Chr 6:17
Mahli, Libni his son, **S** his son, 1 Chr 6:29
of Ethan, son of Zimmah, son of **S**, 1 Chr 6:42
and Shimrath were the sons of **S**. 1 Chr 8:21
sons of Gershon were Ladan and **S**. 1 Chr 23:7
The sons of **S**: Shelomoth, Haziel, and 1 Chr 23:9
And the sons of **S**: Jahath, Zina, and 1 Chr 23:10
These four were the sons of **S**. 1 Chr 23:10
Zeri, Jeshaiah, **S**, Hashabiah, 1 Chr 25:3
the tenth to **S**, his sons and his 1 Chr 25:17
the vineyards was **S** the Ramathite; 1 Chr 27:27
of the sons of Heman, Jehuel and **S**; 2 Chr 29:14
Levite, with **S** his brother as second, 2 Chr 31:12
Conaniah and **S** his brother, 2 Chr 31:13
Jozabad, **S**, Kelaiah (that is, Kelita), Ezr 10:23
Eliphelet, Jeremai, Manasseh, and **S** Ezr 10:33
Of the sons of Binnui: **S**, Ezr 10:38
was Mordecai, the son of Jair, son of **S**, Est 2:5

SHIMEI'S (1)
years that two of **S** servants ran away 1 Kgs 2:39

SHIMEITES (2)
of the Libnites and the clan of the **S**; Nm 3:21
the family of the **S** by itself, and their Zec 12:13

SHIMEON (1)
Isshijah, Malchijah, Shemaiah, **S**, Ezr 10:31

SHIMMERING (1)
with silver, its pinions with **s** gold. Ps 68:13

SHIMON (1)
The sons of **S**: Amnon, Rinnah, 1 Chr 4:20

SHIMRATH (1)
and **S** were the sons of Shimei. 1 Chr 8:21

SHIMRI (4)
son of Allon, son of Jedaiah, son of **S**, 1 Chr 4:37
Jediael the son of **S**, and Joha his 1 Chr 11:45
S the chief (for though he was not 1 Chr 26:10
of the sons of Elizaphan, **S** and Jeuel; 2 Chr 29:13

SHIMRITH (1)
Jehozabad the son of **S** the Moabite. 2 Chr 24:26

SHIMRON (5)
of Issachar: Tola, Puvah, Yob, and **S**. Gn 46:13
the clan of the Jashubites; of **S**, Nm 26:24
king of Madon, and to the king of **S**, Jos 11:1
and Kattath, Nahalal, **S**, Idalah, and Jos 19:15
Tola, Puah, Jashub, and **S**, four. 1 Chr 7:1

SHIMRON-MERON (1)
the king of **S**, one; the king of Jos 12:20

SHIMRONITES (1)
of Shimron, the clan of the **S**. Nm 26:24

SHIMSHAI (4)
the commander and **S** the scribe wrote Ezr 4:8
Rehum the commander, **S** the scribe, Ezr 4:9
the commander and **S** the scribe and Ezr 4:17
read before Rehum and **S** the scribe and Ezr 4:23

SHINAB (1)
king of Gomorrah, **S** king of Admah, Gn 14:2

SHINAR (8)
Accad, and Calneh, in the land of **S**. Gn 10:10
a plain in the land of **S** and settled there. Gn 11:2
In the days of Amraphel king of **S**, Gn 14:1
king of Goiim, Amraphel king of **S**, Gn 14:9
the spoil a beautiful cloak from **S**, Jos 7:21
Pathros, from Cush, from Elam, from **S**, Is 11:11
And he brought them to the land of **S**, to Dn 1:2
He said to me, "To the land of **S**, to build Zec 5:11

SHINE (28)
make his face to **s** upon you and be Nm 6:25
God above not seek it, nor light **s** upon it. Jb 3:4
out, and the flame of his fire does not **s**. Jb 18:5
for you, and light will **s** on your ways. Jb 22:28
causes the lightning of his cloud to **s**? Jb 37:15
Make your face **s** on your servant; save Ps 31:16
bless us and make his face to **s** upon us, Ps 67:1
enthroned upon the cherubim, **s** forth. Ps 80:1
let your face **s**, that we may be saved! Ps 80:3
let your face **s**, that we may be saved! Ps 80:7
let your face **s**, that we may be saved! Ps 80:19
vengeance, O God of vengeance, **s** forth! Ps 94:1
to make his face **s** and bread to Ps 104:15
he has made his light to **s** upon us. Ps 118:27
Make your face **s** upon your servant, Ps 119:135
shame, but on him his crown will **s**." Ps 132:18
A man's wisdom makes his face **s**, and Eccl 8:1
Arise, **s**, for your light has come, and the Is 60:1
your face to **s** upon your sanctuary, Dn 9:17
who are wise shall **s** like the brightness Dn 12:3
of a crown they shall **s** on his land. Zec 9:16
same way, let your light **s** before others, Mt 5:16
Then the righteous will **s** like the sun Mt 13:43
"Let light **s** out of darkness," has shone 2 Cor 4:6
the dead, and Christ will **s** on you." Eph 5:14
among whom you **s** as lights in the Phil 2:15
light of a lamp will **s** in you no more, Rv 18:23
has no need of sun or moon to **s** on it, Rv 21:23

SHINED (1)
land of deep darkness, on them has light **s**. Is 9:2

SHINES (4)
the perfection of beauty, God **s** forth. Ps 50:2
which **s** brighter and brighter until full Prv 4:18
comes from the east and **s** as far as the Mt 24:27
The light **s** in the darkness, and the Jn 1:5

SHINING (13)
that the skin of Moses' face was **s**. Ex 34:35
like the sun **s** forth on a cloudless 2 Sm 23:4
Behind him he leaves a **s** wake; one Jb 41:32
and moon, praise him, all you **s** stars! Ps 148:3
and smoke and the **s** of a flaming fire by Is 4:5

expanse, **s** like awe-inspiring crystal, Ezk 1:22
darkened, and the stars withdraw their **s**. Jl 2:10
darkened, and the stars withdraw their **s**. Jl 3:15
He was a burning and **s** lamp, and you Jn 5:35
attention as to a lamp **s** in a dark place, 2 Pt 1:19
away and the true light is already **s**. 1 Jn 2:8
face was like the sun **s** in full strength. Rv 1:16
a third of the day might be kept from **s**, Rv 8:12

SHION (1)
Hapharaim, **S**, Anaharath, Jos 19:19

SHIP (26)
a rock, the way of a **s** on the high seas, Prv 30:19
oars can go, nor majestic **s** can pass. Is 33:21
to Joppa and found a **s** going to Tarshish. Jon 1:3
sea, so that the **s** threatened to break up. Jon 1:4
cargo that was in the **s** into the sea to Jon 1:5
the inner part of the **s** and had lain down Jon 1:5
But going ahead to the **s**, we set sail Acts 20:13
And they accompanied him to the **s**. Acts 20:38
having found a **s** crossing to Acts 21:2
for there the **s** was to unload its cargo. Acts 21:3
Then we went on board the **s**, and they Acts 21:6
embarking in a **s** of Adramyttium, Acts 27:2
centurion found a **s** of Alexandria Acts 27:6
loss, not only of the cargo and the **s**, Acts 27:10
the owner of the **s** than to what Paul Acts 27:11
And when the **s** was caught and Acts 27:15
they used supports to undergird the **s**. Acts 27:17
of life among you, but only of the **s**. Acts 27:22
were seeking to escape from the **s**, Acts 27:30
"Unless these men stay in the **s**, Acts 27:31
(We were in all 276 persons in the **s**.) Acts 27:37
eaten enough, they lightened the **s**, Acts 27:38
if possible to run the **s** ashore. Acts 27:39
rest on planks or on pieces of the **s**. Acts 27:44
we set sail in a **s** that had wintered in Acts 28:11
in the island, a **s** of Alexandria, Acts 28:11

SHIP'S (4)
with difficulty to secure the **s** boat. Acts 27:16
they threw the **s** tackle overboard Acts 27:19
and had lowered the **s** boat into the Acts 27:30
away the ropes of the **s** boat and let it Acts 27:32

SHIPHI (1)
Ziza the son of **S**, son of Allon, son of 1 Chr 4:37

SHIPHMITE (1)
for the wine cellars was Zabdi the **S**. 1 Chr 27:27

SHIPHRAH (1)
of whom was named **S** and the other Ex 1:15

SHIPHTAN (1)
Ephraim a chief, Kemuel the son of **S**. Nm 34:24

SHIPMASTERS (1)
waste." And all **s** and seafaring men, Rv 18:17

SHIPS (34)
he shall become a haven for **s**, and his Gn 49:13
But **s** shall come from Kittim and Nm 24:24
LORD will bring you back in **s** to Egypt, Dt 28:68
and Dan, why did he stay with the **s**? Jgs 5:17
built a fleet of **s** at Ezion-geber, 1 Kgs 9:26
had a fleet of **s** of Tarshish at sea 1 Kgs 10:22
years the fleet of **s** of Tarshish used 1 Kgs 10:22
Jehoshaphat made **s** of Tarshish to 1 Kgs 22:48
for the **s** were wrecked at 1 Kgs 22:48
servants in the **s**," but Jehoshaphat 1 Kgs 22:49
of his servants **s** and servants 2 Chr 8:18
For the king's **s** went to Tarshish 2 Chr 9:21
three years the **s** of Tarshish used 2 Chr 9:21
joined him in building **s** to go to 2 Chr 20:36
and they built the **s** in Ezion-geber. 2 Chr 20:36
made." And the **s** were wrecked and 2 Chr 20:37
wind you shattered the **s** of Tarshish. Ps 48:7
There go the **s**, and Leviathan, which Ps 104:26
Some went down to the sea in **s**, doing Ps 107:23
She is like the **s** of the merchant; she Prv 31:14
against all the **s** of Tarshish, and against Is 2:16
Wail, O **s** of Tarshish, for Tyre is laid Is 23:1
Wail, O **s** of Tarshish, for your Is 23:14
in the **s** in which they rejoice. Is 43:14
shall hope for me, the **s** of Tarshish first, Is 60:9
all the **s** of the sea with their mariners Ezk 27:9
The **s** of Tarshish traveled for you Ezk 27:25
and down from their **s** come all who Ezk 27:29
out from me in **s** to terrify the Ezk 30:9
For **s** of Kittim shall come against Dn 11:30
and horsemen, and with many **s**. Dn 11:40
Look at the **s** also: though they are so Jas 3:4
died, and a third of the **s** were destroyed. Rv 8:9
where all who had **s** at sea grew rich Rv 18:19

SHIPWRECK (1)
this, some have made **s** of their faith, 1 Tm 1:19

SHIPWRECKED (1)
Three times I was **s**; a night and a 2 Cor 11:25

SHISHA (1)
Ahijah the sons of **S** were secretaries; 1 Kgs 4:3

SHISHAK (7)
fled into Egypt, to **S** king of Egypt, 1 Kgs 11:40
S king of Egypt came up against 1 Kgs 14:25
S king of Egypt came up against 2 Chr 12:2
gathered at Jerusalem because of **S**, 2 Chr 12:5
abandoned you to the hand of **S**.'" 2 Chr 12:5
out on Jerusalem by the hand of **S**. 2 Chr 12:7
So **S** king of Egypt came up against 2 Chr 12:9

SHITRAI (1)
in Sharon was **S** the Sharonite; 1 Chr 27:29

SHITTIM (5)
While Israel lived in **S**, the people Nm 25:1
sent two men secretly from **S** as spies, Jos 2:1
in the morning and they set out from **S**. Jos 3:1
of the LORD and water the Valley of **S**. Jl 3:18
him, and what happened from **S** to Gilgal, Mi 6:5

SHIZA (1)
Adina the son of **S** the Reubenite, a 1 Chr 11:42

SHOA (1)
the Chaldeans, Pekod and **S** and Koa, Ezk 23:23

SHOBAB (4)
Shammua, **S**, Nathan, Solomon, 2 Sm 5:14
were her sons: Jesher, **S**, and Ardon. 1 Chr 2:18
Shimea, **S**, Nathan and Solomon, four 1 Chr 3:5
Shammua, **S**, Nathan, Solomon, 1 Chr 14:4

SHOBACH (2)
with **S** the commander of the army 2 Sm 10:16
and wounded **S** the commander of 2 Sm 10:18

SHOBAI (2)
the sons of Hatita, and the sons of **S**, Ezr 2:42
the sons of Hatita, the sons of **S**, Neh 7:45

SHOBAL (9)
of the land: Lotan, **S**, Zibeon, Anah, Gn 36:20
These are the sons of **S**: Alvan, Gn 36:23
the chiefs Lotan, **S**, Zibeon, Anah, Gn 36:29
Lotan, **S**, Zibeon, Anah, Dishon, Ezer, 1 Chr 1:38
The sons of **S**: Alvan, Manahath, 1 Chr 1:40
S the father of Kiriath-jearim, 1 Chr 2:50
S the father of Kiriath-jearim had 1 Chr 2:52
Perez, Hezron, Carmi, Hur, and **S**. 1 Chr 4:1
Reaiah the son of **S** fathered Jahath, 1 Chr 4:2

SHOBEK (1)
Hallohesh, Pilha, **S**, Neh 10:24

SHOBI (1)
S the son of Nahash from Rabbah of 2 Sm 17:27

SHOCK (1)
He will direct the **s** of his battering Ezk 26:9

SHOCKED (1)
Be appalled, O heavens, at this; be **s**, be Jer 2:12

SHOD (1)
embroidered cloth and **s** you with fine Ezk 16:10

SHOE (2)
my washbasin; upon Edom I cast my **s**; Ps 60:8
my washbasin; upon Edom I cast my **s**; Ps 108:9

SHOES (4)
turban, and put your **s** on your feet; Ezk 24:17
on your heads and your **s** on your feet; Ezk 24:23
a ring on his hand, and **s** on his feet. Lk 15:22
and, as **s** for your feet, having put on Eph 6:15

SHOHAM (1)
of Jaaziah, Beno, **S**, Zaccur and Ibri. 1 Chr 24:27

SHOMER (2)
and Jehozabad the son of **S**, 2 Kgs 12:21
Heber fathered Japhlet, **S**, Hotham, 1 Chr 7:32

SHONE (13)
skin of his face **s** because he had been Ex 34:29
and behold, the skin of his face **s**, Ex 34:30
upon us; he **s** forth from Mount Paran; Dt 33:2
morning and the sun **s** on the water, 2 Kgs 3:22
when his lamp **s** upon my head, and by Jb 29:3
if I have looked at the sun when it **s**, or Jb 31:26
waters, and the earth **s** with his glory. Ezk 43:2
before them, and his face **s** like the sun, Mt 17:2
and the glory of the Lord **s** around them, Lk 2:9
next to him, and a light **s** in the cell. Acts 12:7
from heaven suddenly **s** around me. Acts 22:6
that **s** around me and those who Acts 26:13
out of darkness," has **s** in our hearts to 2 Cor 4:6

SHOOK (11)
I also **s** out the fold of my garment and Neh 5:13
up the world; the earth trembled and **s**. Ps 77:18
foundations of the thresholds **s** at the voice Is 6:4
the heart of his people **s** as the trees of the Is 7:2
the earth tremble, who **s** kingdoms, Is 14:16
the earth; he looked and **s** the nations; Hab 3:6
And the earth **s**, and the rocks were Mt 27:51
But they **s** off the dust from their feet Acts 13:51
he **s** out his garments and said to Acts 18:6
s off the creature into the fire and Acts 28:5
At that time his voice **s** the earth, but Heb 12:26

SHOOT (14)
And I will **s** three arrows to the side 1 Sm 20:20
the arrows that I **s**." As the boy ran, 1 Sm 20:36
that they would **s** from the wall? 2 Sm 11:20
"**S** him also." And they shot him in 2 Kgs 9:27
Then Elisha said, "**S**," and he shot. 2 Kgs 13:17
into this city or **s** an arrow there, 2 Kgs 19:32
bowmen and could **s** arrows and 1 Chr 12:2
to **s** arrows and great stones. 2 Chr 26:15
arrow to the string to **s** in the dark at the Ps 11:2
shall come forth a **s** from the stump of Is 11:1
into this city or **s** an arrow there or Is 37:33
s at her, spare no arrows, for she has Jer 50:14
shall **s** forth your branches and yield Ezk 36:8
off, and you, although a wild olive **s**, Rom 11:17

SHOOTING (2)
s from ambush at the blameless, Ps 64:4
s at him suddenly and without fear. Ps 64:4

SHOOTS (13)
the sun, and his **s** spread over his garden. Jb 8:16
sprout again, and that its **s** will not cease. Jb 14:7
the flame will dry up his **s**, and by the Jb 15:30
But God **s** his arrow at them; they are Ps 64:7
to the sea and its **s** to the River. Ps 80:11
will be like olive **s** around your table. Ps 128:3
Your **s** are an orchard of pomegranates Sg 4:13
its **s** spread abroad and passed over the Is 16:8
he cuts off the **s** with pruning hooks, Is 18:5
blossom and put forth **s** and fill the whole Is 27:6
fire has gone out from the stem of its **s**, Ezk 19:14
long from abundant water in its **s**. Ezk 31:5
his **s** shall spread out; his beauty shall Hos 14:6

SHOPHACH (2)
with **S** the commander of the army 1 Chr 19:16
to death also **S** the commander of 1 Chr 19:18

SHORE (6)
"Zebulun shall dwell at the **s** of the sea; Gn 49:13
is near Eloth on the **s** of the Red Sea, 1 Kgs 9:26
and Eloth on the **s** of the sea, 2 Chr 8:17
land at Gennesaret and moored to the **s**. Mk 6:53
as day was breaking, Jesus stood on the **s**; Jn 21:4
and sailed along Crete, close to the **s**. Acts 27:13

SHORN (4)
their inhabitants, **s** of strength, 2 Kgs 19:26
are like a flock of **s** ewes that have come Sg 4:2
every head is baldness; every beard is **s**; Is 15:2
while their inhabitants, **s** of strength, Is 37:27

SHORT (20)
had gone only a **s** distance from the city. Gn 44:4
too long or too **s** for a freewill offering, Lv 22:23
morning until now, except for a **s** rest." Ru 2:7
had gone from him a **s** distance, 2 Kgs 5:19
that the exulting of the wicked is **s**, and Jb 20:5
You have cut **s** the days of his youth; Ps 89:45
Remember how **s** my time is! For what Ps 89:47
but the years of the wicked will be **s**. Prv 10:27
For the bed is too **s** to stretch oneself on, Is 28:20
And if those days had not been cut **s**, Mt 24:22
of the elect those days will be cut **s**. Mt 24:22
And if the Lord had not cut **s** the days, Mk 13:20
"In a **s** time would you persuade me Acts 26:28
And Paul said, "Whether **s** or long, I Acts 26:29
have sinned and fall **s** of the glory of Rom 3:23
the appointed time has grown very **s**. 1 Cor 7:29
head, then she should cut her hair **s**. 1 Cor 11:6
from you, brothers, for a **s** time, 1 Thes 2:17
disciplined us for a **s** time as it seemed Heb 12:10
because he knows that his time is **s**!" Rv 12:12

SHORT-EARED (2)
the little owl, the cormorant, the **s** owl, Lv 11:17
the little owl and the **s** owl, the barn owl Dt 14:16

SHORTENED (6)
said to Moses, "Is the LORD'S hand **s**? Nm 11:23
His strong steps are **s**, and his own Jb 18:7
in midcourse; he has **s** my days. Ps 102:23
Is my hand **s**, that it cannot redeem? Is 50:2
Behold, the LORD'S hand is not **s**, that it Is 59:1
elect, whom he chose, he **s** the days. Mk 13:20

SHORTLY (4)
by God, and God will **s** bring it about. Gn 41:32
house will now **s** be brought back Jer 27:16
that he himself intended to go there **s**. Acts 25:4
in the Lord that **s** I myself will come Phil 2:24

SHOT (12)
soon as it budded, its blossoms **s** forth, Gn 40:10
bitterly attacked him, **s** at him, Gn 49:23
touch him, but he shall be stoned or **s**; Ex 19:13
the side of it, as though I **s** at a mark. 1 Sm 20:20
boy ran, he **s** an arrow beyond him. 1 Sm 20:36
of the arrow that Jonathan had **s**, 1 Sm 20:37
Then the archers **s** at your servants 2 Sm 11:24
and **s** Joram between the shoulders, 2 Kgs 9:24
him also." And they **s** him in the 2 Kgs 9:27
Then Elisha said, "Shoot," and he **s**. 2 Kgs 13:17
And the archers **s** King Josiah. And 2 Chr 35:23
toward him and **s** forth its branches Ezk 17:7

SHOULDER (45)
gave it to Hagar, putting it on her **s**, Gn 21:14
came out with her water jar on her **s**. Gn 24:15
came out with her water jar on her **s**, Gn 24:45
let down her jar from her **s** and said, Gn 24:46
was pleasant, so he bowed his **s** to bear, Gn 49:15
It shall have two **s** pieces attached to its Ex 28:7
two stones on the **s** pieces of the ephod, Ex 28:12
it in front to the **s** pieces of the ephod. Ex 28:25
part of the two **s** pieces of the ephod, Ex 28:27
made for the ephod attaching **s** pieces, Ex 39:4
he set them on the **s** pieces of the ephod Ex 39:7
it in front to the **s** pieces of the ephod. Ex 39:18
part of the two **s** pieces of the ephod, Ex 39:20
the priest shall take the **s** of the ram, Nm 6:19
things that had to be carried on the **s**. Nm 7:9
down and reach to the **s** of the Sea of Nm 34:11
give to the priest the **s** and the two cheeks Dt 18:3
take up each of you a stone upon his **s**, Jos 4:5
Hinnom at the southern **s** of the Jebusite Jos 15:8
to the northern **s** of Mount Jearim Jos 15:10
goes out to the **s** of the hill north Jos 15:11
goes up to the **s** north of Jericho, Jos 18:12
direction of Luz, to the **s** of Luz (that is, Jos 18:13
Hinnom, south of the **s** of the Jebusites, Jos 18:16
the north of the **s** of Beth-arabah it goes Jos 18:18
on to the north of the **s** of Beth-hoglah. Jos 18:19
and took it up and laid it on his **s**. Jgs 9:48
turned a stubborn **s** and stiffened their Neh 9:29
then let my **s** blade fall from my Jb 31:22
let my shoulder blade fall from my **s**, Jb 31:22
Surely I would carry it on my **s**; I would Jb 31:36
"I relieved your **s** of the burden; your Ps 81:6
yoke of his burden, and the staff for his **s**, Is 9:4
and the government shall be upon his **s**, Is 9:6
day his burden will depart from your **s**, Is 10:27
swoop down on the **s** of the Philistines in Is 11:14
them, and his burden from their **s**." Is 14:25
I will place on his **s** the key of the house Is 22:22
the baggage upon your **s** and carry it Ezk 12:6
dusk, carrying it on my **s** in their sight. Ezk 12:7
lift his baggage upon his **s** at dusk, Ezk 12:12
all the good pieces, the thigh and the **s**; Ezk 24:4
bald, and every **s** was rubbed bare, Ezk 29:18
Because you push with side and **s**, and Ezk 34:21
turned a stubborn **s** and stopped their Zec 7:11

SHOULDERS (17)
took a garment, laid it on both their **s**, Gn 9:23
bound up in their cloaks on their **s**. Ex 12:34
the LORD on his two **s** for remembrance. Ex 28:12
all day long, and dwells between his **s**." Dt 33:12
put them on his **s** and carried them to Jgs 16:3
From his **s** upward he was taller than 1 Sm 9:2
any of the people from his **s** upward. 1 Sm 10:23
javelin of bronze slung between his **s**. 1 Sm 17:6
of Shaphat remains on his **s** today." 2 Kgs 6:31
and shot Joram between the **s**, 2 Kgs 9:24
ark of God on their **s** with the poles, 1 Chr 15:15
You need not carry it on your **s**. 2 Chr 35:3
They lift it to their **s**, they carry it, they set Is 46:7
daughters shall be carried on their **s**. Is 49:22
the hand, you broke and tore all their **s**; Ezk 29:7
hard to bear, and lay them on people's **s**, Mt 23:4
when he has found it, he lays it on his **s**, Lk 15:5

SHOUT (49)
and the **s** of a king is among them. Nm 23:21
all the people shall **s** with a great shout, Jos 6:5
all the people shall shout with a great **s**, Jos 6:5
"You shall not **s** or make your voice Jos 6:10
your mouth, until the day I tell you to **s**. Jos 6:10
I tell you to shout. Then you shall **s**." Jos 6:10
"**S**, for the LORD has given you the city. Jos 6:16
the trumpet, the people shouted a great **s**, Jos 6:20
also on every side of all the camp and **s**, Jgs 7:18
the camp, all Israel gave a mighty **s**, 1 Sm 4:5
Judah rose with a **s** and pursued the 1 Sm 17:52
the men of Judah raised the battle **s**. 2 Chr 13:15
with a great **s** when they praised Ezr 3:11
sound of the joyful **s** from the sound of Ezr 3:13
for the people shouted with a great **s**, Ezr 3:13
they **s** after them as after a thief. Jb 30:5
he sees his face with a **s** of joy, and he Jb 33:26
May we **s** for joy over your salvation, and Ps 20:5
and rejoice, O righteous, and **s** for joy, Ps 32:11
S for joy in the LORD, O you righteous! Ps 33:1
in my righteousness **s** for joy and Ps 35:27
my enemy will not **s** in triumph over Ps 41:11
peoples! **S** to God with loud songs of joy! Ps 47:1
God has gone up with a **s**, the LORD with Ps 47:5
my shoe; over Philistia I **s** in triumph." Ps 60:8
the morning and the evening to **s** for joy. Ps 65:8
grain, they **s** and sing together for joy. Ps 65:13
S for joy to God, all the earth; Ps 66:1
My lips will **s** for joy, when I sing Ps 71:23
strength; **s** for joy to the God of Jacob! Ps 81:1
are the people who know the festal **s**, Ps 89:15
my shoe; over Philistia I **s** in triumph." Ps 108:9
and let your saints **s** for joy. Ps 132:9
salvation, and her saints will **s** for joy. Ps 132:16
S, and sing for joy, O inhabitant of Zion, Is 12:6
fruit and your harvest the **s** has ceased. Is 16:9
majesty of the LORD they **s** from the west. Is 24:14
let them **s** from the top of the Is 42:11
LORD has done it; **s**, O depths of the earth; Is 44:23
Chaldea, declare this with a **s** of joy, Is 48:20
land; they **s** against the cities of Judah. Jer 4:16
For whenever I speak, I cry out, I **s**, Jer 20:8
roar mightily against his fold, and **s**, Jer 25:30
of joy; the shouting is not the **s** of joy. Jer 48:33
Raise a **s** against her all around; she Jer 50:15
they shall raise the **s** of victory over Jer 51:14
and **s** aloud over you and cry out Ezk 27:30
aloud, O daughter of Zion; **s**, O Israel! Zep 3:14
Zion! **S** aloud, O daughter of Jerusalem! Zec 9:9

SHOUTED (16)
heard the noise of the people as they **s**, Ex 32:17
saw it, they **s** and fell on their faces. Lv 9:24
So the people **s**, and the trumpets were Jos 6:20
of the trumpet, the people **s** a great shout, Jos 6:20
And they **s** to the people of Dan, who Jgs 18:23
all the people." And all the people **s**, 1 Sm 10:24
He stood and **s** to the ranks of Israel, 1 Sm 17:8
And when the men of Judah **s**, God 2 Chr 13:15
And they **s** it with a loud voice in 2 Chr 32:18
And all the people **s** with a great shout Ezr 3:11
laid, though many **s** aloud for joy, Ezr 3:12
for the people **s** with a great shout, Ezr 3:13
and the city of Susa **s** and rejoiced. Est 8:15
together and all the sons of God **s** for joy? Jb 38:7
has he done?" But they **s** all the more, Mt 27:23
has he done?" But they **s** all the more, Mk 15:14

SHOUTING (29)
said, "It is not the sound of **s** for victory, Ex 32:18
the Philistines came **s** to meet him. Jgs 15:14
the Philistines heard the noise of the **s**, 1 Sm 4:6
"What does this great **s** in the camp of 1 Sm 4:6
out to the battle line, **s** the war cry. 1 Sm 17:20
of the LORD with **s** and with the sound 2 Sm 6:15
of the covenant of the LORD with **s**, 1 Chr 15:28
voice and with **s** and with trumpets 2 Chr 15:14
with laughter, and your lips with **s**. Jb 8:21
the thunder of the captains, and the **s**. Jb 39:25
like a strong man **s** because of wine. Ps 78:65
are better than the **s** of a ruler among Eccl 9:17
in the presses; I have put an end to the **s**. Is 16:10
down of walls and a **s** to the mountains. Is 22:5
not terrified by their **s** or daunted at their Is 31:4
of joy; the **s** is not the shout of joy. Jer 48:33
and not of joyful **s** on the mountains. Ezk 7:7
murder, to lift up the voice with **s**, Ezk 21:22
strongholds, with **s** on the day of battle, Am 1:14
amid **s** and the sound of the trumpet; Am 2:2
him and that followed him were **s**, Mt 21:9
before and those who followed were **s**, Mk 11:9
but they kept **s**, "Crucify, crucify Lk 23:21
And the people were **s**, "The voice of a Acts 12:22
s, "These men who have turned the Acts 17:6
Some in the crowd were **s** one thing, Acts 21:34
And as they were **s** and throwing off Acts 22:23
out why they were **s** against him like Acts 22:24
s that he ought not to live any longer. Acts 25:24

SHOUTINGS (1)
you who are full of **s**, tumultuous city, Is 22:2

SHOUTS (13)
of the city; he hears not the **s** of the driver. Jb 39:7
offer in his tent sacrifices with **s** of joy; Ps 27:6
you surround me with **s** of deliverance. Ps 32:7
play skillfully on the strings, with loud **s**. Ps 33:3
of God with glad **s** and songs of praise, Ps 42:4
laughter, and our tongue with **s** of joy; Ps 126:2
sow in tears shall reap with **s** of joy! Ps 126:5
sowing, shall come home with **s** of joy, Ps 126:6
wicked perish there are **s** of gladness. Prv 11:10
he cries out, he **s** aloud, he shows Is 42:13
and raise **s** for the chief of the nations; Jer 31:7
no one treads them with **s** of joy; Jer 48:33
forward the top stone amid **s** of 'Grace, Zec 4:7

SHOVEL (1)
has been winnowed with **s** and fork. Is 30:24

SHOVELS (9)
and **s** and basins and forks and fire Ex 27:3
all the utensils of the altar, the pots, the **s**, Ex 38:3
there, the fire pans, the forks, the **s**, Nm 4:14
Hiram also made the pots, the **s**, and 1 Kgs 7:40
Now the pots, the **s**, and the basins, 1 Kgs 7:45
the pots and the **s** and the snuffers 2 Kgs 25:14
Hiram also made the pots, the **s**, and 2 Chr 4:11
The pots, the **s**, the forks, and all the 2 Chr 4:16
the pots and the **s** and the snuffers and Jer 52:18

SHOW (167)
house to the land that I will **s** you. Gn 12:1
success today and **s** steadfast love to Gn 24:12
you are going to **s** steadfast love and Gn 24:49
him to Joseph to **s** the way before him Gn 46:28
I have raised you up, to **s** you my power, Ex 9:16
that I may **s** these signs of mine among Ex 10:1
come near to God to **s** whether or not he Ex 22:8
Exactly as I **s** you concerning the Ex 25:9
your sight, please **s** me now your ways, Ex 33:13
Moses said, "Please **s** me your glory." Ex 33:18
and will **s** mercy on whom I will show Ex 33:19
show mercy on whom I will **s** mercy. Ex 33:19
to **s** when it is unclean and when it is Lv 14:57
the regular **s** bread also shall be on it. Nm 4:7
the morning the LORD will **s** who is his, Nm 16:5
day, to **s** you by what way you should go. Dt 1:33
have only begun to **s** your servant your Dt 3:24
covenant with them and **s** no mercy to Dt 7:2
of his anger and **s** you mercy and have Dt 13:17
You shall not **s** partiality, and you shall Dt 16:19
respect the old or **s** mercy to the young. Dt 28:50
ask your father, and he will **s** you, your Dt 32:7
to him, "Please **s** us the way into the city, Jgs 1:24
and I will **s** you the man whom you are Jgs 4:22
then **s** me a sign that it is you who Jgs 6:17
and they did not **s** steadfast love to the Jgs 8:35
warn them and **s** them the ways 1 Sm 8:9
come to you and **s** you what you shall 1 Sm 10:8
men, and we will **s** ourselves to them. 1 Sm 14:8
and we will **s** you a thing." And 1 Sm 14:12
and I will **s** you what you shall do. 1 Sm 16:3
s me the steadfast love of the LORD, 1 Sm 20:14
Now may the LORD **s** steadfast love and 2 Sm 2:6
that I may **s** him kindness for 2 Sm 9:1
that I may **s** the kindness of God to 2 Sm 9:3
for I will **s** you kindness for the sake of 2 Sm 9:7
that you should **s** regard for a dead dog 2 Sm 9:8
may the LORD **s** steadfast love and 2 Sm 15:20
the merciful you **s** yourself merciful; 2 Sm 22:26
man you **s** yourself blameless; 2 Sm 22:26
"If he will **s** himself a worthy man, 1 Kgs 1:52
earth. Be strong, and **s** yourself a man, 1 Kgs 2:2
year, saying, "Go, **s** yourself to Ahab, 1 Kgs 18:1
So Elijah went to **s** himself to Ahab. 1 Kgs 18:2
I will surely **s** myself to him today." 1 Kgs 18:15
"Will you not **s** me who of us is for 2 Kgs 6:11
realm that Hezekiah did not **s** them. 2 Kgs 20:13
storehouses that I did not **s** them." 2 Kgs 20:15
in order to **s** the peoples and the princes Est 1:11
that he might **s** it to Esther and explain it Est 4:8
together to come to **s** him sympathy and Jb 2:11
Will you **s** partiality toward him? Will Jb 13:8
rebuke you if in secret you **s** partiality. Jb 13:10
"I will **s** you; hear me, and what I have Jb 15:17
me a liar and **s** that there is nothing Jb 24:25
I will not **s** partiality to any man or use Jb 32:21
"Bear with me a little, and I will **s** you, for Jb 36:2
who say, "Who will **s** us some good? Ps 4:6
Wondrously **s** your steadfast love, O Ps 17:7
the merciful you **s** yourself merciful; Ps 18:25
man you **s** yourself blameless; Ps 18:25
with the purified you **s** yourself pure; Ps 18:26
way rightly I will **s** the salvation of Ps 50:23
you judge unjustly and **s** partiality to the Ps 82:2
S us your steadfast love, O LORD, and Ps 85:7
S me a sign of your favor, that those Ps 86:17
satisfy him and **s** him my salvation." Ps 91:16
LORD, when you **s** favor to your people; Ps 106:4
he did not remember to **s** kindness, Ps 109:16
To **s** partiality is not good, but for a Prv 28:21
who formed them will **s** them no favor. Is 27:11
he exalts himself to **s** mercy to you. Is 30:18
his realm that Hezekiah did not **s** them. Is 39:2
in my storehouses that I did not **s** them." Is 39:4
declare this, and **s** us the former things? Is 43:9
and he shall **s** his indignation against Is 66:14
day and night, for I will **s** you no favor.' Jer 16:13
I will **s** them my back, not my face, in Jer 18:17

You **s** steadfast love to thousands, but Jer 32:18
the LORD your God may **s** us the way we Jer 42:3
shall not spare, and you shall **s** no pity. Ezk 9:5
So I will **s** my greatness and my Ezk 38:23
renown on the day that I **s** my glory, Ezk 39:13
your heart upon all that I shall **s** you, Ezk 40:4
here in order that I might **s** it to you. Ezk 40:4
and **s** them how to distinguish Ezk 44:23
dream, and we will **s** the interpretation." Dn 2:4
But if you **s** the dream and its Dn 2:6
Therefore **s** me the dream and its Dn 2:6
dream, and we will **s** its interpretation." Dn 2:7
that you can **s** me its interpretation." Dn 2:9
and no one can **s** it to the king except Dn 2:11
that he might **s** the interpretation to the Dn 2:16
and I will **s** the king the interpretation." Dn 2:24
or astrologers can **s** to the king the Dn 2:27
good to me to **s** the signs and wonders Dn 4:2
called, and he will **s** the interpretation." Dn 5:12
they could not **s** the interpretation of Dn 5:15
"And now I will **s** you the truth. Behold, Dn 11:2
"And I will **s** wonders in the heavens and Jl 2:30
of Egypt, I will **s** them marvelous things. Mi 7:15
You will **s** faithfulness to Jacob and Mi 7:20
yourself, and **s** your uncircumcision! Hab 2:16
me said to me, 'I will **s** you what they are.' Zec 1:9
s kindness and mercy to one another, Zec 7:9
will he accept you or **s** you favor? Mal 1:8
your hand, will he **s** favor to any of you? Mal 1:9
keep my ways but **s** partiality in your Mal 2:9
s yourself to the priest and offer the gift Mt 8:4
they asked him to **s** them a sign from Mt 16:1
time Jesus began to **s** his disciples that Mt 16:21
S me the coin for the tax." And they Mt 22:19
s yourself to the priest and offer for your Mk 1:44
And he will **s** you a large upper room Mk 14:15
to **s** the mercy promised to our fathers Lk 1:72
one, but "go and **s** yourself to the priest, Lk 5:14
does them, I will **s** you what he is like: Lk 6:47
"Go and **s** yourselves to the priests." Lk 17:14
and teach rightly, and **s** no partiality, Lk 20:21
"**S** me a denarius. Whose likeness and Lk 20:24
And he will **s** you a large upper room Lk 22:12
"What sign do you **s** us for doing these Jn 2:18
greater works than these will he **s** him, Jn 5:20
do these things, **s** yourself to the world." Jn 7:4
He said this to **s** by what kind of death Jn 12:33
Philip said to him, "Lord, **s** us the Father, Jn 14:8
How can you say, '**S** us the Father'? Jn 14:9
Jesus had spoken to **s** by what kind of Jn 18:32
(This he said to **s** by what kind of death Jn 21:19
s which one of these two you have Acts 1:24
And I will **s** wonders in the heavens Acts 2:19
and go into the land that I will **s** you.' Acts 7:3
For I will **s** him how much he must Acts 9:16
They **s** that the work of the law is Rom 2:15
serves to **s** the righteousness Rom 3:5
This was to **s** God's righteousness, Rom 3:25
It was to **s** his righteousness at the Rom 3:26
up, that I might **s** my power in you, Rom 9:17
desiring to **s** his wrath and to make Rom 9:22
of the saints and seek to **s** hospitality. Rom 12:13
circumcised to **s** God's truthfulness, Rom 15:8
And I will **s** you a still more 1 Cor 12:31
And you **s** that you are a letter from 2 Cor 3:3
to **s** that the surpassing power belongs 2 Cor 4:7
Lord himself and to **s** our good will. 2 Cor 8:19
may not have to **s** boldness with such 2 Cor 10:2
of the things that **s** my weakness. 2 Cor 11:30
ages he might **s** the immeasurable Eph 2:7
them first learn to **s** godliness to their 1 Tm 5:4
S yourself in all respects to be a model of Ti 2:7
works, and in your teaching **s** integrity, Ti 2:7
and to **s** perfect courtesy toward all people. Ti 3:2
one of you to **s** the same earnestness to Heb 6:11
God desired to **s** more convincingly to Heb 6:17
not neglect to **s** hospitality to strangers, Heb 13:2
s no partiality as you hold the faith in our Jas 2:1
But if you **s** partiality, you are Jas 2:9
and I have works." **S** me your faith apart Jas 2:18
and I will **s** you my faith by my works. Jas 2:18
good conduct let him **s** his works in the Jas 3:13
S hospitality to one another without 1 Pt 4:9
to others **s** mercy with fear, hating Jude 1:23
God gave him to **s** to his servants the Rv 1:1
and I will **s** you what must take place Rv 4:1
I will **s** you the judgment of the great Rv 17:1
me, saying, "Come, I will **s** you the Bride, Rv 21:9
sent his angel to **s** his servants what Rv 22:6

SHOWBREAD (7)
of the Kohathites had charge of the **s**, 1 Chr 9:32
duty was also to assist with the **s**, 1 Chr 23:29
of gold for each table for the **s**, 1 Chr 28:16
for the regular arrangement of the **s**, 2 Chr 2:4
set out the **s** on the table of pure 2 Chr 13:11
the table for the **s** and all its 2 Chr 29:18
for the **s**, the regular grain offering, Neh 10:33

SHOWED (43)
with Joseph and **s** him steadfast love Gn 39:21
to the LORD, and the LORD **s** him a log, Ex 15:25
and **s** them the fruit of the land. Nm 13:26
and through them he **s** himself holy. Nm 20:13
And the LORD **s** signs and wonders, great Dt 6:22
And the LORD **s** him all the land, Gilead Dt 34:1
And he **s** them the way into the city. And Jgs 1:25
So both of them **s** themselves to the 1 Sm 14:11
For you **s** kindness to all the people of 1 Sm 15:6
because you **s** this loyalty to Saul your 2 Sm 2:5
go?" And his sons **s** him the way 1 Kgs 13:12
that he did, and the might that he **s**, 1 Kgs 16:27
and his might that he **s**, 1 Kgs 22:45
did it fall?" When he **s** him the place, 2 Kgs 6:6
LORD, and he **s** them the king's son. 2 Kgs 11:4
and he **s** them all his treasure house, 2 Kgs 20:13
all the Levites who **s** good skill in 2 Chr 30:22
while he **s** the riches of his royal glory Est 1:4
And they **s** him sympathy and Jb 42:11
And he **s** them his treasure house, the Is 39:2
and **s** him the way of understanding? Is 40:14
into your hand; you **s** them no mercy; Is 47:6
and I knew; then you **s** me their deeds. Jer 11:18
to Babylon, the LORD **s** me this vision: Jer 24:1
and envy that you **s** because of your Ezk 35:11
This is what the Lord GOD **s** me: behold, Am 7:1
This is what the Lord GOD **s** me: behold, Am 7:4
This is what he **s** me: behold, the Lord Am 7:7
This is what the Lord GOD **s** me: behold, Am 8:1
Then the LORD **s** me four craftsmen. Zec 1:20
Then he **s** me Joshua the high priest Zec 3:1
very high mountain and **s** him all the Mt 4:8
took him up and **s** him all the kingdoms Lk 4:5
"The one who **s** him mercy." And Jesus Lk 10:37
that the dead are raised, even Moses **s**, Lk 20:37
this, he **s** them his hands and his feet. Lk 24:40
this, he **s** them his hands and his side. Jn 20:20
The native people **s** us unusual Acts 28:2
and the love that you **s** for his sake in Heb 6:10
and so I **s** no concern for them, Heb 8:9
and **s** me the holy city Jerusalem Rv 21:10
Then the angel **s** me the river of the Rv 22:1
at the feet of the angel who **s** them to me, Rv 22:8

SHOWER (2)
"**S**, O heavens, from above, and let the Is 45:8
west, you say at once, 'A **s** is coming.' Lk 12:54

SHOWERS (10)
tender grass, and like **s** upon the herb. Dt 32:2
settling its ridges, softening it with **s**, Ps 65:10
mown grass, like **s** that water the earth! Ps 72:6
Therefore the **s** have been withheld, and Jer 3:3
bring rain? Or can the heavens give **s**? Jer 14:22
I will send down the **s** in their season; Ezk 34:26
season; they shall be **s** of blessing. Ezk 34:26
he will come to us as the **s**, as the spring Hos 6:3
dew from the LORD, like **s** on the grass, Mi 5:7
clouds, and he will give them **s** of rain, Zec 10:1

SHOWING (14)
but **s** steadfast love to thousands of those Ex 20:6
but **s** steadfast love to thousands of those Dt 5:10
To this day I keep **s** steadfast love to the 2 Sm 3:8
keeping covenant and **s** steadfast love 1 Kgs 8:23
keeping covenant and **s** steadfast love 2 Chr 6:14
and your iniquities by **s** mercy to the Dn 4:27
him weeping and **s** tunics and other Acts 9:39
s by the Scriptures that the Christ Acts 18:28
Outdo one another in **s** honor. Rom 12:10
as I count on **s** against some who 2 Cor 10:2
want to make a good **s** in the flesh who Gal 6:12
not pilfering, but **s** all good faith, so that Ti 2:10
s honor to the woman as the weaker 1 Pt 3:7
s favoritism to gain advantage. Jude 1:16

SHOWN (47)
and you have **s** me great kindness in Gn 19:19
know that you have **s** steadfast love to Gn 24:14
that you have **s** to your servant, Gn 32:10
God has **s** to Pharaoh what he is about Gn 41:28
to Joseph, "Since God has **s** you all this, Gn 41:39
which is being **s** you on the mountain. Ex 25:40
for it that you were **s** on the mountain. Ex 26:30
As it has been **s** you on the mountain, Ex 27:8
after he has **s** himself to the priest for his Lv 13:7
spot, then it shall be **s** to the priest. Lv 13:19
disease, and it shall be **s** to the priest. Lv 13:49
to the pattern that the LORD had **s** Moses, Nm 8:4
To you it was **s**, that you might know Dt 4:35
the LORD our God has **s** us his glory and Dt 5:24
at our hands, or **s** us all these things, Jgs 13:23
"You have **s** great and steadfast love to 1 Kgs 3:6
that the LORD had **s** to David his 1 Kgs 8:66
but the LORD has **s** me that he shall 2 Kgs 8:10
"The LORD has **s** me that you are to be 2 Kgs 8:13
and have **s** me future generations, 1 Chr 17:17
"You have **s** great and steadfast love to 2 Chr 1:8
Zechariah's father, had **s** him, 2 Chr 24:22
moment favor has been **s** by the LORD Ezr 9:8
he has wondrously **s** his steadfast love Ps 31:21
and the wonders that he had **s** them. Ps 78:11
Let your work be **s** to your servants, Ps 90:16
He has **s** his people the power of his Ps 111:6
If favor is **s** to the wicked, he does not Is 26:10
"Faithless Israel has **s** herself more Jer 3:11
You have **s** signs and wonders in the Jer 32:20
the vision which the LORD has **s** to me: Jer 38:21
no more; no honor was **s** to the priests, Lam 4:16
hands; no respect is **s** to the elders. Lam 5:12
all the things that the LORD had **s** me. Ezk 11:25
He has **s** strength with his arm; he has Lk 1:51
that the Lord had **s** great mercy to her, Lk 1:58
"I have **s** you many good works from Jn 10:32
but God has **s** me that I should not Acts 10:28
all things I have **s** you that by Acts 20:35
to them, because God has **s** it to them. Rom 1:19
in order that sin might be **s** to be sin, Rom 7:13
I have **s** myself to those who did not Rom 10:20
that by the mercy **s** to you they also Rom 11:31
up children, has **s** hospitality, 1 Tm 5:10
the pattern that was **s** you on the Heb 8:5
mercy to one who has **s** no mercy. Jas 2:13
Do you want to be **s**, you foolish person, Jas 2:20

SHOWS (17)
and whatever he **s** me I will tell you." Nm 23:3
and **s** steadfast love to his anointed, 2 Sm 22:51
who **s** no partiality to princes, nor Jb 34:19
and **s** steadfast love to his anointed, Ps 18:50
the God who **s** me steadfast love. Ps 59:17
As a father **s** compassion to his Ps 103:13
so the LORD **s** compassion to those who Ps 103:13
and the Holy God **s** himself holy in Is 5:16
LORD, or what man **s** him his counsel? Is 40:13
he **s** himself mighty against his foes. Is 42:13
this writing, and **s** me its interpretation, Dn 5:7
every morning he **s** forth his justice; Zep 3:5
loves the Son and **s** him all that he Jn 5:20
I understand that God **s** no partiality, Acts 10:34
For God **s** no partiality. Rom 2:11
but God **s** his love for us in that while Rom 5:8
God **s** no partiality)—those, I say, who Gal 2:6

SHREWD (3)
his son Zechariah, a **s** counselor, 1 Chr 26:14
their own eyes, and **s** in their own sight! Is 5:21
this world are more **s** in dealing with Lk 16:8

SHREWDLY (2)
Come, let us deal **s** with them, lest they Ex 1:10
He dealt **s** with our race and forced our Acts 7:19

SHREWDNESS (1)
the dishonest manager for his **s**. Lk 16:8

SHRINE (1)
And the man Micah had a **s**, and he Jgs 17:5

SHRINES (5)
put them in the **s** of the high places 2 Kgs 17:29
for them in the **s** of the high places. 2 Kgs 17:32
Josiah removed all the **s** also of the 2 Kgs 23:19
and made for yourself colorful **s**, Ezk 16:16
who made silver **s** of Artemis, Acts 19:24

SHRINK (5)
who look at you will **s** from you and say, Na 3:7
how I did not **s** from declaring to you Acts 20:20
for I did not **s** from declaring to you Acts 20:27
not of those who **s** back and are Heb 10:39
have confidence and not **s** from him in 1 Jn 2:28

SHRINKS (1)
shall live by faith, and if he **s** back, Heb 10:38

SHRIVELED (2)
And he has **s** me up, which is a witness Jb 16:8
streets; their skin has **s** on their bones; Lam 4:8

SHRIVELS (1)
The seed **s** under the clods; the Jl 1:17

SHROUD (4)
body and wrapped it in a clean linen **s** Mt 27:59
And Joseph bought a linen **s**, and Mk 15:46
him in the linen **s** and laid him in Mk 15:46
wrapped it in a linen **s** and laid him in Lk 23:53

SHRUB (1)
He is like a **s** in the desert, and shall not Jer 17:6

SHUA (2)
a certain Canaanite whose name was **S**. Gn 38:2
Shomer, Hotham, and their sister **S**. 1 Chr 7:32

SHUA'S (1)
of time the wife of Judah, **S** daughter, Gn 38:12

SHUAH (2)
Jokshan, Medan, Midian, Ishbak, and **S**. Gn 25:2
Medan, Midian, Ishbak, and **S**. 1 Chr 1:32

SHUAL (2)
toward Ophrah, to the land of **S**; 1 Sm 13:17
Suah, Harnepher, **S**, Beri, Imrah. 1 Chr 7:36

SHUBAEL (3)
of Amram, **S**; of the sons of Shubael, 1 Chr 24:20
Shubael; of the sons of **S**, Jehdeiah. 1 Chr 24:20
S, his sons and his brothers, 1 Chr 25:20

SHUDDER (3)
In little more than a year you will **s**, you Is 32:10
who are at ease, **s**, you complacent ones; Is 32:11
well. Even the demons believe—and **s**! Jas 2:19

SHUDDERING (1)
I am dismayed, and **s** seizes my flesh. Jb 21:6

SHUHAH (1)
Chelub, the brother of **S**, fathered 1 Chr 4:11

SHUHAM (1)
of Dan according to their clans: of **S**, Nm 26:42

SHUHAMITES (2)
clans: of Shuham, the clan of the **S**. Nm 26:42
All the clans of the **S**, as they were Nm 26:43

SHUHITE (5)
place, Eliphaz the Temanite, Bildad the **S**, Jb 2:11
Then Bildad the **S** answered and said: Jb 8:1
Then Bildad the **S** answered and said: Jb 18:1
Then Bildad the **S** answered and said: Jb 25:1
and Bildad the **S** and Zophar the Jb 42:9

SHULAMMITE (2)
Return, return, O **S**, return, return, that Sg 6:13
Why should you look upon the **S**, as Sg 6:13

SHUMATHITES (1)
the Ithrites, the Puthites, the **S**, and 1 Chr 2:53

SHUN (2)
have caused my companions to **s** me; Ps 88:8
my beloved and my friend to **s** me; Ps 88:18

SHUNAMMITE (8)
of Israel, and found Abishag the **S**, 1 Kgs 1:3
and Abishag the **S** was attending to 1 Kgs 1:15
to give me Abishag the **S** as my wife." 1 Kgs 2:17
"Let Abishag the **S** be given to 1 Kgs 2:21
you ask Abishag the **S** for Adonijah? 1 Kgs 2:22
"Call this **S**." When he had called 2 Kgs 4:12
his servant, "Look, there is the **S**. 2 Kgs 4:25
said, "Call this **S**." So he called her. 2 Kgs 4:36

SHUNEM (3)
included Jezreel, Chesulloth, **S**, Jos 19:18
and came and encamped at **S**. 1 Sm 28:4
One day Elisha went on to **S**, where a 2 Kgs 4:8

SHUNI (2)
Ziphion, Haggi, **S**, Ezbon, Eri, Arodi, Gn 46:16
of Haggi, the clan of the Haggites; of **S**, Nm 26:15

SHUNITES (1)
Haggites; of Shuni, the clan of the **S**; Nm 26:15

SHUNS (1)
he who swears is as he who **s** an oath. Eccl 9:2

SHUPHAMITES (1)
of Shephupham, the clan of the **S**; of Nm 26:39

SHUPPIM (3)
And **S** and Huppim were the sons of 1 Chr 7:12
took a wife for Huppim and for **S**. 1 Chr 7:15
For **S** and Hosah it came out for the 1 Chr 26:16

SHUR (6)
wilderness, the spring on the way to **S**. Gn 16:7
Negeb and lived between Kadesh and **S**; Gn 20:1
They settled from Havilah to **S**, which Gn 25:18
and they went into the wilderness of **S**. Ex 15:22
Amalekites from Havilah as far as **S**, 1 Sm 15:7
of the land from of old, as far as **S**, 1 Sm 27:8

SHUSHAN (1)
the choirmaster: according to **S** Eduth. Ps 60:T

SHUT (83)
him. And the LORD **s** him in. Gn 7:16
at the entrance, **s** the door after him, Gn 19:6
the house with them and **s** the door. Gn 19:10
the land; the wilderness has **s** them in.' Ex 14:3
the priest shall **s** up the diseased person Lv 13:4
then the priest shall **s** him up for Lv 13:5
He shall not **s** him up, for he is Lv 13:11
then the priest shall **s** him up seven Lv 13:21
the priest shall **s** him up seven days, Lv 13:26
then the priest shall **s** up the person Lv 13:31
and the priest shall **s** up the person with Lv 13:33
the disease and **s** up that which Lv 13:50
and he shall **s** it up for another seven Lv 13:54
of the house and **s** up the house seven Lv 14:38
house while it is **s** up shall be unclean Lv 14:46
Let her be **s** outside the camp seven Nm 12:14
So Miriam was **s** outside the camp Nm 12:15
you, and he will **s** up the heavens, Dt 11:17
your heart or **s** your hand against Dt 15:7
And the gate was **s** as soon as the Jos 2:7
Now Jericho was **s** up inside and outside Jos 6:1
of the city fled to it and **s** themselves in, Jgs 9:51
to the cart and **s** up their calves at 1 Sm 6:10
for he has **s** himself in by entering a 1 Sm 23:7
So they were **s** up until the day of their 2 Sm 20:3
"When heaven is **s** up and there is no 1 Kgs 8:35
Then go in and **s** the door behind 2 Kgs 4:4
went from him and **s** the door behind 2 Kgs 4:5
man of God and **s** the door behind 2 Kgs 4:21
he went in and **s** the door behind the 2 Kgs 4:33
s the door and hold the door fast 2 Kgs 6:32
the king of Assyria **s** him up and 2 Kgs 17:4
"When heaven is **s** up and there is no 2 Chr 6:26
When I **s** up the heavens so that there 2 Chr 7:13
and he **s** up the doors of the house of 2 Chr 28:24
They also **s** the doors of the vestibule 2 Chr 29:7
guard, let them **s** and bar the doors. Neh 7:3
the doors should be **s** and gave orders Neh 13:19
because it did not **s** the doors of my Jb 3:10
houses; by day they **s** themselves up; Jb 24:16
"Or who **s** in the sea with doors when it Jb 38:8
of shields, **s** up closely as with a seal. Jb 41:15
Has he in anger **s** up his compassion?" Ps 77:9
to them. I am **s** in so that I cannot escape; Ps 88:8
on the street are **s**—when the sound Eccl 12:4
He shall open, and none shall **s**; and he Is 22:22
and he shall **s**, and none shall open. Is 22:22
every house is **s** up so that none can Is 24:10
they will be **s** up in a prison, and after Is 24:22
chambers, and **s** your doors behind you; Is 26:20
do they discern, for he has **s** their eyes, Is 44:18
kings shall **s** their mouths because of Is 52:15
day and night they shall not be **s**, that Is 60:11
bring forth, **s** the womb?" says your God. Is 66:9
The cities of the Negeb are **s** up, with Jer 13:19
it were a burning fire **s** up in my bones, Jer 20:9
Jeremiah the prophet was **s** up in the Jer 32:2
while he was still **s** up in the court of the Jer 33:1
Jeremiah while he was **s** up in the court Jer 39:15
me, "Go, **s** yourself within your house. Ezk 3:24
which faces east. And it was **s**. Ezk 44:1
said to me, "This gate shall remain **s**; Ezk 44:2
by it. Therefore it shall remain **s**. Ezk 44:2
faces east shall be **s** on the six working Ezk 46:1
the gate shall not be **s** until evening. Ezk 46:2
he has gone out the gate shall be **s**. Ezk 46:12
sent his angel and **s** the lions' mouths, Dn 6:22
s up the words and seal the book, Dn 12:4
for the words are **s** up and sealed until Dn 12:9
one among you who would **s** the doors, Mal 1:10
into your room and **s** the door and pray Mt 6:6
For you **s** the kingdom of heaven in Mt 23:13
the marriage feast, and the door was **s**. Mt 25:10
when the heavens were **s** up three years Lk 4:25
the door is now **s**, and my children are Lk 11:7
of the house has risen and **s** the door, Lk 13:25
temple, and at once the gates were **s**. Acts 21:30
They want to **s** you out, that you may Gal 4:17
key of David, who opens and no one will **s**, Rv 3:7
an open door, which no one is able to **s**. Rv 3:8
They have the power to **s** the sky, that no Rv 11:6
the pit, and **s** it and sealed it over him, Rv 20:3
its gates will never be **s** by day—and Rv 21:25

SHUTHELAH (4)
according to their clans: of **S**, Nm 26:35
And these are the sons of **S**: of Eran, Nm 26:36
S, and Bered his son, Tahath his son, 1 Chr 7:20
Zabad his son, **S** his son, and Ezer 1 Chr 7:21

SHUTHELAHITES (1)
clans: of Shuthelah, the clan of the **S**; Nm 26:35

SHUTS (6)
have hope, and injustice **s** her mouth. Jb 5:16
rebuild; if he **s** a man in, none can open. Jb 12:14
glad, and all wickedness **s** its mouth. Ps 107:42
of bloodshed and **s** his eyes from Is 33:15
and cry for help, he **s** out my prayer; Lam 3:8
no one will shut, who **s** and no one opens. Rv 3:7

SHUTTLE (1)
swifter than a weaver's **s** and come to their Jb 7:6

SIA (1)
the sons of Keros, the sons of **S**, the Neh 7:47

SIAHA (1)
the sons of Keros, the sons of **S**, the sons Ezr 2:44

SIBBECAI (4)
Then **S** the Hushathite struck down 2 Sm 21:18
S the Hushathite, Ilai the Ahohite, 1 Chr 11:29
Then **S** the Hushathite struck down 1 Chr 20:4
month, was **S** the Hushathite, 1 Chr 27:11

SIBBOLETH (1)
"**S**," for he could not pronounce it right. Jgs 12:6

SIBMAH (5)
(their names were changed), and **S**. Nm 32:38
and Kiriathaim, and **S**, and Jos 13:19
of Heshbon languish, and the vine of **S**; Is 16:8
with the weeping of Jazer for the vine of **S**; Is 16:9
for Jazer I weep for you, O vine of **S**! Jer 48:32

SIBRAIM (1)
S (which lies on the border between Ezk 47:16

SICK (63)
with which the LORD has made it **s**— Dt 29:22
to take David, she said, "He is **s**." 1 Sm 19:14
because I fell **s** three days ago. 1 Sm 30:13
wife bore to David, and he became **s**. 2 Sm 12:15
Abijah the son of Jeroboam fell **s**. 1 Kgs 14:1
of you concerning her son, for he is **s**. 1 Kgs 14:5
upper chamber in Samaria, and lay **s**; 2 Kgs 1:2
Ben-hadad the king of Syria was **s**. 2 Kgs 8:7
of Ahab in Jezreel, because he was **s**. 2 Kgs 8:29
Elisha had fallen **s** with the illness 2 Kgs 13:14
days Hezekiah became **s** and was at 2 Kgs 20:1
he heard that Hezekiah had been **s**. 2 Kgs 20:12
days Hezekiah became **s** and was at 2 Chr 32:24
is your face sad, seeing you are not **s**? Neh 2:2
I, when they were **s**—I wore sackcloth; Ps 35:13
Hope deferred makes the heart **s**, but a Prv 13:12
me with apples, for I am **s** with love. Sg 2:5
beloved, that you tell him I am **s** with love. Sg 5:8
The whole head is **s**, and the whole heart Is 1:5
it will be as when a **s** man wastes away. Is 10:18
And no inhabitant will say, "I am **s**"; the Is 33:24
those days Hezekiah became **s** and was at Is 38:1
after he had been **s** and had recovered Is 38:9
that he had been **s** and had recovered. Is 39:1
is upon me; my heart is **s** within me. Jer 8:18
above all things, and desperately **s**; Jer 17:9
For this our heart has become **s**, for Lam 5:17
strengthened, the **s** you have not healed, Ezk 34:4
was overcome and lay **s** for some days. Dn 8:27
the princes became **s** with the heat of Hos 7:5
when you offer those that are lame or **s**, Mal 1:8
been taken by violence or is lame or **s**, Mal 1:13
all Syria, and they brought him all the **s**, Mt 4:24
his mother-in-law lying **s** with a fever. Mt 8:14
with a word and healed all who were **s**. Mt 8:16
need of a physician, but those who are **s**. Mt 9:12
Heal the **s**, raise the dead, cleanse lepers, Mt 10:8
on them and healed their **s**. Mt 14:14
and brought to him all who were **s** Mt 14:35
clothed me, I was **s** and you visited me, Mt 25:36
when did we see you **s** or in prison and Mt 25:39
s and in prison and you did not visit Mt 25:43
or a stranger or naked or **s** or in prison, Mt 25:44
him all who were **s** or oppressed by Mk 1:32
many who were **s** with various diseases, Mk 1:34
of a physician, but those who are **s**. Mk 2:17
hands on a few **s** people and healed them. Mk 6:5
oil many who were **s** and healed them. Mk 6:13
began to bring the **s** people on their Mk 6:55
they laid the **s** in the marketplaces and Mk 6:56
they will lay their hands on the **s**, and Mk 16:18
any who were **s** with various diseases Lk 4:40
need of a physician, but those who are **s**. Lk 5:31
had a servant who was **s** and at the point Lk 7:2
Heal the **s** in it and say to them, 'The Lk 10:9
The **s** man answered him, "Sir, I have no Jn 5:7
saw the signs that he was doing on the **s**. Jn 6:2
even carried out the **s** into the streets Acts 5:15
bringing the **s** and those afflicted with Acts 5:16
his skin were carried away to the **s**, Acts 19:12
father of Publius lay **s** with fever and Acts 28:8
Is anyone among you **s**? Let him call for Jas 5:14
prayer of faith will save the one who is **s**, Jas 5:15

SICKBED (2)
The LORD sustains him on his **s**; in his Ps 41:3
Behold, I will throw her onto a **s**, and Rv 2:22

SICKLE (13)
weeks from the time the **s** is first put to Dt 16:9
shall not put a **s** to your neighbor's Dt 23:25
his mattock, his axe, or his **s**, 1 Sm 13:20
one who handles the **s** in time of Jer 50:16
Put in the **s**, for the harvest is ripe. Go in, Jl 3:13
the grain is ripe, at once he puts in the **s**, Mk 4:29
on his head, and a sharp **s** in his hand. Rv 14:14
who sat on the cloud, "Put in your **s**, Rv 14:15
the cloud swung his **s** across the earth, Rv 14:16

in heaven, and he too had a sharp **s**. Rv 14:17
voice to the one who had the sharp **s**, Rv 14:18
"Put in your **s** and gather the clusters Rv 14:18
the angel swung his **s** across the earth Rv 14:19

SICKNESS (16)
and I will take **s** away from among you. Ex 23:25
the LORD will take away from you all **s**, Dt 7:15
Every **s** also and every affliction that is Dt 28:61
whatever plague, whatever **s** there is, 1 Kgs 8:37
whether I shall recover from this **s**." 2 Kgs 1:2
saying, 'Shall I recover from this **s**?'" 2 Kgs 8:8
saying, 'Shall I recover from this **s**?'" 2 Kgs 8:9
whatever plague, whatever **s** there is, 2 Chr 6:28
will have a severe **s** with a disease of 2 Chr 21:15
A man's spirit will endure **s**, but a Prv 18:14
in much vexation and **s** and anger. Eccl 5:17
will send wasting **s** among his stout Is 10:16
been sick and had recovered from his **s**: Is 38:9
her; **s** and wounds are ever before me. Jer 6:7
nor have I desired the day of **s**. Jer 17:16
When Ephraim saw his **s**, and Judah Hos 5:13

SICKNESSES (2)
and lasting, and **s** grievous and lasting. Dt 28:59
that land and the **s** with which the LORD Dt 29:22

SIDDIM (3)
joined forces in the Valley of **S** (that is, Gn 14:3
and they joined battle in the Valley of **S** Gn 14:8
Now the Valley of **S** was full of Gn 14:10

SIDE (325)
above, and set the door of the ark in its **s**. Gn 6:16
Fear of Isaac, had not been on my **s**, Gn 31:42
flock to the west **s** of the wilderness and Ex 3:1
Hur held up his hands, one on one **s**, Ex 17:12
one side, and the other on the other **s**. Ex 17:12
its four feet, two rings on the one **s** of it, Ex 25:12
of it, and two rings on the other **s** of it. Ex 25:12
lampstand out of one **s** of it and three Ex 25:32
of the lampstand out of the other **s** of it; Ex 25:32
of the curtains, the cubit on the one **s**, Ex 26:13
one side, and the cubit on the other **s**, Ex 26:13
the tabernacle, on this **s** and that side, Ex 26:13
the tabernacle, on this side and that **s**, Ex 26:13
twenty frames for the south **s**; Ex 26:18
and for the second **s** of the tabernacle, Ex 26:20
on the north **s** twenty frames, Ex 26:20
frames of the one **s** of the tabernacle, Ex 26:26
frames of the other **s** of the tabernacle, Ex 26:27
the frames of the **s** of the tabernacle at Ex 26:27
on the south **s** of the tabernacle Ex 26:35
you shall put the table on the north **s**. Ex 26:35
On the south **s** the court shall have Ex 27:9
linen a hundred cubits long for one **s**. Ex 27:9
length on the north **s** there shall be Ex 27:11
court on the west **s** there shall be Ex 27:12
hangings for the one **s** of the gate shall Ex 27:14
On the other **s** the hangings shall be Ex 27:15
and said, "Who is on the LORD'S **s**? Ex 32:26
'Put your sword on your **s** each of you, Ex 32:27
thus: twenty frames for the south **s**. Ex 36:23
For the second **s** of the tabernacle, on Ex 36:25
side of the tabernacle, on the north **s**, Ex 36:25
frames of the one **s** of the tabernacle, Ex 36:31
frames of the other **s** of the tabernacle, Ex 36:32
two rings on its one **s** and two rings on Ex 37:3
its one side and two rings on its other **s**. Ex 37:3
lampstand out of one **s** of it and three Ex 37:18
of the lampstand out of the other **s** of it; Ex 37:18
For the south **s** the hangings of the court Ex 38:9
for the north **s** there were hangings Ex 38:11
And for the west **s** were hangings of Ex 38:12
The hangings for one **s** of the gate were Ex 38:14
And so for the other **s**. On both sides of Ex 38:15
on the north **s** of the tabernacle, Ex 40:22
table on the south **s** of the tabernacle, Ex 40:24
kill it on the north **s** of the altar before Lv 1:11
shall be drained out on the **s** of the altar. Lv 1:15
and cast it beside the altar on the east **s**, Lv 1:16
of the sin offering on the **s** of the altar, Lv 5:9
the front of the mercy seat on the east **s**, Lv 16:14
facing the tent of meeting on every **s**. Nm 2:2
camp on the east **s** toward the sunrise Nm 2:3
"On the south **s** shall be the standard of Nm 2:10
"On the west **s** shall be the standard of Nm 2:18
"On the north **s** shall be the standard of Nm 2:25
camp on the south **s** of the tabernacle, Nm 3:29
camp on the north **s** of the tabernacle. Nm 3:35
that are on the east **s** shall set out. Nm 10:5
that are on the south **s** shall set out. Nm 10:6
day's journey on this **s** and a day's Nm 11:31
and a day's journey on the other **s**, Nm 11:31
camped on the other **s** of the Arnon, Nm 21:13
the vineyards, with a wall on either **s**. Nm 22:24
them on the other **s** of the Jordan and Nm 32:19
come to us on this **s** of the Jordan to Nm 32:19
your south **s** shall be from the Nm 34:3
to Riblah on the east **s** of Ain. Nm 34:11
city, on the east **s** two thousand cubits, Nm 35:5
on the south **s** two thousand cubits, Nm 35:5
and on the west **s** two thousand cubits, Nm 35:5
on the north **s** two thousand cubits, Nm 35:5
the Arabah on the east **s** of the Jordan as Dt 4:49
Law and put it by the **s** of the ark of the Dt 31:26
city and encamped on the north **s** of Ai, Jos 8:11
in the midst of Israel, some on this **s**, Jos 8:22
some on this side, and some on that **s**. Jos 8:22
defeated on the west **s** of the Jordan, Jos 12:7
boundary on the north **s** runs from the Jos 15:5
which is on the south **s** of the valley. Jos 15:7
the sea, all that were by the **s** of Ashdod, Jos 15:46
which is on the other **s** of the Jordan, Jos 17:5
goes on the north **s** of the brook and Jos 17:9
On the north **s** their boundary began Jos 18:12
on the western **s** southward from the Jos 18:14
of Judah. This forms the western **s**. Jos 18:14
And the southern **s** begins at the Jos 18:15
forms its boundary on the eastern **s**. Jos 18:20
gave them rest on every **s** just as he had Jos 21:44
gave you on the other **s** of the Jordan. Jos 22:4
on the **s** that belongs to the people of Jos 22:11
who lived on the other **s** of the Jordan. Jos 24:8
trumpets also on every **s** of all the camp Jgs 7:18
the hand of all their enemies on every **s**, Jgs 8:34
and arrived on the east **s** of the land of Jgs 11:18
camped on the other **s** of the Arnon. Jgs 11:18
from his seat by the **s** of the gate, 1 Sm 4:18
put in a box at its **s** the figures of gold, 1 Sm 6:8
the hand of your enemies on every **s**, 1 Sm 12:11
garrison on the other **s**." But he did 1 Sm 14:1
crag on the one **s** and a rocky crag 1 Sm 14:4
side and a rocky crag on the other **s**. 1 Sm 14:4
to all Israel, "You shall be on one **s**, 1 Sm 14:40
be on the other **s**." And the people 1 Sm 14:40
against all his enemies on every **s**, 1 Sm 14:47
stood on the mountain on the one **s**, 1 Sm 17:3
stood on the mountain on the other **s**, 1 Sm 17:3
I will shoot three arrows to the **s** of it, 1 Sm 20:20
the arrows are on this **s** of you, 1 Sm 20:21
opposite, and Abner sat by Saul's **s**, 1 Sm 20:25
Saul went on one **s** of the mountain, 1 Sm 23:26
men on the other **s** of the mountain. 1 Sm 23:26
over to the other **s** and stood far off 1 Sm 26:13
were on the other **s** of the valley and 1 Sm 31:7
down, the one on the one **s** of the pool, 2 Sm 2:13
the other on the other **s** of the pool. 2 Sm 2:13
thrust his sword in his opponent's **s**, 2 Sm 2:16
him by the **s** of the mountain. 2 Sm 13:34
So the king stood at the **s** of the gate, 2 Sm 18:4
and on his **s** are Abiathar the priest 1 Kgs 2:22
as far as the other **s** of Jokmeam; 1 Kgs 4:12
my God has given me rest on every **s**. 1 Kgs 5:4
And he made **s** chambers all around. 1 Kgs 6:5
story was on the south **s** of the house, 1 Kgs 6:8
cast with wreaths at the **s** of each. 1 Kgs 7:30
five on the south **s** of the house, 1 Kgs 7:39
and five on the north **s** of the house. 1 Kgs 7:39
five on the south **s** and five on the 1 Kgs 7:49
and on each **s** of the seat were 1 Kgs 10:19
was parted to the one **s** and to the other, 2 Kgs 2:8
parted to the one **s** and to the other, 2 Kgs 2:14
you and I rode **s** by side behind Ahab 2 Kgs 9:25
I rode side by **s** behind Ahab his 2 Kgs 9:25
window and said, "Who is on my **s**? 2 Kgs 9:32
letter, saying, "If you are on my **s**, 2 Kgs 10:6
from the south **s** of the house to the 2 Kgs 11:11
the house to the north **s** of the house, 2 Kgs 11:11
altar on the right **s** as one entered the 2 Kgs 12:9
and put it on the north **s** of his altar. 2 Kgs 16:14
of Gedor, to the east **s** of the valley, 1 Chr 4:39
of the desert this **s** of the Euphrates, 1 Chr 5:9
at Jericho, on the east **s** of the Jordan, 1 Chr 6:78
gate on the east **s** as the gatekeepers of 1 Chr 9:18
he not given you peace on every **s**? 1 Chr 22:18
to wash, and set five on the south **s**, 2 Chr 4:6
the south side, and five on the north **s**. 2 Chr 4:6
five on the south **s** and five on the 2 Chr 4:7
five on the south **s** and five on the 2 Chr 4:8
and on each **s** of the seat were arm 2 Chr 9:18
us peace on every **s**." So they built 2 Chr 14:7
from the south **s** of the house to the 2 Chr 23:10
house to the north **s** of the house, 2 Chr 23:10
and he provided for them on every **s**. 2 Chr 32:22
down to the west **s** of the city of 2 Chr 32:30
sword strapped at his **s** while he built. Neh 4:18
was at the king's **s** in all matters Neh 11:24
his house and all that he has, on every **s**? Jb 1:10
Terrors frighten him on every **s**, and Jb 18:11
He breaks me down on every **s**, and I am Jb 19:10
On every **s** the wicked prowl, as vileness Ps 12:8
whispering of many—terror on every **s**! Ps 31:13
your arrows flashed on every **s**. Ps 77:17
A thousand may fall at your **s**, ten Ps 91:7
The LORD is on my **s**; I will not fear. Ps 118:6
The LORD is on my **s** as my helper; I Ps 118:7
me, surrounded me on every **s**; Ps 118:11
LORD who was on our **s**—let Israel now Ps 124:1
who was on our **s** when people rose up Ps 124:2
On the **s** of their oppressors there was Eccl 4:1
enemy has a sword; terror is on every **s**. Jer 6:25
ancient roads, and to walk into **s** roads, Jer 18:15
name Pashhur, but Terror On Every **S**. Jer 20:3
many whispering. Terror is on every **s**! Jer 20:10
they look not back—terror on every **s**! Jer 46:5
shall cry to them: 'Terror on every **s**!' Jer 49:29
their calamity from every **s** of them, Jer 49:32
against her from every **s** on the day of Jer 51:2
that his city is taken on every **s**; Jer 51:31
to a festival day my terrors on every **s**, Lam 2:22
had the face of a lion on the right **s**, Ezk 1:10
four had the face of an ox on the left **s**, Ezk 1:10
"Then lie on your left **s**, and place the Ezk 4:4
down a second time, but on your right **s**, Ezk 4:6
you cannot turn from one **s** to the other, Ezk 4:8
number of days that you lie on your **s**, Ezk 4:9
standing on the south **s** of the house, Ezk 10:3
that is on the east **s** of the city. Ezk 11:23
you from every **s** with your whorings. Ezk 16:33
you from every **s** and will uncover Ezk 16:37
against him from provinces on every **s**; Ezk 19:8
bring them against you from every **s**: Ezk 23:22
against you on every **s** with buckler, Ezk 23:24
sword that is against her on every **s**. Ezk 28:23
you push with **s** and shoulder, Ezk 34:21
And the **s** rooms, one reed long and one Ezk 40:7
and the space between the **s** rooms, five Ezk 40:7
And there were three **s** rooms on either Ezk 40:10
side rooms on either **s** of the east gate. Ezk 40:10
the jambs on either **s** were of the same Ezk 40:10
was a barrier before the **s** rooms, Ezk 40:12
the side rooms, one cubit on either **s**. Ezk 40:12
And the **s** rooms were six cubits on Ezk 40:12
side rooms were six cubits on either **s**. Ezk 40:12
ceiling of the one **s** room to the ceiling Ezk 40:13
inwards toward the **s** rooms and Ezk 40:16
pavement ran along the **s** of the gates, Ezk 40:18
cubits on the east **s** and on the north Ezk 40:19
on the east side and on the north **s**. Ezk 40:19
Its **s** rooms, three on either side, and its Ezk 40:21
Its side rooms, three on either **s**, and its Ezk 40:21
trees on its jambs, one on either **s**. Ezk 40:26
Its **s** rooms, its jambs, and its Ezk 40:29
me to the inner court on the east **s**, Ezk 40:32
Its **s** rooms, its jambs, and its Ezk 40:33
palm trees on its jambs, on either **s**, Ezk 40:34
Its **s** rooms, its jambs, and its Ezk 40:36
palm trees on its jambs, on either **s**, Ezk 40:37
of the gate were two tables on either **s**, Ezk 40:39
And off to the **s**, on the outside as one Ezk 40:40
and off to the other **s** of the vestibule of Ezk 40:40
tables were on either **s** of the gate, Ezk 40:41
one at the **s** of the north gate facing Ezk 40:44
the other at the **s** of the south gate Ezk 40:44
of the vestibule, five cubits on either **s**. Ezk 40:48
the gate were three cubits on either **s**. Ezk 40:48
beside the jambs, one on either **s**. Ezk 40:49
On each **s** six cubits was the breadth of Ezk 41:1
entrance were five cubits on either **s**. Ezk 41:2
the sidewalls on either **s** of the entrance, Ezk 41:3
and the breadth of the **s** chambers, Ezk 41:5
And the **s** chambers were in three Ezk 41:6
to serve as supports for the **s** chambers, Ezk 41:6
as it wound upward to the **s** chambers, Ezk 41:7
of the **s** chambers measured Ezk 41:8
outer wall of the **s** chambers was five Ezk 41:9
space between the **s** chambers of the Ezk 41:9
all around the temple on every **s**. Ezk 41:10
the doors of the **s** chambers opened on Ezk 41:11
yard on the west **s** was seventy cubits Ezk 41:12
the back and its galleries on either **s**, Ezk 41:15
face toward the palm tree on the one **s**, Ezk 41:19
toward the palm tree on the other **s**. Ezk 41:19
windows and palm trees on either **s**, Ezk 41:26
the **s** chambers of the temple, Ezk 41:26
was an entrance on the east **s**, Ezk 42:9
measured the east **s** with the Ezk 42:16
He measured the north **s**, 500 cubits Ezk 42:17
He measured the south **s**, 500 cubits Ezk 42:18
he turned to the west **s** and measured, Ezk 42:19
which was at the **s** of the gate, Ezk 46:19
water was trickling out on the south **s**. Ezk 47:2
trees on the one **s** and on the other. Ezk 47:7
On the north **s**, from the Great Sea by Ezk 47:15
to the north. This shall be the north **s**. Ezk 47:17
"On the east **s**, the boundary shall run Ezk 47:18

far as Tamar. This shall be the east **s**. Ezk 47:18
"On the south **s**, it shall run from Ezk 47:19
Great Sea. This shall be the south **s**. Ezk 47:19
"On the west **s**, the Great Sea shall be Ezk 47:20
This shall be the west **s**. Ezk 47:20
extending from the east **s** to the west, Ezk 48:1
of Dan, from the east **s** to the west, Ezk 48:2
of Asher, from the east **s** to the west, Ezk 48:3
of Naphtali, from the east **s** to the west, Ezk 48:4
of Manasseh, from the east **s** to the west, Ezk 48:5
of Ephraim, from the east **s** to the west, Ezk 48:6
of Reuben, from the east **s** to the west, Ezk 48:7
of Judah, from the east **s** to the west, Ezk 48:8
portions, from the east **s** to the west, Ezk 48:8
25,000 cubits on the northern **s**, Ezk 48:10
cubits in breadth on the western **s**, Ezk 48:10
10,000 in breadth on the eastern **s**, Ezk 48:10
25,000 in length on the southern **s**, Ezk 48:10
the north **s** 4,500 cubits, Ezk 48:16
side 4,500 cubits, the south **s** 4,500, Ezk 48:16
the south side 4,500, the east **s** 4,500, Ezk 48:16
east side 4,500, and the west **s** 4,500. Ezk 48:16
the tribes: from the east **s** to the west, Ezk 48:23
Benjamin, from the east **s** to the west, Ezk 48:24
of Simeon, from the east **s** to the west, Ezk 48:25
of Issachar, from the east **s** to the west, Ezk 48:26
of Zebulun, from the east **s** to the west, Ezk 48:27
On the north **s**, which is to be 4,500 Ezk 48:30
On the east **s**, which is to be 4,500 Ezk 48:32
On the south **s**, which is to be 4,500 Ezk 48:33
On the west **s**, which is to be 4,500 Ezk 48:34
one, like a bear. It was raised up on one **s**. Dn 7:5
contends by my **s** against these except Dn 10:21
out according to what is on one **s**, Zec 5:3
out according to what is on the other **s**. Zec 5:3
he gave orders to go over to the other **s**. Mt 8:18
And when he came to the other **s**, to the Mt 8:28
boat and go before him to the other **s**, Mt 14:22
When the disciples reached the other **s**, Mt 16:5
them, "Let us go across to the other **s**." Mk 4:35
They came to the other **s** of the sea, to the Mk 5:1
crossed again in the boat to the other **s**, Mk 5:21
boat and go before him to the other **s**, Mk 6:45
the boat again, and went to the other **s**. Mk 8:13
saw a young man sitting on the right **s**, Mk 16:5
standing on the right **s** of the altar of Lk 1:11
go across to the other **s** of the lake." So Lk 8:22
hearts, took a child and put him by his **s** Lk 9:47
he saw him he passed by on the other **s**. Lk 10:31
and saw him, passed by on the other **s**. Lk 10:32
carried by the angels to Abraham's **s**. Lk 16:22
Abraham far off and Lazarus at his **s**. Lk 16:23
up the sky from one **s** to the other, Lk 17:24
you and hem you in on every **s** Lk 19:43
the only God, who is at the Father's **s**, he Jn 1:18
went away to the other **s** of the Sea of Jn 6:1
remained on the other **s** of the sea saw Jn 6:22
they found him on the other **s** of the sea, Jn 6:25
with him two others, one on either **s**, Jn 19:18
of the soldiers pierced his **s** with a spear, Jn 19:34
he showed them his hands and his **s**. Jn 20:20
the nails, and place my hand into his **s**, Jn 20:25
put out your hand, and place it in my **s**. Jn 20:27
"Cast the net on the right **s** of the boat, Jn 21:6
struck Peter on the **s** and woke him, Acts 12:7
with one mind striving **s** by side for the Phil 1:27
mind striving side by **s** for the faith of Phil 1:27
who have labored **s** by side with me in Phil 4:3
have labored side by **s** with me in the Phil 4:3
the throne, on each **s** of the throne, Rv 4:6
also, on either **s** of the river, the tree of Rv 22:2

SIDED (1)
some **s** with the Jews and some with Acts 14:4

SIDES (41)
into the rings on the **s** of the ark to Ex 25:14
shall be six branches going out of its **s**, Ex 25:32
shall hang over the **s** of the tabernacle, Ex 26:13
poles are on the two **s** of the altar when it Ex 27:7
and throw it against the **s** of the altar. Ex 29:16
of the blood against the **s** of the altar. Ex 29:20
its top and around its **s** and its horns. Ex 30:3
molding on two opposite **s** of it you shall Ex 30:4
tablets that were written on both **s**; Ex 32:15
into the rings on the **s** of the ark to carry Ex 37:5
were six branches going out of its **s**, Ex 37:18
its top and around its **s** and its horns. Ex 37:26
its molding, on two opposite **s** of it, Ex 37:27
through the rings on the **s** of the altar to Ex 38:7
On both **s** of the gate of the court were Ex 38:15
the blood against the **s** of the altar that Lv 1:5
throw its blood against the **s** of the altar. Lv 1:11
throw the blood against the **s** of the altar. Lv 3:2
throw its blood against the **s** of the altar. Lv 3:8
throw its blood against the **s** of the altar. Lv 3:13
shall be thrown against the **s** of the altar. Lv 7:2
threw the blood against the **s** of the altar. Lv 8:19
threw the blood against the **s** of the altar. Lv 8:24
and he threw it against the **s** of the altar. Lv 9:12
and he threw it against the **s** of the altar. Lv 9:18
in your eyes and thorns in your **s**, Nm 33:55
stood on opposite **s** of the ark before the Jos 8:33
a whip on your **s** and thorns in your Jos 23:13
but they shall become thorns in your **s**, Jgs 2:3
he had peace on all **s** around him. 1 Kgs 4:24
The gatekeepers were on the four **s**, 1 Chr 9:24
For my **s** are filled with burning, and Ps 38:7
dove that nests in the **s** of the mouth of Jer 48:28
were ninety-six pomegranates on the **s**; Jer 52:23
wings on their four **s** they had human Ezk 1:8
desolate and crushed you from all **s**, Ezk 36:3
He measured it on the four **s**. It had a Ezk 42:20
the land on both **s** of the holy district Ezk 45:7
on the banks, on both **s** of the river, Ezk 47:12
"What remains on both **s** of the holy Ezk 48:21
the covenant covered on all **s** with gold, Heb 9:4

SIDEWALLS (4)
and the **s** of the gate were three cubits Ezk 40:48
and the **s** of the entrance were five Ezk 41:2
and the **s** on either side of the entrance, Ezk 41:3
on either side, on the **s** of the vestibule, Ezk 41:26

SIDING (1)
witness in a lawsuit, **s** with the many, Ex 23:2

SIDON (34)
Canaan fathered **S** his firstborn and Gn 10:15
Canaanites extended from **S** in the Gn 10:19
for ships, and his border shall be at **S**. Gn 49:13
as far as Great **S** and Misrephoth-maim, Jos 11:8
Hammon, Kanah, as far as **S** the Great. Jos 19:28
or the inhabitants of **S** or of Ahlab or of Jgs 1:31
the gods of Syria, the gods of **S**, Jgs 10:6
no deliverer because it was far from **S**, Jgs 18:28
and from Dan they went around to **S**, 2 Sm 24:6
go to Zarephath, which belongs to **S**, 1 Kgs 17:9
Canaan fathered **S** his firstborn and 1 Chr 1:13
the merchants of **S**, who cross the sea, Is 23:2
Be ashamed, O **S**, for the sea has spoken, Is 23:4
exult, O oppressed virgin daughter of **S**; Is 23:12
all the kings of Tyre, all the kings of **S**, Jer 25:22
and the king of **S** by the hand of the Jer 27:3
off from Tyre and **S** every helper that Jer 47:4
The inhabitants of **S** and Arvad were Ezk 27:8
"Son of man, set your face toward **S**, Ezk 28:21
"Behold, I am against you, O **S**, and I Ezk 28:22
"What are you to me, O Tyre and **S**, and all Jl 3:4
also, which borders on it, Tyre and **S**, Zec 9:2
in you had been done in Tyre and **S**, Mt 11:21
judgment for Tyre and **S** than for you. Mt 11:22
withdrew to the district of Tyre and **S**. Mt 15:21
the Jordan and from around Tyre and **S**. Mk 3:8
went away to the region of Tyre and **S**. Mk 7:24
of Tyre and went through **S** to the Sea of Mk 7:31
but only to Zarephath, in the land of **S**, Lk 4:26
and the seacoast of Tyre and **S**, Lk 6:17
in you had been done in Tyre and **S**, Lk 10:13
judgment for Tyre and **S** than for you. Lk 10:14
angry with the people of Tyre and **S**, Acts 12:20
The next day we put in at **S**. And Julius Acts 27:3

SIDONIAN (1)
Edomite, **S**, and Hittite women, 1 Kgs 11:1

SIDONIANS (15)
(the **S** call Hermon Sirion, while the Dt 3:9
and Mearah that belongs to the **S**, Jos 13:4
to Misrephoth-maim, even all the **S**. Jos 13:6
the Canaanites and the **S** and the Hivites Jgs 3:3
The **S** also, and the Amalekites and the Jgs 10:12
in security, after the manner of the **S**, Jgs 18:7
were far from the **S** and had no dealings Jgs 18:7
knows how to cut timber like the **S**." 1 Kgs 5:6
after Ashtoreth the goddess of the **S**, 1 Kgs 11:5
Ashtoreth the goddess of the **S**, 1 Kgs 11:33
daughter of Ethbaal king of the **S**, 1 Kgs 16:31
Ashtoreth the abomination of the **S**, 2 Kgs 23:13
for the **S** and Tyrians brought great 1 Chr 22:4
and oil to the **S** and the Tyrians to bring Ezr 3:7
are there, all of them, and all the **S**, Ezk 32:30

SIEGE (33)
in the **s** and in the distress with which Dt 28:53
in the **s** and in the distress with which Dt 28:55
in the **s** and in the distress with which Dt 28:57
to Lachish and laid **s** to it and fought Jos 10:31
And they laid **s** to it and fought against Jos 10:34
Israel were laying **s** to Gibbethon. 1 Kgs 15:27
or cast up a **s** mound against it. 2 Kgs 19:32
against Jerusalem and laid **s** to it. 2 Kgs 25:1
that you endure the **s** in Jerusalem? 2 Chr 32:10
have cast up their **s** ramp against me Jb 19:12
Go up, O Elam; lay **s**, O Media; all the Is 21:2
They erected their **s** towers, they stripped Is 23:13
a shield or cast up a **s** mound against it. Is 37:33
cast up a **s** mound against Jerusalem. Jer 6:6
the ground, O you who dwell under **s**! Jer 10:17
his neighbor in the **s** and in the distress, Jer 19:9
the **s** mounds have come up to the city Jer 32:24
defense against the **s** mounds and Jer 33:4
army against Jerusalem, and laid **s** to it. Jer 52:4
against it, and build a **s** wall against it, Ezk 4:2
face toward it, and let it be in a state of **s**, Ezk 4:3
a state of siege, and press the **s** against it. Ezk 4:3
set your face toward the **s** of Jerusalem, Ezk 4:7
you have completed the days of your **s**. Ezk 4:8
when the days of the **s** are completed. Ezk 5:2
are cast up and **s** walls built to cut Ezk 17:17
to cast up mounds, to build **s** towers. Ezk 21:22
of Babylon has laid **s** to Jerusalem this Ezk 24:2
He will set up a **s** wall against you and Ezk 26:8
O daughter of troops; **s** is laid against us; Mi 5:1
hasten to the wall; the **s** tower is set up. Na 2:5
Draw water for the **s**; strengthen your Na 3:14
The **s** of Jerusalem will also be against Zec 12:2

SIEGEWORKS (7)
that you may build **s** against the city Dt 20:20
to it. And they built **s** all around it. 2 Kgs 25:1
besieged it, building great **s** against it. Eccl 9:14
with towers and I will raise **s** against you. Is 29:3
siege to it. And they built **s** all around it. Jer 52:4
And put **s** against it, and build a siege Ezk 4:2
come and throw up **s** and take a Dn 11:15

SIEVE (2)
sift the nations with the **s** of destruction, Is 30:28
all the nations as one shakes with a **s**, Am 9:9

SIFT (2)
to **s** the nations with the sieve of Is 30:28
you, that he might **s** you like wheat, Lk 22:31

SIGH (4)
we bring our years to an end like a **s**. Ps 90:9
vine languishes, all the merry-hearted **s**. Is 24:7
of the men who **s** and groan over all Ezk 9:4
S, but not aloud; make no mourning Ezk 24:17

SIGHED (2)
up to heaven, he **s** and said to him, Mk 7:34
And he **s** deeply in his spirit and said, Mk 8:12

SIGHING (6)
For my **s** comes instead of my bread, and Jb 3:24
spent with sorrow, and my years with **s**; Ps 31:10
before you; my **s** is not hidden from you. Ps 38:9
all the **s** she has caused I bring to an end. Is 21:2
joy, and sorrow and **s** shall flee away. Is 35:10
joy, and sorrow and **s** shall flee away. Is 51:11

SIGHT (288)
that is pleasant to the **s** and good for food. Gn 2:9
Now the earth was corrupt in God's **s**, Gn 6:11
"O Lord, if I have found favor in your **s**, Gn 18:3
your servant has found favor in your **s**, Gn 19:19
that I may bury my dead out of my **s**." Gn 23:4
that I should bury my dead out of my **s**, Gn 23:8
In the **s** of the sons of my people I give it Gn 23:11
to him, "If I have found favor in your **s**, Gn 30:27
me, when we are out of one another's **s**. Gn 31:49
order that I may find favor in your **s**.'" Gn 32:5
"To find favor in the **s** of my lord." Gn 33:8
please, if I have found favor in your **s**, Gn 33:10
Let me find favor in the **s** of my lord." Gn 33:15
was wicked in the **s** of the LORD, Gn 38:7
he did was wicked in the **s** of the LORD, Gn 38:10
found favor in his **s** and attended him, Gn 39:4
gave him favor in the **s** of the keeper of Gn 39:21
is nothing left in the **s** of my lord but Gn 47:18
"If now I have found favor in your **s**, Gn 47:29
said, "I will turn aside to see this great **s**, Ex 3:3
people favor in the **s** of the Egyptians; Ex 3:21
and did the signs in the **s** of the people. Ex 4:30
us stink in the **s** of Pharaoh and his Ex 5:21
In the **s** of Pharaoh and in the sight of Ex 7:20
Pharaoh and in the **s** of his servants he Ex 7:20
throw them in the air in the **s** of Pharaoh. Ex 9:8
the people favor in the **s** of the Egyptians. Ex 11:3
in the **s** of Pharaoh's servants and in the Ex 11:3
servants and in the **s** of the people. Ex 11:3
people favor in the **s** of the Egyptians, Ex 12:36
did so, in the **s** of the elders of Israel. Ex 17:6
Mount Sinai in the **s** of all the people. Ex 19:11
of the mountain in the **s** of the people of Ex 24:17
and you have also found favor in my **s**.' Ex 33:12
if I have found favor in your **s**, Ex 33:13
you in order to find favor in your **s**. Ex 33:13
that I have found favor in your **s**, Ex 33:16
do, for you have found favor in my **s**, Ex 33:17
"If now I have found favor in your **s**, Ex 34:9

in the **s** of all the house of Israel Ex 40:38
be cut off in the **s** of the children of Lv 20:17
a defect in his **s** or an itching disease Lv 21:20
not rule ruthlessly over him in your **s**. Lv 25:53
the land of Egypt in the **s** of the nations, Lv 26:45
why have I not found favor in your **s**, Nm 11:11
me at once, if I find favor in your **s**, Nm 11:15
And the heifer shall be burned in his **s**. Nm 19:5
Mount Hor in the **s** of all the Nm 20:27
Now therefore, if it is evil in your **s**, I Nm 22:34
in the **s** of Moses and in the sight of the Nm 25:6
Moses and in the **s** of the whole Nm 25:6
you shall commission him in their **s**. Nm 27:19
said, "If we have found favor in your **s**, Nm 32:5
had done evil in the **s** of the LORD was Nm 32:13
out triumphantly in the **s** of all the Nm 33:3
your understanding in the **s** of the peoples, Dt 4:6
what is evil in the **s** of the LORD your God, Dt 4:25
is right and good in the **s** of the LORD, Dt 6:18
what was evil in the **s** of the LORD to Dt 9:18
you do what is right in the **s** of the LORD. Dt 12:25
good and right in the **s** of the LORD your Dt 12:28
what is right in the **s** of the LORD your Dt 13:18
what is evil in the **s** of the LORD your God, Dt 17:2
you do what is right in the **s** of the LORD. Dt 21:9
your brother be degraded in your **s**. Dt 25:3
and said to him in the **s** of all Israel, Dt 31:7
will do what is evil in the **s** of the LORD, Dt 31:29
that Moses did in the **s** of all Israel. Dt 34:12
begin to exalt you in the **s** of all Israel, Jos 3:7
LORD exalted Joshua in the **s** of all Israel, Jos 4:14
good and right in your **s** to do to us, Jos 9:25
of Israel, and he said in the **s** of Israel, Jos 10:12
before you and drive them out of your **s**. Jos 23:5
great signs in our **s** and preserved us in Jos 24:17
what was evil in the **s** of the LORD and Jgs 2:11
did what was evil in the **s** of the LORD. Jgs 3:7
did what was evil in the **s** of the LORD, Jgs 3:12
done what was evil in the **s** of the LORD. Jgs 3:12
what was evil in the **s** of the LORD after Jgs 4:1
did what was evil in the **s** of the LORD, Jgs 6:1
angel of the LORD vanished from his **s**. Jgs 6:21
what was evil in the **s** of the LORD and Jgs 10:6
did what was evil in the **s** of the LORD, Jgs 13:1
after him in whose **s** I shall find favor." Ru 2:2
was very great in the **s** of the LORD, 1 Sm 2:17
you have done in the **s** of the LORD, 1 Sm 12:17
what was evil in the **s** of the LORD?" 1 Sm 15:19
for he has found favor in my **s**." 1 Sm 16:22
this was good in the **s** of all the people 1 Sm 18:5
and also in the **s** of Saul's servants. 1 Sm 18:5
life was precious this day in my **s**, 1 Sm 26:24
life be precious in the **s** of the LORD, 1 Sm 26:24
as blameless in my **s** as an angel of 1 Sm 29:9
of the LORD, to do what is evil in his **s**? 2 Sm 12:9
with your wives in the **s** of this sun. 2 Sm 12:11
to eat, and prepare the food in my **s**, 2 Sm 13:5
and make a couple of cakes in my **s**, 2 Sm 13:6
made cakes in his **s** and baked the 2 Sm 13:8
that I have found favor in your **s**, 2 Sm 14:22
let me ever find favor in your **s**, my 2 Sm 16:4
concubines in the **s** of all Israel. 2 Sm 16:22
according to my cleanness in his **s**. 2 Sm 22:25
compassion in the **s** of those who 1 Kgs 8:50
for my name I will cast out of my **s**, 1 Kgs 9:7
what was evil in the **s** of the LORD and 1 Kgs 11:6
great favor in the **s** of Pharaoh, 1 Kgs 11:19
is right in my **s** and keeping my 1 Kgs 11:33
what was evil in the **s** of the LORD, 1 Kgs 14:22
was evil in the **s** of the LORD and 1 Kgs 15:26
was evil in the **s** of the LORD and 1 Kgs 15:34
evil that he did in the **s** of the LORD, 1 Kgs 16:7
doing evil in the **s** of the LORD, 1 Kgs 16:19
what was evil in the **s** of the LORD, 1 Kgs 16:25
of Omri did evil in the **s** of the LORD, 1 Kgs 16:30
to do what is evil in the **s** of the LORD. 1 Kgs 21:20
was evil in the **s** of the LORD like 1 Kgs 21:25
what was right in the **s** of the LORD. 1 Kgs 22:43
was evil in the **s** of the LORD and 1 Kgs 22:52
of yours, be precious in your **s**. 2 Kgs 1:13
now let my life be precious in your **s**." 2 Kgs 1:14
did what was evil in the **s** of the LORD, 2 Kgs 3:2
is a light thing in the **s** of the LORD. 2 Kgs 3:18
did what was evil in the **s** of the LORD. 2 Kgs 8:18
did what was evil in the **s** of the LORD, 2 Kgs 8:27
what was evil in the **s** of the LORD and 2 Kgs 13:2
what was evil in the **s** of the LORD. 2 Kgs 13:11
what was evil in the **s** of the LORD. 2 Kgs 14:24
did what was evil in the **s** of the LORD, 2 Kgs 15:9
what was evil in the **s** of the LORD. 2 Kgs 15:18
what was evil in the **s** of the LORD. 2 Kgs 15:24
what was evil in the **s** of the LORD. 2 Kgs 15:28
did what was evil in the **s** of the LORD, 2 Kgs 17:2
to do evil in the **s** of the LORD, 2 Kgs 17:17
and removed them out of his **s**. 2 Kgs 17:18
until he had cast them out of his **s**. 2 Kgs 17:20
the LORD removed Israel out of his **s**, 2 Kgs 17:23
is good in your **s**." And Hezekiah wept 2 Kgs 20:3
did what was evil in the **s** of the LORD, 2 Kgs 21:2
He did much evil in the **s** of the LORD, 2 Kgs 21:6
is evil in my **s** and have provoked 2 Kgs 21:15
what was evil in the **s** of the LORD. 2 Kgs 21:16
what was evil in the **s** of the LORD, 2 Kgs 21:20
will remove Judah also out of my **s**, 2 Kgs 23:27
what was evil in the **s** of the LORD, 2 Kgs 23:32
what was evil in the **s** of the LORD, 2 Kgs 23:37
the LORD, to remove them out of his **s**, 2 Kgs 24:3
did what was evil in the **s** of the LORD, 2 Kgs 24:9
what was evil in the **s** of the LORD, 2 Kgs 24:19
firstborn, was evil in the **s** of the LORD, 1 Chr 2:3
Now therefore in the **s** of all Israel, 1 Chr 28:8
very great in the **s** of all Israel and 1 Chr 29:25
for my name, I will cast out of my **s**, 2 Chr 7:20
what was right in the **s** of the LORD. 2 Chr 20:32
did what was evil in the **s** of the LORD. 2 Chr 21:6
did what was evil in the **s** of the LORD, 2 Chr 22:4
what was evil in the **s** of the LORD our 2 Chr 29:6
was exalted in the **s** of all nations 2 Chr 32:23
did what was evil in the **s** of the LORD, 2 Chr 33:2
He did much evil in the **s** of the LORD, 2 Chr 33:6
what was evil in the **s** of the LORD, 2 Chr 33:22
what was evil in the **s** of the LORD his 2 Chr 36:5
did what was evil in the **s** of the LORD. 2 Chr 36:9
what was evil in the **s** of the LORD his 2 Chr 36:12
him mercy in the **s** of this man." Now Neh 1:11
your servant has found favor in your **s**, Neh 2:5
not their sin be blotted out from your **s**, Neh 4:5
the book in the **s** of all the people, Neh 8:5
and favor in his **s** more than all the Est 2:17
in the court, she won favor in his **s**, Est 5:2
If I have found favor in the **s** of the king, Est 5:8
answered, "If I have found favor in your **s**, Est 7:3
king, and if I have found favor in his **s**, Est 8:5
and the heavens are not pure in his **s**; Jb 15:15
as cattle? Why are we stupid in your **s**? Jb 18:3
they do not hesitate to spit at the **s** of me. Jb 30:10
is false; he is laid low even at the **s** of him. Jb 41:9
your judgments are on high, out of his **s**; Ps 10:5
to the cleanness of my hands in his **s**. Ps 18:24
of my heart be acceptable in your **s**, Ps 19:14
in the **s** of the children of mankind! Ps 31:19
cut off from your **s**." But you heard the Ps 31:22
at the **s** of the enemy and the avenger. Ps 44:16
I sinned and done what is evil in your **s**, Ps 51:4
life, and precious is their blood in his **s**. Ps 72:14
In the **s** of their fathers he performed Ps 78:12
thousand years in your **s** are but as Ps 90:4
his righteousness in the **s** of the nations. Ps 98:2
Precious in the **s** of the LORD is the Ps 116:15
vain is a net spread in the **s** of any bird, Prv 1:17
good success in the **s** of God and man. Prv 3:4
do not lose **s** of these—keep sound Prv 3:21
the only one in the **s** of my mother, Prv 4:3
Let them not escape from your **s**; keep Prv 4:21
Better is the **s** of the eyes than the Eccl 6:9
of your heart and the **s** of your eyes. Eccl 11:9
their own eyes, and shrewd in their own **s**! Is 5:21
is good in your **s**." And Hezekiah wept Is 38:3
And I will cast you out of my **s**, as I cast Jer 7:15
the sons of Judah have done evil in my **s**, Jer 7:30
Send them out of my **s**, and let them go! Jer 15:1
and if it does evil in my **s**, not listening Jer 18:10
nor blot out their sin from your **s**. Jer 18:23
break the flask in the **s** of the men who Jer 19:10
but evil in my **s** from their youth. Jer 32:30
day, so that I will remove it from my **s** Jer 32:31
they are no longer a nation in their **s**. Jer 33:24
Tahpanhes, in the **s** of the men of Judah, Jer 43:9
he did what was evil in the **s** of the LORD, Jer 52:2
baking it in their **s** on human dung." Ezk 4:12
in your midst in the **s** of the nations. Ezk 5:8
around you and in the **s** of all who pass Ezk 5:14
loathsome in their own **s** for the evils Ezk 6:9
and go into exile by day in their **s**. Ezk 12:3
your place to another place in their **s**. Ezk 12:3
out your baggage by day in their **s**, Ezk 12:4
go out yourself at evening in their **s**, Ezk 12:4
In their **s** dig through the wall, and Ezk 12:5
In their **s** you shall lift the baggage Ezk 12:6
carrying it on my shoulder in their **s**. Ezk 12:7
upon you in the **s** of many women. Ezk 16:41
be profaned in the **s** of the nations Ezk 20:9
in whose **s** I made myself known to Ezk 20:9
not be profaned in the **s** of the nations, Ezk 20:14
in whose **s** I had brought them out. Ezk 20:14
not be profaned in the **s** of the nations, Ezk 20:22
in whose **s** I had brought them out. Ezk 20:22
among you in the **s** of the nations. Ezk 20:41
your own doing in the **s** of the nations, Ezk 22:16
on the earth in the **s** of all who saw Ezk 28:18
in them in the **s** of the nations, Ezk 28:25
that it was in the **s** of all who passed Ezk 36:34
my holiness in the **s** of many nations. Ezk 39:27
its laws, and write it down in their **s**, Ezk 43:11
and compassion in the **s** of the chief of Dn 1:9
her lewdness in the **s** of her lovers, Hos 2:10
if they hide from my **s** at the bottom of Am 9:3
I said, 'I am driven away from your **s**; Jon 2:4
it is marvelous in the **s** of the remnant of Zec 8:6
should it also be marvelous in my **s**, Zec 8:6
does evil is good in the **s** of the LORD, Mal 2:17
the blind receive their **s** and the lame Mt 11:5
they recovered their **s** and followed Mt 20:34
he opened his eyes, his **s** was restored, Mk 8:25
to him, "Rabbi, let me recover my **s**." Mk 10:51
he recovered his **s** and followed him Mk 10:52
captives and recovering of **s** to the blind, Lk 4:18
on many who were blind he bestowed **s**. Lk 7:21
the blind receive their **s**, the lame walk, Lk 7:22
men is an abomination in the **s** of God. Lk 16:15
He said, "Lord, let me recover my **s**." Lk 18:41
And Jesus said to him, "Recover your **s**; Lk 18:42
he recovered his **s** and followed him, Lk 18:43
him. And he vanished from their **s**. Lk 24:31
So I went and washed and received my **s**." Jn 9:11
asked him how he had received his **s**. Jn 9:15
he had been blind and had received his **s**, Jn 9:18
of the man who had received his **s** Jn 9:18
up, and a cloud took him out of their **s**. Acts 1:9
it is right in the **s** of God to listen to Acts 4:19
born; and he was beautiful in God's **s**. Acts 7:20
Moses saw it, he was amazed at the **s**, Acts 7:31
found favor in the **s** of God and asked Acts 7:46
And for three days he was without **s**, Acts 9:9
on him so that he might regain his **s**." Acts 9:12
you may regain your **s** and be filled Acts 9:17
from his eyes, and he regained his **s**. Acts 9:18
and burned them in the **s** of all. Acts 19:19
When we had come in **s** of Cyprus, Acts 21:3
to me, 'Brother Saul, receive your **s**.' Acts 22:13
hour I received my **s** and saw him. Acts 22:13
human being will be justified in his **s**, Rom 3:20
to do what is honorable in the **s** of all. Rom 12:17
in the **s** of God we speak in Christ. 2 Cor 2:17
everyone's conscience in the **s** of God. 2 Cor 4:2
for we walk by faith, not by **s**. 2 Cor 5:7
be revealed to you in the **s** of God. 2 Cor 7:12
only in the Lord's **s** but also in the 2 Cor 8:21
Lord's sight but also in the **s** of man. 2 Cor 8:21
It is in the **s** of God that we have 2 Cor 12:19
it is pleasing in the **s** of God our Savior, 1 Tm 2:3
for this is pleasing in the **s** of God. 1 Tm 5:4
And no creature is hidden from his **s**, Heb 4:13
so terrifying was the **s** that Moses said, Heb 12:21
in us that which is pleasing in his **s**, Heb 13:21
by men but in the **s** of God chosen and 1 Pt 2:4
this is a gracious thing in the **s** of God. 1 Pt 2:20
spirit, which in God's **s** is very precious. 1 Pt 3:4
your works complete in the **s** of my God. Rv 3:2

SIGHTS (2)

driven mad by the **s** that your eyes see. Dt 28:34
feel, and the **s** that your eyes shall see. Dt 28:67

SIGN (100)

"This is the **s** of the covenant that I Gn 9:12
it shall be a **s** of the covenant between Gn 9:13
"This is the **s** of the covenant that I have Gn 9:17
it shall be a **s** of the covenant between Gn 17:11
It is a **s** of your innocence in the eyes of Gn 20:16
with you, and this shall be the **s** for you, Ex 3:12
you," God said, "or listen to the first **s**, Ex 4:8
the first sign, they may believe the latter **s**. Ex 4:8
people. Tomorrow this **s** shall happen."'" Ex 8:23
The blood shall be a **s** for you, on the Ex 12:13
be to you as a **s** on your hand and as Ex 13:9
for this is a **s** between me and you Ex 31:13
It is a **s** forever between me and the Ex 31:17
Thus they shall be a **s** to the people of Nm 16:38
to be kept as a **s** for the rebels, Nm 17:10
You shall bind them as a **s** on your hand, Dt 6:8
shall bind them as a **s** on your hand, Dt 11:18
you and gives you a **s** or a wonder, Dt 13:1
and the **s** or wonder that he tells you Dt 13:2
They shall be a **s** and a wonder against Dt 28:46
my father's house, and give me a sure **s** Jos 2:12
that this may be a **s** among you. When Jos 4:6
then show me a **s** that it is you who Jgs 6:17
and Phinehas, shall be the **s** to you: 1 Sm 2:34
And this shall be the **s** to you that the 1 Sm 10:1
hand. And this shall be the **s** to us." 1 Sm 14:10
And he gave a **s** the same day, saying, 1 Kgs 13:3
"This is the **s** that the LORD has 1 Kgs 13:3
according to the **s** that the man of 1 Kgs 13:5
Now the men were watching for a **s**, 1 Kgs 20:33
but there was no sound or **s** of life. 2 Kgs 4:31

"And this shall be the **s** for you: this 2 Kgs 19:29
"What shall be the **s** that the LORD 2 Kgs 20:8
"This shall be the **s** to you from the 2 Kgs 20:9
he answered him and gave him a **s**. 2 Chr 32:24
to inquire about the **s** that had been 2 Chr 32:31
Show me a **s** of your favor, that those Ps 86:17
"Ask a **s** of the LORD your God; let it be Is 7:11
the Lord himself will give you a **s**. Is 7:14
It will be a **s** and a witness to the LORD of Is 19:20
for three years as a **s** and a portent against Is 20:3
"And this shall be the **s** for you: this year Is 37:30
"This shall be the **s** to you from the LORD, Is 38:7
"What is the **s** that I shall go up to the Is 38:22
an everlasting **s** that shall not be cut Is 55:13
and I will set a **s** among them. And from Is 66:19
This shall be the **s** to you, declares the Jer 44:29
it. This is a **s** for the house of Israel. Ezk 4:3
I have made you a **s** for the house of Ezk 12:6
Say, 'I am a **s** for you: as I have done, Ezk 12:11
I will make him a **s** and a byword and Ezk 14:8
as a **s** between me and them, Ezk 20:12
they may be a **s** between me and you, Ezk 20:20
Thus shall Ezekiel be to you a **s**; Ezk 24:24
So you will be a **s** to them, and they Ezk 24:27
bone, then he shall set up a **s** by it, Ezk 39:15
the injunction and **s** the document, Dn 6:8
Did you not **s** an injunction, that Dn 6:12
before you, for they are men who are a **s**: Zec 3:8
"Teacher, we wish to see a **s** from you." Mt 12:38
and adulterous generation seeks for a **s**, Mt 12:39
but no **s** will be given to it except the Mt 12:39
to it except the **s** of the prophet Jonah. Mt 12:39
him to show them a **s** from heaven. Mt 16:1
and adulterous generation seeks for a **s**, Mt 16:4
but no **s** will be given to it except the Mt 16:4
given to it except the **s** of Jonah." So he Mt 16:4
what will be the **s** of your coming and Mt 24:3
will appear in heaven the **s** of the Son of Mt 24:30
Now the betrayer had given them a **s**, Mt 26:48
seeking from him a **s** from heaven to Mk 8:11
"Why does this generation seek a **s**? Mk 8:12
no **s** will be given to this generation." Mk 8:12
what will be the **s** when all these things Mk 13:4
Now the betrayer had given them a **s**, Mk 14:44
And this will be a **s** for you: you will find Lk 2:12
in Israel, and for a **s** that is opposed Lk 2:34
seeking from him a **s** from heaven. Lk 11:16
It seeks for a **s**, but no sign will be Lk 11:29
but no **s** will be given to it except the Lk 11:29
will be given to it except the **s** of Jonah. Lk 11:29
as Jonah became a **s** to the people of Lk 11:30
what will be the **s** when these things are Lk 21:7
was hoping to see some **s** done by him. Lk 23:8
"What **s** do you show us for doing these Jn 2:18
was now the second **s** that Jesus did when Jn 4:54
the people saw the **s** that he had done, Jn 6:14
they said to him, "Then what **s** do you do, Jn 6:30
And they said, "John did no **s**, but Jn 10:41
was that they heard he had done this **s**. Jn 12:18
that a notable **s** has been performed Acts 4:16
man on whom this **s** of healing was Acts 4:22
He received the **s** of circumcision as a Rom 4:11
tongues are a **s** not for believers 1 Cor 14:22
prophecy is a **s** not for unbelievers 1 Cor 14:22
This is a clear **s** to them of their Phil 1:28
This is the **s** of genuineness in every 2 Thes 3:17
And a great **s** appeared in heaven: a Rv 12:1
And another **s** appeared in heaven: Rv 12:3
Then I saw another **s** in heaven, great Rv 15:1

SIGNAL (11)
Now the appointed **s** between the men Jgs 20:38
But when the **s** began to rise out of the Jgs 20:40
He will raise a **s** for nations afar off, and Is 5:26
who shall stand as a **s** for the peoples— Is 11:10
He will raise a **s** for the nations and will Is 11:12
On a bare hill raise a **s**; cry aloud to them; Is 13:2
when a **s** is raised on the mountains, Is 18:3
the top of a mountain, like a **s** on a hill. Is 30:17
nations, and raise my **s** to the peoples; Is 49:22
it of stones; lift up a **s** over the peoples. Is 62:10
Tekoa, and raise a **s** on Beth-haccherem, Jer 6:1

SIGNALED (1)
They **s** to their partners in the other boat Lk 5:7

SIGNALS (1)
winks with his eyes, **s** with his feet, Prv 6:13

SIGNATURE (1)
that I had one to hear me! (Here is my **s**! Jb 31:35

SIGNED (6)
I **s** the deed, sealed it, got witnesses, and Jer 32:10
of the witnesses who **s** the deed of Jer 32:12
and deeds shall be **s** and sealed and Jer 32:44
Therefore King Darius **s** the document Dn 6:9
knew that the document had been **s**, Dn 6:10
O king, or the injunction you have **s**, Dn 6:13

SIGNET (18)
"Your **s** and your cord and your staff Gn 38:18
are, the **s** and the cord and the staff." Gn 38:25
Then Pharaoh took his **s** ring from his Gn 41:42
engrave on it, like the engraving of a **s**, Ex 28:36
and earrings and **s** rings and armlets, Ex 35:22
and engraved like the engravings of a **s**, Ex 39:6
inscription, like the engraving of a **s**, Ex 39:30
of gold, armlets and bracelets, **s** rings, Nm 31:50
the king took his **s** ring from his hand Est 3:10
and sealed with the king's **s** ring. Est 3:12
And the king took off his **s** ring, which Est 8:2
and sealed it with the king's **s** ring. Est 8:10
the **s** rings and nose rings; Is 3:21
were the **s** ring on my right hand, Jer 22:24
"You were the **s** of perfection, full of Ezk 28:12
it with his own **s** and with the signet Dn 6:17
own signet and with the **s** of his lords, Dn 6:17
the LORD, and make you like a **s** ring, Hg 2:23

SIGNETS (3)
As a jeweler engraves **s**, so shall you Ex 28:11
They shall be like **s**, each engraved Ex 28:21
They were like **s**, each engraved with its Ex 39:14

SIGNIFICANT (1)
count others more **s** than yourselves. Phil 2:3

SIGNPOST (1)
And make a **s**; make it at the head of Ezk 21:19

SIGNS (78)
And let them be for **s** and for seasons, Gn 1:14
believe even these two **s** or listen to your Ex 4:9
this staff, with which you shall do the **s**." Ex 4:17
and all the **s** that he had commanded Ex 4:28
to Moses and did the **s** in the sight of the Ex 4:30
though I multiply my **s** and wonders in Ex 7:3
I may show these **s** of mine among them, Ex 10:1
the Egyptians and what **s** I have done Ex 10:2
in spite of all the **s** that I have done Nm 14:11
seen my glory and my **s** that I did in Nm 14:22
midst of another nation, by trials, by **s**, Dt 4:34
And the LORD showed **s** and wonders, Dt 6:22
the great trials that your eyes saw, the **s**, Dt 7:19
his **s** and his deeds that he did in Egypt to Dt 11:3
great deeds of terror, with **s** and wonders. Dt 26:8
the great trials that your eyes saw, the **s**, Dt 29:3
him for all the **s** and the wonders that Dt 34:11
who did those great **s** in our sight and Jos 24:17
Now when these **s** meet you, do what 1 Sm 10:7
And all these **s** came to pass that day. 1 Sm 10:9
and performed **s** and wonders against Neh 9:10
the ends of the earth are in awe at your **s**. Ps 65:8
place; they set up their own **s** for signs. Ps 74:4
place; they set up their own signs for **s**. Ps 74:4
We do not see our **s**; there is no longer Ps 74:9
when he performed his **s** in Egypt and Ps 78:43
They performed his **s** among them Ps 105:27
sent **s** and wonders against Pharaoh Ps 135:9
has given me are **s** and portents in Israel Is 8:18
who frustrates the **s** of liars and makes Is 44:25
be dismayed at the **s** of the heavens Jer 10:2
You have shown **s** and wonders in the Jer 32:20
of the land of Egypt with **s** and wonders, Jer 32:21
to me to show the **s** and wonders that the Dn 4:2
How great are his **s**, how mighty his Dn 4:3
he works **s** and wonders in heaven and Dn 6:27
you cannot interpret the **s** of the times. Mt 16:3
arise and perform great **s** and wonders, Mt 24:24
will arise and perform **s** and wonders, Mk 13:22
And these **s** will accompany those Mk 16:17
the message by accompanying **s**.]] Mk 16:20
And he kept making **s** to them and Lk 1:22
And they made **s** to his father, inquiring Lk 1:62
is not coming with **s** to be observed, Lk 17:20
will be terrors and great **s** from heaven. Lk 21:11
"And there will be **s** in sun and moon Lk 21:25
This, the first of his **s**, Jesus did at Cana Jn 2:11
when they saw the **s** that he was doing. Jn 2:23
no one can do these **s** that you do unless Jn 3:2
"Unless you see **s** and wonders you will Jn 4:48
because they saw the **s** that he was doing Jn 6:2
are seeking me, not because you saw **s**, Jn 6:26
will he do more **s** than this man has Jn 7:31
is a sinner do such **s**?" And there was a Jn 9:16
to do? For this man performs many **s**. Jn 11:47
he had done so many **s** before them, Jn 12:37
Jesus did many other **s** in the presence Jn 20:30
the heavens above and **s** on the earth Acts 2:19
works and wonders and **s** that God did Acts 2:22
many wonders and **s** were being done Acts 2:43
and **s** and wonders are performed Acts 4:30
Now many **s** and wonders were Acts 5:12
great wonders and **s** among the people. Acts 6:8
performing wonders and **s** in Egypt Acts 7:36
heard him and saw the **s** that he did. Acts 8:6
And seeing **s** and great miracles Acts 8:13
granting **s** and wonders to be done by Acts 14:3
they related what **s** and wonders God Acts 15:12
by the power of **s** and wonders, by the Rom 15:19
For Jews demand **s** and Greeks seek 1 Cor 1:22
The **s** of a true apostle were 2 Cor 12:12
with **s** and wonders and mighty 2 Cor 12:12
all power and false **s** and wonders, 2 Thes 2:9
also bore witness by **s** and wonders and Heb 2:4
It performs great **s**, even making fire Rv 13:13
and by the **s** that it is allowed to work Rv 13:14
they are demonic spirits, performing **s**, Rv 16:14
presence had done the **s** by which he Rv 19:20

SIHON (36)
Israel sent messengers to **S** king of the Nm 21:21
But **S** would not allow Israel to pass Nm 21:23
was the city of **S** the king of the Nm 21:26
built; let the city of **S** be established. Nm 21:27
Heshbon, flame from the city of **S**. Nm 21:28
captives, to an Amorite king, **S**. Nm 21:29
as you did to **S** king of the Amorites, Nm 21:34
the kingdom of **S** king of the Nm 32:33
after he had defeated **S** the king of the Dt 1:4
given into your hand **S** the Amorite, Dt 2:24
wilderness of Kedemoth to **S** the king of Dt 2:26
But **S** the king of Heshbon would not let Dt 2:30
I have begun to give **S** and his land over Dt 2:31
Then **S** came out against us, he and all Dt 2:32
him as you did to **S** the king of the Dt 3:2
as we did to **S** the king of Heshbon, Dt 3:6
in the land of **S** the king of the Amorites, Dt 4:46
S the king of Heshbon and Og the king Dt 29:7
will do to them as he did to **S** and Og, Dt 31:4
were beyond the Jordan, to **S** and Og, Jos 2:10
the Jordan, to **S** the king of Heshbon, Jos 9:10
S king of the Amorites who lived at Jos 12:2
to the boundary of **S** king of Heshbon. Jos 12:5
all the cities of **S** king of the Amorites, Jos 13:10
all the kingdom of **S** king of the Jos 13:21
Zur and Hur and Reba, the princes of **S**, Jos 13:21
of the kingdom of **S** king of Heshbon, Jos 13:27
then sent messengers to **S** king of the Jgs 11:19
but **S** did not trust Israel to pass Jgs 11:20
so **S** gathered all his people together Jgs 11:20
gave **S** and all his people into the hand Jgs 11:21
the country of **S** king of the Amorites 1 Kgs 4:19
of the land of **S** king of Heshbon and Neh 9:22
S, king of the Amorites, and Og, king Ps 135:11
S, king of the Amorites, for his Ps 136:19
Heshbon, flame from the house of **S**; Jer 48:45

SIKKUTH (1)
You shall take up **S** your king, and Am 5:26

SILAS (12)
sent Judas called Barsabbas, and **S**, Acts 15:22
We have therefore sent Judas and **S**, Acts 15:27
And Judas and **S**, who were Acts 15:32
but Paul chose **S** and departed, Acts 15:40
seized Paul and **S** and dragged them Acts 16:19
midnight Paul and **S** were praying Acts 16:25
fear he fell down before Paul and **S**. Acts 16:29
were persuaded and joined Paul and **S**, Acts 17:4
sent Paul and **S** away by night Acts 17:10
but **S** and Timothy remained there. Acts 17:14
a command for **S** and Timothy to Acts 17:15
When **S** and Timothy arrived from Acts 18:5

SILENCE (28)
gazed at her in **s** to learn whether the Gn 24:21
priests said to all Israel, "Keep **s** and hear, Dt 27:9
"**S**." And all his attendants went out Jgs 3:19
my eyes; there was **s**, then I heard a voice: Jb 4:16
Should your babble **s** men, and when Jb 11:3
"Let me have **s**, and I will speak, and let Jb 13:13
and waited and kept **s** for my counsel. Jb 29:21
of families terrified me, so that I kept **s**, Jb 31:34
"I will not keep **s** concerning his limbs, Jb 41:12
Our God comes; he does not keep **s**; Ps 50:3
For God alone my soul waits in **s**; from Ps 62:1
For God alone, O my soul, wait in **s**, for Ps 62:5
O God, do not keep **s**; do not hold your Ps 83:1
would soon have lived in the land of **s**. Ps 94:17
LORD, nor do any who go down into **s**. Ps 115:17
a time to keep **s**, and a time to speak; Eccl 3:7
Listen to me in **s**, O coastlands; let the Is 41:1
Sit in **s**, and go into darkness, O daughter Is 47:5
And I will **s** in the cities of Judah and in Jer 7:34
Behold, I will **s** in this place, before your Jer 16:9
also, O Madmen, shall be brought to **s**; Jer 48:2
of Zion sit on the ground in **s**; Lam 2:10
Let him sit alone in **s** when it is laid on Lam 3:28
"**S**! We must not mention the name of Am 6:10
"They are thrown everywhere!" "**S**!" Am 8:3
let all the earth keep **s** before him." Hab 2:20

you should put to **s** the ignorance of 1 Pt 2:15
there was **s** in heaven for about half an Rv 8:1

SILENCED (4)
yet I am not **s** because of the darkness, Jb 23:17
heard that he had **s** the Sadducees, Mt 22:34
mine will not be **s** in the regions of 2 Cor 11:10
They must be **s**, since they are upsetting Ti 1:11

SILENT (56)
for you, and you have only to be **s**." Ex 14:14
If we are **s** and wait until the morning 2 Kgs 7:9
the people were **s** and answered him 2 Kgs 18:36
to us!" They were **s** and could not find Neh 5:8
For if you keep **s** at this time, relief and Est 4:14
men and women, I would have been **s**, Est 7:4
"Teach me, and I will be **s**; make me Jb 6:24
Oh that you would keep **s**, and it would Jb 13:5
with me? For then I would be **s** and die. Jb 13:19
Pay attention, O Job, listen to me; be **s**, Jb 33:31
If not, listen to me; be **s**, and I will teach Jb 33:33
in your own hearts on your beds, and be **s**. Ps 4:4
be not deaf to me, lest, if you be **s** to me, Ps 28:1
may sing your praise and not be **s**. Ps 30:12
For when I kept **s**, my bones wasted away Ps 32:3
You have seen, O LORD; be not **s**! O Lord, Ps 35:22
I was mute and **s**; I held my peace to no Ps 39:2
you have done, and I have been **s**; Ps 50:21
Be not **s**, O God of my praise! Ps 109:1
a man of understanding remains **s**. Prv 11:12
a fool who keeps **s** is considered wise; Prv 17:28
But they were **s** and answered him not a Is 36:21
like a sheep that before its shearers is **s**, Is 53:7
without knowledge; they are all **s** dogs; Is 56:10
For Zion's sake I will not keep **s**, and for Is 62:1
and all the night they shall never be **s**. Is 62:6
Will you keep **s**, and afflict us so Is 64:12
me: "I will not keep **s**, but I will repay; Is 65:6
I cannot keep **s**, for I hear the sound of Jer 4:19
is prudent will keep **s** in such a time, Am 5:13
at traitors and are **s** when the wicked Hab 1:13
thing, Awake; to a **s** stone, Arise! Hab 2:19
Be **s** before the Lord GOD! For the day of Zep 1:7
Be **s**, all flesh, before the LORD, for he has Zec 2:13
rebuked them, telling them to be **s**, Mt 20:31
But Jesus remained **s**. And the high Mt 26:63
But Jesus rebuked him, saying, "Be **s**, Mk 1:25
to save life or to kill?" But they were **s**. Mk 3:4
But they kept **s**, for on the way they had Mk 9:34
rebuked him, telling him to be **s**. Mk 10:48
But he remained **s** and made no Mk 14:61
you will be **s** and unable to speak until Lk 1:20
"Be **s** and come out of him!" And when Lk 4:35
And they kept **s** and told no one in those Lk 9:36
But they remained **s**. Then he took him Lk 14:4
front rebuked him, telling him to be **s**. Lk 18:39
He answered, "I tell you, if these were **s**, Lk 19:40
at his answer they became **s**. Lk 20:26
and like a lamb before its shearer is **s**, Acts 8:32
they heard these things they fell **s**. Acts 11:18
to them with his hand to be **s**, Acts 12:17
And all the assembly fell **s**, and they Acts 15:12
but go on speaking and do not be **s**, Acts 18:9
each of them keep **s** in church and 1 Cor 14:28
sitting there, let the first be **s**. 1 Cor 14:30
women should keep **s** in the 1 Cor 14:34

SILENTLY (1)
be put to shame; let them go **s** to Sheol. Ps 31:17

SILK (3)
in fine linen and covered you with **s**. Ezk 16:10
fine linen and **s** and embroidered Ezk 16:13
fine linen, purple cloth, **s**, scarlet cloth, Rv 18:12

SILLA (1)
on the way that goes down to **S**. 2 Kgs 12:20

SILLY (2)
is like a dove, **s** and without sense, Hos 7:11
nothing to do with irreverent, **s** myths. 1 Tm 4:7

SILOAM (3)
whom the tower in **S** fell and killed Lk 13:4
in the pool of **S**" (which means Sent). Jn 9:7
eyes and said to me, 'Go to **S** and wash.' Jn 9:11

SILVANUS (4)
among you, **S** and Timothy and I, 2 Cor 1:19
Paul, **S**, and Timothy, To the church 1 Thes 1:1
Paul, **S**, and Timothy, To the church 2 Thes 1:1
By **S**, a faithful brother as I regard him, 1 Pt 5:12

SILVER (318)
Abram was very rich in livestock, in **s**, Gn 13:2
your brother a thousand pieces of **s**. Gn 20:16
land worth four hundred shekels of **s**, Gn 23:15
out for Ephron the **s** that he had Gn 23:16
the Hittites, four hundred shekels of **s**, Gn 23:16
given him flocks and herds, **s** and gold, Gn 24:35
brought out jewelry of **s** and of gold, Gn 24:53
the Ishmaelites for twenty shekels of **s**. Gn 37:28
and put my cup, the **s** cup, in the mouth Gn 44:2
then could we steal **s** or gold from your Gn 44:8
hundred shekels of **s** and five changes Gn 45:22
lives in her house, for **s** and gold jewelry, Ex 3:22
of her neighbor, for **s** and gold jewelry." Ex 11:2
the Egyptians for **s** and gold jewelry Ex 12:35
shall not make gods of **s** to be with me, Ex 20:23
give to their master thirty shekels of **s**, Ex 21:32
receive from them: gold, **s**, and bronze, Ex 25:3
and forty bases of **s** you shall make Ex 26:19
and their forty bases of **s**, two bases Ex 26:21
be eight frames, with their bases of **s**, Ex 26:25
with hooks of gold, on four bases of **s**. Ex 26:32
the pillars and their fillets shall be of **s**. Ex 27:10
the pillars and their fillets shall be of **s**. Ex 27:11
the court shall be filleted with **s**. Ex 27:17
Their hooks shall be of **s**, and their Ex 27:17
designs, to work in gold, **s**, and bronze, Ex 31:4
LORD'S contribution: gold, **s**, and bronze; Ex 35:5
a contribution of **s** or bronze brought Ex 35:24
to work in gold and **s** and bronze, Ex 35:32
made forty bases of **s** under the twenty Ex 36:24
and their forty bases of **s**, two bases Ex 36:26
were eight frames with their bases of **s**: Ex 36:30
and he cast for them four bases of **s**. Ex 36:36
of the pillars and their fillets were of **s**. Ex 38:10
of the pillars and their fillets were of **s**. Ex 38:11
of the pillars and their fillets were of **s**. Ex 38:12
of the pillars and their fillets were of **s**. Ex 38:17
of their capitals was also of **s**, Ex 38:17
pillars of the court were filleted with **s**. Ex 38:17
bases were of bronze, their hooks of **s**, Ex 38:19
of their capitals and their fillets of **s**. Ex 38:19
The **s** from those of the congregation Ex 38:25
hundred talents of **s** were for casting Ex 38:27
out of the flock, valued in **s** shekels, Lv 5:15
sixty years old shall be fifty shekels of **s**, Lv 27:3
shall be for a male five shekels of **s**, Lv 27:6
the valuation shall be three shekels of **s**. Lv 27:6
seed shall be valued at fifty shekels of **s**. Lv 27:16
offering was one **s** plate whose weight Nm 7:13
130 shekels, one **s** basin of 70 shekels, Nm 7:13
his offering one **s** plate whose weight Nm 7:19
130 shekels, one **s** basin of 70 shekels, Nm 7:19
offering was one **s** plate whose weight Nm 7:25
130 shekels, one **s** basin of 70 shekels, Nm 7:25
offering was one **s** plate whose weight Nm 7:31
130 shekels, one **s** basin of 70 shekels, Nm 7:31
offering was one **s** plate whose weight Nm 7:37
130 shekels, one **s** basin of 70 shekels, Nm 7:37
offering was one **s** plate whose weight Nm 7:43
130 shekels, one **s** basin of 70 shekels, Nm 7:43
offering was one **s** plate whose weight Nm 7:49
130 shekels, one **s** basin of 70 shekels, Nm 7:49
offering was one **s** plate whose weight Nm 7:55
130 shekels, one **s** basin of 70 shekels, Nm 7:55
offering was one **s** plate whose weight Nm 7:61
130 shekels, one **s** basin of 70 shekels, Nm 7:61
offering was one **s** plate whose weight Nm 7:67
130 shekels, one **s** basin of 70 shekels, Nm 7:67
offering was one **s** plate whose weight Nm 7:73
130 shekels, one **s** basin of 70 shekels, Nm 7:73
offering was one **s** plate whose weight Nm 7:79
130 shekels, one **s** basin of 70 shekels, Nm 7:79
from the chiefs of Israel: twelve **s** plates, Nm 7:84
twelve silver plates, twelve **s** basins, Nm 7:84
each **s** plate weighing 130 shekels and Nm 7:85
all the **s** of the vessels 2,400 shekels Nm 7:85
"Make two **s** trumpets. Of hammered Nm 10:2
you shall fix at five shekels in **s**, Nm 18:16
to give me his house full of **s** and gold, Nm 22:18
give me his house full of **s** and gold, Nm 24:13
only the gold, the **s**, the bronze, the Nm 31:22
You shall not covet the **s** or the gold that Dt 7:25
flocks multiply and your **s** and gold is Dt 8:13
for himself excessive **s** and gold. Dt 17:17
a hundred shekels of **s** and give them to Dt 22:19
of the young woman fifty shekels of **s**, Dt 22:29
idols of wood and stone, of **s** and gold, Dt 29:17
But all **s** and gold, and every vessel of Jos 6:19
and everything in it. Only the **s** and gold, Jos 6:24
cloak from Shinar, and 200 shekels of **s**, Jos 7:21
inside my tent, with the **s** underneath." Jos 7:21
hidden in his tent with the **s** underneath. Jos 7:22
and the **s** and the cloak and the bar of Jos 7:24
and with very much livestock, with **s**, Jos 22:8
of Megiddo; they got no spoils of **s**. Jgs 5:19
him seventy pieces of **s** out of the house Jgs 9:4
we will each give you 1,100 pieces of **s**." Jgs 16:5
"The 1,100 pieces of **s** that were taken Jgs 17:2
it in my ears, behold, the **s** is with me; Jgs 17:2
the 1,100 pieces of **s** to his mother. Jgs 17:3
"I dedicate the **s** to the LORD from my Jgs 17:3
took 200 pieces of **s** and gave it to Jgs 17:4
give you ten pieces of **s** a year and a suit Jgs 17:10
him for a piece of **s** or a loaf of bread 1 Sm 2:36
have with me a quarter of a shekel of **s**, 1 Sm 9:8
Joram brought with him articles of **s**, 2 Sm 8:10
together with the **s** and gold that he 2 Sm 8:11
to give you ten pieces of **s** and a belt." 2 Sm 18:11
the weight of a thousand pieces of **s**, 2 Sm 18:12
is not a matter of **s** or gold between us 2 Sm 21:4
and the oxen for fifty shekels of **s**. 2 Sm 24:24
David his father had dedicated, the **s**, 1 Kgs 7:51
None were of **s**; silver was not 1 Kgs 10:21
s was not considered as anything in 1 Kgs 10:21
used to come bringing gold, **s**, ivory, 1 Kgs 10:22
his present, articles of **s** and gold, 1 Kgs 10:25
And the king made **s** as common in 1 Kgs 10:27
for 600 shekels of **s** and a horse for 1 Kgs 10:29
and his own sacred gifts, **s**, and gold, 1 Kgs 15:15
Asa took all the **s** and the gold that 1 Kgs 15:18
to you a present of **s** and gold. 1 Kgs 15:19
from Shemer for two talents of **s**, 1 Kgs 16:24
'Your **s** and your gold are mine; your 1 Kgs 20:3
"Deliver to me your **s** and your gold, 1 Kgs 20:5
children, and for my **s** and my gold, 1 Kgs 20:7
or else you shall pay a talent of **s**.' 1 Kgs 20:39
went, taking with him ten talents of **s**, 2 Kgs 5:5
them a talent of **s** and two festal 2 Kgs 5:22
tied up two talents of **s** in two bags, 2 Kgs 5:23
head was sold for eighty shekels of **s**, 2 Kgs 6:25
of dove's dung for five shekels of **s**. 2 Kgs 6:25
and they carried off **s** and gold and 2 Kgs 7:8
for the house of the LORD basins of **s**, 2 Kgs 12:13
or any vessels of gold, or of **s**, 2 Kgs 12:13
And he seized all the gold and **s**, and 2 Kgs 14:14
gave Pul a thousand talents of **s**, 2 Kgs 15:19
fifty shekels of **s** from every man, 2 Kgs 15:20
Ahaz also took the **s** and gold that 2 Kgs 16:8
hundred talents of **s** and thirty 2 Kgs 18:14
gave him all the **s** that was found in 2 Kgs 18:15
them all his treasure house, the **s**, 2 Kgs 20:13
a hundred talents of **s** and a talent of 2 Kgs 23:33
Jehoiakim gave the **s** and the gold 2 Kgs 23:35
He exacted the **s** and the gold of the 2 Kgs 23:35
away as gold, and what was of **s**, 2 Kgs 25:15
as gold, and what was of silver, as **s**. 2 Kgs 25:15
sent all sorts of articles of gold, of **s**, 1 Chr 18:10
together with the **s** and gold that he 1 Chr 18:11
sent 1,000 talents of **s** to hire chariots 1 Chr 19:6
talents of gold, a million talents of **s**, 1 Chr 22:14
gold, **s**, bronze, and iron. Arise and 1 Chr 22:16
the weight of **s** vessels for each 1 Chr 28:14
the weight of **s** for a lampstand and 1 Chr 28:15
the **s** for the silver tables, 1 Chr 28:16
the silver for the **s** tables, 1 Chr 28:16
for the **s** bowls and the weight of 1 Chr 28:17
of gold, the **s** for the things of silver, 1 Chr 29:2
of gold, the silver for the things of **s**, 1 Chr 29:2
a treasure of my own of gold and **s**, 1 Chr 29:3
Ophir, and 7,000 talents of refined **s**, 1 Chr 29:4
things of gold and **s** for the things of 1 Chr 29:5
of gold and silver for the things of **s**. 1 Chr 29:5
darics of gold, 10,000 talents of **s**, 1 Chr 29:7
And the king made **s** and gold as 2 Chr 1:15
from Egypt for 600 shekels of **s**, 2 Chr 1:17
man skilled to work in gold, **s**, bronze, 2 Chr 2:7
is trained to work in gold, **s**, bronze, 2 Chr 2:14
father had dedicated, and stored the **s**, 2 Chr 5:1
land brought gold and **s** to Solomon. 2 Chr 9:14
S was not considered as anything in 2 Chr 9:20
used to come bringing gold, **s**, ivory, 2 Chr 9:21
his present, articles of **s** and of gold, 2 Chr 9:24
And the king made **s** as common in 2 Chr 9:27
and his own sacred gifts, **s**, and gold, 2 Chr 15:18
Then Asa took **s** and gold from the 2 Chr 16:2
I am sending to you **s** and gold. 2 Chr 16:3
presents and **s** for tribute, 2 Chr 17:11
father gave them great gifts of **s**, 2 Chr 21:3
for incense and vessels of gold and **s**. 2 Chr 24:14
valor from Israel for 100 talents of **s**. 2 Chr 25:6
And he seized all the gold and **s**, and 2 Chr 25:24
gave him that year 100 talents of **s**, 2 Chr 27:5
he made for himself treasuries for **s**, 2 Chr 32:27
a hundred talents of **s** and a talent of 2 Chr 36:3
by the men of his place with **s** and gold, Ezr 1:4
about them aided them with vessels of **s**, Ezr 1:6
30 basins of gold, 1,000 basins of **s**, 29 Ezr 1:9
30 bowls of gold, 410 bowls of **s**, and Ezr 1:10
the vessels of gold and of **s** were 5,400. Ezr 1:11
61,000 darics of gold, 5,000 minas of **s**, Ezr 2:69
And the gold and **s** vessels of the house Ezr 5:14
also let the gold and **s** vessels of the house Ezr 6:5
and also to carry the **s** and gold that the Ezr 7:15
with all the **s** and gold that you shall Ezr 7:16
to do with the rest of the **s** and gold, Ezr 7:18
up to 100 talents of **s**, 100 cors of wheat, Ezr 7:22

out to them the **s** and the gold and Ezr 8:25
out into their hand 650 talents of **s**, Ezr 8:26
of silver, and **s** vessels worth 200 talents, Ezr 8:26
and the **s** and the gold are a freewill Ezr 8:28
over the weight of the **s** and the gold and Ezr 8:30
the **s** and the gold and the vessels were Ezr 8:33
for their daily ration forty shekels of **s**. Neh 5:15
priests' garments and 500 minas of **s**. Neh 7:70
darics of gold and 2,200 minas of **s**. Neh 7:71
20,000 darics of gold, 2,000 minas of **s**, Neh 7:72
linen and purple to **s** rods and marble Est 1:6
couches of gold and **s** on a mosaic Est 1:6
pay 10,000 talents of **s** into the hands of Est 3:9
had gold, who filled their houses with **s**. Jb 3:15
will be your gold and your precious **s**. Jb 22:25
Though he heap up **s** like dust, and pile Jb 27:16
it, and the innocent will divide the **s**. Jb 27:17
"Surely there is a mine for **s**, and a place Jb 28:1
and **s** cannot be weighed as its price. Jb 28:15
like **s** refined in a furnace on the ground, Ps 12:6
tested us; you have tried us as **s** is tried. Ps 66:10
the wings of a dove covered with **s**, Ps 68:13
he brought out Israel with **s** and gold, Ps 105:37
Their idols are **s** and gold, the work of Ps 115:4
than thousands of gold and **s** pieces. Ps 119:72
The idols of the nations are **s** and gold, Ps 135:15
if you seek it like **s** and search for it as Prv 2:4
better than gain from **s** and her profit Prv 3:14
Take my instruction instead of **s**, and Prv 8:10
fine gold, and my yield than choice **s**. Prv 8:19
tongue of the righteous is choice **s**; Prv 10:20
is to be chosen rather than **s**. Prv 16:16
The crucible is for **s**, and the furnace is Prv 17:3
and favor is better than **s** or gold. Prv 22:1
Take away the dross from the **s**, and the Prv 25:4
is like apples of gold in a setting of **s**. Prv 25:11
The crucible is for **s**, and the furnace Prv 27:21
also gathered for myself **s** and gold and Eccl 2:8
before the **s** cord is snapped, or the Eccl 12:6
you ornaments of gold, studded with **s**. Sg 1:11
He made its posts of **s**, its back of gold, its Sg 3:10
we will build on her a battlement of **s**, Sg 8:9
bring for its fruit a thousand pieces of **s**. Sg 8:11
Your **s** has become dross, your best wine Is 1:22
Their land is filled with **s** and gold, and Is 2:7
cast away their idols of **s** and their idols of Is 2:20
vines, worth a thousand shekels of **s**, Is 7:23
have no regard for **s** and do not delight Is 13:17
idols overlaid with **s** and your Is 30:22
cast away his idols of **s** and his idols of Is 31:7
he showed them his treasure house, the **s**, Is 39:2
it with gold and casts for it **s** chains. Is 40:19
the purse, and weigh out **s** in the scales, Is 46:6
Behold, I have refined you, but not as **s**; I Is 48:10
from afar, their **s** and gold with them, Is 60:9
gold, and instead of iron I will bring **s**; Is 60:17
Rejected **s** they are called, for the LORD Jer 6:30
They decorate it with **s** and gold; they Jer 10:4
Beaten **s** is brought from Tarshish, and Jer 10:9
the money to him, seventeen shekels of **s**. Jer 32:9
took away as gold, and what was of **s**, Jer 52:19
as gold, and what was of silver, as **s**. Jer 52:19
They cast their **s** into the streets, and Ezk 7:19
Their **s** and gold are not able to deliver Ezk 7:19
you were adorned with gold and **s**, Ezk 16:13
jewels of my gold and of my **s**, Ezk 16:17
lead in the furnace; they are dross of **s**. Ezk 22:18
As one gathers **s** and bronze and iron Ezk 22:20
As **s** is melted in a furnace, so you Ezk 22:22
s, iron, tin, and lead they exchanged Ezk 27:12
gathered gold and **s** into your Ezk 28:4
off plunder, to carry away **s** and gold, Ezk 38:13
was of fine gold, its chest and arms of **s**, Dn 2:32
the iron, the clay, the bronze, the **s**, Dn 2:35
the iron, the bronze, the clay, the **s**, Dn 2:45
of gold and of **s** that Nebuchadnezzar his Dn 5:2
wine and praised the gods of gold and **s**, Dn 5:4
you have praised the gods of **s** and gold, Dn 5:23
and their precious vessels of **s** and gold, Dn 11:8
know he shall honor with gold and **s**, Dn 11:38
ruler of the treasures of gold and of **s**, Dn 11:43
oil, and who lavished on her **s** and gold, Hos 2:8
for fifteen shekels of **s** and a homer and Hos 3:2
With their **s** and gold they made idols Hos 8:4
shall possess their precious things of **s**; Hos 9:6
images, idols skillfully made of their **s**, Hos 13:2
For you have taken my **s** and my gold, and Jl 3:5
because they sell the righteous for **s**, Am 2:6
may buy the poor for **s** and the needy for Am 8:6
Plunder the **s**, plunder the gold! There is Na 2:9
Behold, it is overlaid with gold and **s**, Hab 2:19
no more; all who weigh out **s** are cut off. Zep 1:11
Neither their **s** nor their gold shall be Zep 1:18
The **s** is mine, and the gold is mine, Hg 2:8
Take from them **s** and gold, and make Zec 6:11
a rampart and heaped up **s** like dust, Zec 9:3
out as my wages thirty pieces of **s**. Zec 11:12
the thirty pieces of **s** and threw them Zec 11:13
the fire, and refine them as one refines **s**, Zec 13:9
s, and garments in great abundance. Zec 14:14
He will sit as a refiner and purifier of **s**, Mal 3:3
of Levi and refine them like gold and **s**, Mal 3:3
Acquire no gold nor **s** nor copper for Mt 10:9
And they paid him thirty pieces of **s**. Mt 26:15
the thirty pieces of **s** to the chief priests Mt 27:3
down the pieces of **s** into the temple, Mt 27:5
the chief priests, taking the pieces of **s**, Mt 27:6
"And they took the thirty pieces of **s**, Mt 27:9
"Or what woman, having ten **s** coins, if Lk 15:8
But Peter said, "I have no **s** and gold, but Acts 3:6
bought for a sum of **s** from the sons of Acts 7:16
to him, "May your **s** perish with you, Acts 8:20
divine being is like gold or **s** or stone, Acts 17:29
it came to fifty thousand pieces of **s**. Acts 19:19
who made **s** shrines of Artemis, Acts 19:24
I coveted no one's **s** or gold or apparel. Acts 20:33
with gold, **s**, precious stones, 1 Cor 3:12
vessels of gold and **s** but also of wood 2 Tm 2:20
Your gold and **s** have corroded, and their Jas 5:3
perishable things such as **s** or gold, 1 Pt 1:18
idols of gold and **s** and bronze and stone Rv 9:20
cargo of gold, **s**, jewels, pearls, fine Rv 18:12

SILVERSMITH (2)
200 pieces of silver and gave it to the **s**, Jgs 17:4
For a man named Demetrius, a **s**, Acts 19:24

SIMEON (49)
son also." And she called his name **S**. Gn 29:33
two of the sons of Jacob, **S** and Levi, Gn 34:25
Then Jacob said to **S** and Levi, "You Gn 34:30
Reuben (Jacob's firstborn), **S**, Levi, Gn 35:23
And he took **S** from them and bound Gn 42:24
Joseph is no more, and **S** is no more, Gn 42:36
Then he brought **S** out to them. Gn 43:23
The sons of **S**: Jemuel, Jamin, Ohad, Gn 46:10
shall be mine, as Reuben and **S** are. Gn 48:5
"**S** and Levi are brothers; weapons of Gn 49:5
Reuben, **S**, Levi, and Judah, Ex 1:2
The sons of **S**: Jemuel, Jamin, Ohad, Ex 6:15
woman; these are the clans of **S**. Ex 6:15
from **S**, Shelumiel the son of Nm 1:6
Of the people of **S**, their generations, by Nm 1:22
those listed of the tribe of **S** were 59,300. Nm 1:23
next to him shall be the tribe of **S**, Nm 2:12
of the people of **S** being Shelumiel the Nm 2:12
the chief of the people of **S**: Nm 7:36
of the people of **S** was Shelumiel the Nm 10:19
from the tribe of **S**, Shaphat the son of Nm 13:5
The sons of **S** according to their Nm 26:12
Of the tribe of the people of **S**, Shemuel Nm 34:20
S, Levi, Judah, Issachar, Joseph, and Dt 27:12
The second lot came out for **S**, for the Jos 19:1
Simeon, for the tribe of the people of **S**, Jos 19:1
of the people of **S** according to their Jos 19:8
of the people of **S** formed part of the Jos 19:9
the people of **S** obtained an inheritance Jos 19:9
the tribes of Judah, **S**, and Benjamin, Jos 21:4
of the people of **S** they gave the following Jos 21:9
And Judah said to **S** his brother, "Come Jgs 1:3
allotted to you." So **S** went with him. Jgs 1:3
And Judah went with **S** his brother, and Jgs 1:17
Reuben, **S**, Levi, Judah, Issachar, 1 Chr 2:1
The sons of **S**: Nemuel, Jamin, Jarib, 1 Chr 4:24
S, and Benjamin these cities that are 1 Chr 6:65
and **S** who were residing with them, 2 Chr 15:9
cities of Manasseh, Ephraim, and **S**, 2 Chr 34:6
the east side to the west, **S**, one portion. Ezk 48:24
Adjoining the territory of **S**, from the Ezk 48:25
by measure, three gates, the gate of **S**, Ezk 48:33
a man in Jerusalem, whose name was **S**, Lk 2:25
And **S** blessed them and said to Mary his Lk 2:34
the son of **S**, the son of Judah, the son of Lk 3:30
Barnabas, **S** who was called Niger, Acts 13:1
S has related how God first visited the Acts 15:14
S Peter, a servant and apostle of Jesus 2 Pt 1:1
12,000 from the tribe of **S**, 12,000 from the Rv 7:7

SIMEONITES (5)
of a father's house belonging to the **S**. Nm 25:14
These are the clans of the **S**, 22,200. Nm 26:14
of them, five hundred men of the **S**, 1 Chr 4:42
Of the **S**, mighty men of valor for 1 Chr 12:25
for the **S**, Shephatiah the son of 1 Chr 27:16

SIMILAR (3)
And many **s** words were added to them. Jer 36:32
They were **s** to the chambers on the Ezk 42:11
with the workmen in **s** trades, Acts 19:25

SIMILARLY (1)
were carved; **s** the wall of the nave. Ezk 41:20

SIMON (69)
S (who is called Peter) and Andrew his Mt 4:18
first, **S**, who is called Peter, and Andrew Mt 10:2
S the Cananaean, and Judas Iscariot, Mt 10:4
James and Joseph and **S** and Judas? Mt 13:55
S Peter replied, "You are the Christ, the Mt 16:16
him, "Blessed are you, **S** Bar-Jonah! Mt 16:17
S? From whom do kings of the earth Mt 17:25
at Bethany in the house of **S** the leper, Mt 26:6
found a man of Cyrene, **S** by name. Mt 27:32
he saw **S** and Andrew the brother of Mk 1:16
Andrew the brother of **S** casting a net Mk 1:16
and entered the house of **S** and Andrew, Mk 1:29
And **S** and those who were with him Mk 1:36
S (to whom he gave the name Peter); Mk 3:16
and Thaddaeus, and **S** the Cananaean, Mk 3:18
of James and Joses and Judas and **S**? Mk 6:3
at Bethany in the house of **S** the leper, Mk 14:3
and he said to Peter, "**S**, are you asleep? Mk 14:37
compelled a passerby, **S** of Cyrene, Mk 15:21
he had finished speaking, he said to **S**, Lk 5:4
And **S** answered, "Master, we toiled all Lk 5:5
But when **S** Peter saw it, he fell down at Lk 5:8
of Zebedee, who were partners with **S**. Lk 5:10
And Jesus said to **S**, "Do not be afraid; Lk 5:10
S, whom he named Peter, and Andrew Lk 6:14
and **S** who was called the Zealot, Lk 6:15
"**S**, I have something to say to you." And Lk 7:40
S answered, "The one, I suppose, for Lk 7:43
turning toward the woman he said to **S**, Lk 7:44
"**S**, Simon, behold, Satan demanded to Lk 22:31
"Simon, **S**, behold, Satan demanded to Lk 22:31
him away, they seized one **S** of Cyrene, Lk 23:26
risen indeed, and has appeared to **S**!" Lk 24:34
Jesus was Andrew, **S** Peter's brother. Jn 1:40
found his own brother **S** and said to him, Jn 1:41
and said, "So you are **S** the son of John? Jn 1:42
of his disciples, Andrew, **S** Peter's brother, Jn 6:8
S Peter answered him, "Lord, to whom Jn 6:68
He spoke of Judas the son of **S** Iscariot, for Jn 6:71
He came to **S** Peter, who said to him, Jn 13:6
S Peter said to him, "Lord, not my feet Jn 13:9
so **S** Peter motioned to him to ask Jesus Jn 13:24
he gave it to Judas, the son of **S** Iscariot. Jn 13:26
S Peter said to him, "Lord, where are Jn 13:36
Then **S** Peter, having a sword, drew it Jn 18:10
S Peter followed Jesus, and so did Jn 18:15
Now **S** Peter was standing and warming Jn 18:25
she ran and went to **S** Peter and the other Jn 20:2
Then **S** Peter came, following him, and Jn 20:6
S Peter, Thomas (called the Twin), Jn 21:2
S Peter said to them, "I am going Jn 21:3
is the Lord!" When **S** Peter heard that it Jn 21:7
So **S** Peter went aboard and hauled the Jn 21:11
finished breakfast, Jesus said to **S** Peter, Jn 21:15
said to Simon Peter, "**S**, son of John, Jn 21:15
to him a second time, "**S**, son of John, Jn 21:16
to him the third time, "**S**, son of John, Jn 21:17
son of Alphaeus and **S** the Zealot and Acts 1:13
But there was a man named **S**, who had Acts 8:9
Even **S** himself believed, and after Acts 8:13
Now when **S** saw that the Spirit was Acts 8:18
And **S** answered, "Pray for me to the Acts 8:24
in Joppa for many days with one **S**, Acts 9:43
Joppa and bring one **S** who is called Acts 10:5
He is lodging with one **S**, a tanner, Acts 10:6
out to ask whether **S** who was called Acts 10:18
Joppa and ask for **S** who is called Acts 10:32
He is lodging in the house of **S**, a Acts 10:32
to Joppa and bring **S** who is called Acts 11:13

SIMON'S (6)
Now **S** mother-in-law lay ill with a Mk 1:30
left the synagogue and entered **S** house. Lk 4:38
Now **S** mother-in-law was ill with a Lk 4:38
into one of the boats, which was **S**, Lk 5:3
it into the heart of Judas Iscariot, **S** son, Jn 13:2
having made inquiry for **S** house, Acts 10:17

SIMPLE (20)
kills the fool, and jealousy slays the **s**. Jb 5:2
of the LORD is sure, making wise the **s**; Ps 19:7
The LORD preserves the **s**; when I was Ps 116:6
it imparts understanding to the **s**. Ps 119:130
to give prudence to the **s**, knowledge and Prv 1:4
"How long, O **s** ones, will you love being Prv 1:22
O simple ones, will you love being **s**? Prv 1:22
For the **s** are killed by their turning Prv 1:32
and I have seen among the **s**, I have Prv 7:7
O **s** ones, learn prudence; O fools, learn Prv 8:5
"Whoever is **s**, let him turn in here!" To Prv 9:4
Leave your **s** ways, and live, and walk in Prv 9:6
"Whoever is **s**, let him turn in here!" Prv 9:16
The **s** believes everything, but the Prv 14:15
The **s** inherit folly, but the prudent are Prv 14:18
scoffer, and the **s** will learn prudence; Prv 19:25

do not associate with a **s** babbler. Prv 20:19
is punished, the **s** becomes wise; Prv 21:11
himself, but the **s** go on and suffer for it. Prv 22:3
but the **s** go on and suffer for it. Prv 27:12

SIMPLICITY (1)
the world with **s** and godly sincerity, 2 Cor 1:12

SIMPLY (1)
Let what you say be **s** 'Yes' or 'No'; Mt 5:37

SIN (444)
do not do well, **s** is crouching at the door. Gn 4:7
is great and their **s** is very grave, Gn 18:20
on me and my kingdom a great **s**? Gn 20:9
What is my **s**, that you have hotly Gn 31:36
great wickedness and **s** against God?" Gn 39:9
I not tell you not to **s** against the boy? Gn 42:22
of your brothers and their **s**, Gn 50:17
Now therefore, forgive my **s**, please, Ex 10:17
of Israel came to the wilderness of **S**, Ex 16:1
on from the wilderness of **S** by stages, Ex 17:1
be before you, that you may not **s**." Ex 20:20
land, lest they make you **s** against me; Ex 23:33
fire outside the camp; it is a **s** offering. Ex 29:14
a bull as a **s** offering for atonement. Ex 29:36
the blood of the **s** offering of atonement Ex 30:10
brought such a great **s** upon them?" Ex 32:21
the people, "You have sinned a great **s**. Ex 32:30
I can make atonement for your **s**." Ex 32:30
"Alas, this people have sinned a great **s**. Ex 32:31
if you will forgive their **s**—but if not, Ex 32:32
I visit, I will visit their **s** upon them." Ex 32:34
iniquity and transgression and **s**, Ex 34:7
and pardon our iniquity and our **s**, Ex 34:9
shall offer for the **s** that he has committed Lv 4:3
blemish to the LORD for a **s** offering. Lv 4:3
the bull of the **s** offering he shall remove Lv 4:8
when the **s** which they have committed Lv 4:14
the herd for a **s** offering and bring it Lv 4:14
As he did with the bull of the **s** offering, Lv 4:20
bull; it is the **s** offering for the assembly. Lv 4:21
or the **s** which he has committed is Lv 4:23
offering before the LORD; it is a **s** offering. Lv 4:24
the blood of the **s** offering with his finger Lv 4:25
shall make atonement for him for his **s**, Lv 4:26
or the **s** which he has committed is Lv 4:28
for his **s** which he has committed. Lv 4:28
on the head of the **s** offering and kill the Lv 4:29
offering and kill the **s** offering in the Lv 4:29
a lamb as his offering for a **s** offering, Lv 4:32
on the head of the **s** offering and kill it Lv 4:33
and kill it for a **s** offering in the place Lv 4:33
the blood of the **s** offering with his finger Lv 4:34
for him for the **s** which he has Lv 4:35
and confesses the **s** he has committed, Lv 5:5
his compensation for the **s** that he has Lv 5:6
flock, a lamb or a goat, for a **s** offering. Lv 5:6
shall make atonement for him for his **s**. Lv 5:6
his compensation for the **s** that he has Lv 5:7
one for a **s** offering and the other for a Lv 5:7
shall offer first the one for the **s** offering. Lv 5:8
of the blood of the **s** offering on the side of Lv 5:9
at the base of the altar; it is a **s** offering. Lv 5:9
for him for the **s** that he has committed, Lv 5:10
his offering for the **s** that he has Lv 5:11
of an ephah of fine flour for a **s** offering. Lv 5:11
frankincense on it, for it is a **s** offering. Lv 5:11
the LORD'S food offerings; it is a **s** offering. Lv 5:12
for him for the **s** which he has Lv 5:13
the things that people do and **s** thereby— Lv 6:3
like the **s** offering and the guilt offering. Lv 6:17
saying, This is the law of the **s** offering. Lv 6:25
is killed shall the **s** offering be killed Lv 6:25
The priest who offers it for **s** shall eat it. Lv 6:26
But no **s** offering shall be eaten from Lv 6:30
guilt offering is just like the **s** offering; Lv 7:7
of the grain offering, of the **s** offering, Lv 7:37
and the bull of the **s** offering and the two Lv 8:2
he brought the bull of the **s** offering, Lv 8:14
on the head of the bull of the **s** offering. Lv 8:14
a bull calf for a **s** offering and a ram for Lv 9:2
Israel, 'Take a male goat for a **s** offering, Lv 9:3
altar and offer your **s** offering and your Lv 9:7
altar and killed the calf of the **s** offering, Lv 9:8
the liver from the **s** offering he burned Lv 9:10
the goat of the **s** offering that was for Lv 9:15
and killed it and offered it as a **s** offering, Lv 9:15
from offering the **s** offering and the Lv 9:22
about the goat of the **s** offering, Lv 10:16
you not eaten the **s** offering in the place Lv 10:17
have offered their **s** offering and their Lv 10:19
If I had eaten the **s** offering today, would Lv 10:19
a pigeon or a turtledove for a **s** offering, Lv 12:6
offering and the other for a **s** offering. Lv 12:8
where they kill the **s** offering and the Lv 14:13
the guilt offering, like the **s** offering, Lv 14:13
The priest shall offer the **s** offering, to Lv 14:19
one shall be a **s** offering and the other Lv 14:22
one for a **s** offering and the other for a Lv 14:31
one for a **s** offering and the other for a Lv 15:15
use one for a **s** offering and the other Lv 15:30
from the herd for a **s** offering and a ram Lv 16:3
of Israel two male goats for a **s** offering, Lv 16:5
the bull as a **s** offering for himself and Lv 16:6
fell for the LORD and use it as a **s** offering, Lv 16:9
the bull as a **s** offering for himself, Lv 16:11
kill the bull as a **s** offering for himself. Lv 16:11
kill the goat of the **s** offering that is for Lv 16:15
the fat of the **s** offering he shall burn Lv 16:25
the bull for the **s** offering and the goat Lv 16:27
offering and the goat for the **s** offering, Lv 16:27
lest you incur **s** because of him. Lv 19:17
the LORD for his **s** that he has Lv 19:22
be forgiven for the **s** that he has Lv 19:22
nakedness; they shall bear their **s**; Lv 20:20
lest they bear **s** for it and die thereby Lv 22:9
offer one male goat for a **s** offering, Lv 23:19
curses his God shall bear his **s**. Lv 24:15
he shall confess his **s** that he has Nm 5:7
offer one for a **s** offering and the other Nm 6:11
old without blemish as a **s** offering, Nm 6:14
LORD and offer his **s** offering and his Nm 6:16
one male goat for a **s** offering; Nm 7:16
one male goat for a **s** offering; Nm 7:22
one male goat for a **s** offering; Nm 7:28
one male goat for a **s** offering; Nm 7:34
one male goat for a **s** offering; Nm 7:40
one male goat for a **s** offering; Nm 7:46
one male goat for a **s** offering; Nm 7:52
one male goat for a **s** offering; Nm 7:58
one male goat for a **s** offering; Nm 7:64
one male goat for a **s** offering; Nm 7:70
one male goat for a **s** offering; Nm 7:76
one male goat for a **s** offering; Nm 7:82
and twelve male goats for a **s** offering; Nm 7:87
bull from the herd for a **s** offering. Nm 8:8
the one for a **s** offering and the other Nm 8:12
purified themselves from **s** and washed Nm 8:21
time; that man shall bear his **s**. Nm 9:13
"But if you **s** unintentionally, and do Nm 15:22
and one male goat for a **s** offering. Nm 15:24
and their **s** offering before the LORD for Nm 15:25
female goat a year old for a **s** offering. Nm 15:27
the spirits of all flesh, shall one man **s**, Nm 16:22
of theirs and every **s** offering of theirs Nm 18:9
of meeting, lest they bear **s** and die. Nm 18:22
you shall bear no **s** by reason of it, Nm 18:32
of the people of Israel; it is a **s** offering. Nm 19:9
some ashes of the burnt **s** offering, Nm 19:17
of Korah, but died for his own **s**. Nm 27:3
male goat for a **s** offering to the LORD; Nm 28:15
also one male goat for a **s** offering, to Nm 28:22
with one male goat for a **s** offering, to Nm 29:5
also one male goat for a **s** offering, Nm 29:11
besides the **s** offering of atonement, Nm 29:11
also one male goat for a **s** offering, Nm 29:16
also one male goat for a **s** offering, Nm 29:19
also one male goat for a **s** offering, Nm 29:22
also one male goat for a **s** offering, Nm 29:25
also one male goat for a **s** offering; Nm 29:28
also one male goat for a **s** offering; Nm 29:31
also one male goat for a **s** offering; Nm 29:34
also one male goat for a **s** offering; Nm 29:38
and be sure your **s** will find you out. Nm 32:23
Sea and camped in the wilderness of **S**. Nm 33:11
the wilderness of **S** and camped at Nm 33:12
because of all the **s** that you had Dt 9:18
this people, or their wickedness or their **s**, Dt 9:27
LORD against you, and you be guilty of **s**. Dt 15:9
and so you **s** against the LORD your God. Dt 20:18
it of you, and you will be guilty of **s**. Dt 23:21
from vowing, you will not be guilty of **s**. Dt 23:22
you shall not bring **s** upon the land that Dt 24:4
you to the LORD, and you be guilty of **s**. Dt 24:15
one shall be put to death for his own **s**. Dt 24:16
had enough of the **s** at Peor from Jos 22:17
Thus the **s** of the young men was very 1 Sm 2:17
me that I should **s** against the LORD 1 Sm 12:23
and do not **s** against the LORD by 1 Sm 14:34
and see how this **s** has arisen today. 1 Sm 14:38
rebellion is as the **s** of divination, 1 Sm 15:23
please pardon my **s** and return with 1 Sm 15:25
"Let not the king **s** against his servant 1 Sm 19:4
then will you **s** against innocent 1 Sm 19:5
And what is my **s** before your father, 1 Sm 20:1
"The LORD also has put away your **s**; 2 Sm 12:13
and forgive the **s** of your people 1 Kgs 8:34
your name and turn from their **s**, 1 Kgs 8:35
and forgive the **s** of your servants, 1 Kgs 8:36
"If they **s** against you—for there is no 1 Kgs 8:46
no one who does not **s**—and you are 1 Kgs 8:46
Then this thing became a **s**, for the 1 Kgs 12:30
this thing became **s** to the house 1 Kgs 13:34
he sinned and made Israel to **s**." 1 Kgs 14:16
and in his **s** which he made Israel to 1 Kgs 15:26
in his sin which he made Israel to **s**. 1 Kgs 15:26
sinned and that he made Israel to **s**, 1 Kgs 15:30
and in his **s** which he made 1 Kgs 15:34
in his sin which he made Israel to **s**. 1 Kgs 15:34
and have made my people Israel to **s**, 1 Kgs 16:2
and which they made Israel to **s**, 1 Kgs 16:13
and for his **s** which he committed, 1 Kgs 16:19
he committed, making Israel to **s**. 1 Kgs 16:19
in the sins that he made Israel to **s**, 1 Kgs 16:26
to bring my **s** to remembrance and 1 Kgs 17:18
because you have made Israel to **s**. 1 Kgs 21:22
son of Nebat, who made Israel to **s**. 1 Kgs 22:52
he clung to the **s** of Jeroboam the son 2 Kgs 3:3
of Nebat, which he made Israel to **s**; 2 Kgs 3:3
which he made Israel to **s**—that is, 2 Kgs 10:29
which he made Israel to **s**. 2 Kgs 10:31
money from the **s** offerings was not 2 Kgs 12:16
of Nebat, which he made Israel to **s**; 2 Kgs 13:2
Jeroboam, which he made Israel to **s**, 2 Kgs 13:6
of Nebat, which he made Israel to **s**, 2 Kgs 13:11
But each one shall die for his own **s**." 2 Kgs 14:6
of Nebat, which he made Israel to **s**. 2 Kgs 14:24
of Nebat, which he made Israel to **s**. 2 Kgs 15:9
of Nebat, which he made Israel to **s**. 2 Kgs 15:18
of Nebat, which he made Israel to **s**. 2 Kgs 15:24
of Nebat, which he made Israel to **s**. 2 Kgs 15:28
and made them commit great **s**. 2 Kgs 17:21
made Judah also to **s** with his idols, 2 Kgs 21:11
besides the **s** that he made Judah to 2 Kgs 21:16
he made Judah to **s** so that they did 2 Kgs 21:16
he did, and the **s** that he committed, 2 Kgs 21:17
son of Nebat, who made Israel to **s**, 2 Kgs 23:15
and forgive the **s** of your people 2 Chr 6:25
your name and turn from their **s**, 2 Chr 6:26
and forgive the **s** of your servants, 2 Chr 6:27
"If they **s** against you—for there is no 2 Chr 6:36
no one who does not **s**—and you are 2 Chr 6:36
and will forgive their **s** and heal their 2 Chr 7:14
but each one shall die for his own **s**." 2 Chr 25:4
male goats for a **s** offering for the 2 Chr 29:21
goats for the **s** offering were brought 2 Chr 29:23
and made a **s** offering with their 2 Chr 29:24
offering and the **s** offering should be 2 Chr 29:24
and all his **s** and his faithlessness, 2 Chr 33:19
and as a **s** offering for all Israel 12 male Ezr 6:17
and as a **s** offering twelve male goats. Ezr 8:35
and let not their **s** be blotted out from Neh 4:5
be afraid and act in this way and **s**, Neh 6:13
and the **s** offerings to make Neh 10:33
king of Israel **s** on account of Neh 13:26
foreign women made even him to **s**. Neh 13:26
all this Job did not **s** or charge God with Jb 1:22
In all this Job did not **s** with his lips. Jb 2:10
If I **s**, what do I do to you, you watcher of Jb 7:20
out my iniquity and search for my **s**, Jb 10:6
If I **s**, you watch me and do not acquit Jb 10:14
me know my transgression and my **s**. Jb 13:23
you would not keep watch over my **s**; Jb 14:16
not let my mouth **s** by asking for his Jb 31:30
For he adds rebellion to his **s**; he claps Jb 34:37
Be angry, and do not **s**; ponder in your Ps 4:4
is forgiven, whose **s** is covered. Ps 32:1
I acknowledged my **s** to you, and I did Ps 32:5
and you forgave the iniquity of my **s**. Ps 32:5
no health in my bones because of my **s**. Ps 38:3
my iniquity; I am sorry for my **s**. Ps 38:18
ways, that I may not **s** with my tongue; Ps 39:1
discipline a man with rebukes for **s**, Ps 39:11
Burnt offering and **s** offering you have Ps 40:6
my iniquity, and cleanse me from my **s**! Ps 51:2
and my **s** is ever before me. Ps 51:3
and in **s** did my mother conceive me. Ps 51:5
For no transgression or **s** of mine, O Ps 59:3
For the **s** of their mouths, the words of Ps 59:12
of your people; you covered all their **s**. Ps 85:2
guilty; let his prayer be counted as **s**! Ps 109:7
and let not the **s** of his mother be Ps 109:14
heart, that I might not **s** against you. Ps 119:11
and he is held fast in the cords of his **s**. Prv 5:22
leads to life, the gain of the wicked to **s**. Prv 10:16
blameless, but **s** overthrows the wicked. Prv 13:6
but **s** is a reproach to any people. Prv 14:34
his mouth does not **s** in judgment. Prv 16:10
my heart pure; I am clean from my **s**"? Prv 20:9
heart, the lamp of the wicked, are **s**. Prv 21:4
The devising of folly is **s**, and the scoffer Prv 24:9
Let not your mouth lead you into **s**, and Eccl 5:6
them; they proclaim their **s** like Sodom; Is 3:9
falsehood, who draw **s** as with cart ropes, Is 5:18
guilt is taken away, and your **s** atoned for. Is 6:7
be the full fruit of the removal of his **s**: Is 27:9

of my Spirit, that they may add **s** to sin; Is 30:1
of my Spirit, that they may add sin to **s**; Is 30:1
when his soul makes an offering for **s**, Is 53:10
yet he bore the **s** of many, and makes Is 53:12
What is the **s** that we have committed Jer 16:10
doubly repay their iniquity and their **s**, Jer 16:18
"The **s** of Judah is written with a pen of Jer 17:1
high places for **s** throughout all your Jer 17:3
nor blot out their **s** from your sight. Jer 18:23
But everyone shall die for his own **s**. Jer 31:30
and I will remember their **s** no more." Jer 31:34
this abomination, to cause Judah to **s**. Jer 32:35
from all the guilt of their **s** against me, Jer 33:8
the guilt of their **s** and rebellion against Jer 33:8
I may forgive their iniquity and their **s**." Jer 36:3
And **s** in Judah, and none shall be Jer 50:20
not warned him, he shall die for his **s**, Ezk 3:20
you warn the righteous person not to **s**, Ezk 3:21
person not to sin, and he does not **s**, Ezk 3:21
is guilty and the **s** he has committed, Ezk 18:24
if he turns from his **s** and does what is Ezk 33:14
offering and the **s** offering and the Ezk 40:39
—the grain offering, the **s** offering, Ezk 42:13
a bull from the herd for a **s** offering. Ezk 43:19
also take the bull of the **s** offering, Ezk 43:21
goat without blemish for a **s** offering; Ezk 43:22
daily a male goat for a **s** offering; Ezk 43:25
Place, he shall offer his **s** offering, Ezk 44:27
eat the grain offering, the **s** offering, Ezk 44:29
he shall provide the **s** offerings, grain Ezk 45:17
of the blood of the **s** offering and put it Ezk 45:19
the land a young bull for a **s** offering. Ezk 45:22
and a male goat daily for a **s** offering. Ezk 45:23
the same provision for **s** offerings, Ezk 45:25
the guilt offering and the **s** offering, Ezk 46:20
confessing my **s** and the sin of my Dn 9:20
my sin and the **s** of my people Israel, Dn 9:20
the transgression, to put an end to **s**, Dn 9:24
They feed on the **s** of my people; they are Hos 4:8
The high places of Aven, the **s** of Israel, Hos 10:8
they cannot find in me iniquity or **s**." Hos 12:8
And now they **s** more and more, and Hos 13:2
is bound up; his **s** is kept in store. Hos 13:12
was the beginning of **s** to the daughter of Mi 1:13
his transgression and to Israel his **s**. Mi 3:8
the fruit of my body for the **s** of my soul?" Mi 6:7
cleanse them from **s** and uncleanness. Zec 13:1
If your right eye causes you to **s**, tear it Mt 5:29
And if your right hand causes you to **s**, Mt 5:30
every **s** and blasphemy will be forgiven Mt 12:31
all causes of **s** and all law-breakers, Mt 13:41
of these little ones who believe in me to **s**, Mt 18:6
"Woe to the world for temptations to **s**! Mt 18:7
your hand or your foot causes you to **s**, Mt 18:8
And if your eye causes you to **s**, tear it Mt 18:9
often will my brother **s** against me, Mt 18:21
but is guilty of an eternal **s**"— Mk 3:29
these little ones who believe in me to **s**, Mk 9:42
And if your hand causes you to **s**, cut it Mk 9:43
And if your foot causes you to **s**, cut it Mk 9:45
And if your eye causes you to **s**, tear it Mk 9:47
"Temptations to **s** are sure to come, Lk 17:1
should cause one of these little ones to **s**. Lk 17:2
God, who takes away the **s** of the world! Jn 1:29
S no more, that nothing worse may Jn 5:14
him who is without **s** among you be the Jn 8:7
you; go, and from now on **s** no more."]] Jn 8:11
will seek me, and you will die in your **s**. Jn 8:21
everyone who commits **s** is a slave to sin. Jn 8:34
everyone who commits sin is a slave to **s**. Jn 8:34
Which one of you convicts me of **s**? If I Jn 8:46
answered him, "You were born in utter **s**, Jn 9:34
they would not have been guilty of **s**, Jn 15:22
but now they have no excuse for their **s**. Jn 15:22
else did, they would not be guilty of **s**, Jn 15:24
world concerning **s** and righteousness Jn 16:8
concerning **s**, because they do not Jn 16:9
me over to you has the greater **s**." Jn 19:11
do not hold this **s** against them." And Acts 7:60
all, both Jews and Greeks, are under **s**, Rom 3:9
the law comes knowledge of **s**. Rom 3:20
whom the Lord will not count his **s**." Rom 4:8
just as **s** came into the world through Rom 5:12
one man, and death through **s**, Rom 5:12
for **s** indeed was in the world before the Rom 5:13
but **s** is not counted where there is no Rom 5:13
not like the result of that one man's **s**. Rom 5:16
the trespass, but where **s** increased, Rom 5:20
so that, as **s** reigned in death, grace Rom 5:21
we to continue in **s** that grace may Rom 6:1
How can we who died to **s** still live in it? Rom 6:2
that the body of **s** might be brought to Rom 6:6
we would no longer be enslaved to **s**. Rom 6:6
who has died has been set free from **s**. Rom 6:7
For the death he died he died to **s**, once Rom 6:10
yourselves dead to **s** and alive to Rom 6:11
Let not **s** therefore reign in your Rom 6:12
your members to **s** as instruments for Rom 6:13
For **s** will have no dominion over you, Rom 6:14
Are we to **s** because we are not under Rom 6:15
of the one whom you obey, either of **s**, Rom 6:16
once slaves of **s** have become obedient Rom 6:17
and, having been set free from **s**, have Rom 6:18
When you were slaves of **s**, you were Rom 6:20
been set free from **s** and have become Rom 6:22
For the wages of **s** is death, but the free Rom 6:23
then shall we say? That the law is **s**? Rom 7:7
for the law, I would not have known **s**. Rom 7:7
But **s**, seizing an opportunity through Rom 7:8
Apart from the law, **s** lies dead. Rom 7:8
came, **s** came alive and I died. Rom 7:9
For **s**, seizing an opportunity through Rom 7:11
It was **s**, producing death in me Rom 7:13
in order that **s** might be shown to be Rom 7:13
order that sin might be shown to be **s**, Rom 7:13
but I am of the flesh, sold under **s**. Rom 7:14
who do it, but **s** that dwells within me. Rom 7:17
who do it, but **s** that dwells within me. Rom 7:20
to the law of **s** that dwells in my Rom 7:23
but with my flesh I serve the law of **s**. Rom 7:25
Jesus from the law of **s** and death. Rom 8:2
in the likeness of sinful flesh and for **s**, Rom 8:3
for sin, he condemned **s** in the flesh, Rom 8:3
the body is dead because of **s**, Rom 8:10
does not proceed from faith is **s**. Rom 14:23
Every other **s** a person commits is 1 Cor 6:18
he wishes: let them marry—it is no **s**. 1 Cor 7:36
when it is weak, you **s** against Christ. 1 Cor 8:12
The sting of death is **s**, and the 1 Cor 15:56
is sin, and the power of **s** is the law. 1 Cor 15:56
made him to be **s** who knew no sin, 2 Cor 5:21
made him to be sin who knew no **s**, 2 Cor 5:21
did I commit a **s** in humbling myself 2 Cor 11:7
be sinners, is Christ then a servant of **s**? Gal 2:17
imprisoned everything under **s**, Gal 3:22
Be angry and do not **s**; do not let the Eph 4:26
As for those who persist in **s**, rebuke 1 Tm 5:20
be hardened by the deceitfulness of **s**. Heb 3:13
been tempted as we are, yet without **s**. Heb 4:15
ages to put away **s** by the sacrifice of Heb 9:26
not to deal with **s** but to save those who Heb 9:28
no longer have any consciousness of **s**? Heb 10:2
there is a reminder of **s** every year. Heb 10:3
burnt offerings and **s** offerings you Heb 10:6
burnt offerings and **s** offerings" (these Heb 10:8
there is no longer any offering for **s**. Heb 10:18
to enjoy the fleeting pleasures of **s**. Heb 11:25
weight, and **s** which clings so closely, Heb 12:1
In your struggle against **s** you have not Heb 12:4
as a sacrifice for **s** are burned outside Heb 13:11
when it has conceived gives birth to **s**, Jas 1:15
and **s** when it is fully grown brings forth Jas 1:15
you are committing **s** and are convicted Jas 2:9
to do and fails to do it, for him it is **s**. Jas 4:17
is it if, when you **s** and are beaten for it, 1 Pt 2:20
He committed no **s**, neither was deceit 1 Pt 2:22
we might die to **s** and live to 1 Pt 2:24
suffered in the flesh has ceased from **s**, 1 Pt 4:1
eyes full of adultery, insatiable for **s**. 2 Pt 2:14
of Jesus his Son cleanses us from all **s**. 1 Jn 1:7
If we say we have no **s**, we deceive 1 Jn 1:8
things to you so that you may not **s**. 1 Jn 2:1
But if anyone does **s**, we have an 1 Jn 2:1
practices lawlessness; **s** is lawlessness. 1 Jn 3:4
take away sins, and in him there is no **s**. 1 Jn 3:5
brother committing a **s** not leading to 1 Jn 5:16
There is **s** that leads to death; I do not 1 Jn 5:16
All wrongdoing is **s**, but there is sin 1 Jn 5:17
but there is **s** that does not lead to 1 Jn 5:17

SINAI (39)

of Sin, which is between Elim and **S**, Ex 16:1
day they came into the wilderness of **S**. Ex 19:1
and came into the wilderness of **S**, Ex 19:2
come down on Mount **S** in the sight of Ex 19:11
Now Mount **S** was wrapped in smoke Ex 19:18
The LORD came down on Mount **S**, to Ex 19:20
people cannot come up to Mount **S**, Ex 19:23
glory of the LORD dwelt on Mount **S**, Ex 24:16
speaking with him on Mount **S**, Ex 31:18
come up in the morning to Mount **S**, Ex 34:2
the morning and went up on Mount **S**, Ex 34:4
Moses came down from Mount **S**, Ex 34:29
LORD had spoken with him in Mount **S**. Ex 34:32
LORD commanded Moses on Mount **S**, Lv 7:38
to the LORD, in the wilderness of **S**. Lv 7:38
The LORD spoke to Moses on Mount **S**, Lv 25:1
of Israel through Moses on Mount **S**. Lv 26:46
for the people of Israel on Mount **S**. Lv 27:34
spoke to Moses in the wilderness of **S**, Nm 1:1
So he listed them in the wilderness of **S**. Nm 1:19
the LORD spoke with Moses on Mount **S**. Nm 3:1
before the LORD in the wilderness of **S**, Nm 3:4
spoke to Moses in the wilderness of **S**, Nm 3:14
spoke to Moses in the wilderness of **S**, Nm 9:1
at twilight, in the wilderness of **S**; Nm 9:5
out by stages from the wilderness of **S**. Nm 10:12
people of Israel in the wilderness of **S**. Nm 26:64
was ordained at Mount **S** for a pleasing Nm 28:6
and camped in the wilderness of **S**. Nm 33:15
the wilderness of **S** and camped at Nm 33:16
LORD came from **S** and dawned from Dt 33:2
before the LORD, even **S** before the LORD, Jgs 5:5
down on Mount **S** and spoke with Neh 9:13
down rain, before God, the One of **S**, Ps 68:8
among them; **S** is now in the sanctuary. Ps 68:17
to him in the wilderness of Mount **S**, Acts 7:30
angel who spoke to him at Mount **S**, Acts 7:38
One is from Mount **S**, bearing children Gal 4:24
Now Hagar is Mount **S** in Arabia; she Gal 4:25

SINCE (194)

you may pass on—**s** you have come to Gn 18:5
me, **s** the LORD has prospered my way. Gn 24:56
And **s** they bred when they came to Gn 30:38
s I did not give her to my son Shelah." Gn 38:26
Joseph, "**S** God has shown you all this, Gn 41:39
to pieces, and I have never seen him **s**. Gn 44:28
s I have seen your face and know that Gn 46:30
s this one is the firstborn, put your Gn 48:18
either in the past or **s** you have spoken to Ex 4:10
For **s** I came to Pharaoh to speak in your Ex 5:23
the land of Egypt **s** it became a nation. Ex 9:24
people, **s** he has broken faith with her. Ex 21:8
s it is a thing most holy and has been Lv 10:17
your father's family, **s** she is your sister. Lv 18:11
s he has a blemish, he shall not come Lv 21:21
S there is a blemish in them, because of Lv 22:25
s it is for him a most holy portion out of Lv 24:9
him calculate the years **s** he sold it and Lv 25:27
her, **s** she was not taken in the act, Nm 5:13
s the Amalekites and the Canaanites Nm 14:25
s he has defiled the sanctuary of the Nm 19:20
for me, **s** they are too mighty for me. Nm 22:6
S you saw no form on the day that the Dt 4:15
s the day that God created man on the Dt 4:32
And consider today (**s** I am not speaking Dt 11:2
s he has no portion or inheritance with Dt 12:12
household, **s** he is well-off with you, Dt 15:16
many horses, **s** the LORD has said to you, Dt 17:16
s he had not hated his neighbor in the Dt 19:6
as a slave, **s** you have humiliated her. Dt 21:14
not arisen a prophet **s** in Israel like Dt 34:10
has been no day like it before or **s**, Jos 10:14
these forty-five years **s** the time that the Jos 14:10
S you have given me the land of the Jos 15:19
s all along the LORD has blessed me?" Jos 17:14
s the hill country of Ephraim is too Jos 17:15
people of Levi; **s** the lot fell to them first. Jos 21:10
s it is the LORD your God who fights for Jos 23:10
S you have set me in the land of the Jgs 1:15
s this man has come into my house, do Jgs 19:23
s we have sworn by the LORD that we will Jgs 21:7
s the women are destroyed out of Jgs 21:16
take notice of me, **s** I am a foreigner?" Ru 2:10
for your mother-in-law **s** the death of Ru 2:11
comes, **s** he must bless the sacrifice; 1 Sm 9:13
s I have rejected him from being king 1 Sm 16:1
s I am a poor man and have no 1 Sm 18:23
s the LORD has turned from you and 1 Sm 28:16
and **s** he deserted to me I have found 1 Sm 29:3
not lived in a house **s** the day I brought 2 Sm 7:6
about Amnon, **s** he was dead. 2 Sm 13:39
with us, **s** I go I know not where? 2 Sm 15:20
s my lord the king has come safely 2 Sm 19:30
'**S** the day that I brought my people 1 Kgs 8:16
"**S** this has been your practice and 1 Kgs 11:11
"**S** I exalted you out of the dust and 1 Kgs 16:2
s he promised to give a lamp to him 2 Kgs 8:19
s the day their fathers came out of 2 Kgs 21:15
Passover had been kept **s** the days of 2 Kgs 23:22
lived in a house **s** the day I brought 1 Chr 17:5
S more chief men were found among 1 Chr 24:4
is able to build him a house, **s** heaven, 2 Chr 2:6
'**S** the day that I brought my people out 2 Chr 6:5
and **s** he had promised to give a lamp 2 Chr 21:7
for **s** the time of Solomon the son of 2 Chr 30:26
"**S** they began to bring the 2 Chr 31:10
been kept in Israel **s** the days of 2 Chr 35:18
sacrificing to him ever **s** the days of Ezr 4:2
on our way, **s** we had told the king, Ezr 8:22
s the time of the kings of Assyria until Neh 9:32
with contempt, **s** they will say, Est 1:17
s this was the regular period of their Est 2:12
S his days are determined, and the Jb 14:5
S you have closed their hearts to Jb 17:4
from of old, **s** man was placed on earth, Jb 20:4

commanded the morning **s** your days Jb 38:12
beauty. **S** he is your lord, bow to him. Ps 45:11
s the same event happens to the Eccl 9:2
as have not come **s** the day that Ephraim Is 7:17
of Lebanon, saying, '**S** you were laid low, Is 14:8
me, **s** I appointed an ancient people. Is 44:7
dismayed, **s** there is no rain on the land, Jer 14:4
But **s** we left off making offerings to the Jer 44:18
wild beasts, **s** there was no shepherd, Ezk 34:8
as never has been **s** there was a nation Dn 12:1
And **s** you have forgotten the law of your Hos 4:6
S the day that the foundation of the Hg 2:18
sprang up, **s** they had no depth of soil, Mt 13:5
And **s** they had no root, they withered Mt 13:6
has been hidden **s** the foundation of Mt 13:35
And **s** he could not pay, his master Mt 18:25
'**S** there will not be enough for us and for Mt 25:9
into the treasury, **s** it is blood money." Mt 27:6
it sprang up, **s** it had no depth of soil. Mk 4:5
rose it was scorched, and **s** it had no root, Mk 4:6
s it enters not his heart but his Mk 7:19
come, **s** it was the day of Preparation, Mk 15:42
"How will this be, **s** I am a virgin?" Lk 1:34
s my master is taking the management Lk 16:3
s then the good news of the kingdom of Lk 16:16
house, **s** he also is a son of Abraham. Lk 19:9
s you are under the same sentence of Lk 23:40
the third day **s** these things happened. Lk 24:21
Jews said, "Will he kill himself, **s** he says, Jn 8:22
him, **s** he has opened your eyes?" He said, Jn 9:17
Never **s** the world began has it been Jn 9:32
s you have given him authority over all Jn 17:2
S that disciple was known to the high Jn 18:15
S it was the day of Preparation, and so Jn 19:31
s the tomb was close at hand, Jn 19:42
s it is only the third hour of the day. Acts 2:15
S Lydda was near Joppa, the disciples, Acts 9:38
S you thrust it aside and judge Acts 13:46
S we have heard that some persons Acts 15:24
s he himself gives to all mankind life Acts 17:25
But **s** it is a matter of questions about Acts 18:15
s there is no cause that we can give to Acts 19:40
And **s** he would not be persuaded, we Acts 21:14
And **s** I could not see because of the Acts 22:11
"**S** through you we enjoy much peace, Acts 24:2
much peace, and **s** by your foresight, Acts 24:2
more than twelve days **s** I went up to Acts 24:11
S much time had passed, and the Acts 27:9
S we were violently storm-tossed, they Acts 27:18
S they had been without food for a Acts 27:21
s it is because of the hope of Israel Acts 28:20
ever **s** the creation of the world, Rom 1:20
And **s** they did not see fit to Rom 1:28
s through the law comes knowledge of Rom 3:20
s God is one. He will justify the Rom 3:30
was as good as dead (**s** he was about a Rom 4:19
s we have been justified by faith, Rom 5:1
S, therefore, we have now been justified Rom 5:9
s you are not under law but under Rom 6:14
of the Lord, **s** he gives thanks to God, Rom 14:6
s I no longer have any room for work Rom 15:23
and **s** I have longed for many years to Rom 15:23
For **s**, in the wisdom of God, the world 1 Cor 1:21
s then you would need to go out of the 1 Cor 5:10
But **s** it is disgraceful for a wife to cut 1 Cor 11:6
s he is the image and glory of God, 1 Cor 11:7
s you are eager for manifestations of 1 Cor 14:12
S we have such a hope, we are very 2 Cor 3:12
S we have the same spirit of faith 2 Cor 4:13
S we have these promises, beloved, let 2 Cor 7:1
that Achaia has been ready **s** last year. 2 Cor 9:2
S many boast according to the flesh, 2 Cor 11:18
s you seek proof that Christ is 2 Cor 13:3
s we heard of your faith in Christ Jesus Col 1:4
s the day you heard it and understood the Col 1:6
But **s** we were torn away from you, 1 Thes 2:17
For **s** we believe that Jesus died and 1 Thes 4:14
But **s** we belong to the day, let us be 1 Thes 5:8
s indeed God considers it just to repay 2 Thes 1:6
serve all the better **s** those who benefit 1 Tm 6:2
s his aim is to please the one who 2 Tm 2:4
s they are upsetting whole families by Ti 1:11
For **s** the message declared by angels Heb 2:2
S therefore the children share in flesh Heb 2:14
S therefore it remains for some to enter Heb 4:6
S then we have a great high priest who Heb 4:14
s he himself is beset with weakness. Heb 5:2
s you have become dull of hearing. Heb 5:11
word of righteousness, **s** he is a child. Heb 5:13
s they are crucifying once again the Son Heb 6:6
s he had no one greater by whom to Heb 6:13
s he always lives to make intercession Heb 7:25
s he did this once for all when he Heb 7:27
s there are priests who offer gifts Heb 8:4
better, **s** it is enacted on better promises. Heb 8:6
s a death has occurred that redeems Heb 9:15
s it is not in force as long as the one Heb 9:17
to suffer repeatedly **s** the foundation of Heb 9:26
For **s** the law has but a shadow of the Heb 10:1
ceased to be offered, **s** the worshipers, Heb 10:2
s we have confidence to enter the holy Heb 10:19
and **s** we have a great priest over the Heb 10:21
s you knew that you yourselves had a Heb 10:34
s she considered him faithful who Heb 11:11
s God had provided something better Heb 11:40
s we are surrounded by so great a cloud Heb 12:1
mistreated, **s** you also are in the body. Heb 13:3
s it is written, "You shall be holy, for I 1 Pt 1:16
s you have been born again, not of 1 Pt 1:23
s they are heirs with you of the grace of 1 Pt 3:7
S therefore Christ suffered in the flesh, 1 Pt 4:1
s love covers a multitude of sins. 1 Pt 4:8
s I know that the putting off of my 2 Pt 1:14
For ever **s** the fathers fell asleep, all 2 Pt 3:4
S all these things are thus to be 2 Pt 3:11
beloved, **s** you are waiting for these, 2 Pt 3:14
there had never been **s** man was on the Rv 16:18
and mourning, **s** in her heart she says, Rv 18:7
s no one buys their cargo anymore, Rv 18:11

SINCERE (8)
and sent spies, who pretended to be **s**, Lk 20:20
led astray from a **s** and pure devotion 2 Cor 11:3
with fear and trembling, with a **s** heart, Eph 6:5
and a good conscience and a **s** faith. 1 Tm 1:5
I am reminded of your **s** faith, a faith 2 Tm 1:5
mercy and good fruits, impartial and **s**. Jas 3:17
to the truth for a **s** brotherly love, 1 Pt 1:22
I am stirring up your **s** mind by way of 2 Pt 3:1

SINCERELY (2)
and what my lips know they speak **s**. Jb 33:3
not **s** but thinking to afflict me in my Phil 1:17

SINCERITY (5)
and serve him in **s** and in faithfulness. Jos 24:14
the unleavened bread of **s** and truth. 1 Cor 5:8
the world with simplicity and godly **s**, 2 Cor 1:12
of God's word, but as men of **s**, 2 Cor 2:17
as people-pleasers, but with **s** of heart, Col 3:22

SINEW (3)
Israel do not eat the **s** of the thigh that Gn 32:32
of Jacob's hip on the **s** of the thigh. Gn 32:32
neck is an iron **s** and your forehead Is 48:4

SINEWS (4)
and knit me together with bones and **s**. Jb 10:11
the **s** of his thighs are knit together. Jb 40:17
And I will lay **s** upon you, and will Ezk 37:6
and behold, there were **s** on them, Ezk 37:8

SINFUL (16)
your fathers' place, a brood of **s** men, Nm 32:14
Then I took the **s** thing, the calf that you Dt 9:21
Some were fools through their **s** ways, Ps 107:17
Ah, **s** nation, a people laden with iniquity, Is 1:4
bear the penalty for your **s** idolatry, Ezk 23:49
of the Lord GOD are upon the **s** kingdom, Am 9:8
in this adulterous and **s** generation, Mk 8:38
"Depart from me, for I am a **s** man, Lk 5:8
into the hands of **s** men and be crucified Lk 24:7
were living in the flesh, our **s** passions, Rom 7:5
might become **s** beyond measure. Rom 7:13
Son in the likeness of **s** flesh and for sin, Rom 8:3
that such a person is warped and **s**; Ti 3:11
that is in the world because of **s** desire. 2 Pt 1:4
scoffing, following their own **s** desires. 2 Pt 3:3
following their own **s** desires; Jude 1:16

SINFULLY (2)
had made Judah act **s** and had been 2 Chr 28:19
which your hands have **s** made for you. Is 31:7

SING (115)
to the LORD, saying, "I will **s** to the LORD, Ex 15:1
"**S** to the LORD, for he has triumphed Ex 15:21
this song: "Spring up, O well!—**S** to it! Nm 21:17
give ear, O princes; to the LORD I will **s**; Jgs 5:3
Did they not **s** to one another of him 1 Sm 21:11
of whom they **s** to one another in 1 Sm 29:5
nations, and **s** praises to your name. 2 Sm 22:50
S to him; sing praises to him; tell of 1 Chr 16:9
Sing to him; **s** praises to him; tell of 1 Chr 16:9
S to the LORD, all the earth! Tell of 1 Chr 16:23
trees of the forest **s** for joy before the 1 Chr 16:33
those who were to **s** to the LORD and 2 Chr 20:21
when they began to **s** and praise, 2 Chr 20:22
the Levites to **s** praises to the 2 Chr 29:30
They **s** to the tambourine and the lyre Jb 21:12
I caused the widow's heart to **s** for joy. Jb 29:13
let them ever **s** for joy, and spread your Ps 5:11
and I will **s** praise to the name of the Ps 7:17
I will **s** praise to your name, O Most High. Ps 9:2
S praises to the LORD, who sits enthroned Ps 9:11
I will **s** to the LORD, because he has dealt Ps 13:6
among the nations, and **s** to your name. Ps 18:49
We will **s** and praise your power. Ps 21:13
joy; I will **s** and make melody to the LORD. Ps 27:6
S praises to the LORD, O you his saints, Ps 30:4
that my glory may **s** your praise and Ps 30:12
S to him a new song; play skillfully on Ps 33:3
S praises to God, sing praises! Sing Ps 47:6
Sing praises to God, **s** praises! Sing Ps 47:6
S praises to our King, sing praises! Ps 47:6
Sing praises to our King, **s** praises! Ps 47:6
of all the earth; **s** praises with a psalm! Ps 47:7
and my tongue will **s** aloud of your Ps 51:14
is steadfast! I will **s** and make melody! Ps 57:7
I will **s** praises to you among the nations. Ps 57:9
But I will **s** of your strength; I will sing Ps 59:16
I will **s** aloud of your steadfast love in Ps 59:16
O my Strength, I will **s** praises to you, Ps 59:17
So will I ever **s** praises to your name, as I Ps 61:8
the shadow of your wings I will **s** for joy. Ps 63:7
grain, they shout and **s** together for joy. Ps 65:13
s the glory of his name; give to him Ps 66:2
you; they **s** praises to your name." Selah Ps 66:4
Let the nations be glad and **s** for joy, for Ps 67:4
S to God, sing praises to his name; lift up Ps 68:4
Sing to God, **s** praises to his name; lift up Ps 68:4
O kingdoms of the earth, **s** to God; sing Ps 68:32
sing to God; **s** praises to the Lord, Selah Ps 68:32
I will **s** praises to you with the lyre, O Ps 71:22
shout for joy, when I **s** praises to you; Ps 71:23
I will **s** praises to the God of Jacob. Ps 75:9
S aloud to God our strength; shout for Ps 81:1
my heart and flesh **s** for joy to the living Ps 84:2
I will **s** of the steadfast love of the LORD, Ps 89:1
to the LORD, to **s** praises to your name, Ps 92:1
at the works of your hands I **s** for joy. Ps 92:4
Oh come, let us **s** to the LORD; let us make Ps 95:1
Oh **s** to the LORD a new song; sing to the Ps 96:1
a new song; **s** to the LORD, all the earth! Ps 96:1
S to the LORD, bless his name; tell of his Ps 96:2
shall all the trees of the forest **s** for joy Ps 96:12
Oh **s** to the LORD a new song, for he has Ps 98:1
forth into joyous song and **s** praises! Ps 98:4
S praises to the LORD with the lyre, with Ps 98:5
their hands; let the hills **s** for joy together Ps 98:8
I will **s** of steadfast love and justice; to Ps 101:1
dwell; they **s** among the branches. Ps 104:12
I will **s** to the LORD as long as I live; I Ps 104:33
I will **s** praise to my God while I have Ps 104:33
S to him, sing praises to him; tell of all Ps 105:2
Sing to him, **s** praises to him; tell of all Ps 105:2
I will **s** and make melody with all my Ps 108:1
I will **s** praises to you among the Ps 108:3
My tongue will **s** of your word, for all Ps 119:172
is good; **s** to his name, for it is pleasant! Ps 135:3
saying, "**S** us one of the songs of Zion!" Ps 137:3
How shall we **s** the LORD'S song in a Ps 137:4
heart; before the gods I **s** your praise; Ps 138:1
and they shall **s** of the ways of the LORD, Ps 138:5
I will **s** a new song to you, O God; upon Ps 144:9
goodness and shall **s** aloud of your Ps 145:7
I will **s** praises to my God while I have Ps 146:2
For it is good to **s** praises to our God; for Ps 147:1
S to the LORD with thanksgiving; make Ps 147:7
S to the LORD a new song, his praise in Ps 149:1
in glory; let them **s** for joy on their beds. Ps 149:5
Let me **s** for my beloved my love song Is 5:1
"**S** praises to the LORD, for he has done Is 12:5
Shout, and **s** for joy, O inhabitant of Zion, Is 12:6
s many songs, that you may be Is 23:16
They lift up their voices, they **s** for joy; Is 24:14
dwell in the dust, awake and **s** for joy! Is 26:19
In that day, "A pleasant vineyard, **s** of it! Is 27:2
deer, and the tongue of the mute **s** for joy. Is 35:6
S to the LORD a new song, his praise from Is 42:10
let the habitants of Sela **s** for joy, let Is 42:11
S, O heavens, for the LORD has done it; Is 44:23
S for joy, O heavens, and exult, O earth; Is 49:13
lift up their voice; together they **s** for joy; Is 52:8
"**S**, O barren one, who did not bear; break Is 54:1
my servants shall **s** for gladness of heart, Is 65:14
S to the LORD; praise the LORD! For he Jer 20:13
"**S** aloud with gladness for Jacob, and Jer 31:7
They shall come and **s** aloud on the Jer 31:12
of the bride, the voices of those who **s**, Jer 33:11
is in them, shall **s** for joy over Babylon, Jer 51:48
who **s** idle songs to the sound of the harp Am 6:5
S aloud, O daughter of Zion; shout, O Zep 3:14
S and rejoice, O daughter of Zion, for Zec 2:10
the Gentiles, and **s** to your name." Rom 15:9
I will **s** praise with my spirit, but I 1 Cor 14:15
but I will **s** with my mind also. 1 Cor 14:15
the congregation I will **s** your praise." Heb 2:12
Is anyone cheerful? Let him **s** praise. Jas 5:13
And they **s** the song of Moses, the servant Rv 15:3

SINGED (1)
The hair of their heads was not **s**, their Dn 3:27

SINGER (1)
Heman the **s** the son of Joel, son of 1 Chr 6:33

SINGERS (38)
Therefore the ballad **s** say, "Come to Nm 21:27
house, also lyres and harps for the **s**. 1 Kgs 10:12
Now these, the **s**, the heads of fathers' 1 Chr 9:33
brothers as the **s** who should play 1 Chr 15:16
The **s**, Heman, Asaph, and Ethan, 1 Chr 15:19
and the **s** and Chenaniah the leader 1 Chr 15:27
the leader of the music of the **s**. 1 Chr 15:27
and all the Levitical **s**, Asaph, 2 Chr 5:12
the trumpeters and **s** to make 2 Chr 5:13
house, lyres also and harps for the **s**. 2 Chr 9:11
and the **s** with their musical 2 Chr 23:13
and the **s** sang and the trumpeters 2 Chr 29:28
The **s**, the sons of Asaph, were in 2 Chr 35:15
The **s**: the sons of Asaph, 128. Ezr 2:41
and they had 200 male and female **s**. Ezr 2:65
the Levites, some of the people, the **s**, Ezr 2:70
priests and Levites, the **s** and gatekeepers, Ezr 7:7
anyone of the priests, the Levites, the **s**, Ezr 7:24
Of the **s**: Eliashib. Of the gatekeepers: Ezr 10:24
up the doors, and the gatekeepers, the **s**, Neh 7:1
The **s**: the sons of Asaph, 148. Neh 7:44
And they had 245 **s**, male and female. Neh 7:67
the Levites, the gatekeepers, the **s**, Neh 7:73
the Levites, the gatekeepers, the **s**, Neh 10:28
and the gatekeepers and the **s**. Neh 10:39
of Mica, of the sons of Asaph, the **s**, Neh 11:22
them, and a fixed provision for the **s**, Neh 11:23
sons of the **s** gathered together from Neh 12:28
for the **s** had built for themselves Neh 12:29
And the **s** sang with Jezrahiah as their Neh 12:42
as did the **s** and the gatekeepers, Neh 12:45
Asaph there were directors of the **s**, Neh 12:46
portions for the **s** and the gatekeepers; Neh 12:47
to the Levites, **s**, and gatekeepers, Neh 13:5
to them, so that the Levites and the **s**, Neh 13:10
the **s** in front, the musicians last, Ps 68:25
S and dancers alike say, "All my springs Ps 87:7
I got **s**, both men and women, and Eccl 2:8

SINGING (29)
of defeat, but the sound of **s** that I hear." Ex 32:18
all the cities of Israel, **s** and dancing, 1 Sm 18:6
to the voice of **s** men and singing 2 Sm 19:35
voice of singing men and **s** women? 2 Sm 19:35
who were trained in **s** to the LORD, 1 Chr 25:7
of Moses, with rejoicing and with **s**, 2 Chr 23:18
s with all their might to the LORD. 2 Chr 30:21
and all the **s** men and singing 2 Chr 35:25
singing men and **s** women have 2 Chr 35:25
with thanksgivings and with **s**, Neh 12:27
dwell in your house, ever **s** your praise! Ps 84:4
Come into his presence with **s**! Ps 100:2
out with joy, his chosen ones with **s**. Ps 105:43
on the earth, the time of **s** has come, Sg 2:12
at rest and quiet; they break forth into **s**. Is 14:7
No more do they drink wine with **s**; Is 24:9
abundantly and rejoice with joy and **s**. Is 35:2
shall return and come to Zion with **s**; Is 35:10
break forth into **s**, O mountains, O Is 44:23
earth; break forth, O mountains, into **s**! Is 49:13
shall return and come to Zion with **s**; Is 51:11
Break forth together into **s**, you waste Is 52:9
bear; break forth into **s** and cry aloud, Is 54:1
hills before you shall break forth into **s**, Is 55:12
love; he will exult over you with loud **s**. Zep 3:17
were praying and **s** hymns to God, Acts 16:25
s and making melody to the Lord with Eph 5:19
s psalms and hymns and spiritual Col 3:16
and they were **s** a new song before the Rv 14:3

SINGLE (38)
Not a **s** locust was left in all the Ex 10:19
If he comes in **s**, he shall go out single; if Ex 21:3
If he comes in single, he shall go out **s**; if Ex 21:3
whole of it a **s** piece of hammered work Ex 25:36
so that the tabernacle may be a **s** whole. Ex 26:6
tent together that it may be a **s** whole. Ex 26:11
if for a **s** moment I should go up among Ex 33:5
clasps. So the tabernacle was a **s** whole. Ex 36:13
tent together that it might be a **s** whole. Ex 36:18
of it was a **s** piece of hammered work Ex 37:22
your bread in a **s** oven and shall dole Lv 26:26
a branch with a **s** cluster of grapes, Nm 13:23
"A **s** witness shall not suffice against a Dt 19:15
And the LORD will **s** him out from all Dt 29:21
out to seek a **s** flea like one who 1 Sm 26:20
not leave him a **s** male of his 1 Kgs 16:11
you repulse a **s** captain among the 2 Kgs 18:24
Israel were of a **s** mind to make 1 Chr 12:38
counted as a **s** father's house. 1 Chr 23:11
can you repulse a **s** captain among the Is 36:9
put them into a **s** vessel and make your Ezk 4:9
Joshua, on a **s** stone with seven eyes, Zec 3:9
the iniquity of this land in a **s** day. Zec 3:9
anxious can add a **s** hour to his span Mt 6:27
sea and land to make a **s** proselyte, Mt 23:15
him no answer, not even to a **s** charge, Mt 27:14
anxious can add a **s** hour to his span Lk 12:25
it is good for them to remain **s** as I am. 1 Cor 7:8
twenty-three thousand fell in a **s** day. 1 Cor 10:8
If all were a **s** member, where would 1 Cor 12:19
for all time a **s** sacrifice for sins, Heb 10:12
For by a **s** offering he has perfected for Heb 10:14
who sold his birthright for a **s** meal. Heb 12:16
reason her plagues will come in a **s** day, Rv 18:8
For in a **s** hour your judgment has Rv 18:10
For in a **s** hour all this wealth has been Rv 18:17
For in a **s** hour she has been laid waste. Rv 18:19
each of the gates made of a **s** pearl, Rv 21:21

SINGLENESS (1)
war, to help David with **s** of purpose. 1 Chr 12:33

SINGS (5)
He **s** before men and says: 'I sinned and Jb 33:27
earth worships you and **s** praises to you; Ps 66:4
Whoever **s** songs to a heavy heart is Prv 25:20
but a righteous man **s** and rejoices. Prv 29:6
like one who **s** lustful songs with Ezk 33:32

SINITES (2)
the Hivites, the Arkites, the **S**, Gn 10:17
the Hivites, the Arkites, the **S**, 1 Chr 1:15

SINK (10)
who rise against me **s** under me. 2 Sm 22:40
The helpless are crushed, **s** down, and Ps 10:10
those who rise against me **s** under me. Ps 18:39
I **s** in deep mire, where there is no Ps 69:2
and say, 'Thus shall Babylon **s**, to rise Jer 51:64
s into the heart of the seas on the day Ezk 27:27
Nile, and be tossed about and **s** again, Am 8:8
afraid, and beginning to **s** he cried out, Mt 14:30
both the boats, so that they began to **s**. Lk 5:7
"Let these words **s** into your ears: The Lk 9:44

SINKING (1)
Deliver me from **s** in the mire; let me be Ps 69:14

SINKS (4)
for her house **s** down to death, and her Prv 2:18
Through sloth the roof **s** in, and Eccl 10:18
and as dry grass **s** down in the flame, Is 5:24
all of it rises like the Nile, and **s** again, Am 9:5

SINNED (104)
And how have I **s** against you, that you Gn 20:9
and said to them, "This time I have **s**; Ex 9:27
he **s** yet again and hardened his heart, Ex 9:34
"I have **s** against the LORD your God, Ex 10:16
to the people, "You have **s** a great sin. Ex 32:30
"Alas, this people have **s** a great sin. Ex 32:31
to Moses, "Whoever has **s** against me, Ex 32:33
if he has **s** and has realized his guilt and Lv 6:4
because he **s** by reason of the dead Nm 6:11
we have done foolishly and have **s**. Nm 12:11
the LORD has promised, for we have **s**." Nm 14:40
of these men who have **s** at the cost of Nm 16:38
came to Moses and said, "We have **s**, Nm 21:7
said to the angel of the LORD, "I have **s**, Nm 22:34
behold, you have **s** against the LORD, Nm 32:23
me, 'We have **s** against the LORD. Dt 1:41
you had **s** against the LORD your God. Dt 9:16
Israel has **s**; they have transgressed my Jos 7:11
"Truly I have **s** against the LORD God of Jos 7:20
LORD, saying, "We have **s** against you, Jgs 10:10
of Israel said to the LORD, "We have **s**; Jgs 10:15
I therefore have not **s** against you, and Jgs 11:27
"We have **s** against the LORD." And 1 Sm 7:6
out to the LORD and said, 'We have **s**, 1 Sm 12:10
Saul said to Samuel, "I have **s**, for I 1 Sm 15:24
Then he said, "I have **s**; yet honor me 1 Sm 15:30
because he has not **s** against you, 1 Sm 19:4
I have not **s** against you, though you 1 Sm 24:11
Then Saul said, "I have **s**. Return, my 1 Sm 26:21
"I have **s** against the LORD." And 2 Sm 12:13
your servant knows that I have **s**. 2 Sm 19:20
"I have **s** greatly in what I have done. 2 Sm 24:10
people, and said, "Behold, I have **s**, 2 Sm 24:17
because they have **s** against you, 1 Kgs 8:33
rain because they have **s** against you, 1 Kgs 8:35
'We have **s** and have acted perversely 1 Kgs 8:47
your people who have **s** against you, 1 Kgs 8:50
which he **s** and made Israel to sin." 1 Kgs 14:16
of Jeroboam that he **s** and that he 1 Kgs 15:30
which they **s** and which they made 1 Kgs 16:13
And he said, "How have I **s**, that you 1 Kgs 18:9
people of Israel had **s** against the LORD 2 Kgs 17:7
"I have **s** greatly in that I have done 1 Chr 21:8
It is I who have **s** and done great evil. 1 Chr 21:17
because they have **s** against you, 2 Chr 6:24
rain because they have **s** against you, 2 Chr 6:26
'We have **s** and have acted perversely 2 Chr 6:37
your people who have **s** against you. 2 Chr 6:39
of Israel, which we have **s** against you. Neh 1:6
Even I and my father's house have **s**. Neh 1:6
but **s** against your rules, Neh 9:29
said, "It may be that my children have **s**, Jb 1:5
If your children have **s** against him, he Jb 8:4
waters; so does Sheol those who have **s**. Jb 24:19
'I **s** and perverted what was right, and it Jb 33:27
I? How am I better off than if I had **s**?' Jb 35:3
If you have **s**, what do you accomplish Jb 35:6
to me; heal me, for I have **s** against you!" Ps 41:4
have I **s** and done what is evil in your Ps 51:4
Yet they **s** still more against him, Ps 78:17
In spite of all this, they still **s**; despite his Ps 78:32
Both we and our fathers have **s**; we have Ps 106:6
it not the LORD, against whom we have **s**, Is 42:24
Your first father **s**, and your mediators Is 43:27
Behold, you were angry, and we **s**; in our Is 64:5
to judgment for saying, 'I have not **s**.' Jer 2:35
For we have **s** against the LORD our God, Jer 3:25
because we have **s** against the LORD. Jer 8:14
are many; we have **s** against you. Jer 14:7
our fathers, for we have **s** against you. Jer 14:20
Because you **s** against the LORD and did Jer 40:3
and because you **s** against the LORD Jer 44:23
guilty, for they have **s** against the LORD, Jer 50:7
arrows, for she has **s** against the LORD. Jer 50:14
Jerusalem **s** grievously; therefore she Lam 1:8
Our fathers **s**, and are no more; and we Lam 5:7
our head; woe to us, for we have **s**! Lam 5:16
violence in your midst, and you **s**; Ezk 28:16
backslidings in which they have **s**, Ezk 37:23
for anyone who has **s** through error or Ezk 45:20
we have **s** and done wrong and acted Dn 9:5
fathers, because we have **s** against you. Dn 9:8
us, because we have **s** against him. Dn 9:11
for yourself, as at this day, we have **s**, Dn 9:15
increased, the more they **s** against me; Hos 4:7
From the days of Gibeah, you have **s**, O Hos 10:9
of the LORD because I have **s** against him, Mi 7:9
because they have **s** against the LORD; Zep 1:17
"I have **s** by betraying innocent blood." Mt 27:4
I have **s** against heaven and before you. Lk 15:18
I have **s** against heaven and before you. Lk 15:21
his disciples asked him, "Rabbi, who **s**, Jn 9:2
answered, "It was not that this man **s**, Jn 9:3
For all who have **s** without the law Rom 2:12
and all who have **s** under the law will Rom 2:12
for all have **s** and fall short of the glory Rom 3:23
death spread to all men because all **s**— Rom 5:12
But if you do marry, you have not **s**, 1 Cor 7:28
woman marries, she has not **s**. 1 Cor 7:28
of those who **s** earlier and have 2 Cor 12:21
I warned those who **s** before and all 2 Cor 13:2
Was it not with those who **s**, whose Heb 3:17
if God did not spare angels when they **s**, 2 Pt 2:4
If we say we have not **s**, we make him a 1 Jn 1:10

SINNER (20)
how much more the wicked and the **s**! Prv 11:31
Whoever despises his neighbor is a **s**, Prv 14:21
but to the **s** he has given the business Eccl 2:26
escapes her, but the **s** is taken by her. Eccl 7:26
Though a **s** does evil a hundred times Eccl 8:12
As is the good, so is the **s**, and he who Eccl 9:2
of war, but one **s** destroys much good. Eccl 9:18
and the **s** a hundred years old shall be Is 65:20
a woman of the city, who was a **s**, Lk 7:37
is who is touching him, for she is a **s**." Lk 7:39
in heaven over one **s** who repents than Lk 15:7
angels of God over one **s** who repents." Lk 15:10
saying, 'God, be merciful to me, a **s**!' Lk 18:13
in to be the guest of a man who is a **s**." Lk 19:7
a man who is a **s** do such signs?" And Jn 9:16
to God. We know that this man is a **s**." Jn 9:24
"Whether he is a **s** I do not know. Jn 9:25
why am I still being condemned as a **s**? Rom 3:7
brings back a **s** from his wandering Jas 5:20
will become of the ungodly and the **s**?" 1 Pt 4:18

SINNER'S (1)
but the **s** wealth is laid up for the Prv 13:22

SINNERS (46)
were wicked, great **s** against the LORD. Gn 13:13
said, 'Go, devote to destruction the **s**, 1 Sm 15:18
of the wicked, nor stands in the way of **s**, Ps 1:1
nor **s** in the congregation of the righteous; Ps 1:5
LORD; therefore he instructs **s** in the way. Ps 25:8
Do not sweep my soul away with **s**, nor Ps 26:9
your ways, and **s** will return to you. Ps 51:13
Let **s** be consumed from the earth, and Ps 104:35
My son, if **s** entice you, do not consent. Prv 1:10

Disaster pursues **s**, but the righteous Prv 13:21
Let not your heart envy **s**, but Prv 23:17
But rebels and **s** shall be broken together, Is 1:28
a desolation and to destroy its **s** from it. Is 13:9
The **s** in Zion are afraid; trembling has Is 33:14
All the **s** of my people shall die by the Am 9:10
tax collectors and **s** came and were Mt 9:10
teacher eat with tax collectors and **s**?" Mt 9:11
I came not to call the righteous, but **s**." Mt 9:13
a friend of tax collectors and **s**!' Mt 11:19
of Man is betrayed into the hands of **s**. Mt 26:45
tax collectors and **s** were reclining with Mk 2:15
he was eating with **s** and tax collectors, Mk 2:16
does he eat with tax collectors and **s**?" Mk 2:16
I came not to call the righteous, but **s**." Mk 2:17
of Man is betrayed into the hands of **s**. Mk 14:41
eat and drink with tax collectors and **s**?" Lk 5:30
call the righteous but **s** to repentance." Lk 5:32
For even **s** love those who love them. Lk 6:32
is that to you? For even **s** do the same. Lk 6:33
Even **s** lend to sinners, to get back the Lk 6:34
Even sinners lend to **s**, to get back the Lk 6:34
a friend of tax collectors and **s**!' Lk 7:34
these Galileans were worse **s** than all the Lk 13:2
the tax collectors and **s** were all drawing Lk 15:1
"This man receives **s** and eats with Lk 15:2
We know that God does not listen to **s**, Jn 9:31
love for us in that while we were still **s**, Rom 5:8
disobedience the many were made **s**, Rom 5:19
are Jews by birth and not Gentile **s**; Gal 2:15
in Christ, we too were found to be **s**, Gal 2:17
and disobedient, for the ungodly and **s**, 1 Tm 1:9
Jesus came into the world to save **s**, 1 Tm 1:15
innocent, unstained, separated from **s**, Heb 7:26
who endured from **s** such hostility Heb 12:3
Cleanse your hands, you **s**, and purify Jas 4:8
things that ungodly **s** have spoken Jude 1:15

SINNING (16)
it was I who kept you from **s** against me. Gn 20:6
the people are **s** against the LORD by 1 Sm 14:33
Ephraim has multiplied altars for **s**, Hos 8:11
they have become to him altars for **s**. Hos 8:11
even over those whose **s** was not like Rom 5:14
s against your brothers and 1 Cor 8:12
as is right, and do not go on **s**. 1 Cor 15:34
we go on **s** deliberately after receiving Heb 10:26
a practice of **s** also practices lawlessness; 1 Jn 3:4
No one who abides in him keeps on **s**; 1 Jn 3:6
one who keeps on **s** has either seen him 1 Jn 3:6
makes a practice of **s** is of the devil, 1 Jn 3:8
the devil has been **s** from the beginning. 1 Jn 3:8
one born of God makes a practice of **s**, 1 Jn 3:9
he cannot keep on **s** because he has 1 Jn 3:9
been born of God does not keep on **s**, 1 Jn 5:18

SINS (183)
If anyone **s** unintentionally in any of the Lv 4:2
if it is the anointed priest who **s**, thus Lv 4:3
of Israel **s** unintentionally and Lv 4:13
"When a leader **s**, doing unintentionally Lv 4:22
the common people **s** unintentionally in Lv 4:27
"If anyone **s** in that he hears a public Lv 5:1
of faith and **s** unintentionally in any Lv 5:15
"If anyone **s**, doing any of the things that Lv 5:17
"If anyone **s** and commits a breach of Lv 6:2
of their transgressions, all their **s**. Lv 16:16
and all their transgressions, all their **s**. Lv 16:21
clean before the LORD from all your **s**. Lv 16:30
because of all their **s**." And Moses did Lv 16:34
you again sevenfold for your **s**, Lv 26:18
striking you, sevenfold for your **s**. Lv 26:21
will strike you sevenfold for your **s**. Lv 26:24
will discipline you sevenfold for your **s**. Lv 26:28
any of the **s** that people commit Nm 5:6
"If one person **s** unintentionally, he Nm 15:27
a mistake, when he **s** unintentionally, Nm 15:28
you be swept away with all their **s**." Nm 16:26
forgive your transgressions or your **s**. Jos 24:19
If someone **s** against a man, God will 1 Sm 2:25
but if someone **s** against the LORD, 1 Sm 2:25
we have added to all our **s** this evil, 1 Sm 12:19
"If a man **s** against his neighbor and 1 Kgs 8:31
up because of the **s** of Jeroboam, 1 Kgs 14:16
jealousy with their **s** that they 1 Kgs 14:22
walked in all the **s** that his father did 1 Kgs 15:3
It was for the **s** of Jeroboam that he 1 Kgs 15:30
provoking me to anger with their **s**, 1 Kgs 16:2
for all the **s** of Baasha and the sins of 1 Kgs 16:13
of Baasha and the **s** of Elah his son, 1 Kgs 16:13
because of his **s** that he committed, 1 Kgs 16:19
and in the **s** that he made Israel to 1 Kgs 16:26
to walk in the **s** of Jeroboam the son 1 Kgs 16:31
aside from the **s** of Jeroboam the 2 Kgs 10:29
did not turn from the **s** of Jeroboam, 2 Kgs 10:31
and followed the **s** of Jeroboam the 2 Kgs 13:2
not depart from the **s** of the house of 2 Kgs 13:6
depart from all the **s** of Jeroboam the 2 Kgs 13:11
depart from all the **s** of Jeroboam the 2 Kgs 14:24
not depart from the **s** of Jeroboam the 2 Kgs 15:9
days from all the **s** of Jeroboam the 2 Kgs 15:18
away from the **s** of Jeroboam the 2 Kgs 15:24
depart from the **s** of Jeroboam the 2 Kgs 15:28
in all the **s** that Jeroboam did. 2 Kgs 17:22
out of his sight, for the **s** of Manasseh, 2 Kgs 24:3
"If a man **s** against his neighbor and 2 Chr 6:22
Have you not **s** of your own against 2 Chr 28:10
addition to our present **s** and guilt. 2 Chr 28:13
confessing the **s** of the people of Israel, Neh 1:6
and confessed their **s** and the iniquities Neh 9:2
you have set over us because of our **s**. Neh 9:37
How many are my iniquities and my **s**? Jb 13:23
servant also from presumptuous **s**; Ps 19:13
Remember not the **s** of my youth or my Ps 25:7
and my trouble, and forgive all my **s**. Ps 25:18
Hide your face from my **s**, and blot out Ps 51:9
deliver us, and atone for our **s**, for your Ps 79:9
our secret **s** in the light of your presence. Ps 90:8
not deal with us according to our **s**, Ps 103:10
on earth who does good and never **s**. Eccl 7:20
though your **s** are like scarlet, they shall Is 1:18
have cast all my **s** behind your back. Is 38:17
from the LORD'S hand double for all her **s**. Is 40:2
But you have burdened me with your **s**; Is 43:24
sake, and I will not remember your **s**. Is 43:25
like a cloud and your **s** like mist; Is 44:22
to the house of Jacob their **s**. Is 58:1
and your **s** have hidden his face from you Is 59:2
before you, and our **s** testify against us; Is 59:12
in our **s** we have been a long time, and Is 64:5
and your **s** have kept good from you. Jer 5:25
their iniquity and punish their **s**." Jer 14:10
as spoil, without price, for all your **s**, Jer 15:13
is great, because your **s** are flagrant. Jer 30:14
is great, because your **s** are flagrant, Jer 30:15
a man, about the punishment of his **s**? Lam 3:39
This was for the **s** of her prophets and Lam 4:13
he will punish; he will uncover your **s**. Lam 4:22
when a land **s** against me by acting Ezk 14:13
has not committed half your **s**. Ezk 16:51
Because of your **s** in which you acted Ezk 16:52
son is mine: the soul who **s** shall die. Ezk 18:4
who sees all the **s** that his father has Ezk 18:14
The soul who **s** shall die. The son Ezk 18:20
away from all his **s** that he has Ezk 18:21
all your deeds your **s** appear—because Ezk 21:24
transgressions and our **s** are upon us, Ezk 33:10
to live by his righteousness when he **s**. Ezk 33:12
None of the **s** that he has committed Ezk 33:16
break off your **s** by practicing Dn 4:27
your holy hill, because for our **s**, Dn 9:16
their iniquity and punish their **s**; Hos 8:13
their iniquity; he will punish their **s**. Hos 9:9
how great are your **s**—you who afflict Am 5:12
of Jacob and for the **s** of the house of Mi 1:5
making you desolate because of your **s**. Mi 6:13
You will cast all our **s** into the depths of Mi 7:19
for he will save his people from their **s**." Mt 1:21
in the river Jordan, confessing their **s**. Mt 3:6
"Take heart, my son; your **s** are forgiven." Mt 9:2
is easier, to say, 'Your **s** are forgiven,' Mt 9:5
on earth to forgive **s**"—he then said Mt 9:6
"If your brother **s** against you, go and Mt 18:15
out for many for the forgiveness of **s**. Mt 26:28
of repentance for the forgiveness of **s**. Mk 1:4
in the river Jordan, confessing their **s**. Mk 1:5
paralytic, "My son, your **s** are forgiven." Mk 2:5
Who can forgive **s** but God alone?" Mk 2:7
say to the paralytic, 'Your **s** are forgiven,' Mk 2:9
on earth to forgive **s**"—he said to the Mk 2:10
all **s** will be forgiven the children of Mk 3:28
to his people in the forgiveness of their **s**, Lk 1:77
of repentance for the forgiveness of **s**. Lk 3:3
he said, "Man, your **s** are forgiven you." Lk 5:20
Who can forgive **s** but God alone?" Lk 5:21
easier, to say, 'Your **s** are forgiven you,' Lk 5:23
on earth to forgive **s**"—he said to Lk 5:24
Therefore I tell you, her **s**, which are Lk 7:47
he said to her, "Your **s** are forgiven." Lk 7:48
"Who is this, who even forgives **s**?" Lk 7:49
and forgive us our **s**, for we ourselves Lk 11:4
If your brother **s**, rebuke him, and if he Lk 17:3
and if he **s** against you seven times in Lk 17:4
and forgiveness of **s** should be Lk 24:47
I told you that you would die in your **s**, Jn 8:24
that I am he you will die in your **s**." Jn 8:24
If you forgive the **s** of anyone, they are Jn 20:23
Christ for the forgiveness of your **s**, Acts 2:38
again, that your **s** may be blotted out, Acts 3:19
to Israel and forgiveness of **s**. Acts 5:31
receives forgiveness of **s** through his Acts 10:43
man forgiveness of **s** is proclaimed to Acts 13:38
be baptized and wash away your **s**, Acts 22:16
receive forgiveness of **s** and a place Acts 26:18
he had passed over former **s**. Rom 3:25
are forgiven, and whose **s** are covered; Rom 4:7
with them when I take away their **s**." Rom 11:27
immoral person **s** against his 1 Cor 6:18
died for our **s** in accordance with 1 Cor 15:3
is futile and you are still in your **s**. 1 Cor 15:17
gave himself for our **s** to deliver us from Gal 1:4
you were dead in the trespasses and **s** Eph 2:1
have redemption, the forgiveness of **s**. Col 1:14
to fill up the measure of their **s**. 1 Thes 2:16
hands, nor take part in the **s** of others; 1 Tm 5:22
The **s** of some men are conspicuous, 1 Tm 5:24
but the **s** of others appear later. 1 Tm 5:24
burdened with **s** and led astray by 2 Tm 3:6
After making purification for **s**, he sat Heb 1:3
propitiation for the **s** of the people. Heb 2:17
to God, to offer gifts and sacrifices for **s**. Heb 5:1
sacrifice for his own **s** just as he does Heb 5:3
first for his own **s** and then for those of Heb 7:27
and I will remember their **s** no more." Heb 8:12
and for the unintentional **s** of the people. Heb 9:7
of blood there is no forgiveness of **s**. Heb 9:22
been offered once to bear the **s** of many, Heb 9:28
blood of bulls and goats to take away **s**. Heb 10:4
which can never take away **s**. Heb 10:11
for all time a single sacrifice for **s**, Heb 10:12
will remember their **s** and their Heb 10:17
no longer remains a sacrifice for **s**, Heb 10:26
And if he has committed **s**, he will be Jas 5:15
confess your **s** to one another and pray Jas 5:16
death and will cover a multitude of **s**. Jas 5:20
He himself bore our **s** in his body on 1 Pt 2:24
For Christ also suffered once for **s**, the 1 Pt 3:18
since love covers a multitude of **s**. 1 Pt 4:8
that he was cleansed from his former **s**. 2 Pt 1:9
If we confess our **s**, he is faithful and just 1 Jn 1:9
just to forgive us our **s** and to cleanse us 1 Jn 1:9
He is the propitiation for our **s**, and not 1 Jn 2:2
but also for the **s** of the whole world. 1 Jn 2:2
because your **s** are forgiven for his 1 Jn 2:12
know that he appeared to take away **s**, 1 Jn 3:5
his Son to be the propitiation for our **s**. 1 Jn 4:10
to those who commit **s** that do not lead 1 Jn 5:16
and has freed us from our **s** by his blood Rv 1:5
my people, lest you take part in her **s**, Rv 18:4
for her **s** are heaped high as heaven, and Rv 18:5

SIPHMOTH (1)
in Aroer, in **S**, in Eshtemoa, 1 Sm 30:28

SIPPAI (1)
the Hushathite struck down **S**, 1 Chr 20:4

SIR (15)
to him, "Please, **s**, if the LORD is with us, Jgs 6:13
he answered, 'I go, **s**,' but did not go. Mt 21:30
"**S**, we remember how that impostor Mt 27:63
him, '**S**, let it alone this year also, Lk 13:8
'**S**, what you commanded has been Lk 14:22
"**S**, you have nothing to draw water with, Jn 4:11
said to him, "**S**, give me this water, Jn 4:15
him, "**S**, I perceive that you are a prophet. Jn 4:19
"**S**, come down before my child dies." Jn 4:49
"**S**, I have no one to put me into the pool Jn 5:7
to him, "**S**, give us this bread always." Jn 6:34
who is he, **s**, that I may believe in him?" Jn 9:36
and asked him, "**S**, we wish to see Jesus." Jn 12:21
him, "**S**, if you have carried him away, Jn 20:15
him, "**S**, you know." And he said to me, Rv 7:14

SIRAH (1)
him back from the cistern of **S**. 2 Sm 3:26

SIRES (1)
He who **s** a fool gets himself sorrow, Prv 17:21

SIRION (4)
(the Sidonians call Hermon **S**, while the Dt 3:9
of the Arnon, as far as Mount **S** (that is, Dt 4:48
like a calf, and **S** like a young wild ox. Ps 29:6
snow of Lebanon leave the crags of **S**? Jer 18:14

SIRS (2)
said, "**S**, what must I do to be saved?" Acts 16:30
"**S**, I perceive that the voyage will be Acts 27:10

SISERA (21)
The commander of his army was **S**, who Jgs 4:2
And I will draw out **S**, the general of Jgs 4:7
for the LORD will sell **S** into the hand of a Jgs 4:9
When **S** was told that Barak the son of Jgs 4:12
S called out all his chariots, 900 Jgs 4:13
the LORD has given **S** into your hand. Jgs 4:14
And the LORD routed **S** and all his Jgs 4:15
And **S** got down from his chariot and Jgs 4:15
and all the army of **S** fell by the edge of Jgs 4:16
But **S** fled away on foot to the tent of Jael, Jgs 4:17

Jael came out to meet **S** and said to him, Jgs 4:18
And behold, as Barak was pursuing **S**, Jgs 4:22
went in to her tent, and there lay **S** dead, Jgs 4:22
their courses they fought against **S**. Jgs 5:20
to the workmen's mallet; she struck **S**; Jgs 5:26
the mother of **S** wailed through the Jgs 5:28
spoil of dyed materials for **S**, spoil of Jgs 5:30
And he sold them into the hand of **S**, 1 Sm 12:9
the sons of Barkos, the sons of **S**, the Ezr 2:53
the sons of Barkos, the sons of **S**, the Neh 7:55
as to **S** and Jabin at the river Kishon, Ps 83:9

SISMAI (2)
Eleasah fathered **S**, and Sismai 1 Chr 2:40
Sismai, and **S** fathered Shallum. 1 Chr 2:40

SISTER (110)
iron. The **s** of Tubal-cain was Naamah. Gn 4:22
Say you are my **s**, that it may go well Gn 12:13
Why did you say, 'She is my **s**,' so that I Gn 12:19
"She is my **s**." And Abimelech king of Gn 20:2
he not himself say to me, 'She is my **s**'? Gn 20:5
Besides, she is indeed my **s**, the Gn 20:12
and heard the words of Rebekah his **s**, Gn 24:30
away Rebekah their **s** and her nurse, Gn 24:59
Rebekah and said to her, "Our **s**, Gn 24:60
the **s** of Laban the Aramean. Gn 25:20
said, "She is my **s**," for he feared to say, Gn 26:7
say, 'She is my **s**'?" Isaac said to him, Gn 26:9
Abraham's son, the **s** of Nebaioth. Gn 28:9
bore Jacob no children, she envied her **s**. Gn 30:1
wrestled with my **s** and have prevailed." Gn 30:8
because he had defiled their **s** Dinah. Gn 34:13
to give our **s** to one who is Gn 34:14
city, because they had defiled their **s**. Gn 34:27
he treat our **s** like a prostitute?" Gn 34:31
Ishmael's daughter, the **s** of Nebaioth. Gn 36:3
Hemam; and Lotan's **s** was Timna. Gn 36:22
Ishvi, Beriah, with Serah their **s**. Gn 46:17
And his **s** stood at a distance to know Ex 2:4
Then his **s** said to Pharaoh's daughter, Ex 2:7
took as his wife Jochebed his father's **s**, Ex 6:20
of Amminadab and the **s** of Nahshon, Ex 6:23
Miriam the prophetess, the **s** of Aaron, Ex 15:20
not uncover the nakedness of your **s**, Lv 18:9
your father's family, since she is your **s**. Lv 18:11
the nakedness of your father's **s**; Lv 18:12
the nakedness of your mother's **s**, Lv 18:13
take a woman as a rival wife to her **s**, Lv 18:18
her nakedness while her **s** is still alive. Lv 18:18
"If a man takes his **s**, a daughter of his Lv 20:17
nakedness of your mother's **s** or of your Lv 20:19
mother's sister or of your father's **s**, Lv 20:19
or his virgin **s** (who is near to him Lv 21:3
father or for his mother, for brother or **s**, Nm 6:7
of the chief of Midian, their **s**, Nm 25:18
Aaron and Moses and Miriam their **s**. Nm 26:59
"'Cursed be anyone who lies with his **s**, Dt 27:22
not her younger **s** more beautiful than Jgs 15:2
David's son, had a beautiful **s**, 2 Sm 13:1
himself ill because of his **s** Tamar, 2 Sm 13:2
Tamar, my brother Absalom's **s**." 2 Sm 13:4
'Let my **s** Tamar come and give me 2 Sm 13:5
"Please let my **s** Tamar come and 2 Sm 13:6
to her, "Come, lie with me, my **s**." 2 Sm 13:11
you? Now hold your peace, my **s**. 2 Sm 13:20
he had violated his **s** Tamar. 2 Sm 13:22
the day he violated his **s** Tamar. 2 Sm 13:32
daughter of Nahash, **s** of Zeruiah, 2 Sm 17:25
him in marriage the **s** of his own 1 Kgs 11:19
wife, the **s** of Tahpenes the queen. 1 Kgs 11:19
And the **s** of Tahpenes bore him 1 Kgs 11:20
of King Joram, **s** of Ahaziah, 2 Kgs 11:2
Hemam; and Lotan's **s** was Timna. 1 Chr 1:39
concubines, and Tamar was their **s**. 1 Chr 3:9
and Shelomith was their **s**; 1 Chr 3:19
the name of their **s** was Hazzelelponi, 1 Chr 4:3
of the wife of Hodiah, the **s** of Naham, 1 Chr 4:19
The name of his **s** was Maacah. 1 Chr 7:15
And his **s** Hammolecheth bore 1 Chr 7:18
Ishvi, Beriah, and their **s** Serah. 1 Chr 7:30
Shomer, Hotham, and their **s** Shua. 1 Chr 7:32
because she was a **s** of Ahaziah, 2 Chr 22:11
and to the worm, 'My mother,' or 'My **s**,' Jb 17:14
"You are my **s**," and call insight your Prv 7:4
You have captivated my heart, my **s**, my Sg 4:9
How beautiful is your love, my **s**, my Sg 4:10
A garden locked is my **s**, my bride, a Sg 4:12
I came to my garden, my **s**, my bride, I Sg 5:1
"Open to me, my **s**, my love, my dove, my Sg 5:2
We have a little **s**, and she has no breasts. Sg 8:8
shall we do for our **s** on the day when she Sg 8:8
and her treacherous **s** Judah saw it. Jer 3:7
Yet her treacherous **s** Judah did not fear, Jer 3:8
all this her treacherous **s** Judah did not Jer 3:10
'Ah, **s**!' They shall not lament for him, Jer 22:18
and you are the **s** of your sisters, who Ezk 16:45
And your elder **s** is Samaria, who lived Ezk 16:46
and your younger **s**, who lived to the Ezk 16:46
your **s** Sodom and her daughters have Ezk 16:48
this was the guilt of your **s** Sodom: Ezk 16:49
Was not your **s** Sodom a byword in Ezk 16:56
another in you violates his **s**, his Ezk 22:11
elder and Oholibah the name of her **s**. Ezk 23:4
"Her **s** Oholibah saw this, and she Ezk 23:11
more corrupt than her **s** in her lust Ezk 23:11
which was worse than that of her **s**. Ezk 23:11
as I had turned in disgust from her **s**. Ezk 23:18
You have gone the way of your **s**; Ezk 23:31
desolation, the cup of your **s** Samaria; Ezk 23:33
brother or unmarried **s** they may Ezk 44:25
is my brother and **s** and mother." Mt 12:50
he is my brother and **s** and mother." Mk 3:35
And she had a **s** called Mary, who sat at Lk 10:39
you not care that my **s** has left me to Lk 10:40
the village of Mary and her **s** Martha. Jn 11:1
loved Martha and her **s** and Lazarus. Jn 11:5
this, she went and called her **s** Mary, Jn 11:28
stone." Martha, the **s** of the dead man, Jn 11:39
were his mother and his mother's **s**, Jn 19:25
the son of Paul's **s** heard of their Acts 23:16
I commend to you our **s** Phoebe, a Rom 16:1
Philologus, Julia, Nereus and his **s**, Rom 16:15
cases the brother or **s** is not enslaved. 1 Cor 7:15
and Apphia our **s** and Archippus our Phlm 1:2
If a brother or **s** is poorly clothed and Jas 2:15
The children of your elect **s** greet you. 2 Jn 1:13

SISTER'S (4)
ring and the bracelets on his **s** arms, Gn 24:30
heard the news about Jacob, his **s** son, Gn 29:13
He has uncovered his **s** nakedness, and Lv 20:17
"You shall drink your **s** cup that is Ezk 23:32

SISTER-IN-LAW (2)
your **s** has gone back to her people and Ru 1:15
and to her gods; return after your **s**." Ru 1:15

SISTERS (19)
father and mother, my brothers and **s**, Jos 2:13
And their **s** were Zeruiah and 1 Chr 2:16
and invite their three **s** to eat and drink Jb 1:4
all his brothers and **s** and all who had Jb 42:11
and you are the sister of your **s**, who Ezk 16:45
have made your **s** appear righteous by Ezk 16:51
have intervened on behalf of your **s**. Ezk 16:52
have made your **s** appear righteous. Ezk 16:52
As for your **s**, Sodom and her Ezk 16:55
be ashamed when you take your **s**, Ezk 16:61
"You are my people," and to your **s**, Hos 2:1
And are not all his **s** with us? Where Mt 13:56
houses or brothers or **s** or father or Mt 19:29
And are not his **s** here with us?" And Mk 6:3
house or brothers or **s** or mother or Mk 10:29
and brothers and **s** and mothers and Mk 10:30
wife and children and brothers and **s**, Lk 14:26
So the **s** sent to him, saying, "Lord, he Jn 11:3
like mothers, younger women like **s**, 1 Tm 5:2

SIT (116)
now **s** up and eat of my game, that Gn 27:19
Why do you **s** alone, and all the people Ex 18:14
go to the war while you **s** here? Nm 32:6
talk of them when you **s** in your house, Dt 6:7
tools, and when you **s** down outside, Dt 23:13
She used to **s** under the palm of Deborah Jgs 4:5
you who **s** on rich carpets and you who Jgs 5:10
Why did you **s** still among the Jgs 5:16
s down here." And he turned aside and sat Ru 4:1
and said, "**S** down here." So they sat down. Ru 4:2
heap to make them **s** with princes and 1 Sm 2:8
for we will not **s** down till he comes 1 Sm 16:11
I should not fail to **s** at table with the 1 Sm 20:5
me, and he shall **s** on my throne"? 1 Kgs 1:13
me, and he shall **s** on my throne.' 1 Kgs 1:17
tell them who shall **s** on the throne of 1 Kgs 1:20
me, and he shall **s** on my throne'? 1 Kgs 1:24
servants who should **s** on the throne 1 Kgs 1:27
and he shall **s** on my throne in my 1 Kgs 1:30
he shall come and **s** on my throne, 1 Kgs 1:35
granted someone to **s** on my throne 1 Kgs 1:48
given him a son to **s** on his throne this 1 Kgs 3:6
father, and **s** on the throne of Israel, 1 Kgs 8:20
not lack a man to **s** before me on the 1 Kgs 8:25
die there. And if we **s** here, we die also. 2 Kgs 7:4
fourth generation shall **s** on the 2 Kgs 10:30
"Your sons shall **s** on the throne of 2 Kgs 15:12
Solomon my son to **s** on the throne of 1 Chr 28:5
David my father and **s** on the throne 2 Chr 6:10
not lack a man to **s** before me on the 2 Chr 6:16
I do not **s** with men of falsehood, nor do I Ps 26:4
and I will not **s** with the wicked. Ps 26:5
You **s** and speak against your brother; Ps 50:20
I am the talk of those who **s** in the gate, Ps 69:12
"**S** at my right hand, until I make your Ps 110:1
to make them **s** with princes, with the Ps 113:8
though princes **s** plotting against Ps 119:23
also forever shall **s** on your throne." Ps 132:12
You know when I **s** down and when I Ps 139:2
he has made me **s** in darkness like Ps 143:3
When you **s** down to eat with a ruler, Prv 23:1
places, and the rich **s** in a low place. Eccl 10:6
mourn; empty, she shall **s** on the ground. Is 3:26
I bring down those who **s** on thrones. Is 10:13
I will **s** on the mount of assembly in the Is 14:13
and on it will **s** in faithfulness in the tent Is 16:5
from the prison those who **s** in darkness. Is 42:7
Come down and **s** in the dust, O virgin Is 47:1
s on the ground without a throne, O Is 47:1
S in silence, and go into darkness, O Is 47:5
you lover of pleasures, who **s** securely, Is 47:8
I shall not **s** as a widow or know the loss Is 47:8
oneself is this, no fire to **s** before! Is 47:14
who **s** in tombs, and spend the night in Is 65:4
Why do we **s** still? Gather together; let us Jer 8:14
the kings who **s** on David's throne, Jer 13:13
I did not **s** in the company of revelers, Jer 15:17
into the house of feasting to **s** with them, Jer 16:8
kings and princes who **s** on the throne Jer 17:25
this house kings who **s** on the throne of Jer 22:4
never lack a man to **s** on the throne of Jer 33:17
"**S** down and read it." So Baruch read it Jer 36:15
He shall have none to **s** on the throne of Jer 36:30
glory, and **s** on the parched ground, Jer 48:18
the daughter of Zion **s** on the ground Lam 2:10
Let him **s** alone in silence when it is Lam 3:28
are with you and you **s** on scorpions. Ezk 2:6
they will **s** on the ground and tremble Ezk 26:16
'I am a god, I **s** in the seat of the gods, Ezk 28:2
and they **s** before you as my people, Ezk 33:31
Only the prince may **s** in it to eat bread Ezk 44:3
But the court shall **s** in judgment, and Dn 7:26
for there I will **s** to judge all the Jl 3:12
but they shall **s** every man under his vine Mi 4:4
I fall, I shall rise; when I **s** in darkness, Mi 7:8
you and your friends who **s** before you, Zec 3:8
and shall **s** and rule on his throne. Zec 6:13
old women shall again **s** in the streets of Zec 8:4
He will **s** as a refiner and purifier of Mal 3:3
ordered the crowds to **s** down on the Mt 14:19
directing the crowd to **s** down on the Mt 15:35
Son of Man will **s** on his glorious Mt 19:28
me will also **s** on twelve thrones, Mt 19:28
that these two sons of mine are to **s**, Mt 20:21
but to **s** at my right hand and at my left Mt 20:23
said to my Lord, **S** at my right hand, Mt 22:44
and the Pharisees **s** on Moses' seat, Mt 23:2
then he will **s** on his glorious throne. Mt 25:31
and he said to his disciples, "**S** here, Mt 26:36
them all to **s** down in groups Mk 6:39
directed the crowd to **s** down on the Mk 8:6
And they said to him, "Grant us to **s**, Mk 10:37
but to **s** at my right hand or at my left Mk 10:40
said to my Lord, **S** at my right hand, Mk 12:36
to his disciples, "**S** here while I pray." Mk 14:32
light to those who **s** in darkness and in Lk 1:79
"Have them **s** down in groups of about Lk 9:14
they did so, and had them all **s** down. Lk 9:15
feast, do not **s** down in a place of honor, Lk 14:8
are invited, go and **s** in the lowest place, Lk 14:10
presence of all who **s** at table with you. Lk 14:10
does not first **s** down and count the Lk 14:28
will not **s** down first and deliberate Lk 14:31
bill, and **s** down quickly and write fifty.' Lk 16:6
said to my Lord, **S** at my right hand, Lk 20:42
my kingdom and **s** on thrones judging Lk 22:30
"Have the people **s** down." Now there was Jn 6:10
this not the man who used to **s** and beg?" Jn 9:8
said to my Lord, **S** at my right hand, Acts 2:34
Philip to come up and **s** with him. Acts 8:31
"**S** at my right hand until I make your Heb 1:13
"You **s** here in a good place," while you Jas 2:3
stand over there," or, "**S** down at my feet," Jas 2:3
I will grant him to **s** with me on my Rv 3:21
twenty-four elders who **s** on their Rv 11:16
in her heart she says, 'I **s** as a queen, Rv 18:7

SITE (7)
"Give me the **s** of the threshing floor 1 Chr 21:22
shekels of gold by weight for the **s**. 1 Chr 21:25
for the house of God, to erect it on its **s**. Ezr 2:68
let the house of God be rebuilt on its **s**." Ezr 5:15
Jews rebuild this house of God on its **s**. Ezr 6:7
create over the whole **s** of Mount Zion and Is 4:5
remain aloft on its **s** from the Gate of Zec 14:10

SITES (1)
and the **s** on which he built high 2 Chr 33:19

SITHRI (1)
sons of Uzziel: Mishael, Elzaphan, and **S**. Ex 6:22

SITNAH (1)
over that also, so he called its name **S**. Gn 26:21

SITS (35)
of Pharaoh who **s** on his throne, Ex 11:5
on which he **s** shall be unclean. Lv 15:4
And whoever **s** on anything on which Lv 15:6
also on which she **s** shall be unclean. Lv 15:20
on which she **s** shall wash his Lv 15:22
is the bed or anything on which she **s**, Lv 15:23
on which she **s** shall be unclean, Lv 15:26
"And when he **s** on the throne of his Dt 17:18
LORD of hosts who **s** enthroned on the 2 Sm 6:2
Solomon **s** on the royal throne. 1 Kgs 1:46
the LORD who **s** enthroned above the 1 Chr 13:6
Mordecai the Jew who **s** at the king's Est 6:10
way of sinners, nor **s** in the seat of scoffers; Ps 1:1
He who **s** in the heavens laughs; the Lord Ps 2:4
But the LORD **s** enthroned forever; he has Ps 9:7
to the LORD, who **s** enthroned in Zion! Ps 9:11
He **s** in ambush in the villages; in hiding Ps 10:8
The LORD **s** enthroned over the flood; the Ps 29:10
the LORD **s** enthroned as king forever. Ps 29:10
from where he **s** enthroned he looks out Ps 33:14
the nations; God **s** on his holy throne. Ps 47:8
He **s** enthroned upon the cherubim; let Ps 99:1
She **s** at the door of her house; she takes Prv 9:14
A king who **s** on the throne of Prv 20:8
the gates when he **s** among the elders Prv 31:23
of justice to him who **s** in judgment, Is 28:6
I have called her "Rahab who **s** still." Is 30:7
It is he who **s** above the circle of the Is 40:22
of Judah, who **s** on the throne of David, Jer 22:2
the king who **s** on the throne Jer 29:16
How lonely **s** the city that was full of Lam 1:1
of God and by him who **s** upon it. Mt 23:22
"To him who **s** on the throne and to the Rv 5:13
belongs to our God who **s** on the throne, Rv 7:10
and he who **s** on the throne will shelter Rv 7:15

SITTING (76)
and Lot was **s** in the gate of Sodom. Gn 19:1
Now Ephron was **s** among the Hittites, Gn 23:10
of them when you are **s** in your house, Dt 11:19
or eggs and the mother **s** on the young or Dt 22:6
to him as he was **s** alone in his cool roof Jgs 3:20
in the presence of those **s** here and in the Ru 4:4
Eli the priest was **s** on the seat beside 1 Sm 1:9
Eli was **s** on his seat by the road 1 Sm 4:13
Saul was **s** at Gibeah under the 1 Sm 22:6
and his men were **s** in the innermost 1 Sm 24:3
Now David was **s** between the two 2 Sm 18:24
the king is **s** in the gate." And all the 2 Sm 19:8
God and found him **s** under an oak. 1 Kgs 13:14
of Judah were **s** on their thrones, 1 Kgs 22:10
I saw the LORD **s** on his throne, and 1 Kgs 22:19
to Elijah, who was **s** on the top of a hill, 2 Kgs 1:9
of the prophets were **s** before him, 2 Kgs 4:38
Elisha was **s** in his house, and the 2 Kgs 6:32
house, and the elders were **s** with him. 2 Kgs 6:32
"Why are we **s** here until we die? 2 Kgs 7:3
and not to the men **s** on the wall, 2 Kgs 18:27
"But I know your **s** down and your 2 Kgs 19:27
king of Judah were **s** on their thrones, 2 Chr 18:9
And they were **s** at the threshing floor 2 Chr 18:9
I saw the LORD **s** on his throne, and 2 Chr 18:18
said to me (the queen **s** beside him), Neh 2:6
time, Mordecai was **s** at the king's gate. Est 2:19
as Mordecai was **s** at the king's gate, Est 2:21
while the king was **s** on his royal throne Est 5:1
see Mordecai the Jew **s** at the king's Est 5:13
bathed in milk, **s** beside a full pool. Sg 5:12
Uzziah died I saw the Lord **s** upon a throne, Is 6:1
to you, and not to the men **s** on the wall, Is 36:12
"'I know your **s** down and your going Is 37:28
shall succeed in **s** on the throne Jer 22:30
the Judeans who were **s** in the court of Jer 32:12
and all the officials were **s** there: Jer 36:12
and the king was **s** in the winter house, Jer 36:22
—the king was **s** in the Benjamin Gate Jer 38:7
Behold their **s** and their rising; I am Lam 3:63
with the elders of Judah **s** before me, Ezk 8:1
and there was a woman **s** in the basket! Zec 5:7
a man called Matthew **s** at the tax booth, Mt 9:9
It is like children **s** in the marketplaces Mt 11:16
were two blind men **s** by the roadside, Mt 20:30
Now Peter was **s** outside in the Mt 26:69
while he was **s** on the judgment seat, Mt 27:19
Mary were there, **s** opposite the tomb. Mt 27:61
Now some of the scribes were **s** there, Mk 2:6
the son of Alphaeus **s** at the tax booth, Mk 2:14
And a crowd was **s** around him, and Mk 3:32
the one who had had the legion, **s** there, Mk 5:15
son of Timaeus, was **s** by the roadside. Mk 10:46
And he was **s** with the guards and Mk 14:54
saw a young man **s** on the right side, Mk 16:5
him in the temple, **s** among the teachers, Lk 2:46
and teachers of the law were **s** there, Lk 5:17
collector named Levi, **s** at the tax booth. Lk 5:27
are like children **s** in the marketplace Lk 7:32
demons had gone, **s** at the feet of Jesus, Lk 8:35
long ago, **s** in sackcloth and ashes. Lk 10:13
a blind man was **s** by the roadside Lk 18:35
pigeons, and the money-changers **s** there. Jn 2:14
from his journey, was **s** beside the well. Jn 4:6
king is coming, **s** on a donkey's colt!" Jn 12:15
s where the body of Jesus had lain, Jn 20:12
filled the entire house where they were **s**. Acts 2:2
there was a man **s** who could not use Acts 14:8
named Eutychus, **s** at the window, Acts 20:9
Are you **s** to judge me according to the Acts 23:3
and those who were **s** with them. Acts 26:30
is made to another **s** there, 1 Cor 14:30
and I saw a woman **s** on a scarlet beast Rv 17:3
The one **s** on it is called Faithful and Rv 19:11
against him who was **s** on the horse Rv 19:19
mouth of him who was **s** on the horse, Rv 19:21

SITUATION (2)
"Behold, the **s** of this city is pleasant, 2 Kgs 2:19
I have learned in whatever **s** I am to be Phil 4:11

SIVAN (1)
the third month, which is the month of **S**, Est 8:9

SIX (114)
Noah was **s** hundred years old when the Gn 7:6
In the **s** hundredth year of Noah's life, in Gn 7:11
In the **s** hundred and first year, in the Gn 8:13
I have borne him **s** sons." So she called Gn 30:20
daughters, and **s** years for your flock, Gn 31:41
about **s** hundred thousand men on Ex 12:37
and took **s** hundred chosen chariots and Ex 14:7
S days you shall gather it, but on the Ex 16:26
S days you shall labor, and do all your Ex 20:9
For in **s** days the LORD made heaven Ex 20:11
a Hebrew slave, he shall serve **s** years, Ex 21:2
"For **s** years you shall sow your land Ex 23:10
"**S** days you shall do your work, but on Ex 23:12
Sinai, and the cloud covered it **s** days. Ex 24:16
there shall be **s** branches going out Ex 25:32
—so for the **s** branches going out of Ex 25:33
each pair of the **s** branches going out Ex 25:35
and **s** curtains by themselves, Ex 26:9
westward you shall make **s** frames. Ex 26:22
s of their names on the one stone, and Ex 28:10
names of the remaining **s** on the other Ex 28:10
S days shall work be done, but the Ex 31:15
of Israel that in **s** days the LORD made Ex 31:17
"**S** days you shall work, but on the Ex 34:21
S days work shall be done, but on the Ex 35:2
and **s** curtains by themselves. Ex 36:16
tabernacle westward he made **s** frames. Ex 36:27
And there were **s** branches going out of Ex 37:18
—so for the **s** branches going out of Ex 37:19
each pair of the **s** branches going out of Ex 37:21
"**S** days shall work be done, but on the Lv 23:3
shall set them in two piles, **s** in a pile, Lv 24:6
For **s** years you shall sow your field, and Lv 25:3
and for **s** years you shall prune your Lv 25:3
the LORD, **s** wagons and twelve oxen, Nm 7:3
I am number **s** hundred thousand on Nm 11:21
Levites shall be the **s** cities of refuge, Nm 35:6
give shall be your **s** cities of refuge. Nm 35:13
These **s** cities shall be for refuge for Nm 35:15
S days you shall labor and do all your Dt 5:13
is sold to you, he shall serve you **s** years, Dt 15:12
hired servant he has served you **s** years. Dt 15:18
For **s** days you shall eat unleavened Dt 16:8
city once. Thus shall you do for **s** days. Jos 6:3
into the camp. So they did for **s** days. Jos 6:14
and Eltekon: **s** cities with their villages. Jos 15:59
and Engedi: **s** cities with their villages. Jos 15:62
Jephthah judged Israel **s** years. Then Jgs 12:7
he measured out **s** measures of barley Ru 3:15
"These **s** measures of barley he gave to Ru 3:17
chariots and **s** thousand horsemen 1 Sm 13:5
with him, about **s** hundred men. 1 Sm 13:15
with him were about **s** hundred men, 1 Sm 14:2
whose height was **s** cubits and a span. 1 Sm 17:4
head weighed **s** hundred shekels 1 Sm 17:7
his men, who were about **s** hundred, 1 Sm 23:13
he and the **s** hundred men who were 1 Sm 27:2
and the **s** hundred men who were with 1 Sm 30:9
Judah was seven years and **s** months. 2 Sm 2:11
over Judah seven years and **s** months, 2 Sm 5:5
the ark of the LORD had gone **s** steps, 2 Sm 6:13
and all the **s** hundred Gittites who 2 Sm 15:18
who had **s** fingers on each hand, 2 Sm 21:20
each hand, and **s** toes on each foot, 2 Sm 21:20
the middle one was **s** cubits broad, 1 Kgs 6:6
The throne had **s** steps, and at the 1 Kgs 10:19
on each end of a step on the **s** steps. 1 Kgs 10:20
all Israel remained there **s** months, 1 Kgs 11:16
years; **s** years he reigned in Tirzah. 1 Kgs 16:23
of silver, **s** thousand shekels of gold, 2 Kgs 5:5
And he remained with her **s** years, 2 Kgs 11:3
should have struck five or **s** times; 2 Kgs 13:19
over Israel in Samaria **s** months. 2 Kgs 15:8
s were born to him in Hebron, where 1 Chr 3:4
reigned for seven years and **s** months. 1 Chr 3:4
Igal, Bariah, Neariah, and Shaphat, **s**. 1 Chr 3:22
had sixteen sons and **s** daughters; 1 Chr 4:27
Azel had **s** sons, and these are their 1 Chr 8:38
Azel had **s** sons and these are their 1 Chr 9:44
who had **s** fingers on each hand and 1 Chr 20:6
on each hand and **s** toes on each foot, 1 Chr 20:6
s, under the direction of their father 1 Chr 25:3
On the east there were **s** each day, on 1 Chr 26:17
The throne had **s** steps and a 2 Chr 9:18
on each end of a step on the **s** steps. 2 Chr 9:19
And he remained with them **s** years, 2 Chr 22:12
was one ox and **s** choice sheep and Neh 5:18
s months with oil of myrrh and six Est 2:12
oil of myrrh and **s** months with spices Est 2:12
He will deliver you from **s** troubles; in Jb 5:19
There are **s** things that the LORD hates, Prv 6:16
Each had **s** wings: with two he covered his Is 6:2
sold to you and has served you **s** years; Jer 34:14
s men came from the direction of the Ezk 9:2
in the man's hand was **s** long cubits, Ezk 40:5
the side rooms were **s** cubits on either Ezk 40:12
On each side **s** cubits was the breadth Ezk 41:1
two cubits; and the entrance, **s** cubits; Ezk 41:3
the wall of the temple, **s** cubits thick, Ezk 41:5
measured a full reed of **s** long cubits. Ezk 41:8
shall be shut on the **s** working days, Ezk 46:1
day shall be **s** lambs without blemish Ezk 46:4
blemish, and **s** lambs and a ram, Ezk 46:6
was sixty cubits and its breadth **s** cubits. Dn 3:1
And after **s** days Jesus took with him Mt 17:1
And after **s** days Jesus took with him Mk 9:2
were shut up three years and **s** months, Lk 4:25
"There are **s** days in which work ought Lk 13:14
Now there were **s** stone water jars there for Jn 2:6
S days before the Passover, Jesus Jn 12:1
These **s** brothers also accompanied Acts 11:12
And he stayed a year and **s** months, Acts 18:11
for three years and **s** months it did not Jas 5:17
creatures, each of them with **s** wings, Rv 4:8

SIXTEEN (18)
and these she bore to Jacob—**s** persons. Gn 46:18
with their bases of silver, **s** bases; Ex 26:25
s bases, under every frame two bases. Ex 36:30
Makkedah: **s** cities with their villages. Jos 15:41
at the Jordan—**s** cities with their Jos 19:22
in Samaria, and he reigned **s** years. 2 Kgs 13:10
took Azariah, who was **s** years old, 2 Kgs 14:21
He was **s** years old when he began to 2 Kgs 15:2
and he reigned **s** years in Jerusalem. 2 Kgs 15:33
and he reigned **s** years in Jerusalem. 2 Kgs 16:2
Shimei had **s** sons and six daughters; 1 Chr 4:27
organized them under **s** heads of 1 Chr 24:4
twenty-two sons and **s** daughters. 2 Chr 13:21
took Uzziah, who was **s** years old, 2 Chr 26:1
Uzziah was **s** years old when he 2 Chr 26:3
and he reigned **s** years in Jerusalem. 2 Chr 27:1
and he reigned **s** years in Jerusalem. 2 Chr 27:8
and he reigned **s** years in Jerusalem. 2 Chr 28:1

SIXTEENTH (3)
fifteenth to Bilgah, the **s** to Immer, 1 Chr 24:14
to the **s**, to Hananiah, his sons and 1 Chr 25:23
and on the **s** day of the first month 2 Chr 29:17

SIXTH (45)
and there was morning, the **s** day. Gn 1:31
again, and she bore Jacob a **s** son. Gn 30:19
On the **s** day, when they prepare what Ex 16:5
On the **s** day they gathered twice as Ex 16:22
therefore on the **s** day he gives you Ex 16:29
and the **s** curtain you shall double over Ex 26:9
my blessing on you in the **s** year, Lv 25:21
On the **s** day Eliasaph the son of Deuel, Nm 7:42
"On the **s** day eight bulls, two rams, Nm 29:29
The **s** lot came out for the people of Jos 19:32
and the **s**, Ithream, of Eglah, David's 2 Sm 3:5
In the **s** year of Hezekiah, which was 2 Kgs 18:10
Ozem the **s**, David the seventh. 1 Chr 2:15
the fifth, Shephatiah, by Abital; the **s**, 1 Chr 3:3
Attai **s**, Eliel seventh, 1 Chr 12:11
fifth to Malchijah, the **s** to Mijamin, 1 Chr 24:9
the **s** to Bukkiah, his sons and his 1 Chr 25:13
Elam the fifth, Jehohanan the **s**, 1 Chr 26:3
Ammiel the **s**, Issachar the seventh, 1 Chr 26:5
S, for the sixth month, was Ira, the 1 Chr 27:9
Sixth, for the **s** month, was Ira, the 1 Chr 27:9

in the **s** year of the reign of Darius the Ezr 6:15
and Hanun the **s** son of Zalaph Neh 3:30
drink by measure, the **s** part of a hin; Ezk 4:11
In the **s** year, in the sixth month, on the Ezk 8:1
In the sixth year, in the **s** month, on the Ezk 8:1
one **s** of an ephah from each homer of Ezk 45:13
and one **s** of an ephah from each Ezk 45:13
by morning, one **s** of an ephah, Ezk 46:14
year of Darius the king, in the **s** month, Hg 1:1
day of the month, in the **s** month, Hg 1:15
out again about the **s** hour and the Mt 20:5
Now from the **s** hour there was Mt 27:45
And when the **s** hour had come, there Mk 15:33
In the **s** month the angel Gabriel was Lk 1:26
and this is the **s** month with her who Lk 1:36
It was now about the **s** hour, and there Lk 23:44
beside the well. It was about the **s** hour. Jn 4:6
of the Passover. It was about the **s** hour. Jn 19:14
the housetop about the **s** hour to pray. Acts 10:9
When he opened the **s** seal, I looked, and Rv 6:12
Then the **s** angel blew his trumpet, and I Rv 9:13
saying to the **s** angel who had the Rv 9:14
The **s** angel poured out his bowl on the Rv 16:12
the fifth onyx, the **s** carnelian, the Rv 21:20

SIXTY (26)
Isaac was **s** years old when she bore Gn 25:26
years old up to **s** years old shall be Lv 27:3
And if the person is **s** years old or over, Lv 27:7
offerings twenty-four bulls, the rams **s**, Nm 7:88
bulls, the rams sixty, the male goats **s**, Nm 7:88
goats sixty, the male lambs a year old **s**. Nm 7:88
that we did not take from them—**s** cities, Dt 3:4
of Jair, which are in Bashan, **s** cities, Jos 13:30
s great cities with walls and bronze 1 Kgs 4:13
cors of fine flour and **s** cors of meal, 1 Kgs 4:22
built for the LORD was **s** cubits long, 1 Kgs 6:2
and **s** men of the people of the land 2 Kgs 25:19
he married when he was **s** years old, 1 Chr 2:21
Kenath, and its villages, **s** towns. 1 Chr 2:23
of the old standard, was **s** cubits, 2 Chr 3:3
eighteen wives and **s** concubines, 2 Chr 11:21
twenty-eight sons and **s** daughters). 2 Chr 11:21
Its height shall be **s** cubits and its Ezr 6:3
be sixty cubits and its breadth **s** cubits, Ezr 6:3
Around it are **s** mighty men, some of the Sg 3:7
There are **s** queens and eighty Sg 6:8
and **s** men of the people of the land, who Jer 52:25
whose height was **s** cubits and its Dn 3:1
grain, some a hundredfold, some **s**, Mt 13:8
in one case a hundredfold, in another **s**, Mt 13:23
if she is not less than **s** years of age, 1 Tm 5:9

SIXTY-EIGHT (1)
also Obed-edom and his **s** brothers, 1 Chr 16:38

SIXTY-FIVE (1)
(Within **s** years Ephraim will be broken Is 7:8

SIXTY-SIX (2)
sons' wives, were **s** persons in all. Gn 46:26
in the blood of her purifying for **s** days. Lv 12:5

SIXTY-TWO (4)
for the service; **s** of Obed-edom. 1 Chr 26:8
the kingdom, being about **s** years old. Dn 5:31
Then for **s** weeks it shall be built again Dn 9:25
And after the **s** weeks, an anointed one Dn 9:26

SIXTYFOLD (2)
yielding thirtyfold and **s** and a Mk 4:8
thirtyfold and **s** and a hundredfold." Mk 4:20

SIZE (18)
all the curtains shall be the same **s**. Ex 26:2
The eleven curtains shall be the same **s**. Ex 26:8
cubits. All the curtains were the same **s**. Ex 36:9
The eleven curtains were the same **s**. Ex 36:15
by the Jordan, an altar of imposing **s**. Jos 22:10
and all measures of quantity or **s**. 1 Chr 23:29
The three were of the same **s**, and the Ezk 40:10
on either side were of the same **s**. Ezk 40:10
were of the same **s** as those of the Ezk 40:21
trees were of the same **s** as those of the Ezk 40:22
they had the same **s** as the others. Ezk 40:24
gate. It was of the same **s** as the others. Ezk 40:28
were of the same **s** as the others. Ezk 40:29
gate. It was of the same **s** as the others. Ezk 40:32
were of the same **s** as the others, Ezk 40:33
it. It had the same **s** as the others. Ezk 40:35
were of the same **s** as the others, Ezk 40:36
broad; the four were of the same **s**. Ezk 46:22

SKIES (13)
your help, through the **s** in his majesty. Dt 33:26
your dispersed be under the farthest **s**, Neh 1:9
which the **s** pour down and drop on Jb 36:28
Can you, like him, spread out the **s**, Jb 37:18
on the light when it is bright in the **s**, Jb 37:21
over Israel, and whose power is in the **s**. Ps 68:34
out water; the **s** gave forth thunder; Ps 77:17
he commanded the **s** above and opened Ps 78:23
For who in the **s** can be compared to the Ps 89:6
a faithful witness in the **s**." Selah Ps 89:37
when he made firm the **s** above, when Prv 8:28
rot away, and the **s** roll up like a scroll. Is 34:4
and has been lifted up even to the **s**. Jer 51:9

SKIFFS (1)
They go by like **s** of reed, like an eagle Jb 9:26

SKILL (14)
whom I have filled with a spirit of **s**, Ex 28:3
them to use their **s** spun the goats' hair. Ex 35:26
filled him with the Spirit of God, with **s**, Ex 35:31
has filled them with **s** to do every sort Ex 35:35
the LORD has put **s** and intelligence to Ex 36:1
in whose mind the LORD had put **s**, Ex 36:2
and **s** for making any work in 1 Kgs 7:14
willing man who has **s** for any kind 1 Chr 28:21
who showed good **s** in the service 2 Chr 30:22
let my right hand forget its **s**! Ps 137:5
and knowledge and **s** must leave Eccl 2:21
that all toil and all **s** in work come from Eccl 4:4
pride together with the **s** of his hands. Is 25:11
them learning and **s** in all literature Dn 1:17

SKILLED (17)
a breastpiece of judgment, in **s** work. Ex 28:15
carving wood, for work in every **s** craft. Ex 35:33
by any sort of workman or **s** designer. Ex 35:35
into the fine twined linen, in **s** design. Ex 39:3
He made the breastpiece, in **s** work, in Ex 39:8
without number, **s** in working 1 Chr 22:15
now send me a man **s** to work in gold, 2 Chr 2:7
to be with the **s** workers who are with 2 Chr 2:7
"Now I have sent a **s** man, who has 2 Chr 2:13
He was a scribe **s** in the Law of Moses Ezr 7:6
purple; they are all the work of **s** men. Jer 10:9
men of Lud, **s** in handling the bow. Jer 46:9
arrows are like a **s** warrior who does not Jer 50:9
Arvad were your rowers; your **s** men, Ezk 27:8
of Gebal and her **s** men were in you, Ezk 27:9
wailing those who are **s** in lamentation, Am 5:16
like a **s** master builder I laid a 1 Cor 3:10

SKILLFUL (16)
the boys grew up, Esau was a **s** hunter, Gn 25:27
You shall speak to all the **s**, whom I have Ex 28:3
"Let every **s** craftsman among you Ex 35:10
And every **s** woman spun with her Ex 35:25
a man who is **s** in playing the lyre, 1 Sm 16:16
Bethlehemite, who is **s** in playing, 1 Sm 16:18
in singing to the LORD, all who were **s**, 1 Chr 25:7
made engines, invented by **s** men, 2 Chr 26:15
all who were **s** with instruments of 2 Chr 34:12
them and guided them with his **s** hand. Ps 78:72
Do you see a man **s** in his work? He Prv 22:29
the counselor and the **s** magician and the Is 3:3
he seeks out a **s** craftsman to set up an Is 40:20
to come; send for the **s** women to come; Jer 9:17
the hands of brutish men, **s** to destroy. Ezk 21:31
of good appearance and **s** in all wisdom, Dn 1:4

SKILLFULLY (15)
them with cherubim **s** worked into Ex 26:1
made with cherubim **s** worked into it. Ex 26:31
yarns, and of fine twined linen, **s** worked. Ex 28:6
And the **s** woven band on it shall be Ex 28:8
its seam above the **s** woven band of the Ex 28:27
it may lie on the **s** woven band of the Ex 28:28
gird him with the **s** woven band of the Ex 29:5
scarlet yarns, with cherubim **s** worked. Ex 36:8
with cherubim **s** worked into it he Ex 36:35
And the **s** woven band on it was of one Ex 39:5
its seam above the **s** woven band of the Ex 39:20
it should lie on the **s** woven band of the Ex 39:21
on him and tied the **s** woven band of the Lv 8:7
play **s** on the strings, with loud shouts. Ps 33:3
images, idols **s** made of their silver, Hos 13:2

SKIN (87)
took bread and a **s** of water and gave Gn 21:14
When the water in the **s** was gone, she Gn 21:15
went and filled the **s** with water and Gn 21:19
of the bull and its **s** and its dung you Ex 29:14
not know that the **s** of his face shone Ex 34:29
and behold, the **s** of his face shone, Ex 34:30
that the **s** of Moses' face was shining. Ex 34:35
But the **s** of the bull and all its flesh, with Lv 4:11
have for himself the **s** of the burnt Lv 7:8
But the bull and its **s** and its flesh and its Lv 8:17
The flesh and the **s** he burned up with Lv 9:11
of wood or a garment or a **s** or a sack, Lv 11:32
a person has on the **s** of his body a Lv 13:2
of leprous disease on the **s** of his body, Lv 13:2
the diseased area on the **s** of his body. Lv 13:3
to be deeper than the **s** of his body, Lv 13:3
spot is white in the **s** of his body and Lv 13:4
body and appears no deeper than the **s**, Lv 13:4
and the disease has not spread in the **s**, Lv 13:5
and the disease has not spread in the **s**, Lv 13:6
But if the eruption spreads in the **s**, after Lv 13:7
and if the eruption has spread in the **s**, Lv 13:8
white swelling in the **s** that has turned Lv 13:10
leprous disease in the **s** of his body, Lv 13:11
the leprous disease breaks out in the **s**, Lv 13:12
disease covers all the **s** of the diseased Lv 13:12
"If there is in the **s** of one's body a boil Lv 13:18
appears deeper than the **s** and its hair Lv 13:20
hair in it and it is not deeper than the **s**, Lv 13:21
And if it spreads in the **s**, then the priest Lv 13:22
has a burn on its **s** and the raw flesh of Lv 13:24
white and it appears deeper than the **s**, Lv 13:25
in the spot and it is no deeper than the **s**, Lv 13:26
If it is spreading in the **s**, then the priest Lv 13:27
one place and does not spread in the **s**, Lv 13:28
And if it appears deeper than the **s**, and Lv 13:30
no deeper than the **s** and there is no Lv 13:31
itch appears to be no deeper than the **s**, Lv 13:32
has not spread in the **s** and it appears to Lv 13:34
it appears to be no deeper than the **s**, Lv 13:34
itch spreads in the **s** after his cleansing, Lv 13:35
him, and if the itch has spread in the **s**, Lv 13:36
a woman has spots on the **s** of the body, Lv 13:38
if the spots on the **s** of the body are of Lv 13:39
that has broken out in the **s**; Lv 13:39
of leprous disease in the **s** of the body, Lv 13:43
or in a **s** or in anything made of skin, Lv 13:48
or in a skin or in anything made of **s**, Lv 13:48
or in the **s** or in the warp or the woof or Lv 13:49
or the woof or in any article made of **s**, Lv 13:49
in the warp or the woof, or in the **s**, Lv 13:51
in the skin, whatever be the use of the **s**, Lv 13:51
or any article made of **s** that is diseased, Lv 13:52
or the woof or in any article made of **s**, Lv 13:53
of the garment or the **s** or the warp or Lv 13:56
or the woof, or in any article made of **s**, Lv 13:57
any article made of **s** from which the Lv 13:58
or the woof, or in any article made of **s**, Lv 13:59
garment and every **s** on which the Lv 15:17
Their **s** and their flesh and their dung Lv 16:27
heifer shall be burned in his sight. Its **s**, Nm 19:5
every garment, every article of **s**, Nm 31:20
So she opened a **s** of milk and gave Jgs 4:19
an ephah of flour, and a **s** of wine, 1 Sm 1:24
and another carrying a **s** of wine. 1 Sm 10:3
with bread and a **s** of wine and a 1 Sm 16:20
of summer fruits, and a **s** of wine. 2 Sm 16:1
answered the LORD and said, "**S** for skin! Jb 2:4
answered the LORD and said, "Skin for **s**! Jb 2:4
with worms and dirt; my **s** hardens, Jb 7:5
You clothed me with **s** and flesh, and Jb 10:11
sackcloth upon my **s** and have laid Jb 16:15
It consumes the parts of his **s**; the Jb 18:13
My bones stick to my **s** and to my flesh, Jb 19:20
and I have escaped by the **s** of my teeth. Jb 19:20
And after my **s** has been thus destroyed, Jb 19:26
My **s** turns black and falls from me, Jb 30:30
Can you fill his **s** with harpoons or his Jb 41:7
Ethiopian change his **s** or the leopard Jer 13:23
made my flesh and my **s** waste away; Lam 3:4
their **s** has shriveled on their bones; Lam 4:8
Our **s** is hot as an oven with the Lam 5:10
come upon you, and cover you with **s**, Ezk 37:6
upon them, and **s** had covered them. Ezk 37:8
who tear the **s** from off my people and Mi 3:2
my people, and flay their **s** from off them, Mi 3:3
had touched his **s** were carried away Acts 19:12

SKINS (17)
his wife garments of **s** and clothed them. Gn 3:21
And the **s** of the young goats she put on Gn 27:16
tanned rams' **s**, goatskins, acacia wood, Ex 25:5
of tanned rams' **s** and a covering Ex 26:14
tanned rams' **s**, and goatskins; acacia Ex 35:7
or tanned rams' **s** or goatskins brought Ex 35:23
of tanned rams' **s** and goatskins. Ex 36:19
of tanned rams' **s** and goatskins, Ex 39:34
the grapevine, not even the seeds or the **s**. Nm 6:4
loaves and two **s** of wine and 1 Sm 25:18
the **s** burst and the wine is spilled and Mt 9:17
wine is spilled and the **s** are destroyed. Mt 9:17
the wine will burst the **s**—and the wine Mk 2:22
the wine is destroyed, and so are the **s**. Mk 2:22
new wine will burst the **s** and it will be Lk 5:37
be spilled, and the **s** will be destroyed. Lk 5:37
They went about in **s** of sheep and Heb 11:37

SKIP (2)
He makes Lebanon to **s** like a calf, and Ps 29:6
O mountains, that you **s** like rams? O Ps 114:6

SKIPPED (1)
The mountains **s** like rams, the hills Ps 114:4

SKIRT (2)
go away, Saul seized the **s** of his robe, 1 Sm 15:27
instead of a rich robe, a **s** of sackcloth; Is 3:24

SKIRTS (7)
it might take hold of the **s** of the earth, Jb 38:13
Also on your **s** is found the lifeblood of Jer 2:34
your iniquity that your **s** are lifted up Jer 13:22
myself will lift up your **s** over your face, Jer 13:26
Her uncleanness was in her **s**; she took Lam 1:9
and bind them in the **s** of your robe. Ezk 5:3
and will lift up your **s** over your face; Na 3:5

SKULL (7)
on Abimelech's head and crushed his **s**. Jgs 9:53
of her than the **s** and the feet and 2 Kgs 9:35
and on his own **s** his violence descends. Ps 7:16
Golgotha (which means Place of a **S**), Mt 27:33
Golgotha (which means Place of a **S**). Mk 15:22
came to the place that is called The **S**, Lk 23:33
cross, to the place called the place of a **s**, Jn 19:17

SKY (14)
and the **s** above proclaims his Ps 19:1
righteousness looks down from the **s**. Ps 85:11
the way of an eagle in the **s**, the way of Prv 30:19
shine like the brightness of the **s** above; Dn 12:3
'It will be fair weather, for the **s** is red.' Mt 16:2
today, for the **s** is red and threatening.' Mt 16:3
how to interpret the appearance of the **s**, Mt 16:3
interpret the appearance of earth and **s**, Lk 12:56
and lights up the **s** from one side to Lk 17:24
the sacred stone that fell from the **s**? Acts 19:35
and the stars of the **s** fell to the earth as Rv 6:13
The **s** vanished like a scroll that is being Rv 6:14
They have the power to shut the **s**, that Rv 11:6
his presence earth and **s** fled away, Rv 20:11

SLACK (4)
He will not be **s** with one who hates him. Dt 7:10
And take care not to be **s** in this matter. Ezr 4:22
A **s** hand causes poverty, but the hand Prv 10:4
Whoever is **s** in his work is a brother to Prv 18:9

SLACKEN (1)
do not **s** the pace for me unless I tell 2 Kgs 4:24

SLACKNESS (1)
who does the work of the LORD with **s**, Jer 48:10

SLAIN (87)
came upon the **s** and plundered the Gn 34:27
bone, or the **s** or the dead or the grave. Nm 19:18
the prey and drunk the blood of the **s**." Nm 23:24
The name of the **s** man of Israel, who Nm 25:14
kings of Midian with the rest of their **s**, Nm 31:8
and whoever has touched any **s**, Nm 31:19
giving you to possess someone is found **s**, Dt 21:1
that is nearest to the **s** man shall take a Dt 21:3
city nearest to the **s** man shall wash their Dt 21:6
with the blood of the **s** and the captives, Dt 32:42
I will give over all of them, **s**, to Israel. Jos 11:6
of Israel among the rest of their **s**. Jos 13:22
Philistines and fell **s** on Mount 1 Sm 31:1
the Philistines came to strip the **s**, 1 Sm 31:8
O Israel, is **s** on your high places! 2 Sm 1:19
"From the blood of the **s**, from the fat 2 Sm 1:22
"Jonathan lies **s** on your high places. 2 Sm 1:25
returned after him only to strip the **s**. 2 Sm 23:10
of the army went up to bury the **s**, 1 Kgs 11:15
Philistines and fell **s** on Mount 1 Chr 10:1
the Philistines came to strip the **s**, 1 Chr 10:8
so there fell **s** of Israel 500,000 2 Chr 13:17
ones suck up blood, and where the **s** are, Jb 39:30
the dead, like the **s** that lie in the grave, Ps 88:5
low, and all her **s** are a mighty throng. Prv 7:26
among the prisoners or fall among the **s**. Is 10:4
a loathed branch, clothed with the **s**, Is 14:19
your land, you have **s** your people. Is 14:20
Your **s** are not slain with the sword or Is 22:2
Your slain are not **s** with the sword or Is 22:2
shed on it, and will no more cover its **s**. Is 26:21
Or have they been **s** as their slayers were Is 27:7
they been slain as their slayers were **s**? Is 27:7
Their **s** shall be cast out, and the stench Is 34:3
and those **s** by the LORD shall be many. Is 66:16
day and night for the **s** of the daughter of Jer 9:1
the son of Nethaniah filled it with the **s**. Jer 41:9
They shall fall down **s** in the land of the Jer 51:4
and all her **s** shall fall in the midst of Jer 51:47
Babylon must fall for the **s** of Israel, Jer 51:49
Babylon have fallen the **s** of all the Jer 51:49
I will cast down your **s** before your idols. Ezk 6:4
And the **s** shall fall in your midst, and Ezk 6:7
when their **s** lie among their idols Ezk 6:13
the house, and fill the courts with the **s**. Ezk 9:7
You have multiplied your **s** in this city Ezk 11:6
city and have filled its streets with the **s**. Ezk 11:6
Your **s** whom you have laid in the Ezk 11:7
three times, the sword for those to be **s**. Ezk 21:14
die the death of the **s** in the heart of the Ezk 28:8
and the **s** shall fall in her midst, by the Ezk 28:23
be in Cush, when the **s** fall in Egypt, Ezk 30:4
Egypt and fill the land with the **s**. Ezk 30:11
it, to those who are **s** by the sword; Ezk 31:17
with those who are **s** by the sword. Ezk 31:18
amid those who are **s** by the sword. Ezk 32:20
the uncircumcised, **s** by the sword.' Ezk 32:21
its graves all around it, all of them **s**, Ezk 32:22
is all around her grave, all of them **s**, Ezk 32:23
all of them **s**, fallen by the sword, who Ezk 32:24
a bed among the **s** with all her Ezk 32:25
them uncircumcised, **s** by the sword; Ezk 32:25
to the pit; they are placed among the **s**. Ezk 32:25
them uncircumcised, **s** by the sword; Ezk 32:26
with those who are **s** by the sword. Ezk 32:28
have gone down in shame with the **s**, Ezk 32:30
with those who are **s** by the sword, Ezk 32:30
and all his army, **s** by the sword, Ezk 32:31
with those who are **s** by the sword, Ezk 32:32
And I will fill its mountains with the **s**. Ezk 35:8
all your ravines those **s** with the sword Ezk 35:8
winds, O breath, and breathe on these **s**, Ezk 37:9
away, and many shall fall down **s**. Dn 11:26
I have **s** them by the words of my mouth, Hos 6:5
sword and glittering spear, hosts of **s**, Na 3:3
O Cushites, shall be **s** by my sword. Zep 2:12
bring to me **s** beasts and sacrifices, Acts 7:42
a Lamb standing, as though it had been **s**, Rv 5:6
scroll and to open its seals, for you were **s**, Rv 5:9
voice, "Worthy is the Lamb who was **s**, Rv 5:12
of those who had been **s** for the word of Rv 6:9
the book of life of the Lamb that was **s**. Rv 13:8
if anyone is to be **s** with the sword, with Rv 13:10
the sword, with the sword must he be **s**. Rv 13:10
worship the image of the beast to be **s**. Rv 13:15
and of all who have been **s** on earth." Rv 18:24
And the rest were **s** by the sword that Rv 19:21

SLANDER (15)
who does not **s** with his tongue and does Ps 15:3
brother; you **s** your own mother's son. Ps 50:20
lips, and whoever utters **s** is a fool. Prv 10:18
Do not **s** a servant to his master, lest he Prv 30:10
are men in you who **s** to shed blood, Ezk 22:9
immorality, theft, false witness, **s**. Mt 15:19
deceit, sensuality, envy, **s**, pride, Mk 7:22
and dishonor, through **s** and praise. 2 Cor 6:8
jealousy, anger, hostility, **s**, gossip, 2 Cor 12:20
anger and clamor and **s** be put away Eph 4:31
s, and obscene talk from your mouth. Col 3:8
give the adversary no occasion for **s**. 1 Tm 5:14
envy, dissension, **s**, evil suspicions, 1 Tm 6:4
deceit and hypocrisy and envy and all **s**. 1 Pt 2:1
you are rich) and the **s** of those who say Rv 2:9

SLANDERED (3)
He has **s** your servant to my lord the 2 Sm 19:27
when **s**, we entreat. We have become, 1 Cor 4:13
conscience, so that, when you are **s**, 1 Pt 3:16

SLANDERER (3)
go around as a **s** among your people, Lv 19:16
Let not the **s** be established in the land; Ps 140:11
and every neighbor goes about as a **s**. Jer 9:4

SLANDERERS (3)
s, haters of God, insolent, haughty, Rom 1:30
likewise must be dignified, not **s**, 1 Tm 3:11
in behavior, not **s** or slaves to much wine. Ti 2:3

SLANDERING (2)
Whoever goes about **s** reveals secrets, Prv 11:13
Whoever goes about **s** reveals secrets; Prv 20:19

SLANDEROUS (1)
unappeasable, **s**, without self-control, 2 Tm 3:3

SLANDEROUSLY (1)
—as some people **s** charge us with Rom 3:8

SLANDERS (2)
Whoever **s** his neighbor secretly I will Ps 101:5
rebellious, going about with **s**; Jer 6:28

SLAPPED (2)
and after I was instructed, I **s** my thigh; Jer 31:19
face and struck him. And some **s** him, Mt 26:67

SLAPS (1)
But if anyone **s** you on the right cheek, Mt 5:39

SLASHES (1)
He **s** open my kidneys and does not Jb 16:13

SLAUGHTER (46)
hand and took the knife to **s** his son. Gn 22:10
and **s** an animal and make ready, Gn 43:16
you may **s** and eat meat within any of Dt 12:15
And there was a very great **s**, for there 1 Sm 4:10
or his sheep and **s** them here and eat, 1 Sm 14:34
'There has been a **s** among the people 2 Sm 17:9
Levites had to **s** the Passover lamb 2 Chr 30:17
And **s** the Passover lamb, and 2 Chr 35:6
us like sheep for **s** and have scattered us Ps 44:11
he follows her, as an ox goes to the **s**, Prv 7:22
those who are stumbling to the **s**. Prv 24:11
Their bows will **s** the young men; they Is 13:18
Prepare **s** for his sons because of the Is 14:21
with water, in the day of the great **s**, Is 30:25
to destruction, has given them over for **s**. Is 34:2
in Bozrah, a great **s** in the land of Edom. Is 34:6
like a lamb that is led to the **s**, and like a Is 53:7
tree, who **s** your children in the valleys, Is 57:5
and all of you shall bow down to the **s**, Is 65:12
the Son of Hinnom, but the Valley of **S**; Jer 7:32
But I was like a gentle lamb led to the **s**. Jer 11:19
Pull them out like sheep for the **s**, and set Jer 12:3
and set them apart for the day of **s**. Jer 12:3
the Son of Hinnom, but the Valley of **S**. Jer 19:6
the days of your **s** and dispersion have Jer 25:34
of his young men have gone down to **s**, Jer 48:15
all her bulls; let them go down to the **s**. Jer 50:27
bring them down like lambs to the **s**, Jer 51:40
each with his weapon for **s** in his hand, Ezk 9:2
sharpened for **s**, polished to flash like Ezk 21:10
It is the sword for the great **s**, which Ezk 21:14
like lightning; it is taken up for **s**. Ezk 21:15
A sword, a sword is drawn for the **s**. Ezk 21:28
groan, when **s** is made in your midst? Ezk 26:15
with the wool, you **s** the fat ones, Ezk 34:3
of the gate, eight tables, on which to **s**. Ezk 40:41
They shall **s** the burnt offering and Ezk 44:11
And the revolters have gone deep into **s**, Hos 5:2
must lead his children out to **s**. Hos 9:13
from Mount Esau will be cut off by **s**. Ob 1:9
shepherd of the flock doomed to **s**. Zec 11:4
Those who buy them **s** them and go Zec 11:5
them here and **s** them before me.'" Lk 19:27
he was led to the **s** and like a lamb Acts 8:32
returning from the **s** of the kings Heb 7:1
have fattened your hearts in a day of **s**. Jas 5:5

SLAUGHTERED (34)
took Joseph's robe and **s** a goat and Gn 37:31
Shall flocks and herds be **s** for them, Nm 11:22
outside the camp and **s** before him. Nm 19:3
Your ox shall be **s** before your eyes, but Dt 28:31
they seized him and **s** him at the fords Jgs 12:6
Then they **s** the bull, and they 1 Sm 1:25
oxen and calves and **s** them on the 1 Sm 14:32
that night and they **s** them there. 1 Sm 14:34
the brook Kishon and **s** them there. 1 Kgs 18:40
they took the king's sons and **s** them, 2 Kgs 10:7
took them alive and **s** them at the pit 2 Kgs 10:14
They **s** the sons of Zedekiah before 2 Kgs 25:7
So they **s** the bulls, and the priests 2 Chr 29:22
And they **s** the rams and their blood 2 Chr 29:22
And they **s** the lambs and their 2 Chr 29:22
and the priests **s** them and made a 2 Chr 29:24
And they **s** the Passover lamb on 2 Chr 30:15
And they **s** the Passover lamb on the 2 Chr 35:1
And they **s** the Passover lamb, and 2 Chr 35:11
So they **s** the Passover lamb for all the Ezr 6:20
long; we are regarded as sheep to be **s**. Ps 44:22
She has **s** her beasts; she has mixed her Prv 9:2
The king of Babylon **s** the sons of Jer 39:6
the king of Babylon **s** all the nobles of Jer 39:6
the men with him **s** them and cast them Jer 41:7
The king of Babylon **s** the sons of Jer 52:10
and also **s** all the officials of Judah at Jer 52:10
that you **s** my children and delivered Ezk 16:21
For when they had **s** their children in Ezk 23:39
and the guilt offering were to be **s**. Ezk 40:39
offerings and the sacrifices were **s**. Ezk 40:42
flock doomed to be **s** by the sheep Zec 11:7
my oxen and my fat calves have been **s**, Mt 22:4
long; we are regarded as sheep to be **s**." Rom 8:36

SLAUGHTERING (2)
and gladness, killing oxen and **s** sheep, Is 22:13
the day of your anger, **s** without pity. Lam 2:21

SLAUGHTERS (1)
"He who **s** an ox is like one who kills a Is 66:3

SLAVE (70)
"Cast out this **s** woman with her son, Gn 21:10
the son of this **s** woman shall not be Gn 21:10
the boy and because of your **s** woman. Gn 21:12
nation of the son of the **s** woman also, Gn 21:13
the firstborn of the **s** girl who is behind Ex 11:5
but every **s** that is bought for money Ex 12:44
When you buy a Hebrew **s**, he shall Ex 21:2
But if the **s** plainly says, 'I love my Ex 21:5
an awl, and he shall be his **s** forever. Ex 21:6
"When a man sells his daughter as a **s**, Ex 21:7
"When a man strikes his **s**, male or Ex 21:20

a rod and the **s** dies under his hand, Ex 21:20
But if the **s** survives a day or two, he is Ex 21:21
to be avenged, for the **s** is his money. Ex 21:21
"When a man strikes the eye of his **s**, Ex 21:26
he shall let the **s** go free because of his Ex 21:26
If he knocks out the tooth of his **s**, male Ex 21:27
he shall let the **s** go free because of his Ex 21:27
If the ox gores a **s**, male or female, the Ex 21:32
lies sexually with a woman who is a **s**, Lv 19:20
if a priest buys a **s** as his property for Lv 22:11
property for money, the **s** may eat of it, Lv 22:11
you shall not make him serve as a **s**: Lv 25:39
that you were a **s** in the land of Dt 5:15
that you were a **s** in the land of Dt 15:15
the door, and he shall be your **s** forever. Dt 15:17
And to your female **s** you shall do the Dt 15:17
remember that you were a **s** in Egypt; Dt 16:12
money, nor shall you treat her as a **s**, Dt 21:14
to his master a **s** who has escaped from Dt 23:15
and if he treats him as a **s** or sells him, Dt 24:7
that you were a **s** in Egypt and the Dt 24:18
that you were a **s** in the land of Dt 24:22
had an Egyptian **s** whose name was 1 Chr 2:34
daughter in marriage to Jarha his **s**, 1 Chr 2:35
there, and the **s** is free from his master. Jb 3:19
Like a **s** who longs for the shadow, and Jb 7:2
of them, Joseph, who was sold as a **s**. Ps 105:17
much less for a **s** to rule over princes. Prv 19:10
and the borrower is the **s** of the lender. Prv 22:7
a **s** when he becomes king, and a fool Prv 30:22
priest; as with the **s**, so with his master; Is 24:2
"Is Israel a **s**? Is he a homeborn servant? Jer 2:14
and great kings shall make him their **s**. Jer 27:7
that everyone would set free his **s**, Jer 34:10
among the provinces has become a **s**. Lam 1:1
she is carried off, her **s** girls lamenting, Na 2:7
be first among you must be your **s**, Mt 20:27
be first among you must be **s** of all. Mk 10:44
everyone who commits sin is a **s** to sin. Jn 8:34
The **s** does not remain in the house Jn 8:35
we were met by a **s** girl who had a Acts 16:16
Were you a **s** when called? Do not be 1 Cor 7:21
in the Lord as a **s** is a freedman of the 1 Cor 7:22
was free when called is a **s** of Christ. 1 Cor 7:22
nor Greek, there is neither **s** nor free, Gal 3:28
as he is a child, is no different from a **s**, Gal 4:1
So you are no longer a **s**, but a son, and if Gal 4:7
one by a **s** woman and one by a free Gal 4:22
the son of the **s** was born according to Gal 4:23
"Cast out the **s** woman and her son, for Gal 4:30
the son of the **s** woman shall not inherit Gal 4:30
are not children of the **s** but of the free Gal 4:31
from the Lord, whether he is a **s** or free. Eph 6:8
barbarian, Scythian, **s**, free; Col 3:11
no longer as a **s** but more than a Phlm 1:16
longer as a slave but more than a **s**, Phlm 1:16
the powerful, and everyone, **s** and free, Rv 6:15
both rich and poor, both free and **s**, Rv 13:16
and the flesh of all men, both free and **s**, Rv 19:18

SLAVERY (24)
groaned because of their **s** and cried out Ex 2:23
cry for rescue from **s** came up to God. Ex 2:23
and I will deliver you from **s** to them, Ex 6:6
of their broken spirit and harsh **s**. Ex 6:9
out from Egypt, out of the house of **s**, Ex 13:3
us out of Egypt, from the house of **s**. Ex 13:14
of the land of Egypt, out of the house of **s**. Ex 20:2
of the land of Egypt, out of the house of **s**. Dt 5:6
of the land of Egypt, out of the house of **s**. Dt 6:12
and redeemed you from the house of **s**, Dt 7:8
of the land of Egypt, out of the house of **s**, Dt 8:14
and redeemed you out of the house of **s**, Dt 13:5
the land of Egypt, out of the house of **s**. Dt 13:10
the land of Egypt, out of the house of **s**, Jos 24:17
and grant us a little reviving in our **s**. Ezr 9:8
Yet our God has not forsaken us in our **s**, Ezr 9:9
a leader to return to their **s** in Egypt. Neh 9:17
and redeemed you from the house of **s**, Mi 6:4
receive the spirit of **s** to fall back into Rom 8:15
so that they might bring us into **s**— Gal 2:4
Mount Sinai, bearing children for **s**; Gal 4:24
for she is in **s** with her children. Gal 4:25
and do not submit again to a yoke of **s**. Gal 5:1
fear of death were subject to lifelong **s**. Heb 2:15

SLAVES (60)
his wife and female **s** so that they bore Gn 20:17
made the people of Israel work as **s** Ex 1:13
they ruthlessly made them work as **s**. Ex 1:14
of Israel whom the Egyptians hold as **s**, Ex 6:5
Pharaoh hurried his **s** and his livestock Ex 9:20
of the LORD left his **s** and his livestock in Ex 9:21
she shall not go out as the male **s** do. Ex 21:7
your male and female **s** and for your Lv 25:6
of Egypt; they shall not be sold as **s**. Lv 25:42
male and female **s** whom you may Lv 25:44
buy male and female **s** from among the Lv 25:44
You may make **s** of them, but over Lv 25:46
of Egypt, that you should not be their **s**. Lv 26:13
your son, 'We were Pharaoh's **s** in Egypt. Dt 6:21
to your enemies as male and female **s**, Dt 28:68
lest you become **s** to the Hebrews as 1 Sm 4:9
of your flocks, and you shall be his **s**. 1 Sm 8:17
—these Solomon drafted to be **s**, 1 Kgs 9:21
people of Israel Solomon made no **s**. 1 Kgs 9:22
to take my two children to be his **s**." 2 Kgs 4:1
Solomon made no **s** for his work; 2 Chr 8:9
male and female, as your **s**. 2 Chr 28:10
For we are **s**. Yet our God has not Ezr 9:9
our sons and our daughters to be **s**, Neh 5:5
Behold, we are **s** this day; in the land Neh 9:36
fruit and its good gifts, behold, we are **s**. Neh 9:36
If we had been sold merely as **s**, men and Est 7:4
I bought male and female **s**, and had Eccl 2:7
and had **s** who were born in my house. Eccl 2:7
I have seen **s** on horses, and princes Eccl 10:7
princes walking on the ground like **s**. Eccl 10:7
in the LORD'S land as male and female **s**. Is 14:2
great kings shall make **s** even of them, Jer 25:14
everyone should set free his Hebrew **s**, Jer 34:9
the male and female **s** they had set free, Jer 34:11
and brought them into subjection as **s**. Jer 34:11
you took back his male and female **s**, Jer 34:16
them into subjection to be your **s**. Jer 34:16
S rule over us; there is none to deliver us Lam 5:8
yourselves to anyone as obedient **s**, Rom 6:16
you are **s** of the one whom you obey, Rom 6:16
you who were once **s** of sin have Rom 6:17
sin, have become **s** of righteousness. Rom 6:18
your members as **s** to impurity and Rom 6:19
your members as **s** to righteousness Rom 6:19
When you were **s** of sin, you were free Rom 6:20
from sin and have become **s** of God, Rom 6:22
with a price; do not become **s** of men. 1 Cor 7:23
s or free—and all were made to 1 Cor 12:13
bear it if someone makes **s** of you, 2 Cor 11:20
whose **s** you want to be once more? Gal 4:9
S, obey your earthly masters with fear Eph 6:5
S, obey in everything those who are Col 3:22
Masters, treat your **s** justly and fairly, Col 4:1
under a yoke as **s** regard their own 1 Tm 6:1
not slanderers or **s** to much wine. Ti 2:3
S are to be submissive to their own Ti 2:9
s to various passions and pleasures, Ti 3:3
they themselves are **s** of corruption. 2 Pt 2:19
and sheep, horses and chariots, and **s**, Rv 18:13

SLAY (8)
Though he **s** me, I will hope in him; yet Jb 13:15
Affliction will **s** the wicked, and those Ps 34:21
needy, to **s** those whose way is upright; Ps 37:14
Oh that you would **s** the wicked, O Ps 139:19
with famine, and your remnant it will **s**. Is 14:30
and he will **s** the dragon that is in the sea. Is 27:1
god, in the hands of those who **s** you? Ezk 28:9
earth, so that men should **s** one another, Rv 6:4

SLAYER (1)
to be given into the hand of the **s**. Ezk 21:11

SLAYERS (1)
have they been slain as their **s** were slain? Is 27:7

SLAYS (1)
kills the fool, and jealousy **s** the simple. Jb 5:2

SLEDGE (3)
himself like a threshing **s** on the mire. Jb 41:30
Dill is not threshed with a threshing **s**, Is 28:27
Behold, I make of you a threshing **s**, Is 41:15

SLEDGES (3)
and the threshing **s** and the yokes 2 Sm 24:22
and the threshing **s** for the wood 1 Chr 21:23
threshed Gilead with threshing **s** of iron. Am 1:3

SLEEK (3)
and kicked; you grew fat, stout, and **s**; Dt 32:15
until death; their bodies are fat and **s**. Ps 73:4
they have grown fat and **s**. They know Jer 5:28

SLEEP (61)
God caused a deep **s** to fall upon the Gn 2:21
going down, a deep **s** fell on Abram. Gn 15:12
head and lay down in that place to **s**. Gn 28:11
Then Jacob awoke from his **s** and said, Gn 28:16
by night, and my **s** fled from my eyes. Gn 31:40
for his body; in what else shall he **s**? Ex 22:27
poor man, you shall not **s** in his pledge. Dt 24:12
that he may **s** in his cloak and bless Dt 24:13
he awoke from his **s** and pulled away Jgs 16:14
She made him **s** on her knees. And she Jgs 16:19
And he awoke from his **s** and said, Jgs 16:20
Saul on the roof, and he lay down to **s**. 1 Sm 9:25
because a deep **s** from the LORD had 1 Sm 26:12
On that night the king could not **s**. And Est 6:1
of the night, when deep **s** falls on men, Jb 4:13
will not awake or be roused out of his **s**. Jb 14:12
of the night, when deep **s** falls on men, Jb 33:15
In peace I will both lie down and **s**; for you Ps 4:8
up my eyes, lest I **s** the sleep of death, Ps 13:3
up my eyes, lest I sleep the **s** of death, Ps 13:3
stripped of their spoil; they sank into **s**; Ps 76:5
Then the Lord awoke as from **s**, like a Ps 78:65
keeps Israel will neither slumber nor **s**. Ps 121:4
toil; for he gives to his beloved **s**. Ps 127:2
I will not give **s** to my eyes or slumber Ps 132:4
when you lie down, your **s** will be sweet. Prv 3:24
For they cannot **s** unless they have Prv 4:16
they are robbed of **s** unless they have Prv 4:16
Give your eyes no **s** and your eyelids no Prv 6:4
When will you arise from your **s**? Prv 6:9
A little **s**, a little slumber, a little folding Prv 6:10
Slothfulness casts into a deep **s**, and an Prv 19:15
Love not **s**, lest you come to poverty; Prv 20:13
A little **s**, a little slumber, a little Prv 24:33
Sweet is the **s** of a laborer, whether he Eccl 5:12
stomach of the rich will not let him **s**. Eccl 5:12
day nor night do one's eyes see **s**, Eccl 8:16
poured out upon you a spirit of deep **s**, Is 29:10
looked, and my **s** was pleasant to me. Jer 31:26
then **s** a perpetual sleep and not wake, Jer 51:39
then sleep a perpetual **s** and not wake, Jer 51:39
they shall **s** a perpetual sleep and not Jer 51:57
shall sleep a perpetual **s** and not wake, Jer 51:57
in the wilderness and **s** in the woods. Ezk 34:25
his spirit was troubled, and his **s** left him. Dn 2:1
brought to him, and **s** fled from him. Dn 6:18
I fell into a deep **s** with my face to the Dn 8:18
on my face in deep **s** with my face to the Dn 10:9
And many of those who **s** in the dust of Dn 12:2
like a man who is awakened out of his **s**. Zec 4:1
When Joseph woke from **s**, he did as the Mt 1:24
to them, "**S** and take your rest later on. Mt 26:45
who were with him were heavy with **s**, Lk 9:32
thought that he meant taking rest in **s**. Jn 11:13
sank into a deep **s** as Paul talked still Acts 20:9
And being overcome by **s**, he fell down Acts 20:9
has come for you to wake from **s**. Rom 13:11
We shall not all **s**, but we shall all 1 Cor 15:51
So then let us not **s**, as others do, but 1 Thes 5:6
For those who **s**, sleep at night, and 1 Thes 5:7
For those who sleep, **s** at night, and 1 Thes 5:7

SLEEPER (2)
said to him, "What do you mean, you **s**? Jon 1:6
Therefore it says, "Awake, O **s**, and Eph 5:14

SLEEPING (14)
there lay Saul **s** within the 1 Sm 26:7
Awake! Why are you **s**, O Lord? Rouse Ps 44:23
is not dead but **s**." And they laughed at Mt 9:24
but while his men were **s**, his enemy Mt 13:25
came to the disciples and found them **s**. Mt 26:40
And again he came and found them **s**, Mt 26:43
weeping? The child is not dead but **s**." Mk 5:39
And he came and found them **s**, and Mk 14:37
And again he came and found them **s**, Mk 14:40
"Are you still **s** and taking your rest? Mk 14:41
"Do not weep, for she is not dead but **s**." Lk 8:52
disciples and found them **s** for sorrow, Lk 22:45
and he said to them, "Why are you **s**? Lk 22:46
night, Peter was **s** between two soldiers, Acts 12:6

SLEEPLESS (2)
imprisonments, riots, labors, **s** nights, 2 Cor 6:5
hardship, through many a **s** night, 2 Cor 11:27

SLEEPS (5)
and whoever **s** in the house shall wash Lv 14:47
my lord the king **s** with his fathers, 1 Kgs 1:21
but he who **s** in harvest is a son who Prv 10:5
none stumbles, none slumbers or **s**, Is 5:27
He **s** and rises night and day, and the Mk 4:27

SLEEVES (1)
she was wearing a long robe with **s**, 2 Sm 13:18

SLEPT (45)
and while he **s** took one of his ribs and Gn 2:21
So while he **s**, Delilah took the seven Jgs 16:14
But Uriah **s** at the door of the king's 2 Sm 11:9
Then David **s** with his fathers and 1 Kgs 2:10
from beside me, while your servant **s**, 1 Kgs 3:20
Egypt that David **s** with his fathers 1 Kgs 11:21
And Solomon **s** with his fathers and 1 Kgs 11:43
And he **s** with his fathers, and 1 Kgs 14:20
And Rehoboam **s** with his fathers 1 Kgs 14:31
And Abijam **s** with his fathers, and 1 Kgs 15:8
And Asa **s** with his fathers and was 1 Kgs 15:24
And Baasha **s** with his fathers and 1 Kgs 16:6
And Omri **s** with his fathers and 1 Kgs 16:28
he lay down and **s** under a broom 1 Kgs 19:5

So Ahab **s** with his fathers, and 1 Kgs 22:40
And Jehoshaphat **s** with his fathers 1 Kgs 22:50
So Joram **s** with his fathers and was 2 Kgs 8:24
So Jehu **s** with his fathers, and they 2 Kgs 10:35
So Jehoahaz **s** with his fathers, and 2 Kgs 13:9
So Joash **s** with his fathers, and 2 Kgs 13:13
And Jehoash **s** with his fathers and 2 Kgs 14:16
after the king **s** with his fathers. 2 Kgs 14:22
And Jeroboam **s** with his fathers, the 2 Kgs 14:29
And Azariah **s** with his fathers, and 2 Kgs 15:7
And Menahem **s** with his fathers, 2 Kgs 15:22
Jotham **s** with his fathers and was 2 Kgs 15:38
And Ahaz **s** with his fathers and was 2 Kgs 16:20
And Hezekiah **s** with his fathers, 2 Kgs 20:21
And Manasseh **s** with his fathers 2 Kgs 21:18
So Jehoiakim **s** with his fathers, and 2 Kgs 24:6
And Solomon **s** with his fathers and 2 Chr 9:31
And Rehoboam **s** with his fathers 2 Chr 12:16
Abijah **s** with his fathers, and they 2 Chr 14:1
And Asa **s** with his fathers, dying in 2 Chr 16:13
Jehoshaphat **s** with his fathers and 2 Chr 21:1
after the king **s** with his fathers. 2 Chr 26:2
And Uzziah **s** with his fathers, and 2 Chr 26:23
And Jotham **s** with his fathers, and 2 Chr 27:9
And Ahaz **s** with his fathers, and 2 Chr 28:27
And Hezekiah **s** with his fathers, 2 Chr 32:33
So Manasseh **s** with his fathers, and 2 Chr 33:20
lain down and been quiet; I would have **s**; Jb 3:13
I lay down and **s**; I woke again, for the Ps 3:5
I **s**, but my heart was awake. A sound! My Sg 5:2
delayed, they all became drowsy and **s**. Mt 25:5

SLICE (1)
They **s** meat on the right, but are still Is 9:20

SLIGHT (1)
For this **s** momentary affliction is 2 Cor 4:17

SLIME (1)
be like the snail that dissolves into **s**, Ps 58:8

SLING (9)
every one could **s** a stone at a hair and Jgs 20:16
His **s** was in his hand, and he 1 Sm 17:40
the Philistine with a **s** and with a 1 Sm 17:50
your enemies he shall **s** out as from 1 Sm 25:29
sling out as from the hollow of a **s**. 1 Sm 25:29
shoot arrows and **s** stones with either 1 Chr 12:2
for him **s** stones are turned to stubble. Jb 41:28
binds the stone in the **s** is one who gives Prv 26:8
devour, and tread down the **s** stones, Zec 9:15

SLINGERS (1)
and the **s** surrounded and attacked it. 2 Kgs 3:25

SLINGING (2)
coats of mail, bows, and stones for **s**. 2 Chr 26:14
I am **s** out the inhabitants of the land at Jer 10:18

SLIP (7)
for the time when their foot shall **s**; Dt 32:35
steps under me, and my feet did not **s**; 2 Sm 22:37
then let no one **s** out of the city to go 2 Kgs 9:15
it is ready for those whose feet **s**. Jb 12:5
steps under me, and my feet did not **s**. Ps 18:36
God is in his heart; his steps do not **s**. Ps 37:31
the living and has not let our feet **s**. Ps 66:9

SLIPPED (3)
fast to your paths; my feet have not **s**. Ps 17:5
almost stumbled, my steps had nearly **s**. Ps 73:2
secretly brought in—who **s** in to spy out Gal 2:4

SLIPPERY (3)
Let their way be dark and **s**, with the Ps 35:6
Truly you set them in **s** places; you Ps 73:18
be to them like **s** paths in the darkness, Jer 23:12

SLIPS (4)
and the head **s** from the handle and Dt 19:5
who boast against me when my foot **s**!" Ps 38:16
"My foot **s**," your steadfast love, Ps 94:18
is like a bad tooth or a foot that **s**. Prv 25:19

SLOPE (2)
brothers one mountain **s** that I took Gn 48:22
and the **s** of the valleys that extends to Nm 21:15

SLOPES (8)
Sea, under the **s** of Pisgah on the east. Dt 3:17
Sea of the Arabah, under the **s** of Pisgah. Dt 4:49
the Negeb and the lowland and the **s**, Jos 10:40
southward to the foot of the **s** of Pisgah; Jos 12:3
in the lowland, in the Arabah, in the **s**, Jos 12:8
and Beth-peor, and the **s** of Pisgah, and Jos 13:20
of goats leaping down the **s** of Gilead. Sg 4:1
of goats leaping down the **s** of Gilead. Sg 6:5

SLOTH (1)
Through **s** the roof sinks in, and Eccl 10:18

SLOTHFUL (4)
while the **s** will be put to forced labor. Prv 12:24
Whoever is **s** will not roast his game, Prv 12:27
him, 'You wicked and **s** servant! Mt 25:26
Do not be **s** in zeal, be fervent in Rom 12:11

SLOTHFULNESS (1)
S casts into a deep sleep, and an idle Prv 19:15

SLOW (20)
but I am **s** of speech and of tongue." Ex 4:10
a God merciful and gracious, **s** to anger, Ex 34:6
'The LORD is **s** to anger and Nm 14:18
Do not be **s** to go, to enter in and possess Jgs 18:9
s to anger and abounding in steadfast Neh 9:17
s to anger and abounding in steadfast Ps 86:15
s to anger and abounding in steadfast Ps 103:8
s to anger and abounding in steadfast Ps 145:8
Whoever is **s** to anger has great Prv 14:29
but he who is **s** to anger quiets Prv 15:18
Whoever is **s** to anger is better than Prv 16:32
Good sense makes one **s** to anger, and Prv 19:11
he is gracious and merciful, **s** to anger, Jl 2:13
s to anger and abounding in steadfast Jon 4:2
The LORD is **s** to anger and great in power, Na 1:3
If it seems **s**, wait for it; it will surely Hab 2:3
and **s** of heart to believe all that the Lk 24:25
every person be quick to hear, **s** to speak, Jas 1:19
quick to hear, slow to speak, **s** to anger; Jas 1:19
The Lord is not **s** to fulfill his promise as 2 Pt 3:9

SLOWLY (3)
of his servant, and I will lead on **s**, Gn 33:14
I walk **s** all my years because of the Is 38:15
We sailed **s** for a number of days and Acts 27:7

SLOWNESS (1)
to fulfill his promise as some count **s**, 2 Pt 3:9

SLUGGARD (14)
Go to the ant, O **s**; consider her ways, and Prv 6:6
How long will you lie there, O **s**? When Prv 6:9
eyes, so is the **s** to those who send him. Prv 10:26
The soul of the **s** craves and gets Prv 13:4
The way of a **s** is like a hedge of Prv 15:19
The **s** buries his hand in the dish and Prv 19:24
The **s** does not plow in the autumn; he Prv 20:4
The desire of the **s** kills him, for his Prv 21:25
The **s** says, "There is a lion outside! I Prv 22:13
I passed by the field of a **s**, by the Prv 24:30
The **s** says, "There is a lion in the Prv 26:13
on its hinges, so does a **s** on his bed. Prv 26:14
The **s** buries his hand in the dish; it Prv 26:15
The **s** is wiser in his own eyes than Prv 26:16

SLUGGISH (1)
so that you may not be **s**, but imitators Heb 6:12

SLUMBER (10)
falls on men, while they **s** on their beds, Jb 33:15
be moved; he who keeps you will not **s**. Ps 121:3
who keeps Israel will neither **s** nor sleep. Ps 121:4
give sleep to my eyes or **s** to my eyelids, Ps 132:4
your eyes no sleep and your eyelids no **s**; Prv 6:4
A little sleep, a little **s**, a little folding of Prv 6:10
and **s** will clothe them with rags. Prv 23:21
A little sleep, a little **s**, a little folding of Prv 24:33
bark, dreaming, lying down, loving to **s**. Is 56:10
asleep, O king of Assyria; your nobles **s**. Na 3:18

SLUMBERS (1)
is weary, none stumbles, none **s** or sleeps, Is 5:27

SLUNG (2)
javelin of bronze **s** between his 1 Sm 17:6
out a stone and **s** it and struck the 1 Sm 17:49

SMALL (84)
in the land and no **s** plant of the field had Gn 2:5
entrance of the house, both **s** and great, Gn 19:11
"Is it a **s** matter that you have taken Gn 30:15
And if the household is too **s** for a lamb, Ex 12:4
but any **s** matter they shall decide Ex 18:22
but any **s** matter they decided Ex 18:26
You shall beat some of it very **s**, and Ex 30:36
of the house he shall take two **s** birds, Lv 14:49
two handfuls of sweet incense beaten **s**, Lv 16:12
is it too **s** a thing for you that the God of Nm 16:9
Is it a **s** thing that you have brought Nm 16:13
and to a **s** tribe you shall give a small Nm 26:54
tribe you shall give a **s** inheritance; Nm 26:54
and to a **s** tribe you shall give a small Nm 33:54
tribe you shall give a **s** inheritance. Nm 33:54
You shall hear the **s** and the great alike. Dt 1:17
fire and crushed it, grinding it very **s**, Dt 9:21
two kinds of weights, a large and a **s**. Dt 25:13
two kinds of measures, a large and a **s**. Dt 25:14
either great or **s** without disclosing it 1 Sm 20:2
all who were in it, both **s** and great. 1 Sm 30:2
was missing, whether **s** or great, 1 Sm 30:19
yet this was a **s** thing in your eyes, 2 Sm 7:19
"I have one **s** request to make of you; 1 Kgs 2:20
the LORD was too **s** to receive the 1 Kgs 8:64
"Fight with neither **s** nor great, 1 Kgs 22:31
some **s** boys came out of the city and 2 Kgs 2:23
Let us make a **s** room on the roof 2 Kgs 4:10
dwell under your charge is too **s** for us. 2 Kgs 6:1
all the people, both **s** and great. 2 Kgs 23:2
all the people, both **s** and great, 2 Kgs 25:26
And this was a **s** thing in your eyes, 1 Chr 17:17
cast lots for their duties, **s** and great, 1 Chr 25:8
by fathers' houses, **s** and great alike, 1 Chr 26:13
"Fight with neither **s** nor great, 2 Chr 18:30
and the large and **s** shields that had 2 Chr 23:9
all the people both great and **s**. 2 Chr 34:30
of the house of God, great and **s**, 2 Chr 36:18
in Susa, the citadel, both great and **s**, Est 1:5
The **s** and the great are there, and the Jb 3:19
And though your beginning was **s**, your Jb 8:7
Are the comforts of God too **s** for you, or Jb 15:11
and how **s** a whisper do we hear of him! Jb 26:14
"Behold, I am of **s** account; what shall I Jb 40:4
living things both **s** and great. Ps 104:25
fear the LORD, both the **s** and the great. Ps 115:13
I am **s** and despised, yet I do not forget Ps 119:141
the day of adversity, your strength is **s**. Prv 24:10
Four things on earth are **s**, but they Prv 30:24
the offspring and issue, every **s** vessel, Is 22:24
of your foreign foes shall be like **s** dust, Is 29:5
Both great and **s** shall die in this land. Jer 16:6
them honored, and they shall not be **s**. Jer 30:19
I will make you **s** among the nations, Jer 49:15
also the **s** bowls and the fire pans and Jer 52:19
take from these a **s** number and bind Ezk 5:3
Were your whorings so **s** a matter Ezk 16:20
will make them so **s** that they will Ezk 29:15
corners of the court were **s** courts, Ezk 46:22
he shall become strong with a **s** people. Dn 11:23
How can Jacob stand? He is so **s**!" Am 7:2
cease! How can Jacob stand? He is so **s**!" Am 7:5
may make the ephah **s** and the shekel Am 8:5
I will make you **s** among the nations; Ob 1:2
the day of **s** things shall rejoice, Zec 4:10
They said, "Seven, and a few **s** fish." Mt 15:34
And they had a few **s** fish. And having Mk 8:7
came and put in two **s** copper coins, Mk 12:42
are not able to do as **s** a thing as that, Lk 12:26
could not, because he was **s** of stature. Lk 19:3
a poor widow put in two **s** copper coins. Lk 21:2
Barnabas had no **s** dissension and Acts 15:2
here testifying both to **s** and great, Acts 26:22
the lee of a **s** island called Cauda, Acts 27:16
days, and no **s** tempest lay on us, Acts 27:20
me it is a very **s** thing that I should be 1 Cor 4:3
guided by a very **s** rudder wherever the Jas 3:4
So also the tongue is a **s** member, yet it Jas 3:5
great a forest is set ablaze by such a **s** fire! Jas 3:5
who fear your name, both **s** and great, Rv 11:18
Also it causes all, both **s** and great, Rv 13:16
servants, you who fear him, **s** and great." Rv 19:5
both free and slave, both **s** and great." Rv 19:18
And I saw the dead, great and **s**, Rv 20:12

SMALLER (3)
to lot between the larger and the **s**." Nm 26:56
and from the **s** tribes you shall take Nm 35:8
and from the **s** ledge to the larger Ezk 43:14

SMALLEST (3)
a clan, and the **s** one a mighty nation; Is 60:22
It is the **s** of all seeds, but when it has Mt 13:32
ground, is the **s** of all the seeds on earth, Mk 4:31

SMASHED (2)
blew the trumpets and **s** the jars that Jgs 7:19
potter's vessel that is **s** so ruthlessly that Is 30:14

SMEAR (3)
The insolent **s** me with lies, but with Ps 119:69
these prophets **s** it with whitewash, Ezk 13:10
say to those who **s** it with whitewash Ezk 13:11

SMEARED (9)
oil, and unleavened wafers **s** with oil. Ex 29:2
with oil or unleavened wafers **s** with oil. Lv 2:4
with oil, unleavened wafers **s** with oil, Lv 7:12
oil, and unleavened wafers **s** with oil, Nm 6:15
is the coating with which you **s** it?' Ezk 13:12
wall that you have **s** with whitewash, Ezk 13:14
those who have **s** it with whitewash, Ezk 13:15
wall is no more, nor those who **s** it, Ezk 13:15
her prophets have **s** whitewash for Ezk 22:28

SMELL (9)
Isaac smelled the **s** of his garments Gn 27:27
the **s** of my son is as the smell of a field Gn 27:27
of my son is as the **s** of a field that the Gn 27:27
and I will not **s** your pleasing aromas. Lv 26:31
that neither see, nor hear, nor eat, nor **s**. Dt 4:28
but do not hear; noses, but do not **s**. Ps 115:6
and no **s** of fire had come upon them. Dn 3:27

sea; the stench and foul **s** of him will rise, Jl 2:20
ear, where would be the sense of **s**? 1 Cor 12:17

SMELLED (2)
when the LORD **s** the pleasing aroma, Gn 8:21
And Isaac **s** the smell of his garments Gn 27:27

SMELLS (1)
He **s** the battle from afar, the thunder of Jb 39:25

SMELT (1)
against you and will **s** away your dross as Is 1:25

SMELTED (1)
of the earth, and copper is **s** from the ore. Jb 28:2

SMILE (1)
Look away from me, that I may **s** again, Ps 39:13

SMILED (1)
I **s** on them when they had no Jb 29:24

SMITH (2)
and the **s** has material for a vessel; Prv 25:4
I have created the **s** who blows the fire of Is 54:16

SMITHS (1)
and all the craftsmen and the **s**. 2 Kgs 24:14

SMITTEN (1)
yet we esteemed him stricken, **s** by God, Is 53:4

SMOKE (49)
the **s** of the land went up like the Gn 19:28
the land went up like the **s** of a furnace. Gn 19:28
was wrapped in **s** because the LORD Ex 19:18
The **s** of it went up like the smoke of a Ex 19:18
smoke of it went up like the **s** of a kiln, Ex 19:18
his jealousy will **s** against that man, Dt 29:20
the **s** of the city went up to heaven, Jos 8:20
city, and that the **s** of the city went up, Jos 8:21
made a great cloud of **s** rise up out of Jgs 20:38
to rise out of the city in a column of **s**, Jgs 20:40
of the city went up in **s** to heaven. Jgs 20:40
S went up from his nostrils, and 2 Sm 22:9
Out of his nostrils comes forth **s**, as Jb 41:20
S went up from his nostrils, and Ps 18:8
they vanish—like **s** they vanish away. Ps 37:20
with the **s** of the sacrifice of rams; Ps 66:15
As **s** is driven away, so you shall drive Ps 68:2
Why does your anger **s** against the sheep Ps 74:1
For my days pass away like **s**, and my Ps 102:3
touches the mountains and they **s**! Ps 104:32
I have become like a wineskin in the **s**, Ps 119:83
Touch the mountains so that they **s**! Ps 144:5
vinegar to the teeth and **s** to the eyes, Prv 10:26
up from the wilderness like columns of **s**, Sg 3:6
and **s** and the shining of a flaming fire by Is 4:5
who called, and the house was filled with **s**. Is 6:4
and they roll upward in a column of **s**. Is 9:18
For **s** comes out of the north, and there Is 14:31
with his anger, and in thick rising **s**; Is 30:27
be quenched; its **s** shall go up forever. Is 34:10
for the heavens vanish like **s**, the earth Is 51:6
for you." These are a **s** in my nostrils, Is 65:5
and the **s** of the cloud of incense went Ezk 8:11
floor or like **s** from a window. Hos 13:3
earth, blood and fire and columns of **s**. Jl 2:30
hosts, and I will burn your chariots in **s**, Na 2:13
below, blood, and fire, and vapor of **s**; Acts 2:19
and the **s** of the incense, with the prayers Rv 8:4
from the shaft rose **s** like the smoke of Rv 9:2
rose smoke like the **s** of a great furnace, Rv 9:2
were darkened with the **s** from the shaft. Rv 9:2
Then from the **s** came locusts on the Rv 9:3
and fire and **s** and sulfur came out of Rv 9:17
by the fire and **s** and sulfur coming out Rv 9:18
And the **s** of their torment goes up Rv 14:11
was filled with **s** from the glory Rv 15:8
her when they see the **s** of her burning. Rv 18:9
out as they saw the **s** of her burning, Rv 18:18
The **s** from her goes up forever and ever." Rv 19:3

SMOKING (2)
a **s** fire pot and a flaming torch passed Gn 15:17
of the trumpet and the mountain **s**, Ex 20:18

SMOLDERING (2)
of these two **s** stumps of firebrands, Is 7:4
break, and a **s** wick he will not quench, Mt 12:20

SMOLDERS (1)
their intrigue; all night their anger **s**; Hos 7:6

SMOOTH (13)
Esau is a hairy man, and I am a **s** man. Gn 27:11
his hands and on the **s** part of his neck. Gn 27:16
and chose five **s** stones from the 1 Sm 17:40
His speech was **s** as butter, yet war was Ps 55:21
from the adulteress with her **s** words, Prv 2:16
from the **s** tongue of the adulteress. Prv 6:24
from the adulteress with her **s** words. Prv 7:5
him; with her **s** talk she compels him. Prv 7:21
swift messengers, to a nation, tall and **s**, Is 18:2
the LORD of hosts from a people tall and **s**, Is 18:7
speak to us **s** things, prophesy illusions, Is 30:10
Among the **s** stones of the valley is your Is 57:6
and by **s** talk and flattery they Rom 16:18

SMOOTHER (1)
drip honey, and her speech is **s** than oil, Prv 5:3

SMOOTHLY (2)
it sparkles in the cup and goes down **s**. Prv 23:31
best wine. It goes down **s** for my beloved, Sg 7:9

SMOOTHS (1)
and he who **s** with the hammer him who Is 41:7

SMYRNA (2)
to Ephesus and to **S** and to Pergamum Rv 1:11
"And to the angel of the church in **S** write: Rv 2:8

SNAIL (1)
them be like the **s** that dissolves into Ps 58:8

SNAPPED (3)
you, Samson!" But he **s** the bowstrings, Jgs 16:9
But he **s** the ropes off his arms like a Jgs 16:12
before the silver cord is **s**, or the golden Eccl 12:6

SNAPS (1)
as a thread of flax **s** when it touches the Jgs 16:9

SNARE (40)
"How long shall this man be a **s** to us? Ex 10:7
their gods, it will surely be a **s** to you." Ex 23:33
you go, lest it become a **s** in your midst. Ex 34:12
their gods, for that would be a **s** to you. Dt 7:16
but they shall be a **s** and a trap for you, Jos 23:13
sides, and their gods shall be a **s** to you." Jgs 2:3
and it became a **s** to Gideon and to his Jgs 8:27
that she may be a **s** for him and that 1 Sm 18:21
him by the heel; a **s** lays hold of him. Jb 18:9
by his eyes, or pierce his nose with a **s**? Jb 40:24
their own table before them become a **s**; Ps 69:22
deliver you from the **s** of the fowler and Ps 91:3
their idols, which became a **s** to them. Ps 106:36
The wicked have laid a **s** for me, but I Ps 119:110
like a bird from the **s** of the fowlers; Ps 124:7
the **s** is broken, and we have escaped! Ps 124:7
its liver; as a bird rushes into a **s**; Prv 7:23
his ruin, and his lips are a **s** to his soul. Prv 18:7
It is a **s** to say rashly, "It is holy," and Prv 20:25
is a fleeting vapor and a **s** of death. Prv 21:6
his ways and entangle yourself in a **s**. Prv 22:25
The fear of man lays a **s**, but whoever Prv 29:25
and like birds that are caught in a **s**, Eccl 9:12
a trap and a **s** to the inhabitants of Is 8:14
and the pit and the **s** are upon you, Is 24:17
out of the pit shall be caught in the **s**. Is 24:18
and lay a **s** for him who reproves in the Is 29:21
Terror, pit, and **s** are before you, O Jer 48:43
out of the pit shall be caught in the **s**. Jer 48:44
I set a **s** for you and you were taken, O Jer 50:24
him, and he shall be taken in my **s**. Ezk 12:13
him, and he shall be taken in my **s**, Ezk 17:20
for you have been a **s** at Mizpah and a Hos 5:1
yet a fowler's **s** is on all his ways, and Hos 9:8
Does a bird fall in a **s** on the earth, when Am 3:5
Does a **s** spring up from the ground, Am 3:5
"Let their table become a **s** and a trap, Rom 11:9
fall into disgrace, into a **s** of the devil. 1 Tm 3:7
to be rich fall into temptation, into a **s**, 1 Tm 6:9
may escape from the **s** of the devil, 2 Tm 2:26

SNARED (5)
the wicked are **s** in the work of their own Ps 9:16
if you are **s** in the words of your mouth, Prv 6:2
children of man are **s** at an evil time, Eccl 9:12
be broken; they shall be **s** and taken." Is 8:15
fall backward, and be broken, and **s**, Is 28:13

SNARES (13)
me; the **s** of death confronted me. 2 Sm 22:6
Therefore **s** are all around you, and Jb 22:10
me; the **s** of death confronted me. Ps 18:5
Those who seek my life lay their **s**; Ps 38:12
they talk of laying **s** secretly, thinking, Ps 64:5
The **s** of death encompassed me; the Ps 116:3
beside the way they have set **s** for me. Ps 140:5
laid for me and from the **s** of evildoers! Ps 141:9
may turn away from the **s** of death. Prv 13:14
may turn away from the **s** of death. Prv 14:27
Thorns and **s** are in the way of the Prv 22:5
the woman whose heart is **s** and nets, Eccl 7:26
a pit to take me and laid **s** for my feet. Jer 18:22

SNATCH (7)
of the vineyards and **s** each man his Jgs 21:21
are those who **s** the fatherless child Jb 24:9
Drought and heat **s** away the snow Jb 24:19
altogether who seek to **s** away my life; Ps 40:14
he will **s** and tear you from your tent; Ps 52:5
and no one will **s** them out of my hand. Jn 10:28
no one is able to **s** them out of the Jn 10:29

SNATCHED (3)
with a staff and **s** the spear out of 2 Sm 23:21
with a staff and **s** the spear out of 1 Chr 11:23
They were **s** away before their time; Jb 22:16

SNATCHES (3)
Behold, he **s** away; who can turn him Jb 9:12
evil one comes and **s** away what has Mt 13:19
and the wolf **s** them and scatters them. Jn 10:12

SNATCHING (1)
save others by **s** them out of the fire; to Jude 1:23

SNEEZED (1)
upon him. The child **s** seven times, 2 Kgs 4:35

SNEEZINGS (1)
His **s** flash forth light, and his eyes are Jb 41:18

SNIFFING (1)
to the wilderness, in her heat **s** the wind! Jer 2:24

SNORT (1)
a weariness this is,' and you **s** at it, Mal 1:13

SNORTING (2)
the locust? His majestic **s** is terrifying. Jb 39:20
"The **s** of their horses is heard from Dan; Jer 8:16

SNOUT (1)
ring in a pig's **s** is a beautiful woman Prv 11:22

SNOW (24)
it out, behold, his hand was leprous like **s**. Ex 4:6
behold, Miriam was leprous, like **s**. Nm 12:10
in a pit on a day when **s** had fallen. 2 Sm 23:20
out from his presence a leper, like **s**. 2 Kgs 5:27
in a pit on a day when **s** had fallen. 1 Chr 11:22
dark with ice, and where the **s** hides itself. Jb 6:16
I wash myself with **s** and cleanse my Jb 9:30
and heat snatch away the **s** waters; Jb 24:19
For to the **s** he says, 'Fall on the earth,' Jb 37:6
you entered the storehouses of the **s**, Jb 38:22
wash me, and I shall be whiter than **s**. Ps 51:7
kings there, let **s** fall on Zalmon. Ps 68:14
He gives **s** like wool; he scatters Ps 147:16
fire and hail, **s** and mist, stormy wind Ps 148:8
Like the cold of **s** in the time of harvest Prv 25:13
Like **s** in summer or rain in harvest, so Prv 26:1
is not afraid of **s** for her household, Prv 31:21
are like scarlet, they shall be as white as **s**; Is 1:18
the rain and the **s** come down from Is 55:10
Does the **s** of Lebanon leave the crags of Jer 18:14
Her princes were purer than **s**, whiter Lam 4:7
his clothing was white as **s**, and the hair Dn 7:9
lightning, and his clothing white as **s**. Mt 28:3
head were white like wool, as white as **s**. Rv 1:14

SNUFFERS (5)
the cups, **s**, basins, dishes for incense, 1 Kgs 7:50
of the LORD basins of silver, **s**, bowls, 2 Kgs 12:13
the shovels and the **s** and the dishes 2 Kgs 25:14
the **s**, basins, dishes for incense, and 2 Chr 4:22
the shovels and the **s** and the basins Jer 52:18

SO (1) [Proper Noun]
for he had sent messengers to **S**, 2 Kgs 17:4

SO-CALLED (3)
s because they were craftsmen. 1 Chr 4:14
there may be **s** gods in heaven 1 Cor 8:5
himself against every **s** god or object 2 Thes 2:4

SOAK (1)
may it **s** into his body like water, like Ps 109:18

SOAP (2)
wash yourself with lye and use much **s**, Jer 2:22
is like a refiner's fire and like fullers' **s**. Mal 3:2

SOAR (1)
Though you **s** aloft like the eagle, though Ob 1:4

SOARS (1)
that the hawk **s** and spreads his Jb 39:26

SOBER (3)
think, but to think with **s** judgment, Rom 12:3
do, but let us keep awake and be **s**. 1 Thes 5:6
since we belong to the day, let us be **s**, 1 Thes 5:8

SOBER-MINDED (7)
husband of one wife, **s**, self-controlled, 1 Tm 3:2
be dignified, not slanderers, but **s**, 1 Tm 3:11
As for you, always be **s**, endure 2 Tm 4:5
Older men are to be **s**, dignified, Ti 2:2
your minds for action, and being **s**, 1 Pt 1:13
be self-controlled and **s** for the sake 1 Pt 4:7
Be **s**; be watchful. Your adversary the 1 Pt 5:8

SOCKET (4)
against Jacob, he touched his hip **s**, Gn 32:25
sinew of the thigh that is on the hip **s**, Gn 32:32
because he touched the **s** of Jacob's hip Gn 32:32

and let my arm be broken from its **s**. Jb 31:22

SOCKETS (3)
pans, of pure gold; and the **s** of gold, 1 Kgs 7:50
of pure gold, and the **s** of the temple, 2 Chr 4:22
their feet, their eyes will rot in their **s**, Zec 14:12

SOCO (3)
father of Gedor, Heber the father of **S**, 1 Chr 4:18
Beth-zur, **S**, Adullam, 2 Chr 11:7
Gederoth, **S** with its villages, 2 Chr 28:18

SOCOH (5)
Jarmuth, Adullam, **S**, Azekah, Jos 15:35
in the hill country, Shamir, Jattir, **S**, Jos 15:48
And they were gathered at **S**, which 1 Sm 17:1
and encamped between **S** and Azekah, 1 Sm 17:1
(to him belonged **S** and all the 1 Kgs 4:10

SODA (1)
on a cold day, and like vinegar on **s**. Prv 25:20

SODI (1)
tribe of Zebulun, Gaddiel the son of **S**; Nm 13:10

SODOM (48)
as far as Gaza, and in the direction of **S**, Gn 10:19
the LORD destroyed **S** and Gomorrah.) Gn 13:10
valley and moved his tent as far as **S**. Gn 13:12
Now the men of **S** were wicked, great Gn 13:13
kings made war with Bera king of **S**, Gn 14:2
Then the king of **S**, the king of Gn 14:8
as the kings of **S** and Gomorrah fled, Gn 14:10
all the possessions of **S** and Gomorrah, Gn 14:11
brother, who was dwelling in **S**, Gn 14:12
the king of **S** went out to meet him at Gn 14:17
And the king of **S** said to Abram, "Give Gn 14:21
But Abram said to the king of **S**, "I Gn 14:22
there, and they looked down toward **S**. Gn 18:16
the outcry against **S** and Gomorrah is Gn 18:20
turned from there and went toward **S**, Gn 18:22
"If I find at **S** fifty righteous in the city, Gn 18:26
two angels came to **S** in the evening, Gn 19:1
and Lot was sitting in the gate of **S**. Gn 19:1
down, the men of the city, the men of **S**, Gn 19:4
LORD rained on **S** and Gomorrah sulfur Gn 19:24
looked down toward **S** and Gomorrah Gn 19:28
overthrow like that of **S** and Gomorrah, Dt 29:23
from the vine of **S** and from the fields Dt 32:32
few survivors, we should have been like **S**, Is 1:9
Hear the word of the LORD, you rulers of **S**! Is 1:10
them; they proclaim their sin like **S**; Is 3:9
will be like **S** and Gomorrah when God Is 13:19
all of them have become like **S** to me, Jer 23:14
As when **S** and Gomorrah and their Jer 49:18
when God overthrew **S** and Gomorrah Jer 50:40
been greater than the punishment of **S**, Lam 4:6
south of you, is **S** with her daughters. Ezk 16:46
your sister **S** and her daughters have Ezk 16:48
this was the guilt of your sister **S**: Ezk 16:49
the fortunes of **S** and her daughters, Ezk 16:53
S and her daughters shall return to Ezk 16:55
Was not your sister **S** a byword in Ezk 16:56
when God overthrew **S** and Gomorrah, Am 4:11
God of Israel, "Moab shall become like **S**, Zep 2:9
for the land of **S** and Gomorrah than Mt 10:15
works done in you had been done in **S**, Mt 11:23
for the land of **S** than for you." Mt 11:24
on that day for **S** than for that town. Lk 10:12
on the day when Lot went out from **S**, Lk 17:29
have been like **S** and become like Rom 9:29
turning the cities of **S** and Gomorrah to 2 Pt 2:6
just as **S** and Gomorrah and the Jude 1:7
that symbolically is called **S** and Egypt, Rv 11:8

SOFT (8)
to you? Will he speak to you **s** words? Jb 41:3
A **s** answer turns away wrath, but a Prv 15:1
and a **s** tongue will break a bone. Prv 25:15
as you saw iron mixed with the **s** clay. Dn 2:41
As you saw the iron mixed with **s** clay, Dn 2:43
out to see? A man dressed in **s** clothing? Mt 11:8
those who wear **s** clothing are in kings' Mt 11:8
out to see? A man dressed in **s** clothing? Lk 7:25

SOFTENED (1)
not pressed out or bound up or **s** with oil. Is 1:6

SOFTENING (1)
settling its ridges, **s** it with showers, Ps 65:10

SOFTER (1)
his words were **s** than oil, yet they were Ps 55:21

SOFTLY (2)
Then she went **s** to him and drove the Jgs 4:21
Then she came **s** and uncovered his feet Ru 3:7

SOIL (28)
Noah began to be a man of the **s**, and he Gn 9:20
field for tilling the **s** was Ezri the son 1 Chr 27:26
in the fertile lands, for he loved the **s**. 2 Chr 26:10
way, and out of the **s** others will spring. Jb 8:19
in the earth, and its stump die in the **s**, Jb 14:8
torrents wash away the **s** of the earth; Jb 14:19
I had bathed my feet; how could I **s** them? Sg 5:3
for the **s** of my people growing up in Is 32:13
blood, and their **s** shall be gorged with fat. Is 34:7
turned into pitch, and her **s** into sulfur; Is 34:9
of the land and planted it in fertile **s**. Ezk 17:5
planted on good **s** by abundant waters, Ezk 17:8
I will scrape her **s** from her and make Ezk 26:4
stones and timber and **s** they will cast Ezk 26:12
Be ashamed, O tillers of the **s**; wail, O Jl 1:11
'I am no prophet, I am a worker of the **s**, Zec 13:5
it will not destroy the fruits of your **s**, Mal 3:11
where they did not have much **s**, Mt 13:5
sprang up, since they had no depth of **s**, Mt 13:5
seeds fell on good **s** and produced grain, Mt 13:8
As for what was sown on good **s**, this is Mt 13:23
ground, where it did not have much **s**, Mk 4:5
it sprang up, since it had no depth of **s**. Mk 4:5
seeds fell into good **s** and produced grain, Mk 4:8
sown on the good **s** are the ones who Mk 4:20
some fell into good **s** and grew and yielded Lk 8:8
As for that in the good **s**, they are those Lk 8:15
use either for the **s** or for the manure Lk 14:35

SOILED (1)
people who have not **s** their garments, Rv 3:4

SOJOURN (25)
Abram went down to Egypt to **s** there, Gn 12:10
And they said, "This fellow came to **s**, Gn 19:9
S in this land, and I will be with you and Gn 26:3
"We have come to **s** in the land, Gn 47:4
If a stranger shall **s** with you and would Ex 12:48
or of the strangers who **s** among them, Lv 17:8
of the strangers who **s** among them eats Lv 17:10
or of the strangers who **s** among them, Lv 17:13
of the strangers who **s** in Israel who gives Lv 20:2
the strangers who **s** with you and Lv 25:45
Bethlehem in Judah to **s** where he could Jgs 17:8
and I am going to **s** where I may find a Jgs 17:9
in Judah went to **s** in the country of Ru 1:1
even upon the widow with whom I **s**, 1 Kgs 17:20
household, and **s** wherever you can, 2 Kgs 8:1
O LORD, who shall **s** in your tent? Who Ps 15:1
Woe to me, that I **s** in Meshech, that I Ps 120:5
let the outcasts of Moab **s** among you; be Is 16:4
down at the first into Egypt to **s** there, Is 52:4
live many days in the land where you **s**.' Jer 35:7
shall dwell there, no man shall **s** in her. Jer 49:18
dwell there; no man shall **s** in her." Jer 49:33
there, and no son of man shall **s** in her. Jer 50:40
or of the strangers who **s** in Israel, Ezk 14:7
them out of the land where they **s**, Ezk 20:38

SOJOURNED (9)
Kadesh and Shur; and he **s** in Gerar. Gn 20:1
and with the land where you have **s**." Gn 21:23
And Abraham **s** many days in the Gn 21:34
'I have **s** with Laban and stayed until Gn 32:4
where Abraham and Isaac had **s**. Gn 35:27
he went down into Egypt and **s** there, Dt 26:5
Judah, who was a Levite, and he **s** there. Jgs 17:7
with her household and **s** in the land 2 Kgs 8:2
to Egypt; Jacob **s** in the land of Ham. Ps 105:23

SOJOURNER (53)
"I am a **s** and foreigner among you; give Gn 23:4
said, "I have been a **s** in a foreign land." Ex 2:22
whether he is a **s** or a native of the land. Ex 12:19
said, "I have been a **s** in a foreign land"), Ex 18:3
or the **s** who is within your gates. Ex 20:10
shall not wrong a **s** or oppress him, Ex 22:21
"You shall not oppress a **s**. You know Ex 23:9
You know the heart of a **s**, for you were Ex 23:9
by beasts, whether he is a native or a **s**, Lv 17:15
leave them for the poor and for the **s**: Lv 19:10
leave them for the poor and for the **s**: Lv 23:22
The **s** as well as the native, when he Lv 24:16
same rule for the **s** and for the native, Lv 24:22
hired servant and the **s** who lives with Lv 25:6
as though he were a stranger and a **s**, Lv 25:35
with you as a hired servant and as a **s**. Lv 25:40
"If a stranger or **s** with you becomes Lv 25:47
to the stranger or **s** with you or to Lv 25:47
both for the **s** and for the native." Nm 9:14
You and the **s** shall be alike before the Nm 15:15
high hand, whether he is native or a **s**, Nm 15:30
stranger and for the **s** among them, Nm 35:15
or the **s** who is within your gates, Dt 5:14
and the widow, and loves the **s**, Dt 10:18
Love the **s**, therefore, for you were Dt 10:19
may give it to the **s** who is within your Dt 14:21
or inheritance with you, and the **s**, Dt 14:29
Levite who is within your towns, the **s**, Dt 16:11
your female servant, the Levite, the **s**, Dt 16:14
because you were a **s** in his land. Dt 23:7
justice due to the **s** or to the fatherless, Dt 24:17
It shall be for the **s**, the fatherless, and Dt 24:19
It shall be for the **s**, the fatherless, and Dt 24:20
It shall be for the **s**, the fatherless, and Dt 24:21
the Levite, and the **s** who is among you. Dt 26:11
of tithing, giving it to the Levite, the **s**, Dt 26:12
I have given it to the Levite, the **s**, Dt 26:13
who perverts the justice due to the **s**, Dt 27:19
The **s** who is among you shall rise Dt 28:43
wives, and the **s** who is in your camp, Dt 29:11
little ones, and the **s** within your towns, Dt 31:12
And all Israel, **s** as well as native born, Jos 8:33
And he answered, "I am the son of a **s**, 2 Sm 1:13
(the **s** has not lodged in the street; I have Jb 31:32
For I am a **s** with you, a guest, like all Ps 39:12
They kill the widow and the **s**, and Ps 94:6
I am a **s** on the earth; hide not your Ps 119:19
if you do not oppress the **s**, the fatherless, Jer 7:6
the **s** suffers extortion in your midst; Ezk 22:7
extorted from the **s** without justice. Ezk 22:29
In whatever tribe the **s** resides, there Ezk 47:23
oppress the widow, the fatherless, the **s**, Zec 7:10
against those who thrust aside the **s**, Mal 3:5

SOJOURNERS (20)
your offspring will be **s** in a land that Gn 15:13
Canaan, the land in which they lived as **s**. Ex 6:4
him, for you were **s** in the land of Egypt. Ex 22:21
for you were **s** in the land of Egypt. Ex 23:9
of Israel or of the **s** in Israel presents a Lv 22:18
For you are strangers and **s** with me. Lv 25:23
for you were **s** in the land of Egypt. Dt 10:19
brothers or one of the **s** who are in your Dt 24:14
ones, and the **s** who lived among them. Jos 8:35
Gittaim and have been **s** there to this 2 Sm 4:3
and of little account, and **s** in it, 1 Chr 16:19
we are strangers before you and **s**, 1 Chr 29:15
and the **s** who came out of the land 2 Chr 30:25
Israel, and the **s** who lived in Judah, 2 Chr 30:25
number, of little account, and **s** in it, Ps 105:12
The LORD watches over the **s**; he Ps 146:9
and **s** will join them and will attach Is 14:1
and for the **s** who reside among Ezk 47:22
his offspring would be **s** in a land Acts 7:6
I urge you as **s** and exiles to abstain 1 Pt 2:11

SOJOURNING (7)
days of the years of my **s** are 130 years. Gn 47:9
life of my fathers in the days of their **s**." Gn 47:9
And if a stranger is **s** with you, or Nm 15:14
and for the stranger **s** among them, Jos 20:9
a certain Levite was **s** in the remote parts Jgs 19:1
of Ephraim, and he was **s** in Gibeah. Jgs 19:16
been my songs in the house of my **s**. Ps 119:54

SOJOURNINGS (4)
offspring after you the land of your **s**, Gn 17:8
of the land of your **s** that God gave to Gn 28:4
The land of their **s** could not support Gn 36:7
Jacob lived in the land of his father's **s**, Gn 37:1

SOJOURNS (13)
and for the stranger who **s** among you." Ex 12:49
or the stranger who **s** among you. Lv 16:29
any stranger who **s** among you eat Lv 17:12
or the stranger who **s** among you Lv 18:26
"When a stranger **s** with you in your Lv 19:33
treat the stranger who **s** with you as the Lv 19:34
And if a stranger **s** among you and Nm 9:14
and for the stranger who **s** with you, Nm 15:15
and for the stranger who **s** with you." Nm 15:16
and the stranger who **s** among them, Nm 15:26
for the stranger who **s** among them. Nm 15:29
for the stranger who **s** among them. Nm 19:10
let each survivor, in whatever place he **s**, Ezr 1:4

SOLACE (1)
and the **s** of my lips would assuage your Jb 16:5

SOLD (77)
swore to him and **s** his birthright to Gn 25:33
For he has **s** us, and he has indeed Gn 31:15
and **s** him to the Ishmaelites for twenty Gn 37:28
the Midianites had **s** him in Egypt Gn 37:36
the storehouses and **s** to the Egyptians, Gn 41:56
He was the one who **s** to all the people of Gn 42:6
brother, Joseph, whom you **s** into Egypt. Gn 45:4
with yourselves because you **s** me here, Gn 45:5
for all the Egyptians **s** their fields, Gn 47:20
nothing, then he shall be **s** for his theft. Ex 22:3
"The land shall not be **s** in perpetuity, Lv 25:23
and redeem what his brother has **s**. Lv 25:25
the years since he **s** it and pay back Lv 25:27
the balance to the man to whom he **s** it, Lv 25:27
then what he **s** shall remain in the Lv 25:28
then the house that was **s** in a city they Lv 25:33
belonging to their cities may not be **s**, Lv 25:34

of Egypt; they shall not be **s** as slaves. Lv 25:42
then after he is **s** he may be redeemed. Lv 25:48
the year when he **s** himself to him until Lv 25:50
or if he has **s** the field to another man, Lv 27:20
redeemed, it shall be **s** at the valuation. Lv 27:27
inherited field, shall be **s** or redeemed; Lv 27:28
man or a Hebrew woman, is **s** to you, Dt 15:12
to flight, unless their Rock had **s** them, Dt 32:30
And he **s** them into the hand of their Jgs 2:14
and he **s** them into the hand of Jgs 3:8
And the LORD **s** them into the hand of Jgs 4:2
and he **s** them into the hand of the Jgs 10:7
And he **s** them into the hand of Sisera, 1 Sm 12:9
because you have **s** yourself to do 1 Kgs 21:20
was none who **s** himself to do 1 Kgs 21:25
donkey's head was **s** for eighty 2 Kgs 6:25
of fine flour shall be **s** for a shekel, 2 Kgs 7:1
a seah of fine flour was **s** for a shekel, 2 Kgs 7:16
seahs of barley shall be **s** for a shekel, 2 Kgs 7:18
and omens and **s** themselves to do 2 Kgs 17:17
brothers who have been **s** to the nations, Neh 5:8
that they may be **s** to us!" They were Neh 5:8
them on the day when they **s** food. Neh 13:15
kinds of goods and **s** them on the Neh 13:16
For we have been **s**, I and my people, to be Est 7:4
If we had been **s** merely as slaves, men Est 7:4
You have **s** your people for a trifle, Ps 44:12
of them, Joseph, who was **s** as a slave. Ps 105:17
my creditors is it to whom I have **s** you? Is 50:1
Behold, for your iniquities you were **s**, Is 50:1
says the LORD: "You were **s** for nothing, Is 52:3
Hebrew who has been **s** to you and has Jer 34:14
seller shall not return to what he has **s**, Ezk 7:13
and have **s** a girl for wine and have drunk Jl 3:3
You have **s** the people of Judah and Jl 3:6
from the place to which you have **s** them, Jl 3:7
of the soil, for a man **s** me in my youth.' Zec 13:5
Are not two sparrows **s** for a penny? Mt 10:29
went and **s** all that he had and bought Mt 13:46
not pay, his master ordered him to be **s**, Mt 18:25
drove out all who **s** and bought in the Mt 21:12
and the seats of those who **s** pigeons. Mt 21:12
this could have been **s** for a large sum Mt 26:9
drive out those who **s** and those who Mk 11:15
and the seats of those who **s** pigeons. Mk 11:15
could have been **s** for more than Mk 14:5
Are not five sparrows **s** for two pennies? Lk 12:6
and began to drive out those who **s**, Lk 19:45
And he told those who **s** the pigeons, Jn 2:16
this ointment not **s** for three hundred Jn 12:5
of lands or houses **s** them and brought Acts 4:34
brought the proceeds of what was **s** Acts 4:34
s a field that belonged to him and Acts 4:37
his wife Sapphira, **s** a piece of property, Acts 5:1
And after it was **s**, was it not at your Acts 5:4
"Tell me whether you **s** the land for so Acts 5:8
jealous of Joseph, **s** him into Egypt; Acts 7:9
but I am of the flesh, **s** under sin. Rom 7:14
Eat whatever is **s** in the meat market 1 Cor 10:25
who **s** his birthright for a single meal. Heb 12:16

SOLDERING (1)
him who strikes the anvil, saying of the **s**, Is 41:7

SOLDIER (10)
a **s** turned and brought a man to me 1 Kgs 20:39
the mighty man and the **s**, the judge and Is 3:2
them into four parts, one part for each **s**; Jn 19:23
and a devout **s** from among those Acts 10:7
himself, with the **s** that guarded him. Acts 28:16
Who serves as a **s** at his own expense? 1 Cor 9:7
brother and fellow worker and fellow **s**, Phil 2:25
in suffering as a good **s** of Christ Jesus. 2 Tm 2:3
No **s** gets entangled in civilian 2 Tm 2:4
our sister and Archippus our fellow **s**, Phlm 1:2

SOLDIER'S (1)
Now Joab was wearing a **s** garment, 2 Sm 20:8

SOLDIERS (50)
fell of Israel thirty thousand foot **s**. 1 Sm 4:10
him 1,700 horsemen, and 20,000 foot **s**. 2 Sm 8:4
the Syrians of Zobah, 20,000 foot **s**, 2 Sm 10:6
They were the **s**, they were his 1 Kgs 9:22
Syrians 100,000 foot **s** in one day. 1 Kgs 20:29
7,000 horsemen, and 20,000 foot **s**. 1 Chr 18:4
of 7,000 chariots and 40,000 foot **s**, 1 Chr 19:18
they were **s**, and his officers, the 2 Chr 8:9
He had **s**, mighty men of valor, in 2 Chr 17:13
Moreover, Uzziah had an army of **s**, 2 Chr 26:11
for a band of **s** and horsemen to protect Ezr 8:22
the hands of the **s** who are left in Jer 38:4
king of Judah and all the **s** saw them, Jer 39:4
and the Chaldean **s** who happened to be Jer 41:3
down Gedaliah the son of Ahikam—**s**, Jer 41:16
Even her hired **s** in her midst are like Jer 46:21
and all her **s** shall be destroyed in that Jer 49:26
and all her **s** shall be destroyed on that Jer 50:30
burned with fire, and the **s** are in panic. Jer 51:32
with horsemen and a host of many **s**. Ezk 26:7
they charge; like **s** they scale the wall. Jl 2:7
men is red; his **s** are clothed in scarlet. Na 2:3
a man under authority, with **s** under me. Mt 8:9
Then the **s** of the governor took Jesus Mt 27:27
said to them, "You have a guard of **s**. Mt 27:65
gave a sufficient sum of money to the **s** Mt 28:12
And the **s** led him away inside the Mk 15:16
S also asked him, "And we, what shall Lk 3:14
set under authority, with **s** under me: Lk 7:8
And Herod with his **s** treated him with Lk 23:11
The **s** also mocked him, coming up Lk 23:36
procured a band of **s** and some officers Jn 18:3
So the band of **s** and their captain and Jn 18:12
And the **s** twisted together a crown of Jn 19:2
When the **s** had crucified Jesus, they Jn 19:23
they cast lots." So the **s** did these things, Jn 19:24
So the **s** came and broke the legs of the Jn 19:32
But one of the **s** pierced his side with a Jn 19:34
over to four squads of **s** to guard him, Acts 12:4
Peter was sleeping between two **s**, Acts 12:6
disturbance among the **s** over what Acts 12:18
He at once took **s** and centurions and Acts 21:32
when they saw the tribune and the **s**, Acts 21:32
carried by the **s** because of the Acts 21:35
commanded the **s** to go down and Acts 23:10
and said, "Get ready two hundred **s**, Acts 23:23
them with the **s** and rescued him, Acts 23:27
So the **s**, according to their Acts 23:31
Paul said to the centurion and the **s**, Acts 27:31
Then the **s** cut away the ropes of the Acts 27:32

SOLDIERS' (1)
The **s** plan was to kill the prisoners, Acts 27:42

SOLE (12)
not so much as for the **s** of the foot to tread Dt 2:5
place on which the **s** of your foot treads Dt 11:24
from the **s** of your foot to the crown of Dt 28:35
not venture to set the **s** of her foot on the Dt 28:56
be no resting place for the **s** of your foot, Dt 28:65
Every place that the **s** of your foot will Jos 1:3
From the **s** of his foot to the crown of 2 Sm 14:25
I dried up with the **s** of my foot all 2 Kgs 19:24
loathsome sores from the **s** of his foot to Jb 2:7
From the **s** of the foot even to the head, Is 1:6
to dry up with the **s** of my foot all the Is 37:25
of their feet were like the **s** of a calf's foot. Ezk 1:7

SOLEMN (22)
'Tomorrow is a day of **s** rest, a holy Ex 16:23
the seventh day is a Sabbath of **s** rest, Ex 31:15
day you shall have a Sabbath of **s** rest, Ex 35:2
It is a Sabbath of **s** rest to you, and you Lv 16:31
on the seventh day is a Sabbath of **s** rest, Lv 23:3
you shall observe a day of **s** rest, Lv 23:24
It shall be to you a Sabbath of **s** rest, Lv 23:32
It is a **s** assembly; you shall not do any Lv 23:36
On the first day shall be a **s** rest, and on Lv 23:39
and on the eighth day shall be a **s** rest. Lv 23:39
shall be a Sabbath of **s** rest for the land, Lv 25:4
It shall be a year of **s** rest for the land. Lv 25:5
day you shall have a **s** assembly. Nm 29:35
there shall be a **s** assembly to the LORD Dt 16:8
"Sanctify a **s** assembly for Baal." So 2 Kgs 10:20
the eighth day they held a **s** assembly, 2 Chr 7:9
the eighth day there was a **s** assembly, Neh 8:18
I cannot endure iniquity and **s** assembly. Is 1:13
They have sworn **s** oaths, but he Ezk 21:23
Consecrate a fast; call a **s** assembly. Jl 1:14
Zion; consecrate a fast; call a **s** assembly; Jl 2:15
I take no delight in your **s** assemblies. Am 5:21

SOLEMNLY (8)
said to him, "The man **s** warned us, Gn 43:3
had made the sons of Israel **s** swear, Ex 13:19
I **s** warn you today that you shall surely Dt 8:19
only you shall **s** warn them and show 1 Sm 8:9
swear by the LORD and **s** warn you, 1 Kgs 2:42
For I **s** warned your fathers when I Jer 11:7
the angel of the LORD **s** assured Joshua, Zec 3:6
you beforehand and **s** warned you. 1 Thes 4:6

SOLES (7)
And when the **s** of the feet of the priests Jos 3:13
and the **s** of the priests' feet were lifted up Jos 4:18
LORD put them under the **s** of his feet. 1 Kgs 5:3
paths; you set a limit for the **s** of my feet. Jb 13:27
and the **s** of their feet were like the sole of Ezk 1:7
throne and the place of the **s** of my feet, Ezk 43:7
will be ashes under the **s** of your feet, Mal 4:3

SOLICITED (1)
No one **s** you to play the whore, and Ezk 16:34

SOLID (3)
I fed you with milk, not **s** food, for you 1 Cor 3:2
of God. You need milk, not **s** food, Heb 5:12
But **s** food is for the mature, for those Heb 5:14

SOLITARY (2)
God settles the **s** in a home; he leads out Ps 68:6
For the fortified city is **s**, a habitation Is 27:10

SOLOMON (284)
Shammua, Shobab, Nathan, **S**, 2 Sm 5:14
bore a son, and he called his name **S**. 2 Sm 12:24
or the mighty men or **S** his brother. 1 Kgs 1:10
said to Bathsheba the mother of **S**, 1 Kgs 1:11
own life and the life of your son **S**. 1 Kgs 1:12
"**S** your son shall reign after me, 1 Kgs 1:13
'**S** your son shall reign after me, 1 Kgs 1:17
but **S** your servant he has not invited. 1 Kgs 1:19
I and my son **S** will be counted 1 Kgs 1:21
and your servant **S** he has not invited. 1 Kgs 1:26
'**S** your son shall reign after me, 1 Kgs 1:30
your lord and have **S** my son ride on 1 Kgs 1:33
trumpet and say, 'Long live King **S**!' 1 Kgs 1:34
the king, even so may he be with **S**, 1 Kgs 1:37
went down and had **S** ride on King 1 Kgs 1:38
of oil from the tent and anointed **S**. 1 Kgs 1:39
the people said, "Long live King **S**!" 1 Kgs 1:39
lord King David has made **S** king, 1 Kgs 1:43
S sits on the royal throne. 1 Kgs 1:46
the name of **S** more famous than 1 Kgs 1:47
And Adonijah feared **S**. So he arose 1 Kgs 1:50
Then it was told **S**, "Behold, Adonijah 1 Kgs 1:51
"Behold, Adonijah fears King **S**, 1 Kgs 1:51
'Let King **S** swear to me first that he 1 Kgs 1:51
And **S** said, "If he will show himself a 1 Kgs 1:52
So King **S** sent, and they brought him 1 Kgs 1:53
he came and paid homage to King **S**, 1 Kgs 1:53
to King Solomon, and **S** said to him, 1 Kgs 1:53
drew near, he commanded **S** his son, 1 Kgs 2:1
So **S** sat on the throne of David his 1 Kgs 2:12
came to Bathsheba the mother of **S**. 1 Kgs 2:13
"Please ask King **S**—he will not 1 Kgs 2:17
Bathsheba went to King **S** to speak to 1 Kgs 2:19
King **S** answered his mother, "And 1 Kgs 2:22
Then King **S** swore by the LORD, 1 Kgs 2:23
So King **S** sent Benaiah the son of 1 Kgs 2:25
So **S** expelled Abiathar from being 1 Kgs 2:27
And when it was told King **S**, "Joab 1 Kgs 2:29
is beside the altar," **S** sent Benaiah the 1 Kgs 2:29
And when **S** was told that Shimei had 1 Kgs 2:41
But King **S** shall be blessed, and the 1 Kgs 2:45
was established in the hand of **S**. 1 Kgs 2:46
S made a marriage alliance with 1 Kgs 3:1
S loved the LORD, walking in the 1 Kgs 3:3
S used to offer a thousand burnt 1 Kgs 3:4
the LORD appeared to **S** in a dream by 1 Kgs 3:5
And **S** said, "You have shown great 1 Kgs 3:6
the Lord that **S** had asked this. 1 Kgs 3:10
And **S** awoke, and behold, it was a 1 Kgs 3:15
King **S** was king over all Israel, 1 Kgs 4:1
S had twelve officers over all Israel, 1 Kgs 4:7
the daughter of **S** as his wife); 1 Kgs 4:11
the daughter of **S** as his wife); 1 Kgs 4:15
S ruled over all the kingdoms from 1 Kgs 4:21
tribute and served **S** all the days 1 Kgs 4:21
under his fig tree, all the days of **S**. 1 Kgs 4:25
S also had 40,000 stalls of horses for 1 Kgs 4:26
supplied provisions for King **S**, 1 Kgs 4:27
And God gave **S** wisdom and 1 Kgs 4:29
came to hear the wisdom of **S**, 1 Kgs 4:34
sent his servants to **S** when he heard 1 Kgs 5:1
And **S** sent word to Hiram, 1 Kgs 5:2
As soon as Hiram heard the words of **S**, 1 Kgs 5:7
And Hiram sent to **S**, saying, "I have 1 Kgs 5:8
So Hiram supplied **S** with all the 1 Kgs 5:10
while **S** gave Hiram 20,000 cors of 1 Kgs 5:11
oil. **S** gave this to Hiram year by year. 1 Kgs 5:11
And the LORD gave **S** wisdom, as he 1 Kgs 5:12
was peace between Hiram and **S**, 1 Kgs 5:12
King **S** drafted forced labor out of all 1 Kgs 5:13
S also had 70,000 burden-bearers and 1 Kgs 5:15
The house that King **S** built for the 1 Kgs 6:2
Now the word of the LORD came to **S**, 1 Kgs 6:11
So **S** built the house and finished it. 1 Kgs 6:14
And **S** overlaid the inside of the house 1 Kgs 6:21
S was building his own house thirteen 1 Kgs 7:1
S also made a house like this hall for 1 Kgs 7:8
And King **S** sent and brought Hiram 1 Kgs 7:13
He came to King **S** and did all his 1 Kgs 7:14
that he did for King **S** on the house of 1 Kgs 7:40
LORD, which Hiram made for King **S**, 1 Kgs 7:45
And **S** left all the vessels unweighed, 1 Kgs 7:47
So **S** made all the vessels that were in 1 Kgs 7:48
the work that King **S** did on the house 1 Kgs 7:51
And **S** brought in the things that 1 Kgs 7:51
Then **S** assembled the elders of Israel 1 Kgs 8:1
of Israel, before King **S** in Jerusalem, 1 Kgs 8:1
Israel assembled to King **S** at the feast 1 Kgs 8:2

And King **S** and all the congregation 1 Kgs 8:5
Then **S** said, "The LORD has said that 1 Kgs 8:12
Then **S** stood before the altar of the 1 Kgs 8:22
Now as **S** finished offering all this 1 Kgs 8:54
S offered as peace offerings to the 1 Kgs 8:63
So **S** held the feast at that time, and all 1 Kgs 8:65
As soon as **S** had finished building the 1 Kgs 9:1
house and all that **S** desired to build, 1 Kgs 9:1
the LORD appeared to **S** a second time, 1 Kgs 9:2
in which **S** had built the two houses, 1 Kgs 9:10
of Tyre had supplied **S** with cedar and 1 Kgs 9:11
King **S** gave to Hiram twenty cities in 1 Kgs 9:11
to see the cities that **S** had given him, 1 Kgs 9:12
labor that King **S** drafted to build 1 Kgs 9:15
so **S** rebuilt Gezer) and Lower 1 Kgs 9:17
and all the store cities that **S** had, and 1 Kgs 9:19
and whatever **S** desired to build in 1 Kgs 9:19
to destruction—these **S** drafted to be 1 Kgs 9:21
the people of Israel **S** made no slaves. 1 Kgs 9:22
her own house that **S** had built for 1 Kgs 9:24
Three times a year **S** used to offer up 1 Kgs 9:25
King **S** built a fleet of ships at 1 Kgs 9:26
sea, together with the servants of **S**. 1 Kgs 9:27
talents, and they brought it to King **S**. 1 Kgs 9:28
of the fame of **S** concerning the name 1 Kgs 10:1
And when she came to **S**, she told 1 Kgs 10:2
And **S** answered all her questions; 1 Kgs 10:3
of Sheba had seen all the wisdom of **S**, 1 Kgs 10:4
the queen of Sheba gave to King **S**. 1 Kgs 10:10
And King **S** gave to the queen of 1 Kgs 10:13
given her by the bounty of King **S**. 1 Kgs 10:13
gold that came to **S** in one year was 1 Kgs 10:14
King **S** made 200 large shields of 1 Kgs 10:16
as anything in the days of **S**. 1 Kgs 10:21
Thus King **S** excelled all the kings 1 Kgs 10:23
sought the presence of **S** to hear his 1 Kgs 10:24
And **S** gathered together chariots 1 Kgs 10:26
Now King **S** loved many foreign 1 Kgs 11:1
after their gods." **S** clung to these 1 Kgs 11:2
For when **S** was old his wives turned 1 Kgs 11:4
For **S** went after Ashtoreth the 1 Kgs 11:5
So **S** did what was evil in the sight of 1 Kgs 11:6
Then **S** built a high place for 1 Kgs 11:7
And the LORD was angry with **S**, 1 Kgs 11:9
Therefore the LORD said to **S**, "Since 1 Kgs 11:11
raised up an adversary against **S**, 1 Kgs 11:14
adversary of Israel all the days of **S**, 1 Kgs 11:25
of Zeredah, a servant of **S**, 1 Kgs 11:26
S built the Millo, and closed up the 1 Kgs 11:27
and when **S** saw that the young man 1 Kgs 11:28
from the hand of **S** and will give you 1 Kgs 11:31
S sought therefore to kill Jeroboam. 1 Kgs 11:40
was in Egypt until the death of **S**. 1 Kgs 11:40
Now the rest of the acts of **S**, and all 1 Kgs 11:41
written in the Book of the Acts of **S**? 1 Kgs 11:41
the time that **S** reigned in Jerusalem 1 Kgs 11:42
And **S** slept with his fathers and was 1 Kgs 11:43
where he had fled from King **S**), 1 Kgs 12:2
had stood before **S** his father while 1 Kgs 12:6
kingdom to Rehoboam the son of **S**. 1 Kgs 12:21
"Say to Rehoboam the son of **S**, king 1 Kgs 12:23
the son of **S** reigned in Judah. 1 Kgs 14:21
the shields of gold that **S** had made, 1 Kgs 14:26
LORD said to David and to **S** his son, 2 Kgs 21:7
which **S** the king of Israel had built 2 Kgs 23:13
which **S** king of Israel had made, 2 Kgs 24:13
and the stands that **S** had made for 2 Kgs 25:16
Shimea, Shobab, Nathan and **S**, four 1 Chr 3:5
The son of **S** was Rehoboam, Abijah 1 Chr 3:10
the house that **S** built in Jerusalem). 1 Chr 6:10
of meeting until **S** built the house 1 Chr 6:32
Shammua, Shobab, Nathan, **S**, 1 Chr 14:4
With it **S** made the bronze sea and 1 Chr 18:8
"**S** my son is young and 1 Chr 22:5
Then he called for **S** his son and 1 Chr 22:6
David said to **S**, "My son, I had it in 1 Chr 22:7
For his name shall be **S**, and I will 1 Chr 22:9
the leaders of Israel to help **S** his son, 1 Chr 22:17
he made **S** his son king over Israel. 1 Chr 23:1
sons) he has chosen **S** my son to sit 1 Chr 28:5
'It is **S** your son who shall build my 1 Chr 28:6
"And you, **S** my son, know the God of 1 Chr 28:9
Then David gave **S** his son the plan 1 Chr 28:11
Then David said to **S** his son, "Be 1 Chr 28:20
said to all the assembly, "**S** my son, 1 Chr 29:1
Grant to **S** my son a whole heart 1 Chr 29:19
And they made **S** the son of David 1 Chr 29:22
Then **S** sat on the throne of the LORD 1 Chr 29:23
pledged their allegiance to King **S**. 1 Chr 29:24
And the LORD made **S** very great in 1 Chr 29:25
And **S** his son reigned in his place. 1 Chr 29:28
S the son of David established himself 2 Chr 1:1
S spoke to all Israel, to the 2 Chr 1:2
And **S**, and all the assembly with him, 2 Chr 1:3
And **S** and the assembly resorted to it. 2 Chr 1:5
And **S** went up there to the bronze 2 Chr 1:6
In that night God appeared to **S**, and 2 Chr 1:7
And **S** said to God, "You have shown 2 Chr 1:8
God answered **S**, "Because this was in 2 Chr 1:11
So **S** came from the high place at 2 Chr 1:13
S gathered together chariots and 2 Chr 1:14
Now **S** purposed to build a temple for 2 Chr 2:1
And **S** assigned 70,000 men to bear 2 Chr 2:2
And **S** sent word to Hiram the king of 2 Chr 2:3
answered in a letter that he sent to **S**, 2 Chr 2:11
Then **S** counted all the resident 2 Chr 2:17
Then **S** began to build the house of the 2 Chr 3:1
that he did for King **S** on the house of 2 Chr 4:11
bronze for King **S** for the house 2 Chr 4:16
S made all these things in great 2 Chr 4:18
So **S** made all the vessels that were in 2 Chr 4:19
all the work that **S** did for the house 2 Chr 5:1
And **S** brought in the things that 2 Chr 5:1
Then **S** assembled the elders of Israel 2 Chr 5:2
And King **S** and all the congregation 2 Chr 5:6
Then **S** said, "The LORD has said that 2 Chr 6:1
Then **S** stood before the altar of the 2 Chr 6:12
S had made a bronze platform five 2 Chr 6:13
As soon as **S** finished his prayer, fire 2 Chr 7:1
King **S** offered as a sacrifice 22,000 2 Chr 7:5
And **S** consecrated the middle of the 2 Chr 7:7
the bronze altar **S** had made could 2 Chr 7:7
At that time **S** held the feast for seven 2 Chr 7:8
to David and to **S** and to Israel his 2 Chr 7:10
Thus **S** finished the house of the LORD 2 Chr 7:11
All that **S** had planned to do in the 2 Chr 7:11
the LORD appeared to **S** in the night 2 Chr 7:12
in which **S** had built the house of the 2 Chr 8:1
S rebuilt the cities that Hiram had 2 Chr 8:2
And **S** went to Hamath-zobah and 2 Chr 8:3
the store cities that **S** had and all the 2 Chr 8:6
and whatever **S** desired to build in 2 Chr 8:6
destroyed—these **S** drafted as forced 2 Chr 8:8
the people of Israel **S** made no slaves 2 Chr 8:9
these were the chief officers of King **S**, 2 Chr 8:10
S brought Pharaoh's daughter up 2 Chr 8:11
Then **S** offered up burnt offerings to 2 Chr 8:12
all the work of **S** from the day the 2 Chr 8:16
Then **S** went to Ezion-geber and 2 Chr 8:17
the servants of **S** and brought from 2 Chr 8:18
of gold and brought it to King **S**. 2 Chr 8:18
queen of Sheba heard of the fame of **S**, 2 Chr 9:1
And when she came to **S**, she told him 2 Chr 9:1
And **S** answered all her questions. 2 Chr 9:2
nothing hidden from **S** that he could 2 Chr 9:2
of Sheba had seen the wisdom of **S**, 2 Chr 9:3
that the queen of Sheba gave to King **S**. 2 Chr 9:9
of Hiram and the servants of **S**, 2 Chr 9:10
And King **S** gave to the queen of 2 Chr 9:12
of gold that came to **S** in one year was 2 Chr 9:13
the land brought gold and silver to **S**. 2 Chr 9:14
King **S** made 200 large shields of 2 Chr 9:15
as anything in the days of **S**. 2 Chr 9:20
Thus King **S** excelled all the kings of 2 Chr 9:22
sought the presence of **S** to hear his 2 Chr 9:23
And **S** had 4,000 stalls for horses and 2 Chr 9:25
were imported for **S** from Egypt and 2 Chr 9:28
Now the rest of the acts of **S**, from 2 Chr 9:29
S reigned in Jerusalem over all Israel 2 Chr 9:30
And **S** slept with his fathers and was 2 Chr 9:31
where he had fled from King **S**), 2 Chr 10:2
had stood before **S** his father while 2 Chr 10:6
"Say to Rehoboam the son of **S**, king 2 Chr 11:3
Rehoboam the son of **S** secure, 2 Chr 11:17
years in the way of David and **S**. 2 Chr 11:17
the shields of gold that **S** had made, 2 Chr 12:9
a servant of **S** the son of David, 2 Chr 13:6
and defied Rehoboam the son of **S**, 2 Chr 13:7
since the time of **S** the son of David 2 Chr 30:26
God said to David and to **S** his son, 2 Chr 33:7
in the house that **S** the son of David, 2 Chr 35:3
Israel and the document of **S** his son. 2 Chr 35:4
the command of David and his son **S**. Neh 12:45
Did not **S** king of Israel sin on Neh 13:26
Of **S**. Ps 72:T
A Song of Ascents. Of **S**. Ps 127:T
The proverbs of **S**, son of David, king of Prv 1:1
The proverbs of **S**. A wise son makes a Prv 10:1
also are proverbs of **S** which the men of Prv 25:1
the tents of Kedar, like the curtains of **S**. Sg 1:5
Behold, it is the litter of **S**! Around it are Sg 3:7
King **S** made himself a carriage from the Sg 3:9
of Zion, and look upon King **S**, Sg 3:11
S had a vineyard at Baal-hamon; he let Sg 8:11
you, O **S**, may have the thousand, and Sg 8:12
which **S** the king had made for the Jer 52:20
David was the father of **S** by the wife of Mt 1:6
and **S** the father of Rehoboam, and Mt 1:7
even **S** in all his glory was not arrayed Mt 6:29
of the earth to hear the wisdom of **S**, Mt 12:42
something greater than **S** is here. Mt 12:42
of the earth to hear the wisdom of **S**, Lk 11:31
something greater than **S** is here. Lk 11:31
even **S** in all his glory was not arrayed Lk 12:27
in the temple, in the colonnade of **S**. Jn 10:23
But it was **S** who built a house for him. Acts 7:47

SOLOMON'S (21)

S provision for one day was thirty 1 Kgs 4:22
and for all who came to King **S** table, 1 Kgs 4:27
so that **S** wisdom surpassed the 1 Kgs 4:30
besides **S** 3,300 chief officers who 1 Kgs 5:16
So **S** builders and Hiram's builders 1 Kgs 5:18
in the fourth year of **S** reign over Israel, 1 Kgs 6:1
it as dowry to his daughter, **S** wife; 1 Kgs 9:16
chief officers who were over **S** work: 1 Kgs 9:23
All King **S** drinking vessels were of 1 Kgs 10:21
And **S** import of horses was from 1 Kgs 10:28
And **S** import of horses was from 2 Chr 1:16
These are **S** measurements for 2 Chr 3:3
All King **S** drinking vessels were of 2 Chr 9:20
The sons of **S** servants: the sons of Sotai, Ezr 2:55
and the sons of **S** servants were 392. Ezr 2:58
The sons of **S** servants: the sons of Neh 7:57
and the sons of **S** servants were 392. Neh 7:60
and the descendants of **S** servants. Neh 11:3
The Song of Songs, which is **S**. Sg 1:1
to them in the portico called **S**, Acts 3:11
And they were all together in **S** Portico. Acts 5:12

SOLVE (4)

three days they could not **s** the riddle. Jgs 14:14
I will **s** my riddle to the music of the lyre. Ps 49:4
and **s** problems were found in this Dn 5:12
can give interpretations and **s** problems. Dn 5:16

SOME (397)

and she also gave **s** to her husband who Gn 3:6
the LORD and took **s** of every clean Gn 8:20
every clean animal and **s** of every clean Gn 8:20
and Gomorrah fled, **s** fell into them, Gn 14:10
to Jacob, "Let me eat **s** of that red stew, Gn 25:30
"Please give me **s** of your son's Gn 30:14
me leave with you **s** of the people who Gn 33:15
they were still **s** distance from Ephrath, Gn 35:16
S time after this, the cupbearer of the Gn 40:1
They continued for **s** time in custody. Gn 40:4
take **s** of the choice fruits of the land in Gn 43:11
when there was still **s** distance to go to Gn 48:7
you shall take **s** water from the Nile and Ex 4:9
Look, you have **s** evil purpose in mind. Ex 10:10
"Then they shall take **s** of the blood and Ex 12:7
so. They gathered, **s** more, some less. Ex 16:17
so. They gathered, some more, **s** less. Ex 16:17
S left part of it till the morning, and it Ex 16:20
On the seventh day **s** of the people went Ex 16:27
taking with you **s** of the elders of Israel, Ex 17:5
You shall beat **s** of it very small, and Ex 30:36
as its memorial portion **s** of the crushed Lv 2:16
of the crushed grain and **s** of the oil with Lv 2:16
anointed priest shall take **s** of the blood of Lv 4:5
And the priest shall put **s** of the blood on Lv 4:7
anointed priest shall bring **s** of the blood Lv 4:16
And he shall put **s** of the blood on the Lv 4:18
the priest shall take **s** of the blood of Lv 4:25
the priest shall take **s** of its blood with Lv 4:30
the priest shall take **s** of the blood of Lv 4:34
and he shall sprinkle **s** of the blood of the Lv 5:9
and then eats **s** flesh from the sacrifice of Lv 7:21
And he sprinkled **s** of it on the altar Lv 8:11
And he poured **s** of the anointing oil on Lv 8:12
and Moses took **s** of its blood and put it Lv 8:23
and Moses put **s** of the blood on the lobes Lv 8:24
Then Moses took **s** of the anointing oil Lv 8:30
The priest shall take **s** of the blood of Lv 14:14
Then the priest shall take **s** of the log of Lv 14:15
left hand and sprinkle **s** oil with his Lv 14:16
And **s** of the oil that remains in his Lv 14:17
the priest shall take **s** of the blood of Lv 14:25
the priest shall pour **s** of the oil into Lv 14:26
with his right finger **s** of the oil that Lv 14:27
And the priest shall put **s** of the oil that Lv 14:28
seems to me to be **s** case of disease in Lv 14:35
And he shall take **s** of the blood of the Lv 16:14
seat he shall sprinkle **s** of the blood Lv 16:14
and shall take **s** of the blood of the bull Lv 16:18
blood of the bull and **s** of the blood of Lv 16:18
And he shall sprinkle **s** of the blood on Lv 16:19
you will be eating **s** of the old crop; Lv 25:22
for his redemption **s** of his sale Lv 25:51
If a man wishes to redeem **s** of his tithe, Lv 27:31
vessel and take **s** of the dust Nm 5:17
and **s** man other than your husband Nm 5:20
them and consumed **s** outlying parts of Nm 11:1
And I will take **s** of the Spirit that is on Nm 11:17
and took **s** of the Spirit that was on Nm 11:25
good courage and bring **s** of the fruit Nm 13:20

also brought **s** pomegranates and Nm 13:23
S of the first of your dough you shall Nm 15:21
the priest shall take **s** of its blood with Nm 19:4
and sprinkle **s** of its blood toward the Nm 19:4
unclean they shall take **s** ashes of the Nm 19:17
Israel, and took **s** of them captive. Nm 21:1
invest him with **s** of your authority, Nm 27:20
give to the Levites **s** of the inheritance Nm 35:2
they took in their hands **s** of the fruit of Dt 1:25
s of the gods of the peoples who are Dt 13:7
because he has found **s** indecency in her, Dt 24:1
you shall take **s** of the first of all the fruit Dt 26:2
of Judah, took **s** of the devoted things. Jos 7:1
they have taken **s** of the devoted things; Jos 7:11
were in the midst of Israel, **s** on this side, Jos 8:22
some on this side, and **s** on that side. Jos 8:22
So the men took **s** of their provisions, Jos 9:14
and **s** of you shall never be anything but Jos 9:23
in Gath, and in Ashdod did **s** remain. Jos 11:22
After **s** days he returned to take her. And Jgs 14:8
father and mother and gave **s** to them, Jgs 14:9
After **s** days, at the time of wheat harvest, Jgs 15:1
in Judah, and was there **s** four months. Jgs 19:2
to strike and kill **s** of the people in Jgs 20:31
"Come here and eat **s** bread and dip your Ru 2:14
she was satisfied, and she had **s** left over. Ru 2:14
And also pull out **s** from the bundles for Ru 2:16
And he struck **s** of the men of 1 Sm 6:19
a long time passed, **s** twenty years, 1 Sm 7:2
and **s** to plow his ground and to reap 1 Sm 8:12
But **s** worthless fellows said, "How 1 Sm 10:27
and **s** Hebrews crossed the fords of the 1 Sm 13:7
well, and bring **s** token from them." 1 Sm 17:18
And **s** told me to kill you, but I 1 Sm 24:10
"For **s** time past you have been 2 Sm 3:17
he chose **s** of the best men of Israel 2 Sm 10:9
and **s** of the servants of David among 2 Sm 11:17
S of the king's servants are dead, and 2 Sm 11:24
is dead? He may do himself **s** harm." 2 Sm 12:18
in one of the pits or in **s** other place. 2 Sm 17:9
And as soon as **s** of the people fall at 2 Sm 17:9
come upon him in **s** place where he 2 Sm 17:12
Take with you ten loaves, **s** cakes, 1 Kgs 14:3
alive, and not lose **s** of the animals." 1 Kgs 18:5
and stood at **s** distance from them, 2 Kgs 2:7
cast him upon **s** mountain or into 2 Kgs 2:16
mountain or into **s** valley." And he 2 Kgs 2:16
s small boys came out of the city and 2 Kgs 2:23
lived, who urged him to eat **s** food. 2 Kgs 4:8
And they poured out **s** for the men to 2 Kgs 4:40
pot and said, "Pour **s** out for the men, 2 Kgs 4:41
LORD, 'They shall eat and have **s** left.'" 2 Kgs 4:43
And they ate and had **s** left, according 2 Kgs 4:44
"Let **s** men take five of the remaining 2 Kgs 7:13
And **s** of her blood spattered on the 2 Kgs 9:33
them, which killed **s** of them. 2 Kgs 17:25
And **s** of your own sons, who shall 2 Kgs 20:18
of the guard left **s** of the poorest of 2 Kgs 25:12
And **s** of them, five hundred men of 1 Chr 4:42
And **s** of the clans of the sons of 1 Chr 6:66
And **s** of the people of Judah, 1 Chr 9:3
S of them had charge of the utensils 1 Chr 9:28
Also **s** of their kinsmen of the 1 Chr 9:32
And **s** of the men of Benjamin and 1 Chr 12:16
S of the men of Manasseh deserted 1 Chr 12:19
Then he appointed **s** of the Levites as 1 Chr 16:4
he chose **s** of the best men of Israel 1 Chr 19:10
wisely and distributed **s** of his sons 2 Chr 11:23
but I will grant them **s** deliverance, 2 Chr 12:7
inflicted cruelties upon **s** of the 2 Chr 16:10
S of the Philistines brought 2 Chr 17:11
After **s** years he went down to Ahab 2 Chr 18:2
Nevertheless, **s** good is found in you, 2 Chr 19:3
and with them **s** of the Meunites, 2 Chr 20:1
S men came and told Jehoshaphat, 2 Chr 20:2
and also **s** of the princes of Israel. 2 Chr 21:4
However, **s** men of Asher, of 2 Chr 30:11
s of his own sons struck him down 2 Chr 32:21
and **s** of the Levites were scribes and 2 Chr 34:13
S of the heads of families, when they Ezr 2:68
the priests, the Levites, **s** of the people, Ezr 2:70
the king, **s** of the people of Israel, Ezr 7:7
of Israel, and **s** of the priests and Levites, Ezr 7:7
For they have taken **s** of their daughters Ezr 9:2
to grant us **s** reviving to set up the house Ezr 9:9
Now there were found **s** of the sons of Ezr 10:18
s of the sons of Jeshua the son of Ezr 10:18
and **s** of the women had even borne Ezr 10:44
and **s** of our daughters have already Neh 5:5
s at their guard posts and some in front Neh 7:3
their guard posts and **s** in front of their Neh 7:3
Now **s** of the heads of fathers' houses Neh 7:70
And **s** of the heads of fathers' houses Neh 7:71
gatekeepers, the singers, **s** of the people, Neh 7:73
s of the people of Judah lived in Neh 11:25

And after **s** time I asked leave of the Neh 13:6
And I stationed **s** of my servants at the Neh 13:19
cursed them and beat **s** of them and Neh 13:25
S move landmarks; they seize flocks and Jb 24:2
who say, "Who will show us **s** good? Ps 4:6
S trust in chariots and some in horses, Ps 20:7
Some trust in chariots and **s** in horses, Ps 20:7
S wandered in desert wastes, finding no Ps 107:4
S sat in darkness and in the shadow of Ps 107:10
S were fools through their sinful ways, Ps 107:17
S went down to the sea in ships, doing Ps 107:23
or **s** winged creature tell the matter. Eccl 10:20
men, **s** of the mighty men of Israel, Sg 3:7
And **s** of your own sons, who will come Is 39:7
And **s** of them also I will take for priests Is 66:21
and take **s** of the elders of the people and Jer 19:1
elders of the people and **s** of the elders of Jer 19:1
in the land of Judah **s** of the poor people Jer 39:10
shall not return, except **s** fugitives." Jer 44:14
carried away captive **s** of the poorest Jer 52:15
of the guard left **s** of the poorest of Jer 52:16
again you shall take **s** and cast them Ezk 5:4
"Yet I will leave **s** of you alive. When you Ezk 6:8
among the nations **s** who escape the Ezk 6:8
and took **s** of it and put it into the Ezk 10:7
behold, **s** survivors will be left in it, Ezk 14:22
You took **s** of your garments and Ezk 16:16
And you shall take **s** of its blood and Ezk 43:20
The priest shall take **s** of the blood of Ezk 45:19
with **s** of the vessels of the house of God. Dn 1:2
eunuch, to bring **s** of the people of Israel, Dn 1:3
but **s** of the firmness of iron shall be in Dn 2:41
And he ordered **s** of the mighty men of Dn 3:20
And **s** of the host and some of the stars it Dn 8:10
some of the host and **s** of the stars it Dn 8:10
was overcome and lay sick for **s** days. Dn 8:27
After **s** years they shall make an Dn 11:6
and for **s** years he shall refrain from Dn 11:8
And after **s** years he shall come on Dn 11:13
though for **s** days they shall stumble Dn 11:33
and **s** of the wise shall stumble, so that Dn 11:35
earth shall awake, **s** to everlasting life, Dn 12:2
and **s** to shame and everlasting Dn 12:2
And I raised up **s** of your sons for Am 2:11
and **s** of your young men for Nazirites. Am 2:11
"I overthrew **s** of you, as when God Am 4:11
was feeding at **s** distance from them. Mt 8:30
s people brought to him a paralytic, Mt 9:2
behold, **s** of the scribes said to themselves, Mt 9:3
Then **s** of the scribes and Pharisees Mt 12:38
as he sowed, **s** seeds fell along the path, Mt 13:4
and produced grain, **s** a hundredfold, Mt 13:8
grain, some a hundredfold, **s** sixty, Mt 13:8
some a hundredfold, some sixty, **s** thirty. Mt 13:8
And they said, "**S** say John the Baptist, Mt 16:14
there are **s** standing here who will not Mt 16:28
s of whom you will kill and crucify, Mt 23:34
and **s** you will flog in your synagogues Mt 23:34
said to the wise, 'Give us **s** of your oil, Mt 25:8
and struck him. And **s** slapped him, Mt 26:67
price had been set by **s** of the sons of Mt 27:9
And **s** of the bystanders, hearing it, Mt 27:47
s of the guard went into the city and Mt 28:11
they worshiped him, but **s** doubted. Mt 28:17
he returned to Capernaum after **s** days, Mk 2:1
Now **s** of the scribes were sitting there, Mk 2:6
as he sowed, **s** seed fell along the path, Mk 4:4
came from the ruler's house **s** who said, Mk 5:35
S said, "John the Baptist has been raised Mk 6:14
with **s** of the scribes who had come from Mk 7:1
they saw that **s** of his disciples ate with Mk 7:2
And **s** of them have come from far Mk 8:3
And **s** people brought to him a blind Mk 8:22
there are **s** standing here who will not Mk 9:1
And **s** of those standing there said to Mk 11:5
tenants to get from them **s** of the fruit of Mk 12:2
s they beat, and some they killed. Mk 12:5
some they beat, and **s** they killed. Mk 12:5
they sent to him **s** of the Pharisees and Mk 12:13
the Pharisees and **s** of the Herodians, Mk 12:13
There were **s** who said to themselves Mk 14:4
And **s** stood up and bore false witness Mk 14:57
And **s** began to spit on him and to Mk 14:65
And **s** of the bystanders hearing it Mk 15:35
followed all things closely for **s** time past, Lk 1:3
s men were bringing on a bed a man Lk 5:18
disciples plucked and ate **s** heads of grain, Lk 6:1
But **s** of the Pharisees said, "Why are you Lk 6:2
and also **s** women who had been healed of Lk 8:2
s fell along the path and was trampled Lk 8:5
And **s** fell on the rock, and as it grew up, it Lk 8:6
And **s** fell among thorns, and the thorns Lk 8:7
And **s** fell into good soil and grew and Lk 8:8
it was said by **s** that John had been Lk 9:7
by **s** that Elijah had appeared, and by Lk 9:8

there are **s** standing here who will not Lk 9:27
But **s** of them said, "He casts out Lk 11:15
s of whom they will kill and persecute,' Lk 11:49
There were **s** present at that very time Lk 13:1
And behold, **s** are last who will be first, Lk 13:30
be first, and **s** are first who will be last." Lk 13:30
At that very hour **s** Pharisees came and Lk 13:31
told this parable to **s** who trusted in Lk 18:9
And **s** of the Pharisees in the crowd Lk 19:39
they would give him **s** of the fruit of Lk 20:10
There came to him **s** Sadducees, those Lk 20:27
Then **s** of the scribes answered, Lk 20:39
And while **s** were speaking of the temple, Lk 21:5
and **s** of you they will put to death. Lk 21:16
he was hoping to see **s** sign done by him. Lk 23:8
So he questioned him at **s** length, but he Lk 23:9
s women of our company amazed us. Lk 24:22
S of those who were with us went to the Lk 24:24
"Now draw **s** out and take it to the master Jn 2:8
discussion arose between **s** of John's Jn 3:25
But there are **s** of you who do not Jn 6:64
him among the people. While **s** said, Jn 7:12
S of the people of Jerusalem therefore Jn 7:25
heard these words, **s** of the people said, Jn 7:40
said, "This is the Christ." But **s** said, Jn 7:41
S of them wanted to arrest him, but no Jn 7:44
that they might have **s** charge to bring Jn 8:6
S said, "It is he." Others said, "No, but he is Jn 9:9
S of the Pharisees said, "This man is not Jn 9:16
S of the Pharisees near him heard these Jn 9:40
But **s** of them said, "Could not he who Jn 11:37
but **s** of them went to the Pharisees and Jn 11:46
up to worship at the feast were **s** Greeks. Jn 12:20
S thought that, because Judas had the Jn 13:29
So **s** of his disciples said to one another, Jn 16:17
band of soldiers and **s** officers from the Jn 18:3
boat, and you will find **s**." So they cast it, Jn 21:6
"Bring **s** of the fish that you have just Jn 21:10
kept back for himself **s** of the proceeds Acts 5:2
his shadow might fall on **s** of them. Acts 5:15
census and drew away **s** of the people Acts 5:37
Then **s** of those who belonged to the Acts 6:9
along the road they came to **s** water, Acts 8:36
For **s** days he was with the disciples at Acts 9:19
and **s** of the brothers from Joppa Acts 10:23
they asked him to remain for **s** days. Acts 10:48
But there were **s** of them, men of Acts 11:20
violent hands on **s** who belonged to Acts 12:1
s sided with the Jews and some with the Acts 14:4
with the Jews and **s** with the apostles. Acts 14:4
But **s** men came down from Judea and Acts 15:1
Paul and Barnabas and **s** of the others Acts 15:2
But **s** believers who belonged to the Acts 15:5
have heard that **s** persons have gone Acts 15:24
And after they had spent **s** time, they Acts 15:33
And after **s** days Paul said to Acts 15:36
We remained in this city **s** days. Acts 16:12
And **s** of them were persuaded and Acts 17:4
and taking **s** wicked men of the Acts 17:5
dragged Jason and **s** of the brothers Acts 17:6
S of the Epicurean and Stoic Acts 17:18
also conversed with him. And **s** said, Acts 17:18
For you bring **s** strange things to our Acts 17:20
as even **s** of your own poets have said, Acts 17:28
resurrection of the dead, **s** mocked. Acts 17:32
But **s** men joined him and believed, Acts 17:34
After spending **s** time there, he Acts 18:23
to Ephesus. There he found **s** disciples. Acts 19:1
But when **s** became stubborn and Acts 19:9
Then **s** of the itinerant Jewish Acts 19:13
And even **s** of the Asiarchs, who were Acts 19:31
Now **s** cried out one thing, some Acts 19:32
some cried out one thing, **s** another, Acts 19:32
S of the crowd prompted Alexander, Acts 19:33
And **s** of the disciples from Caesarea Acts 21:16
S in the crowd were shouting one Acts 21:34
were shouting one thing, **s** another. Acts 21:34
and **s** of the scribes of the Pharisees' Acts 23:9
came down with **s** elders and a Acts 24:1
or tumult. But **s** Jews from Asia— Acts 24:18
be kept in custody but have **s** liberty, Acts 24:23
After **s** days Felix came with his wife Acts 24:24
Now when **s** days had passed, Acts 25:13
delivered Paul and **s** other prisoners to Acts 27:1
we must run aground on **s** island." Acts 27:26
Paul urged them all to take **s** food, Acts 27:33
Therefore I urge you to take **s** food. It Acts 27:34
and ate **s** food themselves. Acts 27:36
And **s** were convinced by what he Acts 28:24
may impart to you **s** spiritual gift to Rom 1:11
that I may reap **s** harvest among you Rom 1:13
What if **s** were unfaithful? Does their Rom 3:3
—as **s** people slanderously charge us Rom 3:8
Jews jealous, and thus save **s** of them. Rom 11:14
But if **s** of the branches were broken Rom 11:17

But on **s** points I have written to you Rom 15:15
pleased to make **s** contribution for Rom 15:26
S are arrogant, as though I were not 1 Cor 4:18
And such were **s** of you. But you were 1 Cor 6:11
not all possess this knowledge. But **s**, 1 Cor 8:7
a flock without getting **s** of the milk? 1 Cor 9:7
that by all means I might save **s**. 1 Cor 9:22
Do not be idolaters as **s** of them were; 1 Cor 10:7
sexual immorality as **s** of them did, 1 Cor 10:8
as **s** of them did and were destroyed 1 Cor 10:9
as **s** of them did and were destroyed 1 Cor 10:10
are weak and ill, and **s** have died. 1 Cor 11:30
I bring you **s** revelation or knowledge 1 Cor 14:6
still alive, though **s** have fallen asleep. 1 Cor 15:6
how can **s** of you say that there is no 1 Cor 15:12
For **s** have no knowledge of God. 1 Cor 15:34
perhaps of wheat or of **s** other grain. 1 Cor 15:37
I hope to spend **s** time with you, if the 1 Cor 16:7
but in **s** measure—not to put it too 2 Cor 2:5
Or do we need, as **s** do, letters of 2 Cor 3:1
if **s** Macedonians come with me and 2 Cor 9:4
on showing against **s** who suspect us 2 Cor 10:2
compare ourselves with **s** of those 2 Cor 10:12
but there are **s** who trouble you and Gal 1:7
S indeed preach Christ from envy and Phil 1:15
For we hear that **s** among you walk 2 Thes 3:11
s have made shipwreck of their faith, 1 Tm 1:19
that in later times **s** will depart from 1 Tm 4:1
for while bodily training is of **s** value, 1 Tm 4:8
and to make **s** return to their 1 Tm 5:4
For **s** have already strayed after 1 Tm 5:15
The sins of **s** men are conspicuous, 1 Tm 5:24
this craving that **s** have wandered 1 Tm 6:10
by professing it **s** have swerved from 1 Tm 6:21
They are upsetting the faith of **s**. 2 Tm 2:18
of wood and clay, **s** for honorable use, 2 Tm 2:20
for honorable use, **s** for dishonorable. 2 Tm 2:20
I want **s** benefit from you in the Lord. Phlm 1:20
therefore it remains for **s** to enter it, Heb 4:6
to meet together, as is the habit of **s**, Heb 10:25
S were tortured, refusing to accept Heb 11:35
for thereby **s** have entertained angels Heb 13:2
so that even if **s** do not obey the word, 1 Pt 3:1
fulfill his promise as **s** count slowness, 2 Pt 3:9
There are **s** things in them that are 2 Pt 3:16
greatly to find **s** of your children 2 Jn 1:4
is about to throw **s** of you into prison, Rv 2:10
you have **s** there who hold the teaching Rv 2:14
So also you have **s** who hold the Rv 2:15
conquers I will give **s** of the hidden Rv 2:17
have not learned what **s** call the deep Rv 2:24
and a half days **s** from the peoples and Rv 11:9

SOMEBODY (2)
Theudas rose up, claiming to be **s**, Acts 5:36
saying that he himself was **s** great. Acts 8:9

SOMEHOW (5)
on the chance that **s** they could reach Acts 27:12
asking that **s** by God's will I may now Rom 1:10
in order **s** to make my fellow Jews Rom 11:14
yours does not **s** become a stumbling 1 Cor 8:9
for fear that **s** the tempter had 1 Thes 3:5

SOMEONE (59)
he said, "Oh, my Lord, please send **s** else." Ex 4:13
was not a house where **s** was not dead. Ex 12:30
the discharge spits on **s** who is clean, Lv 15:8
And if **s** is too poor to pay the valuation, Lv 27:8
"This is the law when **s** dies in a tent: Nm 19:14
open field touches **s** who was killed Nm 19:16
as when **s** goes into the forest with his Dt 19:5
is giving you to possess **s** is found slain, Dt 21:1
If **s** sins against a man, God will 1 Sm 2:25
for him, but if **s** sins against the LORD, 1 Sm 2:25
"Is there not still **s** of the house of Saul, 2 Sm 9:3
that **s** would give me water to drink 2 Sm 23:15
who has granted **s** to sit on my throne 1 Kgs 1:48
when Naaman saw **s** running after 2 Kgs 5:21
"Oh that **s** would give me water to 1 Chr 11:17
them greatly that **s** had come to Neh 2:10
sleep unless they have made **s** stumble. Prv 4:16
to be enjoyed by **s** who did not toil Eccl 2:21
when **s** sees it, he swallows it as soon as it Is 28:4
And **s** said to the man clothed in linen, Dn 12:6
'If **s** carries holy meat in the fold of his Hg 2:12
"If **s** who is unclean by contact with a Hg 2:13
Or how can **s** enter a strong man's Mt 12:29
And **s** from the crowd answered him, Mk 9:17
we saw **s** casting out demons in your Mk 9:38
And **s** ran and filled a sponge with Mk 15:36
But Jesus said, "**S** touched me, for I Lk 8:46
s from the ruler's house came and said, Lk 8:49
we saw **s** casting out demons in your Lk 9:49
were going along the road, **s** said to him, Lk 9:57
S in the crowd said to him, "Teacher, Lk 12:13
And **s** said to him, "Lord, will those Lk 13:23
you are invited by **s** to a wedding feast, Lk 14:8
lest **s** more distinguished than you be Lk 14:8
but if **s** goes to them from the dead, Lk 16:30
they be convinced if **s** should rise from Lk 16:31
And a little later **s** else saw him and Lk 22:58
that **s** lays down his life for his friends. Jn 15:13
And **s** came and told them, "Look! The Acts 5:25
unless **s** guides me?" And he invited Acts 8:31
this, about himself or about **s** else?" Acts 8:34
are they to hear without **s** preaching? Rom 10:14
lest I build on **s** else's foundation, Rom 15:20
and **s** else is building upon it. 1 Cor 3:10
But if **s** says to you, "This has been 1 Cor 10:28
determined by **s** else's conscience? 1 Cor 10:29
speaks in tongues, unless **s** interprets, 1 Cor 14:5
and each in turn, and let **s** interpret. 1 Cor 14:27
But **s** will ask, "How are the dead 1 Cor 15:35
For if **s** comes and proclaims another 2 Cor 11:4
you bear it if **s** makes slaves of you, 2 Cor 11:20
for if **s** does not know how to manage 1 Tm 3:5
(For every house is built by **s**, but the Heb 3:4
you need **s** to teach you again the basic Heb 5:12
if **s** says he has faith but does not have Jas 2:14
But **s** will say, "You have faith and I Jas 2:18
from the truth and **s** brings him back, Jas 5:19
like a roaring lion, seeking **s** to devour. 1 Pt 5:8
the torment of a scorpion when it stings **s**. Rv 9:5

SOMEONE'S (1)
comes from **s** own interpretation. 2 Pt 1:20

SOMETHING (58)
or has found **s** lost and lied about it, Lv 6:3
But if the LORD creates **s** new, and the Nm 16:30
him out of hatred or hurled **s** at him, Nm 35:20
to them, "Out of the eater came **s** to eat. Jgs 14:14
of the strong came **s** sweet." And in Jgs 14:14
he thought, "**S** has happened to him. 1 Sm 20:26
said, "I have **s** to say to you." She said, 1 Kgs 2:14
him there is found **s** pleasing to the 1 Kgs 14:13
and afterward make **s** for yourself 1 Kgs 17:13
run after him and get **s** from him." 2 Kgs 5:20
for I have yet **s** to say on God's behalf. Jb 36:2
And I find **s** more bitter than death: the Eccl 7:26
his waist was **s** like the appearance Ezk 8:2
appeared above them **s** like a sapphire, Ezk 10:1
of the Holy Place was **s** resembling Ezk 41:21
of Philistia? Are you paying me back for **s**? Jl 3:4
who cry "Peace" when they have **s** to eat, Mi 3:5
that your brother has **s** against you, Mt 5:23
tell you, **s** greater than the temple is here. Mt 12:6
behold, **s** greater than Jonah is here. Mt 12:41
behold, **s** greater than Solomon is here. Mt 12:42
not go away; you give them **s** to eat." Mt 14:16
before him she asked him for **s**. Mt 20:20
this, and told them to give her **s** to eat. Mk 5:43
villages and buy themselves **s** to eat." Mk 6:36
"You give them **s** to eat." And they said Mk 6:37
I have **s** to say to you." And he answered, Lk 7:40
And he directed that **s** should be given Lk 8:55
"You give them **s** to eat." They said, Lk 9:13
behold, **s** greater than Solomon is here. Lk 11:31
behold, **s** greater than Jonah is here. Lk 11:32
him, to catch him in **s** he might say. Lk 11:54
that they might catch him in **s** he said, Lk 20:20
"Has anyone brought him **s** to eat?" Jn 4:33
or that he should give **s** to the poor. Jn 13:29
them, expecting to receive **s** from them. Acts 3:5
And immediately **s** like scales fell Acts 9:18
became hungry and wanted **s** to eat, Acts 10:10
the heavens opened and **s** like a great Acts 10:11
vision, **s** like a great sheet descending, Acts 11:5
except telling or hearing **s** new. Acts 17:21
"May I say **s** to you?" And he said, Acts 21:37
the tribune, for he has **s** to tell him." Acts 23:17
man to you, as he has **s** to say to you." Acts 23:18
examined him, I may have **s** to write. Acts 25:26
by works, he has **s** to boast about, Rom 4:2
if he is thirsty, give him **s** to drink; Rom 12:20
If anyone imagines that he knows **s**, he 1 Cor 8:2
of you is to put **s** aside and store it up, 1 Cor 16:2
For if anyone thinks he is **s**, when he is Gal 6:3
that he may have **s** to share with Eph 4:28
people swear by **s** greater than Heb 6:16
for this priest also to have **s** to offer. Heb 8:3
since God had provided **s** better for us, Heb 11:40
as though **s** strange were happening to 1 Pt 4:12
And we have **s** more sure, the prophetic 2 Pt 1:19
I have written **s** to the church, but 3 Jn 1:9
his trumpet, and **s** like a great mountain, Rv 8:8

SOMETIME (1)
S after the prophet Hananiah had Jer 28:12

SOMETIMES (5)
S the cloud was a few days over the Nm 9:20
And **s** the cloud remained from Nm 9:21
because **s** a person who has toiled with Eccl 2:21
s being publicly exposed to reproach Heb 10:33
and **s** being partners with those so Heb 10:33

SOMEWHAT (1)
going to inquire **s** more closely about Acts 23:20

SOMEWHERE (2)
It has been testified **s**, "What is man, Heb 2:6
For he has **s** spoken of the seventh day Heb 4:4

SON (2342)
name of the city after the name of his **s**, Gn 4:17
and she bore a **s** and called his name Gn 4:25
To Seth also a **s** was born, and he called Gn 4:26
years, he fathered a **s** in his own likeness, Gn 5:3
had lived 182 years, he fathered a **s** Gn 5:28
knew what his youngest **s** had done to Gn 9:24
Terah took Abram his **s** and Lot the Gn 11:31
Abram his son and Lot the **s** of Haran, Gn 11:31
daughter-in-law, his **s** Abram's wife, Gn 11:31
Sarai his wife, and Lot his brother's **s**, Gn 12:5
also took Lot, the **s** of Abram's brother, Gn 14:12
your very own **s** shall be your heir." Gn 15:4
you are pregnant and shall bear a **s**. Gn 16:11
And Hagar bore Abram a **s**, and Gn 16:15
and Abram called the name of his **s**, Gn 16:15
moreover, I will give you a **s** by her. Gn 17:16
but Sarah your wife shall bear you a **s**, Gn 17:19
took Ishmael his **s** and all those Gn 17:23
And Ishmael his **s** was thirteen years Gn 17:25
Abraham and his **s** Ishmael were Gn 17:26
wife shall have a **s**." And Sarah was Gn 18:10
next year, and Sarah shall have a **s**." Gn 18:14
The firstborn bore a **s** and called his Gn 19:37
younger also bore a **s** and called his Gn 19:38
and bore Abraham a **s** in his old age Gn 21:2
the name of his **s** who was born to Gn 21:3
Abraham circumcised his **s** Isaac when Gn 21:4
years old when his **s** Isaac was born to Gn 21:5
Yet I have borne him a **s** in his old age." Gn 21:7
But Sarah saw the **s** of Hagar the Gn 21:9
"Cast out this slave woman with her **s**, Gn 21:10
for the **s** of this slave woman shall not Gn 21:10
shall not be heir with my **s** Isaac." Gn 21:10
to Abraham on account of his **s**. Gn 21:11
a nation of the **s** of the slave woman Gn 21:13
He said, "Take your **s**, your only son Gn 22:2
said, "Take your son, your only **s** Isaac, Gn 22:2
young men with him, and his **s** Isaac. Gn 22:3
burnt offering and laid it on Isaac his **s**. Gn 22:6
And he said, "Here am I, my **s**." He said, Gn 22:7
my **s**." So they went both of them Gn 22:8
and bound Isaac his **s** and laid him on Gn 22:9
and took the knife to slaughter his **s**. Gn 22:10
seeing you have not withheld your **s**, Gn 22:12
not withheld your son, your only **s**, Gn 22:12
up as a burnt offering instead of his **s**. Gn 22:13
this and have not withheld your **s**, Gn 22:16
not withheld your son, your only **s**, Gn 22:16
entreat for me Ephron the **s** of Zohar, Gn 23:8
a wife for my **s** from the daughters of Gn 24:3
kindred, and take a wife for my **s** Isaac." Gn 24:4
Must I then take your **s** back to the land Gn 24:5
it that you do not take my **s** back there. Gn 24:6
shall take a wife for my **s** from there. Gn 24:7
you must not take my **s** back there." Gn 24:8
was born to Bethuel the **s** of Milcah, Gn 24:15
daughter of Bethuel the **s** of Milcah, Gn 24:24
master's wife bore a **s** to my master Gn 24:36
a wife for my **s** from the daughters of Gn 24:37
to my clan and take a wife for my **s**.' Gn 24:38
take a wife for my **s** from my clan and Gn 24:40
LORD has appointed for my master's **s**.' Gn 24:44
'The daughter of Bethuel, Nahor's **s**, Gn 24:47
of my master's kinsman for his **s**. Gn 24:48
let her be the wife of your master's **s**, Gn 24:51
he sent them away from his **s** Isaac, Gn 25:6
field of Ephron the **s** of Zohar the Hittite, Gn 25:9
of Abraham, God blessed Isaac his **s**. Gn 25:11
generations of Ishmael, Abraham's **s**, Gn 25:12
the generations of Isaac, Abraham's **s**: Gn 25:19
called Esau his older **s** and said to him, Gn 27:1
his older son and said to him, "My **s**"; Gn 27:1
when Isaac spoke to his **s** Esau. Gn 27:5
Rebekah said to her **s** Jacob, "I heard Gn 27:6
Now therefore, my **s**, obey my voice as I Gn 27:8
to him, "Let your curse be on me, my **s**; Gn 27:13
the best garments of Esau her older **s**, Gn 27:15
and put them on Jacob her younger **s**. Gn 27:15
prepared, into the hand of her **s** Jacob. Gn 27:17
said, "Here I am. Who are you, my **s**?" Gn 27:18
But Isaac said to his **s**, "How is it that Gn 27:20
it so quickly, my **s**?" He answered, Gn 27:20
come near, that I may feel you, my **s**, Gn 27:21
you are really my **s** Esau or not." Gn 27:21
you really my **s** Esau?" He answered, Gn 27:24

him, "Come near and kiss me, my **s**."	Gn 27:26
the smell of my **s** is as the smell of a	Gn 27:27
are you?" He answered, "I am your **s**,	Gn 27:32
What then can I do for you, my **s**?"	Gn 27:37
of Esau her older **s** were told to	Gn 27:42
called Jacob her younger **s** and said to	Gn 27:42
Now therefore, my **s**, obey my voice.	Gn 27:43
to Laban, the **s** of Bethuel the Aramean,	Gn 28:5
the daughter of Ishmael, Abraham's **s**,	Gn 28:9
you know Laban the **s** of Nahor?" They	Gn 29:5
kinsman, and that he was Rebekah's **s**,	Gn 29:12
the news about Jacob, his sister's **s**,	Gn 29:13
And Leah conceived and bore a **s**, and	Gn 29:32
She conceived again and bore a **s**, and	Gn 29:33
has given me this **s** also." And she	Gn 29:33
Again she conceived and bore a **s**, and	Gn 29:34
And she conceived again and bore a **s**,	Gn 29:35
Bilhah conceived and bore Jacob a **s**.	Gn 30:5
and given me a **s**." Therefore she called	Gn 30:6
again and bore Jacob a second **s**.	Gn 30:7
Leah's servant Zilpah bore Jacob a **s**.	Gn 30:10
servant Zilpah bore Jacob a second **s**.	Gn 30:12
she conceived and bore Jacob a fifth **s**.	Gn 30:17
again, and she bore Jacob a sixth **s**.	Gn 30:19
She conceived and bore a **s** and said,	Gn 30:23
"May the LORD add to me another **s**!"	Gn 30:24
And when Shechem the **s** of Hamor the	Gn 34:2
"The soul of my **s** Shechem longs for	Gn 34:8
Hamor and Hamor's **s** Shechem.	Gn 34:18
So Hamor and his **s** Shechem came to	Gn 34:20
listened to Hamor and his **s** Shechem,	Gn 34:24
Hamor and his **s** Shechem with the	Gn 34:26
"Do not fear, for you have another **s**."	Gn 35:17
Eliphaz the **s** of Adah the wife of Esau,	Gn 36:10
Reuel the **s** of Basemath the wife of	Gn 36:10
was a concubine of Eliphaz, Esau's **s**;	Gn 36:12
These are the sons of Reuel, Esau's **s**:	Gn 36:17
Bela the **s** of Beor reigned in Edom, the	Gn 36:32
and Jobab the **s** of Zerah of Bozrah	Gn 36:33
died, and Hadad the **s** of Bedad,	Gn 36:35
and Baal-hanan the **s** of Achbor	Gn 36:38
Baal-hanan the **s** of Achbor died, and	Gn 36:39
sons, because he was the **s** of his old age.	Gn 37:3
and mourned for his **s** many days.	Gn 37:34
"No, I shall go down to Sheol to my **s**,	Gn 37:35
and she conceived and bore a **s**, and he	Gn 38:3
She conceived again and bore a **s**, and	Gn 38:4
Yet again she bore a **s**, and she called	Gn 38:5
till Shelah my **s** grows up"—for he	Gn 38:11
give her to my **s** Shelah." And he did	Gn 38:26
said, "My **s** shall not go down with you,	Gn 42:38
his brother Benjamin, his mother's **s**,	Gn 43:29
to me? God be gracious to you, my **s**!"	Gn 43:29
say to him, 'Thus says your **s** Joseph,	Gn 45:9
"It is enough; Joseph my **s** is still alive.	Gn 45:28
Shaul, the **s** of a Canaanite woman.	Gn 46:10
he called his **s** Joseph and said to him,	Gn 47:29
"Your **s** Joseph has come to you." Then	Gn 48:2
father refused and said, "I know, my **s**,	Gn 48:19
from the prey, my **s**, you have gone up.	Gn 49:9
also of Machir the **s** of Manasseh were	Gn 50:23
and see them on the birthstool, if it is a **s**,	Ex 1:16
"Every **s** that is born to the Hebrews you	Ex 1:22
The woman conceived and bore a **s**, and	Ex 2:2
daughter, and he became her **s**.	Ex 2:10
She gave birth to a **s**, and he called his	Ex 2:22
says the LORD, Israel is my firstborn **s**,	Ex 4:22
"Let my **s** go that he may serve me." If	Ex 4:23
go, behold, I will kill your firstborn **s**.'"	Ex 4:23
and Shaul, the **s** of a Canaanite woman;	Ex 6:15
Eleazar, Aaron's **s**, took as his wife one of	Ex 6:25
the hearing of your **s** and of your	Ex 10:2
You shall tell your **s** on that day, 'It is	Ex 13:8
when in time to come your **s** asks you,	Ex 13:14
shall not do any work, you, or your **s**,	Ex 20:10
If he designates her for his **s**, he shall	Ex 21:9
If it gores a man's **s** or daughter, he	Ex 21:31
rest, and the **s** of your servant woman,	Ex 23:12
The **s** who succeeds him as priest, who	Ex 29:30
have called by name Bezalel the **s** of Uri,	Ex 31:2
by name Bezalel the son of Uri, **s** of Hur,	Ex 31:2
with him Oholiab, the **s** of Ahisamach,	Ex 31:6
at the cost of his **s** and of his brother,	Ex 32:29
his assistant Joshua the **s** of Nun,	Ex 33:11
has called by name Bezalel the **s** of Uri,	Ex 35:30
name Bezalel the son of Uri, **s** of Hur,	Ex 35:30
and Oholiab the **s** of Ahisamach of	Ex 35:34
direction of Ithamar the **s** of Aaron the	Ex 38:21
Bezalel the **s** of Uri, son of Hur, of the	Ex 38:22
Bezalel the son of Uri, **s** of Hur, of the	Ex 38:22
him was Oholiab the **s** of Ahisamach,	Ex 38:23
whether for a **s** or for a daughter,	Lv 12:6
relatives, his mother, his father, his **s**,	Lv 21:2
Now an Israelite woman's **s**, whose	Lv 24:10
And the Israelite woman's **s** and a man	Lv 24:10
the Israelite woman's **s** blasphemed the	Lv 24:11
From Reuben, Elizur the **s** of Shedeur;	Nm 1:5
Simeon, Shelumiel the **s** of Zurishaddai;	Nm 1:6
Judah, Nahshon the **s** of Amminadab;	Nm 1:7
from Issachar, Nethanel the **s** of Zuar;	Nm 1:8
from Zebulun, Eliab the **s** of Helon;	Nm 1:9
Ephraim, Elishama the **s** of Ammihud,	Nm 1:10
Manasseh, Gamaliel the **s** of Pedahzur;	Nm 1:10
Benjamin, Abidan the **s** of Gideoni;	Nm 1:11
Dan, Ahiezer the **s** of Ammishaddai;	Nm 1:12
from Asher, Pagiel the **s** of Ochran;	Nm 1:13
from Gad, Eliasaph the **s** of Deuel;	Nm 1:14
from Naphtali, Ahira the **s** of Enan."	Nm 1:15
being Nahshon the **s** of Amminadab,	Nm 2:3
Issachar being Nethanel the **s** of Zuar,	Nm 2:5
of Zebulun being Eliab the **s** of Helon,	Nm 2:7
Reuben being Elizur the **s** of Shedeur,	Nm 2:10
being Shelumiel the **s** of Zurishaddai,	Nm 2:12
of Gad being Eliasaph the **s** of Reuel,	Nm 2:14
being Elishama the **s** of Ammihud,	Nm 2:18
being Gamaliel the **s** of Pedahzur,	Nm 2:20
being Abidan the **s** of Gideoni,	Nm 2:22
being Ahiezer the **s** of Ammishaddai,	Nm 2:25
of Asher being Pagiel the **s** of Ochran,	Nm 2:27
of Naphtali being Ahira the **s** of Enan,	Nm 2:29
the **s** of Lael as chief of the fathers'	Nm 3:24
with Elizaphan the **s** of Uzziel as chief	Nm 3:30
And Eleazar the **s** of Aaron the priest	Nm 3:32
of Merari was Zuriel the **s** of Abihail.	Nm 3:35
"And Eleazar the **s** of Aaron the priest	Nm 4:16
direction of Ithamar the **s** of Aaron the	Nm 4:28
direction of Ithamar the **s** of Aaron the	Nm 4:33
direction of Ithamar the **s** of Aaron the	Nm 7:8
was Nahshon the **s** of Amminadab,	Nm 7:12
of Nahshon the **s** of Amminadab.	Nm 7:17
the second day Nethanel the **s** of Zuar,	Nm 7:18
the offering of Nethanel the **s** of Zuar.	Nm 7:23
On the third day Eliab the **s** of Helon,	Nm 7:24
was the offering of Eliab the **s** of Helon.	Nm 7:29
the fourth day Elizur the **s** of Shedeur,	Nm 7:30
the offering of Elizur the **s** of Shedeur.	Nm 7:35
day Shelumiel the **s** of Zurishaddai,	Nm 7:36
of Shelumiel the **s** of Zurishaddai.	Nm 7:41
the sixth day Eliasaph the **s** of Deuel,	Nm 7:42
the offering of Eliasaph the **s** of Deuel.	Nm 7:47
day Elishama the **s** of Ammihud,	Nm 7:48
of Elishama the **s** of Ammihud.	Nm 7:53
eighth day Gamaliel the **s** of Pedahzur,	Nm 7:54
offering of Gamaliel the **s** of Pedahzur.	Nm 7:59
the ninth day Abidan the **s** of Gideoni,	Nm 7:60
the offering of Abidan the **s** of Gideoni.	Nm 7:65
day Ahiezer the **s** of Ammishaddai,	Nm 7:66
of Ahiezer the **s** of Ammishaddai.	Nm 7:71
the eleventh day Pagiel the **s** of Ochran,	Nm 7:72
the offering of Pagiel the **s** of Ochran.	Nm 7:77
On the twelfth day Ahira the **s** of Enan,	Nm 7:78
was the offering of Ahira the **s** of Enan.	Nm 7:83
was Nahshon the **s** of Amminadab.	Nm 10:14
Issachar was Nethanel the **s** of Zuar.	Nm 10:15
of Zebulun was Eliab the **s** of Helon.	Nm 10:16
company was Elizur the **s** of Shedeur.	Nm 10:18
was Shelumiel the **s** of Zurishaddai.	Nm 10:19
of Gad was Eliasaph the **s** of Deuel.	Nm 10:20
was Elishama the **s** of Ammihud.	Nm 10:22
was Gamaliel the **s** of Pedahzur.	Nm 10:23
was Abidan the **s** of Gideoni.	Nm 10:24
was Ahiezer the **s** of Ammishaddai.	Nm 10:25
of Asher was Pagiel the **s** of Ochran.	Nm 10:26
of Naphtali was Ahira the **s** of Enan.	Nm 10:27
said to Hobab the **s** of Reuel the	Nm 10:29
And Joshua the **s** of Nun, the assistant	Nm 11:28
of Reuben, Shammua the **s** of Zaccur;	Nm 13:4
tribe of Simeon, Shaphat the **s** of Hori;	Nm 13:5
of Judah, Caleb the **s** of Jephunneh;	Nm 13:6
tribe of Issachar, Igal the **s** of Joseph;	Nm 13:7
tribe of Ephraim, Hoshea the **s** of Nun;	Nm 13:8
tribe of Benjamin, Palti the **s** of Raphu;	Nm 13:9
tribe of Zebulun, Gaddiel the **s** of Sodi;	Nm 13:10
of Manasseh), Gaddi the **s** of Susi;	Nm 13:11
tribe of Dan, Ammiel the **s** of Gemalli;	Nm 13:12
of Asher, Sethur the **s** of Michael;	Nm 13:13
of Naphtali, Nahbi the **s** of Vophsi;	Nm 13:14
the tribe of Gad, Geuel the **s** of Machi.	Nm 13:15
called Hoshea the **s** of Nun Joshua.	Nm 13:16
And Joshua the **s** of Nun and Caleb the	Nm 14:6
of Nun and Caleb the **s** of Jephunneh,	Nm 14:6
except Caleb the **s** of Jephunneh and	Nm 14:30
Jephunneh and Joshua the **s** of Nun.	Nm 14:30
only Joshua the **s** of Nun and Caleb	Nm 14:38
and Caleb the **s** of Jephunneh	Nm 14:38
Now Korah the **s** of Izhar, son of	Nm 16:1
Korah the son of Izhar, **s** of Kohath,	Nm 16:1
son of Izhar, son of Kohath, **s** of Levi,	Nm 16:1
sons of Eliab, and On the **s** of Peleth,	Nm 16:1
"Tell Eleazar the **s** of Aaron the priest	Nm 16:37
and Eleazar his **s** and bring them	Nm 20:25
and put them on Eleazar his **s**.	Nm 20:26
and put them on Eleazar his **s**.	Nm 20:28
And Balak the **s** of Zippor saw all that	Nm 22:2
of the field." So Balak the **s** of Zippor,	Nm 22:4
messengers to Balaam the **s** of Beor at	Nm 22:5
said to God, "Balak the **s** of Zippor,	Nm 22:10
"Thus says Balak the **s** of Zippor:	Nm 22:16
and hear; give ear to me, O **s** of Zippor:	Nm 23:18
man, that he should lie, or a **s** of man,	Nm 23:19
"The oracle of Balaam the **s** of Beor,	Nm 24:3
"The oracle of Balaam the **s** of Beor,	Nm 24:15
When Phinehas the **s** of Eleazar, son of	Nm 25:7
the son of Eleazar, **s** of Aaron the priest,	Nm 25:7
"Phinehas the **s** of Eleazar, son of	Nm 25:11
son of Eleazar, **s** of Aaron the priest,	Nm 25:11
woman, was Zimri the **s** of Salu,	Nm 25:14
to Moses and to Eleazar the **s** of Aaron,	Nm 26:1
Now Zelophehad the **s** of Hepher had	Nm 26:33
except Caleb the **s** of Jephunneh and	Nm 26:65
Jephunneh and Joshua the **s** of Nun.	Nm 26:65
of Zelophehad the **s** of Hepher,	Nm 27:1
the son of Hepher, **s** of Gilead,	Nm 27:1
of Hepher, son of Gilead, **s** of Machir,	Nm 27:1
Gilead, son of Machir, **s** of Manasseh,	Nm 27:1
the clans of Manasseh the **s** of Joseph.	Nm 27:1
from his clan because he had no **s**?	Nm 27:4
saying, 'If a man dies and has no **s**,	Nm 27:8
to Moses, "Take Joshua the **s** of Nun,	Nm 27:18
with Phinehas the **s** of Eleazar the	Nm 31:6
also killed Balaam the **s** of Beor with	Nm 31:8
except Caleb the **s** of Jephunneh the	Nm 32:12
the Kenizzite and Joshua the **s** of Nun,	Nm 32:12
and to Joshua the **s** of Nun and to	Nm 32:28
half-tribe of Manasseh the **s** of Joseph,	Nm 32:33
of Machir the **s** of Manasseh went	Nm 32:39
Gilead to Machir the **s** of Manasseh,	Nm 32:40
And Jair the **s** of Manasseh went and	Nm 32:41
the priest and Joshua the **s** of Nun.	Nm 34:17
of Judah, Caleb the **s** of Jephunneh.	Nm 34:19
Simeon, Shemuel the **s** of Ammihud.	Nm 34:20
of Benjamin, Elidad the **s** of Chislon.	Nm 34:21
of Dan a chief, Bukki the **s** of Jogli.	Nm 34:22
a chief, Hanniel the **s** of Ephod.	Nm 34:23
a chief, Kemuel the **s** of Shiphtan.	Nm 34:24
a chief, Elizaphan the **s** of Parnach.	Nm 34:25
Issachar a chief, Paltiel the **s** of Azzan.	Nm 34:26
a chief, Ahihud the **s** of Shelomi.	Nm 34:27
a chief, Pedahel the **s** of Ammihud.	Nm 34:28
of the people of Gilead the **s** of Machir,	Nm 36:1
the son of Machir, **s** of Manasseh,	Nm 36:1
the people of Manasseh the **s** of Joseph,	Nm 36:12
God carried you, as a man carries his **s**,	Dt 1:31
except Caleb the **s** of Jephunneh. He shall	Dt 1:36
Joshua the **s** of Nun, who stands before	Dt 1:38
you or your **s** or your daughter or your	Dt 5:14
God, you and your **s** and your son's son,	Dt 6:2
God, you and your son and your son's **s**,	Dt 6:2
"When your **s** asks you in time to come,	Dt 6:20
then you shall say to your **s**, 'We were	Dt 6:21
your heart that, as a man disciplines his **s**,	Dt 8:5
And his **s** Eleazar ministered as priest in	Dt 10:6
Abiram the sons of Eliab, **s** of Reuben,	Dt 11:6
you and your **s** and your daughter,	Dt 12:18
"If your brother, the **s** of your mother, or	Dt 13:6
or your **s** or your daughter or the wife	Dt 13:6
God, you and your **s** and your daughter,	Dt 16:11
you and your **s** and your daughter,	Dt 16:14
who burns his **s** or his daughter	Dt 18:10
and if the firstborn **s** belongs to the	Dt 21:15
he may not treat the **s** of the loved as the	Dt 21:16
in preference to the **s** of the unloved,	Dt 21:16
the firstborn, the **s** of the unloved,	Dt 21:17
stubborn and rebellious **s** who will not	Dt 21:18
'This our **s** is stubborn and rebellious;	Dt 21:20
against you Balaam the **s** of Beor from	Dt 23:4
and one of them dies and has no **s**,	Dt 25:5
And the first **s** whom she bears shall	Dt 25:6
embraces, to her **s** and to her daughter,	Dt 28:56
commissioned Joshua the **s** of Nun and	Dt 31:23
the people, he and Joshua the **s** of Nun.	Dt 32:44
And Joshua the **s** of Nun was full of the	Dt 34:9
the LORD said to Joshua the **s** of Nun,	Jos 1:1
And Joshua the **s** of Nun sent two men	Jos 2:1
over and came to Joshua the **s** of Nun,	Jos 2:23
So Joshua the **s** of Nun called the priests	Jos 6:6
the cost of his youngest **s** shall he set up	Jos 6:26
devoted things, for Achan the **s** of Carmi,	Jos 7:1
for Achan the son of Carmi, **s** of Zabdi,	Jos 7:1
the son of Carmi, son of Zabdi, **s** of Zerah,	Jos 7:1
by man, and Achan the **s** of Carmi,	Jos 7:18
and Achan the son of Carmi, **s** of Zabdi,	Jos 7:18
son of Carmi, son of Zabdi, **s** of Zerah,	Jos 7:18
Then Joshua said to Achan, "My **s**, give	Jos 7:19
with him took Achan the **s** of Zerah,	Jos 7:24

Balaam also, the **s** of Beor, the one who Jos 13:22
people of Machir the **s** of Manasseh for Jos 13:31
priest and Joshua the **s** of Nun and the Jos 14:1
And Caleb the **s** of Jephunneh the Jos 14:6
Hebron to Caleb the **s** of Jephunneh for Jos 14:13
of Caleb the **s** of Jephunneh the Jos 14:14
up to the stone of Bohan the **s** of Reuben. Jos 15:6
by the Valley of the **S** of Hinnom at the Jos 15:8
gave to Caleb the **s** of Jephunneh a Jos 15:13
And Othniel the **s** of Kenaz, the brother Jos 15:17
descendants of Manasseh the **s** of Joseph, Jos 17:2
Now Zelophehad the **s** of Hepher, son of Jos 17:3
the son of Hepher, **s** of Gilead, Jos 17:3
of Hepher, son of Gilead, **s** of Machir, Jos 17:3
of Gilead, son of Machir, **s** of Manasseh, Jos 17:3
priest and Joshua the **s** of Nun and the Jos 17:4
the Valley of the **S** of Hinnom, Jos 18:16
to the stone of Bohan the **s** of Reuben, Jos 18:17
among them to Joshua the **s** of Nun. Jos 19:49
priest and Joshua the **s** of Nun and the Jos 19:51
priest and to Joshua the **s** of Nun and to Jos 21:1
given to Caleb the **s** of Jephunneh as Jos 21:12
Phinehas the **s** of Eleazar the priest, Jos 22:13
Did not Achan the **s** of Zerah break Jos 22:20
And Phinehas the **s** of Eleazar the Jos 22:31
Then Phinehas the **s** of Eleazar the Jos 22:32
Then Balak the **s** of Zippor, king of Jos 24:9
and invited Balaam the **s** of Beor to Jos 24:9
After these things Joshua the **s** of Nun, Jos 24:29
And Eleazar the **s** of Aaron died, and Jos 24:33
at Gibeah, the town of Phinehas his **s**, Jos 24:33
And Othniel the **s** of Kenaz, Caleb's Jgs 1:13
And Joshua the **s** of Nun, the servant of Jgs 2:8
who saved them, Othniel the **s** of Kenaz, Jgs 3:9
years. Then Othniel the **s** of Kenaz died. Jgs 3:11
for them a deliverer, Ehud, the **s** of Gera, Jgs 3:15
After him was Shamgar the **s** of Anath, Jgs 3:31
summoned Barak the **s** of Abinoam from Jgs 4:6
told that Barak the **s** of Abinoam had Jgs 4:12
Deborah and Barak the **s** of Abinoam on Jgs 5:1
"In the days of Shamgar, **s** of Anath, in Jgs 5:6
away your captives, O **s** of Abinoam. Jgs 5:12
while his **s** Gideon was beating out Jgs 6:11
"Gideon the **s** of Joash has done this Jgs 6:29
the town said to Joash, "Bring out your **s**, Jgs 6:30
than the sword of Gideon the **s** of Joash, Jgs 7:14
Then Gideon the **s** of Joash returned Jgs 8:13
one of them resembled the **s** of a king." Jgs 8:18
you and your **s** and your grandson also, Jgs 8:22
you, and my **s** will not rule over you; Jgs 8:23
Jerubbaal the **s** of Joash went and lived Jgs 8:29
who was in Shechem also bore him a **s**, Jgs 8:31
And Gideon the **s** of Joash died in a good Jgs 8:32
Now Abimelech the **s** of Jerubbaal went Jgs 9:1
Jotham the youngest **s** of Jerubbaal was Jgs 9:5
Abimelech, the **s** of his female servant, Jgs 9:18
And Gaal the **s** of Ebed moved into Jgs 9:26
And Gaal the **s** of Ebed said, "Who is Jgs 9:28
Is he not the **s** of Jerubbaal, and is not Jgs 9:28
heard the words of Gaal the **s** of Ebed, Jgs 9:30
Gaal the **s** of Ebed and his relatives have Jgs 9:31
And Gaal the **s** of Ebed went out and Jgs 9:35
the curse of Jotham the **s** of Jerubbaal. Jgs 9:57
arose to save Israel Tola the **s** of Puah, Jgs 10:1
Israel Tola the son of Puah, **s** of Dodo, Jgs 10:1
warrior, but he was the **s** of a prostitute. Jgs 11:1
for you are the **s** of another woman." Jgs 11:2
any better than Balak the **s** of Zippor, Jgs 11:25
her he had neither **s** nor daughter. Jgs 11:34
After him Abdon the **s** of Hillel the Jgs 12:13
Then Abdon the **s** of Hillel the Jgs 12:15
but you shall conceive and bear a **s**. Jgs 13:3
behold, you shall conceive and bear a **s**. Jgs 13:5
'Behold, you shall conceive and bear a **s**. Jgs 13:7
the woman bore a **s** and called his Jgs 13:24
said, "Blessed be my **s** by the LORD." Jgs 17:2
to the LORD from my hand for my **s**, Jgs 17:3
and Jonathan the **s** of Gershom, Jgs 18:30
the son of Gershom, **s** of Moses, Jgs 18:30
and Phinehas the **s** of Eleazar, son of Jgs 20:28
the son of Eleazar, **s** of Aaron, Jgs 20:28
gave her conception, and she bore a **s**. Ru 4:13
"A **s** has been born to Naomi." They Ru 4:17
name was Elkanah the **s** of Jeroham, 1 Sm 1:1
Elkanah the son of Jeroham, **s** of Elihu, 1 Sm 1:1
of Jeroham, son of Elihu, **s** of Tohu, 1 Sm 1:1
son of Elihu, son of Tohu, **s** of Zuph, 1 Sm 1:1
but will give to your servant a **s**, 1 Sm 1:11
time Hannah conceived and bore a **s**, 1 Sm 1:20
and nursed her **s** until she weaned 1 Sm 1:23
me." But he said, "I did not call, my **s**; 1 Sm 3:6
and said, "Samuel, my **s**." And he said, 1 Sm 3:16
And he said, "How did it go, my **s**?" 1 Sm 4:16
you have borne a **s**." But she did not 1 Sm 4:20
they consecrated his **s** Eleazar to have 1 Sm 7:1
The name of his firstborn **s** was Joel, 1 Sm 8:2
whose name was Kish, the **s** of Abiel, 1 Sm 9:1
was Kish, the son of Abiel, **s** of Zeror, 1 Sm 9:1
of Abiel, son of Zeror, **s** of Becorath, 1 Sm 9:1
of Zeror, son of Becorath, **s** of Aphiah, 1 Sm 9:1
And he had a **s** whose name was Saul, a 1 Sm 9:2
So Kish said to Saul his **s**, "Take one of 1 Sm 9:3
"What shall I do about my **s**?"' 1 Sm 10:2
"What has come over the **s** of Kish? 1 Sm 10:11
and Saul the **s** of Kish was taken by 1 Sm 10:21
and Jonathan his **s** and the people 1 Sm 13:16
Saul and Jonathan his **s** had them. 1 Sm 13:22
One day Jonathan the **s** of Saul said to 1 Sm 14:1
including Ahijah the **s** of Ahitub, 1 Sm 14:3
Ichabod's brother, **s** of Phinehas, 1 Sm 14:3
brother, son of Phinehas, **s** of Eli, 1 Sm 14:3
though it be in Jonathan my **s**, 1 Sm 14:39
I and Jonathan my **s** will be on the 1 Sm 14:40
guilt is in me or in Jonathan my **s**, 1 Sm 14:41
me and my **s** Jonathan." And 1 Sm 14:42
of his army was Abner the **s** of Ner, 1 Sm 14:50
father of Abner was the **s** of Abiel. 1 Sm 14:51
I have seen a **s** of Jesse the 1 Sm 16:18
and said, "Send me David your **s**, 1 Sm 16:19
and sent them by David his **s** to Saul. 1 Sm 16:20
David was the **s** of an Ephrathite 1 Sm 17:12
And Jesse said to David his **s**, "Take 1 Sm 17:17
whose **s** is this youth?" And Abner 1 Sm 17:55
said, "Inquire whose **s** the boy is." 1 Sm 17:56
Saul said to him, "Whose **s** are you, 1 Sm 17:58
"I am the **s** of your servant Jesse the 1 Sm 17:58
spoke to Jonathan his **s** and to all his 1 Sm 19:1
But Jonathan, Saul's **s**, delighted 1 Sm 19:1
And Saul said to Jonathan his **s**, 1 Sm 20:27
"Why has not the **s** of Jesse come to 1 Sm 20:27
he said to him, "You **s** of a perverse, 1 Sm 20:30
you have chosen the **s** of Jesse to 1 Sm 20:30
For as long as the **s** of Jesse lives on 1 Sm 20:31
will the **s** of Jesse give every one of you 1 Sm 22:7
to me when my **s** makes a covenant 1 Sm 22:8
makes a covenant with the **s** of Jesse. 1 Sm 22:8
to me that my **s** has stirred up my 1 Sm 22:8
"I saw the **s** of Jesse coming to Nob, 1 Sm 22:9
to Nob, to Ahimelech the **s** of Ahitub, 1 Sm 22:9
the priest, the **s** of Ahitub, 1 Sm 22:11
now, **s** of Ahitub." And he answered, 1 Sm 22:12
against me, you and the **s** of Jesse, 1 Sm 22:13
sons of Ahimelech the **s** of Ahitub, 1 Sm 22:20
When Abiathar the **s** of Ahimelech 1 Sm 23:6
And Jonathan, Saul's **s**, rose and 1 Sm 23:16
my **s** David?" And Saul lifted up his 1 Sm 24:16
to your servants and to your **s** David."' 1 Sm 25:8
is David? Who is the **s** of Jesse? 1 Sm 25:10
David's wife, to Palti the **s** of Laish, 1 Sm 25:44
Saul lay, with Abner the **s** of Ner, 1 Sm 26:5
brother Abishai the **s** of Zeruiah, 1 Sm 26:6
the army, and to Abner the **s** of Ner, 1 Sm 26:14
voice, my **s** David?" And David said, 1 Sm 26:17
Return, my **s** David, for I will no 1 Sm 26:21
David, "Blessed be you, my **s** David! 1 Sm 26:25
with him, to Achish the **s** of Maoch, 1 Sm 27:2
the priest, the **s** of Ahimelech, 1 Sm 30:7
and Saul and his **s** Jonathan are also 2 Sm 1:4
that Saul and his **s** Jonathan are dead?" 2 Sm 1:5
and for Jonathan his **s** and for the 2 Sm 1:12
answered, "I am the **s** of a sojourner, 2 Sm 1:13
over Saul and Jonathan his **s**, 2 Sm 1:17
But Abner the **s** of Ner, commander of 2 Sm 2:8
took Ish-bosheth the **s** of Saul and 2 Sm 2:8
Ish-bosheth, Saul's **s**, was forty years 2 Sm 2:10
Abner the **s** of Ner, and the servants of 2 Sm 2:12
servants of Ish-bosheth the **s** of Saul, 2 Sm 2:12
And Joab the **s** of Zeruiah and the 2 Sm 2:13
and Ish-bosheth the **s** of Saul, 2 Sm 2:15
Absalom the **s** of Maacah the daughter 2 Sm 3:3
the fourth, Adonijah the **s** of Haggith; 2 Sm 3:4
the fifth, Shephatiah the **s** of Abital; 2 Sm 3:4
messengers to Ish-bosheth, Saul's **s**, 2 Sm 3:14
her husband Paltiel the **s** of Laish. 2 Sm 3:15
"Abner the **s** of Ner came to the king, 2 Sm 3:23
know that Abner the **s** of Ner came to 2 Sm 3:25
for the blood of Abner the **s** of Ner. 2 Sm 3:28
will to put to death Abner the **s** of Ner. 2 Sm 3:37
When Ish-bosheth, Saul's **s**, heard that 2 Sm 4:1
Now Saul's **s** had two men who were 2 Sm 4:2
Jonathan, the **s** of Saul, had a son who 2 Sm 4:4
had a **s** who was crippled in his feet. 2 Sm 4:4
is the head of Ish-bosheth, the **s** of Saul, 2 Sm 4:8
a father, and he shall be to me a **s**. 2 Sm 7:14
also defeated Hadadezer the **s** of Rehob, 2 Sm 8:3
Toi sent his **s** Joram to King David, to 2 Sm 8:10
the spoil of Hadadezer the **s** of Rehob, 2 Sm 8:12
Joab the **s** of Zeruiah was over the 2 Sm 8:16
and Jehoshaphat the **s** of Ahilud was 2 Sm 8:16
and Zadok the **s** of Ahitub and 2 Sm 8:17
and Ahimelech the **s** of Abiathar were 2 Sm 8:17
and Benaiah the **s** of Jehoiada was 2 Sm 8:18
the king, "There is still a **s** of Jonathan; 2 Sm 9:3
the house of Machir the **s** of Ammiel, 2 Sm 9:4
the house of Machir the **s** of Ammiel, 2 Sm 9:5
And Mephibosheth the **s** of Jonathan, 2 Sm 9:6
the son of Jonathan, **s** of Saul, 2 Sm 9:6
And Mephibosheth had a young **s**, 2 Sm 9:12
and Hanun his **s** reigned in his place. 2 Sm 10:1
loyally with Hanun the **s** of Nahash, 2 Sm 10:2
Abimelech the **s** of Jerubbesheth? 2 Sm 11:21
became his wife and bore him a **s**. 2 Sm 11:27
and lay with her, and she bore a **s**, 2 Sm 12:24
Now Absalom, David's **s**, had a 2 Sm 13:1
And after a time Amnon, David's **s**, 2 Sm 13:1
name was Jonadab, the **s** of Shimeah, 2 Sm 13:3
And he said to him, "O **s** of the king, 2 Sm 13:4
the king said to Absalom, "No, my **s**, 2 Sm 13:25
But Jonadab the **s** of Shimeah, 2 Sm 13:32
went to Talmai the **s** of Ammihud, 2 Sm 13:37
mourned for his **s** day after day. 2 Sm 13:37
Now Joab the **s** of Zeruiah knew that 2 Sm 14:1
and my **s** be not destroyed." He said, 2 Sm 14:11
not one hair of your **s** shall fall to the 2 Sm 14:11
me and my **s** together from the 2 Sm 14:16
with your two sons, Ahimaaz your **s**, 2 Sm 15:27
son, and Jonathan the **s** of Abiathar. 2 Sm 15:27
them there, Ahimaaz, Zadok's **s**, 2 Sm 15:36
son, and Jonathan, Abiathar's **s**, 2 Sm 15:36
where is your master's **s**?" Ziba said to 2 Sm 16:3
name was Shimei, the **s** of Gera, 2 Sm 16:5
into the hand of your **s** Absalom. 2 Sm 16:8
Then Abishai the **s** of Zeruiah said to 2 Sm 16:9
"Behold, my own **s** seeks my life; 2 Sm 16:11
I serve? Should it not be his **s**? 2 Sm 16:19
Amasa was the **s** of a man named 2 Sm 17:25
Shobi the **s** of Nahash from Rabbah 2 Sm 17:27
and Machir the **s** of Ammiel from 2 Sm 17:27
of Abishai the **s** of Zeruiah, 2 Sm 18:2
out my hand against the king's **s**, 2 Sm 18:12
"I have no **s** to keep my name in 2 Sm 18:18
Then Ahimaaz the **s** of Zadok said, 2 Sm 18:19
news, because the king's **s** is dead." 2 Sm 18:20
Then Ahimaaz the **s** of Zadok said 2 Sm 18:22
Joab said, "Why will you run, my **s**, 2 Sm 18:22
of Ahimaaz the **s** of Zadok." And 2 Sm 18:27
he went, he said, "O my **s** Absalom, 2 Sm 18:33
he said, "O my son Absalom, my **s**, 2 Sm 18:33
Absalom, my son, my **s** Absalom! 2 Sm 18:33
instead of you, O Absalom, my **s**, 2 Sm 18:33
of you, O Absalom, my son, my **s**!" 2 Sm 18:33
day, "The king is grieving for his **s**." 2 Sm 19:2
with a loud voice, "O my **s** Absalom, 2 Sm 19:4
my son Absalom, O Absalom, my **s**, 2 Sm 19:4
Absalom, O Absalom, my son, my **s**!" 2 Sm 19:4
And Shimei the **s** of Gera, the 2 Sm 19:16
And Shimei the **s** of Gera fell down 2 Sm 19:18
Abishai the **s** of Zeruiah answered, 2 Sm 19:21
And Mephibosheth the **s** of Saul 2 Sm 19:24
name was Sheba, the **s** of Bichri, 2 Sm 20:1
have no inheritance in the **s** of Jesse; 2 Sm 20:1
and followed Sheba the **s** of Bichri. 2 Sm 20:2
"Now Sheba the **s** of Bichri will do us 2 Sm 20:6
to pursue Sheba the **s** of Bichri. 2 Sm 20:7
pursued Sheba the **s** of Bichri. 2 Sm 20:10
Joab to pursue Sheba the **s** of Bichri. 2 Sm 20:13
called Sheba the **s** of Bichri, 2 Sm 20:21
head of Sheba the **s** of Bichri and 2 Sm 20:22
and Benaiah the **s** of Jehoiada was in 2 Sm 20:23
and Jehoshaphat the **s** of Ahilud was 2 Sm 20:24
the **s** of Saul's son Jonathan, 2 Sm 21:7
the son of Saul's **s** Jonathan, 2 Sm 21:7
David and Jonathan the **s** of Saul. 2 Sm 21:7
bore to Adriel the **s** of Barzillai the 2 Sm 21:8
the bones of his **s** Jonathan from the 2 Sm 21:12
Saul and the bones of his **s** Jonathan; 2 Sm 21:13
of Saul and his **s** Jonathan in the 2 Sm 21:14
But Abishai the **s** of Zeruiah came to 2 Sm 21:17
and Elhanan the **s** of Jaare-oregim, 2 Sm 21:19
Israel, Jonathan the **s** of Shimei, 2 Sm 21:21
The oracle of David, the **s** of Jesse, the 2 Sm 23:1
men was Eleazar the **s** of Dodo, 2 Sm 23:9
Eleazar the son of Dodo, **s** of Ahohi. 2 Sm 23:9
the **s** of Agee the Hararite. 2 Sm 23:11
the brother of Joab, the **s** of Zeruiah, 2 Sm 23:18
And Benaiah the **s** of Jehoiada was a 2 Sm 23:20
things did Benaiah the **s** of Jehoiada, 2 Sm 23:22
Elhanan the **s** of Dodo of Bethlehem, 2 Sm 23:24
Paltite, Ira the **s** of Ikkesh of Tekoa, 2 Sm 23:26
Heleb the **s** of Baanah of Netophah, 2 Sm 23:29
Ittai the **s** of Ribai of Gibeah of the 2 Sm 23:29
Ahiam the **s** of Sharar the Hararite, 2 Sm 23:33
Eliphelet the **s** of Ahasbai of 2 Sm 23:34
Eliam the **s** of Ahithophel of Gilo, 2 Sm 23:34
Igal the **s** of Nathan of Zobah, Bani 2 Sm 23:36

of Joab the **s** of Zeruiah, 2 Sm 23:37
Now Adonijah the **s** of Haggith exalted 1 Kgs 1:5
with Joab the **s** of Zeruiah and 1 Kgs 1:7
and Benaiah the **s** of Jehoiada and 1 Kgs 1:8
that Adonijah the **s** of Haggith has 1 Kgs 1:11
life and the life of your **s** Solomon. 1 Kgs 1:12
"Solomon your **s** shall reign after me, 1 Kgs 1:13
'Solomon your **s** shall reign after me, 1 Kgs 1:17
that I and my **s** Solomon will be 1 Kgs 1:21
priest, and Benaiah the **s** of Jehoiada, 1 Kgs 1:26
'Solomon your **s** shall reign after me, 1 Kgs 1:30
and Benaiah the **s** of Jehoiada." So 1 Kgs 1:32
and have Solomon my **s** ride on my 1 Kgs 1:33
And Benaiah the **s** of Jehoiada 1 Kgs 1:36
and Benaiah the **s** of Jehoiada, 1 Kgs 1:38
Jonathan the **s** of Abiathar the priest 1 Kgs 1:42
and Benaiah the **s** of Jehoiada, 1 Kgs 1:44
near, he commanded Solomon his **s**, 1 Kgs 2:1
know what Joab the **s** of Zeruiah did to 1 Kgs 2:5
the armies of Israel, Abner the **s** of Ner, 1 Kgs 2:5
son of Ner, and Amasa the **s** of Jether, 1 Kgs 2:5
is also with you Shimei the **s** of Gera, 1 Kgs 2:8
Then Adonijah the **s** of Haggith 1 Kgs 2:13
the priest and Joab the **s** of Zeruiah." 1 Kgs 2:22
sent Benaiah the **s** of Jehoiada, 1 Kgs 2:25
sent Benaiah the **s** of Jehoiada, 1 Kgs 2:29
than himself, Abner the **s** of Ner, 1 Kgs 2:32
of Israel, and Amasa the **s** of Jether, 1 Kgs 2:32
Then Benaiah the **s** of Jehoiada went 1 Kgs 2:34
put Benaiah the **s** of Jehoiada over 1 Kgs 2:35
ran away to Achish, **s** of Maacah, 1 Kgs 2:39
Benaiah the **s** of Jehoiada, 1 Kgs 2:46
and have given him a **s** to sit on his 1 Kgs 3:6
And this woman's **s** died in the night, 1 Kgs 3:19
and took my **s** from beside me, 1 Kgs 3:20
and laid her dead **s** at my breast. 1 Kgs 3:20
one says, 'This is my **s** that is alive, 1 Kgs 3:23
son that is alive, and your **s** is dead'; 1 Kgs 3:23
the other says, 'No; but your **s** is dead, 1 Kgs 3:23
is dead, and my **s** is the living one.'" 1 Kgs 3:23
the woman whose **s** was alive said 1 Kgs 3:26
because her heart yearned for her **s**, 1 Kgs 3:26
Azariah the **s** of Zadok was the priest; 1 Kgs 4:2
Jehoshaphat the **s** of Ahilud was 1 Kgs 4:3
Benaiah the **s** of Jehoiada was in 1 Kgs 4:4
Azariah the **s** of Nathan was over the 1 Kgs 4:5
Zabud the **s** of Nathan was priest and 1 Kgs 4:5
and Adoniram the **s** of Abda was in 1 Kgs 4:6
Baana the **s** of Ahilud, in Taanach, 1 Kgs 4:12
the villages of Jair the **s** of Manasseh, 1 Kgs 4:13
Ahinadab the **s** of Iddo, in 1 Kgs 4:14
Baana the **s** of Hushai, in Asher and 1 Kgs 4:16
Jehoshaphat the **s** of Paruah, in 1 Kgs 4:17
Shimei the **s** of Ela, in Benjamin; 1 Kgs 4:18
Geber the **s** of Uri, in the land of 1 Kgs 4:19
LORD said to David my father, 'Your **s**, 1 Kgs 5:5
given to David a wise **s** to be over this 1 Kgs 5:7
He was the **s** of a widow of the tribe of 1 Kgs 7:14
but your **s** who shall be born to you 1 Kgs 8:19
will tear it out of the hand of your **s**. 1 Kgs 11:12
but I will give one tribe to your **s**, 1 Kgs 11:13
Tahpenes bore him Genubath his **s**, 1 Kgs 11:20
to him, Rezon the **s** of Eliada, 1 Kgs 11:23
Jeroboam the **s** of Nebat, an 1 Kgs 11:26
Yet to his **s** I will give one tribe, that 1 Kgs 11:36
And Rehoboam his **s** reigned in his 1 Kgs 11:43
as Jeroboam the **s** of Nebat heard 1 Kgs 12:2
to Jeroboam the **s** of Nebat. 1 Kgs 12:15
have no inheritance in the **s** of Jesse. 1 Kgs 12:16
to Rehoboam the **s** of Solomon. 1 Kgs 12:21
"Say to Rehoboam the **s** of Solomon, 1 Kgs 12:23
a **s** shall be born to the house of 1 Kgs 13:2
time Abijah the **s** of Jeroboam fell 1 Kgs 14:1
to inquire of you concerning her **s**, 1 Kgs 14:5
and Nadab his **s** reigned in his 1 Kgs 14:20
Now Rehoboam the **s** of Solomon 1 Kgs 14:21
And Abijam his **s** reigned in his 1 Kgs 14:31
year of King Jeroboam the **s** of Nebat, 1 Kgs 15:1
Jerusalem, setting up his **s** after him, 1 Kgs 15:4
And Asa his **s** reigned in his place. 1 Kgs 15:8
to Ben-hadad the **s** of Tabrimmon, 1 Kgs 15:18
son of Tabrimmon, the **s** of Hezion, 1 Kgs 15:18
and Jehoshaphat his **s** reigned in his 1 Kgs 15:24
Nadab the **s** of Jeroboam began to 1 Kgs 15:25
Baasha the **s** of Ahijah, of the house 1 Kgs 15:27
Baasha the **s** of Ahijah began to 1 Kgs 15:33
came to Jehu the **s** of Hanani against 1 Kgs 16:1
the house of Jeroboam the **s** of Nebat. 1 Kgs 16:3
and Elah his **s** reigned in his place. 1 Kgs 16:6
prophet Jehu the **s** of Hanani against 1 Kgs 16:7
Elah the **s** of Baasha began to reign 1 Kgs 16:8
of Baasha and the sins of Elah his **s**, 1 Kgs 16:13
followed Tibni the **s** of Ginath, 1 Kgs 16:21
who followed Tibni the **s** of Ginath. 1 Kgs 16:22
the way of Jeroboam the **s** of Nebat, 1 Kgs 16:26
and Ahab his **s** reigned in his place. 1 Kgs 16:28
Ahab the **s** of Omri began to reign 1 Kgs 16:29
and Ahab the **s** of Omri reigned over 1 Kgs 16:29
And Ahab the **s** of Omri did evil in 1 Kgs 16:30
the sins of Jeroboam the **s** of Nebat, 1 Kgs 16:31
at the cost of his youngest **s** Segub, 1 Kgs 16:34
he spoke by Joshua the **s** of Nun. 1 Kgs 16:34
and prepare it for myself and my **s**, 1 Kgs 17:12
something for yourself and your **s**. 1 Kgs 17:13
After this the **s** of the woman, the 1 Kgs 17:17
and to cause the death of my **s**!" 1 Kgs 17:18
"Give me your **s**." And he took him 1 Kgs 17:19
whom I sojourn, by killing her **s**?" 1 Kgs 17:20
And Elijah said, "See, your **s** lives." 1 Kgs 17:23
And Jehu the **s** of Nimshi you shall 1 Kgs 19:16
and Elisha the **s** of Shaphat of 1 Kgs 19:16
and found Elisha the **s** of Shaphat, 1 Kgs 19:19
house of Jeroboam the **s** of Nebat, 1 Kgs 21:22
the house of Baasha the **s** of Ahijah, 1 Kgs 21:22
of the LORD, Micaiah the **s** of Imlah, 1 Kgs 22:8
quickly Micaiah the **s** of Imlah." 1 Kgs 22:9
And Zedekiah the **s** of Chenaanah 1 Kgs 22:11
Then Zedekiah the **s** of Chenaanah 1 Kgs 22:24
of the city and to Joash the king's **s**, 1 Kgs 22:26
and Ahaziah his **s** reigned in his 1 Kgs 22:40
Jehoshaphat the **s** of Asa began to 1 Kgs 22:41
Then Ahaziah the **s** of Ahab said to 1 Kgs 22:49
and Jehoram his **s** reigned in his 1 Kgs 22:50
Ahaziah the **s** of Ahab began to 1 Kgs 22:51
the way of Jeroboam the **s** of Nebat, 1 Kgs 22:52
year of Jehoram the **s** of Jehoshaphat, 2 Kgs 1:17
of Judah, because Ahaziah had no **s**. 2 Kgs 1:17
Jehoram the **s** of Ahab became king 2 Kgs 3:1
to the sin of Jeroboam the **s** of Nebat, 2 Kgs 3:3
"Elisha the **s** of Shaphat is here, 2 Kgs 3:11
he took his oldest **s** who was to reign 2 Kgs 3:27
the vessels were full, she said to her **s**, 2 Kgs 4:6
Gehazi answered, "Well, she has no **s**, 2 Kgs 4:14
you shall embrace a **s**." And she said, 2 Kgs 4:16
and she bore a **s** about that time the 2 Kgs 4:17
she said, "Did I ask my lord for a **s**? 2 Kgs 4:28
to him, he said, "Pick up your **s**." 2 Kgs 4:36
she picked up her **s** and went out. 2 Kgs 4:37
woman said to me, 'Give your **s**, 2 Kgs 6:28
and we will eat my **s** tomorrow.' 2 Kgs 6:28
So we boiled my **s** and ate him. And 2 Kgs 6:29
the next day I said to her, 'Give your **s**, 2 Kgs 6:29
eat him.' But she has hidden her **s**." 2 Kgs 6:29
of Elisha the **s** of Shaphat remains 2 Kgs 6:31
to the woman whose **s** he had restored 2 Kgs 8:1
the woman whose **s** he had restored to 2 Kgs 8:5
and here is her **s** whom Elisha restored 2 Kgs 8:5
"Your **s** Ben-hadad king of Syria has 2 Kgs 8:9
the fifth year of Joram the **s** of Ahab, 2 Kgs 8:16
Judah, Jehoram the **s** of Jehoshaphat, 2 Kgs 8:16
and Ahaziah his **s** reigned in his 2 Kgs 8:24
twelfth year of Joram the **s** of Ahab, 2 Kgs 8:25
of Israel, Ahaziah the **s** of Jehoram, 2 Kgs 8:25
went with Joram the **s** of Ahab to 2 Kgs 8:28
And Ahaziah the **s** of Jehoram king 2 Kgs 8:29
to see Joram the **s** of Ahab in Jezreel, 2 Kgs 8:29
there for Jehu the **s** of Jehoshaphat, 2 Kgs 9:2
the son of Jehoshaphat, **s** of Nimshi. 2 Kgs 9:2
the house of Jeroboam the **s** of Nebat, 2 Kgs 9:9
the house of Baasha the **s** of Ahijah. 2 Kgs 9:9
Thus Jehu the **s** of Jehoshaphat the 2 Kgs 9:14
of Jehoshaphat the **s** of Nimshi 2 Kgs 9:14
the driving of Jehu the **s** of Nimshi, 2 Kgs 9:20
eleventh year of Joram the **s** of Ahab, 2 Kgs 9:29
met Jehonadab the **s** of Rechab 2 Kgs 10:15
with Jehonadab the **s** of Rechab, 2 Kgs 10:23
the sins of Jeroboam the **s** of Nebat, 2 Kgs 10:29
And Jehoahaz his **s** reigned in his 2 Kgs 10:35
of Ahaziah saw that her **s** was dead, 2 Kgs 11:1
took Joash the **s** of Ahaziah and stole 2 Kgs 11:2
and he showed them the king's **s**. 2 Kgs 11:4
brought out the king's **s** and put the 2 Kgs 11:12
It was Jozacar the **s** of Shimeath and 2 Kgs 12:21
and Jehozabad the **s** of Shomer, 2 Kgs 12:21
and Amaziah his **s** reigned in his 2 Kgs 12:21
year of Joash the **s** of Ahaziah, 2 Kgs 13:1
Jehoahaz the **s** of Jehu began to reign 2 Kgs 13:1
the sins of Jeroboam the **s** of Nebat, 2 Kgs 13:2
hand of Ben-hadad the **s** of Hazael. 2 Kgs 13:3
and Joash his **s** reigned in his place. 2 Kgs 13:9
Jehoash the **s** of Jehoahaz began to 2 Kgs 13:10
the sins of Jeroboam the **s** of Nebat, 2 Kgs 13:11
Ben-hadad his **s** became king in his 2 Kgs 13:24
Then Jehoash the **s** of Jehoahaz took 2 Kgs 13:25
from Ben-hadad the **s** of Hazael the 2 Kgs 13:25
second year of Joash the **s** of Joahaz, 2 Kgs 14:1
king of Israel, Amaziah the **s** of Joash, 2 Kgs 14:1
to Jehoash the **s** of Jehoahaz, 2 Kgs 14:8
Jehoash the son of Jehoahaz, **s** of Jehu, 2 Kgs 14:8
your daughter to my **s** for a wife,' 2 Kgs 14:9
king of Judah, the **s** of Jehoash, 2 Kgs 14:13
the son of Jehoash, **s** of Ahaziah, 2 Kgs 14:13
and Jeroboam his **s** reigned in his 2 Kgs 14:16
Amaziah the **s** of Joash, king of 2 Kgs 14:17
the death of Jehoash **s** of Jehoahaz, 2 Kgs 14:17
year of Amaziah the **s** of Joash, 2 Kgs 14:23
of Judah, Jeroboam the **s** of Joash, 2 Kgs 14:23
the sins of Jeroboam the **s** of Nebat, 2 Kgs 14:24
his servant Jonah the **s** of Amittai, 2 Kgs 14:25
the hand of Jeroboam the **s** of Joash. 2 Kgs 14:27
and Zechariah his **s** reigned in his 2 Kgs 14:29
of Israel, Azariah the **s** of Amaziah, 2 Kgs 15:1
And Jotham the king's **s** was over the 2 Kgs 15:5
and Jotham his **s** reigned in his place. 2 Kgs 15:7
Zechariah the **s** of Jeroboam reigned 2 Kgs 15:8
the sins of Jeroboam the **s** of Nebat, 2 Kgs 15:9
Shallum the **s** of Jabesh conspired 2 Kgs 15:10
Shallum the **s** of Jabesh began to 2 Kgs 15:13
Then Menahem the **s** of Gadi came 2 Kgs 15:14
down Shallum the **s** of Jabesh in 2 Kgs 15:14
Menahem the **s** of Gadi began to 2 Kgs 15:17
the sins of Jeroboam the **s** of Nebat, 2 Kgs 15:18
and Pekahiah his **s** reigned in his 2 Kgs 15:22
Pekahiah the **s** of Menahem began 2 Kgs 15:23
the sins of Jeroboam the **s** of Nebat, 2 Kgs 15:24
And Pekah the **s** of Remaliah, his 2 Kgs 15:25
Pekah the **s** of Remaliah began to 2 Kgs 15:27
the sins of Jeroboam the **s** of Nebat, 2 Kgs 15:28
Then Hoshea the **s** of Elah made a 2 Kgs 15:30
against Pekah the **s** of Remaliah 2 Kgs 15:30
year of Jotham the **s** of Uzziah. 2 Kgs 15:30
year of Pekah the **s** of Remaliah, 2 Kgs 15:32
of Israel, Jotham the **s** of Uzziah, 2 Kgs 15:32
and Pekah the **s** of Remaliah 2 Kgs 15:37
and Ahaz his **s** reigned in his place. 2 Kgs 15:38
year of Pekah the **s** of Remaliah, 2 Kgs 16:1
of Remaliah, Ahaz the **s** of Jotham, 2 Kgs 16:1
He even burned his **s** as an offering, 2 Kgs 16:3
of Syria and Pekah the **s** of Remaliah, 2 Kgs 16:5
"I am your servant and your **s**. 2 Kgs 16:7
and Hezekiah his **s** reigned in his 2 Kgs 16:20
Hoshea the **s** of Elah began to reign 2 Kgs 17:1
made Jeroboam the **s** of Nebat king. 2 Kgs 17:21
In the third year of Hoshea **s** of Elah, 2 Kgs 18:1
king of Israel, Hezekiah the **s** of Ahaz, 2 Kgs 18:1
the seventh year of Hoshea **s** of Elah, 2 Kgs 18:9
to them Eliakim the **s** of Hilkiah, 2 Kgs 18:18
secretary, and Joah the **s** of Asaph, 2 Kgs 18:18
Then Eliakim the **s** of Hilkiah, and 2 Kgs 18:26
Then Eliakim the **s** of Hilkiah, who 2 Kgs 18:37
secretary, and Joah the **s** of Asaph, 2 Kgs 18:37
to the prophet Isaiah the **s** of Amoz. 2 Kgs 19:2
Then Isaiah the **s** of Amoz sent to 2 Kgs 19:20
And Esarhaddon his **s** reigned in his 2 Kgs 19:37
the prophet the **s** of Amoz came 2 Kgs 20:1
Merodach-baladan the **s** of Baladan, 2 Kgs 20:12
and Manasseh his **s** reigned in his 2 Kgs 20:21
And he burned his **s** as an offering 2 Kgs 21:6
said to David and to Solomon his **s**, 2 Kgs 21:7
and Amon his **s** reigned in his place. 2 Kgs 21:18
land made Josiah his **s** king in his 2 Kgs 21:24
and Josiah his **s** reigned in his place. 2 Kgs 21:26
king sent Shaphan the **s** of Azaliah, 2 Kgs 22:3
the son of Azaliah, **s** of Meshullam, 2 Kgs 22:3
and Ahikam the **s** of Shaphan, 2 Kgs 22:12
and Achbor the **s** of Micaiah, 2 Kgs 22:12
the wife of Shallum the **s** of Tikvah, 2 Kgs 22:14
the son of Tikvah, **s** of Harhas, 2 Kgs 22:14
is in the Valley of the **S** of Hinnom, 2 Kgs 23:10
might burn his **s** or his daughter 2 Kgs 23:10
erected by Jeroboam the **s** of Nebat, 2 Kgs 23:15
land took Jehoahaz the **s** of Josiah, 2 Kgs 23:30
made Eliakim the **s** of Josiah king 2 Kgs 23:34
and Jehoiachin his **s** reigned in his 2 Kgs 24:6
Gedaliah the **s** of Ahikam, 2 Kgs 25:22
the son of Ahikam, **s** of Shaphan, 2 Kgs 25:22
namely, Ishmael the **s** of Nethaniah, 2 Kgs 25:23
and Johanan the **s** of Kareah, 2 Kgs 25:23
and Seraiah the **s** of Tanhumeth the 2 Kgs 25:23
and Jaazaniah the **s** of the 2 Kgs 25:23
month, Ishmael the **s** of Nethaniah, 2 Kgs 25:25
the son of Nethaniah, **s** of Elishama, 2 Kgs 25:25
The **s** of Anah: Dishon. The sons of 1 Chr 1:41
the people of Israel: Bela the **s** of Beor, 1 Chr 1:43
and Jobab the **s** of Zerah of Bozrah 1 Chr 1:44
died, and Hadad the **s** of Bedad, 1 Chr 1:46
and Baal-hanan, the **s** of Achbor, 1 Chr 1:49
The **s** of Carmi: Achan, the troubler of 1 Chr 2:7
and Ethan's **s** was Azariah. 1 Chr 2:8
Caleb the **s** of Hezron fathered 1 Chr 2:18
The **s** of Appaim: Ishi. The son of 1 Chr 2:31
Appaim: Ishi. The **s** of Ishi: Sheshan. 1 Chr 2:31
Sheshan. The **s** of Sheshan: Ahlai. 1 Chr 2:31
Ziph. The **s** of Mareshah: Hebron. 1 Chr 2:42
The **s** of Shammai: Maon; and Maon 1 Chr 2:45

The **s** of Solomon was Rehoboam, 1 Chr 3:10
was Rehoboam, Abijah his **s**, 1 Chr 3:10
Rehoboam, Abijah his son, Asa his **s**, 1 Chr 3:10
son, Asa his son, Jehoshaphat his **s**, 1 Chr 3:10
Joram his **s**, Ahaziah his son, Joash 1 Chr 3:11
Joram his son, Ahaziah his **s**, Joash 1 Chr 3:11
his son, Ahaziah his son, Joash his **s**, 1 Chr 3:11
Amaziah his **s**, Azariah his son, 1 Chr 3:12
Amaziah his son, Azariah his **s**, 1 Chr 3:12
son, Azariah his son, Jotham his **s**, 1 Chr 3:12
Ahaz his **s**, Hezekiah his son, 1 Chr 3:13
Ahaz his son, Hezekiah his **s**, 1 Chr 3:13
Hezekiah his son, Manasseh his **s**, 1 Chr 3:13
Amon his **s**, Josiah his son. 1 Chr 3:14
Amon his son, Josiah his **s**. 1 Chr 3:14
Jeconiah his **s**, Zedekiah his son; 1 Chr 3:16
Jeconiah his son, Zedekiah his **s**; 1 Chr 3:16
Jeconiah, the captive: Shealtiel his **s**, 1 Chr 3:17
and Jeshaiah, his **s** Rephaiah, 1 Chr 3:21
his son Rephaiah, his **s** Arnan, 1 Chr 3:21
his son Arnan, his **s** Obadiah, 1 Chr 3:21
his son Obadiah, his **s** Shecaniah. 1 Chr 3:21
The **s** of Shecaniah: Shemaiah. And 1 Chr 3:22
Reaiah the **s** of Shobal fathered Jahath, 1 Chr 4:2
the clans of Aharhel, the **s** of Harum. 1 Chr 4:8
sons of Caleb the **s** of Jephunneh: 1 Chr 4:15
Elah, and Naam; and the **s** of Elah: 1 Chr 4:15
The sons of Shelah the **s** of Judah: Er 1 Chr 4:21
Shallum was his **s**, Mibsam his son, 1 Chr 4:25
Shallum was his son, Mibsam his **s**, 1 Chr 4:25
son, Mibsam his son, Mishma his **s**. 1 Chr 4:25
Hammuel his **s**, Zaccur his son, 1 Chr 4:26
Hammuel his son, Zaccur his **s**, 1 Chr 4:26
his son, Zaccur his son, Shimei his **s**. 1 Chr 4:26
Jamlech, Joshah the **s** of Amaziah, 1 Chr 4:34
Joel, Jehu the **s** of Joshibiah, son of 1 Chr 4:35
the son of Joshibiah, **s** of Seraiah, 1 Chr 4:35
Joshibiah, son of Seraiah, **s** of Asiel, 1 Chr 4:35
Ziza the **s** of Shiphi, son of Allon, son 1 Chr 4:37
Ziza the son of Shiphi, **s** of Allon, son 1 Chr 4:37
of Shiphi, son of Allon, **s** of Jedaiah, 1 Chr 4:37
of Allon, son of Jedaiah, **s** of Shimri, 1 Chr 4:37
son of Shimri, **s** of Shemaiah— 1 Chr 4:37
to the sons of Joseph the **s** of Israel, 1 Chr 5:1
he could not be enrolled as the oldest **s**; 1 Chr 5:1
Shemaiah his **s**, Gog his son, Shimei 1 Chr 5:4
Shemaiah his son, Gog his **s**, Shimei 1 Chr 5:4
his son, Gog his son, Shimei his **s**, 1 Chr 5:4
Micah his **s**, Reaiah his son, Baal his 1 Chr 5:5
Micah his son, Reaiah his **s**, Baal his 1 Chr 5:5
his son, Reaiah his son, Baal his **s**, 1 Chr 5:5
Beerah his **s**, whom Tiglath-pileser 1 Chr 5:6
and Bela the **s** of Azaz, son of Shema, 1 Chr 5:8
and Bela the son of Azaz, **s** of Shema, 1 Chr 5:8
the son of Azaz, son of Shema, **s** of Joel, 1 Chr 5:8
were the sons of Abihail the **s** of Huri, 1 Chr 5:14
Abihail the son of Huri, **s** of Jaroah, 1 Chr 5:14
son of Huri, son of Jaroah, **s** of Gilead, 1 Chr 5:14
of Jaroah, son of Gilead, **s** of Michael, 1 Chr 5:14
Gilead, son of Michael, **s** of Jeshishai, 1 Chr 5:14
Michael, son of Jeshishai, **s** of Jahdo, 1 Chr 5:14
of Jeshishai, son of Jahdo, **s** of Buz. 1 Chr 5:14
Ahi the **s** of Abdiel, son of Guni, was 1 Chr 5:15
Ahi the son of Abdiel, **s** of Guni, was 1 Chr 5:15
Libni his **s**, Jahath his son, Zimmah 1 Chr 6:20
Libni his son, Jahath his **s**, Zimmah 1 Chr 6:20
son, Jahath his son, Zimmah his **s**, 1 Chr 6:20
Joah his **s**, Iddo his son, Zerah his 1 Chr 6:21
Joah his son, Iddo his **s**, Zerah his 1 Chr 6:21
his son, Iddo his son, Zerah his **s**, 1 Chr 6:21
his son, Zerah his son, Jeatherai his **s**. 1 Chr 6:21
Amminadab his **s**, Korah his son, 1 Chr 6:22
Amminadab his son, Korah his **s**, 1 Chr 6:22
his son, Korah his son, Assir his **s**, 1 Chr 6:22
Elkanah his **s**, Ebiasaph his son, 1 Chr 6:23
Elkanah his son, Ebiasaph his **s**, 1 Chr 6:23
his son, Ebiasaph his son, Assir his **s**, 1 Chr 6:23
Tahath his **s**, Uriel his son, Uzziah 1 Chr 6:24
Tahath his son, Uriel his **s**, Uzziah 1 Chr 6:24
his son, Uriel his son, Uzziah his **s**, 1 Chr 6:24
son, Uzziah his son, and Shaul his **s**. 1 Chr 6:24
Elkanah his **s**, Zophai his son, 1 Chr 6:26
Elkanah his son, Zophai his **s**, 1 Chr 6:26
son, Zophai his son, Nahath his **s**, 1 Chr 6:26
Eliab his **s**, Jeroham his son, 1 Chr 6:27
Eliab his son, Jeroham his **s**, 1 Chr 6:27
son, Jeroham his son, Elkanah his **s**. 1 Chr 6:27
Mahli, Libni his **s**, Shimei his son, 1 Chr 6:29
Mahli, Libni his son, Shimei his **s**, 1 Chr 6:29
his son, Shimei his son, Uzzah his **s**, 1 Chr 6:29
Shimea his **s**, Haggiah his son, and 1 Chr 6:30
Shimea his son, Haggiah his **s**, and 1 Chr 6:30
Haggiah his son, and Asaiah his **s**. 1 Chr 6:30
Heman the singer the **s** of Joel, son of 1 Chr 6:33
the singer the son of Joel, **s** of Samuel, 1 Chr 6:33
s of Elkanah, son of Jeroham, son of 1 Chr 6:34
son of Elkanah, **s** of Jeroham, son of 1 Chr 6:34
of Elkanah, son of Jeroham, **s** of Eliel, 1 Chr 6:34
of Jeroham, son of Eliel, **s** of Toah, 1 Chr 6:34
s of Zuph, son of Elkanah, son of 1 Chr 6:35
son of Zuph, **s** of Elkanah, son of 1 Chr 6:35
Zuph, son of Elkanah, **s** of Mahath, 1 Chr 6:35
son of Mahath, **s** of Amasai, 1 Chr 6:35
s of Elkanah, son of Joel, son of 1 Chr 6:36
son of Elkanah, **s** of Joel, son of 1 Chr 6:36
of Elkanah, son of Joel, **s** of Azariah, 1 Chr 6:36
Joel, son of Azariah, **s** of Zephaniah, 1 Chr 6:36
s of Tahath, son of Assir, son of 1 Chr 6:37
son of Tahath, **s** of Assir, son of 1 Chr 6:37
Tahath, son of Assir, **s** of Ebiasaph, 1 Chr 6:37
of Assir, son of Ebiasaph, **s** of Korah, 1 Chr 6:37
s of Izhar, son of Kohath, son of Levi, 1 Chr 6:38
son of Izhar, **s** of Kohath, son of Levi, 1 Chr 6:38
son of Izhar, son of Kohath, **s** of Levi, 1 Chr 6:38
son of Kohath, son of Levi, **s** of Israel; 1 Chr 6:38
namely, Asaph the **s** of Berechiah, 1 Chr 6:39
the son of Berechiah, **s** of Shimea, 1 Chr 6:39
s of Michael, son of Baaseiah, son of 1 Chr 6:40
son of Michael, **s** of Baaseiah, son of 1 Chr 6:40
son of Baaseiah, **s** of Malchijah, 1 Chr 6:40
s of Ethni, son of Zerah, son of 1 Chr 6:41
son of Ethni, **s** of Zerah, son of 1 Chr 6:41
of Ethni, son of Zerah, **s** of Adaiah, 1 Chr 6:41
s of Ethan, son of Zimmah, son of 1 Chr 6:42
son of Ethan, **s** of Zimmah, son of 1 Chr 6:42
Ethan, son of Zimmah, **s** of Shimei, 1 Chr 6:42
s of Jahath, son of Gershom, son of 1 Chr 6:43
son of Jahath, **s** of Gershom, son of 1 Chr 6:43
of Jahath, son of Gershom, **s** of Levi. 1 Chr 6:43
sons of Merari: Ethan the **s** of Kishi, 1 Chr 6:44
Ethan the son of Kishi, **s** of Abdi, son 1 Chr 6:44
of Kishi, son of Abdi, **s** of Malluch, 1 Chr 6:44
s of Hashabiah, son of Amaziah, son 1 Chr 6:45
son of Hashabiah, **s** of Amaziah, son 1 Chr 6:45
son of Amaziah, **s** of Hilkiah, 1 Chr 6:45
s of Amzi, son of Bani, son of Shemer, 1 Chr 6:46
son of Amzi, **s** of Bani, son of Shemer, 1 Chr 6:46
son of Amzi, son of Bani, **s** of Shemer, 1 Chr 6:46
s of Mahli, son of Mushi, son of 1 Chr 6:47
son of Mahli, **s** of Mushi, son of 1 Chr 6:47
of Mahli, son of Mushi, **s** of Merari, 1 Chr 6:47
son of Mushi, son of Merari, **s** of Levi. 1 Chr 6:47
Eleazar his **s**, Phinehas his son, 1 Chr 6:50
Eleazar his son, Phinehas his **s**, 1 Chr 6:50
son, Phinehas his son, Abishua his **s**, 1 Chr 6:50
Bukki his **s**, Uzzi his son, Zerahiah 1 Chr 6:51
Bukki his son, Uzzi his **s**, Zerahiah 1 Chr 6:51
his son, Uzzi his son, Zerahiah his **s**, 1 Chr 6:51
Meraioth his **s**, Amariah his son, 1 Chr 6:52
Meraioth his son, Amariah his **s**, 1 Chr 6:52
son, Amariah his son, Ahitub his **s**, 1 Chr 6:52
Zadok his **s**, Ahimaaz his son. 1 Chr 6:53
Zadok his son, Ahimaaz his **s**. 1 Chr 6:53
gave to Caleb the **s** of Jephunneh. 1 Chr 6:56
The **s** of Uzzi: Izrahiah. And the sons 1 Chr 7:3
The **s** of Jediael: Bilhan. And the sons 1 Chr 7:10
the sons of Ir, Hushim the **s** of Aher. 1 Chr 7:12
Maacah the wife of Machir bore a **s**, 1 Chr 7:16
The **s** of Ulam: Bedan. These were the 1 Chr 7:17
the sons of Gilead the **s** of Machir, 1 Chr 7:17
the son of Machir, **s** of Manasseh. 1 Chr 7:17
Shuthelah, and Bered his **s**, Tahath 1 Chr 7:20
and Bered his son, Tahath his **s**, 1 Chr 7:20
son, Tahath his son, Eleadah his **s**, 1 Chr 7:20
son, Eleadah his son, Tahath his **s**, 1 Chr 7:20
Zabad his **s**, Shuthelah his son, and 1 Chr 7:21
Zabad his son, Shuthelah his **s**, and 1 Chr 7:21
wife, and she conceived and bore a **s**. 1 Chr 7:23
Rephah was his **s**, Resheph his son, 1 Chr 7:25
Rephah was his son, Resheph his **s**, 1 Chr 7:25
his son, Resheph his son, Telah his **s**, 1 Chr 7:25
his son, Telah his son, Tahan his **s**, 1 Chr 7:25
Ladan his **s**, Ammihud his son, 1 Chr 7:26
Ladan his son, Ammihud his **s**, 1 Chr 7:26
Ammihud his son, Elishama his **s**, 1 Chr 7:26
Nun his **s**, Joshua his son. 1 Chr 7:27
Nun his son, Joshua his **s**. 1 Chr 7:27
lived the sons of Joseph the **s** of Israel. 1 Chr 7:29
His firstborn **s**: Abdon, then Zur, 1 Chr 8:30
and the **s** of Jonathan was 1 Chr 8:34
Raphah was his **s**, Eleasah his son, 1 Chr 8:37
Raphah was his son, Eleasah his **s**, 1 Chr 8:37
his son, Eleasah his son, Azel his **s**. 1 Chr 8:37
Uthai the **s** of Ammihud, son of Omri, 1 Chr 9:4
Uthai the son of Ammihud, **s** of Omri, 1 Chr 9:4
of Ammihud, son of Omri, **s** of Imri, 1 Chr 9:4
son of Omri, son of Imri, **s** of Bani, 1 Chr 9:4
from the sons of Perez the **s** of Judah. 1 Chr 9:4
Sallu the **s** of Meshullam, 1 Chr 9:7
the son of Meshullam, **s** of Hodaviah, 1 Chr 9:7
son of Hodaviah, **s** of Hassenuah, 1 Chr 9:7
Ibneiah the **s** of Jeroham, Elah the son 1 Chr 9:8
the son of Jeroham, Elah the **s** of Uzzi, 1 Chr 9:8
Elah the son of Uzzi, **s** of Michri, 1 Chr 9:8
and Meshullam the **s** of Shephatiah, 1 Chr 9:8
the son of Shephatiah, **s** of Reuel, 1 Chr 9:8
Shephatiah, son of Reuel, **s** of Ibnijah; 1 Chr 9:8
and Azariah the **s** of Hilkiah, son of 1 Chr 9:11
the son of Hilkiah, **s** of Meshullam, 1 Chr 9:11
son of Meshullam, **s** of Zadok, 1 Chr 9:11
son of Zadok, **s** of Meraioth, 1 Chr 9:11
Zadok, son of Meraioth, **s** of Ahitub, 1 Chr 9:11
and Adaiah the **s** of Jeroham, son of 1 Chr 9:12
the son of Jeroham, **s** of Pashhur, 1 Chr 9:12
son of Pashhur, **s** of Malchijah, 1 Chr 9:12
Malchijah, and Maasai the **s** of Adiel, 1 Chr 9:12
the son of Adiel, **s** of Jahzerah, 1 Chr 9:12
son of Jahzerah, **s** of Meshullam, 1 Chr 9:12
son of Meshullam, **s** of Meshillemith, 1 Chr 9:12
son of Meshillemith, **s** of Immer; 1 Chr 9:12
Levites: Shemaiah the **s** of Hasshub, 1 Chr 9:14
the son of Hasshub, **s** of Azrikam, 1 Chr 9:14
son of Azrikam, **s** of Hashabiah, 1 Chr 9:14
Galal and Mattaniah the **s** of Mica, 1 Chr 9:15
the son of Mica, **s** of Zichri, 1 Chr 9:15
of Mica, son of Zichri, **s** of Asaph; 1 Chr 9:15
and Obadiah the **s** of Shemaiah, son 1 Chr 9:16
the son of Shemaiah, **s** of Galal, 1 Chr 9:16
son of Galal, **s** of Jeduthun, 1 Chr 9:16
Jeduthun, and Berechiah the **s** of Asa, 1 Chr 9:16
the son of Asa, **s** of Elkanah, 1 Chr 9:16
Shallum the **s** of Kore, son of 1 Chr 9:19
the son of Kore, **s** of Ebiasaph, 1 Chr 9:19
of Kore, son of Ebiasaph, **s** of Korah, 1 Chr 9:19
And Phinehas the **s** of Eleazar was 1 Chr 9:20
Zechariah the **s** of Meshelemiah was 1 Chr 9:21
and his firstborn **s** Abdon, then Zur, 1 Chr 9:36
And the **s** of Jonathan was 1 Chr 9:40
Binea, and Rephaiah was his **s**, 1 Chr 9:43
Rephaiah was his son, Eleasah his **s**, 1 Chr 9:43
his son, Eleasah his son, Azel his **s**. 1 Chr 9:43
kingdom over to David the **s** of Jesse. 1 Chr 10:14
And Joab the **s** of Zeruiah went 1 Chr 11:6
men was Eleazar the **s** of Dodo, 1 Chr 11:12
And Benaiah the **s** of Jehoiada was a 1 Chr 11:22
did Benaiah the **s** of Jehoiada and 1 Chr 11:24
Elhanan the **s** of Dodo of 1 Chr 11:26
Ira the **s** of Ikkesh of Tekoa, Abiezer 1 Chr 11:28
Heled the **s** of Baanah of Netophah, 1 Chr 11:30
Ithai the **s** of Ribai of Gibeah of the 1 Chr 11:31
Jonathan the **s** of Shagee the 1 Chr 11:34
Ahiam the **s** of Sachar the Hararite, 1 Chr 11:35
the Hararite, Eliphal the **s** of Ur, 1 Chr 11:35
of Carmel, Naarai the **s** of Ezbai, 1 Chr 11:37
of Nathan, Mibhar the **s** of Hagri, 1 Chr 11:38
of Joab the **s** of Zeruiah, 1 Chr 11:39
the Hittite, Zabad the **s** of Ahlai, 1 Chr 11:41
Adina the **s** of Shiza the Reubenite, a 1 Chr 11:42
Hanan the **s** of Maacah, and 1 Chr 11:43
Jediael the **s** of Shimri, and Joha his 1 Chr 11:45
freely because of Saul the **s** of Kish. 1 Chr 12:1
O David, and with you, O **s** of Jesse! 1 Chr 12:18
appointed Heman the **s** of Joel; 1 Chr 15:17
brothers Asaph the **s** of Berechiah; 1 Chr 15:17
brothers, Ethan the **s** of Kushaiah; 1 Chr 15:17
while Obed-edom, the **s** of Jeduthun, 1 Chr 16:38
a father, and he shall be to me a **s**. 1 Chr 17:13
he sent his **s** Hadoram to King 1 Chr 18:10
And Abishai, the **s** of Zeruiah, 1 Chr 18:12
And Joab the **s** of Zeruiah was over 1 Chr 18:15
and Jehoshaphat the **s** of Ahilud 1 Chr 18:15
and Zadok the **s** of Ahitub and 1 Chr 18:16
and Ahimelech the **s** of Abiathar 1 Chr 18:16
and Benaiah the **s** of Jehoiada was 1 Chr 18:17
died, and his **s** reigned in his place. 1 Chr 19:1
kindly with Hanun the **s** of Nahash, 1 Chr 19:2
and Elhanan the **s** of Jair struck 1 Chr 20:5
Israel, Jonathan the **s** of Shimea, 1 Chr 20:7
"Solomon my **s** is young and 1 Chr 22:5
for Solomon his **s** and charged him 1 Chr 22:6
David said to Solomon, "My **s**, I had it 1 Chr 22:7
a **s** shall be born to you who shall be 1 Chr 22:9
He shall be my **s**, and I will be his 1 Chr 22:10
"Now, my **s**, the LORD be with you, 1 Chr 22:11
of Israel to help Solomon his **s**, 1 Chr 22:17
made Solomon his **s** king over Israel. 1 Chr 23:1
scribe Shemaiah, the **s** of Nethanel, 1 Chr 24:6
and Ahimelech the **s** of Abiathar and 1 Chr 24:6
Meshelemiah the **s** of Kore, 1 Chr 26:1
Also to his **s** Shemaiah were sons 1 Chr 26:6
cast lots also for his **s** Zechariah, 1 Chr 26:14
and Shebuel the **s** of Gershom, son 1 Chr 26:24
the son of Gershom, **s** of Moses, 1 Chr 26:24
from Eliezer were his **s** Rehabiah, 1 Chr 26:25
son Rehabiah, and his **s** Jeshaiah, 1 Chr 26:25

his son Jeshaiah, and his **s** Joram, 1 Chr 26:25
and his son Joram, and his **s** Zichri, 1 Chr 26:25
his son Zichri, and his **s** Shelomoth. 1 Chr 26:25
seer and Saul the **s** of Kish and 1 Chr 26:28
Kish and Abner the **s** of Ner and 1 Chr 26:28
Ner and Joab the **s** of Zeruiah had 1 Chr 26:28
Jashobeam the **s** of Zabdiel was in 1 Chr 27:2
the **s** of Jehoiada the chief priest; 1 Chr 27:5
Ammizabad his **s** was in charge of 1 Chr 27:6
month, and his **s** Zebadiah after him; 1 Chr 27:7
was Ira, the **s** of Ikkesh the Tekoite; 1 Chr 27:9
Eliezer the **s** of Zichri was chief 1 Chr 27:16
Shephatiah the **s** of Maacah; 1 Chr 27:16
Levi, Hashabiah the **s** of Kemuel; 1 Chr 27:17
for Issachar, Omri the **s** of Michael; 1 Chr 27:18
Ishmaiah the **s** of Obadiah; 1 Chr 27:19
Naphtali, Jeremoth the **s** of Azriel; 1 Chr 27:19
Hoshea the **s** of Azaziah; 1 Chr 27:20
of Manasseh, Joel the **s** of Pedaiah; 1 Chr 27:20
in Gilead, Iddo the **s** of Zechariah; 1 Chr 27:21
for Benjamin, Jaasiel the **s** of Abner; 1 Chr 27:21
for Dan, Azarel the **s** of Jeroham. 1 Chr 27:22
Joab the **s** of Zeruiah began to 1 Chr 27:24
was Azmaveth the **s** of Adiel; 1 Chr 27:25
was Jonathan the **s** of Uzziah; 1 Chr 27:25
the soil was Ezri the **s** of Chelub; 1 Chr 27:26
valleys was Shaphat the **s** of Adlai. 1 Chr 27:29
and Jehiel the **s** of Hachmoni 1 Chr 27:32
by Jehoiada the **s** of Benaiah, 1 Chr 27:34
has chosen Solomon my **s** to sit on 1 Chr 28:5
'It is Solomon your **s** who shall build 1 Chr 28:6
for I have chosen him to be my **s**, 1 Chr 28:6
"And you, Solomon my **s**, know the 1 Chr 28:9
gave Solomon his **s** the plan of 1 Chr 28:11
Then David said to Solomon his **s**, 1 Chr 28:20
to all the assembly, "Solomon my **s**, 1 Chr 29:1
to Solomon my **s** a whole heart 1 Chr 29:19
made Solomon the **s** of David king 1 Chr 29:22
Thus David the **s** of Jesse reigned 1 Chr 29:26
And Solomon his **s** reigned in his 1 Chr 29:28
Solomon the **s** of David established 2 Chr 1:1
bronze altar that Bezalel the **s** of Uri, 2 Chr 1:5
that Bezalel the son of Uri, **s** of Hur, 2 Chr 1:5
who has given King David a wise **s**, 2 Chr 2:12
the **s** of a woman of the daughters of 2 Chr 2:14
but your **s** who shall be born to you 2 Chr 6:9
concerning Jeroboam the **s** of Nebat? 2 Chr 9:29
and Rehoboam his **s** reigned in his 2 Chr 9:31
as Jeroboam the **s** of Nebat heard 2 Chr 10:2
to Jeroboam the **s** of Nebat. 2 Chr 10:15
have no inheritance in the **s** of Jesse. 2 Chr 10:16
"Say to Rehoboam the **s** of Solomon, 2 Chr 11:3
made Rehoboam the **s** of Solomon 2 Chr 11:17
daughter of Jerimoth the **s** of David, 2 Chr 11:18
the daughter of Eliab the **s** of Jesse, 2 Chr 11:18
appointed Abijah the **s** of Maacah 2 Chr 11:22
and Abijah his **s** reigned in his 2 Chr 12:16
Yet Jeroboam the **s** of Nebat, a 2 Chr 13:6
a servant of Solomon the **s** of David, 2 Chr 13:6
defied Rehoboam the **s** of Solomon, 2 Chr 13:7
And Asa his **s** reigned in his place. 2 Chr 14:1
came upon Azariah the **s** of Oded, 2 Chr 15:1
prophecy of Azariah the **s** of Oded, 2 Chr 15:8
Jehoshaphat his **s** reigned in his 2 Chr 17:1
to him Amasiah the **s** of Zichri, 2 Chr 17:16
of the LORD, Micaiah the **s** of Imlah; 2 Chr 18:7
quickly Micaiah the **s** of Imlah." 2 Chr 18:8
And Zedekiah the **s** of Chenaanah 2 Chr 18:10
Then Zedekiah the **s** of Chenaanah 2 Chr 18:23
of the city and to Joash the king's **s**, 2 Chr 18:25
But Jehu the **s** of Hanani the seer 2 Chr 19:2
and Zebadiah the **s** of Ishmael, the 2 Chr 19:11
upon Jahaziel the **s** of Zechariah, 2 Chr 20:14
the son of Zechariah, **s** of Benaiah, 2 Chr 20:14
Zechariah, son of Benaiah, **s** of Jeiel, 2 Chr 20:14
Benaiah, son of Jeiel, **s** of Mattaniah, 2 Chr 20:14
chronicles of Jehu the **s** of Hanani, 2 Chr 20:34
Then Eliezer the **s** of Dodavahu of 2 Chr 20:37
and Jehoram his **s** reigned in his 2 Chr 21:1
so that no **s** was left to him except 2 Chr 21:17
except Jehoahaz, his youngest **s**. 2 Chr 21:17
Ahaziah his youngest **s** king in his 2 Chr 22:1
So Ahaziah the **s** of Jehoram king of 2 Chr 22:1
with Jehoram the **s** of Ahab king 2 Chr 22:5
And Ahaziah the **s** of Jehoram king 2 Chr 22:6
to see Joram the **s** of Ahab in Jezreel, 2 Chr 22:6
to meet Jehu the **s** of Nimshi, 2 Chr 22:7
of Ahaziah saw that her **s** was dead, 2 Chr 22:10
took Joash the **s** of Ahaziah and 2 Chr 22:11
hundreds, Azariah the **s** of Jeroham, 2 Chr 23:1
Jeroham, Ishmael the **s** of Jehohanan, 2 Chr 23:1
of Jehohanan, Azariah the **s** of Obed, 2 Chr 23:1
of Obed, Maaseiah the **s** of Adaiah, 2 Chr 23:1
and Elishaphat the **s** of Zichri. 2 Chr 23:1
said to them, "Behold, the king's **s**! 2 Chr 23:3

brought out the king's **s** and put the 2 Chr 23:11
clothed Zechariah the **s** of Jehoiada 2 Chr 24:20
had shown him, but killed his **s**. 2 Chr 24:22
the blood of the **s** of Jehoiada the 2 Chr 24:25
were Zabad the **s** of Shimeath the 2 Chr 24:26
and Jehozabad the **s** of Shimrith the 2 Chr 24:26
And Amaziah his **s** reigned in his 2 Chr 24:27
and sent to Joash the **s** of Jehoahaz, 2 Chr 25:17
Joash the son of Jehoahaz, **s** of Jehu, 2 Chr 25:17
your daughter to my **s** for a wife,' 2 Chr 25:18
king of Judah, the **s** of Joash, 2 Chr 25:23
the son of Joash, **s** of Ahaziah, 2 Chr 25:23
Amaziah the **s** of Joash, king of 2 Chr 25:25
the death of Joash the **s** of Jehoahaz, 2 Chr 25:25
And Jotham his **s** was over the 2 Chr 26:21
the prophet the **s** of Amoz wrote. 2 Chr 26:22
And Jotham his **s** reigned in his 2 Chr 26:23
and Ahaz his **s** reigned in his place. 2 Chr 27:9
the Valley of the **S** of Hinnom and 2 Chr 28:3
For Pekah the **s** of Remaliah killed 2 Chr 28:6
Maaseiah the king's **s** and Azrikam 2 Chr 28:7
Ephraim, Azariah the **s** of Johanan, 2 Chr 28:12
Berechiah the **s** of Meshillemoth, 2 Chr 28:12
Jehizkiah the **s** of Shallum, 2 Chr 28:12
and Amasa the **s** of Hadlai, 2 Chr 28:12
And Hezekiah his **s** reigned in his 2 Chr 28:27
arose, Mahath the **s** of Amasai, 2 Chr 29:12
of Amasai, and Joel the **s** of Azariah, 2 Chr 29:12
sons of Merari, Kish the **s** of Abdi, 2 Chr 29:12
Abdi, and Azariah the **s** of Jehallelel; 2 Chr 29:12
Gershonites, Joah the **s** of Zimmah, 2 Chr 29:12
of Zimmah, and Eden the **s** of Joah; 2 Chr 29:12
time of Solomon the **s** of David king 2 Chr 30:26
And Kore the **s** of Imnah the Levite, 2 Chr 31:14
Isaiah the prophet, the **s** of Amoz, 2 Chr 32:20
of Isaiah the prophet the **s** of Amoz, 2 Chr 32:32
And Manasseh his **s** reigned in his 2 Chr 32:33
in the Valley of the **S** of Hinnom, 2 Chr 33:6
said to David and to Solomon his **s**, 2 Chr 33:7
and Amon his **s** reigned in his 2 Chr 33:20
land made Josiah his **s** king in his 2 Chr 33:25
he sent Shaphan the **s** of Azaliah, 2 Chr 34:8
of the city, and Joah the **s** of Joahaz, 2 Chr 34:8
Hilkiah, Ahikam the **s** of Shaphan, 2 Chr 34:20
of Shaphan, Abdon the **s** of Micah, 2 Chr 34:20
wife of Shallum the **s** of Tokhath, 2 Chr 34:22
the son of Tokhath, **s** of Hasrah, 2 Chr 34:22
house that Solomon the **s** of David, 2 Chr 35:3
and the document of Solomon his **s**. 2 Chr 35:4
took Jehoahaz the **s** of Josiah and 2 Chr 36:1
And Jehoiachin his **s** reigned in his 2 Chr 36:8
Then arose Jeshua the **s** of Jozadak, with Ezr 3:2
and Zerubbabel the **s** of Shealtiel with Ezr 3:2
Zerubbabel the **s** of Shealtiel and Jeshua Ezr 3:8
and Jeshua the **s** of Jozadak made Ezr 3:8
Haggai and Zechariah the **s** of Iddo, Ezr 5:1
Then Zerubbabel the **s** of Shealtiel and Ezr 5:2
and Jeshua the **s** of Jozadak arose Ezr 5:2
the prophet and Zechariah the **s** of Iddo. Ezr 6:14
king of Persia, Ezra the **s** of Seraiah, Ezr 7:1
Ezra the son of Seraiah, **s** of Azariah, Ezr 7:1
of Seraiah, son of Azariah, **s** of Hilkiah, Ezr 7:1
s of Shallum, son of Zadok, son of Ezr 7:2
son of Shallum, **s** of Zadok, son of Ezr 7:2
of Shallum, son of Zadok, **s** of Ahitub, Ezr 7:2
s of Amariah, son of Azariah, son of Ezr 7:3
son of Amariah, **s** of Azariah, son of Ezr 7:3
Amariah, son of Azariah, **s** of Meraioth, Ezr 7:3
s of Zerahiah, son of Uzzi, son of Bukki, Ezr 7:4
son of Zerahiah, **s** of Uzzi, son of Bukki, Ezr 7:4
son of Zerahiah, son of Uzzi, **s** of Bukki, Ezr 7:4
s of Abishua, son of Phinehas, son of Ezr 7:5
son of Abishua, **s** of Phinehas, son of Ezr 7:5
of Abishua, son of Phinehas, **s** of Eleazar, Ezr 7:5
of Eleazar, **s** of Aaron the chief priest— Ezr 7:5
Eliehoenai the **s** of Zerahiah, Ezr 8:4
sons of Zattu, Shecaniah the **s** of Jahaziel, Ezr 8:5
the sons of Adin, Ebed the **s** of Jonathan, Ezr 8:6
sons of Elam, Jeshaiah the **s** of Athaliah, Ezr 8:7
Shephatiah, Zebadiah the **s** of Michael, Ezr 8:8
the sons of Joab, Obadiah the **s** of Jehiel, Ezr 8:9
of Bani, Shelomith the **s** of Josiphiah, Ezr 8:10
sons of Bebai, Zechariah, the **s** of Bebai, Ezr 8:11
of Azgad, Johanan the **s** of Hakkatan, Ezr 8:12
of the sons of Mahli the **s** of Levi, Ezr 8:18
sons of Mahli the son of Levi, **s** of Israel, Ezr 8:18
of Meremoth the priest, **s** of Uriah, Ezr 8:33
with him was Eleazar the **s** of Phinehas, Ezr 8:33
Jozabad the **s** of Jeshua and Noadiah the Ezr 8:33
of Jeshua and Noadiah the **s** of Binnui. Ezr 8:33
And Shecaniah the **s** of Jehiel, of the Ezr 10:2
of Jehohanan the **s** of Eliashib, Ezr 10:6
Only Jonathan the **s** of Asahel and Ezr 10:15
and Jahzeiah the **s** of Tikvah opposed Ezr 10:15
sons of Jeshua the **s** of Jozadak and his Ezr 10:18

words of Nehemiah the **s** of Hacaliah. Neh 1:1
next to them Zaccur the **s** of Imri built. Neh 3:2
next to them Meremoth the **s** of Uriah, Neh 3:4
the son of Uriah, **s** of Hakkoz repaired. Neh 3:4
to them Meshullam the **s** of Berechiah, Neh 3:4
of Berechiah, **s** of Meshezabel repaired. Neh 3:4
to them Zadok the **s** of Baana repaired. Neh 3:4
Joiada the **s** of Paseah and Meshullam Neh 3:6
and Meshullam the **s** of Besodeiah Neh 3:6
Next to them Uzziel the **s** of Harhaiah, Neh 3:8
Next to them Rephaiah the **s** of Hur, Neh 3:9
them Jedaiah the **s** of Harumaph Neh 3:10
him Hattush the **s** of Hashabneiah Neh 3:10
Malchijah the **s** of Harim and Neh 3:11
and Hasshub the **s** of Pahath-moab Neh 3:11
to him Shallum the **s** of Hallohesh, Neh 3:12
Malchijah the **s** of Rechab, ruler of the Neh 3:14
And Shallum the **s** of Col-hozeh, ruler Neh 3:15
After him Nehemiah the **s** of Azbuk, Neh 3:16
Levites repaired: Rehum the **s** of Bani. Neh 3:17
repaired: Bavvai the **s** of Henadad, Neh 3:18
Next to him Ezer the **s** of Jeshua, ruler Neh 3:19
him Baruch the **s** of Zabbai repaired Neh 3:20
After him Meremoth the **s** of Uriah, Neh 3:21
s of Hakkoz repaired another section Neh 3:21
After them Azariah the **s** of Maaseiah, Neh 3:23
s of Ananiah repaired beside his own Neh 3:23
him Binnui the **s** of Henadad repaired Neh 3:24
Palal the **s** of Uzai repaired opposite the Neh 3:25
After him Pedaiah the **s** of Parosh Neh 3:25
them Zadok the **s** of Immer repaired Neh 3:29
him Shemaiah the **s** of Shecaniah, Neh 3:29
him Hananiah the **s** of Shelemiah and Neh 3:30
Hanun the sixth **s** of Zalaph repaired Neh 3:30
him Meshullam the **s** of Berechiah Neh 3:30
house of Shemaiah the **s** of Delaiah, Neh 6:10
the son of Delaiah, **s** of Mehetabel, Neh 6:10
son-in-law of Shecaniah the **s** of Arah: Neh 6:18
and his **s** Jehohanan had taken the Neh 6:18
of Meshullam the **s** of Berechiah as Neh 6:18
the days of Jeshua the **s** of Nun to that Neh 8:17
the governor, the **s** of Hacaliah, Neh 10:1
the Levites: Jeshua the **s** of Azaniah, Neh 10:9
And the priest, the **s** of Aaron, shall be Neh 10:38
sons of Judah: Athaiah the **s** of Uzziah, Neh 11:4
the son of Uzziah, **s** of Zechariah, Neh 11:4
son of Zechariah, **s** of Amariah, Neh 11:4
son of Amariah, **s** of Shephatiah, Neh 11:4
son of Shephatiah, **s** of Mahalalel, Neh 11:4
and Maaseiah the **s** of Baruch, son of Neh 11:5
the son of Baruch, **s** of Col-hozeh, Neh 11:5
son of Col-hozeh, **s** of Hazaiah, Neh 11:5
Col-hozeh, son of Hazaiah, **s** of Adaiah, Neh 11:5
of Hazaiah, son of Adaiah, **s** of Joiarib, Neh 11:5
Adaiah, son of Joiarib, **s** of Zechariah, Neh 11:5
son of Zechariah, **s** of the Shilonite. Neh 11:5
of Benjamin: Sallu the **s** of Meshullam, Neh 11:7
Sallu the son of Meshullam, **s** of Joed, Neh 11:7
Meshullam, son of Joed, **s** of Pedaiah, Neh 11:7
of Joed, son of Pedaiah, **s** of Kolaiah, Neh 11:7
Pedaiah, son of Kolaiah, **s** of Maaseiah, Neh 11:7
of Kolaiah, son of Maaseiah, **s** of Ithiel, Neh 11:7
of Maaseiah, son of Ithiel, **s** of Jeshaiah, Neh 11:7
Joel the **s** of Zichri was their overseer; Neh 11:9
and Judah the **s** of Hassenuah was Neh 11:9
Of the priests: Jedaiah the **s** of Joiarib, Neh 11:10
Seraiah the **s** of Hilkiah, son of Neh 11:11
the son of Hilkiah, **s** of Meshullam, Neh 11:11
son of Meshullam, **s** of Zadok, Neh 11:11
son of Zadok, **s** of Meraioth, Neh 11:11
Zadok, son of Meraioth, **s** of Ahitub, Neh 11:11
and Adaiah the **s** of Jeroham, son of Neh 11:12
the son of Jeroham, **s** of Pelaliah, Neh 11:12
of Jeroham, son of Pelaliah, **s** of Amzi, Neh 11:12
Pelaliah, son of Amzi, **s** of Zechariah, Neh 11:12
Amzi, son of Zechariah, **s** of Pashhur, Neh 11:12
son of Pashhur, **s** of Malchijah, Neh 11:12
and Amashsai, the **s** of Azarel, son of Neh 11:13
the son of Azarel, **s** of Ahzai, Neh 11:13
son of Ahzai, **s** of Meshillemoth, Neh 11:13
son of Meshillemoth, **s** of Immer, Neh 11:13
was Zabdiel the **s** of Haggedolim. Neh 11:14
Levites: Shemaiah the **s** of Hasshub, Neh 11:15
the son of Hasshub, **s** of Azrikam, Neh 11:15
son of Azrikam, **s** of Hashabiah, Neh 11:15
son of Hashabiah, **s** of Bunni; Neh 11:15
and Mattaniah the **s** of Mica, son of Neh 11:17
the son of Mica, **s** of Zabdi, Neh 11:17
son of Mica, son of Zabdi, **s** of Asaph, Neh 11:17
and Abda the **s** of Shammua, son of Neh 11:17
Abda the son of Shammua, **s** of Galal, Neh 11:17
son of Galal, **s** of Jeduthun. Neh 11:17
in Jerusalem was Uzzi the **s** of Bani, Neh 11:22
Uzzi the son of Bani, **s** of Hashabiah, Neh 11:22
son of Hashabiah, **s** of Mattaniah, Neh 11:22

son of Mattaniah, **s** of Mica, Neh 11:22
And Pethahiah the **s** of Meshezabel, Neh 11:24
of the sons of Zerah the **s** of Judah, Neh 11:24
up with Zerubbabel the **s** of Shealtiel, Neh 12:1
the days of Johanan the **s** of Eliashib. Neh 12:23
and Jeshua the **s** of Kadmiel, Neh 12:24
days of Joiakim the **s** of Jeshua son of Neh 12:26
the son of Jeshua **s** of Jozadak, Neh 12:26
Zechariah the **s** of Jonathan, Neh 12:35
the son of Jonathan, **s** of Shemaiah, Neh 12:35
son of Shemaiah, **s** of Mattaniah, Neh 12:35
son of Mattaniah, **s** of Micaiah, Neh 12:35
son of Micaiah, **s** of Zaccur, Neh 12:35
of Micaiah, son of Zaccur, **s** of Asaph; Neh 12:35
of David and his **s** Solomon. Neh 12:45
their assistant Hanan the **s** of Zaccur, Neh 13:13
the son of Zaccur, **s** of Mattaniah, Neh 13:13
the **s** of Eliashib the high priest, Neh 13:28
whose name was Mordecai, the **s** of Jair, Est 2:5
was Mordecai, the son of Jair, **s** of Shimei, Est 2:5
the son of Jair, son of Shimei, **s** of Kish, Est 2:5
the Agagite, the **s** of Hammedatha, Est 3:1
the Agagite, the **s** of Hammedatha, Est 3:10
the Agagite, the **s** of Hammedatha, Est 8:5
sons of Haman the **s** of Hammedatha, Est 9:10
the Agagite, the **s** of Hammedatha, Est 9:24
as a **s** of man does with his neighbor. Jb 16:21
man, who is a maggot, and the **s** of man, Jb 25:6
Then Elihu the **s** of Barachel the Buzite, Jb 32:2
And Elihu the **s** of Barachel the Buzite Jb 32:6
and your righteousness a **s** of man. Jb 35:8
The LORD said to me, "You are my **S**; Ps 2:7
Kiss the **S**, lest he be angry, and you Ps 2:12
David, when he fled from Absalom his **s**. Ps 3:T
and the **s** of man that you care for him? Ps 8:4
you slander your own mother's **s**. Ps 50:20
and your righteousness to the royal **s**! Ps 72:1
The prayers of David, the **s** of Jesse, are Ps 72:20
and for the **s** whom you made strong Ps 80:15
the **s** of man whom you have made Ps 80:17
and save the **s** of your maidservant. Ps 86:16
servant, the **s** of your maidservant. Ps 116:16
or the **s** of man that you think of him? Ps 144:3
not your trust in princes, in a **s** of man, Ps 146:3
The proverbs of Solomon, **s** of David, Prv 1:1
Hear, my **s**, your father's instruction, Prv 1:8
My **s**, if sinners entice you, do not Prv 1:10
my **s**, do not walk in the way with them; Prv 1:15
My **s**, if you receive my words and Prv 2:1
My **s**, do not forget my teaching, but let Prv 3:1
My **s**, do not despise the LORD'S Prv 3:11
as a father the **s** in whom he delights. Prv 3:12
My **s**, do not lose sight of these—keep Prv 3:21
When I was a **s** with my father, tender, Prv 4:3
Hear, my **s**, and accept my words, that Prv 4:10
My **s**, be attentive to my words; incline Prv 4:20
My **s**, be attentive to my wisdom; incline Prv 5:1
Why should you be intoxicated, my **s**, Prv 5:20
My **s**, if you have put up security for Prv 6:1
then do this, my **s**, and save yourself, for Prv 6:3
My **s**, keep your father's commandment, Prv 6:20
My **s**, keep my words and treasure up my Prv 7:1
A wise **s** makes a glad father, but a Prv 10:1
but a foolish **s** is a sorrow to his Prv 10:1
who gathers in summer is a prudent **s**, Prv 10:5
in harvest is a **s** who brings shame. Prv 10:5
A wise **s** hears his father's instruction, Prv 13:1
Whoever spares the rod hates his **s**, Prv 13:24
A wise **s** makes a glad father, but a Prv 15:20
will rule over a **s** who acts shamefully Prv 17:2
A foolish **s** is a grief to his father and Prv 17:25
A foolish **s** is ruin to his father, and a Prv 19:13
Discipline your **s**, for there is hope; do Prv 19:18
his mother is a **s** who brings shame Prv 19:26
Cease to hear instruction, my **s**, and Prv 19:27
My **s**, if your heart is wise, my heart Prv 23:15
Hear, my **s**, and be wise, and direct Prv 23:19
he who fathers a wise **s** will be glad in Prv 23:24
My **s**, give me your heart, and let your Prv 23:26
My **s**, eat honey, for it is good, and the Prv 24:13
My **s**, fear the LORD and the king, and Prv 24:21
Be wise, my **s**, and make my heart Prv 27:11
keeps the law is a **s** with understanding, Prv 28:7
Discipline your **s**, and he will give you Prv 29:17
The words of Agur **s** of Jakeh. The Prv 30:1
What are you doing, my **s**? What are Prv 31:2
What are you doing, **s** of my womb? Prv 31:2
What are you doing, **s** of my vows? Prv 31:2
words of the Preacher, the **s** of David, Eccl 1:1
who has no other, either **s** or brother, Eccl 4:8
And he is father of a **s**, but he has Eccl 5:14
your king is the **s** of the nobility, Eccl 10:17
My **s**, beware of anything beyond Eccl 12:12
The vision of Isaiah the **s** of Amoz, which Is 1:1
word that Isaiah the **s** of Amoz saw Is 2:1
In the days of Ahaz the **s** of Jotham, son of Is 7:1
of Ahaz the son of Jotham, **s** of Uzziah, Is 7:1
Syria and Pekah the **s** of Remaliah the Is 7:1
meet Ahaz, you and Shear-jashub your **s**, Is 7:3
of Rezin and Syria and the **s** of Remaliah. Is 7:4
with Ephraim and the **s** of Remaliah, Is 7:5
and set up the **s** of Tabeel as king in the Is 7:6
the head of Samaria is the **s** of Remaliah. Is 7:9
the virgin shall conceive and bear a **s**, Is 7:14
priest and Zechariah the **s** of Jeberechiah, Is 8:2
prophetess, and she conceived and bore a **s**. Is 8:3
rejoice over Rezin and the **s** of Remaliah, Is 8:6
For to us a child is born, to us a **s** is given; Is 9:6
Babylon which Isaiah the **s** of Amoz saw. Is 13:1
from heaven, O Day Star, **s** of Dawn! Is 14:12
you say to Pharaoh, "I am a **s** of the wise, Is 19:11
a son of the wise, a **s** of ancient kings"? Is 19:11
the LORD spoke by Isaiah the **s** of Amoz, Is 20:2
my servant Eliakim the **s** of Hilkiah, Is 22:20
out to him Eliakim the **s** of Hilkiah, Is 36:3
the secretary, and Joah the **s** of Asaph, Is 36:3
Then Eliakim the **s** of Hilkiah, who was Is 36:22
the secretary, and Joah the **s** of Asaph, Is 36:22
to the prophet Isaiah the **s** of Amoz. Is 37:2
Then Isaiah the **s** of Amoz sent to Is 37:21
Esarhaddon his **s** reigned in his place. Is 37:38
Isaiah the prophet the **s** of Amoz came to Is 38:1
time Merodach-baladan the **s** of Baladan, Is 39:1
no compassion on the **s** of her womb? Is 49:15
of the **s** of man who is made like grass, Is 51:12
this, and the **s** of man who holds it fast, Is 56:2
her pain came upon her she delivered a **s**. Is 66:7
The words of Jeremiah, the **s** of Hilkiah, Jer 1:1
came in the days of Josiah the **s** of Amon, Jer 1:2
in the days of Jehoiakim the **s** of Josiah, Jer 1:3
eleventh year of Zedekiah, the **s** of Josiah, Jer 1:3
make mourning as for an only **s**, most Jer 6:26
is in the Valley of the **S** of Hinnom, Jer 7:31
or the Valley of the **S** of Hinnom, Jer 7:32
of what Manasseh the **s** of Hezekiah, Jer 15:4
to the Valley of the **S** of Hinnom at the Jer 19:2
or the Valley of the **S** of Hinnom, Jer 19:6
Now Pashhur the priest, the **s** of Immer, Jer 20:1
"A **s** is born to you," making him very Jer 20:15
to him Pashhur the **s** of Malchiah and Jer 21:1
Zephaniah the priest, the **s** of Maaseiah, Jer 21:1
concerning Shallum the **s** of Josiah, Jer 22:11
concerning Jehoiakim the **s** of Josiah, Jer 22:18
though Coniah the **s** of Jehoiakim, Jer 22:24
Jerusalem Jeconiah the **s** of Jehoiakim, Jer 24:1
fourth year of Jehoiakim the **s** of Josiah, Jer 25:1
thirteenth year of Josiah the **s** of Amon, Jer 25:3
of the reign of Jehoiakim the **s** of Josiah, Jer 26:1
Uriah the **s** of Shemaiah from Jer 26:20
Elnathan the **s** of Achbor and others Jer 26:22
hand of Ahikam the **s** of Shaphan was Jer 26:24
of the reign of Zedekiah the **s** of Josiah, Jer 27:1
serve him and his **s** and his grandson, Jer 27:7
to Babylon Jeconiah the **s** of Jehoiakim, Jer 27:20
the fourth year, Hananiah the **s** of Azzur, Jer 28:1
to this place Jeconiah the **s** of Jehoiakim, Jer 28:4
hand of Elasah the **s** of Shaphan and Jer 29:3
Shaphan and Gemariah the **s** of Hilkiah, Jer 29:3
concerning Ahab the **s** of Kolaiah and Jer 29:21
and Zedekiah the **s** of Maaseiah, Jer 29:21
and to Zephaniah the **s** of Maaseiah the Jer 29:25
Is Ephraim my dear **s**? Is he my darling Jer 31:20
Hanamel the **s** of Shallum your uncle Jer 32:7
purchase to Baruch the **s** of Neriah son Jer 32:12
the son of Neriah **s** of Mahseiah, Jer 32:12
of purchase to Baruch the **s** of Neriah, Jer 32:16
Baal in the Valley of the **S** of Hinnom, Jer 32:35
he shall not have a **s** to reign on his Jer 33:21
in the days of Jehoiakim the **s** of Josiah, Jer 35:1
So I took Jaazaniah the **s** of Jeremiah, Jer 35:3
s of Habazziniah and his brothers and Jer 35:3
of the sons of Hanan the **s** of Igdaliah, Jer 35:4
chamber of Maaseiah the **s** of Shallum, Jer 35:4
no wine, for Jonadab the **s** of Rechab, Jer 35:6
the voice of Jonadab the **s** of Rechab, Jer 35:8
that Jonadab the **s** of Rechab gave Jer 35:14
sons of Jonadab the **s** of Rechab have Jer 35:16
Jonadab the **s** of Rechab shall never Jer 35:19
fourth year of Jehoiakim the **s** of Josiah, Jer 36:1
Jeremiah called Baruch the **s** of Neriah, Jer 36:4
And Baruch the **s** of Neriah did all that Jer 36:8
fifth year of Jehoiakim the **s** of Josiah, Jer 36:9
of Gemariah the **s** of Shaphan the Jer 36:10
When Micaiah the **s** of Gemariah, son Jer 36:11
the son of Gemariah, **s** of Shaphan, Jer 36:11
secretary, Delaiah the **s** of Shemaiah, Jer 36:12
Shemaiah, Elnathan the **s** of Achbor, Jer 36:12
of Achbor, Gemariah the **s** of Shaphan, Jer 36:12
Shaphan, Zedekiah the **s** of Hananiah, Jer 36:12
officials sent Jehudi the **s** of Nethaniah, Jer 36:14
the son of Nethaniah, **s** of Shelemiah, Jer 36:14
son of Shelemiah, **s** of Cushi, Jer 36:14
come." So Baruch the **s** of Neriah took Jer 36:14
Jerahmeel the king's **s** and Seraiah the Jer 36:26
son and Seraiah the **s** of Azriel and Jer 36:26
Azriel and Shelemiah the **s** of Abdeel to Jer 36:26
it to Baruch the scribe, the **s** of Neriah, Jer 36:32
Zedekiah the **s** of Josiah, whom Jer 37:1
instead of Coniah the **s** of Jehoiakim. Jer 37:1
sent Jehucal the **s** of Shelemiah, Jer 37:3
Zephaniah the priest, the **s** of Maaseiah, Jer 37:3
there named Irijah the **s** of Shelemiah, Jer 37:13
the son of Shelemiah, **s** of Hananiah, Jer 37:13
Now Shephatiah the **s** of Mattan, Jer 38:1
of Mattan, Gedaliah the **s** of Pashhur, Jer 38:1
of Pashhur, Jucal the **s** of Shelemiah, Jer 38:1
and Pashhur the **s** of Malchiah heard Jer 38:1
the cistern of Malchiah, the king's **s**, Jer 38:6
him to Gedaliah the **s** of Ahikam, Jer 39:14
the son of Ahikam, **s** of Shaphan, Jer 39:14
then return to Gedaliah the **s** of Ahikam, Jer 40:5
the son of Ahikam, **s** of Shaphan, Jer 40:5
went to Gedaliah the **s** of Ahikam, Jer 40:6
appointed Gedaliah the **s** of Ahikam Jer 40:7
at Mizpah—Ishmael the **s** of Nethaniah, Jer 40:8
of Nethaniah, Johanan the **s** of Kareah, Jer 40:8
of Kareah, Seraiah the **s** of Tanhumeth, Jer 40:8
Jezaniah the **s** of the Maacathite, Jer 40:8
Gedaliah the **s** of Ahikam, son of Jer 40:9
the son of Ahikam, **s** of Shaphan, Jer 40:9
appointed Gedaliah the **s** of Ahikam, Jer 40:11
the son of Ahikam, **s** of Shaphan, Jer 40:11
Now Johanan the **s** of Kareah and all Jer 40:13
has sent Ishmael the **s** of Nethaniah to Jer 40:14
But Gedaliah the **s** of Ahikam would Jer 40:14
Then Johanan the **s** of Kareah spoke Jer 40:15
down Ishmael the **s** of Nethaniah, Jer 40:15
But Gedaliah the **s** of Ahikam said to Jer 40:16
said to Johanan the **s** of Kareah, Jer 40:16
month, Ishmael the **s** of Nethaniah, Jer 41:1
the son of Nethaniah, **s** of Elishama, Jer 41:1
ten men to Gedaliah the **s** of Ahikam, Jer 41:1
Ishmael the **s** of Nethaniah and the ten Jer 41:2
struck down Gedaliah the **s** of Ahikam, Jer 41:2
the son of Ahikam, **s** of Shaphan, Jer 41:2
And Ishmael the **s** of Nethaniah came Jer 41:6
"Come in to Gedaliah the **s** of Ahikam." Jer 41:6
Ishmael the **s** of Nethaniah and the men Jer 41:7
Ishmael the **s** of Nethaniah filled it with Jer 41:9
to Gedaliah the **s** of Ahikam. Jer 41:10
Ishmael the **s** of Nethaniah took them Jer 41:10
But when Johanan the **s** of Kareah and Jer 41:11
that Ishmael the **s** of Nethaniah had Jer 41:11
against Ishmael the **s** of Nethaniah. Jer 41:12
saw Johanan the **s** of Kareah and Jer 41:13
and went to Johanan the **s** of Kareah. Jer 41:14
But Ishmael the **s** of Nethaniah escaped Jer 41:15
Then Johanan the **s** of Kareah and all Jer 41:16
from Ishmael the **s** of Nethaniah, Jer 41:16
down Gedaliah the **s** of Ahikam— Jer 41:16
because Ishmael the **s** of Nethaniah Jer 41:18
struck down Gedaliah the **s** of Ahikam, Jer 41:18
and Johanan the **s** of Kareah and Jer 42:1
Kareah and Jezaniah the **s** of Hoshaiah, Jer 42:1
summoned Johanan the **s** of Kareah and Jer 42:8
Azariah the **s** of Hoshaiah and Johanan Jer 43:2
and Johanan the **s** of Kareah and Jer 43:2
but Baruch the **s** of Neriah has set you Jer 43:3
So Johanan the **s** of Kareah and all the Jer 43:4
But Johanan the **s** of Kareah and all the Jer 43:5
had left with Gedaliah the **s** of Ahikam, Jer 43:6
the son of Ahikam, **s** of Shaphan; Jer 43:6
the prophet and Baruch the **s** of Neriah. Jer 43:6
prophet spoke to Baruch the **s** of Neriah, Jer 45:1
fourth year of Jehoiakim the **s** of Josiah, Jer 45:1
fourth year of Jehoiakim the **s** of Josiah, Jer 46:2
and no **s** of man shall sojourn in her. Jer 50:40
and through which no **s** of man passes. Jer 51:43
commanded Seraiah the **s** of Neriah, Jer 51:59
the son of Neriah, **s** of Mahseiah, Jer 51:59
came to Ezekiel the priest, the **s** of Buzi, Ezk 1:3
And he said to me, "**S** of man, stand on Ezk 2:1
And he said to me, "**S** of man, I send you Ezk 2:3
And you, **s** of man, be not afraid of them, Ezk 2:6
"But you, **s** of man, hear what I say to Ezk 2:8
And he said to me, "**S** of man, eat Ezk 3:1
And he said to me, "**S** of man, feed your Ezk 3:3
And he said to me, "**S** of man, go to the Ezk 3:4
Moreover, he said to me, "**S** of man, all Ezk 3:10
"**S** of man, I have made you a Ezk 3:17
And you, O **s** of man, behold, cords will Ezk 3:25
"And you, **s** of man, take a brick and lay Ezk 4:1
Moreover, he said to me, "**S** of man, Ezk 4:16
"And you, O **s** of man, take a sharp Ezk 5:1
"**S** of man, set your face toward the Ezk 6:2

"And you, O **s** of man, thus says the Lord Ezk 7:2
Then he said to me, "**S** of man, lift up Ezk 8:5
And he said to me, "**S** of man, do you see Ezk 8:6
Then he said to me, "**S** of man, dig in the Ezk 8:8
with Jaazaniah the **s** of Shaphan Ezk 8:11
Then he said to me, "**S** of man, have Ezk 8:12
to me, "Have you seen this, O **s** of man? Ezk 8:15
to me, "Have you seen this, O **s** of man? Ezk 8:17
among them Jaazaniah the **s** of Azzur, Ezk 11:1
of Azzur, and Pelatiah the **s** of Benaiah, Ezk 11:1
And he said to me, "**S** of man, these are Ezk 11:2
against them, prophesy, O **s** of man." Ezk 11:4
that Pelatiah the **s** of Benaiah died. Ezk 11:13
"**S** of man, your brothers, even your Ezk 11:15
"**S** of man, you dwell in the midst of a Ezk 12:2
As for you, **s** of man, prepare for Ezk 12:3
"**S** of man, has not the house of Israel, Ezk 12:9
"**S** of man, eat your bread with Ezk 12:18
"**S** of man, what is this proverb that Ezk 12:22
"**S** of man, behold, they of the house of Ezk 12:27
"**S** of man, prophesy against the Ezk 13:2
"And you, **s** of man, set your face Ezk 13:17
"**S** of man, these men have taken their Ezk 14:3
"**S** of man, when a land sins against Ezk 14:13
would deliver neither **s** nor daughter. Ezk 14:20
"**S** of man, how does the wood of the Ezk 15:2
"**S** of man, make known to Jerusalem Ezk 16:2
"**S** of man, propound a riddle, and Ezk 17:2
as well as the soul of the **s** is mine: Ezk 18:4
"If he fathers a **s** who is violent, a Ezk 18:10
this man fathers a **s** who sees all the Ezk 18:14
'Why should not the **s** suffer for the Ezk 18:19
When the **s** has done what is just and Ezk 18:19
The **s** shall not suffer for the iniquity Ezk 18:20
father suffer for the iniquity of the **s**. Ezk 18:20
"**S** of man, speak to the elders of Israel, Ezk 20:3
Will you judge them, **s** of man, will Ezk 20:4
"Therefore, **s** of man, speak to the Ezk 20:27
"**S** of man, set your face toward the Ezk 20:46
"**S** of man, set your face toward Ezk 21:2
"As for you, **s** of man, groan; with Ezk 21:6
"**S** of man, prophesy and say, Thus says Ezk 21:9
You have despised the rod, my **s**, with Ezk 21:10
Cry out and wail, **s** of man, for it is Ezk 21:12
"As for you, **s** of man, prophesy. Clap Ezk 21:14
"As for you, **s** of man, mark two ways Ezk 21:19
"And you, **s** of man, prophesy, and Ezk 21:28
"And you, **s** of man, will you judge, will Ezk 22:2
"**S** of man, the house of Israel has Ezk 22:18
"**S** of man, say to her, You are a land Ezk 22:24
"**S** of man, there were two women, the Ezk 23:2
"**S** of man, will you judge Oholah and Ezk 23:36
"**S** of man, write down the name of this Ezk 24:2
"**S** of man, behold, I am about to take Ezk 24:16
"As for you, **s** of man, surely on the Ezk 24:25
"**S** of man, set your face toward the Ezk 25:2
"**S** of man, because Tyre said Ezk 26:2
"Now you, **s** of man, raise a Ezk 27:2
"**S** of man, say to the prince of Tyre, Ezk 28:2
"**S** of man, raise a lamentation over Ezk 28:12
"**S** of man, set your face toward Sidon, Ezk 28:21
"**S** of man, set your face against Ezk 29:2
"**S** of man, Nebuchadnezzar king of Ezk 29:18
"**S** of man, prophesy, and say, Thus Ezk 30:2
"**S** of man, I have broken the arm of Ezk 30:21
"**S** of man, say to Pharaoh king of Ezk 31:2
"**S** of man, raise a lamentation over Ezk 32:2
"**S** of man, wail over the multitude of Ezk 32:18
"**S** of man, speak to your people and say Ezk 33:2
"So you, **s** of man, I have made a Ezk 33:7
"And you, **s** of man, say to the house Ezk 33:10
"And you, **s** of man, say to your Ezk 33:12
"**S** of man, the inhabitants of these Ezk 33:24
"As for you, **s** of man, your people who Ezk 33:30
"**S** of man, prophesy against the Ezk 34:2
"**S** of man, set your face against Mount Ezk 35:2
"And you, **s** of man, prophesy to the Ezk 36:1
"**S** of man, when the house of Israel Ezk 36:17
And he said to me, "**S** of man, can these Ezk 37:3
prophesy, **s** of man, and say to the Ezk 37:9
Then he said to me, "**S** of man, these Ezk 37:11
"**S** of man, take a stick and write on it, Ezk 37:16
"**S** of man, set your face toward Gog, of Ezk 38:2
"Therefore, **s** of man, prophesy, and Ezk 38:14
"And you, **s** of man, prophesy against Ezk 39:1
"As for you, **s** of man, thus says the Ezk 39:17
And the man said to me, "**S** of man, Ezk 40:4
and he said to me, "**S** of man, this is the Ezk 43:7
"As for you, **s** of man, describe to the Ezk 43:10
And he said to me, "**S** of man, thus Ezk 43:18
And the LORD said to me, "**S** of man, Ezk 44:5
for father or mother, for **s** or daughter, Ezk 44:25
And he said to me, "**S** of man, have you Ezk 47:6
of the fourth is like a **s** of the gods." Dn 3:25
And you his **s**, Belshazzar, have not Dn 5:22
heaven there came one like a **s** of man, Dn 7:13
he said to me, "Understand, O **s** of man, Dn 8:17
first year of Darius the **s** of Ahasuerus, Dn 9:1
LORD that came to Hosea, the **s** of Beeri, Hos 1:1
in the days of Jeroboam the **s** of Joash, Hos 1:1
and she conceived and bore him a **s**. Hos 1:3
No Mercy, she conceived and bore a **s**. Hos 1:8
him, and out of Egypt I called my **s**. Hos 11:1
come for him, but he is an unwise **s**, Hos 13:13
the LORD that came to Joel, the **s** of Pethuel: Jl 1:1
in the days of Jeroboam the **s** of Joash, Am 1:1
"I was no prophet, nor a prophet's **s**, Am 7:14
mourning for an only **s** and the end of Am 8:10
the LORD came to Jonah the **s** of Amittai, Jon 1:1
and what Balaam the **s** of Beor answered Mi 6:5
for the **s** treats the father with contempt, Mi 7:6
that came to Zephaniah the **s** of Cushi, Zep 1:1
the son of Cushi, **s** of Gedaliah, Zep 1:1
of Cushi, son of Gedaliah, **s** of Amariah, Zep 1:1
Gedaliah, son of Amariah, **s** of Hezekiah, Zep 1:1
in the days of Josiah the **s** of Amon, Zep 1:1
prophet to Zerubbabel the **s** of Shealtiel, Hg 1:1
Judah, and to Joshua the **s** of Jehozadak, Hg 1:1
Then Zerubbabel the **s** of Shealtiel, and Hg 1:12
Shealtiel, and Joshua the **s** of Jehozadak, Hg 1:12
spirit of Zerubbabel the **s** of Shealtiel, Hg 1:14
the spirit of Joshua the **s** of Jehozadak, Hg 1:14
now to Zerubbabel the **s** of Shealtiel, Hg 2:2
Judah, and to Joshua the **s** of Jehozadak, Hg 2:2
Be strong, O Joshua, **s** of Jehozadak, the Hg 2:4
my servant, the **s** of Shealtiel, Hg 2:23
prophet Zechariah, the **s** of Berechiah, Zec 1:1
the son of Berechiah, **s** of Iddo, Zec 1:1
prophet Zechariah, the **s** of Berechiah, Zec 1:7
the son of Berechiah, **s** of Iddo, Zec 1:7
the house of Josiah, the **s** of Zephaniah. Zec 6:10
the head of Joshua, the **s** of Jehozadak, Zec 6:11
Jedaiah, and Hen the **s** of Zephaniah. Zec 6:14
"A **s** honors his father, and a servant his Mal 1:6
as a man spares his **s** who serves him. Mal 3:17
genealogy of Jesus Christ, the **s** of David, Mt 1:1
the son of David, the **s** of Abraham. Mt 1:1
in a dream, saying, "Joseph, **s** of David, Mt 1:20
She will bear a **s**, and you shall call his Mt 1:21
the virgin shall conceive and bear a **s**, Mt 1:23
her not until she had given birth to a **s**. Mt 1:25
the prophet, "Out of Egypt I called my **s**." Mt 2:15
from heaven said, "This is my beloved **S**, Mt 3:17
and said to him, "If you are the **S** of God, Mt 4:3
and said to him, "If you are the **S** of God, Mt 4:6
James the **s** of Zebedee and John his Mt 4:21
one of you, if his **s** asks him for bread, Mt 7:9
but the **S** of Man has nowhere to lay his Mt 8:20
have you to do with us, O **S** of God? Mt 8:29
said to the paralytic, "Take heart, my **s**; Mt 9:2
may know that the **S** of Man has Mt 9:6
aloud, "Have mercy on us, **S** of David." Mt 9:27
his brother; James the **s** of Zebedee, Mt 10:2
tax collector; James the **s** of Alphaeus, Mt 10:3
of Israel before the **S** of Man comes. Mt 10:23
and whoever loves **s** or daughter more Mt 10:37
The **S** of Man came eating and Mt 11:19
no one knows the **S** except the Father, Mt 11:27
the Father except the **S** and anyone to Mt 11:27
to whom the **S** chooses to reveal Mt 11:27
For the **S** of Man is lord of the Sabbath." Mt 12:8
and said, "Can this be the **S** of David?" Mt 12:23
a word against the **S** of Man will be Mt 12:32
so will the **S** of Man be three days and Mt 12:40
who sows the good seed is the **S** of Man. Mt 13:37
The **S** of Man will send his angels, and Mt 13:41
Is not this the carpenter's **s**? Is not his Mt 13:55
saying, "Truly you are the **S** of God." Mt 14:33
"Have mercy on me, O Lord, **S** of David; Mt 15:22
do people say that the **S** of Man is?" Mt 16:13
are the Christ, the **S** of the living God." Mt 16:16
For the **S** of Man is going to come with Mt 16:27
until they see the **S** of Man coming in Mt 16:28
the cloud said, "This is my beloved **S**, Mt 17:5
until the **S** of Man is raised from the Mt 17:9
So also the **S** of Man will certainly Mt 17:12
said, "Lord, have mercy on my **s**, for he Mt 17:15
"The **S** of Man is about to be delivered Mt 17:22
when the **S** of Man will sit on his Mt 19:28
And the **S** of Man will be delivered over Mt 20:18
even as the **S** of Man came not to be Mt 20:28
"Lord, have mercy on us, **S** of David!" Mt 20:30
"Lord, have mercy on us, **S** of David!" Mt 20:31
shouting, "Hosanna to the **S** of David! Mt 21:9
"Hosanna to the **S** of David!" they were Mt 21:15
'**S**, go and work in the vineyard today.' Mt 21:28
went to the other **s** and said the same. Mt 21:30
Finally he sent his **s** to them, saying, Mt 21:37
them, saying, 'They will respect my **s**.' Mt 21:37
But when the tenants saw the **s**, they Mt 21:38
king who gave a wedding feast for his **s**, Mt 22:2
Whose **s** is he?" They said to him, "The Mt 22:42
They said to him, "The **s** of David." Mt 22:42
David calls him Lord, how is he his **s**?" Mt 22:45
blood of Zechariah the **s** of Barachiah, Mt 23:35
so will be the coming of the **S** of Man. Mt 24:27
in heaven the sign of the **S** of Man, Mt 24:30
they will see the **S** of Man coming on Mt 24:30
even the angels of heaven, nor the **S**, Mt 24:36
so will be the coming of the **S** of Man. Mt 24:37
so will be the coming of the **S** of Man. Mt 24:39
for the **S** of Man is coming at an hour Mt 24:44
"When the **S** of Man comes in his Mt 25:31
and the **S** of Man will be delivered up to Mt 26:2
The **S** of Man goes as it is written of Mt 26:24
man by whom the **S** of Man is Mt 26:24
and the **S** of Man is betrayed into the Mt 26:45
us if you are the Christ, the **S** of God." Mt 26:63
on you will see the **S** of Man seated at Mt 26:64
If you are the **S** of God, come down Mt 27:40
him. For he said, 'I am the **S** of God.'" Mt 27:43
and said, "Truly this was the **S** of God!" Mt 27:54
the Father and of the **S** and of the Holy Mt 28:19
of the gospel of Jesus Christ, the **S** of God. Mk 1:1
from heaven, "You are my beloved **S**; Mk 1:11
he saw James the **s** of Zebedee and John Mk 1:19
their faith, he said to the paralytic, "My **s**, Mk 2:5
may know that the **S** of Man has Mk 2:10
he saw Levi the **s** of Alphaeus sitting at Mk 2:14
So the **S** of Man is lord even of the Mk 2:28
and cried out, "You are the **S** of God." Mk 3:11
James the **s** of Zebedee and John the Mk 3:17
Thomas, and James the **s** of Alphaeus, Mk 3:18
with me, Jesus, **S** of the Most High God? Mk 5:7
the **s** of Mary and brother of James and Mk 6:3
teach them that the **S** of Man must Mk 8:31
of him will the **S** of Man also be Mk 8:38
out of the cloud, "This is my beloved **S**; Mk 9:7
until the **S** of Man had risen from the Mk 9:9
is it written of the **S** of Man that he Mk 9:12
him, "Teacher, I brought my **s** to you, Mk 9:17
"The **S** of Man is going to be delivered Mk 9:31
and the **S** of Man will be delivered over Mk 10:33
For even the **S** of Man came not to be Mk 10:45
a blind beggar, the **s** of Timaeus, Mk 10:46
to cry out and say, "Jesus, **S** of David, Mk 10:47
he cried out all the more, "**S** of David, Mk 10:48
He had still one other, a beloved **s**. Mk 12:6
them, saying, 'They will respect my **s**.' Mk 12:6
say that the Christ is the **s** of David? Mk 12:35
how is he his **s**?" And the great throng Mk 12:37
they will see the **S** of Man coming in Mk 13:26
even the angels in heaven, nor the **S**, Mk 13:32
For the **S** of Man goes as it is written of Mk 14:21
man by whom the **S** of Man is Mk 14:21
The **S** of Man is betrayed into the Mk 14:41
you the Christ, the **S** of the Blessed?" Mk 14:61
and you will see the **S** of Man seated at Mk 14:62
"Truly this man was the **S** of God!" Mk 15:39
your wife Elizabeth will bear you a **s**, Lk 1:13
conceive in your womb and bear a **s**, Lk 1:31
and will be called the **S** of the Most High. Lk 1:32
born will be called holy—the **S** of God. Lk 1:35
in her old age has also conceived a **s**, Lk 1:36
Elizabeth to give birth, and she bore a **s**. Lk 1:57
birth to her firstborn **s** and wrapped him Lk 2:7
to him, "**S**, why have you treated us so? Lk 2:48
came to John the **s** of Zechariah in the Lk 3:2
from heaven, "You are my beloved **S**; Lk 3:22
being the **s** (as was supposed) of Joseph, Lk 3:23
(as was supposed) of Joseph, the **s** of Heli, Lk 3:23
the **s** of Matthat, the son of Levi, the son Lk 3:24
the son of Matthat, the **s** of Levi, the son Lk 3:24
Matthat, the son of Levi, the **s** of Melchi, Lk 3:24
Levi, the son of Melchi, the **s** of Jannai, Lk 3:24
Melchi, the son of Jannai, the **s** of Joseph, Lk 3:24
the **s** of Mattathias, the son of Amos, the Lk 3:25
the son of Mattathias, the **s** of Amos, the Lk 3:25
the son of Amos, the **s** of Nahum, Lk 3:25
of Amos, the son of Nahum, the **s** of Esli, Lk 3:25
Nahum, the son of Esli, the **s** of Naggai, Lk 3:25
the **s** of Maath, the son of Mattathias, the Lk 3:26
the son of Maath, the **s** of Mattathias, the Lk 3:26
the son of Mattathias, the **s** of Semein, Lk 3:26
the son of Semein, the **s** of Josech, Lk 3:26
Semein, the son of Josech, the **s** of Joda, Lk 3:26
the **s** of Joanan, the son of Rhesa, the son Lk 3:27
the son of Joanan, the **s** of Rhesa, the son Lk 3:27
the son of Rhesa, the **s** of Zerubbabel, Lk 3:27
the son of Zerubbabel, the **s** of Shealtiel, Lk 3:27
the son of Shealtiel, the **s** of Neri, Lk 3:27
the **s** of Melchi, the son of Addi, the son Lk 3:28
the son of Melchi, the **s** of Addi, the son Lk 3:28
Melchi, the son of Addi, the **s** of Cosam, Lk 3:28
the son of Cosam, the **s** of Elmadam, Lk 3:28

Cosam, the son of Elmadam, the **s** of Er, Lk 3:28
the **s** of Joshua, the son of Eliezer, the son Lk 3:29
the son of Joshua, the **s** of Eliezer, the son Lk 3:29
Joshua, the son of Eliezer, the **s** of Jorim, Lk 3:29
the son of Jorim, the **s** of Matthat, Lk 3:29
Jorim, the son of Matthat, the **s** of Levi, Lk 3:29
the **s** of Simeon, the son of Judah, the son Lk 3:30
the son of Simeon, the **s** of Judah, the son Lk 3:30
Simeon, the son of Judah, the **s** of Joseph, Lk 3:30
Judah, the son of Joseph, the **s** of Jonam, Lk 3:30
the son of Jonam, the **s** of Eliakim, Lk 3:30
the **s** of Melea, the son of Menna, the son Lk 3:31
the son of Melea, the **s** of Menna, the son Lk 3:31
the son of Menna, the **s** of Mattatha, Lk 3:31
the son of Mattatha, the **s** of Nathan, Lk 3:31
the son of Nathan, the **s** of David, Lk 3:31
the **s** of Jesse, the son of Obed, the son of Lk 3:32
the son of Jesse, the **s** of Obed, the son of Lk 3:32
of Jesse, the son of Obed, the **s** of Boaz, Lk 3:32
of Obed, the son of Boaz, the **s** of Sala, Lk 3:32
Boaz, the son of Sala, the **s** of Nahshon, Lk 3:32
the **s** of Amminadab, the son of Admin, Lk 3:33
the son of Amminadab, the **s** of Admin, Lk 3:33
the son of Admin, the **s** of Arni, Lk 3:33
Admin, the son of Arni, the **s** of Hezron, Lk 3:33
of Arni, the son of Hezron, the **s** of Perez, Lk 3:33
Hezron, the son of Perez, the **s** of Judah, Lk 3:33
the **s** of Jacob, the son of Isaac, the son of Lk 3:34
the son of Jacob, the **s** of Isaac, the son of Lk 3:34
the son of Isaac, the **s** of Abraham, Lk 3:34
the son of Abraham, the **s** of Terah, Lk 3:34
the son of Terah, the **s** of Nahor, Lk 3:34
the **s** of Serug, the son of Reu, the son of Lk 3:35
the son of Serug, the **s** of Reu, the son of Lk 3:35
of Serug, the son of Reu, the **s** of Peleg, Lk 3:35
son of Reu, the son of Peleg, the **s** of Eber, Lk 3:35
of Peleg, the son of Eber, the **s** of Shelah, Lk 3:35
the **s** of Cainan, the son of Arphaxad, the Lk 3:36
the son of Cainan, the **s** of Arphaxad, the Lk 3:36
the son of Arphaxad, the **s** of Shem, Lk 3:36
the son of Shem, the **s** of Noah, Lk 3:36
Shem, the son of Noah, the **s** of Lamech, Lk 3:36
the **s** of Methuselah, the son of Enoch, Lk 3:37
the son of Methuselah, the **s** of Enoch, Lk 3:37
the son of Enoch, the **s** of Jared, Lk 3:37
the son of Jared, the **s** of Mahalaleel, Lk 3:37
the son of Mahalaleel, the **s** of Cainan, Lk 3:37
the **s** of Enos, the son of Seth, the son of Lk 3:38
the son of Enos, the **s** of Seth, the son of Lk 3:38
of Enos, the son of Seth, the **s** of Adam, Lk 3:38
of Seth, the son of Adam, the **s** of God. Lk 3:38
devil said to him, "If you are the **S** of God, Lk 4:3
and said to him, "If you are the **S** of God, Lk 4:9
And they said, "Is not this Joseph's **s**?" Lk 4:22
"You are the **S** of God!" But he rebuked Lk 4:41
may know that the **S** of Man has Lk 5:24
"The **S** of Man is lord of the Sabbath." Lk 6:5
Thomas, and James the **s** of Alphaeus, Lk 6:15
and Judas the **s** of James, and Judas Lk 6:16
as evil, on account of the **S** of Man! Lk 6:22
carried out, the only **s** of his mother, Lk 7:12
The **S** of Man has come eating and Lk 7:34
with me, Jesus, **S** of the Most High God? Lk 8:28
"The **S** of Man must suffer many things Lk 9:22
of him will the **S** of Man be ashamed Lk 9:26
out of the cloud, saying, "This is my **S**, Lk 9:35
out, "Teacher, I beg you to look at my **s**, Lk 9:38
and bear with you? Bring your **s** here." Lk 9:41
The **S** of Man is about to be delivered Lk 9:44
but the **S** of Man has nowhere to lay his Lk 9:58
And if a **s** of peace is there, your peace Lk 10:6
one knows who the **S** is except the Lk 10:22
Father is except the **S** and anyone to Lk 10:22
to whom the **S** chooses to reveal Lk 10:22
among you, if his **s** asks for a fish, Lk 11:11
so will the **S** of Man be to this Lk 11:30
the **S** of Man also will acknowledge Lk 12:8
a word against the **S** of Man will be Lk 12:10
for the **S** of Man is coming at an hour Lk 12:40
father against **s** and son against father, Lk 12:53
father against son and **s** against father, Lk 12:53
having a **s** or an ox that has fallen into a Lk 14:5
the younger **s** gathered all he had and Lk 15:13
no longer worthy to be called your **s**. Lk 15:19
And the **s** said to him, 'Father, I have Lk 15:21
no longer worthy to be called your **s**.' Lk 15:21
For this my **s** was dead, and is alive Lk 15:24
"Now his older **s** was in the field, and as Lk 15:25
But when this **s** of yours came, who Lk 15:30
said to him, '**S**, you are always with me, Lk 15:31
to see one of the days of the **S** of Man, Lk 17:22
so will the **S** of Man be in his day. Lk 17:24
so will it be in the days of the **S** of Man. Lk 17:26
the day when the **S** of Man is revealed. Lk 17:30
Nevertheless, when the **S** of Man comes, Lk 18:8
is written about the **S** of Man by the Lk 18:31
And he cried out, "Jesus, **S** of David, Lk 18:38
he cried out all the more, "**S** of David, Lk 18:39
house, since he also is a **s** of Abraham. Lk 19:9
For the **S** of Man came to seek and to Lk 19:10
I will send my beloved **s**; perhaps they Lk 20:13
they say that the Christ is David's **s**? Lk 20:41
calls him Lord, so how is he his **s**?" Lk 20:44
they will see the **S** of Man coming in Lk 21:27
and to stand before the **S** of Man." Lk 21:36
For the **S** of Man goes as it has been Lk 22:22
would you betray the **S** of Man with a Lk 22:48
But from now on the **S** of Man shall be Lk 22:69
So they all said, "Are you the **S** of God, Lk 22:70
that the **S** of Man must be delivered into Lk 24:7
glory as of the only **S** from the Father, Jn 1:14
borne witness that this is the **S** of God." Jn 1:34
said, "So you are Simon the **s** of John? Jn 1:42
wrote, Jesus of Nazareth, the **s** of Joseph." Jn 1:45
him, "Rabbi, you are the **S** of God! Jn 1:49
and descending on the **S** of Man." Jn 1:51
descended from heaven, the **S** of Man. Jn 3:13
so must the **S** of Man be lifted up, Jn 3:14
loved the world, that he gave his only **S**, Jn 3:16
God did not send his **S** into the world to Jn 3:17
believed in the name of the only **S** of God. Jn 3:18
The Father loves the **S** and has given all Jn 3:35
believes in the **S** has eternal life; Jn 3:36
does not obey the **S** shall not see life, Jn 3:36
field that Jacob had given to his **s** Joseph. Jn 4:5
there was an official whose **s** was ill. Jn 4:46
asked him to come down and heal his **s**, Jn 4:47
your **s** will live." The man believed the Jn 4:50
and told him that his **s** was recovering. Jn 4:51
"Your **s** will live." And he himself Jn 4:53
the **S** can do nothing of his own accord, Jn 5:19
the Father does, that the **S** does likewise. Jn 5:19
the Father loves the **S** and shows him all Jn 5:20
so also the **S** gives life to whom he will. Jn 5:21
one, but has given all judgment to the **S**, Jn 5:22
that all may honor the **S**, just as they Jn 5:23
does not honor the **S** does not honor the Jn 5:23
dead will hear the voice of the **S** of God, Jn 5:25
so he has granted the **S** also to have life in Jn 5:26
judgment, because he is the **S** of Man. Jn 5:27
life, which the **S** of Man will give to you. Jn 6:27
who looks on the **S** and believes in him Jn 6:40
said, "Is not this Jesus, the **s** of Joseph, Jn 6:42
eat the flesh of the **S** of Man and drink Jn 6:53
you were to see the **S** of Man ascending to Jn 6:62
He spoke of Judas the **s** of Simon Iscariot, Jn 6:71
"When you have lifted up the **S** of Man, Jn 8:28
the house forever; the **s** remains forever. Jn 8:35
So if the **S** sets you free, you will be free Jn 8:36
and asked them, "Is this your **s**, who you Jn 9:19
know that this is our **s** and that he was Jn 9:20
he said, "Do you believe in the **S** of Man?" Jn 9:35
because I said, 'I am the **S** of God'? Jn 10:36
so that the **S** of God may be glorified Jn 11:4
that you are the Christ, the **S** of God, Jn 11:27
hour has come for the **S** of Man to be Jn 12:23
can you say that the **S** of Man must be Jn 12:34
be lifted up? Who is this **S** of Man?" Jn 12:34
into the heart of Judas Iscariot, Simon's **s**, Jn 13:2
gave it to Judas, the **s** of Simon Iscariot. Jn 13:26
said, "Now is the **S** of Man glorified, Jn 13:31
the Father may be glorified in the **S**. Jn 14:13
glorify your **S** that the Son may glorify Jn 17:1
your Son that the **S** may glorify you, Jn 17:1
has been lost except the **s** of destruction, Jn 17:12
he has made himself the **S** of God." Jn 19:7
his mother, "Woman, behold, your **s**!" Jn 19:26
that Jesus is the Christ, the **S** of God, Jn 20:31
said to Simon Peter, "Simon, **s** of John, Jn 21:15
to him a second time, "Simon, **s** of John, Jn 21:16
to him the third time, "Simon, **s** of John, Jn 21:17
James the **s** of Alphaeus and Simon the Acts 1:13
the Zealot and Judas the **s** of James. Acts 1:13
(which means **s** of encouragement), Acts 4:36
him and brought him up as her own **s**. Acts 7:21
and the **S** of Man standing at the right Acts 7:56
saying, "He is the **S** of God." Acts 9:20
and said, "You **s** of the devil, you Acts 13:10
and God gave them Saul the **s** of Kish, Acts 13:21
found in David the **s** of Jesse a man Acts 13:22
in the second Psalm, "'You are my **S**, Acts 13:33
the **s** of a Jewish woman who was a Acts 16:1
of Berea, the **s** of Pyrrhus from Berea, Acts 20:4
I am a Pharisee, a **s** of Pharisees. Acts 23:6
Now the **s** of Paul's sister heard of Acts 23:16
concerning his **S**, who was descended Rom 1:3
was declared to be the **S** of God in power Rom 1:4
with my spirit in the gospel of his **S**, Rom 1:9
reconciled to God by the death of his **S**, Rom 5:10
By sending his own **S** in the likeness of Rom 8:3
to be conformed to the image of his **S**, Rom 8:29
not spare his own **S** but gave him up Rom 8:32
I will return and Sarah shall have a **s**." Rom 9:9
were called into the fellowship of his **S**, 1 Cor 1:9
then the **S** himself will also be 1 Cor 15:28
For the **S** of God, Jesus Christ, whom 2 Cor 1:19
was pleased to reveal his **S** to me, in Gal 1:16
the flesh I live by faith in the **S** of God, Gal 2:20
of time had come, God sent forth his **S**, Gal 4:4
sent the Spirit of his **S** into our hearts, Gal 4:6
So you are no longer a slave, but a **s**, and Gal 4:7
no longer a slave, but a son, and if a **s**, Gal 4:7
But the **s** of the slave was born Gal 4:23
while the **s** of the free woman was born Gal 4:23
"Cast out the slave woman and her **s**, Gal 4:30
for the **s** of the slave woman shall not Gal 4:30
not inherit with the **s** of the free Gal 4:30
and of the knowledge of the **S** of God, Eph 4:13
how as a **s** with a father he has served Phil 2:22
us to the kingdom of his beloved **S**, Col 1:13
and to wait for his **S** from heaven, 1 Thes 1:10
is revealed, the **s** of destruction, 2 Thes 2:3
last days he has spoken to us by his **S**, Heb 1:2
angels did God ever say, "You are my **S**, Heb 1:5
him a father, and he shall be to me a **s**"? Heb 1:5
But of the **S** he says, "Your throne, O Heb 1:8
you are mindful of him, or the **s** of man, Heb 2:6
Christ is faithful over God's house as a **s**. Heb 3:6
the heavens, Jesus, the **S** of God, Heb 4:14
by him who said to him, "You are my **S**, Heb 5:5
Although he was a **s**, he learned Heb 5:8
crucifying once again the **S** of God to Heb 6:6
but resembling the **S** of God he Heb 7:3
appoints a **S** who has been made Heb 7:28
the one who has spurned the **S** of God, Heb 10:29
in the act of offering up his only **s**, Heb 11:17
be called the **s** of Pharaoh's daughter, Heb 11:24
that addresses you as sons? "My **s**, Heb 12:5
and chastises every **s** whom he Heb 12:6
For what **s** is there whom his father Heb 12:7
he offered up his **s** Isaac on the altar? Jas 2:21
you greetings, and so does Mark, my **s**. 1 Pt 5:13
Majestic Glory, "This is my beloved **S**, 2 Pt 1:17
the way of Balaam, the **s** of Beor, 2 Pt 2:15
the Father and with his **S** Jesus Christ. 1 Jn 1:3
blood of Jesus his **S** cleanses us from all 1 Jn 1:7
he who denies the Father and the **S**. 1 Jn 2:22
one who denies the **S** has the Father. 1 Jn 2:23
Whoever confesses the **S** has the 1 Jn 2:23
will abide in the **S** and in the Father. 1 Jn 2:24
The reason the **S** of God appeared was to 1 Jn 3:8
the name of his **S** Jesus Christ and love 1 Jn 3:23
that God sent his only **S** into the world, 1 Jn 4:9
us and sent his **S** to be the propitiation 1 Jn 4:10
Father has sent his **S** to be the Savior 1 Jn 4:14
confesses that Jesus is the **S** of God, 1 Jn 4:15
who believes that Jesus is the **S** of God? 1 Jn 5:5
God that he has borne concerning his **S**. 1 Jn 5:9
Whoever believes in the **S** of God has 1 Jn 5:10
that God has borne concerning his **S**. 1 Jn 5:10
us eternal life, and this life is in his **S**. 1 Jn 5:11
Whoever has the **S** has life; whoever 1 Jn 5:12
does not have the **S** of God does not 1 Jn 5:12
in the name of the **S** of God that you 1 Jn 5:13
we know that the **S** of God has come 1 Jn 5:20
him who is true, in his **S** Jesus Christ. 1 Jn 5:20
and from Jesus Christ the Father's **S**, 2 Jn 1:3
teaching has both the Father and the **S**. 2 Jn 1:9
of the lampstands one like a **s** of man, Rv 1:13
'The words of the **S** of God, who has eyes Rv 2:18
seated on the cloud one like a **s** of man, Rv 14:14
and I will be his God and he will be my **s**. Rv 21:7

SON'S (16)

I may eat of my **s** game and bless you." Gn 27:25
my father arise and eat of his **s** game, Gn 27:31
give me some of your **s** mandrakes." Gn 30:14
take away my **s** mandrakes also?" Gn 30:15
in exchange for your **s** mandrakes." Gn 30:15
you with my **s** mandrakes." So he Gn 30:16
whether it is your **s** robe or not." Gn 37:32
identified it and said, "It is my **s** robe. Gn 37:33
and cut off her **s** foreskin and touched Ex 4:25
the nakedness of your **s** daughter or of Lv 18:10
she is your **s** wife, you shall not Lv 18:15
shall not take her **s** daughter or her Lv 18:17
God, you and your son and your **s** son, Dt 6:2
kingdom out of his **s** hand and will 1 Kgs 11:35
but in his **s** days I will bring the 1 Kgs 21:29
is his name, and what is his **s** name? Prv 30:4

SON-IN-LAW (12)

they said, "Samson, the **s** of the Timnite, Jgs 15:6
to go, but the girl's father said to his **s**, Jgs 19:5
Israel, that I should be **s** to the king?" 1 Sm 18:18
time, "You shall now be my **s**." 1 Sm 18:21

you. Now then become the king's **s**.'" 1 Sm 18:22
a little thing to become the king's **s**, 1 Sm 18:23
pleased David well to be the king's **s**. 1 Sm 18:26
that he might become the king's **s**. 1 Sm 18:27
faithful as David, who is the king's **s**, 1 Sm 22:14
for he was **s** to the house of Ahab. 2 Kgs 8:27
because he was the **s** of Shecaniah the Neh 6:18
was the **s** of Sanballat the Horonite. Neh 13:28

SONG (85)

people of Israel sang this **s** to the LORD, Ex 15:1
The LORD is my strength and my **s**, and Ex 15:2
Then Israel sang this **s**: "Spring up, O Nm 21:17
"Now therefore write this **s** and teach it Dt 31:19
that this **s** may be a witness for me Dt 31:19
this **s** shall confront them as a witness Dt 31:21
So Moses wrote this **s** the same day and Dt 31:22
the words of this **s** until they were Dt 31:30
all the words of this **s** in the hearing of Dt 32:44
Awake, awake, break out in a **s**! Jgs 5:12
the words of this **s** on the day when 2 Sm 22:1
of the service of **s** in the house of 1 Chr 6:31
They ministered with **s** before the 1 Chr 6:32
with **s** and lyres and harps and 1 Chr 13:8
music and instruments for sacred **s**. 1 Chr 16:42
the LORD), and when the **s** was raised, 2 Chr 5:13
began, the **s** to the LORD began also, 2 Chr 29:27
"And now I have become their **s**; I am a Jb 30:9
the words of this **s** to the LORD on Ps 18:T
and with my **s** I give thanks to him. Ps 28:7
A **s** at the dedication of the temple. Ps 30:T
Sing to him a new **s**; play skillfully on Ps 33:3
He put a new **s** in my mouth, a song of Ps 40:3
in my mouth, a **s** of praise to our God. Ps 40:3
love, and at night his **s** is with me, Ps 42:8
A Maskil of the Sons of Korah; a love **s**. Ps 45:T
of Korah. According to Alamoth. A **S**. Ps 46:T
A **S**. A Psalm of the Sons of Korah. Ps 48:T
the choirmaster. A Psalm of David. A **S**. Ps 65:T
To the choirmaster. A **S**. A Psalm. Ps 66:T
stringed instruments. A Psalm. A **S**. Ps 67:T
the choirmaster. A Psalm of David. A **S**. Ps 68:T
lift up a **s** to him who rides through the Ps 68:4
I will praise the name of God with a **s**; I Ps 69:30
Do Not Destroy. A Psalm of Asaph. A **S**. Ps 75:T
instruments. A Psalm of Asaph. A **S**. Ps 76:T
"Let me remember my **s** in the night; Ps 77:6
their young women had no marriage **s**. Ps 78:63
Raise a **s**; sound the tambourine, the Ps 81:2
A **S**. A Psalm of Asaph. Ps 83:T
A Psalm of the Sons of Korah. A **S**. Ps 87:T
A **S**. A Psalm of the Sons of Korah. To Ps 88:T
A Psalm. A **S** for the Sabbath. Ps 92:T
Oh sing to the LORD a new **s**; sing to the Ps 96:1
Oh sing to the LORD a new **s**, for he has Ps 98:1
forth into joyous **s** and sing praises! Ps 98:4
A **S**. A Psalm of David. Ps 108:T
The LORD is my strength and my **s**; he Ps 118:14
A **S** of Ascents. Ps 120:T
A **S** of Ascents. Ps 121:T
A **S** of Ascents. Of David. Ps 122:T
A **S** of Ascents. Ps 123:T
A **S** of Ascents. Of David. Ps 124:T
A **S** of Ascents. Ps 125:T
A **S** of Ascents. Ps 126:T
A **S** of Ascents. Of Solomon. Ps 127:T
A **S** of Ascents. Ps 128:T
A **S** of Ascents. Ps 129:T
A **S** of Ascents. Ps 130:T
A **S** of Ascents. Of David. Ps 131:T
A **S** of Ascents. Ps 132:T
A **S** of Ascents. Of David. Ps 133:T
A **S** of Ascents. Ps 134:T
we sing the LORD'S **s** in a foreign land? Ps 137:4
I will sing a new **s** to you, O God; upon a Ps 144:9
A **S** of Praise. Of David. Ps 145:T
it is pleasant, and a **s** of praise is fitting. Ps 147:1
Sing to the LORD a new **s**, his praise in Ps 149:1
of the wise than to hear the **s** of fools. Eccl 7:5
all the daughters of **s** are brought low Eccl 12:4
The **S** of Songs, which is Solomon's. Sg 1:1
beloved my love **s** concerning his Is 5:1
for the LORD GOD is my strength and my **s**, Is 12:2
to Tyre as in the **s** of the prostitute: Is 23:15
cloud, so the **s** of the ruthless is put down. Is 25:5
In that day this **s** will be sung in the land Is 26:1
You shall have a **s** as in the night when Is 30:29
Sing to the LORD a new **s**, his praise from Is 42:10
in her, thanksgiving and the voice of **s**. Is 51:3
take up a taunt **s** against you and moan Mi 2:4
And they sang a new **s**, saying, "Worthy Rv 5:9
were singing a new **s** before the throne Rv 14:3
one could learn that **s** except the 144,000 Rv 14:3
And they sing the **s** of Moses, the servant Rv 15:3
servant of God, and the **s** of the Lamb, Rv 15:3

SONGS (30)

have sent you away with mirth and **s**, Gn 31:27
Saul, with tambourines, with **s** of joy, 1 Sm 18:6
with **s** and lyres and harps and 2 Sm 6:5
3,000 proverbs, and his **s** were 1,005. 1 Kgs 4:32
was in charge of the **s** of thanksgiving. Neh 12:8
and there were **s** of praise and Neh 12:46
my Maker, who gives **s** in the night, Jb 35:10
of God with glad shouts and **s** of praise, Ps 42:4
peoples! Shout to God with loud **s** of joy! Ps 47:1
and the drunkards make **s** about me. Ps 69:12
a joyful noise to him with **s** of praise! Ps 95:2
and tell of his deeds in **s** of joy! Ps 107:22
Glad **s** of salvation are in the tents of Ps 118:15
statutes have been my **s** in the house Ps 119:54
For there our captors required of us **s**, Ps 137:3
saying, "Sing us one of the **s** of Zion!" Ps 137:3
Whoever sings **s** to a heavy heart is Prv 25:20
The Song of **S**, which is Solomon's. Sg 1:1
field, and in the vineyards no **s** are sung, Is 16:10
sing many **s**, that you may be Is 23:16
the ends of the earth we hear **s** of praise, Is 24:16
of them shall come **s** of thanksgiving, Jer 30:19
And I will stop the music of your **s**, Ezk 26:13
who sings lustful **s** with a beautiful Ezk 33:32
Take away from me the noise of your **s**; Am 5:23
who sing idle **s** to the sound of the harp Am 6:5
The **s** of the temple shall become Am 8:3
and all your **s** into lamentation; Am 8:10
in psalms and hymns and spiritual **s**, Eph 5:19
psalms and hymns and spiritual **s**, Col 3:16

SONS (1324)

years; and he had other **s** and daughters. Gn 5:4
807 years and had other **s** and daughters. Gn 5:7
years and had other **s** and daughters. Gn 5:10
years and had other **s** and daughters. Gn 5:13
years and had other **s** and daughters. Gn 5:16
years and had other **s** and daughters. Gn 5:19
years and had other **s** and daughters. Gn 5:22
years and had other **s** and daughters. Gn 5:26
years and had other **s** and daughters. Gn 5:30
the **s** of God saw that the daughters of Gn 6:2
when the **s** of God came in to the Gn 6:4
And Noah had three **s**, Shem, Ham, and Gn 6:10
you shall come into the ark, you, your **s**, Gn 6:18
And Noah and his **s** and his wife and his Gn 7:7
On the very same day Noah and his **s**, Gn 7:13
three wives of his **s** with them entered Gn 7:13
and your **s** and your sons' wives with Gn 8:16
and his **s** and his wife and his sons' Gn 8:18
blessed Noah and his **s** and said to them, Gn 9:1
God said to Noah and to his **s** with him, Gn 9:8
The **s** of Noah who went forth from the Gn 9:18
These three were the **s** of Noah, and Gn 9:19
are the generations of the **s** of Noah, Gn 10:1
S were born to them after the flood. Gn 10:1
The **s** of Japheth: Gomer, Magog, Madai, Gn 10:2
The **s** of Gomer: Ashkenaz, Riphath, Gn 10:3
The **s** of Javan: Elishah, Tarshish, Gn 10:4
The **s** of Ham: Cush, Egypt, Put, and Gn 10:6
The **s** of Cush: Seba, Havilah, Sabtah, Gn 10:7
The **s** of Raamah: Sheba and Dedan. Gn 10:7
These are the **s** of Ham, by their clans, Gn 10:20
The **s** of Shem: Elam, Asshur, Gn 10:22
The **s** of Aram: Uz, Hul, Gether, and Gn 10:23
To Eber were born two **s**: the name of Gn 10:25
Jobab; all these were the **s** of Joktan. Gn 10:29
These are the **s** of Shem, by their clans, Gn 10:31
These are the clans of the **s** of Noah, Gn 10:32
years and had other **s** and daughters. Gn 11:11
years and had other **s** and daughters. Gn 11:13
years and had other **s** and daughters. Gn 11:15
years and had other **s** and daughters. Gn 11:17
years and had other **s** and daughters. Gn 11:19
years and had other **s** and daughters. Gn 11:21
years and had other **s** and daughters. Gn 11:23
years and had other **s** and daughters. Gn 11:25
Sons-in-law, **s**, daughters, or anyone Gn 19:12
In the sight of the **s** of my people I give Gn 23:11
The **s** of Dedan were Asshurim, Gn 25:3
The **s** of Midian were Ephah, Epher, Gn 25:4
But to the **s** of his concubines Abraham Gn 25:6
Isaac and Ishmael his **s** buried him in Gn 25:9
are the names of the **s** of Ishmael, Gn 25:13
These are the **s** of Ishmael and these Gn 25:16
and may your mother's **s** bow down to Gn 27:29
borne him three **s**." Therefore his Gn 29:34
have borne him six **s**." So she called Gn 30:20
black, and put them in charge of his **s**. Gn 30:35
Jacob heard that the **s** of Laban were Gn 31:1
arose and set his **s** and his wives on Gn 31:17
me to kiss my **s** and my daughters Gn 31:28
And from the **s** of Hamor, Shechem's Gn 33:19
But his **s** were with his livestock in the Gn 34:5
The **s** of Jacob had come in from the Gn 34:7
The **s** of Jacob answered Shechem and Gn 34:13
they were sore, two of the **s** of Jacob, Gn 34:25
The **s** of Jacob came upon the slain Gn 34:27
that they did not pursue the **s** of Jacob. Gn 35:5
of it. Now the **s** of Jacob were twelve. Gn 35:22
The **s** of Leah: Reuben (Jacob's Gn 35:23
The **s** of Rachel: Joseph and Benjamin. Gn 35:24
The **s** of Bilhah, Rachel's servant: Dan Gn 35:25
The **s** of Zilpah, Leah's servant: Gad Gn 35:26
These were the **s** of Jacob who were Gn 35:26
And his **s** Esau and Jacob buried him. Gn 35:29
These are the **s** of Esau who were born Gn 36:5
Then Esau took his wives, his **s**, his Gn 36:6
These are the names of Esau's **s**: Gn 36:10
The **s** of Eliphaz were Teman, Omar, Gn 36:11
These are the **s** of Adah, Esau's wife. Gn 36:12
These are the **s** of Reuel: Nahath, Gn 36:13
These are the **s** of Basemath, Esau's Gn 36:13
These are the **s** of Oholibamah the Gn 36:14
These are the chiefs of the **s** of Esau. Gn 36:15
The **s** of Eliphaz the firstborn of Esau: Gn 36:15
land of Edom; these are the **s** of Adah. Gn 36:16
These are the **s** of Reuel, Esau's son: the Gn 36:17
these are the **s** of Basemath, Esau's Gn 36:17
These are the **s** of Oholibamah, Esau's Gn 36:18
These are the **s** of Esau (that is, Edom), Gn 36:19
These are the **s** of Seir the Horite, the Gn 36:20
the **s** of Seir in the land of Edom. Gn 36:21
The **s** of Lotan were Hori and Hemam; Gn 36:22
These are the **s** of Shobal: Alvan, Gn 36:23
These are the **s** of Zibeon: Aiah and Gn 36:24
These are the **s** of Dishon: Hemdan, Gn 36:26
These are the **s** of Ezer: Bilhan, Zaavan, Gn 36:27
These are the **s** of Dishan: Uz and Gn 36:28
a boy with the **s** of Bilhah and Zilpah, Gn 37:2
Joseph more than any other of his **s**, Gn 37:3
All his **s** and all his daughters rose up Gn 37:35
came, two **s** were born to Joseph. Gn 41:50
grain for sale in Egypt, he said to his **s**, Gn 42:1
Thus the **s** of Israel came to buy among Gn 42:5
We are all **s** of one man. We are honest Gn 42:11
the **s** of one man in the land of Gn 42:13
We are twelve brothers, **s** of our father. Gn 42:32
"Kill my two **s** if I do not bring him Gn 42:37
'You know that my wife bore me two **s**. Gn 44:27
The **s** of Israel did so: and Joseph gave Gn 45:21
The **s** of Israel carried Jacob their father, Gn 46:5
his **s**, and his sons' sons with him, his Gn 46:7
his sons, and his sons' **s** with him, his Gn 46:7
who came into Egypt, Jacob and his **s**. Gn 46:8
and the **s** of Reuben: Hanoch, Pallu, Gn 46:9
The **s** of Simeon: Jemuel, Jamin, Ohad, Gn 46:10
The **s** of Levi: Gershon, Kohath, and Gn 46:11
The **s** of Judah: Er, Onan, Shelah, Gn 46:12
and the **s** of Perez were Hezron and Gn 46:12
The **s** of Issachar: Tola, Puvah, Yob, Gn 46:13
The **s** of Zebulun: Sered, Elon, and Gn 46:14
These are the **s** of Leah, whom she bore Gn 46:15
altogether his **s** and his daughters Gn 46:15
The **s** of Gad: Ziphion, Haggi, Shuni, Gn 46:16
The **s** of Asher: Imnah, Ishvah, Ishvi, Gn 46:17
Serah their sister. And the **s** of Beriah: Gn 46:17
These are the **s** of Zilpah, whom Laban Gn 46:18
The **s** of Rachel, Jacob's wife: Joseph Gn 46:19
And the **s** of Benjamin: Bela, Becher, Gn 46:21
These are the **s** of Rachel, who were Gn 46:22
The **s** of Dan: Hushim. Gn 46:23
The **s** of Naphtali: Jahzeel, Guni, Jezer, Gn 46:24
These are the **s** of Bilhah, whom Gn 46:25
And the **s** of Joseph, who were born to Gn 46:27
is ill." So he took with him his two **s**, Gn 48:1
And now your two **s**, who were born to Gn 48:5
When Israel saw Joseph's **s**, he said, Gn 48:8
Joseph said to his father, "They are my **s**, Gn 48:9
Then Jacob called his **s** and said, Gn 49:1
"Assemble and listen, O **s** of Jacob, Gn 49:2
your father's **s** shall bow down before Gn 49:8
Jacob finished commanding his **s**, Gn 49:33
Thus his **s** did for him as he had Gn 50:12
for his **s** carried him to the land of Gn 50:13
Then Joseph made the **s** of Israel swear, Gn 50:25
are the names of the **s** of Israel who came Ex 1:1
put them on your **s** and on your Ex 3:22
his wife and his **s** and had them ride Ex 4:20
the **s** of Reuben, the firstborn of Israel: Ex 6:14
The **s** of Simeon: Jemuel, Jamin, Ohad, Ex 6:15
the names of the **s** of Levi according to Ex 6:16
The **s** of Gershon: Libni and Shimei, by Ex 6:17
The **s** of Kohath: Amram, Izhar, Hebron, Ex 6:18
The **s** of Merari: Mahli and Mushi. Ex 6:19
The **s** of Izhar: Korah, Nepheg, and Ex 6:21
The **s** of Uzziel: Mishael, Elzaphan, and Ex 6:22
The **s** of Korah: Assir, Elkanah, and Ex 6:24
will go with our **s** and daughters and Ex 10:9
a statute for you and for your **s** forever. Ex 12:24

man among your **s** you shall redeem. Ex 13:13
but all the firstborn of my **s** I redeem.' Ex 13:15
had made the **s** of Israel solemnly Ex 13:19
along with her two **s**. The name of the Ex 18:3
came with his **s** and his wife to Moses in Ex 18:5
with your wife and her two **s** with her," Ex 18:6
a wife and she bears him **s** or daughters, Ex 21:4
The firstborn of your **s** you shall give Ex 22:29
Aaron and his **s** shall tend it from Ex 27:21
Aaron your brother, and his **s** with him, Ex 28:1
me as priests—Aaron and Aaron's **s**, Ex 28:1
your brother and his **s** to serve me as Ex 28:4
on them the names of the **s** of Israel, Ex 28:9
stones with the names of the **s** of Israel. Ex 28:11
of remembrance for the **s** of Israel. Ex 28:12
to the names of the **s** of Israel. Ex 28:21
bear the names of the **s** of Israel in the Ex 28:29
"For Aaron's **s** you shall make coats Ex 28:40
your brother, and on his **s** with him, Ex 28:41
Aaron and on his **s** when they go into Ex 28:43
bring Aaron and his **s** to the entrance of Ex 29:4
you shall bring his **s** and put coats on Ex 29:8
gird Aaron and his **s** with sashes and Ex 29:9
Thus you shall ordain Aaron and his **s**. Ex 29:9
Aaron and his **s** shall lay their hands Ex 29:10
and Aaron and his **s** shall lay their Ex 29:15
and Aaron and his **s** shall lay their Ex 29:19
and on the tips of the right ears of his **s**, Ex 29:20
and on his **s** and his sons' garments Ex 29:21
and his **s** and his sons' garments with Ex 29:21
of Aaron and on the palms of his **s**, Ex 29:24
from what was Aaron's and his **s**. Ex 29:27
for Aaron and his **s** as a perpetual due Ex 29:28
of Aaron shall be for his **s** after him; Ex 29:29
And Aaron and his **s** shall eat the flesh Ex 29:32
you shall do to Aaron and to his **s**, Ex 29:35
Aaron also and his **s** I will consecrate Ex 29:44
which Aaron and his **s** shall wash their Ex 30:19
You shall anoint Aaron and his **s**, and Ex 30:30
the priest and the garments of his **s**, Ex 31:10
that are in the ears of your wives, your **s**, Ex 32:2
me." And all the **s** of Levi gathered Ex 32:26
And the **s** of Levi did according to the Ex 32:28
you take of their daughters for your **s**, Ex 34:16
gods and make your **s** whore after their Ex 34:16
firstborn of your **s** you shall redeem. Ex 34:20
the priest, and the garments of his **s**, Ex 35:19
according to the names of the **s** of Israel. Ex 39:6
of remembrance for the **s** of Israel, Ex 39:7
to the names of the **s** of Israel. Ex 39:14
of fine linen, for Aaron and his **s**, Ex 39:27
the garments of his **s** for their service as Ex 39:41
bring Aaron and his **s** to the entrance Ex 40:12
You shall bring his **s** also and put Ex 40:14
Aaron and his **s** washed their hands Ex 40:31
and Aaron's **s** the priests shall bring the Lv 1:5
and the **s** of Aaron the priest shall put fire Lv 1:7
And Aaron's **s** the priests shall arrange Lv 1:8
and Aaron's **s** the priests shall throw its Lv 1:11
and bring it to Aaron's **s** the priests. And Lv 2:2
offering shall be for Aaron and his **s**; Lv 2:3
offering shall be for Aaron and his **s**; Lv 2:10
and Aaron's **s** the priests shall throw the Lv 3:2
Then Aaron's **s** shall burn it on the altar Lv 3:5
and Aaron's **s** shall throw its blood Lv 3:8
and the **s** of Aaron shall throw its blood Lv 3:13
"Command Aaron and his **s**, saying, This Lv 6:9
The **s** of Aaron shall offer it before the Lv 6:14
the rest of it Aaron and his **s** shall eat. Lv 6:16
that Aaron and his **s** shall offer to the Lv 6:20
The priest from among Aaron's **s**, who is Lv 6:22
"Speak to Aaron and his **s**, saying, This Lv 6:25
shared equally among all the **s** of Aaron. Lv 7:10
the breast shall be for Aaron and his **s**. Lv 7:31
Whoever among the **s** of Aaron offers Lv 7:33
them to Aaron the priest and to his **s**, Lv 7:34
Aaron and of his **s** from the LORD'S food Lv 7:35
"Take Aaron and his **s** with him, and the Lv 8:2
Aaron and his **s** and washed them Lv 8:6
Moses brought Aaron's **s** and clothed Lv 8:13
and Aaron and his **s** laid their hands on Lv 8:14
and Aaron and his **s** laid their hands on Lv 8:18
and Aaron and his **s** laid their hands on Lv 8:22
Then he presented Aaron's **s**, and Moses Lv 8:24
in the hands of his **s** and waved them as Lv 8:27
and also on his **s** and his sons' garments. Lv 8:30
and his **s** and his sons' garments with Lv 8:30
And Moses said to Aaron and his **s**, "Boil Lv 8:31
saying, 'Aaron and his **s** shall eat it.' Lv 8:31
And Aaron and his **s** did all the things Lv 8:36
called Aaron and his **s** and the elders of Lv 9:1
And the **s** of Aaron presented the blood to Lv 9:9
and Aaron's **s** handed him the blood, Lv 9:12
And Aaron's **s** handed him the blood, Lv 9:18
Now Nadab and Abihu, the **s** of Aaron, Lv 10:1
the **s** of Uzziel the uncle of Aaron, Lv 10:4
Aaron and to Eleazar and Ithamar his **s**, Lv 10:6
or strong drink, you or your **s** with you, Lv 10:9
to Eleazar and Ithamar, his surviving **s**: Lv 10:12
you and your **s** and your daughters Lv 10:14
and Ithamar, the surviving **s** of Aaron, Lv 10:16
the priest or to one of his **s** the priests, Lv 13:2
after the death of the two **s** of Aaron, Lv 16:1
"Speak to Aaron and his **s** and to all the Lv 17:2
a grudge against the **s** of your own Lv 19:18
"Speak to the priests, the **s** of Aaron, Lv 21:1
to Aaron and to his **s** and to all the Lv 21:24
to Aaron and his **s** so that they abstain Lv 22:2
to Aaron and his **s** and all the people Lv 22:18
And it shall be for Aaron and his **s**, and Lv 24:9
bequeath them to your **s** after you to Lv 25:46
You shall eat the flesh of your **s**, and Lv 26:29
from the **s** of Joseph, from Ephraim, Nm 1:10
These are the names of the **s** of Aaron: Nm 3:2
These are the names of the **s** of Aaron, Nm 3:3
shall give the Levites to Aaron and his **s**; Nm 3:9
And you shall appoint Aaron and his **s**, Nm 3:10
"List the **s** of Levi, by fathers' houses Nm 3:15
And these were the **s** of Levi by their Nm 3:17
the names of the **s** of Gershon by their Nm 3:18
And the **s** of Kohath by their clans: Nm 3:19
And the **s** of Merari by their clans: Nm 3:20
guard duty of the **s** of Gershon in the Nm 3:25
The clans of the **s** of Kohath were to Nm 3:29
guard duty of the **s** of Merari involved Nm 3:36
were Moses and Aaron and his **s**, Nm 3:38
to Aaron and his **s** as the redemption Nm 3:48
redemption money to Aaron and his **s**, Nm 3:51
a census of the **s** of Kohath from among Nm 4:2
of Kohath from among the **s** of Levi, Nm 4:2
is the service of the **s** of Kohath in the Nm 4:4
Aaron and his **s** shall go in and take Nm 4:5
Aaron and his **s** have finished covering Nm 4:15
after that the **s** of Kohath shall come to Nm 4:15
of meeting that the **s** of Kohath are to Nm 4:15
Aaron and his **s** shall go in and Nm 4:19
a census of the **s** of Gershon also, Nm 4:22
the service of the **s** of the Gershonites Nm 4:27
be at the command of Aaron and his **s**, Nm 4:27
the clans of the **s** of the Gershonites in Nm 4:28
"As for the **s** of Merari, you shall list Nm 4:29
service of the clans of the **s** of Merari, Nm 4:33
congregation listed the **s** of the Nm 4:34
Those listed of the **s** of Gershon, by Nm 4:38
the list of the clans of the **s** of Gershon, Nm 4:41
listed of the clans of the **s** of Merari, Nm 4:42
the list of the clans of the **s** of Merari, Nm 4:45
"Speak to Aaron and his **s**, saying, Nm 6:23
four oxen he gave to the **s** of Gershon, Nm 7:7
and eight oxen he gave to the **s** of Merari, Nm 7:8
But to the **s** of Kohath he gave none, Nm 7:9
set the Levites before Aaron and his **s**, Nm 8:13
to Aaron and his **s** from among the Nm 8:19
tent of meeting before Aaron and his **s**; Nm 8:22
And the **s** of Aaron, the priests, shall Nm 10:8
the **s** of Gershon and the sons of Nm 10:17
sons of Gershon and the **s** of Merari, Nm 10:17
we saw the Nephilim (the **s** of Anak, Nm 13:33
and Dathan and Abiram the **s** of Eliab, Nm 16:1
and On the son of Peleth, **s** of Reuben, Nm 16:1
one. You have gone too far, **s** of Levi!" Nm 16:7
said to Korah, "Hear now, you **s** of Levi: Nm 16:8
all your brothers the **s** of Levi with Nm 16:10
Dathan and Abiram the **s** of Eliab, Nm 16:12
tents, together with their wives, their **s**, Nm 16:27
"You and your **s** and your father's Nm 18:1
and you and your **s** with you shall bear Nm 18:1
while you and your **s** with you are Nm 18:2
And you and your **s** with you shall Nm 18:7
portion and to your **s** as a perpetual Nm 18:8
shall be most holy to you and to your **s**. Nm 18:9
and to your **s** and daughters with you, Nm 18:11
and to your **s** and daughters with you, Nm 18:19
He has made his **s** fugitives, and his Nm 21:29
defeated him and his **s** and all his Nm 21:35
and break down all the **s** of Sheth. Nm 24:17
the firstborn of Israel; the **s** of Reuben: Nm 26:5
And the **s** of Pallu: Eliab. Nm 26:8
The **s** of Eliab: Nemuel, Dathan, and Nm 26:9
But the **s** of Korah did not die. Nm 26:11
The **s** of Simeon according to their Nm 26:12
The **s** of Gad according to their clans: Nm 26:15
are the clans of the **s** of Gad as they Nm 26:18
The **s** of Judah were Er and Onan; and Nm 26:19
And the **s** of Judah according to their Nm 26:20
And the **s** of Perez were: of Hezron, the Nm 26:21
The **s** of Issachar according to their Nm 26:23
The **s** of Zebulun, according to their Nm 26:26
The **s** of Joseph according to their Nm 26:28
The **s** of Manasseh: of Machir, the Nm 26:29
These are the **s** of Gilead: of Iezer, the Nm 26:30
the son of Hepher had no **s**, Nm 26:33
These are the **s** of Ephraim according Nm 26:35
And these are the **s** of Shuthelah: of Nm 26:36
the clans of the **s** of Ephraim as they Nm 26:37
These are the **s** of Joseph according to Nm 26:37
The **s** of Benjamin according to their Nm 26:38
And the **s** of Bela were Ard and Nm 26:40
These are the **s** of Benjamin Nm 26:41
These are the **s** of Dan according to Nm 26:42
The **s** of Asher according to their Nm 26:44
Of the **s** of Beriah: of Heber, the clan of Nm 26:45
are the clans of the **s** of Asher as they Nm 26:47
The **s** of Naphtali according to their Nm 26:48
died for his own sin. And he had no **s**. Nm 27:3
And the **s** of Machir the son of Nm 32:39
to any of the **s** of the other tribes Nm 36:3
were married to **s** of their father's Nm 36:11
we have seen the **s** of the Anakim there."' Dt 1:28
have given it to the **s** of Lot for a Dt 2:19
as the **s** of Esau who live in Seir and the Dt 2:29
defeated him and his **s** and all his people. Dt 2:33
to the land of the **s** of Ammon you did Dt 2:37
your daughters to their **s** or taking their Dt 7:3
sons or taking their daughters for your **s**, Dt 7:3
turn away your **s** from following me, Dt 7:4
people great and tall, the **s** of the Anakim, Dt 9:2
'Who can stand before the **s** of Anak?' Dt 9:2
did to Dathan and Abiram the **s** of Eliab, Dt 11:6
you and your **s** and your daughters, Dt 12:12
even burn their **s** and their daughters Dt 12:31
"You are the **s** of the LORD your God. You Dt 14:1
of the LORD, him and his **s** for all time. Dt 18:5
Then the priests, the **s** of Levi, shall come Dt 21:5
possessions as an inheritance to his **s**, Dt 21:16
and none of the **s** of Israel shall be a Dt 23:17
Your **s** and your daughters shall be Dt 28:32
You shall father **s** and daughters, but Dt 28:41
the flesh of your **s** and daughters, Dt 28:53
and gave it to the priests, the **s** of Levi, Dt 31:9
according to the number of the **s** of God. Dt 32:8
provocation of his **s** and his daughters. Dt 32:19
he said, "Most blessed of **s** be Asher; Dt 33:24
The **s** of Reuben and the sons of Gad and Jos 4:12
sons of Reuben and the **s** of Gad and the Jos 4:12
knives and circumcise the **s** of Israel a Jos 5:2
knives and circumcised the **s** of Israel at Jos 5:3
and his **s** and daughters and his oxen Jos 7:24
the hailstones than the **s** of Israel killed Jos 10:11
gave the Amorites over to the **s** of Israel, Jos 10:12
When Joshua and the **s** of Israel had Jos 10:20
out from there the three **s** of Anak, Jos 15:14
of Machir, son of Manasseh, had no **s**, Jos 17:3
received an inheritance along with his **s**. Jos 17:6
Jacob bought from the **s** of Hamor the Jos 24:32
he drove out from it the three **s** of Anak. Jgs 1:20
their own daughters they gave to their **s**, Jgs 3:6
were my brothers, the **s** of my mother. Jgs 8:19
Now Gideon had seventy **s**, his own Jgs 8:30
all seventy of the **s** of Jerubbaal rule over Jgs 9:2
and killed his brothers the **s** of Jerubbaal, Jgs 9:5
house this day and have killed his **s**, Jgs 9:18
done to the seventy **s** of Jerubbaal might Jgs 9:24
And he had thirty **s** who rode on thirty Jgs 10:4
And Gilead's wife also bore him **s**. And Jgs 11:2
And when his wife's **s** grew up, they Jgs 11:2
He had thirty **s**, and thirty daughters he Jgs 12:9
he brought in from outside for his **s**. Jgs 12:9
He had forty **s** and thirty grandsons, Jgs 12:14
gods, and ordained one of his **s**, Jgs 17:5
man became to him like one of his **s**. Jgs 17:11
and his **s** were priests to the tribe of the Jgs 18:30
of Moab, he and his wife and his two **s**. Ru 1:1
names of his two **s** were Mahlon and Ru 1:2
died, and she was left with her two **s**. Ru 1:3
left without her two **s** and her husband. Ru 1:5
Have I yet **s** in my womb that they may Ru 1:11
a husband this night and should bear **s**, Ru 1:12
you, who is more to you than seven **s**, Ru 4:15
hosts at Shiloh, where the two **s** of Eli, 1 Sm 1:3
his wife and to all her **s** and daughters. 1 Sm 1:4
sad? Am I not more to you than ten **s**?" 1 Sm 1:8
Now the **s** of Eli were worthless men. 1 Sm 2:12
and bore three **s** and two daughters. 1 Sm 2:21
hearing all that his **s** were doing to all 1 Sm 2:22
No, my **s**; it is no good report that I 1 Sm 2:24
and honor your **s** above me by 1 Sm 2:29
this that shall come upon your two **s**, 1 Sm 2:34
because his **s** were blaspheming God, 1 Sm 3:13
And the two **s** of Eli, Hophni and 1 Sm 4:4
God was captured, and the two **s** of Eli, 1 Sm 4:11
Your two **s** also, Hophni and 1 Sm 4:17
old, he made his **s** judges over Israel. 1 Sm 8:1
Yet his **s** did not walk in his ways but 1 Sm 8:3
you are old and your **s** do not walk in 1 Sm 8:5

he will take your **s** and appoint them 1 Sm 8:11
gray; and behold, my **s** are with you. 1 Sm 12:2
Now the **s** of Saul were Jonathan, 1 Sm 14:49
for myself a king among his **s**." 1 Sm 16:1
Jesse and his **s** and invited them 1 Sm 16:5
seven of his **s** pass before Samuel. 1 Sm 16:10
"Are all your **s** here?" And he said, 1 Sm 16:11
Judah, named Jesse, who had eight **s**. 1 Sm 17:12
The three oldest **s** of Jesse had 1 Sm 17:13
names of his three **s** who went to the 1 Sm 17:13
But one of the **s** of Ahimelech the 1 Sm 22:20
you and your **s** shall be with 1 Sm 28:19
their wives and **s** and daughters taken 1 Sm 30:3
in soul, each for his **s** and daughters. 1 Sm 30:6
small or great, **s** or daughters, 1 Sm 30:19
Philistines overtook Saul and his **s**, 1 Sm 31:2
and Malchi-shua, the **s** of Saul. 1 Sm 31:2
Thus Saul died, and his three **s**, and 1 Sm 31:6
fled and that Saul and his **s** were dead, 1 Sm 31:7
Saul and his three **s** fallen on Mount 1 Sm 31:8
the bodies of his **s** from the wall of 1 Sm 31:12
And the three **s** of Zeruiah were there, 2 Sm 2:18
And **s** were born to David at Hebron: 2 Sm 3:2
These men, the **s** of Zeruiah, are more 2 Sm 3:39
s of Rimmon a man of Benjamin from 2 Sm 4:2
Now the **s** of Rimmon the Beerothite, 2 Sm 4:5
the **s** of Rimmon the Beerothite, 2 Sm 4:9
and more **s** and daughters were born 2 Sm 5:13
Uzzah and Ahio, the **s** of Abinadab, 2 Sm 6:3
men, with the stripes of the **s** of men, 2 Sm 7:14
Pelethites, and David's **s** were priests. 2 Sm 8:18
you and your **s** and your servants 2 Sm 9:10
Ziba had fifteen **s** and twenty 2 Sm 9:10
David's table, like one of the king's **s**. 2 Sm 9:11
and Absalom invited all the king's **s**. 2 Sm 13:23
and all the king's **s** go with him. 2 Sm 13:27
Then all the king's **s** arose, and each 2 Sm 13:29
has struck down all the king's **s**, 2 Sm 13:30
killed all the young men the king's **s**, 2 Sm 13:32
suppose that all the king's **s** are dead, 2 Sm 13:33
"Behold, the king's **s** have come; 2 Sm 13:35
the king's **s** came and lifted up their 2 Sm 13:36
And your servant had two **s**, and they 2 Sm 14:6
There were born to Absalom three **s**, 2 Sm 14:27
to the city in peace, with your two **s**, 2 Sm 15:27
their two **s** are with them there, 2 Sm 15:36
I to do with you, you **s** of Zeruiah? 2 Sm 16:10
the lives of your **s** and your daughters 2 Sm 19:5
with his fifteen **s** and his twenty 2 Sm 19:17
I to do with you, you **s** of Zeruiah, 2 Sm 19:22
let seven of his **s** be given to us, so that 2 Sm 21:6
king took the two **s** of Rizpah the 2 Sm 21:8
and the five **s** of Merab the daughter 2 Sm 21:8
the Shaalbonite, the **s** of Jashen, 2 Sm 23:32
he invited all his brothers, the king's **s**, 1 Kgs 1:9
and has invited all the **s** of the king, 1 Kgs 1:19
and has invited all the king's **s**, 1 Kgs 1:25
'If your **s** pay close attention to their 1 Kgs 2:4
deal loyally with the **s** of Barzillai the 1 Kgs 2:7
and Ahijah the **s** of Shisha were 1 Kgs 4:3
Calcol, and Darda, the **s** of Mahol, 1 Kgs 4:31
if only your **s** pay close attention to 1 Kgs 8:25
house among the **s** of Pharaoh. 1 Kgs 11:20
And his **s** came and told him all 1 Kgs 13:11
he go?" And his **s** showed him the 1 Kgs 13:12
And he said to his **s**, "Saddle the 1 Kgs 13:13
And he said to his **s**, "Saddle the 1 Kgs 13:27
he had buried him, he said to his **s**, 1 Kgs 13:31
of the tribes of the **s** of Jacob, 1 Kgs 18:31
certain man of the **s** of the prophets 1 Kgs 20:35
And the **s** of the prophets who were in 2 Kgs 2:3
The **s** of the prophets who were at 2 Kgs 2:5
Fifty men of the **s** of the prophets also 2 Kgs 2:7
Now when the **s** of the prophets who 2 Kgs 2:15
wife of one of the **s** of the prophets cried 2 Kgs 4:1
yourself and your **s** and pour into 2 Kgs 4:4
shut the door behind herself and her **s**. 2 Kgs 4:5
and you and your **s** can live on the 2 Kgs 4:7
And as the **s** of the prophets were 2 Kgs 4:38
boil stew for the **s** of the prophets." 2 Kgs 4:38
young men of the **s** of the prophets. 2 Kgs 5:22
Now the **s** of the prophets said to 2 Kgs 6:1
a lamp to him and to his **s** forever. 2 Kgs 8:19
called one of the **s** of the prophets and 2 Kgs 9:1
the blood of his **s**—declares the LORD 2 Kgs 9:26
Now Ahab had seventy **s** in Samaria. 2 Kgs 10:1
and to the guardians of the **s** of Ahab, 2 Kgs 10:1
seeing your master's **s** are with you, 2 Kgs 10:2
fittest of your master's **s** and set him 2 Kgs 10:3
heads of your master's **s** and come to 2 Kgs 10:6
at this time." Now the king's **s**, 2 Kgs 10:6
took the king's **s** and slaughtered 2 Kgs 10:7
the heads of the king's **s**," he said, 2 Kgs 10:8
royal princes and the **s** of the queen 2 Kgs 10:13
your **s** of the fourth generation shall 2 Kgs 10:30

among the king's **s** who were being 2 Kgs 11:2
"Your **s** shall sit on the throne of 2 Kgs 15:12
they burned their **s** and their 2 Kgs 17:17
Adrammelech and Sharezer, his **s**, 2 Kgs 19:37
And some of your own **s**, who shall 2 Kgs 20:18
They slaughtered the **s** of Zedekiah 2 Kgs 25:7
The **s** of Japheth: Gomer, Magog, 1 Chr 1:5
The **s** of Gomer: Ashkenaz, Riphath, 1 Chr 1:6
The **s** of Javan: Elishah, Tarshish, 1 Chr 1:7
The **s** of Ham: Cush, Egypt, Put, and 1 Chr 1:8
The **s** of Cush: Seba, Havilah, Sabta, 1 Chr 1:9
The **s** of Raamah: Sheba and Dedan. 1 Chr 1:9
The **s** of Shem: Elam, Asshur, 1 Chr 1:17
Lud, and Aram. And the **s** of Aram: 1 Chr 1:17
To Eber were born two **s**: the name of 1 Chr 1:19
Jobab; all these were the **s** of Joktan. 1 Chr 1:23
The **s** of Abraham: Isaac and 1 Chr 1:28
Kedemah. These are the **s** of Ishmael. 1 Chr 1:31
The **s** of Keturah, Abraham's 1 Chr 1:32
The **s** of Jokshan: Sheba and Dedan. 1 Chr 1:32
The **s** of Midian: Ephah, Epher, 1 Chr 1:33
Isaac. The **s** of Isaac: Esau and Israel. 1 Chr 1:34
The **s** of Esau: Eliphaz, Reuel, Jeush, 1 Chr 1:35
The **s** of Eliphaz: Teman, Omar, 1 Chr 1:36
The **s** of Reuel: Nahath, Zerah, 1 Chr 1:37
The **s** of Seir: Lotan, Shobal, Zibeon, 1 Chr 1:38
The **s** of Lotan: Hori and Hemam; 1 Chr 1:39
The **s** of Shobal: Alvan, Manahath, 1 Chr 1:40
The **s** of Zibeon: Aiah and Anah. 1 Chr 1:40
The **s** of Dishon: Hemdan, Eshban, 1 Chr 1:41
The **s** of Ezer: Bilhan, Zaavan, and 1 Chr 1:42
Akan. The **s** of Dishan: Uz and Aran. 1 Chr 1:42
These are the **s** of Israel: Reuben, 1 Chr 2:1
The **s** of Judah: Er, Onan and Shelah; 1 Chr 2:3
and Zerah. Judah had five **s** in all. 1 Chr 2:4
The **s** of Perez: Hezron and Hamul. 1 Chr 2:5
The **s** of Zerah: Zimri, Ethan, Heman, 1 Chr 2:6
The **s** of Hezron that were born to him: 1 Chr 2:9
Nahshon, prince of the **s** of Judah. 1 Chr 2:10
The **s** of Zeruiah: Abishai, Joab, and 1 Chr 2:16
and by Jerioth; and these were her **s**: 1 Chr 2:18
The **s** of Jerahmeel, the firstborn of 1 Chr 2:25
The **s** of Ram, the firstborn of 1 Chr 2:27
The **s** of Onam: Shammai and Jada. 1 Chr 2:28
The **s** of Shammai: Nadab and 1 Chr 2:28
The **s** of Nadab: Seled and Appaim; 1 Chr 2:30
The **s** of Jada, Shammai's brother: 1 Chr 2:32
The **s** of Jonathan: Peleth and Zaza. 1 Chr 2:33
Now Sheshan had no **s**, only 1 Chr 2:34
The **s** of Caleb the brother of 1 Chr 2:42
The **s** of Hebron: Korah, Tappuah, 1 Chr 2:43
The **s** of Jahdai: Regem, Jotham, 1 Chr 2:47
The **s** of Hur the firstborn of 1 Chr 2:50
father of Kiriath-jearim had other **s**: 1 Chr 2:52
The **s** of Salma: Bethlehem, the 1 Chr 2:54
These are the **s** of David who were 1 Chr 3:1
All these were David's **s**, besides the 1 Chr 3:9
sons, besides the **s** of the concubines, 1 Chr 3:9
The **s** of Josiah: Johanan the 1 Chr 3:15
and the **s** of Jeconiah, the captive: 1 Chr 3:17
and the **s** of Pedaiah: Zerubbabel and 1 Chr 3:19
and Shimei; and the **s** of Zerubbabel: 1 Chr 3:19
The **s** of Hananiah: Pelatiah and 1 Chr 3:21
Shemaiah. And the **s** of Shemaiah: 1 Chr 3:22
The **s** of Neariah: Elioenai, Hizkiah, 1 Chr 3:23
The **s** of Elioenai: Hodaviah, 1 Chr 3:24
The **s** of Judah: Perez, Hezron, Carmi, 1 Chr 4:1
These were the **s** of Etam: Jezreel, 1 Chr 4:3
These were the **s** of Hur, the firstborn 1 Chr 4:4
These were the **s** of Naarah. 1 Chr 4:6
The **s** of Helah: Zereth, Izhar, and 1 Chr 4:7
The **s** of Kenaz: Othniel and Seraiah; 1 Chr 4:13
and Seraiah; and the **s** of Othniel: 1 Chr 4:13
The **s** of Caleb the son of Jephunneh: 1 Chr 4:15
The **s** of Jehallelel: Ziph, Ziphah, 1 Chr 4:16
The **s** of Ezrah: Jether, Mered, Epher, 1 Chr 4:17
These are the **s** of Bithiah, the 1 Chr 4:17
The **s** of the wife of Hodiah, the sister 1 Chr 4:19
The **s** of Shimon: Amnon, Rinnah, 1 Chr 4:20
The **s** of Ishi: Zoheth and Ben-zoheth. 1 Chr 4:20
The **s** of Shelah the son of Judah: Er 1 Chr 4:21
The **s** of Simeon: Nemuel, Jamin, 1 Chr 4:24
The **s** of Mishma: Hammuel his son, 1 Chr 4:26
Shimei had sixteen **s** and six 1 Chr 4:27
Rephaiah, and Uzziel, the **s** of Ishi. 1 Chr 4:42
The **s** of Reuben the firstborn of Israel 1 Chr 5:1
was given to the **s** of Joseph the son 1 Chr 5:1
the **s** of Reuben, the firstborn of Israel: 1 Chr 5:3
The **s** of Joel: Shemaiah his son, Gog 1 Chr 5:4
The **s** of Gad lived over against them 1 Chr 5:11
These were the **s** of Abihail the son of 1 Chr 5:14
The **s** of Levi: Gershon, Kohath, and 1 Chr 6:1
The **s** of Kohath: Amram, Izhar, 1 Chr 6:2
The **s** of Aaron: Nadab, Abihu, 1 Chr 6:3
The **s** of Levi: Gershom, Kohath, and 1 Chr 6:16

are the names of the **s** of Gershom: 1 Chr 6:17
The **s** of Kohath: Amram, Izhar, 1 Chr 6:18
The **s** of Merari: Mahli and Mushi. 1 Chr 6:19
The **s** of Kohath: Amminadab his 1 Chr 6:22
The **s** of Elkanah: Amasai and 1 Chr 6:25
The **s** of Samuel: Joel his firstborn, 1 Chr 6:28
The **s** of Merari: Mahli, Libni his 1 Chr 6:29
are the men who served and their **s**. 1 Chr 6:33
Of the **s** of the Kohathites: Heman the 1 Chr 6:33
were their brothers, the **s** of Merari: 1 Chr 6:44
Aaron and his **s** made offerings on 1 Chr 6:49
These are the **s** of Aaron: Eleazar his 1 Chr 6:50
to the **s** of Aaron of the clans of 1 Chr 6:54
To the **s** of Aaron they gave the cities 1 Chr 6:57
the clans of the **s** of Kohath had cities 1 Chr 6:66
The **s** of Issachar: Tola, Puah, Jashub, 1 Chr 7:1
The **s** of Tola: Uzzi, Rephaiah, Jeriel, 1 Chr 7:2
Uzzi: Izrahiah. And the **s** of Izrahiah: 1 Chr 7:3
36,000, for they had many wives and **s**. 1 Chr 7:4
The **s** of Benjamin: Bela, Becher, and 1 Chr 7:6
The **s** of Bela: Ezbon, Uzzi, Uzziel, 1 Chr 7:7
The **s** of Becher: Zemirah, Joash, 1 Chr 7:8
All these were the **s** of Becher. 1 Chr 7:8
Jediael: Bilhan. And the **s** of Bilhan: 1 Chr 7:10
these were the **s** of Jediael according 1 Chr 7:11
and Huppim were the **s** of Ir, 1 Chr 7:12
The **s** of Naphtali: Jahziel, Guni, Jezer 1 Chr 7:13
The **s** of Manasseh: Asriel, whom his 1 Chr 7:14
and his **s** were Ulam and Rakem. 1 Chr 7:16
These were the **s** of Gilead the son of 1 Chr 7:17
The **s** of Shemida were Ahian, 1 Chr 7:19
The **s** of Ephraim: Shuthelah, and 1 Chr 7:20
In these lived the **s** of Joseph the son 1 Chr 7:29
The **s** of Asher: Imnah, Ishvah, Ishvi, 1 Chr 7:30
The **s** of Beriah: Heber, and Malchiel, 1 Chr 7:31
The **s** of Japhlet: Pasach, Bimhal, and 1 Chr 7:33
Ashvath. These are the **s** of Japhlet. 1 Chr 7:33
The **s** of Shemer his brother: Rohgah, 1 Chr 7:34
The **s** of Helem his brother: Zophah, 1 Chr 7:35
The **s** of Zophah: Suah, Harnepher, 1 Chr 7:36
The **s** of Jether: Jephunneh, Pispa, 1 Chr 7:38
The **s** of Ulla: Arah, Hanniel, and 1 Chr 7:39
And Bela had **s**: Addar, Gera, Abihud, 1 Chr 8:3
These are the **s** of Ehud (they were 1 Chr 8:6
And Shaharaim fathered **s** in the 1 Chr 8:8
He fathered **s** by Hodesh his wife: 1 Chr 8:9
These were his **s**, heads of fathers' 1 Chr 8:10
He also fathered **s** by Hushim: 1 Chr 8:11
The **s** of Elpaal: Eber, Misham, and 1 Chr 8:12
Ishpah, and Joha were **s** of Beriah. 1 Chr 8:16
Izliah, and Jobab were the **s** of Elpaal. 1 Chr 8:18
and Shimrath were the **s** of Shimei. 1 Chr 8:21
and Penuel were the **s** of Shashak. 1 Chr 8:25
and Zichri were the **s** of Jeroham. 1 Chr 8:27
The **s** of Micah: Pithon, Melech, 1 Chr 8:35
Azel had six **s**, and these are their 1 Chr 8:38
Hanan. All these were the **s** of Azel. 1 Chr 8:38
The **s** of Eshek his brother: Ulam his 1 Chr 8:39
The **s** of Ulam were men who were 1 Chr 8:40
having many **s** and grandsons, 1 Chr 8:40
from the **s** of Perez the son of Judah. 1 Chr 9:4
Asaiah the firstborn, and his **s**. 1 Chr 9:5
Of the **s** of Zerah: Jeuel and their 1 Chr 9:6
son of Hashabiah, of the **s** of Merari; 1 Chr 9:14
So they and their **s** were in charge of 1 Chr 9:23
Others, of the **s** of the priests, prepared 1 Chr 9:30
The **s** of Micah: Pithon, Melech, 1 Chr 9:41
Azel had six **s** and these are their 1 Chr 9:44
and Hanan; these were the **s** of Azel. 1 Chr 9:44
Philistines overtook Saul and his **s**, 1 Chr 10:2
and Malchi-shua, the **s** of Saul. 1 Chr 10:2
he and his three **s** and all his house 1 Chr 10:6
and that Saul and his **s** were dead, 1 Chr 10:7
found Saul and his **s** fallen on Mount 1 Chr 10:8
body of Saul and the bodies of his **s**, 1 Chr 10:12
Shama and Jeiel the **s** of Hotham the 1 Chr 11:44
and Joshaviah, the **s** of Elnaam, 1 Chr 11:46
Joash, both **s** of Shemaah of Gibeah; 1 Chr 12:3
Jeziel and Pelet, the **s** of Azmaveth; 1 Chr 12:3
Zebadiah, the **s** of Jeroham of Gedor. 1 Chr 12:7
David fathered more **s** and daughters. 1 Chr 14:3
gathered together the **s** of Aaron and 1 Chr 15:4
of the **s** of Kohath, Uriel the chief, 1 Chr 15:5
of the **s** of Merari, Asaiah the chief, 1 Chr 15:6
of the **s** of Gershom, Joel the chief, 1 Chr 15:7
of the **s** of Elizaphan, Shemaiah the 1 Chr 15:8
of the **s** of Hebron, Eliel the chief, 1 Chr 15:9
of the **s** of Uzziel, Amminadab the 1 Chr 15:10
and of the **s** of Merari, their 1 Chr 15:17
of Israel his servant, **s** of Jacob, 1 Chr 16:13
The **s** of Jeduthun were appointed to 1 Chr 16:42
after you, one of your own **s**, 1 Chr 17:11
and David's **s** were the chief officials 1 Chr 18:17
and his four **s** who were with him 1 Chr 21:20
corresponding to the **s** of Levi: 1 Chr 23:6

The **s** of Gershon were Ladan and	1 Chr 23:7
The **s** of Ladan: Jehiel the chief, and	1 Chr 23:8
The **s** of Shimei: Shelomoth, Haziel,	1 Chr 23:9
And the **s** of Shimei: Jahath, Zina,	1 Chr 23:10
These four were the **s** of Shimei.	1 Chr 23:10
and Beriah did not have many **s**,	1 Chr 23:11
The **s** of Kohath: Amram, Izhar,	1 Chr 23:12
The **s** of Amram: Aaron and Moses.	1 Chr 23:13
he and his **s** forever should make	1 Chr 23:13
But the **s** of Moses the man of God	1 Chr 23:14
The **s** of Moses: Gershom and	1 Chr 23:15
The **s** of Gershom: Shebuel the	1 Chr 23:16
The **s** of Eliezer: Rehabiah the chief.	1 Chr 23:17
Eliezer had no other **s**, but the sons	1 Chr 23:17
but the **s** of Rehabiah were very	1 Chr 23:17
The **s** of Izhar: Shelomith the chief.	1 Chr 23:18
The **s** of Hebron: Jeriah the chief,	1 Chr 23:19
The **s** of Uzziel: Micah the chief and	1 Chr 23:20
The **s** of Merari: Mahli and Mushi.	1 Chr 23:21
The **s** of Mahli: Eleazar and Kish.	1 Chr 23:21
Eleazar died having no **s**, but only	1 Chr 23:22
their kinsmen, the **s** of Kish,	1 Chr 23:22
The **s** of Mushi: Mahli, Eder, and	1 Chr 23:23
These were the **s** of Levi by their	1 Chr 23:24
words of David the **s** of Levi were	1 Chr 23:27
was to assist the **s** of Aaron for the	1 Chr 23:28
and to attend the **s** of Aaron,	1 Chr 23:32
The divisions of the **s** of Aaron were	1 Chr 24:1
The **s** of Aaron: Nadab, Abihu,	1 Chr 24:1
the help of Zadok of the **s** of Eleazar,	1 Chr 24:3
and Ahimelech of the **s** of Ithamar,	1 Chr 24:3
found among the **s** of Eleazar than	1 Chr 24:4
Eleazar than among the **s** of Ithamar,	1 Chr 24:4
of fathers' houses of the **s** of Eleazar,	1 Chr 24:4
Eleazar, and eight of the **s** of Ithamar.	1 Chr 24:4
God among both the **s** of Eleazar and	1 Chr 24:5
sons of Eleazar and the **s** of Ithamar.	1 Chr 24:5
And of the rest of the **s** of Levi: of the	1 Chr 24:20
the sons of Levi: of the **s** of Amram,	1 Chr 24:20
Shubael; of the **s** of Shubael,	1 Chr 24:20
Of Rehabiah: of the **s** of Rehabiah,	1 Chr 24:21
Shelomoth; of the **s** of Shelomoth,	1 Chr 24:22
The **s** of Hebron: Jeriah the chief,	1 Chr 24:23
The **s** of Uzziel, Micah; of the sons	1 Chr 24:24
of Uzziel, Micah; of the **s** of Micah,	1 Chr 24:24
Micah, Isshiah; of the **s** of Isshiah,	1 Chr 24:25
The **s** of Merari: Mahli and Mushi.	1 Chr 24:26
and Mushi. The **s** of Jaaziah: Beno.	1 Chr 24:26
The **s** of Merari: of Jaaziah, Beno,	1 Chr 24:27
Of Mahli: Eleazar, who had no **s**.	1 Chr 24:28
Of Kish, the **s** of Kish: Jerahmeel.	1 Chr 24:29
The **s** of Mushi: Mahli, Eder, and	1 Chr 24:30
These were the **s** of the Levites	1 Chr 24:30
just as their brothers the **s** of Aaron,	1 Chr 24:31
apart for the service the **s** of Asaph,	1 Chr 25:1
Of the **s** of Asaph: Zaccur, Joseph,	1 Chr 25:2
and Asharelah, **s** of Asaph,	1 Chr 25:2
Of Jeduthun, the **s** of Jeduthun:	1 Chr 25:3
Of Heman, the **s** of Heman: Bukkiah,	1 Chr 25:4
All these were the **s** of Heman the	1 Chr 25:5
given Heman fourteen **s** and three	1 Chr 25:5
to him and his brothers and his **s**,	1 Chr 25:9
to Zaccur, his **s** and his brothers,	1 Chr 25:10
fourth to Izri, his **s** and his brothers,	1 Chr 25:11
Nethaniah, his **s** and his brothers,	1 Chr 25:12
to Bukkiah, his **s** and his brothers,	1 Chr 25:13
to Jesharelah, his **s** and his brothers,	1 Chr 25:14
to Jeshaiah, his **s** and his brothers,	1 Chr 25:15
Mattaniah, his **s** and his brothers,	1 Chr 25:16
to Shimei, his **s** and his brothers,	1 Chr 25:17
to Azarel, his **s** and his brothers,	1 Chr 25:18
Hashabiah, his **s** and his brothers,	1 Chr 25:19
Shubael, his **s** and his brothers,	1 Chr 25:20
Mattithiah, his **s** and his brothers,	1 Chr 25:21
to Jeremoth, his **s** and his brothers,	1 Chr 25:22
to Hananiah, his **s** and his brothers,	1 Chr 25:23
his **s** and his brothers,	1 Chr 25:24
to Hanani, his **s** and his brothers,	1 Chr 25:25
to Mallothi, his **s** and his brothers,	1 Chr 25:26
to Eliathah, his **s** and his brothers,	1 Chr 25:27
to Hothir, his **s** and his brothers,	1 Chr 25:28
to Giddalti, his **s** and his brothers,	1 Chr 25:29
Mahazioth, his **s** and his brothers,	1 Chr 25:30
his **s** and his brothers,	1 Chr 25:31
the son of Kore, of the **s** of Asaph.	1 Chr 26:1
And Meshelemiah had **s**: Zechariah	1 Chr 26:2
And Obed-edom had **s**: Shemaiah the	1 Chr 26:4
son Shemaiah were **s** born who were	1 Chr 26:6
The **s** of Shemaiah: Othni, Rephael,	1 Chr 26:7
these were of the **s** of Obed-edom with	1 Chr 26:8
Obed-edom with their **s** and brothers,	1 Chr 26:8
Meshelemiah had **s** and brothers,	1 Chr 26:9
And Hosah, of the **s** of Merari, had	1 Chr 26:10
Hosah, of the sons of Merari, had **s**:	1 Chr 26:10
all the **s** and brothers of Hosah were	1 Chr 26:11

and to his **s** was allotted the	1 Chr 26:15
the Korahites and the **s** of Merari.	1 Chr 26:19
The **s** of Ladan, the sons of the	1 Chr 26:21
the **s** of the Gershonites belonging	1 Chr 26:21
The **s** of Jehieli, Zetham, and Joel his	1 Chr 26:22
and his **s** were appointed	1 Chr 26:29
the Pelonite, of the **s** of Ephraim;	1 Chr 27:10
of Pirathon, of the **s** of Ephraim;	1 Chr 27:14
of Hachmoni attended the king's **s**.	1 Chr 27:32
and livestock of the king and his **s**,	1 Chr 28:1
among my father's **s** he took pleasure	1 Chr 28:4
And of all my **s** (for the LORD has	1 Chr 28:5
has given me many **s**) he has chosen	1 Chr 28:5
and also all the **s** of King David,	1 Chr 29:24
and Jeduthun, their **s** and kinsmen,	2 Chr 5:12
if only your **s** pay close attention to	2 Chr 6:16
Jeroboam and his **s** cast them out	2 Chr 11:14
and she bore him **s**, Jeush,	2 Chr 11:19
fathered twenty-eight **s** and sixty	2 Chr 11:21
some of his **s** through all the	2 Chr 11:23
to David and his **s** by a covenant of	2 Chr 13:5
the LORD in the hand of the **s** of David,	2 Chr 13:8
the priests of the LORD, the **s** of Aaron,	2 Chr 13:9
to the LORD who are **s** of Aaron,	2 Chr 13:10
O **s** of Israel, do not fight against the	2 Chr 13:12
and had twenty-two **s** and sixteen	2 Chr 13:21
a Levite of the **s** of Asaph,	2 Chr 20:14
had brothers, the **s** of Jehoshaphat:	2 Chr 21:2
these were the **s** of Jehoshaphat king	2 Chr 21:2
a lamp to him and to his **s** forever.	2 Chr 21:7
house, and also his **s** and his wives,	2 Chr 21:17
to the camp had killed all the older **s**.	2 Chr 22:1
Judah and the **s** of Ahaziah's	2 Chr 22:8
among the king's **s** who were about	2 Chr 22:11
spoke concerning the **s** of David.	2 Chr 23:3
Jehoiada and his **s** anointed him,	2 Chr 23:11
wives, and he had **s** and daughters.	2 Chr 24:3
For the **s** of Athaliah, that wicked	2 Chr 24:7
Accounts of his **s** and of the many	2 Chr 24:27
but for the priests the **s** of Aaron,	2 Chr 26:18
and burned his **s** as an offering,	2 Chr 28:3
relatives, women, **s**, and daughters.	2 Chr 28:8
and our **s** and our daughters and our	2 Chr 29:9
My **s**, do not now be negligent, for	2 Chr 29:11
Azariah, of the **s** of the Kohathites;	2 Chr 29:12
and of the **s** of Merari, Kish the son	2 Chr 29:12
and of the **s** of Elizaphan, Shimri	2 Chr 29:13
and of the **s** of Asaph, Zechariah	2 Chr 29:13
and of the **s** of Heman, Jehuel and	2 Chr 29:14
and of the **s** of Jeduthun, Shemaiah	2 Chr 29:14
the priests the **s** of Aaron to	2 Chr 29:21
little children, their wives, their **s**,	2 Chr 31:18
And for the **s** of Aaron, the priests,	2 Chr 31:19
some of his own **s** struck him down	2 Chr 32:21
part of the tombs of the **s** of David,	2 Chr 32:33
And he burned his **s** as an offering in	2 Chr 33:6
the Levites, of the **s** of Merari,	2 Chr 34:12
of the **s** of the Kohathites,	2 Chr 34:12
the priests the **s** of Aaron were	2 Chr 35:14
and for the priests the **s** of Aaron.	2 Chr 35:14
The singers, the **s** of Asaph, were in	2 Chr 35:15
and to his **s** until the establishment	2 Chr 36:20
the **s** of Parosh, 2,172.	Ezr 2:3
The **s** of Shephatiah, 372.	Ezr 2:4
The **s** of Arah, 775.	Ezr 2:5
The **s** of Pahath-moab, namely the sons	Ezr 2:6
namely the **s** of Jeshua and Joab,	Ezr 2:6
The **s** of Elam, 1,254.	Ezr 2:7
The **s** of Zattu, 945.	Ezr 2:8
The **s** of Zaccai, 760.	Ezr 2:9
The **s** of Bani, 642.	Ezr 2:10
The **s** of Bebai, 623.	Ezr 2:11
The **s** of Azgad, 1,222.	Ezr 2:12
The **s** of Adonikam, 666.	Ezr 2:13
The **s** of Bigvai, 2,056.	Ezr 2:14
The **s** of Adin, 454.	Ezr 2:15
The **s** of Ater, namely of Hezekiah, 98.	Ezr 2:16
The **s** of Bezai, 323.	Ezr 2:17
The **s** of Jorah, 112.	Ezr 2:18
The **s** of Hashum, 223.	Ezr 2:19
The **s** of Gibbar, 95.	Ezr 2:20
The **s** of Bethlehem, 123.	Ezr 2:21
The **s** of Azmaveth, 42.	Ezr 2:24
The **s** of Kiriath-arim, Chephirah, and	Ezr 2:25
The **s** of Ramah and Geba, 621.	Ezr 2:26
The **s** of Nebo, 52.	Ezr 2:29
The **s** of Magbish, 156.	Ezr 2:30
The **s** of the other Elam, 1,254.	Ezr 2:31
The **s** of Harim, 320.	Ezr 2:32
The **s** of Lod, Hadid, and Ono, 725.	Ezr 2:33
The **s** of Jericho, 345.	Ezr 2:34
The **s** of Senaah, 3,630.	Ezr 2:35
the **s** of Jedaiah, of the house of Jeshua,	Ezr 2:36
The **s** of Immer, 1,052.	Ezr 2:37
The **s** of Pashhur, 1,247.	Ezr 2:38

The **s** of Harim, 1,017.	Ezr 2:39
the **s** of Jeshua and Kadmiel, of the sons	Ezr 2:40
and Kadmiel, of the **s** of Hodaviah,	Ezr 2:40
The singers: the **s** of Asaph, 128.	Ezr 2:41
The **s** of the gatekeepers: the sons of	Ezr 2:42
the **s** of Shallum, the sons of Ater, the	Ezr 2:42
the sons of Shallum, the **s** of Ater, the	Ezr 2:42
the sons of Ater, the **s** of Talmon,	Ezr 2:42
the sons of Talmon, the **s** of Akkub,	Ezr 2:42
the sons of Akkub, the **s** of Hatita,	Ezr 2:42
the sons of Hatita, and the **s** of Shobai,	Ezr 2:42
the **s** of Ziha, the sons of Hasupha, the	Ezr 2:43
the sons of Ziha, the **s** of Hasupha, the	Ezr 2:43
the sons of Hasupha, the **s** of Tabbaoth,	Ezr 2:43
the **s** of Keros, the sons of Siaha, the	Ezr 2:44
the sons of Keros, the **s** of Siaha, the	Ezr 2:44
Keros, the sons of Siaha, the **s** of Padon,	Ezr 2:44
the **s** of Lebanah, the sons of Hagabah,	Ezr 2:45
the sons of Lebanah, the **s** of Hagabah,	Ezr 2:45
the sons of Hagabah, the **s** of Akkub,	Ezr 2:45
the **s** of Hagab, the sons of Shamlai, the	Ezr 2:46
the sons of Hagab, the **s** of Shamlai, the	Ezr 2:46
the sons of Shamlai, the **s** of Hanan,	Ezr 2:46
the **s** of Giddel, the sons of Gahar, the	Ezr 2:47
the sons of Giddel, the **s** of Gahar, the	Ezr 2:47
the sons of Gahar, the **s** of Reaiah,	Ezr 2:47
the **s** of Rezin, the sons of Nekoda, the	Ezr 2:48
the sons of Rezin, the **s** of Nekoda, the	Ezr 2:48
the sons of Nekoda, the **s** of Gazzam,	Ezr 2:48
the **s** of Uzza, the sons of Paseah, the	Ezr 2:49
the sons of Uzza, the **s** of Paseah, the	Ezr 2:49
Uzza, the sons of Paseah, the **s** of Besai,	Ezr 2:49
the **s** of Asnah, the sons of Meunim, the	Ezr 2:50
the sons of Asnah, the **s** of Meunim, the	Ezr 2:50
the sons of Meunim, the **s** of Nephisim,	Ezr 2:50
the **s** of Bakbuk, the sons of Hakupha,	Ezr 2:51
the sons of Bakbuk, the **s** of Hakupha,	Ezr 2:51
the sons of Hakupha, the **s** of Harhur,	Ezr 2:51
the **s** of Bazluth, the sons of Mehida, the	Ezr 2:52
the sons of Bazluth, the **s** of Mehida, the	Ezr 2:52
the sons of Mehida, the **s** of Harsha,	Ezr 2:52
the **s** of Barkos, the sons of Sisera, the	Ezr 2:53
the sons of Barkos, the **s** of Sisera, the	Ezr 2:53
the sons of Sisera, the **s** of Temah,	Ezr 2:53
the **s** of Neziah, and the sons of Hatipha.	Ezr 2:54
the sons of Neziah, and the **s** of Hatipha.	Ezr 2:54
The **s** of Solomon's servants: the sons of	Ezr 2:55
the **s** of Sotai, the sons of Hassophereth,	Ezr 2:55
the sons of Sotai, the **s** of Hassophereth,	Ezr 2:55
sons of Hassophereth, the **s** of Peruda,	Ezr 2:55
the **s** of Jaalah, the sons of Darkon, the	Ezr 2:56
the sons of Jaalah, the **s** of Darkon, the	Ezr 2:56
the sons of Darkon, the **s** of Giddel,	Ezr 2:56
the **s** of Shephatiah, the sons of Hattil,	Ezr 2:57
the sons of Shephatiah, the **s** of Hattil,	Ezr 2:57
of Hattil, the **s** of Pochereth-hazzebaim,	Ezr 2:57
Pochereth-hazzebaim, and the **s** of Ami.	Ezr 2:57
servants and the **s** of Solomon's	Ezr 2:58
the **s** of Delaiah, the sons of Tobiah, and	Ezr 2:60
the sons of Delaiah, the **s** of Tobiah, and	Ezr 2:60
the sons of Tobiah, and the **s** of Nekoda,	Ezr 2:60
Also, of the **s** of the priests: the sons of	Ezr 2:61
the **s** of Habaiah, the sons of Hakkoz,	Ezr 2:61
the sons of Habaiah, the **s** of Hakkoz,	Ezr 2:61
and the **s** of Barzillai (who had taken a	Ezr 2:61
And Jeshua with his **s** and his brothers,	Ezr 3:9
and his brothers, and Kadmiel and his **s**,	Ezr 3:9
and Kadmiel and his sons, the **s** of Judah,	Ezr 3:9
along with the **s** of Henadad and the	Ezr 3:9
and the Levites, their **s** and brothers.	Ezr 3:9
and the Levites, the **s** of Asaph,	Ezr 3:10
pray for the life of the king and his **s**.	Ezr 6:10
against the realm of the king and his **s**.	Ezr 7:23
Of the **s** of Phinehas, Gershom. Of the	Ezr 8:2
Phinehas, Gershom. Of the **s** of Ithamar,	Ezr 8:2
of Ithamar, Daniel. Of the **s** of David,	Ezr 8:2
Of the **s** of Shecaniah, who was of the	Ezr 8:3
of Shecaniah, who was of the **s** of Parosh,	Ezr 8:3
Of the **s** of Pahath-moab, Eliehoenai the	Ezr 8:4
Of the **s** of Zattu, Shecaniah the son of	Ezr 8:5
Of the **s** of Adin, Ebed the son of	Ezr 8:6
Of the **s** of Elam, Jeshaiah the son of	Ezr 8:7
Of the **s** of Shephatiah, Zebadiah the son	Ezr 8:8
Of the **s** of Joab, Obadiah the son of	Ezr 8:9
Of the **s** of Bani, Shelomith the son of	Ezr 8:10
Of the **s** of Bebai, Zechariah, the son of	Ezr 8:11
Of the **s** of Azgad, Johanan the son of	Ezr 8:12
Of the **s** of Adonikam, those who came	Ezr 8:13
Of the **s** of Bigvai, Uthai and Zaccur,	Ezr 8:14
I found there none of the **s** of Levi.	Ezr 8:15
of the **s** of Mahli the son of Levi,	Ezr 8:18
Sherebiah with his **s** and kinsmen,	Ezr 8:18
with him Jeshaiah of the **s** of Merari,	Ezr 8:19
of Merari, with his kinsmen and their **s**,	Ezr 8:19
to be wives for themselves and for their **s**,	Ezr 9:2

do not give your daughters to their **s**, Ezr 9:12
neither take their daughters for your **s**, Ezr 9:12
the son of Jehiel, of the **s** of Elam, Ezr 10:2
found some of the **s** of the priests who Ezr 10:18
some of the **s** of Jeshua the son of Ezr 10:18
Of the **s** of Immer: Hanani and Ezr 10:20
Of the **s** of Harim: Maaseiah, Elijah, Ezr 10:21
Of the **s** of Pashhur: Elioenai, Ezr 10:22
And of Israel: of the **s** of Parosh: Ezr 10:25
Of the **s** of Elam: Mattaniah, Ezr 10:26
Of the **s** of Zattu: Elioenai, Eliashib, Ezr 10:27
Of the **s** of Bebai were Jehohanan, Ezr 10:28
Of the **s** of Bani were Meshullam, Ezr 10:29
Of the **s** of Pahath-moab: Adna, Ezr 10:30
Of the **s** of Harim: Eliezer, Isshijah, Ezr 10:31
Of the **s** of Hashum: Mattenai, Ezr 10:33
Of the **s** of Bani: Maadai, Amram, Uel, Ezr 10:34
Of the **s** of Binnui: Shimei, Ezr 10:38
Of the **s** of Nebo: Jeiel, Mattithiah, Ezr 10:43
The **s** of Hassenaah built the Fish Gate. Neh 3:3
and fight for your brothers, your **s**, Neh 4:14
said, "With our **s** and our daughters, Neh 5:2
we are forcing our **s** and our daughters Neh 5:5
the **s** of Parosh, 2,172. Neh 7:8
The **s** of Shephatiah, 372. Neh 7:9
The **s** of Arah, 652. Neh 7:10
The **s** of Pahath-moab, namely the Neh 7:11
namely the **s** of Jeshua and Joab, Neh 7:11
The **s** of Elam, 1,254. Neh 7:12
The **s** of Zattu, 845. Neh 7:13
The **s** of Zaccai, 760. Neh 7:14
The **s** of Binnui, 648. Neh 7:15
The **s** of Bebai, 628. Neh 7:16
The **s** of Azgad, 2,322. Neh 7:17
The **s** of Adonikam, 667. Neh 7:18
The **s** of Bigvai, 2,067. Neh 7:19
The **s** of Adin, 655. Neh 7:20
The **s** of Ater, namely of Hezekiah, 98. Neh 7:21
The **s** of Hashum, 328. Neh 7:22
The **s** of Bezai, 324. Neh 7:23
The **s** of Hariph, 112. Neh 7:24
The **s** of Gibeon, 95. Neh 7:25
The **s** of the other Elam, 1,254. Neh 7:34
The **s** of Harim, 320. Neh 7:35
The **s** of Jericho, 345. Neh 7:36
The **s** of Lod, Hadid, and Ono, 721. Neh 7:37
The **s** of Senaah, 3,930. Neh 7:38
the **s** of Jedaiah, namely the house of Neh 7:39
The **s** of Immer, 1,052. Neh 7:40
The **s** of Pashhur, 1,247. Neh 7:41
The **s** of Harim, 1,017. Neh 7:42
the **s** of Jeshua, namely of Kadmiel of Neh 7:43
namely of Kadmiel of the **s** of Hodevah, Neh 7:43
The singers: the **s** of Asaph, 148. Neh 7:44
the **s** of Shallum, the sons of Ater, the Neh 7:45
the sons of Shallum, the **s** of Ater, the Neh 7:45
the sons of Ater, the **s** of Talmon, Neh 7:45
the sons of Talmon, the **s** of Akkub, Neh 7:45
the sons of Akkub, the **s** of Hatita, Neh 7:45
the sons of Hatita, the **s** of Shobai, Neh 7:45
the **s** of Ziha, the sons of Hasupha, the Neh 7:46
the sons of Ziha, the **s** of Hasupha, the Neh 7:46
sons of Hasupha, the **s** of Tabbaoth, Neh 7:46
the **s** of Keros, the sons of Sia, the sons Neh 7:47
the sons of Keros, the **s** of Sia, the sons Neh 7:47
of Keros, the sons of Sia, the **s** of Padon, Neh 7:47
the **s** of Lebana, the sons of Hagaba, Neh 7:48
the sons of Lebana, the **s** of Hagaba, Neh 7:48
the sons of Hagaba, the **s** of Shalmai, Neh 7:48
the **s** of Hanan, the sons of Giddel, the Neh 7:49
the sons of Hanan, the **s** of Giddel, the Neh 7:49
the sons of Giddel, the **s** of Gahar, Neh 7:49
the **s** of Reaiah, the sons of Rezin, the Neh 7:50
the sons of Reaiah, the **s** of Rezin, the Neh 7:50
the sons of Rezin, the **s** of Nekoda, Neh 7:50
the **s** of Gazzam, the sons of Uzza, the Neh 7:51
the sons of Gazzam, the **s** of Uzza, the Neh 7:51
the sons of Uzza, the **s** of Paseah, Neh 7:51
the **s** of Besai, the sons of Meunim, the Neh 7:52
the sons of Besai, the **s** of Meunim, the Neh 7:52
of Meunim, the **s** of Nephushesim, Neh 7:52
the **s** of Bakbuk, the sons of Hakupha, Neh 7:53
the sons of Bakbuk, the **s** of Hakupha, Neh 7:53
the sons of Hakupha, the **s** of Harhur, Neh 7:53
the **s** of Bazlith, the sons of Mehida, the Neh 7:54
the sons of Bazlith, the **s** of Mehida, the Neh 7:54
the sons of Mehida, the **s** of Harsha, Neh 7:54
the **s** of Barkos, the sons of Sisera, the Neh 7:55
the sons of Barkos, the **s** of Sisera, the Neh 7:55
the sons of Sisera, the **s** of Temah, Neh 7:55
the **s** of Neziah, the sons of Hatipha. Neh 7:56
the sons of Neziah, the **s** of Hatipha. Neh 7:56
The **s** of Solomon's servants: the sons Neh 7:57
the **s** of Sotai, the sons of Sophereth, the Neh 7:57
the sons of Sotai, the **s** of Sophereth, the Neh 7:57
the sons of Sophereth, the **s** of Perida, Neh 7:57
the **s** of Jaala, the sons of Darkon, the Neh 7:58
the sons of Jaala, the **s** of Darkon, the Neh 7:58
the sons of Darkon, the **s** of Giddel, Neh 7:58
the **s** of Shephatiah, the sons of Hattil, Neh 7:59
the sons of Shephatiah, the **s** of Hattil, Neh 7:59
Hattil, the **s** of Pochereth-hazzebaim, Neh 7:59
Pochereth-hazzebaim, the **s** of Amon. Neh 7:59
servants and the **s** of Solomon's Neh 7:60
the **s** of Delaiah, the sons of Tobiah, Neh 7:62
the sons of Delaiah, the **s** of Tobiah, Neh 7:62
the sons of Tobiah, the **s** of Nekoda, Neh 7:62
the **s** of Hobaiah, the sons of Hakkoz, Neh 7:63
the sons of Hobaiah, the **s** of Hakkoz, Neh 7:63
the **s** of Barzillai (who had taken a wife Neh 7:63
of Azaniah, Binnui of the **s** of Henadad, Neh 10:9
to the Law of God, their wives, their **s**, Neh 10:28
land or take their daughters for our **s**. Neh 10:30
the firstborn of our **s** and of our Neh 10:36
of Israel and the **s** of Levi shall bring Neh 10:39
lived certain of the **s** of Judah and of Neh 11:4
sons of Judah and of the **s** of Benjamin. Neh 11:4
the sons of Benjamin. Of the **s** of Judah: Neh 11:4
son of Mahalalel, of the **s** of Perez; Neh 11:4
All the **s** of Perez who lived in Neh 11:6
And these are the **s** of Benjamin: Sallu Neh 11:7
son of Mica, of the **s** of Asaph, Neh 11:22
of the **s** of Zerah the son of Judah, Neh 11:24
As for the **s** of Levi, their heads of Neh 12:23
And the **s** of the singers gathered Neh 12:28
certain of the priests' **s** with trumpets: Neh 12:35
that which was for the **s** of Aaron. Neh 12:47
not give your daughters to their **s**, Neh 13:25
daughters for your **s** or for yourselves. Neh 13:25
And one of the **s** of Jehoiada, the son Neh 13:28
of his riches, the number of his **s**, Est 5:11
the ten **s** of Haman the son of Est 9:10
500 men and also the ten **s** of Haman. Est 9:12
And let the ten **s** of Haman be hanged Est 9:13
and the ten **s** of Haman were hanged. Est 9:14
that he and his **s** should be hanged on Est 9:25
born to him seven **s** and three daughters. Jb 1:2
His **s** used to go and hold a feast in the Jb 1:4
was a day when the **s** of God came to Jb 1:6
a day when his **s** and daughters were Jb 1:13
"Your **s** and daughters were eating and Jb 1:18
was a day when the **s** of God came to Jb 2:1
His **s** come to honor, and he does not Jb 14:21
together and all the **s** of God shouted for Jb 38:7
high; he is king over all the **s** of pride." Jb 41:34
He had also seven **s** and three daughters. Jb 42:13
this Job lived 140 years, and saw his **s**, Jb 42:16
years, and saw his sons, and his sons' **s**, Jb 42:16
choirmaster. A Maskil of the **S** of Korah. Ps 42:T
choirmaster. A Maskil of the **S** of Korah. Ps 44:T
A Maskil of the **S** of Korah; a love song. Ps 45:T
are the most handsome of the **s** of men; Ps 45:2
In place of your fathers shall be your **s**; Ps 45:16
To the choirmaster. Of the **S** of Korah. Ps 46:T
choirmaster. A Psalm of the **S** of Korah. Ps 47:T
A Song. A Psalm of the **S** of Korah. Ps 48:T
choirmaster. A Psalm of the **S** of Korah. Ps 49:T
my brothers, an alien to my mother's **s**. Ps 69:8
I said, "You are gods, **s** of the Most High, Ps 82:6
The Gittith. A Psalm of the **S** of Korah. Ps 84:T
choirmaster. A Psalm of the **S** of Korah. Ps 85:T
A Psalm of the **S** of Korah. A Song. Ps 87:T
A Song. A Psalm of the **S** of Korah. To Ps 88:T
They sacrificed their **s** and their Ps 106:37
the blood of their **s** and daughters, Ps 106:38
"One of the **s** of your body I will set on Ps 132:11
If your **s** keep my covenant and my Ps 132:12
their **s** also forever shall sit on your Ps 132:12
May our **s** in their youth be like plants Ps 144:12
Hear, O **s**, a father's instruction, and be Prv 4:1
And now, O **s**, listen to me, and do not Prv 5:7
And now, O **s**, listen to me, and be Prv 7:24
"And now, O **s**, listen to me: blessed are Prv 8:32
My mother's **s** were angry with me; they Sg 1:6
slaughter for his **s** because of the Is 14:21
the mighty men of the **s** of Kedar will be Is 21:17
god, Adrammelech and Sharezer, his **s**, Is 37:38
And some of your own **s**, who will come Is 39:7
bring my **s** from afar and my daughters Is 43:6
they shall bring your **s** in their bosom, Is 49:22
guide her among all the **s** she has borne; Is 51:18
hand among all the **s** she has brought Is 51:18
Your **s** have fainted; they lie at the head Is 51:20
and a name better than **s** and daughters; Is 56:5
But you, draw near, **s** of the sorceress, Is 57:3
your **s** shall come from afar, and your Is 60:4
The **s** of those who afflicted you shall Is 60:14
woman, so shall your **s** marry you, Is 62:5
"'I said How I would set you among my **s**, Jer 3:19
pleading of Israel's **s** because they have Jer 3:21
"Return, O faithless **s**; I will heal your Jer 3:22
their herds, their **s** and their daughters. Jer 3:24
shall eat up your **s** and your daughters; Jer 5:17
fathers and **s** together, neighbor and Jer 6:21
"For the **s** of Judah have done evil in my Jer 7:30
to burn their **s** and their daughters in Jer 7:31
Egypt, Judah, Edom, the **s** of Ammon, Jer 9:26
their **s** and their daughters shall die by Jer 11:22
against another, fathers and **s** together, Jer 13:14
bury them—them, their wives, their **s**, Jer 14:16
nor shall you have **s** or daughters in this Jer 16:2
LORD concerning the **s** and daughters Jer 16:3
of Baal to burn their **s** in the fire as Jer 19:5
the flesh of their **s** and their daughters, Jer 19:9
Edom, Moab, and the **s** of Ammon; Jer 25:21
of Moab, the king of the **s** of Ammon, Jer 27:3
Take wives and have **s** and daughters; Jer 29:6
take wives for your **s**, and give your Jer 29:6
that they may bear **s** and daughters; Jer 29:6
to offer up their **s** and daughters to Jer 32:35
brothers and all his **s** and the whole Jer 35:3
the chamber of the **s** of Hanan the son Jer 35:4
wine, neither you nor your **s** forever. Jer 35:6
all our days, ourselves, our wives, our **s**, Jer 35:8
the son of Rechab gave to his **s**, Jer 35:14
The **s** of Jonadab the son of Rechab Jer 35:16
your wives and your **s** shall be led out Jer 38:23
Babylon slaughtered the **s** of Zedekiah at Jer 39:6
the **s** of Ephai the Netophathite, Jer 40:8
of Moab, the crown of the **s** of tumult. Jer 48:45
for your **s** have been taken captive, Jer 48:46
Thus says the LORD: "Has Israel no **s**? Jer 49:1
Babylon slaughtered the **s** of Zedekiah Jer 52:10
The precious **s** of Zion, worth their Lam 4:2
fathers shall eat their **s** in your midst, Ezk 5:10
your midst, and **s** shall eat their fathers. Ezk 5:10
would deliver neither **s** nor daughters. Ezk 14:16
would deliver neither **s** nor daughters, Ezk 14:18
s and daughters who will be brought Ezk 14:22
you took your **s** and your daughters, Ezk 16:20
mine, and they bore **s** and daughters. Ezk 23:4
they seized her **s** and her daughters; Ezk 23:10
shall seize your **s** and your daughters, Ezk 23:25
shall kill their **s** and their daughters, Ezk 23:47
and your **s** and your daughters whom Ezk 24:21
desire, and also their **s** and daughters, Ezk 24:25
These are the **s** of Zadok, who alone Ezk 40:46
who alone among the **s** of Levi may Ezk 40:46
the Levitical priests, the **s** of Zadok, Ezk 44:15
a gift to any of his **s** as his inheritance, Ezk 46:16
inheritance, it shall belong to his **s**. Ezk 46:16
inheritance—it shall belong to his **s**. Ezk 46:17
shall give his **s** their inheritance out Ezk 46:18
the consecrated priests, the **s** of Zadok, Ezk 48:11
"His **s** shall wage war and assemble a Dn 11:10
your **s** and your daughters shall Jl 2:28
I will sell your **s** and your daughters into Jl 3:8
I raised up some of your **s** for prophets, Am 2:11
and your **s** and your daughters shall Am 7:17
officials and the king's **s** and all who Zep 1:8
I will stir up your **s**, O Zion, against Zec 9:13
up your sons, O Zion, against your **s**, Zec 9:13
he will purify the **s** of Levi and refine Mal 3:3
for they shall be called **s** of God. Mt 5:9
so that you may be **s** of your Father who Mt 5:45
while the **s** of the kingdom will be Mt 8:12
by whom do your **s** cast them out? Mt 12:27
The weeds are the **s** of the evil one, Mt 13:38
or tax? From their **s** or from others?" Mt 17:25
Jesus said to him, "Then the **s** are free. Mt 17:26
the mother of the **s** of Zebedee came up Mt 20:20
of Zebedee came up to him with her **s**, Mt 20:20
"Say that these two **s** of mine are to sit, Mt 20:21
"What do you think? A man had two **s**. Mt 21:28
yourselves that you are **s** of those who Mt 23:31
him Peter and the two **s** of Zebedee, Mt 26:37
had been set by some of the **s** of Israel, Mt 27:9
and the mother of the **s** of Zebedee. Mt 27:56
name Boanerges, that is, **S** of Thunder); Mk 3:17
And James and John, the **s** of Zebedee, Mk 10:35
also were James and John, **s** of Zebedee, Lk 5:10
great, and you will be **s** of the Most High, Lk 6:35
by whom do your **s** cast them out? Lk 11:19
said, "There was a man who had two **s**. Lk 15:11
For the **s** of this world are more shrewd Lk 16:8
their own generation than the **s** of light. Lk 16:8
"The **s** of this age marry and are given Lk 20:34
are equal to angels and are **s** of God, Lk 20:36
sons of God, being **s** of the resurrection. Lk 20:36
it himself, as did his **s** and his livestock." Jn 4:12
that you may become **s** of light." When Jn 12:36
of Cana in Galilee, the **s** of Zebedee, Jn 21:2
and your **s** and your daughters shall Acts 2:17
You are the **s** of the prophets and of the Acts 3:25
of silver from the **s** of Hamor in Acts 7:16

where he became the father of two **s**. Acts 7:29
s of the family of Abraham, Acts 13:26
Seven **s** of a Jewish high priest named Acts 19:14
led by the Spirit of God are **s** of God. Rom 8:14
received the Spirit of adoption as **s**, Rom 8:15
for the revealing of the **s** of God. Rom 8:19
as we wait eagerly for adoption as **s**, Rom 8:23
they will be called '**s** of the living Rom 9:26
the number of the **s** of Israel be as Rom 9:27
and you shall be **s** and daughters to 2 Cor 6:18
those of faith who are the **s** of Abraham. Gal 3:7
for in Christ Jesus you are all **s** of God, Gal 3:26
so that we might receive adoption as **s**. Gal 4:5
And because you are **s**, God has sent the Gal 4:6
it is written that Abraham had two **s**, Gal 4:22
is now at work in the **s** of disobedience— Eph 2:2
not made known to the **s** of men in other Eph 3:5
God comes upon the **s** of disobedience. Eph 5:6
exist, in bringing many **s** to glory, Heb 2:10
dying, blessed each of the **s** of Joseph, Heb 11:21
the exhortation that addresses you as **s**? Heb 12:5
have to endure. God is treating you as **s**. Heb 12:7
you are illegitimate children and not **s**. Heb 12:8
a stumbling block before the **s** of Israel, Rv 2:14
sealed from every tribe of the **s** of Israel: Rv 7:4
twelve tribes of the **s** of Israel were Rv 21:12

SONS' (15)
your wife, and your **s** wives with you. Gn 6:18
his wife and his **s** wives with him went Gn 7:7
your sons and your **s** wives with you. Gn 8:16
and his wife and his **s** wives with him. Gn 8:18
his sons, and his **s** sons with him, his Gn 46:7
his daughters, and his **s** daughters. Gn 46:7
not including Jacob's **s** wives, Gn 46:26
his sons and his **s** garments with him. Ex 29:21
his sons and his **s** garments with him. Ex 29:21
and also on his sons and his **s** garments. Lv 8:30
his sons and his **s** garments with him. Lv 8:30
because it is your due and your **s** due, Lv 10:13
your due and your **s** due from the Lv 10:14
shall be yours and your **s** with you as a Lv 10:15
years, and saw his sons, and his **s** sons, Jb 42:16

SONS-IN-LAW (3)
S, sons, daughters, or anyone you have Gn 19:12
So Lot went out and said to his **s**, who Gn 19:14
But he seemed to his **s** to be jesting. Gn 19:14

SOON (136)
As **s** as he saw the ring and the Gn 24:30
As **s** as Isaac had finished blessing Gn 27:30
As **s** as Esau heard the words of his Gn 27:34
Now as **s** as Jacob saw Rachel the Gn 29:10
As **s** as Laban heard the news about Gn 29:13
As **s** as Rachel had borne Joseph, Jacob Gn 30:25
in from the field as **s** as they heard of it, Gn 34:7
And as **s** as she saw that he had left his Gn 39:13
And as **s** as he heard that I lifted up my Gn 39:15
But as **s** as I lifted up my voice and Gn 39:18
As **s** as his master heard the words that Gn 39:19
As **s** as it budded, its blossoms shot Gn 40:10
As **s** as the morning was light, the men Gn 44:3
as **s** as I come to your servant my Gn 44:30
as **s** as he sees that the boy is not with Gn 44:31
it that you have come home so **s** today?" Ex 2:18
him, "As **s** as I have gone out of the city, Ex 9:29
And as **s** as Aaron spoke to the whole Ex 16:10
And as **s** as he came near the camp and Ex 32:19
And as **s** as the Spirit rested on them, Nm 11:25
And as **s** as he had finished speaking Nm 16:31
"So as **s** as all the men of war had Dt 2:16
that you will **s** utterly perish from the Dt 4:26
And as **s** as you heard the voice out of the Dt 5:23
the gate was shut as **s** as the pursuers had Jos 2:7
And as **s** as we heard it, our hearts Jos 2:11
"As **s** as you see the ark of the covenant of Jos 3:3
and as **s** as those bearing the ark had Jos 3:15
As **s** as all the kings of the Amorites who Jos 5:1
As **s** as the people heard the sound of the Jos 6:20
And as **s** as you have taken the city, you Jos 8:8
And as **s** as the king of Ai saw this, he Jos 8:14
and as **s** as he had stretched out his Jos 8:19
As **s** as all the kings who were beyond the Jos 9:1
As **s** as Adoni-zedek, king of Jerusalem, Jos 10:1
As **s** as the angel of the LORD spoke these Jgs 2:4
They **s** turned aside from the way in Jgs 2:17
As **s** as Gideon heard the telling of the Jgs 7:15
As **s** as Gideon died, the people of Israel Jgs 8:33
in the morning, as **s** as the sun is up, Jgs 9:33
And as **s** as he saw her, he tore his Jgs 11:35
As **s** as the people saw him, they Jgs 14:11
As **s** as he had finished speaking, he Jgs 15:17
As **s** as you go, you will come to an Jgs 18:10
husband, "As **s** as the child is weaned, 1 Sm 1:22
As **s** as the ark of the covenant of the 1 Sm 4:5
As **s** as he mentioned the ark of God, 1 Sm 4:18
But as **s** as the ark of God came to 1 Sm 5:10
As **s** as you enter the city you will find 1 Sm 9:13
there, as **s** as you come to the city, 1 Sm 10:5
As **s** as he had finished offering the 1 Sm 13:10
As **s** as Saul saw David go out 1 Sm 17:55
And as **s** as David returned from the 1 Sm 17:57
As **s** as he had finished speaking to 1 Sm 18:1
And as **s** as the boy had gone, David 1 Sm 20:41
As **s** as David had finished speaking 1 Sm 24:16
and depart as **s** as you have light." 1 Sm 29:10
And as **s** as he had finished 2 Sm 13:36
"As **s** as you hear the sound of the 2 Sm 15:10
And as **s** as some of the people fall at 2 Sm 17:9
as **s** as they heard of me, they obeyed 2 Sm 22:45
As **s** as Hiram heard the words of 1 Kgs 5:7
As **s** as Solomon had finished building 1 Kgs 9:1
And as **s** as Jeroboam the son of 1 Kgs 12:2
And as **s** as he was king, he killed all 1 Kgs 15:29
as **s** as he had seated himself on his 1 Kgs 16:11
And as **s** as I have gone from you, 1 Kgs 18:12
as **s** as you have gone from me, 1 Kgs 20:36
you down." And as **s** as he had 1 Kgs 20:36
As **s** as Jezebel heard that Naboth 1 Kgs 21:15
And as **s** as Ahab heard that 1 Kgs 21:16
As **s** as they entered Samaria, Elisha 2 Kgs 6:20
As **s** as the king of Israel saw them, he 2 Kgs 6:21
then, as **s** as this letter comes to you, 2 Kgs 10:2
And as **s** as the letter came to them, 2 Kgs 10:7
So as **s** as he had made an end of 2 Kgs 10:25
and as **s** as the man touched the 2 Kgs 13:21
And as **s** as the royal power was 2 Kgs 14:5
As **s** as King Hezekiah heard it, he 2 Kgs 19:1
him at Megiddo, as **s** as he saw him. 2 Kgs 23:29
As **s** as Solomon finished his prayer, 2 Chr 7:1
And as **s** as Jeroboam the son of 2 Chr 10:2
As **s** as Asa heard these words, the 2 Chr 15:8
As **s** as the captains of the chariots 2 Chr 18:31
For as **s** as the captains of the 2 Chr 18:32
And as **s** as the royal power was 2 Chr 25:3
As **s** as the command was spread 2 Chr 31:5
As **s** as I heard this, I tore my garment Ezr 9:3
As **s** as I heard these words I sat down Neh 1:4
As **s** as the people heard the law, they Neh 13:3
As **s** as it began to grow dark at the Neh 13:19
else my Maker would **s** take me away. Jb 32:22
As **s** as they heard of me they obeyed Ps 18:44
For they will **s** fade like the grass and Ps 37:2
As **s** as they saw it, they were astounded; Ps 48:5
I would **s** subdue their enemies and Ps 81:14
they are **s** gone, and we fly away. Ps 90:10
my soul would **s** have lived in the land Ps 94:17
But they **s** forgot his works; they did Ps 106:13
it, he swallows it as **s** as it is in his hand. Is 28:4
cry. As **s** as he hears it, he answers you. Is 30:19
As **s** as King Hezekiah heard it, he tore his Is 37:1
for **s** my salvation will come, Is 56:1
For as **s** as Zion was in labor she brought Is 66:8
Now I will **s** pour out my wrath upon Ezk 7:8
people Israel, for they will **s** come home. Ezk 36:8
as **s** as all the peoples heard the sound of Dn 3:7
And as **s** as he has arisen, his kingdom Dn 11:4
the nations, I will **s** gather them up. Hos 8:10
and princes shall **s** writhe because of Hos 8:10
as **s** as its branch becomes tender and Mt 24:32
name will be able **s** afterward to speak Mk 9:39
as **s** as its branch becomes tender and Mk 13:28
And as **s** as it was morning, the chief Mk 15:1
S afterward he went to a town called Lk 7:11
S afterward he went on through cities and Lk 8:1
As **s** as they come out in leaf, you see Lk 21:30
to come to him as **s** as possible, Acts 17:15
But **s** a tempestuous wind, called the Acts 27:14
of peace will **s** crush Satan under Rom 16:20
But I will come to you **s**, if the Lord 1 Cor 4:19
Lord Jesus to send Timothy to you **s**, Phil 2:19
to send him just as **s** as I see how it Phil 2:23
I hope to come to you **s**, but I am 1 Tm 3:14
Do your best to come to me **s**. 2 Tm 4:9
whom I shall see you if he comes **s**. Heb 13:23
the putting off of my body will be **s**, 2 Pt 1:14
I hope to see you **s**, and we will talk face 3 Jn 1:14
servants the things that must **s** take place. Rv 1:1
will come to you **s** and war against them Rv 2:16
I am coming **s**. Hold fast what you have, Rv 3:11
behold, the third woe is **s** to come. Rv 11:14
his servants what must **s** take place." Rv 22:6
"And behold, I am coming **s**. Blessed is Rv 22:7
"Behold, I am coming **s**, bringing my Rv 22:12
says, "Surely I am coming **s**." Amen. Rv 22:20

SOONER (2)
S than your pots can feel the heat of Ps 58:9
that I may be restored to you the **s**. Heb 13:19

SOOT (3)
Aaron, "Take handfuls of **s** from the kiln, Ex 9:8
So they took **s** from the kiln and stood Ex 9:10
Now their face is blacker than **s**; they Lam 4:8

SOPATER (1)
S of Berea, the son of Pyrrhus from Acts 20:4

SOPHERETH (1)
the sons of Sotai, the sons of **S**, the sons Neh 7:57

SORCERER (1)
tells fortunes or interprets omens, or a **s** Dt 18:10

SORCERERS (7)
summoned the wise men and the **s**, Ex 7:11
they will inquire of the idols and the **s**, Is 19:3
dreamers, your fortune-tellers, or your **s**, Jer 27:9
that the magicians, the enchanters, the **s**, Dn 2:2
I will be a swift witness against the **s**, Mal 3:5
the sexually immoral, **s**, idolaters, Rv 21:8
are the dogs and **s** and the sexually Rv 22:15

SORCERESS (2)
"You shall not permit a **s** to live. Ex 22:18
But you, draw near, sons of the **s**, Is 57:3

SORCERIES (5)
whorings and the **s** of your mother 2 Kgs 9:22
spite of your many **s** and the great power Is 47:9
your enchantments and your many **s**, Is 47:12
and I will cut off **s** from your hand, and Mi 5:12
their murders or their **s** or their sexual Rv 9:21

SORCERY (3)
fortune-telling and omens and **s**, 2 Chr 33:6
idolatry, **s**, enmity, strife, jealousy, fits Gal 5:20
and all nations were deceived by your **s**. Rv 18:23

SORE (1)
On the third day, when they were **s**, two Gn 34:25

SOREK (1)
this he loved a woman in the Valley of **S**, Jgs 16:4

SORES (8)
boils breaking out in **s** on man and beast Ex 9:9
boils breaking out in **s** on man and Ex 9:10
struck Job with loathsome **s** from the sole Jb 2:7
in it, but bruises and **s** and raw wounds; Is 1:6
man named Lazarus, covered with **s**, Lk 16:20
even the dogs came and licked his **s**. Lk 16:21
harmful and painful **s** came upon the Rv 16:2
the God of heaven for their pain and **s**. Rv 16:11

SORREL (1)
behind him were red, **s**, and white horses. Zec 1:8

SORROW (35)
down my gray hairs with **s** to Sheol." Gn 42:38
your servant our father with **s** to Sheol. Gn 44:31
to my **s** Rachel died in the land of Gn 48:7
and his own **s** and stretching out 2 Chr 6:29
for them from **s** into gladness and Est 9:22
in my soul and have **s** in my heart all the Ps 13:2
For my life is spent with **s**, and my Ps 31:10
my eye grows dim through **s**. Every day I Ps 88:9
low through oppression, evil, and **s**, Ps 107:39
My soul melts away for **s**; strengthen Ps 119:28
but a foolish son is a **s** to his mother. Prv 10:1
makes rich, and he adds no **s** with it. Prv 10:22
but by **s** of heart the spirit is crushed. Prv 15:13
He who sires a fool gets himself **s**, and Prv 17:21
Who has woe? Who has **s**? Who has Prv 23:29
who increases knowledge increases **s**. Eccl 1:18
For all his days are full of **s**, and his Eccl 2:23
S is better than laughter, for by sadness Eccl 7:3
joy, and **s** and sighing shall flee away. Is 35:10
joy, and **s** and sighing shall flee away. Is 51:11
out from the womb to see toil and **s**, Jer 20:18
them, and give them gladness for **s**. Jer 31:13
me! For the LORD has added **s** to my pain. Jer 45:3
see if there is any **s** like my sorrow, Lam 1:12
see if there is any sorrow like my **s**, Lam 1:12
will be filled with drunkenness and **s**. Ezk 23:33
disciples and found them sleeping for **s**, Lk 22:45
things to you, **s** has filled your heart. Jn 16:6
sorrowful, but your **s** will turn into joy. Jn 16:20
she has **s** because her hour has come, Jn 16:21
So also you have **s** now, but I will see Jn 16:22
I have great **s** and unceasing anguish Rom 9:2
may be overwhelmed by excessive **s**. 2 Cor 2:7
also, lest I should have **s** upon sorrow. Phil 2:27
also, lest I should have sorrow upon **s**. Phil 2:27

SORROWFUL (10)
young man heard this he went away **s**, Mt 19:22
And they were very **s** and began to say Mt 26:22
Zebedee, he began to be **s** and troubled. Mt 26:37
he said to them, "My soul is very **s**, Mt 26:38
by the saying, he went away **s**, Mk 10:22
They began to be **s** and to say to him Mk 14:19
he said to them, "My soul is very **s**, Mk 14:34
You will be **s**, but your sorrow will turn Jn 16:20

being **s** most of all because of the Acts 20:38
as **s**, yet always rejoicing; as poor, yet 2 Cor 6:10

SORROWS (6)
The **s** of those who run after another god Ps 16:4
Many are the **s** of the wicked, but Ps 32:10
a man of **s**, and acquainted with grief; Is 53:3
he has borne our griefs and carried our **s**; Is 53:4
anguish and **s** have taken hold of her, Jer 49:24
one endures **s** while suffering unjustly. 1 Pt 2:19

SORRY (6)
And the LORD was **s** that he had made Gn 6:6
for I am **s** that I have made them." Gn 6:7
None of you is **s** for me or discloses to 1 Sm 22:8
I confess my iniquity; I am **s** for my sin. Ps 38:18
And the king was **s**, but because of his Mt 14:9
And the king was exceedingly **s**, but Mk 6:26

SORT (21)
shall bring two of every **s** into the ark to Gn 6:19
two of every **s** shall come in to you to Gn 6:20
Also take with you every **s** of food that is Gn 6:21
with skill to do every **s** of work done by Ex 35:35
weaver—by any **s** of workman or Ex 35:35
who were doing every **s** of task on the Ex 36:4
of whatever **s** the uncleanness may be Lv 5:3
good, any **s** of rash oath that people swear, Lv 5:4
make your neighbor a loan of any **s**, Dt 24:10
the Egyptians with every **s** of plague in 1 Sm 4:8
them with every **s** of distress. 2 Chr 15:6
its branches birds of every **s** will nest. Ezk 17:23
of the common **s** drunkards were Ezk 23:42
birds of prey of every **s** and to the beasts Ezk 39:4
to the birds of every **s** and to all beasts Ezk 39:17
saying, "What **s** of man is this, Mt 8:27
tried to discern what **s** of greeting this Lk 1:29
known who and what **s** of woman this is Lk 7:39
fire will test what **s** of work each one 1 Cor 3:13
may fall by the same **s** of disobedience. Heb 4:11
what **s** of people ought you to be in 2 Pt 3:11

SORTED (1)
and sat down and **s** the good into Mt 13:48

SORTS (7)
taking all **s** of choice gifts from his Gn 24:10
basket there were all **s** of baked food Gn 40:17
rings and armlets, all **s** of gold objects, Ex 35:22
among themselves all **s** of people as 2 Kgs 17:32
And he sent all **s** of articles of gold, 1 Chr 18:10
all **s** of precious stones and marble. 1 Chr 29:2
and to do all **s** of engraving and 2 Chr 2:14

SOSIPATER (1)
so do Lucius and Jason and **S**, my Rom 16:21

SOSTHENES (2)
And they all seized **S**, the ruler of the Acts 18:17
of Christ Jesus, and our brother **S**, 1 Cor 1:1

SOTAI (2)
the sons of **S**, the sons of Hassophereth, Ezr 2:55
the sons of **S**, the sons of Sophereth, the Neh 7:57

SOUGHT (92)
his brother, and he **s** a place to weep. Gn 43:30
Pharaoh heard of it, he **s** to kill Moses. Ex 2:15
the LORD met him and **s** to put him to Ex 4:24
And everyone who **s** the LORD would go Ex 33:7
because he **s** to draw you away from the Dt 13:10
But when they **s** him, he could not 1 Sm 10:21
and I have not **s** the favor of the 1 Sm 13:12
The LORD has **s** out a man after his 1 Sm 13:14
by which Jonathan **s** to go over to the 1 Sm 14:4
And Saul **s** to pin David to the wall 1 Sm 19:10
And Saul **s** him every day, but God 1 Sm 23:14
had fled to Gath, he no longer **s** him. 1 Sm 27:4
of Saul, your enemy, who **s** your life. 2 Sm 4:8
David therefore **s** God on behalf of 2 Sm 12:16
And when they had **s** and could not 2 Sm 17:20
year. And David **s** the face of the LORD. 2 Sm 21:1
Saul had **s** to strike them down in his 2 Sm 21:2
a young woman be **s** for my lord the 1 Kgs 1:2
So they **s** for a beautiful young woman 1 Kgs 1:3
the whole earth **s** the presence of 1 Kgs 10:24
Solomon **s** therefore to kill 1 Kgs 11:40
for three days they **s** him but did not 2 Kgs 2:17
Then Jehoahaz **s** the favor of the 2 Kgs 13:4
for the weight of the bronze was not **s**. 2 Chr 4:18
kings of the earth **s** the presence of 2 Chr 9:23
because we have **s** the LORD our God. 2 Chr 14:7
We have **s** him, and he has given us 2 Chr 14:7
the LORD, the God of Israel, and **s** him, 2 Chr 15:4
their heart and had **s** him with their 2 Chr 15:15
LORD, but **s** help from physicians. 2 Chr 16:12
but **s** the God of his father and 2 Chr 17:4
who **s** the LORD with all his heart." 2 Chr 22:9
"Why have you **s** the gods of a 2 Chr 25:15
because they had **s** the gods of 2 Chr 25:20
of God, and as long as he **s** the LORD, 2 Chr 26:5
These **s** their registration among those Ezr 2:62
These **s** their registration among those Neh 7:64
wall of Jerusalem they **s** the Levites in Neh 12:27
beautiful young virgins be **s** out for the Est 2:2
became angry and **s** to lay hands on Est 2:21
Haman **s** to destroy all the Jews, Est 3:6
and who had **s** to lay hands on King Est 6:2
to lay hands on those who **s** their harm. Est 9:2
for he **s** the welfare of his people and Est 10:3
I **s** the LORD, and he answered me and Ps 34:4
though I **s** him, he could not be found. Ps 37:36
of his riches and **s** refuge in his own Ps 52:7
shame and disappointed who **s** to do me Ps 71:24
When he killed them, they **s** him; they Ps 78:34
him; they repented and **s** God earnestly. Ps 78:34
a wide place, for I have **s** your precepts. Ps 119:45
save me, for I have **s** your precepts. Ps 119:94
which my soul has **s** repeatedly, but I Eccl 7:28
but they have **s** out many schemes. Eccl 7:29
The Preacher **s** to find words of Eccl 12:10
my bed by night I **s** him whom my soul Sg 3:1
sought him whom my soul loves; I **s** him, Sg 3:1
seek him whom my soul loves. I **s** him, Sg 3:2
My soul failed me when he spoke. I **s** him, Sg 5:6
O LORD, in distress they **s** you; they Is 26:16
and you shall be called **S** Out, A City Is 62:12
I was ready to be **s** by those who did not Is 65:1
lie down, for my people who have **s** me. Is 65:10
and which they have **s** and worshiped. Jer 8:2
words, the king **s** to put him to death. Jer 26:21
in the wilderness; when Israel **s** for rest, Jer 31:2
who was his enemy and **s** his life." Jer 44:30
the LORD, iniquity shall be **s** in Israel, Jer 50:20
while they **s** food to revive their Lam 1:19
And I **s** for a man among them who Ezk 22:30
Though you be **s** for, you will never Ezk 26:21
brought back, the lost you have not **s**, Ezk 34:4
and they **s** Daniel and his companions, Dn 2:13
My counselors and my lords **s** me, and I Dn 4:36
presidents and the satraps **s** to find a Dn 6:4
had seen the vision, I **s** to understand it. Dn 8:15
and prevailed; he wept and **s** his favor. Hos 12:4
has been pillaged, his treasures **s** out! Ob 1:6
for those who **s** the child's life are dead." Mt 2:20
that moment he **s** an opportunity to Mt 26:16
And he **s** an opportunity to betray Mk 14:11
And the people **s** him and came to him, Lk 4:42
And all the crowd **s** to touch him, for Lk 6:19
I hear such things?" And he **s** to see him. Lk 9:9
and the chief priests **s** to lay hands on Lk 20:19
So he consented and **s** an opportunity to Lk 22:6
Again they **s** to arrest him, but he Jn 10:39
From then on Pilate **s** to release him, Jn 19:12
Barnabas and Saul and **s** to hear the Acts 13:7
immediately we **s** to go on into Acts 16:10
And having **s** out the disciples, we Acts 21:4
to repent, though he **s** it with tears. Heb 12:17

SOUL (247)
that my **s** may bless you before I die." Gn 27:4
my game, that your **s** may bless me." Gn 27:19
And his **s** was drawn to Dinah the Gn 34:3
"The **s** of my son Shechem longs for Gn 34:8
And as her **s** was departing (for she Gn 35:18
in that we saw the distress of his **s**, Gn 42:21
Let my **s** come not into their council; Gn 49:6
that **s** shall be cut off from among his Ex 31:14
you, and my **s** shall not abhor you. Lv 26:11
statutes, and if your **s** abhors my rules, Lv 26:15
of your idols, and my **s** will abhor you. Lv 26:30
rules and their **s** abhorred my statutes. Lv 26:43
take care, and keep your **s** diligently, Dt 4:9
with all your heart and with all your **s**. Dt 4:29
and with all your **s** and with all your Dt 6:5
with all your heart and with all your **s**, Dt 10:12
with all your heart and with all your **s**, Dt 11:13
of mine in your heart and in your **s**, Dt 11:18
with all your heart and with all your **s**. Dt 13:3
is as your own **s** entices you secretly, Dt 13:6
with all your heart and with all your **s**. Dt 26:16
and failing eyes and a languishing **s**. Dt 28:65
with all your heart and with all your **s**, Dt 30:2
with all your heart and with all your **s**, Dt 30:6
with all your heart and with all your **s**. Dt 30:10
with all your heart and with all your **s**." Jos 22:5
Kishon. March on, my **s**, with might! Jgs 5:21
urged him, his **s** was vexed to death. Jgs 16:16
pouring out my **s** before the LORD. 1 Sm 1:15
Behold, I am with you heart and **s**." 1 Sm 14:7
And Abner said, "As your **s** lives, 1 Sm 17:55
the **s** of Jonathan was knit to the soul 1 Sm 18:1
of Jonathan was knit to the **s** of David, 1 Sm 18:1
and Jonathan loved him as his own **s**. 1 Sm 18:1
because he loved him as his own **s**. 1 Sm 18:3
as the LORD lives and as your **s** lives, 1 Sm 20:3
he loved him as he loved his own **s**. 1 Sm 20:17
and everyone who was bitter in **s**, 1 Sm 22:2
as the LORD lives, and as your **s** lives, 1 Sm 25:26
because all the people were bitter in **s**, 1 Sm 30:6
are hated by David's **s**." Therefore it is 2 Sm 5:8
As you live, and as your **s** lives, I will 2 Sm 11:11
who has redeemed my **s** out of every 1 Kgs 1:29
with all their heart and with all their **s**, 1 Kgs 2:4
reign over all that your **s** desires, 1 Kgs 11:37
with all his heart and all his **s**, 2 Kgs 23:3
and with all his **s** and with all his 2 Kgs 23:25
all their heart and with all their **s**, 2 Chr 15:12
with all his heart and all his **s**, 2 Chr 34:31
is in misery, and life to the bitter in **s**, Jb 3:20
I will complain in the bitterness of my **s**. Jb 7:11
I will speak in the bitterness of my **s**. Jb 10:1
Another dies in bitterness of **s**, never Jb 21:25
and the **s** of the wounded cries for help; Jb 24:12
the Almighty, who has made my **s** bitter, Jb 27:2
"And now my **s** is poured out within Jb 30:16
Was not my **s** grieved for the needy? Jb 30:25
he keeps back his **s** from the pit, his life Jb 33:18
His **s** draws near the pit, and his life to Jb 33:22
He has redeemed my **s** from going down Jb 33:28
to bring back his **s** from the pit, that he Jb 33:30
many are saying of my **s**, there is no Ps 3:2
My **s** also is greatly troubled. But you, Ps 6:3
lest like a lion they tear my **s** apart, Ps 7:2
let the enemy pursue my **s** and overtake it, Ps 7:5
the wicked boasts of the desires of his **s**, Ps 10:3
how can you say to my **s**, "Flee like a Ps 11:1
but his **s** hates the wicked and the one Ps 11:5
take counsel in my **s** and have sorrow in Ps 13:2
you will not abandon my **s** to Sheol, Ps 16:10
Deliver my **s** from the wicked by your Ps 17:13
law of the LORD is perfect, reviving the **s**; Ps 19:7
Deliver my **s** from the sword, my Ps 22:20
He restores my **s**. He leads me in paths of Ps 23:3
does not lift up his **s** to what is false and Ps 24:4
To you, O LORD, I lift up my **s**. Ps 25:1
His **s** shall abide in well-being, and his Ps 25:13
Oh, guard my **s**, and deliver me! Let me Ps 25:20
Do not sweep my **s** away with sinners, Ps 26:9
you have brought up my **s** from Sheol; Ps 30:3
you have known the distress of my **s**, Ps 31:7
from grief; my **s** and my body also. Ps 31:9
he may deliver their **s** from death and Ps 33:19
Our **s** waits for the LORD; he is our help Ps 33:20
My **s** makes its boast in the LORD; let the Ps 34:2
Say to my **s**, "I am your salvation!" Ps 35:3
Then my **s** will rejoice in the LORD, Ps 35:9
repay me evil for good; my **s** is bereft. Ps 35:12
flowing streams, so pants my **s** for you, Ps 42:1
My **s** thirsts for God, for the living God. Ps 42:2
things I remember, as I pour out my **s**: Ps 42:4
Why are you cast down, O my **s**, and Ps 42:5
My **s** is cast down within me; therefore I Ps 42:6
Why are you cast down, O my **s**, and Ps 42:11
Why are you cast down, O my **s**, and Ps 43:5
For our **s** is bowed down to the dust; our Ps 44:25
God will ransom my **s** from the power Ps 49:15
his **s** will go to the generation of his Ps 49:19
He redeems my **s** in safety from the Ps 55:18
you have delivered my **s** from death, Ps 56:13
to me, for in you my **s** takes refuge; Ps 57:1
My **s** is in the midst of lions; I lie down Ps 57:4
a net for my steps; my **s** was bowed down. Ps 57:6
For God alone my **s** waits in silence; Ps 62:1
For God alone, O my **s**, wait in silence, Ps 62:5
earnestly I seek you; my **s** thirsts for you; Ps 63:1
My **s** will be satisfied as with fat and rich Ps 63:5
My **s** clings to you; your right hand Ps 63:8
who has kept our **s** among the living and Ps 66:9
I will tell what he has done for my **s**. Ps 66:16
I wept and humbled my **s** with fasting, Ps 69:10
Draw near to my **s**, redeem me; ransom Ps 69:18
when I sing praises to you; my **s** also, Ps 71:23
When my **s** was embittered, when I was Ps 73:21
Do not deliver the **s** of your dove to the Ps 74:19
wearying; my **s** refuses to be comforted. Ps 77:2
My **s** longs, yes, faints for the courts of Ps 84:2
Gladden the **s** of your servant, for to you, Ps 86:4
for to you, O Lord, do I lift up my **s**. Ps 86:4
have delivered my **s** from the depths Ps 86:13
For my **s** is full of troubles, and my life Ps 88:3
O LORD, why do you cast my **s** away? Ps 88:14
Who can deliver his **s** from the power Ps 89:48
my **s** would soon have lived in the land Ps 94:17
many, your consolations cheer my **s**. Ps 94:19
Bless the LORD, O my **s**, and all that is Ps 103:1
Bless the LORD, O my **s**, and forget not Ps 103:2
his dominion. Bless the LORD, O my **s**! Ps 103:22
the LORD, O my **s**! O LORD my God, Ps 104:1
be no more! Bless the LORD, O my **s**! Ps 104:35
and thirsty, their **s** fainted within them. Ps 107:5

For he satisfies the longing **s**, and the Ps 107:9
and the hungry **s** he fills with good Ps 107:9
those who condemn his **s** to death. Ps 109:31
LORD: "O LORD, I pray, deliver my **s**!" Ps 116:4
Return, O my **s**, to your rest; for the Ps 116:7
you have delivered my **s** from death, Ps 116:8
My **s** is consumed with longing for Ps 119:20
My **s** clings to the dust; give me life Ps 119:25
My **s** melts away for sorrow; Ps 119:28
My **s** longs for your salvation; I hope Ps 119:81
therefore my **s** keeps them. Ps 119:129
My **s** keeps your testimonies; I love Ps 119:167
Let my **s** live and praise you, and let Ps 119:175
Our **s** has had more than enough of the Ps 123:4
I wait for the LORD, my **s** waits, and in Ps 130:5
my **s** waits for the Lord more than Ps 130:6
But I have calmed and quieted my **s**, Ps 131:2
like a weaned child is my **s** within me. Ps 131:2
me; my strength of **s** you increased. Ps 138:3
your works; my **s** knows it very well. Ps 139:14
remains to me; no one cares for my **s**. Ps 142:4
For the enemy has pursued my **s**; he Ps 143:3
my **s** thirsts for you like a parched land. Ps 143:6
way I should go, for to you I lift up my **s**. Ps 143:8
righteousness bring my **s** out of Ps 143:11
will destroy all the adversaries of my **s**, Ps 143:12
the LORD! Praise the LORD, O my **s**! Ps 146:1
knowledge will be pleasant to your **s**; Prv 2:10
be life for your **s** and adornment for Prv 3:22
The **s** of the sluggard craves and gets Prv 13:4
while the **s** of the diligent is richly Prv 13:4
A desire fulfilled is sweet to the **s**, but Prv 13:19
sweetness to the **s** and health to the Prv 16:24
ruin, and his lips are a snare to his **s**. Prv 18:7
Whoever gets sense loves his own **s**; Prv 19:8
The **s** of the wicked desires evil; Prv 21:10
whoever guards his **s** will keep far from Prv 22:5
the rod, you will save his **s** from Sheol. Prv 23:14
who keeps watch over your **s** know it, Prv 24:12
Know that wisdom is such to your **s**; Prv 24:14
him; he refreshes the **s** of his masters. Prv 25:13
Like cold water to a thirsty **s**, so is Prv 25:25
but his **s** is not satisfied with life's good Eccl 6:3
which my **s** has sought repeatedly, but Eccl 7:28
Tell me, you whom my **s** loves, where you Sg 1:7
by night I sought him whom my **s** loves; Sg 3:1
squares; I will seek him whom my **s** loves. Sg 3:2
"Have you seen him whom my **s** loves?" Sg 3:3
them when I found him whom my **s** loves. Sg 3:4
and gone. My **s** failed me when he spoke. Sg 5:6
and your appointed feasts my **s** hates; Is 1:14
the LORD will destroy, both **s** and body, Is 10:18
men of Moab cry aloud; his **s** trembles. Is 15:4
and remembrance are the desire of our **s**. Is 26:8
My **s** yearns for you in the night; my Is 26:9
years because of the bitterness of my **s**. Is 38:15
my chosen, in whom my **s** delights; Is 42:1
when his **s** makes an offering for sin, he Is 53:10
of the anguish of his **s** he shall see and Is 53:11
he poured out his **s** to death and was Is 53:12
come to me; hear, that your **s** may live; Is 55:3
my **s** shall exult in my God, for he has Is 61:10
their **s** delights in their abominations; Is 66:3
the beloved of my **s** into the hands of Jer 12:7
my **s** will weep in secret for your pride; Jer 13:17
Judah? Does your **s** loathe Zion? Jer 14:19
I will feast the **s** of the priests with Jer 31:14
For I will satisfy the weary **s**, and every Jer 31:25
and every languishing **s** I will Jer 31:25
with all my heart and all my **s**. Jer 32:41
my **s** is bereft of peace; I have forgotten Lam 3:17
My **s** continually remembers it and is Lam 3:20
"The LORD is my portion," says my **s**, Lam 3:24
wait for him, to the **s** who seeks him. Lam 3:25
but you will have delivered your **s**. Ezk 3:19
and you will have delivered your **s**." Ezk 3:21
the **s** of the father as well as the soul of Ezk 18:4
father as well as the **s** of the son is mine: Ezk 18:4
the son is mine: the **s** who sins shall die. Ezk 18:4
The **s** who sins shall die. The son Ezk 18:20
your eyes, and the yearning of your **s**, Ezk 24:21
malice within your **s** against the land Ezk 25:6
with malice of **s** to destroy in Ezk 25:15
they weep over you in bitterness of **s**, Ezk 27:31
but you will have delivered your **s**. Ezk 33:9
the fruit of my body for the sin of my **s**?" Mi 6:7
to eat, no first-ripe fig that my **s** desires. Mi 7:1
great man utters the evil desire of his **s**; Mi 7:3
"Behold, his **s** is puffed up; it is not Hab 2:4
who kill the body but cannot kill the **s**. Mt 10:28
who can destroy both **s** and body in Mt 10:28
with whom my **s** is well pleased. Mt 12:18
and with all your **s** and with all your Mt 22:37
said to them, "My **s** is very sorrowful, Mt 26:38
and with all your **s** and with all your Mk 12:30
said to them, "My **s** is very sorrowful, Mk 14:34
Mary said, "My **s** magnifies the Lord, Lk 1:46
will pierce through your own **s** also), Lk 2:35
and with all your **s** and with all your Lk 10:27
And I will say to my **s**, Soul, you have Lk 12:19
S, you have ample goods laid up for Lk 12:19
This night your **s** is required of you, Lk 12:20
"Now is my **s** troubled. And what shall I Jn 12:27
you will not abandon my **s** to Hades, Acts 2:27
And awe came upon every **s**, and Acts 2:43
shall be that every **s** who does not Acts 3:23
who believed were of one heart and **s**, Acts 4:32
your whole spirit and **s** and body be 1 Thes 5:23
to the division of **s** and of spirit, Heb 4:12
as a sure and steadfast anchor of the **s**, Heb 6:19
back, my **s** has no pleasure in him." Heb 10:38
will save his **s** from death and Jas 5:20
flesh, which wage war against your **s**. 1 Pt 2:11
tormenting his righteous **s** over their 2 Pt 2:8
good health, as it goes well with your **s**. 3 Jn 1:2
fruit for which your **s** longed has gone Rv 18:14

SOUL'S (1)

delight of their eyes and their **s** desire, Ezk 24:25

SOULS (29)

the altar to make atonement for your **s**, Lv 17:11
and you know in your hearts and **s**, Jos 23:14
of life, and whoever captures **s** is wise. Prv 11:30
is; and walk in it, and find rest for your **s**. Jer 6:16
"As the LORD lives, who made our **s**, Jer 38:16
of every stature, in the hunt for **s**! Ezk 13:18
you hunt down **s** belonging to my Ezk 13:18
my people and keep your own **s** alive? Ezk 13:18
putting to death **s** who should not die Ezk 13:19
and keeping alive **s** who should not Ezk 13:19
with which you hunt the **s** like birds, Ezk 13:20
and I will let the **s** whom you hunt go Ezk 13:20
you hunt go free, the **s** like birds. Ezk 13:20
Behold, all **s** are mine; the soul of the Ezk 18:4
heart, and you will find rest for your **s**. Mt 11:29
added that day about three thousand **s**. Acts 2:41
strengthening the **s** of the disciples, Acts 14:22
gladly spend and be spent for your **s**. 2 Cor 12:15
who have faith and preserve their **s**. Heb 10:39
they are keeping watch over your **s**, Heb 13:17
word, which is able to save your **s**. Jas 1:21
of your faith, the salvation of your **s**. 1 Pt 1:9
Having purified your **s** by your 1 Pt 1:22
to the Shepherd and Overseer of your **s**. 1 Pt 2:25
God's will entrust their **s** to a faithful 1 Pt 4:19
for sin. They entice unsteady **s**. 2 Pt 2:14
saw under the altar the **s** of those who had Rv 6:9
chariots, and slaves, that is, human **s**. Rv 18:13
Also I saw the **s** of those who had been Rv 20:4

SOUND (148)

And they heard the **s** of the LORD God Gn 3:8
said, "I heard the **s** of you in the garden, Gn 3:10
And as the **s** of the trumpet grew louder Ex 19:19
of lightning and the **s** of the trumpet Ex 20:18
and its **s** shall be heard when he goes Ex 28:35
"It is not the **s** of shouting for victory, Ex 32:18
for victory, or the **s** of the cry of defeat, Ex 32:18
defeat, but the **s** of singing that I hear." Ex 32:18
Then you shall **s** the loud trumpet on Lv 25:9
Atonement you shall **s** the trumpet Lv 25:9
The **s** of a driven leaf shall put them to Lv 26:36
blast, but you shall not **s** an alarm. Nm 10:7
then you shall **s** an alarm with the Nm 10:9
You heard the **s** of words, but saw no Dt 4:12
horn, when you hear the **s** of the trumpet, Jos 6:5
as the people heard the **s** of the trumpet, Jos 6:20
To the **s** of musicians at the watering Jgs 5:11
When Eli heard the **s** of the outcry, he 1 Sm 4:14
with a mighty **s** that day against 1 Sm 7:10
when you hear the **s** of marching in 2 Sm 5:24
shouting and with the **s** of the horn. 2 Sm 6:15
as you hear the **s** of the trumpet, 2 Sm 15:10
when Joab heard the **s** of the trumpet, 1 Kgs 1:41
when Ahijah heard the **s** of her feet, 1 Kgs 14:6
for there is a **s** of the rushing of 1 Kgs 18:41
after the fire the **s** of a low whisper. 1 Kgs 19:12
but there was no **s** or sign of life. 2 Kgs 4:31
Is not the **s** of his master's feet behind 2 Kgs 6:32
the Syrians hear the **s** of chariots and 2 Kgs 7:6
and of horses, the **s** of a great army, 2 Kgs 7:6
when you hear the **s** of marching in 1 Chr 14:15
Ethan, were to **s** bronze cymbals; 1 Chr 15:19
with shouting, to the **s** of the horn, 1 Chr 15:28
lyres; Asaph was to **s** the cymbals, 1 Chr 16:5
their battle trumpets to **s** the call to 2 Chr 13:12
could not distinguish the **s** of the joyful Ezr 3:13
joyful shout from the **s** of the people's Ezr 3:13
shout, and the **s** was heard far away. Ezr 3:13
where you hear the **s** of the trumpet, Neh 4:20
With him are strength and **s** wisdom; Jb 12:16
the lyre and rejoice to the **s** of the pipe. Jb 21:12
and plentifully declared **s** knowledge! Jb 26:3
and I have heard the **s** of your words. Jb 33:8
stand still at the **s** of the trumpet. Jb 39:24
Give attention to the **s** of my cry, my King Ps 5:2
the LORD has heard the **s** of my weeping. Ps 6:8
at the **s** of the taunter and reviler, at the Ps 44:16
a shout, the LORD with the **s** of a trumpet. Ps 47:5
O peoples; let the **s** of his praise be heard, Ps 66:8
s the tambourine, the sweet lyre with the Ps 81:2
lyre, with the lyre and the **s** of melody! Ps 98:5
With trumpets and the **s** of the horn Ps 98:6
at the **s** of your thunder they took to Ps 104:7
they do not make a **s** in their throat. Ps 115:7
Praise him with trumpet **s**; praise him Ps 150:3
he stores up **s** wisdom for the upright; he Prv 2:7
of these—keep **s** wisdom and discretion, Prv 3:21
I have counsel and **s** wisdom; I have Prv 8:14
he breaks out against all **s** judgment. Prv 18:1
are shut—when the **s** of the grinding is Eccl 12:4
low, and one rises up at the **s** of a bird, Eccl 12:4
I slept, but my heart was awake. A **s**! My Sg 5:2
The **s** of a tumult is on the mountains as Is 13:4
The **s** of an uproar of kingdoms, of Is 13:4
down to Sheol, the **s** of your harps; Is 14:11
He who flees at the **s** of the terror shall Is 24:18
be gracious to you at the **s** of your cry. Is 30:19
one sets out to the **s** of the flute to go Is 30:29
will be to the **s** of tamborines and lyres. Is 30:32
be heard in it the **s** of weeping and the Is 65:19
"The **s** of an uproar from the city! A Is 66:6
from the city! A **s** from the temple! Is 66:6
The **s** of the LORD, rendering recompense Is 66:6
silent, for I hear the **s** of the trumpet, Jer 4:19
standard and hear the **s** of the trumpet? Jer 4:21
'Pay attention to the **s** of the trumpet!' Jer 6:17
the **s** of them is like the roaring sea; Jer 6:23
at the **s** of the neighing of their stallions Jer 8:16
For a **s** of wailing is heard from Zion: Jer 9:19
see war or hear the **s** of the trumpet or Jer 42:14
"She makes a **s** like a serpent gliding Jer 46:22
At the **s** of their fall the earth shall Jer 49:21
the **s** of their cry shall be heard at the Jer 49:21
The **s** of them is like the roaring of the Jer 50:42
At the **s** of the capture of Babylon the Jer 50:46
I heard the **s** of their wings like the Ezk 1:24
of their wings like the **s** of many waters, Ezk 1:24
waters, like the **s** of the Almighty, Ezk 1:24
a **s** of tumult like the sound of an army. Ezk 1:24
a sound of tumult like the **s** of an army. Ezk 1:24
It was the **s** of the wings of the living Ezk 3:13
and the **s** of the wheels beside them, Ezk 3:13
them, and the **s** of a great earthquake. Ezk 3:13
And the **s** of the wings of the cherubim Ezk 10:5
all who were in it at the **s** of his roaring. Ezk 19:7
The **s** of a carefree multitude was with Ezk 23:42
and the **s** of your lyres shall be heard Ezk 26:13
coastlands shake at the **s** of your fall, Ezk 26:15
At the **s** of the cry of your pilots the Ezk 27:28
the nations quake at the **s** of its fall, Ezk 31:16
anyone who hears the **s** of the trumpet Ezk 33:4
He heard the **s** of the trumpet and did Ezk 33:5
And as I prophesied, there was a **s**, and Ezk 37:7
And the **s** of his coming was like the Ezk 43:2
coming was like the **s** of many waters, Ezk 43:2
that when you hear the **s** of the horn, Dn 3:5
as all the peoples heard the **s** of the horn, Dn 3:7
every man who hears the **s** of the horn, Dn 3:10
ready when you hear the **s** of the horn, Dn 3:15
then because of the **s** of the great words Dn 7:11
and the **s** of his words like the sound of a Dn 10:6
of his words like the **s** of a multitude. Dn 10:6
Then I heard the **s** of his words, and as I Dn 10:9
words, and as I heard the **s** of his words, Dn 10:9
S the alarm at Beth-aven; we follow you, Hos 5:8
in Zion; **s** an alarm on my holy mountain! Jl 2:1
amid shouting and the **s** of the trumpet; Am 2:2
sing idle songs to the **s** of the harp and Am 6:5
and it is **s** wisdom to fear your name: Mi 6:9
body trembles; my lips quiver at the **s**; Hab 3:16
fast; the **s** of the day of the LORD is bitter; Zep 1:14
the Lord GOD will **s** the trumpet and will Zec 9:14
The **s** of the wail of the shepherds, for Zec 11:3
The **s** of the roar of the lions, for the Zec 11:3
give to the needy, **s** no trumpet before you, Mt 6:2
when the **s** of your greeting came to my Lk 1:44
he has received him back safe and **s**.' Lk 15:27
blows where it wishes, and you hear its **s**, Jn 3:8
came from heaven a **s** like a mighty Acts 2:2
And at this **s** the multitude came Acts 2:6
And if the bugle gives an indistinct **s**, 1 Cor 14:8
For the trumpet will **s**, and the dead 1 Cor 15:52
and with the **s** of the trumpet of God. 1 Thes 4:16
else is contrary to **s** doctrine, 1 Tm 1:10
not agree with the **s** words of our Lord 1 Tm 6:3

Light is **s** for the righteous, and joy for Ps 97:11
and all that is **s** by the Nile will be Is 19:7
Scarcely are they planted, scarcely **s**, Is 40:24
a garden causes what is **s** in it to sprout Is 61:11
me in the wilderness, in a land not **s**. Jer 2:2
They have **s** wheat and have reaped Jer 12:13
to you, and you shall be tilled and **s**. Ezk 36:9
You have **s** much, and harvested little. Hg 1:6
away what has been **s** in his heart. Mt 13:19
This is what was **s** along the path. Mt 13:19
As for what was **s** on rocky ground, Mt 13:20
As for what was **s** among thorns, this is Mt 13:22
As for what was **s** on good soil, this is Mt 13:23
ones along the path, where the word is **s**: Mk 4:15
takes away the word that is **s** in them. Mk 4:15
these are the ones **s** on rocky ground: Mk 4:16
others are the ones **s** among thorns. Mk 4:18
But those that were **s** on the good soil Mk 4:20
seed, which, when **s** on the ground, Mk 4:31
yet when it is **s** it grows up and becomes Mk 4:32
If we have **s** spiritual things among 1 Cor 9:11
of the dead. What is **s** is perishable; 1 Cor 15:42
It is **s** in dishonor; it is raised in 1 Cor 15:43
is raised in glory. It is **s** in weakness; 1 Cor 15:43
It is **s** a natural body; it is raised a 1 Cor 15:44
harvest of righteousness is **s** in peace by Jas 3:18

SOWS (12)
and one who **s** discord among brothers. Prv 6:19
but one who **s** righteousness gets a Prv 11:18
Whoever **s** injustice will reap calamity, Prv 22:8
treader of grapes him who **s** the seed; Am 9:13
"The one who **s** the good seed is the Son Mt 13:37
The sower **s** the word. Mk 4:14
holds true, 'One **s** and another reaps.' Jn 4:37
whoever **s** sparingly will also reap 2 Cor 9:6
and whoever **s** bountifully will also 2 Cor 9:6
God is not mocked, for whatever one **s**, Gal 6:7
For the one who **s** to his own flesh will Gal 6:8
but the one who **s** to the Spirit will from Gal 6:8

SPACE (12)
me and put a **s** between drove and Gn 32:16
so as to give light on the **s** in front of it. Ex 25:37
the hill, with a great **s** between them. 1 Sm 26:13
palm trees, according to the **s** of each, 1 Kgs 7:36
lowest parts of the **s** behind the wall, Neh 4:13
are full of filthy vomit, with no **s** left. Is 28:8
and the **s** between the side rooms, five Ezk 40:7
The free **s** between the side chambers of Ezk 41:9
side chambers opened on the free **s**, Ezk 41:11
breadth of the free **s** was five cubits all Ezk 41:11
to the **s** above the door, even to the Ezk 41:17
fifty cubits for an open **s** around it. Ezk 45:2

SPACIOUS (2)
The land is **s**, for God has given it into Jgs 18:10
a great house with **s** upper rooms,' Jer 22:14

SPAIN (2)
hope to see you in passing as I go to **S**, Rom 15:24
I will leave for **S** by way of you. Rom 15:28

SPAN (10)
a **s** its length and a span its breadth. Ex 28:16
a span its length and a **s** its breadth. Ex 28:16
a **s** its length and a span its breadth Ex 39:9
its length and a **s** its breadth when Ex 39:9
whose height was six cubits and a **s**. 1 Sm 17:4
eighty; yet their **s** is but toil and trouble; Ps 90:10
and marked off the heavens with a **s**, Is 40:12
with a rim of one **s** around its edge. Ezk 43:13
can add a single hour to his **s** of life? Mt 6:27
can add a single hour to his **s** of life? Lk 12:25

SPARE (37)
away the place and not **s** it for the fifty Gn 18:24
I will **s** the whole place for their sake." Gn 18:26
your eye pity him, nor shall you **s** him, Dt 13:8
faith against the LORD, do not **s** us today Jos 22:22
Do not **s** them, but kill both man and 1 Sm 15:3
people of Israel had sworn to **s** them, 2 Sm 21:2
of Israel. Perhaps he will **s** your life." 1 Kgs 20:31
If they **s** our lives we shall live, and if 2 Kgs 7:4
and **s** me according to the greatness Neh 13:22
he is in your hand; only **s** his life." Jb 2:6
slashes open my kidneys and does not **s**; Jb 16:13
s none of those who treacherously plot Ps 59:5
his anger; he did not **s** them from death, Ps 78:50
and he will not **s** when he takes revenge. Prv 6:34
and deliver it; he will **s** and rescue it." Is 31:5
I will take vengeance, and I will **s** no one. Is 47:3
I will not pity or **s** or have compassion, Jer 13:14
not pity them or **s** them or have Jer 21:7
shoot at her, **s** no arrows, for she has Jer 50:14
S not her young men; devote to Jer 51:3
My eye will not **s**, and I will have no Ezk 5:11
And my eye will not **s** you, nor will I Ezk 7:4
And my eye will not **s**, nor will I have Ezk 7:9
My eye will not **s**, nor will I have pity. Ezk 8:18
Your eye shall not **s**, and you shall show Ezk 9:5
As for me, my eye will not **s**, nor will I Ezk 9:10
I will not go back; I will not **s**; I will Ezk 24:14
of the LORD, weep and say, "**S** your people, Jl 2:17
and I will **s** them as a man spares his Mal 3:17
He who did not **s** his own Son but gave Rom 8:32
if God did not **s** the natural branches, Rom 11:21
branches, neither will he **s** you. Rom 11:21
troubles, and I would **s** you that. 1 Cor 7:28
me—it was to **s** you that I refrained 2 Cor 1:23
if I come again I will not **s** them— 2 Cor 13:2
if God did not **s** angels when they sinned, 2 Pt 2:4
if he did not **s** the ancient world, but 2 Pt 2:5

SPARED (15)
that my life may be **s** for your sake." Gn 12:13
the Egyptians but **s** our houses.'" And Ex 12:27
my altar shall be **s** to weep his eyes 1 Sm 2:33
Saul and the people **s** Agag and the 1 Sm 15:9
for the people **s** the best of the sheep 1 Sm 15:15
some told me to kill you, but I **s** you. 1 Sm 24:10
be put to death, and one full line to be **s**. 2 Sm 8:2
But the king **s** Mephibosheth, the son 2 Sm 21:7
my master has **s** this Naaman the 2 Kgs 5:20
persons, and he **s** none of them. 2 Kgs 10:14
that the evil man is **s** in the day of Jb 21:30
of Babylon, then your life shall be **s**, Jer 38:17
well with you, and your life shall be **s**. Jer 38:20
Nevertheless, my eye **s** them, and I did Ezk 20:17
loved to thresh, and I **s** her fair neck; Hos 10:11

SPARES (3)
Whoever **s** the rod hates his son, but Prv 13:24
are like fuel for the fire; no one **s** another. Is 9:19
them as a man **s** his son who serves Mal 3:17

SPARING (1)
come in among you, not **s** the flock; Acts 20:29

SPARINGLY (2)
whoever sows **s** will also reap 2 Cor 9:6
sows sparingly will also reap **s**, 2 Cor 9:6

SPARK (1)
shall become tinder, and his work a **s**, Is 1:31

SPARKLED (1)
foot. And they **s** like burnished bronze. Ezk 1:7

SPARKLES (1)
when it **s** in the cup and goes down Prv 23:31

SPARKLING (1)
of the wheels was like **s** beryl. Ezk 10:9

SPARKS (2)
man is born to trouble as the **s** fly upward. Jb 5:7
go flaming torches; **s** of fire leap forth. Jb 41:19

SPARROW (3)
Even the **s** finds a home, and the swallow Ps 84:3
I am like a lonely **s** on the housetop. Ps 102:7
Like a **s** in its flitting, like a swallow in Prv 26:2

SPARROWS (4)
Are not two **s** sold for a penny? And not Mt 10:29
you are of more value than many **s**. Mt 10:31
Are not five **s** sold for two pennies? And Lk 12:6
not; you are of more value than many **s**. Lk 12:7

SPAT (1)
he **s** on the ground and made mud with Jn 9:6

SPATTERED (2)
some of her blood **s** on the wall and 2 Kgs 9:33
their lifeblood **s** on my garments, and Is 63:3

SPEAK (395)
I have undertaken to **s** to the Lord, Gn 18:27
let not the Lord be angry, and I will **s**. Gn 18:30
I have undertaken to **s** to the Lord. Gn 18:31
angry, and I will **s** again but this once. Gn 18:32
what I have to say." He said, "**S** on." Gn 24:33
LORD; we cannot **s** to you bad or good. Gn 24:50
"I heard your father **s** to your brother Gn 27:6
went out to Jacob to **s** with him. Gn 34:6
him and could not **s** peacefully to him. Gn 37:4
"Why does my lord **s** such words as Gn 44:7
we say to my lord? What shall we **s**? Gn 44:16
please let your servant **s** a word in my Gn 44:18
eyes, please **s** in the ears of Pharaoh, Gn 50:4
mouth and teach you what you shall **s**." Ex 4:12
the Levite? I know that he can **s** well. Ex 4:14
You shall **s** to him and put the words in Ex 4:15
He shall **s** for you to the people, and he Ex 4:16
LORD with which he had sent him to **s**, Ex 4:28
I came to Pharaoh to **s** in your name, Ex 5:23
You shall **s** all that I command you, and Ex 7:2
S now in the hearing of the people, that Ex 11:2
the words that you shall **s** to the people of Ex 19:6
the people may hear when I **s** with you, Ex 19:9
and said to Moses, "You **s** to us, and we Ex 20:19
but do not let God **s** to us, lest we die." Ex 20:19
"**S** to the people of Israel, that they take Ex 25:2
I will **s** with you about all that I will Ex 25:22
You shall **s** to all the skillful, whom I Ex 28:3
I will meet with you, to **s** to you there. Ex 29:42
"You are to **s** to the people of Israel and Ex 31:13
tent, and the LORD would **s** with Moses. Ex 33:9
Thus the LORD used to **s** to Moses face to Ex 33:11
went in before the LORD to **s** with him, Ex 34:34
again, until he went in to **s** with him. Ex 34:35
"**S** to the people of Israel and say to them, Lv 1:2
"**S** to the people of Israel, saying, If anyone Lv 4:2
come to know the matter, yet does not **s**, Lv 5:1
"**S** to Aaron and his sons, saying, This is Lv 6:25
"**S** to the people of Israel, saying, You Lv 7:23
"**S** to the people of Israel, saying, Lv 7:29
"**S** to the people of Israel, saying, These Lv 11:2
"**S** to the people of Israel, saying, 'If a Lv 12:2
"**S** to the people of Israel and say to them, Lv 15:2
"**S** to Aaron and his sons and to all the Lv 17:2
"**S** to the people of Israel and say to them, Lv 18:2
"**S** to all the congregation of the people of Lv 19:2
the LORD said to Moses, "**S** to the priests, Lv 21:1
"**S** to Aaron, saying, None of your Lv 21:17
"**S** to Aaron and his sons so that they Lv 22:2
"**S** to Aaron and his sons and all the Lv 22:18
"**S** to the people of Israel and say to them, Lv 23:2
"**S** to the people of Israel and say to Lv 23:10
"**S** to the people of Israel, saying, In the Lv 23:24
"**S** to the people of Israel, saying, On the Lv 23:34
And **s** to the people of Israel, saying, Lv 24:15
"**S** to the people of Israel and say to them, Lv 25:2
"**S** to the people of Israel and say to them, Lv 27:2
"**S** to the people of Israel, When a man or Nm 5:6
"**S** to the people of Israel, If any man's Nm 5:12
"**S** to the people of Israel and say to them, Nm 6:2
"**S** to Aaron and his sons, saying, Thus Nm 6:23
the tent of meeting to **s** with the LORD, Nm 7:89
"**S** to Aaron and say to him, When you Nm 8:2
"**S** to the people of Israel, saying, If any Nm 9:10
in a vision; I **s** with him in a dream. Nm 12:6
With him I **s** mouth to mouth, clearly, Nm 12:8
you not afraid to **s** against my servant Nm 12:8
"**S** to the people of Israel and say to Nm 15:2
"**S** to the people of Israel and say to Nm 15:18
"**S** to the people of Israel, and tell them Nm 15:38
"**S** to the people of Israel, and get from Nm 17:2
you shall **s** and say to the Levites, Nm 18:26
but **s** only the word that I tell you." So Nm 22:35
any power of my own to **s** anything? Nm 22:38
God puts in my mouth, that must I **s**." Nm 22:38
to Balak, and thus you shall **s**." Nm 23:5
I not take care to **s** what the LORD puts Nm 23:12
to Balak, and thus shall you **s**." Nm 23:16
What the LORD speaks, that will I **s**'? Nm 24:13
And you shall **s** to the people of Israel, Nm 27:8
"**S** to the people of Israel and say to Nm 33:51
"**S** to the people of Israel and say to Nm 35:10
you; do not **s** to me of this matter again. Dt 3:26
the rules that I **s** in your hearing today, Dt 5:1
we have seen God **s** with man and man Dt 5:24
our God will say and **s** to us all that the Dt 5:27
us all that the LORD our God will **s** to you, Dt 5:27
and he shall **s** to them all that I Dt 18:18
my words that he shall **s** in my name, Dt 18:19
prophet who presumes to **s** a word in Dt 18:20
that I have not commanded him to **s**, Dt 18:20
shall come forward and **s** to the people Dt 20:2
Then the officers shall **s** to the people, Dt 20:5
And the officers shall **s** further to the Dt 20:8
of his city shall call him and **s** to him, Dt 25:8
So Moses continued to **s** these words to Dt 31:1
that I may **s** these words in their ears Dt 31:28
"Give ear, O heavens, and I will **s**, and let Dt 32:1
against me; let me **s** just once more. Jgs 6:39
to **s** kindly to her and bring her back. Jgs 19:3
day; consider it, take counsel, and **s**." Jgs 19:30
if he calls you, you shall say, '**S**, LORD, 1 Sm 3:9
said, "**S**, for your servant hears." 1 Sm 3:10
this night." And he said to him, "**S**." 1 Sm 15:16
"**S** to David in private and say, 1 Sm 18:22
told him, "Thus and so did David **s**." 1 Sm 18:24
and I will **s** to my father about you. 1 Sm 19:3
man that one cannot **s** to him." 1 Sm 25:17
Please let your servant **s** in your ears, 1 Sm 25:24
of the gate to **s** with him privately, 2 Sm 3:27
did I **s** a word with any of the judges of 2 Sm 7:7
Now therefore, please **s** to the king, 2 Sm 13:13
Go to the king and **s** thus to him." So 2 Sm 14:3
"Please let your servant **s** a word to 2 Sm 14:12
to my lord the king." He said, "**S**." 2 Sm 14:12
servant thought, 'I will **s** to the king; 2 Sm 14:15
said, "Let my lord the king **s**." 2 Sm 14:18
shall we do as he says? If not, you **s**." 2 Sm 17:6

go out and **s** kindly to your servants, 2 Sm 19:7
"Why **s** any more of your affairs? 2 Sm 19:29
not the first to **s** of bringing back 2 Sm 19:43
'Come here, that I may **s** to you.'" 2 Sm 20:16
to say to you." She said, "**S**." 1 Kgs 2:14
not refuse me." She said to him, "**S**." 1 Kgs 2:16
well; I will **s** for you to the king." 1 Kgs 2:18
to King Solomon to **s** to him on 1 Kgs 2:19
and **s** good words to them when you 1 Kgs 12:7
"Thus shall you **s** to this people who 1 Kgs 12:10
of one of them, and **s** favorably." 1 Kgs 22:13
the LORD says to me, that I will **s**." 1 Kgs 22:14
you swear that you **s** to me nothing 1 Kgs 22:16
of the LORD go from me to **s** to you?" 1 Kgs 22:24
words that you **s** in your bedroom." 2 Kgs 6:12
"Please **s** to your servants in 2 Kgs 18:26
Do not **s** to us in the language of 2 Kgs 18:26
master sent me to **s** these words to 2 Kgs 18:27
"Thus shall you **s** to Hezekiah king 2 Kgs 19:10
did I **s** a word with any of the judges 1 Chr 17:6
and please them and **s** good words to 2 Chr 10:7
"Thus shall you **s** to the people who 2 Chr 10:10
of one of them, and **s** favorably." 2 Chr 18:12
what my God says, that I will **s**." 2 Chr 18:13
you swear that you **s** to me nothing 2 Chr 18:15
of the LORD go from me to **s** to you?" 2 Chr 18:23
God of Israel and to **s** against him, 2 Chr 32:17
and they could not **s** the language of Neh 13:24
own household and **s** according to the Est 1:22
of the king's palace to **s** to the king about Est 6:4
"You **s** as one of the foolish women Jb 2:10
as one of the foolish women would **s**. Jb 2:10
I will **s** in the anguish of my spirit; Jb 7:11
Then I would **s** without fear of him, for I Jb 9:35
I will **s** in the bitterness of my soul. Jb 10:1
that God would **s** and open his lips to Jb 11:5
But I would **s** to the Almighty, and I Jb 13:3
Will you **s** falsely for God and speak Jb 13:7
falsely for God and **s** deceitfully for him? Jb 13:7
"Let me have silence, and I will **s**, and let Jb 13:13
answer; or let me **s**, and you reply to me. Jb 13:22
I also could **s** as you do, if you were in my Jb 16:4
"If I **s**, my pain is not assuaged, and if I Jb 16:6
for words? Consider, and then we will **s**. Jb 18:2
Bear with me, and I will **s**, and after I Jb 21:3
my lips will not **s** falsehood, and my Jb 27:4
After I spoke they did not **s** again, and Jb 29:22
Elihu had waited to **s** to Job because they Jb 32:4
I said, 'Let days **s**, and many years teach Jb 32:7
And shall I wait, because they do not **s**, Jb 32:16
I must **s**, that I may find relief; I must Jb 32:20
and what my lips know they **s** sincerely. Jb 33:3
O Job, listen to me; be silent, and I will **s**. Jb 33:31
answer me; **s**, for I desire to justify you. Jb 33:32
Shall it be told him that I would **s**? Did a Jb 37:20
pleas to you? Will he **s** to you soft words? Jb 41:3
'Hear, and I will **s**; I will question you, Jb 42:4
Then he will **s** to them in his wrath, and Ps 2:5
You destroy those who **s** lies; the LORD Ps 5:6
flattering lips and a double heart they **s**. Ps 12:2
with their mouths they **s** arrogantly. Ps 17:10
who **s** peace with their neighbors while Ps 28:3
which **s** insolently against the Ps 31:18
For they do not **s** peace, but against Ps 35:20
who seek my hurt **s** of ruin and Ps 38:12
My mouth shall **s** wisdom; the Ps 49:3
"Hear, O my people, and I will **s**; O Israel, Ps 50:7
You sit and **s** against your brother; you Ps 50:20
For my enemies **s** concerning me; those Ps 71:10
They scoff and **s** with malice; loftily they Ps 73:8
"I will **s** thus," I would have betrayed Ps 73:15
horn on high, or **s** with haughty neck.'" Ps 75:5
open; I am so troubled that I cannot **s**. Ps 77:4
Let me hear what God the LORD will **s**, for Ps 85:8
speak, for he will **s** peace to his people, Ps 85:8
of those who **s** evil against my life! Ps 109:20
They have mouths, but do not **s**; eyes, Ps 115:5
I will also **s** of your testimonies before Ps 119:46
I am for peace, but when I **s**, they are for Ps 120:7
They have mouths, but do not **s**; they Ps 135:16
They **s** against you with malicious Ps 139:20
whose mouths **s** lies and whose right Ps 144:8
whose mouths **s** lies and whose right Ps 144:11
They shall **s** of the might of your Ps 145:6
They shall **s** of the glory of your Ps 145:11
My mouth will **s** the praise of the LORD, Ps 145:21
Hear, for I will **s** noble things, and from Prv 8:6
Do not **s** in the hearing of a fool, for he Prv 23:9
exult when your lips **s** what is right. Prv 23:16
a time to keep silence, and a time to **s**; Eccl 3:7
in that day he will **s** out, saying: "I will not Is 3:7
s a word, but it will not stand, for God is Is 8:10
If they will not **s** according to this word, Is 8:20
and will **s** contemptuously against Is 8:21
land of Egypt that **s** the language of Is 19:18
tongue the LORD will **s** to this people, Is 28:11
from the earth you shall **s**, and from the Is 29:4
s to us smooth things, prophesy Is 30:10
the stammerers will hasten to **s** distinctly. Is 32:4
"Please **s** to your servants in Aramaic, Is 36:11
Do not **s** to us in the language of Judah Is 36:11
master sent me to **s** these words to your Is 36:12
"Thus shall you **s** to Hezekiah king of Is 37:10
S tenderly to Jerusalem, and cry to her Is 40:2
Why do you say, O Jacob, and **s**, O Is 40:27
let them approach, then let them **s**; Is 41:1
I did not **s** in secret, in a land of Is 45:19
I the LORD **s** the truth; I declare what is Is 45:19
that day they shall know that it is I who **s**; Is 52:6
they rely on empty pleas, they **s** lies, they Is 59:4
they shall **s** of you as the ministers of our Is 61:6
Behold, I do not know how to **s**, for I am Jer 1:6
whatever I command you, you shall **s**. Jer 1:7
it is I who **s** in judgment upon them." Jer 4:12
I will go to the great and will **s** to them, for Jer 5:5
To whom shall I **s** and give warning, Jer 6:10
I did not **s** to your fathers or command Jer 7:22
"So you shall **s** all these words to them, Jer 7:27
they have taught their tongue to **s** lies; Jer 9:5
S, "Thus declares the LORD: 'The dead Jer 9:22
in a cucumber field, and they cannot **s**; Jer 10:5
and **s** to the men of Judah and the Jer 11:2
though they **s** friendly words to you." Jer 12:6
"You shall **s** to them this word: 'Thus Jer 13:12
nor did I command them or **s** to them. Jer 14:14
I stood before you to **s** good for them, Jer 18:20
For whenever I **s**, I cry out, I shout, Jer 20:8
or **s** any more in his name," there is in Jer 20:9
the king of Judah and **s** there this word, Jer 22:1
They **s** visions of their own minds, not Jer 23:16
I did not **s** to them, yet they prophesied. Jer 23:21
who has my word **s** my word faithfully. Jer 23:28
and **s** to all the cities of Judah that come Jer 26:2
words that I command you to **s** to them; Jer 26:2
had commanded him to **s** to all the Jer 26:8
sent me to you to **s** all these words in Jer 26:15
this word that I **s** in your hearing and Jer 28:7
For as often as I **s** against him, I do Jer 31:20
and shall **s** with him face to face and see Jer 32:4
Go and **s** to Zedekiah king of Judah and Jer 34:2
eye to eye and **s** with him face to Jer 34:3
of the Rechabites and **s** with them and Jer 35:2
stand on your feet, and I will **s** with you." Ezk 2:1
And you shall **s** my words to them, Ezk 2:7
scroll, and go, **s** to the house of Israel." Ezk 3:1
house of Israel and **s** with my words to Ezk 3:4
my words that I shall **s** to you receive in Ezk 3:10
people, and **s** to them and say to them, Ezk 3:11
nor **s** to warn the wicked from his Ezk 3:18
the valley, and there I will **s** with you." Ezk 3:22
But when I **s** with you, I will open your Ezk 3:27
I will **s** the word that I will speak, and Ezk 12:25
I will speak the word that I will **s**, and Ezk 12:25
house, I will **s** the word and perform it, Ezk 12:25
the word that I **s** will be performed, Ezk 12:28
Therefore **s** to them and say to them, Ezk 14:4
and **s** a parable to the house of Israel; Ezk 17:2
"Son of man, **s** to the elders of Israel, Ezk 20:3
s to the house of Israel and say to Ezk 20:27
and you shall **s** and be no longer Ezk 24:27
s, and say, Thus says the Lord GOD: Ezk 29:3
The mighty chiefs shall **s** of them, Ezk 32:21
man, **s** to your people and say to them, Ezk 33:2
and you do not **s** to warn the wicked to Ezk 33:8
S to the birds of every sort and to all Ezk 39:17
You have agreed to **s** lying and corrupt Dn 2:9
He shall **s** words against the Most High, Dn 7:25
understand the words that I **s** to you, Dn 10:11
strengthened and said, "Let my lord **s**, Dn 10:19
They shall **s** lies at the same table, but Dn 11:27
and shall **s** astonishing things against Dn 11:36
the wilderness, and **s** tenderly to her. Hos 2:14
them, but they **s** lies against me. Hos 7:13
your inhabitants **s** lies, and their tongue Mi 6:12
they shall do no injustice and **s** no lies, Zep 3:13
"**S** now to Zerubbabel the son of Shealtiel, Hg 2:2
"**S** to Zerubbabel, governor of Judah, Hg 2:21
you shall do: **S** the truth to one another; Zec 8:16
off, and he shall **s** peace to the nations; Zec 9:10
for you **s** lies in the name of the LORD.' Zec 13:3
how you are to **s** or what you are Mt 10:19
For it is not you who **s**, but the Spirit of Mt 10:20
Jesus began to **s** to the crowds Mt 11:7
How can you **s** good, when you are Mt 12:34
account for every careless word they **s**, Mt 12:36
stood outside, asking to **s** to him. Mt 12:46
"Why do you **s** to them in parables?" Mt 13:10
This is why I **s** to them in parables, Mt 13:13
that I did not **s** about bread? Mt 16:11
he would not permit the demons to **s**, Mk 1:34
"Why does this man **s** like that? He is Mk 2:7
He did not **s** to them without a parable, Mk 4:34
makes the deaf hear and the mute **s**." Mk 7:37
be able soon afterward to **s** evil of me. Mk 9:39
And he began to **s** to them in parables. Mk 12:1
in that hour, for it is not you who **s**, Mk 13:11
not know this man of whom you **s**." Mk 14:71
demons; they will **s** in new tongues; Mk 16:17
and I was sent to **s** to you and to bring Lk 1:19
silent and unable to **s** until the day that Lk 1:20
he came out, he was unable to **s** to them, Lk 1:22
thanks to God and to **s** of him to all who Lk 2:38
them and would not allow them to **s**, Lk 4:41
to you, when all people **s** well of you, Lk 6:26
And the dead man sat up and began to **s**, Lk 7:15
Jesus began to **s** to the crowds Lk 7:24
provoke him to **s** about many things, Lk 11:53
we know that you **s** and teach rightly, Lk 20:21
two who heard John **s** and followed Jesus Jn 1:40
truly, I say to you, we **s** of what we know, Jn 3:11
Jesus said to her, "I who **s** to you am he." Jn 4:26
but **s** just as the Father taught me. Jn 8:28
I **s** of what I have seen with my Father, Jn 8:38
him; he is of age. He will **s** for himself." Jn 9:21
—what to say and what to **s**. Jn 12:49
to you I do not **s** on my own authority, Jn 14:10
for he will not **s** on his own authority, Jn 16:13
but whatever he hears he will **s**, Jn 16:13
when I will no longer **s** to you in figures Jn 16:25
to you, and these things I **s** in the world, Jn 17:13
said to him, "You will not **s** to me? Jn 19:10
Spirit and began to **s** in other tongues as Acts 2:4
one was hearing them **s** in his own Acts 2:6
us warn them to **s** no more to anyone Acts 4:17
charged them not to **s** or teach at all Acts 4:18
for we cannot but **s** of what we have Acts 4:20
to continue to **s** your word with Acts 4:29
Spirit and continued to **s** the word of Acts 4:31
in the temple and **s** to the people all Acts 5:20
charged them not to **s** in the name of Acts 5:40
have heard him **s** blasphemous words Acts 6:11
never ceases to **s** words against this Acts 6:13
As I began to **s**, the Holy Spirit fell on Acts 11:15
by the Holy Spirit to **s** the word in Asia. Acts 16:6
He began to **s** boldly in the Acts 18:26
beg you, permit me to **s** to the people." Acts 21:39
'You shall not **s** evil of a ruler of your Acts 23:5
the governor had nodded to him to **s**, Acts 24:10
Paul and heard him **s** about faith in Acts 24:24
have permission to **s** for yourself." Acts 26:1
these things, and to him I **s** boldly. Acts 26:26
have asked to see you and **s** with you, Acts 28:20
wrath on us? (I **s** in a human way.) Rom 3:5
not venture to **s** of anything except Rom 15:18
Does he not **s** entirely for our sake? 1 Cor 9:10
I **s** as to sensible people; judge for 1 Cor 10:15
of healing? Do all **s** with tongues? 1 Cor 12:30
If I **s** in the tongues of men and of 1 Cor 13:1
Now I want you all to **s** in tongues, 1 Cor 14:5
thank God that I **s** in tongues more 1 Cor 14:18
I would rather **s** five words with 1 Cor 14:19
of foreigners will I **s** to this people, 1 Cor 14:21
comes together and all **s** in tongues, 1 Cor 14:23
If any **s** in a tongue, let there be only 1 Cor 14:27
in church and **s** to himself and 1 Cor 14:28
Let two or three prophets **s**, and let 1 Cor 14:29
For they are not permitted to **s**, but 1 Cor 14:34
for a woman to **s** in church. 1 Cor 14:35
in the sight of God we **s** in Christ. 2 Cor 2:17
we also believe, and so we also **s**, 2 Cor 4:13
In return (I **s** as to children) widen 2 Cor 6:13
let each one of you **s** the truth with his Eph 4:25
is shameful even to **s** of the things that Eph 5:12
I may declare it boldly, as I ought to **s**. Eph 6:20
much more bold to **s** the word without Phil 1:14
make it clear, which is how I ought to **s**. Col 4:4
be entrusted with the gospel, so we **s**, 1 Thes 2:4
to **s** evil of no one, to avoid quarreling, to Ti 3:2
Though we **s** in this way, yet in your Heb 6:9
these things we cannot now **s** in detail. Heb 9:5
For people who **s** thus make it clear Heb 11:14
every person be quick to hear, slow to **s**, Jas 1:19
So **s** and so act as those who are to be Jas 2:12
Do not **s** evil against one another, Jas 4:11
so that when they **s** against you as 1 Pt 2:12
therefore they **s** from the world, and the 1 Jn 4:5
the beast might even **s** and might cause Rv 13:15

SPEAKER (3)

Hermes, because he was the chief **s**. Acts 14:12
a foreigner to the **s** and the speaker a 1 Cor 14:11
the speaker and the **s** a foreigner to 1 Cor 14:11

SPEAKING (114)

when he had finished **s** to Abraham, Gn 18:33
Before he had finished **s**, behold, Gn 24:15

"Before I had finished **s** in my heart, Gn 24:45
While he was still **s** with them, Rachel Gn 29:9
when he had finished **s** with him on Ex 31:18
when Moses had finished **s** with them, Ex 34:33
he heard the voice **s** to him from above Nm 7:89
as he had finished **s** all these words, Nm 16:31
the voice of a god **s** out of the midst of Dt 4:33
voice of the living God **s** out of the midst Dt 5:26
(since I am not **s** to your children who Dt 11:2
the officers have finished **s** to the people, Dt 20:9
Moses had finished **s** all these words Dt 32:45
As soon as he had finished **s**, he threw Jgs 15:17
Hannah was **s** in her heart; only her 1 Sm 1:13
all along I have been **s** out of my great 1 Sm 1:16
As soon as he had finished **s** to Saul, 1 Sm 18:1
David had finished **s** these words to 1 Sm 24:16
And as soon as he had finished **s**, 2 Sm 13:36
while you are still **s** with the king, 1 Kgs 1:14
While she was still **s** with the king, 1 Kgs 1:22
While he was still **s**, behold, 1 Kgs 1:42
And while he was still **s** with them, 2 Kgs 6:33
But as he was **s**, the king said to 2 Chr 25:16
While he was yet **s**, there came another Jb 1:16
While he was yet **s**, there came another Jb 1:17
While he was yet **s**, there came another Jb 1:18
be impatient? Yet who can keep from **s**? Jb 4:2
from evil and your lips from **s** deceit. Ps 34:13
and lying more than **s** what is right. Ps 52:3
womb; they go astray from birth, **s** lies. Ps 58:3
me, **s** against me with lying tongues. Ps 109:2
pointing of the finger, and **s** wickedness, Is 58:9
our God, **s** oppression and revolt, Is 59:13
"It is I, **s** in righteousness, mighty to Is 63:1
answer; while they are yet **s** I will hear. Is 65:24
people heard Jeremiah **s** these words in Jer 26:7
Jeremiah had finished **s** all that the Jer 26:8
all the people, by **s** such words to them. Jer 38:4
So they stopped **s** with him, for the Jer 38:27
thing, for you are **s** falsely of Ishmael." Jer 40:16
When Jeremiah finished **s** to all the Jer 43:1
my face, and I heard the voice of one **s**. Ezk 1:28
me on my feet, and I heard him **s** to me. Ezk 2:2
I heard one **s** to me out of the temple, Ezk 43:6
of a man, and a mouth **s** great things. Dn 7:8
of the great words that the horn was **s**. Dn 7:11
Then I heard a holy one **s**, and another Dn 8:13
While I was **s** and praying, confessing Dn 9:20
while I was **s** in prayer, the man Gabriel, Dn 9:21
me understand, **s** with me and saying, Dn 9:22
the Spirit of your Father **s** through you. Mt 10:20
While he was still **s** to the people, Mt 12:46
wondered, when they saw the mute **s**, Mt 15:31
He was still **s** when, behold, a bright Mt 17:5
understood that he was **s** to them of Mt 17:13
perceived that he was **s** about them. Mt 21:45
While he was still **s**, Judas came, one of Mt 26:47
While he was still **s**, there came from Mk 5:35
And immediately, while he was still **s**, Mk 14:43
And when he had finished **s**, he said to Lk 5:4
While he was still **s**, someone from the Lk 8:49
While Jesus was **s**, a Pharisee asked Lk 11:37
And while some were **s** of the temple, Lk 21:5
While he was still **s**, there came a Lk 22:47
And immediately, while he was still **s**, Lk 22:60
But he was **s** about the temple of his Jn 2:21
or whether I am **s** on my own authority. Jn 7:17
And here he is, **s** openly, and they say Jn 7:26
that he had been **s** to them about the Jn 8:27
seen him, and it is he who is **s** to you." Jn 9:37
I am not **s** of all of you; I know whom I Jn 13:18
to him to ask Jesus of whom he was **s**. Jn 13:24
now you are **s** plainly and not using Jn 16:29
forty days and **s** about the kingdom Acts 1:3
"Are not all these who are **s** Galileans? Acts 2:7
And as they were **s** to the people, the Acts 4:1
and the Spirit with which he was **s**. Acts 6:10
were hearing them **s** in tongues and Acts 10:46
s the word to no one except Jews. Acts 11:19
for a long time, **s** boldly for the Lord, Acts 14:3
He listened to Paul **s**. And Paul, Acts 14:9
After they finished **s**, James replied, Acts 15:13
afraid, but go on **s** and do not be silent, Acts 18:9
and they began **s** in tongues and Acts 19:6
s evil of the Way before the Acts 19:9
selves will arise men **s** twisted things, Acts 20:30
the voice of the one who was **s** to me. Acts 22:9
but I am **s** true and rational words. Acts 26:25
I am **s** in human terms, because of Rom 6:19
brothers—for I am **s** to those who know Rom 7:1
I am **s** the truth in Christ—I am not Rom 9:1
Now I am **s** to you Gentiles. Rom 11:13
understand that no one **s** in the Spirit 1 Cor 12:3
if I come to you **s** in tongues, 1 Cor 14:6
is said? For you will be **s** into the air. 1 Cor 14:9
and do not forbid **s** in tongues. 1 Cor 14:39
What do I gain if, humanly **s**, I 1 Cor 15:32
Even if I am unskilled in **s**, I am not 2 Cor 11:6
to boast of—I am **s** as a fool—I also 2 Cor 11:21
be a fool, for I would be **s** the truth. 2 Cor 12:6
of God that we have been **s** in Christ, 2 Cor 12:19
you seek proof that Christ is **s** in me. 2 Cor 13:3
Rather, **s** the truth in love, we are to Eph 4:15
Not that I am **s** of being in need, for I Phil 4:11
hindering us from **s** to the Gentiles 1 Thes 2:16
the world to come, of which we are **s**. Heb 2:5
In **s** of a new covenant, he makes the Heb 8:13
the dead, from which, figuratively **s**, Heb 11:19
that you do not refuse him who is **s**. Heb 12:25
from evil and his lips from **s** deceit; 1 Pt 3:10
For, **s** loud boasts of folly, they entice 2 Pt 2:18
I turned to see the voice that was **s** to me, Rv 1:12
which I had heard **s** to me like a trumpet, Rv 4:1

SPEAKS (56)
see, that it is my mouth that **s** to you. Gn 45:12
face to face, as a man **s** to his friend. Ex 33:11
as the LORD **s** to me." So the princes of Nm 22:8
What the LORD **s**, that will I speak'? Nm 24:13
or who **s** in the name of other gods, Dt 18:20
when a prophet **s** in the name of the Dt 18:22
me a sign that it is you who **s** with me. Jgs 6:17
"The Spirit of the LORD **s** by me; his 2 Sm 23:2
my mouth; the tongue in my mouth **s**. Jb 33:2
For God **s** in one way, and in two, Jb 33:14
'Job **s** without knowledge; his words are Jb 34:35
what is right and **s** truth in his heart; Ps 15:2
Transgression **s** to the wicked deep in his Ps 36:1
utters wisdom, and his tongue **s** justice. Ps 37:30
s and summons the earth from the Ps 50:1
to shame when he **s** with his enemies in Ps 127:5
at the entrance of the city gates she **s**: Prv 1:21
Whoever **s** the truth gives honest Prv 12:17
and he loves him who **s** what is right. Prv 16:13
when he **s** graciously, believe him not, Prv 26:25
My beloved **s** and says to me: "Arise, my Sg 2:10
and an evildoer, and every mouth **s** folly. Is 9:17
For the fool **s** folly, and his heart is busy Is 32:6
who walks righteously and **s** uprightly, Is 33:15
his neighbor, and no one **s** the truth; Jer 9:5
tongue is a deadly arrow; it **s** deceitfully; Jer 9:8
with his mouth each **s** peace to his Jer 9:8
Hear the word that the LORD **s** to you, Jer 10:1
the voice of God Almighty when he **s**. Ezk 10:5
if the prophet is deceived and **s** a word, Ezk 14:9
or language that **s** anything against the Dn 3:29
and they abhor him who **s** the truth. Am 5:10
And whoever **s** a word against the Son Mt 12:32
but whoever **s** against the Holy Spirit Mt 12:32
abundance of the heart the mouth **s**. Mt 12:34
"Who is this who **s** blasphemies? Lk 5:21
the abundance of the heart his mouth **s**. Lk 6:45
And everyone who **s** a word against the Lk 12:10
to the earth and **s** in an earthly way. Jn 3:31
The one who **s** on his own authority Jn 7:18
he lies, he **s** out of his own character, Jn 8:44
the law says it **s** to those who are Rom 3:19
just as David also **s** of the blessing of Rom 4:6
For one who **s** in a tongue speaks not 1 Cor 14:2
speaks in a tongue **s** not to men but 1 Cor 14:2
the one who prophesies **s** to people for 1 Cor 14:3
The one who **s** in a tongue builds up 1 Cor 14:4
than the one who **s** in tongues, 1 Cor 14:5
one who **s** in a tongue should pray 1 Cor 14:13
his faith, though he died, he still **s**. Heb 11:4
sprinkled blood that **s** a better word Heb 12:24
The one who **s** against a brother or Jas 4:11
s evil against the law and judges the law. Jas 4:11
whoever **s**, as one who speaks oracles of 1 Pt 4:11
speaks, as one who **s** oracles of God; 1 Pt 4:11
his letters when he **s** in them of these 2 Pt 3:16

SPEAR (49)
congregation and took a **s** in his hand Nm 25:7
Was shield or **s** to be seen among forty Jgs 5:8
was neither sword nor **s** found in the 1 Sm 13:22
The shaft of his **s** was like a weaver's 1 Sm 17:7
sword and with a **s** and with a 1 Sm 17:45
the LORD saves not with sword and **s**. 1 Sm 17:47
by day. Saul had his **s** in his hand. 1 Sm 18:10
And Saul hurled the **s**, for he 1 Sm 18:11
in his house with his **s** in his hand. 1 Sm 19:9
to pin David to the wall with the **s**, 1 Sm 19:10
so that he struck the **s** into the wall. 1 Sm 19:10
But Saul hurled his **s** at him to strike 1 Sm 20:33
have you not here a **s** or a sword at 1 Sm 21:8
on the height with his **s** in his hand, 1 Sm 22:6
with his **s** stuck in the ground at his 1 Sm 26:7
to the earth with one stroke of the **s**, 1 Sm 26:8
But take now the **s** that is at his head 1 Sm 26:11
So David took the **s** and the jar of 1 Sm 26:12
see where the king's **s** is and the jar 1 Sm 26:16
answered and said, "Here is the **s**, 1 Sm 26:22
and there was Saul leaning on his **s**, 2 Sm 1:6
in the stomach with the butt of his **s**, 2 Sm 2:23
so that the **s** came out at his back. 2 Sm 2:23
whose **s** weighed three hundred 2 Sm 21:16
the shaft of whose **s** was like a 2 Sm 21:19
himself with iron and the shaft of a **s**, 2 Sm 23:7
He wielded his **s** against eight 2 Sm 23:8
he wielded his **s** against three 2 Sm 23:18
The Egyptian had a **s** in his hand, 2 Sm 23:21
staff and snatched the **s** out of the 2 Sm 23:21
hand and killed him with his own **s**. 2 Sm 23:21
He wielded his **s** against 300 whom 1 Chr 11:11
he wielded his **s** against 300 men 1 Chr 11:20
in his hand a **s** like a weaver's 1 Chr 11:23
staff and snatched the **s** out of the 1 Chr 11:23
hand and killed him with his own **s**. 1 Chr 11:23
warriors, expert with shield and **s**, 1 Chr 12:8
bearing shield and **s** were 6,800 1 Chr 12:24
men armed with shield and **s**. 1 Chr 12:34
the shaft of whose **s** was like a 1 Chr 20:5
for war, able to handle **s** and shield. 2 Chr 25:5
quiver, the flashing **s** and the javelin. Jb 39:23
reaches him, it does not avail, nor the **s**, Jb 41:26
Draw the **s** and javelin against my Ps 35:3
he breaks the bow and shatters the **s**; Ps 46:9
They lay hold of bow and **s**; they are Jer 50:42
charging, flashing sword and glittering **s**, Na 3:3
sped, at the flash of your glittering **s**. Hab 3:11
of the soldiers pierced his side with a **s**, Jn 19:34

SPEAR'S (1)
and his **s** head weighed six hundred 1 Sm 17:7

SPEARMEN (1)
horsemen and two hundred **s** to go as Acts 23:23

SPEARS (17)
make themselves swords or **s**." 1 Sm 13:19
to the captains the **s** and shields that 2 Kgs 11:10
he put shields and **s** in all the cities 2 Chr 11:12
armed with large shields and **s**, 2 Chr 14:8
to the captains the **s** and the large 2 Chr 23:9
for all the army shields, **s**, helmets, 2 Chr 26:14
their clans, with their swords, their **s**, Neh 4:13
on construction, and half held the **s**, Neh 4:16
of them held the **s** from the break of Neh 4:21
harpoons or his head with fishing **s**? Jb 41:7
of man, whose teeth are **s** and arrows, Ps 57:4
and their **s** into pruning hooks; Is 2:4
with your helmets, polish your **s**, Jer 46:4
bucklers, bow and arrows, clubs and **s**; Ezk 39:9
swords, and your pruning hooks into **s**; Jl 3:10
and their **s** into pruning hooks; Mi 4:3
them; the cypress **s** are brandished. Na 2:3

SPECIAL (4)
If anyone makes a **s** vow to the LORD Lv 27:2
a man or a woman makes a **s** vow, Nm 6:2
coastlands were your own **s** markets; Ezk 27:15
to them as a **s** portion from the holy Ezk 48:12

SPECIFICATIONS (1)
all its parts, and according to all its **s**. 1 Kgs 6:38

SPECK (6)
Why do you see the **s** that is in your Mt 7:3
'Let me take the **s** out of your eye,' Mt 7:4
clearly to take the **s** out of your brother's Mt 7:5
Why do you see the **s** that is in your Lk 6:41
let me take out the **s** that is in your eye,' Lk 6:42
clearly to take out the **s** that is in your Lk 6:42

SPECKLED (5)
from it every **s** and spotted sheep Gn 30:32
and the spotted and **s** among the goats, Gn 30:32
one that is not **s** and spotted among the Gn 30:33
female goats that were **s** and spotted, Gn 30:35
brought forth striped, **s**, and spotted. Gn 30:39

SPECTACLE (3)
you with contempt and make you a **s**. Na 3:6
crowds that had assembled for this **s**, Lk 23:48
we have become a **s** to the world, 1 Cor 4:9

SPECULATIONS (1)
which promote **s** rather than the 1 Tm 1:4

SPED (1)
at the light of your arrows as they **s**, Hab 3:11

SPEECH (50)
may not understand one another's **s**." Gn 11:7
but I am slow of **s** and of tongue." Ex 4:10
drop as the rain, my **s** distill as the dew, Dt 32:2
of valor, a man of war, prudent in **s**, 1 Sm 16:18
when the **s** of a despairing man is wind? Jb 6:26
He deprives of **s** those who are trusted Jb 12:20
"But now, hear my **s**, O Job, and listen to Jb 33:1
Day to day pours out **s**, and night to Ps 19:2
There is no **s**, nor are there words, whose Ps 19:3

His **s** was smooth as butter, yet war was Ps 55:21
the way of evil, from men of perverted **s**, Prv 2:12
Put away from you crooked **s**, and put Prv 4:24
honey, and her **s** is smoother than oil, Prv 5:3
man, goes about with crooked **s**, Prv 6:12
With much seductive **s** she persuades Prv 7:21
the way of evil and perverted **s** I hate. Prv 8:13
sweetness of **s** increases Prv 16:21
wise makes his **s** judicious and adds Prv 16:23
evil, and his **s** is like a scorching fire. Prv 16:27
Fine **s** is not becoming to a fool; still Prv 17:7
to a fool; still less is false **s** to a prince. Prv 17:7
one who is crooked in **s** and is a fool. Prv 19:1
of heart, and whose **s** is gracious, Prv 22:11
because their **s** and their deeds are against Is 3:8
he will punish the **s** of the arrogant Is 10:12
my voice; give attention, and hear my **s**. Is 28:23
from the dust your **s** will be bowed down; Is 29:4
and from the dust your **s** shall whisper. Is 29:4
complacent daughters, give ear to my **s**. Is 32:9
people of an obscure **s** that you cannot Is 33:19
a people of foreign **s** and a hard Ezk 3:5
many peoples of foreign **s** and a hard Ezk 3:6
time I will change the **s** of the peoples to a Zep 3:9
the speech of the peoples to a pure **s**, Zep 3:9
who was deaf and had a **s** impediment, Mk 7:32
This figure of **s** Jesus used with them, but Jn 10:6
said these things to you in figures of **s**. Jn 16:25
to you in figures of **s** but will tell you Jn 16:25
plainly and not using figurative **s**! Jn 16:29
and he prolonged his **s** until midnight. Acts 20:7
in him in all **s** and all knowledge— 1 Cor 1:5
of God with lofty **s** or wisdom. 1 Cor 2:1
and my **s** and my message were not in 1 Cor 2:4
your tongue you utter **s** that is not 1 Cor 14:9
by truthful **s**, and the power of God; 2 Cor 6:7
you excel in everything—in faith, in **s**, 2 Cor 8:7
is weak, and his **s** of no account." 2 Cor 10:10
Let your **s** always be gracious, seasoned Col 4:6
but set the believers an example in **s**, 1 Tm 4:12
and sound **s** that cannot be condemned, Ti 2:8

SPEECHES (1)
and I will not answer him with your **s**. Jb 32:14

SPEECHLESS (4)
own creation when he makes **s** idols! Hab 2:18
a wedding garment?' And he was **s**. Mt 22:12
who were traveling with him stood **s**, Acts 9:7
a **s** donkey spoke with human voice 2 Pt 2:16

SPEED (3)
let him **s** his work that we may see it; Is 5:19
of the Lord may **s** ahead and be 2 Thes 3:1
Do your best to **s** Zenas the lawyer and Ti 3:13

SPEEDILY (10)
Incline your ear to me; rescue me **s**! Be a Ps 31:2
let your compassion come **s** to meet us, Ps 79:8
me; answer me **s** in the day when I call! Ps 102:2
let evil hunt down the violent man **s**! Ps 140:11
against an evil deed is not executed **s**, Eccl 8:11
earth; and behold, quickly, **s** they come! Is 5:26
who is bowed down shall **s** be released; Is 51:14
dawn, and your healing shall spring up **s**; Is 58:8
payment on your own head swiftly and **s**. Jl 3:4
I tell you, he will give justice to them **s**. Lk 18:8

SPEND (39)
servant's house and **s** the night and Gn 19:2
we will **s** the night in the town square." Gn 19:2
father's house for us to **s** the night?" Gn 24:23
and fodder, and room to **s** the night." Gn 24:25
and **s** the money for whatever you Dt 14:26
upon them; I will **s** my arrows on them; Dt 32:23
to the man, "Be pleased to **s** the night, Jgs 19:6
toward evening. Please, **s** the night. Jgs 19:9
But the man would not **s** the night. He Jgs 19:10
of the Jebusites and **s** the night in it." Jgs 19:11
of these places and **s** the night at Jgs 19:13
to go in and **s** the night at Gibeah. Jgs 19:15
took them into his house to **s** the night. Jgs 19:15
Only, do not **s** the night in the square." Jgs 19:20
I and my concubine, to **s** the night. Jgs 20:4
he will not **s** the night with the people. 2 Sm 17:8
They **s** their days in prosperity, and in Jb 21:13
you? Will he **s** the night at your manger? Jb 39:9
Why do you **s** your money for that which Is 55:2
in tombs, and **s** the night in secret places; Is 65:4
and sorrow, and **s** my days in shame? Jer 20:18
"Thus shall my anger **s** itself, and I will Ezk 5:13
jealousy—when I **s** my fury upon Ezk 5:13
Thus I will **s** my fury upon them. Ezk 6:12
upon you, and **s** my anger against you, Ezk 7:8
Thus will I **s** my wrath upon the wall Ezk 13:15
upon them and **s** my anger against Ezk 20:8
upon them and **s** my anger against Ezk 20:21
care of him, and whatever more you **s**, Lk 10:35
who lived there would **s** their time in Acts 17:21
he might not have to **s** time in Asia, Acts 20:16
was not suitable to **s** the winter in, Acts 27:12
and northwest, and **s** the winter there. Acts 27:12
stay with you or even **s** the winter, 1 Cor 16:6
I hope to **s** some time with you, if the 1 Cor 16:7
I will most gladly **s** and be spent for 2 Cor 12:15
for I have decided to **s** the winter there. Ti 3:12
you ask wrongly, to **s** it on your passions. Jas 4:3
and such a town and **s** a year there and Jas 4:13

SPENDING (1)
After **s** some time there, he departed Acts 18:23

SPENT (28)
and drank, and they **s** the night there. Gn 24:54
They ate bread and **s** the night in the Gn 31:54
the money was all **s** in the land of Gn 47:15
from my lord that our money is all **s**. Gn 47:18
And your strength shall be **s** in vain, Lv 26:20
into the camp and **s** the night in the Jos 6:11
but Joshua **s** that night among the people. Jos 8:9
But Joshua **s** that night in the valley. Jos 8:13
they ate and drank and **s** the night there. Jgs 19:4
him, till he **s** the night there again. Jgs 19:7
'The jar of flour shall not be **s**, 1 Kgs 17:14
The jar of flour was not **s**, neither 1 Kgs 17:16
son of Eliashib, where he **s** the night, Ezr 10:6
For my life is **s** with sorrow, and my Ps 31:10
me; I am **s** by the hostility of your hand. Ps 39:10
forsake me not when my strength is **s**. Ps 71:9
I have **s** my strength for nothing and Is 49:4
My eyes are **s** with weeping; my Lam 2:11
to his palace and **s** the night fasting; Dn 6:18
physicians, and had **s** all that she had, Mk 5:26
and though she had **s** all her living on Lk 8:43
And when he had **s** everything, a severe Lk 15:14
the day is now far **s**." So he went in to Lk 24:29
Judea to Caesarea and **s** time there. Acts 12:19
And after they had **s** some time, they Acts 15:33
There he **s** three months, and when a Acts 20:3
s from the beginning among my own Acts 26:4
gladly spend and be **s** for your souls. 2 Cor 12:15

SPICE (3)
the fragrance of your oils than any **s**! Sg 4:10
my bride, I gathered my myrrh with my **s**, Sg 5:1
cinnamon, **s**, incense, myrrh, Rv 18:13

SPICED (1)
I would give you **s** wine to drink, the juice Sg 8:2

SPICES (36)
s for the anointing oil and for the Ex 25:6
"Take the finest **s**: of liquid myrrh 500 Ex 30:23
The LORD said to Moses, "Take sweet **s**, Ex 30:34
sweet **s** with pure frankincense (of each Ex 30:34
s for the anointing oil and for the Ex 35:8
and **s** and oil for the light, and for the Ex 35:28
with camels bearing **s** and very 1 Kgs 10:2
great quantity of **s** and precious 1 Kgs 10:10
an abundance of **s** as these that 1 Kgs 10:10
gold, garments, myrrh, **s**, horses, 1 Kgs 10:25
house, the silver, the gold, the **s**, 2 Kgs 20:13
wine, the oil, the incense, and the **s**. 1 Chr 9:29
priests, prepared the mixing of the **s**, 1 Chr 9:30
of incense of sweet **s** before him, 2 Chr 2:4
and camels bearing **s** and very much 2 Chr 9:1
of gold, and a very great quantity of **s**, 2 Chr 9:9
There were no **s** such as those that the 2 Chr 9:9
of gold, garments, myrrh, **s**, horses, 2 Chr 9:24
offerings and incense of sweet **s**, 2 Chr 13:11
various kinds of **s** prepared by the 2 Chr 16:14
for gold, for precious stones, for **s**, 2 Chr 32:27
six months with **s** and ointments for Est 2:12
myrrh and aloes, with all chief **s**— Sg 4:14
Blow upon my garden, let its **s** flow. Sg 4:16
His cheeks are like beds of **s**, mounds of Sg 5:13
gone down to his garden to the beds of **s**, Sg 6:2
or a young stag on the mountains of **s**. Sg 8:14
treasure house, the silver, the gold, the **s**, Is 39:2
And as **s** were burned for your fathers, Jer 34:5
so people shall burn **s** for you and Jer 34:5
fire, boil the meat well, mix in the **s**, Ezk 24:10
of all kinds of **s** and all precious Ezk 27:22
mother of James and Salome bought **s**, Mk 16:1
returned and prepared **s** and ointments. Lk 23:56
tomb, taking the **s** they had prepared. Lk 24:1
and bound it in linen cloths with the **s**, Jn 19:40

SPIDER'S (2)
is severed, and his trust is a **s** web. Jb 8:14
hatch adders' eggs; they weave the **s** web; Is 59:5

SPIED (7)
they went up and **s** out the land from Nm 13:21
report of the land that they had **s** out, Nm 13:32
among those who had **s** out the land, Nm 14:6
the days in which you **s** out the land, Nm 14:34
came to the Valley of Eshcol and **s** it out. Dt 1:24
to the two men who had **s** out the land, Jos 6:22
land." And the men went up and **s** out Ai. Jos 7:2

SPIES (14)
And he said to them, "You are **s**; you Gn 42:9
Your servants have never been **s**." Gn 42:11
them, "It is as I said to you. You are **s**. Gn 42:14
the life of Pharaoh, surely you are **s**." Gn 42:16
to us and took us to be **s** of the land. Gn 42:30
are honest men; we have never been **s**. Gn 42:31
that you are not **s** but honest men, Gn 42:34
sent two men secretly from Shittim as **s**, Jos 2:1
men who had been **s** went in and Jos 6:23
And the **s** saw a man coming out of the Jgs 1:24
David sent out **s** and learned that Saul 1 Sm 26:4
From there he **s** out the prey; his eyes Jb 39:29
So they watched him and sent **s**, who Lk 20:20
had given a friendly welcome to the **s**. Heb 11:31

SPILLED (4)
we are like water **s** on the ground, 2 Sm 14:14
in the stomach and **s** his entrails to 2 Sm 20:10
burst and the wine is **s** and the skins are Mt 9:17
wine will burst the skins and it will be **s**, Lk 5:37

SPIN (2)
how they grow: they neither toil nor **s**, Mt 6:28
they neither toil nor **s**, yet I tell you, Lk 12:27

SPINDLE (2)
or who holds a **s** or who falls by 2 Sm 3:29
to the distaff, and her hands hold the **s**. Prv 31:19

SPIRIT (568)
And the **S** of God was hovering over the Gn 1:2
"My **S** shall not abide in man forever, Gn 6:3
So in the morning his **s** was troubled, Gn 41:8
like this, in whom is the **S** of God?" Gn 41:38
him, the **s** of their father Jacob revived. Gn 45:27
of their broken **s** and harsh slavery. Ex 6:9
whom I have filled with a **s** of skill, Ex 28:3
and I have filled him with the **S** of God, Ex 31:3
him, and everyone whose **s** moved him, Ex 35:21
and he has filled him with the **S** of God, Ex 35:31
and if the **s** of jealousy comes over him Nm 5:14
or if the **s** of jealousy comes over him Nm 5:14
or when the **s** of jealousy comes over a Nm 5:30
will take some of the **S** that is on you Nm 11:17
took some of the **S** that was on him Nm 11:25
And as soon as the **S** rested on them, Nm 11:25
Medad, and the **S** rested on them. Nm 11:26
the LORD would put his **S** on them!" Nm 11:29
he has a different **s** and has followed Nm 14:24
And the **S** of God came upon him, Nm 24:2
son of Nun, a man in whom is the **S**, Nm 27:18
your God hardened his **s** and made his Dt 2:30
son of Nun was full of the **s** of wisdom, Dt 34:9
and there was no **s** left in any man Jos 2:11
was no longer any **s** in them because of Jos 5:1
The **S** of the LORD was upon him, and he Jgs 3:10
But the **S** of the LORD clothed Gideon, Jgs 6:34
sent an evil **s** between Abimelech and Jgs 9:23
Then the **S** of the LORD was upon Jgs 11:29
And the **S** of the LORD began to stir him Jgs 13:25
Then the **S** of the LORD rushed upon Jgs 14:6
And the **S** of the LORD rushed upon Jgs 14:19
Then the **S** of the LORD rushed upon Jgs 15:14
And when he drank, his **s** returned, Jgs 15:19
my lord, I am a woman troubled in **s**. 1 Sm 1:15
Then the **S** of the LORD will rush upon 1 Sm 10:6
and the **S** of God rushed upon him, 1 Sm 10:10
And the **S** of God rushed upon Saul 1 Sm 11:6
And the **S** of the LORD rushed upon 1 Sm 16:13
Now the **S** of the LORD departed from 1 Sm 16:14
and an evil **s** from the LORD 1 Sm 16:14
an evil **s** from God is tormenting 1 Sm 16:15
and when the evil **s** from God is 1 Sm 16:16
whenever the evil **s** from God was 1 Sm 16:23
and the evil **s** departed from him. 1 Sm 16:23
day a harmful **s** from God rushed 1 Sm 18:10
Then a harmful **s** from the LORD 1 Sm 19:9
the **S** of God came upon the 1 Sm 19:20
And the **S** of God came upon him 1 Sm 19:23
"Divine for me by a **s** and bring up for 1 Sm 28:8
when he had eaten, his **s** revived, 1 Sm 30:12
And the **s** of the king longed to go 2 Sm 13:39
"The **S** of the LORD speaks by me; his 2 Sm 23:2
the **S** of the LORD will carry you I 1 Kgs 18:12
"Why is your **s** so vexed that you eat 1 Kgs 21:5
Then a **s** came forward and stood 1 Kgs 22:21
and will be a lying **s** in the mouth of 1 Kgs 22:22
has put a lying **s** in the mouth of 1 Kgs 22:23
"How did the **S** of the LORD go from 1 Kgs 22:24
be a double portion of your **s** on me." 2 Kgs 2:9
"The **s** of Elijah rests on Elisha." And 2 Kgs 2:15
It may be that the **S** of the LORD has 2 Kgs 2:16
Behold, I will put a **s** in him, so that 2 Kgs 19:7

of Israel stirred up the **s** of Pul king of 1 Chr 5:26
the **s** of Tiglath-pileser king of 1 Chr 5:26
Then the **S** clothed Amasai, chief of 1 Chr 12:18
The **S** of God came upon Azariah the 2 Chr 15:1
Then a **s** came forward and stood 2 Chr 18:20
and will be a lying **s** in the mouth of 2 Chr 18:21
has put a lying **s** in the mouth of 2 Chr 18:22
"Which way did the **S** of the LORD go 2 Chr 18:23
And the **S** of the LORD came upon 2 Chr 20:14
Then the **S** of God clothed 2 Chr 24:20
LORD stirred up the **s** of Cyrus king 2 Chr 36:22
the LORD stirred up the **s** of Cyrus king of Ezr 1:1
everyone whose **s** God had stirred to go Ezr 1:5
You gave your good **S** to instruct them Neh 9:20
them by your **S** through your Neh 9:30
A **s** glided past my face; the hair of my Jb 4:15
are in me; my **s** drinks their poison; Jb 6:4
I will speak in the anguish of my **s**; Jb 7:11
love, and your care has preserved my **s**. Jb 10:12
that you turn your **s** against God and Jb 15:13
My **s** is broken; my days are extinct; the Jb 17:1
out of my understanding a **s** answers me. Jb 20:3
in me, and the **s** of God is in my nostrils, Jb 27:3
But it is the **s** in man, the breath of the Jb 32:8
words; the **s** within me constrains me. Jb 32:18
The **S** of God has made me, and the Jb 33:4
gather to himself his **s** and his breath, Jb 34:14
Into your hand I commit my **s**; you have Ps 31:5
and in whose **s** there is no deceit. Ps 32:2
and saves the crushed in **s**. Ps 34:18
O God, and renew a right **s** within me. Ps 51:10
and take not your Holy **S** from me. Ps 51:11
and uphold me with a willing **s**. Ps 51:12
The sacrifices of God are a broken **s**; a Ps 51:17
who cuts off the **s** of princes, who is to Ps 76:12
I moan; when I meditate, my **s** faints. Ps 77:3
my heart." Then my **s** made a diligent Ps 77:6
whose **s** was not faithful to God. Ps 78:8
When you send forth your **S**, they are Ps 104:30
for they made his **s** bitter, and he Ps 106:33
Where shall I go from your **S**? Or where Ps 139:7
When my **s** faints within me, you Ps 142:3
Therefore my **s** faints within me; my Ps 143:4
Answer me quickly, O LORD! My **s** fails! Ps 143:7
Let your good **S** lead me on level Ps 143:10
behold, I will pour out my **s** to you; Prv 1:23
who is trustworthy in **s** keeps a thing Prv 11:13
life, but perverseness in it breaks the **s**. Prv 15:4
by sorrow of heart the **s** is crushed. Prv 15:13
his own eyes, but the LORD weighs the **s**. Prv 16:2
and a haughty **s** before a fall. Prv 16:18
to be of a lowly **s** with the poor than to Prv 16:19
he who rules his **s** than he who takes Prv 16:32
but a crushed **s** dries up the bones. Prv 17:22
he who has a cool **s** is a man of Prv 17:27
A man's **s** will endure sickness, but a Prv 18:14
but a crushed **s** who can bear? Prv 18:14
The **s** of man is the lamp of the LORD, Prv 20:27
A fool gives full vent to his **s**, but a Prv 29:11
he who is lowly in **s** will obtain honor. Prv 29:23
Who knows whether the **s** of man goes Eccl 3:21
goes upward and the **s** of the beast goes Eccl 3:21
and the patient in **s** is better than the Eccl 7:8
in spirit is better than the proud in **s**. Eccl 7:8
Be not quick in your **s** to become angry, Eccl 7:9
No man has power to retain the **s**, or Eccl 8:8
know the way the **s** comes to the bones Eccl 11:5
and the **s** returns to God who gave it. Eccl 12:7
from its midst by a **s** of judgment and by a Is 4:4
a spirit of judgment and by a **s** of burning. Is 4:4
And the **S** of the LORD shall rest upon him, Is 11:2
him, the **S** of wisdom and understanding, Is 11:2
the **S** of counsel and might, Is 11:2
the **S** of knowledge and the fear of the Is 11:2
and the **s** of the Egyptians within them Is 19:3
has mingled within her a **s** of confusion, Is 19:14
my **s** within me earnestly seeks you. Is 26:9
and a **s** of justice to him who sits in Is 28:6
poured out upon you a **s** of deep sleep, Is 29:10
who go astray in **s** will come to Is 29:24
who make an alliance, but not of my **S**, Is 30:1
God, and their horses are flesh, and not **s**. Is 31:3
until the **S** is poured upon us from on Is 32:15
and his **S** has gathered them. Is 34:16
Behold, I will put a **s** in him, so that he Is 37:7
live, and in all these is the life of my **s**. Is 38:16
Who has measured the **S** of the LORD, or Is 40:13
soul delights; I have put my **S** upon him; Is 42:1
the people on it and **s** to those who walk Is 42:5
I will pour my **S** upon your offspring, and Is 44:3
the Lord GOD has sent me, and his **S**. Is 48:16
you like a wife deserted and grieved in **s**, Is 54:6
him who is of a contrite and lowly **s**, Is 57:15
lowly spirit, to revive the **s** of the lowly, Is 57:15
for the **s** would grow faint before me, Is 57:16
"My **S** that is upon you, and my words Is 59:21
The **S** of the Lord GOD is upon me, Is 61:1
the garment of praise instead of a faint **s**; Is 61:3
But they rebelled and grieved his Holy **S**; Is 63:10
who put in the midst of them his Holy **S**, Is 63:11
valley, the **S** of the LORD gave them rest. Is 63:14
of heart and shall wail for breaking of **s**. Is 65:14
humble and contrite in **s** and trembles at Is 66:2
I will stir up the **s** of a destroyer against Jer 51:1
LORD has stirred up the **s** of the kings of Jer 51:11
is far from me, one to revive my **s**; Lam 1:16
forward. Wherever the **s** would go, Ezk 1:12
Wherever the **s** wanted to go, they went, Ezk 1:20
for the **s** of the living creatures was in Ezk 1:20
for the **s** of the living creatures was in Ezk 1:21
the **S** entered into me and set me on my Ezk 2:2
Then the **S** lifted me up, and I heard Ezk 3:12
The **S** lifted me up and took me away, Ezk 3:14
I went in bitterness in the heat of my **s**, Ezk 3:14
But the **S** entered into me and set me on Ezk 3:24
and the **S** lifted me up between earth and Ezk 8:3
for the **s** of the living creatures was in Ezk 10:17
The **S** lifted me up and brought me to Ezk 11:1
And the **S** of the LORD fell upon me, and Ezk 11:5
and a new **s** I will put within them. Ezk 11:19
And the **S** lifted me up and brought Ezk 11:24
the vision by the **S** of God into Ezk 11:24
prophets who follow their own **s**, Ezk 13:3
yourselves a new heart and a new **s**! Ezk 18:31
every **s** will faint, and all knees will be Ezk 21:7
and a new **s** I will put within you. Ezk 36:26
And I will put my **S** within you, and Ezk 36:27
brought me out in the **S** of the LORD and Ezk 37:1
And I will put my **S** within you, and Ezk 37:14
I pour out my **S** upon the house of Ezk 39:29
the **S** lifted me up and brought me into Ezk 43:5
his **s** was troubled, and his sleep left him. Dn 2:1
and my **s** is troubled to know the dream." Dn 2:3
and in whom is the **s** of the holy gods— Dn 4:8
because I know that the **s** of the holy gods Dn 4:9
able, for the **s** of the holy gods is in you." Dn 4:18
in whom is the **s** of the holy gods. Dn 5:11
because an excellent **s**, knowledge, and Dn 5:12
heard of you that the **s** of the gods is in Dn 5:14
lifted up and his **s** was hardened so that Dn 5:20
because an excellent **s** was in him. Dn 6:3
Daniel, my **s** within me was anxious, Dn 7:15
For a **s** of whoredom has led them Hos 4:12
For the **s** of whoredom is within them, Hos 5:4
the man of the **s** is mad, because of your Hos 9:7
that I will pour out my **S** on all flesh; Jl 2:28
in those days I will pour out my **S**. Jl 2:29
filled with power, with the **S** of the LORD, Mi 3:8
LORD stirred up the **s** of Zerubbabel the Hg 1:14
and the **s** of Joshua the son of Jehozadak, Hg 1:14
and the **s** of all the remnant of the Hg 1:14
out of Egypt. My **S** remains in your midst. Hg 2:5
by might, nor by power, but by my **S**, Zec 4:6
country have set my **S** at rest in the Zec 6:8
had sent by his **S** through the former Zec 7:12
earth and formed the **s** of man within Zec 12:1
of Jerusalem a **s** of grace and Zec 12:10
the prophets and the **s** of uncleanness. Zec 13:2
with a portion of the **S** in their union? Mal 2:15
So guard yourselves in your **s**, and let Mal 2:15
So guard yourselves in your **s**, and do Mal 2:16
found to be with child from the Holy **S**. Mt 1:18
is conceived in her is from the Holy **S**. Mt 1:20
you with the Holy **S** and with fire. Mt 3:11
and he saw the **S** of God descending like Mt 3:16
was led up by the **S** into the wilderness to Mt 4:1
"Blessed are the poor in **s**, for theirs is the Mt 5:3
but the **S** of your Father speaking Mt 10:20
I will put my **S** upon him, and he will Mt 12:18
But if it is by the **S** of God that I cast out Mt 12:28
the blasphemy against the **S** will not be Mt 12:31
speaks against the Holy **S** will not be Mt 12:32
"When the unclean **s** has gone out of a Mt 12:43
"How is it then that David, in the **S**, Mt 22:43
The **s** indeed is willing, but the flesh is Mt 26:41
with a loud voice and yielded up his **s**. Mt 27:50
Father and of the Son and of the Holy **S**, Mt 28:19
but he will baptize you with the Holy **S**." Mk 1:8
opening and the **S** descending on him Mk 1:10
The **S** immediately drove him out into Mk 1:12
synagogue a man with an unclean **s**. Mk 1:23
And the unclean **s**, convulsing him Mk 1:26
perceiving in his **s** that they thus Mk 2:8
against the Holy **S** never has Mk 3:29
they had said, "He has an unclean **s**." Mk 3:30
of the tombs a man with an unclean **s**. Mk 5:2
"Come out of the man, you unclean **s**!" Mk 5:8
possessed by an unclean **s** heard of him Mk 7:25
And he sighed deeply in his **s** and said, Mk 8:12
for he has a **s** that makes him mute. Mk 9:17
And when the **s** saw him, immediately Mk 9:20
together, he rebuked the unclean **s**, Mk 9:25
saying to it, "You mute and deaf **s**, Mk 9:25
David himself, in the Holy **S**, declared, Mk 12:36
it is not you who speak, but the Holy **S**. Mk 13:11
The **s** indeed is willing, but the flesh is Mk 14:38
and he will be filled with the Holy **S**, Lk 1:15
before him in the **s** and power of Elijah, Lk 1:17
her, "The Holy **S** will come upon you, Lk 1:35
And Elizabeth was filled with the Holy **S**, Lk 1:41
and my **s** rejoices in God my Savior, Lk 1:47
filled with the Holy **S** and prophesied, Lk 1:67
the child grew and became strong in **s**, Lk 1:80
of Israel, and the Holy **S** was upon him. Lk 2:25
to him by the Holy **S** that he would not Lk 2:26
And he came in the **S** into the temple, Lk 2:27
you with the Holy **S** and with fire. Lk 3:16
and the Holy **S** descended on him in Lk 3:22
And Jesus, full of the Holy **S**, returned Lk 4:1
and was led by the **S** in the wilderness Lk 4:1
returned in the power of the **S** to Galilee, Lk 4:14
"The **S** of the Lord is upon me, because Lk 4:18
man who had the **s** of an unclean Lk 4:33
commanded the unclean **s** to come out Lk 8:29
And her **s** returned, and she got up at Lk 8:55
And behold, a **s** seizes him, and he Lk 9:39
rebuked the unclean **s** and healed the Lk 9:42
hour he rejoiced in the Holy **S** and said, Lk 10:21
Father give the Holy **S** to those who ask Lk 11:13
"When the unclean **s** has gone out of a Lk 11:24
against the Holy **S** will not be Lk 12:10
for the Holy **S** will teach you in that Lk 12:12
had a disabling **s** for eighteen years. Lk 13:11
I commit my **s**!" And having said Lk 23:46
frightened and thought they saw a **s**. Lk 24:37
For a **s** does not have flesh and bones Lk 24:39
"I saw the **S** descend from heaven like a Jn 1:32
whom you see the **S** descend and remain, Jn 1:33
this is he who baptizes with the Holy **S**.' Jn 1:33
you, unless one is born of water and the **S**, Jn 3:5
and that which is born of the **S** is spirit. Jn 3:6
and that which is born of the Spirit is **s**. Jn 3:6
it is with everyone who is born of the **S**." Jn 3:8
God, for he gives the **S** without measure. Jn 3:34
will worship the Father in **s** and truth, Jn 4:23
God is **s**, and those who worship him Jn 4:24
him must worship in **s** and truth." Jn 4:24
It is the **S** who gives life; the flesh is of no Jn 6:63
that I have spoken to you are **s** and life. Jn 6:63
Now this he said about the **S**, whom Jn 7:39
for as yet the **S** had not been given, Jn 7:39
moved in his **s** and greatly troubled. Jn 11:33
these things, Jesus was troubled in his **s**, Jn 13:21
even the **S** of truth, whom the world Jn 14:17
But the Helper, the Holy **S**, whom the Jn 14:26
to you from the Father, the **S** of truth, Jn 15:26
When the **S** of truth comes, he will Jn 16:13
he bowed his head and gave up his **s**. Jn 19:30
and said to them, "Receive the Holy **S**. Jn 20:22
through the Holy **S** to the apostles Acts 1:2
baptized with the Holy **S** not many days Acts 1:5
power when the Holy **S** has come upon Acts 1:8
which the Holy **S** spoke beforehand by Acts 1:16
filled with the Holy **S** and began to Acts 2:4
tongues as the **S** gave them utterance. Acts 2:4
that I will pour out my **S** on all flesh, Acts 2:17
in those days I will pour out my **S**, Acts 2:18
the Father the promise of the Holy **S**, Acts 2:33
you will receive the gift of the Holy **S**. Acts 2:38
Then Peter, filled with the Holy **S**, said Acts 4:8
your servant, said by the Holy **S**, Acts 4:25
filled with the Holy **S** and continued to Acts 4:31
to lie to the Holy **S** and to keep back for Acts 5:3
agreed together to test the **S** of the Lord? Acts 5:9
to these things, and so is the Holy **S**, Acts 5:32
good repute, full of the **S** and of wisdom, Acts 6:3
a man full of faith and of the Holy **S**, Acts 6:5
the wisdom and the **S** with which he Acts 6:10
and ears, you always resist the Holy **S**. Acts 7:51
But he, full of the Holy **S**, gazed into Acts 7:55
called out, "Lord Jesus, receive my **s**." Acts 7:59
that they might receive the Holy **S**, Acts 8:15
on them and they received the Holy **S**. Acts 8:17
saw that the **S** was given through Acts 8:18
lay my hands may receive the Holy **S**." Acts 8:19
And the **S** said to Philip, "Go over and Acts 8:29
the **S** of the Lord carried Philip away, Acts 8:39
sight and be filled with the Holy **S**." Acts 9:17
Lord and in the comfort of the Holy **S**, Acts 9:31
the vision, the **S** said to him, Acts 10:19
with the Holy **S** and with power. Acts 10:38
the Holy **S** fell on all who heard the Acts 10:44
gift of the Holy **S** was poured out even Acts 10:45
have received the Holy **S** just as we Acts 10:47
And the **S** told me to go with them, Acts 11:12

the Holy **S** fell on them just as on us Acts 11:15
you will be baptized with the Holy **S**.' Acts 11:16
man, full of the Holy **S** and of faith. Acts 11:24
and foretold by the **S** that there would Acts 11:28
the Lord and fasting, the Holy **S** said, Acts 13:2
So, being sent out by the Holy **S**, they Acts 13:4
also called Paul, filled with the Holy **S**, Acts 13:9
filled with joy and with the Holy **S**. Acts 13:52
giving them the Holy **S** just as he did Acts 15:8
seemed good to the Holy **S** and to us to Acts 15:28
forbidden by the Holy **S** to speak the Acts 16:6
but the **S** of Jesus did not allow them. Acts 16:7
girl who had a **s** of divination and Acts 16:16
annoyed, turned and said to the **s**, Acts 16:18
his **s** was provoked within him as he Acts 17:16
And being fervent in **s**, he spoke and Acts 18:25
receive the Holy **S** when you believed?" Acts 19:2
not even heard that there is a Holy **S**." Acts 19:2
on them, the Holy **S** came on them, Acts 19:6
But the evil **s** answered them, "Jesus I Acts 19:15
whom was the evil **s** leaped on them, Acts 19:16
Paul resolved in the **S** to pass through Acts 19:21
to Jerusalem, constrained by the **S**, Acts 20:22
except that the Holy **S** testifies to me Acts 20:23
in which the Holy **S** has made you Acts 20:28
And through the **S** they were telling Acts 21:4
and said, "Thus says the Holy **S**, Acts 21:11
is no resurrection, nor angel, nor **s**, Acts 23:8
What if a **s** or an angel spoke to him?" Acts 23:9
"The Holy **S** was right in saying to Acts 28:25
power according to the **S** of holiness by Rom 1:4
whom I serve with my **s** in the gospel of Rom 1:9
is a matter of the heart, by the **S**, Rom 2:29
through the Holy **S** who has been Rom 5:5
written code but in the new life of the **S**. Rom 7:6
For the law of the **S** of life has set you Rom 8:2
to the flesh but according to the **S**. Rom 8:4
live according to the **S** set their minds Rom 8:5
set their minds on the things of the **S**. Rom 8:5
to set the mind on the **S** is life and peace. Rom 8:6
are not in the flesh but in the **S**, Rom 8:9
if in fact the **S** of God dwells in you. Rom 8:9
does not have the **S** of Christ does not Rom 8:9
the **S** is life because of righteousness. Rom 8:10
If the **S** of him who raised Jesus from Rom 8:11
bodies through his **S** who dwells in Rom 8:11
but if by the **S** you put to death the Rom 8:13
who are led by the **S** of God are sons of Rom 8:14
did not receive the **s** of slavery to fall Rom 8:15
you have received the **S** of adoption as Rom 8:15
The **S** himself bears witness with our Rom 8:16
bears witness with our **s** that we are Rom 8:16
who have the firstfruits of the **S**, Rom 8:23
Likewise the **S** helps us in our Rom 8:26
but the **S** himself intercedes for us Rom 8:26
knows what is the mind of the **S**, Rom 8:27
because the **S** intercedes for the saints Rom 8:27
bears me witness in the Holy **S**— Rom 9:1
written, "God gave them a **s** of stupor, Rom 11:8
not be slothful in zeal, be fervent in **s**, Rom 12:11
and peace and joy in the Holy **S**. Rom 14:17
power of the Holy **S** you may abound Rom 15:13
acceptable, sanctified by the Holy **S**. Rom 15:16
by the power of the **S** of God—so that Rom 15:19
Jesus Christ and by the love of the **S**, Rom 15:30
demonstration of the **S** and of power, 1 Cor 2:4
God has revealed to us through the **S**. 1 Cor 2:10
Spirit. For the **S** searches everything, 1 Cor 2:10
thoughts except the **s** of that person, 1 Cor 2:11
thoughts of God except the **S** of God. 1 Cor 2:11
have received not the **s** of the world, 1 Cor 2:12
the world, but the **S** who is from God, 1 Cor 2:12
human wisdom but taught by the **S**, 1 Cor 2:13
not accept the things of the **S** of God, 1 Cor 2:14
and that God's **S** dwells in you? 1 Cor 3:16
rod, or with love in a **s** of gentleness? 1 Cor 4:21
absent in body, I am present in **s**; 1 Cor 5:3
of the Lord Jesus and my **s** is present, 1 Cor 5:4
so that his **s** may be saved in the day of 1 Cor 5:5
Jesus Christ and by the **S** of our God. 1 Cor 6:11
to the Lord becomes one **s** with him. 1 Cor 6:17
is a temple of the Holy **S** within you, 1 Cor 6:19
Lord, how to be holy in body and **s**. 1 Cor 7:34
I think that I too have the **S** of God. 1 Cor 7:40
one speaking in the **S** of God ever says 1 Cor 12:3
"Jesus is Lord" except in the Holy **S**. 1 Cor 12:3
are varieties of gifts, but the same **S**; 1 Cor 12:4
manifestation of the **S** for the 1 Cor 12:7
given through the **S** the utterance of 1 Cor 12:8
knowledge according to the same **S**, 1 Cor 12:8
to another faith by the same **S**, to 1 Cor 12:9
another gifts of healing by the one **S**, 1 Cor 12:9
empowered by one and the same **S**, 1 Cor 12:11
For in one **S** we were all baptized 1 Cor 12:13
and all were made to drink of one **S**. 1 Cor 12:13
him, but he utters mysteries in the **S**. 1 Cor 14:2
are eager for manifestations of the **S**, 1 Cor 14:12
my **s** prays but my mind is 1 Cor 14:14
I will pray with my **s**, but I will pray 1 Cor 14:15
I will sing praise with my **s**, but I 1 Cor 14:15
if you give thanks with your **s**, 1 Cor 14:16
last Adam became a life-giving **s**. 1 Cor 15:45
for they refreshed my **s** as well as 1 Cor 16:18
us and given us his **S** in our hearts as 2 Cor 1:22
my **s** was not at rest because I did not 2 Cor 2:13
ink but with the **S** of the living God, 2 Cor 3:3
covenant, not of the letter but of the **S**. 2 Cor 3:6
For the letter kills, but the **S** gives life. 2 Cor 3:6
the ministry of the **S** have even more 2 Cor 3:8
Now the Lord is the **S**, and where the 2 Cor 3:17
Spirit, and where the **S** of the Lord is, 2 Cor 3:17
comes from the Lord who is the **S**. 2 Cor 3:18
we have the same **s** of faith according 2 Cor 4:13
who has given us the **S** as a guarantee. 2 Cor 5:5
patience, kindness, the Holy **S**, 2 Cor 6:6
from every defilement of body and **s**, 2 Cor 7:1
because his **s** has been refreshed by 2 Cor 7:13
you receive a different **s** from the one 2 Cor 11:4
of you? Did we not act in the same **s**? 2 Cor 12:18
fellowship of the Holy **S** be with you 2 Cor 13:14
Did you receive the **S** by works of the law Gal 3:2
Having begun by the **S**, are you now Gal 3:3
he who supplies the **S** to you and works Gal 3:5
receive the promised **S** through faith. Gal 3:14
God has sent the **S** of his Son into our Gal 4:6
him who was born according to the **S**, Gal 4:29
For through the **S**, by faith, we ourselves Gal 5:5
But I say, walk by the **S**, and you will Gal 5:16
the desires of the flesh are against the **S**, Gal 5:17
the desires of the **S** are against the flesh, Gal 5:17
But if you are led by the **S**, you are not Gal 5:18
But the fruit of the **S** is love, joy, peace, Gal 5:22
If we live by the **S**, let us also walk by Gal 5:25
by the Spirit, let us also walk by the **S**. Gal 5:25
should restore him in a **s** of gentleness. Gal 6:1
one who sows to the **S** will from the Spirit Gal 6:8
the Spirit will from the **S** reap eternal life. Gal 6:8
of our Lord Jesus Christ be with your **s**, Gal 6:18
were sealed with the promised Holy **S**, Eph 1:13
may give you a **s** of wisdom and of Eph 1:17
the **s** that is now at work in the sons of Eph 2:2
both have access in one **S** to the Father. Eph 2:18
into a dwelling place for God by the **S**. Eph 2:22
his holy apostles and prophets by the **S**. Eph 3:5
with power through his **S** in your inner Eph 3:16
the unity of the **S** in the bond of Eph 4:3
is one body and one **S**—just as you were Eph 4:4
to be renewed in the **s** of your minds, Eph 4:23
And do not grieve the Holy **S** of God, by Eph 4:30
is debauchery, but be filled with the **S**, Eph 5:18
of salvation, and the sword of the **S**, Eph 6:17
praying at all times in the **S**, with all Eph 6:18
the help of the **S** of Jesus Christ this Phil 1:19
that you are standing firm in one **s**, Phil 1:27
from love, any participation in the **S**, Phil 2:1
who worship by the **S** of God and glory Phil 3:3
of the Lord Jesus Christ be with your **s**. Phil 4:23
has made known to us your love in the **S**. Col 1:8
absent in body, yet I am with you in **s**, Col 2:5
and in the Holy **S** and with full 1 Thes 1:5
affliction, with the joy of the Holy **S**, 1 Thes 1:6
but God, who gives his Holy **S** to you. 1 Thes 4:8
Do not quench the **S**. 1 Thes 5:19
and may your whole **s** and soul and 1 Thes 5:23
either by a **s** or a spoken word, 2 Thes 2:2
sanctification by the **S** and belief in 2 Thes 2:13
in the flesh, vindicated by the **S**, 1 Tm 3:16
Now the **S** expressly says that in later 1 Tm 4:1
for God gave us a **s** not of fear but of 2 Tm 1:7
By the Holy **S** who dwells within us, 2 Tm 1:14
The Lord be with your **s**. Grace be 2 Tm 4:22
of regeneration and renewal of the Holy **S**, Ti 3:5
the Lord Jesus Christ be with your **s**. Phlm 1:25
of the Holy **S** distributed according to Heb 2:4
Therefore, as the Holy **S** says, "Today, if Heb 3:7
piercing to the division of soul and of **s**, Heb 4:12
gift, and have shared in the Holy **S**, Heb 6:4
By this the Holy **S** indicates that the way Heb 9:8
through the eternal **S** offered himself Heb 9:14
And the Holy **S** also bears witness to Heb 10:15
and has outraged the **S** of grace? Heb 10:29
For as the body apart from the **s** is dead, Jas 2:26
yearns jealously over the **s** that he has Jas 4:5
the Father, in the sanctification of the **S**, 1 Pt 1:2
person or time the **S** of Christ in them 1 Pt 1:11
to you by the Holy **S** sent from heaven, 1 Pt 1:12
beauty of a gentle and quiet **s**, 1 Pt 3:4
in the flesh but made alive in the **s**, 1 Pt 3:18
might live in the **s** the way God does. 1 Pt 4:6
because the **S** of glory and of God rests 1 Pt 4:14
they were carried along by the Holy **S**. 2 Pt 1:21
in us, by the **S** whom he has given us. 1 Jn 3:24
Beloved, do not believe every **s**, but test 1 Jn 4:1
By this you know the **S** of God: every 1 Jn 4:2
every **s** that confesses that Jesus Christ 1 Jn 4:2
and every **s** that does not confess Jesus is 1 Jn 4:3
from God. This is the **s** of the antichrist, 1 Jn 4:3
By this we know the **S** of truth and the 1 Jn 4:6
the Spirit of truth and the **s** of error. 1 Jn 4:6
in us, because he has given us of his **S**. 1 Jn 4:13
And the **S** is the one who testifies, 1 Jn 5:6
who testifies, because the **S** is the truth. 1 Jn 5:6
the **S** and the water and the blood; and 1 Jn 5:8
worldly people, devoid of the **S**. Jude 1:19
most holy faith; pray in the Holy **S**; Jude 1:20
I was in the **S** on the Lord's day, and I Rv 1:10
hear what the **S** says to the churches. Rv 2:7
hear what the **S** says to the churches. Rv 2:11
hear what the **S** says to the churches. Rv 2:17
hear what the **S** says to the churches.' Rv 2:29
hear what the **S** says to the churches.' Rv 3:6
hear what the **S** says to the churches.' Rv 3:13
hear what the **S** says to the churches.'" Rv 3:22
At once I was in the **S**, and behold, a Rv 4:2
"Blessed indeed," says the **S**, "that they Rv 14:13
me away in the **S** into a wilderness, Rv 17:3
for demons, a haunt for every unclean **s**, Rv 18:2
testimony of Jesus is the **s** of prophecy. Rv 19:10
he carried me away in the **S** to a great, Rv 21:10
The **S** and the Bride say, "Come." And Rv 22:17

SPIRITS (36)

"O God, the God of the **s** of all flesh, Nm 16:22
the LORD, the God of the **s** of all flesh, Nm 27:16
and he cast out the **s** with a word and Mt 8:16
and gave them authority over unclean **s**, Mt 10:1
with it seven other **s** more evil than Mt 12:45
He commands even the unclean **s**, and Mk 1:27
And whenever the unclean **s** saw him, Mk 3:11
And the unclean **s** came out, and Mk 5:13
gave them authority over the unclean **s**. Mk 6:7
and power he commands the unclean **s**, Lk 4:36
troubled with unclean **s** were cured. Lk 6:18
people of diseases and plagues and evil **s**, Lk 7:21
had been healed of evil **s** and infirmities: Lk 8:2
in this, that the **s** are subject to you, Lk 10:20
brings seven other **s** more evil than Lk 11:26
and those afflicted with unclean **s**, Acts 5:16
For unclean **s** came out of many who Acts 8:7
them and the evil **s** came out of them. Acts 19:12
Lord Jesus over those who had evil **s**, Acts 19:13
the ability to distinguish between **s**, 1 Cor 12:10
and the **s** of prophets are subject to 1 Cor 14:32
according to the elemental **s** of the world, Col 2:8
you died to the elemental **s** of the world, Col 2:20
themselves to deceitful **s** and teachings 1 Tm 4:1
they not all ministering **s** sent out to Heb 1:14
be subject to the Father of **s** and live? Heb 12:9
and to the **s** of the righteous made Heb 12:23
went and proclaimed to the **s** in prison, 1 Pt 3:19
but test the **s** to see whether they are 1 Jn 4:1
and from the seven **s** who are before his Rv 1:4
him who has the seven **s** of God and the Rv 3:1
of fire, which are the seven **s** of God, Rv 4:5
which are the seven **s** of God sent out into Rv 5:6
false prophet, three unclean **s** like frogs. Rv 16:13
For they are demonic **s**, performing Rv 16:14
the Lord, the God of the **s** of the prophets, Rv 22:6

SPIRITUAL (29)

impart to you some **s** gift to strengthen Rom 1:11
For we know that the law is **s**, but I am Rom 7:14
to God, which is your **s** worship. Rom 12:1
come to share in their **s** blessings, Rom 15:27
that you are not lacking in any **s** gift, 1 Cor 1:7
interpreting **s** truths to those who are 1 Cor 2:13
spiritual truths to those who are **s**. 1 Cor 2:13
The **s** person judges all things, but is 1 Cor 2:15
could not address you as **s** people, 1 Cor 3:1
If we have sown **s** things among you, 1 Cor 9:11
and all ate the same **s** food, 1 Cor 10:3
and all drank the same **s** drink. For 1 Cor 10:4
drank from the **s** Rock that followed 1 Cor 10:4
Now concerning **s** gifts, brothers, I do 1 Cor 12:1
love, and earnestly desire the **s** gifts, 1 Cor 14:1
thinks that he is a prophet, or **s**, 1 Cor 14:37
a natural body; it is raised a **s** body. 1 Cor 15:44
natural body, there is also a **s** body. 1 Cor 15:44
But it is not the **s** that is first but the 1 Cor 15:46
first but the natural, and then the **s**. 1 Cor 15:46
you who are **s** should restore him in a Gal 6:1
in Christ with every **s** blessing in the Eph 1:3
in psalms and hymns and **s** songs, Eph 5:19
against the **s** forces of evil in the Eph 6:12
will in all **s** wisdom and understanding, Col 1:9
psalms and hymns and **s** songs, Col 3:16

infants, long for the pure **s** milk, 1 Pt 2:2
stones are being built up as a **s** house, 1 Pt 2:5
to offer **s** sacrifices acceptable to God 1 Pt 2:5

SPIRITUALLY (1)
them because they are **s** discerned. 1 Cor 2:14

SPIT (12)
"If her father had but **s** in her face, Nm 12:14
his sandal off his foot and **s** in his face. Dt 25:9
nor leave me alone till I swallow my **s**? Jb 7:19
and I am one before whom men **s**. Jb 17:6
they do not hesitate to **s** at the sight of Jb 30:10
Then they **s** in his face and struck Mt 26:67
And they **s** on him and took the reed Mt 27:30
and when he had **s** on his eyes and laid Mk 8:23
they will mock him and **s** on him, Mk 10:34
And some began to **s** on him and to Mk 14:65
and shamefully treated and **s** upon. Lk 18:32
nor cold, I will **s** you out of my mouth. Rv 3:16

SPITE (10)
And if in **s** of this you will not listen to Lv 26:18
"But if in **s** of this you will not listen to Lv 26:27
in **s** of all the signs that I have done Nm 14:11
Yet in **s** of this word you did not believe Dt 1:32
now there is hope for Israel in **s** of this. Ezr 10:2
in **s** of my right I am counted a liar; my Jb 34:6
In **s** of all this, they still sinned; despite Ps 78:32
contempt, in **s** of all his great multitude, Is 16:14
in **s** of your many sorceries and the great Is 47:9
breaking in. Yet in **s** of all these things Jer 2:34

SPITS (1)
with the discharge **s** on someone who Lv 15:8

SPITTING (3)
I hid not my face from disgrace and **s**. Is 50:6
his ears, and after **s** touched his tongue. Mk 7:33
with a reed and **s** on him and kneeling Mk 15:19

SPITTLE (1)
gate and let his **s** run down his 1 Sm 21:13

SPLASHED (2)
when any of its blood is **s** on a garment, Lv 6:27
that on which it was **s** in a holy place. Lv 6:27

SPLENDID (4)
take on the first day the fruit of **s** trees, Lv 23:40
from Bozrah, he who is **s** in his apparel, Is 63:1
who are dressed in **s** clothing and live in Lk 7:25
Then, arraying him in **s** clothing, he Lk 23:11

SPLENDOR (31)
S and majesty are before him; 1 Chr 16:27
the LORD in the **s** of holiness; 1 Chr 16:29
his royal glory and the **s** and pomp of his Est 1:4
recounted to them the **s** of his riches, Est 5:11
it shone, or the moon moving in **s**, Jb 31:26
Out of the north comes golden **s**; God is Jb 37:22
clothe yourself with glory and **s**. Jb 40:10
s and majesty you bestow on him. Ps 21:5
worship the LORD in the **s** of holiness. Ps 29:2
O mighty one, in your **s** and majesty! Ps 45:3
You have made his **s** to cease and cast Ps 89:44
S and majesty are before him; strength Ps 96:6
Worship the LORD in the **s** of holiness; Ps 96:9
You are clothed with **s** and majesty, Ps 104:1
Full of **s** and majesty is his work, and Ps 111:3
On the glorious **s** of your majesty, and Ps 145:5
and the glorious **s** of your kingdom. Ps 145:12
but the **s** of old men is their gray hair. Prv 20:29
of the LORD, and from the **s** of his majesty. Is 2:10
of the LORD, and from the **s** of his majesty, Is 2:19
of the LORD, and from the **s** of his majesty, Is 2:21
the **s** and pomp of the Chaldeans, Is 13:19
from heaven to earth the **s** of Israel; Lam 2:1
was perfect through the **s** that I had Ezk 16:14
and helmet in you; they gave you **s**. Ezk 27:10
of your wisdom and defile your **s**. Ezk 28:7
your wisdom for the sake of your **s**. Ezk 28:17
my majesty and **s** returned to me. Dn 4:36
children you take away my **s** forever. Mi 2:9
His **s** covered the heavens, and the earth Hab 3:3
present the church to himself in **s**, Eph 5:27

SPLENDORS (1)
your delicacies and your **s** are lost to Rv 18:14

SPLINTERED (1)
It has laid waste my vine and **s** my fig tree; Jl 1:7

SPLIT (14)
words, the ground under them **s** apart. Nm 16:31
And God **s** open the hollow place that is Jgs 15:19
And they **s** up the wood of the cart and 1 Sm 6:14
so that the earth was **s** by their noise. 1 Kgs 1:40
and the cloud is not **s** open under them. Jb 26:8
You **s** open springs and brooks; you Ps 74:15
He **s** rocks in the wilderness and gave Ps 78:15
is utterly broken, the earth is **s** apart, Is 24:19
he **s** the rock and the water gushed out. Is 48:21
under him, and the valleys will **s** open, Mi 1:4
Selah You **s** the earth with rivers. Hab 3:9
of Olives shall be **s** in two from east Zec 14:4
the earth shook, and the rocks were **s**. Mt 27:51
The great city was **s** into three parts, Rv 16:19

SPLITS (1)
and he who **s** logs is endangered by Eccl 10:9

SPOIL (80)
the prey and at evening dividing the **s**." Gn 49:27
pursue, I will overtake, I will divide the **s**, Ex 15:9
and took all the **s** and all the plunder, Nm 31:11
and the plunder and the **s** to Moses, Nm 31:12
remaining of the **s** that the army Nm 31:32
the livestock we took as **s** for ourselves, Dt 2:35
all the livestock and the **s** of the cities we Dt 3:7
shall gather all its **s** into the midst of Dt 13:16
and burn the city and all its **s** with fire, Dt 13:16
and everything else in the city, all its **s**, Dt 20:14
you shall enjoy the **s** of your enemies, Dt 20:14
I saw among the **s** a beautiful cloak Jos 7:21
Only its **s** and its livestock you shall take Jos 8:2
the livestock and the **s** of that city Israel Jos 8:27
And all the **s** of these cities and the Jos 11:14
Divide the **s** of your enemies with your Jos 22:8
'Have they not found and divided the **s**? Jgs 5:30
s of dyed materials for Sisera, spoil of Jgs 5:30
Sisera, **s** of dyed materials embroidered, Jgs 5:30
work embroidered for the neck as **s**?' Jgs 5:30
the earrings from his **s**." (For they had Jgs 8:24
man threw in it the earrings of his **s**. Jgs 8:25
town and took their **s** and gave the Jgs 14:19
freely today of the **s** of their enemies 1 Sm 14:30
pounced on the **s** and took sheep 1 Sm 14:32
you pounce on the **s** and do what 1 Sm 15:19
But the people took of the **s**, sheep 1 Sm 15:21
of all the great **s** they had taken from 1 Sm 30:16
s or anything that had been taken. 1 Sm 30:19
him, and said, "This is David's **s**." 1 Sm 30:20
them any of the **s** that we have 1 Sm 30:22
he sent part of the **s** to his friends, 1 Sm 30:26
for you from the **s** of the enemies of 1 Sm 30:26
and take his **s**." But Asahel would 2 Sm 2:21
a raid, bringing much **s** with them. 2 Sm 3:22
and from the **s** of Hadadezer the son of 2 Sm 8:12
And he brought out the **s** of the city, 2 Sm 12:30
down. Now then, Moab, to the **s**!" 2 Kgs 3:23
a prey and a **s** to all their enemies, 2 Kgs 21:14
And he brought out the **s** of the city, 1 Chr 20:2
From **s** won in battles they 1 Chr 26:27
of Judah carried away very much **s**. 2 Chr 14:13
that day from the **s** that they had 2 Chr 15:11
and his people came to take their **s**, 2 Chr 20:25
were three days in taking the **s**, 2 Chr 20:25
and sent all their **s** to the king of 2 Chr 24:23
people in them and took much **s**. 2 Chr 25:13
also took much **s** from them and 2 Chr 28:8
them and brought the **s** to Samaria. 2 Chr 28:8
captives and the **s** before the princes 2 Chr 28:14
and with the **s** they clothed all who 2 Chr 28:15
and those who hate us have gotten **s**. Ps 44:10
flee!" The women at home divide the **s**— Ps 68:12
The stouthearted were stripped of their **s**; Ps 76:5
your word like one who finds great **s**. Ps 119:162
is wicked covets the **s** of evildoers, Prv 12:12
than to divide the **s** with the proud. Prv 16:19
for us, the little foxes that **s** the vineyards, Sg 2:15
the **s** of the poor is in your houses. Is 3:14
of Damascus and the **s** of Samaria will be Is 8:4
as they are glad when they divide the **s**. Is 9:3
of their right, that widows may be their **s**, Is 10:2
him, to take **s** and seize plunder, Is 10:6
and your **s** is gathered as the caterpillar Is 33:4
Then prey and **s** in abundance will be Is 33:23
with none to rescue, **s** with none to say, Is 42:22
and he shall divide the **s** with the strong, Is 53:12
Even so will I **s** the pride of Judah and the Jer 13:9
and your treasures I will give as **s**, Jer 15:13
treasures I will give for **s** as the price of Jer 17:3
plunder, their herds of livestock a **s**. Jer 49:32
and to the wicked of the earth for **s**, Ezk 7:21
to seize **s** and carry off plunder, to turn Ezk 38:12
say to you, 'Have you come to seize **s**? Ezk 38:13
livestock and goods, to seize great **s**?' Ezk 38:13
They will seize the **s** of those who Ezk 39:10
among them plunder, **s**, and goods. Dn 11:24
tremble? Then you will be **s** for them. Hab 2:7
when the **s** taken from you will be Zec 14:1
in which he trusted and divides his **s**. Lk 11:22

SPOILED (2)
And behold, the loincloth was **s**; it was Jer 13:7
making of clay was **s** in the potter's Jer 18:4

SPOILS (2)
waters of Megiddo; they got no **s** of silver. Jgs 5:19
the patriarch gave a tenth of the **s**! Heb 7:4

SPOKE (339)
Cain **s** to Abel his brother. And when Gn 4:8
the name of the LORD who **s** to her, Gn 16:13
Again he **s** to him and said, "Suppose Gn 18:29
and who **s** to me and swore to me, Gn 24:7
"Thus the man **s** to me," he went to the Gn 24:30
was listening when Isaac **s** to his son Gn 27:5
God of your father **s** to me last night, Gn 31:29
the young woman and **s** tenderly to her. Gn 34:3
So Shechem **s** to his father Hamor, Gn 34:4
But Hamor **s** with them, saying, "The Gn 34:8
gate of their city and **s** to the men of Gn 34:20
And as she **s** to Joseph day after day, he Gn 39:10
heard the words that his wife **s** to him, Gn 39:19
like strangers and **s** roughly to them. Gn 42:7
And he returned to them and **s** to them. Gn 42:24
s roughly to us and took us to be spies Gn 42:30
of Joseph's house and **s** with him at the Gn 43:19
well, the old man of whom you **s**? Gn 43:27
brother, of whom you **s** to me? Gn 43:29
overtook them, he **s** to them these words. Gn 44:6
And God **s** to Israel in visions of the Gn 46:2
Joseph **s** to the household of Pharaoh, Gn 50:4
Joseph wept when they **s** to him. Gn 50:17
comforted them and **s** kindly to them. Gn 50:21
Aaron **s** all the words that the LORD had Ex 4:30
God **s** to Moses and said to him, "I am the Ex 6:2
Moses **s** thus to the people of Israel, but Ex 6:9
But the LORD **s** to Moses and Aaron and Ex 6:13
It was they who **s** to Pharaoh king of Ex 6:27
the day when the LORD **s** to Moses in the Ex 6:28
years old, when they **s** to Pharaoh. Ex 7:7
as soon as Aaron **s** to the whole Ex 16:10
grew louder and louder, Moses **s**, Ex 19:19
And God **s** all these words, saying, Ex 20:1
The LORD **s** to Moses, saying, Ex 40:1
LORD called Moses and **s** to him from the Lv 1:1
And the LORD **s** to Moses, saying, Lv 4:1
The LORD **s** to Moses, saying, Lv 5:14
The LORD **s** to Moses, saying, Lv 6:1
The LORD **s** to Moses, saying, Lv 6:8
The LORD **s** to Moses, saying, Lv 6:19
The LORD **s** to Moses, saying, Lv 6:24
The LORD **s** to Moses, saying, Lv 7:22
The LORD **s** to Moses, saying, Lv 7:28
The LORD **s** to Moses, saying, Lv 8:1
And the LORD **s** to Aaron, saying, Lv 10:8
Moses **s** to Aaron and to Eleazar and Lv 10:12
And the LORD **s** to Moses and Aaron, Lv 11:1
The LORD **s** to Moses, saying, Lv 12:1
The LORD **s** to Moses and Aaron, saying, Lv 13:1
The LORD **s** to Moses, saying, Lv 14:1
The LORD **s** to Moses and Aaron, saying, Lv 14:33
The LORD **s** to Moses and Aaron, saying, Lv 15:1
The LORD **s** to Moses after the death of the Lv 16:1
And the LORD **s** to Moses, saying, Lv 17:1
And the LORD **s** to Moses, saying, Lv 18:1
And the LORD **s** to Moses, saying, Lv 19:1
The LORD **s** to Moses, saying, Lv 20:1
And the LORD **s** to Moses, saying, Lv 21:16
So Moses **s** to Aaron and to his sons Lv 21:24
And the LORD **s** to Moses, saying, Lv 22:1
And the LORD **s** to Moses, saying, Lv 22:17
And the LORD **s** to Moses, saying, Lv 22:26
The LORD **s** to Moses, saying, Lv 23:1
And the LORD **s** to Moses, saying, Lv 23:9
And the LORD **s** to Moses, saying, Lv 23:23
And the LORD **s** to Moses, saying, Lv 23:26
And the LORD **s** to Moses, saying, Lv 23:33
The LORD **s** to Moses, saying, Lv 24:1
Then the LORD **s** to Moses, saying, Lv 24:13
So Moses **s** to the people of Israel, and Lv 24:23
The LORD **s** to Moses on Mount Sinai, Lv 25:1
The LORD **s** to Moses, saying, Lv 27:1
The LORD **s** to Moses in the wilderness of Nm 1:1
For the LORD **s** to Moses, saying, Nm 1:48
The LORD **s** to Moses and Aaron, saying, Nm 2:1
time when the LORD **s** with Moses on Nm 3:1
And the LORD **s** to Moses, saying, Nm 3:5
And the LORD **s** to Moses, saying, Nm 3:11
And the LORD **s** to Moses in the Nm 3:14
And the LORD **s** to Moses, saying, Nm 3:44
The LORD **s** to Moses and Aaron, saying, Nm 4:1
The LORD **s** to Moses and Aaron, Nm 4:17
The LORD **s** to Moses, saying, Nm 4:21
The LORD **s** to Moses, saying, Nm 5:1
And the LORD **s** to Moses, saying, Nm 5:5
And the LORD **s** to Moses, saying, Nm 5:11
And the LORD **s** to Moses, saying, Nm 6:1
The LORD **s** to Moses, saying, Nm 6:22
the two cherubim; and it **s** to him. Nm 7:89
Now the LORD **s** to Moses, saying, Nm 8:1

And the LORD **s** to Moses, saying, Nm 8:5
And the LORD **s** to Moses, saying, Nm 8:23
And the LORD **s** to Moses in the Nm 9:1
The LORD **s** to Moses, saying, Nm 9:9
The LORD **s** to Moses, saying, Nm 10:1
came down in the cloud and **s** to him, Nm 11:25
Miriam and Aaron **s** against Moses Nm 12:1
The LORD **s** to Moses, saying, Nm 13:1
And the LORD **s** to Moses and to Aaron, Nm 14:26
The LORD **s** to Moses, saying, Nm 15:1
The LORD **s** to Moses, saying, Nm 15:17
And the LORD **s** to Moses and to Aaron, Nm 16:20
And the LORD **s** to Moses, saying, Nm 16:23
And he **s** to the congregation, saying, Nm 16:26
Then the LORD **s** to Moses, saying, Nm 16:36
and the LORD **s** to Moses, saying, Nm 16:44
The LORD **s** to Moses, saying, Nm 17:1
Moses **s** to the people of Israel. And all Nm 17:6
Then the LORD **s** to Aaron, "Behold, I Nm 18:8
And the LORD **s** to Moses, saying, Nm 18:25
Now the LORD **s** to Moses and to Aaron, Nm 19:1
and the LORD **s** to Moses, saying, Nm 20:7
And the people **s** against God and Nm 21:5
And the LORD **s** to Moses, saying, Nm 25:16
and Eleazar the priest **s** with them in Nm 26:3
The LORD **s** to Moses, saying, Nm 26:52
Moses **s** to the LORD, saying, Nm 27:15
The LORD **s** to Moses, saying, Nm 28:1
Moses **s** to the heads of the tribes of the Nm 30:1
The LORD **s** to Moses, saying, Nm 31:1
So Moses **s** to the people, saying, "Arm Nm 31:3
And the LORD **s** to Moses in the plains Nm 33:50
The LORD **s** to Moses, saying, Nm 34:1
The LORD **s** to Moses, saying, Nm 34:16
The LORD **s** to Moses in the plains of Nm 35:1
And the LORD **s** to Moses, saying, Nm 35:9
came near and **s** before Moses and Nm 36:1
the words that Moses **s** to all Israel beyond Dt 1:1
Moses **s** to the people of Israel according to Dt 1:3
So I **s** to you, and you would not listen; Dt 1:43
Then the LORD **s** to you out of the midst Dt 4:12
the day that the LORD **s** to you at Horeb Dt 4:15
which Moses **s** to the people of Israel Dt 4:45
The LORD **s** with you face to face at the Dt 5:4
"These words the LORD **s** to all your Dt 5:22
heard your words, when you **s** to me. Dt 5:28
Then Moses **s** the words of this song Dt 31:30
That very day the LORD **s** to Moses, Dt 32:48
At that time Joshua **s** to the LORD in the Jos 10:12
time that the LORD **s** this word to Moses, Jos 14:10
of which the LORD **s** on that day, Jos 14:12
Then the people of Joseph **s** to Joshua, Jos 17:14
of which I **s** to you through Moses, Jos 20:2
of Gad and the people of Manasseh **s**, Jos 22:30
Israel blessed God and **s** no more of Jos 22:33
all the words of the LORD that he **s** to us. Jos 24:27
the angel of the LORD **s** these words to all Jgs 2:4
to Penuel, and **s** to them in the same way, Jgs 8:8
his mother's relatives **s** all these words Jgs 9:3
Gaal **s** again and said, "Look, people are Jgs 9:37
And Jephthah **s** all his words before the Jgs 11:11
you the man who **s** to this woman?" Jgs 13:11
uttered a curse, and also **s** it in my ears, Jgs 17:2
"Here is the man of whom I **s** to you! 1 Sm 9:17
the Philistines and **s** the same words 1 Sm 17:23
brother heard when he **s** to the men. 1 Sm 17:28
another, and **s** in the same way, 1 Sm 17:30
the words that David **s** were heard, 1 Sm 17:31
And Saul's servants **s** those words in 1 Sm 18:23
And Saul **s** to Jonathan his son and to 1 Sm 19:1
And Jonathan **s** well of David to Saul 1 Sm 19:4
Then David sent and **s** to Abigail, 1 Sm 25:39
LORD has done to you as he **s** by me, 1 Sm 28:17
for the people **s** of stoning him, 1 Sm 30:6
Abner also **s** to Benjamin. And then 2 Sm 3:19
all this vision, Nathan **s** to David. 2 Sm 7:17
the child was yet alive, we **s** to him, 2 Sm 12:18
But Absalom **s** to Amnon neither 2 Sm 13:22
called the Gibeonites and **s** to them. 2 Sm 21:2
And David **s** to the LORD the words of 2 Sm 22:1
Then David **s** to the LORD when he 2 Sm 24:17
his word that he **s** concerning me, 1 Kgs 2:4
is mine." Thus they **s** before the king. 1 Kgs 3:22
He also **s** 3,000 proverbs, and his 1 Kgs 4:32
He **s** of trees, from the cedar that is in 1 Kgs 4:33
He **s** also of beasts, and of birds, and 1 Kgs 4:33
you, which I **s** to David your father. 1 Kgs 6:12
You **s** with your mouth, and with 1 Kgs 8:24
which he **s** by Moses his servant. 1 Kgs 8:56
he **s** to them according to the 1 Kgs 12:14
which the LORD **s** by Ahijah the 1 Kgs 12:15
and an angel **s** to me by the word of 1 Kgs 13:18
to the word that the LORD **s** to him." 1 Kgs 13:26
which he **s** by his servant Ahijah 1 Kgs 14:18
the LORD that he **s** by his servant 1 Kgs 15:29
which he **s** against Baasha by Jehu 1 Kgs 16:12
which he **s** by Joshua the son of 1 Kgs 16:34
word of the LORD that he **s** by Elijah. 1 Kgs 17:16
"Because I **s** to Naboth the Jezreelite 1 Kgs 21:6
according to the word that Elisha **s**. 2 Kgs 2:22
"Thus and so **s** the girl from the land 2 Kgs 5:4
And he said, "Thus and so he **s** to me, 2 Kgs 9:12
which he **s** by his servant Elijah the 2 Kgs 9:36
which the LORD **s** concerning the 2 Kgs 10:10
word of the LORD that he **s** to Elijah. 2 Kgs 10:17
which he **s** by his servant Jonah the 2 Kgs 14:25
you heard how I **s** against this place 2 Kgs 22:19
the LORD that he **s** by his servants the 2 Kgs 24:2
And he **s** kindly to him and gave 2 Kgs 25:28
all this vision, Nathan **s** to David. 1 Chr 17:15
And the LORD **s** to Gad, David's seer, 1 Chr 21:9
Solomon **s** to all Israel, to the 2 Chr 1:2
You **s** with your mouth, and with 2 Chr 6:15
King Rehoboam **s** to them 2 Chr 10:14
which he **s** by Ahijah the Shilonite 2 Chr 10:15
as the LORD **s** concerning the sons of 2 Chr 23:3
And Hezekiah **s** encouragingly to 2 Chr 30:22
the city and **s** encouragingly to them, 2 Chr 32:6
And they **s** of the God of Jerusalem 2 Chr 32:19
of Jerusalem as they **s** of the gods of 2 Chr 32:19
The LORD **s** to Manasseh and to his 2 Chr 33:10
of the seers who **s** to him in the 2 Chr 33:18
the Second Quarter) and **s** to her to 2 Chr 34:22
who **s** from the mouth of the LORD. 2 Chr 36:12
came to them and **s** to them thus, Ezr 5:3
we asked those elders and **s** to them thus, Ezr 5:9
Also they **s** of his good deeds in my Neh 6:19
on Mount Sinai and **s** with them from Neh 9:13
of their children **s** the language of Neh 13:24
And when they **s** to him day after day and Est 3:4
Then Esther **s** to Hathach and Est 4:10
Then Esther **s** again to the king. She fell Est 8:3
of his people and **s** peace to all his Est 10:3
seven nights, and no one **s** a word to him, Jb 2:13
After I **s** they did not speak again, and Jb 29:22
For he **s**, and it came to be; he Ps 33:9
the fire burned; then I **s** with my tongue: Ps 39:3
They **s** against God, saying, "Can God Ps 78:19
Of old you **s** in a vision to your godly Ps 89:19
In the pillar of the cloud he **s** to them; Ps 99:7
He **s**, and there came swarms of flies, Ps 105:31
He **s**, and the locusts came, young Ps 105:34
bitter, and he **s** rashly with his lips. Ps 106:33
I believed, even when I **s**, "I am greatly Ps 116:10
and gone. My soul failed me when he **s**. Sg 5:6
Again the LORD **s** to Ahaz, Is 7:10
The LORD **s** to me again: Is 8:5
For the LORD **s** thus to me with his strong Is 8:11
that the LORD **s** concerning Moab in Is 16:13
at that time the LORD **s** by Isaiah the son Is 20:2
when I **s**, you did not listen, but you did Is 65:12
one answered, when I **s** they did not listen; Is 66:4
and when I **s** to you persistently you did Jer 7:13
I **s** to you in your prosperity, but you Jer 22:21
which Jeremiah the prophet **s** to all the Jer 25:2
Then Jeremiah **s** to all the officials and Jer 26:12
the land arose and **s** to all the Jer 26:17
king of Judah I **s** in like manner: Jer 27:12
Then I **s** to the priests and to all this Jer 27:16
Gibeon, **s** to me in the house of the LORD, Jer 28:1
the prophet Jeremiah **s** to Hananiah the Jer 28:5
And Hananiah **s** in the presence of all Jer 28:11
that the LORD **s** concerning Israel and Jer 30:4
What you **s** has come to pass, and Jer 32:24
Jeremiah the prophet **s** all these words Jer 34:6
all the nations, from the day I **s** to you, Jer 36:2
the LORD that he **s** through Jeremiah the Jer 37:2
the son of Kareah **s** secretly to Gedaliah Jer 40:15
Jeremiah the prophet **s** to Baruch the Jer 45:1
word that the LORD **s** to Jeremiah the Jer 46:13
that whenever you **s** of him you wagged Jer 48:27
that the LORD **s** concerning Babylon, Jer 50:1
done what he **s** concerning the Jer 51:12
And he **s** kindly to him, and gave him a Jer 52:32
And as he **s** to me, the Spirit entered into Ezk 2:2
feet, and he **s** with me and said to me, Ezk 3:24
So I **s** to the people in the morning, Ezk 24:18
you he of whom I **s** in former days by Ezk 38:17
And the king **s** with them, and among Dn 1:19
eyes and a mouth that **s** great things, Dn 7:20
another holy one said to the one who **s**, Dn 8:13
who **s** in your name to our kings, Dn 9:6
which he **s** against us and against our Dn 9:12
lips. Then I opened my mouth and **s**. Dn 10:16
of good courage." And as he **s** to me, Dn 10:19
When the LORD first **s** through Hosea, Hos 1:2
God at Bethel, and there God **s** with us— Hos 12:4
I **s** to the prophets; it was I who Hos 12:10
When Ephraim **s**, there was trembling; Hos 13:1
And the LORD **s** to the fish, and it Jon 2:10
s to the people with the LORD'S message, Hg 1:13
who feared the LORD **s** with one another. Mal 3:16
had been cast out, the mute man **s**. Mt 9:33
healed him, so that the man **s** and saw. Mt 12:22
But immediately Jesus **s** to them, Mt 14:27
into the house, Jesus **s** to him first, Mt 17:25
And again Jesus **s** to them in parables, Mt 22:1
many such parables he **s** the word to Mk 4:33
But immediately he **s** to them and said, Mk 6:50
tongue was released, and he **s** plainly. Mk 7:35
about the bush, how God **s** to him, Mk 12:26
as he **s** to our fathers, to Abraham and Lk 1:55
opened and his tongue loosed, and he **s**, Lk 1:64
as he **s** by the mouth of his holy Lk 1:70
understand the saying that he **s** to them. Lk 2:50
And all **s** well of him and marveled at Lk 4:22
he welcomed them and **s** to them of the Lk 9:11
appeared in glory and **s** of his departure, Lk 9:31
demon had gone out, the mute man **s**, Lk 11:14
are my words that I **s** to you while I was Lk 24:44
the word that Jesus **s** to him and went Jn 4:50
He **s** of Judas the son of Simon Iscariot, Jn 6:71
fear of the Jews no one **s** openly of him. Jn 7:13
answered, "No one ever **s** like this man!" Jn 7:46
Again Jesus **s** to them, saying, "I am the Jn 8:12
These words he **s** in the treasury, as he Jn 8:20
because he saw his glory and **s** of him. Jn 12:41
at one another, uncertain of whom he **s**. Jn 13:22
went out and **s** to the servant girl who Jn 18:16
the Holy Spirit **s** beforehand by the Acts 1:16
he foresaw and **s** about the Acts 2:31
about which God **s** by the mouth Acts 3:21
And God **s** to this effect—that his Acts 7:6
with the angel who **s** to him at Mount Acts 7:38
just as he who **s** to Moses directed him Acts 7:44
he had seen the Lord, who **s** to him, Acts 9:27
And he **s** and disputed against the Acts 9:29
When the angel who **s** to him had Acts 10:7
coming to Antioch **s** to the Hellenists Acts 11:20
Barnabas, who, as they **s** with them, Acts 13:43
And Paul and Barnabas **s** out boldly, Acts 13:46
the Jewish synagogue and **s** in such a Acts 14:1
we sat down and **s** to the women who Acts 16:13
And they **s** the word of the Lord to Acts 16:32
he **s** and taught accurately the things Acts 18:25
and for three months **s** boldly, Acts 19:8
What if a spirit or an angel **s** to him?" Acts 23:9
When I was a child, I **s** like a child, I 1 Cor 13:11
"I believed, and so I **s**," we also believe, 2 Cor 4:13
God **s** to our fathers by the prophets, Heb 1:1
those who **s** to you the word of God. Heb 13:7
take the prophets who **s** in the name of Jas 5:10
but men **s** from God as they were 2 Pt 1:21
a speechless donkey **s** with human 2 Pt 2:16
I had heard from heaven **s** to me again, Rv 10:8
like a lamb and it **s** like a dragon. Rv 13:11
full of the seven last plagues and **s** to me, Rv 21:9
And the one who **s** with me had a Rv 21:15

SPOKEN (219)

the city of which you have **s**. Gn 19:21
at the time of which God had **s** to him. Gn 21:2
your master's son, as the LORD has **s**." Gn 24:51
in the place where he had **s** with him. Gn 35:13
in the place where he had **s** with him, Gn 35:14
where God had **s** with him Bethel. Gn 35:15
past or since you have **s** to your servant, Ex 4:10
that the LORD had **s** to Moses and did Ex 4:30
to them, as the LORD had **s** to Moses. Ex 9:12
go, just as the LORD had **s** through Moses. Ex 9:35
"All that the LORD has **s** we will do." And Ex 19:8
the words that the LORD has **s** we will do." Ex 24:3
said, "All that the LORD has **s** we will do, Ex 24:7
disaster that he had **s** of bringing on Ex 32:14
the place about which I have **s** to you; Ex 32:34
very thing that you have **s** I will do, Ex 33:17
that the LORD had **s** with him in Mount Ex 34:32
that the LORD has **s** to them by Moses." Lv 10:11
the LORD indeed **s** only through Moses? Nm 12:2
Has he not **s** through us also?" And the Nm 12:2
I, the LORD, have **s**. Surely this will I do Nm 14:35
that the LORD has **s** to Moses, Nm 15:22
for we have **s** against the LORD and Nm 21:7
said to him, "What has the LORD **s**?" Nm 23:17
Or has he **s**, and will he not fulfill it? Nm 23:19
'The thing that you have **s** is good for us Dt 1:14
of this people, which they have **s** to you. Dt 5:28
They are right in all that they have **s**. Dt 5:28
that the LORD had **s** with you on the Dt 9:10
that the LORD had **s** to you on the Dt 10:4
me, 'They are right in what they have **s**. Dt 18:17
know the word that the LORD has not **s**?' Dt 18:21
that is a word that the LORD has not **s**; Dt 18:22
the prophet has **s** it presumptuously. Dt 18:22
go over at your head, as the LORD has **s**. Dt 31:3
to all that the LORD had **s** to Moses. Jos 11:23

have comforted me and **s** kindly to your Ru 2:13
the redeemer, of whom Boaz had **s**, Ru 4:1
all that I have **s** concerning his house, 1 Sm 3:12
Why then have you **s** to me in this 1 Sm 9:21
kingdom, of which Samuel had **s**, 1 Sm 10:16
the matter of which you and I have **s**, 1 Sm 20:23
that he has **s** concerning you and 1 Sm 25:30
said, "As God lives, if you had not **s**, 2 Sm 2:27
female servants of whom you have **s**, 2 Sm 6:22
You have **s** also of your servant's 2 Sm 7:19
that you have **s** concerning your 2 Sm 7:25
his house, and do as you have **s**. 2 Sm 7:25
For you, O Lord GOD, have **s**, and with 2 Sm 7:29
said to him, "Thus has Ahithophel **s**; 2 Sm 17:6
The God of Israel has **s**; the Rock of 2 Sm 23:3
that he had **s** concerning the house 1 Kgs 2:27
which you have **s** to your servant 1 Kgs 8:26
"This is the sign that the LORD has **s**: 1 Kgs 13:3
the words that he had **s** to the king. 1 Kgs 13:11
shall eat, for the LORD has **s** it."' 1 Kgs 14:11
all the people answered, "It is well **s**." 1 Kgs 18:24
the LORD has not **s** by me." And he 1 Kgs 22:28
to the word of the LORD that he had **s**. 1 Kgs 22:38
the word of the LORD that Elijah had **s**. 2 Kgs 1:17
you have a word **s** on your behalf to 2 Kgs 4:13
a great word the prophet has **s** to you; 2 Kgs 5:13
as he had **s** by all his servants the 2 Kgs 17:23
that the LORD has **s** concerning him: 2 Kgs 19:21
LORD that you have **s** is good." For he 2 Kgs 20:19
You have also **s** of your servant's 1 Chr 17:17
that you have **s** concerning your 1 Chr 17:23
forever, and do as you have **s**, 1 Chr 17:23
which he had **s** in the name of the 1 Chr 21:19
God, as he has **s** concerning you. 1 Chr 22:11
oil and wine, of which my lord has **s**, 2 Chr 2:15
which you have **s** to your servant 2 Chr 6:17
the LORD has not **s** by me." And he 2 Chr 18:27
singing women have **s** of Josiah in 2 Chr 35:25
of the words that the king had **s** to me. Neh 2:18
me, and I will speak, and after I have **s**, Jb 21:3
"Surely you have **s** in my ears, and I have Jb 33:8
I have **s** once, and I will not answer; Jb 40:5
After the LORD had **s** these words to Job, Jb 42:7
for you have not **s** of me what is right, Jb 42:7
For you have not **s** of me what is right, as Jb 42:8
I have **s** of your faithfulness and your Ps 40:10
God has **s** in his holiness: "With Ps 60:6
Once God has **s**; twice have I heard this: Ps 62:11
Glorious things of you are **s**, O city of Ps 87:3
A word fitly **s** is like apples of gold in a Prv 25:11
for our sister on the day when she is **s** for? Sg 8:8
and give ear, O earth; for the LORD has **s**: Is 1:2
sword; for the mouth of the LORD has **s**." Is 1:20
But now the LORD has **s**, saying, "In three Is 16:14
for the LORD, the God of Israel, has **s**." Is 21:17
on it will be cut off, for the LORD has **s**." Is 22:25
Be ashamed, O Sidon, for the sea has **s**, the Is 23:4
plundered; for the LORD has **s** this word. Is 24:3
from all the earth, for the LORD has **s**. Is 25:8
that the LORD has **s** concerning him: Is 37:22
For he has **s** to me, and he himself has Is 38:15
the LORD that you have **s** is good." For he Is 39:8
together, for the mouth of the LORD has **s**." Is 40:5
I have **s**, and I will bring it to pass; I have Is 46:11
I, even I, have **s** and called him; I have Is 48:15
the beginning I have not **s** in secret, Is 48:16
father, for the mouth of the LORD has **s**." Is 58:14
fingers with iniquity; your lips have **s** lies; Is 59:3
Behold, you have **s**, but you have done all Jer 3:5
the heavens above be dark; for I have **s**; Jer 4:28
They have **s** falsely of the LORD and have Jer 5:12
"Because you have **s** this word, behold, I Jer 5:14
and listened, but they have not **s** rightly; Jer 8:6
To whom has the mouth of the LORD **s**, Jer 9:12
ear; be not proud, for the LORD has **s**. Jer 13:15
that nation, concerning which I have **s**, Jer 18:8
answered?' or 'What has the LORD **s**?' Jer 23:35
you?' or 'What has the LORD **s**?' Jer 23:37
to me, and I have **s** persistently to you, Jer 25:3
for he has **s** to us in the name of the Jer 26:16
the LORD has **s** concerning any nation Jer 27:13
and they have **s** in my name lying Jer 29:23
for he has **s** rebellion against the Jer 29:32
a book all the words that I have **s** to you. Jer 30:2
"Alas, lord!"' For I have **s** the word, Jer 34:5
I have **s** to you persistently, but you Jer 35:14
because I have **s** to them and they have Jer 35:17
words that I have **s** to you against Israel Jer 36:2
words of the LORD that he had **s** to him. Jer 36:4
hear that I have **s** with you and come Jer 38:25
the word that you have **s** to us in the Jer 44:16
shall be destroyed, as the LORD has **s**. Jer 48:8
Who has **s** and it came to pass, unless Lam 3:37
LORD—that I have **s** in my jealousy— Ezk 5:13
rebukes—I am the LORD; I have **s**— Ezk 5:15
upon you. I am the LORD; I have **s**." Ezk 5:17
the LORD,' although I have not **s**?" Ezk 13:7
know that I am the LORD; I have **s**." Ezk 17:21
am the LORD; I have **s**, and I will do it." Ezk 17:24
will satisfy my fury; I the LORD have **s**." Ezk 21:17
remembered, for I the LORD have **s**." Ezk 21:32
you? I the LORD have **s**, and I will do it. Ezk 22:14
Lord GOD,' when the LORD has not **s**. Ezk 22:28
for I have **s**, declares the Lord GOD. Ezk 23:34
I have **s**; it shall come to pass; I will do Ezk 24:14
for the spreading of nets, for I have **s**, Ezk 26:5
LORD; I have **s**, declares the Lord GOD. Ezk 26:14
for I have **s**, declares the Lord GOD." Ezk 28:10
of foreigners; I am the LORD; I have **s**. Ezk 30:12
among them. I am the LORD; I have **s**. Ezk 34:24
Surely I have **s** in my hot jealousy Ezk 36:5
Behold, I have **s** in my jealous wrath, Ezk 36:6
I am the LORD; I have **s**, and I will do it. Ezk 36:36
I have **s**, and I will do it, declares the Ezk 37:14
shall fall in the open field, for I have **s**, Ezk 39:5
GOD. That is the day of which I have **s**. Ezk 39:8
"O King Nebuchadnezzar, to you it is **s**: Dn 4:31
And when he had **s** to me, I fell into a Dn 8:18
And when he had **s** this word to me, Dn 10:11
When he had **s** to me according to Dn 10:15
to a nation far away, for the LORD has **s**." Jl 3:8
word that the LORD has **s** against you, Am 3:1
The Lord GOD has **s**; who can but Am 3:8
for the house of Esau, for the LORD has **s**. Ob 1:18
for the mouth of the LORD of hosts has **s**. Mi 4:4
you say, 'How have we **s** against you?' Mal 3:13
what the Lord had **s** by the prophet: Mt 1:22
what the Lord had **s** by the prophet, Mt 2:15
was fulfilled what was **s** by the prophet Mt 2:17
that what was **s** by the prophets might Mt 2:23
this is he who was **s** of by the prophet Mt 3:3
so that what was **s** by the prophet Isaiah Mt 4:14
to fulfill what was **s** by the prophet Mt 8:17
to fulfill what was **s** by the prophet Mt 12:17
was to fulfill what was **s** by the prophet: Mt 13:35
to fulfill what was **s** by the prophet, Mt 21:4
abomination of desolation **s** of by the Mt 24:15
fulfilled what had been **s** by the prophet Mt 27:9
the Lord Jesus, after he had **s** to them, Mk 16:19
fulfillment of what was **s** to her from the Lk 1:45
And when the voice had **s**, Jesus was Lk 9:36
answered, "Teacher, you have **s** well." Lk 20:39
to believe all that the prophets have **s**! Lk 24:25
Scripture and the word that Jesus had **s**. Jn 2:22
The words that I have **s** to you are spirit Jn 6:63
We know that God has **s** to Moses, but as Jn 9:29
Now Jesus had **s** of his death, but they Jn 11:13
Others said, "An angel has **s** to him." Jn 12:29
so that the word **s** by the prophet Isaiah Jn 12:38
the word that I have **s** will judge him on Jn 12:48
For I have not **s** on my own authority, Jn 12:49
"These things I have **s** to you while I am Jn 14:25
because of the word that I have **s** to you. Jn 15:3
These things I have **s** to you, that my Jn 15:11
If I had not come and **s** to them, they Jn 15:22
When Jesus had **s** these words, he lifted Jn 17:1
When Jesus had **s** these words, he went Jn 18:1
This was to fulfill the word that he had **s**: Jn 18:9
him, "I have **s** openly to the world. Jn 18:20
word that Jesus had **s** to show by what Jn 18:32
And all the prophets who have **s**, from Acts 3:24
they had testified and **s** the word of the Acts 8:25
who is well **s** of by the whole Jewish Acts 10:22
to corruption, he has **s** in this way, Acts 13:34
to contradict what was **s** by Paul, Acts 13:45
that the word of God be **s** first to you. Acts 13:46
And when they had **s** the word in Acts 14:25
He was well **s** of by the brothers at Acts 16:2
of all because of the word he had **s**, Acts 20:38
well **s** of by all the Jews who lived Acts 22:12
here has reported or **s** any evil about Acts 28:21
know that everywhere it is **s** against." Acts 28:22
you regard as good be **s** of as evil. Rom 14:16
We have **s** freely to you, Corinthians; 2 Cor 6:11
alarmed, either by a spirit or a **s** word, 2 Thes 2:2
either by our **s** word or by our letter. 2 Thes 2:15
these last days he has **s** to us by his Son, Heb 1:2
to the things that were to be **s** later, Heb 3:5
For he has somewhere **s** of the seventh Heb 4:4
God would not have **s** of another day Heb 4:8
these things are **s** belonged to another Heb 7:13
that no further messages be **s** to them. Heb 12:19
ungodly sinners have **s** against him." Jude 1:15

SPOKES (2)
their axles, their rims, their **s**, and 1 Kgs 7:33
whole body, their rims, and their **s**, Ezk 10:12

SPOKESMAN (1)
came down with some elders and a **s**, Acts 24:1

SPONGE (3)
one of them at once ran and took a **s**, Mt 27:48
ran and filled a **s** with sour wine, Mk 15:36
so they put a **s** full of the sour wine on a Jn 19:29

SPOT (13)
his body a swelling or an eruption or a **s**, Lv 13:2
But if the **s** is white in the skin of his Lv 13:4
a white swelling or a reddish-white **s**, Lv 13:19
But if the **s** remains in one place and Lv 13:23
the raw flesh of the burn becomes a **s**, Lv 13:24
if the hair in the **s** has turned white and Lv 13:25
no white hair in the **s** and it is no deeper Lv 13:26
But if the **s** remains in one place and Lv 13:28
and for a swelling or an eruption or a **s**, Lv 14:56
eyes, and if any **s** has stuck to my hands, Jb 31:7
without **s** or wrinkle or any such Eph 5:27
that of a lamb without blemish or **s**. 1 Pt 1:19
be found by him without **s** or blemish, 2 Pt 3:14

SPOTS (5)
man or a woman has **s** on the skin of Lv 13:38
spots on the skin of the body, white **s**, Lv 13:38
and if the **s** on the skin of the body are Lv 13:39
of the house with greenish or reddish **s**, Lv 14:37
change his skin or the leopard his **s**? Jer 13:23

SPOTTED (10)
it every speckled and **s** sheep and every Gn 30:32
and the **s** and speckled among the Gn 30:32
is not speckled and **s** among the goats Gn 30:33
the male goats that were striped and **s**, Gn 30:35
female goats that were speckled and **s**, Gn 30:35
brought forth striped, speckled, and **s**. Gn 30:39
If he said, 'The **s** shall be your wages,' Gn 31:8
be your wages,' then all the flock bore **s**; Gn 31:8
the flock were striped, **s**, and mottled. Gn 31:10
the flock are striped, **s**, and mottled, Gn 31:12

SPRANG (7)
Then a wind from the LORD **s** up, and Nm 11:31
And fire **s** up from the rock and Jgs 6:21
much soil, and immediately they **s** up, Mt 13:5
have much soil, and immediately it **s** up, Mk 4:5
his cloak, he **s** up and came to Jesus. Mk 10:50
your feet." And he **s** up and began Acts 14:10
And after one day a south wind **s** up, Acts 28:13

SPREAD (126)
the coastland peoples **s** in their lands, Gn 10:5
from these the nations **s** abroad on the Gn 10:32
and you shall **s** abroad to the west and Gn 28:14
when the famine had **s** over all the Gn 41:56
multiplied and the more they **s** abroad. Ex 1:12
"You shall not **s** a false report. You shall Ex 23:1
The cherubim shall **s** out their wings Ex 25:20
The cherubim **s** out their wings above, Ex 37:9
And he **s** the tent over the tabernacle Ex 40:19
and the disease has not **s** in the skin, Lv 13:5
and the disease has not **s** in the skin, Lv 13:6
and if the eruption has **s** in the skin, Lv 13:8
remains in one place and does not **s**, Lv 13:23
in one place and does not **s** in the skin, Lv 13:28
If the itch has not **s**, and there is in it no Lv 13:32
if the itch has not **s** in the skin and it Lv 13:34
him, and if the itch has **s** in the skin, Lv 13:36
If the disease has **s** in the garment, in Lv 13:51
if the disease has not **s** in the garment, Lv 13:53
changed, though the disease has not **s**, Lv 13:55
If the disease has **s** in the walls of the Lv 14:39
And if the disease has **s** in the house, it Lv 14:44
the disease has not **s** in the house after Lv 14:48
covering of goatskin and **s** on top of that Nm 4:6
the Presence they shall **s** a cloth of blue Nm 4:7
Then they shall **s** over them a cloth of Nm 4:8
golden altar they shall **s** a cloth of blue Nm 4:11
from the altar and **s** a purple cloth over Nm 4:13
and they shall **s** on it a covering of Nm 4:14
And they **s** them out for themselves Nm 11:32
as Nophah; fire **s** as far as Medeba." Nm 21:30
And they shall **s** the cloak before the Dt 22:17
willingly give them." And they **s** a cloak, Jgs 8:25
S your wings over your servant, for you Ru 3:9
against Israel, and when the battle **s**, 1 Sm 4:2
city, a bed was **s** for Saul on the roof, 1 Sm 9:25
they were **s** abroad over all the land, 1 Sm 30:16
Philistines had come and **s** out in the 2 Sm 5:18
up yet again and **s** out in the Valley 2 Sm 5:22
woman took and **s** a covering over 2 Sm 17:19
The battle **s** over the face of all the 2 Sm 18:8
took sackcloth and **s** it for herself 2 Sm 21:10
of the cherubim were **s** out so that a 1 Kgs 6:27
them with gold and **s** gold on the 1 Kgs 6:32
For the cherubim **s** out their wings 1 Kgs 8:7
of Israel and **s** out his hands 1 Kgs 8:22
it in water and **s** it over his face, 2 Kgs 8:15
of the LORD and **s** it before the LORD. 2 Kgs 19:14
the cherubim that **s** their wings and 1 Chr 28:18

The cherubim **s** out their wings over 2 Chr 5:8
of Israel and **s** out his hands. 2 Chr 6:12
and **s** out his hands toward heaven, 2 Chr 6:13
and his fame **s** even to the border of 2 Chr 26:8
And his fame **s** far, for he was 2 Chr 26:15
soon as the command was **s** abroad, 2 Chr 31:5
upon my knees and **s** out my hands to Ezr 9:5
people, "The work is great and widely **s**, Neh 4:19
and his fame **s** throughout all the Est 9:4
the sun, and his shoots **s** over his garden. Jb 8:16
nor will his possessions **s** over the earth; Jb 15:29
my roots **s** out to the waters, with the Jb 29:19
Can you, like him, **s** out the skies, hard Jb 37:18
for joy, and **s** your protection over them, Ps 5:11
name of our God or **s** out our hands to a Ps 44:20
"Can God **s** a table in the wilderness? Ps 78:19
you, O LORD; I **s** out my hands to you. Ps 88:9
He **s** a cloud for a covering, and fire to Ps 105:39
to him who **s** out the earth above the Ps 136:6
for me, and with cords they have **s** a net; Ps 140:5
For in vain is a net **s** in the sight of any Prv 1:17
I have **s** my couch with coverings, Prv 7:16
The lips of the wise **s** knowledge; not so Prv 15:7
When you **s** out your hands, I will hide Is 1:15
its shoots **s** abroad and passed over the Is 16:8
they will languish who **s** nets on the Is 19:8
They prepare the table, they **s** the rugs, Is 21:5
peoples, the veil that is **s** over all nations. Is 25:7
And he will **s** out his hands in the midst Is 25:11
firm in its place or keep the sail **s** out. Is 33:23
of the LORD, and **s** it before the LORD. Is 37:14
who **s** out the earth and what comes from Is 42:5
heavens, who **s** out the earth by myself, Is 44:24
and my right hand **s** out the heavens; Is 48:13
For you will **s** abroad to the right and to Is 54:3
and to **s** sackcloth and ashes under him? Is 58:5
I **s** out my hands all the day to a Is 65:2
And they shall be **s** before the sun and the Jer 8:2
there is no one to **s** my tent again and to Jer 10:20
and he will **s** his royal canopy over Jer 43:10
like an eagle and **s** his wings against Jer 48:40
like an eagle and **s** his wings against Jer 49:22
made it descend; he **s** a net for my feet; Lam 1:13
faces. And their wings were **s** out above. Ezk 1:11
crystal, **s** out above their heads. Ezk 1:22
And he **s** it before me. And it had Ezk 2:10
And I will **s** my net over him, and he Ezk 12:13
and I **s** the corner of my garment over Ezk 16:8
I will **s** my net over him, and he shall Ezk 17:20
on every side; they **s** their net over him; Ezk 19:8
with a table **s** before it on which you Ezk 23:41
who **s** terror in the land of the living. Ezk 32:23
who **s** their terror in the land of the Ezk 32:24
for terror of them was **s** in the land of Ezk 32:25
for they **s** their terror in the land of the Ezk 32:26
For I **s** terror in the land of the living; Ezk 32:32
snare at Mizpah and a net **s** upon Tabor. Hos 5:1
As they go, I will **s** over them my net; I Hos 7:12
his shoots shall **s** out; his beauty shall Hos 14:6
blackness there is **s** upon the mountains Jl 2:2
For I have **s** you abroad as the four Zec 2:6
offspring, and **s** dung on your faces, Mal 2:3
So his fame **s** throughout all Syria, and Mt 4:24
they went away and **s** his fame through Mt 9:31
Most of the crowd **s** their cloaks on the Mt 21:8
from the trees and **s** them on the road. Mt 21:8
this story has been **s** among the Jews to Mt 28:15
once his fame **s** everywhere throughout Mk 1:28
to talk freely about it, and to **s** the news, Mk 1:45
And many **s** their cloaks on the road, Mk 11:8
and others **s** leafy branches that they Mk 11:8
report about him **s** through the whole Lk 7:17
along, they **s** their cloaks on the road. Lk 19:36
So the saying **s** abroad among the Jn 21:23
order that it may **s** no further among Acts 4:17
and so death **s** to all men because all Rom 5:12
and their talk will **s** like gangrene. 2 Tm 2:17

SPREADING (12)
the seventh day. If it is **s** in the skin, Lv 13:27
or in any article made of skin, it is **s**. Lv 13:57
flutters over its young, **s** out its wings, Dt 32:11
I hear the people of the LORD **s** abroad. 1 Sm 2:24
anyone understand the **s** of the clouds, Jb 36:29
man, **s** himself like a green laurel tree. Ps 37:35
and the **s** branches he lops off and clears Is 18:5
it sprouted and became a low **s** vine, Ezk 17:6
midst of the sea a place for the **s** of nets, Ezk 26:5
You shall be a place for the **s** of nets. Ezk 26:14
it will be a place for the **s** of nets. Ezk 47:10
the Lord was **s** throughout the whole Acts 13:49

SPREADS (12)
But if the eruption **s** in the skin, after he Lv 13:7
And if it **s** in the skin, then the priest Lv 13:22
But if the itch **s** in the skin after his Lv 13:35
of the full moon and **s** over it his cloud. Jb 26:9
the hawk soars and **s** his wings toward Jb 39:26
he **s** himself like a threshing sledge on Jb 41:30
A dishonest man **s** strife, and a Prv 16:28
who flatters his neighbor **s** a net for his Prv 29:5
of it as a swimmer **s** his hands out to Is 25:11
and **s** them like a tent to dwell in; Is 40:22
The locust **s** its wings and flies away. Na 3:16
and through us **s** the fragrance of the 2 Cor 2:14

SPRIG (1)
myself will take a **s** from the lofty top Ezk 17:22

SPRING (50)
the LORD God made to **s** up every tree that Gn 2:9
LORD found her by a **s** of water in the Gn 16:7
the wilderness, the **s** on the way to Shur. Gn 16:7
Behold, I am standing by the **s** of water, Gn 24:13
went down to the **s** and filled her jar Gn 24:16
ran out toward the man, to the **s**. Gn 24:29
he was standing by the camels at the **s**. Gn 24:30
"I came today to the **s** and said, 'O LORD, Gn 24:42
behold, I am standing by the **s** of water. Gn 24:43
she went down to the **s** and drew water. Gn 24:45
valley and found there a well of **s** water, Gn 26:19
fruitful bough, a fruitful bough by a **s**; Gn 49:22
a **s** or a cistern holding water shall be Lv 11:36
Israel sang this song: "**S** up, O well! Nm 21:17
of the mountain to the **s** of the waters of Jos 15:9
to the **s** of the waters of Nephtoah. Jos 18:15
early and encamped beside the **s** of Harod. Jgs 7:1
were encamped by the **s** that is in 1 Sm 29:1
In the **s** of the year, the time when 2 Sm 11:1
for in the **s** the king of Syria will 1 Kgs 20:22
In the **s**, Ben-hadad mustered the 1 Kgs 20:26
he went to the **s** of water and threw 2 Kgs 2:21
They stopped every **s** of water and 2 Kgs 3:25
a son about that time the following **s**, 2 Kgs 4:17
invade the land in the **s** of the year. 2 Kgs 13:20
In the **s** of the year, the time when 1 Chr 20:1
In the **s** of the year King 2 Chr 36:10
Gate to the Dragon **S** and to the Dung Neh 2:13
his way, and out of the soil others will **s**. Jb 8:19
opened their mouths as for the **s** rain. Jb 29:23
pool of water, the flint into a **s** of water. Ps 114:8
is like the clouds that bring the **s** rain. Prv 16:15
Like a muddied **s** or a polluted Prv 25:26
locked is my sister, my bride, a **s** locked, Sg 4:12
before they **s** forth I tell you of them." Is 42:9
They shall **s** up among the grass like Is 44:4
and your healing shall **s** up speedily; Is 58:8
like a watered garden, like a **s** of water, Is 58:11
withheld, and the **s** rain has not come; Jer 3:3
season, the autumn rain and the **s** rain, Jer 5:24
a righteous Branch to **s** up for David, Jer 33:15
will cause a horn to **s** up for the house Ezk 29:21
as the **s** rains that water the earth." Hos 6:3
shall dry up; his **s** shall be parched; Hos 13:15
Does a snare **s** up from the ground, when Am 3:5
the LORD in the season of the **s** rain, Zec 10:1
become in him a **s** of water welling up Jn 4:14
our appeal does not **s** from error or 1 Thes 2:3
Does a **s** pour forth from the same Jas 3:11
I will give from the **s** of the water of life Rv 21:6

SPRINGS (38)
who found the hot **s** in the wilderness, Gn 36:24
where there were twelve **s** of water and Ex 15:27
Elim there were twelve **s** of water and Nm 33:9
of brooks of water, of fountains and **s**, Dt 8:7
give me also **s** of water." And he gave Jos 15:19
gave her the upper **s** and the lower Jos 15:19
her the upper springs and the lower **s**. Jos 15:19
give me also **s** of water." And Caleb gave Jgs 1:15
gave her the upper **s** and the lower Jgs 1:15
her the upper springs and the lower **s**. Jgs 1:15
the land to all the **s** of water and to all 1 Kgs 18:5
and stop up all **s** of water and ruin 2 Kgs 3:19
the second year what **s** of the same. 2 Kgs 19:29
the water of the **s** that were outside 2 Chr 32:3
they stopped all the **s** and the brook 2 Chr 32:4
"Have you entered into the **s** of the sea, Jb 38:16
You split open **s** and brooks; you dried Ps 74:15
Valley of Baca they make it a place of **s**; Ps 84:6
Faithfulness **s** up from the ground, and Ps 85:11
dancers alike say, "All my **s** are in you." Ps 87:7
You make **s** gush forth in the valleys; Ps 104:10
a desert, **s** of water into thirsty ground, Ps 107:33
water, a parched land into **s** of water. Ps 107:35
vigilance, for from it flow the **s** of life. Prv 4:23
Should your **s** be scattered abroad, Prv 5:16
there were no **s** abounding with water. Prv 8:24
a pool, and the thirsty ground **s** of water; Is 35:7
and in the second year what **s** from that. Is 37:30
pool of water, and the dry land **s** of water. Is 41:18
now it **s** forth, do you not perceive it? Is 43:19
them, and by **s** of water will guide them. Is 49:10
so judgment **s** up like poisonous weeds Hos 10:4
no "root of bitterness" **s** up and causes Heb 12:15
These are waterless **s** and mists driven 2 Pt 2:17
he will guide them to **s** of living water, Rv 7:17
a third of the rivers and on the **s** of water. Rv 8:10
and earth, the sea and the **s** of water." Rv 14:7
bowl into the rivers and the **s** of water, Rv 16:4

SPRINKLE (19)
oil, and **s** it on Aaron and his garments, Ex 29:21
finger in the blood and **s** part of the blood Lv 4:6
in the blood and **s** it seven times before Lv 4:17
and he shall **s** some of the blood of the sin Lv 5:9
And he shall **s** it seven times on him Lv 14:7
in his left hand and **s** some oil with his Lv 14:16
and shall **s** with his right finger some Lv 14:27
the fresh water and **s** the house seven Lv 14:51
blood of the bull and **s** it with his finger Lv 16:14
mercy seat he shall **s** some of the blood Lv 16:14
And he shall **s** some of the blood on it Lv 16:19
s the water of purification upon them, Nm 8:7
You shall **s** their blood on the altar Nm 18:17
and **s** some of its blood toward the front Nm 19:4
it in the water and **s** it on the tent and Nm 19:18
the clean person shall **s** it on the Nm 19:19
so shall he **s** many nations; kings shall Is 52:15
I will **s** clean water on you, and you Ezk 36:25
and the priests shall **s** salt on them Ezk 43:24

SPRINKLED (9)
And he **s** some of it on the altar seven Lv 8:11
was on the altar and **s** it on Aaron and Lv 8:30
tore their robes and **s** dust on their heads Jb 2:12
gray hairs are **s** upon him, and he Hos 7:9
and **s** both the book itself and all the Heb 9:19
the same way he **s** with the blood both Heb 9:21
with our hearts **s** clean from an evil Heb 10:22
he kept the Passover and **s** the blood, Heb 11:28
and to the **s** blood that speaks a better Heb 12:24

SPRINKLES (1)
The one who **s** the water for impurity Nm 19:21

SPRINKLING (3)
s it over the mercy seat and in front of Lv 16:15
For if the **s** of defiled persons with the Heb 9:13
to Jesus Christ and for **s** with his blood: 1 Pt 1:2

SPROUT (14)
God said, "Let the earth **s** vegetation, Gn 1:11
staff of the man whom I choose shall **s**. Nm 17:5
nothing growing, where no plant can **s**, Dt 29:23
that makes grass to **s** from the earth. 2 Sm 23:4
dust, nor does trouble **s** from the ground, Jb 5:6
tree, if it be cut down, that it will **s** again, Jb 14:7
and to make the ground **s** with grass? Jb 38:27
that though the wicked **s** like grass and Ps 92:7
I will make a horn to **s** for David; Ps 132:17
fruit; let the earth cause them both to **s**; Is 45:8
the earth, making it bring forth and **s**, Is 55:10
garden causes what is sown in it to **s** up, Is 61:11
and praise to **s** up before all Is 61:11
the latter growth was just beginning to **s**, Am 7:1

SPROUTED (5)
And behold, after them **s** seven ears, Gn 41:6
blighted by the east wind, **s** after them, Gn 41:23
house of Levi had **s** and put forth buds Nm 17:8
and it **s** and became a low spreading Ezk 17:6
—wither away on the bed where it **s**?" Ezk 17:10

SPROUTING (1)
so that all its fresh **s** leaves wither? Ezk 17:9

SPROUTS (3)
on it, it is gone, for suddenly it **s** wings, Prv 23:5
For as the earth brings forth its **s**, and as Is 61:11
night and day, and the seed **s** and grows; Mk 4:27

SPRUNG (1)
of the field had yet **s** up—for the LORD Gn 2:5

SPUN (3)
every skillful woman **s** with her hands, Ex 35:25
brought what they had **s** in blue and Ex 35:25
them to use their skill **s** the goats' hair. Ex 35:26

SPURN (6)
if you **s** my statutes, and if your soul Lv 26:15
land of their enemies, I will not **s** them, Lv 26:44
"Will the Lord **s** forever, and never again Ps 77:7
You **s** all who go astray from your Ps 119:118
Do not **s** us, for your name's sake; do Jer 14:21
and revile you and **s** your name as evil, Lk 6:22

SPURNED (7)
because they **s** my rules and their soul Lv 26:43
"The LORD saw it and **s** them, because of Dt 32:19
and **s** the counsel of the Most High. Ps 107:11
fierce indignation has **s** king and priest. Lam 2:6
Israel has **s** the good; the enemy shall Hos 8:3
I have **s** your calf, O Samaria. My anger Hos 8:5

by the one who has **s** the Son of God, Heb 10:29

SPY (15)
"Send men to **s** out the land of Canaan, Nm 13:2
whom Moses sent to **s** out the land. Nm 13:16
Moses sent them to **s** out the land of Nm 13:17
which we have gone to **s** it out, Nm 13:32
which we passed through to **s** it out, Nm 14:7
whom Moses sent to **s** out the land, Nm 14:36
those men who went to **s** out the land, Nm 14:38
And Moses sent to **s** out Jazer, and Nm 21:32
whom Joshua sent to **s** out Jericho. Jos 6:25
"Go up and **s** out the land." And the men Jos 7:2
from Kadesh-barnea to **s** out the land, Jos 14:7
to **s** out the land and to explore it. Jgs 18:2
search the city and to **s** it out and to 2 Sm 10:3
to overthrow and to **s** out the land?" 1 Chr 19:3
who slipped in to **s** out our freedom that Gal 2:4

SPYING (1)
they returned from **s** out the land. Nm 13:25

SQUADS (1)
him over to four **s** of soldiers to guard Acts 12:4

SQUANDERED (1)
and there he **s** his property in reckless Lk 15:13

SQUANDERS (1)
a companion of prostitutes **s** his wealth. Prv 29:3

SQUARE (33)
we will spend the night in the town **s**." Gn 19:2
The altar shall be **s**, and its height shall Ex 27:1
It shall be **s** and doubled, a span its Ex 28:16
It shall be **s**, and two cubits shall be its Ex 30:2
It was **s**, and two cubits was its height. Ex 37:25
It was **s**, and three cubits was its height. Ex 38:1
It was **s**. They made the breastpiece Ex 39:9
the midst of its open **s** and burn the city Dt 13:16
and sat down in the open **s** of the city, Jgs 19:15
the traveler in the open **s** of the city. Jgs 19:17
Only, do not spend the night in the **s**." Jgs 19:20
them from the public **s** of Beth-shan, 2 Sm 21:12
of olivewood, in the form of a **s**, 1 Kgs 6:33
doorways and windows had **s** frames, 1 Kgs 7:5
were carvings, and its panels were **s**, 1 Kgs 7:31
assembled them in the **s** on the east 2 Chr 29:4
together to him in the **s** at the gate of 2 Chr 32:6
sat in the open **s** before the house of Ezr 10:9
one man into the **s** before the Water Neh 8:1
from it facing the **s** before the Water Neh 8:3
and in the **s** at the Water Gate and in Neh 8:16
Water Gate and in the **s** at the Gate of Neh 8:16
to Mordecai in the open **s** of the city in Est 4:6
on the horse through the **s** of the city, Est 6:9
and led him through the **s** of the city, Est 6:11
the city, when I prepared my seat in the **s**, Jb 29:7
made yourself a lofty place in every **s**. Ezk 16:24
making your lofty place in every **s**. Ezk 16:31
long and a hundred cubits broad, a **s**. Ezk 40:47
The altar hearth shall be **s**, twelve Ezk 43:16
The ledge also shall be **s**, fourteen Ezk 43:17
Of this a **s** plot of 500 by 500 cubits Ezk 45:2
shall set apart shall be 25,000 cubits **s**, Ezk 48:20

SQUARED (1)
The doorposts of the nave were **s**, and Ezk 41:21

SQUARES (11)
about the city, in the streets and in the **s**; Sg 3:2
housetops and in the **s** everyone wails and Is 15:3
for truth has stumbled in the public **s**, Is 59:14
Search her **s** to see if you can find a man, Jer 5:1
streets and the young men from the **s**. Jer 9:21
Moab and in the **s** there is nothing but Jer 48:38
her young men shall fall in her **s**, Jer 49:26
her young men shall fall in her **s**, Jer 50:30
it shall be built again with **s** and moat, Dn 9:25
"In all the **s** there shall be wailing, and Am 5:16
streets; they rush to and fro through the **s**; Na 2:4

SQUEEZED (1)
rose early next morning and **s** the fleece, Jgs 6:38

STABBED (1)
wheat, and they **s** him in the stomach. 2 Sm 4:6

STABILITY (3)
and knowledge, its **s** will long continue. Prv 28:2
and he will be the **s** of your times, Is 33:6
of lawless people and lose your own **s**. 2 Pt 3:17

STABLE (1)
continue in the faith, **s** and steadfast, Col 1:23

STACHYS (1)
worker in Christ, and my beloved **S**. Rom 16:9

STACKED (2)
thorns so that the **s** grain or the standing Ex 22:6
set fire to the **s** grain and the standing Jgs 15:5

STACTE (1)
"Take sweet spices, **s**, and onycha, Ex 30:34

STADIA (2)
as high as a horse's bridle, for 1,600 **s**. Rv 14:20
the city with his rod, 12,000 **s**. Rv 21:16

STAFF (73)
for with only my **s** I crossed this Gn 32:10
your cord and your **s** that is in your Gn 38:18
are, the signet and the cord and the **s**." Gn 38:25
nor the ruler's **s** from between his feet, Gn 49:10
is that in your hand?" He said, "A **s**." Ex 4:2
caught it, and it became a **s** in his hand— Ex 4:4
And take in your hand this **s**, with Ex 4:17
And Moses took the **s** of God in his hand. Ex 4:20
'Take your **s** and cast it down before Ex 7:9
cast down his **s** before Pharaoh and Ex 7:10
For each man cast down his **s**, and they Ex 7:12
But Aaron's **s** swallowed up their staffs. Ex 7:12
in your hand the **s** that turned into a Ex 7:15
with the **s** that is in my hand I will strike Ex 7:17
'Take your **s** and stretch out your hand Ex 7:19
he lifted up the **s** and struck the water Ex 7:20
out your hand with your **s** over the rivers, Ex 8:5
'Stretch out your **s** and strike the dust of Ex 8:16
his hand with his **s** and struck the dust Ex 8:17
Moses stretched out his **s** toward heaven, Ex 9:23
Moses stretched out his **s** over the land Ex 10:13
on your feet, and your **s** in your hand. Ex 12:11
Lift up your **s**, and stretch out your Ex 14:16
in your hand the **s** with which you Ex 17:5
of the hill with the **s** of God in my hand." Ex 17:9
again and walks outdoors with his **s**, Ex 21:19
of all that pass under the herdsman's **s**, Lv 27:32
staffs. Write each man's name on his **s**, Nm 17:2
write Aaron's name on the **s** of Levi. Nm 17:3
For there shall be one **s** for the head of Nm 17:3
And the **s** of the man whom I choose Nm 17:5
And the **s** of Aaron was among their Nm 17:6
the **s** of Aaron for the house of Levi had Nm 17:8
they looked, and each man took his **s**. Nm 17:9
"Put back the **s** of Aaron before the Nm 17:10
"Take the **s**, and assemble the Nm 20:8
And Moses took the **s** from before the Nm 20:9
and struck the rock with his **s** twice, Nm 20:11
and he struck the donkey with his **s**. Nm 22:27
those who bear the lieutenant's **s**; Jgs 5:14
out the tip of the **s** that was in his hand Jgs 6:21
out the tip of the **s** that was in his 1 Sm 14:27
with the tip of the **s** that was in my 1 Sm 14:43
Then he took his **s** in his hand and 1 Sm 17:40
to him with a **s** and snatched the 2 Sm 23:21
garment and take my **s** in your hand 2 Kgs 4:29
And lay my **s** on the face of the 2 Kgs 4:29
on ahead and laid the **s** on the face of 2 Kgs 4:31
in Egypt, that broken reed of a **s**, 2 Kgs 18:21
to him with a **s** and snatched the 1 Chr 11:23
given orders to all the **s** of his palace to do Est 1:8
your rod and your **s**, they comfort me. Ps 23:4
of his burden, and the **s** for his shoulder, Is 9:4
my anger; the **s** in their hands is my fury! Is 10:5
or as if a **s** should lift him who is not Is 10:15
rod and lift up their **s** against you as the Is 10:24
And his **s** will be over the sea, and he Is 10:26
The LORD has broken the **s** of the wicked, Is 14:5
stroke of the appointed **s** that the LORD Is 30:32
trusting in Egypt, that broken reed of a **s**, Is 36:6
scepter is broken, the glorious **s**.' Jer 48:17
you have been a **s** of reed to the Ezk 29:6
and their walking **s** gives them oracles. Hos 4:12
Shepherd your people with your **s**, the Mi 7:14
each with **s** in hand because of great age. Zec 8:4
And I took my **s** Favor, and I broke it, Zec 11:10
Then I broke my second **s** Union, Zec 11:14
nor two tunics nor sandals nor a **s**, Mt 10:10
for their journey except a **s**—no bread, Mk 6:8
"Take nothing for your journey, no **s**, Lk 9:3
the manna, and Aaron's **s** that budded, Heb 9:4
in worship over the head of his **s**. Heb 11:21
I was given a measuring rod like a **s**, Rv 11:1

STAFFS (10)
But Aaron's staff swallowed up their **s**. Ex 7:12
people of Israel, and get from them **s**, Nm 17:2
to their fathers' houses, twelve **s**. Nm 17:2
And all their chiefs gave him **s**, one for Nm 17:6
to their fathers' houses, twelve **s**. Nm 17:6
the staff of Aaron was among their **s**. Nm 17:6
Moses deposited the **s** before the LORD Nm 17:7
brought out all the **s** from before the Nm 17:9
and with their **s**." And from the Nm 21:18
And I took two **s**, one I named Favor, Zec 11:7

STAG (4)
to the slaughter, or as a **s** is caught fast Prv 7:22
My beloved is like a gazelle or a young **s**. Sg 2:9
gazelle or a young **s** on cleft mountains. Sg 2:17
gazelle or a young **s** on the mountains of Sg 8:14

STAGE (2)
down their starting places, **s** by stage, Nm 33:2
down their starting places, stage by **s**, Nm 33:2

STAGES (4)
on from the wilderness of Sin by **s**, Ex 17:1
Israel set out by **s** from the wilderness Nm 10:12
These are the **s** of the people of Israel, Nm 33:1
and these are their **s** according to their Nm 33:2

STAGGER (9)
and he makes them **s** like a drunken Jb 12:25
given us wine to drink that made us **s**. Ps 60:3
of her tribes have made Egypt **s**. Is 19:13
they will make Egypt **s** in all its deeds, Is 19:14
reel with wine and **s** with strong drink; Is 28:7
by wine, they **s** with strong drink, Is 28:7
with wine; **s**, but not with strong drink! Is 29:9
They shall drink and **s** and be crazed Jer 25:16
mill, and boys **s** under loads of wood. Lam 5:13

STAGGERED (1)
they reeled and **s** like drunken men Ps 107:27

STAGGERING (3)
drunk to the dregs the bowl, the cup of **s**. Is 51:17
have taken from your hand the cup of **s**; Is 51:22
Jerusalem a cup of **s** to all the Zec 12:2

STAGGERS (3)
deeds, as a drunken man **s** in his vomit. Is 19:14
My heart **s**; horror has appalled me; the Is 21:4
The earth **s** like a drunken man; it Is 24:20

STAIN (1)
soap, the **s** of your guilt is still before me, Jer 2:22

STAINED (2)
on my garments, and **s** all my apparel. Is 63:3
hating even the garment **s** by the flesh. Jude 1:23

STAINING (1)
among our members, **s** the whole body, Jas 3:6

STAIRS (4)
one went up by **s** to the middle story, 1 Kgs 6:8
as far as the **s** that go down from the Neh 3:15
On the **s** of the Levites stood Jeshua, Neh 9:4
before them by the **s** of the city of Neh 12:37

STAIRWAY (3)
on its jambs, and its **s** had eight steps. Ezk 40:31
on either side, and its **s** had eight steps. Ezk 40:34
on either side, and its **s** had eight steps. Ezk 40:37

STAKE (1)
done. Turn now; my vindication is at **s**. Jb 6:29

STAKES (2)
tent, whose **s** will never be plucked up, Is 33:20
your cords and strengthen your **s**. Is 54:2

STALK (2)
plump and good, were growing on one **s**. Gn 41:5
my dream seven ears growing on one **s**, Gn 41:22

STALKS (2)
and hid them with the **s** of flax that she Jos 2:6
nor the pestilence that **s** in darkness, nor Ps 91:6

STALL (2)
flock and calves from the midst of the **s**, Am 6:4
go out leaping like calves from the **s**. Mal 4:2

STALLIONS (4)
They were well-fed, lusty **s**, each neighing Jer 5:8
the neighing of their **s** the whole land Jer 8:16
of the stamping of the hoofs of his **s**, Jer 47:3
a heifer in the pasture, and neigh like **s**, Jer 50:11

STALLS (4)
also had 40,000 **s** of horses for 1 Kgs 4:26
Solomon had 4,000 **s** for horses and 2 Chr 9:25
and **s** for all kinds of cattle, and 2 Chr 32:28
the fold and there be no herd in the **s**, Hab 3:17

STAMMERERS (1)
the tongue of the **s** will hasten to speak Is 32:4

STAMMERING (1)
s in a tongue that you cannot understand. Is 33:19

STAMP (1)
"Clap your hands and **s** your foot and Ezk 6:11

STAMPED (4)
crushed them and **s** them down like 2 Sm 22:43
clapped your hands and **s** your feet and Ezk 25:6
broke in pieces and **s** what was left with Dn 7:7
broke in pieces and **s** what was left with Dn 7:19

STAMPING (1)
At the noise of the **s** of the hoofs of his Jer 47:3

STAND (276)
But they said, "**S** back!" And they said, Gn 19:9

of the LORD. Why do you **s** outside? Gn 24:31
S on the bank of the Nile to meet him, Ex 7:15
and also the ground on which they **s**. Ex 8:21
magicians could not **s** before Moses Ex 9:11
said to the people, "Fear not, **s** firm, Ex 14:13
I will **s** before you there on the rock at Ex 17:6
Tomorrow I will **s** on the top of the hill Ex 17:9
and all the people **s** around you from Ex 18:14
and they took their **s** at the foot of the Ex 19:17
a basin of bronze, with its **s** of bronze, Ex 30:18
all its utensils and the basin and its **s**. Ex 30:28
all its utensils, and the basin and its **s**, Ex 31:9
up, and each would **s** at his tent door, Ex 33:8
would descend and **s** at the entrance Ex 33:9
by me where you shall **s** on the rock, Ex 33:21
and all its utensils, the basin and its **s**; Ex 35:16
the basin of bronze and its **s** of bronze, Ex 38:8
and all its utensils; the basin and its **s**; Ex 39:39
shall also anoint the basin and its **s**, Ex 40:11
all its utensils and the basin and its **s**, Lv 8:11
and you shall not **s** up against the life Lv 19:16
"You shall **s** up before the gray head Lv 19:32
have no power to **s** before your enemies. Lv 26:37
he shall be made to **s** before the priest, Lv 27:8
then he shall **s** the animal before the Lv 27:11
bad; as the priest values it, so it shall **s**. Lv 27:14
year of jubilee, the valuation shall **s**, Lv 27:17
let them take their **s** there with you. Nm 11:16
LORD and to **s** before the congregation Nm 16:9
of the LORD took his **s** in the way as his Nm 22:22
to Balak, "**S** beside your burnt offering, Nm 23:3
"**S** here beside your burnt offering, Nm 23:15
Make him **s** before Eleazar the priest Nm 27:19
And he shall **s** before Eleazar the Nm 27:21
and made him **s** before Eleazar the Nm 27:22
to her, then all her vows shall **s**, Nm 30:4
which she has bound herself shall **s**. Nm 30:4
which she has bound herself shall **s**. Nm 30:5
that he hears, then her vows shall **s**, Nm 30:7
which she has bound herself shall **s**. Nm 30:7
has bound herself, shall **s** against her.) Nm 30:9
oppose her, then all her vows shall **s**, Nm 30:11
by which she bound herself shall **s**. Nm 30:11
her pledge of herself shall not **s**. Nm 30:12
everything that can **s** the fire, you Nm 31:23
And whatever cannot **s** the fire, you Nm 31:23
But you, **s** here by me, and I will tell you Dt 5:31
shall be able to **s** against you until you Dt 7:24
said, 'Who can **s** before the sons of Anak?' Dt 9:2
of the LORD to **s** before the LORD to Dt 10:8
No one shall be able to **s** against you. Dt 11:25
of all your tribes to **s** and minister in the Dt 18:5
his fellow Levites who **s** to minister there Dt 18:7
You shall **s** outside, and the man to Dt 24:11
these shall **s** on Mount Gerizim to bless Dt 27:12
And these shall **s** on Mount Ebal for the Dt 27:13
man shall be able to **s** before you all the Jos 1:5
Jordan, you shall **s** still in the Jordan.'" Jos 3:8
down from above shall **s** in one heap." Jos 3:13
of Israel cannot **s** before their enemies. Jos 7:12
You cannot **s** before your enemies until Jos 7:13
Not a man of them shall **s** before you." Jos 10:8
sight of Israel, "Sun, **s** still at Gibeon, Jos 10:12
these cities and shall **s** at the entrance of Jos 20:4
has been able to **s** before you to this Jos 23:9
said to her, "**S** at the opening of the tent, Jgs 4:20
They made him **s** between the pillars. Jgs 16:25
"Who is able to **s** before the LORD, 1 Sm 6:20
Now therefore **s** still that I may plead 1 Sm 12:7
Now therefore **s** still and see this 1 Sm 12:16
you,' then we will **s** still in our place, 1 Sm 14:9
came forward and took his **s**, 1 Sm 17:16
I will go out and **s** beside my father in 1 Sm 19:3
And he said to me '**S** beside me and kill 2 Sm 1:9
group and took their **s** on the top of 2 Sm 2:25
to rise early and **s** beside the way of 2 Sm 15:2
"Turn aside and **s** here." So he 2 Sm 18:30
young men took his **s** by Amasa and 2 Sm 20:11
For does not my house **s** so with God? 2 Sm 23:5
But he took his **s** in the midst of the 2 Sm 23:12
Each **s** was four cubits long, four 1 Kgs 7:27
each **s** had four bronze wheels and 1 Kgs 7:30
supports at the four corners of each **s**. 1 Kgs 7:34
on the top of the **s** there was a round 1 Kgs 7:35
on the top of the **s** its stays and its 1 Kgs 7:35
priests could not **s** to minister 1 Kgs 8:11
who continually **s** before you and 1 Kgs 10:8
God of Israel lives, before whom I **s**, 1 Kgs 17:1
LORD of hosts lives, before whom I **s**, 1 Kgs 18:15
"Go out and **s** on the mount before 1 Kgs 19:11
LORD of hosts lives, before whom I **s**, 2 Kgs 3:14
out to me and **s** and call upon the 2 Kgs 5:11
"As the LORD lives, before whom I **s**, 2 Kgs 5:16
the two kings could not **s** before him. 2 Kgs 10:4
before him. How then can we **s**?" 2 Kgs 10:4

But he took his **s** in the midst of the 1 Chr 11:14
And they were to **s** every morning, 1 Chr 23:30
priests could not **s** to minister 2 Chr 5:14
who continually **s** before you and 2 Chr 9:7
we will **s** before this house and before 2 Chr 20:9
S firm, hold your position, and see 2 Chr 20:17
has chosen you to **s** in his presence, 2 Chr 29:11
Jerusalem and in Benjamin **s** to it. 2 Chr 34:32
And **s** in the Holy Place according to 2 Chr 35:5
for none can **s** before you because of Ezr 9:15
of heavy rain; we cannot **s** in the open. Ezr 10:13
Let our officials **s** for the whole Ezr 10:14
"**S** up and bless the LORD your God from Neh 9:5
to see whether Mordecai's words would **s**, Est 3:4
And no one could **s** against them, for the Est 9:2
leans against his house, but it does not **s**; Jb 8:15
and at the last he will **s** upon the earth. Jb 19:25
for help and you do not answer me; I **s**, Jb 30:20
I **s** up in the assembly and cry for help. Jb 30:28
they do not speak, because they **s** there, Jb 32:16
words in order before me; take your **s**. Jb 33:5
and its features **s** out like a garment. Jb 38:14
he cannot **s** still at the sound of the Jb 39:24
and tread down the wicked where they **s**. Jb 40:12
Who then is he who can **s** before me? Jb 41:10
the wicked will not **s** in the judgment, Ps 1:5
The boastful shall not **s** before your eyes; Ps 5:5
Why, O LORD, do you **s** afar off? Why do Ps 10:1
and fall, but we rise and **s** upright. Ps 20:8
Jacob, glorify him, and **s** in awe of him, Ps 22:23
LORD? And who shall **s** in his holy place? Ps 24:3
LORD, you made my mountain **s** strong; Ps 30:7
inhabitants of the world **s** in awe of him! Ps 33:8
friends and companions **s** aloof from Ps 38:11
my plague, and my nearest kin **s** far off. Ps 38:11
Who can **s** before you when once your Ps 76:7
it, and made the waters **s** like a heap. Ps 78:13
and my covenant will **s** firm for him. Ps 89:28
and you have not made him **s** in battle. Ps 89:43
him; let an accuser **s** at his right hand. Ps 109:6
By your appointment they **s** this day, Ps 119:91
mark iniquities, O Lord, who could **s**? Ps 130:3
who **s** by night in the house of the LORD! Ps 134:1
who **s** in the house of the LORD, in the Ps 135:2
crumbs; who can **s** before his cold? Ps 147:17
the way, at the crossroads she takes her **s**; Prv 8:2
but the house of the righteous will **s**. Prv 12:7
it is the purpose of the LORD that will **s**. Prv 19:21
in his work? He will **s** before kings; Prv 22:29
he will not **s** before obscure men. Prv 22:29
the king's presence or **s** in the place of Prv 25:6
but who can **s** before jealousy? Prv 27:4
youth who was to **s** in the king's place. Eccl 4:15
Do not take your **s** in an evil cause, Eccl 8:3
"'It shall not **s**, and it shall not come to Is 7:7
speak a word, but it will not **s**, for God is Is 8:10
who shall **s** as a signal for the peoples— Is 11:10
it be, and as I have purposed, so shall it **s**, Is 14:24
"Upon a watchtower I **s**, O Lord, Is 21:8
the horsemen took their **s** at the gates. Is 22:7
your agreement with Sheol will not **s**; Is 28:18
One of Jacob and will **s** in awe of the God Is 29:23
but the word of our God will **s** forever. Is 40:8
Let them all assemble, let them **s** forth. Is 44:11
"Remember this and **s** firm, recall it to Is 46:8
not yet done, saying, 'My counsel shall **s**, Is 46:10
S fast in your enchantments and your Is 47:12
let them **s** forth and save you, those who Is 47:13
I call to them, they **s** forth together. Is 48:13
contend with me? Let us **s** up together. Is 50:8
Wake yourself, wake yourself, **s** up, O Is 51:17
Strangers shall **s** and tend your flocks; Is 61:5
"**S** by the roads, and look, and ask for the Jer 6:16
"**S** in the gate of the LORD'S house, and Jer 7:2
and then come and **s** before me in this Jer 7:10
The wild donkeys **s** on the bare heights; Jer 14:6
restore you, and you shall **s** before me. Jer 15:19
"Go and **s** in the People's Gate, by Jer 17:19
S in the court of the LORD'S house, and Jer 26:2
and the palace shall **s** where it used to Jer 30:18
shall never lack a man to **s** before me." Jer 35:19
to live, shall know whose word will **s**, Jer 44:28
my words will surely **s** against you for Jer 44:29
Say, '**S** ready and be prepared, for the Jer 46:14
They do not **s** because the LORD thrust Jer 46:15
they did not **s**, for the day of their Jer 46:21
S by the way and watch, O inhabitant Jer 48:19
me? What shepherd can **s** before me? Jer 49:19
me? What shepherd can **s** before me? Jer 50:44
bow, and let him not **s** up in his armor. Jer 51:3
the LORD'S purposes against Babylon **s**, Jer 51:29
from the sword, go, do not **s** still! Jer 51:50
said to me, "Son of man, **s** on your feet, Ezk 2:1
that it might **s** in battle in the day of the Ezk 13:5
and keep his covenant that it might **s**. Ezk 17:14

up the wall and **s** in the breach before Ezk 22:30
all the pilots of the sea **s** on the land Ezk 27:29
and they shall **s** before the people, Ezk 44:11
And they shall **s** before me to offer me Ezk 44:15
and shall take his **s** by the post of the Ezk 46:2
Fishermen will **s** beside the sea. From Ezk 47:10
and competent to **s** in the king's palace, Dn 1:4
of that time they were to **s** before the king. Dn 1:5
them to an end, and it shall **s** forever, Dn 2:44
the ground and made to **s** on two feet like Dn 7:4
No beast could **s** before him, and there Dn 8:4
the ram had no power to **s** before him, Dn 8:7
But he touched me and made me **s** up. Dn 8:18
that I speak to you, and **s** upright, Dn 10:11
And the forces of the south shall not **s**, Dn 11:15
for there shall be no strength to **s**. Dn 11:15
he wills, and none shall **s** before him. Dn 11:16
And he shall **s** in the glorious land, Dn 11:16
but it shall not **s** or be to his Dn 11:17
and mighty army, but he shall not **s**, Dn 11:25
know their God shall **s** firm and take Dn 11:32
shall rest and shall **s** in your allotted Dn 12:13
he who handles the bow shall not **s**, Am 2:15
GOD, please forgive! How can Jacob **s**? Am 7:2
GOD, please cease! How can Jacob **s**? Am 7:5
Do not **s** at the crossroads to cut off his Ob 1:14
And he shall **s** and shepherd his flock in Mi 5:4
Who can **s** before his indignation? Who Na 1:6
I will take my **s** at my watchpost and Hab 2:1
two anointed ones who **s** by the Lord of Zec 4:14
that day his feet shall **s** on the Mount of Zec 14:4
you, that my covenant with Levi may **s**, Mal 2:4
and who can **s** when he appears? Mal 3:2
and put it under a basket, but on a **s**, Mt 5:15
For they love to **s** and pray in the Mt 6:5
or house divided against itself will **s**. Mt 12:25
himself. How then will his kingdom **s**? Mt 12:26
them, 'Why do you **s** here idle all day?' Mt 20:6
against itself, that kingdom cannot **s**. Mk 3:24
itself, that house will not be able to **s**. Mk 3:25
himself and is divided, he cannot **s**, Mk 3:26
a basket, or under a bed, and not on a **s**? Mk 4:21
And whenever you **s** praying, forgive, Mk 11:25
and you will **s** before governors and Mk 13:9
"Come and **s** here." And he rose and stood Lk 6:8
or puts it under a bed, but puts it on a **s**, Lk 8:16
himself, how will his kingdom **s**? Lk 11:18
a cellar or under a basket, but on a **s**, Lk 11:33
and you begin to **s** outside and to Lk 13:25
place, and to **s** before the Son of Man." Lk 21:36
why do you **s** looking into heaven? Acts 1:11
"Go and **s** in the temple and speak to Acts 5:20
But Peter lifted him up, saying, "**S** up; Acts 10:26
had seen the angel **s** in his house and Acts 11:13
was I that I could **s** in God's way?" Acts 11:17
"**S** upright on your feet." And he Acts 14:10
And now I **s** here on trial because of Acts 26:6
But rise and **s** upon your feet, for I Acts 26:16
and so I **s** here testifying both to Acts 26:22
Paul; you must **s** before Caesar. Acts 27:24
by faith into this grace in which we **s**, Rom 5:2
but you **s** fast through faith. Rom 11:20
do not become proud, but **s** in awe. Rom 11:20
for the Lord is able to make him **s**. Rom 14:4
For we will all **s** before the judgment Rom 14:10
which you received, in which you **s**, 1 Cor 15:1
Be watchful, **s** firm in the faith, act 1 Cor 16:13
your joy, for you **s** firm in your faith. 2 Cor 1:24
s firm therefore, and do not submit Gal 5:1
may be able to **s** against the schemes of Eph 6:11
evil day, and having done all, to **s** firm. Eph 6:13
S therefore, having fastened on the belt Eph 6:14
joy and crown, **s** firm thus in the Lord, Phil 4:1
that you may **s** mature and fully Col 4:12
s firm and hold to the traditions that 2 Thes 2:15
of all, so that the rest may **s** in fear. 1 Tm 5:20
first defense no one came to **s** by me, 2 Tm 4:16
to the poor man, "You **s** over there," or, Jas 2:3
is the true grace of God. **S** firm in it. 1 Pt 5:12
Behold, I **s** at the door and knock. If Rv 3:20
their wrath has come, and who can **s**?" Rv 6:17
I saw the seven angels who **s** before God, Rv 8:2
two lampstands that **s** before the Lord Rv 11:4
They will **s** far off, in fear of her Rv 18:10
gained wealth from her, will **s** far off, Rv 18:15

STANDARD (22)

own camp and each man by his own **s**. Nm 1:52
of Israel shall camp each by his own **s**, Nm 2:2
sunrise shall be of the **s** of the camp of Nm 2:3
south side shall be the **s** of the camp of Nm 2:10
set out, each in position, **s** by standard. Nm 2:17
set out, each in position, standard by **s**. Nm 2:17
west side shall be the **s** of the camp of Nm 2:18
north side shall be the **s** of the camp of Nm 2:25
They shall set out last, **s** by standard." Nm 2:31

They shall set out last, standard by **s**." Nm 2:31
The **s** of the camp of the people of Nm 10:14
And the **s** of the camp of Reuben set Nm 10:18
And the **s** of the camp of the people of Nm 10:22
Then the **s** of the camp of the people of Nm 10:25
the length, in cubits of the old **s**, was 2 Chr 3:3
his officers desert the **s** in panic," declares Is 31:9
Raise a **s** toward Zion, flee for safety, stay Jer 4:6
long must I see the **s** and hear the sound Jer 4:21
"Set up a **s** against the walls of Babylon; Jer 51:12
"Set up a **s** on the earth; blow the Jer 51:27
the homer shall be the **s** measure. Ezk 45:11
the heart to the **s** of teaching to which Rom 6:17

STANDARDS (2)
Moses, so they camped by their **s**, Nm 2:34
you were wise according to worldly **s**, 1 Cor 1:26

STANDING (131)
three men were **s** in front of him. Gn 18:2
Behold, I am **s** by the spring of water, Gn 24:13
he was **s** by the camels at the spring. Gn 24:30
behold, I am **s** by the spring of water. Gn 24:43
dreamed that he was **s** by the Nile, Gn 41:1
in my dream I was **s** on the banks of Gn 41:17
place on which you are **s** is holy ground." Ex 3:5
stacked grain or the **s** grain or the field Ex 22:6
the pillar of cloud **s** at the entrance of Ex 33:10
saw the angel of the LORD **s** in the road, Nm 22:23
saw the angel of the LORD **s** in the way, Nm 22:31
of Moab were **s** beside his burnt Nm 23:6
he was **s** beside his burnt offering, Nm 23:17
time the sickle is first put to the **s** grain. Dt 16:9
If you go into your neighbor's **s** grain, Dt 23:25
put a sickle to your neighbor's **s** grain. Dt 23:25
"You are **s** today all of you before the Dt 29:10
but with whoever is **s** here with us Dt 29:15
a man was **s** before him with his drawn Jos 5:13
place where you are **s** is holy." And Jos 5:15
foxes go into the **s** grain of the Jgs 15:5
fire to the stacked grain and the **s** grain, Jgs 15:5
the woman who was **s** here in your 1 Sm 1:26
and Samuel **s** as head over them, 1 Sm 19:20
and all his servants were **s** about him. 1 Sm 22:6
his servants who were **s** by tore their 2 Sm 13:31
and two lions **s** beside the armrests, 1 Kgs 10:19
Jeroboam was **s** by the altar to make 1 Kgs 13:1
the road and the lion **s** by the body. 1 Kgs 13:25
and the lion **s** beside the body. 1 Kgs 13:28
the host of heaven **s** beside him on 1 Kgs 22:19
as they both were **s** by the Jordan. 2 Kgs 2:7
the watchman was **s** on the tower 2 Kgs 9:17
there was the king **s** by the pillar, 2 Kgs 11:14
of the LORD was **s** by the threshing 1 Chr 21:15
of the LORD **s** between earth and 1 Chr 21:16
rests and two lions **s** beside the arm 2 Chr 9:18
the host of heaven **s** on his right 2 Chr 18:18
there was the king **s** by his pillar at 2 Chr 23:13
And while they are still **s** guard, let them Neh 7:3
Akkub were gatekeepers **s** guard at Neh 12:25
the king saw Queen Esther **s** in the court, Est 5:2
there, **s** in the court." And the king said, Est 6:5
saved the king, is **s** at Haman's house, Est 7:9
Our feet have been **s** within your gates, Ps 122:2
when the reaper gathers **s** grain and his Is 17:5
Asherim or incense altars will remain **s**. Is 27:9
all the people who were **s** in the house of Jer 28:5
the son of Shaphan **s** among them. Ezk 8:11
Now the cherubim were **s** on the south Ezk 10:3
his hand. And he was **s** in the gateway. Ezk 40:3
While the man was **s** beside me, I heard Ezk 43:6
behold, a ram **s** on the bank of the canal. Dn 8:3
which I had seen **s** on the bank of the Dn 8:6
as I was **s** on the bank of the great river Dn 10:4
The **s** grain has no heads; it shall yield Hos 8:7
the Lord was **s** beside a wall built with a Am 7:7
I saw the LORD **s** beside the altar, and he Am 9:1
shall take away from you its **s** place. Mi 1:11
He was **s** among the myrtle trees in the Zec 1:8
the man who was **s** among the myrtle Zec 1:10
the LORD who was **s** among the myrtle Zec 1:11
Joshua the high priest **s** before the angel Zec 3:1
and Satan **s** at his right hand to accuse Zec 3:1
Now Joshua was **s** before the angel, Zec 3:3
said to those who were **s** before him, Zec 3:4
And the angel of the LORD was **s** by. Zec 3:5
of access among those who are **s** here. Zec 3:7
rot while they are still **s** on their feet, Zec 14:12
there are some **s** here who will not taste Mt 16:28
hour he saw others **s** idle in the Mt 20:3
hour he went out and found others **s**. Mt 20:6
s in the holy place (let the reader Mt 24:15
and **s** outside they sent to him and Mk 3:31
there are some **s** here who will not taste Mk 9:1
And some of those **s** there said to them, Mk 11:5
abomination of desolation **s** where it Mk 13:14
an angel of the Lord **s** on the right side of Lk 1:11
God, he was **s** by the lake of Gennesaret, Lk 5:1
and **s** behind him at his feet, weeping, Lk 7:38
mother and your brothers are **s** outside, Lk 8:20
there are some **s** here who will not taste Lk 9:27
The Pharisee, **s** by himself, prayed Lk 18:11
But the tax collector, **s** far off, would Lk 18:13
next day again John was **s** with two of his Jn 1:35
left alone with the woman **s** before him. Jn 8:9
this on account of the people **s** around, Jn 11:42
who betrayed him, was **s** with them. Jn 18:5
and they were **s** and warming Jn 18:18
was with them, **s** and warming himself. Jn 18:18
one of the officers **s** by struck Jesus with Jn 18:22
Simon Peter was **s** and warming Jn 18:25
but **s** by the cross of Jesus were his Jn 19:25
the disciple whom he loved **s** nearby, Jn 19:26
this, she turned around and saw Jesus **s**, Jn 20:14
But Peter, **s** with the eleven, lifted up Acts 2:14
—by him this man is **s** before you well. Acts 4:10
man who was healed **s** beside them, Acts 4:14
locked and the guards **s** at the doors, Acts 5:23
put in prison are **s** in the temple and Acts 5:25
place where you are **s** is holy ground. Acts 7:33
and Jesus **s** at the right hand of God. Acts 7:55
and the Son of Man **s** at the right hand Acts 7:56
reported that Peter was **s** at the gate. Acts 12:14
women of high **s** and the leading Acts 13:50
a man of Macedonia was **s** there, Acts 16:9
Greek women of high **s** as well as Acts 17:12
Paul, **s** in the midst of the Areopagus, Acts 17:22
him permission, Paul, **s** on the steps, Acts 21:40
came to me, and **s** by me said to me, Acts 22:13
I myself was **s** by and approving and Acts 22:20
said to the centurion who was **s** by, Acts 22:25
that I cried out while **s** among them: Acts 24:21
said, "I am **s** before Caesar's tribunal, Acts 25:10
those who have no **s** in the church? 1 Cor 6:4
of you that you are **s** firm in one spirit, Phil 1:27
we live, if you are **s** fast in the Lord. 1 Thes 3:8
gain a good **s** for themselves and 1 Tm 3:13
as long as the first section is still **s** Heb 9:8
judged; behold, the Judge is **s** at the door. Jas 5:9
a faith of equal **s** with ours by the 2 Pt 1:1
and behold, a door **s** open in heaven! Rv 4:1
and among the elders I saw a Lamb **s**, Rv 5:6
this I saw four angels **s** at the four corners Rv 7:1
s before the throne and before the Lamb, Rv 7:9
all the angels were **s** around the throne Rv 7:11
the angel whom I saw **s** on the sea and Rv 10:5
of the angel who is **s** on the sea and on Rv 10:8
s beside the sea of glass with harps of Rv 15:2
Then I saw an angel **s** in the sun, and Rv 19:17
great and small, **s** before the throne, Rv 20:12

STANDS (53)
the land of Egypt, and it **s** to this day, Gn 47:26
and your cloud **s** over them and you Nm 14:14
die until he **s** before the congregation Nm 35:12
Joshua the son of Nun, who **s** before you, Dt 1:38
the priest who **s** to minister there Dt 17:12
heap of stones, which **s** there to this day. Jos 8:29
land where the LORD'S tabernacle **s**, Jos 22:19
our God that **s** before his tabernacle!" Jos 22:29
To this day it still **s** at Ophrah, which Jgs 6:24
He also made the ten **s** of bronze. 1 Kgs 7:27
This was the construction of the **s**: 1 Kgs 7:28
wheels were of one piece with the **s**, 1 Kgs 7:32
supports were of one piece with the **s**. 1 Kgs 7:34
After this manner he made the ten **s**. 1 Kgs 7:37
there was a basin for each of the ten **s**. 1 Kgs 7:38
And he set the **s**, five on the south side 1 Kgs 7:39
the ten **s**, and the ten basins on the 1 Kgs 7:43
stands, and the ten basins on the **s**, 1 Kgs 7:43
the frames of the **s** and removed the 2 Kgs 16:17
and the **s** and the bronze sea that 2 Kgs 25:13
and the **s** that Solomon had made 2 Kgs 25:16
He made the **s** also, and the basins on 2 Chr 4:14
stands also, and the basins on the **s**, 2 Chr 4:14
of the wicked, nor **s** in the way of sinners, Ps 1:1
My foot **s** on level ground; in the great Ps 26:12
The counsel of the LORD **s** forever, the Ps 33:11
Surely all mankind **s** as a mere breath! Ps 39:5
at your right hand **s** the queen in gold of Ps 45:9
On the holy mount **s** the city he founded; Ps 87:1
Who **s** up for me against evildoers? Ps 94:16
For he **s** at the right hand of the needy, Ps 109:31
established the earth, and it **s** fast. Ps 119:90
but my heart **s** in awe of your words. Ps 119:161
Behold, there he **s** behind our wall, gazing Sg 2:9
his place to contend; he **s** to judge peoples. Is 3:13
noble things, and on noble things he **s**. Is 32:8
it, they set it in its place, and it **s** there; Is 46:7
back, and righteousness **s** afar off; Is 59:14
concerning the pillars, the sea, the **s**, Jer 27:19
and the **s** and the bronze sea that were Jer 52:17
bulls that were under the sea, and the **s**, Jer 52:20
the king of Babylon **s** at the parting of Ezk 21:21
answered and said, "The thing **s** fast, Dn 6:12
against the man who **s** next to me," Zec 13:7
Gabriel, who **s** in the presence of God, Lk 1:19
but among you **s** one you do not know, Jn 1:26
of the bridegroom, who **s** and hears him, Jn 3:29
his own master that he **s** or falls. Rom 14:4
who thinks that he **s** take heed lest 1 Cor 10:12
But God's firm foundation **s**, bearing 2 Tm 2:19
the promise of entering his rest still **s**, Heb 4:1
And every priest **s** daily at his service, Heb 10:11
For it **s** in Scripture: "Behold, I am 1 Pt 2:6

STANK (3)
the fish in the Nile died, and the Nile **s**, Ex 7:21
them together in heaps, and the land **s**. Ex 8:14
the morning, and it bred worms and **s**. Ex 16:20

STAR (15)
a **s** shall come out of Jacob, and a Nm 24:17
you are fallen from heaven, O Day **S**, Is 14:12
For we saw his **s** when it rose and have Mt 2:2
from them what time the **s** had appeared. Mt 2:7
the **s** that they had seen when it rose went Mt 2:9
When they saw the **s**, they rejoiced Mt 2:10
of Moloch and the **s** of your god Acts 7:43
stars; for **s** differs from star in glory. 1 Cor 15:41
stars; for star differs from **s** in glory. 1 Cor 15:41
dawns and the morning **s** rises in your 2 Pt 1:19
And I will give him the morning **s**. Rv 2:28
trumpet, and a great **s** fell from heaven, Rv 8:10
The name of the **s** is Wormwood. A Rv 8:11
and I saw a **s** fallen from heaven to earth, Rv 9:1
of David, the bright morning **s**." Rv 22:16

STAR-GOD (1)
and Kiyyun your **s**—your images that Am 5:26

STARE (3)
my bones—they **s** and gloat over me; Ps 22:17
who see you will **s** at you and ponder Is 14:16
wonder at this, or why do you **s** at us, Acts 3:12

STARED (2)
And he fixed his gaze and **s** at him, 2 Kgs 8:11
And he **s** at him in terror and said, Acts 10:4

STARS (51)
lesser light to rule the night—and the **s**. Gn 1:16
toward heaven, and number the **s**, Gn 15:5
your offspring as the **s** of heaven and Gn 22:17
your offspring as the **s** of heaven and Gn 26:4
and eleven **s** were bowing down to me." Gn 37:9
your offspring as the **s** of heaven, Ex 32:13
today as numerous as the **s** of heaven. Dt 1:10
you see the sun and the moon and the **s**, Dt 4:19
you as numerous as the **s** of heaven. Dt 10:22
were as numerous as the **s** of heaven, Dt 28:62
From heaven the **s** fought, from their Jgs 5:20
Israel as many as the **s** of heaven. 1 Chr 27:23
the break of dawn until the **s** came out. Neh 4:21
their children as the **s** of heaven, Neh 9:23
Let the **s** of its dawn be dark; let it hope for Jb 3:9
and it does not rise; who seals up the **s**; Jb 9:7
See the highest **s**, how lofty they are! Jb 22:12
bright, and the **s** are not pure in his eyes; Jb 25:5
when the morning **s** sang together and Jb 38:7
work of your fingers, the moon and the **s**, Ps 8:3
the moon and **s** to rule over the night, Ps 136:9
He determines the number of the **s**; he Ps 147:4
moon, praise him, all you shining **s**! Ps 148:3
the moon and the **s** are darkened and Eccl 12:2
For the **s** of the heavens and their Is 13:10
above the **s** of God I will set my throne Is 14:13
divide the heavens, who gaze at the **s**, Is 47:13
the moon and the **s** for light by night, Jer 31:35
the heavens and make their **s** dark; Ezk 32:7
host and some of the **s** it threw down to Dn 8:10
like the **s** forever and ever. Dn 12:3
and the **s** withdraw their shining. Jl 2:10
and the **s** withdraw their shining. Jl 3:15
though your nest is set among the **s**, Ob 1:4
more than the **s** of the heavens. Na 3:16
light, and the **s** will fall from heaven, Mt 24:29
and the **s** will be falling from heaven, Mk 13:25
will be signs in sun and moon and **s**, Lk 21:25
neither sun nor **s** appeared for many Acts 27:20
moon, and another glory of the **s**; 1 Cor 15:41
as many as the **s** of heaven and as Heb 11:12
foam of their own shame; wandering **s**, Jude 1:13
In his right hand he held seven **s**, from Rv 1:16
mystery of the seven **s** that you saw in Rv 1:20
the seven **s** are the angels of the seven Rv 1:20
who holds the seven **s** in his right hand, Rv 2:1
the seven spirits of God and the seven **s**. Rv 3:1
and the **s** of the sky fell to the earth as the Rv 6:13
a third of the moon, and a third of the **s**, Rv 8:12

feet, and on her head a crown of twelve **s**. Rv 12:1
down a third of the **s** of heaven and cast Rv 12:4

START (1)
you, and **s** early in the morning, 1 Sm 29:10

STARTED (6)
he who **s** the fire shall make full Ex 22:6
the Jews accepted what they had **s** to do, Est 9:23
prison for an insurrection **s** in the city Lk 23:19
boat, and **s** across the sea to Capernaum. Jn 6:17
we urged Titus that as he had **s**, 2 Cor 8:6
who a year ago **s** not only to do this 2 Cor 8:10

STARTING (2)
Moses wrote down their **s** places, stage Nm 33:2
their stages according to their **s** places. Nm 33:2

STARTLED (2)
midnight the man was **s** and turned over, Ru 3:8
But they were **s** and frightened and Lk 24:37

STARTS (1)
come back on him who **s** it rolling. Prv 26:27

STATE (9)
face toward it, and let it be in a **s** of siege, Ezk 4:3
shall return to their former **s**, Ezk 16:55
shall return to their former **s**, Ezk 16:55
shall return to your former **s**. Ezk 16:55
shall be restored to its rightful **s**." Dn 8:14
and the last **s** of that person is worse Mt 12:45
And the last **s** of that person is worse Lk 11:26
his accusers also to **s** before you what Acts 23:30
the last **s** has become worse for them 2 Pt 2:20

STATELY (3)
Three things are **s** in their tread; four Prv 30:29
in their tread; four are **s** in their stride: Prv 30:29
You sat on a **s** couch, with a table Ezk 23:41

STATEMENT (4)
to her, "For this **s** you may go your way; Mk 7:29
When Pilate heard this **s**, he was even Jn 19:8
departed after Paul had made one **s**: Acts 28:25
but by the open **s** of the truth we would 2 Cor 4:2

STATES (1)
The one who **s** his case first seems Prv 18:17

STATION (2)
you will be pulled down from your **s**. Is 22:19
at my watchpost and **s** myself on the Hab 2:1

STATIONED (10)
So they **s** the forces, the main Jos 8:13
whom he **s** in the chariot cities and 1 Kgs 10:26
Now Jehu had **s** eighty men outside 2 Kgs 10:24
whom he **s** in the chariot cities and 2 Chr 1:14
whom he **s** in the chariot cities and 2 Chr 9:25
He **s** the gatekeepers at the gates of 2 Chr 23:19
And he **s** the Levites in the house of 2 Chr 29:25
places, I **s** the people by their clans, Neh 4:13
And I **s** some of my servants at the Neh 13:19
day, and at my post I am **s** whole nights. Is 21:8

STATIONS (2)
them together and set them in their **s**. Neh 13:11
Take your **s** with your helmets, polish Jer 46:4

STATURE (11)
to grow both in **s** and in favor with 1 Sm 2:26
appearance or on the height of his **s**, 1 Sm 16:7
where there was a man of great **s**, 2 Sm 21:20
down an Egyptian, a man of great **s**, 1 Chr 11:23
where there was a man of great **s**, 1 Chr 20:6
Your **s** is like a palm tree, and your Sg 7:7
of Cush, and the Sabeans, men of **s**, Is 45:14
for the heads of persons of every **s**, Ezk 13:18
in wisdom and in **s** and in favor with Lk 2:52
he could not, because he was small of **s**. Lk 19:3
to the measure of the **s** of the fullness of Eph 4:13

STATUTE (42)
Joseph made it a **s** concerning the land Gn 47:26
your generations, as a **s** forever, Ex 12:14
your generations, as a **s** forever. Ex 12:17
observe this rite as a **s** for you and for Ex 12:24
Aaron, "This is the **s** of the Passover: Ex 12:43
therefore keep this **s** at its appointed Ex 13:10
the LORD made for them a **s** and a rule, Ex 15:25
It shall be a **s** forever to be observed Ex 27:21
This shall be a **s** forever for him and Ex 28:43
priesthood shall be theirs by a **s** forever. Ex 29:9
It shall be a **s** forever to them, even to Ex 30:21
It shall be a **s** forever throughout your Lv 3:17
It shall be a **s** forever throughout your Lv 10:9
"And it shall be a **s** to you forever that Lv 16:29
shall afflict yourselves; it is a **s** forever. Lv 16:31
And this shall be a **s** forever for you, Lv 16:34
This shall be a **s** forever for them Lv 17:7
it is a **s** forever throughout your Lv 23:14
It is a **s** forever in all your dwelling Lv 23:21
It is a **s** forever throughout your Lv 23:31
It is a **s** forever throughout your Lv 23:41
It shall be a **s** forever throughout your Lv 24:3
according to all the **s** for the Passover Nm 9:12
according to the **s** of the Passover and Nm 9:14
You shall have one **s**, both for the Nm 9:14
for a perpetual **s** throughout your Nm 10:8
there shall be one **s** for you and for the Nm 15:15
a **s** forever throughout your Nm 15:15
be a perpetual **s** throughout your Nm 18:23
"This is the **s** of the law that the LORD Nm 19:2
shall be a perpetual **s** for the people of Nm 19:10
And it shall be a **s** forever for them. Nm 19:21
be for the people of Israel a **s** and rule, Nm 27:11
"This is the **s** of the law that the LORD Nm 31:21
things shall be for a **s** and rule for you Nm 35:29
And he made it a **s** and a rule for 1 Sm 30:25
which he confirmed as a **s** to Jacob, 1 Chr 16:17
For it is a **s** for Israel, a rule of the God of Ps 81:4
you, those who frame injustice by **s**? Ps 94:20
his testimonies and the **s** that he gave Ps 99:7
which he confirmed to Jacob as a **s**, to Ps 105:10
to the LORD. This is a perpetual **s**. Ezk 46:14

STATUTES (141)
my charge, my commandments, my **s**, Gn 26:5
his commandments and keep all his **s**, Ex 15:26
I make them know the **s** of God and his Ex 18:16
warn them about the **s** and the laws, Ex 18:20
of Israel all the **s** that the LORD has Lv 10:11
you. You shall not walk in their **s**. Lv 18:3
rules and keep my **s** and walk in them. Lv 18:4
shall therefore keep my **s** and my rules; Lv 18:5
you shall keep my **s** and my rules and Lv 18:26
"You shall keep my **s**. You shall not let Lv 19:19
shall observe all my **s** and all my rules, Lv 19:37
Keep my **s** and do them; I am the LORD Lv 20:8
therefore keep all my **s** and all my rules Lv 20:22
you shall do my **s** and keep my rules Lv 25:18
you walk in my **s** and observe my Lv 26:3
if you spurn my **s**, and if your soul Lv 26:15
my rules and their soul abhorred my **s**. Lv 26:43
These are the **s** and rules and laws that Lv 26:46
according to all its **s** and all its rules you Nm 9:3
These are the **s** that the LORD Nm 30:16
listen to the **s** and the rules that I am Dt 4:1
See, I have taught you **s** and rules, as the Dt 4:5
peoples, who, when they hear all these **s**, Dt 4:6
that has **s** and rules so righteous as all Dt 4:8
me at that time to teach you **s** and rules, Dt 4:14
shall keep his **s** and his commandments, Dt 4:40
These are the testimonies, the **s**, and the Dt 4:45
the **s** and the rules that I speak in your Dt 5:1
commandment and the **s** and the rules Dt 5:31
the **s** and the rules that the LORD your God Dt 6:1
keeping all his **s** and his commandments, Dt 6:2
your God, and his testimonies and his **s**, Dt 6:17
the testimonies and the **s** and the rules Dt 6:20
the LORD commanded us to do all these **s**, Dt 6:24
commandment and the **s** and the rules Dt 7:11
commandments and his rules and his **s**, Dt 8:11
the commandments and **s** of the LORD, Dt 10:13
your God and keep his charge, his **s**, Dt 11:1
careful to do all the **s** and the rules that Dt 11:32
"These are the **s** and rules that you shall Dt 12:1
you shall be careful to observe these **s**. Dt 16:12
all the words of this law and these **s**, Dt 17:19
commands you to do these **s** and rules. Dt 26:16
and keep his **s** and his commandments Dt 26:17
keeping his commandments and his **s**, Dt 27:10
commandments and his **s** that I Dt 28:15
commandments and his **s** that he Dt 28:45
commandments and his **s** that are Dt 30:10
commandments and his **s** and his Dt 30:16
and put in place **s** and rules for them at Jos 24:25
and from his **s** I did not turn aside. 2 Sm 22:23
walking in his ways and keeping his **s**, 1 Kgs 2:3
walking in the **s** of David his father, 1 Kgs 3:3
keeping my **s** and my 1 Kgs 3:14
will walk in my **s** and obey my rules 1 Kgs 6:12
to keep his commandments, his **s**, 1 Kgs 8:58
walking in his **s** and keeping his 1 Kgs 8:61
you, and keeping my **s** and my rules, 1 Kgs 9:4
commandments and my **s** that I have 1 Kgs 9:6
my covenant and my **s** that I have 1 Kgs 11:11
and keeping my **s** and my rules, 1 Kgs 11:33
kept my commandments and my **s**. 1 Kgs 11:34
by keeping my **s** and my 1 Kgs 11:38
keep my commandments and my **s**, 2 Kgs 17:13
They despised his **s** and his 2 Kgs 17:15
do not follow the **s** or the rules or 2 Kgs 17:34
And the **s** and the rules and the law 2 Kgs 17:37
his testimonies and his **s** with all his 2 Kgs 23:3
to observe the **s** and the rules 1 Chr 22:13
your testimonies, and your **s**, 1 Chr 29:19
you and keeping my **s** and my rules, 2 Chr 7:17
and forsake my **s** and my 2 Chr 7:19
law or commandment, **s** or rules, 2 Chr 19:10
commanded them, all the law, the **s**, 2 Chr 33:8
and his testimonies and his **s**, 2 Chr 34:31
it and to teach his **s** and rules in Israel. Ezr 7:10
of the LORD and his **s** for Israel: Ezr 7:11
not kept the commandments, the **s**, Neh 1:7
true laws, good **s** and commandments, Neh 9:13
them commandments and **s** and a law Neh 9:14
LORD our Lord and his rules and his **s**. Neh 10:29
and his **s** I did not put away from me. Ps 18:22
you to recite my **s** or take my covenant Ps 50:16
if they violate my **s** and do not keep my Ps 89:31
they might keep his **s** and observe his Ps 105:45
may be steadfast in keeping your **s**! Ps 119:5
I will keep your **s**; do not utterly forsake Ps 119:8
are you, O LORD; teach me your **s**! Ps 119:12
I will delight in your **s**; I will not forget Ps 119:16
your servant will meditate on your **s**. Ps 119:23
you answered me; teach me your **s**! Ps 119:26
Teach me, O LORD, the way of your **s**; Ps 119:33
I love, and I will meditate on your **s**. Ps 119:48
Your **s** have been my songs in the Ps 119:54
of your steadfast love; teach me your **s**! Ps 119:64
are good and do good; teach me your **s**. Ps 119:68
was afflicted, that I might learn your **s**. Ps 119:71
May my heart be blameless in your **s**, Ps 119:80
smoke, yet I have not forgotten your **s**. Ps 119:83
my heart to perform your **s** forever, Ps 119:112
have regard for your **s** continually! Ps 119:117
spurn all who go astray from your **s**, Ps 119:118
steadfast love, and teach me your **s**. Ps 119:124
your servant, and teach me your **s**. Ps 119:135
answer me, O LORD! I will keep your **s**. Ps 119:145
wicked, for they do not seek your **s**. Ps 119:155
forth praise, for you teach me your **s**. Ps 119:171
word to Jacob, his **s** and rules to Israel. Ps 147:19
have transgressed the laws, violated the **s**, Is 24:5
in my law and my **s** that I set before Jer 44:10
law and in his **s** and in his testimonies Jer 44:23
and against my **s** more than the Ezk 5:6
my rules and have not walked in my **s**. Ezk 5:6
not walked in my **s** or obeyed my rules, Ezk 5:7
For you have not walked in my **s**, nor Ezk 11:12
may walk in my **s** and keep my rules Ezk 11:20
walks in my **s**, and keeps my rules by Ezk 18:9
obeys my rules, and walks in my **s**; Ezk 18:17
has been careful to observe all my **s**, Ezk 18:19
and keeps all my **s** and does what is Ezk 18:21
I gave them my **s** and made known to Ezk 20:11
not walk in my **s** but rejected my Ezk 20:13
my rules and did not walk in my **s**, Ezk 20:16
Do not walk in the **s** of your fathers, Ezk 20:18
walk in my **s**, and be careful to obey Ezk 20:19
not walk in my **s** and were not careful Ezk 20:21
had rejected my **s** and profaned my Ezk 20:24
I gave them **s** that were not good and Ezk 20:25
by robbery, and walks in the **s** of life, Ezk 33:15
you to walk in my **s** and be careful to Ezk 36:27
my rules and be careful to obey my **s**. Ezk 37:24
as well all its **s** and its whole design Ezk 43:11
laws and all its **s** and carry them out. Ezk 43:11
you concerning all the **s** of the temple Ezk 44:5
my laws and my **s** in all my appointed Ezk 44:24
law of the LORD, and have not kept his **s**, Am 2:4
For you have kept the **s** of Omri, and all Mi 6:16
But my words and my **s**, which I Zec 1:6
turned aside from my **s** and have not Mal 3:7
the **s** and rules that I commanded him Mal 4:4
all the commandments and **s** of the Lord. Lk 1:6

STAY (56)
his young men, "**S** here with the donkey; Gn 22:5
and **s** with him a while, until your Gn 27:44
give her to any other man; **s** with me." Gn 29:19
let you go, and you shall **s** no longer." Ex 9:28
So you, too, please **s** here tonight, that Nm 22:19
and it shall **s** with you until your Dt 22:2
but do not **s** there yourselves. Pursue Jos 10:19
and Dan, why did he **s** with the ships? Jgs 5:17
And he said, "I will **s** till you return." Jgs 6:18
And Micah said to him, "**S** with me, Jgs 17:10
the girl's father, made him **s**, Jgs 19:4
S in a secret place and hide yourself. 1 Sm 19:2
Do not **s**!" So Jonathan's boy 1 Sm 20:38
my father and my mother **s** with you, 1 Sm 22:3
S with me; do not be afraid, for he 1 Sm 22:23
us? Go back and **s** with the king, 2 Sm 15:19
'Do not **s** tonight at the fords of the 2 Sm 17:16
not a man will **s** with you this night, 2 Sm 19:7
now **s** your hand." And the angel of 2 Sm 24:16
Elijah said to Elisha, "Please **s** here, 2 Kgs 2:2
said to him, "Elisha, please **s** here, 2 Kgs 2:4
Elijah said to him, "Please **s** here, 2 Kgs 2:6
with your glory, and **s** at home, 2 Kgs 14:10
back and did not **s** there in the land. 2 Kgs 15:20

now **s** your hand." And the angel of 1 Chr 21:15
in boastfulness. But now **s** at home. 2 Chr 25:19
with its ways, and do not **s** in its paths. Jb 24:13
bit and bridle, or it will not **s** near you. Ps 32:9
and wayward; her feet do not **s** at home; Prv 7:11
and **s** themselves on the God of Israel; Is 48:2
standard toward Zion, flee for safety, **s** not, Jer 4:6
"They shall **s** with us no longer." Lam 4:15
and none can **s** his hand or say to him, Dn 4:35
worthy in it and **s** there until you Mt 10:11
Therefore, **s** awake, for you do not Mt 24:42
s there until you depart from there. Mk 6:10
commands the doorkeeper to **s** awake. Mk 13:34
Therefore **s** awake—for you do not Mk 13:35
what I say to you I say to all: **S** awake." Mk 13:37
And whatever house you enter, **s** there, Lk 9:4
"**S** dressed for action and keep your Lk 12:35
down, for I must **s** at your house today." Lk 19:5
But **s** awake at all times, praying that Lk 21:36
urged him strongly, saying, "**S** with us, Lk 24:29
far spent." So he went in to **s** with them. Lk 24:29
But **s** in the city until you are clothed Lk 24:49
to him, they asked him to **s** with them, Jn 4:40
people great during their **s** in the land Acts 13:17
my house and **s**." And she prevailed Acts 16:15
they asked him to **s** for a longer Acts 18:20
"Unless these men **s** in the ship, Acts 27:31
and were invited to **s** with them for Acts 28:14
Paul was allowed to **s** by himself, Acts 28:16
and perhaps I will **s** with you or even 1 Cor 16:6
But I will **s** in Ephesus until 1 Cor 16:8
angels who did not **s** within their own Jude 1:6

STAYED (43)
a certain place and **s** there that night, Gn 28:11
my flesh!" And he **s** with him a month. Gn 29:14
sojourned with Laban and **s** until now. Gn 32:4
So he **s** there that night, and from what Gn 32:13
and he himself **s** that night in the Gn 32:21
me." So no one **s** with him when Joseph Gn 45:1
fled from Pharaoh and **s** in the land of Ex 2:15
first month, and the people **s** in Kadesh. Nm 20:1
So the princes of Moab **s** with Balaam. Nm 22:8
'You have **s** long enough at this Dt 1:6
"I myself **s** on the mountain, as at the Dt 10:10
Gilead **s** beyond the Jordan; and Dan, Jgs 5:17
and he went down and **s** in the cleft of Jgs 15:8
were present with them **s** in Geba of 1 Sm 13:16
and they **s** with him all the time that 1 Sm 22:4
where those who were left behind **s**. 1 Sm 30:9
Two hundred **s** behind, who were too 1 Sm 30:10
with food while he **s** at Mahanaim, 2 Sm 19:32
but Haman **s** to beg for his life from Est 7:7
and here shall your proud waves be **s**'? Jb 38:11
and intervened, and the plague was **s**. Ps 106:30
in perfect peace whose mind is **s** on you, Is 26:3
they went and **s** at Geruth Chimham Jer 41:17
he would have **s** awake and would not Mt 24:43
the boy Jesus **s** behind in Jerusalem. Lk 2:43
are those who have **s** with me in my Lk 22:28
staying, and they **s** with him that day, Jn 1:39
disciples, and they **s** there for a few days. Jn 2:12
stay with them, and he **s** there two days. Jn 4:40
he **s** two days longer in the place where Jn 11:6
and there he **s** with the disciples. Jn 11:54
And he **s** in Joppa for many days with Acts 9:43
the same trade he **s** with them and Acts 18:3
And he **s** a year and six months, Acts 18:11
Paul **s** many days longer and then Acts 18:18
he himself **s** in Asia for a while. Acts 19:22
at Troas, where we **s** for seven days. Acts 20:6
the disciples, we **s** there for seven days. Acts 21:4
the brothers and **s** with them for Acts 21:7
was one of the seven, and **s** with him. Acts 21:8
After he **s** among them not more than Acts 25:6
And as they **s** there many days, Acts 25:14
at Syracuse, we **s** there for three days. Acts 28:12

STAYING (8)
at the coast of the sea, **s** by his landings. Jgs 5:17
Saul was **s** in the outskirts of Gibeah 1 Sm 14:2
to him while he was **s** at Jericho, 2 Kgs 2:18
means Teacher), "where are you **s**?" Jn 1:38
So they came and saw where he was **s**, Jn 1:39
And while **s** with them he ordered them Acts 1:4
to the upper room, where they were **s**, Acts 1:13
While we were **s** for many days, a Acts 21:10

STAYS (7)
his share be who **s** by the baggage. 1 Sm 30:24
of the stand its **s** and its panels were 1 Kgs 7:35
the surfaces of its **s** and on its panels, 1 Kgs 7:36
the city, the watchman **s** awake in vain. Ps 127:1
He who **s** in this city shall die by the Jer 21:9
He who **s** in this city shall die by the Jer 38:2
Blessed is the one who **s** awake, keeping Rv 16:15

STEADFAST (208)
success today and show **s** love to my Gn 24:12
that you have shown **s** love to my Gn 24:14
has not forsaken his **s** love and his Gn 24:27
going to show **s** love and faithfulness Gn 24:49
of all the deeds of **s** love and all the Gn 32:10
Joseph and showed him **s** love and gave Gn 39:21
have led in your **s** love the people whom Ex 15:13
but showing **s** love to thousands of those Ex 20:6
and abounding in **s** love and Ex 34:6
keeping **s** love for thousands, forgiving Ex 34:7
to anger and abounding in **s** love, Nm 14:18
to the greatness of your **s** love, Nm 14:19
but showing **s** love to thousands of those Dt 5:10
who keeps covenant and **s** love with those Dt 7:9
the covenant and the **s** love that he swore Dt 7:12
they did not show **s** love to the family Jgs 8:35
alive, show me the **s** love of the LORD, 1 Sm 20:14
not cut off your **s** love from my 1 Sm 20:15
the LORD show **s** love and faithfulness 2 Sm 2:6
day I keep showing **s** love to the house 2 Sm 3:8
but my **s** love will not depart from 2 Sm 7:15
the LORD show **s** love and 2 Sm 15:20
and shows **s** love to his anointed, 2 Sm 22:51
have shown great and **s** love to your 1 Kgs 3:6
him this great and **s** love and have 1 Kgs 3:6
covenant and showing **s** love to your 1 Kgs 8:23
good; for his **s** love endures forever! 1 Chr 16:34
LORD, for his **s** love endures forever. 1 Chr 16:41
I will not take my **s** love from him, 1 Chr 17:13
have shown great and **s** love to David 2 Chr 1:8
for his **s** love endures forever," the 2 Chr 5:13
covenant and showing **s** love to your 2 Chr 6:14
Remember your **s** love for David 2 Chr 6:42
is good, for his **s** love endures forever." 2 Chr 7:3
LORD—for his **s** love endures forever— 2 Chr 7:6
LORD, for his **s** love endures forever." 2 Chr 20:21
for his **s** love endures forever toward Ezr 3:11
extended to me his **s** love before the king Ezr 7:28
extended to us his **s** love before the kings Ezr 9:9
keeps covenant and **s** love with those Neh 1:5
slow to anger and abounding in **s** love, Neh 9:17
God, who keeps covenant and **s** love, Neh 9:32
to the greatness of your **s** love. Neh 13:22
You have granted me life and **s** love, Jb 10:12
I, through the abundance of your **s** love, Ps 5:7
my life; save me for the sake of your **s** love. Ps 6:4
But I have trusted in your **s** love; my Ps 13:5
Wondrously show your **s** love, O Savior Ps 17:7
king, and shows **s** love to his anointed, Ps 18:50
and through the **s** love of the Most High Ps 21:7
your mercy, O LORD, and your **s** love, Ps 25:6
according to your **s** love remember me, Ps 25:7
of the LORD are **s** love and faithfulness, Ps 25:10
For your **s** love is before my eyes, and I Ps 26:3
I will rejoice and be glad in your **s** love, Ps 31:7
on your servant; save me in your **s** love! Ps 31:16
has wondrously shown his **s** love to me Ps 31:21
but **s** love surrounds the one who trusts Ps 32:10
the earth is full of the **s** love of the LORD. Ps 33:5
him, on those who hope in his **s** love, Ps 33:18
Let your **s** love, O LORD, be upon us, Ps 33:22
Your **s** love, O LORD, extends to the Ps 36:5
How precious is your **s** love, O God! The Ps 36:7
continue your **s** love to those who know Ps 36:10
not concealed your **s** love and your Ps 40:10
your **s** love and your faithfulness will Ps 40:11
By day the LORD commands his **s** love, Ps 42:8
Redeem us for the sake of your **s** love! Ps 44:26
We have thought on your **s** love, O God, Ps 48:9
on me, O God, according to your **s** love; Ps 51:1
The **s** love of God endures all the day. Ps 52:1
I trust in the **s** love of God forever and Ps 52:8
will send out his **s** love and his Ps 57:3
My heart is **s**, O God, my heart is Ps 57:7
heart is steadfast, O God, my heart is **s**! Ps 57:7
For your **s** love is great to the heavens, Ps 57:10
My God in his **s** love will meet me; God Ps 59:10
sing aloud of your **s** love in the Ps 59:16
fortress, the God who shows me **s** love. Ps 59:17
appoint **s** love and faithfulness to watch Ps 61:7
and that to you, O Lord, belongs **s** love. Ps 62:12
Because your **s** love is better than life, Ps 63:3
prayer or removed his **s** love from me! Ps 66:20
abundance of your **s** love answer me Ps 69:13
me, O LORD, for your **s** love is good; Ps 69:16
Has his **s** love forever ceased? Are his Ps 77:8
a generation whose heart was not **s**, Ps 78:8
Their heart was not **s** toward him; they Ps 78:37
Show us your **s** love, O LORD, and grant Ps 85:7
S love and faithfulness meet; Ps 85:10
abounding in **s** love to all who call upon Ps 86:5
For great is your **s** love toward me; you Ps 86:13
and abounding in **s** love and Ps 86:15
Is your **s** love declared in the grave, or Ps 88:11
I will sing of the **s** love of the LORD, Ps 89:1
For I said, "**S** love will be built up forever; Ps 89:2
s love and faithfulness go before you. Ps 89:14
My faithfulness and my **s** love shall be Ps 89:24
My **s** love I will keep for him forever, Ps 89:28
remove from him my **s** love or be false Ps 89:33
Lord, where is your **s** love of old, which Ps 89:49
us in the morning with your **s** love, Ps 90:14
to declare your **s** love in the morning, Ps 92:2
I thought, "My foot slips," your **s** love, Ps 94:18
has remembered his **s** love and Ps 98:3
his **s** love endures forever, and his Ps 100:5
I will sing of **s** love and justice; to you, O Ps 101:1
who crowns you with **s** love and mercy, Ps 103:4
slow to anger and abounding in **s** love. Ps 103:8
so great is his **s** love toward those who Ps 103:11
But the **s** love of the LORD is from Ps 103:17
is good, for his **s** love endures forever! Ps 106:1
the abundance of your **s** love, Ps 106:7
to the abundance of his **s** love. Ps 106:45
is good, for his **s** love endures forever! Ps 107:1
Let them thank the LORD for his **s** love, Ps 107:8
Let them thank the LORD for his **s** love, Ps 107:15
Let them thank the LORD for his **s** love, Ps 107:21
Let them thank the LORD for his **s** love, Ps 107:31
let them consider the **s** love of the Ps 107:43
My heart is **s**, O God! I will sing and Ps 108:1
For your **s** love is great above the Ps 108:4
because your **s** love is good, deliver Ps 109:21
Save me according to your **s** love! Ps 109:26
the sake of your **s** love and your Ps 115:1
For great is his **s** love toward us, and the Ps 117:2
is good; for his **s** love endures forever! Ps 118:1
Israel say, "His **s** love endures forever." Ps 118:2
Aaron say, "His **s** love endures forever." Ps 118:3
LORD say, "His **s** love endures forever." Ps 118:4
is good; for his **s** love endures forever! Ps 118:29
my ways may be **s** in keeping your Ps 119:5
Let your **s** love come to me, O LORD, Ps 119:41
earth, O LORD, is full of your **s** love; Ps 119:64
Let your **s** love comfort me according Ps 119:76
In your **s** love give me life, that I may Ps 119:88
servant according to your **s** love, Ps 119:124
my voice according to your **s** love; Ps 119:149
Give me life according to your **s** love. Ps 119:159
For with the LORD there is **s** love, and Ps 130:7
he is good, for his **s** love endures forever. Ps 136:1
of gods, for his **s** love endures forever. Ps 136:2
of lords, for his **s** love endures forever; Ps 136:3
wonders, for his **s** love endures forever; Ps 136:4
heavens, for his **s** love endures forever; Ps 136:5
waters, for his **s** love endures forever; Ps 136:6
lights, for his **s** love endures forever; Ps 136:7
the day, for his **s** love endures forever; Ps 136:8
the night, for his **s** love endures forever; Ps 136:9
of Egypt, for his **s** love endures forever; Ps 136:10
them, for his **s** love endures forever; Ps 136:11
arm, for his **s** love endures forever; Ps 136:12
in two, for his **s** love endures forever; Ps 136:13
of it, for his **s** love endures forever; Ps 136:14
Red Sea, for his **s** love endures forever; Ps 136:15
for his **s** love endures forever; Ps 136:16
kings, for his **s** love endures forever; Ps 136:17
kings, for his **s** love endures forever; Ps 136:18
for his **s** love endures forever; Ps 136:19
Bashan, for his **s** love endures forever; Ps 136:20
heritage, for his **s** love endures forever; Ps 136:21
servant, for his **s** love endures forever. Ps 136:22
estate, for his **s** love endures forever; Ps 136:23
our foes, for his **s** love endures forever; Ps 136:24
all flesh, for his **s** love endures forever. Ps 136:25
heaven, for his **s** love endures forever. Ps 136:26
your name for your **s** love and your Ps 138:2
fulfill his purpose for me; your **s** love, Ps 138:8
me hear in the morning of your **s** love, Ps 143:8
And in your **s** love you will cut off my Ps 143:12
he is my **s** love and my fortress, my Ps 144:2
slow to anger and abounding in **s** love. Ps 145:8
him, in those who hope in his **s** love. Ps 147:11
Let not **s** love and faithfulness forsake Prv 3:3
Whoever is **s** in righteousness will Prv 11:19
devise good meet **s** love and Prv 14:22
By **s** love and faithfulness iniquity is Prv 16:6
What is desired in a man is **s** love, and Prv 19:22
Many a man proclaims his own **s** love, Prv 20:6
S love and faithfulness preserve the Prv 20:28
and by **s** love his throne is upheld. Prv 20:28
then a throne will be established in **s** love, Is 16:5
but my **s** love shall not depart from you, Is 54:10
with you an everlasting covenant, my **s**, Is 55:3
I will recount the **s** love of the LORD, the Is 63:7
according to the abundance of his **s** love. Is 63:7
that I am the LORD who practices **s** love, Jer 9:24
from this people, my **s** love and mercy, Jer 16:5
You show **s** love to thousands, but you Jer 32:18

is good, for his **s** love endures forever!' Jer 33:11
The **s** love of the LORD never ceases; his Lam 3:22
to the abundance of his **s** love; Lam 3:32
who keeps covenant and **s** love with those Dn 9:4
and in justice, in **s** love and in mercy. Hos 2:19
There is no faithfulness or **s** love, and no Hos 4:1
For I desire **s** love and not sacrifice, the Hos 6:6
yourselves righteousness; reap **s** love; Hos 10:12
slow to anger, and abounding in **s** love; Jl 2:13
to vain idols forsake their hope of **s** love. Jon 2:8
slow to anger and abounding in **s** love, Jon 4:2
forever, because he delights in **s** love. Mi 7:18
to Jacob and **s** love to Abraham, Mi 7:20
faithful to the Lord with **s** purpose, Acts 11:23
my beloved brothers, be **s**, 1 Cor 15:58
you continue in the faith, stable and **s**, Col 1:23
this as a sure and **s** anchor of the soul, Heb 6:19
is the man who remains **s** under trial, Jas 1:12
consider those blessed who remained **s**. Jas 5:11

STEADFASTLY (2)
followed their king **s** from the Jordan 2 Sm 20:2
Continue **s** in prayer, being watchful in Col 4:2

STEADFASTNESS (11)
and labor of love and **s** of hope in our 1 Thes 1:3
of God for your **s** and faith in all 2 Thes 1:4
the love of God and to the **s** of Christ. 2 Thes 3:5
godliness, faith, love, **s**, gentleness. 1 Tm 6:11
my faith, my patience, my love, my **s**, 2 Tm 3:10
sound in faith, in love, and in **s**. Ti 2:2
that the testing of your faith produces **s**. Jas 1:3
And let **s** have its full effect, that you may Jas 1:4
You have heard of the **s** of Job, and you Jas 5:11
with self-control, and self-control with **s**, 2 Pt 1:6
with steadfastness, and **s** with godliness, 2 Pt 1:6

STEADILY (1)
And Jehoshaphat grew **s** greater. He 2 Chr 17:12

STEADY (4)
So his hands were **s** until the going Ex 17:12
inhabitants, it is I who keep **s** its pillars. Ps 75:3
His heart is **s**; he will not be afraid, until Ps 112:8
Keep **s** my steps according to your Ps 119:133

STEAL (23)
house, but why did you **s** my gods?" Gn 31:30
How then could we **s** silver or gold from Gn 44:8
"You shall not **s**. Ex 20:15
"You shall not **s**; you shall not deal Lv 19:11
"'And you shall not **s**. Dt 5:19
that day as people **s** in who are 2 Sm 19:3
Let death **s** over them; let them go down Ps 55:15
lies. What I did not **s** must I now restore? Ps 69:4
they **s** away and lie down in their dens. Ps 104:22
I be poor and **s** and profane the name Prv 30:9
Will you **s**, murder, commit adultery, Jer 7:9
who **s** my words from one another. Jer 23:30
would they not **s** only enough for Ob 1:5
and where thieves break in and **s**, Mt 6:19
and where thieves do not break in and **s**. Mt 6:20
not commit adultery, You shall not **s**, Mt 19:18
his disciples go and **s** him away and Mt 27:64
Do not commit adultery, Do not **s**, Mk 10:19
adultery, Do not murder, Do not **s**, Lk 18:20
thief comes only to **s** and kill and Jn 10:10
you preach against stealing, do you **s**? Rom 2:21
You shall not murder, You shall not **s**, Rom 13:9
Let the thief no longer **s**, but rather let Eph 4:28

STEALING (3)
"If a man is found **s** one of his brothers, Dt 24:7
murder, **s**, and committing adultery; Hos 4:2
While you preach against **s**, do you Rom 2:21

STEALS (4)
"Whoever **s** a man and sells him, and Ex 21:16
"If a man **s** an ox or a sheep, and kills it Ex 22:1
a thief if he **s** to satisfy his appetite Prv 6:30
For everyone who **s** shall be cleaned out Zec 5:3

STEALTH (2)
in order to arrest Jesus by **s** and kill him. Mt 26:4
how to arrest him by **s** and kill him, Mk 14:1

STEALTHILY (3)
Then David arose and **s** cut off a 1 Sm 24:4
"Now a word was brought to me **s**; my Jb 4:12
His eyes **s** watch for the helpless; Ps 10:8

STEED (1)
make them like his majestic **s** in battle. Zec 10:3

STEEDS (4)
with the galloping, galloping of his **s**. Jgs 5:22
the horses and swift **s** they brought to 1 Kgs 4:28
away; and, "We will ride upon swift **s**"; Is 30:16
Harness the **s** to the chariots, Mi 1:13

STEEP (5)
will all come and settle in the **s** ravines, Is 7:19
the fire, like waters poured down a **s** place. Mi 1:4
herd rushed down the **s** bank into the Mt 8:32
rushed down the **s** bank into the sea Mk 5:13
herd rushed down the **s** bank into the Lk 8:33

STEERS (1)
them, and young **s** with the mighty bulls. Is 34:7

STEM (6)
its base, its **s**, its cups, its calyxes, and Ex 25:31
Its base, its **s**, its cups, its calyxes, and Ex 37:17
scarcely has their **s** taken root in the Is 40:24
As for its strong **s**, fire consumed it. Ezk 19:12
has gone out from the **s** of its shoots, Ezk 19:14
so that there remains in it no strong **s**, Ezk 19:14

STEMS (1)
Its strong **s** became rulers' scepters; it Ezk 19:11

STENCH (10)
had become a **s** to the Philistines. 1 Sm 13:4
made himself an utter **s** to his people 1 Sm 27:12
that they had become a **s** to David, 2 Sm 10:6
made yourself a **s** to your father, 2 Sm 16:21
that they had become a **s** to David, 1 Chr 19:6
and I am a **s** to the children of my own Jb 19:17
the perfumer's ointment give off a **s**; Eccl 10:1
out, and the **s** of their corpses shall rise; Is 34:3
the **s** and foul smell of him will rise, for he Jl 2:20
and I made the **s** of your camp go up Am 4:10

STEP (8)
there is but a **s** between me and 1 Sm 20:3
on each end of a **s** on the six steps. 1 Kgs 10:20
on each end of a **s** on the six steps. 2 Chr 9:19
if my **s** has turned aside from the way Jb 31:7
you walk, your **s** will not be hampered, Prv 4:12
the east whom victory meets at every **s**? Is 41:2
of the sea will **s** down from their Ezk 26:16
conduct was not in **s** with the truth of Gal 2:14

STEPHANAS (3)
(I did baptize also the household of **S**. 1 Cor 1:16
that the household of **S** were the first 1 Cor 16:15
the coming of **S** and Fortunatus and 1 Cor 16:17

STEPHEN (8)
the whole gathering, and they chose **S**, Acts 6:5
And **S**, full of grace and power, was Acts 6:8
and Asia, rose up and disputed with **S**. Acts 6:9
And **S** said: "Brothers and fathers, hear Acts 7:2
And as they were stoning **S**, he called Acts 7:59
Devout men buried **S** and made great Acts 8:2
that arose over **S** traveled as far Acts 11:19
when the blood of **S** your witness was Acts 22:20

STEPPED (2)
And when Jesus had **s** out of the boat, Mk 5:2
When Jesus had **s** out on land, there met Lk 8:27

STEPS (58)
you shall not go up by **s** to my altar, Ex 20:26
so they followed in your **s**, receiving Dt 33:3
the ark of the LORD had gone six **s**, 2 Sm 6:13
gave a wide place for my **s** under me, 2 Sm 22:37
The throne had six **s**, and at the 1 Kgs 10:19
on each end of a step on the six **s**. 1 Kgs 10:20
and put it under him on the bare **s**, 2 Kgs 9:13
shall the shadow go forward ten **s**, or 2 Kgs 20:9
forward ten steps, or go back ten **s**?" 2 Kgs 20:9
for the shadow to lengthen ten **s**. 2 Kgs 20:10
let the shadow go back ten **s**." 2 Kgs 20:10
he brought the shadow back ten **s**, 2 Kgs 20:11
it had gone down on the **s** of Ahaz. 2 Kgs 20:11
The throne had six **s** and a footstool 2 Chr 9:18
one on each end of a step on the six **s**. 2 Chr 9:19
For then you would number my **s**; you Jb 14:16
His strong **s** are shortened, and his own Jb 18:7
My foot has held fast to his **s**; I have kept Jb 23:11
when my **s** were washed with butter, and Jb 29:6
he see my ways and number all my **s**? Jb 31:4
would give him an account of all my **s**; Jb 31:37
the ways of a man, and he sees all his **s**. Jb 34:21
My **s** have held fast to your paths; my feet Ps 17:5
They have now surrounded our **s**; they Ps 17:11
gave a wide place for my **s** under me, Ps 18:36
The **s** of a man are established by the Ps 37:23
his God is in his heart; his **s** do not slip. Ps 37:31
feet upon a rock, making my **s** secure. Ps 40:2
nor have our **s** departed from your way; Ps 44:18
they watch my **s**, as they have waited for Ps 56:6
They set a net for my **s**; my soul was Ps 57:6
stumbled, my **s** had nearly slipped. Ps 73:2
Direct your **s** to the perpetual ruins; the Ps 74:3
Keep steady my **s** according to your Ps 119:133
to death; her **s** follow the path to Sheol; Prv 5:5
but the prudent gives thought to his **s**. Prv 14:15
his way, but the LORD establishes his **s**. Prv 16:9
A man's **s** are from the LORD; how then Prv 20:24
Guard your **s** when you go to the house Eccl 5:1
it, the feet of the poor, the **s** of the needy." Is 26:6
Ahaz turn back ten **s**." So the sun turned Is 38:8
on the dial the ten **s** by which it had Is 38:8
is not in man who walks to direct his **s**. Jer 10:23
he turned aside my **s** and tore me to Lam 3:11
They dogged our **s** so that we could Lam 4:18
the gateway facing east, going up its **s**, Ezk 40:6
And by seven **s** people would go up to Ezk 40:22
And there were seven **s** leading up to it, Ezk 40:26
its jambs, and its stairway had eight **s**. Ezk 40:31
side, and its stairway had eight **s**. Ezk 40:34
side, and its stairway had eight **s**. Ezk 40:37
and people would go up to it by ten **s**. Ezk 40:49
The **s** of the altar shall face east." Ezk 43:17
I am going another **s** down before me." Jn 5:7
And when he came to the **s**, he was Acts 21:35
permission, Paul, standing on the **s**, Acts 21:40
spirit? Did we not take the same **s**? 2 Cor 12:18
so that you might follow in his **s**. 1 Pt 2:21

STERN (4)
A **s** vision is told to me; the traitor Is 21:2
But he was in the **s**, asleep on the Mk 4:38
anchors from the **s** and prayed for Acts 27:29
and the **s** was being broken up by the Acts 27:41

STERNLY (2)
were opened. And Jesus **s** warned them, Mt 9:30
And Jesus **s** charged him and sent him Mk 1:43

STEW (7)
Once when Jacob was cooking **s**, Esau Gn 25:29
to Jacob, "Let me eat some of that red **s**, Gn 25:30
Jacob gave Esau bread and lentil **s**, Gn 25:34
and boil **s** for the sons of the 2 Kgs 4:38
and cut them up into the pot of **s**, 2 Kgs 4:39
But while they were eating of the **s**, 2 Kgs 4:40
with his fold bread or **s** or wine or oil or Hg 2:12

STEWARD (8)
with them, he said to the **s** of his house, Gn 43:16
went up to the **s** of Joseph's house and Gn 43:19
Then he commanded the **s** of his house, Gn 44:1
Now Joseph said to his **s**, "Up, follow Gn 44:4
Lord GOD of hosts, "Come, go to this **s**, Is 22:15
Daniel said to the **s** whom the chief of Dn 1:11
So the **s** took away their food and the Dn 1:16
For an overseer, as God's **s**, must be above Ti 1:7

STEWARDS (5)
All these were **s** of King David's 1 Chr 27:31
the **s** of all the property and livestock 1 Chr 28:1
of Christ and **s** of the mysteries 1 Cor 4:1
it is required of **s** that they be found 1 Cor 4:2
as good **s** of God's varied grace: 1 Pt 4:10

STEWARDSHIP (4)
own will, I am still entrusted with a **s**. 1 Cor 9:17
have heard of the **s** of God's grace that Eph 3:2
according to the **s** from God that Col 1:25
rather than the **s** from God that 1 Tm 1:4

STICK (19)
the devoted things shall **s** to your hand, Dt 13:17
will make the pestilence **s** to you until Dt 28:21
he cut off a **s** and threw it in there and 2 Kgs 6:6
My bones **s** to my skin and to my flesh, Jb 19:20
and his bones that were not seen **s** out. Jb 33:21
a mass and the clods **s** fast together? Jb 38:38
The folds of his flesh **s** together, firmly Jb 41:23
Let my tongue **s** to the roof of my Ps 137:6
cumin, but dill is beaten out with a **s**, Is 28:27
your mouth wide and **s** out your tongue? Is 57:4
fish of your streams **s** to your scales; Ezk 29:4
of your streams that **s** to your scales. Ezk 29:4
"Son of man, take a **s** and write on it, Ezk 37:16
then take another **s** and write on it, Ezk 37:16
'For Joseph (the **s** of Ephraim) and all Ezk 37:16
join them one to another into one **s**, Ezk 37:17
about to take the **s** of Joseph (that is Ezk 37:19
And I will join with it the **s** of Judah, Ezk 37:19
stick of Judah, and make them one **s**, Ezk 37:19

STICKS (16)
Then Jacob took fresh **s** of poplar and Gn 30:37
in them, exposing the white of the **s**. Gn 30:37
He set the **s** that he had peeled in front Gn 30:38
bred in front of the **s** and so the flocks Gn 30:39
Jacob would lay the **s** in the troughs Gn 30:41
that they might breed among the **s**, Gn 30:41
a man gathering **s** on the Sabbath Nm 15:32
found him gathering **s** brought him Nm 15:33
to me with **s**?" And the Philistine 1 Sm 17:43
a widow was there gathering **s**. 1 Kgs 17:10
gathering a couple of **s** that I may go 1 Kgs 17:12
a potsherd, and my tongue **s** to my jaws; Ps 22:15
is a friend who **s** closer than a brother. Prv 18:24
of the nursing infant **s** to the roof of Lam 4:4
When the **s** on which you write are in Ezk 37:20
gathered a bundle of **s** and put them Acts 28:3

STIFF (1)
He makes his tail **s** like a cedar; the Jb 40:17

STIFF-NECKED (6)
this people, and behold, it is a **s** people. Ex 32:9
you on the way, for you are a **s** people." Ex 33:3
to the people of Israel, 'You are a **s** people; Ex 33:5
go in the midst of us, for it is a **s** people, Ex 34:9
Do not now be **s** as your fathers were, 2 Chr 30:8
"You **s** people, uncircumcised in heart Acts 7:51

STIFFENED (7)
He **s** his neck and hardened his 2 Chr 36:13
acted presumptuously and **s** their neck Neh 9:16
but they **s** their neck and appointed a Neh 9:17
stubborn shoulder and **s** their neck Neh 9:29
me or incline their ear, but **s** their neck. Jer 7:26
or incline their ear, but **s** their neck, Jer 17:23
it, because they have **s** their neck, Jer 19:15

STIFFENS (1)
He who is often reproved, yet **s** his neck, Prv 29:1

STILL (212)
for the waters were **s** on the face of the Gn 8:9
journeyed on, **s** going toward the Negeb. Gn 12:9
but Abraham **s** stood before the LORD. Gn 18:22
and while he was **s** living he sent them Gn 25:6
He said, "Behold, it is **s** high day; it is not Gn 29:7
While he was **s** speaking with them, Gn 29:9
When they were **s** some distance from Gn 35:16
for they were **s** as ugly as at the Gn 41:21
kindred, saying, 'Is your father **s** alive? Gn 43:7
of whom you spoke? Is he **s** alive?" Gn 43:27
he is **s** alive." And they bowed their Gn 43:28
came to Joseph's house, he was **s** there. Gn 44:14
Is my father **s** alive?" But his brothers Gn 45:3
And they told him, "Joseph is **s** alive, Gn 45:26
"It is enough; Joseph my son is **s** alive. Gn 45:28
face and know that you are **s** alive." Gn 46:30
when there was **s** some distance to go to Gn 48:7
see whether they are **s** alive." And Jethro Ex 4:18
but you must **s** deliver the same number Ex 5:18
S Pharaoh's heart was hardened, and he Ex 7:13
you refuse to let them go and **s** hold them, Ex 9:2
You are **s** exalting yourself against my Ex 9:17
of your arm, they are **s** as a stone, Ex 15:16
They **s** kept bringing him freewill Ex 36:3
her nakedness while her sister is **s** alive. Lv 18:18
If there are **s** many years left, he shall Lv 25:51
he shall **s** keep the Passover to the LORD. Nm 9:10
unclean. His uncleanness is **s** on him. Nm 19:13
to increase **s** more the fierce anger of Nm 32:14
of the fire, as you have heard, and **s** live? Dt 4:33
God speak with man and man **s** live. Dt 5:24
midst of fire as we have, and has **s** lived? Dt 5:26
Jordan, you shall stand **s** in the Jordan.'" Jos 3:8
It was **s** warm when we took it from our Jos 9:12
sight of Israel, "Sun, stand **s** at Gibeon, Jos 10:12
And the sun stood **s**, and the moon Jos 10:13
I am **s** as strong today as I was in the Jos 14:11
But when he **s** did not open the doors of Jgs 3:25
Why did you sit **s** among the sheepfolds, Jgs 5:16
Asher sat **s** at the coast of the sea, Jgs 5:17
Between her feet he sank, he fell, he lay **s**; Jgs 5:27
To this day it **s** stands at Ophrah, which Jgs 6:24
to Gideon, "The people are **s** too many. Jgs 7:4
afraid, because he was **s** a young man. Jgs 8:20
"Is there a man **s** to come?" and the 1 Sm 10:22
Now therefore stand **s** that I may 1 Sm 12:7
Now therefore stand **s** and see this 1 Sm 12:16
But if you **s** do wickedly, you shall 1 Sm 12:25
Gad and Gilead. Saul was **s** at Gilgal, 1 Sm 13:7
you,' then we will stand **s** in our place, 1 Sm 14:9
If I am **s** alive, show me the steadfast 1 Sm 20:14
has seized me, and yet my life **s** lingers.' 2 Sm 1:9
Asahel had fallen and died, stood **s**. 2 Sm 2:23
"Is there **s** anyone left of the house of 2 Sm 9:1
"Is there not **s** someone of the house of 2 Sm 9:3
the king, "There is **s** a son of Jonathan; 2 Sm 9:3
He said, "While the child was **s** alive, 2 Sm 12:22
me to be there **s**." Now therefore let 2 Sm 14:32
Absalom while he was **s** alive in the 2 Sm 18:14
here." So he turned aside and stood **s**. 2 Sm 18:30
"How many years have I **s** to live, 2 Sm 19:34
Can I **s** listen to the voice of singing 2 Sm 19:35
the eyes of my lord the king **s** see it, 2 Sm 24:3
while you are **s** speaking with the 1 Kgs 1:14
While she was **s** speaking with the 1 Kgs 1:22
While he was **s** speaking, behold, 1 Kgs 1:42
Hadad **s** being a little child. 1 Kgs 11:17
heard of it (for he was **s** in Egypt, 1 Kgs 12:2
live.'" And he said, "Does he **s** live? 1 Kgs 20:32
and the people **s** sacrificed and made 1 Kgs 22:43
And as they **s** went on and talked, 2 Kgs 2:11
while he was **s** speaking with them, 2 Kgs 6:33
the people **s** sacrificed and made 2 Kgs 14:4
The people **s** sacrificed and made 2 Kgs 15:4
The people **s** sacrificed and made 2 Kgs 15:35
But every nation **s** made gods of its 2 Kgs 17:29
S the LORD did not turn from the 2 Kgs 23:26
The land is **s** ours, because we have 2 Chr 14:7
But the people **s** followed corrupt 2 Chr 27:2
his servants said **s** more against the 2 Chr 32:16
the people **s** sacrificed at the high 2 Chr 33:17
And while they are **s** standing guard, let Neh 7:3
He **s** holds fast his integrity, although you Jb 2:3
to him, "Do you **s** hold fast your integrity? Jb 2:9
It stood **s**, but I could not discern its Jb 4:16
inward parts are in turmoil and never **s**; Jb 30:27
when the earth is **s** because of the south Jb 37:17
he cannot stand **s** at the sound of the Jb 39:24
your foes, to **s** the enemy and the avenger. Ps 8:2
pastures. He leads me beside **s** waters. Ps 23:2
Be **s** before the LORD and wait patiently Ps 37:7
"Be **s**, and know that I am God. I will be Ps 46:10
and I **s** proclaim your wondrous deeds. Ps 71:17
judgment; the earth feared and was **s**, Ps 76:8
Yet they sinned **s** more against him, Ps 78:17
while the food was **s** in their mouths, Ps 78:30
In spite of all this, they **s** sinned; despite Ps 78:32
do not hold your peace or be **s**, O God! Ps 83:1
the sea; when its waves rise, you **s** them. Ps 89:9
They **s** bear fruit in old age; they are Ps 92:14
He made the storm be **s**, and the waves Ps 107:29
the sand. I awake, and I am **s** with you. Ps 139:18
to a wise man, and he will be **s** wiser; Prv 9:9
a fool; **s** less is false speech to a prince. Prv 17:7
wine—my heart **s** guiding me with Eccl 2:3
than the living who are **s** alive. Eccl 4:2
Why will you **s** be struck down? Why will Is 1:5
away, and his hand is stretched out **s**. Is 5:25
away, and his hand is stretched out **s**. Is 9:12
away, and his hand is stretched out **s**. Is 9:17
slice meat on the right, but are **s** hungry, Is 9:20
away, and his hand is stretched out **s**. Is 9:21
away, and his hand is stretched out **s**. Is 10:4
Be **s**, O inhabitants of the coast; the Is 23:2
I have called her "Rahab who sits **s**." Is 30:7
I have kept **s** and restrained myself; Is 42:14
"Therefore I **s** contend with you, declares Jer 2:9
the stain of your guilt is **s** before me, Jer 2:22
Why do we sit **s**? Gather together; let us Jer 8:14
against him, I do remember him **s**. Jer 31:20
while he was **s** shut up in the court of the Jer 33:1
Now Jeremiah was **s** going in and out Jer 37:4
into your scabbard; rest and be **s**! Jer 47:6
from the sword, go, do not stand **s**! Jer 51:50
When they stood **s**, they let down their Ezk 1:24
When they stood **s**, they let down their Ezk 1:25
you will see **s** greater abominations." Ezk 8:6
"You will see **s** greater abominations Ezk 8:13
You will see **s** greater abominations Ezk 8:15
and provoke me **s** further to anger? Ezk 8:17
When they stood **s**, these stood still, Ezk 10:17
When they stood still, these stood **s**, Ezk 10:17
them, and **s** you were not satisfied. Ezk 16:28
Will you **s** say, 'I am a god,' in the Ezk 28:9
'They have come down, they lie **s**, the Ezk 32:21
While the words were **s** in the king's Dn 4:31
and **s** more greatness was added to me. Dn 4:36
end, for it **s** awaits the appointed time. Dn 11:35
but Judah **s** walks with God and is Hos 11:12
"Is there **s** anyone with you?" he shall Am 6:10
For **s** the vision awaits its appointed Hab 2:3
sun and moon stood **s** in their place at Hab 3:11
rot while they are **s** standing on their Zec 14:12
While he was **s** speaking to the people, Mt 12:46
you also **s** without understanding? Mt 15:16
He was **s** speaking when, behold, a Mt 17:5
these I have kept. What do I **s** lack?" Mt 19:20
While he was **s** speaking, Judas came, Mt 26:47
that impostor said, while he was **s** alive, Mt 27:63
in the morning, while it was **s** dark, Mk 1:35
to you, and **s** more will be added to you. Mk 4:24
Be **s**!" And the wind ceased, and there Mk 4:39
are you so afraid? Have you **s** no faith?" Mk 4:40
While he was **s** speaking, there came Mk 5:35
He had **s** one other, a beloved son. Mk 12:6
"Are you **s** sleeping and taking your Mk 14:41
immediately, while he was **s** speaking, Mk 14:43
touched the bier, and the bearers stood **s**. Lk 7:14
While he was **s** speaking, someone from Lk 8:49
has been done, and **s** there is room.' Lk 14:22
But while he was **s** a long way off, Lk 15:20
he said to him, "One thing you **s** lack. Lk 18:22
While he was **s** speaking, there came a Lk 22:47
of about an hour **s** another insisted, Lk 22:59
immediately, while he was **s** speaking, Lk 22:60
he told you, while he was **s** in Galilee, Lk 24:6
other as you walk?" And they stood **s**, Lk 24:17
And while they **s** disbelieved for joy Lk 24:41
I spoke to you while I was **s** with you, Lk 24:44
but was **s** in the place where Martha Jn 11:30
them, they **s** did not believe in him, Jn 12:37
you so long, and you **s** do not know me, Jn 14:9
spoken to you while I am **s** with you. Jn 14:25
"I **s** have many things to say to you, but Jn 16:12
to the tomb early, while it was **s** dark, Jn 20:1
s breathing threats and murder against Acts 9:1
While Peter was **s** saying these Acts 10:44
a deep sleep as Paul talked **s** longer. Acts 20:9
why am I **s** being condemned as a Rom 3:7
faith while he was **s** uncircumcised. Rom 4:11
For while we were **s** weak, at the right Rom 5:6
for us in that while we were **s** sinners, Rom 5:8
How can we who died to sin **s** live in it? Rom 6:2
to me then, "Why does he **s** find fault? Rom 9:19
for you are **s** of the flesh. For while 1 Cor 3:3
We have become, and are **s**, like the 1 Cor 4:13
I am **s** entrusted with a stewardship. 1 Cor 9:17
show you a **s** more excellent way. 1 Cor 12:31
at one time, most of whom are **s** alive, 1 Cor 15:6
is futile and you are **s** in your sins. 1 Cor 15:17
For while we are **s** in this tent, we 2 Cor 5:4
zeal for me, so that I rejoiced **s** more. 2 Cor 7:7
we rejoiced **s** more at the joy of Titus, 2 Cor 7:13
If I were **s** trying to please man, I would Gal 1:10
And I was **s** unknown in person to the Gal 1:22
if I, brothers, **s** preach circumcision, Gal 5:11
why am I **s** being persecuted? Gal 5:11
saw I had and now hear that I **s** have. Phil 1:30
why, as if you were **s** alive in the world, Col 2:20
that when I was **s** with you I told 2 Thes 2:5
the promise of entering his rest **s** stands, Heb 4:1
sake in serving the saints, as you **s** do. Heb 6:10
for he was **s** in the loins of his ancestor Heb 7:10
as long as the first section is **s** standing Heb 9:8
his faith, though he died, he **s** speaks. Heb 11:4
and hates his brother is **s** in darkness. 1 Jn 2:9
Yet you have **s** a few names in Sardis, Rv 3:4
passed; behold, two woes are **s** to come. Rv 9:12
Let the evildoer **s** do evil, and the filthy Rv 22:11
still do evil, and the filthy **s** be filthy, Rv 22:11
be filthy, and the righteous **s** do right, Rv 22:11
still do right, and the holy **s** be holy." Rv 22:11

STILLBORN (3)
Or why was I not as a hidden **s** child, as Jb 3:16
like the **s** child who never sees the sun. Ps 58:8
I say that a **s** child is better off than he. Eccl 6:3

STILLED (3)
By his power he **s** the sea; by his Jb 26:12
The mirth of the tambourines is **s**, the Is 24:8
has ceased, the mirth of the lyre is **s**. Is 24:8

STILLING (1)
Babylon waste and **s** her mighty voice. Jer 51:55

STILLS (1)
who **s** the roaring of the seas, the roaring Ps 65:7

STING (3)
plagues? O Sheol, where is your **s**? Hos 13:14
victory? O death, where is your **s**?" 1 Cor 15:55
The **s** of death is sin, and the power 1 Cor 15:56

STINGS (3)
bites like a serpent and **s** like an adder. Prv 23:32
torment of a scorpion when it **s** someone. Rv 9:5
They have tails and **s** like scorpions, and Rv 9:10

STINGY (2)
Do not eat the bread of a man who is **s**; Prv 23:6
A **s** man hastens after wealth and does Prv 28:22

STINK (6)
me by making me **s** to the inhabitants Gn 34:30
you have made us **s** in the sight of Ex 5:21
in the Nile shall die, and the Nile will **s**, Ex 7:18
commanded them, and it did not **s**, Ex 16:24
My wounds **s** and fester because of my Ps 38:5
their fish **s** for lack of water and die of Is 50:2

STIR (22)
LORD began to **s** him in Mahaneh-dan, Jgs 13:25
one is so fierce that he dares to **s** him up. Jb 41:10
They **s** up strife, they lurk; they watch Ps 56:6
my life; fierce men **s** up strife against me. Ps 59:3
often and did not **s** up all his wrath. Ps 78:38
s up your might and come to save us! Ps 80:2
their heart and **s** up wars continually. Ps 140:2
that you not **s** up or awaken love until it Sg 2:7
that you not **s** up or awaken love until it Sg 3:5
that you not **s** up or awaken love until it Sg 8:4
And I will **s** up Egyptians against Is 19:2
I will **s** up the spirit of a destroyer against Jer 51:1
I will **s** up against you your lovers Ezk 23:22
he shall **s** up all against the kingdom of Dn 11:2
And he shall **s** up his power and his Dn 11:25
oven whose baker ceases to **s** the fire, Hos 7:4

I will **s** them up from the place to which Jl 3:7
Consecrate for war; **s** up the mighty men. Jl 3:9
Let the nations **s** themselves up and come Jl 3:12
I will **s** up your sons, O Zion, against Zec 9:13
us consider how to **s** up one another Heb 10:24
body, to **s** you up by way of reminder, 2 Pt 1:13

STIRRED (29)
they came, everyone whose heart **s** him, Ex 35:21
the women whose hearts **s** them to use Ex 35:26
everyone whose heart **s** him up to come Ex 36:2
They **s** him to jealousy with strange Dt 32:16
the whole town was **s** because of them. Ru 1:19
that my son has **s** up my servant 1 Sm 22:8
the LORD who has **s** you up against 1 Sm 26:19
So the God of Israel **s** up the spirit of 1 Chr 5:26
And the LORD **s** up against Jehoram 2 Chr 21:16
the LORD **s** up the spirit of Cyrus 2 Chr 36:22
the LORD **s** up the spirit of Cyrus king of Ezr 1:1
whose spirit God had **s** to go up to Ezr 1:5
and that sedition was **s** up in it from of Ezr 4:15
Sheol beneath is **s** up to meet you when Is 14:9
Who **s** up one from the east whom Is 41:2
I **s** up one from the north, and he has Is 41:25
I have **s** him up in righteousness, and I Is 45:13
The LORD has **s** up the spirit of the Jer 51:11
And the LORD **s** up the spirit of Hg 1:14
Jerusalem, the whole city was **s** up, Mt 21:10
But the chief priests **s** up the crowd to Mk 15:11
me into the pool when the water is **s** up, Jn 5:7
And they **s** up the people and the elders Acts 6:12
s up persecution against Paul and Acts 13:50
the unbelieving Jews **s** up the Gentiles Acts 14:2
s up the whole crowd and laid hands Acts 21:27
Then all the city was **s** up, and the Acts 21:30
who recently **s** up a revolt and led the Acts 21:38
And your zeal has **s** up most of them. 2 Cor 9:2

STIRRING (11)
and they are **s** up the city against you. Jgs 9:31
I am **s** up the Medes against them, Is 13:17
The **s** of your inner parts and your Is 63:15
a great nation is **s** from the farthest parts Jer 6:22
a great tempest is **s** from the farthest Jer 25:32
I am **s** up and bringing against Babylon Jer 50:9
and many kings are **s** from the farthest Jer 50:41
winds of heaven were **s** up the great sea. Dn 7:2
too, agitating and **s** up the crowds. Acts 17:13
with anyone or **s** up a crowd, Acts 24:12
of them I am **s** up your sincere mind 2 Pt 3:1

STIRS (16)
Like an eagle that **s** up its nest, that Dt 32:11
and the innocent **s** himself up against Jb 17:8
Hatred **s** up strife, but love covers all Prv 10:12
wrath, but a harsh word **s** up anger. Prv 15:1
A hot-tempered man **s** up strife, but he Prv 15:18
A greedy man **s** up strife, but the one Prv 28:25
A man of wrath **s** up strife, and one Prv 29:22
Rezin against him, and **s** up his enemies. Is 9:11
man, like a man of war he **s** up his zeal; Is 42:13
who **s** up the sea so that its waves roar— Is 51:15
If anyone **s** up strife, it is not from me; Is 54:15
whoever **s** up strife with you shall fall Is 54:15
who **s** up the sea so that its waves roar— Jer 31:35
were urgent, saying, "He **s** up the people, Lk 23:5
one who **s** up riots among all the Jews Acts 24:5
As for a person who **s** up division, after Ti 3:10

STOCK (1)
the **s** that your right hand planted, and Ps 80:15

STOCKS (7)
seer and put him in the **s** in prison, 2 Chr 16:10
put my feet in the **s** and watch all my Jb 13:27
puts my feet in the **s** and watches all my Jb 33:11
and put him in the **s** that were in the Jer 20:2
Pashhur released Jeremiah from the **s**, Jer 20:3
to put him in the **s** and neck irons. Jer 29:26
prison and fastened their feet in the **s**. Acts 16:24

STOIC (1)
Epicurean and **S** philosophers also Acts 17:18

STOLE (6)
and Rachel **s** her father's household Gn 31:19
So Absalom **s** the hearts of the men of 2 Sm 15:6
And the people **s** into the city that day 2 Sm 19:3
son of Ahaziah and **s** him away from 2 Kgs 11:2
of Ahaziah and **s** him away from 2 Chr 22:11
came by night and **s** him away while Mt 28:13

STOLEN (12)
if found with me, shall be counted **s**." Gn 30:33
did not know that Rachel had **s** them. Gn 31:32
it, whether **s** by day or stolen by night. Gn 31:39
it, whether stolen by day or **s** by night. Gn 31:39
For I was indeed **s** out of the land of the Gn 40:15
If the **s** beast is found alive in his Ex 22:4
safe, and it is **s** from the man's house, Ex 22:7
But if it is **s** from him, he shall make Ex 22:12
they have **s** and lied and put them Jos 7:11
the men of Judah **s** you away and 2 Sm 19:41
who had **s** them from the public 2 Sm 21:12
"**S** water is sweet, and bread eaten in Prv 9:17

STOMACH (20)
shoulder and the two cheeks and the **s**. Dt 18:3
struck him in the **s** with the butt of 2 Sm 2:23
and there he struck him in the **s**, 2 Sm 3:27
wheat, and they stabbed him in the **s**. 2 Sm 4:6
with it in the **s** and spilled his 2 Sm 20:10
yet his food is turned in his **s**; it is the Jb 20:14
of a man's mouth his **s** is satisfied; Prv 18:20
but the full **s** of the rich will not let Eccl 5:12
with his hands on his **s** like a woman in Jer 30:6
he has filled his **s** with my delicacies; Jer 51:34
LORD, for I am in distress; my **s** churns; Lam 1:20
are spent with weeping; my **s** churns; Lam 2:11
give you and fill your **s** with it." Then I Ezk 3:3
mouth passes into the **s** and is expelled? Mt 15:17
since it enters not his heart but his **s**, Mk 7:19
is meant for the **s** and the stomach 1 Cor 6:13
the stomach and the **s** for food"—and 1 Cor 6:13
the sake of your **s** and your frequent 1 Tm 5:23
it will make your **s** bitter, but in your Rv 10:9
I had eaten it my **s** was made bitter. Rv 10:10

STOMACHS (1)
their hunger or fill their **s** with it. Ezk 7:19

STONE (188)
is good; bdellium and onyx **s** are there. Gn 2:12
thoroughly." And they had brick for **s**, Gn 11:3
morning Jacob took the **s** that he had Gn 28:18
and this **s**, which I have set up for a Gn 28:22
The **s** on the well's mouth was large, Gn 29:2
would roll the **s** from the mouth Gn 29:3
and put the **s** back in its place over the Gn 29:3
together and the **s** is rolled from Gn 29:8
near and rolled the **s** from the well's Gn 29:10
So Jacob took a **s** and set it up as a Gn 31:45
he had spoken with him, a pillar of **s**. Gn 35:14
there is the Shepherd, the **S** of Israel), Gn 49:24
in vessels of wood and in vessels of **s**.'" Ex 7:19
before their eyes, will they not **s** us? Ex 8:26
they went down into the depths like a **s**. Ex 15:5
of your arm, they are still as a **s**, Ex 15:16
people? They are almost ready to **s** me." Ex 17:4
so they took a **s** and put it under him, Ex 17:12
If you make me an altar of **s**, you shall Ex 20:25
strikes the other with a **s** or with his fist Ex 21:18
feet as it were a pavement of sapphire **s**, Ex 24:10
that I may give you the tablets of **s**, Ex 24:12
six of their names on the one **s**, and the Ex 28:10
of the remaining six on the other **s**, Ex 28:10
two tablets of the testimony, tablets of **s**, Ex 31:18
for yourself two tablets of **s** like the first, Ex 34:1
Moses cut two tablets of **s** like the first. Ex 34:4
and took in his hand two tablets of **s**. Ex 34:4
of the land shall **s** him with stones. Lv 20:2
and let all the congregation **s** him. Lv 24:14
death. All the congregation shall **s** him. Lv 24:16
not set up a figured **s** in your land to bow Lv 26:1
congregation said to **s** them with Nm 14:10
the congregation shall **s** him with Nm 15:35
him down with a **s** tool that could Nm 35:17
or used a **s** that could cause death, Nm 35:23
and he wrote them on two tablets of **s**. Dt 4:13
there you will serve gods of wood and **s**, Dt 4:28
on two tablets of **s** and gave them to Dt 5:22
up the mountain to receive the tablets of **s**, Dt 9:9
the two tablets of **s** written with the Dt 9:10
the LORD gave me the two tablets of **s**, Dt 9:11
for yourself two tablets of **s** like the first, Dt 10:1
and cut two tablets of **s** like the first, Dt 10:3
You shall **s** him to death with stones, Dt 13:10
and you shall **s** that man or woman to Dt 17:5
of the city shall **s** him to death with Dt 21:21
men of her city shall **s** her to death with Dt 22:21
and you shall **s** them to death with Dt 22:24
shall serve other gods of wood and **s**. Dt 28:36
shall serve other gods of wood and **s**, Dt 28:64
things, their idols of wood and **s**, Dt 29:17
up each of you a **s** upon his shoulder, Jos 4:5
goes up to the **s** of Bohan the son Jos 15:6
it goes down to the **s** of Bohan the son Jos 18:17
And he took a large **s** and set it up there Jos 24:26
this **s** shall be a witness against us, Jos 24:27
sons of Jerubbaal, seventy men, on one **s**. Jgs 9:5
killed his sons, seventy men on one **s**, Jgs 9:18
every one could sling a **s** at a hair and Jgs 20:16
and stopped there. A great **s** was there. 1 Sm 6:14
figures, and set them upon the great **s** 1 Sm 6:15
The great **s** beside which they set 1 Sm 6:18
Then Samuel took a **s** and set it up 1 Sm 7:12
roll a great **s** to me here." 1 Sm 14:33
and took out a **s** and slung it and 1 Sm 17:49
The **s** sank into his forehead, and he 1 Sm 17:49
Philistine with a sling and with a **s**, 1 Sm 17:50
hand, and remain beside the **s** heap. 1 Sm 20:19
rose from beside the **s** heap and fell 1 Sm 20:41
within him, and he became as a **s**. 1 Sm 25:37
of gold, and in it was a precious **s**, 2 Sm 12:30
were at the great **s** that is in Gibeon, 2 Sm 20:8
and fattened cattle by the Serpent's **S**, 1 Kgs 1:9
the timber and the **s** to build the 1 Kgs 5:18
it was with **s** prepared at the quarry, 1 Kgs 6:7
flowers. All was cedar; no **s** was seen. 1 Kgs 6:18
three courses of cut **s** and one course 1 Kgs 6:36
had three courses of cut **s** all around, 1 Kgs 7:12
the two tablets of **s** that Moses put 1 Kgs 8:9
silver as common in Jerusalem as **s**, 1 Kgs 10:27
take him out and **s** him to death." 1 Kgs 21:10
every man threw a **s** until it was 2 Kgs 3:25
timber and quarried **s** for making 2 Kgs 12:12
under it and put it on a **s** pedestal. 2 Kgs 16:17
work of men's hands, wood and **s**. 2 Kgs 19:18
timber and quarried **s** to repair the 2 Kgs 22:6
of gold, and in it was a precious **s**. 1 Chr 20:2
it; timber and **s**, too, I have provided. 1 Chr 22:14
gold as common in Jerusalem as **s**, 2 Chr 1:15
gold, silver, bronze, iron, **s**, and wood, 2 Chr 2:14
silver as common in Jerusalem as **s**, 2 Chr 9:27
and the builders to buy quarried **s**, 2 Chr 34:11
on it he will break down their **s** wall!" Neh 4:3
the depths, as a **s** into mighty waters. Neh 9:11
His roots entwine the **s** heap; he looks Jb 8:17
The waters become hard like **s**, and the Jb 38:30
His heart is hard as a **s**, hard as the Jb 41:24
up, lest you strike your foot against a **s**. Ps 91:12
The **s** that the builders rejected has Ps 118:22
bribe is like a magic **s** in the eyes of the Prv 17:8
and its **s** wall was broken down. Prv 24:31
Like one who binds the **s** in the sling is Prv 26:8
and a **s** will come back on him who Prv 26:27
A **s** is heavy, and sand is weighty, but a Prv 27:3
like the tower of David, built in rows of **s**; Sg 4:4
a sanctuary and a **s** of offense and a Is 8:14
has laid as a foundation in Zion, a **s**, Is 28:16
a foundation in Zion, a stone, a tested **s**, Is 28:16
the work of men's hands, wood and **s**. Is 37:19
to a tree, 'You are my father,' and to a **s**, Jer 2:27
committing adultery with **s** and tree. Jer 3:9
No **s** shall be taken from you for a Jer 51:26
for a corner and no **s** for a foundation, Jer 51:26
tie a **s** to it and cast it into the midst of Jer 51:63
remove the heart of **s** from their flesh Ezk 11:19
and they shall **s** you and cut you to Ezk 16:40
countries, and worship wood and **s**.' Ezk 20:32
And the host shall **s** them and cut Ezk 23:47
every precious **s** was your covering, Ezk 28:13
remove the heart of **s** from your flesh Ezk 36:26
four tables of hewn **s** for the burnt Ezk 40:42
a **s** was cut out by no human hand, Dn 2:34
But the **s** that struck the image became Dn 2:35
as you saw that a **s** was cut from a Dn 2:45
gold and silver, bronze, iron, wood, and **s**. Dn 5:4
and gold, of bronze, iron, wood, and **s**, Dn 5:23
And a **s** was brought and laid on the Dn 6:17
altars also are like **s** heaps on the Hos 12:11
him, you have built houses of hewn **s**, Am 5:11
For the **s** will cry out from the wall, Hab 2:11
thing, Awake; to a silent **s**, Arise! Hab 2:19
Before **s** was placed upon stone in the Hg 2:15
stone was placed upon **s** in the temple of Hg 2:15
on the **s** that I have set before Joshua, Zec 3:9
Joshua, on a single **s** with seven eyes, Zec 3:9
bring forward the top **s** amid shouts of Zec 4:7
make Jerusalem a heavy **s** for all the Zec 12:3
up, lest you strike your foot against a **s**.'" Mt 4:6
son asks him for bread, will give him a **s**? Mt 7:9
"'The **s** that the builders rejected has Mt 21:42
who falls on this **s** will be broken to Mt 21:44
be left here one **s** upon another that will Mt 24:2
he rolled a great **s** to the entrance of Mt 27:60
secure by sealing the **s** and setting a Mt 27:66
came and rolled back the **s** and sat on it. Mt 28:2
"'The **s** that the builders rejected has Mk 12:10
be left here one **s** upon another that will Mk 13:2
And he rolled a **s** against the entrance Mk 15:46
will roll away the **s** for us from the Mk 16:3
they saw that the **s** had been rolled Mk 16:4
God, command this **s** to become bread." Lk 4:3
up, lest you strike your foot against a **s**.'" Lk 4:11
will not leave one **s** upon another in Lk 19:44
man,' all the people will **s** us to death, Lk 20:6
"'The **s** that the builders rejected has Lk 20:17
who falls on that **s** will be broken to Lk 20:18
be left here one **s** upon another that will Lk 21:6
and laid him in a tomb cut in **s**, Lk 23:53
And they found the **s** rolled away from Lk 24:2

Now there were six **s** water jars there for Jn 2:6
Moses commanded us to **s** such women. Jn 8:5
among you be the first to throw a **s** at her." Jn 8:7
Jews picked up stones again to **s** him. Jn 10:31
which of them are you going to **s** me?" Jn 10:32
we are going to **s** you but for Jn 10:33
the Jews were just now seeking to **s** you, Jn 11:8
It was a cave, and a **s** lay against it. Jn 11:38
Jesus said, "Take away the **s**." Martha, Jn 11:39
So they took away the **s**. And Jesus lifted Jn 11:41
seat at a place called The **S** Pavement, Jn 19:13
and saw that the **s** had been taken away Jn 20:1
This Jesus is the **s** that was rejected by Acts 4:11
rulers, to mistreat them and to **s** them, Acts 14:5
divine being is like gold or silver or **s**, Acts 17:29
and of the sacred **s** that fell from the Acts 19:35
have stumbled over the stumbling **s**, Rom 9:32
I am laying in Zion a **s** of stumbling, Rom 9:33
not on tablets of **s** but on tablets of 2 Cor 3:3
of death, carved in letters on **s**, 2 Cor 3:7
a living **s** rejected by men but in the 1 Pt 2:4
"Behold, I am laying in Zion a **s**, a 1 Pt 2:6
"The **s** that the builders rejected has 1 Pt 2:7
and "A **s** of stumbling, and a rock of 1 Pt 2:8
manna, and I will give him a white **s**, Rv 2:17
name written on the **s** that no one knows Rv 2:17
and silver and bronze and **s** and wood, Rv 9:20
angel took up a **s** like a great millstone Rv 18:21

STONE'S (1)
withdrew from them about a **s** throw, Lk 22:41

STONECUTTERS (4)
burden-bearers and 80,000 **s** in the 1 Kgs 5:15
and to the masons and the **s**, as well 2 Kgs 12:12
and he set **s** to prepare dressed stones 1 Chr 22:2
s, masons, carpenters, and all kinds 1 Chr 22:15

STONED (22)
touch him, but he shall be **s** or shot; Ex 19:13
or a woman to death, the ox shall be **s**, Ex 21:28
a man or a woman, the ox shall be **s**, Ex 21:29
shekels of silver, and the ox shall be **s**. Ex 21:32
They shall be **s** with stones; their blood Lv 20:27
who had cursed and **s** him with stones. Lv 24:23
outside the camp and **s** him to death Nm 15:36
today." And all Israel **s** him with stones. Jos 7:25
them with fire and **s** them with stones. Jos 7:25
and all Israel **s** him to death with 1 Kgs 12:18
outside the city and **s** him to death 1 Kgs 21:13
Jezebel, saying, "Naboth has been **s**; 1 Kgs 21:14
Naboth had been **s** and was dead, 1 Kgs 21:15
the people of Israel **s** him to death 2 Chr 10:18
of the king they **s** him with stones 2 Chr 24:21
beat one, killed another, and **s** another. Mt 21:35
were afraid of being **s** by the people. Acts 5:26
cast him out of the city and **s** him. Acts 7:58
they **s** Paul and dragged him out of Acts 14:19
I was beaten with rods. Once I was **s**. 2 Cor 11:25
They were **s**, they were sawn in two, Heb 11:37
touches the mountain, it shall be **s**." Heb 12:20

STONES (152)
Taking one of the **s** of the place, he put Gn 28:11
"Gather **s**." And they took stones and Gn 31:46
stones." And they took **s** and made a Gn 31:46
stone, you shall not build it of hewn **s**, Ex 20:25
onyx **s**, and stones for setting, for the Ex 25:7
onyx stones, and **s** for setting, for the Ex 25:7
You shall take two onyx **s**, and engrave Ex 28:9
you engrave the two **s** with the names Ex 28:11
shall set the two **s** on the shoulder Ex 28:12
as **s** of remembrance for the sons of Ex 28:12
You shall set in it four rows of **s**. A row Ex 28:17
shall be twelve **s** with their names Ex 28:21
in cutting **s** for setting, and in carving Ex 31:5
and onyx **s** and stones for setting, for the Ex 35:9
and onyx stones and **s** for setting, for the Ex 35:9
leaders brought onyx **s** and stones to Ex 35:27
brought onyx stones and **s** to be set, Ex 35:27
in cutting **s** for setting, and in carving Ex 35:33
They made the onyx **s**, enclosed in Ex 39:6
the ephod to be **s** of remembrance for the Ex 39:7
And they set in it four rows of **s**. A row Ex 39:10
There were twelve **s** with their names Ex 39:14
that they take out the **s** in which is the Lv 14:40
they shall take other **s** and put them in Lv 14:42
and put them in the place of those **s**, Lv 14:42
has taken out the **s** and scraped the Lv 14:43
its **s** and timber and all the plaster of Lv 14:45
people of the land shall stone him with **s**. Lv 20:2
They shall be stoned with **s**; their blood Lv 20:27
who had cursed and stoned him with **s**. Lv 24:23
said to stone them with **s**. Nm 14:10
stone him with **s** outside the camp." Nm 15:35
camp and stoned him to death with **s**, Nm 15:36
all their figured **s** and destroy all Nm 33:52
will lack nothing, a land whose **s** are iron, Dt 8:9
You shall stone him to death with **s**, Dt 13:10
that man or woman to death with **s**. Dt 17:5
the city shall stone him to death with **s**. Dt 21:21
her city shall stone her to death with **s**, Dt 22:21
you shall stone them to death with **s**, Dt 22:24
shall set up large **s** and plaster them with Dt 27:2
over the Jordan, you shall set up these **s**, Dt 27:4
altar to the LORD your God, an altar of **s**. Dt 27:5
an altar to the LORD your God of uncut **s**. Dt 27:6
you shall write on the **s** all the words of Dt 27:8
'Take twelve **s** from here out of the midst Jos 4:3
to come, 'What do those **s** mean to you?' Jos 4:6
So these **s** shall be to the people of Israel a Jos 4:7
and took up twelve **s** out of the midst Jos 4:8
And Joshua set up twelve **s** in the midst of Jos 4:9
And those twelve **s**, which they took out Jos 4:20
times to come, 'What do these **s** mean?' Jos 4:21
today." And all Israel stoned him with **s**. Jos 7:25
them with fire and stoned them with **s**. Jos 7:25
a great heap of **s** that remains to this Jos 7:26
city and raised over it a great heap of **s**, Jos 8:29
of the Law of Moses, "an altar of uncut **s**, Jos 8:31
he wrote on the **s** a copy of the law of Jos 8:32
threw down large **s** from heaven on Jos 10:11
"Roll large **s** against the mouth of the Jos 10:18
and they set large **s** against the mouth Jos 10:27
stronghold here, with **s** laid in due order. Jgs 6:26
chose five smooth **s** from the brook 1 Sm 17:40
And he threw **s** at David and at all the 2 Sm 16:6
he went and threw **s** at him and 2 Sm 16:13
over him a very great heap of **s**. 2 Sm 18:17
costly **s** in order to lay the foundation 1 Kgs 5:17
of the house with dressed **s**. 1 Kgs 5:17
All these were made of costly **s**, cut 1 Kgs 7:9
The foundation was of costly **s**, huge 1 Kgs 7:10
was of costly stones, huge **s**, 1 Kgs 7:10
huge stones, **s** of eight and ten cubits. 1 Kgs 7:10
And above were costly **s**, cut 1 Kgs 7:11
and very much gold and precious **s**. 1 Kgs 10:2
quantity of spices and precious **s**. 1 Kgs 10:10
of almug wood and precious **s**. 1 Kgs 10:11
all Israel stoned him to death with **s**. 1 Kgs 12:18
carried away the **s** of Ramah and 1 Kgs 15:22
Elijah took twelve **s**, according to 1 Kgs 18:31
and with the **s** he built an altar in 1 Kgs 18:32
and the wood and the **s** and the dust, 1 Kgs 18:38
a cake baked on hot **s** and a jar of 1 Kgs 19:6
city and stoned him to death with **s**. 1 Kgs 21:13
ruin every good piece of land with **s**." 2 Kgs 3:19
till only its **s** were left in Kir-hareseth, 2 Kgs 3:25
arrows and sling **s** with either the 1 Chr 12:2
to prepare dressed **s** for building the 1 Chr 22:2
quantities of onyx and **s** for setting, 1 Chr 29:2
for setting, antimony, colored **s**, 1 Chr 29:2
all sorts of precious **s** and marble. 1 Chr 29:2
whoever had precious **s** gave them to 1 Chr 29:8
the house with settings of precious **s**. 2 Chr 3:6
and very much gold and precious **s**. 2 Chr 9:1
quantity of spices, and precious **s**. 2 Chr 9:9
brought algum wood and precious **s**. 2 Chr 9:10
of Israel stoned him to death with **s**. 2 Chr 10:18
carried away the **s** of Ramah and 2 Chr 16:6
they stoned him with **s** in the court 2 Chr 24:21
of mail, bows, and **s** for slinging. 2 Chr 26:14
corners, to shoot arrows and great **s**. 2 Chr 26:15
for silver, for gold, for precious **s**, 2 Chr 32:27
It is being built with huge **s**, and timber Ezr 5:8
three layers of great **s** and one layer of Ezr 6:4
Will they revive the **s** out of the heaps of Neh 4:2
marble, mother-of-pearl and precious **s**. Est 1:6
shall be in league with the **s** of the field, Jb 5:23
Is my strength the strength of **s**, or is my Jb 6:12
stone heap; he looks upon a house of **s**. Jb 8:17
the waters wear away the **s**; the torrents Jb 14:19
of Ophir among the **s** of the torrent bed, Jb 22:24
Its **s** are the place of sapphires, and it has Jb 28:6
for him sling **s** are turned to stubble. Jb 41:28
your servants hold her **s** dear and have Ps 102:14
is gold and abundance of costly **s**, Prv 20:15
a time to cast away **s**, and a time to Eccl 3:5
stones, and a time to gather **s** together; Eccl 3:5
He who quarries **s** is hurt by them, and Eccl 10:9
He dug it and cleared it of **s**, and planted it Is 5:2
fallen, but we will build with dressed **s**; Is 9:10
sword, who go down to the **s** of the pit, Is 14:19
when he makes all the **s** of the altars like Is 27:9
behold, I will set your **s** in antimony, Is 54:11
and all your wall of precious **s**. Is 54:12
Among the smooth **s** of the valley is your Is 57:6
instead of wood, bronze, instead of **s**, Is 60:17
up, build up the highway; clear it of **s**; Is 62:10
in your hands large **s** and hide them in Jer 43:9
his throne above these **s** that I have Jer 43:10
has blocked my ways with blocks of **s**; Lam 3:9
me alive into the pit and cast **s** on me; Lam 3:53
The holy **s** lie scattered at the head of Lam 4:1
Your **s** and timber and soil they will Ezk 26:12
of spices and all precious **s** and gold. Ezk 27:22
in the midst of the **s** of fire you walked. Ezk 28:14
cherub, from the midst of the **s** of fire. Ezk 28:16
silver, with precious **s** and costly gifts. Dn 11:38
I will pour down her **s** into the valley and Mi 1:6
and consume it, both timber and **s**." Zec 5:4
devour, and tread down the sling **s**, Zec 9:15
is able from these **s** to raise up children Mt 3:9
command these **s** to become loaves of Mt 4:3
kills the prophets and **s** those who are Mt 23:37
crying out and bruising himself with **s**. Mk 5:5
what wonderful **s** and what wonderful Mk 13:1
is able from these **s** to raise up children Lk 3:8
kills the prophets and **s** those who are Lk 13:34
were silent, the very **s** would cry out." Lk 19:40
was adorned with noble **s** and offerings, Lk 21:5
So they picked up **s** to throw at him, but Jn 8:59
The Jews picked up **s** again to stone Jn 10:31
with gold, silver, precious **s**, 1 Cor 3:12
yourselves like living **s** are being built 1 Pt 2:5

STONING (2)
for the people spoke of **s** him, 1 Sm 30:6
And as they were **s** Stephen, he called Acts 7:59

STOOD (253)
And he **s** by them under the tree while Gn 18:8
but Abraham still **s** before the LORD. Gn 18:22
place where he had **s** before the LORD. Gn 19:27
behold, the LORD **s** above it and said, Gn 28:13
behold, my sheaf arose and **s** upright. Gn 37:7
and **s** by the other cows on the bank of Gn 41:3
down to Egypt and **s** before Joseph. Gn 43:15
himself before all those who **s** by him. Gn 45:1
his father and **s** him before Pharaoh, Gn 47:7
And his sister **s** at a distance to know Ex 2:4
away, but Moses **s** up and saved them, Ex 2:17
soot from the kiln and **s** before Pharaoh. Ex 9:10
from before them and **s** behind them, Ex 14:19
waters piled up; the floods **s** up in a heap; Ex 15:8
and the people **s** around Moses from Ex 18:13
afraid and trembled, and they **s** far off Ex 20:18
The people **s** far off, while Moses drew Ex 20:21
then Moses **s** in the gate of the camp Ex 32:26
in the cloud and **s** with him there, Ex 34:5
drew near and **s** before the LORD. Lv 9:5
pillar of cloud and **s** at the entrance of Nm 12:5
incense on them and **s** at the entrance Nm 16:18
Abiram came out and **s** at the door of Nm 16:27
And he **s** between the dead and the Nm 16:48
angel of the LORD **s** in a narrow path Nm 22:24
LORD went ahead and **s** in a narrow Nm 22:26
not know that you **s** in the road Nm 22:34
And they **s** before Moses and before Nm 27:2
the day that you **s** before the LORD your Dt 4:10
And you came near and **s** at the foot of Dt 4:11
while I **s** between the LORD and you at that Dt 5:5
the pillar of cloud **s** over the entrance of Dt 31:15
coming down from above **s** and rose up Jos 3:16
covenant of the LORD **s** firmly on dry Jos 3:17
very place where the priests' feet **s** firmly, Jos 4:3
bearing the ark of the covenant had **s**; Jos 4:9
priests bearing the ark **s** in the midst of Jos 4:10
and they **s** in awe of him just as they had Jos 4:14
him just as they had **s** in awe of Moses, Jos 4:14
s on opposite sides of the ark before the Jos 8:33
And the sun **s** still, and the moon Jos 10:13
of the cities that **s** on mounds did Israel Jos 11:13
until he has **s** before the congregation Jos 20:6
blood, till he **s** before the congregation. Jos 20:9
But Joash said to all who **s** against him, Jgs 6:31
Every man **s** in his place around the Jgs 7:21
he went and **s** on top of Mount Gerizim Jgs 9:7
of Ebed went out and **s** in the entrance of Jgs 9:35
rushed forward and **s** at the entrance Jgs 9:44
of war, **s** by the entrance of the gate. Jgs 18:16
while the priest **s** by the entrance of the Jgs 18:17
And the LORD came and **s**, calling as 1 Sm 3:10
And when he **s** among the people, 1 Sm 10:23
And the Philistines **s** on the 1 Sm 17:3
and Israel **s** on the mountain on the 1 Sm 17:3
He **s** and shouted to the ranks of 1 Sm 17:8
David said to the men who **s** by him, 1 Sm 17:26
David ran and **s** over the Philistine 1 Sm 17:51
success, he **s** in fearful awe of him. 1 Sm 18:15
said to his servants who **s** about him, 1 Sm 22:7
who **s** by the servants of Saul, 1 Sm 22:9
said to the guard who **s** about him, 1 Sm 22:17
to the other side and **s** far off on the 1 Sm 26:13
So I **s** beside him and killed him, 2 Sm 1:10
Asahel had fallen and died, **s** still. 2 Sm 2:23
the elders of his house **s** beside him, 2 Sm 12:17
will do." So the king **s** at the side of the 2 Sm 18:4

you yourself would have **s** aloof." 2 Sm 18:13
here." So he turned aside and **s** still. 2 Sm 18:30
the city, and it **s** against the rampart, 2 Sm 20:15
king's presence and **s** before the king. 1 Kgs 1:28
to Jerusalem and **s** before the ark 1 Kgs 3:15
came to the king and **s** before him. 1 Kgs 3:16
and they **s** in awe of the king, 1 Kgs 3:28
It **s** on twelve oxen, three facing 1 Kgs 7:25
while all the assembly of Israel **s**. 1 Kgs 8:14
Then Solomon **s** before the altar of 1 Kgs 8:22
And he **s** and blessed all the assembly 1 Kgs 8:55
while twelve lions **s** there, one on 1 Kgs 10:20
who had **s** before Solomon his father 1 Kgs 12:6
grown up with him and **s** before him. 1 Kgs 12:8
the road, and the donkey **s** beside it; 1 Kgs 13:24
it; the lion also **s** beside the body. 1 Kgs 13:24
and went out and **s** at the entrance 1 Kgs 19:13
came forward and **s** before the LORD, 1 Kgs 22:21
also went and **s** at some distance 2 Kgs 2:7
and went back and **s** on the bank of 2 Kgs 2:13
he had called her, she **s** before him. 2 Kgs 4:12
had called her, she **s** in the doorway. 2 Kgs 4:15
horses and chariots and **s** at the door 2 Kgs 5:9
and he came and **s** before him. 2 Kgs 5:15
He went in and **s** before his master, 2 Kgs 5:25
When he came and **s** before him, he 2 Kgs 8:9
out, he **s** and said to all the people, 2 Kgs 10:9
And the guards **s**, every man with 2 Kgs 11:11
Elisha, he revived and **s** on his feet. 2 Kgs 13:21
they came and **s** by the conduit of 2 Kgs 18:17
Then the Rabshakeh **s** and called 2 Kgs 18:28
And the king **s** by the pillar and 2 Kgs 23:3
Asaph, who **s** on his right hand, 1 Chr 6:39
Then Satan **s** against Israel and 1 Chr 21:1
The cherubim **s** on their feet, facing 2 Chr 3:13
It **s** on twelve oxen, three facing north, 2 Chr 4:4
s east of the altar with 120 priests 2 Chr 5:12
while all the assembly of Israel **s**. 2 Chr 6:3
Then Solomon **s** before the altar of 2 Chr 6:12
had set it in the court, and he **s** on it. 2 Chr 6:13
The priests **s** at their posts; the Levites 2 Chr 7:6
sounded trumpets, and all Israel **s**. 2 Chr 7:6
while twelve lions **s** there, one on 2 Chr 9:19
who had **s** before Solomon his father 2 Chr 10:6
grown up with him and **s** before him. 2 Chr 10:8
Then Abijah **s** up on Mount 2 Chr 13:4
came forward and **s** before the LORD, 2 Chr 18:20
And Jehoshaphat **s** in the assembly 2 Chr 20:5
Meanwhile all Judah **s** before the 2 Chr 20:13
Korahites, **s** up to praise the LORD, 2 Chr 20:19
went out, Jehoshaphat **s** and said, 2 Chr 20:20
the priest, and he **s** above the people, 2 Chr 24:20
s up against those who were coming 2 Chr 28:12
The Levites **s** with the instruments 2 Chr 29:26
the incense altars that **s** above them. 2 Chr 34:4
And the king **s** in his place and 2 Chr 34:31
for, the priests **s** in their place, 2 Chr 35:10
And Ezra the priest **s** up and said to Ezr 10:10
And the leaders **s** behind the whole Neh 4:16
And Ezra the scribe **s** on a wooden Neh 8:4
And beside him **s** Mattithiah, Shema, Neh 8:4
and as he opened it all the people **s**. Neh 8:5
all foreigners and **s** and confessed their Neh 9:2
And they **s** up in their place and read Neh 9:3
On the stairs of the Levites **s** Jeshua, Neh 9:4
and their brothers **s** opposite them in Neh 12:9
their brothers who **s** opposite them, Neh 12:24
those who gave thanks **s** in the house Neh 12:40
her royal robes and **s** in the inner court Est 5:1
Esther rose and **s** before the king. And Est 8:5
past my face; the hair of my flesh **s** up. Jb 4:15
It **s** still, but I could not discern its Jb 4:16
and withdrew, and the aged rose and **s**; Jb 29:8
because I **s** in great fear of the Jb 31:34
to be; he commanded, and it **s** firm. Ps 33:9
the waters **s** above the mountains. Ps 104:6
one, **s** in the breach before him, Ps 106:23
Then Phinehas **s** up and intervened, Ps 106:30
Above him **s** the seraphim. Each had six Is 6:2
And he **s** by the conduit of the upper pool Is 36:2
Then the Rabshakeh **s** and called out in Is 36:13
Moses and Samuel **s** before me, Jer 15:1
Remember how I **s** before you to speak Jer 18:20
and he **s** in the court of the LORD'S Jer 19:14
who among them has **s** in the council Jer 23:18
But if they had **s** in my council, then Jer 23:22
all the officials who **s** beside the king. Jer 36:21
gods, and all the women who **s** by, Jer 44:15
went; and when those **s**, these stood; Ezk 1:21
went; and when those stood, these **s**; Ezk 1:21
When they **s** still, they let down their Ezk 1:24
When they **s** still, they let down their Ezk 1:25
behold, the glory of the LORD **s** there, Ezk 3:23
And before them **s** seventy men of the Ezk 8:11
they went in and **s** beside the bronze Ezk 9:2

he went in and **s** beside a wheel. Ezk 10:6
When they **s** still, these stood still, and Ezk 10:17
When they stood still, these **s** still, and Ezk 10:17
of the house, and **s** over the cherubim. Ezk 10:18
And they **s** at the entrance of the east Ezk 10:19
of the city and **s** on the mountain that Ezk 11:23
him, and its roots remained where it **s**. Ezk 17:6
and they lived and **s** on their feet, Ezk 37:10
Therefore they **s** before the king. Dn 1:19
So they came in and **s** before the king. Dn 2:2
of exceeding brightness, **s** before you, Dn 2:31
And they **s** before the image that Dn 3:3
times ten thousand **s** before him; Dn 7:10
one of those who **s** there and asked him Dn 7:16
there **s** before me one having the Dn 8:15
So he came near where I **s**. And when he Dn 8:17
this word to me, I **s** up trembling. Dn 10:11
I said to him who **s** before me, "O my Dn 10:16
I **s** up to confirm and strengthen him. Dn 11:1
Daniel, looked, and behold, two others **s**, Dn 12:5
On the day that you **s** aloof, on the day Ob 1:11
He **s** and measured the earth; he looked Hab 3:6
The sun and moon **s** still in their place Hab 3:11
he feared me. He **s** in awe of my name. Mal 2:5
his mother and his brothers **s** outside, Mt 12:46
And the whole crowd **s** on the beach. Mt 13:2
And the high priest **s** up and said, Mt 26:62
Now Jesus **s** before the governor, and Mt 27:11
one of those who **s** by drew his sword Mk 14:47
And some **s** up and bore false witness Mk 14:57
And the high priest **s** up in the midst Mk 14:60
the centurion, who **s** facing him, Mk 15:39
on the Sabbath day, and he **s** up to read. Lk 4:16
And he **s** over her and rebuked the fever, Lk 4:39
and stand here." And he rose and **s** there. Lk 6:8
down with them and **s** on a level place, Lk 6:17
touched the bier, and the bearers **s** still. Lk 7:14
glory and the two men who **s** with him. Lk 9:32
a lawyer **s** up to put him to the test, Lk 10:25
met by ten lepers, who **s** at a distance Lk 17:12
And Zacchaeus **s** and said to the Lord, Lk 19:8
And he said to those who **s** by, 'Take Lk 19:24
The chief priests and the scribes **s** by, Lk 23:10
And the people **s** by, watching, but the Lk 23:35
him from Galilee **s** at a distance Lk 23:49
two men **s** by them in dazzling apparel. Lk 24:4
other as you walk?" And they **s** still, Lk 24:17
things, Jesus himself **s** among them, Lk 24:36
the great day, Jesus **s** up and cried out, Jn 7:37
to ask him, he **s** up and said to them, Jn 8:7
Jesus **s** up and said to her, "Woman, Jn 8:10
to one another as they **s** in the temple, Jn 11:56
The crowd that **s** there and heard it said Jn 12:29
but Peter **s** outside at the door. So the Jn 18:16
A jar full of sour wine **s** there, so they Jn 19:29
But Mary **s** weeping outside the tomb, Jn 20:11
Jesus came and **s** among them and said Jn 20:19
Jesus came and **s** among them and said, Jn 20:26
as day was breaking, Jesus **s** on the shore; Jn 21:4
two men **s** by them in white robes, Acts 1:10
In those days Peter **s** up among the Acts 1:15
And leaping up he **s** and began to walk, Acts 3:8
s up and gave orders to put the men Acts 5:34
were traveling with him **s** speechless, Acts 9:7
All the widows **s** beside him weeping Acts 9:39
for Simon's house, **s** at the gate Acts 10:17
a man **s** before me in bright clothing Acts 10:30
them named Agabus **s** up and Acts 11:28
an angel of the Lord **s** next to him, Acts 12:7
So Paul **s** up, and motioning with his Acts 13:16
debate, Peter **s** up and said to them, Acts 15:7
commanded those who **s** by him to Acts 23:2
Those who **s** by said, "Would you Acts 23:4
the Pharisees' party **s** up and Acts 23:9
night the Lord **s** by him and Acts 23:11
found when I **s** before the council, Acts 24:20
down from Jerusalem **s** around him, Acts 25:7
When the accusers **s** up, they Acts 25:18
Paul **s** up among them and said, Acts 27:21
this very night there **s** before me an Acts 27:23
to his face, because he **s** condemned. Gal 2:11
record of debt that **s** against us with its Col 2:14
But the Lord **s** by me and 2 Tm 4:17
for when he has **s** the test he will receive Jas 1:12
Spirit, and behold, a throne **s** in heaven, Rv 4:2
another angel came and **s** at the altar Rv 8:3
them, and they **s** up on their feet, Rv 11:11
And the dragon **s** before the woman who Rv 12:4
of Jesus. And he **s** on the sand of the sea. Rv 12:17
and behold, on Mount Zion **s** the Lamb, Rv 14:1
all whose trade is on the sea, **s** far off Rv 18:17

STOOP (3)
their nobles would not **s** to serve their Neh 3:5
They **s**; they bow down together; they Is 46:2
I am not worthy to **s** down and untie. Mk 1:7

STOOPED (2)
my son, you have gone up. He **s** down; Gn 49:9
and as she wept she **s** to look into the Jn 20:11

STOOPING (2)
s and looking in, he saw the linen Lk 24:12
And **s** to look in, he saw the linen cloths Jn 20:5

STOOPS (1)
Bel bows down; Nebo **s**; their idols are on Is 46:1

STOP (24)
not look back or **s** anywhere in the Gn 19:17
youth, said, "My lord Moses, **s** them." Nm 11:28
passed on, **s** here yourself for a while, 1 Sm 9:27
"**S**! I will tell you what the LORD said 1 Sm 15:16
and go down, lest the rain **s** you.'" 1 Kgs 18:44
every good tree and **s** up all springs of 2 Kgs 3:19
S! Why should you be struck 2 Chr 25:16
his mighty men to **s** the water of the 2 Chr 32:3
and they did not **s** them until the report Ezr 5:5
them and kill them and **s** the work." Neh 4:11
Why should the work **s** while I leave it Neh 6:3
s and consider the wondrous works of Jb 37:14
S regarding man in whose nostrils is Is 2:22
Heshbon fugitives **s** without strength, Jer 48:45
I will make you **s** playing the whore, Ezk 16:41
And I will **s** the music of your songs, Ezk 26:13
hand and put a **s** to their feeding the Ezk 34:10
in your name, and we tried to **s** him, Mk 9:38
But Jesus said, "Do not **s** him, for no one Mk 9:39
in your name, and we tried to **s** him, Lk 9:49
But Jesus said to him, "Do not **s** him, for Lk 9:50
And he commanded the chariot to **s**, Acts 8:38
will you not **s** making crooked the Acts 13:10
same to them, and **s** your threatening, Eph 6:9

STOPPED (29)
the Philistines had **s** and filled with Gn 26:15
the Philistines had **s** after the death Gn 26:18
and the living, and the plague was **s**. Nm 16:48
of meeting, when the plague was **s**. Nm 16:50
the plague on the people of Israel was **s**. Nm 25:8
And the sun stood still, and the moon **s**, Jos 10:13
The sun **s** in the midst of heaven and Jos 10:13
Joshua of Beth-shemesh and **s** there. 1 Sm 6:14
and all the men **s** and pursued Israel 2 Sm 2:28
anyone who came by, seeing him, **s**. 2 Sm 20:12
the man saw that all the people **s**, 2 Sm 20:12
heard of it, he **s** building Ramah, 1 Kgs 15:21
They **s** every spring of water and 2 Kgs 3:25
is not another." Then the oil **s** flowing. 2 Kgs 4:6
And he struck three times and **s**. 2 Kgs 13:18
he **s** building Ramah and let his 2 Chr 16:5
be struck down?" So the prophet **s**, 2 Chr 25:16
and they **s** all the springs and the 2 Chr 32:4
the house of God that is in Jerusalem **s**, Ezr 4:24
exult, for the mouths of liars will be **s**. Ps 63:11
So they **s** speaking with him, for the Jer 38:27
its rivers, and many waters were **s**. Ezk 31:15
stubborn shoulder and **s** their ears that Zec 7:11
And Jesus **s** and said, "Call him." And Mk 10:49
And Jesus **s** and commanded him to be Lk 18:40
a loud voice and **s** their ears and Acts 7:57
and the soldiers, they **s** beating Paul. Acts 21:32
the law, so that every mouth may be **s**, Rom 3:19
promises, **s** the mouths of lions, Heb 11:33

STOPPING (2)
And **s**, Jesus called them and said, Mt 20:32
of no value in **s** the indulgence of the Col 2:23

STOPS (3)
a serpent, like the deaf adder that **s** its ear, Ps 58:4
who **s** his ears from hearing of Is 33:15
and also **s** those who want to and puts 3 Jn 1:10

STORE (17)
sort of food that is eaten, and **s** it up. Gn 6:21
that are coming and **s** up grain under Gn 41:35
They built for Pharaoh **s** cities, Pithom Ex 1:11
You shall eat old **s** long kept, and you Lv 26:10
"'Is not this laid up in **s** with me, sealed Dt 32:34
and all the **s** cities that Solomon had, 1 Kgs 9:19
wilderness and all the **s** cities that he 2 Chr 8:4
and all the **s** cities that Solomon had 2 Chr 8:6
and all the **s** cities of Naphtali. 2 Chr 16:4
built in Judah fortresses and **s** cities, 2 Chr 17:12
you **s** them in your shelter from the Ps 31:20
and oil, and **s** them in your vessels, Jer 40:10
is bound up; his sin is kept in **s**. Hos 13:12
"those who **s** up violence and robbery Am 3:10
I do, for I have nowhere to **s** my crops?' Lk 12:17
and there I will **s** all my grain and my Lk 12:18
is to put something aside and **s** it up, 1 Cor 16:2

STORED (10)
And Joseph **s** up grain in great Gn 41:49
and **s** them in the treasuries of the 1 Kgs 7:51
your fathers have **s** up till this 2 Kgs 20:17

father had dedicated, and **s** the silver, 2 Chr 5:1
the archives where the documents were **s**. Ezr 6:1
which you have **s** up for those who fear Ps 31:19
I have **s** up your word in my heart, Ps 119:11
It will not be **s** or hoarded, but her Is 23:18
which your fathers have **s** up till this day, Is 39:6
and earth that now exist are **s** up for fire, 2 Pt 3:7

STOREHOUSE (4)
of our God, to the chambers of the **s**. Neh 10:38
of the king, to a wardrobe in the **s**, Jer 38:11
Bring the full tithes into the **s**, that Mal 3:10
nor reap, they have neither **s** nor barn, Lk 12:24

STOREHOUSES (16)
Joseph opened all the **s** and sold to the Gn 41:56
armory, all that was found in his **s**. 2 Kgs 20:13
is nothing in my **s** that I did not 2 Kgs 20:15
s also for the yield of grain, wine, 2 Chr 32:28
standing guard at the **s** of the gates. Neh 12:25
of the grain, wine, and oil into the **s**. Neh 13:12
treasurers over the **s** Shelemiah the Neh 13:13
"Have you entered the **s** of the snow, or Jb 38:22
snow, or have you seen the **s** of the hail, Jb 38:22
of the sea as a heap; he puts the deeps in **s**. Ps 33:7
and brings forth the wind from his **s**. Ps 135:7
whole armory, all that was found in his **s**. Is 39:2
There is nothing in my **s** that I did not Is 39:4
he brings forth the wind from his **s**. Jer 10:13
he brings forth the wind from his **s**. Jer 51:16
shrivels under the clods; the **s** are desolate; Jl 1:17

STOREROOMS (1)
day men were appointed over the **s**, Neh 12:44

STORES (6)
and over the **s** of oil was Joash. 1 Chr 27:28
commanders in them, and **s** of food, 2 Chr 11:11
'God **s** up their iniquity for their Jb 21:19
he **s** up sound wisdom for the upright; he Prv 2:7
Migron; at Michmash he **s** his baggage; Is 10:28
put us to death, for we have **s** of wheat, Jer 41:8

STORIES (3)
And the side chambers were in three **s**, Ezk 41:6
was gallery against gallery in three **s**. Ezk 42:3
For they were in three **s**, and they had Ezk 42:6

STORING (2)
impenitent heart you are **s** up wrath for Rom 2:5
thus **s** up treasure for themselves as a 1 Tm 6:19

STORK (5)
the **s**, the heron of any kind, the hoopoe, Lv 11:19
the **s**, the heron of any kind; the hoopoe Dt 14:18
the **s** has her home in the fir trees. Ps 104:17
Even the **s** in the heavens knows her Jer 8:7
They had wings like the wings of a **s**, and Zec 5:9

STORM (20)
the Valley of Salt and took Sela by **s**, 2 Kgs 14:7
and like chaff that the **s** carries away? Jb 21:18
you toss me about in the roar of the **s**. Jb 30:22
He made the **s** be still, and the waves of Ps 107:29
strikes you like a **s** and your calamity Prv 1:27
a refuge and a shelter from the **s** and rain. Is 4:6
the wind and whirling dust before the **s**. Is 17:13
a shelter from the **s** and a shade from the Is 25:4
of the ruthless is like a **s** against a wall, Is 25:4
who is mighty and strong; like a **s** of hail, Is 28:2
a destroying tempest, like a **s** of mighty, Is 28:2
with a cloudburst and **s** and hailstones. Is 30:30
place from the wind, a shelter from the **s**, Is 32:2
Behold, the **s** of the LORD! Wrath has Jer 23:19
Behold the **s** of the LORD! Wrath has Jer 30:23
You will advance, coming on like a **s**. Ezk 38:9
His way is in whirlwind and **s**, and the Na 1:3
from the LORD who makes the **s** clouds, Zec 10:1
behold, there arose a great **s** on the sea, Mt 8:24
springs and mists driven by a **s**. 2 Pt 2:17

STORM-TOSSED (2)
"O afflicted one, **s** and not comforted, Is 54:11
Since we were violently **s**, they began Acts 27:18

STORMS (1)
refuge, till the **s** of destruction pass by. Ps 57:1

STORMY (6)
he commanded and raised the **s** wind, Ps 107:25
and mist, **s** wind fulfilling his word! Ps 148:8
behold, a **s** wind came out of the north, Ezk 1:4
will fall, and a **s** wind break out. Ezk 13:11
I will make a **s** wind break out in my Ezk 13:13
And in the morning, 'It will be **s** today, Mt 16:3

STORY (13)
and she told him the same **s**, saying, Gn 39:17
The lowest **s** was five cubits broad, the 1 Kgs 6:6
entrance for the lowest **s** was on the 1 Kgs 6:8
one went up by stairs to the middle **s**, 1 Kgs 6:8
and from the middle **s** to the third. 1 Kgs 6:8
are written in the **s** of the prophet 2 Chr 13:22
are written in the **S** of the Book of 2 Chr 24:27
one over another, thirty in each **s**. Ezk 41:6
up from the lowest **s** to the top story Ezk 41:7
story to the top **s** through the middle Ezk 41:7
to the top story through the middle **s**. Ezk 41:7
And this **s** has been spread among the Mt 28:15
down from the third **s** and was taken Acts 20:9

STOUT (3)
and kicked; you grew fat, **s**, and sleek; Dt 32:15
wasting sickness among his **s** warriors, Is 10:16
and he who is **s** of heart among the Am 2:16

STOUTHEARTED (1)
The **s** were stripped of their spoil; they Ps 76:5

STOVE (1)
Whether oven or **s**, it shall be broken Lv 11:35

STRAGGLER (1)
the north, and there is no **s** in his ranks. Is 14:31

STRAIGHT (37)
shall go up, everyone **s** before him." Jos 6:5
up into the city, every man **s** before him, Jos 6:20
And the cows went **s** in the direction 1 Sm 6:12
Gate they went up **s** before them by Neh 12:37
my enemies; make your way **s** before me. Ps 5:8
He led them by a **s** way till they reached Ps 107:7
him, and he will make **s** your paths. Prv 3:6
forward, and your gaze be **s** before you. Prv 4:25
They are all **s** to him who understands, Prv 8:9
pass by, who are going **s** on their way, Prv 9:15
of the blameless keeps his way **s**, Prv 11:5
man of understanding walks **s** ahead. Prv 15:21
one whose way is **s** is an abomination Prv 29:27
What is crooked cannot be made **s**, Eccl 1:15
who can make **s** what he has made Eccl 7:13
make **s** in the desert a highway for our Is 40:3
in a **s** path in which they shall not Jer 31:9
shall go out farther, **s** to the hill Gareb, Jer 31:39
be driven out, every man **s** before him, Jer 49:5
Their legs were **s**, and the soles of their Ezk 1:7
Each one of them went **s** forward, Ezk 1:9
And each went **s** forward. Wherever the Ezk 1:12
their wings were stretched out **s**, Ezk 1:23
Each one of them went **s** forward. Ezk 10:22
entered, but each shall go out **s** ahead. Ezk 46:9
through the breaches, each one **s** ahead; Am 4:3
justice and make crooked all that is **s**, Mi 3:9
the way of the Lord; make his paths **s**.'" Mt 3:3
the way of the Lord, make his paths **s**,'" Mk 1:3
the way of the Lord, make his paths **s**. Lk 3:4
low, and the crooked shall become **s**, Lk 3:5
her, and immediately she was made **s**, Lk 13:13
wilderness, 'Make **s** the way of the Lord,' Jn 1:23
him, "Rise and go to the street called **S**, Acts 9:11
making crooked the **s** paths of the Acts 13:10
set sail, we came by a **s** course to Cos, Acts 21:1
and make **s** paths for your feet, so that Heb 12:13

STRAIGHTEN (2)
bent over and could not fully **s** herself. Lk 13:11
to take place, **s** up and raise your heads, Lk 21:28

STRAINING (2)
s out a gnat and swallowing a camel! Mt 23:24
what lies behind and **s** forward to what Phil 3:13

STRANGE (13)
stirred him to jealousy with **s** gods; Dt 32:16
My breath is **s** to my wife, and I am a Jb 19:17
There shall be no **s** god among you; you Ps 81:9
of Jacob from a people of **s** language, Ps 114:1
Your eyes will see **s** things, and your Prv 23:33
For by people of **s** lips and with a foreign Is 28:11
be roused; to do his deed—**s** is his deed! Is 28:21
when there was no **s** god among you; Is 43:12
they would be regarded as a **s** thing. Hos 8:12
For you bring some **s** things to our Acts 17:20
"By people of **s** tongues and by the 1 Cor 14:21
be led away by diverse and **s** teachings, Heb 13:9
as though something **s** were happening 1 Pt 4:12

STRANGER (37)
If a **s** shall sojourn with you and would Ex 12:48
and for the **s** who sojourns among Ex 12:49
the native or the **s** who sojourns among Lv 16:29
neither shall any **s** who sojourns Lv 17:12
the native or the **s** who sojourns among Lv 18:26
"When a **s** sojourns with you in your Lv 19:33
You shall treat the **s** who sojourns with Lv 19:34
as though he were a **s** and a sojourner, Lv 25:35
"If a **s** or sojourner with you becomes Lv 25:47
sells himself to the **s** or sojourner with Lv 25:47
And if a **s** sojourns among you and Nm 9:14
And if a **s** is sojourning with you, or Nm 15:14
you and for the **s** who sojourns with Nm 15:15
you and for the **s** who sojourns with Nm 15:16
and the **s** who sojourns among them, Nm 15:26
and for the **s** who sojourns among Nm 15:29
and for the **s** who sojourns among Nm 19:10
and for the **s** and for the sojourner Nm 35:15
not be married outside the family to a **s**. Dt 25:5
and for the **s** sojourning among them, Jos 20:9
given, and no **s** passed among them). Jb 15:19
and my maidservants count me as a **s**; Jb 19:15
I have become a **s** to my brothers, an Ps 69:8
neighbor, have given your pledge for a **s**, Prv 6:1
up security for a **s** will surely suffer Prv 11:15
own bitterness, and no **s** shares its joy. Prv 14:10
when he has put up security for a **s**, Prv 20:16
you, and not your own mouth; a **s**, Prv 27:2
when he has put up security for a **s**, Prv 27:13
to enjoy them, but a **s** enjoys them. Eccl 6:2
plants and sow the vine-branch of a **s**, Is 17:10
why should you be like a **s** in the land, Jer 14:8
drink, I was a **s** and you welcomed me, Mt 25:35
did we see you a **s** and welcome you, Mt 25:38
I was a **s** and you did not welcome me, Mt 25:43
or thirsty or a **s** or naked or sick Mt 25:44
A **s** they will not follow, but they will flee Jn 10:5

STRANGER'S (1)
with you or to a member of the **s** clan, Lv 25:47

STRANGERS (28)
treated them like **s** and spoke roughly Gn 42:7
or of the **s** who sojourn among them, Lv 17:8
Israel or of the **s** who sojourn among Lv 17:10
or of the **s** who sojourn among them, Lv 17:13
for you were **s** in the land of Egypt: Lv 19:34
of Israel or of the **s** who sojourn in Israel Lv 20:2
For you are **s** and sojourners with me. Lv 25:23
from among the **s** who sojourn with Lv 25:45
For we are **s** before you and 1 Chr 29:15
For **s** have risen against me; ruthless Ps 54:3
may **s** plunder the fruits of his toil! Ps 109:11
lest **s** take their fill of your strength, and Prv 5:10
yourself alone, and not for **s** with you. Prv 5:17
S shall stand and tend your flocks; Is 61:5
inheritance has been turned over to **s**, Lam 5:2
Israel, or of the **s** who sojourn in Israel, Ezk 14:7
who receives **s** instead of her Ezk 16:32
S devour his strength, and he knows it Hos 7:9
flour; if it were to yield, **s** would devour it. Hos 8:7
and **s** shall never again pass through it. Jl 3:17
on the day that **s** carried off his wealth Ob 1:11
the potter's field as a burial place for **s**. Mt 27:7
him, for they do not know the voice of **s**." Jn 10:5
of Israel and **s** to the covenants Eph 2:12
So then you are no longer **s** and aliens, Eph 2:19
that they were **s** and exiles on Heb 11:13
Do not neglect to show hospitality to **s**, Heb 13:2
efforts for these brothers, **s** as they are, 3 Jn 1:5

STRANGLED (4)
for his cubs and **s** prey for his lionesses; Na 2:12
and from what has been **s**, Acts 15:20
blood, and from what has been **s**, Acts 15:29
blood, and from what has been **s**, Acts 21:25

STRANGLING (1)
that I would choose **s** and death rather Jb 7:15

STRAP (8)
thread or a sandal **s** or anything that is Gn 14:23
"Every man **s** on his sword!" And 1 Sm 25:13
waistband is loose, not a sandal **s** broken; Is 5:27
s on your armor and be shattered; Is 8:9
s on your armor and be shattered. Is 8:9
the **s** of whose sandals I am not worthy to Mk 1:7
the **s** of whose sandals I am not worthy Lk 3:16
the **s** of whose sandal I am not worthy to Jn 1:27

STRAPPED (4)
and David **s** his sword over his 1 Sm 17:39
every man of them **s** on his sword. 1 Sm 25:13
his sword. David also **s** on his sword. 1 Sm 25:13
builders had his sword **s** at his side Neh 4:18

STRAPS (3)
'Let not him who **s** on his armor 1 Kgs 20:11
of wickedness, to undo the **s** of the yoke, Is 58:6
to me: "Make yourself **s** and yoke-bars, Jer 27:2

STRATEGY (2)
that mere words are **s** and power for 2 Kgs 18:20
that mere words are **s** and power for war? Is 36:5

STRAW (19)
"We have plenty of both **s** and fodder, Gn 24:25
and gave **s** and fodder to the camels, Gn 24:32
longer give the people **s** to make bricks, Ex 5:7
let them go and gather **s** for themselves. Ex 5:7
says Pharaoh, 'I will not give you **s**. Ex 5:10
and get your **s** yourselves wherever you Ex 5:11
the land of Egypt to gather stubble for **s**. Ex 5:12
task each day, as when there was **s**." Ex 5:13

No **s** is given to your servants, yet they Ex 5:16
No **s** will be given you, but you must Ex 5:18
We have **s** and feed for our donkeys, Jgs 19:19
Barley also and **s** for the horses and 1 Kgs 4:28
That they are like **s** before the wind, and Jb 21:18
He counts iron as **s**, and bronze as Jb 41:27
and the lion shall eat **s** like the ox. Is 11:7
as **s** is trampled down in a dunghill. Is 25:10
the lion shall eat **s** like the ox, and dust Is 65:25
What has **s** in common with wheat? Jer 23:28
silver, precious stones, wood, hay, **s**— 1 Cor 3:12

STRAY (3)
me, but I do not **s** from your precepts. Ps 119:110
to her ways; do not **s** into her paths, Prv 7:25
and you will **s** from the words of Prv 19:27

STRAYED (5)
which reached to Jazer and **s** to the desert; Is 16:8
up, the **s** you have not brought back, Ezk 34:4
the lost, and I will bring back the **s**, Ezk 34:16
Woe to them, for they have **s** from me! Hos 7:13
For some have already **s** after Satan. 1 Tm 5:15

STRAYING (1)
For you were **s** like sheep, but have 1 Pt 2:25

STRAYS (2)
Like a bird that **s** from its nest is a man Prv 27:8
its nest is a man who **s** from his home. Prv 27:8

STREAKS (1)
plane trees, and peeled white **s** in them, Gn 30:37

STREAM (16)
took them and sent them across the **s**, Gn 32:23
The king's heart is a **s** of water in the Prv 21:1
is like an overflowing **s** that reaches up Is 30:28
the breath of the LORD, like a **s** of sulfur, Is 30:33
for he will come like a rushing **s**, which Is 59:19
of the nations like an overflowing **s**; Is 66:12
by water, that sends out its roots by the **s**, Jer 17:8
let tears **s** down like a torrent day and Lam 2:18
A **s** of fire issued and came out from Dn 7:10
on this bank of the **s** and one on that Dn 12:5
stream and one on that bank of the **s**. Dn 12:5
linen, who was above the waters of the **s**, Dn 12:6
linen, who was above the waters of the **s**; Dn 12:7
righteousness like an ever-flowing **s**. Am 5:24
the **s** broke against that house and Lk 6:48
When the **s** broke against it, Lk 6:49

STREAMBED (2)
'I will make this dry **s** full of pools.' 2 Kgs 3:16
but that **s** shall be filled with water, 2 Kgs 3:17

STREAMBEDS (1)
and all the **s** of Judah shall flow with Jl 3:18

STREAMS (35)
the sole of my foot all the **s** of Egypt.' 2 Kgs 19:24
as torrential **s** that pass away, Jb 6:15
the **s** flowing with honey and curds. Jb 20:17
He dams up the **s** so that they do not Jb 28:11
and the rock poured out for me **s** of oil! Jb 29:6
like a tree planted by **s** of water that yields Ps 1:3
As a deer pants for flowing **s**, so pants my Ps 42:1
is a river whose **s** make glad the city Ps 46:4
brooks; you dried up ever-flowing **s**. Ps 74:15
He made **s** come out of the rock and Ps 78:16
that water gushed out and **s** overflowed. Ps 78:20
so that they could not drink of their **s**. Ps 78:44
My eyes shed **s** of tears, because Ps 119:136
fortunes, O LORD, like **s** in the Negeb! Ps 126:4
abroad, **s** of water in the streets? Prv 5:16
All **s** run to the sea, but the sea is not Eccl 1:7
to the place where the **s** flow, there they Eccl 1:7
water, and flowing **s** from Lebanon. Sg 4:15
His eyes are like doves beside **s** of water, Sg 5:12
the fly that is at the end of the **s** of Egypt, Is 7:18
the storm, like **s** of water in a dry place, Is 32:2
be for us a place of broad rivers and **s**, Is 33:21
And the **s** of Edom shall be turned into Is 34:9
forth in the wilderness, and **s** in the desert; Is 35:6
with the sole of my foot all the **s** of Egypt. Is 37:25
the thirsty land, and **s** on the dry ground; Is 44:3
the grass like willows by flowing **s**. Is 44:4
waters run dry, the cold flowing **s**? Jer 18:14
dragon that lies in the midst of his **s**, Ezk 29:3
the fish of your **s** stick to your scales; Ezk 29:4
draw you up out of the midst of your **s**, Ezk 29:4
all the fish of your **s** that stick to your Ezk 29:4
you and all the fish of your **s**; Ezk 29:5
I am against you and against your **s**, Ezk 29:10
sending forth its **s** to all the trees of the Ezk 31:4

STREET (27)
out of the doors of your house into the **s**, Jos 2:19
he and Samuel went out into the **s**. 1 Sm 9:26
the earth, and he has no name in the **s**. Jb 18:17
(the sojourner has not lodged in the **s**; I Jb 31:32
those who see me in the **s** flee from me. Ps 31:11
Wisdom cries aloud in the **s**, in the Prv 1:20
passing along the **s** near her corner, Prv 7:8
now in the **s**, now in the market, and at Prv 7:12
and the doors on the **s** are shut—when Eccl 12:4
lift up his voice, or make it heard in the **s**; Is 42:2
at the head of every **s** like an antelope in Is 51:20
ground and like the **s** for them to pass Is 51:23
"Pour it out upon the children in the **s**, Jer 6:11
was given him daily from the bakers' **s**, Jer 37:21
In the **s** the sword bereaves; in the Lam 1:20
faint for hunger at the head of every **s**." Lam 2:19
lie scattered at the head of every **s**. Lam 4:1
the head of every **s** you built your lofty Ezk 16:25
chamber at the head of every **s**, Ezk 16:31
dashed in pieces at the head of every **s**; Na 3:10
in the synagogues and at the **s** corners, Mt 6:5
a colt tied at a door outside in the **s**, Mk 11:4
"Rise and go to the **s** called Straight, Acts 9:11
they went out and went along one **s**, Acts 12:10
bodies will lie in the **s** of the great city Rv 11:8
and the **s** of the city was pure gold, Rv 21:21
through the middle of the **s** of the city; Rv 22:2

STREETS (55)
publish it not in the **s** of Ashkelon, 2 Sm 1:20
them down like the mire of the **s**. 2 Sm 22:43
I cast them out like the mire of the **s**. Ps 18:42
there be no cry of distress in our **s**! Ps 144:14
at the head of the noisy **s** she cries out; Prv 1:21
abroad, streams of water in the **s**? Prv 5:16
lion outside! I shall be killed in the **s**!" Prv 22:13
in the road! There is a lion in the **s**!" Prv 26:13
and the mourners go about the **s**— Eccl 12:5
about the city, in the **s** and in the squares; Sg 3:2
were as refuse in the midst of the **s**. Is 5:25
to tread them down like the mire of the **s**. Is 10:6
in the **s** they wear sackcloth; on the Is 15:3
is an outcry in the **s** for lack of wine; Is 24:11
Behold, their heroes cry in the **s**; the Is 33:7
the breach, the restorer of **s** to dwell in. Is 58:12
Run to and fro through the **s** of Jerusalem, Jer 5:1
cities of Judah and in the **s** of Jerusalem? Jer 7:17
Judah and in the **s** of Jerusalem the voice Jer 7:34
the children from the **s** and the young Jer 9:21
cities of Judah and in the **s** of Jerusalem: Jer 11:6
as many as the **s** of Jerusalem are the Jer 11:13
shall be cast out in the **s** of Jerusalem, Jer 14:16
of Judah and the **s** of Jerusalem that are Jer 33:10
cities of Judah and in the **s** of Jerusalem, Jer 44:6
land of Judah and in the **s** of Jerusalem? Jer 44:9
of Judah and in the **s** of Jerusalem. Jer 44:17
of Judah and in the **s** of Jerusalem, Jer 44:21
of the Chaldeans, and wounded in her **s**. Jer 51:4
and babies faint in the **s** of the city. Lam 2:11
a wounded man in the **s** of the city, Lam 2:12
In the dust of the **s** lie the young and Lam 2:21
feasted on delicacies perish in the **s**; Lam 4:5
soot; they are not recognized in the **s**; Lam 4:8
They wandered, blind, through the **s**; Lam 4:14
so that we could not walk in our **s**; Lam 4:18
They cast their silver into the **s**, and Ezk 7:19
city and have filled its **s** with the slain. Ezk 11:6
his horses he will trample all your **s**. Ezk 26:11
into her, and blood into her **s**; Ezk 28:23
wailing, and in all the **s** they shall say, Am 5:16
be trampled down like the mire of the **s**. Mi 7:10
The chariots race madly through the **s**; Na 2:4
I have laid waste their **s** so that no one Zep 3:6
shall again sit in the **s** of Jerusalem, Zec 8:4
And the **s** of the city shall be full of boys Zec 8:5
be full of boys and girls playing in its **s**. Zec 8:5
dust, and fine gold like the mud of the **s**. Zec 9:3
trampling the foe in the mud of the **s**; Zec 10:5
do in the synagogues and in the **s**, Mt 6:2
nor will anyone hear his voice in the **s**; Mt 12:19
do not receive you, go into its **s** and say, Lk 10:10
presence, and you taught in our **s**.' Lk 13:26
'Go out quickly to the **s** and lanes of the Lk 14:21
the sick into the **s** and laid them on Acts 5:15

STRENGTH (169)
it shall no longer yield to you its **s**. Gn 4:12
I have served your father with all my **s**, Gn 31:6
Then Israel summoned his **s** and sat up Gn 48:2
my might, and the firstfruits of my **s**, Gn 49:3
The LORD is my **s** and my song, and he Ex 15:2
guided them by your **s** to your holy Ex 15:13
And your **s** shall be spent in vain, for Lv 26:20
But now our **s** is dried up, and there is Nm 11:6
he has, for he is the firstfruits of his **s**. Dt 21:17
and as your days, so shall your **s** be. Dt 33:25
my **s** now is as my strength was then, Jos 14:11
my strength now is as my **s** was then, Jos 14:11
so is his **s**." And Gideon arose and killed Jgs 8:21
him, and see where his great **s** lies, Jgs 16:5
"Please tell me where your great **s** lies, Jgs 16:6
fire. So the secret of his **s** was not known. Jgs 16:9
not told me where your great **s** lies." Jgs 16:15
head is shaved, then my **s** will leave me, Jgs 16:17
to torment him, and his **s** left him. Jgs 16:19
Then he bowed with all his **s**, Jgs 16:30
in the LORD; my **s** is exalted in the LORD. 1 Sm 2:1
are broken, but the feeble bind on **s**. 1 Sm 2:4
he will give **s** to his king and exalt the 1 Sm 2:10
I will cut off your **s** and the strength of 1 Sm 2:31
strength and the **s** of your father's 1 Sm 2:31
And there was no **s** in him, for he 1 Sm 28:20
that you may have **s** when you go on 1 Sm 28:22
wept until they had no more **s** to weep. 1 Sm 30:4
equipped me with **s** for the battle; 2 Sm 22:40
and went in the **s** of that food forty 1 Kgs 19:8
Jehu drew his bow with his full **s**, 2 Kgs 9:24
and there is no **s** to bring them forth. 2 Kgs 19:3
while their inhabitants, shorn of **s**, 2 Kgs 19:26
Seek the LORD and his **s**; seek his 1 Chr 16:11
him; **s** and joy are in his place. 1 Chr 16:27
ascribe to the LORD glory and **s**! 1 Chr 16:28
let us use our **s** for our people and 1 Chr 19:13
is to make great and to give **s** to all. 1 Chr 29:12
"The **s** of those who bear the burdens Neh 4:10
for the joy of the LORD is your **s**." Neh 8:10
What is my **s**, that I should wait? And Jb 6:11
Is my **s** the strength of stones, or is my Jb 6:12
Is my strength the **s** of stones, or is my Jb 6:12
heart and mighty in **s** —who has hardened Jb 9:4
If it is a contest of **s**, behold, he is mighty! Jb 9:19
With him are **s** and sound wisdom; the Jb 12:16
my skin and have laid my **s** in the dust. Jb 16:15
His **s** is famished, and calamity is ready Jb 18:12
you have saved the arm that has no **s**! Jb 26:2
could I gain from the **s** of their hands, Jb 30:2
any; he is mighty in **s** of understanding. Jb 36:5
from distress, or all the force of your **s**? Jb 36:19
depend on him because his **s** is great, Jb 39:11
He paws in the valley and exults in his **s**; Jb 39:21
Behold, his **s** in his loins, and his power Jb 40:16
concerning his limbs, or his mighty **s**, Jb 41:12
In his neck abides **s**, and terror dances Jb 41:22
you have established **s** because of your Ps 8:2
I love you, O LORD, my **s**. Ps 18:1
who equipped me with **s** and made my Ps 18:32
you equipped me with **s** for the battle; Ps 18:39
O LORD, in your **s** the king rejoices, and Ps 21:1
Be exalted, O LORD, in your **s**! We will Ps 21:13
my **s** is dried up like a potsherd, and my Ps 22:15
The LORD is my **s** and my shield; in him Ps 28:7
The LORD is the **s** of his people; he is the Ps 28:8
beings, ascribe to the LORD glory and **s**. Ps 29:1
May the LORD give **s** to his people! May Ps 29:11
my **s** fails because of my iniquity, and Ps 31:10
my **s** was dried up as by the heat of Ps 32:4
a warrior is not delivered by his great **s**. Ps 33:16
my **s** fails me, and the light of my eyes— Ps 38:10
God is our refuge and **s**, a very present Ps 46:1
O my **S**, I will watch for you, for you, O Ps 59:9
But I will sing of your **s**; I will sing Ps 59:16
O my **S**, I will sing praises to you, for Ps 59:17
who by his **s** established the mountains, Ps 65:6
one who gives power and **s** to his people. Ps 68:35
age; forsake me not when my **s** is spent. Ps 71:9
but God is the **s** of my heart and my Ps 73:26
the firstfruits of their **s** in the tents of Ps 78:51
Sing aloud to God our **s**; shout for joy to Ps 81:1
Blessed are those whose **s** is in you, in Ps 84:5
They go from **s** to strength; each one Ps 84:7
They go from strength to **s**; each one Ps 84:7
give your **s** to your servant, and save the Ps 86:16
to the pit; I am a man who has no **s**, Ps 88:4
For you are the glory of their **s**; by your Ps 89:17
seventy, or even by reason of **s** eighty; Ps 90:10
LORD is robed; he has put on **s** as his belt. Ps 93:1
him; **s** and beauty are in his sanctuary. Ps 96:6
peoples, ascribe to the LORD glory and **s**! Ps 96:7
He has broken my **s** in midcourse; he Ps 102:23
Seek the LORD and his **s**; seek his Ps 105:4
their land, the firstfruits of all their **s**. Ps 105:36
The LORD is my **s** and my song; he has Ps 118:14
me; my **s** of soul you increased. Ps 138:3
O LORD, my Lord, the **s** of my salvation, Ps 140:7
His delight is not in the **s** of the horse, Ps 147:10
lest strangers take their fill of your **s**, Prv 5:10
sound wisdom; I have insight; I have **s**. Prv 8:14
abundant crops come by the **s** of the ox. Prv 14:4
The glory of young men is their **s**, but Prv 20:29
A wise man is full of **s**, and a man of Prv 24:5
in the day of adversity, your **s** is small. Prv 24:10
Do not give your **s** to women, your ways Prv 31:3
dresses herself with **s** and makes her Prv 31:17
S and dignity are her clothing, and she Prv 31:25
Wisdom gives **s** to the wise man more Eccl 7:19

sharpen the edge, he must use more **s**, Eccl 10:10
princes feast at the proper time, for **s**, Eccl 10:17
"By the **s** of my hand I have done it, and Is 10:13
for the LORD GOD is my **s** and my song, Is 12:2
and **s** to those who turn back the battle at Is 28:6
trust shall be your **s**." But you were Is 30:15
and there is no **s** to bring them forth. Is 37:3
while their inhabitants, shorn of **s**, are Is 37:27
lift up your voice with **s**, O Jerusalem, Is 40:9
to him who has no might he increases **s**. Is 40:29
wait for the LORD shall renew their **s**; Is 40:31
O coastlands; let the peoples renew their **s**; Is 41:1
He becomes hungry, and his **s** fails; he Is 44:12
be said of me, are righteousness and **s**; Is 45:24
I have spent my **s** for nothing and vanity; Is 49:4
the LORD, and my God has become my **s**— Is 49:5
Awake, awake, put on **s**, O arm of the Is 51:9
Awake, awake, put on your **s**, O Zion; put Is 52:1
you found new life for your **s**, and so you Is 57:10
marching in the greatness of his **s**? Is 63:1
O LORD, my **s** and my stronghold, my Jer 16:19
trusts in man and makes flesh his **s**, Jer 17:5
of Heshbon fugitives stop without **s**, Jer 48:45
in their strongholds; their **s** has failed; Jer 51:30
they fled without **s** before the pursuer. Lam 1:6
treasures for food to revive their **s**. Lam 1:11
upon my neck; he caused my **s** to fail; Lam 1:14
they sought food to revive their **s**. Lam 1:19
this great vision, and no **s** was left in me. Dn 10:8
fearfully changed, and I retained no **s**. Dn 10:8
have come upon me, and I retain no **s**. Dn 10:16
my lord? For now no **s** remains in me, Dn 10:17
But she shall not retain the **s** of her arm, Dn 11:6
troops, for there shall be no **s** to stand. Dn 11:15
to come with the **s** of his whole Dn 11:17
Strangers devour his **s**, and he knows it Hos 7:9
and the strong shall not retain his **s**, Am 2:14
not by our own **s** captured Karnaim for Am 6:13
shepherd his flock in the **s** of the LORD, Mi 5:4
"Though they are at full **s** and many, Na 1:12
road; dress for battle; collect all your **s**. Na 2:1
Cush was her **s**; Egypt too, and that Na 3:9
GOD, the Lord, is my **s**; he makes my Hab 3:19
about to destroy the **s** of the kingdoms of Hg 2:22
of Jerusalem have **s** through the LORD Zec 12:5
pieces. No one had the **s** to subdue him. Mk 5:4
all your mind and with all your **s**.' Mk 12:30
the understanding and with all the **s**, Mk 12:33
He has shown **s** with his arm; he has Lk 1:51
and with all your **s** and with all your Lk 10:27
that you may have **s** to escape all these Lk 21:36
But Saul increased all the more in **s**, Acts 9:22
It will give you **s**, for not a hair is to Acts 27:34
burdened beyond our **s** that we 2 Cor 1:8
may have **s** to comprehend with all the Eph 3:18
in the Lord and in the **s** of his might. Eph 6:10
I thank him who has given me **s**, 1 Tm 1:12
who serves by the **s** that God supplies— 1 Pt 4:11
face was like the sun shining in full **s**. Rv 1:16
poured full **s** into the cup of his anger, Rv 14:10

STRENGTHEN (29)
Joshua, and encourage and **s** him, Dt 3:28
me and please **s** me only this Jgs 16:28
"**S** your heart with a morsel of bread, Jgs 19:5
"**S** your heart and wait until the day Jgs 19:8
S your attack against the city and 2 Sm 11:25
and said to him, "Come, **s** yourself, 1 Kgs 20:22
be done." But now, O God, **s** my hands. Neh 6:9
I could **s** you with my mouth, and the Jb 16:5
of the afflicted; you will **s** their heart; Ps 10:17
with him; my arm also shall **s** him. Ps 89:21
face shine and bread to **s** man's heart. Ps 104:15
sorrow; **s** me according to your word! Ps 119:28
S the weak hands, and make firm the Is 35:3
and they **s** it with nails so that it cannot Is 41:7
I will **s** you, I will help you, I will uphold Is 41:10
lengthen your cords and **s** your stakes. Is 54:2
they **s** the hands of evildoers, so that no Jer 23:14
And I will **s** the arms of the king of Ezk 30:24
I will **s** the arms of the king of Ezk 30:25
up the injured, and I will **s** the weak, Ezk 34:16
Mede, I stood up to confirm and **s** him. Dn 11:1
Draw water for the siege; **s** your forts; go Na 3:14
"I will **s** the house of Judah, and I will Zec 10:6
have turned again, **s** your brothers." Lk 22:32
to you some spiritual gift to **s** you— Rom 1:11
who is able to **s** you according to my Rom 16:25
drooping hands and **s** your weak Heb 12:12
restore, confirm, **s**, and establish you. 1 Pt 5:10
and **s** what remains and is about to die, Rv 3:2

STRENGTHENED (25)
and the LORD **s** Eglon the king of Moab Jgs 3:12
your hands shall be **s** to go down Jgs 7:11
who **s** his hands to kill his brothers. Jgs 9:24
at Horesh, and **s** his hand in God. 1 Sm 23:16
But David **s** himself in the LORD his 1 Sm 30:6
of all who are with you will be **s**." 2 Sm 16:21
They **s** the kingdom of Judah, and 2 Chr 11:17
his place and **s** himself against Israel. 2 Chr 17:1
God to its proper condition and **s** it. 2 Chr 24:13
and he **s** the Millo in the city of 2 Chr 32:5
and build." So they **s** their hands for Neh 2:18
many, and you have **s** the weak hands. Jb 4:3
The weak you have not **s**, the sick you Ezk 34:4
of a man touched me and **s** me. Dn 10:18
And as he spoke to me, I was **s** and said, Dn 10:19
"Let my lord speak, for you have **s** me." Dn 10:19
Although I trained and **s** their arms, yet Hos 7:15
and taking food, he was **s**. For some Acts 9:19
encouraged and **s** the brothers with Acts 15:32
So the churches were **s** in the faith, Acts 16:5
grant you to be **s** with power through Eph 3:16
May you be **s** with all power, according Col 1:11
be **s** by the grace that is in Christ 2 Tm 2:1
But the Lord stood by me and **s** me, so 2 Tm 4:17
it is good for the heart to be **s** by grace, Heb 13:9

STRENGTHENING (5)
and afflicted him instead of **s** him. 2 Chr 28:20
to him an angel from heaven, **s** him. Lk 22:43
s the souls of the disciples, Acts 14:22
Syria and Cilicia, **s** the churches. Acts 15:41
and Phrygia, **s** all the disciples. Acts 18:23

STRENGTHENS (3)
For he **s** the bars of your gates; he Ps 147:13
The craftsman **s** the goldsmith, and he Is 41:7
do all things through him who **s** me. Phil 4:13

STRETCH (44)
So I will **s** out my hand and strike Egypt Ex 3:20
when I **s** out my hand against Egypt and Ex 7:5
'Take your staff and **s** out your hand Ex 7:19
'**S** out your hand with your staff over the Ex 8:5
'**S** out your staff and strike the dust of the Ex 8:16
Moses, "**S** out your hand toward heaven, Ex 9:22
city, I will **s** out my hands to the LORD. Ex 9:29
"**S** out your hand over the land of Egypt Ex 10:12
"**S** out your hand toward heaven, Ex 10:21
and **s** out your hand over the sea and Ex 14:16
to Moses, "**S** out your hand over the sea, Ex 14:26
Like palm groves that **s** afar, like Nm 24:6
"**S** out the javelin that is in your hand Jos 8:18
And I will **s** over Jerusalem the 2 Kgs 21:13
But **s** out your hand and touch all that Jb 1:11
against him do not **s** out your hand." So Jb 1:12
But **s** out your hand and touch his bone Jb 2:5
you will **s** out your hands toward him. Jb 11:13
one in a heap of ruins **s** out his hand, Jb 30:24
Cush shall hasten to **s** out her hands to Ps 68:31
lest the righteous **s** out their hands to do Ps 125:3
you **s** out your hand against the wrath Ps 138:7
I **s** out my hands to you; my soul thirsts Ps 143:6
S out your hand from on high; rescue Ps 144:7
For the bed is too short to **s** oneself on, Is 28:20
He shall **s** the line of confusion over it, Is 34:11
for I will **s** out my hand against the Jer 6:12
I will **s** out my hand against you, and Jer 51:25
And I will **s** out my hand against them Ezk 6:14
and I will **s** out my hand against him Ezk 14:9
and I **s** out my hand against it and Ezk 14:13
I will **s** out my hand against Edom Ezk 25:13
I will **s** out my hand against the Ezk 25:16
and I will **s** out my hand against you, Ezk 35:3
He shall **s** out his hand against the Dn 11:42
beds of ivory and **s** themselves out on Am 6:4
of those who **s** themselves out shall Am 6:7
"I will **s** out my hand against Judah and Zep 1:4
And he will **s** out his hand against the Zep 2:13
"**S** out your hand." And the man Mt 12:13
"**S** out your hand." He stretched it out, Mk 3:5
him, "**S** out your hand." And he did so, Lk 6:10
you are old, you will **s** out your hands, Jn 21:18
while you **s** out your hand to heal, and Acts 4:30

STRETCHED (61)
And Israel **s** out his right hand and Gn 48:14
So Aaron **s** out his hand over the waters of Ex 8:6
Aaron **s** out his hand with his staff and Ex 8:17
Then Moses **s** out his staff toward Ex 9:23
city from Pharaoh and **s** out his hands Ex 9:33
So Moses **s** out his staff over the land of Ex 10:13
So Moses **s** out his hand toward heaven, Ex 10:22
Then Moses **s** out his hand over the sea, Ex 14:21
So Moses **s** out his hand over the sea, Ex 14:27
You **s** out your right hand; the earth Ex 15:12
hand." And Joshua **s** out the javelin Jos 8:18
and as soon as he had **s** out his hand, Jos 8:19
hand with which he **s** out the javelin Jos 8:26
And when the angel **s** out his hand 2 Sm 24:16
Jeroboam **s** out his hand from the 1 Kgs 13:4
hand, which he **s** out against him, 1 Kgs 13:4
Then he **s** himself upon the child 1 Kgs 17:21
And as he **s** himself upon him, 2 Kgs 4:34
and went up and **s** himself upon him. 2 Kgs 4:35
a drawn sword **s** out over Jerusalem. 1 Chr 21:16
who alone **s** out the heavens and trampled Jb 9:8
Because he has **s** out his hand against Jb 15:25
you know! Or who **s** the line upon it? Jb 38:5
My companion **s** out his hand against Ps 55:20
my hand is **s** out without wearying; Ps 77:2
have **s** out my hand and no one has Prv 1:24
and he **s** out his hand against them and Is 5:25
turned away, and his hand is **s** out still. Is 5:25
turned away, and his hand is **s** out still. Is 9:12
turned away, and his hand is **s** out still. Is 9:17
turned away, and his hand is **s** out still. Is 9:21
turned away, and his hand is **s** out still. Is 10:4
is the hand that is **s** out over all the Is 14:26
His hand is **s** out, and who will turn it Is 14:27
He has **s** out his hand over the sea; he Is 23:11
who created the heavens and **s** them out, Is 42:5
all things, who alone **s** out the heavens, Is 44:24
it was my hands that **s** out the heavens, Is 45:12
who **s** out the heavens and laid the Is 51:13
the curtains of your habitations be **s** out; Is 54:2
by his understanding **s** out the Jer 10:12
so I have **s** out my hand against you and Jer 15:6
by his understanding **s** out the Jer 51:15
The enemy has **s** out his hands over Lam 1:10
of Zion; he **s** out the measuring line; Lam 2:8
expanse their wings were **s** out straight, Ezk 1:23
I looked, behold, a hand was **s** out to me, Ezk 2:9
And a cherub **s** out his hand from Ezk 10:7
I **s** out my hand against you and Ezk 16:27
I have **s** out my hand against you, Ezk 25:7
of wine; he **s** out his hand with mockers. Hos 7:5
line shall be **s** out over Jerusalem. Zec 1:16
who **s** out the heavens and founded the Zec 12:1
And Jesus **s** out his hand and touched Mt 8:3
out your hand." And the man **s** it out, Mt 12:13
who were with Jesus **s** out his hand and Mt 26:51
he **s** out his hand and touched him and Mk 1:41
"Stretch out your hand." He **s** it out, Mk 3:5
And Jesus **s** out his hand and touched Lk 5:13
But when they had **s** him out for the Acts 22:25
yourself." Then Paul **s** out his hand Acts 26:1

STRETCHES (7)
He **s** out the north over the void and Jb 26:7
not spirit. When the LORD **s** out his hand, Is 31:3
beauty; they will see a land that **s** afar. Is 33:17
who **s** out the heavens like a curtain, Is 40:22
The carpenter **s** a line; he marks it out Is 44:13
Zion **s** out her hands, but there is none Lam 1:17
of Babylon and he **s** it out against the Ezk 30:25

STRETCHING (5)
his own heart and **s** out his hands 1 Kgs 8:38
his own sorrow and **s** out his hands 2 Chr 6:29
a garment, **s** out the heavens like a tent. Ps 104:2
Zion gasping for breath, **s** out her hands, Jer 4:31
And **s** out his hand toward his Mt 12:49

STREW (1)
I will **s** your flesh upon the mountains Ezk 32:5

STRICKEN (7)
they are not **s** like the rest of mankind. Ps 73:5
long I have been **s** and rebuked every Ps 73:14
needy, and my heart is **s** within me. Ps 109:22
Mourn, utterly **s**, for the raisin cakes of Is 16:7
yet we esteemed him **s**, smitten by God, Is 53:4
s for the transgression of my people? Is 53:8
Ephraim is **s**; their root is dried up; they Hos 9:16

STRICT (1)
according to the **s** manner of the Acts 22:3

STRICTEST (1)
that according to the **s** party of our Acts 26:5

STRICTLY (10)
if only you will **s** obey the voice of the Dt 15:5
"Your father **s** charged the people 1 Sm 14:28
let judgment be **s** executed on him, Ezr 7:26
Then he **s** charged the disciples to tell Mt 16:20
And he **s** ordered them not to make him Mk 3:12
And he **s** charged them that no one Mk 5:43
And he **s** charged them to tell no one Mk 8:30
And he **s** charged and commanded Lk 9:21
"We **s** charged you not to teach in this Acts 5:28
"We have **s** bound ourselves by an Acts 23:14

STRICTNESS (1)
who teach will be judged with greater **s**. Jas 3:1

STRIDE (1)
their tread; four are stately in their **s**: Prv 30:29

STRIFE (31)
and there was **s** between the herdsmen Gn 13:7

“Let there be no **s** between you and me, Gn 13:8
weight and burden of you and your **s**? Dt 1:12
delivered me from **s** with my people; 2 Sm 22:44
bed and with continual **s** in his bones, Jb 33:19
delivered me from **s** with the people; Ps 18:43
in your shelter from the **s** of tongues. Ps 31:20
for I see violence and **s** in the city. Ps 55:9
They stir up **s**, they lurk; they watch my Ps 56:6
my life; fierce men stir up **s** against me. Ps 59:3
Hatred stirs up **s**, but love covers all Prv 10:12
By insolence comes nothing but **s**, but Prv 13:10
A hot-tempered man stirs up **s**, but he Prv 15:18
A dishonest man spreads **s**, and a Prv 16:28
than a house full of feasting with **s**. Prv 17:1
The beginning of **s** is like letting out Prv 17:14
Whoever loves transgression loves **s**; Prv 17:19
honor for a man to keep aloof from **s**, Prv 20:3
Drive out a scoffer, and **s** will go out, Prv 22:10
woe? Who has sorrow? Who has **s**? Prv 23:29
is a quarrelsome man for kindling **s**. Prv 26:21
A greedy man stirs up **s**, but the one Prv 28:25
A man of wrath stirs up **s**, and one Prv 29:22
blood, and pressing anger produces **s**. Prv 30:33
If anyone stirs up **s**, it is not from me; Is 54:15
whoever stirs up **s** with you shall fall Is 54:15
a man of **s** and contention to the whole Jer 15:10
are before me; **s** and contention arise. Hab 1:3
They are full of envy, murder, **s**, deceit, Rom 1:29
there is jealousy and **s** among you, 1 Cor 3:3
idolatry, sorcery, enmity, **s**, jealousy, Gal 5:20

STRIKE (121)
will I ever again **s** down every living Gn 8:21
“Why do you **s** your companion?” Ex 2:13
out my hand and **s** Egypt with all the Ex 3:20
is in my hand I will **s** the water that is in Ex 7:17
out your staff and **s** the dust of the Ex 8:16
and I will **s** all the firstborn in the land Ex 12:12
destroy you, when I **s** the land of Egypt. Ex 12:13
will pass through to **s** the Egyptians, Ex 12:23
destroyer to enter your houses to **s** you. Ex 12:23
rock at Horeb, and you shall **s** the rock, Ex 17:6
and I myself will **s** you sevenfold for Lv 26:24
I will **s** them with the pestilence and Nm 14:12
the Midianites and **s** them down, Nm 25:17
the way is long, and **s** him fatally, Dt 19:6
The LORD will **s** you with wasting Dt 28:22
The LORD will **s** you with the boils of Dt 28:27
The LORD will **s** you with madness and Dt 28:28
The LORD will **s** you on the knees and Dt 28:35
to me and help me, and let us **s** Gibeon. Jos 10:4
and you shall **s** the Midianites as one Jgs 6:16
times they began to **s** and kill some of Jgs 20:31
had begun to **s** and kill about Jgs 20:39
“Go and **s** the inhabitants of Jgs 21:10
And that first **s**, which Jonathan and 1 Sm 14:14
Now go and **s** Amalek and devote to 1 Sm 15:3
and I will **s** you down and cut off 1 Sm 17:46
hurled his spear at him to **s** him. 1 Sm 20:33
out their hand to **s** the priests of the 1 Sm 22:17
“You turn and **s** the priests.” And 1 Sm 22:18
the spear, and I will not **s** him twice.” 1 Sm 26:8
the LORD lives, the LORD will **s** him, 1 Sm 26:10
And David would **s** the land and 1 Sm 27:9
Why should I **s** you to the ground? 2 Sm 2:22
day, “Whoever would **s** the Jebusites, 2 Sm 5:8
out before you to **s** down the army of 2 Sm 5:24
and when I say to you, ‘**S** Amnon,’ 2 Sm 13:28
ruin on us and **s** the city with the 2 Sm 15:14
will flee. I will **s** down only the king, 2 Sm 17:2
then did you not **s** him there to the 2 Sm 18:11
Saul had sought to **s** them down in 2 Sm 21:2
Jehoiada, saying, “Go, **s** him down.” 1 Kgs 2:29
has said, **s** him down and bury him, 1 Kgs 2:31
the LORD will **s** Israel as a reed is 1 Kgs 14:15
at the command of the LORD, “**S** me, 1 Kgs 20:35
But the man refused to **s** him. 1 Kgs 20:35
a lion shall **s** you down.” And as 1 Kgs 20:36
found another man and said, “**S** me, 1 Kgs 20:37
“Please **s** this people with blindness.” 2 Kgs 6:18
“My father, shall I **s** them down? 2 Kgs 6:21
them down? Shall I **s** them down?” 2 Kgs 6:21
“You shall not **s** them down. 2 Kgs 6:22
Would you **s** down those whom you 2 Kgs 6:22
And you shall **s** down the house of 2 Kgs 9:7
officers, “Go in and **s** them down; 2 Kgs 10:25
“**S** the ground with them.” And he 2 Kgs 13:18
but now you will **s** down Syria only 2 Kgs 13:19
out before you to **s** down the army 1 Chr 14:15
a bronze arrow will **s** him through. Jb 20:24
and commands it to **s** the mark. Jb 36:32
For you **s** all my enemies on the cheek; Ps 3:7
is of the earth may **s** terror no more. Ps 10:18
But God will **s** the heads of his enemies, Ps 68:21
that you may **s** your feet in their blood, Ps 68:23
foes before him and **s** down those who Ps 89:23
up, lest you **s** your foot against a stone. Ps 91:12
The sun shall not **s** you by day, nor the Ps 121:6
Let a righteous man **s** me—it is a Ps 141:5
nor to **s** the noble for their Prv 17:26
S a scoffer, and the simple will learn Prv 19:25
if you **s** him with a rod, he will not die. Prv 23:13
If you **s** him with the rod, you will save Prv 23:14
and they **s** hands with the children of Is 2:6
therefore the Lord will **s** with a scab the Is 3:17
the Assyrians when they **s** with the rod Is 10:24
and he shall **s** the earth with the rod of his Is 11:4
breath, and **s** it into seven channels, Is 11:15
And the LORD will **s** Egypt, striking and Is 19:22
scorching wind nor sun shall **s** them, Is 49:10
I gave my back to those who **s**, and my Is 50:6
a lion from the forest shall **s** them down; Jer 5:6
Come, let us **s** him with the tongue, and Jer 18:18
and shall **s** them down with the sword. Jer 20:4
And I will **s** down the inhabitants of this Jer 21:6
He shall **s** them down with the edge of Jer 21:7
and he shall **s** them down before your Jer 29:21
men whom I shall **s** down in my anger Jer 33:5
let me go and **s** down Ishmael the son Jer 40:15
He shall come and **s** the land of Egypt, Jer 43:11
king of Babylon to **s** the land of Egypt: Jer 46:13
you shall take and **s** with the sword all Ezk 5:2
“Pass through the city after him, and **s**. Ezk 9:5
people. **S** therefore upon your thigh. Ezk 21:12
I **s** my hand at the dishonest gain that Ezk 22:13
it, when I **s** down all who dwell in it, Ezk 32:15
Then I will **s** your bow from your left Ezk 39:3
I will **s** the winter house along with the Am 3:15
“**S** the capitals until the thresholds Am 9:1
with a rod they **s** the judge of Israel on the Mi 5:1
Therefore I **s** you with a grievous blow, Mi 6:13
of her possessions and **s** down her power Zec 9:4
sea of troubles and **s** down the waves Zec 10:11
May the sword **s** his arm and his right Zec 11:17
the LORD, I will **s** every horse with panic, Zec 12:4
when I **s** every horse of the peoples with Zec 12:4
“**S** the shepherd, and the sheep will be Zec 13:7
which the LORD will **s** all the peoples Zec 14:12
lest I come and **s** the land with a decree Mal 4:6
up, lest you **s** your foot against a stone.’” Mt 4:6
For it is written, ‘I will **s** the shepherd, Mt 26:31
for it is written, ‘I will **s** the shepherd, Mk 14:27
and to cover his face and to **s** him, Mk 14:65
up, lest you **s** your foot against a stone.’” Lk 4:11
said, “Lord, shall we **s** with the sword?” Lk 22:49
if what I said is right, why do you **s** me?” Jn 18:23
stood by him to **s** him on the mouth. Acts 23:2
said to him, “God is going to **s** you, Acts 23:3
for those who **s** their fathers and 1 Tm 1:9
and I will **s** her children dead. And all Rv 2:23
the sun shall not **s** them, nor any Rv 7:16
into blood and to **s** the earth with every Rv 11:6
with which to **s** down the nations, Rv 19:15

STRIKES (21)
“Whoever **s** a man so that he dies shall Ex 21:12
“Whoever **s** his father or his mother Ex 21:15
men quarrel and one **s** the other with a Ex 21:18
“When a man **s** his slave, male or Ex 21:20
“When a man **s** the eye of his slave, Ex 21:26
from the handle and **s** his neighbor so Dt 19:5
and attacks him and **s** him fatally so Dt 19:11
be anyone who **s** down his neighbor Dt 27:24
“Whoever **s** Kiriath-sepher and Jos 15:16
the manslayer who **s** any person Jos 20:3
“Whoever **s** the Jebusites first shall 1 Chr 11:6
He **s** them for their wickedness in a Jb 34:26
I will mock when terror **s** you, Prv 1:26
when terror **s** you like a storm and your Prv 1:27
voice of the LORD, when he **s** with his rod. Is 30:31
with the hammer him who **s** the anvil, Is 41:7
him give his cheek to the one who **s**, Lam 3:30
you will know that I am the LORD, who **s**. Ezk 7:9
when the east wind **s** it—wither away Ezk 17:10
To one who **s** you on the cheek, offer the Lk 6:29
or puts on airs, or **s** you in the face. 2 Cor 11:20

STRIKING (18)
wounding me, a young man for **s** me. Gn 4:23
not listen to me, I will continue **s** you, Lv 26:21
of Israel had finished **s** them with a Jos 10:20
after capturing it and **s** it with the Jos 19:47
returned from the **s** down of the 1 Sm 17:57
David returned from **s** down the 1 Sm 18:6
had returned from **s** down the 2 Sm 1:1
he returned from **s** down 18,000 2 Sm 8:13
the ground without **s** a second blow, 2 Sm 20:10
saw the angel who was **s** the people, 2 Sm 24:17
forward, **s** the Moabites as they went. 2 Kgs 3:24
Amaziah came from **s** down the 2 Chr 25:14
but he who hates **s** hands in pledge is Prv 11:15
the LORD will strike Egypt, **s** and healing, Is 19:22
And while they were **s**, and I was left Ezk 9:8
And they were **s** his head with a reed Mk 15:19
avenged him by **s** down the Egyptian. Acts 7:24
But **s** a reef, they ran the vessel Acts 27:41

STRING (1)
fitted their arrow to the **s** to shoot in the Ps 11:2

STRINGED (10)
To the choirmaster: with **s** instruments. Ps 4:T
To the choirmaster: with **s** instruments; Ps 6:T
From ivory palaces **s** instruments make Ps 45:8
To the choirmaster: with **s** instruments. Ps 54:T
To the choirmaster: with **s** instruments. Ps 55:T
To the choirmaster: with **s** instruments. Ps 61:T
To the choirmaster: with **s** instruments. Ps 67:T
To the choirmaster: with **s** instruments. Ps 76:T
play my music on **s** instruments all the Is 38:20
the choirmaster: with **s** instruments. Hab 3:19

STRINGS (4)
melody to him with the harp of ten **s**! Ps 33:2
play skillfully on the **s**, with loud shouts. Ps 33:3
and dance; praise him with **s** and pipe! Ps 150:4
ornaments, your neck with **s** of jewels. Sg 1:10

STRIP (19)
you shall not **s** your vineyard bare, Lv 19:10
And **s** Aaron of his garments and put Nm 20:26
vineyard, you shall not **s** it afterward. Dt 24:21
the Philistines came to **s** the slain, 1 Sm 31:8
after him only to **s** the slain. 2 Sm 23:10
the Philistines came to **s** the slain, 1 Chr 10:8
Who can **s** off his outer garment? Who Jb 41:13
s, and make yourselves bare, and tie Is 32:11
flour, put off your veil, **s** off your robe, Is 47:2
s away her branches, for they are not the Jer 5:10
become drunk and **s** yourself bare. Lam 4:21
They shall **s** you of your clothes and Ezk 16:39
They shall also **s** you of your clothes Ezk 23:26
their robes and **s** off their embroidered Ezk 26:16
s off its leaves and scatter its fruit. Dn 4:14
lest I **s** her naked and make her as in the Hos 2:3
it shall **s** his treasury of every precious Hos 13:15
you **s** the rich robe from those who pass Mi 2:8
the Lord will **s** her of her possessions and Zec 9:4

STRIPE (2)
for burn, wound for wound, **s** for stripe. Ex 21:25
for burn, wound for wound, stripe for **s**. Ex 21:25

STRIPED (7)
the male goats that were **s** and spotted, Gn 30:35
and so the flocks brought forth **s**, Gn 30:39
the flocks toward the **s** and all the Gn 30:40
if he said, ‘The **s** shall be your wages,’ Gn 31:8
be your wages,’ then all the flock bore **s**. Gn 31:8
goats that mated with the flock were **s**, Gn 31:10
the goats that mate with the flock are **s**, Gn 31:12

STRIPES (6)
with a number of **s** in proportion to his Dt 25:2
Forty **s** may be given him, but not more, Dt 25:3
on to beat him with more **s** than these, Dt 25:3
of men, with the **s** of the sons of men, 2 Sm 7:14
with the rod and their iniquity with **s**, Ps 89:32
us peace, and with his **s** we are healed. Is 53:5

STRIPPED (26)
to his brothers, they **s** him of his robe, Gn 37:23
the people of Israel **s** themselves of their Ex 33:6
And Moses **s** Aaron of his garments Nm 20:28
And Jonathan **s** himself of the robe 1 Sm 18:4
And he too **s** off his clothes, and he 1 Sm 19:24
off his head and **s** off his armor and 1 Sm 31:9
that time Hezekiah **s** the gold from 2 Kgs 18:16
And they **s** him and took his head 1 Chr 10:9
He leads counselors away **s**, and judges Jb 12:17
leads priests away **s** and overthrows the Jb 12:19
He has **s** from me my glory and taken the Jb 19:9
brothers for nothing and **s** the naked of Jb 22:6
The stouthearted were **s** of their spoil; Ps 76:5
siege towers, they **s** her palaces bare, Is 23:13
But I have **s** Esau bare; I have Jer 49:10
her land will be **s** of all it contains, Ezk 12:19
its fruit; they were **s** off and withered. Ezk 19:12
it has **s** off their bark and thrown it down; Jl 1:7
lament and wail; I will go **s** and naked; Mi 1:8
its mistress is **s**; she is carried off, her Na 2:7
You **s** the sheath from your bow, Hab 3:9
And they **s** him and put a scarlet robe Mt 27:28
they **s** him of the robe and put his own Mt 27:31
they **s** him of the purple cloak and put Mk 15:20
who **s** him and beat him and departed, Lk 10:30
his outer garment, for he was **s** for work, Jn 21:7

STRIPS (3)
the deer give birth and **s** the forests bare, Ps 29:9
there it lies down and **s** its branches. Is 27:10
his hands and feet bound with linen **s**, Jn 11:44

STRIVE (9)
"When men **s** together and hit a — Ex 21:22
those who keep the law **s** against them. — Prv 28:4
those who **s** against you shall be as — Is 41:11
"**S** to enter through the narrow door. — Lk 13:24
to **s** together with me in your prayers — Rom 15:30
s to excel in building up the church. — 1 Cor 14:12
For to this end we toil and **s**, because — 1 Tm 4:10
Let us therefore **s** to enter that rest, so — Heb 4:11
S for peace with everyone, and for the — Heb 12:14

STRIVEN (1)
for you have **s** with God and with men, — Gn 32:28

STRIVES (1)
"Woe to him who **s** with him who formed — Is 45:9

STRIVING (11)
behold, all is vanity and a **s** after wind. — Eccl 1:14
that this also is but a **s** after wind. — Eccl 1:17
all was vanity and a **s** after wind, — Eccl 2:11
me, for all is vanity and a **s** after wind. — Eccl 2:17
all the toil and **s** of heart with which — Eccl 2:22
This also is vanity and a **s** after wind. — Eccl 2:26
This also is vanity and a **s** after wind. — Eccl 4:4
two hands full of toil and a **s** after wind. — Eccl 4:6
this also is vanity and a **s** after wind. — Eccl 4:16
this also is vanity and a **s** after wind. — Eccl 6:9
with one mind **s** side by side for the — Phil 1:27

STROKE (4)
to the earth with one **s** of the spear, — 1 Sm 26:8
Remove your **s** from me; I am spent by — Ps 39:10
And every **s** of the appointed staff that — Is 30:32
of your eyes away from you at a **s**; — Ezk 24:16

STROKES (1)
evil; **s** make clean the innermost parts. — Prv 20:30

STRONG (213)
"Issachar is a **s** donkey, crouching — Gn 49:14
they multiplied and grew exceedingly **s**, so — Ex 1:7
the people multiplied and grew very **s**. — Ex 1:20
for with a **s** hand he will send them out, — Ex 6:1
and with a **s** hand he will drive them out — Ex 6:1
turned the wind into a very **s** west wind, — Ex 10:19
for by a **s** hand the LORD brought you — Ex 13:3
For with a **s** hand the LORD has brought — Ex 13:9
'By a **s** hand the LORD brought us out of — Ex 13:14
for by a **s** hand the LORD brought us out — Ex 13:16
the sea back by a **s** east wind all night — Ex 14:21
"Drink no wine or **s** drink, you or your — Lv 10:9
separate himself from wine and **s** drink. — Nm 6:3
made from wine or **s** drink and shall not — Nm 6:3
that was among them had a **s** craving. — Nm 11:4
people who dwell in it are **s** or weak, — Nm 13:18
the people who dwell in the land are **s**, — Nm 13:28
with a large army and with a **s** force. — Nm 20:20
the border of the Ammonites was **s**. — Nm 21:24
a drink offering of **s** drink to the LORD. — Nm 28:7
command you today, that you may be **s**, — Dt 11:8
—oxen or sheep or wine or **s** drink, — Dt 14:26
and you have not drunk wine or **s** drink, — Dt 29:6
Be **s** and courageous. Do not fear or be in — Dt 31:6
sight of all Israel, "Be **s** and courageous, — Dt 31:7
of Nun and said, "Be **s** and courageous, — Dt 31:23
Be **s** and courageous, for you shall cause — Jos 1:6
Only be **s** and very courageous, being — Jos 1:7
commanded you? Be **s** and courageous. — Jos 1:9
put to death. Only be **s** and courageous." — Jos 1:18
or dismayed; be **s** and courageous. — Jos 10:25
I am still as **s** today as I was in the day — Jos 14:11
Now when the people of Israel grew **s**, — Jos 17:13
of iron, and though they are **s**." — Jos 17:18
be very **s** to keep and to do all that is — Jos 23:6
out before you great and **s** nations. — Jos 23:9
When Israel grew **s**, they put the — Jgs 1:28
time about 10,000 of the Moabites, all **s**, — Jgs 3:29
But there was a **s** tower within the city, — Jgs 9:51
be careful and drink no wine or **s** drink, — Jgs 13:4
So then drink no wine or **s** drink, and — Jgs 13:7
neither let her drink wine or **s** drink, — Jgs 13:14
Out of the **s** came something sweet." — Jgs 14:14
Micah saw that they were too **s** for him, — Jgs 18:26
have drunk neither wine nor **s** drink, — 1 Sm 1:15
And when Saul saw any **s** man, or — 1 Sm 14:52
Now therefore let your hands be **s**, and — 2 Sm 2:7
was making himself **s** in the house — 2 Sm 3:6
said, "If the Syrians are too **s** for me, — 2 Sm 10:11
if the Ammonites are too **s** for you, — 2 Sm 10:11
And the conspiracy grew **s**, and the — 2 Sm 15:12
He rescued me from my **s** enemy, — 2 Sm 22:18
This God is my **s** refuge and has — 2 Sm 22:33
to go the way of all the earth. Be **s**, — 1 Kgs 2:2
and a great and **s** wind tore the — 1 Kgs 19:11
are with your servants fifty **s** men. — 2 Kgs 2:16
1,000, all of them **s** and fit for war. — 2 Kgs 24:16
though Judah became **s** among his — 1 Chr 5:2
who gave him **s** support in his — 1 Chr 11:10
said, "If the Syrians are too **s** for me, — 1 Chr 19:12
if the Ammonites are too **s** for you, — 1 Chr 19:12
Be **s**, and let us use our strength for — 1 Chr 19:13
for Israel. Be **s** and courageous. — 1 Chr 22:13
if he continues **s** in keeping my — 1 Chr 28:7
for the sanctuary; be **s** and do it." — 1 Chr 28:10
son, "Be **s** and courageous and do it. — 1 Chr 28:20
He made the fortresses **s**, and put — 2 Chr 11:11
all the cities and made them very **s**. — 2 Chr 11:12
was established and he was **s**, — 2 Chr 12:1
Rehoboam grew **s** in Jerusalem — 2 Chr 12:13
to give **s** support to those whose heart — 2 Chr 16:9
But go, act, be **s** for the battle. Why — 2 Chr 25:8
border of Egypt, for he became very **s**. — 2 Chr 26:8
marvelously helped, till he was **s**. — 2 Chr 26:15
But when he was **s**, he grew proud, — 2 Chr 26:16
"Be **s** and courageous. Do not be — 2 Chr 32:7
that you may be **s** and eat the good of — Ezr 9:12
and we are with you; be **s** and do it." — Ezr 10:4
your great power and by your **s** hand. — Neh 1:10
The **s** lion perishes for lack of prey, and — Jb 4:11
on princes and loosens the belt of the **s**. — Jb 12:21
His **s** steps are shortened, and his own — Jb 18:7
Their young ones become **s**; they grow — Jb 39:4
rescued me from my **s** enemy and from — Ps 18:17
leaving his chamber, and, like a **s** man, — Ps 19:5
me; **s** bulls of Bashan surround me; — Ps 22:12
The LORD, **s** and mighty, the LORD, — Ps 24:8
Wait for the LORD; be **s**, and let your — Ps 27:14
O LORD, you made my mountain stand **s**; — Ps 30:7
of refuge for me, a **s** fortress to save me! — Ps 31:2
Be **s**, and let your heart take courage, all — Ps 31:24
the poor from him who is too **s** for him, — Ps 35:10
my refuge, a **s** tower against the enemy. — Ps 61:3
to many, but you are my **s** refuge. — Ps 71:7
like a **s** man shouting because of wine. — Ps 78:65
the son whom you made **s** for yourself. — Ps 80:15
whom you have made **s** for yourself! — Ps 80:17
they are the **s** arm of the children of Lot. — Ps 83:8
s is your hand, high your right hand. — Ps 89:13
with a **s** hand and an outstretched — Ps 136:12
persecutors, for they are too **s** for me! — Ps 142:6
A rich man's wealth is his **s** city; the — Prv 10:15
fear of the LORD one has **s** confidence, — Prv 14:26
The name of the LORD is a **s** tower; the — Prv 18:10
A rich man's wealth is his **s** city, and — Prv 18:11
is more unyielding than a **s** city, — Prv 18:19
Wine is a mocker, **s** drink a brawler, — Prv 20:1
anger, and a concealed bribe, **s** wrath. — Prv 21:14
for their Redeemer is **s**; he will plead — Prv 23:11
the ants are a people not **s**, yet they — Prv 30:25
drink wine, or for rulers to take **s** drink, — Prv 31:4
Give **s** drink to the one who is — Prv 31:6
with strength and makes her arms **s**. — Prv 31:17
not to the swift, nor the battle to the **s**, — Eccl 9:11
house tremble, and the **s** men are bent, — Eccl 12:3
seal upon your arm, for love is **s** as death, — Sg 8:6
And the **s** shall become tinder, and his — Is 1:31
morning, that they may run after **s** drink, — Is 5:11
wine, and valiant men in mixing **s** drink, — Is 5:22
thus to me with his **s** hand upon me, — Is 8:11
In that day their **s** cities will be like the — Is 17:9
hurl you away violently, O you **s** man. — Is 22:17
s drink is bitter to those who drink it. — Is 24:9
Therefore **s** peoples will glorify you; cities — Is 25:3
in the land of Judah: "We have a **s** city; — Is 26:1
hard and great and **s** sword will punish — Is 27:1
the Lord has one who is mighty and **s**; — Is 28:2
reel with wine and stagger with **s** drink; — Is 28:7
priest and the prophet reel with **s** drink, — Is 28:7
by wine, they stagger with **s** drink, — Is 28:7
do not scoff, lest your bonds be made **s**; — Is 28:22
with wine; stagger, but not with **s** drink! — Is 29:9
and in horsemen because they are very **s**, — Is 31:1
to those who have an anxious heart, "Be **s**; — Is 35:4
and because he is **s** in power not one is — Is 40:26
neighbor and says to his brother, "Be **s**!" — Is 41:6
hammers and works it with his **s** arm. — Is 44:12
oak and lets it grow **s** among the trees of — Is 44:14
and he shall divide the spoil with the **s**, — Is 53:12
wine; let us fill ourselves with **s** drink; — Is 56:12
scorched places and make your bones **s**; — Is 58:11
and not truth has grown **s** in the land; — Jer 9:3
you with outstretched hand and **s** arm, — Jer 21:5
him from hands too **s** for him. — Jer 31:11
with a **s** hand and outstretched arm, — Jer 32:21
Their Redeemer is **s**; the LORD of hosts is — Jer 50:34
the walls of Babylon; make the watch **s**; — Jer 51:12
though she should fortify her **s** height, — Jer 51:53
the hand of the LORD being **s** upon me. — Ezk 3:14
I will put an end to the pride of the **s**, — Ezk 7:24
It will not take a **s** arm or many people — Ezk 17:9
Its **s** stems became rulers' scepters; it — Ezk 19:11
As for its **s** stem, fire consumed it. — Ezk 19:12
so that there remains in it no **s** stem, — Ezk 19:14
endure, or can your hands be **s**, — Ezk 22:14
that it may become **s** to wield the — Ezk 30:21
both the **s** arm and the one that was — Ezk 30:22
and the fat and the **s** I will destroy. — Ezk 34:16
shall be a fourth kingdom, **s** as iron, — Dn 2:40
shall be partly **s** and partly brittle. — Dn 2:42
The tree grew and became **s**, and its top — Dn 4:11
tree you saw, which grew and became **s**, — Dn 4:20
O king, who have grown and become **s**. — Dn 4:22
terrifying and dreadful and exceedingly **s**. — Dn 7:7
exceedingly great, but when he was **s**, — Dn 8:8
he shall make a **s** covenant with many — Dn 9:27
be **s** and of good courage." And as he — Dn 10:19
he has become **s** through his riches, — Dn 11:2
"Then the king of the south shall be **s**, — Dn 11:5
and he shall become **s** with a small — Dn 11:23
the cedars and who was as **s** as the oaks; — Am 2:9
and the **s** shall not retain his strength, — Am 2:14
destruction flash forth against the **s**, — Am 5:9
to you of wine and **s** drink," he would be — Mi 2:11
and shall decide for **s** nations afar off; — Mi 4:3
and those who were cast off, a **s** nation; — Mi 4:7
Yet now be **s**, O Zerubbabel, declares the — Hg 2:4
O Zerubbabel, declares the LORD. Be **s**, — Hg 2:4
son of Jehozadak, the high priest. Be **s**, — Hg 2:4
chariot dappled horses—all of them **s**. — Zec 6:3
When the **s** horses came out, they were — Zec 6:7
"Let your hands be **s**, you who in these — Zec 8:9
Fear not, but let your hands be **s**." — Zec 8:13
Many peoples and **s** nations shall come — Zec 8:22
I will make them **s** in the LORD, and — Zec 10:12
someone enter a **s** man's house and — Mt 12:29
goods, unless he first binds the **s** man? — Mt 12:29
one can enter a **s** man's house and — Mk 3:27
goods, unless he first binds the **s** man. — Mk 3:27
And he must not drink wine or **s** drink, — Lk 1:15
the child grew and became **s** in spirit, — Lk 1:80
And the child grew and became **s**, filled — Lk 2:40
When a **s** man, fully armed, guards his — Lk 11:21
away from me? I am not **s** enough to dig, — Lk 16:3
rough because a **s** wind was blowing. — Jn 6:18
his feet and ankles were made **s**. — Acts 3:7
has made this man **s** whom you see — Acts 3:16
but he grew **s** in his faith as he gave — Rom 4:20
We who are **s** have an obligation to — Rom 15:1
is weak in the world to shame the **s**; — 1 Cor 1:27
in Christ. We are weak, but you are **s**. — 1 Cor 4:10
his betrothed, if his passions are **s**, — 1 Cor 7:36
firm in the faith, act like men, be **s**. — 1 Cor 16:13
say, "His letters are weighty and **s**, — 2 Cor 10:10
For when I am weak, then I am **s**. — 2 Cor 12:10
glad when we are weak and you are **s**. — 2 Cor 13:9
be **s** in the Lord and in the strength of — Eph 6:10
God sends them a **s** delusion, — 2 Thes 2:11
refuge might have **s** encouragement to — Heb 6:18
sword, were made **s** out of weakness, — Heb 11:34
are so large and are driven by **s** winds, — Jas 3:4
to you, young men, because you are **s**, — 1 Jn 2:14
And I saw a **s** angel proclaiming with a — Rv 5:2

STRONGER (21)
the one shall be **s** than the other, the — Gn 25:23
Whenever the **s** of the flock were — Gn 30:41
would be Laban's, and the **s** Jacob's. — Gn 30:42
the people, for they are **s** than we are." — Nm 13:31
What is **s** than a lion?" And he said to — Jgs 14:18
than eagles; they were **s** than lions. — 2 Sm 1:23
And David grew **s** and stronger, while — 2 Sm 3:1
And David grew stronger and **s**, while — 2 Sm 3:1
listen to her, and being **s** than she, — 2 Sm 13:14
the hills, and so they were **s** than we. — 1 Kgs 20:23
and surely we shall be **s** than they. — 1 Kgs 20:23
surely we shall be **s** than they." And — 1 Kgs 20:25
has clean hands grows **s** and stronger. — Jb 17:9
has clean hands grows stronger and **s**. — Jb 17:9
and made them **s** than their foes. — Ps 105:24
not able to dispute with one **s** than he. — Eccl 6:10
me, and I was deceived; you are **s** than I, — Jer 20:7
his princes shall be **s** than he and shall — Dn 11:5
but when one **s** than he attacks him — Lk 11:22
the weakness of God is **s** than men. — 1 Cor 1:25
Lord to jealousy? Are we **s** than he? — 1 Cor 10:22

STRONGEST (2)
and he killed the **s** of them and laid low — Ps 78:31
shall deal with the **s** fortresses with the — Dn 11:39

STRONGHOLD (38)
LORD your God on the top of the **s** here, — Jgs 6:26
they entered the **s** of the house of — Jgs 9:46
Abimelech put it against the **s**, — Jgs 9:49
and they set the **s** on fire over them, — Jgs 9:49
all the time that David was in the **s**. — 1 Sm 22:4
said to David, "Do not remain in the **s**; — 1 Sm 22:5
David and his men went up to the **s**. — 1 Sm 24:22
Nevertheless, David took the **s** of Zion, — 2 Sm 5:7

David lived in the **s** and called it the 2 Sm 5:9
heard of it and went down to the **s**. 2 Sm 5:17
of my salvation, my **s** and my refuge, 2 Sm 22:3
David was then in the **s**, and the 2 Sm 23:14
David took the **s** of Zion, 1 Chr 11:5
And David lived in the **s**; therefore it 1 Chr 11:7
David was then in the **s**, and the 1 Chr 11:16
to David at the **s** in the wilderness 1 Chr 12:8
and Judah came to the **s** to David. 1 Chr 12:16
his home, on the rocky crag and **s**. Jb 39:28
The LORD is a **s** for the oppressed, a Ps 9:9
for the oppressed, a **s** in times of trouble. Ps 9:9
and the horn of my salvation, my **s**. Ps 18:2
The LORD is the **s** of my life; of whom Ps 27:1
LORD; he is their **s** in the time of trouble. Ps 37:39
But the LORD has become my **s**, and my Ps 94:22
and my fortress, my **s** and my deliverer, Ps 144:2
way of the LORD is a **s** to the blameless, Prv 10:29
and brings down the **s** in which they Prv 21:22
for the sea has spoken, the **s** of the sea, Is 23:4
of Tarshish, for your **s** is laid waste. Is 23:14
For you have been a **s** to the poor, a Is 25:4
to the poor, a **s** to the needy in his distress, Is 25:4
against her and her **s** and distress her, Is 29:7
O LORD, my strength and my **s**, my Jer 16:19
the day when I take from them their **s**, Ezk 24:25
my wrath on Pelusium, the **s** of Egypt, Ezk 30:15
to his people, a **s** to the people of Israel. Jl 3:16
LORD is good, a **s** in the day of trouble; Na 1:7
Return to your **s**, O prisoners of hope; Zec 9:12

STRONGHOLDS (32)
that they dwell in are camps or **s**, Nm 13:19
in the mountains and the caves and the **s**. Jgs 6:2
remained in the **s** in the wilderness, 1 Sm 23:14
hiding among us in the **s** at Horesh, 1 Sm 23:19
there and lived in the **s** of Engedi. 1 Sm 23:29
his walls; you have laid his **s** in ruins. Ps 89:40
concerning Canaan to destroy its **s**. Is 23:11
Thorns shall grow over its **s**, nettles and Is 34:13
up against you; he has destroyed your **s**. Jer 48:18
cities shall be taken and the **s** seized. Jer 48:41
and it shall devour the **s** of Ben-hadad." Jer 49:27
ceased fighting; they remain in their **s**; Jer 51:30
has broken down the **s** of the daughter Lam 2:2
he has laid in ruins its **s**, and he has Lam 2:5
those who are in **s** and in caves shall Ezk 33:27
He shall devise plans against **s**, but Dn 11:24
his cities, and it shall devour her **s**. Hos 8:14
and it shall devour the **s** of Ben-hadad. Am 1:4
wall of Gaza, and it shall devour her **s**. Am 1:7
wall of Tyre, and it shall devour her **s**." Am 1:10
and it shall devour the **s** of Bozrah." Am 1:12
of Rabbah, and it shall devour her **s**, Am 1:14
and it shall devour the **s** of Kerioth, Am 2:2
and it shall devour the **s** of Jerusalem." Am 2:5
Proclaim to the **s** in Ashdod and to the Am 3:9
in Ashdod and to the **s** in the land of Am 3:9
up violence and robbery in their **s**." Am 3:10
you, and your **s** shall be plundered." Am 3:11
abhor the pride of Jacob and hate his **s**, Am 6:8
of your land and throw down all your **s**; Mi 5:11
they shall come trembling out of their **s**; Mi 7:17
but have divine power to destroy **s**. 2 Cor 10:4

STRONGLY (4)
But he pressed them **s**; so they turned Gn 19:3
but they urged him **s**, saying, "Stay Lk 24:29
I **s** urged him to visit you with the 1 Cor 16:12
for he **s** opposed our message. 2 Tm 4:15

STROVE (3)
when he **s** with Aram-naharaim and Ps 60:T
and in his manhood he **s** with God. Hos 12:3
He **s** with the angel and prevailed; he Hos 12:4

STRUCK (273)
And they **s** with blindness the men Gn 19:11
he **s** down the Egyptian and hid him in Ex 2:12
lifted up the staff and **s** the water in the Ex 7:20
days passed after the LORD had **s** the Nile. Ex 7:25
hand with his staff and **s** the dust of the Ex 8:17
out my hand and **s** you and your people Ex 9:15
The hail **s** down everything that was in Ex 9:25
And the hail **s** down every plant of the Ex 9:25
(The flax and the barley were **s** down, for Ex 9:31
wheat and the emmer were not **s** down, Ex 9:32
when he **s** the Egyptians but spared our Ex 12:27
At midnight the LORD **s** down all the Ex 12:29
hand the staff with which you **s** the Nile, Ex 17:5
his staff, he who **s** him shall be clear; Ex 21:19
breaking in and is **s** so that he dies, Ex 22:2
and you shall be **s** down before your Lv 26:17
the day that I **s** down all the firstborn Nm 3:13
the day that I **s** down all the firstborn Nm 8:17
and the LORD **s** down the people with a Nm 11:33
lest you be **s** down before your Nm 14:42
up his hand and **s** the rock with his Nm 20:11
the field. And Balaam **s** the donkey, Nm 22:23
against the wall. So he **s** her again. Nm 22:25
and he **s** the donkey with his staff. Nm 22:27
that you have **s** me these three times?" Nm 22:28
"Why have you **s** your donkey these Nm 22:32
Balaam, and he **s** his hands together. Nm 24:10
land that the LORD **s** down before the Nm 32:4
the LORD had **s** down among them. Nm 33:4
"But if he **s** him down with an iron Nm 35:16
And if he **s** him down with a stone Nm 35:17
Or if he **s** him down with a wooden Nm 35:18
or in enmity **s** him down with his Nm 35:21
then he who **s** the blow shall be put to Nm 35:21
and we **s** him down until he had no Dt 3:3
far as Shebarim and **s** them at the Jos 7:5
they turned back and **s** down the men of Jos 8:21
on that side. And Israel **s** them down, Jos 8:22
returned to Ai and **s** it down with the Jos 8:24
who **s** them with a great blow at Jos 10:10
ascent of Beth-horon and **s** them as far Jos 10:10
And afterward Joshua **s** them and put Jos 10:26
Joshua captured it on that day and **s** it, Jos 10:28
And he **s** it with the edge of the sword, Jos 10:30
on the second day and **s** it with the edge Jos 10:32
And Joshua **s** him and his people, until Jos 10:33
day, and **s** it with the edge of the sword. Jos 10:35
and captured it and **s** it with the edge of Jos 10:37
And they **s** them with the edge of the Jos 10:39
So Joshua **s** the whole land, the hill Jos 10:40
And Joshua **s** them from Jos 10:41
who **s** them and chased them as far as Jos 11:8
And they **s** them until he left none Jos 11:8
and captured Hazor and **s** its king with Jos 11:10
And they **s** with the sword all who were Jos 11:11
and **s** them with the edge of the sword, Jos 11:12
But every man they **s** with the edge of Jos 11:14
all their kings and **s** them and put Jos 11:17
these Moses had **s** and driven out. Jos 13:12
because he **s** his neighbor Jos 20:5
and captured it and **s** it with the edge Jgs 1:8
And they **s** the city with the edge of the Jgs 1:25
to the workmen's mallet; she **s** Sisera; Jgs 5:26
came to the tent and **s** it so that it fell Jgs 7:13
And he **s** them from Aroer to the Jgs 11:33
And the men of Gilead **s** Ephraim, Jgs 12:4
to Ashkelon and **s** down thirty men Jgs 14:19
And he **s** them hip and thigh with a Jgs 15:8
and took it, and with it he **s** 1,000 men. Jgs 15:15
a donkey have I **s** down a thousand Jgs 15:16
and **s** them with the edge of the sword Jgs 18:27
ambush moved out and **s** all the city Jgs 20:37
and 2,000 men of them were **s** down. Jgs 20:45
of Benjamin and **s** them with the Jgs 20:48
are the gods who **s** the Egyptians with 1 Sm 4:8
who did not die were **s** with tumors, 1 Sm 5:12
know that it is not his hand that **s** us; 1 Sm 6:9
And he **s** some of the men of 1 Sm 6:19
He **s** seventy men of them, and the 1 Sm 6:19
the LORD had **s** the people with 1 Sm 6:19
pursued the Philistines and **s** them, 1 Sm 7:11
morning watch and **s** down the 1 Sm 11:11
They **s** down the Philistines that day 1 Sm 14:31
did valiantly and **s** the Amalekites 1 Sm 14:48
after him and **s** him and delivered 1 Sm 17:35
by his beard and **s** him and killed 1 Sm 17:35
Your servant has **s** down both lions 1 Sm 17:36
and slung it and **s** the Philistine on 1 Sm 17:49
and **s** the Philistine and killed him. 1 Sm 17:50
"Saul has **s** down his thousands, 1 Sm 18:7
his hand and he **s** down the Philistine, 1 Sm 19:5
with the Philistines and **s** them with a 1 Sm 19:8
so that he **s** the spear into the wall. 1 Sm 19:10
whom you **s** down in the valley of 1 Sm 21:9
'Saul has **s** down his thousands, 1 Sm 21:11
Edomite turned and **s** down the 1 Sm 22:18
their livestock and **s** them with a 1 Sm 23:5
And afterward David's heart **s** him, 1 Sm 24:5
ten days later the LORD **s** Nabal, 1 Sm 25:38
'Saul has **s** down his thousands, 1 Sm 29:5
And David **s** them down from 1 Sm 30:17
and the Philistines **s** down Jonathan 1 Sm 31:2
execute him." And he **s** him down so 2 Sm 1:15
Therefore Abner **s** him in the 2 Sm 2:23
of David had **s** down of Benjamin 2 Sm 2:31
and there he **s** him in the stomach, 2 Sm 3:27
they **s** him and put him to death and 2 Sm 4:7
and **s** down the Philistines from Geba 2 Sm 5:25
and God **s** him down there because of 2 Sm 6:7
David **s** down 22,000 men of the 2 Sm 8:5
from him, that he may be **s** down, 2 Sm 11:15
You have **s** down Uriah the Hittite 2 Sm 12:9
"Absalom has **s** down all the king's 2 Sm 13:30
and one **s** the other and killed him. 2 Sm 14:6
'Give up the man who **s** his brother, 2 Sm 14:7
surrounded Absalom and **s** him and 2 Sm 18:15
So Joab **s** him with it in the stomach 2 Sm 20:10
the Hushathite **s** down Saph, 2 Sm 21:18
s down Goliath the Gittite, 2 Sm 21:19
David's brother, **s** him down. 2 Sm 21:21
He rose and **s** down the Philistines 2 Sm 23:10
defended it and **s** down the 2 Sm 23:12
deeds. He **s** down two ariels of Moab. 2 Sm 23:20
also went down and **s** down a lion in 2 Sm 23:20
And he **s** down an Egyptian, a 2 Sm 23:21
But David's heart **s** him after he had 2 Sm 24:10
son of Jehoiada, and he **s** him down, 1 Kgs 2:25
went up and **s** him down and 1 Kgs 2:34
and he went out and **s** him down, 1 Kgs 2:46
slain, he **s** down every male in Edom 1 Kgs 11:15
And Baasha **s** him down at 1 Kgs 15:27
Zimri came in and **s** him down and 1 Kgs 16:10
he **s** down all the house of Baasha. 1 Kgs 16:11
And each **s** down his man. The 1 Kgs 20:20
Israel went out and **s** the horses and 1 Kgs 20:21
and **s** the Syrians with a great blow. 1 Kgs 20:21
the people of Israel **s** down of the 1 Kgs 20:29
a lion met him and **s** him down. 1 Kgs 20:36
And the man **s** him—struck 1 Kgs 20:37
struck him—**s** him and wounded 1 Kgs 20:37
came near and **s** Micaiah on the 1 Kgs 22:24
bow at random and **s** the king of 1 Kgs 22:34
cloak and rolled it up and **s** the water, 2 Kgs 2:8
had fallen from him and **s** the water, 2 Kgs 2:14
And when he had **s** the water, 2 Kgs 2:14
fought together and **s** one another 2 Kgs 3:23
the Israelites rose and **s** the Moabites, 2 Kgs 3:24
blindness." So he **s** them with 2 Kgs 6:18
chariot commanders **s** the Edomites 2 Kgs 8:21
killed him, but who **s** down all these? 2 Kgs 10:9
So Jehu **s** down all who remained of 2 Kgs 10:11
he **s** down all who remained to 2 Kgs 10:17
a conspiracy and **s** down Joash in 2 Kgs 12:20
his servants, who **s** him down, 2 Kgs 12:21
them." And he **s** three times and 2 Kgs 13:18
"You should have **s** five or six times; 2 Kgs 13:19
you would have **s** down Syria until 2 Kgs 13:19
he **s** down his servants who had 2 Kgs 14:5
his servants who had **s** down the king 2 Kgs 14:5
He **s** down ten thousand Edomites in 2 Kgs 14:7
You have indeed **s** down Edom, and 2 Kgs 14:10
against him and **s** him down at 2 Kgs 15:10
and he **s** down Shallum the son of 2 Kgs 15:14
Gilead, and **s** him down in Samaria, 2 Kgs 15:25
of Remaliah and **s** him down and 2 Kgs 15:30
He **s** down the Philistines as far as 2 Kgs 18:8
went out and **s** down 185,000 in 2 Kgs 19:35
s him down with the sword and 2 Kgs 19:37
people of the land **s** down all those 2 Kgs 21:24
king of Babylon **s** them down and 2 Kgs 25:21
ten men and **s** down Gedaliah and 2 Kgs 25:25
and the Philistines **s** down Jonathan 1 Chr 10:2
He **s** down two heroes of Moab. 1 Chr 11:22
also went down and **s** down a lion in 1 Chr 11:22
And he **s** down an Egyptian, a man 1 Chr 11:23
and he **s** him down because he put 1 Chr 13:10
and David **s** them down there. 1 Chr 14:11
and they **s** down the Philistine army 1 Chr 14:16
David **s** down 22,000 men of the 1 Chr 18:5
And Joab **s** down Rabbah and 1 Chr 20:1
the Hushathite **s** down Sippai, 1 Chr 20:4
the son of Jair **s** down Lahmi the 1 Chr 20:5
David's brother, **s** him down. 1 Chr 20:7
with this thing, and he **s** Israel. 1 Chr 21:7
and his people **s** them with great 2 Chr 13:17
And the LORD **s** him down, and he 2 Chr 13:20
And they **s** down the tents of those 2 Chr 14:15
came near and **s** Micaiah on the 2 Chr 18:23
bow at random and **s** the king of 2 Chr 18:33
rose by night and **s** the Edomites who 2 Chr 21:9
all this the LORD **s** him in his bowels 2 Chr 21:18
servants who had **s** down the king 2 Chr 25:3
of Salt and **s** down 10,000 men 2 Chr 25:11
and **s** down 3,000 people in them 2 Chr 25:13
Why should you be **s** down?" So the 2 Chr 25:16
You say, 'See, I have **s** down Edom,' 2 Chr 25:19
go out, because the LORD had **s** him. 2 Chr 26:20
of Israel, who **s** him with great force. 2 Chr 28:5
of his own sons **s** him down there 2 Chr 32:21
people of the land **s** down all those 2 Chr 33:25
The Jews **s** all their enemies with the Est 9:5
and took them and **s** down the servants Jb 1:15
and took them and **s** down the servants Jb 1:17
the wilderness and **s** the four corners Jb 1:19
of the LORD and **s** Job with loathsome sores Jb 2:7
they have **s** me insolently on the cheek; Jb 16:10
on his return **s** down twelve thousand Ps 60:T
persecute him whom you have **s** down, Ps 69:26
He **s** the rock so that water gushed out Ps 78:20
He **s** down every firstborn in Egypt, the Ps 78:51

My heart is **s** down like grass and has Ps 102:4
He **s** down their vines and fig trees, and Ps 105:33
He **s** down all the firstborn in their Ps 105:36
He it was who **s** down the firstborn of Ps 135:8
who **s** down many nations and killed Ps 135:10
to him who **s** down the firstborn of Ps 136:10
to him who **s** down great kings, for his Ps 136:17
"They **s** me," you will say, "but I was Prv 23:35
Why will you still be **s** down? Why will Is 1:5
out his hand against them and **s** them, Is 5:25
people did not turn to him who **s** them, Is 9:13
will no more lean on him who **s** them, Is 10:20
as when he **s** Midian at the rock of Oreb. Is 10:26
that **s** the peoples in wrath with Is 14:6
of you, that the rod that **s** you is broken, Is 14:29
of the nations have **s** down its branches, Is 16:8
Has he **s** them as he struck those who Is 27:7
struck them as he **s** those who struck Is 27:7
them as he struck those who **s** them? Is 27:7
LORD went out and **s** down a hundred Is 37:36
his sons, **s** him down with the sword. Is 37:38
of his unjust gain I was angry, I **s** him; Is 57:17
for in my wrath I **s** you, but in my favor Is 60:10
In vain have I **s** your children; they took Jer 2:30
look for truth? You have **s** them down, Jer 5:3
Why have you **s** us down so that there Jer 14:19
their youths be **s** down by the sword in Jer 18:21
who **s** him down with the sword and Jer 26:23
him rose up and **s** down Gedaliah the Jer 41:2
Ishmael also **s** down all the Judeans who Jer 41:3
men whom he had **s** down along with Jer 41:9
after he had **s** down Gedaliah the son of Jer 41:16
of Nethaniah had **s** down Gedaliah the Jer 41:18
before Pharaoh **s** down Gaza. Jer 47:1
king of Babylon **s** down. Jer 49:28
And the king of Babylon **s** them down, Jer 52:27
out." So they went out and **s** in the city. Ezk 9:7
and said, "The city has been **s** down." Ezk 33:21
year after the city was **s** down, Ezk 40:1
and it **s** the image on its feet of iron and Dn 2:34
But the stone that **s** the image became a Dn 2:35
enraged against him and **s** the ram and Dn 8:7
that he may heal us; he has **s** us down, Hos 6:1
"I **s** you with blight and mildew; your Am 4:9
house shall be **s** down into fragments, Am 6:11
I **s** you and all the products of your toil Hg 2:17
drew his sword and **s** the servant of the Mt 26:51
Then they spit in his face and **s** him. Mt 26:67
us, you Christ! Who is it that **s** you?" Mt 26:68
took the reed and **s** him on the head. Mt 27:30
and they **s** him on the head and treated Mk 12:4
drew his sword and **s** the servant of the Mk 14:47
And one of them **s** the servant of the Lk 22:50
him, "Prophesy! Who is it that **s** you?" Lk 22:64
drew it and **s** the high priest's servant Jn 18:10
the officers standing by **s** Jesus with his Jn 18:22
of the Jews!" and **s** him with their hands. Jn 19:3
He **s** Peter on the side and woke him, Acts 12:7
an angel of the Lord **s** him down, Acts 12:23
to the law you order me to be **s**?" Acts 23:3
northeaster, **s** down from the land. Acts 27:14
forsaken; **s** down, but not destroyed; 2 Cor 4:9
his trumpet, and a third of the sun was **s**, Rv 8:12

STRUCTURE (7)
He also built a **s** against the wall of the 1 Kgs 6:5
He built the **s** against the whole 1 Kgs 6:10
to build this house and to finish this **s**?" Ezr 5:3
to build this house and to finish this **s**?' Ezr 5:9
corner pillars cut for the **s** of a palace; Ps 144:12
on which was a **s** like a city to the Ezk 40:2
in whom the whole **s**, being joined Eph 2:21

STRUGGLE (3)
to know how great a **s** I have for you and Col 2:1
you endured a hard **s** with sufferings, Heb 10:32
In your **s** against sin you have not yet Heb 12:4

STRUGGLED (1)
The children **s** together within her, Gn 25:22

STRUGGLING (3)
behold, two Hebrews were **s** together. Ex 2:13
s with all his energy that he powerfully Col 1:29
always **s** on your behalf in his prayers, Col 4:12

STRUTS (1)
and their tongue **s** through the earth. Ps 73:9

STRUTTING (1)
the **s** rooster, the he-goat, and a king Prv 30:31

STUBBLE (13)
all the land of Egypt to gather **s** for straw. Ex 5:12
out your fury; it consumes them like **s**. Ex 15:7
flee; for him sling stones are turned to **s**. Jb 41:28
Clubs are counted as **s**; he laughs at the Jb 41:29
as the tongue of fire devours the **s**, Is 5:24
You conceive chaff; you give birth to **s**; Is 33:11
and the tempest carries them off like **s**. Is 40:24
his sword, like driven **s** with his bow. Is 41:2
Behold, they are like **s**; the fire consumes Is 47:14
crackling of a flame of fire devouring the **s**, Jl 2:5
Joseph a flame, and the house of Esau **s**; Ob 1:18
they are consumed like **s** fully dried. Na 1:10
the arrogant and all evildoers will be **s**. Mal 4:1

STUBBORN (21)
your righteousness, for you are a **s** people. Dt 9:6
this people, and behold, it is a **s** people. Dt 9:13
of your heart, and be no longer **s**. Dt 10:16
a man has a **s** and rebellious son who Dt 21:18
city, 'This our son is **s** and rebellious; Dt 21:20
I know how rebellious and **s** you are. Dt 31:27
any of their practices or their **s** ways. Jgs 2:19
they would not listen, but were **s**, 2 Kgs 17:14
and turned a **s** shoulder and stiffened Neh 9:29
fathers, a **s** and rebellious generation, Ps 78:8
So I gave them over to their **s** hearts, to Ps 81:12
"Ah, **s** children," declares the LORD, "who Is 30:1
"Listen to me, you **s** of heart, you who Is 46:12
this people has a **s** and rebellious heart; Jer 5:23
behold, every one of you follows his **s**, Jer 16:12
descendants also are impudent and **s**: Ezk 2:4
Israel have a hard forehead and a **s** heart. Ezk 3:7
Like a **s** heifer, Israel is stubborn; can Hos 4:16
Like a stubborn heifer, Israel is **s**; can Hos 4:16
and turned a **s** shoulder and stopped Zec 7:11
when some became **s** and continued Acts 19:9

STUBBORNLY (7)
For when Pharaoh **s** refused to let us Ex 13:15
running **s** against him with a thickly Jb 15:26
they shall no more **s** follow their own Jer 3:17
They are all **s** rebellious, going about Jer 6:28
but have **s** followed their own hearts and Jer 9:14
who **s** follow their own heart and have Jer 13:10
and to everyone who **s** follows his own Jer 23:17

STUBBORNNESS (5)
Do not regard the **s** of this people, or their Dt 9:27
safe, though I walk in the **s** of my heart.' Dt 29:19
own counsels and the **s** of their evil Jer 7:24
everyone walked in the **s** of his evil heart. Jer 11:8
act according to the **s** of his evil heart.' Jer 18:12

STUCK (4)
with his spear **s** in the ground at his 1 Sm 26:7
and their tongue **s** to the roof of their Jb 29:10
eyes, and if any spot has **s** to my hands, Jb 31:7
The bow **s** and remained immovable, Acts 27:41

STUD (1)
the king's service, bred from the royal **s**, Est 8:10

STUDDED (1)
for you ornaments of gold, **s** with silver. Sg 1:11

STUDIED (2)
the LORD, **s** by all who delight in them. Ps 111:2
man has learning, when he has never **s**?" Jn 7:15

STUDY (3)
had set his heart to **s** the Law of the Ezr 7:10
the scribe in order to **s** the words of the Neh 8:13
and much **s** is a weariness of the Eccl 12:12

STUDYING (1)
weighing and **s** and arranging many Eccl 12:9

STUMBLE (44)
They shall **s** over one another, as if to Lv 26:37
they **s** and perish before your presence. Ps 9:3
and foes, it is they who **s** and fall. Ps 27:2
your law; nothing can make them **s**. Ps 119:165
way securely, and your foot will not **s**. Prv 3:23
and if you run, you will not **s**. Prv 4:12
sleep unless they have made someone **s**. Prv 4:16
they do not know over what they **s**. Prv 4:19
but the wicked **s** in times of calamity. Prv 24:16
And many shall **s** on it. They shall fall Is 8:15
reel in vision, they **s** in giving judgment. Is 28:7
stretches out his hand, the helper will **s**, Is 31:3
we **s** at noon as in the twilight, among Is 59:10
Like a horse in the desert, they did not **s**. Is 63:13
blocks against which they shall **s**; Jer 6:21
before your feet **s** on the twilight Jer 13:16
gods; they made them **s** in their ways, Jer 18:15
therefore my persecutors will **s**; Jer 20:11
a straight path in which they shall not **s**, Jer 31:9
He made many **s**, and they fell, and they Jer 46:16
The proud one shall **s** and fall, with Jer 50:32
their hearts may melt, and many **s**. Ezk 21:15
and no longer cause your nation to **s**, Ezk 36:15
of his own land, but he shall **s** and fall, Dn 11:19
some days they shall **s** by sword and Dn 11:33
When they **s**, they shall receive a little Dn 11:34
and some of the wise shall **s**, so that Dn 11:35
You shall **s** by day; the prophet also Hos 4:5
the prophet also shall **s** with you by Hos 4:5
Israel and Ephraim shall **s** in his guilt; Hos 5:5
his guilt; Judah also shall **s** with them. Hos 5:5
in them, but transgressors **s** in them. Hos 14:9
they **s** as they go, they hasten to the wall; Na 2:5
without end—they **s** over the bodies! Na 3:3
caused many to **s** by your instruction. Mal 2:8
If anyone walks in the day, he does not **s**, Jn 11:9
did they **s** in order that they might Rom 11:11
to make another **s** by what he Rom 14:20
that causes your brother to **s**. Rom 14:21
if food makes my brother **s**, 1 Cor 8:13
eat meat, lest I make my brother **s**. 1 Cor 8:13
For we all **s** in many ways, and if anyone Jas 3:2
and if anyone does not **s** in what he says, Jas 3:2
of offense." They **s** because they disobey 1 Pt 2:8

STUMBLED (10)
God and took hold of it, for the oxen **s**. 2 Sm 6:6
to take hold of the ark, for the oxen **s**. 1 Chr 13:9
But as for me, my feet had almost **s**, my Ps 73:2
was none among his tribes who **s**. Ps 105:37
For Jerusalem has **s**, and Judah has fallen, Is 3:8
for truth has **s** in the public squares, Is 59:14
river Euphrates they have **s** and fallen. Jer 46:6
cry; for warrior has **s** against warrior; Jer 46:12
for you have **s** because of your iniquity. Hos 14:1
They have **s** over the stumbling stone, Rom 9:32

STUMBLES (3)
let not your heart be glad when he **s**, Prv 24:17
None is weary, none **s**, none slumbers or Is 5:27
But if anyone walks in the night, he **s**, Jn 11:10

STUMBLING (24)
deaf or put a **s** block before the blind, Lv 19:14
Your words have upheld him who was **s**, Jb 4:4
and calamity is ready for his **s**. Jb 18:12
But at my **s** they rejoiced and gathered; Ps 35:15
my eyes from tears, my feet from **s**; Ps 116:8
back those who are **s** to the slaughter. Prv 24:11
offense and a rock of **s** to both houses of Is 8:14
before this people **s** blocks against Jer 6:21
and I lay a **s** block before him, Ezk 3:20
For it was the **s** block of their iniquity. Ezk 7:19
and set the **s** block of their iniquity Ezk 14:3
heart and sets the **s** block of his Ezk 14:4
heart and putting the **s** block of his Ezk 14:7
idols and became a **s** block of iniquity Ezk 44:12
They have stumbled over the **s** stone, Rom 9:32
I am laying in Zion a stone of **s**, Rom 9:33
a **s** block and a retribution for them; Rom 11:9
never to put a **s** block or hindrance Rom 14:13
a **s** block to Jews and folly to Gentiles, 1 Cor 1:23
not somehow become a **s** block to the 1 Cor 8:9
and "A stone of **s**, and a rock of offense." 1 Pt 2:8
and in him there is no cause for **s**. 1 Jn 2:10
to keep you from **s** and to present you Jude 1:24
Balak to put a **s** block before the sons Rv 2:14

STUMP (7)
old in the earth, and its **s** die in the soil, Jb 14:8
whose **s** remains when it is felled." The Is 6:13
when it is felled." The holy seed is its **s**. Is 6:13
come forth a shoot from the **s** of Jesse, Is 11:1
But leave the **s** of its roots in the earth, Dn 4:15
it, but leave the **s** of its roots in the earth, Dn 4:23
commanded to leave the **s** of the roots of Dn 4:26

STUMPS (1)
of these two smoldering **s** of firebrands, Is 7:4

STUNNED (2)
God of Jacob, both rider and horse lay **s**. Ps 76:6
he has left me **s**, faint all the day long. Lam 1:13

STUPID (12)
But a **s** man will get understanding Jb 11:12
as cattle? Why are we **s** in your sight? Jb 18:3
the fool and the **s** alike must perish and Ps 49:10
The **s** man cannot know; the fool cannot Ps 92:6
but he who hates reproof is **s**. Prv 12:1
Surely I am too **s** to be a man. I have not Prv 30:2
counselors of Pharaoh give **s** counsel. Is 19:11
they know me not; they are **s** children; Jer 4:22
They are both **s** and foolish; the Jer 10:8
Every man is **s** and without knowledge; Jer 10:14
For the shepherds are **s** and do not Jer 10:21
Every man is **s** and without knowledge; Jer 51:17

STUPOR (2)
is written, "God gave them a spirit of **s**, Rom 11:8
Wake up from your drunken **s**, as is 1 Cor 15:34

STYLE (2)
In the **s** of the ephod you shall make it Ex 28:15
in skilled work, in the **s** of the ephod, Ex 39:8

SUAH (1)
S, Harnepher, Shual, Beri, Imrah. 1 Chr 7:36

SUBDUE (10)
fill the earth and **s** it and have dominion Gn 1:28
will destroy them and **s** them before you. Dt 9:3
might be bound, that one could **s** you." Jgs 16:6
Israel. And I will **s** all your enemies. 1 Chr 17:10
Arise, O LORD! Confront him, **s** him! Ps 17:13
to themselves, "We will utterly **s** them"; Ps 74:8
I would soon **s** their enemies and turn Ps 81:14
You **s** the noise of the foreigners; as heat Is 25:5
to **s** nations before him and to loose the Is 45:1
pieces. No one had the strength to **s** him. Mk 5:4

SUBDUED (17)
and the land is **s** before the LORD; then Nm 32:22
and the land shall be **s** before you, Nm 32:29
there. The land lay **s** before them. Jos 18:1
So Moab was **s** that day under the hand Jgs 3:30
So on that day God **s** Jabin the king of Jgs 4:23
So Midian was **s** before the people of Jgs 8:28
the Ammonites were **s** before the people Jgs 11:33
So the Philistines were **s** and did not 1 Sm 7:13
defeated the Philistines and **s** them, 2 Sm 8:1
he dedicated from all the nations he **s**, 2 Sm 8:11
defeated the Philistines and **s** them, 1 Chr 18:1
the giants, and the Philistines were **s**. 1 Chr 20:4
and the land is **s** before the LORD and 1 Chr 22:18
the men of Israel were **s** at that time, 2 Chr 13:18
and you **s** before them the inhabitants Neh 9:24
me vengeance and **s** peoples under me, Ps 18:47
He **s** peoples under us, and nations under Ps 47:3

SUBDUES (1)
I take refuge, who **s** peoples under me. Ps 144:2

SUBJECT (18)
them, but became **s** to forced labor. Jgs 1:30
of Beth-anath became **s** to forced labor Jgs 1:33
them, and they became **s** to forced labor. Jgs 1:35
they were in Egypt **s** to the house of 1 Sm 2:27
with Israel and became **s** to them. 2 Sm 10:19
with David and became **s** to him. 1 Chr 19:19
even the demons are **s** to us in your Lk 10:17
in this, that the spirits are **s** to you, Lk 10:20
Let every person be **s** to the governing Rom 13:1
spirits of prophets are **s** to prophets. 1 Cor 14:32
be **s** to such as these, and to every 1 Cor 16:16
enables him even to **s** all things to Phil 3:21
fear of death were **s** to lifelong slavery. Heb 2:15
we not much more be **s** to the Father of Heb 12:9
Be **s** for the Lord's sake to every human 1 Pt 2:13
be **s** to your masters with all respect, 1 Pt 2:18
wives, be **s** to your own husbands, 1 Pt 3:1
you who are younger, be **s** to the elders. 1 Pt 5:5

SUBJECTED (6)
For the creation was **s** to futility, not Rom 8:20
willingly, but because of him who **s** it, Rom 8:20
When all things are **s** to him, then 1 Cor 15:28
himself will also be **s** to him who 1 Cor 15:28
to angels that God **s** the world to come, Heb 2:5
and powers having been **s** to him. 1 Pt 3:22

SUBJECTION (11)
were brought into **s** under their power. Ps 106:42
free, and brought them into **s** as slaves. Jer 34:11
you brought them into **s** to be your Jer 34:16
Therefore one must be in **s**, not only to Rom 13:5
put all things in **s** under his feet." 1 Cor 15:27
things are put in **s**," it is plain that 1 Cor 15:27
who put all things in **s** under him. 1 Cor 15:27
who put all things in **s** under him, 1 Cor 15:28
putting everything in **s** under his feet." Heb 2:8
Now in putting everything in **s** to him, Heb 2:8
we do not yet see everything in **s** to him. Heb 2:8

SUBJUGATE (1)
now you intend to **s** the people of 2 Chr 28:10

SUBMISSION (3)
to speak, but should be in **s**, 1 Cor 14:34
because of your **s** flowing from your 2 Cor 9:13
we did not yield in **s** even for a moment, Gal 2:5

SUBMISSIVE (5)
came to Nazareth and was **s** to them. Lk 2:51
with all dignity keeping his children **s**, 1 Tm 3:4
home, kind, and **s** to their own husbands, Ti 2:5
Slaves are to be **s** to their own masters in Ti 2:9
Remind them to be **s** to rulers and Ti 3:1

SUBMISSIVENESS (1)
Let a woman learn quietly with all **s**. 1 Tm 2:11

SUBMIT (11)
"Return to your mistress and **s** to her." Gn 16:9
to my voice; Israel would not **s** to me. Ps 81:11
to God, for it does not **s** to God's law; Rom 8:7
they did not **s** to God's righteousness. Rom 10:3
and do not **s** again to a yoke of slavery. Gal 5:1
Wives, **s** to your own husbands, as to Eph 5:22
so also wives should **s** in everything to Eph 5:24
in the world, do you **s** to regulations— Col 2:20
Wives, **s** to your husbands, as is fitting Col 3:18
Obey your leaders and **s** to them, for Heb 13:17
S yourselves therefore to God. Resist the Jas 4:7

SUBMITS (1)
Now as the church **s** to Christ, so also Eph 5:24

SUBMITTING (2)
s to one another out of reverence for Eph 5:21
themselves, by **s** to their husbands, 1 Pt 3:5

SUBSEQUENT (1)
sufferings of Christ and the **s** glories. 1 Pt 1:11

SUBSIDED (4)
blow over the earth, and the waters **s**. Gn 8:1
see if the waters had **s** from the face of the Gn 8:8
that the waters had **s** from the earth. Gn 8:11
their anger against him **s** when he said Jgs 8:3

SUBSTANCE (4)
Bless, O LORD, his **s**, and accept the work Dt 33:11
for their livestock and their **s**. Jos 14:4
Your eyes saw my unformed **s**; in your Ps 139:16
to come, but the **s** belongs to Christ. Col 2:17

SUBSTITUTE (6)
shall not exchange it or make a **s** for it, Lv 27:10
he does in fact **s** one animal for Lv 27:10
then both it and the **s** shall be holy. Lv 27:10
or bad, neither shall he make a **s** for it; Lv 27:33
and if he does **s** for it, then both it and Lv 27:33
it, then both it and the **s** shall be holy; Lv 27:33

SUBVERT (1)
to **s** a man in his lawsuit, the Lord Lam 3:36

SUBVERTS (2)
the clear-sighted and **s** the cause of Ex 23:8
eyes of the wise and **s** the cause of the Dt 16:19

SUCATHITES (1)
the Shimeathites and the **S**. 1 Chr 2:55

SUCCEED (25)
caused all that he did to **s** in his hands. Gn 39:3
whatever he did, the LORD made it **s**. Gn 39:23
Aaron's sons, who is anointed to **s** him, Lv 6:22
of the LORD, when that will not **s**? Nm 14:41
whom she bears shall **s** to the name of Dt 25:6
on which we are setting out will **s**." Jgs 18:5
many things and will **s** in them." So 1 Sm 26:25
are to entice him, and you shall **s**; 1 Kgs 22:22
so that you may **s** in building the 1 Chr 22:11
of your fathers, for you cannot **s**." 2 Chr 13:12
are to entice him, and you shall **s**; 2 Chr 18:21
believe his prophets, and you will **s**." 2 Chr 20:20
they devise mischief, they will not **s**. Ps 21:11
fail, but with many advisers they **s**. Prv 15:22
strength, but wisdom helps one to **s**. Eccl 10:10
youth; perhaps you may be able to **s**; Is 47:12
that is fashioned against you shall **s**, Is 54:17
and shall **s** in the thing for which I sent Is 55:11
be greatly shamed, for they will not **s**. Jer 20:11
a man who shall not **s** in his days, Jer 22:30
of his offspring shall **s** in sitting on the Jer 22:30
against the Chaldeans, you shall not **s**'?" Jer 32:5
destruction and shall **s** in what he Dn 8:24
I may now at last **s** in coming to you. Rom 1:10
righteousness did not **s** in reaching Rom 9:31

SUCCEEDED (3)
Ahithophel was **s** by Jehoiada the 1 Chr 27:34
has hardened himself against him, and **s**? Jb 9:4
Felix was **s** by Porcius Festus. Acts 24:27

SUCCEEDS (1)
The son who **s** him as priest, who Ex 29:30

SUCCESS (11)
please grant me **s** today and show Gn 24:12
the LORD your God granted me **s**." Gn 27:20
you may have good **s** wherever you go. Jos 1:7
and then you will have good **s**. Jos 1:8
And David had **s** in all his 1 Sm 18:14
when Saul saw that he had great **s**, 1 Sm 18:15
out David had more **s** than all the 1 Sm 18:30
name, and give **s** to your servant today, Neh 1:11
crafty, so that their hands achieve no **s**. Jb 5:12
O LORD! O LORD, we pray, give us **s**! Ps 118:25
will find favor and good **s** in the sight of Prv 3:4

SUCCESSFUL (2)
with Joseph, and he became a **s** man, Gn 39:2
went out and was **s** wherever Saul sent 1 Sm 18:5

SUCCESSFULLY (1)
in his own house he **s** accomplished. 2 Chr 7:11

SUCCOTH (18)
But Jacob journeyed to **S**, and built Gn 33:17
the name of the place is called **S**. Gn 33:17
of Israel journeyed from Rameses to **S**, Ex 12:37
they moved on from **S** and encamped at Ex 13:20
set out from Rameses and camped at **S**. Nm 33:5
they set out from **S** and camped at Nm 33:6
Beth-nimrah, **S**, and Zaphon, Jos 13:27
So he said to the men of **S**, "Please give Jgs 8:5
And the officials of **S** said, "Are the hands Jgs 8:6
him as the men of **S** had answered. Jgs 8:8
a young man of **S** and questioned him. Jgs 8:14
for him the officials and elders of **S**, Jgs 8:14
And he came to the men of **S** and said, Jgs 8:15
with them taught the men of **S** a lesson. Jgs 8:16
clay ground between **S** and Zarethan. 1 Kgs 7:46
clay ground between **S** and Zeredah. 2 Chr 4:17
Shechem and portion out the Vale of **S**. Ps 60:6
and portion out the Valley of **S**. Ps 108:7

SUCCOTH-BENOTH (1)
The men of Babylon made **S**, the 2 Kgs 17:30

SUCH (178)
Far be it from you to do **s** a thing, to Gn 18:25
prepare for me delicious food, **s** as I love, Gn 27:4
food for your father, **s** as he loves. Gn 27:9
delicious food, **s** as his father loved. Gn 27:14
for **s** a thing must not be done. Gn 34:7
s as I had never seen in all the land of Gn 41:19
does my lord speak **s** words as these? Gn 44:7
be it from your servants to do **s** a thing! Gn 44:7
s as never has been in Egypt from the Ex 9:18
s as had never been in all the land of Ex 9:24
s a dense swarm of locusts as had never Ex 10:14
land of Egypt, **s** as there has never been, Ex 11:6
and place **s** men over the people as Ex 18:21
that you have brought **s** a great sin Ex 32:21
s as have not been created in all the Ex 34:10
and yet **s** things as these have happened Lv 10:19
be drunk from every **s** vessel shall be Lv 11:34
And whoever carries **s** things shall Lv 15:10
the person who touches **s** a thing shall Lv 22:6
of your God any **s** animals gotten from Lv 22:25
earth who can do **s** works and mighty Dt 3:24
whether **s** a great thing as this has ever Dt 4:32
Oh that they had **s** a mind as this always, Dt 5:29
never again do any **s** wickedness as this Dt 13:11
and certain that **s** an abomination has Dt 13:14
and certain that **s** an abomination has Dt 17:4
again commit any **s** evil among you. Dt 19:20
For all who do **s** things, all who act Dt 25:16
S is the inheritance of the tribe of the Jos 16:8
announced to us **s** things as these." Jgs 13:23
that you come with **s** a company?" Jgs 18:23
"**S** a thing has never happened or been Jgs 19:30
to them, "Why do you do **s** things? 1 Sm 2:23
the young men for **s** and such a place. 1 Sm 21:2
the young men for such and **s** a place. 1 Sm 21:2
and he is **s** a worthless man that one 1 Sm 25:17
David has done.'" **S** was his custom 1 Sm 27:11
show regard for a dead dog **s** as I?" 2 Sm 9:8
me, for **s** a thing is not done in Israel; 2 Sm 13:12
have you planned **s** a thing against 2 Sm 14:13
"Your servant is of **s** and such a tribe 2 Sm 15:2
is of such and **s** a tribe in Israel," 2 Sm 15:2
the king repay me with **s** a reward? 2 Sm 19:36
for with **s** loyalty they met me when I 1 Kgs 2:7
you for your servants **s** wages as you 1 Kgs 5:6
Never again came **s** an abundance 1 Kgs 10:10
No **s** almug wood has come or been 1 Kgs 10:12
"At **s** and such a place shall be my 2 Kgs 6:8
"At such and **s** a place shall be my 2 Kgs 6:8
could **s** a thing be?" And he had said, 2 Kgs 7:19
S is Pharaoh king of Egypt to all 2 Kgs 18:21
Jerusalem and Judah **s** disaster that 2 Kgs 21:12
For no **s** Passover had been kept 2 Kgs 23:22
keep forever **s** purposes and 1 Chr 29:18
bestowed on him **s** royal majesty as 1 Chr 29:25
s as none of the kings had who were 2 Chr 1:12
There were no spices **s** as those that 2 Chr 9:9
of Israel had kept **s** a Passover as 2 Chr 35:18
all **s** as know the laws of your God. Ezr 7:25
who put **s** a thing as this into the heart Ezr 7:27
and have given us **s** a remnant as this, Ezr 9:13
burdens were loaded in **s** a way that Neh 4:17
"No **s** things as you say have been done, Neh 6:8
I said, "Should **s** a man as I run away? Neh 6:11
And what man **s** as I could go into the Neh 6:11
of Israel sin on account of **s** women? Neh 13:26
to the kingdom for **s** a time as this?" Est 4:14
S are the paths of all who forget God; the Jb 8:13
Who does not know **s** things as these? Jb 12:3
you open your eyes on **s** a one and bring Jb 14:3
against God and bring **s** words out of Jb 15:13
"I have heard many **s** things; miserable Jb 16:2
Surely **s** are the dwellings of the Jb 18:21
s is the place of him who knows not Jb 18:21
me, and many **s** things are in his mind. Jb 23:14
S is the generation of those who seek Ps 24:6

S knowledge is too wonderful for me; it Ps 139:6
the people to whom **s** blessings fall! Ps 144:15
S are the ways of everyone who is greedy Prv 1:19
Know that wisdom is **s** to your soul; if Prv 24:14
man does not understand **s** knowledge. Prv 29:7
the city where they had done **s** things. Eccl 8:10
upon your father's house **s** days as have Is 7:17
S is Pharaoh king of Egypt to all who Is 36:6
S to you are those with whom you have Is 47:15
Is **s** the fast that I choose, a day for a Is 58:5
Who has heard **s** a thing? Who has seen Is 66:8
such a thing? Who has seen **s** things? Is 66:8
with care; see if there has been **s** a thing. Jer 2:10
I not avenge myself on a nation **s** as this? Jer 5:9
not avenge myself on a nation **s** as this?" Jer 5:29
I not avenge myself on a nation **s** as this? Jer 9:9
make for himself gods? **S** are not gods!" Jer 16:20
I am bringing **s** disaster upon this place Jer 19:3
the people, by speaking **s** words to them. Jer 38:4
S were their faces. And their wings were Ezk 1:11
S was the appearance of the likeness of Ezk 1:28
Surely, if I sent you to **s**, they would Ezk 3:6
Can one escape who does **s** things? Ezk 17:15
trees, **s** as were carved on the walls. Ezk 41:25
powerful king has asked **s** a thing of Dn 2:10
s as never has been since there was a Dn 12:1
Has **s** a thing happened in your days, or in Jl 1:2
is prudent will keep silent in **s** a time, Am 5:13
"one should not preach of **s** things; Mi 2:6
With **s** a gift from your hand, will he Mal 1:9
no one in Israel have I found **s** faith. Mt 8:10
God, who had given **s** authority to men. Mt 9:8
Father, for **s** was your gracious will. Mt 11:26
get enough bread in **s** a desolate place Mt 15:33
"Whoever receives one **s** child in my Mt 18:5
"If **s** is the case of a man with his wife, Mt 19:10
for to **s** belongs the kingdom of Mt 19:14
s as has not been from the beginning Mt 24:21
With many **s** parables he spoke the Mk 4:33
How are **s** mighty works done by his Mk 6:2
s as the washing of cups and pots and Mk 7:4
down. And many **s** things you do." Mk 7:13
"Whoever receives one **s** child in my Mk 9:37
for to **s** belongs the kingdom of God. Mk 10:14
days there will be **s** tribulation as has Mk 13:19
not even in Israel have I found **s** faith." Lk 7:9
about whom I hear **s** things?" And he Lk 9:9
Father, for **s** was your gracious will. Lk 10:21
for to **s** belongs the kingdom of God. Lk 18:16
the Father is seeking **s** people to worship Jn 4:23
Moses commanded us to stone **s** women. Jn 8:5
is a sinner do **s** signs?" And there was Jn 9:16
synagogue and spoke in **s** a way that a Acts 14:1
"Away with **s** a fellow from the earth! Acts 22:22
in his case of **s** evils as I supposed. Acts 25:18
this day might become **s** as I am— Acts 26:29
those who practice **s** things deserve to Rom 1:32
rightly falls on those who do **s** things. Rom 2:2
judge those who do **s** things and yet do Rom 2:3
you to live in **s** harmony with one Rom 15:5
For **s** persons do not serve our Lord Rom 16:18
judgment on the one who did **s** a thing. 1 Cor 5:3
—not even to eat with **s** a one. 1 Cor 5:11
So if you have **s** cases, why do you lay 1 Cor 6:4
And **s** were some of you. But you were 1 Cor 6:11
In **s** cases the brother or sister is not 1 Cor 7:15
things to secure any **s** provision. 1 Cor 9:15
contentious, we have no **s** practice, 1 Cor 11:16
s as the flute or the harp, 1 Cor 14:7
be subject to **s** as these, and to every 1 Cor 16:16
as yours. Give recognition to **s** men. 1 Cor 16:18
He delivered us from **s** a deadly peril, 2 Cor 1:10
For **s** a one, this punishment by the 2 Cor 2:6
S is the confidence that we have 2 Cor 3:4
came with **s** glory that the Israelites 2 Cor 3:7
Since we have **s** a hope, we are very 2 Cor 3:12
show boldness with **s** confidence as I 2 Cor 10:2
Let **s** a person understand that what 2 Cor 10:11
For **s** men are false apostles, 2 Cor 11:13
that those who do **s** things will not Gal 5:21
against **s** things there is no law. Gal 5:23
but only **s** as is good for building up, Eph 4:29
without spot or wrinkle or any **s** thing, Eph 5:27
the Lord with all joy, and honor **s** men, Phil 2:29
Now **s** persons we command and 2 Thes 3:12
but denying its power. Avoid **s** people. 2 Tm 3:5
knowing that **s** a person is warped and Ti 3:11
escape if we neglect **s** a great salvation? Heb 2:3
priests were made **s** without an oath, Heb 7:20
that we should have **s** a high priest, Heb 7:26
we have **s** a high priest, one who is seated Heb 8:1
from sinners **s** hostility against Heb 12:3
for **s** sacrifices are pleasing to God. Heb 13:16
a forest is set ablaze by **s** a small fire! Jas 3:5
we will go into **s** and such a town Jas 4:13
will go into such and **s** a town and spend Jas 4:13
in your arrogance. All **s** boasting is evil. Jas 4:16
not with perishable things **s** as silver or 1 Pt 1:18
S a one is the deceiver and the antichrist. 2 Jn 1:7
have committed in **s** an ungodly way, Jude 1:15
and a great earthquake **s** as there had Rv 16:18
Over **s** the second death has no power, Rv 20:6

SUCK (3)
He will **s** the poison of cobras; the Jb 20:16
His young ones **s** up blood, and where Jb 39:30
You shall **s** the milk of nations; you Is 60:16

SUCKLED (1)
and he **s** him with honey out of the Dt 32:13

SUDDEN (5)
When disaster brings **s** death, he mocks Jb 9:23
you, and **s** terror overwhelms you, Jb 22:10
Do not be afraid of **s** terror or of the Prv 3:25
for a full and **s** end he will make of all Zep 1:18
and security," then **s** destruction will 1 Thes 5:3

SUDDENLY (38)
if any man dies very **s** beside him and he Nm 6:9
And **s** the LORD said to Moses and to Nm 12:4
if he pushed him **s** without enmity, Nm 35:22
So Joshua came upon them **s**, having Jos 10:9
all his warriors came **s** against them by Jos 11:7
people, for the thing came about **s**. 2 Chr 29:36
taking root, but **s** I cursed his dwelling. Jb 5:3
shooting at him **s** and without fear. Ps 64:4
his arrow at them; they are wounded **s**. Ps 64:7
calamity will come upon him **s**; Prv 6:15
on it, it is gone, for **s** it sprouts wings, Prv 23:5
for disaster from them will rise **s**, and Prv 24:22
who is crooked in his ways will **s** fall. Prv 28:18
neck, will **s** be broken beyond healing. Prv 29:1
an evil time, when it **s** falls upon them. Eccl 9:12
like passing chaff. And in an instant, **s**, Is 29:5
to collapse, whose breaking comes **s**, Is 30:13
and ruin shall come upon you **s**, of Is 47:11
then **s** I did them and they came to pass. Is 48:3
S my tents are laid waste, my curtains in Jer 4:20
for **s** the destroyer will come upon us. Jer 6:26
anguish and terror fall upon them **s**. Jer 15:8
you bring the plunderer **s** upon them! Jer 18:22
I will **s** make him run away from her. Jer 49:19
I will **s** make them run away from her, Jer 50:44
S Babylon has fallen and been broken; Jer 51:8
Will not your debtors **s** arise, and those Hab 2:7
whom you seek will **s** come to his Mal 3:1
And **s**, looking around, they no longer Mk 9:8
lest he come **s** and find you asleep. Mk 13:36
And **s** there was with the angel a Lk 2:13
a spirit seizes him, and he **s** cries out. Lk 9:39
that day come upon you **s** like a trap. Lk 21:34
And **s** there came from heaven a sound Acts 2:2
and **s** a light from heaven flashed Acts 9:3
and **s** there was a great earthquake, so Acts 16:26
light from heaven **s** shone around me. Acts 22:6
for him to swell up or **s** fall down dead. Acts 28:6

SUE (1)
And if anyone would **s** you and take Mt 5:40

SUFFER (54)
years and shall **s** for your Nm 14:33
that we may no longer **s** derision." Neh 2:17
of their enemies, who made them **s**. Neh 9:27
they tread the winepresses, but **s** thirst. Jb 24:11
The young lions **s** want and hunger; Ps 34:10
from my youth up, I **s** your terrors; Ps 88:15
for a stranger will surely **s** harm, Prv 11:15
the companion of fools will **s** harm. Prv 13:20
sleep, and an idle person will **s** hunger. Prv 19:15
but the simple go on and **s** for it. Prv 22:3
but the simple go on and **s** for it. Prv 27:12
earth, and its inhabitants **s** for their guilt; Is 24:6
skirts are lifted up and you **s** violence. Jer 13:22
should not the son **s** for the iniquity of Ezk 18:19
The son shall not **s** for the iniquity of Ezk 18:20
nor the father **s** for the iniquity of the Ezk 18:20
and no longer **s** the reproach of the Ezk 34:29
you shall themselves **s** reproach. Ezk 36:7
you may never again **s** the disgrace of Ezk 36:30
account, so that the king might **s** no loss. Dn 6:2
for them; even the flocks of sheep **s**. Jl 1:18
so that you will no longer **s** reproach. Zep 3:18
to Jerusalem and **s** many things from Mt 16:21
of Man will certainly **s** at their hands." Mt 17:12
Son of Man must **s** many things and be Mk 8:31
Man that he should **s** many things and Mk 9:12
Son of Man must **s** many things and be Lk 9:22
But first he must **s** many things and be Lk 17:25
to eat this Passover with you before I **s**. Lk 22:15
the Christ should **s** these things and Lk 24:26
that the Christ should **s** and on the Lk 24:46
the prophets, that his Christ would **s**, Acts 3:18
counted worthy to **s** dishonor for the Acts 5:41
how much he must **s** for the sake of Acts 9:16
for the Christ to **s** and to rise from Acts 17:3
that the Christ must **s** and that, by Acts 26:23
provided we **s** with him in order that Rom 8:17
work is burned up, he will **s** loss, 1 Cor 3:15
for you. Why not rather **s** wrong? 1 Cor 6:7
If one member suffers, all **s** together; 1 Cor 12:26
endure the same sufferings that we **s**. 2 Cor 1:6
came I might not **s** pain from those 2 Cor 2:3
Did you **s** so many things in vain—if Gal 3:4
believe in him but also **s** for his sake, Phil 1:29
that we were to **s** affliction, 1 Thes 3:4
They will **s** the punishment of eternal 2 Thes 1:9
which is why I **s** as I do. But I am not 2 Tm 1:12
have had to **s** repeatedly since the Heb 9:26
you do good and **s** for it you endure, 1 Pt 2:20
if you should **s** for righteousness' sake, 1 Pt 3:14
For it is better to **s** for doing good, if 1 Pt 3:17
But let none of you **s** as a murderer or a 1 Pt 4:15
let those who **s** according to God's 1 Pt 4:19
Do not fear what you are about to **s**. Rv 2:10

SUFFERED (25)
very good to us, and we **s** no harm, 1 Sm 25:15
because of their iniquities **s** affliction; Ps 107:17
hold on me; I **s** distress and anguish. Ps 116:3
because you have **s** the reproach of the Ezk 36:6
a woman who had **s** from a discharge of Mt 9:20
the kingdom of heaven has **s** violence, Mt 11:12
for I have **s** much because of him Mt 27:19
and who had **s** much under many Mk 5:26
Galileans, because they **s** in this way? Lk 13:2
creature into the fire and **s** no harm. Acts 28:5
grief, so that you **s** no loss through us. 2 Cor 7:9
the sake of the one who **s** the wrong, 2 Cor 7:12
For his sake I have **s** the loss of all Phil 3:8
we had already **s** and been 1 Thes 2:2
For you **s** the same things from 1 Thes 2:14
he himself has **s** when tempted, Heb 2:18
he learned obedience through what he **s**. Heb 5:8
Others **s** mocking and flogging, and Heb 11:36
So Jesus also **s** outside the gate in Heb 13:12
called, because Christ also **s** for you, 1 Pt 2:21
when he **s**, he did not threaten, but 1 Pt 2:23
For Christ also **s** once for sins, the 1 Pt 3:18
Since therefore Christ **s** in the flesh, arm 1 Pt 4:1
for whoever has **s** in the flesh has ceased 1 Pt 4:1
And after you have **s** a little while, the 1 Pt 5:10

SUFFERING (21)
in the time of their **s** they cried out to Neh 9:27
for they saw that his **s** was very great. Jb 2:13
I become afraid of all my **s**, for I know Jb 9:28
s no mishap or failure in bearing; Ps 144:14
but hear, all you peoples, and see my **s**; Lam 1:18
is lying paralyzed at home, **s** terribly." Mt 8:6
himself alive after his **s** by many proofs, Acts 1:3
knowing that **s** produces endurance, Rom 5:3
to lose heart over what I am **s** for you, Eph 3:13
of God, for which you are also **s**— 2 Thes 1:5
but share in **s** for the gospel by the 2 Tm 1:8
Share in **s** as a good soldier of Christ 2 Tm 2:3
for which I am **s**, bound with chains 2 Tm 2:9
always be sober-minded, endure **s**, 2 Tm 4:5
and honor because of the **s** of death, Heb 2:9
of their salvation perfect through **s**. Heb 2:10
As an example of **s** and patience, Jas 5:10
Is anyone among you **s**? Let him pray. Is Jas 5:13
one endures sorrows while **s** unjustly. 1 Pt 2:19
same kinds of **s** are being experienced 1 Pt 5:9
s wrong as the wage for their 2 Pt 2:13

SUFFERINGS (13)
of their taskmasters. I know their **s**, Ex 3:7
More than that, we rejoice in our **s**, Rom 5:3
I consider that the **s** of this present Rom 8:18
as we share abundantly in Christ's **s**, 2 Cor 1:5
endure the same **s** that we suffer. 2 Cor 1:6
for we know that as you share in our **s**, 2 Cor 1:7
his resurrection, and may share his **s**, Phil 3:10
Now I rejoice in my **s** for your sake, and Col 1:24
my persecutions and **s** that happened 2 Tm 3:11
you endured a hard struggle with **s**, Heb 10:32
when he predicted the **s** of Christ and 1 Pt 1:11
rejoice insofar as you share Christ's **s**, 1 Pt 4:13
elder and a witness of the **s** of Christ, 1 Pt 5:1

SUFFERS (7)
what he should give, and only **s** want. Prv 11:24
but the belly of the wicked **s** want. Prv 13:25
been afflicted, and she herself **s** bitterly. Lam 1:4
the sojourner **s** extortion in your midst; Ezk 22:7
for he is an epileptic and he **s** terribly. Mt 17:15
If one member **s**, all suffer together; 1 Cor 12:26
Yet if anyone **s** as a Christian, let him 1 Pt 4:16

SUFFICE (4)
witness shall not **s** against a person Dt 19:15
of Samaria shall **s** for handfuls for 1 Kgs 20:10
of their life is costly and can never **s**, Ps 49:8
Lebanon would not **s** for fuel, nor are its Is 40:16

SUFFICES (1)
time that is past **s** for doing what the 1 Pt 4:3

SUFFICIENCY (3)
In the fullness of his **s** he will be in Jb 20:22
from us, but our **s** is from God, 2 Cor 3:5
so that having all **s** in all things at all 2 Cor 9:8

SUFFICIENT (11)
the material they had was **s** to do all the Ex 36:7
it will produce a crop **s** for three years. Lv 25:21
prosperous and finds **s** means to Lv 25:26
But if he has not **s** means to recover it, Lv 25:28
hand to him and lend him **s** for his need, Dt 15:8
consecrated themselves in **s** number, 2 Chr 30:3
for itself. **S** for the day is its own trouble. Mt 6:34
they gave a **s** sum of money to the Mt 28:12
life to life. Who is **s** for these things? 2 Cor 2:16
Not that we are **s** in ourselves to claim 2 Cor 3:5
he said to me, "My grace is **s** for you, 2 Cor 12:9

SUIT (4)
silver a year and a **s** of clothes and your Jgs 17:10
Will he then make repayment to **s** you, Jb 34:33
No one enters **s** justly; no one goes to law Is 59:4
themselves teachers to **s** their own 2 Tm 4:3

SUITABLE (2)
each with the blessing **s** to him. Gn 49:28
the harbor was not **s** to spend the Acts 27:12

SUITS (1)
one of your towns, wherever it **s** him. Dt 23:16

SUKKIIM (1)
Egypt—Libyans, **S**, and Ethiopians. 2 Chr 12:3

SULFUR (14)
Sodom and Gomorrah **s** and fire from Gn 19:24
of his; **s** is scattered over his habitation. Jb 18:15
fire and **s** and a scorching wind shall be Ps 11:6
the breath of the LORD, like a stream of **s**, Is 30:33
be turned into pitch, and her soil into **s**; Is 34:9
rains and hailstones, fire and **s**. Ezk 38:22
fire and **s** rained from heaven and Lk 17:29
the color of fire and of sapphire and of **s**, Rv 9:17
fire and smoke and **s** came out of their Rv 9:17
fire and smoke and **s** coming out of their Rv 9:18
with fire and **s** in the presence Rv 14:10
into the lake of fire that burns with **s**. Rv 19:20
lake of fire and **s** where the beast and Rv 20:10
be in the lake that burns with fire and **s**, Rv 21:8

SULLEN (2)
his house vexed and **s** and came to 1 Kgs 20:43
house vexed and **s** because of what 1 Kgs 21:4

SUM (10)
And Joab gave the **s** of the numbering 2 Sm 24:9
Joab gave the **s** of the numbering 1 Chr 21:5
and the exact **s** of money that Haman Est 4:7
The **s** of your word is truth, and every Ps 119:160
O God! How vast is the **s** of them! Ps 139:17
the dream and told the **s** of the matter. Dn 7:1
been sold for a large **s** and given to the Mt 26:9
they gave a sufficient **s** of money to the Mt 28:12
had bought for a **s** of silver from the Acts 7:16
citizenship for a large **s**." Paul said, Acts 22:28

SUMMED (1)
commandment, are **s** up in this word: Rom 13:9

SUMMER (25)
and harvest, cold and heat, **s** and winter, Gn 8:22
of raisins, a hundred of **s** fruits, 2 Sm 16:1
the bread and **s** fruit for the young 2 Sm 16:2
strength was dried up as by the heat of **s**. Ps 32:4
the earth; you have made **s** and winter. Ps 74:17
prepares her bread in **s** and gathers her Prv 6:8
He who gathers in **s** is a prudent son, Prv 10:5
Like snow in **s** or rain in harvest, so Prv 26:1
yet they provide their food in the **s**; Prv 30:25
for over your **s** fruit and your harvest the Is 16:9
And the birds of prey will **s** on them, and Is 18:6
will be like a first-ripe fig before the **s**: Is 28:4
"The harvest is past, the **s** is ended, and Jer 8:20
you, gather wine and **s** fruits and oil, Jer 40:10
they gathered wine and **s** fruits in great Jer 40:12
on your **s** fruits and your grapes the Jer 48:32
like the chaff of the **s** threshing floors; Dn 2:35
winter house along with the **s** house, Am 3:15
showed me: behold, a basket of **s** fruit. Am 8:1
"A basket of **s** fruit." Then the LORD said Am 8:2
become as when the **s** fruit has been Mi 7:1
sea. It shall continue in **s** as in winter. Zec 14:8
out its leaves, you know that **s** is near. Mt 24:32
out its leaves, you know that **s** is near. Mk 13:28
and know that the **s** is already near. Lk 21:30

SUMMIT (3)
While David was coming to the **s**, 2 Sm 15:32
David had passed a little beyond the **s**, 2 Sm 16:1
like Gilead to me, like the **s** of Lebanon, Jer 22:6

SUMMON (14)
king sent to **s** Ahimelech the priest, 1 Sm 22:11
So Amasa went to **s** Judah, but he 2 Sm 20:5
who went to **s** Micaiah said to 1 Kgs 22:13
who went to **s** Micaiah said to 2 Chr 18:12
If it is a matter of justice, who can **s** him? Jb 9:19
S your power, O God, the power, O God, Ps 68:28
For who is like me? Who will **s** me? Jer 49:19
"**S** archers against Babylon, all those Jer 50:29
For who is like me? Who will **s** me? Jer 50:44
s against her the kingdoms, Ararat, Jer 51:27
And I will **s** the grain and make it Ezk 36:29
I will **s** a sword against Gog on all my Ezk 38:21
I get an opportunity I will **s** you." Acts 24:25
Paul that he **s** him to Jerusalem Acts 25:3

SUMMONED (40)
to you." Then Israel **s** his strength and Gn 48:2
Then Pharaoh **s** the wise men and the Ex 7:11
Then he **s** Moses and Aaron by night Ex 12:31
And Moses **s** all Israel and said to them, Dt 5:1
And Moses **s** all Israel and said to them: Dt 29:2
Then Moses **s** Joshua and said to him in Dt 31:7
Joshua **s** them, and he said to them, Jos 9:22
Joshua **s** all the men of Israel and said Jos 10:24
At that time Joshua **s** the Reubenites and Jos 22:1
Joshua **s** all Israel, its elders and heads, Jos 23:2
of Israel to Shechem and **s** the elders, Jos 24:1
She sent and **s** Barak the son of Abinoam Jgs 4:6
So Saul **s** the people and numbered 1 Sm 15:4
And Saul **s** all the people to war, to go 1 Sm 23:8
Therefore I have **s** you to tell me 1 Sm 28:15
and told him, and he **s** Absalom. 2 Sm 14:33
the king sent and **s** Shimei and said 1 Kgs 2:36
the king sent and **s** Shimei and said 1 Kgs 2:42
the king of Israel **s** an officer and 1 Kgs 22:9
Then he **s** Gehazi and said, "Call this 2 Kgs 4:36
King Jehoash **s** Jehoiada the 2 Kgs 12:7
Then David **s** the priests Zadok and 1 Chr 15:11
the king of Israel **s** an officer and 2 Chr 18:8
So the king **s** Jehoiada the chief and 2 Chr 24:6
delighted in her and she was **s** by name. Est 2:14
king's scribes were **s** on the thirteenth Est 3:12
The king's scribes were **s** at that time, in Est 8:9
If I **s** him and he answered me, I would Jb 9:16
When he **s** a famine on the land and Ps 105:16
and have **s** my mighty men to execute my Is 13:3
Then he **s** Johanan the son of Kareah Jer 42:8
he **s** an assembly against me to crush Lam 1:15
You **s** as if to a festival day my terrors Lam 2:22
and the Chaldeans be **s** to tell the king Dn 2:2
Then Herod **s** the wise men secretly and Mt 2:7
Then his master **s** him and said to Mt 18:32
And the twelve **s** the full number of the Acts 6:2
And Joseph sent and **s** Jacob his father Acts 7:14
who **s** Barnabas and Saul and sought Acts 13:7
And when he had been **s**, Tertullus Acts 24:2

SUMMONING (4)
use them for **s** the congregation and Nm 10:2
for I am **s** a sword against all the Jer 25:29
And **s** the centurion, he asked him Mk 15:44
So, **s** his master's debtors one by one, he Lk 16:5

SUMMONS (2)
through and imprisons and **s** the court, Jb 11:10
speaks and **s** the earth from the rising of Ps 50:1

SUMPTUOUSLY (1)
fine linen and who feasted **s** every day. Lk 16:19

SUMS (1)
box. Many rich people put in large **s**. Mk 12:41

SUN (152)
As the **s** was going down, a deep sleep Gn 15:12
When the **s** had gone down and it was Gn 15:17
The **s** had risen on the earth when Lot Gn 19:23
there that night, because the **s** had set. Gn 28:11
The **s** rose upon him as he passed Gn 32:31
Behold, the **s**, the moon, and eleven stars Gn 37:9
eat; but when the **s** grew hot, it melted. Ex 16:21
steady until the going down of the **s**. Ex 17:12
but if the **s** has risen on him, there shall Ex 22:3
return it to him before the **s** goes down, Ex 22:26
When the **s** goes down he shall be clean, Lv 22:7
and hang them in the **s** before the LORD, Nm 25:4
when you see the **s** and the moon and Dt 4:19
road, toward the going down of the **s**, Dt 11:30
or the **s** or the moon or any of the host of Dt 17:3
bathe himself in water, and as the **s** sets, Dt 23:11
restore to him the pledge as the **s** sets, Dt 24:13
before the **s** sets (for he is poor and Dt 24:15
choicest fruits of the **s** and the rich Dt 33:14
going down of the **s** shall be your Jos 1:4
sight of Israel, "**S**, stand still at Gibeon, Jos 10:12
And the **s** stood still, and the moon Jos 10:13
The **s** stopped in the midst of heaven Jos 10:13
at the time of the going down of the **s**, Jos 10:27
your friends be like the **s** as he rises in Jgs 5:31
in the morning, as soon as the **s** is up, Jgs 9:33
the seventh day before the **s** went down, Jgs 14:18
And the **s** went down on them near Jgs 19:14
'Tomorrow, by the time the **s** is hot, 1 Sm 11:9
And as the **s** was going down they 2 Sm 2:24
or anything else till the **s** goes down!" 2 Sm 3:35
with your wives in the sight of this **s**. 2 Sm 12:11
before all Israel and before the **s**.'" 2 Sm 12:12
like the **s** shining forth on a cloudless 2 Sm 23:4
the morning and the **s** shone on the 2 Kgs 3:22
to the **s** and the moon and the 2 Kgs 23:5
of Judah had dedicated to the **s**, 2 Kgs 23:11
the chariots of the **s** with fire. 2 Kgs 23:11
of Jerusalem be opened until the **s** is hot. Neh 7:3
He is a lush plant before the **s**, and his Jb 8:16
who commands the **s**, and it does not rise; Jb 9:7
I go about darkened, but not by the **s**; I Jb 30:28
if I have looked at the **s** when it shone, Jb 31:26
world. In them he has set a tent for the **s**, Ps 19:4
from the rising of the **s** to its setting. Ps 50:1
the stillborn child who never sees the **s**. Ps 58:8
May they fear you while the **s** endures, Ps 72:5
his fame continue as long as the **s**! Ps 72:17
the heavenly lights and the **s**. Ps 74:16
For the LORD God is a **s** and shield; the Ps 84:11
his throne as long as the **s** before me. Ps 89:36
the **s** knows its time for setting. Ps 104:19
When the **s** rises, they steal away and Ps 104:22
From the rising of the **s** to its setting, Ps 113:3
The **s** shall not strike you by day, nor Ps 121:6
the **s** to rule over the day, for his Ps 136:8
Praise him, **s** and moon, praise him, all Ps 148:3
all the toil at which he toils under the **s**? Eccl 1:3
The **s** rises, and the sun goes down, and Eccl 1:5
The sun rises, and the **s** goes down, and Eccl 1:5
and there is nothing new under the **s**. Eccl 1:9
everything that is done under the **s**, Eccl 1:14
was nothing to be gained under the **s**. Eccl 2:11
is done under the **s** was grievous to me, Eccl 2:17
all my toil in which I toil under the **s**, Eccl 2:18
and used my wisdom under the **s**. Eccl 2:19
all the toil of my labors under the **s**, Eccl 2:20
with which he toils beneath the **s**? Eccl 2:22
I saw under the **s** that in the place of Eccl 3:16
oppressions that are done under the **s**. Eccl 4:1
the evil deeds that are done under the **s**. Eccl 4:3
Again, I saw vanity under the **s**: Eccl 4:7
living who move about under the **s**, Eccl 4:15
evil that I have seen under the **s**: Eccl 5:13
one toils under the **s** the few days of Eccl 5:18
is an evil that I have seen under the **s**, Eccl 6:1
it has not seen the **s** or known anything, Eccl 6:5
what will be after him under the **s**? Eccl 6:12
an advantage to those who see the **s**. Eccl 7:11
my heart to all that is done under the **s**, Eccl 8:9
good thing under the **s** but to eat and Eccl 8:15
that God has given him under the **s**. Eccl 8:15
out the work that is done under the **s**. Eccl 8:17
is an evil in all that is done under the **s**, Eccl 9:3
share in all that is done under the **s**. Eccl 9:6
life that he has given you under the **s**, Eccl 9:9
your toil at which you toil under the **s**. Eccl 9:9
I saw that under the **s** the race is not to Eccl 9:11
this example of wisdom under the **s**, Eccl 9:13
is an evil that I have seen under the **s**, Eccl 10:5
it is pleasant for the eyes to see the **s**. Eccl 11:7
before the **s** and the light and the Eccl 12:2
dark, because the **s** has looked upon me. Sg 1:6
beautiful as the moon, bright as the **s**, Sg 6:10
the **s** will be dark at its rising, and the Is 13:10
will be confounded and the **s** ashamed, Is 24:23
of the moon will be as the light of the **s**, Is 30:26
and the light of the **s** will be sevenfold, Is 30:26
cast by the declining **s** on the dial of Is 38:8
ten steps." So the **s** turned back on the Is 38:8
he has come, from the rising of the **s**, Is 41:25
from the rising of the **s** and from the west, Is 45:6
scorching wind nor **s** shall strike them, Is 49:10
and his glory from the rising of the **s**; Is 59:19
The **s** shall be no more your light by Is 60:19
Your **s** shall no more go down, nor your Is 60:20
be spread before the **s** and the moon and Jer 8:2
her **s** went down while it was yet day; Jer 15:9
who gives the **s** for light by day and the Jer 31:35
east, worshiping the **s** toward the east. Ezk 8:16
I will cover the **s** with a cloud, and the Ezk 32:7
he labored till the **s** went down to rescue Dn 6:14

The **s** and the moon are darkened, and the Jl 2:10
The **s** shall be turned to darkness, and the Jl 2:31
The **s** and the moon are darkened, and the Jl 3:15
"I will make the **s** go down at noon and Am 8:9
When the **s** rose, God appointed a Jon 4:8
and the **s** beat down on the head of Jonah Jon 4:8
The **s** shall go down on the prophets, and Mi 3:6
in a day of cold—when the **s** rises, Na 3:17
The **s** and moon stood still in their Hab 3:11
from the rising of the **s** to its setting my Mal 1:11
the **s** of righteousness shall rise with Mal 4:2
For he makes his **s** rise on the evil and Mt 5:45
but when the **s** rose they were scorched. Mt 13:6
will shine like the **s** in the kingdom of Mt 13:43
them, and his face shone like the **s**, Mt 17:2
of those days the **s** will be darkened, Mt 24:29
And when the **s** rose it was scorched, and Mk 4:6
tribulation, the **s** will be darkened, Mk 13:24
day of the week, when the **s** had risen, Mk 16:2
Now when the **s** was setting, all those Lk 4:40
will be signs in **s** and moon and stars, Lk 21:25
the **s** shall be turned to darkness and Acts 2:20
unable to see the **s** for a time." Acts 13:11
from heaven, brighter than the **s**, Acts 26:13
When neither **s** nor stars appeared Acts 27:20
There is one glory of the **s**, and 1 Cor 15:41
do not let the **s** go down on your anger, Eph 4:26
For the **s** rises with its scorching heat Jas 1:11
face was like the **s** shining in full Rv 1:16
and the **s** became black as sackcloth, Rv 6:12
angel ascending from the rising of the **s**, Rv 7:2
the **s** shall not strike them, nor any Rv 7:16
trumpet, and a third of the **s** was struck, Rv 8:12
and the **s** and the air were darkened with Rv 9:2
over his head, and his face was like the **s**, Rv 10:1
a woman clothed with the **s**, with the Rv 12:1
angel poured out his bowl on the **s**, Rv 16:8
Then I saw an angel standing in the **s**, Rv 19:17
city has no need of **s** or moon to shine Rv 21:23
They will need no light of lamp or **s**, for Rv 22:5

SUN'S (1)
while the **s** light failed. And the curtain Lk 23:45

SUNDOWN (1)
That evening at **s** they brought to him Mk 1:32

SUNG (6)
that thanksgiving be **s** to the LORD 1 Chr 16:7
to extol his work, of which men have **s**. Jb 36:24
and in the vineyards no songs are **s**, Is 16:10
day this song will be **s** in the land of Is 26:1
And when they had **s** a hymn, they Mt 26:30
And when they had **s** a hymn, they Mk 14:26

SUNK (7)
his chosen officers were **s** in the Red Sea. Ex 15:4
On what were its bases **s**, or who laid its Jb 38:6
The nations have **s** in the pit that they Ps 9:15
For your arrows have **s** into me, and Ps 38:2
now that your feet are **s** in the mud, Jer 38:22
Her gates have **s** into the ground; he has Lam 2:9
crew in your midst have **s** with you. Ezk 27:34

SUNRISE (10)
the east side toward the **s** shall be of the Nm 2:3
before the tent of meeting toward the **s**, Nm 3:38
that is opposite Moab, toward the **s**. Nm 21:11
Jordan east of Jericho, toward the **s**." Nm 34:15
you beyond the Jordan toward the **s**." Jos 1:15
land beyond the Jordan toward the **s**, Jos 12:1
Gebalites, and all Lebanon, toward the **s**, Jos 13:5
eastward toward the **s** to the boundary Jos 19:12
on the east toward the **s** to Gath-hepher, Jos 19:13
whereby the **s** shall visit us from on Lk 1:78

SUNSET (4)
Passover sacrifice, in the evening at **s**, Dt 16:6
evening. And at **s** Joshua commanded, Jos 8:29
And about **s** a cry went through the 1 Kgs 22:36
until evening. Then at **s** he died. 2 Chr 18:34

SUNSHINE (1)
from my dwelling like clear heat in **s**, Is 18:4

SUPER-APOSTLES (2)
am not in the least inferior to these **s**. 2 Cor 11:5
I was not at all inferior to these **s**, 2 Cor 12:11

SUPERFLUOUS (1)
Now it is **s** for me to write to you about 2 Cor 9:1

SUPERIOR (2)
having become as much **s** to angels as Heb 1:4
that the inferior is blessed by the **s**. Heb 7:7

SUPERVISE (1)
to **s** the work of the house of the LORD. Ezr 3:8

SUPERVISED (1)
together **s** the workmen in the house of Ezr 3:9

SUPH (1)
the wilderness, in the Arabah opposite **S**, Dt 1:1

SUPHAH (1)
of the Wars of the LORD, "Waheb in **S**, Nm 21:14

SUPPER (7)
not rather say to him, 'Prepare **s** for me, Lk 17:8
During **s**, when the devil had already put Jn 13:2
rose from **s**. He laid aside his outer Jn 13:4
it is not the Lord's **s** that you eat. 1 Cor 11:20
way also he took the cup, after **s**, 1 Cor 11:25
invited to the marriage **s** of the Lamb." Rv 19:9
"Come, gather for the great **s** of God, Rv 19:17

SUPPLEMENT (1)
make every effort to **s** your faith with 2 Pt 1:5

SUPPLICATION (3)
in the Spirit, with all prayer and **s**. Eph 6:18
making **s** for all the saints, Eph 6:18
by prayer and **s** with thanksgiving let Phil 4:6

SUPPLICATIONS (3)
First of all, then, I urge that **s**, prayers, 1 Tm 2:1
and continues in **s** and prayers night 1 Tm 5:5
his flesh, Jesus offered up prayers and **s**, Heb 5:7

SUPPLIED (8)
He **s** them with food in exchange for all Gn 47:17
all the vessels for oil with which it is **s**. Nm 4:9
And those officers **s** provisions for 1 Kgs 4:27
So Hiram **s** Solomon with all the 1 Kgs 5:10
of Tyre had **s** Solomon with cedar 1 Kgs 9:11
while the soul of the diligent is richly **s**. Prv 13:4
came from Macedonia **s** my need. 2 Cor 11:9
I am well **s**, having received from Phil 4:18

SUPPLIES (5)
and he had large **s** in the cities of 2 Chr 17:13
on with a great army and abundant **s**. Dn 11:13
He who **s** seed to the sower and bread 2 Cor 9:10
Does he who **s** the Spirit to you and Gal 3:5
the strength that God **s**—in order that 1 Pt 4:11

SUPPLY (12)
When I break your **s** of bread, ten Lv 26:26
on the land and broke all **s** of bread, Ps 105:16
Jerusalem and from Judah support and **s**, Is 3:1
her merchandise will **s** abundant food Is 23:18
I will break the **s** of bread in Jerusalem. Ezk 4:16
upon you and break your **s** of bread. Ezk 5:16
it and break its **s** of bread and send Ezk 14:13
the present time should **s** their need, 2 Cor 8:14
their abundance may **s** your need, 2 Cor 8:14
for food will **s** and multiply your 2 Cor 9:10
And my God will **s** every need of yours Phil 4:19
face to face and **s** what is lacking in 1 Thes 3:10

SUPPLYING (1)
service is not only **s** the needs of the 2 Cor 9:12

SUPPORT (15)
the land could not **s** both of them Gn 13:6
sojournings could not **s** them because Gn 36:7
you shall **s** him as though he were a Lv 25:35
my calamity, but the LORD was my **s**. 2 Sm 22:19
gave him strong **s** in his kingdom, 1 Chr 11:10
to give strong **s** to those whose heart 2 Chr 16:9
of my calamity, but the LORD was my **s**. Ps 18:18
the sanctuary and give you **s** from Zion! Ps 20:2
Jerusalem and from Judah **s** and supply, Is 3:1
Judah support and supply, all **s** of bread, Is 3:1
all support of bread, and all **s** of water; Is 3:1
Those who **s** Egypt shall fall, and her Ezk 30:6
it is not you who **s** the root, Rom 11:18
churches by accepting **s** from them 2 Cor 11:8
Therefore we ought to **s** people like these, 3 Jn 1:8

SUPPORTED (7)
for Joab had **s** Adonijah although he 1 Kgs 2:28
he had not **s** Absalom—Joab 1 Kgs 2:28
and Shabbethai the Levite **s** them. Ezr 10:15
He gives them security, and they are **s**, Jb 24:23
salvation, and your right hand **s** me, Ps 18:35
that they should not be **s** by the wall of Ezk 41:6
her, and he who **s** her in those times. Dn 11:6

SUPPORTING (2)
in order that the **s** beams should not 1 Kgs 6:6
prophets of God were with them, **s** them. Ezr 5:2

SUPPORTS (9)
at the four corners were **s** for a basin. 1 Kgs 7:30
The **s** were cast with wreaths at the 1 Kgs 7:30
There were four **s** at the four corners 1 Kgs 7:34
The **s** were of one piece with the 1 Kgs 7:34
of the almug wood **s** for the house of 1 Kgs 10:12
from the algum wood **s** for the house 2 Chr 9:11
temple to serve as **s** for the side Ezk 41:6
up, they used **s** to undergird the ship. Acts 27:17
the root, but the root that **s** you. Rom 11:18

SUPPOSE (17)
S there are fifty righteous within the Gn 18:24
S five of the fifty righteous are lacking. Gn 18:28
"**S** forty are found there." He answered, Gn 18:29
S thirty are found there." He answered, Gn 18:30
S twenty are found there." He answered, Gn 18:31
S ten are found there." He answered, Gn 18:32
"Let not my lord **s** that they have 2 Sm 13:32
it to heart as to **s** that all the king's 2 Sm 13:33
Why should you **s** that God will cast 2 Chr 25:8
"Now **s** this man fathers a son who Ezk 18:14
Simon answered, "The one, I **s**, for Lk 7:43
I **s** that the world itself could not Jn 21:25
For these men are not drunk, as you **s**, Acts 2:15
he said, 'What do you **s** that I am? Acts 13:25
Do you **s**, O man—you who judge those Rom 2:3
that person must not **s** that he will receive Jas 1:7
Or do you **s** it is to no purpose that the Jas 4:5

SUPPOSED (6)
of age, being the son (as was **s**) of Joseph, Lk 3:23
and because they **s** that the kingdom of Lk 19:11
He **s** that his brothers would Acts 7:25
where we **s** there was a place of Acts 16:13
and they **s** that Paul had brought Acts 21:29
charge in his case of such evils as I **s**. Acts 25:18

SUPPOSING (6)
but **s** him to be in the group they went a Lk 2:44
s that she was going to the tomb to weep Jn 11:31
Whom are you seeking?" **S** him to be Jn 20:15
out of the city, **s** that he was dead. Acts 14:19
s that the prisoners had escaped. Acts 16:27
s that they had obtained their Acts 27:13

SUPPRESS (1)
by their unrighteousness **s** the truth. Rom 1:18

SUPREME (2)
For the word of the king is **s**, and who Eccl 8:4
whether it be to the emperor as **s**, 1 Pt 2:13

SUPREMELY (1)
the grace of God, and **s** so toward you. 2 Cor 1:12

SUR (1)
third being at the gate **S** and a third at 2 Kgs 11:6

SURE (40)
and be **s** your sin will find you out. Nm 32:23
Only be **s** that you do not eat the blood, Dt 12:23
my father's house, and give me a **s** sign Jos 2:12
And I will build him a **s** house, and he 1 Sm 2:35
Go, make yet more **s**. Know and see 1 Sm 23:22
back to me with **s** information. 1 Sm 23:23
certainly make my lord a **s** house, 1 Sm 25:28
because I was **s** that he could not live 2 Sm 1:10
shall be made **s** forever before me. 2 Sm 7:16
you and will build you a **s** house, 1 Kgs 11:38
the testimony of the LORD is **s**, making Ps 19:7
All your commandments are **s**; they Ps 119:86
swore to David a **s** oath from which he Ps 132:11
of your feet; then all your ways will be **s**. Prv 4:26
sows righteousness gets a **s** reward. Prv 11:18
things, plans formed of old, faithful and **s**. Is 25:1
precious cornerstone, of a **s** foundation: Is 28:16
will be given him; his water will be **s**. Is 33:16
covenant, my steadfast, **s** love for David. Is 55:3
is certain, and its interpretation **s**." Dn 2:45
tribes of Israel I make known what is **s**. Hos 5:9
the LORD; his going out is **s** as the dawn; Hos 6:3
"Temptations to sin are **s** to come, Lk 17:1
"Now I am **s** that the Lord has sent Acts 12:11
the holy and **s** blessings of David.' Acts 13:34
and if you are **s** that you yourself are a Rom 2:19
For I am **s** that neither death nor life, Rom 8:38
Because I was **s** of this, I wanted to 2 Cor 1:15
me rejoice, for I felt **s** of all of you, 2 Cor 2:3
in order to make **s** I was not running or Gal 2:2
For you may be **s** of this, that everyone Eph 5:5
And I am **s** of this, that he who began a Phil 1:6
your mother Eunice and now, I am **s**, 2 Tm 1:5
we feel **s** of better things—things that Heb 6:9
have this as a **s** and steadfast anchor of Heb 6:19
for we are **s** that we have a clear Heb 13:18
to make your calling and election **s**, 2 Pt 1:10
And we have something more **s**, the 2 Pt 1:19
By this we may be **s** that we are in him: 1 Jn 2:5
you may be **s** that everyone who 1 Jn 2:29

SURELY (204)
"You may **s** eat of every tree of the Gn 2:16
the day that you eat of it you shall **s** die." Gn 2:17
said to the woman, "You will not **s** die. Gn 3:4
"I will **s** multiply your pain in Gn 3:16
"I will **s** multiply your offspring so that Gn 16:10
your money, shall **s** be circumcised. Gn 17:13
"I will **s** return to you about this time Gn 18:10
that Abraham shall **s** become a great Gn 18:18
return her, know that you shall **s** die, Gn 20:7

I will **s** bless you, and I will surely Gn 22:17
and I will **s** multiply your offspring as Gn 22:17
or his wife shall **s** be put to death." Gn 26:11
and said, "**S** the LORD is in this place, Gn 28:16
"**S** you are my bone and my flesh!" Gn 29:14
s now you would have sent me away Gn 31:42
But you said, 'I will **s** do you good, and Gn 32:12
by the life of Pharaoh, **s** you are spies." Gn 42:16
and I said, **S** he has been torn to pieces, Gn 44:28
swear, saying, "God will **s** visit you, Gn 50:25
and thought, "**S** the thing is known." Ex 2:14
"I have **s** seen the affliction of my people Ex 3:7
"**S** you are a bridegroom of blood to me!" Ex 4:25
swear, saying, "God will **s** visit you, Ex 13:19
the one who hit her shall **s** be fined, Ex 21:22
be bloodguilt for him. He shall **s** pay. Ex 22:3
cry out to me, I will **s** hear their cry, Ex 22:23
their gods, it will **s** be a snare to you." Ex 23:33
children to Molech shall **s** be put to Lv 20:2
or his mother shall **s** be put to death; Lv 20:9
and the adulteress shall **s** be put to Lv 20:10
both of them shall **s** be put to death; Lv 20:11
both of them shall **s** be put to death; Lv 20:12
they shall **s** be put to death; Lv 20:13
an animal, he shall **s** be put to death, Lv 20:15
the animal; they shall **s** be put to death; Lv 20:16
or a wizard shall **s** be put to death. Lv 20:27
of the LORD shall **s** be put to death. Lv 24:16
a human life shall **s** be put to death. Lv 24:17
be ransomed; he shall **s** be put to death. Lv 27:29
S this will I do to all this wicked Nm 14:35
for I will **s** do you great honor, and Nm 22:17
s just now I would have killed you Nm 22:33
'**S** none of the men who came up out Nm 32:11
'**S** this great nation is a wise and Dt 4:6
warn you today that you shall **s** perish. Dt 8:19
You shall **s** destroy all the places where Dt 12:2
you shall **s** put the inhabitants of that Dt 13:15
LORD your God will **s** require it of you, Dt 23:21
to you today, that you shall **s** perish. Dt 30:18
And I will **s** hide my face in that day Dt 31:18
my death you will **s** act corruptly and Dt 31:29
'**S** the land on which your foot has Jos 14:9
"**S** he is relieving himself in the closet of Jgs 3:24
And she said, "I will **s** go with you. Jgs 4:9
said to his wife, "We shall **s** die, Jgs 13:22
We will **s** not kill you." So they bound Jgs 15:13
said, "**S** they are defeated before us, Jgs 20:39
saying, "He shall **s** be put to death." Jgs 21:5
he shall **s** die." But there was not a 1 Sm 14:39
more also; you shall **s** die, Jonathan." 1 Sm 14:44
"**S** the bitterness of death is past." 1 Sm 15:32
"**S** the LORD'S anointed is before him." 1 Sm 16:6
up? **S** he has come up to defy Israel. 1 Sm 17:25
He is not clean; **s** he is not clean." 1 Sm 20:26
bring him to me, for he shall **s** die." 1 Sm 20:31
And the king said, "You shall **s** die, 1 Sm 22:16
was there, that he would **s** tell Saul. 1 Sm 22:22
your servant has **s** heard that Saul 1 Sm 23:10
I know that you shall **s** be king, 1 Sm 24:20
"**S** in vain have I guarded all that 1 Sm 25:21
For as **s** as the LORD the God of Israel 1 Sm 25:34
"**S** you know what Saul has done, 1 Sm 28:9
for you shall **s** overtake and shall 1 Sm 30:8
surely overtake and shall **s** rescue." 1 Sm 30:8
s the men would not have given up 2 Sm 2:27
answered and said, "As **s** as you live, 2 Sm 14:19
for **s** they will turn away your heart 1 Kgs 11:2
I will **s** tear the kingdom from you 1 Kgs 11:11
of Samaria shall **s** come to pass." 1 Kgs 13:32
I will **s** show myself to him today." 1 Kgs 18:15
and **s** we shall be stronger than they. 1 Kgs 20:23
and **s** we shall be stronger than 1 Kgs 20:25
"It is **s** the king of Israel." So they 1 Kgs 22:32
but you shall **s** die.'" So Elijah went. 2 Kgs 1:4
you have gone up, but you shall **s** die.'" 2 Kgs 1:6
have gone up, but you shall **s** die.'" 2 Kgs 1:16
the kings have **s** fought together and 2 Kgs 3:23
thought that he would **s** come out to 2 Kgs 5:11
'As **s** as I saw yesterday the blood of 2 Kgs 9:26
saying, The LORD will **s** deliver us, 2 Kgs 18:30
S this came upon Judah at the 2 Kgs 24:3
him but will **s** fall before him." Est 6:13
S vexation kills the fool, and jealousy Jb 5:2
s then he will rouse himself for you and Jb 8:6
S then you will lift up your face without Jb 11:15
He will **s** rebuke you if in secret you Jb 13:10
S now God has worn me out; he has Jb 16:7
S there are mockers about me, and my Jb 17:2
S such are the dwellings of the Jb 18:21
S he who is wise is profitable to himself. Jb 22:2
saying, '**S** our adversaries are cut off, Jb 22:20
"**S** there is a mine for silver, and a place Jb 28:1
S I would carry it on my shoulder; I Jb 31:36
"**S** you have spoken in my ears, and I Jb 33:8
S God does not hear an empty cry, nor Jb 35:13
its measurements—**s** you know! Jb 38:5
S goodness and mercy shall follow me Ps 23:6
s in the rush of great waters, they shall Ps 32:6
S all mankind stands as a mere breath! Ps 39:5
S a man goes about as a shadow! Surely Ps 39:6
S for nothing they are in turmoil; man Ps 39:6
to him; **s** all mankind is a mere breath! Ps 39:11
"**S** there is a reward for the righteous; Ps 58:11
s there is a God who judges on earth." Ps 58:11
S the wrath of man shall praise you; the Ps 76:10
S his salvation is near to those who fear Ps 85:9
If I say, "**S** the darkness shall cover me, Ps 139:11
S the righteous shall give thanks to Ps 140:13
for a stranger will **s** suffer harm, Prv 11:15
of the diligent lead **s** to abundance, Prv 21:5
S there is a future, and your hope will Prv 23:18
S I am too stupid to be a man. I have not Prv 30:2
what is his son's name? **S** you know! Prv 30:4
S this also is vanity and a striving after Eccl 4:16
S oppression drives the wise into Eccl 7:7
S there is not a righteous man on earth Eccl 7:20
"**S** many houses shall be desolate, large Is 5:9
"**S** this iniquity will not be atoned for Is 22:14
He will **s** be gracious to you at the sound Is 30:19
by saying, "The LORD will **s** deliver us. Is 36:15
LORD blows on it; **s** the people are grass. Is 40:7
'**S** God is in you, and there is no other, no Is 45:14
that you would **s** deal treacherously, Is 48:8
yet **s** my right is with the LORD, and my Is 49:4
"**S** your waste and your desolate places Is 49:19
your devastated land—**s** now you will be Is 49:19
S he has borne our griefs and carried our Is 53:4
"The LORD will **s** separate me from his Is 56:3
For he said, "**S** they are my people, Is 63:8
s his anger has turned from me.' Jer 2:35
S, as a treacherous wife leaves her Jer 3:20
s you have utterly deceived this people Jer 4:10
Lebanon, yet **s** I will make you a desert, Jer 22:6
I will **s** lift you up and cast you away Jer 23:39
I will **s** have mercy on him, declares the Jer 31:20
but shall **s** be given into the hand of the Jer 32:4
his hand but shall **s** be captured and Jer 34:3
"The Chaldeans will **s** go away from us," Jer 37:9
This city shall **s** be given into the hand Jer 38:3
tell you, will you not **s** put me to death? Jer 38:15
For I will **s** save you, and you shall not Jer 39:18
'We will **s** perform our vows that we Jer 44:25
that my words will **s** stand against you Jer 44:29
S their fold shall be appalled at their Jer 49:20
He will **s** plead their cause, that he may Jer 50:34
S the little ones of their flock shall be Jer 50:45
s their fold shall be appalled at their Jer 50:45
S I will fill you with men, as many as Jer 51:14
is a God of recompense; he will **s** repay. Jer 51:56
s against me he turns his hand again Lam 3:3
S, if I sent you to such, they would listen Ezk 3:6
If I say to the wicked, 'You shall **s** die,' Ezk 3:18
sin, and he does not sin, he shall **s** live, Ezk 3:21
s, because you have defiled my Ezk 5:11
s in the place where the king dwells Ezk 17:16
I live, **s** it is my oath that he despised, Ezk 17:19
he shall **s** live, declares the Lord GOD. Ezk 18:9
all these abominations; he shall **s** die; Ezk 18:13
for his father's iniquity; he shall **s** live. Ezk 18:17
observe all my statutes, he shall **s** live. Ezk 18:19
what is just and right, he shall **s** live; Ezk 18:21
that he had committed, he shall **s** live; Ezk 18:28
s with a mighty hand and an Ezk 20:33
s on the day when I take from them Ezk 24:25
He shall **s** deal with it as its Ezk 31:11
wicked, O wicked one, you shall **s** die, Ezk 33:8
'**S** our transgressions and our sins are Ezk 33:10
to the righteous that he shall **s** live, Ezk 33:13
I say to the wicked, 'You shall **s** die,' Ezk 33:14
life, not doing injustice, he shall **s** live; Ezk 33:15
what is just and right; he shall **s** live. Ezk 33:16
the land is **s** given us to possess.' Ezk 33:24
s those who are in the waste places Ezk 33:27
s because my sheep have become a Ezk 34:8
S I have spoken in my hot jealousy Ezk 36:5
they shall **s** trim the hair of their Ezk 44:20
s it is his inheritance—it shall belong Ezk 46:17
Gilead, they shall **s** come to nothing: Hos 12:11
for Gilgal shall **s** go into exile, Am 5:5
and Israel shall **s** go into exile away Am 7:17
"**S** I will never forget any of their deeds. Am 8:7
I will **s** assemble all of you, O Jacob; I Mi 2:12
If it seems slow, wait for it; it will **s** come; Hab 2:3
I said, '**S** you will fear me; you will accept Zep 3:7
All who lift it will **s** hurt themselves. Zec 12:3
reviles father or mother must **s** die.' Mt 15:4
reviles father or mother must **s** die.' Mk 7:10
they heard this, they said, "**S** not!" Lk 20:16
I have **s** seen the affliction of my people Acts 7:34
As **s** as God is faithful, our word to 2 Cor 1:18
calls you is faithful; he will **s** do it. 1 Thes 5:24
For **s** it is not angels that he helps, but Heb 2:16
"**S** I will bless you and multiply you." Heb 6:14
says, "**S** I am coming soon." Amen. Rv 22:20

SURF (1)
stern was being broken up by the **s**. Acts 27:41

SURFACE (10)
and if it appears to be deeper than the **s**, Lv 14:37
he will twist its **s** and scatter its Is 24:1
When he has leveled its **s**, does he not Is 28:25
shall be as dung on the **s** of the ground. Jer 8:2
shall be as dung on the **s** of the ground. Jer 16:4
shall be dung on the **s** of the ground. Jer 25:33
were very many on the **s** of the valley, Ezk 37:2
and pours them out on the **s** of the earth, Am 5:8
pours them out upon the **s** of the earth— Am 9:6
I will destroy it from the **s** of the ground, Am 9:8

SURFACES (1)
And on the **s** of its stays and on its 1 Kgs 7:36

SURGE (2)
like the Nile, like rivers whose waters **s**? Jer 46:7
like the Nile, like rivers whose waters **s**. Jer 46:8

SURGING (1)
your horses, the **s** of mighty waters. Hab 3:15

SURPASS (6)
wisdom and prosperity **s** the report 1 Kgs 10:7
told me; you **s** the report that I heard. 2 Chr 9:6
done excellently, but you **s** them all." Prv 31:29
does the wood of the vine **s** any wood, Ezk 15:2
'Whom do you **s** in beauty? Go down Ezk 32:19
of Jerusalem may not **s** that of Judah. Zec 12:7

SURPASSED (2)
that Solomon's wisdom **s** the wisdom 1 Kgs 4:30
I became great and **s** all who were Eccl 2:9

SURPASSES (3)
at all, because of the glory that **s** it. 2 Cor 3:10
the love of Christ that **s** knowledge, Eph 3:19
of God, which **s** all understanding, Phil 4:7

SURPASSING (6)
extraordinary, **s** the love of women. 2 Sm 1:26
s all who were over Jerusalem before Eccl 1:16
to show that the **s** power belongs to 2 Cor 4:7
because of the **s** grace of God upon 2 Cor 9:14
too elated by the **s** greatness of the 2 Cor 12:7
loss because of the **s** worth of knowing Phil 3:8

SURPRISE (2)
So it is no **s** if his servants, also, 2 Cor 11:15
for that day to **s** you like a thief. 1 Thes 5:4

SURPRISED (4)
Pilate was **s** to hear that he should Mk 15:44
to this they are **s** when you do not 1 Pt 4:4
do not be **s** at the fiery trial when it 1 Pt 4:12
Do not be **s**, brothers, that the world 1 Jn 3:13

SURRENDER (7)
the men of Keilah **s** me into his 1 Sm 23:11
the men of Keilah **s** me and my men 1 Sm 23:12
And the LORD said, "They will **s** you." 1 Sm 23:12
part shall be to **s** him into the king's 1 Sm 23:20
If you will **s** to the officials of the king Jer 38:17
But if you do not **s** to the officials of the Jer 38:18
But if you refuse to **s**, this is the vision Jer 38:21

SURRENDERED (1)
shout against her all around; she has **s**; Jer 50:15

SURRENDERS (1)
who goes out and **s** to the Chaldeans Jer 21:9

SURROUND (18)
will hear of it and will **s** us and cut off our Jos 7:9
shall **s** the king, each with his 2 Kgs 11:8
these cities and **s** them with walls 2 Chr 14:7
The Levites shall **s** the king, each 2 Chr 23:7
his archers **s** me. He slashes open my Jb 16:13
him; the willows of the brook **s** him. Jb 40:22
violence, my deadly enemies who **s** me. Ps 17:9
me; strong bulls of Bashan **s** me; Ps 22:12
you **s** me with shouts of deliverance. Ps 32:7
They **s** me like a flood all day long; they Ps 88:17
As the mountains **s** Jerusalem, so the Ps 125:2
As for the head of those who **s** me, let Ps 140:9
The righteous will **s** me, for you will Ps 142:7
Now their deeds **s** them; they are before Hos 7:2
"An adversary shall **s** the land and Am 3:11
For the wicked **s** the righteous; so Hab 1:4
the crowds **s** you and are pressing in on Lk 8:45
around you and **s** you and hem Lk 19:43

SURROUNDED (21)
the people to the last man, **s** the house. Gn 19:4
come here." And they **s** the place and set Jgs 16:2

the city, worthless fellows, **s** the house, Jgs 19:22
rose against me and **s** the house against Jgs 20:5
s Absalom and struck him and 2 Sm 18:15
warfare with which his enemies **s** him, 1 Kgs 5:3
and the slingers **s** and attacked it. 2 Kgs 3:25
they came by night and **s** the city. 2 Kgs 6:14
struck the Edomites who had **s** him, 2 Kgs 8:21
the Edomites who had **s** him and his 2 Chr 21:9
They have now **s** our steps; they set Ps 17:11
All nations **s** me; in the name of the Ps 118:10
They **s** me, surrounded me on every Ps 118:11
surrounded me, **s** me on every side; Ps 118:11
They **s** me like bees; they went out like Ps 118:12
Ephraim has **s** me with lies, and the Hos 11:12
the heart of the seas, and the flood **s** me; Jon 2:3
in over me to take my life; the deep **s** me; Jon 2:5
when you see Jerusalem **s** by armies, Lk 21:20
since we are **s** by so great a cloud of Heb 12:1
plain of the earth and **s** the camp of the Rv 20:9

SURROUNDING (27)
shall measure the distance to the **s** cities. Dt 21:2
rest to Israel from all their **s** enemies, Jos 23:1
them into the hand of their **s** enemies, Jgs 2:14
S the Benjaminites, they pursued them Jgs 20:43
from the hand of their **s** enemies. 1 Sm 10:1
given him rest from all his **s** enemies, 2 Sm 7:1
and his fame was in all the **s** nations. 1 Kgs 4:31
land of Judah and its **s** pasturelands, 1 Chr 6:55
give him rest from all his **s** enemies. 1 Chr 22:9
of the LORD, all the **s** chambers, 1 Chr 28:12
him the priests, the men of the **s** area, Neh 3:22
from the district **s** Jerusalem and Neh 12:28
and against all these **s** nations. Jer 25:9
Hasten and come, all you **s** nations, and Jl 3:11
there I will sit to judge all the **s** nations. Jl 3:12
a cup of staggering to all the **s** peoples. Zec 12:2
the right and to the left all the **s** peoples, Zec 12:6
wealth of all the **s** nations shall be Zec 14:14
throughout all the **s** region of Galilee. Mk 1:28
to go into the **s** countryside and villages Mk 6:36
him went out through all the **s** country. Lk 4:14
went out into every place in the **s** region. Lk 4:37
the whole of Judea and all the **s** country. Lk 7:17
the people of the **s** country of the Lk 8:37
to go into the **s** villages and countryside Lk 9:12
of Lycaonia, and to the **s** country, Acts 14:6
Sodom and Gomorrah and the **s** cities, Jude 1:7

SURROUNDS (5)
The High God **s** him all day long, and Dt 33:12
but steadfast love **s** the one who trusts Ps 32:10
the iniquity of those who cheat me **s** me, Ps 49:5
Jerusalem, so the LORD **s** his people, Ps 125:2
for the great slaughter, which **s** them, Ezk 21:14

SURVIVE (4)
Those who **s** him the pestilence buries, Jb 27:15
people in this city who **s** the pestilence, Jer 21:7
Egypt shall escape or **s** or return to the Jer 44:14
and any of you who **s** I will scatter to all Ezk 5:10

SURVIVED (6)
there was left none that **s** or escaped. Jos 8:22
And those who **s** were scattered, so 1 Sm 11:11
Jews who escaped, who had **s** the exile, Neh 1:2
in the province who had **s** the exile is in Neh 1:3
"The people who **s** the sword found grace Jer 31:2
anger of the LORD no one escaped or **s**; Lam 2:22

SURVIVES (3)
But if the slave **s** a day or two, he is not Ex 21:21
Then everyone who **s** of all the nations Zec 14:16
anyone has built on the foundation **s**, 1 Cor 3:14

SURVIVING (5)
and to Eleazar and Ithamar, his **s** sons: Lv 10:12
and Ithamar, the **s** sons of Aaron, Lv 10:16
And the **s** remnant of the house of 2 Kgs 19:30
And the **s** remnant of the house of Judah Is 37:31
from Jerusalem to the **s** elders of the Jer 29:1

SURVIVOR (6)
all his people, until he had no **s** left. Nm 21:35
we struck him down until he had no **s** left. Dt 3:3
And let each **s**, in whatever place he Ezr 1:4
people, and no **s** where he used to live. Jb 18:19
have no remnant or **s** from the disaster Jer 42:17
and there shall be no **s** for the house of Ob 1:18

SURVIVORS (19)
earth, and to keep alive for you many **s**. Gn 45:7
dominion and destroy the **s** of cities!" Nm 24:19
men, women, and children. We left no **s**. Dt 2:34
an inheritance for the **s** of Benjamin, Jgs 21:17
and out of Mount Zion a band of **s**. 2 Kgs 19:31
If the LORD of hosts had not left us a few **s**, Is 1:9
be the pride and honor of the **s** of Israel. Is 4:2
of Israel and the **s** of the house of Is 10:20
and out of Mount Zion a band of **s**. Is 37:32
draw near together, you **s** of the nations! Is 45:20
from them I will send **s** to the nations, Is 66:19
And if any **s** escape, they will be on the Ezk 7:16
But behold, some **s** will be left in it, Ezk 14:22
and the **s** shall be scattered to every Ezk 17:21
and your **s** shall fall by the sword. Ezk 23:25
and your **s** shall be devoured by fire. Ezk 23:25
and among the **s** shall be those whom the Jl 2:32
do not hand over his **s** in the day of Ob 1:14
and the **s** of my nation shall possess Zep 2:9

SUSA (22)
of Erech, the Babylonians, the men of **S**, Ezr 4:9
twentieth year, as I was in **S** the capital, Neh 1:1
Ahasuerus sat on his royal throne in **S**, Est 1:2
king gave for all the people present in **S**, Est 1:5
virgins to the harem in **S** the capital, Est 2:3
was a Jew in **S** the citadel whose name Est 2:5
women were gathered in **S** the citadel in Est 2:8
the decree was issued in **S** the citadel. Est 3:15
but the city of **S** was thrown into Est 3:15
decree issued in **S** for their destruction, Est 4:8
"Go, gather all the Jews to be found in **S**, Est 4:16
the decree was issued in **S** the citadel. Est 8:14
and the city of **S** shouted and rejoiced. Est 8:15
In **S** the citadel itself the Jews killed and Est 9:6
of those killed in **S** the citadel was Est 9:11
"In **S** the citadel the Jews have killed and Est 9:12
Jews who are in **S** be allowed tomorrow Est 9:13
A decree was issued in **S**, and the ten Est 9:14
Jews who were in **S** gathered also on the Est 9:15
of Adar and they killed 300 men in **S**, Est 9:15
Jews who were in **S** gathered on the Est 9:18
and when I saw, I was in **S** the capital, Dn 8:2

SUSANNA (1)
Herod's household manager, and **S**, Lk 8:3

SUSI (1)
of Manasseh), Gaddi the son of **S**; Nm 13:11

SUSPECT (1)
against some who **s** us of walking 2 Cor 10:2

SUSPECTED (1)
midnight the sailors **s** that they were Acts 27:27

SUSPENDED (1)
and he was **s** between heaven and 2 Sm 18:9

SUSPENSE (2)
to him, "How long will you keep us in **s**? Jn 10:24
have continued in **s** and without Acts 27:33

SUSPICIONS (1)
envy, dissension, slander, evil **s**, 1 Tm 6:4

SUSTAIN (4)
burden on the LORD, and he will **s** you; Ps 55:22
S me with raisins; refresh me with apples, Sg 2:5
I may know how to **s** with a word him Is 50:4
who will **s** you to the end, guiltless in 1 Cor 1:8

SUSTAINED (3)
and with grain and wine I have **s** him. Gn 27:37
Forty years you **s** them in the Neh 9:21
and slept; I woke again, for the LORD **s** me. Ps 3:5

SUSTAINS (1)
The LORD **s** him on his sickbed; in his Ps 41:3

SUSTENANCE (1)
and leave no **s** in Israel and no sheep or ox Jgs 6:4

SWADDLING (4)
garment and thick darkness its **s** band, Jb 38:9
with salt, nor wrapped in **s** cloths. Ezk 16:4
and wrapped him in **s** cloths and laid Lk 2:7
a baby wrapped in **s** cloths and lying in Lk 2:12

SWALLOW (16)
for they said, "Lest the earth **s** us up!" Nm 16:34
Why will you **s** up the heritage of the 2 Sm 20:19
be it, that I should **s** up or destroy! 2 Sm 20:20
me, nor leave me alone till I **s** my spit? Jb 7:19
fruit of his toil and will not **s** it down; Jb 20:18
The LORD will **s** them up in his wrath, Ps 21:9
sweep over me, or the deep **s** me up, Ps 69:15
finds a home, and the **s** a nest for herself, Ps 84:3
like Sheol let us **s** them alive, and Prv 1:12
in its flitting, like a **s** in its flying, Prv 26:2
And he will **s** up on this mountain the Is 25:7
He will **s** up death forever; and the Lord Is 25:8
Like a **s** or a crane I chirp; I moan like a Is 38:14
s, and crane keep the time of their Jer 8:7
they shall drink and **s**, and shall be as Ob 1:16
appointed a great fish to **s** up Jonah. Jon 1:17

SWALLOWED (27)
And the thin ears **s** up the seven plump, Gn 41:7
and the thin ears **s** up the seven good Gn 41:24
But Aaron's staff **s** up their staffs. Ex 7:12
out your right hand; the earth **s** them. Ex 15:12
opened its mouth and **s** them up, Nm 16:32
Moab, and **s** the heights of the Arnon. Nm 21:28
its mouth and **s** them up together Nm 26:10
earth opened its mouth and **s** them up, Dt 11:6
people who are with him be **s** up.'" 2 Sm 17:16
a man ever wish that he would be **s** up? Jb 37:20
Let them not say, "We have **s** him up." Ps 35:25
the earth opened and **s** up Dathan, and Ps 106:17
then they would have **s** us up alive, Ps 124:3
you and they have **s** up the course of Is 3:12
those who are guided by them are **s** up. Is 9:16
reel with strong drink, they are **s** by wine, Is 28:7
and those who **s** you up will be far away. Is 49:19
vessel; he has **s** me like a monster; Jer 51:34
take out of his mouth what he has **s**. Jer 51:44
The Lord has **s** up without mercy all Lam 2:2
like an enemy; he has **s** up Israel; Lam 2:5
up Israel; he has **s** up all its palaces; Lam 2:5
their teeth, they cry: "We have **s** her! Lam 2:16
Israel is **s** up; already they are among the Hos 8:8
is written: "Death is **s** up in victory." 1 Cor 15:54
what is mortal may be **s** up by life. 2 Cor 5:4
opened its mouth and **s** the river that Rv 12:16

SWALLOWING (1)
straining out a gnat and **s** a camel! Mt 23:24

SWALLOWS (5)
opens its mouth and **s** them up with Nm 16:30
He **s** down riches and vomits them up Jb 20:15
fierceness and rage he **s** the ground; Jb 39:24
sees it, he **s** it as soon as it is in his hand. Is 28:4
silent when the wicked **s** up the man Hab 1:13

SWAMPED (1)
that the boat was being **s** by the waves; Mt 8:24

SWAMPS (1)
But its **s** and marshes will not become Ezk 47:11

SWARM (9)
"Let the waters **s** with swarms of living Gn 1:20
that moves, with which the waters **s**, Gn 1:21
swarming creatures that **s** on the earth, Gn 7:21
the earth—that they may **s** on the earth, Gn 8:17
The Nile shall **s** with frogs that shall Ex 8:3
such a dense **s** of locusts as had never Ex 10:14
swarming things that **s** on the ground: Lv 11:29
are unclean to you among all that **s**. Lv 11:31
there was a **s** of bees in the body of the Jgs 14:8

SWARMED (1)
Their land **s** with frogs, even in the Ps 105:30

SWARMING (12)
all **s** creatures that swarm on the earth, Gn 7:21
livestock or a carcass of unclean **s** things, Lv 5:2
of the **s** creatures in the waters and of Lv 11:10
to you among the **s** things that swarm Lv 11:29
"Every **s** thing that swarms on the Lv 11:41
any **s** thing that swarms on the ground, Lv 11:42
detestable with any **s** thing that Lv 11:43
yourselves with any **s** thing that crawls Lv 11:44
and whoever touches a **s** thing by which Lv 22:5
cutting locust left, the **s** locust has eaten. Jl 1:4
locust has eaten. What the **s** locust left, Jl 1:4
you the years that the **s** locust has eaten, Jl 2:25

SWARMS (15)
waters swarm with **s** of living creatures, Gn 1:20
I will send **s** of flies on you and your Ex 8:21
Egyptians shall be filled with **s** of flies, Ex 8:21
dwell, so that no **s** of flies shall be there, Ex 8:22
There came great **s** of flies into the house Ex 8:24
the land was ruined by the **s** of flies. Ex 8:24
the LORD that the **s** of flies may depart Ex 8:29
and removed the **s** of flies from Pharaoh, Ex 8:31
swarming thing that **s** on the ground Lv 11:41
swarming thing that **s** on the ground, Lv 11:42
with any swarming thing that **s**, Lv 11:43
every creature that **s** on the ground, Lv 11:46
He sent among them **s** of flies, which Ps 78:45
He spoke, and there came **s** of flies, and Ps 105:31
every living creature that **s** will live, Ezk 47:9

SWAY (3)
are honored, and go hold **s** over the trees?' Jgs 9:9
good fruit and go hold **s** over the trees?' Jgs 9:11
and men and go hold **s** over the trees?' Jgs 9:13

SWAYED (3)
And he **s** the heart of all the men of 2 Sm 19:14
for you are not **s** by appearances. Mt 22:16
For you are not **s** by appearances, but Mk 12:14

SWAYS (1)
like a drunken man; it **s** like a hut; Is 24:20

SWEAR (58)
Now therefore **s** to me here by God that Gn 21:23
And Abraham said, "I will **s**." Gn 21:24
that I may make you **s** by the LORD, the Gn 24:3
My master made me **s**, saying, 'You Gn 24:37

"**S** to me now." So he swore to him and Gn 25:33
And he said, "**S** to me"; and he swore to Gn 47:31
My father made me **s**, saying, 'I am Gn 50:5
bury your father, as he made you **s**." Gn 50:6
Then Joseph made the sons of Israel **s**, Gn 50:25
had made the sons of Israel solemnly **s**, Ex 13:19
good, any sort of rash oath that people **s**, Lv 5:4
You shall not **s** by my name falsely, Lv 19:12
shall serve and by his name you shall **s**. Dt 6:13
to him, and by his name you shall **s**. Dt 10:20
For I lift up my hand to heaven and **s**, Dt 32:40
then, please **s** to me by the LORD that, Jos 2:12
oath of yours that you have made us **s**. Jos 2:17
to your oath that you have made us **s**." Jos 2:20
of their gods or **s** by them or serve Jos 23:7
what you do, I **s** I will be avenged on you, Jgs 15:7
"**S** to me that you will not attack me Jgs 15:12
Therefore I **s** to the house of Eli that 1 Sm 3:14
Jonathan made David **s** again by his 1 Sm 20:17
S to me therefore by the LORD that 1 Sm 24:21
"**S** to me by God that you will not 1 Sm 30:15
to your servants, for I **s** by the LORD, 2 Sm 19:7
my lord the king, **s** to your servant, 1 Kgs 1:13
'Let King Solomon **s** to me first that 1 Kgs 1:51
I not make you **s** by the LORD and 1 Kgs 2:42
shall I make you **s** that you speak to 1 Kgs 22:16
shall I make you **s** that you speak to 2 Chr 18:15
who had made him **s** by God. 2 Chr 36:13
priests and made them **s** to do as they Neh 5:12
to what is false and does not **s** deceitfully. Ps 24:4
all who **s** by him shall exult, for the Ps 63:11
of Canaan and **s** allegiance to the Is 19:18
bow, every tongue shall **s** allegiance.' Is 45:23
who **s** by the name of the LORD and Is 48:1
oath in the land shall **s** by the God of Is 65:16
and if you **s**, 'As the LORD lives,' in truth, Jer 4:2
say, "As the LORD lives," yet they **s** falsely. Jer 5:2
steal, murder, commit adultery, **s** falsely, Jer 7:9
ways of my people, to **s** by my name, Jer 12:16
as they taught my people to **s** by Baal, Jer 12:16
will not obey these words, I **s** by myself, Jer 22:5
I **s** that the nations that are all around Ezk 36:7
nor go up to Beth-aven, and **s** not, Hos 4:15
Those who **s** by the Guilt of Samaria, Am 8:14
who bow down and **s** to the LORD and Zep 1:5
swear to the LORD and yet **s** by Milcom, Zep 1:5
adulterers, against those who **s** falsely, Mal 3:5
to those of old, 'You shall not **s** falsely, Mt 5:33
to invoke a curse on himself and to **s**, Mt 26:74
to invoke a curse on himself and to **s**, Mk 14:71
to whom did he **s** that they would not Heb 3:18
he had no one greater by whom to **s**, Heb 6:13
For people **s** by something greater than Heb 6:16
But above all, my brothers, do not **s**, Jas 5:12

SWEARING (2)
s falsely—in any of all the things that Lv 6:3
there is **s**, lying, murder, stealing, and Hos 4:2

SWEARS (17)
or **s** an oath to bind himself by a Nm 30:2
oath and comes and **s** his oath before 1 Kgs 8:31
oath and comes and **s** his oath before 2 Chr 6:22
who **s** to his own hurt and does not Ps 15:4
and he who **s** is as he who shuns an Eccl 9:2
and everyone who **s** falsely shall be Zec 5:3
house of him who **s** falsely by my name. Zec 5:4
who say, 'If anyone **s** by the temple, Mt 23:16
but if anyone **s** by the gold of the Mt 23:16
And you say, 'If anyone **s** by the altar, it Mt 23:18
but if anyone **s** by the gift that is on the Mt 23:18
So whoever **s** by the altar swears by it Mt 23:20
swears by the altar **s** by it and by Mt 23:20
And whoever **s** by the temple swears by Mt 23:21
swears by the temple **s** by it and by Mt 23:21
And whoever **s** by heaven swears by Mt 23:22
swears by heaven **s** by the throne Mt 23:22

SWEAT (3)
By the **s** of your face you shall eat bread, Gn 3:19
with anything that causes **s**. Ezk 44:18
and his **s** became like great drops of Lk 22:44

SWEEP (19)
"Will you indeed **s** away the righteous Gn 18:23
Will you then **s** away the place and not Gn 18:24
I will utterly **s** away Baasha and his 1 Kgs 16:3
Do not **s** my soul away with sinners, nor Ps 26:9
green or ablaze, may he **s** them away! Ps 58:9
Let not the flood **s** over me, or the deep Ps 69:15
You **s** them away as with a flood; they Ps 90:5
of the wicked will **s** them away, Prv 21:7
the feet, and it will **s** away the beard also. Is 7:20
and it will **s** on into Judah, it will overflow Is 8:8
and I will **s** it with the broom of Is 14:23
As whirlwinds in the Negeb **s** on, it Is 21:1
and hail will **s** away the refuge of lies, Is 28:17
Then they **s** by like the wind and go Hab 1:11
"I will utterly **s** away everything from the Zep 1:2
"I will **s** away man and beast; I will sweep Zep 1:3
I will **s** away the birds of the heavens and Zep 1:3
light a lamp and **s** the house and seek Lk 15:8
the woman, to **s** her away with a flood. Rv 12:15

SWEEPING (1)
will lead to the **s** away of moist and Dt 29:19

SWEEPS (2)
and he is gone; it **s** him out of his place. Jb 27:21
into deep waters, and the flood **s** over me. Ps 69:2

SWEET (37)
into the water, and the water became **s**. Ex 15:25
The LORD said to Moses, "Take **s** spices, Ex 30:34
s spices with pure frankincense (of Ex 30:34
two handfuls of **s** incense beaten small, Lv 16:12
strong came something **s**." And in Jgs 14:14
God of Jacob, the **s** psalmist of Israel: 2 Sm 23:1
of incense of **s** spices before him, 2 Chr 2:4
offerings and incense of **s** spices, 2 Chr 13:11
the fat and drink **s** wine and send Neh 8:10
"Though evil is **s** in his mouth, though Jb 20:12
The clods of the valley are **s** to him; all Jb 21:33
forgets them; the worm finds them **s**; Jb 24:20
We used to take **s** counsel together; Ps 55:14
the tambourine, the **s** lyre with the harp. Ps 81:2
How **s** are your words to my taste, Ps 119:103
when you lie down, your sleep will be **s**. Prv 3:24
"Stolen water is **s**, and bread eaten in Prv 9:17
A desire fulfilled is **s** to the soul, but to Prv 13:19
Bread gained by deceit is **s** to a man, Prv 20:17
of the honeycomb are **s** to your taste. Prv 24:13
who is hungry everything bitter is **s**. Prv 27:7
S is the sleep of a laborer, whether he Eccl 5:12
Light is **s**, and it is pleasant for the eyes Eccl 11:7
shadow, and his fruit was **s** to my taste, Sg 2:3
me hear your voice, for your voice is **s**, Sg 2:14
His mouth is most **s**, and he is altogether Sg 5:16
who put bitter for **s** and sweet for bitter! Is 5:20
who put bitter for sweet and **s** for bitter! Is 5:20
O forgotten prostitute! Make **s** melody; Is 23:16
have not bought me **s** cane with money, Is 43:24
Sheba, or **s** cane from a distant land? Jer 6:20
it, and it was in my mouth as **s** as honey. Ezk 3:3
you drinkers of wine, because of the **s** wine, Jl 1:5
that day the mountains shall drip **s** wine, Jl 3:18
the mountains shall drip **s** wine, and Am 9:13
but in your mouth it will be **s** as honey." Rv 10:9
It was **s** as honey in my mouth, but Rv 10:10

SWEET-SMELLING (2)
and of **s** cinnamon half as much, Ex 30:23
like beds of spices, mounds of **s** herbs. Sg 5:13

SWEETER (3)
went down, "What is **s** than honey? Jgs 14:18
s also than honey and drippings of the Ps 19:10
my taste, **s** than honey to my mouth! Ps 119:103

SWEETNESS (4)
'Shall I leave my **s** and my good fruit Jgs 9:11
and **s** of speech increases Prv 16:21
s to the soul and health to the body. Prv 16:24
and the **s** of a friend comes from his Prv 27:9

SWELL (7)
your thigh fall away and your body **s**. Nm 5:21
make your womb **s** and your thigh Nm 5:22
bitter pain, and her womb shall **s**, Nm 5:27
and your foot did not **s** these forty years. Dt 8:4
did not wear out and their feet did not **s**. Neh 9:21
Their eyes **s** out through fatness; their Ps 73:7
waiting for him to **s** up or suddenly Acts 28:6

SWELLING (8)
skin of his body a **s** or an eruption or a Lv 13:2
if there is a white **s** in the skin that has Lv 13:10
white, and there is raw flesh in the **s**, Lv 13:10
comes a white **s** or a reddish-white Lv 13:19
but has faded, it is a **s** from the burn, Lv 13:28
and if the diseased **s** is reddish-white on Lv 13:43
and for a **s** or an eruption or a spot, Lv 14:56
though the mountains tremble at its **s**. Ps 46:3

SWEPT (18)
lest you be **s** away in the punishment Gn 19:15
Escape to the hills, lest you be **s** away." Gn 19:17
lest you be **s** away with all their sins." Nm 16:26
The torrent Kishon **s** them away, the Jgs 5:21
do wickedly, you shall be **s** away, 1 Sm 12:25
in a moment, **s** away utterly by terrors! Ps 73:19
Your wrath has **s** over me; your Ps 88:16
then the flood would have **s** us away, Ps 124:4
but it is **s** away through injustice. Prv 13:23
in it the beasts and the birds are **s** away, Jer 12:4
shall be utterly **s** away before him Dn 11:22
His army shall be **s** away, and many Dn 11:26
and writhed; the raging waters **s** on; Hab 3:10
the house empty, **s**, and put in order. Mt 12:44
the flood came and **s** them all away, Mt 24:39
it finds the house **s** and put in order. Lk 11:25
waterless clouds, **s** along by winds; Jude 1:12
His tail **s** down a third of the stars of Rv 12:4

SWERVE (3)
but I do not **s** from your testimonies. Ps 119:157
Do not **s** to the right or to the left; turn Prv 4:27
on his way; they do not **s** from their paths. Jl 2:7

SWERVED (2)
it some have **s** from the faith. 1 Tm 6:21
who have **s** from the truth, saying 2 Tm 2:18

SWERVING (1)
Certain persons, by **s** from these, have 1 Tm 1:6

SWIFT (22)
Now Asahel was as **s** of foot as a wild 2 Sm 2:18
the horses and **s** steeds they brought 1 Kgs 4:28
lions and who were **s** as gazelles upon 1 Chr 12:8
couriers riding on **s** horses that were Est 8:10
mounted on their **s** horses that were Est 8:14
say, '**S** are they on the face of the waters; Jb 24:18
has loosed the bonds of the **s** donkey, Jb 39:5
under the sun the race is not to the **s**, Eccl 9:11
seeks justice and is **s** to do righteousness." Is 16:5
Go, you **s** messengers, to a nation, tall and Is 18:2
LORD is riding on a **s** cloud and comes to Is 19:1
away; and, "We will ride upon **s** steeds"; Is 30:16
therefore your pursuers shall be **s**. Is 30:16
and they are **s** to shed innocent blood; Is 59:7
The **s** cannot flee away, nor the warrior Jer 46:6
came to me in **s** flight at the time of the Dn 9:21
Flight shall perish from the **s**, and the Am 2:14
and he who is **s** of foot shall not save Am 2:15
afar; they fly like an eagle **s** to devour. Hab 1:8
I will be a **s** witness against the Mal 3:5
"Their feet are **s** to shed blood; Rom 3:15
bringing upon themselves **s** destruction. 2 Pt 2:1

SWIFTER (6)
not divided; they were **s** than eagles; 2 Sm 1:23
My days are **s** than a weaver's shuttle and Jb 7:6
"My days are **s** than a runner; they flee Jb 9:25
his horses are **s** than eagles—woe to us, Jer 4:13
Our pursuers were **s** than the eagles in Lam 4:19
Their horses are **s** than leopards, more Hab 1:8

SWIFTLY (7)
is at hand, and their doom comes **s**.' Dt 32:35
he came **s** on the wings of the wind. Ps 18:10
to the earth; his word runs **s**. Ps 147:15
at hand, and his affliction hastens **s**. Jer 48:16
one shall fly **s** like an eagle and spread Jer 48:40
mount up and fly **s** like an eagle and Jer 49:22
payment on your own head **s** and speedily. Jl 3:4

SWIM (4)
as a swimmer spreads his hands out to **s**, Is 25:11
It was deep enough to **s** in, a river that Ezk 47:5
lest any should **s** away and escape. Acts 27:42
those who could **s** to jump overboard Acts 27:43

SWIMMER (1)
midst of it as a **s** spreads his hands out to Is 25:11

SWINDLER (1)
or **s**—not even to eat with such a one. 1 Cor 5:11

SWINDLERS (2)
of this world, or the greedy and **s**, 1 Cor 5:10
nor **s** will inherit the kingdom of 1 Cor 6:10

SWING (2)
away from mankind; they **s** to and fro. Jb 28:4
were like those who **s** axes in a forest Ps 74:5

SWINGING (1)
apiece, two **s** leaves for each door. Ezk 41:24

SWINGS (1)
and his hand **s** the axe to cut down a tree, Dt 19:5

SWIRLS (1)
like the chaff that **s** from the threshing Hos 13:3

SWOLLEN (1)
treacherous, reckless, **s** with conceit, 2 Tm 3:4

SWOOP (1)
But they shall **s** down on the shoulder of Is 11:14

SWOOPING (2)
end of the earth, **s** down like the eagle, Dt 28:49
skiffs of reed, like an eagle **s** on the prey. Jb 9:26

SWORD (419)
and a flaming **s** that turned every Gn 3:24
By your **s** you shall live, and you shall Gn 27:40
my daughters like captives of the **s**? Gn 31:26
Shechem with the **s** and took Dinah Gn 34:26
the Amorites with my **s** and with my Gn 48:22

fall upon us with pestilence or with the **s**."	Ex 5:3
and have put a **s** in their hand to kill us."	Ex 5:21
I will draw my **s**; my hand shall destroy	Ex 15:9
Amalek and his people with the **s**.	Ex 17:13
delivered me from the **s** of Pharaoh").	Ex 18:4
will burn, and I will kill you with the **s**,	Ex 22:24
'Put your **s** on your side each of you,	Ex 32:27
and the **s** shall not go through your	Lv 26:6
and they shall fall before you by the **s**.	Lv 26:7
enemies shall fall before you by the **s**.	Lv 26:8
And I will bring a **s** upon you, that	Lv 26:25
and I will unsheathe the **s** after you,	Lv 26:33
they shall flee as one flees from the **s**,	Lv 26:36
over one another, as if to escape a **s**,	Lv 26:37
us into this land, to fall by the **s**?	Nm 14:3
facing you, and you shall fall by the **s**.	Nm 14:43
was killed with a **s** or who died	Nm 19:16
I come out with the **s** against you."	Nm 20:18
the edge of the **s** and took possession	Nm 21:24
the road, with a drawn **s** in his hand.	Nm 22:23
I wish I had a **s** in my hand, for then I	Nm 22:29
the way, with his drawn **s** in his hand.	Nm 22:31
Balaam the son of Beor with the **s**.	Nm 31:8
put the inhabitants of that city to the **s**,	Dt 13:15
in it and its cattle, with the edge of the **s**.	Dt 13:15
you shall put all its males to the **s**,	Dt 20:13
Outdoors the **s** shall bereave, and	Dt 32:25
I sharpen my flashing **s** and my hand	Dt 32:41
and my **s** shall devour flesh—with the	Dt 32:42
of your help, and the **s** of your triumph!	Dt 33:29
him with his drawn **s** in his hand.	Jos 5:13
and donkeys, with the edge of the **s**.	Jos 6:21
very last had fallen by the edge of the **s**,	Jos 8:24
and struck it down with the edge of the **s**.	Jos 8:24
than the sons of Israel killed with the **s**.	Jos 10:11
it, and its king, with the edge of the **s**.	Jos 10:28
And he struck it with the edge of the **s**,	Jos 10:30
day and struck it with the edge of the **s**,	Jos 10:32
day, and struck it with the edge of the **s**.	Jos 10:35
it and struck it with the edge of the **s**,	Jos 10:37
the edge of the **s** and devoted to	Jos 10:39
Hazor and struck its king with the **s**,	Jos 11:10
they struck with the **s** all who were in	Jos 11:11
and struck them with the edge of the **s**,	Jos 11:12
the edge of the **s** until they had	Jos 11:14
was killed with the **s** by the people of	Jos 13:22
it with the **s** they took possession	Jos 19:47
it was not by your **s** or by your bow.	Jos 24:12
it with the edge of the **s** and set the city on	Jgs 1:8
struck the city with the edge of the **s**,	Jgs 1:25
made for himself a **s** with two edges,	Jgs 3:16
hand, took the **s** from his right thigh,	Jgs 3:21
for he did not pull the **s** out of his belly;	Jgs 3:22
army before Barak by the edge of the **s**.	Jgs 4:15
army of Sisera fell by the edge of the **s**;	Jgs 4:16
is no other than the **s** of Gideon the son	Jgs 7:14
out, "A **s** for the LORD and for Gideon!"	Jgs 7:20
set every man's **s** against his comrade	Jgs 7:22
had fallen 120,000 men who drew the **s**.	Jgs 8:10
But the young man did not draw his **s**,	Jgs 8:20
said to him, "Draw your **s** and kill me,	Jgs 9:54
the edge of the **s** and burned the city	Jgs 18:27
400,000 men on foot that drew the **s**.	Jgs 20:2
on that day 26,000 men who drew the **s**,	Jgs 20:15
mustered 400,000 men who drew the **s**;	Jgs 20:17
All these were men who drew the **s**.	Jgs 20:25
day. All these were men who drew the **s**.	Jgs 20:35
struck all the city with the edge of the **s**.	Jgs 20:37
were 25,000 men who drew the **s**,	Jgs 20:46
and struck them with the edge of the **s**,	Jgs 20:48
of Jabesh-gilead with the edge of the **s**;	Jgs 21:10
your house shall die by the **s** of men.	1 Sm 2:33
there was neither **s** nor spear found	1 Sm 13:22
every Philistine's **s** was against his	1 Sm 14:20
all the people with the edge of the **s**.	1 Sm 15:8
"As your **s** has made women	1 Sm 15:33
David strapped his **s** over his armor.	1 Sm 17:39
come to me with a **s** and with a spear	1 Sm 17:45
the LORD saves not with **s** and spear.	1 Sm 17:47
There was no **s** in the hand of David.	1 Sm 17:50
Philistine and took his **s** and drew it	1 Sm 17:51
and even his **s** and his bow and his	1 Sm 18:4
you not here a spear or a **s** at hand?	1 Sm 21:8
brought neither my **s** nor my	1 Sm 21:8
said, "The **s** of Goliath the Philistine,	1 Sm 21:9
and gave him the **s** of Goliath the	1 Sm 22:10
him bread and a **s** and have inquired	1 Sm 22:13
the city of the priests, he put to the **s**;	1 Sm 22:19
ox, donkey and sheep, he put to the **s**.	1 Sm 22:19
man strap on his **s**!" And every man	1 Sm 25:13
every man of them strapped on his **s**.	1 Sm 25:13
sword. David also strapped on his **s**.	1 Sm 25:13
to his armor-bearer, "Draw your **s**,	1 Sm 31:4
Saul took his own **s** and fell upon it.	1 Sm 31:4
also fell upon his **s** and died with him.	1 Sm 31:5
because they had fallen by the **s**.	2 Sm 1:12
and the **s** of Saul returned not empty.	2 Sm 1:22
and thrust his **s** in his opponent's	2 Sm 2:16
to Joab, "Shall the **s** devour forever?	2 Sm 2:26
who falls by the **s** or who lacks	2 Sm 3:29
for the **s** devours now one and now	2 Sm 11:25
the Hittite with the **s** and have taken	2 Sm 12:9
him with the **s** of the Ammonites.	2 Sm 12:9
Now therefore the **s** shall never	2 Sm 12:10
strike the city with the edge of the **s**."	2 Sm 15:14
more people that day than the **s**.	2 Sm 18:8
a belt with a **s** in its sheath fastened	2 Sm 20:8
did not observe the **s** that was in	2 Sm 20:10
and who was armed with a new **s**,	2 Sm 21:16
weary, and his hand clung to the **s**.	2 Sm 23:10
800,000 valiant men who drew the **s**,	2 Sm 24:9
put his servant to death with the **s**.'"	1 Kgs 1:51
'I will not put you to death with the **s**.'	1 Kgs 2:8
and killed with the **s** two men more	1 Kgs 2:32
"Bring me a **s**." So a sword was	1 Kgs 3:24
a sword." So a **s** was brought before	1 Kgs 3:24
had killed all the prophets with the **s**.	1 Kgs 19:1
and killed your prophets with the **s**,	1 Kgs 19:10
and killed your prophets with the **s**,	1 Kgs 19:14
escapes from the **s** of Hazael shall	1 Kgs 19:17
who escapes from the **s** of Jehu shall	1 Kgs 19:17
captive with your **s** and with your	2 Kgs 6:22
young men with the **s** and dash in	2 Kgs 8:12
So when they put them to the **s**,	2 Kgs 10:25
death with the **s** anyone who follows	2 Kgs 11:15
to death with the **s** at the king's	2 Kgs 11:20
him fall by the **s** in his own land.'"	2 Kgs 19:7
down with the **s** and escaped into	2 Kgs 19:37
men who carried shield and **s**,	1 Chr 5:18
"Draw your **s** and thrust me through	1 Chr 10:4
Saul took his own **s** and fell upon it.	1 Chr 10:4
dead, he also fell upon his **s** and died.	1 Chr 10:5
were 1,100,000 men who drew the **s**,	1 Chr 21:5
and in Judah 470,000 who drew the **s**.	1 Chr 21:5
foes while the **s** of your enemies	1 Chr 21:12
or else three days of the **s** of the LORD,	1 Chr 21:12
hand a drawn **s** stretched out over	1 Chr 21:16
and he put his **s** back into its	1 Chr 21:27
he was afraid of the **s** of the angel of	1 Chr 21:30
'If disaster comes upon us, the **s**,	2 Chr 20:9
he killed all his brothers with the **s**,	2 Chr 21:4
to death with the **s**." For the priest	2 Chr 23:14
had been put to death with the **s**.	2 Chr 23:21
our fathers have fallen by the **s**,	2 Chr 29:9
struck him down there with the **s**.	2 Chr 32:21
young men with the **s** in the house	2 Chr 36:17
those who had escaped from the **s**,	2 Chr 36:20
hand of the kings of the lands, to the **s**,	Ezr 9:7
the builders had his **s** strapped at his	Neh 4:18
Jews struck all their enemies with the **s**,	Est 9:5
down the servants with the edge of the **s**,	Jb 1:15
down the servants with the edge of the **s**,	Jb 1:17
the needy from the **s** of their mouth and	Jb 5:15
death, and in war from the power of the **s**.	Jb 5:20
of darkness, and he is marked for the **s**.	Jb 15:22
be afraid of the **s**, for wrath brings the	Jb 19:29
wrath brings the punishment of the **s**,	Jb 19:29
children are multiplied, it is for the **s**,	Jb 27:14
the pit, his life from perishing by the **s**.	Jb 33:18
they perish by the **s** and die without	Jb 36:12
he does not turn back from the **s**.	Jb 39:22
let him who made him bring near his **s**!	Jb 40:19
Though the **s** reaches him, it does not	Jb 41:26
man does not repent, God will whet his **s**;	Ps 7:12
my soul from the wicked by your **s**,	Ps 17:13
Deliver my soul from the **s**, my	Ps 22:20
The wicked draw the **s** and bend their	Ps 37:14
their **s** shall enter their own heart, and	Ps 37:15
for not by their own **s** did they win the	Ps 44:3
my bow do I trust, nor can my **s** save me.	Ps 44:6
Gird your **s** on your thigh, O mighty one,	Ps 45:3
shall be given over to the power of the **s**;	Ps 63:10
the flashing arrows, the shield, the **s**,	Ps 76:3
people over to the **s** and vented his	Ps 78:62
Their priests fell by the **s**, and their	Ps 78:64
have also turned back the edge of his **s**,	Ps 89:43
David his servant from the cruel **s**.	Ps 144:10
as wormwood, sharp as a two-edged **s**.	Prv 5:4
whose rash words are like **s** thrusts,	Prv 12:18
his neighbor is like a war club, or a **s**,	Prv 25:18
expert in war, each with his **s** at his thigh,	Sg 3:8
and rebel, you shall be eaten by the **s**;	Is 1:20
nation shall not lift up **s** against nation,	Is 2:4
shall fall by the **s** and your mighty men	Is 3:25
and whoever is caught will fall by the **s**.	Is 13:15
with the slain, those pierced by the **s**,	Is 14:19
fled from the swords, from the drawn **s**,	Is 21:15
are not slain with the **s** or dead in battle.	Is 22:2
great and strong **s** will punish Leviathan	Is 27:1
"And the Assyrian shall fall by a **s**, not of	Is 31:8
and a **s**, not of man, shall devour him;	Is 31:8
and he shall flee from the **s**, and his	Is 31:8
For my **s** has drunk its fill in the heavens;	Is 34:5
The LORD has a **s**; it is sated with blood; it	Is 34:6
make him fall by the **s** in his own land.'"	Is 37:7
his sons, struck him down with the **s**.	Is 37:38
he makes them like dust with his **s**, like	Is 41:2
He made my mouth like a sharp **s**; in the	Is 49:2
and destruction, famine and **s**;	Is 51:19
I will destine you to the **s**, and all of you	Is 65:12
LORD enter into judgment, and by his **s**,	Is 66:16
your own **s** devoured your prophets like	Jer 2:30
whereas the **s** has reached their very	Jer 4:10
upon us, nor shall we see **s** or famine.	Jer 5:12
trust they shall beat down with the **s**."	Jer 5:17
walk on the road, for the enemy has a **s**;	Jer 6:25
known, and I will send the **s** after them,	Jer 9:16
The young men shall die by the **s**, their	Jer 11:22
for the **s** of the LORD devours from one	Jer 12:12
But I will consume them by the **s**, by	Jer 14:12
say to them, 'You shall not see the **s**,	Jer 14:13
'**S** and famine shall not come upon this	Jer 14:15
By **s** and famine those prophets shall be	Jer 14:15
of Jerusalem, victims of famine and **s**,	Jer 14:16
the field, behold, those pierced by the **s**!	Jer 14:18
to pestilence, and those who are for the **s**,	Jer 15:2
and those who are for the sword, to the **s**;	Jer 15:2
the **s** to kill, the dogs to tear, and the	Jer 15:3
I will give to the **s** before their enemies,	Jer 15:9
shall perish by the **s** and by famine,	Jer 16:4
give them over to the power of the **s**;	Jer 18:21
be struck down by the **s** in battle.	Jer 18:21
to fall by the **s** before their enemies,	Jer 19:7
shall fall by the **s** of their enemies while	Jer 20:4
and shall strike them down with the **s**.	Jer 20:4
s, and famine into the hand of	Jer 21:7
strike them down with the edge of the **s**.	Jer 21:7
who stays in this city shall die by the **s**,	Jer 21:9
And I will send **s**, famine, and	Jer 24:10
crazed because of the **s** that I am	Jer 25:16
because of the **s** that I am sending	Jer 25:27
I am summoning a **s** against all the	Jer 25:29
and the wicked he will put to the **s**,	Jer 25:31
waste because of the **s** of the oppressor,	Jer 25:38
him down with the **s** and dumped his	Jer 26:23
I will punish that nation with the **s**,	Jer 27:8
will you and your people die by the **s**,	Jer 27:13
hosts, behold, I am sending on them **s**,	Jer 29:17
I will pursue them with **s**, famine, and	Jer 29:18
people who survived the **s** found grace in	Jer 31:2
and because of **s** and famine and	Jer 32:24
the hand of the king of Babylon by **s**,	Jer 32:36
the siege mounds and against the **s**:	Jer 33:4
you: 'You shall not die by the **s**.	Jer 34:4
I proclaim to you liberty to the **s**,	Jer 34:17
who stays in this city shall die by the **s**,	Jer 38:2
you, and you shall not fall by the **s**,	Jer 39:18
of Ahikam, son of Shaphan, with the **s**,	Jer 41:2
then the **s** that you fear shall overtake	Jer 42:16
to Egypt to live there shall die by the **s**,	Jer 42:17
a certainty that you shall die by the **s**,	Jer 42:22
and to the **s** those who are doomed to	Jer 43:11
sword those who are doomed to the **s**.	Jer 43:11
by the **s** and by famine they shall be	Jer 44:12
they shall die by the **s** and by famine,	Jer 44:12
I have punished Jerusalem, with the **s**,	Jer 44:13
consumed by the **s** and by famine."	Jer 44:18
be consumed by the **s** and by famine,	Jer 44:27
who escape the **s** shall return from	Jer 44:28
The **s** shall devour and be sated and	Jer 46:10
for the **s** shall devour around you.'	Jer 46:14
birth, because of the **s** of the oppressor.'	Jer 46:16
Ah, **s** of the LORD! How long till you are	Jer 47:6
to silence; the **s** shall pursue you.	Jer 48:2
who keeps back his **s** from bloodshed.	Jer 48:10
I will send the **s** after them, until I have	Jer 49:37
because of the **s** of the oppressor,	Jer 50:16
"A **s** against the Chaldeans, declares	Jer 50:35
A **s** against the diviners, that they may	Jer 50:36
A **s** against her warriors, that they may	Jer 50:36
A **s** against her horses and against her	Jer 50:37
A **s** against all her treasures, that they	Jer 50:37
"You who have escaped from the **s**, go,	Jer 51:50
In the street the **s** bereaves; in the	Lam 1:20
my young men have fallen by the **s**;	Lam 2:21
the victims of the **s** than the victims of	Lam 4:9
lives, because of the **s** in the wilderness.	Lam 5:9
"And you, O son of man, take a sharp **s**.	Ezk 5:1
and strike with the **s** all around the city.	Ezk 5:2
and I will unsheathe the **s** after them.	Ezk 5:2
part shall fall by the **s** all around you;	Ezk 5:12
and will unsheathe the **s** after them.	Ezk 5:12
you, and I will bring the **s** upon you.	Ezk 5:17
Behold, I, even I, will bring a **s** upon you,	Ezk 6:3
the nations some who escape the **s**,	Ezk 6:8

of Israel, for they shall fall by the **s**, Ezk 6:11
and he who is near shall fall by the **s**, Ezk 6:12
The **s** is without; pestilence and famine Ezk 7:15
He who is in the field dies by the **s**, and Ezk 7:15
You have feared the **s**, and I will bring Ezk 11:8
sword, and I will bring the **s** upon you, Ezk 11:8
You shall fall by the **s**. I will judge you Ezk 11:10
and I will unsheathe the **s** after them. Ezk 12:14
let a few of them escape from the **s**, Ezk 12:16
"Or if I bring a **s** upon that land and Ezk 14:17
and say, Let a **s** pass through the land, Ezk 14:17
disastrous acts of judgment, **s**, famine, Ezk 14:21
pick of his troops shall fall by the **s**, Ezk 17:21
and will draw my **s** from its sheath and Ezk 21:3
therefore my **s** shall be drawn from its Ezk 21:4
I have drawn my **s** from its sheath; it Ezk 21:5
Say: "A **s**, a sword is sharpened and also Ezk 21:9
a **s** is sharpened and also polished, Ezk 21:9
So the **s** is given to be polished, that it Ezk 21:11
delivered over to the **s** with my people. Ezk 21:12
hands and let the **s** come down twice, Ezk 21:14
three times, the **s** for those to be slain. Ezk 21:14
It is the **s** for the great slaughter, Ezk 21:14
their gates I have given the glittering **s**. Ezk 21:15
mark two ways for the **s** of the king of Ezk 21:19
a way for the **s** to come to Rabbah Ezk 21:20
say, A **s**, a sword is drawn for the Ezk 21:28
sword, a **s** is drawn for the slaughter. Ezk 21:28
as for her, they killed her with the **s**; Ezk 23:10
and your survivors shall fall by the **s**. Ezk 23:25
you left behind shall fall by the **s**. Ezk 24:21
even to Dedan they shall fall by the **s**. Ezk 25:13
the mainland shall be killed by the **s**. Ezk 26:6
will kill with the **s** your daughters on Ezk 26:8
He will kill your people with the **s**, and Ezk 26:11
by the **s** that is against her on every Ezk 28:23
Behold, I will bring a **s** upon you, and Ezk 29:8
A **s** shall come upon Egypt, and Ezk 30:4
in league, shall fall with them by the **s**. Ezk 30:5
they shall fall within her by the **s**, Ezk 30:6
On and of Pi-beseth shall fall by the **s**, Ezk 30:17
it may become strong to wield the **s**. Ezk 30:21
I will make the **s** fall from his hand. Ezk 30:22
of Babylon and put my **s** in his hand, Ezk 30:24
when I put my **s** into the hand of the Ezk 30:25
with it, to those who are slain by the **s**; Ezk 31:17
with those who are slain by the **s**. Ezk 31:18
when I brandish my **s** before them. Ezk 32:10
The **s** of the king of Babylon shall Ezk 32:11
fall amid those who are slain by the **s**. Ezk 32:20
Egypt is delivered to the **s**; drag her Ezk 32:20
the uncircumcised, slain by the **s**.' Ezk 32:21
it, all of them slain, fallen by the **s**, Ezk 32:22
grave, all of them slain, fallen by the **s**, Ezk 32:23
all of them slain, fallen by the **s**, who Ezk 32:24
them uncircumcised, slain by the **s**; Ezk 32:25
them uncircumcised, slain by the **s**; Ezk 32:26
with those who are slain by the **s**. Ezk 32:28
laid with those who are killed by the **s**; Ezk 32:29
with those who are slain by the **s**, Ezk 32:30
and all his army, slain by the **s**, Ezk 32:31
with those who are slain by the **s**, Ezk 32:32
say to them, If I bring the **s** upon a land, Ezk 33:2
if he sees the **s** coming upon the land Ezk 33:3
and the **s** comes and takes him away, Ezk 33:4
watchman sees the **s** coming and does Ezk 33:6
and the **s** comes and takes any one of Ezk 33:6
You rely on the **s**, you commit Ezk 33:26
in the waste places shall fall by the **s**, Ezk 33:27
to the power of the **s** at the time of their Ezk 35:5
ravines those slain with the **s** shall fall. Ezk 35:8
I will summon a **s** against Gog on all Ezk 38:21
Every man's **s** will be against his Ezk 38:21
adversaries, and they all fell by the **s**. Ezk 39:23
they shall stumble by **s** and flame, Dn 11:33
them by bow or by **s** or by war or by Hos 1:7
And I will abolish the bow, the **s**, and Hos 2:18
shall fall by the **s** because of the Hos 7:16
The **s** shall rage against their cities, Hos 11:6
her God; they shall fall by the **s**; Hos 13:16
his brother with the **s** and cast off all Am 1:11
I killed your young men with the **s**, and Am 4:10
the house of Jeroboam with the **s**." Am 7:9
has said, "'Jeroboam shall die by the **s**, Am 7:11
and your daughters shall fall by the **s**, Am 7:17
who are left of them I will kill with the **s**; Am 9:1
enemies, there I will command the **s**, Am 9:4
sinners of my people shall die by the **s**, Am 9:10
nation shall not lift up **s** against nation, Mi 4:3
shepherd the land of Assyria with the **s**, Mi 5:6
and what you preserve I will give to the **s**. Mi 6:14
and the **s** shall devour your young lions. Na 2:13
charging, flashing **s** and glittering spear, Na 3:3
fire devour you; the **s** will cut you off. Na 3:15
also, O Cushites, shall be slain by my **s**. Zep 2:12
down, every one by the **s** of his brother. Hg 2:22
Greece, and wield you like a warrior's **s**. Zec 9:13
May the **s** strike his arm and his right Zec 11:17
"Awake, O **s**, against my shepherd, Zec 13:7
I have not come to bring peace, but a **s**. Mt 10:34
hand and drew his **s** and struck the Mt 26:51
to him, "Put your **s** back into its place. Mt 26:52
For all who take the **s** will perish by the Mt 26:52
who take the sword will perish by the **s**. Mt 26:52
stood by drew his **s** and struck the Mk 14:47
(and a **s** will pierce through your own Lk 2:35
by the edge of the **s** and be led captive Lk 21:24
the one who has no **s** sell his cloak and Lk 22:36
said, "Lord, shall we strike with the **s**?" Lk 22:49
Then Simon Peter, having a **s**, drew it Jn 18:10
said to Peter, "Put your **s** into its sheath; Jn 18:11
James the brother of John with the **s**, Acts 12:2
he drew his **s** and was about to kill Acts 16:27
famine, or nakedness, or danger, or **s**? Rom 8:35
for he does not bear the **s** in vain. Rom 13:4
of salvation, and the **s** of the Spirit, Eph 6:17
active, sharper than any two-edged **s**, Heb 4:12
power of fire, escaped the edge of the **s**, Heb 11:34
in two, they were killed with the **s**. Heb 11:37
his mouth came a sharp two-edged **s**, Rv 1:16
of him who has the sharp two-edged **s**. Rv 2:12
against them with the **s** of my mouth. Rv 2:16
one another, and he was given a great **s**. Rv 6:4
to kill with **s** and with famine and with Rv 6:8
if anyone is to be slain with the **s**, with Rv 13:10
the sword, with the **s** must he be slain. Rv 13:10
was wounded by the **s** and yet lived. Rv 13:14
mouth comes a sharp **s** with which to Rv 19:15
were slain by the **s** that came from the Rv 19:21

SWORDS (29)
took their **s** and came against the city Gn 34:25
weapons of violence are their **s**. Gn 49:5
make themselves **s** or spears." 1 Sm 13:19
after their custom with **s** and lances, 1 Kgs 18:28
the people by their clans, with their **s**, Neh 4:13
softer than oil, yet they were drawn **s**. Ps 55:21
and arrows, whose tongues are sharp **s**. Ps 57:4
with their mouths with **s** in their lips— Ps 59:7
who whet their tongues like **s**, who aim Ps 64:3
throats and two-edged **s** in their hands, Ps 149:6
There are those whose teeth are **s**, Prv 30:14
all of them wearing **s** and expert in war, Sg 3:8
and they shall beat their **s** into plowshares, Is 2:4
For they have fled from the **s**, from the Is 21:15
you and cut you to pieces with their **s**. Ezk 16:40
them and cut them down with their **s**. Ezk 23:47
shall draw their **s** against the beauty Ezk 28:7
shall draw their **s** against Egypt and Ezk 30:11
to fall by the **s** of mighty ones, Ezk 32:12
whose **s** were laid under their heads, Ezk 32:27
with buckler and shield, wielding **s**. Ezk 38:4
Beat your plowshares into **s**, and your Jl 3:10
they shall beat their **s** into plowshares, Mi 4:3
him a great crowd with **s** and clubs, Mt 26:47
with **s** and clubs to capture me? Mt 26:55
with him a crowd with **s** and clubs, Mk 14:43
with **s** and clubs to capture me? Mk 14:48
here are two **s**." And he said to them, Lk 22:38
as against a robber, with **s** and clubs? Lk 22:52

SWORDSMEN (1)
with him 700 **s** to break through, 2 Kgs 3:26

SWORE (90)
because there both of them **s** an oath. Gn 21:31
and who spoke to me and **s** to me, Gn 24:7
his master and **s** to him concerning Gn 24:9
to me now." So he **s** to him and sold his Gn 25:33
the oath that I **s** to Abraham your Gn 26:3
between us." So Jacob **s** by the Fear of Gn 31:53
he said, "Swear to me"; and he **s** to him. Gn 47:31
land to the land that he **s** to Abraham, Gn 50:24
into the land that I **s** to give to Abraham, Ex 6:8
which he **s** to your fathers to give you, Ex 13:5
as he **s** to you and your fathers, Ex 13:11
to whom you **s** by your own self, Ex 32:13
to the land of which I **s** to Abraham, Ex 33:1
the land that you **s** to give their Nm 11:12
into the land that he **s** to give to them Nm 14:16
see the land that I **s** to give to their Nm 14:23
the land where I **s** that I would make Nm 14:30
was kindled on that day, and he **s**, Nm 32:10
the land that I **s** to give to Abraham, Nm 32:11
of the land that the LORD **s** to your fathers, Dt 1:8
your words and was angered, and he **s**, Dt 1:34
the good land that I **s** to give to your Dt 1:35
and he **s** that I should not cross the Dt 4:21
with your fathers that he **s** to them. Dt 4:31
into the land that he **s** to your fathers, Dt 6:10
good land that the LORD **s** to give to your Dt 6:18
us the land that he **s** to give to our Dt 6:23
keeping the oath that he **s** to your fathers, Dt 7:8
steadfast love that he **s** to your fathers. Dt 7:12
in the land that he **s** to your fathers to Dt 7:13
the land that the LORD **s** to give to your Dt 8:1
his covenant that he **s** to your fathers, Dt 8:18
the word that the LORD **s** to your fathers, Dt 9:5
which I **s** to their fathers to give them.' Dt 10:11
the land that the LORD **s** to your fathers to Dt 11:9
land that the LORD **s** to your fathers to Dt 11:21
multiply you, as he **s** to your fathers, Dt 13:17
the land that the LORD **s** to our fathers to Dt 26:3
have given us, as you **s** to our fathers, Dt 26:15
land that the LORD **s** to your fathers to Dt 28:11
you, and as he **s** to your fathers, Dt 29:13
the land that the LORD **s** to your fathers, Dt 30:20
honey, which I **s** to give to their fathers, Dt 31:20
them into the land that I **s** to give." Dt 31:21
Israel into the land that I **s** to give them. Dt 31:23
is the land of which I **s** to Abraham, Dt 34:4
inherit the land that I **s** to their fathers to Jos 1:6
the LORD **s** to them that he would not let Jos 5:6
all who belong to her, as you **s** to her." Jos 6:22
leaders of the congregation **s** to them. Jos 9:15
because of the oath that we **s** to them." Jos 9:20
And Moses **s** on that day, saying, 'Surely Jos 14:9
all the land that he **s** to give to their Jos 21:43
into the land that I **s** to give to your Jgs 2:1
to the voice of Jonathan. Saul **s**, 1 Sm 19:6
And David **s** this to Saul. Then Saul 1 Sm 24:22
But Saul **s** to her by the LORD, "As the 1 Sm 28:10
But David **s**, saying, "God do so to me 2 Sm 3:35
Then David's men **s** to him, "You 2 Sm 21:17
you **s** to your servant by the LORD 1 Kgs 1:17
And the king **s**, saying, "As the LORD 1 Kgs 1:29
as I **s** to you by the LORD, the God of 1 Kgs 1:30
at the Jordan, I **s** to him by the LORD, 1 Kgs 2:8
Then King Solomon **s** by the LORD, 1 Kgs 2:23
And Gedaliah **s** to them and their 2 Kgs 25:24
They **s** an oath to the LORD with a 2 Chr 15:14
by your faithfulness you **s** to David? Ps 89:49
Therefore I **s** in my wrath, "They shall Ps 95:11
raised his hand and **s** to them that he Ps 106:26
how he **s** to the LORD and vowed to the Ps 132:2
The LORD **s** to David a sure oath from Ps 132:11
as I **s** that the waters of Noah should no Is 54:9
confirm the oath that I **s** to your fathers, Jer 11:5
which you **s** to their fathers to give Jer 32:22
Then King Zedekiah **s** secretly to Jer 38:16
of Shaphan, **s** to them and their men, Jer 40:9
I **s** to the offspring of the house of Jacob, Ezk 20:5
I **s** to them, saying, I am the LORD your Ezk 20:5
On that day I **s** to them that I would Ezk 20:6
I **s** to them in the wilderness that I Ezk 20:15
I **s** to them in the wilderness that I Ezk 20:23
into the land that I **s** to give them, Ezk 20:28
the country that I **s** to give to your Ezk 20:42
divide equally what I **s** to give to your Ezk 47:14
hand toward heaven and **s** by him who Dn 12:7
the oath that he **s** to our father Lk 1:73
As I **s** in my wrath, 'They shall not Heb 3:11
rest, as he has said, "As I **s** in my wrath, Heb 4:3
by whom to swear, he **s** by himself, Heb 6:13
and **s** by him who lives forever and ever, Rv 10:6

SWORN (47)
and said, "By myself I have **s**, declares Gn 22:16
we said, let there be a **s** pact between us, Gn 26:28
or anything about which he has **s** falsely, Lv 6:5
the camp, as the LORD had **s** to them. Dt 2:14
your territory, as he has **s** to your fathers, Dt 19:8
people holy to himself, as he has **s** to you, Dt 28:9
may enter into the **s** covenant of the Dt 29:12
that I am making this **s** covenant, Dt 29:14
he hears the words of this **s** covenant, Dt 29:19
that the LORD has **s** to their fathers to Dt 31:7
land that the LORD had **s** to their fathers to Jos 5:6
of the congregation had **s** to them by the Jos 9:18
"We have **s** to them by the LORD, Jos 9:19
side just as he had **s** to their fathers. Jos 21:44
warned, and as the LORD had **s** to them. Jgs 2:15
Now the men of Israel had **s** at Mizpah, Jgs 21:1
since we have **s** by the LORD that we will Jgs 21:7
For the people of Israel had **s**, Jgs 21:18
because we have **s** both of us in the 1 Sm 20:42
for David what the LORD has **s** to him, 2 Sm 3:9
people of Israel had **s** to spare them, 2 Sm 21:2
Abraham, his **s** promise to Isaac, 1 Chr 16:16
for they had **s** with all their heart 2 Chr 15:15
the land that you had **s** to give them. Neh 9:15
chosen one; I have **s** to David my servant: Ps 89:3
Once for all I have **s** by my holiness; I Ps 89:35
with Abraham, his **s** promise to Isaac, Ps 105:9
The LORD has **s** and will not change his Ps 110:4
I have **s** an oath and confirmed it, to Ps 119:106
The LORD of hosts has **s** in my hearing: Is 5:9
The LORD of hosts has **s**: "As I have Is 14:24

By myself I have **s**; from my mouth has Is 45:23
so I have **s** that I will not be angry with Is 54:9
The LORD has **s** by his right hand and by Is 62:8
forsaken me and have **s** by those who are Jer 5:7
Behold, I have **s** by my great name, says Jer 44:26
For I have **s** by myself, declares the Jer 49:13
The LORD of hosts has **s** by himself: Jer 51:14
divination. They have **s** solemn oaths, Ezk 21:23
therefore I have **s** concerning them, Ezk 44:12
The Lord GOD has **s** by his holiness that, Am 4:2
The Lord GOD has **s** by himself, declares Am 6:8
The LORD has **s** by the pride of Jacob: Am 8:7
as you have **s** to our fathers from the Mi 7:20
perform to the Lord what you have **s**.' Mt 5:33
knowing that God had **s** with an oath Acts 2:30
"The Lord has **s** and will not change Heb 7:21

SWUNG (3)
peoples is broken; it has **s** open to me. Ezk 26:2
sat on the cloud **s** his sickle across the Rv 14:16
So the angel **s** his sickle across the Rv 14:19

SYCAMORE (6)
plentiful as the **s** of the Shephelah. 1 Kgs 10:27
Over the olive and **s** trees in the 1 Chr 27:28
as plentiful as the **s** of the Shephelah. 2 Chr 1:15
as plentiful as the **s** of the Shephelah. 2 Chr 9:27
I was a herdsman and a dresser of **s** figs. Am 7:14
and climbed up into a **s** tree to see him, Lk 19:4

SYCAMORES (2)
vines with hail and their **s** with frost. Ps 78:47
the **s** have been cut down, but we will put Is 9:10

SYCHAR (1)
So he came to a town of Samaria called **S**, Jn 4:5

SYENE (3)
the west, and these from the land of **S**." Is 49:12
and desolation, from Migdol to **S**, Ezk 29:10
from Migdol to **S** they shall fall within Ezk 30:6

SYMBOL (1)
ought to have a **s** of authority on her 1 Cor 11:10

SYMBOLIC (1)
(which is **s** for the present age). Heb 9:9

SYMBOLICALLY (1)
the great city that **s** is called Sodom and Rv 11:8

SYMPATHIZE (1)
is unable to **s** with our weaknesses, Heb 4:15

SYMPATHY (4)
to come to show him **s** and comfort him. Jb 2:11
they showed him **s** and comforted him Jb 42:11
in the Spirit, any affection and **s**, Phil 2:1
have unity of mind, **s**, brotherly love, 1 Pt 3:8

SYNAGOGUE (40)
went on from there and entered their **s**. Mt 12:9
hometown he taught them in their **s**, Mt 13:54
he entered the **s** and was teaching. Mk 1:21
there was in their **s** a man with an Mk 1:23
he left the **s** and entered the Mk 1:29
Again he entered the **s**, and a man was Mk 3:1
Then came one of the rulers of the **s**, Mk 5:22
they said, Jesus said to the ruler of the **s**, Mk 5:36
came to the house of the ruler of the **s**, Mk 5:38
the Sabbath he began to teach in the **s**, Mk 6:2
he went to the **s** on the Sabbath day, Lk 4:16
the eyes of all in the **s** were fixed on him. Lk 4:20
things, all in the **s** were filled with wrath. Lk 4:28
And in the **s** there was a man who had Lk 4:33
arose and left the **s** and entered Simon's Lk 4:38
he entered the **s** and was teaching, Lk 6:6
and he is the one who built us our **s**." Lk 7:5
named Jairus, who was a ruler of the **s**. Lk 8:41
But the ruler of the **s**, indignant Lk 13:14
Jesus said these things in the **s**, as he Jn 6:59
be Christ, he was to be put out of the **s**.) Jn 9:22
that they would not be put out of the **s**; Jn 12:42
who belonged to the **s** of the Freedmen Acts 6:9
day they went into the **s** and sat down. Acts 13:14
the rulers of the **s** sent a message to Acts 13:15
after the meeting of the **s** broke up, Acts 13:43
together into the Jewish **s** and spoke in Acts 14:1
where there was a **s** of the Jews. Acts 17:1
arrived they went into the Jewish **s**. Acts 17:10
he reasoned in the **s** with the Jews and Acts 17:17
he reasoned in the **s** every Sabbath, Acts 18:4
God. His house was next door to the **s**. Acts 18:7
Crispus, the ruler of the **s**, believed in Acts 18:8
all seized Sosthenes, the ruler of the **s**, Acts 18:17
went into the **s** and reasoned with Acts 18:19
He began to speak boldly in the **s**, but Acts 18:26
And he entered the **s** and for three Acts 19:8
know that in one **s** after another I Acts 22:19
are Jews and are not, but are a **s** of Satan. Rv 2:9
will make those of the **s** of Satan who say Rv 3:9

SYNAGOGUES (25)
teaching in their **s** and proclaiming the Mt 4:23
hypocrites do in the **s** and in the streets, Mt 6:2
stand and pray in the **s** and at the street Mt 6:5
teaching in their **s** and proclaiming the Mt 9:35
over to courts and flog you in their **s**, Mt 10:17
honor at feasts and the best seats in the **s** Mt 23:6
will flog in your **s** and persecute from Mt 23:34
preaching in their **s** and casting out Mk 1:39
the best seats in the **s** and the places of Mk 12:39
to councils, and you will be beaten in **s**, Mk 13:9
And he taught in their **s**, being glorified Lk 4:15
And he was preaching in the **s** of Judea. Lk 4:44
best seat in the **s** and greetings in the Lk 11:43
bring you before the **s** and the rulers Lk 12:11
in one of the **s** on the Sabbath. Lk 13:10
the best seats in the **s** and the places of Lk 20:46
delivering you up to the **s** and prisons, Lk 21:12
They will put you out of the **s**. Indeed, the Jn 16:2
have always taught in **s** and in the Jn 18:20
him for letters to the **s** at Damascus, Acts 9:2
he proclaimed Jesus in the **s**, Acts 9:20
the word of God in the **s** of the Jews. Acts 13:5
for he is read every Sabbath in the **s**." Acts 15:21
in the temple or in the **s** or in the city. Acts 24:12
often in all the **s** and tried to make Acts 26:11

SYNTYCHE (1)
I entreat Euodia and I entreat **S** to agree Phil 4:2

SYRACUSE (1)
Putting in at **S**, we stayed there for Acts 28:12

SYRIA (67)
Baals and the Ashtaroth, the gods of **S**, Jgs 10:6
of the Hittites and the kings of **S**. 1 Kgs 10:29
he loathed Israel and reigned over **S**. 1 Kgs 11:25
the son of Hezion, king of **S**, 1 Kgs 15:18
anoint Hazael to be king over **S**. 1 Kgs 19:15
the king of **S** gathered all his 1 Kgs 20:1
Ben-hadad king of **S** escaped on a 1 Kgs 20:20
spring the king of **S** will come up 1 Kgs 20:22
servants of the king of **S** said to him, 1 Kgs 20:23
For three years **S** and Israel 1 Kgs 22:1
it out of the hand of the king of **S**?" 1 Kgs 22:3
the king of **S** had commanded the 1 Kgs 22:31
of the army of the king of **S**, 2 Kgs 5:1
him the LORD had given victory to **S**. 2 Kgs 5:1
And the king of **S** said, "Go now, and I 2 Kgs 5:5
the king of **S** was warring against 2 Kgs 6:8
of the king of **S** was greatly troubled 2 Kgs 6:11
Ben-hadad king of **S** mustered his 2 Kgs 6:24
Ben-hadad the king of **S** was sick. 2 Kgs 8:7
son Ben-hadad king of **S** has sent me 2 Kgs 8:9
me that you are to be king over **S**." 2 Kgs 8:13
Hazael king of **S** at Ramoth-gilead, 2 Kgs 8:28
he fought against Hazael king of **S**. 2 Kgs 8:29
against Hazael king of **S**, 2 Kgs 9:14
he fought with Hazael king of **S**.) 2 Kgs 9:15
time Hazael king of **S** went up and 2 Kgs 12:17
and sent these to Hazael king of **S**. 2 Kgs 12:18
of Hazael king of **S** and into the hand 2 Kgs 13:3
how the king of **S** oppressed them. 2 Kgs 13:4
for the king of **S** had destroyed them 2 Kgs 13:7
victory, the arrow of victory over **S**! 2 Kgs 13:17
have struck down **S** until you had 2 Kgs 13:19
will strike down **S** only three times." 2 Kgs 13:19
Hazael king of **S** oppressed Israel all 2 Kgs 13:22
When Hazael king of **S** died, 2 Kgs 13:24
Rezin the king of **S** and Pekah the 2 Kgs 15:37
Then Rezin king of **S** and Pekah the 2 Kgs 16:5
the king of **S** recovered Elath for 2 Kgs 16:6
recovered Elath for **S** and drove the 2 Kgs 16:6
of the king of **S** and from the hand 2 Kgs 16:7
put garrisons in **S** of Damascus, 1 Chr 18:6
of the Hittites and the kings of **S**. 2 Chr 1:17
sent them to Ben-hadad king of **S**, 2 Chr 16:2
"Because you relied on the king of **S**, 2 Chr 16:7
of the king of **S** has escaped you. 2 Chr 16:7
the king of **S** had commanded the 2 Chr 18:30
Hazael king of **S** at Ramoth-gilead. 2 Chr 22:5
he fought against Hazael king of **S**. 2 Chr 22:6
him into the hand of the king of **S**, 2 Chr 28:5
gods of the kings of **S** helped them, 2 Chr 28:23
Rezin the king of **S** and Pekah the son of Is 7:1
"**S** is in league with Ephraim," the heart of Is 7:2
fierce anger of Rezin and **S** and the son of Is 7:4
Because **S**, with Ephraim and the son of Is 7:5
For the head of **S** is Damascus, and the Is 7:8
and the remnant of **S** will be like the Is 17:3
for the daughters of **S** and all those Ezk 16:57
S did business with you because of Ezk 27:16
and the people of **S** shall go into exile to Am 1:5
So his fame spread throughout all **S**, and Mt 4:24
when Quirinius was governor of **S**. Lk 2:2
in Antioch and **S** and Cilicia, Acts 15:23
And he went through **S** and Cilicia, Acts 15:41
leave of the brothers and set sail for **S**, Acts 18:18
Jews as he was about to set sail for **S**, Acts 20:3
left we sailed to **S** and landed at Tyre, Acts 21:3
I went into the regions of **S** and Cilicia. Gal 1:21

SYRIAN (2)
has spared this Naaman the **S**, 2 Kgs 5:20
was cleansed, but only Naaman the **S**." Lk 4:27

SYRIANS (64)
And when the **S** of Damascus came to 2 Sm 8:5
struck down 22,000 men of the **S**. 2 Sm 8:5
and the **S** became servants to David 2 Sm 8:6
sent and hired the **S** of Beth-rehob, 2 Sm 10:6
of Beth-rehob, and the **S** of Zobah, 2 Sm 10:6
and the **S** of Zobah and of Rehob and 2 Sm 10:8
Israel and arrayed them against the **S**. 2 Sm 10:9
said, "If the **S** are too strong for me, 2 Sm 10:11
drew near to battle against the **S**, 2 Sm 10:13
the Ammonites saw that the **S** fled, 2 Sm 10:14
But when the **S** saw that they had 2 Sm 10:15
brought out the **S** who were beyond 2 Sm 10:16
The **S** arrayed themselves against 2 Sm 10:17
And the **S** fled before Israel, and 2 Sm 10:18
David killed of the **S** the men of 700 2 Sm 10:18
So the **S** were afraid to save the 2 Sm 10:19
struck down his man. The **S** fled, 1 Kgs 20:20
and struck the **S** with a great blow. 1 Kgs 20:21
Ben-hadad mustered the **S** and went 1 Kgs 20:26
of goats, but the **S** filled the country. 1 Kgs 20:27
the LORD, 'Because the **S** have said, 1 Kgs 20:28
down of the **S** 100,000 foot soldiers 1 Kgs 20:29
you shall push the **S** until they are 1 Kgs 22:11
up in his chariot facing the **S**, 1 Kgs 22:35
Now the **S** on one of their raids had 2 Kgs 5:2
place, for the **S** are going down there." 2 Kgs 6:9
And when the **S** came down against 2 Kgs 6:18
And the **S** did not come again on 2 Kgs 6:23
let us go over to the camp of the **S**. 2 Kgs 7:4
at twilight to go to the camp of the **S**. 2 Kgs 7:5
came to the edge of the camp of the **S**, 2 Kgs 7:5
the army of the **S** hear the sound of 2 Kgs 7:6
them, "We came to the camp of the **S**, 2 Kgs 7:10
tell you what the **S** have done to us. 2 Kgs 7:12
sent them after the army of the **S**, 2 Kgs 7:14
equipment that the **S** had thrown 2 Kgs 7:15
out and plundered the camp of the **S**. 2 Kgs 7:16
and the **S** wounded Joram. 2 Kgs 8:28
the wounds that the **S** had given him 2 Kgs 8:29
the wounds that the **S** had given him, 2 Kgs 9:15
they escaped from the hand of the **S**, 2 Kgs 13:5
you shall fight the **S** in Aphek until 2 Kgs 13:17
and bands of the **S** and bands of the 2 Kgs 24:2
And when the **S** of Damascus came 1 Chr 18:5
struck down 22,000 men of the **S**. 1 Chr 18:5
and the **S** became servants to David 1 Chr 18:6
and arrayed them against the **S**. 1 Chr 19:10
said, "If the **S** are too strong for me, 1 Chr 19:12
drew near before the **S** for battle, 1 Chr 19:14
the Ammonites saw that the **S** fled, 1 Chr 19:15
But when the **S** saw that they had 1 Chr 19:16
brought out the **S** who were beyond 1 Chr 19:16
set the battle in array against the **S**, 1 Chr 19:17
And the **S** fled before Israel, and 1 Chr 19:18
David killed of the **S** the men of 1 Chr 19:18
So the **S** were not willing to save the 1 Chr 19:19
you shall push the **S** until they are 2 Chr 18:10
chariot facing the **S** until evening. 2 Chr 18:34
And the **S** wounded Joram, 2 Chr 22:5
the army of the **S** came up against 2 Chr 24:23
the army of the **S** had come with few 2 Chr 24:24
The **S** on the east and the Philistines on Is 9:12
of the Chaldeans and the army of the **S**.' Jer 35:11
from Caphtor and the **S** from Kir? Am 9:7

SYROPHOENICIAN (1)
the woman was a Gentile, a **S** by birth. Mk 7:26

SYRTIS (1)
they would run aground on the **S**, Acts 27:17

T

TAANACH (7)
the king of **T**, one; the king of Megiddo, Jos 12:21
the inhabitants of **T** and its villages, Jos 17:11
of Manasseh, **T** with its pasturelands, Jos 21:25
and its villages, or **T** and its villages, Jgs 1:27
then fought the kings of Canaan, at **T**, Jgs 5:19
Baana the son of Ahilud, in **T**, 1 Kgs 4:12
and its towns, **T** and its towns, 1 Chr 7:29

TAANATH-SHILOH (1)
turns around toward **T** and passes along Jos 16:6

TABBAOTH (2)
the sons of Hasupha, the sons of **T**, Ezr 2:43
the sons of Hasupha, the sons of **T**, Neh 7:46

TABBATH (1)
far as the border of Abel-meholah, by **T**. Jgs 7:22

TABEEL (2)
and Mithredath and **T** and the rest Ezr 4:7
and set up the son of **T** as king in the midst Is 7:6

TABERAH (2)
So the name of that place was called **T**, Nm 11:3
"At **T** also, and at Massah and at Dt 9:22

TABERNACLE (108)
you concerning the pattern of the **t**, Ex 25:9
you shall make the **t** with ten curtains of Ex 26:1
so that the **t** may be a single whole. Ex 26:6
of goats' hair for a tent over the **t**; Ex 26:7
shall hang over the back of the **t**. Ex 26:12
side, shall hang over the sides of the **t**, Ex 26:13
upright frames for the **t** of acacia wood. Ex 26:15
shall you do for all the frames of the **t**. Ex 26:17
You shall make the frames for the **t**: Ex 26:18
and for the second side of the **t**, on the Ex 26:20
the rear of the **t** westward you shall Ex 26:22
frames for corners of the **t** in the rear; Ex 26:23
for the frames of the one side of the **t**, Ex 26:26
for the frames of the other side of the **t**, Ex 26:27
of the side of the **t** at the rear westward. Ex 26:27
you shall erect the **t** according to the Ex 26:30
the south side of the **t** opposite the table, Ex 26:35
"You shall make the court of the **t**. On Ex 27:9
All the utensils of the **t** for every use, Ex 27:19
the **t**, its tent and its covering, its hooks Ex 35:11
screen for the door, at the door of the **t**; Ex 35:15
the pegs of the **t** and the pegs of the Ex 35:18
workmen made the **t** with ten curtains. Ex 36:8
with clasps. So the **t** was a single whole. Ex 36:13
of goats' hair for a tent over the **t**. Ex 36:14
upright frames for the **t** of acacia wood. Ex 36:20
He did this for all the frames of the **t**. Ex 36:22
The frames for the **t** he made thus: Ex 36:23
For the second side of the **t**, on the Ex 36:25
the rear of the **t** westward he made six Ex 36:27
frames for corners of the **t** in the rear. Ex 36:28
for the frames of the one side of the **t**, Ex 36:31
for the frames of the other side of the **t**, Ex 36:32
the frames of the **t** at the rear westward. Ex 36:32
all the pegs for the **t** and for the court Ex 38:20
These are the records of the **t**, the Ex 38:21
of the tabernacle, the **t** of the testimony, Ex 38:21
the gate of the court, all the pegs of the **t**, Ex 38:31
all the work of the **t** of the tent of Ex 39:32
Then they brought the **t** to Moses, the Ex 39:33
all the utensils for the service of the **t**, Ex 39:40
month you shall erect the **t** of the tent of Ex 40:2
and set up the screen for the door of the **t**. Ex 40:5
before the door of the **t** of the tent of Ex 40:6
oil and anoint the **t** and all that is Ex 40:9
first day of the month, the **t** was erected. Ex 40:17
Moses erected the **t**. He laid its bases, Ex 40:18
the tent over the **t** and put the covering Ex 40:19
the ark into the **t** and set up the Ex 40:21
of meeting, on the north side of the **t**, Ex 40:22
the table on the south side of the **t**, Ex 40:24
in place the screen for the door of the **t**. Ex 40:28
at the entrance of the **t** of the tent of Ex 40:29
the court around the **t** and the altar, Ex 40:33
and the glory of the LORD filled the **t**. Ex 40:34
it, and the glory of the LORD filled the **t**. Ex 40:35
the cloud was taken up from over the **t**, Ex 40:36
cloud of the LORD was on the **t** by day, Ex 40:38
oil and anointed the **t** and all that was Lv 8:10
uncleanness by defiling my **t** that is in Lv 15:31
to the LORD in front of the **t** of the LORD, Lv 17:4
the Levites over the **t** of the testimony, Nm 1:50
are to carry the **t** and all its Nm 1:50
care of it and shall camp around the **t**. Nm 1:50
When the **t** is to set out, the Levites Nm 1:51
it down, and when the **t** is to be pitched, Nm 1:51
camp around the **t** of the testimony, Nm 1:53
keep guard over the **t** of the testimony." Nm 1:53
tent of meeting, as they minister at the **t**. Nm 3:7
people of Israel as they minister at the **t**. Nm 3:8
were to camp behind the **t** on the west, Nm 3:23
in the tent of meeting involved the **t**, Nm 3:25
court that is around the **t** and the altar, Nm 3:26
were to camp on the south side of the **t**, Nm 3:29
were to camp on the north side of the **t**. Nm 3:35
of Merari involved the frames of the **t**, Nm 3:36
were to camp before the **t** on the east, Nm 3:38
oversight of the whole **t** and all that is Nm 4:16
the curtains of the **t** and the tent of Nm 4:25
court that is around the **t** and the altar, Nm 4:26
the frames of the **t**, with its bars, pillars, Nm 4:31
is on the floor of the **t** and put it into the Nm 5:17
setting up the **t** and had anointed Nm 7:1
an ox. They brought them before the **t**. Nm 7:3
On the day that the **t** was set up, the Nm 9:15
was set up, the cloud covered the **t**, Nm 9:15
it was over the **t** like the appearance of Nm 9:15
As long as the cloud rested over the **t**, Nm 9:18
cloud continued over the **t** many days, Nm 9:19
the cloud was a few days over the **t**, Nm 9:20
that the cloud continued over the **t**, Nm 9:22
lifted from over the **t** of the testimony, Nm 10:11
And when the **t** was taken down, the Nm 10:17
the sons of Merari, who carried the **t**, Nm 10:17
and the **t** was set up before their Nm 10:21
to do service in the **t** of the LORD and to Nm 16:9
who comes near to the **t** of the LORD, Nm 17:13
himself, defiles the **t** of the LORD, Nm 19:13
keep guard over the **t** of the LORD." Nm 31:30
who kept guard over the **t** of the LORD, Nm 31:47
LORD'S land where the LORD'S **t** stands, Jos 22:19
LORD our God that stands before his **t**!" Jos 22:29
with song before the **t** of the tent of 1 Chr 6:32
all the service of the **t** of the house of 1 Chr 6:48
the priests before the **t** of the LORD in 1 Chr 16:39
For the **t** of the LORD, which Moses 1 Chr 21:29
need to carry the **t** or any of the 1 Chr 23:26
was there before the **t** of the LORD. 2 Chr 1:5

TABITHA (2)
there was in Joppa a disciple named **T**, Acts 9:36
"**T**, arise." And she opened her eyes, Acts 9:40

TABLE (95)
were taken to them from Joseph's **t**, Gn 43:34
"You shall make a **t** of acacia wood. Ex 25:23
as holders for the poles to carry the **t**. Ex 25:27
and the **t** shall be carried with these. Ex 25:28
Presence on the **t** before me regularly. Ex 25:30
And you shall set the **t** outside the veil, Ex 26:35
side of the tabernacle opposite the **t**, Ex 26:35
you shall put the **t** on the north side. Ex 26:35
and the **t** and all its utensils, and the Ex 30:27
the **t** and its utensils, and the pure Ex 31:8
the **t** with its poles and all its utensils, Ex 35:13
He also made the **t** of acacia wood. Two Ex 37:10
as holders for the poles to carry the **t**. Ex 37:14
the poles of acacia wood to carry the **t**, Ex 37:15
of pure gold that were to be on the **t**, Ex 37:16
the **t** with all its utensils, and the bread Ex 39:36
you shall bring in the **t** and arrange it, Ex 40:4
He put the **t** in the tent of meeting, on Ex 40:22
opposite the **t** on the south side of the Ex 40:24
pile, on the **t** of pure gold before the LORD. Lv 24:6
their guard duty involved the ark, the **t**, Nm 3:31
And over the **t** of the bread of the Nm 4:7
cut off used to pick up scraps under my **t**. Jgs 1:7
should not fail to sit at **t** with the king. 1 Sm 20:5
he has not come to the king's **t**." 1 Sm 20:29
rose from the **t** in fierce anger 1 Sm 20:34
and you shall eat at my **t** always." 2 Sm 9:7
always eat at my **t**." Now Ziba had 2 Sm 9:10
do." So Mephibosheth ate at David's **t**, 2 Sm 9:11
for he ate always at the king's **t**. 2 Sm 9:13
among those who eat at your **t**. 2 Sm 19:28
be among those who eat at your **t**, 1 Kgs 2:7
for all who came to King Solomon's **t**, 1 Kgs 4:27
the golden **t** for the bread of the 1 Kgs 7:48
the food of his **t**, the seating of his 1 Kgs 10:5
And as they sat at the **t**, the word of 1 Kgs 13:20
of Asherah, who eat at Jezebel's **t**." 1 Kgs 18:19
walls and put there for him a bed, a **t**, 2 Kgs 4:10
life he dined regularly at the king's **t**, 2 Kgs 25:29
of gold for each **t** for the showbread, 1 Chr 28:16
the food of his **t**, the seating of his 2 Chr 9:4
the showbread on the **t** of pure gold, 2 Chr 13:11
and the **t** for the showbread and all 2 Chr 29:18
Moreover, there were at my **t** 150 men, Neh 5:17
was set on your **t** was full of fatness. Jb 36:16
You prepare a **t** before me in the presence Ps 23:5
Let their own **t** before them become a Ps 69:22
"Can God spread a **t** in the wilderness? Ps 78:19
will be like olive shoots around your **t**. Ps 128:3
mixed her wine; she has also set her **t**. Prv 9:2
They prepare the **t**, they spread the rugs, Is 21:5
who set a **t** for Fortune and fill cups of Is 65:11
life he dined regularly at the king's **t**, Jer 52:33
with a **t** spread before it on which you Ezk 23:41
be filled at my **t** with horses and Ezk 39:20
"This is the **t** that is before the LORD." Ezk 41:22
and they shall approach my **t**, Ezk 44:16
They shall speak lies at the same **t**, but Dn 11:27
saying that the LORD'S **t** may be despised. Mal 1:7
you say that the Lord's **t** is polluted, Mal 1:12
and west and recline at **t** with Abraham, Mt 8:11
And as Jesus reclined at **t** in the house, Mt 9:10
crumbs that fall from their masters' **t**." Mt 15:27
poured it on his head as he reclined at **t**. Mt 26:7
he reclined at **t** with the twelve. Mt 26:20
And as he reclined at **t** in his house, Mk 2:15
the dogs under the **t** eat the children's Mk 7:28
the leper, as he was reclining at **t**, Mk 14:3
as they were reclining at **t** and eating, Mk 14:18
themselves as they were reclining at **t**, Mk 16:14
and others reclining at **t** with them. Lk 5:29
house and took his place at the **t**. Lk 7:36
he was reclining at **t** in the Pharisee's Lk 7:37
those who were at **t** with him began to Lk 7:49
him, so he went in and reclined at **t**. Lk 11:37
for service and have them recline at **t**, Lk 12:37
and recline at **t** in the kingdom of God. Lk 13:29
the presence of all who sit at **t** with you. Lk 14:10
those who reclined at **t** with him heard Lk 14:15
with what fell from the rich man's **t**. Lk 16:21
the field, 'Come at once and recline at **t**'? Lk 17:7
when the hour came, he reclined at **t**, Lk 22:14
who betrays me is with me on the **t**. Lk 22:21
one who reclines at **t** or one who Lk 22:27
Is it not the one who reclines at **t**? Lk 22:27
and drink at my **t** in my kingdom and Lk 22:30
When he was at **t** with them, he took Lk 24:30
one of those reclining with him at the **t**. Jn 12:2
loved, was reclining at **t** close to Jesus, Jn 13:23
Now no one at the **t** knew why he said Jn 13:28
had been reclining at **t** close to him and Jn 21:20
"Let their **t** become a snare and a trap, Rom 11:9
cannot partake of the **t** of the Lord 1 Cor 10:21
of the Lord and the **t** of demons. 1 Cor 10:21
the lampstand and the **t** and the bread of Heb 9:2

TABLELAND (8)
all the cities of the **t** and all Gilead and Dt 3:10
wilderness on the **t** for the Reubenites, Dt 4:43
and all the **t** of Medeba as far as Dibon; Jos 13:9
of the valley, and all the **t** by Medeba; Jos 13:16
and all its cities that are in the **t**; Jos 13:17
that is, all the cities of the **t**, and all the Jos 13:21
Bezer in the wilderness on the **t**, Jos 20:8
"Judgment has come upon the **t**, upon Jer 48:21

TABLES (15)
showbread, the silver for the silver **t**, 1 Chr 28:16
He also made ten **t** and placed them in 2 Chr 4:8
the **t** for the bread of the Presence, 2 Chr 4:19
For all **t** are full of filthy vomit, with no Is 28:8
of the gate were two **t** on either side, Ezk 40:39
entrance of the north gate, were two **t**; Ezk 40:40
of the vestibule of the gate were two **t**. Ezk 40:40
Four **t** were on either side of the gate, Ezk 40:41
were on either side of the gate, eight **t**, Ezk 40:41
And there were four **t** of hewn stone Ezk 40:42
And on the **t** the flesh of the offering Ezk 40:43
he overturned the **t** of the Mt 21:12
he overturned the **t** of the Mk 11:15
money-changers and overturned their **t**. Jn 2:15
up preaching the word of God to serve **t**. Acts 6:2

TABLET (6)
neck; write them on the **t** of your heart. Prv 3:3
fingers; write them on the **t** of your heart. Prv 7:3
"Take a large **t** and write on it in common Is 8:1
it before them on a **t** and inscribe it in a Is 30:8
it is engraved on the **t** of their heart, Jer 17:1
And he asked for a writing **t** and wrote, Lk 1:63

TABLETS (37)
there, that I may give you the **t** of stone, Ex 24:12
Mount Sinai, the two **t** of the testimony, Ex 31:18
two tablets of the testimony, **t** of stone, Ex 31:18
with the two **t** of the testimony Ex 32:15
hand, **t** that were written on both sides; Ex 32:15
The **t** were the work of God, and the Ex 32:16
the writing of God, engraved on the **t**. Ex 32:16
and he threw the **t** out of his hands and Ex 32:19
"Cut for yourself two **t** of stone like the Ex 34:1
I will write on the **t** the words that were Ex 34:1
tablets the words that were on the first **t**, Ex 34:1
So Moses cut two **t** of stone like the first. Ex 34:4
him, and took in his hand two **t** of stone. Ex 34:4
And he wrote on the **t** the words of the Ex 34:28
with the two **t** of the testimony in his Ex 34:29
and he wrote them on two **t** of stone. Dt 4:13
he wrote them on two **t** of stone and gave Dt 5:22
up the mountain to receive the **t** of stone, Dt 9:9
the **t** of the covenant that the LORD made Dt 9:9
gave me the two **t** of stone written with Dt 9:10
the LORD gave me the two **t** of stone, Dt 9:11
two tablets of stone, the **t** of the covenant. Dt 9:11
And the two **t** of the covenant were in my Dt 9:15
hold of the two **t** and threw them out Dt 9:17
'Cut for yourself two **t** of stone like the Dt 10:1
I will write on the **t** the words that were Dt 10:2
that were on the first **t** that you broke, Dt 10:2
wood, and cut two **t** of stone like the first, Dt 10:3

the mountain with the two **t** in my hand. Dt 10:3
And he wrote on the **t**, in the same Dt 10:4
mountain and put the **t** in the ark that Dt 10:5
ark except the two **t** of stone that Moses 1 Kgs 8:9
ark except the two **t** that Moses put 2 Chr 5:10
make it plain on **t**, so he may run who Hab 2:2
not on **t** of stone but on tablets of 2 Cor 3:3
of stone but on **t** of human hearts. 2 Cor 3:3
that budded, and the **t** of the covenant. Heb 9:4

TABOR (10)
The boundary also touches **T**, Jos 19:22
you, 'Go, gather your men at Mount **T**, Jgs 4:6
of Abinoam had gone up to Mount **T**, Jgs 4:12
down from Mount **T** with 10,000 men Jgs 4:14
whom you killed at **T**?" They answered, Jgs 8:18
further and come to the oak of **T**. 1 Sm 10:3
T with its pasturelands, 1 Chr 6:77
T and Hermon joyously praise your Ps 89:12
like **T** among the mountains and like Jer 46:18
at Mizpah and a net spread upon **T**. Hos 5:1

TABRIMMON (1)
sent them to Ben-hadad the son of **T**, 1 Kgs 15:18

TACKLE (1)
threw the ship's **t** overboard with Acts 27:19

TADMOR (1)
He built **T** in the wilderness and all 2 Chr 8:4

TAHAN (2)
the clan of the Becherites; of **T**, Nm 26:35
his son, Telah his son, **T** his son, 1 Chr 7:25

TAHANITES (1)
of Tahan, the clan of the **T**. Nm 26:35

TAHASH (1)
bore Tebah, Gaham, **T**, and Maacah. Gn 22:24

TAHATH (6)
from Makheloth and camped at **T**. Nm 33:26
they set out from **T** and camped at Nm 33:27
T his son, Uriel his son, Uzziah his 1 Chr 6:24
son of **T**, son of Assir, son of 1 Chr 6:37
and Bered his son, **T** his son, 1 Chr 7:20
his son, Eleadah his son, **T** his son, 1 Chr 7:20

TAHCHEMONITE (1)
David had: Josheb-basshebeth a **T**; 2 Sm 23:8

TAHPANHES (6)
men of Memphis and **T** have shaved the Jer 2:16
voice of the LORD. And they arrived at **T**. Jer 43:7
word of the LORD came to Jeremiah in **T**: Jer 43:8
at the entrance to Pharaoh's palace in **T**, Jer 43:9
in the land of Egypt, at Migdol, at **T**, Jer 44:1
Migdol; proclaim in Memphis and **T**; Jer 46:14

TAHPENES (3)
own wife, the sister of **T** the queen. 1 Kgs 11:19
the sister of **T** bore him Genubath 1 Kgs 11:20
whom **T** weaned in Pharaoh's 1 Kgs 11:20

TAHREA (1)
Micah: Pithon, Melech, **T**, and Ahaz. 1 Chr 9:41

TAIL (16)
hand and catch it by the **t**"—so he put out Ex 4:4
the ram and the fat **t** and the fat that Ex 29:22
he shall remove the whole fat **t**, cut off Lv 3:9
And all its fat shall be offered, the fat **t**, the Lv 7:3
the fat and the fat **t** and all the fat that Lv 8:25
the fat **t** and that which covers the Lv 9:19
were faint and weary, and cut off your **t**, Dt 25:18
will make you the head and not the **t**, Dt 28:13
shall be the head, and you shall be the **t**. Dt 28:44
And he turned them **t** to tail and put a Jgs 15:4
he turned them tail to **t** and put a torch Jgs 15:4
He makes his **t** stiff like a cedar; the Jb 40:17
So the LORD cut off from Israel head and **t**, Is 9:14
and the prophet who teaches lies is the **t**; Is 9:15
will be nothing for Egypt that head or **t**, Is 19:15
His **t** swept down a third of the stars of Rv 12:4

TAILS (5)
and put a torch between each pair of **t**. Jgs 15:4
They have **t** and stings like scorpions, Rv 9:10
hurt people for five months is in their **t**. Rv 9:10
horses is in their mouths and in their **t**, Rv 9:19
for their **t** are like serpents with heads, Rv 9:19

TAINTED (4)
It is **t**, and he who eats of it shall bear his Lv 7:18
If it is eaten at all on the third day, it is **t**; Lv 19:7
and broth of **t** meat is in their vessels; Is 65:4
nor has **t** meat come into my mouth." Ezk 4:14

TAKE (855)
reach out his hand and **t** also of the tree Gn 3:22
Also **t** with you every sort of food that is Gn 6:21
T with you seven pairs of all clean Gn 7:2
then, here is your wife; **t** her, and go." Gn 12:19
If you **t** the left hand, then I will go to the Gn 13:9
go to the right, or if you **t** the right hand, Gn 13:9
persons, but **t** the goods for yourself." Gn 14:21
that I would not **t** a thread or a sandal Gn 14:23
I will **t** nothing but what the young Gn 14:24
Eshcol, and Mamre **t** their share." Gn 14:24
T your wife and your two daughters Gn 19:15
ewe lambs you will **t** from my hand, Gn 21:30
He said, "**T** your son, your only son Gn 22:2
that you will not **t** a wife for my son Gn 24:3
kindred, and **t** a wife for my son Isaac." Gn 24:4
Must I then **t** your son back to the land Gn 24:5
it that you do not **t** my son back there. Gn 24:6
and you shall **t** a wife for my son from Gn 24:7
only you must not **t** my son back Gn 24:8
'You shall not **t** a wife for my son from Gn 24:37
and to my clan and **t** a wife for my Gn 24:38
You shall **t** a wife for my son from my Gn 24:40
the right way to **t** the daughter of my Gn 24:48
t her and go, and let her be the wife of Gn 24:51
Now then, **t** your weapons, your quiver Gn 27:3
"You must not **t** a wife from the Gn 28:1
and **t** as your wife from there one of the Gn 28:2
that you may **t** possession of the land of Gn 28:4
away to Paddan-aram to **t** a wife from Gn 28:6
"You must not **t** a wife from the Gn 28:6
Would you **t** away my son's Gn 30:15
that you would **t** your daughters from Gn 31:31
and **t** it." Now Jacob did not know that Gn 31:32
or if you **t** wives besides my daughters, Gn 31:50
us, and **t** our daughters for yourselves. Gn 34:9
and we will **t** your daughters to Gn 34:16
then we will **t** our daughter, Gn 34:17
Let us **t** their daughters as wives, and Gn 34:21
hands, saying, "Let us not **t** his life." Gn 37:21
the Adullamite to **t** back the pledge Gn 38:20
over the land and **t** one-fifth of the Gn 41:34
and **t** grain for the famine of your Gn 42:33
more, and now you would **t** Benjamin. Gn 42:36
t some of the choice fruits of the land Gn 43:11
T double the money with you. Carry Gn 43:12
T also your brother, and arise, go Gn 43:13
If you **t** this one also from me, and Gn 44:29
and **t** your father and your households, Gn 45:18
t wagons from the land of Egypt for Gn 45:19
"**T** this child away and nurse him for me, Ex 2:9
t your sandals off your feet, for the place Ex 3:5
you shall **t** some water from the Nile and Ex 4:9
water that you shall **t** from the Nile will Ex 4:9
And **t** in your hand this staff, with Ex 4:17
why do you **t** the people away from their Ex 5:4
I will **t** you to be my people, and I will be Ex 6:7
'**T** your staff and cast it down before Ex 7:9
and **t** in your hand the staff that turned Ex 7:15
'**T** your staff and stretch out your hand Ex 7:19
house, and he did not **t** even this to heart. Ex 7:23
with the LORD to **t** away the frogs from Ex 8:8
Aaron, "**T** handfuls of soot from the kiln, Ex 9:8
for we must **t** of them to serve the LORD Ex 10:26
t care never to see my face again, for on Ex 10:28
every man shall **t** a lamb according Ex 12:3
nearest neighbor shall **t** according to the Ex 12:4
You may **t** it from the sheep or from the Ex 12:5
"Then they shall **t** some of the blood and Ex 12:7
T a bunch of hyssop and dip it in the Ex 12:22
T your flocks and your herds, as you Ex 12:32
you shall not **t** any of the flesh outside Ex 12:46
You shall each **t** an omer, according to Ex 16:16
And Moses said to Aaron, "**T** a jar, and Ex 16:33
and **t** in your hand the staff with which Ex 17:5
'**T** care not to go up into the mountain Ex 19:12
"You shall not **t** the name of the LORD Ex 20:7
you shall **t** him from my altar, Ex 21:14
If ever you **t** your neighbor's cloak in Ex 22:26
And you shall **t** no bribe, for a bribe Ex 23:8
and I will **t** sickness away from among Ex 23:25
Israel, that they **t** for me a contribution. Ex 25:2
You shall **t** two onyx stones, and engrave Ex 28:9
T one bull of the herd and two rams Ex 29:1
Then you shall **t** the garments, and put Ex 29:5
You shall **t** the anointing oil and pour it Ex 29:7
and shall **t** part of the blood of the bull Ex 29:12
And you shall **t** all the fat that covers Ex 29:13
"Then you shall **t** one of the rams, and Ex 29:15
the ram and shall **t** its blood and throw Ex 29:16
"You shall **t** the other ram, and Aaron Ex 29:19
shall kill the ram and **t** part of its blood Ex 29:20
Then you shall **t** part of the blood that Ex 29:21
"You shall also **t** the fat from the ram Ex 29:22
Then you shall **t** them from their Ex 29:25
"You shall **t** the breast of the ram of Ex 29:26
"You shall **t** the ram of ordination and Ex 29:31
"When you **t** the census of the people of Ex 30:12
You shall **t** the atonement money from Ex 30:16
"**T** the finest spices: of liquid myrrh 500 Ex 30:23
The LORD said to Moses, "**T** sweet spices, Ex 30:34
"**T** off the rings of gold that are in the Ex 32:2
to them, 'Let any who have gold **t** it off.' Ex 32:24
So now **t** off your ornaments, that I may Ex 33:5
Now Moses used to **t** the tent and pitch it Ex 33:7
Then I will **t** away my hand, and you Ex 33:23
our sin, and **t** us for your inheritance." Ex 34:9
T care, lest you make a covenant with Ex 34:12
and you **t** of their daughters for your Ex 34:16
T from among you a contribution to the Ex 35:5
"Then you shall **t** the anointing oil and Ex 40:9
And he shall **t** from it a handful of the Lv 2:2
And the priest shall **t** from the grain Lv 2:9
the anointed priest shall **t** some of the Lv 4:5
all its fat he shall **t** from it and burn on Lv 4:19
Then the priest shall **t** some of the blood Lv 4:25
And the priest shall **t** some of its blood Lv 4:30
Then the priest shall **t** some of the blood Lv 4:34
and the priest shall **t** a handful of it as its Lv 5:12
and he shall **t** up the ashes to which the Lv 6:10
Then he shall **t** off his garments and put Lv 6:11
And one shall **t** from it a handful of the Lv 6:15
"**T** Aaron and his sons with him, and the Lv 8:2
for it will **t** seven days to ordain you. Lv 8:33
"**T** for yourself a bull calf for a sin Lv 9:2
of Israel, '**T** a male goat for a sin offering, Lv 9:3
"**T** the grain offering that is left of the Lv 10:12
then she shall **t** two turtledoves or two Lv 12:8
shall command them to **t** for him who is Lv 14:4
He shall **t** the live bird with the Lv 14:6
eighth day he shall **t** two male lambs Lv 14:10
And the priest shall **t** one of the male Lv 14:12
The priest shall **t** some of the blood of Lv 14:14
Then the priest shall **t** some of the log Lv 14:15
then he shall **t** one male lamb for a Lv 14:21
And the priest shall **t** the lamb of the Lv 14:24
And the priest shall **t** some of the blood Lv 14:25
command that they **t** out the stones Lv 14:40
Then they shall **t** other stones and put Lv 14:42
and he shall **t** other plaster and plaster Lv 14:42
of the house he shall **t** two small birds, Lv 14:49
and shall **t** the cedarwood and the Lv 14:51
eighth day he shall **t** two turtledoves or Lv 15:14
eighth day she shall **t** two turtledoves or Lv 15:29
And he shall **t** from the congregation of Lv 16:5
Then he shall **t** the two goats and set Lv 16:7
And he shall **t** a censer full of coals of Lv 16:12
And he shall **t** some of the blood of the Lv 16:14
and shall **t** some of the blood of the bull Lv 16:18
of meeting and shall **t** off the linen Lv 16:23
and you shall not **t** her son's daughter Lv 18:17
And you shall not **t** a woman as a rival Lv 18:18
You shall not **t** vengeance or bear a Lv 19:18
And he shall **t** a wife in her virginity. Lv 21:13
But he shall **t** as his wife a virgin of his Lv 21:14
from whom he may **t** uncleanness, Lv 22:5
And you shall **t** on the first day the fruit Lv 23:40
"You shall **t** fine flour and bake twelve Lv 24:5
T no interest from him or profit, but Lv 25:36
"**T** a census of all the congregation of Nm 1:2
and you shall not **t** a census of them Nm 1:49
and they shall **t** care of it and shall Nm 1:50
is to set out, the Levites shall **t** it down, Nm 1:51
And you shall **t** the Levites for me—I Nm 3:41
"**T** the Levites instead of all the Nm 3:45
you shall **t** five shekels per head; you Nm 3:47
you shall **t** them according to the Nm 3:47
"**T** a census of the sons of Kohath from Nm 4:2
sons shall go in and **t** down the veil of Nm 4:5
And they shall **t** a cloth of blue and Nm 4:9
And they shall **t** all the vessels of the Nm 4:12
And they shall **t** away the ashes from Nm 4:13
"**T** a census of the sons of Gershon Nm 4:22
And the priest shall **t** holy water in an Nm 5:17
an earthenware vessel and **t** some of the Nm 5:17
the priest shall make her **t** an oath, Nm 5:19
priest make the woman **t** the oath of Nm 5:21
And the priest shall **t** the grain offering Nm 5:25
And the priest shall **t** a handful of the Nm 5:26
of meeting and shall **t** the hair from his Nm 6:18
And the priest shall **t** the shoulder of Nm 6:19
"**T** the Levites from among the people of Nm 8:6
Then let them **t** a bull from the herd and Nm 8:8
and you shall **t** another bull from the Nm 8:8
and let them **t** their stand there with Nm 11:16
And I will **t** some of the Spirit that is Nm 11:17
t censers, Korah and all his company; Nm 16:6
every one of you **t** his censer and put Nm 16:17
Aaron the priest to **t** up the censers Nm 16:37
Moses said to Aaron, "**T** your censer, Nm 16:46
'When you **t** from the people of Israel Nm 18:26
Eleazar the priest shall **t** some of its Nm 19:4
the priest shall **t** cedarwood and hyssop Nm 19:6
the unclean they shall **t** some ashes of Nm 19:17
a clean person shall **t** hyssop and dip Nm 19:18

“**T** the staff, and assemble the Nm 20:8
T Aaron and Eleazar his son and Nm 20:25
that he **t** away the serpents from us.” So Nm 21:7
“Must I not **t** care to speak what the Nm 23:12
now, I will **t** you to another place. Nm 23:27
“**T** all the chiefs of the people and hang Nm 25:4
“**T** a census of all the congregation of Nm 26:2
“**T** a census of the people, from twenty Nm 26:4
to Moses, “**T** Joshua the son of Nun, Nm 27:18
“**T** the count of the plunder that was Nm 31:26
T it from their half and give it to Nm 31:29
Israel's half you shall **t** one drawn out Nm 31:30
Do not **t** us across the Jordan.” Nm 32:5
but we will **t** up arms, ready to go Nm 32:17
if you will **t** up arms to go before the Nm 32:20
And you shall **t** possession of the land Nm 33:53
You shall **t** one chief from every tribe Nm 34:18
the larger tribes you shall **t** many, Nm 35:8
from the smaller tribes you shall **t** few; Nm 35:8
Turn and **t** your journey, and go to the Dt 1:7
Go in and **t** possession of the land that the Dt 1:8
Go up, **t** possession, as the LORD, the God Dt 1:21
Begin to **t** possession, and contend with Dt 2:24
Begin to **t** possession, that you may Dt 2:31
city that we did not **t** from them—sixty Dt 3:4
and go in and **t** possession of the land that Dt 4:1
word that I command you, nor **t** from it, Dt 4:2
that you are entering to **t** possession of it. Dt 4:5
“Only **t** care, and keep your soul Dt 4:9
shall go over and **t** possession of that Dt 4:22
T care, lest you forget the covenant of the Dt 4:23
attempted to go and **t** a nation for Dt 4:34
“‘You shall not **t** the name of the LORD Dt 5:11
then **t** care lest you forget the LORD, who Dt 6:12
may go in and **t** possession of the good Dt 6:18
that you are entering to **t** possession of it, Dt 7:1
And the LORD will **t** away from you all Dt 7:15
gold that is on them or **t** it for yourselves, Dt 7:25
“**T** care lest you forget the LORD your God Dt 8:11
‘Go up and **t** possession of the land that I Dt 9:23
and go in and **t** possession of the land Dt 11:8
you are entering to **t** possession of it is Dt 11:10
T care lest your heart be deceived, and Dt 11:16
you are entering to **t** possession of it, Dt 11:29
to go in to **t** possession of the land Dt 11:31
T care that you do not offer your burnt Dt 12:13
T care that you do not neglect the Dt 12:19
and your vow offerings, you shall **t**, Dt 12:26
t care that you be not ensnared to Dt 12:30
to do. You shall not add to it or **t** from it. Dt 12:32
T care lest there be an unworthy Dt 15:9
then you shall **t** an awl, and put it Dt 15:17
city shall send and **t** him from there, Dt 19:12
die in the battle and another man **t** her.’ Dt 20:7
you shall **t** as plunder for yourselves. Dt 20:14
making war against it in order to **t** it, Dt 20:19
to the slain man shall **t** a heifer that has Dt 21:3
into your hand and you **t** them captive, Dt 21:10
and you desire to **t** her to be your wife, Dt 21:11
And she shall **t** off the clothes in which Dt 21:13
and his mother shall **t** hold of him and Dt 21:19
You shall **t** them back to your brother. Dt 22:1
you shall not **t** the mother with the Dt 22:6
go, but the young you may **t** for yourself, Dt 22:7
and her mother shall **t** and bring out Dt 22:15
of that city shall **t** the man and whip Dt 22:18
“A man shall not **t** his father's wife, so Dt 22:30
you are entering to **t** possession of it. Dt 23:20
away, may not **t** her again to be his wife, Dt 24:4
“No one shall **t** a mill or an upper Dt 24:6
“**T** care, in a case of leprous disease, to be Dt 24:8
or **t** a widow's garment in pledge, Dt 24:17
go in to her and **t** her as his wife and Dt 25:5
man does not wish to **t** his brother's wife, Dt 25:7
he persists, saying, ‘I do not wish to **t** her,’ Dt 25:8
you shall **t** some of the first of all the Dt 26:2
Then the priest shall **t** the basket from Dt 26:4
you are entering to **t** possession of it. Dt 28:21
so the LORD will **t** delight in bringing Dt 28:63
you are entering to **t** possession of it. Dt 28:63
gather you, and from there he will **t** you. Dt 30:4
LORD will again **t** delight in prospering Dt 30:9
you are entering to **t** possession of it. Dt 30:16
“**T** this Book of the Law and put it by Dt 31:26
I will **t** vengeance on my adversaries Dt 32:41
“**T** to heart all the words by which I am Dt 32:46
Jordan to go in to **t** possession of the land Jos 1:11
and they also **t** possession of the land Jos 1:15
“**T** up the ark of the covenant and pass on Jos 3:6
Now therefore **t** twelve men from the Jos 3:12
“**T** twelve men from the people, from each Jos 4:2
‘**T** twelve stones from here out of the Jos 4:3
and **t** up each of you a stone upon his Jos 4:5
“**T** off your sandals from your feet, Jos 5:15
“**T** up the ark of the covenant and let Jos 6:6
have devoted them you **t** any of the Jos 6:18
enemies until you **t** away the devoted Jos 7:13
T all the fighting men with you, and Jos 8:1
its livestock you shall **t** as plunder for Jos 8:2
‘**T** provisions in your hand for the Jos 9:11
Manasseh could not **t** possession of Jos 17:12
off going in to **t** possession of the land, Jos 18:3
Then they shall **t** him into the city and Jos 20:4
and **t** for yourselves a possession Jos 22:19
it, may the LORD himself **t** vengeance. Jos 22:23
to his inheritance to **t** possession of the Jgs 2:6
whether they will **t** care to walk in the Jgs 2:22
“**T** the meat and the unleavened cakes, Jgs 6:20
LORD said to him, “**T** your father's bull, Jgs 6:25
Then **t** the second bull and offer it as a Jgs 6:26
T them down to the water, and I will test Jgs 7:4
then come and **t** refuge in my shade, Jgs 9:15
Israel did not **t** away the land of Moab Jgs 11:15
and are you to **t** possession of them? Jgs 11:23
the LORD, and I cannot **t** back my vow.” Jgs 11:35
that you must go to **t** a wife from the Jgs 14:3
After some days he returned to **t** her. Jgs 14:8
beautiful than she? Please **t** her instead.” Jgs 15:2
“You **t** my gods that I made and the Jgs 18:24
day; consider it, **t** counsel, and speak.” Jgs 19:30
and we will **t** ten men of a hundred Jgs 20:10
because we did not **t** for each man of Jgs 21:22
eyes, that you should **t** notice of me, Ru 2:10
whose wings you have come to **t** refuge!” Ru 2:12
T my right of redemption yourself, for I Ru 4:6
up the priest would **t** for himself. 1 Sm 2:14
and then **t** as much as you wish,” he 1 Sm 2:16
it now, and if not, I will **t** it by force.” 1 Sm 2:16
him a little robe and **t** it to him each 1 Sm 2:19
T courage, and be men, O Philistines, 1 Sm 4:9
t and prepare a new cart and two milk 1 Sm 6:7
to the cart, but **t** their calves home, 1 Sm 6:7
And **t** the ark of the LORD and place it 1 Sm 6:8
LORD. Come down and **t** it up to you.” 1 Sm 6:21
he will **t** your sons and appoint them 1 Sm 8:11
He will **t** your daughters to be 1 Sm 8:13
He will **t** the best of your fields and 1 Sm 8:14
He will **t** the tenth of your grain and of 1 Sm 8:15
He will **t** your male servants and 1 Sm 8:16
He will **t** the tenth of your flocks, and 1 Sm 8:17
son, “**T** one of the young men with you, 1 Sm 9:3
said, “**T** a heifer with you and say, 1 Sm 16:2
“**T** for your brothers an ephah of 1 Sm 17:17
Also **t** these ten cheeses to the 1 Sm 17:18
Saul sent messengers to **t** David, 1 Sm 19:14
Saul sent messengers to **t** David, 1 Sm 19:20
“May the LORD **t** vengeance on 1 Sm 20:16
are on this side of you, **t** them,’ 1 Sm 20:21
If you will **t** that, take it, for there is 1 Sm 21:9
If you will take that, **t** it, for there is 1 Sm 21:9
See therefore and **t** note of all the 1 Sm 23:23
you, though you hunt my life to **t** it. 1 Sm 24:11
Shall I **t** my bread and my water and 1 Sm 25:11
spoke to Abigail, to **t** her as his wife. 1 Sm 25:39
sent us to you to **t** you to him as his 1 Sm 25:40
But **t** now the spear that is at his 1 Sm 26:11
of the young men come over and **t** it. 1 Sm 26:22
alive, but would **t** away the sheep, 1 Sm 27:9
“Will you **t** me down to this band?” 1 Sm 30:15
and I will **t** you down to this band.” 1 Sm 30:15
the young men and **t** his spoil.” But 2 Sm 2:21
was not willing to **t** the ark of the 2 Sm 6:10
he was unwilling to **t** one of his own 2 Sm 12:4
And I will **t** your wives before your 2 Sm 12:11
and encamp against the city and **t** it, 2 Sm 12:28
lest I **t** the city and it be called by my 2 Sm 12:28
do not **t** this to heart.” So Tamar 2 Sm 13:20
my lord the king so **t** it to heart as to 2 Sm 13:33
But God will not **t** away life, and he 2 Sm 14:14
out his hand and **t** hold of him and 2 Sm 15:5
Go back and **t** your brothers with 2 Sm 15:20
Let me go over and **t** off his head.” 2 Sm 16:9
Do not let the king **t** it to heart. 2 Sm 19:19
said to the king, “Oh, let him **t** it all, 2 Sm 19:30
T your lord's servants and pursue 2 Sm 20:6
my God, my rock, in whom I **t** refuge, 2 Sm 22:3
for all those who **t** refuge in him. 2 Sm 22:31
please **t** away the iniquity of your 2 Sm 24:10
my lord the king **t** and offer up what 2 Sm 24:22
“**T** with you the servants of your lord 1 Kgs 1:33
and thus **t** away from me and from 1 Kgs 2:31
and is made to **t** an oath and comes 1 Kgs 8:31
Jeroboam, “**T** for yourself ten pieces, 1 Kgs 11:31
I will not **t** the whole kingdom out of 1 Kgs 11:34
But I will **t** the kingdom out of his 1 Kgs 11:35
And I will **t** you, and you shall reign 1 Kgs 11:37
T with you ten loaves, some cakes, 1 Kgs 14:3
he would **t** an oath of the kingdom 1 Kgs 18:10
now, O LORD, **t** away my life, for I am 1 Kgs 19:4
and they seek my life, to **t** it away.” 1 Kgs 19:10
and they seek my life, to **t** it away.” 1 Kgs 19:14
whatever pleases you and **t** it away.’” 1 Kgs 20:6
“**T** your positions.” And they took 1 Kgs 20:12
come out for peace, **t** them alive. 1 Kgs 20:18
come out for war, **t** them alive.” 1 Kgs 20:18
he hurried to **t** the bandage away 1 Kgs 20:41
Then **t** him out and stone him to 1 Kgs 21:10
t possession of the vineyard of 1 Kgs 21:15
the Jezreelite, to **t** possession of it. 1 Kgs 21:16
where he has gone to **t** possession. 1 Kgs 21:18
keep quiet and do not **t** it out of the 1 Kgs 22:3
and **t** him back to Amon the 1 Kgs 22:26
LORD was about to **t** Elijah up to 2 Kgs 2:1
today the LORD will **t** away your master 2 Kgs 2:3
today the LORD will **t** away your master 2 Kgs 2:5
creditor has come to **t** my two children 2 Kgs 4:1
up your garment and **t** my staff in 2 Kgs 4:29
none.” And he urged him to **t** it, 2 Kgs 5:16
“**T** it up.” So he reached out his hand 2 Kgs 6:7
murderer has sent to **t** off my head? 2 Kgs 6:32
we shall **t** them alive and get into the 2 Kgs 7:12
“Let some men **t** five of the remaining 2 Kgs 7:13
“**T** a present with you and go to meet 2 Kgs 8:8
and **t** this flask of oil in your hand, 2 Kgs 9:1
Then **t** the flask of oil and pour it on 2 Kgs 9:3
“**T** a horseman and send to meet 2 Kgs 9:17
“**T** him up and throw him on the plot 2 Kgs 9:25
Now therefore **t** him up and throw 2 Kgs 9:26
t the heads of your master's sons and 2 Kgs 10:6
“**T** them alive.” And they took them 2 Kgs 10:14
let the priests **t**, each from his donor, 2 Kgs 12:5
Now therefore **t** no more money from 2 Kgs 12:7
that they should **t** no more money 2 Kgs 12:8
“**T** a bow and arrows.” So he took a 2 Kgs 13:15
“**T** the arrows,” and he took them. 2 Kgs 13:18
until I come and **t** you away to a 2 Kgs 18:32
Judah shall again **t** root downward 2 Kgs 19:30
And let them **t** and lay it on the boil, 2 Kgs 20:7
put out his hand to **t** hold of the ark, 1 Chr 13:9
So David did not **t** the ark home into 1 Chr 13:13
I will not **t** my steadfast love from 1 Chr 17:13
please **t** away the iniquity of your 1 Chr 21:8
Then Ornan said to David, “**T** it, 1 Chr 21:23
I will not **t** for the LORD what is 1 Chr 21:24
so that you may **t** it up to Jerusalem.” 2 Chr 2:16
and is made to **t** an oath and comes 2 Chr 6:22
But you, **t** courage! Do not let your 2 Chr 15:7
“Seize Micaiah and **t** him back to 2 Chr 18:25
and his people came to **t** their spoil, 2 Chr 20:25
empty the chest and **t** it and return 2 Chr 24:11
in order that they might **t** the city. 2 Chr 32:18
said to his servants, “**T** me away, 2 Chr 35:23
him in chains to **t** him to Babylon. 2 Chr 36:6
And **t** care not to be slack in this Ezr 4:22
and he said to him, “**T** these vessels, go Ezr 5:15
you are entering, to **t** possession of it, Ezr 9:11
neither **t** their daughters for your sons, Ezr 9:12
Levites and all Israel **t** oath that they Ezr 10:5
now come and let us **t** counsel together.” Neh 6:7
of the land or **t** their daughters for our Neh 10:30
“We also **t** on ourselves the Neh 10:32
And I made them **t** oath in the name Neh 13:25
or **t** their daughters for your sons or Neh 13:25
whatever she desired to **t** with her from Est 2:13
so that he might **t** off his sackcloth, Est 4:4
t the robes and the horse, as you have Est 6:10
on that day to **t** vengeance on their Est 8:13
my transgression and **t** away my Jb 7:21
man, nor **t** the hand of evildoers. Jb 8:20
Let him **t** his rod away from me, and let Jb 9:34
will look around and **t** your rest in Jb 11:18
Why should I **t** my flesh in my teeth Jb 13:14
But he knows the way that I **t**; when he Jb 23:10
they **t** the widow's ox for a pledge. Jb 24:3
and they **t** a pledge against the poor.) Jb 24:9
Will he **t** delight in the Almighty? Will Jb 27:10
else my Maker would soon **t** me away. Jb 32:22
words in order before me; **t** your stand. Jb 33:5
nothing that he should **t** delight in God.’ Jb 34:9
and he does not **t** much note of Jb 35:15
T care; do not turn to iniquity, for this Jb 36:21
that it might **t** hold of the skirts of the Jb 38:13
that you may **t** it to its territory and that Jb 38:20
Can one **t** him by his eyes, or pierce his Jb 40:24
covenant with you to **t** him for your Jb 41:4
Now therefore **t** seven bulls and seven Jb 42:8
and the rulers **t** counsel together, Ps 2:2
Blessed are all who **t** refuge in him. Ps 2:12
But let all who **t** refuge in you rejoice; let Ps 5:11
O LORD my God, in you do I **t** refuge; save Ps 7:1
that you may **t** it into your hands; Ps 10:14
In the LORD I **t** refuge; how can you say to Ps 11:1
How long must I **t** counsel in my soul Ps 13:2
interest and does not **t** a bribe against the Ps 15:5
Preserve me, O God, for in you I **t** refuge. Ps 16:1

will not pour out or **t** their names on my Ps 16:4
my God, my rock, in whom I **t** refuge, Ps 18:2
shield for all those who **t** refuge in him. Ps 18:30
be put to shame, for I **t** refuge in you. Ps 25:20
forsaken me, but the LORD will **t** me in. Ps 27:10
be strong, and let your heart **t** courage; Ps 27:14
In you, O LORD, do I **t** refuge; let me never Ps 31:1
you **t** me out of the net they have hidden Ps 31:4
against me, as they plot to **t** my life. Ps 31:13
worked for those who **t** refuge in you, Ps 31:19
Be strong, and let your heart **t** courage, Ps 31:24
none of those who **t** refuge in him will Ps 34:22
T hold of shield and buckler and rise for Ps 35:2
The children of mankind **t** refuge in the Ps 36:7
them, because they **t** refuge in him. Ps 37:40
For you are the God in whom I **t** refuge; Ps 43:2
recite my statutes or **t** my covenant on Ps 50:16
and **t** not your Holy Spirit from me. Ps 51:11
We used to **t** sweet counsel together; Ps 55:14
the shadow of your wings I will **t** refuge, Ps 57:1
Let me **t** refuge under the shelter of your Ps 61:4
position. They **t** pleasure in falsehood. Ps 62:4
rejoice in the LORD and **t** refuge in him! Ps 64:10
In you, O LORD, do I **t** refuge; let me never Ps 71:1
T it from the fold of your garment and Ps 74:11
"Let us **t** possession for ourselves of the Ps 83:12
"**t** me not away in the midst of my Ps 102:24
when you **t** away their breath, they die Ps 104:29
days be few; may another **t** his office! Ps 109:8
It is better to **t** refuge in the LORD than to Ps 118:8
It is better to **t** refuge in the LORD than to Ps 118:9
T away from me scorn and contempt, Ps 119:22
And **t** not the word of truth utterly out Ps 119:43
of your rules from of old, I **t** comfort, Ps 119:52
If I **t** the wings of the morning and dwell Ps 139:9
your enemies **t** your name in vain! Ps 139:20
my shield and he in whom I **t** refuge, Ps 144:2
lest strangers **t** their fill of your Prv 5:10
let us **t** our fill of love till morning; Prv 7:18
T my instruction instead of silver, and Prv 8:10
but with those who **t** advice is wisdom. Prv 13:10
T a man's garment when he has put Prv 20:16
T away the dross from the silver, and Prv 25:4
t away the wicked from the presence of Prv 25:5
T a man's garment when he has put Prv 27:13
is a shield to those who **t** refuge in him. Prv 30:5
the lizard you can **t** in your hands, yet Prv 30:28
wine, or for rulers to **t** strong drink, Prv 31:4
eat and drink and **t** pleasure in all his Eccl 3:13
who no longer knew how to **t** advice. Eccl 4:13
and shall **t** nothing for his toil that he Eccl 5:15
It is good that you should **t** hold of this, Eccl 7:18
Do not **t** to heart all the things that Eccl 7:21
Do not **t** your stand in an evil cause, for Eccl 8:3
For a man will **t** hold of his brother in the Is 3:6
that day the Lord will **t** away the finery of Is 3:18
And seven women shall **t** hold of one man Is 4:1
by your name; **t** away our reproach." Is 4:1
"**T** a large tablet and write on it in Is 8:1
T counsel together, but it will come to Is 8:10
him, to **t** spoil and seize plunder, Is 10:6
And the peoples will **t** them and bring Is 14:2
They will **t** captive those who were their Is 14:2
you will **t** up this taunt against the king Is 14:4
from your waist and **t** off your sandals Is 20:2
"**T** a harp; go about the city, O forgotten Is 23:16
of his people he will **t** away from all the Is 25:8
In days to come Jacob shall **t** root, Israel Is 27:6
often as it passes through it will **t** you; Is 28:19
to **t** refuge in the protection of Pharaoh Is 30:2
found with which to **t** fire from the Is 30:14
be divided; even the lame will **t** the prey. Is 33:23
until I come and **t** you away to a land Is 36:17
Judah shall again **t** root downward and Is 37:31
"Let them **t** a cake of figs and apply it to Is 38:21
I will **t** you by the hand and keep you; Is 42:6
him up, but he did not **t** it to heart. Is 42:25
your case; let them **t** counsel together! Is 45:21
T the millstones and grind flour, put off Is 47:2
I will **t** vengeance, and I will spare no one. Is 47:3
there is none to **t** her by the hand among Is 51:18
them off, a breath will **t** them away. Is 57:13
ourselves, and you **t** no knowledge of it?' Is 58:3
If you **t** away the yoke from your midst, Is 58:9
then you shall **t** delight in the LORD, and Is 58:14
put the LORD in remembrance, **t** no rest, Is 62:6
our iniquities, like the wind, **t** us away. Is 64:6
who rouses himself to **t** hold of you; Is 64:7
of them also I will **t** for priests and for Is 66:21
I will **t** you, one from a city and two from Jer 3:14
the streets of Jerusalem, look and **t** note! Jer 5:1
them, but they refused to **t** correction. Jer 5:3
object of scorn; they **t** no pleasure in it. Jer 6:10
"I will **t** up weeping and wailing for the Jer 9:10
You plant them, and they **t** root; they Jer 12:2
"**T** the loincloth that you have bought, Jer 13:4
and **t** from there the loincloth that I Jer 13:6
"**T** a lowly seat, for your beautiful Jer 13:18
Will not pangs **t** hold of you like those Jer 13:21
and **t** vengeance for me on my Jer 15:15
In your forbearance **t** me not away; Jer 15:15
"You shall not **t** a wife, nor shall you Jer 16:2
T care for the sake of your lives, and do Jer 17:21
have dug a pit to **t** me and laid snares Jer 18:22
and **t** some of the elders of the people and Jer 19:1
overcome him and **t** our revenge on Jer 20:10
"**T** from my hand this cup of the wine Jer 25:15
king of Babylon did not **t** away, Jer 27:20
T wives and have sons and daughters; Jer 29:6
t wives for your sons, and give your Jer 29:6
fathers, and they shall **t** possession of it." Jer 30:3
And he shall **t** Zedekiah to Babylon, and Jer 32:5
T these deeds, both this sealed deed of Jer 32:14
mounds have come up to the city to **t** it, Jer 32:24
will fight against it and **t** it and burn it Jer 34:22
"**T** a scroll and write on it all the words Jer 36:2
"**T** in your hand the scroll that you Jer 36:14
"**T** another scroll and write on it all the Jer 36:28
"**T** three men with you from here, Jer 38:10
him in chains to **t** him to Babylon. Jer 39:7
"**T** him, look after him well, and do Jer 39:12
Shaphan, that he should **t** him home. Jer 39:14
son of Nethaniah to **t** your life?" But Jer 40:14
Why should he **t** your life, so that all Jer 40:15
they may kill us or **t** us into exile in Jer 43:3
"**T** in your hands large stones and hide Jer 43:9
will send and **t** Nebuchadnezzar the Jer 43:10
I will **t** the remnant of Judah who have Jer 44:12
T your stations with your helmets, Jer 46:4
Go up to Gilead, and **t** balm, O virgin Jer 46:11
of the LORD: **t** vengeance on her; Jer 50:15
T balm for her pain; perhaps she may be Jer 51:8
"Sharpen the arrows! **T** up the shields! Jer 51:11
your cause and **t** vengeance for you. Jer 51:36
and **t** out of his mouth what he has Jer 51:44
of man, **t** a brick and lay it before you, Ezk 4:1
And you, **t** an iron griddle, and place it Ezk 4:3
"And you, **t** wheat and barley, beans and Ezk 4:9
"And you, O son of man, **t** a sharp sword. Ezk 5:1
Then **t** balances for weighing and divide Ezk 5:1
third part you shall **t** and strike with the Ezk 5:2
And you shall **t** from these a small Ezk 5:3
these again you shall **t** some and cast Ezk 5:4
of the nations to **t** possession of their Ezk 7:24
"**T** fire from between the whirling Ezk 10:6
Do people **t** a peg from it to hang any Ezk 15:3
your clothes and **t** your beautiful Ezk 16:39
be ashamed when you **t** your sisters, Ezk 16:61
It will not **t** a strong arm or many Ezk 17:9
"I myself will **t** a sprig from the lofty Ezk 17:22
does not lend at interest or **t** any profit, Ezk 18:8
t up a lamentation for the princes of Ezk 19:1
the turban and **t** off the crown. Ezk 21:26
In you they **t** bribes to shed blood; you Ezk 22:12
you **t** interest and profit and make Ezk 22:12
your clothes and **t** away your Ezk 23:26
you in hatred and **t** away all the fruit Ezk 23:29
all women may **t** warning and not Ezk 23:48
T the choicest one of the flock; pile the Ezk 24:5
T out of it piece after piece, without Ezk 24:6
To rouse my wrath, to **t** vengeance, I Ezk 24:8
I am about to **t** the delight of your eyes Ezk 24:16
the day when I **t** from them their Ezk 24:25
people of the land **t** a man from among Ezk 33:2
of the trumpet does not **t** warning, Ezk 33:4
of the trumpet and did not **t** warning; Ezk 33:5
and we will **t** possession of them'— Ezk 35:10
I will **t** you from the nations and Ezk 36:24
"Son of man, **t** a stick and write on it, Ezk 37:16
then **t** another stick and write on it, Ezk 37:16
I am about to **t** the stick of Joseph Ezk 37:19
I will **t** the people of Israel from the Ezk 37:21
gold, to **t** away livestock and goods, Ezk 38:13
they will not need to **t** wood out of the Ezk 39:10
And you shall **t** some of its blood and Ezk 43:20
You shall also **t** the bull of the sin Ezk 43:21
you shall **t** a bull from the herd Ezk 45:18
The priest shall **t** some of the blood of Ezk 45:19
and shall **t** his stand by the post of the Ezk 46:2
The prince shall not **t** any of the Ezk 46:18
up siegeworks and **t** a well-fortified Dn 11:15
be enraged and **t** action against the Dn 11:30
and shall **t** away the regular burnt Dn 11:31
their God shall stand firm and **t** action. Dn 11:32
t to yourself a wife of whoredom and Hos 1:2
Therefore I will **t** back my grain in its Hos 2:9
and I will **t** away my wool and my flax, Hos 2:9
wine, which **t** away the understanding. Hos 4:11
T with you words and return to the Hos 14:2
LORD; say to him, "**T** away all iniquity; Hos 14:2
he shall **t** root like the trees of Lebanon; Hos 14:5
when they shall **t** you away with hooks, Am 4:2
Hear this word that I **t** up over you in Am 5:1
who afflict the righteous, who **t** a bribe, Am 5:12
and I **t** no delight in your solemn Am 5:21
T away from me the noise of your Am 5:23
You shall **t** up Sikkuth your king, and Am 5:26
shall **t** him up to bring the bones out of Am 6:10
Sheol, from there shall my hand **t** them; Am 9:2
there I will search them out and **t** them; Am 9:3
The waters closed in over me to **t** my life; Jon 2:5
now, O LORD, please **t** my life from me, Jon 4:3
of Beth-ezel shall **t** away from you Mi 1:11
seize them, and houses, and **t** them away; Mi 2:2
In that day they shall **t** up a taunt song Mi 2:4
young children you **t** away my splendor Mi 2:9
he knows those who **t** refuge in him. Na 1:7
the mortar; **t** hold of the brick mold! Na 3:14
fortress, for they pile up earth and **t** it. Hab 1:10
I will **t** my stand at my watchpost and Hab 2:1
Shall not all these **t** up their taunt Hab 2:6
I will **t** joy in the God of my salvation. Hab 3:18
that I may **t** pleasure in it and that I may Hg 1:8
declares the LORD of hosts, I will **t** you, Hg 2:23
"**T** from the exiles Heldai, Tobijah, and Zec 6:10
T from them silver and gold, and make Zec 6:11
of every tongue shall **t** hold of the robe Zec 8:23
I will **t** away its blood from its mouth, Zec 9:7
"**T** once more the equipment of a Zec 11:15
sacrifice may come and **t** of them and Zec 14:21
if you will not **t** it to heart to give honor Mal 2:2
David, do not fear to **t** Mary as your wife, Mt 1:20
said, "Rise, **t** the child and his mother, Mt 2:13
t the child and his mother and go to the Mt 2:20
But I say to you, Do not **t** an oath at all, Mt 5:34
And do not **t** an oath by your head, for Mt 5:36
anyone would sue you and **t** your tunic, Mt 5:40
'Let me **t** the speck out of your eye,' Mt 7:4
first **t** the log out of your own eye, Mt 7:5
you will see clearly to **t** the speck out of Mt 7:5
faith, he said to the paralytic, "**T** heart, Mt 9:2
turned, and seeing her he said, "**T** heart, Mt 9:22
And whoever does not **t** his cross and Mt 10:38
violence, and the violent **t** it by force. Mt 11:12
T my yoke upon you, and learn from Mt 11:29
will not **t** hold of it and lift it out? Mt 12:11
Jesus spoke to them, saying, "**T** heart; Mt 14:27
is not right to **t** the children's bread Mt 15:26
him deny himself and **t** up his cross Mt 16:24
do kings of the earth **t** toll or tax? Mt 17:25
and cast a hook and **t** the first fish that Mt 17:27
T that and give it to them for me and Mt 17:27
t one or two others along with you, Mt 18:16
T what belongs to you and go. I choose Mt 20:14
are not alarmed, for this must **t** place, Mt 24:6
not go down to **t** what is in his Mt 24:17
in the field not turn back to **t** his cloak. Mt 24:18
pass away until all these things **t** place. Mt 24:34
So **t** the talent from him and give it to Mt 25:28
gave it to the disciples, and said, "**T**, eat; Mt 26:26
to them, "Sleep and **t** your rest later on. Mt 26:45
For all who **t** the sword will perish by Mt 26:52
or to say, 'Rise, **t** up your bed and walk'? Mk 2:9
He charged them to **t** nothing for their Mk 6:8
he spoke to them and said, "**T** heart; Mk 6:50
is not right to **t** the children's bread and Mk 7:27
broken pieces did you **t** up?" They said Mk 8:19
broken pieces did you **t** up?" And they Mk 8:20
him deny himself and **t** up his cross Mk 8:34
blind man, saying to him, "**T** heart. Mk 10:49
the man must **t** the widow and raise Mk 12:19
This must **t** place, but the end is not yet. Mk 13:7
nor enter his house, to **t** anything out, Mk 13:15
the field not turn back to **t** his cloak. Mk 13:16
away until all these things **t** place. Mk 13:30
to them, and said, "**T**; this is my body." Mk 14:22
mixed with myrrh, but he did not **t** it. Mk 15:23
for them, to decide what each should **t**. Mk 15:24
Elijah will come to **t** him down." Mk 15:36
until the day that these things **t** place, Lk 1:20
to **t** away my reproach among people." Lk 1:25
let me **t** out the speck that is in your eye,' Lk 6:42
first **t** the log out of your own eye, Lk 6:42
will see clearly to **t** out the speck that Lk 6:42
T care then how you hear, for to the one Lk 8:18
to them, "**T** nothing for your journey, Lk 9:3
him deny himself and **t** up his cross Lk 9:23
the innkeeper, saying, '**T** care of him, Lk 10:35
And he said to them, "**T** care, and be on Lk 12:15
begin with shame to **t** the lowest place. Lk 14:9
He said to him, '**T** your bill, and sit Lk 16:6
He said to him, '**T** your bill, and write Lk 16:7
house, not come down to **t** them away, Lk 17:31
You **t** what you did not deposit, and Lk 19:21
who stood by, '**T** the mina from him, Lk 19:24

the man must **t** the widow and raise up Lk 20:28
when these things are about to **t** place?" Lk 21:7
for these things must first **t** place, Lk 21:9
when these things begin to **t** place, Lk 21:28
these things that are going to **t** place, Lk 21:36
he had given thanks he said, "**T** this, Lk 22:17
let the one who has a moneybag **t** it, Lk 22:36
"Now draw some out and **t** it to the master Jn 2:8
sold the pigeons, "**T** these things away; Jn 2:16
Jesus said to him, "Get up, **t** up your bed, Jn 5:8
it is not lawful for you to **t** up your bed." Jn 5:10
me, that man said to me, '**T** up your bed, Jn 5:11
said to you, '**T** up your bed and walk'?" Jn 5:12
were about to come and **t** him by force to Jn 6:15
they were glad to **t** him into the boat, Jn 6:21
said to them, "Do you **t** offense at this? Jn 6:61
down my life that I may **t** it up again. Jn 10:17
and I have authority to **t** it up again. Jn 10:18
Jesus said, "**T** away the stone." Martha, Jn 11:39
Romans will come and **t** away both our Jn 11:48
that when it does **t** place you may Jn 13:19
will come again and will **t** you to myself, Jn 14:3
that when it does **t** place you may Jn 14:29
for he will **t** what is mine and declare it Jn 16:14
I said that he will **t** what is mine and Jn 16:15
and no one will **t** your joy from you. Jn 16:22
you will have tribulation. But **t** heart; Jn 16:33
do not ask that you **t** them out of the Jn 17:15
"**T** him yourselves and judge him by Jn 18:31
"**T** him yourselves and crucify him, Jn 19:6
Pilate that he might **t** away the body of Jn 19:38
have laid him, and I will **t** him away." Jn 20:15
in it'; and "'Let another **t** his office.' Acts 1:20
to **t** the place in this ministry and Acts 1:25
your plan had predestined to **t** place. Acts 4:28
t care what you are about to do with Acts 5:35
him, '**T** off the sandals from your feet, Acts 7:33
to **t** from them a people for his name. Acts 15:14
Barnabas wanted to **t** with them John Acts 15:37
thought best not to **t** with them one Acts 15:38
them come themselves and **t** us out." Acts 16:37
intending to **t** Paul aboard there, Acts 20:13
t these men and purify yourself along Acts 21:24
toward Damascus to **t** those also who Acts 22:5
to go down and **t** him away from Acts 23:10
stood by him and said, "**T** courage, Acts 23:11
"**T** this young man to the tribune, Acts 23:17
So I always **t** pains to have a clear Acts 24:16
Yet now I urge you to **t** heart, for there Acts 27:22
So **t** heart, men, for I have faith in Acts 27:25
Paul urged them all to **t** some food, Acts 27:33
Therefore I urge you to **t** some food. It Acts 27:34
with them when I **t** away their sins." Rom 11:27
Let each one **t** care how he builds 1 Cor 3:10
Shall I then **t** the members of Christ 1 Cor 6:15
But **t** care that this right of yours does 1 Cor 8:9
have the right to **t** along a believing 1 Cor 9:5
thinks that he stands **t** heed lest he 1 Cor 10:12
We **t** this course so that no one 2 Cor 8:20
and **t** every thought captive to obey 2 Cor 10:5
Did I **t** advantage of you through 2 Cor 12:17
him. Did Titus **t** advantage of you? 2 Cor 12:18
spirit? Did we not **t** the same steps? 2 Cor 12:18
Lord that you will **t** no other view than Gal 5:10
T no part in the unfruitful works of Eph 5:11
Therefore **t** up the whole armor of God, Eph 6:13
In all circumstances **t** up the shield of Eph 6:16
and **t** the helmet of salvation, and the Eph 6:17
in this letter, **t** note of that person, 2 Thes 3:14
hands, nor **t** part in the sins of others; 1 Tm 5:22
and we cannot **t** anything out of the 1 Tm 6:7
T hold of the eternal life to which you 1 Tm 6:12
so that they may **t** hold of that which 1 Tm 6:19
T care, brothers, lest there be in any of Heb 3:12
in the law to **t** tithes from the people, Heb 7:5
blood of bulls and goats to **t** away sins. Heb 10:4
which can never **t** away sins. Heb 10:11
t the prophets who spoke in the name of Jas 5:10
t care that you are not carried away 2 Pt 3:17
know that he appeared to **t** away sins, 1 Jn 3:5
the things that must soon **t** place. Rv 1:1
are and those that are to **t** place after this. Rv 1:19
show you what must **t** place after this." Rv 4:1
"Worthy are you to **t** the scroll and to Rv 5:9
rider was permitted to **t** peace from the Rv 6:4
t the scroll that is open in the hand of the Rv 10:8
And he said to me, "**T** and eat it; it will Rv 10:9
her, my people, lest you **t** part in her sins, Rv 18:4
his servants what must soon **t** place." Rv 22:6
let the one who desires **t** the water of life Rv 22:17
God will **t** away his share in the tree of Rv 22:19

TAKEN (278)

the LORD God had **t** from the man he Gn 2:22
Woman, because she was **t** out of Man." Gn 2:23
to the ground, for out of it you were **t**; Gn 3:19
work the ground from which he was **t**. Gn 3:23
vengeance shall be **t** on him sevenfold." Gn 4:15
the woman was **t** into Pharaoh's Gn 12:15
that his kinsman had been **t** captive, Gn 14:14
of the woman whom you have **t**, Gn 20:3
and he has **t** away your blessing." Gn 27:35
now he has **t** away my blessing." Then Gn 27:36
that you have **t** away my husband? Gn 30:15
said, "God has **t** away my reproach." Gn 30:23
"Jacob has **t** all that was our father's, Gn 31:1
Thus God has **t** away the livestock of Gn 31:9
wealth that God has **t** away from our Gn 31:16
Now Rachel had **t** the household gods Gn 31:34
Portions were **t** to them from Joseph's Gn 43:34
in Egypt that you have **t** us away to die Ex 14:11
Moses' father-in-law, had **t** Zipporah, Ex 18:2
of the ark; they shall not be **t** from it. Ex 25:15
whenever the cloud was **t** up from over Ex 40:36
But if the cloud was not **t** up, then they Ex 40:37
not set out till the day that it was **t** up. Ex 40:37
(just as these are **t** from the ox of the Lv 4:10
is contributed I have **t** from the people of Lv 7:34
after he has **t** out the stones and scraped Lv 14:43
I have **t** the Levites from among the Nm 3:12
her, since she was not **t** in the act, Nm 5:13
of Israel, I have **t** them for myself. Nm 8:16
and I have **t** the Levites instead of all Nm 8:18
And when the tabernacle was **t** down, Nm 10:17
I have not **t** one donkey from them, Nm 16:15
I have **t** your brothers the Levites from Nm 18:6
and it shall be **t** outside the camp and Nm 19:3
king of Moab and **t** all his land out Nm 21:26
of our father be **t** away from his clan Nm 27:4
the count of the plunder that was **t**, Nm 31:26
army had each **t** plunder for himself.) Nm 31:53
inheritance will be **t** from the Nm 36:3
So it will be **t** away from the lot of our Nm 36:3
inheritance will be **t** from the Nm 36:4
But the LORD has **t** you and brought you Dt 4:20
has betrothed a wife and has not **t** her? Dt 20:7
to be happy with his wife whom he has **t**. Dt 24:5
inheritance and have **t** possession of it Dt 26:1
But the woman had **t** the two men and Jos 2:4
they have **t** some of the devoted things; Jos 7:11
And he who is **t** with the devoted things Jos 7:15
by tribe, and the tribe of Judah was **t**. Jos 7:16
and the clan of the Zerahites was **t**. Jos 7:17
Zerahites man by man, and Zabdi was **t**. Jos 7:17
son of Zerah, of the tribe of Judah, was **t**. Jos 7:18
And as soon as you have **t** the city, you Jos 8:8
because he has **t** his wife and given her Jgs 15:6
pieces of silver that were **t** from you, Jgs 17:2
but no one has **t** me into his house. Jgs 19:18
evil is this that has **t** place among you? Jgs 20:12
LORD?" For they had **t** a great oath Jgs 21:5
the Philistines had **t** from Israel were 1 Sm 7:14
the tribe of Benjamin was **t** by lot. 1 Sm 10:20
the clan of the Matrites was **t** by lot; 1 Sm 10:21
and Saul the son of Kish was **t** by lot. 1 Sm 10:21
his anointed. Whose ox have I **t**? 1 Sm 12:3
I taken? Or whose donkey have I **t**? 1 Sm 12:3
whose hand have I **t** a bribe to blind 1 Sm 12:3
oppressed us or **t** anything from any 1 Sm 12:4
And Jonathan and Saul were **t**, 1 Sm 14:41
son Jonathan." And Jonathan was **t**. 1 Sm 14:42
When Saul had **t** the kingship over 1 Sm 14:47
by hot bread on the day it is **t** away. 1 Sm 21:6
I have **t** my life in my hand and have 1 Sm 28:21
and **t** captive the women and all who 1 Sm 30:2
and sons and daughters **t** captive. 1 Sm 30:3
two wives also had been **t** captive, 1 Sm 30:5
And when he had **t** him down, 1 Sm 30:16
great spoil they had **t** from the land 1 Sm 30:16
all that the Amalekites had **t**, 1 Sm 30:18
spoil or anything that had been **t**. 1 Sm 30:19
the sword and have **t** his wife to be 2 Sm 12:9
despised me and have **t** the wife of 2 Sm 12:10
moreover, I have **t** the city of waters. 2 Sm 12:27
in his lifetime had **t** and set up for 2 Sm 18:18
He had neither **t** care of his feet nor 2 Sm 19:24
When he was **t** out of the highway, 2 Sm 20:13
for they cannot be **t** with the hand; 2 Sm 23:6
Naphtali (he had **t** Basemath the 1 Kgs 4:15
daughter whom he had **t** in marriage. 1 Kgs 7:8
But the high places were not **t** away. 1 Kgs 15:14
when Zimri saw that the city was **t**, 1 Kgs 16:18
killed and also **t** possession?"' And 1 Kgs 21:19
Yet the high places were not **t** away, 1 Kgs 22:43
before I am **t** from you." And Elisha 2 Kgs 2:9
you see me as I am being **t** from you, 2 Kgs 2:10
'See, you have **t** all this trouble for us; 2 Kgs 4:13
whom you have **t** captive with your 2 Kgs 6:22
the high places were not **t** away; 2 Kgs 12:3
that he had **t** from Jehoahaz his 2 Kgs 13:25
the high places were not **t** away. 2 Kgs 15:4
king of Israel, Samaria was **t**. 2 Kgs 18:10
be born to you, shall be **t** away, 2 Kgs 20:18
of Babylon had **t** all that belonged 2 Kgs 24:7
So Judah was **t** into exile out of its 2 Kgs 25:21
And Judah was **t** into exile in Babylon 1 Chr 9:1
when they were brought in and **t** out. 1 Chr 9:28
of them that David his father had **t**, 2 Chr 2:17
cities that he had **t** in the hill country 2 Chr 15:8
high places were not **t** out of Israel. 2 Chr 15:17
And when he had **t** counsel with the 2 Chr 20:21
places, however, were not **t** away; 2 Chr 20:33
your relatives whom you have **t**, 2 Chr 28:11
of Judah, and had **t** Beth-shemesh, 2 Chr 28:18
in Jerusalem had **t** counsel to keep 2 Chr 30:2
this same Hezekiah **t** away his high 2 Chr 32:12
of Barzillai (who had **t** a wife from the Ezr 2:61
which Nebuchadnezzar had **t** out of the Ezr 5:14
For they have **t** some of their daughters Ezr 9:2
cities who have **t** foreign wives come Ezr 10:14
son Jehohanan had **t** the daughter of Neh 6:18
of Barzillai (who had **t** a wife of the Neh 7:63
Esther also was **t** into the king's palace Est 2:8
who had **t** her as his own daughter, Est 2:15
when Esther was **t** to King Ahasuerus Est 2:16
signet ring, which he had **t** from Haman, Est 8:2
The LORD gave, and the LORD has **t** away; Jb 1:21
me my glory and **t** the crown from my Jb 19:9
"As God lives, who has **t** away my right, Jb 27:2
Iron is **t** out of the earth, and copper is Jb 28:2
me; days of affliction have **t** hold of me. Jb 30:16
the right, and God has **t** away my right; Jb 34:5
and the mighty are **t** away by no Jb 34:20
God has **t** his place in the divine council; Ps 82:1
for you have **t** me up and thrown me Ps 102:10
the treacherous are **t** captive by their Prv 11:6
should your bed be **t** from under you? Prv 22:27
those who are being **t** away to death; Prv 24:11
be added to it, nor anything **t** from it. Eccl 3:14
escapes her, but the sinner is **t** by her. Eccl 7:26
time. Like fish that are **t** in an evil net, Eccl 9:12
The LORD has **t** his place to contend; he Is 3:13
coal that he had **t** with tongs from the Is 6:6
your guilt is **t** away, and your sin atoned Is 6:7
be broken; they shall be snared and **t**." Is 8:15
joy and gladness are **t** away from the Is 16:10
He has **t** away the covering of Judah. In Is 22:8
from the milk, those **t** from the breast? Is 28:9
and be broken, and snared, and **t**. Is 28:13
and in falsehood we have **t** shelter"; Is 28:15
whom you will father, shall be **t** away, Is 39:7
scarcely has their stem **t** root in the Is 40:24
Can the prey be **t** from the mighty, or Is 49:24
the captives of the mighty shall be **t**, Is 49:25
I have **t** from your hand the cup of Is 51:22
that my people are **t** away for nothing? Is 52:5
oppression and judgment he was **t** away; Is 53:8
devout men are **t** away, while no one Is 57:1
righteous man is **t** away from calamity; Is 57:1
both husband and wife shall be **t**, the Jer 6:11
anguish has **t** hold of us, pain as of a Jer 6:24
to shame; they shall be dismayed and **t**; Jer 8:9
I mourn, and dismay has **t** hold on me. Jer 8:21
the LORD'S flock has been **t** captive. Jer 13:17
all Judah is **t** into exile, wholly taken Jer 13:19
is taken into exile, wholly **t** into exile. Jer 13:19
for I have **t** away my peace from this Jer 16:5
king of Babylon had **t** into exile from Jer 24:1
whom Nebuchadnezzar had **t** into exile Jer 29:1
army of the king of Babylon and be **t**." Jer 38:3
until the day that Jerusalem was **t**. Jer 38:28
And when they had **t** him, they brought Jer 39:5
who had not been **t** into exile to Babylon, Jer 40:7
dwell in your cities that you have **t**." Jer 40:10
Kiriathaim is put to shame, it is **t**; the Jer 48:1
and your treasures, you also shall be **t**; Jer 48:7
and joy have been **t** away from the Jer 48:33
the cities shall be **t** and the strongholds Jer 48:41
for your sons have been **t** captive, Jer 48:46
anguish and sorrows have **t** hold of her, Jer 49:24
Their tents and their flocks shall be **t**, Jer 49:29
'Babylon is **t**, Bel is put to shame, Jer 50:2
against her. From there she shall be **t**. Jer 50:9
I set a snare for you and you were **t**, O Jer 50:24
No stone shall be **t** from you for a Jer 51:26
Babylon that his city is **t** on every side; Jer 51:31
"How Babylon is **t**, the praise of the Jer 51:41
her, upon Babylon; her warriors are **t**; Jer 51:56
So Judah was **t** into exile out of its land. Jer 52:27
"You have **t** up my cause, O Lord; you Lam 3:58
him, and he shall be **t** in my snare. Ezk 12:13
these men have **t** their idols into their Ezk 14:3
Is wood **t** from it to make anything? Do Ezk 15:3
chief men of the land he had **t** away), Ezk 17:13
him, and he shall be **t** in my snare, Ezk 17:20
their net over him; he was **t** in their pit. Ezk 19:8

like lightning; it is **t** up for slaughter. Ezk 21:15
to remembrance, that they may be **t**. Ezk 21:23
remembrance, you shall be **t** in hand. Ezk 21:24
they have **t** treasure and precious Ezk 22:25
But if he had **t** warning, he would have Ezk 33:5
that person is **t** away in his iniquity, Ezk 33:6
gives back what he has **t** by robbery, Ezk 33:15
his father had **t** out of the Dn 5:2
vessels that had been **t** out of the temple, Dn 5:3
throne, and his glory was **t** from him. Dn 5:20
commanded that Daniel be **t** up out of Dn 6:23
So Daniel was **t** up out of the den, and no Dn 6:23
the beasts, their dominion was **t** away, Dn 7:12
and his dominion shall be **t** away, Dn 7:26
burnt offering was **t** away from him, Dn 8:11
And when the multitude is **t** away, his Dn 11:12
burnt offering is **t** away and the Dn 12:11
and even the fish of the sea are **t** away. Hos 4:3
For you have **t** my silver and my gold, and Jl 3:5
every altar on garments **t** in pledge, Am 2:8
cry out from his den, if he has **t** nothing? Am 3:4
from the ground, when it has **t** nothing? Am 3:5
The LORD has **t** away the judgments Zep 3:15
I have **t** your iniquity away from you, Zec 3:4
when the spoil **t** from you will be Zec 14:1
the city shall be **t** and the houses Zec 14:2
bring what has been **t** by violence or is Mal 1:13
and you shall be **t** away with it. Mal 2:3
the bridegroom is **t** away from them, Mt 9:15
not, even what he has will be **t** away. Mt 13:12
fellow servants saw what had **t** place, Mt 18:31
to their master all that had **t** place. Mt 18:31
'Be **t** up and thrown into the sea,' Mt 21:21
of God will be **t** away from you and Mt 21:43
we would not have **t** part with them in Mt 23:30
be in the field; one will be **t** and one left. Mt 24:40
at the mill; one will be **t** and one left. Mt 24:41
not, even what he has will be **t** away. Mt 25:29
But all this has **t** place that the Mt 26:56
the chief priests all that had **t** place. Mt 28:11
with the elders and **t** counsel, Mt 28:12
the bridegroom is **t** away from them, Mk 2:20
not, even what he has will be **t** away." Mk 4:25
And after he had **t** leave of them, he Mk 6:46
'Be **t** up and thrown into the sea,' Mk 11:23
was **t** up into heaven and sat down at Mk 16:19
at the catch of fish that they had **t**, Lk 5:9
the bridegroom is **t** away from them, Lk 5:35
he thinks that he has will be **t** away." Lk 8:18
the days drew near for him to be **t** up, Lk 9:51
which will not be **t** away from her." Lk 10:42
For you have **t** away the key of Lk 11:52
one bed. One will be **t** and the other left. Lk 17:34
One will be **t** and the other left." Lk 17:35
not, even what he has will be **t** away. Lk 19:26
will not pass away until all has **t** place. Lk 21:32
the centurion saw what had **t** place, Lk 23:47
when they saw what had **t** place, Lk 23:48
"It has **t** forty-six years to build this Jn 2:20
Then after he had **t** the morsel, Satan Jn 13:27
broken and that they might be **t** away. Jn 19:31
the stone had been **t** away from the tomb. Jn 20:1
"They have **t** the Lord out of the tomb, Jn 20:2
to them, "They have **t** away my Lord, Jn 20:13
until the day when he was **t** up, after he Acts 1:2
who was **t** up from you into heaven, Acts 1:11
the day when he was **t** up from us— Acts 1:22
For his life is **t** away from the earth." Acts 8:33
and the thing was **t** up at once to Acts 10:16
when they had **t** money as security Acts 17:9
from the third story and was **t** up dead. Acts 20:9
and without food, having **t** nothing. Acts 27:33
And when this had **t** place, the rest of Acts 28:9
only through Christ is it **t** away. 2 Cor 3:14
no one, we have **t** advantage of no one. 2 Cor 7:2
you of everything that has **t** place here. Col 4:9
believed on in the world, **t** up in glory. 1 Tm 3:16
sin offerings you have **t** no pleasure. Heb 10:6
neither desired nor **t** pleasure in Heb 10:8
By faith Enoch was **t** up so that he Heb 11:5
was not found, because God had **t** him. Heb 11:5
before he was **t** he was commended Heb 11:5
And when he had **t** the scroll, the four Rv 5:8
for you have **t** your great power and Rv 11:17
If anyone is to be **t** captive, to captivity Rv 13:10

TAKES (75)

hold him guiltless who **t** his name in Ex 20:7
If he **t** another wife to himself, he shall Ex 21:10
the man does not die but **t** to his bed, Ex 21:18
who **t** in hunting any beast or bird that Lv 17:13
If a man **t** a woman and her mother Lv 20:14
"If a man **t** his sister, a daughter of his Lv 20:17
If a man **t** his brother's wife, it is Lv 20:21
"Whoever **t** a human life shall surely Lv 24:17
Whoever **t** an animal's life shall make Lv 24:18
accordance with the vow that he **t**, Nm 6:21
burned when Asshur **t** you away Nm 24:22
hold him guiltless who **t** his name in Dt 5:11
God, who is not partial and **t** no bribe. Dt 10:17
"If any man **t** a wife and goes in to her Dt 22:13
"When a man **t** a wife and marries her, if Dt 24:1
"'Cursed be anyone who **t** a bribe to Dt 27:25
and my hand **t** hold on judgment, Dt 32:41
of his children and **t** vengeance on his Dt 32:43
tribe that the LORD **t** by lot shall come Jos 7:14
clan that the LORD **t** shall come near by Jos 7:14
that the LORD **t** shall come near Jos 7:14
this Philistine and **t** away the 1 Sm 17:26
boast himself like he who **t** it off.'" 1 Kgs 20:11
his harvest, and he **t** it even out of thorns, Jb 5:5
are trusted and **t** away the discernment Jb 12:20
He **t** away understanding from the Jb 12:24
cuts him off, when God **t** away his life? Jb 27:8
and the pain that gnaws me **t** no rest. Jb 30:17
nor **t** up a reproach against his friend; Ps 15:3
Blessed is the man who **t** refuge in him! Ps 34:8
needy, but the Lord **t** thought for me. Ps 40:17
to me, for in you my soul **t** refuge; Ps 57:1
shall he be who **t** your little ones and Ps 137:9
see: there is none who **t** notice of me; Ps 142:4
but the LORD **t** pleasure in those who Ps 147:11
For the LORD **t** pleasure in his people; he Ps 149:4
gain; it **t** away the life of its possessors. Prv 1:19
and he will not spare when he **t** revenge. Prv 6:34
the way, at the crossroads she **t** her stand; Prv 8:2
she **t** a seat on the highest places of the Prv 9:14
rules his spirit than he who **t** a city. Prv 16:32
A fool **t** no pleasure in understanding, Prv 18:2
is like one who **t** off a garment on Prv 25:20
own is like one who **t** a passing dog by Prv 26:17
There is a vanity that **t** place on earth, Eccl 8:14
he **t** up the coastlands like fine dust. Is 40:15
The ironsmith **t** a cutting tool and Is 44:12
He **t** a part of it and warms himself; he Is 44:15
But he who **t** refuge in me shall possess Is 57:13
and he who **t** an oath in the land shall Is 65:16
and archer every city **t** to flight; Jer 4:29
house of Israel who **t** his idols into his Ezk 14:4
lends at interest, and **t** profit; shall he Ezk 18:13
from iniquity, **t** no interest or profit, Ezk 18:17
and the sword comes and **t** him away, Ezk 33:4
the sword comes and **t** any one of them, Ezk 33:6
the LORD **t** vengeance on his adversaries Na 1:2
before the decree **t** effect —before the day Zep 2:2
immediately comes and **t** away the Mk 4:15
and from one who **t** away your cloak do Lk 6:29
and from one who **t** away your goods do Lk 6:30
the devil comes and **t** away the word Lk 8:12
he **t** away his armor in which he Lk 11:22
of God, who **t** away the sin of the world! Jn 1:29
No one **t** it from me, but I lay it down of Jn 10:18
telling you this now, before it **t** place, Jn 13:19
now I have told you before it **t** place, Jn 14:29
mine that does not bear fruit he **t** away, Jn 15:2
devours you, or **t** advantage of you, 2 Cor 11:20
it that no one **t** you captive by Col 2:8
so that he **t** his seat in the temple of 2 Thes 2:4
And no one **t** this honor for himself, but Heb 5:4
For a will **t** effect only at death, since it Heb 9:17
for whoever greets him **t** part in his 2 Jn 1:11
and if anyone **t** away from the words of Rv 22:19

TAKING (50)

t all sorts of choice gifts from his Gn 24:10
T one of the stones of the place, he put Gn 28:11
and **t** off her veil she put on the Gn 38:19
t with you some of the elders of Israel, Ex 17:5
upward, **t** the number of their names. Nm 3:40
to their sons or **t** their daughters for your Dt 7:3
pledge, for that would be **t** a life in pledge. Dt 24:6
t 10,000 from the people of Naphtali and Jgs 4:6
and **t** hold of his concubine he divided Jgs 19:29
or for my lord **t** vengeance himself. 1 Sm 25:31
as he was **t** his noonday rest. 2 Sm 4:5
went, **t** with him ten talents of silver, 2 Kgs 5:5
our God, or partiality or **t** bribes." 2 Chr 19:7
They were three days in **t** the spoil, it 2 Chr 20:25
While this was **t** place, I was not in Neh 13:6
I have seen the fool **t** root, but suddenly I Jb 5:3
near her corner, **t** the road to her house Prv 7:8
GOD of hosts is **t** away from Jerusalem and Is 3:1
t his idols into his heart and putting the Ezk 14:7
grievously offended in **t** vengeance on Ezk 25:12
with me, "Where are they **t** the basket?" Zec 5:10
and **t** the five loaves and the two fish, Mt 14:19
And **t** with him Peter and the two sons Mt 26:37
But the chief priests, **t** the pieces of silver, Mt 27:6
T her by the hand he said to her, Mk 5:41
And **t** the five loaves and the two fish he Mk 6:41
And **t** him aside from the crowd Mk 7:33
midst of them, and **t** him in his arms, Mk 9:36
And **t** the twelve again, he began to tell Mk 10:32
also, when you see these things **t** place, Mk 13:29
"Are you still sleeping and **t** your rest? Mk 14:41
a linen shroud, and **t** him down, Mk 15:46
But **t** her by the hand he called, saying, Lk 8:54
And **t** the five loaves and the two fish, he Lk 9:16
my master is **t** the management away Lk 16:3
And **t** the twelve, he said to them, "See, Lk 18:31
t what I did not deposit and reaping Lk 19:22
also, when you see these things **t** place, Lk 21:31
the tomb, **t** the spices they had prepared. Lk 24:1
thought that he meant **t** rest in sleep. Jn 11:13
aside his outer garments, and **t** a towel, Jn 13:4
and **t** food, he was strengthened. For Acts 9:19
and **t** some wicked men of the rabble, Acts 17:5
But on **t** leave of them he said, "I will Acts 18:21
bent over him, and **t** him in his arms, Acts 20:10
for the favor of **t** part in the relief 2 Cor 8:4
with Barnabas, **t** Titus along with me. Gal 2:1
himself nothing, **t** the form of a servant, Phil 2:7
like a nursing mother **t** care of her 1 Thes 2:7
but once a year, and not without **t** blood, Heb 9:7

TALE (1)

these words seemed to them an idle **t**, Lk 24:11

TALENT (13)

all these utensils, out of a **t** of pure gold. Ex 25:39
all its utensils out of a **t** of pure gold. Ex 37:24
bases for the hundred talents, a **t** a base. Ex 38:27
The weight of it was a **t** of gold, and 2 Sm 12:30
or else you shall pay a **t** of silver.' 1 Kgs 20:39
Please give them a **t** of silver and two 2 Kgs 5:22
talents of silver and a **t** of gold. 2 Kgs 23:33
He found that it weighed a **t** of gold, 1 Chr 20:2
talents of silver and a **t** of gold. 2 Chr 36:3
had received the one **t** went and dug in Mt 25:18
had received the one **t** came forward, Mt 25:24
I went and hid your **t** in the ground. Mt 25:25
So take the **t** from him and give it to Mt 25:28

TALENTS (53)

was twenty-nine **t** and 730 shekels, Ex 38:24
was a hundred **t** and 1,775 shekels, Ex 38:25
The hundred **t** of silver were for casting Ex 38:27
a hundred bases for the hundred **t**, a Ex 38:27
offered was seventy **t** and 2,400 shekels; Ex 38:29
had sent to the king 120 **t** of gold. 1 Kgs 9:14
and brought from there gold, 420 **t**, 1 Kgs 9:28
Then she gave the king 120 **t** of gold, 1 Kgs 10:10
in one year was 666 **t** of gold, 1 Kgs 10:14
from Shemer for two **t** of silver, 1 Kgs 16:24
went, taking with him ten **t** of silver, 2 Kgs 5:5
pleased to accept two **t**." And he urged 2 Kgs 5:23
him and tied up two **t** of silver in two 2 Kgs 5:23
gave Pul a thousand **t** of silver, 2 Kgs 15:19
Judah three hundred **t** of silver and 2 Kgs 18:14
talents of silver and thirty **t** of gold. 2 Kgs 18:14
tribute of a hundred **t** of silver and a 2 Kgs 23:33
Ammonites sent 1,000 **t** of silver to 1 Chr 19:6
house of the LORD 100,000 **t** of gold, 1 Chr 22:14
talents of gold, a million **t** of silver, 1 Chr 22:14
3,000 **t** of gold, of the gold of Ophir, 1 Chr 29:4
of Ophir, and 7,000 **t** of refined silver, 1 Chr 29:4
of God 5,000 **t** and 10,000 darics 1 Chr 29:7
darics of gold, 10,000 **t** of silver, 1 Chr 29:7
18,000 **t** of bronze and 100,000 talents 1 Chr 29:7
of bronze and 100,000 **t** of iron. 1 Chr 29:7
He overlaid it with 600 **t** of fine gold. 2 Chr 3:8
brought from there 450 **t** of gold and 2 Chr 8:18
Then she gave the king 120 **t** of gold, 2 Chr 9:9
in one year was 666 **t** of gold, 2 Chr 9:13
of valor from Israel for 100 **t** of silver. 2 Chr 25:6
do about the hundred **t** that I have 2 Chr 25:9
gave him that year 100 **t** of silver, 2 Chr 27:5
tribute of a hundred **t** of silver and a 2 Chr 36:3
up to 100 **t** of silver, 100 cors of wheat, Ezr 7:22
out into their hand 650 **t** of silver, Ezr 8:26
of silver, and silver vessels worth 200 **t**, Ezr 8:26
worth 200 talents, and 100 **t** of gold, Ezr 8:26
and I will pay 10,000 **t** of silver into the Est 3:9
to him who owed him ten thousand **t**. Mt 18:24
To one he gave five **t**, to another two, to Mt 25:15
had received the five **t** went at once and Mt 25:16
with them, and he made five **t** more. Mt 25:16
who had the two **t** made two talents Mt 25:17
had the two talents made two **t** more. Mt 25:17
had received the five **t** came forward, Mt 25:20
came forward, bringing five **t** more, Mt 25:20
'Master, you delivered to me five **t**; Mt 25:20
talents; here I have made five **t** more.' Mt 25:20
also who had the two **t** came forward, Mt 25:22
'Master, you delivered to me two **t**; Mt 25:22
talents; here I have made two **t** more.' Mt 25:22
and give it to him who has the ten **t**. Mt 25:28

TALITHA (1)
he said to her, "**T** cumi," which means, Mk 5:41

TALK (35)
I will come down and **t** with you there. Nm 11:17
and shall **t** of them when you sit in your Dt 6:7
T no more so very proudly, let not 1 Sm 2:3
"You know the fellow and his **t**." 2 Kgs 9:11
and a man full of **t** be judged right? Jb 11:2
Should he argue in unprofitable **t**, or in Jb 15:3
me; when I rise they **t** against me. Jb 19:18
Job opens his mouth in empty **t**; he Jb 35:16
they **t** of laying snares secretly, thinking, Ps 64:5
I am the **t** of those who sit in the gate, Ps 69:12
And my tongue will **t** of your righteous Ps 71:24
speech, and put devious **t** far from you. Prv 4:24
when you awake, they will **t** with you. Prv 6:22
with her smooth **t** she compels him. Prv 7:21
profit, but mere **t** tends only to poverty. Prv 14:23
violence, and their lips **t** of trouble. Prv 24:2
and the end of his **t** is evil madness. Eccl 10:13
your people who **t** together about you Ezk 33:30
for with lustful **t** in their mouths they Ezk 33:31
and you became the **t** and evil gossip of Ezk 36:3
can my lord's servant **t** with my lord? Dn 10:17
plotted how to entangle him in his **t**. Mt 22:15
went out and began to **t** freely about it, Mk 1:45
of the Herodians, to trap him in his **t**. Mk 12:13
I will no longer **t** much with you, for the Jn 14:30
and by smooth **t** and flattery they Rom 16:18
find out not the **t** of these arrogant 1 Cor 4:19
does not consist in **t** but in power. 1 Cor 4:20
Let no corrupting **t** come out of your Eph 4:29
filthiness nor foolish **t** nor crude joking, Eph 5:4
slander, and obscene **t** from your mouth. Col 3:8
and their **t** will spread like gangrene. 2 Tm 2:17
not love in word or **t** but in deed and in 1 Jn 3:18
I hope to come to you and **t** face to face, 2 Jn 1:12
see you soon, and we will **t** face to face. 3 Jn 1:14

TALKED (23)
After that his brothers **t** with him. Gn 45:15
yourselves that I have **t** with you from Ex 20:22
to him, and Moses **t** with them. Ex 34:31
he went down and **t** with the woman, Jgs 14:7
As he **t** with them, behold, the 1 Sm 17:23
And as they still went on and **t**, 2 Kgs 2:11
Quarter), and they **t** with her. 2 Kgs 22:14
The angel who **t** with me said to me, 'I Zec 1:9
words to the angel who **t** with me. Zec 1:13
So the angel who **t** with me said to me, Zec 1:14
And I said to the angel who **t** with me, Zec 1:19
the angel who **t** with me came forward, Zec 2:3
And the angel who **t** with me came again Zec 4:1
And I said to the angel who **t** with me, Zec 4:4
Then the angel who **t** with me answered Zec 4:5
Then the angel who **t** with me came Zec 5:5
Then I said to the angel who **t** with me, Zec 5:10
and said to the angel who **t** with me, Zec 6:4
all these things were **t** about through all Lk 1:65
burn within us while he **t** to us on the Lk 24:32
And as he **t** with him, he went in and Acts 10:27
to break bread, Paul **t** with them, Acts 20:7
into a deep sleep as Paul **t** still longer. Acts 20:9

TALKERS (1)
are insubordinate, empty **t** and deceivers, Ti 1:10

TALKING (20)
When he had finished **t** with him, God Gn 17:22
shone because he had been **t** with God. Ex 34:29
t of them when you are sitting in your Dt 11:19
Now while Saul was **t** to the priest, 1 Sm 14:19
Now the king was **t** with Gehazi the 2 Kgs 8:4
While they were yet **t** with him, the Est 6:14
princes refrained from **t** and laid their Jb 29:9
or seeking your own pleasure, or **t** idly; Is 58:13
to them Moses and Elijah, **t** with him. Mt 17:3
with Moses, and they were **t** with Jesus. Mk 9:4
And behold, two men were **t** with him, Lk 9:30
what you are **t** about." And Lk 22:60
and they were **t** with each other about Lk 24:14
While they were **t** and discussing Lk 24:15
As they were **t** about these things, Jesus Lk 24:36
marveled that he was **t** with a woman, Jn 4:27
you seek?" or, "Why are you **t** with her?" Jn 4:27
We do not know what he is **t** about." Jn 16:18
better one—I am **t** like a madman— 2 Cor 11:23
is doing, **t** wicked nonsense against us. 3 Jn 1:10

TALL (9)
great and many, and **t** as the Anakim. Dt 2:10
great and many, and **t** as the Anakim; Dt 2:21
a people great and **t**, the sons of the Dt 9:2
a man of great stature, five cubits **t**. 1 Chr 11:23
messengers, to a nation, **t** and smooth, Is 18:2
LORD of hosts from a people **t** and smooth, Is 18:7
And their rims were **t** and awesome, Ezk 1:18
grew up and became **t** and arrived at Ezk 16:7
the deep made it grow **t**, making its Ezk 31:4

TALLER (3)
"The people are greater and **t** than we. Dt 1:28
shoulders upward he was **t** than any of 1 Sm 9:2
he was **t** than any of the people from 1 Sm 10:23

TALLEST (2)
I felled its **t** cedars, its choicest 2 Kgs 19:23
of Lebanon, to cut down its **t** cedars, Is 37:24

TALMAI (6)
Ahiman, Sheshai, and **T**, the Nm 13:22
of Anak, Sheshai and Ahiman and **T**, Jos 15:14
defeated Sheshai and Ahiman and **T**. Jgs 1:10
the daughter of **T** king of Geshur; 2 Sm 3:3
fled and went to **T** the son of 2 Sm 13:37
was Maacah, the daughter of **T**, 1 Chr 3:2

TALMON (5)
were Shallum, Akkub, **T**, Ahiman, 1 Chr 9:17
Shallum, the sons of Ater, the sons of **T**, Ezr 2:42
the sons of Ater, the sons of **T**, Neh 7:45
Akkub, **T** and their brothers, Neh 11:19
T, and Akkub were gatekeepers Neh 12:25

TAMAR (27)
Er his firstborn, and her name was **T**. Gn 38:6
Judah said to **T** his daughter-in-law, Gn 38:11
So **T** went and remained in her father's Gn 38:11
And when **T** was told, "Your Gn 38:13
"**T** your daughter-in-law has been Gn 38:24
house of Perez, whom **T** bore to Judah, Ru 4:12
a beautiful sister, whose name was **T**. 2 Sm 13:1
himself ill because of his sister **T**, 2 Sm 13:2
me?" Amnon said to him, "I love **T**, 2 Sm 13:4
'Let my sister **T** come and give me 2 Sm 13:5
let my sister **T** come and make 2 Sm 13:6
Then David sent home to **T**, saying, 2 Sm 13:7
So **T** went to her brother Amnon's 2 Sm 13:8
Then Amnon said to **T**, "Bring the 2 Sm 13:10
your hand." And **T** took the cakes 2 Sm 13:10
And **T** put ashes on her head and 2 Sm 13:19
do not take this to heart." So **T** lived, 2 Sm 13:20
because he had violated his sister **T**. 2 Sm 13:22
from the day he violated his sister **T**. 2 Sm 13:32
one daughter whose name was **T**. 2 Sm 14:27
and Baalath and **T** in the wilderness, 1 Kgs 9:18
His daughter-in-law **T** also bore him 1 Chr 2:4
the concubines, and **T** was their sister. 1 Chr 3:9
to the eastern sea and as far as **T**. Ezk 47:18
it shall run from **T** as far as the waters Ezk 47:19
shall run from **T** to the waters Ezk 48:28
Judah the father of Perez and Zerah by **T**, Mt 1:3

TAMARISK (3)
Abraham planted a **t** tree in Beersheba Gn 21:33
at Gibeah under the **t** tree on the 1 Sm 22:6
them under the **t** tree in Jabesh 1 Sm 31:13

TAMBOURINE (8)
with mirth and songs, with **t** and lyre? Gn 31:27
the sister of Aaron, took a **t** in her hand, Ex 15:20
from the high place with harp, **t**, flute, 1 Sm 10:5
They sing to the **t** and the lyre and Jb 21:12
sound the **t**, the sweet lyre with the harp. Ps 81:2
making melody to him with **t** and lyre! Ps 149:3
Praise him with **t** and dance; praise Ps 150:4
harp, **t** and flute and wine at their feasts, Is 5:12

TAMBOURINES (9)
went out after her with **t** and dancing. Ex 15:20
to meet him with **t** and with dances. Jgs 11:34
dancing, to meet King Saul, with **t**, 1 Sm 18:6
and harps and **t** and castanets and 2 Sm 6:5
and harps and **t** and cymbals and 1 Chr 13:8
last, between them virgins playing **t**: Ps 68:25
The mirth of the **t** is stilled, the noise of Is 24:8
them will be to the sound of **t** and lyres. Is 30:32
shall adorn yourself with **t** and shall go Jer 31:4

TAME (1)
but no human being can **t** the tongue. It Jas 3:8

TAMED (2)
can be **t** and has been tamed by Jas 3:7
be tamed and has been **t** by mankind, Jas 3:7

TAMMUZ (1)
behold, there sat women weeping for **T**. Ezk 8:14

TAMPER (1)
cunning or to **t** with God's word, 2 Cor 4:2

TANHUMETH (2)
the son of **T** the Netophathite, 2 Kgs 25:23
the son of Kareah, Seraiah the son of **T**, Jer 40:8

TANNED (6)
t rams' skins, goatskins, acacia wood, Ex 25:5
tent a covering of **t** rams' skins and a Ex 26:14
t rams' skins, and goatskins; acacia Ex 35:7
or goats' hair or **t** rams' skins or Ex 35:23
tent a covering of **t** rams' skins and Ex 36:19
the covering of **t** rams' skins and Ex 39:34

TANNER (3)
for many days with one Simon, a **t**. Acts 9:43
He is lodging with one Simon, a **t**, Acts 10:6
is lodging in the house of Simon, a **t**, Acts 10:32

TAPHATH (1)
Naphath-dor (he had **T** the daughter 1 Kgs 4:11

TAPPUAH (6)
the king of **T**, one; the king of Hepher, Jos 12:17
Zanoah, En-gannim, **T**, Enam, Jos 15:34
From **T** the boundary goes westward to Jos 16:8
The land of **T** belonged to Manasseh, Jos 17:8
but the town of **T** on the boundary of Jos 17:8
Korah, **T**, Rekem, and Shema. 1 Chr 2:43

TARALAH (1)
Rekem, Irpeel, **T**, Jos 18:27

TAREA (1)
Micah: Pithon, Melech, **T**, and Ahaz. 1 Chr 8:35

TARGET (2)
me to pieces; he set me up as his **t**; Jb 16:12
his bow and set me as a **t** for his arrow. Lam 3:12

TARRY (6)
of all Egypt. Come down to me; do not **t**. Gn 45:9
Why **t** the hoofbeats of his chariots?' Jgs 5:28
Weeping may **t** for the night, but joy Ps 30:5
Those who **t** long over wine; those who Prv 23:30
who **t** late into the evening as wine Is 5:11
traveler who turns aside to **t** for a night? Jer 14:8

TARSHISH (28)
Elishah, **T**, Kittim, and Dodanim. Gn 10:4
a fleet of ships of **T** at sea with the 1 Kgs 10:22
fleet of ships of **T** used to come 1 Kgs 10:22
made ships of **T** to go to 1 Kgs 22:48
Elishah, **T**, Kittim, and Rodanim. 1 Chr 1:7
Zethan, **T**, and Ahishahar. 1 Chr 7:10
ships went to **T** with the servants 2 Chr 9:21
years the ships of **T** used to come 2 Chr 9:21
him in building ships to go to **T**, 2 Chr 20:36
and were not able to go to **T**. 2 Chr 20:37
Carshena, Shethar, Admatha, **T**, Meres, Est 1:14
east wind you shattered the ships of **T**. Ps 48:7
May the kings of **T** and of the Ps 72:10
against all the ships of **T**, and against all Is 2:16
Wail, O ships of **T**, for Tyre is laid waste, Is 23:1
Cross over to **T**; wail, O inhabitants of the Is 23:6
your land like the Nile, O daughter of **T**; Is 23:10
Wail, O ships of **T**, for your stronghold Is 23:14
shall hope for me, the ships of **T** first, Is 60:9
I will send survivors to the nations, to **T**, Is 66:19
Beaten silver is brought from **T**, and Jer 10:9
"**T** did business with you because of Ezk 27:12
The ships of **T** traveled for you with Ezk 27:25
and the merchants of **T** and all its Ezk 38:13
rose to flee to **T** from the presence of Jon 1:3
to Joppa and found a ship going to **T**. Jon 1:3
and went on board, to go with them to **T**, Jon 1:3
That is why I made haste to flee to **T**; for I Jon 4:2

TARSUS (5)
Judas look for a man of **T** named Saul, Acts 9:11
to Caesarea and sent him off to **T**. Acts 9:30
So Barnabas went to **T** to look for Acts 11:25
replied, "I am a Jew, from **T** in Cilicia, Acts 21:39
"I am a Jew, born in **T** in Cilicia, but Acts 22:3

TARTAK (1)
the Avvites made Nibhaz and **T**; 2 Kgs 17:31

TARTAN (1)
And the king of Assyria sent the **T**, 2 Kgs 18:17

TASK (11)
your work, your daily **t** each day, Ex 5:13
not done all your **t** of making bricks Ex 5:14
of bricks, your daily **t** each day." Ex 5:19
doing every sort of **t** on the sanctuary Ex 36:4
came, each from the **t** that he was doing, Ex 36:4
them each to his **t** and to his burden, Nm 4:19
each one with his **t** of serving or Nm 4:49
Arise, for it is your **t**, and we are with Ezr 10:4
Nor is this a **t** for one day or for two, Ezr 10:13
this, it seemed to me a wearisome **t**, Ps 73:16
office of overseer, he desires a noble **t**. 1 Tm 3:1

TASKMASTER (3)
who was **t** over the forced labor, 1 Kgs 12:18
who was **t** over the forced labor, 2 Chr 10:18
together; they hear not the voice of the **t**. Jb 3:18

TASKMASTERS (7)
Therefore they set **t** over them to afflict Ex 1:11
have heard their cry because of their **t**. Ex 3:7
Pharaoh commanded the **t** of the people Ex 5:6

So the **t** and the foremen of the people Ex 5:10
The **t** were urgent, saying, "Complete Ex 5:13
whom Pharaoh's **t** had set over them, Ex 5:14
peace and your **t** righteousness. Is 60:17

TASSEL (2)
a cord of blue on the **t** of each corner. Nm 15:38
And it shall be a **t** for you to look at Nm 15:39

TASSELS (2)
tell them to make **t** on the corners of Nm 15:38
"You shall make yourself **t** on the four Dt 22:12

TASTE (22)
and the **t** of it was like wafers made Ex 16:31
And the **t** of it was like the taste of Nm 11:8
of it was like the **t** of cakes baked with Nm 11:8
if I **t** bread or anything else till the sun 2 Sm 3:35
Can your servant **t** what he eats or 2 Sm 19:35
or is there any **t** in the juice of the mallow? Jb 6:6
Oh, **t** and see that the LORD is good! Ps 34:8
How sweet are your words to my **t**, Ps 119:103
of the honeycomb are sweet to your **t**. Prv 24:13
shadow, and his fruit was sweet to my **t**, Sg 2:3
so his **t** remains in him, and his scent Jer 48:11
nor beast, herd nor flock, **t** anything. Jon 3:7
salt of the earth, but if salt has lost its **t**, Mt 5:13
here who will not **t** death until they see Mt 16:28
here who will not **t** death until they see Mk 9:1
here who will not **t** death until they see Lk 9:27
who were invited shall **t** my banquet.'" Lk 14:24
"Salt is good, but if salt has lost its **t**, Lk 14:34
keeps my word, he will never **t** death.' Jn 8:52
by an oath to **t** no food till we Acts 23:14
"Do not handle, Do not **t**, Do not touch" Col 2:21
of God he might **t** death for everyone. Heb 2:9

TASTED (10)
So none of the people had **t** food. 1 Sm 14:24
become bright because I **t** a little of 1 Sm 14:29
"I **t** a little honey with the tip of the 1 Sm 14:43
of soul, never having **t** of prosperity. Jb 21:25
Belshazzar, when he **t** the wine, Dn 5:2
mixed with gall, but when he **t** it, Mt 27:34
master of the feast **t** the water now become Jn 2:9
who have **t** the heavenly gift, Heb 6:4
and have **t** the goodness of the word of Heb 6:5
if indeed you have **t** that the Lord is 1 Pt 2:3

TASTELESS (1)
Can that which is **t** be eaten without salt, Jb 6:6

TASTES (2)
the ear test words as the palate **t** food? Jb 12:11
for the ear tests words as the palate **t** food. Jb 34:3

TATTENAI (4)
At the same time **T** the governor of the Ezr 5:3
of the letter that **T** the governor of the Ezr 5:6
T, governor of the province Beyond the Ezr 6:6
T, the governor of the province Beyond Ezr 6:13

TATTOO (1)
your body for the dead or **t** yourselves: Lv 19:28

TAUGHT (62)
See, I have **t** you statutes and rules, as the Dt 4:5
because he has **t** rebellion against the Dt 13:5
song the same day and **t** it to the people Dt 31:22
briers and with them **t** the men of Jgs 8:16
he said it should be **t** to the people of 2 Sm 1:18
lived in Bethel and **t** them how they 2 Kgs 17:28
And they **t** in Judah, having the Book 2 Chr 17:9
of Judah and **t** among the people. 2 Chr 17:9
to the Levites who **t** all Israel and who 2 Chr 35:3
and the Levites who **t** the people said to Neh 8:9
O God, from my youth you have **t** me, Ps 71:17
from your rules, for you have **t** me. Ps 119:102
he **t** me and said to me, "Let your heart Prv 4:4
I have **t** you the way of wisdom; I have Prv 4:11
An oracle that his mother **t** him: Prv 31:1
the Preacher also **t** the people Eccl 12:9
fear of me is a commandment **t** by men, Is 29:13
Who **t** him the path of justice, and Is 40:14
the path of justice, and **t** him knowledge, Is 40:14
given me the tongue of those who are **t**, Is 50:4
my ear to hear as those who are **t**. Is 50:4
All your children shall be **t** by the LORD, Is 54:13
to wicked women you have **t** your ways. Jer 2:33
they have **t** their tongue to speak lies; Jer 9:5
after the Baals, as their fathers **t** them. Jer 9:14
even as they **t** my people to swear by Jer 12:16
whom you yourself have **t** to be friends Jer 13:21
And though I have **t** them persistently, Jer 32:33
neither have they **t** the difference Ezk 22:26
Yet it was I who **t** Ephraim to walk; I Hos 11:3
And he opened his mouth and **t** them, Mt 5:2
to his hometown he **t** them in their Mt 13:54
for he **t** them as one who had authority, Mk 1:22
told him all that they had done and **t**. Mk 6:30
again, as was his custom, he **t** them. Mk 10:1
And as Jesus **t** in the temple, he said, Mk 12:35
concerning the things you have been **t**. Lk 1:4
And he **t** in their synagogues, being Lk 4:15
And he sat down and **t** the people from the Lk 5:3
teach us to pray, as John **t** his disciples." Lk 11:1
your presence, and you **t** in our streets.' Lk 13:26
Prophets, 'And they will all be **t** by God.' Jn 6:45
in the synagogue, as he **t** at Capernaum. Jn 6:59
So Jesus proclaimed, as he **t** in the temple, Jn 7:28
came to him, and he sat down and **t** them. Jn 8:2
in the treasury, as he **t** in the temple; Jn 8:20
but speak just as the Father **t** me. Jn 8:28
I have always **t** in synagogues and in Jn 18:20
with the church and **t** a great many Acts 11:26
he spoke and **t** accurately the things Acts 18:25
to the doctrine that you have been **t**; Rom 16:17
in words not **t** by human wisdom 1 Cor 2:13
human wisdom but **t** by the Spirit, 1 Cor 2:13
receive it from any man, nor was I **t** it, Gal 1:12
One who is **t** the word must share all Gal 6:6
heard about him and were **t** in him, Eph 4:21
in the faith, just as you were **t**, Col 2:7
you yourselves have been **t** by God to 1 Thes 4:9
the traditions that you were **t** by us, 2 Thes 2:15
hold firm to the trustworthy word as **t**, Ti 1:9
lie, just as it has **t** you—abide in him. 1 Jn 2:27
who **t** Balak to put a stumbling block Rv 2:14

TAUNT (15)
Turn back their **t** on their own heads Neh 4:4
give me a bad name in order to **t** me. Neh 6:13
in my bones, my adversaries **t** me, Ps 42:10
have made us the **t** of our neighbors, Ps 44:13
We have become a **t** to our neighbors, Ps 79:4
All the day my enemies **t** me; those who Ps 102:8
you will take up this **t** against the king of Is 14:4
the earth, to be a reproach, a byword, a **t**, Jer 24:9
an execration, a horror, a curse, and a **t**. Jer 42:18
a curse and a **t** among all the nations Jer 44:8
an oath, a horror, a curse, and a **t**. Jer 44:12
that Bozrah shall become a horror, a **t**, Jer 49:13
You shall be a reproach and a **t**, a Ezk 5:15
shall take up a **t** song against you and Mi 2:4
not all these take up their **t** against him, Hab 2:6

TAUNTED (6)
and Zalmunna, about whom you **t** me, Jgs 8:15
And when he **t** Israel, Jonathan the 2 Sm 21:21
And when he **t** Israel, Jonathan the 1 Chr 20:7
the taunts with which they have **t** you, Ps 79:12
how they have **t** my people and made Zep 2:8
because they **t** and boasted against the Zep 2:10

TAUNTER (1)
at the sound of the **t** and reviler, at the Ps 44:16

TAUNTS (8)
God to prevent the **t** of the nations our Neh 5:9
is not an enemy who **t** me—then I Ps 55:12
of our neighbors the **t** with which they Ps 79:12
I have an answer for him who **t** me, Ps 119:42
the object of their **t** all day long. Lam 3:14
"You have heard their **t**, O LORD, all Lam 3:61
their rising; I am the object of their **t**. Lam 3:63
"I have heard the **t** of Moab and the Zep 2:8

TAVERNS (1)
of Appius and Three **T** to meet us. Acts 28:15

TAWNY (2)
the barn owl, the **t** owl, the carrion Lv 11:18
and the **t** owl, the carrion vulture and Dt 14:17

TAX (34)
and Jerusalem the **t** levied by Moses, 2 Chr 24:6
for the LORD the **t** that Moses the 2 Chr 24:9
and brought their **t** and dropped it 2 Chr 24:10
money for the king's **t** on our fields and Neh 5:4
King Ahasuerus imposed **t** on the land Est 10:1
Do not even the **t** collectors do the same? Mt 5:46
called Matthew sitting at the **t** booth, Mt 9:9
many **t** collectors and sinners came and Mt 9:10
teacher eat with **t** collectors and Mt 9:11
Thomas and Matthew the **t** collector; Mt 10:3
a friend of **t** collectors and sinners!' Mt 11:19
of the half-shekel **t** went up to Mt 17:24
said, "Does your teacher not pay the **t**?" Mt 17:24
do kings of the earth take toll or **t**? Mt 17:25
be to you as a Gentile and a **t** collector. Mt 18:17
the **t** collectors and the prostitutes go Mt 21:31
but the **t** collectors and the prostitutes Mt 21:32
the coin for the **t**." And they brought Mt 22:19
son of Alphaeus sitting at the **t** booth, Mk 2:14
many **t** collectors and sinners were Mk 2:15
eating with sinners and **t** collectors, Mk 2:16
he eat with **t** collectors and sinners?" Mk 2:16
T collectors also came to be baptized Lk 3:12
out and saw a **t** collector named Levi, Lk 5:27
named Levi, sitting at the **t** booth. Lk 5:27
large company of **t** collectors and others Lk 5:29
and drink with **t** collectors and Lk 5:30
heard this, and the **t** collectors too, Lk 7:29
a friend of **t** collectors and sinners!' Lk 7:34
Now the **t** collectors and sinners were all Lk 15:1
a Pharisee and the other a **t** collector. Lk 18:10
adulterers, or even like this **t** collector. Lk 18:11
But the **t** collector, standing far off, Lk 18:13
He was a chief **t** collector and was rich. Lk 19:2

TAXED (1)
but he **t** the land to give the money 2 Kgs 23:35

TAXES (7)
granted a remission of **t** to the provinces Est 2:18
poor and you exact **t** of grain from him, Am 5:11
Is it lawful to pay **t** to Caesar, or not?" Mt 22:17
Is it lawful to pay **t** to Caesar, or not? Mk 12:14
For the same reason you also pay **t**, for Rom 13:6
t to whom taxes are owed, revenue to Rom 13:7
taxes to whom **t** are owed, revenue to Rom 13:7

TEACH (105)
with your mouth and **t** you what you Ex 4:12
his mouth and will **t** you both what to Ex 4:15
And he has inspired him to **t**, both him Ex 35:34
and you are to **t** the people of Israel all Lv 10:11
and that they may **t** their children so.' Dt 4:10
at that time to **t** you statutes and rules, Dt 4:14
and the rules that you shall **t** them, Dt 5:31
LORD your God commanded me to **t** you, Dt 6:1
You shall **t** them diligently to your Dt 6:7
You shall **t** them to your children, Dt 11:19
that they may not **t** you to do according Dt 20:18
write this song and **t** it to the people Dt 31:19
They shall **t** Jacob your rules and Israel Dt 33:10
to **t** war to those who had not known it Jgs 3:2
come again to us and **t** us what we are to Jgs 13:8
when you **t** them the good way in 1 Kgs 8:36
and dwell there and **t** them the law 2 Kgs 17:27
when you **t** them the good way in 2 Chr 6:27
Micaiah, to **t** in the cities of Judah; 2 Chr 17:7
to do it and to **t** his statutes and rules in Ezr 7:10
who do not know them, you shall **t**. Ezr 7:25
"**T** me, and I will be silent; make me Jb 6:24
Will they not **t** you and tell you and utter Jb 8:10
"But ask the beasts, and they will **t** you; Jb 12:7
bushes of the earth, and they will **t** you; Jb 12:8
Will any **t** God knowledge, seeing that Jb 21:22
I will **t** you concerning the hand of God; Jb 27:11
days speak, and many years **t** wisdom.' Jb 32:7
me; be silent, and I will **t** you wisdom." Jb 33:33
t me what I do not see; if I have done Jb 34:32
T us what we shall say to him; we Jb 37:19
your ways, O LORD; **t** me your paths. Ps 25:4
Lead me in your truth and **t** me, for you Ps 25:5
T me your way, O LORD, and lead me on Ps 27:11
I will instruct you and **t** you in the way Ps 32:8
to me; I will **t** you the fear of the LORD. Ps 34:11
let your right hand **t** you awesome deeds! Ps 45:4
and you **t** me wisdom in the secret heart. Ps 51:6
Then I will **t** transgressors your ways, Ps 51:13
our fathers to **t** to their children, Ps 78:5
T me your way, O LORD, that I may Ps 86:11
So **t** us to number our days that we may Ps 90:12
LORD, and whom you **t** out of your law, Ps 94:12
pleasure and to **t** his elders wisdom. Ps 105:22
are you, O LORD; **t** me your statutes! Ps 119:12
you answered me; **t** me your statutes! Ps 119:26
me and graciously **t** me your law! Ps 119:29
T me, O LORD, the way of your statutes; Ps 119:33
your steadfast love; **t** me your statutes! Ps 119:64
T me good judgment and knowledge, Ps 119:66
good and do good; **t** me your statutes. Ps 119:68
of praise, O LORD, and **t** me your rules. Ps 119:108
steadfast love, and **t** me your statutes. Ps 119:124
your servant, and **t** me your statutes. Ps 119:135
praise, for you **t** me your statutes. Ps 119:171
and my testimonies that I shall **t** them, Ps 132:12
T me to do your will, for you are my Ps 143:10
t a righteous man, and he will increase Prv 9:9
of my mother—she who used to **t** me. Sg 8:2
that he may **t** us his ways and that we may Is 2:3
"To whom will he **t** knowledge, and to Is 28:9
t to your daughters a lament, and each Jer 9:20
shall each one **t** his neighbor and Jer 31:34
They shall **t** my people the difference Ezk 44:23
and to **t** them the literature and language Dn 1:4
for a bribe; its priests **t** for a price; Mi 3:11
that he may **t** us his ways and that we Mi 4:2
to a silent stone, Arise! Can this **t**? Hab 2:19
on from there to **t** and preach in their Mt 11:1
that you are true and **t** the way of God Mt 22:16
Again he began to **t** beside the sea. And a Mk 4:1
Sabbath he began to **t** in the synagogue, Mk 6:2
And he began to **t** them many things. Mk 6:34

And he began to **t** them that the Son of Mk 8:31
but truly **t** the way of God. Mk 12:14
disciples said to him, "Lord, **t** us to pray, Lk 11:1
the Holy Spirit will **t** you in that very Lk 12:12
we know that you speak and **t** rightly, Lk 20:21
partiality, but truly **t** the way of God. Lk 20:21
among the Greeks and **t** the Greeks? Jn 7:35
and would you **t** us?" And they cast him Jn 9:34
he will **t** you all things and bring to Jn 14:26
with all that Jesus began to do and **t**, Acts 1:1
them not to speak or **t** at all in the Acts 4:18
the temple at daybreak and began to **t**. Acts 5:21
charged you not to **t** in this name, Acts 5:28
about you that you **t** all the Jews who Acts 21:21
you then who **t** others, do you not Rom 2:21
teach others, do you not **t** yourself? Rom 2:21
as I **t** them everywhere in every 1 Cor 4:17
Does not nature itself **t** you that if a 1 Cor 11:14
persons not to **t** any different doctrine, 1 Tm 1:3
permit a woman to **t** or to exercise 1 Tm 2:12
respectable, hospitable, able to **t**, 1 Tm 3:2
Command and **t** these things. 1 Tm 4:11
and beloved. **T** and urge these things. 1 Tm 6:2
men who will be able to **t** others also. 2 Tm 2:2
but kind to everyone, able to **t**, 2 Tm 2:24
shameful gain what they ought not to **t**. Ti 1:11
you, **t** what accords with sound doctrine. Ti 2:1
to much wine. They are to **t** what is good, Ti 2:3
you need someone to **t** you again the Heb 5:12
And they shall not **t**, each one his Heb 8:11
know that we who **t** will be judged with Jas 3:1
have no need that anyone should **t** you. 1 Jn 2:27

TEACHER (57)
small and great, **t** and pupil alike. 1 Chr 25:8
in his power; who is a **t** like him? Jb 36:22
yet your **T** will not hide himself Is 30:20
anymore, but your eyes shall see your **T**. Is 30:20
has shaped it, a metal image, a **t** of lies? Hab 2:18
"**T**, I will follow you wherever you go." Mt 8:19
"Why does your **t** eat with tax collectors Mt 9:11
"A disciple is not above his **t**, nor a Mt 10:24
enough for the disciple to be like his **t**, Mt 10:25
"**T**, we wish to see a sign from you." Mt 12:38
and said, "Does your **t** not pay the tax?" Mt 17:24
"**T**, what good deed must I do to have Mt 19:16
"**T**, we know that you are true and Mt 22:16
saying, "**T**, Moses said, 'If a man dies Mt 22:24
"**T**, which is the great commandment Mt 22:36
to be called rabbi, for you have one **t**, Mt 23:8
man and say to him, 'The **T** says, Mt 26:18
"**T**, do you not care that we are Mk 4:38
dead. Why trouble the **T** any further?" Mk 5:35
him, "**T**, I brought my son to you, Mk 9:17
"**T**, we saw someone casting out Mk 9:38
before him and asked him, "Good **T**, Mk 10:17
"**T**, all these I have kept from my Mk 10:20
"**T**, we want you to do for us whatever Mk 10:35
"**T**, we know that you are true and do Mk 12:14
"**T**, Moses wrote for us that if a man's Mk 12:19
"You are right, **T**. You have truly said Mk 12:32
T, what wonderful stones and what Mk 13:1
to the master of the house, 'The **T** says, Mk 14:14
and said to him, "**T**, what shall we do?" Lk 3:12
A disciple is not above his **t**, but Lk 6:40
when he is fully trained will be like his **t**. Lk 6:40
to you." And he answered, "Say it, **T**." Lk 7:40
is dead; do not trouble the **T** any more." Lk 8:49
out, "**T**, I beg you to look at my son, Lk 9:38
"**T**, what shall I do to inherit eternal Lk 10:25
"**T**, in saying these things you insult us Lk 11:45
"**T**, tell my brother to divide the Lk 12:13
And a ruler asked him, "Good **T**, what Lk 18:18
said to him, "**T**, rebuke your disciples." Lk 19:39
"**T**, we know that you speak and teach Lk 20:21
"**T**, Moses wrote for us that if a man's Lk 20:28
answered, "**T**, you have spoken well." Lk 20:39
him, "**T**, when will these things be, Lk 21:7
master of the house, 'The **T** says to you, Lk 22:11
said to him, "Rabbi" (which means **T**), Jn 1:38
we know that you are a **t** come from God, Jn 3:2
"Are you the **t** of Israel and yet you do not Jn 3:10
"**T**, this woman has been caught in the Jn 8:4
"The **T** is here and is calling for you." Jn 11:28
You call me **T** and Lord, and you are Jn 13:13
If I then, your Lord and **T**, have washed Jn 13:14
"Rabboni!" (which means **T**). Jn 20:16
a **t** of the law held in honor by all the Acts 5:34
of the foolish, a **t** of children, Rom 2:20
a **t** of the Gentiles in faith and truth. 1 Tm 2:7
a preacher and apostle and **t**, 2 Tm 1:11

TEACHERS (13)
more understanding than all my **t**, Ps 119:99
to the voice of my **t** or incline my ear to Prv 5:13
him in the temple, sitting among the **t**, Lk 2:46
Pharisees and **t** of the law were sitting Lk 5:17
the church at Antioch prophets and **t**, Acts 13:1
apostles, second prophets, third **t**, 1 Cor 12:28
apostles? Are all prophets? Are all **t**? 1 Cor 12:29
the evangelists, the pastors and **t**, Eph 4:11
desiring to be **t** of the law, without 1 Tm 1:7
accumulate for themselves **t** to suit 2 Tm 4:3
though by this time you ought to be **t**, Heb 5:12
Not many of you should become **t**, my Jas 3:1
just as there will be false **t** among you, 2 Pt 2:1

TEACHES (13)
For your iniquity **t** your mouth, and you Jb 15:5
who **t** us more than the beasts of the Jb 35:11
what is right, and **t** the humble his way. Ps 25:9
not rebuke? He who **t** man knowledge— Ps 94:10
head, and the prophet who **t** lies is the tail; Is 9:15
he is rightly instructed; his God **t** him. Is 28:26
the LORD your God, who **t** you to profit, Is 48:17
these commandments and **t** others to do Mt 5:19
whoever does them and **t** them will be Mt 5:19
serving; the one who **t**, in his teaching; Rom 12:7
share all good things with the one who **t**. Gal 6:6
If anyone **t** a different doctrine and 1 Tm 6:3
as his anointing **t** you about 1 Jn 2:27

TEACHING (89)
the statutes and the rules that I am **t** you, Dt 4:1
May my **t** drop as the rain, my speech Dt 32:2
and without a **t** priest and without 2 Chr 15:3
Give ear, O my people, to my **t**; incline Ps 78:1
and forsake not your mother's **t**, Prv 1:8
My son, do not forget my **t**, but let your Prv 3:1
you good precepts; do not forsake my **t**. Prv 4:2
and forsake not your mother's **t**. Prv 6:20
is a lamp and the **t** a light, Prv 6:23
live; keep my **t** as the apple of your eye; Prv 7:2
The **t** of the wise is a fountain of life, Prv 13:14
and the **t** of kindness is on her tongue. Prv 31:26
Give ear to the **t** of our God, you people of Is 1:10
testimony; seal the **t** among my disciples. Is 8:16
To the **t** and to the testimony! If they will Is 8:20
t in their synagogues and proclaiming Mt 4:23
the crowds were astonished at his **t**, Mt 7:28
for he was **t** them as one who had Mt 7:29
t in their synagogues and proclaiming Mt 9:35
t as doctrines the commandments of Mt 15:9
but of the **t** of the Pharisees and Mt 16:12
the people came up to him as he was **t**, Mt 21:23
heard it, they were astonished at his **t**. Mt 22:33
Day after day I sat in the temple **t**, and Mt 26:55
t them to observe all that I have Mt 28:20
he entered the synagogue and was **t**. Mk 1:21
And they were astonished at his **t**, for he Mk 1:22
"What is this? A new **t** with authority! Mk 1:27
was coming to him, and he was **t** them. Mk 2:13
And he was **t** them many things in Mk 4:2
in parables, and in his **t** he said to them: Mk 4:2
And he went about among the villages **t**. Mk 6:6
t as doctrines the commandments of Mk 7:7
for he was **t** his disciples, saying to Mk 9:31
And he was **t** them and saying to Mk 11:17
all the crowd was astonished at his **t**. Mk 11:18
And in his **t** he said, "Beware of the Mk 12:38
day I was with you in the temple **t**, Mk 14:49
And he was **t** them on the Sabbath, Lk 4:31
and they were astonished at his **t**, for his Lk 4:32
On one of those days, as he was **t**, Lk 5:17
he entered the synagogue and was **t**, Lk 6:6
at the Lord's feet and listened to his **t**. Lk 10:39
Now he was **t** in one of the synagogues Lk 13:10
t and journeying toward Jerusalem. Lk 13:22
And he was **t** daily in the temple. The Lk 19:47
as Jesus was **t** the people in the temple Lk 20:1
And every day he was **t** in the temple, Lk 21:37
up the people, **t** throughout all Judea, Lk 23:5
went up into the temple and began **t**. Jn 7:14
Jesus answered them, "My **t** is not mine, Jn 7:16
will know whether the **t** is from God or Jn 7:17
Jesus about his disciples and his **t**. Jn 18:19
to the apostles' **t** and fellowship, Acts 2:42
because they were **t** the people and Acts 4:2
in the temple and **t** the people." Acts 5:25
you have filled Jerusalem with your **t**, Acts 5:28
did not cease **t** and preaching Jesus Acts 5:42
he was astonished at the **t** of the Lord. Acts 13:12
from Judea and were **t** the brothers, Acts 15:1
t and preaching the word of the Lord, Acts 15:35
know what this new **t** is that you are Acts 17:19
t the word of God among them. Acts 18:11
and **t** you in public and from house Acts 20:20
man who is **t** everyone everywhere Acts 21:28
kingdom of God and **t** about the Lord Acts 28:31
to the standard of **t** to which you were Rom 6:17
serving; the one who teaches, in his **t**; Rom 12:7
or knowledge or prophecy or **t**? 1 Cor 14:6
warning everyone and **t** everyone with Col 1:28
t and admonishing one another in all Col 3:16
of Scripture, to exhortation, to **t**. 1 Tm 4:13
close watch on yourself and on the **t**. 1 Tm 4:16
those who labor in preaching and **t**. 1 Tm 5:17
of God and the **t** may not be reviled. 1 Tm 6:1
Christ and the **t** that accords with 1 Tm 6:3
You, however, have followed my **t**, 2 Tm 3:10
out by God and profitable for **t**, 2 Tm 3:16
exhort, with complete patience and **t**. 2 Tm 4:2
when people will not endure sound **t**, 2 Tm 4:3
whole families by **t** for shameful gain Ti 1:11
good works, and in your **t** show integrity, Ti 2:7
and does not abide in the **t** of Christ, 2 Jn 1:9
Whoever abides in the **t** has both the 2 Jn 1:9
comes to you and does not bring this **t**, 2 Jn 1:10
some there who hold the **t** of Balaam, Rv 2:14
some who hold the **t** of the Nicolaitans. Rv 2:15
a prophetess and is **t** and seducing my Rv 2:20
you in Thyatira, who do not hold this **t**, Rv 2:24

TEACHINGS (3)
—according to human precepts and **t**? Col 2:22
to deceitful spirits and **t** of demons, 1 Tm 4:1
be led away by diverse and strange **t**, Heb 13:9

TEAM (1)
I break in pieces the farmer and his **t**; Jer 51:23

TEAR (43)
in a garment, so that it may not **t**. Ex 28:32
You shall **t** down their altars and break Ex 34:13
the opening, so that it might not **t**. Ex 39:23
He shall **t** it open by its wings, but shall Lv 1:17
hang loose, and do not **t** your clothes, Lv 10:6
he shall **t** it out of the garment or the Lv 13:56
of his head hang loose nor **t** his clothes. Lv 21:10
You shall **t** down their altars and dash in Dt 12:3
"**T** your clothes and put on sackcloth 2 Sm 3:31
I will surely **t** the kingdom from you 1 Kgs 11:11
but I will **t** it out of the hand of your 1 Kgs 11:12
I will not **t** away all the kingdom, 1 Kgs 11:13
I am about to **t** the kingdom from 1 Kgs 11:31
You who **t** yourself in your anger, shall Jb 18:4
lest like a lion they **t** my soul apart, Ps 7:2
He is like a lion eager to **t**, as a young Ps 17:12
he will **t** them down and build them up Ps 28:5
you who forget God, lest I **t** you apart, Ps 50:22
he will snatch and **t** you from your tent; Ps 52:5
t out the fangs of the young lions, O Ps 58:6
a time to **t**, and a time to sew; a time to Eccl 3:7
the sword to kill, the dogs to **t**, and the Jer 15:3
on my right hand, yet I would **t** you off Jer 22:24
build them up, and not **t** them down; Jer 24:6
afraid, nor did they **t** their garments. Jer 36:24
and I will **t** them from your arms, Ezk 13:20
veils also I will **t** off and deliver my Ezk 13:21
gnaw its shards, and **t** your breasts; Ezk 23:34
I, even I, will **t** and go away; I will carry Hos 5:14
I will **t** open their breast, and there I will Hos 13:8
who **t** the skin from off my people and Mi 3:2
says, "They may build, but I will **t** down, Mal 1:4
you to sin, **t** it out and throw it away. Mt 5:29
from the garment, and a worse **t** is made. Mt 9:16
you to sin, **t** it out and throw it away. Mt 18:9
new from the old, and a worse **t** is made. Mk 2:21
if your eye causes you to sin, **t** it out. Mk 9:47
If he does, he will **t** the new, and the piece Lk 5:36
I will **t** down my barns and build Lk 12:18
and **t** you down to the ground, you and Lk 19:44
they said to one another, "Let us not **t** it, Jn 19:24
will wipe away every **t** from their eyes." Rv 7:17
He will wipe away every **t** from their eyes, Rv 21:4

TEARING (4)
midst is like a roaring lion **t** the prey; Ezk 22:25
in her midst are like wolves **t** the prey, Ezk 22:27
of the fat ones, **t** off even their hoofs. Zec 11:16
for building up and not for **t** down. 2 Cor 13:10

TEARS (48)
like a lion; he **t** off arm and scalp. Dt 33:20
the lion in pieces as one **t** a young goat. Jgs 14:6
heard your prayer; I have seen your **t**. 2 Kgs 20:5
If he **t** down, none can rebuild; if he Jb 12:14
scorn me; my eye pours out **t** to God, Jb 16:20
every night I flood my bed with **t**; Ps 6:6
to my cry; hold not your peace at my **t**! Ps 39:12
My **t** have been my food day and night, Ps 42:3
of my tossings; put my **t** in your bottle. Ps 56:8
with the bread of **t** and given them tears Ps 80:5
of tears and given them **t** to drink in full Ps 80:5
like bread and mingle **t** with my drink, Ps 102:9
my soul from death, my eyes from **t**, Ps 116:8
My eyes shed streams of **t**, because Ps 119:136
Those who sow in **t** shall reap with Ps 126:5
but folly with her own hands **t** it down. Prv 14:1
The LORD **t** down the house of the Prv 15:25

land, but he who exacts gifts **t** it down. Prv 29:4
And behold, the **t** of the oppressed, and Eccl 4:1
the squares everyone wails and melts in **t**. Is 15:3
I drench you with my **t**, O Heshbon and Is 16:9
"Look away from me; let me weep bitter **t**; Is 22:4
Lord GOD will wipe away **t** from all faces, Is 25:8
heard your prayer; I have seen your **t**. Is 38:5
were waters, and my eyes a fountain of **t**, Jer 9:1
may run down with **t** and our eyelids Jer 9:18
will weep bitterly and run down with **t**, Jer 13:17
my eyes run down with **t** night and day, Jer 14:17
from weeping, and your eyes from **t**, Jer 31:16
in the night, with **t** on her cheeks; Lam 1:2
things I weep; my eyes flow with **t**; Lam 1:16
let **t** stream down like a torrent day Lam 2:18
flow with rivers of **t** because of the Lam 3:48
or weep, nor shall your **t** run down. Ezk 24:16
goes through, treads down and **t** in pieces, Mi 5:8
You cover the LORD'S altar with **t**, with Mal 2:13
for the patch **t** away from the garment, Mt 9:16
If he does, the patch **t** away from it, the Mk 2:21
"No one **t** a piece from a new garment Lk 5:36
his feet with her **t** and wiped them with Lk 7:38
my feet with her **t** and wiped them with Lk 7:44
humility and with **t** and with trials Acts 20:19
or day to admonish everyone with **t**. Acts 20:31
and anguish of heart and with many **t**, 2 Cor 2:4
told you and now tell you even with **t**, Phil 3:18
As I remember your **t**, I long to see you, 2 Tm 1:4
and supplications, with loud cries and **t**, Heb 5:7
to repent, though he sought it with **t**. Heb 12:17

TEBAH (1)
whose name was Reumah, bore **T**, Gn 22:24

TEBALIAH (1)
Hilkiah the second, **T** the third, 1 Chr 26:11

TEBETH (1)
tenth month, which is the month of **T**, Est 2:16

TEEM (1)
t on the earth and multiply in it." Gn 9:7

TEEMS (1)
which **t** with creatures innumerable, Ps 104:25

TEETH (45)
than wine, and his **t** whiter than milk. Gn 49:12
the meat was yet between their **t**, Nm 11:33
I will send the **t** of beasts against them, Dt 32:24
lion, the **t** of the young lions are broken. Jb 4:10
take my flesh in my **t** and put my life in Jb 13:14
and hated me; he has gnashed his **t** at me; Jb 16:9
and I have escaped by the skin of my **t**. Jb 19:20
and made him drop his prey from his **t**. Jb 29:17
doors of his face? Around his **t** is terror. Jb 41:14
the cheek; you break the **t** of the wicked. Ps 3:7
at a feast, they gnash at me with their **t**. Ps 35:16
the righteous and gnashes his **t** at him, Ps 37:12
of man, whose **t** are spears and arrows, Ps 57:4
O God, break the **t** in their mouths; tear Ps 58:6
he gnashes his **t** and melts away; Ps 112:10
who has not given us as prey to their **t**! Ps 124:6
Like vinegar to the **t** and smoke to the Prv 10:26
There are those whose **t** are swords, Prv 30:14
Your **t** are like a flock of shorn ewes that Sg 4:2
Your **t** are like a flock of ewes that have Sg 6:6
for my beloved, gliding over lips and **t**. Sg 7:9
sledge, new, sharp, and having **t**; Is 41:15
and the children's **t** are set on edge.' Jer 31:29
sour grapes, his **t** shall be set on edge. Jer 31:30
they hiss, they gnash their **t**, they cry: Lam 2:16
He has made my **t** grind on gravel, and Lam 3:16
and the children's **t** are set on edge'? Ezk 18:2
had three ribs in its mouth between its **t**; Dn 7:5
It had great iron **t**; it devoured and broke Dn 7:7
with its **t** of iron and claws of bronze, Dn 7:19
its **t** are lions' teeth, and it has the fangs of a Jl 1:6
its teeth are lions' **t**, and it has the fangs of a Jl 1:6
gave you cleanness of **t** in all your cities, Am 4:6
and its abominations from between its **t**; Zec 9:7
there will be weeping and gnashing of **t**." Mt 8:12
will be weeping and gnashing of **t**. Mt 13:42
will be weeping and gnashing of **t**. Mt 13:50
will be weeping and gnashing of **t**.' Mt 22:13
will be weeping and gnashing of **t**. Mt 24:51
will be weeping and gnashing of **t**.' Mt 25:30
and grinds his **t** and becomes rigid. Mk 9:18
will be weeping and gnashing of **t**, Lk 13:28
and they ground their **t** at him. Acts 7:54
women's hair, and their **t** like lions' teeth; Rv 9:8
women's hair, and their teeth like lions' **t**; Rv 9:8

TEHAPHNEHES (1)
At **T** the day shall be dark, when I Ezk 30:18

TEHINNAH (1)
fathered Beth-rapha, Paseah, and **T**, 1 Chr 4:12

TEKEL (2)
inscribed: MENE, MENE, **T**, and PARSIN. Dn 5:25
T, you have been weighed in the Dn 5:27

TEKOA (11)
And Joab sent to **T** and brought from 2 Sm 14:2
When the woman of **T** came to the 2 Sm 14:4
And the woman of **T** said to the king, 2 Sm 14:9
the Paltite, Ira the son of Ikkesh of **T**, 2 Sm 23:26
she bore him Ashhur, the father of **T**. 1 Chr 2:24
Ashhur, the father of **T**, had two wives, 1 Chr 4:5
Ira the son of Ikkesh of **T**, Abiezer of 1 Chr 11:28
He built Bethlehem, Etam, **T**, 2 Chr 11:6
went out into the wilderness of **T**. 2 Chr 20:20
Blow the trumpet in **T**, and raise a signal Jer 6:1
who was among the shepherds of **T**, Am 1:1

TEKOITE (1)
was Ira, the son of Ikkesh the **T**; 1 Chr 27:9

TEKOITES (2)
And next to them the **T** repaired, but Neh 3:5
After him the **T** repaired another Neh 3:27

TEL-ABIB (1)
And I came to the exiles at **T**, who were Ezk 3:15

TEL-HARSHA (2)
came up from Tel-melah, **T**, Cherub, Ezr 2:59
came up from Tel-melah, **T**, Cherub, Neh 7:61

TEL-MELAH (2)
were those who came up from **T**, Ezr 2:59
were those who came up from **T**, Neh 7:61

TELAH (1)
his son, Resheph his son, **T** his son, 1 Chr 7:25

TELAIM (1)
the people and numbered them in **T**, 1 Sm 15:4

TELASSAR (2)
the people of Eden who were in **T**? 2 Kgs 19:12
and the people of Eden who were in **T**? Is 37:12

TELEM (2)
Ziph, **T**, Bealoth, Jos 15:24
the gatekeepers: Shallum, **T**, and Uri. Ezr 10:24

TELL (338)
Why did you not **t** me that she was Gn 12:18
you did not **t** me, and I have not heard Gn 21:26
the mountains of which I shall **t** you." Gn 22:2
"Please **t** me whose daughter you are. Gn 24:23
and faithfulness to my master, **t** me; Gn 24:49
and if not, **t** me, that I may turn to the Gn 24:49
dwell in the land of which I shall **t** you. Gn 26:2
T me, what shall your wages be?" Gn 29:15
secretly and trick me, and did not **t** me, Gn 31:27
I have sent to **t** my lord, in order that I Gn 32:5
"Please **t** me your name." But he said, Gn 32:29
"**T** me, please, where they are pasturing Gn 37:16
belong to God? Please **t** them to me." Gn 40:8
"Did I not **t** you not to sin against the Gn 42:22
me so badly as to **t** the man that you Gn 43:6
You must **t** my father of all my honor Gn 45:13
will go up and **t** Pharaoh and will say Gn 46:31
that I may **t** you what shall happen to Gn 49:1
t Pharaoh king of Egypt to let the people Ex 6:11
t Pharaoh king of Egypt all that I say to Ex 6:29
your brother Aaron shall **t** Pharaoh to let Ex 7:2
and that you may **t** in the hearing of Ex 10:2
T all the congregation of Israel that on Ex 12:3
You shall **t** your son on that day, 'It is Ex 13:8
"**T** the people of Israel to turn back and Ex 14:2
me? **T** the people of Israel to go forward. Ex 14:15
house of Jacob, and **t** the people of Israel: Ex 19:3
the house shall come and **t** the priest, Lv 14:35
"**T** Aaron your brother not to come at Lv 16:2
shall not interpret omens or **t** fortunes. Lv 19:26
and they will **t** the inhabitants of this Nm 14:14
and **t** them to make tassels on the Nm 15:38
"**T** Eleazar the son of Aaron the priest Nm 16:37
T the people of Israel to bring you a red Nm 19:2
and **t** the rock before their eyes to yield Nm 20:8
with them; but only do what I **t** you." Nm 22:20
the word that I **t** you." So Balaam went Nm 22:35
he shows me I will **t** you." And he went Nm 23:3
answered Balak, "Did I not **t** you, Nm 23:26
"Did I not **t** your messengers whom Nm 24:12
and I will **t** you the whole Dt 5:31
you, your elders, and they will **t** you. Dt 32:7
If you do not **t** this business of ours, Jos 2:14
But if you **t** this business of ours, then Jos 2:20
then you shall **t** them that the waters of Jos 4:7
LORD commanded Joshua to **t** the people, Jos 4:10
mouth, until the day I **t** you to shout. Jos 6:10
And **t** me now what you have done; do Jos 7:19
"**T** of it, you who ride on white donkeys, Jgs 5:10
was from, and he did not **t** me his name, Jgs 13:6
But he did not **t** his father or his mother Jgs 14:6
But he did not **t** them that he had Jgs 14:9
If you can **t** me what it is, within the Jgs 14:12
but if you cannot **t** me what it is, then Jgs 14:13
"Entice your husband to **t** us what the Jgs 14:15
nor my mother, and shall I **t** you?" Jgs 14:16
"Please **t** me where your great strength Jgs 16:6
Please **t** me how you might be bound." Jgs 16:10
T me how you might be bound." And Jgs 16:13
And the people of Israel said, "**T** us, how Jgs 20:3
lie down, and he will **t** you what to do." Ru 3:4
So I thought I would **t** you of it and say, Ru 4:4
But if you will not, **t** me, that I may know, Ru 4:4
Samuel was afraid to **t** the vision to 1 Sm 3:15
T us with what we shall send it to its 1 Sm 6:2
Perhaps he can **t** us the way we should 1 Sm 9:6
it to the man of God to **t** us our way." 1 Sm 9:8
"**T** me where is the house of the seer?" 1 Sm 9:18
let you go and will **t** you all that is on 1 Sm 9:19
"**T** the servant to pass on before us, 1 Sm 9:27
"Please **t** me what Samuel said to 1 Sm 10:15
spoken, he did not **t** him anything. 1 Sm 10:16
other side." But he did not **t** his father. 1 Sm 14:1
"**T** me what you have done." And 1 Sm 14:43
I will **t** you what the LORD said to me 1 Sm 15:16
And if I learn anything I will **t** you." 1 Sm 19:3
come to you, would I not **t** you?" 1 Sm 20:9
"Who will **t** me if your father 1 Sm 20:10
there, that he would surely **t** Saul. 1 Sm 22:22
please **t** your servant." And the LORD 1 Sm 23:11
your young men, and they will **t** you. 1 Sm 25:8
she did not **t** her husband Nabal. 1 Sm 25:19
"Lest they should **t** about us and say, 1 Sm 27:11
have summoned you to **t** me what I 1 Sm 28:15
T me." And he answered, "The people 2 Sm 1:4
T it not in Gath, publish it not in the 2 Sm 1:20
it be before you **t** your people to turn 2 Sm 2:26
then Abner went to **t** David at Hebron 2 Sm 3:19
"Go and **t** my servant David, 'Thus 2 Sm 7:5
David all that Joab had sent him to **t**. 2 Sm 11:22
David were afraid to **t** him that the 2 Sm 12:18
Will you not **t** me?" Amnon said to 2 Sm 13:4
t it to Zadok and Abiathar the 2 Sm 15:35
therefore send quickly and **t** David, 2 Sm 17:16
female servant was to go and **t** them, 2 Sm 17:17
they were to go and **t** King David, 2 Sm 17:17
t the king what you have seen." The 2 Sm 18:21
T Joab, 'Come here, that I may speak 2 Sm 20:16
to **t** them who shall sit on the throne 1 Kgs 1:20
He will **t** you what shall happen to the 1 Kgs 14:3
Go, **t** Jeroboam, 'Thus says the LORD, 1 Kgs 14:7
Go, **t** your lord, 'Behold, Elijah is 1 Kgs 18:8
And now you say, 'Go, **t** your lord, 1 Kgs 18:11
when I come and **t** Ahab and he 1 Kgs 18:12
And now you say, 'Go, **t** your lord, 1 Kgs 18:14
of Ben-hadad, "**T** my lord the king, 1 Kgs 20:9
the king of Israel answered, "**T** him, 1 Kgs 20:11
"Did I not **t** you that he would not 1 Kgs 22:18
T me; what have you in the house?" 2 Kgs 4:2
the pace for me unless I **t** you." 2 Kgs 4:24
let us go and **t** the king's household." 2 Kgs 7:9
"I will **t** you what the Syrians have 2 Kgs 7:12
"**T** me all the great things that Elisha 2 Kgs 8:4
t us now." And he said, "Thus and so 2 Kgs 9:12
city to go and **t** the news in Jezreel." 2 Kgs 9:15
and we will do all that you **t** us. 2 Kgs 10:5
'**T** the man who sent you to me, 2 Kgs 22:15
to him; **t** of all his wondrous works! 1 Chr 16:9
T of his salvation from day to day. 1 Chr 16:23
"Go and **t** my servant David, 'Thus 1 Chr 17:4
"Did I not **t** you that he would not 2 Chr 18:17
'**T** the man who sent you to me, 2 Chr 34:23
and in the morning **t** the king to have Est 5:14
sword, and I alone have escaped to **t** you." Jb 1:15
them, and I alone have escaped to **t** you." Jb 1:16
sword, and I alone have escaped to **t** you." Jb 1:17
dead, and I alone have escaped to **t** you." Jb 1:19
not teach you and **t** you and utter words Jb 8:10
and that he would **t** you the secrets of Jb 11:6
birds of the heavens, and they will **t** you; Jb 12:7
earth? **T** me, if you have understanding. Jb 38:4
I will **t** of the decree: The LORD said to me, Ps 2:7
in Zion! **T** among the peoples his deeds! Ps 9:11
I will **t** of your name to my brothers; in Ps 22:22
praise you? Will it **t** of your faithfulness? Ps 30:9
my tongue shall **t** of your righteousness Ps 35:28
I will proclaim and **t** of them, yet they are Ps 40:5
that you may **t** the next generation Ps 48:13
"If I were hungry, I would not **t** you, for Ps 50:12
they **t** what God has brought about and Ps 64:9
and I will **t** what he has done for my Ps 66:16
My mouth will **t** of your righteous acts, Ps 71:15
refuge, that I may **t** of all your works. Ps 73:28
but **t** to the coming generation the Ps 78:4
and arise and **t** them to their children, Ps 78:6
name; **t** of his salvation from day to day. Ps 96:2

to him; **t** of all his wondrous works! Ps 105:2
and **t** of his deeds in songs of joy! Ps 107:22
before him; I **t** my trouble before him. Ps 142:2
of your kingdom and **t** of your power, Ps 145:11
For who can **t** man what will be after Eccl 6:12
to be, for who can **t** him how it will be? Eccl 8:7
and who can **t** him what will be after Eccl 10:14
or some winged creature **t** the matter. Eccl 10:20
T me, you whom my soul loves, where Sg 1:7
that you **t** him I am sick with love. Sg 5:8
T the righteous that it shall be well with Is 3:10
And now I will **t** you what I will do to my Is 5:5
Let them **t** you that they might know Is 19:12
bring them, and **t** us what is to happen. Is 41:22
T us the former things, what they are, Is 41:22
T us what is to come hereafter, that we Is 41:23
before they spring forth I **t** you of them." Is 42:9
"And when you **t** this people all these Jer 16:10
proclaim there the words that I **t** you. Jer 19:2
by their dreams that they **t** one another, Jer 23:27
prophet who has a dream **t** the dream, Jer 23:28
and who **t** them and lead my people Jer 23:32
"Go, **t** Hananiah, 'Thus says the LORD: Jer 28:13
and will **t** you great and hidden things Jer 33:3
Then they asked Baruch, "**T** us, please, Jer 36:17
Jeremiah said to Zedekiah, "If I **t** you, Jer 38:15
'**T** us what you said to the king and Jer 38:25
the LORD answers you I will **t** you. Jer 42:4
in anything that he sent me to **t** you. Jer 42:21
T it beside the Arnon, that Moab is laid Jer 48:20
to **t** the king of Babylon that his city is Jer 51:31
T them therefore, 'Thus says the Lord Ezk 12:23
T them, behold, the king of Babylon Ezk 17:12
"Will you not **t** us what these things Ezk 24:19
'Will you not **t** us what you mean by Ezk 37:18
all that I shall **t** you concerning all the Ezk 44:5
be summoned to **t** the king his Dn 2:2
T your servants the dream, and we will Dn 2:4
"Let the king **t** his servants the dream, Dn 2:7
Therefore **t** me the dream, and I shall Dn 2:9
Now we will **t** the king its interpretation. Dn 2:36
t me the visions of my dream that I saw Dn 4:9
O Belteshazzar, **t** me the interpretation, Dn 4:18
went out, and I have come to **t** it to you, Dn 9:23
But I will **t** you what is inscribed in the Dn 10:21
T your children of it, and let your children Jl 1:3
of it, and let your children **t** their children, Jl 1:3
"**T** us on whose account this evil has Jon 1:8
out against it the message that I **t** you." Jon 3:2
T it not in Gath; weep not at all; in Mi 1:10
they **t** false dreams and give empty Zec 10:2
to Egypt, and remain there until I **t** you, Mt 2:13
have Abraham as our father,' for I **t** you, Mt 3:9
For I **t** you, unless your righteousness Mt 5:20
"Therefore I **t** you, do not be anxious Mt 6:25
yet I **t** you, even Solomon in all his glory Mt 6:29
those who followed him, "Truly, I **t** you, Mt 8:10
I **t** you, many will come from east and Mt 8:11
What I **t** you in the dark, say in the Mt 10:27
"Go and **t** John what you hear and see: Mt 11:4
Yes, I **t** you, and more than a prophet. Mt 11:9
But I **t** you, it will be more bearable on Mt 11:22
But I **t** you that it will be more tolerable Mt 11:24
I **t** you, something greater than the Mt 12:6
Therefore I **t** you, every sin and Mt 12:31
I **t** you, on the day of judgment people Mt 12:36
and at harvest time I will **t** the reapers, Mt 13:30
that he did not **t** them to beware of Mt 16:12
And I **t** you, you are Peter, and on this Mt 16:18
charged the disciples to **t** no one that he Mt 16:20
commanded them, "**T** no one the vision, Mt 17:9
But I **t** you that Elijah has already Mt 17:12
For I **t** you that in heaven their angels Mt 18:10
against you, go and **t** him his fault, Mt 18:15
to listen to them, **t** it to the church. Mt 18:17
Again I **t** you, it is easier for a camel to Mt 19:24
question, and if you **t** me the answer, Mt 21:24
then I also will **t** you by what authority Mt 21:24
"Neither will I **t** you by what authority Mt 21:27
Therefore I **t** you, the kingdom of God Mt 21:43
saying, '**T** those who are invited, Mt 22:4
T us, then, what you think. Is it lawful Mt 22:17
and observe whatever they **t** you—but Mt 23:3
For I **t** you, you will not see me again, Mt 23:39
came to him privately, saying, "**T** us, Mt 24:3
I **t** you I will not drink again of this Mt 26:29
Jesus said to him, "Truly, I **t** you, this Mt 26:34
living God, **t** us if you are the Christ, Mt 26:63
But I **t** you, from now on you will see Mt 26:64
go and steal him away and **t** the people, Mt 27:64
Then go quickly and **t** his disciples that Mt 28:7
and great joy, and ran to **t** his disciples. Mt 28:8
go and **t** my brothers to go to Galilee, Mt 28:10
and said, "**T** people, 'His disciples came Mt 28:13
to your friends and **t** them how much Mk 5:19
And Jesus charged them to **t** no one. But Mk 7:36
strictly charged them to **t** no one about Mk 8:30
he charged them to **t** no one what they Mk 9:9
But I **t** you that Elijah has come, and Mk 9:13
he began to **t** them what was to Mk 10:32
Therefore I **t** you, whatever you ask in Mk 11:24
and I will **t** you by what authority I do Mk 11:29
"Neither will I **t** you by what authority Mk 11:33
"**T** us, when will these things be, and Mk 13:4
And Jesus said to him, "Truly, I **t** you, Mk 14:30
t his disciples and Peter that he is going Mk 16:7
For I **t** you, God is able from these stones Lk 3:8
But in truth, I **t** you, there were many Lk 4:25
And he charged him to **t** no one, but "go Lk 5:14
me 'Lord, Lord,' and not do what I **t** you? Lk 6:46
crowd that followed him, said, "I **t** you, Lk 7:9
"Go and **t** John what you have seen and Lk 7:22
Yes, I **t** you, and more than a prophet. Lk 7:26
I **t** you, among those born of women Lk 7:28
Therefore I **t** you, her sins, which are Lk 7:47
he charged them to **t** no one what had Lk 8:56
and commanded them to **t** this to no Lk 9:21
But I **t** you truly, there are some Lk 9:27
do you want us to **t** fire to come down Lk 9:54
I **t** you, it will be more bearable on that Lk 10:12
For I **t** you that many prophets and Lk 10:24
to serve alone? **T** her then to help me." Lk 10:40
I **t** you, though he will not get up and Lk 11:8
And I **t** you, ask, and it will be given to Lk 11:9
Yes, I **t** you, it will be required of this Lk 11:51
"I **t** you, my friends, do not fear those Lk 12:4
to cast into hell. Yes, I **t** you, fear him! Lk 12:5
"And I **t** you, everyone who Lk 12:8
t my brother to divide the inheritance Lk 12:13
said to his disciples, "Therefore I **t** you, Lk 12:22
they neither toil nor spin, yet I **t** you, Lk 12:27
earth? No, I **t** you, but rather division. Lk 12:51
I **t** you, you will never get out until you Lk 12:59
No, I **t** you; but unless you repent, you Lk 13:3
No, I **t** you; but unless you repent, you Lk 13:5
For many, I **t** you, will seek to enter and Lk 13:24
But he will say, 'I **t** you, I do not know Lk 13:27
And he said to them, "Go and **t** that fox, Lk 13:32
And I **t** you, you will not see me until Lk 13:35
For I **t** you, none of those men who Lk 14:24
Just so, I **t** you, there will be more joy in Lk 15:7
Just so, I **t** you, there is joy before the Lk 15:10
And I **t** you, make friends for yourselves Lk 16:9
I **t** you, in that night there will be two Lk 17:34
I **t** you, he will give justice to them Lk 18:8
I **t** you, this man went down to his Lk 18:14
things, he proceeded to **t** a parable, Lk 19:11
'I **t** you that to everyone who has, more Lk 19:26
He answered, "I **t** you, if these were Lk 19:40
"**T** us by what authority you do these Lk 20:2
also will ask you a question. Now **t** me, Lk 20:3
"Neither will I **t** you by what authority I Lk 20:8
And he began to **t** the people this Lk 20:9
And he said, "Truly, I **t** you, this poor Lk 21:3
and **t** the master of the house, 'The Lk 22:11
For I **t** you I will not eat it until it is Lk 22:16
For I **t** you that from now on I will not Lk 22:18
Jesus said, "I **t** you, Peter, the rooster Lk 22:34
For I **t** you that this Scripture must be Lk 22:37
the Christ, **t** us." But he said to them, Lk 22:67
tell us." But he said to them, "If I **t** you, Lk 22:67
you believe if I **t** you heavenly things? Jn 3:12
When he comes, he will **t** us all things." Jn 4:25
Look, I **t** you, lift up your eyes, and see Jn 4:35
But because I **t** the truth, you do not Jn 8:45
of you convicts me of sin? If I **t** the truth, Jn 8:46
If you are the Christ, **t** us plainly." Jn 10:24
"Did I not **t** you that if you believed you Jn 11:40
Nevertheless, I **t** you the truth: it is to Jn 16:7
of speech but will **t** you plainly about Jn 16:25
away, **t** me where you have laid him, Jn 20:15
"**T** me whether you sold the land for so Acts 5:8
So in the present case I **t** you, keep Acts 5:38
"**T** these things to James and to the Acts 12:17
who themselves will **t** you the same Acts 15:27
Do therefore what we **t** you. We have Acts 21:23
tribune came and said to him, "**T** me, Acts 22:27
for he has something to **t** him." Acts 23:17
"What is it that you have to **t** me?" Acts 23:19
"**T** no one that you have informed me Acts 23:22
For I **t** you that Christ became a Rom 15:8
I **t** you this, brothers: flesh and 1 Cor 15:50
Behold! I **t** you a mystery. We shall 1 Cor 15:51
T me, you who desire to be under the Gal 4:21
in the Lord will **t** you everything. Eph 6:21
Yet which I shall choose I cannot **t**. Phil 1:22
told you and now **t** you even with tears, Phil 3:18
Tychicus will **t** you all about my Col 4:7
They will **t** you of everything that has Col 4:9
"I will **t** of your name to my brothers; Heb 2:12
For time would fail me to **t** of Gideon, Heb 11:32
I will **t** you the mystery of the woman, Rv 17:7

TELLERS (1)
you shall have no more **t** of fortunes; Mi 5:12

TELLING (27)
by not **t** him that he intended to flee. Gn 31:20
a man was **t** a dream to his comrade. Jgs 7:13
as Gideon heard the **t** of the dream and Jgs 7:15
you have finished **t** all the news 2 Sm 11:19
so he sent messengers, **t** them, "Go, 2 Kgs 1:2
And while he was **t** the king how 2 Kgs 8:5
t them what to say to Iddo and his Ezr 8:17
aloud, and **t** all your wondrous deeds. Ps 26:7
men said to Jeremiah, "You are **t** a lie. Jer 43:2
rebuked them, **t** them to be silent, Mt 20:31
many rebuked him, **t** him to be silent. Mk 10:48
are you **t** this parable for us or for all?" Lk 12:41
front rebuked him, **t** him to be silent. Lk 18:39
what I have been **t** you from the Jn 8:25
I am **t** you this now, before it takes Jn 13:19
had the moneybag, Jesus was **t** him, Jn 13:29
he knows that he is **t** the truth—that Jn 19:35
—we hear them **t** in our own tongues Acts 2:11
in nothing except **t** or hearing Acts 17:21
t the people to believe in the one who Acts 19:4
the Spirit they were **t** Paul not to go Acts 21:4
t them not to circumcise their Acts 21:21
become your enemy by **t** you the truth? Gal 4:16
we kept **t** you beforehand that we 1 Thes 3:4
and an apostle (I am **t** the truth, 1 Tm 2:7
t them to make an image for the beast Rv 13:14
voice from the temple **t** the seven angels, Rv 16:1

TELLS (13)
Sarah says to you, do as she **t** you, Gn 21:12
sacrifice to the LORD our God as he **t** us." Ex 8:27
or wonder that he **t** you comes to pass, Dt 13:2
practices divination or **t** fortunes or Dt 18:10
t the king of Israel the words that you 2 Kgs 6:12
famine and by thirst, when he **t** you, 2 Chr 32:11
iniquity; when he goes out, he **t** it abroad. Ps 41:6
harm, but deal with him as he **t** you." Jer 39:12
say, 'If anyone **t** his father or his mother, Mt 15:5
say, 'If a man **t** his father or his mother, Mk 7:11
to the servants, "Do whatever he **t** you." Jn 2:5
listen to him in whatever he **t** you. Acts 3:22
not believe, even if one **t** it to you.'" Acts 13:41

TEMA (5)
Hadad, **T**, Jetur, Naphish, and Gn 25:15
Mishma, Dumah, Massa, Hadad, **T**, 1 Chr 1:30
The caravans of **T** look, the travelers of Jb 6:19
bread, O inhabitants of the land of **T**. Is 21:14
Dedan, **T**, Buz, and all who cut the Jer 25:23

TEMAH (2)
Barkos, the sons of Sisera, the sons of **T**, Ezr 2:53
the sons of Sisera, the sons of **T**, Neh 7:55

TEMAN (11)
The sons of Eliphaz were **T**, Omar, Gn 36:11
the chiefs **T**, Omar, Zepho, Kenaz, Gn 36:15
Kenaz, **T**, Mibzar, Gn 36:42
T, Omar, Zepho, Gatam, Kenaz, and 1 Chr 1:36
Kenaz, **T**, Mibzar, 1 Chr 1:53
LORD of hosts: "Is wisdom no more in **T**? Jer 49:7
formed against the inhabitants of **T**: Jer 49:20
from **T** even to Dedan they shall fall Ezk 25:13
So I will send a fire upon **T**, and it shall Am 1:12
mighty men shall be dismayed, O **T**, Ob 1:9
God came from **T**, and the Holy One Hab 3:3

TEMANITE (6)
each from his own place, Eliphaz the **T**, Jb 2:11
Then Eliphaz the **T** answered and said: Jb 4:1
Then Eliphaz the **T** answered and said: Jb 15:1
Then Eliphaz the **T** answered and said: Jb 22:1
to Job, the LORD said to Eliphaz the **T**: Jb 42:7
So Eliphaz the **T** and Bildad the Shuhite Jb 42:9

TEMANITES (2)
the land of the **T** reigned in his place. Gn 36:34
the land of the **T** reigned in his place. 1 Chr 1:45

TEMENI (1)
Hepher, **T**, and Haahashtari. 1 Chr 4:6

TEMPER (2)
A man of quick **t** acts foolishly, and a Prv 14:17
but he who has a hasty **t** exalts folly. Prv 14:29

TEMPEST (18)
crushes me with a **t** and multiplies my Jb 9:17
a devouring fire, around him a mighty **t**. Ps 50:3
a shelter from the raging wind and **t**." Ps 55:8
them with your **t** and terrify them Ps 83:15
When the **t** passes, the wicked is no Prv 10:25
like a storm of hail, a destroying **t**, like a Is 28:2
and great noise, with whirlwind and **t**, Is 29:6

and the **t** carries them off like stubble. Is 40:24
them away, and the **t** shall scatter them. Is 41:16
the roar of a great **t** he will set fire to Jer 11:16
Wrath has gone forth, a whirling **t**; it Jer 23:19
and a great **t** is stirring from the Jer 25:32
Wrath has gone forth, a whirling **t**; it Jer 30:23
with a **t** in the day of the whirlwind; Am 1:14
sea, and there was a mighty **t** on the sea, Jon 1:4
me that this great **t** has come upon Jon 1:12
many days, and no small **t** lay on us, Acts 27:20
fire and darkness and gloom and a **t** Heb 12:18

TEMPESTUOUS (3)
us?" For the sea grew more and more **t**. Jon 1:11
sea grew more and more **t** against them. Jon 1:13
But soon a **t** wind, called the Acts 27:14

TEMPLE (263)
the peg into his **t** until it went down Jgs 4:21
lay Sisera dead, with the tent peg in his **t**. Jgs 4:22
his head; she shattered and pierced his **t**. Jgs 5:26
beside the doorpost of the **t** of the LORD. 1 Sm 1:9
was lying down in the **t** of the LORD, 1 Sm 3:3
put his armor in the **t** of Ashtaroth, 1 Sm 31:10
From his **t** he heard my voice, and my 2 Sm 22:7
up the pillars at the vestibule of the **t**. 1 Kgs 7:21
and for the doors of the nave of the **t**. 1 Kgs 7:50
offer sacrifices in the **t** of the LORD at 1 Kgs 12:27
the doors of the **t** of the LORD and 2 Kgs 18:16
to bring out of the **t** of the LORD all the 2 Kgs 23:4
vessels of gold in the **t** of the LORD, 2 Kgs 24:13
of bronze used in the **t** service, 2 Kgs 25:14
priests, the Levites, and the **t** servants. 1 Chr 9:2
the chambers of the **t** free from other 1 Chr 9:33
his armor in the **t** of their gods and 1 Chr 10:10
fastened his head in the **t** of Dagon. 1 Chr 10:10
son the plan of the vestibule of the **t**, 1 Chr 28:11
purposed to build a **t** for the name of 2 Chr 2:1
who will build a **t** for the LORD and a 2 Chr 2:12
He set up the pillars in front of the **t**, 2 Chr 3:17
as prescribed, and set them in the **t**, 2 Chr 4:7
ten tables and placed them in the **t**, 2 Chr 4:8
of pure gold, and the sockets of the **t**, 2 Chr 4:22
doors of the nave of the **t** were of gold. 2 Chr 4:22
and the glory of the LORD filled the **t**. 2 Chr 7:1
and the glory of the LORD on the **t**, 2 Chr 7:3
God and entered the **t** of the LORD to 2 Chr 26:16
he did not enter the **t** of the LORD. 2 Chr 27:2
they found in the **t** of the LORD into 2 Chr 29:16
this, when Josiah had prepared the **t**, 2 Chr 35:20
The **t** servants: the sons of Ziha, the Ezr 2:43
All the **t** servants and the sons of Ezr 2:58
and the **t** servants lived in their towns, Ezr 2:70
the foundation of the **t** of the LORD was Ezr 3:6
laid the foundation of the **t** of the LORD, Ezr 3:10
exiles were building a **t** to the LORD, Ezr 4:1
taken out of the **t** that was in Jerusalem Ezr 5:14
and brought into the **t** of Babylon, Ezr 5:14
the king took out of the **t** of Babylon, Ezr 5:14
put them in the **t** that is in Jerusalem, Ezr 5:15
took out of the **t** that is in Jerusalem Ezr 6:5
brought back to the **t** that is in Ezr 6:5
and gatekeepers, and the **t** servants. Ezr 7:7
singers, the doorkeepers, the **t** servants, Ezr 7:24
his brothers and the **t** servants at the Ezr 8:17
besides 220 of the **t** servants, whom Ezr 8:20
for the gates of the fortress of the **t**, Neh 2:8
and the **t** servants living on Ophel Neh 3:26
as the house of the **t** servants and of the Neh 3:31
in the house of God, within the **t**. Neh 6:10
Let us close the doors of the **t**, for they Neh 6:10
such as I could go into the **t** and live? Neh 6:11
The **t** servants: the sons of Ziha, the Neh 7:46
All the **t** servants and the sons of Neh 7:60
some of the people, the **t** servants, Neh 7:73
the singers, the **t** servants, Neh 10:28
the priests, the Levites, the **t** servants, Neh 11:3
But the **t** servants lived on Ophel; and Neh 11:21
and Gishpa were over the **t** servants. Neh 11:21
down toward your holy **t** in the fear of Ps 5:7
The LORD is in his holy **t**; the LORD'S Ps 11:4
From his **t** he heard my voice, and my Ps 18:6
beauty of the LORD and to inquire in his **t**. Ps 27:4
strips the forests bare, and in his **t** all cry, Ps 29:9
David. A song at the dedication of the **t**. Ps 30:T
love, O God, in the midst of your **t**. Ps 48:9
of your house, the holiness of your **t**! Ps 65:4
Because of your **t** at Jerusalem kings Ps 68:29
they have defiled your holy **t**; Ps 79:1
toward your holy **t** and give thanks Ps 138:2
up; and the train of his robe filled the **t**. Is 6:1
He has gone up to the **t**, and to Dibon, to Is 15:2
'She shall be built,' and of the **t**, Is 44:28
uproar from the city! A sound from the **t**! Is 66:6
deceptive words: 'This is the **t** of the LORD, Jer 7:4
is the temple of the LORD, the **t** of the LORD, Jer 7:4
the temple of the LORD, the **t** of the LORD.' Jer 7:4
of figs placed before the **t** of the LORD. Jer 24:1
at the third entrance of the **t** of the LORD. Jer 38:14
incense to present at the **t** of the LORD. Jer 41:5
the LORD our God, vengeance for his **t**. Jer 50:28
of the LORD, the vengeance for his **t**. Jer 51:11
vessels of bronze used in the **t** service; Jer 52:18
at the entrance of the **t** of the LORD, Ezk 8:16
with their backs to the **t** of the LORD, Ezk 8:16
wall all around the outside of the **t** area, Ezk 40:5
the priests who have charge of the **t**, Ezk 40:45
And the altar was in front of the **t**. Ezk 40:47
the vestibule of the **t** and measured the Ezk 40:48
Then he measured the wall of the **t**, six Ezk 41:5
chambers, four cubits, all around the **t**. Ezk 41:5
the wall of the **t** to serve as supports Ezk 41:6
not be supported by the wall of the **t**. Ezk 41:6
because the **t** was enclosed upward all Ezk 41:7
was enclosed upward all around the **t**. Ezk 41:7
Thus the **t** had a broad area upward, Ezk 41:7
saw also that the **t** had a raised Ezk 41:8
the side chambers of the **t** and the Ezk 41:9
cubits all around the **t** on every side. Ezk 41:10
Then he measured the **t**, a hundred Ezk 41:13
of the east front of the **t** and the yard, Ezk 41:14
were carved on the whole **t** all around. Ezk 41:19
vestibule, the side chambers of the **t**, Ezk 41:26
measuring the interior of the **t** area, Ezk 42:15
and measured the **t** area all around. Ezk 42:15
the LORD entered the **t** by the gate facing Ezk 43:4
behold, the glory of the LORD filled the **t**. Ezk 43:5
I heard one speaking to me out of the **t**, Ezk 43:6
describe to the house of Israel the **t**, Ezk 43:10
known to them the design of the **t**, Ezk 43:11
This is the law of the **t**: the whole Ezk 43:12
holy. Behold, this is the law of the **t**. Ezk 43:12
the appointed place belonging to the **t**, Ezk 43:21
of the north gate to the front of the **t**, Ezk 44:4
glory of the LORD filled the **t** of the LORD. Ezk 44:4
all the statutes of the **t** of the LORD and Ezk 44:5
the entrance to the **t** and all the exits Ezk 44:5
to be in my sanctuary, profaning my **t**, Ezk 44:7
the gates of the **t** and ministering in Ezk 44:11
of the temple and ministering in the **t**. Ezk 44:11
appoint them to keep charge of the **t**, Ezk 44:14
be for the Levites who minister at the **t**, Ezk 45:5
and put it on the doorposts of the **t**, Ezk 45:19
so you shall make atonement for the **t**. Ezk 45:20
who minister at the **t** shall boil the Ezk 46:24
he brought me back to the door of the **t**, Ezk 47:1
the threshold of the **t** toward the east Ezk 47:1
toward the east (for the **t** faced east). Ezk 47:1
the south end of the threshold of the **t**, Ezk 47:1
the sanctuary of the **t** shall be in its Ezk 48:21
taken out of the **t** in Jerusalem be Dn 5:2
vessels that had been taken out of the **t**, Dn 5:3
appear and profane the **t** and fortress, Dn 11:31
sanctuary, and it is a **t** of the kingdom." Am 7:13
The songs of the **t** shall become wailings Am 8:3
Yet I shall again look upon your holy **t**.' Jon 2:4
my prayer came to you, into your holy **t**. Jon 2:7
against you, the Lord from his holy **t**. Mi 1:2
But the LORD is in his holy **t**; let all the Hab 2:20
placed upon stone in the **t** of the LORD, Hg 2:15
the foundation of the LORD'S **t** was laid, Hg 2:18
and he shall build the **t** of the LORD. Zec 6:12
he who shall build the **t** of the LORD and Zec 6:13
crown shall be in the **t** of the LORD as a Zec 6:14
come and help to build the **t** of the LORD. Zec 6:15
hosts was laid, that the **t** might be built. Zec 8:9
you seek will suddenly come to his **t**; Mal 3:1
city and set him on the pinnacle of the **t** Mt 4:5
the priests in the **t** profane the Sabbath Mt 12:5
something greater than the **t** is here. Mt 12:6
And Jesus entered the **t** and drove out Mt 21:12
out all who sold and bought in the **t**, Mt 21:12
and the lame came to him in the **t**, Mt 21:14
and the children crying out in the **t**, Mt 21:15
And when he entered the **t**, the chief Mt 21:23
who say, 'If anyone swears by the **t**, Mt 23:16
if anyone swears by the gold of the **t**, Mt 23:16
the gold or the **t** that has made the gold Mt 23:17
whoever swears by the **t** swears by it Mt 23:21
Jesus left the **t** and was going away, Mt 24:1
to point out to him the buildings of the **t**. Mt 24:1
Day after day I sat in the **t** teaching, Mt 26:55
said, 'I am able to destroy the **t** of God, Mt 26:61
down the pieces of silver into the **t**, Mt 27:5
who would destroy the **t** and rebuild it Mt 27:40
the curtain of the **t** was torn in two, Mt 27:51
entered Jerusalem and went into the **t**. Mk 11:11
And he entered the **t** and began to Mk 11:15
sold and those who bought in the **t**, Mk 11:15
to carry anything through the **t**. Mk 11:16
And as he was walking in the **t**, the Mk 11:27
And as Jesus taught in the **t**, he said, Mk 12:35
And as he came out of the **t**, one of his Mk 13:1
on the Mount of Olives opposite the **t**, Mk 13:3
day I was with you in the **t** teaching, Mk 14:49
'I will destroy this **t** that is made with Mk 14:58
who would destroy the **t** and rebuild it Mk 15:29
the curtain of the **t** was torn in two, Mk 15:38
by lot to enter the **t** of the Lord and burn Lk 1:9
they were wondering at his delay in the **t**. Lk 1:21
that he had seen a vision in the **t**. Lk 1:22
And he came in the Spirit into the **t**, and Lk 2:27
She did not depart from the **t**, Lk 2:37
After three days they found him in the **t**, Lk 2:46
on the pinnacle of the **t** and said to him, Lk 4:9
"Two men went up into the **t** to pray, Lk 18:10
And he entered the **t** and began to drive Lk 19:45
And he was teaching daily in the **t**. The Lk 19:47
the people in the **t** and preaching the Lk 20:1
And while some were speaking of the **t**, Lk 21:5
And every day he was teaching in the **t**, Lk 21:37
came to him in the **t** to hear him. Lk 21:38
priests and officers of the **t** and elders, Lk 22:52
I was with you day after day in the **t**, Lk 22:53
the curtain of the **t** was torn in two. Lk 23:45
were continually in the **t** blessing God. Lk 24:53
In the **t** he found those who were selling Jn 2:14
of cords, he drove them all out of the **t**, Jn 2:15
Jesus answered them, "Destroy this **t**, and Jn 2:19
has taken forty-six years to build this **t**, Jn 2:20
he was speaking about the **t** of his body. Jn 2:21
Jesus found him in the **t** and said to him, Jn 5:14
went up into the **t** and began teaching. Jn 7:14
So Jesus proclaimed, as he taught in the **t**, Jn 7:28
in the morning he came again to the **t**. Jn 8:2
in the treasury, as he taught in the **t**; Jn 8:20
Jesus hid himself and went out of the **t**. Jn 8:59
and Jesus was walking in the **t**, in the Jn 10:23
to one another as they stood in the **t**, Jn 11:56
taught in synagogues and in the **t**, Jn 18:20
attending the **t** together and breaking Acts 2:46
were going up to the **t** at the hour of Acts 3:1
at the gate of the **t** that is called the Acts 3:2
Gate to ask alms of those entering the **t**. Acts 3:2
Peter and John about to go into the **t**, Acts 3:3
to walk, and entered the **t** with them, Acts 3:8
who sat at the Beautiful Gate of the **t**, Acts 3:10
the captain of the **t** and the Sadducees Acts 4:1
"Go and stand in the **t** and speak to the Acts 5:20
they entered the **t** at daybreak and Acts 5:21
the captain of the **t** and the chief Acts 5:24
are standing in the **t** and teaching the Acts 5:25
day, in the **t** and from house to house, Acts 5:42
whose **t** was at the entrance to the Acts 14:13
but also that the **t** of the great goddess Acts 19:27
of the Ephesians is **t** keeper of the Acts 19:35
along with them and went into the **t**, Acts 21:26
Jews from Asia, seeing him in the **t**, Acts 21:27
Greeks into the **t** and has defiled Acts 21:28
that Paul had brought him into the **t**. Acts 21:29
Paul and dragged him out of the **t**, Acts 21:30
to Jerusalem and was praying in the **t**, Acts 22:17
He even tried to profane the **t**, but we Acts 24:6
either in the **t** or in the synagogues or Acts 24:12
this, they found me purified in the **t**, Acts 24:18
the law of the Jews, nor against the **t**, Acts 25:8
Jews seized me in the **t** and tried to kill Acts 26:21
that you are God's **t** and that God's 1 Cor 3:16
If anyone destroys God's **t**, God will 1 Cor 3:17
will destroy him. For God's **t** is holy, 1 Cor 3:17
temple is holy, and you are that **t**. 1 Cor 3:17
that your body is a **t** of the Holy Spirit 1 Cor 6:19
have knowledge eating in an idol's **t**, 1 Cor 8:10
are employed in the **t** service get their 1 Cor 9:13
service get their food from the **t**, 1 Cor 9:13
agreement has the **t** of God with 2 Cor 6:16
For we are the **t** of the living God; 2 Cor 6:16
grows into a holy **t** in the Lord. Eph 2:21
that he takes his seat in the **t** of God, 2 Thes 2:4
make him a pillar in the **t** of my God. Rv 3:12
and serve him day and night in his **t**; Rv 7:15
"Rise and measure the **t** of God and the Rv 11:1
do not measure the court outside the **t**; Rv 11:2
Then God's **t** in heaven was opened, Rv 11:19
of his covenant was seen within his **t**. Rv 11:19
And another angel came out of the **t**, Rv 14:15
angel came out of the **t** in heaven, Rv 14:17
loud voice from the **t** telling the seven Rv 16:1
air, and a loud voice came out of the **t**, Rv 16:17
And I saw no **t** in the city, for its temple Rv 21:22
for its **t** is the Lord God the Almighty Rv 21:22

TEMPLES (7)
off the hair on your **t** or mar the edges Lv 19:27
He also made **t** on high places and 1 Kgs 12:31
kindle a fire in the **t** of the gods of Jer 43:12
and the **t** of the gods of Egypt he shall Jer 43:13

have carried my rich treasures into your **t**. Jl 3:5
earth, does not live in **t** made by man, Acts 17:24
You who abhor idols, do you rob **t**? Rom 2:22

TEMPT (1)
that Satan may not **t** you because of 1 Cor 7:5

TEMPTATION (12)
And lead us not into **t**, but deliver us Mt 6:13
woe to the one by whom the **t** comes! Mt 18:7
and pray that you may not enter into **t**. Mt 26:41
and pray that you may not enter into **t**. Mk 14:38
And when the devil had ended every **t**, he Lk 4:13
is indebted to us. And lead us not into **t**." Lk 11:4
"Pray that you may not enter into **t**." Lk 22:40
pray that you may not enter into **t**." Lk 22:46
because of the **t** to sexual immorality, 1 Cor 7:2
No **t** has overtaken you that is not 1 Cor 10:13
but with the **t** he will also provide 1 Cor 10:13
those who desire to be rich fall into **t**, 1 Tm 6:9

TEMPTATIONS (3)
"Woe to the world for **t** to sin! For it is Mt 18:7
For it is necessary that **t** come, but woe Mt 18:7
his disciples, "**T** to sin are sure to come, Lk 17:1

TEMPTED (13)
into the wilderness to be **t** by the devil. Mt 4:1
wilderness forty days, being **t** by Satan. Mk 1:13
for forty days, being **t** by the devil. And he Lk 4:2
not let you be **t** beyond your ability, 1 Cor 10:13
Keep watch on yourself, lest you too be **t**. Gal 6:1
the tempter had **t** you and our 1 Thes 3:5
he himself has suffered when **t**, Heb 2:18
he is able to help those who are being **t**. Heb 2:18
in every respect has been **t** as we are, Heb 4:15
Let no one say when he is **t**, "I am being Jas 1:13
"I am being **t** by God," for God cannot Jas 1:13
by God," for God cannot be **t** with evil, Jas 1:13
But each person is **t** when he is lured Jas 1:14

TEMPTER (2)
And the **t** came and said to him, "If you Mt 4:3
that somehow the **t** had tempted you 1 Thes 3:5

TEMPTS (1)
with evil, and he himself **t** no one. Jas 1:13

TEN (179)
after Abram had lived **t** years in the Gn 16:3
Suppose **t** are found there." He Gn 18:32
"For the sake of **t** I will not destroy it." Gn 18:32
Then the servant took **t** of his master's Gn 24:10
for her arms weighing **t** gold shekels, Gn 24:22
remain with us a while, at least **t** days; Gn 24:55
you become thousands of **t** thousands, Gn 24:60
me and changed my wages **t** times. Gn 31:7
you have changed my wages **t** times. Gn 31:41
and their calves, forty cows and **t** bulls, Gn 32:15
female donkeys and **t** male donkeys. Gn 32:15
So **t** of Joseph's brothers went down to Gn 42:3
t donkeys loaded with the good things Gn 45:23
and **t** female donkeys loaded with Gn 45:23
the tabernacle with **t** curtains of fine Ex 26:1
T cubits shall be the length of a frame, Ex 26:16
fifty cubits, with **t** pillars and ten bases. Ex 27:12
fifty cubits, with ten pillars and **t** bases. Ex 27:12
the covenant, the **T** Commandments. Ex 34:28
made the tabernacle with **t** curtains. Ex 36:8
T cubits was the length of a frame, and Ex 36:21
hangings of fifty cubits, their **t** pillars, Ex 38:12
their ten pillars, and their **t** bases; Ex 38:12
a hundred of you shall chase **t** thousand, Lv 26:8
t women shall bake your bread in a Lv 26:26
shekels, and for a female **t** shekels. Lv 27:5
shekels, and for a female **t** shekels. Lv 27:7
to the **t** thousand thousands of Israel." Nm 10:36
day, or two days, or five days, or **t** days, Nm 11:19
who gathered least gathered **t** homers. Nm 11:32
to the test these **t** times and have not Nm 14:22
"On the fourth day **t** bulls, two rams, Nm 29:23
perform, that is, the **T** Commandments, Dt 4:13
the **T** Commandments that the LORD had Dt 10:4
and two have put **t** thousand to flight, Dt 32:30
he came from the **t** thousands of holy Dt 33:2
they are the **t** thousands of Ephraim, Dt 33:17
Timnah: **t** cities with their villages. Jos 15:57
Thus there fell to Manasseh **t** portions, Jos 17:5
and the half-tribe of Manasseh, **t** cities. Jos 21:5
of the Kohathites were **t** in all with Jos 21:26
and with him **t** chiefs, one from each of Jos 22:14
So Gideon took **t** men of his servants Jgs 6:27
Israel, and he judged Israel **t** years. Jgs 12:11
and I will give you **t** pieces of silver a Jgs 17:10
and we will take **t** men of a hundred Jgs 20:10
and a thousand of **t** thousand, Jgs 20:10
Ruth. They lived there about **t** years, Ru 1:4
And he took **t** men of the elders of the city Ru 4:2
Am I not more to you than **t** sons?" 1 Sm 1:8
on foot, and **t** thousand men of Judah. 1 Sm 15:4
parched grain, and these **t** loaves, 1 Sm 17:17
Also take these **t** cheeses to the 1 Sm 17:18
and David his **t** thousands." 1 Sm 18:7
have ascribed to David **t** thousands, 1 Sm 18:8
and David his **t** thousands'?" 1 Sm 21:11
So David sent **t** young men. And 1 Sm 25:5
And about **t** days later the LORD 1 Sm 25:38
and David his **t** thousands'?" 1 Sm 29:5
the king left **t** concubines to keep 2 Sm 15:16
But you are worth **t** thousand of us. 2 Sm 18:3
glad to give you **t** pieces of silver and 2 Sm 18:11
And **t** young men, Joab's 2 Sm 18:15
"We have **t** shares in the king, 2 Sm 19:43
king took the **t** concubines whom he 2 Sm 20:3
t fat oxen, and twenty pasture-fed 1 Kgs 4:23
and **t** cubits deep in front of the house. 1 Kgs 6:3
of olivewood, each **t** cubits high. 1 Kgs 6:23
it was **t** cubits from the tip of one 1 Kgs 6:24
other cherub also measured **t** cubits; 1 Kgs 6:25
height of one cherub was **t** cubits, 1 Kgs 6:26
stones, stones of eight and **t** cubits. 1 Kgs 7:10
round, **t** cubits from brim to brim, 1 Kgs 7:23
its brim were gourds, for **t** cubits, 1 Kgs 7:24
He also made the **t** stands of bronze. 1 Kgs 7:27
this manner he made the **t** stands. 1 Kgs 7:37
And he made **t** basins of bronze. 1 Kgs 7:38
was a basin for each of the **t** stands. 1 Kgs 7:38
the **t** stands, and the ten basins on the 1 Kgs 7:43
stands, and the **t** basins on the stands; 1 Kgs 7:43
"Take for yourself **t** pieces, 1 Kgs 11:31
Solomon and will give you **t** tribes 1 Kgs 11:31
hand and will give it to you, **t** tribes. 1 Kgs 11:35
Take with you **t** loaves, some cakes, 1 Kgs 14:3
taking with him **t** talents of silver, 2 Kgs 5:5
of gold, and **t** changes of clothes. 2 Kgs 5:5
fifty horsemen and **t** chariots and ten 2 Kgs 13:7
ten chariots and **t** thousand footmen, 2 Kgs 13:7
He struck down **t** thousand Edomites 2 Kgs 14:7
and he reigned **t** years in Samaria. 2 Kgs 15:17
shall the shadow go forward **t** steps, 2 Kgs 20:9
forward ten steps, or go back **t** steps?" 2 Kgs 20:9
for the shadow to lengthen **t** steps. 2 Kgs 20:10
let the shadow go back **t** steps." 2 Kgs 20:10
he brought the shadow back **t** steps, 2 Kgs 20:11
came with **t** men and struck down 2 Kgs 25:25
the half of Manasseh, **t** cities. 1 Chr 6:61
twenty cubits wide and **t** cubits high. 2 Chr 4:1
round, **t** cubits from brim to brim, 2 Chr 4:2
it were figures of gourds, for **t** cubits, 2 Chr 4:3
He also made **t** basins in which to 2 Chr 4:6
And he made **t** golden lampstands as 2 Chr 4:7
He also made **t** tables and placed them 2 Chr 4:8
his days the land had rest for **t** years. 2 Chr 14:1
three months and **t** days in 2 Chr 36:9
and **t** of their kinsmen with them. Ezr 8:24
all directions and said to us **t** times, Neh 4:12
and every **t** days all kinds of wine in Neh 5:18
bring one out of **t** to live in Jerusalem Neh 11:1
while nine out of **t** remained in the Neh 11:1
the **t** sons of Haman the son of Est 9:10
500 men and also the **t** sons of Haman. Est 9:12
And let the **t** sons of Haman be hanged Est 9:13
and the **t** sons of Haman were hanged. Est 9:14
These **t** times you have cast reproach Jb 19:3
melody to him with the harp of **t** strings! Ps 33:2
chariots of God are twice **t** thousand, Ps 68:17
your side, **t** thousand at your right hand, Ps 91:7
forth thousands and **t** thousands in Ps 144:13
wise man more than **t** rulers who are Eccl 7:19
ruddy, distinguished among **t** thousand. Sg 5:10
For **t** acres of vineyard shall yield but one Is 5:10
dial of Ahaz turn back **t** steps." So the sun Is 38:8
back on the dial the **t** steps by which it Is 38:8
came with **t** men to Gedaliah the son of Jer 41:1
of Nethaniah and the **t** men with him Jer 41:2
But there were **t** men among them who Jer 41:8
At the end of **t** days the word of the LORD Jer 42:7
of the opening of the gateway, **t** cubits; Ezk 40:11
and people would go up to it by **t** steps. Ezk 40:49
breadth of the entrance was **t** cubits, Ezk 41:2
t cubits wide and a hundred cubits Ezk 42:4
cor, like the homer, contains **t** baths). Ezk 45:14
"Test your servants for **t** days; let us be Dn 1:12
this matter, and tested them for **t** days. Dn 1:14
At the end of **t** days it was seen that they Dn 1:15
he found them **t** times better than all the Dn 1:20
that were before it, and it had **t** horns. Dn 7:7
and **t** thousand times ten thousand Dn 7:10
ten thousand times **t** thousand stood Dn 7:10
and about the **t** horns that were on its Dn 7:20
As for the **t** horns, out of this kingdom Dn 7:24
out of this kingdom **t** kings shall arise, Dn 7:24
for him my laws by the **t** thousands, Hos 8:12
a hundred shall have **t** left to the house Am 5:3
And if **t** men remain in one house, they Am 6:9
of rams, with **t** thousands of rivers of oil? Mi 6:7
of twenty measures, there were but **t**. Hg 2:16
is twenty cubits, and its width **t** cubits." Zec 5:2
In those days **t** men from the nations of Zec 8:23
him who owed him **t** thousand talents. Mt 18:24
And when the **t** heard it, they were Mt 20:24
heaven will be like **t** virgins who took Mt 25:1
and give it to him who has the **t** talents. Mt 25:28
And when the **t** heard it, they began to Mk 10:41
he is able with **t** thousand to meet him Lk 14:31
"Or what woman, having **t** silver coins, Lk 15:8
entered a village, he was met by **t** lepers, Lk 17:12
Jesus answered, "Were not **t** cleansed? Lk 17:17
Calling **t** of his servants, he gave them Lk 19:13
of his servants, he gave them **t** minas, Lk 19:13
your mina has made **t** minas more.' Lk 19:16
you shall have authority over **t** cities.' Lk 19:17
give it to the one who has the **t** minas.' Lk 19:24
they said to him, 'Lord, he has **t** minas!' Lk 19:25
them not more than eight or **t** days, Acts 25:6
than **t** thousand words in a tongue. 1 Cor 14:19
the Lord came with **t** thousands of his Jude 1:14
and for **t** days you will have tribulation. Rv 2:10
troops was twice **t** thousand times ten Rv 9:16
twice ten thousand times **t** thousand; Rv 9:16
dragon, with seven heads and **t** horns, Rv 12:3
of the sea, with **t** horns and seven heads, Rv 13:1
with **t** diadems on its horns and Rv 13:1
and it had seven heads and **t** horns. Rv 17:3
seven heads and **t** horns that carries Rv 17:7
And the **t** horns that you saw are ten Rv 17:12
that you saw are **t** kings who have not Rv 17:12
And the **t** horns that you saw, they and Rv 17:16

TEN-STRINGED (1)
O God; upon a **t** harp I will play to you, Ps 144:9

TENANTS (15)
in it and built a tower and leased it to **t**, Mt 21:33
sent his servants to the **t** to get his fruit. Mt 21:34
And the **t** took his servants and beat Mt 21:35
But when the **t** saw the son, they said to Mt 21:38
comes, what will he do to those **t**?" Mt 21:40
the vineyard to other **t** who will give Mt 21:41
and leased it to **t** and went into another Mk 12:1
sent a servant to the **t** to get from them Mk 12:2
But those **t** said to one another, 'This is Mk 12:7
come and destroy the **t** and give the Mk 12:9
and let it out to **t** and went into another Lk 20:9
time came, he sent a servant to the **t**, Lk 20:10
But the **t** beat him and sent him away Lk 20:10
But when the **t** saw him, they said to Lk 20:14
come and destroy those **t** and give the Lk 20:16

TEND (4)
and his sons shall **t** it from evening to Ex 27:21
He will **t** his flock like a shepherd; he Is 40:11
Strangers shall stand and **t** your flocks; Is 61:5
love you." He said to him, "**T** my sheep." Jn 21:16

TENDED (1)
other I named Union. And I **t** the sheep. Zec 11:7

TENDER (19)
to the herd and took a calf, **t** and good, Gn 18:7
who is the most **t** and refined among Dt 28:54
The most **t** and refined woman among Dt 28:56
ground because she is so delicate and **t**, Dt 28:56
the dew, like gentle rain upon the **t** grass, Dt 32:2
plants of the field and like **t** grass, 2 Kgs 19:26
your heart was **t** and you humbled 2 Chr 34:27
t, the only one in the sight of my mother, Prv 4:3
like plants of the field and like **t** grass, Is 37:27
shall no more be called **t** and delicate. Is 47:1
womb, the children of their **t** care? Lam 2:20
the topmost of its young twigs a **t** one, Ezk 17:22
and bronze, amid the **t** grass of the field. Dn 4:15
and bronze, in the **t** grass of the field, Dn 4:23
me; my compassion grows warm and **t**. Hos 11:8
as its branch becomes **t** and puts out Mt 24:32
as its branch becomes **t** and puts out Mk 13:28
because of the **t** mercy of our God, Lk 1:78
sympathy, brotherly love, a **t** heart, 1 Pt 3:8

TENDERHEARTED (1)
one another, **t**, forgiving one another, Eph 4:32

TENDERLY (3)
the young woman and spoke **t** to her. Gn 34:3
Speak **t** to Jerusalem, and cry to her that Is 40:2
into the wilderness, and speak **t** to her. Hos 2:14

TENDS (4)
wrath! Fret not yourself; it **t** only to evil. Ps 37:8
profit, but mere talk **t** only to poverty. Prv 14:23
Whoever **t** a fig tree will eat its fruit, Prv 27:18
Or who **t** a flock without getting some 1 Cor 9:7

TENONS (6)

There shall be two **t** in each frame, for Ex 26:17
two bases under one frame for its two **t**, Ex 26:19
bases under the next frame for its two **t**; Ex 26:19
frame had two **t** for fitting together. Ex 36:22
two bases under one frame for its two **t**, Ex 36:24
bases under the next frame for its two **t**. Ex 36:24

TENS (5)

of hundreds, of fifties, and of **t**. Ex 18:21
of hundreds, of fifties, and of **t**. Ex 18:25
commanders of fifties, commanders of **t**, Dt 1:15
and he shall cast down **t** of thousands, Dn 11:12
And **t** of thousands shall fall, but these Dn 11:41

TENT (299)

drunk and lay uncovered in his **t**. Gn 9:21
on the east of Bethel and pitched his **t**, Gn 12:8
to the place where his **t** had been at the Gn 13:3
valley and moved his **t** as far as Sodom. Gn 13:12
So Abram moved his **t** and came and Gn 13:18
sat at the door of his **t** in the heat of the Gn 18:1
he ran from the **t** door to meet them and Gn 18:2
went quickly into the **t** to Sarah and Gn 18:6
your wife?" And he said, "She is in the **t**." Gn 18:9
was listening at the **t** door behind him. Gn 18:10
brought her into the **t** of Sarah his Gn 24:67
of the LORD and pitched his **t** there. Gn 26:25
Jacob had pitched his **t** in the hill Gn 31:25
went into Jacob's **t** and into Leah's Gn 31:33
tent and into Leah's **t** and into the tent Gn 31:33
tent and into the **t** of the two female Gn 31:33
out of Leah's **t** and entered Rachel's. Gn 31:33
Laban felt all about the **t**, but did not Gn 31:34
of land on which he had pitched his **t**. Gn 33:19
on and pitched his **t** beyond the tower Gn 35:21
persons that each of you has in his **t**.'" Ex 16:16
other of their welfare and went into the **t**. Ex 18:7
of goats' hair for a **t** over the tabernacle; Ex 26:7
shall double over at the front of the **t**. Ex 26:9
and couple the **t** together that it may be Ex 26:11
that remains of the curtains of the **t**, Ex 26:12
shall make for the **t** a covering of Ex 26:14
make a screen for the entrance of the **t**, Ex 26:36
In the **t** of meeting, outside the veil that Ex 27:21
they go into the **t** of meeting or when Ex 28:43
the entrance of the **t** of meeting and Ex 29:4
bring the bull before the **t** of meeting. Ex 29:10
LORD at the entrance of the **t** of meeting, Ex 29:11
who comes into the **t** of meeting to Ex 29:30
in the entrance of the **t** of meeting. Ex 29:32
the entrance of the **t** of meeting before Ex 29:42
I will consecrate the **t** of meeting and Ex 29:44
give it for the service of the **t** of meeting, Ex 30:16
put it between the **t** of meeting and the Ex 30:18
When they go into the **t** of meeting, or Ex 30:20
you shall anoint the **t** of meeting and Ex 30:26
the testimony in the **t** of meeting where Ex 30:36
the **t** of meeting, and the ark of the Ex 31:7
is on it, and all the furnishings of the **t**, Ex 31:7
used to take the **t** and pitch it outside Ex 33:7
camp, and he called it the **t** of meeting. Ex 33:7
the LORD would go out to the **t** of meeting, Ex 33:7
Whenever Moses went out to the **t**, all Ex 33:8
up, and each would stand at his **t** door, Ex 33:8
Moses until he had gone into the **t**. Ex 33:8
When Moses entered the **t**, the pillar of Ex 33:9
and stand at the entrance of the **t**, Ex 33:9
cloud standing at the entrance of the **t**, Ex 33:10
rise up and worship, each at his **t** door. Ex 33:10
man, would not depart from the **t**. Ex 33:11
the tabernacle, its **t** and its covering, its Ex 35:11
to be used for the **t** of meeting, Ex 35:21
of goats' hair for a **t** over the tabernacle. Ex 36:14
bronze to couple the **t** together that it Ex 36:18
he made for the **t** a covering of tanned Ex 36:19
made a screen for the entrance of the **t**, Ex 36:37
in the entrance of the **t** of meeting. Ex 38:8
for the entrance of the **t** of meeting, Ex 38:30
the tabernacle of the **t** of meeting was Ex 39:32
to Moses, the **t** and all its utensils, Ex 39:33
and the screen for the entrance of the **t**; Ex 39:38
of the tabernacle, for the **t** of meeting; Ex 39:40
erect the tabernacle of the **t** of meeting. Ex 40:2
door of the tabernacle of the **t** of meeting, Ex 40:6
the basin between the **t** of meeting and Ex 40:7
the entrance of the **t** of meeting and Ex 40:12
And he spread the **t** over the tabernacle Ex 40:19
and put the covering of the **t** over it, Ex 40:19
He put the table in the **t** of meeting, on Ex 40:22
put the lampstand in the **t** of meeting, Ex 40:24
golden altar in the **t** of meeting before Ex 40:26
of the tabernacle of the **t** of meeting, Ex 40:29
the basin between the **t** of meeting and Ex 40:30
When they went into the **t** of meeting, Ex 40:32
the cloud covered the **t** of meeting, Ex 40:34
able to enter the **t** of meeting because Ex 40:35
and spoke to him from the **t** of meeting, Lv 1:1
bring it to the entrance of the **t** of meeting, Lv 1:3
that is at the entrance of the **t** of meeting. Lv 1:5
kill it at the entrance of the **t** of meeting, Lv 3:2
and kill it in front of the **t** of meeting; Lv 3:8
and kill it in front of the **t** of meeting, Lv 3:13
the entrance of the **t** of meeting before the Lv 4:4
the bull and bring it into the **t** of meeting, Lv 4:5
before the LORD that is in the **t** of meeting, Lv 4:7
that is at the entrance of the **t** of meeting. Lv 4:7
and bring it in front of the **t** of meeting. Lv 4:14
blood of the bull into the **t** of meeting, Lv 4:16
altar that is in the **t** of meeting before the Lv 4:18
that is at the entrance of the **t** of meeting. Lv 4:18
In the court of the **t** of meeting they shall Lv 6:16
be eaten, in the court of the **t** of meeting. Lv 6:26
is brought into the **t** of meeting to make Lv 6:30
at the entrance of the **t** of meeting." Lv 8:3
at the entrance of the **t** of meeting. Lv 8:4
flesh at the entrance of the **t** of meeting, Lv 8:31
the entrance of the **t** of meeting for seven Lv 8:33
the entrance of the **t** of meeting you shall Lv 8:35
commanded in front of the **t** of meeting, Lv 9:5
and Aaron went into the **t** of meeting, Lv 9:23
outside the entrance of the **t** of meeting, Lv 10:7
you, when you go into the **t** of meeting, Lv 10:9
the entrance of the **t** of meeting a lamb Lv 12:6
camp, but live outside his **t** seven days. Lv 14:8
LORD, at the entrance of the **t** of meeting. Lv 14:11
to the entrance of the **t** of meeting, Lv 14:23
the entrance of the **t** of meeting and Lv 15:14
to the entrance of the **t** of meeting. Lv 15:29
LORD at the entrance of the **t** of meeting. Lv 16:7
And so he shall do for the **t** of meeting, Lv 16:16
one may be in the **t** of meeting from the Lv 16:17
Holy Place and the **t** of meeting and the Lv 16:20
shall come into the **t** of meeting and Lv 16:23
atonement for the **t** of meeting and Lv 16:33
to the entrance of the **t** of meeting to offer Lv 17:4
priest at the entrance of the **t** of meeting, Lv 17:5
the entrance of the **t** of meeting and Lv 17:6
to the entrance of the **t** of meeting to offer Lv 17:9
LORD, to the entrance of the **t** of meeting, Lv 19:21
veil of the testimony, in the **t** of meeting, Lv 24:3
wilderness of Sinai, in the **t** of meeting, Nm 1:1
shall camp facing the **t** of meeting on Nm 2:2
"Then the **t** of meeting shall set out, Nm 2:17
congregation before the **t** of meeting, Nm 3:7
all the furnishings of the **t** of meeting, Nm 3:8
of Gershon in the **t** of meeting involved Nm 3:25
the tabernacle, the **t** with its covering, Nm 3:25
for the entrance of the **t** of meeting, Nm 3:25
before the **t** of meeting toward the Nm 3:38
duty, to do the work in the **t** of meeting. Nm 4:3
of the sons of Kohath in the **t** of meeting: Nm 4:4
the things of the **t** of meeting that the Nm 4:15
duty, to do service in the **t** of meeting. Nm 4:23
tabernacle and the **t** of meeting with Nm 4:25
for the entrance of the **t** of meeting Nm 4:25
of the Gershonites in the **t** of meeting, Nm 4:28
to do the service of the **t** of meeting. Nm 4:30
of their service in the **t** of meeting: Nm 4:31
of their service in the **t** of meeting, Nm 4:33
on duty, for service in the **t** of meeting; Nm 4:35
all who served in the **t** of meeting, Nm 4:37
on duty for service in the **t** of meeting— Nm 4:39
all who served in the **t** of meeting, Nm 4:41
duty, for service in the **t** of meeting— Nm 4:43
of bearing burdens in the **t** of meeting, Nm 4:47
to the entrance of the **t** of meeting, Nm 6:10
to the entrance of the **t** of meeting, Nm 6:13
the entrance of the **t** of meeting and Nm 6:18
be used in the service of the **t** of meeting, Nm 7:5
Moses went into the **t** of meeting to Nm 7:89
the Levites before the **t** of meeting and Nm 8:9
shall go in to serve at the **t** of meeting, Nm 8:15
of Israel at the **t** of meeting and to Nm 8:19
their service in the **t** of meeting before Nm 8:22
duty in the service of the **t** of meeting. Nm 8:24
their brothers in the **t** of meeting by Nm 8:26
the tabernacle, the **t** of the testimony. Nm 9:15
the cloud lifted from over the **t**, Nm 9:17
you at the entrance of the **t** of meeting. Nm 10:3
clans, everyone at the door of his **t**. Nm 11:10
and bring them to the **t** of meeting, Nm 11:16
people and placed them around the **t**. Nm 11:24
but they had not gone out to the **t**, Nm 11:26
to the **t** of meeting." And the three of Nm 12:4
the entrance of the **t** and called Aaron Nm 12:5
the cloud removed from over the **t**, Nm 12:10
LORD appeared at the **t** of meeting to all Nm 14:10
the entrance of the **t** of meeting with Nm 16:18
at the entrance of the **t** of meeting. Nm 16:19
they turned toward the **t** of meeting. Nm 16:42
came to the front of the **t** of meeting, Nm 16:43
at the entrance of the **t** of meeting, Nm 16:50
deposit them in the **t** of meeting before Nm 17:4
the LORD in the **t** of the testimony. Nm 17:7
Moses went into the **t** of the testimony, Nm 17:8
you are before the **t** of the testimony. Nm 18:2
guard over you and over the whole **t**, Nm 18:3
keep guard over the **t** of meeting for all Nm 18:4
of meeting for all the service of the **t**, Nm 18:4
to do the service of the **t** of meeting. Nm 18:6
do, their service in the **t** of meeting, Nm 18:21
do not come near the **t** of meeting, Nm 18:22
shall do the service of the **t** of meeting, Nm 18:23
for your service in the **t** of meeting. Nm 18:31
the front of the **t** of meeting seven Nm 19:4
is the law when someone dies in a **t**: Nm 19:14
comes into the **t** and everyone who Nm 19:14
who is in the **t** shall be unclean seven Nm 19:14
and sprinkle it on the **t** and on all the Nm 19:18
the entrance of the **t** of meeting and fell Nm 20:6
in the entrance of the **t** of meeting. Nm 25:6
at the entrance of the **t** of meeting, Nm 27:2
and brought it into the **t** of meeting, Nm 31:54
present yourselves in the **t** of meeting, Dt 31:14
themselves in the **t** of meeting. Dt 31:14
the LORD appeared in the **t** in a pillar of Dt 31:15
of cloud stood over the entrance of the **t**. Dt 31:15
they are hidden in the earth inside my **t**, Jos 7:21
sent messengers, and they ran to the **t**; Jos 7:22
was hidden in his **t** with the silver Jos 7:22
them out of the **t** and brought them to Jos 7:23
and sheep and his **t** and all that he Jos 7:24
Shiloh and set up the **t** of meeting there. Jos 18:1
at the entrance of the **t** of meeting. Jos 19:51
and had pitched his **t** as far away as the Jgs 4:11
Sisera fled away on foot to the **t** of Jael, Jgs 4:17
So he turned aside to her into the **t**, Jgs 4:18
said to her, "Stand at the opening of the **t**, Jgs 4:20
But Jael the wife of Heber took a **t** peg, Jgs 4:21
you are seeking." So he went in to her **t**, Jgs 4:22
Sisera dead, with the **t** peg in his temple. Jgs 4:22
sent her hand to the **t** peg and her right Jgs 5:26
all the rest of Israel every man to his **t**, Jgs 7:8
and came to the **t** and struck it so Jgs 7:13
it upside down, so that the **t** lay flat." Jgs 7:13
the way of the **t** dwellers east of Nobah Jgs 8:11
man, saying, "None of us will go to his **t**, Jgs 20:8
at the entrance to the **t** of meeting. 1 Sm 2:22
he sent home, every man to his **t**. 1 Sm 13:2
but he put his armor in his **t**. 1 Sm 17:54
inside the **t** that David had pitched for 2 Sm 6:17
cedar, but the ark of God dwells in a **t**." 2 Sm 7:2
moving about in a **t** for my dwelling. 2 Sm 7:6
So they pitched a **t** for Absalom on 2 Sm 16:22
oil from the **t** and anointed Solomon. 1 Kgs 1:39
—Joab fled to the **t** of the LORD and 1 Kgs 2:28
"Joab has fled to the **t** of the LORD, 1 Kgs 2:29
Benaiah came to the **t** of the LORD and 1 Kgs 2:30
up the ark of the LORD, the **t** of meeting, 1 Kgs 8:4
all the holy vessels that were in the **t**; 1 Kgs 8:4
they went into a **t** and ate and drank, 2 Kgs 7:8
and entered another **t** and carried off 2 Kgs 7:8
tabernacle of the **t** of meeting until 1 Chr 6:32
keepers of the thresholds of the **t**, 1 Chr 9:19
at the entrance of the **t** of meeting. 1 Chr 9:21
of the LORD, that is, the house of the **t**, 1 Chr 9:23
the ark of God and pitched a **t** for it. 1 Chr 15:1
set it inside the **t** that David had 1 Chr 16:1
the covenant of the LORD is under a **t**." 1 Chr 17:1
I have gone from **t** to tent and from 1 Chr 17:5
gone from tent to **t** and from dwelling 1 Chr 17:5
keep charge of the **t** of meeting and 1 Chr 23:32
at Gibeon, for the **t** of meeting of God, 2 Chr 1:3
he had pitched a **t** for it in Jerusalem.) 2 Chr 1:4
LORD, which was at the **t** of meeting, 2 Chr 1:6
Gibeon, from before the **t** of meeting, 2 Chr 1:13
brought up the ark, the **t** of meeting, 2 Chr 5:5
all the holy vessels that were in the **t**; 2 Chr 5:5
of Israel for the **t** of testimony?" 2 Chr 24:6
You shall know that your **t** is at peace, Jb 5:24
and the **t** of the wicked will be no more." Jb 8:22
The light is dark in his **t**, and his lamp Jb 18:6
He is torn from the **t** in which he trusted Jb 18:14
In his **t** dwells that which is none of his; Jb 18:15
against me and encamp around my **t**. Jb 19:12
what is left in his **t** will be consumed. Jb 20:26
Where is the **t** in which the wicked Jb 21:28
the friendship of God was upon my **t**, Jb 29:4
if the men of my **t** have not said, 'Who Jb 31:31
O LORD, who shall sojourn in your **t**? Ps 15:1
world. In them he has set a **t** for the sun, Ps 19:4
will conceal me under the cover of his **t**; Ps 27:5
will offer in his **t** sacrifices with shouts Ps 27:6
he will snatch and tear you from your **t**; Ps 52:5
Let me dwell in your **t** forever! Let me Ps 61:4

the **t** where he dwelt among mankind, Ps 78:60
He rejected the **t** of Joseph; he did not Ps 78:67
befall you, no plague come near your **t**. Ps 91:10
stretching out the heavens like a **t**. Ps 104:2
but the **t** of the upright will flourish. Prv 14:11
no Arab will pitch his **t** there; Is 13:20
in faithfulness in the **t** of David one who Is 16:5
untroubled habitation, an immovable **t**, Is 33:20
removed from me like a shepherd's **t**; Is 38:12
and spreads them like a **t** to dwell in; Is 40:22
"Enlarge the place of your **t**, and let the Is 54:2
My **t** is destroyed, and all my cords are Jer 10:20
no one to spread my **t** again and to set Jer 10:20
only wounded men, every man in his **t**, Jer 37:10
in our eyes in the **t** of the daughter of Lam 2:4
the cornerstone, from him the **t** peg, Zec 10:4
You took up the **t** of Moloch and the Acts 7:43
"Our fathers had the **t** of witness in the Acts 7:44
I will rebuild the **t** of David that has Acts 15:16
For we know that if the **t**, which is our 2 Cor 5:1
For in this **t** we groan, longing to put 2 Cor 5:2
For while we are still in this **t**, we 2 Cor 5:4
places, in the true **t** that the Lord set up, Heb 8:2
For when Moses was about to erect the **t**, Heb 8:5
For a **t** was prepared, the first section, in Heb 9:2
and more perfect **t** (not made with Heb 9:11
the blood both the **t** and all the vessels Heb 9:21
those who serve the **t** have no right to Heb 13:10
the sanctuary of the **t** of witness in Rv 15:5

TENT-CORD (1)
Is not their **t** plucked up within them, do Jb 4:21

TENT-DWELLING (1)
the Kenite, of **t** women most blessed. Jgs 5:24

TENTH (61)
continued to abate until the **t** month; Gn 8:5
in the **t** month, on the first day of the Gn 8:5
Abram gave him a **t** of everything. Gn 14:20
you give me I will give a full **t** to you." Gn 28:22
of Israel that on the **t** day of this month Ex 12:3
(An omer is the **t** part of an ephah.) Ex 16:36
with the first lamb a **t** seah of fine flour Ex 29:40
that he has committed a **t** of an ephah of Lv 5:11
a **t** of an ephah of fine flour as a regular Lv 6:20
and a **t** of an ephah of fine flour mixed Lv 14:21
month, on the **t** day of the month, Lv 16:29
"Now on the **t** day of this seventh Lv 23:27
loud trumpet on the **t** day of the seventh Lv 25:9
every **t** animal of all that pass under the Lv 27:32
of her, a **t** of an ephah of barley flour. Nm 5:15
On the **t** day Ahiezer the son of Nm 7:66
a grain offering of a **t** of an ephah of Nm 15:4
also a **t** of an ephah of fine flour for a Nm 28:5
and a **t** of fine flour mixed with oil as Nm 28:13
a **t** shall you offer for each of the seven Nm 28:21
a **t** for each of the seven lambs; Nm 28:29
and one **t** for each of the seven lambs; Nm 29:4
"On the **t** day of this seventh month Nm 29:7
a **t** for each of the seven lambs: Nm 29:10
and a **t** for each of the fourteen lambs; Nm 29:15
Even to the **t** generation, none of his Dt 23:2
Even to the **t** generation, none of them Dt 23:3
of the Jordan on the **t** day of the first Jos 4:19
He will take the **t** of your grain and of 1 Sm 8:15
He will take the **t** of your flocks, and 1 Sm 8:17
year of his reign, in the **t** month, 2 Kgs 25:1
month, on the **t** day of the month, 2 Kgs 25:1
Jeremiah **t**, Machbannai eleventh. 1 Chr 12:13
ninth to Jeshua, the **t** to Shecaniah, 1 Chr 24:11
the **t** to Shimei, his sons and his 1 Chr 25:17
T, for the tenth month, was 1 Chr 27:13
Tenth, for the **t** month, was 1 Chr 27:13
first day of the **t** month they sat down Ezr 10:16
into his royal palace in the **t** month, Est 2:16
And though a **t** remain in it, it will be Is 6:13
the LORD in the **t** year of Zedekiah king Jer 32:1
Zedekiah king of Judah, in the **t** month, Jer 39:1
ninth year of his reign, in the **t** month, Jer 52:4
tenth month, on the **t** day of the month, Jer 52:4
on the **t** day of the month—that was the Jer 52:12
fifth month, on the **t** day of the month, Ezk 20:1
In the ninth year, in the **t** month, on the Ezk 24:1
tenth month, on the **t** day of the month, Ezk 24:1
In the **t** year, in the tenth month, on the Ezk 29:1
In the tenth year, in the **t** month, on the Ezk 29:1
year of our exile, in the **t** month, Ezk 33:21
of the year, on the **t** day of the month, Ezk 40:1
the bath containing one **t** of a homer, Ezk 45:11
and the ephah one **t** of a homer; Ezk 45:11
one **t** of a bath from each cor (the cor, Ezk 45:14
and the fast of the **t** shall be to the house Zec 8:19
him that day, for it was about the **t** hour. Jn 1:39
Abraham apportioned a **t** part of Heb 7:2
the patriarch gave a **t** of the spoils! Heb 7:4
great earthquake, and a **t** of the city fell. Rv 11:13
the ninth topaz, the **t** chrysoprase, Rv 21:20

TENTHS (19)
a grain offering of three **t** of an ephah of Lv 14:10
with it shall be two **t** of an ephah of fine Lv 23:13
to be waved, made of two **t** of an ephah. Lv 23:17
it; two **t** of an ephah shall be in each loaf. Lv 24:5
for a grain offering two **t** of an ephah of Nm 15:6
grain offering of three **t** of an ephah of Nm 15:9
and two **t** of an ephah of fine flour for a Nm 28:9
also three **t** of an ephah of fine flour Nm 28:12
and two **t** of fine flour for a grain Nm 28:12
three **t** of an ephah shall you offer for Nm 28:20
offer for a bull, and two **t** for a ram; Nm 28:20
oil, three **t** of an ephah for each bull, Nm 28:28
for each bull, two **t** for one ram, Nm 28:28
oil, three **t** of an ephah for the bull, Nm 29:3
an ephah for the bull, two **t** for the ram, Nm 29:3
oil, three **t** of an ephah for the bull, Nm 29:9
for the bull, two **t** for the one ram, Nm 29:9
three **t** of an ephah for each of the Nm 29:14
bulls, two **t** for each of the two rams, Nm 29:14

TENTMAKERS (1)
and worked, for they were **t** by trade. Acts 18:3

TENTS (60)
those who dwell in **t** and have livestock. Gn 4:20
and let him dwell in the **t** of Shem, Gn 9:27
Abram, also had flocks and herds and **t**, Gn 13:5
Jacob was a quiet man, dwelling in **t**. Gn 25:27
with his kinsmen pitched **t** in the hill Gn 31:25
shall pitch their **t** by their companies, Nm 1:52
please, from the **t** of these wicked men, Nm 16:26
out and stood at the door of their **t**, Nm 16:27
How lovely are your **t**, O Jacob, your Nm 24:5
And you murmured in your **t** and said, Dt 1:27
to seek you out a place to pitch your **t**, Dt 1:33
Go and say to them, "Return to your **t**." Dt 5:30
them up, with their households, their **t**, Dt 11:6
morning you shall turn and go to your **t**. Dt 16:7
your going out, and Issachar, in your **t**. Dt 33:18
set out from their **t** to pass over the Jos 3:14
turn and go to your **t** in the land where Jos 22:4
sent them away, and they went to their **t**. Jos 22:6
"Go back to your **t** with much wealth Jos 22:8
come up with their livestock and their **t**; Jgs 6:5
of Jesse; every man to his **t**, O Israel!" 2 Sm 20:1
the son of Jesse. To your **t**, O Israel! 1 Kgs 12:16
David." So Israel went to their **t**. 1 Kgs 12:16
in the twilight and abandoned their **t**, 2 Kgs 7:7
donkeys tied and the **t** as they were." 2 Kgs 7:10
and destroyed their **t** and the 1 Chr 4:41
lived in their **t** throughout all the 1 Chr 5:10
Jesse. Each of you to your **t**, O Israel! 2 Chr 10:16
David." So all Israel went to their **t**. 2 Chr 10:16
they struck down the **t** of those who 2 Chr 14:15
and let not injustice dwell in your **t**. Jb 11:14
The **t** of robbers are at peace, and those Jb 12:6
and fire consumes the **t** of bribery. Jb 15:34
if you remove injustice far from your **t**, Jb 22:23
a desolation; let no one dwell in their **t**. Ps 69:25
of their strength in the **t** of Ham. Ps 78:51
and settled the tribes of Israel in their **t**. Ps 78:55
the **t** of Edom and the Ishmaelites, Moab Ps 83:6
God than dwell in the **t** of wickedness. Ps 84:10
They murmured in their **t**, and did not Ps 106:25
salvation are in the **t** of the righteous: Ps 118:15
that I dwell among the **t** of Kedar! Ps 120:5
daughters of Jerusalem, like the **t** of Kedar, Sg 1:5
your young goats beside the shepherds' **t**. Sg 1:8
Suddenly my **t** are laid waste, my Jer 4:20
her; they shall pitch their **t** around her; Jer 6:3
the fortunes of the **t** of Jacob and have Jer 30:18
but you shall live in **t** all your days, that Jer 35:7
we have lived in **t** and have obeyed and Jer 35:10
Their **t** and their flocks shall be taken, Jer 49:29
pitch his palatial **t** between the sea Dn 11:45
things of silver; thorns shall be in their **t**. Hos 9:6
I will again make you dwell in **t**, as in Hos 12:9
I saw the **t** of Cushan in affliction; the Hab 3:7
will give salvation to the **t** of Judah first, Zec 12:7
the LORD cut off from the **t** of Jacob, Mal 2:12
If you wish, I will make three **t** here, one Mt 17:4
Let us make three **t**, one for you and one Mk 9:5
Let us make three **t**, one for you and one Lk 9:33
land, living in **t** with Isaac and Jacob, Heb 11:9

TERAH (14)
had lived 29 years, he fathered **T**. Gn 11:24
lived after he fathered **T** 119 years and Gn 11:25
When **T** had lived 70 years, he fathered Gn 11:26
Now these are the generations of **T**. Gn 11:27
T fathered Abram, Nahor, and Haran; Gn 11:27
presence of his father **T** in the land of Gn 11:28
T took Abram his son and Lot the son Gn 11:31
The days of **T** were 205 years, and Gn 11:32
were 205 years, and **T** died in Haran. Gn 11:32
set out from Tahath and camped at **T**. Nm 33:27
they set out from **T** and camped at Nm 33:28
T, the father of Abraham and of Nahor; Jos 24:2
Serug, Nahor, **T**; 1 Chr 1:26
Isaac, the son of Abraham, the son of **T**, Lk 3:34

TERAPHIM (1)
shakes the arrows; he consults the **t**; Ezk 21:21

TEREBINTH (7)
hid them under the **t** tree that was near Gn 35:4
it up there under the **t** that was by the Jos 24:26
came and sat under the **t** at Ophrah, Jgs 6:11
to him under the **t** and presented them. Jgs 6:19
under the thick branches of a great **t**, 2 Sm 18:9
it will be burned again, like a **t** or an oak, Is 6:13
on the hills, under oak, poplar, and **t**, Hos 4:13

TEREBINTHS (1)
according to The Dove on Far-off **T**. Ps 56:T

TERESH (2)
sitting at the king's gate, Bigthan and **T**, Est 2:21
had told about Bigthana and **T**, Est 6:2

TERM (1)
called these days Purim, after the **t** Pur. Est 9:26

TERMED (2)
You shall no more be **t** Forsaken, and Is 62:4
your land shall no more be **t** Desolate, Is 62:4

TERMS (9)
to fight against it, offer **t** of peace to it. Dt 20:10
let you go on these **t**." So he made a 1 Kgs 20:34
containing the **t** and conditions and Jer 32:11
did not keep the **t** of the covenant that Jer 34:18
and he shall bring **t** of an agreement Dn 11:17
Come to **t** quickly with your accuser Mt 5:25
a delegation and asks for **t** of peace. Lk 14:32
I am speaking in human **t**, because of Rom 6:19
they work on the same **t** as we do. 2 Cor 11:12

TERRIBLE (3)
to them. And they were in **t** distress. Jgs 2:15
comes from the wilderness, from a **t** land. Is 21:1
of her future; therefore her fall is **t**; Lam 1:9

TERRIBLY (5)
Be not so **t** angry, O LORD, and remember Is 64:9
Will you keep silent, and afflict us so **t**? Is 64:12
is lying paralyzed at home, suffering **t**." Mt 8:6
for he is an epileptic and he suffers **t**. Mt 17:15
after crying out and convulsing him **t**, Mk 9:26

TERRIFIED (16)
and he **t** and afflicted them with 1 Sm 5:6
and when she saw that he was **t**, 1 Sm 28:21
Then Haman was **t** before the king Est 7:6
Therefore I am **t** at his presence; when I Jb 23:15
my heart faint; the Almighty has **t** me; Jb 23:16
and the contempt of families **t** me, Jb 31:34
against him is not **t** by their shouting or Is 31:4
harm, that we may be dismayed and **t**. Is 41:23
They shall be **t**; they shall be put to Is 44:11
destruction of the beasts that **t** them, Hab 2:17
him walking on the sea, they were **t**, Mt 14:26
this, they fell on their faces and were **t**. Mt 17:6
for they all saw him and were **t**. But Mk 6:50
did not know what to say, for they were **t**. Mk 9:6
hear of wars and tumults, do not be **t**, Lk 21:9
and the rest were **t** and gave glory to the Rv 11:13

TERRIFIES (1)
ears of men and **t** them with warnings, Jb 33:16

TERRIFY (16)
on the wall, to frighten and **t** them, 2 Chr 32:18
upon it; let the blackness of the day **t** it. Jb 3:5
me with dreams and **t** me with visions, Jb 7:14
from me, and let not dread of him **t** me. Jb 9:34
Will not his majesty **t** you, and the Jb 13:11
from me, and let not dread of you **t** me. Jb 13:21
distress and anguish **t** him; they prevail Jb 15:24
Behold, no fear of me need **t** you; my Jb 33:7
them in his wrath, and **t** them in his fury, Ps 2:5
with your tempest and **t** them with your Ps 83:15
his majesty, when he rises to **t** the earth. Is 2:19
his majesty, when he rises to **t** the earth. Is 2:21
"Let us go up against Judah and **t** it, and let Is 7:6
I will **t** Elam before their enemies and Jer 49:37
in ships to **t** the unsuspecting people Ezk 30:9
And these have come to **t** them, to cast Zec 1:21

TERRIFYING (8)
all that great and **t** wilderness that you Dt 1:19
you through the great and **t** wilderness, Dt 8:15
you these great and **t** things that your Dt 10:21
the locust? His majestic snorting is **t**. Jb 39:20
hosts will lop the boughs with **t** power; Is 10:33
t and dreadful and exceedingly strong. Dn 7:7

different from all the rest, exceedingly **t**, Dn 7:19
so **t** was the sight that Moses said, Heb 12:21

TERRITORIES (2)

the land and its cities with their **t**, Nm 32:33
distributing the several **t** of the land Jos 19:49

TERRITORY (89)

And the **t** of the Canaanites extended Gn 10:19
The **t** in which they lived extended Gn 10:30
journeyed toward the **t** of the Negeb Gn 20:1
shall be seen with you in all your **t**. Ex 13:7
in Kadesh, a city on the edge of your **t**. Nm 20:16
until we have passed through your **t**." Nm 20:17
to give Israel passage through his **t**, Nm 20:21
until we have passed through your **t**." Nm 21:22
not allow Israel to pass through his **t**. Nm 21:23
at Iye-abarim, in the **t** of Moab. Nm 33:44
to pass through the **t** of your brothers, Dt 2:4
when you approach the **t** of the people of Dt 2:19
and the Gadites the **t** beginning at Aroer, Dt 3:12
the Gadites I gave the **t** from Gilead as far Dt 3:16
Your **t** shall be from the wilderness to Dt 11:24
the LORD your God enlarges your **t**, Dt 12:20
seen with you in all your **t** for seven days, Dt 16:4
And if the LORD your God enlarges your **t**, Dt 19:8
have olive trees throughout all your **t**, Dt 28:40
the going down of the sun shall be your **t**. Jos 1:4
So their **t** was from Aroer, which is on Jos 13:16
Their **t** was Jazer, and all the cities of Jos 13:25
and from Mahanaim to the **t** of Debir, Jos 13:26
along to Ataroth, the **t** of the Archites. Jos 16:2
down westward to the **t** of the Japhletites, Jos 16:3
as far as the **t** of Lower Beth-horon, Jos 16:3
The **t** of the people of Ephraim by their Jos 16:5
The **t** of Manasseh reached from Asher Jos 17:7
shall continue in his **t** on the south, Jos 18:5
shall continue in their **t** on the north. Jos 18:5
and the **t** allotted to it fell between the Jos 18:11
formed part of the **t** of the people of Jos 19:9
And the **t** of their inheritance reached Jos 19:10
Their **t** included Jezreel, Chesulloth, Jos 19:18
Their **t** included Helkath, Hali, Beten, Jos 19:25
And the **t** of its inheritance included Jos 19:41
Rakkon with the **t** over against Joppa. Jos 19:46
When the **t** of the people of Dan was Jos 19:47
up with me into the **t** allotted to me, Jgs 1:3
go with you into the **t** allotted to you." So Jgs 1:3
Judah also captured Gaza with its **t**, and Jgs 1:18
its territory, and Ashkelon with its **t**, Jgs 1:18
with its territory, and Ekron with its **t**. Jgs 1:18
But they did not enter the **t** of Moab, for Jgs 11:18
not trust Israel to pass through his **t**, Jgs 11:20
possession of all the **t** of the Amorites Jgs 11:22
sent her throughout all the **t** of Israel. Jgs 19:29
with tumors, both Ashdod and its **t**. 1 Sm 5:6
and did not again enter the **t** of Israel. 1 Sm 7:13
Israel delivered their **t** from the hand 1 Sm 7:14
Rachel's tomb in the **t** of Benjamin at 1 Sm 10:2
messengers through all the **t** of Israel. 1 Sm 11:3
them throughout all the **t** of Israel by 1 Sm 11:7
have no place in all the **t** of Israel, 2 Sm 21:5
woman throughout all the **t** of Israel, 1 Kgs 1:3
shall eat Jezebel in the **t** of Jezreel, 2 Kgs 9:10
'In the **t** of Jezreel the dogs shall eat 2 Kgs 9:36
the face of the field in the **t** of Jezreel, 2 Kgs 9:37
them throughout the **t** of Israel: 2 Kgs 10:32
were in it and its **t** from Tirzah on, 2 Kgs 15:16
the Philistines as far as Gaza and its **t**, 2 Kgs 18:8
had cities of their **t** out of the tribe 1 Chr 6:66
throughout all the **t** of Israel.' 1 Chr 21:12
built cities in the **t** of Ashdod and 2 Chr 26:6
from all the **t** that belonged to 2 Chr 34:33
may take it to its **t** and that you may Jb 38:20
for all your sins, throughout all your **t**. Jer 15:13
places for sin throughout all your **t**. Jer 17:3
the whole **t** on the top of the mountain Ezk 43:12
Adjoining the **t** of Dan, from the east Ezk 48:2
Adjoining the **t** of Asher, from the east Ezk 48:3
Adjoining the **t** of Naphtali, from the Ezk 48:4
Adjoining the **t** of Manasseh, from the Ezk 48:5
Adjoining the **t** of Ephraim, from the Ezk 48:6
Adjoining the **t** of Reuben, from the Ezk 48:7
"Adjoining the **t** of Judah, from the east Ezk 48:8
place, adjoining the **t** of the Levites. Ezk 48:12
And alongside the **t** of the priests, the Ezk 48:13
shall lie between the **t** of Judah and the Ezk 48:22
of Judah and the **t** of Benjamin. Ezk 48:22
Adjoining the **t** of Benjamin, from the Ezk 48:24
Adjoining the **t** of Simeon, from the Ezk 48:25
Adjoining the **t** of Issachar, from the Ezk 48:26
Adjoining the **t** of Zebulun, from the Ezk 48:27
And adjoining the **t** of Gad to the Ezk 48:28
Or is their **t** greater than your territory, Am 6:2
Or is their territory greater than your **t**, Am 6:2
people and made boasts against their **t**. Zep 2:8
sea, in the **t** of Zebulun and Naphtali, Mt 4:13

TERROR (64)

a **t** from God fell upon the cities that Gn 35:5
T and dread fall upon them; because of Ex 15:16
I will send my **t** before you and will Ex 23:27
outstretched arm, and by great deeds of **t**, Dt 4:34
outstretched arm, with great deeds of **t**, Dt 26:8
the sword shall bereave, and indoors **t**, Dt 32:25
all the great deeds of **t** that Moses did in Dt 34:12
you, and sudden **t** overwhelms you, Jb 22:10
For I was in **t** of calamity from God, and Jb 31:23
doors of his face? Around his teeth is **t**. Jb 41:14
strength, and **t** dances before him. Jb 41:22
is of the earth may strike **t** no more. Ps 10:18
There they are in great **t**, for God is with Ps 14:5
whispering of many—**t** on every side! Ps 31:13
There they are, in great **t**, where there is Ps 53:5
are, in great terror, where there is no **t**! Ps 53:5
like a breath, and their years in **t**. Ps 78:33
You will not fear the **t** of the night, nor Ps 91:5
I will mock when **t** strikes you, Prv 1:26
when **t** strikes you like a storm and Prv 1:27
not be afraid of sudden **t** or of the ruin Prv 3:25
The **t** of a king is like the growling of a Prv 20:2
a joy to the righteous but **t** to evildoers. Prv 21:15
his sword at his thigh, against **t** by night. Sg 3:8
in the dust from before the **t** of the LORD, Is 2:10
the ground, from before the **t** of the LORD, Is 2:19
of the cliffs, from before the **t** of the LORD, Is 2:21
evening time, behold, **t**! Before morning, Is 17:14
Judah will become a **t** to the Egyptians. Is 19:17
T and the pit and the snare are upon Is 24:17
at the sound of the **t** shall fall into the Is 24:18
it will be sheer **t** to understand the Is 28:19
His rock shall pass away in **t**, and his Is 31:9
Your heart will muse on the **t**: "Where is Is 33:18
to succeed; perhaps you may inspire **t**. Is 47:12
and from **t**, for it shall not come near Is 54:14
the enemy has a sword; **t** is on every side. Jer 6:25
for a time of healing, but behold, **t**. Jer 8:15
for a time of healing, but behold, **t**. Jer 14:19
have made anguish and **t** fall upon them Jer 15:8
Be not a **t** to me; you are my refuge in Jer 17:17
name Pashhur, but **T** On Every Side. Jer 20:3
I will make you a **t** to yourself and to all Jer 20:4
many whispering. **T** is on every side! Jer 20:10
kingdoms of the earth, to be a curse, a **t**, Jer 29:18
We have heard a cry of panic, of **t**, and Jer 30:5
and outstretched arm, and with great **t**. Jer 32:21
they look not back—**t** on every side! Jer 46:5
T, pit, and snare are before you, O Jer 48:43
who flees from the **t** shall fall into the Jer 48:44
Behold, I will bring **t** upon you, declares Jer 49:5
shall cry to them: '**T** on every side!' Jer 49:29
the people of the land are paralyzed by **t**. Ezk 7:27
them an object of **t** and a plunder. Ezk 23:46
inhabitants imposed their **t** on all her Ezk 26:17
who spread **t** in the land of the living. Ezk 32:23
who spread their **t** in the land of the Ezk 32:24
for **t** of them was spread in the land of Ezk 32:25
for they spread their **t** in the land of Ezk 32:26
for the **t** of the mighty men was in the Ezk 32:27
for all the **t** that they caused by their Ezk 32:30
For I spread **t** in the land of the living; Ezk 32:32
And he stared at him in **t** and said, Acts 10:4
For rulers are not a **t** to good conduct, Rom 13:3

TERROR-STRICKEN (1)

The Assyrians will be **t** at the voice of Is 30:31

TERRORS (13)

the **t** of God are arrayed against me. Jb 6:4
T frighten him on every side, and chase Jb 18:11
trusted and is brought to the king of **t**. Jb 18:14
of his gallbladder; **t** come upon him. Jb 20:25
are friends with the **t** of deep darkness. Jb 24:17
T overtake him like a flood; in the night Jb 27:20
T are turned upon me; my honor is Jb 30:15
me; the **t** of death have fallen upon me. Ps 55:4
in a moment, swept away utterly by **t**! Ps 73:19
death from my youth up, I suffer your **t**; Ps 88:15
of what is high, and **t** are in the way; Eccl 12:5
if to a festival day my **t** on every side, Lam 2:22
And there will be **t** and great signs Lk 21:11

TERTIUS (1)

I **T**, who wrote this letter, greet you in Rom 16:22

TERTULLUS (2)

some elders and a spokesman, one **T**. Acts 24:1
summoned, **T** began to accuse him, Acts 24:2

TEST (60)

portion every day, that I may **t** them, Ex 16:4
with me? Why do you **t** the LORD?" Ex 17:2
"Do not fear, for God has come to **t** you, Ex 20:20
put me to the **t** these ten times and Nm 14:22
shall not put the LORD your God to the **t**, Dt 6:16
that he might humble you and **t** you, Dt 8:16
in order to **t** Israel by them, whether they Jgs 2:22
that the LORD left, to **t** Israel by them, Jgs 3:1
Please let me **t** just once more with the Jgs 6:39
the water, and I will **t** them for you there, Jgs 7:4
she came to **t** him with hard 1 Kgs 10:1
that you **t** the heart and have 1 Chr 29:17
came to Jerusalem to **t** him with hard 2 Chr 9:1
in order to **t** him and to know all 2 Chr 32:31
every morning and **t** him every moment? Jb 7:18
Does not the ear **t** words as the palate Jb 12:11
righteous—you who **t** the minds and Ps 7:9
his eyes see, his eyelids **t**, the children of Ps 11:4
and try me; **t** my heart and my mind. Ps 26:2
fathers put me to the **t** and put me to the Ps 95:9
and put God to the **t** in the desert; Ps 106:14
"Come now, I will **t** you with pleasure; Eccl 2:1
ask, and I will not put the LORD to the **t**." Is 7:12
that you may know and **t** their ways. Jer 6:27
"Behold, I will refine them and **t** them, for Jer 9:7
you see me, and **t** my heart toward you. Jer 12:3
LORD search the heart and **t** the mind, Jer 17:10
Let us **t** and examine our ways, and Lam 3:40
"**T** your servants for ten days; let us be Dn 1:12
silver, and **t** them as gold is tested. Zec 13:9
And thereby put me to the **t**, says the Mal 3:10
they put God to the **t** and they escape.'" Mal 3:15
shall not put the Lord your God to the **t**.'" Mt 4:7
and to **t** him they asked him to show Mt 16:1
malice, said, "Why put me to the **t**, Mt 22:18
lawyer, asked him a question to **t** him. Mt 22:35
from him a sign from heaven to **t** him. Mk 8:11
came up and in order to **t** him asked, Mk 10:2
he said to them, "Why put me to the **t**? Mk 12:15
not put the Lord your God to the **t**.'" Lk 4:12
a lawyer stood up to put him to the **t**, Lk 10:25
while others, to **t** him, kept seeking Lk 11:16
He said this to **t** him, for he himself knew Jn 6:6
This they said to **t** him, that they might Jn 8:6
have agreed together to **t** the Spirit of the Acts 5:9
putting God to the **t** by placing a yoke Acts 15:10
and the fire will **t** what sort of work 1 Cor 3:13
We must not put Christ to the **t**, as 1 Cor 10:9
that I might **t** you and know whether 2 Cor 2:9
for in a severe **t** of affliction, their 2 Cor 8:2
you are in the faith. **T** yourselves. 2 Cor 13:5
—unless indeed you fail to meet the **t**! 2 Cor 13:5
find out that we have not failed the **t**. 2 Cor 13:6
that we may appear to have met the **t**, 2 Cor 13:7
But let each one **t** his own work, and Gal 6:4
but **t** everything; hold fast what is 1 Thes 5:21
put me to the **t** and saw my works Heb 3:9
he has stood the **t** he will receive the Jas 1:12
trial when it comes upon you to **t** you, 1 Pt 4:12
but **t** the spirits to see whether they are 1 Jn 4:1

TESTED (29)

these things God **t** Abraham and said Gn 22:1
By this you shall be **t**: by the life of Gn 42:15
confined, that your words may be **t**, Gn 42:16
statute and a rule, and there he **t** them, Ex 15:25
and because they **t** the LORD by saying, Ex 17:7
God to the test, as you **t** him at Massah. Dt 6:16
your godly one, whom you **t** at Massah, Dt 33:8
in vain to go, for he had not **t** them. 1 Sm 17:39
for I have not **t** them." So David put 1 Sm 17:39
have visited me by night, you have **t** me, Ps 17:3
For you, O God, have **t** us; you have Ps 66:10
They **t** God in their heart by Ps 78:18
They **t** God again and again and Ps 78:41
Yet they **t** and rebelled against the Most Ps 78:56
thunder; I **t** you at the waters of Meribah. Ps 81:7
to pass, the word of the LORD **t** him. Ps 105:19
for gold, and a man is **t** by his praise. Prv 27:21
All this I have **t** by wisdom. I said, "I Eccl 7:23
a foundation in Zion, a stone, a **t** stone, Is 28:16
in this matter, and **t** them for ten days. Dn 1:14
refines silver, and test them as gold is **t**. Zec 13:9
came up to him and **t** him by asking, Mt 19:3
we have often **t** and found earnest 2 Cor 8:22
And let them also be **t** first; then let 1 Tm 3:10
By faith Abraham, when he was **t**, Heb 11:17
so that the **t** genuineness of your faith— 1 Pt 1:7
that perishes though it is **t** by fire—may 1 Pt 1:7
but have **t** those who call themselves Rv 2:2
of you into prison, that you may be **t**, Rv 2:10

TESTER (1)

have made you a **t** of metals among my Jer 6:27

TESTICLES (3)

itching disease or scabs or crushed **t**. Lv 21:20
that has its **t** bruised or crushed Lv 22:24
"No one whose **t** are crushed or whose Dt 23:1

TESTIFIED (13)
when the LORD has **t** against me and the Ru 1:21
your own mouth has **t** against you, 2 Sm 1:16
These **t** against them, but they 2 Chr 24:19
(For Jesus himself had **t** that a prophet Jn 4:44
Jesus was troubled in his spirit, and **t**, Jn 13:21
Now when they had **t** and spoken the Acts 8:25
be their king, of whom he **t** and said, Acts 13:22
for as you have **t** to the facts about Acts 23:11
because we **t** about God that he 1 Cor 15:15
It has been **t** somewhere, "What is man, Heb 2:6
case, by one of whom it is **t** that he lives. Heb 7:8
the brothers came and **t** to your truth, 3 Jn 1:3
who **t** to your love before the church. 3 Jn 1:6

TESTIFIES (7)
has risen up against me; it **t** to my face. Jb 16:8
heaven, and he who **t** for me is on high. Jb 16:19
The pride of Israel **t** to his face; Israel and Hos 5:5
The pride of Israel **t** to his face; yet they Hos 7:10
that the Holy Spirit **t** to me in every Acts 20:23
And the Spirit is the one who **t**, because 1 Jn 5:6
He who **t** to these things says, "Surely I Rv 22:20

TESTIFY (27)
in that he hears a public adjuration to **t**, Lv 5:1
and they shall **t**, 'Our hands did not shed Dt 21:7
t against me before the LORD and 1 Sm 12:3
T against me and I will restore it to 1 Sm 12:3
and not I; your own lips **t** against you. Jb 15:6
I will speak; O Israel, I will **t** against you. Ps 50:7
before you, and our sins **t** against us; Is 59:12
"Though our iniquities **t** against us, act, Jer 14:7
and **t** against the house of Jacob," Am 3:13
is it that these men **t** against you?" Mt 26:62
how many things they **t** against you?" Mt 27:13
is it that these men **t** against you?" Mk 14:60
it hates me because I **t** about it that its Jn 7:7
to the people and to **t** that he is the one Acts 10:42
to **t** to the gospel of the grace of God. Acts 20:24
Therefore I **t** to you this day that I am Acts 20:26
so you must **t** also in Rome." Acts 23:11
for a long time, if they are willing to **t**, Acts 26:5
according to their means, as I can **t**, 2 Cor 8:3
For I **t** to you that, if possible, you Gal 4:15
I **t** again to every man who accepts Gal 5:3
Now this I say and **t** in the Lord, that Eph 4:17
to **t** to the things that were to be spoken Heb 3:5
and **t** to it and proclaim to you the 1 Jn 1:2
we have seen and **t** that the Father has 1 Jn 4:14
For there are three that **t**: 1 Jn 5:7
sent my angel to **t** to you about these Rv 22:16

TESTIFYING (4)
t to the Jews that the Christ was Jesus. Acts 18:5
t both to Jews and to Greeks of Acts 20:21
so I stand here **t** both to small and Acts 26:22
t to the kingdom of God and trying to Acts 28:23

TESTIMONIES (35)
These are the **t**, the statutes, and the Dt 4:45
LORD your God, and his **t** and his statutes, Dt 6:17
the meaning of the **t** and the statutes and Dt 6:20
commandments, his rules, and his **t**, 1 Kgs 2:3
commandments and his **t** and his 2 Kgs 23:3
keep your commandments, your **t**, 1 Chr 29:19
commandments and his **t** and his 2 Chr 34:31
those who keep his covenant and his **t**. Ps 25:10
Most High God and did not keep his **t**, Ps 78:56
they kept his **t** and the statute that he Ps 99:7
Blessed are those who keep his **t**, who Ps 119:2
In the way of your **t** I delight as much Ps 119:14
and contempt, for I have kept your **t**. Ps 119:22
Your **t** are my delight; they are my Ps 119:24
I cling to your **t**, O LORD; let me not be Ps 119:31
Incline my heart to your **t**, and not to Ps 119:36
also speak of your **t** before kings and Ps 119:46
on my ways, I turn my feet to your **t**; Ps 119:59
to me, that they may know your **t**. Ps 119:79
that I may keep the **t** of your mouth. Ps 119:88
to destroy me, but I consider your **t**. Ps 119:95
teachers, for your **t** are my meditation. Ps 119:99
Your **t** are my heritage forever, for Ps 119:111
like dross, therefore I love your **t**. Ps 119:119
that I may know your **t**! Ps 119:125
Your **t** are wonderful; therefore my Ps 119:129
appointed your **t** in righteousness Ps 119:138
Your **t** are righteous forever; give me Ps 119:144
save me, that I may observe your **t**. Ps 119:146
I known from your **t** that you have Ps 119:152
but I do not swerve from your **t**. Ps 119:157
My soul keeps your **t**; I love them Ps 119:167
I keep your precepts and **t**, for all my Ps 119:168
my covenant and my **t** that I shall Ps 132:12
statutes and in his **t** that this disaster Jer 44:23

TESTIMONY (95)
Aaron placed it before the **t** to be kept. Ex 16:34
put into the ark the **t** that I shall give Ex 25:16
ark you shall put the **t** that I shall give Ex 25:21
cherubim that are on the ark of the **t**, Ex 25:22
the ark of the **t** in there within the Ex 26:33
on the ark of the **t** in the Most Holy Ex 26:34
outside the veil that is before the **t**, Ex 27:21
of the veil that is above the ark of the **t**, Ex 30:6
of the mercy seat that is above the **t**, Ex 30:6
the tent of meeting and the ark of the **t**, Ex 30:26
part of it before the **t** in the tent of Ex 30:36
the tent of meeting, and the ark of the **t**, Ex 31:7
on Mount Sinai, the two tablets of the **t**, Ex 31:18
with the two tablets of the **t** in his hand, Ex 32:15
the two tablets of the **t** in his hand as he Ex 34:29
the tabernacle, the tabernacle of the **t**, Ex 38:21
the ark of the **t** with its poles and the Ex 39:35
And you shall put in it the ark of the **t**, Ex 40:3
altar for incense before the ark of the **t**, Ex 40:5
He took the **t** and put it into the ark, Ex 40:20
the screen, and screened the ark of the **t**, Ex 40:21
cover the mercy seat that is over the **t**, Lv 16:13
Outside the veil of the **t**, in the tent of Lv 24:3
the Levites over the tabernacle of the **t**, Nm 1:50
camp around the tabernacle of the **t**, Nm 1:53
guard over the tabernacle of the **t**." Nm 1:53
screen and cover the ark of the **t** with it. Nm 4:5
mercy seat that was on the ark of the **t**, Nm 7:89
covered the tabernacle, the tent of the **t**. Nm 9:15
lifted from over the tabernacle of the **t**, Nm 10:11
them in the tent of meeting before the **t**, Nm 17:4
staffs before the LORD in the tent of the **t**. Nm 17:7
day Moses went into the tent of the **t**, Nm 17:8
back the staff of Aaron before the **t**, Nm 17:10
with you are before the tent of the **t**. Nm 18:2
be put to death on the **t** of one witness. Nm 35:30
bearing the ark of the **t** to come up out Jos 4:16
crown on him and gave him the **t**. 2 Kgs 11:12
crown on him and gave him the **t**. 2 Chr 23:11
of Israel for the tent of **t**?" 2 Chr 24:6
the roads, and do you not accept their **t** Jb 21:29
the **t** of the LORD is sure, making wise the Ps 19:7
He established a **t** in Jacob and appointed Ps 78:5
choirmaster: according to Lilies. A **T**. Ps 80:T
Bind up the **t**; seal the teaching among Is 8:16
To the teaching and to the **t**! If they will Is 8:20
the whole world as a **t** to all nations, Mt 24:14
were seeking false **t** against Jesus that Mt 26:59
that is on your feet as a **t** against them." Mk 6:11
Council were seeking **t** against Jesus Mk 14:55
against him, but their **t** did not agree. Mk 14:56
even about this their **t** did not agree. Mk 14:59
dust from your feet as a **t** against them." Lk 9:5
they said, "What further **t** do we need? Lk 22:71
And this is the **t** of John, when the Jews Jn 1:19
have seen, but you do not receive our **t**. Jn 3:11
seen and heard, yet no one receives his **t**. Jn 3:32
Whoever receives his **t** sets his seal to Jn 3:33
in him because of the woman's **t**, Jn 4:39
about myself, my **t** is not deemed true. Jn 5:31
and I know that the **t** that he bears about Jn 5:32
Not that the **t** that I receive is from man, Jn 5:34
But the **t** that I have is greater than that Jn 5:36
about yourself; your **t** is not true." Jn 8:13
bear witness about myself, my **t** is true, Jn 8:14
it is written that the **t** of two men is true. Jn 8:17
saw it has borne witness—his **t** is true, Jn 19:35
things, and we know that his **t** is true. Jn 21:24
were giving their **t** to the resurrection Acts 4:33
they will not accept your **t** about me.' Acts 22:18
even as the **t** about Christ was 1 Cor 1:6
proclaiming to you the **t** of God with 1 Cor 2:1
the **t** of our conscience that we 2 Cor 1:12
because our **t** to you was believed. 2 Thes 1:10
which is the **t** given at the proper time. 1 Tm 2:6
who in his **t** before Pontius Pilate 1 Tm 6:13
be ashamed of the **t** about our Lord, 2 Tm 1:8
This **t** is true. Therefore rebuke them Ti 1:13
If we receive the **t** of men, the testimony 1 Jn 5:9
testimony of men, the **t** of God is greater, 1 Jn 5:9
for this is the **t** of God that he has borne 1 Jn 5:9
in the Son of God has the **t** in himself. 1 Jn 5:10
not believed in the **t** that God has borne 1 Jn 5:10
And this is the **t**, that God gave us 1 Jn 5:11
has received a good **t** from everyone, 3 Jn 1:12
We also add our **t**, and you know that 3 Jn 1:12
and you know that our **t** is true. 3 Jn 1:12
word of God and to the **t** of Jesus Christ, Rv 1:2
of the word of God and the **t** of Jesus. Rv 1:9
And when they have finished their **t**, the Rv 11:7
of the Lamb and by the word of their **t**, Rv 12:11
of God and hold to the **t** of Jesus. Rv 12:17
your brothers who hold to the **t** of Jesus. Rv 19:10
Worship God." For the **t** of Jesus is the Rv 19:10
been beheaded for the **t** of Jesus and for Rv 20:4

TESTING (9)
t you to know what was in your heart, Dt 8:2
For the LORD your God is **t** you, to know Dt 13:3
They were for the **t** of Israel, to know Jgs 3:4
man that God is **t** them that they may Eccl 3:18
For it will not be a **t**—what could it do Ezk 21:13
for a while, and in time of **t** fall away. Lk 8:13
that by **t** you may discern what is the Rom 12:2
on the day of **t** in the wilderness, Heb 3:8
you know that the **t** of your faith Jas 1:3

TESTS (6)
for the ear **t** words as the palate tastes Jb 34:3
The LORD **t** the righteous, but his soul Ps 11:5
is for gold, and the LORD **t** hearts. Prv 17:3
who **t** the heart and the mind, Jer 11:20
O LORD of hosts, who **t** the righteous, Jer 20:12
but to please God who **t** our hearts. 1 Thes 2:4

TETRARCH (7)
that time Herod the **t** heard about the Mt 14:1
of Judea, and Herod being **t** of Galilee, Lk 3:1
and his brother Philip **t** of the region of Lk 3:1
Trachonitis, and Lysanias **t** of Abilene, Lk 3:1
But Herod the **t**, who had been reproved Lk 3:19
Now Herod the **t** heard about all that was Lk 9:7
a member of the court of Herod the **t**, Acts 13:1

THADDAEUS (2)
James the son of Alphaeus, and **T**; Mt 10:3
and James the son of Alphaeus, and **T**, Mk 3:18

THANK (29)
the ark of the LORD, to invoke, to **t**, 1 Chr 16:4
And now we **t** you, our God, and 1 Chr 29:13
bring sacrifices and **t** offerings to 2 Chr 29:31
brought sacrifices and **t** offerings, 2 Chr 29:31
I will **t** you in the great congregation; in Ps 35:18
I will **t** you forever, because you have Ps 52:9
O God; I will render **t** offerings to you. Ps 56:12
Let them **t** the LORD for his steadfast Ps 107:8
Let them **t** the LORD for his steadfast Ps 107:15
Let them **t** the LORD for his steadfast Ps 107:21
Let them **t** the LORD for his steadfast Ps 107:31
I **t** you that you have answered me and Ps 118:21
For Sheol does not **t** you; death does not Is 38:18
and bringing **t** offerings to the house of Jer 17:26
as they bring **t** offerings to the house of Jer 33:11
At that time Jesus declared, "I **t** you, Mt 11:25
in the Holy Spirit and said, "I **t** you, Lk 10:21
Does he **t** the servant because he did Lk 17:9
I **t** you that I am not like other men, Lk 18:11
"Father, I **t** you that you have heard me. Jn 11:41
I **t** my God through Jesus Christ for all Rom 1:8
I **t** God that I baptized none of you 1 Cor 1:14
I **t** God that I speak in tongues more 1 Cor 14:18
I **t** my God in all my remembrance of Phil 1:3
We always **t** God, the Father of our Lord Col 1:3
And we also **t** God constantly for 1 Thes 2:13
I **t** him who has given me strength, 1 Tm 1:12
I **t** God whom I serve, as did my 2 Tm 1:3
I **t** my God always when I remember Phlm 1:4

THANKED (1)
them, Paul **t** God and took courage. Acts 28:15

THANKFUL (1)
you were called in one body. And be **t**. Col 3:15

THANKFULNESS (2)
If I partake with **t**, why am I 1 Cor 10:30
songs, with **t** in your hearts to God. Col 3:16

THANKING (1)
morning, **t** and praising the LORD, 1 Chr 23:30

THANKS (98)
Oh give **t** to the LORD; call upon his 1 Chr 16:8
Oh give **t** to the LORD, for he is good; 1 Chr 16:34
that we may give **t** to your holy 1 Chr 16:35
named to give **t** to the LORD, 1 Chr 16:41
and worshiped and gave **t** to the LORD, 2 Chr 7:3
had made for giving **t** to the LORD— 2 Chr 7:6
army, and say, "Give **t** to the LORD, 2 Chr 20:21
offerings and giving **t** to the LORD, 2 Chr 30:22
of the LORD and to give **t** and praise. 2 Chr 31:2
praising and giving **t** to the LORD, Ezr 3:11
the leader of the praise, who gave **t**, Neh 11:17
opposite them, to praise and to give **t**, Neh 12:24
appointed two great choirs that gave **t**. Neh 12:31
of those who gave **t** went to the north, Neh 12:38
of those who gave **t** stood in the house Neh 12:40
to the LORD the **t** due to his righteousness, Ps 7:17
I will give **t** to the LORD with my whole Ps 9:1
exults, and with my song I give **t** to him. Ps 28:7
his saints, and give **t** to his holy name. Ps 30:4
my God, I will give **t** to you forever! Ps 30:12
Give **t** to the LORD with the lyre; make Ps 33:2
and we will give **t** to your name forever. Ps 44:8
to you; I will give **t** to your name, Ps 54:6

I will give **t** to you, O Lord, among the Ps 57:9
We give **t** to you, O God; we give thanks, Ps 75:1
O God; we give **t**, for your name is near. Ps 75:1
your pasture, will give **t** to you forever; Ps 79:13
I give **t** to you, O Lord my God, with my Ps 86:12
It is good to give **t** to the LORD, to sing Ps 92:1
righteous, and give **t** to his holy name! Ps 97:12
A Psalm for giving **t**. Ps 100:T
praise! Give **t** to him; bless his name! Ps 100:4
Oh give **t** to the LORD; call upon his Ps 105:1
Oh give **t** to the LORD, for he is good, for Ps 106:1
that we may give **t** to your holy name Ps 106:47
Oh give **t** to the LORD, for he is good, for Ps 107:1
I will give **t** to you, O LORD, among the Ps 108:3
mouth I will give great **t** to the LORD; Ps 109:30
I will give **t** to the LORD with my whole Ps 111:1
Oh give **t** to the LORD, for he is good; for Ps 118:1
through them and give **t** to the LORD. Ps 118:19
are my God, and I will give **t** to you; Ps 118:28
Oh give **t** to the LORD, for he is good; for Ps 118:29
Israel, to give **t** to the name of the LORD. Ps 122:4
Give **t** to the LORD, for he is good, for his Ps 136:1
Give **t** to the God of gods, for his Ps 136:2
Give **t** to the Lord of lords, for his Ps 136:3
Give **t** to the God of heaven, for his Ps 136:26
I give you **t**, O LORD, with my whole Ps 138:1
holy temple and give **t** to your name for Ps 138:2
the kings of the earth shall give you **t**, Ps 138:4
righteous shall give **t** to your name; Ps 140:13
prison, that I may give **t** to your name! Ps 142:7
All your works shall give **t** to you, O Ps 145:10
"I will give **t** to you, O LORD, for though Is 12:1
"Give **t** to the LORD, call upon his name, Is 12:4
The living, the living, he **t** you, as I do Is 38:19
"'Give **t** to the LORD of hosts, for the LORD Jer 33:11
O God of my fathers, I give **t** and praise, Dn 2:23
and prayed and gave **t** before his God, Dn 6:10
and having given **t** he broke them and Mt 15:36
and when he had given **t** he gave it to Mt 26:27
the seven loaves, and having given **t**, Mk 8:6
and when he had given **t** he gave it to Mk 14:23
hour she began to give **t** to God and to Lk 2:38
on his face at Jesus' feet, giving him **t**. Lk 17:16
a cup, and when he had given **t** he said, Lk 22:17
took bread, and when he had given **t**, Lk 22:19
took the loaves, and when he had given **t**, Jn 6:11
eaten the bread after the Lord had given **t**. Jn 6:23
and giving **t** to God in the presence of Acts 27:35
not honor him as God or give **t** to him, Rom 1:21
But **t** be to God, that you who were Rom 6:17
T be to God through Jesus Christ our Rom 7:25
of the Lord, since he gives **t** to God, Rom 14:6
honor of the Lord and gives **t** to God. Rom 14:6
not only I give **t** but all the churches Rom 16:4
churches of the Gentiles give **t** as well. Rom 16:4
I give **t** to my God always for you 1 Cor 1:4
because of that for which I give **t**? 1 Cor 10:30
and when he had given **t**, he broke 1 Cor 11:24
if you give **t** with your spirit, 1 Cor 14:16
you may be giving **t** well enough, 1 Cor 14:17
But **t** be to God, who gives us the 1 Cor 15:57
that many will give **t** on our behalf 2 Cor 1:11
But **t** be to God, who in Christ always 2 Cor 2:14
But **t** be to God, who put into the 2 Cor 8:16
T be to God for his inexpressible gift! 2 Cor 9:15
I do not cease to give **t** for you, Eph 1:16
giving **t** always and for everything to Eph 5:20
giving **t** to the Father, who has qualified Col 1:12
giving **t** to God the Father through him. Col 3:17
We give **t** to God always for all of you, 1 Thes 1:2
give **t** in all circumstances; for this 1 Thes 5:18
ought always to give **t** to God for you, 2 Thes 1:3
ought always to give **t** to God for 2 Thes 2:13
give glory and honor and **t** to him who is Rv 4:9
saying, "We give **t** to you, Lord God Rv 11:17

THANKSGIVING (35)

If he offers it for a **t**, then he shall offer Lv 7:12
offer with the **t** sacrifice unleavened Lv 7:12
his peace offerings for **t** he shall bring Lv 7:13
his peace offerings for **t** shall be eaten on Lv 7:15
you sacrifice a sacrifice of **t** to the LORD, Lv 22:29
first appointed that **t** be sung to 1 Chr 16:7
with the lyre in **t** and praise to the 1 Chr 25:3
in unison in praise and **t** to the LORD), 2 Chr 5:13
sacrifices of peace offerings and of **t**, 2 Chr 33:16
was in charge of the songs of **t**. Neh 12:8
were songs of praise and **t** to God. Neh 12:46
proclaiming **t** aloud, and telling all your Ps 26:7
Offer to God a sacrifice of **t**, and Ps 50:14
The one who offers **t** as his sacrifice Ps 50:23
with a song; I will magnify him with **t**. Ps 69:30
Let us come into his presence with **t**; let Ps 95:2
Enter his gates with **t**, and his courts Ps 100:4
And let them offer sacrifices of **t**, and Ps 107:22
to you the sacrifice of **t** and call on the Ps 116:17
Sing to the LORD with **t**; make melody to Ps 147:7
be found in her, **t** and the voice of song. Is 51:3
Out of them shall come songs of **t**, and Jer 30:19
offer a sacrifice of **t** of that which is Am 4:5
I with the voice of **t** will sacrifice to you; Jon 2:9
say "Amen" to your **t** when he does 1 Cor 14:16
and more people it may increase **t**, 2 Cor 4:15
through us will produce **t** to God. 2 Cor 9:11
are out of place, but instead let there be **t**. Eph 5:4
and supplication with **t** let your requests Phil 4:6
just as you were taught, abounding in **t**. Col 2:7
in prayer, being watchful in it with **t**. Col 4:2
For what **t** can we return to God for 1 Thes 3:9
to be received with **t** by those who 1 Tm 4:3
is to be rejected if it is received with **t**, 1 Tm 4:4
glory and wisdom and **t** and honor and Rv 7:12

THANKSGIVINGS (3)

gladness, with **t** and with singing, Neh 12:27
is also overflowing in many **t** to God. 2 Cor 9:12
and **t** be made for all people, 1 Tm 2:1

THEATER (2)

and they rushed together into the **t**, Acts 19:29
urging him not to venture into the **t**. Acts 19:31

THEBES (5)

punishment upon Amon of **T**, Jer 46:25
and will execute judgments on **T**. Ezk 30:14
Egypt, and cut off the multitude of **T**. Ezk 30:15
T shall be breached, and Memphis Ezk 30:16
Are you better than **T** that sat by the Na 3:8

THEBEZ (3)

Abimelech went to **T** and encamped Jgs 9:50
and encamped against **T** and captured Jgs 9:50
from the wall, so that he died at **T**? 2 Sm 11:21

THEFT (3)

nothing, then he shall be sold for his **t**. Ex 22:3
sexual immorality, **t**, false witness, Mt 15:19
thoughts, sexual immorality, **t**, murder, Mk 7:21

THEFTS (1)

or their sexual immorality or their **t**. Rv 9:21

THEME (1)

My heart overflows with a pleasing **t**; I Ps 45:1

THEOPHILUS (2)

account for you, most excellent **T**, Lk 1:3
In the first book, O **T**, I have dealt with Acts 1:1

THEREBY (9)

of all the things that people do and sin **t**— Lv 6:3
that one may do and **t** become guilty." Lv 6:7
of semen, becoming unclean **t**; Lv 15:32
sin for it and die **t** when they profane it: Lv 22:9
and be at peace; **t** good will come to you. Jb 22:21
And **t** put me to the test, says the LORD Mal 3:10
myself, but I am not **t** acquitted. 1 Cor 4:4
the cross, **t** killing the hostility. Eph 2:16
for **t** some have entertained angels Heb 13:2

THEREFORE (798)

T a man shall leave his father and his Gn 2:24
t the LORD God sent him out from the Gn 3:23
T it is said, "Like Nimrod a mighty Gn 10:9
T its name was called Babel, because Gn 11:9
T the well was called Beer-lahai-roi; it Gn 16:14
till you arrive there." **T** the name of the Gn 19:22
me. **T** I did not let you touch her. Gn 20:6
Now **t** swear to me here by God that Gn 21:23
T that place was called Beersheba, Gn 21:31
for I am exhausted!" (**T** his name was Gn 25:30
t the name of the city is Beersheba to Gn 26:33
Now **t**, my son, obey my voice as I Gn 27:8
Now **t**, my son, obey my voice. Arise, Gn 27:43
should you **t** serve me for nothing? Gn 29:15
him three sons." **T** his name was Gn 29:34
will praise the LORD." **T** she called his Gn 29:35
given me a son." **T** she called his name Gn 30:6
you and me today." **T** he named it Gn 31:48
T to this day the people of Israel do not Gn 32:32
T the name of the place is called Gn 33:17
made for yourself!" **T** his name was Gn 38:29
Now **t** let Pharaoh select a discerning Gn 41:33
"Now **t**, as soon as I come to your Gn 44:30
Now **t**, please let your servant remain Gn 44:33
gave them; **t** they did not sell their land. Gn 47:22
there shall you bury me.' Now **t**, Gn 50:5
by the Egyptians." **T** the place was Gn 50:11
T they set taskmasters over them to Ex 1:11
Now **t** go, and I will be with your mouth Ex 4:12
T they cry, 'Let us go and offer sacrifice to Ex 5:8
Say **t** to the people of Israel, 'I am the LORD, Ex 6:6
Now **t** send, get your livestock and all Ex 9:19
Now **t**, forgive my sin, please, only this Ex 10:17
T you shall observe this day, Ex 12:17
You shall **t** keep this statute at its Ex 13:10
T I sacrifice to the LORD all the males Ex 13:15
it was bitter; **t** it was named Marah. Ex 15:23
t on the sixth day he gives you bread for Ex 16:29
T the people quarreled with Moses and Ex 17:2
Now **t**, if you will indeed obey my voice Ex 19:5
T the LORD blessed the Sabbath day and Ex 20:11
T you shall not eat any flesh that is Ex 22:31
T the people of Israel shall keep the Ex 31:16
Now **t** let me alone, that my wrath may Ex 32:10
T the people of Israel stripped themselves Ex 33:6
Now **t**, if I have found favor in your Ex 33:13
Consecrate yourselves **t**, and be holy, Lv 11:44
to be your God. You shall **t** be holy, Lv 11:45
T I have said to the people of Israel, No Lv 17:12
T I have said to the people of Israel, You Lv 17:14
You shall **t** keep my statutes and my Lv 18:5
Consecrate yourselves, **t**, and be holy, for Lv 20:7
"You shall **t** keep all my statutes and Lv 20:22
all these things, and **t** I detested them. Lv 20:23
You shall **t** separate the clean beast Lv 20:25
bread of their God; **t** they shall be holy. Lv 21:6
They shall **t** keep my charge, lest they Lv 22:9
"**T** you shall do my statutes and keep Lv 25:18
for us in Egypt." **T** the LORD will give Nm 11:18
T the name of that place was called Nm 11:34
T it is against the LORD that you and Nm 16:11
T I have said of them that they shall Nm 18:24
T you shall say to them, 'When you Nm 18:30
t you shall not bring this assembly Nm 20:12
T the ballad singers say, "Come to Nm 21:27
stood in the road against me. Now **t**, Nm 22:34
T now flee to your own place. I said, 'I Nm 24:11
T say, 'Behold, I give to him my Nm 25:12
Now **t**, kill every male among the Nm 31:17
"**T** watch yourselves very carefully. Dt 4:15
know **t** today, and lay it to your heart, Dt 4:39
T you shall keep his statutes and his Dt 4:40
T the LORD your God commanded you to Dt 5:15
Now **t** why should we die? For this great Dt 5:25
You shall be careful **t** to do as the LORD Dt 5:32
Hear **t**, O Israel, and be careful to do them, Dt 6:3
Know **t** that the LORD your God is God, the Dt 7:9
You shall **t** be careful to do the Dt 7:11
Know **t** today that he who goes over before Dt 9:3
t, that the LORD your God is not giving you Dt 9:6
T Levi has no portion or inheritance Dt 10:9
Circumcise **t** the foreskin of your heart, Dt 10:16
t, for you were sojourners in the land of Dt 10:19
"You shall **t** love the LORD your God and Dt 11:1
"You shall **t** keep the whole Dt 11:8
"You shall **t** lay up these words of mine Dt 11:18
T I command you, 'You shall open Dt 15:11
you; **t** I command you this today. Dt 15:15
T I command you, You shall set apart Dt 19:7
before you, **t** your camp must be holy, Dt 23:14
from there; **t** I command you to do this. Dt 24:18
of Egypt; **t** I command you to do this. Dt 24:22
T when the LORD your God has given Dt 25:19
You shall **t** be careful to do them with Dt 26:16
You shall **t** obey the voice of the LORD Dt 27:10
t you shall serve your enemies whom Dt 28:48
T keep the words of this covenant and do Dt 29:9
T the anger of the LORD was kindled Dt 29:27
T choose life, that you and your Dt 30:19
"Now **t** write this song and teach it to Dt 31:19
"Moses my servant is dead. Now **t** arise, Jos 1:2
Now **t** take twelve men from the tribes of Jos 3:12
T the people of Israel cannot stand Jos 7:12
In the morning **t** you shall be brought Jos 7:14
T, to this day the name of that place is Jos 7:26
Now **t** you are cursed, and some of you Jos 9:23
Now **t** divide this land for an Jos 13:7
T Hebron became the inheritance of Jos 14:14
T turn and go to your tents in the land Jos 22:4
T we said, 'Let us now build an altar, Jos 22:26
T, be very strong to keep and to do all Jos 23:6
careful, **t**, to love the LORD your God. Jos 23:11
"Now **t** fear the LORD and serve him in Jos 24:14
T we also will serve the LORD, for he is Jos 24:18
T it shall be a witness against you, lest Jos 24:27
T the anger of the LORD was kindled Jgs 3:8
T on that day Gideon was called Jgs 6:32
Now **t** proclaim in the ears of the people, Jgs 7:3
"Now **t**, if you acted in good faith and Jgs 9:16
Now **t**, go by night, you and the people Jgs 9:32
other gods; **t** I will save you no more. Jgs 10:13
the Jordan; now **t** restore it peaceably." Jgs 11:13
I **t** have not sinned against you, and Jgs 11:27
T be careful and drink no wine or Jgs 13:4
T the name of it was called Jgs 15:19
image. Now **t** I will restore it to you." Jgs 17:3
Now **t** consider what you will do." Jgs 18:14
Now **t** give up the men, the worthless Jgs 20:13
T they turned their backs before the Jgs 20:42
would you **t** wait till they were grown? Ru 1:13
Would you **t** refrain from marrying? Ru 1:13

Wash **t** and anoint yourself, and put on Ru 3:3
her. **T** Hannah wept and would not eat. 1 Sm 1:7
T Eli took her to be a drunken 1 Sm 1:13
T I have lent him to the LORD. As long 1 Sm 1:28
T the LORD the God of Israel declares: 'I 1 Sm 2:30
T Eli said to Samuel, "Go, lie down, and 1 Sm 3:9
T I swear to the house of Eli that the 1 Sm 3:14
They sent **t** and gathered together all 1 Sm 5:11
who is their father?" **T** it became a 1 Sm 10:12
Now **t** present yourselves before the 1 Sm 10:19
T the men of Jabesh said, 1 Sm 11:10
Now **t** stand still that I may plead with 1 Sm 12:7
Now **t** stand still and see this great 1 Sm 12:16
T Saul said, "O LORD God of Israel, 1 Sm 14:41
now **t** listen to the words of the LORD. 1 Sm 15:1
Now **t**, please pardon my sin and 1 Sm 15:25
T Saul sent messengers to Jesse and 1 Sm 16:19
may be against him." **T** Saul said to 1 Sm 18:21
T be on your guard in the morning. 1 Sm 19:2
T deal kindly with your servant, for 1 Sm 20:8
T send and bring him to me, for he 1 Sm 20:31
T David inquired of the LORD, "Shall I 1 Sm 23:2
See **t** and take note of all the lurking 1 Sm 23:23
T that place was called the Rock of 1 Sm 23:28
May the LORD **t** be judge and give 1 Sm 24:15
Swear to me **t** by the LORD that you 1 Sm 24:21
T let my young men find favor in 1 Sm 25:8
Now **t** know this and consider what 1 Sm 25:17
Now **t** let my lord the king hear the 1 Sm 26:19
Now **t**, let not my blood fall to the 1 Sm 26:20
T Ziklag has belonged to the kings of 1 Sm 27:6
t he shall always be my servant." 1 Sm 27:12
T I have summoned you to tell me 1 Sm 28:15
t the LORD has done this thing to you 1 Sm 28:18
Now **t**, you also obey your servant. 1 Sm 28:22
T Saul took his own sword and fell 1 Sm 31:4
Now **t** let your hands be strong, and be 2 Sm 2:7
T that place was called 2 Sm 2:16
T Abner struck him in the stomach 2 Sm 2:23
are hated by David's soul." **T** it is said, 2 Sm 5:8
like a bursting flood." **T** the name of 2 Sm 5:20
t, thus you shall say to my servant 2 Sm 7:8
T you are great, O LORD God. For there 2 Sm 7:22
T your servant has found courage to 2 Sm 7:27
Now **t** may it please you to bless the 2 Sm 7:29
Now **t** the sword shall never depart 2 Sm 12:10
David **t** sought God on behalf of the 2 Sm 12:16
the outrageous fools in Israel. Now **t**, 2 Sm 13:13
Now **t** let not my lord the king so 2 Sm 13:33
to be there still." Now **t** let me go into 2 Sm 14:32
Now **t** send quickly and tell David, 2 Sm 17:16
T it is better that you send us help 2 Sm 18:3
Now **t** arise, go out and speak kindly 2 Sm 19:7
Now **t** why do you say nothing 2 Sm 19:10
T, behold, I have come this day, the 2 Sm 19:20
of God; do **t** what seems good to you. 2 Sm 19:27
risk of their lives?" **T** he would not 2 Sm 23:17
T his servants said to him, "Let a 1 Kgs 1:2
Now **t** come, let me give you advice, 1 Kgs 1:12
Act **t** according to your wisdom, but 1 Kgs 2:6
Now **t** do not hold him guiltless, for 1 Kgs 2:9
Now **t** as the LORD lives, who has 1 Kgs 2:24
Give your servant **t** an understanding 1 Kgs 3:9
Now **t** command that cedars of 1 Kgs 5:6
Now **t**, O LORD, God of Israel, keep for 1 Kgs 8:25
Now **t**, O God of Israel, let your word 1 Kgs 8:26
Let your heart **t** be wholly true to the 1 Kgs 8:61
T the LORD has brought all this 1 Kgs 9:9
T he said, "What kind of cities are 1 Kgs 9:13
T the LORD said to Solomon, "Since 1 Kgs 11:11
Solomon sought **t** to kill Jeroboam. 1 Kgs 11:40
Now **t** lighten the hard service of 1 Kgs 12:4
t the LORD has given him to the lion, 1 Kgs 13:26
t behold, I will bring harm upon the 1 Kgs 14:10
Arise **t**, go to your house. When 1 Kgs 14:12
killed the king." **T** all Israel made 1 Kgs 16:16
Now **t** send and gather all Israel to 1 Kgs 18:19
a god of the valleys," **t** I will give all 1 Kgs 20:28
t your life shall be for his life, 1 Kgs 20:42
said, "**T** hear the word of the LORD: 1 Kgs 22:19
Now **t** behold, the LORD has put a 1 Kgs 22:23
T he said to the driver of his chariot, 1 Kgs 22:34
Now **t** thus says the LORD, You shall 2 Kgs 1:4
T you shall not come down from the 2 Kgs 1:6
—**t** you shall not come down from the 2 Kgs 1:16
he said, "Send." They sent **t** fifty men. 2 Kgs 2:17
T he returned to meet him and told 2 Kgs 4:31
T the leprosy of Naaman shall cling 2 Kgs 5:27
will overtake us. Now **t** come; 2 Kgs 7:9
T they have gone out of the camp to 2 Kgs 7:12
Now **t** take him up and throw him on 2 Kgs 9:26
Now **t** call to me all the prophets of 2 Kgs 10:19
T King Jehoash summoned Jehoiada 2 Kgs 12:7
Now **t** take no more money from 2 Kgs 12:7
(**T** the LORD gave Israel a savior, so 2 Kgs 13:5
T he sacked it, and he ripped open 2 Kgs 15:16
T the king of Assyria shut him up 2 Kgs 17:4
T the LORD was very angry with 2 Kgs 17:18
T the LORD sent lions among them, 2 Kgs 17:25
T he has sent lions among them, 2 Kgs 17:26
t lift up your prayer for the remnant 2 Kgs 19:4
and stone. **T** they were destroyed. 2 Kgs 19:18
"**T** thus says the LORD concerning 2 Kgs 19:32
t thus says the LORD, the God of 2 Kgs 21:12
t my wrath will be kindled against 2 Kgs 22:17
T, behold, I will gather you to your 2 Kgs 22:20
T Saul took his own sword and fell 1 Chr 10:4
T the LORD put him to death and 1 Chr 10:14
t it was called the city of David. 1 Chr 11:7
they brought it." **T** he would not 1 Chr 11:19
a bursting flood." **T** the name of 1 Chr 14:11
t, thus shall you say to my servant 1 Chr 17:7
T your servant has found courage 1 Chr 17:25
I will **t** make preparation for it." So 1 Chr 22:5
t they became counted as a single 1 Chr 23:11
Now **t** in the sight of all Israel, the 1 Chr 28:8
T David blessed the LORD in the 1 Chr 29:10
Now **t** the wheat and barley, oil and 2 Chr 2:15
Now **t**, O LORD, God of Israel, keep for 2 Chr 6:16
Now **t**, O LORD, God of Israel, let your 2 Chr 6:17
T he has brought all this disaster on 2 Chr 7:22
Now **t** lighten the hard service of 2 Chr 10:4
T the LORD established the kingdom 2 Chr 17:5
said, "**T** hear the word of the LORD: 2 Chr 18:18
Now **t** behold, the LORD has put a 2 Chr 18:22
T he said to the driver of his chariot, 2 Chr 18:33
T the name of that place has been 2 Chr 20:26
T the LORD was angry with 2 Chr 25:15
T the LORD his God gave him into the 2 Chr 28:5
T the wrath of the LORD came on 2 Chr 29:8
T the Levites had to slaughter the 2 Chr 30:17
t, do not let Hezekiah deceive you or 2 Chr 32:15
T wrath came upon him and Judah 2 Chr 32:25
T the LORD brought upon them the 2 Chr 33:11
t my wrath will be poured out on 2 Chr 34:25
T he brought up against them the 2 Chr 36:17
t we send and inform the king, Ezr 4:14
T make a decree that these men be Ezr 4:21
T, if it seems good to the king, let search Ezr 5:17
"Now **t**, Tattenai, governor of the Ezr 6:6
T do not give your daughters to their Ezr 9:12
T let us make a covenant with our God Ezr 10:3
T you gave them into the hand of their Neh 9:27
T you gave them into the hand of the Neh 9:30
"Now, **t**, our God, the great, the mighty, Neh 9:32
Horonite. **T** I chased him from me. Neh 13:28
T the Jews of the villages, who live in the Est 9:19
T they called these days Purim, after the Est 9:26
T, because of all that was written in this Est 9:26
t despise not the discipline of the Jb 5:17
of the sea; **t** my words have been rash. Jb 6:3
"**T** I will not restrain my mouth; I will Jb 7:11
t I say, He destroys both the blameless Jb 9:22
t you will not let them triumph. Jb 17:4
"**T** my thoughts answer me, because of Jb 20:2
eaten; **t** his prosperity will not endure. Jb 20:21
T snares are all around you, and Jb 22:10
T I am terrified at his presence; when I Jb 23:15
t I was timid and afraid to declare my Jb 32:6
T I say, 'Listen to me; let me also declare Jb 32:10
"**T**, hear me, you men of understanding: Jb 34:10
and not I; **t** declare what you know. Jb 34:33
T men fear him; he does not regard any Jb 37:24
T I have uttered what I did not Jb 42:3
t I despise myself, and repent in dust and Jb 42:6
Now **t** take seven bulls and seven rams Jb 42:8
T the wicked will not stand in the Ps 1:5
Now **t**, O kings, be wise; be warned, O Ps 2:10
T my heart is glad, and my whole being Ps 16:9
LORD; **t** he instructs sinners in the way. Ps 25:8
T let everyone who is godly offer prayer Ps 32:6
t I remember you from the land of Ps 42:6
your lips; **t** God has blessed you forever. Ps 45:2
T God, your God, has anointed you with Ps 45:7
t nations will praise you forever and Ps 45:17
T we will not fear though the earth gives Ps 46:2
T pride is their necklace; violence covers Ps 73:6
T his people turn back to them, and Ps 73:10
T, when the LORD heard, he was full of Ps 78:21
T I swore in my wrath, "They shall not Ps 95:11
T he said he would destroy them—had Ps 106:23
T he raised his hand and swore to Ps 106:26
by the way; **t** he will lift up his head. Ps 110:7
me, **t** I will call on him as long as I live. Ps 116:2
t I hate every false way. Ps 119:104
like dross, **t** I love your testimonies. Ps 119:119
T I love your commandments above Ps 119:127
T I consider all your precepts to be Ps 119:128
are wonderful; **t** my soul keeps them. Ps 119:129
T my spirit faints within me; my heart Ps 143:4
t they shall eat the fruit of their way, Prv 1:31
t calamity will come upon him Prv 6:15
t do not associate with a simple Prv 20:19
are on earth. **T** let your words be few. Eccl 5:2
name is oil poured out; **t** virgins love you. Sg 1:3
T the Lord declares, the LORD of hosts, the Is 1:24
t the Lord will strike with a scab the Is 3:17
T my people go into exile for lack of Is 5:13
T Sheol has enlarged its appetite and Is 5:14
T, as the tongue of fire devours the Is 5:24
T the anger of the LORD was kindled Is 5:25
T the Lord himself will give you a sign. Is 7:14
t, behold, the Lord is bringing up against Is 8:7
T the Lord does not rejoice over their Is 9:17
T the Lord GOD of hosts will send Is 10:16
T thus says the Lord GOD of hosts: "O Is 10:24
T all hands will be feeble, and every Is 13:7
T I will make the heavens tremble, and Is 13:13
t the armed men of Moab cry aloud; Is 15:4
T the abundance they have gained and Is 15:7
T let Moab wail for Moab, let everyone Is 16:7
T I weep with the weeping of Jazer for the Is 16:9
T my inner parts moan like a lyre for Is 16:11
t, though you plant pleasant plants and Is 17:10
T my loins are filled with anguish; pangs Is 21:3
T I said: "Look away from me; let me Is 22:4
T a curse devours the earth, and its Is 24:6
t the inhabitants of the earth are Is 24:6
T in the east give glory to the LORD; in Is 24:15
T strong peoples will glorify you; cities of Is 25:3
T by this the guilt of Jacob will be atoned Is 27:9
t he who made them will not have Is 27:11
T hear the word of the LORD, you Is 28:14
t thus says the Lord GOD, "Behold, I am Is 28:16
Now **t** do not scoff, lest your bonds be Is 28:22
t, behold, I will again do wonderful Is 29:14
T thus says the LORD, who redeemed Is 29:22
T shall the protection of Pharaoh turn to Is 30:3
t I have called her "Rahab who sits still." Is 30:7
T thus says the Holy One of Israel, Is 30:12
t this iniquity shall be to you like a Is 30:13
flee upon horses"; **t** you shall flee away; Is 30:16
steeds"; **t** your pursuers shall be swift. Is 30:16
T the LORD waits to be gracious to you, Is 30:18
and **t** he exalts himself to show mercy to Is 30:18
t lift up your prayer for the remnant that Is 37:4
wood and stone. **T** they were destroyed. Is 37:19
"**T** thus says the LORD concerning the Is 37:33
T I will profane the princes of the Is 43:28
Now **t** hear this, you lover of pleasures, Is 47:8
GOD helps me; **t** I have not been disgraced; Is 50:7
t I have set my face like a flint, and I Is 50:7
T hear this, you who are afflicted, who Is 51:21
Now **t** what have I here," declares the Is 52:5
T my people shall know my name. Is 52:6
T in that day they shall know that it is I Is 52:6
T I will divide him a portion with the Is 53:12
T justice is far from us, and Is 59:9
t in their land they shall possess a double Is 61:7
t he turned to be their enemy, and Is 63:10
T thus says the Lord GOD: "Behold, my Is 65:13
"**T** I still contend with you, declares the Jer 2:9
T the showers have been withheld, and Jer 3:3
T a lion from the forest shall strike them Jer 5:6
T thus says the LORD, the God of hosts: Jer 5:14
t they have become great and rich; Jer 5:27
T I am full of the wrath of the LORD; I am Jer 6:11
T they shall fall among those who fall; Jer 6:15
T hear, O nations, and know, O Jer 6:18
T thus says the LORD: 'Behold, I will lay Jer 6:21
t I will do to the house that is called by Jer 7:14
T thus says the Lord GOD: behold, my Jer 7:20
T, behold, the days are coming, declares Jer 7:32
T I will give their wives to others and Jer 8:10
T they shall fall among the fallen; when Jer 8:12
T thus says the LORD of hosts: "Behold, I Jer 9:7
T thus says the LORD of hosts, the God of Jer 9:15
t they have not prospered, and all their Jer 10:21
T I brought upon them all the words of Jer 11:8
T, thus says the LORD, behold, I am Jer 11:11
"**T** do not pray for this people, or lift up Jer 11:14
T thus says the LORD concerning the Jer 11:21
t thus says the LORD of hosts: "Behold, I Jer 11:22
up her voice against me; **t** I hate her. Jer 12:8
feet; **t** the LORD does not accept them; Jer 14:10
T thus says the LORD concerning the Jer 14:15
T thus says the LORD: "If you return, I Jer 15:19
T I will hurl you out of this land into a Jer 16:13
"**T**, behold, the days are coming, Jer 16:14
"**T**, behold, I will make them know, Jer 16:21
t, say to the men of Judah and the Jer 18:11
"**T** thus says the LORD: Ask among the Jer 18:13
T deliver up their children to famine; Jer 18:21
t, behold, days are coming, declares the Jer 19:6
warrior; **t** my persecutors will stumble; Jer 20:11

T thus says the LORD concerning Jer 22:18
T thus says the LORD, the God of Israel, Jer 23:2
"**T**, behold, the days are coming, Jer 23:7
T their way shall be to them like Jer 23:12
T thus says the LORD of hosts Jer 23:15
T, behold, I am against the prophets, Jer 23:30
t, behold, I will surely lift you up and Jer 23:39
"**T** thus says the LORD of hosts: Because Jer 25:8
t, shall prophesy against them all these Jer 25:30
Now **t** mend your ways and your deeds, Jer 26:13
T thus says the LORD: 'Behold, I will Jer 28:16
t thus says the LORD: Behold, I will Jer 29:32
T all who devour you shall be Jer 30:16
t I have continued my faithfulness to Jer 31:3
T my heart yearns for him; I will surely Jer 31:20
T you have made all this disaster come Jer 32:23
T, thus says the LORD: Behold, I am Jer 32:28
"Now **t** thus says the LORD, the God of Jer 32:36
"**T**, thus says the LORD: You have not Jer 34:17
T, thus says the LORD, the God of hosts, Jer 35:17
t thus says the LORD of hosts, the God of Jer 35:19
T thus says the LORD concerning Jer 36:30
Now **t** know for a certainty that you Jer 42:22
T my wrath and my anger were poured Jer 44:6
"**T** thus says the LORD of hosts, the God Jer 44:11
T your land has become a desolation Jer 44:22
T hear the word of the LORD, all you of Jer 44:26
"**T**, behold, the days are coming, Jer 48:12
T I wail for Moab; I cry out for all Jer 48:31
T my heart moans for Moab like a Jer 48:36
T the riches they gained have perished. Jer 48:36
T, behold, the days are coming, declares Jer 49:2
T hear the plan that the LORD has made Jer 49:20
T her young men shall fall in her Jer 49:26
T, thus says the LORD of hosts, the God Jer 50:18
T her young men shall fall in her Jer 50:30
"**T** wild beasts shall dwell with hyenas Jer 50:39
T hear the plan that the LORD has made Jer 50:45
of her wine; **t** the nations went mad. Jer 51:7
T thus says the LORD: "Behold, I will Jer 51:36
"**T**, behold, the days are coming when I Jer 51:47
"**T**, behold, the days are coming, Jer 51:52
sinned grievously; **t** she became filthy; Lam 1:8
of her future; **t** her fall is terrible; Lam 1:9
this I call to mind, and **t** I have hope: Lam 3:21
says my soul, "**t** I will hope in him." Lam 3:24
T thus says the Lord GOD: Because you Ezk 5:7
t thus says the Lord GOD: Behold, I, even Ezk 5:8
T fathers shall eat their sons in your Ezk 5:10
T, as I live, declares the Lord GOD, Ezk 5:11
your abominations, **t** I will withdraw. Ezk 5:11
T I make it an unclean thing to them. Ezk 7:20
T I will act in wrath. My eye will not Ezk 8:18
T prophesy against them, prophesy, O Ezk 11:4
T thus says the Lord GOD: Your slain Ezk 11:7
T say, 'Thus says the Lord GOD: Ezk 11:16
T say, 'Thus says the Lord GOD: I will Ezk 11:17
Tell them **t**, 'Thus says the Lord GOD: I Ezk 12:23
T say to them, Thus says the Lord Ezk 12:28
T thus says the Lord GOD: "Because you Ezk 13:8
and seen lying visions, **t** behold, Ezk 13:8
T thus says the Lord GOD: I will make Ezk 13:13
"**T** thus says the Lord GOD: Behold, I Ezk 13:20
t you shall no more see false visions Ezk 13:23
T speak to them and say to them, Thus Ezk 14:4
"**T** say to the house of Israel, Thus says Ezk 14:6
T thus says the Lord GOD: Like the Ezk 15:6
t, I stretched out my hand against you Ezk 16:27
was given to you; **t** you were different. Ezk 16:34
"**T**, O prostitute, hear the word of the Ezk 16:35
t, behold, I will gather all your lovers Ezk 16:37
me with all these things, **t**, behold, Ezk 16:43
T thus says the Lord GOD: As I live, Ezk 17:19
"**T** I will judge you, O house of Israel, Ezk 18:30
"**T**, son of man, speak to the house of Ezk 20:27
"**T** say to the house of Israel, Thus Ezk 20:30
t my sword shall be drawn from its Ezk 21:4
my people. Strike **t** upon your thigh. Ezk 21:12
"**T** thus says the Lord GOD: Because Ezk 21:24
T I have made you a reproach to the Ezk 22:4
T thus says the Lord GOD: Because Ezk 22:19
you have all become dross, **t**, behold, Ezk 22:19
T I have poured out my indignation Ezk 22:31
T I delivered her into the hands of her Ezk 23:9
T, O Oholibah, thus says the Lord Ezk 23:22
t I will give her cup into your hand. Ezk 23:31
T thus says the Lord GOD: Because Ezk 23:35
"**T** thus says the Lord GOD: Woe to the Ezk 24:6
T thus says the Lord GOD: Woe to the Ezk 24:9
t behold, I am handing you over to the Ezk 25:4
t, behold, I have stretched out my hand Ezk 25:7
t I will lay open the flank of Moab from Ezk 25:9
t thus says the Lord GOD, I will stretch Ezk 25:13
t thus says the Lord GOD, Behold, I will Ezk 25:16
t thus says the Lord GOD: Behold, I am Ezk 26:3
t thus says the Lord GOD: Because you Ezk 28:6
t, behold, I will bring foreigners upon Ezk 28:7
T thus says the Lord GOD: Behold, I will Ezk 29:8
t, behold, I am against you and Ezk 29:10
T thus says the Lord GOD: Behold, I Ezk 29:19
T thus says the Lord GOD: Behold, I Ezk 30:22
"**T** thus says the Lord GOD: Because it Ezk 31:10
T say to them, Thus says the Lord Ezk 33:25
"**T**, you shepherds, hear the word of the Ezk 34:7
t, you shepherds, hear the word of the Ezk 34:9
"**T**, thus says the Lord GOD to them: Ezk 34:20
t, as I live, declares the Lord GOD, I will Ezk 35:6
bloodshed, **t** blood shall pursue you. Ezk 35:6
t, as I live, declares the Lord GOD, I will Ezk 35:11
t prophesy, and say, Thus says the Lord Ezk 36:3
t, O mountains of Israel, hear the word Ezk 36:4
t thus says the Lord GOD: Surely I have Ezk 36:5
T prophesy concerning the land of Ezk 36:6
T thus says the Lord GOD: I swear that Ezk 36:7
t you shall no longer devour people Ezk 36:14
"**T** say to the house of Israel, Thus Ezk 36:22
T prophesy, and say to them, Thus Ezk 37:12
"**T**, son of man, prophesy, and say to Ezk 38:14
"**T** thus says the Lord GOD: Now I will Ezk 39:25
entered by it. **T** it shall remain shut. Ezk 44:2
t I have sworn concerning them, Ezk 44:12
T he asked the chief of the eunuchs to Dn 1:8
Azariah. **T** they stood before the king. Dn 1:19
T show me the dream and its Dn 2:6
T tell me the dream, and I shall know Dn 2:9
T Daniel went in to Arioch, whom the Dn 2:24
T, as soon as all the peoples heard the Dn 3:7
T at that time certain Chaldeans came Dn 3:8
T I make a decree: Any people, nation, Dn 3:29
T, O king, let my counsel be acceptable Dn 4:27
T King Darius signed the document and Dn 6:9
T the LORD has kept ready the calamity Dn 9:14
Now **t**, O our God, listen to the prayer of Dn 9:17
T consider the word and understand the Dn 9:23
Know **t** and understand that from the Dn 9:25
T I will hedge up her way with thorns, Hos 2:6
T I will take back my grain in its time, Hos 2:9
"**T**, behold, I will allure her, and bring Hos 2:14
T the land mourns, and all who dwell in Hos 4:3
T your daughters play the whore, and Hos 4:13
T I have hewn them by the prophets; I Hos 6:5
t the tumult of war shall arise among Hos 10:14
T they shall be like the morning mist Hos 13:3
heart was lifted up; **t** they forgot me. Hos 13:6
t I will punish you for all your iniquities. Am 3:2
T thus says the Lord GOD: "An Am 3:11
"**T** thus I will do to you, O Israel; Am 4:12
T because you trample on the poor and Am 5:11
T he who is prudent will keep silent in Am 5:13
T thus says the LORD, the God of hosts, Am 5:16
T they shall now be the first of those Am 6:7
Now **t** hear the word of the LORD. "You Am 7:16
T thus says the LORD: "'Your wife shall Am 7:17
T they called out to the LORD, "O LORD, Jon 1:14
T now, O LORD, please take my life from Jon 4:3
T I will make Samaria a heap in the open Mi 1:6
T you shall give parting gifts to Mi 1:14
T thus says the LORD: behold, against this Mi 2:3
T you will have none to cast the line by Mi 2:5
T it shall be night to you, without vision, Mi 3:6
T because of you Zion shall be plowed Mi 3:12
T he shall give them up until the time Mi 5:3
T I strike you with a grievous blow, Mi 6:13
T he sacrifices to his net and makes Hab 1:16
T, as I live," declares the LORD of hosts, Zep 2:9
"**T** wait for me," declares the LORD, "for Zep 3:8
Now, **t**, thus says the LORD of hosts: Hg 1:5
T the heavens above you have withheld Hg 1:10
T say to them, Thus declares the LORD of Zec 1:3
T, thus says the LORD, I have returned to Zec 1:16
T great anger came from the LORD of Zec 7:12
cheerful feasts. **T** love truth and peace. Zec 8:19
T the people wander like sheep; they are Zec 10:2
t you, O children of Jacob, are not Mal 3:6
Every tree **t** that does not bear good fruit Mt 3:10
T whoever relaxes one of the least of Mt 5:19
You **t** must be perfect, as your heavenly Mt 5:48
"**T** I tell you, do not be anxious about Mt 6:25
T do not be anxious, saying, 'What Mt 6:31
"**T** do not be anxious about tomorrow, Mt 6:34
t pray earnestly to the Lord of the Mt 9:38
t; you are of more value than many Mt 10:31
them out? **T** they will be your judges. Mt 12:27
T I tell you, every sin and blasphemy Mt 12:31
"**T** every scribe who has been trained Mt 13:52
"**T** the kingdom of heaven may be Mt 18:23
'**T** a man shall leave his father and his Mt 19:5
What **t** God has joined together, let not Mt 19:6
When **t** the owner of the vineyard Mt 21:40
T I tell you, the kingdom of God will be Mt 21:43
Go **t** to the main roads and invite to the Mt 22:9
"**T** render to Caesar the things that are Mt 22:21
In the resurrection, **t**, of the seven, Mt 22:28
T I send you prophets and wise men Mt 23:34
T, stay awake, for you do not know on Mt 24:42
T you also must be ready, for the Son Mt 24:44
Watch **t**, for you know neither the day Mt 25:13
T that field has been called the Field of Mt 27:8
T order the tomb to be made secure Mt 27:64
Go **t** and make disciples of all nations, Mt 28:19
'**T** a man shall leave his father and Mk 10:7
What **t** God has joined together, let not Mk 10:9
T I tell you, whatever you ask in Mk 11:24
T stay awake—for you do not know Mk 13:35
t the child to be born will be called holy Lk 1:35
He said **t** to the crowds that came out to Lk 3:7
Every tree **t** that does not bear good fruit Lk 3:9
T I did not presume to come to you. But Lk 7:7
T I tell you, her sins, which are many, Lk 7:47
T pray earnestly to the Lord of the Lk 10:2
them out? **T** they will be your judges. Lk 11:19
T be careful lest the light in you be Lk 11:35
T also the Wisdom of God said, 'I will Lk 11:49
T whatever you have said in the dark Lk 12:3
he said to his disciples, "**T** I tell you, Lk 12:22
He said **t**, "What is the kingdom of God Lk 13:18
married a wife, and **t** I cannot come.' Lk 14:20
So **t**, any one of you who does not Lk 14:33
He said **t**, "A nobleman went into a far Lk 19:12
t, whose wife will the woman be? Lk 20:33
Settle it **t** in your minds not to meditate Lk 21:14
I will **t** punish and release him." Lk 23:16
death. I will **t** punish and release him." Lk 23:22
When **t** he was raised from the dead, his Jn 2:22
voice. **T** this joy of mine is now complete. Jn 3:29
The Jews **t** marveled, saying, "How is it Jn 7:15
Some of the people of Jerusalem **t** said, "Is Jn 7:25
They said to him **t**, "Where is your Jn 8:19
T his parents said, "He is of age; ask Jn 9:23
Many of the Jews **t**, who had come with Jn 11:45
Jesus **t** no longer walked openly among Jn 11:54
the Passover, Jesus **t** came to Bethany, Jn 12:1
Mary **t** took a pound of expensive Jn 12:3
T they could not believe. For again Jn 12:39
I say, **t**, I say as the Father has told me." Jn 12:50
out of the world, **t** the world hates you. Jn 15:19
t I said that he will take what is mine Jn 16:15
T he who delivered me over to you has Jn 19:11
disciple whom Jesus loved **t** said to Peter, Jn 21:7
t my heart was glad, and my tongue Acts 2:26
Being **t** a prophet, and knowing that Acts 2:30
Being **t** exalted at the right hand of Acts 2:33
the house of Israel **t** know for certain Acts 2:36
Repent **t**, and turn again, that your Acts 3:19
T, brothers, pick out from among you Acts 6:3
Repent, **t**, of this wickedness of yours, Acts 8:22
Send **t** to Joppa and ask for Simon Acts 10:32
Now **t** we are all here in the presence Acts 10:33
T he says also in another psalm, Acts 13:35
Let it be known to you **t**, brothers, Acts 13:38
t, lest what is said in the Prophets Acts 13:40
t, why are you putting God to the test Acts 15:10
T my judgment is that we should not Acts 15:19
We have **t** sent Judas and Silas, who Acts 15:27
go. **T** come out now and go in peace." Acts 16:36
Many of them **t** believed, with not a Acts 17:12
We wish to know **t** what these things Acts 17:20
What **t** you worship as unknown, Acts 17:23
If **t** Demetrius and the craftsmen with Acts 19:38
T I testify to you this day that I am Acts 20:26
T be alert, remembering that for Acts 20:31
Do **t** what we tell you. We have four Acts 21:23
Now **t** you, along with the council, Acts 23:15
T I have brought him before you all, Acts 25:26
T I beg you to listen to me patiently. Acts 26:3
"**T**, O King Agrippa, I was not Acts 26:19
T I urge you to take some food. It will Acts 27:34
t, I have asked to see you and speak Acts 28:20
T let it be known to you that this Acts 28:28
T God gave them up in the lusts of Rom 1:24
T you have no excuse, O man, every Rom 2:1
T, since we have been justified by faith, Rom 5:1
t, we have now been justified by his Rom 5:9
T, just as sin came into the world Rom 5:12
T, as one trespass led to condemnation Rom 5:18
We were buried **t** with him by baptism Rom 6:4
Let not sin **t** reign in your mortal Rom 6:12
There is **t** now no condemnation for Rom 8:1
I appeal to you **t**, brothers, by the Rom 12:1
T whoever resists the authorities Rom 13:2
T one must be in subjection, not only Rom 13:5
t love is the fulfilling of the law. Rom 13:10
T let us not pass judgment on one Rom 14:13
T welcome one another as Christ has Rom 15:7
"**T** I will praise you among the Rom 15:9

When **t** I have completed this and Rom 15:28
T, as it is written, "Let the one who 1 Cor 1:31
T do not pronounce judgment before 1 Cor 4:5
Let us **t** celebrate the festival, not with 1 Cor 5:8
T, as to the eating of food offered to 1 Cor 8:4
T, if food makes my brother stumble, 1 Cor 8:13
T let anyone who thinks that he 1 Cor 10:12
T, my beloved, flee from idolatry. 1 Cor 10:14
t, eats the bread or drinks the cup of 1 Cor 11:27
T I want you to understand that no 1 Cor 12:3
T, one who speaks in a tongue 1 Cor 14:13
t, the whole church comes together 1 Cor 14:23
T, my beloved brothers, be steadfast, 1 Cor 15:58
T, having this ministry by the mercy 2 Cor 4:1
T, knowing the fear of the Lord, we 2 Cor 5:11
one has died for all, **t** all have died; 2 Cor 5:14
t, we regard no one according to the 2 Cor 5:16
T, if anyone is in Christ, he is a new 2 Cor 5:17
T, we are ambassadors for Christ, 2 Cor 5:20
T go out from their midst, and be 2 Cor 6:17
T we are comforted. And besides our 2 Cor 7:13
perfect in weakness." **T** I will boast 2 Cor 12:9
stand firm **t**, and do not submit again to Gal 5:1
T remember that at one time you Eph 2:11
I **t**, a prisoner for the Lord, urge you to Eph 4:1
T it says, "When he ascended on high Eph 4:8
T, having put away falsehood, let each Eph 4:25
T be imitators of God, as beloved Eph 5:1
T do not associate with them; Eph 5:7
T it says, "Awake, O sleeper, and arise Eph 5:14
T do not be foolish, but understand Eph 5:17
"**T** a man shall leave his father and Eph 5:31
T take up the whole armor of God, that Eph 6:13
Stand **t**, having fastened on the belt of Eph 6:14
T God has highly exalted him and Phil 2:9
T, my beloved, as you have always Phil 2:12
I hope **t** to send him just as soon as I see Phil 2:23
t, that you may rejoice at seeing him Phil 2:28
T, my brothers, whom I love and long Phil 4:1
T, as you received Christ Jesus the Lord, Col 2:6
T let no one pass judgment on you in Col 2:16
Put to death **t** what is earthly in you: Col 3:5
T when we could bear it no longer, 1 Thes 3:1
T whoever disregards this, disregards 1 Thes 4:8
T encourage one another with these 1 Thes 4:18
T encourage one another and build 1 Thes 5:11
T we ourselves boast about you in 2 Thes 1:4
T God sends them a strong delusion, 2 Thes 2:11
T an overseer must be above reproach, 1 Tm 3:2
T do not be ashamed of the testimony 2 Tm 1:8
T I endure everything for the sake of 2 Tm 2:10
T, if anyone cleanses himself from 2 Tm 2:21
T rebuke them sharply, that they may Ti 1:13
t God, your God, has anointed you with Heb 1:9
T we must pay much closer attention to Heb 2:1
Since **t** the children share in flesh and Heb 2:14
T he had to be made like his brothers Heb 2:17
T, holy brothers, you who share in a Heb 3:1
T, as the Holy Spirit says, "Today, if you Heb 3:7
T I was provoked with that generation, Heb 3:10
T, while the promise of entering his rest Heb 4:1
Since **t** it remains for some to enter it, Heb 4:6
Let us **t** strive to enter that rest, so that Heb 4:11
T let us leave the elementary doctrine of Heb 6:1
T he is the mediator of a new covenant, Heb 9:15
T not even the first covenant was Heb 9:18
T, brothers, since we have confidence Heb 10:19
T do not throw away your confidence, Heb 10:35
T from one man, and him as good as Heb 11:12
T God is not ashamed to be called Heb 11:16
T, since we are surrounded by so great Heb 12:1
T lift your drooping hands and Heb 12:12
T let us be grateful for receiving a Heb 12:28
T let us go to him outside the camp Heb 13:13
T put away all filthiness and rampant Jas 1:21
T whoever wishes to be a friend of the Jas 4:4
T it says, "God opposes the proud, but Jas 4:6
Submit yourselves **t** to God. Resist the Jas 4:7
Be patient, **t**, brothers, until the coming of Jas 5:7
T, confess your sins to one another and Jas 5:16
T, preparing your minds for action, 1 Pt 1:13
Since **t** Christ suffered in the flesh, arm 1 Pt 4:1
t be self-controlled and sober-minded 1 Pt 4:7
T let those who suffer according to 1 Pt 4:19
t, under the mighty hand of God so that 1 Pt 5:6
T, brothers, be all the more diligent to 2 Pt 1:10
T I intend always to remind you of 2 Pt 1:12
T, beloved, since you are waiting for 2 Pt 3:14
You **t**, beloved, knowing this 2 Pt 3:17
T we know that it is the last hour. 1 Jn 2:18
t they speak from the world, and the 1 Jn 4:5
T we ought to support people like these, 3 Jn 1:8
Write **t** the things that you have seen, Rv 1:19
Remember **t** from where you have fallen; Rv 2:5
T repent. If not, I will come to you soon Rv 2:16
"**T** they are before the throne of God, and Rv 7:15
T, rejoice, O heavens and you who Rv 12:12

THEREIN (1)
thereof, the world and those who dwell **t**, Ps 24:1

THEREOF (2)
The earth is the LORD'S and the fullness **t**, Ps 24:1
is the Lord's, and the fullness **t**." 1 Cor 10:26

THESSALONIANS (3)
and of the **T**, Aristarchus and Acts 20:4
the church of the **T** in God the Father 1 Thes 1:1
the church of the **T** in God our 2 Thes 1:1

THESSALONICA (6)
and Apollonia, they came to **T**, Acts 17:1
were more noble than those in **T**; Acts 17:11
the Jews from **T** learned that the Acts 17:13
Aristarchus, a Macedonian from **T**. Acts 27:2
Even in **T** you sent me help for my Phil 4:16
world, has deserted me and gone to **T**. 2 Tm 4:10

THEUDAS (1)
For before these days **T** rose up, Acts 5:36

THICK (31)
I am coming to you in a **t** cloud, Ex 19:9
and lightnings and a **t** cloud on the Ex 19:16
drew near to the **t** darkness where God Ex 20:21
of the fire, the cloud, and the **t** darkness, Dt 5:22
mule went under the **t** branches of a 2 Sm 18:9
down; **t** darkness was under his feet. 2 Sm 22:10
around him his canopy, **t** clouds, 2 Sm 22:12
that he would dwell in **t** darkness. 1 Kgs 8:12
said that he would dwell in **t** darkness. 2 Chr 6:1
That night—let **t** darkness seize it! Let it Jb 3:6
the land of gloom like **t** darkness, like Jb 10:22
any order, where light is as **t** darkness." Jb 10:22
T clouds veil him, so that he does not Jb 22:14
nor because **t** darkness covers my face. Jb 23:17
He binds up the waters in his **t** clouds, Jb 26:8
He loads the **t** cloud with moisture; the Jb 37:11
its garment and **t** darkness its swaddling Jb 38:9
down; **t** darkness was under his feet. Ps 18:9
around him, **t** clouds dark with water. Ps 18:11
Clouds and **t** darkness are all around Ps 97:2
And they will be thrust into **t** darkness. Is 8:22
with his anger, and in **t** rising smoke; Is 30:27
the earth, and **t** darkness the peoples; Is 60:2
to Israel, or a land of **t** darkness? Jer 2:31
it towered aloft among the **t** boughs; Ezk 19:11
on a day of clouds and **t** darkness. Ezk 34:12
the wall of the temple, six cubits **t**, Ezk 41:5
building was five cubits **t** all around, Ezk 41:12
and gloom, a day of clouds and **t** darkness! Jl 2:2
gloom, a day of clouds and **t** darkness, Zep 1:15
Bashan, for the **t** forest has been felled! Zec 11:2

THICKER (2)
'My little finger is **t** than my father's 1 Kgs 12:10
'My little finger is **t** than my father's 2 Chr 10:10

THICKET (7)
was a ram, caught in a **t** by his horns. Gn 22:13
in their dens or lie in wait in their **t**? Jb 38:40
he lurks in ambush like a lion in his **t**; Ps 10:9
A lion has gone up from his **t**, a destroyer Jer 4:7
what will you do in the **t** of the Jordan? Jer 12:5
coming up from the **t** of the Jordan Jer 50:44
lions, for the **t** of the Jordan is ruined! Zec 11:3

THICKETS (4)
and thorns; it kindles the **t** of the forest, Is 9:18
He will cut down the **t** of the forest with Is 10:34
In the **t** in Arabia you will lodge, O Is 21:13
every city takes to flight; they enter **t**; Jer 4:29

THICKLY (1)
against him with a **t** bossed shield; Jb 15:26

THICKNESS (7)
was hollow, and its **t** was four fingers. 1 Kgs 7:15
Its **t** was a handbreadth, and its brim 1 Kgs 7:26
Its **t** was a handbreadth. And its brim 2 Chr 4:5
twelve cubits, and its **t** was four fingers, Jer 52:21
So he measured the **t** of the wall, one Ezk 40:5
The **t** of the outer wall of the side Ezk 41:9
In the **t** of the wall of the court, on the Ezk 42:10

THIEF (26)
"If a **t** is found breaking in and is struck Ex 22:2
the man's house, then, if the **t** is found, Ex 22:7
If the **t** is not found, the owner of the Ex 22:8
a slave or sells him, then that **t** shall die. Dt 24:7
and needy, and in the night he is like a **t**. Jb 24:14
they shout after them as after a **t**. Jb 30:5
If you see a **t**, you are pleased with him, Ps 50:18
People do not despise a **t** if he steals to Prv 6:30
The partner of a **t** hates his own life; he Prv 29:24
"As a **t** is shamed when caught, so the Jer 2:26
the **t** breaks in, and the bandits raid Hos 7:1
they enter through the windows like a **t**. Jl 2:9
hosts, and it shall enter the house of the **t**, Zec 5:4
part of the night the **t** was coming, Mt 24:43
where no **t** approaches and no moth Lk 12:33
known at what hour the **t** was coming, Lk 12:39
way, that man is a **t** and a robber. Jn 10:1
The **t** comes only to steal and kill and Jn 10:10
about the poor, but because he was a **t**, Jn 12:6
Let the **t** no longer steal, but rather let Eph 4:28
Lord will come like a **t** in the night. 1 Thes 5:2
for that day to surprise you like a **t**. 1 Thes 5:4
as a murderer or a **t** or an evildoer or as 1 Pt 4:15
the day of the Lord will come like a **t**, 2 Pt 3:10
you will not wake up, I will come like a **t**, Rv 3:3
("Behold, I am coming like a **t**! Blessed Rv 16:15

THIEVES (8)
princes are rebels and companions of **t**. Is 1:23
Was he found among **t**, that whenever Jer 48:27
If **t** came by night, would they not Jer 49:9
If **t** came to you, if plunderers came by Ob 1:5
rust destroy and where **t** break in and Mt 6:19
rust destroys and where **t** do not break Mt 6:20
who came before me are **t** and robbers, Jn 10:8
nor **t**, nor the greedy, nor drunkards, 1 Cor 6:10

THIGH (31)
that he had, "Put your hand under my **t**, Gn 24:2
his hand under the **t** of Abraham his Gn 24:9
eat the sinew of the **t** that is on the hip Gn 32:32
of Jacob's hip on the sinew of the **t**. Gn 32:32
your hand under my **t** and promise to Gn 47:29
and the right **t** (for it is a ram of Ex 29:22
is waved and the **t** of the priests' portion Ex 29:27
And the right **t** you shall give to the Lv 7:32
fat shall have the right **t** for a portion. Lv 7:33
is waved and the **t** that is contributed I Lv 7:34
two kidneys with their fat and the right **t**, Lv 8:25
on the pieces of fat and on the right **t**. Lv 8:26
breasts and the right **t** Aaron waved for a Lv 9:21
is waved and the **t** that is contributed Lv 10:14
The **t** that is contributed and the breast Lv 10:15
the LORD makes your **t** fall away and Nm 5:21
your womb swell and your **t** fall away.' Nm 5:22
shall swell, and her **t** shall fall away, Nm 5:27
is waved and the **t** that is contributed. Nm 6:20
is waved and as the right **t** are yours. Nm 18:18
bound it on his right **t** under his clothes. Jgs 3:16
hand, took the sword from his right **t**, Jgs 3:21
struck them hip and **t** with a great blow, Jgs 15:8
a sword in its sheath fastened on his **t**, 2 Sm 20:8
Gird your sword on your **t**, O mighty Ps 45:3
expert in war, each with his sword at his **t**, Sg 3:8
after I was instructed, I slapped my **t**; Jer 31:19
people. Strike therefore upon your **t**. Ezk 21:12
the good pieces, the **t** and the shoulder; Ezk 24:4
laying him bare from **t** to neck. Hab 3:13
his robe and on his **t** he has a name Rv 19:16

THIGHS (6)
They shall reach from the hips to the **t**; Ex 28:42
finger is thicker than my father's **t**. 1 Kgs 12:10
finger is thicker than my father's **t**. 2 Chr 10:10
the sinews of his **t** are knit together. Jb 40:17
Your rounded **t** are like jewels, the work of Sg 7:1
of silver, its middle and **t** of bronze, Dn 2:32

THIN (9)
behold, seven other cows, ugly and **t**, Gn 41:3
ugly, **t** cows ate up the seven attractive, Gn 41:4
ears, **t** and blighted by the east wind. Gn 41:6
And the **t** ears swallowed up the seven Gn 41:7
after them, poor and very ugly and **t**, Gn 41:19
And the **t**, ugly cows ate up the first Gn 41:20
t, and blighted by the east wind, Gn 41:23
and the **t** ears swallowed up the seven Gn 41:24
skin, and the hair in it is yellow and **t**, Lv 13:30

THING (233)
and over every creeping **t** that creeps on Gn 1:26
and over every living **t** that moves on Gn 1:28
And of every living **t** of all flesh, you Gn 6:19
kinds, of every creeping **t** of the ground, Gn 6:20
and every living **t** that I have made I will Gn 7:4
and every creeping **t** that creeps on the Gn 7:14
blotted out every living **t** that was on the Gn 7:23
with you every living **t** that is with you Gn 8:17
and every creeping **t** that creeps on Gn 8:17
Every beast, every creeping **t**, and every Gn 8:19
Every moving **t** that lives shall be food Gn 9:3
Far be it from you to do such a **t**, to put Gn 18:25
"What did you see, that you did this **t**?" Gn 20:10
And the **t** was very displeasing to Gn 21:11
"I do not know who has done this **t**; Gn 21:26
said, "The **t** has come from the LORD; Gn 24:50
shall say the same **t** to Esau when you Gn 32:19
had done an outrageous **t** in Israel by Gn 34:7
daughter, for such a **t** must not be done. Gn 34:7

said to them, "We cannot do this **t**, Gn 34:14
young man did not delay to do the **t**, Gn 34:19
dream means that the **t** is fixed by God, Gn 41:32
be it from your servants to do such a **t**! Gn 44:7
and thought, "Surely the **t** is known." Ex 2:14
the LORD will do this **t** in the land." Ex 9:5
And the next day the LORD did this **t**. All Ex 9:6
Not a green **t** remained, neither tree nor Ex 10:15
face of the wilderness a fine, flake-like **t**, Ex 16:14
out, for the **t** is too heavy for you. Ex 18:18
for a cloak, or for any kind of lost **t**, Ex 22:9
"This very **t** that you have spoken I will Ex 33:17
for it is an awesome **t** that I will do with Ex 34:10
"This is the **t** that the LORD has Ex 35:4
unintentionally and the **t** is hidden from Lv 4:13
or if anyone touches an unclean **t**, Lv 5:2
done amiss in the holy **t** and shall add a Lv 5:16
to him or the lost **t** that he found Lv 6:4
It is a **t** most holy, like the sin offering Lv 6:17
that touches any unclean **t** shall not be Lv 7:19
And if anyone touches an unclean **t**, Lv 7:21
"This is the **t** that the LORD has Lv 8:5
"This is the **t** that the LORD commanded Lv 9:6
since it is a **t** most holy and has been Lv 10:17
"Every swarming **t** that swarms on the Lv 11:41
any swarming **t** that swarms on the Lv 11:42
with any swarming **t** that swarms, Lv 11:43
with any swarming **t** that crawls on Lv 11:44
that they wash the **t** in which is the Lv 13:54
shall examine the diseased **t** after it has Lv 13:55
This is the **t** that the LORD has Lv 17:2
touches a swarming **t** by which he Lv 22:5
who touches such a **t** shall be unclean Lv 22:6
"A lay person shall not eat of a holy **t**; Lv 22:10
or hired servant shall eat of a holy **t**, Lv 22:10
anyone eats of a holy **t** unintentionally, Lv 22:14
to it and give the holy **t** to the priest. Lv 22:14
"But no devoted **t** that a man devotes to Lv 27:28
every devoted **t** is most holy to the LORD. Lv 27:28
is it too small a **t** for you that the God of Nm 16:9
Is it a small **t** that you have brought Nm 16:13
Every devoted **t** in Israel shall be Nm 18:14
'The **t** that you have spoken is good for Dt 1:14
The **t** seemed good to me, and I took Dt 1:23
whether such a great **t** as this has ever Dt 4:32
bring an abominable **t** into your house Dt 7:26
Then I took the sinful **t**, the calf that you Dt 9:21
and every living **t** that followed them, Dt 11:6
for every abominable **t** that the LORD Dt 12:31
man or woman who has done this evil **t**, Dt 17:5
or with any lost **t** of your brother's, Dt 22:3
But if the **t** is true, that evidence of Dt 22:20
has done an outrageous **t** in Israel by Dt 22:21
you shall keep yourself from every evil **t**. Dt 23:9
a **t** made by the hands of a craftsman, Dt 27:15
camp of Israel a **t** for destruction and Jos 6:18
he has done an outrageous **t** in Israel.'" Jos 7:15
our lives because of you and did this **t**. Jos 9:24
"Who has done this **t**?" And after they Jgs 6:29
the son of Joash has done this **t**." Jgs 6:29
to her father, "Let this **t** be done for me: Jgs 11:37
or strong drink, or eat any unclean **t**. Jgs 13:14
into my house, do not do this vile **t**. Jgs 19:23
this man do not do this outrageous **t**." Jgs 19:24
"Such a **t** has never happened or been Jgs 19:30
am about to do a **t** in Israel at which 1 Sm 3:11
But the **t** displeased Samuel when they 1 Sm 8:6
and see this great **t** that the LORD will 1 Sm 12:16
show you a **t**." And Jonathan said 1 Sm 14:12
they told Saul, and the **t** pleased him. 1 Sm 18:20
to you a little **t** to become the king's 1 Sm 18:23
that I should do this **t** to my lord, 1 Sm 24:6
This **t** that you have done is not 1 Sm 26:16
shall come upon you for this **t**." 1 Sm 28:10
LORD has done this **t** to you this day. 1 Sm 28:18
to you because you have done this **t**. 2 Sm 2:6
But one **t** I require of you; that is, you 2 Sm 3:13
yet this was a small **t** in your eyes, 2 Sm 7:19
promised this good **t** to your servant. 2 Sm 7:28
your soul lives, I will not do this **t**." 2 Sm 11:11
But the **t** that David had done 2 Sm 11:27
lamb fourfold, because he did this **t**, 2 Sm 12:6
I will do this **t** before all Israel and 2 Sm 12:12
"What is this **t** that you have done? 2 Sm 12:21
me, for such a **t** is not done in Israel; 2 Sm 13:12
in Israel; do not do this outrageous **t**. 2 Sm 13:12
planned such a **t** against the people 2 Sm 14:13
my lord the king delight in this **t**?" 2 Sm 24:3
Has this **t** been brought about by my 1 Kgs 1:27
commanded him concerning this **t**, 1 Kgs 11:10
for this **t** is from me.'" So they 1 Kgs 12:24
Then this **t** became a sin, for the 1 Kgs 12:30
After this **t** Jeroboam did not turn 1 Kgs 13:33
And this **t** became sin to the house 1 Kgs 13:34
it had been a light **t** for him to walk 1 Kgs 16:31
but this **t** I cannot do.'" And the 1 Kgs 20:9
And one said one **t**, and another said 1 Kgs 22:20
he said, "You have asked a hard **t**; 2 Kgs 2:10
This is a light **t** in the sight of the 2 Kgs 3:18
was greatly troubled because of this **t**, 2 Kgs 6:11
heaven, could this **t** be?" But he said, 2 Kgs 7:2
could such a **t** be?" And he had said, 2 Kgs 7:19
do this great **t**?" Elisha answered, 2 Kgs 8:13
them, "This is the **t** that you shall do: 2 Kgs 11:5
LORD will do the **t** that he has 2 Kgs 20:9
"It is an easy **t** for the shadow to 2 Kgs 20:10
faith in the matter of the devoted **t**; 1 Chr 2:7
for the **t** was right in the eyes of all 1 Chr 13:4
And this was a small **t** in your eyes, 1 Chr 17:17
promised this good **t** to your 1 Chr 17:26
But God was displeased with this **t**, 1 Chr 21:7
greatly in that I have done this **t**. 1 Chr 21:8
for this **t** is from me.'" So they 2 Chr 11:4
And one said one **t**, and another said 2 Chr 18:19
This is the **t** that you shall do: of you 2 Chr 23:4
for the **t** came about suddenly. 2 Chr 29:36
who put such a **t** as this into the heart of Ezr 7:27
"What is this **t** that you are doing? Neh 2:19
"The **t** that you are doing is not good. Neh 5:9
"What is this evil **t** that you are Neh 13:17
and if the **t** seems right before the king, Est 8:5
For the **t** that I fear comes upon me, and Jb 3:25
life of every living **t** and the breath of Jb 12:10
Man wastes away like a rotten **t**, like a Jb 13:28
can bring a clean **t** out of an unclean? Jb 14:4
rocks, and his eye sees every precious **t**. Jb 28:10
and the **t** that is hidden he brings out to Jb 28:11
and he searches after every green **t**. Jb 39:8
One **t** have I asked of the LORD, that will I Ps 27:4
those who seek the LORD lack no good **t**. Ps 34:10
say, "A deadly **t** is poured out on him; Ps 41:8
No good **t** does he withhold from those Ps 84:11
you satisfy the desire of every living **t**. Ps 145:16
trustworthy in spirit keeps a **t** covered. Prv 11:13
wife finds a good **t** and obtains favor Prv 18:22
Is there a **t** of which it is said, "See, this Eccl 1:10
is the end of a **t** than its beginning, Eccl 7:8
while adding one **t** to another to find Eccl 7:27
who knows the interpretation of a **t**? Eccl 8:1
keeps a command will know no evil **t**, Eccl 8:5
man has no good **t** under the sun but Eccl 8:15
into judgment, with every secret **t**, Eccl 12:14
that the **t** made should say of its maker, Is 29:16
or the **t** formed say of him who formed Is 29:16
LORD will do this **t** that he has promised: Is 38:7
Behold, I am doing a new **t**; now it Is 43:19
"It is too light a **t** that you should be my Is 49:6
go out from there; touch no unclean **t**; Is 52:11
shall succeed in the **t** for which I sent Is 55:11
Who has heard such a **t**? Who has seen Is 66:8
with care; see if there has been such a **t**. Jer 2:10
youth the shameful **t** has devoured all Jer 3:24
appalling and horrible **t** has happened Jer 5:30
virgin Israel has done a very horrible **t**. Jer 18:13
land a horror, a **t** to be hissed at forever. Jer 18:16
this city a horror, a **t** to be hissed at. Jer 19:8
of Samaria I saw an unsavory **t**: Jer 23:13
of Jerusalem I have seen a horrible **t**: Jer 23:14
have done an outrageous **t** in Israel, Jer 29:23
LORD has created a new **t** on the earth: Jer 31:22
his voice, this **t** has come upon you. Jer 40:3
son of Kareah, "You shall not do this **t**, Jer 40:16
should go, and the **t** that we should do." Jer 42:3
has become a filthy **t** among them. Lam 1:17
and their gold is like an unclean **t**. Ezk 7:19
I make it an unclean **t** to them. Ezk 7:20
Is it too light a **t** for the house of Judah Ezk 8:17
you as a profane **t** from the mountain Ezk 28:16
and every devoted **t** in Israel shall be Ezk 44:29
has asked such a **t** of any magician or Dn 2:10
The **t** that the king asks is difficult, and Dn 2:11
answered and said, "The **t** stands fast, Dn 6:12
house of Israel I have seen a horrible **t**; Hos 6:10
they would be regarded as a strange **t**. Hos 8:12
themselves to the **t** of shame, Hos 9:10
became detestable like the **t** they loved. Hos 9:10
The **t** itself shall be carried to Assyria Hos 10:6
strip his treasury of every precious **t**. Hos 13:15
Has such a **t** happened in your days, or in Jl 1:2
shall be a deceitful **t** to the kings of Mi 1:14
Woe to him who says to a wooden **t**, Hab 2:19
And this second **t** you do. You cover Mal 2:13
For she has done a beautiful **t** to me. Mt 26:10
him, and said to him, "You lack one **t**: Mk 10:21
her? She has done a beautiful **t** to me. Mk 14:6
and see this **t** that has happened, Lk 2:15
but one **t** is necessary. Mary has Lk 10:42
are not able to do as small a **t** as that, Lk 12:26
he said to him, "One **t** you still lack. Lk 18:22
him was not any **t** made that was made. Jn 1:3
cannot receive even one **t** unless it is Jn 3:27
One **t** I do know, that though I was blind, Jn 9:25
answered, "Why, this is an amazing **t**! Jn 9:30
and the **t** was taken up at once to Acts 10:16
Now some cried out one **t**, some Acts 19:32
in the crowd were shouting one **t**, Acts 21:34
other than this one **t** that I cried out Acts 24:21
what I want, but I do the very **t** I hate. Rom 7:15
of God, attending to this very **t**. Rom 13:6
it is a very small **t** that I should be 1 Cor 4:3
judgment on the one who did such a **t**. 1 Cor 5:3
has prepared us for this very **t** is God, 2 Cor 5:5
the Lord, and touch no unclean **t**; 2 Cor 6:17
the poor, the very **t** I was eager to do. Gal 2:10
without spot or wrinkle or any such **t**, Eph 5:27
equality with God a **t** to be grasped, Phil 2:6
I have made it my own. But one **t** I do: Phil 3:13
knowledge of every good **t** that is in us Phlm 1:6
It is a fearful **t** to fall into the hands of Heb 10:31
whoever knows the right **t** to do and fails Jas 4:17
For this is a gracious **t**, when, mindful 1 Pt 2:19
this is a gracious **t** in the sight of God. 1 Pt 2:20
it is a faithful **t** you do in all your efforts 3 Jn 1:5
and every living **t** died that was in the Rv 16:3

THINGS (738)

—livestock and creeping **t** and beasts of Gn 1:24
and animals and creeping **t** and birds of Gn 6:7
and animals and creeping **t** and birds of Gn 7:23
After these **t** the word of the LORD came Gn 15:1
all his servants and told them all these **t**. Gn 20:8
You have done to me **t** that ought not to Gn 20:9
After these **t** God tested Abraham and Gn 22:1
Now after these **t** it was told to Gn 22:20
the LORD had blessed Abraham in all **t**. Gn 24:1
her mother's household about these **t**. Gn 24:28
told Isaac all the **t** that he had done. Gn 24:66
his house. Jacob told Laban all these **t**, Gn 29:13
replied, "Let her keep the **t** as her own, Gn 38:23
loaded with the good **t** of Egypt, Gn 45:23
if he does not do these three **t** for her, Ex 21:11
guilt from the holy **t** that the people of Ex 28:38
shall eat those **t** with which atonement Ex 29:33
"These are the **t** that the LORD has Ex 35:1
offering that is made of these **t** to the LORD, Lv 2:8
LORD'S commandments about **t** not to be Lv 4:2
do any one of the **t** that by the LORD'S Lv 4:13
one of all the **t** that by the Lv 4:22
doing any one of the **t** that by the LORD'S Lv 4:27
or a carcass of unclean swarming **t**, Lv 5:2
he has committed in any one of these **t**, Lv 5:13
in any of the holy **t** of the LORD, Lv 5:15
doing any of the **t** that by the LORD'S Lv 5:17
—in any of all the **t** that people do and sin Lv 6:3
forgiven for any of the **t** that one may do Lv 6:7
sons did all the **t** that the LORD Lv 8:36
and yet such **t** as these have happened Lv 10:19
These are the living **t** that you may eat Lv 11:2
among the swarming **t** that swarm on Lv 11:29
be cleansed and these **t** before the LORD, Lv 14:11
whoever carries such **t** shall wash his Lv 15:10
whoever touches these **t** shall be Lv 15:27
yourselves unclean by any of these **t**, Lv 18:24
out before you, for they did all these **t**, Lv 20:23
both of the most holy and of the holy **t**, Lv 21:22
abstain from the holy **t** of the people of Lv 22:2
approaches the holy **t** that the people Lv 22:3
may eat of the holy **t** until he is clean. Lv 22:4
not eat of the holy **t** unless he has bathed Lv 22:6
and afterward he may eat of the holy **t**, Lv 22:7
not eat of the contribution of the holy **t**. Lv 22:12
not profane the holy **t** of the people of Lv 22:15
and guilt, by eating their holy **t**: Lv 22:16
in the tent of meeting: the most holy **t**. Nm 4:4
but they must not touch the holy **t**, Nm 4:15
These are the **t** of the tent of meeting Nm 4:15
they come near to the most holy **t**: Nm 4:19
look on the holy **t** even for a moment, Nm 4:20
the service of the holy **t** that had to be Nm 7:9
set out, carrying the holy **t**, Nm 10:21
Israelite shall do these **t** in this way, Nm 15:13
all the consecrated **t** of the people of Nm 18:8
This shall be yours of the most holy **t**, Nm 18:9
not profane the holy **t** of the people of Nm 18:32
And these **t** shall be for a statute and Nm 35:29
at that time all the **t** that you should do. Dt 1:18
lest you forget the **t** that your eyes have Dt 4:9
t that the LORD your God has allotted to Dt 4:19
and all these **t** come upon you in the Dt 4:30
houses full of all good **t** that you did not Dt 6:11
great and terrifying **t** that your eyes Dt 10:21
But the holy **t** that are due from you, Dt 12:26
None of the devoted **t** shall stick to your Dt 13:17
All clean winged **t** you may eat. Dt 14:20
whoever does these **t** is an abomination Dt 18:12
whoever does these **t** is an abomination Dt 22:5

For all who do such **t**, all who act Dt 25:16
heart, because of the abundance of all **t**, Dt 28:47
And you have seen their detestable **t**, Dt 29:17
"The secret **t** belong to the LORD our Dt 29:29
but the **t** that are revealed belong to us Dt 29:29
"And when all these **t** come upon you, Dt 30:1
with the venom of **t** that crawl in the Dt 32:24
Just as we obeyed Moses in all **t**, so we Jos 1:17
yourselves from the **t** devoted to Jos 6:18
any of the devoted **t** and make the camp Jos 6:18
broke faith in regard to the devoted **t**, Jos 7:1
tribe of Judah, took some of the devoted **t**. Jos 7:1
they have taken some of the devoted **t**; Jos 7:11
destroy the devoted **t** from among you. Jos 7:12
"There are devoted **t** in your midst, Jos 7:13
away the devoted **t** from among you." Jos 7:13
taken with the devoted **t** shall be burned Jos 7:15
faith in the matter of the devoted **t**, Jos 22:20
of all the good **t** that the LORD your Jos 23:14
just as all the good **t** that the LORD your Jos 23:15
LORD will bring upon you all the evil **t**, Jos 23:15
After these **t** Joshua the son of Nun, the Jos 24:29
at our hands, or shown us all these **t**, Jgs 13:23
now announced to us such **t** as these." Jgs 13:23
said to them, "Why do you do such **t**? 1 Sm 2:23
the men of Ashdod saw how **t** were, 1 Sm 5:7
aside after empty **t** that cannot profit 1 Sm 12:21
consider what great **t** he has done 1 Sm 12:24
best of the **t** devoted to destruction, 1 Sm 15:21
And David left the **t** in charge of the 1 Sm 17:22
Jonathan reported to him all these **t**. 1 Sm 19:7
of Nabal, his wife told him these **t**, 1 Sm 25:37
You will do many **t** and will succeed 1 Sm 26:25
great and awesome **t** by driving out 2 Sm 7:23
King David heard of all these **t**, 2 Sm 13:21
the course of **t** your servant Joab 2 Sm 14:20
of God to know all **t** that are on the 2 Sm 14:20
covenant, ordered in all **t** and secure. 2 Sm 23:5
it. These **t** the three mighty men did. 2 Sm 23:17
These **t** did Benaiah the son of 2 Sm 23:22
says the LORD, Three **t** I offer you. 2 Sm 24:12
brought in the **t** that David his 1 Kgs 7:51
I have done all these **t** at your word. 1 Kgs 18:36
to meet you and told you these **t**?" 2 Kgs 1:7
tent and carried off **t** from it and went 2 Kgs 7:8
me all the great **t** that Elisha has 2 Kgs 8:4
money of the holy **t** that is brought 2 Kgs 12:4
He did in all **t** as Joash his father had 2 Kgs 14:3
the LORD their God **t** that were not 2 Kgs 17:9
And they did wicked **t**, provoking 2 Kgs 17:11
and has done **t** more evil than 2 Kgs 21:11
who had predicted these **t**. 2 Kgs 23:16
and predicted these **t** that you have 2 Kgs 23:17
it. These **t** did the three mighty men. 1 Chr 11:19
These **t** did Benaiah the son of 1 Chr 11:24
in making known all these great **t**. 1 Chr 17:19
a name for great and awesome **t**, 1 Chr 17:21
says the LORD, Three **t** I offer you; 1 Chr 21:10
set apart to dedicate the most holy **t**, 1 Chr 23:13
or any of the **t** for its service." 1 Chr 23:26
as I was able, the gold for the **t** of gold, 1 Chr 29:2
of gold, the silver for the **t** of silver, 1 Chr 29:2
and the bronze for the **t** of bronze, 1 Chr 29:2
of bronze, the iron for the **t** of iron, 1 Chr 29:2
of iron, and wood for the **t** of wood, 1 Chr 29:2
gold for the **t** of gold and silver for the 1 Chr 29:5
of gold and silver for the **t** of silver. 1 Chr 29:5
For all **t** come from you, and of 1 Chr 29:14
heart I have freely offered all these **t**, 1 Chr 29:17
made all these **t** in great quantities, 2 Chr 4:18
brought in the **t** that David his 2 Chr 5:1
goods, clothing, and precious **t**, 2 Chr 20:25
used all the dedicated **t** of the house of 2 Chr 24:7
tithe of the dedicated **t** that had been 2 Chr 31:6
the tithes, and the dedicated **t**. 2 Chr 31:12
After these **t** and these acts of 2 Chr 32:1
and precious **t** to Hezekiah 2 Chr 32:23
After these **t** had been done, the officials Ezr 9:1
"No such **t** as you say have been done, Neh 6:8
God, according to these **t** that they did, Neh 6:14
possession of houses full of all good **t**, Neh 9:25
the appointed feasts, the holy **t**, Neh 10:33
After these **t**, when the anger of King Est 2:1
After these **t** King Ahasuerus promoted Est 3:1
Mordecai recorded these **t** and sent Est 9:20
who does great **t** and unsearchable, Jb 5:9
marvelous **t** without number: Jb 5:9
"How long will you say these **t**, and the Jb 8:2
who does great **t** beyond searching out, Jb 9:10
out, and marvelous **t** beyond number. Jb 9:10
Yet these **t** you hid in your heart; I know Jb 10:13
"Can you find out the deep **t** of God? Can Jb 11:7
you. Who does not know such **t** as these? Jb 12:3
Only grant me two **t**, then I will not hide Jb 13:20
For you write bitter **t** against me and Jb 13:26

"I have heard many such **t**; miserable Jb 16:2
their houses with good **t**—but the Jb 22:18
me, and many such **t** are in his mind. Jb 23:14
"Behold, God does all these **t**, twice, three Jb 33:29
he does great **t** that we cannot Jb 37:5
"I know that you can do all **t**, and that no Jb 42:2
not understand, **t** too wonderful for me, Jb 42:3
hands; you have put all **t** under his feet, Ps 8:6
He who does these **t** shall never be Ps 15:5
up; they ask me of **t** that I do not know. Ps 35:11
These **t** I remember, as I pour out my Ps 42:4
These **t** you have done, and I have been Ps 50:21
You have made your people see hard **t**; Ps 60:3
You who have done great **t**, O God, who Ps 71:19
of Israel, who alone does wondrous **t**. Ps 72:18
t that we have heard and known, that Ps 78:3
For you are great and do wondrous **t**; Ps 86:10
Glorious **t** of you are spoken, O city of Ps 87:3
a new song, for he has done marvelous **t**! Ps 98:1
living **t** both small and great. Ps 104:25
your hand, they are filled with good **t**. Ps 104:28
Savior, who had done great **t** in Egypt, Ps 106:21
and the hungry soul he fills with good **t**. Ps 107:9
is wise, let him attend to these **t**; Ps 107:43
I may behold wondrous **t** out of your Ps 119:18
my eyes from looking at worthless **t**; Ps 119:37
this day, for all **t** are your servants. Ps 119:91
"The LORD has done great **t** for them." Ps 126:2
The LORD has done great **t** for us; we are Ps 126:3
not occupy myself with **t** too great and Ps 131:1
have exalted above all **t** your name and Ps 138:2
who plan evil **t** in their heart and stir up Ps 140:2
livestock, creeping **t** and flying birds! Ps 148:10
There are six **t** that the LORD hates, Prv 6:16
Hear, for I will speak noble **t**, and from Prv 8:6
mouth of the wicked pours out evil **t**. Prv 15:28
winks his eyes plans dishonest **t**; Prv 16:30
Your eyes will see strange **t**, and your Prv 23:33
things, and your heart utter perverse **t**. Prv 23:33
It is the glory of God to conceal **t**, but Prv 25:2
but the glory of kings is to search **t** out. Prv 25:2
Two **t** I ask of you; deny them not to me Prv 30:7
Three **t** are never satisfied; four never Prv 30:15
Three **t** are too wonderful for me; four Prv 30:18
Under three **t** the earth trembles; Prv 30:21
Four **t** on earth are small, but they are Prv 30:24
Three **t** are stately in their tread; four Prv 30:29
All **t** are full of weariness; a man cannot Eccl 1:8
There is no remembrance of former **t**, Eccl 1:11
any remembrance of later **t** yet to be Eccl 1:11
his soul is not satisfied with life's good **t**, Eccl 6:3
take to heart all the **t** that people say, Eccl 7:21
to seek wisdom and the scheme of **t**, Eccl 7:25
to another to find the scheme of **t**— Eccl 7:27
in the city where they had done such **t**. Eccl 8:10
that for all these **t** God will bring you Eccl 11:9
because they are full of **t** from the east and Is 2:6
name, for you have done wonderful **t**, Is 25:1
again do wonderful **t** with this people, Is 29:14
You turn **t** upside down! Shall the potter Is 29:16
speak to us smooth **t**, prophesy illusions, Is 30:10
You will scatter them as unclean **t**. Is 30:22
But he who is noble plans noble **t**, and on Is 32:8
noble things, and on noble **t** he stands. Is 32:8
O Lord, by these **t** men live, and in all Is 38:16
Tell us the former **t**, what they are, that Is 41:22
outcome; or declare to us the **t** to come. Is 41:22
Behold, the former **t** have come to pass, Is 42:9
come to pass, and new **t** I now declare; Is 42:9
These are the **t** I do, and I do not forsake Is 42:16
He sees many **t**, but does not observe Is 42:20
declare this, and show us the former **t**? Is 43:9
"Remember not the former **t**, nor Is 43:18
former things, nor consider the **t** of old. Is 43:18
and the **t** they delight in do not profit. Is 44:9
Remember these **t**, O Jacob, and Israel, Is 44:21
"I am the LORD, who made all **t**, who Is 44:24
I am the LORD, who does all these **t**. Is 45:7
who formed him: "Ask me of **t** to come; Is 45:11
these **t** you carry are borne as burdens on Is 46:1
remember the former **t** of old; for I am Is 46:9
and from ancient times **t** not yet done, Is 46:10
did not lay these **t** to heart or remember Is 47:7
These two **t** shall come to you in a Is 47:9
"The former **t** I declared of old; they went Is 48:3
this time forth I announce to you new **t**, Is 48:6
hidden **t** that you have not known. Is 48:6
who among them has declared these **t**? Is 48:14
These two **t** have happened to you—who Is 51:19
who choose the **t** that please me and hold Is 56:4
a grain offering. Shall I relent for these **t**? Is 57:6
When you did awesome **t** that we did not Is 64:3
Will you restrain yourself at these **t**, O Is 64:12
and the former **t** shall not be Is 65:17
All these **t** my hand has made, and so all Is 66:2

has made, and so all these **t** came to be, Is 66:2
such a thing? Who has seen such **t**? Is 66:8
land to enjoy its fruits and its good **t**. Jer 2:7
by Baal and went after **t** that do not profit. Jer 2:8
breaking in. Yet in spite of all these **t** Jer 2:34
remove your detestable **t** from my Jer 4:1
Shall I not punish them for these **t**? Jer 5:9
the LORD our God done all these **t** to us?' Jer 5:19
Shall I not punish them for these **t**? Jer 5:29
now, because you have done all these **t**, Jer 7:13
have set their detestable **t** in the house Jer 7:30
Shall I not punish them for these **t**? Jer 9:9
For in these **t** I delight, declares the Jer 9:24
for he is the one who formed all **t**, Jer 10:16
'Why have these **t** come upon me?' Jer 13:22
our hope on you, for you do all these **t**. Jer 14:22
worthless **t** in which there is no profit. Jer 16:19
The heart is deceitful above all **t**, and Jer 17:9
heard Jeremiah prophesying these **t**. Jer 20:1
the officials of Judah heard these **t**, Jer 26:10
are flagrant, I have done these **t** to you. Jer 30:15
you great and hidden **t** that you have not Jer 33:3
And do you seek great **t** for yourself? Jer 45:5
For I will bring these **t** upon Moab, the Jer 48:44
for he is the one who formed all **t**, Jer 51:19
the anger of the LORD **t** came to the point Jer 52:3
bronze of all these **t** was beyond weight. Jer 52:20
all the precious **t** that were hers Lam 1:7
out his hands over all her precious **t**; Lam 1:10
"For these **t** I weep; my eyes flow with Lam 1:16
for these **t** our eyes have grown dim, Lam 5:17
with all your detestable **t** and with all Ezk 5:11
images and their detestable **t** of it. Ezk 7:20
form of creeping **t** and loathsome Ezk 8:10
For I know the **t** that come into your Ezk 11:5
it all its detestable **t** and all its Ezk 11:18
after their detestable **t** and their Ezk 11:21
the exiles all the **t** that the LORD had Ezk 11:25
to do any of these **t** to you out of Ezk 16:5
Lord GOD, because you did all these **t**, Ezk 16:30
but have enraged me with all these **t**, Ezk 16:43
Do you not know what these **t** mean? Ezk 17:12
Can one escape who does such **t**? Ezk 17:15
he gave his hand and did all these **t**; Ezk 17:18
of blood, who does any of these **t** Ezk 18:10
he himself did none of these **t**), Ezk 18:11
away the detestable **t** your eyes feast Ezk 20:7
away the detestable **t** their eyes feasted Ezk 20:8
go whoring after their detestable **t**? Ezk 20:30
crown. **T** shall not remain as they are. Ezk 21:26
despised my holy **t** and profaned my Ezk 22:8
have taken treasure and precious **t**; Ezk 22:25
my law and have profaned my holy **t**. Ezk 22:26
not tell us what these **t** mean for us, Ezk 24:19
with their idols and their detestable **t**, Ezk 37:23
field and all creeping **t** that creep on Ezk 38:20
you have not kept charge of my holy **t**, Ezk 44:8
any of my holy **t** and the things that Ezk 44:13
holy things and the **t** that are most Ezk 44:13
he reveals deep and hidden **t**; he knows Dn 2:22
iron breaks to pieces and shatters all **t**. Dn 2:40
of a man, and a mouth speaking great **t**. Dn 7:8
known to me the interpretation of the **t**. Dn 7:16
had eyes and a mouth that spoke great **t**, Dn 7:20
shall speak astonishing **t** against the Dn 11:36
of silver, and all the precious **t** of Egypt, Dn 11:43
to an end all these **t** would be finished. Dn 12:7
what shall be the outcome of these **t**?" Dn 12:8
and the creeping **t** of the ground. Hos 2:18
shall possess their precious **t** of silver; Hos 9:6
is wise, let him understand these **t**; Hos 14:9
of him will rise, for he has done great **t**. Jl 2:20
and rejoice, for the LORD has done great **t**! Jl 2:21
"one should not preach of such **t**; Mi 2:6
of Egypt, I will show them marvelous **t**. Mi 7:15
a serpent, like the crawling **t** of the earth; Mi 7:17
treasure or of the wealth of all precious **t**. Na 2:9
sea, like crawling **t** that have no ruler. Hab 1:14
despised the day of small **t** shall rejoice, Zec 4:10
of this people to possess all these **t**. Zec 8:12
These are the **t** that you shall do: Speak Zec 8:16
love no false oath, for all these **t** I hate, Zec 8:17
But as he considered these **t**, behold, an Mt 1:20
For the Gentiles seek after all these **t**, and Mt 6:32
and all these **t** will be added to you. Mt 6:33
is in heaven give good **t** to those who ask Mt 7:11
While he was saying these **t** to them, Mt 9:18
you have hidden these **t** from the wise Mt 11:25
All **t** have been handed over to me by Mt 11:27
And he told them many **t** in parables, Mt 13:3
All these **t** Jesus said to the crowds in Mt 13:34
understood all these **t**?" They said to Mt 13:51
then did this man get all these **t**?" Mt 13:56
and suffer many **t** from the elders Mt 16:21
not setting your mind on the **t** of God, Mt 16:23

the things of God, but on the **t** of man." Mt 16:23
does come, and he will restore all **t**. Mt 17:11
but with God all **t** are possible." Mt 19:26
scribes saw the wonderful **t** that he did, Mt 21:15
what authority are you doing these **t**, Mt 21:23
tell you by what authority I do these **t**. Mt 21:24
I tell you by what authority I do these **t**. Mt 21:27
render to Caesar the **t** that are Caesar's, Mt 22:21
and to God the **t** that are God's." Mt 22:21
all these **t** will come upon this Mt 23:36
saying, "Tell us, when will these **t** be, Mt 24:3
So also, when you see all these **t**, you Mt 24:33
pass away until all these **t** take place. Mt 24:34
hear how many **t** they testify against Mt 27:13
do you question these **t** in your hearts? Mk 2:8
was teaching them many **t** in parables, Mk 4:2
the desires for other **t** enter in and Mk 4:19
saying, "Where did this man get these **t**? Mk 6:2
And he began to teach them many **t**. Mk 6:34
down. And many such **t** you do." Mk 7:13
but the **t** that come out of a person are Mk 7:15
All these evil **t** come from within, and Mk 7:23
measure, saying, "He has done all **t** well. Mk 7:37
must suffer many **t** and be rejected Mk 8:31
not setting your mind on the **t** of God, Mk 8:33
the things of God, but on the **t** of man." Mk 8:33
"Elijah does come first to restore all **t**. Mk 9:12
he should suffer many **t** and be treated Mk 9:12
All **t** are possible for one who believes." Mk 9:23
God. For all **t** are possible with God." Mk 10:27
what authority are you doing these **t**, Mk 11:28
tell you by what authority I do these **t**. Mk 11:29
tell you by what authority I do these **t**." Mk 11:33
to Caesar the **t** that are Caesar's, Mk 12:17
and to God the **t** that are God's." And Mk 12:17
"Tell us, when will these **t** be, and what Mk 13:4
the sign when all these **t** are about to be Mk 13:4
guard; I have told you all **t** beforehand. Mk 13:23
also, when you see these **t** taking place, Mk 13:29
pass away until all these **t** take place. Mk 13:30
Father, all **t** are possible for you. Mk 14:36
the chief priests accused him of many **t**. Mk 15:3
After these **t** he appeared in another Mk 16:12
a narrative of the **t** that have been Lk 1:1
having followed all **t** closely for some Lk 1:3
certainty concerning the **t** you have been Lk 1:4
until the day that these **t** take place, Lk 1:20
who is mighty has done great **t** for me, Lk 1:49
he has filled the hungry with good **t**, and Lk 1:53
And all these **t** were talked about Lk 1:65
But Mary treasured up all these **t**, Lk 2:19
treasured up all these **t** in her heart. Lk 2:51
and for all the evil **t** that Herod had done, Lk 3:19
When they heard these **t**, all in the Lk 4:28
"We have seen extraordinary **t** today." Lk 5:26
When Jesus heard these **t**, he marveled at Lk 7:9
of John reported all these **t** to him. Lk 7:18
yielded a hundredfold." As he said these **t**, Lk 8:8
whom I hear such **t**?" And he sought to Lk 9:9
Man must suffer many **t** and be rejected Lk 9:22
As he was saying these **t**, a cloud came Lk 9:34
you have hidden these **t** from the wise Lk 10:21
All **t** have been handed over to me by Lk 10:22
anxious and troubled about many **t**, Lk 10:41
As he said these **t**, a woman in the Lk 11:27
But give as alms those **t** that are within, Lk 11:41
in saying these **t** you insult us also." Lk 11:45
to provoke him to speak about many **t**, Lk 11:53
of you, and the **t** you have prepared, Lk 12:20
nations of the world seek after these **t**, Lk 12:30
and these **t** will be added to you. Lk 12:31
As he said these **t**, all his adversaries Lk 13:17
at all the glorious **t** that were done by Lk 13:17
And they could not reply to these **t**. Lk 14:6
at table with him heard these **t**, Lk 14:15
came and reported these **t** to his master. Lk 14:21
servants and asked what these **t** meant. Lk 15:26
were lovers of money, heard all these **t**, Lk 16:14
in your lifetime received your good **t**, Lk 16:25
and Lazarus in like manner bad **t**; Lk 16:25
he must suffer many **t** and be rejected Lk 17:25
But when he heard these **t**, he became Lk 18:23
But they understood none of these **t**. Lk 18:34
As they heard these **t**, he proceeded to Lk 19:11
And when he had said these **t**, he went Lk 19:28
on this day the **t** that make for peace! Lk 19:42
us by what authority you do these **t**, Lk 20:2
I tell you by what authority I do these **t**." Lk 20:8
render to Caesar the **t** that are Caesar's, Lk 20:25
and to God the **t** that are God's." Lk 20:25
"As for these **t** that you see, the days will Lk 21:6
him, "Teacher, when will these **t** be, Lk 21:7
the sign when these **t** are about to take Lk 21:7
terrified, for these **t** must first take place, Lk 21:9
Now when these **t** begin to take place, Lk 21:28
also, when you see these **t** taking place, Lk 21:31
to escape all these **t** that are going to Lk 21:36
they said many other **t** against him, Lk 22:65
For if they do these **t** when the wood is Lk 23:31
stood at a distance watching these **t**. Lk 23:49
they told all these **t** to the eleven and Lk 24:9
them who told these **t** to the apostles, Lk 24:10
about all these **t** that had happened. Lk 24:14
does not know the **t** that have happened Lk 24:18
them, "What **t**?" And they said to him, Lk 24:19
the third day since these **t** happened. Lk 24:21
should suffer these **t** and enter into Lk 24:26
Scriptures the **t** concerning himself. Lk 24:27
As they were talking about these **t**, Lk 24:36
You are witnesses of these **t**. Lk 24:48
All **t** were made through him, and without Jn 1:3
These **t** took place in Bethany across the Jn 1:28
You will see greater **t** than these." Jn 1:50
who sold the pigeons, "Take these **t** away; Jn 2:16
sign do you show us for doing these **t**?" Jn 2:18
said to him, "How can these **t** be?" Jn 3:9
and yet you do not understand these **t**? Jn 3:10
I have told you earthly **t** and you do not Jn 3:12
can you believe if I tell you heavenly **t**? Jn 3:12
who does wicked **t** hates the light Jn 3:20
the Son and has given all **t** into his hand. Jn 3:35
When he comes, he will tell us all **t**." Jn 4:25
he was doing these **t** on the Sabbath. Jn 5:16
but I say these **t** so that you may be Jn 5:34
Jesus said these **t** in the synagogue, as he Jn 6:59
If you do these **t**, show yourself to the Jn 7:4
the crowd muttering these **t** about him, Jn 7:32
for I always do the **t** that are pleasing to Jn 8:29
As he was saying these **t**, many believed Jn 8:30
Having said these **t**, he spat on the ground Jn 9:6
parents said these **t** because they feared Jn 9:22
of the Pharisees near him heard these **t**, Jn 9:40
After saying these **t**, he said to them, Jn 11:11
When he had said these **t**, he cried out Jn 11:43
did not understand these **t** at first, Jn 12:16
remembered that these **t** had been Jn 12:16
of light." When Jesus had said these **t**, Jn 12:36
Isaiah said these **t** because he saw his Jn 12:41
the Father had given all **t** into his hands, Jn 13:3
If you know these **t**, blessed are you if Jn 13:17
After saying these **t**, Jesus was troubled Jn 13:21
"These **t** I have spoken to you while I Jn 14:25
he will teach you all **t** and bring to your Jn 14:26
These **t** I have spoken to you, that my Jn 15:11
These **t** I command you, so that you Jn 15:17
But all these **t** they will do to you on Jn 15:21
"I have said all these **t** to you to keep you Jn 16:1
they will do these **t** because they have not Jn 16:3
But I have said these **t** to you, that when Jn 16:4
"I did not say these **t** to you from the Jn 16:4
But because I have said these **t** to you, Jn 16:6
"I still have many **t** to say to you, but Jn 16:12
declare to you the **t** that are to come. Jn 16:13
"I have said these **t** to you in figures of Jn 16:25
that you know all **t** and do not need Jn 16:30
I have said these **t** to you, that in me you Jn 16:33
to you, and these **t** I speak in the world, Jn 17:13
When he had said these **t**, one of the Jn 18:22
they cast lots." So the soldiers did these **t**, Jn 19:24
For these **t** took place that the Scripture Jn 19:36
After these **t** Joseph of Arimathea, who Jn 19:38
—and that he had said these **t** to her. Jn 20:18
who is bearing witness about these **t**, Jn 21:24
things, and who has written these **t**, Jn 21:24
are also many other **t** that Jesus did. Jn 21:25
And when he had said these **t**, as they Acts 1:9
together and had all **t** in common. Acts 2:44
for restoring all the **t** about which God Acts 3:21
that any of the **t** that belonged to him Acts 4:32
and upon all who heard of these **t**. Acts 5:11
And we are witnesses to these **t**, and so Acts 5:32
the high priest said, "Are these **t** so?" Acts 7:1
Did not my hand make all these **t**?' Acts 7:50
they heard these **t** they were enraged, Acts 7:54
While Peter was still saying these **t**, Acts 10:44
they heard these **t** they fell silent. Acts 11:18
"Tell these **t** to James and to the Acts 12:17
begged that these **t** might be told Acts 13:42
"Men, why are you doing these **t**? We Acts 14:15
turn from these vain **t** to a living God, Acts 14:15
says the Lord, who makes these **t** Acts 15:17
abstain from the **t** polluted by idols, Acts 15:20
tell you the same **t** by word of mouth. Acts 15:27
disturbed when they heard these **t**. Acts 17:8
daily to see if these **t** were so. Acts 17:11
you bring some strange **t** to our ears. Acts 17:20
to know therefore what these **t** mean." Acts 17:20
I refuse to be a judge of these **t**." Acts 18:15
accurately the **t** concerning Jesus, Acts 18:25
then that these **t** cannot be denied, Acts 19:36
And when he had said these **t**, he Acts 19:41
will arise men speaking twisted **t**, Acts 20:30
In all **t** I have shown you that by Acts 20:35
And when he had said these **t**, he Acts 20:36
one by one the **t** that God had done Acts 21:19
you have informed me of these **t**." Acts 23:22
affirming that all these **t** were so. Acts 24:9
ought to do many **t** in opposing the Acts 26:9
and witness to the **t** in which you Acts 26:16
he was saying these **t** in his defense, Acts 26:24
For the king knows about these **t**, Acts 26:26
that none of these **t** has escaped his Acts 26:26
And when he had said these **t**, he took Acts 27:35
world, in the **t** that have been made. Rom 1:20
who practice such **t** deserve to die, Rom 1:32
you, the judge, practice the very same **t**. Rom 2:1
rightly falls on those who do such **t**. Rom 2:2
those who do such **t** and yet do them Rom 2:3
calls into existence the **t** that do not Rom 4:17
that time from the **t** of which you are Rom 6:21
ashamed? The end of those **t** is death. Rom 6:21
set their minds on the **t** of the flesh, Rom 8:5
set their minds on the **t** of the Spirit. Rom 8:5
who love God all **t** work together for Rom 8:28
What then shall we say to these **t**? If Rom 8:31
also with him graciously give us all **t**? Rom 8:32
in all these **t** we are more than Rom 8:37
nor **t** present nor things to come, Rom 8:38
nor things present nor **t** to come, Rom 8:38
through him and to him are all **t**. Rom 11:36
in the world, even **t** that are not, 1 Cor 1:28
are not, to bring to nothing **t** that are, 1 Cor 1:28
these **t** God has revealed to us 1 Cor 2:10
might understand the **t** freely given 1 Cor 2:12
does not accept the **t** of the Spirit of 1 Cor 2:14
The spiritual person judges all **t**, but 1 Cor 2:15
one boast in men. For all **t** are yours, 1 Cor 3:21
bring to light the **t** now hidden in 1 Cor 4:5
have applied all these **t** to myself and 1 Cor 4:6
scum of the world, the refuse of all **t**. 1 Cor 4:13
do not write these **t** to make you 1 Cor 4:14
"All **t** are lawful for me," but not all 1 Cor 6:12
for me," but not all **t** are helpful. 1 Cor 6:12
"All **t** are lawful for me," but I will 1 Cor 6:12
is anxious about the **t** of the Lord, 1 Cor 7:32
man is anxious about worldly **t**, 1 Cor 7:33
is anxious about the **t** of the Lord, 1 Cor 7:34
woman is anxious about worldly **t**, 1 Cor 7:34
from whom are all **t** and for whom we 1 Cor 8:6
whom are all **t** and through whom 1 Cor 8:6
Do I say these **t** on human authority? 1 Cor 9:8
we have sown spiritual **t** among you, 1 Cor 9:11
much if we reap material **t** from you? 1 Cor 9:11
am I writing these **t** to secure any 1 Cor 9:15
I have become all **t** to all people, that 1 Cor 9:22
athlete exercises self-control in all **t**. 1 Cor 9:25
Now these **t** took place as examples 1 Cor 10:6
t happened to them as an example, 1 Cor 10:11
"All **t** are lawful," but not all things 1 Cor 10:23
are lawful," but not all **t** are helpful. 1 Cor 10:23
"All **t** are lawful," but not all things 1 Cor 10:23
are lawful," but not all **t** build up. 1 Cor 10:23
of woman. And all **t** are from God. 1 Cor 11:12
About the other **t** I will give 1 Cor 11:34
Love bears all **t**, believes all things, 1 Cor 13:7
Love bears all things, believes all **t**, 1 Cor 13:7
things, believes all things, hopes all **t**, 1 Cor 13:7
things, hopes all things, endures all **t**. 1 Cor 13:7
Let all **t** be done for building up. 1 Cor 14:26
acknowledge that the **t** I am writing 1 Cor 14:37
But all **t** should be done decently 1 Cor 14:40
has put all **t** in subjection under 1 Cor 15:27
"all **t** are put in subjection," it is 1 Cor 15:27
who put all **t** in subjection under 1 Cor 15:27
When all **t** are subjected to him, 1 Cor 15:28
who put all **t** in subjection under 1 Cor 15:28
to life. Who is sufficient for these **t**? 2 Cor 2:16
we look not to the **t** that are seen but 2 Cor 4:18
are seen but to the **t** that are unseen. 2 Cor 4:18
For the **t** that are seen are transient, 2 Cor 4:18
but the **t** that are unseen are eternal. 2 Cor 4:18
all sufficiency in all **t** at all times, 2 Cor 9:8
have made this plain to you in all **t**. 2 Cor 11:6
And, apart from other **t**, there is the 2 Cor 11:28
will boast of the **t** that show my 2 Cor 11:30
and he heard **t** that cannot be told, 2 Cor 12:4
reason I write these **t** while I am 2 Cor 13:10
Did you suffer so many **t** in vain—if Gal 3:4
not abide by all **t** written in the Book Gal 3:10
you from doing the **t** you want to do. Gal 5:17
drunkenness, orgies, and **t** like these. Gal 5:21
those who do such **t** will not inherit the Gal 5:21
against such **t** there is no law. Gal 5:23
must share all good **t** with the one who Gal 6:6
fullness of time, to unite all **t** in him, Eph 1:10

him, **t** in heaven and things on earth. Eph 1:10
him, things in heaven and **t** on earth. Eph 1:10
him who works all **t** according to the Eph 1:11
And he put all **t** under his feet and gave Eph 1:22
him as head over all **t** to the church, Eph 1:22
hidden for ages in God who created all **t**, Eph 3:9
all the heavens, that he might fill all **t**.) Eph 4:10
for because of these **t** the wrath of God Eph 5:6
even to speak of the **t** that they do in Eph 5:12
Do all **t** without grumbling or Phil 2:14
To write the same **t** to you is no trouble Phil 3:1
the loss of all **t** and count them as Phil 3:8
shame, with minds set on earthly **t**. Phil 3:19
him even to subject all **t** to himself. Phil 3:21
worthy of praise, think about these **t**. Phil 4:8
heard and seen in me—practice these **t**, Phil 4:9
I can do all **t** through him who Phil 4:13
For by him all **t** were created, in heaven Col 1:16
authorities—all **t** were created through Col 1:16
And he is before all **t**, and in him all Col 1:17
things, and in him all **t** hold together. Col 1:17
him to reconcile to himself all **t**, Col 1:20
These are a shadow of the **t** to come, but Col 2:17
(referring to **t** that all perish as they are Col 2:22
with Christ, seek the **t** that are above, Col 3:1
Set your minds on **t** that are above, not Col 3:2
that are above, not on **t** that are on earth. Col 3:2
suffered the same **t** from your own 1 Thes 2:14
the Lord is an avenger in all these **t**, 1 Thes 4:6
I was still with you I told you these **t**? 2 Thes 2:5
and will do the **t** that we command. 2 Thes 3:4
are saying or the **t** about which they 1 Tm 1:7
but sober-minded, faithful in all **t**. 1 Tm 3:11
I am writing these **t** to you so that, 1 Tm 3:14
If you put these **t** before the brothers, 1 Tm 4:6
Command and teach these **t**. 1 Tm 4:11
Practice these **t**, devote yourself to 1 Tm 4:15
Command these **t** as well, so that they 1 Tm 5:7
and beloved. Teach and urge these **t**. 1 Tm 6:2
as for you, O man of God, flee these **t**. 1 Tm 6:11
presence of God, who gives life to all **t**, 1 Tm 6:13
Remind them of these **t**, and charge 2 Tm 2:14
To the pure, all **t** are pure, but to the Ti 1:15
Declare these **t**; exhort and rebuke with Ti 2:15
and I want you to insist on these **t**, Ti 3:8
These **t** are excellent and profitable for Ti 3:8
Son, whom he appointed the heir of all **t**, Heb 1:2
he, for whom and by whom all **t** exist, Heb 2:10
himself likewise partook of the same **t**, Heb 2:14
someone, but the builder of all **t** is God.) Heb 3:4
to testify to the **t** that were to be spoken Heb 3:5
feel sure of better **t**—things that belong Heb 6:9
of better things—**t** that belong to Heb 6:9
so that by two unchangeable **t**, in Heb 6:18
of whom these **t** are spoken belonged Heb 7:13
a copy and shadow of the heavenly **t**. Heb 8:5
Of these **t** we cannot now speak in detail. Heb 9:5
priest of the good **t** that have come, Heb 9:11
copies of the heavenly **t** to be purified Heb 9:23
but the heavenly **t** themselves with Heb 9:23
hands, which are copies of the true **t**, Heb 9:24
shadow of the good **t** to come instead of Heb 10:1
faith is the assurance of **t** hoped for, Heb 11:1
hoped for, the conviction of **t** not seen. Heb 11:1
was not made out of **t** that are visible. Heb 11:3
not having received the **t** promised, Heb 11:13
the removal of **t** that are shaken Heb 12:27
t that have been made—in order that Heb 12:27
in order that the **t** that cannot be Heb 12:27
desiring to act honorably in all **t**. Heb 13:18
without giving them the **t** needed for the Jas 2:16
is a small member, yet it boasts of great **t**. Jas 3:5
My brothers, these **t** ought not to be so. Jas 3:10
in the **t** that have now been announced 1 Pt 1:12
t into which angels long to look. 1 Pt 1:12
not with perishable **t** such as silver or 1 Pt 1:18
The end of all **t** is at hand; therefore be 1 Pt 4:7
has granted to us all **t** that pertain to life 2 Pt 1:3
be able at any time to recall these **t**. 2 Pt 1:15
all **t** are continuing as they were from 2 Pt 3:4
Since all these **t** are thus to be 2 Pt 3:11
There are some **t** in them that are hard 2 Pt 3:16
we are writing these **t** so that our joy 1 Jn 1:4
I am writing these **t** to you so that you 1 Jn 2:1
not love the world or the **t** in the world. 1 Jn 2:15
I write these **t** to you about those who 1 Jn 2:26
I write these **t** to you who believe in the 1 Jn 5:13
of all the harsh **t** that ungodly sinners Jude 1:15
to his servants the **t** that must soon take Rv 1:1
Write therefore the **t** that you have seen, Rv 1:19
But I have a few **t** against you: you have Rv 2:14
what some call the deep **t** of Satan, Rv 2:24
honor and power, for you created all **t**, Rv 4:11
for the former **t** have passed away." Rv 21:4
I am making all **t** new." Also he said, Rv 21:5
am the one who heard and saw these **t**. Rv 22:8
to you about these **t** for the churches. Rv 22:16
He who testifies to these **t** says, "Surely I Rv 22:20

THINK (57)

'Let them marry whom they **t** best, Nm 36:6
said to Hanun their lord, "Do you **t**, 2 Sm 10:3
"I **t** the running of the first is like the 2 Sm 18:27
Do you **t** that mere words are 2 Kgs 18:20
said to Hanun, "Do you **t**, 1 Chr 19:3
"And now you **t** to withstand the 2 Chr 13:8
"Do not **t** to yourself that in the king's Est 4:13
Do you **t** that you can reprove words, Jb 6:26
"Do you **t** this to be just? Do you say, 'It is Jb 35:2
one would **t** the deep to be white-haired. Jb 41:32
swords in their lips—for "Who," they **t**, Ps 59:7
When I **t** of your rules from of old, I Ps 119:52
When I **t** on my ways, I turn my feet to Ps 119:59
or the son of man that you **t** of him? Ps 144:3
not so intend, and his heart does not so **t**; Is 10:7
Do you **t** that mere words are strategy and Is 36:5
Do you **t** you are a king because you Jer 22:15
who **t** to make my people forget my Jer 23:27
go wherever you **t** it good and right to go. Jer 40:4
Or go wherever you **t** it right to go." So Jer 40:5
the LORD: So you **t**, O house of Israel. Ezk 11:5
and shall **t** to change the times and the Dn 7:25
"Do not **t** that I have come to abolish the Mt 5:17
for they **t** that they will be heard for their Mt 6:7
said, "Why do you **t** evil in your hearts? Mt 9:4
"Do not **t** that I have come to bring Mt 10:34
to him first, saying, "What do you **t**, Mt 17:25
What do you **t**? If a man has a hundred Mt 18:12
"What do you **t**? A man had two sons. Mt 21:28
Tell us, then, what you **t**. Is it lawful to Mt 22:17
"What do you **t** about the Christ? Mt 22:42
Do you **t** that I cannot appeal to my Mt 26:53
Which of these three, do you **t**, proved Lk 10:36
Do you **t** that I have come to give peace Lk 12:51
"Do you **t** that these Galileans were Lk 13:2
do you **t** that they were worse offenders Lk 13:4
the Scriptures because you **t** that in them Jn 5:39
Do not **t** that I will accuse you to the Jn 5:45
stood in the temple, "What do you **t**? Jn 11:56
whoever kills you will **t** he is offering Jn 16:2
we ought not to **t** that the divine Acts 17:29
among you not to **t** of himself more Rom 12:3
more highly than he ought to **t**, Rom 12:3
to think, but to **t** with sober judgment, Rom 12:3
For I **t** that God has exhibited us 1 Cor 4:9
I **t** that in view of the present distress 1 Cor 7:26
And I **t** that I too have the Spirit of 1 Cor 7:40
the body that we **t** less honorable we 1 Cor 12:23
I repeat, let no one **t** me foolish. But 2 Cor 11:16
so that no one may **t** more of me than 2 Cor 12:6
abundantly than all that we ask or **t**, Eph 3:20
those of us who are mature **t** this way, Phil 3:15
and if in anything you **t** otherwise, Phil 3:15
worthy of praise, **t** about these things. Phil 4:8
T over what I say, for the Lord will give 2 Tm 2:7
much worse punishment, do you **t**, Heb 10:29
I **t** it right, as long as I am in this body, 2 Pt 1:13

THINKING (16)

sister," for he feared to say, "My wife," **t**, Gn 26:7
t, "If Esau comes to the one camp and Gn 32:8
t, "Lest they should tell about us and 1 Sm 27:11
t, "He has made himself an utter 1 Sm 27:12
and the lame will ward you off"—**t**, 2 Sm 5:6
t, 'When they come out of the city, 2 Kgs 7:12
cities, **t** to win them for himself. 2 Chr 32:1
t, "Their hands will drop from the work, Neh 6:9
snares secretly, **t**, who can see them? Ps 64:5
him, but they became futile in their **t**, Rom 1:21
do not be children in your **t**. 1 Cor 14:20
in evil, but in your **t** be mature. 1 Cor 14:20
Have you been **t** all along that we 2 Cor 12:19
not sincerely but **t** to afflict me in my Phil 1:17
If they had been **t** of that land from Heb 11:15
arm yourselves with the same way of **t**, 1 Pt 4:1

THINKS (10)

found favor in your eyes, and he **t**, 1 Sm 20:3
even what he **t** that he has will be taken Lk 8:18
unclean for anyone who **t** it unclean. Rom 14:14
If anyone among you **t** that he is wise 1 Cor 3:18
If anyone **t** that he is not behaving 1 Cor 7:36
let anyone who **t** that he stands 1 Cor 10:12
If anyone **t** that he is a prophet, or 1 Cor 14:37
For if anyone **t** he is something, when he Gal 6:3
If anyone else **t** he has reason for Phil 3:4
If anyone **t** he is religious and does not Jas 1:26

THIRD (185)

and there was morning, the **t** day. Gn 1:13
And the name of the **t** river is the Tigris, Gn 2:14
Make it with lower, second, and **t** decks. Gn 6:16
On the **t** day Abraham lifted up his eyes Gn 22:4
told Laban on the **t** day that Jacob had Gn 31:22
the second and the **t** and all who Gn 32:19
On the **t** day, when they were sore, two Gn 34:25
On the **t** day, which was Pharaoh's Gn 40:20
On the **t** day Joseph said to them, "Do Gn 42:18
Ephraim's children of the **t** generation. Gn 50:23
On the **t** new moon after the people of Ex 19:1
and be ready for the **t** day. For on the Ex 19:11
For on the **t** day the LORD will come Ex 19:11
to the people, "Be ready for the **t** day; Ex 19:15
the morning of the **t** day there were Ex 19:16
the children to the **t** and the fourth Ex 20:5
and the **t** row a jacinth, an agate, and Ex 28:19
to the **t** and the fourth generation." Ex 34:7
and the **t** row, a jacinth, an agate, and Ex 39:12
the sacrifice on the **t** day shall be burned Lv 7:17
of his peace offering is eaten on the **t** day, Lv 7:18
left over until the **t** day shall be burned Lv 19:6
If it is eaten at all on the **t** day, it is Lv 19:7
They shall set out **t** on the march. Nm 2:24
On the **t** day Eliab the son of Helon, the Nm 7:24
to the **t** and the fourth generation.' Nm 14:18
fine flour mixed with a **t** of a hin of oil. Nm 15:6
offering you shall offer a **t** of a hin of Nm 15:7
with the water on the **t** day and on the Nm 19:12
cleanse himself on the **t** day and on Nm 19:12
the unclean on the **t** day and on the Nm 19:19
wine for a bull, a **t** of a hin for a ram, Nm 28:14
"On the **t** day eleven bulls, two rams, Nm 29:20
your captives on the **t** day and on the Nm 31:19
the children to the **t** and fourth generation Dt 5:9
to them in the **t** generation may enter the Dt 23:8
the tithe of your produce in the **t** year, Dt 26:12
out and reached their cities on the **t** day. Jos 9:17
and its villages; the **t** is Naphath. Jos 17:11
The **t** lot came up for the people of Jos 19:10
of Benjamin on the **t** day and set Jgs 20:30
LORD called Samuel again the **t** time. 1 Sm 3:8
and a **t** of a shekel for sharpening the 1 Sm 13:21
him Abinadab, and the **t** Shammah. 1 Sm 17:13
sent messengers again the **t** time, 1 Sm 19:21
in the field till the **t** day at evening. 1 Sm 20:5
this time tomorrow, or the **t** day, 1 Sm 20:12
On the **t** day go down quickly to the 1 Sm 20:19
his men came to Ziklag on the **t** day, 1 Sm 30:1
And on the **t** day, behold, a man came 2 Sm 1:2
and the **t**, Absalom the son of Maacah 2 Sm 3:3
one **t** under the command of Joab, 2 Sm 18:2
one **t** under the command of Abishai 2 Sm 18:2
and one **t** under the command of Ittai 2 Sm 18:2
Then on the **t** day after I gave birth, 1 Kgs 3:18
and the **t** was seven cubits broad. 1 Kgs 6:6
and from the middle story to the **t**. 1 Kgs 6:8
people came to Rehoboam the **t** day, 1 Kgs 12:12
said, "Come to me again the **t** day." 1 Kgs 12:12
killed him in the **t** year of Asa king 1 Kgs 15:28
In the **t** year of Asa king of Judah, 1 Kgs 15:33
the LORD came to Elijah, in the **t** year, 1 Kgs 18:1
"Do it a **t** time." And they did it a 1 Kgs 18:34
third time." And they did it a **t** time. 1 Kgs 18:34
But in the **t** year Jehoshaphat the 1 Kgs 22:2
the captain of a **t** fifty with his fifty. 2 Kgs 1:13
And the **t** captain of fifty went up and 2 Kgs 1:13
one **t** of you, those who come off duty 2 Kgs 11:5
(another **t** being at the gate Sur and a 2 Kgs 11:6
the gate Sur and a **t** at the gate behind 2 Kgs 11:6
In the **t** year of Hoshea son of Elah, 2 Kgs 18:1
Then in the **t** year sow and reap and 2 Kgs 19:29
On the **t** day you shall go up to the 2 Kgs 20:5
to the house of the LORD on the **t** day?" 2 Kgs 20:8
Abinadab the second, Shimea the **t**, 1 Chr 2:13
the **t**, Absalom, whose mother was 1 Chr 3:2
the second Jehoiakim, the **t** Zedekiah, 1 Chr 3:15
Ashbel the second, Aharah the **t**, 1 Chr 8:1
Jeush the second, and Eliphelet the **t**. 1 Chr 8:39
the chief, Obadiah second, Eliab **t**, 1 Chr 12:9
Amariah the second, Jahaziel the **t**, 1 Chr 23:19
the **t** to Harim, the fourth to Seorim, 1 Chr 24:8
Amariah the second, Jahaziel the **t**, 1 Chr 24:23
the **t** to Zaccur, his sons and his 1 Chr 25:10
Jediael the second, Zebadiah the **t**, 1 Chr 26:2
Jehozabad the second, Joah the **t**, 1 Chr 26:4
Hilkiah the second, Tebaliah the **t**, 1 Chr 26:11
The **t** commander, for the third 1 Chr 27:5
third commander, for the **t** month, 1 Chr 27:5
people came to Rehoboam the **t** day, 2 Chr 10:12
said, "Come to me again the **t** day." 2 Chr 10:12
at Jerusalem in the **t** month of the 2 Chr 15:10
In the **t** year of his reign he sent his 2 Chr 17:7
Sabbath, one **t** shall be gatekeepers, 2 Chr 23:4
and one **t** shall be at the king's house 2 Chr 23:5
king's house and one **t** at the Gate of 2 Chr 23:5
amount in the second and the **t** years. 2 Chr 27:5
In the **t** month they began to pile up 2 Chr 31:7

was finished on the **t** day of the month Ezr 6:15
to give yearly a **t** part of a shekel Neh 10:32
in the **t** year of his reign he gave a feast Est 1:3
On the **t** day Esther put on her royal Est 5:1
summoned at that time, in the **t** month, Est 8:9
and the name of the **t** Keren-happuch. Jb 42:14
Israel will be the **t** with Egypt and Is 19:24
Then in the **t** year sow and reap, and Is 37:30
received him at the **t** entrance of the Jer 38:14
A **t** part you shall burn in the fire in the Ezk 5:2
And a **t** part you shall take and strike Ezk 5:2
And a **t** part you shall scatter to the Ezk 5:2
A **t** part of you shall die of pestilence Ezk 5:12
a **t** part shall fall by the sword all Ezk 5:12
and a **t** part I will scatter to all the Ezk 5:12
face, and the **t** the face of a lion, Ezk 10:14
In the eleventh year, in the **t** month, on Ezk 31:1
and one **t** of a hin of oil to moisten the Ezk 46:14
In the **t** year of the reign of Jehoiakim Dn 1:1
after you, and yet a **t** kingdom of bronze, Dn 2:39
and shall be the **t** ruler in the kingdom." Dn 5:7
and shall be the **t** ruler in the kingdom." Dn 5:16
he should be the **t** ruler in the kingdom. Dn 5:29
In the **t** year of the reign of King Dn 8:1
In the **t** year of Cyrus king of Persia a Dn 10:1
on the **t** day he will raise us up, that we Hos 6:2
the **t** white horses, and the fourth chariot Zec 6:3
and perish, and one **t** shall be left alive. Zec 13:8
And I will put this **t** into the fire, and Zec 13:9
be killed, and on the **t** day be raised. Mt 16:21
be raised on the **t** day." And they were Mt 17:23
going out about the **t** hour he saw others Mt 20:3
and he will be raised on the **t** day." Mt 20:19
So too the second and **t**, down to the Mt 22:26
he went away and prayed for the **t** time, Mt 26:44
tomb to be made secure until the **t** day, Mt 27:64
no offspring. And the **t** likewise. Mk 12:21
And he came the **t** time and said to Mk 14:41
And it was the **t** hour when they Mk 15:25
be killed, and on the **t** day be raised." Lk 9:22
comes in the second watch, or in the **t**, Lk 12:38
and the **t** day I finish my course. Lk 13:32
kill him, and on the **t** day he will rise." Lk 18:33
And he sent yet a **t**. This one also they Lk 20:12
and the **t** took her, and likewise all Lk 20:31
A **t** time he said to them, "Why, what Lk 23:22
and be crucified and on the **t** day rise." Lk 24:7
it is now the **t** day since these things Lk 24:21
suffer and on the **t** day rise from the Lk 24:46
On the **t** day there was a wedding at Cana Jn 2:1
This was now the **t** time that Jesus was Jn 21:14
He said to him the **t** time, "Simon, son of Jn 21:17
because he said to him the **t** time, Jn 21:17
since it is only the **t** hour of the day. Acts 2:15
raised him on the **t** day and made Acts 10:40
fell down from the **t** story and was Acts 20:9
as Caesarea at the **t** hour of the night. Acts 23:23
And on the **t** day they threw the ship's Acts 27:19
apostles, second prophets, **t** teachers, 1 Cor 12:28
was raised on the **t** day in accordance 1 Cor 15:4
caught up to the **t** heaven—whether 2 Cor 12:2
Here for the **t** time I am ready to 2 Cor 12:14
This is the **t** time I am coming to you. 2 Cor 13:1
the **t** living creature with the face of a Rv 4:7
When he opened the **t** seal, I heard the Rv 6:5
third seal, I heard the **t** living creature say, Rv 6:5
And a **t** of the earth was burned up, and a Rv 8:7
up, and a **t** of the trees were burned up, Rv 8:7
the sea, and a **t** of the sea became blood. Rv 8:8
A **t** of the living creatures in the sea died, Rv 8:9
died, and a **t** of the ships were destroyed. Rv 8:9
The **t** angel blew his trumpet, and a Rv 8:10
and it fell on a **t** of the rivers and on the Rv 8:10
A **t** of the waters became wormwood, Rv 8:11
trumpet, and a **t** of the sun was struck, Rv 8:12
the sun was struck, and a **t** of the moon, Rv 8:12
a third of the moon, and a **t** of the stars, Rv 8:12
so that a **t** of their light might be Rv 8:12
and a **t** of the day might be kept from Rv 8:12
shining, and likewise a **t** of the night. Rv 8:12
year, were released to kill a **t** of mankind. Rv 9:15
these three plagues a **t** of mankind was Rv 9:18
behold, the **t** woe is soon to come. Rv 11:14
His tail swept down a **t** of the stars of Rv 12:4
And another angel, a **t**, followed them, Rv 14:9
The **t** angel poured out his bowl into the Rv 16:4
jasper, the second sapphire, the **t** agate, Rv 21:19

THIRDS (1)
LORD, two **t** shall be cut off and perish, Zec 13:8

THIRST (26)
our children and our livestock with **t**?" Ex 17:3
will send against you, in hunger and **t**, Dt 28:48
shall I now die of **t** and fall into the Jgs 15:18
you over to die by famine and by **t**, 2 Chr 32:11
for them out of the rock for their **t**, Neh 9:15
mouth and gave them water for their **t**. Neh 9:20
they tread the winepresses, but suffer **t**. Jb 24:11
and for my **t** they gave me sour wine to Ps 69:21
field; the wild donkeys quench their **t**. Ps 104:11
and their multitude is parched with **t**. Is 5:13
awakes faint, with his **t** not quenched, Is 29:8
none, and their tongue is parched with **t**, Is 41:17
They did not **t** when he led them Is 48:21
they shall not hunger or **t**, neither Is 49:10
fish stink for lack of water and die of **t**. Is 50:2
going unshod and your throat from **t**. Jer 2:25
sticks to the roof of its mouth for **t**; Lam 4:4
like a parched land, and kill her with **t**. Hos 2:3
not a famine of bread, nor a **t** for water, Am 8:11
and the young men shall faint for **t**. Am 8:13
who hunger and **t** for righteousness, Mt 5:6
and whoever believes in me shall never **t**. Jn 6:35
said (to fulfill the Scripture), "I **t**." Jn 19:28
To the present hour we hunger and **t**, 1 Cor 4:11
a sleepless night, in hunger and **t**, 2 Cor 11:27
hunger no more, neither **t** anymore; Rv 7:16

THIRSTED (1)
But the people **t** there for water, and the Ex 17:3

THIRSTS (5)
My soul **t** for God, for the living God. Ps 42:2
earnestly I seek you; my soul **t** for you; Ps 63:1
my soul **t** for you like a parched land. Ps 143:6
"Come, everyone who **t**, come to the Is 55:1
Jesus stood up and cried out, "If anyone **t**, Jn 7:37

THIRSTY (27)
and scorpions and **t** ground where there Dt 8:15
for I am **t**." So she opened a skin of milk Jgs 4:19
And he was very **t**, and he called upon Jgs 15:18
And when you are **t**, go to the vessels and Ru 2:9
and weary and **t** in the wilderness." 2 Sm 17:29
of thorns, and the **t** pant after his wealth. Jb 5:5
hungry and **t**, their soul fainted within Ps 107:5
a desert, springs of water into **t** ground, Ps 107:33
give him bread to eat, and if he is **t**, Prv 25:21
Like cold water to a **t** soul, so is good Prv 25:25
To the **t** bring water; meet the fugitive Is 21:14
or as when a **t** man dreams he is drinking Is 29:8
unsatisfied, and to deprive the **t** of drink. Is 32:6
a pool, and the **t** ground springs of water; Is 35:7
For I will pour water on the **t** land, and Is 44:3
servants shall drink, but you shall be **t**; Is 65:13
in the wilderness, in a dry and **t** land. Ezk 19:13
me food, I was **t** and you gave me drink, Mt 25:35
and feed you, or **t** and give you drink? Mt 25:37
food, I was **t** and you gave me no drink, Mt 25:42
we see you hungry or **t** or a stranger or Mt 25:44
who drinks of this water will be **t** again, Jn 4:13
I will give him will never be **t** forever. Jn 4:14
that I will not be **t** or have to come here Jn 4:15
if he is **t**, give him something to Rom 12:20
To the **t** I will give from the spring of the Rv 21:6
"Come." And let the one who is **t** come; Rv 22:17

THIRTEEN (13)
Ishmael his son was **t** years old when Gn 17:25
to the LORD, **t** bulls from the herd, Nm 29:13
of an ephah for each of the **t** bulls, Nm 29:14
and Sharuhen—**t** cities with their Jos 19:6
of Judah, Simeon, and Benjamin, **t** cities. Jos 21:4
of Manasseh in Bashan, **t** cities. Jos 21:6
were in all **t** cities with their Jos 21:19
were in all **t** cities with their Jos 21:33
was building his own house **t** years, 1 Kgs 7:1
cities throughout their clans were **t**. 1 Chr 6:60
their clans were allotted **t** cities out of 1 Chr 6:62
sons and brothers of Hosah were **t**. 1 Chr 26:11
and the length of the gateway, **t** cubits. Ezk 40:11

THIRTEENTH (11)
but in the **t** year they rebelled. Gn 14:4
the **t** to Huppah, the fourteenth to 1 Chr 24:13
to the **t**, Shubael, his sons and his 1 Chr 25:20
were summoned on the **t** day of the first Est 3:12
one day, the **t** day of the twelfth month, Est 3:13
on the **t** day of the twelfth month, Est 8:12
month of Adar, on the **t** day of the same, Est 9:1
This was on the **t** day of the month of Est 9:17
in Susa gathered on the **t** day and on the Est 9:18
king of Judah, in the **t** year of his reign. Jer 1:2
from the **t** year of Josiah the son of Jer 25:3

THIRTIETH (1)
In the **t** year, in the fourth month, on the Ezk 1:1

THIRTY (77)
Suppose **t** are found there." He Gn 18:30
"I will not do it, if I find **t** there." Gn 18:30
t milking camels and their calves, Gn 32:15
Joseph was **t** years old when he entered Gn 41:46
give to their master **t** shekels of silver, Ex 21:32
length of each curtain shall be **t** cubits, Ex 26:8
length of each curtain was **t** cubits, Ex 36:15
female, the valuation shall be **t** shekels. Lv 27:4
from **t** years old up to fifty years old, all Nm 4:3
From **t** years old up to fifty years old, Nm 4:23
From **t** years old up to fifty years old, Nm 4:30
from **t** years old up to fifty years old, Nm 4:35
from **t** years old up to fifty years old, Nm 4:39
from **t** years old up to fifty years old, Nm 4:43
from **t** years old up to fifty years old, Nm 4:47
house of Israel wept for Aaron **t** days. Nm 20:29
for Moses in the plains of Moab **t** days. Dt 34:8
And he had **t** sons who rode on thirty Jgs 10:4
had thirty sons who rode on **t** donkeys, Jgs 10:4
on thirty donkeys, and they had **t** cities, Jgs 10:4
He had **t** sons, and thirty daughters he Jgs 12:9
and **t** daughters he gave in marriage Jgs 12:9
and **t** daughters he brought in from Jgs 12:9
He had forty sons and **t** grandsons, who Jgs 12:14
they brought **t** companions to be with Jgs 14:11
I will give you **t** linen garments and Jgs 14:12
linen garments and **t** changes of Jgs 14:12
you shall give me **t** linen garments and Jgs 14:13
linen garments and **t** changes of Jgs 14:13
and struck down **t** men of the Jgs 14:19
the open country, about **t** men of Israel. Jgs 20:31
to strike and kill about **t** men of Israel. Jgs 20:39
fell of Israel **t** thousand foot soldiers. 1 Sm 4:10
invited, who were about **t** persons. 1 Sm 9:22
and the men of Judah **t** thousand. 1 Sm 11:8
t thousand chariots and six thousand 1 Sm 13:5
David was **t** years old when he began to 2 Sm 5:4
the chosen men of Israel, **t** thousand. 2 Sm 6:1
And three of the **t** chief men went 2 Sm 23:13
the son of Zeruiah, was chief of the **t**. 2 Sm 23:18
renowned of the **t** and became their 2 Sm 23:19
He was renowned among the **t**, but 2 Sm 23:23
the brother of Joab was one of the **t**; 2 Sm 23:24
for one day was **t** cors of fine flour 1 Kgs 4:22
twenty cubits wide, and **t** cubits high. 1 Kgs 6:2
fifty cubits and its height **t** cubits, 1 Kgs 7:2
fifty cubits, and its breadth **t** cubits. 1 Kgs 7:6
and a line of **t** cubits measured its 1 Kgs 7:23
talents of silver and **t** talents of gold. 2 Kgs 18:14
Three of the **t** chief men went down 1 Chr 11:15
brother of Joab, was chief of the **t**. 1 Chr 11:20
renowned of the **t** and became their 1 Chr 11:21
He was renowned among the **t**, but 1 Chr 11:25
of the Reubenites, and **t** with him, 1 Chr 11:42
man among the **t** and a leader 1 Chr 12:4
the thirty and a leader over the **t**; 1 Chr 12:4
Spirit clothed Amasai, chief of the **t**, 1 Chr 12:18
The Levites, **t** years old and upward, 1 Chr 23:3
man of the **t** and in command 1 Chr 27:6
the thirty and in command of the **t**; 1 Chr 27:6
and a line of **t** cubits measured its 2 Chr 4:2
to come in to the king these **t** days." Est 4:11
written for you **t** sayings of counsel Prv 22:20
T chambers faced the pavement. Ezk 40:17
one over another, **t** in each story. Ezk 41:6
courts, forty cubits long and **t** broad; Ezk 46:22
petition to any god or man for **t** days, Dn 6:7
god or man within **t** days except to you, Dn 6:12
out as my wages **t** pieces of silver. Zec 11:12
So I took the **t** pieces of silver and Zec 11:13
some a hundredfold, some sixty, some **t**. Mt 13:8
in another sixty, and in another **t**." Mt 13:23
And they paid him **t** pieces of silver. Mt 26:15
and brought back the **t** pieces of silver Mt 27:3
"And they took the **t** pieces of silver, Mt 27:9
his ministry, was about **t** years of age, Lk 3:23
each holding twenty or **t** gallons. Jn 2:6

THIRTY-EIGHT (2)
we crossed the brook Zered was **t** years, Dt 2:14
there who had been an invalid for **t** years. Jn 5:5

THIRTY-EIGHTH (2)
In the **t** year of Asa king of Judah, 1 Kgs 16:29
In the **t** year of Azariah king of Judah, 2 Kgs 15:8

THIRTY-FIFTH (1)
more war until the **t** year of the 2 Chr 15:19

THIRTY-FIRST (1)
In the **t** year of Asa king of Judah, 1 Kgs 16:23

THIRTY-FIVE (3)
Jehoshaphat was **t** years old when he 1 Kgs 22:42
he made two pillars **t** cubits high, 2 Chr 3:15
He was **t** years old when he began to 2 Chr 20:31

THIRTY-NINTH (3)
to reign in the **t** year of Uzziah king 2 Kgs 15:13
In the **t** year of Azariah king of 2 Kgs 15:17
In the **t** year of his reign Asa was 2 Chr 16:12

THIRTY-ONE (3)
the king of Tirzah, one: in all, **t** kings. Jos 12:24

and he reigned **t** years in Jerusalem. 2 Kgs 22:1
and he reigned **t** years in Jerusalem. 2 Chr 34:1

THIRTY-SECOND (2)
year to the **t** year of Artaxerxes Neh 5:14
for in the **t** year of Artaxerxes king of Neh 13:6

THIRTY-SEVEN (1)
Uriah the Hittite: **t** in all. 2 Sm 23:39

THIRTY-SEVENTH (3)
In the **t** year of Joash king of Judah, 2 Kgs 13:10
And in the **t** year of the exile of 2 Kgs 25:27
And in the **t** year of the exile of Jer 52:31

THIRTY-SIX (1)
men of Ai killed about **t** of their men and Jos 7:5

THIRTY-SIXTH (1)
In the **t** year of the reign of Asa, 2 Chr 16:1

THIRTY-THREE (6)
sons and his daughters numbered **t**. Gn 46:15
she shall continue for **t** days in the blood Lv 12:4
over all Israel and Judah **t** years. 2 Sm 5:5
in Hebron and **t** years in Jerusalem. 1 Kgs 2:11
And he reigned **t** years in Jerusalem. 1 Chr 3:4
in Hebron and **t** years in Jerusalem. 1 Chr 29:27

THIRTY-TWO (6)
T kings were with him, and horses 1 Kgs 20:1
he and the **t** kings who helped him. 1 Kgs 20:16
had commanded the **t** captains of 1 Kgs 22:31
He was **t** years old when he became 2 Kgs 8:17
Jehoram was **t** years old when he 2 Chr 21:5
He was **t** years old when he began to 2 Chr 21:20

THIRTYFOLD (2)
increasing and yielding **t** and sixtyfold Mk 4:8
t and sixtyfold and a hundredfold." Mk 4:20

THISTLE (5)
"A **t** on Lebanon sent to a cedar on 2 Kgs 14:9
passed by and trampled down the **t**. 2 Kgs 14:9
"A **t** on Lebanon sent to a cedar on 2 Chr 25:18
passed by and trampled down the **t**. 2 Chr 25:18
Thorn and **t** shall grow up on their Hos 10:8

THISTLES (4)
thorns and **t** it shall bring forth for you; Gn 3:18
nettles and **t** in its fortresses. Is 34:13
from thornbushes, or figs from **t**? Mt 7:16
But if it bears thorns and **t**, it is Heb 6:8

THOMAS (11)
T and Matthew the tax collector; Mt 10:3
and Bartholomew, and Matthew, and **T**, Mk 3:18
and Matthew, and **T**, and James the son Lk 6:15
So **T**, called the Twin, said to his fellow Jn 11:16
T said to him, "Lord, we do not know Jn 14:5
Now **T**, one of the Twelve, called the Jn 20:24
were inside again, and **T** was with them. Jn 20:26
Then he said to **T**, "Put your finger Jn 20:27
T answered him, "My Lord and my Jn 20:28
Simon Peter, **T** (called the Twin), Jn 21:2
and James and Andrew, Philip and **T**, Acts 1:13

THORN (6)
Like a **t** that goes up into the hand of a Prv 26:9
Instead of the **t** shall come up the Is 55:13
to prick or a **t** to hurt them among Ezk 28:24
T and thistle shall grow up on their Hos 10:8
brier, the most upright of them a **t** hedge. Mi 7:4
a **t** was given me in the flesh, 2 Cor 12:7

THORNBUSHES (3)
in the clefts of the rocks, and on all the **t**, Is 7:19
Are grapes gathered from **t**, or figs from Mt 7:16
For figs are not gathered from **t**, nor are Lk 6:44

THORNS (46)
t and thistles it shall bring forth for you; Gn 3:18
out and catches in **t** so that the stacked Ex 22:6
barbs in your eyes and **t** in your sides, Nm 33:55
a whip on your sides and **t** in your eyes, Jos 23:13
but they shall become **t** in your sides, Jgs 2:3
your flesh with the **t** of the wilderness and Jgs 8:7
and he took **t** of the wilderness and Jgs 8:16
men are all like **t** that are thrown 2 Sm 23:6
his harvest, and he takes it even out of **t**, Jb 5:5
let **t** grow instead of wheat, and foul Jb 31:40
than your pots can feel the heat of **t**, Ps 58:9
bees; they went out like a fire among **t**; Ps 118:12
way of a sluggard is like a hedge of **t**, Prv 15:19
T and snares are in the way of the Prv 22:5
behold, it was all overgrown with **t**; Prv 24:31
For as the crackling of **t** under a pot, so Eccl 7:6
or hoed, and briers and **t** shall grow up; Is 5:6
shekels of silver, will become briers and **t**. Is 7:23
there, for all the land will be briers and **t**. Is 7:24
not come there for fear of briers and **t**, Is 7:25
like a fire; it consumes briers and **t**; Is 9:18
burn and devour his **t** and briers in one Is 10:17
Would that I had **t** and briers to battle! Is 27:4
of my people growing up in **t** and briers, Is 32:13
be as if burned to lime, like **t** cut down, Is 33:12
T shall grow over its strongholds, nettles Is 34:13
your fallow ground, and sow not among **t**. Jer 4:3
have sown wheat and have reaped **t**; Jer 12:13
though briers and **t** are with you and Ezk 2:6
Therefore I will hedge up her way with **t**, Hos 2:6
things of silver; **t** shall be in their tents. Hos 9:6
For they are like entangled **t**, like Na 1:10
Other seeds fell among **t**, and the thorns Mt 13:7
and the **t** grew up and choked them. Mt 13:7
As for what was sown among **t**, this is Mt 13:22
and twisting together a crown of **t**, they Mt 27:29
Other seed fell among **t**, and the thorns Mk 4:7
thorns, and the **t** grew up and choked it, Mk 4:7
And others are the ones sown among **t**. Mk 4:18
and twisting together a crown of **t**, Mk 15:17
And some fell among **t**, and the thorns Lk 8:7
and the **t** grew up with it and choked it. Lk 8:7
And as for what fell among the **t**, they Lk 8:14
twisted together a crown of **t** and put it on Jn 19:2
wearing the crown of **t** and the purple Jn 19:5
But if it bears **t** and thistles, it is Heb 6:8

THOROUGHLY (5)
and burn them **t**." And they had brick Gn 11:3
his time, and shall have him **t** healed. Ex 21:19
angel of the LORD, curse its inhabitants **t**, Jgs 5:23
Wash me **t** from my iniquity, and Ps 51:2
"They shall glean **t** as a vine the remnant Jer 6:9

THOUGH (257)
of my father **t** not the daughter Gn 20:12
and **t** I multiply my signs and wonders in Ex 7:3
adjuration to testify, and **t** he is a witness, Lv 5:1
not to be done, **t** he did not know it, Lv 5:17
changed, **t** the disease has not spread, Lv 13:55
shall support him as **t** he were a Lv 25:35
as if to escape a sword, **t** none pursues. Lv 26:37
and she is undetected **t** she has defiled Nm 5:13
of his wife, **t** she has not defiled herself, Nm 5:14
t you are under your husband's Nm 5:20
wife, **t** under her husband's authority, Nm 5:29
counted to you as **t** it were the grain Nm 18:27
"**T** Balak were to give me his house Nm 22:18
t he was not his enemy and did not Nm 35:23
may eat it, as **t** it were a gazelle or a deer. Dt 15:22
fatally, **t** the man did not deserve to die, Dt 19:6
his mother, and, **t** they discipline him, Dt 21:18
did not cry for help **t** she was in the city, Dt 22:24
and **t** the betrothed young woman cried Dt 22:27
t I walk in the stubbornness of my Dt 29:19
T all the people who came out had been Jos 5:5
shall be yours, for **t** it is a forest, Jos 17:18
t they have chariots of iron, Jos 17:18
chariots of iron, and **t** they are strong." Jos 17:18
servant, **t** I am not one of your servants." Ru 2:13
her, **t** the LORD had closed her womb. 1 Sm 1:5
Israel, **t** it be in Jonathan my son, 1 Sm 14:39
"**T** you are little in your own eyes, 1 Sm 15:17
to the side of it, as **t** I shot at a mark. 1 Sm 20:20
you, **t** you hunt my life to take it. 1 Sm 24:11
I was gentle today, **t** anointed king. 2 Sm 3:39
LORD, **t** not like his father and mother, 2 Kgs 3:2
t the Chaldeans were around the city. 2 Kgs 25:4
t Judah became strong among his 1 Chr 5:2
Shimri the chief (for **t** he was not 1 Chr 26:10
T the army of the Syrians had come 2 Chr 24:24
even **t** not according to the 2 Chr 30:19
t they could not prove their fathers' Ezr 2:59
laid, **t** many shouted aloud for joy, Ezr 3:12
t your dispersed be under the farthest Neh 1:9
will go to the king, **t** it is against the law, Est 4:16
And **t** your beginning was small, your Jb 8:7
T I am in the right, I cannot answer him; Jb 9:15
T I am in the right, my own mouth Jb 9:20
t I am blameless, he would prove me Jb 9:20
and were as **t** I had not been, carried Jb 10:19
T he slay me, I will hope in him; yet I Jb 13:15
T its root grow old in the earth, and its Jb 14:8
T his height mount up to the heavens, Jb 20:6
"**T** evil is sweet in his mouth, though he Jb 20:12
mouth, **t** he hides it under his tongue, Jb 20:12
t he is loath to let it go and holds it in Jb 20:13
T he heap up silver like dust, and pile Jb 27:16
and in two, **t** man does not perceive it. Jb 33:14
incurable, **t** I am without transgression.' Jb 34:6
t her labor be in vain, yet she has no Jb 39:16
he is confident **t** Jordan rushes against Jb 40:23
T the sword reaches him, it does not Jb 41:26
T they plan evil against you, though Ps 21:11
evil against you, **t** they devise mischief, Ps 21:11
Even **t** I walk through the valley of the Ps 23:4
T an army encamp against me, my Ps 27:3
t war arise against me, yet I will be Ps 27:3
I went about as **t** I grieved for my friend Ps 35:14
t you look carefully at his place, he will Ps 37:10
t he fall, he shall not be cast headlong, Ps 37:24
t I sought him, he could not be found. Ps 37:36
upon us, **t** we have not forgotten you, Ps 44:17
we will not fear **t** the earth gives way, Ps 46:2
t the mountains be moved into the heart Ps 46:2
t its waters roar and foam, though the Ps 46:3
t the mountains tremble at its swelling. Ps 46:3
t they called lands by their own names. Ps 49:11
For **t**, while he lives, he counts himself Ps 49:18
—and **t** you get praise when you do well Ps 49:18
t you men lie among the sheepfolds— Ps 68:13
that **t** the wicked sprout like grass and Ps 92:7
me to the proof, **t** they had seen my work. Ps 95:9
Even **t** princes sit plotting against me, Ps 119:23
T the cords of the wicked ensnare me, Ps 119:61
For **t** the LORD is high, he regards the Ps 138:6
T I walk in the midst of trouble, you Ps 138:7
he will refuse **t** you multiply gifts. Prv 6:35
t his hatred be covered with deception, Prv 26:26
is not disciplined, for **t** he understands, Prv 29:19
And **t** a man might prevail against one Eccl 4:12
t in his own kingdom he had been Eccl 4:14
Even **t** he should live a thousand years Eccl 6:6
T a sinner does evil a hundred times Eccl 8:12
Even **t** a wise man claims to know, he Eccl 8:17
t the poor man's wisdom is despised Eccl 9:16
words, **t** no man knows what is to be, Eccl 10:14
even **t** you make many prayers, I will not Is 1:15
t your sins are like scarlet, they shall be Is 1:18
t they are red like crimson, they shall Is 1:18
And **t** a tenth remain in it, it will be Is 6:13
For **t** your people Israel be as the sand of Is 10:22
O LORD, for **t** you were angry with me, Is 12:1
t you plant pleasant plants and sow the Is 17:10
t you make them grow on the day that Is 17:11
were captured, **t** they had fled far away. Is 22:3
For **t** his officials are at Zoan and his Is 30:4
And **t** the Lord give you the bread of Is 30:20
name, I name you, **t** you do not know me. Is 45:4
God; I equip you, **t** you do not know me, Is 45:5
Father, **t** Abraham does not know us, Is 63:16
its gods, even **t** they are no gods? Jer 2:11
T you wash yourself with lye and use Jer 2:22
T they say, "As the LORD lives," yet they Jer 5:2
t the waves toss, they cannot prevail; Jer 5:22
t they roar, they cannot pass over it. Jer 5:22
T they cry to me, I will not listen to Jer 11:11
t they speak friendly words to you." Jer 12:6
"**T** our iniquities testify against us, act, Jer 14:7
T they fast, I will not hear their cry, and Jer 14:12
and **t** they offer burnt offering and Jer 14:12
"**T** Moses and Samuel stood before me, Jer 15:1
LORD, **t** Coniah the son of Jehoiakim, Jer 22:24
to you urgently, **t** you have not listened, Jer 26:5
that they broke, **t** I was their husband, Jer 31:32
T you fight against the Chaldeans, you Jer 32:5
and get witnesses"—**t** the city is given Jer 32:25
And **t** I have taught them persistently, Jer 32:33
to Molech, **t** I did not command them, Jer 32:35
declares the LORD, **t** it is impenetrable, Jer 46:23
T you make your nest as high as the Jer 49:16
"**T** you rejoice, though you exult, O Jer 50:11
"Though you rejoice, **t** you exult, O Jer 50:11
t you frolic like a heifer in the pasture, Jer 50:11
T Babylon should mount up to heaven, Jer 51:53
and **t** she should fortify her strong Jer 51:53
t I call and cry for help, he shuts out my Lam 3:8
but, **t** he cause grief, he will have Lam 3:32
t briers and thorns are with you and you Ezk 2:6
And **t** they cry in my ears with a loud Ezk 8:18
T I removed them far off among the Ezk 11:16
and **t** I scattered them among the Ezk 11:16
t they are a rebellious house. Ezk 12:3
t these three men were in it, as I live, Ezk 14:18
T they escape from the fire, the fire Ezk 15:7
(**t** he himself did none of these things), Ezk 18:11
T you be sought for, you will never be Ezk 26:21
t you make your heart like the heart of Ezk 28:2
who kill you, **t** you are but a man, Ezk 28:9
T I say to the righteous that he shall Ezk 33:13
Again, **t** I say to the wicked, 'You shall Ezk 33:14
your heart, **t** you knew all this, Dn 5:22
t for some days they shall stumble by Dn 11:33
t they turn to other gods and love cakes Hos 3:1
T you play the whore, O Israel, let not Hos 4:15
T they hire allies among the nations, I Hos 8:10
Even **t** they give birth, I will put their Hos 9:16
and **t** they call out to the Most High, Hos 11:7
T he may flourish among his Hos 13:15
Even **t** you offer me your burnt Am 5:22
T you soar aloft like the eagle, though Ob 1:4
eagle, **t** your nest is set among the stars, Ob 1:4
and shall be as **t** they had never been. Ob 1:16

"**T** they are at full strength and many, Na 1:12
T I have afflicted you, I will afflict you Na 1:12
T the fig tree should not blossom, nor Hab 3:17
T they build houses, they shall not Zep 1:13
t they plant vineyards, they shall not Zep 1:13
it, Tyre and Sidon, **t** they are very wise. Zec 9:2
and they shall be as **t** I had not rejected Zec 10:6
T I scattered them among the nations, Zec 10:9
t she is your companion and your wife Mal 2:14
And **t** he wanted to put him to death, he Mt 14:5
"**T** they all fall away because of you, Mt 26:33
t many false witnesses came forward. Mt 26:60
said to him, "Even **t** they all fall away, Mk 14:29
and **t** she had spent all her living on Lk 8:43
t he will not get up and give him Lk 11:8
'**T** I neither fear God nor respect man, Lk 18:4
where it came from (**t** the servants who Jn 2:9
One thing I do know, that **t** I was blind, Jn 9:25
I do them, even **t** you do not believe me, Jn 10:38
Whoever believes in me, **t** he die, yet Jn 11:25
T he had done so many signs before Jn 12:37
even **t** the world does not know you, Jn 17:25
as **t** by our own power or piety we have Acts 3:12
offspring after him, **t** he had no child. Acts 7:5
And **t** they found in him no guilt Acts 13:28
hands, as **t** he needed anything, Acts 17:25
t he knew only the baptism of John. Acts 18:25
as **t** you were going to determine his Acts 23:15
as **t** they were going to inquire Acts 23:20
T he has escaped from the sea, Justice Acts 28:4
t I had done nothing against our Acts 28:17
appeal to Caesar—**t** I had no charge Acts 28:19
T they know God's decree that those Rom 1:32
even **t** they do not have the law. Rom 2:14
Let God be true **t** every one were a liar, Rom 3:4
a righteous person—**t** perhaps for a Rom 5:7
But it is not as **t** the word of God has Rom 9:6
t they were not yet born and had done Rom 9:11
"**T** the number of the sons of Israel be Rom 9:27
so we, **t** many, are one body in Christ, Rom 12:5
suffer loss, **t** he himself will be saved, 1 Cor 3:15
For **t** you have countless guides in 1 Cor 4:15
as **t** I were not coming to you. 1 Cor 4:18
For **t** absent in body, I am present in 1 Cor 5:3
have wives live as **t** they had none, 1 Cor 7:29
those who mourn as **t** they were not 1 Cor 7:30
those who rejoice as **t** they were not 1 Cor 7:30
those who buy as **t** they had no goods, 1 Cor 7:30
with the world as **t** they had no 1 Cor 7:31
For **t** I am free from all, I have made 1 Cor 9:19
one under the law (**t** not being myself 1 Cor 9:20
the members of the body, **t** many, 1 Cor 12:12
still alive, **t** some have fallen asleep. 1 Cor 15:6
than any of them, **t** it was not I, 1 Cor 15:10
even **t** a door was opened for me in the 2 Cor 2:12
T our outer nature is wasting away, 2 Cor 4:16
Even **t** we once regarded Christ 2 Cor 5:16
letter, I do not regret it—**t** I did regret it, 2 Cor 7:8
letter grieved you, **t** only for a while. 2 Cor 7:8
Lord Jesus Christ, that **t** he was rich, 2 Cor 8:9
For **t** we walk in the flesh, we are not 2 Cor 10:3
ourselves, as **t** we did not reach you. 2 Cor 10:14
T there is nothing to be gained by it, I 2 Cor 12:1
T if I should wish to boast, I would 2 Cor 12:6
super-apostles, even **t** I am nothing. 2 Cor 12:11
is right, **t** we may seem to have failed. 2 Cor 13:7
set before them (**t** privately before those Gal 2:2
to be circumcised, **t** he was a Greek. Gal 2:3
Cephas before them all, "If you, **t** a Jew, Gal 2:14
a slave, **t** he is the owner of everything, Gal 4:1
and **t** my condition was a trial to you, Gal 4:14
me, **t** I am the very least of all the saints, Eph 3:8
who, **t** he was in the form of God, did not Phil 2:6
t I myself have reason for confidence in Phil 3:4
For **t** I am absent in body, yet I am with Col 2:5
But **t** we had already suffered and 1 Thes 2:2
t we could have made demands as 1 Thes 2:6
t formerly I was a blasphemer, 1 Tm 1:13
t I am bold enough in Christ to Phlm 1:8
For **t** by this time you ought to be Heb 5:12
T we speak in this way, yet in your case, Heb 6:9
t these also are descended from Heb 7:5
And through his faith, **t** he died, he still Heb 11:4
t commended through their faith, Heb 11:39
to repent, **t** he sought it with tears. Heb 12:17
are in prison, as **t** in prison with them, Heb 13:3
t they are so large and are driven by Jas 3:4
this you rejoice, **t** now for a little while, 1 Pt 1:6
than gold that perishes **t** it is tested by 1 Pt 1:7
T you have not seen him, you love him. 1 Pt 1:8
T you do not now see him, you believe 1 Pt 1:8
that **t** judged in the flesh the way people 1 Pt 4:6
as **t** something strange were happening 1 Pt 4:12
t you know them and are established 2 Pt 1:12
angels, **t** greater in might and power, 2 Pt 2:11
dear lady—not as **t** I were writing you a 2 Jn 1:5
T I have much to write to you, I would 2 Jn 1:12
I saw him, I fell at his feet as **t** dead. Rv 1:17
a Lamb standing, as **t** it had been slain, Rv 5:6

THOUGHT (64)

Abraham said, "I did it because I **t**, Gn 20:11
sister'?" Isaac said to him, "Because I **t**, Gn 26:9
for I **t** that you would take your Gn 31:31
servant Jacob is behind us.'" For he **t**, Gn 32:20
saw her, he **t** she was a prostitute, Gn 38:15
Then Moses was afraid, and **t**, Ex 2:14
I will do to you as I **t** to do to them." Nm 33:56
his weapons of war and **t** it easy to go up Dt 1:41
there be an unworthy **t** in your heart and Dt 15:9
And we **t**, If this should be said to us or Jos 22:28
of the roof chamber were locked, they **t**, Jgs 3:24
"I really **t** that you utterly hated her, Jgs 15:2
So I **t** I would tell you of it and say, 'Buy it Ru 4:4
they came, he looked on Eliab and **t**, 1 Sm 16:6
And Saul hurled the spear, for he **t**, "I 1 Sm 18:11
fight the LORD'S battles." For Saul **t**, 1 Sm 18:17
Saul **t**, "Let me give her to him, that 1 Sm 18:21
enemies.'" Now Saul **t** to make David 1 Sm 18:25
not say anything that day, for he **t**, 1 Sm 20:26
whole house of Benjamin **t** good to do. 2 Sm 3:19
and **t** he was bringing good news, 2 Sm 4:10
made me afraid, and your servant **t**, 2 Sm 14:15
And your servant **t**, 'The word of my 2 Sm 14:17
with a new sword, **t** to kill David. 2 Sm 21:16
I **t** that he would surely come out to 2 Kgs 5:11
you have spoken is good." For he **t**, 2 Kgs 20:19
and understands every plan and **t**. 1 Chr 28:9
In the **t** of one who is at ease there is Jb 12:5
Then I **t**, 'I shall die in my nest, and I Jb 29:18
and needy, but the Lord takes **t** for me. Ps 40:17
We have **t** on your steadfast love, O God, Ps 48:9
silent; you **t** that I was one like yourself. Ps 50:21
But when I **t** how to understand this, it Ps 73:16
When I **t**, "My foot slips," your steadfast Ps 94:18
but the prudent gives **t** to his steps. Prv 14:15
Whoever gives **t** to the word will Prv 16:20
but the upright gives **t** to his ways. Prv 21:29
And I **t** the dead who are already dead Eccl 4:2
is no work or **t** or knowledge or Eccl 9:10
Even in your **t**, do not curse the king, Eccl 10:20
that you have spoken is good." For he **t**, Is 39:8
And I **t**, 'After she has done all this she Jer 3:7
And I **t** you would call me, My Father, Jer 3:19
in her skirts; she took no **t** of her future; Lam 1:9
your mind shall never happen—the **t**, Ezk 20:32
wind, and declares to man what is his **t**, Am 4:13
Perhaps the god will give a **t** to us, that we Jon 1:6
who pass by trustingly with no **t** of war. Mi 2:8
came, they **t** they would receive more, Mt 20:10
walking on the sea they **t** it was a ghost, Mk 6:49
and he **t** to himself, 'What shall I do, Lk 12:17
startled and frightened and **t** they saw a Lk 24:37
but they **t** that he meant taking rest in Jn 11:13
Some **t** that, because Judas had the Jn 13:29
because you **t** you could obtain the Acts 8:20
was real, but **t** he was seeing a vision. Acts 12:9
But Paul **t** best not to take with them Acts 15:38
Why is it **t** incredible by any of you Acts 26:8
but give **t** to do what is honorable in Rom 12:17
I spoke like a child, I **t** like a child, 1 Cor 13:11
So I **t** it necessary to urge the brothers 2 Cor 9:5
and take every **t** captive to obey 2 Cor 10:5
I have **t** it necessary to send to you Phil 2:25
he must be well **t** of by outsiders, 1 Tm 3:7

THOUGHTLESS (2)

her vows or any **t** utterance of her lips Nm 30:6
and the **t** utterance of her lips by which Nm 30:8

THOUGHTS (49)

every intention of the **t** of his heart was Gn 6:5
such purposes and **t** in the hearts 1 Chr 29:18
Amid **t** from visions of the night, when Jb 4:13
"Therefore my **t** answer me, because of Jb 20:2
I know your **t** and your schemes to Jb 21:27
seek him; all his **t** are, "There is no God." Ps 10:4
wondrous deeds and your **t** toward us; Ps 40:5
cause; all their **t** are against me for evil. Ps 56:5
works, O LORD! Your **t** are very deep! Ps 92:5
the LORD—knows the **t** of man, that Ps 94:11
I rise up; you discern my **t** from afar. Ps 139:2
How precious to me are your **t**, O God! Ps 139:17
my heart! Try me and know my **t**! Ps 139:23
The **t** of the righteous are just; the Prv 12:5
The **t** of the wicked are an Prv 15:26
his way, and the unrighteous man his **t**; Is 55:7
For my **t** are not your thoughts, neither Is 55:8
For my thoughts are not your **t**, neither Is 55:8
your ways and my **t** than your thoughts. Is 55:9
your ways and my thoughts than your **t**. Is 55:9
blood; their **t** are thoughts of iniquity; Is 59:7
blood; their thoughts are **t** of iniquity; Is 59:7
"For I know their works and their **t**, and Is 66:18
shall your wicked **t** lodge within you? Jer 4:14
The lips and **t** of my assailants are Lam 3:62
that day, **t** will come into your mind, Ezk 38:10
you lay in bed came **t** of what would be Dn 2:29
that you may know the **t** of your mind. Dn 2:30
for a while, and his **t** alarmed him. Dn 4:19
color changed, and his **t** alarmed him; Dn 5:6
Let not your **t** alarm you or your color Dn 5:10
for me, Daniel, my **t** greatly alarmed me, Dn 7:28
But they do not know the **t** of the LORD; Mi 4:12
But Jesus, knowing their **t**, said, "Why do Mt 9:4
Knowing their **t**, he said to them, Mt 12:25
For out of the heart come evil **t**, Mt 15:19
out of the heart of man, come evil **t**, Mk 7:21
the proud in the **t** of their hearts; Lk 1:51
so that **t** from many hearts may be Lk 2:35
When Jesus perceived their **t**, he Lk 5:22
But he knew their **t**, and he said to the Lk 6:8
But he, knowing their **t**, said to them, Lk 11:17
and their conflicting **t** accuse or even Rom 2:15
knows a person's **t** except the spirit 1 Cor 2:11
one comprehends the **t** of God except 1 Cor 2:11
"The Lord knows the **t** of the wise, 1 Cor 3:20
your **t** will be led astray from a 2 Cor 11:3
and discerning the **t** and intentions of Heb 4:12
yourselves and become judges with evil **t**? Jas 2:4

THOUSAND (131)

given your brother a **t** pieces of silver. Gn 20:16
about six hundred **t** men on foot, Ex 12:37
that day about three **t** men of the people Ex 32:28
and a hundred of you shall chase ten **t**, Lv 26:8
LORD, to the ten **t** thousands of Israel." Nm 10:36
I am number six hundred **t** on foot, Nm 11:21
died by the plague were twenty-four **t**. Nm 25:9
You shall send a **t** from each of the Nm 31:4
thousands of Israel, a **t** from each tribe, Nm 31:5
from each tribe, twelve **t** armed for war. Nm 31:5
them to the war, a **t** from each tribe, Nm 31:6
the city outward a **t** cubits all around. Nm 35:4
the city, on the east side two **t** cubits, Nm 35:5
and on the south side two **t** cubits, Nm 35:5
and on the west side two **t** cubits, Nm 35:5
and on the north side two **t** cubits, Nm 35:5
make you a **t** times as many as you are Dt 1:11
his commandments, to a **t** generations, Dt 7:9
How could one have chased a **t**, and two Dt 32:30
and two have put ten **t** to flight, Dt 32:30
let about two or three **t** men go up and Jos 7:3
One man of you puts to flight a **t**, since Jos 23:10
spear to be seen among forty **t** in Israel? Jgs 5:8
a donkey have I struck down a **t** men." Jgs 15:16
the tribes of Israel, and a hundred of a **t**, Jgs 20:10
of a thousand, and a **t** of ten thousand, Jgs 20:10
of a thousand, and a thousand of ten **t**, Jgs 20:10
Eighteen **t** men of Benjamin fell, all of Jgs 20:44
Five **t** men of them were cut down in Jgs 20:45
who killed about four **t** men on the 1 Sm 4:2
there fell of Israel thirty **t** foot soldiers. 1 Sm 4:10
people of Israel were three hundred **t**, 1 Sm 11:8
and the men of Judah thirty **t**. 1 Sm 11:8
Saul chose three **t** men of Israel. Two 1 Sm 13:2
Two **t** were with Saul in Michmash 1 Sm 13:2
and a **t** were with Jonathan in Gibeah 1 Sm 13:2
thirty **t** chariots and six thousand 1 Sm 13:5
chariots and six **t** horsemen and 1 Sm 13:5
in Telaim, two hundred **t** men on foot, 1 Sm 15:4
men on foot, and ten **t** men of Judah. 1 Sm 15:4
the coat was five **t** shekels of bronze. 1 Sm 17:5
cheeses to the commander of their **t**. 1 Sm 17:18
and made him a commander of a **t**. 1 Sm 18:13
Saul took three **t** chosen men out 1 Sm 24:2
he had three **t** sheep and a thousand 1 Sm 25:2
three thousand sheep and a **t** goats. 1 Sm 25:2
of Ziph with three **t** chosen men of 1 Sm 26:2
all the chosen men of Israel, thirty **t**. 2 Sm 6:1
"Let me choose twelve **t** men, 2 Sm 17:1
us. But you are worth ten **t** of us. 2 Sm 18:3
was great on that day, twenty **t** men. 2 Sm 18:7
hand the weight of a **t** pieces of silver, 2 Sm 18:12
him were a **t** men from Benjamin. 2 Sm 19:17
used to offer a **t** burnt offerings on that 1 Kgs 3:4
the flower of a lily. It held two **t** baths. 1 Kgs 7:26
Yet I will leave seven **t** in Israel, all 1 Kgs 19:18
all the people of Israel, seven **t**. 1 Kgs 20:15
talents of silver, six **t** shekels of gold, 2 Kgs 5:5
and ten chariots and ten **t** footmen, 2 Kgs 13:7
He struck down ten **t** Edomites in the 2 Kgs 14:7
gave Pul a **t** talents of silver, 2 Kgs 15:19
I will give you two **t** horses, if you 2 Kgs 18:23
men and the greatest for a **t**. 1 Chr 12:14
he commanded, for a **t** generations, 1 Chr 16:15
"Twenty-four **t** of these," David said, 1 Chr 23:4
and offered a **t** burnt offerings on it. 2 Chr 1:6

Seventy **t** of them he assigned to bear 2 Chr 2:18
and repaired a **t** cubits of the wall, Neh 3:13
could not answer him once in a **t** times. Jb 9:3
him an angel, a mediator, one of the **t**, Jb 33:23
the forest is mine, the cattle on a **t** hills. Ps 50:10
return struck down twelve **t** of Edom in Ps 60:T
The chariots of God are twice ten **t**, Ps 68:17
your courts is better than a **t** elsewhere. Ps 84:10
For a **t** years in your sight are but as Ps 90:4
A **t** may fall at your side, ten thousand at Ps 91:7
fall at your side, ten **t** at your right hand, Ps 91:7
that he commanded, for a **t** generations, Ps 105:8
he should live a **t** years twice over, Eccl 6:6
One man among a **t** I found, but a Eccl 7:28
on it hang a **t** shields, all of them shields Sg 4:4
and ruddy, distinguished among ten **t**. Sg 5:10
to bring for its fruit a **t** pieces of silver. Sg 8:11
you, O Solomon, may have the **t**, and the Sg 8:12
place where there used to be a **t** vines, Is 7:23
vines, worth a **t** shekels of silver, Is 7:23
A **t** shall flee at the threat of one; at the Is 30:17
I will give you two **t** horses, if you are able Is 36:8
a hundred and eighty-five **t** in the camp Is 37:36
his hand, the man measured a **t** cubits, Ezk 47:3
Again he measured a **t**, and led me Ezk 47:4
Again he measured a **t**, and led me Ezk 47:4
Again he measured a **t**, and it was a Ezk 47:5
a great feast for a **t** of his lords and drank Dn 5:1
his lords and drank wine in front of the **t**. Dn 5:1
a **t** thousands served him, and ten Dn 7:10
and ten **t** times ten thousand stood Dn 7:10
thousand times ten **t** stood before him; Dn 7:10
that went out a **t** shall have a hundred Am 5:3
those who ate were about five **t** men, Mt 14:21
Those who ate were four **t** men, besides Mt 15:38
remember the five loaves for the five **t**, Mt 16:9
Or the seven loaves for the four **t**, and Mt 16:10
to him who owed him ten **t** talents. Mt 18:24
and the herd, numbering about two **t**, Mk 5:13
those who ate the loaves were five **t** men. Mk 6:44
And there were about four **t** people. And Mk 8:9
I broke the five loaves for the five **t**, Mk 8:19
"And the seven for the four **t**, how many Mk 8:20
For there were about five **t** men. And he Lk 9:14
he is able with ten **t** to meet him who Lk 14:31
who comes against him with twenty **t**? Lk 14:31
men sat down, about five **t** in number. Jn 6:10
added that day about three **t** souls. Acts 2:41
of the men came to about five **t**. Acts 4:4
found it came to fifty **t** pieces of silver. Acts 19:19
and led the four **t** men of the Acts 21:38
kept for myself seven **t** men who have Rom 11:4
and twenty-three **t** fell in a single day. 1 Cor 10:8
others, than ten **t** words in a tongue. 1 Cor 14:19
that with the Lord one day is as a **t** years, 2 Pt 3:8
thousand years, and a **t** years as one day. 2 Pt 3:8
was twice ten **t** times ten thousand; Rv 9:16
was twice ten thousand times ten **t**; Rv 9:16
Seven **t** people were killed in the Rv 11:13
and Satan, and bound him for a **t** years, Rv 20:2
any longer, until the **t** years were ended. Rv 20:3
life and reigned with Christ for a **t** years. Rv 20:4
come to life until the **t** years were ended. Rv 20:5
they will reign with him for a **t** years. Rv 20:6
And when the **t** years are ended, Satan Rv 20:7

THOUSANDS (61)

may you become **t** of ten thousands, Gn 24:60
may you become thousands of ten **t**, Gn 24:60
such men over the people as chiefs of **t**, Ex 18:21
them heads over the people, chiefs of **t**, Ex 18:25
showing steadfast love to **t** of those who Ex 20:6
keeping steadfast love for **t**, forgiving Ex 34:7
LORD, to the ten thousand **t** of Israel." Nm 10:36
were provided, out of the **t** of Israel, Nm 31:5
the commanders of **t** and the Nm 31:14
who were over the **t** of the army, Nm 31:48
the commanders of **t** and the Nm 31:48
the commanders of **t** and the Nm 31:52
the commanders of **t** and of hundreds, Nm 31:54
as heads over you, commanders of **t**, Dt 1:15
showing steadfast love to **t** of those who Dt 5:10
he came from the ten **t** of holy ones, with Dt 33:2
they are the ten **t** of Ephraim, and they Dt 33:17
and they are the **t** of Manasseh." Dt 33:17
commanders of **t** and commanders 1 Sm 8:12
LORD by your tribes and by your **t**." 1 Sm 10:19
"Saul has struck down his **t**, 1 Sm 18:7
his thousands, and David his ten **t**." 1 Sm 18:7
"They have ascribed to David ten **t**, 1 Sm 18:8
and to me they have ascribed **t**, 1 Sm 18:8
dances, 'Saul has struck down his **t**, 1 Sm 21:11
his thousands, and David his ten **t**'?" 1 Sm 21:11
commanders of **t** and commanders 1 Sm 22:7
him out among all the **t** of Judah." 1 Sm 23:23
passing on by hundreds and by **t**, 1 Sm 29:2
dances, 'Saul has struck down his **t**, 1 Sm 29:5
his thousands, and David his ten **t**'?" 1 Sm 29:5
commanders of **t** and commanders 2 Sm 18:1
marched out by hundreds and by **t**. 2 Sm 18:4
Zillethai, chiefs of **t** in Manasseh. 1 Chr 12:20
the commanders of **t** and of 1 Chr 13:1
the commanders of **t** went to bring 1 Chr 15:25
officers of the **t** and the hundreds 1 Chr 26:26
the commanders of **t** and hundreds, 1 Chr 27:1
served the king, the commanders of **t**, 1 Chr 28:1
the commanders of **t** and of 1 Chr 29:6
the commanders of **t** and of hundreds, 2 Chr 1:2
Of Judah, the commanders of **t**: 2 Chr 17:14
under commanders of **t** and of 2 Chr 25:5
not be afraid of many **t** of people who have Ps 3:6
twice ten thousand, **t** upon thousands; Ps 68:17
twice ten thousand, thousands upon **t**; Ps 68:17
is better to me than **t** of gold and silver Ps 119:72
sheep bring forth **t** and ten thousands Ps 144:13
forth thousands and ten **t** in our fields; Ps 144:13
You show steadfast love to **t**, but you Jer 32:18
before him; a thousand **t** served him, Dn 7:10
and he shall cast down tens of **t**, Dn 11:12
And tens of **t** shall fall, but these shall Dn 11:41
I to write for him my laws by the ten **t**, Hos 8:12
Will the LORD be pleased with **t** of rams, Mi 6:7
of rams, with ten **t** of rivers of oil? Mi 6:7
when so many **t** of the people had Lk 12:1
how many **t** there are among the Jews Acts 21:20
Lord came with ten **t** of his holy ones, Jude 1:14
myriads of myriads and **t** of thousands, Rv 5:11
myriads of myriads and thousands of **t**, Rv 5:11

THREAD (7)

I would not take a **t** or a sandal strap or Gn 14:23
took and tied a scarlet **t** on his hand, Gn 38:28
out with the scarlet **t** on his hand, Gn 38:30
as a **t** of flax snaps when it touches the Jgs 16:9
snapped the ropes off his arms like a **t**. Jgs 16:12
Your lips are like a scarlet **t**, and your Sg 4:3
end has come; the **t** of your life is cut. Jer 51:13

THREADS (1)

and he cut it into **t** to work into the blue Ex 39:3

THREAT (3)

his wealth, but a poor man hears no **t**. Prv 13:8
A thousand shall flee at the **t** of one; at Is 30:17
at the **t** of five you shall flee, till you are Is 30:17

THREATEN (2)

with malice; loftily they **t** oppression. Ps 73:8
when he suffered, he did not **t**, but 1 Pt 2:23

THREATENED (2)

on the sea, so that the ship **t** to break up. Jon 1:4
And when they had further **t** them, Acts 4:21

THREATENING (2)

be stormy today, for the sky is red and **t**.' Mt 16:3
do the same to them, and stop your **t**, Eph 6:9

THREATS (3)

money from anyone by **t** or by false Lk 3:14
look upon their **t** and grant to your Acts 4:29
still breathing **t** and murder against the Acts 9:1

THREE (373)

And Noah had **t** sons, Shem, Ham, and Gn 6:10
Noah's wife and the **t** wives of his sons Gn 7:13
These **t** were the sons of Noah, and from Gn 9:19
to him, "Bring me a heifer **t** years old, Gn 15:9
three years old, a female goat **t** years old, Gn 15:9
goat three years old, a ram **t** years old, Gn 15:9
t men were standing in front of him. Gn 18:2
and said, "Quick! **T** seahs of fine flour! Gn 18:6
behold, **t** flocks of sheep lying beside it, Gn 29:2
I have borne him **t** sons." Therefore his Gn 29:34
a distance of **t** days' journey between Gn 30:36
About **t** months later Judah was told, Gn 38:24
and on the vine there were **t** branches. Gn 40:10
the **t** branches are three days. Gn 40:12
the three branches are **t** days. Gn 40:12
In **t** days Pharaoh will lift up your Gn 40:13
there were **t** cake baskets on my head, Gn 40:16
the **t** baskets are three days. Gn 40:18
the three baskets are **t** days. Gn 40:18
In **t** days Pharaoh will lift up your Gn 40:19
them all together in custody for **t** days. Gn 42:17
Benjamin he gave **t** hundred shekels of Gn 45:22
he was a fine child, she hid him **t** months. Ex 2:2
please let us go a **t** days' journey into the Ex 3:18
Please let us go a **t** days' journey into the Ex 5:3
We must go **t** days' journey into the Ex 8:27
darkness in all the land of Egypt **t** days. Ex 10:22
anyone rise from his place for **t** days, Ex 10:23
They went **t** days in the wilderness and Ex 15:22
if he does not do these **t** things for her, Ex 21:11
"**T** times in the year you shall keep a Ex 23:14
T times in the year shall all your males Ex 23:17
t branches of the lampstand out of one Ex 25:32
side of it and **t** branches of the Ex 25:32
t cups made like almond blossoms, Ex 25:33
and **t** cups made like almond Ex 25:33
square, and its height shall be **t** cubits. Ex 27:1
with their **t** pillars and three bases. Ex 27:14
with their three pillars and **t** bases. Ex 27:14
with their **t** pillars and three bases. Ex 27:15
with their three pillars and **t** bases. Ex 27:15
And that day about **t** thousand men of Ex 32:28
T times in the year shall all your males Ex 34:23
the LORD your God **t** times in the year. Ex 34:24
t branches of the lampstand out of one Ex 37:18
side of it and **t** branches of the Ex 37:18
t cups made like almond blossoms, Ex 37:19
and **t** cups made like almond Ex 37:19
It was square, and **t** cubits was its height. Ex 38:1
with their **t** pillars and three bases. Ex 38:14
with their three pillars and **t** bases. Ex 38:14
with their **t** pillars and their three Ex 38:15
their three pillars and their **t** bases. Ex 38:15
a grain offering of **t** tenths of an ephah Lv 14:10
T years it shall be forbidden to you; it Lv 19:23
produce a crop sufficient for **t** years. Lv 25:21
the valuation shall be **t** shekels of silver. Lv 27:6
the mount of the LORD **t** days' journey. Nm 10:33
went before them **t** days' journey, Nm 10:33
Aaron and Miriam, "Come out, you **t**, Nm 12:4
of meeting." And the **t** of them came Nm 12:4
a grain offering of **t** tenths of an ephah Nm 15:9
you have struck me these **t** times?" Nm 22:28
you struck your donkey these **t** times? Nm 22:32
turned aside before me these **t** times. Nm 22:33
you have blessed them these **t** times. Nm 24:10
also **t** tenths of an ephah of fine flour Nm 28:12
t tenths of an ephah shall you offer for Nm 28:20
oil, **t** tenths of an ephah for each bull, Nm 28:28
oil, **t** tenths of an ephah for the bull, Nm 29:3
oil, **t** tenths of an ephah for the bull, Nm 29:9
t tenths of an ephah for each of the Nm 29:14
and they went a **t** days' journey in the Nm 33:8
You shall give **t** cities beyond the Nm 35:14
and **t** cities in the land of Canaan, Nm 35:14
Then Moses set apart **t** cities in the east Dt 4:41
the end of every **t** years you shall bring Dt 14:28
"**T** times a year all your males shall Dt 16:16
two witnesses or of **t** witnesses the one Dt 17:6
you shall set apart **t** cities for yourselves Dt 19:2
distances and divide into **t** parts the area Dt 19:3
you, You shall set apart **t** cities. Dt 19:7
then you shall add **t** other cities to these Dt 19:9
you shall add three other cities to these **t**, Dt 19:9
two witnesses or of **t** witnesses shall a Dt 19:15
for within **t** days you are to pass over Jos 1:11
and hide there **t** days until the pursuers Jos 2:16
hills and remained there **t** days until the Jos 2:22
At the end of **t** days the officers went Jos 3:2
let about two or **t** thousand men go up Jos 7:3
At the end of **t** days after they had made Jos 9:16
out from there the **t** sons of Anak, Jos 15:14
Provide **t** men from each tribe, and I will Jos 18:4
Kartan with its pasturelands—**t** cities. Jos 21:32
he drove out from it the **t** sons of Anak. Jgs 1:20
the 300 men into **t** companies and put Jgs 7:16
Then the **t** companies blew the trumpets Jgs 7:20
Abimelech ruled over Israel **t** years. Jgs 9:22
divided them into **t** companies and set Jgs 9:43
sweet." And in **t** days they could Jgs 14:14
You have mocked me these **t** times, Jgs 16:15
stay, and he remained with him **t** days. Jgs 19:4
she conceived and bore **t** sons and two 1 Sm 2:21
donkeys that were lost **t** days ago, 1 Sm 9:20
T men going up to God at Bethel will 1 Sm 10:3
you there, one carrying **t** young goats, 1 Sm 10:3
another carrying **t** loaves of bread, 1 Sm 10:3
of Israel were **t** hundred thousand, 1 Sm 11:8
Saul put the people in **t** companies. 1 Sm 11:11
Saul chose **t** thousand men of Israel. 1 Sm 13:2
of the Philistines in **t** companies. 1 Sm 13:17
The **t** oldest sons of Jesse had 1 Sm 17:13
the names of his **t** sons who went to 1 Sm 17:13
youngest. The **t** eldest followed Saul, 1 Sm 17:14
And I will shoot **t** arrows to the side 1 Sm 20:20
to the ground and bowed **t** times. 1 Sm 20:41
Then Saul took **t** thousand chosen 1 Sm 24:2
he had **t** thousand sheep and a 1 Sm 25:2
of Ziph with **t** thousand chosen men 1 Sm 26:2
or drunk water for **t** days and three 1 Sm 30:12
water for three days and **t** nights. 1 Sm 30:12
behind because I fell sick **t** days ago. 1 Sm 30:13
Thus Saul died, and his **t** sons, and 1 Sm 31:6
found Saul and his **t** sons fallen on 1 Sm 31:8
And the **t** sons of Zeruiah were there, 2 Sm 2:18
of Obed-edom the Gittite **t** months, 2 Sm 6:11
to Geshur, and was there **t** years. 2 Sm 13:38

There were born to Absalom **t** sons, 2 Sm 14:27
you." And he took **t** javelins in his 2 Sm 18:14
of Judah together to me within **t** days, 2 Sm 20:4
in the days of David for **t** years, 2 Sm 21:1
spear weighed **t** hundred shekels 2 Sm 21:16
a Tahchemonite; he was chief of the **t**. 2 Sm 23:8
to him among the **t** mighty men was 2 Sm 23:9
And **t** of the thirty chief men went 2 Sm 23:13
Then the **t** mighty men broke 2 Sm 23:16
These things the **t** mighty men did. 2 Sm 23:17
his spear against **t** hundred men and 2 Sm 23:18
them and won a name beside the **t**. 2 Sm 23:18
but he did not attain to the **t**. 2 Sm 23:19
a name beside the **t** mighty men. 2 Sm 23:22
thirty, but he did not attain to the **t**. 2 Sm 23:23
says the LORD, **T** things I offer you. 2 Sm 24:12
"Shall **t** years of famine come to you 2 Sm 24:13
Or will you flee **t** months before your 2 Sm 24:13
Or shall there be **t** days' pestilence in 2 Sm 24:13
at the end of **t** years that two of 1 Kgs 2:39
the inner court with **t** courses of cut 1 Kgs 6:36
There were window frames in **t** rows, 1 Kgs 7:4
and window opposite window in **t** tiers. 1 Kgs 7:4
window was opposite window in **t** tiers. 1 Kgs 7:5
The great court had **t** courses of cut 1 Kgs 7:12
stood on twelve oxen, **t** facing north, 1 Kgs 7:25
three facing north, **t** facing west, 1 Kgs 7:25
three facing west, **t** facing south, 1 Kgs 7:25
three facing south, and **t** facing east. 1 Kgs 7:25
four cubits wide, and **t** cubits high. 1 Kgs 7:27
T times a year Solomon used to offer 1 Kgs 9:25
t minas of gold went into each 1 Kgs 10:17
Once every **t** years the fleet of ships 1 Kgs 10:22
He said to them, "Go away for **t** days, 1 Kgs 12:5
He reigned for **t** years in Jerusalem. 1 Kgs 15:2
upon the child **t** times and cried 1 Kgs 17:21
For **t** years Syria and Israel continued 1 Kgs 22:1
And for **t** days they sought him but 2 Kgs 2:17
LORD has called these **t** kings to give 2 Kgs 3:10
who has called these **t** kings to give 2 Kgs 3:13
Who?" Two or **t** eunuchs looked out 2 Kgs 9:32
And he struck **t** times and stopped. 2 Kgs 13:18
will strike down Syria only **t** times." 2 Kgs 13:19
T times Joash defeated him and 2 Kgs 13:25
and for **t** years he besieged it. 2 Kgs 17:5
and at the end of **t** years he took it. In 2 Kgs 18:10
king of Judah **t** hundred talents of 2 Kgs 18:14
and he reigned **t** months in 2 Kgs 23:31
became his servant **t** years. 2 Kgs 24:1
and he reigned **t** months in 2 Kgs 24:8
height of the capital was **t** cubits. 2 Kgs 25:17
second priest and the **t** keepers of the 2 Kgs 25:18
these **t** Bath-shua the Canaanite bore 1 Chr 2:3
Zeruiah: Abishai, Joab, and Asahel, **t**. 1 Chr 2:16
Elioenai, Hizkiah, and Azrikam, **t**. 1 Chr 3:23
Benjamin: Bela, Becher, and Jediael, **t**. 1 Chr 7:6
he and his **t** sons and all his house 1 Chr 10:6
a Hachmonite, was chief of the **t**. 1 Chr 11:11
him among the **t** mighty men was 1 Chr 11:12
T of the thirty chief men went down 1 Chr 11:15
Then the **t** mighty men broke 1 Chr 11:18
These things did the **t** mighty men. 1 Chr 11:19
them and won a name beside the **t**. 1 Chr 11:20
but he did not attain to the **t**. 1 Chr 11:21
a name beside the **t** mighty men. 1 Chr 11:24
thirty, but he did not attain to the **t**. 1 Chr 11:25
were there with David for **t** days, 1 Chr 12:39
Obed-edom in his house **t** months. 1 Chr 13:14
says the LORD, **T** things I offer you; 1 Chr 21:10
either **t** years of famine, or three 1 Chr 21:12
or **t** months of devastation by your 1 Chr 21:12
or else **t** days of the sword of the 1 Chr 21:12
the chief, and Zetham, and Joel, **t**. 1 Chr 23:8
Shelomoth, Haziel, and Haran, **t**. 1 Chr 23:9
Mushi: Mahli, Eder, and Jeremoth, **t**. 1 Chr 23:23
fourteen sons and **t** daughters. 1 Chr 25:5
It stood on twelve oxen, **t** facing north, 2 Chr 4:4
oxen, three facing north, **t** facing west, 2 Chr 4:4
three facing west, **t** facing south, 2 Chr 4:4
three facing south, and **t** facing east. 2 Chr 4:4
five cubits wide, and **t** cubits high, 2 Chr 6:13
and the **t** annual feasts—the Feast of 2 Chr 8:13
Once every **t** years the ships of 2 Chr 9:21
to me again in **t** days." So the people 2 Chr 10:5
and for **t** years they made 2 Chr 11:17
for they walked for **t** years in the 2 Chr 11:17
He reigned for **t** years in Jerusalem. 2 Chr 13:2
They were **t** days in taking the spoil, 2 Chr 20:25
males from **t** years old and upward 2 Chr 31:16
and he reigned **t** months in 2 Chr 36:2
and he reigned **t** months and ten days 2 Chr 36:9
with **t** layers of great stones and one layer Ezr 6:4
to Ahava, and there we camped **t** days. Ezr 8:15
and there we remained **t** days. Ezr 8:32
if anyone did not come within **t** days, Ezr 10:8
at Jerusalem within the **t** days. Ezr 10:9
went to Jerusalem and was there **t** days. Neh 2:11
and do not eat or drink for **t** days, Est 4:16
born to him seven sons and **t** daughters. Jb 1:2
send and invite their **t** sisters to eat and Jb 1:4
"The Chaldeans formed **t** groups and Jb 1:17
Now when Job's **t** friends heard of all this Jb 2:11
So these **t** men ceased to answer Job, Jb 32:1
anger also at Job's **t** friends because they Jb 32:3
no answer in the mouth of these **t** men, Jb 32:5
God does all these things, twice, **t** times, Jb 33:29
He had also seven sons and **t** daughters. Jb 42:13
T things are never satisfied; four never Prv 30:15
T things are too wonderful for me; Prv 30:18
Under **t** things the earth trembles; Prv 30:21
T things are stately in their tread; four Prv 30:29
the LORD has spoken, saying, "In **t** years, Is 16:14
is beaten—two or **t** berries in the top of Is 17:6
naked and barefoot for **t** years as a sign Is 20:3
As Jehudi read **t** or four columns, the Jer 36:23
"Take **t** men with you from here, Jer 38:10
and the **t** keepers of the threshold; Jer 52:24
even if these **t** men, Noah, Daniel, and Ezk 14:14
even if these **t** men were in it, as I live, Ezk 14:16
though these **t** men were in it, as I live, Ezk 14:18
sword come down twice, yes, **t** times, Ezk 21:14
And there were **t** side rooms on either Ezk 40:10
The **t** were of the same size, and the Ezk 40:10
Its side rooms, **t** on either side, and its Ezk 40:21
of the gate were **t** cubits on either side. Ezk 40:48
And the side chambers were in **t** stories, Ezk 41:6
the galleries all around the **t** of them, Ezk 41:16
an altar of wood, **t** cubits high, two Ezk 41:22
was gallery against gallery in **t** stories. Ezk 42:3
For they were in **t** stories, and they had Ezk 42:6
t gates, the gate of Reuben, the gate of Ezk 48:31
which is to be 4,500 cubits, **t** gates, Ezk 48:32
to be 4,500 cubits by measure, **t** gates, Ezk 48:33
which is to be 4,500 cubits, **t** gates, Ezk 48:34
They were to be educated for **t** years, and Dn 1:5
And these **t** men, Shadrach, Meshach, Dn 3:23
"Did we not cast **t** men bound into the Dn 3:24
and over them **t** presidents, of whom Dn 6:2
got down on his knees **t** times a day and Dn 6:10
but makes his petition **t** times a day." Dn 6:13
It had **t** ribs in its mouth between its Dn 7:5
before which **t** of the first horns were Dn 7:8
came up and before which **t** of them fell, Dn 7:20
former ones, and shall put down **t** kings. Dn 7:24
I, Daniel, was mourning for **t** weeks. Dn 10:2
anoint myself at all, for the full **t** weeks. Dn 10:3
t more kings shall arise in Persia, Dn 11:2
"For **t** transgressions of Damascus, and Am 1:3
"For **t** transgressions of Gaza, and for Am 1:6
"For **t** transgressions of Tyre, and for Am 1:9
"For **t** transgressions of Edom, and for Am 1:11
"For **t** transgressions of the Ammonites, Am 1:13
"For **t** transgressions of Moab, and for Am 2:1
"For **t** transgressions of Judah, and for Am 2:4
"For **t** transgressions of Israel, and for Am 2:6
every morning, your tithes every **t** days; Am 4:4
when there were yet **t** months to the Am 4:7
so two or **t** cities would wander to Am 4:8
belly of the fish **t** days and three nights. Jon 1:17
belly of the fish three days and **t** nights. Jon 1:17
great city, **t** days' journey in breadth. Jon 3:3
one month I destroyed the **t** shepherds. Zec 11:8
just as Jonah was **t** days and three Mt 12:40
was three days and **t** nights in the belly Mt 12:40
Son of Man be **t** days and three nights Mt 12:40
be three days and **t** nights in the heart Mt 12:40
took and hid in **t** measures of flour, Mt 13:33
been with me now **t** days and have Mt 15:32
If you wish, I will make **t** tents here, one Mt 17:4
by the evidence of two or **t** witnesses. Mt 18:16
For where two or **t** are gathered in my Mt 18:20
crows, you will deny me **t** times." Mt 26:34
of God, and to rebuild it in **t** days.'" Mt 26:61
you will deny me **t** times." And he went Mt 26:75
the temple and rebuild it in **t** days, Mt 27:40
was still alive, 'After **t** days I will rise.' Mt 27:63
been with me now **t** days and have Mk 8:2
be killed, and after **t** days rise again. Mk 8:31
Let us make **t** tents, one for you and one Mk 9:5
he is killed, after **t** days he will rise." Mk 9:31
kill him. And after **t** days he will rise." Mk 10:34
for more than **t** hundred denarii and Mk 14:5
crows twice, you will deny me **t** times." Mk 14:30
and in **t** days I will build another, Mk 14:58
you will deny me **t** times." And he Mk 14:72
the temple and rebuild it in **t** days, Mk 15:29
with her about **t** months and returned Lk 1:56
After **t** days they found him in the Lk 2:46
heavens were shut up **t** years and six Lk 4:25
Let us make **t** tents, one for you and one Lk 9:33
Which of these **t**, do you think, proved Lk 10:36
and say to him, 'Friend, lend me **t** loaves, Lk 11:5
t against two and two against three. Lk 12:52
three against two and two against **t**. Lk 12:52
for **t** years now I have come seeking fruit Lk 13:7
took and hid in **t** measures of flour, Lk 13:21
until you deny **t** times that you know Lk 22:34
crows today, you will deny me **t** times." Lk 22:61
temple, and in **t** days I will raise it up." Jn 2:19
and will you raise it up in **t** days?" Jn 2:20
they had rowed about **t** or four miles, Jn 6:19
not sold for **t** hundred denarii and Jn 12:5
crow till you have denied me **t** times. Jn 13:38
added that day about **t** thousand souls. Acts 2:41
an interval of about **t** hours his wife Acts 5:7
was brought up for **t** months in his Acts 7:20
And for **t** days he was without sight, and Acts 9:9
This happened **t** times, and the thing Acts 10:16
"Behold, **t** men are looking for you. Acts 10:19
This happened **t** times, and all was Acts 11:10
at that very moment **t** men arrived at Acts 11:11
and on **t** Sabbath days he reasoned Acts 17:2
synagogue and for **t** months spoke Acts 19:8
There he spent **t** months, and when a Acts 20:3
remembering that for **t** years I did not Acts 20:31
Now **t** days after Festus had arrived in Acts 25:1
entertained us hospitably for **t** days. Acts 28:7
After **t** months we set sail in a ship Acts 28:11
at Syracuse, we stayed there for **t** days. Acts 28:12
of Appius and **T** Taverns to meet Acts 28:15
After **t** days he called together the Acts 28:17
faith, hope, and love abide, these **t**; 1 Cor 13:13
let there be only two or at most **t**, 1 Cor 14:27
Let two or **t** prophets speak, and let 1 Cor 14:29
T times I was beaten with rods. 2 Cor 11:25
T times I was shipwrecked; a night 2 Cor 11:25
T times I pleaded with the Lord about 2 Cor 12:8
by the evidence of two or **t** witnesses. 2 Cor 13:1
Then after **t** years I went up to Gal 1:18
on the evidence of two or **t** witnesses. 1 Tm 5:19
on the evidence of two or **t** witnesses. Heb 10:28
was hidden for **t** months by his Heb 11:23
and for **t** years and six months it did not Jas 5:17
For there are **t** that testify: 1 Jn 5:7
water and the blood; and these **t** agree. 1 Jn 5:8
and **t** quarts of barley for a denarius, Rv 6:6
trumpets that the **t** angels are about Rv 8:13
By these **t** plagues a third of mankind Rv 9:18
For **t** and a half days some from the Rv 11:9
But after the **t** and a half days a breath Rv 11:11
prophet, **t** unclean spirits like frogs. Rv 16:13
The great city was split into **t** parts, and Rv 16:19
on the east **t** gates, on the north three Rv 21:13
the east three gates, on the north **t** gates, Rv 21:13
north three gates, on the south **t** gates, Rv 21:13
three gates, and on the west **t** gates. Rv 21:13

THREE-PRONGED (1)
was boiling, with a **t** fork in his hand, 1 Sm 2:13

THREE-YEAR-OLD (1)
him up with her, along with a **t** bull, 1 Sm 1:24

THREEFOLD (1)
withstand him—a **t** cord is not Eccl 4:12

THRESH (6)
of Egypt the LORD will **t** out the grain, Is 27:12
No, he does not **t** it forever; when he Is 28:28
you shall **t** the mountains and crush Is 41:15
was a trained calf that loved to **t**, Hos 10:11
Arise and **t**, O daughter of Zion, for I will Mi 4:13
hope and the thresher **t** in hope of 1 Cor 9:10

THRESHED (4)
O my **t** and winnowed one, what I have Is 21:10
Dill is not **t** with a threshing sledge, nor Is 28:27
because they have **t** Gilead with Am 1:3
in fury; you **t** the nations in anger. Hab 3:12

THRESHER (1)
in hope and the **t** thresh in hope of 1 Cor 9:10

THRESHING (47)
When they came to the **t** floor of Atad, Gn 50:10
the mourning on the **t** floor of Atad, Gn 50:11
Your **t** shall last to the time of the grape Lv 26:5
like a contribution from the **t** floor, so Nm 15:20
though it were the grain of the **t** floor, Nm 18:27
to the Levites as produce of the **t** floor, Nm 18:30
out of your flock, out of your **t** floor, Dt 15:14
the produce from your **t** floor and your Dt 16:13
am laying a fleece of wool on the **t** floor. Jgs 6:37
is winnowing barley tonight at the **t** floor. Ru 3:2
on your cloak and go down to the **t** floor, Ru 3:3
she went down to the **t** floor and did just Ru 3:6
that the woman came to the **t** floor." Ru 3:14
Keilah and are robbing the **t** floors." 1 Sm 23:1
when they came to the **t** floor of Nacon, 2 Sm 6:6

LORD was by the **t** floor of Araunah 2 Sm 24:16
the LORD on the **t** floor of Araunah 2 Sm 24:18
said, "To buy the **t** floor from you, 2 Sm 24:21
offering and the **t** sledges and the 2 Sm 24:22
So David bought the **t** floor and the 2 Sm 24:24
at the **t** floor at the entrance of the 1 Kgs 22:10
From the **t** floor, or from the 2 Kgs 6:27
and made them like the dust at **t**. 2 Kgs 13:7
they came to the **t** floor of Chidon, 1 Chr 13:9
was standing by the **t** floor of Ornan 1 Chr 21:15
the LORD on the **t** floor of Ornan the 1 Chr 21:18
Now Ornan was **t** wheat. He turned 1 Chr 21:20
went out from the **t** floor and paid 1 Chr 21:21
me the site of the **t** floor that I may 1 Chr 21:22
offerings and the **t** sledges for the 1 Chr 21:23
him at the **t** floor of Ornan 1 Chr 21:28
on the **t** floor of Ornan the Jebusite. 2 Chr 3:1
were sitting at the **t** floor at the 2 Chr 18:9
your grain and gather it to your **t** floor? Jb 39:12
spreads himself like a **t** sledge on the Jb 41:30
Dill is not threshed with a **t** sledge, nor is Is 28:27
Behold, I make of you a **t** sledge, new, Is 41:15
of Babylon is like a **t** floor at the time Jer 51:33
like the chaff of the summer **t** floors; Dn 2:35
loved a prostitute's wages on all **t** floors. Hos 9:1
T floor and wine vat shall not feed them, Hos 9:2
that swirls from the **t** floor or like Hos 13:3
"The **t** floors shall be full of grain; the Jl 2:24
threshed Gilead with **t** sledges of iron. Am 1:3
gathered them as sheaves to the **t** floor. Mi 4:12
he will clear his **t** floor and gather his Mt 3:12
to clear his **t** floor and to gather the Lk 3:17

THRESHOLD (26)
of the house, with her hands on the **t**. Jgs 19:27
his hands were lying cut off on the **t**. 1 Sm 5:4
not tread on the **t** of Dagon in Ashdod 1 Sm 5:5
as she came to the **t** of the house, 1 Kgs 14:17
priests who guarded the **t** put in it all 2 Kgs 12:9
keepers of the **t** have collected from 2 Kgs 22:4
and the keepers of the **t** to bring out of 2 Kgs 23:4
priest and the three keepers of the **t**, 2 Kgs 25:18
which the Levites, the keepers of the **t**, 2 Chr 34:9
the king's eunuchs, who guarded the **t**, Est 2:21
of the king's eunuchs, who guarded the **t**, Est 6:2
the son of Shallum, keeper of the **t**. Jer 35:4
priest, and the three keepers of the **t**; Jer 52:24
on which it rested to the **t** of the house. Ezk 9:3
from the cherub to the **t** of the house, Ezk 10:4
LORD went out from the **t** of the house, Ezk 10:18
its steps, and measured the **t** of the gate, Ezk 40:6
and the **t** of the gate by the vestibule of Ezk 40:7
the three of them, opposite the **t**, Ezk 41:16
by setting their **t** by my threshold and Ezk 43:8
threshold by my **t** and their doorposts Ezk 43:8
and he shall worship at the **t** of the gate. Ezk 46:2
issuing from below the **t** of the temple Ezk 47:1
the south end of the **t** of the temple, Ezk 47:1
punish everyone who leaps over the **t**, Zep 1:9
the window; devastation will be on the **t**; Zep 2:14

THRESHOLDS (6)
the service, keepers of the **t** of the tent, 1 Chr 9:19
were chosen as gatekeepers at the **t**, 1 Chr 9:22
the house with gold—its beams, its **t**, 2 Chr 3:7
the foundations of the **t** shook at the voice Is 6:4
the **t** and the narrow windows and the Ezk 41:16
"Strike the capitals until the **t** shake, and Am 9:1

THREW (58)
it on the ground." So he **t** it on the ground, Ex 4:3
And Moses **t** it in the air, and it became Ex 9:10
Egyptian forces and **t** the Egyptian Ex 14:24
the LORD **t** the Egyptians into the midst Ex 14:27
him a log, and he **t** it into the water, Ex 15:25
half of the blood he **t** against the altar. Ex 24:6
took the blood and **t** it on the people Ex 24:8
and he **t** the tablets out of his hands Ex 32:19
they gave it to me, and I **t** it into the fire, Ex 32:24
and Moses **t** the blood against the sides Lv 8:19
And Moses **t** the blood against the sides Lv 8:24
and he **t** it against the sides of the altar. Lv 9:12
and he **t** it against the sides of the altar. Lv 9:18
of the two tablets and **t** them out of my Dt 9:17
And I **t** the dust of it into the brook that Dt 9:21
from the tree and **t** it at the entrance Jos 8:29
And the LORD **t** them into a panic Jos 10:10
the LORD **t** down large stones from Jos 10:11
from the trees and **t** them into the cave Jos 10:27
and he **t** all the army into a panic. Jgs 8:12
and every man **t** in it the earrings of his Jgs 8:25
a certain woman **t** an upper millstone Jgs 9:53
he **t** away the jawbone out of his hand. Jgs 15:17
the Philistines and **t** them into 1 Sm 7:10
And he **t** stones at David and at all the 2 Sm 16:6
as he went and **t** stones at him and 2 Sm 16:13
they took Absalom and **t** him into a 2 Sm 18:17
into the field and **t** a garment over 2 Sm 20:12
the son of Bichri and **t** it out to Joab. 2 Sm 20:22
the spring of water and **t** salt in it and 2 Kgs 2:21
of land every man **t** a stone until it 2 Kgs 3:25
bring flour." And he **t** it into the pot 2 Kgs 4:41
cut off a stick and **t** it in there and 2 Kgs 6:6
her down." So they **t** her down. 2 Kgs 9:33
his drink offering and **t** the blood of 2 Kgs 16:13
of a rock and **t** them down from the 2 Chr 25:12
the blood and **t** it against the 2 Chr 29:22
took away and **t** into the Kidron 2 Chr 30:14
The priests **t** the blood that they 2 Chr 30:16
and he **t** them outside of the city. 2 Chr 33:15
and the priests **t** the blood that they 2 Chr 35:11
and I **t** all the household furniture of Neh 13:8
some of the stars it **t** down to the ground Dn 8:10
pieces of silver and **t** them into the Zec 11:13
into containers but **t** away the bad. Mt 13:48
And they took him and **t** him out of the Mt 21:39
the colt to Jesus and **t** their cloaks on it, Mk 11:7
and killed him and **t** him out of the Mk 12:8
the demon **t** him to the ground and Lk 9:42
And they **t** him out of the vineyard and Lk 20:15
for work, and **t** himself into the sea. Jn 21:7
upon them, they **t** them into prison, Acts 16:23
the third day they **t** the ship's tackle Acts 27:19
fire from the altar and **t** it on the earth, Rv 8:5
of the earth and **t** it into the great Rv 14:19
And they **t** dust on their heads as they Rv 18:19
a great millstone and **t** it into the sea, Rv 18:21
and **t** him into the pit, and shut it and Rv 20:3

THRILL (1)
your heart shall **t** and exult, because the Is 60:5

THRILLED (1)
the latch, and my heart was **t** within me. Sg 5:4

THRIVE (4)
Why do all who are treacherous **t**? Jer 12:1
"Say, Thus says the Lord GOD: Will it **t**? Ezk 17:9
Behold, it is planted; will it **t**? Will it Ezk 17:10
horses and a large army. Will he **t**? Ezk 17:15

THROAT (6)
self is destruction; their **t** is an open grave; Ps 5:9
with my crying out; my **t** is parched. Ps 69:3
and they do not make a sound in their **t**. Ps 115:7
put a knife to your **t** if you are given to Prv 23:2
going unshod and your **t** from thirst. Jer 2:25
"Their **t** is an open grave; they use Rom 3:13

THROATS (1)
God be in their **t** and two-edged swords Ps 149:6

THROBS (1)
My heart **t**; my strength fails me, and Ps 38:10

THRONE (175)
Only as regards the **t** will I be greater Gn 41:40
firstborn of Pharaoh who sits on his **t**, Ex 11:5
who sat on his **t** to the firstborn of Ex 12:29
saying, "A hand upon the **t** of the LORD! Ex 17:16
when he sits on the **t** of his kingdom, Dt 17:18
and set up the **t** of David over Israel 2 Sm 3:10
I will establish the **t** of his kingdom 2 Sm 7:13
Your **t** shall be established forever.'" 2 Sm 7:16
let the king and his **t** be guiltless." 2 Sm 14:9
after me, and he shall sit on my **t**"? 1 Kgs 1:13
after me, and he shall sit on my **t**.' 1 Kgs 1:17
who shall sit on the **t** of my lord the 1 Kgs 1:20
after me, and he shall sit on my **t**'? 1 Kgs 1:24
who should sit on the **t** of my lord the 1 Kgs 1:27
and he shall sit on my **t** in my place,' 1 Kgs 1:30
and he shall come and sit on my **t**, 1 Kgs 1:35
and make his **t** greater than the 1 Kgs 1:37
throne greater than the **t** of my lord 1 Kgs 1:37
Solomon sits on the royal **t**. 1 Kgs 1:46
and make his **t** greater than your 1 Kgs 1:47
make his throne greater than your **t**.' 1 Kgs 1:47
someone to sit on my **t** this day, 1 Kgs 1:48
shall not lack a man on the **t** of Israel.' 1 Kgs 2:4
Solomon sat on the **t** of David his 1 Kgs 2:12
Then he sat on his **t** and had a seat 1 Kgs 2:19
placed me on the **t** of David my 1 Kgs 2:24
house and for his **t** there shall be 1 Kgs 2:33
and the **t** of David shall be 1 Kgs 2:45
given him a son to sit on his **t** this day. 1 Kgs 3:6
I will set on your **t** in your place, 1 Kgs 5:5
made the Hall of the **T** where he was to 1 Kgs 7:7
my father, and sit on the **t** of Israel, 1 Kgs 8:20
man to sit before me on the **t** of Israel, 1 Kgs 8:25
establish your royal **t** over Israel 1 Kgs 9:5
shall not lack a man on the **t** of Israel.' 1 Kgs 9:5
in you and set you on the **t** of Israel! 1 Kgs 10:9
made a great ivory **t** and overlaid it 1 Kgs 10:18
The **t** had six steps, and at the back 1 Kgs 10:19
at the back of the **t** was a calf's head, 1 Kgs 10:19
as he had seated himself on his **t**, 1 Kgs 16:11
I saw the LORD sitting on his **t**, and 1 Kgs 22:19
him on his father's **t** and fight for 2 Kgs 10:3
shall sit on the **t** of Israel." 2 Kgs 10:30
he took his seat on the **t** of the kings. 2 Kgs 11:19
fathers, and Jeroboam sat on his **t**. 2 Kgs 13:13
sons shall sit on the **t** of Israel to the 2 Kgs 15:12
me, and I will establish his **t** forever. 1 Chr 17:12
and his **t** shall be established 1 Chr 17:14
establish his royal **t** in Israel 1 Chr 22:10
son to sit on the **t** of the kingdom of 1 Chr 28:5
Solomon sat on the **t** of the LORD as 1 Chr 29:23
my father and sit on the **t** of Israel, 2 Chr 6:10
man to sit before me on the **t** of Israel, 2 Chr 6:16
then I will establish your royal **t**, as I 2 Chr 7:18
and set you on his **t** as king for the 2 Chr 9:8
made a great ivory **t** and overlaid it 2 Chr 9:17
The **t** had six steps and a footstool of 2 Chr 9:18
of gold, which were attached to the **t**, 2 Chr 9:18
I saw the LORD sitting on his **t**, and 2 Chr 18:18
had ascended the **t** of his father 2 Chr 21:4
And they set the king on the royal **t**. 2 Chr 23:20
Ahasuerus sat on his royal **t** in Susa, Est 1:2
him and set his **t** above all the officials Est 3:1
sitting on his royal **t** inside the throne Est 5:1
throne inside the **t** room opposite the Est 5:1
with kings on the **t** he sets them forever, Jb 36:7
you have sat on the **t**, giving righteous Ps 9:4
forever; he has established his **t** for justice, Ps 9:7
his holy temple; the LORD'S **t** is in heaven; Ps 11:4
Your **t**, O God, is forever and ever. The Ps 45:6
over the nations; God sits on his holy **t**. Ps 47:8
and build your **t** for all generations.'" Ps 89:4
and justice are the foundation of your **t**; Ps 89:14
offspring forever and his **t** as the days of Ps 89:29
his **t** as long as the sun before me. Ps 89:36
to cease and cast his **t** to the ground. Ps 89:44
Your **t** is established from of old; you are Ps 93:2
and justice are the foundation of his **t**. Ps 97:2
has established his **t** in the heavens, Ps 103:19
sons of your body I will set on your **t**. Ps 132:11
sons also forever shall sit on your **t**." Ps 132:12
the **t** is established by righteousness. Prv 16:12
who sits on the **t** of judgment winnows Prv 20:8
and by steadfast love his **t** is upheld. Prv 20:28
and his **t** will be established in Prv 25:5
poor, his **t** will be established forever. Prv 29:14
For he went from prison to the **t**, Eccl 4:14
Uzziah died I saw the Lord sitting upon a **t**, Is 6:1
on the **t** of David and over his kingdom, Is 9:7
the stars of God I will set my **t** on high; Is 14:13
then a **t** will be established in steadfast Is 16:5
and he will become a **t** of honor to his Is 22:23
sit on the ground without a **t**, O daughter Is 47:1
"Heaven is my **t**, and the earth is my Is 66:1
every one shall set his **t** at the entrance of Jer 1:15
shall be called the **t** of the LORD, Jer 3:17
the kings who sit on David's **t**, the Jer 13:13
sake; do not dishonor your glorious **t**; Jer 14:21
A glorious **t** set on high from the Jer 17:12
and princes who sit on the **t** of David, Jer 17:25
King of Judah, who sits on the **t** of David, Jer 22:2
house kings who sit on the **t** of David, Jer 22:4
in sitting on the **t** of David and ruling Jer 22:30
the king who sits on the **t** of David, Jer 29:16
man to sit on the **t** of the house of Israel, Jer 33:17
he shall not have a son to reign on his **t**, Jer 33:21
shall have none to sit on the **t** of David, Jer 36:30
I will set his **t** above these stones that Jer 43:10
and I will set my **t** in Elam and destroy Jer 49:38
your **t** endures to all generations. Lam 5:19
their heads there was the likeness of a **t**, Ezk 1:26
the likeness of a **t** was a likeness with Ezk 1:26
like a sapphire, in appearance like a **t**. Ezk 10:1
is the place of my **t** and the place of the Ezk 43:7
he was brought down from his kingly **t**, Dn 5:20
like pure wool; his **t** was fiery flames; Dn 7:9
king of Nineveh, and he arose from his **t**, Jon 3:6
and to overthrow the **t** of kingdoms. I Hg 2:22
honor, and shall sit and rule on his **t**. Zec 6:13
And there shall be a priest on his **t**, and Zec 6:13
all, either by heaven, for it is the **t** of God, Mt 5:34
Son of Man will sit on his glorious **t**, Mt 19:28
heaven swears by the **t** of God and by Mt 23:22
him, then he will sit on his glorious **t**. Mt 25:31
will give to him the **t** of his father David, Lk 1:32
set one of his descendants on his **t**, Acts 2:30
"'Heaven is my **t**, and the earth is my Acts 7:49
royal robes, took his seat upon the **t**, Acts 12:21
But of the Son he says, "Your **t**, O God, is Heb 1:8
confidence draw near to the **t** of grace, Heb 4:16
the right hand of the **t** of the Majesty in Heb 8:1
seated at the right hand of the **t** of God. Heb 12:2
from the seven spirits who are before his **t**, Rv 1:4
where you dwell, where Satan's **t** is. Rv 2:13
I will grant him to sit with me on my **t**, Rv 3:21

and sat down with my Father on his **t**. Rv 3:21
the Spirit, and behold, a **t** stood in heaven, Rv 4:2
stood in heaven, with one seated on the **t**. Rv 4:2
and around the **t** was a rainbow that had Rv 4:3
Around the **t** were twenty-four thrones, Rv 4:4
From the **t** came flashes of lightning, and Rv 4:5
and before the **t** were burning seven Rv 4:5
and before the **t** there was as it were a sea Rv 4:6
And around the **t**, on each side of the Rv 4:6
around the throne, on each side of the **t**, Rv 4:6
and thanks to him who is seated on the **t**, Rv 4:9
is seated on the **t** and worship him who Rv 4:10
They cast their crowns before the **t**, Rv 4:10
was seated on the **t** a scroll written within Rv 5:1
And between the **t** and the four living Rv 5:6
hand of him who was seated on the **t**. Rv 5:7
I heard around the **t** and the living Rv 5:11
him who sits on the **t** and to the Lamb Rv 5:13
the face of him who is seated on the **t**, Rv 6:16
standing before the **t** and before the Rv 7:9
belongs to our God who sits on the **t**, Rv 7:10
standing around the **t** and around the Rv 7:11
faces before the **t** and worshiped God, Rv 7:11
"Therefore they are before the **t** of God, Rv 7:15
who sits on the **t** will shelter them with Rv 7:15
the midst of the **t** will be their shepherd, Rv 7:17
the saints on the golden altar before the **t**, Rv 8:3
child was caught up to God and to his **t**, Rv 12:5
his power and his **t** and great authority. Rv 13:2
new song before the **t** and before the four Rv 14:3
out his bowl on the **t** of the beast, Rv 16:10
came out of the temple, from the **t**, Rv 16:17
worshiped God who was seated on the **t**, Rv 19:4
And from the **t** came a voice saying, Rv 19:5
I saw a great white **t** and him who was Rv 20:11
great and small, standing before the **t**, Rv 20:12
I heard a loud voice from the **t** saying, Rv 21:3
And he who was seated on the **t** said, Rv 21:5
flowing from the **t** of God and of the Rv 22:1
but the **t** of God and of the Lamb will be Rv 22:3

THRONES (16)

king of Judah were sitting on their **t**, 1 Kgs 22:10
king of Judah were sitting on their **t**, 2 Chr 18:9
There **t** for judgment were set, the Ps 122:5
were set, the **t** of the house of David. Ps 122:5
a bull I bring down those who sit on **t**. Is 10:13
it raises from their **t** all who were kings of Is 14:9
down from their **t** and remove their Ezk 26:16
As I looked, **t** were placed, and the Dn 7:9
followed me will also sit on twelve **t**, Mt 19:28
mighty from their **t** and exalted those Lk 1:52
and sit on **t** judging the twelve Lk 22:30
whether **t** or dominions or rulers or Col 1:16
Around the throne were twenty-four **t**, Rv 4:4
seated on the **t** were twenty-four elders, Rv 4:4
who sit on their **t** before God fell on Rv 11:16
Then I saw **t**, and seated on them were Rv 20:4

THRONG (8)

in the mighty **t** I will praise you. Ps 35:18
I would go with the **t** and lead them in Ps 42:4
within God's house we walked in the **t**. Ps 55:14
of the wicked, from the **t** of evildoers, Ps 64:2
the lead, the princes of Judah in their **t**, Ps 68:27
I will praise him in the midst of the **t**. Ps 109:30
low, and all her slain are a mighty **t**. Prv 7:26
And the great **t** heard him gladly. Mk 12:37

THRONGED (1)

crowd followed him and **t** about him. Mk 5:24

THROUGHOUT (136)

offspring after you **t** their generations Gn 17:7
offspring after you **t** their generations. Gn 17:9
Every male **t** your generations, Gn 17:12
that were in the field, **t** its whole area, Gn 23:17
years of great plenty **t** all the land of Gn 41:29
I am to be remembered **t** all generations. Ex 3:15
the people were scattered **t** all the land of Ex 5:12
and there shall be blood **t** all the land of Ex 7:19
There was blood **t** all the land of Egypt. Ex 7:21
T all the land of Egypt the land was Ex 8:24
sores on man and beast **t** all the land of Ex 9:9
shall be a great cry **t** all the land of Ex 11:6
t your generations, as a statute forever, Ex 12:14
observe this day, **t** your generations, Ex 12:17
the people of Israel **t** their generations. Ex 12:42
omer of it be kept **t** your generations, Ex 16:32
the LORD to be kept **t** your generations." Ex 16:33
to be observed **t** their generations by Ex 27:21
burnt offering **t** your generations Ex 29:42
before the LORD **t** your generations. Ex 30:8
it once in the year **t** your generations. Ex 30:10
to his offspring **t** their generations." Ex 30:21
holy anointing oil **t** your generations. Ex 30:31
me and you **t** your generations, Ex 31:13
the Sabbath **t** their generations, Ex 31:16
to and fro from gate to gate **t** the camp, Ex 32:27
let no one be seen **t** all the mountain. Ex 34:3
and word was proclaimed **t** the camp, Ex 36:6
perpetual priesthood **t** their Ex 40:15
T all their journeys, whenever the Ex 40:36
the house of Israel **t** all their journeys. Ex 40:38
be a statute forever **t** your generations, Lv 3:17
it, as decreed forever **t** your generations, Lv 6:18
It is a perpetual due **t** their generations." Lv 7:36
be a statute forever **t** your generations. Lv 10:9
forever for them **t** their generations. Lv 17:7
of your offspring **t** their generations Lv 21:17
all your offspring **t** your generations Lv 22:3
is a statute forever **t** your generations in Lv 23:14
dwelling places **t** your generations. Lv 23:21
is a statute forever **t** your generations in Lv 23:31
It is a statute forever **t** your generations; Lv 23:41
be a statute forever **t** your generations. Lv 24:3
shall sound the trumpet **t** all your land. Lv 25:9
and proclaim liberty **t** the land to all its Lv 25:10
to the buyer, **t** his generations; Lv 25:30
a perpetual statute **t** your generations. Nm 10:8
heard the people weeping **t** their clans, Nm 11:10
a statute forever **t** your generations. Nm 15:15
as a contribution **t** your generations. Nm 15:21
and onward **t** your generations, Nm 15:23
of their garments **t** their generations, Nm 15:38
a perpetual statute **t** your generations, Nm 18:23
of each month **t** the months of Nm 28:14
the cities of the land **t** the country. Nm 32:33
and rule for you **t** your generations in Nm 35:29
of tens, and officers, **t** your tribes. Dt 1:15
shall have olive trees **t** all your territory, Dt 28:40
you trusted, come down **t** all your land. Dt 28:52
you in all your towns **t** all your land, Dt 28:52
overflows all its banks **t** the time of Jos 3:15
And he sent messengers **t** all Manasseh, Jgs 6:35
Gideon sent messengers **t** all the hill Jgs 7:24
and sent her **t** all the territory of Israel. Jgs 19:29
in pieces and sent her **t** all the country of Jgs 20:6
ten men of a hundred **t** all the tribes of Jgs 20:10
was a deathly panic **t** the whole city. 1 Sm 5:11
pieces and sent them **t** all the territory 1 Sm 11:7
Saul blew the trumpet **t** all the land, 1 Sm 13:3
blacksmith to be found **t** all the land 1 Sm 13:19
and sent messengers **t** the land of 1 Sm 31:9
t all Edom he put garrisons, and all 2 Sm 8:14
sent secret messengers **t** all the tribes 2 Sm 15:10
the people were arguing **t** all the tribes 2 Sm 19:9
beautiful young woman **t** all the 1 Kgs 1:3
And Jehu sent **t** all Israel, and all the 2 Kgs 10:21
Hazael defeated them **t** the territory 2 Kgs 10:32
lived in their tents **t** all the region east 1 Chr 5:10
All their cities **t** their clans were 1 Chr 6:60
and sent messengers **t** the land of the 1 Chr 10:9
departed and went **t** all Israel and 1 Chr 21:4
the LORD destroying **t** all the 1 Chr 21:12
of fame and glory **t** all lands. 1 Chr 22:5
went, month after month **t** the year, 1 Chr 27:1
LORD run to and fro **t** the whole earth, 2 Chr 16:9
in the fortified cities **t** all Judah. 2 Chr 17:19
and proclaimed a fast **t** all Judah. 2 Chr 20:3
proclamation was made **t** Judah and 2 Chr 24:9
to make a proclamation **t** all Israel, 2 Chr 30:5
So couriers went **t** all Israel and 2 Chr 30:6
places and the altars **t** all Judah and 2 Chr 31:1
Thus Hezekiah did **t** all Judah, and 2 Chr 31:20
all the incense altars **t** all the land of 2 Chr 34:7
made a proclamation **t** all his 2 Chr 36:22
made a proclamation **t** all his kingdom Ezr 1:1
proclamation was made **t** Judah and Ezr 10:7
king is proclaimed **t** all his kingdom, Est 1:20
t the whole kingdom of Ahasuerus. Est 3:6
on one day **t** all the provinces of King Est 8:12
gathered in their cities **t** all the provinces Est 9:2
and his fame spread **t** all the provinces, Est 9:4
and kept **t** every generation, Est 9:28
t all generations I shall not meet Ps 10:6
as long as the moon, **t** all generations! Ps 72:5
you are remembered **t** all generations. Ps 102:12
whose years endure **t** all generations!" Ps 102:24
of flies, and gnats **t** their country. Ps 105:31
your renown, O LORD, **t** all ages. Ps 135:13
dominion endures **t** all generations. Ps 145:13
for all your sins, **t** all your territory. Jer 15:13
high places for sin **t** all your territory. Jer 17:3
and disperse them **t** the countries. Ezk 30:26
broad. It shall be holy **t** its whole extent. Ezk 45:1
120 satraps, to be **t** the whole kingdom; Dn 6:1
And he went **t** all Galilee, teaching in Mt 4:23
So his fame spread **t** all Syria, and they Mt 4:24
And Jesus went **t** all the cities and Mt 9:35
will be proclaimed **t** the whole world Mt 24:14
fame spread everywhere **t** all the Mk 1:28
And he went **t** all Galilee, preaching in Mk 1:39
proclaiming **t** the whole city how much Lk 8:39
stirs up the people, teaching **t** all Judea, Lk 23:5
there came a famine **t** all Egypt and Acts 7:11
they were all scattered **t** the regions of Acts 8:1
So the church **t** all Judea and Galilee Acts 9:31
And it became known **t** all Joppa, and Acts 9:42
know what happened **t** all Judea, Acts 10:37
brothers who were **t** Judea heard that Acts 11:1
Lord was spreading **t** the whole Acts 13:49
among all the Jews **t** the world and is Acts 24:5
then in Jerusalem and **t** all the region Acts 26:20
and in Christ Jesus **t** all generations, Eph 3:21
has become known **t** the whole Phil 1:13
to all the brothers **t** Macedonia. 1 Thes 4:10
yourselves with fear **t** the time of 1 Pt 1:17
by your brotherhood **t** the world. 1 Pt 5:9

THROW (54)

let us kill him and **t** him into one of Gn 37:20
"**T** it on the ground." So he threw it on the Ex 4:3
and let Moses **t** them in the air in the sight Ex 9:8
in the field; you shall **t** it to the dogs. Ex 22:31
before you and will **t** into confusion all Ex 23:27
take its blood and **t** it against the sides Ex 29:16
and **t** the rest of the blood against the Ex 29:20
bring the blood and **t** the blood against Lv 1:5
sons the priests shall **t** its blood against Lv 1:11
sons the priests shall **t** the blood against Lv 3:2
and Aaron's sons shall **t** its blood against Lv 3:8
sons of Aaron shall **t** its blood against Lv 3:13
is the disease and **t** them into an Lv 14:40
And the priest shall **t** the blood on the Lv 17:6
and **t** them into the fire burning the Nm 19:6
over to you and **t** them into great Dt 7:23
and discouraged and **t** him into a 2 Sm 17:2
were battering the wall to **t** it down. 2 Sm 20:15
"Take him up and **t** him on the plot 2 Kgs 9:25
take him up and **t** him on the plot 2 Kgs 9:26
"**T** her down." So they threw her 2 Kgs 9:33
And **t** on it all the blood of the burnt 2 Kgs 16:15
and his own schemes **t** him down. Jb 18:7
t in your lot among us; we will all have Prv 1:14
and **t** you like a ball into a wide land. Is 22:18
off with a knife and **t** them into the fire Jer 36:23
and they shall **t** down your vaulted Ezk 16:39
wall against you and **t** up a mound Ezk 26:8
I will **t** my net over you with a host of Ezk 32:3
and it will **t** truth to the ground, Dn 8:12
shall come and **t** up siegeworks and Dn 11:15
of your land and **t** down all your Mi 5:11
I will **t** filth at you and treat you with Na 3:6
"**T** it to the potter"—the lordly price at Zec 11:13
you are the Son of God, **t** yourself down, Mt 4:6
you to sin, tear it out and **t** it away. Mt 5:29
causes you to sin, cut it off and **t** it away. Mt 5:30
holy, and do not **t** your pearls before pigs, Mt 7:6
and **t** them into the fiery furnace. In Mt 13:42
and **t** them into the fiery furnace. In Mt 13:50
the children's bread and **t** it to the Mt 15:26
causes you to sin, cut it off and **t** it away. Mt 18:8
you to sin, tear it out and **t** it away. Mt 18:9
the children's bread and **t** it to the Mk 7:27
the Son of God, **t** yourself down from here, Lk 4:9
so that they could **t** him down the cliff. Lk 4:29
withdrew from them about a stone's **t**, Lk 22:41
among you be the first to **t** a stone at her." Jn 8:7
So they picked up stones to **t** at him, but Jn 8:59
and do they now **t** us out secretly? Acts 16:37
Therefore do not **t** away your Heb 10:35
the devil is about to **t** some of you into Rv 2:10
Behold, I will **t** her onto a sickbed, and Rv 2:22
with her I will **t** into great tribulation, Rv 2:22

THROWING (6)

upon it and for **t** blood against it, Ezk 43:18
And **t** down the pieces of silver into the Mt 27:5
And **t** off his cloak, he sprang up and Mk 10:50
to Jesus, and **t** their cloaks on the colt, Lk 19:35
were shouting and **t** off their cloaks Acts 22:23
the ship, **t** out the wheat into the sea. Acts 27:38

THROWN (66)

horse and his rider he has **t** into the sea. Ex 15:1
and his rider he has **t** into the sea." Ex 15:21
and its blood shall be **t** against the sides of Lv 7:2
water for impurity was not **t** on him, Nm 19:13
for impurity has not been **t** on him, Nm 19:20
his head shall be **t** to you over the 2 Sm 20:21
are all like thorns that are **t** away, 2 Sm 23:6
And his body was **t** in the road, and 1 Kgs 13:24
and saw the body **t** in the road and 1 Kgs 13:25
and found his body **t** in the road, 1 Kgs 13:28
of the LORD that had been **t** down. 1 Kgs 18:30
your covenant, **t** down your altars, 1 Kgs 19:10
your covenant, **t** down your altars, 1 Kgs 19:14
that the Syrians had **t** away in their 2 Kgs 7:15

and the man was **t** into the grave of 2 Kgs 13:21
their blood was **t** against the altar. 2 Chr 29:22
their blood was **t** against the altar. 2 Chr 29:22
the city of Susa was **t** into confusion. Est 3:15
you have taken me up and **t** me down. Ps 102:10
When their judges are **t** over the cliff, Ps 141:6
into which Ishmael had **t** all the bodies Jer 41:9
have fallen; her walls are **t** down. Jer 50:15
they have **t** dust on their heads and put Lam 2:10
long ago; he has **t** down without pity; Lam 2:17
And the mountains shall be **t** down, Ezk 38:20
and they were **t** into the burning fiery Dn 3:21
it has stripped off their bark and **t** it down; Jl 1:7
"They are **t** everywhere!" "Silence!" Am 8:3
good fruit is cut down and **t** into the fire. Mt 3:10
anything except to be **t** out and trampled Mt 5:13
than that your whole body be **t** into hell. Mt 5:29
is alive and tomorrow is **t** into the oven, Mt 6:30
good fruit is cut down and **t** into the fire. Mt 7:19
the kingdom will be **t** into the outer Mt 8:12
like a net that was **t** into the sea and Mt 13:47
or two feet to be **t** into the eternal fire. Mt 18:8
with two eyes to be **t** into the hell of fire. Mt 18:9
'Be taken up and **t** into the sea,' Mt 21:21
upon another that will not be **t** down." Mt 24:2
his neck and he were **t** into the sea. Mk 9:42
lame than with two feet to be **t** into hell. Mk 9:45
eye than with two eyes to be **t** into hell, Mk 9:47
'Be taken up and **t** into the sea,' Mk 11:23
upon another that will not be **t** down." Mk 13:2
good fruit is cut down and **t** into the fire." Lk 3:9
when the demon had **t** him down in Lk 4:35
today, and tomorrow is **t** into the oven, Lk 12:28
soil or for the manure pile. It is **t** away. Lk 14:35
upon another that will not be **t** down." Lk 21:6
man who had been **t** into prison for an Lk 23:19
man who had been **t** into prison for Lk 23:25
abide in me he is **t** away like a branch Jn 15:6
the branches are gathered, **t** into the fire, Jn 15:6
citizens, and have **t** us into prison; Acts 16:37
blood, and these were **t** upon the earth. Rv 8:7
burning with fire, was **t** into the sea, Rv 8:8
And the great dragon was **t** down, that Rv 12:9
world—he was **t** down to the earth, Rv 12:9
and his angels were **t** down with him. Rv 12:9
of our brothers has been **t** down, Rv 12:10
that he had been **t** down to the earth, Rv 12:13
the great city be **t** down with violence, Rv 18:21
These two were **t** alive into the lake of Rv 19:20
had deceived them was **t** into the lake of Rv 20:10
Death and Hades were **t** into the lake of Rv 20:14
of life, he was **t** into the lake of fire. Rv 20:15

THROWS (4)
to the priest who **t** the blood of the Lv 7:14
wicked; he **t** the wicked down to ruin. Prv 21:12
Like a madman who **t** firebrands, Prv 26:18
whenever it seizes him, it **t** him down, Mk 9:18

THRUST (29)
because they were **t** out of Egypt and Ex 12:39
LORD your God has **t** them out before you, Dt 9:4
And he **t** out the enemy before you and Dt 33:27
his right thigh, and **t** it into his belly. Jgs 3:21
And his young man **t** him through, Jgs 9:54
and he would **t** it into the pan or kettle 1 Sm 2:14
your sword, and **t** me through with it, 1 Sm 31:4
come and **t** me through, 1 Sm 31:4
by the head and **t** his sword in his 2 Sm 2:16
in his hand and **t** them into the heart 2 Sm 18:14
I **t** them through, so that they did not 2 Sm 22:39
your sword and **t** me through with 1 Chr 10:4
He is **t** from light into darkness, and Jb 18:18
They **t** the poor off the road; the poor of Jb 24:4
I **t** them through, so that they were not Ps 18:38
fallen; they are **t** down, unable to rise. Ps 36:12
They only plan to **t** him down from his Ps 62:4
And they will be **t** into thick darkness. Is 8:22
Whoever is found will be **t** through, and Is 13:15
I will **t** you from your office, and you Is 22:19
stand because the LORD **t** them down. Jer 46:15
They shall **t** you down into the pit, and Ezk 28:8
and **t** at all the weak with your horns, Ezk 34:21
is Wickedness." And he **t** her back into Zec 5:8
and **t** down the leaden weight on its Zec 5:8
against those who **t** aside the sojourner, Mal 3:5
wronging his neighbor **t** him aside, Acts 7:27
refused to obey him, but **t** him aside, Acts 7:39
Since you **t** it aside and judge Acts 13:46

THRUSTING (2)
by **t** out all your enemies from before Dt 6:19
the people, **t** them out of their property. Ezk 46:18

THRUSTS (1)
one whose rash words are like sword **t**, Prv 12:18

THUMB (5)
right ear and on the **t** of his right hand Lv 8:23
cleansed and on the **t** of his right hand Lv 14:14
cleansed and on the **t** of his right hand Lv 14:17
and on the **t** of his right hand and on Lv 14:25
cleansed and on the **t** of his right hand Lv 14:28

THUMBS (4)
and on the **t** of their right hands and on Ex 29:20
ears and on the **t** of their right hands Lv 8:24
him and cut off his **t** and his big toes. Jgs 1:6
"Seventy kings with their **t** and their big Jgs 1:7

THUMMIM (6)
you shall put the Urim and the **T**, Ex 28:30
breastpiece he put the Urim and the **T**. Lv 8:8
And of Levi he said, "Give to Levi your **T**, Dt 33:8
give **T**." And Jonathan and Saul were 1 Sm 14:41
be a priest to consult Urim and **T**. Ezr 2:63
a priest with Urim and **T** should arise. Neh 7:65

THUNDER (30)
heaven, and the LORD sent **t** and hail, Ex 9:23
has been enough of God's **t** and hail. Ex 9:28
The **t** will cease, and there will be no Ex 9:29
to the LORD, and the **t** and the hail ceased, Ex 9:33
rain and the hail and the **t** had ceased, Ex 9:34
spoke, and God answered him in **t**. Ex 19:19
the people saw the **t** and the flashes of Ex 20:18
against them he will **t** in heaven. 1 Sm 2:10
LORD, that he may send **t** and rain. 1 Sm 12:17
and the LORD sent **t** and rain that day, 1 Sm 12:18
But the **t** of his power who can Jb 26:14
rain and a way for the lightning of the **t**, Jb 28:26
Keep listening to the **t** of his voice and the Jb 37:2
battle from afar, the **t** of the captains, Jb 39:25
God, and can you **t** with a voice like his? Jb 40:9
poured out water; the skies gave forth **t**; Ps 77:17
The crash of your **t** was in the Ps 77:18
I answered you in the secret place of **t**; Ps 81:7
the sound of your **t** they took to flight. Ps 104:7
Ah, the **t** of many peoples; they thunder Is 17:12
they **t** like the thundering of the sea! Is 17:12
LORD of hosts with **t** and with earthquake Is 29:6
the name Boanerges, that is, Sons of **T**); Mk 3:17
lightning, and rumblings and peals of **t**, Rv 4:5
living creatures say with a voice like **t**, Rv 6:1
it on the earth, and there were peals of **t**, Rv 8:5
of lightning, rumblings, peals of **t**, Rv 11:19
waters and like the sound of loud **t**. Rv 14:2
of lightning, rumblings, peals of **t**, Rv 16:18
and like the sound of mighty peals of **t**, Rv 19:6

THUNDERBOLT (1)
the torrents of rain and a way for the **t**, Jb 38:25

THUNDERBOLTS (1)
cattle to the hail and their flocks to **t**. Ps 78:48

THUNDERED (4)
But the LORD **t** with a mighty sound 1 Sm 7:10
The LORD **t** from heaven, and the 2 Sm 22:14
The LORD also **t** in the heavens, and the Ps 18:13
there and heard it said that it had **t**. Jn 12:29

THUNDERING (1)
they thunder like the **t** of the sea! Is 17:12

THUNDERINGS (1)
of the clouds, the **t** of his pavilion? Jb 36:29

THUNDERS (8)
day there were **t** and lightnings and Ex 19:16
he **t** with his majestic voice, and he does Jb 37:4
God **t** wondrously with his voice; he does Jb 37:5
the God of glory **t**, the LORD, over many Ps 29:3
Mightier than the **t** of many waters, Ps 93:4
When he called out, the seven **t** sounded. Rv 10:3
And when the seven **t** had sounded, I was Rv 10:4
"Seal up what the seven **t** have said, Rv 10:4

THUS (709)
T the heavens and the earth were Gn 2:1
T all the days that Adam lived were 930 Gn 5:5
T all the days of Seth were 912 years, and Gn 5:8
T all the days of Enosh were 905 years, Gn 5:11
T all the days of Kenan were 910 years, Gn 5:14
T all the days of Mahalalel were 895 Gn 5:17
T all the days of Jared were 962 years, Gn 5:20
T all the days of Enoch were 365 years. Gn 5:23
T all the days of Methuselah were 969 Gn 5:27
T all the days of Lamech were 777 years, Gn 5:31
east. **T** they separated from each other. Gn 13:11
T both the daughters of Lot became Gn 19:36
"**T** the man spoke to me," he went to Gn 24:30
T the servant took Rebekah and went Gn 24:61
within her, and she said, "If it is **t**, Gn 25:22
way. **T** Esau despised his birthright. Gn 25:34
T Isaac sent Jacob away. And he went to Gn 28:5
T the man increased greatly and had Gn 30:43
T God has taken away the livestock of Gn 31:9
them, "**T** you shall say to my lord Esau: Gn 32:4
T says your servant Jacob, 'I have Gn 32:4
I have enough." **T** he urged him, Gn 33:11
mourning." **T** his father wept for him. Gn 37:35
"Bow the knee!" **T** he set him over all Gn 41:43
T the sons of Israel came to buy among Gn 42:5
and say to him, '**T** says your son Joseph, Gn 45:9
T Israel settled in the land of Egypt, in Gn 47:27
and as Manasseh.'" **T** he put Ephraim Gn 48:20
T his sons did for him as he had Gn 50:12
your little ones." **T** he comforted them Gn 50:21
and **t** I am to be remembered Ex 3:15
shall say to Pharaoh, '**T** says the LORD, Ex 4:22
and said to Pharaoh, "**T** says the LORD, Ex 5:1
and said to the people, "**T** says Pharaoh, Ex 5:10
Moses spoke **t** to the people of Israel, but Ex 6:9
T says the LORD, "By this you shall know Ex 7:17
Pharaoh and say to him, '**T** says the LORD, Ex 8:1
water, and say to him, '**T** says the LORD, Ex 8:20
T I will put a division between my people Ex 8:23
Pharaoh and say to him, '**T** says the LORD, Ex 9:1
and say to him, '**T** says the LORD, Ex 9:13
and said to him, "**T** says the LORD, Ex 10:3
So Moses said, "**T** says the LORD: About Ex 11:4
asked. **T** they plundered the Egyptians. Ex 12:36
T the LORD saved Israel that day from Ex 14:30
"**T** you shall say to the house of Jacob, Ex 19:3
"**T** you shall say to the people of Israel: Ex 20:22
T shall it be with both of them; they Ex 26:24
T Aaron shall bear the judgment of the Ex 28:30
T you shall ordain Aaron and his sons. Ex 29:9
"**T** you shall do to Aaron and to his Ex 29:35
to them, "**T** says the LORD God of Israel, Ex 32:27
T the LORD used to speak to Moses face Ex 33:11
frames for the tabernacle he made **t**: Ex 36:23
T they attached it in front to the Ex 39:18
T all the work of the tabernacle of the Ex 39:32
who sins, **t** bringing guilt on the people, Lv 4:3
T shall he do with the bull. As he did Lv 4:20
T the priest shall make atonement for Lv 5:13
T the priest shall make atonement for Lv 14:20
T he shall cleanse the house with the Lv 14:52
"**T** you shall keep the people of Israel Lv 15:31
T he shall make atonement for the Lv 16:16
T Moses declared to the people of Israel Lv 23:44
T the people of Israel did as the LORD Lv 24:23
T did the people of Israel; they did Nm 1:54
T did the people of Israel. According to Nm 2:34
but deal **t** with them, that they may live Nm 4:19
T they were listed by him, as the LORD Nm 4:49
T you shall bless the people of Israel: Nm 6:23
T you shall do to them to cleanse them: Nm 8:7
"**T** you shall separate the Levites from Nm 8:14
T did Moses and Aaron and all the Nm 8:20
T shall you do to the Levites in Nm 8:26
"**T** it shall be done for each bull or Nm 15:11
T they shall be a sign to the people of Nm 16:38
T I will make to cease from me the Nm 17:5
T did Moses; as the LORD commanded Nm 17:11
T on the seventh day he shall cleanse Nm 19:19
of Edom: "**T** says your brother Israel: Nm 20:14
T Edom refused to give Israel passage Nm 20:21
T Israel lived in the land of the Nm 21:31
him, "**T** says Balak the son of Zippor: Nm 22:16
to Balak, and **t** you shall speak." Nm 23:5
to Balak, and **t** shall you speak." Nm 23:16
T the plague on the people of Israel was Nm 25:8
But **t** shall you deal with them: you shall Dt 7:5
T you shall do to all the cities that are Dt 20:15
'Why has the LORD done **t** to this land? Dt 29:24
Do you **t** repay the LORD, you foolish and Dt 32:6
T the LORD became king in Jeshurun, Dt 33:5
the city once. **T** shall you do for six days. Jos 6:3
for **t** says the LORD, God of Israel, "There Jos 7:13
For **t** the LORD will do to all your Jos 10:25
T there fell to Manasseh ten portions, Jos 17:5
T the LORD gave to Israel all the land Jos 21:43
"**T** says the whole congregation of the Jos 22:16
said to all the people, "**T** says the LORD, Jos 24:2
And he said to them, "**T** says the LORD, the Jgs 6:8
T God returned the evil of Abimelech, Jgs 9:56
and said to him, "**T** says Jephthah: Jgs 11:15
T the sin of the young men was very 1 Sm 2:17
and said to him, "**T** the LORD has said, 1 Sm 2:27
the people of Israel, "**T** says the LORD, 1 Sm 10:18
and **t** bring disgrace on all Israel." 1 Sm 11:2
"**T** shall you say to the men of 1 Sm 11:9
T says the LORD of hosts, 'I have noted 1 Sm 15:2
him, "**T** and so did David speak." 1 Sm 18:24
Saul said, "**T** shall you say to David, 1 Sm 18:25
have you deceived me **t** and let my 1 Sm 19:17
T it is said, "Is Saul also among the 1 Sm 19:24
And **t** you shall greet him: 'Peace be to 1 Sm 25:6
T Saul died, and his three sons, and 1 Sm 31:6
tell my servant David, '**T** says the LORD: 2 Sm 7:5

t you shall say to my servant David, 2 Sm 7:8
David, '**T** says the LORD of hosts, 2 Sm 7:8
that you have brought me **t** far? 2 Sm 7:18
messenger, "**T** shall you say to Joab, 2 Sm 11:25
T says the LORD, the God of Israel, 'I 2 Sm 12:7
T says the LORD, 'Behold, I will raise 2 Sm 12:11
And **t** he did to all the cities of the 2 Sm 12:31
for **t** were the virgin daughters of the 2 Sm 13:18
the king and speak **t** to him." So Joab 2 Sm 14:3
T they would quench my coal that is 2 Sm 14:7
T Absalom did to all of Israel who 2 Sm 15:6
to him, "**T** has Ahithophel spoken; 2 Sm 17:6
"**T** and so did Ahithophel counsel 2 Sm 17:15
Israel, and **t** and so have I counseled. 2 Sm 17:15
for **t** and so has Ahithophel 2 Sm 17:21
and say to David, '**T** says the LORD, 2 Sm 24:12
"Why have you done **t** and so?" He was 1 Kgs 1:6
t fulfilling the word of the LORD that 1 Kgs 2:27
word again, saying, "**T** said Joab, 1 Kgs 2:30
said Joab, and **t** he answered me." 1 Kgs 2:30
and **t** take away from me and from 1 Kgs 2:31
child is mine." **T** they spoke before 1 Kgs 3:22
T the work of the pillars was finished. 1 Kgs 7:22
T all the work that King Solomon did 1 Kgs 7:51
has the LORD done **t** to this land and 1 Kgs 9:8
T King Solomon excelled all the 1 Kgs 10:23
ten pieces, for **t** says the LORD, 1 Kgs 11:31
"**T** shall you speak to this people 1 Kgs 12:10
it for us,' **t** shall you say to them, 1 Kgs 12:10
'**T** says the LORD, You shall not go 1 Kgs 12:24
said, "O altar, altar, **t** says the LORD: 1 Kgs 13:2
came from Judah, "**T** says the LORD, 1 Kgs 13:21
T and thus shall you say to her." 1 Kgs 14:5
Thus and **t** shall you say to her." 1 Kgs 14:5
Go, tell Jeroboam, '**T** says the LORD, 1 Kgs 14:7
T Zimri destroyed all the house of 1 Kgs 16:12
For **t** says the LORD the God of Israel, 1 Kgs 17:14
and said to him, "**T** says Ben-hadad: 1 Kgs 20:2
again and said, "**T** says Ben-hadad: 1 Kgs 20:5
of Israel and said, "**T** says the LORD, 1 Kgs 20:13
whom?" He said, "**T** says the LORD, 1 Kgs 20:14
the king of Israel, "**T** says the LORD, 1 Kgs 20:28
he said to him, "**T** says the LORD, 1 Kgs 20:42
shall say to him, '**T** says the LORD, 1 Kgs 21:19
shall say to him, '**T** says the LORD: 1 Kgs 21:19
of iron and said, "**T** says the LORD, 1 Kgs 22:11
and say, '**T** says the king, "Put this 1 Kgs 22:27
Now therefore **t** says the LORD, You 2 Kgs 1:4
you, and say to him, **T** says the LORD, 2 Kgs 1:6
and said to him, "**T** says the LORD, 2 Kgs 1:16
salt in it and said, "**T** says the LORD, 2 Kgs 2:21
And he said, "**T** says the LORD, 'I will 2 Kgs 3:16
For **t** says the LORD, 'You shall not see 2 Kgs 3:17
that they may eat, for **t** says the LORD, 2 Kgs 4:43
"**T** and so spoke the girl from the land 2 Kgs 5:4
T he used to warn him, so that he 2 Kgs 6:10
t says the LORD, Tomorrow about this 2 Kgs 7:1
on his head and say, '**T** says the LORD, 2 Kgs 9:3
him, "**T** says the LORD the God of Israel, 2 Kgs 9:6
he said, "**T** and so he spoke to me, 2 Kgs 9:12
spoke to me, saying, '**T** says the LORD, 2 Kgs 9:12
T Jehu the son of Jehoshaphat the son 2 Kgs 9:14
meet him and said, "**T** says the king, 2 Kgs 9:18
them and said, "**T** the king has said, 2 Kgs 9:19
T Jehu wiped out Baal from Israel. 2 Kgs 10:28
T they hid him from Athaliah, so 2 Kgs 11:2
to Hezekiah, '**T** says the great king, 2 Kgs 18:19
T says the king: 'Do not let Hezekiah 2 Kgs 18:29
for **t** says the king of Assyria: 2 Kgs 18:31
They said to him, "**T** says Hezekiah, 2 Kgs 19:3
"Say to your master, '**T** says the LORD: 2 Kgs 19:6
"**T** shall you speak to Hezekiah king 2 Kgs 19:10
Hezekiah, saying, "**T** says the LORD, 2 Kgs 19:20
"Therefore **t** says the LORD 2 Kgs 19:32
and said to him, "**T** says the LORD, 2 Kgs 20:1
leader of my people, **T** says the LORD, 2 Kgs 20:5
therefore **t** says the LORD, the God of 2 Kgs 21:12
she said to them, "**T** says the LORD, 2 Kgs 22:15
T says the LORD, behold, I will bring 2 Kgs 22:16
of the LORD, **t** shall you say to him, 2 Kgs 22:18
you say to him, **T** says the LORD, 2 Kgs 22:18
T Saul died; he and his three sons 1 Chr 10:6
my servant David, '**T** says the LORD: 1 Chr 17:4
t shall you say to my servant David, 1 Chr 17:7
David, '**T** says the LORD of hosts, 1 Chr 17:7
that you have brought me **t** far? 1 Chr 17:16
And **t** David did to all the cities of the 1 Chr 20:3
and say to David, '**T** says the LORD, 1 Chr 21:10
and said to him, "**T** says the LORD, 1 Chr 21:11
T they were to keep charge of the 1 Chr 23:32
should be able **t** to offer willingly? 1 Chr 29:14
T David the son of Jesse reigned over 1 Chr 29:26
T all the work that Solomon did for 2 Chr 5:1
T Solomon finished the house of the 2 Chr 7:11
has the LORD done **t** to this land and 2 Chr 7:21

T was accomplished all the work of 2 Chr 8:16
T King Solomon excelled all the 2 Chr 9:22
"**T** shall you speak to the people 2 Chr 10:10
t shall you say to them, 'My little 2 Chr 10:10
'**T** says the LORD, You shall not go up 2 Chr 11:4
and said to them, "**T** says the LORD, 2 Chr 12:5
T his troops were in front of Judah, 2 Chr 13:13
T the men of Israel were subdued at 2 Chr 13:18
of iron and said, "**T** says the LORD, 2 Chr 18:10
and say, '**T** says the king, Put this 2 Chr 18:26
"**T** you shall do in the fear of the 2 Chr 19:9
T you shall do, and you will not 2 Chr 19:10
T says the LORD to you, 'Do not be 2 Chr 20:15
T Jehoshaphat reigned over Judah. 2 Chr 20:31
prophet, saying, "**T** says the LORD, 2 Chr 21:12
T Jehoshabeath, the daughter of 2 Chr 22:11
T they did day after day, and 2 Chr 24:11
and said to them, "**T** says God, 2 Chr 24:20
T Joash the king did not remember 2 Chr 24:22
T they executed judgment on Joash. 2 Chr 24:24
T the service of the house of the 2 Chr 29:35
T Hezekiah did throughout all 2 Chr 31:20
"**T** says Sennacherib king of 2 Chr 32:10
she said to them, "**T** says the LORD, 2 Chr 34:23
T says the LORD, behold, I will bring 2 Chr 34:24
of the LORD, **t** shall you say to him, 2 Chr 34:26
you say to him, **T** says the LORD, 2 Chr 34:26
"**T** says Cyrus king of Persia, 'The 2 Chr 36:23
"**T** says Cyrus king of Persia: The LORD, Ezr 1:2
came to them and spoke to them **t**, Ezr 5:3
asked those elders and spoke to them **t**, Ezr 5:9
T I cleansed them from everything Neh 13:30
'**T** shall it be done to the man whom the Est 6:9
"**T** shall it be done to the man whom the Est 6:11
in their hearts." **T** Job did continually. Jb 1:5
And after my skin has been **t** destroyed, Jb 19:26
T, knowing their works, he overturns Jb 34:25
and said, '**T** far shall you come, and no Jb 38:11
"I will speak **t**," I would have betrayed Ps 73:15
T they became unclean by their acts, Ps 106:39
t shall the man be blessed who fears the Ps 128:4
He has not dealt **t** with any other Ps 147:20
another beloved, that you **t** adjure us? Sg 5:9
t says the Lord GOD: "'It shall not stand, Is 7:7
For the LORD spoke **t** to me with his strong Is 8:11
Therefore **t** says the Lord GOD of hosts: Is 10:24
For **t** the LORD said to me: "I will quietly Is 18:4
For **t** the Lord said to me: "Go, set a Is 21:6
For **t** the Lord said to me, "Within a Is 21:16
T says the Lord GOD of hosts, "Come, go Is 22:15
For **t** it shall be in the midst of the earth Is 24:13
therefore **t** says the Lord GOD, "Behold, I Is 28:16
Therefore **t** says the LORD, who redeemed Is 29:22
Therefore **t** says the Holy One of Israel, Is 30:12
For **t** said the Lord GOD, the Holy One of Is 30:15
For **t** the LORD said to me, "As a lion or a Is 31:4
"Say to Hezekiah, '**T** says the great king, Is 36:4
T says the king: 'Do not let Hezekiah Is 36:14
For **t** says the king of Assyria: Make Is 36:16
They said to him, "**T** says Hezekiah, 'This Is 37:3
"Say to your master, '**T** says the LORD: Is 37:6
"**T** shall you speak to Hezekiah king of Is 37:10
to Hezekiah, saying, "**T** says the LORD, Is 37:21
"Therefore **t** says the LORD concerning Is 37:33
to him, and said to him, "**T** says the LORD: Is 38:1
"Go and say to Hezekiah, **T** says the LORD, Is 38:5
T says God, the LORD, who created the Is 42:5
But now **t** says the LORD, he who created Is 43:1
T says the LORD, your Redeemer, the Is 43:14
T says the LORD, who makes a way in the Is 43:16
T says the LORD who made you, who Is 44:2
T says the LORD, the King of Israel and his Is 44:6
T says the LORD, your Redeemer, who Is 44:24
T says the LORD to his anointed, to Cyrus, Is 45:1
T says the LORD, the Holy One of Israel, Is 45:11
T says the LORD: "The wealth of Egypt Is 45:14
For **t** says the LORD, who created the Is 45:18
T says the LORD, your Redeemer, the Is 48:17
T says the LORD, the Redeemer of Israel Is 49:7
T says the LORD: "In a time of favor I have Is 49:8
T says the Lord GOD: "Behold, I will lift Is 49:22
For **t** says the LORD: "Even the captives of Is 49:25
T says the LORD: "Where is your mother's Is 50:1
T says your Lord, the LORD, your God Is 51:22
For **t** says the LORD: "You were sold for Is 52:3
For **t** says the Lord GOD: "My people went Is 52:4
T says the LORD: "Keep justice, and do Is 56:1
For **t** says the LORD: "To the eunuchs who Is 56:4
For **t** says the One who is high and lifted Is 57:15
T says the LORD: "As the new wine is Is 65:8
Therefore **t** says the Lord GOD: "Behold, Is 65:13
T says the LORD: "Heaven is my throne, Is 66:1
For **t** says the LORD: "Behold, I will extend Is 66:12
the hearing of Jerusalem, **T** says the LORD, Jer 2:2
T says the LORD: "What wrong did your Jer 2:5

For **t** says the LORD to the men of Judah Jer 4:3
For **t** says the LORD, "The whole land Jer 4:27
not in them. **T** shall it be done to them!" Jer 5:13
Therefore **t** says the LORD, the God of Jer 5:14
For **t** says the LORD of hosts: "Cut down Jer 6:6
T says the LORD of hosts: "They shall Jer 6:9
T says the LORD: "Stand by the roads, and Jer 6:16
Therefore **t** says the LORD: 'Behold, I will Jer 6:21
T says the LORD: "Behold, a people is Jer 6:22
T says the LORD of hosts, the God of Israel: Jer 7:3
Therefore **t** says the Lord GOD: behold, Jer 7:20
T says the LORD of hosts, the God of Jer 7:21
"You shall say to them, **T** says the LORD: Jer 8:4
Therefore **t** says the LORD of hosts: Jer 9:7
Therefore **t** says the LORD of hosts, the Jer 9:15
T says the LORD of hosts: "Consider, and Jer 9:17
Speak, "**T** declares the LORD: 'The dead Jer 9:22
T says the LORD: "Let not the wise man Jer 9:23
T says the LORD: "Learn not the way of Jer 10:2
T shall you say to them: "The gods who Jer 10:11
For **t** says the LORD: "Behold, I am Jer 10:18
You shall say to them, **T** says the LORD, Jer 11:3
Therefore, **t** says the LORD, behold, I am Jer 11:11
Therefore **t** says the LORD concerning Jer 11:21
therefore **t** says the LORD of hosts: Jer 11:22
T says the LORD concerning all my evil Jer 12:14
T says the LORD to me, "Go and buy a Jer 13:1
"**T** says the LORD: Even so will I spoil the Jer 13:9
'**T** says the LORD, the God of Israel, Jer 13:12
you shall say to them, '**T** says the LORD: Jer 13:13
T says the LORD concerning this people: Jer 14:10
people: "They have loved to wander **t**; Jer 14:10
Therefore **t** says the LORD concerning Jer 14:15
you shall say to them, '**T** says the LORD: Jer 15:2
Therefore **t** says the LORD: "If you Jer 15:19
For **t** says the LORD concerning the sons Jer 16:3
"For **t** says the LORD: Do not enter the Jer 16:5
For **t** says the LORD of hosts, the God of Jer 16:9
T says the LORD: "Cursed is the man who Jer 17:5
T said the LORD to me: "Go and stand in Jer 17:19
T says the LORD: Take care for the sake Jer 17:21
'**T** says the LORD, behold, I am shaping Jer 18:11
"Therefore **t** says the LORD: Ask among Jer 18:13
T says the LORD, "Go, buy a potter's Jer 19:1
T says the LORD of hosts, the God of Jer 19:3
say to them, '**T** says the LORD of hosts: Jer 19:11
T will I do to this place, declares the Jer 19:12
"**T** says the LORD of hosts, the God of Jer 19:15
For **t** says the LORD: Behold, I will make Jer 20:4
"**T** you shall say to Zedekiah, 'Thus says Jer 21:4
shall say to Zedekiah, '**T** says the LORD, Jer 21:4
people you shall say: '**T** says the LORD: Jer 21:8
T says the LORD: "'Execute justice in the Jer 21:12
T says the LORD: "Go down to the house Jer 22:1
T says the LORD: Do justice and Jer 22:3
For **t** says the LORD concerning the Jer 22:6
has the LORD dealt **t** with this great city?" Jer 22:8
For **t** says the LORD concerning Jer 22:11
Therefore **t** says the LORD concerning Jer 22:18
T says the LORD: "Write this man down Jer 22:30
Therefore **t** says the LORD, the God of Jer 23:2
Therefore **t** says the LORD of hosts Jer 23:15
T says the LORD of hosts: "Do not listen Jer 23:16
T shall you say, every one to his Jer 23:35
T you shall say to the prophet, 'What Jer 23:37
burden of the LORD,' **t** says the LORD, Jer 23:38
"**T** says the LORD, the God of Israel: Like Jer 24:5
"But **t** says the LORD: Like the bad figs Jer 24:8
"Therefore **t** says the LORD of hosts: Jer 25:8
T the LORD, the God of Israel, said to me: Jer 25:15
say to them, '**T** says the LORD of hosts, Jer 25:27
say to them, '**T** says the LORD of hosts: Jer 25:28
"**T** says the LORD of hosts: Behold, Jer 25:32
"**T** says the LORD: Stand in the court of Jer 26:2
You shall say to them, '**T** says the LORD: Jer 26:4
'**T** says the LORD of hosts, "'Zion shall Jer 26:18
T the LORD said to me: "Make yourself Jer 27:2
'**T** says the LORD of hosts, the God of Jer 27:4
all this people, saying, "**T** says the LORD: Jer 27:16
For **t** says the LORD of hosts concerning Jer 27:19
t says the LORD of hosts, the God of Jer 27:21
"**T** says the LORD of hosts, the God of Jer 28:2
all the people, saying, "**T** says the LORD: Jer 28:11
"Go, tell Hananiah, '**T** says the LORD: Jer 28:13
For **t** says the LORD of hosts, the God of Jer 28:14
Therefore **t** says the LORD: 'Behold, I will Jer 28:16
"**T** says the LORD of hosts, the God of Jer 29:4
For **t** says the LORD of hosts, the God of Jer 29:8
"For **t** says the LORD: When seventy Jer 29:10
t says the LORD concerning the king Jer 29:16
'**T** says the LORD of hosts, behold, I am Jer 29:17
'**T** says the LORD of hosts, the God of Jer 29:21
"**T** says the LORD of hosts, the God of Jer 29:25
'**T** says the LORD concerning Shemaiah Jer 29:31
therefore **t** says the LORD: Behold, I will Jer 29:32

"**T** says the LORD, the God of Israel: Write Jer 30:2
"**T** says the LORD: We have heard a cry of Jer 30:5
"For **t** says the LORD: Your hurt is Jer 30:12
"**T** says the LORD: Behold, I will restore Jer 30:18
T says the LORD: "The people who Jer 31:2
For **t** says the LORD: "Sing aloud with Jer 31:7
T says the LORD: "A voice is heard in Jer 31:15
T says the LORD: "Keep your voice from Jer 31:16
T says the LORD of hosts, the God of Jer 31:23
T says the LORD, who gives the sun for Jer 31:35
T says the LORD: "If the heavens above Jer 31:37
you prophesy and say, '**T** says the LORD: Jer 32:3
'**T** says the LORD of hosts, the God of Jer 32:14
For **t** says the LORD of hosts, the God of Jer 32:15
Therefore, **t** says the LORD: Behold, I am Jer 32:28
"Now therefore **t** says the LORD, the God Jer 32:36
"For **t** says the LORD: Just as I have Jer 32:42
"**T** says the LORD who made the earth, the Jer 33:2
For **t** says the LORD, the God of Israel, Jer 33:4
"**T** says the LORD: In this place of which Jer 33:10
"**T** says the LORD of hosts: In this place Jer 33:12
"For **t** says the LORD: David shall never Jer 33:17
"**T** says the LORD: If you can break my Jer 33:20
T they have despised my people so that Jer 33:24
T says the LORD: If I have not Jer 33:25
"**T** says the LORD, the God of Israel: Go Jer 34:2
Judah and say to him, '**T** says the LORD: Jer 34:2
T says the LORD concerning you: 'You Jer 34:4
"**T** says the LORD, the God of Israel: I Jer 34:13
"Therefore, **t** says the LORD: You have Jer 34:17
"**T** says the LORD of hosts, the God of Jer 35:13
Therefore, **t** says the LORD, the God of Jer 35:17
said, "**T** says the LORD of hosts, Jer 35:18
therefore **t** says the LORD of hosts, the Jer 35:19
of Judah you shall say, '**T** says the LORD, Jer 36:29
Therefore **t** says the LORD concerning Jer 36:30
"**T** says the LORD, God of Israel: Thus Jer 37:7
T shall you say to the king of Judah who Jer 37:7
T says the LORD, Do not deceive Jer 37:9
"**T** says the LORD: He who stays in this Jer 38:2
T says the LORD: This city shall surely be Jer 38:3
said to Zedekiah, "**T** says the LORD, Jer 38:17
the Ethiopian, '**T** says the LORD of hosts, Jer 39:16
and said to them, "**T** says the LORD, the Jer 42:9
T says the LORD of hosts, the God of Jer 42:15
"For **t** says the LORD of hosts, the God of Jer 42:18
say to them, '**T** says the LORD of hosts, Jer 43:10
"**T** says the LORD of hosts, the God of Jer 44:2
And now **t** says the LORD God of hosts, Jer 44:7
"Therefore **t** says the LORD of hosts, the Jer 44:11
T says the LORD of hosts, the God of Jer 44:25
T says the LORD, behold, I will give Jer 44:30
"**T** says the LORD, the God of Israel, to Jer 45:2
T shall you say to him, Thus says the Jer 45:4
shall you say to him, **T** says the LORD: Jer 45:4
"**T** says the LORD: Behold, waters are Jer 47:2
T says the LORD of hosts, the God of Jer 48:1
For **t** says the LORD: "Behold, one shall Jer 48:40
declares the LORD." **T** far is the Jer 48:47
T says the LORD: "Has Israel no sons? Jer 49:1
T says the LORD of hosts: "Is wisdom no Jer 49:7
For **t** says the LORD: "If those who did Jer 49:12
T says the LORD: "Rise up, advance Jer 49:28
T says the LORD of hosts: "Behold, I will Jer 49:35
Therefore, **t** says the LORD of hosts, the Jer 50:18
"**T** says the LORD of hosts: The people of Jer 50:33
T says the LORD: "Behold, I will stir up Jer 51:1
For **t** says the LORD of hosts, the God of Jer 51:33
Therefore **t** says the LORD: "Behold, I Jer 51:36
"**T** says the LORD of hosts: The broad Jer 51:58
and say, '**T** shall Babylon sink, to rise Jer 51:64
shall become exhausted.'" **T** far are the Jer 51:64
and see! With whom have you dealt **t**? Lam 2:20
four had their faces and their wings **t**: Ezk 1:8
shall say to them, '**T** says the Lord GOD.' Ezk 2:4
and say to them, '**T** says the Lord GOD,' Ezk 3:11
shall say to them, '**T** says the Lord GOD.' Ezk 3:27
"**T** shall the people of Israel eat their Ezk 4:13
"**T** says the Lord GOD: This is Jerusalem. Ezk 5:5
Therefore **t** says the Lord GOD: Because Ezk 5:7
therefore **t** says the Lord GOD: Behold, I, Ezk 5:8
"**T** shall my anger spend itself, and I Ezk 5:13
T says the Lord GOD to the mountains Ezk 6:3
T says the Lord GOD: "Clap your hands Ezk 6:11
T I will spend my fury upon them. Ezk 6:12
t says the Lord GOD to the land of Israel: Ezk 7:2
"**T** says the Lord GOD: Disaster after Ezk 7:5
he said to me, "Say, **T** says the LORD: Ezk 11:5
Therefore **t** says the Lord GOD: Your Ezk 11:7
Therefore say, '**T** says the Lord GOD: Ezk 11:16
Therefore say, '**T** says the Lord GOD: I Ezk 11:17
Say to them, '**T** says the Lord GOD: Ezk 12:10
T says the Lord GOD concerning the Ezk 12:19
them therefore, '**T** says the Lord GOD: Ezk 12:23
say to them, **T** says the Lord GOD: Ezk 12:28

T says the Lord GOD, Woe to the foolish Ezk 13:3
Therefore **t** says the Lord GOD: "Because Ezk 13:8
Therefore **t** says the Lord GOD: I will Ezk 13:13
T will I spend my wrath upon the wall Ezk 13:15
and say, **T** says the Lord GOD: Woe to Ezk 13:18
"Therefore **t** says the Lord GOD: Ezk 13:20
and say to them, **T** says the Lord GOD: Ezk 14:4
the house of Israel, **T** says the Lord GOD: Ezk 14:6
"For **t** says the Lord GOD: How much Ezk 14:21
Therefore **t** says the Lord GOD: Like the Ezk 15:6
say, **T** says the Lord GOD to Jerusalem: Ezk 16:3
T you were adorned with gold and Ezk 16:13
T says the Lord GOD, Because your Ezk 16:36
"For **t** says the Lord GOD: I will deal Ezk 16:59
say, **T** says the Lord GOD: A great eagle Ezk 17:3
"Say, **T** says the Lord GOD: Will it Ezk 17:9
Therefore **t** says the Lord GOD: As I Ezk 17:19
T says the Lord GOD: "I myself will Ezk 17:22
and say to them, **T** says the Lord GOD, Ezk 20:3
and say to them, **T** says the Lord GOD: Ezk 20:5
and say to them, **T** says the Lord GOD: Ezk 20:27
house of Israel, **T** says the Lord GOD: Ezk 20:30
O house of Israel, **t** says the Lord GOD: Ezk 20:39
T says the Lord GOD, Behold, I will Ezk 20:47
to the land of Israel, **T** says the LORD: Ezk 21:3
prophesy and say, **T** says the Lord; Ezk 21:9
"Therefore **t** says the Lord GOD: Ezk 21:24
t says the Lord GOD: Remove the Ezk 21:26
T says the Lord GOD concerning the Ezk 21:28
You shall say, **T** says the Lord GOD: A Ezk 22:3
Therefore **t** says the Lord GOD: Ezk 22:19
them, saying, '**T** says the Lord GOD,' Ezk 22:28
T you longed for the lewdness of your Ezk 23:21
O Oholibah, **t** says the Lord GOD: Ezk 23:22
T I will put an end to your lewdness Ezk 23:27
"For **t** says the Lord GOD: Behold, I will Ezk 23:28
T says the Lord GOD: "You shall drink Ezk 23:32
Therefore **t** says the Lord GOD: Ezk 23:35
T they went in to Oholah and to Ezk 23:44
For **t** says the Lord GOD: "Bring up a Ezk 23:46
T will I put an end to lewdness in the Ezk 23:48
and say to them, **T** says the Lord GOD: Ezk 24:3
"Therefore **t** says the Lord GOD: Woe to Ezk 24:6
Therefore **t** says the Lord GOD: Woe to Ezk 24:9
mean for us, that you are acting **t**?" Ezk 24:19
house of Israel, **T** says the Lord GOD: Ezk 24:21
T shall Ezekiel be to you a sign; Ezk 24:24
T says the Lord GOD, Because you said, Ezk 25:3
For **t** says the Lord GOD: Because you Ezk 25:6
"**T** says the Lord GOD: Because Moab Ezk 25:8
"**T** says the Lord GOD: Because Edom Ezk 25:12
therefore **t** says the Lord GOD, I will Ezk 25:13
"**T** says the Lord GOD: Because the Ezk 25:15
therefore **t** says the Lord GOD, Behold, I Ezk 25:16
therefore **t** says the Lord GOD: Behold, I Ezk 26:3
"For **t** says the Lord GOD: Behold, I will Ezk 26:7
"**T** says the Lord GOD to Tyre: Will not Ezk 26:15
"For **t** says the Lord GOD: When I Ezk 26:19
many coastlands, **t** says the Lord GOD: Ezk 27:3
the prince of Tyre, **T** says the Lord GOD: Ezk 28:2
therefore **t** says the Lord GOD: Because Ezk 28:6
and say to him, **T** says the Lord GOD: Ezk 28:12
and say, **T** says the Lord GOD: "Behold, Ezk 28:22
"**T** says the Lord GOD: When I gather Ezk 28:25
speak, and say, **T** says the Lord GOD: Ezk 29:3
Therefore **t** says the Lord GOD: Behold, I Ezk 29:8
"For **t** says the Lord GOD: At the end of Ezk 29:13
Therefore **t** says the Lord GOD: Behold, Ezk 29:19
prophesy, and say, **T** says the Lord GOD: Ezk 30:2
"**T** says the LORD: Those who support Ezk 30:6
"**T** says the Lord GOD: "I will put an Ezk 30:10
"**T** says the Lord GOD: "I will destroy Ezk 30:13
T I will execute judgments on Egypt. Ezk 30:19
Therefore **t** says the Lord GOD: Behold, Ezk 30:22
"Therefore **t** says the Lord GOD: Ezk 31:10
"**T** says the Lord GOD: On the day the Ezk 31:15
"Whom are you **t** like in glory and in Ezk 31:18
T says the Lord GOD: I will throw my Ezk 32:3
"For **t** says the Lord GOD: The sword of Ezk 32:11
to the house of Israel, **T** have you said: Ezk 33:10
say to them, **T** says the Lord GOD: Ezk 33:25
Say this to them, **T** says the Lord GOD: Ezk 33:27
to the shepherds, **T** says the Lord GOD: Ezk 34:2
T says the Lord GOD, Behold, I am Ezk 34:10
"For **t** says the Lord GOD: Behold, I, I Ezk 34:11
for you, my flock, **t** says the Lord GOD: Ezk 34:17
t says the Lord GOD to them: Ezk 34:20
and say to it, **T** says the Lord GOD: Ezk 35:3
T says the Lord GOD: While the whole Ezk 35:14
T says the Lord GOD: Because the Ezk 36:2
prophesy, and say, **T** says the Lord GOD: Ezk 36:3
T says the Lord GOD to the mountains Ezk 36:4
therefore **t** says the Lord GOD: Surely I Ezk 36:5
and valleys, **T** says the Lord GOD: Ezk 36:6
Therefore **t** says the Lord GOD: I swear Ezk 36:7

T says the Lord GOD: Because they say Ezk 36:13
house of Israel, **T** says the Lord GOD: Ezk 36:22
"**T** says the Lord GOD: On the day that Ezk 36:33
"**T** says the Lord GOD: This also I will Ezk 36:37
T says the Lord GOD to these bones: Ezk 37:5
say to the breath, **T** says the Lord GOD: Ezk 37:9
and say to them, **T** says the Lord GOD: Ezk 37:12
say to them, **T** says the Lord GOD: Ezk 37:19
then say to them, **T** says the Lord GOD: Ezk 37:21
and say, **T** says the Lord GOD: Behold, I Ezk 38:3
"**T** says the Lord GOD: On that day, Ezk 38:10
and say to Gog, **T** says the Lord GOD: Ezk 38:14
"**T** says the Lord GOD: Are you he of Ezk 38:17
Gog and say, **T** says the Lord GOD: Ezk 39:1
city.) **T** shall they cleanse the land. Ezk 39:16
you, son of man, **t** says the Lord GOD: Ezk 39:17
"Therefore **t** says the Lord GOD: Now I Ezk 39:25
T the temple had a broad area upward, Ezk 41:7
T the upper chambers were set back Ezk 42:6
me, "Son of man, **t** says the Lord GOD: Ezk 43:18
T you shall purify the altar and make Ezk 43:20
the house of Israel, **T** says the Lord GOD: Ezk 44:6
"**T** says the Lord GOD: No foreigner, Ezk 44:9
"**T** says the Lord GOD: Enough, O Ezk 45:9
"**T** says the Lord GOD: In the first Ezk 45:18
"**T** says the Lord GOD: The gate of the Ezk 46:1
T the lamb and the meal offering and Ezk 46:15
"**T** says the Lord GOD: If the prince Ezk 46:16
T says the Lord GOD: "This is the Ezk 47:13
He went and said **t** to him, "Do not Dn 2:24
the king in haste and said **t** to him: Dn 2:25
He proclaimed aloud and said **t**: 'Chop Dn 4:14
"**T** he said: 'As for the fourth beast, there Dn 7:23
T it shall be done to you, O Bethel, Hos 10:15
T says the LORD: "For three Am 1:3
T says the LORD: "For three Am 1:6
T says the LORD: "For three Am 1:9
T says the LORD: "For three Am 1:11
T says the LORD: "For three Am 1:13
T says the LORD: "For three Am 2:1
T says the LORD: "For three Am 2:4
T says the LORD: "For three Am 2:6
Therefore **t** says the Lord GOD: "An Am 3:11
T says the LORD: "As the shepherd Am 3:12
"Therefore **t** I will do to you, O Israel; Am 4:12
For **t** says the Lord GOD: "The city that Am 5:3
For **t** says the LORD to the house of Israel: Am 5:4
Therefore **t** says the LORD, the God of Am 5:16
For **t** Amos has said, "'Jeroboam shall Am 7:11
Therefore **t** says the LORD: "'Your wife Am 7:17
T says the Lord GOD concerning Edom: Ob 1:1
Therefore **t** says the LORD: behold, against Mi 2:3
"Do not preach"—**t** they preach—"one Mi 2:6
T says the LORD concerning the prophets Mi 3:5
desire of his soul; **t** they weave it together. Mi 7:3
T says the LORD, "Though they are at Na 1:12
"**T** says the LORD of hosts: These people Hg 1:2
Now, therefore, **t** says the LORD of hosts: Hg 1:5
"**T** says the LORD of hosts: Consider your Hg 1:7
For **t** says the LORD of hosts: Yet once Hg 2:6
"**T** says the LORD of hosts: Ask the priests Hg 2:11
say to them, **T** declares the LORD of hosts: Zec 1:3
cried out, '**T** says the LORD of hosts, Zec 1:4
to me, 'Cry out, **T** says the LORD of hosts: Zec 1:14
Therefore, **t** says the LORD, I have Zec 1:16
Cry out again, **T** says the LORD of hosts: Zec 1:17
For **t** said the LORD of hosts, after his Zec 2:8
"**T** says the LORD of hosts: If you will Zec 3:7
say to him, '**T** says the LORD of hosts, Zec 6:12
"**T** says the LORD of hosts, Render true Zec 7:9
T the land they left was desolate, so that Zec 7:14
"**T** says the LORD of hosts: I am jealous Zec 8:2
T says the LORD: I have returned to Zion Zec 8:3
T says the LORD of hosts: Old men and Zec 8:4
T says the LORD of hosts: If it is Zec 8:6
T says the LORD of hosts: behold, I will Zec 8:7
T says the LORD of hosts: "Let your hands Zec 8:9
For **t** says the LORD of hosts: "As I Zec 8:14
"**T** says the LORD of hosts: The fast of the Zec 8:19
"**T** says the LORD of hosts: Peoples shall Zec 8:20
T says the LORD of hosts: In those days Zec 8:23
T said the LORD my God: "Become Zec 11:4
T declares the LORD, who stretched out Zec 12:1
for **t** it is fitting for us to fulfill all Mt 3:15
"**T**, when you give to the needy, sound no Mt 6:2
T you will recognize them by their Mt 7:20
T you witness against yourselves that Mt 23:31
spirit that they **t** questioned within Mk 2:8
t making void the word of God by your Mk 7:13
and is expelled?" (**T** he declared all Mk 7:19
"**T** the Lord has done for me in the days Lk 1:25
Pharisee, standing by himself, prayed **t**: Lk 18:11
David **t** calls him Lord, so how is he his Lk 20:44
and said to them, "**T** it is written, that Lk 24:46
his Christ would suffer, he **t** fulfilled. Acts 3:18

T Joseph, who was also called by the Acts 4:36
and said, "**T** says the Holy Spirit, Acts 21:11
T all will know that there is nothing Acts 21:24
the gear, and **t** they were driven along. Acts 27:17
come to you (but **t** far have been Rom 1:13
T a married woman is bound by law to Rom 7:2
Jews jealous, and **t** save some of them. Rom 11:14
Whoever **t** serves Christ is Rom 14:18
and **t** I make it my ambition to Rom 15:20
T, sinning against your brothers and 1 Cor 8:12
T tongues are a sign not for 1 Cor 14:22
T it is written, "The first man Adam 1 Cor 15:45
the flesh, we regard him **t** no longer. 2 Cor 5:16
joy and crown, stand firm **t** in the Lord, Phil 4:1
t storing up treasure for themselves 1 Tm 6:19
And **t** Abraham, having patiently Heb 6:15
t it is necessary for this priest also to Heb 8:3
These preparations having **t** been made, Heb 9:6
t securing an eternal redemption. Heb 9:12
T it was necessary for the copies of the Heb 9:23
For people who speak **t** make it clear Heb 11:14
and **t** let us offer to God acceptable Heb 12:28
all these things are **t** to be dissolved, 2 Pt 3:11
And everyone who **t** hopes in him 1 Jn 3:3
will be clothed **t** in white garments, Rv 3:5

THWART (1)
discernment of the discerning I will **t**." 1 Cor 1:19

THWARTED (1)
and that no purpose of yours can be **t**. Jb 42:2

THWARTS (1)
but he **t** the craving of the wicked. Prv 10:3

THYATIRA (4)
named Lydia, from the city of **T**, Acts 16:14
to Pergamum and to **T** and to Sardis and Rv 1:11
to the angel of the church in **T** write: Rv 2:18
But to the rest of you in **T**, who do not Rv 2:24

TIBERIAS (3)
of the Sea of Galilee, which is the Sea of **T**. Jn 6:1
Other boats from **T** came near the place Jn 6:23
again to the disciples by the Sea of **T**, Jn 21:1

TIBERIUS (1)
the fifteenth year of the reign of **T** Caesar, Lk 3:1

TIBHATH (1)
And from **T** and from Cun, cities of 1 Chr 18:8

TIBNI (3)
of the people followed **T** the son of 1 Kgs 16:21
the people who followed **T** the son of 1 Kgs 16:22
Tibni the son of Ginath. So **T** died, 1 Kgs 16:22

TIDAL (2)
king of Elam, and **T** king of Goiim, Gn 14:1
king of Elam, **T** king of Goiim, Gn 14:9

TIE (8)
and he shall **t** the linen sash around his Lv 16:4
you shall **t** this scarlet cord in the Jos 2:18
"**T** up your garment and take my 2 Kgs 4:29
and said to him, "**T** up your garments, 2 Kgs 9:1
heart always; **t** them around your neck. Prv 6:21
and **t** sackcloth around your waist. Is 32:11
t a stone to it and cast it into the midst Jer 51:63
They **t** up heavy burdens, hard to bear, Mt 23:4

TIED (16)
the midwife took and **t** a scarlet thread Gn 38:28
And they **t** to it a cord of blue to fasten Ex 39:31
the coat on him and **t** the sash around his Lv 8:7
ephod on him and **t** the skillfully woven Lv 8:7
with coats and **t** sashes around their Lv 8:13
And she **t** the scarlet cord in the window. Jos 2:21
So they **t** sackcloth around their 1 Kgs 20:32
he urged him and **t** up two talents of 2 Kgs 5:23
but the horses **t** and the donkeys 2 Kgs 7:10
tied and the donkeys **t** and the tents as 2 Kgs 7:10
immediately you will find a donkey **t**, Mt 21:2
as you enter it you will find a colt **t**, Mk 11:2
and found a colt **t** at a door outside Mk 11:4
where on entering you will find a colt **t**, Lk 19:30
and taking a towel, **t** it around his waist. Jn 13:4
loosening the ropes that **t** the rudders. Acts 27:40

TIERS (2)
window opposite window in three **t**. 1 Kgs 7:4
was opposite window in three **t**. 1 Kgs 7:5

TIGHT (2)
the web and fasten it **t** with the pin, Jgs 16:13
And she made them **t** with the pin and Jgs 16:14

TIGLATH-PILESER (6)
T king of Assyria came and 2 Kgs 15:29
sent messengers to **T** king of Assyria, 2 Kgs 16:7
Damascus to meet **T** king of 2 Kgs 16:10
whom **T** king of Assyria carried away 1 Chr 5:6
the spirit of **T** king of Assyria, 1 Chr 5:26
So **T** king of Assyria came against 2 Chr 28:20

TIGRIS (2)
And the name of the third river is the **T**, Gn 2:14
bank of the great river (that is, the **T**) Dn 10:4

TIKVAH (2)
the wife of Shallum the son of **T**, 2 Kgs 22:14
and Jahzeiah the son of **T** opposed this, Ezr 10:15

TILES (1)
his bed through the **t** into the midst Lk 5:19

TILL (95)
eat bread, **t** you return to the ground, Gn 3:19
I can do nothing **t** you arrive there." Gn 19:22
t Shelah my son grows up"—for he Gn 38:11
they are still as a stone, **t** your people, Ex 15:16
t the people pass by whom you have Ex 15:16
one leave any of it over **t** the morning." Ex 16:19
Some left part of it **t** the morning, and it Ex 16:20
lay aside to be kept **t** the morning.'" Ex 16:23
So they laid it aside **t** the morning, as Ex 16:24
years, **t** they came to a habitable land. Ex 16:35
They ate the manna **t** they came to the Ex 16:35
around Moses from morning **t** evening. Ex 18:13
around you from morning **t** evening?" Ex 18:14
they did not set out **t** the day that it was Ex 40:37
t the will of the LORD should be clear to Lv 24:12
on the march **t** Miriam was brought Nm 12:15
and overtake you **t** you are destroyed, Dt 28:45
t he stood before the congregation. Jos 20:9
And they waited **t** they were Jgs 3:25
And he said, "I will stay **t** you return." Jgs 6:18
"Let us wait **t** the light of the morning; Jgs 16:2
But Samson lay **t** midnight, and at Jgs 16:3
him, **t** he spent the night there again. Jgs 19:7
and sat there **t** evening before God, Jgs 21:2
you therefore wait **t** they were grown? Ru 1:13
said, "**T** now the LORD has helped us." 1 Sm 7:12
For the people will not eat **t** he comes, 1 Sm 9:13
will not sit down **t** he comes here." 1 Sm 16:11
myself in the field **t** the third day at 1 Sm 20:5
t I know what God will do for me." 1 Sm 22:3
bread or anything else **t** the sun goes 2 Sm 3:35
and your servants shall **t** the land for 2 Sm 9:10
t the two of them could go over on dry 2 Kgs 2:8
they urged him **t** he was ashamed, 2 Kgs 2:17
t the country was filled with water. 2 Kgs 3:20
the Moabites, **t** they fled before them. 2 Kgs 3:24
t only its stones were left in 2 Kgs 3:25
the child sat on her lap **t** noon, 2 Kgs 4:20
and spread it over his face, **t** he died. 2 Kgs 8:15
Samaria, **t** he had wiped them out, 2 Kgs 10:17
fathers have stored up **t** this day, 2 Kgs 20:17
t he had filled Jerusalem from one 2 Kgs 21:16
city was besieged **t** the eleventh year 2 Kgs 25:2
marvelously helped, **t** he was strong. 2 Chr 26:15
not know or see **t** we come among Neh 4:11
month after month **t** the twelfth month, Est 3:7
is long, and I am full of tossing **t** the dawn. Jb 7:4
nor leave me alone **t** I swallow my spit? Jb 7:19
t the heavens are no more he will not Jb 14:12
would wait, **t** my renewal should come. Jb 14:14
t I die I will not put away my integrity Jb 27:5
wickedness to account **t** you find none. Ps 10:15
not turn back **t** they were consumed. Ps 18:37
t the storms of destruction pass by. Ps 57:1
consume them **t** they are no more, that Ps 59:13
peace abound, **t** the moon be no more! Ps 72:7
by a straight way **t** they reached a city Ps 107:7
LORD our God, **t** he has mercy upon us. Ps 123:2
let us take our fill of love **t** morning; Prv 7:18
t an arrow pierces its liver; as a bird Prv 7:23
t I might see what was good for the Eccl 2:3
t you are left like a flagstaff on the top of Is 30:17
your fathers have stored up **t** this day, Is 39:6
or be discouraged **t** he has established Is 42:4
of the LORD! How long **t** you are quiet? Jer 47:6
the city was besieged **t** the eleventh year Jer 52:5
and put him in prison **t** the day of his Jer 52:11
t you have completed the days of your Ezk 4:8
From my youth up **t** now I have never Ezk 4:14
be cleansed anymore **t** I have satisfied Ezk 24:13
t unrighteousness was found in you. Ezk 28:15
t you have scattered them abroad, Ezk 34:21
t the buriers have buried it in the Ezk 39:15
And you shall eat fat **t** you are filled, Ezk 39:19
and drink blood **t** you are drunk, Ezk 39:19
from all the tribes of Israel, shall **t** it. Ezk 48:19
words before me **t** the times change. Dn 2:9
t seven periods of time pass over him,' Dn 4:23
t you know that the Most High rules the Dn 4:25
with the dew of heaven **t** his hair grew as Dn 4:33
And he labored **t** the sun went down to Dn 6:14
He shall prosper **t** the indignation is Dn 11:36
since there was a nation **t** that time. Dn 12:1
"How long shall it be **t** the end of these Dn 12:6
But go your way **t** the end. And you Dn 12:13
I will bereave them **t** none is left. Hos 9:12
t he should see what would become of the Jon 4:5
wolves that leave nothing **t** the morning. Zep 3:3
Lebanon, **t** there is no room for them. Zec 10:10
measures of flour, **t** it was all leavened." Mt 13:33
rooster will not crow **t** you have denied Jn 13:38
to eat nor drink **t** they had killed Acts 23:12
to taste no food **t** we have killed Paul. Acts 23:14
to eat nor drink **t** they have killed Acts 23:21
From morning **t** evening he Acts 28:23

TILLED (2)
to you, and you shall be **t** and sown. Ezk 36:9
the land that was desolate shall be **t**, Ezk 36:34

TILLERS (1)
Be ashamed, O **t** of the soil; wail, O Jl 1:11

TILLING (1)
of the field for **t** the soil was Ezri 1 Chr 27:26

TILON (1)
Amnon, Rinnah, Ben-hanan, and **T**. 1 Chr 4:20

TILT (1)
Or who can **t** the waterskins of the Jb 38:37

TIMAEUS (1)
a blind beggar, the son of **T**, Mk 10:46

TIMBER (22)
its stones and **t** and all the plaster of the Lv 14:45
how to cut **t** like the Sidonians." 1 Kgs 5:6
in the matter of cedar and cypress **t**. 1 Kgs 5:8
Solomon with all the **t** of cedar and 1 Kgs 5:10
and prepared the **t** and the stone 1 Kgs 5:18
with cedar and cypress **t** and gold, 1 Kgs 9:11
away the stones of Ramah and its **t**, 1 Kgs 15:22
well as to buy **t** and quarried stone 2 Kgs 12:12
use it for buying **t** and quarried stone 2 Kgs 22:6
it; **t** and stone, too, I have provided. 1 Chr 22:14
cypress, and algum **t** from Lebanon, 2 Chr 2:8
know how to cut **t** in Lebanon. 2 Chr 2:8
to prepare **t** for me in abundance, for 2 Chr 2:9
servants, the woodsmen who cut **t**, 2 Chr 2:10
we will cut whatever **t** you need from 2 Chr 2:16
away the stones of Ramah and its **t**, 2 Chr 16:6
and **t** for binders and beams for the 2 Chr 34:11
huge stones, and **t** is laid in the walls. Ezr 5:8
layers of great stones and one layer of **t**. Ezr 6:4
he may give me **t** to make beams for Neh 2:8
Your stones and **t** and soil they will Ezk 26:12
and consume it, both **t** and stones." Zec 5:4

TIMBERS (2)
joined to the house with **t** of cedar. 1 Kgs 6:10
and cedar **t** without number, for the 1 Chr 22:4

TIME (599)
In the course of **t** Cain brought to the Gn 4:3
At that **t** people began to call upon the Gn 4:26
At that **t** the Canaanites were in the Gn 12:6
At that **t** the Canaanites and the Gn 13:7
shall bear to you at this **t** next year." Gn 17:21
return to you about this **t** next year, Gn 18:10
At the appointed **t** I will return to you Gn 18:14
return to you about this **t** next year, Gn 18:14
his old age at the **t** of which God had Gn 21:2
At that **t** Abimelech and Phicol the Gn 21:22
to Abraham a second **t** from heaven Gn 22:15
by the well of water at the **t** of evening, Gn 24:11
the **t** when women go out to draw Gn 24:11
When he had been there a long **t**, Gn 26:8
it is not **t** for the livestock to be gathered Gn 29:7
go in to her, for my **t** is completed." Gn 29:21
"Now this **t** my husband will be Gn 29:34
"This **t** I will praise the LORD." Gn 29:35
It happened at that **t** that Judah went Gn 38:1
In the course of **t** the wife of Judah, Gn 38:12
When the **t** of her labor came, there Gn 38:27
From the **t** that he made him overseer in Gn 39:5
And after a **t** his master's wife cast her Gn 39:7
Some **t** after this, the cupbearer of the Gn 40:1
They continued for some **t** in custody. Gn 40:4
he fell asleep and dreamed a second **t**. Gn 41:5
was replaced in our sacks the first **t**, Gn 43:18
we came down the first **t** to buy food. Gn 43:20
And when the **t** drew near that Israel Gn 47:29
Pharaoh hardened his heart this **t** also, Ex 8:32
And the LORD set a **t**, saying, "Tomorrow Ex 9:5
For this **t** I will send all my plagues on Ex 9:14
about this **t** tomorrow I will cause very Ex 9:18
and said to them, "This **t** I have sinned; Ex 9:27
The **t** that the people of Israel lived in Ex 12:40
statute at its appointed **t** from year to Ex 13:10
And when in **t** to come your son asks Ex 13:14
only he shall pay for the loss of his **t**, Ex 21:19
days at the appointed **t** in the month of Ex 23:15

at the **t** appointed in the month Abib, Ex 34:18
In plowing **t** and in harvest you shall Ex 34:21
days. As at the **t** of her menstruation, Lv 12:2
it, shall then be washed a second **t**, Lv 13:58
not at the **t** of her menstrual impurity, Lv 15:25
discharge beyond the **t** of her impurity, Lv 15:25
not to come at any **t** into the Holy Place Lv 16:2
of meeting from the **t** he enters to make Lv 16:17
proclaim at the **t** appointed for them. Lv 23:4
be for you a **t** of holy convocation, Lv 23:27
so that the **t** of the seven weeks of years Lv 25:8
may redeem at any **t** the houses in the Lv 25:32
The **t** he was with his owner shall be Lv 25:50
shall be rated as the **t** of a hired servant. Lv 25:50
shall last to the **t** of the grape harvest, Lv 26:5
harvest shall last to the **t** for sowing. Lv 26:5
and Moses at the **t** when the LORD spoke Nm 3:1
Until the **t** is completed for which he Nm 6:5
when the **t** of his separation has been Nm 6:13
keep the Passover at its appointed **t**. Nm 9:2
you shall keep it at its appointed **t**; Nm 9:3
at its appointed **t** among the people Nm 9:7
the LORD'S offering at its appointed **t**; Nm 9:13
was two days, or a month, or a longer **t**, Nm 9:22
when you blow an alarm the second **t**, Nm 10:6
out for the first **t** at the command of Nm 10:13
the land." Now the **t** was the season of Nm 13:20
Egypt, and we lived in Egypt a long **t**. Nm 20:15
Zippor, who was king of Moab at that **t**, Nm 22:4
careful to offer to me at its appointed **t**.' Nm 28:2
shall at any **t** go beyond the Nm 35:26
"At that **t** I said to you, 'I am not able to Dt 1:9
And I charged your judges at that **t**, 'Hear Dt 1:16
commanded you at that **t** all the things Dt 1:18
And the **t** from our leaving Dt 2:14
his cities at that **t** and devoted to Dt 2:34
all his cities at that **t**—there was not a Dt 3:4
took the land at that **t** out of the hand of Dt 3:8
we took possession of this land at that **t**, Dt 3:12
"And I commanded you at that **t**, saying, Dt 3:18
And I commanded Joshua at that **t**, Dt 3:21
"And I pleaded with the LORD at that **t**, Dt 3:23
commanded me at that **t** to teach you Dt 4:14
the LORD your God is giving you for all **t**." Dt 4:40
being at enmity with him in **t** past; Dt 4:42
I stood between the LORD and you at that **t**, Dt 5:5
"When your son asks you in **t** to come, Dt 6:20
But the LORD listened to me that **t** also. Dt 9:19
I prayed for Aaron also at the same **t**. Dt 9:20
"At that **t** the LORD said to me, 'Cut for Dt 10:1
At that **t** the LORD set apart the tribe of Dt 10:8
stayed on the mountain, as at the first **t**, Dt 10:10
and the LORD listened to me that **t** also. Dt 10:10
at sunset, at the **t** you came out of Egypt. Dt 16:6
seven weeks from the **t** the sickle is first Dt 16:9
of the LORD, him and his sons for all **t**. Dt 18:5
"When you besiege a city for a long **t**, Dt 20:19
who is in office at that **t** and say to him, Dt 26:3
years, at the set **t** in the year of release, Dt 31:10
for the **t** when their foot shall slip; Dt 32:35
its banks throughout the **t** of harvest), Jos 3:15
When your children ask in **t** to come, Jos 4:6
At that **t** the LORD said to Joshua, "Make Jos 5:2
circumcise the sons of Israel a second **t**." Jos 5:2
And at the seventh **t**, when the priests Jos 6:16
Joshua laid an oath on them at that **t**, Jos 6:26
At that **t** Joshua built an altar to the Jos 8:30
At that **t** Joshua spoke to the LORD in Jos 10:12
But at the **t** of the going down of the Jos 10:27
all these kings and their land at one **t**, Jos 10:42
for tomorrow at this **t** I will give over all Jos 11:6
back at that **t** and captured Hazor Jos 11:10
made war a long **t** with all those kings. Jos 11:18
Joshua came at that **t** and cut off the Jos 11:21
forty-five years since the **t** that the LORD Jos 14:10
death of him who is high priest at the **t**. Jos 20:6
At that **t** Joshua summoned the Jos 22:1
from fear that in **t** to come your Jos 22:24
not say to our children in **t** to come, Jos 22:27
us or to our descendants in **t** to come, Jos 22:28
A long **t** afterward, when the LORD had Jos 23:1
And you lived in the wilderness a long **t**. Jos 24:7
they killed at that **t** about 10,000 of the Jgs 3:29
of Lappidoth, was judging Israel at that **t**. Jgs 4:4
them save you in the **t** of your distress." Jgs 10:14
After a **t** the Ammonites made war Jgs 11:4
did you not deliver them within that **t**? Jgs 11:26
At that **t** 42,000 of the Ephraimites fell. Jgs 12:6
At that **t** the Philistines ruled over Israel. Jgs 14:4
some days, at the **t** of wheat harvest, Jgs 15:1
"This **t** I shall be innocent in regard to Jgs 15:3
And Benjamin returned at that **t**. And Jgs 21:14
of Israel departed from there at that **t**, Jgs 21:24
And in due **t** Hannah conceived and 1 Sm 1:20
At that **t** Eli, whose eyesight had begun 1 Sm 3:2

LORD called Samuel again the third **t**. 1 Sm 3:8
And about the **t** of her death the 1 Sm 4:20
at Kiriath-jearim, a long **t** passed, 1 Sm 7:2
"Tomorrow about this **t** I will send to 1 Sm 9:16
'Tomorrow, by the **t** the sun is hot, 1 Sm 11:9
seven days, the **t** appointed by Samuel. 1 Sm 13:8
God went at that **t** with the people of 1 Sm 14:18
Philistines before that **t** and who had 1 Sm 14:21
But at the **t** when Merab, Saul's 1 Sm 18:19
Saul said to David a second **t**, 1 Sm 18:21
son-in-law. Before the **t** had expired, 1 Sm 18:26
sent messengers again the third **t**, 1 Sm 19:21
my father, about this **t** tomorrow, 1 Sm 20:12
with him all the **t** that David was in 1 Sm 22:4
Is today the first **t** that I have 1 Sm 22:15
missed nothing all the **t** they were in 1 Sm 25:7
And the **t** that David was king in 2 Sm 2:11
"For some **t** past you have been 2 Sm 3:17
from the **t** that I appointed judges over 2 Sm 7:11
year, the **t** when kings go out to battle, 2 Sm 11:1
And after a **t** Amnon, David's son, 2 Sm 13:1
And he sent a second **t**, but Joab 2 Sm 14:29
been your father's servant in **t** past, 2 Sm 15:34
"This **t** the counsel that Ahithophel 2 Sm 17:7
"I will not waste **t** like this with you." 2 Sm 18:14
delayed beyond the set **t** that had been 2 Sm 20:5
hundred whom he killed at one **t**. 2 Sm 23:8
and came about harvest **t** to David at 2 Sm 23:13
the morning until the appointed **t**. 2 Sm 24:15
had never at any **t** displeased him by 1 Kgs 1:6
When David's **t** to die drew near, he 1 Kgs 2:1
avenging in **t** of peace for blood that 1 Kgs 2:5
And the **t** that David reigned over 1 Kgs 2:11
I will not at this **t** put you to death, 1 Kgs 2:26
So Solomon held the feast at that **t**, 1 Kgs 8:65
LORD appeared to Solomon a second **t**, 1 Kgs 9:2
and my heart will be there for all **t**. 1 Kgs 9:3
And at that **t**, when Jeroboam went 1 Kgs 11:29
And the **t** that Solomon reigned in 1 Kgs 11:42
At that **t** Abijah the son of Jeroboam 1 Kgs 14:1
And the **t** that Jeroboam reigned was 1 Kgs 14:20
raved on until the **t** of the offering of 1 Kgs 18:29
"Do it a second **t**." And they did it a 1 Kgs 18:34
time." And they did it a second **t**. 1 Kgs 18:34
"Do it a third **t**." And they did it a 1 Kgs 18:34
third time." And they did it a third **t**. 1 Kgs 18:34
And at the **t** of the offering of the 1 Kgs 18:36
And at the seventh **t** he said, 1 Kgs 18:44
of one of them by this **t** tomorrow." 1 Kgs 19:2
again a second **t** and touched him 1 Kgs 19:7
to you tomorrow about this **t**, 1 Kgs 20:6
of Samaria at that **t** and mustered all 2 Kgs 3:6
about the **t** of offering the sacrifice, 2 Kgs 3:20
"At this season, about this **t** next year, 2 Kgs 4:16
son about that **t** the following spring, 2 Kgs 4:17
Was it a **t** to accept money and 2 Kgs 5:26
Tomorrow about this **t** a seah of fine 2 Kgs 7:1
about this **t** tomorrow in the gate of 2 Kgs 7:18
Then Libnah revolted at the same **t**. 2 Kgs 8:22
tomorrow at this **t**." Now the king's 2 Kgs 10:6
The **t** that Jehu reigned over Israel in 2 Kgs 10:36
At that **t** Hazael king of Syria went 2 Kgs 12:17
At that **t** Menahem sacked Tiphsah 2 Kgs 15:16
At that **t** Rezin the king of Syria 2 Kgs 16:6
At that **t** Hezekiah stripped the gold 2 Kgs 18:16
At that **t** Merodach-baladan the son 2 Kgs 20:12
At that **t** the servants of 2 Kgs 24:10
the chief officer over them in **t** past; 1 Chr 9:20
against 300 whom he killed at one **t**. 1 Chr 11:11
you did not carry it the first **t**, 1 Chr 15:13
from the **t** that I appointed judges 1 Chr 17:10
the **t** when kings go out to battle, 1 Chr 20:1
At that **t**, when David saw that the 1 Chr 21:28
offering were at that **t** in the high 1 Chr 21:29
the son of David king the second **t**, 1 Chr 29:22
The **t** that he reigned over Israel was 1 Chr 29:27
At that **t** Solomon held the feast for 2 Chr 7:8
and my heart will be there for all **t**. 2 Chr 7:16
men of Israel were subdued at that **t**, 2 Chr 13:18
For a long **t** Israel was without the 2 Chr 15:3
At that **t** Hanani the seer came to Asa 2 Chr 16:7
some of the people at the same **t**. 2 Chr 16:10
At that **t** Libnah also revolted from 2 Chr 21:10
In course of **t**, at the end of two 2 Chr 21:19
From the **t** when he turned away 2 Chr 25:27
At that **t** King Ahaz sent to the king 2 Chr 28:16
In the **t** of his distress he became yet 2 Chr 28:22
keep it at that **t** because the priests 2 Chr 30:3
for since the **t** of Solomon the son of 2 Chr 30:26
of all nations from that **t** onward. 2 Chr 32:23
present kept the Passover at that **t**, 2 Chr 35:17
At the same **t** Tattenai the governor of Ezr 5:3
and from that **t** until now it has been in Ezr 5:16
At that **t** those who had come from Ezr 8:35
are many, and it is a **t** of heavy rain; Ezr 10:13

to send me when I had given him a **t**. Neh 2:6
At that **t** the Jews who lived near them Neh 4:12
I also said to the people at that **t**, "Let Neh 4:22
from the **t** that I was appointed to be Neh 5:14
it (although up to that **t** I had not set up Neh 6:1
Sanballat for the fifth **t** sent his servant Neh 6:5
And in the **t** of their suffering they Neh 9:27
since the **t** of the kings of Assyria until Neh 9:32
And after some **t** I asked leave of the Neh 13:6
on you." From that **t** on they did not Neh 13:21
were gathered together the second **t**, Est 2:19
For if you keep silent at this **t**, relief and Est 4:14
to the kingdom for such a **t** as this?" Est 4:14
king's scribes were summoned at that **t**, Est 8:9
written and at the **t** appointed every year, Est 9:27
past, that you would appoint me a set **t**, Jb 14:13
It will be paid in full before his **t**, and Jb 15:32
They were snatched away before their **t**; Jb 22:16
I have reserved for the **t** of trouble, Jb 38:23
do you know the **t** when they give birth, Jb 39:2
prayer to you at a **t** when you may be Ps 32:6
he is their stronghold in the **t** of trouble. Ps 37:39
At an acceptable **t**, O God, in the Ps 69:13
Do not cast me off in the **t** of old age; Ps 71:9
"At the set **t** that I appoint I will judge Ps 75:2
Are his promises at an end for all **t**? Ps 77:8
Remember how short my **t** is! For what Ps 89:47
pity on Zion; it is the **t** to favor her; Ps 102:13
to favor her; the appointed **t** has come. Ps 102:13
seasons; the sun knows its **t** for setting. Ps 104:19
LORD from this **t** forth and forevermore! Ps 113:2
LORD from this **t** forth and Ps 115:18
It is **t** for the LORD to act, for your law Ps 119:126
in from this **t** forth and forevermore. Ps 121:8
from this **t** forth and forevermore. Ps 125:2
LORD from this **t** forth and forevermore. Ps 131:3
evening, at the **t** of night and darkness. Prv 7:9
cold of snow in the **t** of harvest is a Prv 25:13
a treacherous man in **t** of trouble is Prv 25:19
and she laughs at the **t** to come. Prv 31:25
and a **t** for every matter under heaven: Eccl 3:1
a **t** to be born, and a time to die; a time Eccl 3:2
a time to be born, and a **t** to die; a time Eccl 3:2
a **t** to plant, and a time to pluck up what Eccl 3:2
and a **t** to pluck up what is planted; Eccl 3:2
a **t** to kill, and a time to heal; a time to Eccl 3:3
a time to kill, and a **t** to heal; a time to Eccl 3:3
a **t** to break down, and a time to build Eccl 3:3
time to break down, and a **t** to build up; Eccl 3:3
a **t** to weep, and a time to laugh; a time Eccl 3:4
a time to weep, and a **t** to laugh; a time Eccl 3:4
a **t** to mourn, and a time to dance; Eccl 3:4
a time to mourn, and a **t** to dance; Eccl 3:4
a **t** to cast away stones, and a time to Eccl 3:5
stones, and a **t** to gather stones together; Eccl 3:5
a **t** to embrace, and a time to refrain Eccl 3:5
and a **t** to refrain from embracing; Eccl 3:5
a **t** to seek, and a time to lose; a time to Eccl 3:6
a time to seek, and a **t** to lose; a time to Eccl 3:6
lose; a **t** to keep, and a time to cast away; Eccl 3:6
lose; a time to keep, and a **t** to cast away; Eccl 3:6
a **t** to tear, and a time to sew; a time to Eccl 3:7
a time to tear, and a **t** to sew; a time to Eccl 3:7
a **t** to keep silence, and a time to speak; Eccl 3:7
a time to keep silence, and a **t** to speak; Eccl 3:7
a **t** to love, and a time to hate; a time for Eccl 3:8
a time to love, and a **t** to hate; a time for Eccl 3:8
to hate; a **t** for war, and a time for peace. Eccl 3:8
to hate; a time for war, and a **t** for peace. Eccl 3:8
has made everything beautiful in its **t**. Eccl 3:11
for there is a **t** for every matter and for Eccl 3:17
Why should you die before your **t**? Eccl 7:17
will know the proper **t** and the just way. Eccl 8:5
For there is a **t** and a way for everything, Eccl 8:6
but **t** and chance happen to them all. Eccl 9:11
For man does not know his **t**. Like fish Eccl 9:12
children of man are snared at an evil **t**, Eccl 9:12
and your princes feast at the proper **t**, Eccl 10:17
on the earth, the **t** of singing has come, Sg 2:12
In the former **t** he brought into contempt Is 9:1
but in the latter **t** he has made glorious the Is 9:1
righteousness from this **t** forth and Is 9:7
hand yet a second **t** to recover the Is 11:11
its **t** is close at hand and its days will not Is 13:22
At evening **t**, behold, terror! Before Is 17:14
At that **t** tribute will be brought to the Is 18:7
at that **t** the LORD spoke by Isaiah the son Is 20:2
Seir, "Watchman, what **t** of the night? Is 21:11
night? Watchman, what **t** of the night?" Is 21:11
it may be for the **t** to come as a witness Is 30:8
our salvation in the **t** of trouble. Is 33:2
At that **t** Merodach-baladan the son of Is 39:1
For a long **t** I have held my peace; I have Is 42:14
will attend and listen for the **t** to come? Is 42:23
From this **t** forth I announce to you new Is 48:6

from the **t** it came to be I have been Is 48:16
LORD: "In a **t** of favor I have answered you; Is 49:8
I not held my peace, even for a long **t**, Is 57:11
"from this **t** forth and forevermore." Is 59:21
I am the LORD; in its **t** I will hasten it. Is 60:22
in our sins we have been a long **t**, and Is 64:5
and the **t** is coming to gather all nations Is 66:18
word of the LORD came to me a second **t**, Jer 1:13
But in the **t** of their trouble they say, Jer 2:27
if they can save you, in your **t** of trouble; Jer 2:28
At that **t** Jerusalem shall be called the Jer 3:17
At that **t** it will be said to this people and Jer 4:11
at the **t** that I punish them, they shall be Jer 6:15
"At that **t**, declares the LORD, the bones of Jer 8:1
and crane keep the **t** of their coming, Jer 8:7
but no good came; for a **t** of healing, Jer 8:15
at the **t** of their punishment they shall Jer 10:15
out the inhabitants of the land at this **t**, Jer 10:18
save them in the **t** of their trouble. Jer 11:12
they call to me in the **t** of their trouble. Jer 11:14
word of the LORD came to me a second **t**, Jer 13:3
hope of Israel, its savior in **t** of trouble, Jer 14:8
but no good came; for a **t** of healing, Jer 14:19
the enemy in the **t** of trouble and in Jer 15:11
time of trouble and in the **t** of distress? Jer 15:11
If at any **t** I declare concerning a nation Jer 18:7
And if at any **t** I declare concerning a Jer 18:9
deal with them in the **t** of your anger. Jer 18:23
until the **t** of his own land comes. Jer 27:7
none like it; it is a **t** of distress for Jacob; Jer 30:7
"At that **t**, declares the LORD, I will be the Jer 31:1
At that **t** the army of the king of Babylon Jer 32:2
vessel, that they may last for a long **t**. Jer 32:14
of the LORD came to Jeremiah a second **t**, Jer 33:1
those days and at that **t** I will cause a Jer 33:15
night will not come at their appointed **t**, Jer 33:20
them vineyards and fields at the same **t**. Jer 39:10
upon them, the **t** of their punishment. Jer 46:21
upon him, the **t** when I punish him. Jer 49:8
"In those days and in that **t**, declares the Jer 50:4
who handles the sickle in **t** of harvest; Jer 50:16
In those days and in that **t**, declares the Jer 50:20
has come, the **t** of their punishment. Jer 50:27
has come, the **t** when I will punish you. Jer 50:31
for this is the **t** of the LORD'S vengeance, Jer 51:6
at the **t** of their punishment they shall Jer 51:18
threshing floor at the **t** when it is Jer 51:33
little while and the **t** of her harvest will Jer 51:33
these, you shall lie down a second **t**, Ezk 4:6
The **t** has come; the day is near, a day of Ezk 7:7
The **t** has come; the day has arrived. Let Ezk 7:12
say, 'The **t** is not near to build houses. Ezk 11:3
within a very little **t** you were more Ezk 16:47
woman in her **t** of menstrual impurity, Ezk 18:6
come, the **t** of your final punishment, Ezk 21:25
come, the **t** of their final punishment. Ezk 21:29
in her midst, so that her **t** may come, Ezk 22:3
the appointed **t** of your years has come. Ezk 22:4
of clouds, a **t** of doom for the nations. Ezk 30:3
my mouth by the **t** the man came to Ezk 33:22
of the sword at the **t** of their calamity, Ezk 35:5
at the **t** of their final punishment, Ezk 35:5
of the city from that **t** on shall be, Ezk 48:35
at the end of that **t** they were to stand Dn 1:5
At the end of the **t**, when the king had Dn 1:18
They answered a second **t** and said, "Let Dn 2:7
certainty that you are trying to gain **t**, Dn 2:8
requested the king to appoint him a **t**, Dn 2:16
Therefore at that **t** certain Chaldeans Dn 3:8
and let seven periods of **t** pass over him. Dn 4:16
till seven periods of **t** pass over him,' Dn 4:23
and seven periods of **t** shall pass over Dn 4:25
for you from the **t** that you know that Dn 4:26
and seven periods of **t** shall pass over Dn 4:32
At the same **t** my reason returned to me, Dn 4:36
lives were prolonged for a season and a **t**. Dn 7:12
and the **t** came when the saints Dn 7:22
they shall be given into his hand for a **t**, Dn 7:25
his hand for a time, times, and half a **t**. Dn 7:25
that the vision is for the **t** of the end." Dn 8:17
for it refers to the appointed **t** of the end. Dn 8:19
swift flight at the **t** of the evening Dn 9:21
squares and moat, but in a troubled **t**. Dn 9:25
And from the **t** that an alliance is Dn 11:23
against strongholds, but only for a **t**. Dn 11:24
the end is yet to be at the **t** appointed. Dn 11:27
"At the **t** appointed he shall return and Dn 11:29
it shall not be this **t** as it was before. Dn 11:29
and made white, until the **t** of the end, Dn 11:35
end, for it still awaits the appointed **t**. Dn 11:35
"At the **t** of the end, the king of the Dn 11:40
"At that **t** shall arise Michael, the great Dn 12:1
And there shall be a **t** of trouble, such as Dn 12:1
been since there was a nation till that **t**. Dn 12:1
But at that **t** your people shall be Dn 12:1

and seal the book, until the **t** of the end. Dn 12:4
who lives forever that it would be for a **t**, Dn 12:7
would be for a time, times, and half a **t**, Dn 12:7
shut up and sealed until the **t** of the end. Dn 12:9
And from the **t** that the regular burnt Dn 12:11
I will take back my grain in its **t**, Hos 2:9
as at the **t** when she came out of the Hos 2:15
ground, for it is the **t** to seek the LORD, Hos 10:12
for at the right **t** he does not present Hos 13:13
"For behold, in those days and at that **t**, Jl 3:1
is prudent will keep silent in such a **t**, Am 5:13
silent in such a time, for it is an evil **t**. Am 5:13
of the LORD came to Jonah the second **t**, Jon 3:1
haughtily, for it will be a **t** of disaster. Mi 2:3
he will hide his face from them at that **t**, Mi 3:4
Zion from this **t** forth and forevermore. Mi 4:7
give them up until the **t** when she who is Mi 5:3
end; trouble will not rise up a second **t**. Na 1:9
For still the vision awaits its appointed **t**; Hab 2:3
At that **t** I will search Jerusalem with Zep 1:12
"For at that **t** I will change the speech of Zep 3:9
at that **t** I will deal with all your Zep 3:19
At that **t** I will bring you in, at the time Zep 3:20
in, at the **t** when I gather you together; Zep 3:20
These people say the **t** has not yet come to Hg 1:2
"Is it a **t** for you yourselves to dwell in Hg 1:4
LORD came a second **t** to Haggai on the Hg 2:20
And a second **t** I answered and said to Zec 4:12
but at evening **t** there shall be light. Zec 14:7
at the **t** of the deportation to Babylon. Mt 1:11
from them what **t** the star had Mt 2:7
according to the **t** that he had Mt 2:16
From that **t** Jesus began to preach, Mt 4:17
come here to torment us before the **t**?" Mt 8:29
At that **t** Jesus declared, "I thank you, Mt 11:25
At that **t** Jesus went through the Mt 12:1
and at harvest **t** I will tell the reapers, Mt 13:30
At that **t** Herod the tetrarch heard about Mt 14:1
but the boat by this **t** was a long way Mt 14:24
From that **t** Jesus began to show his Mt 16:21
At that **t** the disciples came to Jesus, Mt 18:1
to give them their food at the proper **t**? Mt 24:45
Now after a long **t** the master of those Mt 25:19
'The Teacher says, My **t** is at hand. Mt 26:18
Again, for the second **t**, he went away Mt 26:42
he went away and prayed for the third **t**, Mt 26:44
and saying, "The **t** is fulfilled, and the Mk 1:15
God, in the **t** of Abiathar the high priest, Mk 2:26
receive a hundredfold now in this **t**, Mk 10:30
you do not know when the **t** will come. Mk 13:33
he came the third **t** and said to them, Mk 14:41
the rooster crowed a second **t**. Mk 14:72
followed all things closely for some **t** past, Lk 1:3
words, which will be fulfilled in their **t**." Lk 1:20
And when his **t** of service was ended, he Lk 1:23
Now the **t** came for Elizabeth to give Lk 1:57
there, the **t** came for her to give birth. Lk 2:6
And when the **t** came for their Lk 2:22
kingdoms of the world in a moment of **t**, Lk 4:5
departed from him until an opportune **t**. Lk 4:13
in Israel in the **t** of the prophet Elisha, Lk 4:27
but from the **t** I came in she has not Lk 7:45
for a while, and in **t** of testing fall away. Lk 8:13
For a long **t** he had worn no clothes, and Lk 8:27
man. (For many a **t** it had seized him. Lk 8:29
their portion of food at the proper **t**? Lk 12:42
know how to interpret the present **t**? Lk 12:56
present at that very **t** who told him Lk 13:1
And at the **t** for the banquet he sent his Lk 14:17
not receive many times more in this **t**, Lk 18:30
did not know the **t** of your visitation." Lk 19:44
When the **t** came, he sent a servant to Lk 20:10
saying, 'I am he!' and, 'The **t** is at hand!' Lk 21:8
who was himself in Jerusalem at that **t**. Lk 23:7
A third **t** he said to them, "Why, what Lk 23:22
he enter a second **t** into his mother's Jn 3:4
that he had already been there a long **t**, Jn 5:6
Jesus said to them, "My **t** has not yet come, Jn 7:6
not yet come, but your **t** is always here. Jn 7:6
this feast, for my **t** has not yet fully come." Jn 7:8
So for the second **t** they called the man Jn 9:24
At that **t** the Feast of Dedication took Jn 10:22
"Lord, by this **t** there will be an odor, Jn 11:39
was now the third **t** that Jesus was Jn 21:14
He said to him a second **t**, "Simon, son Jn 21:16
He said to him the third **t**, "Simon, son Jn 21:17
because he said to him the third **t**, Jn 21:17
will you at this **t** restore the kingdom to Acts 1:6
us during all the **t** that the Lord Jesus Acts 1:21
receive until the **t** for restoring all Acts 3:21
"But as the **t** of the promise drew near, Acts 7:17
At this **t** Moses was born; and he was Acts 7:20
because for a long **t** he had amazed Acts 8:11
voice came to him again a second **t**, Acts 10:15
answered a second **t** from heaven, Acts 11:9

About that **t** Herod the king laid Acts 12:1
Judea to Caesarea and spent **t** there. Acts 12:19
sun for a **t**." Immediately mist and Acts 13:11
So they remained for a long **t**, speaking Acts 14:3
remained no little **t** with the disciples. Acts 14:28
And after they had spent some **t**, they Acts 15:33
would spend their **t** in nothing except Acts 17:21
After spending some **t** there, he Acts 18:23
About that **t** there arose no little Acts 19:23
he might not have to spend **t** in Asia, Acts 20:16
among you the whole **t** from the first Acts 20:18
At the same **t** he hoped that money Acts 24:26
They have known for a long **t**, if they Acts 26:5
"In a short **t** would you persuade me Acts 26:28
Since much **t** had passed, and the Acts 27:9
had been without food for a long **t**, Acts 27:21
at the same **t** loosening the ropes that Acts 27:40
had waited a long **t** and saw no Acts 28:6
his righteousness at the present **t**, Rom 3:26
at the right **t** Christ died for the Rom 5:6
you getting at that **t** from the things of Rom 6:21
of this present **t** are not worth Rom 8:18
"About this **t** next year I will return and Rom 9:9
too at the present **t** there is a remnant, Rom 11:5
you were at one **t** disobedient to God Rom 11:30
Besides this you know the **t**, that the Rom 13:11
not pronounce judgment before the **t**, 1 Cor 4:5
perhaps by agreement for a limited **t**, 1 Cor 7:5
Was anyone at the **t** of his call 1 Cor 7:18
Was anyone at the **t** of his call 1 Cor 7:18
the appointed **t** has grown very short. 1 Cor 7:29
than five hundred brothers at one **t**, 1 Cor 15:6
I hope to spend some **t** with you, if the 1 Cor 16:7
"Yes, yes" and "No, no" at the same **t**? 2 Cor 1:17
says, "In a favorable **t** I listened to you, 2 Cor 6:2
you." Behold, now is the favorable **t**; 2 Cor 6:2
at the present **t** should supply their 2 Cor 8:14
Here for the third **t** I am ready to 2 Cor 12:14
This is the third **t** I am coming to 2 Cor 13:1
But when the fullness of **t** had come, God Gal 4:4
But just as at that **t** he who was born Gal 4:29
as a plan for the fullness of **t**, to unite Eph 1:10
remember that at one **t** you Gentiles in Eph 2:11
were at that **t** separated from Christ, Eph 2:12
for at one **t** you were darkness, but now Eph 5:8
making the best use of the **t**, because Eph 5:16
At the same **t**, pray also for us, that God Col 4:3
outsiders, making the best use of the **t**. Col 4:5
from you, brothers, for a short **t**, 1 Thes 2:17
so that he may be revealed in his **t**. 2 Thes 2:6
is the testimony given at the proper **t**. 1 Tm 2:6
will display at the proper **t**—he who is 1 Tm 6:15
For the **t** is coming when people will 2 Tm 4:3
and the **t** of my departure has come. 2 Tm 4:6
and at the proper **t** manifested in his word Ti 1:3
At the same **t**, prepare a guest room Phlm 1:22
and find grace to help in **t** of need. Heb 4:16
For though by this **t** you ought to be Heb 5:12
imposed until the **t** of reformation. Heb 9:10
sins of many, will appear a second **t**, Heb 9:28
had offered for all **t** a single sacrifice Heb 10:12
waiting from that **t** until his enemies Heb 10:13
has perfected for all **t** those who are Heb 10:14
For **t** would fail me to tell of Gideon, Heb 11:32
us for a short **t** as it seemed best Heb 12:10
At that **t** his voice shook the earth, Heb 12:26
appears for a little **t** and then vanishes. Jas 4:14
ready to be revealed in the last **t**. 1 Pt 1:5
inquiring what person or **t** the Spirit of 1 Pt 1:11
with fear throughout the **t** of your exile, 1 Pt 1:17
for the rest of the **t** in the flesh no longer 1 Pt 4:2
The **t** that is past suffices for doing what 1 Pt 4:3
For it is **t** for judgment to begin at the 1 Pt 4:17
so that at the proper **t** he may exalt you, 1 Pt 5:6
be able at any **t** to recall these things. 2 Pt 1:15
At the same **t**, it is a new commandment 1 Jn 2:8
you, "In the last **t** there will be scoffers, Jude 1:18
before all **t** and now and forever. Jude 1:25
keep what is written in it, for the **t** is near. Rv 1:3
I gave her **t** to repent, but she refuses to Rv 2:21
and the **t** for the dead to be judged, Rv 11:18
because he knows that his **t** is short!" Rv 12:12
where she is to be nourished for a **t**, Rv 12:14
for a time, and times, and half a **t**. Rv 12:14
prophecy of this book, for the **t** is near. Rv 22:10

TIMES (147)

For he has cheated me these two **t**. Gn 27:36
me and changed my wages ten **t**. Gn 31:7
and you have changed my wages ten **t**. Gn 31:41
bowing himself to the ground seven **t**, Gn 33:3
portion was five **t** as much as Gn 43:34
And let them judge the people at all **t**. Ex 18:22
And they judged the people at all **t**. Any Ex 18:26
"Three **t** in the year you shall keep a Ex 23:14
Three **t** in the year shall all your males Ex 23:17

Three **t** in the year shall all your males Ex 34:23
the LORD your God three **t** in the year. Ex 34:24
part of the blood seven **t** before the LORD in Lv 4:6
and sprinkle it seven **t** before the LORD in Lv 4:17
sprinkled some of it on the altar seven **t**, Lv 8:11
shall sprinkle it seven **t** on him who is Lv 14:7
with his finger seven **t** before the LORD. Lv 14:16
in his left hand seven **t** before the LORD. Lv 14:27
water and sprinkle the house seven **t**. Lv 14:51
of the blood with his finger seven **t**. Lv 16:14
the blood on it with his finger seven **t**, Lv 16:19
shall proclaim as **t** of holy Lv 23:37
seven weeks of years, seven **t** seven years, Lv 25:8
the test these ten **t** and have not Nm 14:22
the front of the tent of meeting seven **t**. Nm 19:4
you have struck me these three **t**?" Nm 22:28
you struck your donkey these three **t**? Nm 22:32
turned aside before me these three **t**. Nm 22:33
bless Israel, he did not go, as at other **t**, Nm 24:1
you have blessed them these three **t**. Nm 24:10
make you a thousand **t** as many as you Dt 1:11
"Three **t** a year all your males shall Dt 16:16
children ask their fathers in **t** to come, Jos 4:21
you shall march around the city seven **t**, Jos 6:4
the city in the same manner seven **t**. Jos 6:15
they marched around the city seven **t**. Jos 6:15
You have mocked me these three **t**, and Jgs 16:15
out as at other **t** and shake myself free." Jgs 16:20
in array against Gibeah, as at other **t**. Jgs 20:30
And as at other **t** they began to strike Jgs 20:31
custom in former **t** in Israel concerning Ru 4:7
came and stood, calling as at other **t**, 1 Sm 3:10
The king sat on his seat, as at other **t**, 1 Sm 20:25
face to the ground and bowed three **t**. 1 Sm 20:41
In **t** past, when Saul was king over us, it 2 Sm 5:2
said, "They used to say in former **t**, 2 Sm 20:18
the people a hundred **t** as many as 2 Sm 24:3
Three **t** a year Solomon used to offer 1 Kgs 9:25
upon the child three **t** and cried to 1 Kgs 17:21
And he said, "Go again," seven **t**. 1 Kgs 18:43
"How many **t** shall I make you 1 Kgs 22:16
The child sneezed seven **t**, and the 2 Kgs 4:35
"Go and wash in the Jordan seven **t**, 2 Kgs 5:10
dipped himself seven **t** in the Jordan, 2 Kgs 5:14
And he struck three **t** and stopped. 2 Kgs 13:18
should have struck five or six **t**; 2 Kgs 13:19
will strike down Syria only three **t**." 2 Kgs 13:19
Three **t** Joash defeated him and 2 Kgs 13:25
In **t** past, even when Saul was king, it 1 Chr 11:2
who had understanding of the **t**, 1 Chr 12:32
his people a hundred **t** as many as 1 Chr 21:3
In those **t** there was no peace to him 2 Chr 15:5
"How many **t** shall I make you 2 Chr 18:15
foreign wives come at appointed **t**, Ezr 10:14
from all directions and said to us ten **t**, Neh 4:12
And they sent to me four **t** in this way, Neh 6:4
and many **t** you delivered them Neh 9:28
to our fathers' houses, at **t** appointed, Neh 10:34
for the wood offering at appointed **t**, Neh 13:31
men who knew the **t** (for this was the Est 1:13
not answer him once in a thousand **t**. Jb 9:3
These ten **t** you have cast reproach upon Jb 19:3
"Why are not **t** of judgment kept by the Jb 24:1
Will he call upon God at all **t**? Jb 27:10
God does all these things, twice, three **t**, Jb 33:29
the oppressed, a stronghold in **t** of trouble. Ps 9:9
do you hide yourself in **t** of trouble? Ps 10:1
His ways prosper at all **t**; your judgments Ps 10:5
a furnace on the ground, purified seven **t**. Ps 12:6
My **t** are in your hand; rescue me from Ps 31:15
I will bless the LORD at all **t**; his praise Ps 34:1
they are not put to shame in evil **t**; in Ps 37:19
Why should I fear in **t** of trouble, when Ps 49:5
Trust in him at all **t**, O people; pour out Ps 62:8
justice, who do righteousness at all **t**! Ps 106:3
Many **t** he delivered them, but they Ps 106:43
with longing for your rules at all **t**. Ps 119:20
Seven **t** a day I praise you for your Ps 119:164
her breasts fill you at all **t** with delight; Prv 5:19
A friend loves at all **t**, and a brother is Prv 17:17
righteous falls seven **t** and rises again, Prv 24:16
the wicked stumble in **t** of calamity. Prv 24:16
knows that many **t** you have yourself Eccl 7:22
does evil a hundred **t** and prolongs his Eccl 8:12
and he will be the stability of your **t**, Is 33:6
and from ancient **t** things not yet Is 46:10
the stork in the heavens knows her **t**, Jer 8:7
and me from ancient **t** prophesied war, Jer 28:8
now, and he prophesies of **t** far off.' Ezk 12:27
sword come down twice, yes, three **t**, Ezk 21:14
to be inhabited as in your former **t**, Ezk 36:11
he found them ten **t** better than all the Dn 1:20
corrupt words before me till the **t** change. Dn 2:9
He changes **t** and seasons; he removes Dn 2:21
the furnace heated seven **t** more than it Dn 3:19
on his knees three **t** a day and prayed Dn 6:10
but makes his petition three **t** a day." Dn 6:13
and ten thousand **t** ten thousand stood Dn 7:10
shall think to change the **t** and the law; Dn 7:25
his hand for a time, **t**, and half a time. Dn 7:25
her, and he who supported her in those **t**. Dn 11:6
"In those **t** many shall rise against the Dn 11:14
it would be for a time, **t**, and half a time, Dn 12:7
you cannot interpret the signs of the **t**. Mt 16:3
I forgive him? As many as seven **t**?" Mt 18:21
said to him, "I do not say to you seven **t**, Mt 18:22
to you seven times, but seventy **t** seven. Mt 18:22
crows, you will deny me three **t**." Mt 26:34
will deny me three **t**." And he went out Mt 26:75
crows twice, you will deny me three **t**." Mk 14:30
will deny me three **t**." And he broke Mk 14:72
if he sins against you seven **t** in the day, Lk 17:4
in the day, and turns to you seven **t**, Lk 17:4
will not receive many **t** more in this Lk 18:30
until the **t** of the Gentiles are fulfilled. Lk 21:24
But stay awake at all **t**, praying that Lk 21:36
until you deny three **t** that you know Lk 22:34
crows today, you will deny me three **t**." Lk 22:61
not crow till you have denied me three **t**. Jn 13:38
not for you to know **t** or seasons that the Acts 1:7
that **t** of refreshing may come from the Acts 3:20
This happened three **t**, and the thing Acts 10:16
This happened three **t**, and all was Acts 11:10
The **t** of ignorance God overlooked, Acts 17:30
all sufficiency in all things at all **t**, 2 Cor 9:8
Five **t** I received at the hands of the 2 Cor 11:24
Three **t** I was beaten with rods. Once 2 Cor 11:25
Three **t** I was shipwrecked; a night 2 Cor 11:25
Three **t** I pleaded with the Lord about 2 Cor 12:8
praying at all **t** in the Spirit, with all Eph 6:18
Now concerning the **t** and the 1 Thes 5:1
give you peace at all **t** in every way. 2 Thes 3:16
says that in later **t** some will depart 1 Tm 4:1
last days there will come **t** of difficulty. 2 Tm 3:1
Long ago, at many **t** and in many ways, Heb 1:1
manifest in the last **t** for your sake, 1 Pt 1:20
was twice ten thousand **t** ten thousand; Rv 9:16
she is to be nourished for a time, and **t**, Rv 12:14

TIMID (1)
therefore I was **t** and afraid to declare my Jb 32:6

TIMNA (6)
(**T** was a concubine of Eliphaz, Esau's Gn 36:12
and Hemam; and Lotan's sister was **T**. Gn 36:22
names: the chiefs **T**, Alvah, Jetheth, Gn 36:40
Zepho, Gatam, Kenaz, and of **T**, 1 Chr 1:36
Hemam; and Lotan's sister was **T**. 1 Chr 1:39
The chiefs of Edom were: chiefs **T**, 1 Chr 1:51

TIMNAH (12)
he went up to **T** to his sheepshearers, Gn 38:12
is going up to **T** to shear his sheep," Gn 38:13
to Enaim, which is on the road to **T**. Gn 38:14
Beth-shemesh and passes along by **T**. Jos 15:10
Kain, Gibeah, and **T**: ten cities with Jos 15:57
Elon, **T**, Ekron, Jos 19:43
Samson went down to **T**, and at Timnah Jgs 14:1
and at **T** he saw one of the daughters of Jgs 14:1
of the daughters of the Philistines at **T**. Jgs 14:2
down with his father and mother to **T**, Jgs 14:5
and they came to the vineyards of **T**. Jgs 14:5
with its villages, **T** with its villages, 2 Chr 28:18

TIMNATH-HERES (1)
the boundaries of his inheritance in **T**, Jgs 2:9

TIMNATH-SERAH (2)
T in the hill country of Ephraim. Jos 19:50
him in his own inheritance at **T**, Jos 24:30

TIMNITE (1)
said, "Samson, the son-in-law of the **T**, Jgs 15:6

TIMON (1)
and Prochorus, and Nicanor, and **T**, Acts 6:5

TIMOTHY (25)
A disciple was there, named **T**, the son Acts 16:1
Paul wanted **T** to accompany him, Acts 16:3
sea, but Silas and **T** remained there. Acts 17:14
command for Silas and **T** to come to Acts 17:15
When Silas and **T** arrived from Acts 18:5
two of his helpers, **T** and Erastus, Acts 19:22
Secundus; and Gaius of Derbe, and **T**; Acts 20:4
T, my fellow worker, greets you; so do Rom 16:21
That is why I sent you **T**, my beloved 1 Cor 4:17
When **T** comes, see that you put 1 Cor 16:10
by the will of God, and **T** our brother, 2 Cor 1:1
among you, Silvanus and **T** and I, 2 Cor 1:19
Paul and **T**, servants of Christ Jesus, To Phil 1:1
in the Lord Jesus to send **T** to you soon, Phil 2:19
by the will of God, and **T** our brother, Col 1:1
Paul, Silvanus, and **T**, To the church 1 Thes 1:1
and we sent **T**, our brother and God's 1 Thes 3:2
But now that **T** has come to us from 1 Thes 3:6
Paul, Silvanus, and **T**, To the church 2 Thes 1:1
To **T**, my true child in the faith: Grace, 1 Tm 1:2
charge I entrust to you, **T**, my child, 1 Tm 1:18
O **T**, guard the deposit entrusted to 1 Tm 6:20
To **T**, my beloved child: Grace, mercy, 2 Tm 1:2
for Christ Jesus, and **T** our brother, Phlm 1:1
that our brother **T** has been released, Heb 13:23

TIMOTHY'S (1)
But you know **T** proven worth, how as Phil 2:22

TIN (4)
the silver, the bronze, the iron, the **t**, Nm 31:22
them are bronze and **t** and iron and Ezk 22:18
and iron and lead and **t** into a furnace, Ezk 22:20
t, and lead they exchanged for your Ezk 27:12

TINDER (1)
And the strong shall become **t**, and his Is 1:31

TINGLE (3)
ears of everyone who hears it will **t**. 1 Sm 3:11
of everyone who hears of it will **t**. 2 Kgs 21:12
the ears of everyone who hears of it will **t**. Jer 19:3

TINKLING (1)
along as they go, **t** with their feet, Is 3:16

TIP (7)
and put it on the **t** of the right ear of Ex 29:20
LORD reached out the **t** of the staff that Jgs 6:21
so he put out the **t** of the staff that 1 Sm 14:27
little honey with the **t** of the staff that 1 Sm 14:43
ten cubits from the **t** of one wing to 1 Kgs 6:24
tip of one wing to the **t** of the other. 1 Kgs 6:24
and touched the **t** of the scepter. Est 5:2

TIPHSAH (2)
west of the Euphrates from **T** to Gaza, 1 Kgs 4:24
time Menahem sacked **T** and all 2 Kgs 15:16

TIPS (1)
of Aaron and on the **t** of the right ears Ex 29:20

TIRAS (2)
Madai, Javan, Tubal, Meshech, and **T**. Gn 10:2
Madai, Javan, Tubal, Meshech, and **T**. 1 Chr 1:5

TIRATHITES (1)
the scribes who lived at Jabez: the **T**, 1 Chr 2:55

TIRED (1)
they have **t** themselves out but profit Jer 12:13

TIRHAKAH (2)
king heard concerning **T** king of 2 Kgs 19:9
king heard concerning **T** king of Cush, Is 37:9

TIRHANAH (1)
concubine, bore Sheber and **T**. 1 Chr 2:48

TIRIA (1)
Ziph, Ziphah, **T**, and Asarel. 1 Chr 4:16

TIRZAH (18)
Noah, Hoglah, Milcah, and **T**. Nm 26:33
Mahlah, Noah, Hoglah, Milcah, and **T**. Nm 27:1
for Mahlah, **T**, Hoglah, Milcah, and Nm 36:11
the king of **T**, one: in all, thirty-one Jos 12:24
Mahlah, Noah, Hoglah, Milcah, and **T**. Jos 17:3
arose and departed and came to **T**. 1 Kgs 14:17
building Ramah, and he lived in **T**. 1 Kgs 15:21
began to reign over all Israel at **T**, 1 Kgs 15:33
with his fathers and was buried at **T**, 1 Kgs 16:6
began to reign over Israel in **T**, 1 Kgs 16:8
When he was at **T**, drinking himself 1 Kgs 16:9
who was over the household in **T**, 1 Kgs 16:9
Zimri reigned seven days in **T**. 1 Kgs 16:15
with him, and they besieged **T**. 1 Kgs 16:17
years; six years he reigned in **T**. 1 Kgs 16:23
Gadi came up from **T** and came to 2 Kgs 15:14
in it and its territory from **T** on, 2 Kgs 15:16
You are beautiful as **T**, my love, lovely as Sg 6:4

TISHBE (1)
Elijah the Tishbite, of **T** in Gilead, 1 Kgs 17:1

TISHBITE (6)
Now Elijah the **T**, of Tishbe in 1 Kgs 17:1
of the LORD came to Elijah the **T**, 1 Kgs 21:17
of the LORD came to Elijah the **T**, 1 Kgs 21:28
angel of the LORD said to Elijah the **T**, 2 Kgs 1:3
waist." And he said, "It is Elijah the **T**." 2 Kgs 1:8
he spoke by his servant Elijah the **T**, 2 Kgs 9:36

TITHE (22)
"Every **t** of the land, whether of the seed Lv 27:30
If a man wishes to redeem some of his **t**, Lv 27:31
And every **t** of herds and flocks, every Lv 27:32
I have given every **t** in Israel for an Nm 18:21
For the **t** of the people of Israel, which Nm 18:24
people of Israel the **t** that I have given Nm 18:26
from it to the LORD, a **t** of the tithe. Nm 18:26
from it to the LORD, a tithe of the **t**. Nm 18:26

within your towns the **t** of your grain or Dt 12:17
"You shall **t** all the yield of your seed Dt 14:22
there, you shall eat the **t** of your grain, Dt 14:23
so that you are not able to carry the **t**, Dt 14:24
bring out all the **t** of your produce in Dt 14:28
paying all the **t** of your produce Dt 26:12
not eaten of the **t** while I was mourning, Dt 26:14
in abundantly the **t** of everything. 2 Chr 31:5
also brought in the **t** of cattle and 2 Chr 31:6
and the **t** of the dedicated things that 2 Chr 31:6
shall bring up the **t** of the tithes to Neh 10:38
all Judah brought the **t** of the grain, Neh 13:12
For you **t** mint and dill and cumin, Mt 23:23
For you **t** mint and rue and every herb, Lk 11:42

TITHES (19)
to the LORD from all your **t**, Nm 18:28
your **t** and the contribution that you Dt 12:6
your **t** and the contribution that you Dt 12:11
brought in the contributions, the **t**, 2 Chr 31:12
to the Levites the **t** from our ground, Neh 10:37
Levites who collect the **t** in all our Neh 10:37
Levites when the Levites receive the **t**. Neh 10:38
up the tithe of the **t** to the house of our Neh 10:38
the firstfruits, and the **t**, Neh 12:44
the vessels, and the **t** of grain, Neh 13:5
every morning, your **t** every three days; Am 4:4
you?' In your **t** and contributions. Mal 3:8
Bring the full **t** into the storehouse, that Mal 3:10
twice a week; I give **t** of all that I get.' Lk 18:12
in the law to take **t** from the people, Heb 7:5
from them received **t** from Abraham Heb 7:6
In the one case **t** are received by mortal Heb 7:8
say that Levi himself, who receives **t**, Heb 7:9
receives tithes, paid **t** through Abraham, Heb 7:9

TITHING (1)
in the third year, which is the year of **t**, Dt 26:12

TITIUS (1)
to the house of a man named **T** Justus, Acts 18:7

TITUS (13)
I did not find my brother **T** there. 2 Cor 2:13
comforted us by the coming of **T**, 2 Cor 7:6
we rejoiced still more at the joy of **T**, 2 Cor 7:13
our boasting before **T** has proved 2 Cor 7:14
we urged **T** that as he had started, 2 Cor 8:6
into the heart of **T** the same earnest 2 Cor 8:16
As for **T**, he is my partner and fellow 2 Cor 8:23
I urged **T** to go, and sent the brother 2 Cor 12:18
him. Did **T** take advantage of you? 2 Cor 12:18
with Barnabas, taking **T** along with me. Gal 2:1
But even **T**, who was with me, was not Gal 2:3
has gone to Galatia, **T** to Dalmatia. 2 Tm 4:10
To **T**, my true child in a common faith: Ti 1:4

TIZITE (1)
Shimri, and Joha his brother, the **T**, 1 Chr 11:45

TOAH (1)
son of Jeroham, son of Eliel, son of **T**, 1 Chr 6:34

TOB (4)
his brothers and lived in the land of **T**, Jgs 11:3
to bring Jephthah from the land of **T**. Jgs 11:5
with 1,000 men, and the men of **T**, 2 Sm 10:6
and the men of **T** and Maacah were 2 Sm 10:8

TOBADONIJAH (1)
Adonijah, Tobijah, and **T**; 2 Chr 17:8

TOBIAH (15)
the sons of Delaiah, the sons of **T**, and Ezr 2:60
when Sanballat the Horonite and **T**, Neh 2:10
the Horonite and **T** the Ammonite Neh 2:19
T the Ammonite was beside him, and Neh 4:3
when Sanballat and **T** and the Arabs Neh 4:7
when Sanballat and **T** and Geshem the Neh 6:1
against me because **T** and Sanballat Neh 6:12
Remember **T** and Sanballat, O my Neh 6:14
nobles of Judah sent many letters to **T**, Neh 6:17
And **T** sent letters to make me afraid. Neh 6:19
the sons of Delaiah, the sons of **T**, the Neh 7:62
of our God, and who was related to **T**, Neh 13:4
prepared for **T** a large chamber where Neh 13:5
the evil that Eliashib had done for **T**, Neh 13:7
the household furniture of **T** out of the Neh 13:8

TOBIAH'S (1)
to Tobiah, and **T** letters came to them. Neh 6:17

TOBIJAH (3)
Adonijah, **T**, and Tobadonijah; 2 Chr 17:8
from the exiles Heldai, **T**, and Jedaiah, Zec 6:10
as a reminder to Helem, **T**, Jedaiah, Zec 6:14

TOCHEN (1)
Etam, Ain, Rimmon, **T**, and Ashan, 1 Chr 4:32

TODAY (173)
you have driven me **t** away from the Gn 4:14
me, and I have not heard of it until **t**." Gn 21:26
grant me success **t** and show steadfast Gn 24:12
"I came **t** to the spring and said, 'O Gn 24:42
let me pass through all your flock **t**, Gn 30:32
you and me **t**." Therefore he named Gn 31:48
"Why are your faces downcast **t**?" Gn 40:7
to Pharaoh, "I remember my offenses **t**. Gn 41:9
should be kept alive, as they are **t**. Gn 50:20
it that you have come home so soon **t**?" Ex 2:18
task of making bricks **t** and yesterday, Ex 5:14
T, in the month of Abib, you are going Ex 13:4
the LORD, which he will work for you **t**. Ex 14:13
For the Egyptians whom you see **t**, you Ex 14:13
Moses said, "Eat it **t**, for today is a Ex 16:25
it today, for **t** is a Sabbath to the LORD; Ex 16:25
LORD; **t** you will not find it in the field. Ex 16:25
and consecrate them **t** and tomorrow, Ex 19:10
"**T** you have been ordained for the Ex 32:29
As has been done **t**, the LORD has Lv 8:34
with oil, for **t** the LORD will appear to you.'" Lv 9:4
t they have offered their sin offering Lv 10:19
If I had eaten the sin offering **t**, would Lv 10:19
you are **t** as numerous as the stars of Dt 1:10
who **t** have no knowledge of good or evil, Dt 1:39
'**T** you are to cross the border of Moab at Dt 2:18
fast to the LORD your God are all alive **t**. Dt 4:4
as all this law that I set before you **t**? Dt 4:8
and earth to witness against you **t**, Dt 4:26
know therefore **t**, and lay it to your heart, Dt 4:39
which I command you **t**, Dt 4:40
the rules that I speak in your hearing **t**, Dt 5:1
but with us, who are all of us here alive **t**. Dt 5:3
that I command you **t** shall be on your Dt 6:6
and the rules that I command you **t**. Dt 7:11
that I command you **t** you shall be Dt 8:1
his statutes, which I command you **t**, Dt 8:11
I solemnly warn you **t** that you shall Dt 8:19
you are to cross over the Jordan **t**, to go in Dt 9:1
Know therefore **t** that he who goes over Dt 9:3
I am commanding you **t** for your good? Dt 10:13
And consider **t** (since I am not speaking Dt 11:2
commandment that I command you **t**, Dt 11:8
commandments that I command you **t**, Dt 11:13
am setting before you **t** a blessing and a Dt 11:26
your God, which I command you **t**, Dt 11:27
the way that I am commanding you **t**, Dt 11:28
the rules that I am setting before you **t**. Dt 11:32
according to all that we are doing here **t**, Dt 12:8
that I am commanding you **t**, Dt 13:18
commandment that I command you **t**. Dt 15:5
you; therefore I command you this **t**. Dt 15:15
which I command you **t**, Dt 19:9
t you are drawing near for battle against Dt 20:3
'I declare **t** to the LORD your God that I Dt 26:3
You have declared **t** that the LORD is Dt 26:17
the LORD has declared **t** that you are a Dt 26:18
commandment that I command you **t**. Dt 27:1
concerning which I command you **t**, Dt 27:4
his statutes, which I command you **t**." Dt 27:10
commandments that I command you **t**, Dt 28:1
your God, which I command you **t**, Dt 28:13
any of the words that I command you **t**, Dt 28:14
and his statutes that I command you **t**, Dt 28:15
"You are standing **t** all of you before the Dt 29:10
LORD your God is making with you **t**, Dt 29:12
he may establish you **t** as his people, Dt 29:13
standing here with us **t** before the LORD Dt 29:15
and with whoever is not here with us **t**. Dt 29:15
heart is turning away **t** from the LORD Dt 29:18
his voice in all that I command you **t**, Dt 30:2
commandments that I command you **t**. Dt 30:8
that I command you **t** is not too hard Dt 30:11
I have set before you **t** life and good, Dt 30:15
LORD your God that I command you **t**, Dt 30:16
I declare to you **t**, that you shall surely Dt 30:18
and earth to witness against you **t**, Dt 30:19
he said to them, "I am 120 years old **t**. Dt 31:2
what they are inclined to do even **t**, Dt 31:21
even **t** while I am yet alive with you, Dt 31:27
words by which I am warning you **t**, Dt 32:46
"**T** I will begin to exalt you in the sight of Jos 3:7
"**T** I have rolled away the reproach of Jos 5:9
brings trouble on you **t**." And all Israel Jos 7:25
I am still as strong **t** as I was in the day Jos 14:11
against the LORD **t** then tomorrow he Jos 22:18
faith against the LORD, do not spare us **t** Jos 22:22
"**T** we know that the LORD is in our Jos 22:31
that **t** there should be one tribe lacking Jgs 21:3
said to her, "Where did you glean **t**? Ru 2:19
name with whom I worked **t** is Boaz." Ru 2:19
will not rest but will settle the matter **t**." Ru 3:18
LORD defeated us **t** before the 1 Sm 4:3
I fled from the battle **t**." And he said, 1 Sm 4:16
people have a sacrifice **t** on the high 1 Sm 9:12
high place, for **t** you shall eat with me, 1 Sm 9:19
When you depart from me **t**, you will 1 Sm 10:2
But **t** you have rejected your God, 1 Sm 10:19
for **t** the LORD has worked salvation 1 Sm 11:13
Is it not wheat harvest **t**? I will call 1 Sm 12:17
people had eaten freely **t** of the spoil 1 Sm 14:30
and see how this sin has arisen **t**. 1 Sm 14:38
to the meal, either yesterday or **t**?" 1 Sm 20:27
How much more **t** will their vessels be 1 Sm 21:5
Is **t** the first time that I have inquired 1 Sm 22:15
the LORD gave you **t** into my hand in 1 Sm 24:10
the LORD gave you into my hand **t**, 1 Sm 26:23
you made a raid **t**?" David would say, 1 Sm 27:10
yet you charge me **t** with a fault 2 Sm 3:8
And I was gentle **t**, though anointed 2 Sm 3:39
the king of Israel honored himself **t**, 2 Sm 6:20
uncovering himself **t** before the eyes 2 Sm 6:20
said to Uriah, "Remain here **t** also, 2 Sm 11:12
"**T** your servant knows that I have 2 Sm 14:22
and shall I **t** make you wander about 2 Sm 15:20
'**T** the house of Israel will give me 2 Sm 16:3
me with good for his cursing **t**." 2 Sm 16:12
to him, "You are not to carry news **t**. 2 Sm 18:20
day, but **t** you shall carry no news, 2 Sm 18:20
"You have **t** covered with shame the 2 Sm 19:5
made it clear **t** that commanders and 2 Sm 19:6
for **t** I know that if Absalom were 2 Sm 19:6
were alive and all of us were dead **t**, 2 Sm 19:6
to this people **t** and serve them, 1 Kgs 12:7
cut off the house of Jeroboam **t**. 1 Kgs 14:14
I will surely show myself to him **t**." 1 Kgs 18:15
"Do you know that **t** the LORD will take 2 Kgs 2:3
"Do you know that **t** the LORD will take 2 Kgs 2:5
he said, "Why will you go to him **t**? 2 Kgs 4:23
'Give your son, that we may eat him **t**, 2 Kgs 6:28
Shaphat remains on his shoulders **t**." 2 Kgs 6:31
and my rules, as he is **t**.' 1 Chr 28:7
consecrating himself **t** to the LORD?" 1 Chr 29:5
plundering, and to utter shame, as it is **t**. Ezr 9:7
left a remnant that has escaped, as it is **t**. Ezr 9:15
and give success to your servant **t**, Neh 1:11
king and Haman come **t** to a feast that Est 5:4
"**T** also my complaint is bitter; my hand Jb 23:2
"You are my Son; **t** I have begotten you. Ps 2:7
of his hand. **T**, if you hear his voice, Ps 95:7
sacrifices, and **t** I have paid my vows; Prv 7:14
I have made them known to you **t**, Prv 22:19
before **t** you have never heard of them, Is 48:7
to you, from the days of Josiah until **t**. Jer 36:2
I release you **t** from the chains on your Jer 40:4
t I declare that I will restore to you Zec 9:12
which **t** is alive and tomorrow is thrown Mt 6:30
And in the morning, 'It will be stormy **t**, Mt 16:3
'Son, go and work in the vineyard **t**.' Mt 21:28
much because of him **t** in a dream." Mt 27:19
"**T** this Scripture has been fulfilled in Lk 4:21
"We have seen extraordinary things **t**." Lk 5:26
the grass, which is alive in the field **t**, Lk 12:28
and perform cures **t** and tomorrow, Lk 13:32
go on my way **t** and tomorrow and the Lk 13:33
down, for I must stay at your house **t**." Lk 19:5
"**T** salvation has come to this house, Lk 19:9
said to him, "Before the rooster crows **t**, Lk 22:61
you, **t** you will be with me in Paradise." Lk 23:43
are being examined **t** concerning a Acts 4:9
are my Son, **t** I have begotten you.' Acts 13:33
of being charged with rioting **t**, Acts 19:40
to make my defense **t** against all the Acts 26:2
"**T** is the fourteenth day that you Acts 27:33
are my Son, **t** I have begotten you"? Heb 1:5
Spirit says, "**T**, if you hear his voice, Heb 3:7
long as it is called "**t**," that none of you Heb 3:13
As it is said, "**T**, if you hear his voice, Heb 3:15
"**T**," saying through David so long Heb 4:7
already quoted, "**T**, if you hear his voice, Heb 4:7
"You are my Son, **t** I have begotten you"; Heb 5:5
is the same yesterday and **t** and forever. Heb 13:8
"**T** or tomorrow we will go into such Jas 4:13

TODAY'S (1)
the seer," for **t** "prophet" was formerly 1 Sm 9:9

TOE (5)
hand and on the big **t** of his right foot. Lv 8:23
hand and on the big **t** of his right foot. Lv 14:14
hand and on the big **t** of his right foot, Lv 14:17
hand and on the big **t** of his right foot. Lv 14:25
hand and on the big **t** of his right foot, Lv 14:28

TOES (8)
and on the great **t** of their right feet, Ex 29:20
hands and on the big **t** of their right feet. Lv 8:24
him and cut off his thumbs and his big **t**. Jgs 1:6
thumbs and their big **t** cut off used to Jgs 1:7
on each hand, and six **t** on each foot, 2 Sm 21:20
on each hand and six **t** on each foot, 1 Chr 20:6
And as you saw the feet and **t**, partly of Dn 2:41
And as the **t** of the feet were partly iron Dn 2:42

TOGARMAH (2)
of Gomer: Ashkenaz, Riphath, and **T**. Gn 10:3
of Gomer: Ashkenaz, Riphath, and **T**. 1 Chr 1:6

TOGETHER (340)
the heavens be gathered **t** into one place, Gn 1:9
that were gathered **t** he called Seas. Gn 1:10
sewed fig leaves **t** and made themselves Gn 3:7
and they went forth **t** from Ur of the Gn 11:31
not support both of them dwelling **t**; Gn 13:6
were so great that they could not dwell **t**, Gn 13:6
the knife. So they went both of them **t**. Gn 22:6
my son." So they went both of them **t**. Gn 22:8
and they arose and went **t** to Beersheba. Gn 22:19
The children struggled **t** within her, Gn 25:22
time for the livestock to be gathered **t**. Gn 29:7
the flocks are gathered **t** and the stone is Gn 29:8
So Laban gathered **t** all the people of Gn 29:22
were too great for them to dwell **t**. Gn 36:7
he put them all **t** in custody for three Gn 42:17
t with his daughter Dinah; Gn 46:15
his sons and said, "Gather yourselves **t**, Gn 49:1
behold, two Hebrews were struggling **t**. Ex 2:13
the elders of Israel **t** and say to them, Ex 3:16
Aaron went and gathered **t** all the elders Ex 4:29
And they gathered them **t** in heaps, and Ex 8:14
All the people answered **t** and said, "All Ex 19:8
"When men strive **t** and hit a pregnant Ex 21:22
and couple the tent **t** that it may be a Ex 26:11
two tenons in each frame, for fitting **t**. Ex 26:17
to its two edges, so that it may be joined **t**. Ex 28:7
people gathered themselves **t** to Aaron Ex 32:1
to couple the tent **t** that it might be Ex 36:18
Each frame had two tenons for fitting **t**. Ex 36:22
assembled the whole congregation **t**, Nm 1:18
t with the breast that is waved and the Nm 6:20
when the assembly is to be gathered **t**, Nm 10:7
fish of the sea be gathered **t** for them, Nm 11:22
who are gathered **t** against me: Nm 14:35
assembled themselves **t** against Moses Nm 16:3
all your company have gathered **t**. Nm 16:11
door of their tents, **t** with their wives, Nm 16:27
assembled themselves **t** against Moses Nm 20:2
gathered the assembly **t** before the Nm 20:10
said to Moses, "Gather the people **t**, Nm 21:16
gathered all his people **t** and went out Nm 21:23
Balaam, and he struck his hands **t**. Nm 24:10
and swallowed them up **t** with Korah, Nm 26:10
who gathered themselves **t** against the Nm 27:3
t with Phinehas the son of Eleazar the Nm 31:6
t with all the Arabah on the east side of Dt 4:49
not plow with an ox and a donkey **t**. Dt 22:10
wear cloth of wool and linen mixed **t**. Dt 22:11
"If brothers dwell **t**, and one of them dies Dt 25:5
were gathered, all the tribes of Israel **t**. Dt 33:5
in the city were called **t** to pursue them, Jos 8:16
they gathered **t** as one to fight against Jos 9:2
and came and encamped **t** at the waters Jos 11:5
t with the towns that were set apart for Jos 16:9
t with all the villages around these cities Jos 19:8
and the people of the East came **t**, Jgs 6:33
And all the leaders of Shechem came **t**, Jgs 9:6
the Tower of Shechem were gathered **t**. Jgs 9:47
And the people of Israel came **t**, and Jgs 10:17
all his people **t** and encamped at Jgs 11:20
the two of them sat and ate and drank **t**. Jgs 19:6
people of Benjamin came **t** out of the Jgs 20:14
Leah, who **t** built up the house of Israel. Ru 4:11
they sent and gathered **t** all the lords of 1 Sm 5:8
therefore and gathered **t** all the lords 1 Sm 5:11
elders of Israel gathered **t** and came to 1 Sm 8:4
called the people **t** to the LORD 1 Sm 10:17
so that no two of them were left **t**. 1 Sm 11:11
Give me a man, that we may fight **t**." 1 Sm 17:10
But his servants, **t** with the woman, 1 Sm 28:23
and all his men, on the same day **t**. 1 Sm 31:6
his opponent's side, so they fell down **t**. 2 Sm 2:16
gathered themselves **t** behind Abner 2 Sm 2:25
when he had gathered all the people **t**, 2 Sm 2:30
t with the silver and gold that he 2 Sm 8:11
by Israel, they gathered themselves **t**. 2 Sm 10:15
gathered all Israel **t** and crossed the 2 Sm 10:17
that his servants were whispering **t**, 2 Sm 12:19
of the people **t** and encamp against 2 Sm 12:28
gathered all the people **t** and went to 2 Sm 12:29
me and my son **t** from the heritage of 2 Sm 14:16
the men of Judah **t** to me within three 2 Sm 20:4
LORD, and the seven of them perished **t**. 2 Sm 21:9
David went down **t** with his servants, 2 Sm 21:15
The Philistines gathered **t** at Lehi, 2 Sm 23:11
sea, **t** with the servants of Solomon. 1 Kgs 9:27
Solomon gathered **t** chariots and 1 Kgs 10:26
t with certain Edomites of his 1 Kgs 11:17
gathered the prophets **t** at Mount 1 Kgs 18:20
king of Syria gathered all his army **t**. 1 Kgs 20:1
king of Israel gathered the prophets **t**, 1 Kgs 22:6
have surely fought **t** and struck one 2 Kgs 3:23
t with all the produce of the fields from 2 Kgs 8:6
t with the elders and the guardians, 2 Kgs 10:5
t with the rest of the multitude, 2 Kgs 25:11
three sons and all his house died **t**. 1 Chr 10:6
Then all Israel gathered **t** to David at 1 Chr 11:1
in his kingdom, **t** with all Israel, 1 Chr 11:10
And David gathered **t** the sons of 1 Chr 15:4
t with the silver and gold that he 1 Chr 18:11
gathered all Israel **t** and crossed the 1 Chr 19:17
commanded to gather **t** the resident 1 Chr 22:2
his sons, **t** with the palace officials, 1 Chr 28:1
Solomon gathered **t** chariots and 2 Chr 1:14
of the cherubim **t** extended twenty 2 Chr 3:11
they went to Ophir **t** with the servants 2 Chr 8:18
king of Israel gathered the prophets **t**, 2 Chr 18:5
t with fortified cities in Judah, 2 Chr 21:3
And Ahaz gathered **t** the vessels of 2 Chr 28:24
many people came **t** in Jerusalem to 2 Chr 30:13
whole assembly agreed **t** to keep the 2 Chr 30:23
people and gathered them **t** to him in 2 Chr 32:6
sent and gathered **t** all the elders 2 Chr 34:29
The whole assembly **t** was 42,360, Ezr 2:64
t with the rest of their kinsmen, Ezr 3:8
t supervised the workmen in the house of Ezr 3:9
the Levites had purified themselves **t**; Ezr 6:20
the wall was joined **t** to half its height, Neh 4:6
And they all plotted **t** to come and fight Neh 4:8
and let us meet **t** at Hakkephirim in the Neh 6:2
So now come and let us take counsel **t**." Neh 6:7
said, "Let us meet **t** in the house of God, Neh 6:10
The whole assembly **t** was 42,360, Neh 7:66
came **t** to Ezra the scribe in order to Neh 8:13
the singers gathered **t** from the Neh 12:28
And I gathered them **t** and set them in Neh 13:11
virgins were gathered **t** the second time, Est 2:19
also I am invited by her **t** with the king. Est 5:12
They made an appointment **t** to come to Jb 2:11
There the prisoners are at ease **t**; they Jb 3:18
him, that we should come to trial **t**. Jb 9:32
and knit me **t** with bones and sinews. Jb 10:11
I could join words **t** against you and Jb 16:4
they mass themselves **t** against me. Jb 16:10
Sheol? Shall we descend **t** into the dust?" Jb 17:16
His troops come on **t**; they have cast up Jb 19:12
they bray; under the nettles they huddle **t**. Jb 30:7
against me and its furrows have wept **t**, Jb 31:38
all flesh would perish **t**, and man would Jb 34:15
the morning stars sang **t** and all the sons Jb 38:7
into a mass and the clods stick fast **t**? Jb 38:38
Hide them all in the dust **t**; bind their Jb 40:13
cedar; the sinews of his thighs are knit **t**. Jb 40:17
The folds of his flesh stick **t**, firmly cast Jb 41:23
themselves, and the rulers take counsel **t**, Ps 2:2
aside; **t** they have become corrupt; Ps 14:3
as they scheme **t** against me, as they plot Ps 31:13
with me, and let us exalt his name **t**! Ps 34:3
gathered; they gathered **t** against me; Ps 35:15
All who hate me whisper **t** about me; Ps 41:7
the kings assembled; they came on **t**. Ps 48:4
both low and high, rich and poor **t**! Ps 49:2
fallen away; **t** they have become corrupt; Ps 53:3
We used to take sweet counsel **t**; within Ps 55:14
go up; they are **t** lighter than a breath. Ps 62:9
grain, they shout and sing **t** for joy. Ps 65:13
those who watch for my life consult **t** Ps 71:10
they consult **t** against your treasured Ps 83:3
flood all day long; they close in on me **t**. Ps 88:17
They band **t** against the life of the Ps 94:21
their hands; let the hills sing for joy **t** Ps 98:8
when peoples gather **t**, and kingdoms, Ps 102:22
—built as a city that is bound firmly **t**, Ps 122:3
you knitted me **t** in my mother's Ps 139:13
Young men and maidens **t**, old men Ps 148:12
The rich and the poor meet **t**; the LORD Prv 22:2
poor man and the oppressor meet **t**; Prv 29:13
stones, and a time to gather stones **t**; Eccl 3:5
Again, if two lie **t**, they keep warm, but Eccl 4:11
"Come now, let us reason **t**, says the LORD: Is 1:18
But rebels and sinners shall be broken **t**, Is 1:28
a spark, and both of them shall burn **t**, Is 1:31
Take counsel **t**, but it will come to Is 8:10
Manasseh; **t** they are against Judah. Is 9:21
calf and the lion and the fattened calf **t**; Is 11:6
shall graze; their young shall lie down **t**; Is 11:7
and **t** they shall plunder the people of the Is 11:14
of kingdoms, of nations gathering **t**! Is 13:4
All your leaders have fled **t**; without the Is 22:3
They will be gathered **t** as prisoners in a Is 24:22
low his pompous pride **t** with the skill of Is 25:11
against them, I would burn them up **t**. Is 27:4
helped will fall, and they will all perish **t**. Is 31:3
be revealed, and all flesh shall see it **t**, Is 40:5
speak; let us **t** draw near for judgment. Is 41:1
the cypress, the plane and the pine **t**, Is 41:19
know, may consider and understand **t**, Is 41:20
All the nations gather **t**, and the peoples Is 43:9
Put me in remembrance; let us argue **t**; Is 43:26
be terrified; they shall be put to shame **t**. Is 44:11
the makers of idols go in confusion **t**. Is 45:16
draw near **t**, you survivors of the Is 45:20
your case; let them take counsel **t**! Is 45:21
They stoop; they bow down **t**; they cannot Is 46:2
when I call to them, they stand forth **t**. Is 48:13
will contend with me? Let us stand up **t**. Is 50:8
they lift up their voice; **t** they sing for joy; Is 52:8
Break forth **t** into singing, you waste Is 52:9
see; they all gather **t**, they come to you; Is 60:4
iniquities and your fathers' iniquities **t**, Is 65:7
The wolf and the lamb shall graze **t**; the Is 65:25
and mice, shall come to an end **t**, Is 66:17
and **t** they shall come from the land of Jer 3:18
over to others, their fields and wives **t**, Jer 6:12
fathers and sons **t**, neighbor and friend Jer 6:21
Why do we sit still? Gather **t**; let us go Jer 8:14
one against another, fathers and sons **t**, Jer 13:14
And I will bring them **t** into the midst of Jer 21:4
of Judah, **t** with the officials of Judah, Jer 24:1
she who is in labor, **t**; a great company, Jer 31:8
and all its cities shall dwell there **t**, Jer 31:24
As they ate bread **t** there at Mizpah, Jer 41:1
warrior; they have both fallen **t**." Jer 46:12
calves; yes, they have turned and fled **t**; Jer 46:21
"Gather yourselves **t** and come against Jer 49:14
and the people of Judah shall come **t**, Jer 50:4
"They shall roar **t** like lions; they shall Jer 51:38
Babylon, **t** with the rest of the artisans. Jer 52:15
yoke; by his hand they were fastened **t**; Lam 1:14
and wall to lament; they languished **t**. Lam 2:8
field, and not be brought **t** or gathered. Ezk 29:5
your people who talk **t** about you by Ezk 33:30
a rattling, and the bones came **t**, Ezk 37:7
is able, **t** with a hin of oil to each ephah. Ezk 46:5
is able, **t** with a hin of oil to each ephah. Ezk 46:7
to give, **t** with a hin of oil to an ephah. Ezk 46:11
the holy portion **t** with the property of Ezk 48:20
and the gold, all **t** were broken in pieces, Dn 2:35
in marriage, but they will not hold **t**, Dn 2:43
king's counselors gathered **t** and saw Dn 3:27
limbs gave way, and his knees knocked **t**. Dn 5:6
given over to it **t** with the regular burnt Dn 8:12
children of Israel shall be gathered **t**, Hos 1:11
in wait for a man, so the priests band **t**; Hos 6:9
he and his princes **t**," says the LORD. Am 1:15
"Do two walk **t**, unless they have agreed Am 3:3
I will set them **t** like sheep in a fold, like Mi 2:12
evil desire of his soul; thus they weave it **t**. Mi 7:3
Gather **t**, yes, gather, O shameless nation, Zep 2:1
you in, at the time when I gather you **t**; Zep 3:20
from him every ruler—all of them **t**. Zec 10:4
before they came **t** she was found to be Mt 1:18
Let both grow **t** until the harvest, and Mt 13:30
What therefore God has joined **t**, let not Mt 19:6
silenced the Sadducees, they gathered **t**. Mt 22:34
while the Pharisees were gathered **t**, Mt 22:41
have gathered your children **t** as a hen Mt 23:37
and plotted **t** in order to arrest Jesus by Mt 26:4
and twisting **t** a crown of thorns, they Mt 27:29
whole city was gathered **t** at the door. Mk 1:33
And many were gathered **t**, so that there Mk 2:2
Jesus saw that a crowd came running **t**, Mk 9:25
What therefore God has joined **t**, let not Mk 10:9
and the elders and the scribes came **t**. Mk 14:53
and they called **t** the whole battalion. Mk 15:16
and twisting **t** a crown of thorns, Mk 15:17
Good measure, pressed down, shaken **t**, Lk 6:38
he called the twelve **t** and gave them Lk 9:1
the people had gathered **t** that they were Lk 12:1
have gathered your children **t** as a hen Lk 13:34
he calls **t** his friends and his neighbors, Lk 15:6
it, she calls **t** her friends and neighbors, Lk 15:9
There will be two women grinding **t**. Lk 17:35
middle of the courtyard and sat down **t**, Lk 22:55
of the elders of the people gathered **t**, Lk 22:66
Pilate then called **t** the chief priests and Lk 23:13
But they all cried out **t**, "Away with this Lk 23:18
they were talking and discussing **t**, Lk 24:15
those who were with them gathered **t**, Lk 24:33
so that sower and reaper may rejoice **t**. Jn 4:36
and in the temple, where all Jews come **t**. Jn 18:20
And the soldiers twisted **t** a crown of Jn 19:2
Both of them were running **t**, but the Jn 20:4
and two others of his disciples were **t**. Jn 21:2
So when they had come **t**, they asked Acts 1:6
t with the women and Mary the Acts 1:14
arrived, they were all **t** in one place. Acts 2:1
And at this sound the multitude came **t**, Acts 2:6
all who believed were **t** and had all Acts 2:44
attending the temple **t** and breaking Acts 2:46
all the people ran **t** to them in the Acts 3:11

and scribes gathered **t** in Jerusalem, Acts 4:5
they lifted their voices **t** to God and Acts 4:24
and the rulers were gathered **t**, Acts 4:26
there were gathered **t** against your holy Acts 4:27
they were gathered **t** was shaken, Acts 4:31
it that you have agreed **t** to test the Spirit Acts 5:9
they were all **t** in Solomon's Portico. Acts 5:12
they called **t** the council and all the Acts 5:21
stopped their ears and rushed **t** at him. Acts 7:57
and had called **t** his relatives and Acts 10:24
many were gathered **t** and were Acts 12:12
Iconium they entered **t** into the Jewish Acts 14:1
arrived and gathered the church **t**, Acts 14:27
elders were gathered **t** to consider this Acts 15:6
having gathered the congregation **t**, Acts 15:30
spoke to the women who had come **t**. Acts 16:13
the Lord, **t** with his entire household. Acts 18:8
brought their books **t** and burned Acts 19:19
These he gathered **t**, with the Acts 19:25
and they rushed **t** into the theater, Acts 19:29
did not know why they had come **t**. Acts 19:32
we were gathered **t** to break bread, Acts 20:7
was stirred up, and the people ran **t**. Acts 21:30
So when they came **t** here, I made no Acts 25:17
three days he called **t** the local leaders Acts 28:17
aside; **t** they have become worthless; Rom 3:12
has been groaning **t** in the pains Rom 8:22
love God all things work **t** for good, Rom 8:28
that **t** you may with one voice glorify Rom 15:6
to strive **t** with me in your prayers to Rom 15:30
called to be saints **t** with all those who 1 Cor 1:2
but then come **t** again, so that Satan 1 Cor 7:5
because when you come **t** it is not 1 Cor 11:17
place, when you come **t** as a church, 1 Cor 11:18
When you come **t**, it is not the 1 Cor 11:20
brothers, when you come **t** to eat, 1 Cor 11:33
that when you come **t** it will not be 1 Cor 11:34
If one member suffers, all suffer **t**; if 1 Cor 12:26
one member is honored, all rejoice **t**. 1 Cor 12:26
whole church comes **t** and all speak 1 Cor 14:23
When you come **t**, each one has a 1 Cor 14:26
t with the church in their house, 1 Cor 16:19
Working **t** with him, then, we appeal 2 Cor 6:1
our hearts, to die **t** and to live together. 2 Cor 7:3
our hearts, to die together and to live **t**. 2 Cor 7:3
made us alive **t** with Christ—by grace Eph 2:5
the whole structure, being joined **t**, Eph 2:21
also are being built **t** into a dwelling Eph 2:22
joined and held **t** by every joint with Eph 4:16
me in the gospel **t** with Clement and the Phil 4:3
all things, and in him all things hold **t**. Col 1:17
may be encouraged, being knit **t** in love, Col 2:2
your flesh, God made alive **t** with him, Col 2:13
nourished and knit **t** through its joints Col 2:19
which binds everything **t** in perfect Col 3:14
will be caught up **t** with them in the 1 Thes 4:17
and our being gathered **t** to him, 2 Thes 2:1
not neglecting to meet **t**, as is the Heb 10:25
as kings for one hour, **t** with the beast. Rv 17:12

TOHU (1)
son of Jeroham, son of Elihu, son of **T**, 1 Sm 1:1

TOI (3)
When **T** king of Hamath heard that 2 Sm 8:9
T sent his son Joram to King David, to 2 Sm 8:10
had often been at war with **T**. 2 Sm 8:10

TOIL (48)
and from the painful **t** of our hands." Gn 5:29
our voice and saw our affliction, our **t**, Dt 26:7
Do not make the whole people **t** up there, Jos 7:3
axes and made them **t** at the brick 2 Sm 12:31
the fruit of his **t** and will not swallow Jb 20:18
in the desert the poor go out to their **t**, Jb 24:5
yet their span is but **t** and trouble; Ps 90:10
possession of the fruit of the peoples' **t**, Ps 105:44
strangers plunder the fruits of his **t**! Ps 109:11
to rest, eating the bread of anxious **t**; Ps 127:2
In all **t** there is profit, but mere talk Prv 14:23
Do not **t** to acquire wealth; be Prv 23:4
man gain by all the **t** at which he toils Eccl 1:3
my heart found pleasure in all my **t**, Eccl 2:10
and this was my reward for all my **t**. Eccl 2:10
had done and the **t** I had expended in Eccl 2:11
I hated all my **t** in which I toil under Eccl 2:18
all my toil in which I **t** under the sun, Eccl 2:18
despair over all the **t** of my labors Eccl 2:20
by someone who did not **t** for it. Eccl 2:21
man from all the **t** and striving of Eccl 2:22
and drink and find enjoyment in his **t**. Eccl 2:24
What gain has the worker from his **t**? Eccl 3:9
take pleasure in all his **t**—this is God's Eccl 3:13
Then I saw that all **t** and all skill in Eccl 4:4
two hands full of **t** and a striving after Eccl 4:6
or brother, yet there is no end to all his **t**, Eccl 4:8
they have a good reward for their **t**. Eccl 4:9
take nothing for his **t** that he may Eccl 5:15
enjoyment in all the **t** with which one Eccl 5:18
lot and rejoice in his **t**—this is the gift Eccl 5:19
All the **t** of man is for his mouth, yet his Eccl 6:7
with him in his **t** through the days of Eccl 8:15
However much man may **t** in seeking, Eccl 8:17
in life and in your **t** at which you toil Eccl 9:9
your toil at which you **t** under the sun. Eccl 9:9
The **t** of a fool wearies him, for he Eccl 10:15
out from the womb to see **t** and sorrow, Jer 20:18
She has wearied herself with **t**; its Ezk 24:12
the products of your **t** with blight and Hg 2:17
how they grow: they neither **t** nor spin, Mt 6:28
how they grow: they neither **t** nor spin, Lk 12:27
in **t** and hardship, through many a 2 Cor 11:27
For this I **t**, struggling with all his Col 1:29
remember, brothers, our labor and **t**: 1 Thes 2:9
but with **t** and labor we worked night 2 Thes 3:8
For to this end we **t** and strive, 1 Tm 4:10
your **t** and your patient endurance, Rv 2:2

TOILED (3)
all for which I **t** and used my wisdom Eccl 2:19
a person who has **t** with wisdom and Eccl 2:21
"Master, we **t** all night and took nothing! Lk 5:5

TOILING (1)
"For whom am I **t** and depriving myself Eccl 4:8

TOILS (4)
all the toil at which he **t** under the sun? Eccl 1:3
with which he **t** beneath the sun? Eccl 2:22
is there to him who **t** for the wind? Eccl 5:16
toil with which one **t** under the sun the Eccl 5:18

TOKEN (1)
well, and bring some **t** from them." 1 Sm 17:18

TOKHATH (1)
the wife of Shallum the son of **T**, 2 Chr 34:22

TOLA (6)
T, Puvah, Yob, and Shimron. Gn 46:13
according to their clans: of **T**, Nm 26:23
arose to save Israel **T** the son of Puah, Jgs 10:1
T, Puah, Jashub, and Shimron, four. 1 Chr 7:1
The sons of **T**: Uzzi, Rephaiah, Jeriel, 1 Chr 7:2
of their fathers' houses, namely of **T**, 1 Chr 7:2

TOLAD (1)
Bilhah, Ezem, **T**, 1 Chr 4:29

TOLAITES (1)
their clans: of Tola, the clan of the **T**; Nm 26:23

TOLD (339)
said, "Who **t** you that you were naked? Gn 3:11
of his father and **t** his two brothers Gn 9:22
So Abram went, as the LORD had **t** him, Gn 12:4
escaped came and **t** Abram the Gn 14:13
all his servants and **t** them all these Gn 20:8
to the place of which God had **t** him. Gn 22:3
to the place of which God had **t** him, Gn 22:9
after these things it was **t** to Abraham, Gn 22:20
woman ran and **t** her mother's Gn 24:28
And the servant **t** Isaac all the things Gn 24:66
servants came and **t** him about the Gn 26:32
I have done as you **t** me; now sit up and Gn 27:19
Esau her older son were **t** to Rebekah. Gn 27:42
And Jacob **t** Rachel that he was her Gn 29:12
son, and she ran and **t** her father. Gn 29:12
house. Jacob **t** Laban all these things, Gn 29:13
When it was **t** Laban on the third day Gn 31:22
and when he **t** it to his brothers they Gn 37:5
dreamed another dream and **t** it to his Gn 37:9
But when he **t** it to his father and to his Gn 37:10
And when Tamar was **t**, "Your Gn 38:13
About three months later Judah was **t**, Gn 38:24
and she **t** him the same story, saying, Gn 39:17
So the chief cupbearer **t** his dream to Gn 40:9
Pharaoh **t** them his dreams, but there Gn 41:8
When we **t** him, he interpreted our Gn 41:12
And I **t** it to the magicians, but there Gn 41:24
It is as I **t** Pharaoh; God has shown to Gn 41:28
they **t** him all that had happened to Gn 42:29
What we **t** him was in answer to these Gn 43:7
man did as Joseph **t** him and brought Gn 43:17
the grain." And he did as Joseph **t** him. Gn 44:2
father, we **t** him the words of my lord. Gn 44:24
And they **t** him, "Joseph is still alive, Gn 45:26
But when they **t** him all the words of Gn 45:27
So Joseph went in and **t** Pharaoh, "My Gn 47:1
After this, Joseph was **t**, "Behold, your Gn 48:1
And it was **t** to Jacob, "Your son Joseph Gn 48:2
And Moses **t** Aaron all the words of the Ex 4:28
of Israel had also done as Moses **t** them, Ex 12:35
king of Egypt was **t** that the people had Ex 14:5
of the congregation came and **t** Moses, Ex 16:22
So Joshua did as Moses **t** him, and Ex 17:10
Then Moses **t** his father-in-law all that Ex 18:8
you forever." When Moses **t** the words of Ex 19:9
went down to the people and **t** them. Ex 19:25
Moses came and **t** the people all the Ex 24:3
he came out and **t** the people of Israel Ex 34:34
So Moses **t** the people of Israel that they Nm 9:4
Moses went out and **t** the people the Nm 11:24
And a young man ran and **t** Moses, Nm 11:27
And they **t** him, "We came to the land Nm 13:27
When Moses **t** these words to all the Nm 14:39
So Moses **t** the people of Israel Nm 29:40
LORD, the God of your fathers, has **t** you. Dt 1:21
direction of the Red Sea, as the LORD **t** me. Dt 2:1
and it is **t** you and you hear of it, then Dt 17:4
And it was **t** to the king of Jericho, Jos 2:2
and they **t** him all that had happened to Jos 2:23
people of Israel, just as the LORD **t** Joshua. Jos 4:8
the people of Israel, as Moses had **t** them. Jos 4:12
"Because it was **t** to your servants for a Jos 9:24
And it was **t** to Joshua, "The five kings Jos 10:17
When Sisera was **t** that Barak the son of Jgs 4:12
servants and did as the LORD had **t** him. Jgs 6:27
When it was **t** to Jotham, he went and Jgs 9:7
that way. And it was **t** to Abimelech. Jgs 9:25
out into the field, and Abimelech was **t**. Jgs 9:42
Abimelech was **t** that all the leaders of Jgs 9:47
the woman came and **t** her husband, Jgs 13:6
ran quickly and **t** her husband, Jgs 13:10
he came up and **t** his father and mother, Jgs 14:2
and you have not **t** me what it is." And Jgs 14:16
I have not **t** my father nor my mother, Jgs 14:16
lasted, and on the seventh day he **t** her, Jgs 14:17
Then she **t** the riddle to her people. Jgs 14:17
garments to those who had **t** the riddle. Jgs 14:19
The Gazites were **t**, "Samson has come Jgs 16:2
you have mocked me and **t** me lies. Jgs 16:10
you have mocked me and **t** me lies. Jgs 16:13
and you have not **t** me where your Jgs 16:15
And he **t** her all his heart, and said to Jgs 16:17
saw that he had **t** her all his heart, Jgs 16:18
for he has **t** me all his heart." Then the Jgs 16:18
of your husband has been fully **t** to me, Ru 2:11
of you." So she **t** her mother-in-law with Ru 2:19
my daughter?" Then she **t** her all that Ru 3:16
Eli said, "What was it that he **t** you? 1 Sm 3:17
from me of all that he **t** you." 1 Sm 3:17
So Samuel **t** him everything and hid 1 Sm 3:18
came into the city and **t** the news, 1 Sm 4:13
the man hurried and came and **t** Eli. 1 Sm 4:14
So Samuel **t** all the words of the LORD 1 Sm 8:10
Samuel saw Saul, the LORD **t** him, 1 Sm 9:17
"He **t** us plainly that the donkeys had 1 Sm 10:16
Then Samuel **t** the people the rights 1 Sm 10:25
are weeping?" So they **t** him the news 1 Sm 11:5
the messengers came and **t** the men of 1 Sm 11:9
Then they **t** Saul, "Behold, the people 1 Sm 14:33
have done." And Jonathan **t** him, 1 Sm 14:43
And it was **t** Samuel, "Saul came to 1 Sm 15:12
And they **t** Saul, and the thing 1 Sm 18:20
And the servants of Saul **t** him, 1 Sm 18:24
when his servants **t** David these 1 Sm 18:26
And Jonathan **t** David, "Saul my 1 Sm 19:2
But Michal, David's wife, **t** him, "If 1 Sm 19:11
Samuel at Ramah and **t** him all that 1 Sm 19:18
And it was **t** Saul, "Behold, David is 1 Sm 19:19
When it was **t** Saul, he sent other 1 Sm 19:21
And Abiathar **t** David that Saul had 1 Sm 22:21
Now they **t** David, "Behold, the 1 Sm 23:1
Now it was **t** Saul that David had 1 Sm 23:7
When Saul was **t** that David had 1 Sm 23:13
for it is **t** me that he is very cunning. 1 Sm 23:22
And David was **t**, so he went down to 1 Sm 23:25
following the Philistines, he was **t**, 1 Sm 24:1
And some **t** me to kill you, but I 1 Sm 24:10
and came back and **t** him all this. 1 Sm 25:12
But one of the young men **t** Abigail, 1 Sm 25:14
So she **t** him nothing at all until the 1 Sm 25:36
of Nabal, his wife **t** him these things, 1 Sm 25:37
And when it was **t** Saul that David 1 Sm 27:4
said to the young man who **t** him, 2 Sm 1:5
And the young man who **t** him said, 2 Sm 1:6
said to the young man who **t** him, 2 Sm 1:13
When they **t** David, "It was the men of 2 Sm 2:4
that was with him came, it was **t** Joab, 2 Sm 3:23
when one **t** me, 'Behold, Saul is dead,' 2 Sm 4:10
And it was **t** King David, "The LORD 2 Sm 6:12
When it was **t** David, he sent to meet 2 Sm 10:5
And when it was **t** David, he gathered 2 Sm 10:17
conceived, and she sent and **t** David, 2 Sm 11:5
When they **t** David, "Uriah did not 2 Sm 11:10
Then Joab sent and **t** David all the 2 Sm 11:18
went and came and **t** David all that 2 Sm 11:22
Joab went to the king and **t** him, 2 Sm 14:33
And it was **t** David, "Ahithophel is 2 Sm 15:31
him curse, for the LORD has **t** him to. 2 Sm 16:11
man saw them and **t** Absalom. 2 Sm 17:18

the well, and went and **t** King David. 2 Sm 17:21
And a certain man saw it and **t** Joab, 2 Sm 18:10
Joab said to the man who **t** him, 2 Sm 18:11
watchman called out and **t** the king. 2 Sm 18:25
It was **t** Joab, "Behold, the king is 2 Sm 19:1
And the people were all **t**, "Behold, the 2 Sm 19:8
When David was **t** what Rizpah the 2 Sm 21:11
So Gad came to David and **t** him, 2 Sm 24:13
And they **t** the king, "Here is Nathan 1 Kgs 1:23
and you have not **t** your servants who 1 Kgs 1:27
Then it was **t** Solomon, "Behold, 1 Kgs 1:51
And when it was **t** King Solomon, 1 Kgs 2:29
And when it was **t** Shimei, "Behold, 1 Kgs 2:39
when Solomon was **t** that Shimei had 1 Kgs 2:41
she **t** him all that was on her mind. 1 Kgs 10:2
it. And behold, the half was not **t** me. 1 Kgs 10:7
his sons came and **t** him all that the 1 Kgs 13:11
They also **t** to their father the words 1 Kgs 13:11
And they came and **t** it in the city 1 Kgs 13:25
Has it not been **t** my lord what I did 1 Kgs 18:13
went to meet Ahab, and **t** him. 1 Kgs 18:16
Ahab **t** Jezebel all that Elijah had 1 Kgs 19:1
to meet you and **t** you these things?" 2 Kgs 1:7
She came and **t** the man of God, and he 2 Kgs 4:7
hidden it from me and has not **t** me." 2 Kgs 4:27
he returned to meet him and **t** him, 2 Kgs 4:31
So Naaman went in and **t** his lord, 2 Kgs 5:4
about which the man of God **t** him. 2 Kgs 6:10
send and seize him." It was **t** him, 2 Kgs 6:13
the gatekeepers of the city and **t** them, 2 Kgs 7:10
and it was **t** within the king's 2 Kgs 7:11
messengers returned and **t** the king. 2 Kgs 7:15
the king asked the woman, she **t** him. 2 Kgs 8:6
And when it was **t** him, "The man of 2 Kgs 8:7
"He **t** me that you would certainly 2 Kgs 8:14
When they came back and **t** him, he 2 Kgs 9:36
the messenger came and **t** him, 2 Kgs 10:8
So the king of Assyria was **t**, "The 2 Kgs 17:26
clothes torn and **t** him the words 2 Kgs 18:37
Shaphan the secretary **t** the king, 2 Kgs 22:10
I see?" And the men of the city **t** him, 2 Kgs 23:17
When David was **t** concerning the 1 Chr 19:5
And when it was **t** to David, he 1 Chr 19:17
she **t** him all that was on her mind. 2 Chr 9:1
of your wisdom was not **t** me; 2 Chr 9:6
Some men came and **t** Jehoshaphat, 2 Chr 20:2
Shaphan the secretary **t** the king, 2 Chr 34:18
The governor **t** them that they were not Ezr 2:63
on our way, since we had **t** the king, Ezr 8:22
And I **t** no one what my God had put Neh 2:12
I was doing, and I had not yet **t** the Jews, Neh 2:16
And I **t** them of the hand of my God Neh 2:18
The governor **t** them that they were not Neh 7:65
And they **t** Ezra the scribe to bring the Neh 8:1
and you **t** them to go in to possess the Neh 9:15
land that you had **t** their fathers to Neh 9:23
of Mordecai, and he **t** it to Queen Esther, Est 2:22
and Esther **t** the king in the name of Est 2:22
would not listen to them, they **t** Haman, Est 3:4
stand, for he had **t** them that he was a Jew. Est 3:4
women and her eunuchs came and **t** her, Est 4:4
and Mordecai **t** him all that had Est 4:7
Hathach went and **t** Esther what Est 4:9
And they **t** Mordecai what Esther had Est 4:12
Then Mordecai **t** them to reply to Est 4:13
Then Esther **t** them to reply to Est 4:15
how Mordecai had **t** about Bigthana and Est 6:2
And the king's young men **t** him, Est 6:5
And Haman **t** his wife Zeresh and all his Est 6:13
king, for Esther had **t** what he was to her. Est 8:1
(what wise men have **t**, without hiding Jb 15:18
Shall it be **t** him that I would speak? Did Jb 37:20
went and did what the LORD had **t** them, Jb 42:9
it shall be **t** of the Lord to the coming Ps 22:30
of them, yet they are more than can be **t**. Ps 40:5
I have **t** the glad news of deliverance in Ps 40:9
with our ears, our fathers have **t** us, Ps 44:1
Doeg, the Edomite, came and **t** Saul, Ps 52:T
when the Ziphites went and **t** Saul, Ps 54:T
and known, that our fathers have **t** us. Ps 78:3
When I **t** of my ways, you answered Ps 119:26
for it is better to be **t**, "Come up here," Prv 25:7
When the house of David was **t**, "Syria is Is 7:2
A stern vision is **t** to me; the traitor Is 21:2
and **t** him the words of the Rabshakeh. Is 36:22
Has it not been **t** you from the Is 40:21
have I not **t** you from of old and declared Is 44:8
counsel together! Who **t** this long ago? Is 45:21
that which has not been **t** them they see, Is 52:15
And Micaiah **t** them all the words that Jer 36:13
And I **t** the exiles all the things that the Ezk 11:25
and **t** them to seek mercy from the God Dn 2:18
came in, and I **t** them the dream, Dn 4:7
of the holy gods—and I **t** him the dream, Dn 4:8
down the dream and **t** the sum of the Dn 7:1
and it was **t**, 'Arise, devour much flesh.' Dn 7:5
So he **t** me and made known to me the Dn 7:16
the mornings that has been **t** is true, Dn 8:26
of the LORD, because he had **t** them. Jon 1:10
He has **t** you, O man, what is good; and Mi 6:8
days that you would not believe if **t**. Hab 1:5
They **t** him, "In Bethlehem of Judea, for so Mt 2:5
and going into the city they **t** everything, Mt 8:33
But he replied to the man who **t** him, Mt 12:48
And he **t** them many things in parables, Mt 13:3
He **t** them another parable. "The Mt 13:33
buried it, and they went and **t** Jesus. Mt 14:12
Then Jesus **t** his disciples, "If anyone Mt 16:24
See, I have **t** you beforehand. Mt 24:25
done will also be **t** in memory of her." Mt 26:13
there you will see him. See, I have **t** you." Mt 28:7
into the city and **t** the chief priests all Mt 28:11
and immediately they **t** him about her. Mk 1:30
And he **t** his disciples to have a boat Mk 3:9
The herdsmen fled and **t** it in the city Mk 5:14
down before him and **t** him the whole Mk 5:33
and **t** them to give her something to eat. Mk 5:43
returned to Jesus and **t** him all that they Mk 6:30
And they **t** him, "John the Baptist; and Mk 8:28
And they **t** them what Jesus had said, Mk 11:6
that he had **t** the parable against Mk 12:12
I have **t** you all things beforehand. Mk 13:23
has done will be **t** in memory of her." Mk 14:9
city and found it just as he had **t** them, Mk 14:16
you will see him, just as he **t** you." Mk 16:7
She went and **t** those who had been Mk 16:10
And they went back and **t** the rest, but Mk 16:13
that had been **t** them concerning this Lk 2:17
wondered at what the shepherds **t** them. Lk 2:18
heard and seen, as it had been **t** them. Lk 2:20
He also **t** them a parable: "No one tears a Lk 5:36
He also **t** them a parable: "Can a blind Lk 6:39
And he was **t**, "Your mother and your Lk 8:20
they fled and **t** it in the city and in the Lk 8:34
who had seen it **t** them how the Lk 8:36
their return the apostles **t** him all that Lk 9:10
they kept silent and **t** no one in those Lk 9:36
And he **t** them a parable, saying, "The Lk 12:16
that very time who **t** him about the Lk 13:1
And he **t** this parable: "A man had a fig Lk 13:6
Now he **t** a parable to those who were Lk 14:7
So he **t** them this parable: Lk 15:3
And he **t** them a parable to the effect that Lk 18:1
He also **t** this parable to some who Lk 18:9
They **t** him, "Jesus of Nazareth is Lk 18:37
and found it just as he had **t** them. Lk 19:32
that he had **t** this parable against Lk 20:19
And he **t** them a parable: "Look at the Lk 21:29
went and found it just as he had **t** them, Lk 22:13
Remember how he **t** you, while he was Lk 24:6
from the tomb they **t** all these things to Lk 24:9
women with them who **t** these things to Lk 24:10
Then they **t** what had happened on the Lk 24:35
And he **t** those who sold the pigeons, Jn 2:16
If I have **t** you earthly things and you do Jn 3:12
see a man who **t** me all that I ever did. Jn 4:29
testimony, "He **t** me all that I ever did." Jn 4:39
servants met him and **t** him that his son Jn 4:51
The man went away and **t** the Jews that it Jn 5:15
they had eaten their fill, he **t** his disciples, Jn 6:12
"This is why I **t** you that no one can Jn 6:65
I **t** you that you would die in your sins, Jn 8:24
a man who has **t** you the truth that I Jn 8:40
He answered them, "I have **t** you already, Jn 9:27
Jesus answered them, "I **t** you, and you Jn 10:25
Then Jesus **t** them plainly, "Lazarus has Jn 11:14
to the Pharisees and **t** them what Jesus Jn 11:46
Philip went and **t** Andrew; Andrew and Jn 12:22
Andrew and Philip went and **t** Jesus. Jn 12:22
therefore, I say as the Father has **t** me." Jn 12:50
would I have **t** you that I go to prepare a Jn 14:2
And now I have **t** you before it takes Jn 14:29
you may remember that I **t** them to you. Jn 16:4
Jesus answered, "I **t** you that I am he. So, Jn 18:8
back outside to the Jews and **t** them, Jn 18:38
So the other disciples **t** him, "We have Jn 20:25
And someone came and **t** them, Acts 5:25
with this Scripture he **t** him the good Acts 8:35
and you will be **t** what you are to do." Acts 9:6
And the Spirit **t** me to go with them, Acts 11:12
And he **t** us how he had seen the Acts 11:13
these things might be **t** them the next Acts 13:42
and they have been **t** about you that Acts 21:21
in what they have been **t** about you, Acts 21:24
there you will be **t** all that is Acts 22:10
and entered the barracks and **t** Paul. Acts 23:16
that it will be exactly as I have been **t**. Acts 27:25
of many nations, as he had been **t**, Rom 4:18
she was **t**, "The older will serve the Rom 9:12
who have never been **t** of him will Rom 15:21
by you, as he **t** us of your longing, 2 Cor 7:7
and he heard things that cannot be **t**, 2 Cor 12:4
whom I have often **t** you and now tell Phil 3:18
as we **t** you beforehand and solemnly 1 Thes 4:6
still with you I **t** you these things? 2 Thes 2:5
given a white robe and **t** to rest a little Rv 6:11
They were **t** not to harm the grass of the Rv 9:4
went to the angel and **t** him to give me Rv 10:9
And I was **t**, "You must again prophesy Rv 10:11
a measuring rod like a staff, and I was **t**, Rv 11:1

TOLERABLE (1)
that it will be more **t** on the day of Mt 11:24

TOLERATE (2)
that it is not to the king's profit to **t** them. Est 3:8
you, that you **t** that woman Jezebel, Rv 2:20

TOLERATED (1)
kind that is not **t** even among pagans, 1 Cor 5:1

TOLL (4)
they will not pay tribute, custom, or **t**, Ezr 4:13
whom tribute, custom, and **t** were paid. Ezr 4:20
custom, or **t** on anyone of the priests, Ezr 7:24
do kings of the earth take **t** or tax? Mt 17:25

TOMB (63)
withhold from you his **t** to hinder you Gn 23:6
and Jacob set up a pillar over her **t**. It is Gn 35:20
It is the pillar of Rachel's **t**, which is Gn 35:20
in my **t** that I hewed out for myself in Gn 50:5
was buried in the **t** of Joash his father, Jgs 8:32
and Eshtaol in the **t** of Manoah his Jgs 16:31
two men by Rachel's **t** in the territory 1 Sm 10:2
and buried him in the **t** of his father, 2 Sm 2:32
buried it in the **t** of Abner at Hebron. 2 Sm 4:12
and was buried in the **t** of his father. 2 Sm 17:23
in Zela, in the **t** of Kish his father. 2 Sm 21:14
not come to the **t** of your fathers.'" 1 Kgs 13:22
buried him in his **t** with his fathers 2 Kgs 9:28
was buried in his **t** in the garden of 2 Kgs 21:26
"It is the **t** of the man of God who 2 Kgs 23:17
and buried him in his own **t**. 2 Kgs 23:30
buried him in the **t** that he had cut 2 Chr 16:14
to the grave, watch is kept over his **t**. Jb 21:32
nations lie in glory, each in his own **t**; Is 14:18
you have cut out here a **t** for yourself, Is 22:16
you who cut out a **t** on the height and Is 22:16
Their quiver is like an open **t**; they are Jer 5:16
and laid it in his own new **t**, which he Mt 27:60
to the entrance of the **t** and went away. Mt 27:60
Mary were there, sitting opposite the **t**. Mt 27:61
Therefore order the **t** to be made secure Mt 27:64
went and made the **t** secure by sealing Mt 27:66
and the other Mary went to see the **t**. Mt 28:1
quickly from the **t** with fear and Mt 28:8
and took his body and laid it in a **t**. Mk 6:29
and laid him in a **t** that had been cut Mk 15:46
a stone against the entrance of the **t**. Mk 15:46
the sun had risen, they went to the **t**. Mk 16:2
stone for us from the entrance of the **t**?" Mk 16:3
And entering the **t**, they saw a young Mk 16:5
And they went out and fled from the **t**, Mk 16:8
shroud and laid him in a **t** cut in stone, Lk 23:53
followed and saw the **t** and how his Lk 23:55
week, at early dawn, they went to the **t**, Lk 24:1
found the stone rolled away from the **t**, Lk 24:2
and returning from the **t** they told all Lk 24:9
But Peter rose and ran to the **t**; stooping Lk 24:12
They were at the **t** early in the Lk 24:22
with us went to the **t** and found it just Lk 24:24
had already been in the **t** four days. Jn 11:17
that she was going to the **t** to weep there. Jn 11:31
Jesus, deeply moved again, came to the **t**. Jn 11:38
Lazarus out of the **t** and raised him Jn 12:17
in the garden a new **t** in which no one Jn 19:41
since the **t** was close at hand, Jn 19:42
Mary Magdalene came to the **t** early, Jn 20:1
stone had been taken away from the **t**. Jn 20:1
"They have taken the Lord out of the **t**, Jn 20:2
and they were going toward the **t**. Jn 20:3
outran Peter and reached the **t** first. Jn 20:4
came, following him, and went into the **t**. Jn 20:6
disciple, who had reached the **t** first, Jn 20:8
But Mary stood weeping outside the **t**, Jn 20:11
she wept she stooped to look into the **t**. Jn 20:11
buried, and his **t** is with us to this day. Acts 2:29
and laid in the **t** that Abraham had Acts 7:16
from the tree and laid him in a **t**. Acts 13:29
and refuse to let them be placed in a **t**, Rv 11:9

TOMBS (24)
Bury your dead in the choicest of our **t**. Gn 23:6
and in rocks and in **t** and in cisterns, 1 Sm 13:6
he saw the **t** there on the mount. 2 Kgs 23:16
bones out of the **t** and burned them 2 Kgs 23:16
David, but not in the **t** of the kings. 2 Chr 21:20

not bury him in the **t** of the kings.	2 Chr 24:25
bring him into the **t** of the kings of	2 Chr 28:27
the upper part of the **t** of the sons of	2 Chr 32:33
was buried in the **t** of his fathers.	2 Chr 35:24
to a point opposite the **t** of David,	Neh 3:16
who sit in **t**, and spend the night in secret	Is 65:4
Jerusalem shall be brought out of their **t**.	Jer 8:1
men met him, coming out of the **t**,	Mt 8:28
For you are like whitewashed **t**, which	Mt 23:27
For you build the **t** of the prophets and	Mt 23:29
The **t** also were opened. And many	Mt 27:52
out of the **t** after his resurrection	Mt 27:53
met him out of the **t** a man with an	Mk 5:2
He lived among the **t**. And no one could	Mk 5:3
and day among the **t** and on the	Mk 5:5
not lived in a house but among the **t**.	Lk 8:27
For you build the **t** of the prophets	Lk 11:47
they killed them, and you build their **t**.	Lk 11:48
all who are in the **t** will hear his voice	Jn 5:28

TOMORROW (55)

And he said, "**T**." Moses said, "Be it as	Ex 8:10
your people. **T** this sign shall happen."'"	Ex 8:23
from his people, **t**. Only let not Pharaoh	Ex 8:29
"**T** the LORD will do this thing in the land."	Ex 9:5
about this time **t** I will cause very heavy	Ex 9:18
t I will bring locusts into your country,	Ex 10:4
'**T** is a day of solemn rest, a holy	Ex 16:23
T I will stand on the top of the hill with	Ex 17:9
and consecrate them today and **t**,	Ex 19:10
and said, "**T** shall be a feast to the LORD."	Ex 32:5
people, 'Consecrate yourselves for **t**,	Nm 11:18
turn **t** and set out for the wilderness	Nm 14:25
put incense on them before the LORD **t**,	Nm 16:7
the LORD, you and they, and Aaron, **t**.	Nm 16:16
for **t** the LORD will do wonders among	Jos 3:5
and say, 'Consecrate yourselves for **t**;	Jos 7:13
for **t** at this time I will give over all of	Jos 11:6
the LORD today then **t** he will be angry	Jos 22:18
and **t** you shall arise early in the	Jgs 19:9
for **t** I will give them into your hand."	Jgs 20:28
"**T** about this time I will send to you a	1 Sm 9:16
'**T**, by the time the sun is hot, you	1 Sm 11:9
"**T** we will give ourselves up to you,	1 Sm 11:10
life tonight, **t** you will be killed."	1 Sm 19:11
Jonathan, "Behold, **t** is the new moon,	1 Sm 20:5
out my father, about this time **t**,	1 Sm 20:12
said to him, "**T** is the new moon,	1 Sm 20:18
and **t** you and your sons shall be	1 Sm 28:19
and **t** I will send you back." So Uriah	2 Sm 11:12
the life of one of them by this time **t**."	1 Kgs 19:2
my servants to you **t** about this time,	1 Kgs 20:6
him today, and we will eat my son **t**.'	2 Kgs 6:28
T about this time a seah of fine flour	2 Kgs 7:1
about this time **t** in the gate of	2 Kgs 7:18
to me at Jezreel **t** at this time." Now	2 Kgs 10:6
T go down against them. Behold,	2 Chr 20:16
T go out against them, and the LORD	2 Chr 20:17
them, and **t** I will do as the king has said."	Est 5:8
And **t** also I am invited by her together	Est 5:12
in Susa be allowed **t** also to do	Est 9:13
t I will give it"—when you have it with	Prv 3:28
Do not boast about **t**, for you do not	Prv 27:1
wine. "Let us eat and drink, for **t** we die."	Is 22:13
and **t** will be like this day, great beyond	Is 56:12
today is alive and **t** is thrown into the	Mt 6:30
"Therefore do not be anxious about **t**,	Mt 6:34
tomorrow, for **t** will be anxious for itself.	Mt 6:34
today, and **t** is thrown into the oven,	Lk 12:28
demons and perform cures today and **t**,	Lk 13:32
my way today and **t** and the day	Lk 13:33
to bring Paul down to the council **t**,	Acts 23:20
to hear the man myself." "**T**," said he,	Acts 25:22
"Let us eat and drink, for **t** we die."	1 Cor 15:32
"Today or **t** we will go into such and	Jas 4:13
yet you do not know what **t** will bring.	Jas 4:14

TONE (2)

was, he cried out in a **t** of anguish.	Dn 6:20
present with you now and change my **t**,	Gal 4:20

TONGS (6)

Its **t** and their trays shall be of pure	Ex 25:38
its seven lamps and its **t** and its trays of	Ex 37:23
for the light, with its lamps, its **t**,	Nm 4:9
the flowers, the lamps, and the **t**, of	1 Kgs 7:49
the flowers, the lamps, and the **t**, of	2 Chr 4:21
that he had taken with **t** from the altar.	Is 6:6

TONGUE (103)

but I am slow of speech and of **t**."	Ex 4:10
a man moved his **t** against any of the	Jos 10:21
"Every one who laps the water with his **t**,	Jgs 7:5
speaks by me; his word is on my **t**.	2 Sm 23:2
shall be hidden from the lash of the **t**,	Jb 5:21
Is there any injustice on my **t**? Cannot	Jb 6:30
and you choose the **t** of the crafty.	Jb 15:5
mouth, though he hides it under his **t**,	Jb 20:12
of cobras; the **t** of a viper will kill him.	Jb 20:16
falsehood, and my **t** will not utter deceit.	Jb 27:4
and their **t** stuck to the roof of their	Jb 29:10
my mouth; the **t** in my mouth speaks.	Jb 33:2
fishhook or press down his **t** with a cord?	Jb 41:1
is an open grave; they flatter with their **t**.	Ps 5:9
under his **t** are mischief and iniquity.	Ps 10:7
lips, the **t** that makes great boasts,	Ps 12:3
who say, "With our **t** we will prevail,	Ps 12:4
not slander with his **t** and does no evil	Ps 15:3
a potsherd, and my **t** sticks to my jaws;	Ps 22:15
Keep your **t** from evil and your lips	Ps 34:13
Then my **t** shall tell of your	Ps 35:28
utters wisdom, and his **t** speaks justice.	Ps 37:30
my ways, that I may not sin with my **t**;	Ps 39:1
the fire burned; then I spoke with my **t**:	Ps 39:3
my **t** is like the pen of a ready scribe.	Ps 45:1
rein for evil, and your **t** frames deceit.	Ps 50:19
and my **t** will sing aloud of your	Ps 51:14
Your **t** plots destruction, like a sharp	Ps 52:2
love all words that devour, O deceitful **t**.	Ps 52:4
mouth, and high praise was on my **t**.	Ps 66:17
And my **t** will talk of your righteous	Ps 71:24
and their **t** struts through the earth.	Ps 73:9
My **t** will sing of your word, for all	Ps 119:172
LORD, from lying lips, from a deceitful **t**.	Ps 120:2
shall be done to you, you deceitful **t**?	Ps 120:3
laughter, and our **t** with shouts of joy;	Ps 126:2
Let my **t** stick to the roof of my mouth,	Ps 137:6
Even before a word is on my **t**, behold,	Ps 139:4
They make their **t** sharp as a serpent's,	Ps 140:3
haughty eyes, a lying **t**, and hands that	Prv 6:17
from the smooth **t** of the adulteress.	Prv 6:24
The **t** of the righteous is choice silver;	Prv 10:20
but the perverse **t** will be cut off.	Prv 10:31
but the **t** of the wise brings healing.	Prv 12:18
but a lying **t** is but for a moment.	Prv 12:19
The **t** of the wise commends knowledge,	Prv 15:2
A gentle **t** is a tree of life, but	Prv 15:4
but the answer of the **t** is from the LORD.	Prv 16:1
and a liar gives ear to a mischievous **t**.	Prv 17:4
with a dishonest **t** falls into calamity.	Prv 17:20
Death and life are in the power of the **t**,	Prv 18:21
treasures by a lying **t** is a fleeting vapor	Prv 21:6
his mouth and his **t** keeps himself out	Prv 21:23
and a soft **t** will break a bone.	Prv 25:15
brings forth rain, and a backbiting **t**,	Prv 25:23
A lying **t** hates its victims, and a	Prv 26:28
favor than he who flatters with his **t**.	Prv 28:23
the teaching of kindness is on her **t**.	Prv 31:26
bride; honey and milk are under your **t**;	Sg 4:11
as the **t** of fire devours the stubble,	Is 5:24
will utterly destroy the **t** of the Sea of	Is 11:15
and with a foreign **t** the LORD will speak	Is 28:11
of fury, and his **t** is like a devouring fire;	Is 30:27
and the **t** of the stammerers will hasten to	Is 32:4
stammering in a **t** that you cannot	Is 33:19
a deer, and the **t** of the mute sing for joy.	Is 35:6
none, and their **t** is parched with thirst,	Is 41:17
bow, every **t** shall swear allegiance.'	Is 45:23
GOD has given me the **t** of those who are	Is 50:4
shall confute every **t** that rises against	Is 54:17
your mouth wide and stick out your **t**?	Is 57:4
spoken lies; your **t** mutters wickedness.	Is 59:3
They bend their **t** like a bow; falsehood	Jer 9:3
they have taught their **t** to speak lies;	Jer 9:5
Their **t** is a deadly arrow; it speaks	Jer 9:8
Come, let us strike him with the **t**, and	Jer 18:18
The **t** of the nursing infant sticks to the	Lam 4:4
And I will make your **t** cling to the roof	Ezk 3:26
because of the insolence of their **t**.	Hos 7:16
and their **t** is deceitful in their mouth.	Mi 6:12
be found in their mouth a deceitful **t**.	Zep 3:13
the nations of every **t** shall take hold of	Zec 8:23
his ears, and after spitting touched his **t**.	Mk 7:33
his ears were opened, his **t** was released,	Mk 7:35
his mouth was opened and his **t** loosed,	Lk 1:64
of his finger in water and cool my **t**,	Lk 16:24
my heart was glad, and my **t** rejoiced;	Acts 2:26
me, and every **t** shall confess to God."	Rom 14:11
who speaks in a **t** speaks not to men	1 Cor 14:2
who speaks in a **t** builds up himself,	1 Cor 14:4
if with your **t** you utter speech that is	1 Cor 14:9
who speaks in a **t** should pray for	1 Cor 14:13
For if I pray in a **t**, my spirit prays	1 Cor 14:14
than ten thousand words in a **t**.	1 Cor 14:19
a hymn, a lesson, a revelation, a **t**,	1 Cor 14:26
If any speak in a **t**, let there be only	1 Cor 14:27
and every **t** confess that Jesus Christ is	Phil 2:11
does not bridle his **t** but deceives his	Jas 1:26
So also the **t** is a small member, yet it	Jas 3:5
And the **t** is a fire, a world of	Jas 3:6
The **t** is set among our members,	Jas 3:6
but no human being can tame the **t**. It is	Jas 3:8
let him keep his **t** from evil and his lips	1 Pt 3:10

TONGUES (33)

them in your shelter from the strife of **t**.	Ps 31:20
Destroy, O Lord, divide their **t**; for I see	Ps 55:9
and arrows, whose **t** are sharp swords.	Ps 57:4
who whet their **t** like swords, who aim	Ps 64:3
with their own **t** turned against them;	Ps 64:8
that the **t** of your dogs may have their	Ps 68:23
mouths; they lied to him with their **t**.	Ps 78:36
me, speaking against me with lying **t**.	Ps 109:2
is coming to gather all nations and **t**.	Is 66:18
the LORD, who use their **t** and declare,	Jer 23:31
and their **t** will rot in their mouths.	Zec 14:12
out demons; they will speak in new **t**;	Mk 16:17
And divided **t** as of fire appeared to them	Acts 2:3
to speak in other **t** as the Spirit gave	Acts 2:4
telling in our own **t** the mighty works	Acts 2:11
them speaking in **t** and extolling God.	Acts 10:46
began speaking in **t** and prophesying.	Acts 19:6
they use their **t** to deceive." "The	Rom 3:13
spirits, to another various kinds of **t**,	1 Cor 12:10
to another the interpretation of **t**.	1 Cor 12:10
and various kinds of **t**.	1 Cor 12:28
gifts of healing? Do all speak with **t**?	1 Cor 12:30
If I speak in the **t** of men and of	1 Cor 13:1
pass away; as for **t**, they will cease;	1 Cor 13:8
Now I want you all to speak in **t**, but	1 Cor 14:5
greater than the one who speaks in **t**,	1 Cor 14:5
if I come to you speaking in **t**,	1 Cor 14:6
that I speak in **t** more than all of	1 Cor 14:18
"By people of strange **t** and by the	1 Cor 14:21
Thus **t** are a sign not for believers	1 Cor 14:22
comes together and all speak in **t**,	1 Cor 14:23
and do not forbid speaking in **t**.	1 Cor 14:39
People gnawed their **t** in anguish	Rv 16:10

TONIGHT (12)

"Where are the men who came to you **t**?	Gn 19:5
Let us make him drink wine **t** also.	Gn 19:34
may lie with you **t** in exchange for	Gn 30:15
And he said to them, "Lodge here **t**, and	Nm 22:8
So you, too, please stay here **t**, that I	Nm 22:19
Israel have come here **t** to search out the	Jos 2:2
down in the place where you lodge **t**.'"	Jos 4:3
he is winnowing barley **t** at the threshing	Ru 3:2
Remain **t**, and in the morning, if he will	Ru 3:13
"If you do not escape with your life **t**,	1 Sm 19:11
and I will arise and pursue David **t**.	2 Sm 17:1
'Do not stay **t** at the fords of the	2 Sm 17:16

TOO (134)

Is anything **t** hard for the LORD? At the	Gn 18:14
their possessions were **t** great for them	Gn 36:7
people of Israel are **t** many and too mighty	Ex 1:9
of Israel are too many and **t** mighty for us.	Ex 1:9
if the household is **t** small for a lamb,	Ex 12:4
out, for the thing is **t** heavy for you.	Ex 18:18
Consider **t** that this nation is your	Ex 33:13
has a mutilated face or a limb **t** long,	Lv 21:18
lamb that has a part **t** long or too short	Lv 22:23
a part too long or **t** short for a freewill	Lv 22:23
And if someone is **t** poor to pay the	Lv 27:8
alone; the burden is **t** heavy for me.	Nm 11:14
and said to them, "You have gone **t** far!	Nm 16:3
one. You have gone **t** far, sons of Levi!"	Nm 16:7
is it **t** small a thing for you that the God	Nm 16:9
for me, since they are **t** mighty for me.	Nm 22:6
So you, **t**, please stay here tonight, that	Nm 22:19
and he **t** shall come to utter	Nm 24:24
And the case that is **t** hard for you, you	Dt 1:17
Gilead, there was not a city **t** high for us.	Dt 2:36
the wild beasts grow **t** numerous for you.	Dt 7:22
to put his name there is **t** far from you,	Dt 12:21
And if the way is **t** long for you, so that	Dt 14:24
you, because the place is **t** far from you,	Dt 14:24
your towns that is **t** difficult for you,	Dt 17:8
you today is not **t** hard for you,	Dt 30:11
of Ephraim is **t** narrow for you."	Jos 17:15
the people of Judah was **t** large for them,	Jos 19:9
that you **t** must turn away this day	Jos 22:18
And if you **t** rebel against the LORD	Jos 22:18
Naphtali, **t**, on the heights of the field.	Jgs 5:18
But because he was **t** afraid of his family	Jgs 6:27
and they **t** were called out to follow him.	Jgs 6:35
people with you are **t** many for me to	Jgs 7:2
to Gideon, "The people are still **t** many.	Jgs 7:4
saw that they were **t** strong for him,	Jgs 18:26
way, for I am **t** old to have a husband.	Ru 1:12
they **t** followed hard after them in the	1 Sm 14:22
And he **t** stripped off his clothes, and	1 Sm 19:24
and he **t** prophesied before Samuel	1 Sm 19:24
who were **t** exhausted to cross the	1 Sm 30:10
who had been **t** exhausted to follow	1 Sm 30:21
"If the Syrians are **t** strong for me,	2 Sm 10:11
the Ammonites are **t** strong for you,	2 Sm 10:11
And if this were **t** little, I would add to	2 Sm 12:8

me, for they were **t** mighty for me. 2 Sm 22:18
t many to be numbered or counted for 1 Kgs 3:8
before the LORD was **t** small to receive 1 Kgs 8:64
eat, for the journey is **t** great for you." 1 Kgs 19:7
neighbors, empty vessels and not **t** few. 2 Kgs 4:3
under your charge is **t** small for us. 2 Kgs 6:1
"If the Syrians are **t** strong for me, 1 Chr 19:12
the Ammonites are **t** strong for you, 1 Chr 19:12
timber and stone, **t**, I have provided. 1 Chr 22:14
But the priests were **t** few and could 2 Chr 29:34
is failing. There is **t** much rubble. Neh 4:10
because the service was **t** heavy on this Neh 5:18
so **t** were the priests in the reign of Neh 12:22
Are the comforts of God **t** small for you, Jb 15:11
I **t** was pinched off from a piece of clay. Jb 33:6
understand, things **t** wonderful for me, Jb 42:3
hated me, for they were **t** mighty for me. Ps 18:17
poor from him who is **t** strong for him, Ps 35:10
a heavy burden, they are **t** heavy for me. Ps 38:4
T long have I had my dwelling among Ps 120:6
lifted up; my eyes are not raised **t** high; Ps 131:1
myself with things **t** great and too Ps 131:1
too great and **t** marvelous for me. Ps 131:1
Such knowledge is **t** wonderful for me; Ps 139:6
persecutors, for they are **t** strong for me! Ps 142:6
and the expectation of wealth perishes **t**. Prv 11:7
heart is wise, my heart **t** will be glad. Prv 23:15
Wisdom is **t** high for a fool; in the gate Prv 24:7
Surely I am **t** stupid to be a man. I have Prv 30:2
Three things are **t** wonderful for me; Prv 30:18
and do not make yourself **t** wise. Eccl 7:16
Is it **t** little for you to weary men, that you Is 7:13
you: 'You **t** have become as weak as we! Is 14:10
For the bed is **t** short to stretch oneself Is 28:20
and the covering **t** narrow to wrap Is 28:20
He who is **t** impoverished for an offering Is 40:20
"It is **t** light a thing that you should be Is 49:6
now you will be **t** narrow for your Is 49:19
your ears: 'The place is **t** narrow for me; Is 49:20
for I am **t** holy for you." These are a Is 65:5
From it **t** you will come away with your Jer 2:37
fear, but she **t** went and played the whore. Jer 3:8
a wind **t** full for this comes for me. Now Jer 4:12
him from hands **t** strong for him. Jer 31:11
arm! Nothing is **t** hard for you. Jer 32:17
of all flesh. Is anything **t** hard for me? Jer 32:27
and he **t** shall be held in derision. Jer 48:26
Is it **t** light a thing for the house of Ezk 8:17
and that no mystery is **t** difficult for you, Dn 4:9
who are **t** little to be among the clans of Mi 5:2
Cush was her strength; Egypt **t**, and that Na 3:9
shall see it, and be afraid; Gaza **t**, Zec 9:5
teeth; it **t** shall be a remnant for our God; Zec 9:7
that I **t** may come and worship him." Mt 2:8
For I **t** am a man under authority, with Mt 8:9
he said, 'You go into the vineyard **t**, Mt 20:4
to them, 'You go into the vineyard **t**.' Mt 20:7
So **t** the second and third, down to the Mt 22:26
Peter, "Certainly you **t** are one of them, Mt 26:73
For I **t** am a man set under authority, Lk 7:8
heard this, and the tax collectors **t**, Lk 7:29
was with him, for he **t** is a Galilean." Lk 22:59
the feast. For they **t** had gone to the feast. Jn 4:45
They replied, "Are you from Galilee **t**? Jn 7:52
of the people after him. He **t** perished, Acts 5:37
up, saying, "Stand up; I **t** am a man." Acts 10:26
Paul at Berea also, they came there **t**, Acts 17:13
we **t** might walk in newness of life. Rom 6:4
for us with groanings **t** deep for words. Rom 8:26
So **t** at the present time there is a Rom 11:5
Otherwise you **t** will be cut off. Rom 11:22
so they **t** have now been disobedient Rom 11:31
And I think that I **t** have the Spirit of 1 Cor 7:40
is it **t** much if we reap material things 1 Cor 9:11
we share abundantly in comfort **t**. 2 Cor 1:5
—not to put it **t** severely—to all of 2 Cor 2:5
I boast a little **t** much of our 2 Cor 10:8
a fool, so that I **t** may boast a little. 2 Cor 11:16
according to the flesh, I **t** will boast. 2 Cor 11:18
I must say, we were **t** weak for that! 2 Cor 11:21
keep me from being **t** elated by the 2 Cor 12:7
me, to keep me from being **t** elated. 2 Cor 12:7
in Christ, we **t** were found to be sinners, Gal 2:17
watch on yourself, lest you **t** be tempted. Gal 6:1
so that I **t** may be cheered by news of Phil 2:19
In these you **t** once walked, when you Col 3:7
so that you **t** may have fellowship with 1 Jn 1:3
then you **t** will abide in the Son and in 1 Jn 2:24
in heaven, and he **t** had a sharp sickle. Rv 14:17

TOOK (705)
The LORD God **t** the man and put him in Gn 2:15
and while he slept **t** one of his ribs and Gn 2:21
to make one wise, she **t** of its fruit and ate, Gn 3:6
And Lamech **t** two wives. The name of Gn 4:19
with God, and he was not, for God **t** him. Gn 5:24
And they **t** as their wives any they chose. Gn 6:2
out his hand and **t** her and brought her Gn 8:9
to the LORD and **t** some of every clean Gn 8:20
Then Shem and Japheth **t** a garment, Gn 9:23
And Abram and Nahor **t** wives. The Gn 11:29
Terah **t** Abram his son and Lot the son Gn 11:31
And Abram **t** Sarai his wife, and Lot his Gn 12:5
is my sister,' so that I **t** her for my wife? Gn 12:19
So the enemy **t** all the possessions of Gn 14:11
They also **t** Lot, the son of Abram's Gn 14:12
Abram's wife, **t** Hagar the Egyptian, Gn 16:3
Then Abraham **t** Ishmael his son and Gn 17:23
Abraham ran to the herd and **t** a calf, Gn 18:7
Then he **t** curds and milk and the calf Gn 18:8
king of Gerar sent and **t** Sarah. Gn 20:2
Then Abimelech **t** sheep and oxen, and Gn 20:14
in the morning and **t** bread and a skin Gn 21:14
and his mother **t** a wife for him from Gn 21:21
So Abraham **t** sheep and oxen and Gn 21:27
and **t** two of his young men with him, Gn 22:3
And Abraham **t** the wood of the burnt Gn 22:6
And he **t** in his hand the fire and the Gn 22:6
out his hand and **t** the knife to Gn 22:10
And Abraham went and **t** the ram and Gn 22:13
who **t** me from my father's house and Gn 24:7
Then the servant **t** ten of his master's Gn 24:10
the man **t** a gold ring weighing a half Gn 24:22
Thus the servant **t** Rebekah and went Gn 24:61
my master." So she **t** her veil and Gn 24:65
of Sarah his mother and **t** Rebekah, Gn 24:67
Abraham **t** another wife, whose name Gn 25:1
years old when he **t** Rebekah to be his Gn 25:20
he **t** Judith the daughter of Beeri the Gn 26:34
So he went and **t** them and brought Gn 27:14
Then Rebekah **t** the best garments of Gn 27:15
He **t** away my birthright, and behold, Gn 27:36
Esau went to Ishmael and **t** as his wife, Gn 28:9
in the morning Jacob **t** the stone that Gn 28:18
in the evening he **t** his daughter Leah Gn 29:23
she **t** her servant Zilpah and gave her to Gn 30:9
Then Jacob **t** fresh sticks of poplar and Gn 30:37
he **t** his kinsmen with him and Gn 31:23
So Jacob **t** a stone and set it up as a Gn 31:45
stones." And they **t** stones and made Gn 31:46
he had with him he **t** a present for his Gn 32:13
night he arose and **t** his two wives, Gn 32:22
He **t** them and sent them across the Gn 32:23
Thus he urged him, and he **t** it. Gn 33:11
t their swords and came against the Gn 34:25
with the sword and **t** Dinah out of Gn 34:26
They **t** their flocks and their herds, Gn 34:28
Esau **t** his wives from the Canaanites: Gn 36:2
Then Esau **t** his wives, his sons, his Gn 36:6
And they **t** him and cast him into a pit. Gn 37:24
of silver. They **t** Joseph to Egypt. Gn 37:28
Then they **t** Joseph's robe and Gn 37:31
was Shua. He **t** her and went in to her, Gn 38:2
And Judah **t** a wife for Er his firstborn, Gn 38:6
she **t** off her widow's garments and Gn 38:14
and the midwife **t** and tied a scarlet Gn 38:28
And Joseph's master **t** him and put Gn 39:20
and I **t** the grapes and pressed them Gn 40:11
Then Pharaoh **t** his signet ring from Gn 41:42
And he **t** Simeon from them and Gn 42:24
spoke roughly to us and **t** us to be spies Gn 42:30
So the men **t** this present, and they took Gn 43:15
and they **t** double the money with Gn 43:15
So Israel **t** his journey with all that he Gn 46:1
They also **t** their livestock and their Gn 46:6
among his brothers he **t** five men and Gn 47:2
father is ill." So he **t** with him his two Gn 48:1
And Joseph **t** them both, Ephraim in Gn 48:13
and he **t** his father's hand to move it Gn 48:17
mountain slope that I **t** from the hand Gn 48:22
house of Levi went and **t** as his wife a Ex 2:1
she **t** for him a basket made of bulrushes Ex 2:3
and sent her servant woman, and she **t** it. Ex 2:5
She **t** pity on him and said, "This is one of Ex 2:6
wages." So the woman **t** the child and Ex 2:9
inside his cloak, and when he **t** it out, Ex 4:6
inside his cloak, and when he **t** it out, Ex 4:7
So Moses **t** his wife and his sons and had Ex 4:20
And Moses **t** the staff of God in his hand. Ex 4:20
Then Zipporah **t** a flint and cut off her Ex 4:25
Amram **t** as his wife Jochebed his Ex 6:20
Aaron **t** as his wife Elisheba, the Ex 6:23
t as his wife one of the daughters of Ex 6:25
So they **t** soot from the kiln and stood Ex 9:10
So the people **t** their dough before it was Ex 12:34
Moses **t** the bones of Joseph with him, Ex 13:19
ready his chariot and **t** his army with Ex 14:6
and **t** six hundred chosen chariots and Ex 14:7
of Aaron, **t** a tambourine in her hand, Ex 15:20
so they **t** a stone and put it under him, Ex 17:12
and they **t** their stand at the foot of the Ex 19:17
And Moses **t** half of the blood and put it Ex 24:6
Then he **t** the Book of the Covenant and Ex 24:7
And Moses **t** the blood and threw it on Ex 24:8
So all the people **t** off the rings of gold Ex 32:3
He **t** the calf that they had made and Ex 32:20
and **t** in his hand two tablets of stone. Ex 34:4
He **t** the testimony and put it into the Ex 40:20
will restore what he **t** by robbery or what Lv 6:4
Then Moses **t** the anointing oil and Lv 8:10
And he killed it, and Moses **t** the blood, Lv 8:15
And he **t** all the fat that was on the Lv 8:16
and Moses **t** some of its blood and put it Lv 8:23
Then he **t** the fat and the fat tail and all Lv 8:25
before the LORD he **t** one unleavened loaf Lv 8:26
Then Moses **t** them from their hands Lv 8:28
And Moses **t** the breast and waved it for a Lv 8:29
Then Moses **t** some of the anointing oil Lv 8:30
the people's offering and **t** the goat of the Lv 9:15
the grain offering, **t** a handful of it, Lv 9:17
each **t** his censer and put fire in it and Lv 10:1
Moses and Aaron **t** these men who had Nm 1:17
So Moses **t** the redemption money from Nm 3:49
of the people of Israel he **t** the money, Nm 3:50
So Moses **t** the wagons and the oxen and Nm 7:6
and **t** some of the Spirit that was on Nm 11:25
son of Peleth, sons of Reuben, **t** men. Nm 16:1
So every man **t** his censer and put fire Nm 16:18
Eleazar the priest **t** the bronze censers, Nm 16:39
So Aaron **t** it as Moses said and ran Nm 16:47
they looked, and each man **t** his staff. Nm 17:9
And Moses **t** the staff from before the Nm 20:9
Israel, and **t** some of them captive. Nm 21:1
of the sword and **t** possession of his Nm 21:24
And Israel **t** all these cities, and Israel Nm 21:25
the angel of the LORD **t** his stand in the Nm 22:22
the morning Balak **t** Balaam and Nm 22:41
And Balaam **t** up his discourse and Nm 23:7
I **t** you to curse my enemies, and Nm 23:11
And he **t** him to the field of Zophim, to Nm 23:14
And Balaam **t** up his discourse and Nm 23:18
So Balak **t** Balaam to the top of Peor, Nm 23:28
and he **t** up his discourse and said, Nm 24:3
And he **t** up his discourse and said, Nm 24:15
on Amalek and **t** up his discourse Nm 24:20
and **t** up his discourse and said, Nm 24:21
And he **t** up his discourse and said, Nm 24:23
left the congregation and **t** a spear in Nm 25:7
He **t** Joshua and made him stand Nm 27:22
the people of Israel **t** captive the women Nm 31:9
and they **t** as plunder all their cattle, Nm 31:9
and **t** all the spoil and all the plunder, Nm 31:11
that the army **t** was 675,000 sheep, Nm 31:32
of Israel's half Moses **t** one of every 50, Nm 31:47
So I **t** the heads of your tribes, wise and Dt 1:15
good to me, and I **t** twelve men from you, Dt 1:23
And they **t** in their hands some of the Dt 1:25
Only the livestock we **t** as spoil for Dt 2:35
And we **t** all his cities at that time—there Dt 3:4
the spoil of the cities we **t** as our plunder. Dt 3:7
So we **t** the land at that time out of the Dt 3:8
"When we **t** possession of this land at Dt 3:12
Jair the Manassite **t** all the region of Dt 3:14
And they **t** possession of his land and the Dt 4:47
So I **t** hold of the two tablets and threw Dt 9:17
Then I **t** the sinful thing, the calf that Dt 9:21
name upon her, saying, 'I **t** this woman, Dt 22:14
latter man dies, who **t** her to be his wife, Dt 24:3
And as the LORD **t** delight in doing you Dt 28:63
We **t** their land and gave it for an Dt 29:8
you, as he **t** delight in your fathers, Dt 30:9
gods, the rock in which they **t** refuge, Dt 32:37
before the people." So they **t** up the ark of Jos 3:6
Joshua commanded and **t** up twelve Jos 4:8
stones, which they **t** out of the Jordan, Jos 4:20
and the priests **t** up the ark of the LORD. Jos 6:12
of Judah, **t** some of the devoted things. Jos 7:1
shekels, then I coveted them and **t** them. Jos 7:21
And they **t** them out of the tent and Jos 7:23
all Israel with him **t** Achan the son of Jos 7:24
He **t** about 5,000 men and set them in Jos 8:12
But the king of Ai they **t** alive, and Jos 8:23
spoil of that city Israel **t** as their plunder, Jos 8:27
and they **t** his body down from the tree Jos 8:29
ready provisions and **t** worn-out sacks for Jos 9:4
still warm when we **t** it from our houses Jos 9:12
So the men **t** some of their provisions, Jos 9:14
until the nation **t** vengeance on their Jos 10:13
and they **t** them down from the trees Jos 10:27
the people of Israel **t** for their plunder. Jos 11:14
So Joshua **t** all that land, the hill Jos 11:16
of Gibeon. They **t** them all in battle. Jos 11:19
So Joshua **t** the whole land, according Jos 11:23
Israel defeated and **t** possession of their Jos 12:1
with the sword they **t** possession of it Jos 19:47
And they **t** possession of it, and they Jos 21:43

Then I **t** your father Abraham from Jos 24:3
hand, and you **t** possession of their land, Jos 24:8
And he **t** a large stone and set it up Jos 24:26
and he **t** possession of the hill country, Jgs 1:19
their daughters they **t** to themselves for Jgs 3:6
And they **t** possession of the city of Jgs 3:13
hand, **t** the sword from his right thigh, Jgs 3:21
they **t** the key and opened them, Jgs 3:25
But Jael the wife of Heber **t** a tent peg, Jgs 4:21
a tent peg, and **t** a hammer in her hand. Jgs 4:21
"That the leaders **t** the lead in Israel, that Jgs 5:2
So Gideon **t** ten men of his servants and Jgs 6:27
So the people **t** provisions in their hands, Jgs 7:8
And he **t** the elders of the city, and he Jgs 8:16
and he **t** thorns of the wilderness and Jgs 8:16
and he **t** the crescent ornaments that Jgs 8:21
He **t** his people and divided them into Jgs 9:43
And Abimelech **t** an axe in his hand Jgs 9:48
bundle of brushwood and **t** it up and Jgs 9:48
coming up from Egypt **t** away my land, Jgs 11:13
So Israel **t** possession of all the land of Jgs 11:21
And they **t** possession of all the Jgs 11:22
I **t** my life in my hand and crossed over Jgs 12:3
So Manoah **t** the young goat with the Jgs 13:19
of the town and **t** their spoil and gave Jgs 14:19
went and caught 300 foxes and **t** torches. Jgs 15:4
a donkey, and put out his hand and **t** it, Jgs 15:15
midnight he arose and **t** hold of the Jgs 16:3
So Delilah **t** new ropes and bound him Jgs 16:12
Delilah **t** the seven locks of his head Jgs 16:14
came down and **t** him and brought Jgs 16:31
I **t** it." And his mother said, "Blessed be Jgs 17:2
his mother **t** 200 pieces of silver and Jgs 17:4
up and entered and **t** the carved image, Jgs 18:17
Micah's house and **t** the carved image, Jgs 18:18
He **t** the ephod and the household gods Jgs 18:20
the people of Dan **t** what Micah had Jgs 18:27
who **t** to himself a concubine from Jgs 19:1
for no one **t** them into his house to Jgs 19:15
when he entered his house, he **t** a knife, Jgs 19:29
So I **t** hold of my concubine and cut her Jgs 20:6
the people, the men of Israel, **t** courage, Jgs 20:22
of Benjamin did so and **t** their wives, Jgs 21:23
These **t** Moabite wives; the name of the Ru 1:4
And she **t** it up and went into the city. Ru 2:18
be the man who **t** notice of you." So Ru 2:19
And he **t** ten men of the elders of the city Ru 4:2
So Boaz **t** Ruth, and she became his wife. Ru 4:13
Then Naomi **t** the child and laid him on Ru 4:16
Therefore Eli **t** her to be a drunken 1 Sm 1:13
weaned him, she **t** him up with her, 1 Sm 1:24
Then the Philistines **t** the ark of God 1 Sm 5:2
So they **t** Dagon and put him back in 1 Sm 5:3
and **t** two milk cows and yoked them 1 Sm 6:10
And the Levites **t** down the ark of the 1 Sm 6:15
Kiriath-jearim came and **t** up the ark 1 Sm 7:1
So Samuel **t** a nursing lamb and 1 Sm 7:9
Then Samuel **t** a stone and set it up 1 Sm 7:12
They **t** bribes and perverted justice. 1 Sm 8:3
Then Samuel **t** Saul and his young 1 Sm 9:22
So the cook **t** up the leg and what was 1 Sm 9:24
Then Samuel **t** a flask of oil and 1 Sm 10:1
Then they ran and **t** him from there. 1 Sm 10:23
He **t** a yoke of oxen and cut them in 1 Sm 11:7
on the spoil and **t** sheep and oxen 1 Sm 14:32
And he **t** Agag the king of the 1 Sm 15:8
But the people **t** of the spoil, sheep 1 Sm 15:21
Then Samuel **t** the horn of oil and 1 Sm 16:13
And Jesse **t** a donkey laden with 1 Sm 16:20
David **t** the lyre and played it with 1 Sm 16:23
came forward and **t** his stand, 1 Sm 17:16
a keeper and **t** the provisions and 1 Sm 17:20
a bear, and **t** a lamb from the flock, 1 Sm 17:34
Then he **t** his staff in his hand and 1 Sm 17:40
in his bag and **t** out a stone and 1 Sm 17:49
the Philistine and **t** his sword and 1 Sm 17:51
And David **t** the head of the 1 Sm 17:54
down of the Philistine, Abner **t** him, 1 Sm 17:57
And Saul **t** him that day and would 1 Sm 18:2
For he **t** his life in his hand and he 1 Sm 19:5
Michal **t** an image and laid it on the 1 Sm 19:13
And David **t** these words to heart and 1 Sm 21:12
Then Saul **t** three thousand chosen 1 Sm 24:2
made haste and **t** two hundred loaves 1 Sm 25:18
David also **t** Ahinoam of Jezreel, and 1 Sm 25:43
So David **t** the spear and the jar of 1 Sm 26:12
and she **t** flour and kneaded it and 1 Sm 28:24
Therefore Saul **t** his own sword and 1 Sm 31:4
went all night and **t** the body of Saul 1 Sm 31:12
And they **t** their bones and buried 1 Sm 31:13
And I **t** the crown that was on his 2 Sm 1:10
Then David **t** hold of his clothes and 2 Sm 1:11
t Ish-bosheth the son of Saul and 2 Sm 2:8
one group and **t** their stand on 2 Sm 2:25
And they **t** up Asahel and buried him 2 Sm 2:32
Ish-bosheth sent and **t** her from her 2 Sm 3:15
Joab **t** him aside into the midst of the 2 Sm 3:27
And all the people **t** notice of it, and it 2 Sm 3:36
Jezreel, and his nurse **t** him up and fled, 2 Sm 4:4
They **t** his head and went by the way of 2 Sm 4:7
But they **t** the head of Ish-bosheth and 2 Sm 4:12
David **t** the stronghold of Zion, 2 Sm 5:7
And David **t** more concubines and 2 Sm 5:13
hand to the ark of God and **t** hold of it, 2 Sm 6:6
But David **t** it aside to the house of 2 Sm 6:10
LORD of hosts, I **t** you from the pasture, 2 Sm 7:8
depart from him, as I **t** it from Saul, 2 Sm 7:15
and David **t** Metheg-ammah out of the 2 Sm 8:1
And David **t** from him 1,700 horsemen, 2 Sm 8:4
And David **t** the shields of gold that 2 Sm 8:7
King David **t** very much bronze. 2 Sm 8:8
So Hanun **t** David's servants and 2 Sm 10:4
So David sent messengers and **t** her, 2 Sm 11:4
but he **t** the poor man's lamb and 2 Sm 12:4
the Ammonites and **t** the royal city. 2 Sm 12:26
and fought against it and **t** it. 2 Sm 12:29
And he **t** the crown of their king 2 Sm 12:30
And she **t** dough and kneaded it and 2 Sm 13:8
And she **t** the pan and emptied it out 2 Sm 13:9
hand." And Tamar **t** the cakes she 2 Sm 13:10
to eat, he **t** hold of her and said to her, 2 Sm 13:11
And the woman **t** and spread a 2 Sm 17:19
with you." And he **t** three javelins in 2 Sm 18:14
And they **t** Absalom and threw him 2 Sm 18:17
the king arose and **t** his seat in the 2 Sm 19:8
And the king **t** the ten concubines 2 Sm 20:3
brother?" And Joab **t** Amasa by the 2 Sm 20:9
of Joab's young men **t** his stand by 2 Sm 20:11
The king **t** the two sons of Rizpah the 2 Sm 21:8
daughter of Aiah **t** sackcloth and 2 Sm 21:10
David went and **t** the bones of Saul 2 Sm 21:12
"He sent from on high, he **t** me; he 2 Sm 22:17
But he **t** his stand in the midst of the 2 Sm 23:12
There Zadok the priest **t** the horn of 1 Kgs 1:39
arose and went and **t** hold of the 1 Kgs 1:50
He **t** Pharaoh's daughter and brought 1 Kgs 3:1
arose at midnight and **t** my son from 1 Kgs 3:20
came, and the priests **t** up the ark. 1 Kgs 8:3
came to Paran and **t** men with them 1 Kgs 11:18
Then King Rehoboam **t** counsel with 1 Kgs 12:6
men gave him and **t** counsel with the 1 Kgs 12:8
So the king **t** counsel and made two 1 Kgs 12:28
And the prophet **t** up the body of the 1 Kgs 13:29
He **t** away the treasures of the house 1 Kgs 14:26
king's house. He **t** away everything. 1 Kgs 14:26
He also **t** away all the shields of gold 1 Kgs 14:26
Then Asa **t** all the silver and the 1 Kgs 15:18
he **t** for his wife Jezebel the daughter 1 Kgs 16:31
your son." And he **t** him from her 1 Kgs 17:19
And Elijah **t** the child and brought 1 Kgs 17:23
Obadiah **t** a hundred prophets and 1 Kgs 18:4
And they **t** the bull that was given 1 Kgs 18:26
Elijah **t** twelve stones, according to 1 Kgs 18:31
following him and **t** the yoke of 1 Kgs 19:21
positions." And they **t** their positions 1 Kgs 20:12
and they quickly **t** it up from him 1 Kgs 20:33
that my father **t** from your father 1 Kgs 20:34
the king." So they **t** him outside the 1 Kgs 21:13
Then Elijah **t** his cloak and rolled it 2 Kgs 2:8
Then he **t** hold of his own clothes and 2 Kgs 2:12
And he **t** up the cloak of Elijah that 2 Kgs 2:13
Then he **t** the cloak of Elijah that had 2 Kgs 2:14
he **t** with him 700 swordsmen to 2 Kgs 3:26
Then he **t** his oldest son who was to 2 Kgs 3:27
he **t** them from their hand and put 2 Kgs 5:24
So he reached out his hand and **t** it. 2 Kgs 6:7
Israel, he **t** counsel with his servants, 2 Kgs 6:8
So they **t** two horsemen, and the king 2 Kgs 7:14
to meet him, and **t** a present with him, 2 Kgs 8:9
the next day he **t** the bed cloth and 2 Kgs 8:15
every man of them **t** his garment and 2 Kgs 9:13
they **t** the king's sons and slaughtered 2 Kgs 10:7
alive." And they **t** them alive and 2 Kgs 10:14
And Jehu **t** him up with him into 2 Kgs 10:15
t Joash the son of Ahaziah and stole 2 Kgs 11:2
And he **t** the captains, the Carites, 2 Kgs 11:19
And he **t** his seat on the throne of the 2 Kgs 11:19
Then Jehoiada the priest **t** a chest and 2 Kgs 12:9
up and fought against Gath and **t** it. 2 Kgs 12:17
king of Judah **t** all the sacred 2 Kgs 12:18
and arrows." So he **t** a bow and 2 Kgs 13:15
"Take the arrows," and he **t** them. 2 Kgs 13:18
son of Jehoahaz **t** again from 2 Kgs 13:25
the Valley of Salt and **t** Sela by storm, 2 Kgs 14:7
all the people of Judah **t** Azariah, 2 Kgs 14:21
Ahaz also **t** the silver and gold that 2 Kgs 16:8
up against Damascus and **t** it, 2 Kgs 16:9
and he **t** down the sea from off the 2 Kgs 16:17
And they **t** possession of Samaria 2 Kgs 17:24
and at the end of three years he **t** it. 2 Kgs 18:10
fortified cities of Judah and **t** them. 2 Kgs 18:13
And he sent and **t** the bones out of 2 Kgs 23:16
people of the land **t** Jehoahaz the son 2 Kgs 23:30
Jehoiakim. But he **t** Jehoahaz away, 2 Kgs 23:34
king of Babylon **t** him prisoner in 2 Kgs 24:12
of the land he **t** into captivity from 2 Kgs 24:15
him in chains and **t** him to Babylon. 2 Kgs 25:7
And they **t** away the pots and the 2 Kgs 25:14
captain of the guard **t** away as gold, 2 Kgs 25:15
of the guard **t** Seraiah the chief 2 Kgs 25:18
from the city he **t** an officer who had 2 Kgs 25:19
of the guard **t** them and brought 2 Kgs 25:20
Geshur and Aram **t** from them 1 Chr 2:23
of Assyria, and he **t** them into exile, 1 Chr 5:26
And Machir **t** a wife for Huppim and 1 Chr 7:15
Therefore Saul **t** his own sword and 1 Chr 10:4
they stripped him and **t** his head and 1 Chr 10:9
men arose and **t** away the body 1 Chr 10:12
David **t** the stronghold of Zion, 1 Chr 11:5
But he **t** his stand in the midst of the 1 Chr 11:14
by the gate and **t** it and brought it 1 Chr 11:18
of the Philistines **t** counsel and sent 1 Chr 12:19
but **t** it aside to the house of 1 Chr 13:13
And David **t** more wives in 1 Chr 14:3
of hosts, I **t** you from the pasture, 1 Chr 17:7
as I **t** it from him who was before 1 Chr 17:13
and he **t** Gath and its villages out of 1 Chr 18:1
And David **t** from him 1,000 chariots, 1 Chr 18:4
And David **t** the shields of gold that 1 Chr 18:7
David **t** a large amount of bronze. 1 Chr 18:8
So Hanun **t** David's servants and 1 Chr 19:4
And David **t** the crown of their king 1 Chr 20:2
my father's sons he **t** pleasure in me 1 Chr 28:4
came, and the Levites **t** up the ark. 2 Chr 5:4
went to Hamath-zobah and **t** it. 2 Chr 8:3
Then King Rehoboam **t** counsel with 2 Chr 10:6
and **t** counsel with the young men 2 Chr 10:8
Rehoboam **t** as wife Mahalath the 2 Chr 11:18
After her he **t** Maacah the daughter 2 Chr 11:20
concubines (he **t** eighteen wives 2 Chr 11:21
And he **t** the fortified cities of Judah 2 Chr 12:4
He **t** away the treasures of the house 2 Chr 12:9
king's house. He **t** away everything. 2 Chr 12:9
He also **t** away the shields of gold that 2 Chr 12:9
pursued Jeroboam and **t** cities from 2 Chr 13:19
And he **t** fourteen wives and had 2 Chr 13:21
He **t** away the foreign altars and the 2 Chr 14:3
He also **t** out of all the cities of Judah 2 Chr 14:5
he **t** courage and put away the 2 Chr 15:8
Then Asa **t** silver and gold from the 2 Chr 16:2
Then King Asa **t** all Judah, and they 2 Chr 16:6
he **t** the high places and the Asherim 2 Chr 17:6
which they **t** for themselves until 2 Chr 20:25
t Joash the son of Ahaziah and stole 2 Chr 22:11
seventh year Jehoiada **t** courage and 2 Chr 23:1
And he **t** the captains, the nobles, 2 Chr 23:20
But Amaziah **t** courage and led out 2 Chr 25:11
10,000 alive and **t** them to the 2 Chr 25:12
people in them and **t** much spoil. 2 Chr 25:13
king of Judah **t** counsel and sent 2 Chr 25:17
And all the people of Judah **t** Uzziah, 2 Chr 26:1
defeated him and **t** captive a great 2 Chr 28:5
The men of Israel **t** captive 200,000 of 2 Chr 28:8
They also **t** much spoil from them 2 Chr 28:8
by name rose and **t** the captives, 2 Chr 28:15
For Ahaz **t** a portion from the house 2 Chr 28:21
And the Levites **t** it and carried it 2 Chr 29:16
burning incense they **t** away and 2 Chr 30:14
They **t** their accustomed posts 2 Chr 30:16
And the people **t** confidence from the 2 Chr 32:8
And he **t** away the foreign gods and 2 Chr 33:15
And Josiah **t** away all the 2 Chr 34:33
So his servants **t** him out of the 2 Chr 35:24
people of the land **t** Jehoahaz the son 2 Chr 36:1
But Neco **t** Jehoahaz his brother and 2 Chr 36:4
He **t** into exile in Babylon those who 2 Chr 36:20
these Cyrus the king **t** out of the temple Ezr 5:14
which Nebuchadnezzar **t** out of the Ezr 6:5
the king's mighty officers. I **t** courage, Ezr 7:28
priests and the Levites **t** over the weight Ezr 8:30
do as had been said. So they **t** the oath. Ezr 10:5
I **t** up the wine and gave it to the king. Neh 2:1
me, none of us **t** off our clothes; Neh 4:23
I **t** counsel with myself, and I brought Neh 5:7
on the people and **t** from them for their Neh 5:15
So they **t** possession of the land of Neh 9:22
and **t** possession of houses full of all Neh 9:25
died, Mordecai **t** her as his own daughter. Est 2:7
So the king **t** his signet ring from his Est 3:10
So Haman **t** the robes and the horse, and Est 6:11
And the king **t** off his signet ring, which Est 8:2
fell upon them and **t** them and struck Jb 1:15
on the camels and **t** them and struck Jb 1:17
And he **t** a piece of broken pottery with Jb 2:8
And Job again **t** up his discourse, and Jb 27:1

And Job again **t** up his discourse, and Jb 29:1
He sent from on high, he **t** me; he drew Ps 18:16
Yet you are he who **t** me from the womb; Ps 22:9
they were in panic; they **t** to flight. Ps 48:5
Trembling **t** hold of them there, anguish Ps 48:6
you are he who **t** me from my mother's Ps 71:6
David his servant and **t** him from the Ps 78:70
for it; it **t** deep root and filled the land. Ps 80:9
sound of your thunder they **t** to flight. Ps 104:7
and they **t** possession of the fruit of the Ps 105:44
he **t** a bag of money with him; at full Prv 7:20
me, they bruised me, they **t** away my veil, Sg 5:7
and the horsemen **t** their stand at the Is 22:7
all the fortified cities of Judah and **t** them. Is 36:1
you whom I **t** from the ends of the earth, Is 41:9
your children; they **t** no correction; Jer 2:30
Because she **t** her whoredom lightly, she Jer 3:9
and I **t** the loincloth from the place Jer 13:7
So I **t** the cup from the LORD'S hand, and Jer 25:17
house of the LORD and **t** their seat in the Jer 26:10
and they **t** Uriah from Egypt and Jer 26:23
when he **t** into exile from Jerusalem to Jer 27:20
king of Babylon **t** away from this Jer 28:3
the prophet Hananiah **t** the yoke-bars Jer 28:10
on the day when I **t** them by the hand to Jer 31:32
Then I **t** the sealed deed of purchase, Jer 32:11
And they entered and **t** possession of it. Jer 32:23
turned around and **t** back the male Jer 34:11
when each of you **t** back his male and Jer 34:16
So I **t** Jaazaniah the son of Jeremiah, son Jer 35:3
the son of Neriah **t** the scroll in his Jer 36:14
and he **t** it from the chamber of Jer 36:21
Then Jeremiah **t** another scroll and Jer 36:32
So they **t** Jeremiah and cast him into the Jer 38:6
So Ebed-melech **t** the men with him Jer 38:11
and **t** from there old rags and worn-out Jer 38:11
sent and **t** Jeremiah from the court of Jer 39:14
when he **t** him bound in chains along Jer 40:1
captain of the guard **t** Jeremiah and said Jer 40:2
Then Ishmael **t** captive all the rest of Jer 41:10
son of Nethaniah **t** them captive and Jer 41:10
they **t** all their men and went to fight Jer 41:12
the forces with him **t** from Mizpah all Jer 41:16
of the forces **t** all the remnant Jer 43:5
All who **t** them captive have held them Jer 50:33
the king of Babylon **t** him to Babylon, Jer 52:11
And they **t** away the pots and the Jer 52:18
the captain of the guard **t** away as gold, Jer 52:19
captain of the guard **t** Seraiah the chief Jer 52:24
from the city he **t** an officer who had Jer 52:25
of the guard **t** them and brought Jer 52:26
skirts; she **t** no thought of her future; Lam 1:9
The Spirit lifted me up and **t** me away, Ezk 3:14
shall surely live, because he **t** warning, Ezk 3:21
the form of a hand and **t** me by a lock of Ezk 8:3
and **t** some of it and put it into the Ezk 10:7
clothed in linen, who **t** it and went out. Ezk 10:7
You **t** some of your garments and Ezk 16:16
You also **t** your beautiful jewels of my Ezk 16:17
And you **t** your embroidered Ezk 16:18
And you **t** your sons and your Ezk 16:20
your lovers with whom you **t** pleasure, Ezk 16:37
came to Lebanon and **t** the top of the Ezk 17:3
Then he **t** of the seed of the land and Ezk 17:5
and **t** her king and her princes and Ezk 17:12
And he **t** one of the royal offspring and Ezk 17:13
she **t** another of her cubs and made Ezk 19:5
was defiled; they both **t** the same way. Ezk 23:13
revengefully and **t** vengeance with Ezk 25:15
they **t** a cedar from Lebanon to make a Ezk 27:5
for the galleries **t** more away from them Ezk 42:5
So the steward **t** away their food and the Dn 1:16
killed those men who **t** up Shadrach, Dn 3:22
placed, and the Ancient of days **t** his seat; Dn 7:9
So he went and **t** Gomer, the daughter of Hos 1:3
I **t** them up by their arms, but they did Hos 11:3
In the womb he **t** his brother by the Hos 12:3
anger, and I **t** him away in my wrath. Hos 13:11
But the LORD **t** me from following the Am 7:15
by the sheep traders. And I **t** two staffs, Zec 11:7
And I **t** my staff Favor, and I broke it, Zec 11:10
So I **t** the thirty pieces of silver and Zec 11:13
birth of Jesus Christ **t** place in this way. Mt 1:18
All this **t** place to fulfill what the Lord Mt 1:22
the Lord commanded him: he **t** his wife, Mt 1:24
And he rose and **t** the child and his Mt 2:14
And he rose and **t** the child and his Mt 2:21
Then the devil **t** him to the holy city and Mt 4:5
the devil **t** him to a very high mountain Mt 4:8
"He **t** our illnesses and bore our Mt 8:17
he went in and **t** her by the hand, Mt 9:25
seed that a man **t** and sowed in his Mt 13:31
leaven that a woman **t** and hid in three Mt 13:33
And they **t** offense at him. But Jesus Mt 13:57
his disciples came and **t** the body and Mt 14:12
And they **t** up twelve baskets full of the Mt 14:20
out his hand and **t** hold of him, Mt 14:31
he **t** the seven loaves and the fish, and Mt 15:36
And they **t** up seven baskets full of the Mt 15:37
And Peter **t** him aside and began to Mt 16:22
after six days Jesus **t** with him Peter and Mt 17:1
he **t** the twelve disciples aside, Mt 20:17
This **t** place to fulfill what was spoken Mt 21:4
And the tenants **t** his servants and beat Mt 21:35
And they **t** him and threw him out of Mt 21:39
like ten virgins who **t** their lamps and Mt 25:1
For when the foolish **t** their lamps, they Mt 25:3
their lamps, they **t** no oil with them, Mt 25:3
but the wise **t** flasks of oil with their Mt 25:4
Now as they were eating, Jesus **t** bread, Mt 26:26
And he **t** a cup, and when he had given Mt 26:27
of the people **t** counsel against Jesus Mt 27:1
So they **t** counsel and bought with them Mt 27:7
"And they **t** the thirty pieces of silver, Mt 27:9
he **t** water and washed his hands before Mt 27:24
soldiers of the governor **t** Jesus into the Mt 27:27
spit on him and **t** the reed and struck Mt 27:30
one of them at once ran and **t** a sponge, Mt 27:48
saw the earthquake and what **t** place, Mt 27:54
And Joseph **t** the body and wrapped it Mt 27:59
And they came up and **t** hold of his feet Mt 28:9
So they **t** the money and did as they Mt 28:15
And he came and **t** her by the hand and Mk 1:31
they **t** him with them in the boat, Mk 4:36
them all outside and **t** the child's father Mk 5:40
here with us?" And they **t** offense at him. Mk 6:3
they came and **t** his body and laid it in Mk 6:29
And they **t** up twelve baskets full of Mk 6:43
And he **t** the seven loaves, and having Mk 8:6
And they **t** up the broken pieces left over, Mk 8:8
And he **t** the blind man by the hand Mk 8:23
And Peter **t** him aside and began to Mk 8:32
after six days Jesus **t** with him Peter and Mk 9:2
But Jesus **t** him by the hand and lifted Mk 9:27
And he **t** a child and put him in the Mk 9:36
And he **t** them in his arms and blessed Mk 10:16
And they **t** him and beat him and sent Mk 12:3
And they **t** him and killed him and Mk 12:8
were seven brothers; the first **t** a wife, Mk 12:20
And the second **t** her, and died, leaving Mk 12:21
And as they were eating, he **t** bread, Mk 14:22
And he **t** a cup, and when he had given Mk 14:23
And he **t** with him Peter and James Mk 14:33
t courage and went to Pilate and asked Mk 15:43
he **t** him up in his arms and blessed God Lk 2:28
And the devil **t** him up and showed him Lk 4:5
And he **t** him to Jerusalem and set him on Lk 4:9
"Master, we toiled all night and **t** nothing! Lk 5:5
the house of God and **t** and ate the bread Lk 6:4
the Pharisee's house and **t** his place at Lk 7:36
And he **t** them and withdrew apart to a Lk 9:10
after these sayings he **t** with him Peter Lk 9:28
hearts, **t** a child and put him by his side Lk 9:47
him to an inn and **t** care of him. Lk 10:34
the next day he **t** out two denarii and Lk 10:35
seed that a man **t** and sowed in his Lk 13:19
leaven that a woman **t** and hid in three Lk 13:21
Then he **t** him and healed him and sent Lk 14:4
all he had and **t** a journey into a Lk 15:13
were seven brothers. The first **t** a wife, Lk 20:29
and the third **t** her, and likewise all Lk 20:31
And he **t** a cup, and when he had given Lk 22:17
And he **t** bread, and when he had given Lk 22:19
Then he **t** it down and wrapped it in a Lk 23:53
he **t** the bread and blessed and broke it Lk 24:30
and he **t** it and ate before them. Lk 24:43
These things **t** place in Bethany across Jn 1:28
it to the master of the feast." So they **t** it. Jn 2:8
healed, and he **t** up his bed and walked. Jn 5:9
Jesus then **t** the loaves, and when he had Jn 6:11
Feast of Dedication **t** place at Jerusalem. Jn 10:22
So they **t** away the stone. And Jesus lifted Jn 11:41
Mary therefore **t** a pound of expensive Jn 12:3
So they **t** branches of palm trees and Jn 12:13
Then Pilate **t** Jesus and flogged him. Jn 19:1
to them to be crucified. So they **t** Jesus, Jn 19:16
they **t** his garments and divided them Jn 19:23
that hour the disciple **t** her to his own Jn 19:27
For these things **t** place that the Jn 19:36
So he came and **t** away his body. Jn 19:38
So they **t** the body of Jesus and bound it Jn 19:40
Jesus came and **t** the bread and gave it Jn 21:13
up, and a cloud **t** him out of their sight. Acts 1:9
And he **t** him by the right hand and Acts 3:7
opposing God!" So they **t** his advice, Acts 5:39
You **t** up the tent of Moloch and the Acts 7:43
but his disciples **t** him by night and let Acts 9:25
But Barnabas **t** him and brought him Acts 9:27
arrived, they **t** him to the upper room. Acts 9:39
all the world (this **t** place in the days Acts 11:28
robes, **t** his seat upon the throne, Acts 12:21
All this **t** about 450 years. And after Acts 13:20
they **t** him down from the tree and Acts 13:29
Barnabas **t** Mark with him and Acts 15:39
and he **t** him and circumcised him Acts 16:3
And he **t** them the same hour of the Acts 16:33
And they **t** them out and asked them Acts 16:39
And they **t** hold of him and brought Acts 17:19
days longer and then **t** leave of the Acts 18:18
they **t** him and explained to him the Acts 18:26
from them and **t** the disciples with Acts 19:9
And they **t** the youth away alive, and Acts 20:12
we **t** him on board and went to Acts 20:14
he **t** Paul's belt and bound his own Acts 21:11
Then Paul **t** the men, and the next Acts 21:26
He at once **t** soldiers and centurions Acts 21:32
So he **t** him and brought him to the Acts 23:18
The tribune **t** him by the hand, and Acts 23:19
t Paul and brought him by night to Acts 23:31
And the next day he **t** his seat on the Acts 25:6
but on the next day **t** my seat on the Acts 25:17
So they **t** a sounding and found Acts 27:28
farther on they **t** a sounding again Acts 27:28
he had said these things, he **t** bread, Acts 27:35
Paul thanked God and **t** courage. Acts 28:15
Now these things **t** place as examples 1 Cor 10:6
night when he was betrayed **t** bread, 1 Cor 11:23
In the same way also he **t** the cup, 1 Cor 11:25
So I **t** leave of them and went on to 2 Cor 2:13
on the day when I **t** them by the hand to Heb 8:9
he **t** the blood of calves and goats, Heb 9:19
And he went and **t** the scroll from the Rv 5:7
Then the angel **t** the censer and filled it Rv 8:5
And I **t** the little scroll from the hand of Rv 10:10
Then a mighty angel **t** up a stone like a Rv 18:21

TOOL (8)
for if you wield your **t** on it you profane Ex 20:25
it with a graving **t** and made a golden Ex 32:4
down with a stone **t** that could cause Nm 35:17
with a wooden **t** that could cause Nm 35:18
You shall wield no iron **t** on them; Dt 27:5
has wielded an iron **t**." And they offered Jos 8:31
nor axe nor any **t** of iron was heard 1 Kgs 6:7
ironsmith takes a cutting **t** and works it Is 44:12

TOOLS (1)
you shall have a trowel with your **t**, Dt 23:13

TOOTH (11)
eye for eye, **t** for tooth, hand for hand, Ex 21:24
eye for eye, tooth for **t**, hand for hand, Ex 21:24
If he knocks out the **t** of his slave, male Ex 21:27
let the slave go free because of his **t**. Ex 21:27
for fracture, eye for eye, **t** for tooth; Lv 24:20
for fracture, eye for eye, tooth for **t**; Lv 24:20
be life for life, eye for eye, **t** for tooth, Dt 19:21
be life for life, eye for eye, tooth for **t**, Dt 19:21
trouble is like a bad **t** or a foot that Prv 25:19
'An eye for an eye and a **t** for a tooth.' Mt 5:38
'An eye for an eye and a tooth for a **t**.' Mt 5:38

TOP (66)
and a tower with its **t** in the heavens, Gn 11:4
laid him on the altar, on **t** of the wood. Gn 22:9
earth, and the **t** of it reached to heaven. Gn 28:12
for a pillar and poured oil on the **t** of it. Gn 28:18
I will stand on the **t** of the hill with the Ex 17:9
and Hur went up to the **t** of the hill. Ex 17:10
Mount Sinai, to the **t** of the mountain. Ex 19:20
called Moses to the **t** of the mountain, Ex 19:20
devouring fire on the **t** of the mountain Ex 24:17
put the mercy seat on the **t** of the ark, Ex 25:21
skins and a covering of goatskins on **t**. Ex 26:14
be separate beneath, but joined at the **t**, Ex 26:24
on the altar on **t** of the burnt offering, Ex 29:25
its **t** and around its sides and its horns. Ex 30:3
there to me on the **t** of the mountain. Ex 34:2
separate beneath but joined at the **t**, Ex 36:29
its **t** and around its sides and its horns. Ex 37:26
it on the altar on **t** of the burnt offering, Lv 3:5
the altar, on **t** of the LORD'S food offerings. Lv 4:35
on **t** of the blood of the guilt offering. Lv 14:17
goatskin and spread on **t** of that a cloth Nm 4:6
of goatskin that is on **t** of it and the Nm 4:25
died there on the **t** of the mountain. Nm 20:28
of Moab by the **t** of Pisgah that looks Nm 21:20
For from the **t** of the crags I see him, Nm 23:9
the field of Zophim, to the **t** of Pisgah, Nm 23:14
So Balak took Balaam to the **t** of Peor, Nm 23:28
Go up to the **t** of Pisgah and lift up your Dt 3:27
Moab to Mount Nebo, to the **t** of Pisgah, Dt 34:1
goes up to the **t** of the mountain that Jos 15:8
extends from the **t** of the mountain Jos 15:9
your God on the **t** of the stronghold here, Jgs 6:26
went and stood on **t** of Mount Gerizim Jgs 9:7
and carried them to the **t** of the hill that Jgs 16:3

and stood far off on the **t** of the hill, 1 Sm 26:13
and took their stand on the **t** of a hill. 2 Sm 2:25
capital that was on the **t** of the pillar, 1 Kgs 7:18
And on the **t** of the stand there was a 1 Kgs 7:35
and on the **t** of the stand its stays and 1 Kgs 7:35
went up to the **t** of Mount Carmel. 1 Kgs 18:42
who was sitting on the **t** of a hill, 2 Kgs 1:9
capital of five cubits on the **t** of each. 2 Chr 3:15
the two capitals on the **t** of the pillars; 2 Chr 4:12
that were on the **t** of the pillars; 2 Chr 4:12
and took them to the **t** of a rock and 2 Chr 25:12
them down from the **t** of the rock, 2 Chr 25:12
like one who lies on the **t** of a mast. Prv 23:34
three berries in the **t** of the highest bough, Is 17:6
like a flagstaff on the **t** of a mountain, Is 30:17
them shout from the **t** of the mountains. Is 42:11
to Lebanon and took the **t** of the cedar. Ezk 17:3
sprig from the lofty **t** of the cedar and Ezk 17:22
towering height, its **t** among the clouds. Ezk 31:3
high and set its **t** among the clouds, Ezk 31:10
lowest story to the **t** story through the Ezk 41:7
territory on the **t** of the mountain Ezk 43:12
strong, and its **t** reached to heaven, Dn 4:11
strong, so that its **t** reached to heaven, Dn 4:20
mourn, and the **t** of Carmel withers." Am 1:2
they hide themselves on the **t** of Carmel, Am 9:3
all of gold, with a bowl on the **t** of it, Zec 4:2
each of the lamps that are on the **t** of it. Zec 4:2
bring forward the **t** stone amid shouts Zec 4:7
was torn in two, from **t** to bottom. Mt 27:51
was torn in two, from **t** to bottom. Mk 15:38
woven in one piece from **t** to bottom, Jn 19:23

TOPAZ (5)
t, and carbuncle shall be the first row; Ex 28:17
t, and carbuncle was the first row; Ex 39:10
The **t** of Ethiopia cannot equal it, nor Jb 28:19
covering, sardius, **t**, and diamond, Ezk 28:13
chrysolite, the eighth beryl, the ninth **t**, Rv 21:20

TOPHEL (1)
opposite Suph, between Paran and **T**, Dt 1:1

TOPHETH (9)
And he defiled **T**, which is in the 2 Kgs 23:10
And they have built the high places of **T**, Jer 7:31
LORD, when it will no more be called **T**, Jer 7:32
for they will bury in **T**, because there is Jer 7:32
this place shall no more be called **T**, Jer 19:6
Men shall bury in **T** because there will Jer 19:11
inhabitants, making this city like **T**. Jer 19:12
—shall be defiled like the place of **T**.'" Jer 19:13
Then Jeremiah came from **T**, where the Jer 19:14

TOPMOST (2)
He broke off the **t** of its young twigs and Ezk 17:4
break off from the **t** of its young twigs Ezk 17:22

TOPS (14)
month, the **t** of the mountains were seen. Gn 8:5
of marching in the **t** of the balsam 2 Sm 5:24
bronze to set on the **t** of the pillars. 1 Kgs 7:16
for the capitals on the **t** of the pillars, 1 Kgs 7:17
that were on the **t** of the pillars in 1 Kgs 7:19
And on the **t** of the pillars was 1 Kgs 7:22
that were on the **t** of the pillars, 1 Kgs 7:41
that were on the **t** of the pillars; 1 Kgs 7:41
of marching in the **t** of the balsam 1 Chr 14:15
and put them on the **t** of the pillars, 2 Chr 3:16
on the **t** of the mountains may it wave; Ps 72:16
height or set their **t** among the clouds, Ezk 31:14
sacrifice on the **t** of the mountains Hos 4:13
they leap on the **t** of the mountains, Jl 2:5

TORCH (5)
and a flaming **t** passed between these Gn 15:17
to tail and put a **t** between each pair of Jgs 15:4
and her salvation as a burning **t**. Is 62:1
wood, like a flaming **t** among sheaves. Zec 12:6
star fell from heaven, blazing like a **t**, Rv 8:10

TORCHES (12)
and empty jars, with **t** inside the jars. Jgs 7:16
They held in their left hands the **t**, and Jgs 7:20
went and caught 300 foxes and took **t**. Jgs 15:4
And when he had set fire to the **t**, he let Jgs 15:5
Out of his mouth go flaming **t**; sparks Jb 41:19
who equip yourselves with burning **t**! Is 50:11
fire, and by the **t** that you have kindled! Is 50:11
like the appearance of **t** moving to and Ezk 1:13
of lightning, his eyes like flaming **t**, Dn 10:6
through the squares; they gleam like **t**; Na 2:4
there with lanterns and **t** and weapons. Jn 18:3
the throne were burning seven **t** of fire, Rv 4:5

TORE (42)
was not in the pit, he **t** his clothes Gn 37:29
Then Jacob **t** his garments and put Gn 37:34
Then they **t** their clothes, and every Gn 44:13
had spied out the land, **t** their clothes Nm 14:6
Then Joshua **t** his clothes and fell to the Jos 7:6
as he saw her, he **t** his clothes and said, Jgs 11:35
he **t** the lion in pieces as one tears a Jgs 14:6
seized the skirt of his robe, and it **t**. 1 Sm 15:27
took hold of his clothes and **t** them, 2 Sm 1:11
on her head and **t** the long robe that 2 Sm 13:19
king arose and **t** his garments and 2 Sm 13:31
were standing by **t** their garments. 2 Sm 13:31
on him, and **t** it into twelve pieces. 1 Kgs 11:30
and **t** the kingdom away from the 1 Kgs 14:8
and strong wind **t** the mountains 1 Kgs 19:11
he **t** his clothes and put sackcloth 1 Kgs 21:27
his own clothes and **t** them in two 2 Kgs 2:12
of the woods and **t** forty-two of the 2 Kgs 2:24
read the letter, he **t** his clothes and said, 2 Kgs 5:7
he **t** his clothes—now he was passing 2 Kgs 6:30
And Athaliah **t** her clothes and 2 Kgs 11:14
to the house of Baal and **t** it down; 2 Kgs 11:18
he **t** his clothes and covered himself 2 Kgs 19:1
the Book of the Law, he **t** his clothes. 2 Kgs 22:11
And Athaliah **t** her clothes and 2 Chr 23:13
to the house of Baal and **t** it down; 2 Chr 23:17
words of the Law, he **t** his clothes. 2 Chr 34:19
I **t** my garment and my cloak and pulled Ezr 9:3
Mordecai **t** his clothes and put on Est 4:1
Then Job arose and **t** his robe and shaved Jb 1:20
and they **t** their robes and sprinkled dust Jb 2:12
I did not know **t** at me without ceasing; Ps 35:15
he **t** his clothes and covered himself with Is 37:1
aside my steps and **t** me to pieces; Lam 3:11
you broke and **t** all their shoulders; Ezk 29:7
off all pity, and his anger **t** perpetually, Am 1:11
The lion **t** enough for his cubs and Na 2:12
Then the high priest **t** his robes and Mt 26:65
And the high priest **t** his garments and Mk 14:63
they **t** their garments and rushed out Acts 14:14
and the magistrates **t** the garments Acts 16:22
For if I rebuild what I **t** down, I prove Gal 2:18

TORMENT (16)
Then she began to **t** him, and his Jgs 16:19
"How long will you **t** me and break me in Jb 19:2
from my hand: you shall lie down in **t**. Is 50:11
you come here to **t** us before the time?" Mt 8:29
God? I adjure you by God, do not **t** me." Mk 5:7
Most High God? I beg you, do not **t** me." Lk 8:28
and in Hades, being in **t**, he lifted up his Lk 16:23
lest they also come into this place of **t**.' Lk 16:28
They were allowed to **t** them for five Rv 9:5
and their **t** was like the torment of a Rv 9:5
torment was like the **t** of a scorpion when Rv 9:5
prophets had been a **t** to those who Rv 11:10
the smoke of their **t** goes up forever and Rv 14:11
her a like measure of **t** and mourning, Rv 18:7
They will stand far off, in fear of her **t**, Rv 18:10
her, will stand far off, in fear of her **t**, Rv 18:15

TORMENTED (4)
an evil spirit from the LORD **t** him. 1 Sm 16:14
And Amnon was so **t** that he made 2 Sm 13:2
and he will be **t** with fire and sulfur in Rv 14:10
and they will be **t** day and night forever Rv 20:10

TORMENTING (2)
now, an evil spirit from God is **t** you. 1 Sm 16:15
he was **t** his righteous soul over their 2 Pt 2:8

TORMENTORS (2)
captors required of us songs, and our **t**, Ps 137:3
and I will put it into the hand of your **t**, Is 51:23

TORN (49)
What was **t** by wild beasts I did not Gn 31:39
Joseph is without doubt **t** to pieces." Gn 37:33
I said, Surely he has been **t** to pieces, Gn 44:28
If it is **t** by beasts, let him bring it as Ex 22:13
make restitution for what has been **t**. Ex 22:13
eat any flesh that is **t** by beasts in the Ex 22:31
fat of one that is **t** by beasts may be put Lv 7:24
the disease shall wear **t** clothes and let Lv 13:45
what dies of itself or what is **t** by beasts, Lv 17:15
not eat what dies of itself or is **t** by beasts, Lv 22:8
bruised or crushed or **t** or cut you shall Lv 22:24
wineskins, worn-out and **t** and mended, Jos 9:4
with his clothes **t** and with dirt on his 1 Sm 4:12
"The LORD has **t** the kingdom of 1 Sm 15:28
for the LORD has **t** the kingdom out of 1 Sm 28:17
with his clothes **t** and dirt on his head. 2 Sm 1:2
him with his coat **t** and dirt on his 2 Sm 15:32
'Behold, the altar shall be **t** down, and 1 Kgs 13:3
The altar also was **t** down, and the 1 Kgs 13:5
which has **t** him and killed him, 1 Kgs 13:26
not eaten the body or **t** the donkey. 1 Kgs 13:28
that the king of Israel had **t** his clothes, 2 Kgs 5:8
saying, "Why have you **t** your clothes? 2 Kgs 5:8
When he had **t** Israel from the 2 Kgs 17:21
with their clothes **t** and told him 2 Kgs 18:37
and you have **t** your clothes and 2 Kgs 22:19
me and have **t** your clothes and 2 Chr 34:27
with my garment and my cloak **t**, Ezr 9:5
He has **t** me in his wrath and hated me; Jb 16:9
He is **t** from the tent in which he trusted Jb 18:14
the land to quake; you have **t** it open; Ps 60:2
came to Hezekiah with their clothes **t**, Is 36:22
who goes out of them shall be **t** in pieces, Jer 5:6
of Judah that were **t** down to make a Jer 33:4
their beards shaved and their clothes **t**, Jer 41:5
what died of itself or was **t** by beasts, Ezk 4:14
away, and her foundations are **t** down. Ezk 30:4
died of itself or is **t** by wild animals. Ezk 44:31
you shall be **t** limb from limb, Dn 2:5
Abednego shall be **t** limb from limb, Dn 3:29
for he has **t** us, that he may heal us; Hos 6:1
the granaries are **t** down because the Jl 1:17
with prey and his dens with **t** flesh. Na 2:12
the curtain of the temple was **t** in two, Mt 27:51
the curtain of the temple was **t** in two, Mk 15:38
the curtain of the temple was **t** in two. Lk 23:45
there were so many, the net was not **t**. Jn 21:11
that Paul would be **t** to pieces by Acts 23:10
But since we were **t** away from you, 1 Thes 2:17

TORRENT (7)
The **t** Kishon swept them away, the Jgs 5:21
Kishon swept them away, the ancient **t**, Jgs 5:21
away, the ancient torrent, the **t** Kishon. Jgs 5:21
of Ophir among the stones of the **t** bed, Jb 22:24
us away, the **t** would have gone over us; Ps 124:4
and shall become an overflowing **t**; Jer 47:2
stream down like a **t** day and night! Lam 2:18

TORRENT-BED (1)
My brothers are treacherous as a **t**, as Jb 6:15

TORRENTIAL (2)
torrent-bed, as **t** streams that pass away, Jb 6:15
are with him **t** rains and hailstones, Ezk 38:22

TORRENTS (5)
me, the **t** of destruction assailed me; 2 Sm 22:5
the **t** wash away the soil of the earth; Jb 14:19
In the gullies of the **t** they must dwell, in Jb 30:6
cleft a channel for the **t** of rain and a Jb 38:25
me; the **t** of destruction assailed me; Ps 18:4

TORTUOUS (2)
crooked you make yourself seem **t**. 2 Sm 22:27
the crooked you make yourself seem **t**. Ps 18:26

TORTURED (1)
Some were **t**, refusing to accept Heb 11:35

TOSS (3)
and you **t** me about in the roar of the Jb 30:22
quiet, and its waters **t** up mire and dirt. Is 57:20
though the waves **t**, they cannot prevail; Jer 5:22

TOSSED (3)
the Nile, and be **t** about and sink again, Am 8:8
t to and fro by the waves and carried Eph 4:14
of the sea that is driven and **t** by the wind. Jas 1:6

TOSSING (2)
is long, and I am full of **t** till the dawn. Jb 7:4
But the wicked are like the **t** sea; for it Is 57:20

TOSSINGS (1)
You have kept count of my **t**; put my Ps 56:8

TOTAL (1)
numbered, and the **t** was 38,000 men. 1 Chr 23:3

TOTTER (2)
The nations rage, the kingdoms **t**; he Ps 46:6
make them **t** by your power and bring Ps 59:11

TOTTERING (1)
batter him, like a leaning wall, a **t** fence? Ps 62:3

TOTTERS (2)
torn it open; repair its breaches, for it **t**. Ps 60:2
When the earth **t**, and all its inhabitants, Ps 75:3

TOU (2)
When **T** king of Hamath heard that 1 Chr 18:9
had often been at war with **T**. 1 Chr 18:10

TOUCH (42)
midst of the garden, neither shall you **t** it, Gn 3:3
me. Therefore I did not let you **t** her. Gn 20:6
and **t** the lintel and the two doorposts Ex 12:22
up into the mountain or **t** the edge of it. Ex 19:12
No hand shall **t** him, but he shall be Ex 19:13
flesh, and you shall not **t** their carcasses; Lv 11:8
She shall not **t** anything holy, nor come Lv 12:4
but they must not **t** the holy things, Nm 4:15
of separation, no razor shall **t** his head. Nm 6:5
wicked men, and **t** nothing of theirs, Nm 16:26
eat, and their carcasses you shall not **t**. Dt 14:8
of Israel, and now we may not **t** them. Jos 9:19
I not charged the young men not to **t** you? Ru 2:9
his life, and no razor shall **t** his head." 1 Sm 1:11

me, and he shall never **t** you again." 2 Sm 14:10
saying, "**T** not my anointed ones, do 1 Chr 16:22
out your hand and **t** all that he has, Jb 1:11
out your hand and **t** his bone and his Jb 2:5
six troubles; in seven no evil shall **t** you. Jb 5:19
My appetite refuses to **t** them; they are as Jb 6:7
saying, "**T** not my anointed ones, do Ps 105:15
T the mountains so that they smoke! Ps 144:5
go out from there; **t** no unclean thing; Is 52:11
evil neighbors who **t** the heritage that Jer 12:14
no one was able to **t** their garments. Lam 4:14
Do not **t**!" So they became fugitives Lam 4:15
but **t** no one on whom is the mark. Ezk 9:6
said to herself, "If I only **t** his garment, Mt 9:21
that they might only **t** the fringe of his Mt 14:36
diseases pressed around him to **t** him. Mk 3:10
For she said, "If I **t** even his garments, I Mk 5:28
him that they might **t** even the fringe of Mk 6:56
a blind man and begged him to **t** him. Mk 8:22
children to him that he might **t** them, Mk 10:13
And all the crowd sought to **t** him, for Lk 6:19
yourselves do not **t** the burdens with Lk 11:46
infants to him that he might **t** them. Lk 18:15
feet, that it is I myself. **T** me, and see. Lk 24:39
the Lord, and **t** no unclean thing; 2 Cor 6:17
"Do not handle, Do not taste, Do not **t**" Col 2:21
of the firstborn might not **t** them. Heb 11:28
him, and the evil one does not **t** him. 1 Jn 5:18

TOUCHED (54)

as we have not **t** you and have done Gn 26:29
against Jacob, he **t** his hip socket, Gn 32:25
because he **t** the socket of Jacob's hip Gn 32:32
her son's foreskin and **t** Moses' feet with Ex 4:25
were there and on whoever **t** the bone, Nm 19:18
person and whoever has **t** any slain, Nm 31:19
was in his hand and **t** the meat and the Jgs 6:21
men of valor whose hearts God had **t**. 1 Sm 10:26
so that a wing of one **t** the one wall, 1 Kgs 6:27
of the other cherub **t** the other wall; 1 Kgs 6:27
their other wings **t** each other in the 1 Kgs 6:27
an angel **t** him and said to him, 1 Kgs 19:5
a second time and **t** him and said, 1 Kgs 19:7
soon as the man **t** the bones of 2 Kgs 13:21
And the LORD **t** the king, so that he 2 Kgs 15:5
of five cubits, **t** the wall of the house, 2 Chr 3:11
t the wing of the other cherub; 2 Chr 3:11
of five cubits, **t** the wall of the house, 2 Chr 3:12
Then Esther approached and **t** the tip of Est 5:2
friends, for the hand of God has **t** me! Jb 19:21
And he **t** my mouth and said: "Behold, this Is 6:7
and said: "Behold, this has **t** your lips; Is 6:7
LORD put out his hand and **t** my mouth. Jer 1:9
their wings **t** one another. Each one of Ezk 1:9
each of which **t** the wing of another, Ezk 1:11
living creatures as they **t** one another, Ezk 3:13
But he **t** me and made me stand up. Dn 8:18
a hand **t** me and set me trembling on Dn 10:10
of the children of man **t** my lips. Dn 10:16
of a man **t** me and strengthened Dn 10:18
Jesus stretched out his hand and **t** him, Mt 8:3
He **t** her hand, and the fever left her, and Mt 8:15
up behind him and **t** the fringe of his Mt 9:20
Then he **t** their eyes, saying, "According Mt 9:29
And as many as **t** it were made well. Mt 14:36
But Jesus came and **t** them, saying, Mt 17:7
And Jesus in pity **t** their eyes, and Mt 20:34
out his hand and **t** him and said to Mk 1:41
him in the crowd and **t** his garment. Mk 5:27
crowd and said, "Who **t** my garments?" Mk 5:30
you, and yet you say, 'Who **t** me?'" Mk 5:31
And as many as **t** it were made well. Mk 6:56
his ears, and after spitting **t** his tongue. Mk 7:33
Jesus stretched out his hand and **t** him, Lk 5:13
Then he came up and **t** the bier, and the Lk 7:14
up behind him and **t** the fringe of his Lk 8:44
"Who was it that **t** me?" When all Lk 8:45
But Jesus said, "Someone **t** me, for I Lk 8:46
of all the people why she had **t** him, Lk 8:47
of this!" And he **t** his ear and healed Lk 22:51
or aprons that had **t** his skin were Acts 19:12
Chios; the next day we **t** at Samos; Acts 20:15
you have not come to what may be **t**, Heb 12:18
looked upon and have **t** with our hands, 1 Jn 1:1

TOUCHES (52)

"Whoever **t** this man or his wife shall Gn 26:11
Whoever **t** the mountain shall be put Ex 19:12
Whatever **t** the altar shall become Ex 29:37
Whatever **t** them will become holy. Ex 30:29
or if anyone **t** an unclean thing, whether Lv 5:2
or if he **t** human uncleanness, of Lv 5:3
Whatever **t** them shall become holy." Lv 6:18
Whatever **t** its flesh shall be holy, and Lv 6:27
"Flesh that **t** any unclean thing shall Lv 7:19
And if anyone **t** an unclean thing, Lv 7:21
Whoever **t** their carcass shall be Lv 11:24
Everyone who **t** them shall be unclean. Lv 11:26
Whoever **t** their carcass shall be Lv 11:27
Whoever **t** them when they are dead Lv 11:31
but whoever **t** a carcass in them shall Lv 11:36
whoever **t** its carcass shall be unclean Lv 11:39
And anyone who **t** his bed shall wash Lv 15:5
And whoever **t** the body of the one with Lv 15:7
And whoever **t** anything that was Lv 15:10
with the discharge **t** without having Lv 15:11
with the discharge **t** shall be broken, Lv 15:12
and whoever **t** her shall be unclean Lv 15:19
And whoever **t** her bed shall wash his Lv 15:21
And whoever **t** anything on which she Lv 15:22
when he **t** it he shall be unclean until Lv 15:23
And whoever **t** these things shall be Lv 15:27
Whoever **t** anything that is unclean Lv 22:4
and whoever **t** a swarming thing by Lv 22:5
the person who **t** such a thing shall be Lv 22:6
"Whoever **t** the dead body of any Nm 19:11
Whoever **t** a dead person, the body of Nm 19:13
in the open field **t** someone who was Nm 19:16
or **t** a human bone or a grave, Nm 19:16
and the one who **t** the water for Nm 19:21
the unclean person **t** shall be Nm 19:22
and anyone who **t** it shall be unclean Nm 19:22
to Ataroth and to Naarah, and **t** Jericho, Jos 16:7
and on to Mareal and **t** Dabbesheth, Jos 19:11
The boundary also **t** Tabor, Jos 19:22
the west it **t** Carmel and Jos 19:26
and **t** Zebulun and the Valley of Jos 19:27
a thread of flax snaps when it **t** the fire. Jgs 16:9
the man who **t** them arms himself 2 Sm 23:7
to you, and you are impatient; it **t** you, Jb 4:5
who **t** the mountains and they smoke! Ps 104:32
none who **t** her will go unpunished. Prv 6:29
of hosts, he who **t** the earth and it melts, Am 9:5
of his garment and **t** with his fold bread Hg 2:12
contact with a dead body **t** any of these, Hg 2:13
for he who **t** you touches the apple of his Zec 2:8
for he who touches you **t** the apple of his Zec 2:8
given, "If even a beast **t** the mountain, Heb 12:20

TOUCHING (6)

were unclean through **t** a dead body, Nm 9:6
"We are unclean through **t** a dead body. Nm 9:7
is unclean through **t** a dead body, Nm 9:10
t Zebulun at the south and Asher on Jos 19:34
of the whole earth, without **t** the ground. Dn 8:5
what sort of woman this is who is **t** him, Lk 7:39

TOWARD (218)

journeyed on, still going **t** the Negeb. Gn 12:9
him outside and said, "Look **t** heaven, Gn 15:5
there, and they looked down **t** Sodom. Gn 18:16
turned from there and went **t** Sodom, Gn 18:22
he looked down **t** Sodom and Gn 19:28
and Gomorrah and **t** all the land Gn 19:28
there Abraham journeyed **t** the territory Gn 20:1
love and his faithfulness **t** my master. Gn 24:27
Laban ran out **t** the man, to the spring. Gn 24:29
out to meditate in the field **t** evening. Gn 24:63
Jacob left Beersheba and went **t** Haran. Gn 28:10
faces of the flocks **t** the striped and all Gn 30:40
and set his face **t** the hill country of Gn 31:21
in his right hand **t** Israel's left hand, Gn 48:13
in his left hand **t** Israel's right hand, Gn 48:13
Moses, "Stretch out your hand **t** heaven, Ex 9:22
Moses stretched out his staff **t** heaven, Ex 9:23
"Stretch out your hand **t** heaven, Ex 10:21
Moses stretched out his hand **t** heaven, Ex 10:22
the way of the wilderness **t** the Red Sea. Ex 13:18
his servants was changed **t** the people, Ex 14:5
of Israel, they looked **t** the wilderness, Ex 16:10
t the mercy seat shall the faces of the Ex 25:20
quickly bowed his head **t** the earth and Ex 34:8
t the mercy seat were the faces of the Ex 37:9
lifted up his hands **t** the people and Lv 9:22
on the east side **t** the sunrise shall be Nm 2:3
before the tent of meeting **t** the sunrise, Nm 3:38
And Aaron turned **t** Miriam, and Nm 12:10
they turned **t** the tent of meeting. Nm 16:42
some of its blood **t** the front of the Nm 19:4
that is opposite Moab, **t** the sunrise. Nm 21:11
omens, but set his face **t** the wilderness. Nm 24:1
Jordan east of Jericho, **t** the sunrise." Nm 34:15
of the road, **t** the going down of the sun, Dt 11:30
to the Great Sea **t** the going down of Jos 1:4
you beyond the Jordan **t** the sunrise." Jos 1:15
and those flowing down **t** the Sea of the Jos 3:16
to the appointed place **t** the Arabah to Jos 8:14
out the javelin that is in your hand **t** Ai, Jos 8:18
javelin that was in his hand **t** the city. Jos 8:18
the coast of the Great Sea **t** Lebanon, Jos 9:1
from Mount Halak, which rises **t** Seir, Jos 11:17
land beyond the Jordan **t** the sunrise, Jos 12:1
that rises **t** Seir (and Joshua gave their Jos 12:7
and all Lebanon, **t** the sunrise, Jos 13:5
and so northward, turning **t** Gilgal, Jos 15:7
south, **t** the boundary of Edom, Jos 15:21
turns around **t** Taanath-shiloh and Jos 16:6
other direction eastward **t** the sunrise Jos 19:12
along on the east **t** the sunrise to Jos 19:13
going on to Rimmon it bends **t** Neah, Jos 19:13
fled as far as Beth-shittah **t** Zererah, Jgs 7:22
the flame went up **t** heaven from the Jgs 13:20
a young lion came **t** him roaring. Jgs 14:5
now the day has waned **t** evening. Jgs 19:9
they turned and fled **t** the wilderness to Jgs 20:45
men turned and fled **t** the wilderness to Jgs 20:47
saw Samuel coming out **t** them on his 1 Sm 9:14
One company turned **t** Ophrah, to 1 Sm 13:17
company turned **t** Beth-horon; 1 Sm 13:18
company turned **t** the border 1 Sm 13:18
the valley of Zeboim **t** the wilderness. 1 Sm 13:18
he turned away from him **t** another, 1 Sm 17:30
David ran quickly **t** the battle line to 1 Sm 17:48
behold, if he is well disposed **t** David, 1 Sm 20:12
David and his men came down **t** her, 1 Sm 25:20
the people passed on **t** the wilderness. 2 Sm 15:23
of the valley, **t** Gad and on to Jazer. 2 Sm 24:5
out his hand **t** Jerusalem to destroy 2 Sm 24:16
and his servants coming on **t** him. 2 Sm 24:20
and in uprightness of heart **t** you. 1 Kgs 3:6
and spread out his hands **t** heaven, 1 Kgs 8:22
be open night and day **t** this house, 1 Kgs 8:29
that your servant offers **t** this place. 1 Kgs 8:29
Israel, when they pray **t** this place. 1 Kgs 8:30
if they pray **t** this place and 1 Kgs 8:35
stretching out his hands **t** this house, 1 Kgs 8:38
he comes and prays **t** this house, 1 Kgs 8:42
pray to the LORD **t** the city that you 1 Kgs 8:44
captive, and pray to you **t** their land, 1 Kgs 8:48
with hands outstretched **t** heaven. 1 Kgs 8:54
look **t** the sea." And he went up and 1 Kgs 18:43
on them, and he turned **t** them, 2 Kgs 13:23
people, and direct their hearts **t** you. 1 Chr 29:18
and spread out his hands **t** heaven, 2 Chr 6:13
be open day and night **t** this house, 2 Chr 6:20
that your servant offers **t** this place. 2 Chr 6:20
Israel, when they pray **t** this place. 2 Chr 6:21
if they pray **t** this place and 2 Chr 6:26
stretching out his hands **t** this house, 2 Chr 6:29
he comes and prays **t** this house, 2 Chr 6:32
they pray to you **t** this city that you 2 Chr 6:34
carried captive, and pray **t** their land, 2 Chr 6:38
those whose heart is blameless **t** him. 2 Chr 16:9
wilderness, they looked **t** the horde, 2 Chr 20:24
in Israel, and **t** God and his house. 2 Chr 24:16
love endures forever **t** Israel." And all Ezr 3:11
was the king's procedure **t** all who were Est 1:13
sprinkled dust on their heads **t** heaven. Jb 2:12
me and increase your vexation **t** me; Jb 10:17
you will stretch out your hands **t** him. Jb 11:13
Will you show partiality **t** him? Will Jb 13:8
land; no treader turns **t** their vineyards. Jb 24:18
"If my heart has been enticed **t** a woman, Jb 31:9
to any man or use flattery **t** any person. Jb 32:21
Behold, I am **t** God as you are; I too was Jb 33:6
soars and spreads his wings **t** the south? Jb 39:26
I will bow down **t** your holy temple in the Ps 5:7
My eyes are ever **t** the LORD, for he will Ps 25:15
lift up my hands **t** your most holy Ps 28:2
of the LORD are **t** the righteous and his Ps 34:15
the righteous and his ears **t** their cry. Ps 34:15
wondrous deeds and your thoughts **t** us; Ps 40:5
awesome in his deeds **t** the children of Ps 66:5
and ignorant; I was like a beast **t** you. Ps 73:22
Their heart was not steadfast **t** him; Ps 78:37
who hate the LORD would cringe **t** him, Ps 81:15
and put away your indignation **t** us! Ps 85:4
For great is your steadfast love **t** me; Ps 86:13
is his steadfast love **t** those who fear Ps 103:11
For great is his steadfast love **t** us, and Ps 117:2
up my hands **t** your commandments, Ps 119:48
I bow down **t** your holy temple and give Ps 138:2
But my eyes are **t** you, O GOD, my Lord; Ps 141:8
T the scorners he is scornful, but to the Prv 3:34
The discerning sets his face **t** wisdom, Prv 17:24
wings, flying like an eagle **t** heaven. Prv 23:5
of Lebanon, which looks **t** Damascus. Sg 7:4
and proclaim these words **t** the north, Jer 3:12
Raise a standard **t** Zion, flee for safety, stay Jer 4:6
heights in the desert **t** the daughter of my Jer 4:11
me; you see me, and test my heart **t** you. Jer 12:3
my heart would not turn **t** this people. Jer 15:1
the corner of the Horse Gate **t** the east, Jer 31:40
two walls; and they went **t** the Arabah. Jer 39:4
the way to Zion, with faces turned **t** it, Jer 50:5
stretched out straight, one **t** another. Ezk 1:23
and set your face **t** it, and let it be in a Ezk 4:3

shall set your face **t** the siege of Ezk 4:7
set your face **t** the mountains of Israel, Ezk 6:2
lift up your eyes now **t** the north." So I Ezk 8:5
north." So I lifted up my eyes **t** the north, Ezk 8:5
of the LORD, and their faces **t** the east, Ezk 8:16
the east, worshiping the sun **t** the east. Ezk 8:16
And I will scatter **t** every wind all who Ezk 12:14
vine, and its branches turned **t** him, Ezk 17:6
vine bent its roots **t** him and shot forth Ezk 17:7
shot forth its branches **t** him from the Ezk 17:7
of man, set your face **t** the southland; Ezk 20:46
set your face **t** Jerusalem and preach Ezk 21:2
set your face **t** the Ammonites and Ezk 25:2
"Son of man, set your face **t** Sidon, and Ezk 28:21
"Son of man, set your face **t** Gog, of the Ezk 38:2
narrowing inwards **t** the side rooms Ezk 40:16
the side rooms and **t** their jambs, Ezk 40:16
As for the gate that faced **t** the north, Ezk 40:20
those of the gate that faced **t** the east. Ezk 40:22
And he led me **t** the south, and behold, Ezk 40:24
from gate to gate **t** the south, Ezk 40:27
on the free space, one door **t** the north, Ezk 41:11
north, and another door **t** the south. Ezk 41:11
a human face **t** the palm tree on the Ezk 41:19
face of a young lion **t** the palm tree on Ezk 41:19
me out into the outer court, **t** the north, Ezk 42:1
to the chambers, **t** the outer court, Ezk 42:7
threshold of the temple **t** the east (for Ezk 47:1
to the outer gate that faces **t** the east; Ezk 47:2
"This water flows **t** the eastern region Ezk 47:8
in his upper chamber open **t** Jerusalem. Dn 6:10
four conspicuous horns **t** the four winds Dn 8:8
which grew exceedingly great **t** the south, Dn 8:9
great toward the south, **t** the east, Dn 8:9
toward the east, and **t** the glorious land. Dn 8:9
I turned my face **t** the ground and was Dn 10:15
be broken and divided **t** the four winds Dn 11:4
turn his face back **t** the fortresses of Dn 11:19
and his left hand **t** heaven and swore by Dn 12:7
black horses goes **t** the north country, Zec 6:6
the dappled ones go **t** the south country." Zec 6:6
those who go **t** the north country have Zec 6:8
stretching out his hand **t** his disciples, Mt 12:49
t the dawn of the first day of the week, Mt 28:1
Then turning **t** the woman he said to Lk 7:44
because his face was set **t** Jerusalem. Lk 9:53
for himself and is not rich **t** God." Lk 12:21
teaching and journeying **t** Jerusalem. Lk 13:22
for it is **t** evening and the day is now far Lk 24:29
The next day he saw Jesus coming **t** him, Jn 1:29
saw Nathanael coming **t** him and said Jn 1:47
that a large crowd was coming **t** him, Jn 6:5
disciple, and they were going **t** the tomb. Jn 20:3
"Rise and go **t** the south to the road Acts 8:26
might feel their way **t** him and find Acts 17:27
to Greeks of repentance **t** God and of Acts 20:21
and I journeyed **t** Damascus to take Acts 22:5
a clear conscience **t** both God and Acts 24:16
do not be arrogant **t** the branches. If Rom 11:18
severity **t** those who have fallen, but Rom 11:22
behaving properly **t** his betrothed, 1 Cor 7:36
and his grace **t** me was not in vain. 1 Cor 15:10
grace of God, and supremely so **t** you. 2 Cor 1:12
that we have through Christ **t** God. 2 Cor 3:4
I am acting with great boldness **t** you; I 2 Cor 7:4
you, but bold **t** you when I am away! 2 Cor 10:1
Jesus and your love **t** all the saints, Eph 1:15
greatness of his power **t** us who believe, Eph 1:19
his grace in kindness **t** us in Christ Eph 2:7
I press on **t** the goal for the prize of the Phil 3:14
Conduct yourselves wisely **t** outsiders, Col 4:5
was our conduct **t** you believers. 1 Thes 2:10
and to show perfect courtesy **t** all people. Ti 3:2
faith that you have **t** the Lord Jesus Phlm 1:5
from dead works and of faith **t** God, Heb 6:1
For I will be merciful **t** their iniquities, Heb 8:12
all of you, with humility **t** one another, 1 Pt 5:5
count slowness, but is patient **t** you, 2 Pt 3:9
is the confidence that we have **t** him, 1 Jn 5:14

TOWEL (2)
aside his outer garments, and taking a **t**, Jn 13:4
wipe them with the **t** that was wrapped Jn 13:5

TOWER (37)
ourselves a city and a **t** with its top in Gn 11:4
LORD came down to see the city and the **t**, Gn 11:5
pitched his tent beyond the **t** of Eder. Gn 35:21
again in peace, I will break down this **t**." Jgs 8:9
he broke down the **t** of Penuel and killed Jgs 8:17
the leaders of the **T** of Shechem heard of Jgs 9:46
the leaders of the **T** of Shechem were Jgs 9:47
the people of the **T** of Shechem also died, Jgs 9:49
But there was a strong **t** within the city, Jgs 9:51
in, and they went up to the roof of the **t**. Jgs 9:51
came to the **t** and fought against Jgs 9:52
to the door of the **t** to burn it with fire. Jgs 9:52
was standing on the **t** in Jezreel, 2 Kgs 9:17
it as far as the **T** of the Hundred, Neh 3:1
the Hundred, as far as the **T** of Hananel. Neh 3:1
another section and the **T** of the Ovens. Neh 3:11
buttress and the **t** projecting from the Neh 3:25
Gate on the east and the projecting **t**. Neh 3:26
opposite the great projecting **t** as far as Neh 3:27
on the wall, above the **T** of the Ovens, Neh 12:38
Fish Gate and the **T** of Hananel and Neh 12:39
of Hananel and the **T** of the Hundred, Neh 12:39
my refuge, a strong **t** against the enemy. Ps 61:3
The name of the LORD is a strong **t**; the Prv 18:10
Your neck is like the **t** of David, built in Sg 4:4
Your neck is like an ivory **t**. Your eyes are Sg 7:4
Your nose is like a **t** of Lebanon, which Sg 7:4
against every high **t**, and against every Is 2:15
the LORD from the **t** of Hananel to the Jer 31:38
And you, O **t** of the flock, hill of the Mi 4:8
hasten to the wall; the siege **t** is set up. Na 2:5
watchpost and station myself on the **t**, Hab 2:1
and from the **T** of Hananel to the Zec 14:10
in it and built a **t** and leased it to Mt 21:33
dug a pit for the winepress and built a **t**, Mk 12:1
eighteen on whom the **t** in Siloam fell Lk 13:4
For which of you, desiring to build a **t**, Lk 14:28

TOWERED (3)
it **t** aloft among the thick boughs; Ezk 19:11
So it **t** high above all the trees of the Ezk 31:5
Because it **t** high and set its top among Ezk 31:10

TOWERING (2)
and forest shade, and of **t** height, Ezk 31:3
waters may grow to **t** height or set Ezk 31:14

TOWERS (19)
the cities, in the villages and in the **t**, 1 Chr 27:25
and surround them with walls and **t**, 2 Chr 14:7
Uzziah built **t** in Jerusalem at the 2 Chr 26:9
And he built **t** in the wilderness and 2 Chr 26:10
men, to be on the **t** and the corners, 2 Chr 26:15
and forts and **t** on the wooded hills. 2 Chr 27:4
broken down and raised **t** upon it, 2 Chr 32:5
Zion, go around her, number her **t**, Ps 48:12
your walls and security within your **t**!" Ps 122:7
I was a wall, and my breasts were like **t**; Sg 8:10
Hyenas will cry in its **t**, and jackals in Is 13:22
They erected their siege **t**, they stripped Is 23:13
and will besiege you with **t** and I will raise Is 29:3
of the great slaughter, when the **t** fall. Is 30:25
Where is he who counted the **t**?" Is 33:18
to cast up mounds, to build siege **t**. Ezk 21:22
the walls of Tyre and break down her **t**, Ezk 26:4
his axes he will break down your **t**. Ezk 26:9
and men of Gamad were in your **t**. Ezk 27:11

TOWN (54)
we will spend the night in the **t** square." Gn 19:2
but the **t** of Tappuah on the boundary of Jos 17:8
return to his own **t** and his own home, Jos 20:6
own home, to the **t** from which he fled.'" Jos 20:6
at Gibeah, the **t** of Phinehas his son, Jos 24:33
and the men of the **t** to do it by day, Jgs 6:27
When the men of the **t** rose early in the Jgs 6:28
Then the men of the **t** said to Joash, Jgs 6:30
thirty men of the **t** and took their spoil Jgs 14:19
man departed from the **t** of Bethlehem in Jgs 17:8
the whole **t** was stirred because of them. Ru 1:19
in by entering a **t** that has gates and 1 Sm 23:7
Jerusalem and Judah, each to his own **t**. Ezr 2:1
to Jerusalem and Judah, each to his **t**. Neh 7:6
beside the gates in front of the **t**, at the Prv 8:3
to call from the highest places in the **t**, Prv 9:3
a seat on the highest places of the **t**, Prv 9:14
of shoutings, tumultuous city, exultant **t**? Is 22:2
him who builds a **t** with blood and Hab 2:12
and enter no **t** of the Samaritans, Mt 10:5
And whatever **t** or village you enter, Mt 10:11
feet when you leave that house or **t**. Mt 10:14
Sodom and Gomorrah than for that **t**. Mt 10:15
When they persecute you in one **t**, flee Mt 10:23
and persecute from **t** to town, Mt 23:34
and persecute from town to **t**, Mt 23:34
Jesus could no longer openly enter a **t**, Mk 1:45
into the hill country, to a **t** in Judah, Lk 1:39
all went to be registered, each to his own **t**. Lk 2:3
up from Galilee, from the **t** of Nazareth, Lk 2:4
into Galilee, to their own **t** of Nazareth. Lk 2:39
him out of the **t** and brought him to Lk 4:29
of the hill on which their **t** was built, Lk 4:29
afterward he went to a **t** called Nain, Lk 7:11
As he drew near to the gate of the **t**, Lk 7:12
crowd from the **t** was with her. Lk 7:12
and people from **t** after town came Lk 8:4
and people from town after **t** came to him, Lk 8:4
when you leave that **t** shake off the dust Lk 9:5
withdrew apart to a **t** called Bethsaida. Lk 9:10
into every **t** and place where he himself Lk 10:1
Whenever you enter a **t** and they receive Lk 10:8
whenever you enter a **t** and they do not Lk 10:10
the dust of your **t** that clings to our Lk 10:11
on that day for Sodom than for that **t**. Lk 10:12
Joseph, from the Jewish **t** of Arimathea. Lk 23:50
he came to a **t** of Samaria called Sychar, Jn 4:5
jar and went away into **t** and said to the Jn 4:28
went out of the **t** and were coming to Jn 4:30
Samaritans from that **t** believed in him Jn 4:39
the wilderness, to a **t** called Ephraim, Jn 11:54
And when the **t** clerk had quieted the Acts 19:35
appoint elders in every **t** as I directed you Ti 1:5
into such and such a **t** and spend a year Jas 4:13

TOWNS (74)
and the Levite that is within your **t**, Dt 12:12
and eat meat within any of your **t**, Dt 12:15
not eat within your **t** the tithe of your Dt 12:17
and the Levite who is within your **t**. Dt 12:18
eat within your **t** whenever you desire. Dt 12:21
it to the sojourner who is within your **t**, Dt 14:21
neglect the Levite who is within your **t**, Dt 14:27
same year and lay it up within your **t**. Dt 14:28
and the widow, who are within your **t**, Dt 14:29
in any of your **t** within your land that Dt 15:7
You shall eat it within your **t**. The Dt 15:22
within any of your **t** that the LORD your Dt 16:5
servant, the Levite who is within your **t**, Dt 16:11
and the widow who are within your **t**. Dt 16:14
officers in all your **t** that the LORD your Dt 16:18
within any of your **t** that the LORD your Dt 17:2
any case within your **t** that is too Dt 17:8
from any of your **t** out of all Israel, Dt 18:6
he shall choose within one of your **t**, Dt 23:16
who are in your land within your **t**. Dt 24:14
they may eat within your **t** and be filled, Dt 26:12
"They shall besiege you in all your **t**, Dt 28:52
you in all your **t** throughout all your Dt 28:52
enemy shall distress you in all your **t**. Dt 28:55
your enemy shall distress you in your **t**. Dt 28:57
ones, and the sojourner within your **t**, Dt 31:12
edge of the sword, and its king and its **t**, Jos 10:37
he captured it with its king and all its **t**. Jos 10:39
Og king of Bashan, and all the **t** of Jair, Jos 13:30
Ekron, with its **t** and its villages; Jos 15:45
Ashdod, its **t** and its villages; Gaza, its Jos 15:47
its villages; Gaza, its **t** and its villages; Jos 15:47
together with the **t** that were set apart for Jos 16:9
all those **t** with their villages. Jos 16:9
a description of it by **t** in seven divisions. Jos 18:9
And all the **t** that they found they set on Jgs 20:48
and rebuilt the **t** and lived in Jgs 21:23
be given me in one of the country **t**, 1 Sm 27:5
and they lived in the **t** of Hebron. 2 Sm 2:3
themselves high places in all their **t**, 2 Kgs 17:9
Kenath, and its villages, sixty **t**. 1 Chr 2:23
lived in Gilead, in Bashan and in its **t**, 1 Chr 5:16
and settlements were Bethel and its **t**, 1 Chr 7:28
and to the west Gezer and its **t**, 1 Chr 7:28
and its towns, Shechem and its **t**, 1 Chr 7:28
and its towns, and Ayyah and its **t**; 1 Chr 7:28
the Manassites, Beth-shean and its **t**, 1 Chr 7:29
and its towns, Taanach and its **t**, 1 Chr 7:29
and its towns, Megiddo and its **t**, 1 Chr 7:29
Megiddo and its towns, Dor and its **t**. 1 Chr 7:29
who built Ono and Lod with its **t**, 1 Chr 8:12
and the temple servants lived in their **t**, Ezr 2:70
towns, and all the rest of Israel in their **t**. Ezr 2:70
and the children of Israel were in the **t**, Ezr 3:1
servants, and all Israel, lived in their **t**. Neh 7:73
the people of Israel were in their **t**. Neh 7:73
it in all their **t** and in Jerusalem, Neh 8:15
the tithes in all our **t** where we labor. Neh 10:37
nine out of ten remained in the other **t**. Neh 11:1
but in the **t** of Judah everyone lived on Neh 11:3
lived on his property in their **t**: Neh 11:3
the Levites, were in all the **t** of Judah, Neh 11:20
Levites according to the fields of the **t**, Neh 12:44
of the villages, who live in the rural **t**, Est 9:19
and upon all its **t** all the disaster that Jer 19:15
Zion, young women in the **t** of Judah. Lam 5:11
gone through all the **t** of Israel before Mt 10:23
it, they followed him on foot from the **t**. Mt 14:13
said to them, "Let us go on to the next **t**, Mk 1:38
foot from all the **t** and got there ahead Mk 6:33
kingdom of God to the other **t** as well; Lk 4:43
went on his way through **t** and villages, Lk 13:22
gathered from the **t** around Jerusalem, Acts 5:16
the gospel to all the **t** until he came to Acts 8:40

TOWNSMEN (1)
for all my fellow **t** know that you are a Ru 3:11

TRACE (1)
so that not a **t** of them could be found. Dn 2:35

TRACHONITIS (1)
tetrarch of the region of Ituraea and **T**, Lk 3:1

TRACKED (1)
Gilead is a city of evildoers, **t** with blood. Hos 6:8

TRACKLESS (1)
and makes them wander in **t** wastes; Ps 107:40

TRACKS (2)
your wagon **t** overflow with Ps 65:11
among women, follow in the **t** of the flock, Sg 1:8

TRADE (15)
shall be open to you. Dwell and **t** in it, Gn 34:10
let them dwell in the land and **t** in it, Gn 34:21
to you, and you shall **t** in the land.'" Gn 42:34
and priest ply their **t** through the land Jer 14:18
they **t** their treasures for food to revive Lam 1:11
carried it to a land of **t** and set it in a Ezk 17:4
wisdom in your **t** you have increased Ezk 28:5
abundance of your **t** you were filled Ezk 28:16
of your **t** you profaned Ezk 28:18
make my Father's house a house of **t**." Jn 2:16
was of the same **t** he stayed with them Acts 18:3
worked, for they were tentmakers by **t**. Acts 18:3
not only that this **t** of ours may come Acts 19:27
a year there and **t** and make a profit" Jas 4:13
sailors and all whose **t** is on the sea, Rv 18:17

TRADED (9)
Tubal, and Meshech **t** with you; Ezk 27:13
The men of Dedan **t** with you. Many Ezk 27:15
and the land of Israel **t** with you; Ezk 27:17
Dedan **t** with you in saddlecloths for Ezk 27:20
of Sheba and Raamah **t** with you; Ezk 27:22
Asshur, and Chilmad **t** with you. Ezk 27:23
In your market these **t** with you in Ezk 27:24
my people, and have **t** a boy for a prostitute, Jl 3:3
talents went at once and **t** with them, Mt 25:16

TRADER (1)
shall no longer be a **t** in the house of Zec 14:21

TRADERS (11)
Then Midianite **t** passed by. And they Gn 37:28
and the king's **t** received them from 1 Kgs 10:28
through the king's **t** they were 1 Kgs 10:29
and the king's **t** would buy them 2 Chr 1:16
Will **t** bargain over him? Will they Jb 41:6
whose **t** were the honored of the earth? Is 23:8
The **t** of Sheba and Raamah traded Ezk 27:22
Haran, Canneh, Eden, **t** of Sheba, Ezk 27:23
of the Mortar! For all the **t** are no more; Zep 1:11
to be slaughtered by the sheep **t**. Zec 11:7
annulled on that day, and the sheep **t**, Zec 11:11

TRADES (1)
with the workmen in similar **t**, Acts 19:25

TRADING (2)
from the profit of his **t** he will get no Jb 20:18
also with the **t** land of Chaldea, Ezk 16:29

TRADITION (10)
your disciples break the **t** of the elders? Mt 15:2
of God for the sake of your **t**? Mt 15:3
the sake of your **t** you have made void Mt 15:6
their hands, holding to the **t** of the elders, Mk 7:3
not walk according to the **t** of the elders, Mk 7:5
of God and hold to the **t** of men." Mk 7:8
of God in order to establish your **t**! Mk 7:9
of God by your **t** that you have handed Mk 7:13
and empty deceit, according to human **t**, Col 2:8
in accord with the **t** that you received 2 Thes 3:6

TRADITIONS (4)
there are many other **t** that they observe, Mk 7:4
and maintain the **t** even as I 1 Cor 11:2
zealous was I for the **t** of my fathers. Gal 1:14
and hold to the **t** that you were 2 Thes 2:15

TRAIN (6)
of captives in your **t** and receiving gifts Ps 68:18
T up a child in the way he should go; Prv 22:6
up; and the **t** of his robe filled the temple. Is 6:1
and the Cushites shall follow in his **t**. Dn 11:43
myths. Rather **t** yourself for godliness; 1 Tm 4:7
and so **t** the young women to love their Ti 2:4

TRAINED (12)
taken captive, he led forth his **t** men, Gn 14:14
who were **t** in singing to the LORD, 1 Chr 25:7
and blue fabrics, **t** also in engraving, 2 Chr 2:7
He is **t** to work in gold, silver, bronze, 2 Chr 2:14
Although I **t** and strengthened their Hos 7:15
Ephraim was a **t** calf that loved to Hos 10:11
scribe who has been **t** for the kingdom Mt 13:52
when he is fully **t** will be like his Lk 6:40
being **t** in the words of the faith and of 1 Tm 4:6
powers of discernment **t** by constant Heb 5:14
to those who have been **t** by it. Heb 12:11

souls. They have hearts **t** in greed. 2 Pt 2:14

TRAINING (3)
for while bodily **t** is of some value, 1 Tm 4:8
correction, and for **t** in righteousness, 2 Tm 3:16
t us to renounce ungodliness and Ti 2:12

TRAINS (3)
He **t** my hands for war, so that my 2 Sm 22:35
He **t** my hands for war, so that my arms Ps 18:34
LORD, my rock, who **t** my hands for war, Ps 144:1

TRAITOR (6)
the righteous, and the **t** for the upright. Prv 21:18
but he overthrows the words of the **t**. Prv 22:12
A stern vision is told to me; the **t** betrays, Is 21:2
yourself have not been destroyed, you **t**, Is 33:1
"Moreover, wine is a **t**, an arrogant man Hab 2:5
and Judas Iscariot, who became a **t**. Lk 6:16

TRAITORS (4)
and increases the **t** among mankind. Prv 23:28
Woe is me! For the **t** have betrayed, with Is 24:16
with betrayal the **t** have betrayed." Is 24:16
you idly look at **t** and are silent when Hab 1:13

TRAMPING (1)
every boot of the **t** warrior in battle tumult Is 9:5

TRAMPLE (14)
and that the wild beast may **t** them. Jb 39:15
and let him **t** my life to the ground and lay Ps 7:5
my enemies **t** on me all day long, for Ps 56:2
T underfoot those who lust after Ps 68:30
and the serpent you will **t** underfoot. Ps 91:13
and on my mountains **t** him underfoot; Is 14:25
he shall **t** on rulers as on mortar, as the Is 41:25
of his horses he will **t** all your streets. Ezk 26:11
devour the whole earth, and **t** it down, Dn 7:23
those who **t** the head of the poor into the Am 2:7
Therefore because you **t** on the poor Am 5:11
you who **t** on the needy and bring the Am 8:4
lest they **t** them underfoot and turn to Mt 7:6
and they will **t** the holy city for forty-two Rv 11:2

TRAMPLED (22)
And the people **t** him in the gate, so 2 Kgs 7:17
for the people **t** him in the gate and he 2 Kgs 7:20
and on the horses, and they **t** on her. 2 Kgs 9:33
passed by and **t** down the thistle. 2 Kgs 14:9
passed by and **t** down the thistle. 2 Chr 25:18
out the heavens and **t** the waves of the Jb 9:8
break down its wall, and it shall be **t** down. Is 5:5
of the pit, like a dead body **t** underfoot. Is 14:19
and Moab shall be **t** down in his place, Is 25:10
place, as straw is **t** down in a dunghill. Is 25:10
in my anger and **t** them in my wrath; Is 63:3
I **t** down the peoples in my anger; I made Is 63:6
our adversaries have **t** down your Is 63:18
vineyard; they have **t** down my portion; Jer 12:10
him down to the ground and **t** on him. Dn 8:7
down to the ground and **t** on them. Dn 8:10
sanctuary and host to be **t** underfoot?" Dn 8:13
now she will be **t** down like the mire of Mi 7:10
You **t** the sea with your horses, the Hab 3:15
be thrown out and **t** under people's feet. Mt 5:13
fell along the path and was **t** underfoot, Lk 8:5
Jerusalem will be **t** underfoot by the Lk 21:24

TRAMPLES (5)
gracious to me, O God, for man **t** on me; Ps 56:1
he will put to shame him who **t** on me. Ps 57:3
and he who **t** underfoot has vanished Is 16:4
The foot **t** it, the feet of the poor, the steps Is 26:6
before him, so that he **t** kings underfoot; Is 41:2

TRAMPLING (4)
has required of you this **t** of my courts? Is 1:12
day of tumult and **t** and confusion in the Is 22:5
battle, **t** the foe in the mud of the streets; Zec 10:5
together that they were **t** one another, Lk 12:1

TRANCE (3)
they were preparing it, he fell into a **t** Acts 10:10
Joppa praying, and in a **t** I saw a vision, Acts 11:5
praying in the temple, I fell into a **t** Acts 22:17

TRANQUIL (1)
A **t** heart gives life to the flesh, but Prv 14:30

TRANSACTION (1)
to confirm a **t**, the one drew off his sandal Ru 4:7

TRANSFER (3)
father's brothers and **t** the inheritance Nm 27:7
then you shall **t** his inheritance to his Nm 27:8
to **t** the kingdom from the house of 2 Sm 3:10

TRANSFERRED (3)
of Israel shall not be **t** from one tribe to Nm 36:7
inheritance shall be **t** from one tribe Nm 36:9
domain of darkness and **t** us to the Col 1:13

TRANSFIGURED (2)
And he was **t** before them, and his face Mt 17:2
by themselves. And he was **t** before them, Mk 9:2

TRANSFORM (1)
who will **t** our lowly body to be like his Phil 3:21

TRANSFORMED (2)
but be **t** by the renewal of your mind, Rom 12:2
are being **t** into the same image from 2 Cor 3:18

TRANSGRESS (7)
if you **t** the covenant of the LORD your Jos 23:16
"Why do you **t** the king's command?" Est 3:3
have purposed that my mouth will not **t**. Ps 17:3
the waters might not **t** his command, Prv 8:29
you, and those who **t** against me. Ezk 20:38
"Come to Bethel, and **t**; to Gilgal, and Am 4:4
that no one **t** and wrong his brother 1 Thes 4:6

TRANSGRESSED (17)
I have not **t** any of your Dt 26:13
they have **t** my covenant that I Jos 7:11
because he has **t** the covenant of the Jos 7:15
this people have **t** my covenant that Jgs 2:20
for I have **t** the commandment of the 1 Sm 15:24
LORD their God but **t** his covenant, 2 Kgs 18:12
for we have greatly **t** in this matter. Ezr 10:13
for they have **t** the laws, violated the Is 24:5
and your mediators **t** against me. Is 43:27
not know me; the shepherds **t** against me; Jer 2:8
You have all **t** against me, declares the Jer 2:29
And the men who **t** my covenant and Jer 34:18
"We have **t** and rebelled, and you have Lam 3:42
and their fathers have **t** against me to Ezk 2:3
All Israel has **t** your law and turned Dn 9:11
But like Adam they **t** the covenant; there Hos 6:7
because they have **t** my covenant and Hos 8:1

TRANSGRESSES (2)
When a land **t**, it has many rulers, but Prv 28:2
shall not deliver him when he **t**, Ezk 33:12

TRANSGRESSING (3)
"Why now are you **t** the command of Nm 14:41
of the LORD your God, in **t** his covenant, Dt 17:2
t, and denying the LORD, and turning Is 59:13

TRANSGRESSION (43)
Please forgive the **t** of your brothers Gn 50:17
please forgive the **t** of the servants of Gn 50:17
him, for he will not pardon your **t**, Ex 23:21
forgiving iniquity and **t** and sin, Ex 34:7
love, forgiving iniquity and **t**, Nm 14:18
you not pardon my **t** and take away my Jb 7:21
has delivered them into the hand of their **t**. Jb 8:4
sins? Make me know my **t** and my sin. Jb 13:23
my **t** would be sealed up in a bag, and Jb 14:17
You say, 'I am pure, without **t**; I am Jb 33:9
is incurable, though I am without **t**.' Jb 34:6
and he does not take much note of **t**, Jb 35:15
be blameless, and innocent of great **t**. Ps 19:13
Blessed is the one whose **t** is forgiven, Ps 32:1
T speaks to the wicked deep in his heart; Ps 36:1
me. For no **t** or sin of mine, O LORD, Ps 59:3
I will punish their **t** with the rod and Ps 89:32
words are many, **t** is not lacking, Prv 10:19
man is ensnared by the **t** of his lips, Prv 12:13
Whoever loves **t** loves strife; he who Prv 17:19
"That is no **t**," is a companion to a Prv 28:24
An evil man is ensnared in his **t**, but a Prv 29:6
the wicked increase, **t** increases, Prv 29:16
and one given to anger causes much **t**. Prv 29:22
its **t** lies heavy upon it, and it falls, and Is 24:20
the living, stricken for the **t** of my people? Is 53:8
Are you not children of **t**, the offspring of Is 57:4
declare to my people their **t**, to the house Is 58:1
who turn from **t**," declares the LORD. Is 59:20
the regular burnt offering because of **t**, Dn 8:12
offering, the **t** that makes desolate, Dn 8:13
people and your holy city, to finish the **t**, Dn 9:24
and transgress; to Gilgal, and multiply **t**; Am 4:4
All this is for the **t** of Jacob and for the Mi 1:5
the house of Israel. What is the **t** of Jacob? Mi 1:5
to declare to Jacob his **t** and to Israel his Mi 3:8
Shall I give my firstborn for my **t**, the Mi 6:7
and passing over **t** for the remnant Mi 7:18
but where there is no law there is no **t**. Rom 4:15
sinning was not like the **t** of Adam, Rom 5:14
Brothers, if anyone is caught in any **t**, Gal 6:1
reliable and every **t** or disobedience Heb 2:2
but was rebuked for his own **t**; a 2 Pt 2:16

TRANSGRESSIONS (48)
people of Israel and because of their **t**, Lv 16:16
of the people of Israel, and all their **t**, Lv 16:21
he will not forgive your **t** or your sins. Jos 24:19
and all their **t** that they have 1 Kgs 8:50
if I have concealed my **t** as others do by Jb 31:33
And if your **t** are multiplied, what do you Jb 35:6

declares to them their work and their **t**, Jb 36:9
the abundance of their **t** cast them out, Ps 5:10
not the sins of my youth or my **t**; Ps 25:7
"I will confess my **t** to the LORD," and you Ps 32:5
Deliver me from all my **t**. Do not make Ps 39:8
to your abundant mercy blot out my **t**. Ps 51:1
For I know my **t**, and my sin is ever Ps 51:3
prevail against me, you atone for our **t**. Ps 65:3
so far does he remove our **t** from us. Ps 103:12
Whoever conceals his **t** will not Prv 28:13
who blots out your **t** for my own sake, Is 43:25
I have blotted out your **t** like a cloud and Is 44:22
and for your **t** your mother was sent Is 50:1
But he was wounded for our **t**; he was Is 53:5
For our **t** are multiplied before you, and Is 59:12
for our **t** are with us, and we know our Is 59:12
torn in pieces, because their **t** are many, Jer 5:6
afflicted her for the multitude of her **t**; Lam 1:5
"My **t** were bound into a yoke; by his Lam 1:14
have dealt with me because of all my **t**; Lam 1:22
themselves anymore with all their **t**, Ezk 14:11
None of the **t** that he has committed Ezk 18:22
away from all the **t** that he had Ezk 18:28
Repent and turn from all your **t**, lest Ezk 18:30
from you all the **t** that you have Ezk 18:31
in that your **t** are uncovered, Ezk 21:24
'Surely our **t** and our sins are upon us, Ezk 33:10
things, or with any of their **t**. Ezk 37:23
to their uncleanness and their **t**, Ezk 39:24
says the LORD: "For three **t** of Damascus, Am 1:3
Thus says the LORD: "For three **t** of Gaza, Am 1:6
Thus says the LORD: "For three **t** of Tyre, Am 1:9
says the LORD: "For three **t** of Edom, Am 1:11
"For three **t** of the Ammonites, and for Am 1:13
says the LORD: "For three **t** of Moab, Am 2:1
says the LORD: "For three **t** of Judah, Am 2:4
Thus says the LORD: "For three **t** of Israel, Am 2:6
"that on the day I punish Israel for his **t**, Am 3:14
how many are your **t** and how great are Am 5:12
for in you were found the **t** of Israel. Mi 1:13
It was added because of **t**, until the Gal 3:19
them from the **t** committed under the Heb 9:15

TRANSGRESSOR (3)
I tore down, I prove myself to be a **t**. Gal 2:18
woman was deceived and became a **t**. 1 Tm 2:14
murder, you have become a **t** of the law. Jas 2:11

TRANSGRESSORS (9)
But **t** shall be altogether destroyed; the Ps 37:38
Then I will teach **t** your ways, and Ps 51:13
and stand firm, recall it to mind, you **t**, Is 46:8
to death and was numbered with the **t**; Is 53:12
many, and makes intercession for the **t**. Is 53:12
when the **t** have reached their limit, Dn 8:23
walk in them, but **t** stumble in them. Hos 14:9
me: 'And he was numbered with the **t**.' Lk 22:37
sin and are convicted by the law as **t**. Jas 2:9

TRANSIENT (1)
For the things that are seen are **t**, but 2 Cor 4:18

TRANSLATED (2)
The letter was written in Aramaic and **t**. Ezr 4:7
Tabitha, which, **t**, means Dorcas. Acts 9:36

TRANSLATION (1)
He is first, by **t** of his name, king of Heb 7:2

TRANSPARENT (1)
of the city was pure gold, **t** as glass. Rv 21:21

TRAP (15)
they shall be a snare and a **t** for you, Jos 23:13
then are you laying a **t** for my life to 1 Sm 28:9
A **t** seizes him by the heel; a snare lays Jb 18:9
in the ground, a **t** for him in the path. Jb 18:10
when they are at peace, let it become a **t**. Ps 69:22
The arrogant have hidden a **t** for me, Ps 140:5
Keep me from the **t** that they have laid Ps 141:9
I walk they have hidden a **t** for me. Ps 142:3
a **t** and a snare to the inhabitants of Is 8:14
in wait. They set a **t**; they catch men. Jer 5:26
on the earth, when there is no **t** for it? Am 3:5
bread have set a **t** beneath you—you Ob 1:7
of the Herodians, to **t** him in his talk. Mk 12:13
day come upon you suddenly like a **t**. Lk 21:34
their table become a snare and a **t**, Rom 11:9

TRAPPED (2)
of their lips, let them be **t** in their pride. Ps 59:12
are all of them **t** in holes and hidden Is 42:22

TRAVEL (7)
that they might **t** by day and by night. Ex 13:21
you not asked those who **t** the roads, Jb 21:29
set apart men to **t** through the land Ezk 39:14
And when these **t** through the land Ezk 39:15
For you **t** across sea and land to make Mt 23:15
who were Paul's companions in **t**. Acts 19:29
by the churches to **t** with us as we 2 Cor 8:19

TRAVELED (3)
for many days we **t** around Mount Seir. Dt 2:1
The ships of Tarshish **t** for you with Ezk 27:25
that arose over Stephen **t** as far as Acts 11:19

TRAVELER (5)
eyes and saw the **t** in the open square Jgs 19:17
Now there came a **t** to the rich man, 2 Sm 12:4
street; I have opened my doors to the **t**), Jb 31:32
The highways lie waste; the **t** ceases. Is 33:8
like a **t** who turns aside to tarry for a Jer 14:8

TRAVELERS (6)
abandoned, and **t** kept to the byways. Jgs 5:6
of Tema look, the **t** of Sheba hope. Jb 6:19
anyone lives; they are forgotten by **t**; Jb 28:4
for burial in Israel, the Valley of the **T**, Ezk 39:11
It will block the **t**, for there Gog and Ezk 39:11
and bury those **t** remaining on the Ezk 39:14

TRAVELERS' (1)
that I had in the desert a **t** lodging place, Jer 9:2

TRAVELING (2)
'You have been **t** around this mountain Dt 2:3
The men who were **t** with him stood Acts 9:7

TRAVELS (1)
who **t** in company with evildoers and Jb 34:8

TRAYS (3)
Its tongs and their **t** shall be of pure Ex 25:38
and its tongs and its **t** of pure gold. Ex 37:23
the light, with its lamps, its tongs, its **t**, Nm 4:9

TREACHEROUS (20)
My brothers are **t** as a torrent-bed, as Jb 6:15
shall be ashamed who are wantonly **t**. Ps 25:3
land, and the **t** will be rooted out of it. Prv 2:22
the crookedness of the **t** destroys them. Prv 11:3
but the **t** are taken captive by their lust. Prv 11:6
but the desire of the **t** is for violence. Prv 13:2
favor, but the way of the **t** is their ruin. Prv 13:15
Trusting in a **t** man in time of trouble Prv 25:19
not return, and her **t** sister Judah saw it. Jer 3:7
Yet her **t** sister Judah did not fear, but she Jer 3:8
Yet for all this her **t** sister Judah did not Jer 3:10
herself more righteous than **t** Judah. Jer 3:11
Surely, as a **t** wife leaves her husband, so Jer 3:20
her husband, so have you been **t** to me, Jer 3:20
house of Judah have been utterly **t** to me, Jer 5:11
are all adulterers, a company of **t** men. Jer 9:2
prosper? Why do all who are **t** thrive? Jer 12:1
but not upward; they are like a **t** bow; Hos 7:16
Her prophets are fickle, **t** men; her priests Zep 3:4
t, reckless, swollen with conceit, lovers 2 Tm 3:4

TREACHEROUSLY (12)
of Israel to act **t** against the LORD in Nm 31:16
of Shechem dealt **t** with Abimelech, Jgs 9:23
And he said, "You have dealt **t**; 1 Sm 14:33
if I had dealt **t** against his life (and 2 Sm 18:13
great evil and act **t** against our God Neh 13:27
spare none of those who **t** plot evil. Ps 59:5
away and acted **t** like their fathers; Ps 78:57
For I knew that you would surely deal **t**, Is 48:8
father, even they have dealt **t** with you; Jer 12:6
her; all her friends have dealt **t** with her; Lam 1:2
blasphemed me, by dealing **t** with me. Ezk 20:27
because they dealt so **t** with me that I Ezk 39:23

TREACHERY (10)
fathers in their **t** that they committed Lv 26:40
saying to Ahaziah, "**T**, O Ahaziah!" 2 Kgs 9:23
king of Assyria found **t** in Hoshea, 2 Kgs 17:4
of ruin and meditate **t** all day long. Ps 38:12
men of blood and **t** shall not live out Ps 55:23
him there for the **t** he has committed Ezk 17:20
for the **t** of which he is guilty and the Ezk 18:24
and all the **t** they have practiced Ezk 39:26
because of the **t** that they have Dn 9:7
the king glad, and the princes by their **t**. Hos 7:3

TREAD (27)
so much as for the sole of the foot to **t** on, Dt 2:5
of you on all the land that you shall **t**, Dt 11:25
you, and you shall **t** upon their backs." Dt 33:29
sole of your foot will **t** upon I have given Jos 1:3
of Dagon do not **t** on the threshold of 1 Sm 5:5
they **t** the winepresses, but suffer thirst. Jb 24:11
bring him low and **t** down the wicked Jb 40:12
through your name we **t** down those who Ps 44:5
it is he who will **t** down our foes. Ps 60:12
You will **t** on the lion and the adder; the Ps 91:13
it is he who will **t** down our foes. Ps 108:13
Three things are stately in their **t**; four Prv 30:29
cattle are let loose and where sheep **t**. Is 7:25
and to **t** them down like the mire of the Is 10:6
fold, and shout, like those who **t** grapes, Jer 25:30
that you must **t** down with your feet Ezk 34:18
is ripe. Go in, **t**, for the winepress is full. Jl 3:13
will come down and **t** upon the high Mi 1:3
you shall **t** olives, but not anoint Mi 6:15
you shall **t** grapes, but not drink wine. Mi 6:15
on us; he will **t** our iniquities under foot. Mi 7:19
your forts; go into the clay; **t** the mortar; Na 3:14
he makes me **t** on my high places. Hab 3:19
devour, and **t** down the sling stones, Zec 9:15
And you shall **t** down the wicked, for Mal 4:3
you authority to **t** on serpents and Lk 10:19
He will **t** the winepress of the fury of the Rv 19:15

TREADER (3)
land; no **t** turns toward their vineyards. Jb 24:18
no **t** treads out wine in the presses; Is 16:10
the reaper and the **t** of grapes him who Am 9:13

TREADING (2)
muzzle an ox when it is **t** out the grain. Dt 25:4
in Judah people **t** winepresses on the Neh 13:15

TREADS (12)
the sole of your foot **t** shall be yours. Dt 11:24
no treader **t** out wine in the presses; Is 16:10
rulers as on mortar, as the potter **t** clay. Is 41:25
no one who **t** on them knows peace. Is 59:8
garments like his who **t** in the winepress? Is 63:2
no one **t** them with shouts of joy; Jer 48:33
and **t** on the heights of the earth—the Am 4:13
comes into our land and **t** in our palaces, Mi 5:5
into our land and **t** within our border. Mi 5:6
goes through, **t** down and tears in pieces, Mi 5:8
an ox when it **t** out the grain." Is 1 Cor 9:9
an ox when it **t** out the grain," and, 1 Tm 5:18

TREASON (5)
there is no wrong or **t** in my hands. 1 Sm 24:11
her clothes and cried, "**T**! Treason!" 2 Kgs 11:14
her clothes and cried, "Treason! **T**!" 2 Kgs 11:14
her clothes and cried, "**T**! Treason!" 2 Chr 23:13
her clothes and cried, "Treason! **T**!" 2 Chr 23:13

TREASURE (31)
your father has put **t** in your sacks for Gn 43:23
and he showed them all his **t** house, 2 Kgs 20:13
I have a **t** of my own of gold and 1 Chr 29:3
You fill their womb with **t**; they are Ps 17:14
my words and **t** up my commandments Prv 2:1
my words and **t** up my commandments Prv 7:1
house of the righteous there is much **t**, Prv 15:6
the LORD than great **t** and trouble with Prv 15:16
Precious **t** and oil are in a wise man's Prv 21:20
and gold and the **t** of kings and Eccl 2:8
knowledge; the fear of the LORD is Zion's **t**. Is 33:6
And he showed them his **t** house, the Is 39:2
they have taken **t** and precious things; Ezk 22:25
There is no end of the **t** or of the wealth of Na 2:9
For where your **t** is, there your heart will Mt 6:21
out of his good **t** brings forth good, Mt 12:35
person out of his evil **t** brings forth evil. Mt 12:35
of heaven is like **t** hidden in a field, Mt 13:44
who brings out of his **t** what is new and Mt 13:52
the poor, and you will have **t** in heaven; Mt 19:21
poor, and you will have **t** in heaven; Mk 10:21
out of the good **t** of his heart produces Lk 6:45
evil person out of his evil **t** produces evil, Lk 6:45
the one who lays up **t** for himself and is Lk 12:21
with a **t** in the heavens that does not Lk 12:33
For where your **t** is, there will your Lk 12:34
the poor, and you will have **t** in heaven; Lk 18:22
who was in charge of all her **t**. Acts 8:27
But we have this **t** in jars of clay, to 2 Cor 4:7
thus storing up **t** for themselves as a 1 Tm 6:19
fire. You have laid up **t** in the last days. Jas 5:3

TREASURED (10)
you shall be my **t** possession among all Ex 19:5
you to be a people for his **t** possession, Dt 7:6
you to be a people for his **t** possession, Dt 14:2
you are a people for his **t** possession, Dt 26:18
I have **t** the words of his mouth more Jb 23:12
consult together against your **t** ones. Ps 83:3
and they shall profane my **t** place. Ezk 7:22
day when I make up my **t** possession, Mal 3:17
But Mary **t** up all these things, Lk 2:19
And his mother **t** up all these things in Lk 2:51

TREASURER (2)
these out in charge of Mithredath the **t**, Ezr 1:8
Erastus, the city **t**, and our brother Rom 16:23

TREASURERS (4)
decree to all the **t** in the province Ezr 7:21
I appointed as **t** over the storehouses Neh 13:13
and the governors, the counselors, the **t**, Dn 3:2
and the governors, the counselors, the **t**, Dn 3:3

TREASURES (41)
of the seas and the hidden **t** of the sand." Dt 33:19

He took away the **t** of the house of	1 Kgs 14:26
the LORD and the **t** of the king's	1 Kgs 14:26
that were left in the **t** of the house of	1 Kgs 15:18
the LORD and the **t** of the king's	1 Kgs 15:18
LORD and in the **t** of the king's house	2 Kgs 16:8
carried off all the **t** of the house of	2 Kgs 24:13
the LORD and the **t** of the king's	2 Kgs 24:13
the chambers and the **t** of the house	1 Chr 9:26
He took away the **t** of the house of the	2 Chr 12:9
the LORD and the **t** of the king's house.	2 Chr 12:9
and gold from the **t** of the house of	2 Chr 16:2
and the **t** of the house of the LORD,	2 Chr 36:18
and the **t** of the king and of his	2 Chr 36:18
not, and dig for it more than for hidden **t**,	Jb 3:21
Utter darkness is laid up for his **t**; a fire	Jb 20:26
silver and search for it as for hidden **t**,	Prv 2:4
T gained by wickedness do not profit,	Prv 10:2
The getting of **t** by a lying tongue is a	Prv 21:6
and gold, and there is no end to their **t**;	Is 2:7
of peoples, and plunder their **t**;	Is 10:13
and their **t** on the humps of camels,	Is 30:6
I will give you the **t** of darkness and the	Is 45:3
"Your wealth and your **t** I will give as	Jer 15:13
Your wealth and all your **t** I will give for	Jer 17:3
and all the **t** of the kings of Judah into	Jer 20:5
you trusted in your works and your **t**,	Jer 48:7
faithless daughter, who trusted in her **t**,	Jer 49:4
A sword against all her **t**, that they may	Jer 50:37
who dwell by many waters, rich in **t**,	Jer 51:13
they trade their **t** for food to revive	Lam 1:11
become ruler of the **t** of gold and of	Dn 11:43
have carried my rich **t** into your temples.	Jl 3:5
Esau has been pillaged, his **t** sought out!	Ob 1:6
forget any longer the **t** of wickedness in	Mi 6:10
so that the **t** of all nations shall come in,	Hg 2:7
Then, opening their **t**, they offered him	Mt 2:11
"Do not lay up for yourselves **t** on earth,	Mt 6:19
but lay up for yourselves **t** in heaven,	Mt 6:20
are hidden all the **t** of wisdom and	Col 2:3
greater wealth than the **t** of Egypt,	Heb 11:26

TREASURIES (23)

up in store with me, sealed up in my **t**?	Dt 32:34
stored them in the **t** of the house of	1 Kgs 7:51
was found in the **t** of the house of	2 Kgs 12:18
LORD and in the **t** of the king's house,	2 Kgs 14:14
LORD and in the **t** of the king's house.	2 Kgs 18:15
had charge of the **t** of the house of	1 Chr 26:20
of God and the **t** of the dedicated	1 Chr 26:20
in charge of the **t** of the house of	1 Chr 26:22
was chief officer in charge of the **t**.	1 Chr 26:24
charge of all the **t** of the dedicated	1 Chr 26:26
Over the king's **t** was Azmaveth the	1 Chr 27:25
Adiel; and over the **t** in the country,	1 Chr 27:25
of the temple, and of its houses, its **t**,	1 Chr 28:11
chambers, the **t** of the house of God,	1 Chr 28:12
of God, and the **t** for dedicated gifts;	1 Chr 28:12
all the vessels in the **t** of the house of	2 Chr 5:1
any matter and concerning the **t**.	2 Chr 8:15
He seized also the **t** of the king's	2 Chr 25:24
and he made for himself **t** for silver,	2 Chr 32:27
that they may put it into the king's **t**."	Est 3:9
pay into the king's **t** for the destruction of	Est 4:7
to those who love me, and filling their **t**.	Prv 8:21
gathered gold and silver into your **t**;	Ezk 28:4

TREASURY (14)

The LORD will open to you his good **t**,	Dt 28:12
they shall go into the **t** of the LORD."	Jos 6:19
they put into the **t** of the house of the	Jos 6:24
gave them to the **t** of the house of	1 Chr 29:8
they gave to the **t** of the work 61,000	Ezr 2:69
Let the cost be paid from the royal **t**.	Ezr 6:4
you may provide it out of the king's **t**.	Ezr 7:20
governor gave to the **t** 1,000 darics of	Neh 7:70
houses gave into the **t** of the work	Neh 7:71
and placed the vessels in the **t** of his god.	Dn 1:2
it shall strip his **t** of every precious	Hos 13:15
"It is not lawful to put them into the **t**,	Mt 27:6
down opposite the **t** and watched the	Mk 12:41
These words he spoke in the **t**, as he	Jn 8:20

TREAT (16)

"Should he **t** our sister like a	Gn 34:31
"Why did you **t** me so badly as to tell the	Gn 43:6
"Why do you **t** your servants like this?	Ex 5:15
You shall **t** the stranger who sojourns	Lv 19:34
He shall **t** him as a servant hired year	Lv 25:53
If you will **t** me like this, kill me at	Nm 11:15
Is it my habit to **t** you this way?" And	Nm 22:30
money, nor shall you **t** her as a slave,	Dt 21:14
he may not **t** the son of the loved as the	Dt 21:16
and because you did not **t** me as holy in	Dt 32:51
so will I **t** Zedekiah the king of Judah,	Jer 24:8
Admah? How can I **t** you like Zeboiim?	Hos 11:8
filth at you and **t** you with contempt and	Na 3:6
T me as one of your hired servants."'	Lk 15:19
Masters, **t** your slaves justly and fairly,	Col 4:1
a father. **T** younger men like brothers,	1 Tm 5:1

TREATED (20)

the way your servant **t** me," his anger	Gn 39:19
but he **t** them like strangers and spoke	Gn 42:7
And the Egyptians **t** us harshly and	Dt 26:6
for the men **t** the offering of the LORD	1 Sm 2:17
and mother are **t** with contempt in	Ezk 22:7
neighbors who have **t** them with	Ezk 28:24
neighbors who have **t** them with	Ezk 28:26
seized his servants, **t** them shamefully,	Mt 22:6
many things and be **t** with contempt?	Mk 9:12
him on the head and **t** him shamefully.	Mk 12:4
said to him, "Son, why have you **t** us so?	Lk 2:48
righteous, and **t** others with contempt:	Lk 18:9
mocked and shamefully **t** and spit	Lk 18:32
they also beat and **t** him shamefully,	Lk 20:11
with his soldiers **t** him with contempt	Lk 23:11
And Julius **t** Paul kindly and gave him	Acts 27:3
parts are **t** with greater	1 Cor 12:23
and praise. We are **t** as impostors,	2 Cor 6:8
and been shamefully **t** at Philippi,	1 Thes 2:2
being partners with those so **t**.	Heb 10:33

TREATING (1)

have to endure. God is **t** you as sons.	Heb 12:7

TREATMENT (1)

also will choose harsh **t** for them and	Is 66:4

TREATS (2)

and if he **t** him as a slave or sells him,	Dt 24:7
for the son **t** the father with contempt, the	Mi 7:6

TREATY (3)

said to Nahash, "Make a **t** with us,	1 Sm 11:1
condition I will make a **t** with you,	1 Sm 11:2
and the two of them made a **t**.	1 Kgs 5:12

TREE (171)

earth, and every **t** with seed in its fruit.	Gn 1:29
to spring up every **t** that is pleasant to	Gn 2:9
The **t** of life was in the midst of the	Gn 2:9
and the **t** of the knowledge of good and	Gn 2:9
may surely eat of every **t** of the garden,	Gn 2:16
but of the **t** of the knowledge of good and	Gn 2:17
shall not eat of any **t** in the garden'?"	Gn 3:1
eat of the fruit of the **t** that is in the midst	Gn 3:3
woman saw that the **t** was good for food,	Gn 3:6
and that the **t** was to be desired to make	Gn 3:6
you eaten of the **t** of which I	Gn 3:11
to be with me, she gave me fruit of the **t**,	Gn 3:12
have eaten of the **t** of which I	Gn 3:17
and take also of the **t** of life and eat,	Gn 3:22
way to guard the way to the **t** of life.	Gn 3:24
feet, and rest yourselves under the **t**,	Gn 18:4
stood by them under the **t** while they ate.	Gn 18:8
planted a tamarisk **t** in Beersheba and	Gn 21:33
under the terebinth **t** that was near	Gn 35:4
—from you!—and hang you on a **t**.	Gn 40:19
of the field and broke every **t** of the field.	Ex 9:25
they shall eat every **t** of yours that grows	Ex 10:5
neither **t** nor plant of the field,	Ex 10:15
land and plant any kind of **t** for food,	Lv 19:23
and on the hills and under every green **t**.	Dt 12:2
shall not plant any **t** as an Asherah	Dt 16:21
his hand swings the axe to cut down a **t**,	Dt 19:5
put to death, and you hang him on a **t**,	Dt 21:22
shall not remain all night on the **t**,	Dt 21:23
a bird's nest in any **t** or on the ground,	Dt 22:6
the king of Ai on a **t** until evening.	Jos 8:29
his body down from the **t** and threw it at	Jos 8:29
over them, and they said to the olive **t**,	Jgs 9:8
But the olive **t** said to them, 'Shall I leave	Jgs 9:9
And the trees said to the fig **t**, 'You come	Jgs 9:10
But the fig **t** said to them, 'Shall I leave	Jgs 9:11
under the tamarisk **t** on the height	1 Sm 22:6
under the tamarisk **t** in Jabesh and	1 Sm 31:13
under his vine and under his fig **t**,	1 Kgs 4:25
high hill and under every green **t**,	1 Kgs 14:23
came and sat down under a broom **t**.	1 Kgs 19:4
lay down and slept under a broom **t**.	1 Kgs 19:5
shall fell every good **t** and stop up all	2 Kgs 3:19
on the hills and under every green **t**.	2 Kgs 16:4
high hill and under every green **t**,	2 Kgs 17:10
vine, and each one of his own fig **t**,	2 Kgs 18:31
on the hills and under every green **t**.	2 Chr 28:4
the firstfruits of all fruit of every **t**,	Neh 10:35
our contributions, the fruit of every **t**,	Neh 10:37
"For there is hope for a **t**, if it be cut	Jb 14:7
and cast off his blossom like the olive **t**.	Jb 15:33
and my hope has he pulled up like a **t**.	Jb 19:10
so wickedness is broken like a **t**.'	Jb 24:20
the roots of the broom **t** for their food.	Jb 30:4
He is like a **t** planted by streams of water	Ps 1:3
spreading himself like a green laurel **t**.	Ps 37:35
am like a green olive **t** in the house of	Ps 52:8
flourish like the palm **t** and grow like a	Ps 92:12
with glowing coals of the broom **t**!	Ps 120:4
She is a **t** of life to those who lay hold of	Prv 3:18
The fruit of the righteous is a **t** of life,	Prv 11:30
sick, but a desire fulfilled is a **t** of life.	Prv 13:12
A gentle tongue is a **t** of life, but	Prv 15:4
Whoever tends a fig **t** will eat its fruit,	Prv 27:18
and if a **t** falls to the south or to the	Eccl 11:3
the north, in the place where the **t** falls,	Eccl 11:3
the almond **t** blossoms, the	Eccl 12:5
As an apple **t** among the trees of the forest,	Sg 2:3
The fig **t** ripens its figs, and the vines are	Sg 2:13
Your stature is like a palm **t**, and your	Sg 7:7
I will climb the palm **t** and lay hold of its	Sg 7:8
Under the apple **t** I awakened you.	Sg 8:5
as when an olive **t** is beaten—two or three	Is 17:6
four or five on the branches of a fruit **t**,	Is 17:6
the nations, as when an olive **t** is beaten,	Is 24:13
the vine, like leaves falling from the fig **t**.	Is 34:4
own vine, and each one of his own fig **t**,	Is 36:16
or he chooses a cypress **t** or an oak and	Is 44:14
O mountains, O forest, and every **t** in it!	Is 44:23
the eunuch say, "Behold, I am a dry **t**."	Is 56:3
lust among the oaks, under every green **t**,	Is 57:5
like the days of a **t** shall the days of my	Is 65:22
and under every green **t** you bowed down	Jer 2:20
who say to a **t**, 'You are my father,' and	Jer 2:27
every high hill and under every green **t**,	Jer 3:6
committing adultery with stone and **t**.	Jer 3:9
among foreigners under every green **t**,	Jer 3:13
grapes on the vine, nor figs on the fig **t**;	Jer 8:13
A **t** from the forest is cut down and	Jer 10:3
LORD once called you 'a green olive **t**,	Jer 11:16
"Let us destroy the **t** with its fruit,	Jer 11:19
beside every green **t** and on the high	Jer 17:2
He is like a **t** planted by water, that sends	Jer 17:8
the mountaintops, under every green **t**,	Ezk 6:13
I bring low the high **t**, and make high	Ezk 17:24
the high tree, and make high the low **t**,	Ezk 17:24
high the low tree, dry up the green **t**,	Ezk 17:24
tree, and make the dry **t** flourish.	Ezk 17:24
they saw any high hill or any leafy **t**,	Ezk 20:28
shall devour every green **t** in you and	Ezk 20:47
every green tree in you and every dry **t**.	Ezk 20:47
no **t** in the garden of God was its equal	Ezk 31:8
the fruit of the **t** and the increase of	Ezk 36:30
a palm **t** between cherub and cherub.	Ezk 41:18
face toward the palm **t** on the one side,	Ezk 41:19
lion toward the palm **t** on the other	Ezk 41:19
and behold, a **t** in the midst of the earth,	Dn 4:10
The **t** grew and became strong, and its	Dn 4:11
'Chop down the **t** and lop off its	Dn 4:14
The **t** you saw, which grew and became	Dn 4:20
saying, 'Chop down the **t** and destroy it,	Dn 4:23
to leave the stump of the roots of the **t**,	Dn 4:26
first fruit on the fig **t** in its first season,	Hos 9:10
laid waste my vine and splintered my fig **t**;	Jl 1:7
The vine dries up; the fig **t** languishes.	Jl 1:12
wilderness are green; the **t** bears its fruit;	Jl 2:22
fruit; the fig **t** and vine give their full yield.	Jl 2:22
man under his vine and under his fig **t**,	Mi 4:4
Though the fig **t** should not blossom,	Hab 3:17
Indeed, the vine, the fig **t**, the	Hg 2:19
and the olive **t** have yielded nothing.	Hg 2:19
under his vine and under his fig **t**."	Zec 3:10
Every **t** therefore that does not bear good	Mt 3:10
So, every healthy **t** bears good fruit, but	Mt 7:17
fruit, but the diseased **t** bears bad fruit.	Mt 7:17
A healthy **t** cannot bear bad fruit, nor	Mt 7:18
nor can a diseased **t** bear good fruit.	Mt 7:18
Every **t** that does not bear good fruit is	Mt 7:19
"Either make the **t** good and its fruit	Mt 12:33
or make the **t** bad and its fruit bad,	Mt 12:33
fruit bad, for the **t** is known by its fruit.	Mt 12:33
all the garden plants and becomes a **t**,	Mt 13:32
And seeing a fig **t** by the wayside, he	Mt 21:19
again!" And the fig **t** withered at once.	Mt 21:19
"How did the fig **t** wither at once?"	Mt 21:20
only do what has been done to the fig **t**,	Mt 21:21
"From the fig **t** learn its lesson: as soon	Mt 24:32
seeing in the distance a fig **t** in leaf,	Mk 11:13
they saw the fig **t** withered away to its	Mk 11:20
The fig **t** that you cursed has	Mk 11:21
"From the fig **t** learn its lesson: as soon	Mk 13:28
Every **t** therefore that does not bear good	Lk 3:9
"For no good **t** bears bad fruit, nor again	Lk 6:43
nor again does a bad **t** bear good fruit,	Lk 6:43
for each **t** is known by its own fruit. For	Lk 6:44
man had a fig **t** planted in his vineyard,	Lk 13:6
I have come seeking fruit on this fig **t**,	Lk 13:7
his garden, and it grew and became a **t**,	Lk 13:19
seed, you could say to this mulberry **t**,	Lk 17:6
climbed up into a sycamore **t** to see him,	Lk 19:4
"Look at the fig **t**, and all the trees.	Lk 21:29
called you, when you were under the fig **t**,	Jn 1:48

I said to you, 'I saw you under the fig **t**,' Jn 1:50
you killed by hanging him on a **t**. Acts 5:30
him to death by hanging him on a **t**, Acts 10:39
him down from the **t** and laid him in Acts 13:29
in the nourishing root of the olive **t**, Rom 11:17
from what is by nature a wild olive **t**, Rom 11:24
to nature, into a cultivated olive **t**, Rom 11:24
be grafted back into their own olive **t**. Rom 11:24
is everyone who is hanged on a **t**"— Gal 3:13
Can a fig **t**, my brothers, bear olives, or a Jas 3:12
bore our sins in his body on the **t**, 1 Pt 2:24
conquers I will grant to eat of the **t** of life, Rv 2:7
the earth as the fig **t** sheds its winter fruit Rv 6:13
blow on earth or sea or against any **t**. Rv 7:1
of the earth or any green plant or any **t**, Rv 9:4
the **t** of life with its twelve kinds of fruit, Rv 22:2
The leaves of the **t** were for the healing of Rv 22:2
have the right to the **t** of life and that Rv 22:14
away his share in the **t** of life and in the Rv 22:19

TREES (132)
and fruit **t** bearing fruit in which is Gn 1:11
and **t** bearing fruit in which is their Gn 1:12
may eat of the fruit of the **t** in the garden, Gn 3:2
the LORD God among the **t** of the garden. Gn 3:8
in it and all the **t** that were in the field, Gn 23:17
of poplar and almond and plane **t**, Gn 30:37
all the fruit of the **t** that the hail had Ex 10:15
springs of water and seventy palm **t**, Ex 15:27
on the first day the fruit of splendid **t**, Lv 23:40
branches of palm **t** and boughs of leafy Lv 23:40
and boughs of leafy **t** and willows of the Lv 23:40
and the **t** of the field shall yield their Lv 26:4
and the **t** of the land shall not yield Lv 26:20
seed of the land or of the fruit of the **t**, Lv 27:30
and whether there are **t** in it or not. Nm 13:20
planted, like cedar **t** beside the waters. Nm 24:6
springs of water and seventy palm **t**, Nm 33:9
and vineyards and olive **t** that you did Dt 6:11
of vines and fig **t** and pomegranates, Dt 8:8
pomegranates, a land of olive **t** and honey, Dt 8:8
shall not destroy its **t** by wielding an Dt 20:19
Are the **t** in the field human, that they Dt 20:19
Only the **t** that you know are not trees Dt 20:20
you know are not **t** for food you may Dt 20:20
When you beat your olive **t**, you shall Dt 24:20
shall have olive **t** throughout all your Dt 28:40
shall possess all your **t** and the fruit of Dt 28:42
is, the Valley of Jericho the city of palm **t**, Dt 34:3
to death, and he hanged them on five **t**. Jos 10:26
And they hung on the **t** until evening. Jos 10:26
them down from the **t** and threw them Jos 10:27
The **t** once went out to anoint a king over Jgs 9:8
are honored, and go hold sway over the **t**?' Jgs 9:9
And the **t** said to the fig tree, 'You come Jgs 9:10
good fruit and go hold sway over the **t**?' Jgs 9:11
And the **t** said to the vine, 'You come Jgs 9:12
and men and go hold sway over the **t**?' Jgs 9:13
Then all the **t** said to the bramble, 'You Jgs 9:14
And the bramble said to the **t**, 'If in good Jgs 9:15
sent messengers to David, and cedar **t**, 2 Sm 5:11
against them opposite the balsam **t**. 2 Sm 5:23
marching in the tops of the balsam **t**, 2 Sm 5:24
He spoke of **t**, from the cedar that is in 1 Kgs 4:33
cherubim and palm **t** and open 1 Kgs 6:29
with carvings of cherubim, palm **t**, 1 Kgs 6:32
on the cherubim and on the palm **t**. 1 Kgs 6:32
cherubim and palm **t** and open 1 Kgs 6:35
carved cherubim, lions, and palm **t**, 1 Kgs 7:36
of water and felled all the good **t**, 2 Kgs 3:25
came to the Jordan, they cut down **t**. 2 Kgs 6:4
a land of olive **t** and honey, 2 Kgs 18:32
messengers to David, and cedar **t**, 1 Chr 14:1
against them opposite the balsam **t**. 1 Chr 14:14
in the tops of the balsam **t**, 1 Chr 14:15
Then shall the **t** of the forest sing for 1 Chr 16:33
olive and sycamore **t** in the 1 Chr 27:28
at Jericho, the city of palm **t**. 2 Chr 28:15
to bring cedar **t** from Lebanon to Ezr 3:7
palm, and other leafy **t** to make booths, Neh 8:15
orchards and fruit **t** in abundance. Neh 9:25
For his shade the lotus **t** cover him; the Jb 40:22
like those who swing axes in a forest of **t**. Ps 74:5
Then shall all the **t** of the forest sing for Ps 96:12
The **t** of the LORD are watered Ps 104:16
the stork has her home in the fir **t**. Ps 104:17
He struck down their vines and fig **t**, Ps 105:33
and shattered the **t** of their country. Ps 105:33
and all hills, fruit **t** and all cedars! Ps 148:9
and planted in them all kinds of fruit **t**. Eccl 2:5
which to water the forest of growing **t**. Eccl 2:6
As an apple tree among the **t** of the forest, Sg 2:3
cinnamon, with all **t** of frankincense, Sg 4:14
his people shook as the **t** of the forest shake Is 7:2
The remnant of the **t** of his forest will be Is 10:19
it grow strong among the **t** of the forest. Is 44:14
and all the **t** of the field shall clap their Is 55:12
shall eat up your vines and your fig **t**; Jer 5:17
says the LORD of hosts: "Cut down her **t**; Jer 6:6
upon the **t** of the field and the fruit of the Jer 7:20
her with axes like those who fell **t**. Jer 46:22
that is among the **t** of the forest? Ezk 15:2
of the vine among the **t** of the forest, Ezk 15:6
And all the **t** of the field shall know Ezk 17:24
all your planks of fir **t** from Senir; Ezk 27:5
forth its streams to all the **t** of the field. Ezk 31:4
towered high above all the **t** of the field; Ezk 31:5
rival it, nor the fir **t** equal its boughs; Ezk 31:8
were the plane **t** like its branches; Ezk 31:8
and all the **t** of Eden envied it, Ezk 31:9
is in order that no **t** by the waters may Ezk 31:14
and that no **t** that drink water may Ezk 31:14
and all the **t** of the field fainted Ezk 31:15
And all the **t** of Eden, the choice and Ezk 31:16
and in greatness among the **t** of Eden? Ezk 31:18
brought down with the **t** of Eden to the Ezk 31:18
And the **t** of the field shall yield their Ezk 34:27
inside, and on the jambs were palm **t**. Ezk 40:16
and its palm **t** were of the same size as Ezk 40:22
them, and it had palm **t** on its jambs, Ezk 40:26
court, and palm **t** were on its jambs, Ezk 40:31
court, and it had palm **t** on its jambs, Ezk 40:34
court, and it had palm **t** on its jambs, Ezk 40:37
It was carved of cherubim and palm **t**, Ezk 41:18
cherubim and palm **t** were carved; Ezk 41:20
were carved cherubim and palm **t**, Ezk 41:25
windows and palm **t** on either side, Ezk 41:26
of the river very many **t** on the one side Ezk 47:7
there will grow all kinds of **t** for food. Ezk 47:12
I will lay waste her vines and her fig **t**, Hos 2:12
he shall take root like the **t** of Lebanon; Hos 14:5
and apple, all the **t** of the field are dried up, Jl 1:12
and flame has burned all the **t** of the field. Jl 1:19
your fig **t** and your olive trees the locust Am 4:9
and your olive **t** the locust devoured; Am 4:9
fortresses are like fig **t** with first-ripe figs Na 3:12
standing among the myrtle **t** in the glen, Zec 1:8
standing among the myrtle **t** answered, Zec 1:10
who was standing among the myrtle **t**, Zec 1:11
And there are two olive **t** by it, one on the Zec 4:3
are these two olive **t** on the right and Zec 4:11
are these two branches of the olive **t**, Zec 4:12
has fallen, for the glorious **t** are ruined! Zec 11:2
now the axe is laid to the root of the **t**. Mt 3:10
branches from the **t** and spread them Mt 21:8
said, "I see men, but they look like **t**, Mk 8:24
now the axe is laid to the root of the **t**. Lk 3:9
"Look at the fig tree, and all the **t**. Lk 21:29
took branches of palm **t** and went out to Jn 12:13
fruitless **t** in late autumn, twice dead, Jude 1:12
"Do not harm the earth or the sea or the **t**, Rv 7:3
up, and a third of the **t** were burned up, Rv 8:7
are the two olive **t** and the two Rv 11:4

TREMBLE (40)
The peoples have heard; they **t**; pangs Ex 15:14
of you and shall **t** and be in anguish Dt 2:25
t before him, all the earth; yes, the 1 Chr 16:30
of those who **t** at the commandment Ezr 10:3
the earth out of its place, and its pillars **t**; Jb 9:6
The dead **t** under the waters and their Jb 26:5
pillars of heaven **t** and are astounded Jb 26:11
though the mountains **t** at its swelling. Ps 46:3
see, and make their loins **t** continually. Ps 69:23
of holiness; **t** before him, all the earth! Ps 96:9
The LORD reigns; let the peoples **t**! He sits Ps 99:1
T, O earth, at the presence of the Lord, Ps 114:7
day when the keepers of the house **t**, Eccl 12:3
Therefore I will make the heavens **t**, and Is 13:13
'Is this the man who made the earth **t**, Is 14:16
the idols of Egypt will **t** at his presence, Is 19:1
and **t** with fear before the hand that the Is 19:16
and the foundations of the earth **t**. Is 24:18
T, you women who are at ease, shudder, Is 32:11
seen and are afraid; the ends of the earth **t**; Is 41:5
that the nations might **t** at your presence! Is 64:2
word of the LORD, you who **t** at his word: Is 66:5
the LORD; Do you not **t** before me? Jer 5:22
They shall fear and **t** because of all the Jer 33:9
the sound of their fall the earth shall **t**; Jer 49:21
the capture of Babylon the earth shall **t**, Jer 50:46
the ground and **t** every moment and Ezk 26:16
Now the coastlands **t** on the day of Ezk 26:18
them. They shall **t** every moment, Ezk 32:10
dominion people are to **t** and fear before Dn 6:26
inhabitants of Samaria **t** for the calf Hos 10:5
Let all the inhabitants of the land **t**, for the Jl 2:1
earth quakes before them; the heavens **t**. Jl 2:10
Shall not the land **t** on this account, and Am 8:8
Hearts melt and knees **t**; anguish is in Na 2:10
and those awake who will make you **t**? Hab 2:7
the curtains of the land of Midian did **t**. Hab 3:7
into my bones; my legs **t** beneath me. Hab 3:16
sight that Moses said, "I **t** with fear." Heb 12:21
they do not **t** as they blaspheme the 2 Pt 2:10

TREMBLED (18)
Then Isaac **t** very violently and said, Gn 27:33
so that all the people in the camp **t**. Ex 19:16
kiln, and the whole mountain **t** greatly. Ex 19:18
smoking, the people were afraid and **t**, Ex 20:18
the earth **t** and the heavens dropped, Jgs 5:4
for his heart **t** for the ark of God. 1 Sm 4:13
The garrison and even the raiders **t**, 1 Sm 14:15
he was afraid, and his heart **t** greatly. 1 Sm 28:5
of the heavens **t** and quaked, 2 Sm 22:8
all the guests of Adonijah **t** and rose, 1 Kgs 1:49
Then all who **t** at the words of the God of Ezr 9:4
that he neither rose nor **t** before him, Est 5:9
also of the mountains **t** and quaked, Ps 18:7
you, they were afraid; indeed, the deep **t**. Ps 77:16
up the world; the earth **t** and shook. Ps 77:18
and languages **t** and feared before him. Dn 5:19
of him the guards **t** and became like Mt 28:4
And Moses **t** and did not dare to look. Acts 7:32

TREMBLES (10)
"At this also my heart **t** and leaps out of Jb 37:1
light up the world; the earth sees and **t**. Ps 97:4
who looks on the earth and it **t**, who Ps 104:32
My flesh **t** for fear of you, and I am Ps 119:120
Under three things the earth **t**; under Prv 30:21
Geba they lodge for the night; Ramah **t**; Is 10:29
armed men of Moab cry aloud; his soul **t**. Is 15:4
and contrite in spirit and **t** at my word. Is 66:2
The land **t** and writhes in pain, for the Jer 51:29
I hear, and my body **t**; my lips quiver at Hab 3:16

TREMBLING (33)
them, and they turned **t** to one another, Gn 42:28
dismayed; **t** seizes the leaders of Moab; Ex 15:15
give you there a **t** heart and failing eyes Dt 28:65
people, saying, 'Whoever is fearful and **t**, Jgs 7:3
and all the people followed him **t**. 1 Sm 13:7
the city came to meet him **t** and said, 1 Sm 16:4
came to meet David **t** and said to him, 1 Sm 21:1
lost heart and came **t** out of their 2 Sm 22:46
t because of this matter and because of Ezr 10:9
dread came upon me, and **t**, which made Jb 4:14
the LORD with fear, and rejoice with **t**. Ps 2:11
lost heart and came **t** out of their Ps 18:45
T took hold of them there, anguish as of Ps 48:6
Fear and **t** come upon me, and horror Ps 55:5
I longed for has been turned for me into **t**. Is 21:4
Zion are afraid; **t** has seized the godless: Is 33:14
drink water with **t** and with anxiety. Ezk 12:18
They will clothe themselves with **t**; Ezk 26:16
the vision, but a great **t** fell upon them, Dn 10:7
me and set me **t** on my hands and Dn 10:10
spoken this word to me, I stood up **t**. Dn 10:11
children shall come **t** from the west; Hos 11:10
they shall come **t** like birds from Hos 11:11
When Ephraim spoke, there was **t**; he Hos 13:1
they shall come **t** out of their Mi 7:17
came in fear and **t** and fell down before Mk 5:33
for **t** and astonishment had seized them, Mk 16:8
saw that she was not hidden, she came **t**, Lk 8:47
and **t** with fear he fell down before Acts 16:29
in weakness and in fear and much **t**, 1 Cor 2:3
how you received him with fear and **t**. 2 Cor 7:15
your earthly masters with fear and **t**, Eph 6:5
out your own salvation with fear and **t**, Phil 2:12

TRENCH (3)
And he made a **t** about the altar, as 1 Kgs 18:32
altar and filled the **t** also with water. 1 Kgs 18:35
licked up the water that was in the **t**. 1 Kgs 18:38

TRESPASS (9)
Please forgive the **t** of your servant. 1 Sm 25:28
But the free gift is not like the **t**. For if Rom 5:15
For if many died through one man's **t**, Rom 5:15
following one **t** brought Rom 5:16
If, because of one man's **t**, death Rom 5:17
as one **t** led to condemnation for all Rom 5:18
Now the law came in to increase the **t**, Rom 5:20
Rather through their **t** salvation has Rom 11:11
Now if their **t** means riches for the Rom 11:12

TRESPASSES (12)
For if you forgive others their **t**, your Mt 6:14
but if you do not forgive others their **t**, Mt 6:15
neither will your Father forgive your **t**. Mt 6:15
is in heaven may forgive you your **t**." Mk 11:25
delivered up for our **t** and raised for Rom 4:25
following many **t** brought Rom 5:16
not counting their **t** against them, 2 Cor 5:19
his blood, the forgiveness of our **t**, Eph 1:7
And you were dead in the **t** and sins Eph 2:1
even when we were dead in our **t**, made Eph 2:5

two and one-half **t** beyond the Jordan, Jos 14:3
For the people of Joseph were two **t**, Jos 14:4
of Israel seven **t** whose inheritance had Jos 18:2
fathers' houses of the **t** of the people of Jos 19:51
fathers' houses of the **t** of the people of Jos 21:1
priest received by lot from the **t** of Judah, Jos 21:4
—nine cities out of these two **t**; Jos 21:16
inheritance for your **t** those nations that Jos 23:4
Joshua gathered all the **t** of Israel to Jos 24:1
no inheritance among the **t** of Israel had Jgs 18:1
of all the people, of all the **t** of Israel, Jgs 20:2
hundred throughout all the **t** of Israel, Jgs 20:10
And the **t** of Israel sent men through all Jgs 20:12
"Which of all the **t** of Israel did not Jgs 21:5
one is there of the **t** of Israel that did not Jgs 21:8
had made a breach in the **t** of Israel. Jgs 21:15
him out of all the **t** of Israel to be my 1 Sm 2:28
from the least of the **t** of Israel? 1 Sm 9:21
the LORD by your **t** and by your 1 Sm 10:19
brought all the **t** of Israel near, 1 Sm 10:20
are you not the head of the **t** of Israel? 1 Sm 15:17
Then all the **t** of Israel came to David at 2 Sm 5:1
throughout all the **t** of Israel, 2 Sm 15:10
arguing throughout all the **t** of Israel, 2 Sm 19:9
passed through all the **t** of Israel to 2 Sm 20:14
him, "Go through all the **t** of Israel, 2 Sm 24:2
of Israel and all the heads of the **t**, 1 Kgs 8:1
city out of all the **t** of Israel in which 1 Kgs 8:16
of Solomon and will give you ten **t** 1 Kgs 11:31
chosen out of all the **t** of Israel), 1 Kgs 11:32
hand and will give it to you, ten **t**. 1 Kgs 11:35
had chosen out of all the **t** of Israel, 1 Kgs 14:21
to the number of the **t** of the sons of 1 Kgs 18:31
I have chosen out of all the **t** of Israel, 2 Kgs 21:7
thirteen cities out of the **t** of Issachar, 1 Chr 6:62
twelve cities out of the **t** of Reuben, 1 Chr 6:63
They gave by lot out of the **t** of Judah, 1 Chr 6:65
Over the **t** of Israel, for the 1 Chr 27:16
were the leaders of the **t** of Israel. 1 Chr 27:22
officials of Israel, the officials of the **t**, 1 Chr 28:1
as did also the leaders of the **t**, 1 Chr 29:6
of Israel and all the heads of the **t**, 2 Chr 5:2
city out of all the **t** of Israel in which to 2 Chr 6:5
them from all the **t** of Israel to 2 Chr 11:16
chosen out of all the **t** of Israel to put 2 Chr 12:13
I have chosen out of all the **t** of Israel, 2 Chr 33:7
to the number of the **t** of Israel. Ezr 6:17
May desert **t** bow down before him and Ps 72:9
possession and settled the **t** of Israel in Ps 78:55
was none among his **t** who stumbled. Ps 105:37
to which the **t** go up, the tribes of the Ps 122:4
which the tribes go up, the **t** of the LORD, Ps 122:4
cornerstones of her **t** have made Egypt Is 19:13
servant to raise up the **t** of Jacob and to Is 49:6
of your servants, the **t** of your heritage. Is 63:17
I am calling all the **t** of the kingdoms of Jer 1:15
I will send for all the **t** of the north, Jer 25:9
and all the mixed **t** among them; all the Jer 25:20
kings of the mixed **t** who dwell in the Jer 25:24
the nations, like the **t** of the countries, Ezk 20:32
Ephraim) and the **t** of Israel Ezk 37:19
have the land according to their **t**. Ezk 45:8
among the twelve **t** of Israel. Ezk 47:13
you according to the **t** of Israel. Ezk 47:21
an inheritance among the **t** of Israel. Ezk 47:22
"These are the names of the **t**: Ezk 48:1
of the city, from all the **t** of Israel, Ezk 48:19
"As for the rest of the **t**: from the east Ezk 48:23
an inheritance among the **t** of Israel, Ezk 48:29
city being named after the **t** of Israel. Ezk 48:31
among the **t** of Israel I make known Hos 5:9
eye on mankind and on all the **t** of Israel, Zec 9:1
thrones, judging the twelve **t** of Israel. Mt 19:28
and then all the **t** of the earth will Mt 24:30
thrones judging the twelve **t** of Israel. Lk 22:30
to which our twelve **t** hope to attain, as Acts 26:7
Christ, To the twelve **t** in the Dispersion: Jas 1:1
and all **t** of the earth will wail on account Rv 1:7
from all **t** and peoples and languages, Rv 7:9
the peoples and **t** and languages and Rv 11:9
the names of the twelve **t** of the sons of Rv 21:12

TRIBULATION (19)
When you are in **t**, and all these things Dt 4:30
and may he deliver me out of all **t**." 1 Sm 26:24
and enveloped me with bitterness and **t**; Lam 3:5
and when **t** or persecution arises on Mt 13:21
will deliver you up to **t** and put you to Mt 24:9
For then there will be great **t**, such as Mt 24:21
"Immediately after the **t** of those days Mt 24:29
when **t** or persecution arises on Mk 4:17
there will be such **t** as has not been Mk 13:19
"But in those days, after that **t**, the sun Mk 13:24
have peace. In the world you will have **t**. Jn 16:33
There will be **t** and distress for every Rom 2:9
us from the love of Christ? Shall **t**, Rom 8:35
Rejoice in hope, be patient in **t**, be Rom 12:12
and partner in the **t** and the kingdom and Rv 1:9
"'I know your **t** and your poverty (but you Rv 2:9
tested, and for ten days you will have **t**. Rv 2:10
with her I will throw into great **t**, Rv 2:22
are the ones coming out of the great **t**. Rv 7:14

TRIBULATIONS (1)
that through many **t** we must enter Acts 14:22

TRIBUNAL (6)
Paul and brought him before the **t**, Acts 18:12
And he drove them from the **t**. Acts 18:16
and beat him in front of the **t**. Acts 18:17
his seat on the **t** and ordered Paul to Acts 25:6
said, "I am standing before Caesar's **t**, Acts 25:10
my seat on the **t** and ordered the man Acts 25:17

TRIBUNE (16)
word came to the **t** of the cohort that Acts 21:31
when they saw the **t** and the soldiers, Acts 21:32
Then the **t** came up and arrested him Acts 21:33
into the barracks, he said to the **t**, Acts 21:37
the **t** ordered him to be brought into Acts 22:24
this, he went to the **t** and said to him, Acts 22:26
So the **t** came and said to him, "Tell Acts 22:27
The **t** answered, "I bought this Acts 22:28
and the **t** also was afraid, Acts 22:29
the dissension became violent, the **t**, Acts 23:10
give notice to the **t** to bring him down Acts 23:15
said, "Take this young man to the **t**, Acts 23:17
and brought him to the **t** and said, Acts 23:18
The **t** took him by the hand, and Acts 23:19
So the **t** dismissed the young man, Acts 23:22
"When Lysias the **t** comes down, Acts 24:22

TRIBUNES (1)
with the military **t** and the prominent Acts 25:23

TRIBUTE (38)
between his feet, until **t** comes to him; Gn 49:10
levy for the LORD a **t** from the men of Nm 31:28
and the LORD'S **t** of sheep was 675. Nm 31:37
36,000, of which the LORD'S **t** was 72. Nm 31:38
30,500, of which the LORD'S **t** was 61. Nm 31:39
of which the LORD'S **t** was 32 persons. Nm 31:40
And Moses gave the **t**, which was the Nm 31:41
your God with the **t** of a freewill offering Dt 16:10
people of Israel sent **t** by him to Eglon Jgs 3:15
And he presented the **t** to Eglon king of Jgs 3:17
Ehud had finished presenting the **t**, Jgs 3:18
sent away the people who carried the **t**. Jgs 3:18
servants to David and brought **t**. 2 Sm 8:2
servants to David and brought **t**. 2 Sm 8:6
They brought **t** and served Solomon 1 Kgs 4:21
became his vassal and paid him **t**. 2 Kgs 17:3
and offered no **t** to the king of 2 Kgs 17:4
on the land a **t** of a hundred talents 2 Kgs 23:33
servants to David and brought **t**. 1 Chr 18:2
servants to David and brought **t**. 1 Chr 18:6
all Judah brought **t** to Jehoshaphat, 2 Chr 17:5
presents and silver for **t**, 2 Chr 17:11
The Ammonites paid **t** to Uzziah, 2 Chr 26:8
and gave **t** to the king of Assyria, 2 Chr 28:21
on the land a **t** of a hundred talents 2 Chr 36:3
the walls finished, they will not pay **t**, Ezr 4:13
province Beyond the River, to whom **t**, Ezr 4:20
the **t** of the province from Beyond the Ezr 6:8
that it shall not be lawful to impose **t**, Ezr 7:24
underfoot those who lust after **t**; Ps 68:30
and of the coastlands render him **t**; Ps 72:10
At that time **t** will be brought to the LORD Is 18:7
counted, where is he who weighed the **t**? Is 33:18
send an exactor of **t** for the glory of Dn 11:20
shall soon writhe because of the **t**. Hos 8:10
carried to Assyria as **t** to the great king. Hos 10:6
Is it lawful for us to give **t** to Caesar, or Lk 20:22
and forbidding us to give **t** to Caesar, Lk 23:2

TRICK (1)
Why did you flee secretly and **t** me, Gn 31:27

TRICKED (3)
And Jacob **t** Laban the Aramean, by Gn 31:20
that you have **t** me and driven away Gn 31:26
saw that he had been **t** by the wise men, Mt 2:16

TRICKLE (1)
up the streams so that they do not **t**, Jb 28:11

TRICKLING (1)
the water was **t** out on the south side. Ezk 47:2

TRIED (23)
The magicians **t** by their secret arts to Ex 8:18
And he **t** in vain to go, for he had not 1 Sm 17:39
when he has **t** me, I shall come out as Jb 23:10
Would that Job were **t** to the end, Jb 34:36
You have **t** my heart, you have visited Ps 17:3
tested us; you have **t** us as silver is tried. Ps 66:10
tested us; you have tried us as silver is **t**. Ps 66:10
When he is **t**, let him come forth guilty; Ps 109:7
Your promise is well **t**, and your Ps 119:140
I have **t** you in the furnace of affliction. Is 48:10
in your name, and we **t** to stop him, Mk 9:38
and **t** to discern what sort of greeting Lk 1:29
in your name, and we **t** to stop him, Lk 9:49
were quarreling and **t** to reconcile Acts 7:26
and **t** to persuade Jews and Greeks. Acts 18:4
He even **t** to profane the temple, but we Acts 24:6
and there be **t** on these charges Acts 25:9
tribunal, where I ought to be **t**. Acts 25:10
Jerusalem and be **t** there regarding Acts 25:20
the synagogues and **t** to make them Acts 26:11
me in the temple and **t** to kill me. Acts 26:21
of God violently and **t** to destroy it. Gal 1:13
the faith he once **t** to destroy." Gal 1:23

TRIFLE (1)
You have sold your people for a **t**, Ps 44:12

TRIGON (4)
the sound of the horn, pipe, lyre, **t**, harp, Dn 3:5
the sound of the horn, pipe, lyre, **t**, harp, Dn 3:7
the sound of the horn, pipe, lyre, **t**, harp, Dn 3:10
the sound of the horn, pipe, lyre, **t**, harp, Dn 3:15

TRIM (1)
they shall surely **t** the hair of their Ezk 44:20

TRIMMED (2)
of his feet nor **t** his beard nor washed 2 Sm 19:24
all those virgins rose and **t** their lamps. Mt 25:7

TRIP (1)
men, who have planned to **t** up my feet. Ps 140:4

TRIUMPH (14)
of your help, and the sword of your **t**! Dt 33:29
said, "Go up to Ramoth-gilead and **t**; 1 Kgs 22:12
And he answered him, "Go up and **t**; 1 Kgs 22:15
said, "Go up to Ramoth-gilead and **t**. 2 Chr 18:11
And he answered, "Go up and **t**; 2 Chr 18:14
therefore you will not let them **t**. Jb 17:4
my enemy will not shout in **t** over me. Ps 41:11
my eye has looked in **t** on my enemies. Ps 54:7
will let me look in **t** on my enemies. Ps 59:10
cast my shoe; over Philistia I shout in **t**." Ps 60:8
my shoe; over Philistia I shout in **t**." Ps 108:9
until he looks in **t** on his adversaries. Ps 112:8
I shall look in **t** on those who hate me. Ps 118:7
When the righteous **t**, there is great Prv 28:12

TRIUMPHAL (1)
always leads us in **t** procession, 2 Cor 2:14

TRIUMPHANT (1)
lest they should say, "Our hand is **t**, Dt 32:27

TRIUMPHANTLY (1)
people of Israel went out **t** in the sight of Nm 33:3

TRIUMPHED (3)
sing to the LORD, for he has **t** gloriously; Ex 15:1
to the LORD, for he has **t** gloriously; Ex 15:21
my affliction, for the enemy has **t**!" Lam 1:9

TRIUMPHING (1)
to open shame, by **t** over them in him. Col 2:15

TRIUMPHS (3)
they repeat the righteous **t** of the LORD, Jgs 5:11
the righteous **t** of his villagers in Israel. Jgs 5:11
no mercy. Mercy **t** over judgment. Jas 2:13

TRIVIAL (1)
are you incompetent to try **t** cases? 1 Cor 6:2

TROAS (6)
by Mysia, they went down to **T**. Acts 16:8
So, setting sail from **T**, we made a Acts 16:11
on ahead and were waiting for us at **T**, Acts 20:5
and in five days we came to them at **T**, Acts 20:6
When I came to **T** to preach the 2 Cor 2:12
the cloak that I left with Carpus at **T**, 2 Tm 4:13

TROD (5)
their vineyards and **t** them and held Jgs 9:27
pursued them and **t** them down from Jgs 20:43
to the old way that wicked men have **t**? Jb 22:15
on safely, by paths his feet have not **t**. Is 41:3
I **t** them in my anger and trampled them Is 63:3

TRODDEN (9)
I will give the land on which he has **t**, Dt 1:36
which your foot has **t** shall be an Jos 14:9
The proud beasts have not **t** it; the lion Jb 28:8
of Ephraim will be **t** underfoot; Is 28:3
"I have **t** the winepress alone, and from Is 63:3
threshing floor at the time when it is **t**; Jer 51:33
the Lord has **t** as in a winepress the Lam 1:15
eat what you have **t** with your feet, Ezk 34:19
the winepress was **t** outside the city, Rv 14:20

TROOP (2)
For by you I can run against a **t**, and 2 Sm 22:30

For by you I can run against a **t**, and by Ps 18:29

TROOPED (1)
committed adultery and **t** to the houses Jer 5:7

TROOPS (25)
And they came out with all their **t**, a Jos 11:4
river Kishon with his chariots and his **t**, Jgs 4:7
And when the **t** came to the camp, the 1 Sm 4:3
thousand horsemen and **t** like the 1 Sm 13:5
and the **t** came back from pursuing 2 Sm 18:16
Now the **t** were encamped against 1 Kgs 16:15
and the **t** who were encamped heard 1 Kgs 16:16
and made them officers of his **t**. 1 Chr 12:18
of the armed **t** who came to 1 Chr 12:23
shield and spear were 6,800 armed **t**. 1 Chr 12:24
Of Zebulun 50,000 seasoned **t**, 1 Chr 12:33
Asher 40,000 seasoned **t** ready for 1 Chr 12:36
Thus his **t** were in front of Judah, 2 Chr 13:13
me; you bring fresh **t** against me. Jb 10:17
His **t** come on together; they have cast Jb 19:12
and I lived like a king among his **t**, Jb 29:25
against all the foreign **t** in her midst, Jer 50:37
around him, his helpers and all his **t**, Ezk 12:14
all the pick of his **t** shall fall by the Ezk 17:21
shall not stand, or even his best **t**, Dn 11:15
Now muster your **t**, O daughter of troops; Mi 5:1
Now muster your troops, O daughter of **t**; Mi 5:1
Behold, your **t** are women in your midst. Na 3:13
and he sent his **t** and destroyed those Mt 22:7
The number of mounted **t** was twice ten Rv 9:16

TROPHIMUS (3)
and the Asians, Tychicus and **T**. Acts 20:4
had previously seen **T** the Ephesian Acts 21:29
remained at Corinth, and I left **T**, 2 Tm 4:20

TROUBLE (106)
"You have brought **t** on me by Gn 34:30
saw that they were in **t** when they said, Ex 5:19
in Jacob, nor has he seen **t** in Israel. Nm 23:21
and they shall **t** you in the land where Nm 33:55
for destruction and bring **t** upon it. Jos 6:18
said, "Why did you bring **t** on us? Jos 7:25
The LORD brings **t** on you today." And Jos 7:25
have become the cause of great **t** to me. Jgs 11:35
that they were in **t** (for the people were 1 Sm 13:6
to Joab, 'Do not let this matter **t** you, 2 Sm 11:25
her, "What is your **t**?" She answered, 2 Sm 14:5
and see how this man is seeking **t**, 1 Kgs 20:7
'See, you have taken all this **t** for us; 2 Kgs 4:13
her, "What is your **t**?" She answered, 2 Kgs 6:28
and said, "This **t** is from the LORD! 2 Kgs 6:33
should you provoke **t** so that you 2 Kgs 14:10
should you provoke **t** so that you 2 Chr 25:19
the exile is in great **t** and shame. Neh 1:3
I said to them, "You see the **t** we are in, Neh 2:17
mother's womb, nor hide **t** from my eyes. Jb 3:10
am I quiet; I have no rest, but **t** comes." Jb 3:26
plow iniquity and sow **t** reap the same. Jb 4:8
dust, nor does **t** sprout from the ground, Jb 5:6
but man is born to **t** as the sparks fly Jb 5:7
of a woman is few of days and full of **t**. Jb 14:1
They conceive **t** and give birth to evil, Jb 15:35
which I have reserved for the time of **t**, Jb 38:23
the oppressed, a stronghold in times of **t**. Ps 9:9
Why do you hide yourself in times of **t**? Ps 10:1
May the LORD answer you in the day of **t**! Ps 20:1
Be not far from me, for **t** is near, and Ps 22:11
Consider my affliction and my **t**, and Ps 25:18
will hide me in his shelter in the day of **t**; Ps 27:5
place for me; you preserve me from **t**; Ps 32:7
The words of his mouth are **t** and deceit; Ps 36:3
He plots **t** while on his bed; he sets Ps 36:4
he is their stronghold in the time of **t**. Ps 37:39
In the day of **t** the LORD delivers him; Ps 41:1
and strength, a very present help in **t**. Ps 46:1
Why should I fear in times of **t**, when the Ps 49:5
and call upon me in the day of **t**; I will Ps 50:15
For he has delivered me from every **t**, and Ps 54:7
For they drop **t** upon me, and in anger Ps 55:3
walls, and iniquity and **t** are within it; Ps 55:10
my mouth promised when I was in **t**. Ps 66:14
They are not in **t** as others are; they are Ps 73:5
In the day of my **t** I seek the Lord; in the Ps 77:2
In the day of my **t** I call upon you, for Ps 86:7
eighty; yet their span is but toil and **t**; Ps 90:10
will answer him; I will be with him in **t**; Ps 91:15
to give him rest from days of **t**, until a Ps 94:13
say so, whom he has redeemed from **t** Ps 107:2
Then they cried to the LORD in their **t**, Ps 107:6
Then they cried to the LORD in their **t**, Ps 107:13
Then they cried to the LORD in their **t**, Ps 107:19
Then they cried to the LORD in their **t**, Ps 107:28
T and anguish have found me out, Ps 119:143
Though I walk in the midst of **t**, you Ps 138:7
before him; I tell my **t** before him. Ps 142:2
righteousness bring my soul out of **t**! Ps 143:11
Whoever winks the eye causes **t**, but a Prv 10:10
The righteous is delivered from **t**, and Prv 11:8
lips, but the righteous escapes from **t**. Prv 12:13
but the wicked are filled with **t**. Prv 12:21
A wicked messenger falls into **t**, but a Prv 13:17
but **t** befalls the income of the wicked. Prv 15:6
LORD than great treasure and **t** with it. Prv 15:16
even the wicked for the day of **t**. Prv 16:4
and his tongue keeps himself out of **t**. Prv 21:23
devise violence, and their lips talk of **t**. Prv 24:2
man in time of **t** is like a bad Prv 25:19
although man's **t** lies heavy on him. Eccl 8:6
Through a land of **t** and anguish, from Is 30:6
morning, our salvation in the time of **t**. Is 33:2
it does not answer or save him from his **t**. Is 46:7
But in the time of their **t** they say, 'Arise Jer 2:27
if they can save you, in your time of **t**; Jer 2:28
Dan and proclaims **t** from Mount Jer 4:15
cannot save them in the time of their **t**. Jer 11:12
they call to me in the time of their **t**. Jer 11:14
you hope of Israel, its savior in time of **t**, Jer 14:8
enemy in the time of **t** and in the time Jer 15:11
stronghold, my refuge in the day of **t**, Jer 16:19
her from every side on the day of **t**. Jer 51:2
All my enemies have heard of my **t**; Lam 1:21
your rivers, **t** the waters with your feet, Ezk 32:2
"I will **t** the hearts of many peoples, Ezk 32:9
no foot of man shall **t** them anymore, Ezk 32:13
nor shall the hoofs of beasts **t** them. Ezk 32:13
And there shall be a time of **t**, such as Dn 12:1
LORD is good, a stronghold in the day of **t**; Na 1:7
end; **t** will not rise up a second time. Na 1:9
for the day of **t** to come upon people Hab 3:16
itself. Sufficient for the day is its own **t**. Mt 6:34
to them, "Why do you **t** the woman? Mt 26:10
will satisfy him and keep you out of **t**." Mt 28:14
dead. Why **t** the Teacher any further?" Mk 5:35
"Leave her alone. Why do you **t** her? Mk 14:6
saying to him, "Lord, do not **t** yourself, Lk 7:6
is dead; do not **t** the Teacher any more." Lk 8:49
that we should not **t** those of the Acts 15:19
there are some who **t** you and want to Gal 1:7
From now on let no one cause me **t**, for Gal 6:17
things to you is no **t** to me and is safe Phil 3:1
Yet it was kind of you to share my **t**. Phil 4:14
of bitterness" springs up and causes **t**, Heb 12:15

TROUBLED (30)
in the morning, he saw that they were **t**. Gn 40:6
So in the morning his spirit was **t**, and Gn 41:8
my lord, I am a woman **t** in spirit. 1 Sm 1:15
said, "My father has **t** the land. 1 Sm 14:29
he answered, "I have not **t** Israel, 1 Kgs 18:18
of Syria was greatly **t** because of this 2 Kgs 6:11
for God **t** them with every sort of 2 Chr 15:6
heal me, O LORD, for my bones are **t**. Ps 6:2
My soul also is greatly **t**. But you, O LORD Ps 6:3
enemies shall be ashamed and greatly **t**; Ps 6:10
open; I am so **t** that I cannot speak. Ps 77:4
they are **t** like the sea that cannot be Jer 49:23
his spirit was **t**, and his sleep left him. Dn 2:1
and my spirit is **t** to know the dream." Dn 2:3
with squares and moat, but in a **t** time. Dn 9:25
Herod the king heard this, he was **t**, Mt 2:3
he began to be sorrowful and **t**. Mt 26:37
began to be greatly distressed and **t**. Mk 14:33
And Zechariah was **t** when he saw him, Lk 1:12
But she was greatly **t** at the saying, and Lk 1:29
those who were **t** with unclean spirits Lk 6:18
are anxious and **t** about many things, Lk 10:41
And he said to them, "Why are you **t**, Lk 24:38
deeply moved in his spirit and greatly **t**. Jn 11:33
"Now is my soul **t**. And what shall I Jn 12:27
these things, Jesus was **t** in his spirit, Jn 13:21
"Let not your hearts be **t**. Believe in God; Jn 14:1
Let not your hearts be **t**, neither let them Jn 14:27
out from us and **t** you with words, Acts 15:24
blessed. Have no fear of them, nor be **t**, 1 Pt 3:14

TROUBLER (2)
to him, "Is it you, you **t** of Israel?" 1 Kgs 18:17
Achan, the **t** of Israel, who broke faith 1 Chr 2:7

TROUBLES (15)
heaven and said to her, "What **t** you, Gn 21:17
And many evils and **t** will come upon Dt 31:17
when many evils and **t** have come upon Dt 31:21
He will deliver you from six **t**; in seven no Jb 5:19
The **t** of my heart are enlarged; bring Ps 25:17
Redeem Israel, O God, out of all his **t**. Ps 25:22
heard him and saved him out of all his **t**. Ps 34:6
and delivers them out of all their **t**. Ps 34:17
me see many **t** and calamities will Ps 71:20
For my soul is full of **t**, and my life draws Ps 88:3
Whoever **t** his own household will Prv 11:29
for unjust gain **t** his own household, Prv 15:27
because the former **t** are forgotten and Is 65:16
through the sea of **t** and strike down Zec 10:11
those who marry will have worldly **t**, 1 Cor 7:28

TROUBLING (2)
There the wicked cease from **t**, and there Jb 3:17
and the one who is **t** you will bear the Gal 5:10

TROUGH (1)
her jar into the **t** and ran again to Gn 24:20

TROUGHS (3)
peeled in front of the flocks in the **t**, Gn 30:38
lay the sticks in the **t** before the eyes of Gn 30:41
water and filled the **t** to water their Ex 2:16

TROWEL (1)
And you shall have a **t** with your tools, Dt 23:13

TRUE (111)
my word will come **t** for you or not." Nm 11:23
if it be **t** and certain that such an Dt 13:14
and if it is **t** and certain that such an Dt 17:4
word does not come to pass or come **t**, Dt 18:22
But if the thing is **t**, that evidence of Dt 22:20
And she said, "**T**, the men came to me, Jos 2:4
said, "Now when your words come **t**, Jgs 13:12
so that, when your words come **t**, Jgs 13:17
And now it is **t** that I am a redeemer. Yet Ru 3:12
held in honor; all that he says comes **t**. 1 Sm 9:6
you are God, and your words are **t**, 2 Sm 7:28
That is not **t**. But a man of the hill 2 Sm 20:21
perfect; the word of the LORD proves **t**; 2 Sm 22:31
heart therefore be wholly **t** to the LORD 1 Kgs 8:61
"The report was **t** that I heard in my 1 Kgs 10:6
heart was not wholly **t** to the LORD his 1 Kgs 11:4
heart was not wholly **t** to the LORD his 1 Kgs 15:3
of Asa was wholly **t** to the LORD all 1 Kgs 15:14
And they said, "That is not **t**; tell us 2 Kgs 9:12
"Is your heart **t** to my heart as mine 2 Kgs 10:15
"The report was **t** that I heard in my 2 Chr 9:5
time Israel was without the **t** God, 2 Chr 15:3
of Asa was wholly **t** all his days. 2 Chr 15:17
and gave them right rules and **t** laws, Neh 9:13
Behold, this we have searched out; it is **t**. Jb 5:27
And even if it be **t** that I have erred, my Jb 19:4
is perfect; the word of the LORD proves **t**; Ps 18:30
the rules of the LORD are **t**, and righteous Ps 19:9
is righteous forever, and your law is **t**. Ps 119:142
and all your commandments are **t**. Ps 119:151
to make you know what is right and **t**, Prv 22:21
you may give a **t** answer to those who Prv 22:21
Every word of God proves **t**; he is a Prv 30:5
right, and let them hear and say, It is **t**. Is 43:9
But the LORD is the **t** God; he is the Jer 10:10
words that you have prophesied come **t**, Jer 28:6
the LORD be a **t** and faithful witness Jer 42:5
executes **t** justice between man and Ezk 18:8
answered and said to them, "Is it **t**, Dn 3:14
and said to the king, "**T**, O king." Dn 3:24
and the mornings that has been told is **t**, Dn 8:26
And the word was **t**, and it was a great Dn 10:1
the LORD of hosts, Render **t** judgments, Zec 7:9
gates judgments that are **t** and make for Zec 8:16
T instruction was in his mouth, and no Mal 2:6
know that you are **t** and teach the way Mt 22:16
we know that you are **t** and do not care Mk 12:14
who will entrust to you the **t** riches? Lk 16:11
The **t** light, which enlightens everyone, Jn 1:9
whoever does what is **t** comes to the light, Jn 3:21
sets his seal to this, that God is **t**. Jn 3:33
your husband. What you have said is **t**." Jn 4:18
when the **t** worshipers will worship the Jn 4:23
For here the saying holds **t**, 'One sows Jn 4:37
myself, my testimony is not deemed **t**. Jn 5:31
the testimony that he bears about me is **t**. Jn 5:32
gives you the **t** bread from heaven. Jn 6:32
For my flesh is **t** food, and my blood is Jn 6:55
is true food, and my blood is **t** drink. Jn 6:55
seeks the glory of him who sent him is **t**, Jn 7:18
He who sent me is **t**, and him you do not Jn 7:28
about yourself; your testimony is not **t**." Jn 8:13
witness about myself, my testimony is **t**, Jn 8:14
Yet even if I do judge, my judgment is **t**, Jn 8:16
that the testimony of two men is **t**. Jn 8:17
much to judge, but he who sent me is **t**, Jn 8:26
that John said about this man was **t**." Jn 10:41
"I am the **t** vine, and my Father is the Jn 15:1
life, that they know you the only **t** God, Jn 17:3
it has borne witness—his testimony is **t**, Jn 19:35
and we know that his testimony is **t**. Jn 21:24
I am speaking **t** and rational words. Acts 26:25
Let God be **t** though every one were a Rom 3:4
That is **t**. They were broken off Rom 11:20
not raise if it is **t** that the dead are 1 Cor 15:15
are treated as impostors, and yet are **t**; 2 Cor 6:8
as everything we said to you was **t**, 2 Cor 7:14
boasting before Titus has proved **t**. 2 Cor 7:14

signs of a **t** apostle were performed 2 Cor 12:12
of God in **t** righteousness and holiness. Eph 4:24
in all that is good and right and **t**), Eph 5:9
Only let us hold **t** to what we have Phil 3:16
Yes, I ask you also, **t** companion, help Phil 4:3
Finally, brothers, whatever is **t**, Phil 4:8
idols to serve the living and **t** God, 1 Thes 1:9
To Timothy, my **t** child in the faith: 1 Tm 1:2
To Titus, my **t** child in a common faith: Ti 1:4
This testimony is **t**. Therefore rebuke Ti 1:13
places, in the **t** tent that the Lord set up, Heb 8:2
hands, which are copies of the **t** things, Heb 9:24
come instead of the **t** form of these Heb 10:1
draw near with a **t** heart in full Heb 10:22
declaring that this is the **t** grace of God. 1 Pt 5:12
What the **t** proverb says has happened 2 Pt 2:22
to you, which is **t** in him and in you, 1 Jn 2:8
passing away and the **t** light is already 1 Jn 2:8
everything—and is **t** and is no lie, 1 Jn 2:27
so that we may know him who is **t**; 1 Jn 5:20
and we are in him who is **t**, in his Son 1 Jn 5:20
Christ. He is the **t** God and eternal life. 1 Jn 5:20
and you know that our testimony is **t**. 3 Jn 1:12
'The words of the holy one, the **t** one, who Rv 3:7
of the Amen, the faithful and **t** witness, Rv 3:14
voice, "O Sovereign Lord, holy and **t**, Rv 6:10
Just and **t** are your ways, O King of the Rv 15:3
t and just are your judgments!" Rv 16:7
for his judgments are **t** and just; for he Rv 19:2
to me, "These are the **t** words of God." Rv 19:9
sitting on it is called Faithful and **T**, Rv 19:11
for these words are trustworthy and **t**." Rv 21:5
me, "These words are trustworthy and **t**. Rv 22:6

TRULY (141)
"**T** here I have seen him who looks Gn 16:13
promise to deal kindly and **t** with me. Gn 47:29
But **t**, as I live, and as all the earth Nm 14:21
"**T** the LORD has given all the land into Jos 2:24
"**T** I have sinned against the LORD God of Jos 7:20
know this, lest he be grieved.' But **t**, 1 Sm 20:3
"**T** women have been kept from us as 1 Sm 21:5
t by morning there had not been left 1 Sm 25:34
T, O LORD, the kings of Assyria have 2 Kgs 19:17
"**T** I know that it is so: But how can a man Jb 9:2
For **t** my words are not false; one who is Jb 36:4
T no man can ransom another, or give Ps 49:7
But **t** God has listened; he has attended Ps 66:19
T God is good to Israel, to those who are Ps 73:1
T you set them in slippery places; you Ps 73:18
are beautiful, my beloved, **t** delightful. Sg 1:16
T, O LORD, the kings of Assyria have laid Is 37:18
T, you are a God who hides yourself, O Is 45:15
T the hills are a delusion, the orgies on Jer 3:23
T in the LORD our God is the salvation of Jer 3:23
"For if you **t** amend your ways and your Jer 7:5
if you **t** execute justice one with another, Jer 7:5
But I said, "**T** this is an affliction, and I Jer 10:19
that the LORD has **t** sent the prophet." Jer 28:9
"**T**, your God is God of gods and Lord of Dn 2:47
For **t**, I say to you, until heaven and Mt 5:18
T, I say to you, you will never get out Mt 5:26
T, I say to you, they have received their Mt 6:2
T, I say to you, they have received their Mt 6:5
T, I say to you, they have received their Mt 6:16
to those who followed him, "**T**, I tell you, Mt 8:10
T, I say to you, it will be more bearable Mt 10:15
you in one town, flee to the next, for **t**, Mt 10:23
because he is a disciple, **t**, I say to you, Mt 10:42
T, I say to you, among those born of Mt 11:11
T, I say to you, many prophets and Mt 13:17
saying, "**T** you are the Son of God." Mt 14:33
T, I say to you, there are some standing Mt 16:28
"Because of your little faith. For **t**, Mt 17:20
and said, "**T**, I say to you, unless you Mt 18:3
And if he finds it, **t**, I say to you, he Mt 18:13
T, I say to you, whatever you bind on Mt 18:18
said to his disciples, "**T**, I say to you, Mt 19:23
Jesus said to them, "**T**, I say to you, in Mt 19:28
Jesus answered them, "**T**, I say to you, Mt 21:21
Jesus said to them, "**T**, I say to you, Mt 21:31
T, I say to you, all these things will Mt 23:36
T, I say to you, there will not be left here Mt 24:2
T, I say to you, this generation will not Mt 24:34
T, I say to you, he will set him over all Mt 24:47
But he answered, '**T**, I say to you, I do Mt 25:12
King will answer them, '**T**, I say to you, Mt 25:40
answer them, saying, '**T**, I say to you, Mt 25:45
T, I say to you, wherever this gospel is Mt 26:13
were eating, he said, "**T**, I say to you, Mt 26:21
Jesus said to him, "**T**, I tell you, this Mt 26:34
and said, "**T** this was the Son of God!" Mt 27:54
"**T**, I say to you, all sins will be forgiven Mk 3:28
T, I say to you, no sign will be given to Mk 8:12
And he said to them, "**T**, I say to you, Mk 9:1
For **t**, I say to you, whoever gives you a Mk 9:41
T, I say to you, whoever does not Mk 10:15
Jesus said, "**T**, I say to you, there is no Mk 10:29
T, I say to you, whoever says to this Mk 11:23
but **t** teach the way of God. Mk 12:14
You have **t** said that he is one, and Mk 12:32
him and said to them, "**T**, I say to you, Mk 12:43
T, I say to you, this generation will not Mk 13:30
And **t**, I say to you, wherever the gospel Mk 14:9
and eating, Jesus said, "**T**, I say to you, Mk 14:18
T, I say to you, I will not drink again Mk 14:25
And Jesus said to him, "**T**, I tell you, Mk 14:30
said, "**T** this man was the Son of God!" Mk 15:39
And he said, "**T**, I say to you, no prophet Lk 4:24
But I tell you **t**, there are some standing Lk 9:27
T, I say to you, he will dress himself for Lk 12:37
T, I say to you, he will set him over all Lk 12:44
T, I say to you, whoever does not Lk 18:17
And he said to them, "**T**, I say to you, Lk 18:29
partiality, but **t** teach the way of God. Lk 20:21
And he said, "**T**, I tell you, this poor Lk 21:3
T, I say to you, this generation will not Lk 21:32
And he said to him, "**T**, I say to you, Lk 23:43
And he said to him, "**T**, truly, I say to Jn 1:51
he said to him, "Truly, **t**, I say to you, Jn 1:51
Jesus answered him, "**T**, truly, I say to you, Jn 3:3
Jesus answered him, "Truly, **t**, I say to you, Jn 3:3
Jesus answered, "**T**, truly, I say to you, Jn 3:5
Jesus answered, "Truly, **t**, I say to you, Jn 3:5
T, truly, I say to you, we speak of what we Jn 3:11
Truly, **t**, I say to you, we speak of what we Jn 3:11
So Jesus said to them, "**T**, truly, I say to Jn 5:19
Jesus said to them, "Truly, **t**, I say to you, Jn 5:19
T, truly, I say to you, whoever hears my Jn 5:24
Truly, **t**, I say to you, whoever hears my Jn 5:24
"**T**, truly, I say to you, an hour is coming, Jn 5:25
"Truly, **t**, I say to you, an hour is coming, Jn 5:25
Jesus answered them, "**T**, truly, I say to Jn 6:26
answered them, "Truly, **t**, I say to you, Jn 6:26
Jesus then said to them, "**T**, truly, I say to Jn 6:32
then said to them, "Truly, **t**, I say to you, Jn 6:32
T, truly, I say to you, whoever believes Jn 6:47
Truly, **t**, I say to you, whoever believes Jn 6:47
So Jesus said to them, "**T**, truly, I say to Jn 6:53
Jesus said to them, "Truly, **t**, I say to you, Jn 6:53
abide in my word, you are **t** my disciples, Jn 8:31
Jesus answered them, "**T**, truly, I say to Jn 8:34
answered them, "Truly, **t**, I say to you, Jn 8:34
T, truly, I say to you, if anyone keeps my Jn 8:51
Truly, **t**, I say to you, if anyone keeps my Jn 8:51
Jesus said to them, "**T**, truly, I say to you, Jn 8:58
Jesus said to them, "Truly, **t**, I say to you, Jn 8:58
"**T**, truly, I say to you, he who does not Jn 10:1
"Truly, **t**, I say to you, he who does not Jn 10:1
So Jesus again said to them, "**T**, truly, I Jn 10:7
again said to them, "Truly, **t**, I say to you, Jn 10:7
T, truly, I say to you, unless a grain of Jn 12:24
Truly, **t**, I say to you, unless a grain of Jn 12:24
T, truly, I say to you, a servant is not Jn 13:16
Truly, **t**, I say to you, a servant is not Jn 13:16
T, truly, I say to you, whoever receives Jn 13:20
Truly, **t**, I say to you, whoever receives Jn 13:20
in his spirit, and testified, "**T**, truly, Jn 13:21
and testified, "Truly, **t**, I say to you, Jn 13:21
T, truly, I say to you, the rooster will not Jn 13:38
Truly, **t**, I say to you, the rooster will not Jn 13:38
"**T**, truly, I say to you, whoever believes Jn 14:12
"Truly, **t**, I say to you, whoever believes Jn 14:12
T, truly, I say to you, you will weep and Jn 16:20
Truly, **t**, I say to you, you will weep and Jn 16:20
T, truly, I say to you, whatever you ask Jn 16:23
Truly, **t**, I say to you, whatever you ask Jn 16:23
T, truly, I say to you, when you were Jn 21:18
Truly, **t**, I say to you, when you were Jn 21:18
for **t** in this city there were gathered Acts 4:27
"**T** I understand that God shows no Acts 10:34
But if we judged ourselves **t**, we 1 Cor 11:31
Honor widows who are **t** widows. 1 Tm 5:3
She who is **t** a widow, left all alone, has 1 Tm 5:5
may take hold of that which is **t** life. 1 Tm 6:19
in him **t** the love of God is perfected. 1 Jn 2:5

TRUMPET (68)
When the **t** sounds a long blast, they Ex 19:13
the mountain and a very loud **t** blast, Ex 19:16
the sound of the **t** grew louder and Ex 19:19
the sound of the **t** and the mountain Ex 20:18
shall sound the loud **t** on the tenth day Lv 25:9
shall sound the **t** throughout all your Lv 25:9
horn, when you hear the sound of the **t**, Jos 6:5
as the people heard the sound of the **t**, Jos 6:20
he sounded the **t** in the hill country of Jgs 3:27
clothed Gideon, and he sounded the **t**, Jgs 6:34
When I blow the **t**, I and all who are Jgs 7:18
Saul blew the **t** throughout all the 1 Sm 13:3
So Joab blew the **t**, and all the men 2 Sm 2:28
soon as you hear the sound of the **t**, 2 Sm 15:10
Then Joab blew the **t**, and the troops 2 Sm 18:16
And he blew the **t** and said, "We have 2 Sm 20:1
So he blew the **t**, and they dispersed 2 Sm 20:22
Then blow the **t** and say, 'Long live 1 Kgs 1:34
Then they blew the **t**, and all the 1 Kgs 1:39
when Joab heard the sound of the **t**, 1 Kgs 1:41
and they blew the **t** and proclaimed, 2 Kgs 9:13
man who sounded the **t** was beside me. Neh 4:18
where you hear the sound of the **t**, Neh 4:20
cannot stand still at the sound of the **t**. Jb 39:24
When the **t** sounds, he says 'Aha!' He Jb 39:25
a shout, the LORD with the sound of a **t**. Ps 47:5
Blow the **t** at the new moon, at the full Ps 81:3
Praise him with **t** sound; praise him Ps 150:3
the mountains, look! When a **t** is blown, Is 18:3
And in that day a great **t** will be blown, Is 27:13
not hold back; lift up your voice like a **t**; Is 58:1
and say, "Blow the **t** through the land; Jer 4:5
keep silent, for I hear the sound of the **t**, Jer 4:19
the standard and hear the sound of the **t**? Jer 4:21
midst of Jerusalem! Blow the **t** in Tekoa, Jer 6:1
'Pay attention to the sound of the **t**!' Jer 6:17
hear the sound of the **t** or be hungry for Jer 42:14
earth; blow the **t** among the nations; Jer 51:27
have blown the **t** and made everything Ezk 7:14
land and blows the **t** and warns the Ezk 33:3
the sound of the **t** does not take Ezk 33:4
the sound of the **t** and did not take Ezk 33:5
sword coming and does not blow the **t**, Ezk 33:6
the horn in Gibeah, the **t** in Ramah. Hos 5:8
Set the **t** to your lips! One like a vulture Hos 8:1
Blow a **t** in Zion; sound an alarm on my Jl 2:1
Blow the **t** in Zion; consecrate a fast; call a Jl 2:15
amid shouting and the sound of the **t**; Am 2:2
Is a **t** blown in a city, and the people are Am 3:6
a day of **t** blast and battle cry against Zep 1:16
GOD will sound the **t** and will march Zec 9:14
give to the needy, sound no **t** before you, Mt 6:2
send out his angels with a loud **t** call, Mt 24:31
the twinkling of an eye, at the last **t**. 1 Cor 15:52
last trumpet. For the **t** will sound, 1 Cor 15:52
and with the sound of the **t** of God. 1 Thes 4:16
and the sound of a **t** and a voice whose Heb 12:19
I heard behind me a loud voice like a **t** Rv 1:10
which I had heard speaking to me like a **t**, Rv 4:1
The first angel blew his **t**, and there Rv 8:7
The second angel blew his **t**, and Rv 8:8
The third angel blew his **t**, and a great Rv 8:10
The fourth angel blew his **t**, and a third Rv 8:12
And the fifth angel blew his **t**, and I saw a Rv 9:1
Then the sixth angel blew his **t**, and I Rv 9:13
saying to the sixth angel who had the **t**, Rv 9:14
in the days of the **t** call to be sounded by Rv 10:7
Then the seventh angel blew his **t**, and Rv 11:15

TRUMPETERS (6)
captains and the **t** beside the king, 2 Kgs 11:14
the altar with 120 priests who were **t**; 2 Chr 5:12
the duty of the **t** and singers to make 2 Chr 5:13
captains and the **t** beside the king, 2 Chr 23:13
the singers sang and the **t** sounded. 2 Chr 29:28
and musicians, of flute players and **t**, Rv 18:22

TRUMPETS (50)
a memorial proclaimed with blast of **t**, Lv 23:24
"Make two silver **t**. Of hammered work Nm 10:2
of Aaron, the priests, shall blow the **t**. Nm 10:8
The **t** shall be to you for a perpetual Nm 10:8
you shall sound an alarm with the **t**, Nm 10:9
you shall blow the **t** over your burnt Nm 10:10
work. It is a day for you to blow the **t**, Nm 29:1
the sanctuary and the **t** for the alarm Nm 31:6
priests shall bear seven **t** of rams' horns Jos 6:4
times, and the priests shall blow the **t**. Jos 6:4
seven priests bear seven **t** of rams' horns Jos 6:6
priests bearing the seven **t** of rams' horns Jos 6:8
the LORD went forward, blowing the **t**, Jos 6:8
before the priests who were blowing the **t**, Jos 6:9
the ark, while the **t** blew continually. Jos 6:9
bearing the seven **t** of rams' horns Jos 6:13
on, and they blew the **t** continually. Jos 6:13
of the LORD, while the **t** blew continually. Jos 6:13
time, when the priests had blown the **t**, Jos 6:16
the people shouted, and the **t** were blown. Jos 6:20
provisions in their hands, and their **t**. Jgs 7:8
companies and put **t** into the hands Jgs 7:16
then blow the **t** also on every side of all Jgs 7:18
And they blew the **t** and smashed the Jgs 7:19
companies blew the **t** and broke the Jgs 7:20
and in their right hands the **t** to blow. Jgs 7:20
When they blew the 300 **t**, the LORD set Jgs 7:22
of the land rejoicing and blowing **t**. 2 Kgs 11:14
bowls, **t**, or any vessels of gold, 2 Kgs 12:13
and tambourines and cymbals and **t**. 1 Chr 13:8
should blow the **t** before the ark of 1 Chr 15:24
sound of the horn, **t**, and cymbals, 1 Chr 15:28

were to blow **t** regularly before the 1 Chr 16:6
and Jeduthun had **t** and cymbals 1 Chr 16:42
with **t** and cymbals and other 2 Chr 5:13
opposite them the priests sounded **t**, 2 Chr 7:6
with their battle **t** to sound the 2 Chr 13:12
the LORD, and the priests blew the **t**. 2 Chr 13:14
shouting and with **t** and with horns. 2 Chr 15:14
with harps and lyres and **t**, 2 Chr 20:28
of the land rejoicing and blowing **t**, 2 Chr 23:13
of David, and the priests with the **t**. 2 Chr 29:26
to the LORD began also, and the **t**, 2 Chr 29:27
in their vestments came forward with **t**, Ezr 3:10
and certain of the priests' sons with **t**: Neh 12:35
Zechariah, and Hananiah, with **t**; Neh 12:41
With **t** and the sound of the horn make a Ps 98:6
God, and seven **t** were given to them. Rv 8:2
who had the seven **t** prepared to blow Rv 8:6
blasts of the other **t** that the three angels Rv 8:13

TRUNK (2)
Only the **t** of Dagon was left to him. 1 Sm 5:4
On its fallen **t** dwell all the birds of the Ezk 31:13

TRUST (85)
For every breach of **t**, whether it is for an Ex 22:9
but Sihon did not **t** Israel to pass Jgs 11:20
On what do you rest this **t** of yours? 2 Kgs 18:19
In whom do you now **t**, that you 2 Kgs 18:20
king of Egypt to all who **t** in him. 2 Kgs 18:21
"We **t** in the LORD our God," is it not 2 Kgs 18:22
when you **t** in Egypt for chariots 2 Kgs 18:24
let Hezekiah make you **t** in the LORD 2 Kgs 18:30
God in whom you **t** deceive you by 2 Kgs 19:10
established them in their office of **t**. 1 Chr 9:22
Even in his servants he puts no **t**, and his Jb 4:18
is severed, and his **t** is a spider's web. Jb 8:14
Behold, God puts no **t** in his holy ones, Jb 15:15
Let him not **t** in emptiness, deceiving Jb 15:31
have made gold my **t** or called fine gold Jb 31:24
sacrifices, and put your **t** in the LORD. Ps 4:5
who know your name put their **t** in you, Ps 9:10
Some **t** in chariots and some in horses, Ps 20:7
but we **t** in the name of the LORD our God. Ps 20:7
you made me **t** you at my mother's Ps 22:9
O my God, in you I **t**; let me not be put to Ps 25:2
to worthless idols, but I **t** in the LORD. Ps 31:6
But I **t** in you, O LORD; I say, "You are Ps 31:14
in him, because we **t** in his holy name. Ps 33:21
T in the LORD, and do good; dwell in the Ps 37:3
way to the LORD; **t** in him, and he will act. Ps 37:5
see and fear, and put their **t** in the LORD. Ps 40:3
is the man who makes the LORD his **t**, Ps 40:4
For not in my bow do I **t**, nor can my Ps 44:6
those who **t** in their wealth and boast of Ps 49:6
I **t** in the steadfast love of God forever and Ps 52:8
out half their days. But I will **t** in you. Ps 55:23
When I am afraid, I put my **t** in you. Ps 56:3
In God, whose word I praise, in God I **t**; I Ps 56:4
in God I **t**; I shall not be afraid. What Ps 56:11
T in him at all times, O people; pour out Ps 62:8
Put no **t** in extortion; set no vain hopes Ps 62:10
For you, O Lord, are my hope, my **t**, O Ps 71:5
in God and did not **t** his saving power. Ps 78:22
and my fortress, my God, in whom I **t**." Ps 91:2
like them; so do all who **t** in them. Ps 115:8
O Israel, **t** in the LORD! He is their help Ps 115:9
O house of Aaron, **t** in the LORD! He is Ps 115:10
You who fear the LORD, **t** in the LORD! Ps 115:11
refuge in the LORD than to **t** in man. Ps 118:8
refuge in the LORD than to **t** in princes. Ps 118:9
who taunts me, for I **t** in your word. Ps 119:42
Those who **t** in the LORD are like Mount Ps 125:1
like them, so do all who **t** in them! Ps 135:18
of your steadfast love, for in you I **t**. Ps 143:8
Put not your **t** in princes, in a son of Ps 146:3
T in the LORD with all your heart, and do Prv 3:5
down the stronghold in which they **t**. Prv 21:22
That your **t** may be in the LORD, I have Prv 22:19
salvation; I will **t**, and will not be afraid; Is 12:2
T in the LORD forever, for the LORD GOD is Is 26:4
this word and **t** in oppression and Is 30:12
in quietness and in **t** shall be your Is 30:15
who **t** in chariots because they are many Is 31:1
of righteousness, quietness and **t** forever. Is 32:17
On what do you rest this **t** of yours? Is 36:4
In whom do you now **t**, that you have Is 36:5
king of Egypt to all who **t** in him. Is 36:6
"We **t** in the LORD our God," is it not he Is 36:7
when you **t** in Egypt for chariots and for Is 36:9
let Hezekiah make you **t** in the LORD by Is 36:15
God in whom you **t** deceive you by Is 37:10
put to shame, who **t** in carved idols, Is 42:17
and has no light **t** in the name of Is 50:10
LORD has rejected those in whom you **t**, Jer 2:37
cities in which you **t** they shall beat Jer 5:17
Do not **t** in these deceptive words: 'This is Jer 7:4
you **t** in deceptive words to no avail. Jer 7:8
called by my name, and in which you **t**, Jer 7:14
his neighbor, and put no **t** in any brother, Jer 9:4
trusts in the LORD, whose **t** is the LORD. Jer 17:7
and you have made this people **t** in a lie. Jer 28:15
send him, and has made you **t** in a lie, Jer 29:31
because you have put your **t** in me, Jer 39:18
upon Pharaoh and those who **t** in him. Jer 46:25
alive; and let your widows **t** in me." Jer 49:11
Put no **t** in a neighbor; have no Mi 7:5
no correction. She does not **t** in the LORD; Zep 3:2
and I **t** in the Lord that shortly I myself Phil 2:24
"I will put my **t** in him." And again, Heb 2:13

TRUSTED (24)
high and fortified walls, in which you **t**, Dt 28:52
because they **t** the men in ambush Jgs 20:36
And Achish **t** David, thinking, "He 1 Sm 27:12
He **t** in the LORD the God of Israel, so 2 Kgs 18:5
urgent plea because they **t** in him. 1 Chr 5:20
speech those who are **t** and takes away Jb 12:20
the tent in which he **t** and is brought to Jb 18:14
But I have **t** in your steadfast love; my Ps 13:5
In you our fathers **t**; they trusted, and Ps 22:4
In you our fathers trusted; they **t**, and Ps 22:4
in you they **t** and were not put to shame. Ps 22:5
and I have **t** in the LORD without Ps 26:1
Even my close friend in whom I **t**, who Ps 41:9
but **t** in the abundance of his riches and Ps 52:7
you have forgotten me and **t** in lies. Jer 13:25
"'Your **t** friends have deceived you and Jer 38:22
because you **t** in your works and your Jer 48:7
daughter, who **t** in her treasures, Jer 49:4
"But you **t** in your beauty and played Ezk 16:15
and delivered his servants, who **t** in him, Dn 3:28
on him, because he had **t** in his God. Dn 6:23
Because you have **t** in your own way Hos 10:13
armor in which he **t** and divides his Lk 11:22
to some who **t** in themselves that Lk 18:9

TRUSTING (6)
Behold, you are **t** now in Egypt, that 2 Kgs 18:21
king of Assyria, 'On what are you **t**, 2 Chr 32:10
news; his heart is firm, **t** in the LORD. Ps 112:7
T in a treacherous man in time of Prv 25:19
Behold, you are **t** in Egypt, that broken Is 36:6
And if in a safe land you are so **t**, what Jer 12:5

TRUSTINGLY (2)
your neighbor, who dwells **t** beside you. Prv 3:29
those who pass by **t** with no thought of Mi 2:8

TRUSTS (19)
For the king **t** in the LORD, and through Ps 21:7
"He **t** in the LORD; let him deliver him; let Ps 22:8
in him my heart **t**, and I am helped; Ps 28:7
surrounds the one who **t** in the LORD. Ps 32:10
of hosts, blessed is the one who **t** in you! Ps 84:12
servant, who **t** in you—you are my God. Ps 86:2
Whoever **t** in his riches will fall, but Prv 11:28
and blessed is he who **t** in the LORD. Prv 16:20
but the one who **t** in the LORD will be Prv 28:25
Whoever **t** in his own mind is a fool, Prv 28:26
but whoever **t** in the LORD is safe. Prv 29:25
The heart of her husband **t** in her, and Prv 31:11
is stayed on you, because he **t** in you. Is 26:3
is the man who **t** in man and makes Jer 17:5
"Blessed is the man who **t** in the LORD, Jer 17:7
yet if he **t** in his righteousness and Ezk 33:13
For its maker **t** in his own creation Hab 2:18
He **t** in God; let God deliver him now, if Mt 27:43
does not work but **t** him who justifies Rom 4:5

TRUSTWORTHY (14)
fear God, who are **t** and hate a bribe, Ex 18:21
Your decrees are very **t**; holiness befits Ps 93:5
faithful and just; all his precepts are **t**; Ps 111:7
but he who is **t** in spirit keeps a thing Prv 11:13
of stewards that they be found **t**. 1 Cor 4:2
as one who by the Lord's mercy is **t**. 1 Cor 7:25
The saying is **t** and deserving of full 1 Tm 1:15
The saying is **t**: If anyone aspires to the 1 Tm 3:1
The saying is **t** and deserving of full 1 Tm 4:9
The saying is **t**, for: If we have died 2 Tm 2:11
He must hold firm to the **t** word as taught, Ti 1:9
The saying is **t**, and I want you to insist on Ti 3:8
down, for these words are **t** and true." Rv 21:5
said to me, "These words are **t** and true. Rv 22:6

TRUTH (141)
may be tested, whether there is **t** in you. Gn 42:16
"In **t** we are guilty concerning our Gn 42:21
of the LORD in your mouth is **t**." 1 Kgs 17:24
me nothing but the **t** in the name of 1 Kgs 22:16
me nothing but the **t** in the name of 2 Chr 18:15
of Ahasuerus, in words of peace and **t**, Est 9:30
Of a **t**, God will not do wickedly, and the Jb 34:12
For there is no **t** in their mouth; their Ps 5:9
what is right and speaks **t** in his heart; Ps 15:2
Lead me in your **t** and teach me, for you Ps 25:5
Send out your light and your **t**; let them Ps 43:3
for the cause of **t** and meekness and Ps 45:4
you delight in **t** in the inward being, Ps 51:6
way, O LORD, that I may walk in your **t**; Ps 86:11
take not the word of **t** utterly out of my Ps 119:43
The sum of your word is **t**, and every Ps 119:160
on him, to all who call on him in **t**. Ps 145:18
for my mouth will utter **t**; wickedness is Prv 8:7
Whoever speaks the **t** gives honest Prv 12:17
Buy **t**, and do not sell it; buy wisdom, Prv 23:23
and uprightly he wrote words of **t**. Eccl 12:10
on the LORD, the Holy One of Israel, in **t**. Is 10:20
I the LORD speak the **t**; I declare what is Is 45:19
the God of Israel, but not in **t** or right. Is 48:1
for **t** has stumbled in the public squares, Is 59:14
T is lacking, and he who departs from Is 59:15
land shall bless himself by the God of **t**, Is 65:16
in the land shall swear by the God of **t**; Is 65:16
and if you swear, 'As the LORD lives,' in **t**, Jer 4:2
a man, one who does justice and seeks **t**, Jer 5:1
O LORD, do not your eyes look for **t**? You Jer 5:3
did not accept discipline; **t** has perished; Jer 7:28
falsehood and not **t** has grown strong in Jer 9:3
his neighbor, and no one speaks the **t**; Jer 9:5
for in **t** the LORD sent me to you to speak Jer 26:15
and asked him the **t** concerning all this. Dn 7:16
desired to know the **t** about the fourth Dn 7:19
and it will throw **t** to the ground, Dn 8:12
iniquities and gaining insight by your **t**. Dn 9:13
you what is inscribed in the book of **t**: Dn 10:21
"And now I will show you the **t**. Behold, Dn 11:2
and they abhor him who speaks the **t**. Am 5:10
you shall do: Speak the **t** to one another; Zec 8:16
feasts. Therefore love **t** and peace. Zec 8:19
before him and told him the whole **t**. Mk 5:33
But in **t**, I tell you, there were many Lk 4:25
Son from the Father, full of grace and **t**. Jn 1:14
grace and **t** came through Jesus Christ. Jn 1:17
will worship the Father in spirit and **t**, Jn 4:23
him must worship in spirit and **t**." Jn 4:24
to John, and he has borne witness to the **t**. Jn 5:33
and you will know the **t**, and the truth Jn 8:32
the truth, and the **t** will set you free." Jn 8:32
who has told you the **t** that I heard from Jn 8:40
and has nothing to do with the **t**, Jn 8:44
the truth, because there is no **t** in him. Jn 8:44
But because I tell the **t**, you do not believe Jn 8:45
If I tell the **t**, why do you not believe me? Jn 8:46
said to him, "I am the way, and the **t**, Jn 14:6
even the Spirit of **t**, whom the world Jn 14:17
to you from the Father, the Spirit of **t**, Jn 15:26
Nevertheless, I tell you the **t**: it is to your Jn 16:7
When the Spirit of **t** comes, he will Jn 16:13
comes, he will guide you into all the **t**, Jn 16:13
have come to know in **t** that I came from Jn 17:8
Sanctify them in the **t**; your word is Jn 17:17
them in the truth; your word is **t**. Jn 17:17
that they also may be sanctified in **t**. Jn 17:19
into the world—to bear witness to the **t**. Jn 18:37
who is of the **t** listens to my voice." Jn 18:37
him, "What is **t**?" After he had said this, Jn 18:38
that he is telling the **t**—that you also Jn 19:35
their unrighteousness suppress the **t**. Rom 1:18
they exchanged the **t** about God for Rom 1:25
are self-seeking and do not obey the **t**, Rom 2:8
the embodiment of knowledge and **t**— Rom 2:20
through my lie God's **t** abounds to his Rom 3:7
I am speaking the **t** in Christ—I am not Rom 9:1
unleavened bread of sincerity and **t**. 1 Cor 5:8
wrongdoing, but rejoices with the **t**. 1 Cor 13:6
statement of the **t** we would commend 2 Cor 4:2
As the **t** of Christ is in me, this 2 Cor 11:10
a fool, for I would be speaking the **t**. 2 Cor 12:6
we cannot do anything against the **t**, 2 Cor 13:8
against the truth, but only for the **t**. 2 Cor 13:8
so that the **t** of the gospel might be Gal 2:5
was not in step with the **t** of the gospel, Gal 2:14
your enemy by telling you the **t**? Gal 4:16
Who hindered you from obeying the **t**? Gal 5:7
you also, when you heard the word of **t**, Eph 1:13
Rather, speaking the **t** in love, we are to Eph 4:15
were taught in him, as the **t** is in Jesus, Eph 4:21
of you speak the **t** with his neighbor, Eph 4:25
having fastened on the belt of **t**, Eph 6:14
every way, whether in pretense or in **t**, Phil 1:18
have heard before in the word of the **t**, Col 1:5
it and understood the grace of God in **t**, Col 1:6
refused to love the **t** and so be saved. 2 Thes 2:10
not believe the **t** but had pleasure 2 Thes 2:12
by the Spirit and belief in the **t**. 2 Thes 2:13
and to come to the knowledge of the **t**. 1 Tm 2:4
and an apostle (I am telling the **t**, 1 Tm 2:7
a teacher of the Gentiles in faith and **t**. 1 Tm 2:7

living God, a pillar and buttress of **t**. 1 Tm 3:15
by those who believe and know the **t**. 1 Tm 4:3
depraved in mind and deprived of the **t**, 1 Tm 6:5
rightly handling the word of **t**. 2 Tm 2:15
who have swerved from the **t**, saying 2 Tm 2:18
leading to a knowledge of the **t**, 2 Tm 2:25
able to arrive at a knowledge of the **t**. 2 Tm 3:7
Moses, so these men also oppose the **t**, 2 Tm 3:8
from listening to the **t** and wander off 2 Tm 4:4
of God's elect and their knowledge of the **t**, Ti 1:1
of people who turn away from the **t**. Ti 1:14
after receiving the knowledge of the **t**, Heb 10:26
will he brought us forth by the word of **t**, Jas 1:18
hearts, do not boast and be false to the **t**. Jas 3:14
wanders from the **t** and someone brings Jas 5:19
your obedience to the **t** for a sincere 1 Pt 1:22
are established in the **t** that you have. 2 Pt 1:12
of them the way of **t** will be blasphemed. 2 Pt 2:2
we lie and do not practice the **t**. 1 Jn 1:6
deceive ourselves, and the **t** is not in us. 1 Jn 1:8
is a liar, and the **t** is not in him, 1 Jn 2:4
not because you do not know the **t**, 1 Jn 2:21
know it, and because no lie is of the **t**. 1 Jn 2:21
in word or talk but in deed and in **t**. 1 Jn 3:18
we are of the **t** and reassure our heart 1 Jn 3:19
we know the Spirit of **t** and the spirit of 1 Jn 4:6
who testifies, because the Spirit is the **t**. 1 Jn 5:6
lady and her children, whom I love in **t**, 2 Jn 1:1
not only I, but also all who know the **t**, 2 Jn 1:1
because of the **t** that abides in us and 2 Jn 1:2
Christ the Father's Son, in **t** and love. 2 Jn 1:3
some of your children walking in the **t**, 2 Jn 1:4
to the beloved Gaius, whom I love in **t**. 3 Jn 1:1
the brothers came and testified to your **t**, 3 Jn 1:3
truth, as indeed you are walking in the **t**. 3 Jn 1:3
that my children are walking in the **t**. 3 Jn 1:4
that we may be fellow workers for the **t**. 3 Jn 1:8
from everyone, and from the **t** itself. 3 Jn 1:12

TRUTHFUL (3)
T lips endure forever, but a lying Prv 12:19
A **t** witness saves lives, but one who Prv 14:25
by **t** speech, and the power of God; with 2 Cor 6:7

TRUTHFULLY (1)
you are true and teach the way of God **t**, Mt 22:16

TRUTHFULNESS (1)
to the circumcised to show God's **t**, Rom 15:8

TRUTHS (1)
interpreting spiritual **t** to those who 1 Cor 2:13

TRY (7)
Prove me, O LORD, and **t** me; test my heart Ps 26:2
heart! **T** me and know my thoughts! Ps 139:23
wine; those who go to **t** mixed wine. Prv 23:30
are you incompetent to **t** trivial cases? 1 Cor 6:2
just as I **t** to please everyone in 1 Cor 10:33
and **t** to discern what is pleasing to the Eph 5:10
world, to **t** those who dwell on the earth. Rv 3:10

TRYING (5)
with certainty that you are **t** to gain time, Dn 2:8
of God and **t** to convince them Acts 28:23
or of God? Or am I **t** to please man? Gal 1:10
If I were still **t** to please man, I would not Gal 1:10
about those who are **t** to deceive you. 1 Jn 2:26

TRYPHAENA (1)
in the Lord, **T** and Tryphosa. Rom 16:12

TRYPHOSA (1)
in the Lord, Tryphaena and **T**. Rom 16:12

TUBAL (7)
Magog, Madai, Javan, **T**, Meshech, Gn 10:2
Magog, Madai, Javan, **T**, Meshech, 1 Chr 1:5
Lud, who draw the bow, to **T** and Javan, Is 66:19
T, and Meshech traded with you; Ezk 27:13
the chief prince of Meshech and **T**, Ezk 38:2
O Gog, chief prince of Meshech and **T**. Ezk 38:3
O Gog, chief prince of Meshech and **T**. Ezk 39:1

TUBAL-CAIN (2)
Zillah also bore **T**; he was the forger of Gn 4:22
and iron. The sister of **T** was Naamah. Gn 4:22

TUBES (1)
His bones are **t** of bronze, his limbs like Jb 40:18

TUMBLE (1)
and every wall shall **t** to the ground. Ezk 38:20

TUMBLED (1)
a cake of barley bread **t** into the camp of Jgs 7:13

TUMORS (8)
of Egypt, and with **t** and scabs and itch, Dt 28:27
he terrified and afflicted them with **t**, 1 Sm 5:6
and old, so that **t** broke out on them. 1 Sm 5:9
who did not die were struck with **t**, 1 Sm 5:12
"Five golden **t** and five golden mice, 1 Sm 6:4
make images of your **t** and images of 1 Sm 6:5
golden mice and the images of their **t**. 1 Sm 6:11
are the golden **t** that the Philistines 1 Sm 6:17

TUMULT (15)
the **t** in the camp of the Philistines 1 Sm 14:19
He scorns the **t** of the city; he hears not Jb 39:7
I groan because of the **t** of my heart. Ps 38:8
of their waves, the **t** of the peoples, Ps 65:7
warrior in battle **t** and every garment Is 9:5
The sound of a **t** is on the mountains as Is 13:4
has a day of **t** and trampling and Is 22:5
there is a **t** of waters in the heavens, Jer 10:13
of Moab, the crown of the sons of **t**. Jer 48:45
his voice there is a **t** of waters in the Jer 51:16
a sound of **t** like the sound of an army. Ezk 1:24
the day is near, a day of **t**, and not of Ezk 7:7
your name is defiled; you are full of **t**. Ezk 22:5
therefore the **t** of war shall arise Hos 10:14
in the temple, without any crowd or **t**. Acts 24:18

TUMULTS (2)
Samaria, and see the great **t** within her, Am 3:9
And when you hear of wars and **t**, do not Lk 21:9

TUMULTUOUS (3)
you who are full of shoutings, **t** city, Is 22:2
At the **t** noise peoples flee; when you lift Is 33:3
Babylon; she is covered with its **t** waves. Jer 51:42

TUNIC (5)
binds me about like the collar of my **t**. Jb 30:18
if anyone would sue you and take your **t**, Mt 5:40
cloak do not withhold your **t** either. Lk 6:29
one part for each soldier; also his **t**. Jn 19:23
also his tunic. But the **t** was seamless, Jn 19:23

TUNICS (6)
men were bound in their cloaks, their **t**, Dn 3:21
nor two **t** nor sandals nor a staff, Mt 10:10
but to wear sandals and not put on two **t**. Mk 6:9
"Whoever has two **t** is to share with him Lk 3:11
bread, nor money; and do not have two **t**. Lk 9:3
weeping and showing **t** and other Acts 9:39

TURBAN (16)
a robe, a coat of checker work, a **t**, Ex 28:4
shall fasten it on the **t** by a cord of blue. Ex 28:37
of blue. It shall be on the front of the **t**. Ex 28:37
and you shall make a **t** of fine linen, Ex 28:39
And you shall set the **t** on his head and Ex 29:6
his head and put the holy crown on the **t**. Ex 29:6
and the **t** of fine linen, and the caps of Ex 39:28
a cord of blue to fasten it on the **t** above, Ex 39:31
And he set the **t** on his head, and on the Lv 8:9
set the turban on his head, and on the **t**, Lv 8:9
around his waist, and wear the linen **t**; Lv 16:4
me; my justice was like a robe and a **t**. Jb 29:14
Remove the **t** and take off the crown. Ezk 21:26
Bind on your **t**, and put your shoes on Ezk 24:17
"Let them put a clean **t** on his head." So Zec 3:5
So they put a clean **t** on his head and Zec 3:5

TURBANS (4)
the mirrors, the linen garments, the **t**, and Is 3:23
waists, with flowing **t** on their heads, Ezk 23:15
Your **t** shall be on your heads and Ezk 24:23
They shall have linen **t** on their heads, Ezk 44:18

TURBULENT (2)
if the river is **t** he is not frightened; Jb 40:23
Because you are more **t** than the nations Ezk 5:7

TURMOIL (6)
My inward parts are in **t** and never still; Jb 30:27
Surely for nothing they are in **t**; man Ps 39:6
soul, and why are you in **t** within me? Ps 42:5
soul, and why are you in **t** within me? Ps 42:11
soul, and why are you in **t** within me? Ps 43:5
from your pain and **t** and the hard service Is 14:3

TURN (313)
please **t** aside to your servant's house Gn 19:2
that I may **t** to the right hand or to the Gn 24:49
said, "I will **t** aside to see this great sight, Ex 3:3
is in the Nile, and it shall **t** into blood. Ex 7:17
people of Israel to **t** back and encamp in Ex 14:2
make all your enemies **t** their backs to Ex 23:27
T from your burning anger and relent Ex 32:12
Do not **t** to idols or make for yourselves Lv 19:4
"Do not **t** to mediums or wizards; do not Lv 19:31
I will **t** to you and make you fruitful and Lv 26:9
t tomorrow and set out for the Nm 14:25
We will not **t** aside to the right hand Nm 20:17
We will not **t** aside into field or Nm 21:22
the donkey, to **t** her into the road. Nm 22:23
was no way to **t** either to the right Nm 22:26
if it is evil in your sight, I will **t** back." Nm 22:34
of the LORD may **t** away from Israel." Nm 25:4
For if you **t** away from following him, Nm 32:15
And your border shall **t** south of the Nm 34:4
And the border shall **t** from Azmon to Nm 34:5
T and take your journey, and go to the Dt 1:7
t, and journey into the wilderness in the Dt 1:40
country long enough. **T** northward Dt 2:3
I will **t** aside neither to the right nor to Dt 2:27
You shall not **t** aside to the right hand or Dt 5:32
for they would **t** away your sons from Dt 7:4
and you **t** aside and serve other gods Dt 11:16
but **t** aside from the way that I am Dt 11:28
that the LORD may **t** from the fierceness Dt 13:17
then you shall **t** it into money and bind Dt 14:25
the morning you shall **t** and go to your Dt 16:7
You shall not **t** aside from the verdict Dt 17:11
wives for himself, lest his heart **t** away, Dt 17:17
that he may not **t** aside from the Dt 17:20
a hole with it and **t** back and cover up Dt 23:13
among you and **t** away from you. Dt 23:14
and if you do not **t** aside from any of the Dt 28:14
when you **t** to the LORD your God with Dt 30:10
they will **t** to other gods and serve them, Dt 31:20
act corruptly and **t** aside from the Dt 31:29
Do not **t** from it to the right hand or to the Jos 1:7
They **t** their backs before their enemies, Jos 7:12
Therefore **t** and go to your tents in the Jos 22:4
that you too must **t** away this day from Jos 22:18
an altar to **t** away from following Jos 22:23
against the LORD and **t** away this day Jos 22:29
For if you **t** back and cling to the Jos 23:12
then he will **t** and do you harm and Jos 24:20
to meet Sisera and said to him, "**T** aside, Jgs 4:18
him, "Turn aside, my lord; **t** aside to me; Jgs 4:18
let us **t** aside to this city of the Jebusites Jgs 19:11
"We will not **t** aside into the city of Jgs 19:12
the men of Israel should **t** in battle. Jgs 20:39
But Naomi said, "**T** back, my Ru 1:11
T back, my daughters; go your way, for Ru 1:12
So Boaz said, "**T** aside, friend; sit down Ru 4:1
his hand does not **t** away from you." 1 Sm 6:3
Yet do not **t** aside from following the 1 Sm 12:20
And do not **t** aside after empty things 1 Sm 12:21
"**T** and kill the priests of the LORD, 1 Sm 22:17
"You **t** and strike the priests." And 1 Sm 22:18
"**T** aside to your right hand or to your 2 Sm 2:21
Asahel would not **t** aside from 2 Sm 2:21
Asahel, "**T** aside from following me. 2 Sm 2:22
But he refused to **t** aside. Therefore 2 Sm 2:23
tell your people to **t** from the pursuit 2 Sm 2:26
one cannot **t** to the right hand or to 2 Sm 14:19
please **t** the counsel of Ahithophel 2 Sm 15:31
"**T** aside and stand here." So he 2 Sm 18:30
from his statutes I did not **t** aside. 2 Sm 22:23
and did not **t** back until they were 2 Sm 22:38
made my enemies **t** their backs to 2 Sm 22:41
in all that you do and wherever you **t**, 1 Kgs 2:3
and if they **t** again to you and 1 Kgs 8:33
your name and **t** from their sin, 1 Kgs 8:35
yet if they **t** their heart in the land to 1 Kgs 8:47
But if you **t** aside from following me, 1 Kgs 9:6
for surely they will **t** away your heart 1 Kgs 11:2
for it was a **t** of affairs brought 1 Kgs 12:15
the kingdom will **t** back to the 1 Kgs 12:26
of this people will **t** again to their 1 Kgs 12:27
Jeroboam did not **t** from his evil 1 Kgs 13:33
and did not **t** aside from anything 1 Kgs 15:5
from here and **t** eastward and hide 1 Kgs 17:3
"**T** around and carry me out of the 1 Kgs 22:34
his father. He did not **t** aside from it, 1 Kgs 22:43
way, he would **t** in there to eat food. 2 Kgs 4:8
T around and ride behind me." And 2 Kgs 9:18
T around and ride behind me." 2 Kgs 9:19
But Jehu did not **t** aside from the 2 Kgs 10:29
He did not **t** from the sins of 2 Kgs 10:31
He did not **t** away from the sins of 2 Kgs 15:24
"**T** from your evil ways and keep my 2 Kgs 17:13
that you should **t** fortified cities into 2 Kgs 19:25
and I will **t** you back on the way by 2 Kgs 19:28
"**T** back, and say to Hezekiah the 2 Kgs 20:5
and he did not **t** aside to the right or to 2 Kgs 22:2
the LORD did not **t** from the burning 2 Kgs 23:26
to come in every seven days, in **t**, 1 Chr 9:25
in Hebron to **t** the kingdom of 1 Chr 12:23
and they **t** again and acknowledge 2 Chr 6:24
your name and **t** from their sin, 2 Chr 6:26
yet if they **t** their heart in the land to 2 Chr 6:37
do not **t** away the face of your 2 Chr 6:42
seek my face and **t** from their wicked 2 Chr 7:14
"But if you **t** aside and forsake my 2 Chr 7:19
And they did not **t** aside from what 2 Chr 8:15
for it was a **t** of affairs brought 2 Chr 10:15
"**T** around and carry me out of the 2 Chr 18:33
his father and did not **t** aside from it, 2 Chr 20:32
fierce anger may **t** away from us. 2 Chr 29:10
that he may **t** again to the remnant of 2 Chr 30:6
fierce anger may **t** away from you. 2 Chr 30:8
merciful and will not **t** away his face 2 Chr 30:9

and he did not **t** aside to the right 2 Chr 34:2
they did not **t** away from following 2 Chr 34:33
Josiah did not **t** away from him, 2 Chr 35:22
T back their taunt on their own heads Neh 4:4
them in order to **t** them back to you, Neh 9:26
them in order to **t** them back to your Neh 9:29
not serve you or **t** from their wicked Neh 9:35
Now when the **t** came for each young Est 2:12
When the **t** came for Esther the Est 2:15
you? To which of the holy ones will you **t**? Jb 5:1
The caravans **t** aside from their course; Jb 6:18
Please **t**; let no injustice be done. Turn Jb 6:29
done. **T** now; my vindication is at stake. Jb 6:29
he snatches away; who can **t** him back? Jb 9:12
"God will not **t** back his anger; beneath Jb 9:13
the court, who can **t** him back? Jb 11:10
that you **t** your spirit against God and Jb 15:13
and who can **t** him back? Jb 23:13
and to **t** away from evil is Jb 28:28
that he may **t** man aside from his deed Jb 33:17
the greatness of the ransom **t** you aside. Jb 36:18
Take care; do not **t** to iniquity, for this Jb 36:21
They **t** around and around by his Jb 37:12
he does not **t** back from the sword. Jb 39:22
T, O LORD, deliver my life; save me for the Ps 6:4
they shall **t** back and be put to shame in Ps 6:10
When my enemies **t** back, they stumble Ps 9:3
and did not **t** back till they were Ps 18:37
You made my enemies **t** their backs to Ps 18:40
earth shall remember and **t** to the LORD, Ps 22:27
T to me and be gracious to me, for I am Ps 25:16
T not your servant away in anger, O you Ps 27:9
T away from evil and do good; seek Ps 34:14
T away from evil and do good; so shall Ps 37:27
his trust, who does not **t** to the proud, Ps 40:4
You have made us **t** back from the foe, Ps 44:10
Then my enemies will **t** back in the day Ps 56:9
to your abundant mercy, **t** to me. Ps 69:16
Let them **t** back because of their shame Ps 70:3
Therefore his people **t** back to them, Ps 73:10
not the downtrodden **t** back in shame; Ps 74:21
T again, O God of hosts! Look down Ps 80:14
Then we shall not **t** back from you; Ps 80:18
their enemies and **t** my hand against Ps 81:14
saints; but let them not **t** back to folly. Ps 85:8
T to me and be gracious to me; give Ps 86:16
to **t** away his wrath from destroying Ps 106:23
you flee? O Jordan, that you **t** back? Ps 114:5
T my eyes from looking at worthless Ps 119:37
T away the reproach that I dread, for Ps 119:39
me, but I do not **t** away from your law. Ps 119:51
ways, I **t** my feet to your testimonies; Ps 119:59
Let those who fear you **t** to me, that Ps 119:79
I do not **t** aside from your rules, for Ps 119:102
T to me and be gracious to me, as is Ps 119:132
But those who **t** aside to their crooked Ps 125:5
do not **t** away the face of your anointed Ps 132:10
oath from which he will not **t** back: Ps 132:11
If you **t** at my reproof, behold, I will Prv 1:23
eyes; fear the LORD, and **t** away from evil. Prv 3:7
and do not **t** away from the words of my Prv 4:5
not go on it; **t** away from it and pass on. Prv 4:15
or to the left; **t** your foot away from evil. Prv 4:27
Let not your heart **t** aside to her ways; Prv 7:25
let him **t** in here!" To him who lacks Prv 9:4
let him **t** in here!" And to him who Prv 9:16
that one may **t** away from the snares Prv 13:14
but to **t** away from evil is an Prv 13:19
that one may **t** away from the snares Prv 14:27
that he may **t** away from Sheol Prv 15:24
and **t** away his anger from him. Prv 24:18
city aflame, but the wise **t** away wrath. Prv 29:8
beasts and does not **t** back before any; Prv 30:30
and the shadows flee, **t**, my beloved, Sg 2:17
T away your eyes from me, for they Sg 6:5
I will **t** my hand against you and will Is 1:25
with their hearts, and **t** and be healed." Is 6:10
and their God, and **t** their faces upward. Is 8:21
The people did not **t** to him who struck Is 9:13
to **t** aside the needy from justice and to Is 10:2
them, each will **t** to his own people, Is 13:14
is stretched out, and who will **t** it back? Is 14:27
strength to those who **t** back the battle at Is 28:6
You **t** things upside down! Shall the Is 29:16
with an empty plea **t** aside him who is Is 29:21
protection of Pharaoh **t** to your shame, Is 30:3
leave the way, **t** aside from the path, let Is 30:11
walk in it," when you **t** to the right or Is 30:21
turn to the right or when you **t** to the left. Is 30:21
T to him from whom people have deeply Is 31:6
and I will **t** you back on the way by Is 37:29
on the dial of Ahaz **t** back ten steps." So Is 38:8
I will **t** the rivers into islands, and dry up Is 42:15
I will **t** the darkness before them into Is 42:16
hand; I work, and who can **t** it back?" Is 43:13

"**T** to me and be saved, all the ends of the Is 45:22
"If you **t** back your foot from the Is 58:13
in Jacob who **t** from transgression," Is 59:20
and would not **t** from following me. Jer 3:19
I have not relented, nor will I **t** back." Jer 4:28
O Jerusalem, lest I **t** from you in disgust, Jer 6:8
my heart would not **t** toward this people. Jer 15:1
Who will **t** aside to ask about your Jer 15:5
people; they did not **t** from their ways. Jer 15:7
be as my mouth. They shall **t** to you, Jer 15:19
turn to you, but you shall not **t** to them. Jer 15:19
those who **t** away from you shall be Jer 17:13
them, to **t** away your wrath from them. Jer 18:20
I will **t** back the weapons of war that are Jer 21:4
of the LORD will not **t** back until he has Jer 23:20
saying, '**T** now, every one of you, from Jer 25:5
listen, and every one **t** from his evil way, Jer 26:3
of the LORD will not **t** back until he has Jer 30:24
I will **t** their mourning into joy; I will Jer 31:13
the hill Gareb, and shall then **t** to Goah. Jer 31:39
that I will not **t** away from doing good Jer 32:40
hearts, that they may not **t** from me. Jer 32:40
'**T** now every one of you from his evil Jer 35:15
that every one may **t** from his evil way, Jer 36:3
that every one will **t** from his evil way, Jer 36:7
in the mud, they **t** away from you.' Jer 38:22
to **t** from their evil and make no Jer 44:5
Flee, **t** back, dwell in the depths, O Jer 49:8
every one shall **t** to his own people, Jer 50:16
and he does not **t** from his wickedness, Ezk 3:19
so that you cannot **t** from one side to the Ezk 4:8
all their multitude; it shall not **t** back; Ezk 7:13
are feeble, and all knees **t** to water. Ezk 7:17
I will **t** my face from them, and they Ezk 7:22
the wheels did not **t** from beside them. Ezk 10:16
that he should not **t** from his evil way Ezk 13:22
Repent and **t** away from your idols, and Ezk 14:6
and **t** away your faces from all your Ezk 14:6
rather that he should **t** from his way Ezk 18:23
Repent and **t** from all your Ezk 18:30
of anyone, declares the Lord GOD; so **t**, Ezk 18:32
iniquity, when they **t** to them for aid. Ezk 29:16
to warn the wicked to **t** from his way, Ezk 33:8
you warn the wicked to **t** from his way, Ezk 33:9
his way, and he does not **t** from his way, Ezk 33:9
but that the wicked **t** from his way Ezk 33:11
t back, turn back from your evil Ezk 33:11
back, **t** back from your evil ways, Ezk 33:11
behold, I am for you, and I will **t** to you, Ezk 36:9
And I will **t** you about and put hooks Ezk 38:4
to **t** your hand against the waste Ezk 38:12
And I will **t** you about and drive you Ezk 39:2
anger and your wrath **t** away from your Dn 9:16
Afterward he shall **t** his face to the Dn 11:18
he shall **t** his insolence back upon Dn 11:18
Then he shall **t** his face back toward Dn 11:19
and shall **t** back and be enraged and Dn 11:30
He shall **t** back and pay attention to Dn 11:30
and those who **t** many to righteousness, Dn 12:3
though they **t** to other gods and love Hos 3:1
knows whether he will not **t** and relent, Jl 2:14
I will **t** my hand against Ekron, and the Am 1:8
dust of the earth and **t** aside the way of Am 2:7
O you who **t** justice to wormwood and Am 5:7
bribe, and **t** aside the needy in the gate. Am 5:12
I will **t** your feasts into mourning and Am 8:10
Let everyone **t** from his evil way and Jon 3:8
God may **t** and relent and turn from his Jon 3:9
turn and relent and **t** from his fierce Jon 3:9
they shall **t** in dread to the LORD our God, Mi 7:17
and with hail, yet you did not **t** to me, Hg 2:17
I will **t** my hand against the little ones. Zec 13:7
And he will **t** the hearts of fathers to Mal 4:6
the right cheek, **t** to him the other also. Mt 5:39
them underfoot and **t** to attack you. Mt 7:6
and understand with their heart and **t**, Mt 13:15
unless you **t** and become like children, Mt 18:3
is in the field not **t** back to take his Mt 24:18
lest they should **t** and be forgiven." Mk 4:12
is in the field not **t** back to take his Mk 13:16
And he will **t** many of the children of Lk 1:16
to **t** the hearts of the fathers to the Lk 1:17
T in the account of your management, Lk 16:2
the one who is in the field not **t** back. Lk 17:31
and understand with their heart, and **t**, Jn 12:40
but your sorrow will **t** into joy. Jn 16:20
Repent therefore, and **t** again, that your Acts 3:19
Our fathers in **t** brought it in with Acts 7:45
seeking to **t** the proconsul away from Acts 13:8
that you should **t** from these vain Acts 14:15
those of the Gentiles who **t** to God, Acts 15:19
so that they may **t** from darkness to Acts 26:18
that they should repent and **t** to God, Acts 26:20
understand with their heart and **t**, Acts 28:27
two or at most three, and each in **t**, 1 Cor 14:27

so you should rather **t** to forgive and 2 Cor 2:7
afflicted at every **t**—fighting without 2 Cor 7:5
how can you **t** back again to the weak Gal 4:9
Jesus Christ this will **t** out for my Phil 1:19
and will **t** away from listening to the 2 Tm 4:4
of people who **t** away from the Ti 1:14
let him **t** away from evil and do good; 1 Pt 3:11
after knowing it to **t** back from the 2 Pt 2:21
over the waters to **t** them into blood and Rv 11:6

TURNED (267)

a flaming sword that **t** every way to Gn 3:24
Their faces were **t** backward, and they Gn 9:23
Then they **t** back and came to Gn 14:7
So the men **t** from there and went Gn 18:22
so they **t** aside to him and entered his Gn 19:3
the LORD has blessed you wherever I **t**. Gn 30:30
from his brothers and **t** aside to a Gn 38:1
He **t** to her at the roadside and said, Gn 38:16
Then he **t** away from them and wept. Gn 42:24
and they **t** trembling to one another, Gn 42:28
When the LORD saw that he **t** aside to see, Ex 3:4
Then Moses **t** to the LORD and said, "O Ex 5:22
your hand the staff that **t** into a serpent. Ex 7:15
and all the water in the Nile **t** into blood. Ex 7:20
Pharaoh **t** and went into his house, and Ex 7:23
this day.'" Then he **t** and went out from Ex 10:6
And the LORD **t** the wind into a very Ex 10:19
They have **t** aside quickly out of the way Ex 32:8
Then Moses **t** and went down from the Ex 32:15
When Moses **t** again into the camp, his Ex 33:11
the diseased area has **t** white and the Lv 13:3
skin, and the hair in it has not **t** white, Lv 13:4
in the skin that has **t** the hair white, Lv 13:10
it has all **t** white, and he is clean. Lv 13:13
him, and if the disease has **t** white, Lv 13:17
than the skin and its hair has **t** white, Lv 13:20
in the spot has **t** white and it appears Lv 13:25
discipline you are not **t** to me but walk Lv 26:23
if you have not **t** aside to uncleanness Nm 5:19
snow. And Aaron **t** toward Miriam, Nm 12:10
Because you have **t** back from Nm 14:43
they **t** toward the tent of meeting. Nm 16:42
territory, so Israel **t** away from him. Nm 20:21
Then they **t** and went up by the way to Nm 21:33
And the donkey **t** aside out of the road Nm 22:23
donkey saw me and **t** aside before me Nm 22:33
If she had not **t** aside from me, surely Nm 22:33
has **t** back my wrath from the people Nm 25:11
from Etham and **t** back to Pi-hahiroth, Nm 33:7
And they **t** and went up into the hill Dt 1:24
"Then we **t** and journeyed into the Dt 2:1
"And we **t** and went in the direction of the Dt 2:8
"Then we **t** and went up the way to Dt 3:1
They have **t** aside quickly out of the way Dt 9:12
So I **t** and came down from the Dt 9:15
You had **t** aside quickly from the way Dt 9:16
Then I **t** and came down from the Dt 10:5
the LORD your God **t** the curse into a Dt 23:5
done, because they have **t** to other gods. Dt 31:18
when Israel has **t** their backs before their Jos 7:8
Then the LORD **t** from his burning Jos 7:26
fled to the wilderness **t** back against the Jos 8:20
then they **t** back and struck down the Jos 8:21
all Israel with him **t** back to Debir and Jos 10:38
And Joshua **t** back at that time and Jos 11:10
They soon **t** aside from the way in Jgs 2:17
they **t** back and were more corrupt than Jgs 2:19
But he himself **t** back at the idols near Jgs 3:19
not be afraid." So he **t** aside to her into Jgs 4:18
And the LORD **t** to him and said, "Go in Jgs 6:14
it so that it fell and **t** it upside down, Jgs 7:13
the people of Israel **t** again and whored Jgs 8:33
"That is why we have **t** to you now, Jgs 11:8
And he **t** aside to see the carcass of the Jgs 14:8
And he **t** them tail to tail and put a torch Jgs 15:4
And they **t** aside and said to him, "Who Jgs 18:3
And they **t** aside there and came to the Jgs 18:15
So they **t** and departed, putting the little Jgs 18:21
Dan, who **t** around and said to Micah, Jgs 18:23
him, he **t** and went back to his home. Jgs 18:26
and they **t** aside there, to go in and Jgs 19:15
Then the men of Israel **t**, and the men Jgs 20:41
Therefore they **t** their backs before the Jgs 20:42
And they **t** and fled toward the Jgs 20:45
But 600 men **t** and fled toward the Jgs 20:47
the men of Israel **t** back against the Jgs 20:48
midnight the man was startled and **t** over, Ru 3:8
down here." And he **t** aside and sat down. Ru 4:1
They **t** neither to the right nor to the 1 Sm 6:12
walk in his ways but **t** aside after gain. 1 Sm 8:3
with them and be **t** into another man. 1 Sm 10:6
When he **t** his back to leave Samuel, 1 Sm 10:9
One company **t** toward Ophrah, 1 Sm 13:17
another company **t** toward 1 Sm 13:18
and another company **t** toward the 1 Sm 13:18

even they also **t** to be with the 1 Sm 14:21
Wherever he **t** he routed them. 1 Sm 14:47
for he has **t** back from following me 1 Sm 15:11
for himself and **t** and passed on 1 Sm 15:12
As Samuel **t** to go away, Saul seized 1 Sm 15:27
So Samuel **t** back after Saul, and 1 Sm 15:31
And he **t** away from him toward 1 Sm 17:30
Doeg the Edomite **t** and struck down 1 Sm 22:18
David's young men **t** away and came 1 Sm 25:12
and God has **t** away from me and 1 Sm 28:15
since the LORD has **t** from you and 1 Sm 28:16
the bow of Jonathan **t** not back, 2 Sm 1:22
he **t** neither to the right hand nor to 2 Sm 2:19
stand here." So he **t** aside and stood 2 Sm 18:30
that day was **t** into mourning for 2 Sm 19:2
the kingdom has **t** about and become 1 Kgs 2:15
Then the king **t** around and blessed 1 Kgs 8:14
So she **t** and went back to her own 1 Kgs 10:13
And his wives **t** away his heart. 1 Kgs 11:3
was old his wives **t** away his heart 1 Kgs 11:4
his heart had **t** away from the 1 Kgs 11:9
that you have **t** their hearts back." 1 Kgs 18:37
a soldier **t** and brought a man to me 1 Kgs 20:39
on his bed and **t** away his face and 1 Kgs 21:4
of Israel." So they **t** to fight against 1 Kgs 22:32
they **t** back from pursuing him. 1 Kgs 22:33
And he **t** around, and when he saw 2 Kgs 2:24
and he **t** into the chamber and rested 2 Kgs 4:11
be clean?" So he **t** and went away in 2 Kgs 5:12
go when the man **t** from his chariot 2 Kgs 5:26
on them, and he **t** toward them, 2 Kgs 13:23
the king of Assyria **t** back and did 2 Kgs 15:20
Then Hezekiah **t** his face to the wall 2 Kgs 20:2
And as Josiah **t**, he saw the tombs 2 Kgs 23:16
who **t** to the LORD with all his heart 2 Kgs 23:25
Then he **t** and rebelled against him. 2 Kgs 24:1
to death and **t** the kingdom over 1 Chr 10:14
He **t** and saw the angel, and his four 1 Chr 21:20
Then the king **t** around and blessed 2 Chr 6:3
So she **t** and went back to her own 2 Chr 9:12
the wrath of the LORD **t** from him, 2 Chr 12:12
in their distress they **t** to the LORD, 2 Chr 15:4
of Israel." So they **t** to fight against 2 Chr 18:31
they **t** back from pursuing him. 2 Chr 18:32
the time when he **t** away from the 2 Chr 25:27
him and have **t** away their faces 2 Chr 29:6
of the LORD and **t** their backs. 2 Chr 29:6
them joyful and had **t** the heart of the Ezr 6:22
over this matter is **t** away from us." Ezr 10:14
and I **t** back and entered by the Valley Neh 2:15
Yet when they **t** and cried to you, you Neh 9:28
and **t** a stubborn shoulder and Neh 9:29
them—yet our God **t** the curse into a Neh 13:2
month that had been **t** for them from Est 9:22
one who feared God and **t** away from evil. Jb 1:1
those whom I loved have **t** against me. Jb 19:19
yet his food is **t** in his stomach; it is the Jb 20:14
I have kept his way and have not **t** aside. Jb 23:11
bread, but underneath it is **t** up as by fire. Jb 28:5
Terrors are **t** upon me; my honor is Jb 30:15
You have **t** cruel to me; with the might Jb 30:21
My lyre is **t** to mourning, and my pipe Jb 30:31
if my step has **t** aside from the way and Jb 31:7
because they **t** aside from following Jb 34:27
for him sling stones are **t** to stubble. Jb 41:28
long shall my honor be **t** into shame? Ps 4:2
They have all **t** aside; together they have Ps 14:3
You have **t** for me my mourning into Ps 30:11
Let them be **t** back and disappointed Ps 35:4
let those be **t** back and brought to Ps 40:14
Our heart has not **t** back, nor have our Ps 44:18
with their own tongues **t** against them; Ps 64:8
He **t** the sea into dry land; they passed Ps 66:6
Let them be **t** back and brought to Ps 70:2
with the bow, **t** back on the day of battle. Ps 78:9
He **t** their rivers to blood, so that they Ps 78:44
but **t** away and acted treacherously like Ps 78:57
your wrath; you **t** from your hot anger. Ps 85:3
You have also **t** back the edge of his Ps 89:43
He **t** their hearts to hate his people, to Ps 105:25
He **t** their waters into blood and Ps 105:29
The sea looked and fled; Jordan **t** back. Ps 114:3
Zion be put to shame and **t** backward! Ps 129:5
So I **t** to consider wisdom and madness Eccl 2:12
So I **t** about and gave my heart up to Eccl 2:20
I **t** my heart to know and to search out Eccl 7:25
beloved, but my beloved had **t** and gone. Sg 5:6
Where has your beloved **t**, that we may Sg 6:1
For all this his anger has not **t** away, and Is 5:25
For all this his anger has not **t** away, and Is 9:12
For all this his anger has not **t** away, and Is 9:17
For all this his anger has not **t** away, and Is 9:21
For all this his anger has not **t** away, and Is 10:4
were angry with me, your anger **t** away, Is 12:1
longed for has been **t** for me into Is 21:4
until Lebanon shall be **t** into a fruitful Is 29:17
the streams of Edom shall be **t** into pitch, Is 34:9
Then Hezekiah **t** his face to the wall and Is 38:2
ten steps." So the sun **t** back on the dial Is 38:8
They are **t** back and utterly put to Is 42:17
I was not rebellious; I **t** not backward. Is 50:5
we have **t** every one to his own way; Is 53:6
they have all **t** to their own way, each to Is 56:11
Justice is **t** back, and righteousness Is 59:14
the abundance of the sea shall be **t** to you, Is 60:5
therefore he **t** to be their enemy, and Is 63:10
then have you **t** degenerate and become Jer 2:21
For they have **t** their back to me, and not Jer 2:27
surely his anger has **t** from me.' Jer 2:35
anger of the LORD has not **t** back from us." Jer 4:8
heart; they have **t** aside and gone away. Jer 5:23
Your iniquities have **t** these away, and Jer 5:25
Their houses shall be **t** over to others, Jer 6:12
then has this people **t** away in perpetual Jer 8:5
They have **t** back to the iniquities of Jer 11:10
and they would have **t** them from their Jer 23:22
in labor? Why has every face **t** pale? Jer 30:6
For after I had **t** away, I relented, and Jer 31:19
They have **t** to me their back and not Jer 32:33
But afterward they **t** around and took Jer 34:11
but then you **t** around and profaned Jer 34:16
the words, they **t** one to another in fear. Jer 36:16
captive from Mizpah **t** around and Jer 41:14
are dismayed and have **t** backward. Jer 46:5
yes, they have **t** and fled together; Jer 46:21
How Moab has **t** his back in shame! Jer 48:39
has become feeble, she **t** to flee, Jer 49:24
the way to Zion, with faces **t** toward it, Jer 50:5
spread a net for my feet; he **t** me back; Lam 1:13
he **t** aside my steps and tore me to Lam 3:11
inheritance has been **t** over to Lam 5:2
our dancing has been **t** to mourning. Lam 5:15
vine, and its branches **t** toward him, Ezk 17:6
he considered and **t** away from all Ezk 18:28
by them, she **t** from them in disgust. Ezk 23:17
her nakedness, I **t** in disgust from her, Ezk 23:18
as I had **t** in disgust from her sister. Ezk 23:18
lovers from whom you **t** in disgust, Ezk 23:22
of those from whom you **t** in disgust, Ezk 23:28
and I **t** you to ashes on the earth in the Ezk 28:18
Then he **t** to the west side and Ezk 42:19
Then I **t** my face to the Lord God, seeking Dn 9:3
has transgressed your law and **t** aside, Dn 9:11
I **t** my face toward the ground and was Dn 10:15
with the peoples; Ephraim is a cake not **t**. Hos 7:8
freely, for my anger has **t** from them. Hos 14:4
The sun shall be **t** to darkness, and the Jl 2:31
But you have **t** justice into poison and Am 6:12
they did, how they **t** from their evil way, Jon 3:10
those who have **t** back from following Zep 1:6
pay attention and **t** a stubborn Zec 7:11
whole land shall be **t** into a plain from Zec 14:10
and he **t** many from iniquity. Mal 2:6
But you have **t** aside from the way. You Mal 2:8
your fathers you have **t** aside from my Mal 3:7
Jesus **t**, and seeing her he said, "Take Mt 9:22
But he **t** and said to Peter, "Get behind Mt 16:23
immediately **t** about in the crowd and Mk 5:30
But he **t** and rebuked them. Lk 9:55
him, and he **t** and said to them, Lk 14:25
he saw that he was healed, **t** back, Lk 17:15
And when you have **t** again, strengthen Lk 22:32
And the Lord **t** and looked at Peter. And Lk 22:61
Jesus **t** and saw them following and said Jn 1:38
many of his disciples **t** back and no Jn 6:66
she **t** around and saw Jesus standing, Jn 20:14
"Mary." She **t** and said to him in Jn 20:16
Peter **t** and saw the disciple whom Jesus Jn 21:20
from which Judas **t** aside to go Acts 1:25
the sun shall be **t** to darkness and the Acts 2:20
and in their hearts they **t** to Egypt, Acts 7:39
But God **t** away and gave them over to Acts 7:42
saw him, and they **t** to the Lord. Acts 9:35
number who believed **t** to the Lord. Acts 11:21
annoyed, **t** and said to the spirit, Acts 16:18
men who have **t** the world upside Acts 17:6
has persuaded and **t** away a great Acts 19:26
All have **t** aside; together they have Rom 3:12
and how you **t** to God from idols to 1 Thes 1:9
all who are in Asia **t** away from me, 2 Tm 1:15
Let your laughter be **t** to mourning and Jas 4:9
Then I **t** to see the voice that was Rv 1:12

TURNING (29)
tribe whose heart is **t** away today from Dt 29:18
and so northward, **t** toward Gilgal, Jos 15:7
t on the western side southward from Jos 18:14
God of Israel in **t** away this day from Jos 22:16
t aside from it neither to the right hand Jos 23:6
dish, wiping it and **t** it upside down. 2 Kgs 21:13
his heart against **t** to the LORD, 2 Chr 36:13
the simple are killed by their **t** away, Prv 1:32
and **t** back from following our God, Is 59:13
astray, **t** them away on the mountains. Jer 50:6
straight forward, without **t** as they went. Ezk 1:9
go, they went, without **t** as they went. Ezk 1:12
four directions without **t** as they went. Ezk 1:17
four directions without **t** as they went, Ezk 10:11
others followed without **t** as they went. Ezk 10:11
t aside from your commandments and Dn 9:5
t from our iniquities and gaining Dn 9:13
My people are bent on **t** away from me, Hos 11:7
But **t** and seeing his disciples, he Mk 8:33
and **t** to the crowd that followed him, Lk 7:9
Then **t** toward the woman he said to Lk 7:44
Then **t** to the disciples he said privately, Lk 10:23
But **t** to them Jesus said, "Daughters of Lk 23:28
to bless you by **t** every one of you from Acts 3:26
and **t** to the body he said, "Tabitha, Acts 9:40
life, behold, we are **t** to the Gentiles. Acts 13:46
of Christ and are **t** to a different gospel Gal 1:6
if by **t** the cities of Sodom and 2 Pt 2:6
and on **t** I saw seven golden lampstands, Rv 1:12

TURNS (53)
until your brother's fury **t** away— Gn 27:44
your brother's anger **t** away from you, Gn 27:45
and it **t** into a case of leprous disease on Lv 13:2
raw flesh recovers and **t** white again, Lv 13:16
"If a person **t** to mediums and wizards, Lv 20:6
But if your heart **t** away, and you will Dt 30:17
Hezron, up to Addar, **t** about to Karka, Jos 15:3
east the boundary **t** around toward Jos 16:6
north the boundary **t** about to Jos 19:14
then it **t** eastward, it goes to Beth-dagon, Jos 19:27
Then the boundary **t** to Ramah, Jos 19:29
Then the boundary **t** to Hosah, and it Jos 19:29
Then the boundary **t** westward to Jos 19:34
until you learn how the matter **t** out, Ru 3:18
who fears God and **t** away from evil?" Jb 1:8
man, who fears God and **t** away from evil? Jb 2:3
he **t** to the right hand, but I do not see Jb 23:9
no treader **t** toward their vineyards. Jb 24:18
My skin **t** black and falls from me, and Jb 30:30
He **t** rivers into a desert, springs of Ps 107:33
He **t** a desert into pools of water, a Ps 107:35
who **t** the rock into a pool of water, the Ps 114:8
wise is cautious and **t** away from evil, Prv 14:16
A soft answer **t** away wrath, but a harsh Prv 15:1
fear of the LORD one **t** away from evil. Prv 16:6
of the upright **t** aside from evil; Prv 16:17
who gives it; wherever he **t** he prospers. Prv 17:8
of the LORD; he **t** it wherever he will. Prv 21:1
As a door **t** on its hinges, so does a Prv 26:14
If one **t** away his ear from hearing the Prv 28:9
who **t** wise men back and makes their Is 44:25
again? If one **t** away, does he not return? Jer 8:4
Everyone **t** to his own course, like a horse Jer 8:6
you look for light he **t** it into gloom and Jer 13:16
like a traveler who **t** aside to tarry for a Jer 14:8
whose heart **t** away from the LORD. Jer 17:5
which I have spoken, **t** from its evil, Jer 18:8
evildoers, so that no one **t** from his evil; Jer 23:14
she herself groans and **t** her face away. Lam 1:8
surely against me he **t** his hand again Lam 3:3
a righteous person **t** from his Ezk 3:20
if a wicked person **t** away from all his Ezk 18:21
a righteous person **t** away from his Ezk 18:24
a righteous person **t** away from his Ezk 18:26
when a wicked person **t** away from the Ezk 18:27
by it when he **t** from his wickedness, Ezk 33:12
yet if he **t** from his sin and does what Ezk 33:14
When the righteous **t** from his Ezk 33:18
when the wicked **t** from his Ezk 33:19
and **t** deep darkness into the morning Am 5:8
"Halt! Halt!" they cry, but none **t** back. Na 2:8
in the day, and **t** to you seven times, Lk 17:4
But when one **t** to the Lord, the veil is 2 Cor 3:16

TURTLEDOVE (4)
three years old, a ram three years old, a **t**, Gn 15:9
and a pigeon or a **t** for a sin offering, Lv 12:6
and the voice of the **t** is heard in our Sg 2:12
in the heavens knows her times, and the **t**, Jer 8:7

TURTLEDOVES (10)
shall bring his offering of **t** or pigeons. Lv 1:14
he has committed two **t** or two pigeons, Lv 5:7
if he cannot afford two **t** or two pigeons, Lv 5:11
then she shall take two **t** or two pigeons, Lv 12:8
also two **t** or two pigeons, whichever he Lv 14:22
And he shall offer, of the **t** or pigeons, Lv 14:30
he shall take two **t** or two pigeons and Lv 15:14
she shall take two **t** or two pigeons and Lv 15:29
he shall bring two **t** or two pigeons to Nm 6:10
is said in the Law of the Lord, "a pair of **t**, Lk 2:24

TUSKS (1)

you in payment ivory **t** and ebony.	Ezk 27:15

TWELFTH (24)

On the **t** day Ahira the son of Enan, the	Nm 7:78
front of him, and he was with the **t**.	1 Kgs 19:19
In the **t** year of Joram the son of	2 Kgs 8:25
In the **t** year of Ahaz king of Judah,	2 Kgs 17:1
king of Judah, in the **t** month,	2 Kgs 25:27
eleventh to Eliashib, the **t** to Jakim,	1 Chr 24:12
the **t** to Hashabiah, his sons and his	1 Chr 25:19
T, for the twelfth month, was Heldai	1 Chr 27:15
Twelfth, for the **t** month, was Heldai	1 Chr 27:15
and in the **t** year he began to purge	2 Chr 34:3
the river Ahava on the **t** day of the first	Ezr 8:31
of Nisan, in the **t** year of King Ahasuerus,	Est 3:7
it month after month till the **t** month,	Est 3:7
day, the thirteenth day of the **t** month,	Est 3:13
on the thirteenth day of the **t** month,	Est 8:12
Now in the **t** month, which is the month	Est 9:1
king of Judah, in the **t** month,	Jer 52:31
tenth month, on the **t** day of the month,	Ezk 29:1
In the **t** year, in the twelfth month, on	Ezk 32:1
In the twelfth year, in the **t** month, on	Ezk 32:1
In the **t** year, in the twelfth month, on	Ezk 32:17
In the twelfth year, in the **t** month, on	Ezk 32:17
In the **t** year of our exile, in the tenth	Ezk 33:21
the eleventh jacinth, the **t** amethyst.	Rv 21:20

TWELVE (161)

T years they had served Chedorlaomer,	Gn 14:4
He shall father **t** princes, and I will	Gn 17:20
t princes according to their tribes.	Gn 25:16
of it. Now the sons of Jacob were **t**.	Gn 35:22
"We, your servants, are **t** brothers,	Gn 42:13
We are **t** brothers, sons of our father.	Gn 42:32
All these are the **t** tribes of Israel. This	Gn 49:28
where there were **t** springs of water and	Ex 15:27
at the foot of the mountain, and **t** pillars,	Ex 24:4
pillars, according to the **t** tribes of Israel.	Ex 24:4
There shall be **t** stones with their	Ex 28:21
engraved with its name, for the **t** tribes.	Ex 28:21
There were **t** stones with their names	Ex 39:14
engraved with its name, for the **t** tribes.	Ex 39:14
take fine flour and bake **t** loaves from it;	Lv 24:5
the help of the chiefs of Israel, **t** men,	Nm 1:44
before the LORD, six wagons and **t** oxen,	Nm 7:3
t silver plates, twelve silver basins,	Nm 7:84
twelve silver plates, **t** silver basins,	Nm 7:84
twelve silver basins, **t** golden dishes,	Nm 7:84
the **t** golden dishes, full of incense,	Nm 7:86
the cattle for the burnt offering **t** bulls,	Nm 7:87
the burnt offering twelve bulls, **t** rams,	Nm 7:87
twelve rams, **t** male lambs a year old,	Nm 7:87
and **t** male goats for a sin offering;	Nm 7:87
to their fathers' houses, **t** staffs.	Nm 17:2
to their fathers' houses, **t** staffs.	Nm 17:6
"On the second day **t** bulls from the	Nm 29:17
each tribe, **t** thousand armed for war.	Nm 31:5
at Elim there were **t** springs of water	Nm 33:9
good to me, and I took **t** men from you,	Dt 1:23
Now therefore take **t** men from the	Jos 3:12
"Take **t** men from the people, from each	Jos 4:2
'Take **t** stones from here out of the midst	Jos 4:3
Then Joshua called the **t** men from the	Jos 4:4
commanded and took up **t** stones out of	Jos 4:8
And Joshua set up **t** stones in the midst of	Jos 4:9
And those **t** stones, which they took out	Jos 4:20
Geba—**t** cities with their villages:	Jos 18:24
and Bethlehem—**t** cities with their	Jos 19:15
of Gad, and the tribe of Zebulun, **t** cities.	Jos 21:7
allotted to them were in all **t** cities.	Jos 21:40
divided her, limb by limb, into **t** pieces,	Jgs 19:29
t for Benjamin and Ish-bosheth the	2 Sm 2:15
of Saul, and **t** of the servants of David.	2 Sm 2:15
"Let me choose **t** thousand men,	2 Sm 17:1
Solomon had **t** officers over all Israel,	1 Kgs 4:7
and a line of **t** cubits measured its	1 Kgs 7:15
It stood on **t** oxen, three facing north,	1 Kgs 7:25
and the **t** oxen underneath the sea.	1 Kgs 7:44
while **t** lions stood there, one on	1 Kgs 10:20
was on him, and tore it into **t** pieces.	1 Kgs 11:30
Israel, and he reigned for **t** years;	1 Kgs 16:23
Elijah took **t** stones, according to	1 Kgs 18:31
was plowing with **t** yoke of oxen	1 Kgs 19:19
in Samaria, and he reigned **t** years.	2 Kgs 3:1
Manasseh was **t** years old when he	2 Kgs 21:1
their clans were allotted **t** cities out of	1 Chr 6:63
him and his brothers and his sons, **t**;	1 Chr 25:9
Zaccur, his sons and his brothers, **t**;	1 Chr 25:10
to Izri, his sons and his brothers, **t**;	1 Chr 25:11
his sons and his brothers, **t**;	1 Chr 25:12
his sons and his brothers, **t**;	1 Chr 25:13
his sons and his brothers, **t**;	1 Chr 25:14
his sons and his brothers, **t**;	1 Chr 25:15
his sons and his brothers, **t**;	1 Chr 25:16
Shimei, his sons and his brothers, **t**;	1 Chr 25:17
Azarel, his sons and his brothers, **t**;	1 Chr 25:18
his sons and his brothers, **t**;	1 Chr 25:19
his sons and his brothers, **t**;	1 Chr 25:20
his sons and his brothers, **t**;	1 Chr 25:21
his sons and his brothers, **t**;	1 Chr 25:22
his sons and his brothers, **t**;	1 Chr 25:23
his sons and his brothers, **t**;	1 Chr 25:24
Hanani, his sons and his brothers, **t**;	1 Chr 25:25
his sons and his brothers, **t**;	1 Chr 25:26
his sons and his brothers, **t**;	1 Chr 25:27
Hothir, his sons and his brothers, **t**;	1 Chr 25:28
his sons and his brothers, **t**;	1 Chr 25:29
his sons and his brothers, **t**;	1 Chr 25:30
his sons and his brothers, **t**.	1 Chr 25:31
It stood on **t** oxen, three facing north,	2 Chr 4:4
one sea, and the **t** oxen underneath it.	2 Chr 4:15
while **t** lions stood there, one on each	2 Chr 9:19
Manasseh was **t** years old when he	2 Chr 33:1
Then I set apart **t** of the leading priests:	Ezr 8:24
to the God of Israel, **t** bulls for all Israel,	Ezr 8:35
and as a sin offering **t** male goats.	Ezr 8:35
year of Artaxerxes the king, **t** years,	Neh 5:14
after being **t** months under the	Est 2:12
return struck down **t** thousand of Edom	Ps 60:T
the **t** bronze bulls that were under the	Jer 52:20
cubits, its circumference was **t** cubits,	Jer 52:21
cubits, and the breadth **t** cubits,	Ezk 40:49
square, **t** cubits long by twelve broad.	Ezk 43:16
square, twelve cubits long by **t** broad.	Ezk 43:16
inheritance among the **t** tribes of	Ezk 47:13
At the end of **t** months he was walking	Dn 4:29
discharge of blood for **t** years came up	Mt 9:20
called to him his **t** disciples and gave	Mt 10:1
The names of the **t** apostles are these:	Mt 10:2
These **t** Jesus sent out, instructing them,	Mt 10:5
had finished instructing his **t** disciples,	Mt 11:1
And they took up **t** baskets full of the	Mt 14:20
followed me will also sit on **t** thrones,	Mt 19:28
thrones, judging the **t** tribes of Israel.	Mt 19:28
Jerusalem, he took the **t** disciples aside,	Mt 20:17
Then one of the **t**, whose name was	Mt 26:14
evening, he reclined at table with the **t**.	Mt 26:20
still speaking, Judas came, one of the **t**,	Mt 26:47
send me more than **t** legions of angels?	Mt 26:53
And he appointed **t** (whom he also	Mk 3:14
He appointed the **t**: Simon (to whom he	Mk 3:16
around him with the **t** asked him about	Mk 4:10
had had a discharge of blood for **t** years,	Mk 5:25
walking (for she was **t** years of age),	Mk 5:42
And he called the **t** and began to send	Mk 6:7
And they took up **t** baskets full of	Mk 6:43
you take up?" They said to him, "**T**."	Mk 8:19
And he sat down and called the **t**. And	Mk 9:35
And taking the **t** again, he began to	Mk 10:32
late, he went out to Bethany with the **t**.	Mk 11:11
Judas Iscariot, who was one of the **t**,	Mk 14:10
it was evening, he came with the **t**.	Mk 14:17
He said to them, "It is one of the **t**, one	Mk 14:20
still speaking, Judas came, one of the **t**,	Mk 14:43
And when he was **t** years old, they went	Lk 2:42
his disciples and chose from them **t**,	Lk 6:13
of God. And the **t** were with him,	Lk 8:1
an only daughter, about **t** years of age,	Lk 8:42
had had a discharge of blood for **t** years,	Lk 8:43
And he called the **t** together and gave	Lk 9:1
away, and the **t** came and said to him,	Lk 9:12
picked up, **t** baskets of broken pieces.	Lk 9:17
And taking the **t**, he said to them, "See,	Lk 18:31
Iscariot, who was of the number of the **t**.	Lk 22:3
on thrones judging the **t** tribes of Israel.	Lk 22:30
and the man called Judas, one of the **t**,	Lk 22:47
up and filled **t** baskets with fragments	Jn 6:13
So Jesus said to the **T**, "Do you want to go	Jn 6:67
them, "Did I not choose you, the **T**?	Jn 6:70
of Simon Iscariot, for he, one of the **T**,	Jn 6:71
"Are there not **t** hours in the day?	Jn 11:9
Now Thomas, one of the **T**, called the	Jn 20:24
And the **t** summoned the full number	Acts 6:2
of Jacob, and Jacob of the **t** patriarchs.	Acts 7:8
There were about **t** men in all.	Acts 19:7
it is not more than **t** days since I went	Acts 24:11
to which our **t** tribes hope to attain, as	Acts 26:7
he appeared to Cephas, then to the **t**.	1 Cor 15:5
Christ, To the **t** tribes in the Dispersion:	Jas 1:1
feet, and on her head a crown of **t** stars.	Rv 12:1
It had a great, high wall, with **t** gates,	Rv 21:12
twelve gates, and at the gates **t** angels,	Rv 21:12
the names of the **t** tribes of the sons	Rv 21:12
the wall of the city had **t** foundations,	Rv 21:14
on them were the **t** names of the twelve	Rv 21:14
twelve names of the **t** apostles of the	Rv 21:14
And the **t** gates were twelve pearls, each	Rv 21:21
And the twelve gates were **t** pearls, each	Rv 21:21
the tree of life with its **t** kinds of fruit,	Rv 22:2

TWENTIETH (9)

month, on the **t** day of the month,	Nm 10:11
In the **t** year of Jeroboam king of	1 Kgs 15:9
in the **t** year of Jotham the son of	2 Kgs 15:30
to Pethahiah, the **t** to Jehezkel,	1 Chr 24:16
to the **t**, to Eliathah, his sons and his	1 Chr 25:27
ninth month, on the **t** day of the month.	Ezr 10:9
in the month of Chislev, in the **t** year,	Neh 1:1
Nisan, in the **t** year of King Artaxerxes,	Neh 2:1
from the **t** year to the thirty-second	Neh 5:14

TWENTY (108)

Suppose **t** are found there." He	Gn 18:31
"For the sake of **t** I will not destroy it."	Gn 18:31
These **t** years I have been with you.	Gn 31:38
These **t** years I have been in your	Gn 31:41
hundred female goats and **t** male goats,	Gn 32:14
goats, two hundred ewes and **t** rams,	Gn 32:14
t female donkeys and ten male	Gn 32:15
to the Ishmaelites for **t** shekels of silver.	Gn 37:28
tabernacle: **t** frames for the south side;	Ex 26:18
you shall make under the **t** frames,	Ex 26:19
tabernacle, on the north side **t** frames,	Ex 26:20
Its **t** pillars and their twenty bases shall	Ex 27:10
twenty pillars and their **t** bases shall be	Ex 27:10
long, its pillars **t** and their bases twenty,	Ex 27:11
long, its pillars twenty and their bases **t**,	Ex 27:11
there shall be a screen **t** cubits long,	Ex 27:16
the sanctuary (the shekel is **t** gerahs),	Ex 30:13
census, from **t** years old and upward,	Ex 30:14
made thus: **t** frames for the south side.	Ex 36:23
forty bases of silver under the **t** frames,	Ex 36:24
on the north side, he made **t** frames	Ex 36:25
their **t** pillars and their twenty bases	Ex 38:10
twenty pillars and their **t** bases were of	Ex 38:10
of a hundred cubits, their **t** pillars,	Ex 38:11
pillars, their **t** bases were of bronze,	Ex 38:11
It was **t** cubits long and five cubits	Ex 38:18
records, from **t** years old and upward,	Ex 38:26
of a male from **t** years old up to	Lv 27:3
is from five years old up to **t** years old,	Lv 27:5
valuation shall be for a male **t** shekels,	Lv 27:5
t gerahs shall make a shekel.	Lv 27:25
From **t** years old and upward, all in	Nm 1:3
number of names from **t** years old and	Nm 1:18
every male from **t** years old and	Nm 1:20
every male from **t** years old and	Nm 1:22
names, from **t** years old and upward,	Nm 1:24
of names, from **t** years old and upward,	Nm 1:26
of names, from **t** years old and upward,	Nm 1:28
of names, from **t** years old and upward,	Nm 1:30
of names, from **t** years old and upward,	Nm 1:32
of names, from **t** years old and upward,	Nm 1:34
of names, from **t** years old and upward,	Nm 1:36
of names, from **t** years old and upward,	Nm 1:38
of names, from **t** years old and upward,	Nm 1:40
of names, from **t** years old and upward,	Nm 1:42
houses, from **t** years old and upward,	Nm 1:45
the sanctuary (the shekel of **t** gerahs),	Nm 3:47
or five days, or ten days, or **t** days,	Nm 11:19
in the census from **t** years old and	Nm 14:29
of the sanctuary, which is **t** gerahs.	Nm 18:16
of Israel, from **t** years old and upward,	Nm 26:2
from **t** years old and upward," as the	Nm 26:4
of Egypt, from **t** years old and upward,	Nm 32:11
the people of Israel cruelly for **t** years.	Jgs 4:3
the neighborhood of Minnith, **t** cities,	Jgs 11:33
in the days of the Philistines **t** years.	Jgs 15:20
his father. He had judged Israel **t** years.	Jgs 16:31
a long time passed, some **t** years,	1 Sm 7:2
killed about **t** men within as it were	1 Sm 14:14
Abner came with **t** men to David	2 Sm 3:20
Ziba had fifteen sons and **t** servants.	2 Sm 9:10
great on that day, **t** thousand men.	2 Sm 18:7
his fifteen sons and his **t** servants,	2 Sm 19:17
at the end of nine months and **t** days.	2 Sm 24:8
ten fat oxen, and **t** pasture-fed cattle, a	1 Kgs 4:23
was sixty cubits long, **t** cubits wide,	1 Kgs 6:2
nave of the house was **t** cubits long,	1 Kgs 6:3
He built **t** cubits of the rear of the	1 Kgs 6:16
inner sanctuary was **t** cubits long,	1 Kgs 6:20
was twenty cubits long, **t** cubits wide,	1 Kgs 6:20
twenty cubits wide, and **t** cubits high,	1 Kgs 6:20
At the end of **t** years, in which	1 Kgs 9:10
Solomon gave to Hiram **t** cities in the	1 Kgs 9:11
t loaves of barley and fresh ears of	2 Kgs 4:42
in Samaria, and he reigned **t** years.	2 Kgs 15:27
Ahaz was **t** years old when he began	2 Kgs 16:2
the individuals from **t** years old and	1 Chr 23:24
were numbered from **t** years old and	1 Chr 23:27
not count those below **t** years of age,	1 Chr 27:23
sixty cubits, and the breadth **t** cubits.	2 Chr 3:3
nave of the house was **t** cubits long,	2 Chr 3:4
the breadth of the house, was **t** cubits,	2 Chr 3:8
cubits, and its breadth was **t** cubits.	2 Chr 3:8
cherubim together extended **t** cubits:	2 Chr 3:11

of these cherubim extended **t** cubits. 2 Chr 3:13
t cubits long and twenty cubits wide 2 Chr 4:1
cubits long and **t** cubits wide and 2 Chr 4:1
At the end of **t** years, in which 2 Chr 8:1
He mustered those **t** years old and 2 Chr 25:5
Ahaz was **t** years old when he began 2 Chr 28:1
of the Levites from **t** years old and upward, 2 Chr 31:17
the Levites, from **t** years old and upward, Ezr 3:8
eat shall be by weight, **t** shekels a day; Ezk 4:10
measured also the vestibule, **t** cubits. Ezk 40:14
length of the vestibule was **t** cubits, Ezk 40:49
forty cubits, and its breadth, **t** cubits. Ezk 41:2
the length of the room, **t** cubits, Ezk 41:4
twenty cubits, and its breadth, **t** cubits, Ezk 41:4
was a breadth of **t** cubits all around Ezk 41:10
Facing the **t** cubits that belonged to the Ezk 42:3
The shekel shall be **t** gerahs; twenty Ezk 45:12
t shekels plus twenty-five shekels plus Ezk 45:12
When one came to a heap of **t** measures, Hg 2:16
to draw fifty measures, there were but **t**. Hg 2:16
Its length is **t** cubits, and its width ten Zec 5:2
comes against him with **t** thousand? Lk 14:31
each holding **t** or thirty gallons. Jn 2:6
a sounding and found **t** fathoms. Acts 27:28

TWENTY-EIGHT (4)
length of each curtain shall be **t** cubits, Ex 26:2
The length of each curtain was **t** cubits, Ex 36:9
over Israel in Samaria was **t** years. 2 Kgs 10:36
and fathered **t** sons and sixty 2 Chr 11:21

TWENTY-FIFTH (3)
was finished on the **t** day of the month Neh 6:15
month, on the **t** day of the month, Jer 52:31
In the **t** year of our exile, at the Ezk 40:1

TWENTY-FIRST (4)
unleavened bread until the **t** day of the Ex 12:18
the **t** to Jachin, the twenty-second to 1 Chr 24:17
to the **t**, to Hothir, his sons and his 1 Chr 25:28
seventh month, on the **t** day of the month, Hg 2:1

TWENTY-FIVE (22)
from **t** years old and upward they shall Nm 8:24
and he reigned **t** years in Jerusalem. 1 Kgs 22:42
He was **t** years old when he began to 2 Kgs 14:2
He was **t** years old when he began to 2 Kgs 15:33
He was **t** years old when he began to 2 Kgs 18:2
Jehoiakim was **t** years old when he 2 Kgs 23:36
and he reigned **t** years in Jerusalem. 2 Chr 20:31
Amaziah was **t** years old when he 2 Chr 25:1
Jotham was **t** years old when he 2 Chr 27:1
He was **t** years old when he began to 2 Chr 27:8
to reign when he was **t** years old, 2 Chr 29:1
Jehoiakim was **t** years old when he 2 Chr 36:5
porch and the altar, were about **t** men, Ezk 8:16
of the gateway there were **t** men. Ezk 11:1
of the other, a breadth of **t** cubits; Ezk 40:13
fifty cubits, and its breadth **t** cubits. Ezk 40:21
fifty cubits, and its breadth **t** cubits. Ezk 40:25
fifty cubits, and its breadth **t** cubits. Ezk 40:29
t cubits long and five cubits broad. Ezk 40:30
fifty cubits, and its breadth **t** cubits. Ezk 40:33
fifty cubits, and its breadth **t** cubits. Ezk 40:36
twenty shekels plus **t** shekels plus Ezk 45:12

TWENTY-FOUR (12)
the sacrifice of peace offerings **t** bulls, Nm 7:88
died by the plague were **t** thousand. Nm 25:9
six toes on each foot, **t** in number, 2 Sm 21:20
at Tirzah, and he reigned **t** years. 1 Kgs 15:33
six toes on each foot, **t** in number, 1 Chr 20:6
"**T** thousand of these," David said, 1 Chr 23:4
Around the throne were **t** thrones, and Rv 4:4
and seated on the thrones were **t** elders, Rv 4:4
the **t** elders fall down before him who is Rv 4:10
living creatures and the **t** elders fell down Rv 5:8
And the **t** elders who sit on their Rv 11:16
And the **t** elders and the four living Rv 19:4

TWENTY-FOURTH (9)
to Delaiah, the **t** to Maaziah. 1 Chr 24:18
to the **t**, to Romamti-ezer, his sons 1 Chr 25:31
Now on the **t** day of this month the Neh 9:1
On the **t** day of the first month, as I was Dn 10:4
on the **t** day of the month, in the sixth Hg 1:15
On the **t** day of the ninth month, in the Hg 2:10
from the **t** day of the ninth month. Hg 2:18
to Haggai on the **t** day of the month, Hg 2:20
On the **t** day of the eleventh month, Zec 1:7

TWENTY-NINE (6)
offering, was **t** talents and 730 shekels, Ex 38:24
in all, **t** cities with their villages. Jos 15:32
and he reigned **t** years in Jerusalem. 2 Kgs 14:2
and he reigned **t** years in Jerusalem. 2 Kgs 18:2
and he reigned **t** years in Jerusalem. 2 Chr 25:1
and he reigned **t** years in Jerusalem. 2 Chr 29:1

TWENTY-ONE (4)
Zedekiah was **t** years old when he 2 Kgs 24:18
Zedekiah was **t** years old when he 2 Chr 36:11
Zedekiah was **t** years old when he Jer 52:1
of Persia withstood me **t** days, Dn 10:13

TWENTY-SECOND (2)
to Jachin, the **t** to Gamul, 1 Chr 24:17
to the **t**, to Giddalti, his sons and his 1 Chr 25:29

TWENTY-SEVENTH (6)
month, on the **t** day of the month, Gn 8:14
in the **t** year of Asa king of Judah, 1 Kgs 16:10
In the **t** year of Asa king of Judah, 1 Kgs 16:15
In the **t** year of Jeroboam king of 2 Kgs 15:1
month, on the **t** day of the month, 2 Kgs 25:27
In the **t** year, in the first month, on the Ezk 29:17

TWENTY-SIXTH (1)
In the **t** year of Asa king of Judah, 1 Kgs 16:8

TWENTY-THIRD (7)
But by the **t** year of King Jehoash, the 2 Kgs 12:6
In the **t** year of Joash the son of 2 Kgs 13:1
the **t** to Delaiah, the twenty-fourth to 1 Chr 24:18
to the **t**, to Mahazioth, his sons and 1 Chr 25:30
On the **t** day of the seventh month he 2 Chr 7:10
which is the month of Sivan, on the **t** day. Est 8:9
in the **t** year of Nebuchadnezzar, Jer 52:30

TWENTY-THREE (6)
And he judged Israel **t** years. Then he Jgs 10:2
Jehoahaz was **t** years old when he 2 Kgs 23:31
who had **t** cities in the land of Gilead. 1 Chr 2:22
Jehoahaz was **t** years old when he 2 Chr 36:2
"For **t** years, from the thirteenth year of Jer 25:3
and **t** thousand fell in a single day. 1 Cor 10:8

TWENTY-TWO (10)
Aphek and Rehob—**t** cities with their Jos 19:30
the Gileadite, who judged Israel **t** years. Jgs 10:3
that Jeroboam reigned was **t** years. 1 Kgs 14:20
over Israel in Samaria **t** years. 1 Kgs 16:29
Ahaziah was **t** years old when he 2 Kgs 8:26
Amon was **t** years old when he 2 Kgs 21:19
and **t** commanders from his own 1 Chr 12:28
wives and had **t** sons and sixteen 2 Chr 13:21
Ahaziah was **t** years old when he 2 Chr 22:2
Amon was **t** years old when he 2 Chr 33:21

TWICE (23)
we would now have returned **t**." Gn 43:10
it will be **t** as much as they gather daily." Ex 16:5
day they gathered **t** as much bread, Ex 16:22
and struck the rock with his staff **t**, Nm 20:11
to the wall." But David evaded him **t**. 1 Sm 18:11
the spear, and I will not strike him **t**." 1 Sm 26:8
of Israel, who had appeared to him **t** 1 Kgs 11:9
himself there more than once or **t**. 2 Kgs 6:10
lodged outside Jerusalem once or **t**. Neh 13:20
God does all these things, **t**, three times, Jb 33:29
answer; **t**, but I will proceed no further." Jb 40:5
And the LORD gave Job **t** as much as he Jb 42:10
God has spoken; **t** have I heard this: Ps 62:11
The chariots of God are **t** ten thousand, Ps 68:17
he should live a thousand years **t** over, Eccl 6:6
hands and let the sword come down **t**, Ezk 21:14
you make him **t** as much a child of Mt 23:15
very night, before the rooster crows **t**, Mk 14:30
to him, "Before the rooster crows **t**, Mk 14:72
I fast **t** a week; I give tithes of all that I Lk 18:12
after warning him once and then **t**, Ti 3:10
fruitless trees in late autumn, **t** dead, Jude 1:12
mounted troops was **t** ten thousand Rv 9:16

TWIG (2)
waters. He set it like a willow **t**, Ezk 17:5
king shall perish like a **t** on the face of Hos 10:7

TWIGS (2)
topmost of its young **t** and carried it to Ezk 17:4
the topmost of its young **t** a tender one, Ezk 17:22

TWILIGHT (19)
of Israel shall kill their lambs at **t**. Ex 12:6
Say to them, 'At **t** you shall eat meat, Ex 16:12
and the other lamb you shall offer at **t**. Ex 29:39
The other lamb you shall offer at **t**, and Ex 29:41
and when Aaron sets up the lamps at **t**, Ex 30:8
on the fourteenth day of the month at **t**, Lv 23:5
the fourteenth day of this month, at **t**, Nm 9:3
on the fourteenth day of the month, at **t**, Nm 9:5
the fourteenth day at **t** they shall keep Nm 9:11
and the other lamb you shall offer at **t**; Nm 28:4
The other lamb you shall offer at **t**. Nm 28:8
them down from **t** until the evening 1 Sm 30:17
So they arose at **t** to go to the camp of 2 Kgs 7:5
fled away in the **t** and abandoned their 2 Kgs 7:7
eye of the adulterer also waits for the **t**, Jb 24:15
in the **t**, in the evening, at the time of Prv 7:9
the **t** I longed for has been turned for me Is 21:4
we stumble at noon as in the **t**, among Is 59:10
your feet stumble on the **t** mountains, Jer 13:16

TWIN (4)
So Thomas, called the **T**, said to his Jn 11:16
one of the Twelve, called the **T**, Jn 20:24
Simon Peter, Thomas (called the **T**), Jn 21:2
with the **t** gods as a figurehead. Acts 28:11

TWINED (28)
purple and scarlet yarns and fine **t** linen, Ex 25:4
ten curtains of fine **t** linen and blue and Ex 26:1
and scarlet yarns and fine **t** linen. Ex 26:31
and scarlet yarns and fine **t** linen, Ex 26:36
have hangings of fine **t** linen a hundred Ex 27:9
and scarlet yarns and fine **t** linen, Ex 27:16
with hangings of fine **t** linen and bases Ex 27:18
and scarlet yarns, and fine **t** linen. Ex 28:5
and scarlet yarns, and of fine **t** linen, Ex 28:6
and scarlet yarns, and fine **t** linen. Ex 28:8
and fine **t** linen shall you make it. Ex 28:15
purple and scarlet yarns and fine **t** linen; Ex 35:6
and scarlet yarns and fine **t** linen. Ex 35:25
and scarlet yarns and fine **t** linen, Ex 35:35
were made of fine **t** linen and blue and Ex 36:8
and scarlet yarns and fine **t** linen; Ex 36:35
and scarlet yarns and fine **t** linen, Ex 36:37
of the court were of fine **t** linen, Ex 38:9
around the court were of fine **t** linen. Ex 38:16
and scarlet yarns and fine **t** linen. Ex 38:18
and scarlet yarns and fine **t** linen. Ex 38:23
and scarlet yarns, and fine **t** linen. Ex 39:2
scarlet yarns, and into the fine **t** linen, Ex 39:3
and scarlet yarns, and fine **t** linen, Ex 39:5
and scarlet yarns, and fine **t** linen. Ex 39:8
and scarlet yarns and fine **t** linen. Ex 39:24
the linen undergarments of fine **t** linen, Ex 39:28
and the sash of fine **t** linen and of blue Ex 39:29

TWINKLING (1)
in a moment, in the **t** of an eye, at 1 Cor 15:52

TWINS (6)
behold, there were **t** in her womb. Gn 25:24
labor came, there were **t** in her womb. Gn 38:27
up from the washing, all of which bear **t**, Sg 4:2
breasts are like two fawns, **t** of a gazelle, Sg 4:5
up from the washing; all of them bear **t**; Sg 6:6
breasts are like two fawns, **t** of a gazelle. Sg 7:3

TWIST (2)
and he will **t** its surface and scatter its Is 24:1
ignorant and unstable **t** to their own 2 Pt 3:16

TWISTED (12)
two chains of pure gold, **t** like cords; Ex 28:14
for the breastpiece **t** chains like cords, Ex 28:22
on the breastpiece **t** chains like cords, Ex 39:15
they are a crooked and **t** generation. Dt 32:5
their fathers; they **t** like a deceitful bow. Ps 78:57
there is nothing **t** or crooked in them. Prv 8:8
sense, but one of **t** mind is despised. Prv 12:8
answered, "O faithless and **t** generation, Mt 17:17
answered, "O faithless and **t** generation, Lk 9:41
And the soldiers **t** together a crown of Jn 19:2
will arise men speaking **t** things, Acts 20:30
midst of a crooked and **t** generation, Phil 2:15

TWISTING (3)
fleeing serpent, Leviathan the **t** serpent, Is 27:1
and **t** together a crown of thorns, they Mt 27:29
and **t** together a crown of thorns, Mk 15:17

TWO (667)
And God made the **t** great lights—the Gn 1:16
And Lamech took **t** wives. The name of Gn 4:19
you shall bring **t** of every sort into the Gn 6:19
t of every sort shall come in to you to Gn 6:20
t and two, male and female, went into the Gn 7:9
two and **t**, male and female, went into the Gn 7:9
t and two of all flesh in which there was Gn 7:15
two and **t** of all flesh in which there was Gn 7:15
father and told his **t** brothers outside. Gn 9:22
To Eber were born **t** sons: the name of Gn 10:25
he fathered Arpachshad **t** years after Gn 11:10
The **t** angels came to Sodom in the Gn 19:1
I have **t** daughters who have not known Gn 19:8
wife and your **t** daughters who are Gn 19:15
his wife and his **t** daughters by the Gn 19:16
lived in the hills with his **t** daughters, Gn 19:30
he lived in a cave with his **t** daughters. Gn 19:30
and the **t** men made a covenant. Gn 21:27
and took **t** of his young men with him, Gn 22:3
and **t** bracelets for her arms weighing Gn 24:22
to her, "**T** nations are in your womb, Gn 25:23
and **t** peoples from within you shall be Gn 25:23
flock and bring me **t** good young goats, Gn 27:9
For he has cheated me these **t** times. Gn 27:36
Now Laban had **t** daughters. The Gn 29:16
into the tent of the **t** female servants, Gn 31:33

that they may decide between us **t**. Gn 31:37
fourteen years for your **t** daughters, Gn 31:41
and herds and camels, into **t** camps, Gn 32:7
and now I have become **t** camps. Gn 32:10
t hundred female goats and twenty Gn 32:14
goats, **t** hundred ewes and twenty rams, Gn 32:14
night he arose and took his **t** wives, Gn 32:22
his two wives, his **t** female servants, Gn 32:22
and Rachel and the **t** female servants. Gn 33:1
they were sore, **t** of the sons of Jacob, Gn 34:25
Pharaoh was angry with his **t** officers, Gn 40:2
After **t** whole years, Pharaoh dreamed Gn 41:1
came, **t** sons were born to Joseph. Gn 41:50
"Kill my **t** sons if I do not bring him Gn 42:37
know that my wife bore me **t** sons. Gn 44:27
has been in the land these **t** years, Gn 45:6
who were born to him in Egypt, were **t**. Gn 46:27
is ill." So he took with him his **t** sons, Gn 48:1
And now your **t** sons, who were born to Gn 48:5
t Hebrews were struggling together. Ex 2:13
not believe even these **t** signs or listen to Ex 4:9
put it on the **t** doorposts and the lintel Ex 12:7
the lintel and the **t** doorposts with the Ex 12:22
on the lintel and on the **t** doorposts, Ex 12:23
twice as much bread, **t** omers each. Ex 16:22
sixth day he gives you bread for **t** days. Ex 16:29
along with her **t** sons. The name of the Ex 18:3
with your wife and her **t** sons with her," Ex 18:6
But if the slave survives a day or **t**, he is Ex 21:21
T cubits and a half shall be its length, Ex 25:10
its four feet, **t** rings on the one side of it, Ex 25:12
of it, and **t** rings on the other side of it. Ex 25:12
T cubits and a half shall be its length, Ex 25:17
you shall make **t** cherubim of gold; Ex 25:18
them, on the **t** ends of the mercy seat. Ex 25:18
you make the cherubim on its **t** ends. Ex 25:19
from between the **t** cherubim that are Ex 25:22
T cubits shall be its length, a cubit its Ex 25:23
There shall be **t** tenons in each frame, Ex 26:17
t bases under one frame for its two Ex 26:19
bases under one frame for its **t** tenons, Ex 26:19
and **t** bases under the next frame for its Ex 26:19
under the next frame for its **t** tenons; Ex 26:19
bases of silver, **t** bases under one frame, Ex 26:21
and **t** bases under the next frame. Ex 26:21
you shall make **t** frames for corners Ex 26:23
of them; they shall form the **t** corners. Ex 26:24
t bases under one frame, and two bases Ex 26:25
and **t** bases under another frame. Ex 26:25
the poles are on the **t** sides of the altar Ex 27:7
It shall have **t** shoulder pieces attached Ex 28:7
shoulder pieces attached to its **t** edges, Ex 28:7
You shall take **t** onyx stones, and Ex 28:9
shall you engrave the **t** stones with the Ex 28:11
you shall set the **t** stones on the Ex 28:12
LORD on his **t** shoulders for Ex 28:12
and **t** chains of pure gold, twisted like Ex 28:14
make for the breastpiece **t** rings of gold, Ex 28:23
and put the **t** rings on the two edges of Ex 28:23
two rings on the **t** edges of the Ex 28:23
And you shall put the **t** cords of gold in Ex 28:24
cords of gold in the **t** rings at the edges Ex 28:24
The **t** ends of the two cords you shall Ex 28:25
two ends of the **t** cords you shall attach Ex 28:25
shall attach to the **t** settings of filigree, Ex 28:25
You shall make **t** rings of gold, and put Ex 28:26
put them at the **t** ends of the Ex 28:26
And you shall make **t** rings of gold, and Ex 28:27
lower part of the **t** shoulder pieces of the Ex 28:27
of the herd and **t** rams without blemish, Ex 29:1
and bring the bull and the **t** rams. Ex 29:3
and the **t** kidneys with the fat that is on Ex 29:13
the liver and the **t** kidneys with the fat Ex 29:22
t lambs a year old day by day regularly. Ex 29:38
square, and **t** cubits shall be its height. Ex 30:2
And you shall make **t** golden rings for it. Ex 30:4
Under its molding on **t** opposite sides of Ex 30:4
Sinai, the **t** tablets of the testimony, Ex 31:18
the mountain with the **t** tablets of the Ex 32:15
"Cut for yourself **t** tablets of stone like Ex 34:1
So Moses cut **t** tablets of stone like the Ex 34:4
and took in his hand **t** tablets of stone. Ex 34:4
with the **t** tablets of the testimony in his Ex 34:29
Each frame had **t** tenons for fitting Ex 36:22
t bases under one frame for its two Ex 36:24
bases under one frame for its **t** tenons, Ex 36:24
and **t** bases under the next frame for its Ex 36:24
under the next frame for its **t** tenons. Ex 36:24
t bases under one frame and two bases Ex 36:26
under one frame and **t** bases under the Ex 36:26
He made **t** frames for corners of the Ex 36:28
He made **t** of them this way for the two Ex 36:29
two of them this way for the **t** corners. Ex 36:29
bases, under every frame **t** bases. Ex 36:30
T cubits and a half was its length, a Ex 37:1

t rings on its one side and two rings on Ex 37:3
on its one side and **t** rings on its other Ex 37:3
T cubits and a half was its length, and a Ex 37:6
And he made **t** cherubim of gold. He Ex 37:7
hammered work on the **t** ends of the Ex 37:7
seat he made the cherubim on its **t** ends. Ex 37:8
T cubits was its length, a cubit its Ex 37:10
was square, and **t** cubits was its height. Ex 37:25
and made **t** rings of gold on it under its Ex 37:27
its molding, on **t** opposite sides of it, Ex 37:27
shoulder pieces, joined to it at its **t** edges. Ex 39:4
And they made **t** settings of gold filigree Ex 39:16
settings of gold filigree and **t** gold rings, Ex 39:16
and put the **t** rings on the two edges of Ex 39:16
two rings on the **t** edges of the Ex 39:16
And they put the **t** cords of gold in the Ex 39:17
cords of gold in the **t** rings at the edges Ex 39:17
They attached the **t** ends of the two Ex 39:18
the two ends of the **t** cords to the two Ex 39:18
the two cords to the **t** settings of filigree. Ex 39:18
Then they made **t** rings of gold, and put Ex 39:19
put them at the **t** ends of the Ex 39:19
And they made **t** rings of gold, and Ex 39:20
lower part of the **t** shoulder pieces of the Ex 39:20
and the **t** kidneys with the fat that is on Lv 3:4
and the **t** kidneys with the fat that is on Lv 3:10
and the **t** kidneys with the fat that is on Lv 3:15
and the **t** kidneys with the fat that is on Lv 4:9
he has committed **t** turtledoves or two Lv 5:7
committed two turtledoves or **t** pigeons, Lv 5:7
if he cannot afford **t** turtledoves or two Lv 5:11
afford two turtledoves or **t** pigeons, Lv 5:11
the **t** kidneys with the fat that is on them Lv 7:4
sin offering and the **t** rams and the basket Lv 8:2
the liver and the **t** kidneys with their fat, Lv 8:16
the liver and the **t** kidneys with their fat Lv 8:25
child, then she shall be unclean **t** weeks, Lv 12:5
then she shall take **t** turtledoves or two Lv 12:8
shall take two turtledoves or **t** pigeons, Lv 12:8
is to be cleansed **t** live clean birds and Lv 14:4
day he shall take **t** male lambs without Lv 14:10
also **t** turtledoves or two pigeons, Lv 14:22
also two turtledoves or **t** pigeons, Lv 14:22
of the house he shall take **t** small birds, Lv 14:49
day he shall take **t** turtledoves or two Lv 15:14
two turtledoves or **t** pigeons and come Lv 15:14
day she shall take **t** turtledoves or two Lv 15:29
two turtledoves or **t** pigeons and bring Lv 15:29
after the death of the **t** sons of Aaron, Lv 16:1
of the people of Israel **t** male goats for a Lv 16:5
he shall take the **t** goats and set them Lv 16:7
Aaron shall cast lots over the **t** goats, Lv 16:8
and **t** handfuls of sweet incense beaten Lv 16:12
not sow your field with **t** kinds of seed, Lv 19:19
of cloth made of **t** kinds of material. Lv 19:19
with it shall be **t** tenths of an ephah Lv 23:13
your dwelling places **t** loaves of bread Lv 23:17
be waved, made of **t** tenths of an ephah. Lv 23:17
and one bull from the herd and **t** rams. Lv 23:18
and **t** male lambs a year old as a Lv 23:19
before the LORD, with the **t** lambs. Lv 23:20
t tenths of an ephah shall be in each Lv 24:5
And you shall set them in **t** piles, six in a Lv 24:6
day he shall bring **t** turtledoves or two Nm 6:10
two turtledoves or **t** pigeons to the Nm 6:10
oxen, a wagon for every **t** of the chiefs, Nm 7:3
T wagons and four oxen he gave to the Nm 7:7
the sacrifice of peace offerings, **t** oxen, Nm 7:17
the sacrifice of peace offerings, **t** oxen, Nm 7:23
the sacrifice of peace offerings, **t** oxen, Nm 7:29
the sacrifice of peace offerings, **t** oxen, Nm 7:35
the sacrifice of peace offerings, **t** oxen, Nm 7:41
the sacrifice of peace offerings, **t** oxen, Nm 7:47
the sacrifice of peace offerings, **t** oxen, Nm 7:53
the sacrifice of peace offerings, **t** oxen, Nm 7:59
the sacrifice of peace offerings, **t** oxen, Nm 7:65
the sacrifice of peace offerings, **t** oxen, Nm 7:71
the sacrifice of peace offerings, **t** oxen, Nm 7:77
the sacrifice of peace offerings, **t** oxen, Nm 7:83
from between the **t** cherubim; Nm 7:89
Whether it was **t** days, or a month, or a Nm 9:22
"Make **t** silver trumpets. Of hammered Nm 10:2
shall not eat just one day, or **t** days, Nm 11:19
Now **t** men remained in the camp, Nm 11:26
and about **t** cubits above the ground. Nm 11:31
carried it on a pole between **t** of them; Nm 13:23
for a grain offering **t** tenths of an ephah Nm 15:6
and his **t** servants were with him. Nm 22:22
t male lambs a year old without Nm 28:3
t male lambs a year old without Nm 28:9
and **t** tenths of an ephah of fine flour Nm 28:9
t bulls from the herd, one ram, seven Nm 28:11
and **t** tenths of fine flour for a grain Nm 28:12
t bulls from the herd, one ram, and Nm 28:19
offer for a bull, and **t** tenths for a ram; Nm 28:20

t bulls from the herd, one ram, seven Nm 28:27
for each bull, **t** tenths for one ram, Nm 28:28
ephah for the bull, **t** tenths for the ram, Nm 29:3
for the bull, **t** tenths for the one ram, Nm 29:9
thirteen bulls from the herd, **t** rams, Nm 29:13
t tenths for each of the two rams, Nm 29:14
two tenths for each of the **t** rams, Nm 29:14
twelve bulls from the herd, **t** rams, Nm 29:17
"On the third day eleven bulls, **t** rams, Nm 29:20
"On the fourth day ten bulls, **t** rams, Nm 29:23
"On the fifth day nine bulls, **t** rams, Nm 29:26
"On the sixth day eight bulls, **t** rams, Nm 29:29
the seventh day seven bulls, **t** rams, Nm 29:32
the plunder into **t** parts between the Nm 31:27
The **t** tribes and the half-tribe have Nm 34:15
city, on the east side **t** thousand cubits, Nm 35:5
on the south side **t** thousand cubits, Nm 35:5
and on the west side **t** thousand cubits, Nm 35:5
on the north side **t** thousand cubits, Nm 35:5
of the hand of the **t** kings of the Amorites Dt 3:8
LORD your God has done to these **t** kings. Dt 3:21
and he wrote them on **t** tablets of stone. Dt 4:13
of Bashan, the **t** kings of the Amorites, Dt 4:47
he wrote them on **t** tablets of stone and Dt 5:22
LORD gave me the **t** tablets of stone Dt 9:10
the LORD gave me the **t** tablets of stone, Dt 9:11
And the **t** tablets of the covenant were in Dt 9:15
of the covenant were in my **t** hands. Dt 9:15
took hold of the **t** tablets and threw them Dt 9:17
them out of my **t** hands and broke them Dt 9:17
'Cut for yourself **t** tablets of stone like the Dt 10:1
and cut **t** tablets of stone like the first, Dt 10:3
the mountain with the **t** tablets in my Dt 10:3
the hoof cloven in **t** and chews the cud, Dt 14:6
On the evidence of **t** witnesses or of three Dt 17:6
the shoulder and the **t** cheeks and the Dt 18:3
on the evidence of **t** witnesses or of three Dt 19:15
"If a man has **t** wives, the one loved and Dt 21:15
sow your vineyard with **t** kinds of seed, Dt 22:9
not have in your bag **t** kinds of weights, Dt 25:13
have in your house **t** kinds of measures, Dt 25:14
and **t** have put ten thousand to flight, Dt 32:30
son of Nun sent **t** men secretly from Jos 2:1
woman had taken the **t** men and hidden Jos 2:4
you did to the **t** kings of the Amorites Jos 2:10
Then the **t** men returned. They came Jos 2:23
But to the **t** men who had spied out the Jos 6:22
but let about **t** or three thousand men go Jos 7:3
that he did to the **t** kings of the Amorites Jos 9:10
inheritance to the **t** and one-half tribes Jos 14:3
For the people of Joseph were **t** tribes, Jos 14:4
and Rabbah: **t** cities with their villages. Jos 15:60
—nine cities out of these **t** tribes; Jos 21:16
with its pasturelands—**t** cities. Jos 21:25
with its pasturelands—**t** cities; Jos 21:27
before you, the **t** kings of the Amorites; Jos 24:12
made for himself a sword with **t** edges, Jgs 3:16
A womb or **t** for every man; spoil of Jgs 5:30
t pieces of dyed work embroidered for Jgs 5:30
they captured the **t** princes of Midian, Jgs 7:25
and captured the **t** kings of Midian, Jgs 8:12
while the **t** companies rushed upon all Jgs 9:44
leave me alone **t** months, that I may go Jgs 11:37
Then he sent her away for **t** months, Jgs 11:38
And at the end of **t** months, she Jgs 11:39
they bound him with **t** new ropes and Jgs 15:13
of the gate of the city and the **t** posts, Jgs 16:3
on the Philistines for my **t** eyes." Jgs 16:28
Samson grasped the **t** middle pillars on Jgs 16:29
So the **t** of them sat and ate and drank Jgs 19:6
of Moab, he and his wife and his **t** sons. Ru 1:1
the names of his **t** sons were Mahlon and Ru 1:2
died, and she was left with her **t** sons. Ru 1:3
was left without her **t** sons and her Ru 1:5
she was with her **t** daughters-in-law, Ru 1:7
But Naomi said to her **t** daughters-in-law, Ru 1:8
So the **t** of them went on until they came Ru 1:19
He had **t** wives. The name of the one 1 Sm 1:2
hosts at Shiloh, where the **t** sons of Eli, 1 Sm 1:3
and bore three sons and **t** daughters. 1 Sm 2:21
this that shall come upon your **t** sons, 1 Sm 2:34
Israel at which the **t** ears of everyone 1 Sm 3:11
And the **t** sons of Eli, Hophni and 1 Sm 4:4
was captured, and the **t** sons of Eli, 1 Sm 4:11
Your **t** sons also, Hophni and 1 Sm 4:17
a new cart and **t** milk cows on which 1 Sm 6:7
and took **t** milk cows and yoked them 1 Sm 6:10
you will meet **t** men by Rachel's tomb 1 Sm 10:2
you and give you **t** loaves of bread, 1 Sm 10:4
so that no **t** of them were left 1 Sm 11:11
he reigned … and **t** years over Israel. 1 Sm 13:1
T thousand were with Saul in 1 Sm 13:2
names of his **t** daughters were these: 1 Sm 14:49
t hundred thousand men on foot, 1 Sm 15:4
and killed **t** hundred of the 1 Sm 18:27

And the **t** of them made a covenant 1 Sm 23:18
while **t** hundred remained with the 1 Sm 25:13
haste and took **t** hundred loaves and 1 Sm 25:18
hundred loaves and **t** skins of wine 1 Sm 25:18
of raisins and **t** hundred cakes of 1 Sm 25:18
and David with his **t** wives, 1 Sm 27:3
and went, he and **t** men with him. 1 Sm 28:8
David's **t** wives also had been taken 1 Sm 30:5
T hundred stayed behind, who were 1 Sm 30:10
cake of figs and **t** clusters of raisins. 1 Sm 30:12
taken, and David rescued his **t** wives. 1 Sm 30:18
came to the **t** hundred men who 1 Sm 30:21
David remained **t** days in Ziklag. 2 Sm 1:1
went up there, and his **t** wives also, 2 Sm 2:2
over Israel, and he reigned **t** years. 2 Sm 2:10
Now Saul's son had **t** men who were 2 Sm 4:2
T lines he measured to be put to death, 2 Sm 8:2
"There were **t** men in a certain city, 2 Sm 12:1
After **t** full years Absalom had 2 Sm 13:23
And your servant had **t** sons, and they 2 Sm 14:6
t hundred shekels by the king's 2 Sm 14:26
So Absalom lived **t** full years in 2 Sm 14:28
With Absalom went **t** hundred men 2 Sm 15:11
to the city in peace, with your **t** sons, 2 Sm 15:27
their **t** sons are with them there, 2 Sm 15:36
bearing **t** hundred loaves of bread, 2 Sm 16:1
David was sitting between the **t** gates, 2 Sm 18:24
The king took the **t** sons of Rizpah the 2 Sm 21:8
He struck down **t** ariels of Moab. 2 Sm 23:20
he dealt with the **t** commanders of the 1 Kgs 2:5
with the sword **t** men more righteous 1 Kgs 2:32
three years that **t** of Shimei's servants 1 Kgs 2:39
Then **t** prostitutes came to the king 1 Kgs 3:16
house; only we **t** were in the house. 1 Kgs 3:18
said, "Divide the living child in **t**, 1 Kgs 3:25
and the **t** of them made a treaty. 1 Kgs 5:12
in Lebanon and **t** months at home. 1 Kgs 5:14
sanctuary he made **t** cherubim of 1 Kgs 6:23
He covered the **t** doors of olivewood 1 Kgs 6:32
and **t** doors of cypress wood. The two 1 Kgs 6:34
The **t** leaves of the one door were 1 Kgs 6:34
and the **t** leaves of the other door were 1 Kgs 6:34
He cast **t** pillars of bronze. Eighteen 1 Kgs 7:15
He also made **t** capitals of cast bronze 1 Kgs 7:16
made pomegranates in **t** rows around 1 Kgs 7:18
capitals were on the **t** pillars and also 1 Kgs 7:20
There were **t** hundred pomegranates 1 Kgs 7:20
hundred pomegranates in **t** rows all 1 Kgs 7:20
The gourds were in **t** rows, cast with 1 Kgs 7:24
of a lily. It held **t** thousand baths. 1 Kgs 7:26
the **t** pillars, the two bowls of the 1 Kgs 7:41
the **t** bowls of the capitals that were 1 Kgs 7:41
and the **t** latticeworks to cover the 1 Kgs 7:41
to cover the **t** bowls of the 1 Kgs 7:41
pomegranates for the **t** latticeworks, 1 Kgs 7:42
t rows of pomegranates for each 1 Kgs 7:42
to cover the **t** bowls of the capitals 1 Kgs 7:42
the ark except the **t** tablets of stone that 1 Kgs 8:9
Solomon had built the **t** houses, 1 Kgs 9:10
were armrests and **t** lions standing 1 Kgs 10:19
and the **t** of them were alone in the 1 Kgs 11:29
counsel and made **t** calves of gold. 1 Kgs 12:28
and he reigned over Israel **t** years. 1 Kgs 15:25
in Tirzah, and he reigned **t** years. 1 Kgs 16:8
of Israel were divided into **t** parts. 1 Kgs 16:21
from Shemer for **t** talents of silver, 1 Kgs 16:24
limping between **t** different 1 Kgs 18:21
Let **t** bulls be given to us, and let 1 Kgs 18:23
as would contain **t** seahs of seed. 1 Kgs 18:32
before them like **t** little flocks of 1 Kgs 20:27
And set **t** worthless men opposite 1 Kgs 21:10
And the **t** worthless men came in 1 Kgs 21:13
and he reigned **t** years over Israel. 1 Kgs 22:51
and consumed the **t** former captains 2 Kgs 1:14
leave you." So the **t** of them went on. 2 Kgs 2:6
till the **t** of them could go over on dry 2 Kgs 2:8
horses of fire separated the **t** of them. 2 Kgs 2:11
own clothes and tore them in **t** pieces. 2 Kgs 2:12
And **t** she-bears came out of the 2 Kgs 2:24
come to take my **t** children to be his 2 Kgs 4:1
the door behind the **t** of them and 2 Kgs 4:33
given to your servant **t** mules' load of 2 Kgs 5:17
country of Ephraim **t** young men of 2 Kgs 5:22
talent of silver and **t** festal garments.'" 2 Kgs 5:22
pleased to accept **t** talents." And he 2 Kgs 5:23
him and tied up **t** talents of silver in 2 Kgs 5:23
tied up two talents of silver in **t** bags, 2 Kgs 5:23
in two bags, with **t** festal garments, 2 Kgs 5:23
and laid them on **t** of his servants. 2 Kgs 5:23
and **t** seahs of barley for a shekel, 2 Kgs 7:1
So they took **t** horsemen, and the 2 Kgs 7:14
and **t** seahs of barley for a shekel, 2 Kgs 7:16
"**T** seahs of barley shall be sold for a 2 Kgs 7:18
Who?" **T** or three eunuchs looked 2 Kgs 9:32
the **t** kings could not stand before 2 Kgs 10:4

"Lay them in **t** heaps at the entrance 2 Kgs 10:8
And the **t** divisions of you, which 2 Kgs 11:7
in Samaria, and he reigned **t** years. 2 Kgs 15:23
themselves metal images of **t** calves; 2 Kgs 17:16
I will give you **t** thousand horses, if 2 Kgs 18:23
of heaven in the **t** courts of the house 2 Kgs 21:5
and he reigned **t** years in Jerusalem. 2 Kgs 21:19
had made in the **t** courts of the 2 Kgs 23:12
way of the gate between the **t** walls, 2 Kgs 25:4
As for the **t** pillars, the one sea, and 2 Kgs 25:16
To Eber were born **t** sons: the name 1 Chr 1:19
the father of Tekoa, had **t** wives, 1 Chr 4:5
He struck down **t** heroes of Moab. 1 Chr 11:22
as well as **t** and two at the gatehouse. 1 Chr 26:17
as well as two and **t** at the gatehouse. 1 Chr 26:17
at the road and **t** at the colonnade. 1 Chr 26:18
Place he made **t** cherubim of wood 2 Chr 3:10
house he made **t** pillars thirty-five 2 Chr 3:15
The gourds were in **t** rows, cast with it 2 Chr 4:3
the **t** pillars, the bowls, and the two 2 Chr 4:12
and the **t** capitals on the top of the 2 Chr 4:12
and the **t** latticeworks to cover the 2 Chr 4:12
to cover the **t** bowls of the 2 Chr 4:12
pomegranates for the **t** latticeworks, 2 Chr 4:13
t rows of pomegranates for each 2 Chr 4:13
to cover the **t** bowls of the capitals 2 Chr 4:13
the ark except the **t** tablets that Moses 2 Chr 5:10
arm rests and **t** lions standing beside 2 Chr 9:18
course of time, at the end of **t** years, 2 Chr 21:19
Jehoiada got for him **t** wives, and he 2 Chr 24:3
of heaven in the **t** courts of the house 2 Chr 33:5
and he reigned **t** years in Jerusalem. 2 Chr 33:21
and **t** vessels of fine bright bronze as Ezr 8:27
Nor is this a task for one day or for **t**, Ezr 10:13
wall and appointed **t** great choirs that Neh 12:31
and Teresh, **t** of the king's eunuchs, Est 2:21
and Teresh, **t** of the king's eunuchs, Est 6:2
would keep these **t** days according to Est 9:27
Only grant me **t** things, then I will not Jb 13:20
For God speaks in one way, and in **t**, Jb 33:14
against you and against your **t** friends, Jb 42:7
bronze and cuts in **t** the bars of iron. Ps 107:16
to him who divided the Red Sea in **t**, for Ps 136:13
T things I ask of you; deny them not to Prv 30:7
The leech has **t** daughters; "Give" and Prv 30:15
of quietness than **t** hands full of Eccl 4:6
T are better than one, because they Eccl 4:9
Again, if **t** lie together, they keep warm, Eccl 4:11
t will withstand him—a threefold cord Eccl 4:12
Your **t** breasts are like two fawns, twins of Sg 4:5
Your two breasts are like **t** fawns, twins of Sg 4:5
as upon a dance before **t** armies? Sg 6:13
Your **t** breasts are like two fawns, twins of Sg 7:3
Your two breasts are like **t** fawns, twins of Sg 7:3
and the keepers of the fruit **t** hundred. Sg 8:12
with **t** he covered his face, and with two he Is 6:2
his face, and with **t** he covered his feet, Is 6:2
two he covered his feet, and with **t** he flew. Is 6:2
because of these **t** smoldering stumps of Is 7:4
the land whose **t** kings you dread will be Is 7:16
will keep alive a young cow and **t** sheep, Is 7:21
olive tree is beaten—**t** or three berries in Is 17:6
a reservoir between the **t** walls for the Is 22:11
I will give you **t** thousand horses, if you Is 36:8
These **t** things shall come to you in a Is 47:9
These **t** things have happened to you— Is 51:19
for my people have committed **t** evils: Jer 2:13
you, one from a city and **t** from a family, Jer 3:14
t baskets of figs placed before the temple Jer 24:1
Within **t** years I will bring back to this Jer 28:3
the nations within **t** years." But Jer 28:11
LORD has rejected the **t** clans that he Jer 33:24
that they cut in **t** and passed between its Jer 34:18
through the gate between the **t** walls; Jer 39:4
by the way of a gate between the **t** walls, Jer 52:7
As for the **t** pillars, the one sea, the Jer 52:20
Each creature had **t** wings, each of Ezk 1:11
of another, while **t** covered their bodies. Ezk 1:11
each creature had **t** wings covering its Ezk 1:23
mark **t** ways for the sword of the king Ezk 21:19
of the way, at the head of the **t** ways, Ezk 21:21
"Son of man, there were **t** women, the Ezk 23:2
'These **t** nations and these two Ezk 35:10
nations and these **t** countries shall be Ezk 35:10
and they shall be no longer **t** nations, Ezk 37:22
no longer divided into **t** kingdoms. Ezk 37:22
eight cubits; and its jambs, **t** cubits; Ezk 40:9
of the gate were **t** tables on either side, Ezk 40:39
of the north gate, were **t** tables; Ezk 40:40
the vestibule of the gate were **t** tables. Ezk 40:40
gateway there were **t** chambers in the Ezk 40:44
the jambs of the entrance, **t** cubits; Ezk 41:3
and cherub. Every cherub had **t** faces: Ezk 41:18
wood, three cubits high, **t** cubits long, Ezk 41:22
two cubits long, and **t** cubits broad. Ezk 41:22

The double doors had **t** leaves apiece, Ezk 41:24
t swinging leaves for each door. Ezk 41:24
the ground to the lower ledge, **t** cubits, Ezk 43:14
sheep from every flock of **t** hundred, Ezk 45:15
of Israel. Joseph shall have **t** portions. Ezk 47:13
and made to stand on **t** feet like a man, Dn 7:4
It had **t** horns, and both horns were high, Dn 8:3
He came to the ram with the **t** horns, Dn 8:6
struck the ram and broke his **t** horns. Dn 8:7
the ram that you saw with the **t** horns, Dn 8:20
And as for the **t** kings, their hearts Dn 11:27
looked, and behold, **t** others stood, Dn 12:5
After **t** days he will revive us; on the third Hos 6:2
of Israel, **t** years before the earthquake. Am 1:1
"Do **t** walk together, unless they have Am 3:3
from the mouth of the lion **t** legs, Am 3:12
so **t** or three cities would wander to Am 4:8
And there are **t** olive trees by it, one on Zec 4:3
"What are these **t** olive trees on the Zec 4:11
"What are these **t** branches of the olive Zec 4:12
are beside the **t** golden pipes from Zec 4:12
"These are the **t** anointed ones who Zec 4:14
and behold, **t** women coming forward! Zec 5:9
came out from between **t** mountains. Zec 6:1
And I took **t** staffs, one I named Favor, Zec 11:7
t thirds shall be cut off and perish, Zec 13:8
shall be split in **t** from east to west Zec 14:4
that region who were **t** years old or Mt 2:16
by the Sea of Galilee, he saw **t** brothers, Mt 4:18
on from there he saw **t** other brothers, Mt 4:21
you to go one mile, go with him **t** miles. Mt 5:41
"No one can serve **t** masters, for either Mt 6:24
t demon-possessed men met him, Mt 8:28
from there, **t** blind men followed him, Mt 9:27
nor **t** tunics nor sandals nor a staff, Mt 10:10
Are not **t** sparrows sold for a penny? Mt 10:29
have only five loaves here and **t** fish." Mt 14:17
taking the five loaves and the **t** fish, Mt 14:19
or lame than with **t** hands or two feet Mt 18:8
with two hands or **t** feet to be thrown Mt 18:8
one eye than with **t** eyes to be thrown Mt 18:9
take one or **t** others along with you, Mt 18:16
by the evidence of **t** or three witnesses. Mt 18:16
if **t** of you agree on earth about Mt 18:19
For where **t** or three are gathered in my Mt 18:20
So they are no longer **t** but one flesh. Mt 19:6
"Say that these **t** sons of mine are to sit, Mt 20:21
it, they were indignant at the **t** brothers. Mt 20:24
there were **t** blind men sitting by the Mt 20:30
of Olives, then Jesus sent **t** disciples, Mt 21:1
do you think? A man had **t** sons. Mt 21:28
Which of the **t** did the will of his Mt 21:31
On these **t** commandments depend all Mt 22:40
Then **t** men will be in the field; one will Mt 24:40
T women will be grinding at the mill; Mt 24:41
To one he gave five talents, to another **t**, Mt 25:15
he who had the **t** talents made two Mt 25:17
the two talents made **t** talents more. Mt 25:17
who had the **t** talents came forward, Mt 25:22
'Master, you delivered to me **t** talents; Mt 25:22
here I have made **t** talents more.' Mt 25:22
"You know that after **t** days the Passover Mt 26:2
him Peter and the **t** sons of Zebedee, Mt 26:37
came forward. At last **t** came forward Mt 26:60
"Which of the **t** do you want me to Mt 27:21
Then **t** robbers were crucified with Mt 27:38
the curtain of the temple was torn in **t**, Mt 27:51
the herd, numbering about **t** thousand, Mk 5:13
and began to send them out **t** by two, Mk 6:7
and began to send them out two by **t**, Mk 6:7
to wear sandals and not put on **t** tunics. Mk 6:9
we go and buy **t** hundred denarii worth Mk 6:37
found out, they said, "Five, and **t** fish." Mk 6:38
five loaves and the **t** fish he looked up Mk 6:41
And he divided the **t** fish among them Mk 6:41
life crippled than with **t** hands to go to Mk 9:43
life lame than with **t** feet to be thrown Mk 9:45
one eye than with **t** eyes to be thrown Mk 9:47
So they are no longer **t** but one flesh. Mk 10:8
of Olives, Jesus sent **t** of his disciples Mk 11:1
came and put in **t** small copper coins, Mk 12:42
It was now **t** days before the Passover Mk 14:1
And he sent **t** of his disciples and said Mk 14:13
with him they crucified **t** robbers, Mk 15:27
the curtain of the temple was torn in **t**, Mk 15:38
appeared in another form to **t** of them, Mk 16:12
pair of turtledoves, or **t** young pigeons." Lk 2:24
"Whoever has **t** tunics is to share with Lk 3:11
and he saw **t** boats by the lake, but the Lk 5:2
calling **t** of his disciples to him, sent Lk 7:19
"A certain moneylender had **t** debtors. Lk 7:41
nor money; and do not have **t** tunics. Lk 9:3
than five loaves and **t** fish—unless we Lk 9:13
And taking the five loaves and the **t** fish, Lk 9:16
behold, **t** men were talking with him, Lk 9:30

his glory and the **t** men who stood with Lk 9:32
and sent them on ahead of him, **t** by two, Lk 10:1
and sent them on ahead of him, two by **t**, Lk 10:1
day he took out **t** denarii and gave Lk 10:35
Are not five sparrows sold for **t** pennies? Lk 12:6
three against **t** and two against three. Lk 12:52
three against two and **t** against three. Lk 12:52
said, "There was a man who had **t** sons. Lk 15:11
No servant can serve **t** masters, for Lk 16:13
in that night there will be **t** in one bed. Lk 17:34
There will be **t** women grinding Lk 17:35
"**T** men went up into the temple to Lk 18:10
called Olivet, he sent **t** of the disciples, Lk 19:29
poor widow put in **t** small copper coins. Lk 21:2
here are **t** swords." And he said to them, Lk 22:38
T others, who were criminals, were led Lk 23:32
the curtain of the temple was torn in **t**. Lk 23:45
t men stood by them in dazzling apparel. Lk 24:4
That very day **t** of them were going to a Lk 24:13
John was standing with **t** of his disciples, Jn 1:35
The **t** disciples heard him say this, and Jn 1:37
One of the **t** who heard John speak and Jn 1:40
with them, and he stayed there **t** days. Jn 4:40
After the **t** days he departed for Galilee. Jn 4:43
"**T** hundred denarii would not buy Jn 6:7
here who has five barley loaves and **t** fish, Jn 6:9
that the testimony of **t** men is true. Jn 8:17
he stayed **t** days longer in the place where Jn 11:6
was near Jerusalem, about **t** miles off, Jn 11:18
crucified him, and with him **t** others, Jn 19:18
And she saw **t** angels in white, sitting Jn 20:12
and **t** others of his disciples were together. Jn 21:2
t men stood by them in white robes, Acts 1:10
And they put forward **t**, Joseph called Acts 1:23
which one of these **t** you have chosen Acts 1:24
where he became the father of **t** sons. Acts 7:29
that Peter was there, sent **t** men to him, Acts 9:38
he called **t** of his servants and a devout Acts 10:7
Peter was sleeping between **t** soldiers, Acts 12:6
two soldiers, bound with **t** chains, Acts 12:6
This continued for **t** years, so that all Acts 19:10
sent into Macedonia **t** of his helpers, Acts 19:22
for about **t** hours they all cried out Acts 19:34
him to be bound with **t** chains. Acts 21:33
Then he called **t** of the centurions Acts 23:23
said, "Get ready **t** hundred soldiers, Acts 23:23
horsemen and **t** hundred spearmen Acts 23:23
When **t** years had elapsed, Felix was Acts 24:27
He lived there **t** whole years at his Acts 28:30
"The **t** will become one flesh." 1 Cor 6:16
let there be only **t** or at most three, 1 Cor 14:27
Let **t** or three prophets speak, and let 1 Cor 14:29
by the evidence of **t** or three witnesses. 2 Cor 13:1
it is written that Abraham had **t** sons, Gal 4:22
these women are **t** covenants. Gal 4:24
himself one new man in place of the **t**, Eph 2:15
wife, and the **t** shall become one flesh." Eph 5:31
I am hard pressed between the **t**. My Phil 1:23
on the evidence of **t** or three witnesses. 1 Tm 5:19
plain to all, as was that of those **t** men. 2 Tm 3:9
so that by **t** unchangeable things, in Heb 6:18
on the evidence of **t** or three witnesses. Heb 10:28
They were stoned, they were sawn in **t**, Heb 11:37
passed; behold, **t** woes are still to come. Rv 9:12
I will grant authority to my **t** witnesses, Rv 11:3
These are the **t** olive trees and the two Rv 11:4
trees and the **t** lampstands that stand Rv 11:4
because these **t** prophets had been a Rv 11:10
woman was given the **t** wings of the Rv 12:14
It had **t** horns like a lamb and it spoke Rv 13:11
These **t** were thrown alive into the lake Rv 19:20

TWO-EDGED (5)
in their throats and **t** swords in their Ps 149:6
bitter as wormwood, sharp as a **t** sword. Prv 5:4
and active, sharper than any **t** sword, Heb 4:12
from his mouth came a sharp **t** sword, Rv 1:16
words of him who has the sharp **t** sword. Rv 2:12

TWO-THIRDS (1)
and the charge was **t** of a shekel for 1 Sm 13:21

TYCHICUS (5)
and the Asians, **T** and Trophimus. Acts 20:4
T the beloved brother and faithful Eph 6:21
T will tell you all about my activities. He Col 4:7
T I have sent to Ephesus. 2 Tm 4:12
When I send Artemas or **T** to you, do Ti 3:12

TYPE (1)
who was a **t** of the one who was to Rom 5:14

TYRANNUS (1)
him, reasoning daily in the hall of **T**. Acts 19:9

TYRANT (2)
mighty, or the captives of a **t** be rescued? Is 49:24
taken, and the prey of the **t** be rescued, Is 49:25

TYRE (56)
reaching to the fortified city of **T**. Jos 19:29
Hiram king of **T** sent messengers to 2 Sm 5:11
came to the fortress of **T** and to all the 2 Sm 24:7
Hiram king of **T** sent his servants 1 Kgs 5:1
sent and brought Hiram from **T**. 1 Kgs 7:13
and his father was a man of **T**, 1 Kgs 7:14
Hiram king of **T** had supplied 1 Kgs 9:11
when Hiram came from **T** to see the 1 Kgs 9:12
Hiram king of **T** sent messengers to 1 Chr 14:1
sent word to Hiram the king of **T**: 2 Chr 2:3
Hiram the king of **T** answered in a 2 Chr 2:11
Dan, and his father was a man of **T**. 2 Chr 2:14
The people of **T** will seek your favor Ps 45:12
Philistia with the inhabitants of **T**; Ps 83:7
behold, Philistia and **T**, with Cush— Ps 87:4
The oracle concerning **T**. Wail, O ships Is 23:1
O ships of Tarshish, for **T** is laid waste, Is 23:1
be in anguish over the report about **T**. Is 23:5
Who has purposed this against **T**, the Is 23:8
In that day **T** will be forgotten for Is 23:15
it will happen to **T** as in the song of the Is 23:15
of seventy years, the LORD will visit **T**, Is 23:17
all the kings of **T**, all the kings of Jer 25:22
of the sons of Ammon, the king of **T**, Jer 27:3
to cut off from **T** and Sidon every helper Jer 47:4
because **T** said concerning Jerusalem, Ezk 26:2
Behold, I am against you, O **T**, and will Ezk 26:3
destroy the walls of **T** and break down Ezk 26:4
I will bring against **T** from the north Ezk 26:7
"Thus says the Lord GOD to **T**: Will Ezk 26:15
son of man, raise a lamentation over **T**, Ezk 27:2
and say to **T**, who dwells at the Ezk 27:3
thus says the Lord GOD: "O **T**, Ezk 27:3
your skilled men, O **T**, were in you; Ezk 27:8
'Who is like **T**, like one destroyed in Ezk 27:32
"Son of man, say to the prince of **T**, Ezk 28:2
raise a lamentation over the king of **T**, Ezk 28:12
made his army labor hard against **T**. Ezk 29:18
army got anything from **T** to pay for Ezk 29:18
"What are you to me, O **T** and Sidon, and Jl 3:4
"For three transgressions of **T**, and for Am 1:9
So I will send a fire upon the wall of **T**, Am 1:10
also, which borders on it, **T** and Sidon, Zec 9:2
T has built herself a rampart and heaped Zec 9:3
in you had been done in **T** and Sidon, Mt 11:21
day of judgment for **T** and Sidon than Mt 11:22
withdrew to the district of **T** and Sidon. Mt 15:21
Jordan and from around **T** and Sidon. Mk 3:8
went away to the region of **T** and Sidon. Mk 7:24
from the region of **T** and went through Mk 7:31
and the seacoast of **T** and Sidon, Lk 6:17
in you had been done in **T** and Sidon, Lk 10:13
in the judgment for **T** and Sidon than Lk 10:14
angry with the people of **T** and Sidon, Acts 12:20
left we sailed to Syria and landed at **T**, Acts 21:3
we had finished the voyage from **T**, Acts 21:7

TYRIANS (3)
the Sidonians and **T** brought great 1 Chr 22:4
the Sidonians and the **T** to bring cedar Ezr 3:7
T also, who lived in the city, brought Neh 13:16

U

UEL (1)
the sons of Bani: Maadai, Amram, **U**, Ezr 10:34

UGLY (6)
behold, seven other cows, **u** and thin, Gn 41:3
And the **u**, thin cows ate up the seven Gn 41:4
after them, poor and very **u** and thin, Gn 41:19
u cows ate up the first seven plump Gn 41:20
they were still as **u** as at the beginning. Gn 41:21
The seven lean and **u** cows that came Gn 41:27

ULAI (2)
in the vision, and I was at the **U** canal. Dn 8:2
man's voice between the banks of the **U**, Dn 8:16

ULAM (4)
and his sons were **U** and Rakem. 1 Chr 7:16
The son of **U**: Bedan. These were the 1 Chr 7:17
U his firstborn, Jeush the second, 1 Chr 8:39
The sons of **U** were men who were 1 Chr 8:40

ULLA (1)
The sons of **U**: Arah, Hanniel, and 1 Chr 7:39

UMMAH (1)
U, Aphek and Rehob—twenty-two Jos 19:30

UNABATED (1)
His eye was undimmed, and his vigor **u**. Dt 34:7

UNABLE (9)
people of Israel were **u** to devote to 1 Kgs 9:21
lie fallen; they are thrust down, **u** to rise. Ps 36:12
the men of war were **u** to use their hands. Ps 76:5
shall be mute and **u** to reprove them, Ezk 3:26
will be silent and **u** to speak until the Lk 1:20
he came out, he was **u** to speak to them, Lk 1:22
you will be blind and **u** to see the sun Acts 13:11
see that they were **u** to enter because of Heb 3:19
high priest who is **u** to sympathize with Heb 4:15

UNANSWERED (1)
"Should a multitude of words go **u**, and a Jb 11:2

UNAPPEASABLE (1)
heartless, **u**, slanderous, without 2 Tm 3:3

UNAPPROACHABLE (1)
immortality, who dwells in **u** light, 1 Tm 6:16

UNAUTHORIZED (4)
You shall not offer **u** incense on it, or a Ex 30:9
on it and offered **u** fire before the LORD, Lv 10:1
LORD when they offered **u** fire before the Nm 3:4
when they offered **u** fire before the Nm 26:61

UNAWARE (1)
and they were **u** until the flood came Mt 24:39

UNAWARES (1)
some have entertained angels **u**. Heb 13:2

UNBEARABLE (1)
I am charged with **u** news for you. 1 Kgs 14:6

UNBELIEF (9)
mighty works there, because of their **u**. Mt 13:58
And he marveled because of their **u**. And Mk 6:6
out and said, "I believe; help my **u**!" Mk 9:24
them for their **u** and hardness of Mk 16:14
became stubborn and continued in **u**, Acts 19:9
were broken off because of their **u**, Rom 11:20
if they do not continue in their **u**, Rom 11:23
because I had acted ignorantly in **u**, 1 Tm 1:13
they were unable to enter because of **u**. Heb 3:19

UNBELIEVER (5)
if any brother has a wife who is an **u**, 1 Cor 7:12
woman has a husband who is an **u**, 1 Cor 7:13
and an **u** or outsider enters, 1 Cor 14:24
does a believer share with an **u**? 2 Cor 6:15
the faith and is worse than an **u**. 1 Tm 5:8

UNBELIEVERS (8)
may be delivered from the **u** in Judea, Rom 15:31
law against brother, and that before **u**? 1 Cor 6:6
If one of the **u** invites you to dinner 1 Cor 10:27
are a sign not for believers but for **u**, 1 Cor 14:22
is a sign not for **u** but for believers. 1 Cor 14:22
in tongues, and outsiders or **u** enter, 1 Cor 14:23
world has blinded the minds of the **u**, 2 Cor 4:4
Do not be unequally yoked with **u**. 2 Cor 6:14

UNBELIEVING (6)
But the **u** Jews stirred up the Gentiles Acts 14:2
For the **u** husband is made holy 1 Cor 7:14
and the **u** wife is made holy because 1 Cor 7:14
But if the **u** partner separates, let it be 1 Cor 7:15
things are pure, but to the defiled and **u**, Ti 1:15
there be in any of you an evil, **u** heart, Heb 3:12

UNBIND (2)
before the LORD and **u** the hair of the Nm 5:18
Jesus said to them, "**U** him, and let him Jn 11:44

UNBORN (2)
his righteousness to a people yet **u**, Ps 22:31
might know them, the children yet **u**, Ps 78:6

UNBOUND (2)
and said, "But I see four men **u**, Dn 3:25
he **u** him and commanded the chief Acts 22:30

UNCEASING (4)
struck the peoples in wrath with **u** blows, Is 14:6
Why is my pain **u**, my wound Jer 15:18
upon whom has not come your **u** evil? Na 3:19
have great sorrow and **u** anguish in my Rom 9:2

UNCERTAIN (1)
at one another, **u** of whom he spoke. Jn 13:22

UNCERTAINTY (1)
to set their hopes on the **u** of riches, 1 Tm 6:17

UNCHANGEABLE (3)
But he is **u**, and who can turn him Jb 23:13
of the promise the **u** character of his Heb 6:17
so that by two **u** things, in which it is Heb 6:18

UNCHANGED (1)
eyes the itch is **u** and black hair has Lv 13:37

UNCIRCUMCISED (43)
Any **u** male who is not circumcised in Gn 17:14
thing, to give our sister to one who is **u**, Gn 34:14
Pharaoh listen to me, for I am of **u** lips?" Ex 6:12
said to the LORD, "Behold, I am of **u** lips. Ex 6:30
the land. But no **u** person shall eat of it. Ex 12:48

—if then their **u** heart is humbled and Lv 26:41
For they were **u**, because they had not Jos 5:7
wife from the **u** Philistines?" But Jgs 14:3
thirst and fall into the hands of the **u**?" Jgs 15:18
us go over to the garrison of these **u**. 1 Sm 14:6
For who is this **u** Philistine, that he 1 Sm 17:26
and this **u** Philistine shall be like 1 Sm 17:36
lest these **u** come and thrust me 1 Sm 31:4
lest the daughters of the **u** exult. 2 Sm 1:20
lest these **u** come and mistreat me." 1 Chr 10:4
come into you the **u** and the unclean. Is 52:1
Behold, their ears are **u**, they cannot Jer 6:10
of their hair, for all these nations are **u**, Jer 9:26
and all the house of Israel is **u** in heart." Jer 9:26
die the death of the **u** by the hand of Ezk 28:10
You shall lie among the **u**, with those Ezk 31:18
down and be laid to rest with the **u**.' Ezk 32:19
have come down, they lie still, the **u**, Ezk 32:21
who went down **u** into the world Ezk 32:24
her graves all around it, all of them **u**, Ezk 32:25
her graves all around it, all of them **u**, Ezk 32:26
mighty, the fallen from among the **u**, Ezk 32:27
shall be broken and lie among the **u**, Ezk 32:28
they lie with the **u**, with those who go Ezk 32:29
they lie **u** with those who are slain by Ezk 32:30
he shall be laid to rest among the **u**, Ezk 32:32
foreigners, **u** in heart and flesh, Ezk 44:7
No foreigner, **u** in heart and flesh, of all Ezk 44:9
stiff-necked people, **u** in heart and ears, Acts 7:51
"You went to **u** men and ate with Acts 11:3
if a man who is **u** keeps the precepts of Rom 2:26
he who is physically **u** but keeps the Rom 2:27
by faith and the **u** through faith. Rom 3:30
for the circumcised, or also for the **u**? Rom 4:9
he had by faith while he was still **u**. Rom 4:11
Was anyone at the time of his call **u**? 1 Cor 7:18
been entrusted with the gospel to the **u**, Gal 2:7
not Greek and Jew, circumcised and **u**, Col 3:11

UNCIRCUMCISION (8)
Drink, yourself, and show your **u**! Hab 2:16
law, your circumcision becomes **u**. Rom 2:25
will not his **u** be regarded as Rom 2:26
counts for anything nor **u**, 1 Cor 7:19
neither circumcision nor **u** counts for Gal 5:6
counts for anything, nor **u**, Gal 6:15
called "the **u**" by what is called the Eph 2:11
your trespasses and the **u** of your flesh, Col 2:13

UNCLE (11)
the sons of Uzziel the **u** of Aaron, Lv 10:4
or his **u** or his cousin may redeem him, Lv 25:49
Saul's **u** said to him and to his 1 Sm 10:14
And Saul's **u** said, "Please tell me 1 Sm 10:15
And Saul said to his **u**, "He told us 1 Sm 10:16
was Abner the son of Ner, Saul's **u**. 1 Sm 14:50
made Mattaniah, Jehoiachin's **u**, 2 Kgs 24:17
Jonathan, David's **u**, was a 1 Chr 27:32
that is Esther, the daughter of his **u**, Est 2:7
daughter of Abihail the **u** of Mordecai, Est 2:15
son of Shallum your **u** will come to you Jer 32:7

UNCLE'S (2)
If a man lies with his **u** wife, he has Lv 20:20
he has uncovered his **u** nakedness; Lv 20:20

UNCLEAN (225)
or if anyone touches an **u** thing, whether Lv 5:2
a carcass of an **u** wild animal or a Lv 5:2
or a carcass of **u** livestock or a carcass Lv 5:2
or a carcass of **u** swarming things, Lv 5:2
is hidden from him and he has become **u**, Lv 5:2
may be with which one becomes **u**, Lv 5:3
that touches any **u** thing shall not Lv 7:19
And if anyone touches an **u** thing, Lv 7:21
uncleanness or an **u** beast or any Lv 7:21
beast or any **u** detestable creature, Lv 7:21
and between the **u** and the clean, Lv 10:10
but does not part the hoof, is **u** to you. Lv 11:4
but does not part the hoof, is **u** to you. Lv 11:5
but does not part the hoof, is **u** to you. Lv 11:6
but does not chew the cud, is **u** to you. Lv 11:7
touch their carcasses; they are **u** to you. Lv 11:8
"And by these you shall become **u**. Lv 11:24
carcass shall be **u** until the evening, Lv 11:24
his clothes and be **u** until the evening. Lv 11:25
or does not chew the cud is **u** to you. Lv 11:26
Everyone who touches them shall be **u**. Lv 11:26
that go on all fours, are **u** to you. Lv 11:27
carcass shall be **u** until the evening, Lv 11:27
his clothes and be **u** until the evening; Lv 11:28
until the evening; they are **u** to you. Lv 11:28
"And these are **u** to you among the Lv 11:29
These are **u** to you among all that Lv 11:31
are dead shall be **u** until the evening. Lv 11:31
falls when they are dead shall be **u**, Lv 11:32
and it shall be **u** until the evening; Lv 11:32
vessel, all that is in it shall be **u**, Lv 11:33
on which water comes, shall be **u**. Lv 11:34
from every such vessel shall be **u**. Lv 11:34
part of their carcass falls shall be **u**. Lv 11:35
They are **u** and shall remain unclean Lv 11:35
unclean and shall remain **u** for you. Lv 11:35
touches a carcass in them shall be **u**. Lv 11:36
of their carcass falls on it, it is **u** to you. Lv 11:38
its carcass shall be **u** until the evening, Lv 11:39
his clothes and be **u** until the evening. Lv 11:40
his clothes and be **u** until the evening. Lv 11:40
them, and become **u** through them. Lv 11:43
distinction between the **u** and the clean Lv 11:47
child, then she shall be **u** seven days. Lv 12:2
time of her menstruation, she shall be **u**. Lv 12:2
child, then she shall be **u** two weeks, Lv 12:5
him, he shall pronounce him **u**. Lv 13:3
then the priest shall pronounce him **u**; Lv 13:8
and the priest shall pronounce him **u**. Lv 13:11
He shall not shut him up, for he is **u**. Lv 13:11
raw flesh appears on him, he shall be **u**. Lv 13:14
the raw flesh and pronounce him **u**. Lv 13:15
Raw flesh is **u**, for it is a leprous disease. Lv 13:15
then the priest shall pronounce him **u**. Lv 13:20
then the priest shall pronounce him **u**; Lv 13:22
and the priest shall pronounce him **u**; Lv 13:25
then the priest shall pronounce him **u**; Lv 13:27
then the priest shall pronounce him **u**. Lv 13:30
not seek for the yellow hair; he is **u**. Lv 13:36
he is a leprous man, he is **u**. The priest Lv 13:44
The priest must pronounce him **u**; his Lv 13:44
his upper lip and cry out, '**U**, unclean.' Lv 13:45
his upper lip and cry out, 'Unclean, **u**.' Lv 13:45
He shall remain **u** as long as he has the Lv 13:46
as long as he has the disease. He is **u**. Lv 13:46
is a persistent leprous disease; it is **u**. Lv 13:51
the disease has not spread, it is **u**. Lv 13:55
to determine whether it is clean or **u**. Lv 13:59
all that is in the house be declared **u**. Lv 14:36
throw them into an **u** place outside the Lv 14:40
pour out in an **u** place outside the city. Lv 14:41
leprous disease in the house; it is **u**. Lv 14:44
carry them out of the city to an **u** place. Lv 14:45
is shut up shall be **u** until the evening, Lv 14:46
to show when it is **u** and when it is Lv 14:57
from his body, his discharge is **u**. Lv 15:2
one with the discharge lies shall be **u**, Lv 15:4
everything on which he sits shall be **u**. Lv 15:4
in water and be **u** until the evening. Lv 15:5
in water and be **u** until the evening. Lv 15:6
in water and be **u** until the evening. Lv 15:7
in water and be **u** until the evening. Lv 15:8
one with the discharge rides shall be **u**. Lv 15:9
under him shall be **u** until the evening. Lv 15:10
in water and be **u** until the evening. Lv 15:10
in water and be **u** until the evening. Lv 15:11
in water and be **u** until the evening. Lv 15:16
with water and be **u** until the evening. Lv 15:17
in water and be **u** until the evening. Lv 15:18
her shall be **u** until the evening. Lv 15:19
her menstrual impurity shall be **u**. Lv 15:20
also on which she sits shall be **u**. Lv 15:20
in water and be **u** until the evening. Lv 15:21
in water and be **u** until the evening. Lv 15:22
it he shall be **u** until the evening. Lv 15:23
upon him, he shall be **u** seven days, Lv 15:24
every bed on which he lies shall be **u**. Lv 15:24
the days of her impurity, she shall be **u**. Lv 15:25
everything on which she sits shall be **u**, Lv 15:26
touches these things shall be **u**, Lv 15:27
in water and be **u** until the evening. Lv 15:27
her before the LORD for her **u** discharge. Lv 15:30
of semen, becoming **u** thereby; Lv 15:32
man who lies with a woman who is **u**. Lv 15:33
in water and be **u** until the evening; Lv 17:15
wife and so make yourself **u** with her. Lv 18:20
animal and so make yourself **u** with it, Lv 18:23
"Do not make yourselves **u** by any of Lv 18:24
driving out before you have become **u**, Lv 18:24
and the land became **u**, so that I Lv 18:25
so that the land became **u**), Lv 18:27
vomit you out when you make it **u**, Lv 18:28
never to make yourselves **u** by them: Lv 18:30
out, and so make yourselves **u** by them: Lv 19:31
to make my sanctuary **u** and to profane Lv 20:3
separate the clean beast from the **u**, Lv 20:25
unclean, and the **u** bird from the clean. Lv 20:25
which I have set apart for you to hold **u**. Lv 20:25
one shall make himself **u** for the dead Lv 21:1
for her he may make himself **u**). Lv 21:3
shall not make himself **u** as a husband Lv 21:4
to any dead bodies nor make himself **u**, Lv 21:11
anything that is **u** through contact with Lv 22:4
he may be made **u** or a person from Lv 22:5
a thing shall be **u** until the evening and Lv 22:6
by beasts, and so make himself **u** by it: Lv 22:8
And if it is any **u** animal that may not Lv 27:11
And if it is an **u** animal, then he shall Lv 27:27
everyone who is **u** through contact with Nm 5:2
if they die, shall he make himself **u**, Nm 6:7
men who were **u** through touching a Nm 9:6
"We are **u** through touching a dead Nm 9:7
descendants is **u** through touching Nm 9:10
the firstborn of **u** animals you shall Nm 18:15
But the priest shall be **u** until evening. Nm 19:7
in water and shall be **u** until evening. Nm 19:8
his clothes and be **u** until evening. Nm 19:10
of any person shall be **u** seven days. Nm 19:11
was not thrown on him, he shall be **u**. Nm 19:13
is in the tent shall be **u** seven days. Nm 19:14
that has no cover fastened on it is **u**. Nm 19:15
bone or a grave, shall be **u** seven days. Nm 19:16
For the **u** they shall take some ashes Nm 19:17
sprinkle it on the **u** on the third day Nm 19:19
the man who is **u** does not cleanse Nm 19:20
has not been thrown on him, he is **u**. Nm 19:20
for impurity shall be **u** until evening. Nm 19:21
And whatever the **u** person touches Nm 19:22
unclean person touches shall be **u**, Nm 19:22
touches it shall be **u** until evening." Nm 19:22
The **u** and the clean may eat of it, as of Dt 12:15
The **u** and the clean alike may eat of it. Dt 12:22
but do not part the hoof, are **u** for you. Dt 14:7
but does not chew the cud, is **u** for you. Dt 14:8
scales you shall not eat; it is **u** for you. Dt 14:10
And all winged insects are **u** for you; Dt 14:19
The **u** and the clean alike may eat it, as Dt 15:22
among you becomes **u** because of a Dt 23:10
or removed any of it while I was **u**, Dt 26:14
now, if the land of your possession is **u**, Jos 22:19
wine or strong drink, and eat nothing **u**, Jgs 13:4
wine or strong drink, and eat nothing **u**, Jgs 13:7
or strong drink, or eat any **u** thing. Jgs 13:14
should enter who was in any way **u**. 2 Chr 23:19
were excluded from the priesthood as **u**. Ezr 2:62
excluded from the priesthood as **u**. Neh 7:64
can bring a clean thing out of an **u**? Jb 14:4
Thus they became **u** by their acts, and Ps 106:39
good and the evil, to the clean and the **u**, Eccl 9:2
for I am a man of **u** lips, and I dwell in the Is 6:5
I dwell in the midst of a people of **u** lips; Is 6:5
You will scatter them as **u** things. Is 30:22
of Holiness; the **u** shall not pass over it. Is 35:8
into you the uncircumcised and the **u**. Is 52:1
go out from there; touch no **u** thing; Is 52:11
We have all become like one who is **u**, Is 64:6
How can you say, 'I am not **u**, I have not Jer 2:23
"Away! **U**!" people cried at them. Lam 4:15
the people of Israel eat their bread **u**, Ezk 4:13
streets, and their gold is like an **u** thing. Ezk 7:19
Therefore I make it an **u** thing to them. Ezk 7:20
women who are **u** in their menstrual Ezk 22:10
difference between the **u** and the Ezk 22:26
On account of your **u** lewdness, Ezk 24:13
distinguish between the **u** and the Ezk 44:23
and they shall eat **u** food in Assyria. Hos 9:3
you yourself shall die in an **u** land, and Am 7:17
"If someone who is **u** by contact with a Hg 2:13
does it become **u**?" The priests answered Hg 2:13
answered and said, "It does become **u**." Hg 2:13
hands. And what they offer there is **u**. Hg 2:14
and gave them authority over **u** spirits, Mt 10:1
"When the **u** spirit has gone out of a Mt 12:43
their synagogue a man with an **u** spirit. Mk 1:23
And the **u** spirit, convulsing him and Mk 1:26
He commands even the **u** spirits, and Mk 1:27
And whenever the **u** spirits saw him, Mk 3:11
for they had said, "He has an **u** spirit." Mk 3:30
out of the tombs a man with an **u** spirit. Mk 5:2
"Come out of the man, you **u** spirit!" Mk 5:8
And the **u** spirits came out, and entered Mk 5:13
gave them authority over the **u** spirits. Mk 6:7
was possessed by an **u** spirit heard of Mk 7:25
together, he rebuked the **u** spirit, Mk 9:25
a man who had the spirit of an **u** demon, Lk 4:33
and power he commands the **u** spirits, Lk 4:36
were troubled with **u** spirits were cured. Lk 6:18
he had commanded the **u** spirit to come Lk 8:29
Jesus rebuked the **u** spirit and healed Lk 9:42
"When the **u** spirit has gone out of a Lk 11:24
sick and those afflicted with **u** spirits, Acts 5:16
For **u** spirits came out of many who Acts 8:7
anything that is common or **u**." Acts 10:14
not call any person common or **u**. Acts 10:28
nothing common or **u** has ever Acts 11:8
Lord Jesus that nothing is **u** in itself, Rom 14:14
but it is **u** for anyone who thinks it Rom 14:14
unclean for anyone who thinks it **u**. Rom 14:14
Otherwise your children would be **u**, 1 Cor 7:14
says the Lord, and touch no **u** thing; 2 Cor 6:17

but **u** what the will of the Lord is. Eph 5:17
But **u** this, that in the last days there 2 Tm 3:1
By faith we **u** that the universe was Heb 11:3
some things in them that are hard to **u**, 2 Pt 3:16
blaspheme all that they do not **u**, Jude 1:10
unreasoning animals, **u** instinctively. Jude 1:10

UNDERSTANDING (125)
your tribes wise, **u**, and experienced men, Dt 1:13
be your wisdom and your **u** in the sight of Dt 4:6
this great nation is a wise and **u** people.' Dt 4:6
of counsel, and there is no **u** in them. Dt 32:28
servant therefore an **u** mind to govern 1 Kgs 3:9
asked for yourself **u** to discern what 1 Kgs 3:11
wisdom and **u** beyond measure, 1 Kgs 4:29
u, and skill for making any work in 1 Kgs 7:14
men who had **u** of the times, 1 Chr 12:32
the LORD grant you discretion and **u**, 1 Chr 22:12
being a man of **u** and a scribe. 1 Chr 27:32
a wise son, who has discretion and **u**, 2 Chr 2:12
I have sent a skilled man, who has **u**, 2 Chr 2:13
all who have knowledge and **u**, Neh 10:28
tell you and utter words out of their **u**? Jb 8:10
of wisdom! For he is manifold in **u**. Jb 11:6
stupid man will get **u** when a wild Jb 11:12
But I have **u** as well as you; I am not Jb 12:3
is with the aged, and **u** in length of days. Jb 12:12
and might; he has counsel and **u**. Jb 12:13
He takes away **u** from the chiefs of the Jb 12:24
Since you have closed their hearts to **u**, Jb 17:4
me, and out of my **u** a spirit answers me. Jb 20:3
the sea; by his **u** he shattered Rahab. Jb 26:12
be found? And where is the place of **u**? Jb 28:12
come? And where is the place of **u**? Jb 28:20
and to turn away from evil is **u**.'" Jb 28:28
"Therefore, hear me, you men of **u**: far Jb 34:10
"If you have **u**, hear this; listen to what I Jb 34:16
Men of **u** will say to me, and the wise Jb 34:34
despise any; he is mighty in strength of **u**. Jb 36:5
of the earth? Tell me, if you have **u**. Jb 38:4
the inward parts or given **u** to the mind? Jb 38:36
wisdom and given her no share in **u**. Jb 39:17
"Is it by your **u** that the hawk soars and Jb 39:26
Be not like a horse or a mule, without **u**, Ps 32:9
the meditation of my heart shall be **u**. Ps 49:3
his pomp yet without **u** is like the Ps 49:20
They have neither knowledge nor **u**, they Ps 82:5
all those who practice it have a good **u**. Ps 111:10
Give me **u**, that I may keep your law Ps 119:34
give me **u** that I may learn your Ps 119:73
I have more **u** than all my teachers, Ps 119:99
Through your precepts I get **u**; Ps 119:104
give me **u**, that I may know your Ps 119:125
gives light; it imparts **u** to the simple. Ps 119:130
forever; give me **u** that I may live. Ps 119:144
give me **u** according to your word! Ps 119:169
to him who by **u** made the heavens, for Ps 136:5
in power; his **u** is beyond measure. Ps 147:5
to wisdom and inclining your heart to **u**; Prv 2:2
out for insight and raise your voice for **u**, Prv 2:3
from his mouth come knowledge and **u**; Prv 2:6
will watch over you, **u** will guard you, Prv 2:11
heart, and do not lean on your own **u**. Prv 3:5
finds wisdom, and the one who gets **u**, Prv 3:13
earth; by **u** he established the heavens; Prv 3:19
to my wisdom; incline your ear to my **u**, Prv 5:1
wisdom call? Does not **u** raise her voice? Prv 8:1
On the lips of him who has **u**, wisdom Prv 10:13
but wisdom is pleasure to a man of **u**. Prv 10:23
sense, but a man of **u** remains silent. Prv 11:12
but knowledge is easy for a man of **u**. Prv 14:6
Whoever is slow to anger has great **u**, Prv 14:29
rests in the heart of a man of **u**, Prv 14:33
of him who has **u** seeks knowledge, Prv 15:14
but a man of **u** walks straight ahead. Prv 15:21
To get **u** is to be chosen rather than Prv 16:16
into a man of **u** than a hundred blows Prv 17:10
he who has a cool spirit is a man of **u**. Prv 17:27
A fool takes no pleasure in **u**, but only Prv 18:2
soul; he who keeps **u** will discover good. Prv 19:8
reprove a man of **u**, and he will gain Prv 19:25
water, but a man of **u** will draw it out. Prv 20:5
No wisdom, no **u**, no counsel can Prv 21:30
sell it; buy wisdom, instruction, and **u**. Prv 23:23
is built, and by **u** it is established; Prv 24:3
but with a man of **u** and knowledge, Prv 28:2
one who keeps the law is a son with **u**, Prv 28:7
poor man who has **u** will find him Prv 28:11
A ruler who lacks **u** is a cruel Prv 28:16
to be a man. I have not the **u** of a man. Prv 30:2
done it, and by my wisdom, for I have **u**; Is 10:13
upon him, the Spirit of wisdom and **u**, Is 11:2
of him who formed it, "He has no **u**"? Is 29:16
who go astray in spirit will come to **u**, Is 29:24
and showed him the way of **u**? Is 40:14
or grow weary; his **u** is unsearchable. Is 40:28
But they are shepherds who have no **u**; Is 56:11
who will feed you with knowledge and **u**. Jer 3:15
they are stupid children; they have no **u**. Jer 4:22
and by his **u** stretched out the heavens. Jer 10:12
and by his **u** stretched out the heavens. Jer 51:15
wisdom and your **u** you have made Ezk 28:4
endowed with knowledge, **u** learning, Dn 1:4
and Daniel had **u** in all visions and Dn 1:17
of wisdom and **u** about which the Dn 1:20
and knowledge to those who have **u**; Dn 2:21
light and **u** and wisdom like the wisdom Dn 5:11
knowledge, and **u** to interpret dreams, Dn 5:12
that light and **u** and excellent wisdom Dn 5:14
now come out to give you insight and **u**. Dn 9:22
the word and had **u** of the vision. Dn 10:1
and new wine, which take away the **u**. Hos 4:11
and a people without **u** shall come to Hos 4:14
set a trap beneath you—you have no **u**. Ob 1:7
out of Edom, and **u** out of Mount Esau? Ob 1:8
from the wise and **u** and revealed them Mt 11:25
he said, "Are you also still without **u**? Mt 15:16
to them, "Then are you also without **u**? Mk 7:18
and with all the **u** and with all the Mk 12:33
were amazed at his **u** and his answers. Lk 2:47
from the wise and **u** and revealed them Lk 10:21
one another, they are without **u**. 2 Cor 10:12
They are darkened in their **u**, alienated Eph 4:18
the peace of God, which surpasses all **u**, Phil 4:7
of his will in all spiritual wisdom and **u**, Col 1:9
of full assurance of **u** and the knowledge Col 2:2
without **u** either what they are saying 1 Tm 1:7
u this, that the law is not laid down for 1 Tm 1:9
the Lord will give you **u** in everything. 2 Tm 2:7
Who is wise and **u** among you? By his Jas 3:13
live with your wives in an **u** way, 1 Pt 3:7
of God has come and has given us **u**, 1 Jn 5:20
one who has **u** calculate the number Rv 13:18

UNDERSTANDS (12)
all hearts and **u** every plan and 1 Chr 28:9
"God **u** the way to it, and he knows its Jb 28:23
and the one who **u** obtain guidance, Prv 1:5
They are all straight to him who **u**, and Prv 8:9
is not disciplined, for though he **u**, Prv 29:19
men are taken away, while no one **u**. Is 57:1
boast in this, that he **u** and knows me, Jer 9:24
a king of bold face, one who **u** riddles, Dn 8:23
is the one who hears the word and **u** it. Mt 13:23
no one **u**; no one seeks for God. Rom 3:11
for no one **u** him, but he utters 1 Cor 14:2
puffed up with conceit and **u** nothing. 1 Tm 6:4

UNDERSTOOD (17)
They did not know that Joseph **u** them, Gn 42:23
people and all Israel **u** that day that it 2 Sm 3:37
David **u** that the child was dead. 2 Sm 12:19
should direct the music, for he **u** it. 1 Chr 15:22
And I **u** and saw that God had not sent Neh 6:12
sense, so that the people **u** the reading. Neh 8:8
because they had **u** the words that were Neh 8:12
seen all this, my ear has heard and **u** it. Jb 13:1
Have you not **u** from the foundations of Is 40:21
And he **u** the word and had Dn 10:1
"Have you **u** all these things?" They Mt 13:51
Then they **u** that he did not tell them to Mt 16:12
Then the disciples **u** that he was Mt 17:13
But they **u** none of these things. This Lk 18:34
None of the rulers of this age **u** this, for 1 Cor 2:8
"For who has **u** the mind of the Lord 1 Cor 2:16
day you heard it and **u** the grace of God Col 1:6

UNDERTAKE (6)
and your households, in all that you **u**, Dt 12:7
the LORD your God in all that you **u**. Dt 12:18
in all your work and in all that you **u**. Dt 15:10
you in all that you **u** in the land that Dt 23:20
you in your barns and in all that you **u**. Dt 28:8
and frustration in all that you **u** to do, Dt 28:20

UNDERTAKEN (3)
"Behold, I have **u** to speak to the Lord, Gn 18:27
"Behold, I have **u** to speak to the Lord. Gn 18:31
Inasmuch as many have **u** to compile a Lk 1:1

UNDERTAKING (1)
for if this plan or this **u** is of man, Acts 5:38

UNDERTAKINGS (1)
And David had success in all his **u**, 1 Sm 18:14

UNDERTOOK (3)
land of Moab, Moses **u** to explain this law, Dt 1:5
every work that he **u** in the service 2 Chr 31:21
itinerant Jewish exorcists **u** to invoke Acts 19:13

UNDETECTED (1)
and she is **u** though she has defiled Nm 5:13

UNDIMMED (1)
His eye was **u**, and his vigor unabated. Dt 34:7

UNDIVIDED (1)
and to secure your **u** devotion to the 1 Cor 7:35

UNDO (1)
of wickedness, to **u** the straps of the yoke, Is 58:6

UNDOING (1)
they were his counselors, to his **u**. 2 Chr 22:4

UNDONE (7)
to Moses, "Behold, we perish, we are **u**, Nm 17:12
we perish, we are undone, we are all **u**. Nm 17:12
You are **u**, O people of Chemosh! Nm 21:29
He left nothing **u** of all that the LORD Jos 11:15
Moab is laid waste in a night, Moab is **u**; Is 15:1
Moab is laid waste in a night, Moab is **u**. Is 15:1
The people of Chemosh are **u**, for your Jer 48:46

UNDRESSED (2)
or gather the grapes of your **u** vine. Lv 25:5
nor gather the grapes from the **u** vines. Lv 25:11

UNEDUCATED (1)
John, and perceived that they were **u**, Acts 4:13

UNEQUAL (3)
U weights and unequal measures are Prv 20:10
Unequal weights and **u** measures are Prv 20:10
U weights are an abomination to the Prv 20:23

UNEQUALLY (1)
Do not be **u** yoked with unbelievers. 2 Cor 6:14

UNEVEN (1)
the **u** ground shall become level, and the Is 40:4

UNFADING (2)
that is imperishable, undefiled, and **u**, 1 Pt 1:4
you will receive the **u** crown of glory. 1 Pt 5:4

UNFAITHFUL (10)
And his concubine was **u** to him, and Jgs 19:2
because they had been **u** to the LORD, 2 Chr 12:2
For he was **u** to the LORD his God 2 Chr 26:16
and had been very **u** to the LORD. 2 Chr 28:19
fathers have been **u** and have done 2 Chr 29:6
people likewise were exceedingly **u**, 2 Chr 36:14
servant Moses, saying, 'If you are **u**, Neh 1:8
put an end to everyone who is **u** to you. Ps 73:27
him in pieces and put him with the **u**. Lk 12:46
What if some were **u**? Does their Rom 3:3

UNFASTENED (1)
opened, and everyone's bonds were **u**. Acts 16:26

UNFEELING (1)
their heart is **u** like fat, but I delight in Ps 119:70

UNFIT (1)
disobedient, **u** for any good work. Ti 1:16

UNFOLDING (1)
The **u** of your words gives light; it Ps 119:130

UNFORGOTTEN (1)
(for it will live **u** in the mouths of Dt 31:21

UNFORMED (1)
Your eyes saw my **u** substance; in Ps 139:16

UNFRUITFUL (7)
the water is bad, and the land is **u**." 2 Kgs 2:19
riches choke the word, and it proves **u**. Mt 13:22
in and choke the word, and it proves **u**. Mk 4:19
my spirit prays but my mind is **u**. 1 Cor 14:14
no part in the **u** works of darkness, Eph 5:11
help cases of urgent need, and not be **u**. Ti 3:14
being ineffective or **u** in the knowledge 2 Pt 1:8

UNGODLINESS (7)
heart is busy with iniquity, to practice **u**, Is 32:6
prophets of Jerusalem **u** has gone out Jer 23:15
against all **u** and unrighteousness Rom 1:18
Zion, he will banish **u** from Jacob"; Rom 11:26
lead people into more and more **u**, 2 Tm 2:16
us to renounce **u** and worldly passions, Ti 2:12
all their deeds of **u** that they have Jude 1:15

UNGODLY (15)
gives me up to the **u** and casts me into Jb 16:11
defend my cause against an **u** people, Ps 43:1
"Both prophet and priest are **u**; even in Jer 23:11
work but trusts him who justifies the **u**, Rom 4:5
at the right time Christ died for the **u**. Rom 5:6
and disobedient, for the **u** and sinners, 1 Tm 1:9
will become of the **u** and the sinner?" 1 Pt 4:18
brought a flood upon the world of the **u**; 2 Pt 2:5
of what is going to happen to the **u**; 2 Pt 2:6
of judgment and destruction of the **u**. 2 Pt 3:7
for this condemnation, **u** people, Jude 1:4
to convict all the **u** of all their deeds Jude 1:15
have committed in such an **u** way, Jude 1:15
harsh things that **u** sinners have Jude 1:15
following their own **u** passions." Jude 1:18

UNGRATEFUL (2)
High, for he is kind to the **u** and the evil. Lk 6:35

disobedient to their parents, **u**, unholy, 2 Tm 3:2

UNHAPPY (2)
It is an **u** business that God has given Eccl 1:13
This also is vanity and an **u** business. Eccl 4:8

UNHARNESSED (1)
came to the house and **u** the camels, Gn 24:32

UNHEALTHY (1)
He has an **u** craving for controversy 1 Tm 6:4

UNHOLY (3)
and sinners, for the **u** and profane, 1 Tm 1:9
to their parents, ungrateful, **u**, 2 Tm 3:2
is sexually immoral or **u** like Esau, Heb 12:16

UNINFORMED (2)
brothers, I do not want you to be **u**. 1 Cor 12:1
But we do not want you to be **u**, 1 Thes 4:13

UNINHABITED (5)
lest I make you a desolation, an **u** land." Jer 6:8
of the wilderness, in an **u** salt land. Jer 17:6
surely I will make you a desert, an **u** city. Jer 22:6
through it; it shall be **u** forty years. Ezk 29:11
perish from Gaza; Ashkelon shall be **u**; Zec 9:5

UNINTENTIONAL (1)
himself and for the **u** sins of the people. Heb 9:7

UNINTENTIONALLY (14)
If anyone sins **u** in any of the LORD'S Lv 4:2
of Israel sins **u** and the thing Lv 4:13
doing **u** any one of all the things that by Lv 4:22
the common people sins **u** in doing any Lv 4:27
breach of faith and sins **u** in any of the Lv 5:15
for him for the mistake that he made **u**, Lv 5:18
And if anyone eats of a holy thing **u**, he Lv 22:14
"But if you sin **u**, and do not observe Nm 15:22
it was done **u** without the knowledge Nm 15:24
"If one person sins **u**, he shall offer a Nm 15:27
makes a mistake, when he sins **u**, Nm 15:28
one law for him who does anything **u**, Nm 15:29
there, anyone who kills his neighbor **u**, Dt 4:42
kills his neighbor **u** without having Dt 19:4

UNION (4)
born of a forbidden **u** may enter the Dt 23:2
I named Favor, the other I named **U**. Zec 11:7
Then I broke my second staff **U**, Zec 11:14
with a portion of the Spirit in their **u**? Mal 2:15

UNIQUE (1)
And there shall be a **u** day, which is Zec 14:7

UNISON (1)
themselves heard in **u** in praise and 2 Chr 5:13

UNITE (2)
truth; **u** my heart to fear your name. Ps 86:11
fullness of time, to **u** all things in him, Eph 1:10

UNITED (6)
against the city, **u** as one man. Jgs 20:11
the Jews made a **u** attack on Paul and Acts 18:12
For if we have been **u** with him in a Rom 6:5
we shall certainly be **u** with him in a Rom 6:5
but that you be **u** in the same mind 1 Cor 1:10
because they were not **u** by faith with Heb 4:2

UNITS (1)
houses, were **u** of the army for war, 1 Chr 7:4

UNITY (4)
pleasant it is when brothers dwell in **u**! Ps 133:1
eager to maintain the **u** of the Spirit in Eph 4:3
we all attain to the **u** of the faith and of Eph 4:13
Finally, all of you, have **u** of mind, 1 Pt 3:8

UNIVERSE (2)
and he upholds the **u** by the word of his Heb 1:3
understand that the **u** was created by Heb 11:3

UNJUST (16)
from the deceitful and **u** man deliver me! Ps 43:1
from the grasp of the **u** and cruel man. Ps 71:4
of everyone who is greedy for **u** gain; Prv 1:19
is greedy for **u** gain troubles his Prv 15:27
but he who hates **u** gain will prolong Prv 28:16
An **u** man is an abomination to the Prv 29:27
of the iniquity of his **u** gain I was angry, Is 57:17
of them, everyone is greedy for **u** gain; Jer 6:13
the greatest everyone is greedy for **u** gain; Jer 8:10
the war against the **u** overtake them in Hos 10:9
does not fail; but the **u** knows no shame. Zep 3:5
and sends rain on the just and on the **u**. Mt 5:45
other men, extortioners, **u**, adulterers, Lk 18:11
of both the just and the **u**. Acts 24:15
For God is not so **u** as to overlook your Heb 6:10
to the good and gentle but also to the **u**. 1 Pt 2:18

UNJUSTLY (2)
will you judge **u** and show partiality Ps 82:2
one endures sorrows while suffering **u**. 1 Pt 2:19

UNKNOWINGLY (2)
without intent or **u** may flee there. Jos 20:3
hand, because he struck his neighbor **u**, Jos 20:5

UNKNOWN (5)
and the plenty will be **u** in the land by Gn 41:31
with this inscription, 'To the **u** god.' Acts 17:23
What therefore you worship as **u**, Acts 17:23
as **u**, and yet well known; as dying, and 2 Cor 6:9
And I was still **u** in person to the Gal 1:22

UNLAWFUL (1)
"You yourselves know how **u** it is for Acts 10:28

UNLEAVENED (62)
made them a feast and baked **u** bread, Gn 19:3
with **u** bread and bitter herbs they shall Ex 12:8
Seven days you shall eat **u** bread. On Ex 12:15
you shall observe the Feast of **U** Bread, Ex 12:17
you shall eat **u** bread until the Ex 12:18
dwelling places you shall eat **u** bread." Ex 12:20
And they baked **u** cakes of the dough Ex 12:39
Seven days you shall eat **u** bread, and on Ex 13:6
U bread shall be eaten for seven days; no Ex 13:7
You shall keep the Feast of **U** Bread. As Ex 23:15
you shall eat **u** bread for seven days at Ex 23:15
and **u** bread, unleavened cakes mixed Ex 29:2
bread, **u** cakes mixed with oil, Ex 29:2
with oil, and **u** wafers smeared with oil. Ex 29:2
of the basket of **u** bread that is before Ex 29:23
"You shall keep the Feast of **U** Bread. Ex 34:18
Seven days you shall eat **u** bread, as I Ex 34:18
it shall be **u** loaves of fine flour mixed Lv 2:4
mixed with oil or **u** wafers smeared with Lv 2:4
on a griddle, it shall be of fine flour **u**, Lv 2:5
eat. It shall be eaten **u** in a holy place. Lv 6:16
thanksgiving sacrifice **u** loaves mixed Lv 7:12
with oil, **u** wafers smeared with oil, Lv 7:12
the two rams and the basket of **u** bread. Lv 8:2
of the basket of **u** bread that was before Lv 8:26
the LORD he took one **u** loaf and one loaf Lv 8:26
offerings, and eat it **u** beside the altar, Lv 10:12
is the Feast of **U** bread to the LORD; Lv 23:6
for seven days you shall eat **u** bread. Lv 23:6
and a basket of **u** bread, loaves of fine Nm 6:15
with oil, and **u** wafers smeared with oil, Nm 6:15
to the LORD, with the basket of **u** bread. Nm 6:17
and one **u** loaf out of the basket and Nm 6:19
loaf out of the basket and one **u** wafer, Nm 6:19
shall eat it with **u** bread and bitter Nm 9:11
Seven days shall **u** bread be eaten. Nm 28:17
Seven days you shall eat it with **u** bread, Dt 16:3
For six days you shall eat **u** bread, and Dt 16:8
at the Feast of **U** Bread, at the Feast of Dt 16:16
of the land, **u** cakes and parched grain. Jos 5:11
a young goat and **u** cakes from an Jgs 6:19
to him, "Take the meat and the **u** cakes, Jgs 6:20
and touched the meat and the **u** cakes. Jgs 6:21
and consumed the flesh and the **u** cakes. Jgs 6:21
kneaded it and baked **u** bread of it, 1 Sm 28:24
but they ate **u** bread among their 2 Kgs 23:9
grain offering, the wafers of **u** bread, 1 Chr 23:29
annual feasts—the Feast of **U** Bread, 2 Chr 8:13
keep the Feast of **U** Bread in the 2 Chr 30:13
kept the Feast of **U** Bread seven days 2 Chr 30:21
and the Feast of **U** Bread seven days. 2 Chr 35:17
kept the Feast of **U** Bread seven days Ezr 6:22
and for seven days **u** bread shall be Ezk 45:21
the first day of **U** Bread the disciples Mt 26:17
the Passover and the Feast of **U** Bread. Mk 14:1
And on the first day of **U** Bread, when Mk 14:12
Now the Feast of **U** Bread drew near, Lk 22:1
Then came the day of **U** Bread, on Lk 22:7
This was during the days of **U** Bread. Acts 12:3
Philippi after the days of **U** Bread, Acts 20:6
be a new lump, as you really are **u**. 1 Cor 5:7
but with the **u** bread of sincerity and 1 Cor 5:8

UNLESS (61)
"I will not let you go **u** you bless me." Gn 32:26
from this place **u** your youngest Gn 42:15
not see my face **u** your brother is with Gn 43:3
my face, **u** your brother is with you.'" Gn 43:5
'**U** your youngest brother comes down Gn 44:23
the man's face **u** our youngest brother Gn 44:26
not let you go **u** compelled by a mighty Ex 3:19
of the holy things **u** he has bathed his Lv 22:6
to flight, **u** their Rock had sold them, Dt 32:30
u you destroy the devoted things from Jos 7:12
u you had hurried and come to meet 1 Sm 25:34
not see my face **u** you first bring 2 Sm 3:13
slacken the pace for me **u** I tell you." 2 Kgs 4:24
u the king delighted in her and she was Est 2:14
U the LORD builds the house, those who Ps 127:1
U the LORD watches over the city, the Ps 127:1
For they cannot sleep **u** they have done Prv 4:16
are robbed of sleep **u** they have made Prv 4:16
to pass, **u** the Lord has commanded it? Lam 3:37
u you have utterly rejected us, and you Lam 5:22
against this Daniel **u** we find it Dn 6:5
together, **u** they have agreed to meet? Am 3:3
come to a city, **u** the LORD has done it? Am 3:6
u your righteousness exceeds that of the Mt 5:20
goods, **u** he first binds the strong man? Mt 12:29
u you turn and become like children, Mt 18:3
Father, if this cannot pass **u** I drink it, Mt 26:42
goods, **u** he first binds the strong man. Mk 3:27
Jews do not eat **u** they wash their hands, Mk 7:3
they do not eat **u** they wash. Mk 7:4
loaves and two fish—**u** we are to go and Lk 9:13
but **u** you repent, you will all likewise Lk 13:3
but **u** you repent, you will all likewise Lk 13:5
signs that you do **u** God is with him." Jn 3:2
u one is born again he cannot see the Jn 3:3
you, **u** one is born of water and the Spirit, Jn 3:5
receive even one thing **u** it is given him Jn 3:27
"**U** you see signs and wonders you will Jn 4:48
can come to me **u** the Father who sent Jn 6:44
u you eat the flesh of the Son of Man and Jn 6:53
one can come to me **u** it is granted him Jn 6:65
for **u** you believe that I am he you will die Jn 8:24
u a grain of wheat falls into the earth Jn 12:24
bear fruit by itself, **u** it abides in the vine, Jn 15:4
vine, neither can you, **u** you abide in me. Jn 15:4
over me at all **u** it had been given Jn 19:11
"**U** I see in his hands the mark of the Jn 20:25
u someone guides me?" And he invited Acts 8:31
"**U** you are circumcised according to Acts 15:1
"**U** these men stay in the ship, Acts 27:31
are they to preach **u** they are sent? Rom 10:15
in tongues, **u** someone interprets, 1 Cor 14:5
will I benefit you **u** I bring you some 1 Cor 14:6
preached to you—**u** you believed in 1 Cor 15:2
sow does not come to life **u** it dies. 1 Cor 15:36
—**u** indeed you fail to meet the test! 2 Cor 13:5
not come, **u** the rebellion comes first, 2 Thes 2:3
is not crowned **u** he competes 2 Tm 2:5
lampstand from its place, **u** you repent. Rv 2:5
tribulation, **u** they repent of her works, Rv 2:22
one can buy or sell **u** he has the mark, Rv 13:17

UNLIFTED (1)
covenant, that same veil remains **u**, 2 Cor 3:14

UNLOAD (1)
for there the ship was to **u** its cargo. Acts 21:3

UNLOVED (6)
two wives, the one loved and the other **u**, Dt 21:15
the loved and the **u** have borne him Dt 21:15
if the firstborn son belongs to the **u**, Dt 21:15
in preference to the son of the **u**, Dt 21:16
the firstborn, the son of the **u**, Dt 21:17
an **u** woman when she gets a Prv 30:23

UNMARKED (1)
For you are like **u** graves, and people Lk 11:44

UNMARRIED (6)
for brother or **u** sister they may defile Ezk 44:25
He had four **u** daughters, who Acts 21:9
To the **u** and the widows I say that it is 1 Cor 7:8
she should remain **u** or else be 1 Cor 7:11
The **u** man is anxious about the 1 Cor 7:32
And the **u** or betrothed woman is 1 Cor 7:34

UNMINDFUL (1)
You were **u** of the Rock that bore you, Dt 32:18

UNMOVED (1)
yet his bow remained **u**; his arms were Gn 49:24

UNNATURAL (1)
immorality and pursued **u** desire, Jude 1:7

UNNI (3)
Shemiramoth, Jehiel, **U**, Eliab, 1 Chr 15:18
Shemiramoth, Jehiel, **U**, Eliab, 1 Chr 15:20
And Bakbukiah and **U** and their Neh 12:9

UNNOTICED (1)
people have crept in **u** who long ago Jude 1:4

UNPRESENTABLE (1)
and our **u** parts are treated with 1 Cor 12:23

UNPROFITABLE (2)
Should he argue in **u** talk, or in words Jb 15:3
the law, for they are **u** and worthless. Ti 3:9

UNPUNISHED (14)
wife; none who touches her will go **u**. Prv 6:29
assured, an evil person will not go **u**, Prv 11:21
to the LORD; be assured, he will not go **u**. Prv 16:5
he who is glad at calamity will not go **u**. Prv 17:5
A false witness will not go **u**, and he Prv 19:5
A false witness will not go **u**, and he Prv 19:9
hastens to be rich will not go **u**. Prv 28:20
by my name, and shall you go **u**? Jer 25:29

You shall not go **u**, for I am Jer 25:29
and I will by no means leave you **u**. Jer 30:11
and I will by no means leave you **u**." Jer 46:28
the cup must drink it, will you go **u**? Jer 49:12
You shall not go **u**, but you must Jer 49:12
buy them slaughter them and go **u**, Zec 11:5

UNQUENCHABLE (3)
but the chaff he will burn with **u** fire." Mt 3:12
two hands to go to hell, to the **u** fire. Mk 9:43
but the chaff he will burn with **u** fire." Lk 3:17

UNREASONABLE (1)
For it seems to me **u**, in sending a Acts 25:27

UNREASONING (1)
by all that they, like **u** animals, Jude 1:10

UNRELENTING (1)
the nations in anger with **u** persecution. Is 14:6

UNREST (1)
but **u** to the inhabitants of Babylon. Jer 50:34

UNRIGHTEOUS (13)
Surely such are the dwellings of the **u**, Jb 18:21
him who rises up against me be as the **u**. Jb 27:7
the fangs of the **u** and made him drop Jb 29:17
Is not calamity for the **u**, and disaster for Jb 31:3
his way, and the **u** man his thoughts; Is 55:7
for yourselves by means of **u** wealth, Lk 16:9
have not been faithful in the **u** wealth, Lk 16:11
Lord said, "Hear what the **u** judge says. Lk 18:6
That God is **u** to inflict wrath on us? Rom 3:5
to law before the **u** instead of the 1 Cor 6:1
not know that the **u** will not inherit 1 Cor 6:9
once for sins, the righteous for the **u**, 1 Pt 3:18
to keep the **u** under punishment until 2 Pt 2:9

UNRIGHTEOUSNESS (13)
he is my rock, and there is no **u** in him. Ps 92:15
to him who builds his house by **u**, Jer 22:13
were created, till **u** was found in you. Ezk 28:15
in the **u** of your trade you profaned Ezk 28:18
against all ungodliness and **u** of men, Rom 1:18
who by their **u** suppress the truth. Rom 1:18
They were filled with all manner of **u**, Rom 1:29
and do not obey the truth, but obey **u**, Rom 2:8
But if our **u** serves to show the Rom 3:5
members to sin as instruments for **u**, Rom 6:13
the truth but had pleasure in **u**. 2 Thes 2:12
And the tongue is a fire, a world of **u**. Jas 3:6
us our sins and to cleanse us from all **u**. 1 Jn 1:9

UNRIPE (1)
will shake off his **u** grape like the vine, Jb 15:33

UNROLLED (1)
He **u** the scroll and found the place Lk 4:17

UNSATISFIED (1)
to leave the craving of the hungry **u**, Is 32:6

UNSAVORY (1)
prophets of Samaria I saw an **u** thing: Jer 23:13

UNSEARCHABLE (7)
who does great things and **u**, marvelous Jb 5:9
him not; the number of his years is **u**. Jb 36:26
to be praised, and his greatness is **u**. Ps 145:3
for depth, so the heart of kings is **u**. Prv 25:3
or grow weary; his understanding is **u**. Is 40:28
How **u** are his judgments and how Rom 11:33
to the Gentiles the **u** riches of Christ, Eph 3:8

UNSEEN (4)
great waters; yet your footprints were **u**. Ps 77:19
are seen but to the things that are **u**. 2 Cor 4:18
but the things that are **u** are eternal. 2 Cor 4:18
by God concerning events as yet **u**, Heb 11:7

UNSETTLE (1)
wish those who **u** you would Gal 5:12

UNSETTLING (1)
you with words, **u** your minds, Acts 15:24

UNSHAKEN (1)
Our hope for you is **u**, for we know 2 Cor 1:7

UNSHEATHE (4)
and I will **u** the sword after you, Lv 26:33
wind, and I will **u** the sword after them. Ezk 5:2
the winds and will **u** the sword after Ezk 5:12
and I will **u** the sword after them. Ezk 12:14

UNSHOD (1)
your feet from going **u** and your throat Jer 2:25

UNSHRUNK (2)
one puts a piece of **u** cloth on an old Mt 9:16
one sews a piece of **u** cloth on an old Mk 2:21

UNSKILLED (2)
Even if I am **u** in speaking, I am not 2 Cor 11:6
who lives on milk is **u** in the word of Heb 5:13

UNSOLD (1)
While it remained **u**, did it not remain Acts 5:4

UNSPARING (1)
I would even exult in pain **u**, for I have Jb 6:10

UNSPIRITUAL (1)
from above, but is earthly, **u**, demonic. Jas 3:15

UNSTABLE (3)
U as water, you shall not have Gn 49:4
a double-minded man, **u** in all his ways. Jas 1:8
which the ignorant and **u** twist to their 2 Pt 3:16

UNSTAINED (3)
keep the commandment **u** and free 1 Tm 6:14
innocent, **u**, separated from sinners, Heb 7:26
and to keep oneself **u** from the world. Jas 1:27

UNSTEADY (1)
insatiable for sin. They entice **u** souls. 2 Pt 2:14

UNSTOPPED (1)
shall be opened, and the ears of the deaf **u**; Is 35:5

UNSUSPECTING (4)
manner of the Sidonians, quiet and **u**, Jgs 18:7
as you go, you will come to an **u** people. Jgs 18:10
came to Laish, to a people quiet and **u**, Jgs 18:27
in ships to terrify the **u** people of Cush, Ezk 30:9

UNTIE (8)
with her. **U** them and bring them to me. Mt 21:2
I am not worthy to stoop down and **u**. Mk 1:7
no one has ever sat. **U** it and bring it. Mk 11:2
of whose sandals I am not worthy to **u**. Lk 3:16
of you on the Sabbath **u** his ox or his Lk 13:15
has ever yet sat. **U** it and bring it here. Lk 19:30
of whose sandal I am not worthy to **u**." Jn 1:27
of whose feet I am not worthy to **u**.' Acts 13:25

UNTIED (1)
door outside in the street, and they **u** it. Mk 11:4

UNTIL (464)
continued to abate **u** the tenth month; Gn 8:5
It went to and fro **u** the waters were dried Gn 8:7
me, and I have not heard of it **u** today." Gn 21:26
also, **u** they have finished drinking." Gn 24:19
"I will not eat **u** I have said what I have Gn 24:33
more and more **u** he became very Gn 26:13
u your brother's fury turns away— Gn 27:44
u your brother's anger turns away Gn 27:45
I will not leave you **u** I have done what Gn 28:15
"We cannot **u** all the flocks are Gn 29:8
with Laban and stayed **u** now. Gn 32:4
wrestled with him **u** the breaking of Gn 32:24
times, **u** he came near to his brother. Gn 33:3
children, **u** I come to my lord in Seir." Gn 33:14
so Jacob held his peace **u** they came. Gn 34:5
you give me a pledge, **u** you send it—" Gn 38:17
his garment by her **u** his master came Gn 39:16
of the sea, **u** he ceased to measure it, Gn 41:49
livestock from our youth even **u** now, Gn 46:34
his feet, **u** tribute comes to him; Gn 49:10
from the day it was founded **u** now. Ex 9:18
must serve the LORD **u** we arrive there." Ex 10:26
you shall keep it **u** the fourteenth day of Ex 12:6
let none of it remain **u** the morning; Ex 12:10
anything that remains **u** the morning Ex 12:10
from the first day **u** the seventh day, Ex 12:15
eat unleavened bread **u** the twenty-first Ex 12:18
of the door of his house **u** the morning. Ex 12:22
his hands were steady **u** the going down Ex 17:12
fat of my feast remain **u** the morning. Ex 23:18
u you have increased and possess the Ex 23:30
"Wait here for us **u** we return to you. Ex 24:14
or of the bread remain **u** the morning, Ex 29:34
and watch Moses **u** he had gone into the Ex 33:8
you with my hand **u** I have passed by. Ex 33:22
of the Passover remain **u** the morning. Ex 34:25
would remove the veil, **u** he came out. Ex 34:34
again, **u** he went in to speak with him. Ex 34:35
on the altar all night **u** the morning, Lv 6:9
shall not leave any of it **u** the morning. Lv 7:15
u the days of your ordination are Lv 8:33
carcass shall be unclean **u** the evening, Lv 11:24
clothes and be unclean **u** the evening. Lv 11:25
carcass shall be unclean **u** the evening, Lv 11:27
clothes and be unclean **u** the evening; Lv 11:28
dead shall be unclean **u** the evening. Lv 11:31
and it shall be unclean **u** the evening; Lv 11:32
carcass shall be unclean **u** the evening, Lv 11:39
clothes and be unclean **u** the evening. Lv 11:40
clothes and be unclean **u** the evening. Lv 11:40
u the days of her purifying are Lv 12:4
shut up shall be unclean **u** the evening, Lv 14:46
in water and be unclean **u** the evening. Lv 15:5
in water and be unclean **u** the evening. Lv 15:6
in water and be unclean **u** the evening. Lv 15:7
in water and be unclean **u** the evening. Lv 15:8
him shall be unclean **u** the evening. Lv 15:10
in water and be unclean **u** the evening. Lv 15:10
in water and be unclean **u** the evening. Lv 15:11
in water and be unclean **u** the evening. Lv 15:16
water and be unclean **u** the evening. Lv 15:17
in water and be unclean **u** the evening. Lv 15:18
her shall be unclean **u** the evening. Lv 15:19
in water and be unclean **u** the evening. Lv 15:21
in water and be unclean **u** the evening. Lv 15:22
it he shall be unclean **u** the evening. Lv 15:23
in water and be unclean **u** the evening. Lv 15:27
in the Holy Place **u** he comes out and Lv 16:17
in water and be unclean **u** the evening; Lv 17:15
and anything left over **u** the third day Lv 19:6
with you all night **u** the morning. Lv 19:13
may eat of the holy things **u** he is clean. Lv 22:4
shall be unclean **u** the evening and Lv 22:6
you shall leave none of it **u** morning: Lv 22:30
grain parched or fresh **u** this same day, Lv 23:14
u you have brought the offering of Lv 23:14
you shall eat the old **u** the ninth year, Lv 25:22
hand of the buyer **u** the year of jubilee. Lv 25:28
He shall serve with you **u** the year of the Lv 25:40
sold himself to him **u** the year of Lv 25:50
but a few years **u** the year of jubilee, Lv 25:52
the years that remain **u** the year of Lv 27:18
U the time is completed for which he Nm 6:5
shall leave none of it **u** the morning, Nm 9:12
like the appearance of fire **u** morning. Nm 9:15
remained from evening **u** morning. Nm 9:21
u it comes out at your nostrils and Nm 11:20
this people, from Egypt **u** now." Nm 14:19
u the last of your dead bodies lies in Nm 14:33
the priest shall be unclean **u** evening. Nm 19:7
water and shall be unclean **u** evening. Nm 19:8
his clothes and be unclean **u** evening. Nm 19:10
impurity shall be unclean **u** evening. Nm 19:21
it shall be unclean **u** evening." Nm 19:22
or to the left **u** we have passed through Nm 20:17
the King's Highway **u** we have passed Nm 21:22
his people, **u** he had no survivor left. Nm 21:35
does not lie down **u** it has devoured Nm 23:24
u all the generation that had done evil Nm 32:13
u we have brought them to their Nm 32:17
return to our homes **u** each of the Nm 32:18
u he has driven out his enemies from Nm 32:21
may not die **u** he stands before Nm 35:12
he shall live in it **u** the death of the Nm 35:25
in his city of refuge **u** the death of the Nm 35:28
the way that you went **u** you came to this Dt 1:31
our leaving Kadesh-barnea **u** we crossed Dt 2:14
years, **u** the entire generation, Dt 2:14
from the camp, **u** they had perished. Dt 2:15
u I go over the Jordan into the land that Dt 2:29
we struck him down **u** he had no survivor Dt 3:3
u the LORD gives rest to your brothers, as Dt 3:20
u those who are left and hide themselves Dt 7:20
great confusion, **u** they are destroyed. Dt 7:23
stand against you **u** you have destroyed Dt 7:24
of the land of Egypt **u** you came to this Dt 9:7
it very small, **u** it was as fine as dust. Dt 9:21
the wilderness, **u** you came to this place, Dt 11:5
the first day remain all night **u** morning. Dt 16:4
city that makes war with you, **u** it falls. Dt 20:20
shall stay with you **u** your brother seeks Dt 22:2
u you are destroyed and perish quickly Dt 28:20
stick to you **u** he has consumed Dt 28:21
They shall pursue you **u** you perish. Dt 28:22
come down on you **u** you are destroyed. Dt 28:24
iron on your neck **u** he has destroyed Dt 28:48
of your ground, **u** you are destroyed; Dt 28:51
flock, **u** they have caused you to perish. Dt 28:51
towns, **u** your high and fortified walls, Dt 28:52
bring upon you, **u** you are destroyed. Dt 28:61
words of this song **u** they were finished, Dt 31:30
u the LORD gives rest to your brothers as Jos 1:15
there three days **u** the pursuers have Jos 2:16
there three days **u** the pursuers returned, Jos 2:22
over on dry ground **u** all the nation Jos 3:17
of the Jordan **u** everything was finished Jos 4:10
of the Jordan for you **u** you passed over, Jos 4:23
he dried up for us **u** we passed over, Jos 4:23
the people of Israel **u** they had crossed Jos 5:1
years in the wilderness, **u** all the nation, Jos 5:6
places in the camp **u** they were healed. Jos 5:8
mouth, **u** the day I tell you to shout. Jos 6:10
before the ark of the LORD **u** the evening, Jos 7:6
before your enemies **u** you take away Jos 7:13
u we have drawn them away from the Jos 8:6
u there was left none that survived or Jos 8:22
out the javelin **u** he had devoted Jos 8:26
the king of Ai on a tree **u** evening. Jos 8:29
u the nation took vengeance on their Jos 10:13
with a great blow **u** they were wiped Jos 10:20
And they hung on the trees **u** evening. Jos 10:26

his people, **u** he left none remaining. Jos 10:33
And they struck them **u** he left none Jos 11:8
edge of the sword **u** they had destroyed Jos 11:14
remain in that city **u** he has stood before Jos 20:6
u the death of him who is high priest at Jos 20:6
u you perish from off this good ground Jos 23:13
u he has destroyed you from off this Jos 23:15
peg into his temple **u** it went down into Jgs 4:21
u they destroyed Jabin king of Canaan. Jgs 4:24
in Israel; they ceased to be **u** I arose; Jgs 5:7
do not depart from here **u** I come to you Jgs 6:18
"**U** now you have mocked me and told Jgs 16:13
for **u** then no inheritance among the Jgs 18:1
the tribe of the Danites **u** the day of the Jgs 18:30
your heart and wait **u** the day declines." Jgs 19:8
abused her all night **u** the morning. Jgs 19:25
where her master was, **u** it was light. Jgs 19:26
up out of the land of Egypt **u** this day; Jgs 19:30
and wept before the LORD **u** the evening. Jgs 20:23
the LORD and fasted that day **u** evening, Jgs 20:26
of them went on **u** they came to Ru 1:19
continued from early morning **u** now, Ru 2:7
grain. And she ate **u** she was satisfied, Ru 2:14
So she gleaned in the field **u** evening. Ru 2:17
by my young men **u** they have finished Ru 2:21
gleaning **u** the end of the barley and Ru 2:23
known to the man **u** he has finished Ru 3:3
redeem you. Lie down **u** the morning." Ru 3:13
So she lay at his feet **u** the morning, but Ru 3:14
u you learn how the matter turns out, Ru 3:18
to you; wait **u** you have weaned him; 1 Sm 1:23
nursed her son **u** she weaned him. 1 Sm 1:23
Samuel lay **u** morning; then he 1 Sm 3:15
kept for you **u** the hour appointed, 1 Sm 9:24
u I come to you and show you what 1 Sm 10:8
down the Ammonites **u** the heat of 1 Sm 11:11
before you from my youth **u** this day. 1 Sm 12:2
say to us, 'Wait **u** we come to you,' 1 Sm 14:9
man who eats food **u** it is evening 1 Sm 14:24
and plunder them **u** the morning 1 Sm 14:36
fight against them **u** they are 1 Sm 15:18
not see Saul again **u** the day of his 1 Sm 15:35
he went he prophesied **u** he came to 1 Sm 19:23
nothing at all **u** the morning light. 1 Sm 25:36
the day I entered your service **u** now, 1 Sm 29:8
their voices and wept **u** they had no 1 Sm 30:4
down from twilight **u** the evening of 1 Sm 30:17
wept and fasted **u** evening for Saul 2 Sm 1:12
of their brothers **u** the morning." 2 Sm 2:27
"Remain at Jericho **u** your beards 2 Sm 10:5
Absalom pressed him **u** he let 2 Sm 13:27
the ark of God **u** the people had all 2 Sm 15:24
of the wilderness **u** word comes from 2 Sm 15:28
u not even a pebble is to be found 2 Sm 17:13
upon you from your youth **u** now." 2 Sm 19:7
day the king departed **u** the day he 2 Sm 19:24
So they were shut up **u** the day of their 2 Sm 20:3
beginning of harvest **u** rain fell 2 Sm 21:10
not turn back **u** they were 2 Sm 22:38
down the Philistines **u** his hand was 2 Sm 23:10
from the morning **u** the appointed 2 Sm 24:15
the city of David **u** he had finished 1 Kgs 3:1
u the LORD put them under the soles of 1 Kgs 5:3
gold, **u** all the house was finished. 1 Kgs 6:22
not believe the reports **u** I came and 1 Kgs 10:7
u he had cut off every male in 1 Kgs 11:16
and was in Egypt **u** the death of 1 Kgs 11:40
man burns up dung **u** it is all gone. 1 Kgs 14:10
that breathed, **u** he had destroyed it, 1 Kgs 15:29
u the day that the LORD sends rain 1 Kgs 17:14
of Baal from morning **u** noon, 1 Kgs 18:26
u the blood gushed out upon them. 1 Kgs 18:28
they raved on **u** the time of the 1 Kgs 18:29
push the Syrians **u** they are 1 Kgs 22:11
and water, **u** I come in peace."'" 1 Kgs 22:27
the Syrians, **u** at evening he died. 1 Kgs 22:35
man threw a stone **u** it was covered. 2 Kgs 3:25
u a donkey's head was sold for eighty 2 Kgs 6:25
"Why are we sitting here **u** we die? 2 Kgs 7:3
silent and wait **u** the morning light, 2 Kgs 7:9
the day that she left the land **u** now." 2 Kgs 8:6
stared at him, **u** he was embarrassed. 2 Kgs 8:11
entrance of the gate **u** the morning." 2 Kgs 10:8
u he left him none remaining. 2 Kgs 10:11
Syrians in Aphek **u** you have made 2 Kgs 13:17
struck down Syria **u** you had made 2 Kgs 13:19
cast them from his presence **u** now. 2 Kgs 13:23
u he had cast them out of his sight. 2 Kgs 17:20
u the LORD removed Israel out of his 2 Kgs 17:23
their own land to Assyria **u** this day. 2 Kgs 17:23
for **u** those days the people of Israel 2 Kgs 18:4
u I come and take you away to a 2 Kgs 18:32
were their cities **u** David reigned. 1 Chr 4:31
they lived in their place **u** the exile. 1 Chr 5:22
tent of meeting **u** Solomon built the 1 Chr 6:32
u then they were in the king's gate on 1 Chr 9:18
help him, **u** there was a great army, 1 Chr 12:22
"Remain at Jericho **u** your beards 1 Chr 19:5
u all the work for the service of the 1 Chr 28:20
of the LORD was laid **u** it was finished. 2 Chr 8:16
not believe the reports **u** I came and 2 Chr 9:6
the Ethiopians fell **u** none remained 2 Chr 14:13
no more war **u** the thirty-fifth year 2 Chr 15:19
push the Syrians **u** they are 2 Chr 18:10
of bread and water **u** I return in 2 Chr 18:26
facing the Syrians **u** evening. 2 Chr 18:34
took for themselves **u** they could 2 Chr 20:25
u your bowels come out because of 2 Chr 21:15
it into the chest **u** they had finished. 2 Chr 24:10
All this continued **u** the burnt 2 Chr 29:28
so **u** other priests had consecrated 2 Chr 29:34
u the work was finished—for the 2 Chr 29:34
u they had destroyed them all. 2 Chr 31:1
offerings and the fat parts **u** night; 2 Chr 35:14
u the wrath of the LORD rose against 2 Chr 36:16
his people, **u** there was no remedy. 2 Chr 36:16
to his sons **u** the establishment of 2 Chr 36:20
u the land had enjoyed its Sabbaths. 2 Chr 36:21
u there should be a priest to consult Ezr 2:63
even **u** the reign of Darius king of Persia. Ezr 4:5
be not rebuilt, **u** a decree is made by me. Ezr 4:21
and it ceased **u** the second year of the Ezr 4:24
did not stop them **u** the report should Ezr 5:5
and from that time **u** now it has been in Ezr 5:16
them and keep them **u** you weigh them Ezr 8:29
I sat appalled **u** the evening sacrifice. Ezr 9:4
be angry with us **u** you consumed us, Ezr 9:14
u the fierce wrath of our God over this Ezr 10:14
let me pass through **u** I come to Judah, Neh 2:7
the break of dawn **u** the stars came Neh 4:21
of Jerusalem be opened **u** the sun is hot. Neh 7:3
the most holy food **u** a priest with Neh 7:65
Gate from early morning **u** midday, Neh 8:3
time of the kings of Assyria **u** this day. Neh 9:32
Book of the Chronicles **u** the days of Neh 12:23
not be opened **u** after the Sabbath. Neh 13:19
you would conceal me **u** your wrath be Jb 14:13
u I proclaim your might to another Ps 71:18
For they have no pangs **u** death; their Ps 73:4
u I went into the sanctuary of God; then Ps 73:17
of trouble, **u** a pit is dug for the wicked. Ps 94:13
work and to his labor **u** the evening. Ps 104:23
u what he had said came to pass, the Ps 105:19
u I make your enemies your footstool." Ps 110:1
u he looks in triumph on his Ps 112:8
u I find a place for the LORD, a dwelling Ps 132:5
shines brighter and brighter **u** full day. Prv 4:18
u the other comes and examines him. Prv 18:17
another, he will be a fugitive **u** death; Prv 28:17
you not stir up or awaken love **u** it pleases. Sg 2:7
U the day breathes and the shadows flee, Sg 2:17
would not let him go **u** I had brought him Sg 3:4
you not stir up or awaken love **u** it pleases. Sg 3:5
U the day breathes and the shadows flee, I Sg 4:6
you not stir up or awaken love **u** it pleases. Sg 8:4
add field to field, **u** there is no more room, Is 5:8
"**U** cities lie waste without inhabitant, Is 6:11
be atoned for you **u** you die," says the Is 22:14
for a little while **u** the fury has passed Is 26:20
a very little while **u** Lebanon shall be Is 29:17
u the Spirit is poured upon us from on Is 32:15
u I come and take you away to a land Is 36:17
I calmed myself **u** morning; like a lion Is 38:13
u her righteousness goes forth as Is 62:1
him no rest **u** he establishes Jerusalem Is 62:7
and **u** the end of the eleventh year of Jer 1:3
u the captivity of Jerusalem in the fifth Jer 1:3
after them, **u** I have consumed them." Jer 9:16
will not turn back **u** he has executed Jer 23:20
u they shall be utterly destroyed from Jer 24:10
u the time of his own land comes. Jer 27:7
LORD, **u** I have consumed it by his hand. Jer 27:8
and remain there **u** the day when Jer 27:22
will not turn back **u** he has executed Jer 30:24
and there he shall remain **u** I visit him, Jer 32:5
to you, from the days of Josiah **u** today. Jer 36:2
u the entire scroll was consumed in the Jer 36:23
u all the bread of the city was gone. Jer 37:21
court of the guard **u** the day that Jer 38:28
by famine, **u** there is an end of them. Jer 44:27
after them, **u** I have consumed them, Jer 49:37
u the day of his death as long as he Jer 52:34
u the LORD from heaven looks down Lam 3:50
This also shall not be, **u** he comes, the Ezk 21:27
the gate shall not be shut **u** evening. Ezk 46:2
And Daniel was there **u** the first year of Dn 1:21
u you know that the Most High rules Dn 4:32
u he knew that the Most High God rules Dn 5:21
u the Ancient of Days came, and Dn 7:22
u the decreed end is poured out on the Dn 9:27
and made white, **u** the time of the end, Dn 11:35
and seal the book, **u** the time of the end. Dn 12:4
are shut up and sealed **u** the time of the Dn 12:9
u they acknowledge their guilt and Hos 5:15
kneading of the dough **u** it is leavened. Hos 7:4
"Strike the capitals **u** the thresholds Am 9:1
shall give them up **u** the time when she Mi 5:3
u he pleads my cause and executes Mi 7:9
I will destroy you **u** no inhabitant is left. Zep 2:5
for you a blessing **u** there is no more Mal 3:10
but knew her not **u** she had given birth Mt 1:25
it rose went before them **u** it came to rest Mt 2:9
to Egypt, and remain there **u** I tell you, Mt 2:13
and remained there **u** the death of Herod. Mt 2:15
to you, **u** heaven and earth pass away, Mt 5:18
from the Law **u** all is accomplished. Mt 5:18
will never get out **u** you have paid the Mt 5:26
in it and stay there **u** you depart. Mt 10:11
of John the Baptist **u** now the kingdom Mt 11:12
and the Law prophesied **u** John, Mt 11:13
it would have remained **u** this day. Mt 11:23
quench, **u** he brings justice to victory; Mt 12:20
Let both grow together **u** the harvest, Mt 13:30
will not taste death **u** they see the Son Mt 16:28
u the Son of Man is raised from the Mt 17:9
put him in prison **u** he should pay the Mt 18:30
the jailers, **u** he should pay all his debt. Mt 18:34
u I put your enemies under your feet'? Mt 22:44
you will not see me again, **u** you say, Mt 23:39
from the beginning of the world **u** now, Mt 24:21
will not pass away **u** all these things Mt 24:34
u the day when Noah entered the ark, Mt 24:38
they were unaware **u** the flood came Mt 24:39
this fruit of the vine **u** that day when I Mt 26:29
over all the land **u** the ninth hour. Mt 27:45
to be made secure **u** the third day, Mt 27:64
stay there **u** you depart from there. Mk 6:10
will not taste death **u** they see the Mk 9:1
u the Son of Man had risen from the Mk 9:9
u I put your enemies under your feet.' Mk 12:36
of the creation that God created **u** now, Mk 13:19
will not pass away **u** all these things Mk 13:30
the fruit of the vine **u** that day when I Mk 14:25
over the whole land **u** the ninth hour. Mk 15:33
and unable to speak **u** the day that these Lk 1:20
he was in the wilderness **u** the day of his Lk 1:80
then as a widow **u** she was eighty-four. Lk 2:37
departed from him **u** an opportune time. Lk 4:13
will not taste death **u** they see the Lk 9:27
is my distress **u** it is accomplished! Lk 12:50
will never get out **u** you have paid the Lk 12:59
u I dig around it and put on manure. Lk 13:8
of flour, **u** it was all leavened." Lk 13:21
I tell you, you will not see me **u** you say, Lk 13:35
go after the one that is lost, **u** he finds it? Lk 15:4
house and seek diligently **u** she finds it? Lk 15:8
Law and the Prophets were **u** John; Lk 16:16
u the day when Noah entered the ark, Lk 17:27
to them, 'Engage in business **u** I come.' Lk 19:13
u I make your enemies your footstool.' Lk 20:43
u the times of the Gentiles are fulfilled. Lk 21:24
will not pass away **u** all has taken Lk 21:32
you I will not eat it **u** it is fulfilled in the Lk 22:16
fruit of the vine **u** the kingdom of God Lk 22:18
u you deny three times that you know Lk 22:34
over the whole land **u** the ninth hour, Lk 23:44
stay in the city **u** you are clothed with Lk 24:49
But you have kept the good wine **u** now." Jn 2:10
them, "My Father is working **u** now, Jn 5:17
u they called the parents of the man who Jn 9:18
U now you have asked nothing in my Jn 16:24
"If it is my will that he remain **u** I come, Jn 21:22
"If it is my will that he remain **u** I come, Jn 21:23
u the day when he was taken up, after Acts 1:2
the baptism of John **u** the day when he Acts 1:22
u I make your enemies your footstool.' Acts 2:35
heaven must receive **u** the time for Acts 3:21
and put them in custody **u** the next day, Acts 4:3
u there arose over Egypt another king Acts 7:18
fathers. So it was **u** the days of David, Acts 7:45
to all the towns **u** he came to Caesarea. Acts 8:40
gave them judges **u** Samuel the Acts 13:20
he prolonged his speech **u** midnight. Acts 20:7
with them a long while, **u** daybreak, Acts 20:11
accompanied us **u** we were outside the Acts 21:5
him to be held **u** I could send him Acts 25:21
in the pains of childbirth **u** now. Rom 8:22
u the fullness of the Gentiles has Rom 11:25
the Lord's death **u** he comes. 1 Cor 11:26
For he must reign **u** he has put all 1 Cor 15:25
I will stay in Ephesus **u** Pentecost, 1 Cor 16:8
u the offspring should come to whom Gal 3:19
imprisoned **u** the coming faith would Gal 3:23
law was our guardian **u** Christ came, Gal 3:24
guardians and managers **u** the date set Gal 4:2

anguish of childbirth **u** Christ is Gal 4:19
of our inheritance **u** we acquire Eph 1:14
u we all attain to the unity of the faith Eph 4:13
in the gospel from the first day **u** now. Phil 1:5
who are left **u** the coming of the 1 Thes 4:15
restrains it will do so **u** he is out of the 2 Thes 2:7
U I come, devote yourself to the 1 Tm 4:13
free from reproach **u** the appearing of 1 Tm 6:14
is able to guard **u** that Day what has 2 Tm 1:12
at my right hand **u** I make your Heb 1:13
the full assurance of hope **u** the end, Heb 6:11
for the body imposed **u** the time of Heb 9:10
from that time **u** his enemies should Heb 10:13
brothers, **u** the coming of the Lord. Jas 5:7
it, **u** it receives the early and the late rains. Jas 5:7
u the day dawns and the morning star 2 Pt 1:19
darkness to be kept **u** the judgment; 2 Pt 2:4
under punishment **u** the day 2 Pt 2:9
being kept **u** the day of judgment and 2 Pt 3:7
under gloomy darkness **u** the judgment Jude 1:6
Only hold fast what you have **u** I come. Rv 2:25
and who keeps my works **u** the end, Rv 2:26
u the number of their fellow servants Rv 6:11
u we have sealed the servants of our God Rv 7:3
enter the sanctuary **u** the seven plagues Rv 15:8
beast, **u** the words of God are fulfilled. Rv 17:17
longer, **u** the thousand years were ended. Rv 20:3
not come to life **u** the thousand years Rv 20:5

UNTIMELY (1)
Last of all, as to one **u** born, he 1 Cor 15:8

UNTO (3)
For **u** you is born this day in the city of Lk 2:11
Be faithful **u** death, and I will give you Rv 2:10
they loved not their lives even **u** death. Rv 12:11

UNTRAINED (1)
and I was disciplined, like an **u** calf; Jer 31:18

UNTROUBLED (1)
eyes will see Jerusalem, an **u** habitation, Is 33:20

UNTYING (4)
them, "What are you doing, **u** the colt?" Mk 11:5
If anyone asks you, 'Why are you **u** it?' Lk 19:31
And as they were **u** the colt, its owners Lk 19:33
said to them, "Why are you **u** the colt?" Lk 19:33

UNUSUAL (1)
native people showed us **u** kindness, Acts 28:2

UNVEILED (1)
And we all, with **u** face, beholding the 2 Cor 3:18

UNWALLED (3)
and bars, besides very many **u** villages. Dt 3:5
both fortified cities and **u** villages. 1 Sm 6:18
go up against the land of **u** villages. Ezk 38:11

UNWASHED (2)
But to eat with **u** hands does not defile Mt 15:20
with hands that were defiled, that is, **u**. Mk 7:2

UNWEIGHED (1)
And Solomon left all the vessels **u**, 1 Kgs 7:47

UNWELL (1)
for her who is **u** with her menstrual Lv 15:33

UNWILLING (6)
also. The LORD was **u** to destroy you. Dt 10:10
and he was **u** to take one of his own 2 Sm 12:4
children **u** to hear the instruction of the Is 30:9
shall be your strength." But you were **u**, Is 30:15
being a just man and **u** to put her to Mt 1:19
And I am **u** to send them away hungry, Mt 15:32

UNWISE (2)
come for him, but he is an **u** son, Hos 13:13
how you walk, not as **u** but as wise, Eph 5:15

UNWORTHY (5)
lest there be an **u** thought in your heart Dt 15:9
commanded, say, 'We are **u** servants; Lk 17:10
and judge yourselves **u** of eternal life, Acts 13:46
the Lord in an **u** manner will be 1 Cor 11:27
the apostles, **u** to be called an apostle, 1 Cor 15:9

UNYIELDING (1)
offended is more **u** than a strong Prv 18:19

UPBUILDING (3)
makes for peace and for mutual **u**. Rom 14:19
people for their **u** and encouragement 1 Cor 14:3
in Christ, and all for your **u**, 2 Cor 12:19

UPHAZ (2)
from Tarshish, and gold from **U**. Jer 10:9
of fine gold from **U** around his waist. Dn 10:5

UPHELD (6)
Your words have **u** him who was Jb 4:4
But you have **u** me because of my Ps 41:12
and by steadfast love his throne is **u**. Prv 20:28
salvation, and his righteousness **u** him. Is 59:16
me salvation, and my wrath **u** me. Is 63:5
And he will be **u**, for the Lord is able to Rom 14:4

UPHOLD (10)
to **u** me as holy in the eyes of the Nm 20:12
failing to **u** me as holy at the waters Nm 27:14
and **u** me with a willing spirit. Ps 51:12
U me according to your promise, Ps 119:116
to establish it and to **u** it with justice and Is 9:7
I will **u** you with my righteous right Is 41:10
Behold my servant, whom I **u**, my Is 42:1
I was appalled, but there was no one to **u**; Is 63:5
There is none to **u** your cause, no Jer 30:13
means! On the contrary, we **u** the law. Rom 3:31

UPHOLDER (1)
is my helper; the Lord is the **u** of my life. Ps 54:4

UPHOLDS (6)
broken, but the LORD **u** the righteous. Ps 37:17
cast headlong, for the LORD **u** his hand. Ps 37:24
soul clings to you; your right hand **u** me. Ps 63:8
The LORD **u** all who are falling and Ps 145:14
he **u** the widow and the fatherless, but Ps 146:9
and he **u** the universe by the word of his Heb 1:3

UPLIFTED (3)
is withheld, and their **u** arm is broken. Jb 38:15
mountains, and against all the **u** hills; Is 2:14
and with **u** arm he led them out of it. Acts 13:17

UPPER (41)
and he shall cover his **u** lip and cry out, Lv 13:45
take a mill or an **u** millstone in pledge, Dt 24:6
he gave her the **u** springs and the lower Jos 15:19
Ataroth-addar as far as **U** Beth-horon, Jos 16:5
Caleb gave her the **u** springs and the Jgs 1:15
woman threw an **u** millstone on Jgs 9:53
woman cast an **u** millstone on him 2 Sm 11:21
up into the **u** chamber where he 1 Kgs 17:19
down from the **u** chamber into the 1 Kgs 17:23
lattice in his **u** chamber in Samaria, 2 Kgs 1:2
He built the **u** gate of the house of 2 Kgs 15:35
stood by the conduit of the **u** pool, 2 Kgs 18:17
the roof of the **u** chamber of Ahaz, 2 Kgs 23:12
built both Lower and **U** Beth-horon, 1 Chr 7:24
houses, its treasuries, its **u** rooms, 1 Chr 28:11
he overlaid the **u** chambers with gold. 2 Chr 3:9
He also built **U** Beth-horon and Lower 2 Chr 8:5
marching through the **u** gate to the 2 Chr 23:20
He built the **u** gate of the house of the 2 Chr 27:3
Hezekiah closed the **u** outlet of the 2 Chr 32:30
buried him in the **u** part of the 2 Chr 32:33
projecting from the **u** house of the Neh 3:25
and to the **u** chamber of the corner. Neh 3:31
And between the **u** chamber of the Neh 3:32
of the conduit of the **u** pool on the highway Is 7:3
the conduit of the **u** pool on the highway Is 36:2
that were in the **u** Benjamin Gate of the Jer 20:2
and his **u** rooms by injustice, Jer 22:13
a great house with spacious **u** rooms,' Jer 22:14
the secretary, which was in the **u** court, Jer 36:10
came from the direction of the **u** gate, Ezk 9:2
Now the **u** chambers were narrower, Ezk 42:5
Thus the **u** chambers were set back Ezk 42:6
windows in his **u** chamber open toward Dn 6:10
who builds his **u** chambers in the Am 9:6
you a large **u** room furnished and Mk 14:15
show you a large **u** room furnished; Lk 22:12
entered, they went up to the **u** room, Acts 1:13
her, they laid her in an **u** room. Acts 9:37
arrived, they took him to the **u** room. Acts 9:39
many lamps in the **u** room where we Acts 20:8

UPPERMOST (1)
and in the **u** basket there were all sorts Gn 40:17

UPRIGHT (67)
and behold, my sheaf arose and stood **u**. Gn 37:7
"You shall make **u** frames for the Ex 26:15
Then he made the **u** frames for the Ex 36:20
Let me die the death of the **u**, and let Nm 23:10
and without iniquity, just and **u** is he. Dt 32:4
and may the LORD be with the **u**!" 2 Chr 19:11
Levites were more **u** in heart than 2 Chr 29:34
Job, and that man was blameless and **u**, Jb 1:1
him on the earth, a blameless and **u** man, Jb 1:8
him on the earth, a blameless and **u** man, Jb 2:3
ever perished? Or where were the **u** cut off? Jb 4:7
How forceful are **u** words! But what does Jb 6:25
if you are pure and **u**, surely then he will Jb 8:6
The **u** are appalled at this, and the Jb 17:8
There an **u** man could argue with him, Jb 23:7
is with God, who saves the **u** in heart. Ps 7:10
to shoot in the dark at the **u** in heart; Ps 11:2
deeds; the **u** shall behold his face. Ps 11:7
collapse and fall, but we rise and stand **u**. Ps 20:8
Good and **u** is the LORD; therefore he Ps 25:8
and shout for joy, all you **u** in heart! Ps 32:11
O you righteous! Praise befits the **u**. Ps 33:1
For the word of the LORD is **u**, and all his Ps 33:4
your righteousness to the **u** of heart! Ps 36:10
and needy, to slay those whose way is **u**; Ps 37:14
Mark the blameless and behold the **u**, Ps 37:37
and the **u** shall rule over them in the Ps 49:14
in him! Let all the **u** in heart exult! Ps 64:10
With **u** heart he shepherded them and Ps 78:72
to declare that the LORD is **u**; he is my Ps 92:15
and all the **u** in heart will follow it. Ps 94:15
the righteous, and joy for the **u** in heart. Ps 97:11
The **u** see it and are glad, and all Ps 107:42
whole heart, in the company of the **u**, Ps 111:1
the generation of the **u** will be blessed. Ps 112:2
Light dawns in the darkness for the **u**; Ps 112:4
I will praise you with an **u** heart, when I Ps 119:7
and to those who are **u** in their hearts! Ps 125:4
the **u** shall dwell in your presence. Ps 140:13
he stores up sound wisdom for the **u**; he Prv 2:7
For the **u** will inhabit the land, and Prv 2:21
LORD, but the **u** are in his confidence. Prv 3:32
The integrity of the **u** guides them, but Prv 11:3
righteousness of the **u** delivers them, Prv 11:6
the blessing of the **u** a city is exalted, Prv 11:11
but the mouth of the **u** delivers them. Prv 12:6
offering, but the **u** enjoy acceptance. Prv 14:9
but the tent of the **u** will flourish. Prv 14:11
the prayer of the **u** is acceptable to him. Prv 15:8
the path of the **u** is a level highway. Prv 15:19
The highway of the **u** turns aside from Prv 16:17
by whether his conduct is pure and **u**. Prv 20:11
but the conduct of the pure is **u**. Prv 21:8
the righteous, and the traitor for the **u**. Prv 21:18
but the **u** gives thought to his ways. Prv 21:29
Whoever misleads the **u** into an evil Prv 28:10
is blameless and seek the life of the **u**. Prv 29:10
alone I found, that God made man **u**, Eccl 7:29
words that I speak to you, and stand **u**, Dn 10:11
LORD are right, and the **u** walk in them, Hos 14:9
and there is no one **u** among mankind; Mi 7:2
a brier, the most **u** of them a thorn hedge. Mi 7:4
it is not **u** within him, but the righteous Hab 2:4
an **u** and God-fearing man, Acts 10:22
"Stand **u** on your feet." And he sprang Acts 14:10
a lover of good, self-controlled, **u**, holy, Ti 1:8
u, and godly lives in the present age, Ti 2:12

UPRIGHTLY (5)
Do you judge the children of man **u**? Ps 58:1
he withhold from those who walk **u**. Ps 84:11
and **u** he wrote words of truth. Eccl 12:10
He who walks righteously and speaks **u**, Is 33:15
my words do good to him who walks **u**? Mi 2:7

UPRIGHTNESS (19)
your righteousness or the **u** of your heart Dt 9:5
and in **u** of heart toward you. 1 Kgs 3:6
walked, with integrity of heart and **u**, 1 Kgs 9:4
the heart and have pleasure in **u**. 1 Chr 29:17
In the **u** of my heart I have freely 1 Chr 29:17
My words declare the **u** of my heart, and Jb 33:3
he judges the peoples with **u**. Ps 9:8
May integrity and **u** preserve me, for I Ps 25:21
scepter of your kingdom is a scepter of **u**; Ps 45:6
be performed with faithfulness and **u**. Ps 111:8
forsake the paths of **u** to walk in the Prv 2:13
wisdom; I have led you in the paths of **u**. Prv 4:11
Whoever walks in **u** fears the LORD, but Prv 14:2
nor to strike the noble for their **u**. Prv 17:26
in the land of **u** he deals corruptly and Is 26:10
rest in their beds who walk in their **u**. Is 57:2
the public squares, and **u** cannot enter. Is 59:14
He walked with me in peace and **u**, and Mal 2:6
the scepter of **u** is the scepter of your Heb 1:8

UPROAR (13)
"What is this **u**?" Then the man 1 Sm 4:14
"What does this **u** in the city mean?" 1 Kgs 1:41
rejoicing, so that the city is in an **u**. 1 Kgs 1:45
foes, the **u** of those who rise against you, Ps 74:23
For behold, your enemies make an **u**; Ps 83:2
The sound of an **u** of kingdoms, of Is 13:4
"The sound of an **u** from the city! A Is 66:6
of Kerioth, and Moab shall die amid **u**, Am 2:2
lest there be an **u** among the people." Mt 26:5
feast, lest there be an **u** from the people." Mk 14:2
they formed a mob, set the city in an **u**, Acts 17:5
After the **u** ceased, Paul sent for the Acts 20:1
not learn the facts because of the **u**, Acts 21:34

UPROOT (2)
he will **u** you from the land of the living. Ps 52:5
down; I will plant them, and not **u** them. Jer 24:6

UPROOTED (6)
and the LORD **u** them from their land in Dt 29:28
shall not be **u** or overthrown anymore Jer 31:40

shall never again be **u** out of the land Am 9:15
out at noon, and Ekron shall be **u**. Zep 2:4
tree, 'Be **u** and planted in the sea,' Lk 17:6
trees in late autumn, twice dead, **u**; Jude 1:12

UPSETTING (2)
They are **u** the faith of some. 2 Tm 2:18
since they are **u** whole families by Ti 1:11

UPSIDE (4)
it so that it fell and turned it **u** down, Jgs 7:13
wiping it and turning it **u** down. 2 Kgs 21:13
You turn things **u** down! Shall the Is 29:16
turned the world **u** down have come Acts 17:6

UPWARD (56)
census, from twenty years old and **u**, Ex 30:14
records, from twenty years old and **u**, Ex 38:26
From twenty years old and **u**, all in Nm 1:3
of names from twenty years old and **u**, Nm 1:18
male from twenty years old and **u**, Nm 1:20
male from twenty years old and **u**, Nm 1:22
names, from twenty years old and **u**, Nm 1:24
of names, from twenty years old and **u**, Nm 1:26
of names, from twenty years old and **u**, Nm 1:28
of names, from twenty years old and **u**, Nm 1:30
of names, from twenty years old and **u**, Nm 1:32
of names, from twenty years old and **u**, Nm 1:34
of names, from twenty years old and **u**, Nm 1:36
of names, from twenty years old and **u**, Nm 1:38
of names, from twenty years old and **u**, Nm 1:40
of names, from twenty years old and **u**, Nm 1:42
houses, from twenty years old and **u**, Nm 1:45
from a month old and **u** you shall list." Nm 3:15
from a month old and **u** was 7,500. Nm 3:22
all the males, from a month old and **u**, Nm 3:28
from a month old and **u** was 6,200. Nm 3:34
all the males from a month old and **u**, Nm 3:39
of Israel, from a month old and **u**, Nm 3:40
a month old and **u** as listed were Nm 3:43
years old and **u** they shall come Nm 8:24
census from twenty years old and **u**, Nm 14:29
of Israel, from twenty years old and **u**, Nm 26:2
twenty years old and **u**," as the LORD Nm 26:4
every male from a month old and **u**. Nm 26:62
of Egypt, from twenty years old and **u**, Nm 32:11
ascent of Akrabbim, from Sela and **u**. Jgs 1:36
From his shoulders **u** he was taller 1 Sm 9:2
of the people from his shoulders **u**. 1 Sm 10:23
a crown that projected **u** one cubit. 1 Kgs 7:31
root downward and bear fruit **u**. 2 Kgs 19:30
The Levites, thirty years old and **u**, 1 Chr 23:3
twenty years old and **u** who were to 1 Chr 23:24
from twenty years old and **u**. 1 Chr 23:27
those twenty years old and **u**, 2 Chr 25:5
three years old and **u**—all who 2 Chr 31:16
years old and **u** was according to 2 Chr 31:17
the Levites, from twenty years old and **u**, Ezr 3:8
man is born to trouble as the sparks fly **u**. Jb 5:7
The path of life leads **u** for the prudent, Prv 15:24
spirit of man goes **u** and the spirit of Eccl 3:21
and their God, and turn their faces **u**. Is 8:21
and they roll **u** in a column of smoke. Is 9:18
take root downward and bear fruit **u**. Is 37:31
dove. My eyes are weary with looking **u**. Is 38:14
And **u** from what had the appearance Ezk 1:27
broader as it wound **u** to the side Ezk 41:7
temple was enclosed **u** all around the Ezk 41:7
Thus the temple had a broad area **u**, Ezk 41:7
from the altar hearth projecting **u**, Ezk 43:15
They return, but not **u**; they are like a Hos 7:16
for the prize of the **u** call of God in Phil 3:14

UR (5)
of his kindred, in **U** of the Chaldeans. Gn 11:28
forth together from **U** of the Chaldeans Gn 11:31
you out from **U** of the Chaldeans Gn 15:7
the Hararite, Eliphal the son of **U**, 1 Chr 11:35
brought him out of **U** of the Chaldeans Neh 9:7

URBANUS (1)
Greet **U**, our fellow worker in Christ, Rom 16:9

URGE (16)
"Do not **u** me to leave you or to return Ru 1:16
said to her servant, "**U** the animal on; 2 Kgs 4:24
Yet now I **u** you to take heart, for Acts 27:22
Therefore I **u** you to take some food. It Acts 27:34
I **u** you, then, be imitators of me. 1 Cor 4:16
Now I **u** you, brothers—you know 1 Cor 16:15
it necessary to **u** the brothers to 2 Cor 9:5
u you to walk in a manner worthy of the Eph 4:1
we ask and **u** you in the Lord Jesus, 1 Thes 4:1
But we **u** you, brothers, to do this 1 Thes 4:10
And we **u** you, brothers, admonish 1 Thes 5:14
First of all, then, I **u** that supplications, 1 Tm 2:1
and beloved. Teach and **u** these things. 1 Tm 6:2
u the younger men to be self-controlled. Ti 2:6

I **u** you the more earnestly to do this Heb 13:19
I **u** you as sojourners and exiles to 1 Pt 2:11

URGED (22)
As morning dawned, the angels **u** Lot, Gn 19:15
I have enough." Thus he **u** him, Gn 33:11
she **u** him to ask her father for a field. Jos 15:18
she **u** him to ask her father for a field. Jgs 1:14
her words day after day, and **u** him, Jgs 16:16
together with the woman, **u** him, 1 Sm 28:23
But when they **u** him till he was 2 Kgs 2:17
lived, who **u** him to eat some food. 2 Kgs 4:8
receive none." And he **u** him to take 2 Kgs 5:16
two talents." And he **u** him and tied 2 Kgs 5:23
hurriedly, **u** by the king's command. Est 8:14
Delaiah and Gemariah **u** the king not Jer 36:25
but they **u** him strongly, saying, "Stay Lk 24:29
u them to continue in the grace of Acts 13:43
and her household as well, she **u** us, Acts 16:15
and the people there **u** him not to go Acts 21:12
case against Paul, and they **u** him, Acts 25:2
Paul **u** them all to take some food, Acts 27:33
I strongly **u** him to visit you with 1 Cor 16:12
we **u** Titus that as he had started, 2 Cor 8:6
I **u** Titus to go, and sent the brother 2 Cor 12:18
As I **u** you when I was going to 1 Tm 1:3

URGENT (8)
The taskmasters were **u**, saying, Ex 5:13
The Egyptians were **u** with the people to Ex 12:33
he granted their **u** plea because they 1 Chr 5:20
of the king so **u**?" Then Arioch made Dn 2:15
the king's order was **u** and the furnace Dn 3:22
But they were **u**, saying, "He stirs up the Lk 23:5
But they were **u**, demanding with loud Lk 23:23
good works, so as to help cases of **u** need, Ti 3:14

URGENTLY (2)
hasten, and plead **u** with your neighbor. Prv 6:3
the prophets whom I send to you **u**, Jer 26:5

URGES (1)
works for him; his mouth **u** him on. Prv 16:26

URGING (4)
Meanwhile the disciples were **u** him, Jn 4:31
was there, sent two men to him, **u** him, Acts 9:38
was standing there, **u** him and saying, Acts 16:9
to him and were **u** him not to venture Acts 19:31

URI (8)
called by name Bezalel the son of **U**, Ex 31:2
called by name Bezalel the son of **U**, Ex 35:30
Bezalel the son of **U**, son of Hur, of the Ex 38:22
Geber the son of **U**, in the land of 1 Kgs 4:19
Hur fathered **U**, and Uri fathered 1 Chr 2:20
fathered Uri, and **U** fathered Bezalel. 1 Chr 2:20
bronze altar that Bezalel the son of **U**, 2 Chr 1:5
gatekeepers: Shallum, Telem, and **U**. Ezr 10:24

URIAH (39)
of Eliam, the wife of **U** the Hittite?" 2 Sm 11:3
"Send me **U** the Hittite." And Joab sent 2 Sm 11:6
the Hittite." And Joab sent **U** to David. 2 Sm 11:6
When **U** came to him, David asked 2 Sm 11:7
Then David said to **U**, "Go down to 2 Sm 11:8
wash your feet." And **U** went out of 2 Sm 11:8
But **U** slept at the door of the king's 2 Sm 11:9
"**U** did not go down to his house," 2 Sm 11:10
down to his house," David said to **U**, 2 Sm 11:10
U said to David, "The ark and Israel 2 Sm 11:11
Then David said to **U**, "Remain here 2 Sm 11:12
you back." So **U** remained in 2 Sm 11:12
to Joab and sent it by the hand of **U**. 2 Sm 11:14
"Set **U** in the forefront of the hardest 2 Sm 11:15
he assigned **U** to the place where he 2 Sm 11:16
the people fell. **U** the Hittite also died. 2 Sm 11:17
'Your servant **U** the Hittite is dead 2 Sm 11:21
and your servant **U** the Hittite is 2 Sm 11:24
the wife of **U** heard that Uriah 2 Sm 11:26
Uriah heard that **U** her husband 2 Sm 11:26
have struck down **U** the Hittite with 2 Sm 12:9
taken the wife of **U** the Hittite to be 2 Sm 12:10
U the Hittite: thirty-seven in all. 2 Sm 23:39
except in the matter of **U** the Hittite. 1 Kgs 15:5
King Ahaz sent to **U** the priest a 2 Kgs 16:10
And **U** the priest built the altar; in 2 Kgs 16:11
Damascus, so **U** the priest made it, 2 Kgs 16:11
Ahaz commanded **U** the priest, 2 Kgs 16:15
U the priest did all this, as King 2 Kgs 16:16
U the Hittite, Zabad the son of 1 Chr 11:41
hands of Meremoth the priest, son of **U**, Ezr 8:33
next to them Meremoth the son of **U**, Neh 3:4
After him Meremoth the son of **U**, son Neh 3:21
Mattithiah, Shema, Anaiah, **U**, Hilkiah, Neh 8:4
U the priest and Zechariah the son of Is 8:2
U the son of Shemaiah from Jer 26:20
But when **U** heard of it, he was afraid Jer 26:21
and they took **U** from Egypt and Jer 26:23

the father of Solomon by the wife of **U**, Mt 1:6

URIAH'S (1)
afflicted the child that **U** wife bore to 2 Sm 12:15

URIEL (4)
Tahath his son, **U** his son, Uzziah 1 Chr 6:24
of the sons of Kohath, **U** the chief, 1 Chr 15:5
and Abiathar, and the Levites **U**, 1 Chr 15:11
the daughter of **U** of Gibeah. 2 Chr 13:2

URIM (8)
shall put the **U** and the Thummim, Ex 28:30
he put the **U** and the Thummim. Lv 8:8
the judgment of the **U** before the LORD. Nm 27:21
and your **U** to your godly one, Dt 33:8
my son, O LORD, God of Israel, give **U**. 1 Sm 14:41
him, either by dreams, or by **U**, 1 Sm 28:6
a priest to consult **U** and Thummim. Ezr 2:63
a priest with **U** and Thummim should Neh 7:65

URINE (2)
dung and to drink their own **u**?" 2 Kgs 18:27
their own dung and drink their own **u**?" Is 36:12

URN (1)
was a golden **u** holding the manna, Heb 9:4

USE (53)
to die; of what **u** is a birthright to me?" Gn 25:32
utensils of the tabernacle for every **u**, Ex 27:19
any like it to **u** as perfume shall be Ex 30:38
acacia wood of any **u** in the work Ex 35:24
hearts stirred them to **u** their skill spun Ex 35:26
by beasts may be put to any other **u**, Lv 7:24
the skin, whatever be the **u** of the skin, Lv 13:51
And the priest shall **u** them, one for a Lv 15:15
And the priest shall **u** one for a sin Lv 15:30
fell for the LORD and **u** it as a sin offering, Lv 16:9
and you shall **u** them for summoning Nm 10:2
and let them **u** it for buying timber 2 Kgs 22:6
and let us **u** our strength for our 1 Chr 19:13
according to the **u** of each 1 Chr 28:15
to any man or **u** flattery toward any Jb 32:21
men of war were unable to **u** their hands. Ps 76:5
those who deride me **u** my name for a Ps 102:8
The poor **u** entreaties, but the rich Prv 18:23
is mad," and of pleasure, "What **u** is it?" Eccl 2:2
the edge, he must **u** more strength, Eccl 10:10
yourself with lye and **u** much soap, Jer 2:22
What **u** to me is frankincense that Jer 6:20
LORD, who **u** their tongues and declare, Jer 23:31
"Once more they shall **u** these words in Jer 31:23
U it as a barber's razor and pass it over Ezk 5:1
they shall no more **u** it as a proverb Ezk 12:23
uses proverbs will **u** this proverb Ezk 16:44
head of the two ways, to **u** divination. Ezk 21:21
they will continue to **u** her for a Ezk 23:43
shall be for common **u** for the city, Ezk 48:15
with the measure you **u** it will be Mt 7:2
with the measure you **u**, it will be Mk 4:24
God, or what parable shall we **u** for it? Mk 4:30
with the measure you **u** it will be Lk 6:38
down. Why should it **u** up the ground?' Lk 13:7
It is of no **u** either for the soil or for the Lk 14:35
a man sitting who could not **u** his feet. Acts 14:8
they **u** their tongues to deceive." "The Rom 3:13
vessel for honored **u** and another for Rom 9:21
use and another for dishonorable **u**? Rom 9:21
to the grace given to us, let us **u** them: Rom 12:6
we have not made **u** of this right, 1 Cor 9:12
But I have made no **u** of any of these 1 Cor 9:15
as not to make full **u** of my right in 1 Cor 9:18
be severe in my **u** of the authority 2 Cor 13:10
Only do not **u** your freedom as an Gal 5:13
making the best **u** of the time, because Eph 5:16
outsiders, making the best **u** of the time. Col 4:5
but **u** a little wine for the sake of your 1 Tm 5:23
wood and clay, some for honorable **u**, 2 Tm 2:20
he will be a vessel for honorable **u**, 2 Tm 2:21
received a gift, **u** it to serve one another, 1 Pt 4:10
I would rather not **u** paper and ink. 2 Jn 1:12

USED (65)
that the LORD **u** against the Egyptians, Ex 14:31
Now Moses **u** to take the tent and pitch it Ex 33:7
Thus the LORD **u** to speak to Moses face Ex 33:11
LORD'S contribution to be **u** for the tent Ex 35:21
All the gold that was **u** for the work, in Ex 38:24
any article that is **u** for any purpose. Lv 11:32
the service that are **u** in the sanctuary Nm 4:12
altar, which are **u** for the service there, Nm 4:14
that they may be **u** in the service of the Nm 7:5
or **u** a stone that could cause death, Nm 35:23
their big toes cut off **u** to pick up scraps Jgs 1:7
She **u** to sit under the palm of Deborah Jgs 4:5
there, for so the young men **u** to do. Jgs 14:10
with new ropes that have not been **u**, Jgs 16:11
Now this man **u** to go up year by year 1 Sm 1:3

And her rival **u** to provoke her 1 Sm 1:6
house of the LORD, she **u** to provoke her. 1 Sm 1:7
And his mother **u** to make for him a 1 Sm 2:19
"Your servant **u** to keep sheep for his 1 Sm 17:34
It **u** to eat of his morsel and drink 2 Sm 12:3
at the end of every year he **u** to cut it; 2 Sm 14:26
And Absalom **u** to rise early and 2 Sm 15:2
said, "They **u** to say in former times, 2 Sm 20:18
Solomon **u** to offer a thousand burnt 1 Kgs 3:4
times a year Solomon **u** to offer up 1 Kgs 9:25
ships of Tarshish **u** to come 1 Kgs 10:22
Thus he **u** to warn him, so that he 2 Kgs 6:10
bands of Moabites **u** to invade the 2 Kgs 13:20
as offerings and **u** divination and 2 Kgs 17:17
an offering and **u** fortune-telling and 2 Kgs 21:6
the vessels of bronze **u** in the temple 2 Kgs 25:14
rinse off what was **u** for the burnt 2 Chr 4:6
ships of Tarshish **u** to come 2 Chr 9:21
and had also **u** all the dedicated 2 Chr 24:7
and **u** fortune-telling and omens and 2 Chr 33:6
swift horses that were **u** in the king's Est 8:10
swift horses that were **u** in the king's Est 8:14
His sons **u** to go and hold a feast in the Jb 1:4
and no survivor where he **u** to live. Jb 18:19
We **u** to take sweet counsel together; Ps 55:14
which I toiled and **u** my wisdom under Eccl 2:19
They **u** to go in and out of the holy Eccl 8:10
of my mother—she who **u** to teach me. Sg 8:2
every place where there **u** to be a Is 7:23
as for all the hills that **u** to be hoed with a Is 7:25
a wild donkey **u** to the wilderness, in her Jer 2:24
this curse shall be **u** by all the exiles Jer 29:22
the palace shall stand where it **u** to be. Jer 30:18
In vain you have **u** many medicines; Jer 46:11
the vessels of bronze **u** in the temple Jer 52:18
beautiful ornament they **u** for pride, Ezk 7:20
when it was whole, it was **u** for nothing. Ezk 15:5
charred, can it ever be **u** for anything! Ezk 15:5
shall no more be **u** by you in Israel. Ezk 18:3
silver and gold, which they **u** for Baal. Hos 2:8
Now at the feast he **u** to release for them Mk 15:6
"Is this not the man who **u** to sit and beg?" Jn 9:8
This figure of speech Jesus **u** with them, Jn 10:6
of the moneybag he **u** to help himself to Jn 12:6
you **u** to dress yourself and walk Jn 21:18
they **u** supports to undergird the ship. Acts 27:17
"He who **u** to persecute us is now Gal 1:23
perish as they are **u**)—according to Col 2:22
tent and all the vessels **u** in worship. Heb 9:21
hoped in God **u** to adorn themselves, 1 Pt 3:5

USEFUL (5)
of it is charred, is it **u** for anything? Ezk 15:4
as holy, **u** to the master of the house, 2 Tm 2:21
for he is very **u** to me for ministry. 2 Tm 4:11
but now he is indeed **u** to you and to Phlm 1:11
and produces a crop **u** to those for whose Heb 6:7

USELESS (4)
Like a lame man's legs, which hang **u**, Prv 26:7
they are among the nations as a **u** vessel. Hos 8:8
(Formerly he was **u** to you, but now Phlm 1:11
person, that faith apart from works is **u**? Jas 2:20

USELESSNESS (1)
set aside because of its weakness and **u** Heb 7:18

USES (2)
everyone who **u** proverbs will use this Ezk 16:44
the law is good, if one **u** it lawfully, 1 Tm 1:8

USING (2)
plainly and not **u** figurative speech! Jn 16:29
not **u** your freedom as a cover-up for 1 Pt 2:16

USUALLY (2)
seven times more than it was **u** heated. Dn 3:19
to ask Pilate to do as he **u** did for them. Mk 15:8

UTENSILS (33)
It shall be made, with all these **u**, out of Ex 25:39
pans. You shall make all its **u** of bronze. Ex 27:3
All the **u** of the tabernacle for every use, Ex 27:19
and the table and all its **u**, and the Ex 30:27
utensils, and the lampstand and its **u**, Ex 30:27
offering with all its **u** and the basin and Ex 30:28
the table and its **u**, and the pure Ex 31:8
and the pure lampstand with all its **u**, Ex 31:8
the altar of burnt offering with all its **u**, Ex 31:9
the table with its poles and all its **u**, and Ex 35:13
for the light, with its **u** and its lamps, Ex 35:14
grating of bronze, its poles, and all its **u**, Ex 35:16
He made it and all its **u** out of a talent of Ex 37:24
And he made all the **u** of the altar, the Ex 38:3
the fire pans. He made all its **u** of bronze. Ex 38:3
grating for it and all the **u** of the altar, Ex 38:30
to Moses, the tent and all its **u**, Ex 39:33
the table with all its **u**, and the bread of Ex 39:36
lamps with the lamps set and all its **u**, Ex 39:37
grating of bronze, its poles, and all its **u**; Ex 39:39
and all the **u** for the service of the Ex 39:40
the altar of burnt offering and all its **u**, Ex 40:10
the altar and all its **u** and the basin and Lv 8:11
put it with all its **u** in a covering of Nm 4:10
they shall put on it all the **u** of the altar, Nm 4:14
and the basins, all the **u** of the altar; Nm 4:14
and consecrated the altar with all its **u**, Nm 7:1
them had charge of the **u** of service, 1 Chr 9:28
the furniture and over all the holy **u**, 1 Chr 9:29
with it were made **u** for the house of 2 Chr 24:14
altar of burnt offering and all its **u**, 2 Chr 29:18
for the showbread and all its **u**. 2 Chr 29:18
All the **u** that King Ahaz discarded 2 Chr 29:19

UTHAI (2)
U the son of Ammihud, son of Omri, 1 Chr 9:4
Of the sons of Bigvai, **U** and Zaccur, Ezr 8:14

UTMOST (1)
among you with **u** patience, 2 Cor 12:12

UTTER (42)
nations, but its end is **u** destruction." Nm 24:20
he too shall come to **u** destruction." Nm 24:24
has made himself an **u** stench to his 1 Sm 27:12
captivity, to plundering, and to **u** shame, Ezr 9:7
you and tell you and **u** words out of their Jb 8:10
U darkness is laid up for his treasures; a Jb 20:26
and my tongue will not **u** deceit. Jb 27:4
and at noon I **u** my complaint and Ps 55:17
For the cursing and lies that they **u**, Ps 59:12
I will **u** dark sayings from of old, Ps 78:2
Who can **u** the mighty deeds of the Ps 106:2
at the brink of **u** ruin in the assembled Prv 5:14
for my mouth will **u** truth; wickedness is Prv 8:7
his lamp will be put out in **u** darkness. Prv 20:20
and your heart **u** perverse things. Prv 23:33
are full of weariness; a man cannot **u** it; Eccl 1:8
heart be hasty to **u** a word before God, Eccl 5:2
to **u** error concerning the LORD, Is 32:6
deliver Jacob to **u** destruction and Israel Is 43:28
If you **u** what is precious, and not what Jer 15:19
from his holy habitation **u** his voice; Jer 25:30
as far as Jahaz they **u** their voice, Jer 48:34
inhabited but shall be an **u** desolation; Jer 50:13
And **u** a parable to the rebellious house Ezk 24:3
of Egypt an **u** waste and desolation, Ezk 29:10
with wholehearted joy and **u** contempt, Ezk 36:5
They **u** mere words; with empty oaths Hos 10:4
should go about and **u** wind and lies, Mi 2:11
and **u** shame will come upon your Hab 2:16
For the household gods **u** nonsense, Zec 10:2
again be a decree of **u** destruction. Zec 14:11
the land with a decree of **u** destruction." Mal 4:6
and persecute you and **u** all kinds of evil Mt 5:11
I will **u** what has been hidden since the Mt 13:35
man, and whatever blasphemies they **u**, Mk 3:28
answered him, "You were born in **u** sin, Jn 9:34
with your tongue you **u** speech that is 1 Cor 14:9
through him that we **u** our Amen to 2 Cor 1:20
be told, which man may not **u**. 2 Cor 12:4
them the gloom of **u** darkness has been 2 Pt 2:17
the gloom of **u** darkness has been Jude 1:13
its mouth to **u** blasphemies against God, Rv 13:6

UTTERANCE (6)
vows or any thoughtless **u** of her lips Nm 30:6
and the thoughtless **u** of her lips by Nm 30:8
life; I will give free **u** to my complaint; Jb 10:1
other tongues as the Spirit gave them **u**. Acts 2:4
through the Spirit the **u** of wisdom, 1 Cor 12:8
to another the **u** of knowledge 1 Cor 12:8

UTTERANCES (1)
nor understand the **u** of the prophets, Acts 13:27

UTTERED (18)
from you, about which you **u** a curse, Jgs 17:2
and the Most High **u** his voice. 2 Sm 22:14
miracles and the judgments he **u**, 1 Chr 16:12
Jeremiah also **u** a lament for Josiah; 2 Chr 35:25
With whose help have you **u** words, and Jb 26:4
Therefore I have **u** what I did not Jb 42:3
heavens, and the Most High **u** his voice, Ps 18:13
that which my lips **u** and my mouth Ps 66:14
From the heavens you **u** judgment; the Ps 76:8
his miracles, and the judgments he **u**, Ps 105:5
all the words that I have **u** against it, Jer 25:13
because you have **u** rebellion against Jer 28:16
a false vision and **u** a lying divination, Ezk 13:7
"Because you have **u** falsehood and Ezk 13:8
revilings that you **u** against the Ezk 35:12
robes and said, "He has **u** blasphemy. Mt 26:65
And Jesus **u** a loud cry and breathed Mk 15:37
this is what was **u** through the prophet Acts 2:16

UTTERING (2)
conceiving and **u** from the heart lying Is 59:13
given a mouth **u** haughty and Rv 13:5

UTTERLY (55)
that I will **u** blot out the memory of Ex 17:14
If her father **u** refuses to give her to Ex 22:17
but you shall **u** overthrow them and Ex 23:24
as to destroy them **u** and break my Lv 26:44
that person shall be **u** cut off; Nm 15:31
that you will soon **u** perish from the land Dt 4:26
live long in it, but will be **u** destroyed. Dt 4:26
You shall **u** detest and abhor it, for it is Dt 7:26
labor, but did not **u** drive them out. Jos 17:13
"I really thought that you **u** hated her, Jgs 15:2
good, and would not **u** destroy them. 1 Sm 15:9
deed you have **u** scorned the LORD, 2 Sm 12:14
heart of a lion, will **u** melt with fear, 2 Sm 17:10
and they are **u** consumed with fire." 2 Sm 23:7
I will **u** sweep away Baasha and his 1 Kgs 16:3
I will **u** burn you up, and will cut off 1 Kgs 21:21
I am **u** bowed down and prostrate; all the Ps 38:6
in a moment, swept away **u** by terrors! Ps 73:19
to themselves, "We will **u** subdue them"; Ps 74:8
full of wrath, and he **u** rejected Israel. Ps 78:59
keep your statutes; do not **u** forsake me! Ps 119:8
the word of truth **u** out of my mouth, Ps 119:43
The insolent **u** deride me, but I do not Ps 119:51
of his house, he would be **u** despised. Sg 8:7
the Holy One of Israel, they are **u** estranged. Is 1:4
And the idols shall **u** pass away. Is 2:18
And the LORD will **u** destroy the tongue Is 11:15
Mourn, **u** stricken, for the raisin cakes of Is 16:7
The princes of Zoan are **u** foolish; the Is 19:11
The earth shall be **u** empty and utterly Is 24:3
shall be utterly empty and **u** plundered; Is 24:3
The earth is **u** broken, the earth is split Is 24:19
down, and the city will be **u** laid low. Is 32:19
are turned back and **u** put to shame, Is 42:17
those nations shall be **u** laid waste. Is 60:12
be shocked, be **u** desolate, declares the Jer 2:12
surely you have **u** deceived this people Jer 4:10
of Judah have been **u** treacherous to me, Jer 5:11
We are **u** shamed, because we have left Jer 9:19
then I will **u** pluck it up and destroy it, Jer 12:17
Have you **u** rejected Judah? Does your Jer 14:19
until they shall be **u** destroyed from the Jer 24:10
your mother shall be **u** shamed, and Jer 50:12
unless you have **u** rejected us, and you Lam 5:22
Will it not **u** wither when the east Ezk 17:10
Armies shall be **u** swept away before Dn 11:22
the king of Israel shall be **u** cut off. Hos 10:15
that I will not **u** destroy the house of Am 9:8
the nations; you shall be **u** despised. Ob 1:2
moan bitterly, and say, "We are **u** ruined; Mi 2:4
pass through you; he is **u** cut off. Na 1:15
"I will **u** sweep away everything from the Zep 1:2
withered, his right eye **u** blinded!" Zec 11:17
ceased. And they were **u** astounded, Mk 6:51
For we were so **u** burdened beyond our 2 Cor 1:8

UTTERMOST (7)
outcasts are in the **u** parts of heaven, Dt 30:4
and dwell in the **u** parts of the sea, Ps 139:9
graves are set in the **u** parts of the pit; Ezk 32:23
Beth-togarmah from the **u** parts of the Ezk 38:6
place out of the **u** parts of the north, Ezk 38:15
you up from the **u** parts of the north, Ezk 39:2
to save to the **u** those who draw near Heb 7:25

UTTERS (16)
or if anyone **u** with his lips a rash oath to Lv 5:4
Everyone **u** lies to his neighbor; with Ps 12:2
The mouth of the righteous **u** wisdom, Ps 37:30
one comes to see me, he **u** empty words, Ps 41:6
totter; he **u** his voice, the earth melts. Ps 46:6
no one who **u** lies shall continue before Ps 101:7
lips, and whoever **u** slander is a fool. Prv 10:18
evidence, but a false witness **u** deceit. Prv 12:17
When he **u** his voice, there is a tumult Jer 10:13
When he **u** his voice there is a tumult Jer 51:16
The LORD **u** his voice before his army, for Jl 2:11
Zion, and **u** his voice from Jerusalem, Jl 3:16
roars from Zion and **u** his voice from Am 1:2
and the great man **u** the evil desire of his Mi 7:3
whom God has sent **u** the words of God, Jn 3:34
him, but he **u** mysteries in the Spirit. 1 Cor 14:2

UZ (8)
of Aram: **U**, Hul, Gether, and Mash. Gn 10:23
U his firstborn, Buz his brother, Gn 22:21
are the sons of Dishan: **U** and Aran. Gn 36:28
Aram: **U**, Hul, Gether, and Meshech. 1 Chr 1:17
The sons of Dishan: **U** and Aran. 1 Chr 1:42
in the land of **U** whose name was Job, Jb 1:1
kings of the land of **U** and all the kings Jer 25:20
Edom, you who dwell in the land of **U**; Lam 4:21

UZAI (1)
Palal the son of **U** repaired opposite the Neh 3:25

UZAL (3)
Hadoram, **U**, Diklah, Gn 10:27
Hadoram, **U**, Diklah, 1 Chr 1:21
of wine from **U** they exchanged for Ezk 27:19

UZZA (5)
of his house, in the garden of **U**, 2 Kgs 21:18
in his tomb in the garden of **U**, 2 Kgs 21:26
Heglam, who fathered **U** and Ahihud. 1 Chr 8:7
the sons of **U**, the sons of Paseah, the Ezr 2:49
the sons of Gazzam, the sons of **U**, the Neh 7:51

UZZAH (9)
And **U** and Ahio, the sons of 2 Sm 6:3
U put out his hand to the ark of God 2 Sm 6:6
of the LORD was kindled against **U**, 2 Sm 6:7
the LORD had burst forth against **U**. 2 Sm 6:8
his son, Shimei his son, **U** his son, 1 Chr 6:29
and **U** and Ahio were driving the 1 Chr 13:7
U put out his hand to take hold of the 1 Chr 13:9
of the LORD was kindled against **U**, 1 Chr 13:10
the LORD had broken out against **U**. 1 Chr 13:11

UZZEN-SHEERAH (1)
Lower and Upper Beth-horon, and **U**. 1 Chr 7:24

UZZI (11)
fathered Bukki, Bukki fathered **U**, 1 Chr 6:5
U fathered Zerahiah, Zerahiah 1 Chr 6:6
Bukki his son, **U** his son, Zerahiah 1 Chr 6:51
U, Rephaiah, Jeriel, Jahmai, Ibsam, 1 Chr 7:2
The son of **U**: Izrahiah. And the sons 1 Chr 7:3
Ezbon, **U**, Uzziel, Jerimoth, and Iri, 1 Chr 7:7
the son of Jeroham, Elah the son of **U**, 1 Chr 9:8
son of Zerahiah, son of **U**, son of Bukki, Ezr 7:4
Levites in Jerusalem was **U** the son of Neh 11:22
of Joiarib, Mattenai; of Jedaiah, **U**; Neh 12:19
Shemaiah, Eleazar, **U**, Jehohanan, Neh 12:42

UZZIA (1)
U the Ashterathite, Shama and Jeiel 1 Chr 11:44

UZZIAH (29)
thirty-ninth year of **U** king of 2 Kgs 15:13
year of Jotham the son of **U**. 2 Kgs 15:30
king of Israel, Jotham the son of **U**, 2 Kgs 15:32
to all that his father **U** had done. 2 Kgs 15:34
his son, Uriel his son, **U** his son, 1 Chr 6:24
towers, was Jonathan the son of **U**; 1 Chr 27:25
And all the people of Judah took **U**, 2 Chr 26:1
U was sixteen years old when he 2 Chr 26:3
The Ammonites paid tribute to **U**, 2 Chr 26:8
U built towers in Jerusalem at the 2 Chr 26:9
U had an army of soldiers, 2 Chr 26:11
And **U** prepared for all the army 2 Chr 26:14
they withstood King **U** and said to 2 Chr 26:18
you, **U**, to burn incense to the LORD, 2 Chr 26:18
Then **U** was angry. Now he had a 2 Chr 26:19
And King **U** was a leper to the day of 2 Chr 26:21
Now the rest of the acts of **U**, from 2 Chr 26:22
And **U** slept with his fathers, and 2 Chr 26:23
to all that his father **U** had done, 2 Chr 27:2
Elijah, Shemaiah, Jehiel, and **U**. Ezr 10:21
Athaiah the son of **U**, son of Neh 11:4
Judah and Jerusalem in the days of **U**, Is 1:1
In the year that King **U** died I saw the Lord Is 6:1
days of Ahaz the son of Jotham, son of **U**, Is 7:1
Hosea, the son of Beeri, in the days of **U**, Hos 1:1
Israel in the days of **U** king of Judah and Am 1:1
in the days of **U** king of Judah. Zec 14:5
of Joram, and Joram the father of **U**, Mt 1:8
and **U** the father of Jotham, and Jotham Mt 1:9

UZZIEL (16)
Amram, Izhar, Hebron, and **U**, the years Ex 6:18
The sons of **U**: Mishael, Elzaphan, and Ex 6:22
the sons of **U** the uncle of Aaron, Lv 10:4
clans: Amram, Izhar, Hebron, and **U**. Nm 3:19
Elizaphan the son of **U** as chief of the Nm 3:30
Pelatiah, Neariah, Rephaiah, and **U**, 1 Chr 4:42
Amram, Izhar, Hebron, and **U**. 1 Chr 6:2
Amram, Izhar, Hebron and **U**. 1 Chr 6:18
Ezbon, Uzzi, **U**, Jerimoth, and Iri, five, 1 Chr 7:7
of the sons of **U**, Amminadab the 1 Chr 15:10
Amram, Izhar, Hebron, and **U**, four. 1 Chr 23:12
The sons of **U**: Micah the chief and 1 Chr 23:20
The sons of **U**, Micah; of the sons of 1 Chr 24:24
Mattaniah, **U**, Shebuel and Jerimoth, 1 Chr 25:4
sons of Jeduthun, Shemaiah and **U**. 2 Chr 29:14
Next to them **U** the son of Harhaiah, Neh 3:8

UZZIELITES (2)
of the Hebronites and the clan of the **U**; Nm 3:27
the Hebronites, and the **U**— 1 Chr 26:23

V

VACILLATING (1)
Was I **v** when I wanted to do this? Do 2 Cor 1:17

VAIN (64)
take the name of the LORD your God in **v**, Ex 20:7
him guiltless who takes his name in **v**. Ex 20:7
And you shall sow your seed in **v**, for Lv 26:16
And your strength shall be spent in **v**, Lv 26:20
take the name of the LORD your God in **v**, Dt 5:11
him guiltless who takes his name in **v**. Dt 5:11
And he tried in **v** to go, for he had not 1 Sm 17:39
"Surely in **v** have I guarded all that 1 Sm 25:21
be condemned; why then do I labor in **v**? Jb 9:29
then have you become altogether **v**? Jb 27:12
though her labor be in **v**, yet she has no Jb 39:16
the nations rage and the peoples plot in **v**? Ps 2:1
long will you love **v** words and seek after Ps 4:2
the foe, for **v** is the salvation of man! Ps 60:11
in extortion; set no **v** hopes on robbery; Ps 62:10
All in **v** have I kept my heart clean and Ps 73:13
the foe, for **v** is the salvation of man! Ps 108:12
statutes, for their cunning is in **v**. Ps 119:118
the house, those who build it labor in **v**. Ps 127:1
city, the watchman stays awake in **v**. Ps 127:1
It is in **v** that you rise up early and go Ps 127:2
your enemies take your name in **v**! Ps 139:20
For in **v** is a net spread in the sight of Prv 1:17
A scoffer seeks wisdom in **v**, but Prv 14:6
Charm is deceitful, and beauty is **v**, Prv 31:30
while he lives the few days of his **v** life, Eccl 6:12
In my **v** life I have seen everything. Eccl 7:15
all the days of your **v** life that he has Eccl 9:9
Bring no more **v** offerings; incense is an Is 1:13
to the offspring of Jacob, 'Seek me in **v**.' Is 45:19
But I said, "I have labored in **v**; I have Is 49:4
shall not labor in **v** or bear children for Is 65:23
In **v** have I struck your children; they Jer 2:30
with paint? In **v** you beautify yourself. Jer 4:30
in **v** the refining goes on, for the wicked Jer 6:29
"But they say, 'That is in **v**! We will Jer 18:12
to you, filling you with **v** hopes. Jer 23:16
In **v** you have used many medicines; Jer 46:11
I have not said in **v** that I would do this Ezk 6:10
When she saw that she waited in **v**, that Ezk 19:5
who pay regard to **v** idols forsake their Jon 2:8
might not kindle fire on my altar in **v**! Mal 1:10
You have said, 'It is **v** to serve God. Mal 3:14
in **v** do they worship me, teaching as Mt 15:9
in **v** do they worship me, teaching as Mk 7:7
Gentiles rage, and the peoples plot in **v**? Acts 4:25
should turn from these **v** things to a Acts 14:15
for he does not bear the sword in **v**. Rom 13:4
to you—unless you believed in **v**. 1 Cor 15:2
his grace toward me was not in **v**. 1 Cor 15:10
our preaching is in **v** and your faith 1 Cor 15:14
is in vain and your faith is in **v**. 1 Cor 15:14
in the Lord your labor is not in **v**. 1 Cor 15:58
not to receive the grace of God in **v**. 2 Cor 6:1
you may not prove **v** in this matter, 2 Cor 9:3
I was not running or had not run in **v**. Gal 2:2
suffer so many things in **v**—if indeed it Gal 3:4
things in vain—if indeed it was in **v**? Gal 3:4
afraid I may have labored over you in **v**. Gal 4:11
that I did not run in **v** or labor in vain. Phil 2:16
that I did not run in vain or labor in **v**. Phil 2:16
that our coming to you was not in **v**. 1 Thes 2:1
you and our labor would be in **v**. 1 Thes 3:5
have wandered away into **v** discussion, 1 Tm 1:6

VAINLY (1)
eyes failed, ever watching **v** for help; Lam 4:17

VAIZATHA (1)
Parmashta and Arisai and Aridai and **V**, Est 9:9

VALE (1)
and portion out the **V** of Succoth. Ps 60:6

VALIANT (16)
saw any strong man, or any **v** man, 1 Sm 14:52
Only be **v** for me and fight the LORD'S 1 Sm 18:17
all the **v** men arose and went all 1 Sm 31:12
let your hands be strong, and be **v**, 2 Sm 2:7
where he knew there were **v** men. 2 Sm 11:16
you? Be courageous and be **v**." 2 Sm 13:28
Then even the **v** man, whose heart is 2 Sm 17:10
those who are with him are **v** men. 2 Sm 17:10
of Jehoiada was a **v** man of Kabzeel, 2 Sm 23:20
there were 800,000 **v** men who drew 2 Sm 24:9
of Manasseh had **v** men who carried 1 Chr 5:18
all the **v** men arose and took away 1 Chr 10:12
of Jehoiada was a **v** man of Kabzeel, 1 Chr 11:22
having an army of **v** men of war, 2 Chr 13:3
lived in Jerusalem were 468 **v** men. Neh 11:6
wine, and **v** men in mixing strong drink, Is 5:22

VALIANTLY (6)
shall be dispossessed. Israel is doing **v**. Nm 24:18
And he did **v** and struck the 1 Sm 14:48
With God we shall do **v**; it is he who Ps 60:12
With God we shall do **v**; it is he who Ps 108:13
"The right hand of the LORD does **v**, Ps 118:15
the right hand of the LORD does **v**!" Ps 118:16

VALLEY (165)
saw that the Jordan **V** was well watered Gn 13:10
Lot chose for himself all the Jordan **V**, Gn 13:11
the cities of the **v** and moved his tent Gn 13:12
joined forces in the **V** of Siddim (that is, Gn 14:3
and they joined battle in the **V** of Siddim Gn 14:8
Now the **V** of Siddim was full of Gn 14:10
to meet him at the **V** of Shaveh (that is, Gn 14:17
of Shaveh (that is, the King's **V**). Gn 14:17
look back or stop anywhere in the **v**. Gn 19:17
he overthrew those cities, and all the **v**, Gn 19:25
and toward all the land of the **v**, Gn 19:28
when God destroyed the cities of the **v**, Gn 19:29
and encamped in the **v** of Gerar and Gn 26:17
servants dug in the **v** and found there a Gn 26:19
So he sent him from the **V** of Hebron, Gn 37:14
they came to the **V** of Eshcol and cut Nm 13:23
That place was called the **V** of Eshcol, Nm 13:24
set out and camped in the **V** of Zered. Nm 21:12
from Bamoth to the **v** lying in the Nm 21:20
went up to the **V** of Eshcol and saw Nm 32:9
and came to the **V** of Eshcol and spied it Dt 1:24
journey and go over the **V** of the Arnon. Dt 2:24
is on the edge of the **V** of the Arnon, Dt 2:36
Arnon, and from the city that is in the **v**, Dt 2:36
from the **V** of the Arnon to Mount Dt 3:8
is on the edge of the **V** of the Arnon, Dt 3:12
from Gilead as far as the **V** of the Arnon, Dt 3:16
with the middle of the **v** as a border, Dt 3:16
we remained in the **v** opposite Beth-peor. Dt 3:29
the Jordan in the **v** opposite Beth-peor, Dt 4:46
is on the edge of the **V** of the Arnon, Dt 4:48
heifer down to a **v** with running water, Dt 21:4
break the heifer's neck there in the **v**. Dt 21:4
heifer whose neck was broken in the **v**, Dt 21:6
is, the **V** of Jericho the city of palm trees, Dt 34:3
he buried him in the **v** in the land of Dt 34:6
they brought them up to the **V** of Achor. Jos 7:24
of that place is called the **V** of Achor. Jos 7:26
But Joshua spent that night in the **v**. Jos 8:13
and moon, in the **V** of Aijalon." Jos 10:12
and eastward as far as the **V** of Mizpeh. Jos 11:8
as Baal-gad in the **V** of Lebanon below Jos 11:17
from the **V** of the Arnon to Mount Jos 12:1
is on the edge of the **V** of the Arnon, Jos 12:2
from the middle of the **v** as far as the Jos 12:2
from Baal-gad in the **V** of Lebanon to Jos 12:7
is on the edge of the **V** of the Arnon, Jos 13:9
and the city that is in the middle of the **v**, Jos 13:9
is on the edge of the **V** of the Arnon, Jos 13:16
the city that is in the middle of the **v**, Jos 13:16
and Zereth-shahar on the hill of the **v**, Jos 13:19
and in the **v** Beth-haram, Beth-nimrah, Jos 13:27
goes up to Debir from the **V** of Achor, Jos 15:7
which is on the south side of the **v**. Jos 15:7
boundary goes up by the **V** of the Son of Jos 15:8
that lies over against the **V** of Hinnom, Jos 15:8
at the northern end of the **V** of Rephaim. Jos 15:8
villages and those in the **V** of Jezreel." Jos 17:16
that overlooks the **V** of the Son Jos 18:16
is at the north end of the **V** of Rephaim. Jos 18:16
it then goes down the **V** of Hinnom, Jos 18:16
and it ends at the **V** of Iphtahel; Jos 19:14
Zebulun and the **V** of Iphtahel Jos 19:27
their root they marched down into the **v**, Jgs 5:14
into the **v** they rushed at his heels. Jgs 5:15
Jordan and encamped in the **V** of Jezreel. Jgs 6:33
of them, by the hill of Moreh, in the **v**. Jgs 7:1
camp of Midian was below him in the **v**. Jgs 7:8
East lay along the **v** like locusts in Jgs 7:12
this he loved a woman in the **V** of Sorek, Jgs 16:4
It was in the **v** that belongs to Jgs 18:28
reaping their wheat harvest in the **v**. 1 Sm 6:13
down on the **v** of Zeboim toward 1 Sm 13:18
of Amalek and lay in wait in the **v**. 1 Sm 15:5
and encamped in the **V** of Elah, 1 Sm 17:2
the other side, with a **v** between them. 1 Sm 17:3
men of Israel were in the **v** of Elah, 1 Sm 17:19
you struck down in the **v** of Elah, 1 Sm 21:9
other side of the **v** and those beyond 1 Sm 31:7
and spread out in the **V** of Rephaim. 2 Sm 5:18
and spread out in the **V** of Rephaim. 2 Sm 5:22
down 18,000 Edomites in the **V** of Salt. 2 Sm 8:13
city, and we shall drag it into the **v**, 2 Sm 17:13
the pillar that is in the King's **V**, 2 Sm 18:18
was encamped in the **V** of Rephaim. 2 Sm 23:13

the city that is in the middle of the **v**, 2 Sm 24:5
or into some **v**." And he said, 2 Kgs 2:16
which is by the **V** of the Arnon, 2 Kgs 10:33
Edomites in the **V** of Salt and 2 Kgs 14:7
which is in the **V** of the Son of 2 Kgs 23:10
of Gedor, to the east side of the **v**, 1 Chr 4:39
who were in the **v** saw that the army 1 Chr 10:7
was encamped in the **V** of Rephaim. 1 Chr 11:15
and made a raid in the **V** of Rephaim. 1 Chr 14:9
yet again made a raid in the **v**. 1 Chr 14:13
18,000 Edomites in the **V** of Salt. 1 Chr 18:12
of battle in the **V** of Zephathah at 2 Chr 14:10
will find them at the end of the **v**, 2 Chr 20:16
they assembled in the **V** of Beracah, 2 Chr 20:26
has been called the **V** of Beracah to 2 Chr 20:26
and went to the **V** of Salt and struck 2 Chr 25:11
Gate and at the **V** Gate and at the 2 Chr 26:9
made offerings in the **V** of the Son of 2 Chr 28:3
away and threw into the Kidron **v**. 2 Chr 30:14
as an offering in the **V** of the Son of 2 Chr 33:6
city of David west of Gihon, in the **v**, 2 Chr 33:14
by night by the **V** Gate to the Dragon Neh 2:13
the night by the **v** and inspected the Neh 2:15
turned back and entered by the **V** Gate, Neh 2:15
of Zanoah repaired the **V** Gate. Neh 3:13
from Beersheba to the **v** of Hinnom. Neh 11:30
Lod, and Ono, the **v** of craftsmen. Neh 11:35
The clods of the **v** are sweet to him; all Jb 21:33
opens shafts in a **v** away from where Jb 28:4
He paws in the **v** and exults in his Jb 39:21
I walk through the **v** of the shadow of Ps 23:4
thousand of Edom in the **V** of Salt. Ps 60:T
they go through the **V** of Baca they make Ps 84:6
and portion out the **V** of Succoth. Ps 108:7
by the ravens of the **v** and eaten by the Prv 30:17
orchard to look at the blossoms of the **v**, Sg 6:11
the ears of grain in the **V** of Rephaim. Is 17:5
The oracle concerning the **v** of vision. Is 22:1
and confusion in the **v** of vision, Is 22:5
head of the rich **v** of those overcome with Is 28:1
beauty, which is on the head of the rich **v**, Is 28:4
as in the **V** of Gibeon he will be roused; Is 28:21
Every **v** shall be lifted up, and every Is 40:4
the smooth stones of the **v** is your portion; Is 57:6
Like livestock that go down into the **v**, Is 63:14
and the **V** of Achor a place for herds to Is 65:10
Look at your way in the **v**; know what Jer 2:23
which is in the **V** of the Son of Hinnom, Jer 7:31
Topheth, or the **V** of the Son of Hinnom, Jer 7:32
Son of Hinnom, but the **V** of Slaughter; Jer 7:32
and go out to the **V** of the Son of Hinnom Jer 19:2
Topheth, or the **V** of the Son of Hinnom, Jer 19:6
Son of Hinnom, but the **V** of Slaughter. Jer 19:6
I am against you, O inhabitant of the **v**, Jer 21:13
The whole **v** of the dead bodies and the Jer 31:40
places of Baal in the **V** of the Son of Jer 32:35
O remnant of their **v**, how long will you Jer 47:5
the **v** shall perish, and the plain shall be Jer 48:8
he said to me, "Arise, go out into the **v**, Ezk 3:22
So I arose and went out into the **v**, and Ezk 3:23
there, like the vision that I saw in the **v**. Ezk 8:4
and set me down in the middle of the **v**; Ezk 37:1
were very many on the surface of the **v**, Ezk 37:2
burial in Israel, the **V** of the Travelers, Ezk 39:11
It will be called the **V** of Hamon-gog. Ezk 39:11
have buried it in the **V** of Hamon-gog. Ezk 39:15
the bow of Israel in the **V** of Jezreel." Hos 1:5
vineyards and make the **V** of Achor a Hos 2:15
bring them down to the **V** of Jehoshaphat. Jl 3:2
up and come up to the **V** of Jehoshaphat; Jl 3:12
multitudes, in the **v** of decision! Jl 3:14
day of the LORD is near in the **v** of decision. Jl 3:14
of the LORD and water the **V** of Shittim. Jl 3:18
off the inhabitants from the **V** of Aven, Am 1:5
her stones into the **v** and uncover her Mi 1:6
two from east to west by a very wide **v**, Zec 14:4
you shall flee to the **v** of my mountains, Zec 14:5
for the **v** of the mountains shall reach Zec 14:5
Every **v** shall be filled, and every Lk 3:5
with his disciples across the Kidron **V**, Jn 18:1

VALLEYS (26)
and the Canaanites dwell in the **v**, Nm 14:25
in Suphah, and the **v** of the Arnon, Nm 21:14
the slope of the **v** that extends to the Nm 21:15
and springs, flowing out in the **v** and hills, Dt 8:7
over to possess is a land of hills and **v**, Dt 11:11
the springs of water and to all the **v**. 1 Kgs 18:5
a god of the **v**," therefore I will give 1 Kgs 20:28
and put to flight all those in the **v**, 1 Chr 12:15
the herds in the **v** was Shaphat the 1 Chr 27:29
ropes, or will he harrow the **v** after you? Jb 39:10
the **v** deck themselves with grain, Ps 65:13
the **v** sank down to the place that you Ps 104:8
You make springs gush forth in the **v**; Ps 104:10
I am a rose of Sharon, a lily of the **v**. Sg 2:1
Your choicest **v** were full of chariots, and Is 22:7
and fountains in the midst of the **v**. Is 41:18
who slaughter your children in the **v**, Is 57:5
Why do you boast of your **v**, O faithless Jer 49:4
and the hills, to the ravines and the **v**: Ezk 6:3
on the mountains, like doves of the **v**, Ezk 7:16
and in all the **v** its branches have Ezk 31:12
and fill the **v** with your carcass. Ezk 32:5
your hills and in your **v** and in all your Ezk 35:8
and the hills, the ravines and the **v**, Ezk 36:4
and hills, to the ravines and **v**, Ezk 36:6
melt under him, and the **v** will split open, Mi 1:4

VALOR (28)
All your men of **v** shall cross over armed Dt 3:18
all the men of **v** among you shall pass Jos 1:14
hand, with its king and mighty men of **v**. Jos 6:2
30,000 mighty men of **v** and sent them Jos 8:3
with him, and all the mighty men of **v**. Jos 10:7
LORD is with you, O mighty man of **v**." Jgs 6:12
of Benjamin fell, all of them men of **v**. Jgs 20:44
drew the sword, all of them men of **v**. Jgs 20:46
him went men of **v** whose hearts God 1 Sm 10:26
is skillful in playing, a man of **v**, 1 Sm 16:18
He was a mighty man of **v**, but he was 2 Kgs 5:1
and all the mighty men of **v**, 2 Kgs 24:14
captive to Babylon all the men of **v**, 2 Kgs 24:16
mighty men of **v** and were 1 Chr 12:21
mighty men of **v** for war, 1 Chr 12:25
Zadok, a young man mighty in **v**, 1 Chr 12:28
20,800, mighty men of **v**, 1 Chr 12:30
All these were mighty men of **v**. 2 Chr 14:8
He had soldiers, mighty men of **v**, in 2 Chr 17:13
with 300,000 mighty men of **v**; 2 Chr 17:14
LORD, with 200,000 mighty men of **v**. 2 Chr 17:16
Eliada, a mighty man of **v**, with 2 Chr 17:17
mighty men of **v** from Israel for 2 Chr 25:6
of mighty men of **v** was 2,600. 2 Chr 26:12
of the LORD who were men of **v**, 2 Chr 26:17
in one day, all of them men of **v**, 2 Chr 28:6
and his brothers, men of **v**, 928. Neh 11:8
and their brothers, mighty men of **v**, Neh 11:14

VALUABLE (1)
gifts of silver, gold, and **v** possessions, 2 Chr 21:3

VALUATION (19)
to the LORD involving the **v** of persons, Lv 27:2
then the **v** of a male from twenty years Lv 27:3
is a female, the **v** shall be thirty shekels. Lv 27:4
the **v** shall be for a male twenty shekels, Lv 27:5
the **v** shall be for a male five shekels of Lv 27:6
for a female the **v** shall be three shekels Lv 27:6
then the **v** for a male shall be fifteen Lv 27:7
And if someone is too poor to pay the **v**, Lv 27:8
to redeem it, he shall add a fifth to the **v**. Lv 27:13
house, he shall add a fifth to the **v** price, Lv 27:15
then the **v** shall be in proportion to its Lv 27:16
the year of jubilee, the **v** shall stand, Lv 27:17
a deduction shall be made from the **v**. Lv 27:18
it, then he shall add a fifth to its **v** price, Lv 27:19
the amount of the **v** for it up to Lv 27:23
the man shall give the **v** on that day as Lv 27:23
Every **v** shall be according to the Lv 27:25
then he shall buy it back at the **v**, Lv 27:27
is not redeemed, it shall be sold at the **v**. Lv 27:27

VALUE (19)
add the fifth of its **v** to it and give the Lv 22:14
the priest, and the priest shall **v** him; Lv 27:8
the priest shall **v** him according to what Lv 27:8
and the priest shall **v** it as either good or Lv 27:12
the priest shall **v** it as either good or Lv 27:14
to you, I will give you its **v** in money." 1 Kgs 21:2
them. Are you not of more **v** than they? Mt 6:26
you are of more **v** than many sparrows. Mt 10:31
Of how much more **v** is a man than a Mt 12:12
who, on finding one pearl of great **v**, Mt 13:46
you are of more **v** than many sparrows. Lk 12:7
Of how much more **v** are you than the Lk 12:24
And they counted the **v** of them and Acts 19:19
my life of any **v** nor as precious to Acts 20:24
indeed is of **v** if you obey Rom 2:25
Jew? Or what is the **v** of circumcision? Rom 3:1
they are of no **v** in stopping the Col 2:23
for while bodily training is of some **v**, 1 Tm 4:8
value, godliness is of **v** in every way, 1 Tm 4:8

VALUED (5)
out of the flock, **v** in silver shekels, Lv 5:15
barley seed shall be **v** at fifty shekels of Lv 27:16
It cannot be **v** in the gold of Ophir, in Jb 28:16
equal it, nor can it be **v** in pure gold. Jb 28:19
point of death, who was highly **v** by him. Lk 7:2

VALUES (2)
or bad; as the priest **v** it, so it shall be. Lv 27:12
bad; as the priest **v** it, so it shall stand. Lv 27:14

VANGUARD (1)
desolate land, his **v** into the eastern sea, Jl 2:20

VANIAH (1)
V, Meremoth, Eliashib, Ezr 10:36

VANISH (8)
when it is hot, they **v** from their place. Jb 6:17
the night, when peoples **v** in their place. Jb 36:20
they **v**—like smoke they vanish away. Ps 37:20
they vanish—like smoke they **v** away. Ps 37:20
Let them **v** like water that runs away; Ps 58:7
So he made their days **v** like a breath, Ps 78:33
for the heavens **v** like smoke, the earth Is 51:6
and growing old is ready to **v** away. Heb 8:13

VANISHED (6)
the angel of the LORD **v** from his sight. Jgs 6:21
for the faithful have **v** from among the Ps 12:1
tramples underfoot has **v** from the land, Is 16:4
from the prudent? Has their wisdom **v**? Jer 49:7
him. And he **v** from their sight. Lk 24:31
The sky **v** like a scroll that is being Rv 6:14

VANISHES (2)
As the cloud fades and **v**, so he who goes Jb 7:9
that appears for a little time and then **v**. Jas 4:14

VANITIES (3)
Vanity of **v**, says the Preacher, vanity of Eccl 1:2
vanities, says the Preacher, vanity of **v**! Eccl 1:2
Vanity of **v**, says the Preacher; all is Eccl 12:8

VANITY (34)
For what **v** you have created all the Ps 89:47
V of vanities, says the Preacher, vanity Eccl 1:2
says the Preacher, **v** of vanities! Eccl 1:2
the Preacher, vanity of vanities! All is **v**. Eccl 1:2
all is **v** and a striving after wind. Eccl 1:14
yourself." But behold, this also was **v**. Eccl 2:1
all was **v** and a striving after wind, Eccl 2:11
I said in my heart that this also is **v**. Eccl 2:15
for all is **v** and a striving after wind. Eccl 2:17
wisdom under the sun. This also is **v**. Eccl 2:19
for it. This also is **v** and a great evil. Eccl 2:21
his heart does not rest. This also is **v**. Eccl 2:23
This also is **v** and a striving after wind. Eccl 2:26
advantage over the beasts, for all is **v**. Eccl 3:19
This also is **v** and a striving after wind. Eccl 4:4
Again, I saw **v** under the sun: Eccl 4:7
This also is **v** and an unhappy Eccl 4:8
Surely this also is **v** and a striving after Eccl 4:16
and words grow many, there is **v**; Eccl 5:7
wealth with his income; this also is **v**. Eccl 5:10
them. This is **v**; it is a grievous evil. Eccl 6:2
For it comes in **v** and goes in darkness, Eccl 6:4
this also is **v** and a striving after wind. Eccl 6:9
The more words, the more **v**, and what Eccl 6:11
is the laughter of the fools; this also is **v**. Eccl 7:6
had done such things. This also is **v**. Eccl 8:10
There is a **v** that takes place on earth, Eccl 8:14
the righteous. I said that this also is **v**. Eccl 8:14
will be many. All that comes is **v**. Eccl 11:8
for youth and the dawn of life are **v**. Eccl 11:10
V of vanities, says the Preacher; all is Eccl 12:8
of vanities, says the Preacher; all is **v**. Eccl 12:8
spent my strength for nothing and **v**; Is 49:4
for the customs of the peoples are **v**. A Jer 10:3

VANQUISH (1)
wisdom; God may **v** him, not a man.' Jb 32:13

VAPOR (2)
tongue is a fleeting **v** and a snare of Prv 21:6
below, blood, and fire, and **v** of smoke; Acts 2:19

VARIATION (1)
whom there is no **v** or shadow due to Jas 1:17

VARIED (1)
as good stewards of God's **v** grace: 1 Pt 4:10

VARIETIES (3)
Now there are **v** of gifts, but the same 1 Cor 12:4
and there are **v** of service, but the 1 Cor 12:5
and there are **v** of activities, but it is 1 Cor 12:6

VARIOUS (15)
been filled with **v** kinds of spices 2 Chr 16:14
those afflicted with **v** diseases and pains, Mt 4:24
be famines and earthquakes in **v** places. Mt 24:7
many who were sick with **v** diseases, Mk 1:34
There will be earthquakes in **v** places; Mk 13:8
were sick with **v** diseases brought them Lk 4:40
and in **v** places famines and Lk 21:11
to another **v** kinds of tongues, 1 Cor 12:10
and **v** kinds of tongues. 1 Cor 12:28
with sins and led astray by **v** passions, 2 Tm 3:6
astray, slaves to **v** passions and pleasures, Ti 3:3
and wonders and **v** miracles and by Heb 2:4
with food and drink and **v** washings, Heb 9:10
brothers, when you meet trials of **v** kinds, Jas 1:2

you have been grieved by **v** trials, 1 Pt 1:6

VARY (1)
of his sale shall **v** with the number of Lv 25:50

VASHTI (10)
Queen **V** also gave a feast for the women Est 1:9
to bring Queen **V** before the king with Est 1:11
But Queen **V** refused to come at the Est 1:12
the law, what is to be done to Queen **V**, Est 1:15
the king has Queen **V** done wrong, Est 1:16
Ahasuerus commanded Queen **V** to be Est 1:17
that **V** is never again to come before Est 1:19
he remembered **V** and what she had done Est 2:1
be queen instead of **V**." This pleased the Est 2:4
head and made her queen instead of **V**. Est 2:17

VASSAL (1)
Hoshea became his **v** and paid him 2 Kgs 17:3

VAST (4)
throughout all his kingdom, for it is **v**, Est 1:20
O God! How **v** is the sum of them! Ps 139:17
For your ruin is **v** as the sea; who can Lam 2:13
GOD: "Bring up a **v** host against them, Ezk 23:46

VAT (3)
the midst of it, and hewed out a wine **v** in it; Is 5:2
floor and wine **v** shall not feed Hos 9:2
came to the wine **v** to draw fifty Hg 2:16

VATS (3)
and your **v** will be bursting with wine. Prv 3:10
the **v** shall overflow with wine and oil. Jl 2:24
for the winepress is full. The **v** overflow, Jl 3:13

VAULT (2)
see, and he walks on the **v** of heaven.' Jb 22:14
and founds his **v** upon the earth; Am 9:6

VAULTED (3)
built yourself a **v** chamber and made Ezk 16:24
building your **v** chamber at the head Ezk 16:31
throw down your **v** chamber and Ezk 16:39

VEGETABLE (1)
that I may have it for a **v** garden, 1 Kgs 21:2

VEGETABLES (4)
seed and irrigated it, like a garden of **v**. Dt 11:10
let us be given **v** to eat and water to Dn 1:12
they were to drink, and gave them **v**. Dn 1:16
while the weak person eats only **v**. Rom 14:2

VEGETATION (8)
And God said, "Let the earth sprout **v**, Gn 1:11
The earth brought forth **v**, plants Gn 1:12
which devoured all the **v** in their land Ps 105:35
appears and the **v** of the mountains Prv 27:25
the grass is withered, the **v** fails, the Is 15:6
and hills, and dry up all their **v**; Is 42:15
their eyes fail because there is no **v**. Jer 14:6
of rain, to everyone the **v** in the field. Zec 10:1

VEHEMENTLY (1)
the scribes stood by, **v** accusing him. Lk 23:10

VEIL (42)
So she took her **v** and covered herself. Gn 24:65
garments and covered herself with a **v**, Gn 38:14
and taking off her **v** she put on the Gn 38:19
you shall make a **v** of blue and purple Ex 26:31
you shall hang the **v** from the clasps, Ex 26:33
of the testimony in there within the **v**. Ex 26:33
And the **v** shall separate for you the Ex 26:33
you shall set the table outside the **v**, Ex 26:35
outside the **v** that is before the Ex 27:21
it in front of the **v** that is above the ark Ex 30:6
with them, he put a **v** over his face. Ex 34:33
speak with him, he would remove the **v**, Ex 34:34
Moses would put the **v** over his face Ex 34:35
the mercy seat, and the **v** of the screen; Ex 35:12
He made the **v** of blue and purple and Ex 36:35
of the sanctuary and the bases of the **v**; Ex 38:27
and goatskins, and the **v** of the screen; Ex 39:34
and you shall screen the ark with the **v**. Ex 40:3
and set up the **v** of the screen, Ex 40:21
side of the tabernacle, outside the **v**, Ex 40:22
altar in the tent of meeting before the **v**, Ex 40:26
the LORD in front of the **v** of the sanctuary. Lv 4:6
times before the LORD in front of the **v**. Lv 4:17
any time into the Holy Place inside the **v**, Lv 16:2
small, and he shall bring it inside the **v** Lv 16:12
its blood inside the **v** and do with its Lv 16:15
not go through the **v** or approach the Lv 21:23
Outside the **v** of the testimony, in the tent Lv 24:3
in and take down the **v** of the screen and Nm 4:5
the altar and that is within the **v**; Nm 18:7
And he made the **v** of blue and purple 2 Chr 3:14
Thick clouds **v** him, so that he does not Jb 22:14
Your eyes are doves behind your **v**. Sg 4:1
halves of a pomegranate behind your **v**. Sg 4:3
they bruised me, they took away my **v**, Sg 5:7
halves of a pomegranate behind your **v**. Sg 6:7
the **v** that is spread over all nations. Is 25:7
millstones and grind flour, put off your **v**, Is 47:2
who would put a **v** over his face so 2 Cor 3:13
that same **v** remains unlifted, 2 Cor 3:14
Moses is read a **v** lies over their 2 Cor 3:15
turns to the Lord, the **v** is removed. 2 Cor 3:16

VEILED (3)
from his hand; and there he **v** his power. Hab 3:4
And even if our gospel is **v**, it is veiled 2 Cor 4:3
it is **v** only to those who are perishing. 2 Cor 4:3

VEILS (5)
'No eye will see me'; and he **v** his face. Jb 24:15
be like one who **v** herself beside the flocks Sg 1:7
linen garments, the turbans, and the **v**. Is 3:23
and make **v** for the heads of persons of Ezk 13:18
Your **v** also I will tear off and deliver Ezk 13:21

VENGEANCE (50)
v shall be taken on him sevenfold." And Gn 4:15
You shall not take **v** or bear a grudge Lv 19:18
that shall execute **v** for the covenant. Lv 26:25
to execute the LORD'S **v** on Midian. Nm 31:3
V is mine, and recompense, for the time Dt 32:35
I will take **v** on my adversaries and will Dt 32:41
children and takes **v** on his adversaries. Dt 32:43
the nation took **v** on their enemies. Jos 10:13
on it, may the LORD himself take **v**. Jos 22:23
the LORD take **v** on David's enemies." 1 Sm 20:16
or for my lord taking **v** himself. 1 Sm 25:31
who gave me **v** and brought down 2 Sm 22:48
on that day to take **v** on their enemies. Est 8:13
who gave me **v** and subdued peoples Ps 18:47
will rejoice when he sees the **v**; Ps 58:10
O LORD, God of **v**, O God of vengeance, Ps 94:1
O LORD, God of vengeance, O God of **v**, Ps 94:1
to execute **v** on the nations and Ps 149:7
For the LORD has a day of **v**, a year of Is 34:8
Behold, your God will come with **v**, with Is 35:4
seen. I will take **v**, and I will spare no one. Is 47:3
he put on garments of **v** for clothing, Is 59:17
LORD'S favor, and the day of **v** of our God; Is 61:2
For the day of **v** was in my heart, and my Is 63:4
the mind, let me see your **v** upon them, Jer 11:20
and take **v** for me on my persecutors. Jer 15:15
the mind, let me see your **v** upon them, Jer 20:12
day of the Lord GOD of hosts, a day of **v**, Jer 46:10
For this is the **v** of the LORD: take Jer 50:15
vengeance of the LORD: take **v** on her; Jer 50:15
to declare in Zion the **v** of the LORD our Jer 50:28
of the LORD our God, **v** for his temple. Jer 50:28
for this is the time of the LORD'S **v**, Jer 51:6
to destroy it, for that is the **v** of the LORD, Jer 51:11
of the LORD, the **v** for his temple. Jer 51:11
plead your cause and take **v** for you. Jer 51:36
You have seen all their **v**, all their Lam 3:60
To rouse my wrath, to take **v**, I have set Ezk 24:8
offended in taking **v** on them, Ezk 25:12
And I will lay my **v** upon Edom by the Ezk 25:14
my wrath, and they shall know my **v**, Ezk 25:14
revengefully and took **v** with malice Ezk 25:15
I will execute great **v** on them with Ezk 25:17
the LORD, when I lay my **v** upon them." Ezk 25:17
wrath I will execute **v** on the nations Mi 5:15
the LORD takes **v** on his adversaries and Na 1:2
for these are days of **v**, to fulfill all that Lk 21:22
of God, for it is written, "**V** is mine, Rom 12:19
inflicting **v** on those who do not 2 Thes 1:8
we know him who said, "**V** is mine; Heb 10:30

VENOM (7)
with the **v** of things that crawl in the Dt 32:24
of serpents and the cruel **v** of asps. Dt 32:33
it is the **v** of cobras within him. Jb 20:14
They have **v** like the venom of a serpent, Ps 58:4
They have venom like the **v** of a serpent, Ps 58:4
and under their lips is the **v** of asps. Ps 140:3
tongues to deceive." "The **v** of asps is Rom 3:13

VENT (4)
my belly is like wine that has no **v**; Jb 32:19
A fool gives full **v** to his spirit, but a Prv 29:11
The LORD gave full **v** to his wrath; he Lam 4:11
and I will **v** my fury upon them and Ezk 5:13

VENTED (1)
over to the sword and **v** his wrath on his Ps 78:62

VENTURE (4)
who would not **v** to set the sole of her Dt 28:56
and those riches were lost in a bad **v**. Eccl 5:14
urging him not to **v** into the theater. Acts 19:31
For I will not **v** to speak of anything Rom 15:18

VENTURES (1)
"If one **v** a word with you, will you be Jb 4:2

VERDICT (1)
turn aside from the **v** that they declare Dt 17:11

VERIFIED (1)
So your words will be **v**, and you shall Gn 42:20

VERIFY (1)
You can **v** that it is not more than Acts 24:11

VERMILION (2)
it with cedar and painting it with **v**. Jer 22:14
of the Chaldeans portrayed in **v**, Ezk 23:14

VERMIN (1)
as a shepherd cleans his cloak of **v**, Jer 43:12

VERSED (1)
toward all who were **v** in law and Est 1:13

VERSES (1)
theme; I address my **v** to the king; Ps 45:1

VESSEL (38)
And the earthenware **v** in which it is Lv 6:28
But if it is boiled in a bronze **v**, that shall Lv 6:28
of them falls into any earthenware **v**, Lv 11:33
from every such **v** shall be unclean. Lv 11:34
in an earthenware **v** over fresh water. Lv 14:5
in an earthenware **v** over fresh water Lv 14:50
And an earthenware **v** that the one with Lv 15:12
and every **v** of wood shall be rinsed in Lv 15:12
in an earthenware **v** and take some Nm 5:17
And every open **v** that has no cover Nm 19:15
and fresh water shall be added in a **v**. Nm 19:17
and gold, and every **v** of bronze and iron, Jos 6:19
said, "Bring me a little water in a **v**, 1 Kgs 17:10
"Bring me another **v**." And he said to 2 Kgs 4:6
and dash them in pieces like a potter's **v**." Ps 2:9
is dead; I have become like a broken **v**. Ps 31:12
and the smith has material for a **v**; Prv 25:4
covering an earthen **v** are fervent lips Prv 26:23
the offspring and issue, every small **v**, Is 22:24
that of a potter's **v** that is smashed so Is 30:14
offering in a clean **v** to the house of Is 66:20
And the **v** he was making of clay was Jer 18:4
hand, and he reworked it into another **v**, Jer 18:4
and this city, as one breaks a potter's **v**, Jer 19:11
broken pot, a **v** no one cares for? Jer 22:28
come, and you shall fall like a choice **v**. Jer 25:34
and put them in an earthenware **v**, Jer 32:14
has not been emptied from **v** to vessel, Jer 48:11
has not been emptied from vessel to **v**, Jer 48:11
broken Moab like a **v** for which no one Jer 48:38
me; he has made me an empty **v**; Jer 51:34
them into a single **v** and make your Ezk 4:9
take a peg from it to hang any **v** on it? Ezk 15:3
are among the nations as a useless **v**. Hos 8:8
a reef, they ran the **v** aground. Acts 27:41
the same lump one **v** for honored use Rom 9:21
he will be a **v** for honorable use, 2 Tm 2:21
honor to the woman as the weaker **v**, 1 Pt 3:7

VESSELS (98)
even in **v** of wood and in vessels of Ex 7:19
in vessels of wood and in **v** of stone.'" Ex 7:19
And he made the **v** of pure gold that Ex 37:16
the **v** of the sanctuary with which the Nm 3:31
and all the **v** for oil with which it is Nm 4:9
shall take all the **v** of the service that Nm 4:12
that is in it, of the sanctuary and its **v**." Nm 4:16
silver of the **v** 2,400 shekels according Nm 7:85
come near to the **v** of the sanctuary or Nm 18:3
with the **v** of the sanctuary and the Nm 31:6
gold, and the **v** of bronze and of iron, Jos 6:24
go to the **v** and drink what the young Ru 2:9
The **v** of the young men are holy even 1 Sm 21:5
more today will their **v** be holy?" 1 Sm 21:5
brought beds, basins, and earthen **v**, 2 Sm 17:28
all these **v** in the house of the LORD, 1 Kgs 7:45
Solomon left all the **v** unweighed, 1 Kgs 7:47
Solomon made all the **v** that were in 1 Kgs 7:48
the silver, the gold, and the **v**, 1 Kgs 7:51
and all the holy **v** that were in the tent; 1 Kgs 8:4
King Solomon's drinking **v** were of 1 Kgs 10:21
and all the **v** of the House of the 1 Kgs 10:21
sacred gifts, silver, and gold, and **v**. 1 Kgs 15:15
borrow **v** from all your neighbors, 2 Kgs 4:3
neighbors, empty **v** and not too few. 2 Kgs 4:3
your sons and pour into all these **v**. 2 Kgs 4:4
she poured they brought the **v** to her. 2 Kgs 4:5
When the **v** were full, she said to her 2 Kgs 4:6
bowls, trumpets, or any **v** of gold, 2 Kgs 12:13
and all the **v** that were found in the 2 Kgs 14:14
of the LORD all the **v** made for Baal, 2 Kgs 23:4
cut in pieces all the **v** of gold in the 2 Kgs 24:13
incense and all the **v** of bronze used 2 Kgs 25:14
of all these **v** was beyond weight 2 Kgs 25:16
and the pillars and the **v** of bronze. 1 Chr 18:8
LORD and the holy **v** of God may be 1 Chr 22:19
for all the **v** for the service in the 1 Chr 28:13

Israel lived in Heshbon and its **v**, Jgs 11:26
and its villages, and in Aroer and its **v**, Jgs 11:26
both fortified cities and unwalled **v**. 1 Sm 6:18
(he had the **v** of Jair the 1 Kgs 4:13
them Havvoth-jair, Kenath, and its **v**, 1 Chr 2:23
And their **v** were Etam, Ain, 1 Chr 4:32
with all their **v** that were around 1 Chr 4:33
the city and its **v** they gave to Caleb 1 Chr 6:56
lived in the **v** of the Netophathites. 1 Chr 9:16
enrolled by genealogies in their **v**. 1 Chr 9:22
who were in their **v** were obligated to 1 Chr 9:25
took Gath and its **v** out of the hand 1 Chr 18:1
the cities, in the **v** and in the towers, 1 Chr 27:25
Bethel with its **v** and Jeshanah with 2 Chr 13:19
Jeshanah with its **v** and Ephron 2 Chr 13:19
its villages and Ephron with its **v**. 2 Chr 13:19
Aijalon, Gederoth, Soco with its **v**, 2 Chr 28:18
with its villages, Timnah with its **v**, 2 Chr 28:18
its villages, and Gimzo with its **v**. 2 Chr 28:18
And as for the **v**, with their fields, Neh 11:25
Judah lived in Kiriath-arba and its **v**, Neh 11:25
its villages, and in Dibon and its **v**, Neh 11:25
its villages, and in Jekabzeel and its **v**, Neh 11:25
Hazar-shual, in Beersheba and its **v**, Neh 11:27
in Ziklag, in Meconah and its **v**, Neh 11:28
Zanoah, Adullam, and their **v**, Neh 11:30
and its fields, and Azekah and its **v**, Neh 11:30
at Michmash, Aija, Bethel and its **v**, Neh 11:31
and from the **v** of the Netophathites; Neh 12:28
for themselves **v** around Jerusalem. Neh 12:29
Therefore the Jews of the **v**, who live in Est 9:19
He sits in ambush in the **v**; in hiding Ps 10:8
go out into the fields and lodge in the **v**; Sg 7:11
up their voice, the **v** that Kedar inhabits; Is 42:11
and its **v** shall be burned with fire; Jer 49:2
go up against the land of unwalled **v**. Ezk 38:11
shall be inhabited as **v** without walls, Zec 2:4
went throughout all the cities and **v**, Mt 9:35
away to go into the **v** and buy food for Mt 14:15
he went about among the **v** teaching. Mk 6:6
countryside and **v** and buy Mk 6:36
And wherever he came, in **v**, cities, or Mk 6:56
disciples to the **v** of Caesarea Philippi. Mk 8:27
he went on through cities and **v**, Lk 8:1
they departed and went through the **v**, Lk 9:6
into the surrounding **v** and countryside Lk 9:12
went on his way through towns and **v**, Lk 13:22
gospel to many **v** of the Samaritans. Acts 8:25

VILLAINY (2)
on the way to Shechem; they commit **v**. Hos 6:9
righteousness, full of all deceit and **v**, Acts 13:10

VINDICATE (9)
For the LORD will **v** his people and have Dt 32:36
V me, O LORD, for I have walked in my Ps 26:1
V me, O LORD, my God, according to Ps 35:24
V me, O God, and defend my cause Ps 43:1
by your name, and **v** me by your might. Ps 54:1
For the LORD will **v** his people and have Ps 135:14
And I will **v** the holiness of my great Ezk 36:23
through you I **v** my holiness before Ezk 36:23
Gog, I **v** my holiness before their eyes. Ezk 38:16

VINDICATED (3)
you, and before everyone you are **v**." Gn 20:16
through them have **v** my holiness in Ezk 39:27
in the flesh, **v** by the Spirit, 1 Tm 3:16

VINDICATES (1)
He who **v** me is near. Who will contend Is 50:8

VINDICATING (2)
and **v** the righteous by rewarding 1 Kgs 8:32
and **v** the righteous by rewarding 2 Chr 6:23

VINDICATION (7)
be done. Turn now; my **v** is at stake. Jb 6:29
From your presence let my **v** come! Let Ps 17:2
Awake and rouse yourself for my **v**, for Ps 35:23
of the LORD and their **v** from me, Is 54:17
The LORD has brought about our **v**; Jer 51:10
for he has given the early rain for your **v**; Jl 2:23
out to the light; I shall look upon his **v**. Mi 7:9

VINE (56)
"In my dream there was a **v** before me, Gn 40:9
and on the **v** there were three branches. Gn 40:10
his foal to the **v** and his donkey's colt Gn 49:11
and his donkey's colt to the choice **v**, Gn 49:11
or gather the grapes of your undressed **v**. Lv 25:5
For their **v** comes from the vine of Dt 32:32
vine comes from the **v** of Sodom and Dt 32:32
And the trees said to the **v**, 'You come Jgs 9:12
But the **v** said to them, 'Shall I leave my Jgs 9:13
eat of anything that comes from the **v**, Jgs 13:14
every man under his **v** and under his 1 Kgs 4:25
and found a wild **v** and gathered from 2 Kgs 4:39
each one of you will eat of his own **v**, 2 Kgs 18:31
shake off his unripe grape like the **v**, Jb 15:33
You brought a **v** out of Egypt; you drove Ps 80:8
heaven, and see; have regard for this **v**, Ps 80:14
be like a fruitful **v** within your house; Ps 128:3
may your breasts be like clusters of the **v**, Sg 7:8
Heshbon languish, and the **v** of Sibmah; Is 16:8
the weeping of Jazer for the **v** of Sibmah; Is 16:9
The wine mourns, the **v** languishes, all Is 24:7
for the pleasant fields, for the fruitful **v**, Is 32:12
host shall fall, as leaves fall from the **v**, Is 34:4
each one of you will eat of his own **v**, Is 36:16
Yet I planted you a choice **v**, wholly of Jer 2:21
turned degenerate and become a wild **v**? Jer 2:21
"Go up through her **v** rows and destroy, Jer 5:10
glean thoroughly as a **v** the remnant of Jer 6:9
the LORD, there are no grapes on the **v**, Jer 8:13
for Jazer I weep for you, O **v** of Sibmah! Jer 48:32
the wood of the **v** surpass any wood, Ezk 15:2
the **v** branch that is among the trees of Ezk 15:2
the wood of the **v** among the trees of Ezk 15:6
and became a low spreading **v**, Ezk 17:6
it became a **v** and produced branches Ezk 17:6
this **v** bent its roots toward him and Ezk 17:7
and bear fruit and become a noble **v**. Ezk 17:8
mother was like a **v** in a vineyard Ezk 19:10
But the **v** was plucked up in fury, cast Ezk 19:12
Israel is a luxuriant **v** that yields its Hos 10:1
the grain; they shall blossom like the **v**; Hos 14:7
It has laid waste my **v** and splintered my fig Jl 1:7
The **v** dries up; the fig tree languishes. Jl 1:12
fruit; the fig tree and **v** give their full yield. Jl 2:22
every man under his **v** and under his fig Mi 4:4
Indeed, the **v**, the fig tree, the Hg 2:19
to come under his **v** and under his fig Zec 3:10
The **v** shall give its fruit, and the Zec 8:12
and your **v** in the field shall not fail to Mal 3:11
of this fruit of the **v** until that day when Mt 26:29
of the fruit of the **v** until that day when Mk 14:25
the fruit of the **v** until the kingdom of Lk 22:18
"I am the true **v**, and my Father is the Jn 15:1
fruit by itself, unless it abides in the **v**, Jn 15:4
I am the **v**; you are the branches. Jn 15:5
the clusters from the **v** of the earth, Rv 14:18

VINE-BRANCH (1)
plants and sow the **v** of a stranger, Is 17:10

VINEDRESSER (2)
And he said to the **v**, 'Look, for three Lk 13:7
am the true vine, and my Father is the **v**. Jn 15:1

VINEDRESSERS (5)
of the land to be **v** and plowmen. 2 Kgs 25:12
he had farmers and **v** in the hills 2 Chr 26:10
foreigners shall be your plowmen and **v**; Is 61:5
of the land to be **v** and plowmen. Jer 52:16
wail, O **v**, for the wheat and the barley, Jl 1:11

VINEGAR (3)
He shall drink no **v** made from wine or Nm 6:3
Like **v** to the teeth and smoke to the Prv 10:26
on a cold day, and like **v** on soda. Prv 25:20

VINES (13)
gather the grapes from the undressed **v**. Lv 25:11
for grain or figs or **v** or pomegranates, Nm 20:5
of **v** and fig trees and pomegranates, Dt 8:8
He destroyed their **v** with hail and their Ps 78:47
He struck down their **v** and fig trees, Ps 105:33
ripens its figs, and the **v** are in blossom; Sg 2:13
valley, to see whether the **v** had budded, Sg 6:11
and see whether the **v** have budded, Sg 7:12
it of stones, and planted it with choice **v**; Is 5:2
place where there used to be a thousand **v**, Is 7:23
shall eat up your **v** and your fig trees; Jer 5:17
I will lay waste her **v** and her fig trees, Hos 2:12
not blossom, nor fruit be on the **v**, Hab 3:17

VINEYARD (70)
be a man of the soil, and he planted a **v**. Gn 9:20
man causes a field or **v** to be grazed over, Ex 22:5
best in his own field and in his own **v**. Ex 22:5
You shall do likewise with your **v**, and Ex 23:11
And you shall not strip your **v** bare, Lv 19:10
you gather the fallen grapes of your **v**. Lv 19:10
you shall prune your **v** and gather in its Lv 25:3
shall not sow your field or prune your **v**. Lv 25:4
We will not pass through field or **v**, or Nm 20:17
We will not turn aside into field or **v**. Nm 21:22
who has planted a **v** and has not enjoyed Dt 20:6
shall not sow your **v** with two kinds of Dt 22:9
that you have sown and the yield of the **v**. Dt 22:9
"If you go into your neighbor's **v**, you Dt 23:24
When you gather the grapes of your **v**, Dt 24:21
You shall plant a **v**, but you shall not Dt 28:30
the Jezreelite had a **v** in Jezreel, 1 Kgs 21:1
said to Naboth, "Give me your **v**, 1 Kgs 21:2
and I will give you a better **v** for it; 1 Kgs 21:2
to him, 'Give me your **v** for money, 1 Kgs 21:6
you, I will give you another **v** for it.' 1 Kgs 21:6
answered, 'I will not give you my **v**.'" 1 Kgs 21:6
will give you the **v** of Naboth the 1 Kgs 21:7
possession of the **v** of Naboth the 1 Kgs 21:15
go down to the **v** of Naboth the 1 Kgs 21:16
behold, he is in the **v** of Naboth, 1 Kgs 21:18
and they glean the **v** of the wicked man. Jb 24:6
by the **v** of a man lacking sense, Prv 24:30
the fruit of her hands she plants a **v**. Prv 31:16
vineyards, but my own **v** I have not kept! Sg 1:6
Solomon had a **v** at Baal-hamon; he let Sg 8:11
Baal-hamon; he let out the **v** to keepers; Sg 8:11
My **v**, my very own, is before me; you, O Sg 8:12
daughter of Zion is left like a booth in a **v**, Is 1:8
"It is you who have devoured the **v**, the Is 3:14
beloved my love song concerning his **v**: Is 5:1
My beloved had a **v** on a very fertile hill. Is 5:1
men of Judah, judge between me and my **v**. Is 5:3
What more was there to do for my **v**, that I Is 5:4
now I will tell you what I will do to my **v**. Is 5:5
For the **v** of the LORD of hosts is the house Is 5:7
For ten acres of **v** shall yield but one Is 5:10
In that day, "A pleasant **v**, sing of it! Is 27:2
Many shepherds have destroyed my **v**; Jer 12:10
sow seed; you shall not plant or have a **v**; Jer 35:7
to dwell in. We have no **v** or field or seed, Jer 35:9
like a vine in a **v** planted by the water, Ezk 19:10
in the morning to hire laborers for his **v**. Mt 20:1
a denarius a day, he sent them into his **v**. Mt 20:2
to them he said, 'You go into the **v** too, Mt 20:4
He said to them, 'You go into the **v** too.' Mt 20:7
the owner of the **v** said to his foreman, Mt 20:8
said, 'Son, go and work in the **v** today.' Mt 21:28
house who planted a **v** and put a fence Mt 21:33
threw him out of the **v** and killed him. Mt 21:39
therefore the owner of the **v** comes, Mt 21:40
and let out the **v** to other tenants who Mt 21:41
"A man planted a **v** and put a fence Mk 12:1
get from them some of the fruit of the **v**. Mk 12:2
killed him and threw him out of the **v**. Mk 12:8
What will the owner of the **v** do? He will Mk 12:9
the tenants and give the **v** to others. Mk 12:9
"A man had a fig tree planted in his **v**, Lk 13:6
"A man planted a **v** and let it out to Lk 20:9
give him some of the fruit of the **v**. Lk 20:10
Then the owner of the **v** said, 'What Lk 20:13
threw him out of the **v** and killed him. Lk 20:15
then will the owner of the **v** do to them? Lk 20:15
tenants and give the **v** to others." When Lk 20:16
Who plants a **v** without eating any of 1 Cor 9:7

VINEYARDS (45)
given us inheritance of fields and **v**. Nm 16:14
stood in a narrow path between the **v**, Nm 22:24
and **v** and olive trees that you did not Dt 6:11
You shall plant **v** and dress them, but Dt 28:39
eat the fruit of **v** and olive orchards Jos 24:13
the grapes from their **v** and trod them Jgs 9:27
and they came to the **v** of Timnah. Jgs 14:5
saying, "Go and lie in ambush in the **v** Jgs 21:20
come out of the **v** and snatch each Jgs 21:21
your fields and **v** and olive orchards 1 Sm 8:14
your grain and of your **v** and give it to 1 Sm 8:15
Jesse give every one of you fields and **v**, 1 Sm 22:7
and garments, olive orchards and **v**, 2 Kgs 5:26
and wine, a land of bread and **v**, 2 Kgs 18:32
third year sow and reap and plant **v**, 2 Kgs 19:29
and over the **v** was Shimei the 1 Chr 27:27
the produce of the **v** for the wine 1 Chr 27:27
"We are mortgaging our fields, our **v**, Neh 5:3
the king's tax on our fields and our **v**. Neh 5:4
other men have our fields and our **v**." Neh 5:5
them this very day their fields, their **v**, Neh 5:11
v, olive orchards and fruit trees in Neh 9:25
land; no treader turns toward their **v**. Jb 24:18
sow fields and plant **v** and get a Ps 107:37
I built houses and planted **v** for myself. Eccl 2:4
they made me keeper of the **v**, but my own Sg 1:6
of henna blossoms in the **v** of Engedi. Sg 1:14
for us, the little foxes that spoil the **v**, Sg 2:15
the vineyards, for our **v** are in blossom." Sg 2:15
go out early to the **v** and see whether the Sg 7:12
field, and in the **v** no songs are sung, Is 16:10
of grain and wine, a land of bread and **v**. Is 36:17
the third year sow and reap, and plant **v**, Is 37:30
they shall plant **v** and eat their fruit. Is 65:21
you shall plant **v** on the mountains Jer 31:5
Houses and fields and **v** shall again be Jer 32:15
and gave them **v** and fields at the same Jer 39:10
they shall build houses and plant **v**. Ezk 28:26
will give her her **v** and make the Valley Hos 2:15
your many gardens and your **v**, your fig Am 4:9
you have planted pleasant **v**, but you Am 5:11
and in all **v** there shall be wailing, for I Am 5:17
they shall plant **v** and drink their wine, Am 9:14

the open country, a place for planting **v**, Mi 1:6
though they plant **v**, they shall not Zep 1:13

VIOLATE (7)
V them and do with them what seems Jgs 19:24
him, "No, my brother, do not **v** me, 2 Sm 13:12
abundant righteousness he will not **v**. Jb 37:23
if they **v** my statutes and do not keep Ps 89:31
I will not **v** my covenant or alter the Ps 89:34
in you they **v** women who are unclean Ezk 22:10
with flattery those who **v** the covenant, Dn 11:32

VIOLATED (8)
man because he **v** his neighbor's wife. Dt 22:24
shall be his wife, because he has **v** her. Dt 22:29
to kill me, and they **v** my concubine, Jgs 20:5
than she, he **v** her and lay with her. 2 Sm 13:14
because he had **v** his sister Tamar. 2 Sm 13:22
from the day he **v** his sister Tamar. 2 Sm 13:32
against his friends; he **v** his covenant. Ps 55:20
have transgressed the laws, **v** the statutes, Is 24:5

VIOLATES (1)
another in you **v** his sister, his father's Ezk 22:11

VIOLATION (1)
the poor and the **v** of justice and Eccl 5:8

VIOLENCE (66)
sight, and the earth was filled with **v**. Gn 6:11
the earth is filled with **v** through them. Gn 6:13
brothers; weapons of **v** are their swords. Gn 49:5
that the **v** done to the seventy sons of Jgs 9:24
my savior; you save me from **v**. 2 Sm 22:3
me; you delivered me from men of **v**. 2 Sm 22:49
although there is no **v** in my hands, and Jb 16:17
I cry out, '**V**!' but I am not answered; Jb 19:7
and on his own skull his **v** descends. Ps 7:16
the wicked and the one who loves **v**. Ps 11:5
from the wicked who do me **v**, my deadly Ps 17:9
me; you rescued me from the man of **v**. Ps 18:48
against me, and they breathe out **v**. Ps 27:12
tongues; for I see **v** and strife in the city. Ps 55:9
wrongs; your hands deal out **v** on earth. Ps 58:2
From oppression and **v** he redeems Ps 72:14
necklace; **v** covers them as a garment. Ps 73:6
the land are full of the habitations of **v**. Ps 74:20
not envy a man of **v** and do not choose Prv 3:31
of wickedness and drink the wine of **v**. Prv 4:17
the mouth of the wicked conceals **v**. Prv 10:6
the mouth of the wicked conceals **v**. Prv 10:11
but the desire of the treacherous is for **v**. Prv 13:2
A man of **v** entices his neighbor and Prv 16:29
He who does **v** to his father and chases Prv 19:26
The **v** of the wicked will sweep them Prv 21:7
for their hearts devise **v**, and their lips Prv 24:2
of the righteous; do no **v** to his home; Prv 24:15
a fool cuts off his own feet and drinks **v**. Prv 26:6
in his death, although he had done no **v**, Is 53:9
iniquity, and deeds of **v** are in their hands. Is 59:6
V shall no more be heard in your land, Is 60:18
v and destruction are heard within her; Jer 6:7
skirts are lifted up and you suffer **v**. Jer 13:22
"**V** and destruction!" For the word of the Jer 20:8
do no wrong or **v** to the resident alien, Jer 22:3
and for practicing oppression and **v**." Jer 22:17
The **v** done to me and to my kinsmen Jer 51:35
in another year, and **v** is in the land, Jer 51:46
V has grown up into a rod of Ezk 7:11
bloody crimes and the city is full of **v**. Ezk 7:23
fill the land with **v** and provoke me still Ezk 8:17
on account of the **v** of all those who Ezk 12:19
Her priests have done **v** to my law and Ezk 22:26
you were filled with **v** in your midst, Ezk 28:16
of Israel! Put away **v** and oppression, Ezk 45:9
long; they multiply falsehood and **v**; Hos 12:1
for the **v** done to the people of Judah, Jl 3:19
"those who store up **v** and robbery in Am 3:10
of disaster and bring near the seat of **v**? Am 6:3
Because of the **v** done to your brother Ob 1:10
evil way and from the **v** that is in his Jon 3:8
Your rich men are full of **v**; your Mi 6:12
Or cry to you "**V**!" and you will not Hab 1:2
Destruction and **v** are before me; strife Hab 1:3
They all come for **v**, all their faces Hab 1:9
for the blood of man and **v** to the earth, Hab 2:8
The **v** done to Lebanon will Hab 2:17
for the blood of man and **v** to the earth, Hab 2:17
their master's house with **v** and fraud. Zep 1:9
profane what is holy; they do **v** to the law. Zep 3:4
what has been taken by **v** or is lame or Mal 1:13
of Israel, covers his garment with **v**, Mal 2:16
the kingdom of heaven has suffered **v**, Mt 11:12
soldiers because of the **v** of the crowd, Acts 21:35
the great city be thrown down with **v**, Rv 18:21

VIOLENT (15)
And **v** men shall afflict them no 2 Sm 7:10
And **v** men shall waste them no 1 Chr 17:9
your lips I have avoided the ways of the **v**. Ps 17:4
and with what **v** hatred they hate me. Ps 25:19
from evil men; preserve me from **v** men, Ps 140:1
preserve me from **v** men, who have Ps 140:4
let evil hunt down the **v** man speedily! Ps 140:11
gets honor, and **v** men get riches. Prv 11:16
"If he fathers a son who is **v**, a shedder Ezk 18:10
and the **v** among your own people Dn 11:14
violence, and the **v** take it by force. Mt 11:12
Herod the king laid **v** hands on some Acts 12:1
And when the dissension became **v**, Acts 23:10
not a drunkard, not **v** but gentle, not 1 Tm 3:3
or a drunkard or **v** or greedy for gain, Ti 1:7

VIOLENTLY (5)
Then Isaac trembled very **v** and said, Gn 27:33
Behold, the LORD will hurl you away **v**, O Is 22:17
earth is split apart, the earth is **v** shaken. Is 24:19
Since we were **v** storm-tossed, they Acts 27:18
the church of God **v** and tried to destroy Gal 1:13

VIOLET (2)
cotton curtains and **v** hangings fastened Est 1:6
their clothing is **v** and purple; Jer 10:9

VIPER (4)
be a serpent in the way, a **v** by the path, Gn 49:17
cobras; the tongue of a **v** will kill him. Jb 20:16
from one that is crushed a **v** is hatched. Is 59:5
a **v** came out because of the heat and Acts 28:3

VIPERS (4)
he said to them, "You brood of **v**! Mt 3:7
You brood of **v**! How can you speak Mt 12:34
You serpents, you brood of **v**, how are Mt 23:33
to be baptized by him, "You brood of **v**! Lk 3:7

VIRGIN (36)
Let the **v** who comes out to draw water, Gn 24:43
a man seduces a **v** who is not engaged Ex 22:16
or his **v** sister (who is near to him Lv 21:3
take as his wife a **v** of his own people, Lv 21:14
brought a bad name upon a **v** of Israel. Dt 22:19
"If there is a betrothed **v**, and a man Dt 22:23
a man meets a **v** who is not betrothed, Dt 22:28
here are my **v** daughter and his Jgs 19:24
of his sister Tamar, for she was a **v**, 2 Sm 13:2
for thus were the **v** daughters of the 2 Sm 13:18
scorns you—the **v** daughter of Zion; 2 Kgs 19:21
no compassion on young man or **v**, 2 Chr 36:17
my eyes; how then could I gaze at a **v**? Jb 31:1
with her **v** companions following Ps 45:14
seas, and the way of a man with a **v**. Prv 30:19
the **v** shall conceive and bear a son, Is 7:14
exult, O oppressed **v** daughter of Sidon; Is 23:12
she scorns you—the **v** daughter of Zion; Is 37:22
sit in the dust, O **v** daughter of Babylon; Is 47:1
Can a **v** forget her ornaments, or a bride Jer 2:32
for the **v** daughter of my people is Jer 14:17
The **v** Israel has done a very horrible Jer 18:13
you, and you shall be built, O **v** Israel! Jer 31:4
Return, O **v** Israel, return to these your Jer 31:21
and take balm, O **v** daughter of Egypt! Jer 46:11
in a winepress the **v** daughter of Judah. Lam 1:15
comfort you, O **v** daughter of Zion? Lam 2:13
pressed and their **v** bosoms handled. Ezk 23:3
and handled her **v** bosom and poured Ezk 23:8
Lament like a **v** wearing sackcloth for the Jl 1:8
"Fallen, no more to rise, is the **v** Israel; Am 5:2
the **v** shall conceive and bear a son, Mt 1:23
to a **v** betrothed to a man whose name Lk 1:27
angel, "How will this be, since I am a **v**?" Lk 1:34
seven years from when she was a **v**, Lk 2:36
to present you as a pure **v** to Christ. 2 Cor 11:2

VIRGIN'S (1)
of David. And the **v** name was Mary. Lk 1:27

VIRGINITY (8)
And he shall take a wife in her **v**. Lv 21:13
her, I did not find in her evidence of **v**,' Dt 22:14
out the evidence of her **v** to the elders of Dt 22:15
daughter evidence of **v**." And yet this Dt 22:17
this is the evidence of my daughter's **v**.' Dt 22:17
that evidence of **v** was not found in the Dt 22:20
on the mountains and weep for my **v**, Jgs 11:37
and wept for her **v** on the mountains. Jgs 11:38

VIRGINS (16)
money equal to the bride-price for **v**. Ex 22:17
Jabesh-gilead 400 young **v** who had not Jgs 21:12
"Let beautiful young **v** be sought out for Est 2:2
all the beautiful young **v** to the harem in Est 2:3
favor in his sight more than all the **v**, Est 2:17
Now when the **v** were gathered together Est 2:19
between them **v** playing tambourines: Ps 68:25
is oil poured out; therefore **v** love you. Sg 1:3
concubines, and **v** without number. Sg 6:8
her **v** have been afflicted, and she Lam 1:4
but only **v** of the offspring of the Ezk 44:22
that day the lovely **v** and the young Am 8:13
will be like ten **v** who took their lamps Mt 25:1
Then all those **v** rose and trimmed their Mt 25:7
Afterward the other **v** came also, Mt 25:11
themselves with women, for they are **v**. Rv 14:4

VIRTUE (2)
effort to supplement your faith with **v**, 2 Pt 1:5
faith with virtue, and **v** with knowledge, 2 Pt 1:5

VISIBLE (6)
and it was **v** to the end of the whole Dn 4:11
and it was **v** to the end of the whole Dn 4:20
is exposed by the light, it becomes **v**, Eph 5:13
for anything that becomes **v** is light. Eph 5:14
in heaven and on earth, **v** and invisible, Col 1:16
was not made out of things that are **v**. Heb 11:3

VISION (80)
word of the LORD came to Abram in a **v**: Gn 15:1
make myself known to him in a **v**; Nm 12:6
of God, who sees the **v** of the Almighty, Nm 24:4
High, who sees the **v** of the Almighty, Nm 24:16
in those days; there was no frequent **v**. 1 Sm 3:1
Samuel was afraid to tell the **v** to Eli. 1 Sm 3:15
and in accordance with all this **v**, 2 Sm 7:17
and in accordance with all this **v**, 1 Chr 17:15
are written in the **v** of Isaiah the 2 Chr 32:32
will be chased away like a **v** of the night. Jb 20:8
In a dream, in a **v** of the night, when Jb 33:15
old you spoke in a **v** to your godly one, Ps 89:19
there is no prophetic **v** the people cast Prv 29:18
The **v** of Isaiah the son of Amoz, which he Is 1:1
A stern **v** is told to me; the traitor betrays, Is 21:2
The oracle concerning the valley of **v**. Is 22:1
and confusion in the valley of **v**, Is 22:5
stagger with strong drink, they reel in **v**, Is 28:7
her, shall be like a dream, a **v** of the night. Is 29:7
And the **v** of all this has become to you Is 29:11
They are prophesying to you a lying **v**, Jer 14:14
to Babylon, the LORD showed me this **v**: Jer 24:1
this is the **v** which the LORD has shown Jer 38:21
her prophets find no **v** from the LORD. Lam 2:9
For the **v** concerns all their multitude; Ezk 7:13
rumor. They seek a **v** from the prophet, Ezk 7:26
there, like the **v** that I saw in the valley. Ezk 8:4
brought me in the **v** by the Spirit of Ezk 11:24
Then the **v** that I had seen went up Ezk 11:24
long, and every **v** comes to nothing'? Ezk 12:22
near, and the fulfillment of every **v**. Ezk 12:23
more any false **v** or flattering Ezk 12:24
'The **v** that he sees is for many days Ezk 12:27
not seen a false **v** and uttered a lying Ezk 13:7
And the **v** I saw was just like the vision Ezk 43:3
saw was just like the **v** that I had seen Ezk 43:3
and just like the **v** that I had seen by the Ezk 43:3
revealed to Daniel in a **v** of the night. Dn 2:19
Daniel declared, "I saw in my **v** by night, Dn 7:2
of King Belshazzar a **v** appeared to me, Dn 8:1
And I saw in the **v**; and when I saw, I was Dn 8:2
And I saw in the **v**, and I was at the Ulai Dn 8:2
long is the **v** concerning the regular Dn 8:13
When I, Daniel, had seen the **v**, I sought Dn 8:15
make this man understand the **v**." Dn 8:16
that the **v** is for the time of the end." Dn 8:17
The **v** of the evenings and the mornings Dn 8:26
has been told is true, but seal up the **v**, Dn 8:26
was appalled by the **v** and did not Dn 8:27
whom I had seen in the **v** at the first, Dn 9:21
consider the word and understand the **v**. Dn 9:23
to seal both **v** and prophet, Dn 9:24
word and had understanding of the **v**. Dn 10:1
And I, Daniel, alone saw the **v**, for the Dn 10:7
men who were with me did not see the **v**, Dn 10:7
So I was left alone and saw this great **v**, Dn 10:8
days. For the **v** is for days yet to come." Dn 10:14
by reason of the **v** pains have come Dn 10:16
themselves up in order to fulfill the **v**, Dn 11:14
The **v** of Obadiah. Thus says the Lord Ob 1:1
it shall be night to you, without **v**, Mi 3:6
The book of the **v** of Nahum of Elkosh. Na 1:1
the LORD answered me: "Write the **v**; Hab 2:2
For still the **v** awaits its appointed time; Hab 2:3
ashamed of his **v** when he prophesies. Zec 13:4
commanded them, "Tell no one the **v**, Mt 17:9
that he had seen a **v** in the temple. Lk 1:22
that they had even seen a **v** of angels, Lk 24:23
The Lord said to him in a **v**, Acts 9:10
has seen in a **v** a man named Ananias Acts 9:12
he saw clearly in a **v** an angel of God Acts 10:3
as to what the **v** that he had seen Acts 10:17
And while Peter was pondering the **v**, Acts 10:19
praying, and in a trance I saw a **v**, Acts 11:5
real, but thought he was seeing a **v**. Acts 12:9
And a **v** appeared to Paul in the night: Acts 16:9
And when Paul had seen the **v**, Acts 16:10

the Lord said to Paul one night in a **v**, Acts 18:9
was not disobedient to the heavenly **v**, Acts 26:19
the horses in my **v** and those who rode Rv 9:17

VISIONS (31)
God spoke to Israel in **v** of the night and Gn 46:2
and in the **v** of Iddo the seer 2 Chr 9:29
Amid thoughts from **v** of the night, when Jb 4:13
me with dreams and terrify me with **v**, Jb 7:14
They speak **v** of their own minds, not Jer 23:16
have seen for you false and deceptive **v**; Lam 2:14
heavens were opened, and I saw **v** of God. Ezk 1:1
and brought me in **v** of God to Ezk 8:3
have seen false **v** and lying divinations. Ezk 13:6
have uttered falsehood and seen lying **v**, Ezk 13:8
prophets who see false **v** and who give Ezk 13:9
Jerusalem and saw **v** of peace for Ezk 13:16
more see false **v** nor practice Ezk 13:23
while they see for you false **v**, while Ezk 21:29
seeing false **v** and divining lies for Ezk 22:28
In **v** of God he brought me to the land Ezk 40:2
had understanding in all **v** and dreams. Dn 1:17
Your dream and the **v** of your head as Dn 2:28
the fancies and the **v** of my head alarmed Dn 4:5
tell me the **v** of my dream that I saw and Dn 4:9
The **v** of my head as I lay in bed were Dn 4:10
"I saw in the **v** of my head as I lay in bed, Dn 4:13
Daniel saw a dream and **v** of his head as Dn 7:1
After this I saw in the night **v**, and Dn 7:7
I saw in the night **v**, and behold, with Dn 7:13
and the **v** of my head alarmed me. Dn 7:15
it was I who multiplied **v**, and through Hos 12:10
dreams, and your young men shall see **v**. Jl 2:28
and your young men shall see **v**, Acts 2:17
I will go on to **v** and revelations of the 2 Cor 12:1
of angels, going on in detail about **v**, Col 2:18

VISIT (32)
but God will **v** you and bring you up Gn 50:24
swear, saying, "God will surely **v** you, Gn 50:25
swear, saying, "God will surely **v** you, Ex 13:19
Nevertheless, in the day when I **v**, I will Ex 32:34
I visit, I will **v** their sin upon them." Ex 32:34
I will **v** you with panic, with wasting Lv 26:16
Samson went to **v** his wife with a young Jgs 15:1
of Judah had come down to **v** Joram. 2 Kgs 9:16
we came down to **v** the royal princes 2 Kgs 10:13
about through his going to **v** Joram. 2 Chr 22:7
v him every morning and test him every Jb 7:18
You **v** the earth and water it; you greatly Ps 65:9
of seventy years, the LORD will **v** Tyre, Is 23:17
remember me and **v** me, and take Jer 15:15
there until the day when I **v** them, Jer 27:22
are completed for Babylon, I will **v** you, Jer 29:10
and there he shall remain until I **v** him, Jer 32:5
we see you sick or in prison and **v** you?' Mt 25:39
and in prison and you did not **v** me.' Mt 25:43
whereby the sunrise shall **v** us from on Lk 1:78
he sent out our fathers on their first **v**. Acts 7:12
on the second **v** Joseph made himself Acts 7:13
it came into his heart to **v** his brothers, Acts 7:23
with or to **v** anyone of another Acts 10:28
"Let us return and **v** the brothers in Acts 15:36
I will **v** you after passing through 1 Cor 16:5
urged him to **v** you with the 1 Cor 16:12
I wanted to **v** you on my way to 2 Cor 1:16
not to make another painful **v** to you. 2 Cor 2:1
as I did when present on my second **v**, 2 Cor 13:2
to Jerusalem to **v** Cephas and remained Gal 1:18
to **v** orphans and widows in their Jas 1:27

VISITATION (2)
you did not know the time of your **v**." Lk 19:44
deeds and glorify God on the day of **v**. 1 Pt 2:12

VISITED (15)
The LORD **v** Sarah as he had said, and Gn 21:1
that the LORD had **v** the people of Israel Ex 4:31
or if they are **v** by the fate of all Nm 16:29
that the LORD had **v** his people and given Ru 1:6
Indeed the LORD **v** Hannah, and she 1 Sm 2:21
tried my heart, you have **v** me by night, Ps 17:3
satisfied; he will not be **v** by harm. Prv 19:23
end you have **v** them with destruction Is 26:14
you will be **v** by the LORD of hosts with Is 29:6
clothed me, I was sick and you **v** me, Mt 25:36
for he has **v** and redeemed his people Lk 1:68
among us!" and "God has **v** his people!" Lk 7:16
related how God first **v** the Gentiles, Acts 15:14
went out of the prison and **v** Lydia. Acts 16:40
And Paul **v** him and prayed, and Acts 28:8

VISITING (4)
v the iniquity of the fathers on the Ex 20:5
v the iniquity of the fathers on the Ex 34:7
v the iniquity of the fathers on the Nm 14:18
v the iniquity of the fathers on the Dt 5:9

VISITOR (1)
"Are you the only **v** to Jerusalem who Lk 24:18

VISITORS (1)
to Cyrene, and **v** from Rome, Acts 2:10

VOICE (396)
have listened to the **v** of your wife and Gn 3:17
The **v** of your brother's blood is crying Gn 4:10
his wives: "Adah and Zillah, hear my **v**; Gn 4:23
And Abram listened to the **v** of Sarai. Gn 16:2
him, she lifted up her **v** and wept. Gn 21:16
And God heard the **v** of the boy, and Gn 21:17
God has heard the **v** of the boy where Gn 21:17
because you have obeyed my **v**." Gn 22:18
Abraham obeyed my **v** and kept my Gn 26:5
my son, obey my **v** as I command you. Gn 27:8
only obey my **v**, and go, bring them to Gn 27:13
him and said, "The **v** is Jacob's voice, Gn 27:22
him and said, "The voice is Jacob's **v**, Gn 27:22
And Esau lifted up his **v** and wept. Gn 27:38
Now therefore, my son, obey my **v**. Gn 27:43
and has also heard my **v** and given me a Gn 30:6
with me, and I cried out with a loud **v**. Gn 39:14
that I lifted up my **v** and cried out, Gn 39:15
as soon as I lifted up my **v** and cried, Gn 39:18
And they will listen to your **v**, and you Ex 3:18
they will not believe me or listen to my **v**, Ex 4:1
even these two signs or listen to your **v**, Ex 4:9
that I should obey his **v** and let Israel go? Ex 5:2
diligently listen to the **v** of the LORD Ex 15:26
Now obey my **v**; I will give you advice, Ex 18:19
listened to the **v** of his father-in-law Ex 18:24
will indeed obey my **v** and keep my Ex 19:5
careful attention to him and obey his **v**; Ex 23:21
you carefully obey his **v** and do all that Ex 23:22
the people answered with one **v** and said, Ex 24:3
he heard the **v** speaking to him from Nm 7:89
ten times and have not obeyed my **v**, Nm 14:22
he heard our **v** and sent an angel and Nm 20:16
the LORD obeyed the **v** of Israel and gave Nm 21:3
did not listen to your **v** or give ear to you. Dt 1:45
but saw no form; there was only a **v**. Dt 4:12
to the LORD your God and obey his **v**. Dt 4:30
people ever hear the **v** of a god speaking Dt 4:33
Out of heaven he let you hear his **v**, that Dt 4:36
and the thick darkness, with a loud **v**; Dt 5:22
soon as you heard the **v** out of the midst Dt 5:23
and we have heard his **v** out of the midst Dt 5:24
If we hear the **v** of the LORD our God any Dt 5:25
that has heard the **v** of the living God Dt 5:26
would not obey the **v** of the LORD your Dt 8:20
and did not believe him or obey his **v**. Dt 9:23
keep his commandments and obey his **v**, Dt 13:4
if you obey the **v** of the LORD your God, Dt 13:18
will strictly obey the **v** of the LORD your Dt 15:5
me not hear again the **v** of the LORD my Dt 18:16
who will not obey the **v** of his father or Dt 21:18
of his father or the **v** of his mother, Dt 21:18
and rebellious; he will not obey our **v**; Dt 21:20
the LORD heard our **v** and saw our Dt 26:7
I have obeyed the **v** of the LORD my God. Dt 26:14
and his rules, and will obey his **v**. Dt 26:17
shall therefore obey the **v** of the LORD Dt 27:10
to all the men of Israel in a loud **v**: Dt 27:14
you faithfully obey the **v** of the LORD Dt 28:1
if you obey the **v** of the LORD your God. Dt 28:2
you will not obey the **v** of the LORD your Dt 28:15
you did not obey the **v** of the LORD your Dt 28:45
you did not obey the **v** of the LORD your Dt 28:62
and obey his **v** in all that I command Dt 30:2
shall again obey the **v** of the LORD and Dt 30:8
when you obey the **v** of the LORD your Dt 30:10
obeying his **v** and holding fast to him, Dt 30:20
"Hear, O LORD, the **v** of Judah, and bring Dt 33:7
they did not obey the **v** of the LORD; Jos 5:6
shall not shout or make your **v** heard, Jos 6:10
when the LORD obeyed the **v** of a man, Jos 10:14
you and have obeyed my **v** in all that I Jos 22:2
we will serve, and his **v** we will obey." Jos 24:24
altars.' But you have not obeyed my **v**. Jgs 2:2
their fathers and have not obeyed my **v**, Jgs 2:20
dwell.' But you have not obeyed my **v**." Jgs 6:10
And God listened to the **v** of Manoah, Jgs 13:9
they recognized the **v** of the young Jgs 18:3
"Do not let your **v** be heard among us, Jgs 18:25
not listen to the **v** of their brothers, Jgs 20:13
lips moved, and her **v** was not heard. 1 Sm 1:13
not listen to the **v** of their father, 1 Sm 2:25
"Obey the **v** of the people in all that 1 Sm 8:7
Now then, obey their **v**; only you shall 1 Sm 8:9
people refused to obey the **v** of Samuel. 1 Sm 8:19
"Obey their **v** and make them a king." 1 Sm 8:22
I have obeyed your **v** in all that you 1 Sm 12:1
him and obey his **v** and not rebel 1 Sm 12:14
if you will not obey the **v** of the LORD, 1 Sm 12:15
did you not obey the **v** of the LORD? 1 Sm 15:19
"I have obeyed the **v** of the LORD. 1 Sm 15:20
as in obeying the **v** of the LORD? 1 Sm 15:22
I feared the people and obeyed their **v**. 1 Sm 15:24
And Saul listened to the **v** of Jonathan. 1 Sm 19:6
to Saul, Saul said, "Is this your **v**, 1 Sm 24:16
And Saul lifted up his **v** and wept. 1 Sm 24:16
See, I have obeyed your **v**, and I have 1 Sm 25:35
Saul recognized David's **v** and said, 1 Sm 26:17
voice and said, "Is this your **v**, 1 Sm 26:17
David?" And David said, "It is my **v**, 1 Sm 26:17
Samuel, she cried out with a loud **v**. 1 Sm 28:12
did not obey the **v** of the LORD and 1 Sm 28:18
the king lifted up his **v** and wept at the 2 Sm 3:32
came and lifted up their **v** and wept. 2 Sm 13:36
face, and the king cried with a loud **v**, 2 Sm 19:4
still listen to the **v** of singing men 2 Sm 19:35
From his temple he heard my **v**, and 2 Sm 22:7
and the Most High uttered his **v**. 2 Sm 22:14
the assembly of Israel with a loud **v**, 1 Kgs 8:55
the LORD listened to the **v** of Elijah. 1 Kgs 17:22
answer us!" But there was no **v**, 1 Kgs 18:26
of the oblation, but there was no **v**. 1 Kgs 18:29
there came a **v** to him and said, 1 Kgs 19:13
And he listened to their **v** and did so. 1 Kgs 20:25
have not obeyed the **v** of the LORD, 1 Kgs 20:36
did not obey the **v** of the LORD their 2 Kgs 18:12
out in a loud **v** in the language of 2 Kgs 18:28
you raised your **v** and lifted your 2 Kgs 19:22
with a loud **v** and with shouting 2 Chr 15:14
the God of Israel, with a very loud **v**. 2 Chr 20:19
the people, and their **v** was heard, 2 Chr 30:27
it with a loud **v** in the language of 2 Chr 32:18
wept with a loud **v** when they saw the Ezr 3:12
the assembly answered with a loud **v**, Ezr 10:12
they cried with a loud **v** to the LORD their Neh 9:4
they hear not the **v** of the taskmaster. Jb 3:18
roar of the lion, the **v** of the fierce lion, Jb 4:10
eyes; there was silence, then I heard a **v**: Jb 4:16
not believe that he was listening to my **v**. Jb 9:16
the **v** of the nobles was hushed, and Jb 29:10
and my pipe to the **v** of those who weep. Jb 30:31
the thunder of his **v** and the rumbling Jb 37:2
After it his **v** roars; he thunders with his Jb 37:4
he thunders with his majestic **v**, and he Jb 37:4
the lightnings when his **v** is heard. Jb 37:4
God thunders wondrously with his **v**; he Jb 37:5
"Can you lift up your **v** to the clouds, Jb 38:34
and can you thunder with a **v** like his? Jb 40:9
O LORD, in the morning you hear my **v**; in Ps 5:3
From his temple he heard my **v**, and my Ps 18:6
and the Most High uttered his **v**, Ps 18:13
nor are there words, whose **v** is not heard. Ps 19:3
Hear the **v** of my pleas for mercy, when I Ps 28:2
for he has heard the **v** of my pleas for Ps 28:6
The **v** of the LORD is over the waters; the Ps 29:3
The **v** of the LORD is powerful; the voice of Ps 29:4
the **v** of the LORD is full of majesty. Ps 29:4
The **v** of the LORD breaks the cedars; the Ps 29:5
The **v** of the LORD flashes forth flames of Ps 29:7
The **v** of the LORD shakes the wilderness; Ps 29:8
The **v** of the LORD makes the deer give Ps 29:9
But you heard the **v** of my pleas for Ps 31:22
totter; he utters his **v**, the earth melts. Ps 46:6
and moan, and he hears my **v**. Ps 55:17
it does not hear the **v** of charmers or of Ps 58:5
Hear my **v**, O God, in my complaint; Ps 64:1
he has attended to the **v** of my prayer. Ps 66:19
behold, he sends out his **v**, his mighty Ps 68:33
he sends out his voice, his mighty **v**. Ps 68:33
"But my people did not listen to my **v**; Ps 81:11
O LORD, the floods have lifted up their **v**; Ps 93:3
of his hand. Today, if you hear his **v**, Ps 95:7
do his word, obeying the **v** of his word! Ps 103:20
and did not obey the **v** of the LORD. Ps 106:25
he has heard my **v** and my pleas for Ps 116:1
Hear my **v** according to your Ps 119:149
O Lord, hear my **v**! Let your ears be Ps 130:2
ears be attentive to the **v** of my pleas for Ps 130:2
give ear to the **v** of my pleas for mercy, Ps 140:6
me! Give ear to my **v** when I call to you! Ps 141:1
With my **v** I cry out to the LORD; with Ps 142:1
with my **v** I plead for mercy to the LORD. Ps 142:1
street, in the markets she raises her **v**; Prv 1:20
and raise your **v** for understanding, Prv 2:3
did not listen to the **v** of my teachers or Prv 5:13
Does not understanding raise her **v**? Prv 8:1
blesses his neighbor with a loud **v**, Prv 27:14
and a fool's **v** with many words. Eccl 5:3
be angry at your **v** and destroy the work Eccl 5:6
for a bird of the air will carry your **v**, Eccl 10:20
The **v** of my beloved! Behold, he comes, Sg 2:8
and the **v** of the turtledove is heard in our Sg 2:12
let me see your face, let me hear your **v**, Sg 2:14
me hear your voice, for your **v** is sweet, Sg 2:14

with companions listening for your **v**; Sg 8:13
thresholds shook at the **v** of him who Is 6:4
And I heard the **v** of the Lord saying, Is 6:8
cry out; their **v** is heard as far as Jahaz; Is 15:4
Give ear, and hear my **v**; give attention, Is 28:23
your **v** shall come from the ground like Is 29:4
from the ground like the **v** of a ghost, Is 29:4
will cause his majestic **v** to be heard and Is 30:30
be terror-stricken at the **v** of the LORD, Is 30:31
you women who are at ease, hear my **v**; Is 32:9
called out in a loud **v** in the language of Is 36:13
have you raised your **v** and lifted your Is 37:23
A **v** cries: "In the wilderness prepare the Is 40:3
A **v** says, "Cry!" And I said, "What shall I Is 40:6
lift up your **v** with strength, O Jerusalem, Is 40:9
He will not cry aloud or lift up his **v**, or Is 42:2
Let the desert and its cities lift up their **v**, Is 42:11
the LORD and obeys the **v** of his servant? Is 50:10
in her, thanksgiving and the **v** of song. Is 51:3
The **v** of your watchmen—they lift up Is 52:8
of your watchmen—they lift up their **v**; Is 52:8
hold back; lift up your **v** like a trumpet; Is 58:1
day will not make your **v** to be heard on Is 58:4
tree, and that you have not obeyed my **v**, Jer 3:13
A **v** on the bare heights is heard, the Jer 3:21
we have not obeyed the **v** of the LORD our Jer 3:25
For a **v** declares from Dan and Jer 4:15
'Obey my **v**, and I will be your God, and Jer 7:23
that did not obey the **v** of the LORD their Jer 7:28
streets of Jerusalem the **v** of mirth and Jer 7:34
the voice of mirth and the **v** of gladness, Jer 7:34
the **v** of the bridegroom and the voice of Jer 7:34
of the bridegroom and the **v** of the bride, Jer 7:34
have not obeyed my **v** or walked in Jer 9:13
When he utters his **v**, there is a tumult Jer 10:13
A **v**, a rumor! Behold, it comes! Jer 10:22
the iron furnace, saying, Listen to my **v**, Jer 11:4
even to this day, saying, Obey my **v**. Jer 11:7
forest; she has lifted up her **v** against me; Jer 12:8
the **v** of mirth and the voice of gladness, Jer 16:9
the voice of mirth and the **v** of gladness, Jer 16:9
the **v** of the bridegroom and the voice of Jer 16:9
of the bridegroom and the **v** of the bride. Jer 16:9
evil in my sight, not listening to my **v**, Jer 18:10
and listen to the **v** of my adversaries. Jer 18:19
cry out, and lift up your **v** in Bashan; Jer 22:20
youth, that you have not obeyed my **v**. Jer 22:21
banish from them the **v** of mirth and Jer 25:10
the voice of mirth and the **v** of gladness, Jer 25:10
the **v** of the bridegroom and the voice of Jer 25:10
the bridegroom and the **v** of the bride, Jer 25:10
from his holy habitation utter his **v**; Jer 25:30
A **v**—the cry of the shepherds, and the Jer 25:36
and obey the **v** of the LORD your God, Jer 26:13
"A **v** is heard in Ramah, lamentation Jer 31:15
the LORD: "Keep your **v** from weeping, Jer 31:16
did not obey your **v** or walk in your Jer 32:23
the **v** of mirth and the voice of gladness, Jer 33:11
the voice of mirth and the **v** of gladness, Jer 33:11
the **v** of the bridegroom and the voice of Jer 33:11
the bridegroom and the **v** of the bride, Jer 33:11
We have obeyed the **v** of Jonadab the son Jer 35:8
Obey now the **v** of the LORD in what I Jer 38:20
against the LORD and did not obey his **v**, Jer 40:3
we will obey the **v** of the LORD our God to Jer 42:6
us when we obey the **v** of the LORD our Jer 42:6
disobeying the **v** of the LORD your God Jer 42:13
have not obeyed the **v** of the LORD your Jer 42:21
the people did not obey the **v** of the LORD, Jer 43:4
for they did not obey the **v** of the LORD. Jer 43:7
and did not obey the **v** of the LORD or Jer 44:23
as far as Jahaz they utter their **v**, Jer 48:34
"A **v**! They flee and escape from the Jer 50:28
When he utters his **v** there is a tumult Jer 51:16
"A **v**! A cry from Babylon! The noise of Jer 51:54
waste and stilling her mighty **v**. Jer 51:55
waters; the noise of their **v** is raised, Jer 51:55
And there came a **v** from above the Ezk 1:25
face, and I heard the **v** of one speaking. Ezk 1:28
heard behind me the **v** of a great Ezk 3:12
they cry in my ears with a loud **v**, Ezk 8:18
Then he cried in my ears with a loud **v**, Ezk 9:1
like the **v** of God Almighty when he Ezk 10:5
and cried out with a loud **v** and said, Ezk 11:13
that his **v** should no more be heard on Ezk 19:9
murder, to lift up the **v** with shouting, Ezk 21:22
with a beautiful **v** and plays well Ezk 33:32
mouth, there fell a **v** from heaven, Dn 4:31
I heard a man's **v** between the banks of Dn 8:16
have not obeyed the **v** of the LORD our Dn 9:10
turned aside, refusing to obey your **v**. Dn 9:11
has done, and we have not obeyed his **v**. Dn 9:14
The LORD utters his **v** before his army, for Jl 2:11
Zion, and utters his **v** from Jerusalem, Jl 3:16
Zion and utters his **v** from Jerusalem; Am 1:2
of Sheol I cried, and you heard my **v**. Jon 2:2
But I with the **v** of thanksgiving will Jon 2:9
mountains, and let the hills hear your **v**. Mi 6:1
The **v** of the LORD cries to the city—and it Mi 6:9
and the **v** of your messengers shall no Na 2:13
swept on; the deep gave forth its **v**; Hab 3:10
capitals; a **v** shall hoot in the window; Zep 2:14
She listens to no **v**; she accepts no Zep 3:2
obeyed the **v** of the LORD their God, Hg 1:12
will diligently obey the **v** of the LORD Zec 6:15
"A **v** was heard in Ramah, weeping and Mt 2:18
"The **v** of one crying in the wilderness: Mt 3:3
and behold, a **v** from heaven said, "This Mt 3:17
will anyone hear his **v** in the streets; Mt 12:19
them, and a **v** from the cloud said, Mt 17:5
hour Jesus cried out with a loud **v**, Mt 27:46
again with a loud **v** and yielded up his Mt 27:50
the **v** of one crying in the wilderness: Mk 1:3
And a **v** came from heaven, "You are Mk 1:11
him and crying out with a loud **v**, Mk 1:26
And crying out with a loud **v**, he said, Mk 5:7
them, and a **v** came out of the cloud, Mk 9:7
ninth hour Jesus cried with a loud **v**, Mk 15:34
"The **v** of one crying in the wilderness: Lk 3:4
and a **v** came from heaven, "You are my Lk 3:22
demon, and he cried out with a loud **v**, Lk 4:33
down before him and said with a loud **v**, Lk 8:28
And a **v** came out of the cloud, saying, Lk 9:35
And when the **v** had spoken, Jesus was Lk 9:36
the crowd raised her **v** and said to him, Lk 11:27
back, praising God with a loud **v**; Lk 17:15
God with a loud **v** for all the mighty Lk 19:37
Then Jesus, calling out with a loud **v**, Lk 23:46
"I am the **v** of one crying out in the Jn 1:23
rejoices greatly at the bridegroom's **v**. Jn 3:29
the dead will hear the **v** of the Son of God, Jn 5:25
all who are in the tombs will hear his **v** Jn 5:28
His **v** you have never heard, his form you Jn 5:37
The sheep hear his **v**, and he calls his Jn 10:3
sheep follow him, for they know his **v**. Jn 10:4
for they do not know the **v** of strangers." Jn 10:5
them also, and they will listen to my **v**. Jn 10:16
My sheep hear my **v**, and I know them, Jn 10:27
these things, he cried out with a loud **v**, Jn 11:43
name." Then a **v** came from heaven: Jn 12:28
"This **v** has come for your sake, Jn 12:30
who is of the truth listens to my **v**." Jn 18:37
lifted up his **v** and addressed them, Acts 2:14
to look, there came the **v** of the Lord: Acts 7:31
out with a loud **v** and stopped their Acts 7:57
to his knees he cried out with a loud **v**, Acts 7:60
were possessed, crying with a loud **v**, Acts 8:7
the ground he heard a **v** saying to him, Acts 9:4
hearing the **v** but seeing no one. Acts 9:7
And there came a **v** to him: "Rise, Acts 10:13
And the **v** came to him again a Acts 10:15
And I heard a **v** saying to me, 'Rise, Acts 11:7
But the **v** answered a second time from Acts 11:9
Recognizing Peter's **v**, in her joy she Acts 12:14
people were shouting, "The **v** of a god, Acts 12:22
said in a loud **v**, "Stand upright on Acts 14:10
But Paul cried with a loud **v**, "Do not Acts 16:28
hours they all cried out with one **v**, Acts 19:34
the ground and heard a **v** saying to me, Acts 22:7
did not understand the **v** of the one Acts 22:9
One and to hear a **v** from his mouth; Acts 22:14
I heard a **v** saying to me in the Acts 26:14
his defense, Festus said with a loud **v**, Acts 26:24
for "Their **v** has gone out to all the Rom 10:18
you may with one **v** glorify the God Rom 15:6
with the **v** of an archangel, 1 Thes 4:16
Spirit says, "Today, if you hear his **v**, Heb 3:7
As it is said, "Today, if you hear his **v**, Heb 3:15
quoted, "Today, if you hear his **v**, Heb 4:7
a trumpet and a **v** whose words made Heb 12:19
At that time his **v** shook the earth, but Heb 12:26
and the **v** was borne to him by the 2 Pt 1:17
heard this very **v** borne from heaven, 2 Pt 1:18
spoke with human **v** and restrained the 2 Pt 2:16
heard behind me a loud **v** like a trumpet Rv 1:10
I turned to see the **v** that was speaking to Rv 1:12
and his **v** was like the roar of many Rv 1:15
If anyone hears my **v** and opens the door, Rv 3:20
And the first **v**, which I had heard Rv 4:1
a strong angel proclaiming with a loud **v**, Rv 5:2
and the elders the **v** of many angels, Rv 5:11
saying with a loud **v**, "Worthy is the Rv 5:12
living creatures say with a **v** like thunder, Rv 6:1
what seemed to be a **v** in the midst of the Rv 6:6
I heard the **v** of the fourth living creature Rv 6:7
They cried out with a loud **v**, "O Rv 6:10
he called with a loud **v** to the four angels Rv 7:2
and crying out with a loud **v**, "Salvation Rv 7:10
crying with a loud **v** as it flew directly Rv 8:13
and I heard a **v** from the four horns of Rv 9:13
and called out with a loud **v**, like a lion Rv 10:3
but I heard a **v** from heaven saying, Rv 10:4
Then the **v** that I had heard from heaven Rv 10:8
they heard a loud **v** from heaven saying Rv 11:12
And I heard a loud **v** in heaven, saying, Rv 12:10
And I heard a **v** from heaven like the Rv 14:2
The **v** I heard was like the sound of Rv 14:2
And he said with a loud **v**, "Fear God and Rv 14:7
followed them, saying with a loud **v**, Rv 14:9
And I heard a **v** from heaven saying, Rv 14:13
calling with a loud **v** to him who sat on Rv 14:15
he called with a loud **v** to the one who Rv 14:18
I heard a loud **v** from the temple telling Rv 16:1
and a loud **v** came out of the temple, Rv 16:17
And he called out with a mighty **v**, Rv 18:2
I heard another **v** from heaven saying, Rv 18:4
and the **v** of bridegroom and bride will Rv 18:23
to be the loud **v** of a great multitude Rv 19:1
And from the throne came a **v** saying, Rv 19:5
seemed to be the **v** of a great multitude, Rv 19:6
and with a loud **v** he called to all the Rv 19:17
I heard a loud **v** from the throne saying, Rv 21:3

VOICES (15)
the people lifted up their **v** and wept. Jgs 2:4
they lifted up their **v** and wept bitterly. Jgs 21:2
them, and they lifted up their **v** and wept. Ru 1:9
they lifted up their **v** and wept again. Ru 1:14
with him raised their **v** and wept until 1 Sm 30:4
And they raised their **v** and wept, and Jb 2:12
They lift up their **v**, they sing for joy; Is 24:14
and the **v** of those who celebrate. Jer 30:19
of the bride, the **v** of those who sing, Jer 33:11
and lifted up their **v**, saying, "Jesus, Lk 17:13
be crucified. And their **v** prevailed. Lk 23:23
they lifted their **v** together to God and Acts 4:24
Paul had done, they lifted up their **v**, Acts 14:11
Then they raised their **v** and said, Acts 22:22
and there were loud **v** in heaven, Rv 11:15

VOID (16)
The earth was without form and **v**, and Gn 1:2
But the previous period shall be **v**, Nm 6:12
then he makes **v** her vow that was on Nm 30:8
makes them null and **v** on the day Nm 30:12
Her husband has made them **v**, and Nm 30:12
or her husband may make **v**. Nm 30:13
makes them null and **v** after he has Nm 30:15
"For they are a nation **v** of counsel, and Dt 32:28
the north over the **v** and hangs the earth Jb 26:7
and behold, it was without form and **v**; Jer 4:23
place I will make **v** the plans of Judah Jer 19:7
tradition you have made **v** the word of Mt 15:6
thus making **v** the word of God by your Mk 7:13
for one dot of the Law to become **v**. Lk 16:17
faith is null and the promise is **v**. Rom 4:14
by God, so as to make the promise **v**. Gal 3:17

VOLUNTARILY (1)
for you have **v** vowed to the LORD your Dt 23:23

VOLUNTEER (1)
a **v** for the service of the LORD, 2 Chr 17:16

VOMIT (10)
lest the land **v** you out when you make Lv 18:28
bringing you to live may not **v** you out. Lv 20:22
You will **v** up the morsels that you have Prv 23:8
lest you have your fill of it and **v** it. Prv 25:16
dog that returns to his **v** is a fool who Prv 26:11
as a drunken man staggers in his **v**. Is 19:14
For all tables are full of filthy **v**, with no Is 28:8
Drink, be drunk and **v**, fall and rise no Jer 25:27
so that Moab shall wallow in his **v**, Jer 48:26
"The dog returns to its own **v**, and the 2 Pt 2:22

VOMITED (3)
and the land **v** out its inhabitants. Lv 18:25
as it **v** out the nation that was before Lv 18:28
and it **v** Jonah out upon the dry land. Jon 2:10

VOMITS (1)
down riches and **v** them up again; Jb 20:15

VOPHSI (1)
tribe of Naphtali, Nahbi the son of **V**; Nm 13:14

VOTE (1)
put to death I cast my **v** against them. Acts 26:10

VOW (47)
Then Jacob made a **v**, saying, "If God Gn 28:20
anointed a pillar and made a **v** to me. Gn 31:13
of his offering is a **v** offering or a freewill Lv 7:16
the LORD to fulfill a **v** or as a freewill Lv 22:21
but for a **v** offering it cannot be Lv 22:23
besides all your **v** offerings and besides Lv 23:38
anyone makes a special **v** to the LORD Lv 27:2
"If the **v** is an animal that may be offered Lv 27:9
a man or a woman makes a special **v**, Nm 6:2
makes a special vow, the **v** of a Nazirite, Nm 6:2

“All the days of his **v** of separation, no Nm 6:5
to the LORD above his Nazirite **v**, Nm 6:21
accordance with the **v** that he takes, Nm 6:21
to fulfill a **v** or as a freewill offering or Nm 15:3
to fulfill a **v** or for peace offerings to the Nm 15:8
And Israel vowed a **v** to the LORD and Nm 21:2
addition to your **v** offerings and your Nm 29:39
If a man vows a **v** to the LORD, or swears Nm 30:2
If a woman vows a **v** to the LORD and Nm 30:3
father hears of her **v** and of her pledge Nm 30:4
the day that he hears of it, no **v** of hers, Nm 30:5
he makes void her **v** that was on her, Nm 30:8
(But any **v** of a widow or of a divorced Nm 30:9
Any **v** and any binding oath to afflict Nm 30:13
that you present, your **v** offerings, Dt 12:6
and all your finest **v** offerings that you Dt 12:11
vow offerings that you **v** to the LORD. Dt 12:11
or any of your **v** offerings that you vow, Dt 12:17
or any of your vow offerings that you **v**, Dt 12:17
are due from you, and your **v** offerings, Dt 12:26
LORD your God in payment for any **v**, Dt 23:18
“If you make a **v** to the LORD your God, Dt 23:21
And Jephthah made a **v** to the LORD and Jgs 11:30
LORD, and I cannot take back my **v**.” Jgs 11:35
her according to his **v** that he had Jgs 11:39
And she vowed a **v** and said, “O LORD 1 Sm 1:11
the yearly sacrifice and to pay his **v**. 1 Sm 1:21
king, “Please let me go and pay my **v**, 2 Sm 15:7
your servant vowed a **v** while I lived at 2 Sm 15:8
When you **v** a vow to God, do not delay Eccl 5:4
When you vow a **v** to God, do not delay Eccl 5:4
no pleasure in fools. Pay what you **v**. Eccl 5:4
that you should not **v** than that you Eccl 5:5
than that you should **v** and not pay. Eccl 5:5
I made my **v** to you and entered into a Ezk 16:8
had cut his hair, for he was under a **v**. Acts 18:18
We have four men who are under a **v**; Acts 21:23

VOWED (12)
And Israel **v** a vow to the LORD and said, Nm 21:2
And if she **v** in her husband's house Nm 30:10
for you have voluntarily **v** to the LORD Dt 23:23
And she **v** a vow and said, “O LORD of 1 Sm 1:11
But David **v** again, saying, “Your 1 Sm 20:3
my vow, which I have **v** to the LORD, 2 Sm 15:7
For your servant **v** a vow while I lived 2 Sm 15:8
v willingly for the house of their God Ezr 7:16
to the LORD and **v** to the Mighty One Ps 132:2
we will do everything that we have **v**, Jer 44:17
sacrifice to you; what I have **v** I will pay. Jon 2:9
And he **v** to her, “Whatever you ask me, Mk 6:23

VOWER (1)
him according to what the **v** can afford. Lv 27:8

VOWING (1)
But if you refrain from **v**, you will not Dt 23:22

VOWS (32)
for any of their **v** or freewill offerings Lv 22:18
But if he **v** an offering to the LORD Nm 6:21
If a man **v** a vow to the LORD, or swears Nm 30:2
If a woman **v** a vow to the LORD and Nm 30:3
to her, then all her **v** shall stand, Nm 30:4
while under her **v** or any thoughtless Nm 30:6
that he hears, then her **v** shall stand, Nm 30:7
oppose her, then all her **v** shall stand, Nm 30:11
lips concerning her **v** or concerning Nm 30:12
he establishes all her **v** or all her Nm 30:14
will hear you, and you will pay your **v**. Jb 22:27
my **v** I will perform before those who Ps 22:25
and perform your **v** to the Most High, Ps 50:14
I must perform my **v** to you, O God; I Ps 56:12
For you, O God, have heard my **v**; you Ps 61:5
name, as I perform my **v** day after day. Ps 61:8
in Zion, and to you shall **v** be performed. Ps 65:1
offerings; I will perform my **v** to you, Ps 66:13
Make your **v** to the LORD your God and Ps 76:11
I will pay my **v** to the LORD in the Ps 116:14
I will pay my **v** to the LORD in the Ps 116:18
sacrifices, and today I have paid my **v**; Prv 7:14
and to reflect only after making **v**. Prv 20:25
What are you doing, son of my **v**? Prv 31:2
and they will make **v** to the LORD and Is 19:21
will surely perform our **v** that we have Jer 44:25
Then confirm your **v** and perform Jer 44:25
your vows and perform your **v**! Jer 44:25
we will pay with bulls the **v** of our lips. Hos 14:2
a sacrifice to the LORD and made **v**. Jon 1:16
fulfill your **v**, for never again shall the Na 1:15
who has a male in his flock, and **v** it, Mal 1:14

VOYAGE (4)
we made a direct **v** to Samothrace, Acts 16:11
we had finished the **v** from Tyre, Acts 21:7
and the **v** was now dangerous because Acts 27:9
I perceive that the **v** will be with Acts 27:10

VULGAR (1)
one of the **v** fellows shamelessly 2 Sm 6:20

VULTURE (7)
the eagle, the bearded **v**, the black Lv 11:13
eagle, the bearded vulture, the black **v**, Lv 11:13
barn owl, the tawny owl, the carrion **v**, Lv 11:18
the eagle, the bearded **v**, the black Dt 14:12
eagle, the bearded vulture, the black **v**, Dt 14:12
owl, the carrion **v** and the cormorant, Dt 14:17
One like a **v** is over the house of the LORD, Hos 8:1

VULTURES (3)
ravens of the valley and eaten by the **v**. Prv 30:17
the corpse is, there the **v** will gather. Mt 24:28
the corpse is, there the **v** will gather.” Lk 17:37

W

WAFER (3)
and one **w** out of the basket of Ex 29:23
with oil and one **w** and placed them on Lv 8:26
of the basket and one unleavened **w**, Nm 6:19

WAFERS (6)
taste of it was like **w** made with honey. Ex 16:31
oil, and unleavened **w** smeared with oil. Ex 29:2
oil or unleavened **w** smeared with oil. Lv 2:4
with oil, unleavened **w** smeared with oil, Lv 7:12
oil, and unleavened **w** smeared with oil, Nm 6:15
offering, the **w** of unleavened bread, 1 Chr 23:29

WAG (4)
make mouths at me; they **w** their heads; Ps 22:7
all who see them will **w** their heads. Ps 64:8
when they see me, they **w** their heads. Ps 109:25
they hiss and **w** their heads at the Lam 2:15

WAGE (14)
came up to **w** war on Jerusalem, 2 Kgs 16:5
soul in safety from the battle that I **w**, Ps 55:18
The **w** of the righteous leads to life, the Prv 10:16
by counsel; by wise guidance **w** war. Prv 20:18
by wise guidance you can **w** your war, Prv 24:6
came up to Jerusalem to **w** war against it, Is 7:1
“His sons shall **w** war and assemble a Dn 11:10
of the south shall **w** war with an Dn 11:25
days there was no **w** for man or any Zec 8:10
no wage for man or any **w** for beast, Zec 8:10
the peoples that **w** war against Zec 14:12
by them you may **w** the good warfare, 1 Tm 1:18
flesh, which **w** war against your soul. 1 Pt 2:11
wrong as the **w** for their wrongdoing. 2 Pt 2:13

WAGED (3)
days of Saul they **w** war against the 1 Chr 5:10
They **w** war against the Hagrites, 1 Chr 5:19
much blood and have **w** great wars. 1 Chr 22:8

WAGER (2)
make a **w** with my master the king 2 Kgs 18:23
make a **w** with my master the king of Is 36:8

WAGES (36)
Tell me, what shall your **w** be?” Gn 29:15
has given me my **w** because I gave my Gn 30:18
Name your **w**, and I will give it.” Gn 30:28
the goats, and they shall be my **w**. Gn 30:32
you come to look into my **w** with you. Gn 30:33
me and changed my **w** ten times. Gn 31:7
If he said, ‘The spotted shall be your **w**,’ Gn 31:8
if he said, ‘The striped shall be your **w**,’ Gn 31:8
and you have changed my **w** ten times. Gn 31:41
will give you your **w**.” So the woman took Ex 2:9
The **w** of a hired servant shall not Lv 19:13
of a prostitute or the **w** of a dog into the Dt 23:18
shall give him his **w** on the same day, Dt 24:15
for your servants such **w** as you set, 1 Kgs 5:6
and like a hired hand who looks for his **w**, Jb 7:2
The wicked earns deceptive **w**, but one Prv 11:18
will return to her **w** and will prostitute Is 23:17
Her merchandise and her **w** will be holy Is 23:18
nothing and does not give him his **w**, Jer 22:13
it; and it shall be the **w** for his army. Ezk 29:19
of which she said, ‘These are my **w**, Hos 2:12
loved a prostitute's **w** on all threshing Hos 9:1
pieces, all her **w** shall be burned with fire, Mi 1:7
And he who earns **w** does so to put them Hg 1:6
“If it seems good to you, give me my **w**; Zec 11:12
weighed out as my **w** thirty pieces of Zec 11:12
who oppress the hired worker in his **w**, Mal 3:5
‘Call the laborers and pay them their **w**, Mt 20:8
and be content with your **w**.” Lk 3:14
provide, for the laborer deserves his **w**. Lk 10:7
reaps is receiving **w** and gathering fruit Jn 4:36
his **w** are not counted as a gift but as Rom 4:4
For the **w** of sin is death, but the free Rom 6:23
will receive his **w** according to his 1 Cor 3:8
and, “The laborer deserves his **w**.” 1 Tm 5:18
the **w** of the laborers who mowed your Jas 5:4

WAGGED (1)
you spoke of him you **w** your head? Jer 48:27

WAGGING (2)
passed by derided him, **w** their heads Mt 27:39
derided him, **w** their heads and saying, Mk 15:29

WAGING (2)
members another law **w** war against Rom 7:23
we are not **w** war according to the 2 Cor 10:3

WAGON (2)
oxen, a **w** for every two of the chiefs, Nm 7:3
your **w** tracks overflow with Ps 65:11

WAGONS (10)
take **w** from the land of Egypt for your Gn 45:19
and Joseph gave them **w**, according to Gn 45:21
when he saw the **w** that Joseph had sent Gn 45:27
in the **w** that Pharaoh had sent to carry Gn 46:5
before the LORD, six **w** and twelve oxen, Nm 7:3
So Moses took the **w** and the oxen and Nm 7:6
Two **w** and four oxen he gave to the sons Nm 7:7
And four **w** and eight oxen he gave to the Nm 7:8
north with chariots and **w** and a host Ezk 23:24
of the horsemen and **w** and chariots, Ezk 26:10

WAGS (2)
she **w** her head behind you—the 2 Kgs 19:21
she **w** her head behind you—the Is 37:22

WAHEB (1)
the Wars of the LORD, “**W** in Suphah, Nm 21:14

WAIL (33)
W, for the day of the LORD is near; as Is 13:6
W, O gate; cry out, O city; melt in fear, O Is 14:31
Therefore let Moab **w** for Moab, let Is 16:7
let Moab wail for Moab, let everyone **w**. Is 16:7
W, O ships of Tarshish, for Tyre is laid Is 23:1
Tarshish; **w**, O inhabitants of the coast! Is 23:6
W, O ships of Tarshish, for your Is 23:14
Their rulers **w**,” declares the LORD, “and Is 52:5
of heart and shall **w** for breaking of Is 65:14
For this put on sackcloth, lament, and **w**, Jer 4:8
“**W**, you shepherds, and cry out, and Jer 25:34
and the **w** of the lords of the flock! Jer 25:36
and every inhabitant of the land shall **w**. Jer 47:2
to shame, for it is broken; **w** and cry! Jer 48:20
Therefore I **w** for Moab; I cry out for all Jer 48:31
How it is broken! How they **w**! How Jer 48:39
“**W**, O Heshbon, for Ai is laid waste! Cry Jer 49:3
has fallen and been broken; **w** for her! Jer 51:8
Cry out and **w**, son of man, for it is Ezk 21:12
the Lord GOD: “**W**, ‘Alas for the day!’ Ezk 30:2
of man, **w** over the multitude of Egypt, Ezk 32:18
the heart, but they **w** upon their beds; Hos 7:14
Awake, you drunkards, and weep, and **w**, Jl 1:5
w, O vinedressers, for the wheat and the Jl 1:11
O priests; **w**, O ministers of the altar. Jl 1:13
For this I will lament and **w**; I will go Mi 1:8
Fish Gate, a **w** from the Second Quarter, Zep 1:10
W, O inhabitants of the Mortar! For all Zep 1:11
W, O cypress, for the cedar has fallen, Zec 11:2
W, oaks of Bashan, for the thick forest Zec 11:2
The sound of the **w** of the shepherds, for Zec 11:3
of the earth will **w** on account of him. Rv 1:7
will weep and **w** over her when they see Rv 18:9

WAILED (1)
mother of Sisera **w** through the lattice: Jgs 5:28

WAILING (10)
land of Moab; her **w** reaches to Eglaim; Is 15:8
to Eglaim; her **w** reaches to Beer-elim. Is 15:8
up weeping and **w** for the mountains, Jer 9:10
them make haste and raise a **w** over us, Jer 9:18
For a sound of **w** is heard from Zion: Jer 9:19
In their **w** they raise a lamentation for Ezk 27:32
“In all the squares there shall be **w**, and Am 5:16
to mourning and to **w** those who are Am 5:16
and in all vineyards there shall be **w**, Am 5:17
people weeping and **w** loudly. Mk 5:38

WAILINGS (1)
the temple shall become **w** in that day,” Am 8:3

WAILS (2)
over Nebo and over Medeba Moab **w**. Is 15:2
in the squares everyone **w** and melts in Is 15:3

WAIST (26)
the sash around his **w** and clothed him Lv 8:7
he shall tie the linen sash around his **w**, Lv 16:4
the belt around his **w** and on the 1 Kgs 2:5
of leather about his **w**.” And he said, 2 Kgs 1:8
with his fat and gathered fat upon his **w** Jb 15:27
Righteousness shall be the belt of his **w**, Is 11:5

the sackcloth from your **w** and take off Is 20:2
bare, and tie sackcloth around your **w**. Is 32:11
loincloth and put it around your **w**, Jer 13:1
of the LORD, and put it around my **w**. Jer 13:2
have bought, which is around your **w**, Jer 13:4
the loincloth clings to the **w** of a man, Jer 13:11
gashes, and around the **w** is sackcloth. Jer 48:37
had the appearance of his **w** I saw as it Ezk 1:27
had the appearance of his **w** I saw as it Ezk 1:27
Below what appeared to be his **w** was fire, Ezk 8:2
and above his **w** was something like the Ezk 8:2
in linen, with a writing case at his **w**. Ezk 9:2
linen, who had the writing case at his **w**. Ezk 9:3
in linen, with the writing case at his **w**, Ezk 9:11
for you and put sackcloth on their **w**, Ezk 27:31
of fine gold from Uphaz around his **w**. Dn 10:5
sackcloth on every **w** and baldness on Am 8:10
hair and a leather belt around his **w**, Mt 3:4
leather belt around his **w** and ate locusts Mk 1:6
and taking a towel, tied it around his **w**. Jn 13:4

WAIST-DEEP (1)
led me through the water, and it was **w**. Ezk 47:4

WAISTBAND (1)
none slumbers or sleeps, not a **w** is loose, Is 5:27

WAISTCLOTH (1)
of kings and binds a **w** on their hips. Jb 12:18

WAISTS (5)
sashes around their **w** and bound caps Lv 8:13
sackcloth around our **w** and ropes 1 Kgs 20:31
sackcloth around their **w** and put 1 Kgs 20:32
wearing belts on their **w**, with flowing Ezk 23:15
linen undergarments around their **w**. Ezk 44:18

WAIT (86)
I **w** for your salvation, O LORD. Gn 49:18
thrust out of Egypt and could not **w**, Ex 12:39
But if he did not lie in **w** for him, but Ex 21:13
up to me on the mountain and **w** there, Ex 24:12
"**W** here for us until we return to you. Ex 24:14
"**W**, that I may hear what the LORD will Nm 9:8
hurled something at him, lying in **w**, Nm 35:20
anything on him without lying in **w** Nm 35:22
neighbor and lies in **w** for him and Dt 19:11
"Let us **w** till the light of the morning; Jgs 16:2
your heart and **w** until the day Jgs 19:8
would you therefore **w** till they were Ru 1:13
She replied, "**W**, my daughter, until you Ru 3:18
to you; **w** until you have weaned him; 1 Sm 1:23
Seven days you shall **w**, until I come 1 Sm 10:8
say to us, '**W** until we come to you,' 1 Sm 14:9
of Amalek and lay in **w** in the valley. 1 Sm 15:5
up my servant against me, to lie in **w**, 1 Sm 22:8
he has risen against me, to lie in **w**, 1 Sm 22:13
I will **w** at the fords of the wilderness 2 Sm 15:28
and let her **w** on the king and be in his 1 Kgs 1:2
Why should I **w** for the LORD any 2 Kgs 6:33
we are silent and **w** until the morning 2 Kgs 7:9
What is my strength, that I should **w**? Jb 6:11
All the days of my service I would **w**, till Jb 14:14
I have lain in **w** at my neighbor's door, Jb 31:9
And shall I **w**, because they do not Jb 32:16
in their dens or lie in **w** in their thicket? Jb 38:40
none who **w** for you shall be put to Ps 25:3
salvation; for you I **w** all the day long. Ps 25:5
uprightness preserve me, for I **w** for you. Ps 25:21
W for the LORD; be strong, and let your Ps 27:14
your heart take courage; **w** for the LORD! Ps 27:14
courage, all you who **w** for the LORD! Ps 31:24
before the LORD and **w** patiently for him; Ps 37:7
but those who **w** for the LORD shall Ps 37:9
W for the LORD and keep his way, and Ps 37:34
But for you, O LORD, do I **w**; it is you, O Ps 38:15
"And now, O Lord, for what do I **w**? My Ps 39:7
I will **w** for your name, for it is good, in Ps 52:9
For behold, they lie in **w** for my life; Ps 59:3
For God alone, O my soul, **w** in silence, Ps 62:5
works; they did not **w** for his counsel. Ps 106:13
The wicked lie in **w** to destroy me, but Ps 119:95
I **w** for the LORD, my soul waits, and in Ps 130:5
"Come with us, let us lie in **w** for blood; Prv 1:11
these men lie in **w** for their own blood; Prv 1:18
and at every corner she lies in **w**. Prv 7:12
words of the wicked lie in **w** for blood, Prv 12:6
w for the LORD, and he will deliver you. Prv 20:22
She lies in **w** like a robber and Prv 23:28
Lie not in **w** as a wicked man against Prv 24:15
I will **w** for the LORD, who is hiding his Is 8:17
of your judgments, O LORD, we **w** for you; Is 26:8
blessed are all those who **w** for him. Is 30:18
O LORD, be gracious to us; we **w** for you. Is 33:2
but they who **w** for the LORD shall renew Is 40:31
earth; and the coastlands **w** for his law. Is 42:4
those who **w** for me shall not be put to Is 49:23
hope for me, and for my arm they **w**. Is 51:5
you, who acts for those who **w** for him. Is 64:4
people; they lurk like fowlers lying in **w**. Jer 5:26
He is a bear lying in **w** for me, a lion in Lam 3:10
LORD is good to those who **w** for him, Lam 3:25
good that one should **w** quietly for the Lam 3:26
they lay in **w** for us in the wilderness. Lam 4:19
As robbers lie in **w** for a man, so the Hos 6:9
and **w** continually for your God." Hos 12:6
inhabitants of Maroth **w** anxiously for Mi 1:12
not for a man nor **w** for the children of Mi 5:7
they all lie in **w** for blood, and each hunts Mi 7:2
LORD; I will **w** for the God of my salvation; Mi 7:7
If it seems slow, **w** for it; it will surely Hab 2:3
Yet I will quietly **w** for the day of Hab 3:16
"Therefore **w** for me," declares the LORD, Zep 3:8
"**W**, let us see whether Elijah will come Mt 27:49
"**W**, let us see whether Elijah will Mk 15:36
lying in **w** for him, to catch him in Lk 11:54
but to **w** for the promise of the Father, Acts 1:4
And now why do you **w**? Rise and be Acts 22:16
inwardly as we **w** eagerly for adoption Rom 8:23
we do not see, we **w** for it with patience. Rom 8:25
as you **w** for the revealing of our Lord 1 Cor 1:7
together to eat, **w** for one another— 1 Cor 11:33
we ourselves eagerly **w** for the hope of Gal 5:5
and to **w** for his Son from heaven, 1 Thes 1:10

WAITED (19)
He **w** another seven days, and again he Gn 8:10
Then he **w** another seven days and sent Gn 8:12
And they **w** till they were embarrassed. Jgs 3:25
He **w** seven days, the time appointed 1 Sm 13:8
the name of David, and then they **w**. 1 Sm 25:9
prophet departed and **w** for the king 1 Kgs 20:38
listened to me and **w** and kept silence Jb 29:21
They **w** for me as for the rain, and they Jb 29:23
good, evil came, and when I **w** for light, Jb 30:26
Now Elihu had **w** to speak to Job because Jb 32:4
"Behold, I **w** for your words, I listened Jb 32:11
I **w** patiently for the LORD; he inclined to Ps 40:1
my steps, as they have **w** for my life. Ps 56:6
this is our God; we have **w** for him, Is 25:9
This is the LORD; we have **w** for him; let us Is 25:9
When she saw that she **w** in vain, that Ezk 19:5
But when they had **w** a long time and Acts 28:6
thus Abraham, having patiently **w**, Heb 6:15
when God's patience **w** in the days of 1 Pt 3:20

WAITING (21)
Moses and Aaron, who were **w** for them, Ex 5:20
and Ahimaaz were **w** at En-rogel. 2 Sm 17:17
is before him, and you are **w** for him! Jb 35:14
My eyes grow dim with **w** for my God. Ps 69:3
daily at my gates, **w** beside my doors. Prv 8:34
And the people were **w** for Zechariah, Lk 1:21
devout, **w** for the consolation of Israel, Lk 2:25
to all who were **w** for the redemption of Lk 2:38
him, for they were all **w** for him. Lk 8:40
like men who are **w** for their master to Lk 12:36
Now while Paul was **w** for them at Acts 17:16
on ahead and were **w** for us at Troas, Acts 20:5
they are ready, **w** for your consent." Acts 23:21
They were **w** for him to swell up or Acts 28:6
w for our blessed hope, the appearing of Ti 2:13
save those who are eagerly **w** for him. Heb 9:28
w from that time until his enemies Heb 10:13
w for and hastening the coming of the 2 Pt 3:12
his promise we are **w** for new heavens 2 Pt 3:13
beloved, since you are **w** for these, 2 Pt 3:14
w for the mercy of our Lord Jesus Jude 1:21

WAITS (9)
of the adulterer also **w** for the twilight, Jb 24:15
Our soul **w** for the LORD; he is our help Ps 33:20
For God alone my soul **w** in silence; Ps 62:1
I wait for the LORD, my soul **w**, and in Ps 130:5
my soul **w** for the Lord more than Ps 130:6
Therefore the LORD **w** to be gracious to Is 30:18
Blessed is he who **w** and arrives at the Dn 12:12
For the creation **w** with eager longing Rom 8:19
See how the farmer **w** for the precious Jas 5:7

WAKE (9)
Behind him he leaves a shining **w**; one Jb 41:32
W yourself, wake yourself, stand up, O Is 51:17
Wake yourself, **w** yourself, stand up, O Is 51:17
then sleep a perpetual sleep and not **w**, Jer 51:39
shall sleep a perpetual sleep and not **w**, Jer 51:57
has come for you to **w** from sleep. Rom 13:11
W up from your drunken stupor, as 1 Cor 15:34
W up, and strengthen what remains and Rv 3:2
If you will not **w** up, I will come like a Rv 3:3

WALK (186)
w through the length and the breadth Gn 13:17
w before me, and be blameless, Gn 17:1
whether they will **w** in my law or not. Ex 16:4
in which they must **w** and what they Ex 18:20
And all that **w** on their paws, among Lv 11:27
you. You shall not **w** in their statutes. Lv 18:3
and keep my statutes and **w** in them. Lv 18:4
And you shall not **w** in the customs of Lv 20:23
"If you **w** in my statutes and observe my Lv 26:3
And I will **w** among you and will be Lv 26:12
of your yoke and made you **w** erect. Lv 26:13
"Then if you **w** contrary to me and will Lv 26:21
not turned to me but **w** contrary to me, Lv 26:23
then I also will **w** contrary to you, and I Lv 26:24
not listen to me, but **w** contrary to me, Lv 26:27
then I will **w** contrary to you in fury, Lv 26:28
You shall **w** in all the way that the LORD Dt 5:33
your house, and when you **w** by the way, Dt 6:7
the LORD your God, to **w** in all his ways, Dt 10:12
You shall **w** after the LORD your God and Dt 13:4
the LORD your God commanded you to **w**. Dt 13:5
God, and that you will **w** in his ways, Dt 26:17
of the LORD your God and **w** in his ways. Dt 28:9
though I **w** in the stubbornness of my Dt 29:19
and to **w** in all his ways and to keep his Jos 22:5
they will take care to **w** in the way of the Jgs 2:22
rich carpets and you who **w** by the way. Jgs 5:10
Yet his sons did not **w** in his ways but 1 Sm 8:3
and your sons do not **w** in your ways. 1 Sm 8:5
to **w** before me in faithfulness with all 1 Kgs 2:4
And if you will **w** in my ways, 1 Kgs 3:14
if you will **w** in my statutes and obey 1 Kgs 6:12
my commandments and **w** in them, 1 Kgs 6:12
your servants who **w** before you with 1 Kgs 8:23
to **w** before me as you have walked 1 Kgs 8:25
the good way in which they should **w**, 1 Kgs 8:36
to **w** in all his ways and to keep his 1 Kgs 8:58
And as for you, if you will **w** before me, 1 Kgs 9:4
you, and will **w** in my ways, 1 Kgs 11:38
thing for him to **w** in the sins of 1 Kgs 16:31
was not careful to **w** in the law of 2 Kgs 10:31
and did not **w** in the way of the LORD. 2 Kgs 21:22
to **w** after the LORD and to keep his 2 Kgs 23:3
are fulfilled to **w** with your fathers, 1 Chr 17:11
your servants who **w** before you with 2 Chr 6:14
to **w** in my law as you have walked 2 Chr 6:16
good way in which they should **w**, 2 Chr 6:27
may fear you and **w** in your ways all 2 Chr 6:31
if you will **w** before me as David your 2 Chr 7:17
to **w** after the LORD and to keep his 2 Chr 34:31
Ought you not to **w** in the fear of our Neh 5:9
and an oath to **w** in God's Law that Neh 10:29
Even though I **w** through the valley of Ps 23:4
my eyes, and I **w** in your faithfulness. Ps 26:3
But as for me, I shall **w** in my integrity; Ps 26:11
W about Zion, go around her, number Ps 48:12
that I may **w** before God in the light of Ps 56:13
but refused to **w** according to his law. Ps 78:10
to me, that Israel would **w** in my ways! Ps 81:13
they **w** about in darkness; Ps 82:5
withhold from those who **w** uprightly. Ps 84:11
way, O LORD, that I may **w** in your truth; Ps 86:11
who know the festal shout, who **w**, Ps 89:15
law and do not **w** according to my Ps 89:30
I will **w** with integrity of heart within Ps 101:2
hands, but do not feel; feet, but do not **w**; Ps 115:7
I will **w** before the LORD in the land of Ps 116:9
who **w** in the law of the LORD! Ps 119:1
also do no wrong, but **w** in his ways! Ps 119:3
and I shall **w** in a wide place, for I have Ps 119:45
Though I **w** in the midst of trouble, you Ps 138:7
the path where I **w** they have hidden a Ps 142:3
my son, do not **w** in the way with them; Prv 1:15
he is a shield to those who **w** in integrity, Prv 2:7
paths of uprightness to **w** in the ways of Prv 2:13
So you will **w** in the way of the good and Prv 2:20
Then you will **w** on your way securely, Prv 3:23
When you **w**, your step will not be Prv 4:12
and do not **w** in the way of the evil. Prv 4:14
When you **w**, they will lead you; when Prv 6:22
Or can one **w** on hot coals and his feet Prv 6:28
I **w** in the way of righteousness, in the Prv 8:20
and live, and **w** in the way of insight." Prv 9:6
A fool's lips **w** into a fight, and his Prv 18:6
W in the ways of your heart and the Eccl 11:9
ways and that we may **w** in his paths." For Is 2:3
come, let us **w** in the light of the LORD. Is 2:5
are haughty and **w** with outstretched Is 3:16
and warned me not to **w** in the way of this Is 8:11
w in it," when you turn to the right or Is 30:21
It shall belong to those who **w** on the way; Is 35:8
there, but the redeemed shall **w** there. Is 35:9
I **w** slowly all my years because of the Is 38:15
not be weary; they shall **w** and not faint. Is 40:31
people on it and spirit to those who **w** in it: Is 42:5
sinned, in whose ways they would not **w**, Is 42:24
when you **w** through fire you shall not be Is 43:2
W by the light of your fire, and by the Is 50:11
in their beds who **w** in their uprightness. Is 57:2

and for brightness, but we **w** in gloom. Is 59:9
people, who **w** in a way that is not good, Is 65:2
and **w** in it, and find rest for your souls. Jer 6:16
souls. But they said, 'We will not **w** in it.' Jer 6:16
not out into the field, nor **w** on the road, Jer 6:25
And **w** in all the way that I command Jer 7:23
have to be carried, for they cannot **w**. Jer 10:5
ancient roads, and to **w** into side roads, Jer 18:15
they commit adultery and **w** in lies; Jer 23:14
to **w** in my law that I have set before you, Jer 26:4
I will make them **w** by brooks of water, Jer 31:9
not obey your voice or **w** in your law. Jer 32:23
voice of the LORD or **w** in his law and in Jer 44:23
so that we could not **w** in our streets; Lam 4:18
that they may **w** in my statutes and Ezk 11:20
Not only did you **w** in their ways and Ezk 16:47
They did not **w** in my statutes but Ezk 20:13
my rules and did not **w** in my statutes, Ezk 20:16
Do not **w** in the statutes of your Ezk 20:18
w in my statutes, and be careful to Ezk 20:19
They did not **w** in my statutes and Ezk 20:21
I will let people **w** on you, even my Ezk 36:12
and cause you to **w** in my statutes and Ezk 36:27
They shall **w** in my rules and be Ezk 37:24
and those who **w** in pride he is able to Dn 4:37
Yet it was I who taught Ephraim to **w**; I Hos 11:3
are right, and the upright **w** in them, Hos 14:9
"Do two **w** together, unless they have Am 3:3
necks, and you shall not **w** haughtily, Mi 2:3
and that we may **w** in his paths." For Mi 4:2
For all the peoples **w** each in the name of Mi 4:5
but we will **w** in the name of the LORD our Mi 4:5
and to **w** humbly with your God? Mi 6:8
so that they shall **w** like the blind, Zep 1:17
If you will **w** in my ways and keep my Zec 3:7
and they shall **w** in his name," Zec 10:12
sins are forgiven,' or to say, 'Rise and **w**'? Mt 9:5
blind receive their sight and the lame **w**, Mt 11:5
or to say, 'Rise, take up your bed and **w**'? Mk 2:9
do your disciples not **w** according to the Mk 7:5
who like to **w** around in long robes Mk 12:38
are forgiven you,' or to say, 'Rise and **w**'? Lk 5:23
the blind receive their sight, the lame **w**, Lk 7:22
and people **w** over them without Lk 11:44
who like to **w** around in long robes, Lk 20:46
each other as you **w**?" And they stood Lk 24:17
to him, "Get up, take up your bed, and **w**." Jn 5:8
said to me, 'Take up your bed, and **w**.'" Jn 5:11
said to you, 'Take up your bed and **w**'?" Jn 5:12
follows me will not **w** in darkness, Jn 8:12
W while you have the light, lest Jn 12:35
dress yourself and **w** wherever you Jn 21:18
Christ of Nazareth, rise up and **w**!" Acts 3:6
leaping up he stood and began to **w**, Acts 3:8
power or piety we have made him **w**? Acts 3:12
all the nations to **w** in their own Acts 14:16
their children or **w** according to our Acts 21:21
but who also **w** in the footsteps Rom 4:12
we too might **w** in newness of life. Rom 6:4
who **w** not according to the flesh but Rom 8:4
Let us **w** properly as in the daytime, Rom 13:13
for we **w** by faith, not by sight. 2 Cor 5:7
among them and **w** among them, 2 Cor 6:16
For though we **w** in the flesh, we are 2 Cor 10:3
But I say, **w** by the Spirit, and you will Gal 5:16
by the Spirit, let us also **w** by the Spirit. Gal 5:25
And as for all who **w** by this rule, peace Gal 6:16
beforehand, that we should **w** in them. Eph 2:10
urge you to **w** in a manner worthy of the Eph 4:1
you must no longer **w** as the Gentiles Eph 4:17
And **w** in love, as Christ loved us and Eph 5:2
light in the Lord. **W** as children of light Eph 5:8
Look carefully then how you **w**, not as Eph 5:15
eyes on those who **w** according to the Phil 3:17
w as enemies of the cross of Christ. Phil 3:18
so as to **w** in a manner worthy of the Col 1:10
Christ Jesus the Lord, so **w** in him, Col 2:6
and charged you to **w** in a manner 1 Thes 2:12
that some among you **w** in idleness, 2 Thes 3:11
with him while we **w** in darkness, 1 Jn 1:6
But if we **w** in the light, as he is in the 1 Jn 1:7
in him ought to **w** in the same way 1 Jn 2:6
that we **w** according to his 2 Jn 1:6
beginning, so that you should **w** in it. 2 Jn 1:6
and they will **w** with me in white, Rv 3:4
wood, which cannot see or hear or **w**, Rv 9:20
By its light will the nations **w**, and the Rv 21:24

WALKED (83)

Enoch **w** with God after he fathered Gn 5:22
Enoch **w** with God, and he was not, for Gn 5:24
in his generation. Noah **w** with God. Gn 6:9
and **w** backward and covered the Gn 9:23
me, 'The LORD, before whom I have **w**, Gn 24:40
my fathers Abraham and Isaac **w**, Gn 48:15
her young women **w** beside the river. Ex 2:5
the people of Israel **w** on dry ground Ex 14:29
the people of Israel **w** on dry ground in Ex 15:19
so that I **w** contrary to them and Lv 26:41
the people of Israel **w** forty years in the Jos 5:6
horns before the ark of the LORD **w** on, Jos 6:13
Moses, while Israel **w** in the wilderness. Jos 14:10
the way in which their fathers had **w**, Jgs 2:17
I have **w** before you from my youth 1 Sm 12:2
because he **w** before you in 1 Kgs 3:6
as your father David **w**, 1 Kgs 3:14
before me as you have **w** before me.' 1 Kgs 8:25
before me, as David your father **w**, 1 Kgs 9:4
and they have not **w** in my ways, 1 Kgs 11:33
And he **w** in all the sins that his 1 Kgs 15:3
sight of the LORD and **w** in the way of 1 Kgs 15:26
sight of the LORD and **w** in the way of 1 Kgs 15:34
and you have **w** in the way of 1 Kgs 16:2
For he **w** in all the way of Jeroboam 1 Kgs 16:26
He **w** in all the way of Asa his father. 1 Kgs 22:43
sight of the LORD and **w** in the way of 1 Kgs 22:52
got up again and **w** once back and 2 Kgs 4:35
And he **w** in the way of the kings of 2 Kgs 8:18
He also **w** in the way of the house of 2 Kgs 8:27
he made Israel to sin, but **w** in them; 2 Kgs 13:6
made Israel to sin, but he **w** in them. 2 Kgs 13:11
but he **w** in the way of the kings of 2 Kgs 16:3
and **w** in the customs of the nations 2 Kgs 17:8
but **w** in the customs that Israel had 2 Kgs 17:19
The people of Israel **w** in all the sins 2 Kgs 17:22
how I have **w** before you in 2 Kgs 20:3
He **w** in all the way in which his 2 Kgs 21:21
in which his father **w** and served the 2 Kgs 21:21
eyes of the LORD and **w** in all the way 2 Kgs 22:2
in my law as you have **w** before me.' 2 Chr 6:16
before me as David your father **w**, 2 Chr 7:17
for they **w** for three years in the way 2 Chr 11:17
because he **w** in the earlier ways of 2 Chr 17:3
his father and **w** in his 2 Chr 17:4
He **w** in the way of Asa his father 2 Chr 20:32
And he **w** in the way of the kings of 2 Chr 21:6
'Because you have not **w** in the ways 2 Chr 21:12
but have **w** in the way of the kings 2 Chr 21:13
He also **w** in the ways of the house of 2 Chr 22:3
but he **w** in the ways of the kings of 2 Chr 28:2
and **w** in the ways of David his father; 2 Chr 34:2
And every day Mordecai **w** in front of Est 2:11
and by his light I **w** through darkness, Jb 29:3
"If I have **w** with falsehood and my foot Jb 31:5
the sea, or **w** in the recesses of the deep? Jb 38:16
me, O LORD, for I have **w** in my integrity, Ps 26:1
within God's house we **w** in the throng. Ps 55:14
The people who **w** in darkness have seen a Is 9:2
servant Isaiah has **w** naked and barefoot Is 20:3
remember how I have **w** before you in Is 38:3
but **w** in their own counsels and the Jer 7:24
obeyed my voice or **w** in accord with it, Jer 9:13
but everyone **w** in the stubbornness of Jer 11:8
nor **w** in my law and my statutes that I Jer 44:10
my rules and have not **w** in my statutes. Ezk 5:6
and have not **w** in my statutes or obeyed Ezk 5:7
For you have not **w** in my statutes, Ezk 11:12
in the midst of the stones of fire you **w**. Ezk 28:14
astray, those after which their fathers **w**. Am 2:4
Ahab; and you have **w** in their counsels, Mi 6:16
He **w** with me in peace and uprightness, Mal 2:6
out of the boat and **w** on the water and Mt 14:29
on from there and **w** beside the Sea of Mt 15:29
he looked at Jesus as he **w** by and said, Jn 1:36
was healed, and he took up his bed and **w**. Jn 5:9
turned back and no longer **w** with him. Jn 6:66
therefore no longer **w** openly among the Jn 11:54
crippled from birth and had never **w**. Acts 14:8
in which you once **w**, following the Eph 2:2
In these you too once **w**, when you were Col 3:7
to walk in the same way in which he **w**. 1 Jn 2:6
For they **w** in the way of Cain and Jude 1:11

WALKING (50)

sound of the LORD God **w** in the garden in Gn 3:8
w in the field to meet us?" The servant Gn 24:65
me, and also in **w** contrary to me, Lv 26:40
the LORD your God by **w** in his ways and Dt 8:6
house, and when you are **w** by the way, Dt 11:19
the LORD your God, **w** in all his ways, Dt 11:22
LORD your God and by **w** ever in his ways Dt 19:9
the LORD your God, by **w** in his ways, Dt 30:16
The armed men were **w** before the priests Jos 6:9
and the rear guard was **w** after the ark, Jos 6:9
And the armed men were **w** before them, Jos 6:13
and the rear guard was **w** after the ark of Jos 6:13
his couch and was **w** on the roof of 2 Sm 11:2
w in his ways and keeping his statutes, 1 Kgs 2:3
w in the statutes of David his father, 1 Kgs 3:3
w in his statutes and keeping his 1 Kgs 8:61
the LORD, **w** in the way of Jeroboam, 1 Kgs 16:19
the earth, and from **w** up and down on it." Jb 1:7
the earth, and from **w** up and down on it." Jb 2:2
and princes **w** on the ground like Eccl 10:7
feet," and he did so, **w** naked and barefoot. Is 20:2
men unbound, **w** in the midst of the fire, Dn 3:25
of twelve months he was **w** on the roof of Dn 4:29
of the LORD our God by **w** in his laws, Dn 9:10
and their **w** staff gives them oracles. Hos 4:12
his charge or of **w** as in mourning Mal 3:14
While **w** by the Sea of Galilee, he saw Mt 4:18
night he came to them, **w** on the sea. Mt 14:25
the disciples saw him **w** on the sea, Mt 14:26
the crippled healthy, the lame **w**, Mt 15:31
got up and began **w** (for she was twelve Mk 5:42
the night he came to them, **w** on the sea. Mk 6:48
when they saw him **w** on the sea they Mk 6:49
"I see men, but they look like trees, **w**." Mk 8:24
and Jesus was **w** ahead of them. Mk 10:32
And as he was **w** in the temple, the Mk 11:27
them, as they were **w** into the country. Mk 16:12
w blamelessly in all the commandments Lk 1:6
they saw Jesus **w** on the sea and coming Jn 6:19
and Jesus was **w** in the temple, in the Jn 10:23
them, **w** and leaping and praising God. Acts 3:8
the people saw him **w** and praising God, Acts 3:9
And **w** in the fear of the Lord and in Acts 9:31
feet." And he sprang up and began **w**. Acts 14:10
you eat, you are no longer **w** in love. Rom 14:15
who suspect us of **w** according to the 2 Cor 10:2
any brother who is **w** in idleness and 2 Thes 3:6
some of your children **w** in the truth, 2 Jn 1:4
truth, as indeed you are **w** in the truth. 3 Jn 1:3
hear that my children are **w** in the truth. 3 Jn 1:4

WALKS (38)

rises again and **w** outdoors with his Ex 21:19
the LORD your God **w** in the midst of Dt 23:14
now, behold, the king **w** before you, 1 Sm 12:2
net by his own feet, and he **w** on its mesh. Jb 18:8
see, and he **w** on the vault of heaven.' Jb 22:14
with evildoers and **w** with wicked men? Jb 34:8
is the man who **w** not in the counsel Ps 1:1
He who **w** blamelessly and does what is Ps 15:2
crown of him who **w** in his guilty ways. Ps 68:21
he who **w** in the way that is blameless Ps 101:6
who fears the LORD, who **w** in his ways! Ps 128:1
Whoever **w** in integrity walks securely, Prv 10:9
Whoever walks in integrity **w** securely, Prv 10:9
and the wicked **w** into it instead. Prv 11:8
Whoever **w** with the wise becomes Prv 13:20
Whoever **w** in uprightness fears the Prv 14:2
of understanding **w** straight ahead. Prv 15:21
a poor person who **w** in his integrity Prv 19:1
The righteous who **w** in his integrity— Prv 20:7
a poor man who **w** in his integrity than Prv 28:6
Whoever **w** in integrity will be Prv 28:18
but he who **w** in wisdom will be Prv 28:26
in his head, but the fool **w** in darkness. Eccl 2:14
Even when the fool **w** on the road, he Eccl 10:3
He who **w** righteously and speaks Is 33:15
Let him who **w** in darkness and has no Is 50:10
is not in man who **w** to direct his steps. Jer 10:23
w in my statutes, and keeps my rules Ezk 18:9
obeys my rules, and **w** in my statutes; Ezk 18:17
robbery, and **w** in the statutes of life, Ezk 33:15
but Judah still **w** with God and is Hos 11:12
words do good to him who **w** uprightly? Mi 2:7
their streets so that no one **w** in them; Zep 3:6
If anyone **w** in the day, he does not Jn 11:9
But if anyone **w** in the night, he Jn 11:10
The one who **w** in the darkness does not Jn 12:35
in the darkness and **w** in the darkness, 1 Jn 2:11
who **w** among the seven golden Rv 2:1

WALL (163)

a spring; his branches run over the **w**. Gn 49:22
the waters being a **w** to them on their Ex 14:22
the waters being a **w** to them on their Ex 14:29
that have no **w** around them shall Lv 25:31
the vineyards, with a **w** on either side. Nm 22:24
pushed against the **w** and pressed Nm 22:25
pressed Balaam's foot against the **w**. Nm 22:25
shall reach from the **w** of the city Nm 35:4
for her house was built into the city **w**, Jos 2:15
the city wall, so that she lived in the **w**. Jos 2:15
and the **w** of the city will fall down flat, Jos 6:5
a great shout, and the **w** fell down flat, Jos 6:20
David to the **w**." But David evaded 1 Sm 18:11
to pin David to the **w** with the spear, 1 Sm 19:10
that he struck the spear into the **w**. 1 Sm 19:10
at other times, on the seat by the **w**. 1 Sm 20:25
They were a **w** to us both by night 1 Sm 25:16
his body to the **w** of Beth-shan. 1 Sm 31:10
of his sons from the **w** of Beth-shan, 1 Sm 31:12
that they would shoot from the **w**? 2 Sm 11:20
upper millstone on him from the **w**, 2 Sm 11:21
Why did you go so near the **w**?' 2 Sm 11:21

shot at your servants from the **w**. 2 Sm 11:24
up to the roof of the gate by the **w**, 2 Sm 18:24
they were battering the **w** to throw it 2 Sm 20:15
shall be thrown to you over the **w**." 2 Sm 20:21
and by my God I can leap over a **w**. 2 Sm 22:30
the LORD and the **w** around Jerusalem. 1 Kgs 3:1
to the hyssop that grows out of the **w**. 1 Kgs 4:33
a structure against the **w** of the house, 1 Kgs 6:5
made offsets on the **w** in order that the 1 Kgs 6:6
that a wing of one touched the one **w**, 1 Kgs 6:27
the other cherub touched the other **w**; 1 Kgs 6:27
the Millo and the **w** of Jerusalem and 1 Kgs 9:15
and the **w** fell upon 27,000 men who 1 Kgs 20:30
him for a burnt offering on the **w**. 2 Kgs 3:27
of Israel was passing by on the **w**, 2 Kgs 6:26
passing by on the **w**—and the people 2 Kgs 6:30
blood spattered on the **w** and on the 2 Kgs 9:33
broke down the **w** of Jerusalem for 2 Kgs 14:13
of the people who are on the **w**." 2 Kgs 18:26
and not to the men sitting on the **w**, 2 Kgs 18:27
his face to the **w** and prayed to the 2 Kgs 20:2
cubits, touched the **w** of the house, 2 Chr 3:11
cubits, touched the **w** of the house, 2 Chr 3:12
broke down the **w** of Jerusalem for 2 Chr 25:23
and broke through the **w** of Gath and 2 Chr 26:6
of Gath and the **w** of Jabneh and the 2 Chr 26:6
wall of Jabneh and the **w** of Ashdod, 2 Chr 26:6
much building on the **w** of Ophel. 2 Chr 27:3
built up all the **w** that was broken 2 Chr 32:5
it, and outside it he built another **w**, 2 Chr 32:5
of Jerusalem who were on the **w**, 2 Chr 32:18
he built an outer **w** for the city of 2 Chr 33:14
broke down the **w** of Jerusalem and 2 Chr 36:19
The **w** of Jerusalem is broken down, and Neh 1:3
of the temple, and for the **w** of the city, Neh 2:8
by the valley and inspected the **w**, Neh 2:15
Come, let us build the **w** of Jerusalem, Neh 2:17
Jerusalem as far as the Broad **W**. Neh 3:8
repaired a thousand cubits of the **w**, Neh 3:13
And he built the **w** of the Pool of Neh 3:15
tower as far as the **w** of Ophel. Neh 3:27
heard that we were building the **w**, Neh 4:1
on it he will break down their stone **w**!" Neh 4:3
So we built the **w**. And all the wall was Neh 4:6
And all the **w** was joined together to half Neh 4:6
we will not be able to rebuild the **w**." Neh 4:10
lowest parts of the space behind the **w**, Neh 4:13
their plan, we all returned to the **w**, Neh 4:15
who were building on the **w**. Those Neh 4:17
spread, and we are separated on the **w**, Neh 4:19
I also persevered in the work on this **w**, Neh 5:16
that I had built the **w** and that there was Neh 6:1
that is why you are building the **w**. Neh 6:6
So the **w** was finished on the Neh 6:15
Now when the **w** had been built and I Neh 7:1
dedication of the **w** of Jerusalem they Neh 12:27
the people and the gates and the **w**. Neh 12:30
up onto the **w** and appointed two Neh 12:31
the south on the **w** to the Dung Gate. Neh 12:31
city of David, at the ascent of the **w**, Neh 12:37
them with half of the people, on the **w**, Neh 12:38
Tower of the Ovens, to the Broad **W**, Neh 12:38
"Why do you lodge outside the **w**? Neh 13:21
and by my God I can leap over a **w**. Ps 18:29
a man to batter him, like a leaning **w**, Ps 62:3
and like a high **w** in his imagination. Prv 18:11
and its stone **w** was broken down. Prv 24:31
will bite him who breaks through a **w**. Eccl 10:8
Behold, there he stands behind our **w**, Sg 2:9
If she is a **w**, we will build on her a Sg 8:9
I was a **w**, and my breasts were like Sg 8:10
high tower, and against every fortified **w**; Is 2:15
I will break down its **w**, and it shall be Is 5:5
broke down the houses to fortify the **w**. Is 22:10
of the ruthless is like a storm against a **w**, Is 25:4
be to you like a breach in a high **w**, Is 30:13
hearing of the people who are on the **w**." Is 36:11
you, and not to the men sitting on the **w**, Is 36:12
turned his face to the **w** and prayed to the Is 38:2
and all your **w** of precious stones. Is 54:12
We grope for the **w** like the blind; we Is 59:10
to this people a fortified **w** of bronze; Jer 15:20
will kindle a fire in the **w** of Damascus, Jer 49:27
to him; the **w** of Babylon has fallen. Jer 51:44
The broad **w** of Babylon shall be Jer 51:58
to lay in ruins the **w** of the daughter of Lam 2:8
he caused rampart and **w** to lament; Lam 2:8
O **w** of the daughter of Zion, let tears Lam 2:18
against it, and build a siege **w** against it, Ezk 4:2
it as an iron **w** between you and the Ezk 4:3
looked, behold, there was a hole in the **w**. Ezk 8:7
man, dig in the **w**." So I dug in the wall, Ezk 8:8
man, dig in the wall." So I dug in the **w**, Ezk 8:8
there, engraved on the **w** all around, Ezk 8:10
In their sight dig through the **w**, and Ezk 12:5
I dug through the **w** with my own Ezk 12:7
shall dig through the **w** to bring him Ezk 12:12
or built up a **w** for the house of Israel, Ezk 13:5
because, when the people build a **w**, Ezk 13:10
And when the **w** falls, will it not be Ezk 13:12
will break down the **w** that you have Ezk 13:14
my wrath upon the **w** and upon those Ezk 13:15
I will say to you, The **w** is no more, Ezk 13:15
should build up the **w** and stand in Ezk 22:30
She saw men portrayed on the **w**, the Ezk 23:14
set up a siege **w** against you and throw Ezk 26:8
and every **w** shall tumble to the Ezk 38:20
there was a **w** all around the outside of Ezk 40:5
So he measured the thickness of the **w**, Ezk 40:5
Then he measured the **w** of the temple, Ezk 41:5
offsets all around the **w** of the temple to Ezk 41:6
not be supported by the **w** of the temple. Ezk 41:6
thickness of the outer **w** of the side Ezk 41:9
and the **w** of the building was five Ezk 41:12
carved; similarly the **w** of the nave. Ezk 41:20
And there was a **w** outside parallel to Ezk 42:7
In the thickness of the **w** of the court, Ezk 42:10
before the corresponding **w** on the east Ezk 42:12
It had a **w** around it, 500 cubits long Ezk 42:20
with only a **w** between me and them. Ezk 43:8
the plaster of the **w** of the king's palace, Dn 5:5
thorns, and I will build a **w** against her, Hos 2:6
they charge; like soldiers they scale the **w**. Jl 2:7
So I will send a fire upon the **w** of Gaza, Am 1:7
So I will send a fire upon the **w** of Tyre, Am 1:10
I will kindle a fire in the **w** of Rabbah, Am 1:14
and leaned his hand against the **w**, Am 5:19
was standing beside a **w** built with a Am 7:7
stumble as they go, they hasten to the **w**; Na 2:5
her, her rampart a sea, and water her **w**? Na 3:8
For the stone will cry out from the **w**, Hab 2:11
And I will be to her a **w** of fire all around, Zec 2:5
down through an opening in the **w**, Acts 9:25
to strike you, you whitewashed **w**! Acts 23:3
a window in the **w** and escaped his 2 Cor 11:33
in his flesh the dividing **w** of hostility Eph 2:14
It had a great, high **w**, with twelve gates, Rv 21:12
And the **w** of the city had twelve Rv 21:14
He also measured its **w**, 144 cubits by Rv 21:17
The **w** was built of jasper, while the city Rv 21:18
The foundations of the **w** of the city Rv 21:19

WALLED (4)
man sells a dwelling house in a **w** city, Lv 25:29
the house in the **w** city shall belong in Lv 25:30
He has **w** up my way, so that I cannot Jb 19:8
He has **w** me about so that I cannot Lam 3:7

WALLOW (3)
so that Moab shall **w** in his vomit, Jer 48:26
dust on their heads and **w** in ashes; Ezk 27:30
herself, returns to **w** in the mire." 2 Pt 2:22

WALLOWING (3)
And Amasa lay **w** in his blood in the 2 Sm 20:12
by you and saw you **w** in your blood, Ezk 16:6
were naked and bare, **w** in your blood. Ezk 16:22

WALLS (71)
the disease is in the **w** of the house with Lv 14:37
disease has spread in the **w** of the house, Lv 14:39
All these were cities fortified with high **w**, Dt 3:5
towns, until your high and fortified **w**, Dt 28:52
great cities with **w** and bronze bars); 1 Kgs 4:13
running around the **w** of the house, 1 Kgs 6:5
not be inserted into the **w** of the house. 1 Kgs 6:6
He lined the **w** of the house on the 1 Kgs 6:15
of the house to the **w** of the ceiling, 1 Kgs 6:15
of cedar from the floor to the **w**, 1 Kgs 6:16
Around all the **w** of the house he 1 Kgs 6:29
eat Jezebel within the **w** of Jezreel.' 1 Kgs 21:23
on the roof with **w** and put there for 2 Kgs 4:10
the way of the gate between the two **w**, 2 Kgs 25:4
down the **w** around Jerusalem. 2 Kgs 25:10
for overlaying the **w** of the house, 1 Chr 29:4
gold—its beams, its thresholds, its **w**, 2 Chr 3:7
—and he carved cherubim on the **w**. 2 Chr 3:7
Beth-horon, fortified cities with **w**, 2 Chr 8:5
surround them with **w** and towers, 2 Chr 14:7
are finishing the **w** and repairing the Ezr 4:12
if this city is rebuilt and the **w** finished, Ezr 4:13
if this city is rebuilt and its **w** finished, Ezr 4:16
huge stones, and timber is laid in the **w**. Ezr 5:8
and I inspected the **w** of Jerusalem that Neh 2:13
the repairing of the **w** of Jerusalem was Neh 4:7
pleasure; build up the **w** of Jerusalem; Ps 51:18
and night they go around it on its **w**, Ps 55:10
Why then have you broken down its **w**, Ps 80:12
You have breached all his **w**; you have Ps 89:40
be within your **w** and security within Ps 122:7
a city broken into and left without **w**. Prv 25:28
away my veil, those watchmen of the **w**. Sg 5:7
a battering down of **w** and a shouting to Is 22:5
reservoir between the two **w** for the water Is 22:11
high fortifications of his **w** he will bring Is 25:12
he sets up salvation as **w** and bulwarks. Is 26:1
your **w** are continually before me. Is 49:16
house and within my **w** a monument and Is 56:5
Foreigners shall build up your **w**, and Is 60:10
you shall call your **w** Salvation, and Is 60:18
On your **w**, O Jerusalem, I have set Is 62:6
against all its **w** all around and against Jer 1:15
city, an iron pillar, and bronze **w**, Jer 1:18
I writhe in pain! Oh the **w** of my heart! Jer 4:19
who are besieging you outside the **w**. Jer 21:4
through the gate between the two **w**; Jer 39:4
and broke down the **w** of Jerusalem. Jer 39:8
have fallen; her **w** are thrown down. Jer 50:15
up a standard against the **w** of Babylon; Jer 51:12
by the way of a gate between the two **w**, Jer 52:7
down all the **w** around Jerusalem. Jer 52:14
hand of the enemy the **w** of her palaces; Lam 2:7
are cast up and siege **w** built to cut off Ezk 17:17
They shall destroy the **w** of Tyre and Ezk 26:4
of his battering rams against your **w**, Ezk 26:9
Your **w** will shake at the noise of the Ezk 26:10
break down your **w** and destroy your Ezk 26:12
Helech were on your **w** all around, Ezk 27:11
their shields on your **w** all around; Ezk 27:11
about you by the **w** and at the doors Ezk 33:30
all of them dwelling without **w**, Ezk 38:11
the yard and the building with its **w**, Ezk 41:13
And on all the **w** all around, inside Ezk 41:17
its base, and its **w** were of wood. Ezk 41:22
trees, such as were carved on the **w**. Ezk 41:25
leap upon the city, they run upon the **w**, Jl 2:9
A day for the building of your **w**! In that Mi 7:11
shall be inhabited as villages without **w**, Zec 2:4
By faith the **w** of Jericho fell down Heb 11:30
to measure the city and its gates and **w**. Rv 21:15

WANDER (22)
God caused me to **w** from my father's Gn 20:13
and he made them **w** in the wilderness Nm 32:13
I today make you **w** about with us, 2 Sm 15:20
feet of Israel to **w** anymore out of the 2 Kgs 21:8
earth and makes them **w** in a pathless Jb 12:24
for help, and **w** about for lack of food? Jb 38:41
yes, I would **w** far away; I would lodge in Ps 55:7
They **w** about for food and growl if they Ps 59:15
and makes them **w** in trackless Ps 107:40
May his children **w** about and beg, Ps 109:10
let me not **w** from your Ps 119:10
who **w** from your commandments. Ps 119:21
her ways **w**, and she does not know it. Prv 5:6
they **w** about each in his own direction; Is 47:15
do you make us **w** from your ways and Is 63:17
this people: "They have loved to **w** thus; Jer 14:10
and those who **w** with their flocks. Jer 31:24
Flee, **w** far away, dwell in the depths, O Jer 49:30
or three cities would **w** to another city to Am 4:8
They shall **w** from sea to sea, and from Am 8:12
Therefore the people **w** like sheep; they Zec 10:2
to the truth and **w** off into myths. 2 Tm 4:4

WANDERED (6)
she departed and **w** in the wilderness Gn 21:14
Some **w** in desert wastes, finding no way Ps 107:4
They **w**, blind, through the streets; Lam 4:14
they **w** over all the mountains and on Ezk 34:6
have **w** away into vain discussion, 1 Tm 1:6
that some have **w** away from the 1 Tm 6:10

WANDERER (2)
shall be a fugitive and a **w** on the earth." Gn 4:12
I shall be a fugitive and a **w** on the earth, Gn 4:14

WANDERERS (2)
So they became fugitives and **w**; Lam 4:15
they shall be **w** among the nations. Hos 9:17

WANDERING (11)
And a man found him **w** in the fields. Gn 37:15
people of Israel, 'They are **w** in the land; Ex 14:3
your God, 'A **w** Aramean was my father. Dt 26:5
w from nation to nation, from one 1 Chr 16:20
w from nation to nation, from one Ps 105:13
of the eyes than the **w** of the appetite: Eccl 6:9
of her affliction and **w** all the precious Lam 1:7
up to Assyria, a wild donkey **w** alone; Hos 8:9
was not worthy—**w** about in deserts Heb 11:38
a sinner from his **w** will save his soul Jas 5:20
w stars, for whom the gloom of utter Jude 1:13

WANDERINGS (1)
Remember my affliction and my **w**, Lam 3:19

WANDERS (3)
He **w** abroad for bread, saying, 'Where Jb 15:23
One who **w** from the way of good sense Prv 21:16
if anyone among you **w** from the truth Jas 5:19

WANED (1)
now the day has **w** toward evening. Jgs 19:9

WANT (70)
Caleb said to her, "What do you **w**?" Jos 15:18
and Caleb said to her, "What do you **w**?" Jgs 1:14
Through **w** and hard hunger they gnaw Jb 30:3
The LORD is my shepherd; I shall not **w**. Ps 23:1
The young lions suffer **w** and hunger; Ps 34:10
a robber, and **w** like an armed man. Prv 6:11
he should give, and only suffers **w**. Prv 11:24
but the belly of the wicked suffers **w**. Prv 13:25
a robber, and **w** like an armed man. Prv 24:34
Whoever gives to the poor will not **w**, Prv 28:27
'Then do you **w** us to go and gather Mt 13:28
her, "What do you **w**?" She said to him, Mt 20:21
"What do you **w** me to do for you?" Mt 20:32
"Whom do you **w** me to release for you: Mt 27:17
of the two do you **w** me to release for Mt 27:21
"I **w** you to give me at once the head of Mk 6:25
guests he did not **w** to break his word Mk 6:26
a house and did not **w** anyone to know, Mk 7:24
And he did not **w** anyone to know, Mk 9:30
we **w** you to do for us whatever we ask Mk 10:35
"What do you **w** me to do for you?" Mk 10:36
"What do you **w** me to do for you?" Mk 10:51
the poor with you, and whenever you **w**, Mk 14:7
"Do you **w** me to release for you the Mk 15:9
do you **w** us to tell fire to come down Lk 9:54
"What do you **w** me to do for you?" He Lk 18:41
'We do not **w** this man to reign over Lk 19:14
who did not **w** me to reign over them, Lk 19:27
he said to him, "Do you **w** to be healed?" Jn 5:6
Twelve, "Do you **w** to go away as well?" Jn 6:67
listen. Why do you **w** to hear it again? Jn 9:27
Do you also **w** to become his disciples?" Jn 9:27
So do you **w** me to release to you the Jn 18:39
carry you where you do not **w** to go." Jn 21:18
Do you **w** to kill me as you killed the Acts 7:28
I **w** you to know, brothers, that I have Rom 1:13
For I do not do what I **w**, but I do the Rom 7:15
Now if I do what I do not **w**, I agree Rom 7:16
For I do not do the good I **w**, but the Rom 7:19
but the evil I do not **w** is what I keep on Rom 7:19
Now if I do what I do not **w**, it is no Rom 7:20
it to be a law that when I **w** to do right, Rom 7:21
I **w** you to understand this mystery, Rom 11:25
but I **w** you to be wise as to what is Rom 16:19
Already you have all you **w**! Already 1 Cor 4:8
I **w** you to be free from anxieties. The 1 Cor 7:32
I **w** you to know, brothers, that our 1 Cor 10:1
I do not **w** you to be participants 1 Cor 10:20
But I **w** you to understand that the 1 Cor 11:3
I do not **w** you to be uninformed. 1 Cor 12:1
Therefore I **w** you to understand that 1 Cor 12:3
Now I **w** you all to speak in tongues, 1 Cor 14:5
For I do not **w** to see you now just in 1 Cor 16:7
For we do not **w** you to be ignorant, 2 Cor 1:8
We **w** you to know, brothers, about 2 Cor 8:1
I do not **w** to appear to be frightening 2 Cor 10:9
who trouble you and **w** to distort the Gal 1:7
whose slaves you **w** to be once more? Gal 4:9
They **w** to shut you out, that you may Gal 4:17
you from doing the things you **w** to do. Gal 5:17
It is those who **w** to make a good Gal 6:12
I **w** you to know, brothers, that what Phil 1:12
For I **w** you to know how great a struggle Col 2:1
But we do not **w** you to be 1 Thes 4:13
and I **w** you to insist on these things, Ti 3:8
I **w** some benefit from you in the Phlm 1:20
Do you **w** to be shown, you foolish Jas 2:20
for doing what the Gentiles **w** to do, 1 Pt 4:3
also stops those who **w** to and puts 3 Jn 1:10
Now I **w** to remind you, although you Jude 1:5

WANTED (22)
For they all **w** to frighten us, thinking, Neh 6:9
of the prophets who **w** to make me Neh 6:14
Wherever the spirit **w** to go, they went, Ezk 1:20
And though he **w** to put him to death, he Mt 14:5
crowd any one prisoner whom they **w**. Mt 27:15
grudge against him and **w** to put him to Mk 6:19
inquiring what he **w** him to be called. Lk 1:62
So also the fish, as much as they **w**. Jn 6:11
Some of them **w** to arrest him, but no one Jn 7:44
Jesus knew that they **w** to ask him, so he Jn 16:19
yourself and walk wherever you **w**, Jn 21:18
they were enraged and **w** to kill them. Acts 5:33
became hungry and **w** something to Acts 10:10
to the gates and **w** to offer sacrifice Acts 14:13
Now Barnabas **w** to take with them Acts 15:37
Paul **w** Timothy to accompany him, Acts 16:3
w to make a defense to the crowd. Acts 19:33
I asked whether he **w** to go to Acts 25:20
sure of this, I **w** to come to you first, 2 Cor 1:15
I **w** to visit you on my way to 2 Cor 1:16
Was I vacillating when I **w** to do this? 2 Cor 1:17
because we **w** to come to you—I, 1 Thes 2:18

WANTING (1)
weighed in the balances and found **w**; Dn 5:27

WANTON (1)
But they had a **w** craving in the Ps 106:14

WANTONLY (2)
be ashamed who are **w** treacherous. Ps 25:3
necks, glancing **w** with their eyes, Is 3:16

WANTS (3)
in her, you shall let her go where she **w**. Dt 21:14
be to you; I will care for all your **w**. Jgs 19:20
from here, for Herod **w** to kill you." Lk 13:31

WAR (210)
these kings made **w** with Bera king of Gn 14:2
lest they multiply, and, if **w** breaks out, Ex 1:10
minds when they see **w** and return to Ex 13:17
The LORD is a man of **w**; the LORD is his Ex 15:3
LORD will have **w** with Amalek from Ex 17:16
"There is a noise of **w** in the camp." Ex 32:17
all in Israel who are able to go to **w**, Nm 1:3
upward, all who were able to go to **w**: Nm 1:20
upward, all who were able to go to **w**: Nm 1:22
upward, all who were able to go to **w**: Nm 1:24
and upward, every man able to go to **w**: Nm 1:26
and upward, every man able to go to **w**: Nm 1:28
and upward, every man able to go to **w**: Nm 1:30
and upward, every man able to go to **w**: Nm 1:32
and upward, every man able to go to **w**: Nm 1:34
and upward, every man able to go to **w**: Nm 1:36
and upward, every man able to go to **w**: Nm 1:38
and upward, every man able to go to **w**: Nm 1:40
and upward, every man able to go to **w**: Nm 1:42
every man able to go to **w** in Israel— Nm 1:45
when you go to **w** in your land against Nm 10:9
all in Israel who are able to go to **w**." Nm 26:2
"Arm men from among you for the **w**, Nm 31:3
each of the tribes of Israel to the **w**." Nm 31:4
tribe, twelve thousand armed for **w**. Nm 31:5
And Moses sent them to the **w**, a Nm 31:6
who had come from service in the **w**. Nm 31:14
from the men of **w** who went out to Nm 31:28
counted the men of **w** who are under Nm 31:49
brothers go to the **w** while you sit here? Nm 32:6
arms to go before the LORD for the **w**, Nm 32:20
over, every man who is armed for **w**, Nm 32:27
on his weapons of **w** and thought it easy Dt 1:41
entire generation, that is, the men of **w**, Dt 2:14
all the men of **w** had perished and were Dt 2:16
by trials, by signs, by wonders, and by **w**, Dt 4:34
you go out to **w** against your enemies, Dt 20:1
with you, but makes **w** against you, Dt 20:12
making **w** against it in order to take it, Dt 20:19
against the city that makes **w** with you, Dt 20:20
you go out to **w** against your enemies, Dt 21:10
40,000 ready for **w** passed over before Jos 4:13
who came out of Egypt, all the men of **w**, Jos 5:4
the men of **w** who came out of Egypt, Jos 5:6
all the men of **w** going around the city Jos 6:3
against Gibeon and made **w** against it. Jos 10:5
he and all the people of **w** with him, Jos 10:7
of the men of **w** who had gone with Jos 10:24
Joshua made **w** a long time with all Jos 11:18
And the land had rest from **w**. Jos 11:23
then, for **w** and for going and coming. Jos 14:11
And the land had rest from **w**. Jos 14:15
and Bashan, because he was a man of **w**. Jos 17:1
at Shiloh to make **w** against them. Jos 22:12
no more of making **w** against them to Jos 22:33
of the people of Israel might know **w**, Jgs 3:2
to teach **w** to those who had not known it Jgs 3:2
He went out to **w**, and the LORD gave Jgs 3:10
gods were chosen, then **w** was in the gates. Jgs 5:8
the Ammonites made **w** against Israel. Jgs 11:4
the Ammonites made **w** against Israel, Jgs 11:5
Israel, or did he ever go to **w** with them? Jgs 11:25
you do me wrong by making **w** on me. Jgs 11:27
tribe of Dan, armed with weapons of **w**, Jgs 18:11
armed with their weapons of **w**, Jgs 18:16
the 600 men armed with weapons of **w**. Jgs 18:17
drew the sword; all these were men of **w**. Jgs 20:17
his implements of **w** and the 1 Sm 8:12
playing, a man of valor, a man of **w**, 1 Sm 16:18
to the battle line, shouting the **w** cry. 1 Sm 17:20
been a man of **w** from his youth." 1 Sm 17:33
that Saul set him over the men of **w**. 1 Sm 18:5
And there was **w** again. And David 1 Sm 19:8
Saul summoned all the people to **w**, 1 Sm 23:8
Philistines gathered their forces for **w**, 1 Sm 28:1
and the weapons of **w** perished!" 2 Sm 1:27
There was a long **w** between the house 2 Sm 3:1
While there was **w** between the house 2 Sm 3:6
had often been at **w** with Toi. 2 Sm 8:10
were doing and how the **w** was going. 2 Sm 11:7
Besides, your father is expert in **w**; he 2 Sm 17:8
There was **w** again between the 2 Sm 21:15
there was again **w** with the 2 Sm 21:18
there was again **w** with the 2 Sm 21:19
And there was again **w** at Gath, 2 Sm 21:20
He trains my hands for **w**, so that my 2 Sm 22:35
for blood that had been shed in **w**, 1 Kgs 2:5
putting the blood of **w** on the belt 1 Kgs 2:5
there was **w** between Rehoboam 1 Kgs 14:30
Now there was **w** between Rehoboam 1 Kgs 15:6
And there was **w** between Abijam 1 Kgs 15:7
And there was **w** between Asa and 1 Kgs 15:16
And there was **w** between Asa and 1 Kgs 15:32
Or if they have come out for **w**, take 1 Kgs 20:18
Syria and Israel continued without **w**. 1 Kgs 22:1
Ahab to make **w** against Hazael king 2 Kgs 8:28
taken from Jehoahaz his father in **w**. 2 Kgs 13:25
came up to wage **w** on Jerusalem, 2 Kgs 16:5
words are strategy and power for **w**? 2 Kgs 18:20
all of them strong and fit for **w**. 2 Kgs 24:16
and all the men of **w** fled by night by 2 Kgs 25:4
been in command of the men of **w**, 2 Kgs 25:19
Saul they waged **w** against the 1 Chr 5:10
sword, and drew the bow, expert in **w**, 1 Chr 5:18
expert in war, 44,760, able to go to **w**. 1 Chr 5:18
They waged **w** against the Hagrites, 1 Chr 5:19
many fell, because the **w** was of God. 1 Chr 5:22
houses, were units of the army for **w**, 1 Chr 7:4
warriors, 17,200, able to go to **w**. 1 Chr 7:11
by genealogies, for service in **w**, 1 Chr 7:40
mighty men who helped him in **w**. 1 Chr 12:1
mighty men of valor for **w**, 1 Chr 12:25
for battle with all the weapons of **w**, 1 Chr 12:33
armed with all the weapons of **w**. 1 Chr 12:37
All these, men of **w**, arrayed in 1 Chr 12:38
had often been at **w** with Tou. 1 Chr 18:10
this there arose **w** with the Philistines 1 Chr 20:4
there was again **w** with the 1 Chr 20:5
And there was again **w** at Gath, 1 Chr 20:6
are a man of **w** and have shed blood.' 1 Chr 28:3
Now there was **w** between Abijah 2 Chr 13:2
having an army of valiant men of **w**, 2 Chr 13:3
had rest. He had no **w** in those years, 2 Chr 14:6
was no more **w** until the thirty-fifth 2 Chr 15:19
made no **w** against Jehoshaphat. 2 Chr 17:10
with 180,000 armed for **w**. 2 Chr 17:18
people. We will be with you in the **w**." 2 Chr 18:3
Israel to make **w** against Hazael king 2 Chr 22:5
were 300,000 choice men, fit for **w**, 2 Chr 25:5
out and made **w** against the 2 Chr 26:6
had an army of soldiers, fit for **w**, 2 Chr 26:11
who could make **w** with mighty 2 Chr 26:13
those who were coming from the **w** 2 Chr 28:12
the house with which I am at **w**. 2 Chr 35:21
and in **w** from the power of the sword. Jb 5:20
of trouble, for the day of battle and **w**? Jb 38:23
He trains my hands for **w**, so that my Ps 18:34
though **w** arise against me, yet I will be Ps 27:3
The **w** horse is a false hope for Ps 33:17
as butter, yet **w** was in his heart; Ps 55:21
scatter the peoples who delight in **w**. Ps 68:30
shield, the sword, and the weapons of **w**. Ps 76:3
all the men of **w** were unable to use their Ps 76:5
peace, but when I speak, they are for **w**! Ps 120:7
my rock, who trains my hands for **w**, Ps 144:1
by counsel; by wise guidance wage **w**. Prv 20:18
by wise guidance you can wage your **w**, Prv 24:6
against his neighbor is like a **w** club, Prv 25:18
hate; a time for **w**, and a time for peace. Eccl 3:8
There is no discharge from **w**, nor will Eccl 8:8
Wisdom is better than weapons of **w**, Eccl 9:18
of them wearing swords and expert in **w**, Sg 3:8
neither shall they learn **w** anymore. Is 2:4
came up to Jerusalem to wage **w** against it, Is 7:1
mere words are strategy and power for **w**? Is 36:5
those who **w** against you shall be as Is 41:12
man, like a man of **w** he stirs up his zeal; Is 42:13
the sound of the trumpet, the alarm of **w**. Jer 4:19
"Prepare **w** against her; arise, and let us Jer 6:4
king of Babylon is making **w** against us. Jer 21:2
back the weapons of **w** that are in your Jer 21:4
live and shall have his life as a prize of **w**. Jer 21:9
me from ancient times prophesied **w**, Jer 28:8
He shall have his life as a prize of **w**, and Jer 38:2
you shall have your life as a prize of **w**, Jer 39:18
we shall not see **w** or hear the sound Jer 42:14
life as a prize of **w** in all places to which Jer 45:5
'We are heroes and mighty men of **w**'? Jer 48:14
are my hammer and weapon of **w**: Jer 51:20
prepare the nations for **w** against her; Jer 51:27
Prepare the nations for **w** against her, Jer 51:28
and all the men of **w** fled and went out Jer 52:7
had been in command of the men of **w**, Jer 52:25
great company will not help him in **w**, Ezk 17:17

were in your army as your men of **w**. Ezk 27:10
they exchanged horses, **w** horses, Ezk 27:14
and all your men of **w** who are in you, Ezk 27:27
to Sheol with their weapons of **w**, Ezk 32:27
against the land that is restored from **w**, Ezk 38:8
this horn made **w** with the saints and Dn 7:21
a flood, and to the end there shall be **w**. Dn 9:26
"His sons shall wage **w** and assemble a Dn 11:10
again shall carry the **w** as far as his Dn 11:10
south shall wage **w** with an Dn 11:25
or by sword or by **w** or by horses or by Hos 1:7
bow, the sword, and **w** from the land, Hos 2:18
Shall not the **w** against the unjust Hos 10:9
the tumult of **w** shall arise among Hos 10:14
of horses, and like **w** horses they run. Jl 2:4
this among the nations: Consecrate for **w**; Jl 3:9
Let all the men of **w** draw near; let them Jl 3:9
pass by trustingly with no thought of **w**. Mi 2:8
but declare **w** against him who puts Mi 3:5
neither shall they learn **w** anymore; Mi 4:3
Ephraim and the **w** horse from Zec 9:10
peoples that wage **w** against Jerusalem: Zec 14:12
out to encounter another king in **w**, Lk 14:31
another law waging **w** against the law Rom 7:23
we are not waging **w** according to the 2 Cor 10:3
out of weakness, became mighty in **w**, Heb 11:34
that your passions are at **w** within you? Jas 4:1
flesh, which wage **w** against your soul. 1 Pt 2:11
to you soon and **w** against them with the Rv 2:16
bottomless pit will make **w** on them and Rv 11:7
Now **w** arose in heaven, Michael and his Rv 12:7
and went off to make **w** on the rest of Rv 12:17
was allowed to make **w** on the saints and Rv 13:7
They will make **w** on the Lamb, and Rv 17:14
righteousness he judges and makes **w**. Rv 19:11
gathered to make **w** against him who Rv 19:19

WARD (1)
and the lame will **w** you off"— 2 Sm 5:6

WARDROBE (4)
to him who was in charge of the **w**, 2 Kgs 10:22
keeper of the **w** (now she lived in 2 Kgs 22:14
keeper of the **w** (now she lived in 2 Chr 34:22
of the king, to a **w** in the storehouse, Jer 38:11

WARES (11)
goods, with beasts, and with costly **w**, Ezr 1:6
all kinds of **w** lodged outside Neh 13:20
were in you to barter for your **w**. Ezk 27:9
and lead they exchanged for your **w**. Ezk 27:12
war horses, and mules for your **w**. Ezk 27:14
they exchanged for your **w** emeralds, Ezk 27:16
from Uzal they exchanged for your **w**; Ezk 27:19
they exchanged for your **w** the best of Ezk 27:22
Your riches, your **w**, your Ezk 27:27
When your **w** came from the seas, Ezk 27:33
The merchants of these **w**, who gained Rv 18:15

WARFARE (4)
God because of the **w** with which his 1 Kgs 5:3
and cry to her that her **w** is ended, Is 40:2
the weapons of our **w** are not of the 2 Cor 10:4
by them you may wage the good **w**, 1 Tm 1:18

WARM (10)
his compassion grew **w** for his brother, Gn 43:30
It was still **w** when we took it from our Jos 9:12
him with clothes, he could not get **w**. 1 Kgs 1:1
that my lord the king may be **w**." 1 Kgs 1:2
him, the flesh of the child became **w**. 2 Kgs 4:34
Again, if two lie together, they keep **w**, Eccl 4:11
warm, but how can one keep **w** alone? Eccl 4:11
warms himself and says, "Aha, I am **w**, Is 44:16
my compassion grows **w** and tender. Hos 11:8
You clothe yourselves, but no one is **w**. Hg 1:6

WARMED (3)
and if he was not **w** with the fleece of my Jb 31:20
earth and lets them be **w** on the ground, Jb 39:14
be **w** and filled," without giving them Jas 2:16

WARMING (6)
the flame. No coal for **w** oneself is this, Is 47:14
with the guards and **w** himself at the Mk 14:54
and seeing Peter **w** himself, she looked Mk 14:67
they were standing and **w** themselves. Jn 18:18
was with them, standing and **w** himself. Jn 18:18
Peter was standing and **w** himself. Jn 18:25

WARMS (2)
He takes a part of it and **w** himself; he Is 44:15
Also he **w** himself and says, "Aha, I am Is 44:16

WARN (20)
and you shall **w** them about the Ex 18:20
to Moses, "Go down and **w** the people, Ex 19:21
I solemnly **w** you today that you shall Dt 8:19
you shall solemnly **w** them and show 1 Sm 8:9
by the LORD and solemnly **w** you, 1 Kgs 2:42
Thus he used to **w** him, so that he 2 Kgs 6:10
or rules, then you shall **w** them, 2 Chr 19:10
W the nations that he is coming; Jer 4:16
nor speak to **w** the wicked from his Ezk 3:18
But if you **w** the wicked, and he does Ezk 3:19
But if you **w** the righteous person not to Ezk 3:21
do not speak to **w** the wicked to turn Ezk 33:8
But if you **w** the wicked to turn from Ezk 33:9
But I will **w** you whom to fear: fear him Lk 12:5
five brothers—so that he may **w** them, Lk 16:28
let us **w** them to speak no more to Acts 4:17
and I **w** them now while absent, 2 Cor 13:2
orgies, and things like these. I **w** you, Gal 5:21
an enemy, but **w** him as a brother. 2 Thes 3:15
I **w** everyone who hears the words of the Rv 22:18

WARNED (29)
So Abimelech **w** all the people, saying, Gn 26:11
said to him, "The man solemnly **w** us, Gn 43:3
to Mount Sinai, for you yourself **w** us, Ex 19:23
its owner has been **w** but has not kept Ex 21:29
them for harm, as the LORD had **w**, Jgs 2:15
Yet the LORD **w** Israel and Judah by 2 Kgs 17:13
who had **w** them in order to turn them Neh 9:26
And you **w** them in order to turn them Neh 9:29
bore with them and **w** them by your Neh 9:30
And I **w** them on the day when they Neh 13:15
But I **w** them and said to them, "Why Neh 13:21
Now therefore, O kings, be wise; be **w**, O Ps 2:10
Moreover, by them is your servant **w**; in Ps 19:11
and **w** me not to walk in the way of this Is 8:11
Be **w**, O Jerusalem, lest I turn from you in Jer 6:8
For I solemnly **w** your fathers when I Jer 11:7
a certainty that I have **w** you this day Jer 42:19
Because you have not **w** him, he shall Ezk 3:20
trumpet, so that the people are not **w**, Ezk 33:6
And being **w** in a dream not to return to Mt 2:12
and being **w** in a dream he withdrew to Mt 2:22
Who **w** you to flee from the wrath to Mt 3:7
And Jesus sternly **w** them, "See that no Mt 9:30
Who **w** you to flee from the wrath to Lk 3:7
I **w** those who sinned before and all 2 Cor 13:2
I warn you, as I **w** you before, that those Gal 5:21
you beforehand and solemnly **w** you. 1 Thes 4:6
being **w** by God concerning events as Heb 11:7
refused him who **w** them on earth, Heb 12:25

WARNING (18)
250 men, and they became a **w**. Nm 26:10
the words by which I am **w** you today, Dt 32:46
To whom shall I speak and give **w**, that Jer 6:10
of the land of Egypt, **w** them persistently, Jer 11:7
mouth, you shall give them **w** from me. Ezk 3:17
surely die,' and you give him no **w**, Ezk 3:18
he shall surely live, because he took **w**, Ezk 3:21
reproach and a taunt, a **w** and a horror, Ezk 5:15
women may take **w** and not commit Ezk 23:48
sound of the trumpet does not take **w**, Ezk 33:4
of the trumpet and did not take **w**; Ezk 33:5
But if he had taken **w**, he would have Ezk 33:5
mouth, you shall give them **w** from me. Ezk 33:7
great. Without **w** he shall destroy many. Dn 8:25
come in without **w** and obtain the Dn 11:21
Without **w** he shall come into the Dn 11:24
w everyone and teaching everyone with Col 1:28
after **w** him once and then twice, Ti 3:10

WARNINGS (3)
their fathers and the **w** that he gave 2 Kgs 17:15
commandments and your **w** that you Neh 9:34
ears of men and terrifies them with **w**, Jb 33:16

WARNS (2)
blows the trumpet and **w** the people, Ezk 33:3
if we reject him who **w** from heaven. Heb 12:25

WARP (9)
in **w** or woof of linen or wool, or in a Lv 13:48
in the skin or in the **w** or the woof or in Lv 13:49
in the garment, in the **w** or the woof, Lv 13:51
burn the garment, or the **w** or the woof, Lv 13:52
in the **w** or the woof or in any article Lv 13:53
or the skin or the **w** or the woof. Lv 13:56
in the garment, in the **w** or the woof, Lv 13:57
But the garment, or the **w** or the woof, Lv 13:58
or linen, either in the **w** or the woof, Lv 13:59

WARPED (1)
that such a person is **w** and sinful; Ti 3:11

WARRED (3)
They **w** against Midian, as the LORD Nm 31:7
how he **w** and how he reigned, 1 Kgs 14:19
that he showed, and how he **w**, 1 Kgs 22:45

WARRING (2)
for the Philistines are **w** against me, 1 Sm 28:15
the king of Syria was **w** against Israel, 2 Kgs 6:8

WARRIOR (14)
Jephthah the Gileadite was a mighty **w**, Jgs 11:1
upon breach; he runs upon me like a **w**. Jb 16:14
a **w** is not delivered by his great Ps 33:16
in the hand of a **w** are the children of Ps 127:4
boot of the tramping **w** in battle tumult Is 9:5
forth chariot and horse, army and **w**; Is 43:17
like a mighty **w** who cannot save? Jer 14:9
But the LORD is with me as a dread **w**; Jer 20:11
swift cannot flee away, nor the **w** escape; Jer 46:6
for **w** has stumbled against warrior; Jer 46:12
for warrior has stumbled against **w**; Jer 46:12
are like a skilled **w** who does not return Jer 50:9
into spears; let the weak say, "I am a **w**." Jl 3:10
Ephraim shall become like a mighty **w**, Zec 10:7

WARRIOR'S (2)
A **w** sharp arrows, with glowing coals Ps 120:4
O Greece, and wield you like a **w** sword. Zec 9:13

WARRIORS (36)
two parts between the **w** who went out Nm 31:27
greater than Ai, and all its men were **w**. Jos 10:2
and all his **w** came suddenly against Jos 11:7
of Benjamin, 180,000 chosen **w**, 1 Kgs 12:21
Hodaviah, and Jahdiel, mighty **w**, 1 Chr 5:24
of Tola, mighty **w** of their generations, 1 Chr 7:2
Issachar were in all 87,000 mighty **w**, 1 Chr 7:5
heads of fathers' houses, mighty **w**. 1 Chr 7:7
of their fathers' houses, mighty **w**, 1 Chr 7:9
of their fathers' houses, mighty **w**, 1 Chr 7:11
fathers' houses, approved, mighty **w**, 1 Chr 7:40
Ulam were men who were mighty **w**, 1 Chr 8:40
mighty and experienced **w**, 1 Chr 12:8
mighty men and all the seasoned **w**. 1 Chr 28:1
and Benjamin, 180,000 chosen **w**, 2 Chr 11:1
him with 800,000 chosen mighty **w**. 2 Chr 13:3
all the mighty **w** and commanders 2 Chr 32:21
thousand shields, all of them shields of **w**. Sg 4:4
wasting sickness among his stout **w**, Is 10:16
an open tomb; they are all mighty **w**. Jer 5:16
with all his **w** and all the officials, Jer 26:21
Their **w** are beaten down and have fled Jer 46:5
and rage, O chariots! Let the **w** go out: Jer 46:9
The heart of the **w** of Moab shall be in Jer 48:41
and the heart of the **w** of Edom shall be Jer 49:22
A sword against her **w**, that they may Jer 50:36
The **w** of Babylon have ceased fighting; Jer 51:30
her, upon Babylon; her **w** are taken; Jer 51:56
her commanders, and her **w**; Jer 51:57
lusted after her lovers the Assyrians, **w** Ezk 23:5
commanders, **w** clothed in full armor, Ezk 23:12
with mighty men and all kinds of **w**,' Ezk 39:20
way and in the multitude of your **w**, Hos 10:13
Like **w** they charge; like soldiers they scale Jl 2:7
there. Bring down your **w**, O LORD. Jl 3:11
with his own arrows the heads of his **w**, Hab 3:14

WARS (13)
said in the Book of the **W** of the LORD, Nm 21:14
had not experienced all the **w** in Canaan. Jgs 3:1
much blood and have waged great **w**. 1 Chr 22:8
were continual **w** between 2 Chr 12:15
for from now on you will have **w**." 2 Chr 16:9
Jotham, and all his **w** and his ways, 2 Chr 27:7
He makes **w** cease to the end of the earth; Ps 46:9
in their heart and stir up **w** continually. Ps 140:2
you will hear of **w** and rumors of wars. Mt 24:6
you will hear of wars and rumors of **w**. Mt 24:6
when you hear of **w** and rumors of Mk 13:7
you hear of wars and rumors of **w**, Mk 13:7
And when you hear of **w** and tumults, Lk 21:9

WASH (78)
little water be brought, and **w** your feet, Gn 18:4
and spend the night and **w** your feet. Gn 19:2
there was water to **w** his feet and the Gn 24:32
and let them **w** their garments Ex 19:10
tent of meeting and **w** them with water. Ex 29:4
pieces, and **w** its entrails and its legs, Ex 29:17
and his sons shall **w** their hands and Ex 30:19
to the LORD, they shall **w** with water, Ex 30:20
They shall **w** their hands and their feet, Ex 30:21
of meeting and shall **w** them with water Ex 40:12
entrails and its legs he shall **w** with water. Lv 1:9
and the legs he shall **w** with water. Lv 1:13
you shall **w** that on which it was Lv 6:27
of their carcass shall **w** his clothes and Lv 11:25
their carcass shall **w** his clothes and Lv 11:28
of its carcass shall **w** his clothes and be Lv 11:40
the carcass shall **w** his clothes and Lv 11:40
And he shall **w** his clothes and be clean. Lv 13:6
And he shall **w** his clothes and be Lv 13:34
command that they **w** the thing in Lv 13:54
to be cleansed shall **w** his clothes and Lv 14:8
and then he shall **w** his clothes and Lv 14:9
sleeps in the house shall **w** his clothes, Lv 14:47

eats in the house shall **w** his clothes. Lv 14:47
touches his bed shall **w** his clothes and Lv 15:5
discharge has sat shall **w** his clothes and Lv 15:6
the discharge shall **w** his clothes and Lv 15:7
then he shall **w** his clothes and bathe Lv 15:8
such things shall **w** his clothes and Lv 15:10
hands in water shall **w** his clothes and Lv 15:11
for his cleansing, and **w** his clothes. Lv 15:13
touches her bed shall **w** his clothes and Lv 15:21
which she sits shall **w** his clothes and Lv 15:22
and shall **w** his clothes and bathe Lv 15:27
go to Azazel shall **w** his clothes and Lv 16:26
burns them shall **w** his clothes and Lv 16:28
shall **w** his clothes and bathe himself Lv 17:15
But if he does not **w** them or bathe his Lv 17:16
in a book and **w** them off into the Nm 5:23
and **w** their clothes and cleanse Nm 8:7
Then the priest shall **w** his clothes and Nm 19:7
burns the heifer shall **w** his clothes in Nm 19:8
of the heifer shall **w** his clothes and be Nm 19:10
and he shall **w** his clothes and bathe Nm 19:19
water for impurity shall **w** his clothes, Nm 19:21
You must **w** your clothes on the Nm 31:24
the slain man shall **w** their hands over Dt 21:6
W therefore and anoint yourself, and put Ru 3:3
is a servant to **w** the feet of the 1 Sm 25:41
to your house and **w** your feet." And 2 Sm 11:8
"Go and **w** in the Jordan seven times, 2 Kgs 5:10
Could I not **w** in them and be clean?" 2 Kgs 5:12
said to you, '**W**, and be clean'?" 2 Kgs 5:13
also made ten basins in which to **w**, 2 Chr 4:6
and the sea was for the priests to **w** in. 2 Chr 4:6
If I **w** myself with snow and cleanse my Jb 9:30
the torrents **w** away the soil of the earth; Jb 14:19
I **w** my hands in innocence and go Ps 26:6
W me thoroughly from my iniquity, Ps 51:2
w me, and I shall be whiter than snow. Ps 51:7
W yourselves; make yourselves clean; Is 1:16
Though you **w** yourself with lye and use Jer 2:22
O Jerusalem, **w** your heart from evil, that Jer 4:14
fast, anoint your head and **w** your face, Mt 6:17
For they do not **w** their hands when they Mt 15:2
Jews do not eat unless they **w** their hands, Mk 7:3
they do not eat unless they **w**. Mk 7:4
see that he did not first **w** before dinner. Lk 11:38
w in the pool of Siloam" (which means Jn 9:7
eyes and said to me, 'Go to Siloam and **w**.' Jn 9:11
basin and began to **w** the disciples' feet Jn 13:5
said to him, "Lord, do you **w** my feet?" Jn 13:6
"You shall never **w** my feet." Jesus Jn 13:8
Jesus answered him, "If I do not **w** you, Jn 13:8
one who has bathed does not need to **w**, Jn 13:10
you also ought to **w** one another's feet. Jn 13:14
be baptized and **w** away your sins, Acts 22:16
Blessed are those who **w** their robes, so Rv 22:14

WASHBASIN (2)
Moab is my **w**; upon Edom I cast my Ps 60:8
Moab is my **w**; upon Edom I cast my Ps 108:9

WASHED (40)
them water, and they had **w** their feet, Gn 43:24
Then he **w** his face and came out. And Gn 43:31
he has **w** his garments in wine and his Gn 49:11
the people; and they **w** their garments. Ex 19:14
Aaron and his sons **w** their hands and Ex 40:31
when they approached the altar, they **w**, Ex 40:32
and his sons and **w** them with water. Lv 8:6
He **w** the entrails and the legs with water, Lv 8:21
And he **w** the entrails and the legs and Lv 9:14
the diseased thing after it has been **w**. Lv 13:55
area has faded after it has been **w**, Lv 13:56
the disease departs when you have **w** it, Lv 13:58
it, shall then be **w** a second time, Lv 13:58
semen comes shall be **w** with water and Lv 15:17
from sin and **w** their clothes, Nm 8:21
the donkeys feed. And they **w** their feet, Jgs 19:21
the earth and **w** and anointed 2 Sm 12:20
trimmed his beard nor **w** his clothes, 2 Sm 19:24
And they **w** the chariot by the pool 1 Kgs 22:38
and the prostitutes **w** themselves in 1 Kgs 22:38
time; their foundation was **w** away. Jb 22:16
when my steps were **w** with butter, and Jb 29:6
my heart clean and **w** my hands in Ps 73:13
own eyes but are not **w** of their filth. Prv 30:12
the Lord shall have **w** away the filth of Is 4:4
nor were you **w** with water to cleanse Ezk 16:4
you with water and **w** off your blood Ezk 16:9
where the burnt offering was to be **w**. Ezk 40:38
he took water and **w** his hands before Mt 27:24
So he went and **w** and came back seeing. Jn 9:7
So I went and **w** and received my sight." Jn 9:11
them, "He put mud on my eyes, and I **w**, Jn 9:15
When he had **w** their feet and put on his Jn 13:12
Lord and Teacher, have **w** your feet, Jn 13:14
ill and died, and when they had **w** her, Acts 9:37
of the night and **w** their wounds; Acts 16:33
But you were **w**, you were sanctified, 1 Cor 6:11
has **w** the feet of the saints, 1 Tm 5:10
and our bodies **w** with pure water. Heb 10:22
They have **w** their robes and made them Rv 7:14

WASHER'S (3)
is on the highway to the **W** Field. 2 Kgs 18:17
upper pool on the highway to the **W** Field. Is 7:3
pool on the highway to the **W** Field. Is 36:2

WASHING (9)
bronze, with its stand of bronze, for **w**. Ex 30:18
and the altar, and put water in it for **w**, Ex 40:30
shorn ewes that have come up from the **w**, Sg 4:2
of ewes that have come up from the **w**; Sg 6:6
such as the **w** of cups and pots and Mk 7:4
gone out of them and were **w** their nets. Lk 5:2
cleansed her by the **w** of water with the Eph 5:26
by the **w** of regeneration and renewal of Ti 3:5
own vomit, and the sow, after **w** herself, 2 Pt 2:22

WASHINGS (2)
and of instruction about **w**, the laying Heb 6:2
with food and drink and various **w**, Heb 9:10

WASTE (102)
brother's wife he would **w** the semen on Gn 38:9
will lay your cities **w** and will make Lv 26:31
desolation, and your cities shall be a **w**. Lv 26:33
and we laid **w** as far as Nophah; Nm 21:30
and in the howling **w** of the wilderness; Dt 32:10
—so that they laid **w** the land as they Jgs 6:5
"I will not **w** time like this with you." 2 Sm 18:14
Assyria have laid **w** the nations and 2 Kgs 19:17
violent men shall **w** them no more, 1 Chr 17:9
old. That was why this city was laid **w**. Ezr 4:15
course; they go up into the **w** and perish. Jb 6:18
makes them wander in a pathless **w**. Jb 12:24
dry ground by night in **w** and desolation; Jb 30:3
to satisfy the **w** and desolate land, and to Jb 38:27
of my iniquity, and my bones **w** away. Ps 31:10
Jacob and laid **w** his habitation. Ps 79:7
wilderness, like an owl of the **w** places; Ps 102:6
a fruitful land into a salty **w**, because Ps 107:34
have eaten, and **w** your pleasant words. Prv 23:8
I will make it a **w**; it shall not be pruned or Is 5:6
"Until cities lie **w** without inhabitant, Is 6:11
people, and the land is a desolate **w**, Is 6:11
Because Ar of Moab is laid **w** in a night, Is 15:1
because Kir of Moab is laid **w** in a night, Is 15:1
O ships of Tarshish, for Tyre is laid **w**, Is 23:1
Tarshish, for your stronghold is laid **w**. Is 23:14
One. But I say, "I **w** away, I waste away. Is 24:16
One. But I say, "I waste away, I **w** away. Is 24:16
The highways lie **w**; the traveler ceases. Is 33:8
generation to generation it shall lie **w**; Is 34:10
of Assyria have laid **w** all the nations Is 37:18
I will lay **w** mountains and hills, and Is 42:15
those who laid you **w** go out from you. Is 49:17
"Surely your **w** and your desolate places Is 49:19
he comforts all her **w** places and makes Is 51:3
into singing, you **w** places of Jerusalem, Is 52:9
those nations shall be utterly laid **w**. Is 60:12
They have made his land a **w**; his cities Jer 2:15
out from his place to make your land a **w**; Jer 4:7
hard on crash; the whole land is laid **w**. Jer 4:20
Suddenly my tents are laid **w**, my Jer 4:20
the bride, for the land shall become a **w**. Jer 7:34
because they are laid **w** so that no one Jer 9:10
land ruined and laid **w** like a wilderness, Jer 9:12
him, and have laid **w** his habitation. Jer 10:25
land shall become a ruin and a **w**, Jer 25:11
making the land an everlasting **w**. Jer 25:12
to make them a desolation and a **w**, Jer 25:18
For the LORD is laying **w** their pasture, Jer 25:36
land has become a **w** because of the Jer 25:38
say, 'It is a **w** without man or beast,' Jer 33:10
In this place that is **w**, without man or Jer 33:12
and they became a **w** and a desolation, Jer 44:6
a desolation and a **w** and a curse, Jer 44:22
For Memphis shall become a **w**, a ruin, Jer 46:19
of Israel: "Woe to Nebo, for it is laid **w**! Jer 48:1
beside the Arnon, that Moab is laid **w**. Jer 48:20
"Wail, O Heshbon, for Ai is laid **w**! Cry Jer 49:3
shall become a horror, a taunt, a **w**, Jer 49:13
a haunt of jackals, an everlasting **w**; Jer 49:33
but you shall be a perpetual **w**, Jer 51:26
is laying Babylon **w** and stilling her Jer 51:55
He has laid **w** his booth like a garden, Lam 2:6
made my flesh and my skin **w** away; Lam 3:4
the cities shall be **w** and the high places Ezk 6:6
so that your altars will be **w** and ruined, Ezk 6:6
and make the land desolate and **w**, Ezk 6:14
the inhabited cities shall be laid **w**, Ezk 12:20
their widows. He laid **w** their cities, Ezk 19:7
be replenished, now that she is laid **w**,' Ezk 26:2
When I make you a city laid **w**, like Ezk 26:19
of Egypt shall be a desolation and a **w**. Ezk 29:9
of Egypt an utter **w** and desolation, Ezk 29:10
years among cities that are laid **w**. Ezk 29:12
be in the midst of cities that are laid **w**. Ezk 30:7
inhabitants of these **w** places in the Ezk 33:24
who are in the **w** places shall fall by Ezk 33:27
make the land a desolation and a **w**, Ezk 33:28
a desolation and a **w** because of all Ezk 33:29
I will make you a desolation and a **w**. Ezk 35:3
I will lay your cities **w**, and you shall Ezk 35:4
make Mount Seir a **w** and a desolation, Ezk 35:7
be inhabited and the **w** places rebuilt. Ezk 36:10
and the **w** places shall be rebuilt. Ezk 36:33
and the **w** and desolate and ruined Ezk 36:35
so shall the **w** cities be filled with Ezk 36:38
Israel, which had been a continual **w**. Ezk 38:8
hand against the **w** places that are Ezk 38:12
And I will lay **w** her vines and her fig Hos 2:12
It has laid **w** my vine and splintered my fig Jl 1:7
the sanctuaries of Israel shall be laid **w**, Am 7:9
with fire, and all her idols I will lay **w**, Mi 1:7
be plundered, and their houses laid **w**. Zep 1:13
by nettles and salt pits, and a **w** forever. Zep 2:9
a desolation, a dry **w** like the desert. Zep 2:13
I have laid **w** their streets so that no one Zep 3:6
I have laid **w** his hill country and left his Mal 1:3
divided against itself is laid **w**, Mt 12:25
were indignant, saying, "Why this **w**? Mt 26:8
divided against itself is laid **w**, Lk 11:17
has been laid **w**." And all shipmasters Rv 18:17
in a single hour she has been laid **w**. Rv 18:19

WASTED (8)
they shall be **w** with hunger, and Dt 32:24
His flesh is so **w** away that it cannot be Jb 33:21
I am in distress; my eye is **w** from grief; Ps 31:9
my bones **w** away through my groaning Ps 32:3
The **w** city is broken down; every house Is 24:10
the victims of hunger, who **w** away, Lam 4:9
shrink from you and say, **W** is Nineveh; Na 3:7
"Why was the ointment **w** like that? Mk 14:4

WASTELAND (1)
game; the **w** yields food for their children. Jb 24:5

WASTES (9)
Man **w** away like a rotten thing, like a Jb 13:28
a lake and a river **w** away and dries up, Jb 14:11
My eye **w** away because of grief; it grows Ps 6:7
nor the destruction that **w** at noonday. Ps 91:6
Some wandered in desert **w**, finding no Ps 107:4
makes them wander in trackless **w**; Ps 107:40
it will be as when a sick man **w** away. Is 10:18
and all her cities shall be perpetual **w**." Jer 49:13
the desolate **w** and the deserted cities, Ezk 36:4

WASTING (6)
with **w** disease and fever that consume Lv 26:16
will strike you with **w** disease and with Dt 28:22
but sent a **w** disease among them. Ps 106:15
of hosts will send **w** sickness among his Is 10:16
that this man was **w** his possessions. Lk 16:1
Though our outer nature is **w** away, 2 Cor 4:16

WATCH (65)
said, "The LORD **w** between you and me, Gn 31:49
And in the morning **w** the LORD in the Ex 14:24
and **w** Moses until he had gone into the Ex 33:8
"Therefore **w** yourselves very carefully. Dt 4:15
camp at the beginning of the middle **w**, Jgs 7:19
watch, when they had just set the **w**. Jgs 7:19
and **w**. If the daughters of Shiloh come Jgs 21:21
and **w**. If it goes up on the way to its 1 Sm 6:9
in the morning **w** and struck down 1 Sm 11:11
to David's house to **w** him, 1 Sm 19:11
have you not kept **w** over your lord 1 Sm 26:15
you have not kept **w** over your lord, 1 Sm 26:16
man who kept the **w** lifted up his 2 Sm 13:34
goes up. **W** corresponded to watch. 1 Chr 26:16
goes up. Watch corresponded to **w**. 1 Chr 26:16
brothers, who kept **w** at the gates, Neh 11:19
of David the man of God, **w** by watch. Neh 12:24
of David the man of God, watch by **w**. Neh 12:24
you **w** me and do not acquit me of my Jb 10:14
feet in the stocks and **w** all my paths; Jb 13:27
you would not keep **w** over my sin; Jb 14:16
to the grave, **w** is kept over his tomb. Jb 21:32
I prepare a sacrifice for you and **w**. Ps 5:3
His eyes stealthily **w** for the helpless; Ps 10:8
they **w** my steps, as they have waited for Ps 56:6
Saul sent men to **w** his house in order Ps 59:T
O my Strength, I will **w** for you, for you, Ps 59:9
love and faithfulness to **w** over him! Ps 61:7
whose eyes keep **w** on the nations—let Ps 66:7
those who **w** for my life consult Ps 71:10
when it is past, or as a **w** in the night. Ps 90:4
mouth; keep **w** over the door of my lips! Ps 141:3

discretion will **w** over you, Prv 2:11
you lie down, they will **w** over you; Prv 6:22
keeping **w** on the evil and the good. Prv 15:3
of the LORD keep **w** over knowledge, Prv 22:12
not he who keeps **w** over your soul Prv 24:12
and all who **w** to do evil shall be cut off, Is 29:20
so I will **w** over them to build and to Jer 31:28
Stand by the way and **w**, O inhabitant Jer 48:19
walls of Babylon; make the **w** strong; Jer 51:12
Man the ramparts; **w** the road; dress for Na 2:1
And in the fourth **w** of the night he Mt 14:25
"**W** and beware of the leaven of the Mt 16:6
W therefore, for you know neither the Mt 25:13
to death; remain here, and **w** with me." Mt 26:38
could you not **w** with me one hour? Mt 26:40
W and pray that you may not enter Mt 26:41
sat down and kept **w** over him there. Mt 27:36
were with him, keeping **w** over Jesus, Mt 27:54
And about the fourth **w** of the night he Mk 6:48
he cautioned them, saying, "**W** out; Mk 8:15
even to death. Remain here and **w**." Mk 14:34
asleep? Could you not **w** one hour? Mk 14:37
W and pray that you may not enter Mk 14:38
field, keeping **w** over their flock by night. Lk 2:8
If he comes in the second **w**, or in the Lk 12:38
"But **w** yourselves lest your hearts be Lk 21:34
the servant girl who kept **w** at the door, Jn 18:16
to **w** out for those who cause Rom 16:17
w out that you are not consumed by Gal 5:15
Keep **w** on yourself, lest you too be Gal 6:1
Keep a close **w** on yourself and on the 1 Tm 4:16
they are keeping **w** over your souls, Heb 13:17
W yourselves, so that you may not lose 2 Jn 1:8

WATCHED (10)
old, as in the days when God **w** over me, Jb 29:2
for the high official is **w** by a higher, Eccl 5:8
that as I have **w** over them to pluck Jer 31:28
in our watching we **w** for a nation Lam 4:17
And they **w** Jesus, to see whether he Mk 3:2
the treasury and **w** the people putting Mk 12:41
And the scribes and the Pharisees **w** him, Lk 6:7
So they **w** him and sent spies, who Lk 20:20
Now I **w** when the Lamb opened one of Rv 6:1
in a cloud, and their enemies **w** them. Rv 11:12

WATCHER (3)
what do I do to you, you **w** of mankind? Jb 7:20
my head as I lay in bed, and behold, a **w**, Dn 4:13
And because the king saw a **w**, a holy Dn 4:23

WATCHERS (1)
The sentence is by the decree of the **w**, Dn 4:17

WATCHES (7)
feet in the stocks and **w** all my paths.' Jb 33:11
The wicked **w** for the righteous and Ps 37:32
meditate on you in the **w** of the night; Ps 63:6
are awake before the **w** of the night, Ps 119:148
in vain. Unless the LORD **w** over the city, Ps 127:1
The LORD **w** over the sojourners; he Ps 146:9
night, at the beginning of the night **w**! Lam 2:19

WATCHFUL (3)
Be **w**, stand firm in the faith, act like 1 Cor 16:13
prayer, being **w** in it with thanksgiving. Col 4:2
Be sober-minded; be **w**. Your adversary 1 Pt 5:8

WATCHING (21)
It was a night of **w** by the LORD, to bring Ex 12:42
night is a night of **w** kept to the LORD by Ex 12:42
and Manoah and his wife were **w**. Jgs 13:19
Now Manoah and his wife were **w**, and Jgs 13:20
was sitting on his seat by the road **w**, 1 Sm 4:13
Now the men were **w** for a sign, and 1 Kgs 20:33
of God, for on them lay the duty of **w**, 1 Chr 9:27
the paths of justice and **w** over the way of Prv 2:8
who listens to me, **w** daily at my gates, Prv 8:34
for I am **w** over my word to perform it." Jer 1:12
A leopard is **w** their cities; everyone who Jer 5:6
say all my close friends, **w** for my fall. Jer 20:10
I am **w** over them for disaster and not Jer 44:27
Our eyes failed, ever **w** vainly for help; Lam 4:17
in our **w** we watched for a nation Lam 4:17
and the sheep traders, who were **w** me, Zec 11:11
Pharisees, they were **w** him carefully. Lk 14:1
by, **w**, but the rulers scoffed at him, Lk 23:35
stood at a distance **w** these things. Lk 23:49
They were **w** the gates day and night in Acts 9:24
and approving and **w** over the Acts 22:20

WATCHMAN (19)
and the **w** went up to the roof of the 2 Sm 18:24
The **w** called out and told the king. 2 Sm 18:25
The **w** saw another man running. 2 Sm 18:26
And the **w** called to the gate and said, 2 Sm 18:26
The **w** said, "I think the running of 2 Sm 18:27
Now the **w** was standing on the tower 2 Kgs 9:17
ride behind me." And the **w** reported, 2 Kgs 9:18
Again the **w** reported, "He reached 2 Kgs 9:20
a moth's, like a booth that a **w** makes. Jb 27:18
over the city, the **w** stays awake in vain. Ps 127:1
For thus the Lord said to me: "Go, set a **w**; Is 21:6
from Seir, "**W**, what time of the night? Is 21:11
the night? **W**, what time of the night?" Is 21:11
The **w** says: "Morning comes, and also Is 21:12
I have made you a **w** for the house of Ezk 3:17
among them, and make him their **w**, Ezk 33:2
But if the **w** sees the sword coming and Ezk 33:6
I have made a **w** for the house of Israel. Ezk 33:7
The prophet is the **w** of Ephraim with Hos 9:8

WATCHMAN'S (1)
his blood I will require at the **w** hand. Ezk 33:6

WATCHMEN (15)
And the **w** of Saul in Gibeah of 1 Sm 14:16
the priest posted **w** over the house 2 Kgs 11:18
And Jehoiada posted **w** for the house 2 Chr 23:18
the Lord more than **w** for the morning, Ps 130:6
more than **w** for the morning. Ps 130:6
The **w** found me as they went about in the Sg 3:3
The **w** found me as they went about in the Sg 5:7
took away my veil, those **w** of the walls. Sg 5:7
The voice of your **w**—they lift up their Is 52:8
His **w** are blind; they are all without Is 56:10
On your walls, O Jerusalem, I have set **w**; Is 62:6
I set **w** over you, saying, 'Pay attention to Jer 6:17
shall be a day when **w** will call in the Jer 31:6
make the watch strong; set up **w**; Jer 51:12
The day of your **w**, of your punishment, Mi 7:4

WATCHPOST (1)
my stand at my **w** and station myself on Hab 2:1

WATCHTOWER (6)
their towns, from **w** to fortified city. 2 Kgs 17:9
its territory, from **w** to fortified city. 2 Kgs 18:8
came to the **w** of the wilderness, 2 Chr 20:24
he built a **w** in the midst of it, and hewed Is 5:2
he who saw cried out: "Upon a **w** I stand, Is 21:8
the hill and the **w** will become dens Is 32:14

WATER (463)
river flowed out of Eden to **w** the garden, Gn 2:10
her by a spring of **w** in the wilderness, Gn 16:7
Let a little **w** be brought, and wash your Gn 18:4
bread and a skin of **w** and gave it to Gn 21:14
When the **w** in the skin was gone, she Gn 21:15
her eyes, and she saw a well of **w**. Gn 21:19
filled the skin with **w** and gave the boy Gn 21:19
a well of **w** that Abimelech's servants Gn 21:25
city by the well of **w** at the time of Gn 24:11
time when women go out to draw **w**. Gn 24:11
I am standing by the spring of **w**, Gn 24:13
of the city are coming out to draw **w**. Gn 24:13
and I will **w** your camels'—let her be Gn 24:14
came out with her **w** jar on her Gn 24:15
give me a little **w** to drink from your Gn 24:17
"I will draw **w** for your camels also, Gn 24:19
and ran again to the well to draw **w**, Gn 24:20
and there was **w** to wash his feet and Gn 24:32
I am standing by the spring of **w**. Gn 24:43
the virgin who comes out to draw **w**, Gn 24:43
give me a little **w** from your jar to Gn 24:43
came out with her **w** jar on her Gn 24:45
went down to the spring and drew **w**. Gn 24:45
again the wells of **w** that had been dug Gn 26:18
and found there a well of spring **w**, Gn 26:19
"The **w** is ours." So he called the name Gn 26:20
and said to him, "We have found **w**." Gn 26:32
the mouth of the well and **w** the sheep, Gn 29:3
W the sheep and go, pasture them." Gn 29:7
mouth of the well; then we **w** the sheep." Gn 29:8
The pit was empty; there was no **w** in it. Gn 37:24
into Joseph's house and given them **w**, Gn 43:24
Unstable as **w**, you shall not have Gn 49:4
she said, "I drew him out of the **w**." Ex 2:10
they came and drew **w** and filled the Ex 2:16
the troughs to **w** their father's flock. Ex 2:16
shepherds and even drew **w** for us and Ex 2:19
you shall take some **w** from the Nile and Ex 4:9
and the **w** that you shall take from the Ex 4:9
the morning, as he is going out to the **w**. Ex 7:15
hand I will strike the **w** that is in the Ex 7:17
weary of drinking **w** from the Nile."" Ex 7:18
and their ponds, and all their pools of **w**, Ex 7:19
up the staff and struck the **w** in the Nile, Ex 7:20
and all the **w** in the Nile turned into Ex 7:20
could not drink **w** from the Nile. Ex 7:21
dug along the Nile for **w** to drink, Ex 7:24
they could not drink the **w** of the Nile. Ex 7:24
to Pharaoh, as he goes out to the **w**, Ex 8:20
Do not eat any of it raw or boiled in **w**, Ex 12:9
that the **w** may come back upon the Ex 14:26
days in the wilderness and found no **w**. Ex 15:22
not drink the **w** of Marah because Ex 15:23
him a log, and he threw it into the **w**, Ex 15:25
into the water, and the **w** became sweet. Ex 15:25
twelve springs of **w** and seventy palm Ex 15:27
and they encamped there by the **w**. Ex 15:27
but there was no **w** for the people to Ex 17:1
"Give us **w** to drink." And Moses said to Ex 17:2
But the people thirsted there for **w**, and Ex 17:3
the rock, and **w** shall come out of it, Ex 17:6
or that is in the **w** under the earth. Ex 20:4
he will bless your bread and your **w**, Ex 23:25
tent of meeting and wash them with **w**. Ex 29:4
and the altar, and you shall put **w** in it, Ex 30:18
to the LORD, they shall wash with **w**, Ex 30:20
scattered it on the **w** and made the Ex 32:20
He neither ate bread nor drank **w**. Ex 34:28
of meeting and the altar, and put **w** in it. Ex 40:7
of meeting and shall wash them with **w** Ex 40:12
the altar, and put **w** in it for washing, Ex 40:30
entrails and its legs he shall wash with **w**. Lv 1:9
and the legs he shall wash with **w**. Lv 1:13
that shall be scoured and rinsed in **w**. Lv 6:28
and his sons and washed them with **w**. Lv 8:6
washed the entrails and the legs with **w**, Lv 8:21
It must be put into **w**, and it shall be Lv 11:32
that could be eaten, on which **w** comes, Lv 11:34
or a cistern holding **w** shall be clean, Lv 11:36
but if **w** is put on the seed and any part Lv 11:38
in an earthenware vessel over fresh **w**. Lv 14:5
the bird that was killed over the fresh **w**. Lv 14:6
off all his hair and bathe himself in **w**, Lv 14:8
his clothes and bathe his body in **w**, Lv 14:9
in an earthenware vessel over fresh **w** Lv 14:50
and in the fresh **w** and sprinkle the Lv 14:51
and with the fresh **w** and with the live Lv 14:52
and bathe himself in **w** and be unclean Lv 15:5
and bathe himself in **w** and be unclean Lv 15:6
and bathe himself in **w** and be unclean Lv 15:7
and bathe himself in **w** and be unclean Lv 15:8
and bathe himself in **w** and be unclean Lv 15:10
rinsed his hands in **w** shall wash his Lv 15:11
and bathe himself in **w** and be unclean Lv 15:11
vessel of wood shall be rinsed in **w**. Lv 15:12
his body in fresh **w** and shall be clean. Lv 15:13
his whole body in **w** and be unclean Lv 15:16
shall be washed with **w** and be unclean Lv 15:17
bathe themselves in **w** and be unclean Lv 15:18
and bathe himself in **w** and be unclean Lv 15:21
and bathe himself in **w** and be unclean Lv 15:22
and bathe himself in **w** and be unclean Lv 15:27
bathe his body in **w** and then put them Lv 16:4
bathe his body in **w** in a holy place Lv 16:24
his clothes and bathe his body in **w**, Lv 16:26
his clothes and bathe his body in **w**, Lv 16:28
and bathe himself in **w** and be unclean Lv 17:15
unless he has bathed his body in **w**. Lv 22:6
shall take holy **w** in an earthenware Nm 5:17
of the tabernacle and put it into the **w**. Nm 5:17
shall have the **w** of bitterness that Nm 5:18
be free from this **w** of bitterness that Nm 5:19
May this **w** that brings the curse pass Nm 5:22
wash them off into the **w** of bitterness. Nm 5:23
woman drink the **w** of bitterness that Nm 5:24
and the **w** that brings the curse shall Nm 5:24
shall make the woman drink the **w**. Nm 5:26
when he has made her drink the **w**, Nm 5:27
the **w** that brings the curse shall enter Nm 5:27
sprinkle the **w** of purification upon Nm 8:7
his clothes and bathe his body in **w**, Nm 19:7
wash his clothes in **w** and bathe his Nm 19:8
bathe his body in **w** and shall be Nm 19:8
be kept for the **w** for impurity for the Nm 19:9
himself with the **w** on the third Nm 19:12
because the **w** for impurity was not Nm 19:13
and fresh **w** shall be added in a vessel. Nm 19:17
and dip it in the **w** and sprinkle it on Nm 19:18
his clothes and bathe himself in **w**, Nm 19:19
Because the **w** for impurity has not Nm 19:20
who sprinkles the **w** for impurity Nm 19:21
who touches the **w** for impurity shall Nm 19:21
there was no **w** for the congregation. Nm 20:2
and there is no **w** to drink." Nm 20:5
the rock before their eyes to yield its **w**. Nm 20:8
So you shall bring **w** out of the rock for Nm 20:8
shall we bring **w** for you out of this Nm 20:10
twice, and **w** came out abundantly, Nm 20:11
or vineyard, or drink **w** from a well. Nm 20:17
highway, and if we drink of your **w**, Nm 20:19
For there is no food and no **w**, and we Nm 21:5
together, so that I may give them **w**." Nm 21:16
We will not drink the **w** of a well. Nm 21:22
W shall flow from his buckets, and his Nm 24:7
be purified with the **w** for impurity. Nm 31:23
the fire, you shall pass through the **w**. Nm 31:23
twelve springs of **w** and seventy palm Nm 33:9
where there was no **w** for the people to Nm 33:14

you shall also buy **w** of them for money, Dt 2:6
that I may eat, and give me **w** for money, Dt 2:28
any fish that is in the **w** under the earth. Dt 4:18
or that is in the **w** under the earth. Dt 5:8
into a good land, a land of brooks of **w**, Dt 8:7
thirsty ground where there was no **w**, Dt 8:15
who brought you **w** out of the flinty Dt 8:15
nights. I neither ate bread nor drank **w**. Dt 9:9
I neither ate bread nor drank **w**, because Dt 9:18
to Jotbathah, a land with brooks of **w**. Dt 10:7
how he made the **w** of the Red Sea flow Dt 11:4
which drinks **w** by the rain from Dt 11:11
shall pour it out on the earth like **w**. Dt 12:16
shall pour it out on the earth like **w**. Dt 12:24
shall pour it out on the ground like **w**. Dt 15:23
heifer down to a valley with running **w**, Dt 21:4
you with bread and with **w** on the way, Dt 23:4
comes, he shall bathe himself in **w**, Dt 23:11
wood to the one who draws your **w**, Dt 29:11
the LORD dried up the **w** of the Red Sea Jos 2:10
the brink of the **w** (now the Jordan Jos 3:15
of the people melted and became as **w**. Jos 7:5
wood and drawers of **w** for all the Jos 9:21
wood and drawers of **w** for the house of Jos 9:23
and drawers of **w** for the congregation Jos 9:27
me also springs of **w**." And he gave her Jos 15:19
me also springs of **w**." And Caleb gave Jgs 1:15
to her, "Please give me a little **w** to drink, Jgs 4:19
dropped, yes, the clouds dropped **w**. Jgs 5:4
He asked **w** and she gave him milk; she Jgs 5:25
dew from the fleece to fill a bowl with **w**. Jgs 6:38
Take them down to the **w**, and I will test Jgs 7:4
So he brought the people down to the **w**. Jgs 7:5
one who laps the **w** with his tongue, Jgs 7:5
rest of the people knelt down to drink **w**. Jgs 7:6
that is at Lehi, and **w** came out from it. Jgs 15:19
at Mizpah and drew **w** and poured it 1 Sm 7:6
coming out to draw **w** and said to 1 Sm 9:11
my bread and my **w** and my meat 1 Sm 25:11
that is at his head and the jar of **w**, 1 Sm 26:11
and the jar of **w** from Saul's head, 1 Sm 26:12
is and the jar of **w** that was at his 1 Sm 26:16
he ate. They gave him **w** to drink, 1 Sm 30:11
bread or drunk **w** for three days 1 Sm 30:12
let him get up the **w** shaft to attack 'the 2 Sm 5:8
we are like **w** spilled on the ground, 2 Sm 14:14
over the brook of **w**." And when they 2 Sm 17:20
"Arise, and go quickly over the **w**, 2 Sm 17:21
thick clouds, a gathering of **w**. 2 Sm 22:12
would give me **w** to drink from 2 Sm 23:15
the Philistines and drew **w** out of the 2 Sm 23:16
not eat bread or drink **w** in this place, 1 Kgs 13:8
eat bread nor drink **w** nor return by 1 Kgs 13:9
eat bread nor drink **w** with you in 1 Kgs 13:16
neither eat bread nor drink **w** there, 1 Kgs 13:17
eat bread and drink **w**.'" But he lied 1 Kgs 13:18
ate bread in his house and drank **w**. 1 Kgs 13:19
bread and drunk **w** in the place 1 Kgs 13:22
and drink no **w**," your body shall 1 Kgs 13:22
Israel as a reed is shaken in the **w**, 1 Kgs 14:15
said, "Bring me a little **w** in a vessel, 1 Kgs 17:10
cave and fed them with bread and **w**.) 1 Kgs 18:4
to all the springs of **w** and to all the 1 Kgs 18:5
and fed them with bread and **w**? 1 Kgs 18:13
"Fill four jars with **w** and pour it on 1 Kgs 18:33
And the **w** ran around the altar and 1 Kgs 18:35
and filled the trench also with **w**. 1 Kgs 18:35
and licked up the **w** that was in the 1 Kgs 18:38
baked on hot stones and a jar of **w**. 1 Kgs 19:6
him meager rations of bread and **w**, 1 Kgs 22:27
and rolled it up and struck the **w**, 2 Kgs 2:8
and the **w** was parted to the one side 2 Kgs 2:8
fallen from him and struck the **w**, 2 Kgs 2:14
And when he had struck the **w**, 2 Kgs 2:14
the **w** was parted to the one side and to 2 Kgs 2:14
as my lord sees, but the **w** is bad, 2 Kgs 2:19
to the spring of **w** and threw salt in 2 Kgs 2:21
says the LORD, I have healed this **w**; 2 Kgs 2:21
So the **w** has been healed to this day, 2 Kgs 2:22
there was no **w** for the army or for the 2 Kgs 3:9
who poured **w** on the hands of 2 Kgs 3:11
that streambed shall be filled with **w**, 2 Kgs 3:17
up all springs of **w** and ruin every 2 Kgs 3:19
w came from the direction of Edom, 2 Kgs 3:20
till the country was filled with **w**. 2 Kgs 3:20
morning and the sun shone on the **w**, 2 Kgs 3:22
Moabites saw the **w** opposite them as 2 Kgs 3:22
every spring of **w** and felled all 2 Kgs 3:25
a log, his axe head fell into the **w**, 2 Kgs 6:5
Set bread and **w** before them, that 2 Kgs 6:22
and dipped it in **w** and spread it over 2 Kgs 8:15
you will drink the **w** of his own 2 Kgs 18:31
conduit and brought **w** into the city, 2 Kgs 20:20
would give me **w** to drink from 1 Chr 11:17
the Philistines and drew **w** out of the 1 Chr 11:18

rations of bread and **w** until I return 2 Chr 18:26
men to stop the **w** of the springs that 2 Chr 32:3
of Assyria come and find much **w**?" 2 Chr 32:4
neither eating bread nor drinking **w**, Ezr 10:6
a point opposite the **W** Gate on the east Neh 3:26
man into the square before the **W** Gate. Neh 8:1
the square before the **W** Gate from early Neh 8:3
in the square at the **W** Gate and in the Neh 8:16
hunger and brought **w** for them out Neh 9:15
and gave them **w** for their thirst. Neh 9:20
of David, to the **W** Gate on the east. Neh 12:37
the people of Israel with bread and **w**, Neh 13:2
and my groanings are poured out like **w**. Jb 3:24
Can reeds flourish where there is no **w**? Jb 8:11
yet at the scent of **w** it will bud and put Jb 14:9
a man who drinks injustice like **w**! Jb 15:16
You have given no **w** to the weary to Jb 22:7
cannot see, and a flood of **w** covers you. Jb 22:11
is like Job, who drinks up scoffing like **w**, Jb 34:7
For he draws up the drops of **w**; they Jb 36:27
planted by streams of **w** that yields its Ps 1:3
around him, thick clouds dark with **w**. Ps 18:11
I am poured out like **w**, and all my Ps 22:14
Let them vanish like **w** that runs away; Ps 58:7
a dry and weary land where there is no **w**. Ps 63:1
You visit the earth and **w** it; you greatly Ps 65:9
enrich it; the river of God is full of **w**; Ps 65:9
You **w** its furrows abundantly, settling Ps 65:10
we went through fire and through **w**; Ps 66:12
grass, like showers that **w** the earth! Ps 72:6
The clouds poured out **w**; the skies gave Ps 77:17
the rock so that **w** gushed out and Ps 78:20
their blood like **w** all around Jerusalem, Ps 79:3
lofty abode you **w** the mountains; Ps 104:13
He opened the rock, and **w** gushed out; Ps 105:41
springs of **w** into thirsty ground, Ps 107:33
He turns a desert into pools of **w**, a Ps 107:35
a parched land into springs of **w**. Ps 107:35
may it soak into his body like **w**, like Ps 109:18
who turns the rock into a pool of **w**, the Ps 114:8
of water, the flint into a spring of **w**. Ps 114:8
Drink **w** from your own cistern, Prv 5:15
cistern, flowing **w** from your own well. Prv 5:15
abroad, streams of **w** in the streets? Prv 5:16
were no springs abounding with **w**. Prv 8:24
"Stolen **w** is sweet, and bread eaten in Prv 9:17
beginning of strife is like letting out **w**, Prv 17:14
purpose in a man's heart is like deep **w**, Prv 20:5
heart is a stream of **w** in the hand of the Prv 21:1
if he is thirsty, give him **w** to drink, Prv 25:21
Like cold **w** to a thirsty soul, so is good Prv 25:25
As in **w** face reflects face, so the heart Prv 27:19
womb, the land never satisfied with **w**, Prv 30:16
pools from which to **w** the forest of Eccl 2:6
a garden fountain, a well of living **w**, and Sg 4:15
eyes are like doves beside streams of **w**, Sg 5:12
dross, your best wine mixed with **w**. Is 1:22
leaf withers, and like a garden without **w**. Is 1:30
all support of bread, and all support of **w**; Is 3:1
joy you will draw **w** from the wells of Is 12:3
of the hedgehog, and pools of **w**, Is 14:23
will languish who spread nets on the **w**. Is 19:8
To the thirsty bring **w**; meet the fugitive Is 21:14
the two walls for the **w** of the old pool. Is 22:11
LORD, am its keeper; every moment I **w** it. Is 27:3
hearth, or to dip up **w** out of the cistern." Is 30:14
of adversity and the **w** of affliction, Is 30:20
there will be brooks running with **w**, Is 30:25
storm, like streams of **w** in a dry place, Is 32:2
will be given him; his **w** will be sure. Is 33:16
pool, and the thirsty ground springs of **w**; Is 35:7
you will drink the **w** of his own cistern, Is 36:16
When the poor and needy seek **w**, and Is 41:17
I will make the wilderness a pool of **w**, Is 41:18
of water, and the dry land springs of **w**. Is 41:18
ostriches, for I give **w** in the wilderness, Is 43:20
For I will pour **w** on the thirsty land, and Is 44:3
fails; he drinks no **w** and is faint. Is 44:12
he made **w** flow for them from the rock; Is 48:21
he split the rock and the **w** gushed out. Is 48:21
and by springs of **w** will guide them. Is 49:10
fish stink for lack of **w** and die of thirst. Is 50:2
and do not return there but **w** the earth, Is 55:10
like a watered garden, like a spring of **w**, Is 58:11
and the fire causes **w** to boil—to Is 64:2
broken cisterns that can hold no **w**. Jer 2:13
As a well keeps its **w** fresh, so she keeps Jer 6:7
and has given us poisoned **w** to drink, Jer 8:14
and give them poisonous **w** to drink. Jer 9:15
with tears and our eyelids flow with **w**. Jer 9:18
your waist, and do not dip it in **w**." Jer 13:1
Her nobles send their servants for **w**; Jer 14:3
they come to the cisterns; they find no **w**; Jer 14:3
He is like a tree planted by **w**, that sends Jer 17:8
the LORD, the fountain of living **w**. Jer 17:13

and give them poisoned **w** to drink, Jer 23:15
I will make them walk by brooks of **w**, Jer 31:9
And there was no **w** in the cistern, but Jer 38:6
your heart like **w** before the presence Lam 2:19
w closed over my head; I said, 'I am Lam 3:54
We must pay for the **w** we drink; the Lam 5:4
And **w** you shall drink by measure, the Ezk 4:11
and they shall drink **w** by measure and Ezk 4:16
do this that they may lack bread and **w**, Ezk 4:17
are feeble, and all knees turn to **w**. Ezk 7:17
and drink **w** with trembling and with Ezk 12:18
with anxiety, and drink **w** in dismay. Ezk 12:19
were you washed with **w** to cleanse you, Ezk 16:4
I bathed you with **w** and washed off Ezk 16:9
where it was planted, that he might **w** it. Ezk 17:7
a vine in a vineyard planted by the **w**, Ezk 19:10
of branches by reason of abundant **w**. Ezk 19:10
faint, and all knees will be weak as **w**. Ezk 21:7
"Set on the pot, set it on; pour in **w** also; Ezk 24:3
long from abundant **w** in its shoots. Ezk 31:5
no trees that drink **w** may reach up to Ezk 31:14
and best of Lebanon, all that drink **w**, Ezk 31:16
and to drink of clear **w**, that you must Ezk 34:18
muddy the rest of the **w** with your feet? Ezk 34:18
I will sprinkle clean **w** on you, and Ezk 36:25
w was issuing from below the Ezk 47:1
The **w** was flowing down from below Ezk 47:1
the **w** was trickling out on the south Ezk 47:2
cubits, and then led me through the **w**, Ezk 47:3
a thousand, and led me through the **w**, Ezk 47:4
a thousand, and led me through the **w**, Ezk 47:4
not pass through, for the **w** had risen. Ezk 47:5
"This **w** flows toward the eastern region Ezk 47:8
when the **w** flows into the sea, the water Ezk 47:8
into the sea, the **w** will become fresh. Ezk 47:8
very many fish. For this **w** goes there, Ezk 47:9
because the **w** for them flows from the Ezk 47:12
given vegetables to eat and **w** to drink. Dn 1:12
lovers, who give me my bread and my **w**, Hos 2:5
them I will pour out my wrath like **w**. Hos 5:10
as the spring rains that **w** the earth." Hos 6:3
for you because the **w** brooks are dried Jl 1:20
streambeds of Judah shall flow with **w**; Jl 3:18
of the LORD and **w** the Valley of Shittim. Jl 3:18
would wander to another city to drink **w**, Am 4:8
a famine of bread, nor a thirst for **w**, Am 8:11
anything. Let them not feed or drink **w**, Jon 3:7
that sat by the Nile, with **w** around her, Na 3:8
her, her rampart a sea, and **w** her wall? Na 3:8
Draw **w** for the siege; strengthen your Na 3:14
"I baptize you with **w** for repentance, but Mt 3:11
immediately he went up from the **w**, Mt 3:16
even a cup of cold **w** because he is a Mt 10:42
me to come to you on the **w**." Mt 14:28
and walked on the **w** and came to Jesus. Mt 14:29
falls into the fire, and often into the **w**. Mt 17:15
he took **w** and washed his hands before Mt 27:24
I have baptized you with **w**, but he will Mk 1:8
And when he came up out of the **w**, Mk 1:10
has often cast him into fire and into **w**, Mk 9:22
you a cup of **w** to drink because you Mk 9:41
man carrying a jar of **w** will meet you. Mk 14:13
them all, saying, "I baptize you with **w**, Lk 3:16
you gave me no **w** for my feet, but she Lk 7:44
they were filling with **w** and were in Lk 8:23
that he commands even winds and **w**, Lk 8:25
the manger and lead it away to **w** it? Lk 13:15
of his finger in **w** and cool my tongue, Lk 16:24
man carrying a jar of **w** will meet you. Lk 22:10
John answered them, "I baptize with **w**, Jn 1:26
for this purpose I came baptizing with **w**, Jn 1:31
who sent me to baptize with **w** said to me, Jn 1:33
there were six stone **w** jars there for the Jn 2:6
"Fill the jars with **w**." And they filled them Jn 2:7
of the feast tasted the **w** now become wine, Jn 2:9
the servants who had drawn the **w** knew), Jn 2:9
you, unless one is born of **w** and the Spirit, Jn 3:5
Salim, because **w** was plentiful there, Jn 3:23
came a woman of Samaria to draw **w**. Jn 4:7
and he would have given you living **w**." Jn 4:10
"Sir, you have nothing to draw **w** with, Jn 4:11
is deep. Where do you get that living **w**? Jn 4:11
who drinks of this **w** will be thirsty Jn 4:13
whoever drinks of the **w** that I will give Jn 4:14
The **w** that I will give him will become in Jn 4:14
in him a spring of **w** welling up to eternal Jn 4:14
woman said to him, "Sir, give me this **w**, Jn 4:15
thirsty or have to come here to draw **w**." Jn 4:15
the woman left her **w** jar and went away Jn 4:28
Galilee, where he had made the **w** wine. Jn 4:46
me into the pool when the **w** is stirred up, Jn 5:7
of his heart will flow rivers of living **w**.'" Jn 7:38
Then he poured **w** into a basin and Jn 13:5
at once there came out blood and **w**. Jn 19:34
for John baptized with **w**, but you will Acts 1:5

along the road they came to some **w**, Acts 8:36
and the eunuch said, "See, here is **w**! Acts 8:36
and they both went down into the **w**, Acts 8:38
And when they came up out of the **w**, Acts 8:39
anyone withhold **w** for baptizing Acts 10:47
how he said, 'John baptized with **w**, Acts 11:16
her by the washing of **w** with the word, Eph 5:26
(No longer drink only **w**, but use a 1 Tm 5:23
with **w** and scarlet wool and hyssop, Heb 9:19
and our bodies washed with pure **w**. Heb 10:22
the same opening both fresh and salt **w**? Jas 3:11
Neither can a salt pond yield fresh **w**. Jas 3:12
were brought safely through **w**. 1 Pt 3:20
was formed out of **w** and through water 2 Pt 3:5
of water and through **w** by the word of 2 Pt 3:5
existed was deluged with **w** and perished. 2 Pt 3:6
is he who came by **w** and blood—Jesus 1 Jn 5:6
not by the **w** only but by the water and 1 Jn 5:6
water only but by the **w** and the blood. 1 Jn 5:6
the Spirit and the **w** and the blood; and 1 Jn 5:8
he will guide them to springs of living **w**, Rv 7:17
of the rivers and on the springs of **w**. Rv 8:10
and many people died from the **w**, Rv 8:11
The serpent poured **w** like a river out of Rv 12:15
and earth, the sea and the springs of **w**." Rv 14:7
bowl into the rivers and the springs of **w**, Rv 16:4
river Euphrates, and its **w** was dried up, Rv 16:12
the spring of the **w** of life without Rv 21:6
angel showed me the river of the **w** of life, Rv 22:1
who desires take the **w** of life without Rv 22:17

WATERED (10)
Valley was well **w** everywhere like the Gn 13:10
it, for out of that well the flocks were **w**. Gn 29:2
the well's mouth and **w** the flock of Gn 29:10
up and saved them, and **w** their flock. Ex 2:17
even drew water for us and **w** the flock." Ex 2:19
trees of the LORD are **w** abundantly, Ps 104:16
and one who waters will himself be **w**. Prv 11:25
and you shall be like a **w** garden, like a Is 58:11
their life shall be like a **w** garden, and Jer 31:12
I planted, Apollos **w**, but God gave the 1 Cor 3:6

WATERFALLS (1)
Deep calls to deep at the roar of your **w**; Ps 42:7

WATERING (4)
the land and was **w** the whole face of Gn 2:6
in the troughs, that is, the **w** places, Gn 30:38
the sound of musicians at the **w** places, Jgs 5:11
from the **w** places of Israel for grain Ezk 45:15

WATERLESS (5)
set your prisoners free from the **w** pit. Zec 9:11
it passes through **w** places seeking rest, Mt 12:43
it passes through **w** places seeking rest, Lk 11:24
These are **w** springs and mists driven 2 Pt 2:17
w clouds, swept along by winds; Jude 1:12

WATERS (215)
God was hovering over the face of the **w**. Gn 1:2
there be an expanse in the midst of the **w**, Gn 1:6
and let it separate the **w** from the waters." Gn 1:6
and let it separate the waters from the **w**." Gn 1:6
and separated the **w** that were under Gn 1:7
the expanse from the **w** that were above Gn 1:7
"Let the **w** under the heavens be gathered Gn 1:9
and the **w** that were gathered together he Gn 1:10
"Let the **w** swarm with swarms of living Gn 1:20
that moves, with which the **w** swarm, Gn 1:21
and multiply and fill the **w** in the seas, Gn 1:22
will bring a flood of **w** upon the earth to Gn 6:17
when the flood of **w** came upon the earth. Gn 7:6
into the ark to escape the **w** of the flood. Gn 7:7
after seven days the **w** of the flood came Gn 7:10
The **w** increased and bore up the ark, Gn 7:17
The **w** prevailed and increased greatly Gn 7:18
and the ark floated on the face of the **w**. Gn 7:18
And the **w** prevailed so mightily on the Gn 7:19
The **w** prevailed above the mountains, Gn 7:20
And the **w** prevailed on the earth 150 Gn 7:24
blow over the earth, and the **w** subsided. Gn 8:1
and the **w** receded from the earth Gn 8:3
At the end of 150 days the **w** had abated, Gn 8:3
And the **w** continued to abate until the Gn 8:5
to and fro until the **w** were dried up from Gn 8:7
to see if the **w** had subsided from the face Gn 8:8
for the **w** were still on the face of the Gn 8:9
knew that the **w** had subsided from Gn 8:11
the **w** were dried from off the earth. Gn 8:13
all flesh be cut off by the **w** of the flood, Gn 9:11
And the **w** shall never again become a Gn 9:15
out your hand over the **w** of Egypt, Ex 7:19
out his hand over the **w** of Egypt, Ex 8:6
the sea dry land, and the **w** were divided. Ex 14:21
the **w** being a wall to them on their Ex 14:22
The **w** returned and covered the Ex 14:28
the **w** being a wall to them on their Ex 14:29
the blast of your nostrils the **w** piled up; Ex 15:8
they sank like lead in the mighty **w**. Ex 15:10
LORD brought back the **w** of the sea Ex 15:19
you may eat, of all that are in the **w**. Lv 11:9
Everything in the **w** that has fins and Lv 11:9
swarming creatures in the **w** and of the Lv 11:10
of the living creatures that are in the **w**, Lv 11:10
Everything in the **w** that has not fins Lv 11:12
moves through the **w** and every Lv 11:46
These are the **w** of Meribah, where the Nm 20:13
my command at the **w** of Meribah. Nm 20:24
planted, like cedar trees beside the **w**. Nm 24:6
and his seed shall be in many **w**; Nm 24:7
as holy at the **w** before their eyes." Nm 27:14
eyes." (These are the **w** of Meribah of Nm 27:14
all that are in the **w** you may eat these: Dt 14:9
of Israel at the **w** of Meribah-kadesh, Dt 32:51
you quarreled at the **w** of Meribah; Dt 33:8
come to the brink of the **w** of the Jordan, Jos 3:8
earth, shall rest in the **w** of the Jordan, Jos 3:13
the **w** of the Jordan shall be cut off from Jos 3:13
and the **w** coming down from above Jos 3:13
the **w** coming down from above stood Jos 3:16
tell them that the **w** of the Jordan were Jos 4:7
Jordan, the **w** of the Jordan were cut off. Jos 4:7
the **w** of the Jordan returned to their Jos 4:18
your God dried up the **w** of the Jordan for Jos 4:23
LORD had dried up the **w** of the Jordan for Jos 5:1
encamped together at the **w** of Merom to Jos 11:5
against them by the **w** of Merom and fell Jos 11:7
passes along to the **w** of En-shemesh and Jos 15:7
to the spring of the **w** of Nephtoah, Jos 15:9
by Jericho, east of the **w** of Jericho, Jos 16:1
to the spring of the **w** of Nephtoah. Jos 18:15
at Taanach, by the **w** of Megiddo; Jgs 5:19
and capture the **w** against them, Jgs 7:24
and they captured the **w** as far as Jgs 7:24
moreover, I have taken the city of **w**. 2 Sm 12:27
took me; he drew me out of many **w**. 2 Sm 22:17
better than all the **w** of Israel? 2 Kgs 5:12
I dug wells and drank foreign **w**, and 2 Kgs 19:24
upper outlet of the **w** of Gihon and 2 Chr 32:30
the depths, as a stone into mighty **w**. Neh 9:11
on the earth and sends **w** on the fields; Jb 5:10
will remember it as **w** that have passed Jb 11:16
If he withholds the **w**, they dry up; if he Jb 12:15
As **w** fail from a lake and a river wastes Jb 14:11
the **w** wear away the stones; the torrents Jb 14:19
say, 'Swift are they on the face of the **w**; Jb 24:18
and heat snatch away the snow **w**; Jb 24:19
tremble under the **w** and their Jb 26:5
He binds up the **w** in his thick clouds, Jb 26:8
the face of the **w** at the boundary Jb 26:10
and apportioned the **w** by measure, Jb 28:25
my roots spread out to the **w**, with the Jb 29:19
is given, and the broad **w** are frozen fast. Jb 37:10
The **w** become hard like stone, and the Jb 38:30
clouds, that a flood of **w** may cover you? Jb 38:34
he took me; he drew me out of many **w**. Ps 18:16
green pastures. He leads me beside still **w**. Ps 23:2
The voice of the LORD is over the **w**; the Ps 29:3
glory thunders, the LORD, over many **w**. Ps 29:3
surely in the rush of great **w**, they shall Ps 32:6
He gathers the **w** of the sea as a heap; he Ps 33:7
though its **w** roar and foam, though the Ps 46:3
For the **w** have come up to my neck. Ps 69:1
I have come into deep **w**, and the flood Ps 69:2
from my enemies and from the deep **w**. Ps 69:14
the heads of the sea monsters on the **w**. Ps 74:13
When the **w** saw you, O God, when the Ps 77:16
saw you, O God, when the **w** saw you, Ps 77:16
the sea, your path through the great **w**; Ps 77:19
it, and made the **w** stand like a heap. Ps 78:13
the rock and caused **w** to flow down Ps 78:16
thunder; I tested you at the **w** of Meribah. Ps 81:7
Mightier than the thunders of many **w**, Ps 93:4
the beams of his chambers on the **w**; Ps 104:3
the **w** stood above the mountains. Ps 104:6
He turned their **w** into blood and Ps 105:29
And the **w** covered their adversaries; Ps 106:11
angered him at the **w** of Meribah, Ps 106:32
ships, doing business on the great **w**; Ps 107:23
they were glad that the **w** were quiet, Ps 107:30
over us would have gone the raging **w**. Ps 124:5
who spread out the earth above the **w**, Ps 136:6
By the **w** of Babylon, there we sat down Ps 137:1
me and deliver me from the many **w**, Ps 144:7
makes his wind blow and the **w** flow. Ps 147:18
heavens, and you **w** above the heavens! Ps 148:4
so that the **w** might not transgress his Prv 8:29
and one who **w** will himself be Prv 11:25
words of a man's mouth are deep **w**; Prv 18:4
has wrapped up the **w** in a garment? Prv 30:4
Cast your bread upon the **w**, for you Eccl 11:1
Many **w** cannot quench love, neither can Sg 8:7
people have refused the **w** of Shiloah that Is 8:6
up against them the **w** of the River, Is 8:7
of the LORD as the **w** cover the sea. Is 11:9
the **w** of Nimrim are a desolation; the Is 15:6
For the **w** of Dibon are full of blood; for I Is 15:9
they roar like the roaring of mighty **w**! Is 17:12
nations roar like the roaring of many **w**, Is 17:13
by the sea, in vessels of papyrus on the **w**! Is 18:2
And the **w** of the sea will be dried up, and Is 19:5
You collected the **w** of the lower pool, Is 22:9
And on many **w** your revenue was the Is 23:3
like a storm of mighty, overflowing **w**, Is 28:2
lies, and **w** will overwhelm the shelter." Is 28:17
Happy are you who sow beside all **w**, Is 32:20
For **w** break forth in the wilderness, and Is 35:6
I dug wells and drank **w**, to dry up with Is 37:25
Who has measured the **w** in the hollow Is 40:12
When you pass through the **w**, I will be Is 43:2
a way in the sea, a path in the mighty **w**, Is 43:16
and who came from the **w** of Judah, Is 48:1
dried up the sea, the **w** of the great deep, Is 51:10
as I swore that the **w** of Noah should no Is 54:9
everyone who thirsts, come to the **w**; Is 55:1
be quiet, and its **w** toss up mire and dirt. Is 57:20
a spring of water, whose **w** do not fail. Is 58:11
who divided the **w** before them to make Is 63:12
forsaken me, the fountain of living **w**, Jer 2:13
going to Egypt to drink the **w** of the Nile? Jer 2:18
Assyria to drink the **w** of the Euphrates? Jer 2:18
Oh that my head were **w**, and my eyes a Jer 9:1
there is a tumult of **w** in the heavens, Jer 10:13
like a deceitful brook, like **w** that fail? Jer 15:18
Do the mountain **w** run dry, the cold Jer 18:14
like the Nile, like rivers whose **w** surge? Jer 46:7
like the Nile, like rivers whose **w** surge. Jer 46:8
Behold, **w** are rising out of the north, and Jer 47:2
For the **w** of Nimrim also have become Jer 48:34
A drought against her **w**, that they may Jer 50:38
O you who dwell by many **w**, rich in Jer 51:13
there is a tumult of **w** in the heavens, Jer 51:16
Their waves roar like many **w**; the Jer 51:55
their wings like the sound of many **w**, Ezk 1:24
soil. He placed it beside abundant **w**. Ezk 17:5
planted on good soil by abundant **w**, Ezk 17:8
they will cast into the midst of the **w**. Ezk 26:12
over you, and the great **w** cover you, Ezk 26:19
by the seas, in the depths of the **w**; Ezk 27:34
The **w** nourished it; the deep made it Ezk 31:4
for its roots went down to abundant **w**. Ezk 31:7
no trees by the **w** may grow to Ezk 31:14
its rivers, and many **w** were stopped. Ezk 31:15
rivers, trouble the **w** with your feet, Ezk 32:2
all its beasts from beside many **w**; Ezk 32:13
Then I will make their **w** clear, and Ezk 32:14
coming was like the sound of many **w**, Ezk 43:2
that the **w** of the sea may become fresh; Ezk 47:9
as far as the **w** of Meribah-kadesh, Ezk 47:19
Tamar to the **w** of Meribah-kadesh, Ezk 48:28
who was above the **w** of the stream, Dn 12:6
who was above the **w** of the stream; Dn 12:7
perish like a twig on the face of the **w**. Hos 10:7
who calls for the **w** of the sea and pours Am 5:8
But let justice roll down like **w**, and Am 5:24
who calls for the **w** of the sea and pours Am 9:6
The **w** closed in over me to take my life; Jon 2:5
the fire, like **w** poured down a steep place. Mi 1:4
Nineveh is like a pool whose **w** run away. Na 2:8
glory of the LORD as the **w** cover the sea. Hab 2:14
and writhed; the raging **w** swept on; Hab 3:10
your horses, the surging of mighty **w**. Hab 3:15
On that day living **w** shall flow out Zec 14:8
bank into the sea and drowned in the **w**. Mt 8:32
who plants nor he who **w** is anything, 1 Cor 3:7
He who plants and he who **w** are one, 1 Cor 3:8
his voice was like the roar of many **w**. Rv 1:15
A third of the **w** became wormwood, and Rv 8:11
have power over the **w** to turn them into Rv 11:6
the roar of many **w** and like the sound Rv 14:2
I heard the angel in charge of the **w** say, Rv 16:5
prostitute who is seated on many **w**, Rv 17:1
angel said to me, "The **w** that you saw, Rv 17:15
the roar of many **w** and like the sound Rv 19:6

WATERSKINS (1)
Or who can tilt the **w** of the heavens, Jb 38:37

WAVE (35)
and **w** them for a wave offering before Ex 29:24
wave them for a **w** offering before the Ex 29:24
of Aaron's ordination and **w** it for a Ex 29:26
wave it for a **w** offering before the LORD, Ex 29:26
the breast of the **w** offering that is Ex 29:27
be waved as a **w** offering before the LORD. Lv 7:30
waved them as a **w** offering before the Lv 8:27
waved it for a **w** offering before the LORD. Lv 8:29
Aaron waved for a **w** offering before the Lv 9:21

of the fat pieces to **w** for a wave offering Lv 10:15
to wave for a **w** offering before the LORD, Lv 10:15
and **w** them for a wave offering before Lv 14:12
wave them for a **w** offering before the Lv 14:12
and the priest shall **w** them for a wave Lv 14:24
wave them for a **w** offering before the Lv 14:24
and he shall **w** the sheaf before the Lv 23:11
after the Sabbath the priest shall **w** it. Lv 23:11
And on the day when you **w** the sheaf, Lv 23:12
you brought the sheaf of the **w** offering. Lv 23:15
And the priest shall **w** them with the Lv 23:20
the firstfruits as a **w** offering before the Lv 23:20
hand and shall **w** the grain offering Nm 5:25
and the priest shall **w** them for a wave Nm 6:20
wave them for a **w** offering before the Nm 6:20
the LORD as a **w** offering from the people Nm 8:11
offer them as a **w** offering to the LORD. Nm 8:13
them and offered them as a **w** offering. Nm 8:15
offered them as a **w** offering before the Nm 8:21
all the **w** offerings of the people of Nm 18:11
and **w** his hand over the place and 2 Kgs 5:11
"The wings of the ostrich **w** proudly, Jb 39:13
on the tops of the mountains may it **w**; Ps 72:16
and will **w** his hand over the River with Is 11:15
w the hand for them to enter the gates of Is 13:2
who doubts is like a **w** of the sea that is Jas 1:6

WAVED (12)
wave offering that is **w** and the thigh of Ex 29:27
the breast may be **w** as a wave offering Lv 7:30
the breast that is **w** and the thigh that Lv 7:34
hands of his sons and **w** them as a wave Lv 8:27
Moses took the breast and **w** it for a wave Lv 8:29
the right thigh Aaron **w** for a wave Lv 9:21
the breast that is **w** and the thigh that Lv 10:14
the breast that is **w** they shall bring Lv 10:15
male lamb for a guilt offering to be **w**, Lv 14:21
places two loaves of bread to be **w**, Lv 23:17
the breast that is **w** and the thigh that Nm 6:20
as the breast that is **w** and as the right Nm 18:18

WAVER (3)
things from my presence, and do not **w**, Jer 4:1
How long will you **w**, O faithless Jer 31:22
distrust made him **w** concerning the Rom 4:20

WAVERING (2)
and I have trusted in the LORD without **w**. Ps 26:1
the confession of our hope without **w**, Heb 10:23

WAVES (26)
"For the **w** of death encompassed me, 2 Sm 22:5
the heavens and trampled the **w** of the sea; Jb 9:8
and here shall your proud **w** be stayed'? Jb 38:11
breakers and your **w** have gone over Ps 42:7
roaring of the seas, the roaring of their **w**, Ps 65:7
and you overwhelm me with all your **w**. Ps 88:7
of the sea; when its **w** rise, you still them. Ps 89:9
waters, mightier than the **w** of the sea, Ps 93:4
wind, which lifted up the **w** of the sea. Ps 107:25
still, and the **w** of the sea were hushed. Ps 107:29
your righteousness like the **w** of the sea; Is 48:18
up the sea so that its **w** roar—the LORD of Is 51:15
though the **w** toss, they cannot prevail; Jer 5:22
the sea so that its **w** roar—the LORD of Jer 31:35
she is covered with its tumultuous **w**. Jer 51:42
Their **w** roar like many waters; the Jer 51:55
against you, as the sea brings up its **w**. Ezk 26:3
all your **w** and your billows passed over Jon 2:3
and strike down the **w** of the sea, Zec 10:11
the boat was being swamped by the **w**; Mt 8:24
way from the land, beaten by the **w**, Mt 14:24
and the **w** were breaking into the boat, Mk 4:37
and rebuked the wind and the raging **w**, Lk 8:24
of the roaring of the sea and the **w**, Lk 21:25
and fro by the **w** and carried about by Eph 4:14
wild **w** of the sea, casting up the foam Jude 1:13

WAVY (1)
gold; his locks are **w**, black as a raven. Sg 5:11

WAX (4)
are out of joint; my heart is like **w**; Ps 22:14
as **w** melts before fire, so the wicked shall Ps 68:2
mountains melt like **w** before the LORD, Ps 97:5
will split open, like **w** before the fire, Mi 1:4

WAY (599)
sword that turned every **w** to guard the Gn 3:24
every way to guard the **w** to the tree of Gn 3:24
flesh had corrupted their **w** on the earth. Gn 6:12
all their provisions, and went their **w**. Gn 14:11
and his possessions, and went their **w**. Gn 14:12
wilderness, the spring on the **w** to Shur. Gn 16:7
The **w** of women had ceased to be with Gn 18:11
went with them to set them on their **w**. Gn 18:16
after him to keep the **w** of the LORD by Gn 18:19
And the LORD went his **w**, when he had Gn 18:33
up early and go on your **w**." They said, Gn 19:2
sat down opposite him a good **w** off, Gn 21:16
has led me in the **w** to the house of my Gn 24:27
his angel with you and prosper your **w**. Gn 24:40
now you are prospering the **w** that I go, Gn 24:42
me by the right **w** to take the daughter Gn 24:48
me, since the LORD has prospered my **w**. Gn 24:56
servant took Rebekah and went his **w**. Gn 24:61
ate and drank and rose and went his **w**. Gn 25:34
And Isaac sent them on their **w**, and Gn 26:31
me and will keep me in this **w** that I go, Gn 28:20
for the **w** of women is upon me." So he Gn 31:35
Jacob went on his **w**, and the angels of Gn 32:1
Esau said, "Let us journey on our **w**, Gn 33:12
Esau returned that day on his **w** to Seir. Gn 33:16
Canaan, on his **w** from Paddan-aram, Gn 33:18
was buried on the **w** to Ephrath (that Gn 35:19
on their **w** to carry it down to Egypt. Gn 37:25
"This is the **w** your servant treated Gn 39:19
of your households, and go your **w**. Gn 42:33
Could we in any **w** know that he would Gn 43:7
to them, "Do not quarrel on the **w**." Gn 45:24
Joseph to show the **w** before him in Gn 46:28
died in the land of Canaan on the **w**, Gn 48:7
her there on the **w** to Ephrath (that is, Gn 48:7
Joseph said to his father, "Not this **w**, Gn 48:18
Dan shall be a serpent in the **w**, a viper Gn 49:17
He looked this **w** and that, and seeing no Ex 2:12
lodging place on the **w** the LORD met him Ex 4:24
did not lead them by **w** of the land of Ex 13:17
around by the **w** of the wilderness Ex 13:18
pillar of cloud to lead them along the **w**, Ex 13:21
that had come upon them in the **w**, Ex 18:8
make them know the **w** in which they Ex 18:20
to guard you on the **w** and to bring you Ex 23:20
quickly out of the **w** that I commanded Ex 32:8
among you, lest I consume you on the **w**, Ex 33:3
two of them this **w** for the two corners. Ex 36:29
But in this **w** Aaron shall come into the Lv 16:3
clear out the old to make **w** for the new. Lv 26:10
the wilderness by the **w** to the Red Nm 14:25
shall do these things in this **w**, Nm 15:13
was coming by the **w** of Atharim, Nm 21:1
Hor they set out by the **w** to the Red Sea, Nm 21:4
the people became impatient on the **w**. Nm 21:4
and went up by the **w** to Bashan. Nm 21:33
his stand in the **w** as his adversary. Nm 22:22
where there was no **w** to turn either to Nm 22:26
to treat you this **w**?" And he said, Nm 22:30
angel of the LORD standing in the **w**, Nm 22:31
you because your **w** is perverse before Nm 22:32
his place. And Balak also went his **w**. Nm 24:25
In the same **w** you shall offer daily, for Nm 28:24
from Horeb by the **w** of Mount Seir to Dt 1:2
on the **w** to the hill country of the Dt 1:19
word again of the **w** by which we must Dt 1:22
all the **w** that you went until you came to Dt 1:31
went before you in the **w** to seek you out Dt 1:33
to show you by what **w** you should go. Dt 1:33
we turned and went up the **w** to Bashan. Dt 3:1
shall walk in all the **w** that the LORD your Dt 5:33
your house, and when you walk by the **w**, Dt 6:7
shall remember the whole **w** that the LORD Dt 8:2
quickly out of the **w** that I commanded Dt 9:12
aside quickly from the **w** that the LORD Dt 9:16
and when you are walking by the **w**, Dt 11:19
turn aside from the **w** that I am Dt 11:28
not worship the LORD your God in that **w**. Dt 12:4
worship the LORD your God in that **w**, Dt 12:31
make you leave the **w** in which the LORD Dt 13:5
And if the **w** is too long for you, so that Dt 14:24
'You shall never return that **w** again.' Dt 17:16
and overtake him, because the **w** is long, Dt 19:6
fallen down by the **w** and ignore them. Dt 22:4
you with bread and with water on the **w**, Dt 23:4
did to Miriam on the **w** as you came out Dt 24:9
did to you on the **w** as you came out of Dt 25:17
attacked you on the **w** when you were Dt 25:18
out against you one **w** and flee before Dt 28:7
shall go out one **w** against them and Dt 28:25
turn aside from the **w** that I have Dt 31:29
then you will make your **w** prosperous, Jos 1:8
after them on the **w** to the Jordan as Jos 2:7
Then afterward you may go your **w**." Jos 2:16
all along the **w** and found nothing. Jos 2:22
that you may know the **w** you shall go, Jos 3:4
go, for you have not passed this **w** before." Jos 3:4
the wilderness on the **w** after they had Jos 5:4
were born on the **w** in the wilderness after Jos 5:5
they had not been circumcised on the **w**. Jos 5:7
they had no power to flee this **w** or that, Jos 8:20
chased them by the **w** of the ascent of Jos 10:10
I am about to go the **w** of all the earth, Jos 23:14
preserved us in all the **w** that we went, Jos 24:17
him, "Please show us the **w** into the city, Jgs 1:24
And he showed them the **w** into the city. Jgs 1:25
turned aside from the **w** in which their Jgs 2:17
care to walk in the **w** of the LORD as their Jgs 2:22
rich carpets and you who walk by the **w**. Jgs 5:10
Penuel, and spoke to them in the same **w**, Jgs 8:8
went up by the **w** of the tent dwellers Jgs 8:11
all who passed by them along that **w**. Jgs 9:25
Then the people of Dan went their **w**. Jgs 18:26
So they passed on and went their **w**. Jgs 19:14
the house and went out to go on his **w**, Jgs 19:27
and they went on the **w** to return to the Ru 1:7
go your **w**, for I am too old to have a Ru 1:12
Then the woman went her **w** and ate, 1 Sm 1:18
Then send it off and let it go its **w** 1 Sm 6:8
If it goes up on the **w** to its own land, to 1 Sm 6:9
he can tell us the **w** we should go." 1 Sm 9:6
it to the man of God to tell us our **w**." 1 Sm 9:8
toward them on his **w** up to the high 1 Sm 9:14
have you spoken to me in this **w**?" 1 Sm 9:21
send you on your **w**." So Saul arose, 1 Sm 9:26
you in the good and the right **w**. 1 Sm 12:23
them on the **w** when they came 1 Sm 15:2
people answered him in the same **w**, 1 Sm 17:27
another, and spoke in the same **w**, 1 Sm 17:30
fell on the **w** from Shaaraim as 1 Sm 17:52
he came to the sheepfolds by the **w**, 1 Sm 24:3
and left the cave and went on his **w**. 1 Sm 24:7
in them." So David went his **w**, 1 Sm 26:25
strength when you go on your **w**." 1 Sm 28:22
but carried them off and went their **w**. 1 Sm 30:2
before Giah on the **w** to the wilderness 2 Sm 2:24
after her all the **w** to Bahurim. 2 Sm 3:16
and went by the **w** of the Arabah all 2 Sm 4:7
While they were on the **w**, news 2 Sm 13:30
and stand beside the **w** of the gate. 2 Sm 15:2
Ahimaaz ran by the **w** of the plain, 2 Sm 18:23
will go a little **w** over the Jordan with 2 Sm 19:36
of Israel, brought the king on his **w**. 2 Sm 19:40
This God—his **w** is perfect; the word 2 Sm 22:31
and has made my **w** blameless. 2 Sm 22:33
and rose, and each went his own **w**. 1 Kgs 1:49
"I am about to go the **w** of all the earth. 1 Kgs 2:2
sons pay close attention to their **w**, 1 Kgs 2:4
sons pay close attention to their **w**, 1 Kgs 8:25
teach them the good **w** in which they 1 Kgs 8:36
by whatever **w** you shall send them, 1 Kgs 8:44
nor return by the **w** that you came.'" 1 Kgs 13:9
So he went another **w** and did not 1 Kgs 13:10
not return by the **w** that he came to 1 Kgs 13:10
"Which **w** did he go?" And his sons 1 Kgs 13:12
showed him the **w** that the man 1 Kgs 13:12
nor return by the **w** that you came.'" 1 Kgs 13:17
him back from the **w** heard of it, 1 Kgs 13:26
did not turn from his evil **w**, 1 Kgs 13:33
and walked in the **w** of his father, 1 Kgs 15:26
walked in the **w** of Jeroboam and 1 Kgs 15:34
walked in the **w** of Jeroboam and 1 Kgs 16:2
LORD, walking in the **w** of Jeroboam, 1 Kgs 16:19
walked in all the **w** of Jeroboam the 1 Kgs 16:26
And as Obadiah was on the **w**, 1 Kgs 18:7
return on your **w** to the wilderness 1 Kgs 19:15
and waited for the king by the **w**, 1 Kgs 20:38
walked in all the **w** of Asa his father. 1 Kgs 22:43
and walked in the **w** of his father 1 Kgs 22:52
father and in the **w** of his mother 1 Kgs 22:52
and in the **w** of Jeroboam the 1 Kgs 22:52
to anger in every **w** that his father 1 Kgs 22:53
Elisha were on their **w** from Gilgal. 2 Kgs 2:1
and while he was going up on the **w**, 2 Kgs 2:23
"By which **w** shall we march?" 2 Kgs 3:8
"By the **w** of the wilderness of Edom." 2 Kgs 3:8
So whenever he passed that **w**, he 2 Kgs 4:8
God who is continually passing our **w**. 2 Kgs 4:9
said to them, "This is not the **w**, 2 Kgs 6:19
all the **w** was littered with garments 2 Kgs 7:15
he walked in the **w** of the kings of 2 Kgs 8:18
also walked in the **w** of the house of 2 Kgs 8:27
On the **w**, when he was at Beth-eked 2 Kgs 10:12
on the **w** that goes down to Silla. 2 Kgs 12:20
but he walked in the **w** of the kings of 2 Kgs 16:3
And the covered **w** for the Sabbath 2 Kgs 16:18
you back on the **w** by which you 2 Kgs 19:28
By the **w** that he came, by the same 2 Kgs 19:33
walked in all the **w** in which his 2 Kgs 21:21
did not walk in the **w** of the LORD. 2 Kgs 21:22
walked in all the **w** of David his 2 Kgs 22:2
by night by the **w** of the gate between 2 Kgs 25:4
sons pay close attention to their **w**, 2 Chr 6:16
teach them the good **w** in which they 2 Chr 6:27
by whatever **w** you shall send them, 2 Chr 6:34
three years in the **w** of David and 2 Chr 11:17
"Which **w** did the Spirit of the LORD 2 Chr 18:23
He walked in the **w** of Asa his father 2 Chr 20:32
he walked in the **w** of the kings of 2 Chr 21:6
have walked in the **w** of the kings of 2 Chr 21:13
enter who was in any **w** unclean. 2 Chr 23:19

protect us against the enemy on our **w**, Ezr 8:22
enemy and from ambushes by the **w**. Ezr 8:31
loaded in such a **w** that each labored Neh 4:17
And they sent to me four times in this **w**, Neh 6:4
In the same **w** Sanballat for the fifth Neh 6:5
be afraid and act in this **w** and sin, Neh 6:13
Then he said to them, "Go your **w**. Eat Neh 8:10
the people went their **w** to eat and drink Neh 8:12
light for them the **w** in which they Neh 9:12
lead them in the **w** did not depart from Neh 9:19
light for them the **w** by which they Neh 9:19
Did not your fathers act in this **w**, and Neh 13:18
woman went in to the king in this **w**, Est 2:13
light given to a man whose **w** is hidden, Jb 3:23
Behold, this is the joy of his **w**, and out of Jb 8:19
all **w** of escape will be lost to them, and Jb 11:20
I shall go the **w** from which I shall Jb 16:22
Yet the righteous holds to his **w**, and he Jb 17:9
He has walled up my **w**, so that I cannot Jb 19:8
Who declares his **w** to his face, and who Jb 21:31
keep to the old **w** that wicked men have Jb 22:15
But he knows the **w** that I take; when he Jb 23:10
I have kept his **w** and have not turned Jb 23:11
"God understands the **w** to it, and he Jb 28:23
for the rain and a **w** for the lightning of Jb 28:26
I chose their **w** and sat as chief, and I Jb 29:25
turned aside from the **w** and my heart Jb 31:7
For God speaks in one **w**, and in two, Jb 33:14
Who has prescribed for him his **w**, or Jb 36:23
"Where is the **w** to the dwelling of light, Jb 38:19
What is the **w** to the place where the Jb 38:24
of rain and a **w** for the thunderbolt, Jb 38:25
the wicked, nor stands in the **w** of sinners, Ps 1:1
for the LORD knows the **w** of the righteous, Ps 1:6
but the **w** of the wicked will perish. Ps 1:6
lest he be angry, and you perish in the **w**, Ps 2:12
enemies; make your **w** straight before me. Ps 5:8
This God—his **w** is perfect; the word of Ps 18:30
strength and made my **w** blameless. Ps 18:32
therefore he instructs sinners in the **w**. Ps 25:8
is right, and teaches the humble his **w**. Ps 25:9
he instruct in the **w** that he should Ps 25:12
Teach me your **w**, O LORD, and lead me Ps 27:11
and teach you in the **w** you should go; Ps 32:8
Let their **w** be dark and slippery, with the Ps 35:6
he sets himself in a **w** that is not good; Ps 36:4
Commit your **w** to the LORD; trust in Ps 37:5
over the one who prospers in his **w**, Ps 37:7
needy, to slay those whose **w** is upright; Ps 37:14
by the LORD, when he delights in his **w**; Ps 37:23
Wait for the LORD and keep his **w**, and Ps 37:34
have our steps departed from your **w**; Ps 44:18
we will not fear though the earth gives **w**, Ps 46:2
one who orders his **w** rightly I will show Ps 50:23
They dug a pit in my **w**, but they have Ps 57:6
that your **w** may be known on earth, Ps 67:2
Your **w**, O God, is holy. What god is Ps 77:13
Your **w** was through the sea, your path Ps 77:19
all who pass along the **w** pluck its fruit? Ps 80:12
before him and make his footsteps a **w**. Ps 85:13
Teach me your **w**, O LORD, that I may Ps 86:11
I will ponder the **w** that is blameless. Oh Ps 101:2
who walks in the **w** that is blameless Ps 101:6
finding no **w** to a city to dwell in; Ps 107:4
them by a straight **w** till they reached a Ps 107:7
He will drink from the brook by the **w**; Ps 110:7
Blessed are those whose **w** is blameless, Ps 119:1
How can a young man keep his **w** pure? Ps 119:9
In the **w** of your testimonies I delight Ps 119:14
me understand the **w** of your precepts, Ps 119:27
I have chosen the **w** of faithfulness; I Ps 119:30
run in the **w** of your commandments Ps 119:32
me, O LORD, the **w** of your statutes; Ps 119:33
I hold back my feet from every evil **w**, Ps 119:101
therefore I hate every false **w**. Ps 119:104
to be right; I hate every false **w**. Ps 119:128
as is your **w** with those who love your Ps 119:132
see if there be any grievous **w** in me, Ps 139:24
me, and lead me in the **w** everlasting! Ps 139:24
beside the **w** they have set snares for me. Ps 140:5
faints within me, you know my **w**! Ps 142:3
Make me know the **w** I should go, for to Ps 143:8
but the **w** of the wicked he brings to Ps 146:9
son, do not walk in the **w** with them; Prv 1:15
they shall eat the fruit of their **w**, Prv 1:31
and watching over the **w** of his saints. Prv 2:8
delivering you from the **w** of evil, from Prv 2:12
you will walk in the **w** of the good and Prv 2:20
Then you will walk on your **w** securely, Prv 3:23
I have taught you the **w** of wisdom; I Prv 4:11
and do not walk in the **w** of the evil. Prv 4:14
The **w** of the wicked is like deep Prv 4:19
Keep your **w** far from her, and do not go Prv 5:8
reproofs of discipline are the **w** of life, Prv 6:23
Her house is the **w** to Sheol, going down Prv 7:27
On the heights beside the **w**, at the Prv 8:2
and arrogance and the **w** of evil and Prv 8:13
I walk in the **w** of righteousness, in the Prv 8:20
and live, and walk in the **w** of insight." Prv 9:6
by, who are going straight on their **w**, Prv 9:15
The **w** of the LORD is a stronghold to Prv 10:29
of the blameless keeps his **w** straight, Prv 11:5
The **w** of a fool is right in his own eyes, Prv 12:15
but the **w** of the wicked leads them Prv 12:26
guards him whose **w** is blameless, Prv 13:6
but the **w** of the treacherous is their Prv 13:15
of the prudent is to discern his **w**, Prv 14:8
There is a **w** that seems right to a man, Prv 14:12
to a man, but its end is the **w** to death. Prv 14:12
The **w** of the wicked is an abomination Prv 15:9
discipline for him who forsakes the **w**; Prv 15:10
The **w** of a sluggard is like a hedge of Prv 15:19
The heart of man plans his **w**, but the Prv 16:9
whoever guards his **w** preserves his Prv 16:17
There is a **w** that seems right to a man, Prv 16:25
to a man, but its end is the **w** to death. Prv 16:25
and leads him in a **w** that is not good. Prv 16:29
makes haste with his feet misses his **w**. Prv 19:2
a man's folly brings his **w** to ruin, Prv 19:3
how then can man understand his **w**? Prv 20:24
Every **w** of a man is right in his own Prv 21:2
The **w** of the guilty is crooked, but the Prv 21:8
who wanders from the **w** of good sense Prv 21:16
and snares are in the **w** of the crooked; Prv 22:5
Train up a child in the **w** he should go; Prv 22:6
be wise, and direct your heart in the **w**. Prv 23:19
man who gives **w** before the wicked. Prv 25:26
upright into an evil **w** will fall into his Prv 28:10
but one whose **w** is straight is an Prv 29:27
the **w** of an eagle in the sky, the way of Prv 30:19
in the sky, the **w** of a serpent on a rock, Prv 30:19
rock, the **w** of a ship on the high seas, Prv 30:19
seas, and the **w** of a man with a virgin. Prv 30:19
This is the **w** of an adulteress: she eats Prv 30:20
But this is gain for a land in every **w**: a Eccl 5:9
know the proper time and the just **w**. Eccl 8:5
there is a time and a **w** for everything, Eccl 8:6
for he does not know the **w** to the city. Eccl 10:15
do not know the **w** the spirit comes to Eccl 11:5
what is high, and terrors are in the **w**; Eccl 12:5
me not to walk in the **w** of this people, Is 8:11
time he has made glorious the **w** of the sea, Is 9:1
of the land, from Sela, by **w** of the desert, Is 16:1
fastened in a secure place will give **w**, Is 22:25
you make level the **w** of the righteous. Is 26:7
leave the **w**, turn aside from the path, let Is 30:11
word behind you, saying, "This is the **w**, Is 30:21
and it shall be called the **W** of Holiness; Is 35:8
shall belong to those who walk on the **w**; Is 35:8
you back on the **w** by which you came.' Is 37:29
By the **w** that he came, by the same he Is 37:34
the wilderness prepare the **w** of the LORD; Is 40:3
showed him the **w** of understanding? Is 40:14
O Israel, "My **w** is hidden from the LORD, Is 40:27
lead the blind in a **w** that they do not Is 42:16
says the LORD, who makes a **w** in the sea, Is 43:16
I will make a **w** in the wilderness and Is 43:19
him, and he will prosper in his **w**. Is 48:15
who leads you in the **w** you should go. Is 48:17
depths of the sea a **w** for the redeemed to Is 51:10
we have turned every one to his own **w**; Is 53:6
let the wicked forsake his **w**, and the Is 55:7
they have all turned to their own **w**, each Is 56:11
were wearied with the length of your **w**, Is 57:10
said, "Build up, build up, prepare the **w**, Is 57:14
every obstruction from my people's **w**." Is 57:14
on backsliding in the **w** of his own Is 57:17
The **w** of peace they do not know, and Is 59:8
the gates; prepare the **w** for the people; Is 62:10
people, who walk in a **w** that is not good, Is 65:2
your God, when he led you in the **w**? Jer 2:17
the Baals'? Look at your **w** in the valley; Jer 2:23
much you go about, changing your **w**! Jer 2:36
because they have perverted their **w**; Jer 3:21
for they do not know the **w** of the LORD, the Jer 5:4
to them, for they know the **w** of the LORD, Jer 5:5
the ancient paths, where the good **w** is; Jer 6:16
walk in all the **w** that I command you, Jer 7:23
the LORD: "Learn not the **w** of the nations, Jer 10:2
that the **w** of man is not in himself, Jer 10:23
Why does the **w** of the wicked prosper? Jer 12:1
Return, every one from his evil **w**, and Jer 18:11
I set before you the **w** of life and the way Jer 21:8
you the way of life and the **w** of death. Jer 21:8
This has been your **w** from your youth, Jer 22:21
Therefore their **w** shall be to them like Jer 23:12
have turned them from their evil **w**, Jer 23:22
of you, from his evil **w** and evil deeds, Jer 25:5
and every one turn from his evil **w**, Jer 26:3
But Jeremiah the prophet went his **w**. Jer 28:11
I will give them one heart and one **w**, Jer 32:39
now every one of you from his evil **w**, Jer 35:15
that every one may turn from his evil **w**, Jer 36:3
that every one will turn from his evil **w**, Jer 36:7
city at night by **w** of the king's garden Jer 39:4
God may show us the **w** we should go, Jer 42:3
Stand by the **w** and watch, O Jer 48:19
They shall ask the **w** to Zion, with faces Jer 50:5
city by night by the **w** of a gate between Jer 52:7
who pass along the **w** clap their hands Lam 2:15
to warn the wicked from his wicked **w**, Ezk 3:18
his wickedness, or from his wicked **w**, Ezk 3:19
According to their **w** I will do to them, Ezk 7:27
In this **w** her land will be stripped of Ezk 12:19
turn from his evil **w** to save his life, Ezk 13:22
he should turn from his **w** and live? Ezk 18:23
you say, 'The **w** of the Lord is not just.' Ezk 18:25
O house of Israel: Is my **w** not just? Ezk 18:25
says, 'The **w** of the Lord is not just.' Ezk 18:29
make it at the head of the **w** to a city. Ezk 21:19
Mark a **w** for the sword to come to Ezk 21:20
Babylon stands at the parting of the **w**, Ezk 21:21
have returned their **w** upon their Ezk 22:31
defiled; they both took the same **w**. Ezk 23:13
You have gone the **w** of your sister; Ezk 23:31
to warn the wicked to turn from his **w**, Ezk 33:8
warn the wicked to turn from his **w**, Ezk 33:9
way, and he does not turn from his **w**, Ezk 33:9
the wicked turn from his **w** and live; Ezk 33:11
say, 'The **w** of the Lord is not just,' Ezk 33:17
when it is their own **w** that is not just. Ezk 33:17
you say, 'The **w** of the Lord is not just.' Ezk 33:20
He shall enter by **w** of the vestibule of Ezk 44:3
gate, and shall go out by the same **w**." Ezk 44:3
he brought me by **w** of the north gate Ezk 44:4
gate, and he shall go out by the same **w**. Ezk 46:8
no one shall return by **w** of the gate by Ezk 46:9
brought me out by **w** of the north gate Ezk 47:2
the Great Sea by **w** of Hethlon to Ezk 47:15
beside the **w** of Hethlon to Ezk 48:1
god who is able to rescue in this **w**." Dn 3:29
his limbs gave **w**, and his knees knocked Dn 5:6
He said, "Go your **w**, Daniel, for the Dn 12:9
But go your **w** till the end. And you Dn 12:13
I will hedge up her **w** with thorns, Hos 2:6
they murder on the **w** to Shechem; Hos 6:9
trusted in your own **w** and in the Hos 10:13
like a leopard I will lurk beside the **w**. Hos 13:7
They march each on his **w**; they do not Jl 2:7
and turn aside the **w** of the afflicted; Am 2:7
and, 'As the **W** of Beersheba lives,' Am 8:14
turn from his evil **w** and from the Jon 3:8
did, how they turned from their evil **w**, Jon 3:10
Pass on your **w**, inhabitants of Shaphir, Mi 1:11
His **w** is in whirlwind and storm, and the Na 1:3
But you have turned aside from the **w**. Mal 2:8
and he will prepare the **w** before me. Mal 3:1
of Jesus Christ took place in this **w**. Mt 1:18
to the king, they went on their **w**. Mt 2:9
to their own country by another **w**. Mt 2:12
the wilderness: 'Prepare the **w** of the Lord; Mt 3:3
the land of Naphtali, the **w** of the sea, Mt 4:15
In the same **w**, let your light shine before Mt 5:16
gate is wide and the **w** is easy that leads Mt 7:13
is narrow and the **w** is hard that leads Mt 7:14
so fierce that no one could pass that **w**. Mt 8:28
who will prepare your **w** before you.' Mt 11:10
this time was a long **w** from the land, Mt 14:24
away hungry, lest they faint on the **w**." Mt 15:32
aside, and on the **w** he said to them, Mt 20:17
came to you in the **w** of righteousness, Mt 21:32
true and teach the **w** of God truthfully, Mt 22:16
him also reviled him in the same **w**. Mt 27:44
your face, who will prepare your **w**, Mk 1:2
'Prepare the **w** of the Lord, make his Mk 1:3
grainfields, and as they made their **w**, Mk 2:23
"You have a fine **w** of rejecting the Mk 7:9
"For this statement you may go your **w**; Mk 7:29
to their homes, they will faint on the **w**. Mk 8:3
And on the **w** he asked his disciples, Mk 8:27
"What were you discussing on the **w**?" Mk 9:33
for on the **w** they had argued with one Mk 9:34
And Jesus said to him, "Go your **w**; Mk 10:52
his sight and followed him on the **w**. Mk 10:52
it and were seeking a **w** to destroy him, Mk 11:18
but truly teach the **w** of God. Mk 12:14
saw that in this **w** he breathed his last, Mk 15:39
to guide our feet into the **w** of peace." Lk 1:79
'Prepare the **w** of the Lord, make his paths Lk 3:4
but finding no **w** to bring him in, Lk 5:19
who will prepare your **w** before you.' Lk 7:27
as they go on their **w** they are choked by Lk 8:14
Go your **w**; behold, I am sending you out Lk 10:3
Now as they went on their **w**, Jesus Lk 10:38
an effort to settle with him on the **w**, Lk 12:58

because they suffered in this **w**? Lk 13:2
He went on his **w** through towns and Lk 13:22
must go on my **w** today and tomorrow Lk 13:33
not, while the other is yet a great **w** off, Lk 14:32
But while he was still a long **w** off, his Lk 15:20
and everyone forces his **w** into it. Lk 16:16
On the **w** to Jerusalem he was passing Lk 17:11
he said to him, "Rise and go your **w**; Lk 17:19
see him, for he was about to pass that **w**. Lk 19:4
—already on the **w** down the Mount of Lk 19:37
partiality, but truly teach the **w** of God. Lk 20:21
'Make straight the **w** of the Lord,' Jn 1:23
to the earth and speaks in an earthly **w**. Jn 3:31
Jesus spoke to him and went on his **w**. Jn 4:50
by the door but climbs in by another **w**, Jn 10:1
And you know the **w** to where I am Jn 14:4
you are going. How can we know the **w**?" Jn 14:5
Jesus said to him, "I am the **w**, and the Jn 14:6
and he revealed himself in this **w**. Jn 21:1
come in the same **w** as you saw him Acts 1:11
them go, finding no **w** to punish them, Acts 4:21
no more, and went on his **w** rejoicing. Acts 8:39
if he found any belonging to the **W**, Acts 9:2
Now as he went on his **w**, he Acts 9:3
was I that I could stand in God's **w**?" Acts 11:17
corruption, he has spoken in this **w**, Acts 13:34
spoke in such a **w** that a great number Acts 14:1
being sent on their **w** by the church, Acts 15:3
went on their **w** through the cities, Acts 16:4
proclaim to you the **w** of salvation." Acts 16:17
sent Paul off on his **w** to the sea, Acts 17:14
perceive that in every **w** you are very Acts 17:22
might feel their **w** toward him and Acts 17:27
been instructed in the **w** of the Lord. Acts 18:25
explained to him the **w** of God more Acts 18:26
evil of the **W** before the congregation, Acts 19:9
little disturbance concerning the **W**. Acts 19:23
working hard in this **w** we must help Acts 20:35
I persecuted this **W** to the death, Acts 22:4
"As I was on my **w** and drew near to Acts 22:6
in every **w** and everywhere we accept Acts 24:3
to you, that according to the **W**, Acts 24:14
rather accurate knowledge of the **W**, Acts 24:22
an ambush to kill him on the **w**. Acts 25:3
I saw on the **w** a light from heaven, Acts 26:13
we gave **w** to it and were driven along. Acts 27:15
Much in every **w**. To begin with, the Rom 3:2
wrath on us? (I speak in a human **w**.) Rom 3:5
and the **w** of peace they have not Rom 3:17
And in this **w** all Israel will be saved, Rom 11:26
or hindrance in the **w** of a brother. Rom 14:13
to you very boldly by **w** of reminder, Rom 15:15
and all the **w** around to Illyricum Rom 15:19
I will leave for Spain by **w** of you. Rom 15:28
in the Lord in a **w** worthy of the saints, Rom 16:2
that in every **w** you were enriched in 1 Cor 1:5
and behaving only in a human **w**? 1 Cor 3:3
an obstacle in the **w** of the gospel of 1 Cor 9:12
In the same **w**, the Lord commanded 1 Cor 9:14
he will also provide the **w** of escape, 1 Cor 10:13
In the same **w** also he took the cup, 1 Cor 11:25
show you a still more excellent **w**. 1 Cor 12:31
It does not insist on its own **w**; it is not 1 Cor 13:5
Help him on his **w** in peace, that he 1 Cor 16:11
to visit you on my **w** to Macedonia, 2 Cor 1:16
have you send me on my **w** to Judea. 2 Cor 1:16
We are afflicted in every **w**, but not 2 Cor 4:8
We put no obstacle in anyone's **w**, so 2 Cor 6:3
we commend ourselves in every **w**: 2 Cor 6:4
be enriched in every **w** for all your 2 Cor 9:11
to come all the **w** to you with the 2 Cor 10:14
in every **w** we have made this plain to 2 Cor 11:6
from burdening you in any **w**. 2 Cor 11:9
In the same **w** we also, when we were Gal 4:3
to grow up in every **w** into him who is Eph 4:15
that is not the **w** you learned Christ! Eph 4:20
In the same **w** husbands should love Eph 5:28
not by the **w** of eye-service, as Eph 6:6
right for me to feel this **w** about you all, Phil 1:7
Only that in every **w**, whether in Phil 1:18
of us who are mature think this **w**, Phil 3:15
earthly masters, not by **w** of eye-service, Col 3:22
our Lord Jesus, direct our **w** to you, 1 Thes 3:11
Let no one deceive you in any **w**. For 2 Thes 2:3
it will do so until he is out of the **w**. 2 Thes 2:7
you peace at all times in every **w**. 2 Thes 3:16
letter of mine; it is the **w** I write. 2 Thes 3:17
life, godly and dignified in every **w**. 1 Tm 2:2
value, godliness is of value in every **w**, 1 Tm 4:8
Zenas the lawyer and Apollos on their **w**; Ti 3:13
spoken of the seventh day in this **w**: Heb 4:4
Though we speak in this **w**, yet in your Heb 6:9
Spirit indicates that the **w** into the holy Heb 9:8
And in the same **w** he sprinkled with Heb 9:21
the new and living **w** that he opened Heb 10:20
Consider the outcome of their **w** of life, Heb 13:7
And in the same **w** was not also Rahab Jas 2:25
and sent them out by another **w**? Jas 2:25
with your wives in an understanding **w**, 1 Pt 3:7
yourselves with the same **w** of thinking, 1 Pt 4:1
judged in the flesh the **w** people are, 1 Pt 4:6
might live in the spirit the **w** God does. 1 Pt 4:6
For in this **w** there will be richly 2 Pt 1:11
body, to stir you up by **w** of reminder, 2 Pt 1:13
because of them the **w** of truth will be 2 Pt 2:2
Forsaking the right **w**, they have gone 2 Pt 2:15
They have followed the **w** of Balaam, 2 Pt 2:15
have known the **w** of righteousness 2 Pt 2:21
up your sincere mind by **w** of reminder, 2 Pt 3:1
walk in the same **w** in which he walked. 1 Jn 2:6
they walked in the **w** of Cain and Jude 1:11
committed in such an ungodly **w**, Jude 1:15
to prepare the **w** for the kings from the Rv 16:12

WAYS (192)

your sight, please show me now your **w**, Ex 33:13
by walking in his **w** and by fearing him. Dt 8:6
the LORD your God, to walk in all his **w**, Dt 10:12
the LORD your God, walking in all his **w**, Dt 11:22
walking ever in his **w**—then you shall Dt 19:9
God, and that you will walk in his **w**, Dt 26:17
you one way and flee before you seven **w**. Dt 28:7
of the LORD your God and walk in his **w**. Dt 28:9
them and flee seven **w** before them. Dt 28:25
and you shall not prosper in your **w**. Dt 28:29
the LORD your God, by walking in his **w**, Dt 30:16
work is perfect, for all his **w** are justice. Dt 32:4
to walk in all his **w** and to keep his Jos 22:5
of their practices or their stubborn **w**. Jgs 2:19
not walk in his **w** but turned aside after 1 Sm 8:3
and your sons do not walk in your **w**. 1 Sm 8:5
and show them the **w** of the king who 1 Sm 8:9
"These will be the **w** of the king who 1 Sm 8:11
For I have kept the **w** of the LORD and 2 Sm 22:22
walking in his **w** and keeping his 1 Kgs 2:3
And if you will walk in my **w**, 1 Kgs 3:14
know, according to all his **w** (for you, 1 Kgs 8:39
to walk in all his **w** and to keep his 1 Kgs 8:58
and they have not walked in my **w**, 1 Kgs 11:33
you, and will walk in my **w**, 1 Kgs 11:38
from your evil **w** and keep my 2 Kgs 17:13
you know, according to all his **w**, 2 Chr 6:30
and walk in your **w** all the days that 2 Chr 6:31
face and turn from their wicked **w**, 2 Chr 7:14
of Abijah, his **w** and his sayings, 2 Chr 13:22
walked in the earlier **w** of his father 2 Chr 17:3
was courageous in the **w** of the LORD. 2 Chr 17:6
walked in the **w** of Jehoshaphat 2 Chr 21:12
or in the **w** of Asa king of Judah, 2 Chr 21:12
also walked in the **w** of the house of 2 Chr 22:3
he ordered his **w** before the LORD 2 Chr 27:6
of Jotham, and all his wars and his **w**, 2 Chr 27:7
but he walked in the **w** of the kings of 2 Chr 28:2
the rest of his acts and all his **w**, 2 Chr 28:26
and walked in the **w** of David his 2 Chr 34:2
and the integrity of your **w** your hope? Jb 4:6
in him; yet I will argue my **w** to his face. Jb 13:15
do not desire the knowledge of your **w**. Jb 21:14
to him if you make your **w** blameless? Jb 22:3
for you, and light will shine on your **w**. Jb 22:28
light, who are not acquainted with its **w**, Jb 24:13
and his eyes are upon their **w**. Jb 24:23
these are but the outskirts of his **w**, Jb 26:14
up against me their **w** of destruction. Jb 30:12
Does not he see my **w** and number all my Jb 31:4
and according to his **w** he will make it Jb 34:11
"For his eyes are on the **w** of a man, and Jb 34:21
him and had no regard for any of his **w**, Jb 34:27
His **w** prosper at all times; your Ps 10:5
lips I have avoided the **w** of the violent. Ps 17:4
For I have kept the **w** of the LORD, and Ps 18:21
Make me to know your **w**, O LORD; teach Ps 25:4
I said, "I will guard my **w**, that I may not Ps 39:1
Then I will teach transgressors your **w**, Ps 51:13
of him who walks in his guilty **w**. Ps 68:21
to me, that Israel would walk in my **w**! Ps 81:13
you to guard you in all your **w**. Ps 91:11
heart, and they have not known my **w**." Ps 95:10
He made known his **w** to Moses, his Ps 103:7
were fools through their sinful **w**, Ps 107:17
also do no wrong, but walk in his **w**! Ps 119:3
Oh that my **w** may be steadfast in Ps 119:5
precepts and fix my eyes on your **w**. Ps 119:15
When I told of my **w**, you answered Ps 119:26
Put false **w** far from me and Ps 119:29
things; and give me life in your **w**. Ps 119:37
When I think on my **w**, I turn my feet Ps 119:59
for all my **w** are before you. Ps 119:168
aside to their crooked **w** the LORD will Ps 125:5
who fears the LORD, who walks in his **w**! Ps 128:1
and they shall sing of the **w** of the LORD, Ps 138:5
and are acquainted with all my **w**. Ps 139:3
righteous in all his **w** and kind in all Ps 145:17
Such are the **w** of everyone who is Prv 1:19
to walk in the **w** of darkness, Prv 2:13
and who are devious in their **w**. Prv 2:15
In all your **w** acknowledge him, and he Prv 3:6
Her **w** are ways of pleasantness, and all Prv 3:17
Her ways are **w** of pleasantness, and all Prv 3:17
and do not choose any of his **w**, Prv 3:31
of your feet; then all your **w** will be sure. Prv 4:26
not ponder the path of life; her **w** wander, Prv 5:6
For a man's **w** are before the eyes of the Prv 5:21
O sluggard; consider her **w**, and be wise. Prv 6:6
Let not your heart turn aside to her **w**; Prv 7:25
to me: blessed are those who keep my **w**. Prv 8:32
Leave your simple **w**, and live, and walk Prv 9:6
he who makes his **w** crooked will be Prv 10:9
those of blameless **w** are his delight. Prv 11:20
he who is devious in his **w** despises him. Prv 14:2
will be filled with the fruit of his **w**, Prv 14:14
will be filled with the fruit of his **w**. Prv 14:14
All the **w** of a man are pure in his own Prv 16:2
When a man's **w** please the LORD, he Prv 16:7
in secret to pervert the **w** of justice. Prv 17:23
his life; he who despises his **w** will die. Prv 19:16
but the upright gives thought to his **w**. Prv 21:29
you learn his **w** and entangle yourself Prv 22:25
heart, and let your eyes observe my **w**. Prv 23:26
a rich man who is crooked in his **w**. Prv 28:6
is crooked in his **w** will suddenly fall. Prv 28:18
your **w** to those who destroy kings. Prv 31:3
looks well to the **w** of her household Prv 31:27
Walk in the **w** of your heart and the Eccl 11:9
he may teach us his **w** and that we may Is 2:3
sinned, in whose **w** they would not walk, Is 42:24
and I will make all his **w** level; Is 45:13
They shall feed along the **w**; on all bare Is 49:9
thoughts, neither are your **w** my ways, Is 55:8
thoughts, neither are your ways my **w**, Is 55:8
so are my **w** higher than your ways and Is 55:9
higher than your **w** and my thoughts Is 55:9
I have seen his **w**, but I will heal him; I Is 57:18
seek me daily and delight to know my **w**, Is 58:2
if you honor it, not going your own **w**, or Is 58:13
us wander from your **w** and harden our Is 63:17
those who remember you in your **w**. Is 64:5
These have chosen their own **w**, and their Is 66:3
wicked women you have taught your **w**. Jer 2:33
Your **w** and your deeds have brought Jer 4:18
that you may know and test their **w**. Jer 6:27
Amend your **w** and your deeds, and I will Jer 7:3
you truly amend your **w** and your deeds, Jer 7:5
will diligently learn the **w** of my people, Jer 12:16
people; they did not turn from their **w**. Jer 15:7
For my eyes are on all their **w**. They are Jer 16:17
to give every man according to his **w**, Jer 17:10
and amend your **w** and your deeds.' Jer 18:11
they made them stumble in their **w**, in Jer 18:15
therefore mend your **w** and your deeds, Jer 26:13
are open to all the **w** of the children of Jer 32:19
according to his **w** and according to Jer 32:19
he has blocked my **w** with blocks of Lam 3:9
Let us test and examine our **w**, and Lam 3:40
I will judge you according to your **w**, Ezk 7:3
pity, but I will punish you for your **w**, Ezk 7:4
you, and judge you according to your **w**, Ezk 7:8
I will punish you according to your **w**, Ezk 7:9
and you see their **w** and their deeds, Ezk 14:22
when you see their **w** and their deeds, Ezk 14:23
you walk in their **w** and do according Ezk 16:47
more corrupt than they in all your **w**. Ezk 16:47
will remember your **w** and be Ezk 16:61
just? Is it not your **w** that are not just? Ezk 18:25
O house of Israel, are my **w** not just? Ezk 18:29
just? Is it not your **w** that are not just? Ezk 18:29
of Israel, every one according to his **w**, Ezk 18:30
shall remember your **w** and all your Ezk 20:43
sake, not according to your evil **w**, Ezk 20:44
mark two **w** for the sword of the king Ezk 21:19
of the way, at the head of the two **w**, Ezk 21:21
according to your **w** and your deeds Ezk 24:14
blameless in your **w** from the day Ezk 28:15
back, turn back from your evil **w**, Ezk 33:11
judge each of you according to his **w**." Ezk 33:20
defiled it by their **w** and their deeds. Ezk 36:17
Their **w** before me were like the Ezk 36:17
accordance with their **w** and their Ezk 36:19
Then you will remember your evil **w**, Ezk 36:31
ashamed and confounded for your **w**, Ezk 36:32
his works are right and his **w** are just; Dn 4:37
your breath, and whose are all your **w**, Dn 5:23
punish them for their **w** and repay them Hos 4:9
yet a fowler's snare is on all his **w**, and Hos 9:8
will punish Jacob according to his **w**; Hos 12:2
for the **w** of the LORD are right, and the Hos 14:9

Now the day began to **w** away, and the Lk 9:12
they will all **w** out like a garment, Heb 1:11

WEARIED (10)
offerings, or **w** you with frankincense. Is 43:23
you have **w** me with your iniquities. Is 43:24
You are **w** with your many counsels; let Is 47:13
You were **w** with the length of your way, Is 57:10
with men on foot, and they have **w** you, Jer 12:5
She has **w** herself with toil; its Ezk 24:12
have I done to you? How have I **w** you? Mi 6:3
You have **w** the LORD with your words. Mal 2:17
say, "How have we **w** him?" By saying, Mal 2:17
so Jesus, **w** as he was from his journey, Jn 4:6

WEARIES (2)
The toil of a fool **w** him, for he does Eccl 10:15
when he **w** himself on the high place, Is 16:12

WEARINESS (4)
while he was lying fast asleep from **w**. Jgs 4:21
All things are full of **w**; a man cannot Eccl 1:8
and much study is a **w** of the flesh. Eccl 12:12
But you say, 'What a **w** this is,' and you Mal 1:13

WEARING (14)
atonement, **w** the holy linen garments. Lv 16:32
the garment you are **w** and hold it out." Ru 3:15
of the LORD in Shiloh, **w** an ephod. 1 Sm 14:3
And David was **w** a linen ephod. 2 Sm 6:14
Now she was **w** a long robe with 2 Sm 13:18
Now Joab was **w** a soldier's garment, 2 Sm 20:8
all of them **w** swords and expert in war, Sg 3:8
for baldness and **w** sackcloth; Is 22:12
w belts on their waists, with flowing Ezk 23:15
Lament like a virgin **w** sackcloth for the Jl 1:8
w the crown of thorns and the purple Jn 19:5
hope of Israel that I am **w** this chain." Acts 28:20
For if a man **w** a gold ring and fine Jas 2:2
—the braiding of hair, the **w** of gold, 1 Pt 3:3

WEARISOME (1)
this, it seemed to me a **w** task, Ps 73:16

WEARS (3)
it **w** him out to bring it back to his Prv 26:15
you that if a man **w** long hair it is a 1 Cor 11:14
to the one who **w** the fine clothing and Jas 2:3

WEARY (44)
Egyptians will grow **w** of drinking water Ex 7:18
But Moses' hands grew **w**, so they took Ex 17:12
on the way when you were faint and **w**, Dt 25:18
with him, arrived **w** at the Jordan. 2 Sm 16:14
while he is **w** and discouraged and 2 Sm 17:2
are hungry and **w** and thirsty in 2 Sm 17:29
the Philistines. And David grew **w**. 2 Sm 21:15
the Philistines until his hand was **w**, 2 Sm 23:10
troubling, and there the **w** are at rest. Jb 3:17
have given no water to the **w** to drink, Jb 22:7
I am **w** with my moaning; every night I Ps 6:6
as in a dry and **w** land where there is no Ps 63:1
I am **w** with my crying out; my throat is Ps 69:3
LORD'S discipline or be **w** of his reproof, Prv 3:11
The man declares, I am **w**, O God; I am Prv 30:1
O God; I am **w**, O God, and worn out. Prv 30:1
a burden to me; I am **w** of bearing them. Is 1:14
None is **w**, none stumbles, none Is 5:27
Is it too little for you to **w** men, that you Is 7:13
to weary men, that you **w** my God also? Is 7:13
has said, "This is rest; give rest to the **w**; Is 28:12
like the shade of a great rock in a **w** land. Is 32:2
My eyes are **w** with looking upward. Is 38:14
He does not faint or grow **w**; his Is 40:28
Even youths shall faint and be **w**, and Is 40:30
like eagles; they shall run and not be **w**; Is 40:31
but you have been **w** of me, O Israel! Is 43:22
carry are borne as burdens on **w** beasts. Is 46:1
how to sustain with a word him who is **w**. Is 50:4
None who seek her need **w** themselves; Jer 2:24
of the LORD; I am **w** of holding it in. Jer 6:11
they **w** themselves committing iniquity. Jer 9:5
and destroyed you—I am **w** of relenting. Jer 15:6
my bones, and I am **w** with holding it in, Jer 20:9
For I will satisfy the **w** soul, and every Jer 31:25
I am **w** with my groaning, and I find no Jer 45:3
and the nations **w** themselves only for Jer 51:58
pursuers are at our necks; we are **w**; Lam 5:5
and nations **w** themselves for nothing? Hab 2:13
And let us not grow **w** of doing good, for Gal 6:9
do not grow **w** in doing good. 2 Thes 3:13
you may not grow **w** or fainthearted. Heb 12:3
Lord, nor be **w** when reproved by him. Heb 12:5
name's sake, and you have not grown **w**. Rv 2:3

WEARYING (1)
my hand is stretched out without **w**; Ps 77:2

WEATHER (1)
it is evening, you say, 'It will be fair **w**, Mt 16:2

WEAVE (4)
"You shall **w** the coat in checker work Ex 28:39
"If you **w** the seven locks of my head Jgs 16:13
adders' eggs; they **w** the spider's web; Is 59:5
desire of his soul; thus they **w** it together. Mi 7:3

WEAVER (2)
or by a **w**—by any sort of workman or Ex 35:35
tent; like a **w** I have rolled up my life; Is 38:12

WEAVER'S (5)
shaft of his spear was like a **w** beam, 1 Sm 17:7
of whose spear was like a **w** beam. 2 Sm 21:19
in his hand a spear like a **w** beam, 1 Chr 11:23
of whose spear was like a **w** beam. 1 Chr 20:5
are swifter than a **w** shuttle and come to Jb 7:6

WEAVERS (1)
be in despair, and the **w** of white cotton. Is 19:9

WEB (5)
my head with the **w** and fasten it tight Jgs 16:13
of his head and wove them into the **w**. Jgs 16:14
away the pin, the loom, and the **w**. Jgs 16:14
is severed, and his trust is a spider's **w**. Jb 8:14
adders' eggs; they weave the spider's **w**; Is 59:5

WEBS (1)
Their **w** will not serve as clothing; men Is 59:6

WEDDING (16)
mother crowned him on the day of his **w**, Sg 3:11
"Can the **w** guests mourn as long as the Mt 9:15
to a king who gave a **w** feast for his son, Mt 22:2
those who were invited to the **w** feast, Mt 22:3
everything is ready. Come to the **w** feast.' Mt 22:4
said to his servants, 'The **w** feast is ready, Mt 22:8
and invite to the **w** feast as many as Mt 22:9
So the **w** hall was filled with guests. Mt 22:10
there a man who had no **w** garment. Mt 22:11
you get in here without a **w** garment?' Mt 22:12
"Can the **w** guests fast while the Mk 2:19
"Can you make **w** guests fast while the Lk 5:34
master to come home from the **w** feast, Lk 12:36
you are invited by someone to a **w** feast, Lk 14:8
third day there was a **w** at Cana in Galilee, Jn 2:1
also was invited to the **w** with his disciples. Jn 2:2

WEEDS (11)
and foul **w** instead of barley." The Jb 31:40
up like poisonous **w** in the furrows Hos 10:4
me; **w** were wrapped about my head Jon 2:5
came and sowed **w** among the wheat Mt 13:25
bore grain, then the **w** appeared also. Mt 13:26
in your field? How then does it have **w**?' Mt 13:27
lest in gathering the **w** you root up the Mt 13:29
Gather the **w** first and bind them in Mt 13:30
to us the parable of the **w** of the field." Mt 13:36
The **w** are the sons of the evil one, Mt 13:38
Just as the **w** are gathered and burned Mt 13:40

WEEK (13)
Complete the **w** of this one, and we will Gn 29:27
Jacob did so, and completed her **w**. Gn 29:28
a strong covenant with many for one **w**, Dn 9:27
and for half of the **w** he shall put an end Dn 9:27
toward the dawn of the first day of the **w**, Mt 28:1
And very early on the first day of the **w**, Mk 16:2
he rose early on the first day of the **w**, Mk 16:9
I fast twice a **w**; I give tithes of all that I Lk 18:12
But on the first day of the **w**, at early Lk 24:1
first day of the **w** Mary Magdalene came Jn 20:1
of that day, the first day of the **w**, Jn 20:19
On the first day of the **w**, when we were Acts 20:7
On the first day of every **w**, each of 1 Cor 16:2

WEEKS (18)
You shall observe the Feast of **W**, the Ex 34:22
child, then she shall be unclean two **w**, Lv 12:5
shall count seven full **w** from the day Lv 23:15
"You shall count seven **w** of years, seven Lv 25:8
the time of the seven **w** of years shall give Lv 25:8
grain to the LORD at your Feast of **W**, Nm 28:26
"You shall count seven **w**. Begin to Dt 16:9
to count the seven **w** from the time the Dt 16:9
keep the Feast of **W** to the LORD your Dt 16:10
of Unleavened Bread, at the Feast of **W**, Dt 16:16
of Unleavened Bread, the Feast of **W**, 2 Chr 8:13
keeps for us the **w** appointed for the Jer 5:24
"Seventy **w** are decreed about your Dn 9:24
one, a prince, there shall be seven **w**. Dn 9:25
Then for sixty-two **w** it shall be built Dn 9:25
And after the sixty-two **w**, an anointed Dn 9:26
I, Daniel, was mourning for three **w**. Dn 10:2
anoint myself at all, for the full three **w**. Dn 10:3

WEEP (51)
in to mourn for Sarah and to **w** for her. Gn 23:2
his brother, and he sought a place to **w**. Gn 43:30
For they **w** before me and say, 'Give us Nm 11:13
the mountains and **w** for my virginity, Jgs 11:37
said to her, "Hannah, why do you **w**? 1 Sm 1:8
shall be spared to **w** his eyes out to 1 Sm 2:33
until they had no more strength to **w**. 1 Sm 30:4
"You daughters of Israel, **w** over Saul, 2 Sm 1:24
"Why does my lord **w**?" He answered, 2 Kgs 8:12
do not mourn or **w**." For all the people Neh 8:9
buries, and his widows do not **w**. Jb 27:15
Did not I **w** for him whose day was Jb 30:25
and my pipe to the voice of those who **w**. Jb 30:31
a time to **w**, and a time to laugh; a time Eccl 3:4
and to Dibon, to the high places to **w**; Is 15:2
Therefore I **w** with the weeping of Jazer for Is 16:9
away from me; let me **w** bitter tears; Is 22:4
Zion, in Jerusalem; you shall **w** no more. Is 30:19
the streets; the envoys of peace **w** bitterly. Is 33:7
that I might **w** day and night for the slain Jer 9:1
my soul will **w** in secret for your pride; Jer 13:17
my eyes will **w** bitterly and run down Jer 13:17
W not for him who is dead, nor grieve Jer 22:10
but **w** bitterly for him who goes away, Jer 22:10
More than for Jazer I **w** for you, O vine Jer 48:32
"For these things I **w**; my eyes flow Lam 1:16
yet you shall not mourn or **w**, nor Ezk 24:16
you shall not mourn or **w**, but you Ezk 24:23
and they **w** over you in bitterness of Ezk 27:31
Awake, you drunkards, and **w**, and wail, Jl 1:5
the ministers of the LORD, **w** and say, Jl 2:17
Tell it not in Gath; **w** not at all; in Mi 1:10
"Should I **w** and abstain in the fifth Zec 7:3
an only child, and **w** bitterly over him, Zec 12:10
"Blessed are you who **w** now, for you Lk 6:21
laugh now, for you shall mourn and **w**. Lk 6:25
on her and said to her, "Do not **w**." Lk 7:13
we sang a dirge, and you did not **w**.' Lk 7:32
for her, but he said, "Do not **w**, Lk 8:52
of Jerusalem, do not **w** for me, Lk 23:28
but **w** for yourselves and for your Lk 23:28
she was going to the tomb to **w** there. Jn 11:31
I say to you, you will **w** and lament, Jn 16:20
who rejoice, **w** with those who weep. Rom 12:15
who rejoice, weep with those who **w**. Rom 12:15
Be wretched and mourn and **w**. Let your Jas 4:9
w and howl for the miseries that are Jas 5:1
and I began to **w** loudly because no one Rv 5:4
one of the elders said to me, "**W** no more; Rv 5:5
will **w** and wail over her when they see Rv 18:9
of the earth **w** and mourn for Rv 18:11

WEEPING (57)
when the days of **w** for him were past, Gn 50:4
heard the people **w** throughout their Nm 11:10
while they were **w** in the entrance of the Nm 25:6
Then the days of **w** and mourning for Dt 34:8
that they are **w**?" So they told him the 1 Sm 11:5
with one another, David **w** the most. 1 Sm 20:41
w after her all the way to Bahurim. 2 Sm 3:16
of the Mount of Olives, **w** as he went, 2 Sm 15:30
and they went up, **w** as they went. 2 Sm 15:30
the king is **w** and mourning for 2 Sm 19:1
shout from the sound of the people's **w**, Ezr 3:13
w and casting himself down before the Ezr 10:1
Jews, with fasting and **w** and lamenting, Est 4:3
My face is red with **w**, and on my eyelids Jb 16:16
with tears; I drench my couch with my **w**. Ps 6:6
for the LORD has heard the sound of my **w**. Ps 6:8
W may tarry for the night, but joy Ps 30:5
He who goes out **w**, bearing the seed for Ps 126:6
For at the ascent of Luhith they go up **w**; Is 15:5
I weep with the **w** of Jazer for the Is 16:9
GOD of hosts called for **w** and mourning, Is 22:12
in it the sound of **w** and the cry of Is 65:19
the **w** and pleading of Israel's sons Jer 3:21
"I will take up **w** and wailing for the Jer 9:10
With **w** they shall come, and with pleas Jer 31:9
in Ramah, lamentation and bitter **w**. Jer 31:15
Rachel is **w** for her children; she refuses Jer 31:15
"Keep your voice from **w**, and your eyes Jer 31:16
Mizpah to meet them, **w** as he came. Jer 41:6
For at the ascent of Luhith they go up **w**; Jer 48:5
shall come together, **w** as they come, Jer 50:4
My eyes are spent with **w**; my stomach Lam 2:11
there sat women **w** for Tammuz. Ezk 8:14
with all your heart, with fasting, with **w**, Jl 2:12
with **w** and groaning because he no Mal 2:13
in Ramah, **w** and loud lamentation, Mt 2:18
lamentation, Rachel **w** for her children; Mt 2:18
place there will be **w** and gnashing of Mt 8:12
place there will be **w** and gnashing of Mt 13:42
place there will be **w** and gnashing of Mt 13:50
place there will be **w** and gnashing of Mt 22:13
place there will be **w** and gnashing of Mt 24:51
place there will be **w** and gnashing of Mt 25:30
people **w** and wailing loudly. Mk 5:38
are you making a commotion and **w**? Mk 5:39
w, she began to wet his feet with her Lk 7:38
And all were **w** and mourning for her, Lk 8:52

place there will be **w** and gnashing of Lk 13:28
When Jesus saw her **w**, and the Jews Jn 11:33
the Jews who had come with her also **w**, Jn 11:33
But Mary stood **w** outside the tomb, and Jn 20:11
why are you **w**?" She said to them, Jn 20:13
said to her, "Woman, why are you **w**? Jn 20:15
stood beside him **w** and showing Acts 9:39
And there was much **w** on the part of Acts 20:37
you doing, **w** and breaking my heart? Acts 21:13
of her torment, **w** and mourning aloud, Rv 18:15

WEEPS (2)
She **w** bitterly in the night, with tears Lam 1:2
over him, as one **w** over a firstborn. Zec 12:10

WEIGH (4)
keep them until you **w** them before the Ezr 8:29
the purse, and **w** out silver in the scales, Is 46:6
more; all who **w** out silver are cut off. Zep 1:11
and let the others **w** what is said. 1 Cor 14:29

WEIGHED (22)
and Abraham **w** out for Ephron the Gn 23:16
knowledge, and by him actions are **w**. 1 Sm 2:3
his spear's head **w** six hundred 1 Sm 17:7
he cut it), he **w** the hair of his head, 2 Sm 14:26
whose spear **w** three hundred shekels 2 Sm 21:16
the money that was **w** out into the 2 Kgs 12:11
He found that it **w** a talent of gold, 1 Chr 20:2
And I **w** out to them the silver and the Ezr 8:25
I **w** out into their hand 650 talents of Ezr 8:26
and the vessels were **w** into the hands of Ezr 8:33
The whole was counted and **w**, and the Ezr 8:34
"Oh that my vexation were **w**, and all my Jb 6:2
gold, and silver cannot be **w** as its price. Jb 28:15
(Let me be **w** in a just balance, and let Jb 31:6
counted, where is he who **w** the tribute? Is 33:18
in a measure and **w** the mountains in Is 40:12
my cousin, and **w** out the money to him, Jer 32:9
witnesses, and **w** the money on scales. Jer 32:10
you have been **w** in the balances and Dn 5:27
keep them." And they **w** out as my Zec 11:12
your hearts be **w** down with dissipation Lk 21:34
they **w** anchor and sailed along Crete, Acts 27:13

WEIGHING (9)
man took a gold ring **w** a half shekel, Gn 24:22
for her arms **w** ten gold shekels, Gn 24:22
each silver plate **w** 130 shekels and Nm 7:85
w 10 shekels apiece according to the Nm 7:86
of silver, and a bar of gold **w** 50 shekels, Jos 7:21
as bronze in quantities beyond **w**, 1 Chr 22:3
and bronze and iron beyond **w**, 1 Chr 22:14
w and studying and arranging many Eccl 12:9
Then take balances for **w** and divide the Ezk 5:1

WEIGHS (4)
Anxiety in a man's heart **w** him down, Prv 12:25
his own eyes, but the LORD **w** the spirit. Prv 16:2
his own eyes, but the LORD **w** the heart. Prv 21:2
does not he who **w** the heart perceive Prv 24:12

WEIGHT (51)
of his sack, our money in full **w**. Gn 43:21
in measures of length or **w** or quantity. Lv 19:35
shall dole out your bread again by **w**, Lv 26:26
silver plate whose **w** was 130 shekels, Nm 7:13
silver plate whose **w** was 130 shekels, Nm 7:19
silver plate whose **w** was 130 shekels, Nm 7:25
silver plate whose **w** was 130 shekels, Nm 7:31
silver plate whose **w** was 130 shekels, Nm 7:37
silver plate whose **w** was 130 shekels, Nm 7:43
silver plate whose **w** was 130 shekels, Nm 7:49
silver plate whose **w** was 130 shekels, Nm 7:55
silver plate whose **w** was 130 shekels, Nm 7:61
silver plate whose **w** was 130 shekels, Nm 7:67
silver plate whose **w** was 130 shekels, Nm 7:73
silver plate whose **w** was 130 shekels, Nm 7:79
I bear by myself the **w** and burden of you Dt 1:12
A full and fair **w** you shall have, a full Dt 25:15
And the **w** of the golden earrings that he Jgs 8:26
and he leaned his **w** against them, Jgs 16:29
and the **w** of the coat was five 1 Sm 17:5
The **w** of it was a talent of gold, and 2 Sm 12:30
two hundred shekels by the king's **w**. 2 Sm 14:26
in my hand the **w** of a thousand 2 Sm 18:12
the **w** of the bronze was not 1 Kgs 7:47
Now the **w** of gold that came to 1 Kgs 10:14
of all these vessels was beyond **w**. 2 Kgs 25:16
600 shekels of gold by **w** for the site. 1 Chr 21:25
the **w** of gold for all golden vessels 1 Chr 28:14
the **w** of silver vessels for each 1 Chr 28:14
the **w** of the golden lampstands and 1 Chr 28:15
the **w** of gold for each lampstand 1 Chr 28:15
the **w** of silver for a lampstand and 1 Chr 28:15
the **w** of gold for each table for the 1 Chr 28:16
the golden bowls and the **w** of each; 1 Chr 28:17
the silver bowls and the **w** of each; 1 Chr 28:17
made of refined gold, and its **w**; 1 Chr 28:18
The **w** of gold for the nails was fifty 2 Chr 3:9
for the **w** of the bronze was not 2 Chr 4:18
Now the **w** of gold that came to 2 Chr 9:13
Levites took over the **w** of the silver and Ezr 8:30
and the **w** of everything was recorded. Ezr 8:34
to the wind its **w** and apportioned the Jb 28:25
to the LORD, but a just **w** is his delight. Prv 11:1
of all these things was beyond **w**. Jer 52:20
sons of Zion, worth their **w** in fine gold, Lam 4:2
your food that you eat shall be by **w**, Ezk 4:10
shall eat bread by **w** and with anxiety, Ezk 4:16
thrust down the leaden **w** on its opening. Zec 5:8
aloes, about seventy-five pounds in **w**. Jn 19:39
for us an eternal **w** of glory beyond 2 Cor 4:17
witnesses, let us also lay aside every **w**, Heb 12:1

WEIGHTIER (1)
and have neglected the **w** matters of the Mt 23:23

WEIGHTS (7)
according to the **w** current among the Gn 23:16
You shall have just balances, just **w**, a Lv 19:36
not have in your bag two kinds of **w**, Dt 25:13
all the **w** in the bag are his work. Prv 16:11
Unequal **w** and unequal measures are Prv 20:10
Unequal **w** are an abomination to the Prv 20:23
scales and with a bag of deceitful **w**? Mi 6:11

WEIGHTY (2)
A stone is heavy, and sand is **w**, but a Prv 27:3
say, "His letters are **w** and strong, 2 Cor 10:10

WELCOME (10)
did we see you a stranger and **w** you, Mt 25:38
I was a stranger and you did not **w** me, Mt 25:43
and wrote to the disciples to **w** him. Acts 18:27
the one who is weak in faith, **w** him, Rom 14:1
Therefore **w** one another as Christ has Rom 15:7
that you may **w** her in the Lord in a Rom 16:2
no unclean thing; then I will **w** you, 2 Cor 6:17
—if he comes to you, **w** him), Col 4:10
she had given a friendly **w** to the spies. Heb 11:31
with that, he refuses to **w** the brothers, 3 Jn 1:10

WELCOMED (12)
And Hezekiah **w** them, and he 2 Kgs 20:13
And Hezekiah **w** them gladly. And he Is 39:2
drink, I was a stranger and you **w** me, Mt 25:35
when Jesus returned, the crowd **w** him, Lk 8:40
and he **w** them and spoke to them of the Lk 9:11
woman named Martha **w** him into her Lk 10:38
he came to Galilee, the Galileans **w** him, Jn 4:45
they were **w** by the church and the Acts 15:4
for they kindled a fire and **w** us all, Acts 28:2
expense, and **w** all who came to him, Acts 28:30
the one who eats, for God has **w** him. Rom 14:3
one another as Christ has **w** you, Rom 15:7

WELFARE (14)
he inquired about their **w** and said, Gn 43:27
each other of their **w** and went into the Ex 18:7
of Micah, and asked him about his **w**. Jgs 18:15
had come to seek the **w** of the people of Neh 2:10
for he sought the **w** of his people and Est 10:3
who delights in the **w** of his servant!" Ps 35:27
it was for my **w** that I had great Is 38:17
"Do not pray for the **w** of this people. Jer 14:11
will turn aside to ask about your **w**? Jer 15:5
But seek the **w** of the city where I have Jer 29:7
for in its **w** you will find your welfare. Jer 29:7
for in its welfare you will find your **w**. Jer 29:7
man is not seeking the **w** of this people, Jer 38:4
be genuinely concerned for your **w**. Phil 2:20

WELL (245)
If you do **w**, will you not be accepted? Gn 4:7
And if you do not do **w**, sin is crouching Gn 4:7
that it may go **w** with me because of Gn 12:13
for her sake he dealt **w** with Abram; Gn 12:16
Valley was **w** watered everywhere Gn 13:10
Therefore the **w** was called Gn 16:14
her eyes, and she saw a **w** of water. Gn 21:19
Abimelech about a **w** of water that Gn 21:25
be a witness for me that I dug this **w**." Gn 21:30
Abraham was old, **w** advanced in years. Gn 24:1
outside the city by the **w** of water at the Gn 24:11
and ran again to the **w** to draw water, Gn 24:20
and found there a **w** of spring water, Gn 26:19
So he called the name of the **w** Esek, Gn 26:20
Then they dug another **w**, and they Gn 26:21
moved from there and dug another **w**, Gn 26:22
And there Isaac's servants dug a **w**. Gn 26:25
told him about the **w** that they had dug Gn 26:32
As he looked, he saw a **w** in the field, and Gn 29:2
for out of that **w** the flocks were watered. Gn 29:2
the mouth of the **w** and water the sheep, Gn 29:3
in its place over the mouth of the **w**. Gn 29:3
to them, "Is it **w** with him?" They said, Gn 29:6
"Is it well with him?" They said, "It is **w**; Gn 29:6
stone is rolled from the mouth of the **w**; Gn 29:8
see if it is **w** with your brothers and Gn 37:14
remember me, when it is **w** with you, Gn 40:14
welfare and said, "Is your father **w**, Gn 43:27
said, "Your servant our father is **w**; Gn 43:28
as **w** as all the household of Joseph, his Gn 50:8
So God dealt **w** with the midwives. And Ex 1:20
land of Midian. And he sat down by a **w**. Ex 2:15
the Levite? I know that he can speak **w**. Ex 4:14
You shall bring it **w** mixed, in baked Lv 6:21
and loaves of fine flour **w** mixed with oil. Lv 7:12
him. The sojourner as **w** as the native, Lv 24:16
it, for we are **w** able to overcome it." Nm 13:30
or vineyard, or drink water from a **w**. Nm 20:17
that is the **w** of which the LORD said to Nm 21:16
Israel sang this song: "Spring up, O **w**! Nm 21:17
the **w** that the princes dug, that the Nm 21:18
We will not drink the water of a **w**. Nm 21:22
that it may go **w** with you and with your Dt 4:40
female servant may rest as **w** as you. Dt 5:14
and that it may go **w** with you in the Dt 5:16
that it might go **w** with them and with Dt 5:29
may live, and that it may go **w** with you, Dt 5:33
to do them, that it may go **w** with you, Dt 6:3
of the LORD, that it may go **w** with you, Dt 6:18
that all may go **w** with you and with Dt 12:25
that it may go **w** with you and with Dt 12:28
Israel, so that it may be **w** with you. Dt 19:13
for yourself, that it may go **w** with you, Dt 22:7
all Israel, sojourner as **w** as native born, Jos 8:33
Joshua was old and **w** advanced in years, Jos 23:1
"I am now old and **w** advanced in years. Jos 23:2
So Gideon said, "**W** then, when the LORD Jgs 8:7
if you have dealt **w** with Jerubbaal and Jgs 9:16
grain, as **w** as the olive orchards. Jgs 15:5
rest for you, that it may be **w** with you? Ru 3:1
And Saul said to his servant, "**W** said; 1 Sm 9:10
the LORD your God, it will be **w**. 1 Sm 12:14
he will play it, and you will be **w**." 1 Sm 16:16
man who can play **w** and bring him 1 Sm 16:17
So Saul was refreshed and was **w**, 1 Sm 16:23
See if your brothers are **w**, and bring 1 Sm 17:18
it pleased David **w** to be the king's 1 Sm 18:26
And Jonathan spoke **w** of David to 1 Sm 19:4
came to the great **w** that is in Secu. 1 Sm 19:22
"Your father knows **w** that I have 1 Sm 20:3
'Good!' it will be **w** with your servant, 1 Sm 20:7
if he is **w** disposed toward David, 1 Sm 20:12
day how you have dealt **w** with me, 1 Sm 24:18
the LORD has dealt **w** with my lord, 1 Sm 25:31
David said to Achish, "Very **w**, you 1 Sm 28:2
And Achish said to David, "Very **w**, 1 Sm 28:2
who had a **w** in his courtyard. 2 Sm 17:18
gone, the men came up out of the **w**, 2 Sm 17:21
"All is **w**." And he bowed before the 2 Sm 18:28
"Is it **w** with the young man 2 Sm 18:29
"Is it **w** with the young man 2 Sm 18:32
Joab said to Amasa, "Is it **w** with you, 2 Sm 20:9
drink from the **w** of Bethlehem that 2 Sm 23:15
water out of the **w** of Bethlehem that 2 Sm 23:16
Bathsheba said, "Very **w**; I will speak 1 Kgs 2:18
you did **w** that it was in your heart. 1 Kgs 8:18
people answered, "It is **w** spoken." 1 Kgs 18:24
and consider **w** what you have to do, 1 Kgs 20:22
Gehazi answered, "**W**, she has no son, 2 Kgs 4:14
nor Sabbath." She said, "All is **w**." 2 Kgs 4:23
her and say to her, 'Is all **w** with you? 2 Kgs 4:26
you? Is all **w** with your husband? 2 Kgs 4:26
Is all **w** with the child?'" And she 2 Kgs 4:26
child?'" And she answered, "All is **w**." 2 Kgs 4:26
to meet him and said, "Is all **w**?" 2 Kgs 5:21
And he said, "All is **w**. My master has 2 Kgs 5:22
his master, they said to him, "Is all **w**? 2 Kgs 9:11
you have done **w** in carrying out 2 Kgs 10:30
as **w** as to buy timber and quarried 2 Kgs 12:12
and it shall be **w** with you." 2 Kgs 25:24
drink from the **w** of Bethlehem that 1 Chr 11:17
water out of the **w** of Bethlehem that 1 Chr 11:18
as **w** as to the priests and Levites in 1 Chr 13:2
as **w** as bronze in quantities beyond 1 Chr 22:3
as **w** as two and two at the 1 Chr 26:17
you did **w** that it was in your heart. 2 Chr 6:8
are, as **w** as the priests who minister, Neh 10:39
But I have understanding as **w** as you; I Jb 12:3
Will it be **w** with you when he searches Jb 13:9
consider **w** her ramparts, go through Ps 48:13
get praise when you do **w** for yourself— Ps 49:18
is a cup with foaming wine, **w** mixed, Ps 75:8
And they ate and were **w** filled, for he Ps 78:29
It is **w** with the man who deals Ps 112:5
You have dealt **w** with your servant, O Ps 119:65
Your promise is **w** tried, and your Ps 119:140
be blessed, and it shall be **w** with you. Ps 128:2
your works; my soul knows it very **w**. Ps 139:14

flowing water from your own **w**. Prv 5:15
When it goes **w** with the righteous, the Prv 11:10
a deep pit; an adulteress is a narrow **w**. Prv 23:27
Know **w** the condition of your flocks, Prv 27:23
She looks **w** to the ways of her Prv 31:27
has made the one as **w** as the other, Eccl 7:14
that it will be **w** with those who fear Eccl 8:12
But it will not be **w** with the wicked, Eccl 8:13
a garden fountain, a **w** of living water, Sg 4:15
are all choice fruits, new as **w** as old, Sg 7:13
the righteous that it shall be **w** with them, Is 3:10
full of marrow, of aged wine **w** refined. Is 25:6
the LORD said to me, "You have seen **w**, Jer 1:12
"How **w** you direct your course to seek Jer 2:33
saying, 'It shall be **w** with you,' Jer 4:10
As a **w** keeps its water fresh, so she keeps Jer 6:7
you, that it may be **w** with you.' Jer 7:23
Then it was **w** with him. Jer 22:15
of the poor and needy; then it was **w**. Jer 22:16
of the LORD, 'It shall be **w** with you'; Jer 23:17
consider **w** the highway, the road by Jer 31:21
I say to you, and it shall be **w** with you, Jer 38:20
"Take him, look after him **w**, and do Jer 39:12
come, and I will look after you **w**, Jer 40:4
of Babylon, and it shall be **w** with you. Jer 40:9
that it may be **w** with us when we obey Jer 42:6
soul of the father as **w** as the soul of the Ezk 18:4
flock; pile the logs under it; boil it **w**; Ezk 24:5
logs, kindle the fire, boil the meat **w**, Ezk 24:10
voice and plays **w** on an instrument, Ezk 33:32
known to them as **w** all its statutes Ezk 43:11
LORD said to me, "Son of man, mark **w**, Ezk 44:5
And mark **w** the entrance to the temple Ezk 44:5
the image that I have made, **w** and good. Dn 3:15
the LORD said, "Do you do **w** to be angry?" Jon 4:4
"Do you do **w** to be angry for the plant?" Jon 4:9
And he said, "Yes, I do **w** to be angry, Jon 4:9
Their hands are on what is evil, to do it **w**; Mi 7:3
Son, with whom I am **w** pleased." Mt 3:17
tunic, let him have your cloak as **w**. Mt 5:40
"Those who are **w** have no need of a Mt 9:12
touch his garment, I will be made **w**." Mt 9:21
has made you **w**." And instantly the Mt 9:22
And instantly the woman was made **w**. Mt 9:22
with whom my soul is **w** pleased. Mt 12:18
as many as touched it were made **w**. Mt 14:36
W did Isaiah prophesy of you, when he Mt 15:7
beloved Son, with whom I am **w** pleased; Mt 17:5
His master said to him, '**W** done, good Mt 25:21
His master said to him, '**W** done, good Mt 25:23
beloved Son; with you I am **w** pleased." Mk 1:11
"Those who are **w** have no need of a Mk 2:17
so that she may be made **w** and live." Mk 5:23
even his garments, I will be made **w**." Mk 5:28
"Daughter, your faith has made you **w**; Mk 5:34
as many as touched it were made **w**. Mk 6:56
"**W** did Isaiah prophesy of you Mk 7:6
saying, "He has done all things **w**. Mk 7:37
has made you **w**." And immediately he Mk 10:52
and seeing that he answered them **w**, Mk 12:28
beloved Son; with you I am **w** pleased." Lk 3:22
And all spoke **w** of him and marveled at Lk 4:22
do here in your hometown as **w**." Lk 4:23
kingdom of God to the other towns as **w**; Lk 4:43
"Those who are **w** have no need of a Lk 5:31
to you, when all people speak **w** of you, Lk 6:26
shake it, because it had been **w** built. Lk 6:48
to the house, they found the servant **w**. Lk 7:10
"Daughter, your faith has made you **w**; Lk 8:48
not fear; only believe, and she will be **w**." Lk 8:50
should bear fruit next year, **w** and good; Lk 13:9
has fallen into a **w** on a Sabbath day, Lk 14:5
your way; your faith has made you **w**." Lk 17:19
sight; your faith has made you **w**." Lk 18:42
And he said to him, '**W** done, good Lk 19:17
"Teacher, you have spoken **w**." Lk 20:39
Jacob's **w** was there; so Jesus, wearied as he Jn 4:6
from his journey, was sitting beside the **w**. Jn 4:6
to draw water with, and the **w** is deep. Jn 4:11
He gave us the **w** and drank from it Jn 4:12
temple and said to him, "See, you are **w**! Jn 5:14
Twelve, "Do you want to go away as **w**?" Jn 6:67
Sabbath I made a man's whole body **w**? Jn 7:23
plans to put Lazarus to death as **w**, Jn 12:10
this man is standing before you **w**. Acts 4:10
who is **w** spoken of by the whole Acts 10:22
seeing that he had faith to be made **w**, Acts 14:9
yourselves from these, you will do **w**. Acts 15:29
He was **w** spoken of by the brothers at Acts 16:2
baptized, and her household as **w**, Acts 16:15
women of high standing as **w** as men. Acts 17:12
w spoken of by all the Jews who lived Acts 22:12
as you yourselves know very **w**. Acts 25:10
harvest among you as **w** as among the Rom 1:13
would be counted to them as **w**, Rom 4:11
a patron of many and of myself as **w**. Rom 16:2
of the Gentiles give thanks as **w**. Rom 16:4
They are **w** known to the apostles, and Rom 16:7
who has been a mother to me as **w**. Rom 16:13
her as his betrothed, he will do **w**. 1 Cor 7:37
he who marries his betrothed does **w**, 1 Cor 7:38
may be giving thanks **w** enough, 1 Cor 14:17
refreshed my spirit as **w** as yours. 1 Cor 16:18
as unknown, and yet **w** known; as 2 Cor 6:9
So now finish doing it as **w**, so that 2 Cor 8:11
You were running **w**. Who hindered you Gal 5:7
"that it may go **w** with you and that you Eph 6:3
I am **w** supplied, having received from Phil 4:18
to you who are afflicted as **w** as to us, 2 Thes 1:7
must manage his own household **w**, 1 Tm 3:4
he must be **w** thought of by outsiders, 1 Tm 3:7
and their own households **w**. 1 Tm 3:12
those who serve **w** as deacons gain 1 Tm 3:13
Command these things as **w**, so that 1 Tm 5:7
elders who rule **w** be considered 1 Tm 5:17
and now, I am sure, dwells in you as **w**. 2 Tm 1:5
—and you **w** know all the service he 2 Tm 1:18
is necessarily a change in the law as **w**. Heb 7:12
neighbor as yourself," you are doing **w**. Jas 2:8
You believe that God is one; you do **w**. Jas 2:19
obey us, we guide their whole bodies as **w**. Jas 3:3
as **w** as a partaker in the glory that is 1 Pt 5:1
Son, with whom I am **w** pleased," 2 Pt 1:17
which you will do **w** to pay attention as 2 Pt 1:19
that all may go **w** with you and that 3 Jn 1:2
good health, as it goes **w** with your soul. 3 Jn 1:2
You will do **w** to send them on their 3 Jn 1:6

WELL'S (3)
The stone on the **w** mouth was large, Gn 29:2
stone from the **w** mouth and watered Gn 29:10
covering over the **w** mouth and 2 Sm 17:19

WELL-AGED (1)
a feast of rich food, a feast of **w** wine, Is 25:6

WELL-BEING (2)
His soul shall abide in **w**, and his Ps 25:13
darkness, I make **w** and create calamity, Is 45:7

WELL-DOING (1)
who by patience in **w** seek for glory and Rom 2:7

WELL-FED (2)
offerings of rams and the fat of **w** beasts; Is 1:11
They were **w**, lusty stallions, each Jer 5:8

WELL-FORTIFIED (1)
throw up siegeworks and take a **w** city. Dn 11:15

WELL-KNOWN (1)
chosen from the assembly, **w** men. Nm 16:2

WELL-OFF (1)
your household, since he is **w** with you, Dt 15:16

WELL-PLEASING (1)
they are to be **w**, not argumentative, Ti 2:9

WELL-SET (1)
a rope; and instead of **w** hair, baldness; Is 3:24

WELLING (1)
a spring of water **w** up to eternal life." Jn 4:14

WELLS (5)
with earth all the **w** that his father's Gn 26:15
Isaac dug again the **w** of water that had Gn 26:18
I dug **w** and drank foreign waters, 2 Kgs 19:24
will draw water from the **w** of salvation. Is 12:3
I dug **w** and drank waters, to dry up with Is 37:25

WENT (1314)
Then Cain **w** away from the presence of Gn 4:16
his sons' wives with him **w** into the ark to Gn 7:7
and female, **w** into the ark with Noah, Gn 7:9
They **w** into the ark with Noah, two and Gn 7:15
flesh, **w** in as God had commanded him. Gn 7:16
It **w** to and fro until the waters were dried Gn 8:7
So Noah **w** out, and his sons and his Gn 8:18
earth, **w** out by families from the ark. Gn 8:19
sons of Noah who **w** forth from the ark Gn 9:18
From that land he **w** into Assyria and Gn 10:11
and they **w** forth together from Ur of Gn 11:31
So Abram **w**, as the LORD had told him, Gn 12:4
LORD had told him, and Lot **w** with him. Gn 12:4
So Abram **w** down to Egypt to sojourn Gn 12:10
So Abram **w** up from Egypt, he and his Gn 13:1
And Lot, who **w** with Abram, also had Gn 13:5
the king of Bela (that is, Zoar) **w** out, Gn 14:8
all their provisions, and **w** their way. Gn 14:11
and his possessions, and **w** their way. Gn 14:12
them, and **w** in pursuit as far as Dan. Gn 14:14
the king of Sodom **w** out to meet him Gn 14:17
the share of the men who **w** with me. Gn 14:24
And he **w** in to Hagar, and she Gn 16:4
with him, God **w** up from Abraham. Gn 17:22
And Abraham **w** quickly into the tent Gn 18:6
And Abraham **w** with them to set Gn 18:16
from there and **w** toward Sodom, Gn 18:22
And the LORD **w** his way, when he had Gn 18:33
Lot **w** out to the men at the entrance, Gn 19:6
So Lot **w** out and said to his Gn 19:14
And Abraham **w** early in the morning Gn 19:27
smoke of the land **w** up like the smoke Gn 19:28
Now Lot **w** up out of Zoar and lived in Gn 19:30
And the firstborn **w** in and lay with Gn 19:33
Then she **w** and sat down opposite him Gn 21:16
And she **w** and filled the skin with Gn 21:19
offering and arose and **w** to the place of Gn 22:3
knife. So they **w** both of them together. Gn 22:6
my son." So they **w** both of them Gn 22:8
And Abraham **w** and took the ram Gn 22:13
they arose and **w** together to Beersheba. Gn 22:19
and Abraham **w** in to mourn for Sarah Gn 23:2
of all who **w** in at the gate of his city, Gn 23:10
before all who **w** in at the gate of his Gn 23:18
and he arose and **w** to Mesopotamia to Gn 24:10
She **w** down to the spring and filled her Gn 24:16
the man spoke to me," he **w** to the man. Gn 24:30
and she **w** down to the spring and drew Gn 24:45
servant took Rebekah and **w** his way. Gn 24:61
And Isaac **w** out to meditate in the field Gn 24:63
to me?" So she **w** to inquire of the Gn 25:22
ate and drank and rose and **w** his way. Gn 25:34
And Isaac **w** to Gerar to Abimelech Gn 26:1
From there he **w** up to Beersheba. Gn 26:23
When Abimelech **w** to him from Gn 26:26
So when Esau **w** to the field to hunt for Gn 27:5
So he **w** and took them and brought Gn 27:14
So he **w** in to his father and said, "My Gn 27:18
So Jacob **w** near to Isaac his father, Gn 27:22
Jacob away. And he **w** to Paddan-aram, Gn 28:5
Esau **w** to Ishmael and took as his wife, Gn 28:9
left Beersheba and **w** toward Haran. Gn 28:10
Then Jacob **w** on his journey and came Gn 29:1
her to Jacob, and he **w** in to her. Gn 29:23
So Jacob **w** in to Rachel also, and he Gn 29:30
Bilhah as a wife, and Jacob **w** in to her. Gn 30:4
wheat harvest Reuben **w** and found Gn 30:14
Leah **w** out to meet him and said, Gn 30:16
So Laban **w** into Jacob's tent and into Gn 31:33
And he **w** out of Leah's tent and entered Gn 31:33
Jacob **w** on his way, and the angels of Gn 32:1
He himself **w** on before them, bowing Gn 33:3
w out to see the women of the land. Gn 34:1
the father of Shechem **w** out to Jacob to Gn 34:6
And all who **w** out of the gate of his Gn 34:24
all who **w** out of the gate of his city. Gn 34:24
out of Shechem's house and **w** away. Gn 34:26
Then God **w** up from him in the place Gn 35:13
from Ephrath, Rachel **w** into labor, Gn 35:16
Reuben **w** and lay with Bilhah his Gn 35:22
He **w** into a land away from his brother Gn 36:6
Now his brothers **w** to pasture their Gn 37:12
Dothan.'" So Joseph **w** after his Gn 37:17
that time that Judah **w** down from his Gn 38:1
was Shua. He took her and **w** in to her, Gn 38:2
So whenever he **w** in to his brother's Gn 38:9
So Tamar **w** and remained in her Gn 38:11
he **w** up to Timnah to his Gn 38:12
So he gave them to her and **w** in to her, Gn 38:18
Then she arose and **w** away, and Gn 38:19
when he **w** into the house to do his Gn 39:11
So Joseph **w** out over the land of Egypt. Gn 41:45
And Joseph **w** out from the presence of Gn 41:46
of Pharaoh and **w** through all the Gn 41:46
ten of Joseph's brothers **w** down to buy Gn 42:3
They arose and **w** down to Egypt and Gn 43:15
So they **w** up to the steward of Joseph's Gn 43:19
Then Judah **w** up to him and said, "O Gn 44:18
"When we **w** back to your servant my Gn 44:24
So they **w** up out of Egypt and came to Gn 45:25
prepared his chariot and **w** up to meet Gn 46:29
So Joseph **w** in and told Pharaoh, "My Gn 47:1
blessed Pharaoh and **w** out from the Gn 47:10
because you **w** up to your father's bed; Gn 49:4
you defiled it—he **w** up to my couch! Gn 49:4
So Joseph **w** up to bury his father. With Gn 50:7
With him **w** up all the servants of Gn 50:7
And there **w** up with him both chariots Gn 50:9
from the house of Levi **w** and took as his Ex 2:1
"Go." So the girl **w** and called the child's Ex 2:8
he **w** out to his people and looked on Ex 2:11
When he **w** out the next day, behold, two Ex 2:13
Moses **w** back to Jethro his father-in-law Ex 4:18
donkey, and **w** back to the land of Egypt. Ex 4:20
to meet Moses." So he **w** and met him at Ex 4:27
Moses and Aaron **w** and gathered Ex 4:29
Afterward Moses and Aaron **w** and said to Ex 5:1
foremen of the people **w** out and said to Ex 5:10
So Moses and Aaron **w** to Pharaoh and Ex 7:10

Pharaoh turned and **w** into his house, Ex 7:23
Moses and Aaron **w** out from Pharaoh, Ex 8:12
So Moses **w** out from Pharaoh and Ex 8:30
So Moses **w** out of the city from Pharaoh Ex 9:33
So Moses and Aaron **w** in to Pharaoh Ex 10:3
he turned and **w** out from Pharaoh. Ex 10:6
So he **w** out from Pharaoh and pleaded Ex 10:18
go out." And he **w** out from Pharaoh in Ex 11:8
Then the people of Israel **w** and did so; Ex 12:28
mixed multitude also **w** up with them, Ex 12:38
hosts of the LORD **w** out from the land Ex 12:41
And the people of Israel **w** up out of the Ex 13:18
And the LORD **w** before them by day in a Ex 13:21
of Israel moved and **w** behind them, Ex 14:19
the people of Israel **w** into the midst of Ex 14:22
Egyptians pursued and **w** in after them Ex 14:23
they **w** down into the depths like a stone. Ex 15:5
and his horsemen **w** into the sea, Ex 15:19
and all the women **w** out after her with Ex 15:20
and they **w** into the wilderness of Shur. Ex 15:22
They **w** three days in the wilderness Ex 15:22
day some of the people **w** out to gather, Ex 16:27
and Hur **w** up to the top of the hill. Ex 17:10
Moses **w** out to meet his father-in-law Ex 18:7
other of their welfare and **w** into the tent. Ex 18:7
and he **w** away to his own country. Ex 18:27
while Moses **w** up to God. The LORD Ex 19:3
So Moses **w** down from the mountain Ex 19:14
The smoke of it **w** up like the smoke of Ex 19:18
top of the mountain, and Moses **w** up. Ex 19:20
So Moses **w** down to the people and told Ex 19:25
and seventy of the elders of Israel **w** up, Ex 24:9
and Moses **w** up into the mountain of Ex 24:13
Then Moses **w** up on the mountain, Ex 24:15
entered the cloud and **w** up on the Ex 24:18
Moses turned and **w** down from the Ex 32:15
Whenever Moses **w** out to the tent, all Ex 33:8
in the morning and **w** up on Mount Ex 34:4
Whenever Moses **w** in before the LORD Ex 34:34
again, until he **w** in to speak with him. Ex 34:35
When they **w** into the tent of meeting, Ex 40:32
And Moses and Aaron **w** into the tent of Lv 9:23
put on when he **w** into the Holy Place Lv 16:23
w out among the people of Israel. Lv 24:10
And when Moses **w** into the tent of Nm 7:89
after that the Levites **w** in to do their Nm 8:22
of the LORD **w** before them three Nm 10:33
The people **w** about and gathered it and Nm 11:8
So Moses **w** out and told the people the Nm 11:24
So they **w** up and spied out the land Nm 13:21
They **w** up into the Negeb and came Nm 13:22
bring into the land into which he **w**, Nm 14:24
Of those men who **w** to spy out the Nm 14:38
in the morning and **w** up to the Nm 14:40
Moses rose and **w** to Dathan and Nm 16:25
belonged to them **w** down alive into Nm 16:33
the next day Moses **w** into the tent of Nm 17:8
Moses and Aaron **w** from the presence Nm 20:6
how our fathers **w** down to Egypt, and Nm 20:15
And they **w** up Mount Hor in the sight Nm 20:27
the wilderness they **w** on to Mattanah, Nm 21:18
people together and **w** out against Nm 21:23
Then they turned and **w** up by the Nm 21:33
of Moab rose and **w** to Balak and said, Nm 22:14
his donkey and **w** with the princes Nm 22:21
anger was kindled because he **w**, Nm 22:22
out of the road and **w** into the field. Nm 22:23
angel of the LORD **w** ahead and stood Nm 22:26
tell you." So Balaam **w** on with the Nm 22:35
he **w** out to meet him at the city of Nm 22:36
Then Balaam **w** with Balak, and they Nm 22:39
tell you." And he **w** to a bare height, Nm 23:3
Then Balaam rose and **w** back to his Nm 24:25
his place. And Balak also **w** his way. Nm 24:25
and **w** after the man of Israel into the Nm 25:8
of the congregation **w** to meet them Nm 31:13
the warriors who **w** out to battle Nm 31:27
the men of war who **w** out to battle, Nm 31:28
For when they **w** up to the Valley of Nm 32:9
the son of Manasseh **w** to Gilead and Nm 32:39
son of Manasseh **w** and captured their Nm 32:41
And Nobah **w** and captured Kenath Nm 32:42
when they **w** out of the land of Egypt by Nm 33:1
people of Israel **w** out triumphantly in Nm 33:3
and they **w** a three days' journey in the Nm 33:8
And Aaron the priest **w** up Mount Hor Nm 33:38
out from Horeb and **w** through all that Dt 1:19
And they turned and **w** up into the hill Dt 1:24
all the way that you **w** until you came to Dt 1:31
who **w** before you in the way to seek you Dt 1:33
LORD and presumptuously **w** up into the Dt 1:43
So we **w** on, away from our brothers, the Dt 2:8
"And we turned and **w** in the direction of Dt 2:8
Zered.' So we **w** over the brook Zered. Dt 2:13
"Then we turned and **w** up the way to Dt 3:1
When I **w** up the mountain to receive the Dt 9:9
and **w** up the mountain with the two Dt 10:3
Your fathers **w** down to Egypt seventy Dt 10:22
And he **w** down into Egypt and Dt 26:5
and **w** and served other gods and Dt 29:26
Moses and Joshua **w** and presented Dt 31:14
Then Moses **w** up from the plains of Dt 34:1
Jericho." And they **w** and came into Jos 2:1
about to be closed at dark, the men **w** out. Jos 2:5
went out. I do not know where the men **w**. Jos 2:5
They departed and **w** into the hills and Jos 2:22
days the officers **w** through the camp Jos 3:2
of the covenant and **w** before the people. Jos 3:6
And Joshua **w** to him and said to him, Jos 5:13
of the people of Israel. None **w** out, Jos 6:1
of rams' horns before the LORD **w** forward, Jos 6:8
flat, so that the people **w** up into the city, Jos 6:20
who had been spies **w** in and brought Jos 6:23
land." And the men **w** up and spied out Jos 7:2
So about 3,000 men **w** up there from the Jos 7:4
And they **w** to the place of ambush and Jos 8:9
and mustered the people and **w** up, Jos 8:10
who were with him **w** up and drew near Jos 8:11
hurried and **w** out early to the appointed Jos 8:14
the smoke of the city **w** up to heaven, Jos 8:20
city, and that the smoke of the city **w** up, Jos 8:21
with cunning and **w** and made ready Jos 9:4
And they **w** to Joshua in the camp at Jos 9:6
gathered their forces and **w** up with all Jos 10:5
So Joshua **w** up from Gilgal, he and all Jos 10:7
all Israel with him **w** up from Eglon to Jos 10:36
But my brothers who **w** up with me Jos 14:8
And he **w** up from there against the Jos 15:15
the people of Joseph **w** from the Jordan Jos 16:1
Then the boundary **w** down to the Jos 17:9
So the men arose and **w**, and Joshua Jos 18:8
Joshua charged those who **w** to write the Jos 18:8
So the men **w** and passed up and down Jos 18:9
the people of Dan **w** up and fought Jos 19:47
which **w** to the descendants of Aaron, Jos 21:10
them away, and they **w** to their tents. Jos 22:6
Jacob and his children **w** down to Egypt. Jos 24:4
And you **w** over the Jordan and came to Jos 24:11
preserved us in all the way that we **w**, Jos 24:17
allotted to you." So Simeon **w** with him. Jgs 1:3
Then Judah **w** up and the LORD gave the Jgs 1:4
the men of Judah **w** down to fight against Jgs 1:9
And Judah **w** against the Canaanites Jgs 1:10
From there they **w** against the Jgs 1:11
w up with the people of Judah from the Jgs 1:16
and they **w** and settled with the people. Jgs 1:16
And Judah **w** with Simeon his brother, Jgs 1:17
house of Joseph also **w** up against Bethel, Jgs 1:22
And the man **w** to the land of the Hittites Jgs 1:26
the angel of the LORD **w** up from Gilgal to Jgs 2:1
the people of Israel **w** each to his Jgs 2:6
They **w** after other gods, from among Jgs 2:12
He **w** out to war, and the LORD gave Jgs 3:10
Amalekites, and **w** and defeated Israel. Jgs 3:13
And all his attendants **w** out from his Jgs 3:19
And the hilt also **w** in after the blade, Jgs 3:22
Then Ehud **w** out into the porch and Jgs 3:23
the people of Israel **w** down with him Jgs 3:27
your hand." So they **w** down after him Jgs 3:28
Then Deborah arose and **w** with Barak to Jgs 4:9
And 10,000 men **w** up at his heels, and Jgs 4:10
his heels, and Deborah **w** up with him. Jgs 4:10
you?" So Barak **w** down from Mount Jgs 4:14
Then she **w** softly to him and drove the Jgs 4:21
his temple until it **w** down into the Jgs 4:21
Jael **w** out to meet him and said to him, Jgs 4:22
you are seeking." So he **w** in to her tent, Jgs 4:22
"LORD, when you **w** out from Seir, when Jgs 5:4
So Gideon **w** into his house and prepared Jgs 6:19
Naphtali, and they **w** up to meet them. Jgs 6:35
the camp." Then he **w** down with Purah Jgs 7:11
call us when you **w** to fight with Jgs 8:1
And from there he **w** up to Penuel, and Jgs 8:8
And Gideon **w** up by the way of the tent Jgs 8:11
the son of Joash **w** and lived in his Jgs 8:29
the son of Jerubbaal **w** to Shechem to his Jgs 9:1
And he **w** to his father's house at Ophrah Jgs 9:5
and they **w** and made Abimelech king, Jgs 9:6
he **w** and stood on top of Mount Gerizim Jgs 9:7
The trees once **w** out to anoint a king Jgs 9:8
away and fled and **w** to Beer and lived Jgs 9:21
And they **w** out into the field and Jgs 9:27
and they **w** into the house of their god Jgs 9:27
Gaal the son of Ebed **w** out and stood in Jgs 9:35
And Gaal **w** out at the head of the leaders Jgs 9:39
day, the people **w** out into the field, Jgs 9:42
And Abimelech **w** up to Mount Zalmon, Jgs 9:48
Then Abimelech **w** to Thebez and Jgs 9:50
in, and they **w** up to the roof of the tower. Jgs 9:51
around Jephthah and **w** out with him. Jgs 11:3
the elders of Gilead **w** to bring Jephthah Jgs 11:5
So Jephthah **w** with the elders of Gilead, Jgs 11:11
Israel **w** through the wilderness to the Jgs 11:16
the wilderness and **w** around the land Jgs 11:18
the daughters of Israel **w** year by year Jgs 11:40
And Manoah arose and **w** after his wife Jgs 13:11
when the flame **w** up toward heaven Jgs 13:20
the angel of the LORD **w** up in the flame Jgs 13:20
Samson **w** down to Timnah, and at Jgs 14:1
Then Samson **w** down with his father Jgs 14:5
Then he **w** down and talked with the Jgs 14:7
scraped it out into his hands and **w** on, Jgs 14:9
his hands and went on, eating as he **w**. Jgs 14:9
His father **w** down to the woman, and Jgs 14:10
the seventh day before the sun **w** down, Jgs 14:18
and he **w** down to Ashkelon and struck Jgs 14:19
In hot anger he **w** back to his father's Jgs 14:19
Samson **w** to visit his wife with a young Jgs 15:1
So Samson **w** and caught 300 foxes and Jgs 15:4
and he **w** down and stayed in the cleft of Jgs 15:8
3,000 men of Judah **w** down to the cleft Jgs 15:11
Samson **w** to Gaza, and there he saw a Jgs 16:1
he saw a prostitute, and he **w** in to her. Jgs 16:1
and your living." And the Levite **w** in. Jgs 17:10
and **w** up and encamped at Jgs 18:12
scout out the land **w** up and entered Jgs 18:17
And when these **w** into Micah's house Jgs 18:18
the carved image and **w** along with the Jgs 18:20
Then the people of Dan **w** their way. Jgs 18:26
he turned and **w** back to his home. Jgs 18:26
and she **w** away from him to her father's Jgs 19:2
her husband arose and **w** after her, Jgs 19:3
So they passed on and **w** their way. And Jgs 19:14
And the sun **w** down on them near Jgs 19:14
And he **w** in and sat down in the open Jgs 19:15
I **w** to Bethlehem in Judah, and I am Jgs 19:18
house, **w** out to them and said to them, Jgs 19:23
doors of the house and **w** out to go on Jgs 19:27
man rose up and **w** away to his home. Jgs 19:28
of Israel arose and **w** up to Bethel and Jgs 20:18
the men of Israel **w** out to fight against Jgs 20:20
the people of Israel **w** up and wept Jgs 20:23
And Benjamin **w** against them out of Jgs 20:25
w up and came to Bethel and wept. Jgs 20:26
the people of Israel **w** up against the Jgs 20:30
people of Benjamin **w** out against the Jgs 20:31
the whole of the city **w** up in smoke to Jgs 20:40
Then they **w** and returned to their Jgs 21:23
and they **w** out from there every man to Jgs 21:24
of Bethlehem in Judah **w** to sojourn in the Ru 1:1
They **w** into the country of Moab and Ru 1:2
and they **w** on the way to return to the Ru 1:7
So the two of them **w** on until they came Ru 1:19
I **w** away full, and the LORD has brought Ru 1:21
So she set out and **w** and gleaned in the Ru 2:3
And she took it up and **w** into the city. Ru 2:18
So she **w** down to the threshing floor and Ru 3:6
he **w** to lie down at the end of the heap of Ru 3:7
put it on her. Then she **w** into the city. Ru 3:15
And he **w** in to her, and the LORD gave Ru 4:13
So it **w** on year by year. As often as she 1 Sm 1:7
As often as she **w** up to the house of the 1 Sm 1:7
Then the woman **w** her way and 1 Sm 1:18
then they **w** back to their house at 1 Sm 1:19
and all his house **w** up to offer to 1 Sm 1:21
Then Elkanah **w** home to Ramah. 1 Sm 2:11
each year when she **w** up with her 1 Sm 2:19
lie down again." So he **w** and lay down. 1 Sm 3:5
and Samuel arose and **w** to Eli and 1 Sm 3:6
And he arose and **w** to Eli and said, 1 Sm 3:8
hears.'" So Samuel **w** and lay down 1 Sm 3:9
Now Israel **w** out to battle against the 1 Sm 4:1
and the cry of the city **w** up to heaven. 1 Sm 5:12
And the cows **w** straight in the 1 Sm 6:12
along one highway, lowing as they **w**. 1 Sm 6:12
lords of the Philistines **w** after them as 1 Sm 6:12
of the Philistines **w** up against Israel. 1 Sm 7:7
the men of Israel **w** out from Mizpah 1 Sm 7:11
And he **w** on a circuit year by year to 1 Sm 7:16
Israel, when a man **w** to inquire of God, 1 Sm 9:9
let us go." So they **w** to the city where 1 Sm 9:10
As they **w** up the hill to the city, they 1 Sm 9:11
So they **w** up to the city. As they were 1 Sm 9:14
both he and Samuel **w** out into the 1 Sm 9:26
'The donkeys that you **w** to seek are 1 Sm 10:2
not to be found, we **w** to Samuel." 1 Sm 10:14
Saul also **w** to his home at Gibeah, 1 Sm 10:26
and with him **w** men of valor whose 1 Sm 10:26
Nahash the Ammonite **w** up and 1 Sm 11:1
So all the people **w** to Gilgal, and 1 Sm 11:15
When Jacob **w** into Egypt, and the 1 Sm 12:8
And Saul **w** out to meet him and 1 Sm 13:10
Samuel arose and **w** up from Gilgal. 1 Sm 13:15
rest of the people **w** up after Saul to 1 Sm 13:15
they **w** up from Gilgal to Gibeah of 1 Sm 13:15

one of the Israelites **w** down to the 1 Sm 13:20
of the Philistines **w** out to the 1 Sm 13:23
the ark of God **w** at that time with 1 Sm 14:18
him rallied and **w** into the battle. 1 Sm 14:20
Then Saul **w** up from pursuing the 1 Sm 14:46
and the Philistines **w** to their own 1 Sm 14:46
passed on and **w** down to Gilgal." 1 Sm 15:12
Then Samuel **w** to Ramah, and Saul 1 Sm 15:34
and Saul **w** up to his house in 1 Sm 15:34
Samuel rose up and **w** to Ramah. 1 Sm 16:13
And his shield-bearer **w** before him. 1 Sm 17:7
his three sons who **w** to the battle 1 Sm 17:13
but David **w** back and forth from 1 Sm 17:15
and took the provisions and **w**, 1 Sm 17:20
to the ranks and **w** and greeted his 1 Sm 17:22
I **w** after him and struck him and 1 Sm 17:35
And David **w** out and was successful 1 Sm 18:5
And he **w** out and came in before the 1 Sm 18:13
for he **w** out and came in before 1 Sm 18:16
David arose and **w**, along with his 1 Sm 18:27
And David **w** out and fought with the 1 Sm 19:8
And he and Samuel **w** and lived at 1 Sm 19:18
Then he himself **w** to Ramah and 1 Sm 19:22
And he **w** there to Naioth in Ramah. 1 Sm 19:23
and as he **w** he prophesied until he 1 Sm 19:23
field." So they both **w** out into the 1 Sm 20:11
the morning Jonathan **w** out into the 1 Sm 20:35
and Jonathan **w** into the city. 1 Sm 20:42
day from Saul and **w** to Achish the 1 Sm 21:10
heard it, they **w** down there to him. 1 Sm 22:1
And David **w** from there to Mizpeh of 1 Sm 22:3
David departed and **w** into the forest 1 Sm 22:5
David and his men **w** to Keilah and 1 Sm 23:5
and they **w** wherever they could go. 1 Sm 23:13
son, rose and **w** to David at Horesh, 1 Sm 23:16
at Horesh, and Jonathan **w** home. 1 Sm 23:18
Then the Ziphites **w** up to Saul at 1 Sm 23:19
And they arose and **w** to Ziph ahead 1 Sm 23:24
Saul and his men **w** to seek him. 1 Sm 23:25
so he **w** down to the rock and lived in 1 Sm 23:25
Saul **w** on one side of the mountain, 1 Sm 23:26
after David and **w** against the 1 Sm 23:28
And David **w** up from there and lived 1 Sm 23:29
of all Israel and **w** to seek David and 1 Sm 24:2
cave, and Saul **w** in to relieve himself. 1 Sm 24:3
up and left the cave and **w** on his way. 1 Sm 24:7
David also arose and **w** out of the 1 Sm 24:8
Then Saul **w** home, but David and 1 Sm 24:22
David and his men **w** up to the 1 Sm 24:22
Then David rose and **w** down to the 1 Sm 25:1
four hundred men **w** up after David, 1 Sm 25:13
the fields, as long as we **w** with them. 1 Sm 25:15
So Saul arose and **w** down to the 1 Sm 26:2
So David and Abishai **w** to the army 1 Sm 26:7
from Saul's head, and they **w** away. 1 Sm 26:12
Then David **w** over to the other side 1 Sm 26:13
in them." So David **w** his way, 1 Sm 26:25
So David arose and **w** over, he and the 1 Sm 27:2
David and his men **w** up and made 1 Sm 27:8
and put on other garments and **w**, 1 Sm 28:8
they rose and **w** away that night. 1 Sm 28:25
But the Philistines **w** up to Jezreel. 1 Sm 29:11
but carried them off and **w** their way. 1 Sm 30:2
And they **w** out to meet David and to 1 Sm 30:21
men arose and **w** all night and 1 Sm 31:12
So David **w** up there, and his two wives 2 Sm 2:2
w out from Mahanaim to Gibeon. 2 Sm 2:12
the servants of David **w** out and met 2 Sm 2:13
Asahel pursued Abner, and as he **w**, 2 Sm 2:19
Abner and his men **w** all that night 2 Sm 2:29
But her husband **w** with her, weeping 2 Sm 3:16
And then Abner **w** to tell David at 2 Sm 3:19
sent Abner away, and he **w** in peace. 2 Sm 3:21
Then Joab **w** to the king and said, 2 Sm 3:24
took his head and **w** by the way of 2 Sm 4:7
and his men **w** to Jerusalem against 2 Sm 5:6
all the Philistines **w** up to search for 2 Sm 5:17
heard of it and **w** down to the 2 Sm 5:17
And David arose and **w** with all the 2 Sm 6:2
ark of God, and Ahio **w** before the ark. 2 Sm 6:4
of God." So David **w** and brought up 2 Sm 6:12
with you wherever you **w** and have cut 2 Sm 7:9
Then King David **w** in and sat before 2 Sm 7:18
on earth whom God **w** to redeem to be 2 Sm 7:23
as he **w** to restore his power at the river 2 Sm 8:3
gave victory to David wherever he **w**. 2 Sm 8:6
gave victory to David wherever he **w**. 2 Sm 8:14
your feet." And Uriah **w** out of the 2 Sm 11:8
And in the evening he **w** out to lie on 2 Sm 11:13
So the messenger **w** and came and 2 Sm 11:22
Then Nathan **w** to his house. And 2 Sm 12:15
And David fasted and **w** in and lay 2 Sm 12:16
And he **w** into the house of the LORD 2 Sm 12:20
He then **w** to his own house. 2 Sm 12:20
and **w** in to her and lay with her, 2 Sm 12:24

people together and **w** to Rabbah and 2 Sm 12:29
So Tamar **w** to her brother Amnon's 2 Sm 13:8
me." So everyone **w** out from him. 2 Sm 13:9
her hand on her head and **w** away, 2 Sm 13:19
went away, crying aloud as she **w**. 2 Sm 13:19
Absalom fled and **w** to Talmai the 2 Sm 13:37
So Absalom fled and **w** to Geshur, 2 Sm 13:38
the king's heart **w** out to Absalom. 2 Sm 14:1
So Joab arose and **w** to Geshur and 2 Sm 14:23
Joab arose and **w** to Absalom at 2 Sm 14:31
Then Joab **w** to the king and told 2 Sm 14:33
peace." So he arose and **w** to Hebron. 2 Sm 15:9
With Absalom **w** two hundred men 2 Sm 15:11
and they **w** in their innocence and 2 Sm 15:11
So the king **w** out, and all his 2 Sm 15:16
And the king **w** out, and all the 2 Sm 15:17
But David **w** up the ascent of the 2 Sm 15:30
Mount of Olives, weeping as he **w**, 2 Sm 15:30
covered their heads, and they **w** up, 2 Sm 15:30
and they went up, weeping as they **w**. 2 Sm 15:30
So David and his men **w** on the road, 2 Sm 16:13
while Shimei **w** along on the hillside 2 Sm 16:13
and cursed as he **w** and threw stones 2 Sm 16:13
And Absalom **w** in to his father's 2 Sm 16:22
So both of them **w** away quickly and 2 Sm 17:18
courtyard. And they **w** down into it. 2 Sm 17:18
the well, and **w** and told King David. 2 Sm 17:21
his donkey and **w** off home to 2 Sm 17:23
So the army **w** out into the field 2 Sm 18:6
and the mule **w** under the thick 2 Sm 18:9
the mule that was under him **w** on. 2 Sm 18:9
and the watchman **w** up to the roof 2 Sm 18:24
was deeply moved and **w** up to the 2 Sm 18:33
And as he **w**, he said, "O my son 2 Sm 18:33
and he **w** on with the king to the 2 Sm 19:31
all the people **w** over the Jordan, 2 Sm 19:39
over the Jordan, and the king **w** over. 2 Sm 19:39
The king **w** on to Gilgal, and 2 Sm 19:40
and Chimham **w** on with him. 2 Sm 19:40
So Amasa **w** to summon Judah, but 2 Sm 20:5
And there **w** out after him Joab's men 2 Sm 20:7
They **w** out from Jerusalem to pursue 2 Sm 20:7
thigh, and as he **w** forward it fell out. 2 Sm 20:8
all the people **w** on after Joab to 2 Sm 20:13
Then the woman **w** to all the people 2 Sm 20:22
David **w** and took the bones of Saul 2 Sm 21:12
and David **w** down together with his 2 Sm 21:15
Smoke **w** up from his nostrils, and 2 Sm 22:9
thirty chief men **w** down and came 2 Sm 23:13
blood of the men who **w** at the risk of 2 Sm 23:17
He also **w** down and struck down a 2 Sm 23:20
but Benaiah **w** down to him with a 2 Sm 23:21
of the army **w** out from the 2 Sm 24:4
from Dan they **w** around to Sidon, 2 Sm 24:6
and they **w** out to the Negeb of Judah 2 Sm 24:7
So David **w** up at Gad's word, as the 2 Sm 24:19
And Araunah **w** out and paid 2 Sm 24:20
So Bathsheba **w** to the king in his 1 Kgs 1:15
and the Pelethites **w** down and had 1 Kgs 1:38
And all the people **w** up after him, 1 Kgs 1:40
and rose, and each **w** his own way. 1 Kgs 1:49
So he arose and **w** and took hold of 1 Kgs 1:50
on the day when I **w** to Mahanaim. 1 Kgs 2:8
So Bathsheba **w** to King Solomon to 1 Kgs 2:19
the son of Jehoiada **w** up and struck 1 Kgs 2:34
saddled a donkey and **w** to Gath to 1 Kgs 2:40
Shimei **w** and brought his servants 1 Kgs 2:40
and he **w** out and struck him down, 1 Kgs 2:46
And the king **w** to Gibeon to sacrifice 1 Kgs 3:4
and one **w** up by stairs to the middle 1 Kgs 6:8
blessed the king and **w** to their homes 1 Kgs 8:66
But Pharaoh's daughter **w** up from 1 Kgs 9:24
And they **w** to Ophir and brought 1 Kgs 9:28
So she turned and **w** back to her 1 Kgs 10:13
shekels of gold **w** into each shield. 1 Kgs 10:16
minas of gold **w** into each shield. 1 Kgs 10:17
For Solomon **w** after Ashtoreth the 1 Kgs 11:5
of the army **w** up to bury 1 Kgs 11:15
And they **w** to Damascus and lived 1 Kgs 11:24
when Jeroboam **w** out of Jerusalem, 1 Kgs 11:29
Rehoboam **w** to Shechem, for all 1 Kgs 12:1
again to me." So the people **w** away. 1 Kgs 12:5
David." So Israel **w** to their tents. 1 Kgs 12:16
word of the LORD and **w** home again, 1 Kgs 12:24
And he **w** out from there and built 1 Kgs 12:25
for the people **w** as far as Dan to be 1 Kgs 12:30
He **w** up to the altar that he had 1 Kgs 12:33
people of Israel and **w** up to the altar 1 Kgs 12:33
So he **w** another way and did not 1 Kgs 13:10
And he **w** after the man of God and 1 Kgs 13:14
So he **w** back with him and ate 1 Kgs 13:19
And as he **w** away a lion met him on 1 Kgs 13:24
And he **w** and found his body 1 Kgs 13:28
She arose and **w** to Shiloh and came 1 Kgs 14:4
often as the king **w** into the house of 1 Kgs 14:28

king of Israel **w** up against Judah 1 Kgs 15:17
So Omri **w** up from Gibbethon, and 1 Kgs 16:17
he **w** into the citadel of the king's 1 Kgs 16:18
and **w** and served Baal and 1 Kgs 16:31
So he **w** and did according to the 1 Kgs 17:5
He **w** and lived by the brook Cherith 1 Kgs 17:5
So he arose and **w** to Zarephath. And 1 Kgs 17:10
And she **w** and did as Elijah said. 1 Kgs 17:15
So Elijah **w** to show himself to Ahab. 1 Kgs 18:2
Ahab **w** in one direction by himself, 1 Kgs 18:6
and Obadiah **w** in another direction 1 Kgs 18:6
So Obadiah **w** to meet Ahab, and 1 Kgs 18:16
him. And Ahab **w** to meet Elijah. 1 Kgs 18:16
So Ahab **w** up to eat and to drink. 1 Kgs 18:42
And Elijah **w** up to the top of Mount 1 Kgs 18:42
the sea." And he **w** up and looked 1 Kgs 18:43
And Ahab rode and **w** to Jezreel. 1 Kgs 18:45
But he himself **w** a day's journey into 1 Kgs 19:4
and **w** in the strength of that food 1 Kgs 19:8
in his cloak and **w** out and stood at 1 Kgs 19:13
he arose and **w** after Elijah and 1 Kgs 19:21
And he **w** up and closed in on 1 Kgs 20:1
And they **w** out at noon, while 1 Kgs 20:16
governors of the districts **w** out first. 1 Kgs 20:17
So these **w** out of the city, the 1 Kgs 20:19
the king of Israel **w** out and struck 1 Kgs 20:21
the Syrians and **w** up to Aphek 1 Kgs 20:26
provisioned and **w** against them. 1 Kgs 20:27
on their heads and **w** to the king of 1 Kgs 20:32
"Your servant **w** out into the midst 1 Kgs 20:39
the king of Israel **w** to his house 1 Kgs 20:43
And Ahab **w** into his house vexed 1 Kgs 21:4
sackcloth and **w** about dejectedly. 1 Kgs 21:27
the messenger who **w** to summon 1 Kgs 22:13
king of Judah **w** up to Ramoth-gilead. 1 Kgs 22:29
disguised himself and **w** into battle. 1 Kgs 22:30
sunset a cry **w** through the army, 1 Kgs 22:36
but you shall surely die.'" So Elijah **w**. 2 Kgs 1:4
He **w** up to Elijah, who was sitting on 2 Kgs 1:9
third captain of fifty **w** up and came 2 Kgs 1:13
So he arose and **w** down with him to 2 Kgs 1:15
leave you." So they **w** down to Bethel. 2 Kgs 2:2
leave you." So the two of them **w** on. 2 Kgs 2:6
of the prophets also **w** and stood at 2 Kgs 2:7
And as they still **w** on and talked, 2 Kgs 2:11
And Elijah **w** up by a whirlwind into 2 Kgs 2:11
from him and **w** back and stood 2 Kgs 2:13
and to the other, and Elisha **w** over. 2 Kgs 2:14
Then he **w** to the spring of water and 2 Kgs 2:21
He **w** up from there to Bethel, and 2 Kgs 2:23
From there he **w** on to Mount 2 Kgs 2:25
And he **w** and sent word to 2 Kgs 3:7
So the king of Israel **w** with the king of 2 Kgs 3:9
and the king of Edom **w** down to him. 2 Kgs 3:12
And they **w** forward, striking the 2 Kgs 3:24
striking the Moabites as they **w**. 2 Kgs 3:24
So she **w** from him and shut the door 2 Kgs 4:5
One day Elisha **w** on to Shunem, 2 Kgs 4:8
he **w** out one day to his father among 2 Kgs 4:18
And she **w** up and laid him on the 2 Kgs 4:21
shut the door behind him and **w** out. 2 Kgs 4:21
Gehazi **w** on ahead and laid the staff 2 Kgs 4:31
So he **w** in and shut the door behind 2 Kgs 4:33
Then he **w** up and lay on the child, 2 Kgs 4:34
and **w** up and stretched himself upon 2 Kgs 4:35
she picked up her son and **w** out. 2 Kgs 4:37
One of them **w** out into the field to 2 Kgs 4:39
So Naaman **w** in and told his lord, 2 Kgs 5:4
a letter to the king of Israel." So he **w**, 2 Kgs 5:5
But Naaman was angry and **w** away, 2 Kgs 5:11
So he turned and **w** away in a rage. 2 Kgs 5:12
So he **w** down and dipped himself 2 Kgs 5:14
He **w** in and stood before his master, 2 Kgs 5:25
he said, "Your servant **w** nowhere." 2 Kgs 5:25
forever." So he **w** out from his 2 Kgs 5:27
So he **w** with them. And when they 2 Kgs 6:4
rose early in the morning and **w** out, 2 Kgs 6:15
away, and they **w** to their master. 2 Kgs 6:23
entire army and **w** up and besieged 2 Kgs 6:24
they **w** into a tent and ate and drank, 2 Kgs 7:8
gold and clothing and **w** and hid them. 2 Kgs 7:8
off things from it and **w** and hid them. 2 Kgs 7:8
So they **w** after them as far as the 2 Kgs 7:15
Then the people **w** out and plundered 2 Kgs 7:16
She **w** with her household and 2 Kgs 8:2
she **w** to appeal to the king for her 2 Kgs 8:3
So Hazael **w** to meet him, and took a 2 Kgs 8:9
He **w** with Joram the son of Ahab to 2 Kgs 8:28
Jehoram king of Judah **w** down to see 2 Kgs 8:29
of the prophet, **w** to Ramoth-gilead. 2 Kgs 9:4
So he arose and **w** into the house. And 2 Kgs 9:6
mounted his chariot and **w** to Jezreel, 2 Kgs 9:16
a man on horseback **w** to meet him 2 Kgs 9:18
in his chariot, and **w** to meet Jehu, 2 Kgs 9:21
Then he **w** in and ate and drank. And 2 Kgs 9:34

But when they **w** to bury her, they 2 Kgs 9:35
Then in the morning, when he **w** out, 2 Kgs 10:9
Then he set out and **w** to Samaria. 2 Kgs 10:12
Then Jehu **w** into the house of Baal 2 Kgs 10:23
Then they **w** in to offer sacrifices 2 Kgs 10:24
cast them out and **w** into the inner 2 Kgs 10:25
she **w** into the house of the LORD to 2 Kgs 11:13
and she **w** through the horses' 2 Kgs 11:16
people of the land **w** to the house of 2 Kgs 11:18
king of Syria **w** up and fought 2 Kgs 12:17
Then Hazael **w** away from 2 Kgs 12:18
Joash king of Israel **w** down to him 2 Kgs 13:14
So Jehoash king of Israel **w** up, and 2 Kgs 14:11
When King Ahaz **w** to Damascus to 2 Kgs 16:10
drew near to the altar and **w** up on it 2 Kgs 16:12
They **w** after false idols and became 2 Kgs 17:15
him; wherever he **w** out, he prospered. 2 Kgs 18:7
And they **w** up and came to 2 Kgs 18:17
with sackcloth and **w** into the house 2 Kgs 19:1
and Hezekiah **w** up to the house of 2 Kgs 19:14
angel of the LORD **w** out and struck 2 Kgs 19:35
Assyria departed and **w** home and 2 Kgs 19:36
and Asaiah **w** to Huldah the 2 Kgs 22:14
And the king **w** up to the house of the 2 Kgs 23:2
Neco king of Egypt **w** up to the king 2 Kgs 23:29
King Josiah **w** to meet him, and 2 Kgs 23:29
And they **w** in the direction of the 2 Kgs 25:4
of the forces arose and **w** to Egypt, 2 Kgs 25:26
Afterward Hezron **w** in to the 1 Chr 2:21
of Hezron, Caleb **w** in to Ephrathah, 1 Chr 2:24
of the Simeonites, **w** to Mount Seir, 1 Chr 4:42
and Jehozadak **w** into exile when the 1 Chr 6:15
And Ephraim **w** in to his wife, and 1 Chr 7:23
David and all Israel **w** to Jerusalem, 1 Chr 11:4
Joab the son of Zeruiah **w** up first, 1 Chr 11:6
the thirty chief men **w** down to the 1 Chr 11:15
He also **w** down and struck down a 1 Chr 11:22
but Benaiah **w** down to him with a 1 Chr 11:23
the Gadites there **w** over to David 1 Chr 12:8
David **w** out to meet them and said 1 Chr 12:17
As he **w** to Ziklag, these men of 1 Chr 12:20
David and all Israel **w** up to Baalah, 1 Chr 13:6
all the Philistines **w** up to search for 1 Chr 14:8
heard of it and **w** out against them. 1 Chr 14:8
And he **w** up to Baal-perazim, and 1 Chr 14:11
the fame of David **w** out into all 1 Chr 14:17
of thousands **w** to bring up the ark 1 Chr 15:25
and David **w** home to bless his 1 Chr 16:43
Then King David **w** in and sat 1 Chr 17:16
on earth whom God **w** to redeem to 1 Chr 17:21
as he **w** to set up his monument at 1 Chr 18:3
gave victory to David wherever he **w**. 1 Chr 18:6
victory to David wherever he **w**. 1 Chr 18:13
Joab departed and **w** throughout all 1 Chr 21:4
So David **w** up at Gad's word, which 1 Chr 21:19
and saw David and **w** out from the 1 Chr 21:21
the divisions that came and **w**, 1 Chr 27:1
w to the high place that was at Gibeon, 2 Chr 1:3
And Solomon **w** up there to the bronze 2 Chr 1:6
And Solomon **w** to Hamath-zobah 2 Chr 8:3
Then Solomon **w** to Ezion-geber and 2 Chr 8:17
and they **w** to Ophir together with the 2 Chr 8:18
So she turned and **w** back to her own 2 Chr 9:12
of beaten gold **w** into each shield. 2 Chr 9:15
shekels of gold **w** into each shield; 2 Chr 9:16
the king's ships **w** to Tarshish with 2 Chr 9:21
Rehoboam **w** to Shechem, for all 2 Chr 10:1
in three days." So the people **w** away. 2 Chr 10:5
David." So all Israel **w** to their tents. 2 Chr 10:16
often as the king **w** into the house of 2 Chr 12:11
Abijah **w** out to battle, having an 2 Chr 13:3
And Asa **w** out to meet him, and 2 Chr 14:10
and he **w** out to meet Asa and said to 2 Chr 15:2
no peace to him who **w** out or to him 2 Chr 15:5
king of Israel **w** up against Judah 2 Chr 16:1
They **w** about through all the cities 2 Chr 17:9
After some years he **w** down to Ahab 2 Chr 18:2
the messenger who **w** to summon 2 Chr 18:12
king of Judah **w** up to 2 Chr 18:28
himself, and they **w** into battle. 2 Chr 18:29
of Hanani the seer **w** out to meet him 2 Chr 19:2
And he **w** out again among the 2 Chr 19:4
in the morning and **w** out into the 2 Chr 20:20
And when they **w** out, Jehoshaphat 2 Chr 20:20
attire, as they **w** before the army, 2 Chr 20:21
their counsel and **w** with Jehoram 2 Chr 22:5
Jehoram king of Judah **w** down to see 2 Chr 22:6
he **w** out with Jehoram to meet Jehu 2 Chr 22:7
And they **w** about through Judah 2 Chr 23:2
she **w** into the house of the LORD to 2 Chr 23:12
and she **w** into the entrance of the 2 Chr 23:15
Then all the people **w** to the house of 2 Chr 23:17
and the repairing **w** forward in their 2 Chr 24:13
out his people and **w** to the Valley of 2 Chr 25:11
So Joash king of Israel **w** up, and he 2 Chr 25:21

He **w** out and made war against the 2 Chr 26:6
Azariah the priest **w** in after him, 2 Chr 26:17
and he **w** out to meet the army that 2 Chr 28:9
consecrated themselves and **w** in as 2 Chr 29:15
The priests **w** into the inner part of 2 Chr 29:16
Then they **w** in to Hezekiah the 2 Chr 29:18
of the city and **w** up to the house 2 Chr 29:20
So couriers **w** throughout all Israel 2 Chr 30:6
So the couriers **w** from city to city 2 Chr 30:10
Israel who were present **w** out to the 2 Chr 31:1
the king had sent **w** to Huldah the 2 Chr 34:22
And the king **w** up to the house of 2 Chr 34:30
Neco king of Egypt **w** up to fight at 2 Chr 35:20
Euphrates and Josiah **w** out to meet 2 Chr 35:20
they **w** in haste to the Jews at Jerusalem Ezr 4:23
to the king that we **w** to the province of Ezr 5:8
this Ezra **w** up from Babylonia. He was a Ezr 7:6
And there **w** up also to Jerusalem, in the Ezr 7:7
genealogy of those who **w** up with me Ezr 8:1
house of God and **w** to the chamber of Ezr 10:6
So I **w** to Jerusalem and was there three Neh 2:11
I **w** out by night by the Valley Gate to Neh 2:13
Then I **w** on to the Fountain Gate and Neh 2:14
Then I **w** up in the night by the valley Neh 2:15
Now when I **w** into the house of Neh 6:10
And all the people **w** their way to eat Neh 8:12
So the people **w** out and brought them Neh 8:16
so that they **w** through the midst of the Neh 9:11
So the descendants **w** in and possessed Neh 9:24
One **w** to the south on the wall to the Neh 12:31
And after them **w** Hoshaiah and half Neh 12:32
And Ezra the scribe **w** before them. Neh 12:36
Fountain Gate they **w** up straight Neh 12:37
those who gave thanks **w** to the north, Neh 12:38
king of Babylon I **w** to the king. Neh 13:6
when the young woman **w** in to the Est 2:13
The couriers **w** out hurriedly by order Est 3:15
and **w** out into the midst of the city, Est 4:1
He **w** up to the entrance of the king's gate, Est 4:2
Hathach **w** out to Mordecai in the open Est 4:6
And Hathach **w** and told Esther what Est 4:9
Mordecai then **w** away and did Est 4:17
And Haman **w** out that day joyful and Est 5:9
Haman restrained himself and **w** home, Est 5:10
So the king and Haman **w** in to feast with Est 7:1
the wine-drinking and **w** into the palace Est 7:7
Then Mordecai **w** out from the presence Est 8:15
your hand." So Satan **w** out from the Jb 1:12
So Satan **w** out from the presence of the Jb 2:7
When I **w** out to the gate of the city, when Jb 29:7
Zophar the Naamathite **w** and did what Jb 42:9
Smoke **w** up from his nostrils, and Ps 18:8
so that he drove him out, and he **w** away. Ps 34:T
I **w** about as though I grieved for my Ps 35:14
when Nathan the prophet **w** to him, Ps 51:T
when the Ziphites **w** and told Saul, Ps 54:T
we **w** through fire and through water; Ps 66:12
God, when you **w** out before your people, Ps 68:7
until I **w** into the sanctuary of God; Ps 73:17
in Joseph when he **w** out over the land Ps 81:5
alter the word that **w** forth from my Ps 89:34
and it **w** ill with Moses on their Ps 106:32
Some **w** down to the sea in ships, doing Ps 107:23
to heaven; they **w** down to the depths; Ps 107:26
When Israel **w** out from Egypt, the Ps 114:1
they **w** out like a fire among thorns; Ps 118:12
Before I was afflicted I **w** astray, but Ps 119:67
For he **w** from prison to the throne, Eccl 4:14
found me as they **w** about in the city. Sg 3:3
found me as they **w** about in the city; Sg 5:7
I **w** down to the nut orchard to look at Sg 6:11
And I **w** to the prophetess, and she Is 8:3
with sackcloth and **w** into the house Is 37:1
and Hezekiah **w** up to the house of the Is 37:14
angel of the LORD **w** out and struck down Is 37:36
they **w** out from my mouth and I Is 48:3
"My people **w** down at the first into Egypt Is 52:4
bed, and there you **w** up to offer sacrifice. Is 57:7
but he **w** on backsliding in the way of Is 57:17
find in me that they **w** far from me, Jer 2:5
far from me, and **w** after worthlessness, Jer 2:5
by Baal and **w** after things that Jer 2:8
how she **w** up on every high hill and Jer 3:6
fear, but she too **w** and played the whore. Jer 3:8
and **w** backward and not forward. Jer 7:24
So I **w** and hid it by the Euphrates, as the Jer 13:5
Then I **w** to the Euphrates, and dug, and Jer 13:7
her sun **w** down while it was yet day; Jer 15:9
So I **w** down to the potter's house, and Jer 18:3
and who **w** away from this place: Jer 22:11
the exiles from Judah who **w** to Babylon, Jer 28:4
But Jeremiah the prophet **w** his way. Jer 28:11
the highway, the road by which you **w**. Jer 31:21
he **w** down to the king's house, into the Jer 36:12
So they **w** into the court to the king, Jer 36:20

Ebed-melech **w** from the king's house Jer 38:8
the men with him and **w** to the house of Jer 38:11
walls; and they **w** toward the Arabah. Jer 39:4
Then Jeremiah **w** to Gedaliah the son of Jer 40:6
they **w** to Gedaliah at Mizpah—Ishmael Jer 40:8
all their men and **w** to fight against Jer 41:12
and **w** to Johanan the son of Kareah. Jer 41:14
eight men, and **w** to the Ammonites. Jer 41:15
And they **w** and stayed at Geruth Jer 41:17
in that they **w** to make offerings and Jer 44:3
of her wine; therefore the nations **w** mad. Jer 51:7
when he **w** with Zedekiah king of Jer 51:59
men of war fled and **w** out from the city Jer 52:7
And they **w** in the direction of the Jer 52:7
Each one of them **w** straight forward, Ezk 1:9
forward, without turning as they **w**. Ezk 1:9
And each **w** straight forward. Ezk 1:12
Wherever the spirit would go, they **w**, Ezk 1:12
they went, without turning as they **w**. Ezk 1:12
and out of the fire **w** forth lightning. Ezk 1:13
When they **w**, they went in any of their Ezk 1:17
they **w** in any of their four directions Ezk 1:17
directions without turning as they **w**. Ezk 1:17
And when the living creatures **w**, the Ezk 1:19
went, the wheels **w** beside them; Ezk 1:19
the spirit wanted to go, they **w**, Ezk 1:20
When those **w**, these went; and when Ezk 1:21
When those went, these **w**; and when Ezk 1:21
And when they **w**, I heard the sound of Ezk 1:24
and I **w** in bitterness in the heat of my Ezk 3:14
So I arose and **w** out into the valley, and Ezk 3:23
So I **w** in and saw. And there, engraved Ezk 8:10
the smoke of the cloud of incense **w** up. Ezk 8:11
And they **w** in and stood beside the Ezk 9:2
Go out." So they **w** out and struck in the Ezk 9:7
the city." And he **w** in before my eyes. Ezk 10:2
side of the house, when the man **w** in, Ezk 10:3
glory of the LORD **w** up from the cherub Ezk 10:4
the cherubim," he **w** in and stood Ezk 10:6
clothed in linen, who took it and **w** out. Ezk 10:7
When they **w**, they went in any of Ezk 10:11
they **w** in any of their four directions Ezk 10:11
directions without turning as they **w**, Ezk 10:11
followed without turning as they **w**. Ezk 10:11
And when the cherubim **w**, the wheels Ezk 10:16
went, the wheels **w** beside them. Ezk 10:16
glory of the LORD **w** out from the Ezk 10:18
the earth before my eyes as they **w** out, Ezk 10:19
Each one of them **w** straight forward. Ezk 10:22
glory of the LORD **w** up from the midst Ezk 11:23
vision that I had seen **w** up from me. Ezk 11:24
And your renown **w** forth among the Ezk 16:14
for their heart **w** after their idols. Ezk 20:16
Thus they **w** in to Oholah and to Ezk 23:44
house of Judah when they **w** into exile, Ezk 25:3
for its roots **w** down to abundant Ezk 31:7
On the day the cedar **w** down to Sheol I Ezk 31:15
They also **w** down to Sheol with it, to Ezk 31:17
who **w** down uncircumcised into the Ezk 32:24
who **w** down to Sheol with their Ezk 32:27
the house of Israel **w** into captivity for Ezk 39:23
Then he **w** into the gateway facing east, Ezk 40:6
Then he **w** into the inner room and Ezk 41:3
and so one **w** up from the lowest story Ezk 41:7
But the Levites who **w** far from me, Ezk 44:10
after their idols when Israel **w** astray, Ezk 44:10
the people of Israel **w** astray from me, Ezk 44:15
As I **w** back, I saw on the bank of the Ezk 47:7
when the people of Israel **w** astray, Ezk 48:11
So the decree **w** out, and the wise men Dn 2:13
And Daniel **w** in and requested the king Dn 2:16
Then Daniel **w** to his house and made Dn 2:17
Therefore Daniel **w** in to Arioch, whom Dn 2:24
He **w** and said thus to him, "Do not Dn 2:24
he **w** to his house where he had windows Dn 6:10
labored till the sun **w** down to rescue Dn 6:14
Then the king **w** to his palace and spent Dn 6:18
the king arose and **w** in haste to the den Dn 6:19
Then I rose and **w** about the king's Dn 8:27
of your pleas for mercy a word **w** out, Dn 9:23
So he **w** and took Gomer, the daughter of Hos 1:3
and **w** after her lovers and forgot me, Hos 2:13
his wound, then Ephraim **w** to Assyria, Hos 5:13
they were called, the more they **w** away; Hos 11:2
"The city that **w** out a thousand shall Am 5:3
and that which **w** out a hundred shall Am 5:3
or **w** into the house and leaned his Am 5:19
He **w** down to Joppa and found a ship Jon 1:3
So he paid the fare and **w** on board, to go Jon 1:3
I **w** down to the land whose bars closed Jon 2:6
So Jonah arose and **w** to Nineveh, Jon 3:3
Jonah **w** out of the city and sat to the east Jon 4:5
lions, where the lion and lioness **w**, Na 2:11
became an exile; she **w** into captivity; Na 3:10
Before him **w** pestilence, and plague Hab 3:5

You **w** out for the salvation of your	Hab 3:13
desolate, so that no one **w** to and fro,	Zec 7:14
the foe for him who **w** out or came in,	Zec 8:10
listening to the king, they **w** on their way.	Mt 2:9
seen when it rose **w** before them until it	Mt 2:9
and his mother and **w** to the land of	Mt 2:21
And he **w** and lived in a city called	Mt 2:23
immediately he **w** up from the water,	Mt 3:16
And leaving Nazareth he **w** and lived in	Mt 4:13
And he **w** throughout all Galilee,	Mt 4:23
the crowds, he **w** up on the mountain,	Mt 5:1
And they **w** and woke him, saying, "Save	Mt 8:25
So they came out and **w** into the pigs,	Mt 8:32
And he rose and **w** home.	Mt 9:7
he **w** in and took her by the hand,	Mt 9:25
the report of this **w** through all that	Mt 9:26
But they **w** away and spread his fame	Mt 9:31
And Jesus **w** throughout all the cities	Mt 9:35
he **w** on from there to teach and preach	Mt 11:1
As they **w** away, Jesus began to speak to	Mt 11:7
that time Jesus **w** through the	Mt 12:1
He **w** on from there and entered their	Mt 12:9
But the Pharisees **w** out and conspired	Mt 12:14
That same day Jesus **w** out of the house	Mt 13:1
parables, saying: "A sower **w** out to sow.	Mt 13:3
weeds among the wheat and **w** away.	Mt 13:25
he left the crowds and **w** into the house.	Mt 13:36
w and sold all that he had and bought	Mt 13:46
these parables, he **w** away from there,	Mt 13:53
buried it, and they **w** and told Jesus.	Mt 14:12
When he **w** ashore he saw a great	Mt 14:14
he **w** up on the mountain by himself to	Mt 14:23
And Jesus **w** away from there and	Mt 15:21
Jesus **w** on from there and walked	Mt 15:29
And he **w** up on the mountain and sat	Mt 15:29
got into the boat and **w** to the region of	Mt 15:39
of the half-shekel tax **w** up to Peter and	Mt 17:24
go in search of the one that **w** astray?	Mt 18:12
the ninety-nine that never **w** astray.	Mt 18:13
But when that same servant **w** out, he	Mt 18:28
He refused and **w** and put him in	Mt 18:30
and they **w** and reported to their master	Mt 18:31
he **w** away from Galilee and entered the	Mt 19:1
he laid his hands on them and **w** away.	Mt 19:15
man heard this he **w** away sorrowful,	Mt 19:22
master of a house who **w** out early in the	Mt 20:1
So they **w**. Going out again about the	Mt 20:5
the eleventh hour he **w** out and found	Mt 20:6
And as they **w** out of Jericho, a great	Mt 20:29
The disciples **w** and did as Jesus had	Mt 21:6
And the crowds that **w** before him and	Mt 21:9
he **w** out of the city to Bethany and	Mt 21:17
he **w** to it and found nothing on it but	Mt 21:19
And he **w** to the first and said, 'Son, go	Mt 21:28
afterward he changed his mind and **w**.	Mt 21:29
And he **w** to the other son and said the	Mt 21:30
to tenants, and **w** into another country.	Mt 21:33
But they paid no attention and **w** off, one	Mt 22:5
And those servants **w** out into the roads	Mt 22:10
Then the Pharisees **w** and plotted how	Mt 22:15
And they left him and **w** away.	Mt 22:22
took their lamps and **w** to meet the	Mt 25:1
those who were ready **w** in with him to	Mt 25:10
to his ability. Then he **w** away.	Mt 25:15
received the five talents **w** at once and	Mt 25:16
received the one talent **w** and dug in the	Mt 25:18
and I **w** and hid your talent in the	Mt 25:25
was Judas Iscariot, **w** to the chief priests	Mt 26:14
they **w** out to the Mount of Olives.	Mt 26:30
Then Jesus **w** with them to a place	Mt 26:36
the second time, he **w** away and prayed,	Mt 26:42
he **w** away and prayed for the third	Mt 26:44
And when he **w** out to the entrance,	Mt 26:71
three times." And he **w** out and wept	Mt 26:75
departed, and he **w** and hanged himself.	Mt 27:5
As they **w** out, they found a man of	Mt 27:32
his resurrection they **w** into the holy	Mt 27:53
He **w** to Pilate and asked for the body of	Mt 27:58
the entrance of the tomb and **w** away.	Mt 27:60
So they **w** and made the tomb secure	Mt 27:66
and the other Mary **w** to see the tomb.	Mt 28:1
some of the guard **w** into the city and	Mt 28:11
Now the eleven disciples **w** to Galilee, to	Mt 28:16
And they **w** into Capernaum, and	Mk 1:21
he departed and **w** out to a desolate	Mk 1:35
And he **w** throughout all Galilee,	Mk 1:39
But he **w** out and began to talk freely	Mk 1:45
up his bed and **w** out before them all,	Mk 2:12
He **w** out again beside the sea, and all	Mk 2:13
The Pharisees **w** out and immediately	Mk 3:6
And he **w** up on the mountain and	Mk 3:13
Then he **w** home, and the crowd	Mk 3:20
family heard it, they **w** out to seize him,	Mk 3:21
"Listen! A sower **w** out to sow.	Mk 4:3
And he **w** away and began to proclaim	Mk 5:20
And he **w** with him. And a great crowd	Mk 5:24
were with him and **w** in where the child	Mk 5:40
He **w** away from there and came to his	Mk 6:1
And he **w** about among the villages	Mk 6:6
So they **w** out and proclaimed that	Mk 6:12
And she **w** out and said to her mother,	Mk 6:24
He **w** and beheaded him in the prison	Mk 6:27
And they **w** away in the boat to a	Mk 6:32
When he **w** ashore he saw a great	Mk 6:34
them, he **w** up on the mountain to pray.	Mk 6:46
there he arose and **w** away to the region	Mk 7:24
And she **w** home and found the child	Mk 7:30
region of Tyre and **w** through Sidon to	Mk 7:31
with his disciples and **w** to the district	Mk 8:10
the boat again, and **w** to the other side.	Mk 8:13
And Jesus **w** on with his disciples to the	Mk 8:27
They **w** on from there and passed	Mk 9:30
And he left there and **w** to the region of	Mk 10:1
by the saying, he **w** away sorrowful,	Mk 10:22
And they **w** away and found a colt tied	Mk 11:4
And those who **w** before and those who	Mk 11:9
entered Jerusalem and **w** into the	Mk 11:11
he **w** out to Bethany with the twelve.	Mk 11:11
he **w** to see if he could find anything	Mk 11:13
when evening came they **w** out of the	Mk 11:19
to tenants and **w** into another country.	Mk 12:1
them. So they left him and **w** away.	Mk 12:12
w to the chief priests in order to betray	Mk 14:10
disciples set out and **w** to the city and	Mk 14:16
they **w** out to the Mount of Olives.	Mk 14:26
And they **w** to a place called	Mk 14:32
And again he **w** away and prayed,	Mk 14:39
came, he **w** up to him at once and said,	Mk 14:45
you mean." And he **w** out into the	Mk 14:68
took courage and **w** to Pilate and	Mk 15:43
the sun had risen, they **w** to the tomb.	Mk 16:2
And they **w** out and fled from the tomb,	Mk 16:8
She **w** and told those who had been	Mk 16:10
And they **w** back and told the rest, but	Mk 16:13
And they **w** out and preached	Mk 16:20
of service was ended, he **w** to his home.	Lk 1:23
days Mary arose and **w** with haste into	Lk 1:39
those days a decree **w** out from Caesar	Lk 2:1
And all **w** to be registered, each to his own	Lk 2:3
And Joseph also **w** up from Galilee, from	Lk 2:4
When the angels **w** away from them	Lk 2:15
And they **w** with haste and found Mary	Lk 2:16
Now his parents **w** to Jerusalem every	Lk 2:41
old, they **w** up according to custom.	Lk 2:42
be in the group they **w** a day's journey,	Lk 2:44
And he **w** down with them and came to	Lk 2:51
And he **w** into all the region around the	Lk 3:3
a report about him **w** out through all	Lk 4:14
he **w** to the synagogue on the Sabbath	Lk 4:16
passing through their midst, he **w** away.	Lk 4:30
And he **w** down to Capernaum, a city of	Lk 4:31
And reports about him **w** out into every	Lk 4:37
he departed and **w** into a desolate place.	Lk 4:42
more the report about him **w** abroad,	Lk 5:15
they **w** up on the roof and let him down	Lk 5:19
what he had been lying on and **w** home,	Lk 5:25
After this he **w** out and saw a tax	Lk 5:27
In these days he **w** out to the mountain	Lk 6:12
And Jesus **w** with them. When he was not	Lk 7:6
Soon afterward he **w** to a town called	Lk 7:11
disciples and a great crowd **w** with him.	Lk 7:11
and he **w** into the Pharisee's house and	Lk 7:36
Soon afterward he **w** on through cities	Lk 8:1
"A sower **w** out to sow his seed. And as he	Lk 8:5
And they **w** and woke him, saying,	Lk 8:24
Then people **w** out to see what had	Lk 8:35
God has done for you." And he **w** away,	Lk 8:39
As Jesus **w**, the people pressed around	Lk 8:42
they departed and **w** through the villages,	Lk 9:6
John and James and **w** up on the	Lk 9:28
who **w** and entered a village of the	Lk 9:52
And they **w** on to another village.	Lk 9:56
He **w** to him and bound up his wounds,	Lk 10:34
Now as they **w** on their way, Jesus	Lk 10:38
And she **w** up to him and said, "Lord,	Lk 10:40
him, so he **w** in and reclined at table.	Lk 11:37
As he **w** away from there, the scribes	Lk 11:53
He **w** on his way through towns and	Lk 13:22
when he **w** to dine at the house of a ruler	Lk 14:1
So he **w** and hired himself out to one of	Lk 15:15
And as they **w** they were cleansed.	Lk 17:14
the day when Lot **w** out from Sodom,	Lk 17:29
"Two men **w** up into the temple to pray,	Lk 18:10
this man **w** down to his house justified,	Lk 18:14
"A nobleman **w** into a far country to	Lk 19:12
had said these things, he **w** on ahead,	Lk 19:28
those who were sent **w** away and found	Lk 19:32
to tenants and **w** into another country	Lk 20:9
but at night he **w** out and lodged on the	Lk 21:37
He **w** away and conferred with the chief	Lk 22:4
And they **w** and found it just as he had	Lk 22:13
And he came out and **w**, as was his	Lk 22:39
And he **w** out and wept bitterly.	Lk 22:62
This man **w** to Pilate and asked for the	Lk 23:52
week, at early dawn, they **w** to the tomb,	Lk 24:1
but when they **w** in they did not find the	Lk 24:3
and he **w** home marveling at what had	Lk 24:12
himself drew near and **w** with them.	Lk 24:15
who were with us **w** to the tomb and	Lk 24:24
now far spent." So he **w** in to stay with	Lk 24:29
After this he **w** down to Capernaum, with	Jn 2:12
was at hand, and Jesus **w** up to Jerusalem.	Jn 2:13
Jesus and his disciples **w** into the Judean	Jn 3:22
her water jar and **w** away into town and	Jn 4:28
They **w** out of the town and were coming	Jn 4:30
he **w** to him and asked him to come	Jn 4:47
Jesus spoke to him and **w** on his way.	Jn 4:50
of the Jews, and Jesus **w** up to Jerusalem.	Jn 5:1
The man **w** away and told the Jews that it	Jn 5:15
After this Jesus **w** away to the other side of	Jn 6:1
Jesus **w** up on the mountain, and there he	Jn 6:3
came, his disciples **w** down to the sea,	Jn 6:16
got into the boats and **w** to Capernaum,	Jn 6:24
After this Jesus **w** about in Galilee. He	Jn 7:1
gone up to the feast, then he also **w** up,	Jn 7:10
of the feast Jesus **w** up into the temple	Jn 7:14
[[They **w** each to his own house,	Jn 7:53
but Jesus **w** to the Mount of Olives.	Jn 8:1
they heard it, they **w** away one by one,	Jn 8:9
Jesus hid himself and **w** out of the temple.	Jn 8:59
So he **w** and washed and came back	Jn 9:7
So I **w** and washed and received my	Jn 9:11
He **w** away again across the Jordan to	Jn 10:40
Jesus was coming, she **w** and met him,	Jn 11:20
this, she **w** and called her sister Mary,	Jn 11:28
heard it, she rose quickly and **w** to him.	Jn 11:29
but some of them **w** to the Pharisees	Jn 11:46
but he **w** from there to the region near the	Jn 11:54
and many **w** up from the country to	Jn 11:55
of palm trees and **w** out to meet him,	Jn 12:13
reason why the crowd **w** to meet him	Jn 12:18
Now among those who **w** up to worship	Jn 12:20
Philip **w** and told Andrew; Andrew and	Jn 12:22
Andrew and Philip **w** and told Jesus.	Jn 12:22
morsel of bread, he immediately **w** out.	Jn 13:30
he **w** out with his disciples across the	Jn 18:1
w there with lanterns and torches and	Jn 18:3
w out and spoke to the servant girl who	Jn 18:16
So Pilate **w** outside to them and said,	Jn 18:29
he **w** back outside to the Jews and told	Jn 18:38
Pilate **w** out again and said to them, "See,	Jn 19:4
and he **w** out, bearing his own cross, to	Jn 19:17
So she ran and **w** to Simon Peter and the	Jn 20:2
So Peter **w** out with the other disciple,	Jn 20:3
following him, and **w** into the tomb.	Jn 20:6
had reached the tomb first, also **w** in,	Jn 20:8
Then the disciples **w** back to their	Jn 20:10
Mary Magdalene **w** and announced to	Jn 20:18
go with you." They **w** out and got into	Jn 21:3
So Simon Peter **w** aboard and hauled	Jn 21:11
they were gazing into heaven as he **w**,	Acts 1:10
entered, they **w** up to the upper room,	Acts 1:13
that the Lord Jesus **w** in and out	Acts 1:21
they **w** to their friends and reported	Acts 4:23
with the officers **w** and brought them,	Acts 5:26
Then he **w** out from the land of the	Acts 7:4
And Jacob **w** down into Egypt, and he	Acts 7:15
who were scattered **w** about preaching	Acts 8:4
Philip **w** down to the city of Samaria	Acts 8:5
And he rose and **w**. And there was an	Acts 8:27
and they both **w** down into the water,	Acts 8:38
no more, and **w** on his way rejoicing.	Acts 8:39
disciples of the Lord, **w** to the high priest	Acts 9:1
Now as he **w** on his way, he approached	Acts 9:3
So he **w** in and out among them at	Acts 9:28
Now as Peter **w** here and there among	Acts 9:32
So Peter rose and **w** with them. And	Acts 9:39
Peter **w** up on the housetop about the	Acts 10:9
And Peter **w** down to the men and	Acts 10:21
day he rose and **w** away with them,	Acts 10:23
he **w** in and found many persons	Acts 10:27
He **w** about doing good and healing	Acts 10:38
So when Peter **w** up to Jerusalem, the	Acts 11:2
"You **w** to uncircumcised men and ate	Acts 11:3
So Barnabas **w** to Tarsus to look for	Acts 11:25
And he **w** out and followed him. He did	Acts 12:9
and they **w** out and went along one	Acts 12:10
they went out and **w** along one street,	Acts 12:10
this, he **w** to the house of Mary,	Acts 12:12
he departed and **w** to another place.	Acts 12:17
Then he **w** down from Judea to	Acts 12:19
Holy Spirit, they **w** down to Seleucia,	Acts 13:4
and he **w** about seeking people to lead	Acts 13:11
but they **w** on from Perga and came	Acts 13:14
Sabbath day they **w** into the	Acts 13:14

As they **w** out, the people begged that Acts 13:42
feet against them and **w** to Iconium. Acts 13:51
the next day he **w** on with Barnabas Acts 14:20
in Perga, they **w** down to Attalia, Acts 14:25
were sent off, they **w** down to Antioch, Acts 15:30
And he **w** through Syria and Cilicia, Acts 15:41
As they **w** on their way through the Acts 16:4
And they **w** through the region of Acts 16:6
by Mysia, they **w** down to Troas. Acts 16:8
the Sabbath day we **w** outside the gate Acts 16:13
So they **w** out of the prison and visited Acts 16:40
And Paul **w** in, as was his custom, and Acts 17:2
they arrived they **w** into the Jewish Acts 17:10
So Paul **w** out from their midst. Acts 17:33
this Paul left Athens and **w** to Corinth. Acts 18:1
to leave Rome. And he **w** to see them, Acts 18:2
And he left there and **w** to the house of Acts 18:7
but he himself **w** into the synagogue Acts 18:19
he **w** up and greeted the church, Acts 18:22
church, and then **w** down to Antioch. Acts 18:22
he departed and **w** from one place to Acts 18:23
These **w** on ahead and were waiting for Acts 20:5
But Paul **w** down and bent over him, Acts 20:10
him on board and **w** to Mitylene. Acts 20:14
and the day after that we **w** to Miletus. Acts 20:15
to Phoenicia, we **w** aboard and set sail. Acts 21:2
we departed and **w** on our journey, Acts 21:5
Then we **w** on board the ship, and they Acts 21:6
we got ready and **w** up to Jerusalem. Acts 21:15
disciples from Caesarea **w** with us, Acts 21:16
the following day Paul **w** in with us Acts 21:18
with them and **w** into the temple, Acts 21:26
he **w** to the tribune and said to him, Acts 22:26
They **w** to the chief priests and elders Acts 23:14
so he **w** and entered the barracks and Acts 23:16
twelve days since I **w** up to worship in Acts 24:11
he **w** up to Jerusalem from Caesarea. Acts 25:1
or ten days, he **w** down to Caesarea. Acts 25:6
leave of them and **w** on to Macedonia. 2 Cor 2:13
before me, but I **w** away into Arabia, Gal 1:17
after three years I **w** up to Jerusalem to Gal 1:18
Then I **w** into the regions of Syria and Gal 1:21
after fourteen years I **w** up again to Gal 2:1
I **w** up because of a revelation and set Gal 2:2
And he **w** out, not knowing where he Heb 11:8
By faith he **w** to live in the land of Heb 11:9
They **w** about in skins of sheep and Heb 11:37
in which he **w** and proclaimed to the 1 Pt 3:19
They **w** out from us, but they were not 1 Jn 2:19
But they **w** out, that it might become 1 Jn 2:19
And he **w** and took the scroll from the Rv 5:7
So I **w** to the angel and told him to give Rv 10:9
up here!" And they **w** up to heaven in Rv 11:12
with the woman and **w** off to make war Rv 12:17
So the first angel **w** and poured out his Rv 16:2

WEPT (71)

him, she lifted up her voice and **w**. Gn 21:16
And Esau lifted up his voice and **w**. Gn 27:38
Jacob kissed Rachel and **w** aloud. Gn 29:11
on his neck and kissed him, and they **w**. Gn 33:4
mourning." Thus his father **w** for him. Gn 37:35
he turned away from them and **w**. Gn 42:24
he entered his chamber and **w** there. Gn 43:30
And he **w** aloud, so that the Egyptians Gn 45:2
his brother Benjamin's neck and **w**, Gn 45:14
wept, and Benjamin **w** upon his neck. Gn 45:14
all his brothers and **w** upon them. Gn 45:15
fell on his neck and **w** on his neck a Gn 46:29
his father's face and **w** over him and Gn 50:1
And the Egyptians **w** for him seventy Gn 50:3
your father." Joseph **w** when they spoke Gn 50:17
people of Israel also **w** again and said, Nm 11:4
for you have **w** in the hearing of the Nm 11:18
is among you and have **w** before him, Nm 11:20
a loud cry, and the people **w** that night. Nm 14:1
the house of Israel **w** for Aaron thirty Nm 20:29
And you returned and **w** before the LORD, Dt 1:45
the people of Israel **w** for Moses in the Dt 34:8
the people lifted up their voices and **w**. Jgs 2:4
and **w** for her virginity on the Jgs 11:38
And Samson's wife **w** over him and Jgs 14:16
She **w** before him the seven days that Jgs 14:17
Israel went up and **w** before the LORD Jgs 20:23
went up and came to Bethel and **w**. Jgs 20:26
they lifted up their voices and **w** bitterly. Jgs 21:2
and they lifted up their voices and **w**. Ru 1:9
they lifted up their voices and **w** again. Ru 1:14
Therefore Hannah **w** and would not 1 Sm 1:7
and prayed to the LORD and **w** bitterly. 1 Sm 1:10
the people, and all the people **w** aloud. 1 Sm 11:4
one another and **w** with one another, 1 Sm 20:41
And Saul lifted up his voice and **w**. 1 Sm 24:16
their voices and **w** until they had 1 Sm 30:4
they mourned and **w** and fasted until 2 Sm 1:12
up his voice and **w** at the grave of 2 Sm 3:32
grave of Abner, and all the people **w**. 2 Sm 3:32
And all the people **w** again over him. 2 Sm 3:34
You fasted and **w** for the child while 2 Sm 12:21
child was still alive, I fasted and **w**, 2 Sm 12:22
came and lifted up their voice and **w**. 2 Sm 13:36
and all his servants **w** very bitterly. 2 Sm 13:36
And all the land **w** aloud as all the 2 Sm 15:23
to the chamber over the gate and **w**. 2 Sm 18:33
embarrassed. And the man of God **w**. 2 Kgs 8:11
down to him and **w** before him, 2 Kgs 13:14
your sight." And Hezekiah **w** bitterly. 2 Kgs 20:3
torn your clothes and **w** before me, 2 Kgs 22:19
torn your clothes and **w** before me, 2 Chr 34:27
w with a loud voice when they saw the Ezr 3:12
out of Israel, for the people **w** bitterly. Ezr 10:1
I sat down and **w** and mourned for days, Neh 1:4
For all the people **w** as they heard the Neh 8:9
at his feet and **w** and pleaded with him Est 8:3
And they raised their voices and **w**, and Jb 2:12
me and its furrows have **w** together, Jb 31:38
When I **w** and humbled my soul with Ps 69:10
of Babylon, there we sat down and **w**, Ps 137:1
in your sight." And Hezekiah **w** bitterly. Is 38:3
prevailed; he **w** and sought his favor. Hos 12:4
times." And he went out and **w** bitterly. Mt 26:75
times." And he broke down and **w**. Mk 14:72
with him, as they mourned and **w**. Mk 16:10
drew near and saw the city, he **w** over it, Lk 19:41
And he went out and **w** bitterly. Lk 22:62
Jesus **w**. Jn 11:35
and as she **w** she stooped to look into the Jn 20:11
on their heads as they **w** and mourned, Rv 18:19

WEST (81)

with Bethel on the **w** and Ai on the east. Gn 12:8
spread abroad to the **w** and to the east Gn 28:14
led his flock to the **w** side of the wilderness Ex 3:1
the wind into a very strong **w** wind, Ex 10:19
of the court on the **w** side there shall be Ex 27:12
And for the **w** side were hangings of Ex 38:12
"On the **w** side shall be the standard of Nm 2:18
camp behind the tabernacle on the **w**, Nm 3:23
and on the **w** side two thousand cubits, Nm 35:5
not beyond the Jordan, **w** of the road, Dt 11:30
who were beyond the Jordan to the **w**, Jos 5:1
lay between Bethel and Ai, to the **w** of Ai, Jos 8:9
Bethel and Ai, to the **w** of the city. Jos 8:12
the city and its rear guard **w** of the city. Jos 8:13
lowland, and in Naphoth-dor on the **w**, Jos 11:2
to the Canaanites in the east and the **w**, Jos 11:3
Israel defeated on the **w** side of the Jos 12:7
against the Valley of Hinnom, on the **w**, Jos 15:8
the boundary circles **w** of Baalah to Jos 15:10
And the **w** boundary was the Great Sea Jos 15:12
On the **w** it touches Carmel and Jos 19:26
and Asher on the **w** and Judah on the Jos 19:34
brothers in the land **w** of the Jordan. Jos 22:7
the Jordan to the Great Sea in the **w**. Jos 23:4
day; behold, it is **w** of Kiriath-jearim. Jgs 18:12
over all the region **w** of the Euphrates 1 Kgs 4:24
over all the kings **w** of the Euphrates. 1 Kgs 4:24
three facing north, three facing **w**, 1 Kgs 7:25
the kings of the **w** and from the 1 Kgs 10:15
and to the **w** Gezer and its towns, 1 Chr 7:28
were on the four sides, east, **w**, north, 1 Chr 9:24
the valleys, to the east and to the **w**. 1 Chr 12:15
and Hosah it came out for the **w**, 1 Chr 26:16
colonnade on the **w** there were four 1 Chr 26:18
three facing north, three facing **w**, 2 Chr 4:4
them down to the **w** side of the city 2 Chr 32:30
for the city of David **w** of Gihon, 2 Chr 33:14
They of the **w** are appalled at his day, Jb 18:20
the east or from the **w** and not from the Ps 75:6
as far as the east is from the **w**, so far Ps 103:12
the lands, from the east and from the **w**, Ps 107:3
Philistines on the **w** devour Israel with Is 9:12
the shoulder of the Philistines in the **w**, Is 11:14
of the LORD they shout from the **w**. Is 24:14
the east, and from the **w** I will gather you. Is 43:5
from the rising of the sun and from the **w**, Is 45:6
these from the north and from the **w**, Is 49:12
fear the name of the LORD from the **w**, Is 59:19
yard on the **w** side was seventy Ezk 41:12
he turned to the **w** side and measured, Ezk 42:19
of the city, on the **w** and on the east, Ezk 45:7
"On the **w** side, the Great Sea shall be Ezk 47:20
This shall be the **w** side Ezk 47:20
extending from the east side to the **w**, Ezk 48:1
of Dan, from the east side to the **w**, Ezk 48:2
of Asher, from the east side to the **w**, Ezk 48:3
of Naphtali, from the east side to the **w**, Ezk 48:4
Manasseh, from the east side to the **w**, Ezk 48:5
of Ephraim, from the east side to the **w**, Ezk 48:6
of Reuben, from the east side to the **w**, Ezk 48:7
of Judah, from the east side to the **w**, Ezk 48:8
portions, from the east side to the **w**, Ezk 48:8
east side 4,500, and the **w** side 4,500. Ezk 48:16
250, on the east 250, and on the **w** 250. Ezk 48:17
cubits to the east, and 10,000 to the **w**, Ezk 48:18
the 25,000 cubits to the **w** border, Ezk 48:21
from the east side to the **w**, Benjamin, Ezk 48:23
Benjamin, from the east side to the **w**, Ezk 48:24
of Simeon, from the east side to the **w**, Ezk 48:25
of Issachar, from the east side to the **w**, Ezk 48:26
of Zebulun, from the east side to the **w**, Ezk 48:27
On the **w** side, which is to be 4,500 Ezk 48:34
goat came from the **w** across the face of Dn 8:5
shall come trembling from the **w**; Hos 11:10
the east country and from the **w** country, Zec 8:7
in two from east to **w** by a very wide Zec 14:4
come from east and **w** and recline at Mt 8:11
from the east and shines as far as the **w**, Mt 24:27
"When you see a cloud rising in the **w**, Lk 12:54
And people will come from east and **w**, Lk 13:29
three gates, and on the **w** three gates. Rv 21:13

WESTERN (11)

"For the **w** border, you shall have the Nm 34:6
its coast. This shall be your **w** border. Nm 34:6
River, the river Euphrates, to the **w** sea. Dt 11:24
all the land of Judah as far as the **w** sea, Dt 34:2
turning on the **w** side southward from Jos 18:14
people of Judah. This forms the **w** side. Jos 18:14
and extending from the **w** to the eastern Ezk 45:7
there at the extreme **w** end of them. Ezk 46:19
10,000 cubits in breadth on the **w** side, Ezk 48:10
sea, and his rear guard into the **w** sea; Jl 2:20
sea and half of them to the **w** sea. Zec 14:8

WESTWARD (14)

and southward and eastward and **w**, Gn 13:14
of the tabernacle **w** you shall make Ex 26:22
the side of the tabernacle at the rear **w**. Ex 26:27
rear of the tabernacle **w** he made six Ex 36:27
frames of the tabernacle at the rear **w**. Ex 36:32
lift up your eyes **w** and northward and Dt 3:27
Then it goes down **w** to the territory of Jos 16:3
the boundary goes **w** to the brook Jos 16:8
then up through the hill country **w**, Jos 18:12
their boundary goes up **w** and on to Jos 19:11
the boundary turns **w** to Aznoth-tabor Jos 19:34
oversight of Israel **w** of the Jordan 1 Chr 26:30
and **w** from the 25,000 cubits to the Ezk 48:21
the ram charging **w** and northward and Dn 8:4

WET (9)

They are **w** with the rain of the Jb 24:8
my perfect one, for my head is **w** with dew, Sg 5:2
Let him be **w** with the dew of heaven. Dn 4:15
and let him be **w** with the dew of heaven, Dn 4:23
and you shall be **w** with the dew of Dn 4:25
and his body was **w** with the dew of Dn 4:33
and his body was **w** with the dew of Dn 5:21
she began to **w** his feet with her tears Lk 7:38
but she has **w** my feet with her tears and Lk 7:44

WHATEVER (162)

And **w** the man called every living Gn 2:19
W Sarah says to you, do as she tells Gn 21:12
Now then, **w** God has said to you, do." Gn 31:16
eyes, and **w** you say to me I will give. Gn 34:11
will, and I will give **w** you say to me. Gn 34:12
and **w** was in the city and in the field. Gn 34:28
W was done there, he was the one who Gn 39:22
And **w** he did, the LORD made it Gn 39:23
W is the first to open the womb among Ex 13:2
redemption of his life **w** is imposed on Ex 21:30
W touches the altar shall become holy. Ex 29:37
W touches them will become holy. Ex 30:29
of **w** sort the uncleanness may be with Lv 5:3
W touches them shall become holy." Lv 6:18
W touches its flesh shall be holy, and Lv 6:27
Moreover, you shall eat no blood **w**, Lv 7:26
W parts the hoof and is cloven-footed Lv 11:3
W goes on its belly, and whatever goes Lv 11:42
on its belly, and **w** goes on all fours, Lv 11:42
goes on all fours, or **w** has many feet, Lv 11:42
or in the skin, **w** be the use of the skin, Lv 13:51
shall burn with fire **w** has the disease. Lv 13:57
w his uncleanness may be— Lv 22:5
w injury he has given a person shall be Lv 24:20
w anyone gives to the priest shall be Nm 5:10
with us, **w** good the LORD will do to us, Nm 10:32
And **w** the unclean person touches Nm 19:22
honor, and **w** you say to me I will do. Nm 22:17
and **w** he shows me I will tell you." And Nm 23:3
then **w** proceeds out of her lips Nm 30:12
And **w** cannot stand the fire, you shall Nm 31:23
w the LORD our God had forbidden us. Dt 2:37
everyone doing **w** is right in his own Dt 12:8
these: **w** has fins and scales you may eat. Dt 14:9
And **w** does not have fins and scales Dt 14:10
spend the money for **w** you desire— Dt 14:26

or strong drink, **w** your appetite craves. Dt 14:26
but **w** of yours is with your brother your Dt 15:3
him sufficient for his need, **w** it may be. Dt 15:8
or blind or has any serious blemish **w**, Dt 15:21
in which is a blemish, any defect **w**, Dt 17:1
your words, **w** you command him, Jos 1:18
W seems good and right in your sight to Jos 9:25
sinned; do to us **w** seems good to you. Jgs 10:15
then **w** comes out from the doors of my Jgs 11:31
may do to us **w** seems good to you." 1 Sm 11:10
"Do **w** seems good to you." But the 1 Sm 14:36
Jonathan said to David, "**W** you say, 1 Sm 20:4
me five loaves of bread, or **w** is here." 1 Sm 21:3
Please give **w** you have at hand to 1 Sm 25:8
are ready to do **w** my lord the king 2 Sm 15:15
So **w** you hear from the king's house, 2 Sm 15:35
"**W** seems best to you I will do." So the 2 Sm 18:4
and do for him **w** seems good to 2 Sm 19:37
will do for him **w** seems good to you, 2 Sm 19:38
not go out from there to any place **w**. 1 Kgs 2:36
day you go out and go to any place **w**, 1 Kgs 2:42
in the land at their gates, **w** plague, 1 Kgs 8:37
whatever plague, **w** sickness there is, 1 Kgs 8:37
w prayer, whatever plea is made by 1 Kgs 8:38
w plea is made by any man or by all 1 Kgs 8:38
by **w** way you shall send them, 1 Kgs 8:44
and **w** Solomon desired to build in 1 Kgs 9:19
w she asked besides what was given 1 Kgs 10:13
and lay hands on **w** pleases you and 1 Kgs 20:6
king. Do **w** is good in your eyes." 2 Kgs 10:5
W you impose on me I will bear." 2 Kgs 18:14
the Hebronites of **w** genealogy or 1 Chr 26:31
And we will cut **w** timber you need 2 Chr 2:16
in the land at their gates, **w** plague, 2 Chr 6:28
whatever plague, **w** sickness there is, 2 Chr 6:28
w prayer, whatever plea is made by 2 Chr 6:29
w plea is made by any man or by all 2 Chr 6:29
by **w** way you shall send them, 2 Chr 6:34
and **w** Solomon desired to build in 2 Chr 8:6
w she asked besides what she had 2 Chr 9:12
let each survivor, in **w** place he sojourns, Ezr 1:4
And **w** is needed—bulls, rams, or sheep Ezr 6:9
W seems good to you and your brothers Ezr 7:18
And **w** else is required for the house of Ezr 7:20
W Ezra the priest, the scribe of the Law Ezr 7:21
W is decreed by the God of heaven, let it Ezr 7:23
she was given **w** she desired to take with Est 2:13
W is under the whole heaven is mine. Jb 41:11
sea, **w** passes along the paths of the seas. Ps 8:8
W the LORD pleases, he does, in heaven Ps 135:6
Get wisdom, and **w** you get, get insight. Prv 4:7
And **w** my eyes desired I did not keep Eccl 2:10
I perceived that **w** God does endures Eccl 3:14
W has come to be has already been Eccl 6:10
an evil cause, for he does **w** he pleases. Eccl 8:3
W your hand finds to do, do it with Eccl 9:10
you, you shall go, and **w** I command you, Jer 1:7
and **w** the LORD answers you I will tell Jer 42:4
and **w** the LORD our God says declare to Jer 42:20
to me, "Son of man, eat **w** you find here. Ezk 3:1
but in **w** direction the front wheel Ezk 10:11
In **w** tribe the sojourner resides, there Ezk 47:23
and **w** beasts may be in those camps. Zec 14:15
"So **w** you wish that others would do to Mt 7:12
And **w** town or village you enter, find Mt 10:11
an oath to give her **w** she might ask. Mt 14:7
you not see that **w** goes into the mouth Mt 15:17
and **w** you bind on earth shall be Mt 16:19
and **w** you loose on earth shall be Mt 16:19
him, but did to him **w** they pleased. Mt 17:12
w you bind on earth shall be bound in Mt 18:18
and **w** you loose on earth shall be Mt 18:18
too, and **w** is right I will give you.' Mt 20:4
And **w** you ask in prayer, you will Mt 21:22
so practice and observe **w** they tell you— Mt 23:3
of man, and **w** blasphemies they utter, Mk 3:28
said to the girl, "Ask me for **w** you wish, Mk 6:22
And he vowed to her, "**W** you ask me, I Mk 6:23
W you would have gained from me is Mk 7:11
Do you not see that **w** goes into a person Mk 7:18
and they did to him **w** they pleased, Mk 9:13
want you to do for us **w** we ask of you." Mk 10:35
I tell you, **w** you ask in prayer, Mk 11:24
but say **w** is given you in that hour, Mk 13:11
And **w** house you enter, stay there, and Lk 9:4
W house you enter, first say, 'Peace be to Lk 10:5
care of him, and **w** more you spend, Lk 10:35
he will rise and give him **w** he needs. Lk 11:8
Therefore **w** you have said in the dark Lk 12:3
said to the servants, "Do **w** he tells you." Jn 2:5
For **w** the Father does, that the Son does Jn 5:19
now I know that **w** you ask from God, Jn 11:22
W you ask in my name, this I will do, Jn 14:13
my words abide in you, ask **w** you wish, Jn 15:7
so that **w** you ask the Father in my Jn 15:16
authority, but **w** he hears he will speak, Jn 16:13
w you ask of the Father in my name, Jn 16:23
shall listen to him in **w** he tells you. Acts 3:22
to do **w** your hand and your plan had Acts 4:28
sail, they put on board **w** we needed. Acts 28:10
Now we know that **w** the law says it Rom 3:19
For **w** does not proceed from faith is Rom 14:23
For **w** was written in former days was Rom 15:4
and help her in **w** she may need from Rom 16:2
in **w** condition each was called, 1 Cor 7:24
Eat **w** is sold in the meat market 1 Cor 10:25
eat **w** is set before you without 1 Cor 10:27
you eat or drink, or **w** you do, 1 Cor 10:31
For **w** boasts I made to him about 2 Cor 7:14
But **w** anyone else dares to boast of— 2 Cor 11:21
God is not mocked, for **w** one sows, that Gal 6:7
knowing that **w** good anyone does, this Eph 6:8
But **w** gain I had, I counted as loss for Phil 3:7
Finally, brothers, **w** is true, whatever is Phil 4:8
whatever is true, **w** is honorable, Phil 4:8
is true, whatever is honorable, **w** is just, Phil 4:8
is honorable, whatever is just, **w** is pure, Phil 4:8
is just, whatever is pure, **w** is lovely, Phil 4:8
whatever is lovely, **w** is commendable, Phil 4:8
I have learned in **w** situation I am to Phil 4:11
And **w** you do, in word or deed, do Col 3:17
W you do, work heartily, as for the Col 3:23
and **w** else is contrary to sound 1 Tm 1:10
For **w** overcomes a person, to that he is 2 Pt 2:19
and **w** we ask we receive from him, 1 Jn 3:22
we know that he hears us in **w** we ask, 1 Jn 5:15

WHEAT (47)

In the days of **w** harvest Reuben went Gn 30:14
But the **w** and the emmer were not Ex 9:32
oil. You shall make them of fine **w** flour. Ex 29:2
of Weeks, the firstfruits of **w** harvest, Ex 34:22
a land of **w** and barley, of vines and fig Dt 8:8
the very finest of the **w**—and you drank Dt 32:14
was beating out **w** in the winepress Jgs 6:11
After some days, at the time of **w** harvest, Jgs 15:1
the end of the barley and **w** harvests. Ru 2:23
were reaping their **w** harvest in the 1 Sm 6:13
Is it not **w** harvest today? I will call 1 Sm 12:17
the midst of the house as if to get **w**, 2 Sm 4:6
and earthen vessels, **w**, barley, 2 Sm 17:28
Hiram 20,000 cors of **w** as food for his 1 Kgs 5:11
Now Ornan was threshing **w**. He 1 Chr 21:20
the wood and the **w** for a grain 1 Chr 21:23
cut timber, 20,000 cors of crushed **w**, 2 Chr 2:10
Now therefore the **w** and barley, oil 2 Chr 2:15
and 10,000 cors of **w** and 10,000 of 2 Chr 27:5
offerings to the God of heaven, **w**, salt, Ezr 6:9
up to 100 talents of silver, 100 cors of **w**, Ezr 7:22
let thorns grow instead of **w**, and foul Jb 31:40
would feed you with the finest of the **w**, Ps 81:16
he fills you with the finest of the **w**. Ps 147:14
Your belly is a heap of **w**, encircled with Sg 7:2
and put in **w** in rows and barley in its Is 28:25
They have sown **w** and have reaped Jer 12:13
What has straw in common with **w**? Jer 23:28
put us to death, for we have stores of **w**, Jer 41:8
"And you, take **w** and barley, beans and Ezk 4:9
for your merchandise **w** of Minnith, Ezk 27:17
of an ephah from each homer of **w**, Ezk 45:13
O vinedressers, for the **w** and the barley, Jl 1:11
Sabbath, that we may offer **w** for sale, Am 8:5
of sandals and sell the chaff of the **w**?" Am 8:6
floor and gather his **w** into the barn, Mt 3:12
weeds among the **w** and went away. Mt 13:25
you root up the **w** along with them. Mt 13:29
but gather the **w** into my barn.'" Mt 13:30
floor and to gather the **w** into his barn, Lk 3:17
He said, 'A hundred measures of **w**.' Lk 16:7
have you, that he might sift you like **w**, Lk 22:31
unless a grain of **w** falls into the earth Jn 12:24
ship, throwing out the **w** into the sea. Acts 27:38
perhaps of **w** or of some other grain. 1 Cor 15:37
saying, "A quart of **w** for a denarius, Rv 6:6
wine, oil, fine flour, **w**, cattle and sheep, Rv 18:13

WHEEL (15)

and the height of a **w** was a cubit and 1 Kgs 7:32
wheels were made like a chariot **w**; 1 Kgs 7:33
the wicked and drives the **w** over them. Prv 20:26
or the **w** broken at the cistern, Eccl 12:6
sledge, nor is a cart **w** rolled over cumin, Is 28:27
he drives his cart **w** over it with his Is 28:28
and there he was working at his **w**. Jer 18:3
I saw a **w** on the earth beside the living Ezk 1:15
being as it were a **w** within a wheel. Ezk 1:16
being as it were a wheel within a **w**. Ezk 1:16
he went in and stood beside a **w**. Ezk 10:6
likeness, as if a **w** were within a wheel. Ezk 10:10
likeness, as if a wheel were within a **w**. Ezk 10:10
whatever direction the front **w** faced, Ezk 10:11
crack of the whip, and rumble of the **w**, Na 3:2

WHEELS (28)

clogging their chariot **w** so that they Ex 14:25
stand had four bronze **w** and axles of 1 Kgs 7:30
And the four **w** were underneath the 1 Kgs 7:32
The axles of the **w** were of one piece 1 Kgs 7:32
The **w** were made like a chariot 1 Kgs 7:33
like flint, and their **w** like the whirlwind. Is 5:28
his chariots, at the rumbling of their **w**, Jer 47:3
appearance of the **w** and their Ezk 1:16
creatures went, the **w** went beside them; Ezk 1:19
rose from the earth, the **w** rose. Ezk 1:19
went, and the **w** rose along with them, Ezk 1:20
of the living creatures was in the **w**. Ezk 1:20
the earth, the **w** rose along with them, Ezk 1:21
of the living creatures was in the **w**. Ezk 1:21
and the sound of the **w** beside them, Ezk 3:13
among the whirling **w** underneath the Ezk 10:2
fire from between the whirling **w**, Ezk 10:6
there were four **w** beside the cherubim, Ezk 10:9
appearance of the **w** was like sparkling Ezk 10:9
and the **w** were full of eyes all around Ezk 10:12
eyes all around—the **w** that the four of Ezk 10:12
As for the **w**, they were called in my Ezk 10:13
in my hearing "the whirling **w**." Ezk 10:13
went, the **w** went beside them. Ezk 10:16
the **w** did not turn from beside them. Ezk 10:16
they went out, with the **w** beside them. Ezk 10:19
their wings, with the **w** beside them, Ezk 11:22
was fiery flames; its **w** were burning fire. Dn 7:9

WHENEVER (43)

W the stronger of the flock were Gn 30:41
So **w** he went in to his brother's wife he Gn 38:9
W Moses held up his hand, Israel Ex 17:11
prevailed, and **w** he lowered his hand, Ex 17:11
W Moses went out to the tent, all the Ex 33:8
W Moses went in before the LORD to Ex 34:34
w the cloud was taken up from over the Ex 40:36
And **w** the cloud lifted from over the Nm 9:17
alarm is to be blown **w** they are to set Nm 10:6
by day, **w** they set out from the camp. Nm 10:34
And **w** the ark set out, Moses said, Nm 10:35
our God is to us, **w** we call upon him? Dt 4:7
meat, you may eat meat **w** you desire. Dt 12:20
eat within your towns **w** you desire. Dt 12:21
W they marched out, the hand of the Jgs 2:15
W the LORD raised up judges for them, Jgs 2:18
But **w** the judge died, they turned back Jgs 2:19
For **w** the Israelites planted crops, the Jgs 6:3
And **w** the evil spirit from God was 1 Sm 16:23
And **w** a man came near to pay 2 Sm 15:5
giving ear to them **w** they call to you. 1 Kgs 8:52
So **w** he passed that way, he would turn 2 Kgs 4:8
and a lamp, so that **w** he comes to us, 2 Kgs 4:10
And **w** they saw that there was 2 Kgs 12:10
and **w** burnt offerings were offered 1 Chr 23:31
endures forever—**w** David offered 2 Chr 7:6
w a case comes to you from your 2 Chr 19:10
And **w** the chest was brought to the 2 Chr 24:11
For **w** I speak, I cry out, I shout, Jer 20:8
that **w** you spoke of him you wagged Jer 48:27
W you hear a word from my mouth, Ezk 3:17
a lying divination, **w** you have said, Ezk 13:7
W you hear a word from my mouth, Ezk 33:7
And **w** the unclean spirits saw him, Mk 3:11
he said to them, "**W** you enter a house, Mk 6:10
And **w** it seizes him, it throws him Mk 9:18
And **w** you stand praying, forgive, if Mk 11:25
the poor with you, and **w** you want, Mk 14:7
W you enter a town and they receive Lk 10:8
But **w** you enter a town and they do not Lk 10:10
to this day **w** Moses is read a veil lies 2 Cor 3:15
for **w** our heart condemns us, God is 1 Jn 3:20
And **w** the living creatures give glory and Rv 4:9

WHERE (524)

whole land of Havilah, **w** there is gold. Gn 2:11
to the man and said to him, "**W** are you?" Gn 3:9
Cain, "**W** is Abel your brother?" He said, Gn 4:9
Bethel to the place **w** his tent had been Gn 13:3
to the place **w** he had made an altar at Gn 13:4
eyes and look from the place **w** you are, Gn 13:14
w have you come from and where are Gn 16:8
you come from and **w** are you going?" Gn 16:8
"**W** is Sarah your wife?" And he said, Gn 18:9
"**W** are the men who came to you Gn 19:5
morning to the place **w** he had stood Gn 19:27
is before you; dwell **w** it pleases you." Gn 20:15
has heard the voice of the boy **w** he is. Gn 21:17
with the land **w** you have sojourned." Gn 21:23
but **w** is the lamb for a burnt offering?" Gn 22:7
w do you come from?" They said, Gn 29:4
places, **w** the flocks came to drink. Gn 30:38
and Leah into the field **w** his flock was Gn 31:4
w you anointed a pillar and made a Gn 31:13

do you belong? **W** are you going? Gn 32:17
him in the place **w** he had spoken with Gn 35:13
pillar in the place **w** he had spoken Gn 35:14
name of the place **w** God had spoken Gn 35:15
w Abraham and Isaac had sojourned. Gn 35:27
please, **w** they are pasturing the flock." Gn 37:16
"The boy is gone, and I, **w** shall I go?" Gn 37:30
"**W** is the cult prostitute who was at Gn 38:21
the place **w** the king's prisoners were Gn 39:20
in the prison **w** Joseph was confined. Gn 40:3
them. "**W** do you come from?" he said. Gn 42:7
brothers remain confined **w** you are in Gn 42:19
He said to his daughters, "Then **w** is he? Ex 2:20
the land of Goshen, **w** my people dwell, Ex 8:22
of Goshen, **w** the people of Israel were, Ex 9:26
people of Israel had light **w** they lived. Ex 10:23
a sign for you, on the houses **w** you are. Ex 12:13
was not a house **w** someone was not Ex 12:30
w there were twelve springs of water Ex 15:27
in the wilderness **w** he was encamped Ex 18:5
near to the thick darkness **w** God was. Ex 20:21
In every place **w** I cause my name to be Ex 20:24
before the LORD, **w** I will meet with you, Ex 29:42
the testimony, **w** I will meet with you. Ex 30:6
the tent of meeting **w** I shall meet with Ex 30:36
is a place by me **w** you shall stand on Ex 33:21
kill it in the place **w** they kill the burnt Lv 4:24
offering in the place **w** they kill the Lv 4:33
In the place **w** the burnt offering is killed Lv 6:25
In the place **w** they kill the burnt offering Lv 7:2
the lamb in the place **w** they kill the sin Lv 14:13
in the place **w** the blood of the guilt Lv 14:28
they do in the land of Egypt, **w** you lived, Lv 18:3
that the land **w** I am bringing you to Lv 20:22
and in the place **w** the cloud settled Nm 9:17
for you know **w** we should camp in Nm 10:31
W am I to get meat to give to all this Nm 11:13
come into the land **w** I swore that I Nm 14:30
the testimony, **w** I meet with you. Nm 17:4
w the people of Israel quarreled with Nm 20:13
w there was no way to turn either to Nm 22:26
their cities in the places **w** they lived, Nm 31:10
w there was no water for the people to Nm 33:14
trouble you in the land **w** you dwell. Nm 33:55
w you shall permit the manslayer to Nm 35:6
W are we going up? Our brothers have Dt 1:28
w you have seen how the LORD your God Dt 1:31
among the nations **w** the LORD will Dt 4:27
and thirsty ground **w** there was no Dt 8:15
w you sowed your seed and irrigated it, Dt 11:10
all the places **w** the nations whom Dt 12:2
w he lives—and he may come when he Dt 18:6
in her, you shall let her go **w** she wants. Dt 21:14
city at the gate of the place **w** he lives, Dt 21:19
among all the peoples **w** the LORD will Dt 28:37
growing, **w** no plant can sprout, Dt 29:23
among all the nations **w** the LORD your Dt 30:1
from all the peoples **w** the LORD your God Dt 30:3
Then he will say, '**W** are their gods, the Dt 32:37
me, but I did not know **w** they were from. Jos 2:4
went out. I do not know **w** the men went. Jos 2:5
from the very place **w** the priests' feet Jos 4:3
down in the place **w** you lodge tonight.'" Jos 4:3
them to the place **w** they lodged and laid Jos 4:8
in the place **w** the feet of the priests Jos 4:9
for the place **w** you are standing is holy." Jos 5:15
the open wilderness **w** they pursued Jos 8:24
are you? And **w** do you come from?" Jos 9:8
them into the cave **w** they had hidden Jos 10:27
tents in the land **w** your possession lies, Jos 22:4
the LORD'S land **w** the LORD'S tabernacle Jos 22:19
to destroy the land **w** the people of Jos 22:33
he fell; **w** he sank, there he fell—dead. Jgs 5:27
And **w** are all his wonderful deeds that Jgs 6:13
"**W** are the men whom you killed at Jgs 8:18
said to him, "**W** is your mouth now, Jgs 9:38
I did not ask him **w** he was from, and he Jgs 13:6
him, and see **w** his great strength lies, Jgs 16:5
"Please tell me **w** your great strength Jgs 16:6
have not told me **w** your great strength Jgs 16:15
in Judah to sojourn **w** he could find a Jgs 17:8
"**W** do you come from?" And he said to Jgs 17:9
I am going to sojourn **w** I may find a Jgs 17:9
a place **w** there is no lack of anything Jgs 18:10
the old man said, "**W** are you going? Jgs 19:17
you going? and **w** do you come from?" Jgs 19:17
of the man's house **w** her master was, Jgs 19:26
in the same place **w** they had formed it Jgs 20:22
set out from the place **w** she was with her Ru 1:7
For **w** you go I will go, and where you Ru 1:16
go I will go, and **w** you lodge I will lodge. Ru 1:16
W you die I will die, and there will I be Ru 1:17
said to her, "**W** did you glean today? Ru 2:19
glean today? And **w** have you worked? Ru 2:19
he lies down, observe the place **w** he lies. Ru 3:4

of hosts at Shiloh, **w** the two sons of Eli, 1 Sm 1:3
of the LORD, **w** the ark of God was. 1 Sm 3:3
they went to the city **w** the man of God 1 Sm 9:10
"Tell me **w** is the house of the seer?" 1 Sm 9:18
w there is a garrison of the Philistines. 1 Sm 10:5
"**W** did you go?" And he said, 1 Sm 10:14
out of the holes **w** they have hidden 1 Sm 14:11
my father in the field **w** you are, 1 Sm 19:3
"**W** are Samuel and David?" And 1 Sm 19:22
to the place **w** you hid yourself 1 Sm 20:19
Know and see the place **w** his foot is, 1 Sm 23:22
of all the lurking places **w** he hides, 1 Sm 23:23
by the way, **w** there was a cave, 1 Sm 24:3
who come from I do not know **w**?" 1 Sm 25:11
to the place **w** Saul had encamped. 1 Sm 26:5
And David saw the place **w** Saul lay, 1 Sm 26:5
And now see **w** the king's spear is 1 Sm 26:16
"**W** have you made a raid today?" 1 Sm 27:10
w those who were left behind stayed. 1 Sm 30:9
And **w** are you from?" He said, "I am 1 Sm 30:13
for all the places **w** David and his 1 Sm 30:31
"**W** do you come from?" And he said to 2 Sm 1:3
"**W** do you come from?" And he 2 Sm 1:13
And he fell there and died **w** he was. 2 Sm 2:23
came to the place **w** Asahel had fallen 2 Sm 2:23
In all places **w** I have moved with all 2 Sm 7:7
"**W** is he?" And Ziba said to the king, 2 Sm 9:4
Uriah to the place **w** he knew there 2 Sm 11:16
Amnon's house, **w** he was lying down. 2 Sm 13:8
for me, **w** could I carry my shame? 2 Sm 13:13
with us, since I go I know not **w**? 2 Sm 15:20
the summit, **w** God was worshiped, 2 Sm 15:32
"And **w** is your master's son?" Ziba 2 Sm 16:3
upon him in some place **w** he is to be 2 Sm 17:12
"**W** are Ahimaaz and Jonathan?" 2 Sm 17:20
w the Philistines had hanged them, 2 Sm 21:12
w there was a man of great stature, 2 Sm 21:20
w there was a plot of ground full of 2 Sm 23:11
to the place **w** it was required, 1 Kgs 4:28
Hall of the Throne **w** he was to 1 Kgs 7:7
His own house **w** he was to dwell, in 1 Kgs 7:8
w the LORD made a covenant with the 1 Kgs 8:9
w he had knelt with hands 1 Kgs 8:54
the city **w** I have chosen to put my 1 Kgs 11:36
w he had fled from King Solomon), 1 Kgs 12:2
it in the city **w** the old prophet lived. 1 Kgs 13:25
into the upper chamber **w** he lodged, 1 Kgs 17:19
nation or kingdom **w** my lord has 1 Kgs 18:10
LORD will carry you I know not **w**. 1 Kgs 18:12
w he has gone to take possession. 1 Kgs 21:18
"In the place **w** dogs licked up the 1 Kgs 21:19
the water, saying, "**W** is the LORD, 2 Kgs 2:14
to Shunem, **w** a wealthy woman lived, 2 Kgs 4:8
said to him, "**W** have you been, 2 Kgs 5:25
the place **w** we dwell under your 2 Kgs 6:1
"**W** did it fall?" When he showed him 2 Kgs 6:6
And he said, "Go and see **w** he is, that 2 Kgs 6:13
of Moses, **w** the LORD commanded, 2 Kgs 14:6
to Elath, **w** they dwell to this day. 2 Kgs 16:6
W are the gods of Hamath and 2 Kgs 18:34
W are the gods of Sepharvaim, 2 Kgs 18:34
W is the king of Hamath, the king 2 Kgs 19:13
And from **w** did they come to you?" 2 Kgs 20:14
w the women wove hangings for the 2 Kgs 23:7
the high places **w** the priests had 2 Kgs 23:8
w he reigned for seven years and six 1 Chr 3:4
w they found rich, good pasture, and 1 Chr 4:40
that is Jebus, **w** the Jebusites were, 1 Chr 11:4
In all places **w** I have moved with all 1 Chr 17:6
w there was a man of great stature, 1 Chr 20:6
w the LORD had appeared to David his 2 Chr 3:1
w the LORD made a covenant with the 2 Chr 5:10
the place **w** you have promised to set 2 Chr 6:20
w he had fled from King Solomon), 2 Chr 10:2
to him from all places **w** they lived. 2 Chr 11:13
of Moses, **w** the LORD commanded, 2 Chr 25:4
of the archives **w** the documents were Ezr 6:1
the place **w** sacrifices were offered, Ezr 6:3
son of Eliashib, **w** he spent the night, Ezr 10:6
officials did not know **w** I had gone or Neh 2:16
plundered in a land **w** they are captives. Neh 4:4
In the place **w** you hear the sound of Neh 4:20
the tithes in all our towns **w** we labor. Neh 10:37
w the vessels of the sanctuary are, Neh 10:39
a large chamber **w** they had previously Neh 13:5
to Queen Esther, "Who is he, and **w** is he, Est 7:5
garden to the place **w** they were drinking Est 7:8
was falling on the couch **w** Esther was. Est 7:8
"From **w** have you come?" Satan Jb 1:7
"From **w** have you come?" Satan Jb 2:2
perished? Or **w** were the upright cut off? Jb 4:7
dark with ice, and **w** the snow hides itself. Jb 6:16
"Can papyrus grow **w** there is no marsh? Jb 8:11
Can reeds flourish **w** there is no water? Jb 8:11
any order, **w** light is as thick darkness." Jb 10:22

low; man breathes his last, and **w** is he? Jb 14:10
abroad for bread, saying, '**W** is it?' Jb 15:23
w then is my hope? Who will see my Jb 17:15
and no survivor **w** he used to live. Jb 18:19
who have seen him will say, '**W** is he?' Jb 20:7
you say, '**W** is the house of the prince? Jb 21:28
W is the tent in which the wicked Jb 21:28
Oh, that I knew **w** I might find him, that I Jb 23:3
in a valley away from **w** anyone lives; Jb 28:4
"But **w** shall wisdom be found? And Jb 28:12
And **w** is the place of understanding? Jb 28:12
"From **w**, then, does wisdom come? And Jb 28:20
And **w** is the place of understanding? Jb 28:20
or deep darkness **w** evildoers may hide Jb 34:22
But none says, '**W** is God my Maker, Jb 35:10
into a broad place **w** there was no Jb 36:16
"**W** were you when I laid the foundation Jb 38:4
"**W** is the way to the dwelling of light, Jb 38:19
of light, and **w** is the place of darkness, Jb 38:19
way to the place **w** the light is Jb 38:24
or **w** the east wind is scattered upon the Jb 38:24
to bring rain on a land **w** no man is, on Jb 38:26
ones suck up blood, and **w** the slain are, Jb 39:30
tread down the wicked **w** they stand. Jb 40:12
yield food for him **w** all the wild beasts Jb 40:20
house and the place **w** your glory dwells. Ps 26:8
from **w** he sits enthroned he looks out Ps 33:14
he will not rise again from **w** he lies." Ps 41:8
say to me continually, "**W** is your God?" Ps 42:3
to me continually, "**W** is your God?" Ps 42:10
are, in great terror, **w** there is no terror! Ps 53:5
a dry and weary land **w** there is no water. Ps 63:1
yes, **w** the LORD will dwell forever? Ps 68:16
sink in deep mire, **w** there is no foothold; Ps 69:2
Mount Zion, **w** you have dwelt. Ps 74:2
the tent **w** he dwelt among mankind, Ps 78:60
"**W** is their God?" Let the avenging of Ps 79:10
for herself, **w** she may lay her young, Ps 84:3
Lord, **w** is your steadfast love of old, Ps 89:49
the nations say, "**W** is their God?" Ps 115:2
the hills. From **w** does my help come? Ps 121:1
W shall I go from your Spirit? Or where Ps 139:7
Or **w** shall I flee from your presence? Ps 139:7
In the path **w** I walk they have hidden a Ps 142:3
W there is no guidance, a people falls, Prv 11:14
W there are no oxen, the manger is Prv 14:4
is a dinner of herbs **w** love is than a Prv 15:17
goes out, and **w** there is no whisperer, Prv 26:20
W there is no prophetic vision the Prv 29:18
down, and hastens to the place **w** it rises. Eccl 1:5
not full; to the place **w** the streams flow, Eccl 1:7
praised in the city **w** they had done Eccl 8:10
the north, in the place **w** the tree falls, Eccl 11:3
my soul loves, **w** you pasture your flock, Sg 1:7
flock, **w** you make it lie down at noon; Sg 1:7
W has your beloved gone, O most Sg 6:1
W has your beloved turned, that we may Sg 6:1
In that day every place **w** there used to be Is 7:23
will become a place **w** cattle are let loose Is 7:25
cattle are let loose and **w** sheep tread. Is 7:25
help, and **w** will you leave your wealth? Is 10:3
W then are your wise men? Let them tell Is 19:12
Ariel, Ariel, the city **w** David encamped! Is 29:1
from **w** come the lioness and the lion, Is 30:6
"**W** is he who counted, where is he who Is 33:18
w is he who weighed the tribute? Is 33:18
W is he who counted the towers?" Is 33:18
streams, **w** no galley with oars can go, Is 33:21
in the haunt of jackals, **w** they lie down, Is 35:7
W are the gods of Hamath and Arpad? Is 36:19
Arpad? **W** are the gods of Sepharvaim? Is 36:19
W is the king of Hamath, the king of Is 37:13
And from **w** did they come to you?" Is 39:3
left alone; from **w** have these come?'" Is 49:21
"**W** is your mother's certificate of Is 50:1
And **w** is the wrath of the oppressor? Is 51:13
W is he who brought them up out of the Is 63:11
W is he who put in the midst of them Is 63:11
W are your zeal and your might? Is 63:15
house, **w** our fathers praised you, Is 64:11
'**W** is the LORD who brought us up from Jer 2:6
none passes through, **w** no man dwells?' Jer 2:6
The priests did not say, '**W** is the LORD?' Jer 2:8
But **w** are your gods that you made for Jer 2:28
and see! **W** have you not been ravished? Jer 3:2
for the ancient paths, **w** the good way is; Jer 6:16
Shiloh, **w** I made my name dwell at first, Jer 7:12
in all the places **w** I have driven them, Jer 8:3
loincloth from the place **w** I had hidden Jer 13:7
W is the flock that was given you, your Jer 13:20
And when they ask you, '**W** shall we go?' Jer 15:2
of all the countries **w** he had driven Jer 16:15
say to me, "**W** is the word of the LORD? Jer 17:15
w the LORD had sent him to prophesy, Jer 19:14
but in the place **w** they have carried Jer 22:12

another country, **w** you were not born, Jer 22:26
of all the countries **w** I have driven them, Jer 23:3
of all the countries **w** he had driven Jer 23:8
in all the places **w** I shall drive them. Jer 24:9
the welfare of the city **w** I have sent you Jer 29:7
and all the places **w** I have driven you, Jer 29:14
among all the nations **w** I have driven Jer 29:18
the palace shall stand **w** it used to be. Jer 30:18
many days in the land **w** you sojourn.' Jer 35:7
and let no one know **w** you are." Jer 36:19
W are your prophets who prophesied to Jer 37:19
w we shall not see war or hear the Jer 42:14
pestilence in the place **w** you desire to Jer 42:22
in the land of Egypt **w** you have come to Jer 44:8
"**W** is bread and wine?" as they faint Lam 2:12
canal, and I sat **w** they were dwelling. Ezk 3:15
among the nations **w** I will drive them." Ezk 4:13
among the nations **w** they are carried Ezk 6:9
w was the seat of the image of jealousy, Ezk 8:3
in the countries **w** they have gone.' Ezk 11:16
out of the countries **w** you have been Ezk 11:17
among the nations **w** they go, Ezk 12:16
'**W** is the coating with which you Ezk 13:12
him, and its roots remained **w** it stood. Ezk 17:6
him from the bed **w** it was planted, Ezk 17:7
wither away on the bed **w** it sprouted?" Ezk 17:10
surely in the place **w** the king dwells Ezk 17:16
of the countries **w** you are scattered, Ezk 20:34
them out of the land **w** they sojourn, Ezk 20:38
out of the countries **w** you have been Ezk 20:41
In the place **w** you were created, Ezk 21:30
them from all places **w** they have been Ezk 34:12
servant Jacob, **w** your fathers lived. Ezk 37:25
w the burnt offering was to be washed. Ezk 40:38
w the priests who approach the LORD Ezk 42:13
w I will dwell in the midst of the people Ezk 43:7
"This is the place **w** the priests shall Ezk 46:20
and **w** they shall bake the grain Ezk 46:20
are the kitchens **w** those who minister Ezk 46:24
so everything will live **w** the river goes. Ezk 47:9
went to his house **w** he had windows in Dn 6:10
he came near to the den **w** Daniel was, Dn 6:20
So he came near **w** I stood. And when he Dn 8:17
And in the place **w** it was said to them, Hos 1:10
W now is your king, to save you in all Hos 13:10
W are all your rulers—those of whom Hos 13:10
Death? O Death, **w** are your plagues? Hos 13:14
plagues? O Sheol, **w** is your sting? Hos 13:14
say among the peoples, '**W** is their God?'" Jl 2:17
occupation? And **w** do you come from? Jon 1:8
"**W** is the LORD your God?" My eyes will Mi 7:10
W is the lions' den, the feeding place of Na 2:11
lions, **w** the lion and lioness went, Na 2:11
lion and lioness went, **w** his cubs were, Na 2:11
her? **W** shall I seek comforters for you? Na 3:7
they fly away; no one knows **w** they are. Na 3:17
Your fathers, **w** are they? And the Zec 1:5
"**W** are you going?" And he said to me, Zec 2:2
me, "**W** are they taking the basket?" Zec 5:10
If then I am a father, **w** is my honor? Mal 1:6
And if I am a master, **w** is my fear? Mal 1:6
by asking, "**W** is the God of justice?" Mal 2:17
"**W** is he who has been born king of the Mt 2:2
he inquired of them **w** the Christ was to Mt 2:4
to rest over the place **w** the child was. Mt 2:9
w moth and rust destroy and where Mt 6:19
and rust destroy and **w** thieves break in Mt 6:19
w neither moth nor rust destroys and Mt 6:20
nor rust destroys and **w** thieves do not Mt 6:20
For **w** your treasure is, there your heart Mt 6:21
to denounce the cities **w** most of his Mt 11:20
ground, **w** they did not have much soil, Mt 13:5
"**W** did this man get this wisdom and Mt 13:54
W then did this man get all these Mt 13:56
"**W** are we to get enough bread in such Mt 15:33
For **w** two or three are gathered in my Mt 18:20
baptism of John, from **w** did it come? Mt 21:25
a hard man, reaping **w** you did not sow, Mt 25:24
and gathering **w** you scattered no seed, Mt 25:24
knew that I reap **w** I have not sowed Mt 25:26
not sowed and gather **w** I scattered no Mt 25:26
"**W** will you have us prepare for you to Mt 26:17
w the scribes and the elders had Mt 26:57
as he said. Come, see the place **w** he lay. Mt 28:6
ground, **w** it did not have much soil, Mk 4:5
ones along the path, **w** the word is sown: Mk 4:15
with him and went in **w** the child was. Mk 5:40
"**W** did this man get these things? Mk 6:2
'**w** their worm does not die and the fire Mk 9:48
of desolation standing **w** it ought not Mk 13:14
"**W** will you have us go and prepare Mk 14:12
Teacher says, **W** is my guest room, Mk 14:14
w I may eat the Passover with my Mk 14:14
the mother of Joses saw **w** he was laid. Mk 15:47
not here. See the place **w** they laid him. Mk 16:6
to Nazareth, **w** he had been brought up. Lk 4:16
and found the place **w** it was written, Lk 4:17
"**W** is your faith?" And they were afraid, Lk 8:25
every town and place **w** he himself was Lk 10:1
as he journeyed, came to **w** he was, Lk 10:33
w no thief approaches and no moth Lk 12:33
For **w** your treasure is, there will your Lk 12:34
you, 'I do not know **w** you come from.' Lk 13:25
you, I do not know **w** you come from. Lk 13:27
not ten cleansed? **W** are the nine? Lk 17:17
to him, "**W**, Lord?" He said to them, Lk 17:37
He said to them, "**W** the corpse is, Lk 17:37
w on entering you will find a colt tied, Lk 19:30
that they did not know **w** it came from. Lk 20:7
w he calls the Lord the God of Lk 20:37
to him, "**W** will you have us prepare it?" Lk 22:9
says to you, **W** is the guest room, Lk 22:11
w I may eat the Passover with my Lk 22:11
stone, **w** no one had ever yet been laid. Lk 23:53
across the Jordan, **w** John was baptizing. Jn 1:28
means Teacher), "**w** are you staying?" Jn 1:38
So they came and saw **w** he was staying, Jn 1:39
and did not know **w** it came from (though Jn 2:9
The wind blows **w** it wishes, and you hear Jn 3:8
but you do not know **w** it comes from or Jn 3:8
know where it comes from or **w** it goes. Jn 3:8
is deep. **W** do you get that living water? Jn 4:11
Jerusalem is the place **w** people ought to Jn 4:20
in Galilee, **w** he had made the water wine. Jn 4:46
said to Philip, "**W** are we to buy bread, Jn 6:5
came near the place **w** they had eaten the Jn 6:23
of Man ascending to **w** he was before? Jn 6:62
him at the feast, and saying, "**W** is he?" Jn 7:11
But we know **w** this man comes from, Jn 7:27
no one will know **w** he comes from." Jn 7:27
know me, and you know **w** I come from? Jn 7:28
not find me. **W** I am you cannot come." Jn 7:34
"**W** does this man intend to go that we Jn 7:35
me,' and, '**W** I am you cannot come'?" Jn 7:36
Bethlehem, the village **w** David was?" Jn 7:42
up and said to her, "Woman, **w** are they? Jn 8:10
for I know **w** I came from and where I am Jn 8:14
where I came from and **w** I am going, Jn 8:14
but you do not know **w** I come from or Jn 8:14
where I come from or **w** I am going. Jn 8:14
"**W** is your Father?" Jesus answered, Jn 8:19
sin. **W** I am going, you cannot come." Jn 8:21
himself, since he says, '**W** I am going, Jn 8:22
They said to him, "**W** is he?" He said, "I Jn 9:12
man, we do not know **w** he comes from." Jn 9:29
You do not know **w** he comes from, and Jn 9:30
Jordan to the place **w** John had been Jn 10:40
two days longer in the place **w** he was. Jn 11:6
still in the place **w** Martha had met Jn 11:30
when Mary came to **w** Jesus was and Jn 11:32
"**W** have you laid him?" They said to Jn 11:34
orders that if anyone knew **w** he was, Jn 11:57
came to Bethany, **w** Lazarus was, Jn 12:1
and **w** I am, there will my servant be Jn 12:26
darkness does not know **w** he is going. Jn 12:35
you, '**W** I am going you cannot come.' Jn 13:33
w are you going?" Jesus answered him, Jn 13:36
"**W** I am going you cannot follow me Jn 13:36
to myself, that **w** I am you may be also. Jn 14:3
And you know the way to **w** I am going." Jn 14:4
"Lord, we do not know **w** you are going. Jn 14:5
none of you asks me, '**W** are you going?' Jn 16:5
have given me, may be with me **w** I am, Jn 17:24
the Kidron Valley, **w** there was a garden, Jn 18:1
in the temple, **w** all Jews come together. Jn 18:20
"**W** are you from?" But Jesus gave him Jn 19:9
for the place **w** Jesus was crucified was Jn 19:20
Now in the place **w** he was crucified Jn 19:41
we do not know **w** they have laid him." Jn 20:2
sitting **w** the body of Jesus had lain, Jn 20:12
I do not know **w** they have laid him." Jn 20:13
him away, tell me **w** you have laid him, Jn 20:15
doors being locked **w** the disciples were Jn 20:19
you and carry you **w** you do not want Jn 21:18
to the upper room, **w** they were staying, Acts 1:13
the entire house **w** they were sitting. Acts 2:2
w he became the father of two sons. Acts 7:29
for the place **w** you are standing is Acts 7:33
w many were gathered together and Acts 12:12
w they had been commended to the Acts 14:26
in every city **w** we proclaimed the Acts 15:36
w we supposed there was a place of Acts 16:13
w there was a synagogue of the Jews. Acts 17:1
at Troas, **w** we stayed for seven days. Acts 20:6
in the upper room **w** we were gathered. Acts 20:8
tribunal, **w** I ought to be tried. Acts 25:10
but **w** there is no law there is no Rom 4:15
sin is not counted **w** there is no law. Rom 5:13
the trespass, but **w** sin increased, Rom 5:20
"And in the very place **w** it was said to Rom 9:26
not **w** Christ has already been Rom 15:20
W is the one who is wise? Where is 1 Cor 1:20
the one who is wise? **W** is the scribe? 1 Cor 1:20
scribe? **W** is the debater of this age? 1 Cor 1:20
w would be the sense of hearing? 1 Cor 12:17
ear, **w** would be the sense of smell? 1 Cor 12:17
member, **w** would the body be? 1 Cor 12:19
"O death, **w** is your victory? O death, 1 Cor 15:55
victory? O death, **w** is your sting?" 1 Cor 15:55
Spirit, and **w** the Spirit of the Lord is, 2 Cor 3:17
the things that are above, **w** Christ is, Col 3:1
w your fathers put me to the test and saw Heb 3:9
w Jesus has gone as a forerunner on Heb 6:20
For **w** a will is involved, the death of the Heb 9:16
W there is forgiveness of these, there Heb 10:18
went out, not knowing **w** he was going. Heb 11:8
For **w** jealousy and selfish ambition Jas 3:16
say, "**W** is the promise of his coming? 2 Pt 3:4
and does not know **w** he is going, 1 Jn 2:11
Remember therefore from **w** you have Rv 2:5
"'I know **w** you dwell, where Satan's Rv 2:13
where you dwell, **w** Satan's throne is. Rv 2:13
was killed among you, **w** Satan dwells. Rv 2:13
robes, and from **w** have they come?" Rv 7:13
and Egypt, **w** their Lord was crucified. Rv 11:8
w she has a place prepared by God, Rv 12:6
to the place **w** she is to be nourished for Rv 12:14
that you saw, **w** the prostitute is seated, Rv 17:15
for the great city **w** all who had ships at Rv 18:19
of fire and sulfur **w** the beast and the Rv 20:10

WHEREAS (11)
w it is because of the wickedness of these Dt 9:4
W you were as numerous as the stars of Dt 28:62
me good, **w** I have repaid you evil. 1 Sm 24:17
'**W** it was in your heart to build a 1 Kgs 8:18
w my father laid on you a heavy 1 Kgs 12:11
'**W** it was in your heart to build a 2 Chr 6:8
w my father laid on you a heavy 2 Chr 10:11
W you have been forsaken and hated, Is 60:15
w the sword has reached their very life." Jer 4:10
w worldly grief produces death. 2 Cor 7:10
w angels, though greater in might and 2 Pt 2:11

WHEREBY (1)
w the sunrise shall visit us from on high Lk 1:78

WHEREFORE (1)
W it is said in the Book of the Wars of Nm 21:14

WHEREVER (51)
with you and will keep you **w** you go, Gn 28:15
the LORD has blessed you **w** I turned. Gn 30:30
and has been with me **w** I have gone." Gn 35:3
get your straw yourselves **w** you can find Ex 5:11
W the lot falls for anyone, that shall Nm 33:54
one of your towns, **w** it suits him. Dt 23:16
you may have good success **w** you go. Jos 1:7
the LORD your God is with you **w** you go." Jos 1:9
we will do, and **w** you send us we will go. Jos 1:16
W he turned he routed them. 1 Sm 14:47
and was successful **w** Saul sent him, 1 Sm 18:5
and they went **w** they could go. 1 Sm 23:13
have been with you **w** you went and 2 Sm 7:9
LORD gave victory to David **w** he went. 2 Sm 8:6
LORD gave victory to David **w** he went. 2 Sm 8:14
lives, **w** my lord the king shall be, 2 Sm 15:21
in all that you do and **w** you turn, 1 Kgs 2:3
household, and sojourn **w** you can, 2 Kgs 8:1
them repair the house **w** any need of 2 Kgs 12:5
him; **w** he went out, he prospered. 2 Kgs 18:7
have been with you **w** you have gone 1 Chr 17:8
LORD gave victory to David **w** he went. 1 Chr 18:6
gave victory to David **w** he went. 1 Chr 18:13
w the king's command and his decree Est 4:3
w the king's command and his edict Est 8:17
one who gives it; **w** he turns he prospers. Prv 17:8
hand of the LORD; he turns it **w** he will. Prv 21:1
go **w** you think it good and right to go. Jer 40:4
Or go **w** you think it right to go." So the Jer 40:5
W the spirit would go, they went, Ezk 1:12
W the spirit wanted to go, they went, Ezk 1:20
W you dwell, the cities shall be waste Ezk 6:6
w they offered pleasing aroma to all Ezk 6:13
then **w** they saw any high hill or any Ezk 20:28
to the left, **w** your face is directed. Ezk 21:16
came to the nations, **w** they came, Ezk 36:20
And **w** the river goes, every living Ezk 47:9
whose hand he has given, **w** they dwell, Dn 2:38
"Teacher, I will follow you **w** you go." Mt 8:19
W the corpse is, there the vultures will Mt 24:28
w this gospel is proclaimed in the Mt 26:13
on their beds to **w** they heard he was. Mk 6:55
And **w** he came, in villages, cities, or Mk 6:56
w the gospel is proclaimed in the whole Mk 14:9
and **w** he enters, say to the master of Mk 14:14
And **w** they do not receive you, when you Lk 9:5

said to him, "I will follow you **w** you go." Lk 9:57
dress yourself and walk **w** you wanted, Jn 21:18
may help me on my journey, **w** I go. 1 Cor 16:6
by a very small rudder **w** the will of the Jas 3:4
is these who follow the Lamb **w** he goes. Rv 14:4

WHET (2)
does not repent, God will **w** his sword; Ps 7:12
who **w** their tongues like swords, who Ps 64:3

WHETHER (127)
w born in your house or bought with Gn 17:12
go down to see **w** they have done Gn 18:21
in silence to learn **w** the LORD had Gn 24:21
to know **w** you are really my son Esau Gn 27:21
it, **w** stolen by day or stolen by night. Gn 31:39
please identify **w** it is your son's robe or Gn 37:32
may be tested, **w** there is truth in you. Gn 42:16
in Egypt to see **w** they are still alive." Ex 4:18
w he is a sojourner or a native of the Ex 12:19
them, **w** they will walk in my law or not. Ex 16:4
shot; **w** beast or man, he shall not live.' Ex 19:13
w it is an ox or a donkey or a sheep, Ex 22:4
near to God to show **w** or not he has put Ex 22:8
every breach of trust, **w** it is for an ox, Ex 22:9
them both to see **w** or not he has Ex 22:11
w he has seen or come to know the Lv 5:1
w a carcass of an unclean wild animal or Lv 5:2
w human uncleanness or an unclean Lv 7:21
blood whatever, **w** of fowl or of animal, Lv 7:26
and scales, **w** in the seas or in the rivers, Lv 11:9
w it is an article of wood or a garment Lv 11:32
W oven or stove, it shall be broken in Lv 11:35
completed, **w** for a son or for a daughter, Lv 12:6
w a woolen or a linen garment, Lv 13:47
w the rot is on the back or on the front. Lv 13:55
to determine **w** it is clean or unclean. Lv 13:59
w his body runs with his discharge, or Lv 15:3
W it is the bed or anything on which Lv 15:23
beasts, **w** he is a native or a sojourner, Lv 17:15
w brought up in the family or in Lv 18:9
dedicate; **w** ox or sheep, it is the LORD'S. Lv 27:26
anything that he has, **w** man or beast, Lv 27:28
w of the seed of the land or of the fruit of Lv 27:30
W it was two days, or a month, or a Nm 9:22
Now you shall see **w** my word will Nm 11:23
and **w** the people who dwell in it are Nm 13:18
or weak, **w** they are few or many, Nm 13:18
and **w** the land that they dwell in is Nm 13:19
and **w** the cities that they dwell in are Nm 13:19
and **w** the land is rich or poor, and Nm 13:20
poor, and **w** there are trees in it or not. Nm 13:20
hand, **w** he is native or a sojourner, Nm 15:30
the womb of all flesh, **w** man or beast, Nm 18:15
w such a great thing as this has ever Dt 4:32
w you would keep his commandments or Dt 8:2
to know **w** you love the LORD your God Dt 13:3
you, **w** near you or far off from you, Dt 13:7
offering a sacrifice, **w** an ox or a sheep: Dt 18:3
w he is one of your brothers or one of Dt 24:14
w the daughter of his father or the Dt 27:22
w the gods your fathers served in the Jos 24:15
w they will take care to walk in the way Jgs 2:22
to know **w** Israel would obey the Jgs 3:4
that we may know **w** the journey on Jgs 18:5
gone after young men, **w** poor or rich. Ru 3:10
was missing, **w** small or great, 1 Sm 30:19
'Who knows **w** the LORD will be 2 Sm 12:22
king shall be, **w** for death or for life, 2 Sm 15:21
w I shall recover from this sickness." 2 Kgs 1:2
be put to death, **w** young or old, 2 Chr 15:13
their descent, **w** they belonged to Israel: Ezr 2:59
to see **w** a decree was issued by Cyrus Ezr 5:17
w for death or for banishment or for Ezr 7:26
their descent, **w** they belonged to Israel: Neh 7:61
in order to see **w** Mordecai's words would Est 3:4
And who knows **w** you have not come Est 4:14
behold him, **w** it be a nation or a man? Jb 34:29
W for correction or for his land or for Jb 37:13
feel the heat of thorns, **w** green or ablaze, Ps 58:9
by **w** his conduct is pure and upright. Prv 20:11
and who knows **w** he will be wise or a Eccl 2:19
Who knows **w** the spirit of man goes Eccl 3:21
of a laborer, **w** he eats little or much, Eccl 5:12
W it is love or hate, man does not know; Eccl 9:1
or that, or **w** both alike will be good. Eccl 11:6
every secret thing, **w** good or evil. Eccl 12:14
the valley, to see **w** the vines had budded, Sg 6:11
w the pomegranates were in bloom. Sg 6:11
the vineyards and see **w** the vines have Sg 7:12
w the grape blossoms have opened and Sg 7:12
W it is good or bad, we will obey the Jer 42:6
And **w** they hear or refuse to hear (for Ezk 2:5
to them, **w** they hear or refuse to hear, Ezk 2:7
GOD,' **w** they hear or refuse to hear." Ezk 3:11
not eat of anything, **w** bird or beast, Ezk 44:31
Who knows **w** he will not turn and relent, Jl 2:14
let us see **w** Elijah will come to save Mt 27:49
to see **w** he would heal him on the Mk 3:2
let us see **w** Elijah will come to take Mk 15:36
he asked him **w** he was already dead. Mk 15:44
John, **w** he might be the Christ, Lk 3:15
to see **w** he would heal on the Sabbath, Lk 6:7
cost, **w** he has enough to complete it? Lk 14:28
down first and deliberate **w** he is able Lk 14:31
this, he asked **w** the man was a Galilean. Lk 23:6
he will know **w** the teaching is from God Jn 7:17
is from God or **w** I am speaking on Jn 7:17
"**W** he is a sinner I do not know. Jn 9:25
"**W** it is right in the sight of God to Acts 4:19
"Tell me **w** you sold the land for so Acts 5:8
called out to ask **w** Simon who was Acts 10:18
I asked **w** he wanted to go to Acts 25:20
And Paul said, "**W** short or long, I Acts 26:29
So then, **w** we live or whether we die, Rom 14:8
So then, whether we live or **w** we die, Rom 14:8
I do not know **w** I baptized anyone 1 Cor 1:16
w Paul or Apollos or Cephas or the 1 Cor 3:22
how do you know **w** you will save 1 Cor 7:16
how do you know **w** you will save 1 Cor 7:16
So, **w** you eat or drink, or whatever 1 Cor 10:31
W then it was I or they, so we preach 1 Cor 15:11
test you and know **w** you are obedient 2 Cor 2:9
So **w** we are at home or away, we make 2 Cor 5:9
has done in the body, **w** good or evil. 2 Cor 5:10
to the third heaven—**w** in the body or 2 Cor 12:2
up into paradise—**w** in the body or 2 Cor 12:3
to see **w** you are in the faith. 2 Cor 13:5
from the Lord, **w** he is a slave or free. Eph 6:8
in every way, **w** in pretense or in truth, Phil 1:18
in my body, **w** by life or by death. Phil 1:20
so that **w** I come and see you or am Phil 1:27
w thrones or dominions or rulers or Col 1:16
all things, **w** on earth or in heaven, Col 1:20
people, **w** from you or from others, 1 Thes 2:6
died for us so that **w** we are awake or 1 Thes 5:10
w it be to the emperor as supreme, 1 Pt 2:13
the spirits to see **w** they are from God, 1 Jn 4:1

WHICHEVER (3)
W of your servants is found with it Gn 44:9
or two pigeons, **w** he can afford. Lv 14:22
turtledoves or pigeons, **w** he can afford, Lv 14:30

WHILE (353)
and **w** he slept took one of his ribs and Gn 2:21
W the earth remains, seedtime and Gn 8:22
w Lot settled among the cities of the Gn 13:12
w I bring a morsel of bread, that you Gn 18:5
stood by them under the tree **w** they ate. Gn 18:8
the young woman remain with us a **w**, Gn 24:55
and **w** he was still living he sent them Gn 25:6
of the field, **w** Jacob was a quiet man, Gn 25:27
and stay with him a **w**, until your Gn 27:44
W he was still speaking with them, Gn 29:9
came against the city **w** it felt secure Gn 34:25
W Israel lived in that land, Reuben Gn 35:22
your brother, **w** you remain confined, Gn 42:16
neck and wept on his neck a good **w**. Gn 46:29
w her young women walked beside the Ex 2:5
the people of Israel **w** the people of Israel Ex 14:8
and fought with Amalek, **w** Moses, Ex 17:10
it, **w** Aaron and Hur held up his hands, Ex 17:12
w Moses went up to God. The LORD called Ex 19:3
w Moses drew near to the thick Ex 20:21
and **w** my glory passes by I will put you Ex 33:22
w the rest of the blood shall be drained Lv 5:9
LORD'S peace offerings **w** an uncleanness Lv 7:20
whoever enters the house **w** it is shut up Lv 14:46
uncovering her nakedness **w** her sister Lv 18:18
to uncover her nakedness **w** she is in Lv 18:19
to the LORD, **w** he has an uncleanness, Lv 22:3
w you are in your enemies' land; Lv 26:34
and enjoy its Sabbaths **w** it lies desolate Lv 26:43
aside to uncleanness **w** you were under Nm 5:19
W the meat was yet between their Nm 11:33
W the people of Israel were in the Nm 15:32
and minister to you **w** you and your Nm 18:2
offering, **w** I meet the LORD over there." Nm 23:15
W Israel lived in Shittim, the people Nm 25:1
w they were weeping in the entrance of Nm 25:6
w within her father's house in her Nm 30:3
w under her vows or any thoughtless Nm 30:6
father and his daughter **w** she is in Nm 30:16
brothers go to the war **w** you sit here? Nm 32:6
w the Egyptians were burying all their Nm 33:4
Sirion, **w** the Amorites call it Senir), Dt 3:9
w the mountain burned with fire to the Dt 4:11
w I stood between the LORD and you at that Dt 5:5
w the mountain was burning with fire, Dt 5:23
not eaten of the tithe **w** I was mourning, Dt 26:14
or removed any of it **w** I was unclean, Dt 26:14
w your eyes look on and fail with Dt 28:32
even today **w** I am yet alive with you, Dt 31:27
W the people of Israel were encamped at Jos 5:10
the ark, **w** the trumpets blew continually. Jos 6:9
LORD, **w** the trumpets blew continually. Jos 6:13
w they were going down the ascent of Jos 10:11
w Israel walked in the wilderness. Jos 14:10
Ehud escaped **w** they delayed, and he Jgs 3:26
down into the ground **w** he was lying Jgs 4:21
w his son Gideon was beating out wheat Jgs 6:11
w the two companies rushed upon all Jgs 9:44
W Israel lived in Heshbon and its Jgs 11:26
So **w** he slept, Delilah took the seven Jgs 16:14
who looked on **w** Samson entertained. Jgs 16:27
w the priest stood by the entrance of the Jgs 18:17
would come, **w** the meat was boiling, 1 Sm 2:13
passed on, stop here yourself for a **w**, 1 Sm 9:27
Now **w** Saul was talking to the priest, 1 Sm 14:19
within his house **w** David was 1 Sm 18:10
w two hundred remained with the 1 Sm 25:13
all the **w** we were with them keeping 1 Sm 25:16
w the army was encamped around 1 Sm 26:5
his custom all the **w** he lived in the 1 Sm 27:11
w the house of Saul became weaker 2 Sm 3:1
W there was war between the house of 2 Sm 3:6
David to eat bread **w** it was yet day. 2 Sm 3:35
servant's house for a great **w** to come, 2 Sm 7:19
"Behold, **w** the child was yet alive, 2 Sm 12:18
and wept for the child **w** he was alive; 2 Sm 12:21
He said, "**W** the child was still alive, I 2 Sm 12:22
W they were on the way, news came 2 Sm 13:30
servant vowed a vow **w** I lived at 2 Sm 15:8
And **w** Absalom was offering the 2 Sm 15:12
W David was coming to the 2 Sm 15:32
w Shimei went along on the hillside 2 Sm 16:13
will come upon him **w** he is weary 2 Sm 17:2
w all the army marched out by 2 Sm 18:4
w the mule that was under him went 2 Sm 18:9
the heart of Absalom **w** he was still 2 Sm 18:14
the king with food **w** he stayed at 2 Sm 19:32
w the eyes of my lord the king still see 2 Sm 24:3
before your foes **w** they pursue you? 2 Sm 24:13
Then **w** you are still speaking with 1 Kgs 1:14
W she was still speaking with the 1 Kgs 1:22
W he was still speaking, behold, 1 Kgs 1:42
gave birth to a child **w** she was in the 1 Kgs 3:17
from beside me, **w** your servant slept, 1 Kgs 3:20
w Solomon gave Hiram 20,000 cors 1 Kgs 5:11
heard in the house **w** it was being 1 Kgs 6:7
w all the assembly of Israel stood. 1 Kgs 8:14
w twelve lions stood there, one on 1 Kgs 10:20
Solomon his father **w** he was yet 1 Kgs 12:6
And after a **w** the brook dried up, 1 Kgs 17:7
And in a little **w** the heavens grew 1 Kgs 18:45
w Ben-hadad was drinking himself 1 Kgs 20:16
came back to him **w** he was staying 2 Kgs 2:18
and **w** he was going up on the way, 2 Kgs 2:23
But **w** they were eating of the stew, 2 Kgs 4:40
And **w** he was still speaking with 2 Kgs 6:33
And **w** he was telling the king how 2 Kgs 8:5
w Athaliah reigned over the land. 2 Kgs 11:3
w their inhabitants, shorn of 2 Kgs 19:26
came to the city **w** his servants were 2 Kgs 24:11
w he could not move about freely 1 Chr 12:1
sixty-eight brothers, **w** Obed-edom, 1 Chr 16:38
house for a great **w** to come, 1 Chr 17:17
by your foes **w** the sword of 1 Chr 21:12
w all the assembly of Israel stood. 2 Chr 6:3
w twelve lions stood there, one on 2 Chr 9:19
Solomon his father **w** he was yet 2 Chr 10:6
LORD is with you **w** you are with him. 2 Chr 15:2
he was captured **w** hiding in 2 Chr 22:9
w Athaliah reigned over the land. 2 Chr 22:12
w Jehiel, Azaziah, Nahath, Asahel, 2 Chr 31:13
year of his reign, **w** he was yet a boy, 2 Chr 34:3
W they were bringing out the 2 Chr 34:14
received from them **w** the Levites 2 Chr 35:11
gathered around me **w** I sat appalled Ezr 9:4
W Ezra prayed and made confession, Ezr 10:1
sword strapped at his side **w** he built. Neh 4:18
should the work stop **w** I leave it and Neh 6:3
And **w** they are still standing guard, let Neh 7:3
w the people remained in their places. Neh 8:7
w nine out of ten remained in the other Neh 11:1
W this was taking place, I was not in Neh 13:6
w he showed the riches of his royal glory Est 1:4
w the king was sitting on his royal Est 5:1
W they were yet talking with him, the Est 6:14
W he was yet speaking, there came Jb 1:16
W he was yet speaking, there came Jb 1:17
W he was yet speaking, there came Jb 1:18
which to scrape himself **w** he sat in the Jb 2:8
w your eyes are on me, I shall be gone. Jb 7:8
W yet in flower and not cut down, they Jb 8:12
They are exalted a little **w**, and then are Jb 24:24

w you searched out what to say. Jb 32:11
on men, **w** they slumber on their beds, Jb 33:15
peace with their neighbors **w** evil is in Ps 28:3
He plots trouble **w** on his bed; he sets Ps 36:4
In just a little **w**, the wicked will be no Ps 37:10
words, **w** his heart gathers iniquity; Ps 41:6
and night, **w** they say to me continually, Ps 42:3
taunt me, **w** they say to me continually, Ps 42:10
For though, **w** he lives, he counts Ps 49:18
May they fear you **w** the sun endures, Ps 72:5
w the food was still in their mouths, Ps 78:30
Hear, O my people, **w** I admonish you! O Ps 81:8
sing praise to my God **w** I have being. Ps 104:33
into their own nets, **w** I pass by safely. Ps 141:10
praises to my God **w** I have my being. Ps 146:2
w the slothful will be put to forced Prv 12:24
w the soul of the diligent is richly Prv 13:4
She rises **w** it is yet night and provides Prv 31:15
what is good for man **w** he lives the few Eccl 6:12
w adding one thing to another to find Eccl 7:27
All this I observed **w** applying my heart Eccl 8:9
madness is in their hearts **w** they live, Eccl 9:3
W the king was on his couch, my nard Sg 1:12
For in a very little **w** my fury will come Is 10:25
yourselves for a little **w** until the fury Is 26:20
their lips, **w** their hearts are far from me, Is 29:13
yet a very little **w** until Lebanon shall be Is 29:17
w their inhabitants, shorn of strength, Is 37:27
"Seek the LORD **w** he may be found; call Is 55:6
be found; call upon him **w** he is near; Is 55:6
are taken away, **w** no one understands. Is 57:1
holy people held possession for a little **w**; Is 63:18
w they are yet speaking I will hear. Is 65:24
and **w** you look for light he turns it into Jer 13:16
her sun went down **w** it was yet day; Jer 15:9
w their children remember their altars Jer 17:2
sword of their enemies **w** you look on. Jer 20:4
w he was still shut up in the court of the Jer 33:1
w I wrote them with ink on the scroll." Jer 36:18
LORD came to Jeremiah **w** he was shut Jer 39:15
yet a little **w** and the time of her harvest Jer 51:33
W they are inflamed I will prepare Jer 51:39
w the Chaldeans were around the city. Jer 52:7
w they sought food to revive their Lam 1:19
of another, **w** two covered their bodies. Ezk 1:11
w your abominations are in your midst. Ezk 7:4
w your abominations are in your midst. Ezk 7:9
return to what he has sold, **w** they live. Ezk 7:13
w the law perishes from the priest and Ezk 7:26
And **w** they were striking, and I was left Ezk 9:8
it came to pass, **w** I was prophesying, Ezk 11:13
to them for a **w** in the countries where Ezk 11:16
w no payment was given to you; Ezk 16:34
w they see for you false visions, while Ezk 21:29
w they divine lies for you—to place Ezk 21:29
played the whore **w** she was mine, Ezk 23:5
W the whole earth rejoices, I will Ezk 35:14
w those opposite the nave were a Ezk 42:8
W the man was standing beside me, I Ezk 43:6
w they minister at the gates of the Ezk 44:17
was Belteshazzar, was dismayed for a **w**, Dn 4:19
W the words were still in the king's Dn 4:31
W I was speaking and praying, Dn 9:20
w I was speaking in prayer, the man Dn 9:21
for in just a little **w** I will punish the Hos 1:4
houses, **w** this house lies in ruins? Hg 1:4
w each of you busies himself with his Hg 1:9
Yet once more, in a little **w**, I will shake Hg 2:6
for **w** I was angry but a little, they Zec 1:15
w Jerusalem shall again be inhabited Zec 12:6
their flesh will rot **w** they are still Zec 14:12
W walking by the Sea of Galilee, he saw Mt 4:18
with your accuser **w** you are going Mt 5:25
w the sons of the kingdom will be Mt 8:12
W he was saying these things to them, Mt 9:18
W he was still speaking to the people, Mt 12:46
no root in himself, but endures for a **w**, Mt 13:21
but **w** his men were sleeping, his Mt 13:25
other side, **w** he dismissed the crowds. Mt 14:22
w the rest seized his servants, treated Mt 22:6
Now **w** the Pharisees were gathered Mt 22:41
And **w** they were going to buy, the Mt 25:10
"Sit here, **w** I go over there and pray." Mt 26:36
W he was still speaking, Judas came, Mt 26:47
After a little **w** the bystanders came up Mt 26:73
w he was sitting on the judgment seat, Mt 27:19
that impostor said, **w** he was still alive, Mt 27:63
W they were going, behold, some of the Mt 28:11
and stole him away **w** we were asleep.' Mt 28:13
in the morning, **w** it was still dark, Mk 1:35
wedding guests fast **w** the bridegroom is Mk 2:19
root in themselves, but endure for a **w**; Mk 4:17
W he was still speaking, there came Mk 5:35
place and rest a **w**." For many were Mk 6:31
to Bethsaida, **w** he dismissed the crowd. Mk 6:45

And **w** he was at Bethany in the house Mk 14:3
said to his disciples, "Sit here **w** I pray." Mk 14:32
immediately, **w** he was still speaking, Mk 14:43
after a little **w** the bystanders again Mk 14:70
w the Lord worked with them and Mk 16:20
Now **w** he was serving as priest before Lk 1:8
And **w** they were there, the time came for Lk 2:6
w the crowd was pressing in on him to Lk 5:1
W he was in one of the cities, there came Lk 5:12
wedding guests fast **w** the bridegroom is Lk 5:34
w he was going through the grainfields, Lk 6:1
they believe for a **w**, and in time of Lk 8:13
W he was still speaking, someone from Lk 8:49
W he was coming, the demon threw Lk 9:42
But **w** they were all marveling at Lk 9:43
w others, to test him, kept seeking from Lk 11:16
W Jesus was speaking, a Pharisee Lk 11:37
if not, **w** the other is yet a great way off, Lk 14:32
But **w** he was still a long way off, his Lk 15:20
properly, and serve me **w** I eat and drink, Lk 17:8
For a **w** he refused, but afterward he said Lk 18:4
went into another country for a long **w**. Lk 20:9
And **w** some were speaking of the Lk 21:5
W he was still speaking, there came a Lk 22:47
immediately, **w** he was still speaking, Lk 22:60
w the sun's light failed. And the Lk 23:45
W they were perplexed about this, Lk 24:4
he told you, **w** he was still in Galilee, Lk 24:6
W they were talking and discussing Lk 24:15
hearts burn within us **w** he talked to us Lk 24:32
road, **w** he opened to us the Scriptures?" Lk 24:32
And **w** they still disbelieved for joy and Lk 24:41
that I spoke to you **w** I was still with Lk 24:44
W he blessed them, he parted from Lk 24:51
and **w** I am going another steps down Jn 5:7
were willing to rejoice for a **w** in his light. Jn 5:35
W some said, "He is a good man," others Jn 7:12
the works of him who sent me **w** it is day; Jn 9:4
light is among you for a little **w** longer. Jn 12:35
Walk **w** you have the light, lest Jn 12:35
W you have the light, believe in the Jn 12:36
children, yet a little **w** I am with you. Jn 13:33
Yet a little **w** and the world will see me Jn 14:19
I have spoken to you **w** I am still with Jn 14:25
"A little **w**, and you will see me no Jn 16:16
and again a little **w**, and you will see Jn 16:16
is this that he says to us, 'A little **w**, Jn 16:17
you will not see me, and again a little **w**, Jn 16:17
"What does he mean by 'a little **w**'? Jn 16:18
'A little **w** and you will not see me, Jn 16:19
and again a little **w** and you will see Jn 16:19
W I was with them, I kept them in your Jn 17:12
to the tomb early, **w** it was still dark, Jn 20:1
And **w** staying with them he ordered Acts 1:4
And **w** they were gazing into heaven as Acts 1:10
W he clung to Peter and John, all the Acts 3:11
w you stretch out your hand to heal, Acts 4:30
W it remained unsold, did it not remain Acts 5:4
to put the men outside for a little **w**. Acts 5:34
that Dorcas made **w** she was with Acts 9:39
to eat, but **w** they were preparing it, Acts 10:10
Now **w** Peter was inwardly perplexed Acts 10:17
And **w** Peter was pondering the Acts 10:19
W Peter was still saying these things, Acts 10:44
W they were worshiping the Lord and Acts 13:2
Now **w** Paul was waiting for them at Acts 17:16
And it happened that **w** Apollos was at Acts 19:1
he himself stayed in Asia for a **w**. Acts 19:22
he conversed with them a long **w**, Acts 20:11
W we were staying for many days, a Acts 21:10
W I was doing this, they found me Acts 24:18
I cried out **w** standing among them: Acts 24:21
w their conscience also bears witness, Rom 2:15
W you preach against stealing, do you Rom 2:21
he had by faith **w** he was still Rom 4:11
For **w** we were still weak, at the right Rom 5:6
for us in that **w** we were still sinners, Rom 5:8
For if **w** we were enemies we were Rom 5:10
by law to her husband **w** he lives, Rom 7:2
with another man **w** her husband is Rom 7:3
For **w** we were living in the flesh, our Rom 7:5
w the weak person eats only Rom 14:2
w another esteems all days alike. Rom 14:5
to God, **w** the one who abstains, Rom 14:6
I have enjoyed your company for a **w**. Rom 15:24
For **w** there is jealousy and strife 1 Cor 3:3
w prophecy is a sign not for 1 Cor 14:22
For **w** we are still in this tent, we groan, 2 Cor 5:4
We know that **w** we are at home in the 2 Cor 5:6
letter grieved you, though only for a **w**. 2 Cor 7:8
w they long for you and pray for you, 2 Cor 9:14
and I warn them now **w** absent, 2 Cor 13:2
I write these things **w** I am away 2 Cor 13:10
w the son of the free woman was born Gal 4:23
w we proclaimed to you the gospel of 1 Thes 2:9

W people are saying, "There is peace 1 Thes 5:3
for **w** bodily training is of some value, 1 Tm 4:8
self-indulgent is dead even **w** she lives. 1 Tm 5:6
w evil people and impostors will go 2 Tm 3:13
why he was parted from you for a **w**, Phlm 1:15
w God also bore witness by signs and Heb 2:4
him for a little **w** lower than the angels; Heb 2:7
who for a little **w** was made lower than Heb 2:9
w the promise of entering his rest still Heb 4:1
For, "Yet a little **w**, and the coming Heb 10:37
here in a good place," **w** you say to the Jas 2:3
you rejoice, though now for a little **w**, 1 Pt 1:6
endures sorrows **w** suffering unjustly. 1 Pt 2:19
of Noah, **w** the ark was being prepared, 1 Pt 3:20
to a faithful Creator **w** doing good. 1 Pt 4:19
And after you have suffered a little **w**, 1 Pt 5:10
their deceptions, **w** they feast with you. 2 Pt 2:13
have fellowship with him **w** we walk in 1 Jn 1:6
come he must remain only a little **w**. Rv 17:10
that he must be released for a little **w**. Rv 20:3
built of jasper, **w** the city was pure gold, Rv 21:18

WHIP (7)
that city shall take the man and **w** him, Dt 22:18
a **w** on your sides and thorns in your Jos 23:13
A **w** for the horse, a bridle for the Prv 26:3
of hosts will wield against them a **w**, Is 10:26
the overwhelming **w** passes through Is 28:15
The crack of the **w**, and rumble of the Na 3:2
And making a **w** of cords, he drove them Jn 2:15

WHIPPED (1)
brood, they have been **w** out of the land. Jb 30:8

WHIPS (5)
My father disciplined you with **w**, 1 Kgs 12:11
My father disciplined you with **w**, 1 Kgs 12:14
My father disciplined you with **w**, 2 Chr 10:11
My father disciplined you with **w**, 2 Chr 10:14
they had stretched him out for the **w**, Acts 22:25

WHIRL (1)
and **w** you around and around, and Is 22:18

WHIRLING (7)
O my God, make them like **w** dust, like Ps 83:13
before the wind and **w** dust before the Is 17:13
Wrath has gone forth, a **w** tempest; it Jer 23:19
Wrath has gone forth, a **w** tempest; it Jer 30:23
in among the **w** wheels underneath the Ezk 10:2
"Take fire from between the **w** wheels, Ezk 10:6
called in my hearing "the **w** wheels." Ezk 10:13

WHIRLWIND (18)
to take Elijah up to heaven by a **w**, 2 Kgs 2:1
Elijah went up by a **w** into heaven. 2 Kgs 2:11
a flood; in the night a **w** carries him off. Jb 27:20
From its chamber comes the **w**, and cold Jb 37:9
LORD answered Job out of the **w** and said: Jb 38:1
LORD answered Job out of the **w** and said: Jb 40:6
crash of your thunder was in the **w**; Ps 77:18
and your calamity comes like a **w**, Prv 1:27
like flint, and their wheels like the **w**. Is 5:28
and great noise, with **w** and tempest, Is 29:6
come in fire, and his chariots like the **w**, Is 66:15
up like clouds; his chariots like the **w**; Jer 4:13
north shall rush upon him like a **w**, Dn 11:40
sow the wind, and they shall reap the **w**. Hos 8:7
with a tempest in the day of the **w**; Am 1:14
His way is in **w** and storm, and the clouds Na 1:3
who came like a **w** to scatter me, Hab 3:14
scattered them with a **w** among all the Zec 7:14

WHIRLWINDS (2)
As **w** in the Negeb sweep on, it comes Is 21:1
will march forth in the **w** of the south. Zec 9:14

WHIRRING (1)
land of **w** wings that is beyond the rivers Is 18:1

WHISPER (5)
after the fire the sound of a low **w**. 1 Kgs 19:12
me stealthily; my ear received the **w** of it. Jb 4:12
and how small a **w** do we hear of him! Jb 26:14
All who hate me **w** together about me; Ps 41:7
and from the dust your speech shall **w**. Is 29:4

WHISPERED (3)
they poured out a **w** prayer when your Is 26:16
say in the light, and what you hear **w**, Mt 10:27
and what you have **w** in private rooms Lk 12:3

WHISPERER (4)
strife, and a **w** separates close friends. Prv 16:28
The words of a **w** are like delicious Prv 18:8
fire goes out, and where there is no **w**, Prv 26:20
The words of a **w** are like delicious Prv 26:22

WHISPERING (3)
that his servants were **w** together, 2 Sm 12:19
For I hear the **w** of many—terror on Ps 31:13
For I hear many **w**. Terror is on every Jer 20:10

WHISTLE (3)
and **w** for them from the ends of the earth; Is 5:26
that day the LORD will **w** for the fly that is Is 7:18
"I will **w** for them and gather them in, Zec 10:8

WHISTLING (1)
sheepfolds, to hear the **w** for the flocks? Jgs 5:16

WHITE (59)
and spotted, every one that had **w** on it, Gn 30:35
trees, and peeled **w** streaks in them, Gn 30:37
in them, exposing the **w** of the sticks. Gn 30:37
w, and the taste of it was like wafers Ex 16:31
area has turned **w** and the disease Lv 13:3
But if the spot is **w** in the skin of his Lv 13:4
skin, and the hair in it has not turned **w**, Lv 13:4
And if there is a **w** swelling in the skin Lv 13:10
in the skin that has turned the hair **w**, Lv 13:10
it has all turned **w**, and he is clean. Lv 13:13
raw flesh recovers and turns **w** again, Lv 13:16
him, and if the disease has turned **w**, Lv 13:17
boil there comes a **w** swelling or a Lv 13:19
than the skin and its hair has turned **w**, Lv 13:20
it and there is no **w** hair in it and it Lv 13:21
becomes a spot, reddish-white or **w**, Lv 13:24
the spot has turned **w** and it appears Lv 13:25
it and there is no **w** hair in the spot and Lv 13:26
spots on the skin of the body, **w** spots, Lv 13:38
on the skin of the body are of a dull **w**, Lv 13:39
"Tell of it, you who ride on **w** donkeys, Jgs 5:10
There were **w** cotton curtains and violet Est 1:6
of the king in royal robes of blue and **w**, Est 8:15
Let your garments be always **w**. Let not Eccl 9:8
like scarlet, they shall be as **w** as snow; Is 1:18
be in despair, and the weavers of **w** cotton. Is 19:9
his clothing was **w** as snow, and the hair Dn 7:9
may be refined, purified, and made **w**, Dn 11:35
and make themselves **w** and be refined, Dn 12:10
it down; their branches are made **w**. Jl 1:7
him were red, sorrel, and **w** horses. Zec 1:8
the third **w** horses, and the fourth Zec 6:3
north country, the **w** ones go after them, Zec 6:6
you cannot make one hair **w** or black. Mt 5:36
sun, and his clothes became **w** as light. Mt 17:2
lightning, and his clothing **w** as snow. Mt 28:3
his clothes became radiant, intensely **w**, Mk 9:3
on the right side, dressed in a **w** robe, Mk 16:5
and his clothing became dazzling **w**. Lk 9:29
and see that the fields are **w** for harvest. Jn 4:35
And she saw two angels in **w**, sitting Jn 20:12
two men stood by them in **w** robes, Acts 1:10
The hairs of his head were **w** like wool, Rv 1:14
head were white like wool, as **w** as snow. Rv 1:14
manna, and I will give him a **w** stone, Rv 2:17
and they will walk with me in **w**, Rv 3:4
will be clothed thus in **w** garments, Rv 3:5
and **w** garments so that you may clothe Rv 3:18
twenty-four elders, clothed in **w** garments, Rv 4:4
And I looked, and behold, a **w** horse! And Rv 6:2
they were each given a **w** robe and told to Rv 6:11
and before the Lamb, clothed in **w** robes, Rv 7:9
"Who are these, clothed in **w** robes, Rv 7:13
robes and made them **w** in the blood of Rv 7:14
Then I looked, and behold, a **w** cloud, Rv 14:14
heaven opened, and behold, a **w** horse! Rv 19:11
arrayed in fine linen, **w** and pure, Rv 19:14
pure, were following him on **w** horses. Rv 19:14
I saw a great **w** throne and him who Rv 20:11

WHITE-HAIRED (1)
wake; one would think the deep to be **w**. Jb 41:32

WHITER (3)
than wine, and his teeth **w** than milk. Gn 49:12
wash me, and I shall be **w** than snow. Ps 51:7
were purer than snow, **w** than milk; Lam 4:7

WHITEWASH (6)
As for you, you **w** with lies; worthless Jb 13:4
a wall, these prophets smear it with **w**, Ezk 13:10
who smear it with **w** that it shall fall! Ezk 13:11
wall that you have smeared with **w**, Ezk 13:14
those who have smeared it with **w**, Ezk 13:15
prophets have smeared **w** for them, Ezk 22:28

WHITEWASHED (2)
For you are like **w** tombs, which Mt 23:27
is going to strike you, you **w** wall! Acts 23:3

WHOLE (287)
and was watering the **w** face of the Gn 2:6
flowed around the **w** land of Havilah, Gn 2:11
that flowed around the **w** land of Cush. Gn 2:13
mountains under the **w** heaven were Gn 7:19
were still on the face of the **w** earth. Gn 8:9
the people of the **w** earth were dispersed. Gn 9:19
Now the **w** earth had one language and Gn 11:1
dispersed over the face of the **w** earth." Gn 11:4
Is not the **w** land before you? Separate Gn 13:9
I will spare the **w** place for their sake." Gn 18:26
Will you destroy the **w** city for lack of Gn 18:28
were in the field, throughout its **w** area, Gn 23:17
After two **w** years, Pharaoh dreamed Gn 41:1
and settled on the **w** country of Egypt, Ex 10:14
They covered the face of the **w** land, so Ex 10:15
when the **w** assembly of the Ex 12:6
And the **w** congregation of the people of Ex 16:2
to kill this **w** assembly with hunger." Ex 16:3
"Say to the **w** congregation of the people Ex 16:9
spoke to the **w** congregation of the Ex 16:10
and the **w** mountain trembled greatly. Ex 19:18
the **w** of it a single piece of hammered Ex 25:36
so that the tabernacle may be a single **w**. Ex 26:6
tent together that it may be a single **w**. Ex 26:11
and burn the **w** ram on the altar. It is a Ex 29:18
So the tabernacle was a single **w**. Ex 36:13
tent together that it might be a single **w**. Ex 36:18
The **w** of it was a single piece of Ex 37:22
he shall remove the **w** fat tail, cut off close Lv 3:9
"If the **w** congregation of Israel sins Lv 4:13
forever. The **w** of it shall be burned. Lv 6:22
and Moses burned the **w** ram on the Lv 8:21
let your brothers, the **w** house of Israel, Lv 10:6
he shall bathe his **w** body in water and Lv 15:16
assembled the **w** congregation Nm 1:18
and over the **w** congregation before the Nm 3:7
oversight of the **w** tabernacle and all Nm 4:16
as the **w** of their service in the tent of Nm 4:31
the **w** of their service in the tent of Nm 4:33
and assemble the **w** congregation of the Nm 8:9
but a **w** month, until it comes out at Nm 11:20
meat, that they may eat a **w** month!' Nm 11:21
The **w** congregation said to them, Nm 14:2
because the **w** population was Nm 15:26
guard over you and over the **w** tent, Nm 18:3
the people of Israel, the **w** congregation, Nm 20:1
people of Israel, the **w** congregation, Nm 20:22
the sight of the **w** congregation of the Nm 25:6
Israel with him, the **w** congregation." Nm 27:21
the priest and the **w** congregation, Nm 27:22
the peoples who are under the **w** heaven, Dt 2:25
them—sixty cities, the **w** region of Argob, Dt 3:4
to all the peoples under the **w** heaven. Dt 4:19
tell you the **w** commandment and the Dt 5:31
"The **w** commandment that I command Dt 8:1
you shall remember the **w** way that the Dt 8:2
therefore keep the **w** commandment that Dt 11:8
as a **w** burnt offering to the LORD your Dt 13:16
kinds of seed, lest the **w** yield be forfeited, Dt 22:9
"Keep the **w** commandment that I Dt 27:1
the **w** land burned out with brimstone Dt 29:23
according to the **w** commandment that I Dt 31:5
before you and **w** burnt offerings on Dt 33:10
circumcising of the **w** nation was Jos 5:8
Do not make the **w** people toil up there, Jos 7:3
did not hurry to set for about a **w** day. Jos 10:13
So Joshua struck the **w** land, the hill Jos 10:40
So Joshua took the **w** land, according Jos 11:23
the **w** kingdom of Og king of Bashan, Jos 13:30
Then the **w** congregation of the people of Jos 18:1
the **w** assembly of the people of Israel Jos 22:12
"Thus says the **w** congregation of the Jos 22:16
angry with the **w** congregation of Jos 22:18
to them and to the **w** clan of his mother's Jgs 9:1
able men from the **w** number of their Jgs 18:2
all the people of Israel, the **w** army, Jgs 20:26
the **w** of the city went up in smoke to Jgs 20:40
Then the **w** congregation sent word to Jgs 21:13
the **w** town was stirred because of them. Ru 1:19
deathly panic throughout the **w** city. 1 Sm 5:11
offered it as a **w** burnt offering to the 1 Sm 7:9
and marching the **w** morning, 2 Sm 2:29
Israel and the **w** house of Benjamin 2 Sm 3:19
the people, the **w** multitude of Israel, 2 Sm 6:19
had defeated the **w** army of Hadadezer, 2 Sm 8:9
And now the **w** clan has risen against 2 Sm 14:7
the structure against the **w** house, 1 Kgs 6:10
he overlaid the **w** house with gold, 1 Kgs 6:22
Also the **w** altar that belonged to the 1 Kgs 6:22
And the **w** earth sought the presence 1 Kgs 10:24
will not take the **w** kingdom out of 1 Kgs 11:34
will fare like the **w** multitude of Israel 2 Kgs 7:13
For the **w** house of Ahab shall perish, 2 Kgs 9:8
in faithfulness and with a **w** heart, 2 Kgs 20:3
had defeated the **w** army of 1 Chr 18:9
serve him with a **w** heart and with a 1 Chr 28:9
for with a **w** heart they had offered 1 Chr 29:9
Solomon my son a **w** heart that he 1 Chr 29:19
had sought him with their **w** desire, 2 Chr 15:15
to and fro throughout the **w** earth, 2 Chr 16:9
faithfulness, and with your **w** heart: 2 Chr 19:9
of the LORD, yet not with a **w** heart. 2 Chr 25:2
The **w** number of the heads of 2 Chr 26:12
The **w** assembly worshiped, and the 2 Chr 29:28
Then the **w** assembly agreed 2 Chr 30:23
The **w** assembly of Judah, and the 2 Chr 30:25
and the **w** assembly that came out 2 Chr 30:25
their daughters, the **w** assembly, 2 Chr 31:18
The **w** assembly together was 42,360, Ezr 2:64
ruled over the **w** province Beyond the Ezr 4:20
find in the **w** province of Babylonia, Ezr 7:16
The **w** was counted and weighed, and Ezr 8:34
our officials stand for the **w** assembly. Ezr 10:14
stood behind the **w** house of Judah, Neh 4:16
The **w** assembly together was 42,360, Neh 7:66
throughout the **w** kingdom of Est 3:6
and who laid on him the **w** world? Jb 34:13
Under the **w** heaven he lets it go, and his Jb 37:3
is under the **w** heaven is mine. Jb 41:11
give thanks to the LORD with my **w** heart; Ps 9:1
heart is glad, and my **w** being rejoices; Ps 16:9
burnt offerings and **w** burnt offerings; Ps 51:19
may the **w** earth be filled with his glory! Ps 72:19
you, O Lord my God, with my **w** heart, Ps 86:12
thanks to the LORD with my **w** heart, Ps 111:1
who seek him with their **w** heart, Ps 119:2
With my **w** heart I seek you; let me not Ps 119:10
law and observe it with my **w** heart. Ps 119:34
but with my **w** heart I keep your Ps 119:69
With my **w** heart I cry; answer me, O Ps 119:145
you thanks, O LORD, with my **w** heart; Ps 138:1
Sheol let us swallow them alive, and **w**, Prv 1:12
for this is the **w** duty of man. Eccl 12:13
The **w** head is sick, and the whole heart Is 1:5
whole head is sick, and the **w** heart faint. Is 1:5
will create over the **w** site of Mount Zion Is 4:5
of hosts; the **w** earth is full of his glory!" Is 6:3
of his indignation, to destroy the **w** land. Is 13:5
The **w** earth is at rest and quiet; they Is 14:7
that is purposed concerning the **w** earth, Is 14:26
and at my post I am stationed **w** nights. Is 21:8
hang on him the **w** honor of his father's Is 22:24
shoots and fill the **w** world with fruit. Is 27:6
the Lord GOD of hosts against the **w** land. Is 28:22
you in faithfulness and with a **w** heart, Is 38:3
the spices, the precious oil, his **w** armory, Is 39:2
the God of the **w** earth he is called. Is 54:5
and bronze walls, against the **w** land, Jer 1:18
did not return to me with her **w** heart, Jer 3:10
hard on crash; the **w** land is laid waste. Jer 4:20
LORD, "The **w** land shall be a desolation; Jer 4:27
of their stallions the **w** land quakes. Jer 8:16
The **w** land is made desolate, but no Jer 12:11
so I made the **w** house of Israel and the Jer 13:11
of Israel and the **w** house of Judah cling Jer 13:11
of strife and contention to the **w** land! Jer 15:10
shall return to me with their **w** heart. Jer 24:7
This **w** land shall become a ruin and a Jer 25:11
The **w** valley of the dead bodies and the Jer 31:40
his sons and the **w** house of the Jer 35:3
should defeat the **w** army of Chaldeans Jer 37:10
See, the **w** land is before you; go wherever Jer 40:4
I am plucking up—that is, the **w** land. Jer 45:4
the hammer of the **w** earth is cut down Jer 50:23
the LORD, which destroys the **w** earth; Jer 51:25
is taken, the praise of the **w** earth seized! Jer 51:41
her **w** land shall be put to shame, and Jer 51:47
hand again and again the **w** day long. Lam 3:3
And their **w** body, their rims, and Ezk 10:12
your kinsmen, the **w** house of Israel, Ezk 11:15
Behold, when it was **w**, it was used for Ezk 15:5
the beasts of the **w** earth with you. Ezk 32:4
Lord GOD: While the **w** earth rejoices, Ezk 35:14
people on you, the **w** house of Israel, Ezk 36:10
these bones are the **w** house of Israel. Ezk 37:11
have mercy on the **w** house of Israel, Ezk 39:25
carved on the **w** temple all around. Ezk 41:19
and its entrances, that is, its **w** design; Ezk 43:11
its statutes and its **w** design and all its Ezk 43:11
the **w** territory on the top of the Ezk 43:12
It shall be holy throughout its **w** extent. Ezk 45:1
It shall belong to the **w** house of Israel. Ezk 45:6
The **w** length shall be 25,000 cubits Ezk 48:13
The **w** portion that you shall set apart Ezk 48:20
a great mountain and filled the **w** earth. Dn 2:35
ruler over the **w** province of Babylon Dn 2:48
it was visible to the end of the **w** earth. Dn 4:11
it was visible to the end of the **w** earth, Dn 4:20
satraps, to be throughout the **w** kingdom; Dn 6:1
planned to set him over the **w** kingdom. Dn 6:3
and it shall devour the **w** earth, Dn 7:23
kingdoms under the **w** heaven shall be Dn 7:27
the west across the face of the **w** earth, Dn 8:5
For under the **w** heaven there has not Dn 9:12
with the strength of his **w** kingdom, Dn 11:17
carried into exile a **w** people to deliver Am 1:6
they delivered up a **w** people to Edom, Am 1:9
against the **w** family that I brought up Am 3:1
their wealth to the Lord of the **w** earth. Mi 4:13

which range through the **w** earth." Zec 4:10
who stand by the Lord of the **w** earth." Zec 4:14
that goes out over the face of the **w** land. Zec 5:3
In the **w** land, declares the LORD, two Zec 13:8
The **w** land shall be turned into a Zec 14:10
are robbing me, the **w** nation of you. Mal 3:9
than that your **w** body be thrown Mt 5:29
members than that your **w** body go into Mt 5:30
your **w** body will be full of light, Mt 6:22
your **w** body will be full of darkness. Mt 6:23
the **w** herd rushed down the steep bank Mt 8:32
And the **w** crowd stood on the beach. Mt 13:2
if he gains the **w** world and forfeits his Mt 16:26
Jerusalem, the **w** city was stirred up, Mt 21:10
proclaimed throughout the **w** world as Mt 24:14
gospel is proclaimed in the **w** world, Mt 26:13
priests and the **w** Council were seeking Mt 26:59
they gathered the **w** battalion before Mt 27:27
And the **w** city was gathered together at Mk 1:33
and the **w** crowd was beside the sea on Mk 4:1
before him and told him the **w** truth. Mk 5:33
and ran about the **w** region and began Mk 6:55
man to gain the **w** world and forfeit his Mk 8:36
more than all **w** burnt offerings and Mk 12:33
the gospel is proclaimed in the **w** world, Mk 14:9
priests and the **w** Council were Mk 14:55
elders and scribes and the **w** Council. Mk 15:1
they called together the **w** battalion. Mk 15:16
was darkness over the **w** land until the Mk 15:33
proclaim the gospel to the **w** creation. Mk 16:15
And the **w** multitude of the people were Lk 1:10
him spread through the **w** of Judea and Lk 7:17
proclaiming throughout the **w** city how Lk 8:39
man if he gains the **w** world and loses or Lk 9:25
is healthy, your **w** body is full of light, Lk 11:34
If then your **w** body is full of light, Lk 11:36
of Olives—the **w** multitude of his Lk 19:37
all who dwell on the face of the **w** earth. Lk 21:35
Then the **w** company of them arose and Lk 23:1
was darkness over the **w** land until the Lk 23:44
the Sabbath I made a man's **w** body well? Jn 7:23
not that the **w** nation should perish." Jn 11:50
came upon the **w** church and upon Acts 5:11
what they said pleased the **w** gathering, Acts 6:5
spoken of by the **w** Jewish nation, Acts 10:22
For a **w** year they met with the Acts 11:26
had gone through the **w** island as far Acts 13:6
Sabbath almost the **w** city gathered Acts 13:44
spreading throughout the **w** region. Acts 13:49
and the elders, with the **w** church, Acts 15:22
lived among you the **w** time from the Acts 20:18
to you the **w** counsel of God. Acts 20:27
stirred up the **w** crowd and laid hands Acts 21:27
high priest and the **w** council of elders Acts 22:5
about whom the **w** Jewish people Acts 25:24
He lived there two **w** years at his own Acts 28:30
and the **w** world may be held Rom 3:19
we know that the **w** creation has been Rom 8:22
as firstfruits is holy, so is the **w** lump, Rom 11:16
is host to me and to the **w** church, Rom 16:23
that a little leaven leavens the **w** lump? 1 Cor 5:6
If the **w** body were an eye, where 1 Cor 12:17
If the **w** body were an ear, where 1 Cor 12:17
the **w** church comes together and 1 Cor 14:23
the saints who are in the **w** of Achaia: 2 Cor 1:1
that he is obligated to keep the **w** law. Gal 5:3
A little leaven leavens the **w** lump. Gal 5:9
For the **w** law is fulfilled in one word: Gal 5:14
in whom the **w** structure, being joined Eph 2:21
from whom the **w** body, joined and Eph 4:16
Put on the **w** armor of God, that you Eph 6:11
Therefore take up the **w** armor of God, Eph 6:13
throughout the **w** imperial guard Phil 1:13
as indeed in the **w** world it is bearing Col 1:6
For in him the **w** fullness of deity dwells Col 2:9
to the Head, from whom the **w** body, Col 2:19
and may your **w** spirit and soul and 1 Thes 5:23
they are upsetting **w** families by Ti 1:11
For whoever keeps the **w** law but fails in Jas 2:10
man, able also to bridle his **w** body. Jas 3:2
obey us, we guide their **w** bodies as well. Jas 3:3
our members, staining the **w** body, Jas 3:6
only but also for the sins of the **w** world. 1 Jn 2:2
and the **w** world lies in the power of the 1 Jn 5:19
of trial that is coming on the **w** world, Rv 3:10
the deceiver of the **w** world—he was Rv 12:9
and the **w** earth marveled as they Rv 13:3
go abroad to the kings of the **w** world, Rv 16:14

WHOLEHEARTED (1)
as a possession with **w** joy and utter Ezk 36:5

WHOLENESS (1)
the LORD, plans for **w** and not for evil, Jer 29:11

WHOLLY (22)
offering of a priest shall be **w** burned. Lv 6:23
they are **w** given to him from among the Nm 3:9
For they are **w** given to me from Nm 8:16
because they have not **w** followed me, Nm 32:11
for they have **w** followed the LORD.' Nm 32:12
because he has **w** followed the LORD!' Dt 1:36
melt; yet I **w** followed the LORD my God. Jos 14:8
because you have **w** followed the LORD Jos 14:9
day, because he **w** followed the LORD, Jos 14:14
your heart therefore be **w** true to the 1 Kgs 8:61
his heart was not **w** true to the LORD 1 Kgs 11:4
LORD and did not **w** follow the LORD, 1 Kgs 11:6
his heart was not **w** true to the LORD 1 Kgs 15:3
heart of Asa was **w** true to the LORD 1 Kgs 15:14
people will be **w** at your command." 1 Chr 28:21
heart of Asa was **w** true all his days. 2 Chr 15:17
who knew me are **w** estranged from me. Jb 19:13
full vigor, being **w** at ease and secure, Jb 21:23
planted you a choice vine, **w** of pure seed. Jer 2:21
is taken into exile, **w** taken into exile. Jer 13:19
Let his arm be **w** withered, his right Zec 11:17
no part dark, it will be **w** bright, Lk 11:36

WHOMEVER (6)
and bring up for me **w** I shall name to 1 Sm 28:8
and I give it to **w** it seems right to me. Jer 27:5
And I will appoint over her **w** I choose. Jer 49:19
and I will appoint over her **w** I choose. Jer 50:44
So then he has mercy on **w** he wills, Rom 9:18
he wills, and he hardens **w** he wills. Rom 9:18

WHORE (37)
and when they **w** after their gods and Ex 34:15
and their daughters **w** after their gods Ex 34:16
and make your sons **w** after their gods. Ex 34:16
to goat demons, after whom they **w**. Lv 17:7
which you are inclined to **w** after. Nm 15:39
people began to **w** with the daughters Nm 25:1
people will rise and **w** after the foreign Dt 31:16
acts, and played the **w** in their deeds. Ps 106:39
How the faithful city has become a **w**, she Is 1:21
green tree you bowed down like a **w**. Jer 2:20
You have played the **w** with many lovers; Jer 3:1
come; yet you have the forehead of a **w**; Jer 3:3
every green tree, and there played the **w**? Jer 3:6
fear, but she too went and played the **w**. Jer 3:8
and played the **w** because of your Ezk 16:15
shrines, and on them played the **w**. Ezk 16:16
of men, and with them played the **w**. Ezk 16:17
also played the **w** with the Egyptians, Ezk 16:26
You played the **w** also with the Ezk 16:28
yes, you played the **w** with them, and Ezk 16:28
No one solicited you to play the **w**, and Ezk 16:34
I will make you stop playing the **w**, Ezk 16:41
They played the **w** in Egypt; they played Ezk 23:3
Egypt; they played the **w** in their youth; Ezk 23:3
"Oholah played the **w** while she was Ezk 23:5
when she played the **w** in the land of Ezk 23:19
you played the **w** with the nations Ezk 23:30
they will continue to use her for a **w**, Ezk 23:43
For their mother has played the **w**; she Hos 2:5
You shall not play the **w**, or belong to Hos 3:3
they shall play the **w**, but not multiply, Hos 4:10
they have left their God to play the **w**. Hos 4:12
Therefore your daughters play the **w**, Hos 4:13
your daughters when they play the **w**, Hos 4:14
Though you play the **w**, O Israel, let not Hos 4:15
now, O Ephraim, you have played the **w**; Hos 5:3
for you have played the **w**, forsaking Hos 9:1

WHORED (4)
for they **w** after other gods and bowed Jgs 2:17
in Ophrah. And all Israel **w** after it there, Jgs 8:27
Israel turned again and **w** after the Baals Jgs 8:33
and **w** after the gods of the peoples of 1 Chr 5:25

WHOREDOM (13)
of Jerusalem into **w** and made Judah 2 Chr 21:11
the inhabitants of Jerusalem into **w**, 2 Chr 21:13
the house of Ahab led Israel into **w**, 2 Chr 21:13
have polluted the land with your vile **w**. Jer 3:2
Because she took her **w** lightly, she Jer 3:9
yourself a wife of **w** and have children of Hos 1:2
of whoredom and have children of **w**, Hos 1:2
land commits great **w** by forsaking the Hos 1:2
mercy, because they are children of **w**. Hos 2:4
w, wine, and new wine, which take Hos 4:11
For a spirit of **w** has led them astray, Hos 4:12
For the spirit of **w** is within them, and Hos 5:4
a horrible thing; Ephraim's **w** is there; Hos 6:10

WHORES (1)
adultery and trooped to the houses of **w**. Jer 5:7

WHORING (26)
all who follow him in **w** after Molech. Lv 20:5
to mediums and wizards, **w** after them, Lv 20:6
of any priest, if she profanes herself by **w**, Lv 21:9
thing in Israel by **w** in her father's Dt 22:21
been broken over their **w** heart that has Ezk 6:9
over their eyes that go **w** after their idols. Ezk 6:9
any passerby and multiplying your **w**. Ezk 16:25
neighbors, multiplying your **w**, Ezk 16:26
You multiplied your **w** also with the Ezk 16:29
fathers and go **w** after their detestable Ezk 20:30
She bestowed her **w** upon them, the Ezk 23:7
not give up her **w** that she had begun Ezk 23:8
and poured out their **w** lust upon her. Ezk 23:8
her sister in her lust and in her **w**, Ezk 23:11
But she carried her **w** further. She saw Ezk 23:14
and they defiled her with their **w** lust. Ezk 23:17
she carried on her **w** so openly and Ezk 23:18
Yet she increased her **w**, remembering Ezk 23:19
lewdness and your **w** begun in the Ezk 23:27
nakedness of your **w** shall be Ezk 23:29
uncovered. Your lewdness and your **w** Ezk 23:29
of your lewdness and **w**." Ezk 23:35
by their **w** and by the dead bodies of Ezk 43:7
them put away their **w** and the dead Ezk 43:9
that she put away her **w** from her face, Hos 2:2
is gone, they give themselves to **w**; Hos 4:18

WHORINGS (10)
so long as the **w** and the sorceries of 2 Kgs 9:22
adulteries and neighings, your lewd **w**, Jer 13:27
and lavished your **w** on any passerby; Ezk 16:15
Were your **w** so small a matter Ezk 16:20
abominations and your **w** you did not Ezk 16:22
to you from every side with your **w**. Ezk 16:33
different from other women in your **w**. Ezk 16:34
uncovered in your **w** with your lovers, Ezk 16:36
all for the countless **w** of the prostitute, Na 3:4
charms, who betrays nations with her **w**, Na 3:4

WHY (466)
The LORD said to Cain, "**W** are you angry, Gn 4:6
you angry, and **w** has your face fallen? Gn 4:6
W did you not tell me that she was Gn 12:18
W did you say, 'She is my sister,' so Gn 12:19
"**W** did Sarah laugh and say, Gn 18:13
of the LORD. **W** do you stand outside? Gn 24:31
w is this happening to me?" So she Gn 25:22
said to them, "**W** have you come to me, Gn 26:27
W should I be bereft of you both in Gn 27:45
W then have you deceived me?" Gn 29:25
W did you flee secretly and trick me, Gn 31:27
And **w** did you not permit me to kiss Gn 31:28
house, but **w** did you steal my gods?" Gn 31:30
"**W** is it that you ask my name?" And Gn 32:29
"**W** are your faces downcast today?" Gn 40:7
sons, "**W** do you look at one another?" Gn 42:1
That is **w** this distress has come upon Gn 42:21
"**W** did you treat me so badly as to tell Gn 43:6
them, '**W** have you repaid evil for good? Gn 44:4
"**W** does my lord speak such words as Gn 44:7
W should we die before your eyes? Gn 47:15
W should we die before your eyes, both Gn 47:19
said to them, "**W** have you done this, Ex 1:18
"**W** do you strike your companion?" Ex 2:13
where is he? **W** have you left the man? Ex 2:20
great sight, **w** the bush is not burned." Ex 3:3
w do you take the people away from their Ex 5:4
"**W** have you not done all your task of Ex 5:14
"**W** do you treat your servants like this? Ex 5:15
are idle, you are idle; that is **w** you say, Ex 5:17
w have you done evil to this people? Ex 5:22
to this people? **W** did you ever send me? Ex 5:22
said to Moses, "**W** do you cry to me? Ex 14:15
to them, "**W** do you quarrel with me? Ex 17:2
with me? **W** do you test the LORD?" Ex 17:2
"**W** did you bring us up out of Egypt, Ex 17:3
W do you sit alone, and all the people Ex 18:14
w does your wrath burn hot against Ex 32:11
W should the Egyptians say, 'With evil Ex 32:12
"**W** have you not eaten the sin offering Lv 10:17
W are we kept from bringing the LORD'S Nm 9:7
"**W** have you dealt ill with your Nm 11:11
And **w** have I not found favor in your Nm 11:11
"**W** did we come out of Egypt?"'" Nm 11:20
W then were you not afraid to speak Nm 12:8
W is the LORD bringing us into this Nm 14:3
"**W** now are you transgressing the Nm 14:41
W then do you exalt yourselves above Nm 16:3
W have you brought the assembly of Nm 20:4
And **w** have you made us come up out Nm 20:5
"**W** have you brought us up out of Nm 21:5
"**W** have you struck your donkey Nm 22:32
call you? **W** did you not come to me? Nm 22:37
W should the name of our father be Nm 27:4
W will you discourage the heart of the Nm 32:7
Now therefore **w** should we die? For this Dt 5:25
'**W** has the LORD done thus to this land? Dt 29:24
is the reason **w** Joshua circumcised them: Jos 5:4
w have you brought this people over the Jos 7:7
up! **W** have you fallen on your face? Jos 7:10

said, “**W** did you bring trouble on us? Jos 7:25
he said to them, “**W** did you deceive us, Jos 9:22
“**W** have you given me but one lot and Jos 17:14
W did you sit still among the sheepfolds, Jgs 5:16
and Dan, **w** did he stay with the ships? Jgs 5:17
‘**W** is his chariot so long in coming? Jgs 5:28
W tarry the hoofbeats of his chariots?’ Jgs 5:28
us, **w** then has all this happened to us? Jgs 6:13
of Shechem; but **w** should we serve him? Jgs 9:28
W have you come to me now when you Jgs 11:7
“That is **w** we have turned to you now, Jgs 11:8
w did you not deliver them within that Jgs 11:26
“**W** did you cross over to fight against Jgs 12:1
W then have you come up to me this Jgs 12:3
said to him, “**W** do you ask my name, Jgs 13:18
“**W** have you come up against us?” Jgs 15:10
of Israel, **w** has this happened in Israel, Jgs 21:3
my daughters; **w** will you go with me? Ru 1:11
W call me Naomi, when the LORD has Ru 1:21
“**W** have I found favor in your eyes, Ru 2:10
said to her, “Hannah, **w** do you weep? 1 Sm 1:8
do you weep? And **w** do you not eat? 1 Sm 1:8
you not eat? And **w** is your heart sad? 1 Sm 1:8
to them, “**W** do you do such things? 1 Sm 2:23
W then do you scorn my sacrifices 1 Sm 2:29
“**W** has the LORD defeated us today 1 Sm 4:3
This is **w** the priests of Dagon and all 1 Sm 5:5
be known to you **w** his hand does not 1 Sm 6:3
W should you harden your hearts as 1 Sm 6:6
W then have you spoken to me in this 1 Sm 9:21
w have you not answered your 1 Sm 14:41
W then did you not obey the voice of 1 Sm 15:19
W did you pounce on the spoil and 1 Sm 15:19
“**W** have you come out to draw up for 1 Sm 17:8
he said, “**W** have you come down? 1 Sm 17:28
W then will you sin against innocent 1 Sm 19:5
“**W** have you deceived me thus and 1 Sm 19:17
‘Let me go. **W** should I kill you?’” 1 Sm 19:17
And **w** should my father hide this 1 Sm 20:2
for **w** should you bring me to your 1 Sm 20:8
“**W** has not the son of Jesse come to 1 Sm 20:27
“**W** should he be put to death? 1 Sm 20:32
and said to him, “**W** are you alone, 1 Sm 21:1
W then have you brought him to 1 Sm 21:14
“**W** have you conspired against me, 1 Sm 22:13
“**W** do you listen to the words of men 1 Sm 24:9
W then have you not kept watch 1 Sm 26:15
“**W** does my lord pursue after his 1 Sm 26:18
For **w** should your servant dwell in 1 Sm 27:5
W then are you laying a trap for my 1 Sm 28:9
to Saul, “**W** have you deceived me? 1 Sm 28:12
“**W** have you disturbed me by 1 Sm 28:15
said, “**W** then do you ask me, 1 Sm 28:16
W should I strike you to the ground? 2 Sm 2:22
“**W** have you gone in to my father's 2 Sm 3:7
W is it that you have sent him away, 2 Sm 3:24
“**W** have you not built me a house of 2 Sm 7:7
W did you not go down to your 2 Sm 11:10
‘**W** did you go so near the city to 2 Sm 11:20
W did you go so near the wall?’ 2 Sm 11:21
W have you despised the word of the 2 Sm 12:9
But now he is dead. **W** should I fast? 2 Sm 12:23
w are you so haggard morning after 2 Sm 13:4
to him, “**W** should he go with you?” 2 Sm 13:26
“**W** then have you planned such a 2 Sm 14:13
“**W** have your servants set my field 2 Sm 14:31
ask, “**W** have I come from Geshur? 2 Sm 14:32
Gittite, “**W** do you also go with us? 2 Sm 15:19
“**W** have you brought these?” Ziba 2 Sm 16:2
“**W** should this dead dog curse my 2 Sm 16:9
shall say, ‘**W** have you done so?’” 2 Sm 16:10
W did you not go with your friend?” 2 Sm 16:17
W then did you not strike him there 2 Sm 18:11
And Joab said, “**W** will you run, 2 Sm 18:22
Now therefore **w** do you say nothing 2 Sm 19:10
‘**W** should you be the last to bring 2 Sm 19:11
W then should you be the last to 2 Sm 19:12
to him, “**W** did you not go with me, 2 Sm 19:25
“**W** speak any more of your affairs? 2 Sm 19:29
W then should your servant be an 2 Sm 19:35
W should the king repay me with 2 Sm 19:36
“**W** have our brothers the men of 2 Sm 19:41
W then are you angry over this 2 Sm 19:42
you. **W** then did you despise us? 2 Sm 19:43
W will you swallow up the heritage 2 Sm 20:19
but **w** does my lord the king delight in 2 Sm 24:3
“**W** has my lord the king come to 2 Sm 24:21
“**W** have you done thus and so?” He 1 Kgs 1:6
throne”? **W** then is Adonijah king?’ 1 Kgs 1:13
“And **w** do you ask Abishag the 1 Kgs 2:22
W then have you not kept your oath 1 Kgs 2:43
‘**W** has the LORD done thus to this land 1 Kgs 9:8
this was the reason **w** he lifted up his 1 Kgs 11:27
W do you pretend to be another? 1 Kgs 14:6
“**W** is your spirit so vexed that you 1 Kgs 21:5

said to them, “**W** have you returned?” 2 Kgs 1:5
he said, “**W** will you go to him today? 2 Kgs 4:23
“**W** have you torn your clothes? 2 Kgs 5:8
W should I wait for the LORD any 2 Kgs 6:33
“**W** are we sitting here until we die? 2 Kgs 7:3
“**W** does my lord weep?” He answered, 2 Kgs 8:12
W did this mad fellow come to you?” 2 Kgs 9:11
“**W** are you not repairing the house? 2 Kgs 12:7
for **w** should you provoke trouble so 2 Kgs 14:10
is good.” For he thought, “**W** not, 2 Kgs 20:19
“**W** have you not built me a house of 1 Chr 17:6
W then should my lord require this? 1 Chr 21:3
W should it be a cause of guilt for 1 Chr 21:3
‘**W** has the LORD done thus to this 2 Chr 7:21
“**W** have you not required the Levites 2 Chr 24:6
‘**W** do you break the commandments 2 Chr 24:20
W should you suppose that God will 2 Chr 25:8
“**W** have you sought the gods of a 2 Chr 25:15
W should you be struck down?” So 2 Chr 25:16
W should you provoke trouble so 2 Chr 25:19
“**W** should the kings of Assyria 2 Chr 32:4
old. That was **w** this city was laid waste. Ezr 4:15
W should damage grow to the hurt of Ezr 4:22
the king said to me, “**W** is your face sad, Neh 2:2
W should not my face be sad, when the Neh 2:3
W should the work stop while I leave it Neh 6:3
that is **w** you are building the wall. Neh 6:6
“**W** is the house of God forsaken?” Neh 13:11
“**W** do you lodge outside the wall? Neh 13:21
“**W** do you transgress the king's Est 3:3
to learn what this was and **w** it was. Est 4:5
“**W** did I not die at birth, come out from Jb 3:11
W did the knees receive me? Or why the Jb 3:12
Or **w** the breasts, that I should nurse? Jb 3:12
Or **w** was I not as a hidden stillborn Jb 3:16
“**W** is light given to him who is in Jb 3:20
W is light given to a man whose way is Jb 3:23
W have you made me your mark? Jb 7:20
W have I become a burden to you? Jb 7:20
W do you not pardon my transgression Jb 7:21
be condemned; **w** then do I labor in vain? Jb 9:29
let me know **w** you contend against me. Jb 10:2
“**W** did you bring me out from the Jb 10:18
W should I take my flesh in my teeth Jb 13:14
W do you hide your face and count me Jb 13:24
W does your heart carry you away, and Jb 15:12
you away, and **w** do your eyes flash, Jb 15:12
W are we counted as cattle? Why are we Jb 18:3
as cattle? **W** are we stupid in your sight? Jb 18:3
W do you, like God, pursue me? Why Jb 19:22
W are you not satisfied with my flesh? Jb 19:22
man? **W** should I not be impatient? Jb 21:4
W do the wicked live, reach old age, and Jb 21:7
“**W** are not times of judgment kept by Jb 24:1
and **w** do those who know him never see Jb 24:1
w then have you become altogether Jb 27:12
W do you contend against him, saying, Jb 33:13
W do the nations rage and the peoples plot Ps 2:1
W, O LORD, do you stand afar off? Why Ps 10:1
W do you hide yourself in times of Ps 10:1
W does the wicked renounce God and Ps 10:13
God, my God, **w** have you forsaken me? Ps 22:1
W are you so far from saving me, from Ps 22:1
W are you cast down, O my soul, and Ps 42:5
and **w** are you in turmoil within me? Ps 42:5
my rock: “**W** have you forgotten me? Ps 42:9
W do I go mourning because of the Ps 42:9
W are you cast down, O my soul, and Ps 42:11
and **w** are you in turmoil within me? Ps 42:11
I take refuge; **w** have you rejected me? Ps 43:2
W do I go about mourning because of Ps 43:2
W are you cast down, O my soul, and Ps 43:5
and **w** are you in turmoil within me? Ps 43:5
Awake! **W** are you sleeping, O Lord? Ps 44:23
W do you hide your face? Why do you Ps 44:24
W do you forget our affliction and Ps 44:24
W should I fear in times of trouble, Ps 49:5
W do you boast of evil, O mighty man? Ps 52:1
W do you look with hatred, O Ps 68:16
O God, **w** do you cast us off forever? Why Ps 74:1
W does your anger smoke against the Ps 74:1
W do you hold back your hand, your Ps 74:11
W should the nations say, “Where is Ps 79:10
W then have you broken down its Ps 80:12
O LORD, **w** do you cast my soul away? Ps 88:14
W do you hide your face from me? Ps 88:14
W should the nations say, “Where is Ps 115:2
W should you be intoxicated, my son, Prv 5:20
W should a fool have money in his Prv 17:16
w should your bed be taken from Prv 22:27
W then have I been so very wise?” And Eccl 2:15
W should God be angry at your voice Eccl 5:6
“**W** were the former days better than Eccl 7:10
wise. **W** should you destroy yourself? Eccl 7:16
W should you die before your time? Eccl 7:17

for **w** should I be like one who veils herself Sg 1:7
W should you look upon the Sg 6:13
W will you still be struck down? Why will Is 1:5
down? **W** will you continue to rebel? Is 1:5
it to yield grapes, **w** did it yield wild grapes? Is 5:4
W do you say, O Jacob, and speak, O Is 40:27
W, when I came, was there no man; why, Is 50:2
w, when I called, was there no one to Is 50:2
W do you spend your money for that Is 55:2
‘**W** have we fasted, and you see it not? Is 58:3
W have we humbled ourselves, and you Is 58:3
W is your apparel red, and your Is 63:2
w do you make us wander from your Is 63:17
servant? **W** then has he become a prey? Jer 2:14
“**W** do you contend with me? You have Jer 2:29
W then do my people say, ‘We are free, Jer 2:31
‘**W** has the LORD our God done all these Jer 5:19
W then has this people turned away in Jer 8:5
W do we sit still? Gather together; let us Jer 8:14
not in her?” “**W** have they provoked Jer 8:19
W then has the health of the daughter of Jer 8:22
W is the land ruined and laid waste like Jer 9:12
W does the way of the wicked prosper? Jer 12:1
W do all who are treacherous thrive? Jer 12:1
‘**W** have these things come upon me?’ Jer 13:22
w should you be like a stranger in the Jer 14:8
W should you be like a man confused, Jer 14:9
W have you struck us down so that Jer 14:19
W is my pain unceasing, my wound Jer 15:18
‘**W** has the LORD pronounced all this Jer 16:10
W did I come out from the womb to see Jer 20:18
“**W** has the LORD dealt thus with this Jer 22:8
W are he and his children hurled and Jer 22:28
W have you prophesied in the name of Jer 26:9
W will you and your people die by the Jer 27:13
W should this city become a Jer 27:17
Now **w** have you not rebuked Jeremiah Jer 29:27
W then do I see every man with his Jer 30:6
in labor? **W** has every face turned pale? Jer 30:6
W do you cry out over your hurt? Your Jer 30:15
saying, “**W** do you prophesy and say, Jer 32:3
“**W** have you written in it that the king Jer 36:29
W should he take your life, so that all Jer 40:15
W do you commit this great evil against Jer 44:7
W do you provoke me to anger with the Jer 44:8
W have I seen it? They are dismayed and Jer 46:5
W are your mighty ones face down? Jer 46:15
W then has Milcom dispossessed Gad, Jer 49:1
W do you boast of your valleys, O Jer 49:4
W should a living man complain, a Lam 3:39
W do you forget us forever, why do Lam 5:20
w do you forsake us for so many days? Lam 5:20
‘**W** should not the son suffer for the Ezk 18:19
W will you die, O house of Israel? Ezk 18:31
they say to you, ‘**W** do you groan?’ Ezk 21:7
your evil ways, for **w** will you die, Ezk 33:11
for **w** should he see that you were in Dn 1:10
“**W** is the decree of the king so urgent?” Dn 2:15
“Do you know **w** I have come to you? Dn 10:20
W should they say among the peoples, Jl 2:17
W would you have the day of the LORD? Am 5:18
That is **w** I made haste to flee to Jon 4:2
Now **w** do you cry aloud? Is there no king Mi 4:9
W do you make me see iniquity, and Hab 1:3
and **w** do you idly look at wrong? Hab 1:3
w do you idly look at traitors and are Hab 1:13
it away. **W**? declares the LORD of hosts. Hg 1:9
W then are we faithless to one another, Mal 2:10
“**W** does he not?” Because the LORD was Mal 2:14
And **w** are you anxious about clothing? Mt 6:28
W do you see the speck that is in your Mt 7:3
And he said to them, “**W** are you afraid, Mt 8:26
“**W** do you think evil in your hearts? Mt 9:4
“**W** does your teacher eat with tax Mt 9:11
saying, “**W** do we and the Pharisees fast, Mt 9:14
“**W** do you speak to them in parables?” Mt 13:10
This is **w** I speak to them in parables, Mt 13:13
that is **w** these miraculous powers are at Mt 14:2
“O you of little faith, **w** did you doubt?” Mt 14:31
“**W** do your disciples break the tradition Mt 15:2
“And **w** do you break the Mt 15:3
w are you discussing among yourselves Mt 16:8
“Then **w** do the scribes say that first Mt 17:10
and said, “**W** could we not cast it out?” Mt 17:19
“**W** then did Moses command one to Mt 19:7
“**W** do you ask me about what is good? Mt 19:17
them, ‘**W** do you stand here idle all day?’ Mt 20:6
us, ‘**W** then did you not believe him?’ Mt 21:25
malice, said, “**W** put me to the test, Mt 22:18
were indignant, saying, “**W** this waste? Mt 26:8
them, “**W** do you trouble the woman? Mt 26:10
“**W**, what evil has he done?” But they Mt 27:23
my God, **w** have you forsaken me?” Mt 27:46
there also, for that is **w** I came out.” Mk 1:38
“**W** does this man speak like that? He is Mk 2:7

“**W** do you question these things in your Mk 2:8
“**W** does he eat with tax collectors and Mk 2:16
“**W** do John's disciples and the disciples Mk 2:18
w are they doing what is not lawful on Mk 2:24
He said to them, “**W** are you so afraid? Mk 4:40
W trouble the Teacher any further?” Mk 5:35
“**W** are you making a commotion and Mk 5:39
That is **w** these miraculous powers are Mk 6:14
“**W** do your disciples not walk Mk 7:5
“**W** does this generation seek a sign? Mk 8:12
“**W** are you discussing the fact that you Mk 8:17
“**W** do the scribes say that first Elijah Mk 9:11
privately, “**W** could we not cast it out?” Mk 9:28
said to him, “**W** do you call me good? Mk 10:18
says to you, ‘**W** are you doing this?’ Mk 11:3
say, ‘**W** then did you not believe him?’ Mk 11:31
he said to them, “**W** put me to the test? Mk 12:15
“**W** was the ointment wasted like that? Mk 14:4
her alone. **W** do you trouble her? Mk 14:6
“**W**, what evil has he done?” But they Mk 15:14
my God, **w** have you forsaken me?” Mk 15:34
And **w** is this granted to me that the Lk 1:43
to him, “Son, **w** have you treated us so? Lk 2:48
to them, “**W** were you looking for me? Lk 2:49
“**W** do you question in your hearts? Lk 5:22
“**W** do you eat and drink with tax Lk 5:30
“**W** are you doing what is not lawful to do Lk 6:2
W do you see the speck that is in your Lk 6:41
“**W** do you call me ‘Lord, Lord,’ and not Lk 6:46
of all the people **w** she had touched him, Lk 8:47
W, even the hairs of your head are all Lk 12:7
that, **w** are you anxious about the rest? Lk 12:26
but **w** do you not know how to Lk 12:56
“And **w** do you not judge for yourselves Lk 12:57
it down. **W** should it use up the ground?’ Lk 13:7
said to him, “**W** do you call me good? Lk 18:19
W then did you not put my money in Lk 19:23
asks you, ‘**W** are you untying it?’ Lk 19:31
to them, “**W** are you untying the colt?” Lk 19:33
he will say, ‘**W** did you not believe him?’ Lk 20:5
he said to them, “**W** are you sleeping? Lk 22:46
to them, “**W**, what evil has he done? Lk 23:22
“**W** do you seek the living among the Lk 24:5
he said to them, “**W** are you troubled, Lk 24:38
and **w** do doubts arise in your hearts? Lk 24:38
asked him, “Then **w** are you baptizing, Jn 1:25
seek?” or, “**W** are you talking with her?” Jn 4:27
And this was **w** the Jews were persecuting Jn 5:16
This was **w** the Jews were seeking all the Jn 5:18
“This is **w** I told you that no one can Jn 6:65
keeps the law. **W** do you seek to kill me?” Jn 7:19
to them, “**W** did you not bring him?” Jn 7:45
W do you not understand what I say? It Jn 8:43
I tell the truth, **w** do you not believe me? Jn 8:46
The reason **w** you do not hear them is Jn 8:47
listen. **W** do you want to hear it again? Jn 9:27
answered, “**W**, this is an amazing thing! Jn 9:30
demon, and is insane; **w** listen to him?” Jn 10:20
“**W** was this ointment not sold for three Jn 12:5
The reason **w** the crowd went to meet Jn 12:18
was to betray him; that was **w** he said, Jn 13:11
one at the table knew **w** he said this to Jn 13:28
him, “Lord, **w** can I not follow you now? Jn 13:37
this is **w** we believe that you came from Jn 16:30
W do you ask me? Ask those who have Jn 18:21
I said is right, **w** do you strike me?” Jn 18:23
w are you weeping?” She said to them, Jn 20:13
to her, “Woman, **w** are you weeping? Jn 20:15
w do you stand looking into heaven? Acts 1:11
of Israel, **w** do you wonder at this, Acts 3:12
wonder at this, or **w** do you stare at us, Acts 3:12
Holy Spirit, “‘**W** did the Gentiles rage, Acts 4:25
w has Satan filled your heart to lie to the Acts 5:3
W is it that you have contrived this Acts 5:4
W do you wrong each other?’ Acts 7:26
“Saul, Saul, **w** are you persecuting me?” Acts 9:4
I ask then **w** you sent for me.” Acts 10:29
“Men, **w** are you doing these things? Acts 14:15
w are you putting God to the test by Acts 15:10
them did not know **w** they had come Acts 19:32
‘Saul, Saul, **w** are you persecuting me?’ Acts 22:7
And now **w** do you wait? Rise and be Acts 22:16
to find out **w** they were shouting Acts 22:24
know the real reason **w** he was being Acts 22:30
W is it thought incredible by any of Acts 26:8
Saul, **w** are you persecuting me? Acts 26:14
w am I still being condemned as a Rom 3:7
And **w** not do evil that good may come? Rom 3:8
That is **w** it depends on faith, in order Rom 4:16
That is **w** his faith was “counted to Rom 4:22
to me then, “**W** does he still find fault? Rom 9:19
“**W** have you made me like this?” Rom 9:20
W? Because they did not pursue it by Rom 9:32
W do you pass judgment on your Rom 14:10
you, **w** do you despise your brother? Rom 14:10
This is the reason **w** I have so often Rom 15:22
w do you boast as if you did not receive 1 Cor 4:7
That is **w** I sent you Timothy, my 1 Cor 4:17
w do you lay them before those who 1 Cor 6:4
for you. **W** not rather suffer wrong? 1 Cor 6:7
wrong? **W** not rather be defrauded? 1 Cor 6:7
For **w** should my liberty be 1 Cor 10:29
w am I denounced because of that 1 Cor 10:30
That is **w** a wife ought to have a 1 Cor 11:10
That is **w** many of you are weak and 1 Cor 11:30
w are people baptized on their 1 Cor 15:29
W am I in danger every hour? 1 Cor 15:30
That is **w** it is through him that we 2 Cor 1:20
For this is **w** I wrote, that I might test 2 Cor 2:9
And **w**? Because I do not love you? 2 Cor 11:11
W then the law? It was added because Gal 3:19
w am I still being persecuted? Gal 5:11
w, as if you were still alive in the world, Col 2:20
which is **w** I suffer as I do. But I am 2 Tm 1:12
This is **w** I left you in Crete, so that you Ti 1:5
For this perhaps is **w** he was parted Phlm 1:15
That is **w** he is not ashamed to call Heb 2:11
For this is **w** the gospel was preached 1 Pt 4:6
The reason **w** the world does not know 1 Jn 3:1
his brother. And **w** did he murder him? 1 Jn 3:12
the angel said to me, “**W** do you marvel? Rv 17:7

WICK (3)
and a faintly burning **w** he will not Is 42:3
are extinguished, quenched like a **w**: Is 43:17
and a smoldering **w** he will not Mt 12:20

WICKED (303)
Now the men of Sodom were **w**, great Gn 13:13
sweep away the righteous with the **w**? Gn 18:23
put the righteous to death with the **w**, Gn 18:25
so that the righteous fare as the **w**! Gn 18:25
firstborn, was **w** in the sight of the LORD, Gn 38:7
And what he did was **w** in the sight of Gn 38:10
not join hands with a **w** man to be a Ex 23:1
and righteous, for I will not acquit the **w**. Ex 23:7
shall this **w** congregation grumble Nm 14:27
do to all this **w** congregation who are Nm 14:35
please, from the tents of these **w** men, Nm 16:26
but the **w** shall be cut off in darkness, 1 Sm 2:9
‘Out of the **w** comes wickedness.’ 1 Sm 24:13
Then all the **w** and worthless fellows 1 Sm 30:22
falls before the **w** you have fallen.” 2 Sm 3:34
when **w** men have killed a righteous 2 Sm 4:11
And they did **w** things, provoking 2 Kgs 17:11
my face and turn from their **w** ways, 2 Chr 7:14
you help the **w** and love those 2 Chr 19:2
the sons of Athaliah, that **w** woman, 2 Chr 24:7
rebuilding that rebellious and **w** city. Ezr 4:12
serve you or turn from their **w** works. Neh 9:35
This **w** Haman!” Then Haman was Est 7:6
There the **w** cease from troubling, and Jb 3:17
and the tent of the **w** will be no more.” Jb 8:22
destroys both the blameless and the **w**. Jb 9:22
The earth is given into the hand of the **w**; Jb 9:24
hands and favor the designs of the **w**? Jb 10:3
But the eyes of the **w** will fail; all way of Jb 11:20
The **w** man writhes in pain all his days, Jb 15:20
and casts me into the hands of the **w**. Jb 16:11
“Indeed, the light of the **w** is put out, and Jb 18:5
that the exulting of the **w** is short, and the Jb 20:5
This is the **w** man's portion from God, Jb 20:29
Why do the **w** live, reach old age, and Jb 21:7
The counsel of the **w** is far from me. Jb 21:16
is it that the lamp of the **w** is put out? Jb 21:17
Where is the tent in which the **w** lived?’ Jb 21:28
to the old way that **w** men have trod? Jb 22:15
but the counsel of the **w** is far from me. Jb 22:18
they glean the vineyard of the **w** man. Jb 24:6
the olive rows of the **w** they make oil; Jb 24:11
“Let my enemy be as the **w**, and let him Jb 27:7
is the portion of a **w** man with God, Jb 27:13
with evildoers and walks with **w** men? Jb 34:8
one,’ and to nobles, ‘**W** man,’ Jb 34:18
the end, because he answers like **w** men. Jb 34:36
He does not keep the **w** alive, but gives the Jb 36:6
you are full of the judgment on the **w**; Jb 36:17
the earth, and the **w** be shaken out of it? Jb 38:13
From the **w** their light is withheld, and Jb 38:15
and tread down the **w** where they stand. Jb 40:12
who walks not in the counsel of the **w**, Ps 1:1
The **w** are not so, but are like chaff that Ps 1:4
Therefore the **w** will not stand in the Ps 1:5
righteous, but the way of the **w** will perish. Ps 1:6
on the cheek; you break the teeth of the **w**. Ps 3:7
Oh, let the evil of the **w** come to an end, Ps 7:9
the **w** man conceives evil and is Ps 7:14
the nations; you have made the **w** perish; Ps 9:5
the **w** are snared in the work of their own Ps 9:16
The **w** shall return to Sheol, all the Ps 9:17
In arrogance the **w** hotly pursue the Ps 10:2
For the **w** boasts of the desires of his soul, Ps 10:3
pride of his face the **w** does not seek him; Ps 10:4
Why does the **w** renounce God and say Ps 10:13
Break the arm of the **w** and evildoer; Ps 10:15
for behold, the **w** bend the bow; they Ps 11:2
but his soul hates the **w** and the one who Ps 11:5
Let him rain coals on the **w**; fire and Ps 11:6
On every side the **w** prowl, as vileness is Ps 12:8
from the **w** who do me violence, my Ps 17:9
my soul from the **w** by your sword, Ps 17:13
of evildoers, and I will not sit with the **w**. Ps 26:5
Do not drag me off with the **w**, with the Ps 28:3
upon you; let the **w** be put to shame; Ps 31:17
Many are the sorrows of the **w**, but Ps 32:10
Affliction will slay the **w**, and those Ps 34:21
speaks to the **w** deep in his Ps 36:1
nor the hand of the **w** drive me away. Ps 36:11
just a little while, the **w** will be no more; Ps 37:10
The **w** plots against the righteous and Ps 37:12
but the Lord laughs at the **w**, for he sees Ps 37:13
The **w** draw the sword and bend their Ps 37:14
has than the abundance of many **w**. Ps 37:16
For the arms of the **w** shall be broken, Ps 37:17
But the **w** will perish; the enemies of the Ps 37:20
The **w** borrows but does not pay back, Ps 37:21
the children of the **w** shall be cut off. Ps 37:28
The **w** watches for the righteous and Ps 37:32
you will look on when the **w** are cut off. Ps 37:34
I have seen a **w**, ruthless man, Ps 37:35
the future of the **w** shall be cut off. Ps 37:38
them from the **w** and saves them, Ps 37:40
so long as the **w** are in my presence.” Ps 39:1
But to the **w** God says: “What right Ps 50:16
because of the oppression of the **w**. Ps 55:3
The **w** are estranged from the womb; Ps 58:3
will bathe his feet in the blood of the **w**. Ps 58:10
Hide me from the secret plots of the **w**, Ps 64:2
fire, so the **w** shall perish before God! Ps 68:2
me, O my God, from the hand of the **w**, Ps 71:4
when I saw the prosperity of the **w**. Ps 73:3
Behold, these are the **w**; always at ease, Ps 73:12
the boastful, ‘Do not boast,’ and to the **w**, Ps 75:4
and all the **w** of the earth shall drain it Ps 75:8
All the horns of the **w** I will cut off, but Ps 75:10
unjustly and show partiality to the **w**? Ps 82:2
deliver them from the hand of the **w**.” Ps 82:4
him; the **w** shall not humble him. Ps 89:22
eyes and see the recompense of the **w**. Ps 91:8
that though the **w** sprout like grass and Ps 92:7
O LORD, how long shall the **w**, how long Ps 94:3
the wicked, how long shall the **w** exult? Ps 94:3
of trouble, until a pit is dug for the **w**. Ps 94:13
Who rises up for me against the **w**? Ps 94:16
Can **w** rulers be allied with you, those Ps 94:20
delivers them from the hand of the **w**. Ps 97:10
I will destroy all the **w** in the land, Ps 101:8
the earth, and let the **w** be no more! Ps 104:35
company; the flame burned up the **w**. Ps 106:18
For **w** and deceitful mouths are opened Ps 109:2
Appoint a **w** man against him; let an Ps 109:6
The **w** man sees it and is angry; he Ps 112:10
away; the desire of the **w** will perish! Ps 112:10
seizes me because of the **w**, Ps 119:53
the cords of the **w** ensnare me, Ps 119:61
The **w** lie in wait to destroy me, but I Ps 119:95
The **w** have laid a snare for me, but I Ps 119:110
All the **w** of the earth you discard like Ps 119:119
Salvation is far from the **w**, for they Ps 119:155
righteous; he has cut the cords of the **w**. Ps 129:4
Oh that you would slay the **w**, O God! Ps 139:19
me, O LORD, from the hands of the **w**; Ps 140:4
Grant not, O LORD, the desires of the **w**; Ps 140:8
busy myself with **w** deeds in company Ps 141:4
Let the **w** fall into their own nets, while Ps 141:10
love him, but all the **w** he will destroy. Ps 145:20
but the way of the **w** he brings to ruin. Ps 146:9
humble; he casts the **w** to the ground. Ps 147:6
but the **w** will be cut off from the land, Prv 2:22
of sudden terror or of the ruin of the **w**, Prv 3:25
LORD'S curse is on the house of the **w**, Prv 3:33
Do not enter the path of the **w**, and do Prv 4:14
The way of the **w** is like deep darkness; Prv 4:19
The iniquities of the **w** ensnare him, Prv 5:22
A worthless person, a **w** man, goes Prv 6:12
a heart that devises **w** plans, feet that Prv 6:18
he who reproves a **w** man incurs injury. Prv 9:7
but he thwarts the craving of the **w**. Prv 10:3
the mouth of the **w** conceals violence. Prv 10:6
blessing, but the name of the **w** will rot. Prv 10:7
the mouth of the **w** conceals violence. Prv 10:11
leads to life, the gain of the **w** to sin. Prv 10:16
the heart of the **w** is of little worth. Prv 10:20
What the **w** dreads will come upon Prv 10:24
the tempest passes, the **w** is no more, Prv 10:25
but the years of the **w** will be short. Prv 10:27

the expectation of the **w** will perish. Prv 10:28
but the **w** will not dwell in the land. Prv 10:30
is acceptable, but the mouth of the **w**, Prv 10:32
but the **w** falls by his own wickedness. Prv 11:5
When the **w** dies, his hope will perish, Prv 11:7
trouble, and the **w** walks into it instead. Prv 11:8
and when the **w** perish there are Prv 11:10
the mouth of the **w** it is overthrown. Prv 11:11
The **w** earns deceptive wages, but one Prv 11:18
the expectation of the **w** in wrath. Prv 11:23
how much more the **w** and the sinner! Prv 11:31
just; the counsels of the **w** are deceitful. Prv 12:5
The words of the **w** lie in wait for blood, Prv 12:6
The **w** are overthrown and are no more, Prv 12:7
beast, but the mercy of the **w** is cruel. Prv 12:10
Whoever is **w** covets the spoil of Prv 12:12
but the **w** are filled with trouble. Prv 12:21
but the way of the **w** leads them astray. Prv 12:26
but the **w** brings shame and disgrace. Prv 13:5
is blameless, but sin overthrows the **w**. Prv 13:6
but the lamp of the **w** will be put out. Prv 13:9
A **w** messenger falls into trouble, but a Prv 13:17
but the belly of the **w** suffers want. Prv 13:25
The house of the **w** will be destroyed, Prv 14:11
the **w** at the gates of the righteous. Prv 14:19
The **w** is overthrown through his Prv 14:32
but trouble befalls the income of the **w**. Prv 15:6
sacrifice of the **w** is an abomination Prv 15:8
The way of the **w** is an abomination to Prv 15:9
thoughts of the **w** are an abomination Prv 15:26
the mouth of the **w** pours out evil Prv 15:28
The LORD is far from the **w**, but he Prv 15:29
even the **w** for the day of trouble. Prv 16:4
An evildoer listens to **w** lips, and a liar Prv 17:4
He who justifies the **w** and he who Prv 17:15
The **w** accepts a bribe in secret to Prv 17:23
to be partial to the **w** or to deprive the Prv 18:5
the mouth of the **w** devours iniquity. Prv 19:28
king winnows the **w** and drives the Prv 20:26
and a proud heart, the lamp of the **w**, Prv 21:4
The violence of the **w** will sweep them Prv 21:7
The soul of the **w** desires evil; his Prv 21:10
One observes the house of the **w**; Prv 21:12
wicked; he throws the **w** down to ruin. Prv 21:12
The **w** is a ransom for the righteous, Prv 21:18
sacrifice of the **w** is an abomination; Prv 21:27
A **w** man puts on a bold face, but the Prv 21:29
in wait as a **w** man against the Prv 24:15
but the **w** stumble in times of Prv 24:16
evildoers, and be not envious of the **w**, Prv 24:19
the lamp of the **w** will be put out. Prv 24:20
Whoever says to the **w**, "You are in the Prv 24:24
who rebuke the **w** will have delight, Prv 24:25
take away the **w** from the presence of Prv 25:5
man who gives way before the **w**. Prv 25:26
The **w** flee when no one pursues, but Prv 28:1
Those who forsake the law praise the **w**, Prv 28:4
is great glory, but when the **w** rise, Prv 28:12
charging bear is a **w** ruler over a poor Prv 28:15
When the **w** rise, people hide Prv 28:28
the people rejoice, but when the **w** rule, Prv 29:2
a **w** man does not understand such Prv 29:7
to falsehood, all his officials will be **w**. Prv 29:12
When the **w** increase, transgression Prv 29:16
is straight is an abomination to the **w**. Prv 29:27
God will judge the righteous and the **w**, Eccl 3:17
and there is a **w** man who prolongs his Eccl 7:15
Be not overly **w**, neither be a fool. Why Eccl 7:17
Then I saw the **w** buried. They used to Eccl 8:10
But it will not be well with the **w**, Eccl 8:13
according to the deeds of the **w**, Eccl 8:14
and there are **w** people to whom it Eccl 8:14
happens to the righteous and the **w**, Eccl 9:2
Woe to the **w**! It shall be ill with him, for Is 3:11
the breath of his lips he shall kill the **w**. Is 11:4
for its evil, and the **w** for their iniquity; Is 13:11
The LORD has broken the staff of the **w**, Is 14:5
If favor is shown to the **w**, he does not Is 26:10
he plans **w** schemes to ruin the poor with Is 32:7
is no peace," says the LORD, "for the **w**." Is 48:22
his grave with the **w** and with a rich Is 53:9
let the **w** forsake his way, and the Is 55:7
But the **w** are like the tossing sea; for it Is 57:20
is no peace," says my God, "for the **w**." Is 57:21
and to fight and to hit with a **w** fist. Is 58:4
So that even to **w** women you have Jer 2:33
long shall your **w** thoughts lodge within Jer 4:14
For **w** men are found among my people; Jer 5:26
goes on, for the **w** are not removed. Jer 6:29
you. Why does the way of the **w** prosper? Jer 12:1
deliver you out of the hand of the **w**, Jer 15:21
it will burst upon the head of the **w**. Jer 23:19
flesh, and the **w** he will put to the sword, Jer 25:31
it will burst upon the head of the **w**. Jer 30:23
If I say to the **w**, 'You shall surely die,' Ezk 3:18
speak to warn the **w** from his wicked Ezk 3:18
to warn the wicked from his **w** way, Ezk 3:18
that **w** person shall die for his iniquity, Ezk 3:18
But if you warn the **w**, and he does not Ezk 3:19
his wickedness, or from his **w** way, Ezk 3:19
prey, and to the **w** of the earth for spoil, Ezk 7:21
iniquity and who give **w** counsel in this Ezk 11:2
him, and you have encouraged the **w**, Ezk 13:22
the wickedness of the **w** shall be upon Ezk 18:20
"But if a **w** person turns away from all Ezk 18:21
I any pleasure in the death of the **w**, Ezk 18:23
abominations that the **w** person does, Ezk 18:24
when a **w** person turns away from the Ezk 18:27
cut off from you both righteous and **w**. Ezk 21:3
cut off from you both righteous and **w**, Ezk 21:4
And you, O profane **w** one, prince of Ezk 21:25
you on the necks of the profane **w**, Ezk 21:29
If I say to the **w**, O wicked one, you shall Ezk 33:8
If I say to the wicked, O **w** one, you shall Ezk 33:8
speak to warn the **w** to turn from his Ezk 33:8
that **w** person shall die in his iniquity, Ezk 33:8
But if you warn the **w** to turn from his Ezk 33:9
have no pleasure in the death of the **w**, Ezk 33:11
but that the **w** turn from his way and Ezk 33:11
and as for the wickedness of the **w**, Ezk 33:12
Again, though I say to the **w**, 'You Ezk 33:14
if the **w** restores the pledge, gives back Ezk 33:15
And when the **w** turns from his Ezk 33:19
refined, but the **w** shall act wickedly. Dn 12:10
And none of the **w** shall understand, Dn 12:10
of wickedness in the house of the **w**, Mi 6:10
acquit the man with **w** scales and with a Mi 6:11
For the **w** surround the righteous; so Hab 1:4
are silent when the **w** swallows up the Hab 1:13
crushed the head of the house of the **w**, Hab 3:13
fish of the sea, and the rubble with the **w**. Zep 1:3
and they will be called 'the **w** country,' Mal 1:4
between the righteous and the **w**, Mal 3:18
And you shall tread down the **w**, for they Mal 4:3
him and said to him, 'You **w** servant! Mt 18:32
But if that **w** servant says to himself, Mt 24:48
him, 'You **w** and slothful servant! Mt 25:26
with your own words, you **w** servant! Lk 19:22
For everyone who does **w** things hates the Jn 3:20
and taking some **w** men of the rabble, Acts 17:5
and with all **w** deception for those 2 Thes 2:10
be delivered from **w** and evil men. 2 Thes 3:2
by the sensual conduct of the **w** 2 Pt 2:7
greets him takes part in his **w** works. 2 Jn 1:11
doing, talking **w** nonsense against us. 3 Jn 1:10

WICKEDLY (15)

"I beg you, my brothers, do not act so **w**. Gn 19:7
"No, my brothers, do not act so **w**; Jgs 19:23
But if you still do **w**, you shall be 1 Sm 12:25
and have not **w** departed from my 2 Sm 22:22
I have sinned, and I have done **w**. 2 Sm 24:17
and have acted perversely and **w**,' 1 Kgs 8:47
and have acted perversely and **w**,' 2 Chr 6:37
Ahaziah king of Israel, who acted **w**. 2 Chr 20:35
was his counselor in doing **w**. 2 Chr 22:3
dealt faithfully and we have acted **w**. Neh 9:33
Of a truth, God will not do **w**, and the Jb 34:12
and have not **w** departed from my God. Ps 18:21
done wrong and acted **w** and rebelled, Dn 9:5
day, we have sinned, we have done **w**. Dn 9:15
be refined, but the wicked shall act **w**. Dn 12:10

WICKEDNESS (61)

LORD saw that the **w** of man was great Gn 6:5
I do this great **w** and sin against God?" Gn 39:9
it is because of the **w** of these nations that Dt 9:4
but because of the **w** of these nations the Dt 9:5
of this people, or their **w** or their sin, Dt 9:27
again do any such **w** as this among Dt 13:11
know and see that your **w** is great, 1 Sm 12:17
says, 'Out of the wicked comes **w**.' 1 Sm 24:13
the evildoer according to his **w**!" 2 Sm 3:39
to the earth, but if **w** is found in him, 1 Kgs 1:52
remembered, so **w** is broken like a tree.' Jb 24:20
far be it from God that he should do **w**, Jb 34:10
He strikes them for their **w** in a place for Jb 34:26
Your **w** concerns a man like yourself, Jb 35:8
For you are not a God who delights in **w**; Ps 5:4
call his **w** to account till you find none. Ps 10:15
have loved righteousness and hated **w**. Ps 45:7
of my God than dwell in the tents of **w**. Ps 84:10
iniquity and wipe them out for their **w**; Ps 94:23
committed iniquity; we have done **w**. Ps 106:6
are glad, and all **w** shuts its mouth. Ps 107:42
For the scepter of **w** shall not rest on the Ps 125:3
eat the bread of **w** and drink the wine Prv 4:17
truth; **w** is an abomination to my lips. Prv 8:7
Treasures gained by **w** do not profit, Prv 10:2
but the wicked falls by his own **w**. Prv 11:5
No one is established by **w**, but the root Prv 12:3
When **w** comes, contempt comes also, Prv 18:3
his **w** will be exposed in the assembly. Prv 26:26
the place of justice, even there was **w**, Eccl 3:16
of righteousness, even there was **w**. Eccl 3:16
and to know the **w** of folly and the Eccl 7:25
nor will **w** deliver those who are given to Eccl 8:8
For **w** burns like a fire; it consumes Is 9:18
You felt secure in your **w**, you said, "No Is 47:10
to loose the bonds of **w**, to undo the straps Is 58:6
pointing of the finger, and speaking **w**, Is 58:9
have spoken lies; your tongue mutters **w**. Is 59:3
We acknowledge our **w**, O LORD, and Jer 14:20
and he does not turn from his **w**, Ezk 3:19
my rules by doing **w** more than the Ezk 5:6
Violence has grown up into a rod of **w**. Ezk 7:11
"And after all your **w** (woe, woe to Ezk 16:23
before your **w** was uncovered? Now Ezk 16:57
and the **w** of the wicked shall be upon Ezk 18:20
away from the **w** he has committed Ezk 18:27
surely deal with it as its **w** deserves. Ezk 31:11
and as for the **w** of the wicked, Ezk 33:12
fall by it when he turns from his **w**, Ezk 33:12
turns from his **w** and does what Ezk 33:19
Because of the **w** of their deeds I will Hos 9:15
to those who devise **w** and work evil on Mi 2:1
longer the treasures of **w** in the house of Mi 6:10
"This is **W**." And he thrust her back Zec 5:8
coveting, **w**, deceit, sensuality, envy, Mk 7:22
but inside you are full of greed and **w**. Lk 11:39
bought a field with the reward of his **w**, Acts 1:18
every one of you from your **w**." Acts 3:26
Repent, therefore, of this **w** of yours, Acts 8:22
have loved righteousness and hated **w**; Heb 1:9
filthiness and rampant **w** and receive Jas 1:21

WIDE (31)

a rim around it a handbreadth **w**, Ex 25:25
made a rim around it a handbreadth **w**, Ex 37:12
Then scatter the fire far and **w**, for Nm 16:37
'You shall open **w** your hand to your Dt 15:11
You gave a **w** place for my steps 2 Sm 22:37
was sixty cubits long, twenty cubits **w**, 1 Kgs 6:2
twenty cubits long, twenty cubits **w**, 1 Kgs 6:20
was four cubits long, four cubits **w**, 1 Kgs 7:27
and twenty cubits **w** and ten cubits 2 Chr 4:1
five cubits long, five cubits **w**, 2 Chr 6:13
The city was **w** and large, but the people Neh 7:4
As through a **w** breach they come; Jb 30:14
You gave a **w** place for my steps under Ps 18:36
they open **w** their mouths at me, like a Ps 22:13
They open **w** their mouths against me; Ps 35:21
Open your mouth **w**, and I will fill it. Ps 81:10
Here is the sea, great and **w**, which Ps 104:25
he will shatter chiefs over the **w** earth. Ps 110:6
and I shall walk in a **w** place, for I Ps 119:45
he who opens **w** his lips comes to ruin. Prv 13:3
and throw you like a ball into a **w** land. Is 22:18
is made ready, its pyre made deep and **w**, Is 30:33
you open your mouth **w** and stick out Is 57:4
have gone up to it, you have made it **w**; Is 57:8
ten cubits **w** and a hundred cubits Ezk 42:4
of your land are **w** open to your enemies; Na 3:13
His greed is as **w** as Sheol; like death he Hab 2:5
two from east to west by a very **w** valley, Zec 14:4
For the gate is **w** and the way is easy that Mt 7:13
for a **w** door for effective work has 1 Cor 16:9
Corinthians; our heart is **w** open. 2 Cor 6:11

WIDELY (1)

"The work is great and **w** spread, Neh 4:19

WIDEN (1)

as to children) **w** your hearts also. 2 Cor 6:13

WIDOW (58)

"Remain a **w** in your father's house, Gn 38:11
not mistreat any **w** or fatherless child. Ex 22:22
A **w**, or a divorced woman, or a woman Lv 21:14
(But any vow of a **w** or of a divorced Nm 30:9
justice for the fatherless and the **w**, Dt 10:18
the sojourner, the fatherless, and the **w**, Dt 14:29
and the **w** who are among you, Dt 16:11
and the **w** who are within your towns. Dt 16:14
the sojourner, the fatherless, and the **w**, Dt 24:19
the sojourner, the fatherless, and the **w**. Dt 24:20
the sojourner, the fatherless, and the **w**. Dt 24:21
the sojourner, the fatherless, and the **w**, Dt 26:12
the sojourner, the fatherless, and the **w**, Dt 26:13
the sojourner, the fatherless, and the **w**.' Dt 27:19
Ruth the Moabite, the **w** of the dead, Ru 4:5
Also Ruth the Moabite, the **w** of Mahlon, Ru 4:10
and Abigail of Carmel, Nabal's **w**. 1 Sm 27:3
Jezreel and Abigail the **w** of Nabal of 1 Sm 30:5
Jezreel and Abigail the **w** of Nabal of 2 Sm 2:2
of Abigail the **w** of Nabal of Carmel; 2 Sm 3:3
She answered, "Alas, I am a **w**; 2 Sm 14:5
was the son of a **w** of the tribe of 1 Kgs 7:14

mother's name was Zeruah, a **w**, 1 Kgs 11:26
I have commanded a **w** there to feed 1 Kgs 17:9
a **w** was there gathering sticks. 1 Kgs 17:10
even upon the **w** with whom I 1 Kgs 17:20
woman, and do no good to the **w**. Jb 24:21
or have caused the eyes of the **w** to fail, Jb 31:16
my mother's womb I guided the **w**), Jb 31:18
They kill the **w** and the sojourner, and Ps 94:6
children be fatherless and his wife a **w**! Ps 109:9
he upholds the **w** and the fatherless, Ps 146:9
I shall not sit as a **w** or know the loss of Is 47:8
the sojourner, the fatherless, or the **w**, Jer 7:6
resident alien, the fatherless, and the **w**, Jer 22:3
of people! How like a **w** has she become, Lam 1:1
the fatherless and the **w** are wronged in Ezk 22:7
shall not marry a **w** or a divorced Ezk 44:22
or a **w** who is the widow of a priest. Ezk 44:22
or a widow who is the **w** of a priest. Ezk 44:22
do not oppress the **w**, the fatherless, the Zec 7:10
in his wages, the **w** and the fatherless, Mal 3:5
brother must marry the **w** and raise up Mt 22:24
man must take the **w** and raise up Mk 12:19
And a poor **w** came and put in two Mk 12:42
this poor **w** has put in more than all Mk 12:43
and then as a **w** until she was Lk 2:37
land of Sidon, to a woman who was a **w**. Lk 4:26
only son of his mother, and she was a **w**, Lk 7:12
And there was a **w** in that city who kept Lk 18:3
yet because this **w** keeps bothering me, I Lk 18:5
man must take the **w** and raise up Lk 20:28
and he saw a poor **w** put in two small Lk 21:2
this poor **w** has put in more than all of Lk 21:3
But if a **w** has children or 1 Tm 5:4
She who is truly a **w**, left all alone, has 1 Tm 5:5
Let a **w** be enrolled if she is not less 1 Tm 5:9
she says, 'I sit as a queen, I am no **w**, Rv 18:7

WIDOW'S (7)
took off her **w** garments and covered Gn 38:14
or take a **w** garment in pledge, Dt 24:17
fatherless; they take the **w** ox for a pledge. Jb 24:3
and I caused the **w** heart to sing for joy. Jb 29:13
but maintains the **w** boundaries. Prv 15:25
justice to the fatherless, plead the **w** cause. Is 1:17
and the **w** cause does not come to them. Is 1:23

WIDOWED (2)
a priest's daughter is **w** or divorced and Lv 22:13
let their wives become childless and **w**. Jer 18:21

WIDOWHOOD (4)
veil she put on the garments of her **w**. Gn 38:19
the day of their death, living as if in **w**. 2 Sm 20:3
loss of children and **w** shall come upon Is 47:9
reproach of your **w** you will remember Is 54:4

WIDOWS (24)
wives shall become **w** and your Ex 22:24
You have sent **w** away empty, and the Jb 22:9
pestilence buries, and his **w** do not weep. Jb 27:15
fatherless and protector of **w** is God in Ps 68:5
and their **w** made no lamentation. Ps 78:64
no compassion on their fatherless and **w**; Is 9:17
of their right, that **w** may be their spoil, Is 10:2
I have made their **w** more in number Jer 15:8
them alive; and let your **w** trust in me." Jer 49:11
fatherless; our mothers are like **w**. Lam 5:3
and seized their **w**. He laid waste their Ezk 19:7
they have made many **w** in her midst. Ezk 22:25
who devour **w**' houses and for a Mk 12:40
there were many **w** in Israel in the days Lk 4:25
who devour **w**' houses and for a Lk 20:47
Hebrews because their **w** were being Acts 6:1
All the **w** stood beside him weeping Acts 9:39
Then calling the saints and **w**, he Acts 9:41
the unmarried and the **w** I say that it 1 Cor 7:8
Honor **w** who are truly widows. 1 Tm 5:3
Honor widows who are truly **w**. 1 Tm 5:3
But refuse to enroll younger **w**, for 1 Tm 5:11
So I would have younger **w** marry, 1 Tm 5:14
woman has relatives who are **w**, 1 Tm 5:16
may care for those who are really **w**. 1 Tm 5:16
to visit orphans and **w** in their affliction, Jas 1:27

WIDOWS' (2)
who devour **w** houses and for a Mk 12:40
who devour **w** houses and for a Lk 20:47

WIDTH (7)
long, equal to the **w** of the house, 1 Kgs 6:3
long, equal to the **w** of the house, 2 Chr 3:4
he measured the **w** of the opening Ezk 40:11
to see what is its **w** and what is its Zec 2:2
is twenty cubits, and its **w** ten cubits." Zec 5:2
foursquare; its length the same as its **w**. Rv 21:16
Its length and **w** and height are equal. Rv 21:16

WIELD (6)
for if you **w** your tool on it you profane Ex 20:25
stones. You shall **w** no iron tool on them; Dt 27:5
As if a rod should **w** him who lifts it, or Is 10:15
LORD of hosts will **w** against them a Is 10:26
it may become strong to **w** the sword. Ezk 30:21
and **w** you like a warrior's sword. Zec 9:13

WIELDED (5)
which no man has **w** an iron tool." And Jos 8:31
He **w** his spear against eight hundred 2 Sm 23:8
And he **w** his spear against three 2 Sm 23:18
He **w** his spear against 300 whom he 1 Chr 11:11
And he **w** his spear against 300 men 1 Chr 11:20

WIELDING (2)
destroy its trees by **w** an axe against Dt 20:19
with buckler and shield, **w** swords. Ezk 38:4

WIELDS (1)
magnify itself against him who **w** it? Is 10:15

WIFE (383)
and his mother and hold fast to his **w**, Gn 2:24
the man and his **w** were both naked and Gn 2:25
the man and his **w** hid themselves from Gn 3:8
to the voice of your **w** and have eaten of Gn 3:17
Adam and for his **w** garments of skins Gn 3:21
Now Adam knew Eve his **w**, and she Gn 4:1
Cain knew his **w**, and she conceived Gn 4:17
And Adam knew his **w** again, and she Gn 4:25
into the ark, you, your sons, your **w**, Gn 6:18
his sons and his **w** and his sons' wives Gn 7:7
and Noah's **w** and the three wives of his Gn 7:13
"Go out from the ark, you and your **w**, Gn 8:16
his sons and his **w** and his sons' wives Gn 8:18
The name of Abram's **w** was Sarai, Gn 11:29
was Sarai, and the name of Nahor's **w**, Gn 11:29
daughter-in-law, his son Abram's **w**, Gn 11:31
And Abram took Sarai his **w**, and Lot Gn 12:5
to enter Egypt, he said to Sarai his **w**, Gn 12:11
see you, they will say, 'This is his **w**.' Gn 12:12
plagues because of Sarai, Abram's **w**. Gn 12:17
you not tell me that she was your **w**? Gn 12:18
my sister,' so that I took her for my **w**? Gn 12:19
Now then, here is your **w**; take her, and Gn 12:19
him away with his **w** and all that he Gn 12:20
Egypt, he and his **w** and all that he had, Gn 13:1
Now Sarai, Abram's **w**, had borne him Gn 16:1
the land of Canaan, Sarai, Abram's **w**, Gn 16:3
gave her to Abram her husband as a **w**. Gn 16:3
said to Abraham, "As for Sarai your **w**, Gn 17:15
but Sarah your **w** shall bear you a son, Gn 17:19
"Where is Sarah your **w**?" And he said, Gn 18:9
and Sarah your **w** shall have a son." Gn 18:10
Take your **w** and your two daughters Gn 19:15
seized him and his **w** and his two Gn 19:16
But Lot's **w**, behind him, looked back, Gn 19:26
And Abraham said of Sarah his **w**, "She Gn 20:2
you have taken, for she is a man's **w**." Gn 20:3
Now then, return the man's **w**, for he is Gn 20:7
and they will kill me because of my **w**. Gn 20:11
of my mother, and she became my **w**. Gn 20:12
and returned Sarah his **w** to him. Gn 20:14
also healed his **w** and female slaves Gn 20:17
because of Sarah, Abraham's **w**. Gn 20:18
his mother took a **w** for him from the Gn 21:21
buried Sarah his **w** in the cave Gn 23:19
you will not take a **w** for my son from Gn 24:3
kindred, and take a **w** for my son Isaac." Gn 24:4
and you shall take a **w** for my son from Gn 24:7
the son of Milcah, the **w** of Nahor, Gn 24:15
And Sarah my master's **w** bore a son to Gn 24:36
shall not take a **w** for my son from Gn 24:37
to my clan and take a **w** for my son.' Gn 24:38
You shall take a **w** for my son from Gn 24:40
let her be the **w** of your master's son, Gn 24:51
took Rebekah, and she became his **w**, Gn 24:67
Abraham took another **w**, whose name Gn 25:1
was buried, with Sarah his **w**. Gn 25:10
old when he took Rebekah to be his **w**, Gn 25:20
And Isaac prayed to the LORD for his **w**, Gn 25:21
prayer, and Rebekah his **w** conceived. Gn 25:21
men of the place asked him about his **w**, Gn 26:7
for he feared to say, "My **w**," thinking, Gn 26:7
saw Isaac laughing with Rebekah his **w**. Gn 26:8
Isaac and said, "Behold, she is your **w**. Gn 26:9
might easily have lain with your **w**, Gn 26:10
this man or his **w** shall surely be put Gn 26:11
daughter of Beeri the Hittite to be his **w**, Gn 26:34
must not take a **w** from the Canaanite Gn 28:1
and take as your **w** from there one of the Gn 28:2
to Paddan-aram to take a **w** from there, Gn 28:6
must not take a **w** from the Canaanite Gn 28:6
Esau went to Ishmael and took as his **w**, Gn 28:9
"Give me my **w** that I may go in to her, Gn 29:21
him his daughter Rachel to be his **w**. Gn 29:28
She gave him her servant Bilhah as a **w**, Gn 30:4
Zilpah and gave her to Jacob as a **w**. Gn 30:9
saying, "Get me this girl for my **w**." Gn 34:4
Please give her to him to be his **w**. Gn 34:8
me the young woman to be my **w**." Gn 34:12
Eliphaz the son of Adah the **w** of Esau, Gn 36:10
the son of Basemath the **w** of Esau. Gn 36:10
These are the sons of Adah, Esau's **w**. Gn 36:12
are the sons of Basemath, Esau's **w**. Gn 36:13
the daughter of Zibeon, Esau's **w**: Gn 36:14
are the sons of Basemath, Esau's **w**. Gn 36:17
are the sons of Oholibamah, Esau's **w**: Gn 36:18
the daughter of Anah, Esau's **w**. Gn 36:18
And Judah took a **w** for Er his firstborn, Gn 38:6
in to your brother's **w** and perform the Gn 38:8
in to his brother's **w** he would waste the Gn 38:9
In the course of time the **w** of Judah, Gn 38:12
a time his master's **w** cast her eyes on Gn 39:7
he refused and said to his master's **w**, Gn 39:8
except yourself, because you are his **w**. Gn 39:9
the words that his **w** spoke to him, Gn 39:19
'You know that my **w** bore me two Gn 44:27
The sons of Rachel, Jacob's **w**: Joseph Gn 46:19
buried Abraham and Sarah his **w**. Gn 49:31
they buried Isaac and Rebekah his **w**, Gn 49:31
went and took as his **w** a Levite woman. Ex 2:1
So Moses took his **w** and his sons and Ex 4:20
took as his **w** Jochebed his father's Ex 6:20
Aaron took as his **w** Elisheba, the Ex 6:23
took as his **w** one of the daughters of Ex 6:25
had taken Zipporah, Moses' **w**, Ex 18:2
with his sons and his **w** to Moses in the Ex 18:5
to you with your **w** and her two sons Ex 18:6
you shall not covet your neighbor's **w**, Ex 20:17
then his **w** shall go out with him. Ex 21:3
master gives him a **w** and she bears him Ex 21:4
the **w** and her children shall be her Ex 21:4
plainly says, 'I love my master, my **w**, Ex 21:5
If he takes another **w** to himself, he Ex 21:10
bride-price for her and make her his **w**. Ex 22:16
the nakedness of your father's **w**; Lv 18:8
that is, you shall not approach his **w**; Lv 18:14
she is your son's **w**, you shall not Lv 18:15
the nakedness of your brother's **w**; Lv 18:16
take a woman as a rival **w** to her sister, Lv 18:18
with your neighbor's **w** and so make Lv 18:20
adultery with the **w** of his neighbor, Lv 20:10
If a man lies with his father's **w**, he has Lv 20:11
If a man lies with his uncle's **w**, he has Lv 20:20
If a man takes his brother's **w**, it is Lv 20:21
And he shall take a **w** in her virginity. Lv 21:13
he shall take as his **w** a virgin of his Lv 21:14
If any man's **w** goes astray and breaks Nm 5:12
is jealous of his **w** who has defiled Nm 5:14
over him and he is jealous of his **w**, Nm 5:14
man shall bring his **w** to the priest and Nm 5:15
the law in cases of jealousy, when a **w**, Nm 5:29
over a man and he is jealous of his **w**. Nm 5:30
name of Amram's **w** was Jochebed the Nm 26:59
a man and his **w** and about a father Nm 30:16
people of Israel shall be **w** to one of the Nm 36:8
you shall not covet your neighbor's **w**. Dt 5:21
your daughter or the **w** you embrace or Dt 13:6
who has betrothed a **w** and has not taken Dt 20:7
and you desire to take her to be your **w**, Dt 21:11
her husband, and she shall be your **w**. Dt 21:13
"If any man takes a **w** and goes in to her Dt 22:13
virgin of Israel. And she shall be his **w**. Dt 22:19
found lying with the **w** of another man, Dt 22:22
because he violated his neighbor's **w**. Dt 22:24
shekels of silver, and she shall be his **w**, Dt 22:29
"A man shall not take his father's **w**, so Dt 22:30
a man takes a **w** and marries her, Dt 24:1
she goes and becomes another man's **w**, Dt 24:2
latter man dies, who took her to be his **w**, Dt 24:3
may not take her again to be his **w**, Dt 24:4
be happy with his **w** whom he has taken. Dt 24:5
the **w** of the dead man shall not be Dt 25:5
take her as his **w** and perform the duty Dt 25:5
does not wish to take his brother's **w**, Dt 25:7
then his brother's **w** shall go up to the Dt 25:7
then his brother's **w** shall go up to him Dt 25:9
one another and the **w** of the one draws Dt 25:11
be anyone who lies with his father's **w**, Dt 27:20
You shall betroth a **w**, but another Dt 28:30
to his brother, to the **w** he embraces, Dt 28:54
will I give Achsah my daughter as **w**." Jos 15:16
he gave him Achsah his daughter as **w**. Jos 15:17
give him Achsah my daughter for a **w**." Jgs 1:12
gave him Achsah his daughter for a **w**. Jgs 1:13
a prophetess, the **w** of Lappidoth, Jgs 4:4
the tent of Jael, the **w** of Heber the Kenite, Jgs 4:17
But Jael the **w** of Heber took a tent peg, Jgs 4:21
be Jael, the **w** of Heber the Kenite, Jgs 5:24
And Gilead's **w** also bore him sons. And Jgs 11:2
And his **w** was barren and had no Jgs 13:2
and went after his **w** and came to the Jgs 13:11

and Manoah and his **w** were watching. Jgs 13:19
Manoah and his **w** were watching, Jgs 13:20
no more to Manoah and to his **w**. Jgs 13:21
And Manoah said to his **w**, "We shall Jgs 13:22
But his **w** said to him, "If the LORD had Jgs 13:23
Timnah. Now get her for me as my **w**." Jgs 14:2
go to take a **w** from the uncircumcised Jgs 14:3
the fourth day they said to Samson's **w**, Jgs 14:15
And Samson's **w** wept over him and Jgs 14:16
And Samson's **w** was given to his Jgs 14:20
went to visit his **w** with a young goat. Jgs 15:1
will go in to my **w** in the chamber." But Jgs 15:1
he has taken his **w** and given her to Jgs 15:6
be he who gives a **w** to Benjamin." Jgs 21:18
each man his **w** from the daughters Jgs 21:21
for each man of them his **w** in battle, Jgs 21:22
of Moab, he and his **w** and his two sons. Ru 1:1
Elimelech and the name of his **w** Naomi, Ru 1:2
of Mahlon, I have bought to be my **w**, Ru 4:10
Boaz took Ruth, and she became his **w**. Ru 4:13
portions to Peninnah his **w** and to all 1 Sm 1:4
And Elkanah knew Hannah his **w**, 1 Sm 1:19
Eli would bless Elkanah and his **w**, 1 Sm 2:20
daughter-in-law, the **w** of Phinehas, 1 Sm 4:19
name of Saul's **w** was Ahinoam the 1 Sm 14:50
Merab. I will give her to you for a **w**. 1 Sm 18:17
to Adriel the Meholathite for a **w**. 1 Sm 18:19
him his daughter Michal for a **w**. 1 Sm 18:27
But Michal, David's **w**, told him, "If 1 Sm 19:11
Nabal, and the name of his **w** Abigail. 1 Sm 25:3
young men told Abigail, Nabal's **w**, 1 Sm 25:14
Nabal, his **w** told him these things, 1 Sm 25:37
spoke to Abigail, to take her as his **w**. 1 Sm 25:39
to you to take you to him as his **w**." 1 Sm 25:40
of David and became his **w**. 1 Sm 25:42
Michal his daughter, David's **w**, 1 Sm 25:44
may lead away his **w** and children, 1 Sm 30:22
the sixth, Ithream, of Eglah, David's **w**. 2 Sm 3:5
son, saying, "Give me my **w** Michal, 2 Sm 3:14
of Eliam, the **w** of Uriah the Hittite?" 2 Sm 11:3
and to drink and to lie with my **w**? 2 Sm 11:11
When the **w** of Uriah heard that 2 Sm 11:26
and she became his **w** and bore him 2 Sm 11:27
and have taken his **w** to be your wife 2 Sm 12:9
wife to be your **w** and have killed him 2 Sm 12:9
and have taken the **w** of Uriah the 2 Sm 12:10
of Uriah the Hittite to be your **w**.' 2 Sm 12:10
child that Uriah's **w** bore to David, 2 Sm 12:15
Then David comforted his **w**, 2 Sm 12:24
Abishag the Shunammite as my **w**." 1 Kgs 2:17
to Adonijah your brother as his **w**." 1 Kgs 2:21
the daughter of Solomon as his **w**); 1 Kgs 4:11
the daughter of Solomon as his **w**); 1 Kgs 4:15
dowry to his daughter, Solomon's **w**; 1 Kgs 9:16
in marriage the sister of his own **w**, 1 Kgs 11:19
And Jeroboam said to his **w**, "Arise, 1 Kgs 14:2
that you are the **w** of Jeroboam, 1 Kgs 14:2
Jeroboam's **w** did so. She arose and 1 Kgs 14:4
the **w** of Jeroboam is coming to 1 Kgs 14:5
he said, "Come in, **w** of Jeroboam. 1 Kgs 14:6
Then Jeroboam's **w** arose and 1 Kgs 14:17
took for his **w** Jezebel the daughter 1 Kgs 16:31
But Jezebel his **w** came to him and 1 Kgs 21:5
And Jezebel his **w** said to him, "Do 1 Kgs 21:7
Ahab, whom Jezebel his **w** incited. 1 Kgs 21:25
Now the **w** of one of the sons of the 2 Kgs 4:1
worked in the service of Naaman's **w**. 2 Kgs 5:2
for the daughter of Ahab was his **w**. 2 Kgs 8:18
your daughter to my son for a **w**,' 2 Kgs 14:9
the **w** of Shallum the son of Tikvah, 2 Kgs 22:14
fathered children by his **w** Azubah, 1 Chr 2:18
the **w** of Hezron his father, 1 Chr 2:24
Jerahmeel also had another **w**, whose 1 Chr 2:26
name of Abishur's **w** was Abihail, 1 Chr 2:29
the sixth, Ithream, by his **w** Eglah; 1 Chr 3:3
And his Judahite **w** bore Jered the 1 Chr 4:18
The sons of the **w** of Hodiah, the 1 Chr 4:19
Machir took a **w** for Huppim and 1 Chr 7:15
And Maacah the **w** of Machir bore a 1 Chr 7:16
And Ephraim went in to his **w**, and 1 Chr 7:23
He fathered sons by Hodesh his **w**: 1 Chr 8:9
and the name of his **w** was Maacah. 1 Chr 8:29
and the name of his **w** was Maacah, 1 Chr 9:35
"My **w** shall not live in the house of 2 Chr 8:11
Rehoboam took as **w** Mahalath the 2 Chr 11:18
for the daughter of Ahab was his **w**. 2 Chr 21:6
King Jehoram and **w** of Jehoiada the 2 Chr 22:11
your daughter to my son for a **w**,' 2 Chr 25:18
the **w** of Shallum the son of 2 Chr 34:22
(who had taken a **w** from the daughters Ezr 2:61
the son of Berechiah as his **w**. Neh 6:18
(who had taken a **w** of the daughters of Neh 7:63
brought his friends and his **w** Zeresh. Est 5:10
Then his **w** Zeresh and all his friends Est 5:14
And Haman told his **w** Zeresh and all Est 6:13
wise men and his **w** Zeresh said to him, Est 6:13
Then his **w** said to him, "Do you still hold Jb 2:9
My breath is strange to my **w**, and I am Jb 19:17
then let my **w** grind for another, and let Jb 31:10
be fatherless and his **w** a widow! Ps 109:9
Your **w** will be like a fruitful vine Ps 128:3
and rejoice in the **w** of your youth, Prv 5:18
So is he who goes in to his neighbor's **w**; Prv 6:29
An excellent **w** is the crown of her Prv 12:4
He who finds a **w** finds a good thing Prv 18:22
but a prudent **w** is from the LORD. Prv 19:14
a house shared with a quarrelsome **w**. Prv 21:9
a house shared with a quarrelsome **w**. Prv 25:24
day and a quarrelsome **w** are alike; Prv 27:15
An excellent **w** who can find? She is Prv 31:10
Enjoy life with the **w** whom you love, all Eccl 9:9
called you like a **w** deserted and grieved in Is 54:6
like a **w** of youth when she is cast off, Is 54:6
a man divorces his **w** and she goes from Jer 3:1
from him and becomes another man's **w**, Jer 3:1
as a treacherous **w** leaves her husband, Jer 3:20
each neighing for his neighbor's **w**. Jer 5:8
both husband and **w** shall be taken, Jer 6:11
"You shall not take a **w**, nor shall you Jer 16:2
Adulterous **w**, who receives strangers Ezk 16:32
defile his neighbor's **w** or approach a Ezk 18:6
mountains, defiles his neighbor's **w**, Ezk 18:11
Israel, does not defile his neighbor's **w**, Ezk 18:15
abomination with his neighbor's **w**; Ezk 22:11
morning, and at evening my **w** died. Ezk 24:18
each of you defiles his neighbor's **w**; Ezk 33:26
take to yourself a **w** of whoredom and Hos 1:2
your mother, plead—for she is not my **w**, Hos 2:2
there Israel served for a **w**, and for a Hos 12:12
a wife, and for a **w** he guarded sheep. Hos 12:12
"'Your **w** shall be a prostitute in the Am 7:17
between you and the **w** of your youth, Mal 2:14
companion and your **w** by covenant. Mal 2:14
you be faithless to the **w** of your youth. Mal 2:15
the father of Solomon by the **w** of Uriah, Mt 1:6
do not fear to take Mary as your **w**, Mt 1:20
Lord commanded him: he took his **w**, Mt 1:24
was also said, 'Whoever divorces his **w**, Mt 5:31
to you that everyone who divorces his **w**, Mt 5:32
sake of Herodias, his brother Philip's **w**, Mt 14:3
with his **w** and children and all that he Mt 18:25
lawful to divorce one's **w** for any cause?" Mt 19:3
and his mother and hold fast to his **w**, Mt 19:5
whoever divorces his **w**, except for Mt 19:9
"If such is the case of a man with his **w**, Mt 19:10
no children left his **w** to his brother. Mt 22:25
of the seven, whose **w** will she be? Mt 22:28
judgment seat, his **w** sent word to him, Mt 27:19
sake of Herodias, his brother Philip's **w**, Mk 6:17
for you to have your brother's **w**." Mk 6:18
it lawful for a man to divorce his **w**?" Mk 10:2
and mother and hold fast to his **w**, Mk 10:7
"Whoever divorces his **w** and marries Mk 10:11
if a man's brother dies and leaves a **w**, Mk 12:19
the first took a **w**, and when he died left Mk 12:20
they rise again, whose **w** will she be? Mk 12:23
she be? For the seven had her as **w**." Mk 12:23
And he had a **w** from the daughters of Lk 1:5
and your **w** Elizabeth will bear you a Lk 1:13
man, and my **w** is advanced in years." Lk 1:18
these days his **w** Elizabeth conceived, Lk 1:24
by him for Herodias, his brother's **w**, Lk 3:19
and Joanna, the **w** of Chuza, Herod's Lk 8:3
And another said, 'I have married a **w**, Lk 14:20
and mother and **w** and children and Lk 14:26
who divorces his **w** and marries Lk 16:18
Remember Lot's **w**. Lk 17:32
has left house or **w** or brothers or Lk 18:29
dies, having a **w** but no children, Lk 20:28
The first took a **w**, and died without Lk 20:29
therefore, whose **w** will the woman be? Lk 20:33
be? For the seven had her as **w**." Lk 20:33
mother's sister, Mary the **w** of Clopas, Jn 19:25
named Ananias, with his **w** Sapphira, Acts 5:1
of about three hours his **w** came in, Acts 5:7
come from Italy with his **w** Priscilla, Acts 18:2
days Felix came with his **w** Drusilla, Acts 24:24
pagans, for a man has his father's **w**. 1 Cor 5:1
have his own **w** and each woman 1 Cor 7:2
give to his **w** her conjugal rights, 1 Cor 7:3
and likewise the **w** to her husband. 1 Cor 7:3
For the **w** does not have authority over 1 Cor 7:4
over his own body, but the **w** does. 1 Cor 7:4
the **w** should not separate from her 1 Cor 7:10
husband should not divorce his **w**. 1 Cor 7:11
any brother has a **w** who is an 1 Cor 7:12
is made holy because of his **w**, 1 Cor 7:14
and the unbelieving **w** is made holy 1 Cor 7:14
W, how do you know whether you 1 Cor 7:16
know whether you will save your **w**? 1 Cor 7:16
Are you bound to a **w**? Do not seek to 1 Cor 7:27
seek to be free. Are you free from a **w**? 1 Cor 7:27
you free from a wife? Do not seek a **w**. 1 Cor 7:27
worldly things, how to please his **w**, 1 Cor 7:33
A **w** is bound to her husband as long 1 Cor 7:39
the right to take along a believing **w**, 1 Cor 9:5
the head of a **w** is her husband, 1 Cor 11:3
but every **w** who prays or prophesies 1 Cor 11:5
For if a **w** will not cover her head, 1 Cor 11:6
it is disgraceful for a **w** to cut off her 1 Cor 11:6
That is why a **w** ought to have a 1 Cor 11:10
is it proper for a **w** to pray to God 1 Cor 11:13
is the head of the **w** even as Christ is the Eph 5:23
He who loves his **w** loves himself. Eph 5:28
and mother and hold fast to his **w**, Eph 5:31
each one of you love his **w** as himself, Eph 5:33
and let the **w** see that she respects her Eph 5:33
above reproach, the husband of one **w**, 1 Tm 3:2
each be the husband of one **w**, 1 Tm 3:12
having been the **w** of one husband, 1 Tm 5:9
is above reproach, the husband of one **w**, Ti 1:6
show you the Bride, the **w** of the Lamb." Rv 21:9

WIFE'S (7)
The man called his **w** name Eve, Gn 3:20
his **w** name was Mehetabel, the Gn 36:39
nakedness of your father's **w** daughter, Lv 18:11
him sons. And when his **w** sons grew up, Jgs 11:2
and his **w** name was Mehetabel, the 1 Chr 1:50
and a **w** quarreling is a continual Prv 19:13
and with his **w** knowledge he kept back Acts 5:2

WILD (64)
He shall be a **w** donkey of a man, his Gn 16:12
What was torn by **w** beasts I did not Gn 31:39
desolate and the **w** beasts multiply Ex 23:29
carcass of an unclean **w** animal or a Lv 5:2
cattle and for the **w** animals that are in Lv 25:7
I will let loose the **w** beasts against you, Lv 26:22
is for them like the horns of the **w** ox. Nm 23:22
is for him like the horns of the **w** ox; Nm 24:8
lest the **w** beasts grow too numerous for Dt 7:22
deer, the gazelle, the roebuck, the **w** goat, Dt 14:5
and his horns are the horns of a **w** ox; Dt 33:17
air and to the **w** beasts of the earth, 1 Sm 17:46
was as swift of foot as a **w** gazelle. 2 Sm 2:18
and found a **w** vine and gathered 2 Kgs 4:39
from it his lap full of **w** gourds, 2 Kgs 4:39
and a **w** beast of Lebanon passed by 2 Kgs 14:9
and a **w** beast of Lebanon passed by 2 Chr 25:18
and bring branches of olive, **w** olive, Neh 8:15
Does the **w** donkey bray when he has Jb 6:5
understanding when a **w** donkey's colt Jb 11:12
like **w** donkeys in the desert the poor go Jb 24:5
"Who has let the **w** donkey go free? Who Jb 39:5
"Is the **w** ox willing to serve you? Will he Jb 39:9
them and that the **w** beast may trample Jb 39:15
food for him where all the **w** beasts play. Jb 40:20
me from the horns of the **w** oxen! Ps 22:21
like a calf, and Sirion like a young **w** ox. Ps 29:6
the soul of your dove to the **w** beasts; Ps 74:19
exalted my horn like that of the **w** ox; Ps 92:10
the **w** donkeys quench their thirst. Ps 104:11
high mountains are for the **w** goats; Ps 104:18
it to yield grapes, but it yielded **w** grapes. Is 5:2
it to yield grapes, why did it yield **w** grapes? Is 5:4
But **w** animals will lie down there, and Is 13:21
will dwell, and there **w** goats will dance. Is 13:21
was not; Assyria destined it for **w** beasts. Is 23:13
become dens forever, a joy of **w** donkeys, Is 32:14
W oxen shall fall with them, and young Is 34:7
And **w** animals shall meet with hyenas; Is 34:14
the **w** goat shall cry to his fellow; Is 34:14
The **w** beasts will honor me, the jackals Is 43:20
turned degenerate and become a **w** vine? Jer 2:21
a **w** donkey used to the wilderness, in her Jer 2:24
Go, assemble all the **w** beasts; bring Jer 12:9
The **w** donkeys stand on the bare Jer 14:6
"Therefore **w** beasts shall dwell with Jer 50:39
send famine and **w** beasts against you, Ezk 5:17
"If I cause **w** beasts to pass through Ezk 14:15
of judgment, sword, famine, **w** beasts, Ezk 14:21
they became food for all the **w** beasts. Ezk 34:5
have become food for all the **w** beasts, Ezk 34:8
of peace and banish **w** beasts from the Ezk 34:25
died of itself or is torn by **w** animals. Ezk 44:31
his dwelling was with the **w** donkeys. Dn 5:21
to Assyria, a **w** donkey wandering alone; Hos 8:9
lion, as a **w** beast would rip them open. Hos 13:8
she has become, a lair for **w** beasts! Zep 2:15
and his food was locusts and **w** honey. Mt 3:4
his waist and ate locusts and **w** honey. Mk 1:6
And he was with the **w** animals, and the Mk 1:13
and you, although a **w** olive shoot, Rom 11:17
from what is by nature a **w** olive tree, Rom 11:24
w waves of the sea, casting up the foam Jude 1:13

with pestilence and by **w** beasts of the Rv 6:8

WILDERNESS (280)

as far as El-paran on the border of the **w**. Gn 14:6
found her by a spring of water in the **w**, Gn 16:7
and wandered in the **w** of Beersheba. Gn 21:14
He lived in the **w** and became an expert Gn 21:20
He lived in the **w** of Paran, and his Gn 21:21
who found the hot springs in the **w**, Gn 36:24
cast him into this pit here in the **w**, but Gn 37:22
the west side of the **w** and came to Horeb, Ex 3:1
let us go a three days' journey into the **w**, Ex 3:18
"Go into the **w** to meet Moses." So he Ex 4:27
they may hold a feast to me in the **w**.'" Ex 5:1
days' journey into the **w** that we may Ex 5:3
go, that they may serve me in the **w**. Ex 7:16
days' journey into the **w** and sacrifice to Ex 8:27
sacrifice to the LORD your God in the **w**; Ex 8:28
by the way of the **w** toward the Red Sea. Ex 13:18
at Etham, on the edge of the **w**. Ex 13:20
in the land; the **w** has shut them in.' Ex 14:3
you have taken us away to die in the **w**? Ex 14:11
the Egyptians than to die in the **w**." Ex 14:12
Sea, and they went into the **w** of Shur. Ex 15:22
three days in the **w** and found no water. Ex 15:22
the people of Israel came to the **w** of Sin, Ex 16:1
against Moses and Aaron in the **w**, Ex 16:2
us out into this **w** to kill this whole Ex 16:3
of Israel, they looked toward the **w**, Ex 16:10
up, there was on the face of the **w** a fine, Ex 16:14
the bread with which I fed you in the **w**, Ex 16:32
moved on from the **w** of Sin by stages, Ex 17:1
to Moses in the **w** where he was Ex 18:5
that day they came into the **w** of Sinai. Ex 19:1
Rephidim and came into the **w** of Sinai, Ex 19:2
of Sinai, and they encamped in the **w**. Ex 19:2
and from the **w** to the Euphrates, Ex 23:31
offerings to the LORD, in the **w** of Sinai. Lv 7:38
may be sent away into the **w** to Azazel. Lv 16:10
send it away into the **w** by the hand of a Lv 16:21
and he shall let the goat go free in the **w**. Lv 16:22
LORD spoke to Moses in the **w** of Sinai, Nm 1:1
So he listed them in the **w** of Sinai. Nm 1:19
fire before the LORD in the **w** of Sinai, Nm 3:4
LORD spoke to Moses in the **w** of Sinai, Nm 3:14
LORD spoke to Moses in the **w** of Sinai, Nm 9:1
the month, at twilight, in the **w** of Sinai; Nm 9:5
set out by stages from the **w** of Sinai. Nm 10:12
cloud settled down in the **w** of Paran. Nm 10:12
know where we should camp in the **w**, Nm 10:31
and camped in the **w** of Paran. Nm 12:16
Moses sent them from the **w** of Paran, Nm 13:3
the land from the **w** of Zin to Rehob, Nm 13:21
the people of Israel in the **w** of Paran, Nm 13:26
Or would that we had died in this **w**! Nm 14:2
that he has killed them in the **w**.' Nm 14:16
signs that I did in Egypt and in the **w**, Nm 14:22
and set out for the **w** by the way to the Nm 14:25
your dead bodies shall fall in this **w**, Nm 14:29
your dead bodies shall fall in this **w**. Nm 14:32
be shepherds in the **w** forty years and Nm 14:33
last of your dead bodies lies in the **w**. Nm 14:33
in this **w** they shall come to a full end, Nm 14:35
the people of Israel were in the **w**, Nm 15:32
milk and honey, to kill us in the **w**, Nm 16:13
came into the **w** of Zin in the first Nm 20:1
the assembly of the LORD into this **w**, Nm 20:4
us up out of Egypt to die in the **w**? Nm 21:5
in the **w** that is opposite Moab, Nm 21:11
which is in the **w** that extends from Nm 21:13
staffs." And from the **w** they went on Nm 21:18
against Israel to the **w** and came to Nm 21:23
omens, but set his face toward the **w**. Nm 24:1
the people of Israel in the **w** of Sinai. Nm 26:64
shall die in the **w**." Not one of them Nm 26:65
"Our father died in the **w**. He was not Nm 27:3
my word in the **w** of Zin when the Nm 27:14
of Meribah of Kadesh in the **w** of Zin.) Nm 27:14
them wander in the **w** forty years, Nm 32:13
he will again abandon them in the **w**, Nm 32:15
at Etham, which is on the edge of the **w**. Nm 33:6
through the midst of the sea into the **w**, Nm 33:8
days' journey in the **w** of Etham and Nm 33:8
Red Sea and camped in the **w** of Sin. Nm 33:11
set out from the **w** of Sin and camped Nm 33:12
and camped in the **w** of Sinai. Nm 33:15
set out from the **w** of Sinai and Nm 33:16
and camped in the **w** of Zin (that is, Nm 33:36
shall be from the **w** of Zin alongside Nm 34:3
to all Israel beyond the Jordan in the **w**, Dt 1:1
that great and terrifying **w** that you saw, Dt 1:19
and in the **w**, where you have seen how Dt 1:31
and journey into the **w** in the direction of Dt 1:40
and journeyed into the **w** in the direction Dt 2:1
knows your going through this great **w**. Dt 2:7
went in the direction of the **w** of Moab. Dt 2:8
messengers from the **w** of Kedemoth to Dt 2:26
Bezer in the **w** on the tableland for the Dt 4:43
God has led you these forty years in the **w**, Dt 8:2
you through the great and terrifying **w**, Dt 8:15
fed you in the **w** with manna that your Dt 8:16
the LORD your God to wrath in the **w**. Dt 9:7
them out to put them to death in the **w**." Dt 9:28
and what he did to you in the **w**, until Dt 11:5
shall be from the **w** to the Lebanon and Dt 11:24
I have led you forty years in the **w**. Your Dt 29:5
land, and in the howling waste of the **w**; Dt 32:10
of Meribah-kadesh, in the **w** of Zin, Dt 32:51
From the **w** and this Lebanon as far as Jos 1:4
had died in the **w** on the way after they Jos 5:4
on the way in the **w** after they had come Jos 5:5
of Israel walked forty years in the **w**, Jos 5:6
them and fled in the direction of the **w**. Jos 8:15
who fled to the **w** turned back against Jos 8:20
Ai in the open **w** where they pursued Jos 8:24
in the Arabah, in the slopes, in the **w**, Jos 12:8
to Moses, while Israel walked in the **w**. Jos 14:10
to the **w** of Zin at the farthest south. Jos 15:1
In the **w**, Beth-arabah, Middin, Jos 15:61
east of the waters of Jericho, into the **w**, Jos 16:1
and it ends at the **w** of Beth-aven. Jos 18:12
Bezer in the **w** on the tableland, Jos 20:8
And you lived in the **w** a long time. Jos 24:7
the city of palms into the **w** of Judah, Jgs 1:16
with the thorns of the **w** and with briers." Jgs 8:7
took thorns of the **w** and briers and with Jgs 8:16
Israel went through the **w** to the Red Jgs 11:16
journeyed through the **w** and went Jgs 11:18
Jabbok and from the **w** to the Jordan. Jgs 11:22
men of Israel in the direction of the **w**, Jgs 20:42
and fled toward the **w** to the rock of Jgs 20:45
and fled toward the **w** to the rock of Jgs 20:47
with every sort of plague in the **w**. 1 Sm 4:8
the valley of Zeboim toward the **w**. 1 Sm 13:18
you left those few sheep in the **w**? 1 Sm 17:28
in the strongholds in the **w**, 1 Sm 23:14
in the hill country of the **W** of Ziph. 1 Sm 23:14
David was in the **W** of Ziph at 1 Sm 23:15
and his men were in the **w** of Maon, 1 Sm 23:24
the rock and lived in the **w** of Maon. 1 Sm 23:25
after David in the **w** of Maon. 1 Sm 23:25
"Behold, David is in the **w** of Engedi." 1 Sm 24:1
rose and went down to the **w** of Paran. 1 Sm 25:1
David heard in the **w** that Nabal was 1 Sm 25:4
messengers out of the **w** to greet our 1 Sm 25:14
all that this fellow has in the **w**, 1 Sm 25:21
went down to the **w** of Ziph with three 1 Sm 26:2
Israel to seek David in the **w** of Ziph. 1 Sm 26:2
But David remained in the **w**. 1 Sm 26:3
that Saul came after him into the **w**, 1 Sm 26:3
Giah on the way to the **w** of Gibeon. 2 Sm 2:24
all the people passed on toward the **w**. 2 Sm 15:23
the fords of the **w** until word comes 2 Sm 15:28
for those who faint in the **w** to drink." 2 Sm 16:2
not stay tonight at the fords of the **w**, 2 Sm 17:16
and weary and thirsty in the **w**." 2 Sm 17:29
was buried in his own house in the **w**. 1 Kgs 2:34
and Baalath and Tamar in the **w**, in 1 Kgs 9:18
journey into the **w** and came and 1 Kgs 19:4
on your way to the **w** of Damascus. 1 Kgs 19:15
"By the way of the **w** of Edom." 2 Kgs 3:8
Bezer in the **w** with its pasturelands, 1 Chr 6:78
stronghold in the **w** mighty and 1 Chr 12:8
which Moses had made in the **w**, 1 Chr 21:29
servant of the LORD had made in the **w**, 2 Chr 1:3
built Tadmor in the **w** and all the 2 Chr 8:4
of the valley, east of the **w** of Jeruel. 2 Chr 20:16
and went out into the **w** of Tekoa. 2 Chr 20:20
came to the watchtower of the **w**, 2 Chr 20:24
servant of God laid on Israel in the **w**. 2 Chr 24:9
built towers in the **w** and cut out 2 Chr 26:10
mercies did not forsake them in the **w**. Neh 9:19
years you sustained them in the **w**, Neh 9:21
wind came across the **w** and struck the Jb 1:19
The voice of the LORD shakes the **w**; the Ps 29:8
the LORD shakes the **w** of Kadesh. Ps 29:8
wander far away; I would lodge in the **w**; Ps 55:7
of David, when he was in the **w** of Judah. Ps 63:T
The pastures of the **w** overflow, the hills Ps 65:12
when you marched through the **w**, Ps 68:7
him as food for the creatures of the **w**. Ps 74:14
and not from the **w** comes lifting up, Ps 75:6
split rocks in the **w** and gave them Ps 78:15
"Can God spread a table in the **w**? Ps 78:19
against him in the **w** and grieved him Ps 78:40
and guided them in the **w** like a flock. Ps 78:52
as on the day at Massah in the **w**, Ps 95:8
I am like a desert owl of the **w**, like an Ps 102:6
they had a wanton craving in the **w**, Ps 106:14
that he would make them fall in the **w**, Ps 106:26
him who led his people through the **w**, Ps 136:16
coming up from the **w** like columns of Sg 3:6
Who is that coming up from the **w**, Sg 8:5
The oracle concerning the **w** of the sea. Is 21:1
the Negeb sweep on, it comes from the **w**, Is 21:1
deserted and forsaken, like the **w**; Is 27:10
high, and the **w** becomes a fruitful field, Is 32:15
Then justice will dwell in the **w**, and Is 32:16
The **w** and the dry land shall be glad; the Is 35:1
For waters break forth in the **w**, and Is 35:6
"In the **w** prepare the way of the LORD; Is 40:3
valleys. I will make the **w** a pool of water, Is 41:18
I will put in the **w** the cedar, the acacia, Is 41:19
make a way in the **w** and rivers in the Is 43:19
the ostriches, for I give water in the **w**, Is 43:20
waste places and makes her **w** like Eden, Is 51:3
Your holy cities have become a **w**; Zion Is 64:10
Zion has become a **w**, Jerusalem a Is 64:10
as a bride, how you followed me in the **w**, Jer 2:2
the land of Egypt, who led us in the **w**, Jer 2:6
a wild donkey used to the **w**, in her heat Jer 2:24
Have I been a **w** to Israel, or a land of Jer 2:31
sat awaiting lovers like an Arab in the **w**. Jer 3:2
a lamentation for the pastures of the **w**, Jer 9:10
the land ruined and laid waste like a **w**, Jer 9:12
made my pleasant portion a desolate **w**. Jer 12:10
dwell in the parched places of the **w**, Jer 17:6
and the pastures of the **w** are dried up. Jer 23:10
survived the sword found grace in the **w**; Jer 31:2
she shall be the last of the nations, a **w**, Jer 50:12
cruel, like the ostriches in the **w**. Lam 4:3
they lay in wait for us in the **w**. Lam 4:19
our lives, because of the sword in the **w**. Lam 5:9
dwelling places, from the **w** to Riblah. Ezk 6:14
Now it is planted in the **w**, in a dry and Ezk 19:13
of Egypt and brought them into the **w**. Ezk 20:10
of Israel rebelled against me in the **w**. Ezk 20:13
out my wrath upon them in the **w**, Ezk 20:13
to them in the **w** that I would not Ezk 20:15
or make a full end of them in the **w**. Ezk 20:17
"And I said to their children in the **w**, Ezk 20:18
my anger against them in the **w**. Ezk 20:21
to them in the **w** that I would scatter Ezk 20:23
bring you into the **w** of the peoples, Ezk 20:35
your fathers in the **w** of the land of Ezk 20:36
drunkards were brought from the **w**; Ezk 23:42
And I will cast you out into the **w**, you Ezk 29:5
dwell securely in the **w** and sleep in Ezk 34:25
she was born, and make her like a **w**, Hos 2:3
allure her, and bring her into the **w**, Hos 2:14
Like grapes in the **w**, I found Israel. Hos 9:10
It was I who knew you in the **w**, in the Hos 13:5
LORD, shall come, rising from the **w**, Hos 13:15
fire has devoured the pastures of the **w**, Jl 1:19
fire has devoured the pastures of the **w**. Jl 1:20
before them, but behind them a desolate **w**, Jl 2:3
field, for the pastures of the **w** are green; Jl 2:22
a desolation and Edom a desolate **w**, Jl 3:19
Egypt and led you forty years in the **w**, Am 2:10
during the forty years in the **w**, Am 5:25
Baptist came preaching in the **w** of Judea, Mt 3:1
he said, "The voice of one crying in the **w**: Mt 3:3
by the Spirit into the **w** to be tempted by Mt 4:1
"What did you go out into the **w** to see? Mt 11:7
if they say to you, 'Look, he is in the **w**,' Mt 24:26
the voice of one crying in the **w**: 'Prepare Mk 1:3
baptizing in the **w** and proclaiming a Mk 1:4
immediately drove him out into the **w**. Mk 1:12
And he was in the **w** forty days, being Mk 1:13
and he was in the **w** until the day of his Lk 1:80
to John the son of Zechariah in the **w**. Lk 3:2
"The voice of one crying in the **w**: Lk 3:4
Jordan and was led by the Spirit in the **w** Lk 4:1
"What did you go out into the **w** to see? Lk 7:24
am the voice of one crying out in the **w**, Jn 1:23
as Moses lifted up the serpent in the **w**, Jn 3:14
Our fathers ate the manna in the **w**; as it Jn 6:31
Your fathers ate the manna in the **w**, and Jn 6:49
from there to the region near the **w**, Jn 11:54
to him in the **w** of Mount Sinai, Acts 7:30
the Red Sea and in the **w** for forty years. Acts 7:36
congregation in the **w** with the angel Acts 7:38
during the forty years in the **w**, Acts 7:42
fathers had the tent of witness in the **w**, Acts 7:44
years he put up with them in the **w**. Acts 13:18
men of the Assassins out into the **w**?" Acts 21:38
for they were overthrown in the **w**. 1 Cor 10:5
danger in the city, danger in the **w**, 2 Cor 11:26
rebellion, on the day of testing in the **w**, Heb 3:8
who sinned, whose bodies fell in the **w**? Heb 3:17
and the woman fled into the **w**, where Rv 12:6
might fly from the serpent into the **w**, Rv 12:14
he carried me away in the Spirit into a **w**, Rv 17:3

WILDGOATS' (1)

and his men in front of the **W** Rocks. 1 Sm 24:2

WILDLY (1)
My heart is beating **w**; I cannot keep Jer 4:19

WILES (1)
they have harassed you with their **w**, Nm 25:18

WILL (102) [Noun, or Verb of Volition]
of the people of the land, "But if you **w**, Gn 23:13
as great a bride price and gift as you **w**, Gn 34:12
till the **w** of the LORD should be clear to Lv 24:12
for it was the **w** of the LORD to put 1 Sm 2:25
not been the king's **w** to put to death 2 Sm 3:37
may do, according to the **w** of your God. Ezr 7:18
the God of your fathers and do his **w**. Ezr 10:11
I desire to do your **w**, O my God; your law Ps 40:8
not give him up to the **w** of his enemies. Ps 41:2
his hosts, his ministers, who do his **w**! Ps 103:21
Teach me to do your **w**, for you are my Ps 143:10
Yet it was the **w** of the LORD to crush Is 53:10
the **w** of the LORD shall prosper in his Is 53:10
does according to his **w** among the host Dn 4:35
he shall work his **w** and return to his Dn 11:28
Your kingdom come, your **w** be done, Mt 6:10
one who does the **w** of my Father who Mt 7:21
Father, for such was your gracious **w**. Mt 11:26
For whoever does the **w** of my Father in Mt 12:50
So it is not the **w** of my Father who is in Mt 18:14
of the two did the **w** of his father?" They Mt 21:31
nevertheless, not as I **w**, but as you Mt 26:39
not as I will, but as you **w**." Mt 26:39
pass unless I drink it, your **w** be done." Mt 26:42
Whoever does the **w** of God, he is my Mk 3:35
Yet not what I **w**, but what you will." Mk 14:36
Yet not what I will, but what you **w**." Mk 14:36
his face and begged him, "Lord, if you **w**, Lk 5:12
his hand and touched him, saying, "I **w**; Lk 5:13
who knew his master's **w** but did not Lk 12:47
not get ready or act according to his **w**, Lk 12:47
Nevertheless, not my **w**, but yours, be Lk 22:42
but he delivered Jesus over to their **w**. Lk 23:25
of blood nor of the **w** of the flesh nor of Jn 1:13
the will of the flesh nor of the **w** of man, Jn 1:13
food is to do the **w** of him who sent me Jn 4:34
I seek not my own **w** but the will of him Jn 5:30
my own will but the **w** of him who sent Jn 5:30
not to do my own **w** but the will of him Jn 6:38
my own will but the **w** of him who sent Jn 6:38
And this is the **w** of him who sent me, Jn 6:39
For this is the **w** of my Father, that Jn 6:40
If anyone's **w** is to do God's will, he will Jn 7:17
If anyone's will is to do God's **w**, he will Jn 7:17
and your **w** is to do your father's desires. Jn 8:44
is a worshiper of God and does his **w**, Jn 9:31
"If it is my **w** that he remain until I Jn 21:22
"If it is my **w** that he remain until I Jn 21:23
after my heart, who will do all my **w**.' Acts 13:22
said, "Let the **w** of the Lord be done." Acts 21:14
fathers appointed you to know his **w**, Acts 22:14
that somehow by God's **w** I may now Rom 1:10
and know his **w** and approve what is Rom 2:18
the saints according to the **w** of God. Rom 8:27
depends not on human **w** or exertion, Rom 9:16
find fault? For who can resist his **w**?" Rom 9:19
you may discern what is the **w** of God, Rom 12:2
so that by God's **w** I may come to you Rom 15:32
called by the **w** of God to be an apostle 1 Cor 1:1
For if I do this of my own **w**, I have a 1 Cor 9:17
I have a reward, but not of my own **w**, 1 Cor 9:17
it was not at all his **w** to come now. 1 Cor 16:12
apostle of Christ Jesus by the **w** of God, 2 Cor 1:1
their means, of their own free **w**, 2 Cor 8:3
Lord and then by the **w** of God to us. 2 Cor 8:5
Lord himself and to show our good **w**. 2 Cor 8:19
according to the **w** of our God and Gal 1:4
apostle of Christ Jesus by the **w** of God, Eph 1:1
according to the purpose of his **w**, Eph 1:5
known to us the mystery of his **w**, Eph 1:9
according to the counsel of his **w**, Eph 1:11
but understand what the **w** of the Lord Eph 5:17
doing the **w** of God from the heart, Eph 6:6
service with a good **w** as to the Lord Eph 6:7
and rivalry, but others from good **w**. Phil 1:15
both to **w** and to work for his good Phil 2:13
apostle of Christ Jesus by the **w** of God, Col 1:1
the knowledge of his **w** in all spiritual Col 1:9
and fully assured in all the **w** of God. Col 4:12
For this is the **w** of God, your 1 Thes 4:3
for this is the **w** of God in Christ 1 Thes 5:18
Christ Jesus by the **w** of God according 2 Tm 1:1
being captured by him to do his **w**. 2 Tm 2:26
compulsion but of your own free **w**. Phlm 1:14
Spirit distributed according to his **w**. Heb 2:4
For where a **w** is involved, the death of Heb 9:16
For a **w** takes effect only at death, since Heb 9:17
said, 'Behold, I have come to do your **w**, Heb 10:7
come to do your **w**." He abolishes the Heb 10:9
And by that **w** we have been Heb 10:10
you have done the **w** of God you may Heb 10:36
good that you may do his **w**, Heb 13:21
Of his own **w** he brought us forth by the Jas 1:18
small rudder wherever the **w** of the pilot Jas 3:4
For this is the **w** of God, that by doing 1 Pt 2:15
doing good, if that should be God's **w**, 1 Pt 3:17
human passions but for the **w** of God. 1 Pt 4:2
according to God's **w** entrust their 1 Pt 4:19
was ever produced by the **w** of man, 2 Pt 1:21
but whoever does the **w** of God abides 1 Jn 2:17
according to his **w** he hears us. 1 Jn 5:14
and by your **w** they existed and were Rv 4:11

WILLFUL (1)
Bold and **w**, they do not tremble as they 2 Pt 2:10

WILLFULLY (1)
But if a man **w** attacks another to kill Ex 21:14

WILLFULNESS (1)
and in their **w** they hamstrung oxen. Gn 49:6

WILLING (31)
"If you are **w** that I should bury my dead Gn 23:8
woman may not be **w** to follow me to Gn 24:5
But if the woman is not **w** to follow you, Gn 24:8
were of a **w** heart brought brooches Ex 35:22
The LORD will not be **w** to forgive him, Dt 29:20
But if he is not **w** to redeem you, then, as Ru 3:13
So David was not **w** to take the ark of 2 Sm 6:10
ships," but Jehoshaphat was not **w**. 1 Kgs 22:49
the LORD was not **w** to destroy Judah, 2 Kgs 8:19
the Syrians were not **w** to save the 1 Chr 19:19
a whole heart and with a **w** mind, 1 Chr 28:9
work will be every **w** man who has 1 Chr 28:21
the LORD was not **w** to destroy the 2 Chr 21:7
were of a **w** heart brought burnt 2 Chr 29:31
"Is the wild ox **w** to serve you? Will he Jb 39:9
and uphold me with a **w** spirit. Ps 51:12
and flax, and works with **w** hands. Prv 31:13
If you are **w** and obedient, you shall eat Is 1:19
of Israel will not be **w** to listen to you, Ezk 3:7
to you, for they are not **w** to listen to me. Ezk 3:7
me and were not **w** to listen to me. Ezk 20:8
and if you are **w** to accept it, he is Mt 11:14
they themselves are not **w** to move them Mt 23:4
The spirit indeed is **w**, but the flesh is Mt 26:41
The spirit indeed is **w**, but the flesh is Mk 14:38
saying, "Father, if you are **w**, remove Lk 22:42
and you were **w** to rejoice for a while in Jn 5:35
for a long time, if they are **w** to testify, Acts 26:5
so that it may be ready as a **w** gift, 2 Cor 9:5
we were **w** to be left behind at Athens 1 Thes 3:1
If anyone is not **w** to work, let him 2 Thes 3:10

WILLINGLY (12)
that the people offered themselves **w**, Jgs 5:2
who offered themselves **w** among the Jgs 5:9
"We will **w** give them." And they spread Jgs 8:25
Who then will offer **w**, consecrating 1 Chr 29:5
rejoiced because they had given **w**, 1 Chr 29:9
we should be able thus to offer **w**? 1 Chr 29:14
his officials contributed **w** to the 2 Chr 35:8
vowed **w** for the house of their God that Ezr 7:16
all the men who **w** offered to live in Neh 11:2
for he does not **w** afflict or grieve the Lam 3:33
was subjected to futility, not **w**, Rom 8:20
oversight, not under compulsion, but **w**, 1 Pt 5:2

WILLOW (1)
abundant waters. He set it like a **w** twig, Ezk 17:5

WILLOWS (5)
of leafy trees and **w** of the brook, Lv 23:40
him; the **w** of the brook surround him. Jb 40:22
On the **w** there we hung up our lyres. Ps 137:2
they carry away over the Brook of the **W**. Is 15:7
the grass like **w** by flowing streams. Is 44:4

WILLS (9)
with great dominion and do as he **w**. Dn 11:3
comes against him shall do as he **w**, Dn 11:16
"And the king shall do as he **w**. He Dn 11:36
to you if God **w**," and he set sail Acts 18:21
then he has mercy on whomever he **w**, Rom 9:18
wills, and he hardens whomever he **w**. Rom 9:18
I will come to you soon, if the Lord **w**, 1 Cor 4:19
to each one individually as he **w**. 1 Cor 12:11
Instead you ought to say, "If the Lord **w**, Jas 4:15

WILY (2)
the schemes of the **w** are brought to a Jb 5:13
him, dressed as a prostitute, **w** of heart. Prv 7:10

WIN (9)
thinking to **w** them for himself. 2 Chr 32:1
by their own sword did they **w** the land, Ps 44:3
of a wise man's mouth **w** him favor, Eccl 10:12
to all, that I might **w** more of them. 1 Cor 9:19
I became as a Jew, in order to **w** Jews. 1 Cor 9:20
law) that I might **w** those under the 1 Cor 9:20
that I might **w** those outside the 1 Cor 9:21
weak, that I might **w** the weak. 1 Cor 9:22
worked for, but may **w** a full reward. 2 Jn 1:8

WIND (135)
And God made a **w** blow over the earth, Gn 8:1
ears, thin and blighted by the east **w**. Gn 41:6
thin, and blighted by the east **w**, Gn 41:23
blighted by the east **w** are also seven Gn 41:27
LORD brought an east **w** upon the land Ex 10:13
the east **w** had brought the locusts. Ex 10:13
the LORD turned the **w** into a very strong Ex 10:19
the wind into a very strong west **w**, Ex 10:19
by a strong east **w** all night and made Ex 14:21
You blew with your **w**; the sea covered Ex 15:10
Then a **w** from the LORD sprang up, Nm 11:31
he was seen on the wings of the **w**. 2 Sm 22:11
grew black with clouds and **w**, 1 Kgs 18:45
great and strong **w** tore the 1 Kgs 19:11
LORD, but the LORD was not in the **w**. 1 Kgs 19:11
And after the **w** an earthquake, but 1 Kgs 19:11
the LORD, 'You shall not see **w** or rain, 2 Kgs 3:17
a great **w** came across the wilderness and Jb 1:19
the speech of a despairing man is **w**? Jb 6:26
and the words of your mouth be a great **w**? Jb 8:2
and fill his belly with the east **w**? Jb 15:2
That they are like straw before the **w**, Jb 21:18
By his **w** the heavens were made fair; his Jb 26:13
The east **w** lifts him up and he is gone; it Jb 27:21
he gave to the **w** its weight and Jb 28:25
my honor is pursued as by the **w**, and Jb 30:15
You lift me up on the **w**; you make me Jb 30:22
the earth is still because of the south **w**? Jb 37:17
when the **w** has passed and cleared Jb 37:21
or where the east **w** is scattered upon the Jb 38:24
but are like chaff that the **w** drives away. Ps 1:4
sulfur and a scorching **w** shall be the Ps 11:6
he came swiftly on the wings of the **w**. Ps 18:10
I beat them fine as dust before the **w**; I Ps 18:42
Let them be like chaff before the **w**, with Ps 35:5
By the east **w** you shattered the ships of Ps 48:7
a shelter from the raging **w** and tempest." Ps 55:8
He caused the east **w** to blow in the Ps 78:26
and by his power he led out the south **w**; Ps 78:26
a **w** that passes and comes not again. Ps 78:39
whirling dust, like chaff before the **w**. Ps 83:13
for the **w** passes over it, and it is gone, Ps 103:16
chariot; he rides on the wings of the **w**; Ps 104:3
commanded and raised the stormy **w**, Ps 107:25
brings forth the **w** from his Ps 135:7
he makes his **w** blow and the waters Ps 147:18
and mist, stormy **w** fulfilling his word! Ps 148:8
his own household will inherit the **w**, Prv 11:29
Like clouds and **w** without rain is a Prv 25:14
The north **w** brings forth rain, and a Prv 25:23
her is to restrain the **w** or to grasp oil Prv 27:16
Who has gathered the **w** in his fists? Prv 30:4
The **w** blows to the south and goes Eccl 1:6
around and around goes the **w**, and on Eccl 1:6
wind, and on its circuits the **w** returns. Eccl 1:6
all is vanity and a striving after **w**. Eccl 1:14
that this also is but a striving after **w**. Eccl 1:17
all was vanity and a striving after **w**, Eccl 2:11
for all is vanity and a striving after **w**. Eccl 2:17
also is vanity and a striving after **w**. Eccl 2:26
also is vanity and a striving after **w**. Eccl 4:4
hands full of toil and a striving after **w**. Eccl 4:6
also is vanity and a striving after **w**. Eccl 4:16
is there to him who toils for the **w**? Eccl 5:16
this also is vanity and a striving after **w**. Eccl 6:9
He who observes the **w** will not sow, Eccl 11:4
Awake, O north **w**, and come, O south Sg 4:16
O north wind, and come, O south **w**! Sg 4:16
as the trees of the forest shake before the **w**. Is 7:2
mountains before the **w** and whirling Is 17:13
writhed, but we have given birth to **w**. Is 26:18
his fierce breath in the day of the east **w**. Is 27:8
will be like a hiding place from the **w**, Is 32:2
them, and the **w** shall carry them away, Is 41:16
their metal images are empty **w**. Is 41:29
neither scorching **w** nor sun shall strike Is 49:10
The **w** will carry them off, a breath will Is 57:13
stream, which the **w** of the LORD drives. Is 59:19
like a leaf, and our iniquities, like the **w**, Is 64:6
wilderness, in her heat sniffing the **w**! Jer 2:24
"A hot **w** from the bare heights in the Jer 4:11
a **w** too full for this comes for me. Now it Jer 4:12
The prophets will become **w**; the word is Jer 5:13
brings forth the **w** from his Jer 10:13
chaff driven by the **w** from the desert. Jer 13:24
Like the east **w** I will scatter them Jer 18:17
The **w** shall shepherd all your Jer 22:22
will scatter to every **w** those who cut the Jer 49:32
brings forth the **w** from his Jer 51:16
a stormy **w** came out of the north, Ezk 1:4

a third part you shall scatter to the **w**, Ezk 5:2
will scatter toward every **w** all who are Ezk 12:14
will fall, and a stormy **w** break out. Ezk 13:11
will make a stormy **w** break out in Ezk 13:13
wither when the east **w** strikes it— Ezk 17:10
survivors shall be scattered to every **w**, Ezk 17:21
ground; the east **w** dried up its fruit; Ezk 19:12
The east **w** has wrecked you in the Ezk 27:26
and the **w** carried them away, so that Dn 2:35
A **w** has wrapped them in its wings, and Hos 4:19
For they sow the **w**, and they shall reap Hos 8:7
feeds on the **w** and pursues the Hos 12:1
and pursues the east **w** all day long; Hos 12:1
among his brothers, the east **w**, Hos 13:15
the east wind, the **w** of the LORD, Hos 13:15
forms the mountains and creates the **w**, Am 4:13
the LORD hurled a great **w** upon the sea, Jon 1:4
rose, God appointed a scorching east **w**, Jon 4:8
should go about and utter **w** and lies, Mi 2:11
they sweep by like the **w** and go on, Hab 1:11
forward! The **w** was in their wings. Zec 5:9
to see? A reed shaken by the **w**? Mt 11:7
the waves, for the **w** was against them. Mt 14:24
But when he saw the **w**, he was afraid, Mt 14:30
they got into the boat, the **w** ceased. Mt 14:32
awoke and rebuked the **w** and said to Mk 4:39
Be still!" And the **w** ceased, and there Mk 4:39
is this, that even **w** and sea obey him?" Mk 4:41
painfully, for the **w** was against them. Mk 6:48
the boat with them, and the **w** ceased. Mk 6:51
to see? A reed shaken by the **w**? Lk 7:24
and rebuked the **w** and the raging Lk 8:24
when you see the south **w** blowing, Lk 12:55
The **w** blows where it wishes, and you Jn 3:8
rough because a strong **w** was blowing. Jn 6:18
a sound like a mighty rushing **w**, Acts 2:2
and as the **w** did not allow us to go Acts 27:7
Now when the south **w** blew gently, Acts 27:13
But soon a tempestuous **w**, called the Acts 27:14
was caught and could not face the **w**, Acts 27:15
the foresail to the **w** they made for the Acts 27:40
after one day a south **w** sprang up, Acts 28:13
carried about by every **w** of doctrine, Eph 4:14
the sea that is driven and tossed by the **w**. Jas 1:6
that no **w** might blow on earth or sea or Rv 7:1

WINDOW (22)
days Noah opened the **w** of the ark that Gn 8:6
looked out of a **w** and saw Isaac Gn 26:8
let them down by a rope through the **w**, Jos 2:15
scarlet cord in the **w** through which you Jos 2:18
And she tied the scarlet cord in the **w**. Jos 2:21
"Out of the **w** she peered, the mother of Jgs 5:28
let David down through the **w**, 1 Sm 19:12
looked out of the **w** and saw King 2 Sm 6:16
There were **w** frames in three rows, 1 Kgs 7:4
and **w** opposite window in three tiers. 1 Kgs 7:4
and window opposite **w** in three tiers. 1 Kgs 7:4
and **w** was opposite window in three 1 Kgs 7:5
window was opposite **w** in three tiers. 1 Kgs 7:5
her head and looked out of the **w**. 2 Kgs 9:30
he lifted up his face to the **w** and said, 2 Kgs 9:32
"Open the **w** eastward," and he 2 Kgs 13:17
looked out of the **w** and saw King 1 Chr 15:29
For at the **w** of my house I have looked Prv 7:6
threshing floor or like smoke from a **w**. Hos 13:3
her capitals; a voice shall hoot in the **w**; Zep 2:14
man named Eutychus, sitting at the **w**, Acts 20:9
a basket through a **w** in the wall 2 Cor 11:33

WINDOWS (27)
and the **w** of the heavens were opened. Gn 7:11
of the deep and the **w** of the heavens were Gn 8:2
for the house **w** with recessed frames. 1 Kgs 6:4
the doorways and **w** had square 1 Kgs 7:5
himself should make **w** in heaven, 2 Kgs 7:2
himself should make **w** in heaven, 2 Kgs 7:19
who look through the **w** are dimmed, Eccl 12:3
behind our wall, gazing through the **w**, Sg 2:9
For the **w** of heaven are opened, and the Is 24:18
fly like a cloud, and like doves to their **w**? Is 60:8
For death has come up into our **w**; it has Jer 9:21
upper rooms,' who cuts out **w** for it, Jer 22:14
And the gateway had **w** all around, Ezk 40:16
the vestibule had **w** all around inside, Ezk 40:16
And its **w**, its vestibule, and its palm Ezk 40:22
it and its vestibule had **w** all around, Ezk 40:25
all around, like the **w** of the others. Ezk 40:25
it and its vestibule had **w** all around. Ezk 40:29
it and its vestibule had **w** all around. Ezk 40:33
as the others, and it had **w** all around. Ezk 40:36
and the narrow **w** and the galleries Ezk 41:16
floor up to the **w** (now the windows Ezk 41:16
windows (now the **w** were covered), Ezk 41:16
there were narrow **w** and palm trees Ezk 41:26
house where he had **w** in his upper Dn 6:10
they enter through the **w** like a thief. Jl 2:9
I will not open the **w** of heaven for you Mal 3:10

WINDS (24)
and cold from the scattering **w**. Jb 37:9
he makes his messengers **w**, his Ps 104:4
upon Elam the four **w** from the four Jer 49:36
And I will scatter them to all those **w**, Jer 49:36
who survive I will scatter to all the **w**. Ezk 5:10
scatter to all the **w** and will unsheathe Ezk 5:12
Come from the four **w**, O breath, and Ezk 37:9
the four **w** of heaven were stirring up the Dn 7:2
horns toward the four **w** of heaven. Dn 8:8
and divided toward the four **w** of heaven, Dn 11:4
you abroad as the four **w** of the heavens, Zec 2:6
are going out to the four **w** of heaven, Zec 6:5
and the **w** blew and beat on that house, Mt 7:25
and the **w** blew and beat against that Mt 7:27
he rose and rebuked the **w** and the sea, Mt 8:26
is this, that even **w** and sea obey him?" Mt 8:27
will gather his elect from the four **w**, Mt 24:31
and gather his elect from the four **w**, Mk 13:27
that he commands even **w** and water, Lk 8:25
Cyprus, because the **w** were against us. Acts 27:4
angels he says, "He makes his angels **w**, Heb 1:7
are so large and are driven by strong **w**, Jas 3:4
waterless clouds, swept along by **w**; Jude 1:12
holding back the four **w** of the earth, Rv 7:1

WINDSTORM (2)
And a great **w** arose, and the waves were Mk 4:37
And a **w** came down on the lake, and Lk 8:23

WINDY (2)
a wise man answer with **w** knowledge, Jb 15:2
Shall **w** words have an end? Or what Jb 16:3

WINE (236)
He drank of the **w** and became drunk Gn 9:21
Noah awoke from his **w** and knew what Gn 9:24
of Salem brought out bread and **w**. Gn 14:18
Come, let us make our father drink **w**, Gn 19:32
made their father drink **w** that night. Gn 19:33
Let us make him drink **w** tonight also. Gn 19:34
their father drink **w** that night also. Gn 19:35
and he brought him **w**, and he drank. Gn 27:25
of the earth and plenty of grain and **w**. Gn 27:28
and with grain and **w** I have sustained Gn 27:37
his garments in **w** and his vesture Gn 49:11
His eyes are darker than **w**, and his Gn 49:12
fourth of a hin of **w** for a drink offering. Ex 29:40
"Drink no **w** or strong drink, you or Lv 10:9
the drink offering with it shall be of **w**, Lv 23:13
separate himself from **w** and strong Nm 6:3
no vinegar made from **w** or strong drink Nm 6:3
after that the Nazirite may drink **w**. Nm 6:20
of a hin of **w** for the drink offering Nm 15:5
you shall offer a third of a hin of **w**, Nm 15:7
for the drink offering half a hin of **w**, Nm 15:10
all the best of the **w** and of the grain, Nm 18:12
shall be half a hin of **w** for a bull, Nm 28:14
your grain and your **w** and your oil, Dt 7:13
in your grain and your **w** and your oil. Dt 11:14
of your grain or of your **w** or of your oil, Dt 12:17
eat the tithe of your grain, of your **w**, Dt 14:23
—oxen or sheep or **w** or strong drink, Dt 14:26
of your grain, of your **w** and of your oil, Dt 18:4
neither drink of the **w** nor gather the Dt 28:39
also shall not leave you grain, **w**, or oil, Dt 28:51
you have not drunk **w** or strong drink, Dt 29:6
you drank foaming **w** made from the Dt 32:14
their **w** is the poison of serpents and the Dt 32:33
and drank the **w** of their drink Dt 32:38
lived alone, in a land of grain and **w**, Dt 33:28
'Shall I leave my **w** that cheers God and Jgs 9:13
careful and drink no **w** or strong drink, Jgs 13:4
So then drink no **w** or strong drink, and Jgs 13:7
neither let her drink **w** or strong drink, Jgs 13:14
with bread and **w** for me and your Jgs 19:19
your morsel in the **w**." So she sat beside Ru 2:14
drunk? Put away your **w** from you." 1 Sm 1:14
have drunk neither **w** nor strong 1 Sm 1:15
an ephah of flour, and a skin of **w**, 1 Sm 1:24
and another carrying a skin of **w**. 1 Sm 10:3
and a skin of **w** and a young goat 1 Sm 16:20
and two skins of **w** and five sheep 1 Sm 25:18
when the **w** had gone out of Nabal, 1 Sm 25:37
Amnon's heart is merry with **w**, 2 Sm 13:28
of summer fruits, and a skin of **w**. 2 Sm 16:1
and the **w** for those who faint in the 2 Sm 16:2
own land, a land of grain and **w**, 2 Kgs 18:32
also over the fine flour, the **w**, 1 Chr 9:29
clusters of raisins, and **w** and oil, 1 Chr 12:40
vineyards for the **w** cellars was 1 Chr 27:27
cors of barley, 20,000 baths of **w**, 2 Chr 2:10
the wheat and barley, oil and **w**, 2 Chr 2:15
them, and stores of food, oil, and **w**. 2 Chr 11:11
the firstfruits of grain, **w**, oil, 2 Chr 31:5
also for the yield of grain, **w**, and oil; 2 Chr 32:28
to the God of heaven, wheat, salt, **w**, or oil, Ezr 6:9
silver, 100 cors of wheat, 100 baths of **w**, Ezr 7:22
Artaxerxes, when **w** was before him, Neh 2:1
I took up the **w** and gave it to the king. Neh 2:1
w, and oil that you have been exacting Neh 5:11
ten days all kinds of **w** in abundance. Neh 5:18
and drink sweet **w** and send portions Neh 8:10
fruit of every tree, the **w** and the oil, Neh 10:37
of grain, **w**, and oil to the chambers, Neh 10:39
and the tithes of grain, **w**, and oil, Neh 13:5
grain, **w**, and oil into the storehouses. Neh 13:12
loading them on donkeys, and also **w**, Neh 13:15
and the royal **w** was lavished according Est 1:7
the heart of the king was merry with **w**, Est 1:10
as they were drinking **w** after the feast, Est 5:6
as they were drinking **w** after the feast, Est 7:2
to the place where they were drinking **w**, Est 7:8
eating and drinking **w** in their oldest Jb 1:13
eating and drinking **w** in their oldest Jb 1:18
my belly is like **w** that has no vent; Jb 32:19
have when their grain and **w** abound. Ps 4:7
you have given us **w** to drink that made Ps 60:3
my thirst they gave me sour **w** to drink. Ps 69:21
the LORD there is a cup with foaming **w**, Ps 75:8
a strong man shouting because of **w**. Ps 78:65
and **w** to gladden the heart of man, oil Ps 104:15
and your vats will be bursting with **w**. Prv 3:10
wickedness and drink the **w** of violence. Prv 4:17
her beasts; she has mixed her **w**; Prv 9:2
bread and drink of the **w** I have mixed. Prv 9:5
W is a mocker, strong drink a brawler, Prv 20:1
he who loves **w** and oil will not be Prv 21:17
Those who tarry long over **w**; those Prv 23:30
wine; those who go to try mixed **w**. Prv 23:30
Do not look at **w** when it is red, when it Prv 23:31
O Lemuel, it is not for kings to drink **w**, Prv 31:4
and **w** to those in bitter distress; Prv 31:6
cheer my body with **w**—my heart still Eccl 2:3
and drink your **w** with a merry heart, Eccl 9:7
for laughter, and **w** gladdens life, Eccl 10:19
his mouth! For your love is better than **w**; Sg 1:2
you; we will extol your love more than **w**; Sg 1:4
How much better is your love than **w**, Sg 4:10
my honey, I drank my **w** with my milk. Sg 5:1
a rounded bowl that never lacks mixed **w**. Sg 7:2
and your mouth like the best **w**. It goes Sg 7:9
I would give you spiced **w** to drink, the Sg 8:2
dross, your best **w** mixed with water. Is 1:22
the midst of it, and hewed out a **w** vat in it; Is 5:2
late into the evening as **w** inflames them! Is 5:11
and flute and **w** at their feasts, Is 5:12
to those who are heroes at drinking **w**, Is 5:22
no treader treads out **w** in the presses; Is 16:10
sheep, eating flesh and drinking **w**. Is 22:13
The **w** mourns, the vine languishes, all Is 24:7
No more do they drink **w** with singing; Is 24:9
is an outcry in the streets for lack of **w**; Is 24:11
a feast of rich food, a feast of well-aged **w**, Is 25:6
full of marrow, of aged **w** well refined. Is 25:6
the rich valley of those overcome with **w**! Is 28:1
These also reel with **w** and stagger with Is 28:7
strong drink, they are swallowed by **w**, Is 28:7
Be drunk, but not with **w**; stagger, but not Is 29:9
your own land, a land of grain and **w**, Is 36:17
drunk with their own blood as with **w**. Is 49:26
afflicted, who are drunk, but not with **w**: Is 51:21
buy **w** and milk without money and Is 55:1
"Come," they say, "let me get **w**; let us fill Is 56:12
shall not drink your **w** for which you Is 62:8
"As the new **w** is found in the cluster, and Is 65:8
and fill cups of mixed **w** for Destiny, Is 65:11
shall be filled with **w**."' And they will Jer 13:12
that every jar will be filled with **w**?' Jer 13:12
man, like a man overcome by **w**, Jer 23:9
my hand this cup of the **w** of wrath, Jer 25:15
of the LORD, over the grain, the **w**, Jer 31:12
chambers; then offer them **w** to drink." Jer 35:2
before the Rechabites pitchers full of **w**, Jer 35:5
and cups, and I said to them, "Drink **w**." Jer 35:5
But they answered, "We will drink no **w**, Jer 35:6
commanded us, 'You shall not drink **w**, Jer 35:6
us, to drink no **w** all our days, Jer 35:8
Rechab gave to his sons, to drink no **w**, Jer 35:14
gather **w** and summer fruits and oil, Jer 40:10
And they gathered **w** and summer Jer 40:12
I have made the **w** cease from the Jer 48:33
drunken; the nations drank of her **w**; Jer 51:7
"Where is bread and **w**?" as they faint Lam 2:12
kind; **w** of Helbon and wool of Sahar Ezk 27:18
and casks of **w** from Uzal they Ezk 27:19
priest shall drink **w** when he enters Ezk 44:21
the king ate, and of the **w** that he drank. Dn 1:5
king's food, or with the **w** that he drank. Dn 1:8

their food and the **w** they were to drink, Dn 1:16
of his lords and drank **w** in front of the Dn 5:1
Belshazzar, when he tasted the **w**, Dn 5:2
They drank **w** and praised the gods of Dn 5:4
concubines have drunk **w** from them. Dn 5:23
no meat or **w** entered my mouth, Dn 10:3
it was I who gave her the grain, the **w**, Hos 2:8
grain in its time, and my **w** in its season, Hos 2:9
the earth shall answer the grain, the **w**, Hos 2:22
whoredom, **w**, and new wine, which Hos 4:11
whoredom, wine, and new **w**, which Hos 4:11
princes became sick with the heat of **w**; Hos 7:5
for grain and **w** they gash themselves; Hos 7:14
Threshing floor and **w** vat shall not feed Hos 9:2
feed them, and the new **w** shall fail them. Hos 9:2
not pour drink offerings of **w** to the LORD, Hos 9:4
fame shall be like the **w** of Lebanon. Hos 14:7
and weep, and wail, all you drinkers of **w**, Jl 1:5
drinkers of wine, because of the sweet **w**, Jl 1:5
the grain is destroyed, the **w** dries up, Jl 1:10
I am sending to you grain, **w**, and oil, Jl 2:19
the vats shall overflow with **w** and oil. Jl 2:24
have sold a girl for **w** and have drunk it. Jl 3:3
day the mountains shall drip sweet **w**, Jl 3:18
God they drink the **w** of those who have Am 2:8
"But you made the Nazirites drink **w**, Am 2:12
but you shall not drink their **w**. Am 5:11
who drink **w** in bowls and anoint Am 6:6
the mountains shall drip sweet **w**, and Am 9:13
plant vineyards and drink their **w**, Am 9:14
preach to you of **w** and strong drink," he Mi 2:11
you shall tread grapes, but not drink **w**. Mi 6:15
"Moreover, **w** is a traitor, an arrogant Hab 2:5
they shall not drink **w** from them." Zep 1:13
and the hills, on the grain, the new **w**, Hg 1:11
fold bread or stew or **w** or oil or any kind Hg 2:12
one came to the **w** vat to draw fifty Hg 2:16
shall drink and roar as if drunk with **w**, Zec 9:15
flourish, and new **w** the young women. Zec 9:17
and their hearts shall be glad as with **w**. Zec 10:7
Neither is new **w** put into old wineskins. Mt 9:17
skins burst and the **w** is spilled and the Mt 9:17
But new **w** is put into fresh wineskins, Mt 9:17
they offered him **w** to drink, mixed Mt 27:34
and took a sponge, filled it with sour **w**, Mt 27:48
no one puts new **w** into old wineskins. Mk 2:22
the **w** will burst the skins—and the Mk 2:22
burst the skins—and the **w** is destroyed, Mk 2:22
But new **w** is for fresh wineskins." Mk 2:22
they offered him **w** mixed with myrrh, Mk 15:23
ran and filled a sponge with sour **w**, Mk 15:36
he must not drink **w** or strong drink, Lk 1:15
no one puts new **w** into old wineskins. Lk 5:37
the new **w** will burst the skins and it will Lk 5:37
But new **w** must be put into fresh Lk 5:38
no one after drinking old **w** desires new, Lk 5:39
eating no bread and drinking no **w**, Lk 7:33
up his wounds, pouring on oil and **w**. Lk 10:34
coming up and offering him sour **w** Lk 23:36
When the **w** ran out, the mother of Jesus Jn 2:3
of Jesus said to him, "They have no **w**." Jn 2:3
of the feast tasted the water now become **w**, Jn 2:9
to him, "Everyone serves the good **w** first, Jn 2:10
have drunk freely, then the poor **w**. Jn 2:10
But you have kept the good **w** until now." Jn 2:10
Galilee, where he had made the water **w**. Jn 4:46
A jar full of sour **w** stood there, so they Jn 19:29
full of the sour **w** on a hyssop branch Jn 19:29
When Jesus had received the sour **w**, he Jn 19:30
said, "They are filled with new **w**." Acts 2:13
eat meat or drink **w** or do anything Rom 14:21
And do not get drunk with **w**, for that is Eph 5:18
not addicted to much **w**, 1 Tm 3:8
but use a little **w** for the sake of your 1 Tm 5:23
not slanderers or slaves to much **w**. Ti 2:3
denarius, and do not harm the oil and **w**!" Rv 6:6
all nations drink the **w** of the passion of Rv 14:8
he also will drink the **w** of God's wrath, Rv 14:10
drain the cup of the **w** of the fury of his Rv 16:19
and with the **w** of whose sexual Rv 17:2
nations have drunk the **w** of the passion Rv 18:3
incense, myrrh, frankincense, **w**, oil, Rv 18:13

WINE-DRINKING (1)
in his wrath from the **w** and went into the Est 7:7

WINEPRESS (17)
floor, and as the fullness of the **w**. Nm 18:27
floor, and as produce of the **w**. Nm 18:30
your threshing floor, and out of your **w**. Dt 15:14
from your threshing floor and your **w**. Dt 16:13
out wheat in the **w** to hide it from Jgs 6:11
and Zeeb they killed at the **w** of Zeeb. Jgs 7:25
the threshing floor, or from the **w**?" 2 Kgs 6:27
garments like his who treads in the **w**? Is 63:2
"I have trodden the **w** alone, and from the Is 63:3
trodden as in a **w** the virgin daughter Lam 1:15
is ripe. Go in, tread, for the **w** is full. Jl 3:13
around it and dug a **w** in it and built a Mt 21:33
dug a pit for the **w** and built a tower, Mk 12:1
threw it into the great **w** of the wrath of Rv 14:19
And the **w** was trodden outside the city, Rv 14:20
the city, and blood flowed from the **w**, Rv 14:20
He will tread the **w** of the fury of the Rv 19:15

WINEPRESSES (4)
Judah people treading **w** on the Neh 13:15
oil; they tread the **w**, but suffer thirst. Jb 24:11
I have made the wine cease from the **w**; Jer 48:33
the Tower of Hananel to the king's **w**. Zec 14:10

WINESKIN (1)
I have become like a **w** in the smoke, Ps 119:83

WINESKINS (9)
worn-out sacks for their donkeys, and **w**, Jos 9:4
These **w** were new when we filled them, Jos 9:13
has no vent; like new **w** ready to burst. Jb 32:19
Neither is new wine put into old **w**. If it Mt 9:17
But new wine is put into fresh **w**, and so Mt 9:17
And no one puts new wine into old **w**. If Mk 2:22
the skins. But new wine is for fresh **w**." Mk 2:22
And no one puts new wine into old **w**. If Lk 5:37
But new wine must be put into fresh **w**. Lk 5:38

WING (14)
was the length of one **w** of the cherub, 1 Kgs 6:24
length of the other **w** of the cherub; 1 Kgs 6:24
from the tip of one **w** to the tip of the 1 Kgs 6:24
out so that a **w** of one touched the 1 Kgs 6:27
and a **w** of the other cherub touched 1 Kgs 6:27
one **w** of the one, of five cubits, 2 Chr 3:11
the wall of the house, and its other **w**, 2 Chr 3:11
touched the **w** of the other cherub; 2 Chr 3:11
and of this cherub, one **w**, of five 2 Chr 3:12
the wall of the house, and the other **w**, 2 Chr 3:12
was joined to the **w** of the first 2 Chr 3:12
none that moved a **w** or opened the Is 10:14
of which touched the **w** of another, Ezk 1:11
And on the **w** of abominations shall Dn 9:27

WINGED (10)
and every **w** bird according to its kind. Gn 1:21
according to its kind, every **w** creature. Gn 7:14
"All **w** insects that go on all fours are Lv 11:20
Yet among the **w** insects that go on all Lv 11:21
But all other **w** insects that have four Lv 11:23
the likeness of any **w** bird that flies in the Dt 4:17
And all **w** insects are unclean for you; Dt 14:19
All clean **w** things you may eat. Dt 14:20
dust, **w** birds like the sand of the seas; Ps 78:27
or some **w** creature tell the matter. Eccl 10:20

WINGS (76)
bore you on eagles' **w** and brought you Ex 19:4
shall spread out their **w** above, Ex 25:20
the mercy seat with their **w**, Ex 25:20
The cherubim spread out their **w** above, Ex 37:9
the mercy seat with their **w**, Ex 37:9
He shall tear it open by its **w**, but shall Lv 1:17
over its young, spreading out its **w**, Dt 32:11
under whose **w** you have come to take Ru 2:12
Spread your **w** over your servant, for you Ru 3:9
he was seen on the **w** of the wind. 2 Sm 22:11
And the **w** of the cherubim were 1 Kgs 6:27
their other **w** touched each other in 1 Kgs 6:27
underneath the **w** of the cherubim. 1 Kgs 8:6
spread out their **w** over the place 1 Kgs 8:7
that spread their **w** and covered the 1 Chr 28:18
The **w** of the cherubim together 2 Chr 3:11
The **w** of these cherubim extended 2 Chr 3:13
underneath the **w** of the cherubim. 2 Chr 5:7
spread out their **w** over the place 2 Chr 5:8
"The **w** of the ostrich wave proudly, but Jb 39:13
and spreads his **w** toward the south? Jb 39:26
eye; hide me in the shadow of your **w**, Ps 17:8
he came swiftly on the **w** of the wind. Ps 18:10
take refuge in the shadow of your **w**. Ps 36:7
And I say, "Oh, that I had **w** like a dove! I Ps 55:6
the shadow of your **w** I will take refuge, Ps 57:1
take refuge under the shelter of your **w**! Ps 61:4
in the shadow of your **w** I will sing for Ps 63:7
the sheepfolds—the **w** of a dove covered Ps 68:13
and under his **w** you will find refuge; Ps 91:4
chariot; he rides on the **w** of the wind; Ps 104:3
If I take the **w** of the morning and dwell Ps 139:9
it, it is gone, for suddenly it sprouts **w**, Prv 23:5
Each had six **w**: with two he covered his Is 6:2
and its outspread **w** will fill the breadth of Is 8:8
land of whirring **w** that is beyond the Is 18:1
they shall mount up with **w** like eagles; Is 40:31
"Give **w** to Moab, for she would fly away; Jer 48:9
eagle and spread his **w** against Moab; Jer 48:40
eagle and spread his **w** against Bozrah, Jer 49:22
four faces, and each of them had four **w**. Ezk 1:6
Under their **w** on their four sides they Ezk 1:8
the four had their faces and their **w** thus: Ezk 1:8
their **w** touched one another. Each one Ezk 1:9
And their **w** were spread out above. Ezk 1:11
Each creature had two **w**, each of Ezk 1:11
the expanse their **w** were stretched out Ezk 1:23
creature had two **w** covering its body. Ezk 1:23
the sound of their **w** like the sound of Ezk 1:24
they stood still, they let down their **w**. Ezk 1:24
they stood still, they let down their **w**. Ezk 1:25
the sound of the **w** of the living Ezk 3:13
the sound of the **w** of the cherubim was Ezk 10:5
form of a human hand under their **w**. Ezk 10:8
their rims, and their spokes, their **w**, Ezk 10:12
lifted up their **w** to mount up Ezk 10:16
lifted up their **w** and mounted up Ezk 10:19
Each had four faces, and each four **w**, Ezk 10:21
and underneath their **w** the likeness of Ezk 10:21
Then the cherubim lifted up their **w**, Ezk 11:22
eagle with great **w** and long pinions, Ezk 17:3
eagle with great **w** and much plumage, Ezk 17:7
first was like a lion and had eagles' **w**. Dn 7:4
Then as I looked its **w** were plucked off, Dn 7:4
leopard, with four **w** of a bird on its back. Dn 7:6
A wind has wrapped them in its **w**, and Hos 4:19
The locust spreads its **w** and flies away. Na 3:16
forward! The wind was in their **w**. Zec 5:9
They had **w** like the wings of a stork, and Zec 5:9
They had wings like the **w** of a stork, and Zec 5:9
shall rise with healing in its **w**. Mal 4:2
a hen gathers her brood under her **w**, Mt 23:37
a hen gathers her brood under her **w**, Lk 13:34
living creatures, each of them with six **w**, Rv 4:8
and the noise of their **w** was like the noise Rv 9:9
was given the two **w** of the great eagle Rv 12:14

WINK (1)
and let not those **w** the eye who hate me Ps 35:19

WINKS (3)
w with his eyes, signals with his feet, Prv 6:13
Whoever **w** the eye causes trouble, but Prv 10:10
Whoever **w** his eyes plans dishonest Prv 16:30

WINNING (1)
Now Esther was **w** favor in the eyes of Est 2:15

WINNOW (3)
you shall **w** them, and the wind shall Is 41:16
of my people, not to **w** or cleanse, Jer 4:11
winnowers, and they shall **w** her, Jer 51:2

WINNOWED (3)
O my threshed and **w** one, what I have Is 21:10
which has been **w** with shovel and fork. Is 30:24
I have **w** them with a winnowing fork in Jer 15:7

WINNOWERS (1)
and I will send to Babylon **w**, and they Jer 51:2

WINNOWING (4)
he is **w** barley tonight at the threshing Ru 3:2
winnowed them with a **w** fork in the Jer 15:7
His **w** fork is in his hand, and he will Mt 3:12
His **w** fork is in his hand, to clear his Lk 3:17

WINNOWS (2)
the throne of judgment **w** all evil with Prv 20:8
A wise king **w** the wicked and drives Prv 20:26

WINS (1)
Good sense **w** favor, but the way of the Prv 13:15

WINTER (16)
harvest, cold and heat, summer and **w**, Gn 8:22
earth; you have made summer and **w**. Ps 74:17
for behold, the **w** is past; the rain is over Sg 2:11
all the beasts of the earth will **w** on them. Is 18:6
and the king was sitting in the **w** house, Jer 36:22
I will strike the **w** house along with the Am 3:15
It shall continue in summer as in **w**. Zec 14:8
flight may not be in **w** or on a Sabbath. Mt 24:20
Pray that it may not happen in **w**. Mk 13:18
took place at Jerusalem. It was **w**, Jn 10:22
was not suitable to spend the **w** in, Acts 27:12
and northwest, and spend the **w** there. Acts 27:12
stay with you or even spend the **w**, 1 Cor 16:6
Do your best to come before **w**. 2 Tm 4:21
for I have decided to spend the **w** there. Ti 3:12
fig tree sheds its **w** fruit when shaken by Rv 6:13

WINTERED (1)
sail in a ship that had **w** in the island, Acts 28:11

WIPE (11)
I will **w** them from human memory," Dt 32:26
and I will **w** Jerusalem as one wipes 2 Kgs 21:13
and do not **w** out my good deeds that I Neh 13:14
"Come, let us **w** them out as a nation; Ps 83:4
them their iniquity and **w** them out for Ps 94:23
the LORD our God will **w** them out. Ps 94:23

the Lord GOD will **w** away tears from all Is 25:8
clings to our feet we **w** off against you. Lk 10:11
disciples' feet and to **w** them with the Jn 13:5
and God will **w** away every tear from Rv 7:17
He will **w** away every tear from their Rv 21:4

WIPED (10)
with a great blow until they were **w** out, Jos 10:20
in Samaria, till he had **w** them out, 2 Kgs 10:17
Thus Jehu **w** out Baal from Israel. 2 Kgs 10:28
get, and his disgrace will not be **w** away. Prv 6:33
with destruction and **w** out all Is 26:14
altars cut down, and your works **w** out. Ezk 6:6
with her tears and **w** them with the hair Lk 7:38
with her tears and **w** them with her hair. Lk 7:44
Lord with ointment and **w** his feet with Jn 11:2
the feet of Jesus and **w** his feet with her Jn 12:3

WIPES (2)
will wipe Jerusalem as one **w** a dish, 2 Kgs 21:13
she eats and **w** her mouth and says, "I Prv 30:20

WIPING (1)
w it and turning it upside down. 2 Kgs 21:13

WISDOM (212)
will be your **w** and your understanding Dt 4:6
the son of Nun was full of the spirit of **w**, Dt 34:9
But my lord has **w** like the wisdom 2 Sm 14:20
has wisdom like the **w** of the angel of 2 Sm 14:20
went to all the people in her **w**. 2 Sm 20:22
Act therefore according to your **w**, but 1 Kgs 2:6
they perceived that the **w** of God was 1 Kgs 3:28
gave Solomon **w** and understanding 1 Kgs 4:29
so that Solomon's **w** surpassed the 1 Kgs 4:30
wisdom surpassed the **w** of all the 1 Kgs 4:30
of the east and all the **w** of Egypt. 1 Kgs 4:30
came to hear the **w** of Solomon, 1 Kgs 4:34
of the earth, who had heard of his **w**. 1 Kgs 4:34
And the LORD gave Solomon **w**, as he 1 Kgs 5:12
And he was full of **w**, understanding, 1 Kgs 7:14
Sheba had seen all the **w** of Solomon, 1 Kgs 10:4
land of your words and of your **w**, 1 Kgs 10:6
Your **w** and prosperity surpass the 1 Kgs 10:7
stand before you and hear your **w**! 1 Kgs 10:8
of the earth in riches and in **w**. 1 Kgs 10:23
presence of Solomon to hear his **w**, 1 Kgs 10:24
and all that he did, and his **w**, 1 Kgs 11:41
Give me now **w** and knowledge to go 2 Chr 1:10
but have asked **w** and knowledge for 2 Chr 1:11
w and knowledge are granted to you. 2 Chr 1:12
of Sheba had seen the **w** of Solomon, 2 Chr 9:3
own land of your words and of your **w**, 2 Chr 9:5
the greatness of your **w** was not told 2 Chr 9:6
stand before you and hear your **w**! 2 Chr 9:7
kings of the earth in riches and in **w**. 2 Chr 9:22
presence of Solomon to hear his **w**, 2 Chr 9:23
according to the **w** of your God that is Ezr 7:25
do they not die, and that without **w**?' Jb 4:21
that he would tell you the secrets of **w**! Jb 11:6
are the people, and **w** will die with you. Jb 12:2
W is with the aged, and understanding Jb 12:12
"With God are **w** and might; he has Jb 12:13
With him are strength and sound **w**; Jb 12:16
keep silent, and it would be your **w**! Jb 13:5
of God? And do you limit **w** to yourself? Jb 15:8
you have counseled him who has no **w**, Jb 26:3
"But where shall **w** be found? And Jb 28:12
of crystal; the price of **w** is above pearls. Jb 28:18
"From where, then, does **w** come? And Jb 28:20
'Behold, the fear of the Lord, that is **w**, Jb 28:28
'Let days speak, and many years teach **w**.' Jb 32:7
Beware lest you say, 'We have found **w**; Jb 32:13
to me; be silent, and I will teach you **w**." Jb 33:33
Who has put **w** in the inward parts or Jb 38:36
Who can number the clouds by **w**? Or Jb 38:37
has made her forget **w** and given her no Jb 39:17
The mouth of the righteous utters **w**, Ps 37:30
My mouth shall speak **w**; the meditation Ps 49:3
and you teach me **w** in the secret heart. Ps 51:6
our days that we may get a heart of **w**. Ps 90:12
In **w** have you made them all; the Ps 104:24
his pleasure and to teach his elders **w**. Ps 105:22
fear of the LORD is the beginning of **w**; Ps 111:10
To know **w** and instruction, to Prv 1:2
fools despise **w** and instruction. Prv 1:7
W cries aloud in the street, in the Prv 1:20
ear attentive to **w** and inclining your Prv 2:2
For the LORD gives **w**; from his mouth Prv 2:6
he stores up sound **w** for the upright; he Prv 2:7
for **w** will come into your heart, and Prv 2:10
Blessed is the one who finds **w**, and the Prv 3:13
The LORD by **w** founded the earth; by Prv 3:19
of these—keep sound **w** and discretion, Prv 3:21
Get **w**; get insight; do not forget, and do Prv 4:5
The beginning of **w** is this: Get wisdom, Prv 4:7
The beginning of wisdom is this: Get **w**, Prv 4:7
I have taught you the way of **w**; I have Prv 4:11
My son, be attentive to my **w**; incline Prv 5:1
Say to **w**, "You are my sister," and call Prv 7:4
Does not **w** call? Does not understanding Prv 8:1
for **w** is better than jewels, and all that Prv 8:11
"I, **w**, dwell with prudence, and I find Prv 8:12
I have counsel and sound **w**; I have Prv 8:14
W has built her house; she has hewn her Prv 9:1
fear of the LORD is the beginning of **w**, Prv 9:10
who has understanding, **w** is found, Prv 10:13
but **w** is pleasure to a man of Prv 10:23
mouth of the righteous brings forth **w**, Prv 10:31
disgrace, but with the humble is **w**. Prv 11:2
but with those who take advice is **w**. Prv 13:10
A scoffer seeks **w** in vain, but Prv 14:6
The **w** of the prudent is to discern his Prv 14:8
W rests in the heart of a man of Prv 14:33
fear of the LORD is instruction in **w**, Prv 15:33
How much better to get **w** than gold! Prv 16:16
in his hand to buy **w** when he has no Prv 17:16
The discerning sets his face toward **w**, Prv 17:24
the fountain of **w** is a bubbling brook. Prv 18:4
that you may gain **w** in the future. Prv 19:20
No **w**, no understanding, no counsel Prv 21:30
Buy truth, and do not sell it; buy **w**, Prv 23:23
By **w** a house is built, and by Prv 24:3
W is too high for a fool; in the gate he Prv 24:7
Know that **w** is such to your soul; if Prv 24:14
he who walks in **w** will be delivered. Prv 28:26
He who loves **w** makes his father glad, Prv 29:3
The rod and reproof give **w**, but a Prv 29:15
I have not learned **w**, nor have I Prv 30:3
She opens her mouth with **w**, and the Prv 31:26
and to search out by **w** all that is done Eccl 1:13
in my heart, "I have acquired great **w**, Eccl 1:16
great experience of **w** and knowledge." Eccl 1:16
my heart to know **w** and to know Eccl 1:17
For in much **w** is much vexation, and Eccl 1:18
still guiding me with **w**—and how to Eccl 2:3
Also my **w** remained with me. Eccl 2:9
turned to consider **w** and madness and Eccl 2:12
there is more gain in **w** than in folly, Eccl 2:13
I toiled and used my **w** under the sun. Eccl 2:19
has toiled with **w** and knowledge and Eccl 2:21
God has given **w** and knowledge and Eccl 2:26
For it is not from **w** that you ask this. Eccl 7:10
W is good with an inheritance, an Eccl 7:11
For the protection of **w** is like the Eccl 7:12
knowledge is that **w** preserves the life Eccl 7:12
W gives strength to the wise man Eccl 7:19
All this I have tested by **w**. I said, "I will Eccl 7:23
out and to seek **w** and the scheme of Eccl 7:25
A man's **w** makes his face shine, and Eccl 8:1
When I applied my heart to know **w**, Eccl 8:16
or thought or knowledge or **w** in Sheol, Eccl 9:10
seen this example of **w** under the sun, Eccl 9:13
and he by his **w** delivered the city. Eccl 9:15
But I say that **w** is better than might, Eccl 9:16
the poor man's **w** is despised and Eccl 9:16
W is better than weapons of war, but Eccl 9:18
so a little folly outweighs **w** and honor. Eccl 10:1
strength, but **w** helps one to succeed. Eccl 10:10
of my hand I have done it, and by my **w**, Is 10:13
him, the Spirit of **w** and understanding, Is 11:2
wonderful in counsel and excellent in **w**. Is 28:29
and the **w** of their wise men shall perish, Is 29:14
of salvation, **w**, and knowledge; Is 33:6
your **w** and your knowledge led you Is 47:10
word of the LORD, so what **w** is in them? Jer 8:9
"Let not the wise man boast in his **w**, let Jer 9:23
who established the world by his **w**, Jer 10:12
LORD of hosts: "Is **w** no more in Teman? Jer 49:7
from the prudent? Has their **w** vanished? Jer 49:7
who established the world by his **w**, Jer 51:15
by your **w** and your understanding you Ezk 28:4
by your great **w** in your trade you have Ezk 28:5
the beauty of your **w** and defile your Ezk 28:7
full of **w** and perfect in beauty. Ezk 28:12
you corrupted your **w** for the sake of Ezk 28:17
of good appearance and skillful in all **w**, Dn 1:4
and skill in all literature and **w**, Dn 1:17
every matter of **w** and understanding Dn 1:20
and ever, to whom belong **w** and might. Dn 2:20
he gives **w** to the wise and knowledge to Dn 2:21
for you have given me **w** and might, Dn 2:23
not because of any **w** that I have more Dn 2:30
and understanding and **w** like the Dn 5:11
and wisdom like the **w** of the gods were Dn 5:11
and excellent **w** are found Dn 5:14
and it is sound **w** to fear your name: Mi 6:9
Yet **w** is justified by her deeds." Mt 11:19
of the earth to hear the **w** of Solomon, Mt 12:42
this man get this **w** and these mighty Mt 13:54
things? What is the **w** given to him? Mk 6:2
and the disobedient to the **w** of the just, Lk 1:17
grew and became strong, filled with **w**. Lk 2:40
And Jesus increased in **w** and in stature Lk 2:52
Yet **w** is justified by all her children." Lk 7:35
of the earth to hear the **w** of Solomon, Lk 11:31
Therefore also the **W** of God said, 'I will Lk 11:49
for I will give you a mouth and **w**, Lk 21:15
of good repute, full of the Spirit and of **w**, Acts 6:3
not withstand the **w** and the Spirit Acts 6:10
gave him favor and **w** before Pharaoh, Acts 7:10
in all the **w** of the Egyptians, Acts 7:22
of the riches and **w** and knowledge of Rom 11:33
and not with words of eloquent **w**, 1 Cor 1:17
"I will destroy the **w** of the wise, 1 Cor 1:19
God made foolish the **w** of the world? 1 Cor 1:20
For since, in the **w** of God, the world 1 Cor 1:21
world did not know God through **w**, 1 Cor 1:21
demand signs and Greeks seek **w**, 1 Cor 1:22
the power of God and the **w** of God. 1 Cor 1:24
God made our **w** and our 1 Cor 1:30
of God with lofty speech or **w**. 1 Cor 2:1
were not in plausible words of **w**, 1 Cor 2:4
might not rest in the **w** of men but in 1 Cor 2:5
Yet among the mature we do impart **w**, 1 Cor 2:6
although it is not a **w** of this age or of 1 Cor 2:6
impart a secret and hidden **w** of God, 1 Cor 2:7
taught by human **w** but taught by 1 Cor 2:13
For the **w** of this world is folly with 1 Cor 3:19
through the Spirit the utterance of **w**, 1 Cor 12:8
not by earthly **w** but by the grace of 2 Cor 1:12
he lavished upon us, in all **w** and insight Eph 1:8
you a spirit of **w** and of revelation in Eph 1:17
church the manifold **w** of God might Eph 3:10
in all spiritual **w** and understanding, Col 1:9
and teaching everyone with all **w**, Col 1:28
all the treasures of **w** and knowledge. Col 2:3
an appearance of **w** in promoting Col 2:23
and admonishing one another in all **w**, Col 3:16
If any of you lacks **w**, let him ask God, Jas 1:5
show his works in the meekness of **w**. Jas 3:13
This is not the **w** that comes down from Jas 3:15
But the **w** from above is first pure, then Jas 3:17
to you according to the **w** given him, 2 Pt 3:15
power and wealth and **w** and might and Rv 5:12
and glory and **w** and thanksgiving and Rv 7:12
This calls for **w**: let the one who has Rv 13:18
This calls for a mind with **w**: the seven Rv 17:9

WISE (186)
the tree was to be desired to make one **w**, Gn 3:6
magicians of Egypt and all its **w** men. Gn 41:8
select a discerning and **w** man, Gn 41:33
is none so discerning and **w** as you are. Gn 41:39
Pharaoh summoned the **w** men and the Ex 7:11
Choose for your tribes **w**, understanding, Dt 1:13
of your tribes, **w** and experienced men, Dt 1:15
nation is a **w** and understanding people.' Dt 4:6
the eyes of the **w** and subverts the cause Dt 16:19
If they were **w**, they would understand Dt 32:29
from there a **w** woman and said 2 Sm 14:2
Then a **w** woman called from the 2 Sm 20:16
him guiltless, for you are a **w** man. 1 Kgs 2:9
I give you a **w** and discerning mind, 1 Kgs 3:12
has given to David a **w** son to be over 1 Kgs 5:7
who has given King David a **w** son, 2 Chr 2:12
king said to the **w** men who knew the Est 1:13
Then his **w** men and his wife Zeresh Est 6:13
He catches the **w** in their own craftiness, Jb 5:13
He is **w** in heart and mighty in strength— Jb 9:4
"Should a **w** man answer with windy Jb 15:2
(what **w** men have told, without hiding Jb 15:18
I shall not find a **w** man among you. Jb 17:10
Surely he who is **w** is profitable to Jb 22:2
It is not the old who are **w**, nor the aged Jb 32:9
words, I listened for your **w** sayings, Jb 32:11
"Hear my words, you **w** men, and give ear Jb 34:2
and the **w** man who hears me will say: Jb 34:34
regard any who are **w** in their own Jb 37:24
Now therefore, O kings, be **w**; be warned, Ps 2:10
of the LORD is sure, making **w** the simple; Ps 19:7
For he sees that even the **w** die; the fool Ps 49:10
of the people! Fools, when will you be **w**? Ps 94:8
Whoever is **w**, let him attend to these Ps 107:43
to receive instruction in **w** dealing, in Prv 1:3
Let the **w** hear and increase in learning, Prv 1:5
the words of the **w** and their riddles. Prv 1:6
Be not **w** in your own eyes; fear the LORD, Prv 3:7
The **w** will inherit honor, but fools get Prv 3:35
O sluggard; consider her ways, and be **w**. Prv 6:6
Hear instruction and be **w**, and do not Prv 8:33
reprove a **w** man, and he will love you. Prv 9:8
Give instruction to a **w** man, and he will Prv 9:9
If you are **w**, you are wise for yourself; if Prv 9:12
If you are wise, you are **w** for yourself; if Prv 9:12
A **w** son makes a glad father, but a Prv 10:1
The **w** of heart will receive Prv 10:8
The **w** lay up knowledge, but the Prv 10:14

fool will be servant to the **w** of heart. Prv 11:29
life, and whoever captures souls is **w**. Prv 11:30
eyes, but a **w** man listens to advice. Prv 12:15
the tongue of the **w** brings healing. Prv 12:18
A **w** son hears his father's instruction, Prv 13:1
The teaching of the **w** is a fountain of Prv 13:14
walks with the **w** becomes wise, Prv 13:20
walks with the wise becomes **w**, Prv 13:20
but the lips of the **w** will preserve them. Prv 14:3
One who is **w** is cautious and turns Prv 14:16
The crown of the **w** is their wealth, but Prv 14:24
tongue of the **w** commends knowledge, Prv 15:2
The lips of the **w** spread knowledge; not Prv 15:7
to be reproved; he will not go to the **w**. Prv 15:12
A **w** son makes a glad father, but a Prv 15:20
reproof will dwell among the **w**. Prv 15:31
of death, and a **w** man will appease it. Prv 16:14
The **w** of heart is called discerning, Prv 16:21
The heart of the **w** makes his speech Prv 16:23
a fool who keeps silent is considered **w**; Prv 17:28
and the ear of the **w** seeks knowledge. Prv 18:15
and whoever is led astray by it is not **w**. Prv 20:1
by counsel; by **w** guidance wage war. Prv 20:18
A **w** king winnows the wicked and Prv 20:26
is punished, the simple becomes **w**; Prv 21:11
when a **w** man is instructed, he gains Prv 21:11
and oil are in a **w** man's dwelling, Prv 21:20
A **w** man scales the city of the mighty Prv 21:22
your ear, and hear the words of the **w**, Prv 22:17
My son, if your heart is **w**, my heart Prv 23:15
Hear, my son, and be **w**, and direct Prv 23:19
he who fathers a **w** son will be glad in Prv 23:24
A **w** man is full of strength, and a man Prv 24:5
for by **w** guidance you can wage your Prv 24:6
These also are sayings of the **w**. Prv 24:23
of gold is a **w** reprover to a listening Prv 25:12
to his folly, lest he be **w** in his own eyes. Prv 26:5
see a man who is **w** in his own eyes? Prv 26:12
Be **w**, my son, and make my heart Prv 27:11
A rich man is **w** in his own eyes, but a Prv 28:11
city aflame, but the **w** turn away wrath. Prv 29:8
If a **w** man has an argument with a Prv 29:9
but a **w** man quietly holds it back. Prv 29:11
are small, but they are exceedingly **w**: Prv 30:24
The **w** person has his eyes in his head, Eccl 2:14
have I been so very **w**?" And I said in Eccl 2:15
For of the **w** as of the fool there is no Eccl 2:16
How the **w** dies just like the fool! Eccl 2:16
knows whether he will be **w** or a fool? Eccl 2:19
was a poor and **w** youth than an old Eccl 4:13
what advantage has the **w** man over the Eccl 6:8
The heart of the **w** is in the house of Eccl 7:4
the rebuke of the **w** than to hear the Eccl 7:5
oppression drives the **w** into madness, Eccl 7:7
and do not make yourself too **w**. Eccl 7:16
gives strength to the **w** man more than Eccl 7:19
"I will be **w**," but it was far from me. Eccl 7:23
Who is like the **w**? And who knows the Eccl 8:1
and the **w** heart will know the proper Eccl 8:5
Even though a **w** man claims to know, Eccl 8:17
the righteous and the **w** and their deeds Eccl 9:1
battle to the strong, nor bread to the **w**, Eccl 9:11
there was found in it a poor, **w** man, Eccl 9:15
The words of the **w** heard in quiet are Eccl 9:17
A **w** man's heart inclines him to the Eccl 10:2
The words of a **w** man's mouth win Eccl 10:12
Besides being **w**, the Preacher also Eccl 12:9
The words of the **w** are like goads, Eccl 12:11
Woe to those who are **w** in their own eyes, Is 5:21
you say to Pharaoh, "I am a son of the **w**, Is 19:11
Where then are your **w** men? Let them Is 19:12
the wisdom of their **w** men shall perish, Is 29:14
And yet he is **w** and brings disaster; he Is 31:2
who turns **w** men back and makes their Is 44:25
They are '**w**'—in doing evil! Jer 4:22
"How can you say, 'We are **w**, and the law Jer 8:8
The **w** men shall be put to shame; they Jer 8:9
is the man so **w** that he can understand Jer 9:12
"Let not the **w** man boast in his wisdom, Jer 9:23
for among all the **w** ones of the nations Jer 10:7
from the priest, nor counsel from the **w**, Jer 18:18
against her officials and her **w** men! Jer 50:35
drunk her officials and her **w** men, Jer 51:57
that all the **w** men of Babylon Dn 2:12
and the **w** men were about to be killed; Dn 2:13
gone out to kill the **w** men of Babylon. Dn 2:14
with the rest of the **w** men of Babylon. Dn 2:18
gives wisdom to the **w** and knowledge to Dn 2:21
to destroy the **w** men of Babylon. Dn 2:24
"Do not destroy the **w** men of Babylon; Dn 2:24
answered the king and said, "No **w** men, Dn 2:27
prefect over all the **w** men of Babylon. Dn 2:48
decree that all the **w** men of Babylon Dn 4:6
because all the **w** men of my kingdom Dn 4:18
king declared to the **w** men of Babylon, Dn 5:7
Then all the king's **w** men came in, but Dn 5:8
Now the **w** men, the enchanters, have Dn 5:15
And the **w** among the people shall Dn 11:33
and some of the **w** shall stumble, so Dn 11:35
And those who are **w** shall shine like the Dn 12:3
but those who are **w** shall understand. Dn 12:10
Whoever is **w**, let him understand these Hos 14:9
the LORD, destroy the **w** men out of Edom, Ob 1:8
Tyre and Sidon, though they are very **w**. Zec 9:2
w men from the east came to Jerusalem, Mt 2:1
Herod summoned the **w** men secretly and Mt 2:7
that he had been tricked by the **w** men, Mt 2:16
that he had ascertained from the **w** men. Mt 2:16
them will be like a **w** man who built his Mt 7:24
so be **w** as serpents and innocent as Mt 10:16
things from the **w** and understanding Mt 11:25
you prophets and **w** men and scribes, Mt 23:34
then is the faithful and **w** servant, Mt 24:45
of them were foolish, and five were **w**. Mt 25:2
but the **w** took flasks of oil with their Mt 25:4
And the foolish said to the **w**, 'Give us Mt 25:8
But the **w** answered, saying, 'Since there Mt 25:9
things from the **w** and understanding Lk 10:21
then is the faithful and **w** manager, Lk 12:42
both to the **w** and to the foolish. Rom 1:14
Claiming to be **w**, they became fools, Rom 1:22
Lest you be **w** in your own conceits, I Rom 11:25
I want you to be **w** as to what is good Rom 16:19
to the only **w** God be glory Rom 16:27
"I will destroy the wisdom of the **w**, 1 Cor 1:19
Where is the one who is **w**? Where is 1 Cor 1:20
of you were **w** according to worldly 1 Cor 1:26
is foolish in the world to shame the **w**; 1 Cor 1:27
you thinks that he is **w** in this age, 1 Cor 3:18
become a fool that he may become **w**. 1 Cor 3:18
"He catches the **w** in their craftiness," 1 Cor 3:19
Lord knows the thoughts of the **w**, 1 Cor 3:20
sake, but you are **w** in Christ. 1 Cor 4:10
no one among you **w** enough to settle a 1 Cor 6:5
bear with fools, being **w** yourselves! 2 Cor 11:19
how you walk, not as unwise but as **w**, Eph 5:15
to make you **w** for salvation through 2 Tm 3:15
Who is **w** and understanding among Jas 3:13

WISELY (8)

And he dealt **w** and distributed 2 Chr 11:23
he has ceased to act **w** and do good. Ps 36:3
A servant who deals **w** has the king's Prv 14:35
A servant who deals **w** will rule over a Prv 17:2
Behold, my servant shall act **w**; he shall Is 52:13
and he shall reign as king and deal **w**, Jer 23:5
when Jesus saw that he answered **w**, Mk 12:34
Conduct yourselves **w** toward outsiders, Col 4:5

WISER (8)

For he was **w** than all other men, 1 Kgs 4:31
men, **w** than Ethan the Ezrahite, 1 Kgs 4:31
earth and makes us **w** than the birds of Jb 35:11
commandment makes me **w** than my Ps 119:98
to a wise man, and he will be still **w**; Prv 9:9
The sluggard is **w** in his own eyes Prv 26:16
you are indeed **w** than Daniel; no secret Ezk 28:3
the foolishness of God is **w** than men, 1 Cor 1:25

WISEST (3)

Her **w** princesses answer, indeed, she Jgs 5:29
The **w** of women builds her house, but Prv 14:1
the **w** counselors of Pharaoh give stupid Is 19:11

WISH (34)

But if he does not **w** to redeem the field, Lv 27:20
I **w** I had a sword in my hand, for then Nm 22:29
your fill of grapes, as many as you **w**, Dt 23:24
the man does not **w** to take his brother's Dt 25:7
persists, saying, 'I do not **w** to take her,' Dt 25:8
as much as you **w**," he would say, 1 Sm 2:16
all that is in your heart. Do as you **w**. 1 Sm 14:7
to these reports you **w** to become their Neh 6:6
the king said to Esther, "What is your **w**? Est 5:6
answered, "My **w** and my request is: Est 5:7
king to grant my **w** and fulfill my Est 5:8
again said to Esther, "What is your **w**, Est 7:2
king, let my life be granted me for my **w**, Est 7:3
king's provinces! Now what is your **w**? Est 9:12
Did a man ever **w** that he would be Jb 37:20
"So whatever you **w** that others would do Mt 7:12
"Teacher, we **w** to see a sign from you." Mt 12:38
If you **w**, I will make three tents here, one Mt 17:4
to the girl, "Ask me for whatever you **w**, Mk 6:22
And as you **w** that others would do to Lk 6:31
and asked him, "Sir, we **w** to see Jesus." Jn 12:21
words abide in you, ask whatever you **w**, Jn 15:7
does this babbler **w** to say?" Others Acts 17:18
We **w** to know therefore what these Acts 17:20
"Do you **w** to go up to Jerusalem and Acts 25:9
For I could **w** that I myself were Rom 9:3
What do you **w**? Shall I come to you 1 Cor 4:21
I **w** that all were as I myself am. But 1 Cor 7:7
I **w** you would bear with me in a little 2 Cor 11:1
Though if I should **w** to boast, I 2 Cor 12:6
I come I may find you not as I **w**, 2 Cor 12:20
me not as you **w**—that perhaps 2 Cor 12:20
I **w** I could be present with you now and Gal 4:20
I **w** those who unsettle you would Gal 5:12

WISHED (5)

If one **w** to contend with him, one could Jb 9:3
to a king who **w** to settle accounts with Mt 18:23
And when he **w** to cross to Achaia, Acts 18:27
But when Paul **w** to go in among the Acts 19:30
me, they **w** to set me at liberty, Acts 28:18

WISHES (10)

But if he **w** to redeem it, he shall add a Lv 27:13
And if the donor **w** to redeem his house, Lv 27:15
who dedicates the field **w** to redeem it, Lv 27:19
If a man **w** to redeem some of his tithe, Lv 27:31
you, and he **w** to offer a food offering, Nm 15:14
shall meet my **w** by providing food 1 Kgs 5:9
The wind blows where it **w**, and you hear Jn 3:8
and it has to be, let him do as he **w**: 1 Cor 7:36
is free to be married to whom she **w**, 1 Cor 7:39
Therefore whoever **w** to be a friend of the Jas 4:4

WISHING (4)

So Pilate, **w** to satisfy the crowd, Mk 15:15
But Festus, **w** to do the Jews a favor, Acts 25:9
But the centurion, **w** to save Paul, Acts 27:43
you, not **w** that any should perish, 2 Pt 3:9

WITHDRAW (15)

fifty years they shall **w** from the duty of Nm 8:25
said to the priest, "**W** your hand." 1 Sm 14:19
and I will **w** from the city." And the 2 Sm 20:21
of Israel, that he may **w** from me." 1 Kgs 15:19
"I have done wrong; **w** from me. 2 Kgs 18:14
of Israel, that he may **w** from me." 2 Chr 16:3
w your hand far from me, and let not Jb 13:21
He does not **w** his eyes from the Jb 36:7
more go down, nor your moon **w** itself; Is 60:20
deeds and will make him **w** from us." Jer 21:2
your abominations, therefore I will **w**. Ezk 5:11
him, and he shall be afraid and **w**, Dn 11:30
darkened, and the stars **w** their shining. Jl 2:10
darkened, and the stars **w** their shining. Jl 3:15
But he would **w** to desolate places and Lk 5:16

WITHDRAWN (7)

of Babylon which has **w** from you. Jer 34:21
Chaldean army had **w** from Jerusalem Jer 37:11
he has **w** from them his right hand in Lam 2:3
will not find him; he has **w** from them. Hos 5:6
did not know who it was, for Jesus had **w**, Jn 5:13
them one who had **w** from them in Acts 15:38
And when they had **w**, they said to Acts 26:31

WITHDRAWS (1)

If he **w** into a city, then all Israel will 2 Sm 17:13

WITHDREW (18)

the men of Israel **w** from David and 2 Sm 20:2
for battle, and the men of Israel **w**. 2 Sm 23:9
And they **w** from him and returned to 2 Kgs 3:27
Then Ezra **w** from before the house of Ezr 10:6
the young men saw me and **w**, and the Jb 29:8
You **w** all your wrath; you turned from Ps 85:3
about them, they **w** from Jerusalem. Jer 37:5
warned in a dream he **w** to the district of Mt 2:22
had been arrested, he **w** into Galilee. Mt 4:12
Jesus, aware of this, **w** from there. And Mt 12:15
he **w** from there in a boat to a desolate Mt 14:13
away from there and **w** to the district of Mt 15:21
Jesus **w** with his disciples to the sea, and Mk 3:7
And he took them and **w** apart to a town Lk 9:10
And he **w** from them about a stone's Lk 22:41
Jesus **w** again to the mountain by Jn 6:15
he **w** from them and took the disciples Acts 19:9
to examine him **w** from him Acts 22:29

WITHER (14)

cut down, they **w** before any other plant. Jb 8:12
up beneath, and his branches **w** above. Jb 18:16
fruit in its season, and its leaf does not **w**. Ps 1:3
like the grass and **w** like the green herb. Ps 37:2
evening shadow; I **w** away like grass. Ps 102:11
when he blows on them, and they **w**, Is 40:24
mourn and the grass of every field **w**? Jer 12:4
so that all its fresh sprouting leaves **w**? Ezk 17:9
Will it not utterly **w** when the east Ezk 17:10
wind strikes it—**w** away on the bed Ezk 17:10
Their leaves will not **w**, nor their fruit Ezk 47:12
field on which it did not rain would **w**; Am 4:7
up all the rivers; Bashan and Carmel **w**; Na 1:4
"How did the fig tree **w** at once?" Mt 21:20

WITHERED (18)

Seven ears, **w**, thin, and blighted by the Gn 41:23

is struck down like grass and has **w**; Ps 102:4
the grass is **w**, the vegetation fails, the Is 15:6
even the leaves are **w**, and what I gave Jer 8:13
its fruit; they were stripped off and **w**. Ezk 19:12
that attacked the plant, so that it **w**. Jon 4:7
Let his arm be wholly **w**, his right eye Zec 11:17
And a man was there with a **w** hand. Mt 12:10
since they had no root, they **w** away. Mt 13:6
you again!" And the fig tree **w** at once. Mt 21:19
and a man was there with a **w** hand. Mk 3:1
And he said to the man with the **w** hand, Mk 3:3
and since it had no root, it **w** away. Mk 4:6
saw the fig tree **w** away to its roots. Mk 11:20
The fig tree that you cursed has **w**." Mk 11:21
a man was there whose right hand was **w**. Lk 6:6
and he said to the man with the **w** hand, Lk 6:8
on the rock, and as it grew up, it **w** away, Lk 8:6

WITHERS (15)
He comes out like a flower and **w**; he flees Jb 14:2
is renewed; in the evening it fades and **w**. Ps 90:6
housetops, which **w** before it grows up, Ps 129:6
For you shall be like an oak whose leaf **w**, Is 1:30
The earth mourns and **w**; the world Is 24:4
and withers; the world languishes and **w**; Is 24:4
Lebanon is confounded and **w** away; Is 33:9
The grass **w**, the flower fades when the Is 40:7
The grass **w**, the flower fades, but the Is 40:8
its roots and cut off its fruit, so that it **w**, Ezk 17:9
mourn, and the top of Carmel **w**." Am 1:2
Carmel wither; the bloom of Lebanon **w**. Na 1:4
he is thrown away like a branch and **w**; Jn 15:6
with its scorching heat and **w** the grass; Jas 1:11
grass. The grass **w**, and the flower falls, 1 Pt 1:24

WITHHELD (14)
God, seeing you have not **w** your son, Gn 22:12
done this and have not **w** your son, Gn 22:16
who has **w** from you the fruit of the Gn 30:2
and you have **w** bread from the hungry. Jb 22:7
"If I have **w** anything that the poor Jb 31:16
From the wicked their light is **w**, and Jb 38:15
desire and have not **w** the request of his Ps 21:2
Therefore the showers have been **w**, and Jer 3:3
But I **w** my hand and acted for the Ezk 20:22
and drink offering are **w** from the house Jl 1:13
"I also **w** the rain from you when there Am 4:7
the heavens above you have **w** the dew, Hg 1:10
the dew, and the earth has **w** its produce. Hg 1:10
forgiveness from anyone, it is **w**." Jn 20:23

WITHHOLD (12)
None of us will **w** from you his tomb to Gn 23:6
king, for he will not **w** me from you." 2 Sm 13:13
them and did not **w** your manna from Neh 9:20
good thing does he **w** from those who Ps 84:11
Do not **w** good from those to whom it is Prv 3:27
Do not **w** discipline from a child; if Prv 23:13
of this, and from that **w** not your hand, Eccl 7:18
seed, and at evening **w** not your hand, Eccl 11:6
Give up, and to the south, Do not **w**; Is 43:6
your cloak do not **w** your tunic either. Lk 6:29
if you **w** forgiveness from anyone, it is Jn 20:23
"Can anyone **w** water for baptizing Acts 10:47

WITHHOLDS (5)
"He who **w** kindness from a friend Jb 6:14
If he **w** the waters, they dry up; if he Jb 12:15
another **w** what he should give, and Prv 11:24
any profit, **w** his hand from injustice, Ezk 18:8
w his hand from iniquity, takes no Ezk 18:17

WITHIN (173)
there are fifty righteous **w** the city. Gn 18:24
The children struggled together **w** her, Gn 25:22
and two peoples from **w** you shall be Gn 25:23
"Go, sacrifice to your God **w** the land." Ex 8:25
or the sojourner who is **w** your gates. Ex 20:10
ark of the testimony in there **w** the veil. Ex 26:33
LORD; you shall not do it **w** your land, Lv 22:24
he may redeem it **w** a year of its sale. Lv 25:29
If it is not redeemed **w** a full year, then Lv 25:30
And if you gather **w** your cities, I will Lv 26:25
the altar and that is **w** the veil; Nm 18:7
while **w** her father's house in her Nm 30:3
is in her youth **w** her father's house. Nm 30:16
only they shall marry **w** the clan of the Nm 36:6
or the sojourner who is **w** your gates, Dt 5:14
and the Levite that is **w** your towns, Dt 12:12
slaughter and eat meat **w** any of your Dt 12:15
You may not eat **w** your towns the tithe Dt 12:17
and the Levite who is **w** your towns. Dt 12:18
you may eat **w** your towns whenever Dt 12:21
it to the sojourner who is **w** your towns, Dt 14:21
neglect the Levite who is **w** your towns, Dt 14:27
same year and lay it up **w** your towns. Dt 14:28
and the widow, who are **w** your towns, Dt 14:29
any of your towns **w** your land that the Dt 15:7
You shall eat it **w** your towns. The Dt 15:22
offer the Passover sacrifice **w** any of your Dt 16:5
servant, the Levite who is **w** your towns, Dt 16:11
and the widow who are **w** your towns. Dt 16:14
w any of your towns that the LORD your Dt 17:2
any case **w** your towns that is too Dt 17:8
that he shall choose **w** one of your Dt 23:16
who are in your land **w** your towns. Dt 24:14
that they may eat **w** your towns and be Dt 26:12
w the land that the LORD swore to your Dt 28:11
ones, and the sojourner **w** your towns, Dt 31:12
for **w** three days you are to pass over this Jos 1:11
city and all that is **w** it shall be devoted Jos 6:17
people of Ephraim **w** the inheritance of Jos 16:9
And they buried him **w** the boundaries of Jgs 2:9
But there was a strong tower **w** the city, Jgs 9:51
did you not deliver them **w** that time? Jgs 11:26
what it is, **w** the seven days of the feast, Jgs 14:12
did not come **w** the days appointed, 1 Sm 13:11
W the passes, by which Jonathan 1 Sm 14:4
killed about twenty men **w** as it were 1 Sm 14:14
and he raved **w** his house while 1 Sm 18:10
Nabal's heart was merry **w** him, 1 Sm 25:36
things, and his heart died **w** him, 1 Sm 25:37
Saul was lying **w** the encampment, 1 Sm 26:5
lay Saul sleeping **w** the encampment, 1 Sm 26:7
me any longer **w** the borders of 1 Sm 27:1
of Judah together to me **w** three days, 2 Sm 20:4
and he built this **w** as an inner 1 Kgs 6:16
The cedar **w** the house was carved in 1 Kgs 6:18
Its opening was **w** a crown that 1 Kgs 7:31
dogs shall eat Jezebel **w** the walls of 1 Kgs 21:23
it was told **w** the king's household. 2 Kgs 7:11
language of Judah **w** the hearing of 2 Kgs 18:26
to their settlements **w** their borders: 1 Chr 6:54
w the chambers of the house of the Ezr 8:29
the fourth day, **w** the house of our God, Ezr 8:33
to give us a secure hold **w** his holy place, Ezr 9:8
if anyone did not come **w** three days, Ezr 10:8
assembled at Jerusalem **w** the three Ezr 10:9
his servant pass the night **w** Jerusalem, Neh 4:22
in the house of God, **w** the temple. Neh 6:10
and large, but the people **w** it were few, Neh 7:4
enraged, and his anger burned **w** him. Est 1:12
Is not their tent-cord plucked up **w** them, Jb 4:21
and not another. My heart faints **w** me! Jb 19:27
answer me, because of my haste **w** me. Jb 20:2
it is the venom of cobras **w** him. Jb 20:14
"And now my soul is poured out **w** me; Jb 30:16
of words; the spirit **w** me constrains me. Jb 32:18
is like wax; it is melted **w** my breast; Ps 22:14
My heart became hot **w** me. As I mused, Ps 39:3
will, O my God; your law is **w** my heart." Ps 40:8
hidden your deliverance **w** my heart; Ps 40:10
soul, and why are you in turmoil **w** me? Ps 42:5
My soul is cast down **w** me; therefore I Ps 42:6
soul, and why are you in turmoil **w** me? Ps 42:11
soul, and why are you in turmoil **w** me? Ps 43:5
W her citadels God has made himself Ps 48:3
O God, and renew a right spirit **w** me. Ps 51:10
My heart is in anguish **w** me; the terrors Ps 55:4
walls, and iniquity and trouble are **w** it; Ps 55:10
w God's house we walked in the throng. Ps 55:14
with integrity of heart **w** my house; Ps 101:2
LORD, O my soul, and all that is **w** me, Ps 103:1
and thirsty, their soul fainted **w** them. Ps 107:5
needy, and my heart is stricken **w** me. Ps 109:22
feet have been standing **w** your gates, Ps 122:2
Peace be **w** your walls and security Ps 122:7
your walls and security **w** your towers!" Ps 122:7
sake I will say, "Peace be **w** you!" Ps 122:8
be like a fruitful vine **w** your house; Ps 128:3
like a weaned child is my soul **w** me. Ps 131:2
When my spirit faints **w** me, you know Ps 142:3
Therefore my spirit faints **w** me; my Ps 143:4
within me; my heart **w** me is appalled. Ps 143:4
gates; he blesses your children **w** you. Ps 147:13
your sight; keep them **w** your heart. Prv 4:21
be pleasant if you keep them **w** you, Prv 22:18
the latch, and my heart was thrilled **w** me. Sg 5:4
(**W** sixty-five years Ephraim will be Is 7:8
heart of the Egyptians will melt **w** them. Is 19:1
spirit of the Egyptians **w** them will be Is 19:3
The LORD has mingled **w** her a spirit of Is 19:14
For thus the Lord said to me, "**W** a year, Is 21:16
night; my spirit **w** me earnestly seeks you. Is 26:9
the language of Judah **w** the hearing of Is 36:11
in my house and **w** my walls a Is 56:5
or destruction **w** your borders; Is 60:18
your wicked thoughts lodge **w** you? Jer 4:14
there is nothing but oppression **w** her. Jer 6:6
violence and destruction are heard **w** her; Jer 6:7
grief is upon me; my heart is sick **w** me. Jer 8:18
the prophets: My heart is broken **w** me; Jer 23:9
W two years I will bring back to this Jer 28:3
of all the nations **w** two years." But Jer 28:11
I will put my law **w** them, and I will Jer 31:33
my heart is wrung **w** me, because I Lam 1:20
it and is bowed down **w** me. Lam 3:20
being as it were a wheel **w** a wheel. Ezk 1:16
to me, "Go, shut yourself **w** your house. Ezk 3:24
is without; pestilence and famine are **w**. Ezk 7:15
likeness, as if a wheel were **w** a wheel. Ezk 10:10
and a new spirit I will put **w** them. Ezk 11:19
or flattering divination **w** the house of Ezk 12:24
w a very little time you were more Ezk 16:47
with all the malice **w** your soul against Ezk 25:6
Syene they shall fall **w** her by the Ezk 30:6
and a new spirit I will put **w** you. Ezk 36:26
And I will put my Spirit **w** you, and Ezk 36:27
And I will put my Spirit **w** you, and Ezk 37:14
long, were fastened all around **w**. Ezk 40:43
at the gates of the inner court, and **w**. Ezk 44:17
any god or man **w** thirty days except to Dn 6:12
me, Daniel, my spirit **w** me was anxious, Dn 7:15
But **w** a few days he shall be broken, Dn 11:20
For the spirit of whoredom is **w** them, Hos 5:4
My heart recoils **w** me; my compassion Hos 11:8
and see the great tumults **w** her, Am 3:9
into our land and treads **w** our border. Mi 5:6
and there shall be hunger **w** you; Mi 6:14
it is not upright **w** him, but the Hab 2:4
Her officials **w** her are roaring lions; her Zep 3:3
The LORD **w** her is righteous; he does no Zep 3:5
and formed the spirit of man **w** him: Zec 12:1
but **w** are full of dead people's bones Mt 23:27
but **w** you are full of hypocrisy and Mt 23:28
that they thus questioned **w** themselves, Mk 2:8
For from **w**, out of the heart of man, Mk 7:21
All these evil things come from **w**, and Mk 7:23
and he will answer from **w**, 'Do not Lk 11:7
give as alms those things that are **w**, Lk 11:41
ground, you and your children **w** you. Lk 19:44
not our hearts burn **w** us while he Lk 24:32
you do not have the love of God **w** you. Jn 5:42
his spirit was provoked **w** him as he Acts 17:16
I who do it, but sin that dwells **w** me. Rom 7:17
I who do it, but sin that dwells **w** me. Rom 7:20
is a temple of the Holy Spirit **w** you, 1 Cor 6:19
turn—fighting without and fear **w**. 2 Cor 7:5
according to the power at work **w** us, Eph 3:20
energy that he powerfully works **w** me. Col 1:29
By the Holy Spirit who dwells **w** us, 2 Tm 1:14
this, that your passions are at war **w** you? Jas 4:1
who did not stay **w** their own position of Jude 1:6
wings, are full of eyes all around and **w**, Rv 4:8
throne a scroll written **w** and on the back, Rv 5:1
of his covenant was seen **w** his temple. Rv 11:19

WITHOUT (315)
The earth was **w** form and void, and Gn 1:2
him. Joseph is **w** doubt torn to pieces." Gn 37:33
and **w** your consent no one shall lift up Gn 41:44
Your lamb shall be **w** blemish, a male a Ex 12:5
lit up the night **w** one coming near the Ex 14:20
out for nothing, **w** payment of money. Ex 21:11
or is driven away, **w** anyone seeing it, Ex 22:10
of the herd and two rams **w** blemish, Ex 29:1
the herd, he shall offer a male **w** blemish. Lv 1:3
goats, he shall bring a male **w** blemish, Lv 1:10
he shall offer it **w** blemish before the Lv 3:1
or female, he shall offer it **w** blemish. Lv 3:6
bull from the herd **w** blemish to the LORD Lv 4:3
as his offering a goat, a male **w** blemish, Lv 4:23
his offering a goat, a female **w** blemish, Lv 4:28
he shall bring a female **w** blemish Lv 4:32
a ram **w** blemish out of the flock, Lv 5:15
to the priest a ram **w** blemish out of the Lv 5:18
to the LORD a ram **w** blemish out of the Lv 6:6
ram for a burnt offering, both **w** blemish, Lv 9:2
and a lamb, both a year old **w** blemish, Lv 9:3
shall take two male lambs **w** blemish, Lv 14:10
one ewe lamb a year old **w** blemish, Lv 14:10
the discharge touches **w** having rinsed Lv 15:11
for you it shall be a male **w** blemish, Lv 22:19
lamb a year old **w** blemish as a burnt Lv 23:12
seven lambs a year old **w** blemish, Lv 23:18
Sabbaths while it lies desolate **w** them, Lv 26:43
lamb a year old **w** blemish for a burnt Nm 6:14
ewe lamb a year old **w** blemish as a sin Nm 6:14
and one ram **w** blemish as a peace Nm 6:14
done unintentionally **w** the Nm 15:24
Israel to bring you a red heifer **w** defect, Nm 19:2
two male lambs a year old **w** blemish, Nm 28:3
two male lambs a year old **w** blemish, Nm 28:9
male lambs a year old **w** blemish; Nm 28:11
a year old; see that they are **w** blemish; Nm 28:19
offering. See that they are **w** blemish Nm 28:31
male lambs a year old **w** blemish; Nm 29:2
a year old: see that they are **w** blemish. Nm 29:8
a year old; they shall be **w** blemish; Nm 29:13

male lambs a year old **w** blemish, Nm 29:17
male lambs a year old **w** blemish, Nm 29:20
male lambs a year old **w** blemish, Nm 29:23
male lambs a year old **w** blemish, Nm 29:26
male lambs a year old **w** blemish, Nm 29:29
male lambs a year old **w** blemish, Nm 29:32
male lambs a year old **w** blemish, Nm 29:36
kills any person **w** intent may flee Nm 35:11
kills any person **w** intent may flee Nm 35:15
if he pushed him suddenly **w** enmity, Nm 35:22
anything on him **w** lying in wait Nm 35:22
and **w** seeing him dropped it on him, Nm 35:23
w being at enmity with him in time past; Dt 4:42
in which you will eat bread **w** scarcity, Dt 8:9
neighbor unintentionally **w** having Dt 19:4
A God of faithfulness and **w** iniquity, Dt 32:4
and that he will **w** fail drive out from Jos 3:10
strikes any person **w** intent or Jos 20:3
who killed a person **w** intent could flee Jos 20:9
and their camels were **w** number, Jgs 7:12
the woman was left **w** her two sons and Ru 1:5
has not left you this day **w** a redeemer, Ru 4:14
blood by killing David **w** cause?" 1 Sm 19:5
either great or small **w** disclosing it to 1 Sm 20:2
for having shed blood **w** cause or for 1 Sm 25:31
of Joab never be **w** one who has a 2 Sm 3:29
w coming into the king's presence. 2 Sm 14:28
to the ground **w** striking a second 2 Sm 20:10
for the blood that Joab shed **w** cause. 1 Kgs 2:31
w the knowledge of my father David, 1 Kgs 2:32
Syria and Israel continued **w** war. 1 Kgs 22:1
is it **w** the LORD that I have come up 2 Kgs 18:25
and cedar timbers **w** number, for the 1 Chr 22:4
all kinds of craftsmen **w** number, 1 Chr 22:15
w regard to their divisions, 2 Chr 5:11
the people were **w** number who came 2 Chr 12:3
a long time Israel was **w** the true God, 2 Chr 15:3
and **w** a teaching priest and without 2 Chr 15:3
without a teaching priest and **w** law, 2 Chr 15:3
men in full and **w** delay from the royal Ezr 6:8
that be given to them day by day **w** fail, Ezr 6:9
oil, and salt **w** prescribing how much. Ezr 7:22
inside the inner court **w** being called, Est 4:11
that **w** fail they would keep these two Est 9:27
me against him to destroy him **w** reason." Jb 2:3
they perish forever **w** anyone regarding Jb 4:20
do they not die, and that **w** wisdom?' Jb 4:21
marvelous things **w** number: Jb 5:9
Can that which is tasteless be eaten **w** salt, Jb 6:6
shuttle and come to their end **w** hope. Jb 7:6
and multiplies my wounds **w** cause; Jb 9:17
Then I would speak **w** fear of him, for I Jb 9:35
darkness, like deep shadow **w** any order, Jb 10:22
you will lift up your face **w** blemish; Jb 11:15
They grope in the dark **w** light, and he Jb 12:25
have told, **w** hiding it from their fathers, Jb 15:18
Their bull breeds **w** fail; their cow Jb 21:10
They lie all night naked, **w** clothing, and Jb 24:7
They go about naked, **w** clothing; Jb 24:10
It hurls at him **w** pity; he flees from its Jb 27:22
of clothing, or the needy **w** covering, Jb 31:19
eaten its yield **w** payment and made Jb 31:39
You say, 'I am pure, **w** transgression; I Jb 33:9
incurable, though I am **w** transgression.' Jb 34:6
shatters the mighty **w** investigation and Jb 34:24
'Job speaks **w** knowledge; his words are Jb 34:35
knowledge; his words are **w** insight.' Jb 34:35
talk; he multiplies words **w** knowledge." Jb 35:16
by the sword and die **w** knowledge. Jb 36:12
darkens counsel by words **w** knowledge? Jb 38:2
there is not his like, a creature **w** fear. Jb 41:33
is this that hides counsel **w** knowledge?' Jb 42:3
with evil or plundered my enemy **w** cause, Ps 7:4
I have trusted in the LORD **w** wavering. Ps 26:1
like a horse or a mule, **w** understanding, Ps 32:9
For **w** cause they hid their net for me; Ps 35:7
for me; **w** cause they dug a pit for my life. Ps 35:7
I did not know tore at me **w** ceasing; Ps 35:15
wink the eye who hate me **w** cause. Ps 35:19
in his pomp yet **w** understanding is like Ps 49:20
shooting at him suddenly and **w** fear. Ps 64:4
my head are those who hate me **w** cause; Ps 69:4
my hand is stretched out **w** wearying; Ps 77:2
came, young locusts **w** number, Ps 105:34
words of hate, and attack me **w** cause. Ps 109:3
Princes persecute me **w** cause, but Ps 119:161
let us ambush the innocent **w** reason; Prv 1:11
and will be at ease, **w** dread of disaster." Prv 1:33
W having any chief, officer, or ruler, Prv 6:7
is a beautiful woman **w** discretion. Prv 11:22
a king, but **w** people a prince is ruined. Prv 14:28
W counsel plans fail, but with many Prv 15:22
Desire **w** knowledge is not good, and Prv 19:2
Who has wounds **w** cause? Prv 23:29
against your neighbor **w** cause, Prv 24:28
Like clouds and wind **w** rain is a man Prv 25:14
A man **w** self-control is like a city Prv 25:28
a city broken into and left **w** walls. Prv 25:28
concubines, and virgins **w** number. Sg 6:8
leaf withers, and like a garden **w** water. Is 1:30
large and beautiful houses, **w** inhabitant. Is 5:9
"Until cities lie waste **w** inhabitant, and Is 6:11
without inhabitant, and houses **w** people, Is 6:11
together; **w** the bow they were captured. Is 22:3
for Tyre is laid waste, **w** house or harbor! Is 23:1
For this is a people **w** discernment; Is 27:11
down to Egypt, **w** asking for my direction, Is 30:2
be missing; none shall be **w** her mate. Is 34:16
is it **w** the LORD that I have come up Is 36:10
sit on the ground **w** a throne, O daughter Is 47:1
and you shall be redeemed **w** money." Is 52:3
buy wine and milk **w** money and without Is 55:1
and milk without money and **w** price. Is 55:1
are blind; they are all **w** knowledge; Is 56:10
his cities are in ruins, **w** inhabitant. Jer 2:15
have forgotten me days **w** number. Jer 2:32
your cities will be ruins **w** inhabitant. Jer 4:7
and behold, it was **w** form and void; Jer 4:23
of Judah a desolation, **w** inhabitant." Jer 9:11
Every man is stupid and **w** knowledge; Jer 10:14
treasures I will give as spoil, **w** price, Jer 15:13
cities that the LORD overthrew **w** pity; Jer 20:16
w inhabitant'?" And all the people Jer 26:9
'It is a desolation, **w** man or beast; Jer 32:43
you say, 'It is a waste **w** man or beast,' Jer 33:10
desolate, **w** man or inhabitant or beast, Jer 33:10
this place that is waste, **w** man or beast, Jer 33:12
of Judah a desolation **w** inhabitant." Jer 34:22
was it **w** our husbands' approval that Jer 44:19
and a waste and a curse, **w** inhabitant, Jer 44:22
become a waste, a ruin, **w** inhabitant. Jer 46:19
than locusts; they are **w** number. Jer 46:23
of Heshbon fugitives stop **w** strength, Jer 48:45
Every man is stupid and **w** knowledge; Jer 51:17
of Babylon a desolation, **w** inhabitant. Jer 51:29
a horror and a hissing, **w** inhabitant. Jer 51:37
they fled **w** strength before the pursuer. Lam 1:6
Lord has swallowed up **w** mercy all the Lam 2:2
long ago; he has thrown down **w** pity; Lam 2:17
day of your anger, slaughtering **w** pity. Lam 2:21
brought me into darkness **w** any light; Lam 3:2
anger and pursued us, killing **w** pity; Lam 3:43
"My eyes will flow **w** ceasing, without Lam 3:49
will flow without ceasing, **w** respite, Lam 3:49
those who were my enemies **w** cause; Lam 3:52
straight forward, **w** turning as they went. Ezk 1:9
go, they went, **w** turning as they went. Ezk 1:12
their four directions **w** turning as they Ezk 1:17
The sword is **w**; pestilence and famine Ezk 7:15
their four directions **w** turning as they Ezk 10:11
the others followed **w** turning as they Ezk 10:11
that I have not done **w** cause all that I Ezk 14:23
extorted from the sojourner **w** justice. Ezk 22:29
piece after piece, **w** making any choice. Ezk 24:6
securely, all of them dwelling **w** walls, Ezk 38:11
into the outer court **w** laying there the Ezk 42:14
offer a male goat **w** blemish for a sin Ezk 43:22
bull from the herd **w** blemish and a Ezk 43:23
and a ram from the flock **w** blemish. Ezk 43:23
and a ram from the flock, **w** blemish. Ezk 43:25
take a bull from the herd **w** blemish, Ezk 45:18
bulls and seven rams **w** blemish, Ezk 45:23
shall be six lambs **w** blemish and a Ezk 46:4
without blemish and a ram **w** blemish. Ezk 46:4
offer a bull from the herd **w** blemish, Ezk 46:6
and a ram, which shall be **w** blemish. Ezk 46:6
lamb a year old **w** blemish for a burnt Ezk 46:13
youths **w** blemish, of good appearance Dn 1:4
the whole earth, **w** touching the ground. Dn 8:5
W warning he shall destroy many. Dn 8:25
shall come in **w** warning and obtain Dn 11:21
W warning he shall come into the Dn 11:24
shall dwell many days **w** king or prince, Hos 3:4
king or prince, **w** sacrifice or pillar, Hos 3:4
or pillar, **w** ephod or household gods. Hos 3:4
and a people **w** understanding shall Hos 4:14
is like a dove, silly and **w** sense, Hos 7:11
GOD does nothing **w** revealing his secret Am 3:7
it shall be night to you, **w** vision, Mi 3:6
vision, and darkness to you, **w** divination. Mi 3:6
dead bodies **w** end—they stumble over Na 3:3
her strength; Egypt too, and that **w** limit; Na 3:9
cities have been made desolate, **w** a man, Zep 3:6
without a man, **w** an inhabitant. Zep 3:6
shall be inhabited as villages **w** walls, Zec 2:4
and helpless, like sheep **w** a shepherd. Mt 9:36
You received **w** paying; give without Mt 10:8
received without paying; give **w** pay. Mt 10:8
he said nothing to them **w** a parable. Mt 13:34
"A prophet is not **w** honor except in his Mt 13:57
"Are you also still **w** understanding? Mt 15:16
you get in here **w** a wedding garment?' Mt 22:12
to have done, **w** neglecting the others. Mt 23:23
He did not speak to them **w** a parable, Mk 4:34
said to them, "A prophet is not **w** honor, Mk 6:4
they were like sheep **w** a shepherd. Mk 6:34
"Then are you also **w** understanding? Mk 7:18
of our enemies, might serve him **w** fear, Lk 1:74
a house on the ground **w** a foundation. Lk 6:49
to have done, **w** neglecting the others. Lk 11:42
people walk over them **w** knowing it." Lk 11:44
first took a wife, and died **w** children. Lk 20:29
and **w** him was not any thing made that Jn 1:3
of God, for he gives the Spirit **w** measure. Jn 3:34
our law judge a man **w** first giving him a Jn 7:51
"Let him who is **w** sin among you be the Jn 8:7
be fulfilled: 'They hated me **w** a cause.' Jn 15:25
And for three days he was **w** sight, and Acts 9:9
him, "Please come to us **w** delay." Acts 9:38
and accompany them **w** hesitation, Acts 10:20
I was sent for, I came **w** objection. Acts 10:29
he did not leave himself **w** witness, Acts 14:17
in the temple, **w** any crowd or tumult. Acts 24:18
Since they had been **w** food for a long Acts 27:21
continued in suspense and **w** food, Acts 27:33
with all boldness and **w** hindrance. Acts 28:31
his Son, that **w** ceasing I mention you Rom 1:9
have been made. So they are **w** excuse. Rom 1:20
all who have sinned **w** the law will Rom 2:12
the law will also perish **w** the law, Rom 2:12
all who believe **w** being circumcised, Rom 4:11
upon the earth fully and **w** delay." Rom 9:28
they to hear **w** someone preaching? Rom 10:14
rich! **W** us you have become kings! 1 Cor 4:8
Who plants a vineyard **w** eating any of 1 Cor 9:7
who tends a flock **w** getting some of 1 Cor 9:7
the meat market **w** raising any 1 Cor 10:25
set before you **w** raising any 1 Cor 10:27
eats and drinks **w** discerning the 1 Cor 11:29
the world, and none is **w** meaning, 1 Cor 14:10
turn—fighting **w** and fear within. 2 Cor 7:5
that leads to salvation **w** regret, 2 Cor 7:10
another, they are **w** understanding. 2 Cor 10:12
w boasting of work already done in 2 Cor 10:16
in hunger and thirst, often **w** food, 2 Cor 11:27
having no hope and **w** God in the Eph 2:12
w spot or wrinkle or any such thing, Eph 5:27
that she might be holy and **w** blemish. Eph 5:27
more bold to speak the word **w** fear. Phil 1:14
Do all things **w** grumbling or Phil 2:14
children of God **w** blemish in the Phil 2:15
with a circumcision made **w** hands, Col 2:11
puffed up **w** reason by his sensuous Col 2:18
pray **w** ceasing, 1 Thes 5:17
we eat anyone's bread **w** paying for it, 2 Thes 3:8
w understanding either what they are 1 Tm 1:7
lifting holy hands **w** anger or 1 Tm 2:8
well, so that they may be **w** reproach. 1 Tm 5:7
you to keep these rules **w** prejudging, 1 Tm 5:21
slanderous, **w** self-control, 2 Tm 3:3
to do nothing **w** your consent in Phlm 1:14
has been tempted as we are, yet **w** sin. Heb 4:15
He is **w** father or mother or genealogy, Heb 7:3
And it was not **w** an oath. For those Heb 7:20
priests were made such **w** an oath, Heb 7:20
but once a year, and not **w** taking blood, Heb 9:7
Spirit offered himself **w** blemish to Heb 9:14
covenant was inaugurated **w** blood. Heb 9:18
and **w** the shedding of blood there is no Heb 9:22
confession of our hope **w** wavering, Heb 10:23
law of Moses dies **w** mercy on the Heb 10:28
And **w** faith it is impossible to please Heb 11:6
If you are left **w** discipline, in which all Heb 12:8
and for the holiness **w** which no one Heb 12:14
who gives generously to all **w** reproach, Jas 1:5
For judgment is **w** mercy to one who Jas 2:13
warmed and filled," **w** giving them the Jas 2:16
like that of a lamb **w** blemish or spot. 1 Pt 1:19
they may be won **w** a word by the 1 Pt 3:1
hospitality to one another **w** grumbling. 1 Pt 4:9
to be found by him **w** spot or blemish, 2 Pt 3:14
feasts, as they feast with you **w** fear, Jude 1:12
the spring of the water of life **w** payment. Rv 21:6
desires take the water of life **w** price. Rv 22:17

WITHSTAND (9)

they could no longer **w** their enemies. Jgs 2:14
and irresolute and could not **w** them. 2 Chr 13:7
now you think to **w** the kingdom of 2 Chr 13:8
might, so that none is able to **w** you. 2 Chr 20:6
two will **w** him—a threefold cord is Eccl 4:12
the hands of those whom I cannot **w**. Lam 1:14
will be able to **w** or contradict. Lk 21:15
But they could not **w** the wisdom and Acts 6:10
you may be able to **w** in the evil day, Eph 6:13

WITHSTOOD (3)
one of all their enemies had **w** them, Jos 21:44
and they **w** King Uzziah and said to 2 Chr 26:18
kingdom of Persia **w** me twenty-one Dn 10:13

WITNESS (130)
that this may be a **w** for me that I dug Gn 21:30
And let it be a **w** between you and me." Gn 31:44
"This heap is a **w** between you and me Gn 31:48
us, see, God is **w** between you and me." Gn 31:50
This heap is a **w**, and the pillar is a Gn 31:52
heap is a witness, and the pillar is a **w**, Gn 31:52
not bear false **w** against your neighbor. Ex 20:16
with a wicked man to be a malicious **w**. Ex 23:1
evil, nor shall you bear **w** in a lawsuit, Ex 23:2
adjuration to testify, and though he is a **w**, Lv 5:1
herself, and there is no **w** against her, Nm 5:13
to death on the testimony of one **w**. Nm 35:30
heaven and earth to **w** against you today, Dt 4:26
not bear false **w** against your neighbor. Dt 5:20
be put to death on the evidence of one **w**. Dt 17:6
"A single **w** shall not suffice against a Dt 19:15
If a malicious **w** arises to accuse a Dt 19:16
and if the **w** is a false witness and has Dt 19:18
witness is a false **w** and has accused his Dt 19:18
and earth to **w** against you today, Dt 30:19
this song may be a **w** for me against the Dt 31:19
confront them as a **w** (for it will live Dt 31:21
that it may be there for a **w** against you. Dt 31:26
heaven and earth to **w** against them. Dt 31:28
but to be a **w** between us and you, and Jos 22:27
but to be a **w** between us and you.' Jos 22:28
the people of Gad called the altar **W**, Jos 22:34
"it is a **w** between us that the LORD is Jos 22:34
this stone shall be a **w** against us, Jos 24:27
Therefore it shall be a **w** against you, Jos 24:27
"The LORD will be **w** between us, Jgs 11:10
ark of the LORD is a **w** to this day in the 1 Sm 6:18
to them, "The LORD is **w** against you, 1 Sm 12:5
you, and his anointed is **w** this day, 1 Sm 12:5
in my hand." And they said, "He is **w**." 1 Sm 12:5
said to the people, "The LORD is **w**, 1 Sm 12:6
"The LORD, the God of Israel, be **w**! 1 Sm 20:12
fitting for us to **w** the king's dishonor, Ezr 4:14
me up, which is a **w** against me, Jb 16:8
Even now, behold, my **w** is in heaven, Jb 16:19
forever, a faithful **w** in the skies." Selah Ps 89:37
a false **w** who breathes out lies, and one Prv 6:19
evidence, but a false **w** utters deceit. Prv 12:17
A faithful **w** does not lie, but a false Prv 14:5
not lie, but a false **w** breathes out lies. Prv 14:5
A truthful **w** saves lives, but one who Prv 14:25
A false **w** will not go unpunished, and Prv 19:5
A false **w** will not go unpunished, and Prv 19:9
A worthless **w** mocks at justice, and Prv 19:28
A false **w** will perish, but the word of a Prv 21:28
Be not a **w** against your neighbor Prv 24:28
who bears false **w** against his Prv 25:18
look on their faces bears **w** against them; Is 3:9
be a sign and a **w** to the LORD of hosts Is 19:20
be for the time to come as a **w** forever. Is 30:8
Behold, I made him a **w** to the peoples, a Is 55:4
I am the one who knows, and I am **w**, Jer 29:23
be a true and faithful **w** against us if we Jer 42:5
and let the Lord GOD be a **w** against you, Mi 1:2
the LORD was **w** between you and Mal 2:14
I will be a swift **w** against the sorcerers, Mal 3:5
to bear **w** before them and the Gentiles. Mt 10:18
sexual immorality, theft, false **w**, Mt 15:19
not steal, You shall not bear false **w**, Mt 19:18
Thus you **w** against yourselves that Mt 23:31
Do not steal, Do not bear false **w**, Mk 10:19
for my sake, to bear **w** before them. Mk 13:9
For many bore false **w** against him, Mk 14:56
stood up and bore false **w** against him, Mk 14:57
Do not steal, Do not bear false **w**, Lk 18:20
will be your opportunity to bear **w**. Lk 21:13
He came as a **w**, to bear witness about the Jn 1:7
as a witness, to bear **w** about the light, Jn 1:7
light, but came to bear **w** about the light. Jn 1:8
(John bore **w** about him, and cried out, Jn 1:15
And John bore **w**: "I saw the Spirit Jn 1:32
seen and have borne **w** that this is the Jn 1:34
and needed no one to bear **w** about man, Jn 2:25
know, and bear **w** to what we have seen, Jn 3:11
the Jordan, to whom you bore **w**—look, Jn 3:26
You yourselves bear me **w**, that I said, 'I Jn 3:28
He bears **w** to what he has seen and Jn 3:32
If I alone bear **w** about myself, my Jn 5:31
There is another who bears **w** about me, Jn 5:32
to John, and he has borne **w** to the truth. Jn 5:33
bear **w** about me that the Father has sent Jn 5:36
sent me has himself borne **w** about me. Jn 5:37
life; and it is they that bear **w** about me, Jn 5:39
him, "You are bearing **w** about yourself; Jn 8:13
"Even if I do bear **w** about myself, Jn 8:14
I am the one who bears **w** about myself, Jn 8:18
Father who sent me bears **w** about me." Jn 8:18
in my Father's name bear **w** about me, Jn 10:25
him from the dead continued to bear **w**. Jn 12:17
the Father, he will bear **w** about me. Jn 15:26
And you also will bear **w**, because you Jn 15:27
I said is wrong, bear **w** about the wrong; Jn 18:23
into the world—to bear **w** to the truth. Jn 18:37
saw it has borne **w**—his testimony is Jn 19:35
who is bearing **w** about these things, Jn 21:24
with us a **w** to his resurrection." Acts 1:22
words he bore **w** and continued to Acts 2:40
had the tent of **w** in the wilderness, Acts 7:44
the prophets bear **w** that everyone Acts 10:43
who bore **w** to the word of his grace, Acts 14:3
he did not leave himself without **w**, Acts 14:17
who knows the heart, bore **w** to them, Acts 15:8
whole council of elders can bear me **w**. Acts 22:5
you will be a **w** for him to everyone Acts 22:15
of Stephen your **w** was being shed, Acts 22:20
as a servant and **w** to the things in Acts 26:16
For God is my **w**, whom I serve with my Rom 1:9
while their conscience also bears **w**, Rom 2:15
Law and the Prophets bear **w** to it— Rom 3:21
Spirit himself bears **w** with our spirit Rom 8:16
my conscience bears me **w** in the Holy Rom 9:1
I bear them **w** that they have a zeal for Rom 10:2
But I call God to **w** against me—it 2 Cor 1:23
For God is my **w**, how I yearn for you all Phil 1:8
For I bear him **w** that he has worked Col 4:13
with a pretext for greed—God is **w**. 1 Thes 2:5
while God also bore **w** by signs and Heb 2:4
And the Holy Spirit also bears **w** to us; Heb 10:15
a fellow elder and a **w** of the sufferings of 1 Pt 5:1
who bore **w** to the word of God and to the Rv 1:2
and from Jesus Christ the faithful **w**, the Rv 1:5
in the days of Antipas my faithful **w**, Rv 2:13
of the Amen, the faithful and true **w**, Rv 3:14
word of God and for the **w** they had borne. Rv 6:9
of the tent of **w** in heaven was opened, Rv 15:5

WITNESSED (2)
deeds shall be signed and sealed and **w**, Jer 32:44
For it is **w** of him, "You are a priest Heb 7:17

WITNESSES (46)
be put to death on the evidence of **w**. Nm 35:30
the evidence of two **w** or of three Dt 17:6
two witnesses or of three **w** the one who is Dt 17:6
The hand of the **w** shall be first against Dt 17:7
the evidence of two **w** or of three Dt 19:15
witnesses or of three **w** shall a charge be Dt 19:15
"You are **w** against yourselves that you Jos 24:22
serve him." And they said, "We are **w**." Jos 24:22
"You are **w** this day that I have bought Ru 4:9
of his native place. You are **w** this day." Ru 4:10
the gate and the elders said, "We are **w**. Ru 4:11
You renew your **w** against me and Jb 10:17
for false **w** have risen against me, and Ps 27:12
Malicious **w** rise up; they ask me of Ps 35:11
And I will get reliable **w**, Uriah the priest Is 8:2
Let them bring their **w** to prove them Is 43:9
"You are my **w**," declares the LORD, "and Is 43:10
and you are my **w**," declares the LORD, Is 43:12
of old and declared it? And you are my **w**! Is 44:8
Their **w** neither see nor know, that they Is 44:9
I signed the deed, sealed it, got **w**, and Jer 32:10
the presence of the **w** who signed the Jer 32:12
for money and get **w**"—though the city Jer 32:25
by the evidence of two or three **w**. Mt 18:16
though many false **w** came forward. Mt 26:60
What further **w** do we need? Mt 26:65
and said, "What further **w** do we need? Mk 14:63
So you are **w** and you consent to the Lk 11:48
You are **w** of these things. Lk 24:48
you will be my **w** in Jerusalem and in Acts 1:8
God raised up, and of that we all are **w**. Acts 2:32
raised from the dead. To this we are **w**. Acts 3:15
And we are **w** to these things, and so is Acts 5:32
and they set up false **w** who said, "This Acts 6:13
And the **w** laid down their garments at Acts 7:58
And we are **w** of all that he did both Acts 10:39
us who had been chosen by God as **w**, Acts 10:41
who are now his **w** to the people. Acts 13:31
by the evidence of two or three **w**. 2 Cor 13:1
You are **w**, and God also, how holy 1 Thes 2:10
on the evidence of two or three **w**. 1 Tm 5:19
in the presence of many **w**. 1 Tm 6:12
presence of many **w** entrust to faithful 2 Tm 2:2
on the evidence of two or three **w**. Heb 10:28
surrounded by so great a cloud of **w**, Heb 12:1
And I will grant authority to my two **w**, Rv 11:3

WITS' (1)
drunken men and were at their **w** end. Ps 107:27

WIVES (120)
And Lamech took two **w**. The name of Gn 4:19
Lamech said to his **w**: "Adah and Zillah, Gn 4:23
you **w** of Lamech, listen to what I say: Gn 4:23
And they took as their **w** any they chose. Gn 6:2
your wife, and your sons' **w** with you. Gn 6:18
wife and his sons' **w** with him went into Gn 7:7
wife and the three **w** of his sons with Gn 7:13
your sons and your sons' **w** with you. Gn 8:16
and his wife and his sons' **w** with him. Gn 8:18
And Abram and Nahor took **w**. The Gn 11:29
took as his wife, besides the **w** he had, Gn 28:9
Give me my **w** and my children for Gn 30:26
and set his sons and his **w** on camels. Gn 31:17
or if you take **w** besides my daughters, Gn 31:50
night he arose and took his two **w**, Gn 32:22
Let us take their daughters as **w**, and Gn 34:21
wealth, all their little ones and their **w**, Gn 34:29
Esau took his **w** from the Canaanites: Gn 36:2
Then Esau took his **w**, his sons, his Gn 36:6
of Bilhah and Zilpah, his father's **w**. Gn 37:2
for your little ones and for your **w**, Gn 45:19
their father, their little ones, and their **w**, Gn 46:5
not including Jacob's sons' **w**, Gn 46:26
and your **w** shall become widows and Ex 22:24
of gold that are in the ears of your **w**, Ex 32:2
Our **w** and our little ones will become a Nm 14:3
of their tents, together with their **w**, Nm 16:27
Our little ones, our **w**, our livestock, Nm 32:26
Only your **w**, your little ones, and your Dt 3:19
shall not acquire many **w** for himself, Dt 17:17
"If a man has two **w**, the one loved and Dt 21:15
your little ones, your **w**, and the Dt 29:11
Your **w**, your little ones, and your Jos 1:14
daughters they took to themselves for **w**, Jgs 3:6
his own offspring, for he had many **w**. Jgs 8:30
shall we do for **w** for those who are Jgs 21:7
give them any of our daughters for **w**?" Jgs 21:7
shall we do for **w** for those who are Jgs 21:16
cannot give them **w** from our Jgs 21:18
of Benjamin did so and took their **w**, Jgs 21:23
These took Moabite **w**; the name of the Ru 1:4
He had two **w**. The name of the one was 1 Sm 1:2
and both of them became his **w**. 1 Sm 25:43
household, and David with his two **w**, 1 Sm 27:3
and their **w** and sons and daughters 1 Sm 30:3
David's two **w** also had been taken 1 Sm 30:5
taken, and David rescued his two **w**. 1 Sm 30:18
went up there, and his two **w** also, 2 Sm 2:2
concubines and **w** from Jerusalem, 2 Sm 5:13
and your master's **w** into your arms 2 Sm 12:8
I will take your **w** before your eyes 2 Sm 12:11
shall lie with your **w** in the sight of 2 Sm 12:11
lives of your **w** and your concubines, 2 Sm 19:5
He had 700 **w**, princesses, and 300 1 Kgs 11:3
And his **w** turned away his heart. 1 Kgs 11:3
was old his **w** turned away his 1 Kgs 11:4
And so he did for all his foreign **w**, 1 Kgs 11:8
your best **w** and children also are 1 Kgs 20:3
gold, your **w** and your children." 1 Kgs 20:5
sent to me for my **w** and my children, 1 Kgs 20:7
The king's mother, the king's **w**, his 2 Kgs 24:15
the father of Tekoa, had two **w**, 1 Chr 4:5
36,000, for they had many **w** and sons. 1 Chr 7:4
sent away Hushim and Baara his **w**. 1 Chr 8:8
David took more **w** in Jerusalem, 1 Chr 14:3
Happy are your **w**! Happy are these 2 Chr 9:7
above all his **w** and concubines (he 2 Chr 11:21
(he took eighteen **w** and sixty 2 Chr 11:21
and procured **w** for them. 2 Chr 11:23
he took fourteen **w** and had 2 Chr 13:21
LORD, with their little ones, their **w**, 2 Chr 20:13
your people, your children, your **w**, 2 Chr 21:14
house, and also his sons and his **w**, 2 Chr 21:17
Jehoiada got for him two **w**, and he 2 Chr 24:3
daughters and our **w** are in captivity 2 Chr 29:9
with all their little children, their **w**, 2 Chr 31:18
daughters to be **w** for themselves and Ezr 9:2
put away all these **w** and their children, Ezr 10:3
of the land and from the foreign **w**." Ezr 10:11
have taken foreign **w** come at Ezr 10:14
themselves to put away their **w**, Ezr 10:19
your sons, your daughters, your **w**, Neh 4:14
and of their **w** against their Jewish Neh 5:1
of the lands to the Law of God, their **w**, Neh 10:28
will be plundered and their **w** ravished. Is 13:16
over to others, their fields and **w** together, Jer 6:12
I will give their **w** to others and their Jer 8:10
none to bury them—them, their **w**, Jer 14:16
let their **w** become childless and Jer 18:21
Take **w** and have sons and daughters; Jer 29:6
take **w** for your sons, and give your Jer 29:6
adultery with their neighbors' **w**, Jer 29:23
no wine all our days, ourselves, our **w**, Jer 35:8
All your **w** and your sons shall be led Jer 38:23

of the kings of Judah, the evil of their **w**, Jer 44:9
your own evil, and the evil of your **w**, Jer 44:9
knew that their **w** had made offerings Jer 44:15
You and your **w** have declared with Jer 44:25
that the king and his lords, his **w**, Dn 5:2
and the king and his lords, his **w**, Dn 5:3
you, and you and your lords, your **w**, Dn 5:23
lions—they, their children, and their **w**. Dn 6:24
by itself, and their **w** by themselves; Zec 12:12
by itself, and their **w** by themselves; Zec 12:12
by itself, and their **w** by themselves; Zec 12:13
by itself, and their **w** by themselves; Zec 12:13
by itself, and their **w** by themselves. Zec 12:14
Moses allowed you to divorce your **w**, Mt 19:8
and they all, with **w** and children, Acts 21:5
let those who have **w** live as though 1 Cor 7:29
W, submit to your own husbands, as Eph 5:22
so also **w** should submit in everything Eph 5:24
Husbands, love your **w**, as Christ loved Eph 5:25
should love their **w** as their own Eph 5:28
W, submit to your husbands, as is Col 3:18
Husbands, love your **w**, and do not be Col 3:19
Their **w** likewise must be dignified, 1 Tm 3:11
w, be subject to your own husbands, 1 Pt 3:1
a word by the conduct of their **w**— 1 Pt 3:1
live with your **w** in an understanding 1 Pt 3:7

WIZARD (2)
is a medium or a **w** shall surely be put Lv 20:27
or a medium or a **w** or a necromancer, Dt 18:11

WIZARDS (4)
"Do not turn to mediums or **w**; do not Lv 19:31
"If a person turns to mediums and **w**, Lv 20:6
and dealt with mediums and with **w**. 2 Kgs 21:6
and dealt with mediums and with **w**. 2 Chr 33:6

WOE (94)
W to you, O Moab! You are undone, Nm 21:29
the camp." And they said, "**W** to us! 1 Sm 4:7
W to us! Who can deliver us from the 1 Sm 4:8
If I am guilty, **w** to me! If I am in the Jb 10:15
W to me, that I sojourn in Meshech, Ps 120:5
Who has **w**? Who has sorrow? Who Prv 23:29
But **w** to him who is alone when he Eccl 4:10
W to you, O land, when your king is Eccl 10:16
like Sodom; they do not hide it. **W** to them! Is 3:9
W to the wicked! It shall be ill with him, Is 3:11
W to those who join house to house, who Is 5:8
W to those who rise early in the morning, Is 5:11
W to those who draw iniquity with cords Is 5:18
W to those who call evil good and good Is 5:20
W to those who are wise in their own Is 5:21
W to those who are heroes at drinking Is 5:22
And I said: "**W** is me! For I am lost; for I Is 6:5
W to those who decree iniquitous decrees, Is 10:1
"I waste away, I waste away. **W** is me! Is 24:16
W to those who go down to Egypt for help Is 31:1
"**W** to him who strives with him who Is 45:9
W to him who says to a father, 'What Is 45:10
horses are swifter than eagles—**w** to us, Jer 4:13
stretching out her hands, "**W** is me! Jer 4:31
W to us, for the day declines, for the Jer 6:4
W is me because of my hurt! My Jer 10:19
in the field. **W** to you, O Jerusalem! Jer 13:27
W is me, my mother, that you bore me, Jer 15:10
"**W** to him who builds his house by Jer 22:13
"**W** to the shepherds who destroy and Jer 23:1
You said, '**W** is me! For the LORD has Jer 45:3
of Israel: "**W** to Nebo, for it is laid waste! Jer 48:1
W to you, O Moab! The people of Jer 48:46
W to them, for their day has come, the Jer 50:27
our head; **w** to us, for we have sinned! Lam 5:16
of lamentation and mourning and **w**. Ezk 2:10
W to the foolish prophets who follow Ezk 13:3
W to the women who sew magic Ezk 13:18
"And after all your wickedness (**w**, Ezk 16:23
all your wickedness (woe, **w** to you! Ezk 16:23
W to the bloody city, to the pot whose Ezk 24:6
the Lord GOD: **W** to the bloody city! Ezk 24:9
W to them, for they have strayed from Hos 7:13
W to them when I depart from them! Hos 9:12
W to you who desire the day of the Am 5:18
"**W** to those who are at ease in Zion, and Am 6:1
"**W** to those who lie on beds of ivory and Am 6:4
W to those who devise wickedness and Mi 2:1
W is me! For I have become as when the Mi 7:1
W to the bloody city, all full of lies and Na 3:1
"**W** to him who heaps up what is not his Hab 2:6
"**W** to him who gets evil gain for his Hab 2:9
"**W** to him who builds a town with Hab 2:12
"**W** to him who makes his neighbors Hab 2:15
W to him who says to a wooden thing, Hab 2:19
W to you inhabitants of the seacoast, Zep 2:5
W to her who is rebellious and defiled, Zep 3:1
"**W** to my worthless shepherd, who Zec 11:17
"**W** to you, Chorazin! Woe to you, Mt 11:21
to you, Chorazin! **W** to you, Bethsaida! Mt 11:21
"**W** to the world for temptations to sin! Mt 18:7
but **w** to the one by whom the Mt 18:7
"But **w** to you, scribes and Pharisees, Mt 23:13
W to you, scribes and Pharisees, Mt 23:15
"**W** to you, blind guides, who say, 'If Mt 23:16
"**W** to you, scribes and Pharisees, Mt 23:23
"**W** to you, scribes and Pharisees, Mt 23:25
"**W** to you, scribes and Pharisees, Mt 23:27
"**W** to you, scribes and Pharisees, Mt 23:29
but **w** to that man by whom the Son of Mt 26:24
but **w** to that man by whom the Son of Mk 14:21
"But **w** to you who are rich, for you have Lk 6:24
"**W** to you who are full now, for you Lk 6:25
"**W** to you who laugh now, for you shall Lk 6:25
"**W** to you, when all people speak well of Lk 6:26
"**W** to you, Chorazin! Woe to you, Lk 10:13
to you, Chorazin! **W** to you, Bethsaida! Lk 10:13
"But **w** to you Pharisees! For you tithe Lk 11:42
W to you Pharisees! For you love the Lk 11:43
W to you! For you are like unmarked Lk 11:44
And he said, "**W** to you lawyers also! Lk 11:46
W to you! For you build the tombs of Lk 11:47
W to you lawyers! For you have taken Lk 11:52
but **w** to the one through whom they Lk 17:1
but **w** to that man by whom he is Lk 22:22
W to me if I do not preach the gospel! 1 Cor 9:16
W to them! For they walked in the way Jude 1:11
as it flew directly overhead, "**W**, woe, Rv 8:13
w, woe to those who dwell on the earth, Rv 8:13
woe, **w** to those who dwell on the earth, Rv 8:13
The first **w** has passed; behold, two woes Rv 9:12
The second **w** has passed; behold, the Rv 11:14
behold, the third **w** is soon to come. Rv 11:14
But **w** to you, O earth and sea, for the Rv 12:12

WOES (1)
passed; behold, two **w** are still to come. Rv 9:12

WOKE (8)
I lay down and slept; I **w** again, for the Ps 3:5
talked with me came again and **w** me, Zec 4:1
When Joseph **w** from sleep, he did as the Mt 1:24
And they went and **w** him, saying, "Save Mt 8:25
And they **w** him and said to him, Mk 4:38
And they went and **w** him, saying, Lk 8:24
He struck Peter on the side and **w** him, Acts 12:7
When the jailer **w** and saw that the Acts 16:27

WOLF (6)
"Benjamin is a ravenous **w**, in the Gn 49:27
The **w** shall dwell with the lamb, and the Is 11:6
The **w** and the lamb shall graze Is 65:25
a **w** from the desert shall devastate them. Jer 5:6
sees the **w** coming and leaves the sheep Jn 10:12
and the **w** snatches them and scatters Jn 10:12

WOLVES (7)
her midst are like **w** tearing the prey, Ezk 22:27
more fierce than the evening **w**; Hab 1:8
judges are evening **w** that leave nothing Zep 3:3
clothing but inwardly are ravenous **w**. Mt 7:15
you out as sheep in the midst of **w**, Mt 10:16
you out as lambs in the midst of **w**. Lk 10:3
my departure fierce **w** will come in Acts 20:29

WOMAN (380)
he made into a **w** and brought her to Gn 2:22
she shall be called **W**, because she was Gn 2:23
He said to the **w**, "Did God actually say, Gn 3:1
And the **w** said to the serpent, "We may Gn 3:2
But the serpent said to the **w**, "You will Gn 3:4
So when the **w** saw that the tree was good Gn 3:6
"The **w** whom you gave to be with me, Gn 3:12
Then the LORD God said to the **w**, "What Gn 3:13
is this that you have done?" The **w** said, Gn 3:13
I will put enmity between you and the **w**, Gn 3:15
To the **w** he said, "I will surely multiply Gn 3:16
you are a **w** beautiful in appearance, Gn 12:11
saw that the **w** was very beautiful. Gn 12:14
And the **w** was taken into Pharaoh's Gn 12:15
man because of the **w** whom you have Gn 20:3
"Cast out this slave **w** with her son, Gn 21:10
the son of this slave **w** shall not be heir Gn 21:10
of the boy and because of your slave **w**. Gn 21:12
a nation of the son of the slave **w** also, Gn 21:13
"Perhaps the **w** may not be willing to Gn 24:5
But if the **w** is not willing to follow you, Gn 24:8
Let the young **w** to whom I shall say, Gn 24:14
The young **w** was very attractive in Gn 24:16
Then the young **w** ran and told her Gn 24:28
'Perhaps the **w** will not follow me.' Gn 24:39
let her be the **w** whom the LORD has Gn 24:44
"Let the young **w** remain with us a Gn 24:55
"Let us call the young **w** and ask her." Gn 24:57
loved the young **w** and spoke tenderly Gn 34:3
give me the young **w** to be my wife." Gn 34:12
and Shaul, the son of a Canaanite **w**. Gn 46:10
Levi went and took as his wife a Levite **w**. Ex 2:1
The **w** conceived and bore a son, and Ex 2:2
among the reeds and sent her servant **w**, Ex 2:5
your wages." So the **w** took the child and Ex 2:9
but each **w** shall ask of her neighbor, Ex 3:22
and any **w** who lives in her house, Ex 3:22
and Shaul, the son of a Canaanite **w**; Ex 6:15
neighbor and every **w** of her neighbor, Ex 11:2
for the third day; do not go near a **w**." Ex 19:15
strive together and hit a pregnant **w**, Ex 21:22
an ox gores a man or a **w** to death, Ex 21:28
not kept it in, and it kills a man or a **w**, Ex 21:29
rest, and the son of your servant **w**, Ex 23:12
And every skillful **w** spun with her Ex 35:25
"Let no man or **w** do anything more for Ex 36:6
'If a **w** conceives and bears a male child, Lv 12:2
"When a man or **w** has a disease on the Lv 13:29
"When a man or a **w** has spots on the Lv 13:38
man lies with a **w** and has an emission Lv 15:18
"When a **w** has a discharge, and the Lv 15:19
"If a **w** has a discharge of blood for Lv 15:25
man who lies with a **w** who is unclean. Lv 15:33
the nakedness of a **w** and of her Lv 18:17
you shall not take a **w** as a rival wife to Lv 18:18
shall not approach a **w** to uncover her Lv 18:19
shall not lie with a male as with a **w**; Lv 18:22
neither shall any **w** give herself to an Lv 18:23
lies sexually with a **w** who is a slave, Lv 19:20
If a man lies with a male as with a **w**, Lv 20:13
If a man takes a **w** and her mother also, Lv 20:14
If a **w** approaches any animal and lies Lv 20:16
it, you shall kill the **w** and the animal; Lv 20:16
lies with a **w** during her menstrual Lv 20:18
"A man or a **w** who is a medium or a Lv 20:27
a prostitute or a **w** who has been defiled, Lv 21:7
shall they marry a **w** divorced from her Lv 21:7
A widow, or a divorced **w**, or a woman Lv 21:14
woman, or a **w** who has been defiled, Lv 21:14
When a man or **w** commits any of the Nm 5:6
priest shall set the **w** before the LORD Nm 5:18
the priest make the **w** take the oath of Nm 5:21
and say to the **w**) 'the LORD make you a Nm 5:21
thigh fall away.' And the **w** shall say, Nm 5:22
he shall make the **w** drink the water of Nm 5:24
shall make the **w** drink the water. Nm 5:26
and the **w** shall become a curse among Nm 5:27
But if the **w** has not defiled herself and Nm 5:28
Then he shall set the **w** before the LORD, Nm 5:30
but the **w** shall bear her iniquity." Nm 5:31
a man or a **w** makes a special vow, Nm 6:2
because of the Cushite **w** whom he had Nm 12:1
for he had married a Cushite **w**. Nm 12:1
brought a Midianite **w** to his family, Nm 25:6
of Israel and the **w** through her belly. Nm 25:8
who was killed with the Midianite **w**, Nm 25:14
of the Midianite **w** who was killed Nm 25:15
If a **w** vows a vow to the LORD and binds Nm 30:3
any vow of a widow or of a divorced **w**, Nm 30:9
and kill every **w** who has known man Nm 31:17
brother, a Hebrew man or a Hebrew **w**, Dt 15:12
a man or **w** who does what is evil in the Dt 17:2
gates that man or **w** who has done this Dt 17:5
stone that man or **w** to death with stones. Dt 17:5
see among the captives a beautiful **w**, Dt 21:11
"A **w** shall not wear a man's garment, Dt 22:5
name upon her, saying, 'I took this **w**, Dt 22:14
father of the young **w** and her mother Dt 22:15
father of the young **w** shall say to the Dt 22:16
give them to the father of the young **w**, Dt 22:19
virginity was not found in the young **w**, Dt 22:20
bring out the young **w** to the door of Dt 22:21
shall die, the man who lay with the **w**, Dt 22:22
who lay with the woman, and the **w**. Dt 22:22
the young **w** because she did not cry for Dt 22:24
man meets a young **w** who is betrothed, Dt 22:25
you shall do nothing to the young **w**; Dt 22:26
the betrothed young **w** cried for help Dt 22:27
father of the young **w** fifty shekels of Dt 22:29
most tender and refined **w** among you, Dt 28:56
among you a man or **w** or clan or tribe Dt 29:18
terror, for young man and **w** alike, Dt 32:25
But the **w** had taken the two men and Jos 2:4
out from there the **w** and all who belong Jos 6:22
the hand of a **w**." Then Deborah arose Jgs 4:9
And a certain **w** threw an upper Jgs 9:53
'A **w** killed him.'" And his young man Jgs 9:54
house, for you are the son of another **w**." Jgs 11:2
LORD appeared to the **w** and said to her, Jgs 13:3
Then the **w** came and told her husband, Jgs 13:6
God came again to the **w** as she sat in Jgs 13:9
So the **w** ran quickly and told her Jgs 13:10
who spoke to this **w**?" And he said, Jgs 13:11
all that I said to the **w** let her be careful. Jgs 13:13
And the **w** bore a son and called his Jgs 13:24
"Is there not a **w** among the daughters of Jgs 14:3

he went down and talked with the **w**, Jgs 14:7
His father went down to the **w**, and Jgs 14:10
After this he loved a **w** in the Valley of Jgs 16:4
the **w** came and fell down at the door of Jgs 19:26
husband of the **w** who was murdered, Jgs 20:4
every male and every **w** that has lain Jgs 21:11
so that the **w** was left without her two Ru 1:5
of the reapers, "Whose young **w** is this?" Ru 2:5
answered, "She is the young Moabite **w**, Ru 2:6
over, and behold, a **w** lay at his feet! Ru 3:8
know that you are a worthy **w**. Ru 3:11
be known that the **w** came to the Ru 3:14
May the LORD make the **w**, who is Ru 4:11
the LORD will give you by this young **w**." Ru 4:12
Eli took her to be a drunken **w**. 1 Sm 1:13
my lord, I am a **w** troubled in spirit. 1 Sm 1:15
regard your servant as a worthless **w**, 1 Sm 1:16
your eyes." Then the **w** went her way 1 Sm 1:18
word." So the **w** remained and nursed 1 Sm 1:23
I am the **w** who was standing here in 1 Sm 1:26
you children by this **w** for the petition 1 Sm 2:20
spare them, but kill both man and **w**, 1 Sm 15:3
"You son of a perverse, rebellious **w**, 1 Sm 20:30
both man and **w**, child and infant, 1 Sm 22:19
The **w** was discerning and beautiful, 1 Sm 25:3
would leave neither man nor **w** alive, 1 Sm 27:9
neither man nor **w** alive to bring 1 Sm 27:11
out for me a **w** who is a medium, 1 Sm 28:7
And they came to the **w** by night. 1 Sm 28:8
The **w** said to him, "Surely you know 1 Sm 28:9
Then the **w** said, "Whom shall I 1 Sm 28:11
When the **w** saw Samuel, she cried 1 Sm 28:12
And the **w** said to Saul, "Why have 1 Sm 28:12
do you see?" And the **w** said to Saul, 1 Sm 28:13
And the **w** came to Saul, and when 1 Sm 28:21
But his servants, together with the **w**, 1 Sm 28:23
Now the **w** had a fattened calf in the 1 Sm 28:24
me today with a fault concerning a **w**. 2 Sm 3:8
that he saw from the roof a **w** bathing; 2 Sm 11:2
and the **w** was very beautiful. 2 Sm 11:2
David sent and inquired about the **w**. 2 Sm 11:3
And the **w** conceived, and she sent 2 Sm 11:5
Did not a **w** cast an upper millstone 2 Sm 11:21
"Put this **w** out of my presence and 2 Sm 13:17
heart." So Tamar lived, a desolate **w**, 2 Sm 13:20
from there a wise **w** and said to her, 2 Sm 14:2
but behave like a **w** who has been 2 Sm 14:2
When the **w** of Tekoa came to the 2 Sm 14:4
Then the king said to the **w**, "Go to 2 Sm 14:8
And the **w** of Tekoa said to the king, 2 Sm 14:9
Then the **w** said, "Please let your 2 Sm 14:12
And the **w** said, "Why then have you 2 Sm 14:13
Then the king answered the **w**, "Do 2 Sm 14:18
anything I ask you." And the **w** said, 2 Sm 14:18
all this?" The **w** answered and said, 2 Sm 14:19
was Tamar. She was a beautiful **w**. 2 Sm 14:27
And the **w** took and spread a 2 Sm 17:19
servants came to the **w** at the house, 2 Sm 17:20
Jonathan?" And the **w** said to them, 2 Sm 17:20
Then a wise **w** called from the city, 2 Sm 20:16
he came near her, and the **w** said, 2 Sm 20:17
the city." And the **w** said to Joab, 2 Sm 20:21
Then the **w** went to all the people in 2 Sm 20:22
"Let a young **w** be sought for my lord 1 Kgs 1:2
a beautiful young **w** throughout all 1 Kgs 1:3
The young **w** was very beautiful, and 1 Kgs 1:4
The one **w** said, "Oh, my lord, this 1 Kgs 3:17
this **w** and I live in the same house, 1 Kgs 3:17
I gave birth, this **w** also gave birth. 1 Kgs 3:18
But the other **w** said, "No, the living 1 Kgs 3:22
Then the **w** whose son was alive said 1 Kgs 3:26
"Give the living child to the first **w**, 1 Kgs 3:27
came, she pretended to be another **w**. 1 Kgs 14:5
After this the son of the **w**, the 1 Kgs 17:17
And the **w** said to Elijah, "Now I 1 Kgs 17:24
to Shunem, where a wealthy **w** lived, 2 Kgs 4:8
But the **w** conceived, and she bore a 2 Kgs 4:17
by on the wall, a **w** cried out to him, 2 Kgs 6:26
She answered, "This **w** said to me, 2 Kgs 6:28
the king heard the words of the **w**, 2 Kgs 6:30
had said to the **w** whose son he had 2 Kgs 8:1
So the **w** arose and did according to the 2 Kgs 8:2
when the **w** returned from the land of 2 Kgs 8:3
the **w** whose son he had restored to life 2 Kgs 8:5
said, "My lord, O king, here is the **w**, 2 Kgs 8:5
And when the king asked the **w**, she 2 Kgs 8:6
now to this cursed **w** and bury her, 2 Kgs 9:34
the son of a **w** of the daughters of 2 Chr 2:14
whether young or old, man or **w**. 2 Chr 15:13
the sons of Athaliah, that wicked **w**, 2 Chr 24:7
And let the young **w** who pleases the king Est 2:4
The young **w** had a beautiful figure and Est 2:7
And the young **w** pleased him and won Est 2:9
turn came for each young **w** to go in to Est 2:12
when the young **w** went in to the king in Est 2:13
that if any man or **w** goes to the king Est 4:11
who is born of a **w** is few of days and Jb 14:1
Or he who is born of a **w**, that he can be Jb 15:14
"They wrong the barren childless **w**, Jb 24:21
How can he who is born of **w** be pure? Jb 25:4
"If my heart has been enticed toward a **w**, Jb 31:9
of them there, anguish as of a **w** in labor. Ps 48:6
He gives the barren **w** a home, making Ps 113:9
will be delivered from the forbidden **w**, Prv 2:16
For the lips of a forbidden **w** drip honey, Prv 5:3
with a forbidden **w** and embrace the Prv 5:20
to preserve you from the evil **w**, from Prv 6:24
but a married **w** hunts down a precious Prv 6:26
to keep you from the forbidden **w**, from Prv 7:5
And behold, the **w** meets him, dressed Prv 7:10
The **w** Folly is loud; she is seductive Prv 9:13
A gracious **w** gets honor, and violent Prv 11:16
is a beautiful **w** without discretion. Prv 11:22
than with a quarrelsome and fretful **w**. Prv 21:19
an unloved **w** when she gets a Prv 30:23
but a **w** who fears the LORD is to be Prv 31:30
the **w** whose heart is snares and nets, Eccl 7:26
but a **w** among all these I have not Eccl 7:28
bones in the womb of a **w** with child, Eccl 11:5
they will be in anguish like a **w** in labor. Is 13:8
seized me, like the pangs of a **w** in labor; Is 21:3
Like a pregnant **w** who writhes and cries Is 26:17
now I will cry out like a **w** in labor; Is 42:14
or to a **w**, 'With what are you in labor?'" Is 45:10
"Can a **w** forget her nursing child, that Is 49:15
offspring of the adulterer and the loose **w**. Is 57:3
For as a young man marries a young **w**, Is 62:5
For I heard a cry as of a **w** in labor, Jer 4:31
taken hold of us, pain as of a **w** in labor. Jer 6:24
hold of you like those of a **w** in labor? Jer 13:21
upon you, pain as of a **w** in labor!" Jer 22:23
hands on his stomach like a **w** in labor? Jer 30:6
the pregnant **w** and she who is in labor, Jer 31:8
on the earth: a **w** encircles a man." Jer 31:22
to cut off from you man and **w**, Jer 44:7
like the heart of a **w** in her birth pains; Jer 48:41
like the heart of a **w** in her birth pains." Jer 49:22
taken hold of her, as of a **w** in labor. Jer 49:24
seized him, pain as of a **w** in labor. Jer 50:43
with you I break in pieces man and **w**; Jer 51:22
pieces the young man and the young **w**; Jer 51:22
wife or approach a **w** in her time of Ezk 18:6
uncleanness of a **w** in her menstrual Ezk 36:17
not marry a widow or a divorced **w**, Ezk 44:22
love a **w** who is loved by another man Hos 3:1
that pain seized you like a **w** in labor? Mi 4:9
O daughter of Zion, like a **w** in labor, Mi 4:10
and there was a **w** sitting in the basket! Zec 5:7
who looks at a **w** with lustful intent has Mt 5:28
marries a divorced **w** commits adultery. Mt 5:32
a **w** who had suffered from a discharge Mt 9:20
And instantly the **w** was made well. Mt 9:22
is like leaven that a **w** took and hid in Mt 13:33
a Canaanite **w** from that region came Mt 15:22
Then Jesus answered her, "O **w**, great is Mt 15:28
After them all, the **w** died. Mt 22:27
a **w** came up to him with an alabaster Mt 26:7
to them, "Why do you trouble the **w**? Mt 26:10
And there was a **w** who had had a Mk 5:25
But the **w**, knowing what had happened Mk 5:33
But immediately a **w** whose little Mk 7:25
Now the **w** was a Gentile, a Mk 7:26
no offspring. Last of all the **w** also died. Mk 12:22
a **w** came with an alabaster flask of Mk 14:3
land of Sidon, to a **w** who was a widow. Lk 4:26
And behold, a **w** of the city, who was a Lk 7:37
who and what sort of **w** this is who is Lk 7:39
Then turning toward the **w** he said to Lk 7:44
he said to Simon, "Do you see this **w**? Lk 7:44
And he said to the **w**, "Your faith has Lk 7:50
And there was a **w** who had had a Lk 8:43
And when the **w** saw that she was not Lk 8:47
And a **w** named Martha welcomed him Lk 10:38
a **w** in the crowd raised her voice and Lk 11:27
And there was a **w** who had had a Lk 13:11
"**W**, you are freed from your Lk 13:12
And ought not this **w**, a daughter of Lk 13:16
is like leaven that a **w** took and hid in Lk 13:21
"Or what **w**, having ten silver coins, if Lk 15:8
he who marries a **w** divorced from her Lk 16:18
Afterward the **w** also died. Lk 20:32
therefore, whose wife will the **w** be? Lk 20:33
it, saying, "**W**, I do not know him." Lk 22:57
"**W**, what does this have to do with me? Jn 2:4
There came a **w** of Samaria to draw water. Jn 4:7
The Samaritan **w** said to him, "How is it Jn 4:9
a **w** of Samaria?" (For Jews have no Jn 4:9
The **w** said to him, "Sir, you have Jn 4:11
The **w** said to him, "Sir, give me this Jn 4:15
The **w** answered him, "I have no Jn 4:17
The **w** said to him, "Sir, I perceive that Jn 4:19
Jesus said to her, "**W**, believe me, the Jn 4:21
The **w** said to him, "I know that Messiah Jn 4:25
marveled that he was talking with a **w**, Jn 4:27
So the **w** left her water jar and went away Jn 4:28
They said to the **w**, "It is no longer Jn 4:42
the Pharisees brought a **w** who had been Jn 8:3
this **w** has been caught in the act of Jn 8:4
left alone with the **w** standing before him. Jn 8:9
up and said to her, "**W**, where are they? Jn 8:10
When a **w** is giving birth, she has Jn 16:21
he said to his mother, "**W**, behold, Jn 19:26
"**W**, why are you weeping?" She said to Jn 20:13
said to her, "**W**, why are you weeping? Jn 20:15
son of a Jewish **w** who was a believer, Acts 16:1
who heard us was a **w** named Lydia, Acts 16:14
Areopagite and a **w** named Damaris Acts 17:34
Thus a married **w** is bound by law to Rom 7:2
not to have sexual relations with a **w**." 1 Cor 7:1
wife and each **w** her own husband. 1 Cor 7:2
If any **w** has a husband who is an 1 Cor 7:13
sinned, and if a betrothed **w** marries, 1 Cor 7:28
unmarried or betrothed **w** is anxious 1 Cor 7:34
But the married **w** is anxious about 1 Cor 7:34
of God, but **w** is the glory of man. 1 Cor 11:7
For man was not made from **w**, but 1 Cor 11:8
made from woman, but **w** from man. 1 Cor 11:8
Neither was man created for **w**, but 1 Cor 11:9
created for woman, but **w** for man. 1 Cor 11:9
in the Lord **w** is not independent of 1 Cor 11:11
independent of man nor man of **w**; 1 Cor 11:11
for as **w** was made from man, so 1 Cor 11:12
from man, so man is now born of **w**. 1 Cor 11:12
but if a **w** has long hair, it is her 1 Cor 11:15
is shameful for a **w** to speak in 1 Cor 14:35
come, God sent forth his Son, born of **w**, Gal 4:4
one by a slave **w** and one by a free Gal 4:22
by a slave woman and one by a free **w**. Gal 4:22
son of the free **w** was born through Gal 4:23
"Cast out the slave **w** and her son, for Gal 4:30
son of the slave **w** shall not inherit with Gal 4:30
not inherit with the son of the free **w**." Gal 4:30
children of the slave but of the free **w**. Gal 4:31
labor pains come upon a pregnant **w**, 1 Thes 5:3
Let a **w** learn quietly with all 1 Tm 2:11
I do not permit a **w** to teach or to 1 Tm 2:12
but the **w** was deceived and became a 1 Tm 2:14
If any believing **w** has relatives who 1 Tm 5:16
showing honor to the **w** as the weaker 1 Pt 3:7
you, that you tolerate that **w** Jezebel, Rv 2:20
a **w** clothed with the sun, with the moon Rv 12:1
stood before the **w** who was about Rv 12:4
and the **w** fled into the wilderness, where Rv 12:6
he pursued the **w** who had given birth Rv 12:13
But the **w** was given the two wings of Rv 12:14
like a river out of his mouth after the **w**, Rv 12:15
But the earth came to the help of the **w**, Rv 12:16
became furious with the **w** and went off Rv 12:17
and I saw a **w** sitting on a scarlet beast Rv 17:3
The **w** was arrayed in purple and scarlet, Rv 17:4
And I saw the **w**, drunk with the blood of Rv 17:6
I will tell you the mystery of the **w**, and of Rv 17:7
mountains on which the **w** is seated; Rv 17:9
And the **w** that you saw is the great city Rv 17:18

WOMAN'S (10)

take back the pledge from the **w** hand, Gn 38:20
as the **w** husband shall impose on him, Ex 21:22
Now an Israelite **w** son, whose father Lv 24:10
And the Israelite **w** son and a man of Lv 24:10
and the Israelite **w** son blasphemed the Lv 24:11
the hair of the **w** head and place in Nm 5:18
jealousy out of the **w** hand and shall Nm 5:25
nor shall a man put on a **w** cloak, Dt 22:5
And this **w** son died in the night, 1 Kgs 3:19
in him because of the **w** testimony, Jn 4:39

WOMB (80)

to her, "Two nations are in your **w**, Gn 25:23
behold, there were twins in her **w**. Gn 25:24
that Leah was hated, he opened her **w**, Gn 29:31
withheld from you the fruit of the **w**?" Gn 30:2
God listened to her and opened her **w**. Gn 30:22
labor came, there were twins in her **w**. Gn 38:27
blessings of the breasts and of the **w**. Gn 49:25
first to open the **w** among the people of Ex 13:2
to the LORD all that first opens the **w**. Ex 13:12
LORD all the males that first open the **w**, Ex 13:15
All that open the **w** are mine, all your Ex 34:19
who opens the **w** among the people Nm 3:12
and make your **w** swell and your Nm 5:22
cause bitter pain, and her **w** shall swell, Nm 5:27
Instead of all who open the **w**, the Nm 8:16
he comes out of his mother's **w**." Nm 12:12
that opens the **w** of all flesh, Nm 18:15
bless the fruit of your **w** and the fruit of Dt 7:13

be the fruit of your **w** and the fruit of Dt 28:4
in the fruit of your **w** and in the fruit of Dt 28:11
be the fruit of your **w** and the fruit of Dt 28:18
And you shall eat the fruit of your **w**, Dt 28:53
in the fruit of your **w** and in the fruit of Dt 30:9
A **w** or two for every man; spoil of dyed Jgs 5:30
shall be a Nazirite to God from the **w**, Jgs 13:5
Nazirite to God from the **w** to the day of Jgs 13:7
a Nazirite to God from my mother's **w**. Jgs 16:17
yet sons in my **w** that they may become Ru 1:11
her, though the LORD had closed her **w**. 1 Sm 1:5
her, because the LORD had closed her **w**. 1 Sm 1:6
"Naked I came from my mother's **w**, Jb 1:21
did not shut the doors of my mother's **w**, Jb 3:10
at birth, come out from the **w** and expire? Jb 3:11
did you bring me out from the **w**? Jb 10:18
been, carried from the **w** to the grave. Jb 10:19
to evil, and their **w** prepares deceit." Jb 15:35
The **w** forgets them; the worm finds Jb 24:20
he who made me in the **w** make him? Jb 31:15
And did not one fashion us in the **w**? Jb 31:15
and from my mother's **w** I guided the Jb 31:18
with doors when it burst out from the **w**, Jb 38:8
From whose **w** did the ice come forth, Jb 38:29
You fill their **w** with treasure; they are Ps 17:14
Yet you are he who took me from the **w**; Ps 22:9
and from my mother's **w** you have been Ps 22:10
The wicked are estranged from the **w**; Ps 58:3
are he who took me from my mother's **w**. Ps 71:6
from the **w** of the morning, the dew of Ps 110:3
the LORD, the fruit of the **w** a reward. Ps 127:3
knitted me together in my mother's **w**. Ps 139:13
Sheol, the barren **w**, the land never Prv 30:16
son? What are you doing, son of my **w**? Prv 31:2
came from his mother's **w** he shall go Eccl 5:15
to the bones in the **w** of a woman with Eccl 11:5
will have no mercy on the fruit of the **w**; Is 13:18
formed you from the **w** and will help you: Is 44:2
Redeemer, who formed you from the **w**: Is 44:24
before your birth, carried from the **w**; Is 46:3
The LORD called me from the **w**, from the Is 49:1
formed me from the **w** to be his servant, Is 49:5
no compassion on the son of her **w**? Is 49:15
bring forth, shut the **w**?" says your God. Is 66:9
"Before I formed you in the **w** I knew you, Jer 1:5
because he did not kill me in the **w**; so Jer 20:17
been my grave, and her **w** forever great. Jer 20:17
I come out from the **w** to see toil and Jer 20:18
Should women eat the fruit of their **w**, Lam 2:20
them a miscarrying **w** and dry breasts. Hos 9:14
In the **w** he took his brother by the heel, Hos 12:3
himself at the opening of the **w**. Hos 13:13
Holy Spirit, even from his mother's **w**. Lk 1:15
will conceive in your **w** and bear a son, Lk 1:31
of Mary, the baby leaped in her **w**. Lk 1:41
and blessed is the fruit of your **w**! Lk 1:42
ears, the baby in my **w** leaped for joy. Lk 1:44
angel before he was conceived in the **w**. Lk 2:21
who first opens the **w** shall be called Lk 2:23
to him, "Blessed is the **w** that bore you, Lk 11:27
time into his mother's **w** and be born?" Jn 3:4
the barrenness of Sarah's **w**. Rom 4:19

WOMBS (2)
had closed all the **w** of the house of Gn 20:18
the barren and the **w** that never bore Lk 23:29

WOMEN (225)
possessions, and the **w** and the people. Gn 14:16
The way of **w** had ceased to be with Gn 18:11
the time when **w** go out to draw water. Gn 24:11
and her young **w** arose and rode Gn 24:61
loathe my life because of the Hittite **w**. Gn 27:46
marries one of the Hittite **w** like these, Gn 27:46
like these, one of the **w** of the land, Gn 27:46
not take a wife from the Canaanite **w**. Gn 28:1
not take a wife from the Canaanite **w**," Gn 28:6
saw that the Canaanite **w** did not please Gn 28:8
For **w** have called me happy." So she Gn 30:13
for the way of **w** is upon me." So he Gn 31:35
up his eyes and saw the **w** and children, Gn 33:5
Jacob, went out to see the **w** of the land. Gn 34:1
midwife to the Hebrew **w** and see them Ex 1:16
"Because the Hebrew **w** are not like the Ex 1:19
women are not like the Egyptian **w**, Ex 1:19
while her young **w** walked beside the Ex 2:5
nurse from the Hebrew **w** to nurse the Ex 2:7
men on foot, besides **w** and children. Ex 12:37
and all the **w** went out after her with Ex 15:20
So they came, both men and **w**. All who Ex 35:22
All the **w** whose hearts stirred them to Ex 35:26
All the men and **w**, the people of Israel, Ex 35:29
of the ministering **w** who ministered in Ex 38:8
ten **w** shall bake your bread in a single Lv 26:26
Israel took captive the **w** of Midian and Nm 31:9
to them, "Have you let all the **w** live? Nm 31:15
w who had not known man by lying Nm 31:35
every city, men, **w**, and children. Dt 2:34
every city, men, **w**, and children. Dt 3:6
but the **w** and the little ones, the Dt 20:14
the people, men, **w**, and little ones, Dt 31:12
the city to destruction, both men and **w**, Jos 6:21
all who fell that day, both men and **w**, Jos 8:25
all the assembly of Israel, and the **w**, Jos 8:35
"Most blessed of **w** be Jael, the wife of Jgs 5:24
Kenite, of tent-dwelling **w** most blessed. Jgs 5:24
also died, about 1,000 men and **w**. Jgs 9:49
all the men and **w** and all the leaders Jgs 9:51
Now the house was full of men and **w**. Jgs 16:27
roof there were about 3,000 men and **w**, Jgs 16:27
the sword; also the **w** and the little ones. Jgs 21:10
they gave them the **w** whom they had Jgs 21:14
saved alive of the **w** of Jabesh-gilead, Jgs 21:14
since the **w** are destroyed out of Jgs 21:16
them. And the **w** said, "Is this Naomi?" Ru 1:19
this one, but keep close to my young **w**. Ru 2:8
that you go out with his young **w**, Ru 2:22
So she kept close to the young **w** of Boaz, Ru 2:23
relative, with whose young **w** you were? Ru 3:2
Then the **w** said to Naomi, "Blessed be Ru 4:14
And the **w** of the neighborhood gave Ru 4:17
they lay with the **w** who were serving 1 Sm 2:22
of her death the **w** attending her said 1 Sm 4:20
they met young **w** coming out to draw 1 Sm 9:11
your sword has made **w** childless, 1 Sm 15:33
be childless among **w**." And Samuel 1 Sm 15:33
the **w** came out of all the cities of 1 Sm 18:6
And the **w** sang to one another as they 1 Sm 18:7
men have kept themselves from **w**." 1 Sm 21:4
"Truly **w** have been kept from us as 1 Sm 21:5
and her five young **w** attended her. 1 Sm 25:42
and taken captive the **w** and all who 1 Sm 30:2
surpassing the love of **w**. 2 Sm 1:26
multitude of Israel, both men and **w**, 2 Sm 6:19
voice of singing men and singing **w**? 2 Sm 19:35
King Solomon loved many foreign **w**, 1 Kgs 11:1
Edomite, Sidonian, and Hittite **w**, 1 Kgs 11:1
ones and rip open their pregnant **w**." 2 Kgs 8:12
ripped open all the **w** in it who were 2 Kgs 15:16
where the **w** wove hangings for the 2 Kgs 23:7
to all Israel, both men and **w**, 1 Chr 16:3
200,000 of their relatives, **w**, sons, 2 Chr 28:8
men and singing **w** have spoken of 2 Chr 35:25
great assembly of men, **w**, and children, Ezr 10:1
have married foreign **w** from the Ezr 10:2
broken faith and married foreign **w**, Ezr 10:10
the men who had married foreign **w**. Ezr 10:17
the priests who had married foreign **w**: Ezr 10:18
All these had married foreign **w**, and Ezr 10:44
and some of the **w** had even borne Ezr 10:44
both men and **w** and all who could Neh 8:2
the men and the **w** and those who could Neh 8:3
joy; the **w** and children also rejoiced. Neh 12:43
Jews who had married **w** of Ashdod, Neh 13:23
of Israel sin on account of such **w**? Neh 13:26
foreign **w** made even him to sin. Neh 13:26
our God by marrying foreign **w**?" Neh 13:27
gave a feast for the **w** in the palace that Est 1:9
behavior will be made known to all **w**, Est 1:17
very day the noble **w** of Persia and Est 1:18
all **w** will give honor to their husbands, Est 1:20
king's eunuch, who is in charge of the **w**. Est 2:3
when many young **w** were gathered in Est 2:8
of Hegai, who had charge of the **w**. Est 2:8
seven chosen young **w** from the king's Est 2:9
her and her young **w** to the best place Est 2:9
months under the regulations for the **w**, Est 2:12
with spices and ointments for **w**— Est 2:12
eunuch, who had charge of the **w**, Est 2:15
king loved Esther more than all the **w**, Est 2:17
all Jews, young and old, **w** and children, Est 3:13
When Esther's young **w** and her Est 4:4
I and my young **w** will also fast as you Est 4:16
been sold merely as slaves, men and **w**, Est 7:4
attack them, children and **w** included, Est 8:11
as one of the foolish **w** would speak. Jb 2:10
land there were no **w** so beautiful as Jb 42:15
the **w** who announce the news are a Ps 68:11
they flee!" The **w** at home divide the Ps 68:12
and their young **w** had no marriage Ps 78:63
has sent out her young **w** to call from the Prv 9:3
The wisest of **w** builds her house, but Prv 14:1
The mouth of forbidden **w** is a deep Prv 22:14
Do not give your strength to **w**, your Prv 31:3
"Many **w** have done excellently, but Prv 31:29
I got singers, both men and **w**, and Eccl 2:8
do not know, O most beautiful among **w**, Sg 1:8
so is my love among the young **w**. Sg 2:2
beloved, O most beautiful among **w**? Sg 5:9
beloved gone, O most beautiful among **w**? Sg 6:1
The young **w** saw her and called her Sg 6:9
their oppressors, and **w** rule over them. Is 3:12
And seven **w** shall take hold of one man in Is 4:1
In that day the Egyptians will be like **w**, Is 19:16
young men nor brought up young **w**." Is 23:4
w come and make a fire of them. Is 27:11
Rise up, you **w** who are at ease, hear my Is 32:9
you will shudder, you complacent **w**; Is 32:10
Tremble, you **w** who are at ease, Is 32:11
that even to wicked **w** you have taught Jer 2:33
kindle fire, and the **w** knead dough, Jer 7:18
and call for the mourning **w** to come; Jer 9:17
to come; send for the skillful **w** to come; Jer 9:17
Hear, O **w**, the word of the LORD, and let Jer 9:20
Then shall the young **w** rejoice in the Jer 31:13
all the **w** left in the house of the king of Jer 38:22
committed to him men, **w**, and children, Jer 40:7
son of Ahikam—soldiers, **w**, children, Jer 41:16
the men, the **w**, the children, the Jer 43:6
other gods, and all the **w** who stood by, Jer 44:15
And the **w** said, "When we made Jer 44:19
said to all the people, men and **w**, Jer 44:20
said to all the people and all the **w**, Jer 44:24
in her midst, that they may become **w**! Jer 50:37
has failed; they have become **w**; Jer 51:30
my young **w** and my young men have Lam 1:18
the young **w** of Jerusalem have bowed Lam 2:10
Should **w** eat the fruit of their womb, Lam 2:20
my young **w** and my young men have Lam 2:21
hands of compassionate **w** have boiled Lam 4:10
W are raped in Zion, young women in Lam 5:11
Zion, young **w** in the towns of Judah. Lam 5:11
there sat **w** weeping for Tammuz. Ezk 8:14
men and maidens, little children and **w**, Ezk 9:6
Woe to the **w** who sew magic bands Ezk 13:18
different from other **w** in your Ezk 16:34
judge you as **w** who commit adultery Ezk 16:38
upon you in the sight of many **w**. Ezk 16:41
in you they violate **w** who are unclean Ezk 22:10
"Son of man, there were two **w**, the Ezk 23:2
and she became a byword among **w**, Ezk 23:10
put bracelets on the hands of the **w**, Ezk 23:42
in to Oholah and to Oholibah, lewd **w**! Ezk 23:44
the sentence of **w** who shed blood, Ezk 23:45
that all **w** may take warning and not Ezk 23:48
and the **w** shall go into captivity. Ezk 30:17
him the daughter of **w** to destroy the Dn 11:17
his fathers, or to the one beloved by **w**. Dn 11:37
and their pregnant **w** ripped open. Hos 13:16
have ripped open pregnant **w** in Gilead, Am 1:13
The **w** of my people you drive out from Mi 2:9
Behold, your troops are **w** in your midst. Na 3:13
saw, and behold, two **w** coming forward! Zec 5:9
Old men and old **w** shall again sit in the Zec 8:4
flourish, and new wine the young **w**. Zec 9:17
the houses plundered and the **w** raped. Zec 14:2
those born of **w** there has arisen Mt 11:11
thousand men, besides **w** and children. Mt 14:21
thousand men, besides **w** and children. Mt 15:38
And alas for **w** who are pregnant and Mt 24:19
Two **w** will be grinding at the mill; one Mt 24:41
There were also many **w** there, looking Mt 27:55
But the angel said to the **w**, "Do not be Mt 28:5
And alas for **w** who are pregnant and Mk 13:17
There were also **w** looking on from a Mk 15:40
were also many other **w** who came up Mk 15:41
a loud cry, "Blessed are you among **w**, Lk 1:42
among those born of **w** none is greater Lk 7:28
and also some **w** who had been healed of Lk 8:2
There will be two **w** grinding together. Lk 17:35
Alas for **w** who are pregnant and for Lk 21:23
people and of **w** who were mourning Lk 23:27
acquaintances and the **w** who had Lk 23:49
The **w** who had come with him from Lk 23:55
James and the other **w** with them who Lk 24:10
some **w** of our company amazed us. Lk 24:22
and found it just as the **w** had said, Lk 24:24
Moses commanded us to stone such **w**. Jn 8:5
together with the **w** and Mary the Acts 1:14
Lord, multitudes of both men and **w**, Acts 5:14
off men and **w** and committed them Acts 8:3
they were baptized, both men and **w**. Acts 8:12
any belonging to the Way, men or **w**, Acts 9:2
incited the devout **w** of high standing Acts 13:50
and spoke to the **w** who had come Acts 16:13
Greeks and not a few of the leading **w**. Acts 17:4
not a few Greek **w** of high standing as Acts 17:12
delivering to prison both men and **w**, Acts 22:4
For their **w** exchanged natural Rom 1:26
natural relations with **w** and were Rom 1:27
the **w** should keep silent in the 1 Cor 14:34
these **w** are two covenants. Gal 4:24
you also, true companion, help these **w**, Phil 4:3
likewise also that **w** should adorn 1 Tm 2:9
is proper for **w** who profess godliness 1 Tm 2:10
older **w** like mothers, younger women 1 Tm 5:2

like mothers, younger **w** like sisters, 1 Tm 5:2
into households and capture weak **w**, 2 Tm 3:6
Older **w** likewise are to be reverent in Ti 2:3
so train the young **w** to love their Ti 2:4
W received back their dead by Heb 11:35
this is how the holy **w** who hoped in God 1 Pt 3:5
who have not defiled themselves with **w**, Rv 14:4

WOMEN'S (1)
their hair like **w** hair, and their teeth like Rv 9:8

WON (10)
killed them and **w** a name beside 2 Sm 23:18
and **w** a name beside the three 2 Sm 23:22
killed them and **w** a name beside 1 Chr 11:20
of Jehoiada and **w** a name beside 1 Chr 11:24
From spoil **w** in battles they 1 Chr 26:27
woman pleased him and **w** his favor. Est 2:9
and she **w** grace and favor in his sight Est 2:17
in the court, she **w** favor in his sight, Est 5:2
mountain which his right hand had **w**. Ps 78:54
they may be **w** without a word by the 1 Pt 3:1

WONDER (9)
among you and gives you a sign or a **w**, Dt 13:1
and the sign or **w** that he tells you comes Dt 13:2
be a sign and a **w** against you and your Dt 28:46
with this people, with **w** upon wonder; Is 29:14
with this people, with wonder upon **w**; Is 29:14
nations, and see; **w** and be astounded. Hab 1:5
were filled with **w** and amazement at Acts 3:10
"Men of Israel, why do you **w** at this, or Acts 3:12
And no **w**, for even Satan disguises 2 Cor 11:14

WONDERED (4)
and **w** that there was no one to intercede; Is 59:16
so that the crowd **w**, when they saw the Mt 15:31
"His name is John." And they all **w**. Lk 1:63
all who heard it **w** at what the shepherds Lk 2:18

WONDERFUL (17)
where are all his **w** deeds that our fathers Jgs 6:13
do you ask my name, seeing it is **w**?" Jgs 13:18
I am to build will be great and **w**. 2 Chr 2:9
I did not understand, things too **w** for me, Jb 42:3
heart; I will recount all of your **w** deeds. Ps 9:1
Your testimonies are **w**; therefore my Ps 119:129
Such knowledge is too **w** for me; it is Ps 139:6
W are your works; my soul knows it Ps 139:14
Three things are too **w** for me; four I Prv 30:18
his name shall be called **W** Counselor, Is 9:6
your name, for you have done **w** things, Is 25:1
he is **w** in counsel and excellent in Is 28:29
I will again do **w** things with this people, Is 29:14
according to all his **w** deeds and will Jer 21:2
the scribes saw the **w** things that he Mt 21:15
what **w** stones and what wonderful Mk 13:1
stones and what **w** buildings!" Mk 13:1

WONDERFULLY (1)
you, for I am fearfully and **w** made. Ps 139:14

WONDERING (2)
and they were **w** at his delay in the Lk 1:21
them, **w** what this would come to. Acts 5:24

WONDERS (50)
strike Egypt with all the **w** that I will do Ex 3:20
I multiply my signs and **w** in the land of Ex 7:3
that my **w** may be multiplied in the land Ex 11:9
Aaron did all these **w** before Pharaoh, Ex 11:10
awesome in glorious deeds, doing **w**? Ex 15:11
another nation, by trials, by signs, by **w**, Dt 4:34
And the LORD showed signs and **w**, great Dt 6:22
trials that your eyes saw, the signs, the **w**, Dt 7:19
great deeds of terror, with signs and **w**. Dt 26:8
eyes saw, the signs, and those great **w**. Dt 29:3
the signs and the **w** that the LORD sent Dt 34:11
the LORD will do **w** among you." Jos 3:5
to the LORD, to the one who works **w**, Jgs 13:19
signs and **w** against Pharaoh Neh 9:10
mindful of the **w** that you performed Neh 9:17
a lion and again work **w** against me. Jb 10:16
yes, I will remember your **w** of old. Ps 77:11
You are the God who works **w**; you Ps 77:14
his might, and the **w** that he has done. Ps 78:4
his works and the **w** that he had shown Ps 78:11
their fathers he performed **w** in the land Ps 78:12
despite his **w**, they did not believe. Ps 78:32
Do you work **w** for the dead? Do the Ps 88:10
Are your **w** known in the darkness, or Ps 88:12
Let the heavens praise your **w**, O LORD, Ps 89:5
sent signs and **w** against Pharaoh and Ps 135:9
to him who alone does great **w**, for his Ps 136:4
have shown signs and **w** in the land of Jer 32:20
of the land of Egypt with signs and **w**, Jer 32:21
show the signs and **w** that the Most High Dn 4:2
great are his signs, how mighty his **w**! Dn 4:3
he works signs and **w** in heaven and on Dn 6:27
long shall it be till the end of these **w**?" Dn 12:6
"And I will show **w** in the heavens and on Jl 2:30
arise and perform great signs and **w**, Mt 24:24
will arise and perform signs and **w**, Mk 13:22
you see signs and **w** you will not believe." Jn 4:48
And I will show **w** in the heavens Acts 2:19
mighty works and **w** and signs that Acts 2:22
and many **w** and signs were being Acts 2:43
and signs and **w** are performed Acts 4:30
many signs and **w** were regularly done Acts 5:12
was doing great **w** and signs among the Acts 6:8
performing **w** and signs in Egypt and Acts 7:36
granting signs and **w** to be done by Acts 14:3
what signs and **w** God had done Acts 15:12
by the power of signs and **w**, by the Rom 15:19
with signs and **w** and mighty works. 2 Cor 12:12
with all power and false signs and **w**, 2 Thes 2:9
by signs and **w** and various miracles Heb 2:4

WONDROUS (23)
praises to him; tell of all his **w** works! 1 Chr 16:9
Remember the **w** works that he has 1 Chr 16:12
stop and consider the **w** works of God. Jb 37:14
the **w** works of him who is perfect in Jb 37:16
aloud, and telling all your **w** deeds. Ps 26:7
your **w** deeds and your thoughts toward Ps 40:5
me, and I still proclaim your **w** deeds. Ps 71:17
God of Israel, who alone does **w** things. Ps 72:18
name is near. We recount your **w** deeds. Ps 75:1
For you are great and do **w** things; you Ps 86:10
praises to him; tell of all his **w** works! Ps 105:2
Remember the **w** works that he has Ps 105:5
Egypt, did not consider your **w** works; Ps 106:7
w works in the land of Ham, and Ps 106:22
for his **w** works to the children of men! Ps 107:8
for his **w** works to the children of Ps 107:15
for his **w** works to the children of Ps 107:21
of the LORD, his **w** works in the deep. Ps 107:24
for his **w** works to the children of Ps 107:31
He has caused his **w** works to be Ps 111:4
that I may behold **w** things out of your Ps 119:18
and I will meditate on your **w** works. Ps 119:27
of your majesty, and on your **w** works, Ps 145:5

WONDROUSLY (4)
God thunders **w** with his voice; he does Jb 37:5
W show your steadfast love, O Savior of Ps 17:7
for he has **w** shown his steadfast love to Ps 31:21
LORD your God, who has dealt **w** with you. Jl 2:26

WOOD (116)
Make yourself an ark of gopher **w**. Gn 6:14
And he cut the **w** for the burnt offering Gn 22:3
And Abraham took the **w** of the burnt Gn 22:6
son." He said, "Behold, the fire and the **w**, Gn 22:7
there and laid the **w** in order and bound Gn 22:9
laid him on the altar, on top of the **w**. Gn 22:9
even in vessels of **w** and in vessels of Ex 7:19
tanned rams' skins, goatskins, acacia **w**, Ex 25:5
"They shall make an ark of acacia **w**. Ex 25:10
poles of acacia **w** and overlay them Ex 25:13
"You shall make a table of acacia **w**. Ex 25:23
You shall make the poles of acacia **w**, Ex 25:28
frames for the tabernacle of acacia **w**. Ex 26:15
"You shall make bars of acacia **w**, five Ex 26:26
"You shall make the altar of acacia **w**, Ex 27:1
poles for the altar, poles of acacia **w**, Ex 27:6
incense; you shall make it of acacia **w**. Ex 30:1
the poles of acacia **w** and overlay them Ex 30:5
stones for setting, and in carving **w**, Ex 31:5
rams' skins, and goatskins; acacia **w**, Ex 35:7
one who possessed acacia **w** of any use Ex 35:24
stones for setting, and in carving **w**, Ex 35:33
frames for the tabernacle of acacia **w**. Ex 36:20
He made bars of acacia **w**, five for the Ex 36:31
Bezalel made the ark of acacia **w**. Two Ex 37:1
poles of acacia **w** and overlaid them Ex 37:4
He also made the table of acacia **w**. Ex 37:10
the poles of acacia **w** to carry the table, Ex 37:15
made the altar of incense of acacia **w**. Ex 37:25
the poles of acacia **w** and overlaid them Ex 37:28
the altar of burnt offering of acacia **w**. Ex 38:1
the poles of acacia **w** and overlaid them Ex 38:6
fire on the altar and arrange **w** on the fire. Lv 1:7
fat, on the **w** that is on the fire on the altar; Lv 1:8
arrange them on the **w** that is on the Lv 1:12
it on the altar, on the **w** that is on the fire. Lv 1:17
offering, which is on the **w** on the fire; Lv 3:5
heap, and shall burn it up on a fire of **w**. Lv 4:12
The priest shall burn **w** on it every Lv 6:12
it is an article of **w** or a garment or a Lv 11:32
and every vessel of **w** shall be rinsed in Lv 15:12
of goats' hair, and every article of **w**." Nm 31:20
there you will serve gods of **w** and stone, Dt 4:28
on the mountain and make an ark of **w**. Dt 10:1
So I made an ark of acacia **w**, and cut Dt 10:3
the forest with his neighbor to cut **w**, Dt 19:5
shall serve other gods of **w** and stone. Dt 28:36
shall serve other gods of **w** and stone, Dt 28:64
one who chops your **w** to the one who Dt 29:11
things, their idols of **w** and stone, Dt 29:17
they became cutters of **w** and drawers of Jos 9:21
cutters of **w** and drawers of water for the Jos 9:23
that day cutters of **w** and drawers of Jos 9:27
burnt offering with the **w** of the Asherah Jgs 6:26
And they split up the **w** of the cart and 1 Sm 6:14
and the yokes of the oxen for the **w**. 2 Sm 24:22
he covered them on the inside with **w**, 1 Kgs 6:15
and two doors of cypress **w**. The two 1 Kgs 6:34
amount of almug **w** and precious 1 Kgs 10:11
of the almug **w** supports for the 1 Kgs 10:12
No such almug **w** has come or been 1 Kgs 10:12
cut it in pieces and lay it on the **w**, 1 Kgs 18:23
and lay it on the **w** and put no fire to 1 Kgs 18:23
And he put the **w** in order and cut 1 Kgs 18:33
bull in pieces and laid it on the **w**. 1 Kgs 18:33
on the burnt offering and on the **w**." 1 Kgs 18:33
offering and the **w** and the stones 1 Kgs 18:38
work of men's hands, **w** and stone. 2 Kgs 19:18
sledges for the **w** and the wheat 1 Chr 21:23
of iron, and **w** for the things of wood, 1 Chr 29:2
of iron, and wood for the things of **w**, 1 Chr 29:2
silver, bronze, iron, stone, and **w**, 2 Chr 2:14
two cherubim of **w** and overlaid 2 Chr 3:10
brought algum **w** and precious 2 Chr 9:10
from the algum **w** supports for the 2 Chr 9:11
likewise cast lots for the **w** offering, Neh 10:34
provided for the **w** offering at Neh 13:31
iron as straw, and bronze as rotten **w**. Jb 41:27
And all its carved **w** they broke down Ps 74:6
For lack of **w** the fire goes out, and Prv 26:20
charcoal to hot embers and **w** to fire, Prv 26:21
himself a carriage from the **w** of Lebanon. Sg 3:9
as if a staff should lift him who is not **w**! Is 10:15
and wide, with fire and **w** in abundance; Is 30:33
the work of men's hands, **w** and stone. Is 37:19
for an offering chooses **w** that will not Is 40:20
Shall I fall down before a block of **w**?" Is 44:19
instead of **w**, bronze, instead of stones, Is 60:17
in your mouth a fire, and this people **w**, Jer 5:14
The children gather **w**, the fathers Jer 7:18
foolish; the instruction of idols is but **w**! Jer 10:8
their bones; it has become as dry as **w**. Lam 4:8
we drink; the **w** we get must be bought. Lam 5:4
and boys stagger under loads of **w**. Lam 5:13
how does the **w** of the vine surpass any Ezk 15:2
the wood of the vine surpass any **w**, Ezk 15:2
Is **w** taken from it to make anything? Ezk 15:3
Like the **w** of the vine among the trees Ezk 15:6
countries, and worship **w** and stone.' Ezk 20:32
the rod, my son, with everything of **w**.) Ezk 21:10
will not need to take **w** out of the field Ezk 39:10
were paneled with **w** all around, Ezk 41:16
an altar of **w**, three cubits high, two Ezk 41:22
its base, and its walls were of **w**. Ezk 41:22
there was a canopy of **w** in front of the Ezk 41:25
and silver, bronze, iron, **w**, and stone. Dn 5:4
and gold, of bronze, iron, **w**, and stone, Dn 5:23
My people inquire of a piece of **w**, and Hos 4:12
the hills and bring **w** and build the Hg 1:8
like a blazing pot in the midst of **w**, Zec 12:6
do these things when the **w** is green, Lk 23:31
gold, silver, precious stones, **w**, hay, 1 Cor 3:12
gold and silver but also of **w** and clay, 2 Tm 2:20
and silver and bronze and stone and **w**, Rv 9:20
scarlet cloth, all kinds of scented **w**, Rv 18:12
of ivory, all kinds of articles of costly **w**, Rv 18:12

WOODCUTTER (1)
were laid low, no **w** comes up against us.' Is 14:8

WOODED (4)
and forts and towers on the **w** hills. 2 Chr 27:4
deserted places of the **w** heights and the Is 17:9
the mountain of the house a **w** height.' Jer 26:18
the mountain of the house a **w** height. Mi 3:12

WOODEN (5)
him down with a **w** tool that could Nm 35:18
scribe stood on a **w** platform that they Neh 8:4
who carry about their **w** idols, Is 45:20
You have broken **w** bars, but you have Jer 28:13
Woe to him who says to a **w** thing, Hab 2:19

WOODS (2)
came out of the **w** and tore forty-two 2 Kgs 2:24
in the wilderness and sleep in the **w**. Ezk 34:25

WOODSMEN (1)
your servants, the **w** who cut timber, 2 Chr 2:10

WOODWORK (1)
and the beam from the **w** respond. Hab 2:11

WOOF (9)
in warp or **w** of linen or wool, or in a Lv 13:48
in the warp or the **w** or in any article Lv 13:49

in the garment, in the warp or the **w**, Lv 13:51
burn the garment, or the warp or the **w**, Lv 13:52
in the warp or the **w** or in any article Lv 13:53
or the skin or the warp or the **w**. Lv 13:56
in the garment, in the warp or the **w**, Lv 13:57
But the garment, or the warp or the **w**, Lv 13:58
or linen, either in the warp or the **w**, Lv 13:59

WOOL (18)
in warp or woof of linen or **w**, or in a Lv 13:48
the warp or the woof, the **w** or the linen, Lv 13:52
disease in a garment of **w** or linen, Lv 13:59
not wear cloth of **w** and linen mixed Dt 22:11
laying a fleece of **w** on the threshing Jgs 6:37
lambs and the **w** of 100,000 rams. 2 Kgs 3:4
He gives snow like **w**; he scatters Ps 147:16
She seeks **w** and flax, and works with Prv 31:13
like crimson, they shall become like **w**. Is 1:18
and the worm will eat them like **w**; Is 51:8
kind; wine of Helbon and **w** of Sahar Ezk 27:18
fat, you clothe yourselves with the **w**, Ezk 34:3
shall have nothing of **w** on them, Ezk 44:17
and the hair of his head like pure **w**; Dn 7:9
bread and my water, my **w** and my flax, Hos 2:5
and I will take away my **w** and my flax, Hos 2:9
with water and scarlet **w** and hyssop, Heb 9:19
The hairs of his head were white like **w**, Rv 1:14

WOOLEN (1)
whether a **w** or a linen garment, Lv 13:47

WORD (701)
After these things the **w** of the LORD Gn 15:1
behold, the **w** of the LORD came to him: Gn 15:4
and bring me **w**." So he sent him from Gn 37:14
out, she sent **w** to her father-in-law, Gn 38:25
your servant speak a **w** in my lord's Gn 44:18
the LORD did according to the **w** of Moses. Ex 8:13
Then whoever feared the **w** of the LORD Ex 9:20
not pay attention to the **w** of the LORD left Ex 9:21
And when he sent **w** to Moses, "I, your Ex 18:6
of Levi did according to the **w** of Moses. Ex 32:28
the people heard this disastrous **w**, Ex 33:4
and **w** was proclaimed throughout the Ex 36:6
they did according to the **w** of Moses. Lv 10:7
them according to the **w** of the LORD, Nm 3:16
sons, according to the **w** of the LORD, Nm 3:51
shall see whether my **w** will come true Nm 11:23
They brought back **w** to them and to Nm 13:26
have pardoned, according to your **w**. Nm 14:20
he has despised the **w** of the LORD and Nm 15:31
tonight, and I will bring back **w** to you, Nm 22:8
but speak only the **w** that I tell you." Nm 22:35
The **w** that God puts in my mouth, Nm 22:38
the LORD put a **w** in Balaam's mouth Nm 23:5
Balaam and put a **w** in his mouth and Nm 23:16
be able to go beyond the **w** of the LORD, Nm 24:13
rebelled against my **w** in the Nm 27:14
At his **w** they shall go out, and at his Nm 27:21
out, and at his **w** they shall come in, Nm 27:21
by a pledge, he shall not break his **w**. Nm 30:2
of Israel according to the **w** of the LORD, Nm 36:5
for us and bring us **w** again of the way Dt 1:22
to us, and brought us **w** again and said, Dt 1:25
Yet in spite of this **w** you did not believe Dt 1:32
not add to the **w** that I command you, Dt 4:2
time, to declare to you the **w** of the LORD. Dt 5:5
man lives by every **w** that comes from the Dt 8:3
he may confirm the **w** that the LORD swore Dt 9:5
presumes to speak a **w** in my name that Dt 18:20
may we know the **w** that the LORD has Dt 18:21
if the **w** does not come to pass or come Dt 18:22
that is a **w** that the LORD has not spoken; Dt 18:22
and by their **w** every dispute and every Dt 21:5
But the **w** is very near you. It is in your Dt 30:14
For it is no empty **w** for you, but your Dt 32:47
and by this **w** you shall live long in the Dt 32:47
For they observed your **w** and kept your Dt 33:9
of Moab, according to the **w** of the LORD, Dt 34:5
"Remember the **w** that Moses the Jos 1:13
neither shall any **w** go out of your Jos 6:10
shall do according to the **w** of the Lord. Jos 8:8
according to the **w** of the LORD that he Jos 8:27
There was not a **w** of all that Moses Jos 8:35
and I brought him **w** again as it was in Jos 14:7
that the LORD spoke this **w** to Moses, Jos 14:10
Not one **w** of all the good promises that Jos 21:45
of Israel, and brought back **w** to them. Jos 22:32
that not one **w** has failed of all the good Jos 23:14
whole congregation sent **w** to the Jgs 21:13
LORD establish his **w**." So the woman 1 Sm 1:23
And the **w** of the LORD was rare in those 1 Sm 3:1
and the **w** of the LORD had not yet been 1 Sm 3:7
Samuel at Shiloh by the **w** of the LORD. 1 Sm 3:21
And the **w** of Samuel came to all Israel. 1 Sm 4:1
make known to you the **w** of God." 1 Sm 9:27
The **w** of the LORD came to Samuel: 1 Sm 15:10
you have rejected the **w** of the LORD, 1 Sm 15:23
you have rejected the **w** of the LORD, 1 Sm 15:26
I done now? Was it not but a **w**?" 1 Sm 17:29
could not answer Abner another **w**, 2 Sm 3:11
that same night the **w** of the LORD came 2 Sm 7:4
did I speak a **w** with any of the judges of 2 Sm 7:7
confirm forever the **w** that you have 2 Sm 7:25
So David sent **w** to Joab, "Send me 2 Sm 11:6
have you despised the **w** of the LORD, 2 Sm 12:9
your servant speak a **w** to my lord 2 Sm 14:12
'The **w** of my lord the king will set 2 Sm 14:17
Joab, "Behold, I sent **w** to you, 2 Sm 14:32
the wilderness until **w** comes from 2 Sm 15:28
was as if one consulted the **w** of God; 2 Sm 16:23
when the **w** of all Israel has come to 2 Sm 19:11
man, so that they sent **w** to the king, 2 Sm 19:14
perfect; the **w** of the LORD proves true; 2 Sm 22:31
speaks by me; his **w** is on my tongue. 2 Sm 23:2
But the king's **w** prevailed against 2 Sm 24:4
the **w** of the LORD came to the prophet 2 Sm 24:11
So David went up at Gad's **w**, as the 2 Sm 24:19
may establish his **w** that he spoke 1 Kgs 2:4
more also if this **w** does not cost 1 Kgs 2:23
thus fulfilling the **w** of the LORD that 1 Kgs 2:27
Benaiah brought the king **w** again, 1 Kgs 2:30
behold, I now do according to your **w**. 1 Kgs 3:12
And Solomon sent **w** to Hiram, 1 Kgs 5:2
Now the **w** of the LORD came to 1 Kgs 6:11
then I will establish my **w** with you, 1 Kgs 6:12
of Israel, let your **w** be confirmed, 1 Kgs 8:26
Not one **w** has failed of all his good 1 Kgs 8:56
the LORD that he might fulfill his **w**, 1 Kgs 12:15
But the **w** of God came to Shemaiah 1 Kgs 12:22
they listened to the **w** of the LORD and 1 Kgs 12:24
according to the **w** of the LORD. 1 Kgs 12:24
out of Judah by the **w** of the LORD to 1 Kgs 13:1
the altar by the **w** of the LORD and 1 Kgs 13:2
of God had given by the **w** of the LORD. 1 Kgs 13:5
commanded me by the **w** of the LORD, 1 Kgs 13:9
was said to me by the **w** of the LORD, 1 Kgs 13:17
spoke to me by the **w** of the LORD, 1 Kgs 13:18
the **w** of the LORD came to the 1 Kgs 13:20
have disobeyed the **w** of the LORD 1 Kgs 13:21
who disobeyed the **w** of the LORD; 1 Kgs 13:26
according to the **w** that the LORD 1 Kgs 13:26
called out by the **w** of the LORD 1 Kgs 13:32
him, according to the **w** of the LORD, 1 Kgs 14:18
according to the **w** of the LORD that 1 Kgs 15:29
And the **w** of the LORD came to Jehu 1 Kgs 16:1
the **w** of the LORD came by the prophet 1 Kgs 16:7
according to the **w** of the LORD, 1 Kgs 16:12
according to the **w** of the LORD, 1 Kgs 16:34
nor rain these years, except by my **w**." 1 Kgs 17:1
And the **w** of the LORD came to him, 1 Kgs 17:2
did according to the **w** of the LORD. 1 Kgs 17:5
Then the **w** of the LORD came to him, 1 Kgs 17:8
according to the **w** of the LORD that 1 Kgs 17:16
and that the **w** of the LORD in your 1 Kgs 17:24
After many days the **w** of the LORD 1 Kgs 18:1
the people did not answer him a **w**. 1 Kgs 18:21
to whom the **w** of the LORD came, 1 Kgs 18:31
have done all these things at your **w**. 1 Kgs 18:36
the **w** of the LORD came to him, 1 Kgs 19:9
departed and brought him **w** again. 1 Kgs 20:9
did as Jezebel had sent **w** to them. 1 Kgs 21:11
Then the **w** of the LORD came to 1 Kgs 21:17
And the **w** of the LORD came to 1 Kgs 21:28
"Inquire first for the **w** of the LORD." 1 Kgs 22:5
Let your **w** be like the word of one of 1 Kgs 22:13
word be like the **w** of one of them, 1 Kgs 22:13
"Therefore hear the **w** of the LORD: 1 Kgs 22:19
according to the **w** of the LORD that 1 Kgs 22:38
is no God in Israel to inquire of his **w**? 2 Kgs 1:16
died according to the **w** of the LORD 2 Kgs 1:17
according to the **w** that Elisha spoke. 2 Kgs 2:22
went and sent **w** to Jehoshaphat king 2 Kgs 3:7
"The **w** of the LORD is with him." So 2 Kgs 3:12
Would you have a **w** spoken on your 2 Kgs 4:13
left, according to the **w** of the LORD. 2 Kgs 4:44
that this man sends **w** to me to cure a 2 Kgs 5:7
it is a great **w** the prophet has spoken 2 Kgs 5:13
according to the **w** of the man of God, 2 Kgs 5:14
the man of God sent **w** to the king of 2 Kgs 6:9
Elisha said, "Hear the **w** of the LORD: 2 Kgs 7:1
according to the **w** of the LORD. 2 Kgs 7:16
did according to the **w** of the man of 2 Kgs 8:2
And he said, "I have a **w** for you, O 2 Kgs 9:5
accordance with the **w** of the LORD." 2 Kgs 9:26
he said, "This is the **w** of the LORD, 2 Kgs 9:36
earth nothing of the **w** of the LORD, 2 Kgs 10:10
according to the **w** of the LORD that 2 Kgs 10:17
king of Israel sent **w** to Amaziah king 2 Kgs 14:9
according to the **w** of the LORD, 2 Kgs 14:25
"Hear the **w** of the great king, the 2 Kgs 18:28
silent and answered him not a **w**, 2 Kgs 18:36
This is the **w** that the LORD has 2 Kgs 19:21
court, the **w** of the LORD came to him: 2 Kgs 20:4
to Hezekiah, "Hear the **w** of the LORD: 2 Kgs 20:16
"The **w** of the LORD that you have 2 Kgs 20:19
they brought back **w** to the king. 2 Kgs 22:20
according to the **w** of the LORD that 2 Kgs 23:16
according to the **w** of the LORD that he 2 Kgs 24:2
according to the **w** of the LORD by 1 Chr 11:3
according to the **w** of the LORD 1 Chr 11:10
him, according to the **w** of the LORD. 1 Chr 12:23
according to the **w** of the LORD. 1 Chr 15:15
forever, the **w** that he commanded, 1 Chr 16:15
that same night the **w** of the LORD 1 Chr 17:3
did I speak a **w** with any of the judges 1 Chr 17:6
let the **w** that you have spoken 1 Chr 17:23
But the king's **w** prevailed against 1 Chr 21:4
So David went up at Gad's **w**, which 1 Chr 21:19
But the **w** of the LORD came to me, 1 Chr 22:8
let your **w** to David my father be now 2 Chr 1:9
And Solomon sent **w** to Hiram the 2 Chr 2:3
of Israel, let your **w** be confirmed, 2 Chr 6:17
that the LORD might fulfill his **w**, 2 Chr 10:15
But the **w** of the LORD came to 2 Chr 11:2
they listened to the **w** of the LORD and 2 Chr 11:4
the **w** of the LORD came to Shemaiah: 2 Chr 12:7
"Inquire first for the **w** of the LORD." 2 Chr 18:4
Let your **w** be like the word of one of 2 Chr 18:12
word be like the **w** of one of them, 2 Chr 18:12
"Therefore hear the **w** of the LORD: 2 Chr 18:18
of Israel sent **w** to Amaziah king 2 Chr 25:18
commanded by the **w** of the LORD. 2 Chr 30:12
have not kept the **w** of the LORD, 2 Chr 34:21
they brought back **w** to the king. 2 Chr 34:28
do according to the **w** of the LORD by 2 Chr 35:6
to fulfill the **w** of the LORD by the 2 Chr 36:21
that the **w** of the LORD by the mouth 2 Chr 36:22
that the **w** of the LORD by the mouth of Ezr 1:1
according to the **w** sent by Darius the Ezr 6:13
Remember the **w** that you commanded Neh 1:8
were silent and could not find a **w** to say. Neh 5:8
own house?" As the **w** left the mouth of Est 7:8
for Mordecai, whose **w** saved the king, Est 7:9
nights, and no one spoke a **w** to him, Jb 2:13
"If one ventures a **w** with you, will you be Jb 4:2
"Now a **w** was brought to me stealthily; Jb 4:12
you, or the **w** that deals gently with you? Jb 15:11
again, and my **w** dropped upon them. Jb 29:22
no more; they have not a **w** to say. Jb 32:15
by the **w** of your lips I have avoided the Ps 17:4
is perfect; the **w** of the LORD proves true; Ps 18:30
For the **w** of the LORD is upright, and all Ps 33:4
By the **w** of the LORD the heavens were Ps 33:6
In God, whose **w** I praise, in God I trust; I Ps 56:4
In God, whose **w** I praise, in the LORD, Ps 56:10
I praise, in the LORD, whose **w** I praise, Ps 56:10
The Lord gives the **w**; the women who Ps 68:11
covenant or alter the **w** that went forth Ps 89:34
angels, you mighty ones who do his **w**, Ps 103:20
his word, obeying the voice of his **w**! Ps 103:20
forever, the **w** that he commanded, Ps 105:8
to pass, the **w** of the LORD tested him. Ps 105:19
He sent out his **w** and healed them, Ps 107:20
By guarding it according to your **w**. Ps 119:9
I have stored up your **w** in my heart, Ps 119:11
your statutes; I will not forget your **w**. Ps 119:16
that I may live and keep your **w**. Ps 119:17
dust; give me life according to your **w**! Ps 119:25
strengthen me according to your **w**! Ps 119:28
who taunts me, for I trust in your **w**. Ps 119:42
And take not the **w** of truth utterly out Ps 119:43
Remember your **w** to your servant, in Ps 119:49
servant, O LORD, according to your **w**. Ps 119:65
I went astray, but now I keep your **w**. Ps 119:67
because I have hoped in your **w**. Ps 119:74
for your salvation; I hope in your **w**. Ps 119:81
your **w** is firmly fixed in the heavens. Ps 119:89
evil way, in order to keep your **w**. Ps 119:101
Your **w** is a lamp to my feet and a Ps 119:105
me life, O LORD, according to your **w**! Ps 119:107
and my shield; I hope in your **w**. Ps 119:114
The sum of your **w** is truth, and Ps 119:160
I rejoice at your **w** like one who finds Ps 119:162
understanding according to your **w**! Ps 119:169
you; deliver me according to your **w**. Ps 119:170
My tongue will sing of your **w**, for all Ps 119:172
my soul waits, and in his **w** I hope; Ps 130:5
all things your name and your **w**. Ps 138:2
Even before a **w** is on my tongue, Ps 139:4
to the earth; his **w** runs swiftly. Ps 147:15
He sends out his **w**, and melts them; he Ps 147:18
He declares his **w** to Jacob, his statutes Ps 147:19
and mist, stormy wind fulfilling his **w**! Ps 148:8
down, but a good **w** makes him glad. Prv 12:25
despises the **w** brings destruction Prv 13:13
wrath, but a harsh **w** stirs up anger. Prv 15:1

is a joy to a man, and a **w** in season,	Prv 15:23
thought to the **w** will discover good,	Prv 16:20
but the **w** of a man who hears will	Prv 21:28
A **w** fitly spoken is like apples of gold	Prv 25:11
Every **w** of God proves true; he is a	Prv 30:5
heart be hasty to utter a **w** before God,	Eccl 5:2
For the **w** of the king is supreme, and	Eccl 8:4
Hear the **w** of the LORD, you rulers of	Is 1:10
The **w** that Isaiah the son of Amoz saw	Is 2:1
law, and the **w** of the LORD from Jerusalem.	Is 2:3
and have despised the **w** of the Holy One	Is 5:24
speak a **w**, but it will not stand, for God is	Is 8:10
If they will not speak according to this **w**,	Is 8:20
The Lord has sent a **w** against Jacob, and it	Is 9:8
This is the **w** that the LORD spoke	Is 16:13
plundered; for the LORD has spoken this **w**.	Is 24:3
And the **w** of the LORD will be to them	Is 28:13
Therefore hear the **w** of the LORD, you	Is 28:14
who by a **w** make a man out to be an	Is 29:21
"Because you despise this **w** and trust in	Is 30:12
your ears shall hear a **w** behind you,	Is 30:21
were silent and answered him not a **w**,	Is 36:21
this is the **w** that the LORD has spoken	Is 37:22
Then the **w** of the LORD came to Isaiah:	Is 38:4
"Hear the **w** of the LORD of hosts:	Is 39:5
"The **w** of the LORD that you have spoken	Is 39:8
but the **w** of our God will stand forever.	Is 40:8
who confirms the **w** of his servant and	Is 44:26
out in righteousness a **w** that shall not	Is 45:23
to sustain with a **w** him who is weary.	Is 50:4
so shall my **w** be that goes out from my	Is 55:11
contrite in spirit and trembles at my **w**.	Is 66:2
Hear the **w** of the LORD, you who tremble	Is 66:5
of the LORD, you who tremble at his **w**:	Is 66:5
to whom the **w** of the LORD came in the	Jer 1:2
Now the **w** of the LORD came to me,	Jer 1:4
And the **w** of the LORD came to me,	Jer 1:11
I am watching over my **w** to perform it."	Jer 1:12
The **w** of the LORD came to me a second	Jer 1:13
The **w** of the LORD came to me, saying,	Jer 2:1
Hear the **w** of the LORD, O house of Jacob,	Jer 2:4
O generation, behold the **w** of the LORD.	Jer 2:31
will become wind; the **w** is not in them.	Jer 5:13
"Because you have spoken this **w**,	Jer 5:14
the **w** of the LORD is to them an object of	Jer 6:10
The **w** that came to Jeremiah from the	Jer 7:1
LORD'S house, and proclaim there this **w**,	Jer 7:2
this word, and say, Hear the **w** of the LORD,	Jer 7:2
they have rejected the **w** of the LORD,	Jer 8:9
Hear, O women, the **w** of the LORD, and let	Jer 9:20
let your ear receive the **w** of his mouth;	Jer 9:20
Hear the **w** that the LORD speaks to you, O	Jer 10:1
The **w** that came to Jeremiah from the	Jer 11:1
loincloth according to the **w** of the LORD,	Jer 13:2
And the **w** of the LORD came to me a	Jer 13:3
Then the **w** of the LORD came to me:	Jer 13:8
"You shall speak to them this **w**: 'Thus	Jer 13:12
The **w** of the LORD that came to Jeremiah	Jer 14:1
"You shall say to them this **w**: 'Let my	Jer 14:17
The **w** of the LORD came to me:	Jer 16:1
say to me, "Where is the **w** of the LORD?	Jer 17:15
'Hear the **w** of the LORD, you kings of	Jer 17:20
The **w** that came to Jeremiah from the	Jer 18:1
Then the **w** of the LORD came to me:	Jer 18:5
the wise, nor the **w** from the prophet.	Jer 18:18
You shall say, 'Hear the **w** of the LORD, O	Jer 19:3
and destruction!" For the **w** of the LORD	Jer 20:8
This is the **w** that came to Jeremiah	Jer 21:1
of Judah say, 'Hear the **w** of the LORD,	Jer 21:11
the king of Judah and speak there this **w**,	Jer 22:1
and say, 'Hear the **w** of the LORD, O King	Jer 22:2
For if you will indeed obey this **w**, then	Jer 22:4
land, land, land, hear the **w** of the LORD!	Jer 22:29
to those who despise the **w** of the LORD,	Jer 23:17
of the LORD to see and to hear his **w**,	Jer 23:18
paid attention to his **w** and listened?	Jer 23:18
him who has my **w** speak my word	Jer 23:28
has my word speak my **w** faithfully.	Jer 23:28
Is not my **w** like fire, declares the LORD,	Jer 23:29
for the burden is every man's own **w**,	Jer 23:36
Then the **w** of the LORD came to me:	Jer 24:4
The **w** that came to Jeremiah	Jer 25:1
day, the **w** of the LORD has come to me,	Jer 25:3
of Judah, this **w** came from the LORD:	Jer 26:1
to speak to them; do not hold back a **w**.	Jer 26:2
this **w** came to Jeremiah from the LORD.	Jer 27:1
Send **w** to the king of Edom, the king of	Jer 27:3
and if the **w** of the LORD is with them,	Jer 27:18
Yet hear now this **w** that I speak in your	Jer 28:7
when the **w** of that prophet comes to	Jer 28:9
the **w** of the LORD came to Jeremiah:	Jer 28:12
Hear the **w** of the LORD, all you exiles	Jer 29:20
Then the **w** of the LORD came to	Jer 29:30
The **w** that came to Jeremiah from the	Jer 30:1
"Hear the **w** of the LORD, O nations, and	Jer 31:10
The **w** that came to Jeremiah from the	Jer 32:1
said, "The **w** of the LORD came to me:	Jer 32:6
in accordance with the **w** of the LORD,	Jer 32:8
I knew that this was the **w** of the LORD.	Jer 32:8
The **w** of the LORD came to Jeremiah:	Jer 32:26
The **w** of the LORD came to Jeremiah a	Jer 33:1
The **w** of the LORD came to Jeremiah:	Jer 33:19
The **w** of the LORD came to Jeremiah:	Jer 33:23
The **w** that came to Jeremiah from the	Jer 34:1
Yet hear the **w** of the LORD, O Zedekiah	Jer 34:4
"Alas, lord!"' For I have spoken the **w**,	Jer 34:5
The **w** that came to Jeremiah from the	Jer 34:8
The **w** of the LORD came to Jeremiah	Jer 34:12
The **w** that came to Jeremiah from the	Jer 35:1
Then the **w** of the LORD came to	Jer 35:12
this **w** came to Jeremiah from the LORD:	Jer 36:1
the **w** of the LORD came to Jeremiah:	Jer 36:27
Then the **w** of the LORD came to Jeremiah	Jer 37:6
"Is there any **w** from the LORD?"	Jer 37:17
The **w** of the LORD came to Jeremiah	Jer 39:15
The **w** that came to Jeremiah from the	Jer 40:1
according to all the **w** with which the	Jer 42:5
end of ten days the **w** of the LORD came to	Jer 42:7
then hear the **w** of the LORD, O remnant	Jer 42:15
Then the **w** of the LORD came to Jeremiah	Jer 43:8
The **w** that came to Jeremiah	Jer 44:1
"As for the **w** that you have spoken to	Jer 44:16
all the women, "Hear the **w** of the LORD,	Jer 44:24
Therefore hear the **w** of the LORD, all	Jer 44:26
to live, shall know whose **w** will stand,	Jer 44:28
The **w** that Jeremiah the prophet spoke	Jer 45:1
The **w** of the LORD that came to Jeremiah	Jer 46:1
The **w** that the LORD spoke to Jeremiah	Jer 46:13
The **w** of the LORD that came to Jeremiah	Jer 47:1
The **w** of the LORD that came to	Jer 49:34
The **w** that the LORD spoke concerning	Jer 50:1
The **w** that Jeremiah the prophet	Jer 51:59
right, for I have rebelled against his **w**;	Lam 1:18
he has carried out his **w**, which he	Lam 2:17
the **w** of the LORD came to Ezekiel the	Ezk 1:3
days, the **w** of the LORD came to me:	Ezk 3:16
you hear a **w** from my mouth,	Ezk 3:17
The **w** of the LORD came to me:	Ezk 6:1
of Israel, hear the **w** of the Lord GOD!	Ezk 6:3
The **w** of the LORD came to me:	Ezk 7:1
case at his waist, brought back **w**,	Ezk 9:11
And the **w** of the LORD came to me:	Ezk 11:14
The **w** of the LORD came to me:	Ezk 12:1
In the morning the **w** of the LORD came	Ezk 12:8
And the **w** of the LORD came to me:	Ezk 12:17
And the **w** of the LORD came to me:	Ezk 12:21
I will speak the **w** that I will speak,	Ezk 12:25
I will speak the **w** and perform it,	Ezk 12:25
And the **w** of the LORD came to me:	Ezk 12:26
but the **w** that I speak will be	Ezk 12:28
The **w** of the LORD came to me:	Ezk 13:1
own hearts: 'Hear the **w** of the LORD!'	Ezk 13:2
yet they expect him to fulfill their **w**.	Ezk 13:6
And the **w** of the LORD came to me:	Ezk 14:2
the prophet is deceived and speaks a **w**,	Ezk 14:9
And the **w** of the LORD came to me:	Ezk 14:12
And the **w** of the LORD came to me:	Ezk 15:1
Again the **w** of the LORD came to me:	Ezk 16:1
O prostitute, hear the **w** of the LORD:	Ezk 16:35
The **w** of the LORD came to me:	Ezk 17:1
Then the **w** of the LORD came to me:	Ezk 17:11
The **w** of the LORD came to me:	Ezk 18:1
And the **w** of the LORD came to me:	Ezk 20:2
And the **w** of the LORD came to me:	Ezk 20:45
of the Negeb, Hear the **w** of the LORD:	Ezk 20:47
The **w** of the LORD came to me:	Ezk 21:1
And the **w** of the LORD came to me:	Ezk 21:8
The **w** of the LORD came to me again:	Ezk 21:18
And the **w** of the LORD came to me,	Ezk 22:1
And the **w** of the LORD came to me:	Ezk 22:17
And the **w** of the LORD came to me:	Ezk 22:23
The **w** of the LORD came to me:	Ezk 23:1
month, the **w** of the LORD came to me:	Ezk 24:1
The **w** of the LORD came to me:	Ezk 24:15
them, "The **w** of the LORD came to me:	Ezk 24:20
The **w** of the LORD came to me:	Ezk 25:1
Hear the **w** of the Lord GOD:	Ezk 25:3
month, the **w** of the LORD came to me:	Ezk 26:1
The **w** of the LORD came to me:	Ezk 27:1
The **w** of the LORD came to me:	Ezk 28:1
the **w** of the LORD came to me:	Ezk 28:11
The **w** of the LORD came to me:	Ezk 28:20
month, the **w** of the LORD came to me:	Ezk 29:1
month, the **w** of the LORD came to me:	Ezk 29:17
The **w** of the LORD came to me:	Ezk 30:1
month, the **w** of the LORD came to me:	Ezk 30:20
month, the **w** of the LORD came to me:	Ezk 31:1
month, the **w** of the LORD came to me:	Ezk 32:1
month, the **w** of the LORD came to me:	Ezk 32:17
The **w** of the LORD came to me:	Ezk 33:1
you hear a **w** from my mouth,	Ezk 33:7
The **w** of the LORD came to me:	Ezk 33:23
and hear what the **w** is that comes	Ezk 33:30
The **w** of the LORD came to me:	Ezk 34:1
you shepherds, hear the **w** of the LORD:	Ezk 34:7
you shepherds, hear the **w** of the LORD:	Ezk 34:9
The **w** of the LORD came to me:	Ezk 35:1
of Israel, hear the **w** of the LORD.	Ezk 36:1
of Israel, hear the **w** of the Lord GOD:	Ezk 36:4
The **w** of the LORD came to me:	Ezk 36:16
O dry bones, hear the **w** of the LORD.	Ezk 37:4
The **w** of the LORD came to me:	Ezk 37:15
The **w** of the LORD came to me:	Ezk 38:1
the Chaldeans, "The **w** from me is firm:	Dn 2:5
you see that the **w** from me is firm	Dn 2:8
the decision by the **w** of the holy ones,	Dn 4:17
Immediately the **w** was fulfilled against	Dn 4:33
according to the **w** of the LORD to	Dn 9:2
of your pleas for mercy a **w** went out,	Dn 9:23
consider the **w** and understand	Dn 9:23
going out of the **w** to restore and build	Dn 9:25
king of Persia a **w** was revealed to	Dn 10:1
Belteshazzar. And the **w** was true,	Dn 10:1
he understood the **w** and had	Dn 10:1
And when he had spoken this **w** to me,	Dn 10:11
The **w** of the LORD that came to Hosea,	Hos 1:1
Hear the **w** of the LORD, O children of	Hos 4:1
The **w** of the LORD that came to Joel, the son	Jl 1:1
great; he who executes his **w** is powerful.	Jl 2:11
Hear this **w** that the LORD has spoken	Am 3:1
"Hear this **w**, you cows of Bashan, who	Am 4:1
Hear this **w** that I take up over you in	Am 5:1
Now therefore hear the **w** of the LORD.	Am 7:16
run to and fro, to seek the **w** of the LORD,	Am 8:12
Now the **w** of the LORD came to Jonah the	Jon 1:1
Then the **w** of the LORD came to Jonah the	Jon 3:1
Nineveh, according to the **w** of the LORD.	Jon 3:3
The **w** reached the king of Nineveh, and	Jon 3:6
The **w** of the LORD that came to Micah of	Mi 1:1
and the **w** of the LORD from Jerusalem.	Mi 4:2
The **w** of the LORD that came to	Zep 1:1
The **w** of the LORD is against you, O	Zep 2:5
the **w** of the LORD came by the hand of	Hg 1:1
Then the **w** of the LORD came by the hand	Hg 1:3
the **w** of the LORD came by the hand of	Hg 2:1
the **w** of the LORD came by Haggai the	Hg 2:10
The **w** of the LORD came a second time to	Hg 2:20
the **w** of the LORD came to the prophet	Zec 1:1
the **w** of the LORD came to the prophet	Zec 1:7
"This is the **w** of the LORD to Zerubbabel:	Zec 4:6
Then the **w** of the LORD came to me,	Zec 4:8
And the **w** of the LORD came to me:	Zec 6:9
the **w** of the LORD came to Zechariah on	Zec 7:1
Then the **w** of the LORD of hosts came to	Zec 7:4
And the **w** of the LORD came to	Zec 7:8
And the **w** of the LORD of hosts came,	Zec 8:1
And the **w** of the LORD of hosts came to	Zec 8:18
The burden of the **w** of the LORD is	Zec 9:1
me, knew that it was the **w** of the LORD.	Zec 11:11
The burden of the **w** of the LORD	Zec 12:1
The oracle of the **w** of the LORD to Israel	Mal 1:1
when you have found him, bring me **w**,	Mt 2:8
but by every **w** that comes from the	Mt 4:4
come under my roof, but only say the **w**,	Mt 8:8
the spirits with a **w** and healed all who	Mt 8:16
of the Christ, he sent **w** by his disciples	Mt 11:2
whoever speaks a **w** against the Son	Mt 12:32
for every careless **w** they speak,	Mt 12:36
anyone hears the **w** of the kingdom	Mt 13:19
who hears the **w** and immediately	Mt 13:20
persecution arises on account of the **w**,	Mt 13:21
thorns, this is the one who hears the **w**,	Mt 13:22
the deceitfulness of riches choke the **w**,	Mt 13:22
who hears the **w** and understands it.	Mt 13:23
you have made void the **w** of God.	Mt 15:6
But he did not answer her a **w**. And his	Mt 15:23
no one was able to answer him a **w**,	Mt 22:46
judgment seat, his wife sent **w** to him,	Mt 27:19
And he was preaching the **w** to them.	Mk 2:2
The sower sows the **w**.	Mk 4:14
along the path, where the **w** is sown:	Mk 4:15
and takes away the **w** that is sown in	Mk 4:15
the ones who, when they hear the **w**,	Mk 4:16
persecution arises on account of the **w**,	Mk 4:17
thorns. They are those who hear the **w**,	Mk 4:18
other things enter in and choke the **w**,	Mk 4:19
ones who hear the **w** and accept it and	Mk 4:20
such parables he spoke the **w** to them,	Mk 4:33
he did not want to break his **w** to her.	Mk 6:26
thus making void the **w** of God by your	Mk 7:13
ministers of the **w** have delivered them	Lk 1:2
me according to your **w**." And the angel	Lk 1:38
depart in peace, according to your **w**;	Lk 2:29
the **w** of God came to John the son of	Lk 3:2
teaching, for his **w** possessed authority.	Lk 4:32

said to one another, "What is this **w**? Lk 4:36
pressing in on him to hear the **w** of God, Lk 5:1
But at your **w** I will let down the nets." Lk 5:5
But say the **w**, and let my servant be Lk 7:7
parable is this: The seed is the **w** of God. Lk 8:11
and takes away the **w** from their hearts, Lk 8:12
are those who, when they hear the **w**, Lk 8:13
soil, they are those who, hearing the **w**, Lk 8:15
are those who hear the **w** of God and do Lk 8:21
those who hear the **w** of God and keep Lk 11:28
who speaks a **w** against the Son Lk 12:10
mighty in deed and **w** before God and Lk 24:19
In the beginning was the **W**, and the Jn 1:1
was the Word, and the **W** was with God, Jn 1:1
Word was with God, and the **W** was God. Jn 1:1
And the **W** became flesh and dwelt Jn 1:14
the Scripture and the **w** that Jesus had Jn 2:22
many more believed because of his **w**. Jn 4:41
The man believed the **w** that Jesus spoke Jn 4:50
whoever hears my **w** and believes him Jn 5:24
you do not have his **w** abiding in you, Jn 5:38
believed in him, "If you abide in my **w**, Jn 8:31
kill me because my **w** finds no place in Jn 8:37
because you cannot bear to hear my **w**. Jn 8:43
truly, I say to you, if anyone keeps my **w**, Jn 8:51
yet you say, 'If anyone keeps my **w**, Jn 8:52
you, but I do know him and I keep his **w**. Jn 8:55
gods to whom the **w** of God came— Jn 10:35
so that the **w** spoken by the prophet Jn 12:38
the **w** that I have spoken will judge him Jn 12:48
"If anyone loves me, he will keep my **w**, Jn 14:23
And the **w** that you hear is not mine but Jn 14:24
clean because of the **w** that I have spoken Jn 15:3
Remember the **w** that I said to you: 'A Jn 15:20
If they kept my **w**, they will also keep Jn 15:20
But the **w** that is written in their Law Jn 15:25
them to me, and they have kept your **w**. Jn 17:6
I have given them your **w**, and the world Jn 17:14
them in the truth; your **w** is truth. Jn 17:17
who will believe in me through their **w**, Jn 17:20
was to fulfill the **w** that he had spoken: Jn 18:9
was to fulfill the **w** that Jesus had Jn 18:32
who received his **w** were baptized, Acts 2:41
of those who had heard the **w** believed, Acts 4:4
to speak your **w** with all boldness, Acts 4:29
continued to speak the **w** of God with Acts 4:31
give up preaching the **w** of God to serve Acts 6:2
to prayer and to the ministry of the **w**." Acts 6:4
And the **w** of God continued to increase, Acts 6:7
scattered went about preaching the **w**. Acts 8:4
Samaria had received the **w** of God, Acts 8:14
testified and spoken the **w** of the Lord, Acts 8:25
As for the **w** that he sent to Israel, Acts 10:36
Spirit fell on all who heard the **w**. Acts 10:44
also had received the **w** of God. Acts 11:1
And I remembered the **w** of the Lord, Acts 11:16
speaking the **w** to no one except Jews. Acts 11:19
But the **w** of God increased and Acts 12:24
they proclaimed the **w** of God in the Acts 13:5
Saul and sought to hear the **w** of God. Acts 13:7
if you have any **w** of exhortation for Acts 13:15
gathered to hear the **w** of the Lord. Acts 13:44
was necessary that the **w** of God be Acts 13:46
and glorifying the **w** of the Lord, Acts 13:48
And the **w** of the Lord was spreading Acts 13:49
who bore witness to the **w** of his grace, Acts 14:3
when they had spoken the **w** in Perga, Acts 14:25
should hear the **w** of the gospel Acts 15:7
you the same things by **w** of mouth. Acts 15:27
and preaching the **w** of the Lord, Acts 15:35
we proclaimed the **w** of the Lord, Acts 15:36
the Holy Spirit to speak the **w** in Asia. Acts 16:6
And they spoke the **w** of the Lord to Acts 16:32
they received the **w** with all eagerness, Acts 17:11
learned that the **w** of God was Acts 17:13
Paul was occupied with the **w**, Acts 18:5
teaching the **w** of God among them. Acts 18:11
of Asia heard the **w** of the Lord, Acts 19:10
So the **w** of the Lord continued to Acts 19:20
you to God and to the **w** of his grace, Acts 20:32
of all because of the **w** he had spoken, Acts 20:38
w came to the tribune of the cohort Acts 21:31
Up to this **w** they listened to him. Acts 22:22
is not as though the **w** of God has failed. Rom 9:6
"The **w** is near you, in your mouth Rom 10:8
is, the **w** of faith that we proclaim); Rom 10:8
and hearing through the **w** of Christ. Rom 10:17
are summed up in this **w**: Rom 13:9
to obedience—by **w** and deed, Rom 15:18
For the **w** of the cross is folly to those 1 Cor 1:18
it from you that the **w** of God came? 1 Cor 14:36
hold fast to the **w** I preached to you 1 Cor 15:2
our **w** to you has not been Yes and 2 Cor 1:18
not, like so many, peddlers of God's **w**, 2 Cor 2:17
cunning or to tamper with God's **w**, 2 Cor 4:2
For the whole law is fulfilled in one **w**: Gal 5:14
who is taught the **w** must share all good Gal 6:6
also, when you heard the **w** of truth, Eph 1:13
her by the washing of water with the **w**, Eph 5:26
of the Spirit, which is the **w** of God, Eph 6:17
more bold to speak the **w** without fear. Phil 1:14
holding fast to the **w** of life, so that in Phil 2:16
have heard before in the **w** of the truth, Col 1:5
you, to make the **w** of God fully known, Col 1:25
Let the **w** of Christ dwell in you richly, Col 3:16
And whatever you do, in **w** or deed, do Col 3:17
that God may open to us a door for the **w**, Col 4:3
our gospel came to you not only in **w**, 1 Thes 1:5
you received the **w** in much 1 Thes 1:6
not only has the **w** of the Lord 1 Thes 1:8
that when you received the **w** of God, 1 Thes 2:13
it not as the **w** of men but as 1 Thes 2:13
but as what it really is, the **w** of God, 1 Thes 2:13
declare to you by a **w** from the Lord, 1 Thes 4:15
either by a spirit or a spoken **w**, 2 Thes 2:2
either by our spoken **w** or by our 2 Thes 2:15
them in every good work and **w**. 2 Thes 2:17
that the **w** of the Lord may speed 2 Thes 3:1
made holy by the **w** of God and prayer. 1 Tm 4:5
But the **w** of God is not bound! 2 Tm 2:9
rightly handling the **w** of truth. 2 Tm 2:15
preach the **w**; be ready in season and 2 Tm 4:2
manifested in his **w** through the Ti 1:3
hold firm to the trustworthy **w** as taught, Ti 1:9
that the **w** of God may not be reviled. Ti 2:5
the universe by the **w** of his power. Heb 1:3
For the **w** of God is living and active, Heb 4:12
is unskilled in the **w** of righteousness, Heb 5:13
the goodness of the **w** of God and the Heb 6:5
as high priests, but the **w** of the oath, Heb 7:28
universe was created by the **w** of God, Heb 11:3
that speaks a better **w** than the blood Heb 12:24
those who spoke to you the **w** of God. Heb 13:7
bear with my **w** of exhortation, Heb 13:22
he brought us forth by the **w** of truth, Jas 1:18
receive with meekness the implanted **w**, Jas 1:21
But be doers of the **w**, and not hearers Jas 1:22
is a hearer of the **w** and not a doer, Jas 1:23
the living and abiding **w** of God; 1 Pt 1:23
but the **w** of the Lord remains forever." 1 Pt 1:25
forever." And this **w** is the good 1 Pt 1:25
stumble because they disobey the **w**, 1 Pt 2:8
so that even if some do not obey the **w**, 1 Pt 3:1
be won without a **w** by the conduct of 1 Pt 3:1
something more sure, the prophetic **w**, 2 Pt 1:19
and through water by the **w** of God, 2 Pt 3:5
But by the same **w** the heavens and 2 Pt 3:7
our hands, concerning the **w** of life— 1 Jn 1:1
make him a liar, and his **w** is not in us. 1 Jn 1:10
but whoever keeps his **w**, in him truly 1 Jn 2:5
commandment is the **w** that you have 1 Jn 2:7
strong, and the **w** of God abides in you, 1 Jn 2:14
let us not love in **w** or talk but in deed 1 Jn 3:18
who bore witness to the **w** of God and to Rv 1:2
on account of the **w** of God and the Rv 1:9
you have kept my **w** and have not denied Rv 3:8
have kept my **w** about patient Rv 3:10
had been slain for the **w** of God and for Rv 6:9
Lamb and by the **w** of their testimony, Rv 12:11
by which he is called is The **W** of God. Rv 19:13
testimony of Jesus and for the **w** of God, Rv 20:4

WORDS (535)

earth had one language and the same **w**. Gn 11:1
and heard the **w** of Rebekah his sister, Gn 24:30
Abraham's servant heard their **w**, Gn 24:52
soon as Esau heard the **w** of his father, Gn 27:34
But the **w** of Esau her older son were Gn 27:42
Their **w** pleased Hamor and Hamor's Gn 34:18
even more for his dreams and for his **w**. Gn 37:8
his master heard the **w** that his wife Gn 39:19
confined, that your **w** may be tested, Gn 42:16
So your **w** will be verified, and you Gn 42:20
them, he spoke to them these **w**. Gn 44:6
does my lord speak such **w** as these? Gn 44:7
father, we told him the **w** of my lord. Gn 44:24
when they told him all the **w** of Joseph, Gn 45:27
to him and put the **w** in his mouth, Ex 4:15
told Aaron all the **w** of the LORD with Ex 4:28
Aaron spoke all the **w** that the LORD had Ex 4:30
labor at it and pay no regard to lying **w**." Ex 5:9
These are the **w** that you shall speak to Ex 19:6
before them all these **w** that the LORD had Ex 19:7
And Moses reported the **w** of the people to Ex 19:8
When Moses told the **w** of the people to Ex 19:9
And God spoke all these **w**, saying, Ex 20:1
told the people all the **w** of the LORD and Ex 24:3
"All the **w** that the LORD has spoken we Ex 24:3
Moses wrote down all the **w** of the LORD. Ex 24:4
you in accordance with all these **w**." Ex 24:8
on the tablets the **w** that were on the Ex 34:1
the LORD said to Moses, "Write these **w**, Ex 34:27
accordance with these **w** I have made Ex 34:27
on the tablets the **w** of the covenant, Ex 34:28
and told the people the **w** of the LORD. Nm 11:24
And he said, "Hear my **w**: If there is a Nm 12:6
When Moses told these **w** to all the Nm 14:39
he had finished speaking all these **w**, Nm 16:31
oracle of him who hears the **w** of God, Nm 24:4
oracle of him who hears the **w** of God, Nm 24:16
These are the **w** that Moses spoke to all Dt 1:1
the LORD heard your **w** and was angered, Dt 1:34
the king of Heshbon, with **w** of peace, Dt 2:26
to me, that I may let them hear my **w**, Dt 4:10
You heard the sound of **w**, but saw no Dt 4:12
and you heard his **w** out of the midst of Dt 4:36
"These **w** the LORD spoke to all your Dt 5:22
"And the LORD heard your **w**, when you Dt 5:28
to me, 'I have heard the **w** of this people, Dt 5:28
And these **w** that I command you today Dt 6:6
on them were all the **w** that the LORD had Dt 9:10
on the tablets the **w** that were on the Dt 10:2
therefore lay up these **w** of mine in your Dt 11:18
to obey all these **w** that I command you, Dt 12:28
shall not listen to the **w** of that prophet or Dt 13:3
God by keeping all the **w** of this law and Dt 17:19
And I will put my **w** in his mouth, and Dt 18:18
not listen to my **w** that he shall speak Dt 18:19
shall write on them all the **w** of this law, Dt 27:3
on the stones all the **w** of this law very Dt 27:8
does not confirm the **w** of this law by Dt 27:26
from any of the **w** that I command you Dt 28:14
careful to do all the **w** of this law that Dt 28:58
These are the **w** of the covenant that the Dt 29:1
Therefore keep the **w** of this covenant Dt 29:9
when he hears the **w** of this sworn Dt 29:19
that we may do all the **w** of this law. Dt 29:29
continued to speak these **w** to all Israel. Dt 31:1
be careful to do all the **w** of this law, Dt 31:12
had finished writing the **w** of this law in Dt 31:24
I may speak these **w** in their ears and Dt 31:28
Then Moses spoke the **w** of this song Dt 31:30
let the earth hear the **w** of my mouth. Dt 32:1
and recited all the **w** of this song in Dt 32:44
speaking all these **w** to all Israel, Dt 32:45
"Take to heart all the **w** by which I am Dt 32:46
be careful to do all the **w** of this law. Dt 32:46
commandment and disobeys your **w**, Jos 1:18
And she said, "According to your **w**, so Jos 2:21
here and listen to the **w** of the LORD your Jos 3:9
afterward he read all the **w** of the law, Jos 8:34
heard the **w** that the people of Reuben Jos 22:30
And Joshua wrote these **w** in the Book Jos 24:26
it has heard all the **w** of the LORD that Jos 24:27
of the LORD spoke these **w** to all the people Jgs 2:4
relatives spoke all these **w** on his behalf Jgs 9:3
of the city heard the **w** of Gaal the son of Jgs 9:30
spoke all his **w** before the LORD Jgs 11:11
not listen to the **w** of Jephthah that he Jgs 11:28
said, "Now when your **w** come true, Jgs 13:12
name, so that, when your **w** come true, Jgs 13:17
him hard with her **w** day after day, Jgs 16:16
let none of his **w** fall to the ground. 1 Sm 3:19
So Samuel told all the **w** of the LORD to 1 Sm 8:10
had heard all the **w** of the people, 1 Sm 8:21
upon Saul when he heard these **w**, 1 Sm 11:6
therefore listen to the **w** of the LORD. 1 Sm 15:1
of the LORD and your **w**, 1 Sm 15:24
Israel heard these **w** of the Philistine, 1 Sm 17:11
and spoke the same **w** as before. 1 Sm 17:23
When the **w** that David spoke were 1 Sm 17:31
servants spoke those **w** in the ears 1 Sm 18:23
his servants told David these **w**, 1 Sm 18:26
And David took these **w** to heart and 1 Sm 21:12
his men with these **w** and did not 1 Sm 24:7
do you listen to the **w** of men who say, 1 Sm 24:9
finished speaking these **w** to Saul, 1 Sm 24:16
ears, and hear the **w** of your servant. 1 Sm 25:24
the king hear the **w** of his servant. 1 Sm 26:19
with fear because of the **w** of Samuel. 1 Sm 28:20
urged him, and he listened to their **w**. 1 Sm 28:23
angry over the **w** of Ish-bosheth and 2 Sm 3:8
In accordance with all these **w**, and in 2 Sm 7:17
GOD, you are God, and your **w** are true, 2 Sm 7:28
him." So Joab put the **w** in her mouth. 2 Sm 14:3
who put all these **w** in the mouth of 2 Sm 14:19
our king?" But the **w** of the men of 2 Sm 19:43
were fiercer than the **w** of the men of 2 Sm 19:43
"Listen to the **w** of your servant." 2 Sm 20:17
spoke to the LORD the **w** of this song on 2 Sm 22:1
Now these are the last **w** of David: The 2 Sm 23:1
in after you and confirm your **w**." 1 Kgs 1:14
as Hiram heard the **w** of Solomon, 1 Kgs 5:7
Let these **w** of mine, with which I 1 Kgs 8:59
own land of your **w** and of your 1 Kgs 10:6
and speak good **w** to them when you 1 Kgs 12:7

to their father the **w** that he had	1 Kgs 13:11
And when Ahab heard those **w**, he	1 Kgs 21:27
the **w** of the prophets with one	1 Kgs 22:13
king of Israel the **w** that you speak in	2 Kgs 6:12
the king heard the **w** of the woman,	2 Kgs 6:30
think that mere **w** are strategy and	2 Kgs 18:20
me to speak these **w** to your master	2 Kgs 18:27
told him the **w** of the Rabshakeh.	2 Kgs 18:37
heard all the **w** of the Rabshakeh,	2 Kgs 19:4
and will rebuke the **w** that the LORD	2 Kgs 19:4
afraid because of the **w** that you have	2 Kgs 19:6
and hear the **w** of Sennacherib,	2 Kgs 19:16
the king heard the **w** of the Book of	2 Kgs 22:11
concerning the **w** of this book that	2 Kgs 22:13
have not obeyed the **w** of this book,	2 Kgs 22:13
all the **w** of the book that the king of	2 Kgs 22:16
Regarding the **w** that you have	2 Kgs 22:18
their hearing all the **w** of the Book of	2 Kgs 23:2
to perform the **w** of this covenant that	2 Kgs 23:3
he might establish the **w** of the law	2 Kgs 23:24
In accordance with all these **w**, and	1 Chr 17:15
For by the last **w** of David the sons	1 Chr 23:27
own land of your **w** and of your	2 Chr 9:5
them and speak good **w** to them,	2 Chr 10:7
As soon as Asa heard these **w**, the	2 Chr 15:8
the **w** of the prophets with one	2 Chr 18:12
commanded, by the **w** of the LORD,	2 Chr 29:15
the LORD with the **w** of David and of	2 Chr 29:30
confidence from the **w** of Hezekiah	2 Chr 32:8
and the **w** of the seers who spoke to	2 Chr 33:18
the king heard the **w** of the Law,	2 Chr 34:19
concerning the **w** of the book that	2 Chr 34:21
Regarding the **w** that you have	2 Chr 34:26
you heard his **w** against this place	2 Chr 34:27
their hearing all the **w** of the Book	2 Chr 34:30
to perform the **w** of the covenant	2 Chr 34:31
not listen to the **w** of Neco from the	2 Chr 35:22
despising his **w** and scoffing at his	2 Chr 36:16
all who trembled at the **w** of the God of	Ezr 9:4
The **w** of Nehemiah the son of	Neh 1:1
soon as I heard these **w** I sat down and	Neh 1:4
and also of the **w** that the king had	Neh 2:18
when I heard their outcry and these **w**.	Neh 5:6
presence and reported my **w** to him.	Neh 6:19
wept as they heard the **w** of the Law.	Neh 8:9
had understood the **w** that were	Neh 8:12
in order to study the **w** of the Law.	Neh 8:13
to see whether Mordecai's **w** would stand,	Est 3:4
of Ahasuerus, in **w** of peace and truth,	Est 9:30
Your **w** have upheld him who was	Jb 4:4
of the sea; therefore my **w** have been rash.	Jb 6:3
I have not denied the **w** of the Holy One.	Jb 6:10
How forceful are upright **w**! But what	Jb 6:25
Do you think that you can reprove **w**,	Jb 6:26
and the **w** of your mouth be a great wind?	Jb 8:2
tell you and utter **w** out of their	Jb 8:10
I answer him, choosing my **w** with him?	Jb 9:14
"Should a multitude of **w** go unanswered,	Jb 11:2
not the ear test **w** as the palate tastes	Jb 12:11
Keep listening to my **w**, and let my	Jb 13:17
or in **w** with which he can do no good?	Jb 15:3
God and bring such **w** out of your	Jb 15:13
Shall windy **w** have an end? Or what	Jb 16:3
I could join **w** together against you and	Jb 16:4
"How long will you hunt for **w**?	Jb 18:2
me and break me in pieces with **w**?	Jb 19:2
"Oh that my **w** were written! Oh that	Jb 19:23
"Keep listening to my **w**, and let this be	Jb 21:2
mouth, and lay up his **w** in your heart.	Jb 22:22
I have treasured the **w** of his mouth	Jb 23:12
With whose help have you uttered **w**, and	Jb 26:4
instead of barley." The **w** of Job are	Jb 31:40
"Behold, I waited for your **w**, I listened	Jb 32:11
who refuted Job or who answered his **w**.	Jb 32:12
He has not directed his **w** against me,	Jb 32:14
For I am full of **w**; the spirit within me	Jb 32:18
my speech, O Job, and listen to all my **w**.	Jb 33:1
My **w** declare the uprightness of my	Jb 33:3
if you can; set your **w** in order before me;	Jb 33:5
and I have heard the sound of your **w**.	Jb 33:8
'He will answer none of man's **w**'?	Jb 33:13
If you have any **w**, answer me; speak, for	Jb 33:32
"Hear my **w**, you wise men, and give ear	Jb 34:2
for the ear tests **w** as the palate tastes food.	Jb 34:3
knowledge; his **w** are without insight.'	Jb 34:35
us and multiplies his **w** against God."	Jb 34:37
he multiplies **w** without knowledge."	Jb 35:16
For truly my **w** are not false; one who is	Jb 36:4
counsel by **w** without knowledge?	Jb 38:2
pleas to you? Will he speak to you soft **w**?	Jb 41:3
After the LORD had spoken these **w** to Job,	Jb 42:7
will you love vain **w** and seek after lies?	Ps 4:2
Give ear to my **w**, O LORD; consider my	Ps 5:1
to the LORD concerning the **w** of Cush,	Ps 7:T
The **w** of the LORD are pure words, like	Ps 12:6
The words of the LORD are pure **w**, like	Ps 12:6
God; incline your ear to me; hear my **w**.	Ps 17:6
who addressed the **w** of this song to the	Ps 18:T
There is no speech, nor are there **w**,	Ps 19:3
earth, and their **w** to the end of the world.	Ps 19:4
Let the **w** of my mouth and the	Ps 19:14
saving me, from the **w** of my groaning?	Ps 22:1
quiet in the land they devise **w** of deceit.	Ps 35:20
The **w** of his mouth are trouble and	Ps 36:3
one comes to see me, he utters empty **w**,	Ps 41:6
and you cast my **w** behind you.	Ps 50:17
be justified in your **w** and blameless in	Ps 51:4
You love all **w** that devour, O deceitful	Ps 52:4
prayer; give ear to the **w** of my mouth.	Ps 54:2
his **w** were softer than oil, yet they were	Ps 55:21
sin of their mouths, the **w** of their lips,	Ps 59:12
swords, who aim bitter **w** like arrows,	Ps 64:3
incline your ears to the **w** of my mouth!	Ps 78:1
They pour out their arrogant **w**; all the	Ps 94:4
dark; they did not rebel against his **w**.	Ps 105:28
Then they believed his **w**; they sang	Ps 106:12
they had rebelled against the **w** of God,	Ps 107:11
They encircle me with **w** of hate, and	Ps 109:3
my portion; I promise to keep your **w**.	Ps 119:57
How sweet are your **w** to my taste,	Ps 119:103
The unfolding of your **w** gives light;	Ps 119:130
me, because my foes forget your **w**.	Ps 119:139
and cry for help; I hope in your **w**.	Ps 119:147
my heart stands in awe of your **w**.	Ps 119:161
they have heard the **w** of your mouth,	Ps 138:4
the cliff, then they shall hear my **w**,	Ps 141:6
is faithful in all his **w** and kind in all	Ps 145:13
instruction, to understand **w** of insight,	Prv 1:2
the **w** of the wise and their riddles.	Prv 1:6
to you; I will make my **w** known to you.	Prv 1:23
if you receive my **w** and treasure up my	Prv 2:1
from the adulteress with her smooth **w**,	Prv 2:16
to me, "Let your heart hold fast my **w**;	Prv 4:4
not turn away from the **w** of my mouth.	Prv 4:5
Hear, my son, and accept my **w**, that the	Prv 4:10
My son, be attentive to my **w**; incline	Prv 4:20
do not depart from the **w** of my mouth.	Prv 5:7
if you are snared in the **w** of your mouth,	Prv 6:2
mouth, caught in the **w** of your mouth,	Prv 6:2
keep my **w** and treasure up my	Prv 7:1
from the adulteress with her smooth **w**.	Prv 7:5
and be attentive to the **w** of my mouth.	Prv 7:24
All the **w** of my mouth are righteous;	Prv 8:8
When **w** are many, transgression is	Prv 10:19
The **w** of the wicked lie in wait for	Prv 12:6
is one whose rash **w** are like sword	Prv 12:18
there you do not meet **w** of knowledge.	Prv 14:7
to the LORD, but gracious **w** are pure.	Prv 15:26
Gracious **w** are like a honeycomb,	Prv 16:24
restrains his **w** has knowledge,	Prv 17:27
The **w** of a man's mouth are deep	Prv 18:4
The **w** of a whisperer are like delicious	Prv 18:8
He pursues them with **w**, but does not	Prv 19:7
will stray from the **w** of knowledge.	Prv 19:27
but he overthrows the **w** of the traitor.	Prv 22:12
your ear, and hear the **w** of the wise,	Prv 22:17
have eaten, and waste your pleasant **w**.	Prv 23:8
he will despise the good sense of your **w**.	Prv 23:9
and your ear to **w** of knowledge.	Prv 23:12
The **w** of a whisperer are like delicious	Prv 26:22
By mere **w** a servant is not disciplined,	Prv 29:19
you see a man who is hasty in his **w**?	Prv 29:20
The **w** of Agur son of Jakeh. The oracle.	Prv 30:1
Do not add to his **w**, lest he rebuke you	Prv 30:6
The **w** of King Lemuel. An oracle that	Prv 31:1
The **w** of the Preacher, the son of David,	Eccl 1:1
on earth. Therefore let your **w** be few.	Eccl 5:2
and a fool's voice with many **w**.	Eccl 5:3
dreams increase and **w** grow many,	Eccl 5:7
The more **w**, the more vanity, and	Eccl 6:11
is despised and his **w** are not heard.	Eccl 9:16
The **w** of the wise heard in quiet are	Eccl 9:17
The **w** of a wise man's mouth win	Eccl 10:12
The beginning of the **w** of his mouth	Eccl 10:13
A fool multiplies **w**, though no man	Eccl 10:14
Preacher sought to find **w** of delight,	Eccl 12:10
and uprightly he wrote **w** of truth.	Eccl 12:10
The **w** of the wise are like goads, and	Eccl 12:11
become to you like the **w** of a book that	Is 29:11
day the deaf shall hear the **w** of a book,	Is 29:18
he does not call back his **w**, but will arise	Is 31:2
schemes to ruin the poor with lying **w**,	Is 32:7
you think that mere **w** are strategy and	Is 36:5
me to speak these **w** to your master and	Is 36:12
"Hear the **w** of the great king, the king of	Is 36:13
and told him the **w** of the Rabshakeh.	Is 36:22
God will hear the **w** of the Rabshakeh,	Is 37:4
and will rebuke the **w** that the LORD your	Is 37:4
afraid because of the **w** that you have	Is 37:6
and hear all the **w** of Sennacherib,	Is 37:17
proclaimed, none who heard your **w**.	Is 41:26
And I have put my **w** in your mouth and	Is 51:16
and uttering from the heart lying **w**.	Is 59:13
and my **w** that I have put in your	Is 59:21
The **w** of Jeremiah, the son of Hilkiah, one	Jer 1:1
"Behold, I have put my **w** in your mouth.	Jer 1:9
and proclaim these **w** toward the north,	Jer 3:12
I am making my **w** in your mouth a fire,	Jer 5:14
they have not paid attention to my **w**;	Jer 6:19
Do not trust in these deceptive **w**: 'This is	Jer 7:4
you trust in deceptive **w** to no avail.	Jer 7:8
"So you shall speak all these **w** to them,	Jer 7:27
"Hear the **w** of this covenant, and speak	Jer 11:2
who does not hear the **w** of this covenant	Jer 11:3
"Proclaim all these **w** in the cities of	Jer 11:6
Hear the **w** of this covenant and do them.	Jer 11:6
upon them all the **w** of this covenant,	Jer 11:8
forefathers, who refused to hear my **w**.	Jer 11:10
though they speak friendly **w** to you."	Jer 12:6
evil people, who refuse to hear my **w**,	Jer 13:10
Your **w** were found, and I ate them, and	Jer 15:16
and your **w** became to me a joy and the	Jer 15:16
when you tell this people all these **w**,	Jer 16:10
and there I will let you hear my **w**."	Jer 18:2
let us not pay attention to any of his **w**."	Jer 18:18
and proclaim there the **w** that I tell you.	Jer 19:2
their neck, refusing to hear my **w**."	Jer 19:15
But if you will not obey these **w**, I swear	Jer 22:5
of the LORD and because of his holy **w**.	Jer 23:9
not listen to the **w** of the prophets who	Jer 23:16
have proclaimed my **w** to my people,	Jer 23:22
who steal my **w** from one another.	Jer 23:30
and you pervert the **w** of the living God,	Jer 23:36
LORD, 'Because you have said these **w**,	Jer 23:38
Because you have not obeyed my **w**,	Jer 25:8
that land all the **w** that I have uttered	Jer 25:13
prophesy against them all these **w**,	Jer 25:30
the LORD all the **w** that I command you	Jer 26:2
and to listen to the **w** of my servants the	Jer 26:5
Jeremiah speaking these **w** in the house	Jer 26:7
and this city all the **w** you have heard.	Jer 26:12
you to speak all these **w** in your ears."	Jer 26:15
against this land in **w** like those of	Jer 26:20
and all the officials, heard his **w**,	Jer 26:21
not listen to the **w** of the prophets who	Jer 27:14
not listen to the **w** of your prophets who	Jer 27:16
the LORD make the **w** that you have	Jer 28:6
These are the **w** of the letter that	Jer 29:1
they did not pay attention to my **w**,	Jer 29:19
in my name lying **w** that I did not	Jer 29:23
in a book all the **w** that I have spoken to	Jer 30:2
These are the **w** that the LORD spoke	Jer 30:4
they shall use these **w** in the land of	Jer 31:23
spoke all these **w** to Zedekiah king	Jer 34:6
receive instruction and listen to my **w**?	Jer 35:13
write on it all the **w** that I have spoken to	Jer 36:2
of Jeremiah all the **w** of the LORD that	Jer 36:4
you shall read the **w** of the LORD from	Jer 36:6
from the scroll the **w** of the LORD in	Jer 36:8
Baruch read the **w** of Jeremiah from the	Jer 36:10
heard all the **w** of the LORD from the	Jer 36:11
told them all the **w** that he had heard,	Jer 36:13
When they heard all the **w**, they turned	Jer 36:16
must report all these **w** to the king."	Jer 36:16
please, how did you write all these **w**?	Jer 36:17
them, "He dictated all these **w** to me,	Jer 36:18
and they reported all the **w** to the king.	Jer 36:20
who heard all these **w** was afraid,	Jer 36:24
the scroll with the **w** that Baruch wrote	Jer 36:27
on it all the former **w** that were in the	Jer 36:28
of Jeremiah all the **w** of the scroll that	Jer 36:32
And many similar **w** were added to	Jer 36:32
the land listened to the **w** of the LORD that	Jer 37:2
Malchiah heard the **w** that Jeremiah was	Jer 38:1
the people, by speaking such **w** to them.	Jer 38:4
Jeremiah, "Let no one know of these **w**,	Jer 38:24
I will fulfill my **w** against this city for	Jer 39:16
all the people all these **w** of the LORD their	Jer 43:1
may know that my **w** will surely stand	Jer 44:29
when he wrote these **w** in a book at the	Jer 45:1
all these **w** that are written concerning	Jer 51:60
Babylon, see that you read all these **w**,	Jer 51:61
Thus far are the **w** of Jeremiah.	Jer 51:64
afraid of them, nor be afraid of their **w**,	Ezk 2:6
Be not afraid of their **w**, nor be dismayed	Ezk 2:6
And you shall speak my **w** to them,	Ezk 2:7
were written on it **w** of lamentation and	Ezk 2:10
of Israel and speak with my **w** to them.	Ezk 3:4
whose **w** you cannot understand.	Ezk 3:6
all my **w** that I shall speak to you	Ezk 3:10
None of my **w** will be delayed any	Ezk 12:28
and multiplied your **w** against me;	Ezk 35:13
speak lying and corrupt **w** before me till	Dn 2:9
While the **w** were still in the king's	Dn 4:31
because of the **w** of the king and his	Dn 5:10

Then the king, when he heard these **w**, Dn 6:14
sound of the great **w** that the horn was Dn 7:11
He shall speak **w** against the Most High, Dn 7:25
He has confirmed his **w**, which he spoke Dn 9:12
and the sound of his **w** like the sound of Dn 10:6
Then I heard the sound of his **w**, and as I Dn 10:9
words, and as I heard the sound of his **w**, Dn 10:9
understand the **w** that I speak to you, Dn 10:11
your God, your **w** have been heard, Dn 10:12
and I have come because of your **w**. Dn 10:12
had spoken to me according to these **w**, Dn 10:15
Daniel, shut up the **w** and seal the book, Dn 12:4
for the **w** are shut up and sealed until Dn 12:9
I have slain them by the **w** of my mouth, Hos 6:5
They utter mere **w**; with empty oaths Hos 10:4
Take with you **w** and return to the Hos 14:2
The **w** of Amos, who was among the Am 1:1
The land is not able to bear all his **w**. Am 7:10
water, but of hearing the **w** of the LORD. Am 8:11
Do not my **w** do good to him who walks Mi 2:7
God, and the **w** of Haggai the prophet, Hg 1:12
But my **w** and my statutes, which I Zec 1:6
gracious and comforting **w** to the angel Zec 1:13
Were not these the **w** that the LORD Zec 7:7
hear the law and the **w** that the LORD of Zec 7:12
been hearing these **w** from the mouth Zec 8:9
have wearied the LORD with your **w**. Mal 2:17
"Your **w** have been hard against me, Mal 3:13
that they will be heard for their many **w**. Mt 6:7
then who hears these **w** of mine and does Mt 7:24
everyone who hears these **w** of mine and Mt 7:26
will not receive you or listen to your **w**, Mt 10:14
for by your **w** you will be justified, and Mt 12:37
and by your **w** you will be Mt 12:37
away, but my **w** will not pass away. Mt 24:35
third time, saying the same **w** again. Mt 26:44
me and of my **w** in this adulterous and Mk 8:38
the disciples were amazed at his **w**. Mk 10:24
away, but my **w** will not pass away. Mk 13:31
away and prayed, saying the same **w**. Mk 14:39
place, because you did not believe my **w**, Lk 1:20
in the book of the **w** of Isaiah the prophet, Lk 3:4
at the gracious **w** that were coming Lk 4:22
to me and hears my **w** and does them, Lk 6:47
whoever is ashamed of me and of my **w**, Lk 9:26
"Let these **w** sink into your ears: The Lk 9:44
'I will condemn you with your own **w**, Lk 19:22
all the people were hanging on his **w**. Lk 19:48
away, but my **w** will not pass away. Lk 21:33
And they remembered his **w**, Lk 24:8
but these **w** seemed to them an idle tale, Lk 24:11
"These are my **w** that I spoke to you Lk 24:44
whom God has sent utters the **w** of God, Jn 3:34
writings, how will you believe my **w**?" Jn 5:47
The **w** that I have spoken to you are spirit Jn 6:63
we go? You have the **w** of eternal life, Jn 6:68
When they heard these **w**, some of the Jn 7:40
These **w** he spoke in the treasury, as he Jn 8:20
Whoever is of God hears the **w** of God. Jn 8:47
among the Jews because of these **w**. Jn 10:19
"These are not the **w** of one who is Jn 10:21
If anyone hears my **w** and does not keep Jn 12:47
and does not receive my **w** has a judge; Jn 12:48
The **w** that I say to you I do not speak on Jn 14:10
does not love me does not keep my **w**. Jn 14:24
you abide in me, and my **w** abide in you, Jn 15:7
When Jesus had spoken these **w**, he lifted Jn 17:1
have given them the **w** that you gave me, Jn 17:8
When Jesus had spoken these **w**, he went Jn 18:1
So when Pilate heard these **w**, he Jn 19:13
be known to you, and give ear to my **w**. Acts 2:14
"Men of Israel, hear these **w**: Jesus of Acts 2:22
with many other **w** he bore witness Acts 2:40
When Ananias heard these **w**, he fell Acts 5:5
to the people all the **w** of this Life." Acts 5:20
and the chief priests heard these **w**, Acts 5:24
speak blasphemous **w** against Moses Acts 6:11
ceases to speak **w** against this holy Acts 6:13
and he was mighty in his **w** and deeds. Acts 7:22
Even with these **w** they scarcely Acts 14:18
And with this the **w** of the prophets Acts 15:15
out from us and troubled you with **w**, Acts 15:24
the brothers with many **w**. Acts 15:32
the jailer reported these **w** to Paul, Acts 16:36
police reported these **w** to the Acts 16:38
of questions about **w** and names and Acts 18:15
and remember the **w** of the Lord Acts 20:35
I am speaking true and rational **w**. Acts 26:25
"That you may be justified in your **w**, Rom 3:4
But the **w** "it was counted to him" were Rom 4:23
for us with groanings too deep for **w**. Rom 8:26
and their **w** to the ends of the world." Rom 10:18
and not with **w** of eloquent wisdom, 1 Cor 1:17
were not in plausible **w** of wisdom, 1 Cor 2:4
we impart this in **w** not taught by 1 Cor 2:13
rather speak five **w** with my mind 1 Cor 14:19
than ten thousand **w** in a tongue. 1 Cor 14:19
Let no one deceive you with empty **w**, for Eph 5:6
that **w** may be given to me in opening Eph 6:19
For we never came with **w** of flattery, 1 Thes 2:5
encourage one another with these **w**. 1 Thes 4:18
being trained in the **w** of the faith and 1 Tm 4:6
agree with the sound **w** of our Lord 1 Tm 6:3
controversy and for quarrels about **w**, 1 Tm 6:4
pattern of the sound **w** that you have 2 Tm 1:13
before God not to quarrel about **w**, 2 Tm 2:14
long afterward, in the **w** already quoted, Heb 4:7
and a voice whose **w** made the hearers Heb 12:19
greed they will exploit you with false **w**. 2 Pt 2:3
who reads aloud the **w** of this prophecy, Rv 1:3
'The **w** of him who holds the seven stars Rv 2:1
'The **w** of the first and the last, who died Rv 2:8
'The **w** of him who has the sharp Rv 2:12
'The **w** of the Son of God, who has eyes Rv 2:18
'The **w** of him who has the seven spirits of Rv 3:1
'The **w** of the holy one, the true one, who Rv 3:7
'The **w** of the Amen, the faithful and true Rv 3:14
uttering haughty and blasphemous **w**, Rv 13:5
beast, until the **w** of God are fulfilled. Rv 17:17
said to me, "These are the true **w** of God." Rv 19:9
for these **w** are trustworthy and true." Rv 21:5
me, "These **w** are trustworthy and true. Rv 22:6
one who keeps the **w** of the prophecy of Rv 22:7
with those who keep the **w** of this book. Rv 22:9
"Do not seal up the **w** of the prophecy of Rv 22:10
who hears the **w** of the prophecy Rv 22:18
takes away from the **w** of the book of Rv 22:19

WORE (10)
so that they **w** themselves out groping Gn 19:11
the robe of many colors that he **w**. Gn 37:23
eighty-five persons who **w** the linen 1 Sm 22:18
and tore the long robe that she **w**. 2 Sm 13:19
him, "He **w** a garment of hair, 2 Kgs 1:8
singers. And David **w** a linen ephod. 1 Chr 15:27
I, when they were sick—I **w** sackcloth; Ps 35:13
Now John **w** a garment of camel's hair Mt 3:4
with camel's hair and **w** a leather belt Mk 1:6
they **w** breastplates the color of fire and Rv 9:17

WORK (363)
day God finished his **w** that he had done, Gn 2:2
day from all his **w** that he had done. Gn 2:2
rested from all his **w** that he had done Gn 2:3
and there was no man to **w** the ground, Gn 2:5
in the garden of Eden to **w** it and keep it. Gn 2:15
garden of Eden to **w** the ground from Gn 3:23
When you **w** the ground, it shall no Gn 4:12
us relief from our **w** and from the Gn 5:29
the house to do his **w** and none of the Gn 39:11
made the people of Israel **w** as slaves Ex 1:13
brick, and in all kinds of **w** in the field. Ex 1:14
In all their **w** they ruthlessly made them Ex 1:14
they ruthlessly made them **w** as slaves. Ex 1:14
do you take the people away from their **w**? Ex 5:4
Let heavier **w** be laid on the men that they Ex 5:9
but your **w** will not be reduced in the Ex 5:11
were urgent, saying, "Complete your **w**, Ex 5:13
Go now and **w**. No straw will be given Ex 5:18
No **w** shall be done on those days. Ex 12:16
the LORD, which he will **w** for you today. Ex 14:13
days you shall labor, and do all your **w**, Ex 20:9
On it you shall not do any **w**, you, or Ex 20:10
"Six days you shall do your **w**, but on Ex 23:12
of hammered **w** shall you make them, Ex 25:18
shall be made of hammered **w**: Ex 25:31
piece of hammered **w** of pure gold. Ex 25:36
an ephod, a robe, a coat of checker **w**, Ex 28:4
a breastpiece of judgment, in skilled **w**. Ex 28:15
the coat in checker **w** of fine linen, Ex 28:39
to devise artistic designs, to **w** in gold, Ex 31:4
and in carving wood, to **w** in every craft. Ex 31:5
Whoever does any **w** on it, that soul Ex 31:14
Six days shall **w** be done, but the Ex 31:15
Whoever does any **w** on the Sabbath Ex 31:15
The tablets were the **w** of God, and the Ex 32:16
you are shall see the **w** of the LORD, Ex 34:10
"Six days you shall **w**, but on the Ex 34:21
Six days **w** shall be done, but on the Ex 35:2
Whoever does any **w** on it shall be put to Ex 35:2
wood of any use in the **w** brought it. Ex 35:24
bring anything for the **w** that the LORD Ex 35:29
to **w** in gold and silver and bronze, Ex 35:32
wood, for **w** in every skilled craft. Ex 35:33
do every sort of **w** done by an engraver Ex 35:35
how to do any **w** in the construction of Ex 36:1
the sanctuary shall **w** in accordance Ex 36:1
heart stirred him up to come to do the **w**. Ex 36:2
for doing the **w** on the sanctuary. Ex 36:3
enough for doing the **w** that the LORD has Ex 36:5
they had was sufficient to do all the **w**, Ex 36:7
made them of hammered **w** on the two Ex 37:7
made the lampstand of hammered **w**. Ex 37:17
piece of hammered **w** of pure gold. Ex 37:22
All the gold that was used for the **w**, in Ex 38:24
cut it into threads to **w** into the blue and Ex 39:3
He made the breastpiece, in skilled **w**, in Ex 39:8
Thus all the **w** of the tabernacle of the Ex 39:32
the people of Israel had done all the **w**. Ex 39:42
And Moses saw all the **w**, and behold, Ex 39:43
of the court. So Moses finished the **w**. Ex 40:33
afflict yourselves and shall do no **w**, Lv 16:29
"Six days shall **w** be done, but on the Lv 23:3
a holy convocation. You shall do no **w**. Lv 23:3
you shall not do any ordinary **w**. Lv 23:7
you shall not do any ordinary **w**." Lv 23:8
You shall not do any ordinary **w**. Lv 23:21
You shall not do any ordinary **w**, and Lv 23:25
shall not do any **w** on that very day, Lv 23:28
And whoever does any **w** on that very Lv 23:30
You shall not do any **w**. It is a statute Lv 23:31
you shall not do any ordinary **w**. Lv 23:35
you shall not do any ordinary **w**. Lv 23:36
duty, to do the **w** in the tent of meeting. Nm 4:3
of the lampstand, hammered **w** of gold. Nm 8:4
base to its flowers, it was hammered **w**; Nm 8:4
Of hammered **w** you shall make them, Nm 10:2
You shall not do any ordinary **w**, Nm 28:18
You shall not do any ordinary **w**. Nm 28:25
You shall not do any ordinary **w**, Nm 28:26
You shall not do any ordinary **w**. Nm 29:1
afflict yourselves. You shall do no **w**, Nm 29:7
You shall not do any ordinary **w**, and Nm 29:12
You shall not do any ordinary **w**, Nm 29:35
article of skin, all **w** of goats' hair, Nm 31:20
has blessed you in all the **w** of your hands. Dt 2:7
wood and stone, the **w** of human hands, Dt 4:28
days you shall labor and do all your **w**, Dt 5:13
On it you shall not do any **w**, you or your Dt 5:14
have seen all the great **w** of the LORD that Dt 11:7
you in all the **w** of your hands that Dt 14:29
bless you in all your **w** and in all that Dt 15:10
You shall do no **w** with the firstborn of Dt 15:19
LORD your God. You shall do no **w** on it. Dt 16:8
produce and in all the **w** of your hands, Dt 16:15
bless you in all the **w** of your hands. Dt 24:19
and to bless all the **w** of your hands. Dt 28:12
prosperous in all the **w** of your hand, Dt 30:9
to anger through the **w** of your hands." Dt 31:29
"The Rock, his **w** is perfect, for all his Dt 32:4
and accept the **w** of his hands; Dt 33:11
had known all the **w** that the LORD did Jos 24:31
had seen all the great **w** that the LORD had Jgs 2:7
know the LORD or the **w** that he had done Jgs 2:10
two pieces of dyed **w** embroidered for the Jgs 5:30
was coming from his **w** in the field at Jgs 19:16
your donkeys, and put them to his **w**. 1 Sm 8:16
It may be that the LORD will **w** for us, 1 Sm 14:6
chief officers who were over the **w**, 1 Kgs 5:16
of the people who carried on the **w**. 1 Kgs 5:16
gold evenly applied on the carved **w**. 1 Kgs 6:35
skill for making any **w** in bronze. 1 Kgs 7:14
to King Solomon and did all his **w**. 1 Kgs 7:14
lattices of checker **w** with wreaths of 1 Kgs 7:17
wreaths of chain **w** for the capitals 1 Kgs 7:17
Thus the **w** of the pillars was 1 Kgs 7:22
oxen, there were wreaths of beveled **w**. 1 Kgs 7:29
Hiram finished all the **w** that he did 1 Kgs 7:40
Thus all the **w** that King Solomon 1 Kgs 7:51
officers who were over Solomon's **w**: 1 Kgs 9:23
of the people who carried on the **w**. 1 Kgs 9:23
him to anger with the **w** of his hands, 1 Kgs 16:7
not gods, but the **w** of men's hands, 2 Kgs 19:18
anger with all the **w** of their hands, 2 Kgs 22:17
incense for all the **w** of the Most Holy 1 Chr 6:49
mighty men for the **w** of the service 1 Chr 9:13
were in charge of the **w** of the service, 1 Chr 9:19
bronze, and iron. Arise and **w**! 1 Chr 22:16
have charge of the **w** in the house of 1 Chr 23:4
were to do the **w** for the service of 1 Chr 23:24
and any **w** for the service of the 1 Chr 23:28
those who did the **w** and of their 1 Chr 25:1
Jordan for all the **w** of the LORD and 1 Chr 26:30
those who did the **w** of the field for 1 Chr 27:26
and all the **w** of the service in the 1 Chr 28:13
all the **w** to be done according to the 1 Chr 28:19
until all the **w** for the service of the 1 Chr 28:20
you in all the **w** will be every willing 1 Chr 28:21
and inexperienced, and the **w** is great, 1 Chr 29:1
and for all the **w** to be done by 1 Chr 29:5
and the officers over the king's **w**. 1 Chr 29:6
send me a man skilled to **w** in gold, 2 Chr 2:7
He is trained to **w** in gold, silver, 2 Chr 2:14
as overseers to make the people **w**. 2 Chr 2:18
So Hiram finished the **w** that he did 2 Chr 4:11
Thus all the **w** that Solomon did for 2 Chr 5:1

Solomon made no slaves for his **w**; 2 Chr 8:9
accomplished all the **w** of Solomon 2 Chr 8:16
weak, for your **w** shall be rewarded." 2 Chr 15:7
building Ramah and let his **w** cease. 2 Chr 16:5
had charge of the **w** of the house of 2 Chr 24:12
who were engaged in the **w** labored, 2 Chr 24:13
until the **w** was finished—for the 2 Chr 29:34
They set to **w** and removed the 2 Chr 30:14
And every **w** that he undertook in 2 Chr 31:21
He set to **w** resolutely and built up all 2 Chr 32:5
which are the **w** of men's hands. 2 Chr 32:19
And the men did the **w** faithfully. 2 Chr 34:12
directed all who did **w** in every kind 2 Chr 34:13
the treasury of the **w** 61,000 darics of Ezr 2:69
to supervise the **w** of the house of the Ezr 3:8
Then the **w** on the house of God that is Ezr 4:24
This **w** goes on diligently and prospers in Ezr 5:8
Let the **w** on this house of God alone. Let Ezr 6:7
he aided them in the **w** of the house of Ezr 6:22
and the rest who were to do the **w**. Neh 2:16
their hands for the good **w**. Neh 2:18
height, for the people had a mind to **w**. Neh 4:6
them and kill them and stop the **w**." Neh 4:11
all returned to the wall, each to his **w**. Neh 4:15
each labored on the **w** with one hand Neh 4:17
"The **w** is great and widely spread, Neh 4:19
So we labored at the **w**, and half of Neh 4:21
I also persevered in the **w** on this wall, Neh 5:16
servants were gathered there for the **w**. Neh 5:16
am doing a great **w** and I cannot come Neh 6:3
Why should the **w** stop while I leave it Neh 6:3
"Their hands will drop from the **w**, Neh 6:9
perceived that this **w** had been Neh 6:16
heads of fathers' houses gave to the **w**. Neh 7:70
the treasury of the **w** 20,000 darics of Neh 7:71
and for all the **w** of the house of our Neh 10:33
brothers who did the **w** of the house, Neh 11:12
were over the outside **w** of the house of Neh 11:16
over the **w** of the house of God. Neh 11:22
Levites and the singers, who did the **w**, Neh 13:10
the priests and Levites, each in his **w**; Neh 13:30
You have blessed the **w** of his hands, and Jb 1:10
to despise the **w** of your hands and favor Jb 10:3
a lion and again **w** wonders against me. Jb 10:16
you would long for the **w** of your hands. Jb 14:15
For according to the **w** of a man he will Jb 34:11
poor, for they are all the **w** of his hands? Jb 34:19
to them their **w** and their transgressions, Jb 36:9
"Remember to extol his **w**, of which Jb 36:24
at your heavens, the **w** of your fingers, Ps 8:3
are snared in the **w** of their own hands. Ps 9:16
according to their **w** and according to Ps 28:4
them according to the **w** of their hands; Ps 28:4
works of the LORD or the **w** of his hands, Ps 28:5
and all his **w** is done in faithfulness. Ps 33:4
Have those who **w** evil no knowledge, Ps 53:4
deliver me from those who **w** evil, and Ps 59:2
will render to a man according to his **w**. Ps 62:12
I will ponder all your **w**, and meditate Ps 77:12
Do you **w** wonders for the dead? Do the Ps 88:10
Let your **w** be shown to your servants, Ps 90:16
and establish the **w** of our hands upon Ps 90:17
us; yes, establish the **w** of our hands! Ps 90:17
O LORD, have made me glad by your **w**; Ps 92:4
to the proof, though they had seen my **w**. Ps 95:9
I hate the **w** of those who fall away; it Ps 101:3
the heavens are the **w** of your hands. Ps 102:25
is satisfied with the fruit of your **w**. Ps 104:13
Man goes out to his **w** and to his labor Ps 104:23
Full of splendor and majesty is his **w**, Ps 111:3
silver and gold, the **w** of human hands. Ps 115:4
and gold, the **w** of human hands. Ps 135:15
Do not forsake the **w** of your hands. Ps 138:8
in company with men who **w** iniquity, Ps 141:4
done; I ponder the **w** of your hands. Ps 143:5
possessed me at the beginning of his **w**, Prv 8:22
and the **w** of a man's hand comes Prv 12:14
Commit your **w** to the LORD, and your Prv 16:3
all the weights in the bag are his **w**. Prv 16:11
is slack in his **w** is a brother to Prv 18:9
Do you see a man skillful in his **w**? He Prv 22:29
he not repay man according to his **w**? Prv 24:12
Prepare your **w** outside; get everything Prv 24:27
full of sorrow, and his **w** is a vexation. Eccl 2:23
a time for every matter and for every **w**. Eccl 3:17
that a man should rejoice in his **w**, Eccl 3:22
and all skill in **w** come from a man's Eccl 4:4
voice and destroy the **w** of your hands? Eccl 5:6
Consider the **w** of God: who can make Eccl 7:13
then I saw all the **w** of God, that man Eccl 8:17
cannot find out the **w** that is done Eccl 8:17
for there is no **w** or thought or Eccl 9:10
do not know the **w** of God who makes Eccl 11:5
are like jewels, the **w** of a master hand. Sg 7:1
shall become tinder, and his **w** a spark, Is 1:31
they bow down to the **w** of their hands, to Is 2:8
of the LORD, or see the **w** of his hands. Is 5:12
let him speed his **w** that we may see it; Is 5:19
has finished all his **w** on Mount Zion Is 10:12
not look to the altars, the **w** of his hands, Is 17:8
and all who **w** for pay will be grieved. Is 19:10
people, and Assyria the **w** of my hands, Is 19:25
and to **w** his work—alien is his work! Is 28:21
and to work his **w**—alien is his work! Is 28:21
and to work his work—alien is his **w**! Is 28:21
he sees his children, the **w** of my hands, Is 29:23
and the donkeys that **w** the ground will Is 30:24
the helpers of those who **w** iniquity. Is 31:2
were no gods, but the **w** of men's hands, Is 37:19
and your **w** is less than nothing; Is 41:24
who can deliver from my hand; I **w**, Is 43:13
making?' or 'Your **w** has no handles'? Is 45:9
my children and the **w** of my hands? Is 45:11
of my planting, the **w** of my hands, Is 60:21
our potter; we are all the **w** of your hand. Is 64:8
shall long enjoy the **w** of their hands. Is 65:22
But you, dress yourself for **w**; arise, and Jer 1:17
They are the **w** of the craftsman and of Jer 10:9
purple; they are all the **w** of skilled men. Jer 10:9
They are worthless, a **w** of delusion; at Jer 10:15
houses on the Sabbath or do any **w**, Jer 17:22
the Sabbath day holy and do no **w** on it, Jer 17:24
me to anger with the **w** of your hands. Jer 25:6
me to anger with the **w** of your hands to Jer 25:7
to their deeds and the **w** of their hands." Jer 25:14
I begin to **w** disaster at the city that is Jer 25:29
on its own land, to **w** it and dwell there, Jer 27:11
tears, for there is a reward for your **w**, Jer 31:16
me to anger by the **w** of their hands, Jer 32:30
is he who does the **w** of the LORD with Jer 48:10
GOD of hosts has a **w** to do in the land Jer 50:25
us declare in Zion the **w** of the LORD our Jer 51:10
They are worthless, a **w** of delusion; at Jer 51:18
according to the **w** of their hands. Lam 3:64
earthen pots, the **w** of a potter's hands! Lam 4:2
emeralds, purple, embroidered **w**, Ezk 27:16
in clothes of blue and embroidered **w**, Ezk 27:24
And he shall **w** his will and return to Dn 11:28
silver, all of them the **w** of craftsmen. Hos 13:2
more, 'Our God,' to the **w** of our hands. Hos 14:3
devise wickedness and **w** evil on their Mi 2:1
down no more to the **w** of your hands; Mi 5:13
For I am doing a **w** in your days that Hab 1:5
heard the report of you, and your **w**, Hab 3:2
for her cedar **w** will be laid bare. Zep 2:14
W, for I am with you, declares the LORD of Hg 2:4
LORD, and so with every **w** of their hands. Hg 2:14
miraculous powers are at **w** in him." Mt 14:2
'Son, go and **w** in the vineyard today.' Mt 21:28
And he could do no mighty **w** there, Mk 6:5
miraculous powers are at **w** in him." Mk 6:14
who does a mighty **w** in my name will Mk 9:39
servants in charge, each with his **w**, Mk 13:34
six days in which **w** ought to be done. Lk 13:14
who sent me and to accomplish his **w**. Jn 4:34
answered them, "This is the **w** of God, Jn 6:29
believe you? What **w** do you perform? Jn 6:30
We must **w** the works of him who sent me Jn 9:4
day; night is coming, when no one can **w**. Jn 9:4
is not for a good **w** that we are going to Jn 10:33
having accomplished the **w** that you Jn 17:4
outer garment, for he was stripped for **w**, Jn 21:7
and Saul for the **w** to which I have Acts 13:2
for I am doing a **w** in your days, a Acts 13:41
days, a **w** that you will not believe, Acts 13:41
of God for the **w** that they had Acts 14:26
and had not gone with them to the **w**. Acts 15:38
They show that the **w** of the law is Rom 2:15
one who does not **w** but trusts him who Rom 4:5
were at **w** in our members to bear fruit Rom 7:5
God all things **w** together for good, Rom 8:28
the sake of food, destroy the **w** of God. Rom 14:20
reason to be proud of my **w** for God. Rom 15:17
have any room for **w** in these regions, Rom 15:23
each one's **w** will become manifest, 1 Cor 3:13
test what sort of **w** each one has done. 1 Cor 3:13
If the **w** that anyone has built on the 1 Cor 3:14
If anyone's **w** is burned up, he will 1 Cor 3:15
Are all teachers? Do all **w** miracles? 1 Cor 12:29
abounding in the **w** of the Lord, 1 Cor 15:58
door for effective **w** has opened to 1 Cor 16:9
for he is doing the **w** of the Lord, 1 Cor 16:10
faith, but we **w** with you for your joy, 2 Cor 1:24
So death is at **w** in us, but life in you. 2 Cor 4:12
not only to do this **w** but also to desire 2 Cor 8:10
you may abound in every good **w**. 2 Cor 9:8
without boasting of **w** already done 2 Cor 10:16
boasted mission they **w** on the same 2 Cor 11:12
But let each one test his own **w**, and then Gal 6:4
spirit that is now at **w** in the sons of Eph 2:2
according to the power at **w** within us, Eph 3:20
equip the saints for the **w** of ministry, Eph 4:12
doing honest **w** with his own hands, Eph 4:28
who began a good **w** in you will bring Phil 1:6
w out your own salvation with fear Phil 2:12
to will and to **w** for his good pleasure. Phil 2:13
for he nearly died for the **w** of Christ, Phil 2:30
fruit in every good **w** and increasing in Col 1:10
Whatever you do, **w** heartily, as for the Col 3:23
God and Father your **w** of faith and 1 Thes 1:3
God, which is at **w** in you believers. 1 Thes 2:13
affairs, and to **w** with your hands, 1 Thes 4:11
highly in love because of their **w**. 1 Thes 5:13
for good and every **w** of faith by his 2 Thes 1:11
of lawlessness is already at **w**. 2 Thes 2:7
them in every good **w** and word. 2 Thes 2:17
If anyone is not willing to **w**, let him 2 Thes 3:10
you walk in idleness, not busy at **w**, 2 Thes 3:11
Christ to do their **w** quietly and to 2 Thes 3:12
has devoted herself to every good **w**. 1 Tm 5:10
of the house, ready for every good **w**. 2 Tm 2:21
competent, equipped for every good **w**. 2 Tm 3:17
suffering, do the **w** of an evangelist, 2 Tm 4:5
disobedient, unfit for any good **w**. Ti 1:16
be obedient, to be ready for every good **w**, Ti 3:1
the heavens are the **w** of your hands; Heb 1:10
as to overlook your **w** and the love that Heb 6:10
that it is allowed to **w** in the presence of Rv 13:14

WORKED (40)

with cherubim skillfully **w** into them. Ex 26:1
with cherubim skillfully **w** into it. Ex 26:31
and of fine twined linen, skillfully **w**. Ex 28:6
and the finely **w** garments, the holy Ex 31:10
the finely **w** garments for ministering Ex 35:19
yarns, with cherubim skillfully **w**. Ex 36:8
with cherubim skillfully **w** into it he Ex 36:35
the finely **w** garments for ministering Ex 39:41
that has never been **w** and that has not Dt 21:3
glean today? And where have you **w**? Ru 2:19
with whom she had **w** and said, Ru 2:19
name with whom I **w** today is Boaz." Ru 2:19
the LORD has **w** salvation in Israel." 1 Sm 11:13
who has **w** this great salvation in 1 Sm 14:45
for he has **w** with God this day." So 1 Sm 14:45
and the LORD **w** a great salvation for 1 Sm 19:5
and the LORD **w** a great victory. 2 Sm 23:12
and she **w** in the service of Naaman's 2 Kgs 5:2
the builders who **w** on the house 2 Kgs 12:11
fine linen, and he **w** cherubim on it. 2 Chr 3:14
half of my servants **w** on construction, Neh 4:16
who fear you and **w** for those who take Ps 31:19
O God, by which you have **w** for us. Ps 68:28
his holy arm have **w** salvation for him. Ps 98:1
forest is cut down and **w** with an axe by Jer 10:3
he labored, because they **w** for me, Ezk 29:20
And they came and **w** on the house of Hg 1:14
saying, 'These last **w** only one hour, Mt 20:12
while the Lord **w** with them and Mk 16:20
same trade he stayed with them and **w**, Acts 18:3
Greet Mary, who has **w** hard for you. Rom 16:6
Persis, who has **w** hard in the Lord. Rom 16:12
I **w** harder than any of them, 1 Cor 15:10
(for he who **w** through Peter for his Gal 2:8
to the circumcised **w** also through me Gal 2:8
that he **w** in Christ when he raised him Eph 1:20
witness that he has **w** hard for you and Col 4:13
we **w** night and day, that we might 1 Thes 2:9
toil and labor we **w** night and day, 2 Thes 3:8
you may not lose what we have **w** for, 2 Jn 1:8

WORKER (16)

of sheep, and Cain a **w** of the ground. Gn 4:2
was a man of Tyre, a **w** in bronze. 1 Kgs 7:14
like a sharp razor, you **w** of deceit. Ps 52:2
What gain has the **w** from his toil? Eccl 3:9
three years, like the years of a hired **w**, Is 16:14
year, according to the years of a hired **w**, Is 21:16
'I am no prophet, I am a **w** of the soil, Zec 13:5
who oppress the hired **w** in his wages, Mal 3:5
to give to this last **w** as I give to you. Mt 20:14
Greet Urbanus, our fellow **w** in Christ, Rom 16:9
Timothy, my fellow **w**, greets you; so Rom 16:21
and to every fellow **w** and laborer. 1 Cor 16:16
partner and fellow **w** for your benefit. 2 Cor 8:23
brother and fellow **w** and fellow Phil 2:25
a **w** who has no need to be ashamed, 2 Tm 2:15
To Philemon our beloved fellow **w** Phlm 1:1

WORKER'S (1)

A **w** appetite works for him; his mouth Prv 16:26

WORKERS (22)

and the craftsmen and the metal **w**, 2 Kgs 24:16
the house of linen **w** at Beth-ashbea; 1 Chr 4:21
be with the skilled **w** who are with me 2 Chr 2:7
and also **w** in iron and bronze to 2 Chr 24:12

and disaster for the **w** of iniquity? Jb 31:3
Depart from me, all you **w** of evil, for the Ps 6:8
me off with the wicked, with the **w** of evil, Ps 28:3
The **w** in combed flax will be in despair, Is 19:9
own pleasure, and oppress all your **w**. Is 58:3
of Judah, the craftsmen, and the metal **w**, Jer 24:1
and the metal **w** had departed from Jer 29:2
shall be food for the **w** of the city. Ezk 48:18
And the **w** of the city, from all the Ezk 48:19
depart from me, you **w** of lawlessness.' Mt 7:23
Depart from me, all you **w** of evil!' Lk 13:27
Aquila, my fellow **w** in Christ Jesus, Rom 16:3
Greet those **w** in the Lord, Tryphaena Rom 16:12
For we are God's fellow **w**. You are 1 Cor 3:9
Clement and the rest of my fellow **w**, Phil 4:3
among my fellow **w** for the kingdom Col 4:11
Demas, and Luke, my fellow **w**. Phlm 1:24
that we may be fellow **w** for the truth. 3 Jn 1:8

WORKING (25)
to you, 'Prove yourselves by **w** a miracle,' Ex 7:9
angel who was **w** destruction among 2 Sm 24:16
to the angel who was **w** destruction, 1 Chr 21:15
without number, skilled in **w** 1 Chr 22:15
workmen who were **w** in the house 2 Chr 34:10
workmen who were **w** in the house 2 Chr 34:10
on the left hand when he is **w**, I do not Jb 23:9
w salvation in the midst of the earth. Ps 74:12
house, and there he was **w** at his wheel. Jer 18:3
east shall be shut on the six **w** days, Ezk 46:1
them, "My Father is **w** until now, Jn 5:17
is working until now, and I am **w**." Jn 5:17
shown you that by **w** hard in this Acts 20:35
and we labor, **w** with our own hands. 1 Cor 4:12
no right to refrain from **w** for a living? 1 Cor 9:6
to another the **w** of miracles, to 1 Cor 12:10
W together with him, then, we appeal 2 Cor 6:1
anything, but only faith **w** through love. Gal 5:6
according to the **w** of his great might Eph 1:19
was given me by the **w** of his power. Eph 3:7
equipped, when each part is **w** properly, Eph 4:16
through faith in the powerful **w** of God, Col 2:12
to be self-controlled, pure, **w** at home, Ti 2:5
w in us that which is pleasing in his Heb 13:21
person has great power as it is **w**. Jas 5:16

WORKMAN (2)
—by any sort of **w** or skilled designer. Ex 35:35
then I was beside him, like a master **w**, Prv 8:30

WORKMANSHIP (4)
And this was the **w** of the lampstand, Nm 8:4
court back of the hall, was of like **w**. 1 Kgs 7:8
Lord? Are not you my **w** in the Lord? 1 Cor 9:1
For we are his **w**, created in Christ Eph 2:10

WORKMEN (14)
craftsmen among the **w** made the Ex 36:8
the hands of the **w** who had the 2 Kgs 12:11
given to the **w** who were repairing 2 Kgs 12:14
the money to pay out to the **w**, 2 Kgs 12:15
the hand of the **w** who have the 2 Kgs 22:5
them give it to the **w** who are at the 2 Kgs 22:5
the hand of the **w** who have the 2 Kgs 22:9
You have an abundance of **w**: 1 Chr 22:15
gave it to the **w** who were working 2 Chr 34:10
And the **w** who were working in the 2 Chr 34:10
the hand of the overseers and the **w**." 2 Chr 34:17
together supervised the **w** in the house of Ezr 3:9
together, with the **w** in similar trades, Acts 19:25
men are false apostles, deceitful **w**, 2 Cor 11:13

WORKMEN'S (1)
peg and her right hand to the **w** mallet; Jgs 5:26

WORKS (178)
the LORD has sent me to do all these **w**, Nm 16:28
who can do such **w** and mighty acts as Dt 3:24
to the LORD, to the one who **w** wonders, Jgs 13:19
to him; tell of all his wondrous **w**! 1 Chr 16:9
Remember the wondrous **w** that he 1 Chr 16:12
his marvelous **w** among all the 1 Chr 16:24
Hezekiah prospered in all his **w**. 2 Chr 32:30
anger with all the **w** of their hands, 2 Chr 34:25
serve you or turn from their wicked **w**. Neh 9:35
Thus, knowing their **w**, he overturns Jb 34:25
and consider the wondrous **w** of God. Jb 37:14
the wondrous **w** of him who is perfect in Jb 37:16
"He is the first of the **w** of God; let him Jb 40:19
him dominion over the **w** of your hands; Ps 8:6
With regard to the **w** of man, by the Ps 17:4
they do not regard the **w** of the LORD or Ps 28:5
Come, behold the **w** of the LORD, how he Ps 46:8
my refuge, that I may tell of all your **w**. Ps 73:28
You are the God who **w** wonders; you Ps 77:14
hope in God and not forget the **w** of God, Ps 78:7
They forgot his **w** and the wonders that Ps 78:11
O Lord, nor are there any **w** like yours. Ps 86:8
at the **w** of your hands I sing for joy. Ps 92:4
How great are your **w**, O LORD! Your Ps 92:5
his marvelous **w** among all the peoples! Ps 96:3
The LORD **w** righteousness and justice Ps 103:6
Bless the LORD, all his **w**, in all places Ps 103:22
O LORD, how manifold are your **w**! In Ps 104:24
forever; may the LORD rejoice in his **w**, Ps 104:31
to him; tell of all his wondrous **w**! Ps 105:2
Remember the wondrous **w** that he has Ps 105:5
did not consider your wondrous **w**; Ps 106:7
But they soon forgot his **w**; they did Ps 106:13
wondrous **w** in the land of Ham, and Ps 106:22
for his wondrous **w** to the children of Ps 107:8
for his wondrous **w** to the children of Ps 107:15
for his wondrous **w** to the children of Ps 107:21
the LORD, his wondrous **w** in the deep. Ps 107:24
for his wondrous **w** to the children of Ps 107:31
Great are the **w** of the LORD, studied by Ps 111:2
caused his wondrous **w** to be Ps 111:4
shown his people the power of his **w**, Ps 111:6
The **w** of his hands are faithful and Ps 111:7
I will meditate on your wondrous **w**. Ps 119:27
Wonderful are your **w**; my soul Ps 139:14
shall commend your **w** to another, Ps 145:4
your majesty, and on your wondrous **w**, Ps 145:5
All your **w** shall give thanks to you, O Ps 145:10
in all his words and kind in all his **w**.] Ps 145:13
in all his ways and kind in all his **w**. Ps 145:17
Whoever **w** his land will have plenty Prv 12:11
A worker's appetite **w** for him; his Prv 16:26
and a flattering mouth **w** ruin. Prv 26:28
Whoever **w** his land will have plenty Prv 28:19
and flax, and **w** with willing hands. Prv 31:13
and let her **w** praise her in the gates. Prv 31:31
I made great **w**. I built houses and Eccl 2:4
for us; you have done for us all our **w**. Is 26:12
are all a delusion; their **w** are nothing; Is 41:29
a cutting tool and **w** it over the coals. Is 44:12
it with hammers and **w** it with his Is 44:12
Their **w** are works of iniquity, and deeds Is 59:6
Their works are **w** of iniquity, and deeds Is 59:6
meet him who joyfully **w** righteousness, Is 64:5
"For I know their **w** and their thoughts, Is 66:18
gods and worshiped the **w** of their own Jer 1:16
me to anger with the **w** of your hands, Jer 44:8
trusted in your **w** and your treasures, Jer 48:7
altars cut down, and your **w** wiped out. Ezk 6:6
for all his **w** are right and his ways are Dn 4:37
he **w** signs and wonders in heaven and Dn 6:27
righteous in all the **w** that he has done, Dn 9:14
and all the **w** of the house of Ahab; Mi 6:16
may see your good **w** and give glory to Mt 5:16
and do many mighty **w** in your name?' Mt 7:22
most of his mighty **w** had been done, Mt 11:20
For if the mighty **w** done in you had Mt 11:21
For if the mighty **w** done in you had Mt 11:23
get this wisdom and these mighty **w**? Mt 13:54
he did not do many mighty **w** there, Mt 13:58
How are such mighty **w** done by his Mk 6:2
For if the mighty **w** done in you had Lk 10:13
for all the mighty **w** that they had seen, Lk 19:37
And greater **w** than these will he show Jn 5:20
For the **w** that the Father has given me to Jn 5:36
accomplish, the very **w** that I am doing, Jn 5:36
must we do, to be doing the **w** of God?" Jn 6:28
disciples also may see the **w** you are doing. Jn 7:3
For no one **w** in secret if he seeks to be Jn 7:4
because I testify about it that its **w** are evil. Jn 7:7
but that the **w** of God might be displayed Jn 9:3
We must work the **w** of him who sent me Jn 9:4
The **w** that I do in my Father's name Jn 10:25
you many good **w** from the Father; Jn 10:32
If I am not doing the **w** of my Father, Jn 10:37
you do not believe me, believe the **w**, Jn 10:38
the Father who dwells in me does his **w**. Jn 14:10
believe on account of the **w** themselves. Jn 14:11
in me will also do the **w** that I do; Jn 14:12
and greater **w** than these will he do, Jn 14:12
done among them the **w** that no one else Jn 15:24
own tongues the mighty **w** of God." Acts 2:11
God with mighty **w** and wonders and Acts 2:22
were rejoicing in the **w** of their hands. Acts 7:41
was full of good **w** and acts of charity. Acts 9:36
render to each one according to his **w**: Rom 2:6
For by **w** of the law no human being Rom 3:20
By what kind of law? By a law of **w**? Rom 3:27
by faith apart from **w** of the law. Rom 3:28
For if Abraham was justified by **w**, he Rom 4:2
Now to the one who **w**, his wages are Rom 4:4
counts righteousness apart from **w**: Rom 4:6
not because of **w** but because of his Rom 9:11
it by faith, but as if it were based on **w**. Rom 9:32
grace, it is no longer on the basis of **w**; Rom 11:6
us cast off the **w** of darkness and put Rom 13:12
signs and wonders and mighty **w**. 2 Cor 12:12
is not justified by **w** of the law but Gal 2:16
faith in Christ and not by **w** of the law, Gal 2:16
because by **w** of the law no one will be Gal 2:16
you receive the Spirit by **w** of the law or Gal 3:2
Spirit to you and **w** miracles among you Gal 3:5
among you do so by **w** of the law, Gal 3:5
For all who rely on **w** of the law are Gal 3:10
Now the **w** of the flesh are evident: Gal 5:19
of him who **w** all things according Eph 1:11
not a result of **w**, so that no one may Eph 2:9
created in Christ Jesus for good **w**, Eph 2:10
no part in the unfruitful **w** of darkness, Eph 5:11
for it is God who **w** in you, both to will Phil 2:13
energy that he powerfully **w** within me. Col 1:29
who profess godliness—with good **w**. 1 Tm 2:10
and having a reputation for good **w**: if 1 Tm 5:10
So also good **w** are conspicuous, and 1 Tm 5:25
are to do good, to be rich in good **w**, 1 Tm 6:18
not because of our **w** but because of 2 Tm 1:9
know God, but they deny him by their **w**. Ti 1:16
in all respects to be a model of good **w**, Ti 2:7
possession who are zealous for good **w**. Ti 2:14
not because of **w** done by us in Ti 3:5
be careful to devote themselves to good **w**. Ti 3:8
learn to devote themselves to good **w**, Ti 3:14
fathers put me to the test and saw my **w** Heb 3:9
rest,'" although his **w** were finished from Heb 4:3
on the seventh day from all his **w**." Heb 4:4
also rested from his **w** as God did from Heb 4:10
of repentance from dead **w** and of faith Heb 6:1
conscience from dead **w** to serve the Heb 9:14
up one another to love and good **w**, Heb 10:24
says he has faith but does not have **w**? Jas 2:14
also faith by itself, if it does not have **w**, Jas 2:17
faith and I have **w**." Show me your faith Jas 2:18
Show me your faith apart from your **w**, Jas 2:18
and I will show you my faith by my **w**. Jas 2:18
that faith apart from **w** is useless? Jas 2:20
our father justified by **w** when he offered Jas 2:21
that faith was active along with his **w**, Jas 2:22
and faith was completed by his **w**; Jas 2:22
person is justified by **w** and not by faith Jas 2:24
prostitute justified by **w** when she Jas 2:25
dead, so also faith apart from **w** is dead. Jas 2:26
let him show his **w** in the meekness of Jas 3:13
the earth and the **w** that are done on 2 Pt 3:10
was to destroy the **w** of the devil. 1 Jn 3:8
greets him takes part in his wicked **w**. 2 Jn 1:11
"'I know your **w**, your toil and your Rv 2:2
fallen; repent, and do the **w** you did at first. Rv 2:5
have: you hate the **w** of the Nicolaitans, Rv 2:6
"'I know your **w**, your love and faith and Rv 2:19
and that your latter **w** exceed the first. Rv 2:19
tribulation, unless they repent of her **w**, Rv 2:22
give to each of you as your **w** deserve. Rv 2:23
and who keeps my **w** until the end, Rv 2:26
God and the seven stars. "'I know your **w**. Rv 3:1
have not found your **w** complete in the Rv 3:2
"'I know your **w**. Behold, I have set before Rv 3:8
"'I know your **w**: you are neither cold Rv 3:15
did not repent of the **w** of their hands nor Rv 9:20

WORLD (255)
LORD'S, and on them he has set the **w**. 1 Sm 2:8
foundations of the **w** were laid bare, 2 Sm 22:16
the earth; yes, the **w** is established; 1 Chr 16:30
into darkness, and driven out of the **w**. Jb 18:18
and who laid on him the whole **w**? Jb 34:13
them on the face of the habitable **w**. Jb 37:12
bind their faces in the **w** below. Jb 40:13
and he judges the **w** with righteousness; Ps 9:8
from men of the **w** whose portion is in Ps 17:14
the foundations of the **w** were laid bare Ps 18:15
earth, and their words to the end of the **w**. Ps 19:4
the **w** and those who dwell therein, Ps 24:1
the inhabitants of the **w** stand in awe of Ps 33:8
Give ear, all inhabitants of the **w**, Ps 49:1
you, for the **w** and its fullness are mine. Ps 50:12
your lightnings lighted up the **w**; Ps 77:18
the **w** and all that is in it, you have Ps 89:11
ever you had formed the earth and the **w**, Ps 90:2
Yes, the **w** is established; it shall never be Ps 93:1
Yes, the **w** is established; it shall never Ps 96:10
He will judge the **w** in righteousness, Ps 96:13
His lightnings light up the **w**; the earth Ps 97:4
fills it; the **w** and those who dwell in it! Ps 98:7
He will judge the **w** with righteousness, Ps 98:9
its fields, or the first of the dust of the **w**. Prv 8:26
in his inhabited **w** and delighting in Prv 8:31
I will punish the **w** for its evil, and the Is 13:11
who made the **w** like a desert and Is 14:17
and fill the face of the **w** with cities." Is 14:21
All you inhabitants of the **w**, you who Is 18:3
all the kingdoms of the **w** on the face of Is 23:17
withers; the **w** languishes and withers; Is 24:4
inhabitants of the **w** learn righteousness. Is 26:9

the inhabitants of the **w** have not fallen. Is 26:18
shoots and fill the whole **w** with fruit. Is 27:6
the earth hear, and all that fills it; the **w**, Is 34:1
more among the inhabitants of the **w**. Is 38:11
who established the **w** by his wisdom, Jer 10:12
the kingdoms of the **w** that are on the Jer 25:26
who established the **w** by his wisdom, Jer 51:15
nor any of the inhabitants of the **w**, Lam 4:12
will make you to dwell in the **w** below, Ezk 26:20
all given over to death, to the **w** below, Ezk 31:14
water, were comforted in the **w** below. Ezk 31:16
with the trees of Eden to the **w** below. Ezk 31:18
of majestic nations, to the **w** below, Ezk 32:18
uncircumcised into the **w** below, Ezk 32:24
before him, the **w** and all who dwell in it. Na 1:5
all the kingdoms of the **w** and their glory. Mt 4:8
"You are the light of the **w**. A city set on Mt 5:14
the cares of the **w** and the deceitfulness Mt 13:22
hidden since the foundation of the **w**." Mt 13:35
The field is the **w**, and the good seed is Mt 13:38
he gains the whole **w** and forfeits his Mt 16:26
"Woe to the **w** for temptations to sin! Mt 18:7
"Truly, I say to you, in the new **w**, Mt 19:28
throughout the whole **w** as a testimony Mt 24:14
from the beginning of the **w** until now, Mt 24:21
for you from the foundation of the **w**. Mt 25:34
gospel is proclaimed in the whole **w**, Mt 26:13
the cares of the **w** and the deceitfulness Mk 4:19
to gain the whole **w** and forfeit his life? Mk 8:36
the gospel is proclaimed in the whole **w**, Mk 14:9
"Go into all the **w** and proclaim the Mk 16:15
that all the **w** should be registered. Lk 2:1
all the kingdoms of the **w** in a moment of Lk 4:5
he gains the whole **w** and loses or forfeits Lk 9:25
shed from the foundation of the **w**, Lk 11:50
the nations of the **w** seek after these Lk 12:30
the sons of this **w** are more shrewd in Lk 16:8
foreboding of what is coming on the **w**. Lk 21:26
everyone, was coming into the **w**. Jn 1:9
He was in the **w**, and the world was made Jn 1:10
world, and the **w** was made through him, Jn 1:10
him, yet the **w** did not know him. Jn 1:10
of God, who takes away the sin of the **w**! Jn 1:29
"For God so loved the **w**, that he gave his Jn 3:16
his Son into the **w** to condemn the world, Jn 3:17
his Son into the world to condemn the **w**, Jn 3:17
in order that the **w** might be saved Jn 3:17
the light has come into the **w**, and people Jn 3:19
that this is indeed the Savior of the **w**." Jn 4:42
the Prophet who is to come into the **w**!" Jn 6:14
from heaven and gives life to the **w**." Jn 6:33
I will give for the life of the **w** is my flesh." Jn 6:51
do these things, show yourself to the **w**." Jn 7:4
The **w** cannot hate you, but it hates me Jn 7:7
to them, saying, "I am the light of the **w**. Jn 8:12
You are of this **w**; I am not of this world. Jn 8:23
You are of this world; I am not of this **w**. Jn 8:23
and I declare to the **w** what I have heard Jn 8:26
As long as I am in the **w**, I am the light of Jn 9:5
I am in the world, I am the light of the **w**." Jn 9:5
Never since the **w** began has it been Jn 9:32
said, "For judgment I came into this **w**, Jn 9:39
Father consecrated and sent into the **w**, Jn 10:36
because he sees the light of this **w**. Jn 11:9
Son of God, who is coming into the **w**." Jn 11:27
Look, the **w** has gone after him." Jn 12:19
hates his life in this **w** will keep it for Jn 12:25
Now is the judgment of this **w**; now will Jn 12:31
now will the ruler of this **w** be cast out. Jn 12:31
I have come into the **w** as light, so that Jn 12:46
not come to judge the **w** but to save the Jn 12:47
to judge the world but to save the **w**. Jn 12:47
come to depart out of this **w** to the Father, Jn 13:1
having loved his own who were in the **w**, Jn 13:1
of truth, whom the **w** cannot receive, Jn 14:17
a little while and the **w** will see me no Jn 14:19
yourself to us, and not to the **w**?" Jn 14:22
you. Not as the **w** gives do I give to you. Jn 14:27
you, for the ruler of this **w** is coming. Jn 14:30
so that the **w** may know that I love the Jn 14:31
"If the **w** hates you, know that it has Jn 15:18
If you were of the **w**, the world would Jn 15:19
world, the **w** would love you as its own; Jn 15:19
but because you are not of the **w**, but I Jn 15:19
the world, but I chose you out of the **w**, Jn 15:19
of the world, therefore the **w** hates you. Jn 15:19
he will convict the **w** concerning sin and Jn 16:8
because the ruler of this **w** is judged. Jn 16:11
weep and lament, but the **w** will rejoice. Jn 16:20
human being has been born into the **w**. Jn 16:21
the Father and have come into the **w**, Jn 16:28
now I am leaving the **w** and going to the Jn 16:28
In the **w** you will have tribulation. Jn 16:33
But take heart; I have overcome the **w**." Jn 16:33
that I had with you before the **w** existed. Jn 17:5
people whom you gave me out of the **w**. Jn 17:6
not praying for the **w** but for those whom Jn 17:9
And I am no longer in the **w**, but they Jn 17:11
in the world, but they are in the **w**, Jn 17:11
to you, and these things I speak in the **w**, Jn 17:13
and the **w** has hated them because they Jn 17:14
them because they are not of the **w**, Jn 17:14
of the world, just as I am not of the **w**. Jn 17:14
not ask that you take them out of the **w**, Jn 17:15
They are not of the **w**, just as I am not of Jn 17:16
of the world, just as I am not of the **w**. Jn 17:16
As you sent me into the **w**, so I have sent Jn 17:18
world, so I have sent them into the **w**. Jn 17:18
so that the **w** may believe that you have Jn 17:21
so that the **w** may know that you sent Jn 17:23
loved me before the foundation of the **w**. Jn 17:24
even though the **w** does not know you, Jn 17:25
him, "I have spoken openly to the **w**. Jn 18:20
answered, "My kingdom is not of this **w**. Jn 18:36
If my kingdom were of this **w**, my Jn 18:36
But my kingdom is not from the **w**." Jn 18:36
I have come into the **w**—to bear witness Jn 18:37
I suppose that the **w** itself could not Jn 21:25
famine over all the **w** (this took place Acts 11:28
have turned the **w** upside down have Acts 17:6
who made the **w** and everything in Acts 17:24
will judge the **w** in righteousness by Acts 17:31
whom all Asia and the **w** worship." Acts 19:27
the Jews throughout the **w** and is a Acts 24:5
your faith is proclaimed in all the **w**. Rom 1:8
ever since the creation of the **w**, Rom 1:20
For then how could God judge the **w**? Rom 3:6
and the whole **w** may be held Rom 3:19
be heir of the **w** did not come through Rom 4:13
sin came into the **w** through one man, Rom 5:12
indeed was in the **w** before the law was Rom 5:13
and their words to the ends of the **w**." Rom 10:18
their trespass means riches for the **w**, Rom 11:12
means the reconciliation of the **w**, Rom 11:15
Do not be conformed to this **w**, but be Rom 12:2
made foolish the wisdom of the **w**? 1 Cor 1:20
the **w** did not know God through 1 Cor 1:21
is foolish in the **w** to shame the wise; 1 Cor 1:27
is weak in the **w** to shame the strong; 1 Cor 1:27
what is low and despised in the **w**, 1 Cor 1:28
have received not the spirit of the **w**, 1 Cor 2:12
the wisdom of this **w** is folly with 1 Cor 3:19
or Cephas or the **w** or life or death 1 Cor 3:22
we have become a spectacle to the **w**, 1 Cor 4:9
and are still, like the scum of the **w**, 1 Cor 4:13
the sexually immoral of this **w**, 1 Cor 5:10
you would need to go out of the **w**. 1 Cor 5:10
know that the saints will judge the **w**? 1 Cor 6:2
And if the **w** is to be judged by you, are 1 Cor 6:2
who deal with the **w** as though they 1 Cor 7:31
form of this **w** is passing away. 1 Cor 7:31
not be condemned along with the **w**. 1 Cor 11:32
many different languages in the **w**, 1 Cor 14:10
behaved in the **w** with simplicity and 2 Cor 1:12
the god of this **w** has blinded the 2 Cor 4:4
God was reconciling the **w** to himself, 2 Cor 5:19
to the elementary principles of the **w**. Gal 4:3
worthless elementary principles of the **w**, Gal 4:9
by which the **w** has been crucified to Gal 6:14
has been crucified to me, and I to the **w**. Gal 6:14
in him before the foundation of the **w**, Eph 1:4
walked, following the course of this **w**, Eph 2:2
no hope and without God in the **w**. Eph 2:12
whom you shine as lights in the **w**, Phil 2:15
indeed in the whole **w** it is bearing fruit Col 1:6
to the elemental spirits of the **w**, Col 2:8
died to the elemental spirits of the **w**, Col 2:20
why, as if you were still alive in the **w**, Col 2:20
Jesus came into the **w** to save sinners, 1 Tm 1:15
the nations, believed on in the **w**, 1 Tm 3:16
for we brought nothing into the **w**, and 1 Tm 6:7
we cannot take anything out of the **w**. 1 Tm 6:7
Demas, in love with this present **w**, 2 Tm 4:10
through whom also he created the **w**. Heb 1:2
when he brings the firstborn into the **w**, Heb 1:6
angels that God subjected the **w** to come, Heb 2:5
finished from the foundation of the **w**. Heb 4:3
since the foundation of the **w**. Heb 9:26
when Christ came into the **w**, Heb 10:5
he condemned the **w** and became an Heb 11:7
of whom the **w** was not worthy— Heb 11:38
to keep oneself unstained from the **w**. Jas 1:27
who are poor in the **w** to be rich in faith Jas 2:5
tongue is a fire, a **w** of unrighteousness. Jas 3:6
that friendship with the **w** is enmity with Jas 4:4
a friend of the **w** makes himself an enemy Jas 4:4
the foundation of the **w** but was made 1 Pt 1:20
by your brotherhood throughout the **w**. 1 Pt 5:9
that is in the **w** because of sinful desire. 2 Pt 1:4
if he did not spare the ancient **w**, but 2 Pt 2:5
a flood upon the **w** of the ungodly; 2 Pt 2:5
defilements of the **w** through the 2 Pt 2:20
means of these the **w** that then existed 2 Pt 3:6
only but also for the sins of the whole **w**. 1 Jn 2:2
Do not love the **w** or the things in the 1 Jn 2:15
love the world or the things in the **w**. 1 Jn 2:15
If anyone loves the **w**, the love of the 1 Jn 2:15
all that is in the **w**—the desires of the 1 Jn 2:16
not from the Father but is from the **w**. 1 Jn 2:16
And the **w** is passing away along with 1 Jn 2:17
The reason why the **w** does not know us 1 Jn 3:1
brothers, that the **w** hates you. 1 Jn 3:13
false prophets have gone out into the **w**. 1 Jn 4:1
was coming and now is in the **w** already. 1 Jn 4:3
in you is greater than he who is in the **w**. 1 Jn 4:4
They are from the **w**; therefore they 1 Jn 4:5
therefore they speak from the **w**, and the 1 Jn 4:5
the world, and the **w** listens to them. 1 Jn 4:5
us, that God sent his only Son into the **w**, 1 Jn 4:9
sent his Son to be the Savior of the **w**. 1 Jn 4:14
as he is so also are we in this **w**. 1 Jn 4:17
has been born of God overcomes the **w**. 1 Jn 5:4
that has overcome the **w**—our faith. 1 Jn 5:4
it that overcomes the **w** except the one 1 Jn 5:5
and the whole **w** lies in the power of the 1 Jn 5:19
deceivers have gone out into the **w**, 2 Jn 1:7
of trial that is coming on the whole **w**, Rv 3:10
"The kingdom of the **w** has become the Rv 11:15
deceiver of the whole **w**—he was thrown Rv 12:9
the foundation of the **w** in the book of Rv 13:8
go abroad to the kings of the whole **w**, Rv 16:14
the foundation of the **w** will marvel to Rv 17:8

WORLD'S (1)
if anyone has the **w** goods and sees his 1 Jn 3:17

WORLDLY (7)
were wise according to **w** standards, 1 Cor 1:26
who marry will have **w** troubles, 1 Cor 7:28
man is anxious about **w** things, 1 Cor 7:33
woman is anxious about **w** things, 1 Cor 7:34
whereas **w** grief produces death. 2 Cor 7:10
to renounce ungodliness and **w** passions, Ti 2:12
is these who cause divisions, **w** people, Jude 1:19

WORM (10)
the grapes, for the **w** shall eat them. Dt 28:39
the pit, 'You are my father,' and to the **w**, Jb 17:14
forgets them; the **w** finds them sweet; Jb 24:20
maggot, and the son of man, who is a **w**!" Jb 25:6
But I am a **w** and not a man, scorned by Ps 22:6
Fear not, you **w** Jacob, you men of Is 41:14
and the **w** will eat them like wool; Is 51:8
For their **w** shall not die, their fire shall Is 66:24
God appointed a **w** that attacked the Jon 4:7
'where their **w** does not die and the fire Mk 9:48

WORMS (6)
the morning, and it bred **w** and stank. Ex 16:20
did not stink, and there were no **w** in it. Ex 16:24
My flesh is clothed with **w** and dirt; my Jb 7:5
alike in the dust, and the **w** cover them. Jb 21:26
bed beneath you, and **w** are your covers. Is 14:11
he was eaten by **w** and breathed his Acts 12:23

WORMWOOD (7)
but in the end she is bitter as **w**, sharp as Prv 5:4
bitterness; he has sated me with **w**. Lam 3:15
my wanderings, the **w** and the gall! Lam 3:19
who turn justice to **w** and cast down Am 5:7
and the fruit of righteousness into **w**— Am 6:12
The name of the star is **W**. A third of the Rv 8:11
A third of the waters became **w**, and Rv 8:11

WORN (10)
to herself, saying, "After I am **w** out, Gn 18:12
Your clothes have not **w** out on you, and Dt 29:5
your sandals have not **w** off your feet. Dt 29:5
sandals of ours are **w** out from the very Jos 9:13
and the purple garments **w** by the kings Jgs 8:26
robes be brought, which the king has **w**, Est 6:8
Surely now God has **w** me out; he has Jb 16:7
O God; I am weary, O God, and **w** out. Prv 30:1
said of her who was **w** out by adultery, Ezk 23:43
For a long time he had **w** no clothes, and Lk 8:27

WORN-OUT (5)
provisions and took **w** sacks for their Jos 9:4
and wineskins, **w** and torn and mended, Jos 9:4
with **w**, patched sandals on their feet, and Jos 9:5
sandals on their feet, and **w** clothes. Jos 9:5
took from there old rags and **w** clothes, Jer 38:11

WORRIED (1)
and what you are to drink, nor be **w**. Lk 12:29

WORSE (22)
Now we will deal **w** with you than with Gn 19:9
and this will be **w** for you than all the 2 Sm 19:7
to no avail, and my distress grew **w**. Ps 39:2

neck. They did **w** than their fathers. Jer 7:26
you have done **w** than your fathers, Jer 16:12
which was **w** than that of her sister. Ezk 23:11
that you were in **w** condition than the Dn 1:10
from the garment, and a **w** tear is made. Mt 9:16
state of that person is **w** than the first. Mt 12:45
the last fraud will be **w** than the first." Mt 27:64
new from the old, and a **w** tear is made. Mk 2:21
and was no better but rather grew **w**. Mk 5:26
state of that person is **w** than the first." Lk 11:26
these Galileans were **w** sinners than all Lk 13:2
think that they were **w** offenders than all Lk 13:4
that nothing **w** may happen to you." Jn 5:14
We are no **w** off if we do not eat, and no 1 Cor 8:8
it is not for the better but for the **w**. 1 Cor 11:17
the faith and is **w** than an unbeliever. 1 Tm 5:8
impostors will go on from bad to **w**, 2 Tm 3:13
How much **w** punishment, do you Heb 10:29
last state has become **w** for them than 2 Pt 2:20

WORSHIP (111)
go over there and **w** and come again to Gn 22:5
of the elders of Israel, and **w** from afar. Ex 24:1
tent, all the people would rise up and **w**, Ex 33:10
(for you shall **w** no other god, for the Ex 34:14
other gods and serve them and **w** them, Dt 8:19
aside and serve other gods and **w** them; Dt 11:16
You shall not **w** the LORD your God in Dt 12:4
You shall not **w** the LORD your God in Dt 12:31
LORD your God and **w** before the LORD Dt 26:10
are drawn away to **w** other gods and Dt 30:17
make our children cease to **w** the LORD. Jos 22:25
from his city to **w** and to sacrifice to 1 Sm 1:3
with me that I may **w** the LORD." 1 Sm 15:25
then I will offer **w** to the LORD.'" 2 Sm 15:8
go and serve other gods and **w** them, 1 Kgs 9:6
into the house of Rimmon to **w** there, 2 Kgs 5:18
"You shall **w** before this altar in 2 Kgs 18:22
W the LORD in the splendor of 1 Chr 16:29
go and serve other gods and **w** them, 2 Chr 7:19
"Before one altar you shall **w**, 2 Chr 32:12
with you, for we **w** your God as you do, Ezr 4:2
of the peoples of the land to **w** the LORD, Ezr 6:21
of the nations shall **w** before you. Ps 22:27
the prosperous of the earth eat and **w**; Ps 22:29
w the LORD in the splendor of holiness. Ps 29:2
have made shall come and **w** before you, Ps 86:9
Oh come, let us **w** and bow down; let us Ps 95:6
W the LORD in the splendor of holiness; Ps 96:9
in worthless idols; **w** him, all you gods! Ps 97:7
the LORD our God; **w** at his footstool! Ps 99:5
our God, and **w** at his holy mountain; Ps 99:9
together, and kingdoms, to **w** the LORD. Ps 102:22
dwelling place; let us **w** at his footstool!" Ps 132:7
which they made for themselves to **w**, Is 2:20
in that day and **w** with sacrifice and Is 19:21
the Egyptians will **w** with the Assyrians. Is 19:23
Egypt will come and **w** the LORD on the Is 27:13
"You shall **w** before this altar"? Is 36:7
it into a god; then they fall down and **w**! Is 46:6
all flesh shall come to **w** before me, Is 66:23
Judah who enter these gates to **w** the LORD. Jer 7:2
other gods to serve them and **w** them, Jer 13:10
go after other gods to serve and **w** them, Jer 25:6
of Judah that come to **w** in the house of Jer 26:2
the countries, and **w** wood and stone.' Ezk 20:32
and he shall **w** at the threshold of the Ezk 46:2
by the north gate to **w** shall go out by Ezk 46:9
to fall down and **w** the golden image that Dn 3:5
not fall down and **w** shall immediately be Dn 3:6
shall fall down and **w** the golden image. Dn 3:10
not fall down and **w** shall be cast into Dn 3:11
serve your gods or **w** the golden image Dn 3:12
serve my gods or **w** the golden image Dn 3:14
to fall down and **w** the image that I have Dn 3:15
But if you do not **w**, you shall Dn 3:15
serve your gods or **w** the golden image Dn 3:18
rather than serve and **w** any god except Dn 3:28
go up year after year to **w** the King, Zec 14:16
not go up to Jerusalem to **w** the King, Zec 14:17
when it rose and have come to **w** him." Mt 2:2
word, that I too may come and **w** him." Mt 2:8
give you, if you will fall down and **w** me." Mt 4:9
"'You shall **w** the Lord your God and Mt 4:10
in vain do they **w** me, teaching as Mt 15:9
in vain do they **w** me, teaching as Mk 7:7
If you, then, will **w** me, it will all be Lk 4:7
written, "'You shall **w** the Lord your God, Lk 4:8
is the place where people ought to **w**." Jn 4:20
nor in Jerusalem will you **w** the Father. Jn 4:21
You **w** what you do not know; we Jn 4:22
we **w** what we know, for salvation is from Jn 4:22
the true worshipers will **w** the Father in Jn 4:23
Father is seeking such people to **w** him. Jn 4:23
and those who **w** him must worship in Jn 4:24
who worship him must **w** in spirit and Jn 4:24
those who went up to **w** at the feast were Jn 12:20
shall come out and **w** me in this place.' Acts 7:7
gave them over to **w** the host of heaven, Acts 7:42
the images that you made to **w**; Acts 7:43
He had come to Jerusalem to **w** Acts 8:27
and observed the objects of your **w**, Acts 17:23
What therefore you **w** as unknown, Acts 17:23
persuading people to **w** God contrary Acts 18:13
she whom all Asia and the world **w**." Acts 19:27
since I went up to **w** in Jerusalem, Acts 24:11
call a sect, I **w** the God of our fathers, Acts 24:14
as they earnestly **w** night and day. Acts 26:7
God to whom I belong and whom I **w**, Acts 27:23
covenants, the giving of the law, the **w**, Rom 9:4
to God, which is your spiritual **w**. Rom 12:1
he will **w** God and declare that God 1 Cor 14:25
who **w** by the Spirit of God and glory in Phil 3:3
insisting on asceticism and **w** of angels, Col 2:18
every so-called god or object of **w**, 2 Thes 2:4
he says, "Let all God's angels **w** him." Heb 1:6
had regulations for **w** and an earthly Heb 9:1
the tent and all the vessels used in **w**. Heb 9:21
bowing in **w** over the head of his staff. Heb 11:21
thus let us offer to God acceptable **w**, Heb 12:28
on the throne and **w** him who lives Rv 4:10
God and the altar and those who **w** there, Rv 11:1
and all who dwell on earth will **w** it, Rv 13:8
and its inhabitants **w** the first beast, Rv 13:12
those who would not **w** the image of the Rv 13:15
and **w** him who made heaven and earth, Rv 14:7
All nations will come and **w** you, for Rv 15:4
Then I fell down at his feet to **w** him, Rv 19:10
W God." For the testimony of Jesus is Rv 19:10
will be in it, and his servants will **w** him. Rv 22:3
I fell down to **w** at the feet of the angel Rv 22:8
keep the words of this book. **W** God." Rv 22:9

WORSHIPED (55)
man bowed his head and **w** the LORD Gn 24:26
bowed my head and **w** the LORD and Gn 24:48
affliction, they bowed their heads and **w**. Ex 4:31
the people bowed their heads and **w**. Ex 12:27
golden calf and have **w** it and sacrificed Ex 32:8
bowed his head toward the earth and **w**. Ex 34:8
gone and served other gods and **w** them, Dt 17:3
went and served other gods and **w** them, Dt 29:26
face to the earth and **w** and said to him, Jos 5:14
of the dream and its interpretation, he **w**. Jgs 7:15
in the morning and **w** before the LORD; 1 Sm 1:19
to the LORD." And he **w** the LORD there. 1 Sm 1:28
into the house of the LORD and **w**. 2 Sm 12:20
to the summit, where God was **w**, 2 Sm 15:32
on other gods and **w** them and served 1 Kgs 9:9
forsaken me and **w** Ashtoreth the 1 Kgs 11:33
went and served Baal and **w** him. 1 Kgs 16:31
served Baal and **w** him and 1 Kgs 22:53
made an Asherah and **w** all the host 2 Kgs 17:16
and **w** all the host of heaven and 2 Kgs 21:3
that his father served and **w** them. 2 Kgs 21:21
the pavement and **w** and gave thanks 2 Chr 7:3
on other gods and **w** them and served 2 Chr 7:22
set them up as his gods and **w** them, 2 Chr 25:14
The whole assembly **w**, and the 2 Chr 29:28
with him bowed themselves and **w**. 2 Chr 29:29
and they bowed down and **w**. 2 Chr 29:30
and **w** all the host of heaven and 2 Chr 33:3
bowed their heads and **w** the LORD with Neh 8:6
made confession and **w** the LORD their Neh 9:3
his head and fell on the ground and **w**. Jb 1:20
a calf in Horeb and **w** a metal image. Ps 106:19
to other gods and **w** the works of their Jer 1:16
after, and which they have sought and **w**. Jer 8:2
other gods and have served and **w** them, Jer 16:11
LORD their God and **w** other gods and Jer 22:9
fell down and **w** the golden image Dn 3:7
mother, and they fell down and **w** him. Mt 2:11
And those in the boat **w** him, saying, Mt 14:33
up and took hold of his feet and **w** him. Mt 28:9
And when they saw him they **w** him, Mt 28:17
And they **w** him and returned to Lk 24:52
Our fathers **w** on this mountain, but you Jn 4:20
He said, "Lord, I believe," and he **w** him. Jn 9:38
and fell down at his feet and **w** him. Acts 10:25
for a lie and **w** and served the creature Rom 1:25
"Amen!" and the elders fell down and **w**. Rv 5:14
their faces before the throne and **w** God, Rv 7:11
God fell on their faces and **w** God, Rv 11:16
And they **w** the dragon, for he had given Rv 13:4
to the beast, and they **w** the beast, Rv 13:4
the mark of the beast and **w** its image. Rv 16:2
creatures fell down and **w** God who was Rv 19:4
of the beast and those who **w** its image. Rv 19:20
and who had not **w** the beast or its image Rv 20:4

WORSHIPER (4)
but if anyone is a **w** of God and does his Jn 9:31
of purple goods, who was a **w** of God. Acts 16:14
man named Titius Justus, a **w** of God. Acts 18:7
cannot perfect the conscience of the **w**, Heb 9:9

WORSHIPERS (11)
of Baal, all his **w** and all his priests. 2 Kgs 10:19
in order to destroy the **w** of Baal. 2 Kgs 10:19
all Israel, and all the **w** of Baal came, 2 Kgs 10:21
vestments for all the **w** of Baal." So 2 Kgs 10:22
Rechab, and he said to the **w** of Baal, 2 Kgs 10:23
among you, but only the **w** of Baal." 2 Kgs 10:23
All **w** of images are put to shame, who Ps 97:7
From beyond the rivers of Cush my **w**, Zep 3:10
when the true **w** will worship the Father Jn 4:23
have ceased to be offered, since the **w**, Heb 10:2
these **w** of the beast and its image, Rv 14:11

WORSHIPING (7)
And as he was **w** in the house of 2 Kgs 19:37
down before the LORD, **w** the LORD. 2 Chr 20:18
And as he was **w** in the house of Nisroch Is 37:38
the east, **w** the sun toward the east. Ezk 8:16
w with fasting and prayer night and day. Lk 2:37
While they were **w** the Lord and Acts 13:2
hands nor give up **w** demons and idols of Rv 9:20

WORSHIPS (5)
of them; and the host of heaven **w** you. Neh 9:6
All the earth **w** you and sings praises to Ps 66:4
Also he makes a god and **w** it; he makes Is 44:15
his idol, and falls down to it and **w** it. Is 44:17
"If anyone **w** the beast and its image and Rv 14:9

WORST (2)
about me; they imagine the **w** for me. Ps 41:7
I will bring the **w** of the nations to take Ezk 7:24

WORTH (13)
a piece of land **w** four hundred shekels Gn 23:15
us. But you are **w** ten thousand of us. 2 Sm 18:3
of silver, and silver vessels **w** 200 talents, Ezr 8:26
20 bowls of gold **w** 1,000 darics, and two Ezr 8:27
Yet all this is **w** nothing to me, so long Est 5:13
Man does not know its **w**, and it is not Jb 28:13
the heart of the wicked is of little **w**. Prv 10:20
vines, **w** a thousand shekels of silver, Is 7:23
sons of Zion, **w** their weight in fine gold, Lam 4:2
two hundred denarii **w** of bread and Mk 6:37
time are not **w** comparing with the Rom 8:18
But you know Timothy's proven **w**, Phil 2:22
of the surpassing **w** of knowing Christ Phil 3:8

WORTHILY (1)
May you act **w** in Ephrathah and be Ru 4:11

WORTHLESS (49)
no water, and we loathe this **w** food." Nm 21:5
that certain **w** fellows have gone out Dt 13:13
which Abimelech hired **w** and reckless Jgs 9:4
and **w** fellows collected around Jephthah Jgs 11:3
behold, the men of the city, **w** fellows, Jgs 19:22
up the men, the **w** fellows in Gibeah, Jgs 20:13
regard your servant as a **w** woman, 1 Sm 1:16
Now the sons of Eli were **w** men. They 1 Sm 2:12
But some **w** fellows said, "How can 1 Sm 10:27
was despised and **w** they devoted to 1 Sm 15:9
he is such a **w** man that one cannot 1 Sm 25:17
Let not my lord regard this **w** fellow, 1 Sm 25:25
the wicked and **w** fellows among the 1 Sm 30:22
out, you man of blood, you **w** man! 2 Sm 16:7
there happened to be there a **w** man, 2 Sm 20:1
But **w** men are all like thorns that are 2 Sm 23:6
And set two **w** men opposite him, 1 Kgs 21:10
And the two **w** men came in and sat 1 Kgs 21:13
And the **w** men brought a charge 1 Kgs 21:13
and certain **w** scoundrels gathered 2 Chr 13:7
For he knows **w** men; when he sees Jb 11:11
with lies; **w** physicians are you all. Jb 13:4
who says to a king, '**W** one,' and to Jb 34:18
I hate those who pay regard to **w** idols, Ps 31:6
For all the gods of the peoples are **w** idols, Ps 96:5
shame, who make their boast in **w** idols; Ps 97:7
set before my eyes anything that is **w**. Ps 101:3
my eyes from looking at **w** things; Ps 119:37
A **w** person, a wicked man, goes about Prv 6:12
he who follows **w** pursuits lacks sense. Prv 12:11
A **w** man plots evil, and his speech is Prv 16:27
A **w** witness mocks at justice, and the Prv 19:28
he who follows **w** pursuits will have Prv 28:19
Egypt's help is **w** and empty; therefore I Is 30:7
went after worthlessness, and became **w**? Jer 2:5
They are **w**, a work of delusion; at the Jer 10:15
to you a lying vision, **w** divination, Jer 14:14
what is precious, and not what is **w**, Jer 15:19
w things in which there is no profit. Jer 16:19
They are **w**, a work of delusion; at the Jer 51:18
evil against the LORD, a **w** counselor. Na 1:11
again shall the **w** pass through you; Na 1:15
"Woe to my **w** shepherd, who deserts Zec 11:17

And cast the **w** servant into the outer Mt 25:30
aside; together they have become **w**; Rom 3:12
the weak and **w** elementary principles of Gal 4:9
the law, for they are unprofitable and **w**. Ti 3:9
thistles, it is **w** and near to being cursed, Heb 6:8
his heart, this person's religion is **w**. Jas 1:26

WORTHLESSNESS (1)
they went far from me, and went after **w**, Jer 2:5

WORTHY (46)
I am not **w** of the least of all the deeds of Gn 32:10
a **w** man of the clan of Elimelech, Ru 2:1
know that you are a **w** woman. Ru 3:11
upon the LORD, who is **w** to be praised, 2 Sm 22:4
for you are a **w** man and bring good 1 Kgs 1:42
"If he will show himself a **w** man, 1 Kgs 1:52
upon the LORD, who is **w** to be praised, Ps 18:3
I, whose sandals I am not **w** to carry. Mt 3:11
I am not **w** to have you come under my Mt 8:8
find out who is **w** in it and stay there Mt 10:11
And if the house is **w**, let your peace Mt 10:13
peace come upon it, but if it is not **w**, Mt 10:13
mother more than me is not **w** of me, Mt 10:37
daughter more than me is not **w** of me. Mt 10:37
his cross and follow me is not **w** of me. Mt 10:38
is ready, but those invited were not **w**. Mt 22:8
sandals I am not **w** to stoop down and Mk 1:7
of whose sandals I am not **w** to untie. Lk 3:16
"He is **w** to have you do this for him, Lk 7:4
for I am not **w** to have you come under Lk 7:6
I am no longer **w** to be called your son. Lk 15:19
I am no longer **w** to be called your son.' Lk 15:21
those who are considered **w** to attain to Lk 20:35
of whose sandal I am not **w** to untie." Jn 1:27
they were counted **w** to suffer dishonor Acts 5:41
of whose feet I am not **w** to untie.' Acts 13:25
found in him no guilt **w** of death, Acts 13:28
in the Lord in a way **w** of the saints, Rom 16:2
to walk in a manner **w** of the calling to Eph 4:1
manner of life be **w** of the gospel of Phil 1:27
if there is anything **w** of praise, Phil 4:8
so as to walk in a manner **w** of the Lord, Col 1:10
you to walk in a manner **w** of God, 1 Thes 2:12
may be considered **w** of the kingdom 2 Thes 1:5
God may make you **w** of his calling 2 Thes 1:11
well be considered **w** of double honor, 1 Tm 5:17
their own masters as **w** of all honor, 1 Tm 6:1
Jesus has been counted **w** of more glory Heb 3:3
world was not **w**—wandering about Heb 11:38
on their journey in a manner **w** of God. 3 Jn 1:6
will walk with me in white, for they are **w**. Rv 3:4
"**W** are you, our Lord and God, to receive Rv 4:11
"Who is **w** to open the scroll and break its Rv 5:2
no one was found **w** to open the scroll Rv 5:4
"**W** are you to take the scroll and to open Rv 5:9
voice, "**W** is the Lamb who was slain, Rv 5:12

WOUND (24)
burn for burn, **w** for wound, stripe for Ex 21:25
burn for burn, wound for **w**, stripe for Ex 21:25
I kill and I make alive; I **w** and I heal; Dt 32:39
the blood of the **w** flowed into the 1 Kgs 22:35
my **w** is incurable, though I am without Jb 34:6
As with a deadly **w** in my bones, my Ps 42:10
Blows that **w** cleanse away evil; Prv 20:30
They have healed the **w** of my people Jer 6:14
They have healed the **w** of my people Jer 8:11
For the **w** of the daughter of my people is Jer 8:21
because of my hurt! My **w** is grievous. Jer 10:19
of my people is shattered with a great **w**, Jer 14:17
is my pain unceasing, my **w** incurable, Jer 15:18
is incurable, and your **w** is grievous. Jer 30:12
your cause, no medicine for your **w**, Jer 30:13
became broader as it **w** upward to the Ezk 41:7
saw his sickness, and Judah his **w**, Hos 5:13
is not able to cure you or heal your **w**. Hos 5:13
For her **w** is incurable, and it has come to Mi 1:9
no easing your hurt; your **w** is grievous. Na 3:19
heads, and by means of them they **w**. Rv 9:19
of its heads seemed to have a mortal **w**, Rv 13:3
wound, but its mortal **w** was healed, Rv 13:3
first beast, whose mortal **w** was healed. Rv 13:12

WOUNDED (27)
And many fell **w**, up to the entrance of Jgs 9:40
so that the **w** Philistines fell on the 1 Sm 17:52
and he was badly **w** by the archers. 1 Sm 31:3
and **w** Shobach the commander of 2 Sm 10:18
him—struck him and **w** him. 1 Kgs 20:37
me out of the battle, for I am **w**." 1 Kgs 22:34
and the Syrians **w** Joram. 2 Kgs 8:28
him, and he was **w** by the archers. 1 Chr 10:3
me out of the battle, for I am **w**." 2 Chr 18:33
And the Syrians **w** Joram, 2 Chr 22:5
of Ahab in Jezreel, because he was **w**. 2 Chr 22:6
from him, leaving him severely **w**, 2 Chr 24:25

"Take me away, for I am badly **w**." 2 Chr 35:23
and the soul of the **w** cries for help; Jb 24:12
his arrow at them; they are **w** suddenly. Ps 64:7
recount the pain of those you have **w**. Ps 69:26
But he was **w** for our transgressions; he Is 53:5
the daughter of my people is my heart **w**; Jer 8:21
there remained of them only **w** men, Jer 37:10
of the Chaldeans, and **w** in her streets. Jer 51:4
through all her land the **w** shall groan. Jer 51:52
they faint like a **w** man in the streets Lam 2:12
sound of your fall, when the **w** groan, Ezk 26:15
before him like a man mortally **w**. Ezk 30:24
This one also they **w** and cast out. Lk 20:12
fled out of that house naked and **w**. Acts 19:16
the beast that was **w** by the sword and Rv 13:14

WOUNDING (2)
I have killed a man for **w** me, a young Gn 4:23
your brothers and **w** their conscience 1 Cor 8:12

WOUNDS (22)
in Jezreel of the **w** that the Syrians 2 Kgs 8:29
in Jezreel of the **w** that the Syrians 2 Kgs 9:15
in Jezreel of the **w** that he had 2 Chr 22:6
For he **w**, but he binds up; he shatters, Jb 5:18
and multiplies my **w** without cause; Jb 9:17
My **w** stink and fester because of my Ps 38:5
brokenhearted and binds up their **w**. Ps 147:3
W and dishonor will he get, and his Prv 6:33
Who has **w** without cause? Prv 23:29
Like an archer who **w** everyone is one Prv 26:10
Faithful are the **w** of a friend; profuse Prv 27:6
in it, but bruises and sores and raw **w**; Is 1:6
and heals the **w** inflicted by his blow. Is 30:26
her; sickness and **w** are ever before me. Jer 6:7
and will hiss because of all its **w**. Jer 19:8
health to you, and your **w** I will heal, Jer 30:17
appalled, and hiss because of all her **w**. Jer 50:13
him, 'What are these **w** on your back?' Zec 13:6
'The **w** I received in the house of my Zec 13:6
He went to him and bound up his **w**, Lk 10:34
hour of the night and washed their **w**; Acts 16:33
By his **w** you have been healed. 1 Pt 2:24

WOVE (2)
of his head and **w** them into the web. Jgs 16:14
where the women **w** hangings for the 2 Kgs 23:7

WOVEN (14)
And the skillfully **w** band on it shall be Ex 28:8
seam above the skillfully **w** band of the Ex 28:27
lie on the skillfully **w** band of the Ex 28:28
with a **w** binding around the opening, Ex 28:32
him with the skillfully **w** band of the Ex 29:5
yarns they made finely **w** garments, Ex 39:1
And the skillfully **w** band on it was of Ex 39:5
seam above the skillfully **w** band of the Ex 39:20
lie on the skillfully **w** band of the Ex 39:21
the robe of the ephod **w** all of blue, Ex 39:22
also made the coats, **w** of fine linen, Ex 39:27
and tied the skillfully **w** band of the ephod Lv 8:7
intricately **w** in the depths of the earth. Ps 139:15
w in one piece from top to bottom, Jn 19:23

WRAP (2)
the covering too narrow to **w** oneself in. Is 28:20
"**W** your cloak around you and follow Acts 12:8

WRAPPED (24)
Mount Sinai was **w** in smoke because Ex 19:18
fire to the heart of heaven, **w** in darkness, Dt 4:11
it is here **w** in a cloth behind the 1 Sm 21:9
and he is **w** in a robe." And Saul 1 Sm 28:14
he **w** his face in his cloak and went 1 Kgs 19:13
may they be **w** in their own shame as Ps 109:29
Who has **w** up the waters in a garment? Prv 30:4
and **w** himself in zeal as a cloak. Is 59:17
"You have **w** yourself with anger and Lam 3:43
you have **w** yourself with a cloud so Lam 3:44
mourns, the prince is **w** in despair, Ezk 7:27
with salt, nor **w** in swaddling cloths. Ezk 16:4
I **w** you in fine linen and covered you Ezk 16:10
A wind has **w** them in its wings, and Hos 4:19
me; weeds were **w** about my head Jon 2:5
took the body and **w** it in a clean Mt 27:59
w him in the linen shroud and laid Mk 15:46
firstborn son and **w** him in swaddling Lk 2:7
will find a baby **w** in swaddling cloths Lk 2:12
he took it down and **w** it in a linen Lk 23:53
linen strips, and his face **w** with a cloth. Jn 11:44
with the towel that was **w** around him. Jn 13:5
young men rose and **w** him up and Acts 5:6
down from heaven, **w** in a cloud, Rv 10:1

WRAPPING (1)
herself with a veil, **w** herself up, Gn 38:14

WRAPS (1)
like a garment that he **w** around him, Ps 109:19

WRATH (212)
their anger, for it is fierce, and their **w**, Gn 49:7
and my **w** will burn, and I will kill you Ex 22:24
that my **w** may burn hot against them Ex 32:10
why does your **w** burn hot against your Ex 32:11
and **w** come upon all the congregation; Lv 10:6
there may be no **w** on the congregation Nm 1:53
for **w** has gone out from the LORD; Nm 16:46
may never again be **w** on the people of Nm 18:5
turned back my **w** from the people Nm 25:11
the LORD your God to **w** in the wilderness. Dt 9:7
at Horeb you provoked the LORD to **w**, Dt 9:8
you provoked the LORD to **w**. Dt 9:22
LORD overthrew in his anger and **w**— Dt 29:23
land in anger and fury and great **w**, Dt 29:28
let them live, lest **w** be upon us, because Jos 9:20
and **w** fell upon all the congregation of Jos 22:20
out his fierce **w** against Amalek, 1 Sm 28:18
there came great **w** against Israel. 2 Kgs 3:27
For great is the **w** of the LORD that is 2 Kgs 22:13
therefore my **w** will be kindled 2 Kgs 22:17
from the burning of his great **w**, 2 Kgs 23:26
Yet **w** came upon Israel for this, and 1 Chr 27:24
and my **w** shall not be poured out on 2 Chr 12:7
humbled himself the **w** of the LORD 2 Chr 12:12
w has gone out against you from the 2 Chr 19:2
the LORD and **w** may not come 2 Chr 19:10
And **w** came upon Judah and 2 Chr 24:18
for the fierce **w** of the LORD is upon 2 Chr 28:11
and there is fierce **w** against Israel." 2 Chr 28:13
Therefore the **w** of the LORD came on 2 Chr 29:8
Therefore **w** came upon him and 2 Chr 32:25
so that the **w** of the LORD did not 2 Chr 32:26
For great is the **w** of the LORD that is 2 Chr 34:21
therefore my **w** will be poured out 2 Chr 34:25
until the **w** of the LORD rose against 2 Chr 36:16
lest his **w** be against the realm of the Ezr 7:23
the power of his **w** is against all who Ezr 8:22
until the fierce **w** of our God over this Ezr 10:14
you are bringing more **w** on Israel by Neh 13:18
there will be contempt and **w** in plenty. Est 1:18
he was filled with **w** against Mordecai. Est 5:9
arose in his **w** from the wine-drinking Est 7:7
Then the **w** of the king abated. Est 7:10
would conceal me until your **w** be past, Jb 14:13
He has torn me in his **w** and hated me; he Jb 16:9
He has kindled his **w** against me and Jb 19:11
for **w** brings the punishment of the Jb 19:29
away, dragged off in the day of God's **w**. Jb 20:28
let them drink of the **w** of the Almighty. Jb 21:20
that he is rescued in the day of **w**? Jb 21:30
Beware lest **w** entice you into scoffing, Jb 36:18
Then he will speak to them in his **w**, and Ps 2:5
in the way, for his **w** is quickly kindled. Ps 2:12
your anger, nor discipline me in your **w**. Ps 6:1
The LORD will swallow them up in his **w**, Ps 21:9
Refrain from anger, and forsake **w**! Fret Ps 37:8
your anger, nor discipline me in your **w**! Ps 38:1
In **w** cast down the peoples, O God! Ps 56:7
consume them in **w**; consume them till Ps 59:13
Surely the **w** of man shall praise you; Ps 76:10
the remnant of **w** you will put on like a Ps 76:10
when the LORD heard, he was full of **w**; Ps 78:21
anger often and did not stir up all his **w**. Ps 78:38
his burning anger, **w**, indignation, Ps 78:49
When God heard, he was full of **w**, and Ps 78:59
sword and vented his **w** on his heritage. Ps 78:62
You withdrew all your **w**; you turned Ps 85:3
Your **w** lies heavy upon me, and you Ps 88:7
Your **w** has swept over me; your Ps 88:16
you are full of **w** against your anointed. Ps 89:38
How long will your **w** burn like fire? Ps 89:46
your anger; by your **w** we are dismayed. Ps 90:7
For all our days pass away under your **w**; Ps 90:9
and your **w** according to the fear of Ps 90:11
Therefore I swore in my **w**, "They shall Ps 95:11
turn away his **w** from destroying Ps 106:23
will shatter kings on the day of his **w**. Ps 110:5
your hand against the **w** of my enemies, Ps 138:7
Riches do not profit in the day of **w**, but Prv 11:4
the expectation of the wicked in **w**. Prv 11:23
but his **w** falls on one who acts Prv 14:35
A soft answer turns away **w**, but a Prv 15:1
A king's **w** is a messenger of death, Prv 16:14
A king's **w** is like the growling of a Prv 19:12
A man of great **w** will pay the penalty, Prv 19:19
and a concealed bribe, strong **w**. Prv 21:14
W is cruel, anger is overwhelming, but Prv 27:4
a city aflame, but the wise turn away **w**. Prv 29:8
A man of **w** stirs up strife, and one Prv 29:22
Through the **w** of the LORD of hosts the Is 9:19
the people of my **w** I command him, Is 10:6
comes, cruel, with **w** and fierce anger, Is 13:9
at the **w** of the LORD of hosts in the day of Is 13:13
the peoples in **w** with unceasing blows, Is 14:6

I have no **w**. Would that I had thorns and Is 27:4
day because of the **w** of the oppressor, Is 51:13
And where is the **w** of the oppressor? Is 51:13
the hand of the LORD the cup of his **w**, Is 51:17
they are full of the **w** of the LORD, the Is 51:20
the bowl of my **w** you shall drink no Is 51:22
so will he repay, **w** to his adversaries, Is 59:18
to you; for in my **w** I struck you, Is 60:10
in my anger and trampled them in my **w**; Is 63:3
me salvation, and my **w** upheld me. Is 63:5
I made them drunk in my **w**, and I poured Is 63:6
lest my **w** go forth like fire, and burn with Jer 4:4
Therefore I am full of the **w** of the LORD; I Jer 6:11
my anger and my **w** will be poured out Jer 7:20
and forsaken the generation of his **w**.' Jer 7:29
At his **w** the earth quakes, and the Jer 10:10
Pour out your **w** on the nations that Jer 10:25
them, to turn away your **w** from them. Jer 18:20
arm, in anger and in fury and in great **w**. Jer 21:5
robbed, lest my **w** go forth like fire, Jer 21:12
W has gone forth, a whirling tempest; Jer 23:19
my hand this cup of the wine of **w**, Jer 25:15
W has gone forth, a whirling tempest; Jer 30:23
This city has aroused my anger and **w**, Jer 32:31
my anger and my **w** and in great Jer 32:37
strike down in my anger and my **w**, Jer 33:5
is the anger and **w** that the LORD has Jer 36:7
my anger and my **w** were poured out on Jer 42:18
so my **w** will be poured out on you Jer 42:18
Therefore my **w** and my anger were Jer 44:6
Because of the **w** of the LORD she shall Jer 50:13
and brought out the weapons of his **w**, Jer 50:25
in his **w** he has broken down the Lam 2:2
seen affliction under the rod of his **w**; Lam 3:1
The LORD gave full vent to his **w**; he Lam 4:11
I will soon pour out my **w** upon you, Ezk 7:8
for **w** is upon all their multitude. Ezk 7:12
for my **w** is upon all their multitude. Ezk 7:14
them in the day of the **w** of the LORD. Ezk 7:19
Therefore I will act in **w**. My eye will Ezk 8:18
the outpouring of your **w** on Jerusalem?" Ezk 9:8
a stormy wind break out in my **w**, Ezk 13:13
and great hailstones in **w** to make a Ezk 13:13
will I spend my **w** upon the wall and Ezk 13:15
and pour out my **w** upon it with Ezk 14:19
upon you the blood of **w** and jealousy. Ezk 16:38
So will I satisfy my **w** on you, and my Ezk 16:42
would pour out my **w** upon them and Ezk 20:8
would pour out my **w** upon them in Ezk 20:13
would pour out my **w** upon them and Ezk 20:21
arm and with **w** poured out I Ezk 20:33
arm, and with **w** poured out. Ezk 20:34
blow upon you with the fire of my **w**, Ezk 21:31
gather you in my anger and in my **w**, Ezk 22:20
and blow on you with the fire of my **w**, Ezk 22:21
I have poured out my **w** upon you." Ezk 22:22
consumed them with the fire of my **w**. Ezk 22:31
To rouse my **w**, to take vengeance, I Ezk 24:8
to my anger and according to my **w**, Ezk 25:14
I will pour out my **w** on Pelusium, Ezk 30:15
Behold, I have spoken in my jealous **w**, Ezk 36:6
I poured out my **w** upon them for the Ezk 36:18
GOD, my **w** will be roused in my anger. Ezk 38:18
and in my blazing **w** I declare, Ezk 38:19
and he ran at him in his powerful **w**. Dn 8:6
your anger and your **w** turn away from Dn 9:16
them I will pour out my **w** like water. Hos 5:10
in your midst, and I will not come in **w**. Hos 11:9
anger, and I took him away in my **w**. Hos 13:11
perpetually, and he kept his **w** forever. Am 1:11
And in anger and **w** I will execute Mi 5:15
adversaries and keeps **w** for his enemies. Na 1:2
His **w** is poured out like fire, and the Na 1:6
you pour out your **w** and make them Hab 2:15
make it known; in **w** remember mercy. Hab 3:2
Was your **w** against the rivers, O LORD? Hab 3:8
A day of **w** is that day, a day of distress Zep 1:15
them on the day of the **w** of the LORD. Zep 1:18
and I am jealous for her with great **w**. Zec 8:2
when your fathers provoked me to **w**, Zec 8:14
warned you to flee from the **w** to come? Mt 3:7
warned you to flee from the **w** to come? Lk 3:7
all in the synagogue were filled with **w**. Lk 4:28
the earth and **w** against this people. Lk 21:23
see life, but the **w** of God remains on him. Jn 3:36
For the **w** of God is revealed from Rom 1:18
you are storing up **w** for yourself on the Rom 2:5
on the day of **w** when God's righteous Rom 2:5
there will be **w** and fury. Rom 2:8
God is unrighteous to inflict **w** on us? Rom 3:5
For the law brings **w**, but where there Rom 4:15
we be saved by him from the **w** of God. Rom 5:9
desiring to show his **w** and to make Rom 9:22
patience vessels of **w** prepared for Rom 9:22
but leave it to the **w** of God, Rom 12:19
carries out God's **w** on the wrongdoer. Rom 13:4
only to avoid God's **w** but also for the Rom 13:5
mind, and were by nature children of **w**, Eph 2:3
Let all bitterness and **w** and anger and Eph 4:31
of these things the **w** of God comes upon Eph 5:6
account of these the **w** of God is coming. Col 3:6
anger, **w**, malice, slander, and obscene Col 3:8
who delivers us from the **w** to come. 1 Thes 1:10
But God's **w** has come upon them at 1 Thes 2:16
For God has not destined us for **w**, 1 Thes 5:9
As I swore in my **w**, 'They shall not Heb 3:11
rest, as he has said, "As I swore in my **w**, Heb 4:3
the throne, and from the **w** of the Lamb, Rv 6:16
for the great day of their **w** has come, Rv 6:17
The nations raged, but your **w** came, Rv 11:18
devil has come down to you in great **w**, Rv 12:12
he also will drink the wine of God's **w**, Rv 14:10
into the great winepress of the **w** of God. Rv 14:19
for with them the **w** of God is finished. Rv 15:1
bowls full of the **w** of God who lives Rv 15:7
earth the seven bowls of the **w** of God." Rv 16:1
the cup of the wine of the fury of his **w**. Rv 16:19
the fury of the **w** of God the Almighty. Rv 19:15

WRATHFUL (3)
given to anger, nor go with a **w** man, Prv 22:24
vengeance on them with **w** rebukes. Ezk 25:17
God; the LORD is avenging and **w**; Na 1:2

WREATH (1)
They do it to receive a perishable **w**, 1 Cor 9:25

WREATHS (4)
checker work with **w** of chain work 1 Kgs 7:17
oxen, there were **w** of beveled work. 1 Kgs 7:29
supports were cast with **w** at the side 1 Kgs 7:30
the space of each, with **w** all around. 1 Kgs 7:36

WRECKED (4)
for the ships were **w** at Ezion-geber. 1 Kgs 22:48
And the ships were **w** and were not 2 Chr 20:37
The east wind has **w** you in the heart Ezk 27:26
Now you are **w** by the seas, in the Ezk 27:34

WRENCHED (1)
and chains, but he **w** the chains apart, Mk 5:4

WRESTLE (1)
For we do not **w** against flesh and Eph 6:12

WRESTLED (3)
wrestlings I have **w** with my sister Gn 30:8
And a man **w** with him until the Gn 32:24
was put out of joint as he **w** with him. Gn 32:25

WRESTLINGS (1)
"With mighty **w** I have wrestled with Gn 30:8

WRETCHED (3)
W man that I am! Who will deliver Rom 7:24
Be **w** and mourn and weep. Let your Jas 4:9
nothing, not realizing that you are **w**, Rv 3:17

WRETCHEDNESS (1)
your sight, that I may not see my **w**." Nm 11:15

WRETCHES (2)
w whom I did not know tore at me Ps 35:15
"He will put those **w** to a miserable Mt 21:41

WRING (2)
it to the altar and **w** off its head and burn Lv 1:15
He shall **w** its head from its neck but Lv 5:8

WRINKLE (1)
without spot or **w** or any such thing, Eph 5:27

WRISTS (2)
who sew magic bands upon all **w**, Ezk 13:18
put bracelets on your **w** and a chain Ezk 16:11

WRITE (85)
"**W** this as a memorial in a book and Ex 17:14
and I will **w** on the tablets the words that Ex 34:1
the LORD said to Moses, "**W** these words, Ex 34:27
"Then the priest shall **w** these curses in Nm 5:23
staffs. **W** each man's name on his staff, Nm 17:2
and **w** Aaron's name on the staff of Nm 17:3
You shall **w** them on the doorposts of Dt 6:9
And I will **w** on the tablets the words that Dt 10:2
You shall **w** them on the doorposts of Dt 11:20
he shall **w** for himself in a book a copy Dt 17:18
And you shall **w** on them all the words of Dt 27:3
And you shall **w** on the stones all the Dt 27:8
"Now therefore **w** this song and teach it Dt 31:19
They shall **w** a description of it with a Jos 18:4
those who went to **w** the description of Jos 18:8
in the land and **w** a description and Jos 18:8
that we might **w** down the names of Ezr 5:10
But you may **w** as you please with regard Est 8:8
For you **w** bitter things against me and Jb 13:26
neck; **w** them on the tablet of your heart. Prv 3:3
w them on the tablet of your heart. Prv 7:3
a large tablet and **w** on it in common Is 8:1
be so few that a child can **w** them down. Is 10:19
w it before them on a tablet and inscribe Is 30:8
of Jacob, and another will **w** on his hand, Is 44:5
"**W** this man down as childless, a man Jer 22:30
W in a book all the words that I have Jer 30:2
them, and I will **w** it on their hearts. Jer 31:33
"Take a scroll and **w** on it all the words Jer 36:2
please, how did you **w** all these words? Jer 36:17
"Take another scroll and **w** on it all the Jer 36:28
of man, **w** down the name of this day, Ezk 24:2
"Son of man, take a stick and **w** on it, Ezk 37:16
then take another stick and **w** on it, Ezk 37:16
sticks on which you **w** are in your Ezk 37:20
its laws, and **w** it down in their sight, Ezk 43:11
Were I to **w** for him my laws by the ten Hos 8:12
the LORD answered me: "**W** the vision; Hab 2:2
allowed a man to **w** a certificate of Mk 10:4
past, to **w** an orderly account for you, Lk 1:3
bill, and sit down quickly and **w** fifty.' Lk 16:6
to him, 'Take your bill, and **w** eighty.' Lk 16:7
of the Jews said to Pilate, "Do not **w**, Jn 19:21
but should **w** to them to abstain from Acts 15:20
have nothing definite to **w** to my lord Acts 25:26
him, I may have something to **w**. Acts 25:26
I do not **w** these things to make you 1 Cor 4:14
w this greeting with my own hand. 1 Cor 16:21
superfluous for me to **w** to you about 2 Cor 9:1
this reason I **w** these things while 2 Cor 13:10
To **w** the same things to you is no Phil 3:1
w this greeting with my own hand. Col 4:18
have no need for anyone to **w** to you, 1 Thes 4:9
w this greeting with my own hand. 2 Thes 3:17
every letter of mine; it is the way I **w**. 2 Thes 3:17
I, Paul, **w** this with my own hand: I Phlm 1:19
of your obedience, I **w** to you, Phlm 1:21
minds, and **w** them on their hearts, Heb 8:10
hearts, and **w** them on their minds," Heb 10:16
I **w** to you, children, because you know 1 Jn 2:13
I **w** to you, fathers, because you know 1 Jn 2:14
I **w** to you, young men, because you are 1 Jn 2:14
I **w** to you, not because you do not 1 Jn 2:21
I **w** these things to you about those who 1 Jn 2:26
I **w** these things to you who believe in 1 Jn 5:13
Though I have much to **w** to you, I 2 Jn 1:12
I had much to **w** to you, but I would 3 Jn 1:13
I would rather not **w** with pen and ink. 3 Jn 1:13
I was very eager to **w** to you about our Jude 1:3
found it necessary to **w** appealing to you Jude 1:3
"**W** what you see in a book and send it to Rv 1:11
W therefore the things that you have Rv 1:19
"To the angel of the church in Ephesus **w**: Rv 2:1
to the angel of the church in Smyrna **w**: Rv 2:8
the angel of the church in Pergamum **w**: Rv 2:12
to the angel of the church in Thyatira **w**: Rv 2:18
to the angel of the church in Sardis **w**: Rv 3:1
angel of the church in Philadelphia **w**: Rv 3:7
and I will **w** on him the name of my God, Rv 3:12
to the angel of the church in Laodicea **w**: Rv 3:14
thunders had sounded, I was about to **w**, Rv 10:4
have said, and do not **w** it down." Rv 10:4
a voice from heaven saying, "**W** this: Rv 14:13
And the angel said to me, "**W** this: Rv 19:9
things new." Also he said, "**W** this down, Rv 21:5

WRITERS (1)
and the **w** who keep writing oppression, Is 10:1

WRITES (3)
and he **w** her a certificate of divorce and Dt 24:1
man hates her and **w** her a certificate of Dt 24:3
For Moses **w** about the righteousness Rom 10:5

WRITHE (4)
My anguish, my anguish! I **w** in pain! Jer 4:19
and princes shall soon **w** because of the Hos 8:10
W and groan, O daughter of Zion, like a Mi 4:10
afraid; Gaza too, and shall **w** in anguish; Zec 9:5

WRITHED (2)
we were pregnant, we **w**, but we have Is 26:18
The mountains saw you and **w**; the Hab 3:10

WRITHES (3)
The wicked man **w** in pain all his days, Jb 15:20
a pregnant woman who **w** and cries out Is 26:17
The land trembles and **w** in pain, for Jer 51:29

WRITING (41)
God, and the **w** was the writing of God, Ex 32:16
God, and the writing was the **w** of God, Ex 32:16
on the tablets, in the same **w** as before, Dt 10:4
Moses had finished **w** the words of Dt 31:24
clear to me in **w** from the hand of 1 Chr 28:19
as prescribed in the **w** of David king 2 Chr 35:4
all his kingdom and also put it in **w**: 2 Chr 36:22
all his kingdom and also put it in **w**: Ezr 1:1
all this we make a firm covenant in **w**; Neh 9:38
he gave orders in **w** that his evil plan Est 9:25

of Purim, and it was recorded in **w**. Est 9:32
and the writers who keep **w** oppression, Is 10:1
A **w** of Hezekiah king of Judah, after he Is 38:9
And it had **w** on the front and on the Ezk 2:10
in linen, with a **w** case at his waist. Ezk 9:2
in linen, who had the **w** case at his waist. Ezk 9:3
in linen, with the **w** case at his waist, Ezk 9:11
men of Babylon, "Whoever reads this **w**, Dn 5:7
could not read the **w** or make known to Dn 5:8
me to read this **w** and make known to Dn 5:15
you can read the **w** and make known to Dn 5:16
I will read the **w** to the king and make Dn 5:17
was sent, and this **w** was inscribed. Dn 5:24
And this is the **w** that was inscribed: Dn 5:25
And he asked for a **w** tablet and wrote, Lk 1:63
But now I am **w** to you not to 1 Cor 5:11
nor am I **w** these things to secure any 1 Cor 9:15
that the things I am **w** to you are a 1 Cor 14:37
For we are not **w** to you anything 2 Cor 1:13
(In what I am **w** to you, before God, I do Gal 1:20
large letters I am **w** to you with my Gal 6:11
but I am **w** these things to you so 1 Tm 3:14
now the second letter that I am **w** to you, 2 Pt 3:1
And we are **w** these things so that our 1 Jn 1:4
I am **w** these things to you so that you 1 Jn 2:1
I am **w** you no new commandment, 1 Jn 2:7
new commandment that I am **w** to you, 1 Jn 2:8
I am **w** to you, little children, because 1 Jn 2:12
I am **w** to you, fathers, because you 1 Jn 2:13
is from the beginning. I am **w** to you, 1 Jn 2:13
as though I were **w** you a new 2 Jn 1:5

WRITINGS (3)
But if you do not believe his **w**, how will Jn 5:47
through the prophetic **w** has been Rom 16:26
been acquainted with the sacred **w**, 2 Tm 3:15

WRITTEN (250)
which I have **w** for their instruction." Ex 24:12
of stone, **w** with the finger of God. Ex 31:18
hand, tablets that were **w** on both sides; Ex 32:15
the front and on the back they were **w**. Ex 32:15
me out of your book that you have **w**." Ex 32:32
two tablets of stone **w** with the finger of Dt 9:10
of this law that are **w** in this book, Dt 28:58
and the curses **w** in this book will settle Dt 29:20
curses of the covenant **w** in this Book of Dt 29:21
upon it all the curses **w** in this book, Dt 29:27
his statutes that are **w** in this Book of Dt 30:10
to do according to all that is **w** in it. Jos 1:8
as it is **w** in the Book of the Law of Jos 8:31
of the law of Moses, which he had **w**. Jos 8:32
according to all that is **w** in the Book of Jos 8:34
Is this not **w** in the Book of Jashar? Jos 10:13
and to do all that is **w** in the Book of the Jos 23:6
behold, it is **w** in the Book of Jashar. 2 Sm 1:18
as it is **w** in the Law of Moses, 1 Kgs 2:3
are they not **w** in the Book of the 1 Kgs 11:41
they are **w** in the Book of the 1 Kgs 14:19
are they not **w** in the Book of the 1 Kgs 14:29
are they not **w** in the Book of the 1 Kgs 15:7
are they not **w** in the Book of the 1 Kgs 15:23
are they not **w** in the Book of the 1 Kgs 15:31
are they not **w** in the Book of the 1 Kgs 16:5
are they not **w** in the Book of the 1 Kgs 16:14
are they not **w** in the Book of the 1 Kgs 16:20
are they not **w** in the Book of the 1 Kgs 16:27
As it was **w** in the letters that she 1 Kgs 21:11
are they not **w** in the Book of the 1 Kgs 22:39
are they not **w** in the Book of the 1 Kgs 22:45
are they not **w** in the Book of the 2 Kgs 1:18
are they not **w** in the Book of the 2 Kgs 8:23
are they not **w** in the Book of the 2 Kgs 10:34
are they not **w** in the Book of the 2 Kgs 12:19
are they not **w** in the Book of the 2 Kgs 13:8
are they not **w** in the Book of the 2 Kgs 13:12
according to what is **w** in the Book of 2 Kgs 14:6
are they not **w** in the Book of the 2 Kgs 14:15
are they not **w** in the Book of the 2 Kgs 14:18
are they not **w** in the Book of the 2 Kgs 14:28
are they not **w** in the Book of the 2 Kgs 15:6
they are **w** in the Book of the 2 Kgs 15:11
they are **w** in the Book of the 2 Kgs 15:15
are they not **w** in the Book of the 2 Kgs 15:21
they are **w** in the Book of the 2 Kgs 15:26
they are **w** in the Book of the 2 Kgs 15:31
are they not **w** in the Book of the 2 Kgs 15:36
are they not **w** in the Book of the 2 Kgs 16:19
are they not **w** in the Book of the 2 Kgs 20:20
are they not **w** in the Book of the 2 Kgs 21:17
are they not **w** in the Book of the 2 Kgs 21:25
to all that is **w** concerning us." 2 Kgs 22:13
covenant that were **w** in this book. 2 Kgs 23:3
as it is **w** in this Book of the 2 Kgs 23:21
the law that were **w** in the book that 2 Kgs 23:24
are they not **w** in the Book of the 2 Kgs 23:28
are they not **w** in the Book of the 2 Kgs 24:5
and these are **w** in the Book of the 1 Chr 9:1
to do all that is **w** in the Law of the 1 Chr 16:40
are **w** in the Chronicles of Samuel 1 Chr 29:29
are they not **w** in the history of 2 Chr 9:29
are they not **w** in the chronicles of 2 Chr 12:15
are **w** in the story of the prophet 2 Chr 13:22
are **w** in the Book of the Kings of 2 Chr 16:11
are **w** in the chronicles of Jehu the 2 Chr 20:34
LORD, as it is **w** in the Law of Moses, 2 Chr 23:18
house of God are **w** in the Story of 2 Chr 24:27
according to what is **w** in the Law, 2 Chr 25:4
are they not **w** in the Book of the 2 Chr 25:26
they are **w** in the Book of the Kings of 2 Chr 27:7
they are **w** in the Book of the Kings 2 Chr 28:26
as it is **w** in the Law of the LORD. 2 Chr 31:3
they are **w** in the vision of Isaiah the 2 Chr 32:32
they are **w** in the Chronicles of the 2 Chr 33:19
to all that is **w** in this book." 2 Chr 34:21
the curses that are **w** in the book 2 Chr 34:24
covenant that were **w** in this book. 2 Chr 34:31
LORD, as it is **w** in the Book of Moses. 2 Chr 35:12
behold, they are **w** in the Laments. 2 Chr 35:25
according to what is **w** in the Law of 2 Chr 35:26
they are **w** in the Book of the Kings 2 Chr 35:27
they are **w** in the Book of the Kings of 2 Chr 36:8
as it is **w** in the Law of Moses the man of Ezr 3:2
they kept the Feast of Booths, as it is **w**, Ezr 3:4
The letter was **w** in Aramaic and Ezr 4:7
him a report, in which was **w** as follows: Ezr 5:7
a scroll was found on which this was **w**: Ezr 6:2
as it is **w** in the Book of Moses. Ezr 6:18
In it was **w**, "It is reported among the Neh 6:6
came up at the first, and I found **w** in it: Neh 7:5
And they found it **w** in the Law that the Neh 8:14
leafy trees to make booths, as it is **w**." Neh 8:15
LORD our God, as it is **w** in the Law. Neh 10:34
and of our cattle, as it is **w** in the Law, Neh 10:36
of fathers' houses were **w** in the Book Neh 12:23
in it was found **w** that no Ammonite or Neh 13:1
and let it be **w** among the laws of the Est 1:19
was **w** to the king's satraps and to the Est 3:12
It was **w** in the name of King Ahasuerus Est 3:12
him a copy of the **w** decree issued in Susa Est 4:8
And it was found **w** how Mordecai had Est 6:2
let an order be **w** to revoke the letters Est 8:5
for an edict **w** in the name of the king Est 8:8
And an edict was **w**, according to all that Est 8:9
A copy of what was **w** was to be issued Est 8:13
do, and what Mordecai had **w** to them. Est 9:23
because of all that was **w** in this letter, Est 9:26
according to what was **w** and at the time Est 9:27
Mordecai the Jew gave full **w** authority, Est 9:29
are they not **w** in the Book of the Est 10:2
"Oh that my words were **w**! Oh that they Jb 19:23
had the indictment **w** by my adversary! Jb 31:35
in the scroll of the book it is **w** of me: Ps 40:7
in your book were **w**, every one of Ps 139:16
to execute on them the judgment **w**! Ps 149:9
Have I not **w** for you thirty sayings of Prv 22:20
Behold, it is **w** before me: "I will not keep Is 65:6
"The sin of Judah is **w** with a pen of iron; Jer 17:1
away from you shall be **w** in the earth, Jer 17:13
against it, everything **w** in this book, Jer 25:13
scroll that you have **w** at my dictation. Jer 36:6
"Why have you **w** in it that the king of Jer 36:29
words that are **w** concerning Babylon. Jer 51:60
and there were **w** on it words of Ezk 2:10
curse and oath that are **w** in the Law of Dn 9:11
As it is **w** in the Law of Moses, all this Dn 9:13
name shall be found **w** in the book. Dn 12:1
of remembrance was **w** before him of Mal 3:16
of Judea, for so it is **w** by the prophet: Mt 2:5
But he answered, "It is **w**, "'Man shall not Mt 4:4
of God, throw yourself down, for it is **w**, Mt 4:6
Jesus said to him, "Again it is **w**, 'You Mt 4:7
For it is **w**, "'You shall worship the Lord Mt 4:10
This is he of whom it is **w**, "'Behold, I Mt 11:10
He said to them, "It is **w**, 'My house Mt 21:13
The Son of Man goes as it is **w** of him, Mt 26:24
For it is **w**, 'I will strike the shepherd, Mt 26:31
As it is **w** in Isaiah the prophet, "Behold, I Mk 1:2
prophesy of you hypocrites, as it is **w**, Mk 7:6
And how is it **w** of the Son of Man that Mk 9:12
whatever they pleased, as it is **w** of him." Mk 9:13
them and saying to them, "Is it not **w**, Mk 11:17
the Son of Man goes as it is **w** of him, Mk 14:21
"You will all fall away, for it is **w**, Mk 14:27
(as it is **w** in the Law of the Lord, "Every Lk 2:23
As it is **w** in the book of the words of Lk 3:4
And Jesus answered him, "It is **w**, 'Man Lk 4:4
And Jesus answered him, "It is **w**, "'You Lk 4:8
for it is **w**, "'He will command his angels Lk 4:10
and found the place where it was **w**, Lk 4:17
This is he of whom it is **w**, "'Behold, I Lk 7:27
that your names are **w** in heaven." Lk 10:20
He said to him, "What is **w** in the Law? Lk 10:26
and everything that is **w** about the Son Lk 18:31
saying to them, "It is **w**, 'My house Lk 19:46
and said, "What then is this that is **w**: Lk 20:17
of vengeance, to fulfill all that is **w**. Lk 21:22
For what is **w** about me has its Lk 22:37
that everything **w** about me in the Law Lk 24:44
and said to them, "Thus it is **w**, that the Lk 24:46
His disciples remembered that it was **w**, Jn 2:17
as it is **w**, 'He gave them bread from Jn 6:31
It is **w** in the Prophets, 'And they will all Jn 6:45
In your Law it is **w** that the testimony of Jn 8:17
answered them, "Is it not **w** in your Law, Jn 10:34
donkey and sat on it, just as it is **w**, Jn 12:14
these things had been **w** about him and Jn 12:16
the word that is **w** in their Law must Jn 15:25
near the city, and it was **w** in Aramaic, Jn 19:20
"What I have **w** I have written." Jn 19:22
"What I have written I have **w**." Jn 19:22
disciples, which are not **w** in this book; Jn 20:30
but these are **w** so that you may believe Jn 20:31
things, and who has **w** these things, Jn 21:24
Were every one of them to be **w**, I Jn 21:25
not contain the books that would be **w**. Jn 21:25
"For it is **w** in the Book of Psalms, Acts 1:20
as it is **w** in the book of the prophets: Acts 7:42
had carried out all that was **w** of him, Acts 13:29
as also it is **w** in the second Psalm, Acts 13:33
of the prophets agree, just as it is **w**, Acts 15:15
that he was the high priest, for it is **w**, Acts 23:5
by the Law and **w** in the Prophets, Acts 24:14
revealed from faith for faith, as it is **w**, Rom 1:17
work of the law is **w** on their hearts, Rom 2:15
For, as it is **w**, "The name of God is Rom 2:24
who have the **w** code and Rom 2:27
though every one were a liar, as it is **w**, Rom 3:4
as it is **w**: "None is righteous, no, not Rom 3:10
as it is **w**, "I have made you the father Rom 4:17
to him" were not **w** for his sake alone, Rom 4:23
not under the old **w** code but in the Rom 7:6
As it is **w**, "For your sake we are being Rom 8:36
As it is **w**, "Jacob I loved, but Esau I Rom 9:13
as it is **w**, "Behold, I am laying in Zion Rom 9:33
As it is **w**, "How beautiful are the feet Rom 10:15
as it is **w**, "God gave them a spirit of Rom 11:8
way all Israel will be saved, as it is **w**, Rom 11:26
leave it to the wrath of God, for it is **w**, Rom 12:19
for it is **w**, "As I live, says the Lord, Rom 14:11
did not please himself, but as it is **w**, Rom 15:3
For whatever was **w** in former days Rom 15:4
former days was **w** for our instruction, Rom 15:4
As it is **w**, "Therefore I will praise you Rom 15:9
some points I have **w** to you very Rom 15:15
but as it is **w**, "Those who have never Rom 15:21
For it is **w**, "I will destroy the wisdom 1 Cor 1:19
Therefore, as it is **w**, "Let the one who 1 Cor 1:31
But, as it is **w**, "What no eye has seen, 1 Cor 2:9
For it is **w**, "He catches the wise in 1 Cor 3:19
learn by us not to go beyond what is **w**, 1 Cor 4:6
For, as it is **w**, "The two will become 1 Cor 6:16
For it is **w** in the Law of Moses, "You 1 Cor 9:9
It was **w** for our sake, because the 1 Cor 9:10
as it is **w**, "The people sat down to eat 1 Cor 10:7
but they were **w** down for our 1 Cor 10:11
In the Law it is **w**, "By people of 1 Cor 14:21
Thus it is **w**, "The first man Adam 1 Cor 15:45
come to pass the saying that is **w**: 1 Cor 15:54
of recommendation, **w** on our hearts, 2 Cor 3:2
w not with ink but with the Spirit of 2 Cor 3:3
faith according to what has been **w**, 2 Cor 4:13
As it is **w**, "Whoever gathered much 2 Cor 8:15
As it is **w**, "He has distributed freely, he 2 Cor 9:9
for it is **w**, "Cursed be everyone who Gal 3:10
not abide by all things **w** in the Book of Gal 3:10
by becoming a curse for us—for it is **w**, Gal 3:13
For it is **w** that Abraham had two sons, Gal 4:22
For it is **w**, "Rejoice, O barren one who Gal 4:27
to me by revelation, as I have **w** briefly. Eph 3:3
no need to have anything **w** to you. 1 Thes 5:1
as it is **w** of me in the scroll of the Heb 10:7
for I have **w** to you briefly. Heb 13:22
since it is **w**, "You shall be holy, for I 1 Pt 1:16
as I regard him, I have **w** briefly to you, 1 Pt 5:12
I have **w** something to the church, but 3 Jn 1:9
who hear, and who keep what is **w** in it, Rv 1:3
with a new name **w** on the stone that no Rv 2:17
on the throne a scroll **w** within and on the Rv 5:1
has not been **w** before the foundation Rv 13:8
his Father's name **w** on their foreheads. Rv 14:1
on her forehead was **w** a name of Rv 17:5
names have not been **w** in the book of Rv 17:8
he has a name **w** that no one knows Rv 19:12
robe and on his thigh he has a name **w**, Rv 19:16
judged by what was **w** in the books, Rv 20:12

name was not found **w** in the book of Rv 20:15
only those who are **w** in the Lamb's Rv 21:27

WRONG (76)
"May the **w** done to me be on you! Gn 16:5
And he said to the man in the **w**, "Why Ex 2:13
right, and I and my people are in the **w**. Ex 9:27
"You shall not **w** a sojourner or oppress Ex 22:21
in your land, you shall not do him **w**. Lv 19:33
"You shall do no **w** in judgment, in Lv 19:35
neighbor, you shall not **w** one another. Lv 25:14
You shall not **w** one another, but you Lv 25:17
he shall make full restitution for his **w**, Nm 5:7
giving it to him to whom he did the **w**. Nm 5:7
restitution may be made for the **w**, Nm 5:8
the restitution for **w** shall go to the LORD Nm 5:8
crime or for any **w** in connection with Dt 19:15
it suits him. You shall not **w** him. Dt 23:16
and you do me **w** by making war on Jgs 11:27
Saul said, "What is **w** with the people, 1 Sm 11:5
that there is no **w** or treason in my 1 Sm 24:11
I have found nothing **w** in you from 1 Sm 29:6
for this **w** in sending me away is 2 Sm 13:16
LORD will look on the **w** done to me, 2 Sm 16:12
how your servant did **w** on the day 2 Sm 19:19
at Lachish, saying, "I have done **w**; 2 Kgs 18:14
although there is no **w** in my hands, 1 Chr 12:17
the sanctuary, for you have done **w**, 2 Chr 26:18
the king has Queen Vashti done **w**, Est 1:16
this Job did not sin or charge God with **w**. Jb 1:22
upon me; are you not ashamed to **w** me? Jb 19:3
has put me in the **w** and closed his net Jb 19:6
thoughts and your schemes to **w** me. Jb 21:27
for help; yet God charges no one with **w**. Jb 24:12
"They **w** the barren childless woman, Jb 24:21
they had declared Job to be in the **w**. Jb 32:3
from the Almighty that he should do **w**. Jb 34:10
or who can say, 'You have done **w**'? Jb 36:23
Will you even put me in the **w**? Will you Jb 40:8
I have done this, if there is **w** in my hands, Ps 7:3
who also do no **w**, but walk in his ways! Ps 119:3
stretch out their hands to do **w**. Ps 125:3
cannot sleep unless they have done **w**; Prv 4:16
Doing **w** is like a joke to a fool, but Prv 10:23
for a piece of bread a man will do **w**. Prv 28:21
mouth and says, "I have done no **w**." Prv 30:20
LORD love justice; I hate robbery and **w**; Is 61:8
"What **w** did your fathers find in me that Jer 2:5
And do no **w** or violence to the resident Jer 22:3
"What **w** have I done to you or your Jer 37:18
but if it seems **w** to you to come with me Jer 40:4
You have seen the **w** done to me, O Lam 3:59
sinned and done **w** and acted wickedly Dn 9:5
iniquity, and why do you idly look at **w**? Hab 1:3
than to see evil and cannot look at **w**, Hab 1:13
mouth, and no **w** was found on his lips. Mal 2:6
of them, 'Friend, I am doing you no **w**. Mt 20:13
But Jesus answered them, "You are **w**, Mt 22:29
them, "Is this not the reason you are **w**, Mk 12:24
but of the living. You are quite **w**." Mk 12:27
but this man has done nothing **w**." Lk 23:41
Jesus answered him, "If what I said is **w**, Jn 18:23
said is wrong, bear witness about the **w**; Jn 18:23
brothers. Why do you **w** each other?' Acts 7:26
"We find nothing **w** in this man. Acts 23:9
if there is anything **w** about the man, Acts 25:5
To the Jews I have done no **w**, as you Acts 25:10
But if you do **w**, be afraid, for he does Rom 13:4
Love does no **w** to a neighbor; Rom 13:10
but it is **w** for anyone to make Rom 14:20
for you. Why not rather suffer **w**? 1 Cor 6:7
But you yourselves **w** and defraud— 1 Cor 6:8
for the sake of the one who did the **w**, 2 Cor 7:12
sake of the one who suffered the **w**, 2 Cor 7:12
not burden you? Forgive me this **w**! 2 Cor 12:13
that you may not do **w**—not that we 2 Cor 13:7
become as you are. You did me no **w**. Gal 4:12
will be paid back for the **w** he has done, Col 3:25
one transgress and **w** his brother in 1 Thes 4:6
suffering **w** as the wage for their 2 Pt 2:13

WRONGDOER (3)
then I am a **w** and have committed Acts 25:11
who carries out God's wrath on the **w**. Rom 13:4
For the **w** will be paid back for the Col 3:25

WRONGDOERS (1)
because of evildoers; be not envious of **w**! Ps 37:1

WRONGDOING (8)
witness arises to accuse a person of **w**, Dt 19:16
has kept back his servant from **w**. 1 Sm 25:39
it were a matter of **w** or vicious crime, Acts 18:14
themselves say what **w** they found Acts 24:20
it does not rejoice at **w**, but rejoices 1 Cor 13:6
suffering wrong as the wage for their **w**. 2 Pt 2:13
the son of Beor, who loved gain from **w**, 2 Pt 2:15
All **w** is sin, but there is sin that does 1 Jn 5:17

WRONGDOINGS (1)
God to them, but an avenger of their **w**. Ps 99:8

WRONGED (5)
because they have **w** me with Ps 119:78
fatherless and the widow are **w** in you. Ezk 22:7
And seeing one of them being **w**, he Acts 7:24
your hearts for us. We have **w** no one, 2 Cor 7:2
If he has **w** you at all, or owes you Phlm 1:18

WRONGFULLY (2)
rejoice over me who are **w** my foes, Ps 35:19
and many are those who hate me **w**. Ps 38:19

WRONGING (1)
man who was **w** his neighbor thrust Acts 7:27

WRONGLY (1)
and do not receive, because you ask **w**, Jas 4:3

WRONGS (2)
No, in your hearts you devise **w**; your Ps 58:2
the **w** I have done are not hidden from Ps 69:5

WROTE (59)
And Moses **w** down all the words of the Ex 24:4
And he **w** on the tablets the words of the Ex 34:28
of pure gold, and **w** on it an inscription, Ex 39:30
Moses **w** down their starting places, Nm 33:2
and he **w** them on two tablets of stone. Dt 4:13
And he **w** them on two tablets of stone Dt 5:22
And he **w** on the tablets, in the same Dt 10:4
Then Moses **w** this law and gave it to the Dt 31:9
So Moses **w** this song the same day and Dt 31:22
he **w** on the stones a copy of the law of Jos 8:32
down in the land and **w** in a book a Jos 18:9
And Joshua **w** these words in the Book Jos 24:26
And he **w** down for him the officials and Jgs 8:14
and he **w** them in a book and laid it 1 Sm 10:25
In the morning David **w** a letter to 2 Sm 11:14
In the letter he **w**, "Set Uriah in the 2 Sm 11:15
So she **w** letters in Ahab's name and 1 Kgs 21:8
And she **w** in the letters, "Proclaim a 1 Kgs 21:9
So Jehu **w** letters and sent them to 2 Kgs 10:1
Then he **w** to them a second letter, 2 Kgs 10:6
commandment that he **w** for you, 2 Kgs 17:37
the prophet the son of Amoz **w**. 2 Chr 26:22
and **w** letters also to Ephraim and 2 Chr 30:1
And he **w** letters to cast contempt on 2 Chr 32:17
they **w** an accusation against the Ezr 4:6
of their associates **w** to Artaxerxes king Ezr 4:7
Shimshai the scribe **w** a letter against Ezr 4:8
which he **w** to destroy the Jews who are in Est 8:5
And he **w** in the name of King Est 8:10
and uprightly he **w** words of truth. Eccl 12:10
and Baruch **w** on a scroll at the Jer 36:4
while I **w** them with ink on the scroll." Jer 36:18
words that Baruch **w** at Jeremiah's Jer 36:27
who **w** on it at the dictation of Jeremiah Jer 36:32
when he **w** these words in a book at the Jer 45:1
Jeremiah **w** in a book all the disaster Jer 51:60
hand appeared and **w** on the plaster Dn 5:5
And the king saw the hand as it **w**. Dn 5:5
Then King Darius **w** to all the peoples, Dn 6:25
Then he **w** down the dream and told the Dn 7:1
of heart he **w** you this commandment. Mk 10:5
Moses **w** for us that if a man's brother Mk 12:19
And he asked for a writing tablet and **w**, Lk 1:63
Moses **w** for us that if a man's brother Lk 20:28
in the Law and also the prophets **w**, Jn 1:45
you would believe me; for he **w** of me. Jn 5:46
Jesus bent down and **w** with his finger on Jn 8:6
more he bent down and **w** on the ground. Jn 8:8
Pilate also **w** an inscription and put it Jn 19:19
encouraged him and **w** to the Acts 18:27
And he **w** a letter to this effect: Acts 23:25
I Tertius, who **w** this letter, greet you Rom 16:22
I **w** to you in my letter not to associate 1 Cor 5:9
the matters about which you **w**: 1 Cor 7:1
And I **w** as I did, so that when I came I 2 Cor 2:3
For I **w** to you out of much affliction 2 Cor 2:4
For this is why I **w**, that I might test 2 Cor 2:9
So although I **w** to you, it was not for 2 Cor 7:12
brother Paul also **w** to you according 2 Pt 3:15

WROUGHT (2)
of Jacob and Israel, 'What has God **w**!' Nm 23:23
w iron, cassia, and calamus were Ezk 27:19

WRUNG (3)
he **w** enough dew from the fleece to fill a Jgs 6:38
my heart is **w** within me, because I Lam 1:20
moment, and no hands were **w** for her. Lam 4:6

Y

YARD (7)
was facing the separate **y** on the west Ezk 41:12
and the **y** and the building with its Ezk 41:13
the east front of the temple and the **y**, Ezk 41:14
the building facing the **y** that was at Ezk 41:15
opposite the separate **y** and opposite the Ezk 42:1
opposite the **y** and opposite the Ezk 42:10
chambers opposite the **y** are the holy Ezk 42:13

YARDS (1)
from the land, but about a hundred **y** off. Jn 21:8

YARN (6)
and cedarwood and scarlet **y** and hyssop. Lv 14:4
and the scarlet **y** and the hyssop, Lv 14:6
cedarwood and scarlet **y** and hyssop, Lv 14:49
and the hyssop and the scarlet **y**, Lv 14:51
cedarwood and hyssop and scarlet **y**. Lv 14:52
cedarwood and hyssop and scarlet **y**, Nm 19:6

YARNS (26)
and purple and scarlet **y** and fine twined Ex 25:4
linen and blue and purple and scarlet **y**; Ex 26:1
purple and scarlet **y** and fine twined Ex 26:31
purple and scarlet **y** and fine twined Ex 26:36
purple and scarlet **y** and fine twined Ex 27:16
gold, blue and purple and scarlet **y**, Ex 28:5
of gold, of blue and purple and scarlet **y**, Ex 28:6
it, of gold, blue and purple and scarlet **y**, Ex 28:8
—of gold, blue and purple and scarlet **y**, Ex 28:15
of blue and purple and scarlet **y**, Ex 28:33
and purple and scarlet **y** and fine twined Ex 35:6
or purple or scarlet **y** or fine linen or Ex 35:23
purple and scarlet **y** and fine twined Ex 35:25
purple and scarlet **y** and fine twined Ex 35:35
linen and blue and purple and scarlet **y**, Ex 36:8
purple and scarlet **y** and fine twined Ex 36:35
purple and scarlet **y** and fine twined Ex 36:37
purple and scarlet **y** and fine twined Ex 38:18
purple and scarlet **y** and fine twined Ex 38:23
purple and scarlet **y** they made finely Ex 39:1
of gold, blue and purple and scarlet **y**, Ex 39:2
the blue and purple and the scarlet **y**, Ex 39:3
it, of gold, blue and purple and scarlet **y**, Ex 39:5
of gold, blue and purple and scarlet **y**, Ex 39:8
purple and scarlet **y** and fine twined Ex 39:24
and of blue and purple and scarlet **y**, Ex 39:29

YEAR (373)
In the six hundredth **y** of Noah's life, in Gn 7:11
In the six hundred and first **y**, in the first Gn 8:13
but in the thirteenth **y** they rebelled. Gn 14:4
In the fourteenth **y** Chedorlaomer and Gn 14:5
shall bear to you at this time next **y**." Gn 17:21
return to you about this time next **y**, Gn 18:10
return to you about this time next **y**, Gn 18:14
reaped in the same **y** a hundredfold. Gn 26:12
Before the **y** of famine came, two sons Gn 41:50
exchange for all their livestock that **y**. Gn 47:17
And when that **y** was ended, they came Gn 47:18
to him the following **y** and said to him, Gn 47:18
shall be the first month of the **y** for you. Ex 12:2
shall be without blemish, a male a **y** old Ex 12:5
at its appointed time from **y** to year. Ex 13:10
at its appointed time from year to **y**. Ex 13:10
but the seventh **y** you shall let it rest Ex 23:11
"Three times in the **y** you shall keep a Ex 23:14
Feast of Ingathering at the end of the **y**, Ex 23:16
Three times in the **y** shall all your Ex 23:17
them out from before you in one **y**, Ex 23:29
two lambs a **y** old day by day regularly. Ex 29:38
make atonement on its horns once a **y**. Ex 30:10
once in the **y** throughout your Ex 30:10
Three times in the **y** shall all your Ex 34:23
the LORD your God three times in the **y**. Ex 34:24
In the first month in the second **y**, on Ex 40:17
a lamb, both a **y** old without blemish, Lv 9:3
of meeting a lamb a **y** old for a burnt Lv 12:6
one ewe lamb a **y** old without blemish, Lv 14:10
Israel once in the **y** because of all their Lv 16:34
And in the fourth **y** all its fruit shall be Lv 19:24
But in the fifth **y** you may eat of its Lv 19:25
a male lamb a **y** old without blemish Lv 23:12
seven lambs a **y** old without blemish, Lv 23:18
two male lambs a **y** old as a sacrifice Lv 23:19
feast to the LORD for seven days in the **y**. Lv 23:41
but in the seventh **y** there shall be a Lv 25:4
It shall be a **y** of solemn rest for the land. Lv 25:5
And you shall consecrate the fiftieth **y**, Lv 25:10
That fiftieth **y** shall be a jubilee for Lv 25:11
"In this **y** of jubilee each of you shall Lv 25:13
say, 'What shall we eat in the seventh **y**, Lv 25:20
my blessing on you in the sixth **y**, Lv 25:21

When you sow in the eighth **y**, you will Lv 25:22
you shall eat the old until the ninth **y**, Lv 25:22
hand of the buyer until the **y** of jubilee. Lv 25:28
he may redeem it within a **y** of its sale. Lv 25:29
For a full **y** he shall have the right of Lv 25:29
If it is not redeemed within a full **y**, then Lv 25:30
serve with you until the **y** of the jubilee. Lv 25:40
his buyer from the **y** when he sold Lv 25:50
himself to him until the **y** of jubilee, Lv 25:50
but a few years until the **y** of jubilee, Lv 25:52
treat him as a servant hired **y** by year. Lv 25:53
treat him as a servant hired year by **y**. Lv 25:53
him shall be released in the **y** of jubilee. Lv 25:54
dedicates his field from the **y** of jubilee, Lv 27:17
years that remain until the **y** of jubilee, Lv 27:18
valuation for it up to the **y** of jubilee, Lv 27:23
In the **y** of jubilee the field shall return Lv 27:24
in the second **y** after they had come out Nm 1:1
bring a male lamb a **y** old for a guilt Nm 6:12
male lamb a **y** old without blemish Nm 6:14
one ewe lamb a **y** old without blemish Nm 6:14
herd, one ram, one male lamb a **y** old, Nm 7:15
goats, and five male lambs a **y** old. Nm 7:17
herd, one ram, one male lamb a **y** old, Nm 7:21
goats, and five male lambs a **y** old. Nm 7:23
herd, one ram, one male lamb a **y** old, Nm 7:27
goats, and five male lambs a **y** old. Nm 7:29
herd, one ram, one male lamb a **y** old, Nm 7:33
goats, and five male lambs a **y** old. Nm 7:35
herd, one ram, one male lamb a **y** old, Nm 7:39
goats, and five male lambs a **y** old. Nm 7:41
herd, one ram, one male lamb a **y** old, Nm 7:45
goats, and five male lambs a **y** old. Nm 7:47
herd, one ram, one male lamb a **y** old, Nm 7:51
goats, and five male lambs a **y** old. Nm 7:53
herd, one ram, one male lamb a **y** old, Nm 7:57
goats, and five male lambs a **y** old. Nm 7:59
herd, one ram, one male lamb a **y** old, Nm 7:63
goats, and five male lambs a **y** old. Nm 7:65
herd, one ram, one male lamb a **y** old, Nm 7:69
goats, and five male lambs a **y** old. Nm 7:71
herd, one ram, one male lamb a **y** old, Nm 7:75
goats, and five male lambs a **y** old. Nm 7:77
herd, one ram, one male lamb a **y** old, Nm 7:81
goats, and five male lambs a **y** old. Nm 7:83
twelve rams, twelve male lambs a **y** old, Nm 7:87
sixty, the male lambs a **y** old sixty. Nm 7:88
month of the second **y** after they had Nm 9:1
In the second **y**, in the second month, Nm 10:11
the land, forty days, a **y** for each day, Nm 14:34
offer a female goat a **y** old for a sin Nm 15:27
male lambs a **y** old without blemish, Nm 28:3
male lambs a **y** old without blemish, Nm 28:9
male lambs a **y** old without blemish; Nm 28:11
throughout the months of the **y**. Nm 28:14
ram, and seven male lambs a **y** old; Nm 28:19
one ram, seven male lambs a **y** old; Nm 28:27
male lambs a **y** old without blemish; Nm 29:2
one ram, seven male lambs a **y** old: Nm 29:8
rams, fourteen male lambs a **y** old; Nm 29:13
male lambs a **y** old without blemish, Nm 29:17
male lambs a **y** old without blemish, Nm 29:20
male lambs a **y** old without blemish, Nm 29:23
male lambs a **y** old without blemish, Nm 29:26
male lambs a **y** old without blemish, Nm 29:29
male lambs a **y** old without blemish, Nm 29:32
male lambs a **y** old without blemish, Nm 29:36
in the fortieth **y** after the people of Nm 33:38
In the fortieth **y**, on the first day of the Dt 1:3
the beginning of the **y** to the end of Dt 11:12
beginning of the year to the end of the **y**. Dt 11:12
seed that comes from the field **y** by year. Dt 14:22
seed that comes from the field year by **y**. Dt 14:22
produce in the same **y** and lay it up Dt 14:28
your heart and you say, 'The seventh **y**, Dt 15:9
seventh year, the **y** of release is near,' Dt 15:9
and in the seventh **y** you shall let him Dt 15:12
the LORD your God **y** by year at the Dt 15:20
your God year by **y** at the place that Dt 15:20
"Three times a **y** all your males shall Dt 16:16
be free at home one **y** to be happy with Dt 24:5
the tithe of your produce in the third **y**, Dt 26:12
the third year, which is the **y** of tithing, Dt 26:12
years, at the set time in the **y** of release, Dt 31:10
of the fruit of the land of Canaan that **y**. Jos 5:12
and oppressed the people of Israel that **y**. Jgs 10:8
daughters of Israel went **y** by year to Jgs 11:40
Israel went year by **y** to lament the Jgs 11:40
the Gileadite four days in the **y**. Jgs 11:40
ten pieces of silver a **y** and a suit of Jgs 17:10
man used to go up **y** by year from his 1 Sm 1:3
to go up year by **y** from his city to 1 Sm 1:3
So it went on **y** by year. As often as she 1 Sm 1:7
So it went on year by **y**. As often as she 1 Sm 1:7
it to him each **y** when she went up 1 Sm 2:19

went on a circuit **y** by year to Bethel, 1 Sm 7:16
went on a circuit year by **y** to Bethel, 1 Sm 7:16
Philistines was a **y** and four months. 1 Sm 27:7
In the spring of the **y**, the time when 2 Sm 11:1
at the end of every **y** he used to cut it; 2 Sm 14:26
of David for three years, **y** after year. 2 Sm 21:1
of David for three years, year after **y**. 2 Sm 21:1
provision for one month in the **y**. 1 Kgs 4:7
gave this to Hiram **y** by year. 1 Kgs 5:11
gave this to Hiram year by **y**. 1 Kgs 5:11
hundred and eightieth **y** after the 1 Kgs 6:1
in the fourth **y** of Solomon's reign over 1 Kgs 6:1
In the fourth **y** the foundation of the 1 Kgs 6:37
And in the eleventh **y**, in the month 1 Kgs 6:38
Three times a **y** Solomon used to offer 1 Kgs 9:25
to Solomon in one **y** was 666 talents 1 Kgs 10:14
and mules, so much **y** by year. 1 Kgs 10:25
and mules, so much year by **y**. 1 Kgs 10:25
In the fifth **y** of King Rehoboam, 1 Kgs 14:25
in the eighteenth **y** of King Jeroboam 1 Kgs 15:1
In the twentieth **y** of Jeroboam king 1 Kgs 15:9
Israel in the second **y** of Asa king of 1 Kgs 15:25
him in the third **y** of Asa king of 1 Kgs 15:28
In the third **y** of Asa king of Judah, 1 Kgs 15:33
In the twenty-sixth **y** of Asa king of 1 Kgs 16:8
in the twenty-seventh **y** of Asa king 1 Kgs 16:10
In the twenty-seventh **y** of Asa king 1 Kgs 16:15
In the thirty-first **y** of Asa king of 1 Kgs 16:23
In the thirty-eighth **y** of Asa king of 1 Kgs 16:29
LORD came to Elijah, in the third **y**, 1 Kgs 18:1
in the third **y** Jehoshaphat the king 1 Kgs 22:2
Judah in the fourth **y** of Ahab king 1 Kgs 22:41
in the seventeenth **y** of Jehoshaphat 1 Kgs 22:51
place in the second **y** of Jehoram the 2 Kgs 1:17
In the eighteenth **y** of Jehoshaphat 2 Kgs 3:1
this season, about this time next **y**, 2 Kgs 4:16
In the fifth **y** of Joram the son of 2 Kgs 8:16
In the twelfth **y** of Joram the son of 2 Kgs 8:25
and he reigned one **y** in Jerusalem. 2 Kgs 8:26
In the eleventh **y** of Joram the son of 2 Kgs 9:29
in the seventh **y** Jehoiada sent and 2 Kgs 11:4
In the seventh **y** of Jehu, Jehoash 2 Kgs 12:1
by the twenty-third **y** of King 2 Kgs 12:6
In the twenty-third **y** of Joash the son 2 Kgs 13:1
In the thirty-seventh **y** of Joash king 2 Kgs 13:10
the land in the spring of the **y**. 2 Kgs 13:20
In the second **y** of Joash the son of 2 Kgs 14:1
In the fifteenth **y** of Amaziah the son 2 Kgs 14:23
In the twenty-seventh **y** of Jeroboam 2 Kgs 15:1
In the thirty-eighth **y** of Azariah king 2 Kgs 15:8
in the thirty-ninth **y** of Uzziah king 2 Kgs 15:13
In the thirty-ninth **y** of Azariah 2 Kgs 15:17
In the fiftieth **y** of Azariah king of 2 Kgs 15:23
In the fifty-second **y** of Azariah king 2 Kgs 15:27
in the twentieth **y** of Jotham the son 2 Kgs 15:30
In the second **y** of Pekah the son of 2 Kgs 15:32
In the seventeenth **y** of Pekah the son 2 Kgs 16:1
In the twelfth **y** of Ahaz king of 2 Kgs 17:1
of Assyria, as he had done **y** by year. 2 Kgs 17:4
of Assyria, as he had done year by **y**. 2 Kgs 17:4
In the ninth **y** of Hoshea, the king of 2 Kgs 17:6
In the third **y** of Hoshea son of Elah, 2 Kgs 18:1
In the fourth **y** of King Hezekiah, 2 Kgs 18:9
was the seventh **y** of Hoshea son 2 Kgs 18:9
In the sixth **y** of Hezekiah, which 2 Kgs 18:10
was the ninth **y** of Hoshea king 2 Kgs 18:10
In the fourteenth **y** of King 2 Kgs 18:13
this **y** eat what grows of itself, and in 2 Kgs 19:29
and in the second **y** what springs of 2 Kgs 19:29
Then in the third **y** sow and reap 2 Kgs 19:29
In the eighteenth **y** of King Josiah, the 2 Kgs 22:3
in the eighteenth **y** of King Josiah 2 Kgs 23:23
prisoner in the eighth **y** of his reign 2 Kgs 24:12
And in the ninth **y** of his reign, in the 2 Kgs 25:1
till the eleventh **y** of King Zedekiah. 2 Kgs 25:2
was the nineteenth **y** of King 2 Kgs 25:8
in the thirty-seventh **y** of the exile 2 Kgs 25:27
in the **y** that he began to reign, 2 Kgs 25:27
In the spring of the **y**, the time when 1 Chr 20:1
(In the fortieth **y** of David's reign 1 Chr 26:31
after month throughout the **y**, 1 Chr 27:1
month of the fourth **y** of his reign. 2 Chr 3:2
to Solomon in one **y** was 666 talents 2 Chr 9:13
and mules, so much **y** by year. 2 Chr 9:24
and mules, so much year by **y**. 2 Chr 9:24
In the fifth **y** of King Rehoboam, 2 Chr 12:2
In the eighteenth **y** of King Jeroboam, 2 Chr 13:1
month of the fifteenth **y** of the reign 2 Chr 15:10
until the thirty-fifth **y** of the reign 2 Chr 15:19
In the thirty-sixth **y** of the reign of 2 Chr 16:1
In the thirty-ninth **y** of his reign 2 Chr 16:12
dying in the forty-first **y** of his reign. 2 Chr 16:13
In the third **y** of his reign he sent his 2 Chr 17:7
and he reigned one **y** in Jerusalem. 2 Chr 22:2
in the seventh **y** Jehoiada took 2 Chr 23:1

the house of your God from **y** to year, 2 Chr 24:5
the house of your God from year to **y**, 2 Chr 24:5
At the end of the **y** the army of the 2 Chr 24:23
gave him that **y** 100 talents of 2 Chr 27:5
In the first **y** of his reign, in the first 2 Chr 29:3
For in the eighth **y** of his reign, while 2 Chr 34:3
and in the twelfth **y** he began to 2 Chr 34:3
Now in the eighteenth **y** of his reign, 2 Chr 34:8
In the eighteenth **y** of the reign of 2 Chr 35:19
of the **y** King Nebuchadnezzar 2 Chr 36:10
Now in the first **y** of Cyrus king of 2 Chr 36:22
In the first **y** of Cyrus king of Persia, that Ezr 1:1
Now in the second **y** after their coming Ezr 3:8
ceased until the second **y** of the reign of Ezr 4:24
in the first **y** of Cyrus king of Babylon, Ezr 5:13
In the first **y** of Cyrus the king, Cyrus the Ezr 6:3
in the sixth **y** of the reign of Darius the Ezr 6:15
in the seventh **y** of Artaxerxes the king, Ezr 7:7
which was in the seventh **y** of the king. Ezr 7:8
the month of Chislev, in the twentieth **y**, Neh 1:1
in the twentieth **y** of King Artaxerxes, Neh 2:1
from the twentieth **y** to the Neh 5:14
to the thirty-second **y** of Artaxerxes the Neh 5:14
of the seventh **y** and the exaction Neh 10:31
houses, at times appointed, **y** by year, Neh 10:34
houses, at times appointed, year by **y**, Neh 10:34
of all fruit of every tree, **y** by year, Neh 10:35
of all fruit of every tree, year by **y**, Neh 10:35
in the thirty-second **y** of Artaxerxes Neh 13:6
in the third **y** of his reign he gave a feast Est 1:3
of Tebeth, in the seventh **y** of his reign, Est 2:16
in the twelfth **y** of King Ahasuerus, Est 3:7
the fifteenth day of the same, **y** by year, Est 9:21
the fifteenth day of the same, year by **y**, Est 9:21
and at the time appointed every **y**, Est 9:27
Let it not rejoice among the days of the **y**; Jb 3:6
You crown the **y** with your bounty; Ps 65:11
In the **y** that King Uzziah died I saw the Is 6:1
In the **y** that King Ahaz died came this Is 14:28
In the **y** that the commander in chief, Is 20:1
thus the Lord said to me, "Within a **y**, Is 21:16
Add **y** to year; let the feasts run their Is 29:1
Add year to **y**; let the feasts run their Is 29:1
In little more than a **y** you will shudder, Is 32:10
a **y** of recompense for the cause of Zion. Is 34:8
In the fourteenth **y** of King Hezekiah, Is 36:1
this **y** you shall eat what grows of itself, Is 37:30
and in the second **y** what springs from Is 37:30
Then in the third **y** sow and reap, and Is 37:30
to proclaim the **y** of the LORD'S favor, and Is 61:2
heart, and my **y** of redemption had come. Is 63:4
of Judah, in the thirteenth **y** of his reign. Jer 1:2
the end of the eleventh **y** of Zedekiah, Jer 1:3
Anathoth, the **y** of their punishment." Jer 11:23
and is not anxious in the **y** of drought, Jer 17:8
them in the **y** of their punishment, Jer 23:12
in the fourth **y** of Jehoiakim the son of Jer 25:1
was the first **y** of Nebuchadnezzar king Jer 25:1
from the thirteenth **y** of Josiah the son of Jer 25:3
In that same **y**, at the beginning of the Jer 28:1
Judah, in the fifth month of the fourth **y**, Jer 28:1
This **y** you shall die, because you have Jer 28:16
In that same **y**, in the seventh month, Jer 28:17
LORD in the tenth **y** of Zedekiah king of Jer 32:1
the eighteenth **y** of Nebuchadnezzar. Jer 32:1
In the fourth **y** of Jehoiakim the son of Jer 36:1
In the fifth **y** of Jehoiakim the son of Jer 36:9
In the ninth **y** of Zedekiah king of Judah, Jer 39:1
In the eleventh **y** of Zedekiah, in the Jer 39:2
in the fourth **y** of Jehoiakim the son of Jer 45:1
defeated in the fourth **y** of Jehoiakim the Jer 46:2
upon Moab, the **y** of their punishment, Jer 48:44
report comes in one **y** and afterward a Jer 51:46
and afterward a report in another **y**, Jer 51:46
to Babylon, in the fourth **y** of his reign. Jer 51:59
And in the ninth **y** of his reign, in the Jer 52:4
till the eleventh **y** of King Zedekiah. Jer 52:5
was the nineteenth **y** of King Jer 52:12
captive: in the seventh **y**, 3,023 Judeans; Jer 52:28
in the eighteenth **y** of Nebuchadnezzar Jer 52:29
the twenty-third **y** of Nebuchadnezzar, Jer 52:30
And in the thirty-seventh **y** of the exile Jer 52:31
Babylon, in the **y** that he became king, Jer 52:31
In the thirtieth **y**, in the fourth month, Ezk 1:1
month (it was the fifth **y** of the exile of Ezk 1:2
Forty days I assign you, a day for each **y**. Ezk 4:6
In the sixth **y**, in the sixth month, on the Ezk 8:1
In the seventh **y**, in the fifth month, on Ezk 20:1
In the ninth **y**, in the tenth month, on Ezk 24:1
In the eleventh **y**, on the first day of the Ezk 26:1
In the tenth **y**, in the tenth month, on Ezk 29:1
In the twenty-seventh **y**, in the first Ezk 29:17
In the eleventh **y**, in the first month, Ezk 30:20
In the eleventh **y**, in the third month, Ezk 31:1
In the twelfth **y**, in the twelfth month, Ezk 32:1

In the twelfth **y**, in the twelfth month, Ezk 32:17
In the twelfth **y** of our exile, in the Ezk 33:21
In the twenty-fifth **y** of our exile, at the Ezk 40:1
of our exile, at the beginning of the **y**, Ezk 40:1
in the fourteenth **y** after the city was Ezk 40:1
a lamb a **y** old without blemish Ezk 46:13
it shall be his to the **y** of liberty. Ezk 46:17
In the third **y** of the reign of Jehoiakim Dn 1:1
was there until the first **y** of King Cyrus. Dn 1:21
In the second **y** of the reign of Dn 2:1
In the first **y** of Belshazzar king of Dn 7:1
In the third **y** of the reign of King Dn 8:1
In the first **y** of Darius the son of Dn 9:1
in the first **y** of his reign, I, Daniel, Dn 9:2
In the third **y** of Cyrus king of Persia a Dn 10:1
for me, in the first **y** of Darius the Mede, Dn 11:1
with burnt offerings, with calves a **y** old? Mi 6:6
In the second **y** of Darius the king, in the Hg 1:1
in the second **y** of Darius the king. Hg 1:15
ninth month, in the second **y** of Darius, Hg 2:10
eighth month, in the second **y** of Darius, Zec 1:1
of Shebat, in the second **y** of Darius, Zec 1:7
In the fourth **y** of King Darius, the word Zec 7:1
Jerusalem shall go up **y** after year to Zec 14:16
go up year after **y** to worship the King, Zec 14:16
went to Jerusalem every **y** at the Feast of Lk 2:41
In the fifteenth **y** of the reign of Tiberius Lk 3:1
to proclaim the **y** of the Lord's favor." Lk 4:19
him, 'Sir, let it alone this **y** also, Lk 13:8
Then if it should bear fruit next **y**, well Lk 13:9
Caiaphas, who was high priest that **y**, Jn 11:49
high priest that **y** he prophesied that Jn 11:51
of Caiaphas, who was high priest that **y**. Jn 18:13
For a whole **y** they met with the Acts 11:26
And he stayed a **y** and six months, Acts 18:11
"About this time next **y** I will return Rom 9:9
who a **y** ago started not only to do this 2 Cor 8:10
Achaia has been ready since last **y**. 2 Cor 9:2
the high priest goes, and he but once a **y**, Heb 9:7
the holy places every **y** with blood not Heb 9:25
that are continually offered every **y**, Heb 10:1
there is a reminder of sin every **y**. Heb 10:3
a town and spend a **y** there and trade and Jas 4:13
the hour, the day, the month, and the **y**, Rv 9:15

YEAR'S (1)
the Feast of Ingathering at the **y** end. Ex 34:22

YEARLY (5)
there is the **y** feast of the LORD at Shiloh, Jgs 21:19
to the LORD the **y** sacrifice and to pay 1 Sm 1:21
her husband to offer the **y** sacrifice. 1 Sm 2:19
for there is a **y** sacrifice there for all 1 Sm 20:6
the obligation to give **y** a third part of Neh 10:32

YEARN (1)
how I **y** for you all with the affection of Phil 1:8

YEARNED (1)
king, because her heart **y** for her son, 1 Kgs 3:26

YEARNING (1)
of your eyes, and the **y** of your soul, Ezk 24:21

YEARNS (3)
My soul **y** for you in the night; my spirit Is 26:9
Therefore my heart **y** for him; I will Jer 31:20
"He **y** jealously over the spirit that he has Jas 4:5

YEARS (543)
and for seasons, and for days and **y**, Gn 1:14
When Adam had lived 130 **y**, he fathered Gn 5:3
of Adam after he fathered Seth were 800 **y**; Gn 5:4
all the days that Adam lived were 930 **y**, Gn 5:5
When Seth had lived 105 **y**, he fathered Gn 5:6
he fathered Enosh 807 **y** and had other Gn 5:7
Thus all the days of Seth were 912 **y**, and Gn 5:8
When Enosh had lived 90 **y**, he fathered Gn 5:9
he fathered Kenan 815 **y** and had other Gn 5:10
Thus all the days of Enosh were 905 **y**, Gn 5:11
When Kenan had lived 70 **y**, he fathered Gn 5:12
fathered Mahalalel 840 **y** and had other Gn 5:13
Thus all the days of Kenan were 910 **y**, Gn 5:14
When Mahalalel had lived 65 **y**, he Gn 5:15
he fathered Jared 830 **y** and had other Gn 5:16
all the days of Mahalalel were 895 **y**, Gn 5:17
Jared had lived 162 **y** he fathered Enoch. Gn 5:18
he fathered Enoch 800 **y** and had other Gn 5:19
Thus all the days of Jared were 962 **y**, Gn 5:20
When Enoch had lived 65 **y**, he fathered Gn 5:21
fathered Methuselah 300 **y** and had Gn 5:22
Thus all the days of Enoch were 365 **y**. Gn 5:23
When Methuselah had lived 187 **y**, he Gn 5:25
he fathered Lamech 782 **y** and had other Gn 5:26
all the days of Methuselah were 969 **y**, Gn 5:27
When Lamech had lived 182 **y**, he Gn 5:28
he fathered Noah 595 **y** and had other Gn 5:30
Thus all the days of Lamech were 777 **y**, Gn 5:31
After Noah was 500 **y** old, Noah Gn 5:32
for he is flesh: his days shall be 120 **y**." Gn 6:3
Noah was six hundred **y** old when the Gn 7:6
After the flood Noah lived 350 **y**. Gn 9:28
All the days of Noah were 950 **y**, and he Gn 9:29
When Shem was 100 **y** old, he fathered Gn 11:10
fathered Arpachshad two **y** after the Gn 11:10
fathered Arpachshad 500 **y** and had Gn 11:11
When Arpachshad had lived 35 **y**, he Gn 11:12
he fathered Shelah 403 **y** and had other Gn 11:13
When Shelah had lived 30 **y**, he Gn 11:14
he fathered Eber 403 **y** and had other Gn 11:15
When Eber had lived 34 **y**, he fathered Gn 11:16
he fathered Peleg 430 **y** and had other Gn 11:17
When Peleg had lived 30 **y**, he fathered Gn 11:18
he fathered Reu 209 **y** and had other Gn 11:19
When Reu had lived 32 **y**, he fathered Gn 11:20
he fathered Serug 207 **y** and had other Gn 11:21
When Serug had lived 30 **y**, he fathered Gn 11:22
he fathered Nahor 200 **y** and had other Gn 11:23
When Nahor had lived 29 **y**, he Gn 11:24
he fathered Terah 119 **y** and had other Gn 11:25
When Terah had lived 70 **y**, he Gn 11:26
The days of Terah were 205 **y**, and Gn 11:32
Abram was seventy-five **y** old when he Gn 12:4
Twelve **y** they had served Gn 14:4
to him, "Bring me a heifer three **y** old, Gn 15:9
three years old, a female goat three **y** old, Gn 15:9
goat three years old, a ram three **y** old, Gn 15:9
will be afflicted for four hundred **y**. Gn 15:13
Abram had lived ten **y** in the land of Gn 16:3
Abram was eighty-six **y** old when Gn 16:16
Abram was ninety-nine **y** old the LORD Gn 17:1
born to a man who is a hundred **y** old? Gn 17:17
Shall Sarah, who is ninety **y** old, bear a Gn 17:17
Abraham was ninety-nine **y** old when Gn 17:24
his son was thirteen **y** old when he was Gn 17:25
and Sarah were old, advanced in **y**. Gn 18:11
Abraham was a hundred **y** old when his Gn 21:5
Sarah lived 127 **y**; these were the years of Gn 23:1
these were the **y** of the life of Sarah. Gn 23:1
Abraham was old, well advanced in **y**. Gn 24:1
are the days of the **y** of Abraham's life, Gn 25:7
of the years of Abraham's life, 175 **y**. Gn 25:7
a good old age, an old man and full of **y**, Gn 25:8
(These are the **y** of the life of Ishmael: Gn 25:17
the years of the life of Ishmael: 137 **y**. Gn 25:17
and Isaac was forty **y** old when he took Gn 25:20
Isaac was sixty **y** old when she bore Gn 25:26
When Esau was forty **y** old, he took Gn 26:34
will serve you seven **y** for your younger Gn 29:18
So Jacob served seven **y** for Rachel, and Gn 29:20
return for serving me another seven **y**." Gn 29:27
and served Laban for another seven **y**. Gn 29:30
These twenty **y** I have been with you. Gn 31:38
These twenty **y** I have been in your Gn 31:41
I served you fourteen **y** for your two Gn 31:41
two daughters, and six **y** for your flock, Gn 31:41
Now the days of Isaac were 180 **y**. Gn 35:28
Joseph, being seventeen **y** old, was Gn 37:2
After two whole **y**, Pharaoh dreamed Gn 41:1
The seven good cows are seven **y**, and Gn 41:26
and the seven good ears are seven **y**; Gn 41:26
that came up after them are seven **y**, Gn 41:27
east wind are also seven **y** of famine. Gn 41:27
There will come seven **y** of great plenty Gn 41:29
them there will arise seven **y** of famine, Gn 41:30
of Egypt during the seven plentiful **y**. Gn 41:34
food of these good **y** that are coming Gn 41:35
land against the seven **y** of famine that Gn 41:36
Joseph was thirty **y** old when he entered Gn 41:46
the seven plentiful **y** the earth Gn 41:47
up all the food of these seven **y**, Gn 41:48
The seven **y** of plenty that occurred in Gn 41:53
and the seven **y** of famine began to Gn 41:54
famine has been in the land these two **y**, Gn 45:6
there are yet five **y** in which there will Gn 45:6
there are yet five **y** of famine to come, Gn 45:11
many are the days of the **y** of your life?" Gn 47:8
"The days of the **y** of my sojourning are Gn 47:9
of the years of my sojourning are 130 **y**. Gn 47:9
have been the days of the **y** of my life, Gn 47:9
to the days of the **y** of the life of my Gn 47:9
lived in the land of Egypt seventeen **y**. Gn 47:28
So the days of Jacob, the **y** of his life, Gn 47:28
Jacob, the years of his life, were 147 **y**. Gn 47:28
his father's house. Joseph lived 110 **y**. Gn 50:22
So Joseph died, being 110 **y** old. They Gn 50:26
the **y** of the life of Levi being 137 years. Ex 6:16
the years of the life of Levi being 137 **y**. Ex 6:16
the **y** of the life of Kohath being 133 Ex 6:18
years of the life of Kohath being 133 **y**. Ex 6:18
the **y** of the life of Amram being 137 Ex 6:20
years of the life of Amram being 137 **y**. Ex 6:20
Now Moses was eighty **y** old, and Aaron Ex 7:7
years old, and Aaron eighty-three **y** old, Ex 7:7
people of Israel lived in Egypt was 430 **y**. Ex 12:40
At the end of 430 **y**, on that very day, all Ex 12:41
people of Israel ate the manna forty **y**, Ex 16:35
buy a Hebrew slave, he shall serve six **y**, Ex 21:2
"For six **y** you shall sow your land and Ex 23:10
census, from twenty **y** old and upward, Ex 30:14
records, from twenty **y** old and upward, Ex 38:26
Three **y** it shall be forbidden to you; it Lv 19:23
For six **y** you shall sow your field, and Lv 25:3
and for six **y** you shall prune your Lv 25:3
"You shall count seven weeks of **y**, seven Lv 25:8
weeks of years, seven times seven **y**, Lv 25:8
the seven weeks of **y** shall give you Lv 25:8
of years shall give you forty-nine **y**. Lv 25:8
to the number of **y** after the jubilee, Lv 25:15
according to the number of **y** for crops. Lv 25:15
If the **y** are many, you shall increase Lv 25:16
increase the price, and if the **y** are few, Lv 25:16
produce a crop sufficient for three **y**. Lv 25:21
let him calculate the **y** since he sold it Lv 25:27
sale shall vary with the number of **y**. Lv 25:50
If there are still many **y** left, he shall Lv 25:51
remain but a few **y** until the year of Lv 25:52
in proportion to his **y** of service. Lv 25:52
of a male from twenty **y** old up to sixty Lv 27:3
years old up to sixty **y** old shall be fifty Lv 27:3
the person is from five **y** old up to twenty Lv 27:5
is from five years old up to twenty **y** old, Lv 27:5
is from a month old up to five **y** old, Lv 27:6
And if the person is sixty **y** old or over, Lv 27:7
according to the **y** that remain until Lv 27:18
From twenty **y** old and upward, all in Nm 1:3
names from twenty **y** old and upward, Nm 1:18
male from twenty **y** old and upward, Nm 1:20
male from twenty **y** old and upward, Nm 1:22
names, from twenty **y** old and upward, Nm 1:24
names, from twenty **y** old and upward, Nm 1:26
names, from twenty **y** old and upward, Nm 1:28
names, from twenty **y** old and upward, Nm 1:30
names, from twenty **y** old and upward, Nm 1:32
names, from twenty **y** old and upward, Nm 1:34
names, from twenty **y** old and upward, Nm 1:36
names, from twenty **y** old and upward, Nm 1:38
names, from twenty **y** old and upward, Nm 1:40
names, from twenty **y** old and upward, Nm 1:42
houses, from twenty **y** old and upward, Nm 1:45
from thirty **y** old up to fifty years old, all Nm 4:3
from thirty years old up to fifty **y** old, all Nm 4:3
From thirty **y** old up to fifty years old, Nm 4:23
From thirty years old up to fifty **y** old, Nm 4:23
From thirty **y** old up to fifty years old, Nm 4:30
From thirty years old up to fifty **y** old, Nm 4:30
from thirty **y** old up to fifty years old, Nm 4:35
from thirty years old up to fifty **y** old, Nm 4:35
from thirty **y** old up to fifty years old, Nm 4:39
from thirty years old up to fifty **y** old, Nm 4:39
from thirty **y** old up to fifty years old, Nm 4:43
from thirty years old up to fifty **y** old, Nm 4:43
from thirty **y** old up to fifty years old, Nm 4:47
from thirty years old up to fifty **y** old, Nm 4:47
from twenty-five **y** old and upward they Nm 8:24
the age of fifty **y** they shall withdraw Nm 8:25
was built seven **y** before Zoan in Nm 13:22
census from twenty **y** old and upward, Nm 14:29
the wilderness forty **y** and shall suffer Nm 14:33
you shall bear your iniquity forty **y**, Nm 14:34
Israel, from twenty **y** old and upward, Nm 26:2
from twenty **y** old and upward," as the Nm 26:4
Egypt, from twenty **y** old and upward, Nm 32:11
them wander in the wilderness forty **y**, Nm 32:13
And Aaron was 123 **y** old when he Nm 33:39
These forty **y** the LORD your God has been Dt 2:7
the brook Zered was thirty-eight **y**, Dt 2:14
has led you these forty **y** in the wilderness, Dt 8:2
and your foot did not swell these forty **y**. Dt 8:4
end of every three **y** you shall bring out Dt 14:28
the end of every seven **y** you shall grant a Dt 15:1
is sold to you, he shall serve you six **y**, Dt 15:12
a hired servant he has served you six **y**. Dt 15:18
I have led you forty **y** in the wilderness. Dt 29:5
he said to them, "I am 120 **y** old today. Dt 31:2
them, "At the end of every seven **y**, Dt 31:10
old; consider the **y** of many generations; Dt 32:7
Moses was 120 **y** old when he died. His Dt 34:7
of Israel walked forty **y** in the wilderness, Jos 5:6
Now Joshua was old and advanced in **y**, Jos 13:1
to him, "You are old and advanced in **y**, Jos 13:1
I was forty **y** old when Moses the servant Jos 14:7
these forty-five **y** since the time that the Jos 14:10
behold, I am this day eighty-five **y** old. Jos 14:10
Joshua was old and well advanced in **y**, Jos 23:1
"I am now old and well advanced in **y**. Jos 23:2
of the LORD, died, being 110 **y** old. Jos 24:29
of the LORD, died at the age of 110 **y**. Jgs 2:8
Israel served Cushan-rishathaim eight **y**. Jgs 3:8

So the land had rest forty **y**. Then Jgs 3:11
Eglon the king of Moab eighteen **y**. Jgs 3:14
Israel. And the land had rest for eighty **y**. Jgs 3:30
the people of Israel cruelly for twenty **y**. Jgs 4:3
might." And the land had rest for forty **y**. Jgs 5:31
them into the hand of Midian seven **y**. Jgs 6:1
bull, and the second bull seven **y** old, Jgs 6:25
the land had rest forty **y** in the days of Jgs 8:28
Abimelech ruled over Israel three **y**. Jgs 9:22
And he judged Israel twenty-three **y**. Jgs 10:2
who judged Israel twenty-two **y**. Jgs 10:3
For eighteen **y** they oppressed all the Jgs 10:8
are on the banks of the Arnon, 300 **y**, Jgs 11:26
Jephthah judged Israel six **y**. Then Jgs 12:7
his sons. And he judged Israel seven **y**. Jgs 12:9
Israel, and he judged Israel ten **y**. Jgs 12:11
donkeys, and he judged Israel eight **y**. Jgs 12:14
the hand of the Philistines for forty **y**. Jgs 13:1
in the days of the Philistines twenty **y**. Jgs 15:20
father. He had judged Israel twenty **y**. Jgs 16:31
other Ruth. They lived there about ten **y**, Ru 1:4
Eli was ninety-eight **y** old and his 1 Sm 4:15
heavy. He had judged Israel forty **y**. 1 Sm 4:18
a long time passed, some twenty **y**, 1 Sm 7:2
Saul was … **y** old when he began to 1 Sm 13:1
he reigned … and two **y** over Israel. 1 Sm 13:1
was already old and advanced in **y**. 1 Sm 17:12
has been with me now for days and **y**, 1 Sm 29:3
was forty **y** old when he began to 2 Sm 2:10
reign over Israel, and he reigned two **y**. 2 Sm 2:10
of Judah was seven **y** and six months. 2 Sm 2:11
He was five **y** old when the news about 2 Sm 4:4
David was thirty **y** old when he began 2 Sm 5:4
began to reign, and he reigned forty **y**. 2 Sm 5:4
over Judah seven **y** and six months, 2 Sm 5:5
over all Israel and Judah thirty-three **y**. 2 Sm 5:5
After two full **y** Absalom had 2 Sm 13:23
to Geshur, and was there three **y**. 2 Sm 13:38
lived two full **y** in Jerusalem, 2 Sm 14:28
the end of four **y** Absalom said to the 2 Sm 15:7
was a very aged man, eighty **y** old. 2 Sm 19:32
"How many **y** have I still to live, 2 Sm 19:34
I am this day eighty **y** old. Can I 2 Sm 19:35
in the days of David for three **y**, 2 Sm 21:1
"Shall three **y** of famine come to you 2 Sm 24:13
King David was old and advanced in **y**. 1 Kgs 1:1
David reigned over Israel was forty **y**. 1 Kgs 2:11
He reigned seven **y** in Hebron and 1 Kgs 2:11
and thirty-three **y** in Jerusalem. 1 Kgs 2:11
the end of three **y** that two of Shimei's 1 Kgs 2:39
He was seven **y** in building it. 1 Kgs 6:38
was building his own house thirteen **y**, 1 Kgs 7:1
At the end of twenty **y**, in which 1 Kgs 9:10
Once every three **y** the fleet of ships 1 Kgs 10:22
Jerusalem over all Israel was forty **y**. 1 Kgs 11:42
Jeroboam reigned was twenty-two **y**. 1 Kgs 14:20
Rehoboam was forty-one **y** old when 1 Kgs 14:21
he reigned seventeen **y** in Jerusalem, 1 Kgs 14:21
He reigned for three **y** in Jerusalem. 1 Kgs 15:2
he reigned forty-one **y** in Jerusalem. 1 Kgs 15:10
and he reigned over Israel two **y**. 1 Kgs 15:25
and he reigned twenty-four **y**. 1 Kgs 15:33
Israel in Tirzah, and he reigned two **y**. 1 Kgs 16:8
Israel, and he reigned for twelve **y**; 1 Kgs 16:23
years; six **y** he reigned in Tirzah. 1 Kgs 16:23
over Israel in Samaria twenty-two **y**. 1 Kgs 16:29
shall be neither dew nor rain these **y**, 1 Kgs 17:1
For three **y** Syria and Israel 1 Kgs 22:1
was thirty-five **y** old when 1 Kgs 22:42
reigned twenty-five **y** in Jerusalem. 1 Kgs 22:42
and he reigned two **y** over Israel. 1 Kgs 22:51
in Samaria, and he reigned twelve **y**. 2 Kgs 3:1
it will come upon the land for seven **y**." 2 Kgs 8:1
in the land of the Philistines seven **y**. 2 Kgs 8:2
And at the end of the seven **y**, when the 2 Kgs 8:3
He was thirty-two **y** old when he 2 Kgs 8:17
and he reigned eight **y** in Jerusalem. 2 Kgs 8:17
Ahaziah was twenty-two **y** old when 2 Kgs 8:26
in Samaria was twenty-eight **y**. 2 Kgs 10:36
And he remained with her six **y**, 2 Kgs 11:3
Jehoash was seven **y** old when he 2 Kgs 11:21
and he reigned forty **y** in Jerusalem. 2 Kgs 12:1
Samaria, and he reigned seventeen **y**. 2 Kgs 13:1
Samaria, and he reigned sixteen **y**. 2 Kgs 13:10
He was twenty-five **y** old when he 2 Kgs 14:2
reigned twenty-nine **y** in Jerusalem. 2 Kgs 14:2
lived fifteen **y** after the death of 2 Kgs 14:17
took Azariah, who was sixteen **y** old, 2 Kgs 14:21
Samaria, and he reigned forty-one **y**. 2 Kgs 14:23
He was sixteen **y** old when he began 2 Kgs 15:2
he reigned fifty-two **y** in Jerusalem. 2 Kgs 15:2
and he reigned ten **y** in Samaria. 2 Kgs 15:17
in Samaria, and he reigned two **y**. 2 Kgs 15:23
in Samaria, and he reigned twenty **y**. 2 Kgs 15:27
He was twenty-five **y** old when he 2 Kgs 15:33
he reigned sixteen **y** in Jerusalem. 2 Kgs 15:33
Ahaz was twenty **y** old when he 2 Kgs 16:2
and he reigned sixteen **y** in Jerusalem. 2 Kgs 16:2
over Israel, and he reigned nine **y**. 2 Kgs 17:1
and for three **y** he besieged it. 2 Kgs 17:5
He was twenty-five **y** old when he 2 Kgs 18:2
reigned twenty-nine **y** in Jerusalem. 2 Kgs 18:2
and at the end of three **y** he took it. 2 Kgs 18:10
and I will add fifteen **y** to your life. I 2 Kgs 20:6
Manasseh was twelve **y** old when he 2 Kgs 21:1
he reigned fifty-five **y** in Jerusalem. 2 Kgs 21:1
Amon was twenty-two **y** old when 2 Kgs 21:19
and he reigned two **y** in Jerusalem. 2 Kgs 21:19
Josiah was eight **y** old when he began 2 Kgs 22:1
he reigned thirty-one **y** in Jerusalem. 2 Kgs 22:1
was twenty-three **y** old when 2 Kgs 23:31
was twenty-five **y** old when 2 Kgs 23:36
he reigned eleven **y** in Jerusalem. 2 Kgs 23:36
became his servant three **y**. 2 Kgs 24:1
Jehoiachin was eighteen **y** old when 2 Kgs 24:8
was twenty-one **y** old when 2 Kgs 24:18
he reigned eleven **y** in Jerusalem. 2 Kgs 24:18
he married when he was sixty **y** old, 1 Chr 2:21
he reigned for seven **y** and six months. 1 Chr 3:4
he reigned thirty-three **y** in Jerusalem. 1 Chr 3:4
either three **y** of famine, or three 1 Chr 21:12
The Levites, thirty **y** old and upward, 1 Chr 23:3
individuals from twenty **y** old and 1 Chr 23:24
numbered from twenty **y** old and 1 Chr 23:27
count those below twenty **y** of age, 1 Chr 27:23
he reigned over Israel was forty **y**. 1 Chr 29:27
He reigned seven **y** in Hebron and 1 Chr 29:27
and thirty-three **y** in Jerusalem. 1 Chr 29:27
At the end of twenty **y**, in which 2 Chr 8:1
Once every three **y** the ships of 2 Chr 9:21
in Jerusalem over all Israel forty **y**. 2 Chr 9:30
and for three **y** they made 2 Chr 11:17
they walked for three **y** in the way of 2 Chr 11:17
was forty-one **y** old when 2 Chr 12:13
he reigned seventeen **y** in Jerusalem, 2 Chr 12:13
He reigned for three **y** in Jerusalem. 2 Chr 13:2
In his days the land had rest for ten **y**. 2 Chr 14:1
He had no war in those **y**, for the LORD 2 Chr 14:6
After some **y** he went down to Ahab 2 Chr 18:2
He was thirty-five **y** old when he 2 Chr 20:31
reigned twenty-five **y** in Jerusalem. 2 Chr 20:31
Jehoram was thirty-two **y** old when 2 Chr 21:5
and he reigned eight **y** in Jerusalem. 2 Chr 21:5
In course of time, at the end of two **y**, 2 Chr 21:19
He was thirty-two **y** old when he 2 Chr 21:20
and he reigned eight **y** in Jerusalem. 2 Chr 21:20
Ahaziah was twenty-two **y** old when 2 Chr 22:2
And he remained with them six **y**, 2 Chr 22:12
Joash was seven **y** old when he began 2 Chr 24:1
and he reigned forty **y** in Jerusalem. 2 Chr 24:1
died. He was 130 **y** old at his death. 2 Chr 24:15
Amaziah was twenty-five **y** old when 2 Chr 25:1
reigned twenty-nine **y** in Jerusalem. 2 Chr 25:1
mustered those twenty **y** old and 2 Chr 25:5
lived fifteen **y** after the death of 2 Chr 25:25
took Uzziah, who was sixteen **y** old, 2 Chr 26:1
Uzziah was sixteen **y** old when he 2 Chr 26:3
he reigned fifty-two **y** in Jerusalem. 2 Chr 26:3
Jotham was twenty-five **y** old when 2 Chr 27:1
he reigned sixteen **y** in Jerusalem. 2 Chr 27:1
in the second and the third **y**. 2 Chr 27:5
He was twenty-five **y** old when he 2 Chr 27:8
he reigned sixteen **y** in Jerusalem. 2 Chr 27:8
Ahaz was twenty **y** old when he 2 Chr 28:1
he reigned sixteen **y** in Jerusalem. 2 Chr 28:1
reign when he was twenty-five **y** old, 2 Chr 29:1
reigned twenty-nine **y** in Jerusalem. 2 Chr 29:1
males from three **y** old and upward 2 Chr 31:16
Levites from twenty **y** old and 2 Chr 31:17
Manasseh was twelve **y** old when he 2 Chr 33:1
he reigned fifty-five **y** in Jerusalem. 2 Chr 33:1
Amon was twenty-two **y** old when 2 Chr 33:21
and he reigned two **y** in Jerusalem. 2 Chr 33:21
Josiah was eight **y** old when he began 2 Chr 34:1
he reigned thirty-one **y** in Jerusalem. 2 Chr 34:1
was twenty-three **y** old when 2 Chr 36:2
was twenty-five **y** old when 2 Chr 36:5
and he reigned eleven **y** in Jerusalem. 2 Chr 36:5
Jehoiachin was eight **y** old when he 2 Chr 36:9
was twenty-one **y** old when 2 Chr 36:11
he reigned eleven **y** in Jerusalem. 2 Chr 36:11
it kept Sabbath, to fulfill seventy **y**. 2 Chr 36:21
Levites, from twenty **y** old and upward, Ezr 3:8
the house that was built many **y** ago, Ezr 5:11
year of Artaxerxes the king, twelve **y**, Neh 5:14
Forty **y** you sustained them in the Neh 9:21
Many **y** you bore with them and Neh 9:30
days of man, or your **y** as a man's years, Jb 10:5
days of man, or your years as a man's **y**, Jb 10:5
through all the **y** that are laid up for the Jb 15:20
For when a few **y** have come I shall go Jb 16:22
said: "I am young in **y**, and you are aged; Jb 32:6
days speak, and many **y** teach wisdom.' Jb 32:7
prosperity, and their **y** in pleasantness. Jb 36:11
the number of his **y** is unsearchable. Jb 36:26
And after this Job lived 140 **y**, and saw Jb 42:16
with sorrow, and my **y** with sighing; Ps 31:10
may his **y** endure to all generations! Ps 61:6
I consider the days of old, the **y** long ago. Ps 77:5
to the **y** of the right hand of the Most Ps 77:10
like a breath, and their **y** in terror. Ps 78:33
For a thousand **y** in your sight are but as Ps 90:4
we bring our **y** to an end like a sigh. Ps 90:9
The **y** of our life are seventy, or even by Ps 90:10
and for as many **y** as we have seen evil. Ps 90:15
For forty **y** I loathed that generation Ps 95:10
you whose **y** endure throughout all Ps 102:24
are the same, and your **y** have no end. Ps 102:27
for length of days and **y** of life and peace Prv 3:2
that the **y** of your life may be many. Prv 4:10
to others and your **y** to the merciless, Prv 5:9
and **y** will be added to your life. Prv 9:11
but the **y** of the wicked will be short. Prv 10:27
a hundred children and lives many **y**, Eccl 6:3
years, so that the days of his **y** are many, Eccl 6:3
he should live a thousand **y** twice over, Eccl 6:6
So if a person lives many **y**, let him Eccl 11:8
days come and the **y** draw near of Eccl 12:1
(Within sixty-five **y** Ephraim will be Is 7:8
the LORD has spoken, saying, "In three **y**, Is 16:14
three years, like the **y** of a hired worker, Is 16:14
and barefoot for three **y** as a sign and Is 20:3
according to the **y** of a hired worker, Is 21:16
day Tyre will be forgotten for seventy **y**, Is 23:15
At the end of seventy **y**, it will happen to Is 23:15
At the end of seventy **y**, the LORD will Is 23:17
Behold, I will add fifteen **y** to your life. Is 38:5
to the gates of Sheol for the rest of my **y**. Is 38:10
walk slowly all my **y** because of the Is 38:15
young man shall die a hundred **y** old, Is 65:20
the sinner a hundred **y** old shall be Is 65:20
"For twenty-three **y**, from the thirteenth Jer 25:3
serve the king of Babylon seventy **y**. Jer 25:11
Then after seventy **y** are completed, I Jer 25:12
Within two **y** I will bring back to this Jer 28:3
nations within two **y**." But Jeremiah the Jer 28:11
When seventy **y** are completed for Jer 29:10
'At the end of seven **y** each of you must Jer 34:14
sold to you and has served you six **y**; Jer 34:14
Zedekiah was twenty-one **y** old when he Jer 52:1
and he reigned eleven **y** in Jerusalem. Jer 52:1
number of the **y** of their punishment. Ezk 4:5
the appointed time of your **y** has come. Ezk 22:4
it; it shall be uninhabited forty **y**. Ezk 29:11
a desolation forty **y** among cities that Ezk 29:12
At the end of forty **y** I will gather the Ezk 29:13
In the latter **y** you will go against the Ezk 38:8
days prophesied for **y** that I would Ezk 38:17
they will make fires of them for seven **y**, Ezk 39:9
They were to be educated for three **y**, and Dn 1:5
kingdom, being about sixty-two **y** old. Dn 5:31
in the books the number of **y** that, Dn 9:2
of Jerusalem, namely, seventy **y**. Dn 9:2
After some **y** they shall make an Dn 11:6
and for some **y** he shall refrain from Dn 11:8
And after some **y** he shall come on Dn 11:13
after them through the **y** of all generations. Jl 2:2
restore to you the **y** that the swarming Jl 2:25
of Israel, two **y** before the earthquake. Am 1:1
and led you forty **y** in the wilderness, Am 2:10
during the forty **y** in the wilderness, Am 5:25
In the midst of the **y** revive it; in the Hab 3:2
it; in the midst of the **y** make it known; Hab 3:2
you have been angry these seventy **y**?' Zec 1:12
month, as I have done for so many **y**?" Zec 7:3
and in the seventh, for these seventy **y**, Zec 7:5
as in the days of old and as in former **y**. Mal 3:4
that region who were two **y** old or under, Mt 2:16
of blood for twelve **y** came up behind Mt 9:20
had a discharge of blood for twelve **y**, Mk 5:25
walking (for she was twelve **y** of age), Mk 5:42
was barren, and both were advanced in **y**. Lk 1:7
old man, and my wife is advanced in **y**." Lk 1:18
She was advanced in **y**, having lived Lk 2:36
her husband seven **y** from when she Lk 2:36
And when he was twelve **y** old, they went Lk 2:42
his ministry, was about thirty **y** of age, Lk 3:23
were shut up three **y** and six months, Lk 4:25
an only daughter, about twelve **y** of age, Lk 8:42
had a discharge of blood for twelve **y**, Lk 8:43
have ample goods laid up for many **y**; Lk 12:19
for three **y** now I have come seeking Lk 13:7
had a disabling spirit for eighteen **y**. Lk 13:11
whom Satan bound for eighteen **y**, Lk 13:16
'Look, these many **y** I have served you, Lk 15:29

“It has taken forty-six **y** to build this Jn 2:20
who had been an invalid for thirty-eight **y**. Jn 5:5
said to him, “You are not yet fifty **y** old, Jn 8:57
performed was more than forty **y** old. Acts 4:22
them and afflict them four hundred **y**. Acts 7:6
“When he was forty **y** old, it came into Acts 7:23
“Now when forty **y** had passed, an Acts 7:30
Sea and in the wilderness for forty **y**. Acts 7:36
during the forty **y** in the wilderness, Acts 7:42
named Aeneas, bedridden for eight **y**, Acts 9:33
And for about forty **y** he put up with Acts 13:18
All this took about 450 **y**. And after Acts 13:20
of the tribe of Benjamin, for forty **y**. Acts 13:21
This continued for two **y**, so that all Acts 19:10
that for three **y** I did not Acts 20:31
that for many **y** you have been Acts 24:10
Now after several **y** I came to bring Acts 24:17
When two **y** had elapsed, Felix was Acts 24:27
lived there two whole **y** at his own Acts 28:30
(since he was about a hundred **y** old), Rom 4:19
have longed for many **y** to come to Rom 15:23
Christ who fourteen **y** ago was 2 Cor 12:2
Then after three **y** I went up to Gal 1:18
Then after fourteen **y** I went up again to Gal 2:1
the law, which came 430 **y** afterward, Gal 3:17
days and months and seasons and **y**! Gal 4:10
if she is not less than sixty **y** of age, 1 Tm 5:9
the same, and your **y** will have no end.” Heb 1:12
for forty **y**. Therefore I was provoked Heb 3:10
whom was he provoked for forty **y**? Heb 3:17
and for three **y** and six months it did not Jas 5:17
with the Lord one day is as a thousand **y**, 2 Pt 3:8
years, and a thousand **y** as one day. 2 Pt 3:8
Satan, and bound him for a thousand **y**, Rv 20:2
longer, until the thousand **y** were ended. Rv 20:3
reigned with Christ for a thousand **y**. Rv 20:4
to life until the thousand **y** were ended. Rv 20:5
will reign with him for a thousand **y**. Rv 20:6
And when the thousand **y** are ended, Rv 20:7

YELLOW (3)
the skin, and the hair in it is **y** and thin, Lv 13:30
not spread, and there is in it no **y** hair, Lv 13:32
the priest need not seek for the **y** hair; Lv 13:36

YES (63)
“**Y**, I know that you have done this in Gn 20:6
him? **Y**, and he shall be blessed.” Gn 27:33
Y, he loved his people, all his holy ones Dt 33:3
dropped, **y**, the clouds dropped water. Jgs 5:4
“**Y**, your brother Ben-hadad.” Then 1 Kgs 20:33
over you?” And he said, “**Y**, I know it; 2 Kgs 2:3
you?” And he answered, “**Y**, I know it; 2 Kgs 2:5
the earth; **y**, the world is established; 1 Chr 16:30
“**Y**, what they are building—if a fox Neh 4:3
y, you exalted me above those who rose Ps 18:48
y, I would wander far away; I would lodge Ps 55:7
soul from death, **y**, my feet from falling, Ps 56:13
y, where the LORD will dwell forever? Ps 68:16
y, I will remember your wonders of old. Ps 77:11
longs, **y**, faints for the courts of the LORD; Ps 84:2
Y, the LORD will give what is good, and Ps 85:12
us; **y**, establish the work of our hands! Ps 90:17
Y, the world is established; it shall never Ps 93:1
Y, the world is established; it shall Ps 96:10
y, if you call out for insight and raise Prv 2:3
y, for all the joyous houses in the Is 32:13
y, on every high hill and under every Jer 2:20
y, they have turned and fled together; Jer 46:21
y, you played the whore with them, Ezk 16:28
come down twice, **y**, three times, Ezk 21:14
y, those who were its arm, who lived Ezk 31:17
And he said, “**Y**, I do well to be angry, Jon 4:9
Gather together, **y**, gather, O shameless Zep 2:1
Let what you say be simply ‘**Y**’ or ‘No’; Mt 5:37
to do this?” They said to him, “**Y**, Lord.” Mt 9:28
Y, I tell you, and more than a prophet. Mt 11:9
y, Father, for such was your gracious Mt 11:26
these things?” They said to him, “**Y**.” Mt 13:51
She said, “**Y**, Lord, yet even the dogs eat Mt 15:27
“**Y**.” And when he came into the house, Mt 17:25
said to them, “**Y**; have you never read, Mt 21:16
But she answered him, “**Y**, Lord; yet Mk 7:28
Y, I tell you, and more than a prophet. Lk 7:26
y, Father, for such was your gracious Lk 10:21
Y, I tell you, it will be required of this Lk 11:51
to cast into hell. **Y**, I tell you, fear him! Lk 12:5
and sisters, **y**, and even his own life, Lk 14:26
Y, and besides all this, it is now the Lk 24:21
She said to him, “**Y**, Lord; I believe that Jn 11:27
than these?” He said to him, “**Y**, Lord; Jn 21:15
you love me?” He said to him, “**Y**, Lord; Jn 21:16
much.” And she said, “**Y**, for so much.” Acts 5:8
a Roman citizen?” And he said, “**Y**.” Acts 22:27
of Gentiles also? **Y**, of Gentiles also, Rom 3:29
to the flesh, ready to say “**Y**, 2 Cor 1:17
flesh, ready to say “Yes, **y**” and “No, 2 Cor 1:17
word to you has not been **Y** and No. 2 Cor 1:18
Timothy and I, was not **Y** and No, 2 Cor 1:19
and No, but in him it is always **Y**. 2 Cor 1:19
promises of God find their **Y** in him. 2 Cor 1:20
Y, to this day whenever Moses is read 2 Cor 3:15
Y, we are of good courage, and we 2 Cor 5:8
in that I rejoice. **Y**, and I will rejoice, Phil 1:18
Y, I ask you also, true companion, help Phil 4:3
Y, brother, I want some benefit from Phlm 1:20
but let your “**y**” be yes and your “no” be Jas 5:12
but let your “yes” be **y** and your “no” be Jas 5:12
altar saying, “**Y**, Lord God the Almighty, Rv 16:7

YESHANAH (2)
son of Besodeiah repaired the Gate of **Y**. Neh 3:6
of Ephraim, and by the Gate of **Y**, Neh 12:39

YESTERDAY (9)
your task of making bricks today and **y**, Ex 5:14
come to the meal, either **y** or today?” 1 Sm 20:27
You came only **y**, and shall I today 2 Sm 15:20
surely as I saw **y** the blood of Naboth 2 Kgs 9:26
For we are but of **y** and know nothing, for Jb 8:9
in your sight are but as **y** when it is past, Ps 90:4
“**Y** at the seventh hour the fever left him.” Jn 4:52
kill me as you killed the Egyptian **y**?’ Acts 7:28
Christ is the same **y** and today and Heb 13:8

YIELD (41)
it shall no longer **y** to you its strength. Gn 4:12
be rich, and he shall **y** royal delicacies. Gn 49:20
shall sow your land and gather in its **y**, Ex 23:10
eat of its fruit, to increase its **y** for you: Lv 19:25
in your land: all its **y** shall be for food. Lv 25:7
The land will **y** its fruit, and you will Lv 25:19
season, and the land shall **y** its increase, Lv 26:4
the trees of the field shall **y** their fruit. Lv 26:4
for your land shall not **y** its increase, Lv 26:20
trees of the land shall not **y** their fruit. Lv 26:20
the rock before their eyes to **y** its water. Nm 20:8
be no rain, and the land will **y** no fruit, Dt 11:17
you shall not **y** to him or listen to him, Dt 13:8
shall tithe all the **y** of your seed that Dt 14:22
kinds of seed, lest the whole **y** be forfeited, Dt 22:9
you have sown and the **y** of the vineyard. Dt 22:9
of the sun and the rich **y** of the months, Dt 33:14
but **y** yourselves to the LORD and 2 Chr 30:8
storehouses also for the **y** of grain, 2 Chr 32:28
And its rich **y** goes to the kings whom Neh 9:37
I have eaten its **y** without payment and Jb 31:39
For the mountains **y** food for him Jb 40:20
is good, and our land will **y** its increase. Ps 85:12
plant vineyards and get a fruitful **y**. Ps 107:37
fine gold, and my **y** than choice silver. Prv 8:19
of the poor would **y** much food, Prv 13:23
he is satisfied by the **y** of his lips. Prv 18:20
and he looked for it to **y** grapes, but it Is 5:2
When I looked for it to **y** grapes, why did it Is 5:4
it to yield grapes, why did it **y** wild grapes? Is 5:4
acres of vineyard shall **y** but one bath, Is 5:10
a homer of seed shall **y** but an ephah.” Is 5:10
the trees of the field shall **y** their fruit, Ezk 34:27
fruit, and the earth shall **y** its increase, Ezk 34:27
forth your branches and **y** your fruit to Ezk 36:8
grain has no heads; it shall **y** no flour; Hos 8:7
if it were to **y**, strangers would devour it. Hos 8:7
fruit; the fig tree and vine give their full **y**. Jl 2:22
of the olive fail and the fields **y** no food, Hab 3:17
them we did not **y** in submission even Gal 2:5
Neither can a salt pond **y** fresh water. Jas 3:12

YIELDED (7)
The earth has **y** its increase; God, our Ps 67:6
for it to yield grapes, but it **y** wild grapes. Is 5:2
and **y** up their bodies rather than serve Dn 3:28
and the olive tree have **y** nothing. Hg 2:19
with a loud voice and **y** up his spirit. Mt 27:50
grew up and choked it, and it **y** no grain. Mk 4:7
soil and grew and **y** a hundredfold.” As he Lk 8:8

YIELDING (5)
earth sprout vegetation, plants **y** seed, Gn 1:11
plants **y** seed according to their own Gn 1:12
given you every plant **y** seed that is on Gn 1:29
and increasing and **y** thirtyfold and Mk 4:8
kinds of fruit, **y** its fruit each month. Rv 22:2

YIELDS (5)
the wasteland **y** food for their children. Jb 24:5
by streams of water that **y** its fruit in its Ps 1:3
Israel is a luxuriant vine that **y** its fruit. Hos 10:1
He indeed bears fruit and **y**, in one case Mt 13:23
but later it **y** the peaceful fruit of Heb 12:11

YIRON (1)
Y, Migdal-el, Horem, Beth-anath, and Jos 19:38

YOB (1)
Tola, Puvah, **Y**, and Shimron. Gn 46:13

YOKE (58)
you shall break his **y** from your neck.” Gn 27:40
the bars of your **y** and made you walk Lv 26:13
and on which a **y** has never come. Nm 19:2
worked and that has not pulled in a **y**. Dt 21:3
And he will put a **y** of iron on your Dt 28:48
on which there has never come a **y**, 1 Sm 6:7
come a yoke, and **y** the cows to the cart, 1 Sm 6:7
He took a **y** of oxen and cut them in 1 Sm 11:7
“Your father made our **y** heavy. Now 1 Kgs 12:4
of your father and his heavy **y** on us, 1 Kgs 12:4
‘Lighten the **y** that your father put on 1 Kgs 12:9
you, ‘Your father made our **y** heavy, 1 Kgs 12:10
my father laid on you a heavy **y**, 1 Kgs 12:11
a heavy yoke, I will add to your **y**. 1 Kgs 12:11
“My father made your **y** heavy, 1 Kgs 12:14
yoke heavy, but I will add to your **y**. 1 Kgs 12:14
was plowing with twelve **y** of oxen in 1 Kgs 19:19
him and took the **y** of oxen and 1 Kgs 19:21
“Your father made our **y** heavy. Now 2 Chr 10:4
of your father and his heavy **y** on us, 2 Chr 10:4
‘Lighten the **y** that your father put on 2 Chr 10:9
you, ‘Your father made our **y** heavy, 2 Chr 10:10
my father laid on you a heavy **y**, 2 Chr 10:11
a heavy yoke, I will add to your **y**. 2 Chr 10:11
“My father made your **y** heavy, 2 Chr 10:14
7,000 sheep, 3,000 camels, 500 **y** of oxen, Jb 1:3
sheep, 6,000 camels, 1,000 **y** of oxen, Jb 42:12
For the **y** of his burden, and the staff for Is 9:4
shoulder, and his **y** from your neck; Is 10:27
and the **y** will be broken because of the Is 10:27
and his **y** shall depart from them, and Is 14:25
aged you made your **y** exceedingly heavy. Is 47:6
of wickedness, to undo the straps of the **y**, Is 58:6
oppressed go free, and to break every **y**? Is 58:6
If you take away the **y** from your midst, Is 58:9
ago I broke your **y** and burst your Jer 2:20
God.” But they all alike had broken the **y**; Jer 5:5
put its neck under the **y** of the king of Jer 27:8
its neck under the **y** of the king of Jer 27:11
your necks under the **y** of the king of Jer 27:12
I have broken the **y** of the king of Jer 28:2
for I will break the **y** of the king of Jer 28:4
I break the **y** of Nebuchadnezzar king Jer 28:11
nations an iron **y** to serve Jer 28:14
I will break his **y** from off your neck, Jer 30:8
transgressions were bound into a **y**; Lam 1:14
a man that he bear the **y** in his youth. Lam 3:27
when I break there the **y** bars of Egypt, Ezk 30:18
LORD, when I break the bars of their **y**, Ezk 34:27
neck; but I will put Ephraim to the **y**; Hos 10:11
as one who eases the **y** on their jaws, Hos 11:4
now I will break his **y** from off you and Na 1:13
Take my **y** upon you, and learn from Mt 11:29
For my **y** is easy, and my burden is Mt 11:30
said, ‘I have bought five **y** of oxen, Lk 14:19
the test by placing a **y** on the neck of Acts 15:10
do not submit again to a **y** of slavery. Gal 5:1
who are under a **y** as slaves regard 1 Tm 6:1

YOKE-BARS (3)
“Make yourself straps and **y**, and put Jer 27:2
Hananiah took the **y** from the neck Jer 28:10
had broken the **y** from off the Jer 28:12

YOKED (5)
So Israel **y** himself to Baal of Peor. And Nm 25:3
his men who have **y** themselves to Baal Nm 25:5
two milk cows and **y** them to the cart 1 Sm 6:10
Then they **y** themselves to the Baal of Ps 106:28
not be unequally **y** with unbelievers. 2 Cor 6:14

YOKES (2)
sledges and the **y** of the oxen 2 Sm 24:22
their flesh with the **y** of the oxen and 1 Kgs 19:21

YOUNG (332)
wounding me, a **y** man for striking me. Gn 4:23
but what the **y** men have eaten, Gn 14:24
years old, a turtledove, and a **y** pigeon.” Gn 15:9
tender and good, and gave it to a **y** man, Gn 18:7
city, the men of Sodom, both **y** and old, Gn 19:4
and took two of his **y** men with him, Gn 22:3
Then Abraham said to his **y** men, “Stay Gn 22:5
So Abraham returned to his **y** men, Gn 22:19
Let the **y** woman to whom I shall say, Gn 24:14
The **y** woman was very attractive in Gn 24:16
Then the **y** woman ran and told her Gn 24:28
“Let the **y** woman remain with us a Gn 24:55
“Let us call the **y** woman and ask her.” Gn 24:57
Rebekah and her **y** women arose and Gn 24:61
flock and bring me two good **y** goats, Gn 27:9
And the skins of the **y** goats she put on Gn 27:16
He loved the **y** woman and spoke Gn 34:3
Only give me the **y** woman to be my Gn 34:12
And the **y** man did not delay to do the Gn 34:19
will send you a **y** goat from the flock.” Gn 38:17

When Judah sent the **y** goat by his Gn 38:20
You see, I sent this **y** goat, and you did Gn 38:23
A **y** Hebrew was there with us, a Gn 41:12
a father, an old man, and a **y** brother, Gn 44:20
while her **y** women walked beside the Ex 2:5
said, "We will go with our **y** and our old. Ex 10:9
shall not boil a **y** goat in its mother's Ex 23:19
And he sent **y** men of the people of Israel, Ex 24:5
Joshua the son of Nun, a **y** man, Ex 33:11
shall not boil a **y** goat in its mother's Ex 34:26
an ox or a sheep and her **y** in one day. Lv 22:28
And a **y** man ran and told Moses, Nm 11:27
or ram, or for each lamb or **y** goat. Nm 15:11
But all the **y** girls who have not Nm 31:18
of your herds and the **y** of your flock, Dt 7:13
shall not boil a **y** goat in its mother's Dt 14:21
with **y** ones or eggs and the mother Dt 22:6
mother sitting on the **y** or on the eggs, Dt 22:6
you shall not take the mother with the **y**. Dt 22:6
go, but the **y** you may take for yourself, Dt 22:7
the father of the **y** woman and her Dt 22:15
the father of the **y** woman shall say to Dt 22:16
give them to the father of the **y** woman, Dt 22:19
was not found in the **y** woman, Dt 22:20
shall bring out the **y** woman to the door Dt 22:21
the **y** woman because she did not cry Dt 22:24
a man meets a **y** woman who is Dt 22:25
you shall do nothing to the **y** woman; Dt 22:26
though the betrothed **y** woman cried Dt 22:27
the father of the **y** woman fifty shekels Dt 22:29
of your herds and the **y** of your flock. Dt 28:4
of your herds and the **y** of your flock. Dt 28:18
respect the old or show mercy to the **y**. Dt 28:50
of your herds or the **y** of your flock, Dt 28:51
stirs up its nest, that flutters over its **y**, Dt 32:11
terror, for **y** man and woman alike, Dt 32:25
both men and women, **y** and old, Jos 6:21
So the **y** men who had been spies went in Jos 6:23
and prepared a **y** goat and unleavened Jgs 6:19
And he captured a **y** man of Succoth Jgs 8:14
kill them!" But the **y** man did not draw Jgs 8:20
was afraid, because he was still a **y** man. Jgs 8:20
quickly to the **y** man his armor-bearer Jgs 9:54
killed him.'" And his **y** man thrust him Jgs 9:54
you and prepare a **y** goat for you." Jgs 13:15
So Manoah took the **y** goat with the Jgs 13:19
name Samson. And the **y** man grew, Jgs 13:24
a **y** lion came toward him roaring. Jgs 14:5
the lion in pieces as one tears a **y** goat. Jgs 14:6
feast there, for so the **y** men used to do. Jgs 14:10
went to visit his wife with a **y** goat. Jgs 15:1
Samson said to the **y** man who held Jgs 16:26
Now there was a **y** man of Bethlehem in Jgs 17:7
and the **y** man became to him like one Jgs 17:11
and the **y** man became his priest, Jgs 17:12
they recognized the voice of the **y** Levite. Jgs 18:3
and came to the house of the **y** Levite, Jgs 18:15
And he said to his **y** man, "Come and Jgs 19:13
servant and the **y** man with your Jgs 19:19
of Jabesh-gilead 400 **y** virgins who had Jgs 21:12
Then Boaz said to his **y** man who was in Ru 2:5
of the reapers, "Whose **y** woman is this?" Ru 2:5
answered, "She is the **y** Moabite woman, Ru 2:6
this one, but keep close to my **y** women. Ru 2:8
I not charged the **y** men not to touch Ru 2:9
and drink what the **y** men have drawn." Ru 2:9
rose to glean, Boaz instructed his **y** men, Ru 2:15
keep close by my **y** men until they have Ru 2:21
that you go out with his **y** women, Ru 2:22
So she kept close to the **y** women of Boaz, Ru 2:23
relative, with whose **y** women you were? Ru 3:2
in that you have not gone after **y** men, Ru 3:10
the LORD will give you by this **y** woman." Ru 4:12
LORD at Shiloh. And the child was **y**. 1 Sm 1:24
the sin of the **y** men was very great 1 Sm 2:17
And the **y** man Samuel grew in the 1 Sm 2:21
Now the **y** man Samuel continued to 1 Sm 2:26
Now the **y** man Samuel was 1 Sm 3:1
that the LORD was calling the **y** man. 1 Sm 3:8
the men of the city, both **y** and old, 1 Sm 5:9
the best of your **y** men and your 1 Sm 8:16
name was Saul, a handsome **y** man. 1 Sm 9:2
son, "Take one of the **y** men with you, 1 Sm 9:3
they met **y** women coming out to 1 Sm 9:11
took Saul and his **y** man and brought 1 Sm 9:22
you there, one carrying three **y** goats, 1 Sm 10:3
Saul said to the **y** man who carried 1 Sm 14:1
said to the **y** man who carried 1 Sm 14:6
One of the **y** men answered, "Behold, 1 Sm 16:18
of wine and a **y** goat and sent them 1 Sm 16:20
you, **y** man?" And David answered, 1 Sm 17:58
And behold, I will send the **y** man, 1 Sm 20:21
If I say to the **y** man, 'Look, the 1 Sm 20:21
appointment with the **y** men for such 1 Sm 21:2
bread—if the **y** men have kept 1 Sm 21:4
The vessels of the **y** men are holy even 1 Sm 21:5
So David sent ten **y** men. And David 1 Sm 25:5
And David said to the **y** men, "Go up 1 Sm 25:5
Ask your **y** men, and they will tell 1 Sm 25:8
Therefore let my **y** men find favor in 1 Sm 25:8
When David's **y** men came, they said 1 Sm 25:9
So David's **y** men turned away and 1 Sm 25:12
But one of the **y** men told Abigail, 1 Sm 25:14
And she said to her **y** men, "Go on 1 Sm 25:19
did not see the **y** men of my lord, 1 Sm 25:25
be given to the **y** men who follow my 1 Sm 25:27
and her five **y** women attended her. 1 Sm 25:42
Let one of the **y** men come over and 1 Sm 26:22
He said, "I am a **y** man of Egypt, 1 Sm 30:13
escaped, except four hundred **y** men, 1 Sm 30:17
David said to the **y** man who told him, 2 Sm 1:5
And the **y** man who told him said, "By 2 Sm 1:6
David said to the **y** man who told him, 2 Sm 1:13
called one of the **y** men and said, 2 Sm 1:15
"Let the **y** men arise and compete 2 Sm 2:14
seize one of the **y** men and take his 2 Sm 2:21
And David commanded his **y** men, 2 Sm 4:12
And Mephibosheth had a **y** son, 2 Sm 9:12
He called the **y** man who served him 2 Sm 13:17
have killed all the **y** men the king's 2 Sm 13:32
And the **y** man who kept the watch 2 Sm 13:34
go, bring back the **y** man Absalom." 2 Sm 14:21
and summer fruit for the **y** men to eat, 2 Sm 16:2
But a **y** man saw them and told 2 Sm 17:18
sake with the **y** man Absalom." And 2 Sm 18:5
sake protect the **y** man Absalom.' 2 Sm 18:12
And ten **y** men, Joab's 2 Sm 18:15
well with the **y** man Absalom?" 2 Sm 18:29
well with the **y** man Absalom?" And 2 Sm 18:32
you for evil be like that **y** man." 2 Sm 18:32
And one of Joab's **y** men took his 2 Sm 20:11
"Let a **y** woman be sought for my lord 1 Kgs 1:2
for a beautiful **y** woman throughout 1 Kgs 1:3
The **y** woman was very beautiful, and 1 Kgs 1:4
saw that the **y** man was industrious 1 Kgs 11:28
took counsel with the **y** men who had 1 Kgs 12:8
And the **y** men who had grown up 1 Kgs 12:10
to the counsel of the **y** men, 1 Kgs 12:14
country of Ephraim two **y** men of the 2 Kgs 5:22
the LORD opened the eyes of the **y** man, 2 Kgs 6:17
you will kill their **y** men with the 2 Kgs 8:12
So the **y** man, the servant of the 2 Kgs 9:4
And the **y** man poured the oil on his 2 Kgs 9:6
Zadok, a **y** man mighty in valor, 1 Chr 12:28
my son is **y** and inexperienced, 1 Chr 22:5
has chosen, is **y** and inexperienced, 1 Chr 29:1
counsel with the **y** men who had 2 Chr 10:8
And the **y** men who had grown up 2 Chr 10:10
to the counsel of the **y** men, 2 Chr 10:14
Rehoboam was **y** and irresolute 2 Chr 13:7
for ordination with a **y** bull or seven 2 Chr 13:9
be put to death, whether **y** or old, 2 Chr 15:13
to their brothers, old and **y** alike, 2 Chr 31:15
lambs and **y** goats from the flock to 2 Chr 35:7
5,000 lambs and **y** goats and 500 2 Chr 35:9
who killed their **y** men with the 2 Chr 36:17
no compassion on **y** man or virgin, 2 Chr 36:17
Then the king's **y** men who attended him Est 2:2
"Let beautiful **y** virgins be sought out for Est 2:2
gather all the beautiful **y** virgins to the Est 2:3
And let the **y** woman who pleases the Est 2:4
The **y** woman had a beautiful figure and Est 2:7
and when many **y** women were gathered Est 2:8
And the **y** woman pleased him and won Est 2:9
and with seven chosen **y** women from the Est 2:9
advanced her and her **y** women to the Est 2:9
turn came for each **y** woman to go in Est 2:12
when the **y** woman went in to the king Est 2:13
and to annihilate all Jews, **y** and old, Est 3:13
When Esther's **y** women and her Est 4:4
I and my **y** women will also fast as you Est 4:16
for this?" The king's **y** men who attended Est 6:3
And the king's **y** men told him, "Haman Est 6:5
of the house, and it fell upon the **y** people, Jb 1:19
lion, the teeth of the **y** lions are broken. Jb 4:10
bud and put out branches like a **y** plant. Jb 14:9
Even **y** children despise me; when I rise Jb 19:18
the **y** men saw me and withdrew, and the Jb 29:8
answered and said: "I am **y** in years, Jb 32:6
lion, or satisfy the appetite of the **y** lions, Jb 38:39
prey, when its **y** ones cry to God for help, Jb 38:41
offspring, and are delivered of their **y**? Jb 39:3
Their **y** ones become strong; they grow Jb 39:4
She deals cruelly with her **y**, as if they Jb 39:16
His **y** ones suck up blood, and where the Jb 39:30
to tear, as a **y** lion lurking in ambush. Ps 17:12
like a calf, and Sirion like a **y** wild ox. Ps 29:6
The **y** lions suffer want and hunger; Ps 34:10
I have been **y**, and now am old, yet I Ps 37:25
tear out the fangs of the **y** lions, O LORD! Ps 58:6
of them and laid low the **y** men of Israel. Ps 78:31
Fire devoured their **y** men, and their Ps 78:63
and their **y** women had no marriage Ps 78:63
nest for herself, where she may lay her **y**, Ps 84:3
the **y** lion and the serpent you will Ps 91:13
The **y** lions roar for their prey, seeking Ps 104:21
came, **y** locusts without number, Ps 105:34
How can a **y** man keep his way pure? Ps 119:9
may our cattle be heavy with **y**, Ps 144:14
their food, and to the **y** ravens that cry. Ps 147:9
Y men and maidens together, old men Ps 148:12
the youths, a **y** man lacking sense, Prv 7:7
has sent out her **y** women to call from Prv 9:3
The glory of **y** men is their strength, Prv 20:29
Rejoice, O **y** man, in your youth, and Eccl 11:9
and pasture your **y** goats beside the Sg 1:8
so is my love among the **y** women. Sg 2:2
forest, so is my beloved among the **y** men. Sg 2:3
My beloved is like a gazelle or a **y** stag. Sg 2:9
a gazelle or a **y** stag on cleft mountains. Sg 2:17
and not one among them has lost its **y**. Sg 4:2
twins; not one among them has lost its **y**. Sg 6:6
The **y** women saw her and called her Sg 6:9
a gazelle or a **y** stag on the mountains Sg 8:14
is like a lion, like **y** lions they roar; Is 5:29
will keep alive a **y** cow and two sheep, Is 7:21
the Lord does not rejoice over their **y** men, Is 9:17
the leopard shall lie down with the **y** goat, Is 11:6
graze; their **y** shall lie down together; Is 11:7
Their bows will slaughter the **y** men; Is 13:18
the Cushite exiles, both the **y** and the old, Is 20:4
I have neither reared **y** men nor brought Is 23:4
young men nor brought up **y** women." Is 23:4
"As a lion or a **y** lion growls over his prey, Is 31:4
and his **y** men shall be put to forced Is 31:8
them, and **y** steers with the mighty bulls. Is 34:7
and gathers her **y** in her shadow; Is 34:15
with which the **y** men of the king of Is 37:6
and gently lead those that are with **y**. Is 40:11
weary, and **y** men shall fall exhausted; Is 40:30
For he grew up before him like a **y** plant, Is 53:2
you, the **y** camels of Midian and Ephah; Is 60:6
For as a **y** man marries a young woman, Is 62:5
For as a young man marries a **y** woman, Is 62:5
for the **y** man shall die a hundred years Is 65:20
done—a restless **y** camel running here Jer 2:23
street, and upon the gatherings of **y** men, Jer 6:11
the streets and the **y** men from the Jer 9:21
The **y** men shall die by the sword, their Jer 11:22
against the mothers of **y** men a destroyer Jer 15:8
and over the **y** of the flock and the herd; Jer 31:12
Then shall the **y** women rejoice in the Jer 31:13
and the **y** men and the old shall be Jer 31:13
the choicest of his **y** men have gone Jer 48:15
Therefore her **y** men shall fall in her Jer 49:26
Therefore her **y** men shall fall in her Jer 50:30
Spare not her **y** men; devote to Jer 51:3
break in pieces the **y** man and the Jer 51:22
the young man and the **y** woman; Jer 51:22
against me to crush my **y** men; Lam 1:15
my **y** women and my young men have Lam 1:18
women and my **y** men have gone Lam 1:18
the **y** women of Jerusalem have bowed Lam 2:10
dust of the streets lie the **y** and the old; Lam 2:21
my **y** women and my young men have Lam 2:21
women and my **y** men have fallen Lam 2:21
they nurse their **y**, but the daughter of Lam 4:3
Zion, **y** women in the towns of Judah. Lam 5:11
Y men are compelled to grind at the Lam 5:13
the city gate, the **y** men their music. Lam 5:14
old men outright, **y** men and maidens, Ezk 9:6
the topmost of its **y** twigs and carried it Ezk 17:4
the topmost of its **y** twigs a tender one, Ezk 17:22
in the midst of **y** lions she reared her Ezk 19:2
he became a **y** lion, and he learned to Ezk 19:3
of her cubs and made him a **y** lion. Ezk 19:5
he became a **y** lion, and he learned to Ezk 19:6
all of them desirable **y** men, Ezk 23:6
on horses, all of them desirable **y** men. Ezk 23:12
bosom and pressed your **y** breasts." Ezk 23:21
Assyrians with them, desirable **y** men, Ezk 23:23
The **y** men of On and of Pi-beseth Ezk 30:17
beasts of the field gave birth to their **y**, Ezk 31:6
the face of a **y** lion toward the palm Ezk 41:19
people of the land a **y** bull for a sin Ezk 45:22
to the LORD seven **y** bulls and seven Ezk 45:23
grain offering with a **y** bull shall be Ezk 46:11
and like a **y** lion to the house of Judah. Hos 5:14
was like a **y** palm planted in a meadow; Hos 9:13
dreams, and your **y** men shall see visions. Jl 2:28
and some of your **y** men for Nazirites. Am 2:11
Does a **y** lion cry out from his den, if he Am 3:4
I killed your **y** men with the sword, and Am 4:10
lovely virgins and the **y** men shall faint Am 8:13
from their **y** children you take away my Mi 2:9

like a **y** lion among the flocks of sheep, Mi 5:8
den, the feeding place of the **y** lions, Na 2:11
and the sword shall devour your **y** lions. Na 2:13
and said to him, "Run, say to that **y** man, Zec 2:4
Grain shall make the **y** men flourish, Zec 9:17
flourish, and new wine the **y** women. Zec 9:17
or seek the **y** or heal the maimed or Zec 11:16
The **y** man said to him, "All these I Mt 19:20
When the **y** man heard this he went Mt 19:22
And a **y** man followed him, with Mk 14:51
they saw a **y** man sitting on the right Mk 16:5
"a pair of turtledoves, or two **y** pigeons." Lk 2:24
And he said, "**Y** man, I say to you, arise." Lk 7:14
yet you never gave me a **y** goat, Lk 15:29
And Jesus found a **y** donkey and sat on Jn 12:14
truly, I say to you, when you were **y**, Jn 21:18
and your **y** men shall see visions, Acts 2:17
The **y** men rose and wrapped him up Acts 5:6
When the **y** men came in they found Acts 5:10
at the feet of a **y** man named Saul. Acts 7:58
And a **y** man named Eutychus, sitting Acts 20:9
said, "Take this **y** man to the tribune, Acts 23:17
asked me to bring this **y** man to you, Acts 23:18
So the tribune dismissed the **y** man, Acts 23:22
and so train the **y** women to love their Ti 2:4
I am writing to you, **y** men, because 1 Jn 2:13
I write to you, **y** men, because you are 1 Jn 2:14

YOUNGER (30)
And the firstborn said to the **y**, "Our Gn 19:31
next day, the firstborn said to the **y**, Gn 19:34
And the **y** arose and lay with him, and Gn 19:35
The **y** also bore a son and called his Gn 19:38
the other, the older shall serve the **y**." Gn 25:23
and put them on Jacob her **y** son. Gn 27:15
and called Jacob her **y** son and said to Gn 27:42
and the name of the **y** was Rachel. Gn 29:16
years for your **y** daughter Rachel." Gn 29:18
to give the **y** before the firstborn. Gn 29:26
on the head of Ephraim, who was the **y**, Gn 48:14
his **y** brother shall be greater than he, Gn 48:19
the son of Kenaz, Caleb's **y** brother, Jgs 1:13
the son of Kenaz, Caleb's **y** brother. Jgs 3:9
Is not her **y** sister more beautiful than Jgs 15:2
and the name of the **y** Michal. 1 Sm 14:49
house and his **y** brother alike, 1 Chr 24:31
they laugh at me, men who are **y** than I, Jb 30:1
and your **y** sister, who lived to the Ezk 16:46
sisters, both your elder and your **y**, Ezk 16:61
the mother of James the **y** and of Joses, Mk 15:40
And the **y** of them said to his father, Lk 15:12
the **y** son gathered all he had and took Lk 15:13
was told, "The older will serve the **y**." Rom 9:12
a father. Treat **y** men like brothers, 1 Tm 5:1
like mothers, **y** women like sisters, 1 Tm 5:2
But refuse to enroll **y** widows, for 1 Tm 5:11
So I would have **y** widows marry, 1 Tm 5:14
urge the **y** men to be self-controlled. Ti 2:6
Likewise, you who are **y**, be subject to 1 Pt 5:5

YOUNGEST (22)
and knew what his **y** son had done to Gn 9:24
the **y** is this day with our father, Gn 42:13
place unless your **y** brother comes Gn 42:15
and bring your **y** brother to me. So Gn 42:20
and the **y** is this day with our father in Gn 42:32
Bring your **y** brother to me. Then I Gn 42:34
son, and said, "Is this your **y** brother, Gn 43:29
birthright and the **y** according to his Gn 43:33
cup, in the mouth of the sack of the **y**, Gn 44:2
with the eldest and ending with the **y**. Gn 44:12
'Unless your **y** brother comes down Gn 44:23
If our **y** brother goes with us, then we Gn 44:26
man's face unless our **y** brother is with Gn 44:26
at the cost of his **y** son shall he set up Jos 6:26
But Jotham the **y** son of Jerubbaal was Jgs 9:5
he said, "There remains yet the **y**, 1 Sm 16:11
David was the **y**. The three eldest 1 Sm 17:14
gates at the cost of his **y** son Segub, 1 Kgs 16:34
put on armor, from the **y** to the oldest, 2 Kgs 3:21
to him except Jehoahaz, his **y** son. 2 Chr 21:17
made Ahaziah his **y** son king in 2 Chr 22:1
greatest among you become as the **y**, Lk 22:26

YOUTH (74)
of man's heart is evil from his **y**. Gn 8:21
and the youngest according to his **y**. Gn 43:33
of livestock from our **y** even until now, Gn 46:34
to her father's house, as in her **y**, Lv 22:13
the assistant of Moses from his **y**, Nm 11:28
within her father's house in her **y**, Nm 30:3
she is in her **y** within her father's Nm 30:16
before you from my **y** until this day. 1 Sm 12:2
to fight with him, for you are but a **y**, 1 Sm 17:33
has been a man of war from his **y**." 1 Sm 17:33
he disdained him, for he was but a **y**, 1 Sm 17:42
son is this **y**?" And Abner said, 1 Sm 17:55
But if I say to the **y**, 'Look, the arrows 1 Sm 20:22
upon you from your **y** until now." 2 Sm 19:7
have feared the LORD from my **y**. 1 Kgs 18:12
make me inherit the iniquities of my **y**. Jb 13:26
(for from my **y** the fatherless grew up Jb 31:18
let his flesh become fresh with **y**; let Jb 33:25
They die in **y**, and their life ends among Jb 36:14
the sins of my **y** or my transgressions; Ps 25:7
my hope, my trust, O LORD, from my **y**. Ps 71:5
O God, from my **y** you have taught me, Ps 71:17
and close to death from my **y** up, Ps 88:15
You have cut short the days of his **y**; Ps 89:45
good so that your **y** is renewed like the Ps 103:5
the dew of your **y** will be yours. Ps 110:3
of a warrior are the children of one's **y**. Ps 127:4
afflicted me from my **y**"—let Israel now Ps 129:1
have they afflicted me from my **y**, Ps 129:2
our sons in their **y** be like plants full Ps 144:12
knowledge and discretion to the **y**— Prv 1:4
the companion of her **y** and forgets the Prv 2:17
and rejoice in the wife of your **y**, Prv 5:18
was a poor and wise **y** than an old and Eccl 4:13
along with that **y** who was to stand in Eccl 4:15
Rejoice, O young man, in your **y**, and Eccl 11:9
heart cheer you in the days of your **y**. Eccl 11:9
for **y** and the dawn of life are vanity. Eccl 11:10
also your Creator in the days of your **y**, Eccl 12:1
the **y** will be insolent to the elder, and the Is 3:5
which you have labored from your **y**; Is 47:12
done business with you from your **y**; Is 47:15
for you will forget the shame of your **y**, Is 54:4
spirit, like a wife of **y** when she is cast off, Is 54:6
not know how to speak, for I am only a **y**." Jer 1:6
said to me, "Do not say, 'I am only a **y**'; Jer 1:7
LORD, "I remember the devotion of your **y**, Jer 2:2
'My father, you are the friend of my **y**— Jer 3:4
"But from our **y** the shameful thing has Jer 3:24
our fathers, from our **y** even to this day, Jer 3:25
This has been your way from your **y**, Jer 22:21
because I bore the disgrace of my **y**.' Jer 31:19
but evil in my sight from their **y**. Jer 32:30
at ease from his **y** and has settled on Jer 48:11
I break in pieces the old man and the **y**; Jer 51:22
a man that he bear the yoke in his **y**. Lam 3:27
From my **y** up till now I have never Ezk 4:14
did not remember the days of your **y**, Ezk 16:22
not remembered the days of your **y**, Ezk 16:43
with you in the days of your **y**, Ezk 16:60
Egypt; they played the whore in their **y**; Ezk 23:3
for in her **y** men had lain with her and Ezk 23:8
remembering the days of her **y**, Ezk 23:19
you longed for the lewdness of your **y**, Ezk 23:21
she shall answer as in the days of her **y**, Hos 2:15
sackcloth for the bridegroom of her **y**. Jl 1:8
of the soil, for a man sold me in my **y**.' Zec 13:5
between you and the wife of your **y**, Mal 2:14
of you be faithless to the wife of your **y**. Mal 2:15
all these I have kept from my **y**." Mk 10:20
said, "All these I have kept from my **y**." Lk 18:21
And they took the **y** away alive, and Acts 20:12
"My manner of life from my **y**, spent Acts 26:4
Let no one despise you for your **y**, but 1 Tm 4:12

YOUTHFUL (3)
His bones are full of his **y** vigor, but it Jb 20:11
let him return to the days of his **y** vigor'; Jb 33:25
So flee **y** passions and pursue 2 Tm 2:22

YOUTHS (8)
the simple, I have perceived among the **y**, Prv 7:7
Even **y** shall faint and be weary, and Is 40:30
their **y** be struck down by the sword in Jer 18:21
y without blemish, of good appearance Dn 1:4
worse condition than the **y** who are of Dn 1:10
the appearance of the **y** who eat the Dn 1:13
in flesh than all the **y** who ate the king's Dn 1:15
As for these four **y**, God gave them Dn 1:17

Z

ZAANAN (1)
the inhabitants of **Z** do not come out; Mi 1:11

ZAANANNIM (2)
ran from Heleph, from the oak in **Z**, Jos 19:33
his tent as far away as the oak in **Z**, Jgs 4:11

ZAAVAN (2)
the sons of Ezer: Bilhan, **Z**, and Akan. Gn 36:27
sons of Ezer: Bilhan, **Z**, and Akan. 1 Chr 1:42

ZABAD (8)
Nathan, and Nathan fathered **Z**. 1 Chr 2:36
Z fathered Ephlal, and Ephlal 1 Chr 2:37
Z his son, Shuthelah his son, and 1 Chr 7:21
Uriah the Hittite, **Z** the son of Ahlai, 1 Chr 11:41
against him were **Z** the son of 2 Chr 24:26
Mattaniah, Jeremoth, **Z**, and Aziza. Ezr 10:27
Mattenai, Mattattah, **Z**, Eliphelet, Ezr 10:33
Jeiel, Mattithiah, **Z**, Zebina, Jaddai, Ezr 10:43

ZABBAI (2)
Jehohanan, Hananiah, **Z**, and Athlai. Ezr 10:28
the son of **Z** repaired another section Neh 3:20

ZABDI (6)
for Achan the son of Carmi, son of **Z**, Jos 7:1
man by man, and **Z** was taken. Jos 7:17
and Achan the son of Carmi, son of **Z**, Jos 7:18
Jakim, Zichri, **Z**, 1 Chr 8:19
wine cellars was **Z** the Shiphmite. 1 Chr 27:27
Mattaniah the son of Mica, son of **Z**, Neh 11:17

ZABDIEL (2)
the son of **Z** was in charge 1 Chr 27:2
their overseer was **Z** the son of Neh 11:14

ZABUD (1)
Z the son of Nathan was priest and 1 Kgs 4:5

ZACCAI (2)
The sons of **Z**, 760. Ezr 2:9
The sons of **Z**, 760. Neh 7:14

ZACCHAEUS (3)
And there was a man named **Z**. He was a Lk 19:2
said to him, "**Z**, hurry and come down, Lk 19:5
And **Z** stood and said to the Lord, Lk 19:8

ZACCUR (10)
of Reuben, Shammua the son of **Z**; Nm 13:4
Hammuel his son, **Z** his son, Shimei 1 Chr 4:26
Jaaziah, Beno, Shoham, **Z** and Ibri. 1 Chr 24:27
Z, Joseph, Nethaniah, and Asharelah, 1 Chr 25:2
the third to **Z**, his sons and his 1 Chr 25:10
Of the sons of Bigvai, Uthai and **Z**, and Ezr 8:14
And next to them **Z** the son of Imri Neh 3:2
Z, Sherebiah, Shebaniah, Neh 10:12
Mattaniah, son of Micaiah, son of **Z**, Neh 12:35
as their assistant Hanan the son of **Z**, Neh 13:13

ZADOK (54)
and **Z** the son of Ahitub and 2 Sm 8:17
Z came also with all the Levites, 2 Sm 15:24
Then the king said to **Z**, "Carry the 2 Sm 15:25
The king also said to **Z** the priest, 2 Sm 15:27
So **Z** and Abiathar carried the ark of 2 Sm 15:29
Are not **Z** and Abiathar the priests 2 Sm 15:35
tell it to **Z** and Abiathar the priests. 2 Sm 15:35
Hushai said to **Z** and Abiathar the 2 Sm 17:15
Then Ahimaaz the son of **Z** said, 2 Sm 18:19
Ahimaaz the son of **Z** said again to 2 Sm 18:22
Ahimaaz the son of **Z**." And the king 2 Sm 18:27
this message to **Z** and Abiathar the 2 Sm 19:11
and **Z** and Abiathar were priests; 2 Sm 20:25
But **Z** the priest and Benaiah the son of 1 Kgs 1:8
me, your servant, and **Z** the priest, 1 Kgs 1:26
David said, "Call to me **Z** the priest, 1 Kgs 1:32
And let **Z** the priest and Nathan the 1 Kgs 1:34
So **Z** the priest, Nathan the prophet, 1 Kgs 1:38
There **Z** the priest took the horn of oil 1 Kgs 1:39
king has sent with him **Z** the priest, 1 Kgs 1:44
And **Z** the priest and Nathan the 1 Kgs 1:45
and the king put **Z** the priest in the 1 Kgs 2:35
Azariah the son of **Z** was the priest; 1 Kgs 4:2
the army; **Z** and Abiathar were priests; 1 Kgs 4:4
name was Jerusha the daughter of **Z**. 2 Kgs 15:33
Ahitub fathered **Z**, Zadok fathered 1 Chr 6:8
fathered Zadok, **Z** fathered Ahimaaz, 1 Chr 6:8
Ahitub fathered **Z**, Zadok fathered 1 Chr 6:12
fathered Zadok, **Z** fathered Shallum, 1 Chr 6:12
Z his son, Ahimaaz his son. 1 Chr 6:53
Hilkiah, son of Meshullam, son of **Z**, 1 Chr 9:11
Z, a young man mighty in valor, 1 Chr 12:28
the priests **Z** and Abiathar, 1 Chr 15:11
And he left **Z** the priest and his 1 Chr 16:39
and **Z** the son of Ahitub and 1 Chr 18:16
With the help of **Z** of the sons of 1 Chr 24:3
and the princes and **Z** the priest and 1 Chr 24:6
of King David, **Z**, Ahimelech, 1 Chr 24:31
the son of Kemuel; for Aaron, **Z**; 1 Chr 27:17
prince for the LORD, and **Z** as priest. 1 Chr 29:22
was Jerushah the daughter of **Z**. 2 Chr 27:1
priest, who was of the house of **Z**, 2 Chr 31:10
son of Shallum, son of **Z**, son of Ahitub, Ezr 7:2
And next to them **Z** the son of Baana Neh 3:4
After them **Z** the son of Immer repaired Neh 3:29
Meshezabel, **Z**, Jaddua, Neh 10:21
Hilkiah, son of Meshullam, son of **Z**, Neh 11:11
Shelemiah the priest, **Z** the scribe, Neh 13:13
These are the sons of **Z**, who alone Ezk 40:46
the Levitical priests of the family of **Z**, Ezk 43:19
the Levitical priests, the sons of **Z**, Ezk 44:15
the consecrated priests, the sons of **Z**, Ezk 48:11
and Azor the father of **Z**, and Zadok the Mt 1:14

of Zadok, and **Z** the father of Achim, Mt 1:14

ZADOK'S (1)
are with them there, Ahimaaz, **Z** son, 2 Sm 15:36

ZAHAM (1)
him sons, Jeush, Shemariah, and **Z**. 2 Chr 11:19

ZAIR (1)
Joram passed over to **Z** with all his 2 Kgs 8:21

ZALAPH (1)
sixth son of **Z** repaired another section. Neh 3:30

ZALMON (3)
And Abimelech went up to Mount **Z**, he Jgs 9:48
Z the Ahohite, Maharai of 2 Sm 23:28
scatters kings there, let snow fall on **Z**. Ps 68:14

ZALMONAH (2)
from Mount Hor and camped at **Z**. Nm 33:41
they set out from **Z** and camped at Nm 33:42

ZALMUNNA (12)
and I am pursuing after Zebah and **Z**, Jgs 8:5
hands of Zebah and **Z** already in your Jgs 8:6
has given Zebah and **Z** into my hand, Jgs 8:7
Now Zebah and **Z** were in Karkor with Jgs 8:10
And Zebah and **Z** fled, and he pursued Jgs 8:12
the two kings of Midian, Zebah and **Z**, Jgs 8:12
Succoth and said, "Behold Zebah and **Z**, Jgs 8:15
hands of Zebah and **Z** already in your Jgs 8:15
Then he said to Zebah and **Z**, "Where Jgs 8:18
Then Zebah and **Z** said, "Rise yourself Jgs 8:21
Gideon arose and killed Zebah and **Z**, Jgs 8:21
Zeeb, all their princes like Zebah and **Z**, Ps 83:11

ZAMZUMMIM (1)
—but the Ammonites call them **Z**— Dt 2:20

ZANOAH (5)
Z, En-gannim, Tappuah, Enam, Jos 15:34
Jezreel, Jokdeam, **Z**, Jos 15:56
of Soco, and Jekuthiel the father of **Z**. 1 Chr 4:18
the inhabitants of **Z** repaired the Neh 3:13
Z, Adullam, and their villages, Neh 11:30

ZAPHENATH-PANEAH (1)
And Pharaoh called Joseph's name **Z**. Gn 41:45

ZAPHON (2)
Beth-nimrah, Succoth, and **Z**, Jos 13:27
and they crossed to **Z** and said to Jgs 12:1

ZAREPHATH (4)
"Arise, go to **Z**, which belongs to 1 Kgs 17:9
So he arose and went to **Z**. And when 1 Kgs 17:10
the land of the Canaanites as far as **Z**, Ob 1:20
was sent to none of them but only to **Z**, Lk 4:26

ZARETHAN (3)
away, at Adam, the city that is beside **Z**, Jos 3:16
that is beside **Z** below Jezreel, 1 Kgs 4:12
clay ground between Succoth and **Z**. 1 Kgs 7:46

ZATTU (5)
The sons of **Z**, 945. Ezr 2:8
Of the sons of **Z**, Shecaniah the son of Ezr 8:5
Of the sons of **Z**: Elioenai, Eliashib, Ezr 10:27
The sons of **Z**, 845. Neh 7:13
Parosh, Pahath-moab, Elam, **Z**, Bani, Neh 10:14

ZAZA (1)
The sons of Jonathan: Peleth and **Z**. 1 Chr 2:33

ZEAL (19)
them down in his **z** for the people of 2 Sm 21:2
and see my **z** for the LORD." So he had 2 Kgs 10:16
The **z** of the LORD will do this. 2 Kgs 19:31
For **z** for your house has consumed me, Ps 69:9
My **z** consumes me, because my foes Ps 119:139
The **z** of the LORD of hosts will do this. Is 9:7
Let them see your **z** for your people, and Is 26:11
The **z** of the LORD of hosts will do this. Is 37:32
man, like a man of war he stirs up his **z**; Is 42:13
and wrapped himself in **z** as a cloak. Is 59:17
Where are your **z** and your might? Is 63:15
"**Z** for your house will consume me." Jn 2:17
witness that they have a **z** for God, Rom 10:2
generosity; the one who leads, with **z**; Rom 12:8
Do not be slothful in **z**, be fervent in Rom 12:11
your mourning, your **z** for me, 2 Cor 7:7
what fear, what longing, what **z**, 2 Cor 7:11
And your **z** has stirred up most of 2 Cor 9:2
as to **z**, a persecutor of the church; as to Phil 3:6

ZEALOT (2)
and Simon who was called the **Z**, Lk 6:15
and Simon the **Z** and Judas the Acts 1:13

ZEALOUS (6)
believed. They are all **z** for the law, Acts 21:20
being **z** for God as all of you are this Acts 22:3
so extremely **z** was I for the traditions of Gal 1:14
possession who are **z** for good works. Ti 2:14
harm you if you are **z** for what is good? 1 Pt 3:13
and discipline, so be **z** and repent. Rv 3:19

ZEALOUSLY (1)
them, the more **z** they proclaimed it. Mk 7:36

ZEBADIAH (9)
Z, Arad, Eder, 1 Chr 8:15
Z, Meshullam, Hizki, Heber, 1 Chr 8:17
And Joelah and **Z**, the sons of 1 Chr 12:7
Jediael the second, **Z** the third, 1 Chr 26:2
month, and his son **Z** after him; 1 Chr 27:7
Shemaiah, Nethaniah, **Z**, Asahel, 2 Chr 17:8
and **Z** the son of Ishmael, the 2 Chr 19:11
sons of Shephatiah, **Z** the son of Michael, Ezr 8:8
Of the sons of Immer: Hanani and **Z**. Ezr 10:20

ZEBAH (12)
I am pursuing after **Z** and Zalmunna, Jgs 8:5
the hands of **Z** and Zalmunna already Jgs 8:6
the LORD has given **Z** and Zalmunna into Jgs 8:7
Now **Z** and Zalmunna were in Karkor Jgs 8:10
And **Z** and Zalmunna fled, and he Jgs 8:12
two kings of Midian, **Z** and Zalmunna, Jgs 8:12
and said, "Behold **Z** and Zalmunna, Jgs 8:15
the hands of **Z** and Zalmunna already Jgs 8:15
Then he said to **Z** and Zalmunna, Jgs 8:18
Then **Z** and Zalmunna said, "Rise Jgs 8:21
arose and killed **Z** and Zalmunna, Jgs 8:21
all their princes like **Z** and Zalmunna, Ps 83:11

ZEBEDEE (12)
James the son of **Z** and John his brother, Mt 4:21
brother, in the boat with **Z** their father, Mt 4:21
James the son of **Z**, and John his brother; Mt 10:2
mother of the sons of **Z** came up to him Mt 20:20
with him Peter and the two sons of **Z**, Mt 26:37
Joseph and the mother of the sons of **Z**. Mt 27:56
James the son of **Z** and John his Mk 1:19
they left their father **Z** in the boat with Mk 1:20
James the son of **Z** and John the brother Mk 3:17
And James and John, the sons of **Z**, Mk 10:35
so also were James and John, sons of **Z**, Lk 5:10
of Cana in Galilee, the sons of **Z**, Jn 21:2

ZEBIDAH (1)
mother's name was **Z** the daughter 2 Kgs 23:36

ZEBINA (1)
Jeiel, Mattithiah, Zabad, **Z**, Jaddai, Joel, Ezr 10:43

ZEBOIIM (5)
of Sodom, Gomorrah, Admah, and **Z**, Gn 10:19
king of Admah, Shemeber king of **Z**, Gn 14:2
the king of Admah, the king of **Z**, Gn 14:8
Sodom and Gomorrah, Admah, and **Z**, Dt 29:23
Admah? How can I treat you like **Z**? Hos 11:8

ZEBOIM (2)
the valley of **Z** toward the wilderness. 1 Sm 13:18
Hadid, **Z**, Neballat, Neh 11:34

ZEBUL (6)
of Jerubbaal, and is not **Z** his officer? Jgs 9:28
When **Z** the ruler of the city heard the Jgs 9:30
when Gaal saw the people, he said to **Z**, Jgs 9:36
the mountaintops!" And **Z** said to him, Jgs 9:36
Then **Z** said to him, "Where is your Jgs 9:38
and **Z** drove out Gaal and his relatives, Jgs 9:41

ZEBULUN (48)
six sons." So she called his name **Z**. Gn 30:20
Simeon, Levi, Judah, Issachar, and **Z**. Gn 35:23
The sons of **Z**: Sered, Elon, and Jahleel. Gn 46:14
"**Z** shall dwell at the shore of the sea; he Gn 49:13
Issachar, **Z**, and Benjamin, Ex 1:3
from **Z**, Eliab the son of Helon; Nm 1:9
Of the people of **Z**, their generations, by Nm 1:30
those listed of the tribe of **Z** were 57,400. Nm 1:31
Then the tribe of **Z**, the chief of the Nm 2:7
of the people of **Z** being Eliab the son Nm 2:7
of Helon, the chief of the people of **Z**: Nm 7:24
of the people of **Z** was Eliab the son Nm 10:16
from the tribe of **Z**, Gaddiel the son of Nm 13:10
The sons of **Z**, according to their Nm 26:26
Of the tribe of the people of **Z** a chief, Nm 34:25
Reuben, Gad, Asher, **Z**, Dan, and Dt 27:13
And of **Z** he said, "Rejoice, Zebulun, in Dt 33:18
he said, "Rejoice, **Z**, in your going out, Dt 33:18
third lot came up for the people of **Z**, Jos 19:10
is the inheritance of the people of **Z**, Jos 19:16
and touches **Z** and the Valley of Jos 19:27
touching **Z** at the south and Asher on Jos 19:34
the tribe of Gad, and the tribe of **Z**, Jos 21:7
clans, were given out of the tribe of **Z**, Jos 21:34
Z did not drive out the inhabitants of Jgs 1:30
the people of Naphtali and the people of **Z**. Jgs 4:6
And Barak called out **Z** and Naphtali to Jgs 4:10
and from **Z** those who bear the Jgs 5:14
Z is a people who risked their lives to the Jgs 5:18
messengers to Asher, **Z**, and Naphtali, Jgs 6:35
was buried at Aijalon in the land of **Z**. Jgs 12:12
Simeon, Levi, Judah, Issachar, **Z**, 1 Chr 2:1
of the tribes of Reuben, Gad and **Z**. 1 Chr 6:63
were allotted out of the tribe of **Z**: 1 Chr 6:77
Of **Z** 50,000 seasoned troops, 1 Chr 12:33
far as Issachar and **Z** and Naphtali, 1 Chr 12:40
for **Z**, Ishmaiah the son of Obadiah; 1 Chr 27:19
and Manasseh, and as far as **Z**, 2 Chr 30:10
and of **Z** humbled themselves and 2 Chr 30:11
Manasseh, Issachar, and **Z**, 2 Chr 30:18
Judah in their throng, the princes of **Z**, Ps 68:27
into contempt the land of **Z** and the land of Is 9:1
the east side to the west, **Z**, one portion. Ezk 48:26
Adjoining the territory of **Z**, from the Ezk 48:27
the gate of Issachar, and the gate of **Z**. Ezk 48:33
sea, in the territory of **Z** and Naphtali, Mt 4:13
"The land of **Z** and the land of Naphtali, Mt 4:15
12,000 from the tribe of **Z**, 12,000 from the Rv 7:8

ZEBULUNITE (2)
After him Elon the **Z** judged Israel, and Jgs 12:11
Then Elon the **Z** died and was buried at Jgs 12:12

ZEBULUNITES (1)
the clans of the **Z** as they were listed, Nm 26:27

ZECHARIAH (54)
and **Z** his son reigned in his place. 2 Kgs 14:29
Z the son of Jeroboam reigned over 2 Kgs 15:8
Now the rest of the deeds of **Z**, 2 Kgs 15:11
name was Abi the daughter of **Z**. 2 Kgs 18:2
was recorded: the chief, Jeiel, and **Z**, 1 Chr 5:7
Z the son of Meshelemiah was 1 Chr 9:21
Gedor, Ahio, **Z**, and Mikloth; 1 Chr 9:37
of the second order, **Z**, Jaaziel, 1 Chr 15:18
Z, Aziel, Shemiramoth, Jehiel, Unni, 1 Chr 15:20
Nethanel, Amasai, **Z**, Benaiah, 1 Chr 15:24
the chief, and second to him were **Z**, 1 Chr 16:5
Isshiah; of the sons of Isshiah, **Z**. 1 Chr 24:25
Z the firstborn, Jediael the second, 1 Chr 26:2
Tebaliah the third, **Z** the fourth: 1 Chr 26:11
They cast lots also for his son **Z**, a 1 Chr 26:14
in Gilead, Iddo the son of **Z**; 1 Chr 27:21
Ben-hail, Obadiah, **Z**, Nethanel, 2 Chr 17:7
came upon Jahaziel the son of **Z**, 2 Chr 20:14
Azariah, Jehiel, **Z**, Azariah, Michael, 2 Chr 21:2
Spirit of God clothed **Z** the son of 2 Chr 24:20
himself to seek God in the days of **Z**, 2 Chr 26:5
name was Abijah the daughter of **Z**. 2 Chr 29:1
the sons of Asaph, **Z** and Mattaniah; 2 Chr 29:13
of Merari, and **Z** and Meshullam, 2 Chr 34:12
Hilkiah, **Z**, and Jehiel, the chief 2 Chr 35:8
prophets, Haggai and **Z** the son of Iddo, Ezr 5:1
Haggai the prophet and **Z** the son of Ezr 6:14
Z, with whom were registered 150 men. Ezr 8:3
Of the sons of Bebai, **Z**, the son of Bebai, Ezr 8:11
Elnathan, Nathan, **Z**, and Meshullam, Ezr 8:16
Mattaniah, **Z**, Jehiel, Abdi, Jeremoth, Ezr 10:26
Z, and Meshullam on his left hand. Neh 8:4
Athaiah the son of Uzziah, son of **Z**, Neh 11:4
son of Adaiah, son of Joiarib, son of **Z**, Neh 11:5
son of Pelaliah, son of Amzi, son of **Z**, Neh 11:12
of Iddo, **Z**; of Ginnethon, Meshullam; Neh 12:16
Z the son of Jonathan, son of Neh 12:35
Micaiah, Elioenai, **Z**, and Hananiah, Neh 12:41
Uriah the priest and **Z** the son of Is 8:2
word of the LORD came to the prophet **Z**, Zec 1:1
word of the LORD came to the prophet **Z**, Zec 1:7
of the LORD came to **Z** on the fourth day Zec 7:1
And the word of the LORD came to **Z**, Zec 7:8
to the blood of **Z** the son of Barachiah, Mt 23:35
king of Judea, there was a priest named **Z**, Lk 1:5
And **Z** was troubled when he saw him, Lk 1:12
Z, for your prayer has been heard, Lk 1:13
And **Z** said to the angel, "How shall I Lk 1:18
And the people were waiting for **Z**, and Lk 1:21
the house of **Z** and greeted Elizabeth. Lk 1:40
would have called him **Z** after his father, Lk 1:59
And his father **Z** was filled with the Holy Lk 1:67
to John the son of **Z** in the wilderness. Lk 3:2
the blood of Abel to the blood of **Z**, Lk 11:51

ZECHARIAH'S (1)
the kindness that Jehoiada, **Z** father, 2 Chr 24:22

ZECHER (1)
Gedor, Ahio, **Z**, 1 Chr 8:31

ZEDAD (2)
the limit of the border shall be at **Z**. Nm 34:8
Hethlon to Lebo-hamath, and on to **Z**, Ezk 47:15

ZEDEKIAH (64)
And **Z** the son of Chenaanah made 1 Kgs 22:11
Then **Z** the son of Chenaanah came 1 Kgs 22:24
place, and changed his name to **Z**. 2 Kgs 24:17
Z was twenty-one years old when he 2 Kgs 24:18
And **Z** rebelled against the king of 2 Kgs 24:20
till the eleventh year of King **Z**. 2 Kgs 25:2

ZIBEON (8)
of Anah the daughter of **Z** the Hivite, Gn 36:2
daughter of Anah the daughter of **Z**, Gn 36:14
of the land: Lotan, Shobal, **Z**, Anah, Gn 36:20
These are the sons of **Z**: Aiah and Gn 36:24
he pastured the donkeys of **Z** his father. Gn 36:24
the chiefs Lotan, Shobal, **Z**, Anah, Gn 36:29
Lotan, Shobal, **Z**, Anah, Dishon, 1 Chr 1:38
The sons of **Z**: Aiah and Anah. 1 Chr 1:40

ZIBIA (1)
his wife: Jobab, **Z**, Mesha, Malcam, 1 Chr 8:9

ZIBIAH (2)
mother's name was **Z** of Beersheba. 2 Kgs 12:1
mother's name was **Z** of Beersheba. 2 Chr 24:1

ZICHRI (12)
The sons of Izhar: Korah, Nepheg, and **Z**. Ex 6:21
Jakim, **Z**, Zabdi, 1 Chr 8:19
Abdon, **Z**, Hanan, 1 Chr 8:23
and **Z** were the sons of Jeroham. 1 Chr 8:27
Mattaniah the son of Mica, son of **Z**, 1 Chr 9:15
and his son Joram, and his son **Z**, 1 Chr 26:25
Eliezer the son of **Z** was chief officer; 1 Chr 27:16
next to him Amasiah the son of **Z**, 2 Chr 17:16
Adaiah, and Elishaphat the son of **Z**. 2 Chr 23:1
And **Z**, a mighty man of Ephraim, 2 Chr 28:7
Joel the son of **Z** was their overseer; and Neh 11:9
of Abijah, **Z**; of Miniamin, of Neh 12:17

ZIDDIM (1)
The fortified cities are **Z**, Zer, Jos 19:35

ZIHA (3)
the sons of **Z**, the sons of Hasupha, the Ezr 2:43
the sons of **Z**, the sons of Hasupha, the Neh 7:46
and **Z** and Gishpa were over the Neh 11:21

ZIKLAG (15)
Z, Madmannah, Sansannah, Jos 15:31
Z, Beth-marcaboth, Hazar-susah, Jos 19:5
So that day Achish gave him **Z**. 1 Sm 27:6
Therefore **Z** has belonged to the kings 1 Sm 27:6
his men came to **Z** on the third day, 1 Sm 30:1
raid against the Negeb and against **Z**. 1 Sm 30:1
They had overcome **Z** and burned it 1 Sm 30:1
of Caleb, and we burned **Z** with fire." 1 Sm 30:14
When David came to **Z**, he sent part 1 Sm 30:26
David remained two days in **Z**. 2 Sm 1:1
news, I seized him and killed him at **Z**, 2 Sm 4:10
Bethuel, Hormah, **Z**, 1 Chr 4:30
are the men who came to David at **Z**, 1 Chr 12:1
As he went to **Z**, these men of 1 Chr 12:20
in **Z**, in Meconah and its villages, Neh 11:28

ZILLAH (3)
was Adah, and the name of the other **Z**. Gn 4:19
Z also bore Tubal-cain; he was the Gn 4:22
his wives: "Adah and **Z**, hear my voice; Gn 4:23

ZILLETHAI (2)
Elienai, **Z**, Eliel, 1 Chr 8:20
Michael, Jozabad, Elihu, and **Z**, 1 Chr 12:20

ZILPAH (7)
his female servant **Z** to his daughter Gn 29:24
she took her servant **Z** and gave her to Gn 30:9
Then Leah's servant **Z** bore Jacob a Gn 30:10
Leah's servant **Z** bore Jacob a second Gn 30:12
The sons of **Z**, Leah's servant: Gad and Gn 35:26
was a boy with the sons of Bilhah and **Z**, Gn 37:2
These are the sons of **Z**, whom Laban Gn 46:18

ZIMMAH (3)
his son, Jahath his son, **Z** his son, 1 Chr 6:20
son of Ethan, son of **Z**, son of Shimei, 1 Chr 6:42
of the Gershonites, Joah the son of **Z**, 2 Chr 29:12

ZIMRAN (2)
She bore him **Z**, Jokshan, Medan, Gn 25:2
she bore **Z**, Jokshan, Medan, Midian, 1 Chr 1:32

ZIMRI (15)
woman, was **Z** the son of Salu, Nm 25:14
But his servant **Z**, commander of half 1 Kgs 16:9
Z came in and struck him down 1 Kgs 16:10
Thus **Z** destroyed all the house of 1 Kgs 16:12
Z reigned seven days in Tirzah. 1 Kgs 16:15
heard it said, "**Z** has conspired, 1 Kgs 16:16
And when **Z** saw that the city was 1 Kgs 16:18
Now the rest of the acts of **Z**, and the 1 Kgs 16:20
the gate, she said, "Is it peace, you **Z**, 2 Kgs 9:31
Z, Ethan, Heman, Calcol, and Dara, 1 Chr 2:6
fathered Alemeth, Azmaveth, and **Z**. 1 Chr 8:36
and Zimri. **Z** fathered Moza. 1 Chr 8:36
fathered Alemeth, Azmaveth, and **Z**. 1 Chr 9:42
and Zimri. And **Z** fathered Moza. 1 Chr 9:42
all the kings of **Z**, all the kings of Elam, Jer 25:25

ZIN (10)
from the wilderness of **Z** to Rehob, Nm 13:21
into the wilderness of **Z** in the first Nm 20:1
the wilderness of **Z** when the Nm 27:14
of Kadesh in the wilderness of **Z**.) Nm 27:14
camped in the wilderness of **Z** (that is, Nm 33:36
the wilderness of **Z** alongside Edom, Nm 34:3
ascent of Akrabbim, and cross to **Z**, Nm 34:4
Meribah-kadesh, in the wilderness of **Z**, Dt 32:51
to the wilderness of **Z** at the farthest Jos 15:1
ascent of Akrabbim, passes along to **Z**, Jos 15:3

ZINA (1)
Jahath, **Z**, and Jeush and Beriah. 1 Chr 23:10

ZION (161)
David took the stronghold of **Z**, 2 Sm 5:7
out of the city of David, which is **Z**. 1 Kgs 8:1
you—the virgin daughter of **Z**; 2 Kgs 19:21
and out of Mount **Z** a band of 2 Kgs 19:31
David took the stronghold of **Z**, 1 Chr 11:5
out of the city of David, which is **Z**. 2 Chr 5:2
"As for me, I have set my King on **Z**, my Ps 2:6
to the LORD, who sits enthroned in **Z**! Ps 9:11
of the daughter of **Z** I may rejoice in Ps 9:14
salvation for Israel would come out of **Z**! Ps 14:7
sanctuary and give you support from **Z**! Ps 20:2
is the joy of all the earth, Mount **Z**, Ps 48:2
Let Mount **Z** be glad! Let the daughters Ps 48:11
Walk about **Z**, go around her, number Ps 48:12
Out of **Z**, the perfection of beauty, God Ps 50:2
Do good to **Z** in your good pleasure; Ps 51:18
salvation for Israel would come out of **Z**! Ps 53:6
Praise is due to you, O God, in **Z**, and to Ps 65:1
For God will save **Z** and build up the Ps 69:35
Remember Mount **Z**, where you have Ps 74:2
in Salem, his dwelling place in **Z**. Ps 76:2
he chose the tribe of Judah, Mount **Z**, Ps 78:68
in whose heart are the highways to **Z**. Ps 84:5
each one appears before God in **Z**. Ps 84:7
loves the gates of **Z** more than all the Ps 87:2
And of **Z** it shall be said, "This one and Ps 87:5
Z hears and is glad, and the daughters of Ps 97:8
The LORD is great in **Z**; he is exalted over Ps 99:2
You will arise and have pity on **Z**; it is Ps 102:13
For the LORD builds up **Z**; he appears Ps 102:16
they may declare in **Z** the name of the Ps 102:21
sends forth from **Z** your mighty scepter. Ps 110:2
who trust in the LORD are like Mount **Z**, Ps 125:1
the LORD restored the fortunes of **Z**, Ps 126:1
The LORD bless you from **Z**! May you Ps 128:5
May all who hate **Z** be put to shame Ps 129:5
For the LORD has chosen **Z**; he has Ps 132:13
which falls on the mountains of **Z**! Ps 133:3
May the LORD bless you from **Z**, he who Ps 134:3
Blessed be the LORD from **Z**, he who Ps 135:21
and wept, when we remembered **Z**. Ps 137:1
saying, "Sing us one of the songs of **Z**!" Ps 137:3
LORD will reign forever, your God, O **Z**, Ps 146:10
O Jerusalem! Praise your God, O **Z**! Ps 147:12
let the children of **Z** rejoice in their Ps 149:2
Go out, O daughters of **Z**, and look upon Sg 3:11
And the daughter of **Z** is left like a booth in Is 1:8
Z shall be redeemed by justice, and those Is 1:27
in his paths." For out of **Z** shall go the law, Is 2:3
the daughters of **Z** are haughty and Is 3:16
a scab the heads of the daughters of **Z**, Is 3:17
who is left in **Z** and remains in Jerusalem Is 4:3
of the daughters of **Z** and cleansed the Is 4:4
whole site of Mount **Z** and over her Is 4:5
the LORD of hosts, who dwells on Mount **Z**. Is 8:18
his work on Mount **Z** and on Jerusalem, Is 10:12
"O my people, who dwell in **Z**, be not Is 10:24
fist at the mount of the daughter of **Z**, Is 10:32
Shout, and sing for joy, O inhabitant of **Z**, Is 12:6
"The LORD has founded **Z**, and in her the Is 14:32
desert, to the mount of the daughter of **Z**. Is 16:1
whose land the rivers divide, to Mount **Z**, Is 18:7
reigns on Mount **Z** and in Jerusalem, Is 24:23
one who has laid as a foundation in **Z**, Is 28:16
nations be that fight against Mount **Z**. Is 29:8
For a people shall dwell in **Z**, in Is 30:19
down to fight on Mount **Z** and on its hill. Is 31:4
declares the LORD, whose fire is in **Z**, Is 31:9
he will fill **Z** with justice and Is 33:5
The sinners in **Z** are afraid; trembling Is 33:14
Behold **Z**, the city of our appointed Is 33:20
a year of recompense for the cause of **Z**. Is 34:8
shall return and come to **Z** with singing; Is 35:10
scorns you—the virgin daughter of **Z**; Is 37:22
and out of Mount **Z** a band of survivors. Is 37:32
Get you up to a high mountain, O **Z**, Is 40:9
I was the first to say to **Z**, "Behold, here Is 41:27
I will put salvation in **Z**, for Israel my Is 46:13
But **Z** said, "The LORD has forsaken me; Is 49:14
For the LORD comforts **Z**; he comforts all Is 51:3
shall return and come to **Z** with singing; Is 51:11
of the earth, and saying to **Z**, Is 51:16
Awake, awake, put on your strength, O **Z**; Is 52:1
from your neck, O captive daughter of **Z**. Is 52:2
who publishes salvation, who says to **Z**, Is 52:7
to eye they see the return of the LORD to **Z**. Is 52:8
"And a Redeemer will come to **Z**, to those Is 59:20
the LORD, the **Z** of the Holy One of Israel. Is 60:14
to those who mourn in **Z**—to give them a Is 61:3
Say to the daughter of **Z**, "Behold, your Is 62:11
Z has become a wilderness, Jerusalem a Is 64:10
For as soon as **Z** was in labor she Is 66:8
from a family, and I will bring you to **Z**. Jer 3:14
Raise a standard toward **Z**, flee for safety, Jer 4:6
of the daughter of **Z** gasping for breath, Jer 4:31
bred I will destroy, the daughter of **Z**. Jer 6:2
for battle, against you, O daughter of **Z**!" Jer 6:23
of the land: "Is the LORD not in **Z**? Jer 8:19
For a sound of wailing is heard from **Z**: Jer 9:19
Judah? Does your soul loathe **Z**? Jer 14:19
of hosts, "'**Z** shall be plowed as a field; Jer 26:18
outcast: 'It is **Z**, for whom no one cares!' Jer 30:17
'Arise, and let us go up to **Z**, to the LORD Jer 31:6
come and sing aloud on the height of **Z**, Jer 31:12
They shall ask the way to **Z**, with faces Jer 50:5
to declare in **Z** the vengeance of the Jer 50:28
let us declare in **Z** the work of the LORD Jer 51:10
for all the evil that they have done in **Z**, Jer 51:24
Babylon," let the inhabitant of **Z** say. Jer 51:35
The roads to **Z** mourn, for none come Lam 1:4
From the daughter of **Z** all her majesty Lam 1:6
Z stretches out her hands, but there is Lam 1:17
has set the daughter of **Z** under a cloud! Lam 2:1
our eyes in the tent of the daughter of **Z**; Lam 2:4
the LORD has made **Z** forget festival and Lam 2:6
in ruins the wall of the daughter of **Z**; Lam 2:8
of the daughter of **Z** sit on the ground Lam 2:10
comfort you, O virgin daughter of **Z**? Lam 2:13
O wall of the daughter of **Z**, let tears Lam 2:18
The precious sons of **Z**, worth their Lam 4:2
kindled a fire in **Z** that consumed its Lam 4:11
of your iniquity, O daughter of **Z**, Lam 4:22
Women are raped in **Z**, young women Lam 5:11
for Mount **Z** which lies desolate; Lam 5:18
Blow a trumpet in **Z**; sound an alarm on Jl 2:1
Blow the trumpet in **Z**; consecrate a fast; Jl 2:15
"Be glad, O children of **Z**, and rejoice in Jl 2:23
For in Mount **Z** and in Jerusalem there Jl 2:32
The LORD roars from **Z**, and utters his Jl 3:16
I am the LORD your God, who dwells in **Z**, Jl 3:17
not avenged, for the LORD dwells in **Z**." Jl 3:21
"The LORD roars from **Z** and utters his Am 1:2
"Woe to those who are at ease in **Z**, and Am 6:1
But in Mount **Z** there shall be those who Ob 1:17
go up to Mount **Z** to rule Mount Esau, Ob 1:21
beginning of sin to the daughter of **Z**, Mi 1:13
who build **Z** with blood and Jerusalem Mi 3:10
because of you **Z** shall be plowed Mi 3:12
his paths." For out of **Z** shall go forth the Mi 4:2
over them in Mount **Z** from this time Mi 4:7
of the flock, hill of the daughter of **Z**, Mi 4:8
Writhe and groan, O daughter of **Z**, like Mi 4:10
be defiled, and let our eyes gaze upon **Z**." Mi 4:11
Arise and thresh, O daughter of **Z**, for I Mi 4:13
Sing aloud, O daughter of **Z**; shout, O Zep 3:14
be said to Jerusalem: "Fear not, O **Z**; Zep 3:16
jealous for Jerusalem and for **Z**. Zec 1:14
will again comfort **Z** and again choose Zec 1:17
Escape to **Z**, you who dwell with the Zec 2:7
Sing and rejoice, O daughter of **Z**, for Zec 2:10
I am jealous for **Z** with great jealousy, Zec 8:2
I have returned to **Z** and will dwell in the Zec 8:3
Rejoice greatly, O daughter of **Z**! Shout Zec 9:9
I will stir up your sons, O **Z**, against Zec 9:13
"Say to the daughter of **Z**, 'Behold, your Mt 21:5
"Fear not, daughter of **Z**; behold, your Jn 12:15
I am laying in **Z** a stone of stumbling, Rom 9:33
"The Deliverer will come from **Z**, Rom 11:26
have come to Mount **Z** and to the city Heb 12:22
"Behold, I am laying in **Z** a stone, a 1 Pt 2:6
behold, on Mount **Z** stood the Lamb, Rv 14:1

ZION'S (2)
the fear of the LORD is **Z** treasure. Is 33:6
For **Z** sake I will not keep silent, and for Is 62:1

ZIOR (1)
Kiriath-arba (that is, Hebron), and **Z**: Jos 15:54

ZIPH (10)
Z, Telem, Bealoth, Jos 15:24
Maon, Carmel, **Z**, Juttah, Jos 15:55
hill country of the Wilderness of **Z**. 1 Sm 23:14
in the Wilderness of **Z** at Horesh. 1 Sm 23:15
arose and went to **Z** ahead of Saul. 1 Sm 23:24
the wilderness of **Z** with three 1 Sm 26:2

to seek David in the wilderness of **Z**. 1 Sm 26:2
his firstborn, who fathered **Z**. 1 Chr 2:42
Z, Ziphah, Tiria, and Asarel. 1 Chr 4:16
Gath, Mareshah, **Z**, 2 Chr 11:8

ZIPHAH (1)
Jehallelel: Ziph, **Z**, Tiria, and Asarel. 1 Chr 4:16

ZIPHION (1)
Z, Haggi, Shuni, Ezbon, Eri, Arodi, and Gn 46:16

ZIPHITES (3)
Then the **Z** went up to Saul at 1 Sm 23:19
Then the **Z** came to Saul at Gibeah, 1 Sm 26:1
of David, when the **Z** went and told Saul, Ps 54:T

ZIPHRON (1)
Then the border shall extend to **Z**, and Nm 34:9

ZIPPOR (7)
Balak the son of **Z** saw all that Israel Nm 22:2
of the field." So Balak the son of **Z**, Nm 22:4
said to God, "Balak the son of **Z**, Nm 22:10
to him, "Thus says Balak the son of **Z**: Nm 22:16
and hear; give ear to me, O son of **Z**: Nm 23:18
Then Balak the son of **Z**, king of Moab, Jos 24:9
you any better than Balak the son of **Z**, Jgs 11:25

ZIPPORAH (3)
man, and he gave Moses his daughter **Z**. Ex 2:21
Then **Z** took a flint and cut off her son's Ex 4:25
Moses' father-in-law, had taken **Z**, Ex 18:2

ZIV (2)
reign over Israel, in the month of **Z**, 1 Kgs 6:1
the LORD was laid, in the month of **Z**. 1 Kgs 6:37

ZIZ (1)
will come up by the ascent of **Z**. 2 Chr 20:16

ZIZA (2)
Z the son of Shiphi, son of Allon, son 1 Chr 4:37
Abijah, Attai, **Z**, and Shelomith. 2 Chr 11:20

ZIZAH (1)
was the chief, and **Z** the second; 1 Chr 23:11

ZOAN (7)
built seven years before **Z** in Egypt.) Nm 13:22
in the land of Egypt, in the fields of **Z**. Ps 78:12
Egypt and his marvels in the fields of **Z**. Ps 78:43
The princes of **Z** are utterly foolish; the Is 19:11
The princes of **Z** have become fools, and Is 19:13
his officials are at **Z** and his envoys reach Is 30:4
will set fire to **Z** and will execute Ezk 30:14

ZOAR (10)
the land of Egypt, in the direction of **Z**. Gn 13:10
and the king of Bela (that is, **Z**). Gn 14:2
the king of Bela (that is, **Z**) went out, Gn 14:8
the name of the city was called **Z**. Gn 19:22
risen on the earth when Lot came to **Z**. Gn 19:23
Lot went up out of **Z** and lived in the Gn 19:30
for he was afraid to live in **Z**. Gn 19:30
Jericho the city of palm trees, as far as **Z**. Dt 34:3
her fugitives flee to **Z**, to Is 15:5
from **Z** to Horonaim and Jer 48:34

ZOBAH (11)
Edom, against the kings of **Z**, 1 Sm 14:47
Hadadezer the son of Rehob, king of **Z**, 2 Sm 8:3
came to help Hadadezer king of **Z**, 2 Sm 8:5
Hadadezer the son of Rehob, king of **Z**. 2 Sm 8:12
of Beth-rehob, and the Syrians of **Z**, 2 Sm 10:6
and the Syrians of **Z** and of Rehob and 2 Sm 10:8
Igal the son of Nathan of **Z**, Bani the 2 Sm 23:36
his master Hadadezer king of **Z**. 1 Kgs 11:23
came to help Hadadezer king of **Z**, 1 Chr 18:5
whole army of Hadadezer, king of **Z**, 1 Chr 18:9
from Aram-maacah and from **Z**. 1 Chr 19:6

ZOBAH-HAMATH (1)
also defeated Hadadezer king of **Z**, 1 Chr 18:3

ZOBEBAH (1)
Anub, **Z**, and the clans of Aharhel, 1 Chr 4:8

ZOHAR (4)
and entreat for me Ephron the son of **Z**, Gn 23:8
field of Ephron the son of **Z** the Hittite, Gn 25:9
Jamin, Ohad, Jachin, **Z**, and Shaul, Gn 46:10
Jamin, Ohad, Jachin, **Z**, and Shaul, Ex 6:15

ZOHETH (1)
The sons of Ishi: **Z** and Ben-zoheth. 1 Chr 4:20

ZOPHAH (2)
brother: **Z**, Imna, Shelesh, and Amal. 1 Chr 7:35
The sons of **Z**: Suah, Harnepher, 1 Chr 7:36

ZOPHAI (1)
Elkanah his son, **Z** his son, Nahath 1 Chr 6:26

ZOPHAR (4)
the Shuhite, and **Z** the Naamathite. Jb 2:11
Then **Z** the Naamathite answered and Jb 11:1
Then **Z** the Naamathite answered and Jb 20:1
the Shuhite and **Z** the Naamathite went Jb 42:9

ZOPHIM (1)
And he took him to the field of **Z**, to Nm 23:14

ZORAH (10)
in the lowland, Eshtaol, **Z**, Ashnah, Jos 15:33
territory of its inheritance included **Z**, Jos 19:41
There was a certain man of **Z**, of the Jgs 13:2
Mahaneh-dan, between **Z** and Eshtaol. Jgs 13:25
buried him between **Z** and Eshtaol in Jgs 16:31
of their tribe, from **Z** and from Eshtaol, Jgs 18:2
came to their brothers at **Z** and Eshtaol, Jgs 18:8
of war, set out from **Z** and Eshtaol, Jgs 18:11
Z, Aijalon, and Hebron, fortified 2 Chr 11:10
in En-rimmon, in **Z**, in Jarmuth, Neh 11:29

ZORATHITES (2)
these came the **Z** and the Eshtaolites. 1 Chr 2:53
Lahad. These were the clans of the **Z**. 1 Chr 4:2

ZORITES (1)
and half of the Manahathites, the **Z**. 1 Chr 2:54

ZUAR (5)
from Issachar, Nethanel the son of **Z**; Nm 1:8
of Issachar being Nethanel the son of **Z**, Nm 2:5
the second day Nethanel the son of **Z**, Nm 7:18
the offering of Nethanel the son of **Z**. Nm 7:23
of Issachar was Nethanel the son of **Z**. Nm 10:15

ZUPH (3)
son of Elihu, son of Tohu, son of **Z**, 1 Sm 1:1
When they came to the land of **Z**, Saul 1 Sm 9:5
son of **Z**, son of Elkanah, son of 1 Chr 6:35

ZUR (5)
killed was Cozbi the daughter of **Z**, Nm 25:15
rest of their slain, Evi, Rekem, **Z**, Hur, Nm 31:8
Evi and Rekem and **Z** and Hur and Jos 13:21
Abdon, then **Z**, Kish, Baal, Nadab, 1 Chr 8:30
and his firstborn son Abdon, then **Z**, 1 Chr 9:36

ZURIEL (1)
clans of Merari was **Z** the son of Nm 3:35

ZURISHADDAI (5)
from Simeon, Shelumiel the son of **Z**; Nm 1:6
Simeon being Shelumiel the son of **Z**, Nm 2:12
On the fifth day Shelumiel the son of **Z**, Nm 7:36
the offering of Shelumiel the son of **Z**. Nm 7:41
of Simeon was Shelumiel the son of **Z**. Nm 10:19

ZUZIM (1)
in Ashteroth-karnaim, the **Z** in Ham, Gn 14:5

NUMERALS

10 (13)
one golden dish of **10** shekels, full of Nm 7:14
one golden dish of **10** shekels, full of Nm 7:20
one golden dish of **10** shekels, full of Nm 7:26
one golden dish of **10** shekels, full of Nm 7:32
one golden dish of **10** shekels, full of Nm 7:38
one golden dish of **10** shekels, full of Nm 7:44
one golden dish of **10** shekels, full of Nm 7:50
one golden dish of **10** shekels, full of Nm 7:56
one golden dish of **10** shekels, full of Nm 7:62
one golden dish of **10** shekels, full of Nm 7:68
one golden dish of **10** shekels, full of Nm 7:74
one golden dish of **10** shekels, full of Nm 7:80
weighing **10** shekels apiece according to Nm 7:86

12 (1)
a sin offering for all Israel **12** male goats, Ezr 6:17

18 (1)
with his sons and kinsmen, **18**; Ezr 8:18

20 (2)
with his kinsmen and their sons, **20**; Ezr 8:19
20 bowls of gold worth 1,000 darics, Ezr 8:27

28 (1)
the son of Bebai, and with him **28** men. Ezr 8:11

29 (2)
When Nahor had lived **29** years, he Gn 11:24
of gold, 1,000 basins of silver, **29** censers, Ezr 1:9

30 (7)
50 cubits, and its height **30** cubits. Gn 6:15
When Shelah had lived **30** years, he Gn 11:14
When Peleg had lived **30** years, he Gn 11:18
When Serug had lived **30** years, he Gn 11:22
30 basins of gold, 1,000 basins of silver, Ezr 1:9
30 bowls of gold, 410 bowls of silver, and Ezr 1:10
30 priests' garments and 500 minas of Neh 7:70

32 (2)
When Reu had lived **32** years, he Gn 11:20
the LORD'S tribute was **32** persons. Nm 31:40

34 (1)
When Eber had lived **34** years, he Gn 11:16

35 (1)
When Arpachshad had lived **35** years, Gn 11:12

42 (2)
The sons of Azmaveth, **42**. Ezr 2:24
The men of Beth-azmaveth, **42**. Neh 7:28

50 (5)
the ark 300 cubits, its breadth **50** cubits, Gn 6:15
Israel's half Moses took one of every **50**, Nm 31:47
and a bar of gold weighing **50** shekels, Jos 7:21
son of Jonathan, and with him **50** men. Ezr 8:6
treasury 1,000 darics of gold, **50** basins, Neh 7:70

52 (2)
The sons of Nebo, **52**. Ezr 2:29
The men of the other Nebo, **52**. Neh 7:33

56 (1)
The men of Netophah, **56**. Ezr 2:22

60 (1)
and Shemaiah, and with them **60** men. Ezr 8:13

61 (1)
of which the LORD'S tribute was **61**. Nm 31:39

65 (2)
When Mahalalel had lived **65** years, he Gn 5:15
When Enoch had lived **65** years, he Gn 5:21

67 (1)
of silver, and **67** priests' garments. Neh 7:72

70 (18)
When Kenan had lived **70** years, he Gn 5:12
When Terah had lived **70** years, he Gn 11:26
shekels, one silver basin of **70** shekels, Nm 7:13
shekels, one silver basin of **70** shekels, Nm 7:19
shekels, one silver basin of **70** shekels, Nm 7:25
shekels, one silver basin of **70** shekels, Nm 7:31
shekels, one silver basin of **70** shekels, Nm 7:37
shekels, one silver basin of **70** shekels, Nm 7:43
shekels, one silver basin of **70** shekels, Nm 7:49
shekels, one silver basin of **70** shekels, Nm 7:55
shekels, one silver basin of **70** shekels, Nm 7:61
shekels, one silver basin of **70** shekels, Nm 7:67
shekels, one silver basin of **70** shekels, Nm 7:73
shekels, one silver basin of **70** shekels, Nm 7:79
130 shekels and each basin **70**, Nm 7:85
the assembly brought was **70** bulls, 2 Chr 29:32
son of Athaliah, and with him **70** men. Ezr 8:7
and Zaccur, and with them **70** men. Ezr 8:14

72 (1)
of which the LORD'S tribute was **72**. Nm 31:38

74 (2)
and Kadmiel, of the sons of Hodaviah, **74**. Ezr 2:40
of Kadmiel of the sons of Hodevah, **74**. Neh 7:43

80 (2)
Eliel the chief, with **80** of his brothers; 1 Chr 15:9
the son of Michael, and with him **80** men. Ezr 8:8

90 (1)
When Enosh had lived **90** years, he Gn 5:9

95 (2)
The sons of Gibbar, **95**. Ezr 2:20
The sons of Gibeon, **95**. Neh 7:25

98 (2)
The sons of Ater, namely of Hezekiah, **98**. Ezr 2:16
sons of Ater, namely of Hezekiah, **98**. Neh 7:21

100 (12)
When Shem was **100** years old, he Gn 11:10
horses, but left enough for **100** chariots. 1 Chr 18:4
from Israel for **100** talents of silver. 2 Chr 25:6
gave him that year **100** talents of silver, 2 Chr 27:5
brought was 70 bulls, **100** rams, 2 Chr 29:32
of silver, and **100** priests' garments. Ezr 2:69
dedication of this house of God **100** bulls, Ezr 6:17
up to **100** talents of silver, 100 cors of Ezr 7:22
to 100 talents of silver, **100** cors of wheat, Ezr 7:22
100 cors of wheat, **100** baths of wine, Ezr 7:22
wheat, 100 baths of wine, **100** baths of oil, Ezr 7:22
worth 200 talents, and **100** talents of gold, Ezr 8:26

105 (1)
When Seth had lived **105** years, he fathered Gn 5:6

110 (5)
his father's house. Joseph lived **110** years. Gn 50:22
So Joseph died, being **110** years old. Gn 50:26
of the LORD, died, being **110** years old. Jos 24:29
of the LORD, died at the age of **110** years. Jgs 2:8
son of Hakkatan, and with him **110** men. Ezr 8:12

112 (3)
the chief, with **112** of his brothers. 1 Chr 15:10
The sons of Jorah, **112**. Ezr 2:18
The sons of Hariph, **112**. Neh 7:24

119 (1)
after he fathered Terah **119** years and had Gn 11:25

120 (12)
for he is flesh: his days shall be **120** years." Gn 6:3
the gold of the dishes being **120** shekels; Nm 7:86
he said to them, "I am **120** years old today. Dt 31:2
Moses was **120** years old when he died. Dt 34:7
had sent to the king **120** talents of gold. 1 Kgs 9:14
she gave the king **120** talents of gold, 1 Kgs 10:10
Uriel the chief, with **120** of his brothers; 1 Chr 15:5
the house, and its height was **120** cubits. 2 Chr 3:4
of the altar with **120** priests who were 2 Chr 5:12
she gave the king **120** talents of gold, 2 Chr 9:9
Darius to set over the kingdom **120** satraps, Dn 6:1
of persons was in all about **120**) and said, Acts 1:15

122 (2)
The men of Michmas, **122**. Ezr 2:27
The men of Michmas, **122**. Neh 7:31

123 (3)
And Aaron was **123** years old when he Nm 33:39
The sons of Bethlehem, **123**. Ezr 2:21
The men of Bethel and Ai, **123**. Neh 7:32

127 (4)
Sarah lived **127** years; these were the years Gn 23:1
from India to Ethiopia over **127** provinces, Est 1:1
from India to Ethiopia, **127** provinces, Est 8:9
to the **127** provinces of the kingdom of Est 9:30

128 (4)
The men of Anathoth, **128**. Ezr 2:23
The singers: the sons of Asaph, **128**. Ezr 2:41
The men of Anathoth, **128**. Neh 7:27
brothers, mighty men of valor, **128**; Neh 11:14

130 (17)
When Adam had lived **130** years, he Gn 5:3
the years of my sojourning are **130** years. Gn 47:9
silver plate whose weight was **130** shekels, Nm 7:13
silver plate whose weight was **130** shekels, Nm 7:19
silver plate whose weight was **130** shekels, Nm 7:25
silver plate whose weight was **130** shekels, Nm 7:31
silver plate whose weight was **130** shekels, Nm 7:37
silver plate whose weight was **130** shekels, Nm 7:43
silver plate whose weight was **130** shekels, Nm 7:49
silver plate whose weight was **130** shekels, Nm 7:55
silver plate whose weight was **130** shekels, Nm 7:61
silver plate whose weight was **130** shekels, Nm 7:67
silver plate whose weight was **130** shekels, Nm 7:73
silver plate whose weight was **130** shekels, Nm 7:79
silver plate weighing **130** shekels and Nm 7:85
Joel the chief, with **130** of his brothers; 1 Chr 15:7
He was **130** years old at his death. 2 Chr 24:15

133 (1)
years of the life of Kohath being **133** years. Ex 6:18

137 (3)
the years of the life of Ishmael: **137** years. Gn 25:17
the years of the life of Levi being **137** years. Ex 6:16
years of the life of Amram being **137** years. Ex 6:20

138 (1)
sons of Hatita, the sons of Shobai, **138**. Neh 7:45

139 (1)
Hatita, and the sons of Shobai, in all **139**. Ezr 2:42

140 (1)
And after this Job lived **140** years, and saw Jb 42:16

144 (1)
measured its wall, **144** cubits by human Rv 21:17

147 (1)
the years of his life, were **147** years. Gn 47:28

148 (1)
The singers: the sons of Asaph, **148**. Neh 7:44

150 (7)
waters prevailed on the earth **150** days. Gn 7:24
At the end of **150** days the waters had Gn 8:3
shekels of silver and a horse for **150**, 1 Kgs 10:29
having many sons and grandsons, **150**. 1 Chr 8:40
shekels of silver, and a horse for **150**. 2 Chr 1:17
with whom were registered **150** men. Ezr 8:3
there were at my table **150** men, Neh 5:17

153 (1)
net ashore, full of large fish, **153** of them. Jn 21:11

156 (1)
The sons of Magbish, **156**. Ezr 2:30

160 (1)
son of Josiphiah, and with him **160** men. Ezr 8:10

162 (1)
Jared had lived **162** years he fathered Gn 5:18

172 (1)
who kept watch at the gates, were **172**. Neh 11:19

175 (1)
of the years of Abraham's life, **175** years. Gn 25:7

180 (2)
Now the days of Isaac were **180** years. Gn 35:28
of his greatness for many days, **180** days. Est 1:4

182 (1)
When Lamech had lived **182** years, he Gn 5:28

187 (1)
When Methuselah had lived **187** years, he Gn 5:25

188 (1)
men of Bethlehem and Netophah, **188**. Neh 7:26

200 (12)
he fathered Nahor **200** years and had Gn 11:23
from Shinar, and **200** shekels of silver, Jos 7:21
his mother took **200** pieces of silver and Jgs 17:4
King Solomon made **200** large shields 1 Kgs 10:16
what Israel ought to do, **200** chiefs, 1 Chr 12:32
the chief, with **200** of his brothers; 1 Chr 15:8
King Solomon made **200** large shields 2 Chr 9:15
70 bulls, 100 rams, and **200** lambs; 2 Chr 29:32
they had **200** male and female singers. Ezr 2:65
of this house of God 100 bulls, **200** rams, Ezr 6:17
son of Zerahiah, and with him **200** men. Ezr 8:4
silver, and silver vessels worth **200** talents, Ezr 8:26

205 (1)
The days of Terah were **205** years, and Gn 11:32

207 (1)
after he fathered Serug **207** years and Gn 11:21

209 (1)
after he fathered Reu **209** years and had Gn 11:19

212 (1)
gatekeepers at the thresholds, were **212**. 1 Chr 9:22

218 (1)
the son of Jehiel, and with him **218** men. Ezr 8:9

220 (2)
the chief, with **220** of his brothers; 1 Chr 15:6
besides **220** of the temple servants, Ezr 8:20

223 (2)
The sons of Hashum, **223**. Ezr 2:19
The men of Bethel and Ai, **223**. Ezr 2:28

232 (1)
of the districts, and they were **232**. 1 Kgs 20:15

242 (1)
of fathers' houses, **242**; and Amashsai, Neh 11:13

245 (3)
horses were 736, their mules were **245**, Ezr 2:66
And they had **245** singers, male and Neh 7:67
Their horses were 736, their mules **245**, Neh 7:68

250 (11)
that is, **250**, and 250 of aromatic cane, Ex 30:23
that is, 250, and **250** of aromatic cane, Ex 30:23
of Israel, **250** chiefs of the congregation, Nm 16:2
before the LORD his censer, **250** censers; Nm 16:17
and consumed the **250** men offering the Nm 16:35
died, when the fire devoured **250** men, Nm 26:10
250, who exercised authority over the 2 Chr 8:10
on the north **250** cubits, on the south Ezk 48:17
the north 250 cubits, on the south **250**, Ezk 48:17
on the south 250, on the east **250**, Ezk 48:17
on the east 250, and on the west **250**. Ezk 48:17

273 (1)
price for the **273** of the firstborn Nm 3:46

276 (1)
(We were in all **276** persons in the Acts 27:37

284 (1)
All the Levites in the holy city were **284**. Neh 11:18

288 (1)
all who were skillful, was **288**. 1 Chr 25:7

300 (20)
he fathered Methuselah **300** years and had Gn 5:22
the length of the ark **300** cubits, its Gn 6:15
their hands to their mouths, was **300** men, Jgs 7:6
"With the **300** men who lapped I will save Jgs 7:7
man to his tent, but retained the **300** men. Jgs 7:8
And he divided the **300** men into three Jgs 7:16
When they blew the **300** trumpets, the Jgs 7:22
he and the **300** men who were with him, Jgs 8:4
are on the banks of the Arnon, **300** years, Jgs 11:26
went and caught **300** foxes and took Jgs 15:4
And he made **300** shields of beaten 1 Kgs 10:17
wives, princesses, and **300** concubines. 1 Kgs 11:3
his spear against **300** whom he killed 1 Chr 11:11
his spear against **300** men and killed 1 Chr 11:20
he made **300** shields of beaten gold; 2 Chr 9:16
300 shekels of gold went into each 2 Chr 9:16
of a million men and **300** chariots, 2 Chr 14:9
2,600 Passover lambs and **300** bulls. 2 Chr 35:8
the son of Jahaziel, and with him **300** men. Ezr 8:5
of Adar and they killed **300** men in Susa, Est 9:15

318 (1)
men, born in his house, **318** of them, Gn 14:14

320 (2)
The sons of Harim, **320**. Ezr 2:32
The sons of Harim, **320**. Neh 7:35

323 (1)
The sons of Bezai, **323**. Ezr 2:17

324 (1)
The sons of Bezai, **324**. Neh 7:23

328 (1)
The sons of Hashum, **328**. Neh 7:22

345 (2)
The sons of Jericho, **345**. Ezr 2:34
The sons of Jericho, **345**. Neh 7:36

350 (1)
After the flood Noah lived **350** years. Gn 9:28

360 (1)
down of Benjamin **360** of Abner's men. 2 Sm 2:31

365 (1)
Thus all the days of Enoch were **365** years. Gn 5:23

372 (2)
The sons of Shephatiah, **372**. Ezr 2:4
The sons of Shephatiah, **372**. Neh 7:9

390 (2)
I assign to you a number of days, **390** days, Ezk 4:5
of days that you lie on your side, **390** days, Ezk 4:9

392 (2)
the sons of Solomon's servants were **392**. Ezr 2:58
the sons of Solomon's servants were **392**. Neh 7:60

400 (5)
of Jabesh-gilead **400** young virgins Jgs 21:12
Baal and the **400** prophets of Asherah, 1 Kgs 18:19
and the **400** pomegranates for the two 2 Chr 4:13
the wall of Jerusalem for **400** cubits, 2 Chr 25:23
of God 100 bulls, 200 rams, **400** lambs, Ezr 6:17

403 (2)
he fathered Shelah **403** years and had Gn 11:13
after he fathered Eber **403** years and had Gn 11:15

410 (1)
30 bowls of gold, **410** bowls of silver, and Ezr 1:10

420 (1)
brought from there gold, **420** talents, 1 Kgs 9:28

430 (4)
after he fathered Peleg **430** years and had Gn 11:17
of Israel lived in Egypt was **430** years. Ex 12:40
At the end of **430** years, on that very day, Ex 12:41
the law, which came **430** years afterward, Gal 3:17

435 (2)
their camels were **435**, and their donkeys Ezr 2:67
their camels **435**, and their donkeys Neh 7:69

450 (4)
and the **450** prophets of Baal and the 1 Kgs 18:19
LORD, but Baal's prophets are **450** men. 1 Kgs 18:22
brought from there **450** talents of gold 2 Chr 8:18
All this took about **450** years. And after Acts 13:20

454 (1)
The sons of Adin, **454**. Ezr 2:15

468 (1)
lived in Jerusalem were **468** valiant men. Neh 11:6

500 (18)
After Noah was **500** years old, Noah Gn 5:32
he fathered Arpachshad **500** years and Gn 11:11
of liquid myrrh **500** shekels, and of Ex 30:23
and **500** of cassia, according to the shekel Ex 30:24
lambs and young goats and **500** bulls. 2 Chr 35:9
priests' garments and **500** minas of silver. Neh 7:70
the Jews killed and destroyed **500** men, Est 9:6
killed and destroyed **500** men and also Est 9:12
sheep, 3,000 camels, **500** yoke of oxen, Jb 1:3
yoke of oxen, and **500** female donkeys, Jb 1:3
500 cubits by the measuring reed all Ezk 42:16
500 cubits by the measuring reed all Ezk 42:17
side, **500** cubits by the measuring reed. Ezk 42:18
500 cubits by the measuring reed. Ezk 42:19
it, **500** cubits long and 500 cubits broad, Ezk 42:20
it, 500 cubits long and **500** cubits broad, Ezk 42:20
a square plot of **500** by 500 cubits shall Ezk 45:2
plot of 500 by **500** cubits shall be for Ezk 45:2

550 (1)
over Solomon's work: **550** who had 1 Kgs 9:23

595 (1)
after he fathered Noah **595** years and had Gn 5:30

600 (12)
who killed **600** of the Philistines with an Jgs 3:31
So **600** men of the tribe of Dan, armed Jgs 18:11
Now the **600** men of the Danites, armed Jgs 18:16
the gate with the **600** men armed with Jgs 18:17
But **600** men turned and fled toward the Jgs 20:47
600 shekels of gold went into each 1 Kgs 10:16
from Egypt for **600** shekels of silver 1 Kgs 10:29
David paid Ornan **600** shekels of gold 1 Chr 21:25
from Egypt for **600** shekels of silver, 2 Chr 1:17
He overlaid it with **600** talents of fine 2 Chr 3:8
600 shekels of beaten gold went into 2 Chr 9:15
offerings were **600** bulls and 2 Chr 29:33

621 (2)
The sons of Ramah and Geba, **621**. Ezr 2:26
The men of Ramah and Geba, **621**. Neh 7:30

623 (1)
The sons of Bebai, **623**. Ezr 2:11

628 (1)
The sons of Bebai, **628**. Neh 7:16

642 (2)
The sons of Bani, **642**. Ezr 2:10
sons of Tobiah, the sons of Nekoda, **642**. Neh 7:62

648 (1)
The sons of Binnui, **648**. Neh 7:15

650 (1)
out into their hand **650** talents of silver, Ezr 8:26

652 (2)
of Tobiah, and the sons of Nekoda, **652**. Ezr 2:60
The sons of Arah, **652**. Neh 7:10

655 (1)
The sons of Adin, **655**. Neh 7:20

666 (4)
in one year was **666** talents of gold, 1 Kgs 10:14
in one year was **666** talents of gold, 2 Chr 9:13
The sons of Adonikam, **666**. Ezr 2:13
number of a man, and his number is **666**. Rv 13:18

667 (1)
The sons of Adonikam, **667**. Neh 7:18

675 (1)
the LORD'S tribute of sheep was **675**. Nm 31:37

690 (1)
of Zerah: Jeuel and their kinsmen, **690**. 1 Chr 9:6

700 (6)
Gibeah, who mustered **700** chosen men. Jgs 20:15
all these were **700** chosen men who Jgs 20:16
of the Syrians the men of **700** chariots, 2 Sm 10:18
He had **700** wives, princesses, and 300 1 Kgs 11:3
took with him **700** swordsmen to break 2 Kgs 3:26
they had brought **700** oxen and 7,000 2 Chr 15:11

721 (1)
The sons of Lod, Hadid, and Ono, **721**. Neh 7:37

725 (1)
The sons of Lod, Hadid, and Ono, **725**. Ezr 2:33

730 (1)
was twenty-nine talents and **730** shekels, Ex 38:24

736 (2)
Their horses were **736**, their mules were Ezr 2:66
Their horses were **736**, their mules 245, Neh 7:68

743 (2)
Chephirah, and Beeroth, **743**. Ezr 2:25
Chephirah, and Beeroth, **743**. Neh 7:29

745 (1)
away captive of the Judeans **745** persons; Jer 52:30

760 (2)
The sons of Zaccai, **760**. Ezr 2:9
The sons of Zaccai, **760**. Neh 7:14

775 (1)
The sons of Arah, **775**. Ezr 2:5

777 (1)
all the days of Lamech were **777** years, Gn 5:31

782 (1)
he fathered Lamech **782** years and had Gn 5:26

800 (2)
Adam after he fathered Seth were **800** years; Gn 5:4
after he fathered Enoch **800** years and had Gn 5:19

807 (1)
after he fathered Enosh **807** years and had Gn 5:7

815 (1)
after he fathered Kenan **815** years and had Gn 5:10

822 (1)
who did the work of the house, **822**; Neh 11:12

830 (1)
after he fathered Jared **830** years and had Gn 5:16

832 (1)
away captive from Jerusalem **832** persons; Jer 52:29

840 (1)
he fathered Mahalalel **840** years and had Gn 5:13

845 (1)
The sons of Zattu, **845**. Neh 7:13

895 (1)
all the days of Mahalalel were **895** years, Gn 5:17

900 (2)
for he had **900** chariots of iron and he Jgs 4:3
out all his chariots, **900** chariots of iron, Jgs 4:13

905 (1)
Thus all the days of Enosh were **905** years, Gn 5:11

910 (1)
Thus all the days of Kenan were **910** years, Gn 5:14

912 (1)
Thus all the days of Seth were **912** years, Gn 5:8

928 (1)
and his brothers, men of valor, **928**. Neh 11:8

930 (1)
all the days that Adam lived were **930** years, Gn 5:5

945 (1)
The sons of Zattu, **945**. Ezr 2:8

950 (1)
All the days of Noah were **950** years, and Gn 9:29

956 (1)
according to their generations, **956**. 1 Chr 9:9

962 (1)
Thus all the days of Jared were **962** years, Gn 5:20

969 (1)
all the days of Methuselah were **969** years, Gn 5:27

973 (2)
of Jedaiah, of the house of Jeshua, **973**. Ezr 2:36
Jedaiah, namely the house of Jeshua, **973**. Neh 7:39

1,000 (18)
also died, about **1,000** men and women. Jgs 9:49
took it, and with it he struck **1,000** men. Jgs 15:15
and the king of Maacah with **1,000** men, 2 Sm 10:6
and the metal workers, **1,000**, all of 2 Kgs 24:16
Of Naphtali **1,000** commanders with 1 Chr 12:34
David took from him **1,000** chariots, 1 Chr 18:4
the Ammonites sent **1,000** talents of 1 Chr 19:6
offerings to the LORD, **1,000** bulls, 1 Chr 29:21
to the LORD, 1,000 bulls, **1,000** rams, 1 Chr 29:21
bulls, 1,000 rams, and **1,000** lambs, 1 Chr 29:21
gave the assembly **1,000** bulls and 2 Chr 30:24
gave the assembly **1,000** bulls and 2 Chr 30:24
30 basins of gold, **1,000** basins of silver, Ezr 1:9
bowls of silver, and **1,000** other vessels; Ezr 1:10
20 bowls of gold worth **1,000** darics, Ezr 8:27
gave to the treasury **1,000** darics of gold, Neh 7:70
sheep, 6,000 camels, **1,000** yoke of oxen, Jb 42:12
yoke of oxen, and **1,000** female donkeys. Jb 42:12

1,005 (1)
and his songs were **1,005**. 1 Kgs 4:32

1,017 (2)
The sons of Harim, **1,017**. Ezr 2:39
The sons of Harim, **1,017**. Neh 7:42

1,052 (2)
The sons of Immer, **1,052**. Ezr 2:37
The sons of Immer, **1,052**. Neh 7:40

1,100 (3)
will each give you **1,100** pieces of silver." Jgs 16:5
"The **1,100** pieces of silver that were taken Jgs 17:2
he restored the **1,100** pieces of silver to Jgs 17:3

1,200 (1)
with **1,200** chariots and 60,000 2 Chr 12:3

1,222 (1)
The sons of Azgad, **1,222**. Ezr 2:12

1,247 (2)
The sons of Pashhur, **1,247**. Ezr 2:38
The sons of Pashhur, **1,247**. Neh 7:41

1,254 (4)
The sons of Elam, **1,254**. Ezr 2:7
The sons of the other Elam, **1,254**. Ezr 2:31
The sons of Elam, **1,254**. Neh 7:12
The sons of the other Elam, **1,254**. Neh 7:34

1,260 (2)
and they will prophesy for **1,260** days, Rv 11:3
she is to be nourished for **1,260** days. Rv 12:6

1,290 (1)
is set up, there shall be **1,290** days. Dn 12:11

1,335 (1)
who waits and arrives at the **1,335** days. Dn 12:12

1,365 (1)
Israel he took the money, **1,365** shekels, Nm 3:50

1,400 (2)
He had **1,400** chariots and 12,000 1 Kgs 10:26
He had **1,400** chariots and 12,000 2 Chr 1:14

1,600 (1)
high as a horse's bridle, for **1,600** stadia. Rv 14:20

1,700 (3)
he requested was **1,700** shekels of gold, Jgs 8:26
David took from him **1,700** horsemen, 2 Sm 8:4
and his brothers, **1,700** men of ability, 1 Chr 26:30

1,760 (1)
heads of their fathers' houses, **1,760**, 1 Chr 9:13

1,775 (2)
was a hundred talents and **1,775** shekels, Ex 38:25
of the **1,775** shekels he made hooks for Ex 38:28

2,000 (4)
you and it, about **2,000** cubits in length. Jos 3:4
2,000 men of them were struck down. Jgs 20:45
camels, 250,000 sheep, **2,000** donkeys, 1 Chr 5:21
darics of gold, **2,000** minas of silver, Neh 7:72

2,056 (1)
The sons of Bigvai, **2,056**. Ezr 2:14

2,067 (1)
The sons of Bigvai, **2,067**. Neh 7:19

2,172 (2)
the sons of Parosh, **2,172**. Ezr 2:3
the sons of Parosh, **2,172**. Neh 7:8

2,200 (1)
darics of gold and **2,200** minas of silver. Neh 7:71

2,300 (1)
to me, "For **2,300** evenings and mornings. Dn 8:14

2,322 (1)
The sons of Azgad, **2,322**. Neh 7:17

2,400 (2)
was seventy talents and **2,400** shekels; Ex 38:29
of the vessels **2,400** shekels according to Nm 7:85

2,600 (2)
of mighty men of valor was **2,600**. 2 Chr 26:12
Passover offerings **2,600** Passover lambs 2 Chr 35:8

2,630 (1)
and their fathers' houses were **2,630**. Nm 4:40

2,700 (1)
and his brothers, **2,700** men of ability, 1 Chr 26:32

2,750 (1)
and those listed by clans were **2,750**. Nm 4:36

2,812 (1)
namely the sons of Jeshua and Joab, **2,812**. Ezr 2:6

2,818 (1)
the sons of Jeshua and Joab, **2,818**. Neh 7:11

3,000 (11)
So about **3,000** men went up there from the Jos 7:4
Then **3,000** men of Judah went down to Jgs 15:11
there were about **3,000** men and women, Jgs 16:27
He also spoke **3,000** proverbs, and his 1 Kgs 4:32
the kinsmen of Saul, **3,000**, of whom 1 Chr 12:29
3,000 talents of gold, of the gold of 1 Chr 29:4
the flower of a lily. It held **3,000** baths. 2 Chr 4:5
struck down **3,000** people in them 2 Chr 25:13
were 600 bulls and **3,000** sheep. 2 Chr 29:33
the number of 30,000, and **3,000** bulls; 2 Chr 35:7
He possessed 7,000 sheep, **3,000** camels, Jb 1:3

3,023 (1)
in the seventh year, **3,023** Judeans; Jer 52:28

3,200 (1)
those listed by clans were **3,200**. Nm 4:44

3,300 (1)
besides Solomon's **3,300** chief officers 1 Kgs 5:16

3,600 (2)
hill country, and **3,600** to oversee them. 2 Chr 2:2
and **3,600** as overseers to make the 2 Chr 2:18

3,630 (1)
The sons of Senaah, **3,630**. Ezr 2:35

3,700 (1)
house of Aaron, and with him **3,700**. 1 Chr 12:27

3,930 (1)
The sons of Senaah, **3,930**. Neh 7:38

4,000 (3)
4,000 gatekeepers, and 4,000 shall offer 1 Chr 23:5
4,000 shall offer praises to the LORD 1 Chr 23:5
Solomon had **4,000** stalls for horses 2 Chr 9:25

4,500 (8)
north side **4,500** cubits, the south side Ezk 48:16
side 4,500 cubits, the south side **4,500**, Ezk 48:16
the south side 4,500, the east side **4,500**, Ezk 48:16
east side 4,500, and the west side **4,500**. Ezk 48:16
which is to be **4,500** cubits by measure, Ezk 48:30
east side, which is to be **4,500** cubits, Ezk 48:32
which is to be **4,500** cubits by measure, Ezk 48:33
west side, which is to be **4,500** cubits, Ezk 48:34

4,600 (2)
Of the Levites **4,600**. 1 Chr 12:26
745 persons; all the persons were **4,600**. Jer 52:30

5,000 (6)
He took about **5,000** men and set them in Jos 8:12
house of God **5,000** talents and 10,000 1 Chr 29:7
the Passover offerings **5,000** lambs and 2 Chr 35:9
darics of gold, **5,000** minas of silver, Ezr 2:69
the city an area **5,000** cubits broad and Ezk 45:6
5,000 cubits in breadth and 25,000 in Ezk 48:15

5,400 (1)
vessels of gold and of silver were **5,400**. Ezr 1:11

6,000 (2)
of the LORD, **6,000** shall be officers and 1 Chr 23:4
And he had 14,000 sheep, **6,000** camels, Jb 42:12

6,200 (1)
from a month old and upward was **6,200**. Nm 3:34

6,720 (2)
were 435, and their donkeys were **6,720**. Ezr 2:67
camels 435, and their donkeys **6,720**. Neh 7:69

6,800 (1)
and spear were **6,800** armed troops. 1 Chr 12:24

7,000 (7)
to Babylon all the men of valor, **7,000**, 2 Kgs 24:16
1,000 chariots, **7,000** horsemen, and 1 Chr 18:4
the men of **7,000** chariots and 40,000 1 Chr 19:18
and **7,000** talents of refined silver, 1 Chr 29:4
brought 700 oxen and **7,000** sheep. 2 Chr 15:11
1,000 bulls and **7,000** sheep for 2 Chr 30:24
He possessed **7,000** sheep, 3,000 camels, Jb 1:3

7,100 (1)
mighty men of valor for war, **7,100**. 1 Chr 12:25

7,337 (2)
servants, of whom there were **7,337**, Ezr 2:65
servants, of whom there were **7,337**. Neh 7:67

7,500 (1)
from a month old and upward was **7,500**. Nm 3:22

7,700 (2)
Arabians also brought him **7,700** rams 2 Chr 17:11
him 7,700 rams and **7,700** goats. 2 Chr 17:11

8,580 (1)
those listed were **8,580**. Nm 4:48

8,600 (1)
month old and upward, there were **8,600**, Nm 3:28

10,000 (24)
and they defeated **10,000** of them at Bezek. Jgs 1:4
at that time about **10,000** of the Moabites, Jgs 3:29
taking **10,000** from the people of Naphtali Jgs 4:6
And **10,000** men went up at his heels, and Jgs 4:10
Mount Tabor with **10,000** men following Jgs 4:14
the people returned, and **10,000** remained. Jgs 7:3
came against Gibeah **10,000** chosen men Jgs 20:34
to Lebanon, **10,000** a month in shifts. 1 Kgs 5:14
mighty men of valor, **10,000** captives, 2 Kgs 24:14
5,000 talents and **10,000** darics of gold, 1 Chr 29:7
darics of gold, **10,000** talents of silver, 1 Chr 29:7
and struck down **10,000** men of Seir. 2 Chr 25:11
Judah captured another **10,000** alive 2 Chr 25:12
10,000 cors of wheat and 10,000 of 2 Chr 27:5
cors of wheat and **10,000** of barley. 2 Chr 27:5
1,000 bulls and **10,000** sheep. 2 Chr 30:24
I will pay **10,000** talents of silver into Est 3:9
25,000 cubits long and **10,000** broad, Ezk 45:3
cubits long and **10,000** cubits broad, Ezk 45:5
10,000 cubits in breadth on the western Ezk 48:10
10,000 in breadth on the eastern side, Ezk 48:10
cubits in length and **10,000** in breadth. Ezk 48:13
holy portion shall be **10,000** cubits to Ezk 48:18
to the east, and **10,000** to the west, Ezk 48:18

12,000 (20)
day, both men and women, were **12,000**, Jos 8:25
congregation sent **12,000** of their bravest Jgs 21:10
men, and the men of Tob, **12,000** men. 2 Sm 10:6
for his chariots, and **12,000** horsemen. 1 Kgs 4:26
1,400 chariots and **12,000** horsemen, 1 Kgs 10:26
1,400 chariots and **12,000** horsemen, 2 Chr 1:14
and chariots, and **12,000** horsemen, 2 Chr 9:25
12,000 from the tribe of Judah were sealed, Rv 7:5
sealed, **12,000** from the tribe of Reuben, Rv 7:5
of Reuben, **12,000** from the tribe of Gad, Rv 7:5
12,000 from the tribe of Asher, 12,000 from Rv 7:6
of Asher, **12,000** from the tribe of Naphtali, Rv 7:6
12,000 from the tribe of Manasseh, Rv 7:6
12,000 from the tribe of Simeon, 12,000 Rv 7:7
of Simeon, **12,000** from the tribe of Levi, Rv 7:7
of Levi, **12,000** from the tribe of Issachar, Rv 7:7
12,000 from the tribe of Zebulun, 12,000 Rv 7:8
of Zebulun, **12,000** from the tribe of Joseph, Rv 7:8
12,000 from the tribe of Benjamin were Rv 7:8
the city with his rod, **12,000** stadia. Rv 21:16

14,000 (1)
he had **14,000** sheep, 6,000 camels, Jb 42:12

14,700 (1)
who died in the plague were **14,700**, Nm 16:49

15,000 (1)
Karkor with their army, about **15,000** men, Jgs 8:10

16,000 (2)
The persons were **16,000**, of which the Nm 31:40
and **16,000** persons— Nm 31:46

16,750 (1)
of hundreds, was **16,750** shekels. Nm 31:52

17,200 (1)
warriors, **17,200**, able to go to war. 1 Chr 7:11

18,000 (6)
destroyed **18,000** men of the people of Jgs 20:25
striking down **18,000** Edomites in the 2 Sm 8:13
Of the half-tribe of Manasseh **18,000**, 1 Chr 12:31
killed **18,000** Edomites in the Valley 1 Chr 18:12
18,000 talents of bronze and 100,000 1 Chr 29:7
of the city shall be **18,000** cubits. Ezk 48:35

20,000 (14)
horsemen, and **20,000** foot soldiers. 2 Sm 8:4
Syrians of Zobah, **20,000** foot soldiers, 2 Sm 10:6
gave Hiram **20,000** cors of wheat 1 Kgs 5:11
and **20,000** cors of beaten oil. 1 Kgs 5:11
horsemen, and **20,000** foot soldiers. 1 Chr 18:4
timber, **20,000** cors of crushed wheat, 2 Chr 2:10
of crushed wheat, **20,000** cors of barley, 2 Chr 2:10
cors of barley, **20,000** baths of wine, 2 Chr 2:10
baths of wine, and **20,000** baths of oil." 2 Chr 2:10
of the work **20,000** darics of gold Neh 7:71
people gave was **20,000** darics of gold, Neh 7:72
cubits long and **20,000** cubits broad. Ezk 45:1
cubits in length, and **20,000** in breadth. Ezk 48:9
25,000 cubits and the breadth **20,000**. Ezk 48:13

20,800 (1)
the Ephraimites **20,800**, mighty men 1 Chr 12:30

22,000 (7)
a month old and upward, were **22,000**. Nm 3:39
Mount Gilead.'" Then **22,000** of the people Jgs 7:3
destroyed on that day **22,000** men of the Jgs 20:21
David struck down **22,000** men of the 2 Sm 8:5
to the LORD **22,000** oxen and 120,000 1 Kgs 8:63
David struck down **22,000** men of the 1 Chr 18:5
as a sacrifice **22,000** oxen and 120,000 2 Chr 7:5

22,034 (1)
enrollment by genealogies was **22,034**. 1 Chr 7:7

22,200 (2)
are the clans of the Simeonites, **22,200**. Nm 26:14
houses, mighty warriors, was **22,200**. 1 Chr 7:9

22,273 (1)
old and upward as listed were **22,273**. Nm 3:43

22,600 (1)
in the days of David being **22,600**. 1 Chr 7:2

23,000 (1)
those listed were **23,000**, every male Nm 26:62

24,000 (13)
year, each division numbering **24,000**: 1 Chr 27:1
first month; in his division were **24,000**. 1 Chr 27:2
month; in his division were **24,000**. 1 Chr 27:4
chief priest; in his division were **24,000**. 1 Chr 27:5
after him; in his division were **24,000**. 1 Chr 27:7
Izrahite; in his division were **24,000**. 1 Chr 27:8
Tekoite; in his division were **24,000**. 1 Chr 27:9
Ephraim; in his division were **24,000**. 1 Chr 27:10
Zerahites; in his division were **24,000**. 1 Chr 27:11
in his division were **24,000**. 1 Chr 27:12
Zerahites; in his division were **24,000**. 1 Chr 27:13
Ephraim; in his division were **24,000**. 1 Chr 27:14
Othniel; in his division were **24,000**. 1 Chr 27:15

25,000 (15)
of Benjamin were **25,000** men who drew Jgs 20:46
25,000 cubits long and 20,000 cubits Ezk 45:1
measure off a section **25,000** cubits long Ezk 45:3
25,000 cubits long and 10,000 cubits Ezk 45:5
cubits broad and **25,000** cubits long. Ezk 45:6
shall set apart, **25,000** cubits in breadth, Ezk 48:8
for the LORD shall be **25,000** cubits in Ezk 48:9
allotment measuring **25,000** cubits on Ezk 48:10
25,000 in length on the southern side, Ezk 48:10
an allotment **25,000** cubits in length Ezk 48:13
whole length shall be **25,000** cubits and Ezk 48:13
cubits in breadth and **25,000** in length, Ezk 48:15
set apart shall be **25,000** cubits square, Ezk 48:20
Extending from the **25,000** cubits of the Ezk 48:21
westward from the **25,000** cubits to the Ezk 48:21

25,100 (1)
Israel destroyed **25,100** men of Benjamin Jgs 20:35

26,000 (2)
cities on that day **26,000** men who drew Jgs 20:15
for service in war, was **26,000** men. 1 Chr 7:40

27,000 (1)
wall fell upon **27,000** men who were 1 Kgs 20:30

28,600 (1)
Of the Danites **28,600** men equipped 1 Chr 12:35

30,000 (3)
Joshua chose **30,000** mighty men of valor Jos 8:3
and the draft numbered **30,000** men. 1 Kgs 5:13
the flock to the number of **30,000**, 2 Chr 35:7

30,500 (2)
The donkeys were **30,500**, of which the Nm 31:39
and **30,500** donkeys, Nm 31:45

32,000 (2)
and **32,000** persons in all, women who Nm 31:35
They hired **32,000** chariots and the 1 Chr 19:7

32,200 (2)
of the tribe of Manasseh were **32,200**. Nm 1:35
his company as listed being **32,200**. Nm 2:21

32,500 (1)
of Ephraim as they were listed, **32,500**. Nm 26:37

35,400 (2)
of the tribe of Benjamin were **35,400**. Nm 1:37
his company as listed being **35,400**. Nm 2:23

36,000 (3)
cattle were **36,000**, of which the LORD'S Nm 31:38
36,000 cattle, Nm 31:44
36,000, for they had many wives and 1 Chr 7:4

37,000 (1)
with whom were **37,000** men armed 1 Chr 12:34

38,000 (1)
and the total was **38,000** men. 1 Chr 23:3

40,000 (5)
About **40,000** ready for war passed over Jos 4:13
of 700 chariots, and **40,000** horsemen, 2 Sm 10:18
Solomon also had **40,000** stalls of 1 Kgs 4:26
Asher **40,000** seasoned troops ready 1 Chr 12:36
chariots and **40,000** foot soldiers, 1 Chr 19:18

40,500 (3)
of the tribe of Ephraim were **40,500**. Nm 1:33
his company as listed being **40,500**. Nm 2:19
sons of Gad as they were listed, **40,500**. Nm 26:18

41,500 (2)
listed of the tribe of Asher were **41,500**. Nm 1:41
his company as listed being **41,500**. Nm 2:28

42,000 (1)
that time **42,000** of the Ephraimites fell. Jgs 12:6

42,360 (2)
whole assembly together was **42,360**, Ezr 2:64
whole assembly together was **42,360**, Neh 7:66

43,730 (1)
Reubenites, and those listed were **43,730**. Nm 26:7

44,760 (1)
expert in war, **44,760**, able to go to war. 1 Chr 5:18

45,400 (1)
clans, and those listed were **45,400**. Nm 26:50

45,600 (1)
clans, and those listed were **45,600**. Nm 26:41

45,650 (2)
listed of the tribe of Gad were **45,650**. Nm 1:25
his company as listed being **45,650**. Nm 2:15

46,500 (2)
listed of the tribe of Reuben were **46,500**. Nm 1:21
his company as listed being **46,500**. Nm 2:11

50,000 (2)
their livestock: **50,000** of their camels, 1 Chr 5:21
Of Zebulun **50,000** seasoned troops, 1 Chr 12:33

52,700 (1)
Manasseh, and those listed were **52,700**. Nm 26:34

53,400 (3)
of the tribe of Naphtali were **53,400**. Nm 1:43
his company as listed being **53,400**. Nm 2:30